W9-AWP-718

is presented to

by

on

Church Record

EVENT

MINISTER

CHURCH DATE

EVENT

MINISTER

CHURCH DATE

EVENT

MINISTER

CHURCH DATE

EVENT

MINISTER

CHURCH DATE

EVENT

MINISTER

CHURCH DATE

EVENT

MINISTER

CHURCH DATE

Marriages

HUSBAND

WIFE

PLACE DATE

HUSBAND

WIFE

PLACE DATE

HUSBAND

WIFE

PLACE DATE

HUSBAND

WIFE

PLACE DATE

HUSBAND

WIFE

PLACE DATE

HUSBAND

WIFE

PLACE DATE

Wife's Family Tree

NAME

BIRTHPLACE DATE

BROTHERS AND SISTERS

PARENTS

FATHER

NAME

BIRTHPLACE DATE

MOTHER

NAME

BIRTHPLACE DATE

GRANDPARENTS

PATERNAL

GRANDFATHER

BIRTHPLACE DATE

GRANDMOTHER

BIRTHPLACE DATE

MATERNAL

GRANDFATHER

BIRTHPLACE DATE

GRANDMOTHER

BIRTHPLACE DATE

GREAT-GRANDPARENTS

PATERNAL

GRANDFATHER'S FATHER

BIRTHPLACE DATE

GRANDFATHER'S MOTHER

BIRTHPLACE DATE

GRANDMOTHER'S FATHER

BIRTHPLACE DATE

GRANDMOTHER'S MOTHER

BIRTHPLACE DATE

MATERNAL

GRANDFATHER'S FATHER

BIRTHPLACE DATE

GRANDFATHER'S MOTHER

BIRTHPLACE DATE

GRANDMOTHER'S FATHER

BIRTHPLACE DATE

GRANDMOTHER'S MOTHER

BIRTHPLACE DATE

Husband's Family Tree

NAME

BIRTHPLACE DATE

BROTHERS AND SISTERS

PARENTS

FATHER

NAME

BIRTHPLACE DATE

MOTHER

NAME

BIRTHPLACE DATE

GRANDPARENTS

PATERNAL

GRANDFATHER

BIRTHPLACE DATE

GRANDMOTHER

BIRTHPLACE DATE

MATERNAL

GRANDFATHER

BIRTHPLACE DATE

GRANDMOTHER

BIRTHPLACE DATE

GREAT-GRANDPARENTS

PATERNAL

GRANDFATHER'S FATHER

BIRTHPLACE DATE

GRANDFATHER'S MOTHER

BIRTHPLACE DATE

GRANDMOTHER'S FATHER

BIRTHPLACE DATE

GRANDMOTHER'S MOTHER

BIRTHPLACE DATE

MATERNAL

GRANDFATHER'S FATHER

BIRTHPLACE DATE

GRANDFATHER'S MOTHER

BIRTHPLACE DATE

GRANDMOTHER'S FATHER

BIRTHPLACE DATE

GRANDMOTHER'S MOTHER

BIRTHPLACE DATE

Births

NAME DATE

BORN TO

NAME DATE

BORN TO

NAME DATE

BORN TO

NAME DATE

BORN TO

NAME DATE

BORN TO

NAME DATE

BORN TO

NAME DATE

BORN TO

NAME DATE

BORN TO

NAME DATE

BORN TO

Deaths

NAME

DATE

NAME

DATE

NAME

DATE

NAME

DATE

NAME

DATE

NAME

DATE

NAME

DATE

NAME

DATE

NAME

DATE

Special Events

EVENT

PLACE DATE

EVENT

PLACE DATE

EVENT

PLACE DATE

EVENT

PLACE DATE

EVENT

PLACE DATE

EVENT

PLACE DATE

THE HOLY BIBLE

Updated New American Standard Bible

THE HOLY BIBLE

Updated New American Standard Bible

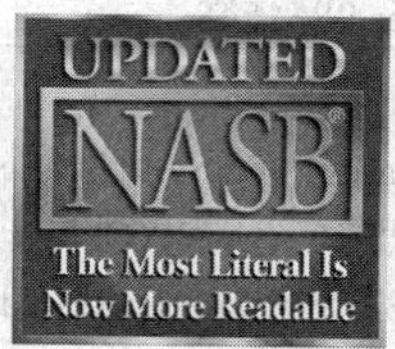

UPDATED
NASB
The Most Literal Is
Now More Readable

Containing The Old Testament and The New Testament

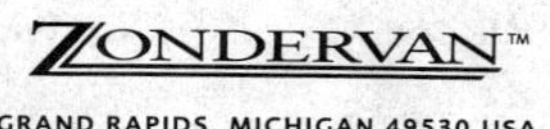

GRAND RAPIDS, MICHIGAN 49530 USA

ZONDERVAN™

Classic Reference Bible, New American Standard Bible – Updated Edition

Published by Zondervan
Grand Rapids, Michigan 49530, U.S.A.

www.zondervan.com

Library of Congress Catalog Card Number 9861548

Printed in the United States of America

05 06 /❖ DC/ 10 9 8 7 6 5

Contents

THE BOOKS OF THE OLD TESTAMENT

THE BOOKS OF THE NEW TESTAMENT

Maps and Charts

Book Abbreviations

Genesis	Gen	Nahum	Nah
Exodus	Ex	Habakkuk	Hab
Leviticus	Lev	Zephaniah	Zeph
Numbers	Num	Haggai	Hag
Deuteronomy	Deut	Zechariah	Zech
Joshua	Josh	Malachi	Mal
Judges	Judg	Matthew	Matt
Ruth	Ruth	Mark	Mark
1 Samuel	1 Sam	Luke	Luke
2 Samuel	2 Sam	John	John
1 Kings	1 Kin	Acts	Acts
2 Kings	2 Kin	Romans	Rom
1 Chronicles	1 Chr	1 Corinthians	1 Cor
2 Chronicles	2 Chr	2 Corinthians	2 Cor
Ezra	Ezra	Galatians	Gal
Nehemiah	Neh	Ephesians	Eph
Esther	Esth	Philippians	Phil
Job	Job	Colossians	Col
Psalms	Ps	1 Thessalonians	1 Thess
Proverbs	Prov	2 Thessalonians	2 Thess
Ecclesiastes	Eccl	1 Timothy	1 Tim
Song of Solomon	Song	2 Timothy	2 Tim
Isaiah	Is	Titus	Titus
Jeremiah	Jer	Philemon	Philem
Lamentations	Lam	Hebrews	Heb
Ezekiel	Ezek	James	James
Daniel	Dan	1 Peter	1 Pet
Hosea	Hos	2 Peter	2 Pet
Joel	Joel	1 John	1 John
Amos	Amos	2 John	2 John
Obadiah	Obad	3 John	3 John
Jonah	Jon	Jude	Jude
Micah	Mic	Revelation	Rev

Foreword

Scriptural Promise

"The grass withers, the flower fades, but the word of our God stands forever."

Isaiah 40:8

The New American Standard Bible has been produced with the conviction that the words of Scripture as originally penned in the Hebrew, Aramaic, and Greek were inspired by God. Since they are the eternal Word of God, the Holy Scriptures speak with fresh power to each generation, to give wisdom that leads to salvation, that men may serve Christ to the glory of God.

The Fourfold Aim of The Lockman Foundation

1. These publications shall be true to the original Hebrew, Aramaic, and Greek.
2. They shall be grammatically correct.
3. They shall be understandable.
4. They shall give the Lord Jesus Christ His proper place, the place which the Word gives Him; therefore, no work will ever be personalized.

Preface

TO THE

NEW AMERICAN STANDARD BIBLE

In the history of English Bible translations, the King James Version is the most prestigious. This time-honored version of 1611, itself a revision of the Bishops' Bible of 1568, became the basis for the English Revised Version appearing in 1881 (New Testament) and 1885 (Old Testament). The American counterpart of this last work was published in 1901 as the American Standard Version. The ASV, a product of both British and American scholarship, has been highly regarded for its scholarship and accuracy. Recognizing the values of the American Standard Version, The Lockman Foundation felt an urgency to preserve these and other lasting values of the ASV by incorporating recent discoveries of Hebrew and Greek textual sources and by rendering it into more current English. Therefore, in 1959 a new translation project was launched, based on the time-honored principles of translation of the ASV and KJV. The result is the New American Standard Bible.

Translation work for the NASB was begun in 1959. In the preparation of this work numerous other translations have been consulted along with the linguistic tools and literature of biblical scholarship. Decisions about English renderings were made by consensus of a team composed of educators and pastors. Subsequently, review and evaluation by other Hebrew and Greek scholars outside the Editorial Board were sought and carefully considered.

The Editorial Board has continued to function since publication of the complete Bible in 1971. This edition of the NASB represents revisions and refinements recommended over the last several years as well as thorough research based on modern English usage.

Principles of Translation

MODERN ENGLISH USAGE: The attempt has been made to render the grammar and terminology in contemporary English. When it was felt that the word-for-word literalness was unacceptable to the modern reader, a change was made in the direction of a more current English idiom. In the instances where this has been done, the more literal rendering has been indicated in the notes. There are a few exceptions to this procedure. In particular, frequently "And" is not translated at the beginning of sentences because of differences in style between ancient and modern writing. Punctuation is a relatively modern invention, and ancient writers often linked most of their sentences with "and" or other connectives. Also, the Hebrew idiom "answered and said" is sometimes reduced to "answered" or "said" as demanded by the context. For current English the idiom "it came about that" has not been translated in the New Testament except when a major transition is needed.

ALTERNATIVE READINGS: In addition to the more literal renderings, notations have been made to include alternate translations, reading of variant manuscripts and explanatory equivalents of the text. Only such notations have been used as have been felt justified in assisting the reader's comprehension of the terms used by the original author.

HEBREW TEXT: In the present translation the latest edition of Rudolf Kittel's *BIBLIA HEBRAICA* has been employed together with the most recent light from lexicography, cognate languages, and the Dead Sea Scrolls.

HEBREW TENSES: Consecution of tenses in Hebrew remains a puzzling factor in translation. The translators have been guided by the requirements of a literal translation, the sequence of tenses, and the immediate and broad contexts.

THE PROPER NAME OF GOD IN THE OLD TESTAMENT: In the Scriptures, the name of God is most significant and understandably so. It is inconceivable to think of spiritual matters without a proper designation for the Supreme Deity. Thus the most common name for the Deity is God, a translation of the original *Elohim.* One of the titles for God is Lord, a translation of *Adonai.* There is yet another name which is particularly assigned to God as His special or proper name, that is, the four letters YHWH (Exodus 3:14 and Isaiah 42:8). This name has not been pronounced by the Jews because of reverence for the great sacredness of the divine name. Therefore, it has been consistently translated LORD. The only exception to this translation of YHWH is when it occurs in immediate proximity to the word Lord, that is, *Adonai.* In that case it is regularly translated GOD in order to avoid confusion.

It is known that for many years YHWH has been transliterated as Yahweh, however no complete certainty attaches to this pronunciation.

GREEK TEXT: Consideration was given to the latest available manuscripts with a view to determining the best Greek text. In most instances the 26th edition of Eberhard Nestle's *NOVUM TESTAMENTUM GRAECE* was followed.

GREEK TENSES: A careful distinction has been made in the treatment of the Greek aorist tense (usually translated as the English past, "He did") and the Greek imperfect tense (normally rendered either as English past progressive, "He was doing"; or, if inceptive, as "He began to do" or "He started to do"; or else if customary past, as "He used to do"). "Began" is italicized if it renders an imperfect tense, in order to distinguish it from the Greek verb for "begin." In some contexts the difference between the Greek imperfect and the English past is conveyed better by the choice of vocabulary or by other words in the context, and in such cases the Greek imperfect may be rendered as a simple past tense (e.g. "had an illness for many years" would be preferable to "was having an illness for many years" and would be understood in the same way).

On the other hand, not all aorists have been rendered as English pasts ("He did"), for some of them are clearly to be rendered as English perfects ("He has done"), or even as past perfects ("He had done"), judging from the context in which they occur. Such aorists have been rendered as perfects or past perfects in this translation.

As for the distinction between aorist and present imperatives, the translators have usually rendered these imperatives in the customary manner, rather than attempting any such fine distinction as "Begin to do!" (for the aorist imperative), or, "Continually do!" (for the present imperative).

As for sequence of tenses, the translators took care to follow English rules rather than Greek in translating Greek presents, imperfects and aorists. Thus, where English says, "We knew that he was doing," Greek puts it, "We knew that he does"; similarly, "We knew that he had done" is the Greek, "We knew that he did." Likewise, the English, "When he had come, they met him," is represented in Greek by, "When he came, they met him." In all cases a consistent transfer has been made from the Greek tense in the subordinate clause to the appropriate tense in English.

In the rendering of negative questions introduced by the particle *mē* (which always expects the answer "No") the wording has been altered from a mere, "Will he not do this?" to a more accurate, "He will not do this, will he?"

THE LOCKMAN FOUNDATION

Explanation of General Format

NOTES AND CROSS REFERENCES are placed in a column adjoining the text on the page and listed under verse numbers to which they refer. Superior numbers refer to literal renderings, alternate translations, or explanations. Superior letters refer to cross references. Cross references in italics are parallel passages.

PARAGRAPHS are designated by a paragraph symbol and bold face verse numbers or letters.

QUOTATION MARKS are used in the text in accordance with modern English usage.

"THOU," "THEE" AND "THY" are not used in this edition and have been rendered as "You" and "Your."

PERSONAL PRONOUNS are capitalized when pertaining to Deity.

ITALICS are used in the text to indicate words which are not found in the original Hebrew, Aramaic, or Greek but implied by it. Italics are used in the marginal notes to signify alternate readings for the text. Roman text in the marginal alternate readings is the same as italics in the Bible text.

SMALL CAPS in the New Testament are used in the text to indicate Old Testament quotations or obvious references to Old Testament texts. Variations of Old Testament wording are found in New Testament citations depending on whether the New Testament writer translated from a Hebrew text, used existing Greek or Aramaic translations, or paraphrased the material. It should be noted that modern rules for the indication of direct quotation were not used in biblical times; thus, the ancient writer would use exact quotations or references to quotation without specific indication of such.

ASTERISKS are used to mark verbs that are historical presents in the Greek which have been translated with an English past tense in order to conform to modern usage. The translators recognized that in some contexts the present tense seems more unexpected and unjustified to the English reader than a past tense would have been. But Greek authors frequently used the present tense for the sake of heightened vividness, thereby transporting their readers in imagination to the actual scene at the time of occurrence. However, the translators felt that it would be wise to change these historical presents to English past tenses.

Abbreviations and Special Markings

Aram = Aramaic

DSS = Dead Sea Scrolls

Gr = Greek translation of O.T. (Septuagint or LXX) or Greek text of N.T.

Heb = Hebrew text, usually Masoretic

Lat = Latin

M.T. = Masoretic text

Syr = Syriac

Lit = A literal translation

Or = An alternate translation justified by the Hebrew, Aramaic, or Greek

[ ] = In text, brackets indicate words probably not in the original writings

[ ] = In margin, brackets indicate references to a name, place or thing similar to, but not identical with that in the text

cf = compare

f, ff = following verse or verses

mg = Refers to a marginal reading on another verse

ms, mss = manuscript, manuscripts

v, vv = verse, verses

OLD TESTAMENT

Genesis

Title and Background

The first phrase in the Hebrew text of Genesis 1:1 means "In the beginning." The book of Genesis is about many beginnings—the beginning of the universe, the beginning of man and woman, the beginning of human sin, and the beginning of God's promises and plans for salvation.

Author and Date of Writing

Jews and Christians alike hold that Moses was the author/compiler of Genesis, the first of the five books of the Old Testament known as the Pentateuch (meaning "five-volumed book").

The historical period during which Moses lived is most likely that referred to in 1 Kings 6:1, which states that "the fourth year of Solomon's reign over Israel" was the same as "the four hundred and eightieth year after the sons of Israel came out of the land of Egypt." Since the former was about 966 B.C., the latter—and thus the date of the exodus—was about 1446 B.C. The forty-year period of Israel's wanderings in the wilderness, which lasted from about 1446 to about 1406 B.C., would have been the most likely time for Moses to write Genesis.

Theme and Message

The message of Genesis is rich and complex, but it is mainly a book of relationships—between God and nature, God and man, and man and man. It stresses the fact that the one true God is sovereign over all that exists, whether good or evil. It introduces us to the way in which God initiates and enters into covenants with His chosen people, pledging His love and faithfulness to them.

Outline

- I. Primeval History: Four Great Events (1:1—11:32)
  - A. The Creation of the Universe, Adam and Eve (1:1—2:25)
  - B. Man's Fall and the Results of Sin (3:1—5:32)
  - C. The Flood (6:1—9:29)
  - D. The Scattering of the Nations (10:1—11:32)
- II. Patriarchal History: Four Great Characters (12:1—50:26)
  - A. Abraham (12:1—20:18)
  - B. Isaac (21:1—26:35)
  - C. Jacob (27:1—37:1)
  - D. Joseph (37:2—50:26)

The Creation

1 [a]In the beginning [b]God [c]created
the heavens and the earth.
2 The earth was [1a]formless and
void, and [b]darkness was over the [2]sur-
face of the deep, and [c]the Spirit of God
[d]was [3]moving over the [2]surface of the
waters.
3 Then [a]God said, "Let there be
light"; and there was light.
4 God saw that the light was [a]good;
and God [b]separated the light from the
darkness.
5 [a]God called the light day, and the
darkness He called night. And [b]there
was evening and there was morning, one
day.
6 ¶ Then God said, "Let there be [1]an
[a]expanse in the midst of the waters, and
let it separate the waters from the waters."
7 God made the [1]expanse, and separated [a]the waters which were below the
[1]expanse from the waters [b]which were
above the [1]expanse; and it was so.
8 God called the [1]expanse heaven.
And there was evening and there was
morning, a second day.
9 ¶ Then God said, "[a]Let the waters
below the heavens be gathered into one
place, and let [b]the dry land appear"; and
it was so.
10 God called the dry land earth, and

1:1 [a]Ps 102:25; Is 40:21; John 1:1; Heb 1:10 [b]Ps 89:11; Acts 17:24; Rom 1:20; Heb 11:3 [c]Job 38:4; Is 42:5; Rev 4:11
2 [1]Or *a waste and emptiness* [2]Lit *face of* [3]Or *hovering* [a]Jer 4:23 [b]Job 38:9 [c]Ps 104:30; Is 40:13 [d]Deut 32:11; Is 31:5
3 [a]Ps 33:6; 2 Cor 4:6
4 [a]Ps 145:9 [b]Is 45:7
5 [a]Ps 74:16 [b]Ps 65:8
6 [1]Or *a firmament* [a]Is 40:22; Jer 10:12; 2 Pet 3:5
7 [1]Or *firmament* [a]Job 38:8-11 [b]Ps 148:4
8 [1]Or *firmament* **9** [a]Ps 104:6-9; Jer 5:22; 2 Pet 3:5 [b]Ps 24:1

the [a]gathering of the waters He called seas; and God saw that it was good.

11 Then God said, "Let the earth sprout [1a]vegetation: [2]plants yielding seed, *and* fruit trees on the earth bearing fruit after [3]their kind [4]with seed in them"; and it was so.

12 The earth brought forth [1]vegetation, [2]plants yielding seed after [3]their kind, and trees bearing fruit [4]with seed in them, after [3]their kind; and God saw that it was good.

13 There was evening and there was morning, a third day.

14 ¶ Then God said, "Let there be [1a]lights in the [2b]expanse of the heavens to separate the day from the night, and let them be for [c]signs and for [d]seasons and for days and years;

15 and let them be for [1]lights in the [2]expanse of the heavens to give light on the earth"; and it was so.

16 God made the two [1]great lights, the [a]greater [2]light [3]to govern the day, and the lesser [2]light [3]to govern the night; *He made* [b]the stars also.

17 [a]God placed them in the [1]expanse of the heavens to give light on the earth,

18 and [1]to [a]govern the day and the night, and to separate the light from the darkness; and God saw that it was good.

19 There was evening and there was morning, a fourth day.

20 ¶ Then God said, "Let the waters [1]teem with swarms of living creatures, and let birds fly above the earth [2]in the open [3]expanse of the heavens."

21 God created [a]the great sea monsters and every living creature that moves, with which the waters swarmed after their kind, and every winged bird after its kind; and God saw that it was good.

22 God blessed them, saying, "Be fruitful and multiply, and fill the waters in the seas, and let birds multiply on the earth."

23 There was evening and there was morning, a fifth day.

24 ¶ [a]Then God said, "Let the earth bring forth living creatures after [1]their kind: cattle and creeping things and beasts of the earth after [1]their kind"; and it was so.

25 God made the [a]beasts of the earth after [1]their kind, and the cattle after [1]their kind, and everything that creeps on the ground after its kind; and God saw that it was good.

26 ¶ Then God said, "Let [a]Us make [b]man in Our image, according to Our likeness; and let them [c]rule over the fish of the sea and over the birds of the [1]sky and over the cattle and over all the earth, and over every creeping thing that creeps on the earth."

27 God created man [a]in His own image, in the image of God He created him; [b]male and female He created them.

28 God blessed them; and God said to them, "[a]Be fruitful and multiply, and fill the earth, and subdue it; and rule over the fish of the sea and over the birds of the [1]sky and over every living thing that [2]moves on the earth."

29 Then God said, "Behold, [a]I have given you every plant yielding seed that is on the [1]surface of all the earth, and every tree [2]which has fruit yielding seed; it shall be food for you;

30 and [a]to every beast of the earth and to every bird of the [1]sky and to every thing that [2]moves on the earth [3]which has life, *I have given* every green plant for food"; and it was so.

31 God saw all that He had made, and behold, it was very [a]good. And there was evening and there was morning, the sixth day.

The Creation of Man and Woman

2 Thus the heavens and the earth were completed, and all [a]their hosts.

2 By [a]the seventh day God completed His work which He had done, and [b]He rested on the seventh day from all His work which He had done.

3 Then God blessed the seventh day and sanctified it, because in it He rested from all His work which God had created [1]and made.

4 ¶ [1a]This is the account of the heavens and the earth when they were created, in [b]the day that the LORD God made earth and heaven.

5 [a]Now no shrub of the field was yet in the earth, and no plant of the field had yet sprouted, [b]for the LORD God had not sent rain upon the earth, and there was no man to [1]cultivate the ground.

6 But a [1]mist used to rise from the earth and water the whole [2]surface of the ground.

7 Then the LORD God formed man of [a]dust from the ground, and breathed into his nostrils the breath of life; and [b]man became a living [1]being.

8 The LORD God planted a [a]garden toward the east, in Eden; and there He placed the man whom He had formed.

9 Out of the ground the LORD God caused to grow [a]every tree that is pleasing to the sight and good for food; [b]the tree of life also in the midst of the garden, and the tree of the knowledge of good and evil.

10 ¶ Now a [a]river [1]flowed out of

10 [a]Ps 33:7
11 [1]Or *grass* [2]Or *herbs* [3]Lit *its* [4]Lit *in which is its seed* [a]Ps 65:9-13; Heb 6:7
12 [1]Or *grass* [2]Or *herbs* [3]Lit *its* [4]Lit *in which is its seed*
14 [1]Or *luminaries, light-bearers* [2]Or *firmament* [a]Ps 74:16 [b]Ps 19:1 [c]Jer 10:2 [d]Ps 104:19
15 [1]Or *luminaries, light-bearers* [2]Or *firmament*
16 [1]Or *luminaries, light-bearers* [2]Or *luminary, light-bearer* [3]Lit *for the dominion of* [a]Ps 136:8 [b]Job 38:7; Ps 8:3; Is 40:26
17 [1]Or *firmament* [a]Jer 33:20
18 [1]Lit *for the dominion of* [a]Jer 31:35
20 [1]Or *swarm* [2]Lit *on the face of* [3]Or *firmament*
21 [a]Ps 104:25-28
24 [1]Lit *its* [a]Gen 2:19
25 [1]Lit *its* [a]Gen 7:21; Jer 27:5
26 [1]Lit *heavens* [a]Gen 3:22 [b]Gen 5:1; 1 Cor 11:7; Eph 4:24; James 3:9 [c]Ps 8:6-8
27 [a]Gen 5:1f; 1 Cor 11:7; Eph 4:24; Col 3:10 [b]Matt 19:4; Mark 10:6
28 [1]Lit *heavens* [2]Or *creeps* [a]Gen 9:1; Lev 26:9; Ps 127:3
29 [1]Lit *face of* [2]Lit *in which is the fruit of a tree yielding seed* [a]Ps 104:14
30 [1]Lit *heavens* [2]Or *creeps* [3]Lit *in which is a living soul* [a]Ps 145:15
31 [a]Ps 104:24; 1 Tim 4:4
2:1 [a]Deut 4:19
2 [a]Ex 20:8-11 [b]Heb 4:4
3 [1]Lit *to make*
4 [1]Lit *These are the generations* [a]Job 38:4-11 [b]Gen 1:3-31
5 [1]Lit *work, serve* [a]Gen 1:11 [b]Ps 65:9; Jer 10:12
6 [1]Or *flow* [2]Lit *face of*
7 [1]Lit *soul* [a]Gen 3:19 [b]1 Cor 15:45
8 [a]Gen 13:10; Is 51:3; Ezek 28:13
9 [a]Ezek 47:12 [b]Gen 3:22; Rev 2:7
10 [1]Lit *was going out* [a]Ps 46:4

Eden to water the garden; and from there
it divided and became four [2]rivers.
11 The name of the first is Pishon; it
[1]flows around the whole land of [a]Havi-
lah, where there is gold.
12 The gold of that land is good; the
bdellium and the onyx stone are there.
13 The name of the second river is Gihon; it [1]flows around the whole land of
Cush.
14 The name of the third river is [1a]Ti-
gris; it [2]flows east of Assyria. And the
fourth river is the [3b]Euphrates.
15 ¶ Then the LORD God took the man
and put him into the garden of Eden to
cultivate it and keep it.
16 The LORD God [a]commanded the
man, saying, "From any tree of the garden you may eat freely;
17 but from the tree of the knowledge
of good and evil you shall not [1]eat, for in
the day that you eat from it [a]you will
surely die."
18 ¶ Then the LORD God said, "It is not
good for the man to be alone; [a]I will
make him a helper [1]suitable for him."
19 [a]Out of the ground the LORD God
formed every beast of the field and every
bird of the [1]sky, and [b]brought *them* to
the man to see what he would call them;
and whatever the man called a living
creature, that was its name.
20 The man gave names to all the cattle, and to the birds of the [1]sky, and to
every beast of the field, but for [2]Adam
there was not found [a]a helper [3]suitable
for him.
21 So the LORD God caused a [a]deep
sleep to fall upon the man, and he slept;
then He took one of his ribs and closed up
the flesh at that place.
22 The LORD God [1]fashioned into a
woman [a]the rib which He had taken
from the man, and brought her to the
man.
23 The man said,

"[a]This is now bone of my bones,
And flesh of my flesh;
[1]She shall be called [2]Woman,
Because [1]she was taken out
of [3]Man."

24 [a]For this reason a man shall leave
his father and his mother, and be joined
to his wife; and they shall become one
flesh.
25 [a]And the man and his wife were
both naked and were not ashamed.

The Fall of Man

3 Now [a]the serpent was more crafty
than any beast of the field which the
LORD God had made. And he said to the
woman, "Indeed, has God said, 'You shall
not eat from [1]any tree of the garden'?"

10 [2]Lit *heads*
11 [1]Lit *surrounds* [a]Gen 25:18
13 [1]Lit *is the one surrounding*
14 [1]Heb *Hiddekel* [2]Lit *is the one going* [3]Heb *Perath* [a]Dan 10:4 [b]Gen 15:18
16 [a]Gen 3:2,3
17 [1]Lit *eat from it* [a]Deut 30:15, 19,20; Rom 6:23; 1 Tim 5:6; James 1:15
18 [1]Lit *corresponding to* [a]1 Cor 11:9
19 [1]Lit *heavens* [a]Gen 1:24 [b]Gen 1:26
20 [1]Lit *heavens* [2]Or *man* [3]Lit *corresponding to* [a]Gen 2:18
21 [a]Gen 15:12
22 [1]Lit *built* [a]1 Cor 11:8,9
23 [1]Lit *This one* [2]Heb *Ishshah* [3]Heb *Ish* [a]Gen 29:14; Eph 5:28, 29
24 [a]Matt 19:5; Mark 10:7,8; 1 Cor 6:16; Eph 5:31
25 [a]Gen 3:7,10, 11
3:1 [1]Or *every* [a]2 Cor 11:3; Rev 12:9; 20:2
2 [a]Gen 2:16,17
4 [a]John 8:44; 2 Cor 11:3
5 [a]Is 14:14; Ezek 28:2,12-17
6 [a]Rom 5:12-19; 1 Tim 2:14; James 1:14,15; 1 John 2:16
7 [1]Or *girdles* [a]Is 47:3; Lam 1:8
8 [1]Lit *wind, breeze* [a]Gen 18:33; Lev 26:12; Deut 23:14 [b]Job 31:33; Ps 139:1-12; Hos 10:8; Amos 9:3; Rev 6:15-17
9 [a]Gen 4:9; 18:9
10 [a]Ex 20:18, 19; Deut 5:25
12 [a]Job 31:33; Prov 28:13
13 [a]2 Cor 11:3; 1 Tim 2:14
14 [a]Deut 28:15-20 [b]Is 65:25; Mic 7:17
15 [1]Or *crush* [a]Rev 12:17 [b]Rom 16:20

2 The woman said to the serpent,
"[a]From the fruit of the trees of the garden we may eat;
3 but from the fruit of the tree which
is in the middle of the garden, God has
said, 'You shall not eat from it or touch it,
or you will die.' "
4 [a]The serpent said to the woman,
"You surely will not die!
5 "For God knows that in the day you
eat from it your eyes will be opened, and
[a]you will be like God, knowing good and
evil."
6 [a]When the woman saw that the
tree was good for food, and that it was a
delight to the eyes, and that the tree was
desirable to make *one* wise, she took
from its fruit and ate; and she gave also to
her husband with her, and he ate.
7 Then the eyes of both of them were
opened, and they [a]knew that they were
naked; and they sewed fig leaves together
and made themselves [1]loin coverings.
8 ¶ They heard the sound of [a]the
LORD God walking in the garden in the
[1]cool of the day, [b]and the man and his
wife hid themselves from the presence of
the LORD God among the trees of the garden.
9 Then the LORD God called to the
man, and said to him, "[a]Where are you?"
10 He said, "[a]I heard the sound of You
in the garden, and I was afraid because I
was naked; so I hid myself."
11 And He said, "Who told you that
you were naked? Have you eaten from
the tree of which I commanded you not
to eat?"
12 [a]The man said, "The woman
whom You gave *to be* with me, she gave
me from the tree, and I ate."
13 Then the LORD God said to the
woman, "What is this you have done?"
And the woman said, "[a]The serpent deceived me, and I ate."
14 The LORD God said to the serpent,

"[a]Because you have done this,
Cursed are you more than all
cattle,
And more than every beast of
the field;
On your belly you will go,
And [b]dust you will eat
All the days of your life;
15 And I will put [a]enmity
Between you and the woman,
And between your seed and her
seed;
[b]He shall [1]bruise you on the
head,
And you shall bruise him on the
heel."

16 To the woman He said,

"I will greatly multiply

Your pain [1]in childbirth,
In pain you will [a]bring forth
children;
Yet your desire will be for your
husband,
And [b]he will rule over you."
17 Then to Adam He said, "Because
you have listened to the voice of your
wife, and have eaten from the tree about
which I commanded you, saying, 'You
shall not eat from it';
[a]Cursed is the ground because
of you;
[b]In [1]toil you will eat of it
All the days of your life.
18 "Both thorns and thistles it shall
grow for you;
And you will eat the [1]plants of
the field;
19 By the sweat of your face
You will eat bread,
Till you [a]return to the ground,
Because [b]from it you were
taken;
For you are dust,
And to dust you shall return."
20 ¶ Now the man called his wife's
name [1a]Eve, because she was the mother of all *the* living.
21 The LORD God made garments of
skin for Adam and his wife, and clothed
them.
22 ¶ Then the LORD God said, "Behold, the man has become like one of
[a]Us, knowing good and evil; and now, he
might stretch out his hand, and take also
from [b]the tree of life, and eat, and live
forever"—
23 therefore the LORD God sent him
out from the garden of Eden, to cultivate
the ground from which he was taken.
24 So [a]He drove the man out; and at
the [b]east of the garden of Eden He stationed the [c]cherubim and the flaming
sword which turned every direction to
guard the way to [d]the tree of life.

Cain and Abel

4 Now the man [1]had relations with
his wife Eve, and she conceived and
gave birth to [2]Cain, and she said, "I have
gotten a [3]manchild with *the help of* the
LORD."
2 Again, she gave birth to his brother
Abel. And [a]Abel was [b]a keeper of flocks,
but Cain was a tiller of the ground.
3 So it came about [1]in the course of
time that Cain brought an offering to the
LORD of the fruit of the ground.
4 [a]Abel, on his part also brought of
the firstlings of his flock and of their fat
portions. And [b]the LORD had regard for
Abel and for his offering;
5 but [a]for Cain and for his offering
He had no regard. So [b]Cain became very
angry and his countenance fell.
6 Then the LORD said to Cain, "[a]Why
are you angry? And why has your countenance fallen?
7 "[a]If you do well, [1]will not *your
countenance* be lifted up? [b]And if you do
not do well, sin is crouching at the door;
and its desire is for you, [c]but you must
master it."
8 Cain [1]told Abel his brother. And it
came about when they were in the field,
that Cain rose up against Abel his brother
and [a]killed him.
9 ¶ Then the LORD said to Cain,
"[a]Where is Abel your brother?" And he
said, "I do not know. Am I my brother's
keeper?"
10 He said, "What have you done?
[a]The voice of your brother's blood is crying to Me from the ground.
11 "Now [a]you are cursed from the
ground, which has opened its mouth to
receive your brother's blood from your
hand.
12 "[a]When you cultivate the ground, it
will no longer yield its strength to you;
[b]you will be a vagrant and a wanderer on
the earth."
13 Cain said to the LORD, "My punishment is too great to bear!
14 "Behold, You have [a]driven me this
day from the face of the ground; and from
Your face I will be hidden, and [b]I will be
a vagrant and a wanderer on the earth,
and [c]whoever finds me will kill me."
15 So the LORD said to him, "Therefore
whoever kills Cain, vengeance will be
taken on him [a]sevenfold." And the LORD
[1b]appointed a sign for Cain, so that no
one finding him would slay him.
16 ¶ Then Cain went out from the
presence [a]of the LORD, and [1]settled in
the land of [2]Nod, east of Eden.
17 ¶ Cain [1]had relations with his wife
and she conceived, and gave birth to
Enoch; and he built a city, and called the
name of the city Enoch, after the name of
his son.
18 Now to Enoch was born Irad, and
Irad [1]became the father of Mehujael, and
Mehujael [1]became the father of Methushael, and Methushael [1]became the father of Lamech.
19 Lamech took to himself [a]two
wives: the name of the one was Adah,
and the name of the other, Zillah.
20 Adah gave birth to Jabal; he was the
father of those who dwell in tents and
have livestock.
21 His brother's name was Jubal; he
was the father of all those who play the
lyre and pipe.
22 As for Zillah, she also gave birth to

16 [1]Lit *and your pregnancy, conception* [a]John 16:21; 1 Tim 2:15 [b]1 Cor 14:34
17 [1]Or *sorrow* [a]Gen 5:29; Rom 8:20-22; Heb 6:8 [b]Job 5:7; 14:1; Eccl 2:23
18 [1]Lit *plant*
19 [a]Ps 90:3; 104:29; Eccl 12:7 [b]Gen 2:7
20 [1]I.e. living; or life [a]2 Cor 11:3; 1 Tim 2:13
22 [a]Gen 1:26 [b]Gen 2:9; Rev 22:14
24 [a]Ezek 31:11 [b]Gen 2:8 [c]Ex 25:18-22; Ps 104:4; Ezek 10:1-20; Heb 1:7 [d]Gen 2:9
4:1 [1]Lit *knew* [2]I.e. gotten one [3]Or *man, the* LORD
2 [a]Luke 11:50, 51 [b]Gen 46:32; 47:3
3 [1]Lit *at the end of days*
4 [a]Heb 11:4 [b]1 Sam 15:22
5 [a]1 Sam 16:7 [b]Is 3:9; Jude 11
6 [a]Jon 4:4
7 [1]Or *surely you will be accepted* [a]Jer 3:12; Mic 7:18 [b]Num 32:23 [c]Job 11:14,15; Rom 6:12,16
8 [1]Lit *said to* [a]Matt 23:35; Luke 11:51; 1 John 3:12-15; Jude 11
9 [a]Gen 3:9
10 [a]Num 35:33; Deut 21:1-9; Heb 12:24; Rev 6:9,10
11 [a]Gen 3:14; Deut 28:15-20; Gal 3:10
12 [a]Deut 28:15-24; Joel 1:10-20 [b]Lev 26:17,36
14 [a]Gen 3:24; Jer 52:3 [b]Deut 28:64-67 [c]Num 35:19
15 [1]Or *set a mark on* [a]Gen 4:24 [b]Ezek 9:4,6
16 [1]Lit *dwelt* [2]I.e. wandering [a]2 Kin 24:20; Jer 23:39; 52:3
17 [1]Lit *knew*
18 [1]Lit *begot*
19 [a]Gen 2:24

Tubal-cain, the forger of all implements of bronze and iron; and the sister of Tubal-cain was Naamah.

23 ¶ Lamech said to his wives,
“Adah and Zillah,
Listen to my voice,
You wives of Lamech,
Give heed to my speech,
[a]For I [1]have killed a man for
wounding me;
And a boy for striking me;
24 If Cain is avenged [a]sevenfold,
Then Lamech seventy-sevenfold.”

25 ¶ [a]Adam [1]had relations with his wife again; and she gave birth to a son, and named him [2]Seth, for, *she said,* “God [3]has appointed me another [4]offspring in place of Abel, [b]for Cain killed him.”

26 To Seth, to him also [a]a son was born; and he called his name Enosh. Then *men* began [b]to call [1]upon the name of the LORD.

Descendants of Adam

5 This is the book of the generations of Adam. In the day when God created man, He made him [a]in the likeness of God.

2 He created them [a]male and female, and He [b]blessed them and named them [1]Man in the day when they were created.

3 ¶ When Adam had lived one hundred and thirty years, he [1]became the father of *a son* in his own likeness, according to his image, and named him Seth.

4 Then the days of Adam after he became the father of Seth were eight hundred years, and he had *other* sons and daughters.

5 So all the days that Adam lived were nine hundred and thirty years, and he died.

6 ¶ Seth lived one hundred and five years, and became the father of Enosh.

7 Then Seth lived eight hundred and seven years after he became the father of Enosh, and he had *other* sons and daughters.

8 So all the days of Seth were nine hundred and twelve years, and he died.

9 ¶ Enosh lived ninety years, and became the father of Kenan.

10 Then Enosh lived eight hundred and fifteen years after he became the father of Kenan, and he had *other* sons and daughters.

11 So all the days of Enosh were nine hundred and five years, and he died.

12 ¶ Kenan lived seventy years, and became the father of Mahalalel.

13 Then Kenan lived eight hundred and forty years after he became the father of Mahalalel, and he had *other* sons and daughters.

14 So all the days of Kenan were nine hundred and ten years, and he died.

15 ¶ Mahalalel lived sixty-five years, and became the father of Jared.

16 Then Mahalalel lived eight hundred and thirty years after he became the father of Jared, and he had *other* sons and daughters.

17 So all the days of Mahalalel were eight hundred and ninety-five years, and he died.

18 ¶ Jared lived one hundred and sixty-two years, and became the father of Enoch.

19 Then Jared lived eight hundred years after he became the father of Enoch, and he had *other* sons and daughters.

20 So all the days of Jared were nine hundred and sixty-two years, and he died.

21 ¶ Enoch lived sixty-five years, and became the father of Methuselah.

22 Then Enoch [a]walked with God three hundred years after he became the father of Methuselah, and he had *other* sons and daughters.

23 So all the days of Enoch were three hundred and sixty-five years.

24 [a]Enoch walked with God; and he was not, for God [b]took him.

25 ¶ Methuselah lived one hundred and eighty-seven years, and became the father of Lamech.

26 Then Methuselah lived seven hundred and eighty-two years after he became the father of Lamech, and he had *other* sons and daughters.

27 So all the days of Methuselah were nine hundred and sixty-nine years, and he died.

28 ¶ Lamech lived one hundred and eighty-two years, and became the father of a son.

29 Now he called his name Noah, saying, “This one will [1]give us rest from our work and from the toil of our hands *arising* from [a]the ground which the LORD has cursed.”

30 Then Lamech lived five hundred and ninety-five years after he became the father of Noah, and he had *other* sons and daughters.

31 So all the days of Lamech were seven hundred and seventy-seven years, and he died.

32 ¶ Noah was [a]five hundred years old, and Noah became the father of Shem, Ham, and Japheth.

---

23 [1]Or *kill* [a]Ex 20:13; Lev 19:18; Deut 32:35; Ps 94:1
24 [a]Gen 4:15
25 [1]Lit *knew* [2]Heb *Sheth* [3]Heb *shath* [4]Lit *seed* [a]Gen 5:3 [b]Gen 4:8
26 [1]Or *by* [a]Luke 3:38 [b]Gen 12:8; 26:25; 1 Kin 18:24; Ps 116:17; Joel 2:32; Zeph 3:9; 1 Cor 1:2
5:1 [a]Gen 1:26, 27; Eph 4:24; Col 3:10
2 [1]Lit *Adam* [a]Matt 19:4; Mark 10:6 [b]Gen 1:28
3 [1]Lit *begot,* and so throughout the ch
22 [a]Gen 6:9; 17:1; 24:40; 48:15; Mic 6:8; Mal 2:6; 1 Thess 2:12
24 [a]2 Kin 2:11; Jude 14 [b]2 Kin 2:10; Ps 49:15; 73:24; Heb 11:5
29 [1]Lit *comfort us in* [a]Gen 3:17-19; 4:11
32 [a]Gen 7:6

The Corruption of Mankind

6 Now it came about, when men began
to multiply on the face of the land,
and daughters were born to them,
2 that the sons of God saw that the
daughters of men were [1]beautiful; and
they took wives for themselves, whomever they chose.
3 Then the LORD said, "[a]My Spirit
shall not [1]strive with man forever,
[2][b]because he also is flesh; [3]neverthe-
less his days shall be one hundred and
twenty years."
4 The [a]Nephilim were on the earth
in those days, and also afterward, when
the sons of God came in to the daughters
of men, and they bore *children* to them.
Those were the mighty men who *were* of
old, men of renown.
5 ¶ Then the LORD saw that the wickedness of man was great on the earth, and
that [a]every intent of the thoughts of his
heart was only evil continually.
6 [a]The LORD was sorry that He had
made man on the earth, and He was
[b]grieved [1]in His heart.
7 The LORD said, "[a]I will blot out
man whom I have created from the face
of the land, from man to animals to creeping things and to birds of the [1]sky; for [b]I
am sorry that I have made them."
8 But [a]Noah [b]found favor in the
eyes of the LORD.
9 ¶ These are *the records of* the generations of Noah. Noah was a [a]righteous
man, [1][b]blameless in his [2]time; Noah
[c]walked with God.
10 Noah [1]became the father of three
sons: Shem, Ham, and Japheth.
11 ¶ Now the earth was [a]corrupt in
the sight of God, and the earth was
[b]filled with violence.
12 God looked on the earth, and behold, it was corrupt; for [a]all flesh had
corrupted their way upon the earth.
13 ¶ Then God said to Noah, "[a]The
end of all flesh has come before Me; for
the earth is filled with violence because
of them; and behold, I am about to destroy them with the earth.
14 "Make for yourself an ark of gopher
wood; you shall make the ark with rooms,
and shall [1]cover it inside and out with
pitch.
15 "This is how you shall make it: the
length of the ark three hundred [1]cubits,
its breadth fifty [1]cubits, and its height
thirty [1]cubits.
16 "You shall make a [1]window for the
ark, and finish it to a cubit from [2]the top;
and set the door of the ark in the side of
it; you shall make it with lower, second,
and third decks.

6:2 [1]Lit *good*
3 [1]Or *rule in*; some ancient versions read *abide in* [2]Or *in his going astray he is flesh* [3]Or *therefore* [a]Gal 5:16,17; 1 Pet 3:20 [b]Ps 78:39
4 [a]Num 13:33
5 [a]Gen 8:21; Ps 14:1-3; Prov 6:18; Matt 15:19; Rom 1:28-32
6 [1]Lit *to* [a]Gen 6:7; Jer 18:7-10 [b]Is 63:10; Eph 4:30
7 [1]Lit *heavens* [a]Deut 28:63; 29:20 [b]Gen 6:6; Amos 7:3,6
8 [a]Matt 24:37; Luke 17:26; 1 Pet 3:20 [b]Gen 19:19; Ex 33:17; Luke 1:30
9 [1]Lit *complete, perfect*; or *having integrity* [2]Lit *generations* [a]Ps 37:39; 2 Pet 2:5 [b]Gen 17:1; Deut 18:13; Job 1:1 [c]Gen 5:24
10 [1]Lit *begot*
11 [a]Deut 31:29; Judg 2:19 [b]Ezek 8:17
12 [a]Ps 14:1-3
13 [a]Is 34:1-4; Ezek 7:2,3; Amos 8:2; 1 Pet 4:7
14 [1]Or *pitch*
15 [1]I.e. One cubit equals approx 18 in.
16 [1]Or *roof* [2]Lit *above*
17 [a]2 Pet 2:5
18 [a]Gen 9:9-16; 17:7 [b]Gen 7:7
19 [a]Gen 7:2,14, 15
20 [a]Gen 7:3
21 [a]Gen 1:29, 30
22 [a]Gen 7:5; Heb 11:7
7:1 [1]Lit *generation* [a]Gen 6:9
2 [1]Lit *to* [2]Lit *seven seven* [a]Lev 11:1-31; Deut 14:3-20
3 [1]Lit *heavens* [2]Lit *seven seven* [3]Lit *seed*
4 [a]Gen 7:10 [b]Gen 7:12,17 [c]Gen 6:7,13
5 [a]Gen 6:22
6 [1]Lit *was* [a]Gen 5:32
7 [a]Gen 6:18; 7:13; Matt 24:38f; Luke 17:27
8 [a]Gen 6:19,20; 7:2,3
9 [1]Lit *two two*
10 [1]Lit *were* [a]Gen 7:4
11 [a]Gen 7:6 [b]Gen 8:2

17 "Behold, [a]I, even I am bringing the
flood of water upon the earth, to destroy
all flesh in which is the breath of life,
from under heaven; everything that is on
the earth shall perish.
18 "But I will establish [a]My covenant
with you; and [b]you shall enter the ark—
you and your sons and your wife, and
your sons' wives with you.
19 "[a]And of every living thing of all
flesh, you shall bring two of every *kind*
into the ark, to keep *them* alive with you;
they shall be male and female.
20 "[a]Of the birds after their kind, and
of the animals after their kind, of every
creeping thing of the ground after its
kind, two of every *kind* will come to you
to keep *them* alive.
21 "As for you, take for yourself some of
all [a]food which is edible, and gather *it* to
yourself; and it shall be for food for you
and for them."
22 [a]Thus Noah did; according to all
that God had commanded him, so he did.

The Flood

7 Then the LORD said to Noah, "Enter
the ark, you and all your household,
for you *alone* I have seen *to be* [a]righ-
teous before Me in this [1]time.
2 "You shall take [1]with you of every
[a]clean animal [2]by sevens, a male and his
female; and of the animals that are not
clean two, a male and his female;
3 also of the birds of the [1]sky, [2]by
sevens, male and female, to keep [3]off-
spring alive on the face of all the earth.
4 "For after [a]seven more days, I will
send rain on the earth [b]forty days and
forty nights; and I will blot out from the
face of the land [c]every living thing that
I have made."
5 [a]Noah did according to all that the
LORD had commanded him.
6 ¶ Now Noah was [a]six hundred
years old when the flood of water [1]came
upon the earth.
7 Then [a]Noah and his sons and his
wife and his sons' wives with him entered the ark because of the water of the
flood.
8 [a]Of clean animals and animals that
are not clean and birds and everything
that creeps on the ground,
9 there went into the ark to Noah
[1]by twos, male and female, as God had
commanded Noah.
10 It came about after [a]the seven
days, that the water of the flood [1]came
upon the earth.
11 In the [a]six hundredth year of
Noah's life, in the second month, on the
seventeenth day of the month, on the
same day all [b]the fountains of the great

deep burst open, and the [1]floodgates of
the sky were opened.
12 [a]The rain [1]fell upon the earth for
forty days and forty nights.
13 ¶ On the very same day [a]Noah and
Shem and Ham and Japheth, the sons of
Noah, and Noah's wife and the three
wives of his sons with them, entered the
ark,
14 they and every beast after its kind,
and all the cattle after [1]their kind, and
every creeping thing that creeps on the
earth after its kind, and every bird after
its kind, [2]all sorts of birds.
15 So they went into the ark to Noah,
[a]by twos of all flesh in which was the
breath of life.
16 Those that entered, male and female of all flesh, entered as God had commanded him; and the LORD closed *it* behind him.
17 ¶ Then the flood [1]came upon the
earth for [a]forty days, and the water increased and lifted up the ark, so that it
rose above the earth.
18 The water prevailed and increased
greatly upon the earth, and the ark [1]float-
ed on the [2]surface of the water.
19 The water prevailed more and
more upon the earth, so that all the high
mountains [1]everywhere under the heavens were covered.
20 The water prevailed fifteen [1]cubits
higher, [a]and the mountains were covered.
21 [a]All flesh that [1]moved on the
earth perished, birds and cattle and
beasts and every swarming thing that
swarms upon the earth, and all mankind;
22 of all that was on the dry land, all
[a]in whose nostrils was the breath of the
spirit of life, died.
23 Thus He blotted out [1]every living
thing that was upon the face of the land,
from man to animals to creeping things
and to birds of the [2]sky, and they were
blotted out from the earth; and only
[a]Noah was left, together with those that
were with him in the ark.
24 [a]The water prevailed upon the
earth one hundred and fifty days.

The Flood Subsides

8 But [a]God remembered Noah and all
the beasts and all the cattle that were
with him in the ark; and [b]God caused a
wind to pass over the earth, and the water subsided.
2 Also [a]the fountains of the deep and
the [1]floodgates of the sky were closed,
and [b]the rain from the sky was restrained;
3 and the water receded steadily
from the earth, and at the end [a]of one
hundred and fifty days the water decreased.
4 In the seventh month, on the seventeenth day of the month, [a]the ark rested upon the mountains of Ararat.
5 The water decreased steadily until
the tenth month; in the tenth month, on
the first day of the month, the tops of the
mountains became visible.
6 ¶ Then it came about at the end of
forty days, that Noah opened the [a]win-
dow of the ark which he had made;
7 and he sent out a raven, and it
[1]flew here and there until the water was
dried up [2]from the earth.
8 Then he sent out a dove from him,
to see if the water was abated from the
face of the land;
9 but the dove found no resting place
for the sole of her foot, so she returned to
him into the ark, for the water was on the
[1]surface of all the earth. Then he put out
his hand and took her, and brought her
into the ark to himself.
10 So he waited yet another seven
days; and again he sent out the dove from
the ark.
11 The dove came to him toward
[1]evening, and behold, in her [2]beak was
a freshly picked olive leaf. So Noah knew
that the water was abated from the earth.
12 Then he waited yet another seven
days, and sent out [a]the dove; but she did
not return to him again.
13 ¶ Now it came about in the [a]six
hundred and first year, in the first *month,*
on the first of the month, the water was
dried up [1]from the earth. Then Noah
removed the covering of the ark, and
looked, and behold, the [2]surface of the
ground was dried up.
14 In the second month, on the
twenty-seventh day of the month, the
earth was dry.
15 Then God spoke to Noah, saying,
16 "Go out of the ark, you and your wife
and your sons and your sons' wives with
you.
17 "Bring out with you every living
thing of all flesh that is with you, birds
and animals and every creeping thing
that creeps on the earth, that they may
[1a]breed abundantly on the earth, and be
fruitful and multiply on the earth."
18 So Noah went out, and his sons and
his wife and his sons' wives with him.
19 Every beast, every creeping thing,
and every bird, everything that moves on
the earth, went out [1]by their families
from the ark.
20 ¶ Then Noah built [a]an altar to the
LORD, and took of every [b]clean animal
and of every clean bird and offered
[c]burnt offerings on the altar.

11 [1]Or *windows of the heavens*

12 [1]Lit *was* [a]Gen 7:4,17

13 [a]Gen 6:18; 7:7

14 [1]Lit *its* [2]Lit *every bird, every wing*

15 [a]Gen 6:19; 7:9

17 [1]Lit *was* [a]Gen 7:4

18 [1]Lit *went* [2]Lit *face*

19 [1]Lit *which were under all the heavens*

20 [1]I.e. One cubit equals approx 18 in. [a]Gen 8:4

21 [1]Or *crept* [a]Gen 6:7,13,17; 7:4

22 [a]Gen 2:7

23 [1]Lit *all existence* [2]Lit *heavens* [a]Matt 24:38, 39; Luke 17:26, 27; Heb 11:7; 1 Pet 3:20; 2 Pet 2:5

24 [a]Gen 8:3

8:1 [a]Gen 19:29; Ex 2:24; 1 Sam 1:19; Ps 105:42 [b]Ex 14:21; 15:10; Job 12:15; Ps 29:10; Is 44:27; Nah 1:4

2 [1]Or *windows of the heavens* [a]Gen 7:11 [b]Gen 7:4,12

3 [a]Gen 7:24

4 [a]Gen 7:20

6 [a]Gen 6:16

7 [1]Lit *went out, going and returning* [2]Lit *from upon*

9 [1]Lit *face*

11 [1]Lit *the time of evening* [2]Lit *mouth*

12 [a]Jer 48:28

13 [1]Lit *from upon* [2]Lit *face* [a]Gen 7:6

17 [1]Or *swarm* [a]Gen 1:22,28

19 [1]Or *according to their kind*

20 [a]Gen 12:7,8; 13:18; 22:9 [b]Gen 7:2; Lev 11:1-47 [c]Gen 22:2; Ex 10:25

21 The LORD [a]smelled the soothing
aroma; and the LORD said [1]to Himself, "I
will never again [b]curse the ground on
account of man, for [c]the [2]intent of
man's heart is evil from his youth; [d]and
I will never again [3]destroy every living
thing, as I have done.
22 "While the earth remains,
Seedtime and harvest,
And cold and heat,
And [a]summer and winter,
And [b]day and night
Shall not cease."

Covenant of the Rainbow

9 And God blessed Noah and his sons
and said to them, "[a]Be fruitful and
multiply, and fill the earth.
2 "The fear of you and the terror of you
will be on every beast of the earth and on
every bird of the [1]sky; with everything
that creeps on the ground, and all the fish
of the sea, into your hand they are given.
3 "Every moving thing that is alive
shall be food for you; I give all to you, [a]as
I gave the green plant.
4 "Only you shall not eat flesh with its
life, *that is,* [a]its blood.
5 "Surely I will require [1a]your lifeblood; [2b]from every beast I will require
it. And [2]from *every* man, [2]from every
man's brother I will require the life of
man.
6 "[a]Whoever sheds man's blood,
By man his blood shall be shed,
For [b]in the image of God
He made man.
7 "As for you, [a]be fruitful and
multiply;
[1]Populate the earth abundantly
and multiply in it."
8 ¶ Then God spoke to Noah and to
his sons with him, saying,
9 "Now behold, [a]I Myself do establish
My covenant with you, and with your
[1]descendants after you;
10 and with every living creature that
is with you, the birds, the cattle, and every beast of the earth with you; of all that
comes out of the ark, even every beast of
the earth.
11 "I establish My covenant with you;
and all flesh shall [a]never again be cut off
by the water of the flood, [b]neither shall
there again be a flood to destroy the
earth."
12 God said, "This is [a]the sign of the
covenant which I am making between
Me and you and every living creature that
is with you, for [1]all successive generations;
13 I set My [a]bow in the cloud, and it
shall be for a sign of a covenant between
Me and the earth.

21 [1]Lit *to His heart* [2]Or *inclination* [3]Lit *smite* [a]Ex 29:18,25 [b]Gen 3:17; 6:7, 13,17; Is 54:9 [c]Gen 6:5; Ps 51:5; Jer 17:9; Rom 1:21; 3:23; Eph 2:1-3 [d]Gen 9:11,15
22 [a]Ps 74:17 [b]Jer 33:20,25
9:1 [a]Gen 1:28; 9:7
2 [1]Lit *heavens*
3 [a]Gen 1:29
4 [a]Lev 7:26f; 17:10-16; 19:26; Deut 12:16,23; 15:23; 1 Sam 14:34; Acts 15:20,29
5 [1]Lit *your blood of your lives* [2]Lit *from the hand of* [a]Ex 20:13; 21:12 [b]Ex 21:28,29
6 [a]Ex 21:12-14; Lev 24:17; Num 35:33; Matt 26:52 [b]Gen 1:26,27
7 [1]Lit *Swarm in the earth* [a]Gen 9:1
9 [1]Lit *seed* [a]Gen 6:18
11 [a]Gen 8:21 [b]Is 54:9
12 [1]Or *everlasting generations* [a]Gen 9:13,17; 17:11
13 [a]Ezek 1:28
15 [a]Lev 26:42, 45; Deut 7:9; Ezek 16:60 [b]Gen 9:11
16 [a]Gen 17:13, 19; 2 Sam 23:5
18 [a]Gen 9:25-27; 10:6
19 [1]Lit *scattered* [a]Gen 9:1,7; 10:32; 1 Chr 1:4
20 [1]Lit *to be a farmer*
21 [a]Prov 20:1
22 [a]Hab 2:15
23 [1]Lit *backward*
25 [1]I.e. The lowest of servants [a]Deut 27:16 [b]Josh 9:23
26 [1]Or *their* [a]Gen 14:20; 24:27
27 [1]Or *their* [a]Gen 10:2-5; Is 66:19

14 "It shall come about, when I bring a
cloud over the earth, that the bow will be
seen in the cloud,
15 and [a]I will remember My covenant, which is between Me and you and
every living creature of all flesh; and
[b]never again shall the water become a
flood to destroy all flesh.
16 "When the bow is in the cloud, then
I will look upon it, to remember the
[a]everlasting covenant between God and
every living creature of all flesh that is on
the earth."
17 And God said to Noah, "This is the
sign of the covenant which I have established between Me and all flesh that is on
the earth."
18 ¶ Now the sons of Noah who came
out of the ark were Shem and Ham and
Japheth; and [a]Ham was the father of Canaan.
19 These three *were* the sons of Noah,
and [a]from these the whole earth was
[1]populated.
20 ¶ Then Noah began [1]farming and
planted a vineyard.
21 He drank of the wine and [a]became
drunk, and uncovered himself inside his
tent.
22 Ham, the father of Canaan, [a]saw
the nakedness of his father, and told his
two brothers outside.
23 But Shem and Japheth took a garment and laid it upon both their shoulders and walked backward and covered
the nakedness of their father; and their
faces were [1]turned away, so that they did
not see their father's nakedness.
24 When Noah awoke from his wine,
he knew what his youngest son had done
to him.
25 So he said,
"[a]Cursed be Canaan;
[1b]A servant of servants
He shall be to his brothers."
26 He also said,
"[a]Blessed be the LORD,
The God of Shem;
And let Canaan be [1]his servant.
27 "[a]May God enlarge Japheth,
And let him dwell in the tents of
Shem;
And let Canaan be [1]his
servant."
28 ¶ Noah lived three hundred and fifty years after the flood.
29 So all the days of Noah were nine
hundred and fifty years, and he died.

Descendants of Noah

10 Now these are *the records of* the
generations of Shem, Ham, and
Japheth, the sons of Noah; and sons were
born to them after the flood.

2 ¶ [a]The sons of Japheth *were* [b]Gomer and Magog and [c]Madai and [d]Javan and Tubal and [e]Meshech and Tiras.

3 The sons of Gomer *were* [a]Ashkenaz and [1]Riphath and [b]Togarmah.

4 The sons of Javan *were* Elishah and [a]Tarshish, Kittim and [1]Dodanim.

5 From these the coastlands of the nations [1]were separated into their lands, every one according to his language, according to their families, into their nations.

6 ¶ [a]The sons of Ham *were* Cush and Mizraim and Put and Canaan.

7 The sons of Cush *were* [a]Seba and Havilah and Sabtah and [b]Raamah and Sabteca; and the sons of Raamah *were* [b]Sheba and [c]Dedan.

8 Now Cush [1]became the father of Nimrod; he [2]became a mighty one on the earth.

9 He was a mighty hunter before the LORD; therefore it is said, "Like Nimrod a mighty hunter before the LORD."

10 The beginning of his kingdom was [1a]Babel and Erech and Accad and Calneh, in the land of [b]Shinar.

11 From that land he went forth [a]into Assyria, and built Nineveh and Rehoboth-Ir and Calah,

12 and Resen between Nineveh and Calah; that is the great city.

13 Mizraim [1]became the father of [a]Ludim and Anamim and Lehabim and Naphtuhim

14 and [a]Pathrusim and Casluhim (from which came the Philistines) and Caphtorim.

15 ¶ Canaan [1]became the father of [a]Sidon, his firstborn, and [b]Heth

16 and [a]the Jebusite and the Amorite and the Girgashite

17 and the Hivite and the Arkite and the Sinite

18 and the Arvadite and the Zemarite and the Hamathite; and afterward the families of the Canaanite were spread abroad.

19 [a]The territory of the Canaanite [1]extended from Sidon as you go toward Gerar, as far as Gaza; as you go toward [b]Sodom and Gomorrah and Admah and Zeboiim, as far as Lasha.

20 These are the sons of Ham, according to their families, according to their languages, by their lands, by their nations.

21 ¶ Also to Shem, the father of all the children of Eber, *and* the [1]older brother of Japheth, children were born.

22 [a]The sons of Shem *were* [b]Elam and Asshur and [c]Arpachshad and [d]Lud and Aram.

23 The sons of Aram *were* [a]Uz and Hul and Gether and Mash.

24 Arpachshad [1]became the father of [a]Shelah; and Shelah [1]became the father of Eber.

25 [a]Two sons were born to Eber; the name of the one *was* [1]Peleg, for in his days the earth was divided; and his brother's name *was* Joktan.

26 Joktan [1]became the father of Almodad and Sheleph and Hazarmaveth and Jerah

27 and Hadoram and Uzal and Diklah

28 and [1]Obal and Abimael and Sheba

29 and Ophir and Havilah and Jobab; all these were the sons of Joktan.

30 Now their [1]settlement [2]extended from Mesha as you go toward Sephar, the hill country of the east.

31 These are the sons of Shem, according to their families, according to their languages, by their lands, according to their nations.

32 ¶ These are the families of the sons of Noah, according to their genealogies, by their nations; and [a]out of these the nations were separated on the earth after the flood.

Universal Language, Babel, Confusion

11 Now the whole earth [1]used the same language and [2]the same words.

2 It came about as they journeyed east, that they found a plain in the land [a]of Shinar and [1]settled there.

3 They said to one another, "Come, let us make bricks and burn *them* thoroughly." And they used brick for stone, and they used [a]tar for mortar.

4 They said, "Come, let us build for ourselves a city, and a tower whose top [a]*will reach* into heaven, and let us make for ourselves [b]a name, otherwise we [c]will be scattered abroad over the face of the whole earth."

5 [a]The LORD came down to see the city and the tower which the sons of men had built.

6 The LORD said, "Behold, they are one people, and they all have [1a]the same language. And this is what they began to do, and now nothing which they purpose to do will be [2]impossible for them.

7 "Come, [a]let Us go down and there [b]confuse their [1]language, so that they will not understand one another's [1]speech."

8 So the LORD [a]scattered them abroad from there over the face of the

10:2 [a]1 Chr 1:5-7 [b]Ezek 38:2,6 [c]2 Kin 17:6 [d]Is 66:19 [e]Ezek 38:2

3 [1]I.e. In 1 Chr 1:6, *Diphath* [a]Jer 51:27 [b]Ezek 27:14

4 [1]I.e. In 1 Chr 1:7, *Rodanim* [a]Ezek 27:12,25

5 [1]Or *separated themselves*

6 [a]1 Chr 1:8-10

7 [a]Is 43:3 [b]Ezek 27:22 [c]Ezek 27:15,20

8 [1]Lit *begot* [2]Lit *began to be*

10 [1]Or *Babylon* [a]Gen 11:9 [b]Gen 11:2; 14:1

11 [a]Mic 5:6

13 [1]Lit *begot* [a]Jer 46:9

14 [a]1 Chr 1:12

15 [1]Lit *begot* [a]1 Chr 1:13; Jer 47:4 [b]Gen 23:3

16 [a]Gen 15:19-21

19 [1]Lit *was* [a]Num 34:2-12 [b]Gen 14:2,3

21 [1]Or *the brother of Japheth the elder*

22 [a]1 Chr 1:17 [b]Gen 14:1,9 [c]Gen 11:10 [d]Is 66:19

23 [a]Job 1:1; Jer 25:20

24 [1]Lit *begot* [a]Gen 11:12; Luke 3:35

25 [1]I.e. division [a]1 Chr 1:19

26 [1]Lit *begot*

28 [1]I.e. In 1 Chr 1:22, *Ebal*

30 [1]Lit *dwelling* [2]Lit *was*

32 [a]Gen 9:19

11:1 [1]Lit *was one lip* [2]Or *few* or *one* set of *words*

2 [1]Lit *dwelt* [a]Gen 10:10; 14:1; Dan 1:2

3 [a]Gen 14:10

4 [a]Deut 1:28; 9:1; Ps 107:26 [b]Gen 6:4; 2 Sam 8:13 [c]Deut 4:27

5 [a]Gen 18:21; Ex 3:8; 19:11, 18,20

6 [1]Lit *one lip* [2]Lit *withheld from* [a]Gen 11:1

7 [1]Lit *lip* [a]Gen 1:26 [b]Gen 42:23; Ex 4:11; Deut 28:49; Is 33:19; Jer 5:15

8 [a]Gen 11:4; Ps 92:9; Luke 1:51

whole earth; and they stopped building the city.

9 Therefore its name was called [1a]Babel, because there the LORD confused the [2]language of the whole earth; and from there the LORD scattered them abroad over the face of the whole earth.

Descendants of Shem

10 ¶ [a]These are *the records of* the generations of Shem. Shem was one hundred years old, and [1]became the father of Arpachshad two years after the flood;

11 and Shem lived five hundred years after he became the father of Arpachshad, and he had *other* sons and daughters.

12 ¶ Arpachshad lived thirty-five years, and became the father of Shelah;

13 and Arpachshad lived four hundred and three years after he became the father of Shelah, and he had *other* sons and daughters.

14 ¶ Shelah lived thirty years, and became the father of Eber;

15 and Shelah lived four hundred and three years after he became the father of Eber, and he had *other* sons and daughters.

16 ¶ Eber lived thirty-four years, and became the father of Peleg;

17 and Eber lived four hundred and thirty years after he became the father of Peleg, and he had *other* sons and daughters.

18 ¶ Peleg lived thirty years, and became the father of Reu;

19 and Peleg lived two hundred and nine years after he became the father of Reu, and he had *other* sons and daughters.

20 ¶ Reu lived thirty-two years, and became the father of Serug;

21 and Reu lived two hundred and seven years after he became the father of Serug, and he had *other* sons and daughters.

22 ¶ Serug lived thirty years, and became the father of Nahor;

23 and Serug lived two hundred years after he became the father of Nahor, and he had *other* sons and daughters.

24 ¶ Nahor lived twenty-nine years, and became the father of [a]Terah;

25 and Nahor lived one hundred and nineteen years after he became the father of Terah, and he had *other* sons and daughters.

26 ¶ Terah lived seventy years, and became [a]the father of Abram, Nahor and Haran.

27 ¶ Now these are *the records of* the generations of Terah. Terah became the father of Abram, Nahor and Haran; and [a]Haran became the father of [b]Lot.

28 Haran died [1]in the presence of his father Terah in the land of his birth, in [a]Ur of the Chaldeans.

29 Abram and [a]Nahor took wives for themselves. The name of Abram's wife was [b]Sarai; and the name of Nahor's wife was [c]Milcah, the daughter of Haran, the father of Milcah [1]and Iscah.

30 [a]Sarai was barren; she had no child.

31 ¶ Terah took Abram his son, and Lot the son of Haran, his grandson, and Sarai his daughter-in-law, his son Abram's wife; and they went out [1]together from [a]Ur of the Chaldeans in order to enter the land of Canaan; and they went as far as Haran, and [2]settled there.

32 The days of Terah were two hundred and five years; and Terah died in Haran.

Abram Journeys to Egypt

12 Now [a]the LORD said to Abram,
"[1]Go forth from your country,
And from your relatives
And from your father's house,
To the land which I will show
you;
2 And [a]I will make you a great
nation,
And [b]I will bless you,
And make your name great;
And so [1c]you shall be a
blessing;
3 And [a]I will bless those who
bless you,
And the one who [1]curses you I
will [2]curse.
[b]And in you all the families of
the earth will be blessed."

4 ¶ So Abram went forth as the LORD had spoken to him; and [a]Lot went with him. Now Abram was seventy-five years old when he departed from Haran.

5 Abram took Sarai his wife and Lot his nephew, and all their [a]possessions which they had accumulated, and [b]the [1]persons which they had acquired in Haran, and they [2]set out for the land of Canaan; [c]thus they came to the land of Canaan.

6 Abram passed through the land as far as the site of [a]Shechem, to the [1]oak of Moreh. Now the Canaanite *was* then in the land.

7 The LORD [a]appeared to Abram and said, "[b]To your [1]descendants I will give this land." So he built [c]an altar there to the LORD who had appeared to him.

8 Then he proceeded from there to the mountain on the east of Bethel, and pitched his tent, with [a]Bethel on the west and Ai on the east; and there he

9 [1]Or *Babylon;* cf Heb *balal,* confuse [2]Lit *lip* [a]Gen 10:10

10 [1]Lit *begot,* and so throughout the ch [a]Gen 10:22-25

24 [a]Josh 24:2

26 [a]Josh 24:2

27 [a]Gen 11:31; 12:4 [b]Gen 13:10; 14:12; 19:1,29

28 [1]Or *during the lifetime of* [a]Gen 11:31

29 [1]Lit *and the father of* [a]Gen 24:10 [b]Gen 17:15; 20:12 [c]Gen 22:20,23; 24:15

30 [a]Gen 16:1

31 [1]Lit *with them* [2]Lit *dwelt* [a]Gen 15:7; Neh 9:7; Acts 7:4

12:1 [1]Lit *Go for yourself* [a]Gen 15:7; Acts 7:3; Heb 11:8

2 [1]Lit *be a blessing* [a]Gen 17:4-6; 18:18; 46:3; Deut 26:5 [b]Gen 22:17 [c]Zech 8:13

3 [1]Or *reviles* [2]Or *bind under a curse* [a]Gen 24:35; 27:29; Num 24:9 [b]Gen 22:18; 26:4; 28:14; Acts 3:25; Gal 3:8

4 [a]Gen 11:27,31

5 [1]Lit *souls* [2]Lit *went forth to go to* [a]Gen 13:6 [b]Gen 14:14; Lev 22:11 [c]Gen 11:31; Heb 11:8

6 [1]Or *terebinth* [a]Gen 35:4; Deut 11:30

7 [1]Lit *seed* [a]Gen 17:1; 18:1 [b]Gen 13:15; 15:18; Deut 34:4; Ps 105: 9-12; Acts 7:5; Gal 3:16 [c]Gen 13:4,18; 22:9

8 [a]Josh 8:9,12

built an altar to the LORD and [b]called upon the name of the LORD.

9 Abram journeyed on, continuing toward [a]the [1]Negev.

10 ¶ Now there was [a]a famine in the land; so Abram went down to Egypt to sojourn there, for the famine was [b]severe in the land.

11 It came about when he [1]came near to Egypt, that he said to Sarai his wife, "See now, I know that you are a [2a]beautiful woman;

12 [a]and when the Egyptians see you, they will say, 'This is his wife'; and they will kill me, but they will let you live.

13 "Please say that you are [a]my sister so that it may go well with me because of you, and that [1b]I may live on account of you."

14 It came about when Abram came into Egypt, the Egyptians [1]saw that the woman was very beautiful.

15 Pharaoh's officials saw her and praised her to Pharaoh; and [a]the woman was taken into Pharaoh's house.

16 Therefore [a]he treated Abram well for her sake; and [1b]gave him sheep and oxen and donkeys and male and female servants and female donkeys and camels.

17 ¶ But the LORD [a]struck Pharaoh and his house with great plagues because of Sarai, Abram's wife.

18 Then Pharaoh called Abram and said, "[a]What is this you have done to me? Why did you not tell me that she was your wife?

19 "Why did you say, 'She is my sister,' so that I took her for my wife? Now then, [1]here is your wife, take her and go."

20 Pharaoh commanded *his* men concerning him; and they [1]escorted him away, with his wife and all that belonged to him.

Abram and Lot

13 So Abram went up from Egypt to [a]the [1]Negev, he and his wife and all that belonged to him, and Lot with him.

2 ¶ Now Abram was [a]very rich in livestock, in silver and in gold.

3 He went [1]on his journeys from the [2]Negev as far as Bethel, to the place where his tent had been at the beginning, [a]between Bethel and Ai,

4 to the place of the [a]altar which he had made there formerly; and there Abram called on the name of the LORD.

5 Now [a]Lot, who went with Abram, also had flocks and herds and tents.

6 And [a]the land could not [1]sustain them [2]while dwelling together, [b]for their possessions were so great that they were not able to remain together.

8 [b]Gen 4:26
9 [1]I.e. South country [a]Gen 13:1
10 [a]Gen 26:1 [b]Gen 43:1
11 [1]Lit *drew near to enter* [2]Lit *woman of beautiful appearance* [a]Gen 26:7
12 [a]Gen 20:11
13 [1]Lit *my soul* [a]Gen 20:2 [b]Jer 38:17
14 [1]Lit *saw the woman that she was*
15 [a]Gen 20:2
16 [1]Lit *he had* [a]Gen 20:14 [b]Gen 13:2
17 [a]Gen 20:18; 1 Chr 16:21; Ps 105:14
18 [a]Gen 20:9
19 [1]Or *behold*
20 [1]Lit *sent*
13:1 [1]I.e. South country [a]Gen 12:9
2 [a]Gen 24:35
3 [1]Lit *by his stages* [2]I.e. South country [a]Gen 12:8
4 [a]Gen 12:7
5 [a]Gen 12:5
6 [1]Lit *bear* [2]Lit *to dwell* [a]Gen 36:7 [b]Gen 12:5
7 [a]Gen 26:20 [b]Gen 12:6
8 [a]Prov 15:18
10 [1]Lit *circle* [a]Gen 19:17-29; Deut 34:3 [b]Gen 19:24 [c]Gen 2:8 [d]Gen 47:6 [e]Gen 14:2; Deut 34:3
11 [1]Lit *circle*
12 [1]Lit *dwelt* [2]Lit *circle* [a]Gen 14:2
13 [1]Lit *wicked and sinners exceedingly* [a]Gen 18:20; Ezek 16:49 [b]Gen 39:9; Num 32:23; 2 Pet 2:7
14 [a]Deut 3:27; Is 49:18 [b]Gen 28:14
15 [1]Lit *seed* [a]Gen 12:7 [b]Gen 13:17; 2 Chr 20:7; Acts 7:5
16 [1]Lit *seed* [a]Gen 16:10; Num 23:10
17 [a]Num 13:17-24 [b]Gen 13:15
18 [1]Or *terebinths* [a]Gen 14:13 [b]Gen 8:20
14:1 [1]Or *nations* [a]Gen 10:10 [b]Gen 10:22; Is 11:11; Dan 8:2
2 [a]Gen 10:19 [b]Deut 29:23 [c]Gen 13:10
3 [1]Lit *joined together* [a]Gen 14:8 [b]Num 34:12; Deut 3:17; Josh 3:16

7 [a]And there was strife between the herdsmen of Abram's livestock and the herdsmen of Lot's livestock. Now [b]the Canaanite and the Perizzite were dwelling then in the land.

8 ¶ [a]So Abram said to Lot, "Please let there be no strife between you and me, nor between my herdsmen and your herdsmen, for we are brothers.

9 "Is not the whole land before you? Please separate from me; if *to* the left, then I will go to the right; or if *to* the right, then I will go to the left."

10 Lot lifted up his eyes and saw all the [1a]valley of the Jordan, that it was well watered everywhere—*this was* before the LORD [b]destroyed Sodom and Gomorrah—like [c]the garden of the LORD, [d]like the land of Egypt as you go to [e]Zoar.

11 So Lot chose for himself all the [1]valley of the Jordan, and Lot journeyed eastward. Thus they separated from each other.

12 Abram [1]settled in the land of Canaan, while Lot [1]settled in [a]the cities of the [2]valley, and moved his tents as far as Sodom.

13 Now [a]the men of Sodom were wicked [1]exceedingly and [b]sinners against the LORD.

14 ¶ The LORD said to Abram, after Lot had separated from him, "[a]Now lift up your eyes and look from the place where you are, [b]northward and southward and eastward and westward;

15 [a]for all the land which you see, [b]I will give it to you and to your [1]descendants forever.

16 "I will make your [1]descendants [a]as the dust of the earth, so that if anyone can number the dust of the earth, then your [1]descendants can also be numbered.

17 "Arise, [a]walk about the land through its length and breadth; for [b]I will give it to you."

18 Then Abram moved his tent and came and dwelt by the [1a]oaks of Mamre, which are in Hebron, and there he built [b]an altar to the LORD.

War of the Kings

14 And it came about in the days of Amraphel king of [a]Shinar, Arioch king of Ellasar, Chedorlaomer king of [b]Elam, and Tidal king of [1]Goiim,

2 *that* they made war with Bera king of Sodom, and with Birsha king of Gomorrah, Shinab king of [a]Admah, and Shemeber king of [b]Zeboiim, and the king of Bela (that is, [c]Zoar).

3 All these [1]came as allies to [a]the valley of Siddim (that is, [b]the Salt Sea).

4 Twelve years they had served
Chedorlaomer, but the thirteenth year
they rebelled.
5 In the fourteenth year Chedorlaomer and the kings that were with
him, came and [1]defeated the [a]Rephaim
in [b]Ashteroth-karnaim and the Zuzim
in Ham and the Emim in [2c]Shaveh-
kiriathaim,
6 and the [a]Horites in their Mount
Seir, as far as [b]El-paran, which is by the
wilderness.
7 Then they turned back and came to
En-mishpat (that is, [a]Kadesh), and [1]con-
quered all the country of the Amalekites,
and also the Amorites, who lived in
[b]Hazazon-tamar.
8 And the king of Sodom and the king
of Gomorrah and the king of Admah and
the king of Zeboiim and the king of Bela
(that is, Zoar) came out; and they arrayed
for battle against them in [a]the valley of
Siddim,
9 against Chedorlaomer king of Elam
and Tidal king of [1]Goiim and Amraphel
king of Shinar and Arioch king of Ellasar—four kings against five.
10 Now the valley of Siddim was full of
tar pits; and [a]the kings of Sodom and
Gomorrah fled, and they fell [1]into them.
But those who survived fled to the [b]hill
country.
11 Then they took all the goods of Sodom and Gomorrah and all their food supply, and departed.
12 They also took Lot, [a]Abram's nephew, and his possessions and departed,
[b]for he was living in Sodom.
13 ¶ Then [1]a fugitive came and told
Abram the [a]Hebrew. Now he was [2]liv-
ing by the [3b]oaks of Mamre the Amorite, brother of Eshcol and brother of
Aner, and these were [4c]allies with
Abram.
14 When Abram heard that [a]his [1]rel-
ative had been taken captive, he [2]led out
his trained men, [b]born in his house,
three hundred and eighteen, and went in
pursuit as far as [c]Dan.
15 [a]He divided [1]his forces against
them by night, he and his servants, and
[2]defeated them, and pursued them as far
as Hobah, which is [3]north of [b]Damas-
cus.
16 He [a]brought back all the goods,
and also brought back [b]his [1]relative Lot
with his possessions, and also the wom-
en, and the people.

God's Promise to Abram

17 ¶ Then after his return from the
[1]defeat of Chedorlaomer and the kings
who were with him, [a]the king of Sodom
went out to meet him at the valley of
Shaveh (that is, [b]the King's Valley).
18 And [a]Melchizedek king of Salem
brought out [b]bread and wine; now he
was a [c]priest of [1]God Most High.
19 He blessed him and said,
"Blessed be Abram of [1]God Most
High,
[2a]Possessor of heaven and
earth;
20 And blessed be [1]God Most High,
Who has delivered your enemies
into your hand."
[a]He gave him a tenth of all.
21 The king of Sodom said to Abram,
"Give the [1]people to me and take the
goods for yourself."
22 Abram said to the king of Sodom, "I
have [1]sworn to the LORD [2a]God Most
High, [3b]possessor of heaven and earth,
23 that [a]I will not take a thread or a
sandal thong or anything that is yours, for
fear you would say, 'I have made Abram
rich.'
24 "[1]I will take nothing except what
the young men have eaten, and the share
of the men who went with me, [a]Aner,
Eshcol, and Mamre; let them take their
share."

Abram Promised a Son

15 After these things [a]the word of
the LORD came to Abram in a vision, saying,
"[b]Do not fear, Abram,
I am [c]a shield to you;
[1]Your [d]reward shall be very
great."
2 Abram said, "O Lord [1]GOD, what
will You give me, since I [2]am childless,
and the [3]heir of my house is Eliezer of
Damascus?"
3 And Abram said, "[1]Since You have
given no [2]offspring to me, [3]one [a]born
in my house is my heir."
4 Then behold, the word of the LORD
came to him, saying, "This man will not
be your heir; [a]but one who will come
forth from your own [1]body, he shall be
your heir."
5 And He took him outside and said,
"Now look toward the heavens, and
[a]count the stars, if you are able to count
them." And He said to him, "[b]So shall
your [1]descendants be."
6 [a]Then he believed in the LORD;
and He reckoned it to him as righteousness.
7 And He said to him, "I am the LORD
who brought you out of [a]Ur of the Chaldeans, to [b]give you this land to [1]pos-
sess it."

5 [1]Lit *smote* [2]Or *the plain of Kiriathaim* [a]Deut 3:11 [b]Deut 1:4; Josh 9:10 [c]Num 32:37
6 [a]Gen 36:20; Deut 2:12 [b]Gen 21:21; Num 10:12
7 [1]Lit *smote* [a]Num 13:26 [b]2 Chr 20:2
8 [a]Gen 14:3
9 [1]Or *nations*
10 [1]Lit *there* [a]Gen 14:17 [b]Gen 19:17
12 [a]Gen 11:27 [b]Gen 13:12
13 [1]Lit *the* [2]Lit *abiding* [3]Or *terebinths* [4]Lit *possessors of the covenant* [a]Gen 40:15; Ex 3:18 [b]Gen 13:18 [c]Gen 21:27
14 [1]Lit *brother* [2]Or *mustered* [a]Gen 14:12 [b]Gen 12:5; Eccl 2:7 [c]Deut 34:1; Judg 18:29; 1 Kin 15:20
15 [1]Lit *himself* [2]Lit *smote* [3]Lit *on the left* [a]Judg 7:16 [b]Gen 15:2
16 [1]Lit *brother* [a]1 Sam 30:8 [b]Gen 14:12
17 [1]Lit *smiting* [a]Gen 14:10 [b]2 Sam 18:18
18 [1]Heb *El Elyon* [a]Heb 7:1-10 [b]Ps 104:15 [c]Ps 110:4; Heb 5:6
19 [1]Heb *El Elyon* [2]Or *Creator* [a]Gen 14:22
20 [1]Heb *El Elyon* [a]Heb 7:4
21 [1]Lit *soul*
22 [1]Lit *lifted up my hand* [2]Heb *El Elyon* [3]Or *Creator* [a]Gen 14:19 [b]Ps 24:1
23 [a]2 Kin 5:16
24 [1]Lit *Not to me except* [a]Gen 14:13
15:1 [1]Or *Your very great reward* [a]Gen 15:4; 1 Sam 15:10 [b]Gen 21:17; Is 41:10 [c]Deut 33:29 [d]Num 18:20; Ps 58:11
2 [1]Heb *YHWH,* usually rendered *LORD* [2]Lit *go* [3]Lit *son of acquisition*
3 [1]Lit *Behold* [2]Lit *seed* [3]Lit *and behold, a son of* [a]Gen 14:14
4 [1]Lit *inward parts* [a]Gal 4:28
5 [1]Lit *seed* [a]Gen 22:17; Deut 1:10 [b]Ex 32:13; Rom 4:18; Heb 11:12
6 [a]Rom 4:3; Gal 3:6; James 2:23
7 [1]Or *inherit* [a]Gen 11:31 [b]Gen 13:15

8 He said, "O Lord [1]GOD, [a]how may
I know that I will [2]possess it?"
9 So He said to him, "[1]Bring Me a
three year old heifer, and a three year old
female goat, and a three year old ram, and
a turtledove, and a young pigeon."
10 Then he [1]brought all these to Him
and [a]cut them [2]in two, and laid each
half opposite the other; but he [b]did not
cut the birds.
11 The birds of prey came down upon
the carcasses, and Abram drove them
away.
12 ¶ Now when the sun was going
down, [a]a deep sleep fell upon Abram;
and behold, [1]terror *and* great darkness
fell upon him.
13 *God* said to Abram, "Know for certain that [a]your [1]descendants will be
strangers in a land that is not theirs,
[2]where [b]they will be enslaved and oppressed [c]four hundred years.
14 "But I will also judge the nation
whom they will serve, and afterward they
will come out [a]with [1]many possessions.
15 "As for you, [a]you shall go to your
fathers in peace; you will be buried at a
good old age.
16 "Then in [a]the fourth generation
they will return here, for [b]the iniquity of
the Amorite is not yet complete."
17 ¶ It came about when the sun had
set, that it was very dark, and behold,
there appeared a smoking oven and a
flaming torch which [a]passed between
these pieces.
18 On that day the LORD made a covenant with Abram, saying,
"[a]To your [1]descendants I have
given this land,
From [b]the river of Egypt as far
as the great river, the river
Euphrates:
19 [a]the Kenite and the Kenizzite and
the Kadmonite
20 and the Hittite and the Perizzite
and the Rephaim
21 and the Amorite and the Canaanite
and the Girgashite and the Jebusite."

Sarai and Hagar

16 Now [a]Sarai, Abram's wife had
borne him no *children,* and she
had [b]an Egyptian maid whose name was
Hagar.
2 So Sarai said to Abram, "Now behold, the LORD has prevented me from
bearing *children.* [a]Please go in to my
maid; perhaps I will [1]obtain children
through her." And Abram listened to the
voice of Sarai.
3 After Abram had [1]lived [a]ten years
in the land of Canaan, Abram's wife Sarai
took Hagar the Egyptian, her maid, and
gave her to her husband Abram as his
wife.
4 He went in to Hagar, and she conceived; and when she saw that she had
conceived, her mistress was despised in
her sight.
5 And Sarai said to Abram, "[a]May
the wrong done me be upon you. I gave
my maid into your [1]arms, but when she
saw that she had conceived, I was despised in her [2]sight. [b]May the LORD
judge between [3]you and me."
6 But Abram said to Sarai, "Behold,
your maid is in your [1]power; do to her
what is good in your [2]sight." So Sarai
treated her harshly, and [a]she fled from
her presence.
7 ¶ Now [a]the angel of the LORD
found her by a spring of water in the
wilderness, by the spring on the way to
[b]Shur.
8 He said, "Hagar, Sarai's maid,
[a]where have you come from and where
are you going?" And she said, "I am fleeing from the presence of my mistress Sarai."
9 Then the angel of the LORD said to
her, "Return to your mistress, and submit
yourself [1]to her authority."
10 Moreover, the [a]angel of the LORD
said to her, "[b]I will greatly multiply your
[1]descendants so that [2]they will be too
many to count."
11 The angel of the LORD said to her
further,
"Behold, you are with child,
And you will bear a son;
And you shall call his name
[1]Ishmael,
Because [a]the LORD [2]has given
heed to your affliction.
12 "He will be a [a]wild donkey of a
man,
His hand *will be* against
everyone,
And everyone's hand *will be*
against him;
And he will [1]live [2b]to the east
of all his brothers."
13 Then she called the name of the
LORD who spoke to her, "[1]You are [2]a
God who sees"; for she said, "[a]Have I
even [3]remained alive here after seeing
Him?"
14 Therefore the well was called
[1]Beer-lahai-roi; behold, it is between
[a]Kadesh and Bered.
15 ¶ So Hagar bore Abram a son; and
Abram called the name of his son, whom
Hagar bore, Ishmael.
16 Abram was [a]eighty-six years old
when Hagar bore Ishmael to [1]him.

8 [1]Heb *YHWH,* usually rendered LORD [2]Or *inherit* [a]Judg 6:36-40; Luke 1:18
9 [1]Lit *Take*
10 [1]Lit *took* [2]Lit *in the midst* [a]Gen 15:17 [b]Lev 1:17
12 [1]Or *a terror of great darkness* [a]Gen 2:21; 28:11; Job 33:15
13 [1]Lit *seed* [2]Lit *and shall serve them; and they shall afflict them* [a]Acts 7:6,17 [b]Ex 1:11; Deut 5:15 [c]Ex 12:40; Gal 3:17
14 [1]Lit *great* [a]Ex 12:32-38
15 [a]Gen 25:8; 47:30
16 [a]Gen 15:13 [b]Lev 18:24-28
17 [a]Jer 34:18,19
18 [1]Lit *seed* [a]Gen 17:8; Josh 21:43; Acts 7:5 [b]Ex 23:31; Num 34:1-15; Deut 1:7,8
19 [a]Ex 3:17; 23:28; Josh 24:11; Neh 9:8
16:1 [a]Gen 11:30 [b]Gen 12:16
2 [1]Lit *be built from her* [a]Gen 30:3,4,9,10
3 [1]Lit *dwelt* [a]Gen 12:4
5 [1]Lit *bosom* [2]Lit *eyes* [3]Lit *me and you* [a]Jer 51:35 [b]Gen 31:53; Ex 5:21
6 [1]Lit *hand* [2]Lit *eyes* [a]Gen 16:9
7 [a]Gen 21:17, 18; 22:11,15; 31:11 [b]Gen 20:1; 25:18
8 [a]Gen 3:9; 1 Kin 19:9,13
9 [1]Lit *under her hands*
10 [1]Lit *seed* [2]Or *it shall not be counted for multitude* [a]Gen 22:15-18 [b]Gen 17:20
11 [1]I.e. God hears [2]Lit *has heard* [a]Ex 2:23, 24; 3:7,9
12 [1]Lit *dwell* [2]Lit *before the face of;* or *in defiance of* [a]Job 24:5; 39:5-8 [b]Gen 25:18
13 [1]Or *You, God, see me* [2]Heb *Elroi* [3]Lit *seen here after the one who saw me* [a]Gen 32:30; Ps 139:1-12
14 [1]I.e. the well of the living one who sees me [a]Gen 14:7
16 [1]Lit *Abram* [a]Gen 12:4; 16:3

Abraham and the Covenant of Circumcision

17 Now when Abram was ninety-
nine years old, [a]the LORD appeared to Abram and said to him,
"I am [1]God [b]Almighty;
Walk before Me, and be
[2c]blameless.
2 "I will [1]establish My [a]covenant
between Me and you,
And I will [b]multiply you
exceedingly."
3 Abram [a]fell on his face, and God
talked with him, saying,
4 "As for Me, behold, My covenant
is with you,
And you will be the father of a
[a]multitude of nations.
5 "No longer shall your name be
called [1]Abram,
But [a]your name shall be
[2]Abraham;
For [b]I will make you the father
of a multitude of nations.
6 "I will make you exceedingly fruitful, and I will make nations of you, and
[a]kings will come forth from you.
7 "I will establish My covenant between Me and you and your [1]descen-
dants after you throughout their generations for an [a]everlasting covenant, [b]to
be God to you and [c]to your [1]descen-
dants after you.
8 "[a]I will give to you and to your
[1]descendants after you, the land of your
sojournings, all the land of Canaan, for an
everlasting possession; and [b]I will be
their God."
9 ¶ God said further to Abraham,
"Now as for you, [a]you shall keep My
covenant, you and your [1]descendants after you throughout their generations.
10 "[a]This is My covenant, which you
shall keep, between Me and you and your
[1]descendants after you: every male
among you shall be circumcised.
11 "And [a]you shall be circumcised in
the flesh of your foreskin, and it shall be
the sign of the covenant between Me and
you.
12 "And every male among you who
is [a]eight days old shall be circumcised
throughout your generations, a *servant*
who is born in the house or who is
bought with money from any foreigner,
who is not of your [1]descendants.
13 "A *servant* who is born in your
house or [a]who is bought with your money shall surely be circumcised; thus shall
My covenant be in your flesh for an everlasting covenant.
14 "But an uncircumcised male who is
not circumcised in the flesh of his foreskin, that person shall be [a]cut off from
his people; he has broken My covenant."
15 ¶ Then God said to Abraham, "As
for Sarai your wife, you shall not call her
name Sarai, but [1]Sarah *shall be* her
name.
16 "I will bless her, and indeed I will
give you [a]a son by her. Then I will bless
her, and she shall be *a mother of* nations;
[b]kings of peoples will [1]come from her."
17 Then Abraham [a]fell on his face and
laughed, and said in his heart, "Will a
child be born to a man one hundred years
old? And [b]will Sarah, who is ninety years
old, bear *a child?*"
18 And Abraham said to God, "Oh that
Ishmael might live before You!"
19 But God said, "No, but Sarah your
wife will bear you [a]a son, and you shall
call his name [1]Isaac; and [b]I will establish
My covenant with him for an everlasting
covenant for his [2]descendants after him.
20 "As for Ishmael, I have heard you;
behold, I will bless him, and [a]will make
him fruitful and will multiply him exceedingly. [b]He shall [1]become the father of
twelve princes, and I will make him a
[c]great nation.
21 "But My covenant I will establish
with [a]Isaac, whom [b]Sarah will bear to
you at this season next year."
22 When He finished talking with
him, [a]God went up from Abraham.
23 ¶ Then Abraham took Ishmael his
son, and all *the servants* who were [a]born
in his house and all who were bought
with his money, every male among the
men of Abraham's household, and circumcised the flesh of their foreskin in the
very same day, [b]as God had said to him.
24 Now Abraham was ninety-nine
years old when [a]he was circumcised in
the flesh of his foreskin.
25 And [a]Ishmael his son was thirteen
years old when he was circumcised in the
flesh of his foreskin.
26 In the very same day Abraham was
circumcised, and Ishmael his son.
27 All the men of his household, who
were [a]born in the house or bought with
money from a foreigner, were circumcised with him.

Birth of Isaac Promised

18 Now [a]the LORD appeared to him
by the [1b]oaks of Mamre, while
he was sitting at the tent door in the heat
of the day.
2 When he lifted up his eyes and
looked, behold, three [a]men were standing opposite him; and when he saw *them,*
he ran from the tent door to meet them
and bowed himself to the earth,
3 and said, "[1]My lord, if now I have

17:1 [1]Heb *El Shaddai* [2]Lit *complete, perfect;* or *having integrity* [a]Gen 12:7; 18:1 [b]Gen 28:3; 35:11 [c]Gen 6:9; Deut 18:13
2 [1]Lit *give* [a]Gen 15:18 [b]Gen 13:16; 15:5
3 [a]Gen 17:17; 18:2
4 [a]Gen 35:11; 48:19
5 [1]I.e. exalted father [2]I.e. father of a multitude [a]Neh 9:7 [b]Rom 4:17
6 [a]Gen 17:16; 35:11
7 [1]Lit *seed* [a]Gen 17:13,19; Ps 105:9,10; Luke 1:55 [b]Gen 26:24; Lev 11:45; 26:12,45; Heb 11:16 [c]Gen 28:13; Gal 3:16
8 [1]Lit *seed* [a]Gen 12:7; 13:15,17; Acts 7:5 [b]Ex 6:7; 29:45; Lev 26:12; Deut 29:13; Rev 21:7
9 [1]Lit *seed* [a]Ex 19:5
10 [1]Lit *seed* [a]John 7:22; Acts 7:8; Rom 4:11
11 [a]Ex 12:48; Deut 10:16; Acts 7:8; Rom 4:11
12 [1]Lit *seed* [a]Lev 12:3
13 [a]Ex 12:44
14 [a]Ex 4:24-26
15 [1]I.e. princess
16 [1]Lit *be* [a]Gen 18:10 [b]Gen 17:6; 36:31
17 [a]Gen 17:3; 18:12; 21:6 [b]Gen 21:7
19 [1]I.e. he laughs [2]Lit *seed* [a]Gen 17:16; 18:10; 21:2 [b]Gen 26:2-5
20 [1]Lit *beget twelve princes* [a]Gen 16:10 [b]Gen 25:12-16 [c]Gen 21:18
21 [a]Gen 17:19; 18:10,14 [b]Gen 21:2
22 [a]Gen 18:33; 35:13
23 [a]Gen 14:14 [b]Gen 17:9-11
24 [a]Rom 4:11
25 [a]Gen 16:16
27 [a]Gen 14:14
18:1 [1]Or *terebinths* [a]Gen 12:7; 17:1 [b]Gen 13:18; 14:13
2 [a]Gen 18:16, 22; 32:24; Josh 5:13; Judg 13:6-11; Heb 13:2
3 [1]Or *O Lord*

found favor in your sight, please do not [2]pass your servant by.

4 "Please let a little water be brought and [a]wash your feet, and [1]rest yourselves under the tree;

5 and I will [1a]bring a piece of bread, that you may [2]refresh yourselves; after that you may go on, since you have [3]visited your servant." And they said, "So do, as you have said."

6 So Abraham hurried into the tent to Sarah, and said, "[1]Quickly, prepare three [2]measures of fine flour, knead *it* and make bread cakes."

7 Abraham also ran to the herd, and took a tender and [1]choice calf and gave *it* to the servant, and he hurried to prepare it.

8 He took curds and milk and the calf which he had prepared, and placed *it* before them; and he was standing by them under the tree [1]as they ate.

9 ¶ Then they said to him, "Where is Sarah your wife?" And he said, "There, in the tent."

10 He said, "[a]I will surely return to you [1]at this time next year; and behold, Sarah your wife will have a son." And Sarah was listening at the tent door, which was behind him.

11 Now [a]Abraham and Sarah were old, advanced in age; Sarah was [b]past [1]childbearing.

12 Sarah laughed [1]to herself, saying, "[a]After I have become old, shall I have pleasure, my [b]lord being old also?"

13 And the LORD said to Abraham, "Why did Sarah laugh, saying, 'Shall I indeed [1]bear *a child,* when I am *so* old?'

14 "[a]Is anything too [1]difficult for the LORD? At the [b]appointed time I will return to you, [2]at this time next year, and Sarah will have a son."

15 Sarah denied *it* however, saying, "I did not laugh"; for she was afraid. And He said, "No, but you did laugh."

16 ¶ Then [a]the men rose up from there, and looked down toward Sodom; and Abraham was walking with them to send them off.

17 [a]The LORD said, "Shall I hide from Abraham [b]what I am about to do,

18 since Abraham will surely become a great and [1]mighty nation, and in him [a]all the nations of the earth will be blessed?

19 "For I have [1a]chosen him, so that he may [b]command his children and his household after him to [c]keep the way of the LORD by doing righteousness and justice, so that the LORD may bring upon Abraham [d]what He has spoken about him."

20 And the LORD said, "[a]The outcry of Sodom and Gomorrah is indeed great, and their sin is exceedingly grave.

21 "I will [a]go down now, and see if they have done entirely according to its outcry, which has come to Me; and if not, I will know."

22 ¶ Then [a]the men turned away from there and went toward Sodom, while Abraham was still standing before [b]the LORD.

23 Abraham came near and said, "[a]Will You indeed sweep away the righteous with the wicked?

24 "Suppose there are fifty righteous within the city; will You indeed sweep *it* away and not [1]spare the place for the sake of the fifty righteous who are in it?

25 "Far be it from You to do [1]such a thing, to slay the righteous with the wicked, so that the righteous and the wicked are *treated* alike. Far be it from You! Shall not [a]the Judge of all the earth [2]deal justly?"

26 So the LORD said, "[a]If I find in Sodom fifty righteous within the city, then I will [1]spare the whole place on their account."

27 And Abraham replied, "Now behold, I have [1]ventured to speak to the Lord, although I am *but* [a]dust and ashes.

28 "Suppose the fifty righteous are lacking five, will You destroy the whole city because of five?" And He said, "I will not destroy *it* if I find forty-five there."

29 He spoke to Him yet again and said, "Suppose forty are found there?" And He said, "I will not do *it* on account of the forty."

30 Then he said, "Oh may the Lord not be angry, and I shall speak; suppose thirty are found there?" And He said, "I will not do *it* if I find thirty there."

31 And he said, "Now behold, I have [1]ventured to speak to the Lord; suppose twenty are found there?" And He said, "I will not destroy *it* on account of the twenty."

32 Then he said, "[a]Oh may the Lord not be angry, and I shall speak only this once; suppose ten are found there?" And He said, "I will not destroy *it* on account of the ten."

33 As soon as He had finished speaking to Abraham [a]the LORD departed, and Abraham returned to his place.

The Doom of Sodom

19 Now the [a]two angels came to Sodom in the evening as Lot was sitting in the gate of Sodom. When [b]Lot saw *them,* he rose to meet them and [1]bowed down *with his* face to the ground.

2 And he said, "Now behold, my

3 [2]Lit *pass away from your servant*
4 [1]Lit *support* [a]Gen 19:2; 24:32; 43:24
5 [1]Lit *take* [2]Lit *sustain your heart* [3]Lit *come to* [a]Judg 6:18,19; 13:15,16
6 [1]Lit *Hasten three measures* [2]Heb *seah;* i.e. one seah equals approx eleven qts
7 [1]Lit *good*
8 [1]Lit *and*
10 [1]Lit *when the time revives* [a]Gen 21:2; Rom 9:9
11 [1]Lit *the manner of women* [a]Gen 17:17; Rom 4:19 [b]Heb 11:11
12 [1]Lit *within* [a]Gen 17:17; Luke 1:18 [b]1 Pet 3:6
13 [1]Lit *surely bear*
14 [1]Or *wonderful* [2]Lit *when the time revives* [a]Jer 32:17,27; Zech 8:6; Matt 19:26; Luke 1:37; Rom 4:21 [b]Gen 17:21; 18:10
16 [a]Gen 18:2, 22; 19:1
17 [a]Gen 18:22, 26,33; Amos 3:7 [b]Gen 18:21; 19:24
18 [1]Or *populous* [a]Gen 12:3; 22:18; Acts 3:25; Gal 3:8
19 [1]Lit *known* [a]Neh 9:7; Amos 3:2 [b]Deut 6:6,7 [c]Gen 17:9 [d]Gen 12:2,3
20 [a]Gen 19:13; Ezek 16:49,50
21 [a]Gen 11:5; Ex 3:8; Ps 14:2
22 [a]Gen 18:16; 19:1 [b]Gen 18:1, 17
23 [a]Ex 23:7; Num 16:22; 2 Sam 24:17; Ps 11:4-7
24 [1]Or *forgive*
25 [1]Lit *after this manner* [2]Lit *do justice* [a]Deut 1:16,17; 32:4; Job 8:3,20; Ps 58:11; 94:2; Is 3:10,11; Rom 3:5,6
26 [1]Or *forgive* [a]Jer 5:1
27 [1]Lit *undertaken* [a]Gen 3:19; Job 30:19; 42:6
31 [1]Lit *undertaken*
32 [a]Judg 6:39
33 [a]Gen 17:22; 35:13
19:1 [1]Lit *bowed himself* [a]Gen 18:2,22 [b]Gen 18:2-5

lords, please turn aside into your servant's house, and spend the night, and
wash your feet; then you may rise early
and go on your way." They said however,
"No, but we shall spend the night in the
square."
3 Yet he urged them strongly, so they
turned aside to him and entered his
house; [a]and he prepared a feast for them,
and baked unleavened bread, and they
ate.
4 Before they lay down, [a]the men of
the city, the men of Sodom, surrounded
the house, both young and old, all the
people [1]from every quarter;
5 and they called to Lot and said to
him, "[a]Where are the men who came to
you tonight? Bring them out to us that we
may [1]have relations with them."
6 But Lot went out to them at the
doorway, and shut the door behind him,
7 and said, "Please, my brothers, do
not act wickedly.
8 "Now behold, [a]I have two daughters who have not [1]had relations with
man; please let me bring them out to you,
and do to them [2]whatever you like; only
do nothing to these men, inasmuch as
they have come under the [3]shelter of my
roof."
9 But they said, "Stand aside." Furthermore, they said, "This one came in
[1]as an alien, and already [a]he is acting
like a judge; now we will treat you worse
than them." So they pressed hard against
[2]Lot and came near to break the door.
10 But [a]the men reached out their
[1]hands and brought Lot into the house
[2]with them, and shut the door.
11 [a]They [1]struck the men who were
at the doorway of the house with blindness, both small and great, so that they
wearied *themselves trying* to find the
doorway.
12 ¶ Then the *two* men said to Lot,
"Whom else have you here? A son-in-
law, and your sons, and your daughters,
and whomever you have in the city, bring
them out of the place;
13 for we are about to destroy this
place, because [a]their outcry has become
so great before the LORD that [b]the LORD
has sent us to destroy it."
14 Lot went out and spoke to his sons-
in-law, who [1]were to marry his daughters, and said, "Up, [a]get out of this place,
for the LORD will destroy the city." [b]But
he appeared to his sons-in-law [2]to be
jesting.
15 ¶ When morning dawned, the angels urged Lot, saying, "Up, take your
wife and your two daughters who are
here, or you will be swept away in the
[1]punishment of the city."
16 But he hesitated. So the men
[a]seized his hand and the hand of his wife
and the [1]hands of his two daughters, for
[b]the compassion of the LORD *was* upon
him; and they brought him out, and put
him outside the city.
17 When they had brought them outside, [1]one said, "[a]Escape for your life!
[b]Do not look behind you, and do not stay
[2]anywhere in the [c]valley; escape to
[d]the [3]mountains, or you will be swept
away."
18 But Lot said to them, "Oh no, my
lords!
19 "Now behold, your servant has
found favor in your sight, and you have
magnified your lovingkindness, which
you have shown me by saving my life; but
I cannot escape to the [1]mountains, for
the disaster will overtake me and I will
die;
20 now behold, this town is near
enough to flee to, and it is small. Please,
let me escape there (is it not small?)
[1]that my life may be saved."
21 He said to him, "Behold, I grant you
this [1]request also, not to overthrow the
town of which you have spoken.
22 "Hurry, escape there, for I cannot do
anything until you arrive there." Therefore the name of the town was called
[1a]Zoar.
23 ¶ The sun had risen over the earth
when Lot came to Zoar.
24 Then the LORD [a]rained on Sodom
and Gomorrah brimstone and fire from
the LORD out of heaven,
25 and [a]He overthrew those cities,
and all the [1]valley, and all the inhabitants of the cities, and what grew on the
ground.
26 But his wife, from behind him,
[a]looked *back*, and she became a pillar of
salt.
27 ¶ Now Abraham arose early in the
morning *and went* to [a]the place where
he had stood before the LORD;
28 and he looked down toward Sodom
and Gomorrah, and toward all the land
of the [1]valley, and he saw, and behold,
[a]the smoke of the land ascended like the
smoke of a [2]furnace.
29 ¶ Thus it came about, when God
destroyed the cities of the [1]valley, that
[a]God remembered Abraham, and [b]sent
Lot out of the midst of the overthrow,
when He overthrew the cities in which
Lot lived.

Lot Is Debased

30 ¶ Lot went up from Zoar, and
[1a]stayed in the [2]mountains, and his two
daughters with him; for he was afraid to

3 [a]Gen 18:6-8
4 [1]Or *without exception*; lit *from every end* [a]Gen 13:13; 18:20
5 [1]I.e. have intercourse [a]Lev 18:22; Judg 19:22
8 [1]I.e. had intercourse [2]Lit *as is good in your sight* [3]Lit *shadow* [a]Judg 19:24
9 [1]Lit *to sojourn* [2]Lit *the man, against Lot* [a]Ex 2:14
10 [1]Lit *hand* [2]Lit *to* [a]Gen 19:1
11 [1]Lit *smote* [a]Deut 28:28,29; 2 Kin 6:18; Acts 13:11
13 [a]Gen 18:20 [b]Lev 26:30-33; Deut 4:26; 28:45; 1 Chr 21:15
14 [1]Or *had married*; lit *were taking* [2]Lit *like one who was jesting* [a]Num 16:21,45; Rev 18:4 [b]Jer 43:1,2
15 [1]Or *iniquity*
16 [1]Lit *hand* [a]Deut 5:15; 6:21; 7:8; 2 Pet 2:7 [b]Ex 34:7; Ps 32:10; 33:18,19
17 [1]Lit *he* [2]Lit *in all the circle* [3]Lit *mountain* [a]Jer 48:6 [b]Gen 19:26 [c]Gen 13:10 [d]Gen 14:10
19 [1]Lit *mountain*
20 [1]Lit *and my soul will live*
21 [1]Lit *thing*
22 [1]I.e. small [a]Gen 13:10; 14:2
24 [a]Deut 29:23; Ps 11:6; Is 13:19; Ezek 16:49,50; Luke 17:29; Jude 7
25 [1]Lit *circle* [a]Deut 29:23; Ps 107:34; Is 13:19; Lam 4:6; 2 Pet 2:6
26 [a]Gen 19:17; Luke 17:32
27 [a]Gen 18:22
28 [1]Lit *circle* [2]Lit *kiln* [a]Rev 9:2; 18:9
29 [1]Lit *circle* [a]Deut 7:8; 9:5, 27 [b]2 Pet 2:7
30 [1]Lit *dwelt* [2]Lit *mountain* [a]Gen 19:17,19

[3]stay in Zoar; and he [4]stayed in a cave,
he and his two daughters.
31 Then the firstborn said to the younger, "Our father is old, and there is not a
man [1]on earth to [a]come in to us after
the manner of the earth.
32 "Come, [a]let us make our father
drink wine, and let us lie with him that
we may preserve [1]our family through
our father."
33 So they made their father drink
wine that night, and the firstborn went in
and lay with her father; and he did not
know when she lay down or when she
arose.
34 On the following day, the firstborn
said to the younger, "Behold, I lay last
night with my father; let us make him
drink wine tonight also; then you go in
and lie with him, that we may preserve
[1]our family through our father."
35 So they made their father drink
wine that night also, and the younger
arose and lay with him; and he did not
know when she lay down or when she
arose.
36 Thus both the daughters of Lot
were with child by their father.
37 The firstborn bore a son, and called
his name [a]Moab; he is the father of the
Moabites to this day.
38 As for the younger, she also bore a
son, and called his name Ben-ammi; he is
the father of the [1]sons of [a]Ammon to
this day.

Abraham's Treachery

20 Now Abraham journeyed from
[a]there toward the land of [b]the
[1]Negev, and [2]settled between Kadesh
and Shur; then he sojourned in [c]Gerar.
2 Abraham said of Sarah his wife,
"[a]She is my sister." So [b]Abimelech king
of Gerar sent and took Sarah.
3 [a]But God came to Abimelech in a
dream of the night, and said to him, "Behold, [b]you are a dead man because of the
woman whom you have taken, for she is
[1]married."
4 Now Abimelech had not come near
her; and he said, "Lord, [a]will You slay a
nation, even *though* [1]blameless?
5 "Did he not himself say to me, 'She
is my sister'? And she [a]herself said, 'He
is my brother.' In [b]the integrity of my
heart and the innocence of my [1]hands I
have done this."
6 Then God said to him in the dream,
"Yes, I know that in the integrity of your
heart you have done this, and I also
[1a]kept you from sinning against Me;
therefore I did not let you touch her.
7 "Now therefore, restore the man's
wife, for [a]he is a prophet, and he will
pray for you and you will live. But if you
do not restore *her,* know that you shall
surely die, you and all who are yours."
8 ¶ So Abimelech arose early in the
morning and called all his servants and
told all these things in their hearing; and
the men were greatly frightened.
9 [a]Then Abimelech called Abraham
and said to him, "What have you done to
us? And [1]how have I sinned against you,
that you have brought on me and on my
kingdom [b]a great sin? You have done to
me [2]things that ought not to be done."
10 And Abimelech said to Abraham,
"What have you [1]encountered, that you
have done this thing?"
11 Abraham said, "Because I thought,
surely there is no [a]fear of God in this
place, and [b]they will kill me because of
my wife.
12 "Besides, she actually is my sister,
the daughter of my father, but not the
daughter of my mother, and she became
my wife;
13 and it came about, when [a]God
caused me to wander from my father's
house, that I said to her, 'This is [1]the
kindness which you will show to me:
[2]everywhere we go, [b]say of me, "He is
my brother." ' "
14 [a]Abimelech then took sheep and
oxen and male and female servants, and
gave them to Abraham, and restored his
wife Sarah to him.
15 Abimelech said, "[a]Behold, my land
is before you; [1]settle wherever [2]you
please."
16 To Sarah he said, "Behold, I have
given your [a]brother a thousand pieces of
silver; behold, it is [1]your vindication before all who are with you, and before all
men you are cleared."
17 [a]Abraham prayed to God, and God
healed Abimelech and his wife and his
maids, so that they bore *children.*
18 [a]For the LORD had closed fast all
the wombs of the household of Abimelech because of Sarah, Abraham's wife.

Isaac Is Born

21 [a]Then the LORD took note of Sarah as He had said, and the LORD
did for Sarah as He had [1]promised.
2 [a]So Sarah conceived and bore a
son to Abraham in his old age, at [b]the
appointed time of which God had spoken
to him.
3 Abraham called the name of his son
who was born to him, whom Sarah bore
to him, [a]Isaac.
4 Then Abraham circumcised his son
Isaac when he was [a]eight days old, as
God had commanded him.
5 Now Abraham was [a]one hundred

30 [3]Lit *dwell* [4]Lit *dwelt*
31 [1]Or *in the land* [a]Gen 16:2, 4; 38:8; Deut 25:5
32 [1]Lit *seed from our father* [a]Luke 21:34
34 [1]Lit *seed from our father*
37 [a]Deut 2:9
38 [1]Heb *Bene-Ammon* [a]Deut 2:19
20:1 [1]I.e. South country [2]Lit *dwelt* [a]Gen 18:1 [b]Gen 12:9 [c]Gen 26:1,6
2 [a]Gen 12:11-13; 20:12; 26:7 [b]Gen 12:15
3 [1]Lit *married to a husband* [a]Gen 12:17,18 [b]Gen 20:7
4 [1]Lit *righteous* [a]Gen 18:23-25
5 [1]Lit *palms* [a]Gen 20:13 [b]1 Kin 9:4; Ps 7:8; 26:6
6 [1]Lit *restrained* [a]1 Sam 25:26,34
7 [a]1 Sam 7:5; 2 Kin 5:11; Job 42:8
9 [1]Lit *what* [2]Lit *deeds* [a]Gen 12:18 [b]Gen 39:9
10 [1]Lit *seen*
11 [a]Neh 5:15; Prov 16:6 [b]Gen 12:12; 26:7
13 [1]Lit *your* [2]Lit *at every place where* [a]Gen 12:1-9 [b]Gen 12:13; 20:5
14 [a]Gen 12:16
15 [1]Lit *dwell* [2]Lit *it is good in your sight* [a]Gen 13:9; 34:10; 47:6
16 [1]Lit *for you a covering of the eyes* [a]Gen 20:5
17 [a]Num 12:13; 21:7; James 5:16
18 [a]Gen 12:17
21:1 [1]Lit *spoken* [a]Gen 17:16,21; 18:10,14; Gal 4:23
2 [a]Acts 7:8; Gal 4:22; Heb 11:11 [b]Gen 17:21; 18:10,14
3 [a]Gen 17:19,21
4 [a]Gen 17:12; Acts 7:8
5 [a]Gen 17:17

years old when his son Isaac was born to
him.
6 Sarah said, "God has made [a]laugh-
ter for me; everyone who hears will laugh
[1]with me."
7 And she said, "[a]Who would have
said to Abraham that Sarah would nurse
children? Yet I have borne him a son in
his old age."
8 ¶ The child grew and was weaned,
and Abraham made a great feast on the
day that Isaac was weaned.

Sarah Turns against Hagar

9 Now Sarah saw [a]the son of Hagar
the Egyptian, whom she had borne to
Abraham, [1b]mocking.
10 Therefore she said to Abraham,
"[a]Drive out this maid and her son, for
the son of this maid shall not be an heir
with my son [1]Isaac."
11 [a]The matter [1]distressed Abraham
greatly because of his son.
12 But God said to Abraham, "[1]Do not
be distressed because of the lad and your
maid; whatever Sarah tells you, listen to
her, for [a]through Isaac [2]your descendants shall be named.
13 "And of [a]the son of the maid I will
make a nation also, because he is your
[1]descendant."
14 So Abraham rose early in the morning and took bread and a [1]skin of water
and gave *them* to Hagar, putting *them* on
her shoulder, and *gave her* the boy, and
sent her away. And she departed and
wandered about in the wilderness of Beersheba.
15 ¶ When the water in the skin was
used up, she [1]left the boy under one of
the bushes.
16 Then she went and sat down opposite him, about a bowshot away, for she
said, "Do not let me [1]see the boy die."
And she sat opposite him, and [a]lifted up
her voice and wept.
17 God [a]heard the lad crying; and the
angel of God called to Hagar from heaven
and said to her, "What is the matter with
you, Hagar? [b]Do not fear, for God has
heard the voice of the lad where he is.
18 "Arise, lift up the lad, and hold him
by [1]the hand, [a]for I will make a great
nation of him."
19 Then God [a]opened her eyes and
she saw [b]a well of water; and she went
and filled the [1]skin with water and gave
the lad a drink.
20 ¶ [a]God was with the lad, and he
grew; and he [1]lived in the wilderness
and became an archer.
21 [a]He [1]lived in the wilderness of Paran, and his mother took a wife for him
from the land of Egypt.

Covenant with Abimelech

22 ¶ Now it came about at that time
that [a]Abimelech and Phicol, the commander of his army, spoke to Abraham,
saying, "[b]God is with you in all that
you do;
23 now therefore, [a]swear to me here
by God that you will not deal falsely with
me or with my offspring or with my posterity, but according to the kindness that
I have shown to you, you shall show to
me and to the land in which you have
sojourned."
24 Abraham said, "I swear it."
25 But Abraham [1]complained to
Abimelech because of the well of water
which the servants of Abimelech [a]had
seized.
26 And Abimelech said, "I do not
know who has done this thing; you did
not tell me, nor did I hear of it [1]until
today."
27 ¶ Abraham took sheep and oxen
and gave them to Abimelech, and [a]the
two of them made a covenant.
28 Then Abraham set seven ewe
lambs of the flock by themselves.
29 Abimelech said to Abraham, "What
do these seven ewe lambs mean, which
you have set by themselves?"
30 He said, "You shall take these sev-
en ewe lambs from my hand so that it
may be a [a]witness to me, that I dug this
well."
31 Therefore he called that place [a]Be-
ersheba, because there the two of them
took an oath.
32 So they made a covenant at Beersheba; and Abimelech and Phicol, the
commander of his army, arose and returned to the land of the Philistines.
33 *Abraham* planted a tamarisk tree at
Beersheba, and there [a]he called on the
name of the LORD, the [b]Everlasting God.
34 And Abraham sojourned [a]in the
land of the Philistines for many days.

The Offering of Isaac

22 Now it came about after these
things, that [a]God tested Abraham, and said to him, "[b]Abraham!" And
he said, "Here I am."
2 He said, "Take now [a]your son,
your only son, whom you love, Isaac, and
go to the land of [b]Moriah, and offer him
there as a [c]burnt offering on one of the
mountains of which I will tell you."
3 So Abraham rose early in the morning and saddled his donkey, and took two
of his young men with him and Isaac his
son; and he split wood for the burnt offering, and arose and went to the place of
which God had told him.

6 [1]Lit *for* [a]Gen 18:13; Ps 126:2; Is 54:1
7 [a]Gen 18:11,13
9 [1]Or *playing* [a]Gen 16:1,4,15 [b]Gal 4:29
10 [1]Lit *with Isaac* [a]Gal 4:30
11 [1]Lit *was very grievous in Abraham's sight* [a]Gen 17:18
12 [1]Lit *Do not let it be grievous in your sight* [2]Lit *your seed will be called* [a]Rom 9:7; Heb 11:18
13 [1]Lit *seed* [a]Gen 16:10; 21:18; 25:12-18
14 [1]I.e. a skin used as a bottle
15 [1]Lit *cast*
16 [1]Lit *look upon the death of the child* [a]Jer 6:26; Amos 8:10
17 [a]Ex 3:7; Deut 26:7; Ps 6:8 [b]Gen 26:24
18 [1]Lit *your* [a]Gen 16:10; 21:13; 25:12-16
19 [1]V 14, note 1 [a]Num 22:31; 2 Kin 6:17 [b]Gen 16:7,14
20 [1]Lit *dwelt* [a]Gen 28:15; 39:2,3,21
21 [1]Lit *dwelt* [a]Gen 25:18
22 [a]Gen 20:2, 14; 26:26 [b]Gen 26:28; Is 8:10
23 [a]Josh 2:12; 1 Sam 24:21
25 [1]Lit *reproved* [a]Gen 26:15,18, 20-22
26 [1]Lit *except*
27 [a]Gen 26:31
30 [a]Gen 31:48
31 [a]Gen 21:14; 26:33
33 [a]Gen 12:8 [b]Ex 15:18; Deut 32:40; Ps 90:2; 93:2; Is 40:28; Jer 10:10; Hab 1:12; Heb 13:8
34 [a]Gen 22:19
22:1 [a]Deut 8:2, 16; Heb 11:17; James 1:12-14 [b]Gen 22:11
2 [a]Gen 22:12, 16; John 3:16; 1 John 4:9 [b]2 Chr 3:1 [c]Gen 8:20

4 On the third day Abraham raised his eyes and saw the place from a distance.

5 Abraham said to his young men, "Stay here with the donkey, and I and the lad will go over there; and we will worship and return to you."

6 Abraham took the wood of the burnt offering and [a]laid it on Isaac his son, and he took in his hand the fire and the knife. So the two of them walked on together.

7 Isaac spoke to Abraham his father and said, "My father!" And he said, "Here I am, my son." And he said, "Behold, the fire and the wood, but where is the [a]lamb for the burnt offering?"

8 Abraham said, "God will [1]provide for Himself the lamb for the burnt offering, my son." So the two of them walked on together.

9 ¶ Then they came to [a]the place of which God had told him; and Abraham built [b]the altar there and arranged the wood, and bound his son Isaac and [c]laid him on the altar, on top of the wood.

10 Abraham stretched out his hand and took the knife to slay his son.

11 But [a]the angel of the LORD called to him from heaven and said, "Abraham, Abraham!" And he said, "Here I am."

12 He said, "Do not stretch out your hand against the lad, and do nothing to him; for now [a]I know that you [1]fear God, since you have not withheld [b]your son, your only son, from Me."

13 Then Abraham raised his eyes and looked, and behold, behind *him* a ram caught in the thicket by his horns; and Abraham went and took the ram and offered him up for a burnt offering in the place of his son.

14 Abraham called the name of that place [1]The LORD Will Provide, as it is said to this day, "In the mount of the LORD [a]it will [2]be provided."

15 ¶ Then the angel of the LORD called to Abraham a second time from heaven,

16 and said, "[a]By Myself I have sworn, declares the LORD, because you have done this thing and have not withheld your son, your only son,

17 indeed I will greatly bless you, and I will greatly [a]multiply your [1]seed as the stars of the heavens and as [b]the sand which is on the seashore; and [c]your seed shall possess the gate of [2]their enemies.

18 "[a]In your [1]seed all the nations of the earth shall [2]be blessed, because you have [b]obeyed My voice."

19 [a]So Abraham returned to his young men, and they arose and went together to Beersheba; and Abraham lived at Beersheba.

20 ¶ Now it came about after these things, that it was told Abraham, saying, "Behold, [a]Milcah [1]also has borne children to your brother Nahor:

21 Uz his firstborn and Buz his brother and Kemuel the father of Aram

22 and Chesed and Hazo and Pildash and Jidlaph and Bethuel."

23 Bethuel [1]became the father of [a]Rebekah; these eight Milcah bore to Nahor, Abraham's brother.

24 His concubine, whose name was Reumah, [1]also bore Tebah and Gaham and Tahash and Maacah.

Death and Burial of Sarah

23 Now [1]Sarah lived one hundred and twenty-seven years; *these were* the years of the life of Sarah.

2 Sarah died in [a]Kiriath-arba (that is, Hebron) in the land of Canaan; and Abraham [1]went in to mourn for Sarah and to weep for her.

3 Then Abraham rose from before his dead, and spoke to the [a]sons of Heth, saying,

4 "I am [a]a stranger and a sojourner among you; [b]give me [1]a [c]burial site among you that I may bury my dead out of my sight."

5 The sons of Heth answered Abraham, saying to him,

6 "Hear us, my lord, you are a [1a]mighty prince among us; bury your dead in the choicest of our graves; none of us will refuse you his grave for burying your dead."

7 So Abraham rose and bowed to the people of the land, the sons of Heth.

8 And he spoke with them, saying, "If it is your [1]wish *for me* to bury my dead out of my sight, hear me, and approach [a]Ephron the son of Zohar for me,

9 that he may give me the cave of Machpelah which he owns, which is at the end of his field; for the full price let him give it to me in [1]your presence for [2]a burial site."

10 Now Ephron was sitting among the sons of Heth; and Ephron the Hittite answered Abraham in the hearing of the sons of Heth; *even* [a]of all who went in at the gate of his city, saying,

11 "No, my lord, hear me; [a]I give you the field, and I give you the cave that is in it. In the presence of the sons of my people I give it to you; bury your dead."

12 And Abraham bowed before the people of the land.

13 He spoke to Ephron in the hearing of the people of the land, saying, "If you will only please listen to me; I will give

6 [a]John 19:17

7 [a]Ex 29:38-42; John 1:29,36; Rev 13:8

8 [1]Lit *see*

9 [a]Gen 22:2 [b]Gen 12:7,8; 13:18 [c]Heb 11:17-19; James 2:21

11 [a]Gen 16:7-11; 21:17,18

12 [1]Or *reverence*; lit *are a fearer of God* [a]James 2:21,22 [b]Gen 22:2,16

14 [1]Heb *YHWH-jireh* [2]Lit *be seen* [a]Gen 22:8

16 [a]Ps 105:9; Luke 1:73; Heb 6:13,14

17 [1]Or *descendants* [2]Lit *his* [a]Gen 15:5; 26:4; Jer 33:22; Heb 11:12 [b]Gen 32:12 [c]Gen 24:60

18 [1]Or *descendants* [2]Or *bless themselves* [a]Gen 12:3; 18:18; Acts 3:25; Gal 3:8,16 [b]Gen 18:19; 22:3,10; 26:5

19 [a]Gen 22:5

20 [1]Lit *she also* [a]Gen 11:29

23 [1]Lit *begot* [a]Gen 24:15

24 [1]Lit *she also*

23:1 [1]Lit *the life of Sarah was*

2 [1]Or *proceeded* [a]Josh 14:15; 15:13; 21:11

3 [a]Gen 10:15; 15:20

4 [1]Lit *possession of a grave* [a]Gen 17:8; Lev 25:23; 1 Chr 29:15; Ps 39:12; 105:12; 119:19; Heb 11:9,13 [b]Acts 7:16 [c]Gen 49:30

6 [1]Lit *prince of God* [a]Gen 14:14; 20:7

8 [1]Lit *soul* [a]Gen 25:9

9 [1]Lit *the midst of you* [2]Lit *possession of a burial place*

10 [a]Gen 23:18; 34:20,24; Ruth 4:1,11

11 [a]2 Sam 24:21-24

the price of the field, accept *it* from me
that I may bury my dead there."
14 Then Ephron answered Abraham,
saying to him,
15 "My lord, listen to me; a piece of
land worth four hundred [a]shekels of silver, what is that between me and you? So
bury your dead."
16 Abraham listened to Ephron; and
Abraham [a]weighed out for Ephron the
silver which he had named in the [1]hear-
ing of the sons of Heth, four hundred
shekels of silver, [2]commercial standard.
17 ¶ So [a]Ephron's field, which was
in Machpelah, which faced Mamre, the
field and cave which was in it, and all the
trees which were in the field, that were
[1]within all the confines of its border,
[2]were deeded over
18 to Abraham for a possession [a]in
the presence of the sons of Heth, before
all who went in at the gate of his city.
19 After this, Abraham buried Sarah
his wife in the cave of the field at Machpelah facing Mamre (that is, Hebron) in
the land of Canaan.
20 So the field and the cave that is in
it, [1]were [a]deeded over to Abraham for
[2]a burial site by the sons of Heth.

A Bride for Isaac

24 Now [a]Abraham was old, advanced in age; and the LORD had
[b]blessed Abraham in every way.
2 Abraham said to his servant, the
oldest of his household, who had [a]charge
of all that he owned, "[b]Please place your
hand under my thigh,
3 and I will make you swear by the
LORD, [a]the God of heaven and the God of
earth, that you [b]shall not take a wife for
my son from the daughters of [c]the Canaanites, among whom I live,
4 but you will go to [a]my country and
to my relatives, and take a wife for my son
Isaac."
5 The servant said to him, "Suppose
the woman is not willing to follow me to
this land; should I take your son back to
the land from where you came?"
6 Then Abraham said to him, "[a]Be-
ware that you do not take my son back
there!
7 "[a]The LORD, the God of heaven,
who took me from my father's house and
from the land of my birth, and who spoke
to me and who swore to me, saying, '[b]To
your [1]descendants I will give this land,'
He will send [c]His angel before you, and
you will take a wife for my son from
there.
8 "But if the woman is not willing to
follow you, then you will [a]be free from
this my oath; [b]only do not take my son
back there."
9 So the servant [a]placed his hand under the thigh of Abraham his master, and
swore to him concerning this matter.
10 ¶ Then the servant took ten camels
from the camels of his master, and set out
with a variety of [a]good things of his master's in his hand; and he arose and went
to [1]Mesopotamia, to [b]the city of Nahor.
11 He made the camels kneel down
outside the city by [a]the well of water at
evening time, [b]the time when women go
out to draw water.
12 He said, "[a]O LORD, the God of my
master Abraham, please [1b]grant me success today, and show lovingkindness to
my master Abraham.
13 "Behold, [a]I am standing by the
[1]spring, and the daughters of the men of
the city are coming out to draw water;
14 now may it be that the girl to whom
I say, 'Please let down your jar so that I
may drink,' and [1]who answers, 'Drink,
and I will water your camels also'—*may*
she *be the one* whom You have appointed
for Your servant Isaac; and by this I will
know that You have shown lovingkindness to my master."

Rebekah Is Chosen

15 ¶ [a]Before he had finished speaking, behold, [b]Rebekah who was born to
Bethuel the son of [c]Milcah, the wife of
Abraham's brother Nahor, came out with
her jar on her shoulder.
16 The girl was [a]very beautiful, a virgin, and no man had [1]had relations with
her; and she went down to the spring and
filled her jar and came up.
17 Then the servant ran to meet her
and said, "[a]Please let me drink a little
water from your jar."
18 [a]She said, "Drink, my lord"; and
she quickly lowered her jar to her hand
and gave him a drink.
19 Now when she had finished giving
him a drink, [a]she said, "I will draw also
for your camels until they have finished
drinking."
20 So she quickly emptied her jar into
the trough, and ran back to the well to
draw, and she drew for all his camels.
21 [a]Meanwhile, the man was gazing
at her [1]in silence, to know whether the
LORD had made his journey successful or
not.
22 ¶ When the camels had finished
drinking, the man took a [a]gold ring
weighing a half-shekel and two bracelets
for her [1]wrists weighing ten shekels in
gold,
23 and said, "Whose daughter are

15 [a]Ex 30:13; Ezek 45:12
16 [1]Lit *ears* [2]Lit *current according to the merchant* [a]2 Sam 14:26; Jer 32:9, 10; Zech 11:12
17 [1]Lit *in all its border around* [2]Or *were ratified* [a]Gen 25:9; 49:29,30; 50:13
18 [a]Gen 23:10
20 [1]Or *were ratified* [2]Lit *possession of a burial place* [a]Jer 32:10-14
24:1 [a]Gen 18:11 [b]Gen 12:2; 13:2; 24:35; Gal 3:9
2 [a]Gen 39:4-6 [b]Gen 24:9; 47:29
3 [a]Gen 14:19,22 [b]Deut 7:3; 2 Cor 6:14-17 [c]Gen 10:15-19; 26:34, 35; 28:1,8
4 [a]Gen 12:1; Heb 11:15
6 [a]Gen 24:8
7 [1]Lit *seed* [a]Gen 24:3 [b]Gen 12:7; 13:15; 15:18; Ex 32:13 [c]Gen 16:7; 21:17; 22:11; Ex 23:20, 23
8 [a]Josh 2:17-20 [b]Gen 24:6
9 [a]Gen 24:2
10 [1]Heb *Aram-naharaim, Aram of the two rivers* [a]Gen 24:22,53 [b]Gen 11:31,32
11 [a]Gen 24:42 [b]Ex 2:16; 1 Sam 9:11
12 [1]Lit *cause to occur for me* [a]Gen 24:27,42, 48; 26:24; Ex 3:6,15 [b]Gen 27:20
13 [1]Lit *fountain of water* [a]Gen 24:43
14 [1]Lit *she will say*
15 [a]Gen 24:45 [b]Gen 22:20,23 [c]Gen 11:29
16 [1]Lit *known* [a]Gen 12:11; 26:7; 29:17
17 [a]John 4:7
18 [a]Gen 24:14, 46
19 [a]Gen 24:14
21 [1]Lit *keeping silent* [a]Gen 24:12-14,27,52
22 [1]Lit *hands* [a]Gen 24:47; Ex 32:2,3

you? Please tell me, is there room for us
to lodge in your father's house?"
24 She said to him, "[a]I am the daughter of Bethuel, the son of Milcah, whom
she bore to Nahor."
25 Again she said to him, "We have
plenty of both straw and feed, and room
to lodge in."
26 Then the man [a]bowed low and
worshiped the LORD.
27 He said, "[a]Blessed be the LORD,
the God of my master Abraham, who has
not forsaken [b]His lovingkindness and His
truth toward my master; as for me, [c]the
LORD has guided me in the way to the
house of my master's brothers."
28 ¶ Then [a]the girl ran and told her
mother's household about these things.
29 Now Rebekah had a brother whose
name was [a]Laban; and Laban ran outside
to the man at the spring.
30 When he saw the ring and the
bracelets on his sister's [1]wrists, and
when he heard the words of Rebekah his
sister, saying, "[2]This is what the man
said to me," he went to the man; and
behold, he was standing by the camels at
the spring.
31 And he said, "[a]Come in, [b]blessed
of the LORD! Why do you stand outside
since [c]I have prepared the house, and a
place for the camels?"
32 So the man entered the house.
Then [1a]Laban unloaded the camels, and
he gave straw and feed to the camels, and
water to wash his feet and the feet of the
men who were with him.
33 But when *food* was set before him
to eat, he said, "I will not eat until I
have told my business." And he said,
"Speak on."
34 So he said, "I am [a]Abraham's servant.
35 "The LORD has greatly [a]blessed my
master, so that he has become [1]rich; and
He has given him [b]flocks and herds, and
silver and gold, and servants and maids,
and camels and donkeys.
36 "Now [a]Sarah my master's wife bore
a son to my master [1]in her old age, and
[b]he has given him all that he has.
37 "[a]My master made me swear, saying, 'You shall not take a wife for my son
from the daughters of the Canaanites, in
whose land I [1]live;
38 but you shall go to my father's
house and to my relatives, and take a wife
for my son.'
39 "[a]I said to my master, 'Suppose the
woman does not follow me.'
40 "He said to me, '[a]The LORD, before
whom I have [b]walked, will send [c]His
angel with you to make your journey successful, and you will take a wife for my
son from my relatives and from my father's house;
41 [a]then you will be free from my
oath, when you come to my relatives; and
if they do not give her to you, you will be
free from my oath.'
42 ¶ "So [a]I came today to the spring,
and said, 'O LORD, the God of my master
Abraham, if now You will make my journey on which I go [b]successful;
43 behold, [a]I am standing by the
[1]spring, and may it be that the maiden
who comes out to draw, and to whom I
say, "[b]Please let me drink a little water
from your jar";
44 and she will say to me, "You drink,
and I will draw for your camels also"; let
her be the woman whom the LORD has
appointed for my master's son.'
45 ¶ "Before I had finished [a]speaking
in my heart, behold, [b]Rebekah came out
with her jar on her shoulder, and went
down to the spring and drew, and [c]I said
to her, 'Please let me drink.'
46 "She quickly lowered her jar from
her *shoulder,* and said, '[a]Drink, and I
will water your camels also'; so I drank,
and she watered the camels also.
47 "[a]Then I asked her, and said,
'Whose daughter are you?' And she said,
'The daughter of Bethuel, Nahor's son,
whom Milcah bore to him'; and I put the
[b]ring on her nose, and the bracelets on
her [1]wrists.
48 "And I [a]bowed low and worshiped
the LORD, and blessed the LORD, the God
of my master Abraham, [b]who had guided
me in the right way to take the daughter
of my master's [1]kinsman for his son.
49 "So now if you are going to [1a]deal
kindly and truly with my master, tell me;
and if not, let me know, that I may turn
to the right hand or the left."
50 ¶ Then Laban and Bethuel replied,
"[a]The matter comes from the LORD; [b]*so*
we cannot speak to you bad or good.
51 "Here is Rebekah before you, take
her and go, and let her be the wife of your
master's son, as the LORD has spoken."
52 ¶ When Abraham's servant heard
their words, he [a]bowed himself to the
ground [1]before the LORD.
53 The servant brought out [a]articles
of silver and articles of gold, and garments, and gave them to Rebekah; he
also gave precious things to her brother
and to her mother.
54 Then he and the men who were
with him ate and drank and spent the
night. When they arose in the morning,
he said, "[a]Send me away to my master."
55 But her brother and her mother
said, "[a]Let the girl stay with us *a few*
days, say ten; afterward she may go."

24 [a]Gen 24:15
26 [a]Gen 24:48, 52; Ex 4:31
27 [a]Gen 24:12, 42,48; Ex 18:10; Ruth 4:14; 1 Sam 25:32; 2 Sam 18:28; Luke 1:68 [b]Gen 32:10; Ps 98:3 [c]Gen 24:21,48
28 [a]Gen 29:12
29 [a]Gen 29:5, 13
30 [1]Lit *hands* [2]Lit *Thus the man*
31 [a]Gen 29:13 [b]Gen 26:29; Ruth 3:10; Ps 115:15 [c]Gen 18:3-5; 19:2,3
32 [1]Lit *he* [a]Gen 43:24; Judg 19:21
34 [a]Gen 24:2
35 [1]Lit *great* [a]Gen 24:1 [b]Gen 13:2
36 [1]Lit *after she was old* [a]Gen 21:1-7 [b]Gen 25:5
37 [1]Lit *dwell* [a]Gen 24:2-4
39 [a]Gen 24:5
40 [a]Gen 24:7 [b]Gen 5:22,24; 17:1 [c]Ex 23:20
41 [a]Gen 24:8
42 [a]Gen 24:11, 12 [b]Neh 1:11
43 [1]Lit *fountain of water* [a]Gen 24:13 [b]Gen 24:14
45 [a]1 Sam 1:13 [b]Gen 24:15 [c]Gen 24:17
46 [a]Gen 24:18, 19
47 [1]Lit *hands* [a]Gen 24:23,24 [b]Ezek 16:11,12
48 [1]Lit *brother* [a]Gen 24:26,52 [b]Gen 24:27; Ps 32:8; 48:14; Is 48:17
49 [1]Lit *show lovingkindness and truth* [a]Gen 47:29; Josh 2:14
50 [a]Ps 118:23; Mark 12:11 [b]Gen 31:24,29
52 [1]Lit *to* [a]Gen 24:26,48
53 [a]Gen 24:10, 22; Ex 3:22; 11:2; 12:35
54 [a]Gen 24:56, 59; 30:25
55 [a]Judg 19:4

56 He said to them, "Do not delay me,
since [a]the LORD has prospered my way.
Send me away that I may go to my master."
57 And they said, "We will call the girl
and [1]consult her wishes."
58 Then they called Rebekah and said
to her, "Will you go with this man?" And
she said, "I will go."
59 Thus they sent away their sister Rebekah and [a]her nurse with Abraham's
servant and his men.
60 They blessed Rebekah and said to
her,

"May you, our sister,
[a]Become thousands of ten
thousands,
And may [b]your [1]descendants
possess
The gate of those who hate
them."

61 Then Rebekah arose with her
maids, and they mounted the camels and
followed the man. So the servant took
Rebekah and departed.

Isaac Marries Rebekah

62 ¶ Now Isaac had come from going
to [a]Beer-lahai-roi; for he [1]was living in
[b]the [2]Negev.
63 Isaac went out [a]to [1]meditate in
the field toward evening; and [b]he lifted
up his eyes and looked, and behold, camels were coming.
64 Rebekah lifted up her eyes, and
when she saw Isaac she dismounted from
the camel.
65 She said to the servant, "Who is
that man walking in the field to meet us?"
And the servant said, "He is my master."
Then she took her [1]veil and covered herself.
66 The servant told Isaac all the things
that he had done.
67 Then Isaac brought her into his
mother Sarah's tent, and [a]he took Rebekah, and she became his wife, and [b]he
loved her; thus Isaac was comforted after
[c]his mother's death.

Abraham's Death

25 Now Abraham took another wife,
[1]whose name was Keturah.
2 [a]She bore to him Zimran and Jokshan and Medan and Midian and Ishbak
and Shuah.
3 Jokshan [1]became the father of Sheba and Dedan. And the sons of Dedan
were Asshurim and Letushim and Leum-
mim.
4 The sons of Midian *were* Ephah and
Epher and Hanoch and Abida and Eldaah.
All these *were* the sons of Keturah.

56 [a]Gen 24:40
57 [1]Lit *ask her mouth*
59 [a]Gen 35:8
60 [1]Lit *seed* [a]Gen 17:16 [b]Gen 22:17
62 [1]Lit *was dwelling* [2]I.e. South country [a]Gen 16:14; 25:11 [b]Gen 20:1
63 [1]Or *stroll*; meaning uncertain [a]Josh 1:8; Ps 1:2; 77:12; 119:15,27,48; 143:5; 145:5 [b]Gen 18:2
65 [1]Or *shawl*
67 [a]Gen 25:20 [b]Gen 29:18 [c]Gen 23:1,2
25:1 [1]Lit *and her name*
2 [a]1 Chr 1:32, 33
3 [1]Lit *begot*
5 [a]Gen 24:35,36
6 [1]Lit *concubines which belonged to Abraham* [a]Gen 21:14
7 [1]Lit *the days of* [a]Gen 12:4
8 [1]Lit *good* [a]Gen 15:15; 47:8,9 [b]Gen 25:17; 35:29; 49:29,33
9 [a]Gen 23:17, 18; 49:29,30; 50:13
10 [a]Gen 23:3-16
11 [1]Lit *dwelt* [a]Gen 12:2,3; 22:17; 26:3 [b]Gen 16:14; 24:62
12 [a]Gen 16:15
13 [1]Lit *in regard to their generations* [a]1 Chr 1:29-31
16 [1]Or *peoples* [a]Gen 17:20
17 [a]Gen 16:16 [b]Gen 25:8; 49:33
18 [1]Lit *dwelt* [2]Lit *before* [3]Lit *as you go* [4]Lit *fell over against* [5]Lit *brothers* [a]1 Sam 15:7 [b]Gen 20:1 [c]Gen 16:12
19 [1]Lit *begot* [a]Matt 1:2
20 [1]I.e. Syrian [a]Gen 24:15,29, 67 [b]Gen 22:23 [c]Gen 24:29

5 [a]Now Abraham gave all that he
had to Isaac;
6 but to the sons of [1]his concubines,
Abraham gave gifts while he was still living, and [a]sent them away from his son
Isaac eastward, to the land of the east.
7 ¶ These are [1]all the years of Abraham's life that he lived, [a]one hundred
and seventy-five years.
8 Abraham breathed his last and died
[a]in a [1]ripe old age, an old man and satisfied *with life;* and he was [b]gathered to
his people.
9 Then his sons Isaac and Ishmael
buried him in [a]the cave of Machpelah, in
the field of Ephron the son of Zohar the
Hittite, facing Mamre,
10 [a]the field which Abraham purchased from the sons of Heth; there Abraham was buried with Sarah his wife.
11 It came about after the death of
Abraham, that [a]God blessed his son
Isaac; and Isaac [1]lived by [b]Beer-lahai-
roi.

Descendants of Ishmael

12 ¶ Now these are *the records of* the
generations of [a]Ishmael, Abraham's son,
whom Hagar the Egyptian, Sarah's maid,
bore to Abraham;
13 and these are the names of [a]the
sons of Ishmael, by their names, [1]in the
order of their birth: Nebaioth, the firstborn of Ishmael, and Kedar and Adbeel
and Mibsam
14 and Mishma and Dumah and
Massa,
15 Hadad and Tema, Jetur, Naphish
and Kedemah.
16 These are the sons of Ishmael and
these are their names, by their villages,
and by their camps; [a]twelve princes according to their [1]tribes.
17 These are the years of the life of
Ishmael, [a]one hundred and thirty-seven
years; and he breathed his last and died,
and was [b]gathered to his people.
18 They [1]settled from [a]Havilah to
[b]Shur which is [2]east of Egypt [3]as one
goes toward Assyria; [c]he [4]settled in defiance of all his [5]relatives.

Isaac's Sons

19 ¶ Now these are *the records of*
[a]the generations of Isaac, Abraham's
son: Abraham [1]became the father of
Isaac;
20 and Isaac was forty years old when
he took [a]Rebekah, the [b]daughter of Bethuel the [1]Aramean of Paddan-aram, the
[c]sister of Laban the [1]Aramean, to be his
wife.
21 Isaac prayed to the LORD on behalf
of his wife, because she was barren; and

[a]the LORD [1]answered him and Rebekah
his wife [b]conceived.
22 But the children struggled together
within her; and she said, "If it is so, why
then am I *this way?*" So she went to [a]in-
quire of the LORD.
23 The LORD said to her,
"[a]Two nations are in your womb;
[b]And two peoples will be
separated from your body;
And one people shall be stronger
than the other;
And [c]the older shall serve the
younger."
24 When her days to be delivered
were fulfilled, behold, there were twins
in her womb.
25 Now the first came forth red, [a]all
over like a hairy garment; and they
named him Esau.
26 Afterward his brother came forth
with [a]his hand holding on to Esau's heel,
so [b]his name was called [1]Jacob; and
Isaac was [c]sixty years old when she gave
birth to them.
27 ¶ When the boys grew up, Esau became a skillful hunter, a man of the field,
but Jacob was a [1]peaceful man, [2a]living
in tents.
28 Now Isaac loved Esau, because [1]he
had [a]a taste for game, [b]but Rebekah
loved Jacob.
29 When Jacob had cooked [a]stew,
Esau came in from the field and he was
[1]famished;
30 and Esau said to Jacob, "Please let
me have a swallow of [1]that red stuff
there, for I am [2]famished." Therefore his
name was called [3]Edom.
31 But Jacob said, "[1]First sell me your
[a]birthright."
32 Esau said, "Behold, I am about to
die; so of what *use* then is the birthright
to me?"
33 And Jacob said, "[1]First swear to
me"; so he swore to him, and [a]sold his
birthright to Jacob.
34 Then Jacob gave Esau bread and
lentil stew; and he ate and drank, and
rose and went on his way. Thus Esau despised his birthright.

Isaac Settles in Gerar

26 Now there was [a]a famine in the
land, besides the previous famine
that had occurred in the days of Abraham. So Isaac went to Gerar, to [b]Abime-
lech king of the Philistines.
2 The LORD [a]appeared to him and
said, "Do not go down to Egypt; [1b]stay
in the land of which I shall tell you.
3 "Sojourn in this land and [a]I will be
with you and [b]bless you, for [c]to you and
to your [1]descendants I will give all these
lands, and I will establish [d]the oath
which I swore to your father Abraham.
4 "[a]I will multiply your [1]descendants
as the stars of heaven, and will give your
[1]descendants all these lands; and [b]by
your [1]descendants all the nations of the
earth [2]shall be blessed;
5 because Abraham [1a]obeyed Me
and kept My charge, My commandments,
My statutes and My laws."
6 ¶ So Isaac [1]lived in Gerar.
7 When the men of the place asked
about his wife, he said, "[a]She is my sister," for he was [b]afraid to say, "my wife,"
thinking, "[1]the men of the place might
kill me on account of Rebekah, for she is
[c]beautiful."
8 It came about, when he had been
there a long time, that Abimelech king of
the Philistines looked out through a window, and saw, and behold, Isaac was ca-
ressing his wife Rebekah.
9 Then Abimelech called Isaac and
said, "Behold, certainly she is your wife!
How then did you say, 'She is my sister'?"
And Isaac said to him, "Because I said, 'I
might die on account of her.' "
10 [a]Abimelech said, "What is this you
have done to us? One of the people might
easily have lain with your wife, and you
would have brought guilt upon us."
11 So Abimelech charged all the people, saying, "He who [a]touches this man
or his wife shall surely be put to death."
12 ¶ Now Isaac sowed in that land and
[1]reaped in the same year a hundredfold.
And [a]the LORD blessed him,
13 and the man [a]became rich, and
continued to grow [1]richer until he became very [1]wealthy;
14 for [a]he had possessions of flocks
[1]and herds and a great household, so that
the Philistines envied him.
15 Now [a]all the wells which his father's servants had dug in the days of
Abraham his father, the Philistines
stopped up [1]by filling them with earth.
16 Then Abimelech said to Isaac, "Go
away from us, for you are [1a]too powerful
for us."
17 And Isaac departed from there and
camped in the valley of Gerar, and [1]set-
tled there.

Quarrel over the Wells

18 ¶ Then Isaac dug again the wells of
water which [1]had been dug in the days
of his father Abraham, for the Philistines
had stopped them up after the death of
Abraham; and he [2]gave them the same
names which his father had [3]given them.
19 But when Isaac's servants dug in
the valley and found there a well of
[1]flowing water,

21 [1]Lit *was entreated of him* [a]1 Sam 1:17; 1 Chr 5:20; 2 Chr 33:13; Ezra 8:23; Ps 127:3 [b]Rom 9:10
22 [a]1 Sam 9:9; 10:22
23 [a]Gen 17:4-6, 16; Num 20:14; Deut 2:4,8 [b]Gen 27:29 [c]Gen 27:40; Mal 1:2, 3; Rom 9:12
25 [a]Gen 27:11
26 [1]I.e. one who takes by the heel or supplants [a]Hos 12:3 [b]Gen 27:36 [c]Gen 25:20
27 [1]Lit *complete* [2]Lit *dwelling* [a]Heb 11:9
28 [1]Lit *game was in his mouth* [a]Gen 27:19 [b]Gen 27:6-10
29 [1]Lit *weary* [a]2 Kin 4:38
30 [1]Lit *the red, this red* [2]Lit *weary* [3]I.e. red
31 [1]Lit *Today* [a]Deut 21:16,17; 1 Chr 5:1,2
33 [1]Lit *Today* [a]Heb 12:16
26:1 [a]Gen 12:10 [b]Gen 20:1,2
2 [1]Lit *dwell* [a]Gen 12:7; 17:1; 18:1 [b]Gen 12:1
3 [1]Lit *seed* [a]Gen 26:24; 28:15; 31:3 [b]Gen 12:2 [c]Gen 12:7; 13:15; 15:18 [d]Gen 22:16-18; Ps 105:9
4 [1]Lit *seed* [2]Or *bless themselves* [a]Gen 15:5; 22:17; Ex 32:13 [b]Gen 22:18; Gal 3:8
5 [1]Lit *hearkened to My voice* [a]Gen 22:16
6 [1]Lit *dwelt*
7 [1]Lit *lest...place* [a]Gen 12:13; 20:2,12 [b]Prov 29:25 [c]Gen 12:11; 24:16; 29:17
10 [a]Gen 20:9
11 [a]Ps 105:15
12 [1]Lit *found* [a]Gen 24:1; 26:3; Job 42:12; Prov 10:22
13 [1]Lit *great* [a]Prov 10:22
14 [1]Lit *and possessions of herds* [a]Gen 24:35; 25:5
15 [1]Lit *and filled them* [a]Gen 21:25,30
16 [1]Lit *much mightier than we* [a]Ex 1:9
17 [1]Lit *dwelt*
18 [1]Lit *they had dug* [2]Lit *called their names as the names* [3]Lit *called*
19 [1]Lit *living*

20 the herdsmen of Gerar [a]quarreled with the herdsmen of Isaac, saying, "The water is ours!" So he named the well [1]Esek, because they contended with him.
21 Then they dug another well, and they quarreled over it too, so he named it [1]Sitnah.
22 He moved away from there and dug another well, and they did not quarrel over it; so he named it [1]Rehoboth, for he said, "[2a]At last the LORD has made [3]room for us, and we will be [b]fruitful in the land."
23 ¶ Then he went up from there to [a]Beersheba.
24 The LORD [a]appeared to him the same night and said,

"[b]I am the God of your father
Abraham;
[c]Do not fear, for I am with you.
I [d]will bless you, and multiply
your [1]descendants,
For the sake of My servant
Abraham."

25 So he built an [a]altar there and called upon the name of the LORD, and pitched his tent there; and there Isaac's servants dug a well.

Covenant with Abimelech

26 ¶ Then [a]Abimelech came to him from Gerar [1]with his adviser Ahuzzath and Phicol the commander of his army.
27 Isaac said to them, "[a]Why have you come to me, since you hate me and have sent me away from you?"
28 They said, "We see plainly [a]that the LORD has been with you; so we said, 'Let there now be an oath between us, *even* between [1]you and us, and let us make a covenant with you,
29 that you will do us no harm, just as we have not touched you [1]and have done to you nothing but good and have sent you away in peace. You are now the [a]blessed of the LORD.' "
30 Then [a]he made them a feast, and they ate and drank.
31 In the morning they arose early and [1a]exchanged oaths; then Isaac sent them away and they departed from him in peace.
32 Now it came about on the same day, that Isaac's servants came in and told him about the well which they had dug, and said to him, "We have found water."
33 So he called it Shibah; therefore the name of the city is [a]Beersheba to this day.
34 ¶ When Esau was forty years old [a]he [1]married Judith the daughter of Beeri the Hittite, and Basemath the daughter of Elon the Hittite;
35 and [a]they [1]brought grief to Isaac and Rebekah.

Jacob's Deception

27 Now it came about, when Isaac was old and [a]his eyes were too dim to see, that he called his [b]older son Esau and said to him, "My son." And he said to him, "Here I am."
2 [1a]Isaac said, "Behold now, I am old *and* I do not know the day of my death.
3 "Now then, please take your gear, your quiver and your bow, and go out to the field and [a]hunt game for me;
4 and prepare a savory dish for me such as I love, and bring it to me that I may eat, so that [a]my soul may bless you before I die."
5 ¶ Rebekah was listening while Isaac spoke to his son Esau. So when Esau went to the field to hunt for game to bring *home,*
6 [a]Rebekah said to her son Jacob, "Behold, I heard your father speak to your brother Esau, saying,
7 'Bring me *some* game and prepare a savory dish for me, that I may eat, and bless you in the presence of the LORD before my death.'
8 "Now therefore, my son, [a]listen to [1]me [2]as I command you.
9 "Go now to the flock and [1]bring me two choice [2]young goats from there, that I may prepare them *as* a savory dish for your father, such as he loves.
10 "Then you shall bring *it* to your father, that he may eat, so that he may bless you before his death."
11 Jacob [1]answered his mother Rebekah, "Behold, Esau my brother is a [a]hairy man and I am a smooth man.
12 "[a]Perhaps my father will feel me, then I will be as a [1]deceiver in his sight, and I will bring upon myself a curse and not a blessing."
13 But his mother said to him, "Your curse be on me, my son; only [a]obey my voice, and go, get *them* for me."
14 So he went and got *them,* and brought *them* to his mother; and his mother made savory food such as his father loved.
15 Then Rebekah took the [1]best [a]garments of Esau her elder son, which were with her in the house, and put them on Jacob her younger son.
16 And she put the skins of the [1]young goats on his hands and on the smooth part of his neck.
17 She also gave the savory food and the bread, which she had made, [1]to her son Jacob.
18 ¶ Then he came to his father and

20 [1]I.e. contention [a]Gen 21:25
21 [1]I.e. enmity
22 [1]I.e. broad places [2]Lit *Truly now* [3]Or *broad* [a]Ps 4:1; Is 54:2, 3 [b]Gen 17:6; Ex 1:7
23 [a]Gen 22:19
24 [1]Lit *seed* [a]Gen 26:2 [b]Gen 17:7,8; 24:12; Ex 3:6; Acts 7:32 [c]Gen 15:1 [d]Gen 22:17; 26:3,4
25 [a]Gen 12:7,8; 13:4,18; Ps 116:17
26 [1]Lit *and his confidential friend* [a]Gen 21:22
27 [a]Judg 11:7
28 [1]Lit *us and you* [a]Gen 21:22, 23
29 [1]Lit *and just as we* [a]Gen 24:31; Ps 115:15
30 [a]Gen 19:3
31 [1]Lit *swore one to another* [a]Gen 21:31
33 [a]Gen 21:31
34 [1]Lit *took as wife* [a]Gen 28:8; 36:2
35 [1]Lit *were a bitterness of spirit to* [a]Gen 27:46
27:1 [a]Gen 48:10; 1 Sam 3:2 [b]Gen 25:25,33, 34
2 [1]Lit *He* [a]Gen 47:29
3 [a]Gen 25:28
4 [a]Gen 27:19, 25,31; 48:9,15, 16; Deut 33:1; Heb 11:20
6 [a]Gen 25:28
8 [1]Lit *my voice* [2]Lit *according to what* [a]Gen 27:13,43
9 [1]Lit *take* [2]Lit *kids of goats*
11 [1]Lit *said to* [a]Gen 25:25
12 [1]Lit *mocker* [a]Gen 27:21,22
13 [a]Gen 27:8
15 [1]Lit *desirable*; or *choice* [a]Gen 27:27
16 [1]Lit *kids of the goats*
17 [1]Lit *into the hand of*

said, "My father." And he said, "Here I
am. Who are you, my son?"
19 Jacob said to his father, "I am Esau
your firstborn; I have done as you told
me. [a]Get up, please, sit and eat of my
game, that [1b]you may bless me."
20 Isaac said to his son, "How is it that
you have *it* so quickly, my son?" And
he said, "[a]Because the LORD your God
caused *it* to happen to me."
21 Then Isaac said to Jacob, "Please
come close, that [a]I may feel you, my son,
whether you are really my son Esau or
not."
22 So Jacob came close to Isaac his father, and he felt him and said, "The voice
is the voice of Jacob, but the hands are
the hands of Esau."
23 He did not recognize him, because
his hands were [a]hairy like his brother
Esau's hands; so he blessed him.
24 And he said, "Are you really my son
Esau?" And he said, "I am."
25 So he said, "Bring *it* to me, and I
will eat of my son's game, that [1a]I may
bless you." And he brought *it* to him, and
he ate; he also brought him wine and he
drank.
26 Then his father Isaac said to him,
"Please come close and kiss me, my son."
27 So he came close and kissed him;
and when he smelled the smell of his
garments, he [a]blessed him and said,

"See, [b]the smell of my son
Is like the smell of a field
[c]which the LORD has
blessed;
28 Now may [a]God give you of the
dew of heaven,
And of the [b]fatness of the earth,
And an abundance of grain and
new wine;
29 [a]May peoples serve you,
And nations bow down to you;
[b]Be master of your brothers,
[c]And may your mother's sons
bow down to you.
[d]Cursed be those who curse
you,
And blessed be those who bless
you."

The Stolen Blessing

30 ¶ Now it came about, as soon as
Isaac had finished blessing Jacob, and Jacob had hardly gone out from the presence of Isaac his father, that Esau his
brother came in from his hunting.
31 Then he also made savory food, and
brought it to his father; and he said to
his father, "[a]Let my father arise and eat
of his son's game, that [1b]you may
bless me."
32 Isaac his father said to him, "[a]Who
are you?" And he said, "I am your son,
[b]your firstborn, Esau."
33 Then Isaac [1]trembled violently,
and said, "[a]Who was he then that hunted game and brought *it* to me, so that I ate
of all *of it* before you came, and blessed
him? [b]Yes, and he shall be blessed."
34 When Esau heard the words of his
father, [a]he cried out with an exceedingly
great and bitter cry, and said to his father,
"Bless me, *even* me also, O my father!"
35 And he said, "[a]Your brother came
deceitfully and has taken away your blessing."
36 Then he said, "[1]Is he not rightly
named [a]Jacob, for he has supplanted me
these two times? He took away my birthright, and behold, now he has taken away
my blessing." And he said, "Have you not
reserved a blessing for me?"
37 But Isaac replied to Esau, "Behold,
I have made him [a]your master, and all
his [1]relatives I have given to him [2]as
servants; and with grain and new wine I
have sustained him. Now as for you then,
what can I do, my son?"
38 Esau said to his father, "Do you
have only one blessing, my father? Bless
me, *even* me also, O my father." So Esau
lifted his voice and [a]wept.
39 ¶ Then [a]Isaac his father answered
and said to him,

"Behold, [1b]away from the
[2]fertility of the earth shall
be your dwelling,
And [1]away from the dew of
heaven from above.
40 "By your sword you shall live,
And your brother [a]you shall
serve;
But it shall come about [b]when
you become restless,
That you will [1]break his yoke
from your neck."

41 ¶ So Esau [a]bore a grudge against
Jacob because of the blessing with which
his father had blessed him; and Esau said
[1]to himself, "[b]The days of mourning for
my father are near; then I will kill my
brother Jacob."
42 Now when the words of her elder
son Esau were reported to Rebekah, she
sent and called her younger son Jacob,
and said to him, "Behold your brother
Esau is consoling himself concerning you
by planning to kill you.
43 "Now therefore, my son, [a]obey my
voice, and arise, [1]flee to [b]Haran, to my
brother [c]Laban!
44 "Stay with him [a]a few days, until
your brother's fury [1]subsides,
45 until your brother's anger [1]against
you subsides and he forgets [a]what you
did to him. Then I will send and get you

19 [1]Lit *your soul* [a]Gen 27:31 [b]Gen 27:4
20 [a]Gen 24:12
21 [a]Gen 27:12
23 [a]Gen 27:16
25 [1]Lit *my soul* [a]Gen 27:4
27 [a]Heb 11:20 [b]Song 4:11 [c]Ps 65:10
28 [a]Gen 27:39; Deut 33:13,28; Prov 3:20; Zech 8:12 [b]Num 18:12
29 [a]Gen 25:23; Is 45:14; 49:7, 23; 60:12,14 [b]Gen 9:26,27; 27:37 [c]Gen 37:7,10 [d]Gen 12:3; Num 24:9
31 [1]Lit *your soul* [a]Gen 27:19 [b]Gen 27:4
32 [a]Gen 27:18 [b]Gen 25:33,34
33 [1]Lit *trembled with a very great trembling* [a]Gen 27:35 [b]Gen 25:23; 28:3,4; Num 23:20
34 [a]Heb 12:17
35 [a]Gen 27:19
36 [1]Or *Was he then named Jacob that he has* [a]Gen 25:26, 32-34
37 [1]Lit *brothers* [2]Lit *for* [a]Gen 27:28,29
38 [a]Heb 12:17
39 [1]Or *of* [2]Lit *fatness* [a]Heb 11:20 [b]Gen 27:28; Deut 33:13,28
40 [1]Lit *tear off* [a]Gen 25:23; 27:29 [b]2 Kin 8:20-22
41 [1]Lit *in his heart* [a]Gen 32:3-11; 37:4,8 [b]Gen 50:2-4,10
43 [1]Lit *flee for yourself* [a]Gen 27:8,13 [b]Gen 11:31 [c]Gen 24:29
44 [1]Lit *turns away* [a]Gen 31:41
45 [1]Lit *turns away from you* [a]Gen 27:12,19, 35

from there. Why should I be bereaved of you both in one day?"

46 ¶ Rebekah said to Isaac, "I am tired of [1]living because of [a]the daughters of Heth; [b]if Jacob takes a wife from the daughters of Heth, like these, from the daughters of the land, what good will my life be to me?"

Jacob Is Sent Away

28 So Isaac called Jacob and [a]blessed him and charged him, and said to him, "[b]You shall not take a wife from the daughters of Canaan.

2 "Arise, go to Paddan-aram, to the house of [a]Bethuel your mother's father; and from there take to yourself a wife from the daughters of Laban your mother's brother.

3 "May [1a]God Almighty [b]bless you and [c]make you fruitful and [d]multiply you, that you may become a [e]company of peoples.

4 "May He also give you the [a]blessing of Abraham, to you and to your [1]descendants with you, that you may [b]possess the land of your [c]sojournings, which God gave to Abraham."

5 Then [a]Isaac sent Jacob away, and he went to Paddan-aram to Laban, son of Bethuel the Aramean, the brother of Rebekah, the mother of Jacob and Esau.

6 ¶ Now Esau saw that Isaac had blessed Jacob and sent him away to Paddan-aram to take to himself a wife from there, *and that* when he blessed him he charged him, saying, "[a]You shall not take a wife from the daughters of Canaan,"

7 and that Jacob had obeyed his father and his mother and had gone to Paddan-aram.

8 So Esau saw that [a]the daughters of Canaan displeased [1]his father Isaac;

9 and Esau went to Ishmael, and [1]married, [a]besides the wives that he had, Mahalath the daughter of Ishmael, Abraham's son, the sister of Nebaioth.

Jacob's Dream

10 ¶ Then Jacob departed from [a]Beersheba and went toward [b]Haran.

11 He [1]came to [2]a [a]certain place and spent the night there, because the sun had set; and he took one of the stones of the place and put it [3]under his head, and lay down in that place.

12 [a]He had a dream, and behold, a ladder was set on the earth with its top reaching to heaven; and behold, [b]the angels of God were ascending and descending on it.

13 And behold, [a]the LORD stood [1]above it and said, "I am the LORD, [b]the God of your father Abraham and the God of Isaac; the land on which you lie, I will give it [c]to you and to [d]your [2]descendants.

14 "Your [1]descendants will also be like [a]the dust of the earth, and you will [2]spread out [b]to the west and to the east and to the north and to the south; and [c]in you and in your [1]descendants shall all the families of the earth be blessed.

15 "Behold, [a]I am with you and [b]will keep you wherever you go, and [c]will bring you back to this land; for [d]I will not leave you until I have done what I have [1]promised you."

16 Then Jacob [a]awoke from his sleep and said, "[b]Surely the LORD is in this place, and I did not know it."

17 He was afraid and said, "[a]How awesome is this place! This is none other than the house of God, and this is the gate of heaven."

18 ¶ So Jacob rose early in the morning, and took [a]the stone that he had put [1]under his head and set it up as a pillar and poured oil on its top.

19 He called the name of that place [1a]Bethel; however, [2]previously the name of the city had been [b]Luz.

20 Then Jacob [a]made a vow, saying, "[b]If God will be with me and will keep me on this journey that I [1]take, and will give me [2c]food to eat and garments to wear,

21 and [a]I return to my father's house in [1]safety, [b]then the LORD will be my God.

22 "This stone, which I have set up as a pillar, [a]will be God's house, and [b]of all that You give me I will surely give a tenth to You."

Jacob Meets Rachel

29 Then Jacob [1]went on his journey, and came to the land of [a]the sons of the east.

2 He looked, and [1]saw [a]a well in the field, and behold, three flocks of sheep were lying there beside it, for from that well they watered the flocks. Now the stone on the mouth of the well was large.

3 When all the flocks were gathered there, they would then roll the stone from the mouth of the well and water the sheep, and put the stone back in its place on the mouth of the well.

4 ¶ Jacob said to them, "My brothers, where are you from?" And they said, "We are from [a]Haran."

5 He said to them, "Do you know Laban the [a]son of Nahor?" And they said, "We know *him.*"

6 And he said to them, "Is it well with him?" And they said, "It is well, and

46 [1]Lit *my life* [a]Gen 26:34,35; 28:8 [b]Gen 24:3
28:1 [a]Gen 27:33 [b]Gen 24:3,4
2 [a]Gen 25:20
3 [1]Heb *El Shaddai* [a]Gen 17:1; 35:11; 48:3 [b]Gen 22:17 [c]Gen 17:6,20 [d]Gen 17:2; 26:4,24 [e]Gen 35:11; 48:4
4 [1]Lit *seed* [a]Gen 12:2; 22:17 [b]Gen 15:7,8; 17:8 [c]1 Chr 29:15; Ps 39:12
5 [a]Gen 27:43
6 [a]Gen 28:1
8 [1]Lit *in the eyes of his* [a]Gen 24:3; 26:34,35; 27:46
9 [1]Lit *took for his wife* [a]Gen 26:34; 36:2
10 [a]Gen 26:23 [b]Gen 12:4,5; 27:43
11 [1]Lit *lighted on* [2]Lit *the place* [3]Lit *at his head-place* [a]Gen 28:19
12 [a]Gen 41:1; Num 12:6 [b]John 1:51
13 [1]Or *beside him* [2]Lit *seed* [a]Gen 35:1; Amos 7:7 [b]Gen 26:3,24 [c]Gen 13:15,17; 26:3 [d]Gen 12:7; 15:18
14 [1]Lit *seed* [2]Lit *break through* [a]Gen 13:16; 22:17 [b]Gen 13:14,15 [c]Gen 12:3; 18:18; 22:18; 26:4
15 [1]Lit *spoken to* [a]Gen 26:3,24; 31:3 [b]Num 6:24; Ps 121:5,7,8 [c]Gen 48:21; Deut 30:3 [d]Num 23:19; Deut 7:9; 31:6,8
16 [a]1 Kin 3:15; Jer 31:26 [b]Ex 3:4-6; Josh 5:13-15; Ps 139:7-12
17 [a]Ps 68:35
18 [1]Lit *at his head-place* [a]Gen 28:11; 35:14
19 [1]I.e. the house of God [2]Lit *at the first* [a]Judg 1:23 [b]Gen 35:6; 48:3
20 [1]Lit *go* [2]Lit *bread* [a]Gen 31:13; Judg 11:30; 2 Sam 15:8 [b]Gen 28:15 [c]1 Tim 6:8
21 [1]Lit *peace* [a]Judg 11:31 [b]Deut 26:17
22 [a]Gen 35:7 [b]Lev 27:30; Deut 14:22
29:1 [1]Lit *lifted up his feet* [a]Judg 6:3,33
2 [1]Lit *behold* [a]Gen 24:10,11; Ex 2:15,16
4 [a]Gen 28:10
5 [a]Gen 24:24,29

here is [a]Rachel his daughter coming
with the sheep."
7 He said, "Behold, it is still high day;
it is not time for the livestock to be gathered. Water the sheep, and go, pasture
them."
8 But they said, "We cannot, until all
the flocks are gathered, and they roll the
stone from the mouth of the well; then
we water the sheep."
9 ¶ While he was still speaking with
them, Rachel came with her father's
sheep, for she was a shepherdess.
10 When Jacob saw Rachel the daughter of Laban his mother's brother, and the
sheep of Laban his mother's brother, Jacob went up and rolled the stone from the
mouth of the well and watered the flock
of Laban his mother's brother.
11 Then Jacob [a]kissed Rachel, and lifted his voice and wept.
12 Jacob told Rachel that he was a
[1a]relative of her father and that he was
Rebekah's son, and [b]she ran and told her
father.
13 ¶ So when [a]Laban heard the news
of Jacob his sister's son, he ran to meet
him, and [b]embraced him and kissed him
and brought him to his house. Then he
related to Laban all these things.
14 Laban said to him, "Surely you are
[a]my bone and my flesh." And he stayed
with him a month.
15 ¶ Then Laban said to Jacob, "Because you are my [1]relative, should you
therefore serve me for nothing? Tell me,
what shall [a]your wages be?"
16 Now Laban had two daughters; the
name of the older was Leah, and the
name of the younger was Rachel.
17 And Leah's eyes were weak, but Rachel was [a]beautiful of form and [1]face.
18 Now Jacob [a]loved Rachel, so he
said, "[b]I will serve you seven years for
your younger daughter Rachel."
19 Laban said, "It is better that I give
her to you than to give her to another
man; stay with me."
20 So Jacob served seven years for Rachel and they seemed to him but a few
days [a]because of his love for her.

Laban's Treachery

21 ¶ Then Jacob said to Laban, "Give
me my wife, for my [1]time is completed,
that I may [a]go in to her."
22 Laban gathered all the men of the
place and made a feast.
23 Now in the evening he took his
daughter Leah, and brought her to him;
and *Jacob* went in to her.
24 Laban also gave his maid Zilpah to
his daughter Leah as a maid.
25 So it came about in the morning
that, behold, it was Leah! And he said to
Laban, "[a]What is this you have done to
me? Was it not for Rachel that I served
with you? Why then have you [b]de-
ceived me?"
26 But Laban said, "It is not [1]the practice in our place to [2]marry off the younger before the firstborn.
27 "Complete the week of this one, and
we will give you the other also for the
service which [a]you shall serve with me
for another seven years."
28 Jacob did so and completed her
week, and he gave him his daughter Rachel as his wife.
29 Laban also gave his maid Bilhah to
his daughter Rachel as her maid.
30 So *Jacob* went in to Rachel also, and
indeed [a]he loved Rachel more than
Leah, and he served with [1]Laban for
[b]another seven years.
31 ¶ Now the LORD saw that Leah was
[1]unloved, and He opened her womb, but
Rachel was barren.
32 Leah conceived and bore a son and
named him [1]Reuben, for she said, "Because the LORD has [2a]seen my affliction;
surely now my husband will love me."
33 Then she conceived again and bore
a son and said, "[a]Because the LORD has
[1]heard that I am [2]unloved, He has therefore given me this *son* also." So she
named him Simeon.
34 She conceived again and bore a son
and said, "Now this time my husband
will become [1]attached to me, because I
have borne him three sons." Therefore
he was named [a]Levi.
35 And she conceived again and bore
a son and said, "This time I will [1]praise
the LORD." Therefore she named him
[2a]Judah. Then she stopped bearing.

The Sons of Jacob

30 Now when Rachel saw that [a]she
bore Jacob no children, [1]she became jealous of her sister; and she said to
Jacob, "[b]Give me children, or else I die."
2 Then Jacob's anger burned against
Rachel, and he said, "Am I in the place of
God, who has [a]withheld from you the
fruit of the womb?"
3 She said, "[a]Here is my maid Bilhah, go in to her that she may [b]bear on
my knees, that [1a]through her I too may
have children."
4 So [a]she gave him her maid Bilhah
as a wife, and Jacob went in to her.
5 Bilhah conceived and bore Jacob a
son.
6 Then Rachel said, "God has [1a]vin-
dicated me, and has indeed heard my
voice and has given me a son." Therefore
she named him [2]Dan.

6 [a]Ex 2:16
11 [a]Gen 33:4
12 [1]Lit *brother* [a]Gen 28:5 [b]Gen 24:28
13 [a]Gen 24:29-31 [b]Gen 33:4
14 [a]Gen 2:23; Judg 9:2; 2 Sam 5:1; 19:12,13
15 [1]Lit *brother* [a]Gen 31:41
17 [1]Lit *beautiful of appearance* [a]Gen 12:11,14; 26:7
18 [a]Gen 24:67 [b]Hos 12:12
20 [a]Song 8:7
21 [1]Lit *days are* [a]Judg 15:1
25 [a]Gen 12:18; 20:9; 26:10 [b]1 Sam 28:12
26 [1]Lit *done thus in* [2]Lit *give*
27 [a]Gen 31:41
30 [1]Lit *him* [a]Gen 29:17,18 [b]Gen 31:41
31 [1]Lit *hated*
32 [1]I.e. see, a son [2]Lit *looked upon* [a]Gen 16:11; 31:42; Ex 3:7; 4:31; Deut 26:7; Ps 25:18
33 [1]Heb *shama,* related to Simeon [2]Lit *hated* [a]Deut 21:15
34 [1]Heb *lavah,* related to Levi [a]Gen 49:5
35 [1]Heb *Jadah,* related to Judah [2]Heb *Jehudah* [a]Gen 49:8; Matt 1:2
30:1 [1]Lit *Rachel* [a]Gen 29:31 [b]1 Sam 1:5,6
2 [a]Gen 20:18; 29:31
3 [1]Lit *from her I too may be built* [a]Gen 16:2 [b]Gen 50:23; Job 3:12
4 [a]Gen 16:3,4
6 [1]Lit *judged* [2]I.e. He judged [a]Ps 35:24; 43:1; Lam 3:59

7 Rachel's maid Bilhah conceived
again and bore Jacob a second son.
8 So Rachel said, "With [1]mighty
wrestlings I have [2]wrestled with my sister, *and* I have indeed prevailed." And
she named him Naphtali.
9 ¶ When Leah saw that she had
stopped bearing, she took her maid Zilpah and gave her to Jacob as a wife.
10 Leah's maid Zilpah bore Jacob a
son.
11 Then Leah said, "[1]How fortunate!"
So she named him [2]Gad.
12 Leah's maid Zilpah bore Jacob a second son.
13 Then Leah said, "[1]Happy am I! For
women [a]will call me happy." So she
named him [2]Asher.
14 ¶ Now in the days of wheat harvest
Reuben went and found [a]mandrakes in
the field, and brought them to his mother
Leah. Then Rachel said to Leah, "Please
give me some of your son's mandrakes."
15 But she said to her, "Is it a small
matter for you to take my husband? And
would you take my son's mandrakes
also?" So Rachel said, "Therefore he may
lie with you tonight in return for your
son's mandrakes."
16 When Jacob came in from the field
in the evening, then Leah went out to
meet him and said, "You must come in to
me, for I have surely hired you with my
son's mandrakes." So he lay with her that
night.
17 God gave heed to Leah, and she
conceived and bore Jacob a fifth son.
18 Then Leah said, "God has given me
my [1]wages because I gave my maid to my
husband." So she named him Issachar.
19 Leah conceived again and bore a
sixth son to Jacob.
20 Then Leah said, "God has endowed
me with a good gift; now my husband
[1]will dwell with me, because I have
borne him six sons." So she named him
Zebulun.
21 Afterward she bore a daughter and
named her Dinah.
22 ¶ Then [a]God remembered Rachel,
and God gave heed to her and [b]opened
her womb.
23 So she conceived and bore a son
and said, "God has [a]taken away my reproach."
24 She named him Joseph, saying,
"[a]May the LORD [1]give me another son."

Jacob Prospers

25 ¶ Now it came about when Rachel
had borne Joseph, that Jacob said to Laban, "[a]Send me away, that I may go to
my own place and to my own country.
26 "Give *me* my wives and my children
[a]for whom I have served you, and let me
depart; for you yourself know my service
which I have [1]rendered you."
27 But Laban said to him, "If now [1]it
pleases you, *stay with me;* I have divined
[a]that the LORD has blessed me on your
account."
28 He [1]continued, "[a]Name me your
wages, and I will give it."
29 But he said to him, "[a]You yourself
know how I have served you and how
your cattle have [1]fared with me.
30 "For you had little before [1]I came
and it has [2]increased to a multitude, and
the LORD has blessed you [3]wherever I
turned. But now, when shall I provide for
my own household also?"
31 So he said, "What shall I give you?"
And Jacob said, "You shall not give me
anything. If you will do this *one* thing for
me, I will again pasture *and* keep your
flock:
32 let me pass through your entire
flock today, removing from there every
[a]speckled and spotted sheep and every
black [1]one among the lambs and the
spotted and speckled among the goats;
and *such* shall be my wages.
33 "So my [1]honesty will answer for me
later, when you come concerning my
[2]wages. Every one that is not speckled
and spotted among the goats and black
among the lambs, *if found* with me, will
be considered stolen."
34 Laban said, "[1]Good, let it be according to your word."
35 So he removed on that day the
striped and spotted male goats and all the
speckled and spotted female goats, every
one with white in it, and all the black
ones among the sheep, and gave them
into the [1]care of his sons.
36 And he put *a distance of* three days'
journey between himself and Jacob, and
Jacob fed the rest of Laban's flocks.
37 ¶ Then Jacob [1]took fresh rods of
poplar and almond and plane trees, and
peeled white stripes in them, exposing
the white which *was* [2]in the rods.
38 He set the rods which he had
peeled in front of the flocks in the gutters,
even in the watering troughs, where the
flocks came to drink; and they [1]mated
when they came to drink.
39 So the flocks [1]mated by the rods,
and the flocks brought forth striped,
speckled, and spotted.
40 Jacob separated the lambs, and
[1]made the flocks face toward the striped
and all the black in the flock of Laban; and
he put his own herds apart, and did not
put them with Laban's flock.
41 Moreover, whenever the [1]stronger
of the flock [2]were mating, Jacob would

8 [1]Lit *wrestlings of God* [2]Heb *niphtal,* related to Naphtali
11 [1]Lit *With fortune!* Some versions read *Fortune has come* [2]I.e. Fortune
13 [1]Lit *With my happiness!* [2]I.e. happy [a]Luke 1:48
14 [a]Song 7:13
18 [1]Heb *sachar,* related to Issachar
20 [1]Heb *zabal,* related to Zebulun. Some translate *will honor*
22 [a]1 Sam 1:19, 20 [b]Gen 29:31
23 [a]Is 4:1; Luke 1:25
24 [1]Lit *add to me;* Heb *Joseph* [a]Gen 35:17
25 [a]Gen 24:54, 56
26 [1]Lit *served* [a]Gen 29:18,20, 27; Hos 12:12
27 [1]Lit *I have found favor in your eyes* [a]Gen 26:24; 39:3,5; Is 61:9
28 [1]Lit *said* [a]Gen 29:15; 31:7,41
29 [1]Lit *been* [a]Gen 31:6
30 [1]Lit *me* [2]Lit *broken forth* [3]Lit *at my foot*
32 [1]Lit *sheep* [a]Gen 31:8
33 [1]Lit *righteousness* [2]Lit *wages which are before you*
34 [1]Lit *Behold, would that it might be*
35 [1]Lit *hand*
37 [1]Lit *took to himself* [2]Lit *on*
38 [1]Or *conceived*
39 [1]Or *conceived*
40 [1]Lit *set the faces*
41 [1]Lit *bound ones;* i.e. firm and compact [2]Or *conceived*

place the rods in the sight of the flock in the gutters, so that they might [3]mate by the rods;

42 but when the flock was feeble, he did not put *them* in; so the feebler were Laban's and the [1]stronger Jacob's.

43 So [a]the man [1]became exceedingly prosperous, and had large flocks and female and male servants and camels and donkeys.

Jacob Leaves Secretly for Canaan

31 Now [1]Jacob heard the words of Laban's sons, saying, "Jacob has taken away all that was our father's, and from what belonged to our father he has made all this [2]wealth."

2 Jacob saw the [1]attitude of Laban, and behold, it was not *friendly* toward him as formerly.

3 Then the LORD said to Jacob, "[a]Return to the land of your fathers and to your relatives, and [b]I will be with you."

4 So Jacob sent and called Rachel and Leah to his flock in the field,

5 and said to them, "[a]I see your father's [1]attitude, that it is not *friendly* toward me as formerly, but [b]the God of my father has been with me.

6 "[a]You know that I have served your father with all my strength.

7 "Yet your father has [a]cheated me and [b]changed my wages ten times; however, [c]God did not allow him to hurt me.

8 "If [a]he spoke thus, 'The speckled shall be your wages,' then all the flock brought forth speckled; and if he spoke thus, 'The striped shall be your wages,' then all the flock brought forth striped.

9 "Thus God has [a]taken away your father's livestock and given *them* to me.

10 "And it came about at the time when the flock were [1]mating that I lifted up my eyes and saw in a dream, and behold, the male goats which were [2]mating *were* striped, speckled, and mottled.

11 "Then [a]the angel of God said to me in the dream, 'Jacob,' and I said, 'Here I am.'

12 "He said, 'Lift up now your eyes and see *that* all the male goats which are [1]mating are striped, speckled, and mottled; for [a]I have seen all that Laban has been doing to you.

13 'I am [a]the God *of* Bethel, where you [b]anointed a pillar, where you made a vow to Me; now arise, [1]leave this land, and [c]return to the land of your birth.' "

14 Rachel and Leah said to him, "Do we still have any portion or inheritance in our father's house?

15 "Are we not reckoned by him as foreigners? For [a]he has sold us, and has also [1]entirely consumed [2]our purchase price.

16 "Surely all the wealth which God has taken away from our father belongs to us and our children; now then, do whatever God has said to you."

17 ¶ Then Jacob arose and put his children and his wives upon camels;

18 and he drove away all his livestock and all his property which he had gathered, his acquired livestock which he had gathered in Paddan-aram, [a]to go to the land of Canaan to his father Isaac.

19 When Laban had gone to shear his flock, then Rachel stole the [1a]household idols that were her father's.

20 And Jacob [1]deceived Laban the Aramean by not telling him that he was fleeing.

21 So he fled with all that he had; and he arose and crossed the *Euphrates* River, and set his face toward the hill country of [a]Gilead.

Laban Pursues Jacob

22 ¶ When it was told Laban on the third day that Jacob had fled,

23 then he took his [1]kinsmen with him and pursued him *a distance of* seven days' journey, and he overtook him in the hill country of Gilead.

24 [a]God came to Laban the Aramean in a [b]dream of the night and said to him, "[1c]Be careful that you do not speak to Jacob either good or bad."

25 ¶ Laban caught up with Jacob. Now Jacob had pitched his tent in the hill country, and Laban with his [1]kinsmen camped in the hill country of Gilead.

26 Then Laban said to Jacob, "What have you done [1]by deceiving me and carrying away my daughters like captives of the sword?

27 "Why did you flee secretly and [1]deceive me, and did not tell me so that I might have sent you away with joy and with songs, with [a]timbrel and with [b]lyre;

28 and did not allow me [a]to kiss my sons and my daughters? Now you have done foolishly.

29 "It is in [1]my power to do you harm, but [a]the God of your father spoke to me last night, saying, '[2b]Be careful not to speak either good or bad to Jacob.'

30 "Now you have indeed gone away because you longed greatly for your father's house; *but* why did you steal [a]my gods?"

31 Then Jacob replied to Laban, "Because I was afraid, for I thought that you would take your daughters from me by force.

32 "[a]The one with whom you find your

---

41 [3]Or *conceive*
42 [1]Lit *bound ones*; i.e. firm and compact
43 [1]Lit *broke forth* [a]Gen 12:16; 13:2; 24:35; 26:13,14; 30:30
31:1 [1]Lit *he* [2]Lit *glory*
2 [1]Lit *face*
3 [a]Gen 32:9 [b]Gen 28:15
5 [1]Lit *face* [a]Gen 31:2 [b]Gen 21:22; 28:13,15; 31:29,42,53; Is 41:10; Heb 13:5
6 [a]Gen 30:29
7 [a]Gen 29:25 [b]Gen 31:41 [c]Gen 15:1; 31:29
8 [a]Gen 30:32
9 [a]Gen 31:1,16
10 [1]Or *conceiving* [2]Lit *leaping upon the flock*
11 [a]Gen 16:7-11; 22:11, 15; 31:13; 48:16
12 [1]Lit *leaping upon the flock* [a]Ex 3:7
13 [1]Lit *go out from* [a]Gen 28:13,19 [b]Gen 28:18,20 [c]Gen 28:15; 32:9
15 [1]I.e. enjoyed the benefit of [2]Lit *our money* [a]Gen 29:20,23, 27
18 [a]Gen 35:27
19 [1]Heb *teraphim* [a]Gen 31:30,34; 35:2; Judg 17:5; 1 Sam 19:13; Hos 3:4
20 [1]Lit *stole the heart of*
21 [a]Gen 37:25
23 [1]Lit *brothers*
24 [1]Lit *Take heed to yourself* [a]Gen 20:3; 31:29 [b]Gen 20:3,6; 31:11 [c]Gen 24:50; 31:7,29
25 [1]Lit *brothers*
26 [1]Lit *and you have stolen my heart*
27 [1]Lit *steal me* [a]Ex 15:20 [b]Gen 4:21
28 [a]Gen 31:55
29 [1]Lit *the power of my hand* [2]Lit *Take heed to yourself* [a]Gen 31:5,24,42,53 [b]Gen 31:24
30 [a]Gen 31:19; Josh 24:2; Judg 18:24
32 [a]Gen 44:9

Jacob's Journeys

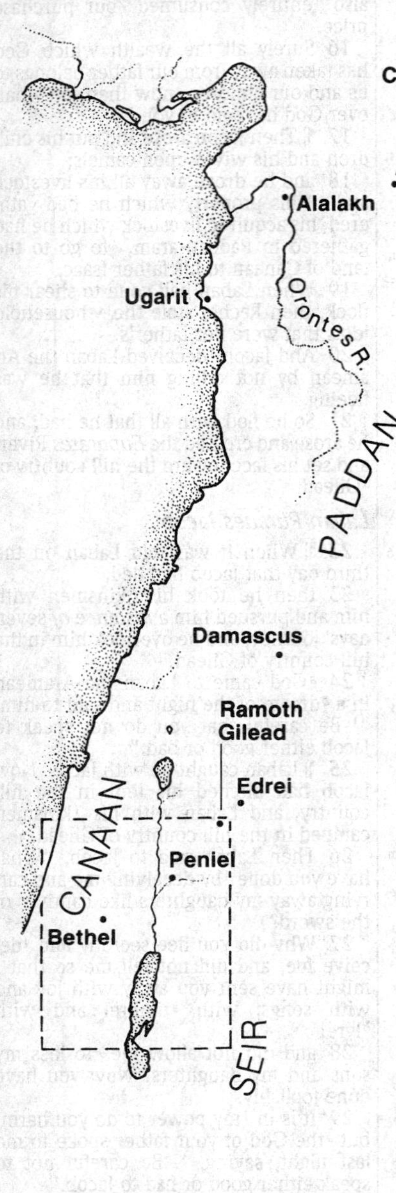

Jacob's journey took him from Beersheba in Canaan to the home of his uncle Laban near Haran and back to Canaan. His route back (after twenty years in Haran) likely took him toward Aleppo, then to Damascus and Edrei before reaching Peniel on the Jabbok River. From Peniel he camped at Succoth, finally reentering Canaan and settling at Shechem, where he built an altar to the Lord.

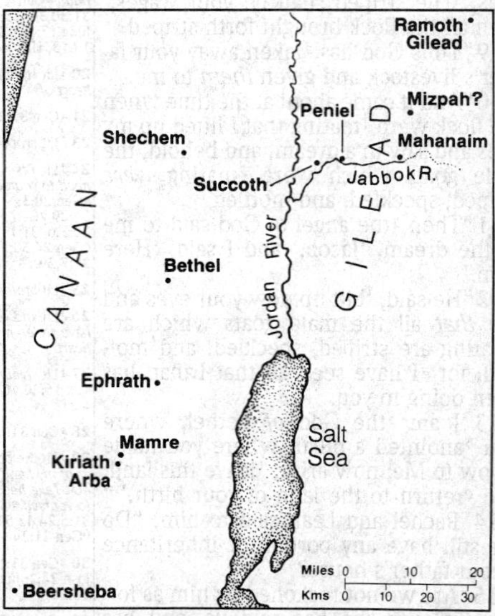

gods shall not live; in the presence of
our [1]kinsmen [2]point out what is yours
[3]among my belongings and take *it* for
yourself." For Jacob did not know that
Rachel had stolen them.
33 ¶ So Laban went into Jacob's tent
and into Leah's tent and into the tent of
the two maids, but he did not find *them.*
Then he went out of Leah's tent and entered Rachel's tent.
34 Now Rachel had taken the [1]house-
hold idols and put them in the camel's
saddle, and she sat on them. And Laban
felt through all the tent but did not find
them.
35 She said to her father, "Let not my
lord be angry that I cannot [a]rise before
you, for the manner of women is upon
me." So he searched but did not find the
[1b]household idols.
36 ¶ Then Jacob became angry and
contended with Laban; and Jacob said to
Laban, "What is my transgression? What
is my sin that you have hotly pursued me?
37 "Though you have felt through all
my goods, what have you found of all
your household goods? Set *it* here before
my [1]kinsmen and your [1]kinsmen, that
they may decide between us two.
38 "These twenty years I *have been*
with you; your ewes and your female
goats have not miscarried, nor have I eat-
en the rams of your flocks.
39 "That which was torn *of beasts* I did
not bring to you; I bore the loss of it
myself. You required it of my hand
whether stolen by day or stolen by night.
40 "*Thus* I was: by day the [1]heat consumed me and the frost by night, and my
sleep fled from my eyes.
41 "These twenty years I have been in
your house; [a]I served you fourteen years
for your two daughters and six years for
your flock, and you [b]changed my wages
ten times.
42 "If [a]the God of my father, the God
of Abraham, and the fear of Isaac, had not
been for me, surely now you would have
sent me away empty-handed. [b]God has
seen my affliction and the toil of my
hands, so He [c]rendered judgment last
night."

The Covenant of Mizpah

43 ¶ Then Laban replied to Jacob,
"The daughters are my daughters, and
the children are my children, and [a]the
flocks are my flocks, and all that you see
is mine. But what can I do this day to
these my daughters or to their children
whom they have borne?
44 "So now come, let us [a]make a covenant, [1]you and I, and [b]let it be a witness between [2]you and me."
45 Then Jacob took [a]a stone and set it
up *as* a pillar.
46 Jacob said to his [1]kinsmen, "Gather stones." So they took stones and made
a heap, and they ate there by the heap.
47 Now Laban [a]called it [1]Jegar-
sahadutha, but Jacob called it [2]Galeed.
48 Laban said, "[a]This heap is a witness between [1]you and me this day."
Therefore it was named Galeed,
49 and [1a]Mizpah, for he said, "May
the LORD watch between [2]you and me
when we are [3]absent one from the other.
50 "If you mistreat my daughters, or if
you take wives besides my daughters, *al-*
though no man is with us, see, [a]God is
witness between [1]you and me."
51 Laban said to Jacob, "Behold this
heap and behold the pillar which I have
set between [1]you and me.
52 "This heap is a witness, and the pillar is a witness, that I will not pass by this
heap to you for harm, and you will not
pass by this heap and this pillar to me, for
harm.
53 "[a]The God of Abraham and the God
of Nahor, the God of their father, [b]judge
between us." So Jacob swore by [c]the fear
of his father Isaac.
54 Then Jacob [a]offered a sacrifice on
the mountain, and called his [1]kinsmen to
[2]the meal; and they ate [3]the meal and
spent the night on the mountain.
55 [1]Early in the morning Laban arose,
and [a]kissed his sons and his daughters
and blessed them. Then Laban departed
and returned to his place.

Jacob's Fear of Esau

32 Now as Jacob went on his way,
[a]the angels of God met him.
2 Jacob said when he saw them,
"This is God's [1]camp." So he named that
place [2a]Mahanaim.
3 ¶ Then Jacob [a]sent messengers before him to his brother Esau in the land
of [b]Seir, the [1]country of [c]Edom.
4 He also commanded them saying,
"Thus you shall say to my lord Esau:
'Thus says your servant Jacob, "I have
sojourned with Laban, and [a]stayed until
now;
5 [a]I have oxen and donkeys *and*
flocks and male and female servants; and
I have sent to tell my lord, [b]that I may
find favor in your sight." ' "
6 ¶ The messengers returned to Jacob, saying, "We came to your brother
Esau, and furthermore [a]he is coming to
meet you, and four hundred men are
with him."
7 Then Jacob was [a]greatly afraid and

32 [1]Lit *brothers* [2]Lit *recognize* [3]Lit *with me*

34 [1]Heb *teraphim*

35 [1]Heb *teraphim* [a]Lev 19:32 [b]Gen 31:19

37 [1]Lit *brothers*

40 [1]Or *drought*

41 [a]Gen 29:27, 30 [b]Gen 31:7

42 [a]Gen 31:5, 29,53 [b]Gen 29:32; Ex 3:7 [c]Gen 31:24,29

43 [a]Gen 31:1

44 [1]Lit *I and you* [2]Lit *me and you* [a]Gen 21:27, 32; 26:28 [b]Josh 24:27

45 [a]Gen 28:18; Josh 24:26,27

46 [1]Lit *brothers*

47 [1]I.e. the heap of witness, in Aram [2]I.e. the heap of witness, in Heb [a]Josh 22:34

48 [1]Lit *me and you* [a]Josh 24:27

49 [1]Lit *the Mizpah*; i.e. the watchtower [2]Lit *me and you* [3]Lit *hidden* [a]Judg 11:29; 1 Sam 7:5,6

50 [1]Lit *me and you* [a]Jer 29:23; 42:5

51 [1]Lit *me and you*

53 [a]Gen 28:13 [b]Gen 16:5 [c]Gen 31:42

54 [1]Lit *brothers* [2]Lit *eat bread* [3]Lit *bread* [a]Ex 18:12

55 [1]Ch 32:1 in Heb [a]Gen 31:28, 43

32:1 [a]2 Kin 6:16,17; Ps 34:7

2 [1]Or *company* [2]I.e. Two Camps, or Two Companies [a]Josh 21:38; 2 Sam 2:8

3 [1]Lit *field* [a]Gen 27:41,42; 32:7, 11 [b]Gen 14:6; 33:14 [c]Gen 25:30; 36:8,9

4 [a]Gen 31:41

5 [a]Gen 30:43 [b]Gen 33:8

6 [a]Gen 33:1

7 [a]Gen 32:11

distressed; and he divided the people who were with him, and the flocks and the herds and the camels, into two companies;

8 for he said, “If Esau comes to the one company and [1]attacks it, then the company which is left will escape.”

9 ¶ Jacob said, “O [a]God of my father Abraham and God of my father Isaac, O LORD, who said to me, ‘[b]Return to your country and to your relatives, and I will [1]prosper you,’

10 [1]I am unworthy [a]of all the lovingkindness and of all the [2]faithfulness which You have shown to Your servant; for with my staff *only* I crossed this Jordan, and now I have become two companies.

11 “[a]Deliver me, I pray, [b]from the hand of my brother, from the hand of Esau; for I fear him, that he will come and [1]attack me *and* the [c]mothers with the children.

12 “For You said, ‘[a]I will surely [1]prosper you and [b]make your [2]descendants as the sand of the sea, which is too great to be numbered.’ ”

13 ¶ So he spent the night there. Then he [1]selected from what [2]he had with him a [a]present for his brother Esau:

14 two hundred female goats and twenty male goats, two hundred ewes and twenty rams,

15 thirty milking camels and their colts, forty cows and ten bulls, twenty female donkeys and ten male donkeys.

16 He delivered *them* into the hand of his servants, every drove by itself, and said to his servants, “Pass on before me, and put a space between droves.”

17 He commanded the [1]one in front, saying, “When my brother Esau meets you and asks you, saying, ‘To whom do you belong, and where are you going, and to whom do these *animals* in front of you belong?’

18 then you shall say, ‘*These* belong to your servant Jacob; it is a present sent to my lord Esau. And behold, he also is behind us.’ ”

19 Then he commanded also the second and the third, and all those who followed the droves, saying, “After this manner you shall speak to Esau when you find him;

20 and you shall say, ‘Behold, your servant Jacob also is behind us.’ ” For he said, “I will appease him with the present that goes before me. Then afterward I will see his face; perhaps he will accept me.”

21 So the present passed on before him, while he himself spent that night in the camp.

22 ¶ Now he arose that same night and took his two wives and his two maids and his eleven children, and crossed the ford of the [a]Jabbok.

23 He took them and sent them across the stream. And he sent across whatever he had.

Jacob Wrestles

24 Then Jacob was left alone, and a man [a]wrestled with him until daybreak.

25 When he saw that he had not prevailed against him, he touched the socket of his thigh; so the socket of Jacob's thigh was dislocated while he wrestled with him.

26 Then he said, “Let me go, for the dawn is breaking.” But he said, “[a]I will not let you go unless you bless me.”

27 So he said to him, “What is your name?” And he said, “Jacob.”

28 [a]He said, “Your name shall no longer be Jacob, but [1]Israel; for you have striven with God and with men and have prevailed.”

29 Then [a]Jacob asked him and said, “Please tell me your name.” But he said, “Why is it that you ask my name?” And he blessed him there.

30 So Jacob named the place [1]Peniel, for *he said,* “[a]I have seen God face to face, yet my [2]life has been preserved.”

31 Now the sun rose upon him just as he crossed over [a]Penuel, and he was limping on his thigh.

32 Therefore, to this day the sons of Israel do not eat the sinew of the hip which is on the socket of the thigh, because he touched the socket of Jacob's thigh in the sinew of the hip.

Jacob Meets Esau

33 Then Jacob lifted his eyes and looked, and behold, [a]Esau was coming, and four hundred men with him. So he divided the children [1]among Leah and Rachel and the two maids.

2 He put the maids and their children [1]in front, and Leah and her children [2]next, and Rachel and Joseph [2]last.

3 But he himself passed on ahead of them and [a]bowed down to the ground seven times, until he came near to his brother.

4 ¶ Then Esau ran to meet him and embraced him, and [a]fell on his neck and kissed him, and they wept.

5 He lifted his eyes and saw the women and the children, and said, “[1]Who are these with you?” So he said, “[a]The children whom God has graciously given your servant.”

6 Then the maids came near [1]with their children, and they bowed down.

8 [1]Lit *smites*

9 [1]Lit *do good with you* [a]Gen 28:13; 31:42 [b]Gen 28:15; 31:3,13

10 [1]Lit *I am less than all* [2]Or *truth* [a]Gen 24:27

11 [1]Lit *smite* [a]Ps 59:1,2 [b]Gen 27:41,42; 33:4 [c]Hos 10:14

12 [1]Lit *do good with* [2]Lit *seed* [a]Gen 28:14 [b]Gen 22:17

13 [1]Lit *took* [2]Lit *had come to his hand* [a]Gen 43:11

17 [1]Lit *first*

22 [a]Deut 3:16; Josh 12:2

24 [a]Hos 12:3,4

26 [a]Hos 12:4

28 [1]I.e. he who strives with God; or God strives [a]Gen 35:10; 1 Kin 18:31

29 [a]Judg 13:17, 18

30 [1]I.e. the face of God [2]Lit *soul* [a]Gen 16:13; Ex 24:10,11; 33:20; Num 12:8; Judg 6:22; 13:22

31 [a]Judg 8:8

33:1 [1]Or *to* [a]Gen 32:6

2 [1]Lit *first* [2]Lit *behind*

3 [a]Gen 42:6; 43:26

4 [a]Gen 45:14,15

5 [1]Or *What relation are these to you?* [a]Gen 48:9; Ps 127:3; Is 8:18

6 [1]Lit *they and*

7 Leah likewise came near with her
children, and they bowed down; and afterward Joseph came near with Rachel,
and they bowed down.
8 And he said, "What do you mean by
[a]all this company which I have met?"
And he said, "[b]To find favor in the sight
of my lord."
9 But Esau said, "[a]I have plenty, my
brother; let what you have be your own."
10 Jacob said, "No, please, if now I
have found favor in your sight, then take
my present from my hand, [1]for I see your
face as one sees the face of God, and you
have received me favorably.
11 "Please take my [1a]gift which has
been brought to you, [b]because God has
dealt graciously with me and because I
have [2]plenty." Thus he urged him and
he took *it.*
12 ¶ Then [1]Esau said, "Let us take our
journey and go, and I will go before you."
13 But he said to him, "My lord knows
that the children are frail and that the
flocks and herds which are nursing are
[1]a care to me. And if they are driven hard
one day, all the flocks will die.
14 "Please let my lord pass on before
his servant, and I will proceed at my lei-
sure, according to the pace of the cattle
that are before me and according to the
pace of the children, until I come to my
lord at [a]Seir."
15 ¶ Esau said, "Please let me leave
with you some of the people who are
with me." But he said, "[1]What need is
there? [a]Let me find favor in the sight of
my lord."
16 So Esau returned that day on his
way to Seir.
17 Jacob journeyed to [1a]Succoth, and
built for himself a house and made booths
for his livestock; therefore the place is
named Succoth.

Jacob Settles in Shechem

18 ¶ Now Jacob came safely to the city
of [a]Shechem, which is in the land of
Canaan, when he came from [b]Paddan-
aram, and camped before the city.
19 [a]He bought the piece of land
where he had pitched his tent from the
hand of the sons of Hamor, Shechem's
father, for one hundred [1]pieces of
money.
20 Then he erected there an altar and
called it [1]El-Elohe-Israel.

The Treachery of Jacob's Sons

34 Now [a]Dinah the daughter of
Leah, whom she had borne to Ja-
cob, went out to [1]visit the daughters of
the land.
2 When Shechem the son of Hamor
[a]the Hivite, the prince of the land, saw
her, he took her and lay with her [1]by
force.
3 [1]He was deeply attracted to Dinah
the daughter of Jacob, and he loved the
girl and [2]spoke tenderly to her.
4 So Shechem [a]spoke to his father
Hamor, saying, "Get me this young girl
for a wife."
5 Now Jacob heard that he had defiled Dinah his daughter; but his sons
were with his livestock in the field, so
Jacob kept silent until they came in.
6 Then Hamor the father of Shechem
went out to Jacob to speak with him.
7 Now the sons of Jacob came in from
the field when they heard *it;* and the men
were grieved, and they were very angry
because he had done a [1a]disgraceful
thing in Israel [2]by lying with Jacob's
daughter, for such a thing ought not to be
done.
8 ¶ But Hamor spoke with them, saying, "The soul of my son Shechem longs
for your daughter; please give her to him
[1]in marriage.
9 "Intermarry with us; give your
daughters to us and take our daughters
for yourselves.
10 "Thus you shall [1]live with us, and
[a]the land shall be *open* before you; [1]live
and [b]trade in it and [c]acquire property
in it."
11 Shechem also said to her father and
to her brothers, "If I find favor in your
sight, then I will give whatever you say
to me.
12 "Ask me ever so much bridal payment and gift, and I will give according as
you say to me; but give me the girl [1]in
marriage."
13 ¶ But Jacob's sons answered Shechem and his father Hamor with deceit,
because he had defiled Dinah their sister.
14 They said to them, "We cannot do
this thing, to give our sister to [a]one who
is uncircumcised, for that would be a disgrace to us.
15 "Only on this *condition* will we consent to you: if you will become like us, in
that every male of you be circumcised,
16 then we will give our daughters to
you, and we will take your daughters for
ourselves, and we will [1]live with you and
become one people.
17 "But if you will not listen to us to
be circumcised, then we will take our
daughter and go."
18 ¶ Now their words seemed [1]rea-
sonable to Hamor and Shechem, Hamor's
son.
19 The young man did not delay to do
the thing, because he was delighted with
Jacob's daughter. Now he was more re-

8 [a]Gen 32:13-16 [b]Gen 32:5
9 [a]Gen 27:39,40
10 [1]Lit *for therefore I have seen your face like seeing God's face*
11 [1]Lit *blessing* [2]Lit *all* [a]1 Sam 25:27 [b]Gen 30:43
12 [1]Lit *he*
13 [1]Lit *upon me*
14 [a]Gen 32:3
15 [1]Lit *Why this?* [a]Ruth 2:13
17 [1]I.e. booths [a]Josh 13:27; Judg 8:5,14; Ps 60:6
18 [a]Gen 12:6; Josh 24:1; Judg 9:1 [b]Gen 25:20; 28:2
19 [1]Heb *qesitah* [a]Josh 24:32; John 4:5
20 [1]I.e. God, the God of Israel
34:1 [1]Lit *see* [a]Gen 30:21
2 [1]Lit *and humbled her* [a]Gen 34:30
3 [1]Lit *His soul clung* [2]Lit *spoke to the heart of the girl*
4 [a]Judg 14:2
7 [1]Lit *senseless* [2]Lit *to lie* [a]Deut 22:20-30; Judg 20:6; 2 Sam 13:12
8 [1]Lit *for a wife*
10 [1]Lit *dwell* [a]Gen 13:9; 20:15 [b]Gen 42:34 [c]Gen 47:27
12 [1]Lit *for a wife*
14 [a]Gen 17:14
16 [1]Lit *dwell*
18 [1]Lit *good*

spected than all the household of his father.
20 So Hamor and his son Shechem
came to the [a]gate of their city and spoke
to the men of their city, saying,
21 "These men are [1]friendly with us;
therefore let them [2]live in the land and
trade in it, for behold, the land is [3]large
enough for them. Let us take their daughters [4]in marriage, and give our daughters
to them.
22 "Only on this *condition* will the men
consent to us to [1]live with us, to become
one people: that every male among us be
circumcised as they are circumcised.
23 "Will not their livestock and their
property and all their animals be ours?
Only let us consent to them, and they will
[1]live with us."
24 [a]All who went out of the gate of his
city listened to Hamor and to his son Shechem, and every male was circumcised,
all who went out of the gate of his city.
25 ¶ Now it came about on the third
day, when they were in pain, that two of
Jacob's sons, [a]Simeon and Levi, Dinah's
brothers, each took his sword and came
upon the city unawares, and killed every
male.
26 They killed Hamor and his son Shechem with the edge of the sword, and
took Dinah from Shechem's house, and
went forth.
27 Jacob's sons came upon the slain
and looted the city, because they had defiled their sister.
28 They took their flocks and their
herds and their donkeys, and that which
was in the city and that which was in the
field;
29 and they captured and looted all
their wealth and all their little ones and
their wives, even all that *was* in the
houses.
30 Then Jacob said to Simeon and
Levi, "You have [a]brought trouble on me
by [b]making me odious among the inhabitants of the land, among [c]the Canaanites
and the Perizzites; and [1d]my men being
few in number, they will gather together
against me and [2]attack me and I will be
destroyed, I and my household."
31 But they said, "Should he [1]treat
our sister as a harlot?"

Jacob Moves to Bethel

35 Then God said to Jacob, "Arise, go
up to [a]Bethel and [1]live there,
and make an altar there to [b]God, who
appeared to you [c]when you fled [2]from
your brother Esau."
2 So Jacob said to his [a]household and
to all who were with him, "Put away
[b]the foreign gods which are among you,
and [c]purify yourselves and change your
garments;
3 and let us arise and go up to Bethel,
and I will make [a]an altar there to God,
[b]who answered me in the day of my distress and [c]has been with me [1]wherever
I have gone."
4 So they gave to Jacob all the foreign
gods which [1]they had and the rings
which were in their ears, and Jacob hid
them under the [2]oak which was near
Shechem.
5 ¶ As they journeyed, there was
[1a]a great terror upon the cities which
were around them, and they did not pursue the sons of Jacob.
6 So Jacob came to [a]Luz (that is,
Bethel), which is in the land of Canaan,
he and all the people who were with him.
7 [a]He built an altar there, and called
the place [1]El-bethel, because there God
had revealed Himself to him when he fled
[2]from his brother.
8 Now [a]Deborah, Rebekah's nurse,
died, and she was buried below Bethel
under the oak; it was named [1]Allon-
bacuth.

Jacob Is Named Israel

9 ¶ Then God appeared to Jacob
again when he came from Paddan-aram,
and He [a]blessed him.
10 [a]God said to him,
"Your name is Jacob;
[1]You shall no longer be called
Jacob,
But Israel shall be your name."
Thus He called [2]him Israel.
11 God also said to him,
"I am [1a]God Almighty;
[b]Be fruitful and multiply;
A nation and a [c]company of
nations shall [2]come from
you,
And [d]kings shall [2]come forth
from [3]you.
12 "[a]The land which I gave to
Abraham and Isaac,
I will give it to you,
And I will give the land to your
[1]descendants after you."
13 Then [a]God went up from him in
the place where He had spoken with him.
14 Jacob set up [a]a pillar in the place
where He had spoken with him, a pillar
of stone, and he poured out a drink offering on it; he also poured oil on it.
15 So Jacob named the place where
God had spoken with him, [1a]Bethel.
16 ¶ Then they journeyed from Bethel; and when there was still some distance to go to [a]Ephrath, Rachel began to
give birth and she [1]suffered severe labor.
17 When she was in severe labor the

20 [a]Ruth 4:1; 2 Sam 15:2
21 [1]Lit *peaceful* [2]Lit *dwell* [3]Lit *wide of hands before them* [4]Lit *to us for wives*
22 [1]Lit *dwell*
23 [1]Lit *dwell*
24 [a]Gen 23:10
25 [a]Gen 49:5-7
30 [1]Lit *I, few in number* [2]Lit *smite* [a]Josh 7:25 [b]Ex 5:21; 1 Sam 13:4; 2 Sam 10:6 [c]Gen 13:7; 34:2 [d]Gen 46:26,27; Deut 4:27; 1 Chr 16:19; Ps 105:12
31 [1]Or *make*
35:1 [1]Lit *dwell* [2]Lit *from the face of* [a]Gen 28:19 [b]Gen 28:13 [c]Gen 27:43
2 [a]Gen 18:19; Josh 24:15 [b]Gen 31:19,30,34 [c]Ex 19:10,14
3 [1]Lit *in the way which* [a]Gen 28:20-22 [b]Ps 107:6 [c]Gen 28:15; 31:3,42
4 [1]Lit *were in their hand* [2]Or *terebinth*
5 [1]Or *a terror of God* [a]Ex 15:16; 23:27; Deut 2:25
6 [a]Gen 28:19; 48:3
7 [1]I.e. the God of Bethel [2]Lit *from the face of* [a]Gen 35:3
8 [1]I.e. oak of weeping [a]Gen 24:59
9 [a]Gen 32:29
10 [1]Lit *Your name* [2]Lit *his name* [a]Gen 17:5; 32:28
11 [1]Heb *El Shaddai* [2]Or *come into being* [3]Lit *your loins* [a]Gen 17:1; 28:3; Ex 6:3 [b]Gen 9:1, 7 [c]Gen 48:4 [d]Gen 17:6,16; 36:31
12 [1]Lit *seed* [a]Gen 12:7; 13:15; 26:3,4; 28:13; Ex 32:13
13 [a]Gen 17:22; 18:33
14 [a]Gen 28:18, 19; 31:45
15 [1]I.e. the house of God [a]Gen 28:19
16 [1]Lit *had difficulty in her giving birth* [a]Gen 35:19; 48:7; Ruth 4:11; Mic 5:2

midwife said to her, "Do not fear, for now
[a]you have another son."
18 It came about as her soul was departing (for she died), that she named
him [1]Ben-oni; but his father called him
[2]Benjamin.
19 So [a]Rachel died and was buried on
the way to [b]Ephrath (that is, Bethlehem).
20 Jacob set up a pillar over her grave;
that is the [a]pillar of Rachel's grave to this
day.
21 Then Israel journeyed on and
pitched his tent beyond the [1a]tower of
[2]Eder.
22 ¶ It came about while Israel was
dwelling in that land, that [a]Reuben went
and lay with Bilhah his father's concubine, and Israel heard *of it.*

The Sons of Israel

¶ Now there were twelve sons of Jacob—
23 [a]the sons of Leah: Reuben, Jacob's
firstborn, then Simeon and Levi and Judah and Issachar and Zebulun;
24 [a]the sons of Rachel: Joseph and
Benjamin;
25 and [a]the sons of Bilhah, Rachel's
maid: Dan and Naphtali;
26 and [a]the sons of Zilpah, Leah's
maid: Gad and Asher. These are the sons
of Jacob who were born to him in Paddan-
aram.
27 ¶ Jacob came to his father Isaac at
[a]Mamre of [b]Kiriath-arba (that is, Hebron), where Abraham and Isaac had sojourned.
28 ¶ Now the days of Isaac were [a]one
hundred and eighty years.
29 Isaac breathed his last and died and
was [a]gathered to his people, an [b]old
man [1]of ripe age; and [c]his sons Esau and
Jacob buried him.

Esau Moves

36 Now these are *the records of* the
generations of [a]Esau (that is,
Edom).
2 ¶ Esau [a]took his wives from the
daughters of Canaan: Adah the daughter
of Elon the Hittite, and [b]Oholibamah the
daughter of Anah and the [c]granddaugh-
ter of Zibeon the Hivite;
3 also Basemath, Ishmael's daughter,
the sister of Nebaioth.
4 Adah bore [a]Eliphaz to Esau, and
Basemath bore Reuel,
5 and Oholibamah bore Jeush and Jalam and Korah. These are the sons of
Esau who were born to him in the land of
Canaan.
6 ¶ [a]Then Esau took his wives and
his sons and his daughters and all [1]his
household, and his livestock and all his
cattle and all his goods which he had acquired in the land of Canaan, and went to
another land away from his brother Jacob.
7 [a]For their property had become
too great for them to [1]live together, and
the [b]land where they [c]sojourned could
not sustain them because of their livestock.
8 So Esau lived in the hill country of
[a]Seir; Esau is [b]Edom.

Descendants of Esau

9 ¶ These then are *the records of* the
generations of Esau the father of [1]the
Edomites in the hill country of Seir.
10 These are the names of Esau's sons:
Eliphaz the son of Esau's wife Adah, Reuel the son of Esau's wife Basemath.
11 The sons of Eliphaz were Teman,
Omar, [1]Zepho and Gatam and Kenaz.
12 Timna was a concubine of Esau's
son Eliphaz and she bore [a]Amalek to Eliphaz. These are the sons of Esau's wife
Adah.
13 These are the sons of Reuel: Nahath
and Zerah, Shammah and Mizzah. These
were the sons of Esau's wife Basemath.
14 These were the sons of Esau's wife
Oholibamah, the daughter of Anah and
the [1]granddaughter of Zibeon: [2]she bore
to Esau, Jeush and Jalam and Korah.
15 ¶ These are the chiefs of the sons of
Esau. The sons of Eliphaz, the firstborn of
Esau, are chief Teman, chief Omar, chief
Zepho, chief Kenaz,
16 chief Korah, chief Gatam, chief Amalek. These are the chiefs [1]descended
from Eliphaz in the land of Edom; these
are the sons of Adah.
17 These are the sons of Reuel, Esau's
son: chief Nahath, chief Zerah, chief
Shammah, chief Mizzah. These are the
chiefs [1]descended from Reuel in the land
of Edom; these are the sons of Esau's wife
Basemath.
18 These are the sons of Esau's wife
Oholibamah: chief Jeush, chief Jalam,
chief Korah. These are the chiefs [1]de-
scended from Esau's wife Oholibamah,
the daughter of Anah.
19 These are the sons of Esau (that is,
Edom), and these are their chiefs.
20 ¶ These are the sons of Seir [a]the
Horite, the inhabitants of the land: Lotan
and Shobal and Zibeon and Anah,
21 and Dishon and Ezer and Dishan.
These are the chiefs [1]descended from
the Horites, the sons of Seir in the land of
Edom.
22 The sons of Lotan were Hori and
[1]Hemam; and Lotan's sister was Timna.
23 These are the sons of Shobal: [1]Al-

17 [a]Gen 30:24
18 [1]I.e. the son of my sorrow [2]I.e. the son of the right hand
19 [a]Gen 48:7 [b]Ruth 1:2; 4:11; Mic 5:2
20 [a]1 Sam 10:2
21 [1]Heb *Migdal-eder* [2]Or *flock* [a]Mic 4:8
22 [a]Gen 49:4; 1 Chr 5:1
23 [a]Gen 29:31-35; 30:18-20; 46:8; Ex 1:1-4
24 [a]Gen 30:22-24; 35:18
25 [a]Gen 30:5-8
26 [a]Gen 30:10-13
27 [a]Gen 13:18; 18:1; 23:19 [b]Josh 14:15
28 [a]Gen 25:26
29 [1]Lit *and satisfied with days* [a]Gen 25:8; 49:33 [b]Gen 15:15 [c]Gen 25:9
36:1 [a]Gen 25:30
2 [a]Gen 28:9 [b]Gen 36:25 [c]Gen 36:24
4 [a]1 Chr 1:35
6 [1]Lit *the souls of his house* [a]Gen 12:5
7 [1]Lit *dwell* [a]Gen 13:6 [b]Gen 17:8; Heb 11:9 [c]1 Chr 29:15; Ps 39:12
8 [a]Gen 32:3 [b]Gen 36:1,19
9 [1]Lit *Edom*
11 [1]In 1 Chr 1:36, *Zephi*
12 [a]Ex 17:8-16; Num 24:20; Deut 25:17-19; 1 Sam 15:2,3
14 [1]Gr *son* [2]Lit *and she*
16 [1]Lit *of Eliphaz*
17 [1]Lit *of Reuel*
18 [1]Lit *of Oholibamah, Esau's wife*
20 [a]Gen 14:6; Deut 2:12,22; 1 Chr 1:38-42
21 [1]Lit *of the Horites*
22 [1]In 1 Chr 1:39, *Homam*
23 [1]In 1 Chr 1:40, *Alian*

van and Manahath and Ebal, [2]Shepho
and Onam.
24 These are the sons of Zibeon: Aiah
and Anah—he is the Anah who found the
hot springs in the wilderness when he
was pasturing the donkeys of his father
Zibeon.
25 These are the children of Anah: Dishon, and Oholibamah, the daughter of
Anah.
26 These are the sons of [1a]Dishon:
[2]Hemdan and Eshban and Ithran and
Cheran.
27 These are the sons of Ezer: Bilhan
and Zaavan and [1]Akan.
28 These are the sons of Dishan: Uz
and Aran.
29 These are the chiefs [1]descended
from the Horites: chief Lotan, chief Shobal, chief Zibeon, chief Anah,
30 chief Dishon, chief Ezer, chief Dishan. These are the chiefs [1]descended
from the Horites, according to their *various* chiefs in the land of Seir.
31 ¶ Now these are the kings who
reigned in the land of Edom before any
[a]king reigned over the sons of Israel.
32 [1a]Bela the son of Beor reigned in
Edom, and the name of his city was Dinhabah.
33 Then Bela died, and Jobab the son
of Zerah of Bozrah became king in his
place.
34 Then Jobab died, and Husham of
the land of the Temanites became king in
his place.
35 Then Husham died, and Hadad the
son of Bedad, who [1]defeated Midian in
the field of Moab, became king in his
place; and the name of his city was Avith.
36 Then Hadad died, and Samlah of
Masrekah became king in his place.
37 Then Samlah died, and Shaul of Re-
hoboth on the *Euphrates* River became
king in his place.
38 Then Shaul died, and Baal-hanan
the son of Achbor became king in his
place.
39 Then Baal-hanan the son of Achbor
died, and [1]Hadar became king in his
place; and the name of his city was [2]Pau;
and his wife's name was Mehetabel, the
daughter of Matred, daughter of Mezahab.
40 ¶ Now these are the names of the
chiefs [1]descended from Esau, according
to their families *and* their localities, by
their names: chief Timna, chief [2]Alvah,
chief Jetheth,
41 chief Oholibamah, chief Elah, chief
Pinon,
42 chief Kenaz, chief Teman, chief
Mibzar,
43 chief Magdiel, chief Iram. These
are the chiefs of Edom (that is, Esau, the
father of [1]the Edomites), according to
their habitations in the land of their possession.

Joseph's Dream

37 Now Jacob lived in [a]the land
[1]where his father had sojourned,
in the land of Canaan.
2 These are *the records of* the generations of Jacob.
¶ Joseph, when [a]seventeen years of
age, was pasturing the flock with his
brothers while he was *still* a youth, along
with [b]the sons of Bilhah and the sons of
Zilpah, his father's wives. And Joseph
brought back a [c]bad report about them to
their father.
3 Now Israel loved Joseph more than
all his sons, because he was [a]the son of
his old age; and he made him a [1b]vari-
colored tunic.
4 His brothers saw that their father
loved him more than all his brothers; and
so they [a]hated him and could not speak
to him [1]on friendly terms.
5 ¶ Then Joseph [1a]had a dream, and
when he told it to his brothers, they hated him even more.
6 He said to them, "Please listen to
this dream which I have [1]had;
7 for behold, we were binding
sheaves in the field, and lo, my sheaf rose
up and also stood erect; and behold, your
sheaves gathered around and [a]bowed
down to my sheaf."
8 Then his brothers said to him,
"[a]Are you actually going to reign over
us? Or are you really going to rule over
us?" So they hated him even more for his
dreams and for his words.
9 ¶ Now he [1]had still another
dream, and related it to his brothers, and
said, "Lo, I have [1]had still another
dream; and behold, the sun and the moon
and eleven stars were bowing down
to me."
10 He related *it* to his father and to his
brothers; and his father rebuked him and
said to him, "What is this dream that you
have [1]had? Shall I and your mother and
[a]your brothers actually come to bow ourselves down before you to the ground?"
11 [a]His brothers were jealous of him,
but his father [b]kept the saying *in mind.*
12 ¶ Then his brothers went to pasture their father's flock in Shechem.
13 Israel said to Joseph, "Are not your
brothers pasturing *the flock* in [a]She-
chem? Come, and I will send you to
them." And he said to him, "[1]I will go."
14 Then he said to him, "Go now and
see about the welfare of your brothers
and the welfare of the flock, and bring

23 [2]In 1 Chr 1:40, *Shephi*
26 [1]Heb *Dishan* [2]In 1 Chr 1:41, *Hamran* [a]1 Chr 1:41
27 [1]In 1 Chr 1:42, *Jaakan*
29 [1]Lit *of the Horites*
30 [1]Lit *of the Horites*
31 [a]Gen 17:6, 16; 35:11; 1 Chr 1:43
32 [1]Lit *And Bela* [a]1 Chr 1:43
35 [1]Or *smote*
39 [1]In 1 Chr 1:50, *Hadad* [2]In 1 Chr 1:50, *Pai*
40 [1]Lit *of Esau* [2]In 1 Chr 1:51, *Aliah*
43 [1]Heb *Edom*
37:1 [1]Lit *of his father's sojournings* [a]Gen 17:8; 28:4
2 [a]Gen 41:46 [b]Gen 35:25,26 [c]1 Sam 2:22-24
3 [1]Or *full-length robe* [a]Gen 44:20 [b]Gen 37:23,32
4 [1]Lit *in peace* [a]Gen 27:41; 1 Sam 17:28
5 [1]Lit *dreamed* [a]Gen 28:12; 31:10,11,24
6 [1]Lit *dreamed*
7 [a]Gen 42:6,9; 43:26; 44:14
8 [a]Gen 49:26; Deut 33:16
9 [1]Lit *dreamed*
10 [1]Lit *dreamed* [a]Gen 27:29
11 [a]Acts 7:9 [b]Dan 7:28; Luke 2:19,51
13 [1]Lit *Behold me* [a]Gen 33:18-20

word back to me." So he sent him from the valley of [a]Hebron, and he came to Shechem.

15 ¶ A man found him, and behold, he was wandering in the field; and the man asked him, "[1]What are you looking for?"

16 He said, "I am looking for my brothers; please tell me where they are pasturing *the flock.*"

17 Then the man said, "They have moved from here; for I heard *them* say, 'Let us go to [a]Dothan.' " So Joseph went after his brothers and found them at Dothan.

The Plot against Joseph

18 ¶ [1]When they saw him from a distance and before he came close to them, they [a]plotted against him to put him to death.

19 They said to one another, "[1]Here comes this dreamer!

20 "Now then, come and let us kill him and throw him into one of the pits; and [a]we will say, 'A wild beast devoured him.' Then let us see what will become of his dreams!"

21 But [a]Reuben heard *this* and rescued him out of their hands and said, "Let us not [1]take his life."

22 Reuben further said to them, "Shed no blood. Throw him into this pit that is in the wilderness, but do not lay hands on him"—that he might rescue him out of their hands, to restore him to his father.

23 So it came about, when Joseph [1]reached his brothers, that they stripped Joseph of his [2]tunic, the varicolored tunic that was on him;

24 and they took him and threw him into the pit. Now the pit was empty, without any water in it.

25 ¶ Then they sat down to eat [1]a meal. And as they raised their eyes and looked, behold, a caravan of [a]Ishmaelites was coming from Gilead, with their camels bearing [2b]aromatic gum and [3c]balm and [4]myrrh, [5]on their way to bring *them* down to Egypt.

26 Judah said to his brothers, "What profit is it for us to kill our brother and [a]cover up his blood?

27 "[a]Come and let us sell him to the Ishmaelites and not lay our hands on him, for he is our brother, our *own* flesh." And his brothers listened *to him.*

28 Then some [a]Midianite traders passed by, so they pulled *him* up and lifted Joseph out of the pit, and [b]sold [1]him to the Ishmaelites for twenty *shekels* of silver. Thus [c]they brought Joseph into Egypt.

29 ¶ Now Reuben returned to the pit, and behold, Joseph was not in the pit; so he [a]tore his garments.

30 He returned to his brothers and said, "[a]The boy is not *there;* as for me, where am I to go?"

31 So [a]they took Joseph's tunic, and slaughtered a male goat and dipped the tunic in the blood;

32 and they sent the varicolored tunic and brought it to their father and said, "We found this; please [1]examine *it* to *see* whether it is your son's tunic or not."

33 Then he [1]examined it and said, "It is my son's tunic. [a]A wild beast has devoured him; [b]Joseph has surely been torn to pieces!"

34 So Jacob [a]tore his clothes, and put sackcloth on his loins and mourned for his son many days.

35 Then all his sons and all his daughters arose to comfort him, but he refused to be comforted. And he said, "Surely I will [a]go down to Sheol in mourning for my son." So his father wept for him.

36 Meanwhile, the [1]Midianites [a]sold him in Egypt to Potiphar, Pharaoh's officer, the captain of the bodyguard.

Judah and Tamar

38 And it came about at that time, that Judah [1]departed from his brothers and [2]visited a certain [a]Adullamite, whose name was Hirah.

2 Judah saw there a daughter of a certain Canaanite whose name was [a]Shua; and he took her and went in to her.

3 So she conceived and bore a son and he named him [a]Er.

4 Then she conceived again and bore a son and named him [a]Onan.

5 She bore still another son and named him [a]Shelah; and it was at Chezib [1]that she bore him.

6 ¶ Now Judah took a wife for Er his firstborn, and her name *was* Tamar.

7 But [a]Er, Judah's firstborn, was evil in the sight of the LORD, so the LORD took his life.

8 Then Judah said to Onan, "[a]Go in to your brother's wife, and perform your duty as a brother-in-law to her, and raise up [1]offspring for your brother."

9 Onan knew that the [1a]offspring would not be his; so when he went in to his brother's wife, he [2]wasted his seed on the ground in order not to give [1]offspring to his brother.

10 But what he did was displeasing in the sight of the LORD; so He [a]took his life also.

11 Then Judah said to his daughter-in-law Tamar, "[a]Remain a widow in your father's house until my son Shelah grows up"; for he [1]thought, "*I am afraid* that he

14 [a]Gen 13:18; 23:2,19; 35:27; Josh 14:14,15; Judg 1:10
15 [1]Lit *saying, "What...?"*
17 [a]2 Kin 6:13
18 [1]Or *And* [a]Ps 31:13; 37:12,32; Mark 14:1; John 11:53; Acts 23:12
19 [1]Lit *Behold, this master of dreams comes*
20 [a]Gen 37:32, 33
21 [1]Lit *smite his soul* [a]Gen 42:22
23 [1]Lit *came to* [2]Or *full-length robe*
25 [1]Lit *bread* [2]Or *ladanum spice* [3]Or *mastic* [4]Or *resinous bark* [5]Lit *going* [a]Gen 16:11,12; 37:28; 39:1 [b]Gen 43:11 [c]Jer 8:22; 46:11
26 [a]Gen 37:20
27 [a]Gen 42:21
28 [1]Lit *Joseph* [a]Gen 37:25; Judg 6:1-3; 8:22, 24 [b]Gen 45:4,5; Ps 105:17; Acts 7:9 [c]Gen 39:1
29 [a]Gen 37:34; 44:13
30 [a]Gen 42:13, 36
31 [a]Gen 37:3, 23
32 [1]Or *recognize*
33 [1]Or *recognized* [a]Gen 37:20 [b]Gen 44:28
34 [a]Gen 37:29
35 [a]Gen 25:8; 35:29; 42:38; 44:29,31
36 [1]Lit *Medanites* [a]Gen 39:1
38:1 [1]Lit *went down* [2]Lit *turned aside to* [a]Josh 15:35; 1 Sam 22:1
2 [a]1 Chr 2:3
3 [a]Gen 46:12; Num 26:19
4 [a]Gen 46:12
5 [1]Lit *when* [a]Num 26:20
7 [a]Gen 46:12; Num 26:19; 1 Chr 2:3
8 [1]Lit *seed* [a]Deut 25:5,6; Matt 22:24
9 [1]Lit *seed* [2]Lit *spilled on the ground* [a]Deut 25:6
10 [a]Gen 46:12; Num 26:19
11 [1]Lit *said* [a]Ruth 1:12,13

too may die like his brothers." So Tamar went and lived in her father's house.

12 ¶ Now [1]after a considerable time Shua's daughter, the wife of Judah, died; and when [2]the time of mourning was ended, Judah went up to his sheepshearers at [a]Timnah, he and his friend Hirah the Adullamite.

13 It was told to Tamar, "[1]Behold, your father-in-law is going up to [a]Timnah to shear his sheep."

14 So she [1]removed her widow's garments and [a]covered *herself* with a [2]veil, and wrapped herself, and sat in the gateway of [3]Enaim, which is on the road to Timnah; for she saw that Shelah had grown up, and [b]she had not been given to him as a wife.

15 When Judah saw her, he thought she *was* a harlot, for she had covered her face.

16 So he turned aside to her by the road, and said, "[1]Here now, let me come in to you"; for he did not know that she was his daughter-in-law. And she said, "What will you give me, that you may come in to me?"

17 He said, therefore, "I will send you a [1]young goat from the flock." She said, moreover, "Will you give a pledge until you send *it?*"

18 He said, "What pledge shall I give you?" And she said, "[a]Your seal and your cord, and your staff that is in your hand." So he gave *them* to her and went in to her, and she conceived by him.

19 Then she arose and departed, and [1]removed her [2]veil and put on her widow's garments.

20 ¶ When Judah sent the [1]young goat by his friend the Adullamite, to receive the pledge from the woman's hand, he did not find her.

21 He asked the men of her place, saying, "Where is the temple prostitute who was by the road at Enaim?" But they said, "There has been no temple prostitute here."

22 So he returned to Judah, and said, "I did not find her; and furthermore, the men of the place said, 'There has been no temple prostitute here.' "

23 Then Judah said, "Let her [1]keep them, otherwise we will become a laughingstock. [2]After all, I sent this young goat, but you did not find her."

24 ¶ Now it was about three months later that Judah was informed, "[1]Your daughter-in-law Tamar has played the harlot, and behold, she is also with child by harlotry." Then Judah said, "Bring her out and [a]let her be burned!"

25 It was while she was being brought out that she sent to her father-in-law, saying, "I am with child by the man to whom these things belong." And she said, "[a]Please examine and see, whose signet ring and cords and staff are these?"

26 Judah recognized *them,* and said, "[a]She is more righteous than I, inasmuch as [b]I did not give her to my son Shelah." And he did not [1]have relations with her again.

27 ¶ It came about at the time she was giving birth, that behold, there were [a]twins in her womb.

28 Moreover, it took place while she was giving birth, one put out a hand, and the midwife took and tied a scarlet *thread* on his hand, saying, "This one came out first."

29 But it came about as he drew back his hand, that behold, his brother came out. Then she said, "What a breach you have made for yourself!" So he was named [1a]Perez.

30 Afterward his brother came out who had the scarlet *thread* on his hand; and he was named [1a]Zerah.

Joseph's Success in Egypt

39 Now Joseph had been taken down to Egypt; and Potiphar, an Egyptian officer of Pharaoh, the captain of the bodyguard, bought him [1]from the [a]Ishmaelites, who had taken him down there.

2 [a]The LORD was with Joseph, so he became a [1]successful man. And he was in the house of his master, the Egyptian.

3 Now his master [a]saw that the LORD was with him and *how* the LORD [b]caused all that he did to prosper in his hand.

4 So Joseph [a]found favor in his sight and [1]became his personal servant; and he made him overseer over his house, and [b]all that he owned he put in his [2]charge.

5 It came about that from the time he made him overseer in his house and over all that he owned, the LORD [a]blessed the Egyptian's house on account of Joseph; thus [b]the LORD'S blessing was upon all that he owned, in the house and in the field.

6 So he left everything he owned in Joseph's [1]charge; and with him *there* he did not [2]concern himself with anything except the [3]food which he [4]ate.

¶ Now Joseph was [a]handsome in form and appearance.

7 It came about after these events [a]that his master's wife [1]looked with desire at Joseph, and she said, "[b]Lie with me."

8 But [a]he refused and said to his master's wife, "Behold, with me *here,* my master [1]does not concern himself with

12 [1]Lit *the days became many and* [2]Lit *Judah was comforted, he* [a]Josh 15:10, 57

13 [1]Lit *saying, Behold* [a]Josh 15:10,57; Judg 14:1

14 [1]Lit *removed from herself* [2]Or *shawl* [3]In Josh 15:34, *Enam* [a]Gen 24:65 [b]Gen 38:11,26

16 [1]Or *Come, now*

17 [1]Lit *kid of goats*

18 [a]Gen 38:25; 41:42

19 [1]Lit *removed from herself* [2]Or *shawl*

20 [1]Lit *kid of goats by the hand of*

23 [1]Lit *take for herself* [2]Lit *Behold*

24 [1]Lit *saying, Your* [a]Lev 21:9

25 [a]Gen 37:32

26 [1]Lit *know her yet again* [a]1 Sam 24:17 [b]Gen 38:14

27 [a]Gen 25:24-26

29 [1]I.e. a breach [a]Gen 46:12; Ruth 4:12

30 [1]I.e. a dawning or brightness [a]1 Chr 2:4

39:1 [1]Lit *from the hand of* [a]Gen 37:25,28, 36; Ps 105:17

2 [1]Or *prosperous* [a]Gen 39:3, 21,23; Acts 7:9

3 [a]Gen 21:22; 26:28 [b]Ps 1:3

4 [1]Or *ministered to him* [2]Lit *hand* [a]Gen 18:3; 19:19 [b]Gen 24:2; 39:8,22

5 [a]Gen 30:27 [b]Deut 28:3,4,11

6 [1]Lit *hand* [2]Lit *know* [3]Lit *bread* [4]Or *used to eat* [a]Gen 29:17; 1 Sam 16:12

7 [1]Lit *lifted up her eyes at* [a]Prov 7:15-20 [b]2 Sam 13:11

8 [1]Lit *does not know what is in the house* [a]Prov 6:23,24

anything in the house, and he has put all that he owns in my [2]charge.
9 "[1a]There is no one greater in this house than I, and he has withheld nothing from me except you, because you are his wife. How then could I do this great evil and [b]sin against God?"
10 As she spoke to Joseph day after day, he did not listen to her to lie beside her *or* be with her.
11 Now it happened [1]one day that he went into the house to do his work, and none of the men of the household was there inside.
12 She caught him by his garment, saying, "Lie with me!" And he left his garment in her hand and fled, and went outside.
13 [1]When she saw that he had left his garment in her hand and had fled outside,
14 she called to the men of her household and said to them, "See, he has brought in a [1]Hebrew to us to make sport of us; he came in to me to lie with me, and I [2]screamed.
15 "When he heard that I raised my voice and [1]screamed, he left his garment beside me and fled and went outside."
16 So she [1]left his garment beside her until his master came home.
17 Then she [a]spoke to him [1]with these words, "[2]The Hebrew slave, whom you brought to us, came in to me to make sport of me;
18 and as I raised my voice and [1]screamed, he left his garment beside me and fled outside."

Joseph Imprisoned

19 ¶ Now when his master heard the words of his wife, which she spoke to him, saying, "[1]This is what your slave did to me," [a]his anger burned.
20 So Joseph's master took him and [a]put him into the jail, the place where the king's prisoners were confined; and he was there in the jail.
21 But [a]the LORD was with Joseph and extended kindness to him, and [b]gave him favor in the sight of the chief jailer.
22 The chief jailer [a]committed to Joseph's [1]charge all the prisoners who were in the jail; so that whatever was done there, he was [2]responsible *for it.*
23 [a]The chief jailer did not supervise anything under [1]Joseph's charge because [b]the LORD was with him; and whatever he did, [c]the LORD made to prosper.

Joseph Interprets a Dream

40 Then it came about after these things, [a]the cupbearer and the baker for the king of Egypt offended their lord, the king of Egypt.
2 Pharaoh was [a]furious with his two officials, the chief cupbearer and the chief baker.
3 So he put them in confinement in the house of the [a]captain of the bodyguard, in the jail, the *same* place where Joseph was imprisoned.
4 The captain of the bodyguard put Joseph in charge of them, and he [1]took care of them; and they were in confinement for [2]some time.
5 Then the cupbearer and the baker for the king of Egypt, who were confined in jail, both had a dream the same night, each man with his *own* dream *and* each dream with its *own* interpretation.
6 [1]When Joseph came to them in the morning and observed them, [2]behold, they were dejected.
7 He asked Pharaoh's officials who were with him in confinement in his master's house, "[1a]Why are your faces so sad today?"
8 Then they said to him, "[a]We have [1]had a dream and there is no one to interpret it." Then Joseph said to them, "[b]Do not interpretations belong to God? Tell *it* to me, please."
9 ¶ So the chief cupbearer told his dream to Joseph, and said to him, "In my dream, [1]behold, *there was* a vine in front of me;
10 and on the vine *were* three branches. And as it was budding, its blossoms came out, *and* its clusters produced ripe grapes.
11 "Now Pharaoh's cup was in my hand; so I took the grapes and squeezed them into Pharaoh's cup, and I put the cup into Pharaoh's [1]hand."
12 Then Joseph said to him, "This is the [a]interpretation of it: the three branches are three days;
13 within three more days Pharaoh will [1]lift up your head and restore you to your [2]office; and you will put Pharaoh's cup into his hand according to your former custom when you were his cupbearer.
14 "Only [1]keep me in mind when it goes well with you, and please [a]do me a kindness [2]by mentioning me to Pharaoh and get me out of this house.
15 "For [a]I was in fact kidnapped from the land of the Hebrews, and even here I have done nothing that they should have put me into the [1]dungeon."
16 ¶ When the chief baker saw that he had interpreted favorably, he said to Joseph, "I also *saw* in my dream, and behold, *there were* three baskets of white bread on my head;
17 and in the top basket *there were* some of all [1]sorts of baked food for Phar-

8 [2]Lit *hand*
9 [1]Or *He is not greater* [a]Gen 41:40 [b]Gen 20:6; 42:18; 2 Sam 12:13; Ps 51:4
11 [1]Lit *about this day*
13 [1]Lit *And it came about when*
14 [1]Lit *Hebrew man* [2]Lit *called with a great voice*
15 [1]Lit *called out*
16 [1]Lit *let...lie beside*
17 [1]Lit *according to* [2]Lit *saying, "The* [a]Ex 23:1; Prov 26:28
18 [1]Lit *called out*
19 [1]Lit *According to these things your slave* [a]Prov 6:34
20 [a]Gen 40:3; Ps 105:18
21 [a]Gen 39:2; Ps 105:19; Acts 7:9 [b]Ex 3:21; 11:3; 12:36
22 [1]Lit *hand* [2]Lit *the doer* [a]Gen 39:4; 40:3, 4
23 [1]Lit *his hand* [a]Gen 39:3,8 [b]Gen 39:2,3 [c]Gen 39:3
40:1 [a]Gen 40:11,13; Neh 1:11
2 [a]Prov 16:14
3 [a]Gen 39:1,20
4 [1]Lit *ministered to* [2]Lit *days*
6 [1]Or *And* [2]Lit *and behold*
7 [1]Lit *saying, Why* [a]Neh 2:2
8 [1]Lit *dreamed* [a]Gen 41:15 [b]Gen 41:16; Dan 2:27,28
9 [1]Lit *and behold*
11 [1]Lit *palm*
12 [a]Dan 2:36; 4:18,19
13 [1]Or possibly *forgive you* [2]Lit *place*
14 [1]Lit *remember me with yourself* [2]Lit *and mention* [a]Josh 2:12; 1 Sam 20:14; 1 Kin 2:7
15 [1]Or *pit* [a]Gen 37:26-28
17 [1]Lit *food for Pharaoh made by a baker*

aoh, and the birds were eating them out
of the basket on my head."
18 Then Joseph answered and said,
"This is its interpretation: the three baskets are three days;
19 within three more days Pharaoh
will lift up your head from you and will
hang you on a tree, and the birds will eat
your flesh off you."
20 ¶ Thus it came about on the third
day, *which was* [a]Pharaoh's birthday, that
he made a feast for all his servants; [b]and
he lifted up the head of the chief cupbearer and the head of the chief baker among
his servants.
21 He restored the chief cupbearer to
his [1]office, and [a]he put the cup into
Pharaoh's [2]hand;
22 but [a]he hanged the chief baker,
just as Joseph had interpreted to them.
23 Yet the chief cupbearer did not remember Joseph, but [a]forgot him.

Pharaoh's Dream

41 Now it happened at the end of
two full years that Pharaoh had a
dream, and behold, he was standing by
the Nile.
2 And lo, from the Nile there came
up seven cows, sleek and [1]fat; and they
grazed in the [a]marsh grass.
3 Then behold, seven other cows
came up after them from the Nile, ugly
and [1]gaunt, and they stood by the *other*
cows on the bank of the Nile.
4 The ugly and [1]gaunt cows ate up
the seven sleek and fat cows. Then Pharaoh awoke.
5 He fell asleep and dreamed a second time; and behold, seven ears of grain
came up on a single stalk, plump and
good.
6 Then behold, seven ears, thin and
scorched by the east wind, sprouted up
after them.
7 The thin ears swallowed up the sev-
en plump and full ears. Then Pharaoh
awoke, and behold, *it was* a dream.
8 Now in the morning [a]his spirit was
troubled, so he sent and called for all the
[1b]magicians of Egypt, and all its [c]wise
men. And Pharaoh told them his
[2]dreams, but [d]there was no one who
could interpret them to Pharaoh.
9 ¶ Then the chief cupbearer spoke
to Pharaoh, saying, "I would make mention today of [a]my *own* [1]offenses.
10 "Pharaoh was [a]furious with his servants, and [b]he put me in confinement in
the house of the captain of the bodyguard, *both* me and the chief baker.
11 "[a]We had a dream [1]on the same
night, [2]he and I; each of us dreamed according to the interpretation of his *own*
dream.
12 "Now a Hebrew youth *was* with us
there, a [a]servant of the captain of the
bodyguard, and we related *them* to him,
and [b]he interpreted our dreams for us.
To each one he interpreted according to
his *own* dream.
13 "And just [a]as he interpreted for us,
so it happened; he restored me in my
[1]office, but he hanged him."

Joseph Interprets

14 ¶ Then Pharaoh sent and [a]called
for Joseph, and they [b]hurriedly brought
him out of the dungeon; and when he had
shaved himself and changed his clothes,
he came to Pharaoh.
15 Pharaoh said to Joseph, "I have had
a dream, [a]but no one can interpret it;
and [b]I have heard [1]it said about you,
that [2]when you hear a dream you can
interpret it."
16 Joseph then answered Pharaoh,
saying, "[1a]It is not in me; [b]God will
[2]give Pharaoh a favorable answer."
17 So Pharaoh spoke to Joseph, "In my
dream, behold, I was standing on the
bank of the Nile;
18 and behold, seven cows, [1]fat and
sleek came up out of the Nile, and they
grazed in the marsh grass.
19 "Lo, seven other cows came up after
them, poor and very ugly and [1]gaunt,
such as I had never seen for [2]ugliness in
all the land of Egypt;
20 and the lean and [1]ugly cows ate up
the first seven fat cows.
21 "Yet when they had [1]devoured
them, it could not be [2]detected that they
had [1]devoured them, [3]for they were just
as ugly as [4]before. Then I awoke.
22 "I saw also in my dream, and behold,
seven ears, full and good, came up on a
single stalk;
23 and lo, seven ears, withered, thin,
and scorched by the east wind, sprouted
up after them;
24 and the thin ears swallowed the
seven good ears. Then [a]I told it to the
[1]magicians, but there was no one who
could explain it to me."
25 ¶ Now Joseph said to Pharaoh,
"Pharaoh's [1]dreams are one *and the
same;* [a]God has told to Pharaoh what He
is about to do.
26 "The seven good cows are seven
years; and the seven good ears are seven
years; the [1]dreams are one *and the same.*
27 "The seven lean and ugly cows that
came up after them are seven years, and
the seven thin ears scorched by the east
wind [a]will be seven years of famine.
28 "[1]It is as I have spoken to Pharaoh

20 [a]Matt 14:6 [b]2 Kin 25:27; Jer 52:31
21 [1]Lit *wine-pouring* [2]Lit *palm* [a]Gen 40:13
22 [a]Gen 40:19; Esth 7:10
23 [a]Job 19:14; Ps 31:12; Eccl 9:15
41:2 [1]Lit *fat of flesh* [a]Job 8:11; Is 19:6,7
3 [1]Lit *lean of flesh*
4 [1]Lit *lean of flesh*
8 [1]Or *soothsayer priests* [2]Lit *dream* [a]Dan 2:1, 3 [b]Ex 7:11,22; Dan 1:20; 2:2 [c]Matt 2:1 [d]Dan 2:27; 4:7
9 [1]Or *sins* [a]Gen 40:14,23
10 [a]Gen 40:2,3 [b]Gen 39:20
11 [1]Lit *one night* [2]Lit *I and he* [a]Gen 40:5
12 [a]Gen 37:36 [b]Gen 40:12
13 [1]Lit *place* [a]Gen 40:21,22
14 [a]Ps 105:20 [b]Dan 2:25
15 [1]Lit *about you, saying* [2]Lit *you hear a dream to interpret it* [a]Gen 41:8 [b]Dan 5:16
16 [1]Lit *Apart from me* [2]Lit *answer the peace of Pharaoh* [a]Dan 2:30; Zech 4:6; Acts 3:12; 2 Cor 3:5 [b]Gen 40:8; 41:25,28,32; Deut 29:29; Dan 2:22,28,47
18 [1]Lit *fat of flesh*
19 [1]Lit *lean of flesh* [2]Lit *badness*
20 [1]Lit *bad*
21 [1]Lit *entered their inward parts* [2]Or *known* [3]Lit *and* [4]Lit *in the beginning*
24 [1]Or *soothsayer priests* [a]Is 8:19; Dan 4:7
25 [1]Lit *dream is* [a]Gen 41:28,32; Dan 2:28,29,45
26 [1]Lit *dream is*
27 [a]2 Kin 8:1
28 [1]Lit *That is the thing which I spoke*

[a]God has shown to Pharaoh what He is about to do.

29 "Behold, [a]seven years of great abundance are coming in all the land of Egypt;

30 and after them [a]seven years of famine will [1]come, and all the abundance will be forgotten in the land of Egypt, and the famine will [2]ravage the land.

31 "So the abundance will be unknown in the land because of that subsequent famine; for it *will be* very severe.

32 "Now as for the repeating of the dream to Pharaoh twice, *it means* that [a]the matter is determined by God, and God will quickly bring it about.

33 "Now let Pharaoh look for a man [a]discerning and wise, and set him over the land of Egypt.

34 "Let Pharaoh take action to appoint overseers [1]in charge of the land, and let him exact a fifth *of the produce* of the land of Egypt in the seven years of abundance.

35 "Then let them [a]gather all the food of these good years that are coming, and store up the grain for food in the cities under Pharaoh's authority, and let them guard *it.*

36 "Let the food become as a reserve for the land for the seven years of famine which will occur in the land of Egypt, so that the land will not perish during the famine."

37 ¶ Now the [1]proposal seemed good [2]to Pharaoh and [2]to all his servants.

Joseph Is Made a Ruler of Egypt

38 Then Pharaoh said to his servants, "Can we find a man like this, [a]in whom is a divine spirit?"

39 So Pharaoh said to Joseph, "Since God has informed you of all this, there is no one so [a]discerning and wise as you are.

40 "[a]You shall be over my house, and according to your [1]command all my people shall [2]do homage; only in the throne I will be greater than you."

41 Pharaoh said to Joseph, "See, I have set you [a]over all the land of Egypt."

42 Then Pharaoh [a]took off his signet ring from his hand and put it on Joseph's hand, and clothed him in garments of fine linen and [b]put the gold necklace around his neck.

43 He had him ride in [1]his second chariot; and they proclaimed before him, "[2]Bow the knee!" And he set him over all the land of Egypt.

44 Moreover, Pharaoh said to Joseph, "*Though* I am Pharaoh, yet [a]without [1]your permission no one shall raise his hand or foot in all the land of Egypt."

45 Then Pharaoh named Joseph [1]Zaphenath-paneah; and he gave him Asenath, the daughter of Potiphera priest of [2a]On, as his wife. And Joseph went forth over the land of Egypt.

46 ¶ Now Joseph was [a]thirty years old when he [1]stood before Pharaoh, king of Egypt. And Joseph went out from the presence of Pharaoh and went through all the land of Egypt.

47 During the seven years of plenty the land brought forth [1]abundantly.

48 So he gathered all the food of *these* seven years which occurred in the land of Egypt and placed the food in the cities; he placed in every city the food from its own surrounding fields.

49 Thus Joseph stored up grain [1]in great abundance like the sand of the sea, until he stopped [2]measuring *it,* for it was [3]beyond measure.

The Sons of Joseph

50 ¶ Now before the year of famine came, [a]two sons were born to Joseph, whom Asenath, the daughter of Potiphera priest of [1]On, bore to him.

51 Joseph named the firstborn [1]Manasseh, "For," *he said,* "God has made me forget all my trouble and all my father's household."

52 He named the second [1]Ephraim, "For," *he said,* "[a]God has made me fruitful in the land of my affliction."

53 ¶ When the seven years of plenty which had been in the land of Egypt came to an end,

54 and [a]the seven years of famine began to come, just as Joseph had said, then there was famine in all the lands, but in all the land of Egypt there was bread.

55 So when all the land of Egypt was famished, the people cried out to Pharaoh for bread; and Pharaoh said to all the Egyptians, "Go to Joseph; [a]whatever he says to you, you shall do."

56 When the famine was *spread* over all the face of the earth, then Joseph opened all [1]the storehouses, and sold to the Egyptians; and the famine was severe in the land of Egypt.

57 *The people of* all the earth came to Egypt to buy grain from Joseph, because [a]the famine was severe in all the earth.

Joseph's Brothers Sent to Egypt

42 Now [a]Jacob saw that there was grain in Egypt, and Jacob said to his sons, "Why are you staring at one another?"

2 He said, "Behold, [a]I have heard that there is grain in Egypt; go down there and buy *some* for us [1]from that place, [b]so that we may live and not die."

28 [a]Gen 41:25, 32
29 [a]Gen 41:47
30 [1]Lit *arise* [2]Lit *destroy* [a]Gen 41:54,56; 47:13; Ps 105:16
32 [a]Gen 41:25, 28
33 [a]Gen 41:39
34 [1]Lit *over*
35 [a]Gen 41:48
37 [1]Lit *word* [2]Lit *in the sight of*
38 [a]Job 32:8; Dan 4:8,9,18; 5:11,14
39 [a]Gen 41:33
40 [1]Lit *mouth* [2]Lit *kiss* [a]Ps 105:21; Acts 7:10
41 [a]Gen 42:6; Ps 105:21; Dan 6:3; Acts 7:10
42 [a]Esth 3:10; 8:2 [b]Dan 5:7,16, 29
43 [1]Lit *the second...which was his* [2]Heb *Abreck: Attention* or *Make way*
44 [1]Lit *you no one* [a]Ps 105:22
45 [1]Probably Egyptian for "God speaks; he lives" [2]Or *Heliopolis* [a]Jer 43:13; Ezek 30:17
46 [1]Or *entered the service of* [a]Gen 37:2
47 [1]Lit *by handfuls*
49 [1]Lit *very much* [2]Lit *numbering* [3]Or *without number*
50 [1]Or *Heliopolis* [a]Gen 48:5
51 [1]I.e. making to forget
52 [1]I.e. fruitfulness [a]Gen 17:6; 28:3; 49:22
54 [a]Gen 41:30; Ps 105:16; Acts 7:11
55 [a]John 2:5
56 [1]Lit *that which was in them*
57 [a]Gen 12:10
42:1 [a]Acts 7:12
2 [1]Lit *from there* [a]Acts 7:12 [b]Gen 43:8; Ps 33:18, 19

3 Then ten brothers of Joseph went
down to buy grain from Egypt.
4 But Jacob did not send Joseph's
brother [a]Benjamin with his brothers, for
he said, "[b]I am afraid that harm may befall him."
5 So the sons of Israel came to buy
grain among those who were coming,
[a]for the famine was in the land of Canaan *also.*
6 ¶ Now [a]Joseph was the ruler over
the land; he was the one who sold to
all the people of the land. And Joseph's
brothers came and [b]bowed down to him
with *their* faces to the ground.
7 When Joseph saw his brothers he
recognized them, but he disguised himself to them and [a]spoke to them harshly.
And he said to them, "Where have you
come from?" And they said, "From the
land of Canaan, to buy food."
8 ¶ But Joseph had recognized his
brothers, although [a]they did not recognize him.
9 Joseph [a]remembered the dreams
which he [1]had about them, and said to
them, "You are spies; you have come
to look at the [2]undefended parts of our
land."
10 Then they said to him, "No, [a]my
lord, but your servants have come to buy
food.
11 "We are all sons of one man; we
are [a]honest men, your servants are not
spies."
12 Yet he said to them, "No, but you
have come to look at the [1]undefended
parts of our land!"
13 But they said, "Your servants are
twelve brothers *in all,* the sons of one
man in the land of Canaan; and behold,
the youngest is with [a]our father today,
and [b]one is no longer alive."
14 Joseph said to them, "It is as I said
[1]to you, you are spies;
15 by this you will be tested: [a]by the
life of Pharaoh, you shall not go from
this place unless your youngest brother
comes here!
16 "Send one of you that he may get
your brother, while you remain confined,
that your words may be tested, whether
there is [a]truth in you. But if not, by the
life of Pharaoh, surely you are spies."
17 So he put them all together in
[a]prison for three days.
18 ¶ Now Joseph said to them on the
third day, "Do this and live, for [a]I fear
God:
19 if you are honest men, let one of
your brothers be confined in [1]your prison; but as for *the rest of* you, go, carry
grain for the famine of your households,
20 and [a]bring your youngest brother
to me, so your words may be verified, and
you will not die." And they did so.
21 Then they said to one another,
"[a]Truly we are guilty concerning our
brother, because we saw the distress of
his soul when he pleaded with us, yet we
would not listen; therefore this distress
has come upon us."
22 Reuben answered them, saying,
"[a]Did I not tell [1]you, 'Do not sin against
the boy'; and you would not listen?
[2][b]Now comes the reckoning for his
blood."
23 They did not know, however, that
Joseph understood, for there was an interpreter between them.
24 He turned away from them and
[a]wept. But when he returned to them
and spoke to them, he [b]took Simeon
from them and bound him before their
eyes.
25 [a]Then Joseph gave orders to fill
their bags with grain and to restore every
man's money in his sack, and to give
them provisions for the journey. And
thus it was done for them.
26 ¶ So they loaded their donkeys
with their grain and departed from there.
27 As one *of them* opened his sack
to give his donkey fodder at the lodging
place, he saw his [a]money; and behold, it
was in the mouth of his sack.
28 Then he said to his brothers, "My
money has been returned, and behold, it
is even in my sack." And their hearts
[1]sank, and they *turned* [2]trembling to
one another, saying, "[a]What is this that
God has done to us?"

Simeon Is Held Hostage

29 ¶ When they came to their father
Jacob in the land of Canaan, they told him
all that had happened to them, saying,
30 "The man, the lord of the land,
[a]spoke harshly with us, and took us for
spies of the country.
31 "But we said to him, 'We are [a]hon-
est men; we are not spies.
32 'We are twelve brothers, sons of our
father; one is no longer alive, and the
youngest is with our father today in the
land of Canaan.'
33 "The man, the lord of the land, said
to us, '[a]By this I will know that you are
honest men: leave one of your brothers
with me and take *grain for* the famine of
your households, and go.
34 'But bring your youngest brother to
me that I may know that you are not
spies, but [1]honest men. I will give your
brother to you, and you may [a]trade in the
land.'"
35 ¶ Now it came about as they were
emptying their sacks, that behold, [a]every

4 [a]Gen 35:24 [b]Gen 42:38
5 [a]Gen 12:10; 26:1; 41:57; Acts 7:11
6 [a]Gen 41:41,55 [b]Gen 37:7-10; 41:43; Is 60:14
7 [a]Gen 42:30
8 [a]Gen 37:2; 41:46
9 [1]Lit *had dreamed* [2]Lit *nakedness of the land* [a]Gen 37:6-9
10 [a]Gen 37:8
11 [a]Gen 42:16, 19,31,34
12 [1]Lit *nakedness of the land*
13 [a]Gen 43:7 [b]Gen 37:30; 42:32; 44:20
14 [1]Lit *to you, saying*
15 [a]1 Sam 17:55
16 [a]Gen 42:11
17 [a]Gen 40:4,7
18 [a]Gen 39:9; Lev 25:43; Neh 5:15
19 [1]Lit *the house of your prison*
20 [a]Gen 42:34; 43:5; 44:23
21 [a]Gen 37:26-28; 45:3; Hos 5:15
22 [1]Lit *you saying* [2]Lit *And behold, his blood also is required* [a]Gen 37:21,22 [b]Gen 9:5,6; 1 Kin 2:32; 2 Chr 24:22; Ps 9:12
24 [a]Gen 43:30; 45:14,15 [b]Gen 43:14,23
25 [a]Gen 44:1; Rom 12:17,20, 21; 1 Pet 3:9
27 [a]Gen 43:21, 22
28 [1]Lit *went out* [2]Lit *trembled* [a]Gen 43:23
30 [a]Gen 42:7
31 [a]Gen 42:11
33 [a]Gen 42:19, 20
34 [1]Lit *you are honest* [a]Gen 34:10
35 [a]Gen 43:12, 15,21

man's bundle of money *was* in his sack;
and when they and their father saw their
bundles of money, they were dismayed.
36 Their father Jacob said to them,
"You have [a]bereaved me of my children:
Joseph is no more, and Simeon is no
more, and you would take Benjamin; all
these things are against me."
37 Then Reuben spoke to his father,
saying, "You may put my two sons to
death if I do not bring him *back* to you;
put him in my [1]care, and I will return
him to you."
38 But [1]Jacob said, "My son shall not
go down with you; for his [a]brother is
dead, and he alone is left. [b]If harm
should befall him on the journey [2]you
are taking, then you will [c]bring my gray
hair down to Sheol in sorrow."

The Return to Egypt

43 [a]Now the famine was severe in
the land.
2 So it came about when they had
finished eating the grain which they had
brought from Egypt, that their father said
to them, "Go back, buy us a little food."
3 Judah spoke to him, however, saying, "[a]The man solemnly warned [1]us,
'You shall not see my face unless your
brother is with you.'
4 "If you send our brother with us, we
will go down and buy you food.
5 "But if you do not send *him,* we will
not go down; for the man said to us, 'You
will not see my face unless your brother
is with you.' "
6 Then Israel said, "Why did you
treat me so badly [1]by telling the man
whether you still had *another* brother?"
7 But they said, "The man questioned particularly about us and our relatives, saying, '[a]Is your father still alive?
Have you *another* brother?' So we [1]an-
swered his questions. Could we possibly
know that he would say, 'Bring your
brother down'?"
8 Judah said to his father Israel,
"Send the lad with me and we will arise
and go, [a]that we may live and not die, we
as well as you and our little ones.
9 "[a]I myself will be surety for him;
[1]you may hold me responsible for him. If
I do not bring him *back* to you and set
him before you, then [2]let me bear the
blame before you forever.
10 "For if we had not delayed, surely by
now we could have returned twice."
11 ¶ Then their father Israel said to
them, "If *it must be* so, then do this: take
some of the best products of the land in
your [1]bags, and carry down to the man
[a]as a present, a little [2b]balm and a little
honey, [3]aromatic gum and [4]myrrh, pis-
tachio nuts and almonds.
12 "Take double *the* money in your
hand, and take back in your hand [a]the
money that was returned in the mouth of
your sacks; perhaps it was a mistake.
13 "Take your brother also, and arise,
return to the man;
14 and may [1a]God Almighty [b]grant
you compassion in the sight of the man,
so that he will release to you [c]your other
brother and Benjamin. And as for me, [d]if
I am bereaved of my children, I am bereaved."
15 So the men took [a]this present, and
they took double *the* money in their
hand, and Benjamin; then they arose and
went down to Egypt and stood before Joseph.

Joseph Sees Benjamin

16 ¶ When Joseph saw Benjamin with
them, he said to his [a]house steward,
"Bring the men into the house, and slay
an animal and make ready; for the men
are to dine with me at noon."
17 So the man did as Joseph said, and
[1]brought the men to Joseph's house.
18 Now the men were afraid, because
they were brought to Joseph's house; and
they said, "*It is* because of the money that
was returned in our sacks the first time
that we are being brought in, that he may
[1]seek occasion against us and fall upon
us, and take us for slaves with our donkeys."
19 So they came near to Joseph's
house steward, and spoke to him at the
entrance of the house,
20 and said, "Oh, my lord, we indeed
came down the first time to buy food,
21 and it came about when we came to
the lodging place, that we opened our
sacks, and behold, [a]each man's money
was in the mouth of his sack, our money
in [1]full. So [b]we have brought it back in
our hand.
22 "We have also brought down other
money in our hand to buy food; we do not
know who put our money in our sacks."
23 He said, "[1]Be at ease, do not be
afraid. [a]Your God and the God of your
father has given you treasure in your
sacks; [2]I had your money." Then [b]he
brought Simeon out to them.
24 Then the man brought the men
into Joseph's house and [a]gave them water, and they [b]washed their feet; and he
gave their donkeys fodder.
25 So they prepared [a]the present [1]for
Joseph's coming at noon; for they had
heard that they were to eat [2]a meal
there.
26 ¶ When Joseph came home, they

---

36 [a]Gen 43:14
37 [1]Lit *hand*
38 [1]Lit *he* [2]Lit *on which you are going* [a]Gen 37:33,34; 42:13; 44:27,28 [b]Gen 42:4 [c]Gen 37:35; 44:29,31
43:1 [a]Gen 12:10; 26:1; 41:56,57
3 [1]Lit *us, saying* [a]Gen 43:5; 44:23
6 [1]Lit *to tell*
7 [1]Lit *told him according to these words* [a]Gen 42:13; 43:27
8 [a]Gen 42:2
9 [1]Lit *from my hand you may require him* [2]Lit *I shall have sinned before you all the days* [a]Gen 42:37; 44:32; Philem 18,19
11 [1]Or *vessels* [2]Or *mastic* [3]Or *ladanum spice* [4]Or *resinous bark* [a]Gen 32:20; 43:25,26 [b]Gen 37:25; Jer 8:22; Ezek 27:17
12 [a]Gen 42:25, 35; 43:21,22
14 [1]Heb *El Shaddai* [a]Gen 17:1; 28:3; 35:11 [b]Ps 106:46 [c]Gen 42:24 [d]Gen 42:36
15 [a]Gen 43:11
16 [a]Gen 44:1
17 [1]Lit *the man brought*
18 [1]Lit *roll himself upon us*
21 [1]Lit *its weight* [a]Gen 42:27,35 [b]Gen 43:12,15
23 [1]Lit *Peace be to you* [2]Lit *your money had come to me* [a]Gen 42:28 [b]Gen 42:24
24 [a]Gen 18:4; 19:2; 24:32 [b]Luke 7:44; John 13:5; 1 Tim 5:10
25 [1]Lit *until* [2]Lit *bread* [a]Gen 43:11,15

brought into the house to him the present which was in their hand and [a]bowed to the ground before him.

27 Then he asked them about their welfare, and said, "[a]Is your old father well, of whom you spoke? Is he still alive?"

28 They said, "Your servant our father is well; he is still alive." [a]They bowed down [1]in homage.

29 As he lifted his eyes and saw his brother Benjamin, his mother's son, he said, "Is this [a]your youngest brother, of whom you spoke to me?" And he said, "[b]May God be gracious to you, my son."

30 Joseph hurried *out* for [1a]he was deeply stirred over his brother, and he sought *a place* to weep; and he entered his chamber and [b]wept there.

31 Then he washed his face and came out; and he [a]controlled himself and said, "[1]Serve the meal."

32 So they served him by himself, and them by themselves, and the Egyptians who ate with him by themselves, because the Egyptians could not eat bread with the Hebrews, for that is [1a]loathsome to the Egyptians.

33 Now they [1]were seated before him, [a]the firstborn according to his birthright and the youngest according to his youth, and the men looked at one another in astonishment.

34 He took portions to them from [1]his own table, [a]but Benjamin's portion was five times as much as any of theirs. So they feasted and drank freely with him.

The Brothers Are Brought Back

44 [a]Then he commanded his house steward, saying, "Fill the men's sacks with food, as much as they can carry, and put each man's money in the mouth of his sack.

2 "Put my cup, the silver cup, in the mouth of the sack of the youngest, and his money for the grain." And he did [1]as Joseph had told *him*.

3 [1]As soon as it was light, the men were sent away, they with their donkeys.

4 They had *just* gone out of [a]the city, *and* were not far off, when Joseph said to his house steward, "Up, follow the men; and when you overtake them, say to them, 'Why have you repaid evil for good?

5 'Is not this the one from which my lord drinks and which he indeed uses for [a]divination? You have done wrong in doing this.' "

6 ¶ So he overtook them and spoke these words to them.

7 They said to him, "Why does my lord speak such words as these? Far be it from your servants to do such a thing.

8 "Behold, [a]the money which we found in the mouth of our sacks we have brought back to you from the land of Canaan. How then could we steal silver or gold from your lord's house?

9 "[a]With whomever of your servants it is found, let him die, and we also will be my lord's [b]slaves."

10 So he said, "Now let it also be according to your words; he with whom it is found shall be my slave, and *the rest of* you shall be innocent."

11 Then they hurried, each man lowered his sack to the ground, and each man opened his sack.

12 He searched, beginning with the oldest and ending with the youngest, and [a]the cup was found in Benjamin's sack.

13 Then they [a]tore their clothes, and when each man loaded his donkey, they returned to [b]the city.

14 ¶ When Judah and his brothers came to Joseph's house, he was still there, and [a]they fell to the ground before him.

15 Joseph said to them, "What is this deed that you have done? Do you not know that such a man as I can indeed practice [a]divination?"

16 So Judah said, "What can we say to my lord? What can we speak? And how can we justify ourselves? God has found out the iniquity of your servants; behold, we are my lord's [a]slaves, both we and the one in whose [1]possession the cup has been found."

17 But he said, "Far be it from me to do this. The man in whose [1]possession the cup has been found, he shall be my slave; but as for you, go up in peace to your father."

18 ¶ Then Judah approached him, and said, "Oh my lord, may your servant please speak a word in my lord's ears, and [1a]do not be angry with your servant; for [b]you are equal to Pharaoh.

19 "[a]My lord asked his servants, saying, 'Have you a father or a brother?'

20 "We said to my lord, 'We have an old father and [a]a little child of *his* old age. Now [b]his brother is dead, so he alone is left of his mother, and his father loves him.'

21 "Then you said to your servants, '[a]Bring him down to me that I may set my eyes on him.'

22 "But we said to my lord, 'The lad cannot leave his father, for if he should leave his father, [1]his father would die.'

23 "You said to your servants, however, '[a]Unless your youngest brother comes

26 [a]Gen 37:7, 10

27 [a]Gen 43:7; 45:3

28 [1]Lit *and prostrated themselves* [a]Gen 37:7,10

29 [a]Gen 42:13 [b]Num 6:25; Ps 67:1

30 [1]Lit *his compassion grew warm* [a]1 Kin 3:26 [b]Gen 42:24; 45:2,14, 15; 46:29

31 [1]Lit *Set on bread* [a]Gen 45:1

32 [1]Lit *an abomination* [a]Gen 46:34; Ex 8:26

33 [1]Lit *sat* [a]Gen 42:7

34 [1]Lit *his face* [a]Gen 35:24; 45:22

44:1 [a]Gen 42:25

2 [1]Or *according to the word*

3 [1]Lit *The morning was light*

4 [a]Gen 44:13

5 [a]Gen 30:27; 44:15; Lev 19:26; Deut 18:10-14

8 [a]Gen 43:21

9 [a]Gen 31:32 [b]Gen 44:16

12 [a]Gen 44:2

13 [a]Gen 37:29, 34; Num 14:6; 2 Sam 1:11 [b]Gen 44:4

14 [a]Gen 37:7, 10

15 [a]Gen 44:5

16 [1]Lit *hand* [a]Gen 44:9

17 [1]Lit *hand*

18 [1]Lit *let not your anger burn against* [a]Gen 18:30,32; Ex 32:22 [b]Gen 37:7,8; 41:40-44

19 [a]Gen 43:7

20 [a]Gen 37:3; 43:8; 44:30 [b]Gen 37:33; 42:13,38

21 [a]Gen 42:15, 20

22 [1]Lit *he would*

23 [a]Gen 43:3,5

down with you, you will not see my face again.'

24 "Thus it came about when we went up to your servant my father, we told him the words of my lord.

25 "[a]Our father said, 'Go back, buy us a little food.'

26 "But we said, 'We cannot go down. If our youngest brother is with us, then we will go down; for we cannot see the man's face unless our youngest brother is with us.'

27 "Your servant my father said to us, 'You know that [a]my wife bore me two sons;

28 and the one went out from me, and [a]I said, "Surely he is torn in pieces," and I have not seen him since.

29 'If you take this one also from [1]me, and harm befalls him, you will [a]bring my gray hair down to Sheol in [2]sorrow.'

30 "Now, therefore, when I come to your servant my father, and the lad is not with us, since [1a]his life is bound up in the lad's life,

31 when he sees that the lad is not *with us,* he will die. Thus your servants will [a]bring the gray hair of your servant our father down to Sheol in sorrow.

32 "For your servant [a]became surety for the lad to my father, saying, 'If I do not bring him *back* to you, then [1]let me bear the blame before my father forever.'

33 "Now, therefore, please let your servant remain instead of the lad a slave to my lord, and let the lad go up with his brothers.

34 "For how shall I go up to my father if the lad is not with me—for fear that I see the evil that would [1]overtake my father?"

Joseph Deals Kindly with His Brothers

45 Then Joseph could not control himself before all those who stood by him, and he cried, "Have everyone go out from me." So there [1]was no man with him [a]when Joseph made himself known to his brothers.

2 [a]He [1]wept so loudly that the Egyptians heard *it,* and the household of Pharaoh heard *of it.*

3 Then Joseph said to his brothers, "[a]I am Joseph! [b]Is my father still alive?" But his brothers could not answer him, for [c]they were dismayed at his presence.

4 ¶ Then Joseph said to his brothers, "Please come [1]closer to me." And they came [1]closer. And he said, "I am your brother Joseph, whom you [a]sold into Egypt.

5 "Now do not be grieved or angry [1]with yourselves, because [a]you sold me here, for [b]God sent me before you to preserve life.

6 "For the famine *has been* in the land [a]these two years, and there are still five years in which there will be neither plowing nor harvesting.

7 "[a]God sent me before you to preserve for you a remnant in the earth, and to keep you alive by a great [1]deliverance.

8 "Now, therefore, it was not you who sent me here, but God; and He has made me a [a]father to Pharaoh and lord of all his household and ruler over all the land of Egypt.

9 "Hurry and go up to my father, and [a]say to him, 'Thus says your son Joseph, "God has made me lord of all Egypt; come down to me, do not delay.

10 "You shall [1]live in the land of [a]Goshen, and you shall be near me, you and your children and your children's children and your flocks and your herds and all that you have.

11 "There I will also [a]provide for you, for there are still five years of famine *to come,* and you and your household and all that you have would be impoverished." '

12 "Behold, your eyes see, and the eyes of my brother Benjamin *see,* that it is my mouth which is speaking to you.

13 "Now you must tell my father of all my splendor in Egypt, and all that you have seen; and you must hurry and [a]bring my father down here."

14 Then he fell on his brother Benjamin's neck and [a]wept, and Benjamin wept on his neck.

15 He kissed all his brothers and wept on them, and afterward his brothers talked with him.

16 ¶ Now when [a]the [1]news was heard in Pharaoh's house [2]that Joseph's brothers had come, it [3]pleased Pharaoh and his servants.

17 Then Pharaoh said to Joseph, "Say to your brothers, 'Do this: load your beasts and [1]go to the land of Canaan,

18 and take your father and your households and come to me, and [a]I will give you the [1]best of the land of Egypt and you will eat the fat of the land.'

19 "Now you are ordered, 'Do this: [1]take [a]wagons from the land of Egypt for your little ones and for your wives, and bring your father and come.

20 'Do not [1]concern yourselves with your goods, for the [2]best of all the land of Egypt is yours.' "

21 ¶ Then the sons of Israel did so; and Joseph gave them [a]wagons according to the [1]command of Pharaoh, and gave them provisions for the journey.

---

25 [a]Gen 43:2
27 [a]Gen 46:19
28 [a]Gen 37:31-35
29 [1]Lit *my face* [2]Lit *evil* [a]Gen 42:38; 44:31
30 [1]Lit *his soul is bound with his soul* [a]1 Sam 18:1
31 [a]Gen 44:29
32 [1]Lit *and I shall have sinned for all the days before my father* [a]Gen 43:9
34 [1]Lit *find*
45:1 [1]Lit *stood* [a]Acts 7:13
2 [1]Lit *gave forth his voice in weeping* [a]Gen 45:14,15; 46:29
3 [a]Acts 7:13 [b]Gen 43:27 [c]Gen 37:20-28; 42:21,22
4 [1]Lit *near* [a]Gen 37:28
5 [1]Lit *in your eyes* [a]Gen 37:28 [b]Gen 45:7,8; 50:20; Ps 105:17
6 [a]Gen 37:2; 41:46,53
7 [1]Lit *escaped company* [a]Gen 45:5
8 [a]Judg 17:10
9 [a]Acts 7:14
10 [1]Lit *dwell* [a]Gen 46:28,34; 47:1
11 [a]Gen 47:12
13 [a]Acts 7:14
14 [a]Gen 45:2
16 [1]Lit *voice* [2]Lit *saying, "Joseph's brothers have come"* [3]Lit *was good in the eyes of* [a]Acts 7:13
17 [1]Lit *come, go*
18 [1]Lit *good* [a]Gen 27:28
19 [1]Lit *take for yourselves* [a]Gen 45:21,27; 46:5; Num 7:3-8
20 [1]Lit *let your eye look with regret upon your vessels* [2]Lit *good*
21 [1]Lit *mouth* [a]Gen 45:19

22 To [1]each of them he gave
[a]changes of garments, but to Benjamin
he gave three hundred *pieces of* silver
and [b]five changes of garments.
23 To his father he sent [1]as follows:
ten donkeys loaded with the [2]best things
of Egypt, and ten female donkeys loaded
with grain and bread and sustenance for
his father [3]on the journey.
24 ¶ So he sent his brothers away, and
[1]as they departed, he said to them, "Do
not [2]quarrel on the journey."
25 Then they went up from Egypt, and
came to the land of Canaan to their father
Jacob.
26 They told him, saying, "Joseph is
still alive, and indeed he is ruler over all
the land of Egypt." But [1]he was stunned,
for [a]he did not believe them.
27 When they told him all the words
of Joseph that he had spoken to them, and
when he saw the [a]wagons that Joseph
had sent to carry him, the spirit of their
father Jacob revived.
28 Then Israel said, "It is enough; my
son Joseph is still alive. I will go and see
him before I die."

Jacob Moves to Egypt

46 So Israel set out with all that he
had, and came to [a]Beersheba,
and offered sacrifices to the [b]God of his
father Isaac.
2 [a]God spoke to Israel [1]in visions of
the night and said, "[b]Jacob, Jacob." And
he said, "Here I am."
3 He said, "[a]I am God, the God of
your father; do not be afraid to go down
to Egypt, for I will [b]make you a great
nation there.
4 "[a]I will go down with you to Egypt,
and [b]I will also surely bring you up again;
and [c]Joseph will [1]close your eyes."
5 ¶ Then Jacob arose from Beersheba; and the sons of Israel carried their
father Jacob and their little ones and their
wives in the [a]wagons which Pharaoh
had sent to carry him.
6 They took their livestock and their
property, which they had acquired in the
land of Canaan, and [a]came to Egypt, Jacob and all his [1]descendants with him:
7 his sons and his grandsons with
him, his daughters and his granddaugh-
ters, and all his [1]descendants he brought
with him to Egypt.

Those Who Came to Egypt

8 ¶ Now these are the [a]names of the
sons of Israel, Jacob and his sons, who
went to Egypt: Reuben, Jacob's firstborn.
9 The sons of Reuben: Hanoch and
Pallu and Hezron and Carmi.
10 The [a]sons of Simeon: [1]Jemuel and
Jamin and Ohad and [2]Jachin and [3]Zohar
and Shaul the son of a Canaanite woman.
11 The sons of Levi: [1]Gershon, Kohath, and Merari.
12 The sons of Judah: Er and Onan and
Shelah and Perez and Zerah (but Er and
Onan died in the land of Canaan). And
the [a]sons of Perez were Hezron and Hamul.
13 The sons of Issachar: Tola and
[1]Puvvah and [2]Iob and Shimron.
14 The sons of Zebulun: Sered and
Elon and Jahleel.
15 These are the sons of Leah, whom
she bore to Jacob in Paddan-aram, with
his daughter Dinah; [1]all his sons and his
daughters *numbered* thirty-three.
16 The [a]sons of Gad: [1]Ziphion and
Haggi, Shuni and [2]Ezbon, Eri and [3]Arodi
and Areli.
17 The [a]sons of Asher: Imnah and Ishvah and Ishvi and Beriah and their sister
Serah. And the [b]sons of Beriah: Heber
and Malchiel.
18 These are the sons of Zilpah, whom
Laban gave to his daughter Leah; and she
bore to Jacob these sixteen persons.
19 The sons of Jacob's wife Rachel: Joseph and Benjamin.
20 [a]Now to Joseph in the land of
Egypt were born Manasseh and Ephraim,
whom Asenath, the daughter of Potiphera, priest of On, bore to him.
21 The [a]sons of Benjamin: Bela and
Becher and Ashbel, Gera and Naaman,
[1]Ehi and Rosh, [2]Muppim and [3]Huppim
and Ard.
22 These are the sons of Rachel, who
were born to Jacob; *there were* fourteen
persons in all.
23 The sons of Dan: [1]Hushim.
24 The sons of Naphtali: [1]Jahzeel and
Guni and Jezer and [2]Shillem.
25 These are the [a]sons of Bilhah,
whom [b]Laban gave to his daughter Rachel, and she bore these to Jacob; *there
were* seven persons in all.
26 [a]All the persons belonging to Jacob, who came to Egypt, [1]his direct
descendants, not including the wives of
Jacob's sons, *were* sixty-six persons in all,
27 and the sons of Joseph, who were
born to him in Egypt were [1]two; [a]all the
persons of the house of Jacob, who came
to Egypt, *were* seventy.
28 ¶ Now he sent Judah before him to
Joseph, to point out *the way* before him
to [a]Goshen; and they came into the land
of Goshen.
29 Joseph [1]prepared his chariot and
went up to Goshen to meet his father
Israel; as soon as he appeared [2]before
him, he fell on his neck and [a]wept on his
neck a long time.

22 [1]Lit *all of them he gave each man* [a]2 Kin 5:5 [b]Gen 43:34
23 [1]Lit *like this* [2]Lit *good* [3]Lit *for*
24 [1]Lit *they departed; and he said* [2]Lit *be agitated*
26 [1]Lit *his heart grew numb* [a]Gen 37:31-35
27 [a]Gen 45:19
46:1 [a]Gen 21:31; 28:10 [b]Gen 26:24; 28:13; 31:42
2 [1]Lit *in the visions* [a]Gen 15:1; Num 12:6; Job 33:14,15 [b]Gen 22:11; 31:11
3 [a]Gen 17:1; 28:13 [b]Gen 12:2; Ex 1:9; Deut 26:5
4 [1]Lit *put his hand on* [a]Gen 28:15; 48:21 [b]Gen 50:24; Ex 3:8 [c]Gen 50:1
5 [a]Gen 45:21
6 [1]Lit *seed* [a]Deut 26:5; Josh 24:4; Ps 105:23; Is 52:4; Acts 7:15
7 [1]Lit *seed*
8 [a]Ex 1:1-4; Num 26:4,5; 1 Chr 2:1ff
10 [1]In Num 26:12 and 1 Chr 4:24, *Nemuel* [2]In 1 Chr 4:24, *Jarib* [3]In Num 26:13 and 1 Chr 4:24, *Zerah* [a]Ex 6:15
11 [1]In 1 Chr 6:16, *Gershom*
12 [a]1 Chr 2:5
13 [1]In Num 26:23, *Puvah*; in 1 Chr 7:1, *Puah* [2]In Num 26:24 and 1 Chr 7:1, *Jashub*
15 [1]Lit *all the souls of*
16 [1]In Num 26:15, *Zephon* [2]In Num 26:16, *Ozni* [3]In Num 26:17, *Arod* [a]Num 26:15-18
17 [a]1 Chr 7:30 [b]1 Chr 7:31
20 [a]Gen 41:50-52
21 [1]In Num 26:38, *Ahiram* [2]In Num 26:39, *Shephupham*; in 1 Chr 7:12, *Shuppim* [3]In Num 26:39, *Hupham* [a]1 Chr 7:6
23 [1]In Num 26:42, *Shuham*
24 [1]In 1 Chr 7:13, *Jahziel* [2]In 1 Chr 7:13, *Shallum*
25 [a]Gen 30:5,7 [b]Gen 29:29
26 [1]Lit *who came out of his loins* [a]Ex 1:5
27 [1]Lit *two souls* [a]Ex 1:5; Deut 10:22; Acts 7:14
28 [a]Gen 45:10
29 [1]Lit *tied, harnessed* [2]Lit *to* [a]Gen 45:14,15

30 Then Israel said to Joseph, "Now let me die, since I have seen your face, that you are still alive."

31 Joseph said to his brothers and to his father's household, "[a]I will go up and tell Pharaoh, and will say to him, 'My brothers and my father's household, who *were* in the land of Canaan, have come to me;

32 and the men are shepherds, for they have been [1]keepers of livestock; and they have brought their flocks and their herds and all that they have.'

33 "When Pharaoh calls you and says, '[a]What is your occupation?'

34 you shall say, 'Your servants have been [1a]keepers of livestock from our youth even until now, both we and our fathers,' that you may [2]live in the land of [b]Goshen; for every shepherd is [3c]loathsome to the Egyptians."

Jacob's Family Settles in Goshen

47 Then [a]Joseph went in and told Pharaoh, and said, "My father and my brothers and their flocks and their herds and all that they have, have come out of the land of Canaan; and behold, they are in the land of [b]Goshen."

2 He took five men from among his brothers and [a]presented them to Pharaoh.

3 Then Pharaoh said to his brothers, "[a]What is your occupation?" So they said to Pharaoh, "Your servants are [b]shepherds, both we and our fathers."

4 They said to Pharaoh, "[a]We have come to sojourn in the land, for there is no pasture for your servants' flocks, for [b]the famine is severe in the land of Canaan. Now, therefore, please let your servants [1c]live in the land of Goshen."

5 Then Pharaoh said to [1]Joseph, "Your father and your brothers have come to you.

6 "The land of Egypt is [1]at your disposal; [2]settle your father and your brothers in [a]the best of the land, let them [3]live in the land of Goshen; and if you know any [b]capable men among them, then [4]put them in charge of my livestock."

7 ¶ Then Joseph brought his father Jacob and [1]presented him to Pharaoh; and Jacob [a]blessed Pharaoh.

8 Pharaoh said to Jacob, "How many [1]years have you lived?"

9 So Jacob said to Pharaoh, "The [1a]years of my sojourning are one hundred and [2]thirty; few and [3]unpleasant have been the [1]years of my life, nor have they [4]attained [b]the [1]years [5]that my fathers lived during the days of their sojourning."

10 And Jacob [a]blessed Pharaoh, and went out from [1]his presence.

11 So Joseph [1]settled his father and his brothers and gave them a possession in the land of Egypt, in [a]the best of the land, in the land of [b]Rameses, as Pharaoh had ordered.

12 Joseph [a]provided his father and his brothers and all his father's household with [1]food, according to their little ones.

13 ¶ Now there was no [1]food in all the land, because the famine was very severe, so that [a]the land of Egypt and the land of Canaan languished because of the famine.

14 [a]Joseph gathered all the money that was found in the land of Egypt and in the land of Canaan for the grain which they bought, and Joseph brought the money into Pharaoh's house.

15 When the money was all spent in the land of Egypt and in the land of Canaan, all the Egyptians came to Joseph [1]and said, "Give us [2]food, for [a]why should we die in your presence? For *our* money [3]is gone."

16 Then Joseph said, "Give up your livestock, and I will give you *food* for your livestock, since *your* money [1]is gone."

17 So they brought their livestock to Joseph, and Joseph gave them [1]food in exchange for the horses and the [2]flocks and the herds and the donkeys; and he [3]fed them with [1]food in exchange for all their livestock [4]that year.

18 When that year was ended, they came to him the [1]next year and said to him, "We will not hide from my lord that our money is all spent, and the [2]cattle are my lord's. There is nothing left [3]for my lord except our bodies and our lands.

19 "Why should we die before your eyes, both we and our land? Buy us and our land for [1]food, and we and our land will be slaves to Pharaoh. So give us seed, that we may live and not die, and that the land may not be desolate."

Result of the Famine

20 ¶ So Joseph bought all the land of Egypt for Pharaoh, for [1]every Egyptian sold his field, because the famine was severe upon them. Thus the land became Pharaoh's.

21 As for the people, he removed them to the cities from one end of Egypt's border to the other.

22 Only the land of the priests he did not buy, for the priests had an allotment from Pharaoh, and they [1]lived off the allotment which Pharaoh gave them. Therefore, they did not sell their land.

23 Then Joseph said to the people, "Behold, I have today bought you and

31 [a]Gen 47:1
32 [1]Lit *men*
33 [a]Gen 47:2,3
34 [1]Lit *men* [2]Lit *dwell* [3]Lit *an abomination* [a]Gen 13:7,8; 26:20; 37:2 [b]Gen 45:10,18; 47:6,11 [c]Gen 43:32; Ex 8:26
47:1 [a]Gen 46:31 [b]Gen 45:10; 46:28
2 [a]Acts 7:13
3 [a]Gen 46:33 [b]Gen 46:34
4 [1]Lit *dwell* [a]Gen 15:13; Deut 26:5; Ps 105:23 [b]Gen 43:1; Acts 7:11 [c]Gen 46:34
5 [1]Lit *Joseph, saying*
6 [1]Lit *before you* [2]Lit *cause them to dwell* [3]Lit *dwell* [4]Lit *appoint them rulers* [a]Gen 45:10,18; 47:11 [b]Ex 18:21,25; 1 Kin 11:28; Prov 22:29
7 [1]Lit *set him before* [a]Gen 47:10; 2 Sam 14:22; 1 Kin 8:66
8 [1]Lit *are the days of the years of your life*
9 [1]Lit *days of the years* [2]Lit *thirty years* [3]Lit *evil* [4]Lit *reached* [5]Lit *of the life of my fathers* [a]Heb 11:9,13 [b]Gen 25:7; 35:28
10 [1]Lit *Pharaoh's* [a]Gen 47:7
11 [1]Lit *caused to dwell* [a]Gen 47:6,27 [b]Ex 1:11; 12:37
12 [1]Or *bread* [a]Gen 45:11
13 [1]Or *bread* [a]Gen 41:30; Acts 7:11
14 [a]Gen 41:56
15 [1]Lit *saying* [2]Or *bread* [3]Lit *ceases* [a]Gen 47:19
16 [1]Lit *ceases*
17 [1]Or *bread* [2]Lit *livestock of the flocks and livestock of the herds* [3]Lit *led them as a shepherd* [4]Lit *in that year*
18 [1]Lit *second* [2]Lit *livestock of the cattle* [3]Lit *in the presence of*
19 [1]Or *bread*
20 [1]Lit *Egypt, every man*
22 [1]Lit *ate their allotment*

your land for Pharaoh; now, *here* is seed
for you, and you may sow the land.
24 "[1]At the harvest you shall give a
[a]fifth to Pharaoh, and [2]four-fifths shall
be your own for seed of the field and for
your food and for those of your households and as food for your little ones."
25 So they said, "You have saved our
lives! Let us find favor in the sight of my
lord, and we will be Pharaoh's slaves."
26 Joseph made it a statute concerning
the land of Egypt *valid* to this day, that
Pharaoh should have the fifth; [a]only the
land of the priests [1]did not become Pharaoh's.
27 ¶ Now Israel [1]lived in the land of
Egypt, in [2]Goshen, and they [a]acquired
property in it and [b]were fruitful and became very numerous.
28 Jacob lived in the land of Egypt
[a]seventeen years; so the [1]length of Jacob's life was one hundred and forty-
seven years.
29 ¶ When [1a]the time for Israel to
die drew near, he called his son Joseph
and said to him, "Please, if I have found
favor in your sight, [b]place now your hand
under my thigh and [c]deal with me in
kindness and [2]faithfulness. Please do not
bury me in Egypt,
30 but when I [a]lie down with my fathers, you shall carry me out of Egypt and
bury me in [b]their burial place." And he
said, "I will do as you have said."
31 He said, "[a]Swear to me." So he
swore to him. Then [b]Israel bowed *in
worship* at the head of the bed.

Israel's Last Days

48 Now it came about after these
things that [1]Joseph was told, "Behold, your father is sick." So he took his
two sons [a]Manasseh and Ephraim with
him.
2 When [1]it was told to Jacob, "Behold, your son Joseph has come to you,"
Israel [2]collected his strength and sat [3]up
in the bed.
3 Then Jacob said to Joseph, "[1a]God
Almighty appeared to me at [b]Luz in the
land of Canaan and blessed me,
4 and He said to me, 'Behold, I will
make you fruitful and numerous, and I
will make you a company of peoples, and
will give this land to your [1]descendants
after you for [a]an everlasting possession.'
5 "Now your two sons, who were born
to you in the land of Egypt before I came
to you in Egypt, are mine; [a]Ephraim and
Manasseh shall be mine, as [b]Reuben and
Simeon are.
6 "But your offspring that [1]have been
born after them shall be yours; they shall
be called by the [2]names of their brothers
in their inheritance.
7 "Now as for me, when I came from
[a]Paddan, [b]Rachel died, [1]to my sorrow,
in the land of Canaan on the journey,
when there was still some distance to go
to Ephrath; and I buried her there on the
way to Ephrath (that is, Bethlehem)."
8 ¶ When Israel [a]saw Joseph's sons,
he said, "Who are these?"
9 Joseph said to his father, "[a]They
are my sons, whom God has given me
here." So he said, "Bring them to me,
please, that [b]I may bless them."
10 Now [a]the eyes of Israel were *so*
dim from age *that* he could not see. Then
[1]Joseph brought them close to him, and
he [b]kissed them and embraced them.
11 Israel said to Joseph, "I never [1]ex-
pected to see your face, and behold, God
has let me see your [2]children as well."
12 Then Joseph [1]took them from his
knees, and [a]bowed with his face to the
ground.
13 Joseph took them both, Ephraim
with his right hand toward Israel's left,
and Manasseh with his left hand toward
Israel's right, and brought them close to
him.
14 But Israel stretched out his right
hand and laid it on the head of Ephraim,
who was the younger, and his left hand
on Manasseh's head, [1]crossing his
hands, [2]although [a]Manasseh was the
firstborn.
15 He blessed Joseph, and said,
"[a]The God before whom my
fathers Abraham and Isaac
walked,
[b]The God who has been my
shepherd [1]all my life to this
day,
16 [a]The angel who has redeemed
me from all evil,
[b]Bless the lads;
And may my name [1]live on in
them,
And the [2]names of my fathers
Abraham and Isaac;
And [c]may they grow into a
multitude in the midst of
the earth."
17 ¶ When Joseph saw that his father
[a]laid his right hand on Ephraim's head,
it displeased him; and he grasped his father's hand to remove it from Ephraim's
head to Manasseh's head.
18 Joseph said to his father, "Not so,
my father, for this one is the firstborn.
Place your right hand on his head."
19 But his father refused and said, "I
know, my son, I know; he also will become a people and he also will be great.
However, his younger brother shall be

24 [1]Lit *It shall come about...that you shall* [2]Lit *four parts* [a]Gen 41:34

26 [1]Lit *alone did* [a]Gen 47:22

27 [1]Lit *dwelt* [2]Lit *in the land of Goshen* [a]Gen 47:11 [b]Gen 17:6; 26:4; 35:11; Ex 1:7; Deut 26:5; Acts 7:17

28 [1]Lit *days of Jacob, the years of his life* [a]Gen 47:9

29 [1]Lit *the days of Israel to die drew near* [2]Lit *truth* [a]Deut 31:14; 1 Kin 2:1 [b]Gen 24:2 [c]Gen 24:49

30 [a]Gen 15:15; Deut 31:16 [b]Gen 23:17-20; 25:9,10; 35:29; 49:29-32; 50:5, 13; Acts 7:15,16

31 [a]Gen 21:23, 24; 24:3; 31:53; 50:25 [b]1 Kin 1:47

48:1 [1]Lit *one said to Joseph* [a]Gen 41:51,52; Josh 14:4

2 [1]Lit *one told Jacob and said* [2]Lit *strengthened himself* [3]Lit *upon the bed*

3 [1]Heb *El Shaddai* [a]Gen 28:13f; 35:9-12 [b]Gen 28:19; 35:6

4 [1]Lit *seed* [a]Gen 17:8

5 [a]Gen 41:50-52; 46:20; 48:1; Josh 14:4 [b]1 Chr 5:1,2

6 [1]Lit *you have begotten* [2]Lit *name*

7 [1]Lit *upon me* [a]Gen 33:18 [b]Gen 35:19,20

8 [a]Gen 48:10

9 [a]Gen 33:5 [b]Gen 27:4

10 [1]Lit *he* [a]Gen 27:1 [b]Gen 27:27

11 [1]Lit *meditated, judged* [2]Lit *seed*

12 [1]Lit *made them come out* [a]Gen 42:6

14 [1]Or *consciously directing* [2]Lit *when* [a]Gen 41:51,52

15 [1]Lit *from the continuance of me* [a]Gen 17:1 [b]Gen 49:24

16 [1]Lit *be called* [2]Lit *name* [a]Gen 22:11,15-18; 28:13-15; 31:11 [b]Heb 11:21 [c]Gen 28:14; 46:3

17 [a]Gen 48:14

greater than he, and [a]his [1]descendants
shall become a [2]multitude of nations."
20 [a]He blessed them that day, saying,
"By you Israel will pronounce
blessing, saying,
'May God make you like Ephraim
and Manasseh!' "
Thus he put Ephraim before Manasseh.
21 Then Israel said to Joseph, "Behold,
I am about to die, but [a]God will be with
you, and [b]bring you back to the land of
your fathers.
22 "I give you one [1]portion more than
your brothers, [a]which I took from the
hand of the Amorite with my sword and
my bow."

Israel's Prophecy concerning His Sons

49 Then Jacob summoned his sons and said, "Assemble yourselves that I may tell you what will befall you [a]in the [1]days to come.
2 "Gather together and hear, O sons
of Jacob;
And [a]listen to Israel your father.

3 ¶ "Reuben, you are my firstborn;
My might and [a]the beginning of
my strength,
[1]Preeminent in dignity and
[1]preeminent in power.
4 "[1]Uncontrolled as water, you
shall not have preeminence,
[a]Because you went up to your
father's bed;
Then you defiled *it*—he went up
to my couch.

5 ¶ "[a]Simeon and Levi are
brothers;
Their swords are implements of
violence.
6 "[a]Let my soul not enter into their
council;
Let not my glory be united with
their assembly;
Because in their anger they
slew [1]men,
And in their self-will they lamed
[2]oxen.
7 "Cursed be their anger, for it is
fierce;
And their wrath, for it is cruel.
[a]I will [1]disperse them in Jacob,
And scatter them in Israel.

8 ¶ "Judah, your brothers shall
praise you;
Your hand shall be on the neck
of your enemies;
[a]Your father's sons shall bow
down to you.
9 "Judah is a [a]lion's whelp;
From the prey, my son, you have
gone up.
[b]He [1]couches, he lies down as
a lion,
And as a [2]lion, who [3]dares
rouse him up?
10 "[a]The scepter shall not depart
from Judah,
Nor the ruler's staff from
between his feet,
[1]Until Shiloh comes,
And [b]to him *shall be* the
obedience of the peoples.
11 "[1a]He ties *his* foal to the vine,
And his donkey's colt to the
choice vine;
[b]He washes his garments in
wine,
And his robes in the blood of
grapes.
12 "His eyes are [1]dull from wine,
And his teeth [2]white from milk.

13 ¶ "[a]Zebulun will dwell at the
seashore;
And he *shall be* [1]a haven for
ships,
And his flank *shall be* toward
Sidon.

14 ¶ "Issachar is [1]a strong donkey,
[a]Lying down between the
[2]sheepfolds.
15 "When he saw that a resting place
was good
And that the land was pleasant,
He bowed his shoulder to bear
burdens,
And became a slave at forced
labor.

16 ¶ "[a]Dan shall [b]judge his people,
As one of the tribes of Israel.
17 "Dan shall be a serpent in the
way,
A horned snake in the path,
That bites the horse's heels,
So that his rider falls backward.
18 "[a]For Your salvation I wait,
O LORD.

19 ¶ "[a]As for Gad, [1]raiders shall
raid him,
But he will raid *at* their [2]heels.

20 ¶ "[1a]As for [b]Asher, his [2]food
shall be [3]rich,
And he will yield royal dainties.

21 ¶ "[a]Naphtali is a doe let loose,
He gives beautiful words.

22 ¶ "[a]Joseph is a fruitful [1]bough,
A fruitful [1]bough by a spring;
Its [2]branches run over a wall.
23 "The archers bitterly attacked
him,

---

19 [1]Lit *seed* [2]Lit *fullness* [a]Gen 28:14; 46:3
20 [a]Heb 11:21
21 [a]Gen 26:3 [b]Gen 28:15; 46:4; 50:24
22 [1]Or *ridge;* lit *shoulder;* Heb *Shechem* [a]Josh 24:32; John 4:5
49:1 [1]Lit *end of the days* [a]Num 24:14
2 [a]Ps 34:11
3 [1]Lit *preeminence* [a]Deut 21:17; Ps 78:51; 105:36
4 [1]Or *Boiling over;* lit *Recklessness* [a]Gen 35:22; Deut 27:20; 1 Chr 5:1
5 [a]Gen 34:25-30
6 [1]Lit *a man* [2]Lit *an ox* [a]Ps 64:2
7 [1]Lit *divide* [a]Josh 19:1,9; 21:1-42
8 [a]Gen 27:29; 1 Chr 5:2
9 [1]Lit *bows down* [2]Or *lioness* [3]Lit *shall* [a]Ezek 19:5-7; Mic 5:8 [b]Num 24:9
10 [1]Or *Until he comes to Shiloh;* or *Until he comes to whom it belongs* [a]Num 24:17; Ps 60:7; 108:8 [b]Ps 2:6-9; 72:8-11; Is 42:1, 4; 49:6
11 [1]Lit *Binding of* [a]Deut 8:7,8; 2 Kin 18:32 [b]Is 63:2
12 [1]Or *darker than* [2]Or *whiter than*
13 [1]Lit *for a shore of ships* [a]Deut 33:18,19
14 [1]Lit *a donkey of bone* [2]Or *saddlebags* [a]Judg 5:16; Ps 68:13
16 [a]Deut 33:22; Judg 18:26,27 [b]Gen 30:6
18 [a]Ex 15:2; Ps 25:5; 40:1-3; 119:166,174; Is 25:9; Mic 7:7
19 [1]Lit *a raiding band* [2]Lit *heel* [a]Deut 33:20
20 [1]Lit *From* [2]Or *bread* [3]Lit *fat* [a]Deut 33:24, 25 [b]Gen 30:13
21 [a]Deut 33:23
22 [1]Lit *son* [2]Lit *daughters* [a]Deut 33:13-17

And shot *at him* and harassed
him;
24 But his [a]bow remained [1]firm,
And [2b]his arms were agile,
From the hands of the [c]Mighty
One of Jacob
(From there is [d]the Shepherd,
[e]the Stone of Israel),
25 From [a]the God of your father
who helps you,
And [1b]by the [2]Almighty who
blesses you
With [c]blessings of heaven above,
Blessings of the deep that lies
beneath,
Blessings of the breasts and of
the womb.
26 "The blessings of your father
Have surpassed the blessings of
my ancestors
Up to the [1]utmost bound of
[a]the everlasting hills;
May they be on the head of
Joseph,
And on the crown of the head of
the one distinguished among
his brothers.

27 ¶ "Benjamin is a [1]ravenous wolf;
In the morning he devours the
prey,
And in the evening he divides
the spoil."
28 ¶ All these are the twelve tribes of
Israel, and this is what their father said
to them [1]when he blessed them. He
blessed them, every one [2]with the blessing appropriate to him.
29 Then he charged them and said to
them, "I am about to be [a]gathered to my
people; [b]bury me with my fathers in the
cave that is in [c]the field of Ephron the
Hittite,
30 in the [a]cave that is in the field of
Machpelah, which is before Mamre, in
the land of Canaan, which Abraham
bought along with the field from Ephron
the Hittite for a [1]burial site.
31 "There they buried [a]Abraham and
his wife [b]Sarah, there they buried [c]Isaac
and his wife Rebekah, and there I buried
Leah—
32 the field and the cave that is in it,
purchased from the sons of Heth."
33 When Jacob finished charging his
sons, he drew his feet into the bed and
[a]breathed his last, and was [b]gathered to
his people.

The Death of Israel

50 Then Joseph fell on his father's
face, and wept over him and
kissed him.

24 [1]I.e. in an unyielding position [2]Lit *the arms of his hands* [a]Job 29:20 [b]Ps 18:34; 73:23; Is 41:10 [c]Ps 132:2,5; Is 1:24; 49:26 [d]Ps 23:1; 80:1 [e]Ps 118:22; Is 28:16; 1 Pet 2:6-8

25 [1]Or *with* [2]Heb *Shaddai* [a]Gen 28:13; 32:9 [b]Gen 28:3; 48:3 [c]Gen 27:28

26 [1]Lit *limit*; or *desire* [a]Deut 33:15,16

27 [1]Lit *a wolf that tears*

28 [1]Lit *and* [2]Lit *according to his blessing*

29 [a]Gen 25:8 [b]Gen 47:30 [c]Gen 23:16-20; 50:13

30 [1]Lit *possession of a burial place* [a]Gen 23:3-20

31 [a]Gen 25:9 [b]Gen 23:19 [c]Gen 35:29

33 [a]Gen 25:8; Acts 7:15 [b]Gen 49:29

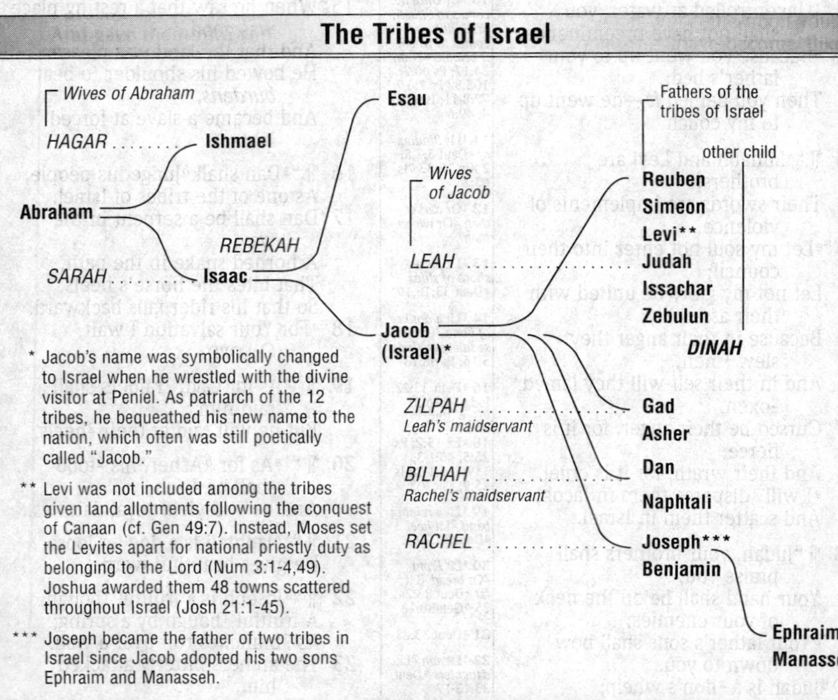

* Jacob's name was symbolically changed to Israel when he wrestled with the divine visitor at Peniel. As patriarch of the 12 tribes, he bequeathed his new name to the nation, which often was still poetically called "Jacob."

** Levi was not included among the tribes given land allotments following the conquest of Canaan (cf. Gen 49:7). Instead, Moses set the Levites apart for national priestly duty as belonging to the Lord (Num 3:1-4,49). Joshua awarded them 48 towns scattered throughout Israel (Josh 21:1-45).

*** Joseph became the father of two tribes in Israel since Jacob adopted his two sons Ephraim and Manasseh.

2 Joseph commanded his servants the physicians to embalm his father. So the physicians [a]embalmed Israel.

3 Now forty days were [1]required for [2]it, for [3]such is the period required for embalming. And the Egyptians [a]wept for him seventy days.

4 ¶ When the days of [1]mourning for him were past, Joseph spoke to the household of Pharaoh, saying, "If now I have found favor in your sight, please speak [2]to Pharaoh, saying,

5 '[a]My father made me swear, saying, "Behold, I am about to die; in my grave [b]which I dug for myself in the land of Canaan, there you shall bury me." Now therefore, please let me go up and bury my father; then I will return.' "

6 Pharaoh said, "Go up and bury your father, as he made you swear."

7 ¶ So Joseph went up to bury his father, and with him went up all the servants of Pharaoh, the elders of his household and all the elders of the land of Egypt,

8 and all the household of Joseph and his brothers and his father's household; they left only their little ones and their flocks and their herds in the land of Goshen.

9 There also went up with him both chariots and horsemen; and it was a very great company.

10 When they came to the [1]threshing floor of Atad, which is beyond the Jordan, they [a]lamented there with a very great and [2]sorrowful lamentation; and he [3]observed seven days mourning for his father.

11 Now when the inhabitants of the land, the Canaanites, saw the mourning at [1]the threshing floor of Atad, they said, "This is a [2]grievous [3]mourning for the Egyptians." Therefore it was named [4]Abel-mizraim, which is beyond the Jordan.

Burial at Machpelah

12 Thus his sons did for him as he had charged them;

13 for his sons carried him to the land of Canaan and buried him in [a]the cave of the field of Machpelah before Mamre, which Abraham had bought along with the field for a [1]burial site from Ephron the Hittite.

14 After he had buried his father, Joseph returned to Egypt, he and his brothers, and all who had gone up with him to bury his father.

15 ¶ When Joseph's brothers saw that their father was dead, they said, "[a]What if Joseph bears a grudge against us and pays us back in full for all the wrong which we did to him!"

16 So they [1]sent *a message* to Joseph, saying, "Your father charged before he died, saying,

17 'Thus you shall say to Joseph, "Please forgive, I beg you, the transgression of your brothers and their sin, for they did you wrong." ' And now, please forgive the transgression of the servants of the God of your father." And Joseph wept when they spoke to him.

18 Then his brothers also came and [a]fell down before him and said, "Behold, we are your servants."

19 But Joseph said to them, "Do not be afraid, for am I in God's place?

20 "As for you, [a]you meant evil against me, *but* God meant it for good in order to bring about [1]this present result, to preserve many people alive.

21 "So therefore, do not be afraid; [a]I will provide for you and your little ones." So he comforted them and spoke [1]kindly to them.

Death of Joseph

22 ¶ Now Joseph stayed in Egypt, he and his father's household, and Joseph lived one hundred and ten years.

23 Joseph saw the third generation of Ephraim's sons; also the sons of Machir, the son of Manasseh, were [a]born on Joseph's knees.

24 Joseph said to his brothers, "[a]I am about to die, but God will surely [1]take care of you and bring you up from this land to the land which He [2]promised on oath to [b]Abraham, to [c]Isaac and to [d]Jacob."

25 Then Joseph made the sons of Israel swear, saying, "God will surely [1]take care of you, and [a]you shall carry my bones up from here."

26 So Joseph died at the age of one hundred and ten years; and [1]he was [a]embalmed and placed in a coffin in Egypt.

50:2 [a]Gen 50:26; 2 Chr 16:14; Matt 26:12; Mark 16:1; John 19:39,40

3 [1]Lit *fulfilled* [2]Or *him* [3]Lit *so are fulfilled the days of embalming* [a]Gen 50:10; Num 20:29; Deut 34:8

4 [1]Lit *weeping* [2]Lit *In the ears of*

5 [a]Gen 47:29-31 [b]2 Chr 16:14; Is 22:16; Matt 27:60

10 [1]Heb *Goren ha-Atad* [2]Lit *heavy* [3]Lit *made a mourning for seven days* [a]Acts 8:2

11 [1]Heb *Goren ha-Atad* [2]Lit *heavy* [3]Heb *ebel* [4]I.e. the meadow (or mourning) of Egypt

13 [1]Lit *possession of a burial place* [a]Gen 23:16-20; Acts 7:16

15 [a]Gen 37:28; 42:21,22

16 [1]Lit *commanded*

18 [a]Gen 37:8-10; 41:43

20 [1]Lit *as it is this day* [a]Gen 37:26,27; 45:5,7

21 [1]Lit *to their heart* [a]Gen 45:11; 47:12

23 [a]Gen 30:3

24 [1]Or *visit* [2]Lit *swore* [a]Gen 48:21; Ex 3:16, 17; Heb 11:22 [b]Gen 13:15,17; 15:7,8,18 [c]Gen 26:3 [d]Gen 28:13; 35:12

25 [1]Or *visit* [a]Gen 47:29,30; Ex 13:19; Josh 24:32; Heb 11:22

26 [1]Lit *they embalmed him* [a]Gen 50:2

Exodus

Title and Background

"Exodus" is a Latin word (derived from the Greek) that means "exit," "departure," and describes the greatest miracle in the Old Testament record of Israel's history—the "going out" from Egypt and slavery. While the story of the Israelites began with Abraham in Genesis, Exodus is the history of their early years as God's chosen nation, committed to Him according to the terms of the Mosaic covenant given at Mount Sinai. The book of Exodus was not intended to exist separately, but was thought of as a continuation of a narrative that began in Genesis and continues through Leviticus, Numbers and Deuteronomy.

Author and Date of Writing

Several statements in Exodus indicate that Moses wrote certain sections of the book (see 17:14; 24:4; 34:27). The New Testament also claims Mosaic authorship for various passages in Exodus (see, for example, Mark 7:10; 12:26; Luke 2:22–23). Taken together these references strongly suggest that Moses was largely responsible for writing the book of Exodus.

According to 1 Kings 6:1, the exodus took place 480 years before "the fourth year of Solomon's reign over Israel." Since that year was about 966 B.C., the exodus occurred in about 1446 B.C. The book of Exodus was most likely written after the exodus from Egypt (about 1446 B.C.) and before the death of Moses (about 1406 B.C.).

Theme and Message

Exodus lays the foundation for a theology of God's revelation of His name, His attributes, His redemption, His law and His worship. It also reports the appointment and work of the first covenant mediator (Moses), describes the beginning of the priesthood, defines the role of the prophet and relates how the ancient covenant relationship between God and His people came under a new administration (the Sinai covenant).

Outline

I. Preparation for Israel's Deliverance From Bondage (1:1—4:31)
II. Israel's Deliverance From Egyptian Bondage (5:1—18:27)
  A. Pharaoh's Resistance and the Lord's Reassurance (5:1—6:27)
  B. Plagues on Egypt (6:28—12:36)
  C. The Exodus: From Egypt to Mount Sinai (12:37—18:27)
III. Covenant at Sinai (19:1—24:18)
IV. The Tabernacle for Worship (25:1—40:38)

Israel Multiplies in Egypt

1 Now these are the [a]names of the
sons of Israel who came to Egypt
with Jacob; they came each one [1]with
his household:
2 Reuben, Simeon, Levi and Judah;
3 Issachar, Zebulun and Benjamin;
4 Dan and Naphtali, Gad and Asher.
5 All the [1]persons who came from
the loins of Jacob were [a]seventy [2]in
number, but Joseph was *already* in Egypt.
6 [a]Joseph died, and all his brothers
and all that generation.
7 But the sons of Israel [a]were fruitful
and [1]increased greatly, and multiplied,
and became exceedingly [2]mighty, so that
the land was filled with them.
8 ¶ Now a new [a]king arose over
Egypt, who did not know Joseph.
9 [a]He said to his people, "Behold,
the people of the sons of Israel are [1]more
and mightier than we.
10 "Come, let us [a]deal wisely with
them, or else they will multiply and [1]in
the event of war, they will also join themselves to those who hate us, and fight
against us and [2]depart from the land."
11 So they appointed [a]taskmasters
over them to afflict them with [1b]hard
labor. And they built for Pharaoh [c]stor-
age cities, Pithom and [d]Raamses.
12 But the more they afflicted them,
[a]the more they multiplied and the more

1:1 [1]Lit *and* [a]Gen 46:8-27
5 [1]Lit *souls* [2]Lit *as to souls* [a]Gen 46:26; Deut 10:22
6 [a]Gen 50:26
7 [1]Lit *swarmed* [2]Or *numerous* [a]Gen 12:2; Deut 26:5; Ps 105:24; Acts 7:17
8 [a]Acts 7:18
9 [1]Or *too many and too mighty for us* [a]Ps 105:24
10 [1]Lit *it came about when war befalls that* [2]Lit *go up from* [a]Acts 7:19
11 [1]Lit *their burdens* [a]Gen 15:13; Ex 3:7 [b]Ex 1:14 [c]1 Kin 9:19; 2 Chr 8:4 [d]Gen 47:11
12 [a]Ex 1:7

they [1]spread out, so that they were in
dread of the sons of Israel.
13 The Egyptians compelled the sons
of Israel [a]to labor rigorously;
14 and they made [a]their lives bitter
with hard labor in mortar and bricks and
at all *kinds* of labor in the field, all their
labors which they rigorously [1]imposed
on them.
15 ¶ Then the king of Egypt spoke to
the Hebrew midwives, one of whom
[1]was named Shiphrah and the other
[1]was named Puah;
16 and he said, "When you are helping
the Hebrew women to give birth and see
them upon the birthstool, [a]if it is a son,
then you shall put him to death; but if it
is a daughter, then she shall live."
17 But the midwives [1a]feared God,
and [b]did not do as the king of Egypt had
[2]commanded them, but let the boys live.
18 So the king of Egypt called for the
midwives and said to them, "Why have
you done this thing, and let the boys
live?"
19 The midwives said to Pharaoh, "Because the Hebrew women are not as the
Egyptian women; for they are vigorous
and give birth before the midwife [1]can
get to them."
20 So [a]God was good to the midwives,
and [b]the people multiplied, and became
very [1]mighty.
21 Because the midwives [1a]feared
God, He [2b]established [3]households for
them.
22 Then Pharaoh commanded all his
people, saying, "[a]Every son who is born
[1]you are to cast into [b]the Nile, and every
daughter you are to keep alive."

The Birth of Moses

2 Now a man from [a]the house of Levi
went and [1]married a daughter of
Levi.
2 The woman conceived and bore
a son; and when she saw [1]that he
was [2a]beautiful, she hid him for three
months.
3 But when she could hide him no
longer, she got him a [1a]wicker [2]basket
and covered it over with tar and pitch.
Then she put the child into it and set *it*
among the [b]reeds by the bank of the
Nile.
4 [a]His sister stood at a distance to
[1]find out what would [2]happen to him.
5 ¶ The daughter of Pharaoh came
down [a]to bathe at the Nile, with her
maidens walking alongside the Nile; and
she saw the [1]basket among the reeds and
sent her maid, and she brought it *to her.*
6 When she opened *it,* she [1]saw the
child, and behold, *the* [2]boy was crying.
And she had pity on him and said, "This
is one of the Hebrews' children."
7 Then his sister said to Pharaoh's
daughter, "Shall I go and call [1]a nurse for
you from the Hebrew women that she
may nurse the child for you?"
8 Pharaoh's daughter said to her, "Go
ahead." So the girl went and called the
child's mother.
9 Then Pharaoh's daughter said to
her, "Take this child away and nurse him
for me and I will give *you* your wages." So
the woman took the child and nursed
him.
10 The child grew, and she brought
him to Pharaoh's daughter and [a]he became her son. And she named him [1]Mo-
ses, and said, "Because I [2]drew him out
of the water."
11 ¶ Now it came about in those days,
[a]when Moses had grown up, that he
went out to his brethren and looked on
their [1b]hard labors; and [c]he saw an
Egyptian beating a Hebrew, one of his
brethren.
12 So he [1]looked this way and that,
and when he saw there was no one
around, he [a]struck down the Egyptian
and hid him in the sand.
13 He went out [a]the next day, and
behold, two Hebrews were [1]fighting
with each other; and he said to the [2]of-
fender, "Why are you striking your companion?"
14 But he said, "[a]Who made you a
[1]prince or a judge over us? Are you [2]in-
tending to kill me as you killed the Egyptian?" Then Moses was afraid and said,
"Surely the matter has become known."

Moses Escapes to Midian

15 When Pharaoh heard of this matter, he tried to kill Moses. But [a]Moses
fled from the presence of Pharaoh and
[1]settled in the land of Midian, and he sat
down [b]by a well.
16 ¶ Now [a]the priest of Midian had
seven daughters; and [b]they came to draw
water and filled the troughs to water their
father's flock.
17 Then the shepherds came and
drove them away, but [a]Moses stood up
and helped them and watered their flock.
18 When they came to [a]Reuel their
father, he said, "Why have you come
back so soon today?"
19 So they said, "An Egyptian delivered us from the hand of the shepherds,
and what is more, he even drew the water for us and watered the flock."
20 He said to his daughters, "Where is
he then? Why is it that you have left the
man behind? Invite him [1]to have something to eat."

12 [1]Lit *broke forth*
13 [a]Gen 15:13; Deut 4:20
14 [1]Lit *worked through them* [a]Ex 2:23; 6:9; Num 20:15; Acts 7:19
15 [1]Lit *the name was*
16 [a]Acts 7:19
17 [1]Or *revered* [2]Lit *spoken to* [a]Ex 1:21; Prov 16:6 [b]Acts 4:18-20; 5:29
19 [1]Lit *comes to*
20 [1]Or *numerous* [a]Prov 11:18; Eccl 8:12; Heb 6:10 [b]Ex 1:12; Is 3:10
21 [1]Or *revered* [2]Lit *made* [3]Or *families* [a]Ex 1:17 [b]1 Sam 2:35; 2 Sam 7:11,27; 1 Kin 2:24; 11:38
22 [1]Some versions insert *to the Hebrews* [a]Acts 7:19 [b]Gen 41:1
2:1 [1]Lit *took* [a]Ex 6:16,18,20
2 [1]Lit *him that* [2]Lit *good* [a]Acts 7:20; Heb 11:23
3 [1]I.e. papyrus reeds [2]Or *chest* [a]Is 18:2 [b]Is 19:6
4 [1]Lit *know* [2]Lit *be done* [a]Ex 15:20; Num 26:59
5 [1]Or *chest* [a]Ex 7:15; 8:20
6 [1]Heb *saw it, the child* [2]Or *lad*
7 [1]Lit *a woman giving suck*
10 [1]Heb *Mosheh,* from *mashah* [2]Heb *mashah* [a]Acts 7:21
11 [1]Lit *burdens* [a]Acts 7:23; Heb 11:24-26 [b]Ex 1:11; 5:4,5; 6:6,7 [c]Acts 7:24
12 [1]Lit *turned* [a]Acts 7:24,25
13 [1]Or *quarreling* [2]Or *the guilty one* [a]Acts 7:26-28
14 [1]Lit *man, a prince* [2]Lit *saying in your heart* [a]Gen 19:9; Acts 7:27,28
15 [1]Lit *dwelt* [a]Acts 7:29; Heb 11:27 [b]Gen 24:11; 29:2
16 [a]Ex 3:1; 18:12 [b]Gen 24:11,13,19; 29:9,10; 1 Sam 9:11
17 [a]Gen 29:3,10
18 [a]Ex 3:1; Num 10:29
20 [1]Lit *that he may eat bread*

21 [a]Moses was willing to dwell with
the man, and he gave his daughter [b]Zip-
porah to Moses.
22 Then she gave birth to [a]a son, and
he named him [1]Gershom, for he said, "I
have been [b]a [2]sojourner in a foreign
land."
23 ¶ Now it came about in *the course
of* those many days that the king of Egypt
died. And the sons of Israel [a]sighed because of the bondage, and they cried out;
and [b]their cry for help because of *their*
bondage rose up to God.
24 So [a]God heard their groaning; and
God remembered [b]His covenant with
Abraham, Isaac, and Jacob.
25 [a]God saw the sons of Israel, and
God [1]took notice *of them.*

The Burning Bush

3 Now Moses was pasturing the flock
of [a]Jethro his father-in-law, the
priest of Midian; and he led the flock to
the [1]west side of the wilderness and
came to [b]Horeb, the [c]mountain of God.
2 [a]The angel of the LORD appeared to
him in a blazing fire from the midst of [1]a
[b]bush; and he looked, and behold, the
bush was burning with fire, yet the bush
was not consumed.
3 So Moses said, "[1][a]I must turn
aside now and see this [2]marvelous sight,
why the bush is not burned up."
4 When the LORD saw that he turned
aside to look, [a]God called to him from
the midst of the bush and said, "Moses,
Moses!" And he said, "Here I am."
5 Then He said, "Do not come near
here; [a]remove your sandals from your
feet, for the place on which you are standing is holy ground."
6 He said also, "[a]I am the God of
your father, the God of Abraham, the God
of Isaac, and the God of Jacob." [b]Then
Moses hid his face, for he was [c]afraid to
look at God.
7 ¶ The LORD said, "I have surely
[a]seen the affliction of My people who are
in Egypt, and have given heed to their cry
because of their taskmasters, for I am
aware of their sufferings.
8 "So I have come down [a]to deliver
them from the [1]power of the Egyptians,
and to bring them up from that land to a
[b]good and spacious land, to a land flowing with milk and honey, to the place of
[c]the Canaanite and the Hittite and the
Amorite and the Perizzite and the Hivite
and the Jebusite.
9 "Now, behold, [a]the cry of the sons
of Israel has come to Me; furthermore, I
have seen the oppression with which the
Egyptians are oppressing them.

The Mission of Moses

10 "Therefore, come now, and I will
send you to Pharaoh, [a]so that you may
bring My people, the sons of Israel, out of
Egypt."
11 But Moses said to God, "[a]Who am
I, that I should go to Pharaoh, and that I
should bring the sons of Israel out of
Egypt?"
12 And He said, "Certainly [a]I will be
with you, and this shall be the sign to you
that it is I who have sent you: [b]when you
have brought the people out of Egypt,
[c]you shall [1]worship God at this mountain."
13 ¶ Then Moses said to God, "Behold, I am going to the sons of Israel, and
I will say to them, 'The God of your fathers has sent me to you.' Now they may
say to me, 'What is His name?' What shall
I say to them?"
14 God said to Moses, "[1][a]I AM
WHO [1]I AM"; and He said, "Thus you
shall say to the sons of Israel, '[1]I AM has
sent me to you.' "
15 God, furthermore, said to Moses,
"Thus you shall say to the sons of Israel,
'[a]The LORD, the God of your fathers, the
God of Abraham, the God of Isaac, and
the God of Jacob, has sent me to you.'
This is My name forever, and this is My
[b]memorial-name [1]to all generations.
16 "Go and [a]gather the elders of Israel
together and say to them, '[b]The LORD,
the God of your fathers, the God of Abraham, Isaac and Jacob, has appeared to
me, saying, "[1][c]I am indeed concerned
about you and what has been done to you
in Egypt.
17 "So [a]I said, I will bring you up out
of the affliction of Egypt to the land of
[b]the Canaanite and the Hittite and the
Amorite and the Perizzite and the Hivite
and the Jebusite, to a land [c]flowing with
milk and honey." '
18 "[a]They will [1]pay heed to what you
say; and [b]you with the elders of Israel
will come to the king of Egypt and you
will say to him, 'The LORD, the God of
the Hebrews, has met with us. So now,
please, let us go a [c]three days' journey
into the wilderness, that we may sacrifice
to the LORD our God.'
19 "But I know that the king of Egypt
[a]will not permit you to go, [b]except [1]un-
der compulsion.
20 "So I will stretch out [a]My hand and
strike Egypt with all My [b]miracles which
I shall do in the midst of it; and [c]after
that he will let you go.

21 [a]Acts 7:29 [b]Ex 4:25
22 [1]Cf Heb *ger sham, a stranger there* [2]Heb *ger* [a]Ex 4:20 [b]Gen 23:4; Lev 25:23; Acts 7:29; Heb 11:13
23 [a]Ex 6:5 [b]Ex 3:7; Deut 26:7; James 5:4
24 [a]Ex 6:5; Acts 7:34 [b]Gen 15:13f; Ps 105:8
25 [1]Lit *knew* them [a]Ex 3:7; Acts 7:34
3:1 [1]Or *rear part* [a]Ex 2:18; Num 10:29 [b]Ex 3:12; 1 Kin 19:8 [c]Ex 4:27
2 [1]Lit *the* [a]Gen 16:7-11; Ex 3:4-11; Judg 13:13-21; Acts 7:30 [b]Deut 33:16; Mark 12:26; Luke 20:37; Acts 7:30
3 [1]Lit *Let me turn* [2]Lit *great* [a]Acts 7:31
4 [a]Ex 4:5
5 [a]Josh 5:15; Acts 7:33
6 [a]Gen 28:13; Ex 3:16; Matt 22:32; Mark 12:26; Luke 20:37 [b]Acts 7:32 [c]Judg 13:22; Rev 1:17
7 [a]Ex 2:25; Neh 9:9; Ps 106:44; Is 63:9; Acts 7:34
8 [1]Lit *hand* [a]Gen 15:13-16; Ex 6:6-8 [b]Ex 3:17; Num 13:27; Deut 1:25; Jer 11:5; Ezek 20:6 [c]Gen 15:19-21; Josh 24:11
9 [a]Ex 2:23
10 [a]Gen 15:13; Ex 12:40; Mic 6:4; Acts 7:6
11 [a]Ex 4:10; 1 Sam 18:18
12 [1]Or *serve* [a]Gen 31:3; Ex 4:12; Deut 31:23; Josh 1:5; Is 43:2 [b]Ex 19:1 [c]Ex 19:2; Acts 7:7
14 [1]Related to the name of God, *YHWH,* rendered *LORD,* which is derived from the verb *HAYAH, to be* [a]Ex 6:3; John 8:24; Heb 13:8; Rev 1:8
15 [1]Lit *to generation of generation* [a]Ex 3:6 [b]Ps 30:4; Hos 12:5
16 [1]Lit *Visiting I have visited* [a]Ex 4:29 [b]Gen 28:13; Ex 3:2 [c]Ex 4:31; Ps 33:18f
17 [a]Gen 15:13-21 [b]Josh 24:11 [c]Ex 3:8
18 [1]Lit *hear your voice* [a]Ex 4:31 [b]Ex 5:1 [c]Ex 5:3
19 [1]Lit *by a strong hand* [a]Ex 5:2 [b]Ex 6:1
20 [a]Ex 6:1 [b]Ex 7:3; Deut 6:22; Neh 9:10; Ps 105:27; Jer 32:20; Acts 7:36 [c]Ex 11:1

21 "I will grant this people [a]favor in the sight of the Egyptians; and it shall be that when you go, you will not go empty-handed.

22 "But every woman [a]shall ask of her neighbor and the woman who lives in her house, articles of silver and articles of gold, and clothing; and you will put them on your sons and daughters. Thus you will [b]plunder the Egyptians."

Moses Given Powers

4 Then Moses said, "What if they will not believe me or [a]listen [1]to what I say? For they may say, '[b]The LORD has not appeared to you.' "

2 The LORD said to him, "What is that in your hand?" And he said, "[a]A staff."

3 Then He said, "Throw it on the ground." So he threw it on the ground, and [a]it became a serpent; and Moses fled from it.

4 But the LORD said to Moses, "Stretch out your hand and grasp *it* by its tail"—so he stretched out his hand and caught it, and it became a staff in his [1]hand—

5 "that [a]they may believe that [b]the LORD, the God of their fathers, the God of Abraham, the God of Isaac, and the God of Jacob, has appeared to you."

6 ¶ The LORD furthermore said to him, "Now put your hand into your bosom." So he put his hand into his bosom, and when he took it out, behold, his hand was [a]leprous like snow.

7 Then He said, "Put your hand into your bosom again." So he put his hand into his bosom again, and when he took it out of his bosom, behold, [a]it was restored like *the rest of* his flesh.

8 "If they will not believe you or [1]heed the [2]witness of the first sign, they may believe the [2]witness of the last sign.

9 "But if they will not believe even these two signs or heed what you say, then you shall take some water from the Nile and pour it on the dry ground; and the water which you take from the Nile [a]will become blood on the dry ground."

10 ¶ Then Moses said to the LORD, "Please, Lord, [a]I have never been [1]eloquent, neither [2]recently nor in time past, nor since You have spoken to Your servant; for I am [3]slow of speech and [3]slow of tongue."

11 The LORD said to him, "Who has made man's mouth? Or [a]who makes *him* mute or deaf, or seeing or blind? Is it not I, the LORD?

12 "Now then go, and [a]I, even I, will be with your mouth, and [b]teach you what you are to say."

13 But he said, "Please, Lord, now [1]send *the message* by whomever You will."

Aaron to Be Moses' Mouthpiece

14 Then the anger of the LORD burned against Moses, and He said, "Is there not your brother Aaron the Levite? I know that [1]he speaks fluently. And moreover, behold, [a]he is coming out to meet you; when he sees you, he will be glad in his heart.

15 "You are to speak to him and [a]put the words in his mouth; and I, even I, will be with your mouth and his mouth, and I will teach you what you are to do.

16 "Moreover, [a]he shall speak for you to the people; and he will be as a mouth for you and you will be as God to him.

17 "You shall take in your hand [a]this staff, [b]with which you shall perform the signs."

18 ¶ Then Moses departed and returned to [1]Jethro [a]his father-in-law and said to him, "Please, let me go, that I may return to my brethren who are in Egypt, and see if they are still alive." And Jethro said to Moses, "Go in peace."

19 Now the LORD said to Moses in Midian, "Go [1]back to Egypt, for [a]all the men who were seeking your life are dead."

20 So Moses took his wife and his [a]sons and mounted them on a donkey, and returned to the land of Egypt. Moses also took the [b]staff of God in his hand.

21 ¶ The LORD said to Moses, "When you go [1]back to Egypt see that you perform before Pharaoh all [a]the wonders which I have put in your [2]power; but [b]I will harden his heart so that he will not let the people go.

22 "Then you shall say to Pharaoh, 'Thus says the LORD, "[a]Israel is My son, My firstborn.

23 "So I said to you, '[a]Let My son go that he may serve Me'; but you have refused to let him go. Behold, [b]I will kill your son, your firstborn." ' "

24 ¶ Now it came about at the lodging place on the way that the LORD met him and [a]sought to put him to death.

25 Then Zipporah took [a]a flint and cut off her son's foreskin and [1]threw it at Moses' feet, and she said, "You are indeed a bridegroom of blood to me."

26 So He let him alone. At that time she said, "*You are* a bridegroom of blood"—[1]because of the circumcision.

27 ¶ [a]Now the LORD said to Aaron, "Go to meet Moses in the wilderness." So he went and met him at the [b]mountain of God and kissed him.

28 [a]Moses told Aaron all the words of the LORD with which He had sent him,

21 [a]Ex 11:3; 12:36; 1 Kin 8:50; Ps 105:37f; 106:46; Prov 16:7
22 [a]Gen 15:14; Ex 11:2; 12:35 [b]Ezek 39:10
4:1 [1]Lit *to my voice* [a]Ex 3:18; 6:30 [b]Ex 3:15, 16
2 [a]Ex 4:17,20
3 [a]Ex 7:10-12
4 [1]Lit *palm*
5 [a]Ex 4:31; 19:9 [b]Gen 28:13; 48:15; Ex 3:6,15
6 [a]Num 12:10; 2 Kin 5:27
7 [a]Num 12:13-15; Deut 32:39; 2 Kin 5:14; Matt 8:3; Luke 17:12-14
8 [1]Lit *listen to* [2]Lit *voice*
9 [a]Ex 7:19,20
10 [1]Lit *a man of words* [2]Lit *yesterday* [3]Lit *heavy* [a]Ex 3:11; 4:1; 6:12; Jer 1:6
11 [a]Ps 94:9; 146:8; Matt 11:5; Luke 1:20, 64
12 [a]Ex 4:15,16; Deut 18:18; Is 50:4; Jer 1:9 [b]Matt 10:19,20; Mark 13:11; Luke 12:11,12; 21:14,15
13 [1]Lit *send by the hand which You send*
14 [1]Lit *speaking he speaks* [a]Ex 4:27
15 [a]Ex 4:12,30; 7:1f; Num 23:5, 12,16; Deut 18:18; Is 51:16; 59:21; Jer 1:9
16 [a]Ex 7:1,2
17 [a]Ex 4:2,20; 17:9 [b]Ex 7:9-20; 14:16
18 [1]Heb *Jether* [a]Ex 2:21; 3:1
19 [1]Lit *return* [a]Ex 2:15,23
20 [a]Ex 18:3,4; Acts 7:29 [b]Ex 4:17; 17:9; Num 20:8,9,11
21 [1]Lit *to return* [2]Lit *hand* [a]Ex 3:20; 11:9,10 [b]Ex 7:3,13; 9:12,35; 10:1, 20,27; 14:4,8; Deut 2:30; Josh 11:20; 1 Sam 6:6; Is 63:17; John 12:40; Rom 9:18
22 [a]Is 63:16; 64:8; Jer 31:9; Hos 11:1; Rom 9:4
23 [a]Ex 5:1; 6:11; 7:16 [b]Ex 11:5; 12:29; Ps 105:36; 135:8; 136:10
24 [a]Num 22:22
25 [1]Lit *made it touch at his feet* [a]Gen 17:14; Josh 5:2,3
26 [1]Lit *with reference to*
27 [a]Ex 4:14 [b]Ex 3:1; 18:5; 24:13
28 [a]Ex 4:15f

and [b]all the signs that He had commanded him *to do.*

29 Then Moses and Aaron went and [a]assembled all the elders of the sons of Israel;

30 and [a]Aaron spoke all the words which the LORD had spoken to Moses. He then performed the [b]signs in the sight of the people.

31 So [a]the people believed; and when they heard that the LORD [1b]was concerned about the sons of Israel and that He had seen their affliction, then [c]they bowed low and worshiped.

Israel's Labor Increased

5 And afterward Moses and Aaron came and said to Pharaoh, "[a]Thus says the LORD, the God of Israel, '[b]Let My people go that they may celebrate a feast to Me in the wilderness.' "

2 But Pharaoh said, "[a]Who is the LORD that I should obey His voice to let Israel go? I do not know the LORD, and besides, [b]I will not let Israel go."

3 Then they said, "[a]The God of the Hebrews has met with us. Please, let us go a three days' journey into the wilderness that we may sacrifice to the LORD our God, otherwise He will fall upon us with pestilence or with the sword."

4 But the king of Egypt said to them, "Moses and Aaron, why do you [1]draw the people away from their [2]work? Get *back* to your [3a]labors!"

5 Again Pharaoh said, "Look, [a]the people of the land are now many, and you would have them cease from their labors!"

6 So the same day Pharaoh commanded [a]the taskmasters over the people and their [b]foremen, saying,

7 "You are no longer to give the people straw to make brick as previously; let them go and gather straw for themselves.

8 "But the quota of bricks which they were making previously, you shall impose on them; you are not to reduce any of it. Because they are [a]lazy, therefore they cry out, '[1]Let us go and sacrifice to our God.'

9 "Let the labor be heavier on the men, and let them work at it so that they will pay no attention to false words."

10 ¶ So [a]the taskmasters of the people and their foremen went out and spoke to the people, saying, "Thus says Pharaoh, 'I am not going to give you *any* straw.

11 'You go *and* get straw for yourselves wherever you can find *it,* but none of your labor will be reduced.' "

12 So the people scattered through all the land of Egypt to gather stubble for straw.

13 The taskmasters pressed them, saying, "Complete your [1]work quota, [2]*your* daily amount, just as when [3]you had straw."

14 Moreover, [a]the foremen of the sons of Israel, whom Pharaoh's taskmasters had set over them, [b]were beaten [1]and were asked, "Why have you not completed your required amount either yesterday or today in making brick as previously?"

15 ¶ Then the foremen of the sons of Israel came and cried out to Pharaoh, saying, "Why do you deal this way with your servants?

16 "There is no straw given to your servants, yet they keep saying to us, 'Make bricks!' And behold, your servants are being beaten; but it is the fault of your *own* people."

17 But he said, "You are [a]lazy, *very* lazy; therefore you say, 'Let us go *and* sacrifice to the LORD.'

18 "So go now *and* work; for you will be given no straw, yet you must deliver the quota of bricks."

19 The foremen of the sons of Israel saw that they were in trouble [1]because they were told, "You must not reduce [2]*your* daily amount of bricks."

20 When they left Pharaoh's presence, they met Moses and Aaron as they were [1]waiting for them.

21 [a]They said to them, "[b]May the LORD look upon you and judge *you,* for you have [c]made [1]us odious in Pharaoh's sight and in the sight of his servants, to put a sword in their hand to kill us."

22 ¶ Then Moses returned to the LORD and said, "[a]O Lord, why have You brought harm to this people? Why did You ever send me?

23 "Ever since I came to Pharaoh to speak in Your name, he has done harm to this people, [a]and You have not delivered Your people at all."

God Promises Action

6 Then the LORD said to Moses, "Now you shall see what I will do to Pharaoh; for [1a]under compulsion he will let them go, and [1]under compulsion he will drive them out of his land."

2 ¶ God spoke further to Moses and said to him, "I am [a]the LORD;

3 and I appeared to Abraham, Isaac, and Jacob, as [1a]God Almighty, but *by* [b]My name, [2]LORD, I did not make Myself known to them.

4 "I also established [a]My covenant with them, to give them the land of Canaan, the [1]land in which they sojourned.

5 "Furthermore I have [a]heard the groaning of the sons of Israel, because the

28 [b]Ex 4:8f
29 [a]Ex 3:16
30 [a]Ex 4:15,16 [b]Ex 4:1-9
31 [1]Lit *had visited* [a]Ex 3:18; 4:8f; 19:9 [b]Gen 50:24; Ex 3:16 [c]Gen 24:26; Ex 12:27; 1 Chr 29:20
5:1 [a]Ex 3:18 [b]Ex 4:23; 6:11; 7:16
2 [a]2 Kin 18:35; 2 Chr 32:14; Job 21:15 [b]Ex 3:19
3 [a]Ex 3:18
4 [1]Lit *loose* [2]Lit *works* [3]Lit *burdens* [a]Ex 1:11; 2:11; 6:5-7
5 [a]Ex 1:7,9
6 [a]Ex 1:11; 3:7; 5:10,13,14 [b]Ex 5:10,14,15,19
8 [1]Lit *saying, 'Let* [a]Ex 5:17
10 [a]Ex 1:11; 3:7; 5:6
13 [1]Lit *works* [2]Lit *the matter of a day in its day* [3]Lit *there was*
14 [1]Lit *saying* [a]Ex 5:6 [b]Is 10:24
17 [a]Ex 5:8
19 [1]Lit *saying* [2]Lit *from your bricks the matter of a day in its day*
20 [1]Lit *standing to meet*
21 [1]Lit *our savor to stink* [a]Ex 14:11; 15:24; 16:2 [b]Gen 16:5; 31:53 [c]Gen 34:30; 1 Sam 13:4; 27:12; 2 Sam 10:6; 1 Chr 19:6
22 [a]Num 11:11; Jer 4:10
23 [a]Ex 3:8
6:1 [1]Lit *by a strong hand* [a]Ex 3:19,20; 7:4,5; 11:1; 12:31,33, 39; 13:3
2 [a]Ex 3:14,15
3 [1]Heb *El Shaddai* [2]Heb *YHWH,* usually rendered LORD [a]Gen 17:1; 35:11; 48:3 [b]Ps 68:4; 83:18; Is 52:6; Jer 16:21; Ezek 37:6,13
4 [1]Lit *land of their sojournings in which...* [a]Gen 12:7; 15:18; 17:4,7; 26:3,4; 28:4,13
5 [a]Ex 2:24

Egyptians are holding them in bondage, and I have remembered My covenant.

6 “Say, therefore, to the sons of Israel, ‘[a]I am the LORD, and [b]I will bring you out from under the burdens of the Egyptians, and I will deliver you from their bondage. I will also [c]redeem you with [d]an outstretched arm and with great judgments.

7 ‘Then I will take you [1][a]for My people, and [b]I will be [2]your God; and [c]you shall know that I am the LORD your God, who brought you out from under the burdens of the Egyptians.

8 ‘I will bring you to the land which [a]I [1]swore to give to Abraham, Isaac, and Jacob, and [b]I will give it to you *for* a possession; [c]I am the LORD.’ ”

9 So Moses spoke thus to the sons of Israel, but they did not listen to Moses on [a]account of *their* [1]despondency and cruel bondage.

10 ¶ Now the LORD spoke to Moses, saying,

11 “[a]Go, [1]tell Pharaoh king of Egypt [2]to let the sons of Israel go out of his land.”

12 But Moses spoke before the LORD, saying, “Behold, the sons of Israel have not listened to me; [a]how then will Pharaoh listen to me, for I am [1][b]unskilled in speech?”

13 Then the LORD spoke to Moses and to Aaron, and gave them a charge to the sons of Israel and to Pharaoh king of Egypt, to bring the sons of Israel out of the land of Egypt.

The Heads of Israel

14 ¶ These are the heads of their fathers’ households. [a]The sons of Reuben, Israel’s firstborn: Hanoch and Pallu, Hezron and Carmi; these are the families of Reuben.

15 The [a]sons of Simeon: Jemuel and Jamin and Ohad and Jachin and Zohar and Shaul the son of a Canaanite woman; these are the families of Simeon.

16 These are the names of [a]the sons of Levi according to their generations: Gershon and Kohath and Merari; and the [1]length of Levi’s life was one hundred and thirty-seven years.

17 [a]The sons of Gershon: [1]Libni and Shimei, according to their families.

18 [a]The sons of Kohath: Amram and Izhar and Hebron and Uzziel; and the [1]length of Kohath’s life was one hundred and thirty-three years.

19 [a]The sons of Merari: Mahli and Mushi. These are the families of the Levites according to their generations.

20 [a]Amram [1]married his father’s sister Jochebed, and she bore him Aaron and Moses; and the [2]length of Amram’s life was one hundred and thirty-seven years.

21 [a]The sons of Izhar: Korah and Nepheg and Zichri.

22 [a]The sons of Uzziel: Mishael and [1]Elzaphan and Sithri.

23 Aaron [1]married Elisheba, the daughter of [a]Amminadab, the sister of [b]Nahshon, and she bore him [c]Nadab and Abihu, Eleazar and Ithamar.

24 The [a]sons of Korah: Assir and Elkanah and [1]Abiasaph; these are the families of the Korahites.

25 Aaron’s son [a]Eleazar [1]married one of the daughters of Putiel, and she bore him [b]Phinehas. These are the heads of the fathers’ *households* of the Levites according to their families.

26 It was *the same* Aaron and Moses to whom the LORD said, “[a]Bring out the sons of Israel from the land of Egypt according to their [b]hosts.”

27 They were the ones [a]who spoke to Pharaoh king of Egypt [1]about bringing out the sons of Israel from Egypt; it was *the same* Moses and Aaron.

28 ¶ Now it came about on the day when the LORD spoke to Moses in the land of Egypt,

29 that the LORD spoke to Moses, saying, “[a]I am the LORD; [b]speak to Pharaoh king of Egypt all that I speak to you.”

30 But Moses said before the LORD, “Behold, I am [1][a]unskilled in speech; how then will Pharaoh listen to me?”

“I Will Stretch Out My Hand”

7 Then the LORD said to Moses, “[a]See, I make you *as* God to Pharaoh, and your brother Aaron shall be your prophet.

2 “You shall speak all that I command you, and your brother [a]Aaron shall speak to Pharaoh that he let the sons of Israel go out of his land.

3 “But [a]I will harden Pharaoh’s heart that I may [b]multiply My signs and My wonders in the land of Egypt.

4 “When [a]Pharaoh does not listen to you, then I will lay My hand on Egypt and [b]bring out My hosts, My people the sons of Israel, from the land of Egypt by [c]great judgments.

5 “[a]The Egyptians shall know that I am the LORD, when I [b]stretch out My hand on Egypt and bring out the sons of Israel from their midst.”

6 So Moses and Aaron did *it;* [a]as the LORD commanded them, thus they did.

7 Moses was [a]eighty years old and Aaron [1]eighty-three, when they spoke to Pharaoh.

7 [1]Lit *83 years old* [a]Deut 29:5; Acts 7:23

6 [a]Ex 13:3; Deut 6:12 [b]Ex 3:17; Deut 26:8; Ps 136:11 [c]Ex 15:13; Deut 7:8; 1 Chr 17:21; Neh 1:10 [d]Deut 4:34; Ps 136:11f
7 [1]Lit *to Me for a people* [2]Lit *to you for a God* [a]Ex 19:5; Deut 4:20; 2 Sam 7:24 [b]Gen 17:7f; Ex 29:45f; Lev 11:45; Deut 29:13 [c]Ex 16:12; Is 41:20
8 [1]Lit *lifted up My hand* [a]Gen 15:18; Num 14:30; Neh 9:15; Ezek 20:5 [b]Josh 24:13; Ps 136:21 [c]Ex 6:6
9 [1]Lit *shortness of spirit* [a]Ex 2:23
11 [1]Lit *speak to* [2]Lit *that he let* [a]Ex 4:22
12 [1]Lit *uncircumcised of lips* [a]Ex 4:1 [b]Jer 1:6
14 [a]Gen 46:9; Num 26:5-11; 1 Chr 5:3
15 [a]Gen 46:10; 1 Chr 4:24
16 [1]Lit *years* [a]Gen 46:11; Num 3:17; 1 Chr 6:1
17 [1]In 1 Chr 23:7, *Ladan* [a]Num 3:18-20; 1 Chr 6:17-19
18 [1]Lit *years* [a]Num 3:19; 1 Chr 6:2
19 [a]Num 3:20; 1 Chr 6:19
20 [1]Lit *took to him to wife* [2]Lit *years* [a]Ex 2:1; Num 26:59
21 [a]Num 16:1; 1 Chr 6:37
22 [1]In Num 3:30, *Elizaphan* [a]Lev 10:4; Num 3:30
23 [1]Lit *took to him to wife* [a]Ruth 4:19; 1 Chr 2:10 [b]Num 1:7 [c]Lev 10:1; Num 3:2; 1 Chr 6:3
24 [1]In 1 Chr 6:23 and 9:19, *Ebiasaph* [a]Num 26:11; 1 Chr 6:22
25 [1]Lit *took to him to wife* [a]Josh 24:33 [b]Num 25:7-13; Josh 24:33; Ps 106:30
26 [a]Ex 3:10 [b]Ex 7:4
27 [1]Lit *to bring out* [a]Ex 5:1
29 [a]Ex 6:2 [b]Ex 6:11
30 [1]Lit *uncircumcised of lips* [a]Ex 4:10; Jer 1:6
7:1 [a]Ex 4:16
2 [a]Ex 4:15
3 [a]Ex 4:21 [b]Ex 11:9; Acts 7:36
4 [a]Ex 3:19 [b]Ex 12:51 [c]Ex 6:6
5 [a]Ex 7:17 [b]Ex 3:20
6 [a]Gen 6:22; Ex 7:2

Aaron's Rod Becomes a Serpent

8 ¶ Now the LORD spoke to Moses and Aaron, saying,

9 "When Pharaoh speaks to you, saying, '[1][a]Work a miracle,' then you shall say to Aaron, '[b]Take your staff and throw *it* down before Pharaoh, *that* it may become a serpent.' "

10 So Moses and Aaron came to Pharaoh, and thus they did just as the LORD had commanded; and Aaron threw his staff down before Pharaoh and [1]his servants, and it [a]became a serpent.

11 Then Pharaoh also [a]called for *the* wise men and *the* sorcerers, and they also, the [1][b]magicians of Egypt, did [2]the same with [c]their secret arts.

12 For each one threw down his staff and they turned into serpents. But Aaron's staff swallowed up their staffs.

13 Yet [a]Pharaoh's heart was [1]hardened, and he did not listen to them, as the LORD had said.

Water Is Turned to Blood

14 ¶ Then the LORD said to Moses, "Pharaoh's heart is [1]stubborn; he refuses to let the people go.

15 "Go to Pharaoh in the morning [1]as [a]he is going out to the water, and station yourself to meet him on the bank of the Nile; and you shall take in your hand [b]the staff that was turned into a serpent.

16 "[a]You shall say to him, 'The LORD, the God of the Hebrews, sent me to you, saying, "[b]Let My people go, that they may serve Me in the wilderness. But behold, you have not listened until now."

17 'Thus says the LORD, "[a]By this you shall know that I am the LORD: behold, I will strike [1]the water that is in the Nile with the staff that is in my hand, and [b]it will be turned to blood.

18 "[a]The fish that are in the Nile will die, and the Nile will [1]become foul, and the Egyptians will [2][b]find difficulty in drinking water from the Nile." ' "

19 Then the LORD said to Moses, "Say to Aaron, 'Take your staff and [a]stretch out your hand over the waters of Egypt, over their rivers, over their [1]streams, and over their pools, and over all their reservoirs of water, that they may become blood; and there will be blood throughout all the land of Egypt, both in *vessels of* wood and in *vessels of* stone.' "

20 ¶ So Moses and Aaron did even as the LORD had commanded. And he lifted up [1][a]the staff and struck the water that *was* in the Nile, in the sight of Pharaoh and in the sight of his servants, and [b]all the water that *was* in the Nile was turned to blood.

21 The fish that *were* in the Nile died, and the Nile [1]became foul, so that the Egyptians could not drink water from the Nile. And the blood was through all the land of Egypt.

22 [a]But the [1]magicians of Egypt did [2]the same with their secret arts; and Pharaoh's heart was [3]hardened, and he did not listen to them, as the LORD had said.

23 Then Pharaoh turned and went into his house [1]with no concern even for this.

24 So all the Egyptians dug around the Nile for water to drink, for they could not drink of the water of the Nile.

25 Seven days [1]passed after the LORD had struck the Nile.

Frogs over the Land

8 [1]Then the LORD said to Moses, "Go to Pharaoh and say to him, 'Thus says the LORD, "[a]Let My people go, that they may serve Me.

2 "But if you refuse to let *them* go, behold, I will smite your whole territory with frogs.

3 "The Nile will [a]swarm with frogs, which will come up and go into your house and into your bedroom and on your bed, and into the houses of your servants and on your people, and into your ovens and into your kneading bowls.

4 "So the frogs will come up on you and your people and all your servants." ' "

5 [1]Then the LORD said to Moses, "Say to Aaron, '[a]Stretch out your hand with your staff over the rivers, over the [2]streams and over the pools, and make frogs come up on the land of Egypt.' "

6 So Aaron stretched out his hand over the waters of Egypt, and the [1][a]frogs came up and covered the land of Egypt.

7 [a]The [1]magicians did [2]the same with their secret arts, [3]making frogs come up on the land of Egypt.

8 ¶ Then Pharaoh [a]called for Moses and Aaron and said, "[b]Entreat the LORD that He remove the frogs from me and from my people; and [c]I will let the people go, that they may sacrifice to the LORD."

9 Moses said to Pharaoh, "[1]The honor is yours to tell me: when shall I entreat for you and your servants and your people, that the frogs be [2]destroyed from you and your houses, *that* they may be left only in the Nile?"

10 ¶ Then he said, "Tomorrow." So he said, "*May it be* according to your word, that you may know that there is [a]no one like the LORD our God.

11 "The [a]frogs will depart from you

---

9 [1]Lit *Show a wonder for yourselves* [a]Is 7:11; John 2:18; 6:30 [b]Ex 4:2,17
10 [1]Lit *before his* [a]Ex 4:3; 7:9
11 [1]Or *soothsayer priests* [2]Lit *thus* [a]Dan 2:2; 4:6; 5:7 [b]Gen 41:8; Ex 7:22; Dan 2:2; 2 Tim 3:8 [c]Ex 7:22; 8:7,18; 2 Tim 3:9; Rev 13:13, 14
13 [1]Lit *strong* [a]Ex 4:21; 7:3, 22; 8:15,19,32; 9:7,12,34,35; 10:1,20,27
14 [1]Or *hard;* lit *heavy*
15 [1]Lit *behold* [a]Ex 2:5; 8:20 [b]Ex 4:2,3; 7:10
16 [a]Ex 3:13,18; 4:22; 5:1 [b]Ex 4:23; 5:1,3
17 [1]Lit *upon the waters* [a]Ex 5:2; 7:5; 10:2; Ps 9:16; Ezek 25:17 [b]Ex 4:9; 7:20; Rev 11:6; 16:4,6
18 [1]I.e. have a bad smell [2]Or *be weary of* [a]Ex 7:21 [b]Ex 7:24
19 [1]Or *canals* [a]Ex 8:5,6,16; 9:22; 10:12,21; 14:21,26
20 [1]Lit *with the staff* [a]Ex 17:5 [b]Ps 78:44; 105:29
21 [1]I.e. had a bad smell
22 [1]Or *soothsayer priests* [2]Lit *thus* [3]Lit *strong* [a]Ex 7:11; 8:7
23 [1]Lit *and he did not set his heart even to this*
25 [1]Lit *were fulfilled*
8:1 [1]Ch 7:26 in Heb [a]Ex 3:18; 4:23; 5:1,3
3 [a]Ps 105:30
5 [1]Ch 8:1 in Heb [2]Or *canals* [a]Ex 7:19
6 [1]Lit *frog* [a]Ps 78:45; 105:30
7 [1]Or *soothsayer priests* [2]Lit *thus* [3]Lit *and made* [a]Ex 7:11,22
8 [a]Ex 8:25; 9:27; 10:16 [b]Ex 8:28; 9:28; 10:17; Num 21:7; 1 Kin 13:6 [c]Ex 8:15,29,32
9 [1]Lit *Glory over me* [2]Lit *cut off*
10 [a]Ex 9:14; Deut 4:35,39; 33:26; 2 Sam 7:22; 1 Chr 17:20; Ps 86:8; Is 46:9; Jer 10:6, 7
11 [a]Ex 8:13

and your houses and your servants and your people; they will be left only in the Nile."

12 Then Moses and Aaron went out from Pharaoh, and [a]Moses cried to the LORD concerning the frogs which He had [1]inflicted upon Pharaoh.

13 The LORD did according to the word of Moses, and the frogs died out of the houses, the courts, and the fields.

14 So they piled them in heaps, and the land [1]became foul.

15 But when Pharaoh saw that there was relief, he [1]hardened his heart and [a]did not listen to them, as the LORD had said.

The Plague of Insects

16 ¶ Then the LORD said to Moses, "Say to Aaron, 'Stretch out your staff and strike the dust of the earth, that it may become [1]gnats through all the land of Egypt.' "

17 They did so; and Aaron stretched out his hand with his staff, and struck the dust of the earth, and there were [1]gnats on man and beast. All the dust of the earth became [1a]gnats through all the land of Egypt.

18 The [1]magicians tried with their secret arts to bring forth [2]gnats, but [a]they could not; so there were [2]gnats on man and beast.

19 Then the [1]magicians said to Pharaoh, "[a]This is the finger of God." But Pharaoh's heart was [2]hardened, and he did not listen to them, as the LORD had said.

20 ¶ Now the LORD said to Moses, "[a]Rise early in the morning and present yourself before Pharaoh, [1]as [b]he comes out to the water, and say to him, 'Thus says the LORD, "[c]Let My people go, that they may serve Me.

21 "For if you do not let My people go, behold, I will send swarms of insects on you and on your servants and on your people and into your houses; and the houses of the Egyptians will be full of swarms of insects, and also the ground on which they *dwell.*

22 "[a]But on that day I will set apart the land of Goshen, where My people are [1]living, so that no swarms of insects will be there, in order that you may know that [2b]I, the LORD, am in the midst of the land.

23 "I will [1]put a division between My people and your people. Tomorrow this sign will occur." ' "

24 Then the LORD did so. And there came [1]great swarms of insects into the house of Pharaoh and the houses of his servants and the land was [a]laid waste because of the swarms of insects in all the land of Egypt.

25 ¶ Pharaoh [a]called for Moses and Aaron and said, "[b]Go, sacrifice to your God within the land."

26 But Moses said, "It is not right to do so, for we will sacrifice to the LORD our God [1]what is [a]an abomination to the Egyptians. If we sacrifice [1]what is an abomination to the Egyptians before their eyes, will they not then stone us?

27 "We must go a [a]three days' journey into the wilderness and sacrifice to the LORD our God as He [1]commands us."

28 Pharaoh said, "[a]I will let you go, that you may sacrifice to the LORD your God in the wilderness; only you shall not go very far away. [b]Make supplication for me."

29 Then Moses said, "Behold, I am going out from you, and I shall make supplication to the LORD that the swarms of insects may depart from Pharaoh, from his servants, and from his people tomorrow; only do not let Pharaoh [a]deal deceitfully again in not letting the people go to sacrifice to the LORD."

30 ¶ So [a]Moses went out from Pharaoh and made supplication to the LORD.

31 The LORD did [1]as Moses asked, and removed the swarms of insects from Pharaoh, from his servants and from his people; not one remained.

32 But Pharaoh [1]hardened his heart this time also, and [a]he did not let the people go.

Egyptian Cattle Die

9 Then the LORD said to Moses, "Go to Pharaoh and speak to him, 'Thus says the LORD, the God of the Hebrews, "[a]Let My people go, that they may serve Me.

2 "For [a]if you refuse to let *them* go and [1]continue to hold them,

3 behold, [a]the hand of the LORD [1]will come *with* a very severe pestilence on your livestock which are in the field, on the horses, on the donkeys, on the camels, on the herds, and on the flocks.

4 "[a]But the LORD will make a distinction between the livestock of Israel and the livestock of Egypt, so that [b]nothing will die of all that belongs to the sons of Israel." ' "

5 The LORD set a definite time, saying, "Tomorrow the LORD will do this thing in the land."

6 So the LORD did this thing on the next day, and [a]all the livestock of Egypt died; [b]but of the livestock of the sons of Israel, not one died.

7 Pharaoh sent, and behold, there was not even one of the livestock of Israel dead. But [a]the heart of Pharaoh was

12 [1]Lit *placed* [a]Ex 8:30; 9:33; 10:18

14 [1]I.e. had a bad smell

15 [1]Lit *made heavy* [a]Ex 7:4

16 [1]Or *lice*

17 [1]Or *lice* [a]Ps 105:31

18 [1]Or *soothsayer priests* [2]Or *lice* [a]Ex 7:11,12; 8:7; 9:11

19 [1]Or *soothsayer priests* [2]Lit *strong* [a]Ex 7:5; 10:7; Ps 8:3; Luke 11:20

20 [1]Lit *behold* [a]Ex 7:15; 9:13 [b]Ex 2:5; 7:15 [c]Ex 3:18; 4:23; 5:1,3; 8:1

22 [1]Lit *standing* [2]Or *I am the LORD in the midst of the earth* [a]Ex 9:4,6,24; 10:23; 11:7 [b]Ex 9:29; 19:5; 20:11

23 [1]Lit *set a ransom*

24 [1]Lit *heavy* [a]Ps 78:45; 105:31

25 [a]Ex 8:8; 9:27; 10:16 [b]Ex 9:28; 10:8,24; 12:31

26 [1]Lit *the abomination of Egypt* [a]Gen 43:32; 46:34; Deut 7:25f

27 [1]Lit *says to us* [a]Ex 3:18; 5:3

28 [a]Ex 8:8,15, 29,32 [b]Ex 8:8; 9:28; 1 Kin 13:6

29 [a]Ex 8:8,15

30 [a]Ex 8:12

31 [1]Lit *according to the word of Moses*

32 [1]Lit *made heavy* [a]Ex 4:21; 8:8,15

9:1 [a]Ex 4:23; 8:1

2 [1]Lit *still hold* [a]Ex 8:2

3 [1]Lit *will be* [a]Ex 7:4; 1 Sam 5:6; Ps 39:10; Acts 13:11

4 [a]Ex 8:22 [b]Ex 9:6

6 [a]Ex 9:19,20, 25; Ps 78:48 [b]Ex 9:4

7 [a]Ex 7:14; 8:32

[1]hardened, and he did not let the people go.

The Plague of Boils

8 ¶ Then the LORD said to Moses and
Aaron, “Take for yourselves handfuls of
soot from a kiln, and let Moses throw it
toward the sky in the sight of Pharaoh.
9 “It will become fine dust over all the
land of Egypt, and will become [a]boils
breaking out with sores on man and beast
through all the land of Egypt.”
10 So they took soot from a kiln, and
stood before Pharaoh; and Moses threw
it toward the sky, and it became boils
breaking out with sores on man and
beast.
11 [a]The [1]magicians could not stand
before Moses because of the boils, for the
boils were on the magicians [2]as well as
on all the Egyptians.
12 And [a]the LORD [1]hardened Pharaoh’s heart, and he did not listen to them,
just as the LORD had spoken to Moses.
13 ¶ Then the LORD said to Moses,
“[a]Rise up early in the morning and stand
before Pharaoh and say to him, ‘Thus says
the LORD, the God of the Hebrews, “[b]Let
My people go, that they may serve Me.
14 “For this time I will send all My
plagues [1]on you and your servants and
your people, so that [a]you may know that
there is no one like Me in all the earth.
15 “For *if by* now I had put forth My
hand and struck you and your people
with pestilence, you would then have
been cut off from the earth.
16 “But, indeed, [a]for this reason I have
allowed you to [1]remain, in order to show
you My power and in order to proclaim
My name through all the earth.
17 “Still you exalt yourself against My
people [1]by not letting them go.

The Plague of Hail

18 “Behold, about this time tomorrow,
[a]I will [1]send a very heavy hail, such as
has not been *seen* in Egypt from the day
it was founded [2]until now.
19 “Now therefore send, bring [a]your
livestock and whatever you have in the
field to safety. [b]Every man and beast that
is found in the field and is not brought
home, when the hail comes down on
them, will die.” ’ ”
20 [a]The one among the servants of
Pharaoh who [1]feared the word of the
LORD made his servants and his livestock
flee into the houses;
21 but he who [1]paid no regard to the
word of the LORD [2]left his servants and
his livestock in the field.
22 ¶ Now the LORD said to Moses,
“Stretch out your hand toward the sky,
that [1a]hail may fall on all the land of
Egypt, on man and on beast and on every
plant of the field, throughout the land of
Egypt.”
23 Moses stretched out his staff toward the sky, and the LORD [1]sent [2]thun-
der and [a]hail, and fire ran down to the
earth. And the LORD rained hail on the
land of Egypt.
24 So there was hail, and fire [1]flash-
ing continually in the midst of the hail,
very severe, such as had not been in all
the land of Egypt since it became a nation.
25 [a]The hail struck all that was in the
field through all the land of Egypt, both
man and beast; the hail also struck every
plant of the field and shattered every tree
of the field.
26 [a]Only in the land of Goshen,
where the sons of Israel *were,* there was
no hail.
27 ¶ Then Pharaoh [1a]sent for Moses
and Aaron, and said to them, “[b]I have
sinned this time; the LORD is the righteous one, and I and my people are the
wicked ones.
28 “[a]Make supplication to the LORD,
for there has been enough of God’s
[1]thunder and hail; and [b]I will let you go,
and you shall stay no longer.”
29 Moses said to him, “As soon as I go
out of the city, I will [a]spread out my
[1]hands to the LORD; the [2]thunder will
cease and there will be hail no longer,
that you may know that [b]the earth is the
LORD’S.
30 “[a]But as for you and your servants,
I know that [b]you do not yet [1]fear [2]the
LORD God.”
31 (Now the flax and the [a]barley were
[1]ruined, for the barley was in the ear and
the flax was in bud.
32 But the wheat and the spelt were
not [1]ruined, for they *ripen* late.)
33 [a]So Moses went out of the city
from Pharaoh, and spread out his [1]hands
to the LORD; and the [2]thunder and the
hail ceased, and rain [3]no longer poured
on the earth.
34 But when Pharaoh saw that the rain
and the hail and the [1]thunder had
ceased, he sinned again and [2]hardened
his heart, he and his servants.
35 Pharaoh’s heart was [1]hardened,
and he did not let the sons of Israel go,
just as the [a]LORD had spoken through
Moses.

The Plague of Locusts

10 Then the LORD said to Moses, “Go
to Pharaoh, for [a]I have [1]hard-
ened his heart and the heart of his ser-

7 [1]Lit *heavy*
9 [a]Deut 28:27; Rev 16:2
11 [1]Or *soothsayer priests* [2]Lit *and on all* [a]Ex 8:18
12 [1]Lit *made strong* [a]Ex 4:21; 10:1,20; 14:8; Josh 11:20; John 12:40
13 [a]Ex 8:20 [b]Ex 4:23
14 [1]Lit *to your heart* [a]Ex 8:10; Deut 3:24; 2 Sam 7:22; 1 Chr 17:20; Ps 86:8; Is 45:5-8; 46:9; Jer 10:6,7
16 [1]Lit *stand* [a]Prov 16:4; Rom 9:17
17 [1]Lit *so as not to let*
18 [1]Lit *cause to rain* [2]Lit *and until now* [a]Ex 9:23,24
19 [a]Ex 9:6 [b]Ex 9:25
20 [1]Or *revered* [a]Prov 13:13
21 [1]Lit *did not set his heart to* [2]Lit *then left*
22 [1]Lit *there may be hail* [a]Rev 16:21
23 [1]Lit *gave* [2]Lit *sounds* [a]Gen 19:24; Josh 10:11; Ps 18:13; 78:47; 105:32; Is 30:30; Ezek 38:22; Rev 8:7
24 [1]Lit *taking hold of itself*
25 [a]Ex 9:19; Ps 78:47,48; 105:32,33
26 [a]Ex 8:22; 9:4,6; 11:7
27 [1]Lit *sent and called* [a]Ex 8:8 [b]Ex 10:16,17; 2 Chr 12:6; Ps 129:4; 145:17; Lam 1:18
28 [1]Lit *sounds* [a]Ex 8:8,28; 10:17 [b]Ex 8:25; 10:8,24
29 [1]Lit *palms* [2]Lit *sounds* [a]1 Kin 8:22,38; Ps 143:6; Is 1:15 [b]Ex 8:22; 19:5; 20:11; Ps 24:1; 1 Cor 10:26
30 [1]Or *reverence* [2]Lit *before the LORD* [a]Ex 8:29 [b]Is 26:10
31 [1]Lit *smitten* [a]Ruth 1:22; 2:23
32 [1]Lit *smitten*
33 [1]Lit *palms* [2]Lit *sounds* [3]Lit *was not poured* [a]Ex 8:12; 9:29
34 [1]Lit *sounds* [2]Lit *made heavy*
35 [1]Lit *strong* [a]Ex 4:21
10:1 [1]Lit *made heavy* [a]Ex 4:21; 7:13; Josh 11:20; John 12:40; Rom 9:18

vants, that I may [2]perform these signs of Mine [3]among them,

2 and [a]that you may tell in the [1]hearing of your son, and of your grandson, how I made a mockery of the Egyptians and how I [2]performed My signs among them, [b]that you may know that I am the LORD."

3 ¶ Moses and Aaron went to Pharaoh and said to him, "Thus says the LORD, the God of the Hebrews, 'How long will you refuse to [a]humble yourself before Me? [b]Let My people go, that they may serve Me.

4 'For if you refuse to let My people go, behold, tomorrow I will bring locusts into your territory.

5 'They shall cover the surface of the land, so that no one will be able to see the land. [a]They will also eat the rest of what has escaped—what is left to you from the hail—and they will eat every tree which sprouts for you out of the field.

6 'Then [a]your houses shall be filled and the houses of all your servants and the houses of all the Egyptians, *something* which neither your fathers nor your grandfathers have seen, from the day that they [1]came upon the earth until this day.' " And he turned and went out from Pharaoh.

7 [a]Pharaoh's servants said to him, "How long will this man be [b]a snare to us? Let the men go, that they may serve the LORD their God. Do you not [1]realize that Egypt is destroyed?"

8 So Moses and Aaron [a]were brought back to Pharaoh, and he said to them, "[b]Go, serve the LORD your God! [1]Who are the ones that are going?"

9 Moses said, "[a]We shall go with our young and our old; with our sons and our daughters, [b]with our flocks and our herds we shall go, for we [1]must hold a feast to the LORD."

10 Then he said to them, "Thus may the LORD be with you, [1]if ever I let you and your little ones go! Take heed, for evil is [2]in your mind.

11 "Not so! Go now, the men *among you,* and serve the LORD, for [1]that is what you desire." So [a]they were driven out from Pharaoh's presence.

12 ¶ Then the LORD said to Moses, "[a]Stretch out your hand over the land of Egypt for the locusts, that they may come up on the land of Egypt and [b]eat every plant of the land, *even* all that the hail has left."

13 So Moses stretched out his staff over the land of Egypt, and the LORD directed an east wind on the land all that day and all that night; and when it was morning, the east wind [1]brought the [a]locusts.

14 [a]The locusts came up over all the land of Egypt and settled in all the territory of Egypt; *they were* very [1]numerous. There had never been so *many* [2]locusts, nor would there be so *many* [3]again.

15 For they covered the surface of the whole land, so that the land was darkened; and they [a]ate every plant of the land and all the fruit of the trees that the hail had left. Thus nothing green was left on tree or plant of the field through all the land of Egypt.

16 Then Pharaoh hurriedly [a]called for Moses and Aaron, and he said, "[b]I have sinned against the LORD your God and against you.

17 "Now therefore, please forgive my sin only this once, and [a]make supplication to the LORD your God, that He would only remove this death from me."

18 [a]He went out from Pharaoh and made supplication to the LORD.

19 So the LORD shifted *the wind* to a very strong west wind which took up the locusts and drove them into the [1]Red Sea; not one locust was left in all the territory of Egypt.

20 But [a]the LORD [1]hardened Pharaoh's heart, and he did not let the sons of Israel go.

Darkness over the Land

21 ¶ Then the LORD said to Moses, "[a]Stretch out your hand toward the sky, that there may be darkness over the land of Egypt, even a darkness [b]which may be felt."

22 So Moses stretched out his hand toward the sky, and there was [a]thick darkness in all the land of Egypt for three days.

23 They did not see one another, nor did anyone rise from his place for three days, [a]but all the sons of Israel had light in their dwellings.

24 Then Pharaoh [a]called to Moses, and said, "Go, serve the LORD; only let your flocks and your herds be detained. Even [b]your little ones may go with you."

25 But Moses said, "You must also [1]let us have sacrifices and burnt offerings, that we may [2]sacrifice *them* to the LORD our God.

26 "[a]Therefore, our livestock too shall go with us; not a hoof shall be left behind, for we shall take some of them to serve the LORD our God. And until we arrive there, we ourselves do not know with what we shall serve the LORD."

27 But [a]the LORD [1]hardened Pharaoh's heart, and he was not willing to let them go.

1 [2]Lit *put* [3]Lit *in his midst*
2 [1]Lit *ears* [2]Lit *put* [a]Ex 12:26, 27; 13:8,14,15; Deut 4:9; Ps 44:1; 78:5; Joel 1:3 [b]Ex 7:5,17
3 [a]1 Kin 21:29; 2 Chr 34:27; James 4:10; 1 Pet 5:6 [b]Ex 4:23
5 [a]Joel 1:4; 2:25
6 [1]Lit *were* [a]Ex 8:3,21
7 [1]Lit *know* [a]Ex 7:5; 8:19; 12:33 [b]Ex 23:33; Josh 23:13; 1 Sam 18:21; Eccl 7:26
8 [1]Lit *Who and who are* [a]Ex 8:8 [b]Ex 8:25
9 [1]Lit *have a feast* [a]Ex 12:37, 38 [b]Ex 10:26
10 [1]Lit *when I* [2]Lit *before your face*
11 [1]Lit *you desire it* [a]Ex 10:28
12 [a]Ex 7:19 [b]Ex 10:5,15
13 [1]Lit *carried* [a]Ps 78:46; 105:34
14 [1]Lit *heavy* [2]Lit *locusts like them before them* [3]Lit *after them* [a]Deut 28:38; Ps 78:46; 105:34; Joel 1:4, 7; 2:1-11; Rev 9:3
15 [a]Ex 10:5; Ps 105:34f
16 [a]Ex 8:8 [b]Ex 9:27
17 [a]Ex 8:8,28; 9:28; 1 Kin 13:6
18 [a]Ex 8:30
19 [1]Lit *Sea of Reeds*
20 [1]Lit *made strong* [a]Ex 4:21; 11:10
21 [a]Ex 9:22 [b]Deut 28:29
22 [a]Ps 105:28; Rev 16:10
23 [a]Ex 8:22
24 [a]Ex 8:8,25 [b]Ex 10:10
25 [1]Lit *give into our hand* [2]Lit *make*
26 [a]Ex 10:9
27 [1]Lit *made strong* [a]Ex 4:21; 10:20; 14:4,8

Hebrew Calendar and Selected Events

NUMBER of MONTH		HEBREW NAME	MODERN EQUIVALENT	BIBLICAL REFERENCES	AGRICULTURE	FEASTS
1 Sacred sequence begins	7	**Abib; Nisan**	March–April	Ex 12:2; 13:4; 23:15; 34:18; Deut 16:1; Neh 2:1; Esth 3:7	Spring (later) rains; barley and flax harvest begins	Passover; Unleavened Bread; Firstfruits
2	8	**Ziv (Iyyar)***	April–May	1 Kin 6:1,37	Barley harvest; dry season begins	
3	9	**Sivan**	May–June	Esth 8:9	Wheat harvest	Pentecost (Weeks)
4	10	**(Tammuz)***	June–July		Tending vines	
5	11	**(Ab)***	July–August		Ripening of grapes, figs and olives	
6	12	**Elul**	August–September	Neh 6:15	Processing grapes, figs and olives	
7	1 Civil sequence	**Ethanim (Tishri)***	September–October	1 Kin 8:2	Autumn (early) rains begin; plowing	Trumpets; Atonement; Tabernacles (Booths)
8	2	**Bul (Marcheshvan)***	October–November	1 Kin 6:38	Sowing of wheat and barley	
9	3	**Chislev**	November–December	Neh 1:1; Zech 7:1	Winter rains begin (snow in some areas)	Hanukkah ("Dedication")
10	4	**Tebeth**	December–January	Esth 2:16		
11	5	**Shebat**	January–February	Zech 1:7		
12	6	**Adar**	February–March	Ezra 6:15; Esth 3:7,13; 8:12; 9:1,15,17,19,21	Almond trees bloom; citrus fruit harvest	Purim
		(Adar Sheni)* — Second Adar	This intercalary month was added about every three years so the lunar calendar would correspond to the solar year.			

**Names in parentheses are not in the Bible*

28 Then Pharaoh said to him, "[a]Get
away from me! [1]Beware, do not see my
face again, for in the day you see my face
you shall die!"
29 Moses said, "You are right; [a]I shall
never see your face again!"

The Last Plague

11 Now the LORD said to Moses,
"One more plague I will bring on
Pharaoh and on Egypt; [a]after that he will
let you go from here. When he lets you
go, he will surely drive you out from here
completely.
2 "Speak now in the [1]hearing of the
people that [a]each man ask from his
neighbor and each woman from her
neighbor for articles of silver and articles
of gold."
3 [a]The LORD gave the people favor in
the sight of the Egyptians. [b]Furthermore,
the man Moses *himself* was [1]greatly esteemed in the land of Egypt, *both* in the
sight of Pharaoh's servants and in the
sight of the people.
4 ¶ Moses said, "Thus says the LORD,
'About [a]midnight I am going out into the
midst of Egypt,
5 and [a]all the firstborn in the land of
Egypt shall die, from the firstborn of the
Pharaoh who sits on his throne, even to
the firstborn of the slave girl who is behind the millstones; all the firstborn of
the cattle as well.
6 'Moreover, there shall be [a]a great
cry in all the land of Egypt, such as there
has not been *before* and such as shall
never be again.
7 '[a]But against any of the sons of Israel a dog will not *even* [1]bark, whether
against man or beast, that you may [2]un-
derstand how the LORD makes a distinction between Egypt and Israel.'
8 "[a]All these your servants will come
down to me and bow themselves [1]before
me, saying, 'Go out, you and all the people who [2]follow you,' and after that I will
go out." [b]And he went out from Pharaoh
in hot anger.
9 ¶ Then the LORD said to Moses,
"[a]Pharaoh will not listen to you, so [b]that
My wonders will be multiplied in the
land of Egypt."
10 [a]Moses and Aaron performed all
these wonders before Pharaoh; yet [b]the
LORD [1]hardened Pharaoh's heart, and he
did not let the sons of Israel go out of his
land.

The Passover Lamb

12 Now the LORD said to Moses and
Aaron in the land of [1]Egypt,
2 "[a]This month shall be the beginning of months for you; it is to be the first
month of the year to you.
3 "Speak to all the congregation of Israel, saying, 'On the tenth of this month
they are each one to take a [1]lamb for
themselves, according to their fathers'
households, a [1]lamb for [2]each household.
4 'Now if the household is too small
for a [1]lamb, then he and his neighbor
nearest to his house are to take one according to the [2]number of persons *in*
them; according to [3]what each man
should eat, you are to [4]divide the lamb.
5 'Your [1]lamb shall be [a]an unblemished male a year old; you may take it
from the sheep or from the goats.
6 '[1]You shall keep it until the [a]four-
teenth day of the same month, then the
whole assembly of the congregation of
Israel is to kill it [2b]at twilight.
7 '[a]Moreover, they shall take some of
the blood and put it on the two doorposts
and on the lintel [1]of the houses in which
they eat it.
8 'They shall eat the flesh [a]that *same*
night, [b]roasted with fire, and they shall
eat it with [c]unleavened bread [1d]and bitter herbs.
9 'Do not eat any of it raw or boiled at
all with water, but rather [a]roasted with
fire, *both* its head and its legs along with
[b]its entrails.
10 '[a]And you shall not leave any of it
over until morning, but whatever is left of
it until morning, you shall burn with fire.
11 'Now you shall eat it in this manner:
with your loins girded, your sandals on
your feet, and your staff in your hand; and
you shall eat it in haste—it is [a]the LORD'S
Passover.
12 'For [a]I will go through the land of
Egypt on that night, and will strike down
all the firstborn in the land of Egypt, both
man and beast; and [b]against all the gods
of Egypt I will execute judgments—[c]I
am the LORD.
13 '[a]The blood shall be a sign for you
on the houses where you [1]live; and
when I see the blood I will pass over you,
and no plague will befall you [2]to destroy
you when I strike the land of Egypt.

Feast of Unleavened Bread

14 ¶ 'Now [a]this day will be [b]a memorial to you, and you shall celebrate it *as* a
feast to the LORD; throughout your generations you are to celebrate it *as* [1c]a permanent ordinance.
15 '[a]Seven days you shall eat unleavened bread, but on the first day you shall
[1]remove leaven from your houses; for
whoever eats anything leavened from the

28 [1]Lit *Take heed to yourself* [a]Ex 10:11
29 [a]Ex 11:8; Heb 11:27
11:1 [a]Ex 12:31, 33,39
2 [1]Lit *ears* [a]Ex 3:22; 12:35,36
3 [1]Lit *very great* [a]Ex 3:21; 12:36; Ps 106:46 [b]Deut 34:10-12
4 [a]Ex 12:29
5 [a]Ex 12:12,29; Ps 78:51; 105:36; 135:8; 136:10
6 [a]Ex 12:30
7 [1]Lit *sharpen his tongue* [2]Lit *know* [a]Ex 8:22; Josh 10:21
8 [1]Lit *to* [2]Lit *are at your feet* [a]Ex 12:31-33 [b]Heb 11:27
9 [a]Ex 7:4 [b]Ex 7:3
10 [1]Lit *made strong* [a]Ex 4:21 [b]Ex 7:3; 9:12; 10:20,27; Josh 11:20; Is 63:17; John 12:40
12:1 [1]Lit *Egypt, saying*
2 [a]Ex 13:4; 23:15; 34:18; Deut 16:1
3 [1]Or *kid* [2]Lit *the*
4 [1]Or *kid* [2]Or *amount* [3]Lit *each man's eating* [4]Lit *compute for*
5 [1]Or *kid* [a]Lev 22:18-21; 23:12; Heb 9:14; 1 Pet 1:19
6 [1]Lit *It shall be to you for a guarding* [2]Lit *between the two evenings* [a]Ex 12:14,17; Lev 23:5; Num 9:1-3,11; 28:16 [b]Ex 16:12; Deut 16:4,6
7 [1]Lit *upon* [a]Ex 12:22
8 [1]Lit *in addition to* [a]Ex 34:25; Num 9:12 [b]Deut 16:7 [c]Deut 16:3,4; 1 Cor 5:8 [d]Num 9:11
9 [a]Ex 12:8 [b]Ex 29:13,17,22
10 [a]Ex 16:19; 23:18; 34:25
11 [a]Ex 12:13, 21,27,43
12 [a]Ex 11:4,5 [b]Num 33:4; Ps 82:1 [c]Ex 6:2
13 [1]Lit *are* [2]Lit *for destruction* [a]Heb 11:28
14 [1]Or *an eternal* [a]Ex 12:6; Lev 23:4,5; 2 Kin 23:21 [b]Ex 13:9 [c]Ex 12:17, 24; 13:10
15 [1]Lit *cause to cease* [a]Ex 13:6, 7; 23:15; 34:18; Lev 23:6; Num 28:17; Deut 16:3,8

first day until the seventh day, [b]that [2]person shall be cut off from Israel.

16 '[a]On the first day you shall have a holy assembly, and *another* holy assembly on the seventh day; no work at all shall be done on them, except what must be eaten [1]by every person, that alone may be [2]prepared by you.

17 'You shall also observe [a]the *Feast of* Unleavened Bread, for on this [b]very day I brought your hosts out of the land of Egypt; therefore you shall observe this day throughout your generations as [c]a [1]permanent ordinance.

18 '[a]In the first *month,* on the fourteenth day of the month at evening, you shall eat unleavened bread, until the twenty-first day of the month at evening.

19 '[a]Seven days there shall be no leaven found in your houses; for whoever eats what is leavened, that [1][b]person shall be cut off from the congregation of Israel, whether *he is* an alien or a native of the land.

20 'You shall not eat anything leavened; in all your dwellings you shall eat unleavened bread.' "

21 ¶ Then [a]Moses called for all the elders of Israel and said to them, "[1]Go and [b]take for yourselves [2]lambs according to your families, and slay [c]the Passover *lamb.*

22 "[a]You shall take a bunch of hyssop and dip it in the blood which is in the basin, and [1]apply some of the blood that is in the basin to the lintel and the two doorposts; and none of you shall go outside the door of his house until morning.

A Memorial of Redemption

23 "For [a]the LORD will pass through to smite the Egyptians; and when He sees the blood on the lintel and on the two doorposts, the LORD will pass over the door and will [b]not allow the [c]destroyer to come in to your houses to smite *you.*

24 "And [a]you shall observe this event as an ordinance for you and your children forever.

25 "When you enter the land which the LORD will give you, as He has [1]promised, you shall observe this [2]rite.

26 "[a]And when your children say to you, '[1]What does this rite mean to you?'

27 you shall say, 'It is a Passover sacrifice to [a]the LORD [1]who passed over the houses of the sons of Israel in Egypt when He smote the Egyptians, but [2]spared our homes.' " [b]And the people bowed low and worshiped.

28 ¶ Then the sons of Israel went and did *so;* just as the LORD had commanded Moses and Aaron, so they did.

29 ¶ Now it came about at [a]midnight that [b]the LORD struck all [c]the firstborn in the land of Egypt, from the firstborn of Pharaoh who sat on his throne to the firstborn of the captive who was in the dungeon, and all the firstborn of [d]cattle.

30 Pharaoh arose in the night, he and all his servants and all the Egyptians, and there was [a]a great cry in Egypt, for there was no home where there was not someone dead.

31 Then [a]he called for Moses and Aaron at night and said, "Rise up, [b]get out from among my people, both you and the sons of Israel; and go, [1]worship the LORD, as you have said.

32 "Take [a]both your flocks and your herds, as you have said, and go, and bless me also."

Exodus of Israel

33 [a]The Egyptians urged the people, to send them out of the land in haste, for they said, "We will all be dead."

34 So the people took [a]their dough before it was leavened, *with* their kneading bowls bound up in the clothes on their shoulders.

35 ¶ [a]Now the sons of Israel had done according to the word of Moses, for they had requested from the Egyptians articles of silver and articles of gold, and clothing;

36 and the LORD had given the people favor in the sight of the Egyptians, so that they let them have their request. Thus they [a]plundered the Egyptians.

37 ¶ Now the [a]sons of Israel journeyed from [b]Rameses to Succoth, about [c]six hundred thousand men on foot, aside from children.

38 A [a]mixed multitude also went up with them, [1]along with flocks and herds, a [b]very large number of livestock.

39 They baked the dough which they had brought out of Egypt into cakes of unleavened bread. For it had not become leavened, since they were [a]driven out of Egypt and could not delay, nor had they [1]prepared any provisions for themselves.

40 ¶ Now the time [1]that the sons of Israel lived in Egypt was [a]four hundred and thirty years.

41 And at the end of four hundred and thirty years, [1]to [a]the very day, [b]all the hosts of the LORD went out from the land of Egypt.

Ordinance of the Passover

42 [a]It is a night [1]to be observed for the LORD for having brought them out from the land of Egypt; this night is for the LORD, [1]to be observed [2]by all the sons of Israel throughout their generations.

43 ¶ The LORD said to Moses and Aar-

15 [2]Lit *soul* [b]Gen 17:14; Ex 12:19; Num 9:13

16 [1]Lit *pertaining to* [2]Lit *done* [a]Lev 23:7; Num 28:18

17 [1]Or *eternal* [a]Deut 16:3-8 [b]Ex 12:41 [c]Ex 12:14

18 [a]Ex 12:2; Lev 23:5-8; Num 28:16-25

19 [1]Lit *soul* [a]Ex 12:15 [b]Num 9:13

21 [1]Lit *Draw out* [2]Lit *sheep* [a]Num 9:4; Heb 11:28 [b]Ex 12:3 [c]Ex 12:11

22 [1]Lit *cause to touch* [a]Ex 12:7

23 [a]Ex 11:4 [b]Rev 7:3 [c]1 Cor 10:10; Heb 11:28

24 [a]Ex 12:14

25 [1]Lit *spoken* [2]Lit *service*

26 [1]Lit *What is this service to you?* [a]Ex 10:2; Deut 32:7; Josh 4:6; Ps 78:6

27 [1]Lit *because He* [2]Lit *delivered* [a]Ex 12:11 [b]Ex 4:31

29 [a]Ex 11:4 [b]Num 8:17; Ps 135:8 [c]Ex 4:23; Ps 78:51 [d]Ex 9:6

30 [a]Ex 11:6

31 [1]Or *serve* [a]Ex 8:8 [b]Ex 8:25

32 [a]Ex 10:9

33 [a]Ex 10:7; Ps 105:38

34 [a]Ex 12:39

35 [a]Ex 3:21; Ps 105:37

36 [a]Ex 3:22

37 [a]Num 33:3 [b]Gen 47:11 [c]Ex 38:26; Num 1:46

38 [1]Lit *and* [a]Num 11:4 [b]Ex 17:3; Num 20:19; Deut 3:19

39 [1]Lit *made* [a]Ex 6:1

40 [1]Or *of the sons of Israel who dwelt* [a]Gen 15:13; Acts 7:6; Gal 3:17

41 [1]Lit *that it happened on this very day* [a]Ex 12:17 [b]Ex 3:8

42 [1]Or *of vigil* [2]Lit *to the sons* [a]Ex 13:10; Deut 16:1

on, "This is the ordinance of [a]the Passover: no [1b]foreigner is to eat of it;
44 but every man's [a]slave purchased
with money, after you have circumcised
him, then he may eat of it.
45 "[a]A sojourner or a hired servant
shall not eat of it.
46 "It is to be eaten in a single house;
you are not to bring forth any of the flesh
outside of the house, [a]nor are you to
break any bone of it.
47 "[a]All the congregation of Israel are
to [1]celebrate this.
48 "But [a]if a [1]stranger sojourns with
you, and [2]celebrates the Passover to the
LORD, let all his males be circumcised,
and then let him come near to [3]celebrate
it; and he shall be like a native of the land.
But no uncircumcised person may eat
of it.
49 "[1a]The same law shall [2]apply to
the native as to the [3]stranger who sojourns among you."
50 ¶ Then all the sons of Israel did *so;*
they did just as the LORD had commanded
Moses and Aaron.
51 And on that same day [a]the LORD
brought the sons of Israel out of the land
of Egypt [1b]by their hosts.

Consecration of the Firstborn

13 Then the LORD spoke to Moses,
saying,
2 "[a]Sanctify to Me every firstborn, the
first [1]offspring of every womb among the
sons of Israel, both of man and beast; it
belongs to Me."
3 ¶ Moses said to the people, "[a]Re-
member this day in which you went out
from Egypt, from the house of [1]slavery;
for [b]by [2]a powerful hand the LORD
brought you out from this place. [c]And
nothing leavened shall be eaten.
4 "On this day in the [a]month of Abib,
you are about to go forth.
5 "It shall be when the LORD [a]brings
you to the land of the Canaanite, the Hittite, the Amorite, the Hivite and the Jebusite, which [b]He swore to your fathers to
give you, a land flowing with milk and
honey, [c]that you shall [1]observe this rite
in this month.
6 "For [a]seven days you shall eat unleavened bread, and on the seventh day
there shall be a feast to the LORD.
7 "Unleavened bread shall be eaten
throughout the seven days; and [a]nothing
leavened shall be seen [1]among you, nor
shall any leaven be seen [1]among you in
all your borders.
8 "[a]You shall tell your son on that day,
saying, 'It is because of what the LORD did
for me when I came out of Egypt.'
9 "And [a]it shall [1]serve as a sign to
you on your hand, and as a reminder [2]on
your forehead, that the law of the LORD
may be in your mouth; for with [b]a powerful hand the LORD brought you out of
Egypt.
10 "Therefore, you shall [a]keep this ordinance at its appointed time from [1]year
to year.
11 ¶ "Now when [a]the LORD brings
you to the land of the Canaanite, as [b]He
swore to you and to your fathers, and
gives it to you,
12 [a]you shall [1]devote to the LORD the
first [2]offspring of every womb, and [3]the
first offspring of every beast that you
own; the males belong to the LORD.
13 "But [a]every first [1]offspring of a donkey you shall redeem with a lamb, but
if you do not redeem *it,* then you shall
break its neck; and [b]every firstborn of
man among your sons you shall redeem.
14 "[a]And it shall be when your son
asks you in time to come, saying, 'What
is this?' then you shall say to him, '[b]With
a [1]powerful hand the LORD brought us
out of Egypt, from the house of [2]slavery.
15 'It came about, when Pharaoh was
stubborn about letting us go, that the
[a]LORD killed every firstborn in the land
of Egypt, both the firstborn of man and
the firstborn of beast. Therefore, I sacrifice to the LORD the males, the first [1]off-
spring of every womb, but every firstborn
of my sons I redeem.'
16 "So [a]it shall [1]serve as a sign on your
hand and as [2]phylacteries [3]on your forehead, for with a [4]powerful hand the
LORD brought us out of Egypt."

God Leads the People

17 ¶ Now when Pharaoh had let the
people go, God did not lead them by the
way of the land of the Philistines, even
though it was near; for God said, "[a]The
people might change their minds when
they see war, and return to Egypt."
18 Hence God led the people around
by the way of the wilderness to the [1]Red
Sea; and the sons of Israel went up [a]in
martial array from the land of Egypt.
19 Moses took [a]the bones of Joseph
with him, for he had made the sons of
Israel solemnly swear, saying, "God will
surely [1]take care of you, and you shall
carry my bones from here with you."
20 Then they set out from [a]Succoth
and camped in Etham on the edge of the
wilderness.
21 [a]The LORD was going before them
in a pillar of cloud by day to lead them on
the way, and in a pillar of fire by night to
give them light, that they might [1]travel
by day and by night.

43 [1]Lit *son of a stranger* [a]Ex 12:11; Num 9:14 [b]Ex 12:48
44 [a]Gen 17:12; Lev 22:11
45 [a]Lev 22:10
46 [a]Num 9:12; Ps 34:20; John 19:33
47 [1]Lit *do* [a]Ex 12:6; Num 9:13
48 [1]Lit *sojourner* [2]Lit *does* [3]Lit *do* [a]Num 9:14
49 [1]Lit *One law* [2]Lit *be* [3]Lit *sojourner* [a]Lev 24:22; Num 15:15
51 [1]Lit *according to* [a]Ex 12:41 [b]Ex 6:26
13:2 [1]Lit *opening* [a]Ex 13:12; Lev 27:26; Num 3:13; Deut 15:19; Luke 2:23
3 [1]Lit *slaves* [2]Lit *strength of hand* [a]Ex 12:42; Deut 16:3 [b]Ex 3:20 [c]Ex 12:19
4 [a]Ex 12:2; Deut 16:1
5 [1]Lit *serve this service* [a]Ex 3:8; Josh 24:11 [b]Ex 6:8 [c]Ex 12:25
6 [a]Ex 12:15-20
7 [1]Lit *to* [a]Ex 12:19
8 [a]Ex 10:2; Ps 44:1
9 [1]Lit *be for* [2]Lit *between your eyes* [a]Ex 12:14; Num 15:39; Deut 6:8 [b]Ex 13:3
10 [1]Lit *days to days* [a]Ex 12:24
11 [a]Ex 13:5 [b]Gen 15:18; Ps 105:42-45
12 [1]Lit *cause to pass over* [2]Lit *opening* [3]Lit *every issue the offspring of a beast* [a]Ex 13:1; Lev 27:26; Num 18:15; Ezek 44:30; Luke 2:23
13 [1]Lit *opening* [a]Ex 34:20; Num 18:15 [b]Num 3:46
14 [1]Lit *strength of hand* [2]Lit *slaves* [a]Ex 10:2; Deut 6:20; Josh 4:6 [b]Ex 13:3
15 [1]Lit *opening* [a]Ex 12:29
16 [1]Lit *be for* [2]Or *frontlet-bands* [3]Lit *between your eyes* [4]Lit *strength of hand* [a]Ex 13:9; Deut 6:8
17 [a]Ex 14:11; Num 14:1-4; Deut 17:16
18 [1]Lit *Sea of Reeds* [a]Josh 1:14
19 [1]Lit *visit* [a]Gen 50:24; Josh 24:32; Acts 7:15
20 [a]Ex 12:37; Num 33:6
21 [1]Lit *go* [a]Ex 14:19; Num 9:15; Deut 1:33; Neh 9:12; Ps 78:14; Is 4:5; 1 Cor 10:1

22 [1]He [a]did not take away the pillar
of cloud by day, nor the pillar of fire by
night, from before the people.

Pharaoh in Pursuit

14 Now the LORD spoke to Moses,
saying,
2 "Tell the sons of Israel to turn back
and camp before [a]Pi-hahiroth, between
[b]Migdol and the sea; you shall camp in
front of Baal-zephon, opposite it, by the
sea.
3 "For Pharaoh will say of the sons
of Israel, 'They are wandering aimlessly
in the land; the wilderness has shut
them in.'
4 "Thus [a]I will [1]harden Pharaoh's
heart, and [b]he will chase after them; and
I will be honored through Pharaoh and all
his army, and [c]the Egyptians will know
that I am the LORD." And they did so.
5 ¶ When the king of Egypt was told
that the people had fled, [1]Pharaoh and
his servants had a change of heart toward
the people, and they said, "What is this
we have done, that we have let Israel go
from serving us?"
6 So he made his chariot ready and
took his people with him;
7 and he took six hundred select
chariots, and all the *other* chariots of
Egypt with officers over all of them.
8 [a]The LORD [1]hardened the heart of
Pharaoh, king of Egypt, and he chased
after the sons of Israel as the sons of Israel
were going out [2b]boldly.
9 Then [a]the Egyptians chased after
them *with* all the horses *and* chariots of
Pharaoh, his horsemen and his army, and
they overtook them camping by the sea,
[b]beside Pi-hahiroth, in front of Baal-
zephon.
10 ¶ As Pharaoh drew near, the sons
of Israel [1]looked, and behold, the Egyptians were marching after them, and they
became very frightened; [a]so the sons of
Israel cried out to the LORD.
11 Then [a]they said to Moses, "Is it
because there were no graves in Egypt
that you have taken us away to die in the
wilderness? Why have you dealt with us
in this way, [1]bringing us out of Egypt?
12 "[a]Is this not the word that we spoke
to you in Egypt, saying, '[1]Leave us alone
that we may serve the Egyptians'? For it
would have been better for us to serve
the Egyptians than to die in the wilderness."

The Sea Is Divided

13 But Moses said to the people, "[a]Do
not fear! [1]Stand by and see [b]the salvation of the LORD which He will accomplish for you today; for the Egyptians
whom you have seen today, you will never see them again forever.
14 "[a]The LORD will fight for you while
[b]you keep silent."
15 ¶ Then the LORD said to Moses,
"Why are you crying out to Me? Tell the
sons of Israel to go forward.
16 "As for you, lift up [a]your staff and
stretch out your hand over the sea and
divide it, and the sons of Israel shall [1]go
through the midst of the sea on dry land.
17 "As for Me, behold, [a]I will [1]harden
the hearts of the Egyptians so that they
will go in after them; and I will be honored through Pharaoh and all his army,
through his chariots and his horsemen.
18 "[a]Then the Egyptians will know
that I am the LORD, when I am honored
through Pharaoh, through his chariots
and his horsemen."
19 ¶ [a]The angel of God, who had
been going before the camp of Israel,
moved and went behind them; and the
pillar of cloud moved from before them
and stood behind them.
20 So it came between the camp of
Egypt and the camp of Israel; and there
was the cloud [1]along with the darkness,
yet it gave light at night. Thus the one did
not come near the other all night.
21 ¶ [a]Then Moses stretched out his
hand over the sea; and the LORD [1]swept
the sea *back* by a strong east wind all
night and turned the sea into [b]dry land,
so [c]the waters were divided.
22 [a]The sons of Israel [1]went through
the midst of the sea on the dry land, and
[b]the waters *were like* a wall to them on
their right hand and on their left.
23 Then [a]the Egyptians took up the
pursuit, and all Pharaoh's horses, his
chariots and his horsemen went in after
them into the midst of the sea.
24 At the morning watch, [a]the LORD
looked down on the [1]army of the Egyptians [2]through the pillar of fire and cloud
and brought the [1]army of the Egyptians
into confusion.
25 He [1]caused their chariot wheels to
swerve, and He made them drive with
difficulty; so the Egyptians said, "Let [2]us
flee from Israel, [a]for the LORD is fighting
for them against the Egyptians."
26 ¶ Then the LORD said to Moses,
"[a]Stretch out your hand over the sea so
that the waters may come back over the
Egyptians, over their chariots and their
horsemen."
27 So Moses stretched out his hand
over the sea, and [a]the sea returned to its
normal state at daybreak, while the Egyptians were fleeing [1]right into it; then the
LORD [2b]overthrew the Egyptians in the
midst of the sea.

---

22 [1]Or *The pillar of cloud by day and the pillar of fire by night did not depart* [a]Neh 9:19
14:2 [a]Num 33:7 [b]Jer 44:1
4 [1]Lit *make strong* [a]Ex 4:21; 7:3; 14:17 [b]Ex 14:23 [c]Ex 7:5; 14:25
5 [1]Lit *the heart of Pharaoh...was changed*
8 [1]Lit *made strong* [2]Lit *with a high hand* [a]Ex 14:4 [b]Num 33:3; Acts 13:17
9 [a]Ex 15:9; Josh 24:6 [b]Ex 14:2
10 [1]Lit *lifted up their eyes* [a]Josh 24:7; Neh 9:9; Ps 34:17; 107:6
11 [1]Lit *so as to bring* [a]Ex 5:21; 15:24; 16:2; Ps 106:7,8
12 [1]Lit *Cease from us* [a]Ex 6:9
13 [1]Or *Take your stand* [a]Gen 15:1; 46:3; Ex 20:20; 2 Chr 20:15,17; Is 41:10,13,14 [b]Ex 14:30; 15:2
14 [a]Ex 14:25; 15:3; Deut 1:30; 3:22; Josh 23:3; 2 Chr 20:29; Neh 4:20 [b]Is 30:15
16 [1]Lit *enter the* [a]Ex 4:17,20; 7:19; 14:21,26; 17:5,6,9; Num 20:8,9,11; Is 10:26
17 [1]Lit *make strong* [a]Ex 14:4, 8
18 [a]Ex 14:25
19 [a]Ex 13:21,22
20 [1]Lit *and the darkness*
21 [1]Lit *caused to go* [a]Ex 7:19; 14:16 [b]Ps 66:6; 106:9; 136:13, 14 [c]Ex 15:8; Josh 3:16; 4:23; Neh 9:11; Ps 74:13; 78:13; 114:3,5; Is 63:12,13
22 [1]Lit *entered the* [a]Ex 15:19; Josh 3:17; 4:22; Neh 9:11; Ps 66:6; 78:13; Heb 11:29 [b]Ex 14:29; 15:8
23 [a]Ex 14:4,17
24 [1]Lit *camp* [2]Or *in* [a]Ex 13:21
25 [1]Or *removed* [2]Lit *me* [a]Ex 14:4,14,18
26 [a]Ex 14:16
27 [1]Lit *to meet it* [2]Lit *shook off* [a]Josh 4:18 [b]Ex 15:1,7; Deut 11:4; Neh 9:11; Ps 78:53; Heb 11:29

28 The waters returned and covered
the chariots and the horsemen, [1]even
Pharaoh's entire army that had gone into
the sea after them; [a]not even one of
them remained.
29 But the sons of Israel walked on
[a]dry land through the midst of the sea,
and the waters *were like* a wall to them
on their right hand and on their left.
30 ¶ [a]Thus the LORD saved Israel that
day from the hand of the Egyptians, and
Israel [b]saw the Egyptians dead on the
seashore.
31 When Israel saw the great [1]power
which the LORD had [2]used against the
Egyptians, the people [3]feared the LORD,
and [a]they believed in the LORD and in
His servant Moses.

The Song of Moses and Israel

15 [a]Then Moses and the sons of Israel sang this song to the LORD,
[1]and said,
"[2][b]I will sing to the LORD, for He
[3]is highly exalted;
[c]The horse and its rider He has
hurled into the sea.
2 "[1][a]The LORD is my strength and
song,
And He has become my
salvation;
[b]This is my God, and I will
praise Him;
[c]My father's God, and I will
[d]extol Him.
3 "[a]The LORD is a warrior;
[1][b]The LORD is His name.
4 "[a]Pharaoh's chariots and his army
He has cast into the sea;
And the choicest of his officers
are [1]drowned in the
[2]Red Sea.
5 "The deeps cover them;
[a]They went down into the
depths like a stone.
6 "[a]Your right hand, O LORD, is
majestic in power,
[b]Your right hand, O LORD,
shatters the enemy.
7 "And in the greatness of Your
[1]excellence You [a]overthrow
those who rise up
against You;
[b]You send forth Your burning
anger, *and* it [c]consumes
them as chaff.
8 "[a]At the blast of Your nostrils the
waters were piled up,
[b]The flowing waters stood up
like a heap;
The deeps were congealed in the
heart of the sea.
9 "[a]The enemy said, 'I will pursue,
I will overtake, I will
[b]divide the spoil;
My [1]desire shall be [2]gratified
against them;
I will draw out my sword, my
hand will [3]destroy them.'
10 "[a]You blew with Your wind, the
sea covered them;
[b]They sank like lead in the
[1]mighty waters.
11 "[a]Who is like You among the
gods, O LORD?
Who is like You, [b]majestic in
holiness,
[c]Awesome in praises, [d]working
wonders?
12 "[a]You stretched out Your right
hand,
The earth swallowed them.
13 "In Your lovingkindness You have
[a]led the people whom You
have [b]redeemed;
In Your strength You have
guided *them* [c]to Your holy
habitation.
14 "[a]The peoples have heard, they
tremble;
Anguish has gripped the
inhabitants of Philistia.
15 "Then the [a]chiefs of Edom were
dismayed;
[b]The leaders of Moab, trembling
grips them;
[c]All the inhabitants of Canaan
have melted away.
16 "[a]Terror and dread fall upon
them;
[b]By the greatness of Your arm
they are motionless as stone;
Until Your people pass over,
O LORD,
Until the people pass over whom
You [c]have purchased.
17 "[a]You will bring them and [b]plant
them in [c]the mountain of
Your inheritance,
[d]The place, O LORD, which You
have made for Your
dwelling,
[e]The sanctuary, O Lord, which
Your hands have established.
18 "[a]The LORD shall reign forever
and ever."
19 ¶ [a]For the horses of Pharaoh with
his chariots and his horsemen went into
the sea, and the LORD brought back the
waters of the sea on them, but the sons of
Israel walked on [b]dry land through the
midst of the sea.
20 ¶ [a]Miriam the prophetess, Aaron's
sister, took the [b]timbrel in her hand, and

28 [1]Lit *in respect to* [a]Ps 78:53
29 [a]Ex 14:22; Ps 66:6; Is 11:15
30 [a]Ex 14:13; Ps 106:8; Is 63:8 [b]Ps 58:10
31 [1]Lit *hand* [2]Lit *done* [3]Or *revered* [a]Ex 4:31; Ps 106:12; John 2:11
15:1 [1]Lit *and said, saying* [2]Or *Let me sing* [3]Or *triumphed gloriously* [a]Ps 106:12; Rev 15:3 [b]Is 12:5 [c]Jer 51:21
2 [1]Heb *YAH* [a]Ps 18:1; Is 12:2; Hab 3:18f [b]Ps 48:14 [c]Ex 3:6 [d]2 Sam 22:47; Ps 99:5; Is 25:1
3 [1]Heb *YHWH,* usually rendered *LORD* [a]Ex 14:14; Rev 19:11 [b]Ex 3:15; Ps 24:8
4 [1]Lit *sunk* [2]Lit *Sea of Reeds* [a]Ex 14:6
5 [a]Ex 15:10; Neh 9:11
6 [a]Ex 3:20 [b]Ps 118:15
7 [1]Or *exaltation* [a]Ex 14:27 [b]Ps 78:49 [c]Deut 4:24; Is 5:24; Heb 12:29
8 [a]Ex 14:22; Job 4:9 [b]Ps 78:13
9 [1]Lit *soul* [2]Lit *be filled with them* [3]Or *dispossess, bring to ruin* [a]Ex 14:5 [b]Judg 5:30; Is 53:12; Luke 11:22
10 [1]Or *majestic* [a]Ex 14:27 [b]Ex 15:5
11 [a]Ex 8:10; Deut 3:24; 2 Sam 7:22; 1 Kin 8:23; Ps 71:19; Mic 7:18 [b]Is 6:3; Rev 4:8 [c]Ps 22:23 [d]Ps 72:18
12 [a]Ex 15:6
13 [a]Neh 9:12; Ps 77:20 [b]Ex 15:16; Ps 77:15 [c]Ex 15:17; Ps 78:54
14 [a]Deut 2:25; Hab 3:7
15 [a]Gen 36:15 [b]Num 22:3 [c]Josh 2:9
16 [a]Ex 23:27; Deut 2:25; Josh 2:9 [b]Ex 15:5 [c]Ex 15:13; Ps 74:2; Is 43:1; Jer 31:11; Titus 2:14; 2 Pet 2:1
17 [a]Ex 23:20 [b]Ps 44:2 [c]Ps 2:6 [d]Ps 68:16 [e]Ps 78:69
18 [a]Ps 10:16; Is 57:15
19 [a]Ex 14:23 [b]Ex 14:22
20 [a]Ex 2:4; Num 26:59; 1 Chr 6:3; Mic 6:4 [b]Judg 11:34; 1 Sam 18:6; 1 Chr 15:16; Ps 68:25; Jer 31:4

all the women went out after her with timbrels and with [1c]dancing.

21 Miriam answered them,
"[a]Sing to the LORD, for He [1]is
highly exalted;
The horse and his rider He has
hurled into the sea."

The LORD Provides Water

22 ¶ [a]Then Moses [1]led Israel from the [2]Red Sea, and they went out into [b]the wilderness of [c]Shur; and they went three days in the wilderness and found no water.

23 When they came to [a]Marah, they could not drink the waters [1]of Marah, for they were [2]bitter; therefore it was named [3]Marah.

24 So the people [a]grumbled at Moses, saying, "What shall we drink?"

25 Then he [a]cried out to the LORD, and the LORD showed him [b]a tree; and he threw *it* into the waters, and the waters became sweet.

¶ There He [c]made for them a statute and regulation, and there He [d]tested them.

26 And He said, "[a]If you will give earnest heed to the voice of the LORD your God, and do what is right in His sight, and give ear [b]to His commandments, and keep all His statutes, [c]I will put none of the diseases on you which I have put on the Egyptians; for I, [d]the LORD, am your healer."

27 ¶ Then they came to [a]Elim where there *were* twelve springs of water and seventy date palms, and they camped there beside the waters.

The LORD Provides Manna

16 Then they set out from Elim, and all the congregation of the sons of Israel came to the wilderness of [a]Sin, which is between Elim and Sinai, on [b]the fifteenth day of the second month after their departure from the land of Egypt.

2 The whole congregation of the sons of Israel [a]grumbled against Moses and Aaron in the wilderness.

3 The sons of Israel said to them, "[a]Would that we had died by the LORD's hand in the land of Egypt, [b]when we sat by the pots of [1]meat, when we ate bread to the full; for you have brought us out into this wilderness to kill this whole assembly with hunger."

4 ¶ Then the LORD said to Moses, "Behold, [a]I will rain bread from heaven for you; and the people shall go out and gather a day's portion every day, that I may [b]test them, whether or not they will walk in My [1]instruction.

5 "[a]On the sixth day, when they prepare what they bring in, it will be twice as much as they gather daily."

6 So Moses and Aaron said to all the sons of Israel, "At evening [1a]you will know that the LORD has brought you out of the land of Egypt;

7 and in the morning [1]you will see [a]the glory of the LORD, for [b]He hears your grumblings against the LORD; and [c]what are we, that you grumble against us?"

The LORD Provides Meat

8 Moses said, "*This will happen* when the LORD gives you [1]meat to eat in the evening, and bread to the full in the morning; for the LORD hears your grumblings which you grumble against Him. And what are we? Your grumblings are [a]not against us but against the LORD."

9 ¶ Then Moses said to Aaron, "Say to all the congregation of the sons of Israel, '[a]Come near before the LORD, for He has heard your grumblings.' "

10 It came about as Aaron spoke to the whole congregation of the sons of Israel, that they [1]looked toward the wilderness, and behold, [a]the glory of the LORD appeared in the cloud.

11 And the LORD spoke to Moses, saying,

12 "[a]I have heard the grumblings of the sons of Israel; speak to them, saying, '[1]At twilight you shall eat [2]meat, and in the morning you shall be filled with bread; and [b]you shall know that I am the LORD your God.' "

13 ¶ So it came about at evening that [a]the quails came up and covered the camp, and in the morning [b]there was a layer of dew around the camp.

14 [a]When the layer of dew [1]evaporated, behold, on the [2]surface of the wilderness [b]there was a fine flake-like thing, fine as the frost on the ground.

15 When the sons of Israel saw *it,* they said to one another, "[1]What is it?" For they did not know what it was. And Moses said to them, "[a]It is the bread which the LORD has given you to eat.

16 "This is [1]what the LORD has commanded, 'Gather of it every man [2]as much as he should eat; you shall take [3a]an omer apiece according to the number of persons each of you has in his tent.' "

17 The sons of Israel did so, and *some* gathered much and *some* little.

18 When they measured it with an omer, [a]he who had gathered much had no excess, and he who had gathered little had no lack; every man gathered [1]as much as he should eat.

20 [1]Lit *dances* [c]Judg 11:34; 1 Sam 18:6; Ps 30:11
21 [1]Or *has triumphed gloriously* [a]Ex 15:1
22 [1]Lit *caused Israel to journey* [2]Lit *Sea of Reeds* [a]Ps 77:20 [b]Num 33:8 [c]Gen 16:7
23 [1]Lit *from* [2]Heb *Marim* [3]I.e. bitterness [a]Num 33:8; Ruth 1:20
24 [a]Ex 14:11; Ps 106:13
25 [a]Ex 14:10 [b]Ezek 47:7 [c]Josh 24:25 [d]Ex 16:4; Deut 8:2; Judg 2:22; Ps 66:10
26 [a]Ex 19:5; Deut 7:12 [b]Ex 20:2-17 [c]Deut 7:15 [d]Ex 23:25; Deut 32:39; Ps 41:3
27 [a]Num 33:9
16:1 [a]Num 33:10; Ezek 30:15 [b]Ex 12:6
2 [a]Ex 14:11; Ps 106:25; 1 Cor 10:10
3 [1]Or *flesh* [a]Ex 17:3; Num 14:2; Lam 4:9 [b]Num 11:4
4 [1]Or *law* [a]Neh 9:15; Ps 78:23-25; John 6:31; 1 Cor 10:3 [b]Ex 15:25; Deut 8:2
5 [a]Ex 16:22
6 [1]Lit *and you* [a]Ex 6:7
7 [1]Lit *and you* [a]Ex 16:10; Is 35:2; John 11:4 [b]Num 14:27 [c]Num 16:11
8 [1]Or *flesh* [a]1 Sam 8:7; Luke 10:16; Rom 13:2; 1 Thess 4:8
9 [a]Num 16:16
10 [1]Lit *turned* [a]Ex 13:21; Num 16:19; 1 Kin 8:10f
12 [1]Lit *Between the two evenings* [2]Or *flesh* [a]Ex 16:8; Num 14:27 [b]Ex 6:7; 1 Kin 20:28; Joel 3:17
13 [a]Num 11:31; Ps 78:27-29 [b]Num 11:9
14 [1]Lit *had gone up* [2]Lit *face of* [a]Num 11:7-9 [b]Ex 16:31; Neh 9:15; Ps 78:24
15 [1]Heb *Man hu,* cf v 31 [a]Ex 16:4; Neh 9:15; Ps 78:24; John 6:31; 1 Cor 10:3
16 [1]Lit *the thing which* [2]Lit *according to his eating* [3]Lit *an omer for a head* [a]Ex 16:32
18 [1]Lit *according to his eating* [a]2 Cor 8:15

19 Moses said to them, "[a]Let no man
leave any of it until morning."
20 But they did not listen to Moses,
and some left part of it until morning, and
it bred worms and became foul; and Moses was angry with them.
21 They gathered it morning by morning, every man [1]as much as he should
eat; but when the sun grew hot, it would
melt.

The Sabbath Observed

22 ¶ [a]Now on the sixth day they gathered twice as much bread, two omers for
each one. When all the [b]leaders of the
congregation came and told Moses,
23 then he said to them, "This is what
the LORD [1]meant: [a]Tomorrow is a sabbath observance, a holy sabbath to the
LORD. Bake what you will bake and boil
what you will boil, and [b]all that is left
over [2]put aside to be kept until morning."
24 So they [1]put it aside until morning,
as Moses had ordered, and [a]it did not
become foul nor was there any worm
in it.
25 Moses said, "Eat it today, for today
is a sabbath to the LORD; today you will
not find it in the field.
26 "[a]Six days you shall gather it, but on
the seventh day, *the* sabbath, there will
be [1]none."
27 ¶ It came about on the seventh day
that some of the people went out to gather, but they found none.
28 Then the LORD said to Moses,
"[a]How long do you refuse to keep My
commandments and My [1]instructions?
29 "See, [1]the LORD has given you the
sabbath; therefore He gives you bread for
two days on the sixth day. Remain every
man in his place; let no man go out of his
place on the seventh day."
30 So the people rested on the seventh
day.
31 ¶ The house of [a]Israel named it
[1]manna, and it was like [b]coriander seed,
white, and its taste was like wafers with
honey.
32 Then Moses said, "This is [1]what
the LORD has commanded, 'Let an omerful of it be kept throughout your generations, that they may see the bread that I
fed you in the wilderness, when I brought
you out of the land of Egypt.'"
33 Moses said to Aaron, "[a]Take a jar
and put an omerful of manna in it, and
place it before the LORD to be kept
throughout your generations."
34 As the LORD commanded Moses, so
Aaron placed it before [a]the Testimony,
to be kept.
35 [a]The sons of Israel ate the manna
forty years, until they came to an inhabited land; they ate the manna until they
came to the border of the land of Canaan.
36 (Now [a]an omer is a tenth of an
[1]ephah.)

Water in the Rock

17 Then all the congregation of the
sons of Israel journeyed by
[1]stages from the wilderness of [a]Sin, according to the [2]command of the LORD,
and camped at [b]Rephidim, and there was
no water for the people to drink.
2 Therefore the people [a]quarreled
with Moses and said, "Give us water that
we may drink." And Moses said to them,
"[b]Why do you quarrel with me? [c]Why
do you test the LORD?"
3 But the people thirsted there for
water; and [1]they [a]grumbled against Moses and said, "Why, now, have you
brought us up from Egypt, to kill [2]us and
[3]our children and [3b]our livestock with
thirst?"
4 So Moses cried out to the LORD, saying, "What shall I do to this people? A
[a]little more and they will stone me."
5 Then the LORD said to Moses, "Pass
before the people and take with you some
of [a]the elders of Israel; and take in your
hand your staff with which [b]you struck
the Nile, and go.
6 "Behold, I will stand before you
there on the rock at [a]Horeb; and [b]you
shall strike the rock, and water will come
out of it, that the people may drink." And
Moses did so in the sight of the elders of
Israel.
7 He named the place [1a]Massah and
[2b]Meribah because of the quarrel of the
sons of Israel, and because they [c]tested
the LORD, saying, "Is the LORD among us,
or not?"

Amalek Fought

8 ¶ Then [a]Amalek came and fought
against Israel at [b]Rephidim.
9 So Moses said to [a]Joshua, "Choose
men for us and go out, fight against Amalek. Tomorrow I will station myself on
the top of the hill with [b]the staff of God
in my hand."
10 Joshua did as Moses [1]told him,
[2]and fought against Amalek; and Moses,
Aaron, and [a]Hur went up to the top of
the hill.
11 So it came about when Moses held
his hand up, that Israel prevailed, and
when he let his hand [1]down, Amalek
prevailed.
12 But Moses' hands were heavy.
Then they took a stone and put it under
him, and he sat on it; and Aaron and Hur
[a]supported his hands, one on one side

19 [a]Ex 12:10; 16:23; 23:18
21 [1]Lit *according to his eating*
22 [a]Ex 16:5 [b]Ex 34:31
23 [1]Lit *spoke* [2]Lit *lay up for you* [a]Gen 2:3; Ex 20:8-11; 23:12; 31:15; 35:2; Lev 23:3; Neh 9:13,14 [b]Ex 16:19
24 [1]Lit *laid it up* [a]Ex 16:20
26 [1]Lit *none on it* [a]Ex 20:9,10
28 [1]Or *laws* [a]2 Kin 17:14; Ps 78:10; 106:13
29 [1]Lit *for the LORD*
31 [1]Heb *man*, cf v 15 [a]Num 11:7-9; Deut 8:3, 16 [b]Ex 16:14
32 [1]Lit *the thing which*
33 [a]Heb 9:4; Rev 2:17
34 [a]Ex 25:16, 21; 27:21; 40:20; Num 17:10
35 [a]Deut 8:2f; Josh 5:12; Neh 9:20,21
36 [1]I.e. Approx one bu [a]Ex 16:16
17:1 [1]Lit *their journeyings* [2]Lit *mouth* [a]Ex 16:1; Num 33:12 [b]Ex 19:2; Num 33:14
2 [a]Ex 14:11; Num 20:2,3,13 [b]Ex 16:8 [c]Deut 6:16; Ps 78:18, 41; Matt 4:7; 1 Cor 10:9
3 [1]Lit *the people* [2]Lit *me* [3]Lit *my* [a]Ex 16:2,3 [b]Ex 12:38
4 [a]Num 14:10; 1 Sam 30:6
5 [a]Ex 3:16,18 [b]Ex 7:20
6 [a]Ex 3:1 [b]Num 20:10,11; Deut 8:15; Neh 9:15; Ps 78:15; 105:41; 114:8; 1 Cor 10:4
7 [1]I.e. test [2]I.e. quarrel [a]Deut 6:16; 9:22; Ps 95:8 [b]Num 20:13,24; 27:14; Ps 81:7 [c]Num 14:22; Deut 33:8
8 [a]Gen 36:12; Num 24:20; Deut 25:17-19; 1 Sam 15:2 [b]Ex 17:1
9 [a]Ex 24:13 [b]Ex 4:20
10 [1]Lit *said to* [2]Lit *to fight* [a]Ex 24:14; 31:2
11 [1]Lit *rest*
12 [a]Is 35:3

and one on the other. Thus his hands were steady until the sun set.

13 So Joshua [1]overwhelmed Amalek and his people with the edge of the sword.

14 ¶ Then the LORD said to Moses, "[a]Write this in [1]a book as a memorial and [2]recite it to Joshua, [3]that [b]I will utterly blot out the memory of Amalek from under heaven."

15 Moses built an [a]altar and named it [b]The LORD is My Banner;

16 and he said, "[1a]The LORD has sworn; the LORD will have war against Amalek from generation to generation."

Jethro, Moses' Father-in-law

18 Now [a]Jethro, the priest of Midian, Moses' father-in-law, heard of all that God had done for Moses and for Israel His people, how the LORD had brought Israel out of Egypt.

2 Jethro, Moses' father-in-law, took Moses' wife [a]Zipporah, after he had sent her away,

3 and her [a]two sons, of whom [1]one was named Gershom, for Moses said, "I have been [b]a [2]sojourner in a foreign land."

4 [1]The other was named [2a]Eliezer, for *he said,* "[b]The God of my father was my help, and delivered me from the sword of Pharaoh."

5 ¶ Then Jethro, Moses' father-in-law, came with his sons and his wife to Moses [1]in the wilderness where he was camped, at [a]the mount of God.

6 He [1]sent word to Moses, "I, your father-in-law Jethro, am coming to you with your wife and her two sons with her."

7 Then Moses went out to meet his father-in-law, and [a]he bowed down and [b]kissed him; and they [c]asked each other of their welfare and went into the tent.

8 Moses told his father-in-law all that the LORD had done to Pharaoh and to the Egyptians [a]for Israel's sake, all the [b]hardship that had befallen them on the journey, and *how* [c]the LORD had delivered them.

9 Jethro rejoiced over all [a]the goodness which the LORD had done to Israel, [1]in delivering [2]them from the hand of the Egyptians.

10 So Jethro said, "[a]Blessed be the LORD who delivered you from the hand of the Egyptians and from the hand of Pharaoh, *and* who delivered the people from under the hand of the Egyptians.

11 "Now I know that [a]the LORD is greater than all the gods; [1]indeed, [b]it was proven when they dealt proudly against [2]the people."

12 [a]Then Jethro, Moses' father-in-law, took a burnt offering and sacrifices for God, and Aaron came with all the elders of Israel to eat [1]a meal with Moses' father-in-law before God.

13 ¶ It came about the next day that Moses sat to judge the people, and the people stood about Moses from the morning until the evening.

14 Now when Moses' father-in-law saw all that he was doing for the people, he said, "What is this thing that you are doing for the people? Why do you alone sit *as judge* and all the people stand about you from morning until evening?"

15 Moses said to his father-in-law, "Because the people come to me [a]to inquire of God.

16 "When they have a [1a]dispute, it comes to me, and I judge between a man and his neighbor and make known the statutes of God and His laws."

Jethro Counsels Moses

17 Moses' father-in-law said to him, "The thing that you are doing is not good.

18 "[a]You will surely wear out, both yourself and [1]these people who are with you, for the [2]task is too heavy for you; [b]you cannot do it alone.

19 "Now listen to [1]me: I will give you counsel, and God be with you. [2]You be the people's representative before God, and you [a]bring the [3]disputes to God,

20 [a]then teach them the statutes and the laws, and make known to them [b]the way in which they are to walk and the work they are to do.

21 "Furthermore, you shall [1]select out of all the people [a]able men [b]who fear God, men of truth, those who [c]hate dishonest gain; and you shall place *these* over them *as* leaders of thousands, [2]of hundreds, [2]of fifties and [2]of tens.

22 "Let them judge the people at all times; and let it be [a]that every major [1]dispute they will bring to you, but every minor [1]dispute they themselves will judge. So it will be easier for you, and [b]they will bear *the burden* with you.

23 "If you do this thing and God *so* commands you, then you will be able to [1]endure, and all [2]these people also will go to [3]their place in peace."

24 ¶ So Moses listened [1]to his father-in-law and did all that he had said.

25 Moses chose [a]able men out of all Israel and made them heads over the people, leaders of thousands, [1]of hundreds, [1]of fifties and [1]of tens.

26 They judged the people at all times; [a]the difficult [1]dispute they would bring to Moses, but every minor [1]dispute they themselves would judge.

13 [1]Lit *weakened*
14 [1]Lit *the book* [2]Lit *place it in the ears of* [3]Or *for* [a]Ex 24:4; Num 33:2 [b]Deut 25:19; 1 Sam 15:3
15 [a]Ex 24:4 [b]Gen 22:14; Judg 6:24
16 [1]Or *Because a hand is against the throne of the LORD;* lit *Because a hand upon the throne of YAH* [a]Gen 22:16
18:1 [a]Ex 2:16
2 [a]Ex 2:21
3 [1]Lit *the name of the one was* [2]Heb *ger* [a]Ex 2:22; Acts 7:29 [b]Ex 2:22
4 [1]Lit *The name of the other was* [2]Heb *El-ezer;* i.e. my God is help [a]1 Chr 23:15 [b]Gen 49:25
5 [1]Lit *unto* [a]Ex 3:1
6 [1]Lit *said*
7 [a]Gen 43:26 [b]Gen 29:13; Ex 4:27 [c]Gen 43:27; 2 Sam 11:7
8 [a]Ex 4:23 [b]Num 20:14; Neh 9:32 [c]Ex 15:6
9 [1]Lit *in that He had delivered* [2]Lit *him* [a]Is 63:7-14
10 [a]Gen 14:20; 2 Sam 18:28; 1 Kin 8:56; Ps 68:19
11 [1]Lit *indeed, in the thing in which they* [2]Lit *them* [a]Ex 12:12; 2 Chr 2:5; Ps 95:3 [b]Luke 1:51
12 [1]Lit *bread* [a]Gen 31:54; Ex 24:5
15 [a]Num 9:6; Deut 17:8-13
16 [1]Lit *matter* [a]Ex 24:14
18 [1]Lit *this* [2]Lit *matter* [a]Num 11:14; Deut 1:12 [b]Deut 1:9
19 [1]Lit *my voice* [2]Lit *You be for the people in front of God* [3]Lit *matters* [a]Num 27:5
20 [a]Deut 1:18 [b]Ps 143:8
21 [1]Lit *see* [2]Lit *leaders of* [a]Ex 18:25; Deut 1:13; 2 Chr 19:5-10; Ps 15:1-5; Acts 6:3 [b]Gen 42:18; 2 Sam 23:3 [c]Deut 16:19
22 [1]Lit *matter* [a]Deut 1:17 [b]Num 11:17
23 [1]Lit *stand* [2]Lit *this* [3]Lit *his*
24 [1]Lit *to the voice of*
25 [1]Lit *leaders of* [a]Ex 18:21; Deut 1:15
26 [1]Lit *matter* [a]Ex 18:22

27 Then Moses [1][a]bade his father-in-law farewell, and he went his way into his own land.

Moses on Sinai

19 [a]In the third month after the sons of Israel had gone out of the land of Egypt, [1]on that very day they came into the wilderness of [b]Sinai.

2 When they set out from [a]Rephidim, they came to the wilderness of Sinai and camped in the wilderness; and there Israel camped in front of [b]the mountain.

3 Moses went up to God, and [a]the LORD called to him from the mountain, saying, "Thus you shall say to the house of Jacob and tell the sons of Israel:

4 '[a]You yourselves have seen what I did to the Egyptians, and *how* I bore you on [b]eagles' wings, and brought you to Myself.

5 'Now then, [a]if you will indeed obey My voice and [b]keep My covenant, then you shall be [c]My [1]own possession among all the peoples, for [d]all the earth is Mine;

6 and you shall be to Me [a]a kingdom of priests and [b]a holy nation.' These are the words that you shall speak to the sons of Israel."

7 ¶ [a]So Moses came and called the elders of the people, and set before them all these words which the LORD had commanded him.

8 [a]All the people answered together and said, "All that the LORD has spoken we will do!" And Moses brought back the words of the people to the LORD.

9 The LORD said to Moses, "Behold, I will come to you in [a]a thick cloud, so that the [b]people may hear when I speak with you and may also believe in you forever." Then Moses told the words of the people to the LORD.

10 ¶ The LORD also said to Moses, "Go to the people and [a]consecrate them today and tomorrow, and let them [b]wash their garments;

11 and let them be ready for the third day, for on [a]the third day the LORD will come down on Mount Sinai in the sight of all the people.

12 "You shall set bounds for the people all around, saying, '[1]Beware that you do not go up on the mountain or touch the border of it; [a]whoever touches the mountain shall surely be put to death.

13 'No hand shall touch him, but [a]he shall surely be stoned or [1]shot through; whether beast or man, he shall not live.' When the ram's horn sounds a long blast, they shall come up to [b]the mountain."

14 So Moses went down from the mountain to the people and consecrated the people, and they washed their garments.

15 He said to the people, "Be ready for the third day; do not go near a woman."

16 ¶ [a]So it came about on the third day, when it was morning, that there were [1]thunder and lightning flashes and a thick cloud upon the mountain and a very loud trumpet sound, so that all the people who *were* in the camp trembled.

17 And Moses brought the people out of the camp to meet God, and they stood at the [1]foot of the mountain.

The LORD Visits Sinai

18 [a]Now Mount Sinai *was* all in smoke because the LORD descended upon it [b]in fire; and its smoke ascended like [c]the smoke of a furnace, and [d]the whole mountain [1]quaked violently.

19 When the sound of the trumpet grew louder and louder, Moses spoke and [a]God answered him with [1]thunder.

20 [a]The LORD came down on Mount Sinai, to the top of the mountain; and the LORD called Moses to the top of the mountain, and Moses went up.

21 Then the LORD spoke to Moses, "Go down, [1]warn the people, so that [a]they do not break through to the LORD to gaze, and many of them [2]perish.

22 "Also let the [a]priests who come near to the LORD consecrate themselves, or else the LORD will break out against them."

23 Moses said to the LORD, "The people cannot come up to Mount Sinai, for You [1]warned us, saying, '[a]Set bounds about the mountain and consecrate it.' "

24 Then the LORD said to him, "[1]Go down and come up *again,* [a]you and Aaron with you; but do not let the [b]priests and the people break through to come up to the LORD, or He will break forth upon them."

25 So Moses went down to the people and told them.

The Ten Commandments

20 Then God spoke all these words, saying,

2 ¶ "[a]I am the LORD your God, [b]who brought you out of the land of Egypt, out of the house of [1]slavery.

3 ¶ "[a]You shall have no other [b]gods [1]before Me.

4 ¶ "[a]You shall not make for yourself [1]an idol, or any likeness of what is in heaven above or on the earth beneath or in the water under the earth.

5 "[a]You shall not worship them or serve them; for I, the LORD your God, am a [b]jealous God, [c]visiting the iniquity of the fathers on the children, on the third

27 [1]Lit *sent off his father-in-law* [a]Num 10:29
19:1 [1]Lit *on this day* [a]Ex 12:6 [b]Deut 1:6
2 [a]Ex 17:1; Num 33:15 [b]Ex 3:1
3 [a]Ex 3:4
4 [a]Deut 29:2 [b]Deut 32:11; Rev 12:14
5 [1]Or *special treasure* [a]Ex 15:26; Deut 5:2f [b]Ps 78:10 [c]Deut 4:20; Ps 135:4; Titus 2:14; 1 Pet 2:9 [d]Ex 9:29; Deut 10:14; Job 41:11; Ps 50:12; 1 Cor 10:26
6 [a]1 Pet 2:5; Rev 1:6 [b]Deut 7:6; Is 62:12
7 [a]Ex 4:29
8 [a]Ex 4:31; Deut 5:27
9 [a]Ex 19:16; Deut 4:11; Ps 99:7 [b]Deut 4:12
10 [a]Lev 11:44 [b]Gen 35:2; Lev 15:5; Num 8:7; Rev 22:14
11 [a]Ex 19:16
12 [1]Lit *Take heed to yourselves* [a]Heb 12:20
13 [1]I.e. with arrows [a]Heb 12:20 [b]Ex 19:17
16 [1]Lit *sounds* [a]Heb 12:18
17 [1]Lit *lower part*
18 [1]Or *trembled* [a]Deut 4:11; Ps 104:32 [b]Ex 3:2; Deut 5:4; 2 Chr 7:1-3; Heb 12:18 [c]Gen 15:17 [d]Judg 5:5; Ps 68:7; Jer 4:24
19 [1]Or *a voice;* lit *a sound* [a]Ps 81:7
20 [a]Neh 9:13
21 [1]Lit *testify to* [2]Lit *fall* [a]Ex 3:5; 1 Sam 6:19
22 [a]Ex 19:24; Lev 10:3
23 [1]Lit *testified to* [a]Ex 19:12
24 [1]Lit *Go, descend* [a]Ex 24:1 [b]Ex 19:22
20:2 [1]Lit *slaves* [a]Lev 26:1; Deut 5:6; Ps 81:10 [b]Ex 13:3; Deut 7:8
3 [1]Or *besides Me* [a]Deut 6:14; 2 Kin 17:35; Jer 25:6 [b]Ex 15:11
4 [1]Or *a graven image* [a]Lev 19:4; Deut 4:15-19
5 [a]Ex 23:24; Josh 23:7; 2 Kin 17:35 [b]Ex 34:14; Deut 4:24; Josh 24:19; Nah 1:2 [c]Ex 34:6; Num 14:18; Deut 5:9; 1 Kin 21:29; Jer 32:18

and the fourth generations of those who hate Me,

6 but showing lovingkindness to [a]thousands, to those who love Me and keep My commandments.

7 ¶ "[a]You shall not take the name of the LORD your God in vain, for the LORD will not [1]leave him unpunished who takes His name in vain.

8 ¶ "Remember [a]the sabbath day, to keep it holy.

9 "[a]Six days you shall labor and do all your work,

10 but the seventh day is a sabbath of the LORD your God; *in it* [a]you shall not do any work, you or your son or your daughter, your male or your female servant or your cattle or your sojourner who [1]stays with you.

11 "[a]For in six days the LORD made the heavens and the earth, the sea and all that is in them, and rested on the seventh day; therefore the LORD blessed the sabbath day and made it holy.

12 ¶ "[a]Honor your father and your mother, that your [b]days may be prolonged in the land which the LORD your God gives you.

13 ¶ "[a]You shall not murder.

14 ¶ "[a]You shall not commit adultery.

15 ¶ "[a]You shall not steal.

16 ¶ "[a]You shall not bear false witness against your [b]neighbor.

17 ¶ "[a]You shall not covet your neighbor's house; [b]you shall not covet your neighbor's wife or his male servant or his female servant or his ox or his donkey or anything that belongs to your neighbor."

18 ¶ [a]All the people perceived the [1]thunder and the lightning flashes and the sound of the trumpet and the mountain smoking; and when the people saw *it,* they trembled and stood at a distance.

19 [a]Then they said to Moses, "Speak [1]to us yourself and we will listen; but let not God speak [1]to us, or we will die."

20 Moses said to the people, "[a]Do not be afraid; for God has come in order [b]to test you, and in order that [c]the fear of Him may [1]remain with you, so that you may not sin."

21 So the people stood at a distance, while Moses approached [a]the thick cloud where God *was.*

22 ¶ Then the LORD said to Moses, "Thus you shall say to the sons of Israel, 'You yourselves have seen that [a]I have spoken [1]to you from heaven.

23 '[a]You shall not make *other gods* besides Me; [b]gods of silver or gods of gold, you shall not make for yourselves.

24 'You shall make [a]an altar of earth for Me, and you shall sacrifice on it your [b]burnt offerings and your [c]peace offerings, [d]your sheep and your oxen; in every place [e]where I cause My name to be remembered, I will come to you and bless you.

25 'If you make an altar of stone for Me, [a]you shall not build it of cut stones, for if you wield your tool on it, you will profane it.

26 'And you shall not go up by steps to My altar, so that [a]your nakedness will not be exposed on it.'

Ordinances for the People

21 "Now these are the [a]ordinances which you are to set before them:

2 ¶ "If you buy [a]a Hebrew slave, he shall serve for six years; but on the seventh he shall go out as a free man without payment.

3 "If he comes [1]alone, he shall go out [1]alone; if he is the husband of a wife, then his wife shall go out with him.

4 "If his master gives him a wife, and she bears him sons or daughters, the wife and her children shall belong to her master, and he shall go out [1]alone.

5 "But [a]if the slave plainly says, 'I love my master, my wife and my children; I will not go out as a free man,'

6 then his master shall bring him to [1]God, then he shall bring him to the door or the doorpost. And his master shall pierce his ear with an awl; and he shall serve him permanently.

7 ¶ "[a]If a man sells his daughter as a female slave, she is not to [1]go free [b]as the male slaves [1]do.

8 "If she is [1]displeasing in the eyes of her master [2]who designated her for himself, then he shall let her be redeemed. He does not have authority to sell her to a foreign people because of his [3]unfairness to her.

9 "If he designates her for his son, he shall deal with her according to the custom of daughters.

10 "If he takes to himself another woman, he may not reduce her [1]food, her clothing, or [a]her conjugal rights.

11 "If he will not do these three *things* for her, then she shall go out for nothing, without *payment of* money.

Personal Injuries

12 ¶ "[a]He who strikes a man so that he dies shall surely be put to death.

13 "[a]But [1]if he did not lie in wait *for him,* but [b]God let *him* fall into his hand, then I will appoint you a place to which he may flee.

14 "[a]If, however, a man acts presump-

6 [a]Deut 7:9
7 [1]Or *hold him guiltless* [a]Lev 19:12; Deut 6:13
8 [a]Ex 23:12; Lev 26:2; Deut 5:12
9 [a]Ex 34:21; Lev 23:3; Deut 5:13; Luke 13:14
10 [1]Lit *is in your gates* [a]Neh 13:16-19
11 [a]Gen 2:2; Ex 31:17
12 [a]Lev 19:3; Deut 27:16; Matt 15:4; Mark 7:10; Luke 18:20; Eph 6:2 [b]Deut 5:16; Jer 35:7
13 [a]Gen 9:6; Ex 21:12; Lev 24:17; Matt 5:21; Mark 10:19; Luke 18:20; Rom 13:9; James 2:11
14 [a]Lev 20:10; Deut 5:18; Matt 5:27; Rom 13:9
15 [a]Ex 21:16; Lev 19:11; Matt 19:18; Rom 13:9
16 [a]Ex 23:1; Deut 5:20; Matt 19:18 [b]Lev 19:18
17 [a]Deut 5:21; Rom 7:7; Eph 5:3 [b]Prov 6:29; Matt 5:28
18 [1]Lit *sounds* [a]Ex 19:16; Heb 12:18
19 [1]Lit *with* [a]Deut 5:5; Gal 3:19; Heb 12:19
20 [1]Lit *be before* [a]Ex 14:13; Is 41:10 [b]Ex 15:25; Deut 13:3 [c]Deut 4:10; Prov 3:7; Is 8:13
21 [a]Ex 19:16; Deut 5:22
22 [1]Lit *with* [a]Deut 4:36; Neh 9:13
23 [a]Ex 20:3 [b]Ex 32:1; Deut 29:17
24 [a]Ex 20:25 [b]Ex 10:25 [c]Ex 24:5; Lev 1:2 [d]Deut 12:5; 2 Chr 6:6 [e]Deut 12:5
25 [a]Deut 27:5; Josh 8:31
26 [a]Ex 28:42
21:1 [a]Ex 24:3; Deut 4:14
2 [a]Lev 25:39-43; Deut 15:12-18; Jer 34:14
3 [1]Lit *by himself*
4 [1]Lit *by himself*
5 [a]Deut 15:16
6 [1]Or *the judges who acted in God's name*
7 [1]Lit *go out* [a]Neh 5:5 [b]Ex 21:2
8 [1]Lit *bad* [2]Another reading is *so that he did not designate her* [3]Lit *dealing treacherously*
10 [1]Lit *flesh* [a]1 Cor 7:3
12 [a]Gen 9:6; Lev 24:17; Num 35:30; Matt 26:52
13 [1]Lit *he who* [a]Num 35:10-34; Deut 19:1-13; Josh 20:1-9 [b]1 Sam 24:4 **14** [a]Deut 19:11; 1 Kin 2:28-34

tuously toward his neighbor, so as to kill
him craftily, you are to take him *even*
from My altar, that he may die.
15 ¶ "He who strikes his father or his
mother shall surely be put to death.
16 ¶ "[a]He who [1]kidnaps a man,
whether he sells him or he is found in his
[2]possession, shall surely be put to death.
17 ¶ "[a]He who curses his father or his
mother shall surely be put to death.
18 ¶ "If men have a quarrel and one
strikes the other with a stone or with *his*
fist, and he does not die but [1]remains in
bed,
19 if he gets up and walks around outside on his staff, then he who struck him
shall go unpunished; he shall only pay for
his [1]loss of time, and [2]shall take care of
him until he is completely healed.
20 ¶ "If a man strikes his male or female slave with a rod and he dies [1]at his
hand, he shall [2]be punished.
21 "If, however, he [1]survives a day or
two, no vengeance shall be taken; [a]for he
is his [2]property.
22 ¶ "If men struggle with each other
and strike a woman with child so that
[1]she gives birth prematurely, yet there is
no injury, he shall surely be fined as the
woman's husband [2]may demand of him,
and he shall [a]pay [3]as the judges *decide.*
23 "But if there is *any further* injury,
[a]then you shall appoint *as a penalty* life
for life,
24 [a]eye for eye, tooth for tooth, hand
for hand, foot for foot,
25 burn for burn, wound for wound,
[1]bruise for bruise.
26 ¶ "If a man strikes the eye of his
male or female slave, and destroys it, he
shall let him go free on account of his eye.
27 "And if he [1]knocks out a tooth of his
male or female slave, he shall let him go
free on account of his tooth.
28 ¶ "If an ox gores a man or a woman
[1]to death, [a]the ox shall surely be stoned
and its flesh shall not be eaten; but the
owner of the ox shall go unpunished.
29 "If, however, an ox was previously
in the habit of goring and its owner has
been warned, yet he does not confine it
and it kills a man or a woman, the ox shall
be stoned and its owner also shall be put
to death.
30 "If a ransom is [1]demanded of him,
then he shall give for the redemption of
his life whatever is [1]demanded of him.
31 "Whether it gores a son or [1]a daughter, it shall be done to him according to
[2]the same rule.
32 "If the ox gores a male or female
slave, [1]the owner shall give his *or her*
master [a]thirty shekels of silver, and the
ox shall be stoned.
33 ¶ "If a man opens a pit, or [1]digs a
pit and does not cover it over, and an ox
or a donkey falls into it,
34 the owner of the pit shall make restitution; he shall [1]give money to its owner, and the dead *animal* shall become his.
35 ¶ "If one man's ox hurts another's
so that it dies, then they shall sell the live
ox and divide its price equally; and also
they shall divide the dead *ox.*
36 "Or *if* it is known that the ox was
previously in the habit of goring, yet its
owner has not confined it, he shall surely
pay ox for ox, and the dead *animal* shall
become his.

Property Rights

22 "[1]If a man steals an ox or a sheep
and slaughters it or sells it, he
shall pay five oxen for the ox and [a]four
sheep for the sheep.
2 ¶ "[1]If the [a]thief is [2]caught while
breaking in and is struck so that he dies,
there will be no bloodguiltiness on his
account.
3 "*But* if the sun has risen on him,
there will be bloodguiltiness on his account. He shall surely make restitution; if
he owns nothing, then he shall be [a]sold
for his theft.
4 "If what he stole is actually found
alive in his [1]possession, whether an ox
or a donkey or a sheep, [a]he shall pay
double.
5 ¶ "If a man lets a field or vineyard
be grazed *bare* and lets his animal loose
so that it grazes in another man's field, he
shall make restitution from the best of his
own field and the best of his own vineyard.
6 ¶ "If a fire breaks out and spreads
to thorn bushes, so that stacked grain or
the standing grain or the field *itself* is
consumed, he who started the fire shall
surely make restitution.
7 ¶ "[a]If a man gives his neighbor
money or goods to keep *for him* and it is
stolen from the man's house, if the thief
is [1]caught, he shall pay double.
8 "If the thief is not [1]caught, then the
owner of the house shall [2]appear before
[3a]the judges, *to* determine whether he
[4]laid his hands on his neighbor's property.
9 "For every [1]breach of trust, *whether*
it is for ox, for donkey, for sheep, for
clothing, *or* for any lost thing about
which one says, 'This is it,' the [2]case
of both parties shall come before [3a]the
judges; he whom [3]the judges condemn
shall pay double to his neighbor.
10 ¶ "If a man gives his neighbor a
donkey, an ox, a sheep, or any animal to

16 [1]Lit *steals* [2]Lit *hand* [a]Deut 24:7
17 [a]Lev 20:9; Prov 20:20; Matt 15:4; Mark 7:10
18 [1]Lit *lies*
19 [1]Lit *his sitting* [2]Lit *healing, he shall cause to be healed*
20 [1]Lit *under* [2]Lit *suffer vengeance*
21 [1]Lit *stands* [2]Lit *money* [a]Lev 25:44-46
22 [1]Or *an untimely birth occurs;* lit *her children come out* [2]Lit *lays on him* [3]Lit *by arbitration* [a]Ex 21:30; Deut 22:18,19
23 [a]Lev 24:19; Deut 19:21
24 [a]Lev 24:20; Deut 19:21; Matt 5:38
25 [1]Lit *welt*
27 [1]Lit *causes to fall*
28 [1]Lit *so that he dies* [a]Gen 9:5; Ex 21:32
30 [1]Lit *laid on him*
31 [1]Lit *gores a daughter* [2]Lit *this judgment*
32 [1]Lit *he* [a]Zech 11:12; Matt 26:15; 27:3,9
33 [1]Lit *if a man digs*
34 [1]Lit *give back*
22:1 [1]Ch 21:37 in Heb [a]2 Sam 12:6; Luke 19:8
2 [1]Ch 22:1 in Heb [2]Lit *found* [a]Matt 6:19; 24:43; 1 Pet 4:15
3 [a]Matt 18:25
4 [1]Lit *hand* [a]Ex 22:7
7 [1]Lit *found* [a]Lev 6:1-7
8 [1]Lit *found* [2]Lit *approach to* [3]Or *God* [4]Lit *stretched his hand* [a]Ex 22:9; Deut 17:8,9; 19:17
9 [1]Or *matter of transgression* [2]Lit *matter* [3]Or *God* [a]Ex 22:8, 28; Deut 25:1

keep *for him,* and it dies or is hurt or is driven away while no one is looking,

11 an [a]oath before the LORD shall be made by the two of them [1]that he has not [2]laid hands on his neighbor's property; and its owner shall accept *it,* and he shall not make restitution.

12 "But if it is actually stolen from him, he shall make restitution to its owner.

13 "If it is all torn to pieces, let him bring it as evidence; he shall not make restitution for what has been torn to pieces.

14 ¶ "If a man [1]borrows *anything* from his neighbor, and it is injured or dies while its owner is not with it, he shall make full restitution.

15 "If its owner is with it, he shall not make restitution; if it is hired, it came for its hire.

Sundry Laws

16 ¶ "[a]If a man seduces a virgin who is not engaged, and lies with her, he must pay a dowry for her *to be* his wife.

17 "If her father absolutely refuses to give her to him, he shall [1]pay money equal to the [a]dowry for virgins.

18 ¶ "You shall not allow a [a]sorceress to live.

19 ¶ "[a]Whoever lies with an animal shall surely be put to death.

20 ¶ "[a]He who sacrifices to [1]any god, other than to the LORD alone, shall be [2]utterly destroyed.

21 ¶ "[a]You shall not wrong a stranger or oppress him, for you were strangers in the land of Egypt.

22 "[a]You shall not afflict any widow or orphan.

23 "If you afflict him at all, *and* [a]if he does cry out to Me, [b]I will surely hear his cry;

24 and My anger will be kindled, and I will kill you with the sword, [a]and your wives shall become widows and your children fatherless.

25 ¶ "[a]If you lend money to My people, to the poor [1]among you, you are not to [2]act as a creditor to him; you shall not [3]charge him [b]interest.

26 "If you ever take your neighbor's cloak [a]as a pledge, you are to return it to him before the sun sets,

27 for that is his only covering; it is his cloak for his [1]body. What else shall he sleep in? And it shall come about that [a]when he cries out to Me, I will hear *him,* for [b]I am gracious.

28 ¶ "You shall not [1a]curse God, [b]nor curse a ruler of your people.

29 ¶ "[a]You shall not delay *the offering from* [1]your harvest and your vintage. [b]The firstborn of your sons you shall give to Me.

30 "[a]You shall do the same with your oxen *and* with your sheep. It shall be with its mother seven days; [b]on the eighth day you shall give it to Me.

31 ¶ "[a]You shall be holy men to Me, therefore [b]you shall not eat *any* flesh torn to pieces in the field; you shall throw it to the dogs.

Sundry Laws

23 "[a]You shall not bear a false report; do not join your hand with a wicked man to be a [b]malicious witness.

2 "You shall not follow [1]the masses in doing evil, nor shall you [2]testify in a dispute so as to turn aside after [1]a multitude in order to [a]pervert *justice;*

3 [a]nor shall you [1]be partial to a poor man in his dispute.

4 ¶ "[a]If you meet your enemy's ox or his donkey wandering away, you shall surely return it to him.

5 "[a]If you see the donkey of one who hates you lying *helpless* under its load, you shall refrain from leaving it to him, you shall surely release *it* with him.

6 ¶ "[a]You shall not pervert the justice *due* to your needy *brother* in his dispute.

7 "[a]Keep far from a false charge, and [b]do not kill the innocent or the righteous, for [c]I will not acquit the guilty.

8 ¶ "[a]You shall not take a bribe, for a bribe blinds the clear-sighted and [1]subverts the cause of the just.

9 ¶ "[a]You shall not oppress a [1]stranger, since you yourselves know the [2]feelings of a [1]stranger, for you *also* were [1]strangers in the land of Egypt.

The Sabbath and Land

10 ¶ "[a]You shall sow your land for six years and gather in its yield,

11 but *on* the seventh year you shall let it [1]rest and lie fallow, so that the needy of your people may eat; and whatever they leave the beast of the field may eat. You are to do the same with your vineyard *and* your olive grove.

12 ¶ "[a]Six days you are to do your work, but on the seventh day you shall cease *from labor* so that your ox and your donkey may rest, and the son of your female slave, as well as [1]your stranger, may refresh themselves.

13 "Now [a]concerning everything which I have said to you, be on your guard; and [b]do not mention the name of

11 [1]Lit *whether* [2]Lit *stretched his hand* [a]Heb 6:16
14 [1]Lit *asks*
16 [a]Deut 22:28
17 [1]Lit *weigh out silver* [a]Gen 34:12; 1 Sam 18:25
18 [a]Lev 19:31; Deut 18:10; 1 Sam 28:3; Jer 27:9
19 [a]Lev 18:23; Deut 27:21
20 [1]Lit *the gods* [2]Lit *put under the ban* [a]Ex 32:8; Lev 17:7; Num 25:2; Deut 17:2; 1 Kin 18:40; 2 Kin 10:25
21 [a]Ex 23:9; Lev 19:33; Deut 1:16; Zech 7:10
22 [a]Deut 24:17; Prov 23:10; Jer 7:6
23 [a]Deut 15:9; Job 35:9; Luke 18:7 [b]Deut 10:18; Job 34:28; Ps 10:14; James 5:4
24 [a]Ps 109:2
25 [1]Lit *with* [2]Lit *be* [3]Lit *lay upon* [a]Lev 25:35-37; Deut 15:7-11 [b]Deut 23:19; Neh 5:7; Ps 15:5; Ezek 18:8
26 [a]Deut 24:6; Job 24:3; Prov 20:16; Amos 2:8
27 [1]Lit *skin* [a]Ex 22:23 [b]Ex 34:6
28 [1]Or *revile* [a]Lev 24:15 [b]Eccl 10:20; Acts 23:5
29 [1]Lit *your fullness and your tears* [a]Ex 23:16; Deut 26:2-11; Prov 3:9 [b]Ex 13:2
30 [a]Deut 15:19; Lev 22:27 [b]Gen 17:12; Lev 12:3
31 [a]Ex 19:6; Lev 11:44 [b]Lev 7:24; Ezek 4:14
23:1 [a]Ex 20:16; Lev 19:11f; Deut 5:20; Ps 101:5; Prov 10:18 [b]Deut 19:16-21; Ps 35:11; Prov 19:5; Acts 6:11
2 [1]Lit *many men* [2]Or *answer* [a]Deut 16:19
3 [1]Lit *honor* [a]Ex 23:6; Lev 19:15; Deut 1:17
4 [a]Deut 22:1-4
5 [a]Deut 22:4
6 [a]Ex 23:2; Lev 19:15
7 [a]Ex 20:16; Ps 119:29; Eph 4:25 [b]Ex 20:13; Deut 27:25 [c]Ex 34:7; Deut 25:1; Rom 1:18
8 [1]Or *distorts the words* [a]Deut 10:17; Prov 15:27; Is 5:22
9 [1]Or *sojourner(s)* [2]Lit *soul* [a]Ex 22:21; Lev 19:33f; Deut 24:17f
10 [a]Lev 25:1-7
11 [1]Lit *drop*
12 [1]Lit *the sojourner* [a]Ex 20:8-11; Lev 23:3; Deut 5:13f **13** [a]Deut 4:9; 1 Tim 4:16 [b]Josh 23:7; Ps 16:4; Hos 2:17

other gods, nor let *them* be heard [1]from
your mouth.

Three National Feasts

14 ¶ "[a]Three times a year you shall
celebrate a feast to Me.
15 "You shall observe [a]the Feast of Unleavened Bread; for seven days you are to
eat unleavened bread, as I commanded
you, at the appointed time in the [b]month
Abib, for in it you came out of Egypt. And
[1c]none shall appear before Me empty-
handed.
16 "Also *you shall observe* [a]the Feast of
the Harvest *of* the first fruits of your labors *from* what you sow in the field; also
the Feast of the Ingathering at the end of
the year [b]when you gather in *the fruit of*
your labors from the field.
17 "[a]Three times a year all your males
shall appear before the Lord [1]GOD.
18 ¶ "[a]You shall not offer the blood of
My sacrifice with leavened bread; [b]nor is
the fat of My [1]feast to remain overnight
until morning.
19 ¶ "You shall bring [a]the choice first
fruits of your soil into the house of the
LORD your God.
¶ "[b]You are not to boil a young goat in
the milk of its mother.

Conquest of the Land

20 ¶ "Behold, I am going to send [a]an
angel before you to guard you along the
way and [b]to bring you into the place
which I have prepared.
21 "Be on your guard before him and
obey his voice; [a]do not be rebellious toward him, for he will not pardon your
transgression, since [b]My name is in him.
22 "But if you truly obey his voice and
do all that I say, then [a]I will be an enemy
to your enemies and an adversary to your
adversaries.
23 "[a]For My angel will go before you
and bring you in to *the land of* the Amorites, the Hittites, the Perizzites, the Canaanites, the Hivites and the Jebusites;
and I will completely destroy them.
24 "[a]You shall not worship their gods,
nor serve them, nor do according to their
deeds; [b]but you shall utterly overthrow
them and break their [c]*sacred* pillars in
pieces.
25 "[a]But you shall serve the LORD your
God, [1]and He will bless your bread and
your water; and [b]I will remove sickness
from your midst.
26 "There shall be no one miscarrying
or [a]barren in your land; [b]I will fulfill the
number of your days.
27 "I will [a]send My terror ahead of
you, and [b]throw into confusion all the
people among whom you come, and I will
[c]make all your enemies turn *their* backs
to you.
28 "I will send [a]hornets ahead of you
so that they will [b]drive out the Hivites,
the Canaanites, and the Hittites before
you.
29 "[a]I will not drive them out before
you in a single year, that the land may not
become desolate and the beasts of the
field become too numerous for you.
30 "I will drive them out before you
[a]little by little, until you become fruitful
and take possession of the land.
31 "[a]I will fix your boundary from the
[1]Red Sea to the sea of the Philistines, and
from the wilderness to the River *Euphrates;* [b]for I will deliver the inhabitants of
the land into your hand, and you will
[c]drive them out before you.
32 "[a]You shall [1]make no covenant
with them [b]or with their gods.
33 "[a]They shall not live in your land,
because they will make you sin against
Me; for *if* you serve their gods, [b]it will
surely be a snare to you."

People Affirm Their Covenant with God

24 Then He said to Moses, "[a]Come
up to the LORD, you and Aaron,
[b]Nadab and Abihu and [c]seventy of the
elders of Israel, and you shall worship at
a distance.
2 "Moses alone, however, shall come
near to the LORD, but they shall not come
near, nor shall the people come up with
him."
3 ¶ Then Moses came and recounted
to the people all the words of the LORD
and all the [1]ordinances; and all the people answered with one voice and said,
"[a]All the words which the LORD has spoken we will do!"
4 [a]Moses wrote down all the words
of the LORD. Then he arose early in the
morning, and built an [b]altar [1]at the foot
of the mountain with twelve pillars for
the twelve tribes of Israel.
5 He sent young men of the sons of
Israel, [a]and they offered burnt offerings
and sacrificed young bulls as peace offerings to the LORD.
6 [a]Moses took half of the blood and
put *it* in basins, and the *other* half of the
blood he sprinkled on the altar.
7 Then he took [a]the book of the covenant and read *it* in the hearing of the
people; and they said, "[b]All that the
LORD has spoken we will do, and we will
be obedient!"
8 So [a]Moses took the blood and
sprinkled *it* on the people, and said, "Behold [b]the blood of the covenant, which

13 [1]Lit *on*
14 [a]Ex 23:17; Deut 16:16
15 [1]Lit *they...not* [a]Ex 12:14-20; Lev 23:6-8; Num 28:16-25 [b]Ex 12:2 [c]Ex 22:29
16 [a]Ex 34:22; Lev 23:10; Num 28:26 [b]Lev 23:39
17 [1]Heb *YHWH,* usually rendered *LORD* [a]Ex 23:14; Deut 16:16
18 [1]Or *festival* [a]Ex 34:25; Lev 2:11 [b]Ex 12:10; Lev 7:15; Deut 16:4
19 [a]Ex 22:29; Deut 26:2; Neh 10:35; Prov 3:9 [b]Deut 14:21
20 [a]Ex 3:2 [b]Ex 15:16
21 [a]Deut 9:7; Ps 78:40 [b]Ex 3:14
22 [a]Gen 12:3; Num 24:9; Deut 30:7
23 [a]Ex 23:20; Josh 24:8
24 [a]Ex 20:5; Deut 12:30f [b]Num 33:52; Deut 7:5; 2 Kin 18:4 [c]Ex 34:13; Lev 26:1; 2 Kin 3:2
25 [1]Or *that He may bless* [a]Lev 26:3-13; Deut 6:13; Josh 22:5; 1 Sam 12:20; Matt 4:10 [b]Ex 15:26; Deut 7:15
26 [a]Deut 7:14 [b]Deut 4:40; Job 5:26
27 [a]Gen 35:5; Ex 15:16; Deut 2:25; Josh 2:9 [b]Deut 7:23 [c]Ps 18:40
28 [a]Deut 7:20; Josh 24:12 [b]Ex 33:2
29 [a]Deut 7:22
30 [a]Deut 7:22
31 [1]Lit *Sea of Reeds* [a]Gen 15:18; Deut 1:7 [b]Deut 2:36; Josh 21:44 [c]Josh 24:12
32 [1]Lit *cut* [a]Ex 34:12; Deut 7:2 [b]Ex 23:13
33 [a]Deut 7:1-5 [b]Ex 34:12; Deut 12:30; Josh 23:13; Judg 2:3; Ps 106:36
24:1 [a]Ex 19:24 [b]Ex 6:23; Lev 10:1 [c]Num 11:16
3 [1]Or *judgments* [a]Ex 19:8; Deut 5:27
4 [1]Lit *under* [a]Ex 17:14; Deut 31:9 [b]Ex 17:15
5 [a]Ex 18:12
6 [a]Heb 9:18
7 [a]Ex 24:4; Heb 9:19 [b]Ex 24:3
8 [a]Heb 9:19 [b]Zech 9:11; Matt 26:28; Mark 14:24; Luke 22:20; 1 Cor 11:25; Heb 13:20

the LORD has [1]made with you [2]in accordance with all these words."

9 ¶ Then Moses went up [1]with Aaron, [a]Nadab and Abihu, and seventy of the elders of Israel,

10 and [a]they saw the God of Israel; and under His feet [1b]there appeared to be a pavement of sapphire, [2]as clear as the sky itself.

11 Yet He did not stretch out His hand against the nobles of the sons of Israel; and [a]they saw God, and they ate and drank.

12 ¶ Now the LORD said to Moses, "Come up to Me on the mountain and [1]remain there, and [a]I will give you the stone tablets [2]with the law and the commandment which I have written for their instruction."

13 So Moses arose [1]with [a]Joshua his [2]servant, and Moses went up to [b]the mountain of God.

14 But to the elders he said, "[a]Wait here for us until we return to you. And behold, [b]Aaron and Hur are with you; whoever [1]has a legal matter, let him approach them."

15 Then Moses went up to the mountain, and [a]the cloud covered the mountain.

16 [a]The glory of the LORD [1]rested on Mount Sinai, and the cloud covered it for six days; and on the seventh day He [b]called to Moses from the midst of the cloud.

17 [a]And to the eyes of the sons of Israel the appearance of the glory of the LORD was like a [b]consuming fire on the mountain top.

18 Moses entered the midst of the cloud [1]as he went up to the mountain; and Moses was on the mountain [a]forty days and forty nights.

Offerings for the Sanctuary

25 Then the LORD spoke to Moses, saying,

2 "[a]Tell the sons of Israel to [1]raise a [2]contribution for Me; [b]from every man whose heart moves him you shall [1]raise My [2]contribution.

3 "This is the [1]contribution which you are to [2]raise from them: gold, silver and bronze,

4 [1a]blue, purple and scarlet *material,* fine linen, goat *hair,*

5 rams' skins dyed red, porpoise skins, acacia wood,

6 [a]oil for lighting, [b]spices for the anointing oil and for the fragrant incense,

7 onyx stones and setting stones for the [a]ephod and for the [1b]breastpiece.

8 "Let them [a]construct a sanctuary for Me, [b]that I may dwell among them.

9 "[a]According to all that I am going to show you, *as* the pattern of the tabernacle and the pattern of all its furniture, just so you shall construct *it.*

Ark of the Covenant

10 ¶ "[a]They shall construct an ark of acacia wood two and a half [1]cubits [2]long, and one and a half cubits [3]wide, and one and a half cubits [4]high.

11 "You shall [a]overlay it with pure gold, inside and out you shall overlay it, and you shall make a gold molding [1]around it.

12 "You shall cast four gold rings for it and [1]fasten them on its four feet, and two rings shall be on one side of it and two rings on the other side of it.

13 "You shall make poles of acacia wood and overlay them with gold.

14 "You shall put the poles into the rings on the sides of the ark, to carry the ark with them.

15 "The [a]poles shall [1]remain in the rings of the ark; they shall not be removed from it.

16 "You shall [a]put into the ark the testimony which I shall give you.

17 ¶ "You shall [a]make a [1]mercy seat of pure gold, two and a half [2]cubits [3]long and one and a half cubits [4]wide.

18 "You shall make two cherubim of gold, make them of hammered work [1]at the two ends of the mercy seat.

19 "Make one cherub [1]at one end and one cherub [1]at the other end; you shall make the cherubim *of one piece* with the mercy seat at its two ends.

20 "[a]The cherubim shall have *their* wings spread upward, covering the mercy seat with their wings and [1]facing one another; the faces of the cherubim are to be *turned* toward the mercy seat.

21 "[a]You shall put the mercy seat [1]on top of the ark, and [b]in the ark you shall put the testimony which I will give to you.

22 "[a]There I will meet with you; and from above the mercy seat, from [b]between the two cherubim which are upon the ark of the testimony, I will speak to you about all that I will give you in commandment for the sons of Israel.

The Table of Showbread

23 ¶ "[a]You shall make a table of acacia wood, two cubits [1]long and one cubit [2]wide and one and a half cubits [3]high.

24 "You shall overlay it with pure gold and make a gold [a]border around it.

25 "You shall make for it a rim of a handbreadth around *it;* and you shall

---

8 [1]Lit *cut* [2]Lit *on all*
9 [1]Lit *and* [a]Ex 24:1
10 [1]Lit *like a pavement* [2]Lit *and as* [a]Ex 24:11; Num 12:8; Is 6:5; John 1:18 [b]Ezek 1:26; Rev 4:3
11 [a]Gen 16:13; Ex 24:10
12 [1]Lit *be* [2]Lit *and* [a]Ex 31:18; Deut 5:22
13 [1]Lit *and* [2]Or *minister* [a]Ex 17:9-14 [b]Ex 3:1
14 [1]Lit *is a master of matters* [a]Gen 22:5 [b]Ex 17:10
15 [a]Ex 19:9
16 [1]Lit *dwelt* [a]Ex 16:10; Num 14:10 [b]Ps 99:7
17 [a]Ex 3:2; Ezek 1:28 [b]Deut 4:24; Heb 12:29
18 [1]Lit *and* [a]Ex 34:28; Deut 9:9
25:2 [1]Lit *take* [2]Or *heave offering* [a]Ex 35:4-9 [b]Ex 35:21; 1 Chr 29:3; Ezra 2:68; 2 Cor 8:11
3 [1]Or *heave offering* [2]Lit *take*
4 [1]Or *violet* [a]Ex 28:5
6 [a]Ex 27:20 [b]Ex 30:23f
7 [1]Or *pouch* [a]Ex 28:4 [b]Ex 28:4
8 [a]Ex 36:1-5 [b]Ex 29:45; Num 5:3; Deut 12:11; 1 Kin 6:13; 2 Cor 6:16; Rev 21:3
9 [a]Ex 25:40; Acts 7:44; Heb 8:2
10 [1]I.e. One cubit equals approx 18 in. [2]Lit *its length* [3]Lit *its width* [4]Lit *its height* [a]Ex 37:1-9; Deut 10:3; Heb 9:4
11 [1]Lit *on it round about* [a]Heb 9:4
12 [1]Or *put*
15 [1]Lit *be* [a]1 Kin 8:8
16 [a]Ex 40:20; Deut 10:2; 1 Kin 8:9; Heb 9:4
17 [1]Lit *propitiatory,* and so through v 22 [2]I.e. One cubit equals approx 18 in. [3]Lit *its length* [4]Lit *its width* [a]Ex 37:6
18 [1]Lit *from*
19 [1]Lit *from*
20 [1]Lit *their faces to* [a]1 Kin 8:7; 1 Chr 28:18; Heb 9:5
21 [1]Lit *above, upon* [a]Ex 26:34 [b]Ex 25:16
22 [a]Ex 29:42; Lev 16:2; Num 17:4 [b]Num 7:89; 1 Sam 4:4; 2 Sam 6:2; 2 Kin 19:15; Ps 80:1; Is 37:16
23 [1]Lit *its length* [2]Lit *its width* [3]Lit *its height* [a]Ex 37:10-16 **24** [a]Ex 25:11

make a gold border for the rim around it.
26 "You shall make four gold rings for it
and put rings on the four corners which
are on its four feet.
27 "The rings shall be close to the rim
as holders for the poles to carry the table.
28 "You shall make the poles of acacia
wood and overlay them with gold, so that
with them the table may be carried.
29 "You shall make its [1a]dishes and its
pans and its jars and its [2]bowls with
which to pour drink offerings; you shall
make them of pure gold.
30 "You shall set [a]the bread of the
[1]Presence on the table before Me [2]at all
times.

The Golden Lampstand

31 ¶ "[a]Then you shall make a lampstand of pure gold. The lampstand *and* its
base and its shaft are to be made of hammered work; its cups, its [1]bulbs and its
flowers shall be *of one piece* with it.
32 "[a]Six branches shall go out from its
sides; three branches of the lampstand
from its one side and three branches of
the lampstand from its [1]other side.
33 "[a]Three cups *shall be* shaped like
almond *blossoms* in the one branch, a
[1]bulb and a flower, and three cups
shaped like almond *blossoms* in the [2]oth-
er branch, a [1]bulb and a flower—so for
six branches going out from the lampstand;
34 and [a]in the lampstand four cups
shaped like almond *blossoms,* its [1]bulbs
and its flowers.
35 "[a]A [1]bulb shall be under the *first*
pair of branches *coming* out of it, and a
[1]bulb under the *second* pair of branches
coming out of it, and a [1]bulb under the
third pair of branches *coming* out of it, for
the six branches coming out of the lampstand.
36 "[a]Their [1]bulbs and their branches
shall be of one piece with it; all of it shall
be one piece of hammered work of pure
gold.
37 "Then you shall make its lamps sev-
en *in number;* and [a]they shall [1]mount
its lamps so as to shed light on the space
in front of it.
38 "Its snuffers and [1]their trays *shall be*
of pure gold.
39 "It shall be made from a talent of
pure gold, with all these utensils.
40 "[a]See that you make *them* [b]after
the pattern for them, which was shown
to you on the mountain.

Curtains of Linen

26 "[a]Moreover you shall make the
tabernacle with ten curtains of
fine twisted linen and [1]blue and purple
and scarlet *material;* you shall make them
with cherubim, the work of a skillful
workman.
2 "The length of each curtain shall be
twenty-eight [1]cubits, and the width of
each curtain four [1]cubits; all the curtains
shall have [2]the same measurements.
3 "Five curtains shall be [1]joined to
one another, and *the other* five curtains
shall be [1]joined to one another.
4 "You shall make loops of [1]blue on
the edge of the [2]outermost curtain in the
first set, and likewise you shall make
them on the edge of the curtain that is
outermost in the second [3]set.
5 "You shall make fifty loops in the
one curtain, and you shall make fifty
loops on the [1]edge of the curtain that is
in the second [2]set; the loops shall be
opposite each other.
6 "You shall make fifty clasps of gold,
and [1]join the curtains to one another
with the clasps so that the [2]tabernacle
will be a unit.

Curtains of Goats' Hair

7 ¶ "Then [a]you shall make curtains
of goats' *hair* for a tent over the tabernacle; you shall make eleven curtains in all.
8 "The length of each curtain *shall be*
thirty [1]cubits, and the width of each curtain four cubits; the eleven curtains shall
have [2]the same measurements.
9 "You shall [1]join five curtains by
themselves and the *other* six curtains by
themselves, and you shall double over the
sixth curtain [2]at the front of the tent.
10 "You shall make fifty loops on the
edge of the [1]curtain that is outermost in
the *first* [2]set, and fifty loops on the edge
of the curtain *that is outermost in* the
second [2]set.
11 ¶ "You shall make fifty clasps of
[1]bronze, and you shall put the clasps into
the loops and [2]join the tent together so
that it will be [3]a unit.
12 "The [1]overlapping part that is left
over in the curtains of the tent, the half
curtain that is left over, shall lap over the
back of the tabernacle.
13 "The cubit on one side and the cubit
on the other, of what is left over in the
length of the curtains of the tent, shall lap
over the sides of the tabernacle on one
side and on the other, to cover it.
14 "[a]You shall make a covering for the
tent of rams' skins [1]dyed red and a covering of porpoise skins above.

Boards and Sockets

15 ¶ "Then you shall make [a]the
boards for the tabernacle of acacia wood,
standing upright.
16 "Ten cubits *shall be* the length of

29 [1]Or *platters* [2]Lit *libation bowls* [a]Ex 37:16; Num 4:7
30 [1]Lit *Face* [2]Or *continually* [a]Ex 39:36; 40:23; Lev 24:5-9
31 [1]Or *calyx* [a]Ex 37:17-24; 1 Kin 7:49; Zech 4:2
32 [1]Lit *second* [a]Ex 37:18
33 [1]Or *calyx* [2]Lit *one branch* [a]Ex 37:19
34 [1]Or *calyxes* [a]Ex 37:20
35 [1]Or *calyx* [a]Ex 37:21
36 [1]Or *calyxes* [a]Ex 37:22
37 [1]Lit *raise up* [a]Num 8:2
38 [1]Lit *its snuff dishes*
40 [a]Heb 8:5 [b]Ex 25:9; 26:30; Num 8:4; Acts 7:44
26:1 [1]Or *violet* [a]Ex 36:8-19
2 [1]I.e. One cubit equals approx 18 in. [2]Lit *one measure*
3 [1]Or *coupled*
4 [1]Or *violet* [2]Lit *one curtain from the end in the coupling* [3]Lit *coupling*
5 [1]Lit *end* [2]Lit *coupling*
6 [1]Or *couple* [2]Or *dwelling place,* and so throughout the ch
7 [a]Ex 36:14
8 [1]I.e. One cubit equals approx 18 in. [2]Lit *one measure*
9 [1]Or *couple* [2]Lit *toward the front of the face of the tent*
10 [1]Lit *one curtain* [2]Lit *coupling*
11 [1]Or *copper* [2]Or *couple* [3]Lit *one*
12 [1]Lit *excess*
14 [1]Or *tanned* [a]Ex 36:19
15 [a]Ex 36:20-34

[1]each board and one and a half cubits the width of each board.

17 "*There shall be* two tenons for each board, [1]fitted to one another; thus you shall do for all the boards of the tabernacle.

18 "You shall make the boards for the tabernacle: twenty boards [1]for the south side.

19 "You shall make forty [1][a]sockets of silver under the twenty boards, two [1]sockets under one board for its two tenons and two [1]sockets under another board for its two tenons;

20 and for the second side of the tabernacle, on the north side, twenty boards,

21 and their forty [1]sockets of silver; two [1]sockets under one board and two [1]sockets under another board.

22 "For the [1]rear of the tabernacle, to the west, you shall make six boards.

23 "You shall make two boards for the corners of the tabernacle at the [1]rear.

24 "They shall be double beneath, and together they shall be complete [1]to its top [2]to the first ring; thus it shall be with both of them: they shall form the two corners.

25 "There shall be eight boards with their [1]sockets of silver, sixteen [1]sockets; two [1]sockets under one board and two [1]sockets under another board.

26 ¶ "Then you shall make [a]bars of acacia wood, five for the boards of one side of the tabernacle,

27 and five bars for the boards of the [1]other side of the tabernacle, and five bars for the boards of the side of the tabernacle for the [2]rear *side* to the west.

28 "The middle bar in the [1]center of the boards shall pass through from end to end.

29 "You shall overlay the boards with gold and make their rings of gold *as* holders for the bars; and you shall overlay the bars with gold.

30 "Then you shall erect the tabernacle [a]according to its plan which you have been shown in the mountain.

The Veil and Screen

31 ¶ "You shall make [a]a veil of [1]blue and purple and scarlet *material* and fine twisted linen; it shall be made with cherubim, the work of a skillful workman.

32 "You shall [1]hang it on four pillars of acacia overlaid with gold, their hooks *also being of* gold, on four [2]sockets of silver.

33 "You shall [1]hang up the veil under the clasps, and shall bring in [a]the ark of the testimony there within the veil; and the veil shall [2]serve for you as a partition [b]between the holy place and the holy of holies.

34 "[a]You shall put the mercy seat on the ark of the testimony in the holy of holies.

35 "[a]You shall set the table outside the veil, and the [b]lampstand opposite the table on the side of the tabernacle toward the south; and you shall put the table on the north side.

36 ¶ "[a]You shall make a screen for the doorway of the tent of [1]blue and purple and scarlet *material* and fine twisted linen, the work of a [2]weaver.

37 "[a]You shall make five pillars of acacia for the screen and overlay them with gold, their hooks *also being of* gold; and you shall cast five [1]sockets of [2]bronze for them.

The Bronze Altar

27 "And you shall make [a]the altar of acacia wood, five [1]cubits long and five cubits wide; the altar shall be square, and its height shall be three cubits.

2 "You shall make [a]its horns on its four corners; its horns shall be of one piece with it, and you shall overlay it with [1]bronze.

3 "You shall make its pails for removing its ashes, and its shovels and its basins and its forks and its firepans; you shall make all its utensils of bronze.

4 "You shall make for it a grating of network of bronze, and on the net you shall make four bronze rings [1]at its four corners.

5 "You shall put it beneath, under the ledge of the altar, so that the net will reach halfway up the altar.

6 "You shall make poles for the altar, poles of acacia wood, and overlay them with bronze.

7 "Its poles shall be inserted into the rings, so that the poles shall be on the two sides of the altar [a]when it is carried.

8 "You shall make it hollow with planks; [a]as it was shown to you in the mountain, so they shall make *it*.

Court of the Tabernacle

9 ¶ "You shall make [a]the court of the [1]tabernacle. [2]On the south side *there shall be* hangings for the court of fine twisted linen one hundred cubits long for one side;

10 and its pillars *shall be* twenty, with their twenty [1]sockets of bronze; the hooks of the pillars and their [2]bands *shall be* of silver.

11 "Likewise for the north side in length *there shall be* hangings one hundred *cubits* long, and its twenty pillars with their twenty [1]sockets of bronze; the

16 [1]Lit *the*
17 [1]Lit *bound*
18 [1]Lit *toward the side of the Negev to the south*
19 [1]Or *bases* [a]Ex 38:27
21 [1]Or *bases*
22 [1]Lit *extreme parts*
23 [1]Lit *extreme parts*
24 [1]Or *at its head* [2]Or *with reference to*
25 [1]Or *bases*
26 [a]Ex 36:31
27 [1]Lit *second* [2]Lit *extreme parts*
28 [1]Lit *midst*
30 [a]Ex 25:9,40; Acts 7:44; Heb 8:5
31 [1]Or *violet* [a]Ex 36:35,36; 2 Chr 3:14; Matt 27:51; Heb 9:3
32 [1]Lit *put* [2]Or *bases*
33 [1]Lit *put* [2]Lit *separate for you between* [a]Ex 25:16; 40:21 [b]Heb 9:2f
34 [a]Ex 25:21; 40:20; Lev 16:2
35 [a]Ex 40:22 [b]Ex 40:24
36 [1]Or *violet* [2]Lit *variegator;* i.e. a weaver in colors [a]Ex 36:37
37 [1]Or *bases* [2]Or *copper* [a]Ex 36:38
27:1 [1]I.e. One cubit equals approx 18 in. [a]Ex 38:1-7
2 [1]Or *copper,* and so for *bronze* throughout the ch [a]Ps 118:27
4 [1]Lit *on*
7 [a]Num 4:15
8 [a]Ex 25:40; 26:30; Acts 7:44; Heb 8:5
9 [1]Or *dwelling place* [2]Lit *For the side of the Negev to the south* [a]Ex 38:9-20
10 [1]Or *bases* [2]Or *fillets, rings*
11 [1]Or *bases*

hooks of the pillars and their bands *shall be* of silver.

12 "*For* the width of the court on the west side *shall be* hangings of fifty cubits *with* their ten pillars and their ten [1]sockets.

13 "The width of the court on the [1]east side *shall be* fifty cubits.

14 "The hangings for the *one* [1]side *of the gate shall be* fifteen cubits *with* their three pillars and their three [2]sockets.

15 "And for the [1]other [2]side *shall be* hangings of fifteen cubits *with* their three pillars and their three [3]sockets.

16 "For the gate of the court *there shall be* a screen of twenty cubits, of [1]blue and purple and scarlet *material* and fine twisted linen, the work of a [2]weaver, *with* their four pillars and their four [3]sockets.

17 "All the pillars around the court shall be furnished with silver bands *with* their hooks of silver and their [1]sockets of bronze.

18 "The length of the court *shall be* one hundred cubits, and the width fifty throughout, and the height five cubits of fine twisted linen, and their [1]sockets of bronze.

19 "All the utensils of the tabernacle *used* in all its service, and all its pegs, and all the pegs of the court, *shall be* of bronze.

20 ¶ "You shall charge the sons of Israel, that they bring you [a]clear oil of beaten olives for the [1]light, to make a lamp [2]burn continually.

21 "In the [a]tent of meeting, outside [b]the veil which is before the testimony, [c]Aaron and his sons shall keep it in order from evening to morning before the LORD; *it shall be* a perpetual [d]statute throughout their generations [1]for the sons of Israel.

Garments of the Priests

28 "Then [a]bring near to yourself Aaron your brother, and his sons with him, from among the sons of Israel, to minister as priest to Me—Aaron, [b]Nadab and Abihu, Eleazar and Ithamar, Aaron's sons.

2 "You shall make [a]holy garments for Aaron your brother, for glory and for beauty.

3 "You shall speak to all the [1a]skillful persons [b]whom I have endowed with [2]the spirit of wisdom, that they make Aaron's garments to consecrate him, that he may minister as priest to Me.

4 "These are the garments which they shall make: a [1a]breastpiece and an ephod and a robe and a tunic of checkered work, a turban and a sash, and they shall make holy garments for Aaron your brother and his sons, that he may minister as priest to Me.

5 "They shall take [a]the gold and the [1]blue and the purple and the scarlet *material* and the fine linen.

6 ¶ "They shall also make [a]the ephod of gold, of [1]blue and purple *and* scarlet *material* and fine twisted linen, the work of the skillful workman.

7 "It shall have two shoulder pieces joined to its two ends, that it may be joined.

8 "The skillfully woven band, which is on it, shall be like its workmanship, [1]of the same material: of gold, of [2]blue and purple and scarlet *material* and fine twisted linen.

9 "You shall take two onyx stones and engrave on them the names of the sons of Israel,

10 six of their names on the one stone and the names of the remaining six on the [1]other stone, according to their birth.

11 "[1]As a jeweler engraves a signet, you shall engrave the two stones according to the names of the sons of Israel; you shall [2]set them in filigree *settings* of gold.

12 "You shall put the two stones on the shoulder pieces of the ephod, *as* stones of memorial for the sons of Israel, and Aaron shall [a]bear their names before the LORD on his two shoulders [b]for a memorial.

13 "[a]You shall make filigree *settings* of gold,

14 and two chains of pure gold; you shall make them of twisted cordage work, and you shall put the corded chains on the filigree *settings*.

15 ¶ "[a]You shall make a [1]breastpiece of judgment, the work of a skillful workman; like the work of the ephod you shall make it: of gold, of [2]blue and purple and scarlet *material* and fine twisted linen you shall make it.

16 "It shall be square *and* folded double, a span [1]in length and a span [1]in width.

17 "You shall [1]mount on it four rows of stones; the first row *shall be* a row of ruby, topaz and emerald;

18 and the second row a turquoise, a sapphire and a diamond;

19 and the third row a jacinth, an agate and an amethyst;

20 and the fourth row a beryl and an onyx and a jasper; they shall be [1]set in gold filigree.

21 "The stones shall be according to the names of the sons of Israel: twelve, according to their names; they shall be *like* the engravings of a seal, each [a]according to his name for the twelve tribes.

---

12 [1]Or *bases*

13 [1]Lit *east side eastward*

14 [1]Lit *shoulder* [2]Or *bases*

15 [1]Lit *second* [2]Lit *shoulder* [3]Or *bases*

16 [1]Or *violet* [2]Lit *variegator;* i.e. a weaver in colors [3]Or *bases*

17 [1]Or *bases*

18 [1]Or *bases*

20 [1]Or *luminary* [2]Lit *ascend* [a]Ex 35:8,28; Lev 24:1-4

21 [1]Lit *from* [a]Ex 25:22; 29:42; 30:36 [b]Ex 26:31,33 [c]Ex 30:8; 1 Sam 3:3; 2 Chr 13:11 [d]Ex 28:43; 29:9; Lev 3:17; 16:34; Num 18:23; 19:21; 1 Sam 30:25

28:1 [a]Num 18:7; Ps 99:6; Heb 5:1,4 [b]Ex 24:1,9

2 [a]Ex 29:5,29; 31:10; 39:1-31; Lev 8:7-9,30

3 [1]Lit *wise of heart* [2]I.e. artistic skill [a]Ex 31:6; 35:25, 31-35; 36:1 [b]Ex 31:3; Is 11:2; 1 Cor 12:7-11; Eph 1:17

4 [1]Or *pouch* [a]Ex 28:15-43

5 [1]Or *violet* [a]Ex 25:3

6 [1]Or *violet* [a]Ex 39:2-7; Lev 8:7

8 [1]Lit *from it* [2]Or *violet*

10 [1]Lit *second*

11 [1]Lit *A work of a lapidary, engravings of a seal* [2]Lit *make them to be surrounded*

12 [a]Ex 28:29; 39:6f [b]Ex 39:7; Lev 24:7; Num 31:54; Josh 4:7; 1 Cor 11:24f

13 [a]Ex 39:16-18

15 [1]Or *pouch* [2]Or *violet* [a]Ex 39:8-21

16 [1]Lit *its*

17 [1]Lit *fill in a setting of stones, four rows of stones*

20 [1]Lit *interwoven with gold in their settings*

21 [a]Rev 7:4-8; 21:12

22 "You shall make on the [1]breastpiece chains of twisted cordage work in pure gold.

23 "You shall make on the breastpiece two rings of gold, and shall put the two rings on the two ends of the breastpiece.

24 "You shall put the two cords of gold on the two rings at the ends of the breastpiece.

25 "You shall put the *other* two ends of the two cords on the two filigree *settings,* and put them on the shoulder pieces of the ephod, at the front of it.

26 "You shall make two rings of gold and shall place them on the two ends of the breastpiece, on the edge of it, which is toward the inner side of the ephod.

27 "You shall make two rings of gold and put them on the bottom of the two shoulder pieces of the ephod, on the front of it close to the place where it is joined, above the skillfully woven band of the ephod.

28 "They shall bind the breastpiece by its rings to the rings of the ephod with a [1]blue cord, so that it will be on the skillfully woven band of the ephod, and that the breastpiece will not come loose from the ephod.

29 "Aaron shall carry the names of the sons of Israel in the breastpiece of judgment over his heart when he enters the holy place, for a memorial before the LORD continually.

30 "[a]You shall put in the breastpiece of judgment the [1b]Urim and the Thummim, and they shall be over Aaron's heart when he goes in before the LORD; and Aaron shall carry the judgment of the sons of Israel over his heart before the LORD continually.

31 ¶ "[a]You shall make the robe of the ephod all of [1]blue.

32 "There shall be an opening [1]at its top in the middle of it; around its opening there shall be a binding of woven work, as like the opening of a coat of mail, so that it will not be torn.

33 "You shall make on its hem pomegranates of blue and purple and scarlet *material,* all around on its hem, and bells of gold between them all around:

34 a golden bell and a pomegranate, a golden bell and a pomegranate, all around on the hem of the robe.

35 "It shall be on Aaron [1]when he ministers; and [2]its tinkling shall be heard when he enters and [3]leaves the holy place before the LORD, so that he will not die.

36 ¶ "You shall also make [a]a plate of pure gold and shall engrave on it, like the engravings of a seal, '[b]Holy to the LORD.'

37 "You shall [1]fasten it on a [2]blue cord, and it shall be on the turban; it shall be at the front of the turban.

38 "It shall be on Aaron's forehead, and Aaron shall [1a]take away the iniquity of the holy things which the sons of Israel consecrate, with regard to all their holy gifts; and it shall always be on his forehead, that [b]they may be accepted before the LORD.

39 ¶ "You shall weave [a]the tunic of checkered work of fine linen, and shall make a turban of fine linen, and you shall make a sash, the work of a [1]weaver.

40 ¶ "For Aaron's sons you shall make [a]tunics; you shall also make sashes for them, and you shall make [1b]caps for them, for glory and for beauty.

41 "You shall put them on Aaron your brother and on his sons with him; and you shall [a]anoint them and [1]ordain them and consecrate them, that they may serve Me as priests.

42 "You shall make for them [a]linen breeches to cover *their* bare flesh; they shall [1]reach from the loins even to the thighs.

43 "They shall be on Aaron and on his sons when they enter the tent of meeting, or [a]when they approach the altar to minister in the holy place, so that they do not incur [1]guilt and die. [b]It *shall be* a statute forever to him and to his [2]descendants after him.

Consecration of the Priests

29 "[a]Now this is [1]what you shall do to them to consecrate them to minister as priests to Me: take one young bull and two rams without blemish,

2 and [a]unleavened bread and unleavened cakes mixed with oil, and unleavened wafers [1]spread with oil; you shall make them of fine wheat flour.

3 "You shall put them in one basket, and present them in the basket along with the bull and the two rams.

4 "Then [a]you shall bring Aaron and his sons to the doorway of the tent of meeting and wash them with water.

5 "You shall take the garments, and put on Aaron the [a]tunic and [b]the robe of the ephod and [c]the ephod and [d]the [1]breastpiece, and gird him with the skillfully [e]woven band of the ephod;

6 and you shall set the [a]turban on his head and put [b]the holy crown on the turban.

7 "Then you shall take [a]the anointing oil and pour it on his head and anoint him.

8 "You shall bring his sons and put [a]tunics on them.

9 "You shall gird them with [a]sashes, Aaron and his sons, and bind [1]caps on

---

22 [1]Or *pouch,* and so through v 30

28 [1]Or *violet*

30 [1]I.e. lights and perfections [a]Lev 8:8 [b]Num 27:21; Deut 33:8; Ezra 2:63; Neh 7:65

31 [1]Or *violet* [a]Ex 39:22-26

32 [1]Or *for his head*

35 [1]Lit *for ministering* [2]Lit *its sound* [3]Lit *comes out* from

36 [a]Ex 39:30, 31; Lev 8:9 [b]Zech 14:20

37 [1]Lit *place* [2]Or *violet*

38 [1]Or *bear* [a]Lev 10:17; 22:16; Num 18:1 [b]Lev 1:4; 22:27; 23:11; Is 56:7

39 [1]Lit *variegator;* i.e. a weaver in colors [a]Ex 39:27-29

40 [1]Lit *headgear* [a]Ex 28:4; 39:27, 41 [b]Ex 29:9; 39:28; Lev 8:13; Ezek 44:18

41 [1]Lit *fill their hand* [a]Ex 29:7,9; 30:30; 40:15; Lev 8:1-36; 10:7

42 [1]Lit *be* [a]Ex 39:28; Lev 6:10; 16:4; Ezek 44:18

43 [1]Or *iniquity* [2]Lit *seed* [a]Ex 20:26 [b]Ex 27:21

29:1 [1]Lit *the thing which* [a]Lev 8:1-34

2 [1]Or *anointed* [a]Lev 2:4; 6:19-23

4 [a]Ex 40:12; Lev 8:6

5 [1]Or *pouch* [a]Ex 28:39; Lev 8:7 [b]Ex 28:31 [c]Ex 28:6 [d]Ex 28:15 [e]Ex 28:8

6 [a]Ex 28:4,39 [b]Ex 28:36,37; Lev 8:9

7 [a]Ex 30:25; Lev 8:12; 21:10; Num 35:25; Ps 133:2

8 [a]Ex 28:39,40; Lev 8:13

9 [1]Lit *headgear* [a]Ex 28:40

them, and they shall have [b]the priesthood by a perpetual statute. So you shall [2c]ordain Aaron and his sons.

The Sacrifices

10 ¶ "Then you shall bring the bull before the tent of meeting, and Aaron and his sons shall [a]lay their hands on the head of the bull.

11 "You shall slaughter the bull before the Lord at the doorway of the tent of meeting.

12 "You shall [a]take some of the blood of the bull and put *it* on [b]the horns of the altar with your finger; and you shall pour out all the blood at the base of the altar.

13 "You shall [a]take all the fat that covers the entrails and the [1]lobe of the liver, and the two kidneys and the fat that is on them, and offer them up in smoke on the altar.

14 "But [a]the flesh of the bull and its hide and its refuse, you shall burn with fire outside the camp; it is a sin offering.

15 ¶ "[a]You shall also take the one ram, and Aaron and his sons shall lay their hands on the head of the ram;

16 and you shall slaughter the ram and shall take its blood and sprinkle it around on the altar.

17 "Then you shall cut the ram into its pieces, and wash its entrails and its legs, and put *them* [1]with its pieces and [2]its head.

18 "You shall offer up in smoke the whole ram on the altar; it is a burnt offering to the Lord: [a]it is a soothing aroma, an offering by fire to the Lord.

19 ¶ "Then [a]you shall take the [1]other ram, and Aaron and his sons shall lay their hands on the head of the ram.

20 "You shall slaughter the ram, and take some of its blood and put *it* on the lobe of Aaron's right ear and on the lobes of his sons' right ears and on the thumbs of their right hands and on the big toes of their right feet, and sprinkle the *rest of the* blood around on the altar.

21 "Then you shall take some of the blood that is on the altar and some of the [a]anointing oil, and sprinkle *it* on Aaron and on his garments and on his sons and on his sons' garments with him; so he and his garments shall be consecrated, as well as his sons and his sons' garments with him.

22 ¶ "You shall also take the fat from the ram and the fat tail, and the fat that covers the entrails and the [1]lobe of the liver, and the two kidneys and the fat that is on them and the right thigh (for it is a ram of [2]ordination),

23 and one cake of bread and [a]one cake of bread *mixed with* oil and one wafer from the basket of unleavened bread which is *set* before the Lord;

24 and you shall put [1]all these [2]in the [3]hands of Aaron and [2]in the [3]hands of his sons, and shall wave them as a wave offering before the Lord.

25 "[a]You shall take them from their hands, and offer them up in smoke on the altar on the burnt offering for a soothing aroma before the Lord; it is an offering by fire to the Lord.

26 ¶ "Then you shall take [a]the breast of Aaron's ram of [1]ordination, and wave it as a wave offering before the Lord; and it shall be your portion.

27 "You shall consecrate the breast of the wave offering and the thigh of the heave offering which was waved and which was [1]offered from the ram of [2]ordination, from the one which was for Aaron and from the one which was for his sons.

28 "It shall be for Aaron and his sons as *their* portion forever from the sons of Israel, for it is a heave offering; and it shall be a heave offering from the sons of Israel from the sacrifices of their peace offerings, *even* their heave offering to the Lord.

29 ¶ "[a]The holy garments of Aaron shall be for his sons after him, [1]that in them they may be anointed and ordained.

30 "For seven days the one of his sons who is priest in his stead shall put them on when he enters the tent of meeting to minister in the holy place.

Food of the Priests

31 ¶ "You shall take the ram of [1]ordination and [a]boil its flesh in a holy place.

32 "Aaron and his sons shall eat the flesh of the ram and the bread that is in the basket, at the doorway of the tent of meeting.

33 "Thus [a]they shall eat [1]those things by which atonement was made [2]at their ordination *and* consecration; but a [3b]layman shall not eat *them*, because they are holy.

34 "[a]If any of the flesh of [1]ordination or any of the bread remains until morning, then you shall burn the remainder with fire; it shall not be eaten, because it is holy.

35 ¶ "Thus you shall do to Aaron and to his sons, according to all that I have commanded you; you shall [1]ordain them through [a]seven days.

36 "[a]Each day you shall offer a bull as a sin offering for atonement, and you shall [1]purify the altar when you make atonement [2]for it, and [b]you shall anoint it to consecrate it.

37 "For seven days you shall make

9 [2]Lit *fill the hand of* [b]Ex 40:15; Num 3:10; 18:7; 25:13; Deut 18:5 [c]Ex 28:41; Lev 8:1-36
10 [a]Lev 1:4; 8:14
12 [a]Lev 8:15 [b]Ex 27:2; 30:2
13 [1]Or *appendage on* [a]Lev 3:3, 4
14 [a]Lev 4:11, 12,21; Heb 13:11
15 [a]Lev 8:18
17 [1]Lit *on* [2]Lit *on its*
18 [a]Gen 8:21; Ex 29:25
19 [1]Lit *second* [a]Lev 8:22f
21 [a]Ex 30:25, 31; Lev 8:30
22 [1]Or *appendage on* [2]Lit *filling*
23 [a]Lev 8:26
24 [1]Lit *the whole* [2]Lit *on* [3]Lit *palms*
25 [a]Lev 8:28
26 [1]Lit *filling* [a]Lev 7:31,34; 8:29
27 [1]Lit *heaved; or lifted up* [2]Lit *filling*
29 [1]Lit *for anointing in them and filling their hand in them* [a]Num 20:26,28
31 [1]Lit *filling* [a]Lev 8:31
33 [1]Lit *them* [2]Lit *to fill their hand to sanctify them* [3]Lit *stranger* [a]Lev 10:14 [b]Lev 22:10,13
34 [1]Lit *filling* [a]Ex 12:10; 23:18; 34:25; Lev 8:32
35 [1]Lit *fill their hand* [a]Lev 8:33
36 [1]Or *offer a sin offering on the altar* [2]Lit *upon* [a]Heb 10:11 [b]Ex 40:10

atonement [1]for the altar and consecrate it; then [a]the altar shall be most holy, *and* whatever touches the altar shall be holy.

38 ¶ "Now [a]this is what you shall offer on the altar: two one year old lambs each day, continuously.

39 "The [a]one lamb you shall offer in the morning and the [1]other lamb you shall offer at [2]twilight;

40 and there *shall be* one-tenth *of an ephah* of fine flour mixed with one-fourth of a hin of beaten oil, and one-fourth of a hin of wine for a drink offering with one lamb.

41 "The [1]other lamb you shall offer at [2]twilight, and shall offer with it [3]the same grain offering and [4]the same drink offering as in the morning, for a soothing aroma, an offering by fire to the LORD.

42 "It shall be a continual burnt offering throughout your generations at the doorway of the tent of meeting before the LORD, [a]where I will meet with you, to speak to you there.

43 "I will meet there with the sons of Israel, and it shall be consecrated by My glory.

44 "I will consecrate the tent of meeting and the altar; I will also consecrate Aaron and his sons to minister as priests to Me.

45 "[a]I will dwell among the sons of Israel and will be their God.

46 "They shall know that [a]I am the LORD their God who brought them out of the land of Egypt, that I might dwell among them; I am the LORD their God.

The Altar of Incense

30 "Moreover, you shall make [a]an altar as a place for burning incense; you shall make it of acacia wood.

2 "Its length *shall be* a [1]cubit, and its width a cubit, it shall be square, and its height *shall be* two cubits; its horns *shall be* [2]of one piece with it.

3 "You shall overlay it with pure gold, its top and its [1]sides all around, and its horns; and you shall make a gold molding all around for it.

4 "You shall make two gold rings for it under its molding; you shall make *them* on its two side walls—on [1]opposite sides—and [2]they shall be holders for poles with which to carry it.

5 "You shall make the poles of acacia wood and overlay them with gold.

6 "You shall put [1]this altar in front of the veil that is [2]near the ark of the testimony, in front of the [3a]mercy seat that is over *the ark of* the testimony, where I will meet with you.

7 "Aaron shall burn fragrant incense on it; he shall burn it every morning when he trims the lamps.

8 "When Aaron [1]trims the lamps at [2]twilight, he shall burn incense. *There shall be* perpetual incense before the LORD throughout your generations.

9 "You shall not offer any strange incense on [1]this altar, or burnt offering or meal offering; and you shall not pour out a drink offering on it.

10 "Aaron shall [a]make atonement on its horns once a year; he shall make atonement on it with the blood of the sin offering of atonement once a year throughout your generations. It is most holy to the LORD."

11 ¶ The LORD also spoke to Moses, saying,

12 "When you take [a]a [1]census of the sons of Israel [2]to number them, then each one of them shall give [b]a ransom for [3]himself to the LORD, when you [4]number them, so that there will be no plague among them when you [4]number them.

13 "This is what everyone who [1]is numbered shall give: half a shekel according to the shekel of the sanctuary ([a]the shekel is twenty gerahs), half a shekel as a [2]contribution to the LORD.

14 "Everyone who [1]is numbered, from twenty years old and over, shall give the [2]contribution to the LORD.

15 "The rich shall not pay more and the poor shall not pay less than the half shekel, when you give the [1]contribution to the LORD to make atonement for [2]yourselves.

16 "You shall take the atonement money from the sons of Israel and shall give it for the service of the tent of meeting, that it may be a memorial for the sons of Israel before the LORD, to make atonement for [1]yourselves."

17 ¶ The LORD spoke to Moses, saying,

18 "You shall also make [a]a laver of [1]bronze, with its base of bronze, for washing; and you shall [b]put it between the tent of meeting and the altar, and you shall put water in it.

19 "Aaron and his sons shall [a]wash their hands and their feet from it;

20 when they enter the tent of meeting, they shall wash with water, so that they will not die; or when they approach the altar to minister, by offering up in smoke a fire *sacrifice* to the LORD.

21 "So they shall wash their hands and their feet, so that they will not die; and [a]it shall be a perpetual statute for them, for [1]Aaron and his [2]descendants throughout their generations."

37 [1]Lit *upon* [a]Ex 30:28f

38 [a]Num 28:3-31; 29:6-38

39 [1]Lit *second* [2]Lit *between the two evenings* [a]Ezek 46:13-15

41 [1]Lit *second* [2]Lit *between the two evenings* [3]Lit *according to the grain offering of the morning* [4]Lit *according to its*

42 [a]Ex 25:22; Num 17:4

45 [a]Ex 25:8; Lev 26:12; Num 5:3; Deut 12:11; Zech 2:10; 2 Cor 6:16; Rev 21:3

46 [a]Ex 20:2

30:1 [a]Ex 37:25-29

2 [1]I.e. One cubit equals approx 18 in. [2]Lit *from itself*

3 [1]Lit *walls*

4 [1]Lit *its two* [2]Lit *it*

6 [1]Lit *it* [2]Lit *upon* or *over* [3]Lit *propitiatory* [a]Ex 25:21f

8 [1]Lit *causes to ascend* [2]Lit *between the two evenings*

9 [1]Lit *it*

10 [a]Lev 16:18

12 [1]Lit *sum* [2]Lit *for their being mustered* [3]Lit *his soul* [4]Lit *muster* [a]Ex 38:25,26; Num 1:2; 26:2 [b]Num 31:50

13 [1]Lit *passes over to those who are mustered* [2]Lit *heave offering* [a]Lev 27:25; Num 3:47; Ezek 45:12

14 [1]V 13, note 1 [2]Lit *heave offering of the LORD*

15 [1]Lit *heave offering of the LORD* [2]Lit *your souls*

16 [1]Lit *your souls*

18 [1]Or *copper* [a]Ex 38:8 [b]Ex 40:30

19 [a]Ex 40:31f; Is 52:11

21 [1]Lit *him* [2]Lit *seed* [a]Ex 28:43

The Anointing Oil

22 ¶ Moreover, the LORD spoke to Moses, saying,
23 "Take also for yourself the finest of
spices: of flowing myrrh five hundred
shekels, and of fragrant cinnamon half as
much, two hundred and fifty, and of fragrant cane two hundred and fifty,
24 and of cassia five hundred, according to the shekel of the sanctuary, and of
olive oil a hin.
25 "You shall make [1]of these a holy
anointing oil, a perfume mixture, the
work of a perfumer; it shall be [a]a holy
anointing oil.
26 "With it [a]you shall anoint the tent of
meeting and the ark of the testimony,
27 and the table and all its utensils,
and the lampstand and its utensils, and
the altar of incense,
28 and the altar of burnt offering and
all its utensils, and the laver and its stand.
29 "You shall also consecrate them, that
they may be most holy; whatever touches
them shall be holy.
30 "[a]You shall anoint Aaron and his
sons, and consecrate them, that they may
minister as priests to Me.
31 "You shall speak to the sons of Israel,
saying, 'This shall be a holy anointing oil
to Me throughout your generations.
32 'It shall not be poured on [1]anyone's
body, nor shall you make *any* like it in
[2]the same proportions; [a]it is holy, *and* it
shall be holy to you.
33 '[a]Whoever shall mix *any* like it or
whoever puts any of it on a [1]layman
[2b]shall be cut off from his people.'"

The Incense

34 ¶ Then the LORD said to Moses,
"Take for yourself spices, stacte and ony-
cha and galbanum, spices with pure
frankincense; there shall be an equal part
of each.
35 "With it you shall make incense, a
perfume, the work of a perfumer, salted,
pure, *and* holy.
36 "You shall beat some of it very fine,
and put part of it before the testimony in
the tent of meeting [a]where I will meet
with you; it shall be most holy to you.
37 "The incense which you shall make,
[a]you shall not make in [1]the same proportions for yourselves; it shall be holy to
you for the LORD.
38 "[a]Whoever shall make *any* like it, to
[1]use as perfume, [2]shall be cut off from
his people."

The Skilled Craftsmen

31 [a]Now the LORD spoke to Moses,
saying,
2 "See, I have called by name Bezalel,
the [a]son of Uri, the son of Hur, of the
tribe of Judah.
3 "I have [a]filled him with the Spirit
of God in wisdom, in understanding, in
knowledge, and in all *kinds of* [1]crafts-
manship,
4 to [1]make artistic designs for work
in gold, in silver, and in [2]bronze,
5 and in the cutting of stones [1]for
settings, and in the carving of wood, that
he may work in all *kinds of* [2]craftsman-
ship.
6 "And behold, I Myself have [1]ap-
pointed with him [a]Oholiab, the son of
Ahisamach, of the tribe of Dan; and in the
hearts of all who are [2]skillful I have put
[3]skill, that they may make all that I have
commanded you:
7 [a]the tent of meeting, and [b]the ark
of testimony, and [c]the [1]mercy seat upon
it, and all the furniture of the tent,
8 [a]the table also and its [1]utensils,
and the [b]pure *gold* lampstand with all its
[1]utensils, and [c]the altar of incense,
9 [a]the altar of burnt offering also
with all its [1]utensils, and [b]the laver and
its stand,
10 the [1a]woven garments as well,
and the holy garments for Aaron the
priest, and the garments of his sons, *with*
which to [2]carry on their priesthood;
11 [a]the anointing oil also, and the
[b]fragrant incense for the holy place, they
are to make *them* according to all that I
have commanded you."

The Sign of the Sabbath

12 ¶ The LORD spoke to Moses, saying,
13 "But as for you, speak to the sons of
Israel, saying, '[a]You shall surely observe
My sabbaths; for *this* is [b]a sign between
Me and you throughout your generations,
that you may know that I am the LORD
who sanctifies you.
14 'Therefore you are to observe the
sabbath, for it is holy to you. [a]Everyone
who profanes it shall surely be put to
death; for whoever does any work on it,
that person shall be cut off from among
his people.
15 '[a]For six days work may be done,
but on the seventh day there is a [b]sab-
bath of complete rest, holy to the LORD;
[c]whoever does any work on the sabbath
day shall surely be put to death.
16 'So the sons of Israel shall observe
the sabbath, to [1]celebrate the sabbath
throughout their generations as a perpetual covenant.'
17 "[a]It is a sign between Me and the
sons of Israel forever; [b]for in six days the
LORD made heaven and earth, but on the

---

25 [1]Lit *it* [a]Ex 37:29; 40:9; Lev 8:10
26 [a]Ex 40:9; Lev 8:10; Num 7:1
30 [a]Ex 29:7; Lev 8:12
32 [1]Lit *the flesh of man* [2]Lit *its proportion* [a]Ex 30:25,37
33 [1]Lit *stranger* [2]Lit *even he shall* [a]Ex 30:38 [b]Gen 17:14; Ex 12:15; Lev 7:20f
36 [a]Ex 29:42
37 [1]Lit *its proportion* [a]Ex 30:32
38 [1]Lit *smell of it* [2]Lit *even he shall* [a]Ex 30:33
31:1 [a]Ex 35:30-36:1
2 [a]1 Chr 2:20
3 [1]Or *workmanship* [a]Ex 35:31; 1 Kin 7:14; 1 Cor 12:4-8
4 [1]Lit *devise devices* [2]Or *copper*
5 [1]Lit *to fill in (for a setting)* [2]Or *workmanship*
6 [1]Lit *given* [2]Lit *wise of heart* [3]Lit *wisdom* [a]Ex 35:34
7 [1]Lit *propitiatory* [a]Ex 36:8-38 [b]Ex 37:1-5 [c]Ex 37:6-9
8 [1]Or *vessels* [a]Ex 37:10-16 [b]Ex 37:17-24; Lev 24:4 [c]Ex 37:25-29
9 [1]Or *vessels* [a]Ex 38:1-7 [b]Ex 38:8
10 [1]Or *service garments* [2]Lit *minister as priests* [a]Ex 39:1
11 [a]Ex 30:23-32 [b]Ex 30:34-38
13 [a]Ex 20:8 [b]Ex 31:17; Ezek 20:12,20
14 [a]Ex 31:15; 35:2; Num 15:32,35; John 7:23
15 [a]Ex 20:9-11; 23:12; 34:21; 35:2; Lev 23:3; Deut 5:12-14 [b]Gen 2:2f; Ex 16:23; 20:8; 35:2,3 [c]Ex 31:14
16 [1]Lit *do*
17 [a]Ex 31:13; Ezek 20:12 [b]Gen 1:31; 2:2,3; Ex 20:11

seventh day He ceased *from labor,* and was refreshed."

18 ¶ When He had finished speaking with him upon Mount Sinai, He gave Moses [a]the two tablets of the testimony, tablets of stone, [b]written by the finger of God.

The Golden Calf

32 Now when the people saw that Moses [a]delayed to come down from the mountain, the people assembled about Aaron and said to him, "Come, [b]make us [1]a god who will go before us; as for [c]this Moses, the man who brought us up from the land of Egypt, we do not know what has become of him."

2 Aaron said to them, "[a]Tear off the gold rings which are in the ears of your wives, your sons, and your daughters, and bring *them* to me."

3 Then all the people tore off the gold rings which were in their ears and brought *them* to Aaron.

4 He took *this* from their hand, and fashioned it with a graving tool and made it into a [a]molten calf; and they said, "[1]This is your god, O Israel, who brought you up from the land of Egypt."

5 Now when Aaron saw *this,* he built an altar before it; and Aaron made a proclamation and said, "Tomorrow *shall be* a feast to the LORD."

6 So the next day they rose early and [a]offered burnt offerings, and brought peace offerings; and [b]the people sat down to eat and to drink, and rose up [c]to play.

7 ¶ Then the LORD spoke to Moses, "Go [1]down at once, for your people, whom [a]you brought up from the land of Egypt, have [b]corrupted *themselves.*

8 "They have quickly turned aside from the way which I commanded them. [a]They have made for themselves a molten calf, and have worshiped it and [b]have sacrificed to it and said, '[1c]This is your god, O Israel, who brought you up from the land of Egypt!' "

9 [a]The LORD said to Moses, "I have seen this people, and behold, they are [1b]an obstinate people.

10 "Now then [a]let Me alone, that My anger may burn against them and that I may destroy them; and [b]I will make of you a great nation."

Moses' Entreaty

11 ¶ Then [a]Moses entreated the LORD his God, and said, "O LORD, why does Your anger burn against Your people whom You have brought out from the land of Egypt with great power and with a mighty hand?

12 "Why should [a]the Egyptians speak, saying, 'With evil *intent* He brought them out to kill them in the mountains and to destroy them from the face of the earth'? Turn from Your burning anger and change Your mind about *doing* harm to Your people.

13 "Remember Abraham, Isaac, and Israel, Your servants to whom You [a]swore by Yourself, and said to them, 'I will [b]multiply your [1]descendants as the stars of the heavens, and [c]all this land of which I have spoken I will give to your [1]descendants, and they shall inherit *it* forever.' "

14 [a]So the LORD changed His mind about the harm which He said He would do to His people.

15 ¶ [a]Then Moses turned and went down from the mountain with the two tablets of the testimony in his hand, [b]tablets which were written on both [1]sides; they were written on one *side* and the other.

16 The tablets were God's work, and the writing was God's writing engraved on the tablets.

17 Now when Joshua heard the sound of the people [1]as they shouted, he said to Moses, "There is a sound of war in the camp."

18 But he said,

"It is not the sound of the cry of triumph,
Nor is it the sound of the cry of defeat;
But the sound of singing I hear."

Moses' Anger

19 It came about, as soon as [1]Moses came near the camp, that [a]he saw the calf and *the* dancing; and Moses' anger burned, and [b]he threw the tablets from his hands and shattered them [2]at the foot of the mountain.

20 [a]He took the calf which they had made and burned *it* with fire, and ground it to powder, and scattered it over the surface of the water and made the sons of Israel drink *it.*

21 ¶ Then Moses said to Aaron, "What did this people do to you, that you have brought *such* great sin upon them?"

22 Aaron said, "Do not let the anger of my lord burn; you know the people yourself, [a]that they are [1]prone to evil.

23 "For [a]they said to me, 'Make [1]a god for us who will go before us; for this Moses, the man who brought us up from the land of Egypt, we do not know what has become of him.'

24 "I said to them, 'Whoever has any gold, let them tear it off.' So they gave *it*

---

18 [a]Ex 24:12; 34:29; Deut 4:13; 5:22; 9:10f [b]Ex 32:15,16; 34:1,28; Deut 9:10

32:1 [1]Or *gods* [a]Ex 24:18; Deut 9:11,12 [b]Acts 7:40 [c]Ex 14:11

2 [a]Ex 35:22

4 [1]Or *These are your gods* [a]Deut 9:16; Neh 9:18; Ps 106:19; Acts 7:41

6 [a]Acts 7:41 [b]1 Cor 10:7 [c]Ex 32:17-19; Num 25:2

7 [1]Lit *go down* [a]Ex 32:4,11; Deut 9:12 [b]Gen 6:11f

8 [1]Or *These are your gods* [a]Ex 20:3,4,23 [b]Ex 22:20; 34:15; Deut 32:17 [c]1 Kin 12:28

9 [1]Or *a stiff-necked* [a]Num 14:11-20 [b]Ex 33:3,5; 34:9; Is 48:4; Acts 7:51

10 [a]Deut 9:14 [b]Num 14:12

11 [a]Deut 9:18, 26

12 [a]Num 14:13-19; Deut 9:28; Josh 7:9

13 [1]Lit *seed* [a]Gen 22:16-18; Heb 6:13 [b]Gen 15:5; 26:4 [c]Gen 12:7; 13:15; 15:18; 17:8; 35:12; Ex 13:5, 11; 33:1

14 [a]Ps 106:45

15 [1]Lit *their sides* [a]Deut 9:15 [b]Ex 31:18

17 [1]Lit *in its shouting*

19 [1]Lit *he* [2]Lit *beneath* [a]Ex 32:6; Deut 9:16 [b]Deut 9:17

20 [a]Deut 9:21

22 [1]Lit *in evil* [a]Deut 9:24

23 [1]Or *gods* [a]Ex 32:1-4

to me, and [a]I threw it into the fire, and out came this calf."

25 ¶ Now when Moses saw that the people were [1]out of control—for Aaron had [a]let them [2]get out of control to be a derision among [3]their enemies—

26 then Moses stood in the gate of the camp, and said, "Whoever is for the LORD, *come* to me!" And all the sons of Levi gathered together to him.

27 He said to them, "Thus says the LORD, the God of Israel, 'Every man *of you* put his sword upon his thigh, and go back and forth from gate to gate in the camp, and kill every man his brother, and every man his friend, and every man his [1]neighbor.' "

28 So [a]the sons of Levi did [1]as Moses instructed, and about three thousand men of the people fell that day.

29 Then Moses said, "[1]Dedicate yourselves today to the LORD—for every man has been against his son and against his brother—in order that He may bestow a blessing upon you today."

30 ¶ On the next day Moses said to the people, "[a]You yourselves have [1]committed a great sin; and now I am going up to the LORD, perhaps I can [b]make atonement for your sin."

31 Then Moses returned to the LORD, and said, "Alas, this people has [1]committed a great sin, and they have made [2]a [a]god of gold for themselves.

32 "But now, if You will, forgive their sin—and if not, please blot me out from Your [a]book which You have written!"

33 The LORD said to Moses, "Whoever has sinned against Me, [a]I will blot him out of My book.

34 "But go now, lead the people [a]where I told you. Behold, [b]My angel shall go before you; nevertheless [c]in the day when I [1]punish, [d]I will [2]punish them for their sin."

35 [a]Then the LORD smote the people, because of [b]what they did with the calf which Aaron had made.

The Journey Resumed

33 Then the LORD spoke to Moses, "Depart, go up from here, you and the people whom you have brought up from the land of Egypt, to the land of which [a]I swore to Abraham, [b]Isaac, and [c]Jacob, saying, '[d]To your [1]descendants I will give it.'

2 "I will send [a]an angel before you and [b]I will drive out the Canaanite, the Amorite, the Hittite, the Perizzite, the Hivite and the Jebusite.

3 "*Go up* to a land [a]flowing with milk and honey; for I will not go up in your midst, because you are [1b]an obstinate people, and [c]I might destroy you on the way."

4 ¶ When the people heard this [1]sad word, [a]they went into mourning, and none of them put on his ornaments.

5 For the LORD had said to Moses, "Say to the sons of Israel, 'You are [1a]an obstinate people; should I go up in your midst for one moment, I would destroy you. Now therefore, put off your ornaments from you, that I may know what I shall do with you.' "

6 So the sons of Israel stripped themselves of their ornaments, from Mount Horeb *onward*.

7 ¶ Now Moses used to take [a]the tent and pitch it outside the camp, a good distance from the camp, and he called it the tent of meeting. And [b]everyone who sought the LORD would go out to the tent of meeting which was outside the camp.

8 And it came about, whenever Moses went out to the tent, that all the people would arise and stand, each at the entrance of his tent, and gaze after Moses until he entered the tent.

9 Whenever Moses entered the tent, [a]the pillar of cloud would descend and stand at the entrance of the tent; [b]and [1]the LORD would speak with Moses.

10 When all the people saw the pillar of cloud standing at the entrance of the tent, all the people would arise and worship, each at the entrance of his tent.

11 Thus [a]the LORD used to speak to Moses face to face, just as a man speaks to his friend. When [1]Moses returned to the camp, [b]his servant Joshua, the son of Nun, a young man, would not depart from the tent.

Moses Intercedes

12 ¶ Then Moses said to the LORD, "See, You say to me, '[a]Bring up this people!' But You Yourself have not let me know [b]whom You will send with me. [c]Moreover, You have said, 'I have known you by name, and you have also found favor in My sight.'

13 "Now therefore, I pray You, if I have found favor in Your sight, [a]let me know Your ways that I may know You, so that I may find favor in Your sight. [b]Consider too, that this nation is Your people."

14 And He said, "[a]My presence shall go *with you*, and [b]I will give you rest."

15 Then he said to Him, "[a]If Your presence does not go *with us*, do not lead us up from here.

16 "For how then can it be known that I have found favor in Your sight, I and Your people? Is it not by Your going with us, so that [a]we, I and Your people, may

---

24 [a]Ex 32:4
25 [1]Lit *let loose* [2]Lit *go loose* [3]Lit *those who rise against them* [a]1 Kin 12:28-30; 14:16
27 [1]Or *kin*
28 [1]Lit *according to Moses' word* [a]Num 25:7-13; Deut 33:9
29 [1]Lit *Fill your hand*
30 [1]Lit *sinned* [a]1 Sam 12:20,23 [b]Num 25:13
31 [1]Lit *sinned* [2]Or *gods* [a]Ex 20:23
32 [a]Ps 69:28; Is 4:3; Dan 12:1; Mal 3:16,17; Phil 4:3; Rev 3:5; 21:27
33 [a]Ex 17:14; Deut 29:20; Ps 9:5; Rev 3:5
34 [1]Lit *visit* [2]Lit *visit their sin upon them* [a]Ex 3:17 [b]Ex 23:20 [c]Deut 32:35; Rom 2:5,6 [d]Ps 99:8
35 [a]Ex 32:28 [b]Ex 32:4,24
33:1 [1]Lit *seed* [a]Ex 32:13 [b]Gen 26:1-3 [c]Gen 28:10 [d]Gen 12:7
2 [a]Ex 32:34 [b]Ex 23:27-31; Josh 24:11
3 [1]Lit *a stiff-necked* [a]Ex 3:8, 17 [b]Ex 32:9; 33:5 [c]Ex 32:10
4 [1]Lit *evil* [a]Num 14:1,39
5 [1]Lit *a stiff-necked* [a]Ex 33:3
7 [a]Ex 18:7, 12-16 [b]Ex 29:42f
9 [1]Lit *He* [a]Ex 13:21 [b]Ps 99:7
11 [1]Lit *he* [a]Num 12:8; Deut 34:10 [b]Ex 24:13
12 [a]Ex 3:10; 32:34 [b]Ex 33:2 [c]Ex 33:17
13 [a]Ps 25:4; 27:11; 51:13; 86:11; 119:33 [b]Ex 3:7,10; 5:1; 32:12,14; Deut 9:26,29
14 [a]Deut 4:37; Is 63:9 [b]Deut 12:10; 25:19; Josh 21:44; 22:4
15 [a]Ps 80:3,7, 19
16 [a]Lev 20:24, 26

be distinguished from all the *other* people
who are upon the face of the [1]earth?"
17 ¶ The LORD said to Moses, "I will
also do this thing of which you have spoken; [a]for you have found favor in My
sight and I have known you by name."
18 [a]Then [1]Moses said, "I pray You,
show me Your glory!"
19 And He said, "[a]I Myself will make
all My goodness pass before you, and will
proclaim the name of the LORD before
you; and [b]I will be gracious to whom I
will be gracious, and will show compassion on whom I will show compassion."
20 But He said, "You cannot see My
face, [a]for no man can see Me and live!"
21 Then the LORD said, "Behold, there
is a place [1]by Me, and [a]you shall stand
there on the rock;
22 and it will come about, while My
glory is passing by, that I will put you in
the cleft of the rock and [a]cover you with
My hand until I have passed by.
23 "Then I will take My hand away and
you shall see My back, but [a]My face shall
not be seen."

The Two Tablets Replaced

34 Now the LORD said to Moses,
"Cut out for yourself [a]two stone
tablets like the former ones, and [b]I will
write on the tablets the words that were
on the former tablets which you shattered.
2 "So be ready by morning, and come
up in the morning to [a]Mount Sinai, and
[1]present yourself there to Me on the top
of the mountain.
3 "[a]No man is to come up with you,
nor let any man be seen [1]anywhere on
the mountain; even the flocks and the
herds may not graze in front of that
mountain."
4 So he cut out [a]two stone tablets
like the former ones, and Moses rose up
early in the morning and went up to
Mount Sinai, as the LORD had commanded him, and he took two stone tablets in
his hand.
5 [a]The LORD descended in the cloud
and stood there with him as [1]he called
upon the name of the LORD.
6 Then the LORD passed by in front
of him and proclaimed, "The LORD, the
LORD God, [a]compassionate and gracious,
slow to anger, and abounding in lovingkindness and [1]truth;
7 who [a]keeps lovingkindness for
thousands, who forgives iniquity, transgression and sin; yet He [b]will by no
means leave *the guilty* unpunished, [c]vis-
iting the iniquity of fathers on the children and on the grandchildren to the
third and fourth generations."
8 Moses made haste [1a]to bow low
toward the earth and worship.
9 He said, "[a]If now I have found favor in Your sight, O Lord, I pray, let the
Lord go along in our midst, even though
[1b]the people are so obstinate, and [c]par-
don our iniquity and our sin, and [d]take
us as Your own [2]possession."

The Covenant Renewed

10 ¶ Then [1]God said, "Behold, [a]I am
going to make a covenant. Before all your
people [b]I will perform miracles which
have not been [2]produced in all the earth
nor among any of the nations; and all the
people [3]among whom you live will see
the working of the LORD, for it is a fearful
thing that I am going to perform with
you.
11 ¶ "[1]Be sure to observe what I am
commanding you this day: behold, [a]I am
going to drive out the Amorite before
you, and the Canaanite, the Hittite, the
Perizzite, the Hivite and the Jebusite.
12 "[a]Watch yourself that you make no
covenant with the inhabitants of the land
into which you are going, or it will become a snare in your midst.
13 "[a]But *rather,* you are to tear down
their altars and smash their *sacred* pillars
and cut down their [1b]Asherim
14 —for [a]you shall not worship any
other god, for the LORD, whose name is
Jealous, is a jealous God—
15 otherwise you might make a covenant with the inhabitants of the land
and they would play the harlot with their
gods and [a]sacrifice to their gods, and
someone [b]might invite you [1]to eat of his
sacrifice,
16 and [a]you might take some of his
daughters for your sons, and his daughters might play the harlot with their gods
and cause your sons *also* to play the harlot with their gods.
17 "[a]You shall make for yourself no
molten gods.
18 ¶ "You shall observe [a]the Feast of
Unleavened Bread. For [b]seven days you
are to eat unleavened bread, [1]as I commanded you, at the appointed time in the
[c]month of Abib, for in the month of Abib
you came out of Egypt.
19 ¶ "[a]The first offspring from every
womb belongs to Me, and all your male
livestock, the first offspring from [1]cattle
and sheep.
20 "[a]You shall redeem with a lamb the
[1]first offspring from a donkey; and if you
do not redeem *it,* then you shall break its
neck. You shall redeem [b]all the firstborn
of your sons. [2c]None shall appear before
Me empty-handed.
21 ¶ "You shall work [a]six days, but on

16 [1]Lit *ground*
17 [a]Ex 33:12
18 [1]Lit *he* [a]Ex 33:20-23
19 [a]Ex 34:6 [b]Rom 9:15
20 [a]Is 6:5; 1 Tim 6:16
21 [1]Lit *with* [a]Ps 18:2
22 [a]Ps 91:1; Is 49:2
23 [a]Ex 33:20; John 1:18
34:1 [a]Ex 24:12 [b]Deut 10:2
2 [1]Or *place yourself before* [a]Ex 19:11
3 [1]Lit *on all* [a]Ex 19:12
4 [a]Ex 34:1
5 [1]Or *he called out with the name of the LORD* [a]Ex 19:9
6 [1]Or *faithfulness* [a]Num 14:18; Deut 4:31; Neh 9:17; Ps 86:15; Joel 2:13; Rom 2:4
7 [a]Ex 20:5; Deut 5:10; Ps 103:3; 1 John 1:9 [b]Ex 23:7; Deut 7:10; Job 10:14; Nah 1:3 [c]Deut 5:9
8 [1]Lit *and bowed... worshiped* [a]Ex 4:31
9 [1]Lit *it is a people stiff-necked* [2]Or *inheritance* [a]Ex 33:13 [b]Ex 32:9 [c]Ex 34:7 [d]Deut 4:20; Ps 33:12
10 [1]Lit *He* [2]Lit *created* [3]Lit *in whose midst you are* [a]Ex 34:27; Deut 5:2 [b]Deut 4:32; Ps 72:18
11 [1]Lit *Observe for yourself* [a]Ex 33:2
12 [a]Ex 23:32
13 [1]I.e. wooden symbols of a female deity [a]Ex 23:24; Deut 12:3 [b]Deut 16:21; Judg 6:25; 2 Kin 18:4; 2 Chr 34:3f
14 [a]Ex 20:3; Deut 4:24
15 [1]Lit *and you eat* [a]Ex 22:20 [b]Num 25:1; Deut 32:37
16 [a]Deut 7:3; Josh 23:12; 1 Kin 11:1-4
17 [a]Ex 20:4; Lev 19:4; Deut 5:8
18 [1]Or *which* [a]Ex 12:17; Lev 23:6; Num 28:16f [b]Ex 12:15 [c]Ex 12:2
19 [1]Or *oxen* [a]Ex 13:2
20 [1]Lit *first opening of* [2]Lit *They shall not* [a]Ex 13:13 [b]Ex 13:15; Num 3:45 [c]Ex 22:29; Deut 16:16
21 [a]Ex 20:9f; Lev 23:3; Deut 5:13f

the seventh day you shall rest; *even* during plowing time and harvest you shall rest.

22 "You shall celebrate [a]the Feast of Weeks, *that is,* the first fruits of the wheat harvest, and the Feast of Ingathering at the turn of the year.

23 "[a]Three times a year all your males are to appear before the Lord [1]GOD, the God of Israel.

24 "For I will [1a]drive out nations before you and enlarge your borders, and no man shall covet your land when you go up three times a year to appear before the LORD your God.

25 ¶ "[a]You shall not [1]offer the blood of My sacrifice with leavened bread, [b]nor is the sacrifice of the Feast of the Passover to [2]be left over until morning.

26 ¶ "You shall bring [a]the very first of the first fruits of your soil into the house of the LORD your God.

¶ "You shall not boil a young goat in its mother's milk."

27 ¶ Then the LORD said to Moses, "[a]Write [1]down these words, for in accordance with these words I have made [b]a covenant with you and with Israel."

28 So he was there with the LORD [a]forty days and forty nights; he did not eat bread or drink water. And [b]he wrote on the tablets the words of the covenant, [c]the Ten [1]Commandments.

Moses' Face Shines

29 ¶ It came about when Moses was coming down from Mount Sinai (and the [a]two tablets of the testimony *were* in Moses' hand as he was coming down from the mountain), that Moses did not know that [b]the skin of his face shone because of his speaking with Him.

30 So when Aaron and all the sons of Israel saw Moses, behold, the skin of his face shone, and [a]they were afraid to come near him.

31 Then Moses called to them, and Aaron and all the rulers in the congregation returned to him; and Moses spoke to them.

32 Afterward all the sons of Israel came near, and he commanded them *to do* everything that the LORD had spoken [1]to him on Mount Sinai.

33 When Moses had finished speaking with them, [a]he put a veil over his face.

34 But whenever Moses went in before the LORD to speak with Him, [a]he would take off the veil until he came out; and whenever he came out and spoke to the sons of Israel what he had been commanded,

35 [a]the sons of Israel would see the face of Moses, that the skin of Moses' face shone. So Moses would replace the veil over his face until he went in to speak with Him.

The Sabbath Emphasized

35 Then Moses assembled all the congregation of the sons of Israel, and said to them, "[a]These are the things that the LORD has commanded *you* to [1]do:

2 ¶ "[a]For six days work may be done, but on the seventh day you shall have a holy *day,* [b]a sabbath of complete rest to the LORD; [c]whoever does any work on it shall be put to death.

3 "[a]You shall not kindle a fire in any of your dwellings on the sabbath day."

4 ¶ Moses spoke to all the congregation of the sons of Israel, saying, "This is the thing which the LORD has commanded, saying,

5 '[a]Take from among you a [1]contribution to the LORD; whoever is of a willing heart, let him bring it as the LORD'S [1]contribution: gold, silver, and [2]bronze,

6 and [1]blue, purple and scarlet *material,* fine linen, goats' *hair,*

7 and rams' skins [1]dyed red, and porpoise skins, and acacia wood,

8 and oil for lighting, and spices for the anointing oil, and for the fragrant incense,

9 and onyx stones and setting stones for the ephod and for the [1]breastpiece.

Tabernacle Workmen

10 ¶ '[a]Let every skillful man among you come, and make all that the LORD has commanded:

11 the [1a]tabernacle, its tent and its covering, its hooks and its boards, its bars, its pillars, and its [2]sockets;

12 the [a]ark and its poles, the [1]mercy seat, and the curtain of the screen;

13 the [a]table and its poles, and all its [1]utensils, and the bread of the [2]Presence;

14 the [a]lampstand also for the light and its utensils and its lamps and the oil for the light;

15 and the [a]altar of incense and its poles, and the [b]anointing oil and the [c]fragrant incense, and the screen for the doorway at the [1]entrance of the tabernacle;

16 [a]the altar of burnt offering with its [1]bronze grating, its poles, and all its [2]utensils, the [3]basin and its stand;

17 [a]the hangings of the court, its pillars and its [1]sockets, and the screen for the gate of the court;

18 the pegs of the tabernacle and the pegs of the court and their cords;

19 the [1a]woven garments for minis-

22 [a]Ex 23:16; Num 28:26
23 [1]Heb *YHWH,* usually rendered LORD [a]Ex 23:14-17
24 [1]Or *dispossess* [a]Ex 33:2; Ps 78:55
25 [1]Lit *slaughter* [2]Lit *remain overnight* [a]Ex 23:18 [b]Ex 12:10
26 [a]Ex 23:19; Deut 26:2
27 [1]Lit *for yourself* [a]Ex 17:14; 24:4 [b]Ex 34:10
28 [1]Lit *Words* [a]Ex 24:18 [b]Ex 31:18; 34:1 [c]Deut 4:13; 10:4
29 [a]Ex 32:15 [b]Matt 17:2; 2 Cor 3:7
30 [a]2 Cor 3:7
32 [1]Lit *with*
33 [a]2 Cor 3:13
34 [a]2 Cor 3:16
35 [a]2 Cor 3:13
35:1 [1]Lit *do them* [a]Ex 34:32
2 [a]Ex 20:9,10; 23:12; 31:15; 34:21; Lev 23:3; Deut 5:13f [b]Ex 16:23 [c]Num 15:32-36
3 [a]Ex 12:16; 16:23
5 [1]Or *heave offering* [2]Or *copper* [a]Ex 25:1-9
6 [1]Or *violet*
7 [1]Or *tanned*
9 [1]Or *pouch*
10 [a]Ex 31:6
11 [1]Lit *dwelling place* [2]Or *bases* [a]Ex 26:1-30
12 [1]Lit *propitiatory* [a]Ex 25:10-22
13 [1]Or *vessels* [2]Lit *Face* [a]Ex 25:23-30
14 [a]Ex 25:31ff
15 [1]Or *doorway* [a]Ex 30:1-6 [b]Ex 30:25 [c]Ex 30:34-38
16 [1]Or *copper* [2]Or *vessels* [3]Or *laver* [a]Ex 27:1-8
17 [1]Or *bases* [a]Ex 27:9-18
19 [1]Or *service garments* [a]Ex 31:10; 39:1

tering in the holy place, the holy garments for Aaron the priest and the garments of his sons, to minister as priests.' "

Gifts Received

20 ¶ Then all the congregation of the sons of Israel departed from Moses' presence.

21 [a]Everyone whose heart [1]stirred him and everyone whose spirit [2]moved him came *and* brought the LORD'S [3]contribution for the work of the tent of meeting and for all its service and for the holy garments.

22 Then all [1]whose hearts moved them, both men and women, came *and* brought brooches and [2]earrings and signet rings and bracelets, all articles of gold; so *did* every man who [3]presented an offering of gold to the LORD.

23 Every man, [1]who had in his possession [2]blue and purple and scarlet *material* and fine linen and goats' *hair* and rams' skins [3]dyed red and porpoise skins, brought them.

24 Everyone who could make a [1]contribution of silver and [2]bronze brought the LORD'S [1]contribution; and every man [3]who had in his possession acacia wood for any work of the service brought it.

25 All the [1]skilled women spun with their hands, and brought what they had spun, *in* [2]blue and purple *and* scarlet *material* and *in* fine linen.

26 All the women whose heart [1]stirred with a skill spun the goats' *hair.*

27 The rulers brought the onyx stones and the stones for setting for the ephod and for the [1]breastpiece;

28 and [a]the spice and the oil for the light and for the anointing oil and for the fragrant incense.

29 The [1]Israelites, all the men and women, whose heart [2]moved them to bring *material* for all the work, which the LORD had commanded through Moses to be done, brought a [a]freewill offering to the LORD.

30 ¶ [a]Then Moses said to the sons of Israel, "See, the LORD has called by name Bezalel the son of Uri, the son of Hur, of the tribe of Judah.

31 "And He has filled him with the Spirit of God, in wisdom, in understanding and in knowledge and in all [1]craftsmanship;

32 [1]to make designs for working in gold and in silver and in [2]bronze,

33 and in the cutting of stones for settings and in the carving of wood, so as to perform in every inventive work.

34 "He also has put in his heart to teach, both he and [a]Oholiab, the son of Ahisamach, of the tribe of Dan.

35 "[a]He has filled them with [1]skill to perform every work of an engraver and of a designer and of an embroiderer, in [2]blue and in purple *and* in scarlet *material,* and in fine linen, and of a weaver, as performers of every work and makers of designs.

The Tabernacle Underwritten

36 "Now Bezalel and Oholiab, and every [1]skillful person in whom the LORD has put [2]skill and understanding to know how to perform all the work [3]in the construction of the sanctuary, shall perform in accordance with all that the LORD has commanded."

2 ¶ Then Moses called Bezalel and Oholiab and every [1]skillful person in [2]whom the LORD had put [3]skill, [a]everyone whose heart stirred him, to come to the work to perform it.

3 They received from Moses all the [1]contributions which the sons of Israel had brought [2]to perform the work [3]in the construction of the sanctuary. And they still *continued* bringing to him freewill offerings every morning.

4 And all the [1]skillful men who were performing all the work of the sanctuary came, each from [2]the work which [3]he was performing,

5 and they said to [1]Moses, "[a]The people are bringing much more than enough for the [2]construction work which the LORD commanded *us* to [3]perform."

6 So Moses issued a command, and a [1]proclamation was circulated throughout the camp, saying, "Let no man or woman any longer perform work for the [2]contributions of the sanctuary." Thus the people were restrained from bringing *any more.*

7 [a]For the [1]material they had was sufficient and more than enough for all the work, to perform it.

Construction Proceeds

8 ¶ [a]All the [1]skillful men among those who were performing the work made the [2]tabernacle with ten curtains; of fine twisted linen and [3]blue and purple and scarlet *material,* with cherubim, the work of a skillful workman, [4]Bezalel made them.

9 The length of each curtain was twenty-eight [1]cubits and the width of each curtain four [1]cubits; all the curtains had [2]the same measurements.

10 He [1]joined five curtains to one another and *the other* five curtains he [1]joined to one another.

21 [1]Lit *lifted up* [2]Or *made him willing* [3]Or *heave offering* [a]Ex 25:2; 35:5, 22,26,29; 36:2

22 [1]Or *who were willing-hearted* [2]Or *nose rings* [3]Lit *waved a wave offering*

23 [1]Lit *with whom was found* [2]Or *violet* [3]Or *tanned*

24 [1]Or *heave offering* [2]Or *copper* [3]Lit *with whom was found*

25 [1]Lit *women wise of heart* [2]Or *violet*

26 [1]Lit *lifted them up in wisdom*

27 [1]Or *pouch*

28 [a]Ex 30:23ff

29 [1]Lit *sons of Israel* [2]Lit *made them willing* [a]Ex 35:21; 1 Chr 29:9

30 [a]Ex 31:1-6

31 [1]Or *work*

32 [1]Lit *devise devices* [2]Or *copper*

34 [a]Ex 31:6

35 [1]Lit *wisdom of heart* [2]Or *violet* [a]Ex 31:3,6; 35:31; 1 Kin 7:14

36:1 [1]Lit *man wise of heart* [2]Lit *wisdom* [3]Or *connected with the service of;* lit *of the service of*

2 [1]Lit *man wise of heart* [2]Lit *whose heart* [3]Lit *wisdom* [a]Ex 35:21,26

3 [1]Lit *lifted offering* [2]Lit *to perform it for the work* [3]Lit *of the service of*

4 [1]Lit *wise* [2]Lit *his* [3]Lit *they were*

5 [1]Lit *Moses, saying,* [2]Lit *service for the work* [3]Lit *perform it* [a]2 Chr 24:14; 31:6-10

6 [1]Lit *voice* [2]Lit *heave offering*

7 [1]Lit *work* [a]1 Kin 8:64

8 [1]Lit *wise of heart* [2]Lit *dwelling place* [3]Or *violet* [4]Lit *he* [a]Ex 26:1-14

9 [1]I.e. One cubit equals approx 18 in. [2]Lit *one measure*

10 [1]Or *coupled*

11 He made loops of [1]blue on the
edge of the [2]outermost curtain in the
first [3]set; he did likewise on the edge of
the curtain that was [2]outermost in the
second [3]set.
12 He made [a]fifty loops in the one
curtain and he made fifty loops on the
[1]edge of the curtain that was in the second [2]set; the loops were opposite each
other.
13 He made [a]fifty clasps of gold and
[1]joined the curtains to one another with
the clasps, so the tabernacle was [2]a unit.
14 ¶ Then [a]he made curtains of goats'
hair for a tent over the tabernacle; he
made eleven curtains [1]in all.
15 The length of each curtain *was* thirty cubits and four cubits the width of each
curtain; the eleven curtains had [1]the
same measurements.
16 He [1]joined five curtains by themselves and *the other* six curtains by themselves.
17 Moreover, he made fifty loops on
the edge of the curtain that was outermost in the *first* [1]set, and he made fifty
loops on the edge of the curtain *that was
outermost in* the second [1]set.
18 He made fifty clasps of [1]bronze to
[2]join the tent together so that it would be
[3]a unit.
19 He made a covering for the tent of
rams' skins [1]dyed red, and a covering of
porpoise skins above.
20 ¶ [a]Then he made the boards for
the tabernacle of acacia wood, standing
upright.
21 Ten cubits *was* the length of [1]each
board and one and a half cubits the width
of each board.
22 *There were* two tenons for each
board, [1]fitted to one another; thus he did
for all the boards of the tabernacle.
23 He made the boards for the tabernacle: twenty boards [1]for the south side;
24 and he made forty [1]sockets of silver under the twenty boards; two [1]sock-
ets under one board for its two tenons
and two [1]sockets under another board
for its two tenons.
25 Then for the second side of the tabernacle, on the north side, he made twenty boards,
26 and their forty [1]sockets of silver;
two [1]sockets under one board and two
[1]sockets under another board.
27 For the [1]rear of the tabernacle, to
the west, he made six boards.
28 He made two boards for the corners
of the [1]tabernacle at the [2]rear.
29 They were double beneath, and together they were complete to its [1]top
[2]to the first ring; thus he did with both
of them for the two corners.
30 There were eight boards with their
[1]sockets of silver, sixteen [1]sockets,
[2]two under every board.
31 ¶ Then he made [a]bars of acacia
wood, five for the boards of one side of
the tabernacle,
32 and five bars for the boards of the
[1]other side of the tabernacle, and five
bars for the boards of the tabernacle for
the [2]rear *side* to the west.
33 He made the middle bar to pass
through in the [1]center of the boards from
end to end.
34 He overlaid the boards with gold
and made their rings of gold *as* holders for
the bars, and overlaid the bars with gold.
35 ¶ [a]Moreover, he made the veil of
[1]blue and purple and scarlet *material,*
and fine twisted linen; he made it with
cherubim, the work of a skillful workman.
36 He made four pillars of acacia for it,
and overlaid them with gold, with their
hooks of gold; and he cast four [1]sockets
of silver for them.
37 He made a [a]screen for the doorway
of the tent, of [1]blue and purple and scarlet *material,* and fine twisted linen, the
work of a [2]weaver;
38 and *he made* its [a]five pillars with
their hooks, and he overlaid their tops
and their [1]bands with gold; but their five
[2]sockets were of [3]bronze.

Construction Continues

37 [a]Now Bezalel made the ark of
acacia wood; its length was two
and a half [1]cubits, and its width one and
a half cubits, and its height one and a half
cubits;
2 and he overlaid it with pure gold
inside and out, and made a gold molding
for it all around.
3 He cast four rings of gold for it on
its four feet; even two rings on one side
of it, and two rings on the [1]other side
of it.
4 He made poles of acacia wood and
overlaid them with gold.
5 He put the poles into the rings on
the sides of the ark, to carry [1]it.
6 He made a [1]mercy seat of pure
gold, two and a half cubits [2]long and one
and a half cubits [3]wide.
7 He made two cherubim of gold; he
made them of hammered work [1]at the
two ends of the mercy seat;
8 one cherub [1]at the one end and
one cherub [1]at the other end; he made
the cherubim *of one piece* with the mercy seat [1]at the two ends.
9 The cherubim had *their* wings
spread upward, covering the [1]mercy seat
with their wings, with their faces toward

11 [1]Or *violet* [2]Lit *one curtain from the end in the coupling* [3]Lit *coupling*

12 [1]Lit *end* [2]Lit *coupling* [a]Ex 26:5

13 [1]Or *coupled* [2]Lit *one* [a]Ex 26:6

14 [1]Lit *in number* [a]Ex 26:7-14

15 [1]Lit *one measure*

16 [1]Or *coupled*

17 [1]Lit *coupling*

18 [1]Or *copper* [2]Or *couple* [3]Lit *one*

19 [1]Or *tanned*

20 [a]Ex 26:15-29

21 [1]Lit *the*

22 [1]Lit *bound*

23 [1]Lit *to the side of the Negev, to the south*

24 [1]Or *bases*

26 [1]Or *bases*

27 [1]Lit *extreme parts*

28 [1]Lit *dwelling place* [2]Lit *extreme parts*

29 [1]Or *head* [2]Or *with reference to*

30 [1]Or *bases* [2]Lit *two sockets*

31 [a]Ex 26:26-29

32 [1]Or *second* [2]Lit *extreme parts*

33 [1]Lit *midst*

35 [1]Or *violet* [a]Ex 26:31-37

36 [1]Or *bases*

37 [1]Or *violet* [2]Lit *variegator;* i.e. a weaver in colors [a]Ex 26:36

38 [1]Or *fillets, rings* [2]Or *bases* [3]Or *copper* [a]Ex 26:37

37:1 [1]I.e. One cubit equals approx 18 in. [a]Ex 25:10-20

3 [1]Lit *second*

5 [1]Lit *the ark*

6 [1]Lit *propitiatory* [2]Lit *its length* [3]Lit *its width*

7 [1]Lit *from*

8 [1]Lit *from*

9 [1]Lit *propitiatory*

each other; the faces of the cherubim
were toward the mercy seat.
10 ¶ [a]Then he made the table of acacia wood, two [1]cubits [2]long and a cubit
[3]wide and one and a half cubits [4]high.
11 He overlaid it with pure gold, and
made a gold molding for it all around.
12 He made a rim for it of a handbreadth all around, and made a gold
molding for its rim all around.
13 He cast four gold rings for it and put
the rings on the four corners that were on
its four feet.
14 Close by the rim were the rings,
the holders for the poles to carry the table.
15 He made the poles of acacia wood
and overlaid them with gold, to carry the
table.
16 He made the utensils which were
on the table, its [1]dishes and its pans and
its [2]bowls and its jars, with which to
pour out drink offerings, of pure gold.
17 ¶ [a]Then he made the lampstand
of pure gold. He made the lampstand of
hammered work, its base and its shaft; its
cups, its [1]bulbs and its flowers were *of
one piece* with it.
18 There were six branches going out
of its sides; three branches of the lampstand from the one side of it and three
branches of the lampstand from the [1]oth-
er side of it;
19 three cups shaped like almond *blossoms,* a [1]bulb and a flower in one
branch, and three cups shaped like almond *blossoms,* a [1]bulb and a flower
in the other branch—so for the six
branches going out of the lampstand.
20 In the lampstand *there were* four
cups shaped like almond *blossoms,* its
[1]bulbs and its flowers;
21 and a [1]bulb was under the *first* pair
of branches *coming* out of it, and a [1]bulb
under the *second* pair of branches *coming* out of it, and a [1]bulb under the *third*
pair of branches *coming* out of it, for the
six branches coming out of the lampstand.
22 Their [1]bulbs and their branches
were *of one piece* with it; the whole of
it *was* a single hammered work of pure
gold.
23 He made its seven lamps with its
snuffers and its [1]trays of pure gold.
24 He made it and all its utensils from
a talent of pure gold.
25 ¶ [a]Then he made the altar of incense of acacia wood: a cubit [1]long and
a cubit [2]wide, square, and two cubits
[3]high; its horns were *of one piece*
with it.
26 He overlaid it with pure gold, its
top and its [1]sides all around, and its
horns; and he made a gold molding for it
all around.
27 He made two golden rings for it under its molding, on its two sides—on opposite sides—as holders for poles with
which to carry it.
28 He made the poles of acacia wood
and overlaid them with gold.
29 [a]And he made the holy anointing
oil and the pure, fragrant incense of
spices, the work of a perfumer.

The Tabernacle Completed

38 [a]Then he made the altar of burnt
offering of acacia wood, five [1]cu-
bits [2]long, and five cubits [3]wide, square,
and three cubits [4]high.
2 He made its horns on its four corners, its horns [1]being *of one piece* with
it, and he overlaid it with [2]bronze.
3 He made all the utensils of the altar,
the pails and the shovels and the basins,
the flesh hooks and the firepans; he made
all its utensils of bronze.
4 He made for the altar a grating of
bronze network beneath, under its ledge,
reaching halfway up.
5 He cast four rings on the four ends
of the bronze grating *as* holders for the
poles.
6 He made the poles of acacia wood
and overlaid them with bronze.
7 He inserted the poles into the rings
on the sides of the altar, with which to
carry it. He made it hollow with planks.
8 ¶ [a]Moreover, he made the laver of
bronze with its base of bronze, [1]from
the mirrors of the serving women who
served at the doorway of the tent of meeting.
9 ¶ [a]Then he made the court: [1]for
the south side the hangings of the court
were of fine twisted linen, one hundred
cubits;
10 their twenty pillars, and their twenty [1]sockets, *made* of bronze; the hooks of
the pillars and their [2]bands *were* of silver.
11 For the north side *there were* one
hundred cubits; their twenty pillars and
their twenty [1]sockets *were* of bronze,
the hooks of the pillars and their [2]bands
were of silver.
12 For the west side *there were* hangings of fifty cubits *with* their ten pillars
and their ten [1]sockets; the hooks of the
pillars and their [2]bands *were* of silver.
13 For the [1]east side fifty cubits.
14 The hangings for the *one* [1]side *of
the gate were* fifteen cubits, *with* their
three pillars and their three [2]sockets,
15 and so for the [1]other [2]side. [3]On
both sides of the gate of the court *were*

10 [1]I.e. One cubit equals approx 18 in. [2]Lit *its length* [3]Lit *its width* [4]Lit *its height* [a]Ex 25:23-29
16 [1]Or *platters* [2]Lit *libation bowls*
17 [1]Or *calyxes* [a]Ex 25:31-39
18 [1]Lit *second*
19 [1]Or *calyx*
20 [1]Or *calyxes*
21 [1]Or *calyx*
22 [1]Or *calyxes*
23 [1]Lit *snuff dishes*
25 [1]Lit *its length* [2]Lit *its width* [3]Lit *its height* [a]Ex 30:1-5
26 [1]Lit *walls*
29 [a]Ex 30:23-25,34,35
38:1 [1]I.e. One cubit equals approx 18 in. [2]Lit *its length* [3]Lit *its width* [4]Lit *its height* [a]Ex 27:1-8
2 [1]Lit *were* [2]Or *copper,* and so for *bronze* throughout the ch
8 [1]Lit *with* [a]Ex 30:18
9 [1]Lit *to the side of the Negev, to the south* [a]Ex 27:9-19
10 [1]Or *bases* [2]Or *fillets, rings*
11 [1]Or *bases* [2]Or *fillets, rings*
12 [1]Or *bases* [2]Or *fillets, rings*
13 [1]Lit *east side, eastward*
14 [1]Lit *shoulder* [2]Or *bases*
15 [1]Lit *second* [2]Lit *shoulder* [3]Lit *On this side and on that side*

hangings of fifteen cubits, *with* their three pillars and their three [4]sockets.

16 All the hangings of the court all around *were* of fine twisted linen.

17 The [1]sockets for the pillars *were* of [2]bronze, the hooks of the pillars and their [3]bands, of silver; and the overlaying of their tops, of silver, and all the pillars of the court were furnished with silver [3]bands.

18 The screen of the gate of the court was the work of the [1]weaver, of [2]blue and purple and scarlet *material* and fine twisted linen. And the length *was* twenty cubits and the [3]height *was* five cubits, corresponding to the hangings of the court.

19 Their four pillars and their four [1]sockets *were* of bronze; their hooks *were* of silver, and the overlaying of their tops and their [2]bands *were* of silver.

20 All the pegs of the [1]tabernacle and of the court all around *were* of bronze.

The Cost of the Tabernacle

21 ¶ [1]This is the number of the things for the [2]tabernacle, the [2]tabernacle of the testimony, as they were [3]numbered according to the [4]command of Moses, for the service of the Levites, by the hand of Ithamar the son of Aaron the priest.

22 Now [a]Bezalel the son of Uri, the son of Hur, of the tribe of Judah, made all that the LORD had commanded Moses.

23 With him *was* [a]Oholiab the son of Ahisamach, of the tribe of Dan, an engraver and a skillful workman and a [1]weaver in [2]blue and in purple and in scarlet *material,* and fine linen.

24 ¶ All the gold that was used for the work, in all the work of the sanctuary, even the gold of the wave offering, was 29 talents and 730 shekels, according to [a]the shekel of the sanctuary.

25 [a]The silver of those of the congregation who were [1]numbered was 100 talents and 1,775 shekels, according to the shekel of the sanctuary;

26 [a]a beka a head (*that is,* half a shekel according to the shekel of the sanctuary), for each one who passed over to those who were [1]numbered, from twenty years old and upward, for [b]603,550 men.

27 The hundred talents of silver were for casting the [1]sockets of the sanctuary and the [1]sockets of the veil; one hundred [1]sockets for the hundred talents, a talent for a [1]socket.

28 Of the 1,775 *shekels,* he made hooks for the pillars and overlaid their tops and made [1]bands for them.

29 The bronze of the wave offering was 70 talents and 2,400 shekels.

30 With it he made the [1]sockets to the doorway of the tent of meeting, and the bronze altar and its bronze grating, and all the utensils of the altar,

31 and the [1]sockets of the court all around and the [1]sockets of the gate of the court, and all the pegs of the [2]tabernacle and all the pegs of the court all around.

The Priestly Garments

39 Moreover, from the [1a]blue and purple and scarlet *material,* they made finely [b]woven garments for ministering in the holy place [2]as well as the holy garments which were for Aaron, just as the LORD had commanded Moses.

2 ¶ [a]He made the ephod of gold, *and* of [1]blue and purple and scarlet *material,* and fine twisted linen.

3 Then they hammered out gold sheets and cut *them* into threads [1]to be woven in *with* the [2]blue and the purple and the scarlet *material,* and the fine linen, the work of a skillful workman.

4 They made attaching shoulder pieces for [1]the ephod; it was attached at its two *upper* ends.

5 The skillfully woven band which was on it was like its workmanship, [1]of the same material: of gold *and* of [2]blue and purple and scarlet *material,* and fine twisted linen, just as the LORD had commanded Moses.

6 ¶ [a]They made the onyx stones, set in gold filigree *settings;* they were engraved *like* the engravings of a signet, according to the names of the sons of Israel.

7 And [a]he placed them on the shoulder pieces of the ephod, *as* memorial stones for the sons of Israel, just as the LORD had commanded Moses.

8 ¶ [a]He made the breastpiece, the work of a skillful workman, like the workmanship of the ephod: of gold *and* of [1]blue and purple and scarlet *material* and fine twisted linen.

9 It was square; they made the breastpiece folded double, a span [1]long and a span [2]wide when folded double.

10 And they [1]mounted four rows of stones on it. The first row *was* a row of ruby, topaz, and emerald;

11 and the second row, a turquoise, a sapphire and a diamond;

12 and the third row, a jacinth, an agate, and an amethyst;

13 and the fourth row, a beryl, an onyx, and a jasper. They were set in gold filigree *settings* when they were [1]mounted.

14 The stones were corresponding to the names of the sons of Israel; they were

15 [4]Or *bases*

17 [1]Or *bases* [2]Or *copper* [3]Or *fillets, rings*

18 [1]Lit *variegator;* i.e. a weaver in colors [2]Or *violet* [3]Lit *height in width*

19 [1]Or *bases* [2]Or *fillets, rings*

20 [1]Lit *dwelling place*

21 [1]Lit *These are the appointed things of the tabernacle* [2]Lit *dwelling place* [3]Lit *appointed* [4]Lit *mouth*

22 [a]Ex 31:2

23 [1]Lit *variegator;* i.e. a weaver in colors [2]Or *violet* [a]Ex 31:6

24 [a]Ex 30:13; Lev 27:25; Num 3:47; 18:16

25 [1]Lit *mustered* [a]Ex 30:11-16

26 [1]Lit *mustered* [a]Ex 30:13,15 [b]Ex 12:37; Num 1:46; 26:51

27 [1]Or *bases*

28 [1]Or *fillets, rings*

30 [1]Or *bases*

31 [1]Or *bases* [2]Lit *dwelling place*

39:1 [1]Or *violet* [2]Lit *and they made* [a]Ex 35:23 [b]Ex 31:10; 35:19

2 [1]Or *violet* [a]Ex 28:6-12

3 [1]Lit *to work* [2]Or *violet*

4 [1]Lit *it*

5 [1]Lit *from it* [2]Or *violet*

6 [a]Ex 28:9-11

7 [a]Ex 28:12

8 [1]Or *violet* [a]Ex 28:15-28

9 [1]Lit *its length* [2]Lit *its width*

10 [1]Lit *filled*

13 [1]Lit *filled*

twelve, corresponding to their names,
engraved with the engravings of a signet,
each with its name for the twelve tribes.
15 They made on the breastpiece
chains like cords, of twisted cordage
work in pure gold.
16 They made two gold filigree *settings* and two gold rings, and put the two
rings on the two ends of the breastpiece.
17 Then they put the two gold cords in
the two rings at the ends of the breastpiece.
18 They put the *other* two ends of the
two cords on the two filigree *settings,*
and put them on the shoulder pieces of
the ephod at the front of it.
19 They made two gold rings and
placed *them* on the two ends of the
breastpiece, on its inner edge which was
next to the ephod.
20 Furthermore, they made two gold
rings and placed them on the bottom of
the two shoulder pieces of the ephod, on
the front of it, close to the place where
it joined, above the woven band of the
ephod.
21 They bound the breastpiece by its
rings to the rings of the ephod with a
[1]blue cord, so that it would be on the
woven band of the ephod, and that the
breastpiece would not come loose from
the ephod, just as the LORD had commanded Moses.
22 ¶ [a]Then he made the robe of the
ephod of woven work, all of [1]blue;
23 [a]and the opening of the robe was
at the top in the center, as the opening of
a coat of mail, with a binding all around
its opening, so that it would not be torn.
24 They made pomegranates of [1]blue
and purple and scarlet *material and* twisted *linen* on the hem of the robe.
25 They also made bells of pure gold,
and put the bells between the pomegranates all around on the hem of the [1]robe,
26 [1]alternating a bell and a pomegranate all around on the hem of the robe for
the service, just as the LORD had commanded Moses.
27 ¶ [a]They made the tunics of finely
woven linen for Aaron and his sons,
28 and the turban of fine linen, and
the decorated [1]caps of fine linen, and the
linen breeches of fine twisted linen,
29 and the sash of fine twisted linen,
and [1]blue and purple and scarlet *material,* the work of the [2]weaver, just as the
LORD had commanded Moses.
30 ¶ [a]They made the plate of the holy
crown of pure gold, and [1]inscribed it like
the engravings of a signet, "Holy to the
LORD."
31 They [1]fastened a [2]blue cord to it,
to [1]fasten it on the turban above, just as
the LORD had commanded Moses.
32 ¶ Thus all the work of the [1]taber-
nacle of the tent of meeting was completed; and the sons of Israel did according to
all that the LORD had commanded Moses;
so they did.
33 They brought the tabernacle to Moses, the tent and all its [1]furnishings: its
clasps, its boards, its bars, and its pillars
and its [2]sockets;
34 and the covering of rams' skins
[1]dyed red, and the covering of porpoise
skins, and the screening veil;
35 the ark of the testimony and its
poles and the [1]mercy seat;
36 the table, all its utensils, and the
bread of the [1]Presence;
37 the pure *gold* lampstand, [1]with its
arrangement of lamps and all its utensils,
and the oil for the light;
38 and the gold altar, and the anointing oil and the fragrant incense, and the
veil for the doorway of the tent;
39 the [1]bronze altar and its [1]bronze
grating, its poles and all its utensils, the
laver and its stand;
40 the hangings for the court, its pillars and its [1]sockets, and the screen for
the gate of the court, its cords and its pegs
and all the [2]equipment for the service of
the tabernacle, for the tent of meeting;
41 the woven garments for ministering in the holy place and the holy garments for Aaron the priest and the garments of his sons, to minister as priests.
42 So the sons of Israel did all the work
according to all that the LORD had commanded Moses.
43 And Moses [1]examined all the work
and behold, they had done it; just as the
LORD had commanded, this they had
done. So Moses [a]blessed them.

The Tabernacle Erected

40 Then the LORD spoke to Moses,
saying,
2 "[a]On the first day of the first month
you shall set up the [1]tabernacle of the
tent of meeting.
3 "[a]You shall place the ark of the testimony there, and you shall screen the ark
with the veil.
4 "You shall [a]bring in the table and
[1b]arrange what belongs on it; and you
shall [c]bring in the lampstand and
[2]mount its lamps.
5 "Moreover, you shall [a]set the gold
altar of incense before the ark of the testimony, and set up the veil for the doorway
to the tabernacle.
6 "You shall set the altar of burnt offering in front of the doorway of the tabernacle of the tent of meeting.

21 [1]Or *violet*
22 [1]Or *violet* [a]Ex 28:31,34
23 [a]Ex 28:32
24 [1]Or *violet*
25 [1]Lit *robe, between the pomegranates*
26 [1]Lit *a bell and a pomegranate, a bell...*
27 [a]Ex 28:39, 40,42
28 [1]Lit *headgear*
29 [1]Or *violet* [2]Lit *variegator;* i.e. a weaver in colors
30 [1]Lit *wrote on it a writing* [a]Ex 28:36,37
31 [1]Lit *put* [2]Or *violet*
32 [1]Lit *dwelling place*
33 [1]Or *utensils* [2]Or *bases*
34 [1]Or *tanned*
35 [1]Lit *propitiatory*
36 [1]Lit *Face*
37 [1]Lit *its lamps, the lamps set in order*
39 [1]Or *copper*
40 [1]Or *bases* [2]Or *utensils*
43 [1]Lit *saw* [a]Lev 9:22,23; Num 6:23-26
40:2 [1]Lit *dwelling place* [a]Ex 19:1; 40:17; Num 1:1
3 [a]Ex 26:33; 40:21; Num 4:5
4 [1]Lit *arrange its arrangement* [2]Or *light* [a]Ex 26:35; 40:22 [b]Ex 25:30; 40:23 [c]Ex 40:24f
5 [a]Ex 40:26

7 "You shall [a]set the laver between the tent of meeting and the altar and put water [1]in it.

8 "You shall set up the court all around and [1]hang up the veil for the gateway of the court.

9 "Then you shall take the anointing oil and [a]anoint the tabernacle and all that is in it, and shall consecrate it and all its [1]furnishings; and it shall be holy.

10 "You shall anoint the altar of burnt offering and all its utensils, and consecrate the altar, and [a]the altar shall be most holy.

11 "You shall anoint the laver and its stand, and consecrate it.

12 "Then you shall [a]bring Aaron and his sons to the doorway of the tent of meeting and wash them with water.

13 "[a]You shall put the holy garments on Aaron and anoint him and consecrate him, that he may minister as a priest to Me.

14 "You shall bring his sons and put tunics on them;

15 and you shall anoint them even as you have anointed their father, that they may minister as priests to Me; and their anointing will [1]qualify them for a [a]perpetual priesthood throughout their generations."

16 Thus Moses did; according to all that the LORD had commanded him, so he did.

17 ¶ Now [a]in the first month [1]of the second year, on the first *day* of the month, the [2]tabernacle was erected.

18 Moses erected the tabernacle and [1]laid its [2]sockets, and set up its boards, and [1]inserted its bars and erected its pillars.

19 He spread the tent over the tabernacle and put the covering of the tent [1]on top of it, just as the LORD had commanded Moses.

20 Then he took [a]the testimony and put *it* into the ark, and [1]attached the poles to the ark, and put the [2]mercy seat [3]on top of the ark.

21 He brought the ark into the tabernacle, and [a]set up a veil for the screen, and screened off the ark of the testimony, just as the LORD had commanded Moses.

22 Then he [a]put the table in the tent of meeting on the north side of the tabernacle, outside the veil.

23 He set the arrangement of [a]bread in order on it before the LORD, just as the LORD had commanded Moses.

24 Then he placed the lampstand in the tent of meeting, opposite the table, on the south side of the tabernacle.

25 He [a]lighted the lamps before the LORD, just as the LORD had commanded Moses.

26 Then he [a]placed the gold altar in the tent of meeting in front of the veil;

27 and he [a]burned fragrant incense on it, just as the LORD had commanded Moses.

28 Then he set up the [1]veil for the doorway of the tabernacle.

29 He [a]set the altar of burnt offering *before* the doorway of the tabernacle of the tent of meeting, and [b]offered on it the burnt offering and the meal offering, just as the LORD had commanded Moses.

30 He placed the laver between the tent of meeting and the altar and put water in it for washing.

31 [a]From it Moses and Aaron and his sons washed their hands and their feet.

32 When they entered the tent of meeting, and when they approached the altar, they washed, just as the LORD had commanded Moses.

33 He [a]erected the court all around the [1]tabernacle and the altar, and [2]hung up the veil for the gateway of the court. Thus Moses finished the work.

The Glory of the LORD

34 ¶ [a]Then the cloud covered the tent of meeting, and the [b]glory of the LORD filled the tabernacle.

35 Moses [a]was not able to enter the tent of meeting because the cloud had settled on it, and the glory of the LORD filled the tabernacle.

36 Throughout all their journeys [a]whenever the cloud was taken up from over the tabernacle, the sons of Israel would set out;

37 but [a]if the cloud was not taken up, then they did not set out until the day when it was taken up.

38 For throughout all their journeys, [a]the cloud of the LORD was on the tabernacle by day, and there was fire in it by night, in the sight of all the house of Israel.

---

7 [1]Lit *there* [a]Ex 30:18; 40:30
8 [1]Lit *put the screen*
9 [1]Or *utensils* [a]Ex 30:26; Lev 8:10
10 [a]Ex 29:37
12 [a]Lev 8:1-6
13 [a]Ex 28:41; Lev 8:13
15 [1]Lit *be for them* [a]Ex 29:9; Num 25:13
17 [1]Lit *in* [2]Lit *dwelling place* [a]Ex 40:2
18 [1]Lit *put* [2]Or *bases*
19 [1]Lit *over it above*
20 [1]Lit *set* [2]Lit *propitiatory* [3]Lit *over the ark above* [a]Ex 25:16; Deut 10:5; 1 Kin 8:9; 2 Chr 5:10; Heb 9:4
21 [a]Ex 26:33
22 [a]Ex 26:35
23 [a]Ex 25:30; Lev 24:5,6
25 [a]Ex 25:37; 40:4
26 [a]Ex 30:6; 40:5
27 [a]Ex 30:7
28 [1]Or *screen*
29 [a]Ex 40:6 [b]Ex 29:38-42
31 [a]Ex 30:19,20
33 [1]Or *dwelling place* [2]Lit *put the screen* [a]Ex 27:9-18; 40:8
34 [a]Num 9:15-23 [b]1 Kin 8:11; Ezek 43:4f; Rev 15:8
35 [a]1 Kin 8:11; 2 Chr 5:13,14
36 [a]Num 9:17; Neh 9:19
37 [a]Num 9:19-22
38 [a]Ex 13:21; Num 9:12,15; Ps 78:14; Is 4:5

Leviticus

Title and Background

Leviticus receives its name from the *Septuagint* (the Greek translation of the Old Testament) and means "relating to the Levites." Although Leviticus does not deal only with the special duties of the Levites, it is so named because it is concerned mainly with the service of worship at the tabernacle. Exodus had given the directions for building the tabernacle. Leviticus gives the laws and regulations for worship at the tabernacle, along with instructions on ceremonial cleanness, moral laws, holy days, the sabbath year, and the Year of Jubilee.

Author and Date of Writing

Leviticus 1:1 states that the contents of Leviticus were given to Moses by God. In more than fifty places in the book it is said that the Lord spoke to Moses. The date for the writing of the book by Moses would appear to be between about 1446 and about 1406 B.C.

Theme and Message

The key thought of Leviticus is holiness—the holiness of God and of man. The command to be holy is stated in 11:45—"thus you shall be holy, for I am holy." The instructions or laws in the book were given to help the Israelites worship and live as God's holy people. Some of the instructions deal with such things as offering sacrifices, handling everyday problems concerning cleanliness, and observing special holidays. The Levitical priests are also given special instructions for making sacrifices and carrying out God's commands.

Outline

I. Laws and Instructions for Offerings (1:1—7:38)
II. Appointment of Aaron and His Sons as God's Priests (8:1—10:20)
III. Rules for Holy Living (11:1—15:33)
IV. The Day of Atonement (16:1–34)
V. Practical Holiness (17:1—22:33)
VI. The Sabbath, Feasts and Seasons (23:1—25:55)
VII. Conditions for God's Blessings (26:1—27:34)

The Law of Burnt Offerings

1 Then [a]the LORD called to Moses and
spoke to him from the tent of meeting, saying,
2 "Speak to the sons of Israel and say
to them, 'When any man of you brings an
[1a]offering to the LORD, you shall bring
your [1]offering of animals from [b]the herd
or the flock.
3 'If his offering is a [a]burnt offering
from the herd, he shall offer it, a male
[b]without defect; he shall offer it [c]at the
doorway of the tent of meeting, that he
may be accepted before the LORD.
4 '[a]He shall lay his hand on the head
of the burnt offering, that it may be accepted for him to make [b]atonement on
his behalf.
5 '[a]He shall slay the [1]young bull before the LORD; and Aaron's sons the
priests shall offer up [b]the blood and
[c]sprinkle the blood around on the altar
that is at the doorway of the tent of meeting.
6 '[a]He shall then skin the burnt offering and cut it into its pieces.
7 '[a]The sons of Aaron the priest shall
put fire on the altar and arrange wood on
the fire.
8 'Then Aaron's sons the priests shall
arrange the pieces, the head and the
[a]suet over the wood which is on the fire
that is on the altar.
9 'Its [a]entrails, however, and its legs
he shall wash with water. And [b]the
priest shall offer up in smoke all of it
on the altar for a burnt offering, an offering by fire of [c]a soothing aroma to the
LORD.
10 ¶ 'But if his offering is from the
flock, of the sheep or of the goats, for a
burnt offering, he shall offer it a [a]male
without defect.
11 '[a]He shall slay it on the side of the

1:1 [a]Ex 19:3; Num 7:89
2 [1]Heb *qorban* [a]Mark 7:11 [b]Lev 22:18f
3 [a]Lev 6:8-13 [b]Ex 12:5; Lev 22:20-24; Deut 15:21 [c]Lev 17:8; Deut 12:5
4 [a]Ex 29:10; Lev 3:2 [b]Ex 29:33; Lev 4:20; 2 Chr 29:23
5 [1]Or *one of the herd*; lit *son of the herd* [a]Ex 29:11 [b]Lev 17:11 [c]Lev 1:11; Heb 12:24; 1 Pet 1:2
6 [a]Lev 7:8
7 [a]Lev 6:8-13
8 [a]Lev 1:12
9 [a]Ex 12:9 [b]Num 15:8-10 [c]Gen 8:21; Ex 29:18; Lev 1:13; Num 15:3; Eph 5:2
10 [a]Ex 12:5; Lev 1:3; Ezek 43:22; 1 Pet 1:19
11 [a]Ex 24:6; Lev 1:5

altar northward before the LORD, and Aaron's sons the priests shall sprinkle its
blood around on the altar.
12 'He shall then cut it into its pieces
with its head and its [a]suet, and the priest
shall arrange them on the wood which is
on the fire that is on the altar.
13 'The entrails, however, and the legs
he shall wash with water. And [a]the
priest shall offer all of it, and offer it up in
smoke on the altar; it is a burnt offering,
an offering by fire of a soothing aroma to
the LORD.
14 ¶ 'But if his offering to the LORD is
a burnt offering of birds, then he shall
bring his offering from the [a]turtledoves
or from young pigeons.
15 'The priest shall bring it to the altar,
and wring off its head and offer it up in
smoke on the altar; and its blood is to be
drained out [a]on the side of the altar.
16 'He shall also take away its crop
with its feathers and cast it beside the
altar eastward, to the place of the
[1a]ashes.
17 'Then he shall tear it by its wings,
but [a]shall not sever *it.* And the priest
shall offer it up in smoke on the altar on
the wood which is on the fire; [b]it is a
burnt offering, an offering by fire of a
soothing aroma to the LORD.

The Law of Grain Offerings

2 'Now when anyone presents a
[a]grain offering as an offering to the
LORD, his offering shall be of fine flour,
and he shall pour oil on it and put frankincense on it.
2 'He shall then bring it to Aaron's
sons the priests; and shall take from it
[a]his handful of its fine flour and of its
oil with all of its frankincense. And the
priest shall offer *it* up in smoke *as* its
[b]memorial portion on the altar, an offering by fire of a soothing aroma to the
LORD.
3 '[a]The remainder of the grain offering belongs to [b]Aaron and his sons: a
thing most holy, of the offerings to the
LORD by fire.
4 ¶ 'Now when you bring an offering
of a grain offering baked in an oven, *it
shall be* [a]unleavened cakes of fine flour
mixed with oil, or unleavened wafers
[1]spread with oil.
5 'If your offering is a grain offering
made [a]on the griddle, *it shall be* of fine
flour, unleavened, mixed with oil;
6 you shall break it into bits and pour
oil on it; it is a grain offering.
7 'Now if your offering is a grain offering *made* [a]in a [1]pan, it shall be made of
fine flour with oil.
8 'When you bring in the grain offering which is made of these things to the
LORD, it shall be presented to the priest
and he shall bring it to the altar.
9 'The priest then shall take up from
the grain offering [a]its memorial portion,
and shall offer *it* up in smoke on the altar
as an offering by fire of a soothing aroma
to the LORD.
10 '[a]The remainder of the grain offering belongs to Aaron and his sons: a thing
most holy of the offerings to the LORD by
fire.
11 ¶ '[a]No grain offering, which you
bring to the LORD, shall be made with
leaven, for you shall not offer [1]up in
smoke any leaven or any honey as an [b]of-
fering by fire to the LORD.
12 '[a]As an offering of first fruits you
shall bring them to the LORD, but they
shall not ascend for a soothing aroma on
the altar.
13 'Every grain offering of yours, moreover, you shall season with salt, so that
[a]the salt of the covenant of your God
shall not be lacking from your grain offering; with all your offerings you shall offer
salt.
14 ¶ 'Also if you bring a grain offering
of early ripened things to the LORD, you
shall bring [a]fresh heads of grain roasted
in the fire, grits of new growth, for the
grain offering of your early ripened
things.
15 'You shall then put oil on it and lay
incense on it; it is a grain offering.
16 'The priest shall offer up in smoke
[a]its memorial portion, part of its grits
and its oil with all its incense as an offering by fire to the LORD.

The Law of Peace Offerings

3 'Now if his offering is a [a]sacrifice of
peace offerings, if he is going to offer
out of the herd, whether male or female,
he shall offer it [b]without defect before
the LORD.
2 '[a]He shall lay his hand on the head
of his offering and [b]slay it at the doorway of the tent of meeting, and Aaron's
sons the priests shall sprinkle the blood
around on the altar.
3 'From the sacrifice of the peace offerings he shall present an offering by fire
to the LORD, the fat that covers the entrails and all the fat that is on the entrails,
4 and the two kidneys with the fat
that is on them, which is on the loins, and
the [1]lobe of the liver, which he shall
remove with the kidneys.
5 'Then [a]Aaron's sons shall offer *it* up
in smoke on the altar [b]on the burnt offering, which is on the wood that is on the
fire; [c]it is an offering by fire of a soothing
aroma to the LORD.

12 [a]Lev 3:3,4
13 [a]Num 15:4-7; 28:11-14
14 [a]Gen 15:9; Lev 5:7,11; 12:8; Luke 2:24
15 [a]Lev 5:9
16 [1]Or *fat ashes* [a]Lev 6:10
17 [a]Gen 15:10; Lev 5:8 [b]Lev 9:13
2:1 [a]Lev 6:14-18; Num 15:4
2 [a]Lev 5:12; 6:15 [b]Lev 2:9, 16; 5:12; 24:7; Acts 10:4
3 [a]Lev 2:10; 6:16 [b]Lev 10:12, 13
4 [1]Lit *anointed* [a]Ex 29:2
5 [a]Lev 6:21; 7:9
7 [1]Lit *lidded cooking pan* [a]Lev 7:9
9 [a]Lev 2:2,16; 5:12
10 [a]Lev 2:3; 6:16
11 [1]Lit *up from it* [a]Ex 23:18; 34:25; Lev 6:16, 17 [b]Ex 29:25; Lev 1:13
12 [a]Ex 34:22; Lev 7:13; 23:10, 17,18
13 [a]Num 18:19; 2 Chr 13:5; Ezek 43:24
14 [a]Lev 23:14
16 [a]Lev 2:2
3:1 [a]Lev 7:11-34; 17:5 [b]Lev 1:3; 22:20-24
2 [a]Lev 1:4 [b]Ex 29:11,16,20
4 [1]Or *appendage on*
5 [a]Lev 7:28-34 [b]Ex 29:38-42; Num 28:3-10 [c]Num 15:8-10; 28:12-14

6 ‘But if his offering for a sacrifice of peace offerings to the LORD is from the flock, he shall offer it, male or female, [a]without defect.

7 ‘If he is going to offer [a]a lamb for his offering, then he shall offer it [b]before the LORD,

8 and [a]he shall lay his hand on the head of his offering and [b]slay it before the tent of meeting, and Aaron’s sons shall [c]sprinkle its blood around on the altar.

9 ‘From the [a]sacrifice of peace offerings he shall bring as an offering by fire to the LORD, its fat, [1]the entire fat tail which he shall remove close to the backbone, and the fat that covers the entrails and all the fat that is on the entrails,

10 and the two kidneys with the fat that is on them, which is on the loins, and the [1]lobe of the liver, which he shall remove [a]with the kidneys.

11 ‘Then the priest shall offer *it* up in smoke [a]on the altar *as* [b]food, an offering by fire to the LORD.

12 ¶ ‘Moreover, if his offering is [a]a goat, then he shall offer it before the LORD,

13 and he shall lay his hand on its head and slay it before the tent of meeting, and the sons of Aaron shall sprinkle its blood around on the altar.

14 ‘From it he shall present his offering as an offering by fire to the LORD, the fat that covers the entrails and all the fat that is on the entrails,

15 and the two kidneys with the fat that is on them, which is on the loins, and the [1]lobe of the liver, which he shall remove [a]with the kidneys.

16 ‘The priest shall offer them up in smoke on the altar *as* food, an offering by fire for a soothing aroma; [a]all fat is the LORD’S.

17 ‘It is a [a]perpetual statute throughout your generations in all your dwellings: you shall not eat any fat [b]or any blood.’ ”

The Law of Sin Offerings

4 Then the LORD spoke to Moses, saying,

2 “Speak to the sons of Israel, saying, ‘If a person sins [a]unintentionally in any of the [1]things which the LORD has [b]commanded not to be done, and commits any of them,

3 [a]if the anointed priest sins so as to bring guilt on the people, then let him offer to the LORD a [1]bull without defect as a sin offering for the sin he has [2]committed.

4 ‘He shall bring the bull to the doorway of the tent of meeting before the LORD, and [a]he shall lay his hand on the head of the bull and slay the bull before the LORD.

5 ‘Then the [a]anointed priest is to take some of the blood of the bull and bring it to the tent of meeting,

6 and the priest shall dip his finger in the blood and sprinkle some of the blood seven times before the LORD, in front of [a]the veil of the sanctuary.

7 ‘The priest shall also put some of the blood on the horns of [a]the altar of fragrant incense which is before the LORD in the tent of meeting; and all the blood of the bull he shall pour out at the base of the altar of burnt offering which is at the doorway of the tent of meeting.

8 ‘[a]He shall remove from it all the fat of the bull of the sin offering: the fat that covers the entrails, and all the fat which is on the entrails,

9 and the two kidneys with the fat that is on them, which is on the loins, and the [1]lobe of the liver, which he shall remove [a]with the kidneys

10 (just as it is removed from the ox of the sacrifice of peace offerings), and the priest is to offer them up in smoke on the altar of burnt offering.

11 ‘But [a]the hide of the bull and all its flesh with its head and its legs and its entrails and its refuse,

12 [1]that is, all *the rest of* the bull, he is to bring out to [a]a clean place outside the camp where the [2]ashes are poured out, and burn it on wood with fire; where the [2]ashes are poured out it shall be burned.

13 ¶ ‘[a]Now if the whole congregation of Israel commits error and the matter [1]escapes the notice of the assembly, and they commit any of the [2]things which the LORD has commanded not to be done, and they become guilty;

14 [a]when the sin [1]which they have [2]committed becomes known, then the assembly shall offer [b]a [3]bull of the herd for a sin offering and bring it before the tent of meeting.

15 ‘Then [a]the elders of the congregation shall lay their hands on the head of the bull before the LORD, and the bull shall be slain [b]before the LORD.

16 ‘Then the anointed priest is to bring some of the blood of the bull to the tent of meeting;

17 and [a]the priest shall dip his finger in the blood and sprinkle *it* seven times before the LORD, in front of the veil.

18 ‘He shall put some of the blood on the horns of [a]the altar which is before the LORD [1]in the tent of meeting; and all the blood he shall pour out at the base of

---

6 [a]Lev 3:1; 22:20-24

7 [a]Num 15:4,5; 28:4-8 [b]Lev 17:8,9; 1 Kin 8:62

8 [a]Lev 1:4 [b]Lev 3:2 [c]Lev 1:5

9 [1]Lit *the fat tail, entire* [a]Lev 17:5; Num 7:88; 1 Sam 10:8; 2 Sam 6:17; 1 Kin 3:15; 8:63, 64; 1 Chr 16:1

10 [1]Or *appendage on* [a]Lev 3:4, 15

11 [a]Lev 3:5 [b]Lev 3:16; 21:6, 8,17,22

12 [a]Num 15:6-11

15 [1]Or *appendage on* [a]Lev 3:4; 7:4

16 [a]Lev 7:23-25

17 [a]Lev 6:18, 22; 7:34,36; 10:9,15; 16:29; 17:7; 23:14,21; 24:3 [b]Lev 7:26; 17:10-16

4:2 [1]Lit *commands of the* LORD *which are not to be done* [a]Lev 4:22,27; 5:15-18; 22:14 [b]Lev 4:13

3 [1]Or *bull of the herd* [2]Lit *sinned* [a]Lev 4:14,23,28

4 [a]Lev 1:4; 4:15; Num 8:12

5 [a]Lev 4:3,17

6 [a]Ex 40:21,26

7 [a]Lev 4:18,25, 30,34; 8:15; 9:9; 16:18

8 [a]Lev 3:3,4

9 [1]Or *appendage on* [a]Lev 3:4

11 [a]Lev 9:11; Num 19:5

12 [1]Lit *and* [2]Or *fat ashes are* [a]Lev 4:21; 6:10, 11; 16:27

13 [1]Lit *is hidden from the eyes of* [2]Lit *commands of the* LORD *which are not to be done* [a]Num 15:24-26

14 [1]Lit *concerning which* [2]Lit *sinned* [3]Lit *son of the herd* [a]Lev 4:3 [b]Lev 4:3,23, 28

15 [a]Lev 8:14, 18,22; Num 8:10,12 [b]Lev 1:3

17 [a]Lev 4:6

18 [1]Lit *which is in* [a]Lev 4:7,25, 30,34

Old Testament Sacrifices

SACRIFICE	OT REFERENCES	ELEMENTS	PURPOSE
Burnt Offering	Lev 1; 6:8-13; 8:18-21; 16:24	Bull, ram or male bird (dove or young pigeon for the poor); wholly consumed; no defect	Voluntary act of worship; atonement for unintentional sin in general; expression of devotion, commitment and complete surrender to God
Grain Offering	Lev 2; 6:14-23	Grain, fine flour, olive oil, incense, baked bread (cakes or wafers), salt; no yeast or honey; accompanied burnt offering and fellowship offering (along with drink offering)	Voluntary act of worship; recognition of God's goodness and provisions; devotion to God
Peace Offering	Lev 3; 7:11-34	Any animal without defect from herd or flock; variety of breads	Voluntary act of worship; thanksgiving and fellowship (it included a communal meal)
Sin Offering	Lev 4:1–5:13; 6:24-30; 8:14-17; 16:3-22	1. Young bull: for high priest and congregation 2. Male goat: for leader 3. Female goat or lamb: for common person 4. Dove or pigeon: for the poor 5. Tenth of an ephah of fine flour: for the very poor	Mandatory atonement for specific unintentional sin; confession of sin; forgiveness of sin; cleansing from defilement
Guilt Offering	Lev. 5:14–6:7; 7:1-6	Ram or lamb	Mandatory atonement for unintentional sin requiring restitution; cleansing from defilement; make restitution; pay 20% fine

When more than one kind of offering was presented (as in Num 7:16,17), the procedure was usually as follows: (1) sin offering or guilt offering, (2) burnt offering, (3) peace offering and grain offering (along with a drink offering). This sequence furnishes part of the spiritual significance of the sacrificial system. First, sin had to be dealt with (sin offering or guilt offering). Second, the worshiper committed himself completely to God (burnt offering and grain offering). Third, fellowship or communion between the Lord, the priest and the worshiper (peace offering) was established.

the altar of burnt offering which is at the doorway of the tent of meeting.

19 ‘[a]He shall remove all its fat from it and offer it up in smoke on the altar.

20 ‘He shall also do with the bull just as he did with [a]the bull of the sin offering; thus he shall do with it. So [b]the priest shall make atonement for them, and they will be forgiven.

21 ‘Then he is to bring out the bull to *a place* outside the camp and burn it as he burned the first bull; it is [a]the sin offering for the assembly.

22 ¶ ‘When [a]a leader [b]sins and unintentionally does any one of all the [1]things which the LORD his God has commanded not to be done, and he becomes guilty,

23 [1a]if his sin [2]which he has committed is made known to him, he shall bring for his offering a [3b]goat, [c]a male without defect.

24 ‘He shall lay his hand on the head of the male goat and slay it in the place where [1]they slay the burnt offering before the LORD; it is a sin offering.

25 ‘Then the priest is to take some of the blood of the sin offering with his finger and put it on [a]the horns of the altar of burnt offering; and *the rest of* its blood he shall pour out at the base of the altar of burnt offering.

26 ‘[a]All its fat he shall offer up in smoke on the altar as *in the case of* the fat of the sacrifice of peace offerings. Thus [b]the priest shall make atonement for him in regard to his sin, and he will be forgiven.

27 ¶ ‘Now if [1]anyone of [2]the common people sins [a]unintentionally in doing any of the [3]things which the LORD has commanded not to be done, and becomes guilty,

28 [1a]if his sin which he has [2]committed is made known to him, then he shall bring for his offering a [3b]goat, a [c]female without defect, for his sin which he has [2]committed.

29 ‘[a]He shall lay his hand on the head of the sin offering and [b]slay the sin offering at the place of the burnt offering.

30 ‘The priest shall take some of its blood with his finger and put it on the horns of [a]the altar of burnt offering; and [b]all *the rest of* its blood he shall pour out at the base of the altar.

31 ‘[a]Then he shall remove all its fat, just as the fat was removed from the sacrifice of peace offerings; and the priest shall offer it up in smoke on the altar for [b]a soothing aroma to the LORD. Thus the priest shall make atonement for him, [1]and he will be forgiven.

32 ¶ ‘But if he brings [a]a lamb as his offering for a sin offering, he shall bring it, a female without defect.

33 ‘[a]He shall lay his hand on the head of the sin offering and slay it for a sin offering [b]in the place where [1]they slay the burnt offering.

34 ‘The priest is to take some of the blood of the sin offering with his finger and put it on the horns of [a]the altar of burnt offering, and [b]all *the rest of* its blood he shall pour out at the base of the altar.

35 ‘Then he shall remove [a]all its fat, just as the fat of the lamb is removed from the sacrifice of the peace offerings, and the priest shall offer them up in smoke on the altar, on the offerings by fire to the LORD. Thus [b]the priest shall make atonement for him in regard to his sin which he has [1]committed, and he will be forgiven.

The Law of Guilt Offerings

5 ‘Now if a person sins after he hears a [1]public [a]adjuration *to testify* when he is a witness, whether he has seen or *otherwise* known, if he does not tell *it,* then he will bear his [2]guilt.

2 ‘Or if a person touches [a]any unclean thing, whether a carcass of an unclean beast or the carcass of unclean cattle or a carcass of unclean swarming things, though it is hidden from him and he is unclean, then he will be guilty.

3 ‘Or if he touches human uncleanness, of whatever *sort* his uncleanness *may* be with which he becomes unclean, and it is hidden from him, and then he comes to know *it,* he will be guilty.

4 ‘Or if a person [a]swears thoughtlessly with his lips to do evil or to do good, in whatever matter a man may speak thoughtlessly with an oath, and it is hidden from him, and then he comes to know *it,* he will be guilty in one of these.

5 ‘So it shall be when he becomes guilty in one of these, that he shall [a]confess that in which he has sinned.

6 ‘He shall also bring his guilt offering to the LORD for his sin which he has [1]committed, [a]a female from the flock, a lamb or a [2]goat as a sin offering. So the priest shall make atonement on his behalf for his sin.

7 ¶ ‘But if [1]he cannot afford a lamb, then he shall bring to the LORD his guilt offering for that in which he has sinned, two turtledoves or two young pigeons, [a]one for a sin offering and the other for a burnt offering.

8 ‘He shall bring them to the priest, who shall offer first that which is for the sin offering and shall nip its head at the

19 [a]Lev 4:8

20 [a]Lev 4:8,21 [b]Num 15:25,28

21 [a]Lev 4:13f; 16:15-17; Num 15:24-26

22 [1]Lit *commands of the LORD which are not to be done* [a]Num 31:13; 32:2 [b]Lev 4:2,27

23 [1]Lit *or* [2]Lit *in which he has sinned* [3]Lit *buck of the goats* [a]Lev 4:3 [b]Lev 4:3,14, 28 [c]Lev 4:28

24 [1]Lit *one slays*

25 [a]Lev 4:7,18, 30,34

26 [a]Lev 4:19 [b]Lev 4:20,31; 5:10,13,16,18; 6:7

27 [1]Lit *one soul* [2]Lit *the people of the land* [3]Lit *commands of the LORD which are not to be done* [a]Lev 4:2; Num 15:27

28 [1]Lit *or* [2]Lit *sinned* [3]Or *female goat* [a]Lev 4:3 [b]Lev 4:3,14, 23,32 [c]Lev 4:23

29 [a]Lev 1:4; 4:4,24 [b]Lev 1:5, 11

30 [a]Lev 4:7,18, 25,34 [b]Lev 4:7

31 [1]Or *so that he may be* [a]Lev 4:8 [b]Gen 8:21; Ex 29:18; Lev 1:9,13; 2:2,9,12

32 [a]Lev 4:28

33 [1]Lit *one slays* [a]Lev 1:4,5 [b]Lev 4:29

34 [a]Lev 4:7,18, 25,30 [b]Lev 4:7

35 [1]Lit *sinned* [a]Lev 4:26,31 [b]Lev 4:20

5:1 [1]Lit *voice of an oath* [2]Or *iniquity* [a]Prov 29:24; Jer 23:10

2 [a]Lev 11:8,11, 24-40; Num 19:11-16; Deut 14:8

4 [a]Num 30:6,8; Ps 106:33

5 [a]Lev 16:21; 26:40; Num 5:7; Prov 28:13

6 [1]Lit *sinned* [2]Lit *female goat* [a]Lev 4:28,32

7 [1]Lit *his hand does not reach enough for* [a]Lev 12:6,8; 14:22, 30,31

front of its neck, but he [a]shall not sever *it.*

9 'He shall also sprinkle some of the blood of the sin offering [a]on the side of the altar, while the rest of the blood shall be drained out [b]at the base of the altar: it is a sin offering.

10 'The second he shall then prepare as a burnt offering [a]according to the ordinance. [b]So the priest shall make atonement on his behalf for his sin which he has [1]committed, and it will be forgiven him.

11 ¶ 'But [a]if his [1]means are insufficient for two turtledoves or two young pigeons, then for his offering for that which he has sinned, he shall bring the tenth of an [2]ephah of fine flour for a sin offering; [b]he shall not put oil on it or place incense on it, for it is a sin offering.

12 'He shall bring it to the priest, and the priest shall take his handful of it as its memorial portion and offer *it* up in smoke on the altar, [1]with the offerings of the LORD by fire: it is a sin offering.

13 'So the priest shall make atonement for him concerning his sin which he has [1]committed from [a]one of these, and it will be forgiven him; then [b]*the rest* shall become the priest's, like the grain offering.' "

14 ¶ Then the LORD spoke to Moses, saying,

15 "[a]If a person acts unfaithfully and sins [b]unintentionally against the LORD'S holy things, then he shall bring his [c]guilt offering to the LORD: [d]a ram without defect from the flock, according to your valuation in silver by shekels, in *terms of* the [e]shekel of the sanctuary, for a guilt offering.

16 "[a]He shall make restitution for that which he has sinned against the holy thing, and shall add to it a fifth part of it and give it to the priest. [b]The priest shall then make atonement for him with the ram of the guilt offering, and it will be forgiven him.

17 ¶ "Now if a person sins and does any of the things [1]which the LORD has commanded not to be done, [a]though he was unaware, still he is guilty and shall bear his punishment.

18 "He is then to bring to the priest [a]a ram without defect from the flock, according to your valuation, for a guilt offering. So the priest shall make atonement for him concerning his error in which he sinned [b]unintentionally and did not know *it,* and it will be forgiven him.

19 "It is a guilt offering; he was certainly guilty before the LORD."

Guilt Offering

6 [1]Then the LORD spoke to Moses, saying,

2 "[a]When a person sins and acts unfaithfully against the LORD, and deceives his companion in regard to a deposit or a security entrusted *to him,* or through robbery, or *if* he has extorted from his companion,

3 or [a]has found what was lost and lied about it and sworn falsely, so that he sins in regard to any one of the things a man may do;

4 then it shall be, when he sins and becomes guilty, that he shall [a]restore what he took by robbery or what he got by extortion, or the deposit which was [1]entrusted to him or the lost thing which he found,

5 or anything about which he swore falsely; [a]he shall make restitution for it [1]in full and add to it one-fifth more. [b]He shall give it to the one to whom it belongs on the day *he presents* his guilt offering.

6 "Then he shall bring to the priest his guilt offering to the LORD, [a]a ram without defect from the flock, according to your valuation, for a guilt offering,

7 and [a]the priest shall make atonement for him before the LORD, and he will be forgiven for any one of the things which he may have done to incur guilt."

The Priest's Part in the Offerings

8 ¶ [1]Then the LORD spoke to Moses, saying,

9 "Command Aaron and his sons, saying, 'This is [a]the law for the burnt offering: the burnt offering itself *shall remain* on the hearth on the altar all night until the morning, and [b]the fire on the altar is to be kept burning on it.

10 'The priest is to put on [a]his linen robe, and he shall put on undergarments next to his flesh; and he shall take up the [1]ashes *to* which the fire [2]reduces the burnt offering on the altar and place them beside the altar.

11 'Then he shall take off his garments and put on other garments, and carry the [1]ashes outside the camp to a clean place.

12 'The fire on the altar shall be kept burning on it. It shall not go out, but the priest shall burn wood on it every morning; and he shall lay out the burnt offering on it, and offer up in smoke the fat portions of the peace offerings [a]on it.

13 'Fire shall be kept burning continually on the altar; it is not to go out.

14 ¶ 'Now this is the law of the grain offering: the sons of Aaron shall present it before the LORD in front of the altar.

15 '[a]Then one *of them* shall lift up

8 [a]Lev 1:17
9 [a]Lev 1:15 [b]Lev 4:7,18
10 [1]Lit *sinned* [a]Lev 1:14-17 [b]Lev 4:20,26; 5:13,16
11 [1]Lit *hand does not reach* [2]I.e. Approx one bu [a]Lev 14:21-32; 27:8 [b]Lev 2:1,2
12 [1]Lit *upon*
13 [1]Lit *sinned* [a]Lev 5:4,5 [b]Lev 2:3
15 [a]Num 5:5-8 [b]Lev 4:2; 22:14 [c]Lev 7:1-10 [d]Lev 6:6 [e]Ex 30:13
16 [a]Lev 6:5; 22:14; Num 5:7, 8 [b]Lev 7:2-7
17 [1]Lit *the commands of the* LORD *which are* [a]Lev 4:2; 5:19
18 [a]Lev 5:15 [b]Lev 5:17
6:1 [1]Ch 5:20 in Heb
2 [a]Ex 22:7-15
3 [a]Ex 23:4; Deut 22:1-4
4 [1]Or *deposited with* [a]Lev 24:18, 21
5 [1]Lit *in its sum* [a]Lev 5:16 [b]Num 5:8
6 [a]Lev 5:15
7 [a]Lev 7:2-5
8 [1]Ch 6:1 in Heb
9 [a]Ex 29:38-42; Num 28:3-10 [b]Lev 6:12,13
10 [1]Or *fat ashes* [2]Lit *consumes* [a]Ex 28:39,42; 39:27,28
11 [1]Or *fat ashes*
12 [a]Lev 3:5
15 [a]Lev 2:2,9

from it a handful of the fine flour of the
grain offering, [1]with its oil and all the
incense that is on the grain offering, and
he shall offer *it* up in smoke on the altar,
a soothing aroma, as its memorial offering
to the LORD.
16 '[a]What is left of it Aaron and his
sons are to eat. It shall be eaten as unleavened cakes in a holy place; they are to eat
it in the court of the tent of meeting.
17 '[a]It shall not be baked with leaven.
I have given it as their share from My
offerings by fire; [b]it is most holy, like the
sin offering and [c]the guilt offering.
18 '[a]Every male among the sons of
Aaron may eat it; it is a permanent ordinance throughout your generations, from
the offerings by fire to the LORD. [b]Who-
ever touches them will become consecrated.' "
19 ¶ Then the LORD spoke to Moses,
saying,
20 "This is the offering which Aaron
and his sons are to present to the LORD on
the day when he is anointed; the tenth of
an [a]ephah of fine flour as [b]a [1]regular
grain offering, half of it in the morning
and half of it in the evening.
21 "It shall be prepared with oil on a
[a]griddle. When it is *well* stirred, you
shall bring it. You shall present the grain
offering in baked pieces as a soothing aroma to the LORD.
22 "The anointed priest who will be in
his place [1]among his sons shall [2]offer it.
By a permanent ordinance it shall be entirely offered up in smoke to the LORD.
23 "So every grain offering of the priest
shall be burned entirely. It shall not be
eaten."
24 ¶ Then the LORD spoke to Moses,
saying,
25 "Speak to Aaron and to his sons, saying, 'This is the law of the sin offering:
[a]in the place where the burnt offering is
slain the sin offering shall be slain before
the LORD; it is most holy.
26 '[a]The priest who offers it for sin
shall eat it. It shall be eaten in a holy
place, in the court of the tent of meeting.
27 '[a]Anyone who touches its flesh will
become consecrated; and when any of
its blood [1]splashes on a garment, in a
holy place you shall wash what was
splashed on.
28 'Also [a]the earthenware vessel in
which it was boiled shall be broken; and
if it was boiled in a bronze vessel, then it
shall be scoured and rinsed in water.
29 '[a]Every male among the priests
may eat of it; [b]it is most holy.
30 'But no sin offering [a]of which any of
the blood is brought into the tent of meeting to make atonement [b]in the holy place
shall be eaten; [c]it shall be burned with
fire.

The Priest's Part in the Offerings

7 'Now this is the law of the [a]guilt
offering; it is most holy.
2 'In [a]the place where they slay the
burnt offering they are to slay the guilt
offering, and he shall sprinkle its blood
around on the altar.
3 'Then he shall offer from it all its fat:
the [a]fat tail and the fat that covers the
entrails,
4 and the two kidneys with the fat
that is on them, which is on the loins, and
the lobe on the liver he shall remove
[a]with the kidneys.
5 'The priest shall offer them up in
smoke on the altar as an offering by fire
to the LORD; it is a guilt offering.
6 '[a]Every male among the priests
may eat of it. It shall be eaten in a holy
place; it is most holy.
7 'The guilt offering is like the [a]sin
offering, there is one law for them; the
[b]priest who makes atonement with it
[1]shall have it.
8 'Also the priest who presents any
man's burnt offering, [1]that priest shall
have for himself the skin of the burnt
offering which he has presented.
9 'Likewise, every grain offering that
is baked in the oven and everything prepared in a [1]pan or on a [a]griddle [2]shall
belong to the priest who presents it.
10 'Every grain offering, mixed with oil
or dry, shall [1]belong to all the sons of
Aaron, [2]to all alike.
11 ¶ 'Now this is the law of the [a]sacri-
fice of peace offerings which shall be presented to the LORD.
12 'If he offers it by way of [a]thanksgiv-
ing, then along with the sacrifice of
thanksgiving he shall offer [b]unleavened
cakes mixed with oil, and unleavened
wafers [1]spread with oil, and cakes *of*
well stirred fine flour mixed with oil.
13 'With the sacrifice of his peace offerings for thanksgiving, he shall present his
offering with cakes of [a]leavened bread.
14 'Of [1]this he shall present one of every offering as a [2]contribution to the
LORD; [a]it shall [3]belong to the priest who
sprinkles the blood of the peace offerings.
15 ¶ '[a]Now *as for* the flesh of the sacrifice of his thanksgiving peace offerings,
it shall be eaten on the day of his offering;
he shall not leave any of it over until
morning.
16 'But if the sacrifice of his offering is
a [a]votive or a freewill offering, it shall be
eaten on the day that he offers his sacrifice, and on the [1]next day what is left of
it may be eaten;

15 [1]Lit *and some of*
16 [a]Lev 2:3; 10:12-14; Ezek 44:29
17 [a]Lev 2:11 [b]Ex 40:10; Lev 6:25,26,29,30; Num 18:9 [c]Lev 7:7; 10:16-18
18 [a]Lev 6:29; 7:6; Num 18:10; 1 Cor 9:13 [b]Lev 6:27
20 [1]Lit *grain offering continually* [a]Lev 5:11 [b]Num 4:16
21 [a]Lev 2:5
22 [1]Lit *from among* [2]Lit do
25 [a]Lev 1:11
26 [a]Lev 6:29
27 [1]Lit *one sprinkles* [a]Lev 7:19
28 [a]Lev 11:33; 15:12
29 [a]Lev 6:18 [b]Lev 6:17,25
30 [a]Lev 4:1-21 [b]Lev 4:7,18 [c]Lev 4:11,12,21
7:1 [a]Lev 5:14-6:7
2 [a]Lev 1:11
3 [a]Lev 3:9
4 [a]Lev 3:4
6 [a]Lev 6:18,29; Num 18:9
7 [1]Lit *it shall be for him* [a]Lev 6:25,26,30 [b]1 Cor 9:13; 10:18
8 [1]Lit *for the priest, it shall be for him*
9 [1]Lit *lidded cooking pan* [2]Lit *for the priest, it shall be for him* [a]Lev 2:5
10 [1]Lit *be* [2]Lit *a man as his brother*
11 [a]Lev 3:1
12 [1]Or *anointed* [a]Lev 7:15 [b]Lev 2:4; Num 6:15
13 [a]Lev 2:12; 23:17,18; Amos 4:5
14 [1]Lit *it* [2]Or *heave offering* [3]Lit *be for* [a]Num 18:8,11,19
15 [a]Lev 22:29, 30
16 [1]Lit *morrow and what* [a]Lev 19:5-8

17 [a]but what is left over from the
flesh of the sacrifice on the third day shall
be burned with fire.
18 'So if any of the flesh of the sacrifice
of his peace offerings should *ever* be eat-
en on the third day, he who offers it will
not be accepted, *and* it will not be reckoned to his *benefit.* It shall be an [a]offen-
sive thing, and the person who eats of it
will bear his *own* iniquity.
19 ¶ 'Also the flesh that touches anything unclean shall not be eaten; it shall
be burned with fire. [1]As for *other* flesh,
anyone who is clean may eat *such* flesh.
20 '[a]But the person who eats the flesh
of the sacrifice of peace offerings which
belong to the LORD, [1]in his uncleanness,
that person [b]shall be cut off from his people.
21 '[a]When anyone touches anything
unclean, whether human uncleanness, or
an unclean animal, or any unclean [1]de-
testable thing, and eats of the flesh of the
sacrifice of peace offerings which belong
to the LORD, that person shall be cut off
from his people.' "
22 ¶ Then the LORD spoke to Moses,
saying,
23 "Speak to the sons of Israel, saying,
'You shall not eat [a]any fat *from* an ox, a
sheep or a goat.
24 'Also the fat of *an animal* which dies
and the fat of an animal [a]torn *by beasts*
may be put to any other use, but you must
certainly not eat it.
25 'For whoever eats the fat of the animal from which [1]an offering by fire is
offered to the LORD, even the person who
eats shall be cut off from his people.
26 '[a]You are not to eat any blood, either of bird or animal, in any of your
dwellings.
27 'Any person who eats any blood,
even that person shall be cut off from his
people.' "
28 ¶ Then the LORD spoke to Moses,
saying,
29 "Speak to the sons of Israel, saying,
'He who offers [a]the sacrifice of his peace
offerings to the LORD shall bring his offering to the LORD from the sacrifice of his
peace offerings.
30 'His own hands are to bring offerings by fire to the LORD. He shall bring
the fat with the breast, that the [a]breast
may be [1]presented as a wave offering
before the LORD.
31 'The priest shall offer up the fat in
smoke on the altar, but [a]the breast shall
belong to Aaron and his sons.
32 'You shall give [a]the right thigh to
the priest as a [1]contribution from the
sacrifices of your peace offerings.
33 'The one among the sons of Aaron
who offers the blood of the peace offerings and the fat, the right thigh shall be
his as *his* portion.
34 'For I have taken [a]the breast of the
wave offering and the thigh of the [1]con-
tribution from the sons of Israel from the
sacrifices of their peace offerings, and
have given them to Aaron the priest and
to his sons as *their* due forever from the
sons of Israel.
35 ¶ 'This is [1]that which is consecrated to Aaron and [1]that [a]which is consecrated to his sons from the offerings by
fire to the LORD, in that day when he
presented them to serve as priests to the
LORD.
36 '[1]These the LORD had commanded
to be given them from the sons of Israel
in the day that He [a]anointed them. It is
their due forever throughout their generations.' "
37 ¶ This is the law of the burnt offering, the grain offering and the sin offering
and the guilt offering and [a]the ordination
offering and the sacrifice of peace offerings,
38 [a]which the LORD commanded
Moses at Mount Sinai in the day that
He commanded the sons of Israel to
[1]present their offerings to the LORD in
the wilderness of Sinai.

The Consecration of Aaron and His Sons

8 Then the LORD spoke to Moses, saying,
2 "[a]Take Aaron and his sons with
him, and the [b]garments and [c]the anointing oil and the bull of the sin offering, and
the two rams and the basket of unleavened bread,
3 and assemble all the congregation
at the doorway of the tent of meeting."
4 So Moses did just as the LORD commanded him. When the congregation
was assembled at the doorway of the tent
of meeting,
5 Moses said to the congregation,
"This is the thing which the LORD has
commanded to do."
6 ¶ Then [a]Moses had Aaron and his
sons come near and [b]washed them with
water.
7 He [a]put the tunic on him and girded him with the sash, and clothed him
with the robe and put the ephod on him;
and he girded him with the artistic band
of the ephod, [1]with which he tied *it* to
him.
8 He then placed the [1]breastpiece
on him, and in the [1]breastpiece he put
[2a]the Urim and the Thummim.
9 He also placed the turban on his

17 [a]Ex 12:10
18 [a]Lev 19:7; Prov 15:8
19 [1]Lit *And the flesh*
20 [1]Lit *and his uncleanness is on him* [a]Lev 22:3-7; Num 19:13 [b]Lev 7:25
21 [1]Some mss read *swarming thing* [a]Lev 5:2,3
23 [a]Lev 3:17
24 [a]Ex 22:31; Lev 17:15; 22:8
25 [1]Lit *he offers an offering by fire*
26 [a]Gen 9:4; Lev 17:10-16; 19:26; Deut 12:23; 1 Sam 14:33; Acts 15:20
29 [a]Lev 3:1
30 [1]Lit *waved* [a]Ex 29:26,27; Lev 8:29; Num 6:20
31 [a]Num 18:11; Deut 18:3
32 [1]Or *heave offering* [a]Ex 29:27; Lev 7:34; 9:21; Num 6:20
34 [1]Or *heave offering* [a]Ex 29:27; Lev 10:14,15; Num 18:18
35 [1]Lit *the anointed portion of* [a]Num 18:8
36 [1]Lit *Which* [a]Ex 40:13-15; Lev 8:12,30
37 [a]Ex 29:22-34; Lev 8:22,23
38 [1]Or *offer* [a]Lev 1:1; 26:46; 27:34; Deut 4:5
8:2 [a]Ex 28:1 [b]Lev 6:10 [c]Ex 30:25
6 [a]Ex 29:4-6 [b]Ex 30:19,20; Ps 26:6; 1 Cor 6:11; Eph 5:26
7 [1]Lit *and with it* [a]Ex 28:4
8 [1]Lit *pouch* [2]I.e. the lights and perfections [a]Ex 28:30; Num 27:21; Deut 33:8; 1 Sam 28:6; Ezra 2:63; Neh 7:65

head, and on the turban, at its front, he
placed [a]the golden plate, the holy crown,
just as the LORD had commanded Moses.
10 ¶ Moses then took [a]the anointing
oil and anointed the [1]tabernacle and all
that was in it, and consecrated them.
11 He sprinkled some of it on the altar
seven times and anointed the altar and all
its utensils, and the basin and its stand, to
[a]consecrate them.
12 Then he poured some of the
[a]anointing oil on Aaron's head and
anointed him, to consecrate him.
13 [a]Next Moses had Aaron's sons
come near and clothed them with tunics,
and girded them with sashes and bound
[1]caps on them, just as the LORD had commanded Moses.
14 ¶ Then he brought [a]the bull of the
sin offering, and Aaron and his sons laid
their hands on the head of the bull of the
sin offering.
15 Next [1]Moses slaughtered *it* and
took the blood and with his finger [a]put
some of it around on the horns of the
altar, and purified the altar. Then he
poured out *the rest of* the blood at the
base of the altar and consecrated it, to
make atonement for it.
16 He also [a]took all the fat that was on
the entrails and the [1]lobe of the liver,
and the two kidneys and their fat; and
Moses offered it up in smoke on the altar.
17 [a]But the bull and its hide and its
flesh and its refuse he burned in the fire
outside the camp, just as the LORD had
commanded Moses.
18 ¶ Then he presented [a]the ram of
the burnt offering, and Aaron and his
sons laid their hands on the head of the
ram.
19 [1]Moses slaughtered *it* and sprinkled the blood around on the altar.
20 When he had cut the ram into its
pieces, Moses [a]offered up the head and
the pieces and the suet in smoke.
21 After he had washed the entrails
and the legs with water, Moses [a]offered
up the whole ram in smoke on the altar.
It was a burnt offering for a soothing aroma; it was an offering by fire to the LORD,
just as the LORD had commanded Moses.
22 ¶ Then he presented the second
ram, [a]the ram of [1]ordination, and Aaron
and his sons laid their hands on the head
of the ram.
23 [1]Moses slaughtered *it* and took
some of its blood and [a]put it on the lobe
of Aaron's right ear, and on the thumb of
his right hand and on the big toe of his
right foot.
24 He also had Aaron's sons come
near; and Moses put some of the blood on
the lobe of their right ear, and on the
thumb of their right hand and on the big
toe of their right foot. Moses then [a]sprin-
kled *the rest of* the blood around on the
altar.
25 He took the fat, and the fat tail, and
all the fat that was on the entrails, and the
[1]lobe of the liver and the two kidneys
and their fat and the right thigh.
26 [a]From the basket of unleavened
bread that was before the LORD, he took
one unleavened cake and one cake of
bread *mixed with* oil and one wafer, and
placed *them* on the portions of fat and on
the right thigh.
27 He then [a]put all *these* on the hands
of Aaron and on the hands of his sons and
presented them as a wave offering before
the LORD.
28 Then Moses [a]took them from their
hands and offered them up in smoke on
the altar with the burnt offering. They
were an ordination offering for [b]a soothing aroma; it was an offering by fire to the
LORD.
29 Moses also took [a]the breast and
presented it for a wave offering before the
LORD; it was [b]Moses' portion of the ram
of ordination, just as the LORD had commanded Moses.
30 ¶ So Moses [a]took some of the
anointing oil and some of the blood
which was on the altar and sprinkled it
on Aaron, on his garments, on his sons,
and on the garments of his sons with him;
and he consecrated Aaron, his garments,
and his sons, and the garments of his sons
with him.
31 ¶ Then Moses said to Aaron and to
his sons, "[a]Boil the flesh at the doorway
of the tent of meeting, and eat it there
together with the bread which is in the
basket of the ordination offering, just as
I commanded, [b]saying, 'Aaron and his
sons shall eat it.'
32 "[a]The remainder of the flesh and of
the bread you shall burn in the fire.
33 "[a]You shall not go outside the doorway of the tent of meeting for seven days,
until the day that the period of your ordination is fulfilled; for he will [1]ordain you
through seven days.
34 "The LORD has commanded to do as
has been done this day, to make atonement on your behalf.
35 "At the doorway of the tent of meeting, moreover, you shall remain day and
night for seven days and [a]keep the
charge of the LORD, so that you will not
die, for so I have been commanded."
36 Thus Aaron and his sons did all the
things which the LORD had commanded
through Moses.

9 [a]Ex 28:36
10 [1]Or *dwelling place* [a]Ex 30:26-29; Lev 8:2
11 [a]Ex 29:36, 37; 30:29
12 [a]Ex 29:7; 30:30; Lev 21:10,12; Ps 133:2
13 [1]Lit *headgear* [a]Ex 29:8,9
14 [a]Ex 29:10; Lev 4:4; Ps 66:15; Ezek 43:19
15 [1]Lit *he slaughtered it and Moses took* [a]Ex 29:12; Lev 4:7; Ezek 43:20
16 [1]Or *appendage on* [a]Ex 29:13
17 [a]Ex 29:14; Lev 4:11,12
18 [a]Ex 29:15; Lev 8:2
19 [1]Lit *He slaughtered it and Moses sprinkled*
20 [a]Lev 1:8
21 [a]Ex 29:18
22 [1]Lit *filling,* and so throughout the ch [a]Ex 29:31; Lev 8:2
23 [1]Lit *He slaughtered it and Moses took* [a]Ex 29:20,21
24 [a]Heb 9:18-22
25 [1]Or *appendage on*
26 [a]Ex 29:23
27 [a]Ex 29:24
28 [a]Ex 29:25 [b]Gen 8:21
29 [a]Lev 7:31-34 [b]Ex 29:26; Ps 99:6
30 [a]Ex 29:21
31 [a]Ex 29:31 [b]Ex 29:32
32 [a]Ex 29:34
33 [1]Lit *fill your hands* [a]Ex 29:35
35 [a]Num 3:7; 9:19; Deut 11:1; 1 Kin 2:3; Ezek 48:11

Aaron Offers Sacrifices

9 Now it came about [a]on the eighth day that Moses called Aaron and his sons and the elders of Israel;

2 and he said to Aaron, "[a]Take for yourself a calf, a bull, for a sin offering and a ram for a burnt offering, *both* without defect, and offer *them* before the LORD.

3 "Then to the sons of Israel you shall speak, saying, 'Take a male goat for a sin offering, and a calf and a lamb, both one year old, without defect, for a burnt offering,

4 and an ox and a ram for peace offerings, to sacrifice before the LORD, and a grain offering mixed with oil; for today [a]the LORD will appear to you.' "

5 So they took what Moses had commanded to the front of the tent of meeting, and the whole congregation came near and stood before the LORD.

6 Moses said, "This is the thing which the LORD has commanded you to do, that [a]the glory of the LORD may appear to you."

7 Moses then said to Aaron, "Come near to the altar and [1a]offer your sin offering and your burnt offering, that you may make atonement for yourself and for the people; then make the offering [2]for the people, that you may make atonement for them, just as the LORD has commanded."

8 ¶ [a]So Aaron came near to the altar and slaughtered the calf of the sin offering which was for himself.

9 [a]Aaron's sons presented the blood to him; and he dipped his finger in the blood and [b]put *some* on the horns of the altar, and poured out *the rest of* the blood at the base of the altar.

10 The fat and the kidneys and the [1]lobe of the liver of the sin offering, he then offered up in smoke on the altar just as the LORD had commanded Moses.

11 [a]The flesh and the skin, however, he burned with fire outside the camp.

12 ¶ Then he slaughtered the burnt offering; and Aaron's sons handed the blood to him and he sprinkled it around on the altar.

13 They handed the burnt offering to him in [1]pieces, with the head, and he offered *them* up in smoke on the altar.

14 He also washed the entrails and the legs, and offered *them* up in smoke with the burnt offering on the altar.

15 ¶ Then he presented the people's offering, and took the [a]goat of the sin offering which was for the people, and slaughtered it and offered it for sin, like the first.

16 He also presented the burnt offering, and [1]offered it according to [a]the ordinance.

17 Next he presented [a]the grain offering, and filled his [1]hand with some of it and offered *it* up in smoke on the altar, [b]besides the burnt offering of the morning.

18 ¶ Then [a]he slaughtered the ox and the ram, the sacrifice of peace offerings which was for the people; and Aaron's sons handed the blood to him and he sprinkled it around on the altar.

19 As for the portions of fat from the ox and from the ram, the fat tail, and the *fat* [a]covering, and the kidneys and the [1]lobe of the liver,

20 they now placed the portions of fat on the breasts; and he offered [1]them up in smoke on the altar.

21 But [a]the breasts and the right thigh Aaron [1]presented as a wave offering before the LORD, just as Moses had commanded.

22 ¶ Then Aaron lifted up his hands toward the people and [a]blessed them, and he stepped down after making the sin offering and the burnt offering and the peace offerings.

23 Moses and Aaron went into the tent of meeting. When they came out and blessed the people, [a]the glory of the LORD appeared to all the people.

24 [a]Then fire came out from before the LORD and consumed the burnt offering and the portions of fat on the altar; and when all the people saw *it,* they shouted and fell on their faces.

The Sin of Nadab and Abihu

10 Now [a]Nadab and Abihu, the sons of Aaron, took their respective [b]firepans, and after putting fire in them, placed incense on it and offered strange fire before the LORD, which He had not commanded them.

2 [a]And fire came out from the presence of the LORD and consumed them, and they died before the LORD.

3 Then Moses said to Aaron, "It is what the LORD spoke, saying,

'By those who [a]come near Me I
[1b]will be treated as holy,
And before all the people I will
[c]be honored.' "

So Aaron, therefore, kept silent.

4 ¶ Moses called also to [a]Mishael and Elzaphan, the sons of Aaron's uncle Uzziel, and said to them, "Come forward, carry your [1]relatives away from the front of the sanctuary to the outside of the camp."

5 So they came forward and carried

9:1 [a]Ezek 43:27
2 [a]Ezek 29:1; Lev 4:3
4 [a]Ex 29:43
6 [a]Ex 24:16; Lev 9:23
7 [1]Lit *make* [2]Lit *of* [a]Heb 5:3; 7:27
8 [a]Lev 4:1-12
9 [a]Lev 9:12,18 [b]Lev 4:7
10 [1]Or *appendage on*
11 [a]Lev 4:11, 12; 8:17
13 [1]Lit *its pieces*
15 [a]Lev 4:27-31
16 [1]Lit *made* [a]Lev 1:1-13
17 [1]Lit *palm* [a]Lev 2:1-3 [b]Lev 3:5
18 [a]Lev 3:1-11
19 [1]Or *appendage on* [a]Lev 3:9
20 [1]Lit *the portions of fat*
21 [1]Lit *waved* [a]Ex 29:26,27; Lev 7:30-34
22 [a]Num 6:22-26; Deut 21:5; Luke 24:50
23 [a]Lev 9:6; Num 16:19
24 [a]1 Kin 18:38,39; 2 Chr 7:1
10:1 [a]Ex 24:1,9; Num 3:2; 26:61 [b]Lev 16:12
2 [a]Num 3:4; 16:35; 26:61
3 [1]Or *will show Myself holy* [a]Ex 19:22; Lev 21:6 [b]Ex 30:30; Ezek 38:16 [c]Ex 14:4, 17; Is 49:3; Ezek 28:22
4 [1]Lit *brothers* [a]Ex 6:22

them still in their [a]tunics to the outside
of the camp, as Moses had said.
6 Then Moses said to Aaron and to
his sons Eleazar and Ithamar, "[a]Do not
[1]uncover your heads nor tear your
clothes, so that you will not die and that
He will not [b]become wrathful against all
the congregation. But your [2]kinsmen,
the whole house of Israel, shall bewail
the burning which the LORD has
[3]brought about.
7 "You shall not even go out from the
doorway of the tent of meeting, or you
will die; for [a]the LORD'S anointing oil is
upon you." So they did according to the
word of Moses.
8 ¶ The LORD then spoke to Aaron,
saying,
9 "[a]Do not drink wine or strong
drink, neither you nor your sons with
you, when you come into the tent of
meeting, so that you will not die—it is a
perpetual statute throughout your generations—
10 and [a]so as to make a distinction
between the holy and the profane, and
between the unclean and the clean,
11 and [a]so as to teach the sons of Israel all the statutes which the LORD has
spoken to them through Moses."
12 ¶ Then Moses spoke to Aaron, and
to his surviving sons, [a]Eleazar and Ithamar, "[b]Take the grain offering that is left
over from the LORD'S offerings by fire and
eat it unleavened beside the altar, for it is
most holy.
13 "You shall eat it, moreover, in a holy
place, because it is your due and your
sons' due out of the LORD'S offerings by
fire; for thus I have been commanded.
14 "[a]The breast of the wave offering,
however, and the thigh of the offering
you may eat in a clean place, you and your
sons and your daughters with you; for
they have been given as your due and
your sons' due out of the sacrifices of the
peace offerings of the sons of Israel.
15 "[a]The thigh offered by lifting up and
the breast offered by waving they shall
bring along with the offerings by fire of
the portions of fat, to present as a wave
offering before the LORD; so it shall be a
thing perpetually due you and your sons
with you, just as the LORD has commanded."
16 ¶ But Moses searched carefully for
the [a]goat of the sin offering, and behold,
it had been burned up! So he was angry
with Aaron's surviving sons Eleazar and
Ithamar, saying,
17 "Why [a]did you not eat the sin offering at the holy place? For it is most holy,
and [1]He gave it to you to bear away [b]the
guilt of the congregation, to make atonement for them before the LORD.
18 "Behold, [a]since its blood had not
been brought inside, into the sanctuary,
you should certainly have [b]eaten it in the
sanctuary, just as I commanded."
19 But Aaron spoke to Moses, "Behold, this very day they [a]presented their
sin offering and their burnt offering before the LORD. When things like these
happened to me, if I had eaten a sin offering today, would it have been good in the
sight of the LORD?"
20 When Moses heard *that,* it seemed
good in his sight.

Laws about Animals for Food

11 The LORD spoke again to Moses
and to Aaron, saying to them,
2 "Speak to the sons of Israel, saying,
'[a]These are the creatures which you may
eat from all the animals that are on the
earth.
3 'Whatever divides a hoof, thus making split hoofs, *and* chews the cud, among
the animals, that you may eat.
4 'Nevertheless, [a]you are not to eat of
these, among those which chew the cud,
or among those which divide the hoof:
the camel, for though it chews cud, it
does not divide the hoof, it is unclean to
you.
5 'Likewise, the [1]shaphan, for though
it chews cud, it does not divide the hoof,
it is unclean to you;
6 the [1]rabbit also, for though it
chews cud, it does not divide the hoof, it
is unclean to you;
7 and the pig, for though it divides
the hoof, thus making a split hoof, it does
not chew cud, it is unclean to you.
8 'You shall not eat of their flesh nor
touch their carcasses; they are unclean to
you.
9 ¶ '[a]These you may eat, whatever is
in the water: all that have fins and scales,
those in the water, in the seas or in the
rivers, you may eat.
10 '[a]But whatever is in the seas and in
the rivers that does not have fins and
scales among all the teeming life of the
water, and among all the living creatures
that are in the water, they are detestable
things to you,
11 and they shall be [1]abhorrent to
you; you may not eat of their flesh, and
their carcasses you shall detest.
12 'Whatever in the water does not
have fins and scales is [1]abhorrent to you.

Avoid the Unclean

13 ¶ 'These, moreover, [a]you shall detest among the birds; they are [1]abhor-

5 [a]Ex 29:5; Lev 8:13
6 [1]Lit *unbind* [2]Lit *brothers* [3]Lit *burned* [a]Lev 21:1-5,10-12 [b]Num 1:53; 16:22,46; 18:5; Josh 7:1; 22:18, 20; 2 Sam 24:1
7 [a]Ex 28:41; Lev 21:12
9 [a]Prov 20:1; 31:5; Is 28:7; Ezek 44:21; Hos 4:11; Luke 1:15; Eph 5:18; 1 Tim 3:3; Titus 1:7
10 [a]Lev 11:47; 20:25; Ezek 22:26
11 [a]Deut 17:10, 11; 33:10
12 [a]Ex 6:23; Num 3:2 [b]Lev 6:14-18
14 [a]Lev 7:30-34; Num 18:11
15 [a]Lev 7:34
16 [a]Lev 9:3,15
17 [1]Or *was given* [a]Lev 6:24-30 [b]Ex 28:38; Lev 22:16; Num 18:1
18 [a]Lev 6:30 [b]Lev 6:26
19 [a]Lev 9:8,12
11:2 [a]Deut 14:3-21
4 [a]Acts 10:14
5 [1]A small, shy, furry animal *(Hyrax syriacus)* found in the peninsula of the Sinai, northern Israel, and the region round the Dead Sea; KJV *coney,* orig NASB *rock badger*
6 [1]Or *hare*
9 [a]Deut 14:9
10 [a]Deut 14:10
11 [1]Lit *detestable things*
12 [1]Lit *detestable things*
13 [1]Lit *a detestable thing* [a]Deut 14:12-19

rent, not to be eaten: the [2]eagle and the
vulture and the [3]buzzard,
14 and the kite and the falcon in its
kind,
15 every raven in its kind,
16 and the ostrich and the owl and the
sea gull and the hawk in its kind,
17 and the little owl and the cormorant and the [1]great owl,
18 and the white owl and the [1]pelican
and the carrion vulture,
19 and the stork, the heron in its
kinds, and the hoopoe, and the bat.
20 ¶ 'All the [1]winged insects that
walk on *all* fours are detestable to you.
21 'Yet these you may eat among all the
[1]winged insects which walk on *all* fours:
those which have above their feet jointed
legs with which to jump on the earth.
22 'These of them you may eat: the locust in its kinds, and the devastating locust in its kinds, and the cricket in its
kinds, and the grasshopper in its kinds.
23 'But all other [1]winged insects
which are four-footed are detestable to
you.
24 ¶ 'By these, moreover, you will be
made unclean: whoever touches their
carcasses becomes unclean until evening,
25 and [a]whoever picks up any of their
carcasses shall wash his clothes and be
unclean until evening.
26 'Concerning all the animals which
divide the hoof but do not make a split
hoof, or which do not chew cud, they are
unclean to you: whoever touches them
becomes unclean.
27 'Also whatever walks on its paws,
among all the creatures that walk on *all*
fours, are unclean to you; whoever
touches their carcasses becomes unclean
until evening,
28 and the one who picks up their carcasses shall wash his clothes and be unclean until evening; they are unclean to
you.
29 ¶ 'Now these are to you the unclean among the swarming things which
swarm on the earth: the mole, and the
mouse, and the [1]great lizard in its kinds,
30 and the gecko, and the [1]crocodile,
and the lizard, and the [2]sand reptile, and
the chameleon.
31 'These are to you the unclean
among all the swarming things; whoever
touches them when they are dead becomes unclean until evening.
32 'Also anything on which one of
them may fall when they are dead becomes unclean, including any wooden article, or clothing, or a skin, or a sack—
any article [1]of which use is made—[a]it
shall be put in the water and be unclean
until evening, then it becomes clean.

13 [2]Or *vulture* [3]Or *black vulture*
17 [1]Specifically, *great horned owl*
18 [1]Or *owl* or *jackdaw*
20 [1]Lit *swarming things with wings*
21 [1]V 20, note 1
23 [1]V 20, note 1
25 [a]Lev 11:40
29 [1]Or *thorn-tailed lizard*
30 [1]Or *lizard* [2]Species as yet undefined
32 [1]Lit *with which work is done* [a]Lev 15:12
33 [1]Lit *it* [a]Lev 6:28; 15:12
34 [1]I.e. if touched by a carcass; cf vv 29-32
35 [1]Lit *hearth for supporting (two) pots*
36 [1]Lit *of a gathering of*
40 [a]Lev 17:15; 22:8; Deut 14:21; Ezek 44:31
41 [a]Lev 11:29
43 [1]Lit *your souls* [a]Lev 20:25
44 [a]Ex 6:7; 16:12; 23:25; Is 43:3; 51:15 [b]Lev 19:2; 1 Pet 1:16
45 [a]Ex 6:7; 20:2; Lev 22:33; 25:38; 26:45 [b]Lev 19:2; 1 Pet 1:16
47 [a]Lev 10:10; Ezek 22:26; 44:23

33 'As for any [a]earthenware vessel
into which one of them may fall, whatever is in it becomes unclean and you
shall break [1]the vessel.
34 'Any of the [1]food which may be eat-
en, on which water comes, shall become
unclean, and any [1]liquid which may be
drunk in every vessel shall become unclean.
35 'Everything, moreover, on which
part of their carcass may fall becomes
unclean; an oven or a [1]stove shall be
smashed; they are unclean and shall continue as unclean to you.
36 'Nevertheless a spring or a cistern
[1]collecting water shall be clean, though
the one who touches their carcass shall
be unclean.
37 'If a part of their carcass falls on any
seed for sowing which is to be sown, it is
clean.
38 'Though if water is put on the seed
and a part of their carcass falls on it, it is
unclean to you.
39 ¶ 'Also if one of the animals dies
which you have for food, the one who
touches its carcass becomes unclean until
evening.
40 '[a]He too, who eats some of its carcass shall wash his clothes and be unclean until evening, and the one who
picks up its carcass shall wash his clothes
and be unclean until evening.
41 ¶ '[a]Now every swarming thing
that swarms on the earth is detestable,
not to be eaten.
42 'Whatever crawls on its belly, and
whatever walks on *all* fours, whatever
has many feet, in respect to every swarming thing that swarms on the earth, you
shall not eat them, for they are detestable.
43 '[a]Do not render [1]yourselves detestable through any of the swarming
things that swarm; and you shall not
make yourselves unclean with them so
that you become unclean.
44 'For [a]I am the LORD your God. Consecrate yourselves therefore, and [b]be
holy, for I am holy. And you shall not
make yourselves unclean with any of the
swarming things that swarm on the
earth.
45 '[a]For I am the LORD who brought
you up from the land of Egypt to be your
God; thus [b]you shall be holy, for I am
holy.' "
46 ¶ This is the law regarding the animal and the bird, and every living thing
that moves in the waters and everything
that swarms on the earth,
47 [a]to make a distinction between the
unclean and the clean, and between the

edible creature and the creature which is not to be eaten.

Laws of Motherhood

12 Then the LORD spoke to Moses, saying,

2 "Speak to the sons of Israel, saying: ¶ 'When a woman [1]gives birth and bears a male *child,* then she shall be unclean for seven days, [a]as in the days of [2]her menstruation she shall be unclean.

3 'On [a]the eighth day the flesh of his foreskin shall be circumcised.

4 'Then she shall remain in the blood of *her* purification for thirty-three days; she shall not touch any consecrated thing, nor enter the sanctuary until the days of her purification are completed.

5 'But if she bears a female *child,* then she shall be unclean for two weeks, as in her [1]menstruation; and she shall remain in the blood of *her* purification for sixty-six days.

6 ¶ '[a]When the days of her purification are completed, for a son or for a daughter, she shall bring to the priest at the doorway of the tent of meeting a one year old lamb for a burnt offering and a young pigeon or a turtledove [b]for a sin offering.

7 'Then he shall offer it before the LORD and make atonement for her, and she shall be cleansed from the [1]flow of her blood. This is the law for her who bears *a child, whether* a male or a female.

8 'But if [1]she cannot afford a lamb, then she shall take [a]two turtledoves or two young pigeons, [b]the one for a burnt offering and the other for a sin offering; and the [c]priest shall make atonement for her, and she will be clean.' "

The Test for Leprosy

13 Then the LORD spoke to Moses and to Aaron, saying,

2 "When a man has on the skin of his [1]body a swelling or a scab or a bright spot, and it becomes [2]an infection of leprosy on the skin of his [1]body, [a]then he shall be brought to Aaron the priest or to one of his sons the priests.

3 "The priest shall look at the mark on the skin of the [1]body, and if the hair in the infection has turned white and the infection appears to be deeper than the skin of his [1]body, it is an infection of leprosy; when the priest has looked at him, he shall pronounce him unclean.

4 "But if the bright spot is white on the skin of his [1]body, and [2]it does not appear to be deeper than the skin, and the hair on it has not turned white, then the priest shall [3]isolate *him who has* the infection for seven days.

5 "The priest shall look at him on the seventh day, and if in his eyes the infection [1]has not changed *and* the infection has not spread on the skin, then the priest shall [2]isolate him for seven more days.

6 "The priest shall look at him again on the seventh day, and if the infection has faded and the mark has not spread on the skin, then the priest shall pronounce him clean; it is *only* a scab. And he shall [a]wash his clothes and be clean.

7 ¶ "But if the scab spreads farther on the skin after he has shown himself to the priest for his cleansing, he shall appear again to the priest.

8 "The priest shall look, and if the scab has spread on the skin, then the priest shall pronounce him unclean; it is leprosy.

9 ¶ "When the infection of leprosy is on a man, then he shall be brought to the priest.

10 "The priest shall then look, and if there is a [a]white swelling in the skin, and it has turned the hair white, and there is quick raw flesh in the swelling,

11 it is [1]a chronic leprosy on the skin of his [2]body, and the priest shall pronounce him unclean; he shall not [3]isolate him, for he is unclean.

12 "If the leprosy breaks out farther on the skin, and the leprosy covers all the skin of *him who has* the infection from his head even to his feet, [1]as far as the priest can see,

13 then the priest shall look, and behold, *if* the leprosy has covered all his [1]body, he shall pronounce clean *him who has* the infection; it has all turned white *and* he is clean.

14 "But whenever raw flesh appears on him, he shall be unclean.

15 "The priest shall look at the raw flesh, and he shall pronounce him unclean; the raw flesh is unclean, it is leprosy.

16 "Or if the raw flesh turns again and is changed to white, then he shall [a]come to the priest,

17 and the priest shall look at him, and behold, *if* the infection has turned to white, then the priest shall pronounce clean *him who has* the infection; he is clean.

18 ¶ "When the [1]body has a boil on its skin and it is healed,

19 and in the place of the boil there is a white swelling or a reddish-white, bright spot, then it shall be shown to the priest;

20 and the priest shall look, and behold, *if* [1]it appears to be lower than the skin, and the hair on it has turned white,

12:2 [1]Lit *produces seed* [2]Lit *the impurity of her sickness* [a]Lev 15:19; 18:19
3 [a]Gen 17:12; Luke 1:59; 2:21
5 [1]Lit *impurity*
6 [a]Luke 2:22 [b]Lev 5:7
7 [1]Lit *fountain*
8 [1]Lit *her hand does not find a sufficiency of a lamb* [a]Luke 2:22-24 [b]Lev 5:7 [c]Lev 4:26
13:2 [1]Lit *flesh* [2]Lit *a mark, stroke,* and so throughout the ch [a]Deut 24:8
3 [1]Lit *flesh*
4 [1]Lit *flesh* [2]Lit *the appearance of it is not deeper* [3]Lit *shut up*
5 [1]Lit *has stood* [2]Lit *shut up*
6 [a]Lev 11:25; 14:8
10 [a]Num 12:10; 2 Kin 5:27; 2 Chr 26:19,20
11 [1]Lit *an old* [2]Lit *flesh* [3]Lit *shut up*
12 [1]Lit *with regard to the whole sight of the priest's eyes*
13 [1]Lit *flesh*
16 [a]Luke 5:12-14
18 [1]Lit *flesh*
20 [1]Lit *the appearance of it is lower*

then the priest shall pronounce him unclean; it is the infection of leprosy, it has
broken out in the boil.
21 "But if the priest looks at it, and behold, there are no white hairs in it and it
is not lower than the skin and is faded,
then the priest shall [1]isolate him for sev-
en days;
22 and if it spreads farther on the skin,
then the priest shall pronounce him unclean; it is an infection.
23 "But if the bright spot remains in its
place and does not spread, it is *only* the
scar of the boil; and the priest shall pronounce him clean.
24 ¶ "Or if the [1]body sustains in its
skin a burn by fire, and the raw *flesh* of
the burn becomes a bright spot, reddish-
white, or white,
25 then the priest shall look at it. And
if the hair in the bright spot has [a]turned
white and it appears to be deeper than
the skin, it is leprosy; it has broken out in
the burn. Therefore, the priest shall pronounce him unclean; it is an infection of
leprosy.
26 "But if the priest looks at it, and indeed, there is no white hair in the bright
spot and it is no [1]deeper than the skin,
but is dim, then the priest shall [2]isolate
him for seven days;
27 and the priest shall look at him on
the seventh day. If it spreads farther in
the skin, then the priest shall pronounce
him unclean; it is an infection of leprosy.
28 "But if the bright spot remains in its
place and has not spread in the skin, but
is dim, it is the swelling from the burn;
and the priest shall pronounce him clean,
for it is *only* the scar of the burn.
29 ¶ "Now if a man or woman has an
infection on the head or on the beard,
30 then the priest shall look at the infection, and if it appears to be deeper
than the skin and there is thin yellowish
hair in it, then the priest shall pronounce
him unclean; it is a scale, it is leprosy of
the head or of the beard.
31 "But if the priest looks at the infection of the scale, and indeed, it appears to
be no deeper than the skin and there is
no black hair in it, then the priest shall
[1]isolate *the person* with the scaly infection for seven days.
32 "On the seventh day the priest shall
look at the infection, and if the scale has
not spread and no yellowish hair has
[1]grown in it, and the appearance of the
scale is no deeper than the skin,
33 then he shall shave himself, but he
shall not shave the scale; and the priest
shall [1]isolate *the person* with the scale
seven more days.
34 "Then on the seventh day the priest
shall look at the scale, and if the scale has
not spread in the skin and it appears to be
no deeper than the skin, the priest shall
pronounce him clean; and he shall wash
his clothes and be clean.
35 "But if the scale spreads farther in
the skin after his cleansing,
36 then the priest shall look at him,
and if the scale has spread in the skin, the
priest need not seek for the yellowish
hair; he is unclean.
37 "If in his sight the scale has remained, however, and black hair has
grown in it, the scale has healed, he is
clean; and the priest shall pronounce him
clean.
38 ¶ "When a man or a woman has
bright spots on the skin of the [1]body,
even white bright spots,
39 then the priest shall look, and if the
bright spots on the skin of their [1]bodies
are a faint white, it is [2]eczema that has
broken out on the skin; he is clean.
40 ¶ "Now if a [1]man loses the hair of
his head, he is [a]bald; he is clean.
41 "If his head becomes bald at the
[1]front and sides, he is bald on the forehead; he is clean.
42 "But if on the bald head or the bald
forehead, there occurs a reddish-white
infection, it is leprosy breaking out on his
bald head or on his bald forehead.
43 "Then [a]the priest shall look at him;
and if the swelling of the infection is
reddish-white on his bald head or on his
bald forehead, like the appearance of leprosy in the skin of the [1]body,
44 he is a leprous man, he is unclean.
The priest shall surely pronounce him unclean; his infection is on his head.
45 ¶ "As for the leper who has the
infection, his clothes shall be torn, and
[a]the hair of his head shall be [1]uncov-
ered, and he shall [b]cover his mustache
and cry, '[c]Unclean! Unclean!'
46 "He shall remain unclean all the
days during which he has the infection;
he is unclean. He shall live alone; his
dwelling shall be [a]outside the camp.
47 ¶ "When a garment has a [1]mark of
leprosy in it, whether it is a wool garment
or a linen garment,
48 whether in [1]warp or woof, of linen
or of wool, whether in leather or in any
article made of leather,
49 if the mark is greenish or reddish in
the garment or in the leather, or in the
[1]warp or in the woof, or in any article of
leather, it is a leprous mark and shall be
shown to the priest.
50 "Then [a]the priest shall look at the
mark and shall [1]quarantine the article
with the mark for seven days.
51 "He shall then look at the mark on

21 [1]Lit *shut up*
24 [1]Lit *flesh*
25 [a]Ex 4:6; Num 12:10; 2 Kin 5:27
26 [1]Lit *lower* [2]Lit *shut up*
31 [1]Lit *shut up*
32 [1]Lit *been*
33 [1]Lit *shut up*
38 [1]Lit *flesh*
39 [1]Lit *flesh* [2]Lit *tetter*
40 [1]Lit *man's head becomes bald* [a]2 Kin 2:23; Is 15:2; Amos 8:10
41 [1]Lit *border of his face*
43 [1]Lit *flesh* [a]Lev 10:10; Ezek 22:26
45 [1]Or *disheveled* [a]Lev 10:6 [b]Ezek 24:17,22; Mic 3:7 [c]Lam 4:15
46 [a]Num 5:1-4; 12:14
47 [1]Lit *infection,* and so throughout the ch
48 [1]Or *weaving or texture*
49 [1]Or *weaving or texture*
50 [1]Lit *shut up* [a]Ezek 44:23

the seventh day; if the mark has spread in the garment, whether in the warp or in the woof, or in the leather, whatever the purpose for which the leather is used, the mark is a [1]leprous malignancy, it is unclean.

52 "So he shall burn the garment, whether the warp or the woof, in wool or in linen, or any article of leather in which the mark occurs, for it is a [1]leprous malignancy; it shall be burned in the fire.

53 ¶ "But if the priest shall look, and indeed the mark has not spread in the garment, either in the warp or in the woof, or in any article of leather,

54 then the priest shall order them to wash the thing in which the mark occurs and he shall [1]quarantine it for seven more days.

55 "After the article with the mark has been washed, the priest shall again look, and if the mark has not changed its appearance, even though the mark has not spread, it is unclean; you shall burn it in the fire, whether an eating away has produced bareness on the top or on the front of it.

56 ¶ "Then if the priest looks, and if the mark has faded after it has been washed, then he shall tear it out of the garment or out of the leather, whether from the warp or from the woof;

57 and if it appears again in the garment, whether in the warp or in the woof, or in any article of leather, it is an outbreak; the article with the mark shall be burned in the fire.

58 "The garment, whether the warp or the woof, or any article of leather from which the mark has departed when you washed it, it shall then be washed a second time and will be clean."

59 ¶ This is the law for the mark of leprosy in a garment of wool or linen, whether in the warp or in the woof, or in any article of leather, for pronouncing it clean or unclean.

Law of Cleansing a Leper

14 Then the LORD spoke to Moses, saying,

2 "This shall be the law of the leper in the day of his cleansing. [a]Now he shall be brought to the priest,

3 and the priest shall go [a]out to the outside of the camp. Thus the priest shall look, and if the [1]infection of leprosy has been healed in the leper,

4 then the priest shall give orders to take two live clean birds and [a]cedar wood and a [1]scarlet string and hyssop for the one who is to be cleansed.

5 "The priest shall also give orders to slay the one bird in an earthenware vessel over [1]running water.

6 "*As for* the live bird, he shall take it together with [a]the cedar wood and the [1]scarlet string and the [b]hyssop, and shall dip them and the live bird in the blood of the bird that was slain over the [2]running water.

7 "[a]He shall then sprinkle seven times the one who is to be cleansed from the leprosy and shall pronounce him clean, and shall let the live bird go free over the open field.

8 "[a]The one to be cleansed shall then wash his clothes and shave off all his hair and bathe in water and [b]be clean. Now afterward, he may enter the camp, but he [c]shall stay outside his tent for seven days.

9 "It will be on the seventh day that he shall shave off all his hair: he shall shave his head and his beard and his eyebrows, even all his hair. He shall then wash his clothes and bathe his [1]body in water and [a]be clean.

10 ¶ "Now on the eighth day he is to take two male lambs without defect, and a yearling ewe lamb without defect, and three-tenths *of an* [1]*ephah* of fine flour mixed with oil for a grain offering, and one [2a]log of oil;

11 and the priest who pronounces him clean shall present the man to be cleansed and the [1]aforesaid before the LORD at the doorway of the tent of meeting.

12 "Then the priest shall take the one male lamb and bring it for a [a]guilt offering, with the [1b]log of oil, and present them as a [c]wave offering before the LORD.

13 "Next he shall slaughter the male lamb in [a]the place where they slaughter the sin offering and the burnt offering, at the place of the sanctuary—for the guilt offering, [b]like the sin offering, belongs to the priest; it is most holy.

14 "The priest shall then take some of the blood of the [a]guilt offering, and the priest shall put *it* on [b]the lobe of the right ear of the one to be cleansed, and on the thumb of his right hand and on the big toe of his right foot.

15 "The priest shall also take some of the [1a]log of oil, and pour *it* into his left palm;

16 the priest shall then dip his right-hand finger into the oil that is in his left palm, and with his finger sprinkle some of the oil seven times before the LORD.

17 "Of the remaining oil which is in his palm, the priest shall put some on the right ear lobe of the one to be cleansed, and on the thumb of his right hand, and

---

51 [1]Lit *malignant leprosy*
52 [1]Lit *malignant leprosy*
54 [1]Lit *shut up*
14:2 [a]Matt 8:4; Mark 1:44; Luke 5:14; 17:14
3 [1]Lit *mark, stroke,* and so throughout the ch [a]Lev 13:46
4 [1]Lit *scarlet color and* [a]Lev 14:6,49,51,52; Num 19:6
5 [1]Lit *living*
6 [1]Lit *scarlet color and* [2]Lit *living* [a]Lev 14:4 [b]Ps 51:7
7 [a]Ezek 36:25
8 [a]Lev 11:25; 13:6; Num 8:7 [b]Lev 14:9,20 [c]Num 5:2,3; 12:14,15; 2 Chr 26:21
9 [1]Lit *flesh* [a]Lev 14:8,20
10 [1]I.e. Approx one bu [2]I.e. Approx one pt [a]Lev 14:12,15,21,24
11 [1]Lit *them*
12 [1]I.e. Approx one pt [a]Lev 5:6, 18; 6:6; 14:19 [b]Lev 14:10 [c]Ex 29:22-24,26
13 [a]Ex 29:11; Lev 1:11; 4:24 [b]Lev 6:24-30; 7:7
14 [a]Lev 14:19 [b]Ex 29:20; Lev 8:23,24
15 [1]I.e. Approx one pt [a]Lev 14:10

on the big toe of his right foot, on the
blood of the guilt offering;
18 while the rest of the oil that is in
the priest's palm, he shall put on the head
of the one to be cleansed. So the priest
shall make [a]atonement on his behalf before the LORD.
19 "The priest shall next offer the [a]sin
offering and make atonement for the one
to be cleansed from his uncleanness.
Then afterward, he shall slaughter the
burnt offering.
20 "The priest shall offer up the burnt
offering and the grain offering on the altar. Thus the priest shall make atonement
for him, and [a]he will be clean.
21 ¶ "[a]But if he is poor and his
[1]means are insufficient, then he is to
take one male lamb for a [b]guilt offering
as a wave offering to make atonement for
him, and one-tenth *of an* [2]*ephah* of fine
flour mixed with oil for a grain offering,
and a [3c]log of oil,
22 and two turtledoves or two young
pigeons which [1]are within his means,
[a]the one shall be a [b]sin offering and the
other a burnt offering.
23 "[a]Then the eighth day he shall bring
them for his cleansing to the priest, at the
doorway of the tent of meeting, before
the LORD.
24 "The priest shall take the lamb of the
guilt offering and [a]the [1]log of oil, and
the priest shall offer them for a wave offering before the LORD.
25 "Next he shall slaughter the lamb of
the guilt offering; and the priest is to take
some of the blood of the guilt offering and
put *it* on [a]the lobe of the right ear of the
one to be cleansed and on the thumb of
his right hand and on the big toe of his
right foot.
26 "The priest shall also pour some of
the oil into his left palm;
27 and with his right-hand finger the
priest shall sprinkle some of the oil that is
in his left palm seven times before the
LORD.
28 "The priest shall then put some of
the oil that is in his palm on the lobe of
the right ear of the one to be cleansed,
and on the thumb of his right hand and
on the big toe of his right foot, on the
place of the blood of the guilt offering.
29 "Moreover, the rest of the oil that is
in the priest's palm he shall put on the
head of the one to be cleansed, to make
atonement on his behalf before the LORD.
30 "He shall then offer one of the turtledoves or young pigeons, [1]which are
within his means.
31 "*He shall offer* what [1]he can afford,
[a]the one for a sin offering and the other
for a burnt offering, together with the
grain offering. So the priest shall make
atonement before the LORD on behalf of
the one to be cleansed.
32 "This is the law *for him* in whom
there is an infection of leprosy, whose
[1]means are limited for his cleansing."

Cleansing a Leprous House

33 ¶ The LORD further spoke to Moses
and to Aaron, saying:
34 ¶ "[a]When you enter the land of
Canaan, which I give you for a possession, and I put a mark of leprosy on a
house in the land of your possession,
35 then the one who owns the house
shall come and tell the priest, saying,
'*Something* like [a]a mark *of leprosy* has
become visible to me in the house.'
36 "The priest shall then command that
they empty the house before the priest
goes in to look at the mark, so that everything in the house need not become unclean; and afterward the priest shall go in
to look at the house.
37 "So he shall look at the mark, and if
the mark on the walls of the house has
greenish or reddish depressions and appears deeper than the [1]surface,
38 then the priest shall come out of
the house, to the [1]doorway, and [2]quar-
antine the house for seven days.
39 "The priest shall return on the seventh day and [1]make an inspection. If the
mark has indeed spread in the walls of
the house,
40 then the priest shall order them to
tear out the stones with the mark in them
and throw them away [1]at an unclean
place outside the city.
41 "He shall have the house scraped all
around [1]inside, and they shall dump the
plaster that they scrape off at an unclean
place outside the city.
42 "Then they shall take other stones
and replace *those* stones, and he shall
take other plaster and replaster the
house.
43 ¶ "If, however, the mark breaks out
again in the house after he has torn out
the stones and scraped the house, and
after it has been replastered,
44 then the priest shall come in and
[1]make an inspection. If he sees that the
mark has indeed spread in the house, it is
[a]a malignant mark in the house; it is unclean.
45 "He shall therefore tear down the
house, its stones, and its timbers, and all
the plaster of the house, and he shall take
them outside the city to an [a]unclean
place.
46 "Moreover, whoever goes into the
house during the time that he has [1]quar-

18 [a]Lev 4:26; Num 15:28; Heb 2:17
19 [a]Lev 14:12
20 [a]Lev 14:8,9
21 [1]Lit *hand is not reaching* [2]I.e. Approx one bu [3]I.e. Approx one pt [a]Lev 5:11; 12:8; 27:8 [b]Lev 14:22 [c]Lev 14:10
22 [1]Lit *his hand reaches* [a]Lev 5:7 [b]Lev 14:21,24, 25
23 [a]Lev 14:10, 11
24 [1]I.e. Approx one pt [a]Lev 14:10
25 [a]Lev 14:14
30 [1]Lit *from those which his hand can reach*
31 [1]Lit *his hand can reach* [a]Lev 5:7
32 [1]Lit *hand does not reach*
34 [a]Gen 17:8; Num 32:22; Deut 7:1; 32:49
35 [a]Ps 91:10
37 [1]Lit *wall*
38 [1]Lit *doorway of the house* [2]Lit *shut up*
39 [1]Lit *look*
40 [1]Lit *to*
41 [1]Lit *from the house around*
44 [1]Lit *look* [a]Lev 13:51
45 [a]Lev 14:41
46 [1]Lit *shut up*

antined it, becomes [a]unclean until evening.

47 "Likewise, whoever lies down in the house shall wash his clothes, and whoever eats in the house shall wash his clothes.

48 ¶ "If, on the other hand, the priest comes in and [1]makes an inspection and the mark has not indeed spread in the house after the house has been replastered, then the priest shall pronounce the house clean because the mark has [2]not reappeared.

49 "To cleanse the house then, he shall take [a]two birds and cedar wood and a [1]scarlet string and hyssop,

50 and he shall slaughter the one bird in an earthenware vessel over [1]running water.

51 "Then he shall take the cedar wood and the [a]hyssop and the [1]scarlet string, with the live bird, and dip them in the blood of the slain bird as well as in the [2]running water, and sprinkle the house seven times.

52 "He shall thus cleanse the house with the blood of the bird and with the [1]running water, along with the live bird and with the cedar wood and with the hyssop and with the [2]scarlet string.

53 "However, he shall let the live bird go free outside the city into the open field. So he shall make atonement for the house, and it will be clean."

54 ¶ This is the law for any mark of leprosy—even for a [a]scale,

55 and for the [a]leprous garment or house,

56 and [a]for a swelling, and for a scab, and for a bright spot—

57 to teach [1]when they are unclean and [2]when they are clean. This is the law of leprosy.

Cleansing Unhealthiness

15 The LORD also spoke to Moses and to Aaron, saying,

2 "Speak to the sons of Israel, and say to them, '[a]When any man has a discharge from his [1]body, [2]his discharge is unclean.

3 'This, moreover, shall be his uncleanness in his discharge: it is his uncleanness whether his body allows its discharge to flow or whether his body obstructs its discharge.

4 'Every bed on which the person with the discharge lies becomes unclean, and everything on which he sits becomes unclean.

5 'Anyone, moreover, who touches his bed shall wash his clothes and bathe in water and be unclean until evening;

6 and whoever sits on the thing on which the man with the discharge has been sitting, shall wash his clothes and bathe in water and be unclean until evening.

7 'Also whoever touches the [1]person with the discharge shall wash his clothes and bathe in water and be unclean until evening.

8 'Or if the man with the discharge spits on one who is clean, he too shall wash his clothes and bathe in water and be unclean until evening.

9 'Every saddle on which the person with the discharge rides becomes unclean.

10 'Whoever then touches any of the things which were under him shall be unclean until evening, and he who carries them shall wash his clothes and bathe in water and be unclean until evening.

11 'Likewise, whomever the one with the discharge touches without having rinsed his hands in water shall wash his clothes and bathe in water and be unclean until evening.

12 'However, an [a]earthenware vessel which the person with the discharge touches shall be broken, and every wooden vessel shall be rinsed in water.

13 ¶ 'Now when the man with the discharge becomes cleansed from his discharge, then he [a]shall count off for himself seven days for his cleansing; he shall then wash his clothes and bathe his body in [1]running water and will become clean.

14 'Then on the eighth day he shall take for himself [a]two turtledoves or two young pigeons, and come before the LORD to the doorway of the tent of meeting and give them to the priest;

15 and the priest shall offer them, [a]one for a sin offering and the other for a burnt offering. So [b]the priest shall make atonement on his behalf before the LORD because of his discharge.

16 ¶ '[a]Now if a [1]man has a seminal emission, he shall bathe all his body in water and be unclean until evening.

17 'As for any garment or any leather on which there is seminal emission, it shall be washed with water and be unclean until evening.

18 'If a man lies with a woman *so that* there is a seminal emission, they shall both bathe in water and be [a]unclean until evening.

19 ¶ '[a]When a woman has a discharge, *if* her discharge in her body is blood, she shall continue in her menstrual impurity for seven days; and whoever touches her shall be unclean until evening.

46 [a]Num 19:7, 10,21,22
48 [1]Lit *looks* [2]Lit *healed*
49 [1]Lit *scarlet color* [a]Lev 14:4
50 [1]Lit *living*
51 [1]Lit *scarlet color* [2]Lit *living* [a]1 Kin 4:33; Ps 51:7
52 [1]Lit *living* [2]Lit *scarlet color*
54 [a]Lev 13:30
55 [a]Lev 13:47-52
56 [a]Lev 13:2
57 [1]Lit *in the day of uncleanness* [2]Lit *in the day of cleanness*
15:2 [1]Lit *flesh*, and so throughout the ch [2]Or *by his discharge, he is unclean* [a]Lev 22:4; Num 5:2; 2 Sam 3:29
7 [1]Lit *flesh*
12 [a]Lev 6:28; 11:33
13 [1]Lit *living* [a]Lev 8:33; 14:8
14 [a]Lev 14:22, 23
15 [a]Lev 5:7; 14:31 [b]Lev 14:19,31
16 [1]Lit *man's...goes out from him* [a]Lev 22:4; Deut 23:10,11
18 [a]1 Sam 21:4
19 [a]Lev 12:2

20 'Everything also on which she lies during her menstrual impurity shall be unclean, and everything on which she sits shall be unclean.

21 'Anyone who touches her bed shall wash his clothes and bathe in water and be unclean until evening.

22 'Whoever touches any thing on which she sits shall wash his clothes and bathe in water and be unclean until evening.

23 'Whether it be on the bed or on the thing on which she is sitting, when he touches it, he shall be unclean until evening.

24 '[a]If a man actually lies with her so that her menstrual impurity is on him, he shall be unclean seven days, and every bed on which he lies shall be unclean.

25 ¶ '[a]Now if a woman has a discharge of her blood many days, not at the period of her menstrual impurity, or if she has a discharge beyond [1]that period, all the days of her impure discharge she shall continue as though [2]in her menstrual impurity; she is unclean.

26 'Any bed on which she lies all the days of her discharge shall be to her like [1]her bed at menstruation; and every thing on which she sits shall be unclean, like [2]her uncleanness at that time.

27 'Likewise, whoever touches them shall be unclean and shall wash his clothes and bathe in water and be unclean until evening.

28 'When she becomes clean from her discharge, she shall count off for herself seven days; and afterward she will be clean.

29 'Then on the eighth day she shall take for herself two turtledoves or two young pigeons and bring them in to the priest, to the doorway of the tent of meeting.

30 'The priest shall offer the [a]one for a sin offering and the other for a burnt offering. So the priest shall make atonement on her behalf before the LORD because of her impure discharge.'

31 ¶ "Thus you shall keep the sons of Israel separated from their uncleanness, so that they will not die in their uncleanness by their [a]defiling My [1]tabernacle that is among them."

32 This is the law for the one with a discharge, and for the man [1]who has a seminal emission so that he is unclean by it,

33 and for the woman who is ill because of menstrual impurity, and for the one who has a discharge, whether a male or a female, or a man who lies with an unclean woman.

Law of Atonement

16 Now the LORD spoke to Moses after [a]the death of the two sons of Aaron, when they had approached the presence of the LORD and died.

2 The LORD said to Moses:

¶ "Tell your brother Aaron that he shall not enter [a]at any time into the holy place inside the veil, before the [1]mercy seat which is on the ark, or he will die; for [b]I will appear in the cloud over the [1]mercy seat.

3 "Aaron shall enter the holy place with this: with a [1]bull for a [a]sin offering and a ram for a burnt offering.

4 "He shall put on the [a]holy linen tunic, and the linen undergarments shall be next to his [1]body, and he shall be girded with the linen sash and attired with the linen turban (these are holy garments). Then he shall [b]bathe his [1]body in water and put them on.

5 "He shall take from the congregation of the sons of Israel [a]two male goats for a sin offering and one ram for a burnt offering.

6 "Then [a]Aaron shall offer the bull for the sin offering which is for himself, that he may make atonement for himself and for his household.

7 "He shall take the two goats and present them before the LORD at the doorway of the tent of meeting.

8 "Aaron shall cast lots for the two goats, one lot for the LORD and the other lot for the [1]scapegoat.

9 "Then Aaron shall offer the goat on which the lot for the LORD fell, and make it a sin offering.

10 "But the goat on which the lot for the [1]scapegoat fell shall be presented alive before the LORD, to make [a]atonement upon it, to send it into the wilderness as the [1]scapegoat.

11 ¶ "Then Aaron shall offer the bull of the sin offering [a]which is for himself and make atonement for himself and [b]for his household, and he shall slaughter the bull of the sin offering which is for himself.

12 "He shall take a [a]firepan full of coals of fire from upon the altar before the LORD and [1]two handfuls of finely ground [b]sweet incense, and bring *it* inside the veil.

13 "He shall put the incense on the fire before the LORD, that the cloud of incense may cover the [1a]mercy seat that is on *the ark of* the testimony, [b]otherwise he will die.

14 "Moreover, [a]he shall take some of the blood of the bull and sprinkle *it* [b]with his finger on the [1]mercy seat on the east

24 [a]Lev 18:19; 20:18
25 [1]Lit *her menstrual impurity* [2]Lit *in the days of* [a]Matt 9:20; Mark 5:25; Luke 8:43
26 [1]Lit *the bed of her menstrual impurity* [2]Lit *the uncleanness of her menstrual impurity*
30 [a]Lev 5:7
31 [1]Or *dwelling place* [a]Lev 20:3; Num 19:13,20; Ezek 5:11; 36:17
32 [1]Lit *whose seminal emission goes out from him*
16:1 [a]Lev 10:1, 2
2 [1]Lit *propitiatory* [a]Ex 30:10; Heb 6:19; 9:7,25 [b]Ex 25:21,22; 40:34; 1 Kin 8:10-12
3 [1]Or *bull of the herd* [a]Lev 4:1-12; 16:6; Heb 9:7
4 [1]Lit *flesh* [a]Ex 28:39,42 [b]Ex 30:20; Lev 16:24; Heb 10:22
5 [a]Lev 4:13-21; 2 Chr 29:21; Ezek 45:22
6 [a]Heb 5:3
8 [1]Lit *goat of removal,* or else a name: *Azazel*
10 [1]Lit *goat of removal,* or else a name: *Azazel* [a]Is 53:4-10; Rom 3:25; 1 John 2:2
11 [a]Heb 7:27; 9:7 [b]Lev 16:33
12 [1]Lit *the filling of the hollow of his hands* [a]Lev 10:1; Num 16:18 [b]Ex 30:34-38
13 [1]Lit *propitiatory* [a]Ex 25:21 [b]Ex 28:43; Lev 22:9; Num 4:15, 20
14 [1]Lit *propitiatory* [a]Heb 9:25 [b]Lev 4:6,17

side; also in front of the [2]mercy seat he
shall sprinkle some of the blood with his
finger seven times.
15 ¶ "Then he shall slaughter the goat
of the sin offering [a]which is for the people, and bring its blood inside the veil and
do with its blood as he did with the blood
of the bull, and sprinkle it on the [1]mercy
seat and in front of the [1]mercy seat.
16 "[a]He shall make atonement for the
holy place, because of the impurities of
the sons of Israel and because of their
transgressions in regard to all their sins;
and thus he shall do for the tent of meeting which abides with them in the midst
of their impurities.
17 "When he goes in to make atonement in the holy place, no one shall be in
the tent of meeting until he comes out,
that he may make atonement for himself
and for his household and for all the assembly of Israel.
18 "Then he shall go out to the altar
that is before the LORD and make atonement for it, and shall take some of the
blood of the bull and of the blood of the
goat and [a]put it on the horns of the altar
on all sides.
19 "[a]With his finger he shall sprinkle
some of the blood on it seven times and
cleanse it, and from the impurities of the
sons of Israel consecrate it.
20 ¶ "When he finishes atoning for
the holy place and the tent of meeting
and the altar, he shall offer the live goat.
21 "Then Aaron shall lay both of his
hands on the head of the live goat, and
[a]confess over it all the iniquities of the
sons of Israel and all their transgressions
[1]in regard to all their sins; and he shall
lay them on the head of the goat and send
it away into the wilderness by the hand
of a man who *stands* in readiness.
22 "The goat shall bear on itself all their
iniquities to a solitary land; and he shall
release the goat in the wilderness.
23 ¶ "Then Aaron shall come into the
tent of meeting and take off [a]the linen
garments which he put on when he went
into the holy place, and shall leave them
there.
24 "[a]He shall bathe his [1]body with
water in a holy place and put on [b]his
clothes, and come forth and offer his
burnt offering and the burnt offering of
the people and make atonement for himself and for the people.
25 "Then he shall offer up in smoke the
fat of the sin offering on the altar.
26 "The one who released the goat as
the [1]scapegoat [a]shall wash his clothes
and bathe his [2]body with water; then
afterward he shall come into the camp.
27 "But the bull of the sin offering and
the goat of the sin offering, [a]whose blood
was brought in to make atonement in the
holy place, shall be taken outside the
camp, and they shall burn their hides,
their flesh, and their refuse in the fire.
28 "Then the [a]one who burns them
shall wash his clothes and bathe his body
with water, then afterward he shall come
into the camp.

An Annual Atonement

29 ¶ "*This* shall be a permanent statute for you: [a]in the seventh month, on
the tenth day of the month, you shall
humble your souls and not [b]do any work,
whether the native, or the alien who sojourns among you;
30 for it is on this day that [1]atonement
shall be made for you to [a]cleanse you;
you will be clean from all your sins before
the LORD.
31 "It is to be a sabbath of solemn rest
for you, that you may [a]humble your
souls; it is a permanent statute.
32 "So the priest who is anointed and
[1]ordained to serve as priest in his father's place shall make atonement: he
shall thus put on [a]the linen garments,
the holy garments,
33 and make atonement for the holy
sanctuary, and he shall make atonement
for the tent of meeting and for the altar.
He shall also make atonement for [a]the
priests and for all the people of the assembly.
34 "Now you shall have this as a [a]per-
manent statute, to [b]make atonement for
the sons of Israel for all their sins once
every year." And just as the LORD had
commanded Moses, *so* he did.

Blood for Atonement

17 Then the LORD spoke to Moses,
saying,
2 "Speak to Aaron and to his sons and
to all the sons of Israel and say to them,
'This is what the LORD has commanded,
saying,
3 "Any man from the house of Israel
who slaughters an ox or a lamb or a goat
in the camp, or who slaughters it outside
the camp,
4 and [a]has not brought it to the doorway of the tent of meeting to present *it* as
an offering to the LORD before the [1]taber-
nacle of the LORD, bloodguiltiness is to be
reckoned to that man. He has shed blood
and that man shall be cut off from among
his people.
5 "[1]The reason is so that the sons of
Israel may bring their sacrifices which
they were sacrificing in the open field,
that they may bring them in to the LORD,
at the doorway of the tent of meeting to

14 [2]Lit *propitiatory*
15 [1]Lit *propitiatory* [a]Heb 7:27; 9:7,12
16 [a]Ex 29:36, 37; 30:10; Heb 2:17
18 [a]Lev 4:25; Ezek 43:20,22
19 [a]Lev 16:14; Ezek 43:20
21 [1]Lit *in addition to* [a]Lev 5:5
23 [a]Lev 16:4; Ezek 42:14; 44:19
24 [1]Lit *flesh* [a]Lev 16:4 [b]Ex 28:40,41
26 [1]Lit *goat of removal,* or else a name: *Azazel* [2]Lit *flesh* [a]Lev 11:25,40
27 [a]Lev 6:30; Heb 13:11
28 [a]Num 19:8
29 [a]Lev 23:27; Num 29:7 [b]Ex 31:14,15
30 [1]Lit *he shall make atonement* [a]Ps 51:2; Jer 33:8; Eph 5:26
31 [a]Lev 23:32; Ezra 8:21; Is 58:3,5; Dan 10:12
32 [1]Lit *whose hand is filled* [a]Lev 16:4
33 [a]Lev 16:11
34 [a]Lev 23:31 [b]Heb 9:7
17:4 [1]Lit *dwelling place* [a]Deut 12:5-21
5 [1]Lit *In order that*

the priest, and sacrifice them as sacrifices
of peace offerings to the LORD.
6 "The priest shall sprinkle the blood
on the altar of the LORD at the doorway of
the tent of meeting, and [a]offer up the
fat in smoke as a soothing aroma to the
LORD.
7 "[a]They shall no longer sacrifice
their sacrifices to the [1]goat demons with
which they play the harlot. This shall be
a permanent statute to them throughout
their generations." '
8 ¶ "Then you shall say to them, 'Any
man from the house of Israel, or from the
aliens who sojourn among them, who offers a burnt offering or sacrifice,
9 and [a]does not bring it to the doorway of the tent of meeting to [1]offer it to
the LORD, that man also shall be cut off
from his people.
10 ¶ '[a]And any man from the house of
Israel, or from the aliens who sojourn
among them, who eats any blood, [b]I will
set My face against that person who eats
blood and will cut him off from among his
people.
11 'For [a]the [1]life of the flesh is in the
blood, and I have given it to you on the
altar to make atonement for your souls;
for [b]it is the blood by reason of the [1]life
that makes atonement.'
12 "Therefore I said to the sons of Israel, 'No person among you may eat blood,
nor may any alien who sojourns among
you eat blood.'
13 "So when any man from the sons of
Israel, or from the aliens who sojourn
among them, [1]in hunting catches a beast
or a bird which may be eaten, [a]he shall
pour out its blood and cover it with earth.
14 ¶ "[a]For *as for the* [1]life of all flesh,
its blood is *identified* with its [1]life.
Therefore I said to the sons of Israel, 'You
are not to eat the blood of any flesh, for
the [1]life of all flesh is its blood; whoever
eats it shall be cut off.'
15 "[a]When any person eats *an animal*
which dies or is torn *by beasts,* whether
he is a native or an alien, he shall wash
his clothes and bathe in water, and remain unclean until evening; then he will
become clean.
16 "But if he does not wash *them* or
bathe his body, then [a]he shall bear his
guilt."

Laws on Immoral Relations

18 Then the LORD spoke to Moses,
saying,
2 "Speak to the sons of Israel and say
to them, '[a]I am the LORD your God.
3 'You shall not do [1]what is [a]done in
the land of Egypt where you lived, nor are
you to do [1]what is [b]done in the land of
Canaan where I am bringing you; you
shall not walk in their statutes.
4 'You are to perform My judgments
and keep My statutes, [1]to live in accord
with them; [a]I am the LORD your God.
5 'So you shall keep My statutes and
My judgments, [a]by which a man may
live if he does them; I am the LORD.
6 ¶ 'None of you shall approach any
blood relative [1]of his to uncover nakedness; I am the LORD.
7 '[a]You shall not uncover the nakedness of your father, that is, the nakedness
of your mother. She is your mother; you
are not to uncover her nakedness.
8 '[a]You shall not uncover the nakedness of your father's wife; it is your father's nakedness.
9 '[a]The nakedness of your sister, *either* your father's daughter or your mother's daughter, whether born at home or
born outside, their nakedness you shall
not uncover.
10 'The nakedness of your son's daughter or your daughter's daughter, their nakedness you shall not uncover; for [1]their
nakedness is yours.
11 'The nakedness of your father's
wife's daughter, [1]born to your father,
she is your sister, you shall not uncover
her nakedness.
12 '[a]You shall not uncover the nakedness of your father's sister; she is your
father's blood relative.
13 'You shall not uncover the nakedness of your mother's sister, for she is
your mother's blood relative.
14 '[a]You shall not uncover the nakedness of your father's brother; you shall
not approach his wife, she is your aunt.
15 '[a]You shall not uncover the nakedness of your daughter-in-law; she is your
son's wife, you shall not uncover her nakedness.
16 '[a]You shall not uncover the nakedness of your brother's wife; it is your
brother's nakedness.
17 '[a]You shall not uncover the nakedness of a woman and of her daughter, nor
shall you take her son's daughter or her
daughter's daughter, to uncover her nakedness; they are blood relatives. It is
[1]lewdness.
18 'You shall not [1]marry a woman in
addition to [2]her sister [3]as a rival while
she is alive, to uncover her nakedness.
19 ¶ '[a]Also you shall not approach a
woman to uncover her nakedness during
her [b]menstrual impurity.
20 '[a]You shall not have intercourse
with your neighbor's wife, to be defiled
with her.
21 'You shall not give any of your offspring [a]to [1]offer them to Molech, nor

6 [a]Num 18:17
7 [1]Or *goat-idols* [a]Ex 22:20; 32:8; 34:15; Deut 32:17; 2 Chr 11:15; Ps 106:37f; 1 Cor 10:20
9 [1]Lit *do* [a]Ex 20:24; Lev 17:4
10 [a]Gen 9:4; Lev 3:17; 7:26, 27; Deut 12:16, 23-25; 1 Sam 14:33 [b]Lev 20:3, 6; Jer 44:11
11 [1]Lit *soul* [a]Gen 9:4; Lev 17:14 [b]Heb 9:22
13 [1]Lit *who in hunting* [a]Deut 12:16
14 [1]Lit *soul* [a]Gen 9:4; Lev 17:11
15 [a]Ex 22:31; Lev 7:24; 22:8; Deut 14:21
16 [1]Or *iniquity* [a]Num 19:20
18:2 [a]Ex 6:7; Lev 11:44; Ezek 20:5
3 [1]Lit *according to the deed of* [a]Ezek 20:7,8 [b]Lev 18:24-30; 20:23
4 [1]Lit *to walk in them* [a]Lev 18:2
5 [a]Neh 9:29; Ezek 18:9; 20:11; Luke 10:28; Rom 10:5; Gal 3:12
6 [1]Lit *of his flesh*
7 [a]Lev 20:11; Deut 27:20; Ezek 22:10
8 [a]Lev 20:11; Deut 22:30; 27:20; 1 Cor 5:1
9 [a]Lev 18:11; 20:17; Deut 27:22
10 [1]Lit *they are your nakedness*
11 [1]Lit *begotten of*
12 [a]Lev 20:19
14 [a]Lev 20:20
15 [a]Lev 20:12
16 [a]Lev 20:21
17 [1]Or *wickedness* [a]Lev 20:14
18 [1]Lit *take a wife* [2]Or *another* [3]Lit *to be*
19 [a]Lev 15:24; 20:18 [b]Lev 12:2
20 [a]Lev 20:10; Prov 6:29; Matt 5:27,28; 1 Cor 6:9; Heb 13:4
21 [1]Lit *cause to pass over* [a]Lev 20:2-5; Deut 12:31

shall you [b]profane the name of your God; I am the LORD.

22 ‘[a]You shall not lie with a male as [1]one lies with a female; it is an abomination.

23 ‘[a]Also you shall not have intercourse with any animal to be defiled with it, nor shall any woman stand before an animal to [1]mate with it; it is a perversion.

24 ¶ ‘Do not defile yourselves by any of these things; for by all these [a]the nations which I am casting out before you have become defiled.

25 ‘For the land has become defiled, [a]therefore I have brought its [1]punishment upon it, so the land [b]has spewed out its inhabitants.

26 ‘But as for you, you are to keep My statutes and My judgments and shall not do any of these abominations, *neither* the native, nor the alien who sojourns among you

27 (for the men of the land who have been before you have done all these abominations, and the land has become defiled);

28 so that the land will not spew you out, should you defile it, as it has spewed out the nation which has been before you.

29 ‘For whoever does any of these abominations, [1]those persons who do *so* shall be cut off from among their people.

30 ‘Thus you are to keep [a]My charge, that you do not practice any of the abominable customs which have been practiced before you, so as not to defile yourselves with them; [b]I am the LORD your God.’ ”

Idolatry Forbidden

19 Then the LORD spoke to Moses, saying:

2 ¶ “Speak to all the congregation of the sons of Israel and say to them, ‘[a]You shall be holy, for I the LORD your God am holy.

3 ‘Every one of you [a]shall reverence his mother and his father, and you shall keep [b]My sabbaths; [c]I am the LORD your God.

4 ‘Do not turn to [a]idols or make for yourselves molten [b]gods; I am the LORD your God.

5 ¶ ‘Now when you offer a sacrifice of peace offerings to the LORD, you shall offer it so that you may be accepted.

6 ‘It shall be eaten the same day you offer *it,* and the next day; but what remains until the third day shall be burned with fire.

7 ‘So if it is eaten at all on the third day, it is an offense; it will not be accepted.

8 ‘Everyone who eats it will bear his iniquity, for he has profaned the holy thing of the LORD; and that person shall be cut off from his people.

Sundry Laws

9 ¶ ‘[a]Now when you reap the harvest of your land, you shall not reap to the very corners of your field, nor shall you gather the gleanings of your harvest.

10 ‘Nor shall you glean your vineyard, nor shall you gather the fallen fruit of your vineyard; you shall leave them for the needy and for the stranger. I am the LORD your God.

11 ¶ ‘[a]You shall not steal, nor deal falsely, [b]nor lie to one another.

12 ‘[a]You shall not swear falsely by My name, so as to [b]profane the name of your God; I am the LORD.

13 ¶ ‘[a]You shall not oppress your neighbor, nor rob *him.* [b]The wages of a hired man are not to remain with you all night until morning.

14 ‘You shall not curse a deaf man, nor [a]place a stumbling block before the blind, but you shall revere your God; I am the LORD.

15 ¶ ‘[a]You shall do no injustice in judgment; you shall not be partial to the poor nor defer to the great, but you are to judge your neighbor fairly.

16 ‘You shall not go about as [a]a slanderer among your people, and you are not to [1]act against the [2b]life of your neighbor; I am the LORD.

17 ¶ ‘You [a]shall not hate your [1]fellow countryman in your heart; you [b]may surely reprove your neighbor, but shall not incur sin because of him.

18 ‘[a]You shall not take vengeance, [b]nor bear any grudge against the sons of your people, but [c]you shall love your neighbor as yourself; I am the LORD.

19 ¶ ‘You are to keep My statutes. You shall not breed together two kinds of your cattle; [a]you shall not sow your field with two kinds of seed, nor wear a garment upon you of two kinds of material mixed together.

20 ¶ ‘[a]Now if a man lies carnally with a woman who is a slave acquired for *another* man, but who has in no way been redeemed nor given her freedom, there shall be punishment; they shall not, *however,* be put to death, because she was not free.

21 ‘He shall bring his guilt offering to the LORD to the doorway of the tent of meeting, [a]a ram for a guilt offering.

22 ‘The priest shall also make atonement for him with the ram of the guilt offering before the LORD for his sin which

21 [b]Lev 19:12; 20:3; 21:6; Ezek 36:20; Mal 1:12
22 [1]Lit *those who lie* [a]Lev 20:13; Deut 23:18 mg; Rom 1:27
23 [1]Or *lie* [a]Ex 22:19; Lev 20:15,16; Deut 27:21
24 [a]Lev 18:3; Deut 18:12
25 [1]Lit *iniquity* [a]Lev 20:23; Deut 9:5; 18:12 [b]Lev 18:28; 20:22
29 [1]Or *and the*
30 [a]Lev 22:9; Deut 11:1 [b]Lev 18:2
19:2 [a]Ex 19:6; Lev 11:44; 20:7, 26; Eph 1:4; 1 Pet 1:16
3 [a]Ex 20:12; 31:13; Deut 5:16 [b]Ex 20:8 [c]Lev 11:44
4 [a]Lev 26:1; Ps 96:5; 115:4-7 [b]Ex 20:23; 34:17
9 [a]Lev 23:22; Deut 24:20-22
11 [a]Ex 20:15,16 [b]Jer 9:3-5; Eph 4:25
12 [a]Ex 20:7; Deut 5:11; Matt 5:33 [b]Lev 18:21
13 [a]Ex 22:7-15, 21-27 [b]Deut 24:15; James 5:4
14 [a]Deut 27:18
15 [a]Ex 23:3,6; Deut 1:17; 10:17; 16:19
16 [1]Lit *stand* [2]Lit *blood* [a]Ps 15:3; Jer 6:28; 9:4; Ezek 22:9 [b]Ex 23:7; Deut 27:25
17 [1]Lit *brother* [a]1 John 2:9,11; 3:15 [b]Matt 18:15; Luke 17:3
18 [a]Deut 32:35; Rom 12:19; Heb 10:30 [b]Ps 103:9 [c]Matt 19:19; Mark 12:31; Luke 10:27; Rom 13:9; Gal 5:14; James 2:8
19 [a]Deut 22:9, 11
20 [a]Deut 22:23-27
21 [a]Lev 6:1-7

he has committed, and the sin which he has committed will be forgiven him.

23 ¶ 'When you enter the land and plant all kinds of trees for food, then you shall count their fruit as [1]forbidden. Three years it shall be [1]forbidden to you; *it* shall not be eaten.

24 'But in the fourth year all its fruit shall be holy, an offering of praise to the LORD.

25 'In the fifth year you are to eat of its fruit, that its yield may increase for you; I am the LORD your God.

26 ¶ 'You shall not eat *anything* [a]with the blood, nor practice [b]divination or soothsaying.

27 '[a]You shall not round off the side-growth of your heads nor harm the edges of your beard.

28 'You shall not make any cuts in your [1]body for the [2]dead nor make any tattoo marks on yourselves: I am the LORD.

29 ¶ '[a]Do not [1]profane your daughter by making her a harlot, so that the land will not fall to harlotry and the land become full of lewdness.

30 'You shall [a]keep My sabbaths and [b]revere My sanctuary; I am the LORD.

31 ¶ 'Do not turn to [1a]mediums or spiritists; do not seek them out to be defiled by them. I am the LORD your God.

32 ¶ '[a]You shall rise up before the grayheaded and honor the [1]aged, and you shall revere your God; I am the LORD.

33 ¶ '[a]When a stranger resides with you in your land, you shall not do him wrong.

34 'The stranger who resides with you shall be to you as the native among you, and [a]you shall love him as yourself, for you were aliens in the land of Egypt; I am the LORD your God.

35 ¶ '[a]You shall do no wrong in judgment, in measurement of weight, or capacity.

36 'You shall have [a]just balances, just weights, a just [1]ephah, and a just [2]hin; I am the LORD your God, who brought you out from the land of Egypt.

37 'You shall thus observe all My statutes and all My ordinances and do them; I am the LORD.' "

On Human Sacrifice and Immoralities

20 Then the LORD spoke to Moses, saying,

2 "You shall also say to the sons of Israel:

¶ 'Any man from the sons of Israel or from the aliens sojourning in Israel [a]who gives any of his [1]offspring to Molech, shall surely be put to death; [b]the people of the land shall stone him with stones.

3 'I will also set My face against that man and will cut him off from among his people, because he has given some of his [1]offspring to Molech, [a]so as to defile My sanctuary and [b]to profane My holy name.

4 'If the people of the land, however, [1]should ever disregard that man when he gives any of his [2]offspring to Molech, so as not to put him to death,

5 then I Myself will set My face against that man and against his family, and I will cut off from among their people both him and all those who play the harlot after him, by playing the harlot after Molech.

6 ¶ 'As for the person who turns to [1a]mediums and to spiritists, to play the harlot after them, I will also set My face against that person and will cut him off from among his people.

7 'You shall consecrate yourselves therefore and [a]be holy, for I am the LORD your God.

8 '[a]You shall keep My statutes and practice them; I am the LORD who sanctifies you.

9 ¶ '[a]If *there is* anyone who curses his father or his mother, he shall surely be put to death; he has cursed his father or his mother, his bloodguiltiness is upon him.

10 ¶ '[a]If *there is* a man who commits adultery with another man's wife, one who commits adultery with his friend's wife, the adulterer and the adulteress shall surely be put to death.

11 '[a]If *there is* a man who lies with his father's wife, he has uncovered his father's nakedness; both of them shall surely be put to death, their bloodguiltiness is upon them.

12 '[a]If *there is* a man who lies with his daughter-in-law, both of them shall surely be put to death; they have committed [1]incest, their bloodguiltiness is upon them.

13 '[a]If *there is* a man who lies with a male as those who lie with a woman, both of them have committed a detestable act; they shall surely be put to death. Their bloodguiltiness is upon them.

14 '[a]If *there is* a man who [1]marries a woman and her mother, it is immorality; both he and they shall be burned with fire, so that there will be no immorality in your midst.

15 '[a]If *there is* a man who lies with an animal, he shall surely be put to death; you shall also kill the animal.

16 'If *there is* a woman who approaches any animal to [1]mate with it, you shall kill the woman and the animal;

23 [1]Lit *uncircumcised*
26 [a]Gen 9:4; Lev 7:26f; 17:10; Deut 12:16,23 [b]Deut 18:10; 2 Kin 17:17
27 [a]Lev 21:5; Deut 14:1
28 [1]Lit *flesh* [2]Lit *soul*
29 [1]Or *degrade* [a]Lev 21:9; Deut 22:21; 23:17,18
30 [a]Lev 19:3 [b]Lev 26:2
31 [1]Or *ghosts or spirits* [a]Lev 20:6, 27; Deut 18:11; 1 Sam 28:3; Is 8:19
32 [1]Lit *face of the aged* [a]Prov 23:22; Lam 5:12; 1 Tim 5:1
33 [a]Ex 22:21; Deut 24:17,18
34 [a]Lev 19:18
35 [a]Deut 25:13-16; Ezek 45:10
36 [1]I.e. Approx one bu [2]I.e. Approx one gal. [a]Deut 25:13-15; Prov 20:10
20:2 [1]Lit *seed* [a]Lev 18:21 [b]Lev 20:27; 24:14-23; Num 15:35,36; Deut 21:21
3 [1]Lit *seed* [a]Lev 15:31 [b]Lev 18:21
4 [1]Lit *hiding they hide their eyes from* [2]Lit *seed*
6 [1]Or *ghosts and spirits* [a]Lev 19:31
7 [a]Eph 1:4; 1 Pet 1:16
8 [a]Ex 31:13
9 [a]Ex 21:17; Deut 27:16
10 [a]Ex 20:14; Lev 18:20; Deut 5:18
11 [a]Lev 18:7,8; Deut 27:20
12 [1]Lit *confusion*; i.e. a violation of divine order [a]Lev 18:15
13 [a]Lev 18:22
14 [1]Lit *takes* [a]Lev 18:17; Deut 27:23
15 [a]Lev 18:23; Deut 27:21
16 [1]Lit *lie*

they shall surely be put to death. Their bloodguiltiness is upon them.

17 ¶ '[a]If *there is* a man who takes his sister, his father's daughter or his mother's daughter, so that he sees her nakedness and she sees his nakedness, it is a disgrace; and they shall be cut off in the sight of the sons of their people. He has uncovered his sister's nakedness; he bears his guilt.

18 '[a]If *there is* a man who lies with a [1]menstruous woman and uncovers her nakedness, he has laid bare her flow, and she has [2]exposed the flow of her blood; thus both of them shall be cut off from among their people.

19 '[a]You shall also not uncover the nakedness of your mother's sister or of your father's sister, for such a one has made naked his [1]blood relative; they will bear their guilt.

20 '[a]If *there is* a man who lies with his uncle's wife he has uncovered his uncle's nakedness; they will bear their sin. They will die childless.

21 '[a]If *there is* a man who takes his brother's wife, it is [1]abhorrent; he has uncovered his brother's nakedness. They will be childless.

22 ¶ 'You are therefore to keep all My statutes and all My ordinances and do them, so that the land to which I am bringing you to [1]live will not [a]spew you out.

23 'Moreover, you shall not [1]follow [a]the customs of the nation which I will drive out before you, for they did all these things, and [b]therefore I have abhorred them.

24 'Hence I have said to you, "[a]You are to possess their land, and I Myself will give it to you to possess it, a land flowing with milk and honey." I am the LORD your God, who has [b]separated you from the peoples.

25 '[a]You are therefore to make a distinction between the clean animal and the unclean, and between the unclean bird and the clean; and you shall not make [1]yourselves detestable by animal or by bird or by anything [2]that creeps on the ground, which I have separated for you as unclean.

26 'Thus you are to be holy to Me, for I the LORD am holy; and I [a]have set you apart from the peoples to be Mine.

27 ¶ 'Now a man or a woman [a]who is a medium or a [1]spiritist shall surely be put to death. They shall be stoned with stones, their bloodguiltiness is upon them.' "

Regulations concerning Priests

21 Then the LORD said to Moses, "Speak to the priests, the sons of Aaron, and say to them:

¶ '[a]No one shall defile himself for a *dead* person among his people,

2 [a]except for his relatives who are nearest to him, his mother and his father and his son and his daughter and his brother,

3 also for his virgin sister, who is near to him [1]because she has had no husband; for her he may defile himself.

4 'He shall not defile himself as a [1]relative by marriage among his people, and so profane himself.

5 '[a]They shall not make any baldness on their heads, [b]nor shave off the edges of their beards, [c]nor make any cuts in their flesh.

6 'They shall be holy to their God and [a]not profane the name of their God, for they present the offerings by fire [1]to the LORD, [b]the food of their God; so they shall be holy.

7 '[a]They shall not take a woman who is profaned by harlotry, nor shall they take a woman divorced from her husband; for he is holy to his God.

8 'You shall consecrate him, therefore, for he offers [a]the food of your God; he shall be holy to you; for I the LORD, who sanctifies you, am holy.

9 '[a]Also the daughter of any priest, if she profanes herself by harlotry, she profanes her father; she shall be burned with fire.

10 ¶ 'The priest who is the highest among his brothers, on whose head the anointing oil has been poured and [1]who has been consecrated to wear the garments, [a]shall not [2]uncover his head nor tear his clothes;

11 [a]nor shall he approach any dead person, nor defile himself *even* for his father or his mother;

12 [a]nor shall he go out of the sanctuary nor profane the sanctuary of his God, for [b]the consecration of the anointing oil of his God is on him; I am the LORD.

13 'He shall take a wife in her virginity.

14 '[a]A widow, or a divorced woman, or one who is profaned by harlotry, these he may not take; but rather he is to [1]marry a virgin of his own people,

15 so that he will not profane his [1]offspring among his people; for I am the LORD who sanctifies him.' "

16 ¶ Then the LORD spoke to Moses, saying,

17 "Speak to Aaron, saying, 'No man of your [1]offspring throughout their genera-

17 [a]Lev 18:9; Deut 27:22
18 [1]Lit *sick* [2]Or *uncovered* [a]Lev 15:24; 18:19
19 [1]Lit *flesh* [a]Lev 18:12,13
20 [a]Lev 18:14
21 [1]Or *an impure deed* [a]Lev 18:16
22 [1]Lit *dwell in it* [a]Lev 18:28
23 [1]Lit *walk in the statutes* [a]Lev 18:3 [b]Lev 18:25
24 [a]Ex 13:5; 33:1-3 [b]Ex 33:16; Lev 20:26
25 [1]Lit *your souls* [2]Lit *with which the ground creeps* [a]Lev 10:10; 11:1-47; Deut 14:3-21
26 [a]Lev 20:24
27 [1]Lit *spiritist among them* [a]Lev 19:31
21:1 [a]Lev 19:28; Ezek 44:25
2 [a]Lev 21:11
3 [1]Or *whom no man has had*
4 [1]Lit *husband among*
5 [a]Deut 14:1; Ezek 44:20 [b]Lev 19:27 [c]Deut 14:1
6 [1]Lit *of* [a]Lev 18:21 [b]Lev 3:11
7 [a]Lev 21:13,14
8 [a]Lev 21:6
9 [a]Gen 38:24; Lev 19:29
10 [1]Lit *whose hand has been filled* [2]Lit *unbind* [a]Lev 10:6
11 [a]Lev 19:28; Num 19:14
12 [a]Lev 10:7 [b]Ex 29:6,7
14 [1]Lit *take as wife* [a]Lev 21:7; Ezek 44:22
15 [1]Lit *seed*
17 [1]Lit *seed*

tions who has a defect shall approach to
offer the [a]food of his God.
18 '[a]For no one who has a defect shall
approach: a blind man, or a lame man, or
he who has a [1a]disfigured *face,* or any
deformed *limb,*
19 or a man who has a broken foot or
broken hand,
20 or a hunchback or a dwarf, or *one*
who has a [1]defect in his eye or eczema
or scabs or [a]crushed testicles.
21 'No man among the [1]descendants
of Aaron the priest who has a defect is to
come near to offer the LORD'S offerings by
fire; *since* he has a defect, he shall not
come near to offer [a]the food of his God.
22 'He may eat [a]the food of his God,
both of the most holy and of the holy,
23 only he shall not go in to the veil or
come near the altar because he has a defect, so that he will not profane My sanctuaries. For I am the LORD who sanctifies
them.' "
24 So Moses spoke to Aaron and to his
sons and to all the sons of Israel.

Sundry Rules for Priests

22 Then the LORD spoke to Moses,
saying,
2 "Tell Aaron and his sons to be careful with the holy *gifts* of the sons of Israel,
which they dedicate to Me, so as not to
profane My holy name; I am the LORD.
3 "Say to them, '[a]If any man among
all your [1]descendants throughout your
generations approaches the holy *gifts*
which the sons of Israel dedicate to the
LORD, while he has an uncleanness, that
person shall be cut off from before Me; I
am the LORD.
4 '[a]No man of the [1]descendants of
Aaron, who is a leper or who has a discharge, may eat of the holy *gifts* until he
is clean. [b]And if one touches anything
made unclean by a corpse or if [c]a man
has a seminal emission,
5 or [a]if a man touches any teeming
things by which he is made unclean, or
any man by whom he is made unclean,
whatever his uncleanness;
6 a [1]person who touches any such
shall be unclean until evening, and shall
not eat of the holy *gifts* unless he has
bathed his [2]body in water.
7 'But when the sun sets, he will be
clean, and afterward he shall eat of the
holy *gifts,* for [a]it is his [1]food.
8 'He shall not eat [a]*an animal* which
dies or is torn *by beasts,* becoming unclean by it; I am the LORD.
9 'They shall therefore keep [a]My
charge, so that [b]they will not bear sin
because of it and die thereby because
they profane it; I am the LORD who sanctifies them.
10 ¶ '[a]No [1]layman, however, is to eat
the holy *gift;* a sojourner with the priest
or a hired man shall not eat of the holy
gift.
11 '[a]But if a priest buys a [1]slave as *his*
property with his money, [2]that one may
eat of it, and those who are born in his
house may eat of his [3]food.
12 'If a priest's daughter is married to a
[1]layman, she shall not eat of the [2]offer-
ing of the *gifts.*
13 'But if a priest's daughter becomes a
widow or divorced, and has no child and
returns to her father's house as in her
youth, she shall eat of her father's [1]food;
[a]but no [2]layman shall eat of it.
14 '[a]But if a man eats a holy *gift* unintentionally, then he shall add to it a fifth
of it and shall give the holy *gift* to the
priest.
15 '[a]They shall not profane the holy
gifts of the sons of Israel which they offer
to the LORD,
16 and *so* cause them [a]to bear [1]pun-
ishment for guilt by eating their holy
gifts; for I am the LORD who sanctifies
them.' "

Flawless Animals for Sacrifice

17 ¶ Then the LORD spoke to Moses,
saying,
18 "Speak to Aaron and to his sons and
to all the sons of Israel and say to them,
'[a]Any man of the house of Israel or of the
aliens in Israel who presents his offering,
whether it is any of their [1]votive or any
of their freewill offerings, which they
present to the LORD for a burnt offering—
19 [a]for you to be accepted—*it must*
be a male without defect from the cattle,
the sheep, or the goats.
20 '[a]Whatever has a defect, you shall
not offer, for it will not be accepted for
you.
21 'When a man offers a sacrifice of
peace offerings to the LORD [a]to [1]fulfill a
special vow or for a freewill offering, of
the herd or of the flock, it must be perfect
to be accepted; there shall be no defect
in it.
22 'Those *that are* blind or fractured or
maimed or having a running sore or eczema or scabs, you shall not offer to the
LORD, nor make of them an offering by
fire on the altar to the LORD.
23 'In respect to an ox or a lamb which
has an [1]overgrown or stunted *member,*
you may present it for a freewill offering,
but for a vow it will not be accepted.
24 'Also [a]anything *with its testicles*
bruised or crushed or torn or cut, you

17 [a]Lev 21:6
18 [1]Lit *slit* [a]Lev 22:19-25
20 [1]Lit *obscurity* [a]Deut 23:1; Is 56:3-5
21 [1]Lit *seed* [a]Lev 21:6
22 [a]1 Cor 9:13
22:3 [1]Lit *seed* [a]Lev 7:20,21; Num 19:13
4 [1]Lit *seed* [a]Lev 14:1-32 [b]Lev 11:24-28,39,40 [c]Lev 15:16,17
5 [a]Lev 11:23-28
6 [1]Lit *soul* [2]Lit *flesh*
7 [1]Lit *bread* [a]Num 18:11
8 [a]Lev 7:24; 11:39,40; 17:15
9 [a]Lev 18:30 [b]Ex 28:43; Lev 22:16; Num 18:22
10 [1]Lit *stranger* [a]Ex 29:33; Lev 22:13; Num 3:10
11 [1]Lit *soul* [2]Lit *he may* [3]Lit *bread* [a]Gen 17:13; Ex 12:44
12 [1]Lit *stranger* [2]Lit *heave offering*
13 [1]Lit *bread* [2]Lit *stranger* [a]Lev 22:10
14 [a]Lev 5:15,16
15 [a]Num 18:32
16 [1]Or *iniquity requiring a guilt offering* [a]Lev 10:17; 22:9
18 [1]Lit *vows* [a]Num 15:14
19 [a]Lev 21:18-21; Deut 15:21
20 [a]Deut 15:21; 17:1; Mal 1:8, 14; Heb 9:14; 1 Pet 1:19
21 [1]Or *make a special votive offering* [a]Num 15:3,8
23 [1]Or *a deformed*
24 [a]Lev 21:20

shall not offer to the LORD, or [1]sacrifice
in your land,
25 nor shall you accept any such from
the hand of a foreigner for offering [a]as
the [1]food of your God; for their corruption is in them, they have a defect, they
shall not be accepted for you.' "
26 ¶ Then the LORD spoke to Moses,
saying,
27 "When an ox or a sheep or a goat is
born, it shall [1]remain [a]seven days [2]with
its mother, and from the eighth day on it
shall be accepted as a sacrifice of an offering by fire to the LORD.
28 "[a]But, *whether* it is an ox or a
sheep, you shall not kill *both* it and its
young in one day.
29 "When you sacrifice [a]a sacrifice of
thanksgiving to the LORD, you shall sacrifice it so that you may be accepted.
30 "It shall be eaten on the same day,
you shall leave none of it until morning;
I am the LORD.
31 "[a]So you shall keep My commandments, and do them; I am the LORD.
32 ¶ "You shall not profane My holy
name, but I will be sanctified among the
sons of Israel; I am the LORD who sanctifies you,
33 [a]who brought you out from the
land of Egypt, to be your God; I am the
LORD."

Laws of Religious Festivals

23 The LORD spoke again to Moses,
saying,
2 "Speak to the sons of Israel and say
to them, '[a]The LORD'S appointed times
which you shall [b]proclaim as holy convocations—My appointed times are these:
3 ¶ '[a]For six days work may be done,
but on the seventh day there is a sabbath
of complete rest, a holy convocation. You
shall not do any work; it is a sabbath to
the LORD in all your dwellings.
4 ¶ 'These are the [a]appointed times
of the LORD, holy convocations which you
shall proclaim at the times appointed for
them.
5 '[a]In the first month, on the fourteenth day of the month [1]at twilight is
the LORD'S Passover.
6 'Then on the fifteenth day of the
same month there is the [a]Feast of Unleavened Bread to the LORD; for seven
days you shall eat unleavened bread.
7 'On the first day you shall have a
holy convocation; you shall [a]not do any
laborious work.
8 'But for seven days you shall present
an offering by fire to the LORD. On the
seventh day is a holy convocation; you
shall not do any laborious work.' "

24 [1]Lit *do*

25 [1]Lit *bread* [a]Lev 21:22

27 [1]Lit *be* [2]Lit *under* [a]Ex 22:30

28 [a]Deut 22:6,7

29 [a]Lev 7:12

31 [a]Lev 19:37; Num 15:40; Deut 4:40

33 [a]Lev 11:45

23:2 [a]Lev 23:4, 37,44; Num 29:39 [b]Lev 23:21

3 [a]Ex 20:9,10; 23:12; 31:13-17; 35:2,3; Lev 19:3; Deut 5:13,14

4 [a]Ex 23:14; Lev 23:2

5 [1]Lit *between the two evenings* [a]Ex 12:18,19; Num 28:16-25; Deut 16:1; Josh 5:10

6 [a]Ex 12:14-20; 23:15; 34:18; Deut 16:3-8

7 [a]Lev 23:8,21, 25,35,36

10 [a]Ex 23:19; 34:26

13 [1]I.e. Approx one gal. [a]Lev 6:20

14 [a]Ex 34:26; Num 15:20,21

15 [a]Num 28:26-31; Deut 16:9-12

16 [a]Num 28:26

17 [1]I.e. Approx one bu [a]Lev 2:12; 7:13

19 [a]Lev 4:23; Num 28:30

21 [a]Lev 23:2,4 [b]Lev 23:7

22 [a]Lev 19:9, 10; Deut 24:19; Ruth 2:15f

9 ¶ Then the LORD spoke to Moses,
saying,
10 "Speak to the sons of Israel and say
to them, 'When you enter the land which
I am going to give to you and [a]reap its
harvest, then you shall bring in the sheaf
of the first fruits of your harvest to the
priest.
11 'He shall wave the sheaf before the
LORD for you to be accepted; on the day
after the sabbath the priest shall wave it.
12 'Now on the day when you wave the
sheaf, you shall offer a male lamb one
year old without defect for a burnt offering to the LORD.
13 'Its [a]grain offering shall then be
two-tenths *of an ephah* of fine flour
mixed with oil, an offering by fire to the
LORD *for* a soothing aroma, with its drink
offering, a fourth of a [1]hin of wine.
14 'Until this same day, until you have
brought in the offering of your God, [a]you
shall eat neither bread nor roasted grain
nor new growth. It is to be a perpetual
statute throughout your generations in all
your dwelling places.
15 ¶ '[a]You shall also count for yourselves from the day after the sabbath,
from the day when you brought in the
sheaf of the wave offering; there shall be
seven complete sabbaths.
16 'You shall count fifty days to the day
after the seventh sabbath; then you shall
present a [a]new grain offering to the
LORD.
17 'You shall bring in from your dwelling places two *loaves* of bread for a wave
offering, made of two-tenths *of an*
[1]*ephah;* they shall be of a fine flour,
baked [a]with leaven as first fruits to the
LORD.
18 'Along with the bread you shall
present seven one year old male lambs
without defect, and a bull of the herd and
two rams; they are to be a burnt offering
to the LORD, with their grain offering and
their drink offerings, an offering by fire of
a soothing aroma to the LORD.
19 'You shall also offer [a]one male goat
for a sin offering and two male lambs one
year old for a sacrifice of peace offerings.
20 'The priest shall then wave them
with the bread of the first fruits for a
wave offering with two lambs before the
LORD; they are to be holy to the LORD for
the priest.
21 'On this same day you shall [a]make
a proclamation as well; you are to have a
holy convocation. You shall do no laborious [b]work. It is to be a perpetual statute
in all your dwelling places throughout
your generations.
22 ¶ '[a]When you reap the harvest of
your land, moreover, you shall not reap to

the very corners of your field nor gather the gleaning of your harvest; you are to leave them for the needy and the alien. I am the LORD your God.' "

23 ¶ Again the LORD spoke to Moses, saying,

24 "Speak to the sons of Israel, saying, '[a]In the seventh month on the first of the month you shall have a [1]rest, a [b]reminder by blowing *of trumpets,* a holy convocation.

25 'You shall [a]not do any laborious work, but you shall present an offering by fire to the LORD.' "

The Day of Atonement

26 ¶ The LORD spoke to Moses, saying,

27 "On exactly [a]the tenth day of this seventh month is [b]the day of atonement; it shall be a holy convocation for you, and you shall humble your souls and present an offering by fire to the LORD.

28 "You shall not do any work on this same day, for it is a [a]day of atonement, [b]to make atonement on your behalf before the LORD your God.

29 "If there is any [1]person who will not humble himself on this same day, [a]he shall be cut off from his people.

30 "As for any person who does any work on this same day, that person I will destroy from among his people.

31 "You shall do no work at all. It is to be a perpetual statute throughout your generations in all your dwelling places.

32 "It is to be a sabbath of complete rest to you, and you shall humble your souls; on the ninth of the month at evening, from evening until evening you shall keep your sabbath."

33 ¶ Again the LORD spoke to Moses, saying,

34 "Speak to the sons of Israel, saying, 'On [a]the fifteenth of this seventh month is the [b]Feast of Booths for seven days to the LORD.

35 'On the first day is a holy convocation; you shall do [a]no laborious work of any kind.

36 '[a]For seven days you shall present an offering by fire to the LORD. On [b]the eighth day you shall have a holy convocation and present an offering by fire to the LORD; it is an assembly. You shall do no laborious work.

37 ¶ 'These are [a]the appointed times of the LORD which you shall proclaim as holy convocations, to present offerings by fire to the LORD—burnt offerings and grain offerings, sacrifices and drink offerings, [b]*each* day's matter on its own day—

38 besides *those of* the sabbaths of the LORD, and besides your gifts and besides all your [1]votive and freewill offerings, which you give to the LORD.

39 ¶ 'On exactly the fifteenth day of the seventh month, [a]when you have gathered in the crops of the land, you shall celebrate the feast of the LORD for seven days, with a [1]rest on the first day and a [1]rest on the eighth day.

40 'Now on the first day you shall take for yourselves the [1]foliage of beautiful trees, palm branches and boughs of leafy trees and willows of the brook, and you shall rejoice before the LORD your God for seven days.

41 'You shall thus celebrate it *as* a feast to the LORD for seven days in the year. It *shall be* a perpetual statute throughout your generations; you shall celebrate it in the seventh month.

42 'You shall [1]live [a]in booths for seven days; all the native-born in Israel shall [1]live in booths,

43 so that [a]your generations may know that I had the sons of Israel live in booths when I brought them out from the land of Egypt. I am the LORD your God.' "

44 So Moses declared to the sons of Israel [a]the appointed times of the LORD.

The Lamp and the Bread of the Sanctuary

24 Then the LORD spoke to Moses, saying,

2 "Command the sons of Israel that they bring to you [a]clear oil from beaten olives for the [1]light, to make a lamp [2]burn continually.

3 "Outside the veil of testimony in the tent of meeting, Aaron shall keep it in order from evening to morning before the LORD continually; *it shall be* a perpetual statute throughout your generations.

4 "He shall keep the lamps in order on the [a]pure *gold* lampstand before the LORD continually.

5 ¶ "[a]Then you shall take fine flour and bake twelve cakes with it; two-tenths *of an ephah* shall be *in* each cake.

6 "You shall set them *in* two rows, six *to* a row, on the [a]pure *gold* table before the LORD.

7 "You shall put pure frankincense on each row that it may be [a]a memorial portion for the bread, *even* an offering by fire to the LORD.

8 "[a]Every sabbath day he shall set it in order before the LORD [b]continually; it is an everlasting covenant [1]for the sons of Israel.

9 "[a]It shall be for Aaron and his sons, and they shall eat it in a holy place; for it is most holy to him from the LORD's offerings by fire, *his* portion forever."

24 [1]Lit *sabbath rest* [a]Num 29:1 [b]Num 10:9,10
25 [a]Lev 23:21
27 [a]Lev 16:29; 25:9; Num 29:7 [b]Ex 30:10; Lev 16:30; 23:28; Num 29:7-11
28 [a]Lev 23:27 [b]Lev 16:34
29 [1]Lit *soul* [a]Gen 17:14; Lev 13:46; Num 5:2
34 [a]Num 29:12 [b]Lev 23:42,43; Deut 16:13,16; Ezra 3:4; Neh 8:14; Zech 14:16; John 7:2
35 [a]Lev 23:25
36 [a]Num 29:12-34 [b]Num 29:35-38
37 [a]Lev 23:2 [b]Num 28:1-29:38
38 [1]Lit *vows, and besides all your*
39 [1]Lit *sabbath rest* [a]Ex 23:16
40 [1]Lit *products, fruit*
42 [1]Lit *dwell* [a]Lev 23:34
43 [a]Deut 31:13; Ps 78:5f
44 [a]Lev 23:37
24:2 [1]Or *luminary* [2]Lit *ascend* [a]Ex 27:20,21
4 [a]Ex 25:31; 31:8; 37:17
5 [a]Ex 25:30; 39:36; 40:23
6 [a]Ex 25:24; 1 Kin 7:48
7 [a]Lev 2:2,9,16
8 [1]Lit *from* [a]Matt 12:5 [b]Ex 25:30; Num 4:7; 2 Chr 2:4
9 [a]Matt 12:4; Mark 2:26; Luke 6:4

10 ¶ Now the son of an Israelite woman, whose father was an Egyptian, went
out among the sons of Israel; and the Israelite woman's son and a man of Israel
struggled with each other in the camp.
11 The son of the Israelite woman
blasphemed the [a]Name and cursed. So
they brought him to Moses. (Now his
mother's name was Shelomith, the
daughter of Dibri, of the tribe of Dan.)
12 They put him in [1]custody [2]so that
[a]the command of the LORD might be
made clear to them.
13 ¶ Then the LORD spoke to Moses,
saying,
14 "Bring the one who has cursed outside the camp, and let all who heard him
[a]lay their hands on his head; then [b]let
all the congregation stone him.
15 "You shall speak to the sons of Israel,
saying, '[a]If anyone curses his God, then
he will bear his sin.
16 'Moreover, the one who [a]blas-
phemes the name of the LORD shall surely
be put to death; all the congregation shall
certainly stone him. The alien as well
as the native, when he blasphemes the
Name, shall be put to death.

"An Eye for an Eye"

17 ¶ '[a]If a man [1]takes the life of any
human being, he shall surely be put to
death.
18 '[a]The one who [1]takes the life of an
animal shall make it good, life for life.
19 'If a man [1]injures his neighbor, just
as he has done, so it shall be done to him:
20 [a]fracture for fracture, [b]eye for eye,
tooth for tooth; just as he has [1]injured a
man, so it shall be [2]inflicted on him.
21 'Thus the one who [1]kills an animal
shall make it good, but [a]the one who
[1]kills a man shall be put to death.
22 'There shall be [a]one [1]standard for
you; it shall be for the stranger as well as
the native, for I am the LORD your God.' "
23 Then Moses spoke to the sons of
Israel, and they brought the one who had
cursed outside the camp and stoned him
with stones. Thus the sons of Israel did,
just as the LORD had commanded Moses.

The Sabbatic Year and Year of Jubilee

25 The LORD then spoke to Moses
[1]at Mount Sinai, saying,
2 "Speak to the sons of Israel and say
to them, 'When you come into the land
which I shall give you, then the land shall
have a sabbath to the LORD.
3 '[a]Six years you shall sow your field,
and six years you shall prune your vineyard and gather in its crop,
4 but during [a]the seventh year the
land shall have a sabbath rest, a sabbath
to the LORD; you shall not sow your field
nor prune your vineyard.
5 'Your harvest's [1]aftergrowth you
shall not reap, and your grapes of un-
trimmed vines you shall not gather; the
land shall have a sabbatical year.
6 '[a]All of you shall have the sabbath
products of the land for food; yourself,
and your male and female slaves, and
your hired man and your foreign resident, those who live as aliens with you.
7 'Even your cattle and the animals
that are in your land shall have all its
crops to eat.
8 ¶ 'You are also to count off seven
sabbaths of years for yourself, seven
times seven years, so that you have the
time of the seven sabbaths of years,
namely, forty-nine years.
9 'You shall then sound a ram's horn
abroad on [a]the tenth day of the seventh
month; on the day of atonement you shall
sound a horn all through your land.
10 'You shall thus consecrate the fiftieth year and [a]proclaim [1]a release
through the land to all its inhabitants. It
shall be a jubilee for you, [2]and [b]each
of you shall return to his own property,
[2]and each of you shall return to his family.
11 'You shall have the fiftieth year as a
jubilee; you shall not sow, nor reap its
aftergrowth, nor gather in *from* its un-
trimmed vines.
12 'For it is a jubilee; it shall be holy to
you. You shall eat its crops out of the
field.
13 ¶ '[a]On this year of jubilee each of
you shall return to his own property.
14 'If you make a sale, moreover, to
your friend or buy from your friend's
hand, [a]you shall not wrong one another.
15 'Corresponding to the number of
years after the jubilee, you shall buy from
your [1]friend; he is to sell to you according to the number of years of crops.
16 '[a]In proportion to the [1]extent of
the years you shall increase its price, and
in proportion to the fewness of the years
you shall diminish its price, for *it is* a
number of crops he is selling to you.
17 'So [a]you shall not wrong one another, but you shall [1]fear your God; for I am
the LORD your God.
18 ¶ 'You shall thus observe My statutes and keep My judgments, so as to
carry them out, that [a]you may live securely on the land.
19 'Then the land will yield its produce, so that you can eat your fill and live
securely on it.
20 'But if you say, "[a]What are we go-

11 [a]Ex 3:15; 22:28; Job 2:5,9; Is 8:21
12 [1]Or *prison* [2]Lit *to declare distinctly to them according to the mouth of the LORD* [a]Ex 18:15; Num 15:34
14 [a]Deut 13:9; 17:7 [b]Lev 20:2, 27; Deut 21:21
15 [a]Ex 22:28
16 [a]1 Kin 21:10; Matt 12:31; Mark 3:28f
17 [1]Lit *smites* [a]Gen 9:6; Ex 21:12; Num 35:30,31; Deut 27:24
18 [1]Lit *smites* [a]Lev 24:21
19 [1]Lit *gives a blemish*
20 [1]Lit *given a blemish* [2]Lit *given* [a]Ex 21:23; Deut 19:21 [b]Matt 5:38
21 [1]Lit *smites* [a]Lev 24:17
22 [1]Lit *judgment* [a]Ex 12:49; Num 9:14; 15:15,16,29
25:1 [1]Or *on*
3 [a]Ex 23:10,11
4 [a]Lev 25:20
5 [1]Lit *growth from spilled kernels*
6 [a]Lev 25:20,21
9 [a]Lev 23:27
10 [1]Or *liberty* [2]Or *when* [a]Jer 34:8,15,17 [b]Lev 25:13,28,54
13 [a]Lev 25:10; 27:24
14 [a]Lev 25:17
15 [1]Lit *friend's hands*
16 [1]Lit *multitude* [a]Lev 25:27, 51,52
17 [1]Or *reverence* [a]Lev 25:14; Prov 14:31; 22:22; Jer 7:5,6; 1 Thess 4:6
18 [a]Lev 26:5; Deut 12:10; Jer 23:6
20 [a]Lev 25:4

ing to eat on the seventh year [1]if we do not sow or gather in our crops?"

21 then [a]I will so order My blessing for you in the sixth year that it will bring forth the crop for three years.

22 'When you are sowing the eighth year, you can still eat [a]old things from the crop, eating *the old* until the ninth year when its crop comes in.

The Law of Redemption

23 ¶ 'The land, moreover, shall not be sold permanently, for [a]the land is Mine; for [b]you are *but* aliens and sojourners with Me.

24 'Thus for every [1]piece of your property, you are to provide for the redemption of the land.

25 ¶ '[a]If a [1]fellow countryman of yours becomes so poor he has to sell part of his property, then his nearest kinsman is to come and buy back what his [1]relative has sold.

26 'Or in case a man has no kinsman, but so [1]recovers his means as to find sufficient for its redemption,

27 [a]then he shall calculate the years since its sale and refund the balance to the man to whom he sold it, and so return to his property.

28 'But if [1]he has not found sufficient means to get it back for himself, then what he has sold shall remain in the hands of its purchaser until the year of jubilee; but at the jubilee it shall [2]revert, that [a]he may return to his property.

29 ¶ 'Likewise, if a man sells a dwelling house in a walled city, then his redemption right remains valid until a full year from its sale; his right of redemption lasts a full year.

30 'But if it is not bought back for him within the space of a full year, then the house that is in the walled city passes permanently to its purchaser throughout his generations; it does not [1]revert in the jubilee.

31 'The houses of the villages, however, which have no surrounding wall shall be considered [1]as open fields; they have redemption rights and [2]revert in the jubilee.

32 'As for [a]cities of the Levites, the Levites have a permanent right of redemption for the houses of the cities which are their possession.

33 'What, therefore, [1]belongs to the Levites may be redeemed and a house sale [2]in the city of this possession [3]reverts in the jubilee, for the houses of the cities of the Levites are their possession among the sons of Israel.

34 '[a]But pasture fields of their cities shall not be sold, for that is their perpetual possession.

Of Poor Countrymen

35 ¶ '[a]Now in case a [1]countryman of yours becomes poor and his [2]means with regard to you falter, then you are to sustain him, like a stranger or a sojourner, that he may live with you.

36 '[a]Do not take [1]usurious interest from him, but revere your God, that your [2]countryman may live with you.

37 'You shall not give him your silver at interest, nor your food for gain.

38 '[a]I am the LORD your God, who brought you out of the land of Egypt to give you the land of Canaan *and* [b]to be your God.

39 ¶ '[a]If a [1]countryman of yours becomes so poor with regard to you that he sells himself to you, you shall not subject him to a slave's service.

40 'He shall be with you as a hired man, as [a]if he were a sojourner; he shall serve with you until the year of jubilee.

41 'He shall then go out from you, he and his sons with him, and shall go back to his family, that he may return to the property of his forefathers.

42 'For they are My servants whom I brought out from the land of Egypt; they are not to be sold *in* a slave sale.

43 '[a]You shall not rule over him with severity, but are to revere your God.

44 'As for your male and female slaves whom you may have—you may acquire male and female slaves from the pagan nations that are around you.

45 'Then, too, *it is* out of the sons of the sojourners who live as aliens among you that you may gain acquisition, and out of their families who are with you, whom they will have [1]produced in your land; they also may become your possession.

46 'You may even bequeath them to your sons after you, to receive as a possession; you can use them as permanent slaves. [a]But in respect to your [1]countrymen, the sons of Israel, you shall not rule with severity over one another.

Of Redeeming a Poor Man

47 ¶ 'Now if the [1]means of a stranger or of a sojourner with you becomes sufficient, and a [2]countryman of yours becomes so poor with regard to him as to sell himself to a stranger who is sojourning with you, or to the descendants of a stranger's family,

48 then he shall have redemption right after he has been sold. One of his brothers may redeem him,

49 or his uncle, or his uncle's son, may redeem him, or one of his blood relatives

---

20 [1]Or *behold*
21 [a]Deut 28:8
22 [a]Lev 26:10
23 [a]Ex 19:5 [b]Gen 23:4; 1 Chr 29:15; Ps 39:12; Heb 11:13; 1 Pet 2:11
24 [1]Lit *land*
25 [1]Lit *brother* [a]Ruth 2:20; 4:4, 6
26 [1]Lit *his hand reaches*
27 [a]Lev 25:16
28 [1]Lit *his hand has not found sufficient to* [2]Lit *go out* [a]Lev 25:10,13
30 [1]Lit *go out*
31 [1]Lit *according to* [2]Lit *go out*
32 [a]Num 35:1-8; Josh 21:2
33 [1]Lit *is from* [2]Lit *and* [3]Lit *goes out*
34 [a]Num 35:2-5
35 [1]Lit *brother* [2]Lit *hand* [a]Deut 15:7-11; 24:14, 15
36 [1]Lit *interest and usury* [2]Lit *brother* [a]Ex 22:25; Deut 23:19,20
38 [a]Lev 11:45 [b]Gen 17:7
39 [1]Lit *brother* [a]Ex 21:2-6; Deut 15:12-18; 1 Kin 9:22
40 [a]Ex 21:2
43 [a]Ex 1:13,14; Lev 25:46,53; Ezek 34:4; Col 4:1
45 [1]Lit *begotten*
46 [1]Lit *brothers* [a]Lev 25:43
47 [1]Lit *hand...reaches* [2]Lit *brother*

from his family may redeem him; or [1a]if he prospers, he may redeem himself.

50 'He then with his purchaser shall calculate from the year when he sold himself to him up to the year of jubilee; and the price of his sale shall correspond to the number of years. *It is* like the days of a hired man *that* he shall be with him.

51 'If there are still many years, [a]he shall refund part of his purchase price in proportion to them for his own redemption;

52 and if few years remain until the year of jubilee, he shall so calculate with him. In proportion to his years he is to refund *the amount for* his redemption.

53 'Like a man hired year by year he shall be with him; [a]he shall not rule over him with severity in your sight.

54 'Even if he is not redeemed by [1]these *means,* [a]he shall still go out in the year of jubilee, he and his sons with him.

55 'For the sons of Israel are My servants; they are My servants whom I brought out from the land of Egypt. I am the LORD your God.

Blessings of Obedience

26 'You shall not make for yourselves [1a]idols, nor shall you set up for yourselves [b]an image or [c]a *sacred* pillar, nor shall you place a [d]figured stone in your land to bow down [2]to it; for I am the LORD your God.

2 '[a]You shall keep My sabbaths and reverence My sanctuary; I am the LORD.

3 '[a]If you walk in My statutes and keep My commandments so as to carry them out,

4 then [a]I shall give you rains in their season, so that the land will yield its produce and the trees of the field will bear their fruit.

5 '[a]Indeed, your threshing will last for you until grape gathering, and grape gathering will last until sowing time. You will thus eat your [1]food to the full and [b]live securely in your land.

6 '[a]I shall also grant peace in the land, so that [b]you may lie down with no one making *you* tremble. [c]I shall also eliminate harmful beasts from the land, and [d]no sword will pass through your land.

7 'But you will chase your enemies and they will fall before you by the sword;

8 [a]five of you will chase a hundred, and a hundred of you will chase ten thousand, and your enemies will fall before you by the sword.

9 'So I will turn toward you and [a]make you fruitful and multiply you, and I will [b]confirm My covenant with you.

10 '[a]You will eat the old supply and clear out the old because of the new.

11 '[a]Moreover, I will make My [1]dwelling among you, and My soul will not [2]reject you.

12 '[a]I will also walk among you and be your God, and you shall be My people.

13 '[a]I am the LORD your God, who brought you out of the land of Egypt so that *you* would not be their slaves, and [b]I broke the bars of your yoke and made you walk erect.

Penalties of Disobedience

14 ¶ '[a]But if you do not obey Me and do not carry out all these commandments,

15 if, instead, you [a]reject My statutes, and if your soul abhors My ordinances so as not to carry out all My commandments, *and* so [b]break My covenant,

16 I, in turn, will do this to you: I will appoint over you a [a]sudden terror, consumption and fever that will waste away the eyes and cause the [b]soul to pine away; also, [c]you will sow your seed uselessly, for your enemies will eat it up.

17 'I will set My face against you so that you will be struck down before your enemies; and [a]those who hate you will rule over you, and [b]you will flee when no one is pursuing you.

18 'If also after these things you do not obey Me, then I will punish you [a]seven times more for your sins.

19 'I will also [a]break down your pride of power; I will also make your sky like iron and your earth like bronze.

20 '[a]Your strength will be spent uselessly, for your land will not yield its produce and the trees of the land will not yield their fruit.

21 ¶ 'If then, you [1a]act with hostility against Me and are unwilling to obey Me, I will increase the plague on you [b]seven times according to your sins.

22 '[a]I will let loose among you the beasts of the field, which will bereave you of your children and destroy your cattle and reduce your number so that [b]your roads lie deserted.

23 ¶ '[a]And if by these things you are not turned to Me, but act with hostility against Me,

24 then I will [a]act with hostility against you; and I, even I, will strike you [b]seven times for your sins.

25 'I will also bring upon you a sword which will execute [a]vengeance for the covenant; and when you gather together into your cities, I will send [b]pestilence among you, so that you shall be delivered into enemy hands.

26 '[a]When I break your staff of bread,

49 [1]Lit *if his hand has reached and* [a]Lev 25:26,27
51 [a]Lev 25:16
53 [a]Lev 25:43
54 [1]Or *these years* [a]Lev 25:10,13,28
26:1 [1]Or *graven images* [2]Lit *over* [a]Lev 19:4; Deut 5:8 [b]Ex 20:4; Deut 16:21f [c]Ex 23:24 [d]Num 33:52
2 [a]Lev 19:30
3 [a]Deut 7:12-26; 11:13; 28:1-14
4 [a]Deut 11:14
5 [1]Lit *bread* [a]Deut 11:15; Joel 2:19,26; Amos 9:13 [b]Lev 25:18,19; Ezek 34:25
6 [a]Ps 29:11; 85:8; 147:14 [b]Zeph 3:13 [c]Lev 26:22 [d]Lev 26:25
8 [a]Deut 32:30
9 [a]Gen 17:6; 22:17; 48:4 [b]Gen 17:7
10 [a]Lev 25:22
11 [1]Or *tabernacle* [2]Lit *abhor* [a]Ex 25:8; 29:45, 46; Ezek 37:26
12 [a]Gen 3:8; Deut 23:14; 2 Cor 6:16
13 [a]Ex 20:2 [b]Ezek 34:27
14 [a]Deut 28:15-68; Josh 23:15
15 [a]Lev 26:11; 2 Kin 17:15 [b]Lev 26:9
16 [a]Deut 28:22; Ps 78:33 [b]1 Sam 2:33; Ezek 24:23; 33:10 [c]Judg 6:3-6; Job 31:8
17 [a]Ps 106:41 [b]Lev 26:36,37; Ps 53:5; Prov 28:1
18 [a]Lev 26:21, 24,28
19 [a]Is 28:1-3; Ezek 24:21
20 [a]Ps 127:1; Is 17:10,11; 49:4; Jer 12:13
21 [1]Lit *walk,* and so throughout the ch [a]Lev 26:23,27,40 [b]Lev 26:18
22 [a]2 Kin 17:25 [b]Judg 5:6
23 [a]Lev 26:21; Jer 5:3
24 [a]Lev 26:28, 41 [b]Lev 26:21
25 [a]Jer 50:28; 51:11 [b]Num 14:12
26 [a]Is 3:1; Ezek 4:16,17; 5:16

ten women will bake your bread in one
oven, and they will bring back your bread
[1]in rationed amounts, so that you will
[b]eat and not be satisfied.
27 ¶ 'Yet if in spite of this you do
not obey Me, but act with hostility
against Me,
28 then [a]I will act with wrathful hostility against you, and I, even I, will punish you seven times for your sins.
29 'Further, [a]you will eat the flesh of
your sons and the flesh of your daughters
you will eat.
30 'I then [a]will destroy your high
places, and cut down your [b]incense altars, and heap your [1]remains on the [1]re-
mains of your idols, for My soul shall abhor you.
31 'I will [1]lay [a]waste your cities as
well and will make your [b]sanctuaries
desolate, and I will not [c]smell your
soothing aromas.
32 'I will make [a]the land desolate [b]so
that your enemies who settle in it will be
appalled over it.
33 'You, however, I [a]will scatter
among the nations and will draw out a
sword after you, as your land becomes
desolate and your cities become waste.
34 ¶ '[a]Then the land will [1]enjoy its
sabbaths all the days of the desolation,
while you are in your enemies' land; then
the land will rest and [1]enjoy its sabbaths.
35 'All the days of *its* desolation it will
observe the rest which it did not observe
on your sabbaths, while you were living
on it.
36 'As for those of you who may be left,
I will also bring [a]weakness into their
hearts in the lands of their enemies. And
the sound of a driven leaf will chase
them, and even when no one is pursuing
they will flee [1]as though from the sword,
and they will fall.
37 '[a]They will therefore stumble over
each other as if *running* from the sword,
although no one is pursuing; and you will
have *no strength* [1]to stand up before
your enemies.
38 'But [a]you will perish among the nations, and your enemies' land will consume you.
39 '[a]So those of you who may be left
will rot away because of their iniquity in
the lands of your enemies; and also because of the iniquities of their forefathers
they will rot away with them.
40 ¶ '[a]If they confess their iniquity
and the iniquity of their forefathers, in
their unfaithfulness which they committed against Me, and also in their acting
with hostility against Me—
41 I also was acting with hostility
against them, to bring them into the land
of their enemies—[a]or if their uncircumcised heart becomes humbled so that
[b]they then make amends for their iniquity,
42 then I will remember [a]My covenant with Jacob, and I will remember
also [b]My covenant with Isaac, and [c]My
covenant with Abraham as well, and I
will remember the land.
43 '[a]For the land will be abandoned by
them, and will make up for its sabbaths
while it is made desolate without them.
They, meanwhile, will be making
amends for their iniquity, [1]because they
rejected My ordinances and their [b]soul
abhorred My statutes.
44 'Yet in spite of this, when they are
in the land of their enemies, I will not
reject them, nor will I so [a]abhor them as
[b]to destroy them, [c]breaking My covenant with them; for I am the LORD their
God.
45 'But I will remember for them the
[a]covenant with their ancestors, whom I
brought out of the land of Egypt in the
sight of the nations, that [b]I might be
their God. I am the LORD.' "
46 ¶ [a]These are the statutes and ordinances and laws which the LORD established between Himself and the sons of
Israel [1]through Moses at Mount Sinai.

Rules concerning Valuations

27 Again, the LORD spoke to Moses,
saying,
2 "Speak to the sons of Israel and say
to them, '[a]When a man makes a difficult
vow, he *shall be valued* according to your
valuation of persons belonging to the
LORD.
3 'If your valuation is of the male from
twenty years even to sixty years old, then
your valuation shall be fifty shekels of silver, after [a]the shekel of the sanctuary.
4 'Or if it is a female, then your valuation shall be thirty shekels.
5 'If it be from five years even to twenty years old then your valuation for the
male shall be twenty shekels and for the
female ten shekels.
6 'But if *they are* from a month even
up to five years old, then your valuation
shall be [a]five shekels of silver for the
male, and for the female your valuation
shall be three shekels of silver.
7 'If *they are* from sixty years old and
upward, if it is a male, then your valuation shall be fifteen shekels, and for the
female ten shekels.
8 'But if he is poorer than your valuation, then he shall be placed before the
priest and the priest shall value him; [a]ac-
cording to [1]the means of the one who
vowed, the priest shall value him.

26 [1]Lit *by weight* [b]Mic 6:14
28 [a]Lev 26:24, 41; Is 59:18
29 [a]2 Kin 6:29
30 [1]Lit *corpses* [a]2 Kin 23:20; Ezek 6:3,6; Amos 7:9 [b]2 Chr 34:4,7; Is 27:9
31 [1]Lit *give desolation to* [a]Neh 2:3; Jer 44:2,6, 22 [b]Is 63:18; Lam 2:7 [c]Amos 5:21
32 [a]Jer 9:11; 12:11; 25:11; 33:10 [b]Jer 18:16; 19:8
33 [a]Deut 4:27; 28:64; Ps 44:11; 106:27; Jer 31:10; Ezek 12:15; 20:23; Zech 7:14
34 [1]Lit *satisfy* [a]Lev 26:43; 2 Chr 36:21
36 [1]Lit *the flight of the sword* [a]Is 30:17; Lam 1:3, 6; 4:19; Ezek 21:7
37 [1]Lit *you will stand* [a]Jer 6:21; Nah 3:3
38 [a]Deut 4:26
39 [a]Ezek 4:17; 33:10
40 [a]Jer 3:12-15; 14:20; Hos 5:15
41 [a]Jer 4:4; 9:25,26; Ezek 44:7,9; Acts 7:51 [b]Ezek 20:43
42 [a]Gen 28:13-15; 35:11, 12 [b]Gen 26:2-5 [c]Gen 22:15-18
43 [1]Lit *because and by the cause* [a]Lev 26:34 [b]Lev 26:11
44 [a]Lev 26:11 [b]Deut 4:31; Jer 30:11 [c]Jer 33:20-26
45 [a]Ex 6:6-8 [b]Gen 17:7
46 [1]Lit *by the hand of* [a]Lev 7:38; 27:34; Deut 4:5; 29:1
27:2 [a]Num 6:2; Deut 23:21-23
3 [a]Ex 30:13; Lev 27:25; Num 3:47; 18:16
6 [a]Num 18:16
8 [1]Lit *what the hand reaches* [a]Lev 5:11; 14:21-24

9 ¶ 'Now if it is an animal of the kind
which [1]men can present as an offering to
the LORD, any such that one gives to the
LORD shall be holy.
10 '[a]He shall not replace it or exchange it, a good for a bad, or a bad for a
good; or if he does exchange animal for
animal, then both it and its substitute
shall become holy.
11 'If, however, it is any unclean animal of the kind which [1]men do not
present as an offering to the LORD, then
he shall place the animal before the
priest.
12 'The priest shall value it [1]as either
good or bad; as you, the priest, value it,
so it shall be.
13 'But if he should ever *wish to* redeem it, then he shall add one-fifth of it
to your valuation.
14 ¶ 'Now if a man consecrates his
house as holy to the LORD, then the priest
shall value it [1]as either good or bad; as
the priest values it, so it shall stand.
15 'Yet if the one who consecrates it
should *wish to* redeem his house, then he
shall add one-fifth of your valuation price
to it, so that it may be his.
16 ¶ 'Again, if a man consecrates to
the LORD part of the fields of his own
property, then your valuation shall be
[1]proportionate to the seed needed for it:
a homer of barley seed at fifty shekels of
silver.
17 'If he consecrates his field as of the
year of jubilee, according to your valuation it shall stand.
18 'If he consecrates his field after the
jubilee, however, then the priest shall
calculate the price for [1]him [2]proportion-
ate to the years that are left until the year
of jubilee; and it shall be deducted from
your valuation.
19 'If the one who consecrates it
should ever wish to redeem the field,
then he shall add one-fifth of your valuation price to it, so that it may pass to him.
20 'Yet if he will not redeem the field,
[1]but has sold the field to another man, it
may no longer be redeemed;
21 and when it [1]reverts in the jubilee,
the field shall be holy to the LORD, like a
field [2]set apart; [a]it shall be for the priest
as his [3]property.
22 'Or if he consecrates to the LORD a
field which he has bought, which is not
a part of the field of his own [1]property,
23 then the priest shall calculate for
[1]him the amount of your valuation up to
the year of jubilee; and he shall on that
day give your valuation as holy to the
LORD.
24 'In the year of jubilee the field shall
return to the one from whom he bought
it, to whom the possession of the land
belongs.
25 'Every valuation of yours, moreover,
shall be after [a]the shekel of the sanctuary. The shekel shall be twenty gerahs.
26 ¶ '[a]However, a firstborn among
animals, which as a firstborn belongs to
the LORD, no man may consecrate it;
whether ox or sheep, it is the LORD'S.
27 'But if *it is* among the unclean animals, then he shall [1]redeem it according
to your valuation and add to it one-fifth of
it; and if it is not redeemed, then it shall
be sold according to your valuation.
28 ¶ 'Nevertheless, [a]anything which
a man [1]sets apart to the LORD out of all
that he has, of man or animal or of the
fields of his own property, shall not be
sold or redeemed. Anything [2]devoted to
destruction is most holy to the LORD.
29 'No [1]one who may have been [2]set
apart among men shall be ransomed; he
shall surely be put to death.
30 ¶ 'Thus [a]all the tithe of the land, of
the seed of the land or of the fruit of the
tree, is the LORD'S; it is holy to the LORD.
31 'If, therefore, a man wishes to redeem part of his tithe, he shall add to it
one-fifth of it.
32 'For every tenth part of herd or
flock, whatever [a]passes under the rod,
the tenth one shall be holy to the LORD.
33 '[a]He is not to be concerned whether *it is* good or bad, nor shall he exchange
it; or if he does exchange it, then both it
and its substitute shall become holy. It
shall not be redeemed.' "
34 ¶ [a]These are the commandments
which the LORD commanded Moses for
the sons of Israel at Mount Sinai.

9 [1]Lit *they*
10 [a]Lev 27:33
11 [1]Lit *they*
12 [1]Lit *between*
14 [1]Lit *between good*
16 [1]Lit *according to its seed*
18 [1]Or *it* [2]Lit *according to the years*
20 [1]Or *if he*
21 [1]Lit *goes out* [2]Or *devoted, banned* [3]Lit *possession* [a]Num 18:14; Ezek 44:29
22 [1]Lit *possession*
23 [1]Or *it*
25 [a]Ex 30:13; Lev 27:3; Num 3:47; 18:16
26 [a]Ex 13:2
27 [1]Or *ransom*
28 [1]Lit *anything devoted*; or *banned* [2]Or *puts under the ban* [a]Num 18:14; Josh 6:17-19
29 [1]Lit *one devoted*; or *banned* [2]Or *put under the ban*
30 [a]Gen 28:22; 2 Chr 31:5; Neh 13:12
32 [a]Jer 33:13; Ezek 20:37
33 [a]Lev 27:10
34 [a]Lev 26:46; Deut 4:5

Numbers

Title and Background

The book of Numbers gets its name from the two numberings or countings of the Israelites during their 38 years of wandering in the wilderness. These countings are found in chapters 1 and 26. Numbers presents an account of that wandering in the wilderness following the establishment of the covenant of Sinai.

Author and Date of Writing

Numbers has been traditionally ascribed to Moses. This assignment is based on: (1) the statements concerning Moses' writing activity (e.g., 33:1–2; Exodus 17:14; 24:4; 34:27); (2) the assumption that the Pentateuch is a unity and comes from one great author; and (3) the New Testament's ascription of quotations from the Pentateuch to Moses (e.g., Matthew 19:8; John 5:46–47; Romans 10:5). Numbers was written by Moses shortly before his death in about 1406 B.C.

Theme and Message

Numbers relates the story of Israel's journey from Mount Sinai to the plains of Moab on the border of Canaan. It tells of the murmuring and rebellion of God's people and of their subsequent judgment. They were condemned to live out their lives in the wilderness; only their children would enjoy the fulfillment of the promise that had originally been theirs. Throughout the years in the wilderness, one thing became clear to Israel—God's constant care for them. Not only did He meet their needs, but He also loved and forgave His people continually.

Outline

I. Israel at Sinai, Preparing to Go to Canaan (1:1—10:10)
II. From Sinai to Kadesh-barnea (10:11—12:16)
III. Israel at Kadesh, the Delay Resulting From Rebellion (13:1—20:13)
IV. From Kadesh to the Plains of Moab (20:14—22:1)
V. Israel on the Plains of Moab, Anticipating the Taking of Canaan (22:2—32:42)
VI. Supplements Dealing With Various Matters (33:1—36:13)

The Census of Israel's Warriors

1 Then the LORD spoke to Moses in the
wilderness of Sinai, in the tent of
meeting, on [a]the first of the second
month, in the second year after they had
come out of the land of Egypt, saying,
2 "[a]Take a [1]census of all the congregation of the sons of Israel, by their families, by their fathers' households, according to the number of names, every male,
head by head
3 from [a]twenty years old and upward, whoever *is able to* go out to war
in Israel, you and Aaron shall [1]number
them by their armies.
4 "With you, moreover, there shall be
a man of each tribe, [a]each one head of
his father's household.
5 "These then are the names of the
men who shall stand with you: [a]of Reuben, Elizur the son of Shedeur;
6 of Simeon, Shelumiel the son of Zurishaddai;
7 of Judah, [a]Nahshon the son of Amminadab;
8 of Issachar, Nethanel the son of
Zuar;
9 of Zebulun, Eliab the son of Helon;
10 of the sons of Joseph: of Ephraim,
Elishama the son of Ammihud; of Manasseh, Gamaliel the son of Pedahzur;
11 of Benjamin, Abidan the son of Gideoni;
12 of Dan, Ahiezer the son of Ammishaddai;
13 of Asher, Pagiel the son of Ochran;
14 of Gad, Eliasaph the son of [a]Deuel;
15 of Naphtali, Ahira the son of Enan.
16 "These are they who were [a]called of
the congregation, the leaders of their fathers' tribes; they were the [b]heads of
[1]divisions of Israel."

1:1 [a]Ex 40:2,17
2 [1]Lit *sum* [a]Ex 12:37; 38:25,26; Num 26:2
3 [1]Lit *muster,* and so throughout the ch [a]Ex 30:14; 38:26
4 [a]Ex 18:21,25; Num 1:16; Deut 1:15
5 [a]Gen 29:32; Ex 1:2; Deut 33:6; Rev 7:5
7 [a]Ruth 4:20; 1 Chr 2:10; Luke 3:32
14 [a]Num 2:14
16 [1]Lit *thousands;* or *clans* [a]Ex 18:21; Num 7:2; 16:2; 26:9 [b]Ex 18:25

17 ¶ So Moses and Aaron took these men who had been designated by name,

18 and they assembled all the congregation together on the [a]first of the second month. Then they registered by [b]ancestry in their families, by their fathers' households, according to the number of names, from twenty years old and upward, head by head,

19 just as [a]the LORD had commanded Moses. So he numbered them in the wilderness of Sinai.

20 ¶ [a]Now the sons of Reuben, Israel's firstborn, their genealogical registration by their families, by their fathers' households, according to the number of names, head by head, every male from twenty years old and upward, whoever *was able to* go out to war,

21 their numbered men of the tribe of Reuben *were* 46,500.

22 ¶ [a]Of the sons of Simeon, their genealogical registration by their families, by their fathers' households, their numbered men, according to the number of names, head by head, every male from twenty years old and upward, [b]whoever *was able to* go out to war,

23 their numbered men of the tribe of Simeon *were* 59,300.

24 ¶ [a]Of the sons of Gad, their genealogical registration by their families, by their fathers' households, according to the number of names, from twenty years old and upward, whoever *was able to* go out to war,

25 their numbered men of the tribe of Gad *were* 45,650.

26 ¶ [a]Of the sons of Judah, their genealogical registration by their families, by their fathers' households, according to the number of names, from twenty years old and upward, whoever *was able to* go out to war,

27 their numbered men of the tribe of Judah *were* 74,600.

28 ¶ [a]Of the sons of Issachar, their genealogical registration by their families, by their fathers' households, according to the number of names, from twenty years old and upward, whoever *was able to* go out to war,

29 their numbered men of the tribe of Issachar *were* 54,400.

30 ¶ [a]Of the sons of Zebulun, their genealogical registration by their families, by their fathers' households, according to the number of names, from twenty years old and upward, whoever *was able to* go out to war,

31 their numbered men of the tribe of Zebulun *were* 57,400.

32 ¶ [a]Of the sons of Joseph, *namely,* of the sons of Ephraim, their genealogical registration by their families, by their fathers' households, according to the number of names, from twenty years old and upward, whoever *was able to* go out to war,

33 their numbered men of the tribe of Ephraim *were* 40,500.

34 ¶ [a]Of the sons of Manasseh, their genealogical registration by their families, by their fathers' households, according to the number of names, from twenty years old and upward, whoever *was able to* go out to war,

35 their numbered men of the tribe of Manasseh *were* 32,200.

36 ¶ [a]Of the sons of Benjamin, their genealogical registration by their families, by their fathers' households, according to the number of names, from twenty years old and upward, whoever *was able to* go out to war,

37 their numbered men of the tribe of Benjamin *were* 35,400.

38 ¶ [a]Of the sons of Dan, their genealogical registration by their families, by their fathers' households, according to the number of names, from twenty years old and upward, whoever *was able to* go out to war,

39 their numbered men of the tribe of Dan *were* 62,700.

40 ¶ [a]Of the sons of Asher, their genealogical registration by their families, by their fathers' households, according to the number of names, from twenty years old and upward, whoever *was able to* go out to war,

41 their numbered men of the tribe of Asher *were* 41,500.

42 ¶ [a]Of the sons of Naphtali, their genealogical registration by their families, by their fathers' households, according to the number of names, from twenty years old and upward, whoever *was able to* go out to war,

43 their numbered men of the tribe of Naphtali *were* 53,400.

44 ¶ These are the ones who were numbered, whom Moses and Aaron numbered, with the leaders of Israel, twelve men, each of whom was of his father's household.

45 So all the numbered men of the sons of Israel by their fathers' households, from twenty years old and upward, whoever *was able to* go out to war in Israel,

46 even all the numbered men were [a]603,550.

Levites Exempted

47 ¶ [a]The Levites, however, were not numbered among them by their fathers' tribe.

18 [a]Num 1:1 [b]Ezra 2:59; Heb 7:3
19 [a]2 Sam 24:1
20 [a]Num 26:5-7
22 [a]Num 26:12-14 [b]Ps 144:1
24 [a]Gen 30:11; Num 26:15-18; Josh 4:12; Jer 49:1
26 [a]Gen 29:35; Num 26:19-22; 2 Sam 24:9; Ps 78:68; Matt 1:2
28 [a]Num 26:23-25
30 [a]Num 26:26, 27
32 [a]Num 26:35-37; Deut 33:13-17; Jer 7:15; Obad 19
34 [a]Num 26:28-34
36 [a]Gen 49:27; Num 26:38-41; 2 Chr 17:17; Rev 7:8
38 [a]Gen 30:6; 46:23; Num 2:25; 26:42,43
40 [a]Num 26:44-47
42 [a]Num 26:48-50
46 [a]Ex 12:37; 38:26; Num 2:32; 26:51
47 [a]Num 2:33; 3:14-39; 4:49; 26:57-64

48 For the LORD had spoken to Moses,
saying,
49 "Only the tribe of Levi [a]you shall
not number, nor shall you take their
[1]census among the sons of Israel.
50 "But you shall [a]appoint the Levites
over the [1]tabernacle of the testimony,
and over all its furnishings and over all
that belongs to it. They shall carry the
tabernacle and all its furnishings, and
they shall take care of it; they shall also
camp around the [1]tabernacle.
51 "[a]So when the tabernacle is to set
out, the Levites shall take it down; and
when the tabernacle encamps, the Levites shall set it up. But [b]the [1]layman
who comes near shall be put to death.
52 "[a]The sons of Israel shall camp,
each man by his own camp, and each
man by his own standard, according to
their armies.
53 "[a]But the Levites shall camp around
the tabernacle of the testimony, so that
there will be [b]no wrath on the congregation of the sons of Israel. [c]So the Levites
shall keep charge of the tabernacle of the
testimony."
54 Thus the sons of Israel did; according to all which the LORD had commanded Moses, so they did.

Arrangement of the Camps

2 Now the LORD spoke to Moses and to
Aaron, saying,
2 "[a]The sons of Israel shall camp,
each by his own standard, with the [1]ban-
ners of their fathers' households; they
shall camp around the tent of meeting
[2]at a distance.
3 "Now those who camp on the east
side toward the sunrise *shall be* of the
standard of the camp of Judah, by their
armies, and the leader of the sons of Judah: [a]Nahshon the son of Amminadab,
4 and his army, even their [1]num-
bered men, 74,600.
5 "Those who camp next to him *shall
be* the tribe of Issachar, and the leader of
the sons of Issachar: [a]Nethanel the son
of Zuar,
6 and his army, even their numbered
men, 54,400.
7 "*Then comes* the tribe of Zebulun,
and the leader of the sons of Zebulun:
[a]Eliab the son of Helon,
8 and his army, even his numbered
men, 57,400.
9 "The total of the numbered men of
the camp of Judah: 186,400, by their armies. [a]They shall set out first.
10 ¶ "On the south side *shall be* the
standard of the camp of Reuben by their
armies, and the leader of the sons of Reuben: [a]Elizur the son of Shedeur,
11 and his army, even their numbered
men, 46,500.
12 "Those who camp next to him *shall
be* the tribe of Simeon, and the leader of
the sons of Simeon: [a]Shelumiel the son
of Zurishaddai,
13 and his army, even their numbered
men, 59,300.
14 "Then *comes* the tribe of Gad, and
the leader of the sons of Gad: [a]Eliasaph
the son of [1]Deuel,
15 and his army, even their numbered
men, 45,650.
16 "The total of the numbered men of
the camp of Reuben: 151,450 by their
armies. And [a]they shall set out second.
17 ¶ "[a]Then the tent of meeting shall
set out *with* the camp of the Levites in the
midst of the camps; just as they camp, so
they shall set out, every man in his place
by their standards.
18 ¶ "On the west side *shall be* the
standard of the camp of [a]Ephraim by
their armies, and the leader of the sons of
Ephraim *shall be* [b]Elishama the son of
Ammihud,
19 and his army, even their numbered
men, 40,500.
20 "Next to him *shall be* the tribe of
Manasseh, and the leader of the sons of
Manasseh: [a]Gamaliel the son of Pedahzur,
21 and his army, even their numbered
men, 32,200.
22 "Then *comes* the tribe of [a]Benja-
min, and the leader of the sons of Benjamin: [b]Abidan the son of Gideoni,
23 and his army, even their numbered
men, 35,400.
24 "The total of the numbered men of
the camp of Ephraim: 108,100, by their
armies. And [a]they shall set out third.
25 ¶ "On the north side *shall be* the
standard of the camp of Dan by their armies, and the leader of the sons of Dan:
[a]Ahiezer the son of Ammishaddai,
26 and his army, even their numbered
men, 62,700.
27 "Those who camp next to him *shall
be* the tribe of Asher, and the leader of
the sons of Asher: [a]Pagiel the son of Ochran,
28 and his army, even their numbered
men, 41,500.
29 "Then *comes* the tribe of [a]Naphtali,
and the leader of the sons of Naphtali:
[b]Ahira the son of Enan,
30 and his army, even their numbered
men, 53,400.
31 "The total of the numbered men of
the camp of Dan *was* 157,600. [a]They
shall set out last by their standards."
32 ¶ These are the numbered men of
the sons of Israel by their fathers' house-

49 [1]Lit *sum* [a]Num 26:62
50 [1]Lit *dwelling place,* and so throughout the ch [a]Ex 38:21; Num 3:6-8, 25-37; 4:15, 25-27,31,32
51 [1]Lit *stranger* [a]Num 4:1-33 [b]Num 3:10,38; 4:15,19,20
52 [a]Num 2:2,34
53 [a]Num 3:23, 29,35,38 [b]Lev 10:6; Num 16:46; 18:5 [c]Num 8:24; 18:2-4; 1 Chr 23:32
2:2 [1]Lit *signs* [2]Or *facing it* [a]Num 1:52; 24:2
3 [a]Num 1:7; 10:14; Ruth 4:20; 1 Chr 2:10; Luke 3:32, 33
4 [1]Lit *mustered,* and so throughout the ch
5 [a]Num 1:8; 7:18,23
7 [a]Num 1:9
9 [a]Num 10:14
10 [a]Num 1:5
12 [a]Num 1:6
14 [1]Many mss read *Reuel* [a]Num 1:14; 7:42
16 [a]Num 10:18
17 [a]Num 1:53
18 [a]Gen 48:14-20; Jer 31:9,18-20 [b]Num 1:10
20 [a]Num 1:10
22 [a]Ps 68:27 [b]Num 1:11
24 [a]Num 10:22
25 [a]Num 1:12
27 [a]Num 1:13
29 [a]Gen 30:8 [b]Num 1:15
31 [a]Num 10:25

holds; the total of the numbered men of the camps by their armies, [a]603,550.

33 [a]The Levites, however, were not numbered among the sons of Israel, just as the LORD had commanded Moses.

34 Thus the sons of Israel did; according to all that the LORD commanded Moses, so they camped by their standards, and so they set out, every one by his family according to his father's household.

Levites to Be Priesthood

3 [a]Now these are *the records of* the generations of Aaron and Moses at the time when the LORD spoke with Moses on Mount Sinai.

2 [a]These then are the names of the sons of Aaron: Nadab the firstborn, and Abihu, Eleazar and Ithamar.

3 These are the names of the sons of Aaron, the [a]anointed priests, whom he [1]ordained to serve as priests.

4 [a]But Nadab and Abihu died before the LORD when they offered strange fire before the LORD in the wilderness of Sinai; and they had no children. So Eleazar and Ithamar served as priests [1]in the lifetime of their father Aaron.

5 ¶ Then the LORD spoke to Moses, saying,

6 "[a]Bring the tribe of Levi near and set them before Aaron the priest, that they may serve him.

7 "They shall perform the duties for [1]him and for the whole congregation before the tent of meeting, to do the [a]service of the tabernacle.

8 "They shall also keep all the furnishings of the tent of meeting, along with the duties of the sons of Israel, to do the service of the tabernacle.

9 "You shall thus [a]give the Levites to Aaron and to his sons; they are wholly given to him from among the sons of Israel.

10 "So you shall appoint Aaron and his sons that [a]they may keep their priesthood, but [b]the [1]layman who comes near shall be put to death."

11 ¶ Again the LORD spoke to Moses, saying,

12 "Now, behold, I [a]have taken the Levites from among the sons of Israel instead of every [b]firstborn, the first issue of the womb among the sons of Israel. So the Levites shall be Mine.

13 "For [a]all the firstborn are Mine; on the day that I struck down all the firstborn in the land of Egypt, I sanctified to Myself all the firstborn in Israel, from man to beast. They shall be Mine; I am the LORD."

14 ¶ Then the LORD spoke to Moses [a]in the wilderness of Sinai, saying,

32 [a]Ex 38:26; Num 1:46
33 [a]Num 1:47; 26:57-62
3:1 [a]Ex 6:20-27
2 [a]Ex 6:23; Num 26:60
3 [1]Lit *filled their hand* [a]Ex 28:41
4 [1]Lit *before the face* [a]Lev 10:1,2; Num 26:61
6 [a]Num 8:6-22; 18:1-7; Deut 10:8
7 [1]Lit *him and the duties of the whole congregation* [a]Num 1:50
9 [a]Num 18:6
10 [1]Lit *stranger* [a]Ex 29:9 [b]Num 1:51
12 [a]Num 3:45; 8:14 [b]Ex 13:2
13 [a]Ex 13:2; Lev 27:26; Neh 10:36
14 [a]Ex 19:1
15 [1]Lit *muster,* and so throughout the ch [a]Num 1:47
16 [1]Lit *mouth*
17 [a]Ex 6:16-22
18 [a]Ex 6:17
23 [1]Lit *dwelling place,* and so throughout the ch
25 [a]Num 4:24-26 [b]Ex 26:1,7,14 [c]Ex 26:36
26 [1]Lit *of it* [a]Ex 27:9,12,14,15 [b]Ex 27:16
30 [1]In Ex 6:22, *Elzaphan*
31 [a]Num 4:15 [b]Ex 25:10-22 [c]Ex 25:23-28 [d]Ex 25:31-40 [e]Ex 27:1,2; 30:1-5

15 "[1][a]Number the sons of Levi by their fathers' households, by their families; every male from a month old and upward you shall number."

16 So Moses numbered them according to the [1]word of the LORD, just as he had been commanded.

17 [a]These then are the sons of Levi by their names: Gershon and Kohath and Merari.

18 These are the names of the [a]sons of Gershon by their families: Libni and Shimei;

19 and the sons of Kohath by their families: Amram and Izhar, Hebron and Uzziel;

20 and the sons of Merari by their families: Mahli and Mushi. These are the families of the Levites according to their fathers' households.

21 ¶ Of Gershon *was* the family of the Libnites and the family of the Shimeites; these *were* the families of the Gershonites.

22 Their numbered men, in the numbering of every male from a month old and upward, *even* their numbered men *were* 7,500.

23 The families of the Gershonites were to camp behind the [1]tabernacle westward,

24 and the leader of the fathers' households of the Gershonites *was* Eliasaph the son of Lael.

Duties of the Priests

25 Now [a]the duties of the sons of Gershon in the tent of meeting *involved* the tabernacle and [b]the tent, its covering, and [c]the screen for the doorway of the tent of meeting,

26 and [a]the hangings of the court, and [b]the screen for the doorway of the court which is around the tabernacle and the altar, and its cords, according to all the service [1]concerning them.

27 ¶ Of Kohath *was* the family of the Amramites and the family of the Izharites and the family of the Hebronites and the family of the Uzzielites; these were the families of the Kohathites.

28 In the numbering of every male from a month old and upward, *there were* 8,600, performing the duties of the sanctuary.

29 The families of the sons of Kohath were to camp on the southward side of the tabernacle,

30 and the leader of the fathers' households of the Kohathite families was [1]Elizaphan the son of Uzziel.

31 Now [a]their duties *involved* [b]the ark, [c]the table, [d]the lampstand, [e]the altars, and the utensils of the sanctuary

with which they minister, and the
screen, and all the service [1]concerning
them;
32 and Eleazar the son of Aaron the
priest *was* the chief of the leaders of Levi,
and had the oversight of those who perform the duties of the sanctuary.
33 ¶ Of Merari *was* the family of the
Mahlites and the family of the Mushites;
these *were* the families of Merari.
34 Their numbered men in the numbering of every male from a month old
and upward, *were* 6,200.
35 The leader of the fathers' households of the families of Merari *was* Zuriel
the son of Abihail. They *were* to [a]camp
on the northward side of the tabernacle.
36 Now the appointed duties of the
sons of Merari *involved* the frames of the
tabernacle, its bars, its pillars, its sockets,
all its equipment, and the service concerning them,
37 and the pillars around the court
with their sockets and their pegs and
their cords.
38 ¶ Now those who were to [a]camp
before the tabernacle eastward, before
the tent of meeting toward the sunrise,
are Moses and Aaron and his sons, performing the duties of the sanctuary for
the obligation of the sons of Israel; but
[b]the [1]layman coming near was to be put
to death.
39 All the numbered men of the Levites, whom Moses and Aaron numbered
at the [1]command of the LORD by their
families, every male from a month old
and upward, *were* [a]22,000.

Firstborn Redeemed

40 ¶ Then the LORD said to Moses,
"[a]Number every firstborn male of the
sons of Israel from a month old and upward, and [1]make a list of their names.
41 "You [a]shall take the Levites for Me,
I am the LORD, instead of all the firstborn
among the sons of Israel, and the cattle of
the Levites instead of all the firstborn
among the cattle of the sons of Israel."
42 So Moses numbered all the firstborn among the sons of Israel, just as the
LORD had commanded him;
43 and all the firstborn males by the
number of names from a month old and
upward, for their numbered men were
[a]22,273.
44 ¶ Then the LORD spoke to Moses,
saying,
45 "[a]Take the Levites instead of all the
firstborn among the sons of Israel and the
cattle of the Levites. And the Levites shall
be Mine; I am the LORD.
46 "[a]For the ransom of the 273 of the
firstborn of the sons of Israel who are in
excess beyond the Levites,
47 you shall take [a]five shekels apiece,
per head; you shall take *them* in [b]terms
of the shekel of the sanctuary ([c]the shekel is twenty [1]gerahs),
48 and give the money, the ransom of
those who are in excess among them, to
Aaron and to his sons."
49 So Moses took the ransom money
from those who were in excess, beyond
those ransomed by the Levites;
50 from the firstborn of the sons of Israel he took the money in terms of the
shekel of the sanctuary, 1,365.
51 Then Moses gave the ransom money to Aaron and to his sons, at the [1]com-
mand of the LORD, just as the LORD had
commanded Moses.

Duties of the Kohathites

4 Then the LORD spoke to Moses and to
Aaron, saying,
2 "Take [1]a census of the [2]descen-
dants of Kohath from among the sons of
Levi, by their families, by their fathers'
households,
3 from [a]thirty years and upward,
even to fifty years old, all who enter the
service to do the work in the tent of meeting.
4 "This is the work of the [1]descen-
dants of Kohath in the tent of meeting,
concerning the most holy things.
5 ¶ "When the camp sets out, Aaron
and his sons shall go in and they shall
take down [a]the veil of the screen and
cover the [b]ark of the testimony with it;
6 and they shall lay a [a]covering of
porpoise skin on it, and shall spread over
it a cloth of pure [1]blue, and shall insert
its poles.
7 "Over the table of the bread of the
Presence they shall also spread a cloth of
[1]blue and put on it the dishes and the
pans and the sacrificial bowls and the jars
for the drink offering, and [a]the continual
bread shall be on it.
8 "They shall spread over them a cloth
of scarlet *material,* and cover the same
with a covering of porpoise skin, and they
shall insert its poles.
9 "Then they shall take a [1]blue cloth
and cover the [a]lampstand for the light,
[b]along with its lamps and its snuffers,
and its [2]trays and all its oil vessels, by
which they serve it;
10 and they shall put it and all its utensils in a covering of porpoise skin, and
shall put it on the carrying bars.
11 "Over the golden altar they shall
spread a [1]blue cloth and cover it with a
covering of porpoise skin, and shall insert
its poles;

31 [1]Lit *of it*
35 [a]Num 1:53; 2:25
38 [1]Lit *stranger* [a]Num 1:53; 2:3 [b]Num 1:51
39 [1]Lit *word* [a]Num 3:43; 4:48; 26:62
40 [1]Lit *take the number* [a]Num 3:15
41 [a]Num 3:12, 45
43 [a]Num 3:39
45 [a]Num 3:12
46 [a]Ex 13:13, 15; Num 18:15, 16
47 [1]I.e. A gerah equals approx one-fortieth oz [a]Lev 27:6; Num 18:16 [b]Ex 30:13 [c]Lev 27:25; Ezek 45:12
51 [1]Lit *mouth*
4:2 [1]Lit *the sum* [2]Lit *sons*
3 [a]Num 4:23, 30,35; 8:24; 1 Chr 23:3,24, 27; Ezra 3:8
4 [1]Lit *sons*
5 [a]Ex 40:5; Lev 16:2; 2 Chr 3:14; Matt 27:51; Heb 9:3 [b]Ex 25:10-16
6 [1]Or *violet* [a]Num 4:25
7 [1]Or *violet* [a]Ex 25:30; Lev 24:5-9
9 [1]Or *violet* [2]Lit *snuff dishes* [a]Ex 25:31 [b]Ex 25:37,38
11 [1]Or *violet*

12 and they shall take all the utensils of service, with which they serve in the sanctuary, and put them in a [1]blue cloth and cover them with a covering of porpoise skin, and put them on the carrying bars.

13 "Then they shall take away the [1]ashes from the [a]altar, and spread a purple cloth over it.

14 "They shall also put on it all its utensils by which they serve in connection with it: the firepans, the forks and shovels and the basins, all the utensils of the altar; and they shall spread a cover of porpoise skin over it and insert its poles.

15 "When Aaron and his sons have finished covering the holy *objects* and all the furnishings of the sanctuary, when the camp is to set out, after that the sons of Kohath shall come to carry *them,* so that they will not touch the holy *objects* [a]and die. These are the [1]things in the tent of meeting which the sons of Kohath are to carry.

16 ¶ "The responsibility of Eleazar the son of Aaron the priest is [a]the oil for the light and the [b]fragrant incense and [c]the continual grain offering and [d]the anointing oil—the responsibility of all the [1]tabernacle and of all that is in it, with the sanctuary and its furnishings."

17 ¶ Then the LORD spoke to Moses and to Aaron, saying,

18 "Do not let the tribe of the families of the Kohathites be cut off from among the Levites.

19 "But do this to them that they may live and [a]not die when they approach the most holy *objects:* Aaron and his sons shall go in and assign each of them to his work and to his load;

20 but [a]they shall not go in to see the holy *objects* even for a moment, or they will die."

Duties of the Gershonites

21 ¶ Then the LORD spoke to Moses, saying,

22 "Take [1]a census of the sons of Gershon [2]also, by their fathers' households, by their families;

23 from [a]thirty years and upward to fifty years old, you shall [1]number them; all who enter to perform the service to do the work in the tent of meeting.

24 "This is the service of the families of the Gershonites, in serving and in carrying:

25 they shall carry [a]the curtains of the tabernacle and the tent of meeting *with* its covering and [b]the covering of porpoise skin that is on top of it, and the screen for the doorway of the tent of meeting,

26 and [a]the hangings of the court, and the screen for the doorway of the gate of the court which is around the tabernacle and the altar, and their cords and all the equipment for their service; and all that is to be done, [1]they shall perform.

27 "All the service of the sons of the Gershonites, in all their loads and in all their work, shall be *performed* at the [1]command of Aaron and his sons; and you shall assign to them as a duty all their loads.

28 "This is the service of the families of the sons of the Gershonites in the tent of meeting, and their duties *shall be* [1]under the direction of Ithamar the son of Aaron the priest.

Duties of the Merarites

29 ¶ "*As for* the sons of Merari, you shall number them by their families, by their fathers' households;

30 from [a]thirty years and upward even to fifty years old, you shall number them, everyone who enters the service to do the work of the tent of meeting.

31 "Now this is the duty of their loads, for all their service in the tent of meeting: the boards of the tabernacle and its bars and its pillars and its [1]sockets,

32 and the pillars around the court and their [1]sockets and their pegs and their cords, with all their equipment and with all their service; and you shall assign *each man* by name the items [2]he is to carry.

33 "This is the service of the families of the sons of Merari, according to all their service in the tent of meeting, [1]under the direction of Ithamar the son of Aaron the priest."

34 ¶ So Moses and Aaron and the leaders of the congregation numbered the sons of the Kohathites by their families and by their fathers' households,

35 from [a]thirty years and upward even to fifty years old, everyone who entered the service for work in the tent of meeting.

36 Their numbered men by their families were 2,750.

37 These are the numbered men of the Kohathite families, everyone who was serving in the tent of meeting, whom Moses and Aaron numbered according to the [1]commandment of the LORD [2]through Moses.

38 ¶ The numbered men of the sons of Gershon by their families and by their fathers' households,

39 from thirty years and upward even to fifty years old, everyone who entered the service for work in the tent of meeting.

40 Their numbered men by their fami-

12 [1]Or *violet*

13 [1]Or *fat ashes;* i.e. soaked with fat [a]Ex 27:1-8

15 [1]Lit *burden...of the sons* [a]Num 1:51; 4:19,20; 2 Sam 6:6,7

16 [1]Lit *dwelling place,* and so throughout the ch [a]Lev 24:1-3 [b]Ex 30:34-38 [c]Lev 6:20 [d]Ex 30:22-33

19 [a]Num 4:15

20 [a]Ex 19:21; 1 Sam 6:19

22 [1]Lit *the sum* [2]Lit *also them*

23 [1]Lit *muster,* and so throughout the ch [a]Num 4:3; 1 Chr 23:3, 24,27

25 [a]Ex 40:19 [b]Ex 26:14; Num 4:6

26 [1]Lit *so they shall serve* [a]Ex 38:9

27 [1]Lit *mouth*

28 [1]Lit *in the hand*

30 [a]Num 4:3; 8:24-26

31 [1]Or *bases*

32 [1]Or *bases* [2]Lit *of the duty of their loads*

33 [1]Lit *in the hand*

35 [a]1 Chr 23:24

37 [1]Lit *mouth* [2]Lit *by the hand of*

lies, by their fathers' households, were 2,630.

41 These are the numbered men of the families of the sons of Gershon, everyone who was serving in the tent of meeting, whom Moses and Aaron numbered according to the [1]commandment of the LORD.

42 ¶ The numbered men of the families of the sons of Merari by their families, by their fathers' households,

43 from [a]thirty years and upward even to fifty years old, everyone who entered the service for work in the tent of meeting.

44 Their numbered men by their families were 3,200.

45 These are the numbered men of the families of the sons of Merari, whom Moses and Aaron numbered according to the [1]commandment of the LORD [2]through Moses.

46 ¶ All the numbered men of the Levites, whom Moses and Aaron and the leaders of Israel numbered, by their families and by their fathers' households,

47 from thirty years and upward even to fifty years old, everyone who could enter to do the work of service and the work of carrying in the tent of meeting.

48 Their numbered men were [a]8,580.

49 According to the [1]commandment of the LORD [2]through Moses, they [a]were numbered, everyone by his serving or carrying; thus *these were* his numbered men, just as the LORD had commanded Moses.

On Defilement

5 Then the LORD spoke to Moses, saying,

2 "Command the sons of Israel that they [a]send away from the camp every leper and everyone having a [b]discharge and everyone who is [c]unclean because of a *dead* person.

3 "You shall send away both male and female; you shall send them outside the camp so that they will not defile their camp where I dwell [a]in their midst."

4 The sons of Israel did so and sent them outside the camp; just as the LORD had spoken to Moses, thus the sons of Israel did.

5 ¶ Then the LORD spoke to Moses, saying,

6 "Speak to the sons of Israel, '[a]When a man or woman commits any of the sins of mankind, acting unfaithfully against the LORD, and that person is guilty,

7 then [1]he shall [a]confess [2]his sins which [3]he has committed, and he [b]shall make restitution in full for his wrong and add to it one-fifth of it, and give *it* to him whom he has wronged.

8 'But if the man has no [1]relative to whom restitution may be made for the wrong, the restitution which is made for the wrong *must go* to the LORD for the priest, besides the ram of atonement, by which atonement is made for him.

9 '[a]Also every [1]contribution pertaining to all the holy *gifts* of the sons of Israel, which they offer to the priest, shall be his.

10 'So every man's holy *gifts* shall be his; whatever any man gives to the priest, it [a]becomes his.' "

The Adultery Test

11 ¶ Then the LORD spoke to Moses, saying,

12 "Speak to the sons of Israel and say to them, 'If any man's wife [a]goes astray and is unfaithful to him,

13 and a man has [a]intercourse with her and it is hidden from the eyes of her husband and she is [1]undetected, although she has defiled herself, and there is no witness against her and she has not been caught in the act,

14 [1]if a spirit of [a]jealousy comes over him and he is jealous of his wife when she has defiled herself, or if a spirit of jealousy comes over him and he is jealous of his wife when she has not defiled herself,

15 the man shall then bring his wife to the priest, and shall bring *as* [1]an offering for her one-tenth of an [2]ephah of barley meal; he shall not pour oil on it nor put frankincense on it, for it is a grain offering of jealousy, a grain offering of memorial, [a]a reminder of iniquity.

16 ¶ 'Then the priest shall bring her near and have her stand before the LORD,

17 and the priest shall take holy water in an earthenware vessel; and [1]he shall take some of the dust that is on the floor of the tabernacle and put *it* into the water.

18 'The priest shall then have the woman stand before the LORD and let *the hair of* the woman's head go loose, and place the grain offering of memorial [1]in her hands, which is the grain offering of jealousy, and in the hand of the priest is to be the water of bitterness that brings a curse.

19 'The priest shall have her take an oath and shall say to the woman, "If no man has lain with you and if you have not [a]gone astray into uncleanness, *being* under *the authority of* your husband, be [1]immune to this water of bitterness that brings a curse;

20 if you, however, have [a]gone astray,

---

41 [1]Lit *mouth*
43 [a]Num 8:24-26
45 [1]Lit *mouth* [2]Lit *by the hand of*
48 [a]Num 3:39
49 [1]Lit *mouth* [2]Lit *by the hand of* [a]Num 1:47
5:2 [a]Lev 13:8, 46; Num 12:10, 14,15 [b]Lev 15:2 [c]Lev 21:1; Num 9:6-10; 19:11
3 [a]Lev 26:12; Num 35:34
6 [a]Lev 5:14-6:7
7 [1]Lit *they* [2]Lit *their* [3]Lit *they have* [a]Lev 5:5; 26:40,41; Josh 7:19 [b]Lev 6:4,5
8 [1]Lit *redeemer*
9 [1]Lit *heave offering* [a]Lev 7:32, 34; 10:14,15
10 [a]Lev 10:13
12 [a]Num 5:19-21,29
13 [1]Lit *concealed* [a]Lev 18:20; 20:10
14 [1]Lit *and* [a]Prov 6:34; Song 8:6
15 [1]Lit *her* [2]I.e. Approx one bu [a]1 Kin 17:18; Ezek 29:16
17 [1]Lit *the priest*
18 [1]Lit *on her palms*
19 [1]Lit *free from* [a]Num 5:12
20 [a]Num 5:12

being under *the authority of* your husband, and if you have defiled yourself and
a man other than your husband has had
intercourse with you"
21 (then the priest shall have the
woman [a]swear with the oath of the
curse, and the priest shall say to the woman), "the LORD make you a curse and an
oath among your people by the LORD'S
making your thigh [1]waste away and your
abdomen swell;
22 and this water that brings a curse
shall go into your [1]stomach, and make
your abdomen swell and your thigh
[2]waste away." And the woman [a]shall
say, "Amen. Amen."
23 ¶ 'The priest shall then write these
curses on a scroll, and he shall [1]wash
them off into the water of bitterness.
24 'Then he shall make the woman
drink the water of bitterness that brings
a curse, so that the water which brings a
curse will go into her [1]and *cause* bitterness.
25 'The priest shall take the grain offering of jealousy from the woman's hand,
and he shall wave the grain offering before the LORD and bring it to the altar;
26 and [a]the priest shall take a handful
of the grain offering as its memorial offering and offer *it* up in smoke on the altar,
and afterward he shall make the woman
drink the water.
27 'When he has made her drink the
water, then it shall come about, if she has
defiled herself and has been unfaithful to
her husband, that the water which brings
a curse will go into her [1]and *cause* bitterness, and her abdomen will swell and her
thigh will [2]waste away, and the woman
will become [a]a curse among her people.
28 'But if the woman has not defiled
herself and is clean, she will then be free
and conceive [1]children.
29 ¶ 'This is the law of jealousy: when
a wife, *being* under *the authority of* her
husband, [a]goes astray and defiles herself,
30 or when a spirit of jealousy comes
over a man and he is jealous of his wife,
he shall then make the woman stand before the LORD, and the priest shall apply
all this law to her.
31 'Moreover, the man will be free
from [1]guilt, but that woman shall [a]bear
her [1]guilt.' "

Law of the Nazirites

6 Again the LORD spoke to Moses, saying,
2 "Speak to the sons of Israel and say
to them, 'When a man or woman makes
a [1]special vow, the vow of [a]a [2]Nazirite,
to [3]dedicate himself to the LORD,
3 he shall [a]abstain from wine and
strong drink; he shall drink no vinegar,
whether made from wine or strong drink,
nor shall he drink any grape juice nor eat
fresh or dried grapes.
4 'All the days of his [1]separation he
shall not eat anything that is produced by
the grape vine, from *the* seeds even to *the*
skin.
5 ¶ 'All the days of his vow of separation [a]no razor shall pass over his head.
He shall be holy until the days are fulfilled
for which he separated himself to the
LORD; he shall let the locks of hair on his
head grow long.
6 ¶ '[a]All the days of his separation to
the LORD he shall not go near to a dead
person.
7 'He [a]shall not make himself unclean for his father or for his mother, for
his brother or for his sister, when they
die, because his separation to God is on
his head.
8 'All the days of his separation he is
holy to the LORD.
9 ¶ 'But if a man dies very suddenly
beside him and he defiles his dedicated
head *of hair,* then [a]he shall shave his
head on the day when he becomes clean;
[b]he shall shave it on the seventh day.
10 'Then on the eighth day he shall
bring [a]two turtledoves or two young pigeons to the priest, to the doorway of the
tent of meeting.
11 'The priest shall offer [a]one for a sin
offering and *the* other for a burnt offering,
and make atonement for him [1]concern-
ing his sin because of the *dead* person.
And that same day he shall consecrate his
head,
12 and shall dedicate to the LORD his
days [1]as a [2]Nazirite, and shall bring a
male lamb a year old for a guilt offering;
but the former days will be void because
his separation was defiled.
13 ¶ 'Now this is the law of the Nazirite [a]when the days of his separation are
fulfilled, he shall bring [1]the offering to
the doorway of the tent of meeting.
14 'He shall present his offering to the
LORD: one male lamb a year old without
defect for a burnt offering and one [a]ewe-
lamb a year old without defect for a sin
offering and one ram without defect for a
peace offering,
15 and a basket of [a]unleavened cakes
of fine flour mixed with oil and unleavened wafers spread with oil, along with
[b]their grain offering and their drink offering.
16 'Then the priest shall present *them*
before the LORD and shall offer his sin
offering and his burnt offering.
17 'He shall also offer the ram for a
sacrifice of peace offerings to the LORD,

21 [1]Lit *fall* [a]Josh 6:26; 1 Sam 14:24; Neh 10:29
22 [1]Or *inward parts* [2]Lit *fall* [a]Deut 27:15
23 [1]Lit *wipe*
24 [1]Lit *to*
26 [a]Lev 2:2,9
27 [1]Lit *to* [2]Lit *fall* [a]Jer 29:18; 42:18; 44:12
28 [1]Lit *seed*
29 [a]Num 5:12
31 [1]Or *iniquity* [a]Lev 20:17
6:2 [1]Or *difficult* [2]I.e. one separated [3]Or *live as a Nazirite* [a]Judg 13:5; 16:17; Amos 2:11,12
3 [a]Luke 1:15
4 [1]Or *living as a Nazirite,* and so through v 21
5 [a]1 Sam 1:11
6 [a]Lev 21:1-3; Num 19:11-22
7 [a]Num 9:6
9 [a]Lev 14:8,9 [b]Num 6:18
10 [a]Lev 5:7; 14:22
11 [1]Lit *because of that which he sinned* [a]Lev 5:7
12 [1]Or *of dedication* [2]I.e. one separated
13 [1]Lit *it* [a]Acts 21:26
14 [a]Lev 14:10; Num 15:27
15 [a]Ex 29:2; Lev 2:4 [b]Num 15:1-7

together with the basket of unleavened
cakes; the priest shall likewise offer its
grain offering and its drink offering.
18 ‘[a]The Nazirite shall then shave his
dedicated head *of hair* at the doorway of
the tent of meeting, and take the dedicated hair of his head and put *it* on the fire
which is under the sacrifice of peace offerings.
19 ‘[a]The priest shall take the ram’s
shoulder *when it has been* boiled, and
one unleavened cake out of the basket
and one unleavened wafer, and shall put
them on the [1]hands of the Nazirite after
he has shaved his [2]dedicated *hair.*
20 ‘Then the priest shall wave them for
a wave offering before the LORD. It is holy
for the priest, together with the breast
offered by waving and the thigh offered
by lifting up; and [a]afterward the Nazirite
may drink wine.’
21 ¶ “This is the law of the Nazirite
who vows his offering to the LORD according to his separation, in addition to what
else [1]he can afford; according to his vow
which he takes, so he shall do according
to the law of his separation.”

Aaron’s Benediction

22 ¶ Then the LORD spoke to Moses,
saying,
23 “Speak to Aaron and to his sons, saying, ‘Thus [a]you shall bless the sons of
Israel. You shall say to them:
24 ¶ The LORD [a]bless you, and [b]keep
you;
25 ¶ The LORD [a]make His face shine
on you,
And [b]be gracious to you;
26 ¶ The LORD [a]lift up His countenance on you,
And [b]give you peace.’
27 “So they shall [1a]invoke My name
on the sons of Israel, and I *then* will bless
them.”

Offerings of the Leaders

7 Now on [a]the day that Moses had
finished setting up the tabernacle, he
[b]anointed it and consecrated it with all
its furnishings and the altar and all its
utensils; he anointed them and consecrated them also.
2 Then [a]the leaders of Israel, the
heads of their fathers’ households,
[b]made an offering (they were the leaders
of the tribes; they were the ones who
[1]were over the [2]numbered men).
3 When they brought their offering
before the LORD, six [a]covered carts and
twelve oxen, a cart for *every* two of the
leaders and an ox for each one, then they
presented them before the tabernacle.

18 [a]Num 6:9; Acts 21:23,24
19 [1]Lit *palms* [2]Or *separated* [a]Lev 7:28-34
20 [a]Eccl 9:7
21 [1]Lit *his hand can reach*
23 [a]1 Chr 23:13
24 [a]Deut 28:3-6; Ps 28:9 [b]1 Sam 2:9; Ps 17:8
25 [a]Ps 80:3,7, 19 [b]Ps 86:16
26 [a]Ps 4:6; 44:3 [b]Ps 29:11; 37:37
27 [1]Lit *put* [a]2 Sam 7:23; 2 Chr 7:14
7:1 [a]Ex 40:17 [b]Ex 40:9-11; Num 7:10,84,88
2 [1]Lit *stood* [2]Lit *mustered* [a]Num 1:5-16 [b]2 Chr 35:8
3 [a]Is 66:20
5 [1]Lit *for serving*
7 [a]Num 4:24-26
8 [1]Lit *hand* [a]Num 4:31,32
9 [a]Num 4:5-15
10 [1]Lit *of* [2]Lit *in the day that* [a]Num 7:1; 2 Chr 7:9
13 [1]Or *platter,* and so through v 85 [2]I.e. Approx one-half oz, and so through v 86 [a]Ex 25:29; 37:16 [b]Num 3:47
15 [1]Or *bull of the herd,* and so through v 81
16 [a]Lev 4:23
17 [a]Luke 3:32, 33
23 [a]Lev 7:11-13

4 Then the LORD spoke to Moses, saying,
5 “Accept *these things* from them,
that they may be [1]used in the service of
the tent of meeting, and you shall give
them to the Levites, *to* each man according to his service.”
6 So Moses took the carts and the
oxen and gave them to the Levites.
7 Two carts and four oxen he gave to
the sons of Gershon, according to [a]their
service,
8 and four carts and eight oxen he
gave to the sons of Merari, according to
[a]their service, under the [1]direction of
Ithamar the son of Aaron the priest.
9 But he did not give *any* to the sons
of Kohath because theirs *was* [a]the service of the holy *objects, which* they carried on the shoulder.
10 ¶ The leaders offered the dedication *offering* [1]for the altar [2]when [a]it
was anointed, so the leaders offered their
offering before the altar.
11 Then the LORD said to Moses, “Let
them present their offering, one leader
each day, for the dedication of the altar.”
12 ¶ Now the one who presented his
offering on the first day was Nahshon the
son of Amminadab, of the tribe of Judah;
13 and his offering *was* one silver
[1a]dish whose weight *was* one hundred
and thirty *shekels,* one silver bowl of seventy shekels, [b]according to [2]the shekel
of the sanctuary, both of them full of fine
flour mixed with oil for a grain offering;
14 one gold pan of ten *shekels,* full of
incense;
15 one [1]bull, one ram, one male lamb
one year old, for a burnt offering;
16 [a]one male goat for a sin offering;
17 and for the sacrifice of peace offerings, two oxen, five rams, five male goats,
five male lambs one year old. This *was*
the offering of [a]Nahshon the son of Amminadab.
18 ¶ On the second day Nethanel the
son of Zuar, leader of Issachar, presented
an offering;
19 he presented as his offering one silver dish whose weight *was* one hundred
and thirty *shekels,* one silver bowl of seventy shekels, according to the shekel of
the sanctuary, both of them full of fine
flour mixed with oil for a grain offering;
20 one gold pan of ten *shekels,* full of
incense;
21 one bull, one ram, one male lamb
one year old, for a burnt offering;
22 one male goat for a sin offering;
23 and for the sacrifice of [a]peace offerings, two oxen, five rams, five male
goats, five male lambs one year old. This

was the offering of Nethanel the son of
Zuar.
24 ¶ On the third day *it was* Eliab the
son of Helon, leader of the sons of Zebulun;
25 his offering *was* one silver dish
whose weight *was* one hundred and thirty *shekels,* one silver bowl of seventy
shekels, according to the shekel of the
sanctuary, both of them full of fine flour
mixed with oil for a grain offering;
26 one gold pan of ten *shekels,* full of
incense;
27 one young bull, one ram, one
[a]male lamb one year old, for a burnt offering;
28 one male goat for a sin offering;
29 and for the sacrifice of peace offerings, two oxen, five rams, five male goats,
five male lambs one year old. This *was*
the offering of Eliab the son of Helon.
30 ¶ On the fourth day *it was* Elizur
the son of Shedeur, leader of the sons of
Reuben;
31 his offering *was* one silver dish
whose weight *was* one hundred and thirty *shekels,* one silver bowl of seventy
shekels, according to the shekel of the
sanctuary, both of them full of fine flour
mixed with oil for a grain offering;
32 one gold pan of ten *shekels,* full of
incense;
33 one bull, one ram, one [a]male lamb
one year old, for a burnt offering;
34 one male goat for a sin offering;
35 and for the sacrifice of peace offerings, two oxen, five rams, five male goats,
five male lambs one year old. This *was*
the offering of Elizur the son of Shedeur.
36 ¶ On the fifth day *it was* Shelumiel
the son of Zurishaddai, leader of the children of Simeon;
37 his offering *was* one silver dish
whose weight *was* one hundred and thirty *shekels,* one silver bowl of seventy
shekels, according to the shekel of the
sanctuary, both of them full of fine flour
mixed with oil for a grain offering;
38 one gold pan of ten *shekels,* full of
incense;
39 one bull, one ram, one male lamb
one year old, for a burnt offering;
40 one male goat for a sin offering;
41 and for the sacrifice of peace offerings, two oxen, five rams, five male goats,
five male lambs one year old. This *was*
the offering of Shelumiel the son of Zurishaddai.
42 ¶ On the sixth day *it was* [a]Eliasaph
the son of Deuel, leader of the sons
of Gad;
43 his offering *was* one silver dish
whose weight *was* one hundred and thirty *shekels,* one silver bowl of seventy

27 [a]Is 53:7; John 1:29; 1 Pet 1:19
33 [a]Heb 9:28
42 [a]Num 1:14; 10:20
43 [a]Lev 2:5; 14:10
45 [a]Ps 50:8-14; Is 1:11
48 [a]Num 1:10; 2:18; 1 Chr 7:26
50 [a]Deut 33:10; Ezek 8:11; Luke 1:10
51 [a]Mic 6:6-8
54 [a]Num 2:20
56 [a]Ex 30:7
57 [a]Ex 12:5; Acts 8:32; Rev 5:6
59 [a]Lev 3:1-17
60 [a]Num 1:11; 2:22
62 [a]Rev 5:8; 8:3,4
64 [a]2 Cor 5:21

shekels, according to the shekel of the
sanctuary, both of them full of [a]fine flour
mixed with oil for a grain offering;
44 one gold pan of ten *shekels,* full of
incense;
45 [a]one bull, one ram, one male lamb
one year old, for a burnt offering;
46 one male goat for a sin offering;
47 and for the sacrifice of peace offerings, two oxen, five rams, five male goats,
five male lambs one year old. This *was*
the offering of Eliasaph the son of Deuel.
48 ¶ On the seventh day *it was* [a]Elish-
ama the son of Ammihud, leader of the
sons of Ephraim;
49 his offering *was* one silver dish
whose weight *was* one hundred and thirty *shekels,* one silver bowl of seventy
shekels, according to the shekel of the
sanctuary, both of them full of fine flour
mixed with oil for a grain offering;
50 one gold pan of ten *shekels,* full of
[a]incense;
51 [a]one bull, one ram, one male lamb
one year old, for a burnt offering;
52 one male goat for a sin offering;
53 and for the sacrifice of peace offerings, two oxen, five rams, five male goats,
five male lambs one year old. This *was*
the offering of Elishama the son of Ammihud.
54 ¶ On the eighth day *it was* [a]Gama-
liel the son of Pedahzur, leader of the
sons of Manasseh;
55 his offering *was* one silver dish
whose weight *was* one hundred and thirty *shekels,* one silver bowl of seventy
shekels, according to the shekel of the
sanctuary, both of them full of fine flour
mixed with oil for a grain offering;
56 one gold pan of ten *shekels,* full of
[a]incense;
57 one bull, one ram, one [a]male lamb
one year old, for a burnt offering;
58 one male goat for a sin offering;
59 and for the [a]sacrifice of peace offerings, two oxen, five rams, five male
goats, five male lambs one year old. This
was the offering of Gamaliel the son of
Pedahzur.
60 ¶ On the ninth day *it was* [a]Abidan
the son of Gideoni, leader of the sons of
Benjamin;
61 his offering *was* one silver dish
whose weight *was* one hundred and thirty *shekels,* one silver bowl of seventy
shekels, according to the shekel of the
sanctuary, both of them full of fine flour
mixed with oil for a grain offering;
62 one gold pan of ten *shekels,* full of
[a]incense;
63 one bull, one ram, one male lamb
one year old, for a burnt offering;
64 one male goat for a [a]sin offering;

65 and for the sacrifice of [a]peace offerings, two oxen, five rams, five male
goats, five male lambs one year old. This
was the offering of Abidan the son of Gideoni.
66 ¶ On the tenth day *it was* [a]Ahiezer
the son of Ammishaddai, leader of the
sons of Dan;
67 his offering *was* one silver dish
whose weight *was* one hundred and thirty *shekels,* one silver bowl of seventy
shekels, according to the [a]shekel of the
sanctuary, both of them full of fine flour
mixed with oil for a grain offering;
68 one gold pan of ten *shekels,* full of
[a]incense;
69 one bull, one ram, one male lamb
one year old, for a burnt offering;
70 one male goat for a sin offering;
71 and for the sacrifice of peace offerings, two oxen, five rams, five male goats,
five male lambs one year old. This *was*
the offering of Ahiezer the son of Ammishaddai.
72 ¶ On the eleventh day *it was* [a]Pagi-
el the son of Ochran, leader of the sons of
Asher;
73 his offering *was* one silver dish
whose weight *was* one hundred and thirty *shekels,* one silver bowl of seventy
shekels, according to the shekel of the
sanctuary, both of them full of fine flour
mixed with oil for a grain offering;
74 one gold pan of ten *shekels,* full of
[a]incense;
75 one bull, one ram, one male lamb
one year old, for a burnt offering;
76 one male goat for a sin offering;
77 and for the sacrifice of peace offerings, two oxen, five rams, five male goats,
five male lambs one year old. This *was*
the offering of Pagiel the son of Ochran.
78 ¶ On the twelfth day *it was* [a]Ahira
the son of Enan, leader of the sons of
Naphtali;
79 his offering *was* one [a]silver dish
whose weight *was* one hundred and thirty *shekels,* one silver bowl of seventy
shekels, according to the shekel of the
sanctuary, both of them full of fine flour
mixed with oil for a grain offering;
80 one gold pan of ten *shekels,* full of
incense;
81 one bull, one ram, one male lamb
one year old, for a burnt offering;
82 one male goat for a sin offering;
83 and for the sacrifice of peace offerings, two oxen, five rams, five male goats,
five male lambs one year old. This *was*
the offering of Ahira the son of Enan.
84 ¶ This *was* [a]the dedication *offering*
[1]for the altar from the leaders of Israel
[2]when [b]it was anointed: twelve silver
dishes, twelve silver bowls, twelve gold
pans,
85 each silver dish *weighing* one hundred and thirty *shekels* and each bowl
seventy; all the silver of the utensils *was*
2,400 *shekels,* according to the shekel of
the sanctuary;
86 the twelve gold pans, full of incense, *weighing* ten *shekels* apiece, according to the [a]shekel of the sanctuary,
all the gold of the pans 120 *shekels;*
87 all the oxen for the burnt offering
twelve bulls, *all* the rams twelve, the
male lambs one year old with their grain
offering twelve, and the male goats for a
sin offering twelve;
88 and all the oxen for the sacrifice of
peace offerings 24 bulls, *all* the rams 60,
the male goats 60, the male lambs one
year old 60. [a]This *was* the dedication
offering for the altar after it was anointed.
89 ¶ Now when [a]Moses went into the
tent of meeting to speak with Him, he
heard the voice speaking to him from
above [b]the [1]mercy seat that was on the
ark of the testimony, from [c]between the
two cherubim, so He spoke to him.

The Seven Lamps

8 Then the LORD spoke to Moses, saying,
2 "Speak to Aaron and say to him,
'When you [1]mount the lamps, the seven
lamps will [a]give light in the front of the
lampstand.' "
3 Aaron therefore did so; he [1]mount-
ed its lamps at the front of the lampstand,
just as the LORD had commanded Moses.
4 [a]Now this was the workmanship of
the lampstand, hammered work of gold;
from its base to its flowers it was hammered work; [b]according to the pattern
which the LORD had showed Moses, so he
made the lampstand.

Cleansing the Levites

5 ¶ Again the LORD spoke to Moses,
saying,
6 "Take the Levites from among the
sons of Israel and [a]cleanse them.
7 "Thus you shall do to them, for their
[1]cleansing: *sprinkle* [2]purifying [a]water
on them, and let them [3b]use a razor over
their whole [4]body and [c]wash their
clothes, and they will be clean.
8 "Then let them take a [1]bull with
[a]its grain offering, fine flour mixed with
oil; and a second [1]bull you shall take for
a sin offering.
9 "So [a]you shall present the Levites
before the tent of meeting. [b]You shall
also assemble the whole congregation of
the sons of Israel,
10 and present the Levites before the

---

65 [a]Col 1:20
66 [a]Num 1:12; 2:25
67 [a]Ex 30:13; Lev 27:25
68 [a]Ps 141:2
72 [a]Num 1:13; 2:27
74 [a]Mal 1:11
78 [a]Num 1:15; 2:29
79 [a]Ezra 1:9,10; Dan 5:2
84 [1]Lit *of* [2]Lit *in the day that* [a]Num 7:10 [b]Num 7:1
86 [a]Ex 30:13
88 [a]Num 7:1,10
89 [1]Lit *propitiatory* [a]Ex 40:34, 35 [b]Ex 25:21,22 [c]Ps 80:1; 99:1
8:2 [1]Lit *raise up* [a]Ex 25:37; Lev 24:2,4
3 [1]Lit *raised up*
4 [a]Ex 25:31-40 [b]Ex 25:9,31-40; 26:30; 37:17-24
6 [a]Is 52:11
7 [1]Lit *this their cleansing* [2]Lit *water of sin* [3]Lit *cause to pass* [4]Lit *flesh* [a]Num 19:9,13,20 [b]Lev 14:8,9 [c]Num 8:21
8 [1]Or *bull of the herd* [a]Lev 2:1; Num 15:8-10
9 [a]Ex 29:4; 40:12 [b]Lev 8:3

LORD; and the sons of Israel [a]shall lay
their hands on the Levites.
11 "Aaron then shall [1]present the Levites before the LORD as a [a]wave offering
from the sons of Israel, that they may
[2]qualify to perform the service of the
LORD.
12 "Now [a]the Levites shall lay their
hands on the heads of the bulls; then offer
the one for a sin offering and the other for
a burnt offering to the LORD, to make
atonement for the Levites.
13 "You shall have the Levites stand before Aaron and before his sons so as to
present them as a wave offering to the
LORD.
14 ¶ "Thus you shall separate the Levites from among the sons of Israel, and
[a]the Levites shall be Mine.
15 "Then after that the Levites may go
in to serve the tent of meeting. But you
shall cleanse them and [a]present them as
a wave offering;
16 for they are [a]wholly given to Me
from among the sons of Israel. I have tak-
en them for Myself [b]instead of every first
issue of the womb, the firstborn of all the
sons of Israel.
17 "For [a]every firstborn among the
sons of Israel is Mine, among the men
and among the animals; on the day that I
struck down all the firstborn in the land
of Egypt I sanctified them for Myself.
18 "But I have taken the Levites instead
of every firstborn among the sons of Israel.
19 "[a]I have given the Levites as [1]a gift
to Aaron and to his sons from among the
sons of Israel, to perform the service of
the sons of Israel at the tent of meeting
and to make atonement on behalf of the
sons of Israel, so that there will be no
[b]plague among the sons of Israel by
[2]their coming near to the sanctuary."
20 ¶ Thus did Moses and Aaron and all
the congregation of the sons of Israel to
the Levites; according to all that the LORD
had commanded Moses concerning the
Levites, so the sons of Israel did to them.
21 [a]The Levites, too, purified themselves from sin and washed their clothes;
and Aaron presented them as a wave offering before the LORD. Aaron also made
atonement for them to cleanse them.
22 Then after that the Levites went in
to perform their service in the tent of
meeting before Aaron and before his
sons; just as the LORD had commanded
Moses concerning the Levites, so they
did to them.

Retirement

23 ¶ Now the LORD spoke to Moses,
saying,
24 "This is what *applies* to the Levites:
from [a]twenty-five years old and upward
[1]they shall enter to perform service in
the work of the tent of meeting.
25 "But at the age of fifty years they
shall [1]retire from service in the work and
not work any more.
26 "They may, however, [1]assist their
brothers in the tent of meeting, [a]to keep
an obligation, but they *themselves* shall
do no work. Thus you shall deal with the
Levites concerning their obligations."

The Passover

9 Thus the LORD spoke to Moses in the
wilderness of Sinai, in [a]the first
month of the second year after they had
come out of the land of Egypt, saying,
2 "Now, let the sons of Israel observe
the Passover at [a]its appointed time.
3 "On the fourteenth day of this
month, [1]at twilight, you shall observe it
at its appointed time; you shall observe it
according to all its statutes and according
to all its ordinances."
4 So Moses [1]told the sons of Israel to
observe the Passover.
5 [a]They observed the Passover in
the first *month*, on the fourteenth day of
the month, at twilight, in the wilderness
of Sinai; [b]according to all that the LORD
had commanded Moses, so the sons of
Israel did.
6 But there were *some* men who
were [a]unclean because of *the* [1]dead person, so that they could not observe Passover on that day; so [b]they came before
Moses and Aaron on that day.
7 Those men said to him, "*Though*
we are unclean because of *the* [1]dead person, why are we restrained from presenting the offering of the LORD at its appointed time among the sons of Israel?"
8 Moses therefore said to them,
"[1a]Wait, and I will listen to what the
LORD will command concerning you."
9 ¶ Then the LORD spoke to Moses,
saying,
10 "Speak to the sons of Israel, saying,
'If any one of you or of your generations
becomes unclean because of a *dead* [1]per-
son, or is on a distant journey, he may,
however, observe the Passover to the
LORD.
11 'In the second month on the [a]four-
teenth day at twilight, they shall observe
it; they [b]shall eat it with unleavened
bread and bitter herbs.
12 'They [a]shall leave none of it until
morning, [b]nor break a bone of it; according to all the statute of the Passover they
shall observe it.
13 '[a]But the man who is clean and is
not on a journey, and yet [1]neglects to

10 [a]Lev 1:4
11 [1]Lit *wave*, and so throughout the ch [2]Lit *be able* [a]Lev 7:30,34
12 [a]Ex 29:10
14 [a]Num 3:12; 16:9
15 [a]Ex 29:24
16 [a]Num 3:9 [b]Ex 13:2; Num 3:12,45
17 [a]Ex 13:2,12, 13,15; Luke 2:23
19 [1]Lit *given ones* [2]Lit *the sons of Israel's* [a]Num 3:9 [b]Num 1:53; 16:46
21 [a]Num 8:7
24 [1]Lit *he* [a]Num 4:3; 1 Chr 23:3, 24,27
25 [1]Lit *return*
26 [1]Lit *serve* [a]Num 1:53
9:1 [a]Ex 40:2,17; Num 1:1
2 [a]Ex 12:6; Lev 23:5; Deut 16:1, 2
3 [1]Lit *between the two evenings*, and so throughout the ch
4 [1]Lit *spoke to*
5 [a]Josh 5:10 [b]Ex 12:1-13
6 [1]Lit *soul of man* [a]Num 5:2; 19:11-22 [b]Ex 18:15; Num 27:2
7 [1]Lit *soul of man*
8 [1]Lit *Stand* [a]Ex 18:15; Ps 85:8
10 [1]Lit *soul*
11 [a]2 Chr 30:2, 15 [b]Ex 12:8
12 [a]Ex 12:10 [b]Ex 12:46; John 19:36
13 [1]Or *ceases* [a]Gen 17:14; Ex 12:15,47

observe the Passover, that [2]person shall then be cut off from his people, for he did not present the offering of the LORD at its appointed time. That man [b]will bear his sin.

14 '[a]If an alien sojourns among you and [1]observes the Passover to the LORD, according to the statute of the Passover and according to its ordinance, so he shall do; you shall have [b]one statute, both for the alien and for the native of the land.' "

The Cloud on the Tabernacle

15 ¶ Now on [a]the day that the tabernacle was erected [b]the cloud covered the tabernacle, the [c]tent of the testimony, and [d]in the evening it was like the appearance of fire over the tabernacle, until morning.

16 So it was continuously; [a]the cloud would cover it *by day,* and the appearance of fire by night.

17 [a]Whenever the cloud was lifted from over the tent, afterward the sons of Israel would then set out; and in the place where the cloud settled down, there the sons of Israel would camp.

18 At the [1]command of the LORD the sons of Israel would set out, and at the [1]command of the LORD they would camp; [a]as long as the cloud settled over the tabernacle, they remained camped.

19 Even when the cloud lingered over the tabernacle for many days, [1]the sons of Israel would keep the LORD'S charge and not set out.

20 If [1]sometimes the cloud remained a few days over the tabernacle, [a]according to the [2]command of the LORD they remained camped. Then according to the [2]command of the LORD they set out.

21 If [1]sometimes the cloud [2]remained from evening until morning, when the cloud was lifted in the morning, they would move out; or *if it remained* in the daytime and at night, whenever the cloud was lifted, they would set out.

22 Whether it was two days or a month or a year that the cloud lingered over the tabernacle, staying above it, the sons of Israel remained camped and did not set out; but [a]when it was lifted, they did set out.

23 [a]At the [1]command of the LORD they camped, and at the [1]command of the LORD they set out; they kept the LORD'S charge, according to the [1]command of the LORD through Moses.

The Silver Trumpets

10 The LORD spoke further to Moses, saying,

2 "Make yourself two trumpets of silver, of hammered work you shall make them; and you shall use them for [a]summoning the congregation and for having the camps set out.

3 "[a]When both are blown, all the congregation shall gather themselves to you at the doorway of the tent of meeting.

4 "Yet if *only* one is blown, then the [a]leaders, the heads of the [1]divisions of Israel, shall assemble before you.

5 "But when you blow an alarm, the camps that are pitched [a]on the east side shall set out.

6 "When you blow an alarm the second time, the camps that are pitched on [a]the south side shall set out; an alarm is to be blown for them to set out.

7 "When convening the assembly, however, you shall blow without [a]sounding an alarm.

8 "[a]The priestly sons of Aaron, moreover, shall blow the trumpets; and [1]this shall be for you a perpetual statute throughout your generations.

9 "When you go to war in your land against the adversary who [a]attacks you, then you shall sound an alarm with the trumpets, that you may be [b]remembered before the LORD your God, and be saved from your enemies.

10 "Also in the day of your gladness and in your appointed [1]feasts, and on the first *days* of your months, [a]you shall blow the trumpets over your burnt offerings, and over the sacrifices of your peace offerings; and they shall be as a reminder of you before your God. I am the LORD your God."

The Tribes Leave Sinai

11 ¶ Now in [a]the second year, in the second month, on the twentieth of the month, the cloud was lifted from over the [1]tabernacle of the testimony;

12 and the sons of Israel set out on [a]their journeys from the wilderness of Sinai. Then the cloud settled down in the [b]wilderness of Paran.

13 [a]So they moved out for the first time according to the [1]commandment of the LORD through Moses.

14 The standard of the camp of the sons of Judah, according to their armies, [a]set out first, with Nahshon the son of Amminadab, over its army,

15 and Nethanel the son of Zuar, over the tribal army of the sons of Issachar;

16 and Eliab the son of Helon over the tribal army of the sons of Zebulun.

17 ¶ [a]Then the tabernacle was taken down; and the sons of Gershon and the sons of Merari, who were carrying the tabernacle, set out.

18 Next [a]the standard of the camp of

---

13 [2]Lit *soul* [b]Num 5:31
14 [1]Or *would observe* [a]Ex 12:48 [b]Ex 12:49; Lev 24:22; Num 15:15,16,29
15 [a]Ex 40:2,17 [b]Ex 40:34 [c]Num 17:7 [d]Ex 13:21, 22
16 [a]Ex 40:34; Neh 9:12
17 [a]Ex 40:36-38; Num 10:11,12
18 [1]Lit *mouth* [a]1 Cor 10:1
19 [1]Lit *and the*
20 [1]Lit *it was that* [2]Lit *mouth* [a]Ps 48:14; Prov 3:5,6
21 [1]Lit *it was that* [2]Lit *was*
22 [a]Ex 40:36,37
23 [1]Lit *mouth* [a]Ps 73:24; 107:7; Is 63:14
10:2 [a]Is 1:13
3 [a]Jer 4:5; Joel 2:15
4 [1]Lit *thousands*; or *clans* [a]Ex 18:21; Num 1:16; 7:2
5 [a]Num 10:14
6 [a]Num 10:18
7 [a]Joel 2:1
8 [1]Lit *it* [a]Num 31:6; Josh 6:4; 2 Chr 13:12
9 [a]Judg 2:18; 1 Sam 10:18; Ps 106:42 [b]Gen 8:1; Ps 106:4
10 [1]Or *times* [a]Ps 81:3-5
11 [1]Lit *dwelling place,* and so throughout the ch [a]Ex 40:17
12 [a]Ex 40:36 [b]Gen 21:21; Num 12:16
13 [1]Lit *mouth* [a]Deut 1:6
14 [a]Num 2:3-9
17 [a]Num 4:21-32
18 [a]Num 2:10-16

Reuben, according to their armies, set out with Elizur the son of Shedeur, over its army,

19 and Shelumiel the son of Zurishaddai over the tribal army of the sons of Simeon,

20 and Eliasaph the son of Deuel was over the tribal army of the sons of Gad.

21 ¶ [a]Then the Kohathites set out, carrying the holy *objects;* and [b]the tabernacle was set up before their arrival.

22 [a]Next the standard of the camp of the sons of Ephraim, according to their armies, was set out, with Elishama the son of Ammihud over its army,

23 and Gamaliel the son of Pedahzur over the tribal army of the sons of Manasseh;

24 and Abidan the son of Gideoni over the tribal army of the sons of Benjamin.

25 ¶ [a]Then the standard of the camp of the sons of Dan, according to their armies, *which formed* the [b]rear guard for all the camps, set out, with Ahiezer the son of Ammishaddai over its army,

26 and Pagiel the son of Ochran over the tribal army of the sons of Asher;

27 and Ahira the son of Enan over the tribal army of the sons of Naphtali.

28 [1]This was the order of march of the sons of Israel by their armies as they set out.

29 ¶ Then Moses said to [a]Hobab the son of [b]Reuel the Midianite, Moses' father-in-law, "We are setting out to the place of which the LORD said, '[c]I will give it to you'; [d]come with us and we will do you good, for the LORD [e]has [1]promised good concerning Israel."

30 But he said to him, "[a]I will not come, but rather will go to my *own* land and relatives."

31 Then he said, "Please do not leave us, inasmuch as you know where we should camp in the wilderness, and you [a]will be as eyes for us.

32 "So it will be, if you go with us, that [1a]whatever good the LORD [2]does for us, [b]we will [3]do for you."

33 ¶ [a]Thus they set out from the mount of the LORD three days' journey, with [b]the ark of the covenant of the LORD journeying in front of them for the [1]three days, to seek out [c]a resting place for them.

34 [a]The cloud of the LORD was over them by day when they set out from the camp.

35 ¶ Then it came about when the ark set out that Moses said,

"[a]Rise up, O LORD!
And let Your enemies be scattered,
And let those [b]who hate You flee [1]before You."

36 When it came to rest, he said,

"[a]Return, O LORD,
To the myriad [b]thousands of Israel."

The People Complain

11 Now the people became like [a]those who complain of adversity [b]in the hearing of the LORD; and when the LORD heard *it,* His anger was kindled, and the fire of the LORD burned among them and consumed *some* of the outskirts of the camp.

2 [a]The people therefore cried out to Moses, and Moses prayed to the LORD and the fire [1]died out.

3 So the name of that place was called [1a]Taberah, because the fire of the LORD burned among them.

4 ¶ The [a]rabble who were among them [1]had greedy desires; and also the sons of Israel wept again and said, "[b]Who will give us [2]meat to eat?

5 "[a]We remember the fish which we used to eat free in Egypt, the cucumbers and the melons and the leeks and the onions and the garlic,

6 but now [a]our [1]appetite is gone. There is nothing at all [2]to look at except this manna."

7 ¶ [a]Now the manna was like coriander seed, and its appearance like that of [b]bdellium.

8 The people would go about and gather *it* and grind *it* [1]between two millstones or beat *it* in the mortar, and boil *it* in the pot and make cakes with it; and its taste was as the taste of [2]cakes baked with oil.

9 [a]When the dew fell on the camp at night, the manna would fall [1]with it.

The Complaint of Moses

10 ¶ Now Moses heard the people weeping throughout their families, each man at the doorway of his tent; and the anger of the LORD was kindled greatly, and [1]Moses was displeased.

11 [a]So Moses said to the LORD, "Why have You [1]been so hard on Your servant? And why have I not found favor in Your sight, that You have laid the burden of all this people on me?

12 "Was it I who conceived all this people? Was it I who brought them forth, that You should say to me, 'Carry them in your bosom as a [1a]nurse carries a nursing infant, to the land which [b]You swore to their fathers'?

13 "Where am I to get meat to give to [a]all this people? For they weep before

---

21 [a]Num 4:4-20 [b]Num 10:17
22 [a]Num 2:18-24
25 [a]Num 2:25-31 [b]Josh 6:9,13
28 [1]Lit *These are the settings out of the sons*
29 [1]Lit *spoken* [a]Judg 4:11 [b]Ex 2:18; 3:1; 18:12 [c]Gen 12:7; Ex 6:4-8 [d]Ps 95:1-7; 100:1-5 [e]Deut 4:40; 30:5
30 [a]Judg 1:16; Matt 21:28,29
31 [a]Job 29:15
32 [1]Lit *that good which* [2]Lit *does good* [3]Lit *do good* [a]Ps 22:27-31; 67:5-7 [b]Lev 19:34; Deut 10:18
33 [1]Lit *three days' journey* [a]Num 10:12 [b]Deut 1:33 [c]Is 11:10
34 [a]Num 9:15-23
35 [1]Or *from Your presence* [a]Ps 68:1,2; Is 17:12-14 [b]Deut 7:10; 32:41
36 [a]Is 63:17 [b]Deut 1:10
11:1 [a]Num 14:2; 16:11; 17:5 [b]Num 11:18; 14:28
2 [1]Lit *sank down* [a]Num 12:11,13; 21:7
3 [1]I.e. burning [a]Deut 9:22
4 [1]Lit *desired a desire* [2]Lit *flesh,* and so throughout the ch [a]Ex 12:38; 1 Cor 10:6 [b]Ps 78:20
5 [a]Ex 16:3
6 [1]Lit *soul is dried up* [2]Lit *for our eyes* [a]Num 21:5
7 [a]Ex 16:31 [b]Gen 2:12
8 [1]Lit *with* [2]Lit *juice of oil*
9 [1]Lit *on* [a]Ex 16:13,14
10 [1]Lit it was *evil in Moses' sight*
11 [1]Lit *dealt ill with* [a]Ex 5:22; Deut 1:12
12 [1]Or *foster-father* [a]2 Kin 10:1,5; Is 49:23 [b]Gen 24:7; Ex 13:5,11; 33:1
13 [a]Num 11:21,22; John 6:5-9

me, saying, 'Give us meat that we may eat!'

14 "[a]I alone am not able to carry all this people, because it is too [1]burdensome for me.

15 "[a]So if You are going to deal thus with me, please kill me at once, if I have found favor in Your sight, and do not let me see my wretchedness."

Seventy Elders to Assist

16 ¶ The LORD therefore said to Moses, "Gather for Me [a]seventy men from the elders of Israel, [b]whom you know to be the elders of the people and their officers and bring them to the tent of meeting, and let them take their stand there with you.

17 "[a]Then I will come down and speak with you there, and I will take of [b]the Spirit who is upon you, and will put *Him* upon them; and they shall bear the burden of the people with you, so that you will not bear *it* all alone.

18 "Say to the people, '[a]Consecrate yourselves for tomorrow, and you shall eat meat; for you have wept [b]in the ears of the LORD, saying, "Oh that someone would give us meat to eat! For we were well-off in Egypt." Therefore the LORD will give you meat and you shall eat.

19 'You shall eat, not one day, nor two days, nor five days, nor ten days, nor twenty days,

20 [1]but a whole month, until it comes out of your nostrils and becomes loathsome to you; because [a]you have rejected the LORD who is among you and have wept before Him, saying, "Why did we ever leave Egypt?" ' "

21 But Moses said, "The people, among whom I am, are 600,000 on foot; yet You have said, 'I will give them meat, so that they may eat for a whole month.'

22 "Should flocks and herds be slaughtered for them, to be sufficient for them? Or should all the fish of the sea be gathered together for them, to be sufficient for them?"

23 The LORD said to Moses, "Is [a]the LORD'S [1]power limited? Now you shall see whether [b]My word will [2]come true for you or not."

24 ¶ So Moses went out and [a]told the people the words of the LORD. Also, he gathered seventy men of the elders of the people, and stationed them around the tent.

25 [a]Then the LORD came down in the cloud and spoke to him; and He took of the Spirit who was upon him and placed *Him* upon the seventy elders. And when the Spirit rested upon them, they prophesied. But they did not do *it* again.

26 ¶ But two men had remained in the camp; the name of one was Eldad and the name of the [1]other Medad. And [a]the Spirit rested upon them (now they were among those who had been registered, but had not gone out to the tent), and they prophesied in the camp.

27 So a young man ran and told Moses and said, "Eldad and Medad are prophesying in the camp."

28 Then [a]Joshua the son of Nun, the attendant of Moses from his youth, said, "[b]Moses, my lord, restrain them."

29 But Moses said to him, "Are you jealous for my sake? [a]Would that all the LORD'S people were prophets, that the LORD would put His Spirit upon them!"

30 Then Moses [1]returned to the camp, *both* he and the elders of Israel.

The Quail and the Plague

31 ¶ [a]Now there went forth a wind from the LORD and it brought quail from the sea, and let *them* fall beside the camp, about a day's journey on this side and a day's journey on the other side, all around the camp and [1]about two [2]cubits *deep* on the surface of the ground.

32 The people [1]spent all day and all night and all the next day, and gathered the quail (he who gathered least gathered ten [2a]homers) and they spread *them* out for themselves all around the camp.

33 [a]While the meat was still between their teeth, before it was chewed, the anger of the LORD was kindled against the people, and the LORD struck the people with a very severe plague.

34 So the name of that place was called [1a]Kibroth-hattaavah, because there they buried the people who had been greedy.

35 From Kibroth-hattaavah [a]the people set out for Hazeroth, and they [1]remained at Hazeroth.

The Murmuring of Miriam and Aaron

12 Then Miriam and Aaron spoke against Moses because of the Cushite woman whom he had married (for he had married a [a]Cushite woman);

2 [a]and they said, "Has the LORD indeed spoken only through Moses? Has He not spoken through us as well?" And the LORD heard it.

3 (Now the man Moses was [a]very humble, more than any man who was on the face of the earth.)

4 Suddenly the LORD said to Moses and Aaron and to Miriam, "You three come out to the tent of meeting." So the three of them came out.

5 [a]Then the LORD came down in a

---

14 [1]Lit *heavy* [a]Ex 18:18; Deut 1:12
15 [a]Ex 32:32
16 [a]Ex 24:1,9 [b]Ex 18:25
17 [a]Num 11:25 [b]1 Sam 10:6; Joel 2:28
18 [a]Ex 19:10,22 [b]Num 11:1
20 [1]Lit *until* [a]Josh 24:27; 1 Sam 10:19
23 [1]Lit *hand short* [2]Lit *befall you* [a]Is 50:2; 59:1 [b]Ezek 12:25; 24:14
24 [a]Num 11:16
25 [a]Num 11:17; 12:5
26 [1]Lit *second* [a]Num 24:2; 1 Sam 10:6; 2 Chr 15:1; Neh 9:30
28 [a]Ex 33:11; Josh 1:1 [b]Mark 9:38-40
29 [a]1 Cor 14:5
30 [1]Lit *removed himself*
31 [1]Or *from about two cubits above* [2]I.e. One cubit equals approx 18 in. [a]Ex 16:13; Ps 78:26-28; 105:40
32 [1]Lit *rose* [2]I.e. One homer equals approx 11 bu [a]Ezek 45:11
33 [a]Ps 78:29-31; 106:15
34 [1]I.e. the graves of greediness [a]Deut 9:22
35 [1]Lit *were* [a]Num 33:17
12:1 [a]Ex 2:21
2 [a]Num 16:3
3 [a]Matt 11:29
5 [a]Ex 19:9; 34:5

pillar of cloud and stood at the doorway of
the tent, and He called [1]Aaron and Miriam. When they had both come forward,
6 He said,
"Hear now My words:
If there is a prophet among you,
I, the LORD, shall make Myself
known to him in a [a]vision.
I shall speak with him in a
[b]dream.
7 "Not so, with [a]My servant
Moses,
[b]He is faithful in all My
household;
8 [a]With him I speak mouth to
mouth,
Even openly, and not in dark
sayings,
And he beholds [b]the form of the
LORD.
Why then were you not afraid
To speak against My servant,
against Moses?"
9 ¶ So the anger of the LORD burned
against them and [a]He departed.
10 But when the cloud had withdrawn
from over the tent, behold, [a]Miriam *was*
leprous, as [b]*white as* snow. As Aaron
turned toward Miriam, behold, she *was*
leprous.
11 Then Aaron said to Moses, "Oh, my
lord, I beg you, [a]do not account *this* sin
to us, in which we have acted foolishly
and in which we have sinned.
12 "Oh, do not let her be like one dead,
whose flesh is half eaten away when he
comes from his mother's womb!"
13 Moses cried out to the LORD, saying, "O God, [a]heal her, I pray!"
14 But the LORD said to Moses, "If her
father had but [a]spit in her face, would
she not bear her shame for seven days?
Let her be shut up for seven days [b]out-
side the camp, and afterward she may be
received again."
15 So [a]Miriam was shut up outside
the camp for seven days, and the people
did not move on until Miriam was received again.
16 ¶ Afterward, however, the people
moved out from Hazeroth and camped in
the wilderness of Paran.

Spies View the Land

13 Then [a]the LORD spoke to Moses
saying,
2 "[a]Send out for yourself men so that
they may spy out the land of Canaan,
which I am going to give to the sons of
Israel; you shall send a man from each of
their fathers' tribes, every one a leader
among them."
3 So Moses sent them from the wilderness of Paran at the [1]command of the
LORD, all of them men who were heads of
the sons of Israel.
4 These then *were* their names: from
the tribe of Reuben, Shammua the son of
Zaccur;
5 from the tribe of Simeon, Shaphat
the son of Hori;
6 from the tribe of Judah, [a]Caleb the
son of Jephunneh;
7 from the tribe of Issachar, Igal the
son of Joseph;
8 from the tribe of Ephraim, [a]Ho-
shea the son of Nun;
9 from the tribe of Benjamin, Palti
the son of Raphu;
10 from the tribe of Zebulun, Gaddiel
the son of Sodi;
11 from the tribe of Joseph, from the
tribe of Manasseh, Gaddi the son of Susi;
12 from the tribe of Dan, Ammiel the
son of Gemalli;
13 from the tribe of Asher, Sethur the
son of Michael;
14 from the tribe of Naphtali, Nahbi
the son of Vophsi;
15 from the tribe of Gad, Geuel the
son of Machi.
16 These are the names of the men
whom Moses sent to spy out the land; but
Moses called [a]Hoshea the son of Nun,
Joshua.
17 ¶ When Moses sent them to spy
out the land of Canaan, he said to them,
"Go up [1]there into [a]the [2]Negev; then
go up into the hill country.
18 "See what the land is like, and
whether the people who live in it are
strong *or* weak, whether they are few or
many.
19 "How is the land in which they live,
is it good or bad? And how are the cities
in which they live, are *they* [1]like *open*
camps or with fortifications?
20 "[a]How is the land, is it fat or lean?
Are there trees in it or not? [1]Make an
[b]effort then to get some of the fruit of the
land." Now the time was the time of the
first ripe grapes.
21 ¶ So they went up and spied out the
land from [a]the wilderness of Zin as far as
Rehob, [1b]at Lebo-hamath.
22 When they had gone up into [a]the
Negev, [1]they came to Hebron where
[b]Ahiman, Sheshai and Talmai, the
[2]descendants of [c]Anak were. (Now Hebron was built seven years before [d]Zoan
in Egypt.)
23 ¶ Then they came to the [1]valley of
[2a]Eshcol and from there cut down a
branch with a single cluster of grapes;
and they carried it on a pole between two
men, with some of the pomegranates and
the figs.
24 That place was called the valley of

5 [1]Or *"Aaron and Miriam!"*
6 [a]Gen 46:2; 1 Sam 3:15 [b]Gen 31:11; 1 Kin 3:5,15
7 [a]Josh 1:1 [b]Heb 3:2,5
8 [a]Deut 34:10; Hos 12:13 [b]Ex 20:4; 24:10,11; Deut 5:8; Ps 17:15
9 [a]Gen 17:22; 18:33
10 [a]Deut 24:9 [b]Ex 4:6; 2 Kin 5:27
11 [a]2 Sam 19:19; 24:10
13 [a]Ps 30:2; 41:4; Is 30:26; Jer 17:14
14 [a]Deut 25:9; Job 17:6; 30:10; Is 50:6 [b]Num 5:1-4
15 [a]Deut 24:9
13:1 [a]Deut 1:22,23
2 [a]Deut 1:22; 9:23
3 [1]Lit *mouth*
6 [a]Num 14:6, 30; Josh 14:6
8 [a]Num 13:16; Deut 32:44
16 [a]Num 13:8; Deut 32:44
17 [1]Lit *here* [2]I.e. South country, and so throughout the ch [a]Gen 12:9; 13:1,3
19 [1]Lit *in*
20 [1]Lit *Use your strength* [a]Deut 1:24,25 [b]Deut 31:6,23
21 [1]Or *to the entrance of Hamath* [a]Num 20:1; 27:14; 33:36 [b]Josh 13:5
22 [1]Lit Most mss read *one came* [2]Lit *children* [a]Num 13:17 [b]Josh 15:14 [c]Num 13:28,33 [d]Ps 78:12,43
23 [1]Or *wadi* [2]I.e. cluster [a]Gen 14:13; Num 13:24; 32:9; Deut 1:24

[1]Eshcol, because of the cluster which the
sons of Israel cut down from there.

The Spies' Reports

25 ¶ When they returned from spying
out the land, at the end of forty days,
26 they proceeded to come to Moses
and Aaron and to all the congregation of
the sons of Israel [1]in the wilderness of
Paran, at [a]Kadesh; and they brought
back word to them and to all the congregation and showed them the fruit of the
land.
27 Thus they told him, and said, "We
went in to the land where you sent us;
and [a]it certainly does flow with milk and
honey, and [b]this is its fruit.
28 "Nevertheless, [a]the people who live
in the land are strong, and the cities are
fortified *and* very large; and moreover,
we saw [b]the [1]descendants of Anak
there.
29 "Amalek is living in the land of [a]the
Negev and the Hittites and the Jebusites
and [b]the Amorites are living in the hill
country, and [c]the Canaanites are living
by the sea and by the side of the Jordan."
30 ¶ Then Caleb quieted the people
[1]before Moses and said, "We should by
all means go up and take possession of it,
for we will surely overcome it."
31 But the men who had gone up with
him said, "[a]We are not able to go up
against the people, for they are too strong
for us."
32 So they gave out to the sons of Israel [a]a bad report of the land which they
had spied out, saying, "The land through
which we have gone, in spying it out, is
[b]a land that devours its [1]inhabitants;
and [c]all the people whom we saw in it
are men of *great* size.
33 "There also we saw the [a]Nephilim
(the sons of Anak are part of the Nephilim); and [b]we became like grasshoppers
in our own sight, and so we were in their
sight."

The People Rebel

14 Then all the congregation [1]lifted
up their voices and cried, and the
people wept [2]that night.
2 All the sons of Israel [a]grumbled
against Moses and Aaron; and the whole
congregation said to them, "[b]Would that
we had died in the land of Egypt! Or
would that we had died in this wilderness!
3 "Why is the LORD bringing us into
this land, [a]to fall by the sword? [b]Our
wives and our little ones will become
plunder; would it not be better for us to
return to Egypt?"
4 So they said to one another, "[a]Let
us appoint a leader and return to Egypt."
5 ¶ [a]Then Moses and Aaron fell on
their faces in the presence of all the assembly of the congregation of the sons of
Israel.
6 Joshua the son of Nun and Caleb
the son of Jephunneh, of those who had
spied out the land, tore their clothes;
7 and they spoke to all the congregation of the sons of Israel, saying, "[a]The
land which we passed through to spy out
is an exceedingly good land.
8 "[a]If the LORD is pleased with us,
then He will bring us into this land and
give it to us—[b]a land which flows with
milk and honey.
9 "Only [a]do not rebel against the
LORD; and do not [b]fear the people of the
land, for they will be our [1]prey. Their
[2]protection has been removed from
them, and the LORD is with us; do not fear
them."
10 [a]But all the congregation said to
stone them with stones. Then [b]the glory
of the LORD appeared in the tent of meeting to all the sons of Israel.

Moses Pleads for the People

11 ¶ [a]The LORD said to Moses, "How
long will this people spurn Me? And how
long will [b]they not believe in Me, despite
all the signs which I have performed in
their midst?
12 "I will smite them with [1a]pesti-
lence and dispossess them, and I [b]will
make you into a nation greater and mightier than they."
13 ¶ [a]But Moses said to the LORD,
"Then the Egyptians will hear of it, for by
Your strength You brought up this people
from their midst,
14 and they will tell *it* to the inhabitants of this land. They have heard that
You, O LORD, are in the midst of this people, for [a]You, O LORD, are seen eye to
eye, while Your cloud stands over them;
and You go before them in a pillar of
cloud by day and in a pillar of fire by
night.
15 "Now if You slay this people as one
man, [a]then the nations who have heard
of Your fame will [1]say,
16 'Because the LORD [a]could not bring
this people into the land which He promised them by oath, therefore He slaughtered them in the wilderness.'
17 "But now, I pray, let the power of
the Lord be great, just as You have [1]de-
clared,
18 '[a]The LORD is slow to anger and
abundant in lovingkindness, forgiving iniquity and transgression; but [b]He will by
no means clear *the guilty,* [c]visiting the

24 [1]I.e. cluster
26 [1]Lit *to* [a]Num 20:1,14; 32:8
27 [a]Ex 3:8,17; 13:5 [b]Deut 1:25
28 [1]Lit *born ones* [a]Deut 1:28; 9:1,2 [b]Num 13:33
29 [a]Num 13:17; 14:25,45 [b]Josh 10:6 [c]Num 14:43,45
30 [1]Lit *toward*
31 [a]Deut 1:28; 9:1-3
32 [1]Or *settlers* [a]Num 14:36,37; Ps 106:24 [b]Ezek 36:13,14 [c]Amos 2:9
33 [a]Gen 6:4 [b]Deut 1:28; 9:2; Josh 11:21
14:1 [1]Lit *lifted and gave their voice* [2]Lit *in that*
2 [a]Num 11:1 [b]Num 11:5; 16:13; 20:3,4; 21:5
3 [a]Ex 5:21; 16:3 [b]Num 14:31; Deut 1:39
4 [a]Neh 9:17
5 [a]Num 16:4
7 [a]Num 13:27; Deut 1:25
8 [a]Deut 10:15 [b]Ex 3:8; Num 13:27
9 [1]Lit *food* [2]Lit *shadow* [a]Deut 1:26; 9:23,24 [b]Deut 1:21,29
10 [a]Ex 17:4 [b]Ex 16:10; Lev 9:23
11 [a]Ex 32:9-13 [b]Ps 106:24
12 [1]Lit *the pestilence* [a]Lev 26:25; Deut 28:21 [b]Ex 32:10
13 [a]Ex 32:11-14; Ps 106:23
14 [a]Ex 13:21; Deut 5:4
15 [1]Lit *speak, saying* [a]Ex 32:12
16 [a]Josh 7:7
17 [1]Lit *spoken, saying*
18 [a]Ex 20:6; 34:6,7; Deut 5:10; 7:9; Ps 103:8; 145:8; Jon 4:2 [b]Ex 20:5; Deut 5:9; 7:10 [c]Ex 34:7

iniquity of the fathers on the children [1]to the third and the fourth *generations.*'

19 "[a]Pardon, I pray, the iniquity of this people according to the greatness of Your lovingkindness, just as You also have forgiven this people, from Egypt even until now."

The LORD Pardons and Rebukes

20 ¶ So the LORD said, "[a]I have pardoned *them* according to your word;

21 but indeed, [a]as I live, [1][b]all the earth will be filled with the glory of the LORD.

22 "Surely [a]all the men who have seen My glory and My signs which I performed in Egypt and in the wilderness, yet [b]have put Me to the test these ten times and have not listened to My voice,

23 [a]shall by no means see the land which I swore to their fathers, nor shall any of those who spurned Me see it.

24 "But My servant Caleb, [a]because he has had a different spirit and has followed Me fully, [1][b]I will bring into the land [2]which he entered, and his [3]descendants shall take possession of it.

25 "[a]Now the Amalekites and the Canaanites live in the valleys; turn tomorrow and set out to the wilderness by the way of the [1]Red Sea."

26 ¶ The LORD spoke to Moses and Aaron, saying,

27 "How long *shall I bear* with this evil congregation who are [a]grumbling against Me? I have heard the complaints of the sons of Israel, which they are [1]making against Me.

28 "Say to them, '[a]As I live,' says the LORD, 'just as [b]you have spoken in My hearing, so I will surely do to you;

29 [a]your corpses will fall in this wilderness, even all [b]your [1]numbered men, according to your complete number from twenty years old and upward, who have grumbled against Me.

30 'Surely you shall not come into the land in which I [1]swore to settle you, [a]except Caleb the son of Jephunneh and Joshua the son of Nun.

31 '[a]Your children, however, whom you said would become a prey—I will bring them in, and they will know the land which you have rejected.

32 '[a]But as for you, your corpses will fall in this wilderness.

33 'Your sons shall be shepherds for [a]forty years in the wilderness, and they will [1]suffer *for* your [2]unfaithfulness, until your corpses [3]lie in the wilderness.

34 'According to the [a]number of days which you spied out the land, forty days, for every day you shall bear your [1]guilt a year, *even* forty years, and you will know My opposition.

35 '[a]I, the LORD, have spoken, surely this I will do to all this evil congregation who are gathered together against Me. In this wilderness they shall be destroyed, and there they will die.' "

36 ¶ [a]As for the men whom Moses sent to spy out the land and who returned and made all the congregation grumble against him by bringing out a bad report concerning the land,

37 even [a]those men who brought out the very bad report of the land died by a [b]plague before the LORD.

38 But Joshua the son of Nun and Caleb the son of Jephunneh remained alive out of those men who went to spy out the land.

Israel Repulsed

39 ¶ When Moses spoke [a]these words to all the sons of Israel, [b]the people mourned greatly.

40 In the morning, however, they rose up early and went up to the [1]ridge of the hill country, saying, "[a]Here we are; [2]we have indeed sinned, but we will go up to the place which the LORD has promised."

41 But Moses said, "[a]Why then are you transgressing the [1]commandment of the LORD, when it will not succeed?

42 "[a]Do not go up, or you will be struck down before your enemies, for the LORD is not among you.

43 "For the Amalekites and the Canaanites will be there in front of you, and you will fall by the sword, inasmuch as you have turned back from following the LORD. And the LORD will not be with you."

44 But they went up heedlessly to the [1]ridge of the hill country; neither [a]the ark of the covenant of the LORD nor Moses left the camp.

45 Then the Amalekites and the Canaanites who lived in that hill country came down, and struck them and beat them down as far as [a]Hormah.

Laws for Canaan

15 Now the LORD spoke to Moses, saying,

2 "[a]Speak to the sons of Israel and say to them, 'When you enter the land [1]where you are to live, which I am giving you,

3 then make [a]an offering by fire to the LORD, a burnt offering or a sacrifice to [1][b]fulfill a special vow, or as a freewill offering or in your [c]appointed times, to make a [d]soothing aroma to the LORD, from the herd or from the flock.

4 '[a]The one who presents his offering

18 [1]Lit *on*
19 [a]Ex 32:32; 34:9
20 [a]Mic 7:18-20
21 [1]Lit *and all* [a]Num 14:28; Deut 32:40; Is 49:18 [b]Is 6:3; Hab 2:14
22 [a]1 Cor 10:5 [b]Ex 5:21; 14:11; 15:24; 16:2; 17:2,3; 32:1; Num 11:1,4; 12:1; 14:2
23 [a]Num 26:65; 32:11; Heb 3:18
24 [1]Lit *him I* [2]Lit *where* [3]Lit *seed* [a]Num 14:6-9 [b]Num 26:65; 32:12; Deut 1:36; Josh 14:6-15
25 [1]Lit *Sea of Reeds* [a]Num 13:29
27 [1]Lit *complaining* [a]Num 11:1
28 [a]Num 14:21 [b]Num 14:2; Deut 2:14,15; Heb 3:17
29 [1]Lit *mustered* [a]Heb 3:17 [b]Num 1:45,46
30 [1]Lit *raised My hand* [a]Num 14:24
31 [a]Num 14:3
32 [a]Num 26:64, 65; 32:13; 1 Cor 10:5
33 [1]Lit *bear* [2]Lit *fornications* [3]Lit *are finished* [a]Deut 2:7; 8:2,4; 29:5
34 [1]Or *iniquities* [a]Num 13:25
35 [a]Num 23:19
36 [a]Num 13:4-16,32
37 [a]1 Cor 10:10; Heb 3:17, 18 [b]Num 16:49
39 [a]Num 14:28-35 [b]Ex 33:4
40 [1]Or *top of the mountain* [2]Or *and we will go up...for we have sinned* [a]Deut 1:41-44
41 [1]Lit *mouth* [a]2 Chr 24:20
42 [a]Deut 1:42
44 [1]Or *top of the mountain* [a]Num 31:6
45 [a]Num 21:3
15:2 [1]Lit *of your dwellings* [a]Lev 23:10
3 [1]Or *make a special votive offering* [a]Lev 1:2,3 [b]Lev 22:21 [c]Lev 23:1-44 [d]Gen 8:21; 2 Cor 2:15,16; Phil 4:18
4 [a]Num 28:1-29:40

shall present to the LORD a grain offering
of one-tenth *of an ephah* of fine flour
mixed with one-fourth of a [1]hin of oil,
5 and you shall prepare wine for the
drink offering, one-fourth of a hin, with
the burnt offering or for the sacrifice, for
[a]each lamb.
6 'Or for a ram you shall prepare as a
grain offering two-tenths *of an ephah* of
fine flour mixed with one-third of a hin of
oil;
7 and for the drink offering you shall
offer one-third of a hin of wine as a soothing aroma to the LORD.
8 'When you prepare [a]a bull as a
burnt offering or a sacrifice, to [1]fulfill a
special vow, or for peace offerings to the
LORD,
9 then you shall offer with the bull a
grain offering of three-tenths *of an ephah*
of fine flour mixed with one-half a hin of
oil;
10 and you shall offer as the drink offering one-half a hin of wine as an offering by fire, as a soothing aroma to the
LORD.
11 ¶ 'Thus it shall be done for each ox,
or for each ram, or for each of the male
lambs, or of the goats.
12 'According to the number that you
prepare, so you shall do for everyone according to their number.
13 'All who are native shall do these
things in this manner, in presenting an
offering by fire, as a soothing aroma to the
LORD.

Law of the Sojourner

14 'If an alien sojourns with you, or one
who may be among you throughout your
generations, and he *wishes to* make an
offering by fire, as a soothing aroma to the
LORD, just as you do so he shall do.
15 '*As for* the assembly, there shall be
[a]one statute for you and for the alien
who sojourns *with you,* a perpetual statute throughout your generations; as you
are, so shall the alien be before the LORD.
16 'There is to be [a]one law and one
ordinance for you and for the alien who
sojourns with you.' "
17 ¶ Then the LORD spoke to Moses,
saying,
18 "Speak to the sons of Israel and say
to them, 'When you enter the land where
I bring you,
19 then it shall be, that when you eat
of the [1a]food of the land, you shall lift up
[2]an offering to the LORD.
20 '[a]Of the first of your [1]dough you
shall lift up a cake as an [2]offering; as
[b]the [2]offering of the threshing floor, so
you shall lift it up.
21 'From the first of your [1]dough
you shall give to the LORD an [2]offering
throughout your generations.
22 ¶ 'But when you [a]unwittingly fail
and do not observe all these commandments, which the LORD has spoken to
Moses,
23 *even* all that the LORD has commanded you [1]through Moses, from the
day when the LORD gave commandment
and onward throughout your generations,
24 then it shall be, if it is done [a]unin-
tentionally, [1]without the knowledge of
the congregation, that all the congregation shall offer one bull for a burnt offering, as a soothing aroma to the LORD,
[b]with its grain offering and its drink offering, according to the ordinance, and
one male goat for a sin offering.
25 'Then [a]the priest shall make atonement for all the congregation of the sons
of Israel, and they will be forgiven; for it
was an error, and they have brought their
offering, an offering by fire to the LORD,
and their sin offering before the LORD, for
their error.
26 'So all the congregation of the sons
of Israel will be forgiven, with the alien
who sojourns among them, for *it happened* to all the people through [a]error.
27 ¶ 'Also if one person sins [a]unin-
tentionally, then he shall offer a one year
old female goat for a sin offering.
28 '[a]The priest shall make atonement
before the LORD for the person who goes
astray when he sins unintentionally,
making atonement for him [1]that he may
be forgiven.
29 'You shall have one law for him who
does *anything* unintentionally, for him
who is native among the sons of Israel
and for the alien who sojourns among
them.
30 'But the person who does *anything*
[a]defiantly, whether he is native or an
alien, that one is blaspheming the LORD;
and that person shall be cut off from
among his people.
31 'Because he has [a]despised the word
of the LORD and has broken His commandment, that person shall be completely cut off; [b]his [1]guilt *will be*
on him.' "

Sabbath-breaking Punished

32 ¶ Now while the sons of Israel
were in the wilderness, they found a man
[a]gathering wood on the sabbath day.
33 Those who found him gathering
wood brought him to Moses and Aaron
and to all the congregation;
34 and they put him in [1]custody [a]be-
cause it had not been [2]declared what
should be done to him.

4 [1]I.e. Approx one gal., and so through v 10
5 [a]Lev 1:10; 3:6; Num 15:11
8 [1]Or *make a special votive offering* [a]Lev 1:3; 3:1
15 [a]Num 9:14; 15:29
16 [a]Lev 24:22
19 [1]Lit *bread* [2]Or *a heave offering* [a]Josh 5:11,12
20 [1]Or *coarse meal* [2]Or *heave offering* [a]Ex 34:26; Lev 23:14 [b]Deut 14:22,23; 16:13
21 [1]Or *coarse meal* [2]Or *offering lifted up*
22 [a]Lev 4:2
23 [1]Lit *by the hand of*
24 [1]Lit *from the eyes of the congregation* [a]Lev 4:2,22,27; 5:15,18 [b]Num 15:8-10
25 [a]Lev 4:20; Heb 2:17
26 [a]Num 15:24
27 [a]Lev 4:27-31; Luke 12:48
28 [1]Or *and he shall* [a]Lev 4:35
30 [a]Num 14:40-44; Deut 1:43; 17:12,13
31 [1]Or *iniquity* [a]2 Sam 12:9; Prov 13:13 [b]Ezek 18:20
32 [a]Ex 31:14,15; 35:2,3
34 [1]Or *prison* [2]Lit *declared distinctly* [a]Num 9:8

35 Then the LORD said to Moses, "The man shall surely be put to death; [a]all the congregation shall stone him with stones outside the camp."

36 So all the congregation brought him outside the camp and stoned him [1]to death with stones, just as the LORD had commanded Moses.

37 ¶ The LORD also spoke to Moses, saying,

38 "Speak to the sons of Israel, and tell them that they shall make for themselves [a]tassels on the corners of their garments throughout their generations, and that they shall put on the tassel of each corner a cord of blue.

39 "It shall be a tassel for you [1]to look at and [a]remember all the commandments of the LORD, so as to do them and not [2]follow after your own heart and your own eyes, after which you played the harlot,

40 so that you may remember to do all My commandments and [a]be holy to your God.

41 "I am the LORD your God who brought you out from the land of Egypt to be your God; I am the LORD your God."

Korah's Rebellion

16 Now [a]Korah the son of Izhar, the son of Kohath, the son of Levi, with [b]Dathan and Abiram, the sons of Eliab, and On the son of Peleth, sons of Reuben, took *action,*

2 and they rose up before Moses, [1]together with some of the sons of Israel, two hundred and fifty leaders of the congregation, [2a]chosen in the assembly, men of renown.

3 They assembled together [a]against Moses and Aaron, and said to them, "[1b]You have gone far enough, for all the congregation are holy, every one of them, and [c]the LORD is in their midst; so why do you exalt yourselves above the assembly of the LORD?"

4 ¶ When Moses heard *this,* [a]he fell on his face;

5 and he spoke to Korah and all his company, saying, "Tomorrow morning the LORD will show who is His, and [a]who is holy, and will bring *him* near to Himself; even [b]the one whom He will choose, He will bring near to Himself.

6 "Do this: take censers for yourselves, Korah and all [1]your company,

7 and put fire in them, and lay incense upon them in the presence of the LORD tomorrow; and the man whom the LORD chooses *shall be* the one who is holy. [1a]You have gone far enough, you sons of Levi!"

8 ¶ Then Moses said to Korah, "Hear now, you sons of Levi,

9 [a]is it [1]not enough for you that the God of Israel has separated you from the *rest of* the congregation of Israel, [b]to bring you near to Himself, to do the service of the tabernacle of the LORD, and to stand before the congregation to minister to them;

10 and that He has brought you near, *Korah,* and all your brothers, sons of Levi, with you? And are you [a]seeking for the priesthood also?

11 "Therefore you and all your company are gathered together [a]against the LORD; but as for Aaron, [1]who is he that [b]you grumble against him?"

12 ¶ Then Moses sent [1]a summons to Dathan and Abiram, the sons of Eliab; but they said, "We will not come up.

13 "Is it [1]not enough that you have brought us up out of a [a]land flowing with milk and honey [b]to have us die in the wilderness, but you would also lord it over us?

14 "Indeed, you have not brought us [a]into a land flowing with milk and honey, nor have you given us an inheritance of [b]fields and vineyards. Would you [1c]put out the eyes of [2]these men? We will not come up!"

15 ¶ Then Moses became very angry and said to the LORD, "[a]Do not regard their offering! [b]I have not taken a single donkey from them, nor have I done harm to any of them."

16 Moses said to Korah, "You and all your company be present before the LORD tomorrow, both you and they along with Aaron.

17 "Each of you take his firepan and put incense on [1]it, and each of you bring his censer before the LORD, two hundred and fifty firepans; also you and Aaron *shall* each *bring* his firepan."

18 So they each took his *own* censer and put fire on [1]it, and laid incense on [1]it; and they stood at the doorway of the tent of meeting, with Moses and Aaron.

19 Thus Korah assembled all the congregation against them at the doorway of the tent of meeting. And [a]the glory of the LORD appeared to all the congregation.

20 ¶ Then the LORD spoke to Moses and Aaron, saying,

21 "[a]Separate yourselves from among this congregation, [b]that I may consume them instantly."

22 But they fell on their faces and said, "O God, [a]God of the spirits of all flesh, [b]when one man sins, will You be angry with the entire congregation?"

23 ¶ Then the LORD spoke to Moses, saying,

35 [a]Lev 20:2, 27; 24:14-23; Deut 21:21
36 [1]Lit *with stones and he died*
38 [a]Deut 22:12; Matt 23:5
39 [1]Lit *and you shall look at it* [2]Lit *seek* [a]Deut 4:23; 6:12; 8:11, 14,19
40 [a]Lev 11:44, 45
16:1 [a]Ex 6:21; Jude 11 [b]Num 26:9; Deut 11:6
2 [1]Lit *and men from* [2]Lit *called ones of* [a]Num 1:16; 26:9
3 [1]Lit *It is much for you* [a]Num 12:2; Ps 106:16 [b]Num 16:7 [c]Num 5:3
4 [a]Num 14:5
5 [a]Lev 10:3; Ps 65:4 [b]Num 17:5, 8
6 [1]Lit *his*
7 [1]Lit *It is much for you* [a]Num 16:3
9 [1]Or *too little for you* [a]Is 7:13 [b]Num 3:6,9; Deut 10:8
10 [a]Num 3:10; 18:1-7
11 [1]Lit *what* [a]Ex 16:7 [b]1 Cor 10:10
12 [1]Lit *to call*
13 [1]Lit *a little thing* [a]Ex 16:3; Num 11:4-6 [b]Num 14:2,3
14 [1]Lit *bore out* [2]Lit *those* [a]Num 13:27; 14:8 [b]Ex 22:5; 23:10,11; Num 20:5 [c]Judg 16:21; 1 Sam 11:2
15 [a]Gen 4:4,5 [b]1 Sam 12:3
17 [1]Lit *them*
18 [1]Lit *them*
19 [a]Num 14:10; 16:42; 20:6
21 [a]Num 16:45 [b]Ex 32:10,12
22 [a]Num 27:16 [b]Gen 18:23-32; Lev 4:3

24 "Speak to the congregation, saying,
'[a]Get back from around the dwellings of
Korah, Dathan and Abiram.' "
25 ¶ Then Moses arose and went to
Dathan and Abiram, with the elders of
Israel following him,
26 and he spoke to the congregation,
saying, "[a]Depart now from the tents of
these wicked men, and touch nothing
that belongs to them, [b]or you will be
swept away in all their sin."
27 So they got back from around the
dwellings of Korah, Dathan and Abiram;
and Dathan and Abiram came out *and*
stood at the doorway of their tents, along
with their wives and [a]their sons and
their little ones.
28 Moses said, "By this you shall know
that [a]the LORD has sent me to do all these
deeds; for this is not [1]my doing.
29 "If these men die [1]the death of all
men or [2]if they suffer the [a]fate of all
men, *then* the LORD has not sent me.
30 "But [a]if the LORD [1]brings about an
entirely new thing and the ground opens
its mouth and swallows them up with all
that is theirs, and they [b]descend alive
into [2]Sheol, then you will understand
that these men have spurned the LORD."
31 ¶ As he finished speaking all these
words, the ground that was under them
split open;
32 and [a]the earth opened its mouth
and swallowed them up, and their households, and [b]all the men who belonged to
Korah with *their* possessions.
33 So they and all that belonged to
them went down alive to [1]Sheol; and the
earth closed over them, and they perished from the midst of the assembly.
34 All Israel who *were* around them
fled at their [1]outcry, for they said, "The
earth may swallow us up!"
35 [a]Fire also came forth from the
LORD and consumed the [b]two hundred
and fifty men who were offering the incense.
36 ¶ [1]Then the LORD spoke to Moses,
saying,
37 "Say to Eleazar, the son of Aaron the
priest, that he shall take up the censers
out of the midst of the [1]blaze, for they
are holy; and you scatter the [2]burning
coals abroad.
38 "As for the censers of these [1]men
who have sinned at the cost of their lives,
let them be made into hammered sheets
for a plating of the altar, since they did
present them before the LORD and they
are holy; and [a]they shall be for a sign to
the sons of Israel."
39 So Eleazar the priest took the
bronze censers which the men who were
burned had offered, and they hammered
them out as a plating for the altar,
40 as a [1]reminder to the sons of Israel
that [a]no [2]layman who is not of the
[3]descendants of Aaron should come near
[b]to burn incense before the LORD; so that
he will not become like Korah and his
company—just as the LORD had spoken to
him [4]through Moses.

Murmuring and Plague

41 ¶ But on the next day all the congregation of the sons of Israel [a]grumbled
against Moses and Aaron, saying, "You
are the ones who have caused the death
of the LORD's people."
42 It came about, however, when the
congregation had assembled against Moses and Aaron, that they turned toward
the tent of meeting, and behold, the
cloud covered it and [a]the glory of the
LORD appeared.
43 Then Moses and Aaron came to the
front of the tent of meeting,
44 and the LORD spoke to Moses, saying,
45 "[1][a]Get away from among this congregation, that I may consume them instantly." Then they fell on their faces.
46 Moses said to Aaron, "Take your
censer and put in it fire from the altar,
and lay incense *on it;* then bring it quickly to the congregation and [a]make atonement for them, for [b]wrath has gone forth
from the LORD, the plague has begun!"
47 Then Aaron took *it* as Moses had
spoken, and ran into the midst of the assembly, for behold, the plague had begun
among the people. [a]So he put *on* the
incense and made atonement for the people.
48 He took his stand between the dead
and the living, so that the plague was
checked.
49 [a]But those who died by the plague
were 14,700, besides those who [b]died
on account of Korah.
50 Then Aaron returned to Moses at
the doorway of the tent of meeting, for
the plague had been checked.

Aaron's Rod Buds

17 [1]Then the LORD spoke to Moses,
saying,
2 "Speak to the sons of Israel, and get
from them a rod for each father's household: twelve rods, from all their leaders
according to their fathers' households.
You shall write each name on his rod,
3 and write Aaron's name on the rod
of Levi; for there is one rod for the head
of each of their fathers' households.
4 "You shall then deposit them in the

24 [a]Num 16:45
26 [a]Is 52:11 [b]Gen 19:15,17
27 [a]Num 26:11
28 [1]Lit *from my heart* [a]Ex 3:12-15; 4:12,15
29 [1]Lit *like the death* [2]Lit *the visitation of all men be visited upon them* [a]Eccl 3:19
30 [1]Lit *creates a new creation* [2]I.e. the nether world [a]Job 31:2, 3 [b]Ps 55:15
32 [a]Num 26:10; Deut 11:6; Ps 106:17 [b]Num 26:11
33 [1]I.e. the nether world
34 [1]Or *voice*
35 [a]Num 11:1-3; 26:10 [b]Num 16:2
36 [1]Ch 17:1 in Heb
37 [1]Or *place of burning* [2]Lit *the fire*
38 [1]Lit *sinners against their lives* [a]Ezek 14:8; 2 Pet 2:6
40 [1]Or *memorial* [2]Lit *stranger* [3]Lit *seed* [4]Lit *by the hand of* [a]Num 1:51 [b]Ex 30:7-10
41 [a]Num 16:3
42 [a]Num 16:19
45 [1]Or *Arise* [a]Num 16:21,24
46 [a]Num 25:13; Is 6:6,7 [b]Num 18:5; Deut 9:22
47 [a]Num 25:6-8,13
49 [a]Num 25:9 [b]Num 16:32,35
17:1 [1]Ch 17:16 in Heb

tent of meeting in front of [a]the testimony, where I meet with you.

5 "It will come about that the rod of [a]the man whom I choose will sprout. Thus I will lessen from upon Myself the grumblings of the sons of Israel, who are grumbling against you."

6 Moses therefore spoke to the sons of Israel, and all their leaders gave him a rod apiece, for each leader according to their fathers' households, twelve rods, with the rod of Aaron among their rods.

7 So Moses deposited the rods before the LORD in [a]the tent of the testimony.

8 ¶ Now on the next day Moses went into the tent of the testimony; and behold, [a]the rod of Aaron for the house of Levi had sprouted and put forth buds and produced blossoms, and it bore ripe almonds.

9 Moses then brought out all the rods from the presence of the LORD to all the sons of Israel; and they looked, and each man took his rod.

10 But the LORD said to Moses, "Put back the rod of Aaron [a]before the testimony [1]to be kept as a sign against the [2b]rebels, that you may put an end to their grumblings against Me, so that they will not die."

11 Thus Moses did; just as the LORD had commanded him, so he did.

12 ¶ Then the sons of Israel spoke to Moses, saying, "[a]Behold, we perish, we are dying, we are all dying!

13 "[a]Everyone who comes near, who comes near to the tabernacle of the LORD, must die. Are we to perish completely?"

Duties of Levites

18 So the LORD said to Aaron, "You and your sons and your father's household with you shall [a]bear the guilt [1]in connection with the sanctuary, and you and your sons with you shall bear the guilt [2]in connection with your priesthood.

2 "But bring with you also your brothers, the tribe of Levi, the tribe of your father, that they may be [a]joined with you and serve you, while you and your sons with you are before the tent of the testimony.

3 "And they shall thus attend to your obligation and the obligation of all the tent, but [a]they shall not come near to the furnishings of the sanctuary and [b]the altar, or both they and you will die.

4 "They shall be joined with you and attend to the obligations of the tent of meeting, for all the service of the tent; but an [1]outsider may not come near you.

5 "So you shall attend to the [a]obligations of the sanctuary and the obligations of the altar, [b]so that there will no longer be wrath on the sons of Israel.

6 "Behold, I Myself [a]have taken your [1]fellow Levites from among the sons of Israel; they are [b]a gift to you, [2]dedicated to the LORD, to perform the service for the tent of meeting.

7 "But you and your sons with you shall [a]attend to your priesthood for everything concerning the altar and inside the veil, and you are to perform service. I am giving you the priesthood as [b]a [1]bestowed service, but [c]the [2]outsider who comes near shall be put to death."

The Priests' Portion

8 ¶ Then the LORD spoke to Aaron, "Now behold, I Myself have given you charge of My [1a]offerings, even all the holy gifts of the sons of Israel I have given them to you as a portion and to your sons as a perpetual allotment.

9 "This shall be yours from the most holy *gifts reserved* from the fire; every offering of theirs, even [a]every grain offering and every [b]sin offering and every guilt offering, which they shall render to Me, shall be most holy for you and for your sons.

10 "As the most holy *gifts* you shall eat it; every male shall eat it. It shall be holy to you.

11 "This also is yours, [a]the offering of their gift, even all the wave offerings of the sons of Israel; I have [b]given them to you and to your sons and daughters with you as a perpetual allotment. Everyone of your household who is clean may eat it.

12 "[a]All the [1]best of the fresh oil and all the [1]best of the fresh wine and of the grain, the first fruits of those which they give to the LORD, I give them to you.

13 "[a]The first ripe fruits of all that is in their land, which they bring to the LORD, shall be yours; everyone of your household who is clean may eat it.

14 "[a]Every devoted thing in Israel shall be yours.

15 "[1a]Every first issue of the womb of all flesh, whether man or animal, which they offer to the LORD, shall be yours; nevertheless the firstborn of man you shall surely redeem, and the firstborn of unclean animals you shall redeem.

16 "As to their redemption price, from a month old you shall redeem them, by your valuation, five [1]shekels in silver, according to the [1]shekel of the sanctuary, which is twenty gerahs.

17 "But [a]the firstborn of an ox or the firstborn of a sheep or the firstborn of a goat, you shall not redeem; they are holy. [b]You shall sprinkle their blood on the altar and shall offer up their fat in smoke

4 [a]Ex 25:16,21, 22; Num 17:7
5 [a]Num 16:5
7 [a]Num 1:50, 53; 9:15
8 [a]Ezek 17:24; Heb 9:4
10 [1]Lit *for preserving* [2]Lit *sons of rebellion* [a]Num 17:4 [b]Deut 9:7,24
12 [a]Is 6:5
13 [a]Num 1:51
18:1 [1]Lit *of the sanctuary* [2]Lit *of your priesthood* [a]Ex 28:38; Lev 10:17; 22:16
2 [a]Num 3:5-10
3 [a]Num 4:15-20 [b]Num 1:51; 18:7
4 [1]Lit *a stranger*
5 [a]Ex 27:21; Lev 24:3 [b]Num 16:46
6 [1]Lit *brethren the* [2]Lit *given* [a]Num 3:12,45 [b]Num 3:9
7 [1]Lit *service of gift* [2]Lit *stranger* [a]Ex 29:9 [b]Num 18:20; Deut 18:2; Matt 10:8; 1 Pet 5:2,3 [c]Num 1:51
8 [1]Lit *heave offerings*, and so throughout the ch [a]Lev 6:16,18; 7:28-34
9 [a]Lev 2:1-16 [b]Lev 6:30
11 [a]Num 18:1; Deut 18:3 [b]Lev 22:1-16
12 [1]Lit *fat* [a]Deut 18:4; 32:14; Ps 81:16; 147:14
13 [a]Ex 22:29; 23:19; 34:26
14 [a]Lev 27:1-33
15 [1]Lit *Everything that opens* [a]Ex 13:13,15; Num 3:46
16 [1]I.e. A shekel equals approx one-half oz
17 [a]Deut 15:19 [b]Lev 3:2

as an offering by fire, for a soothing aroma to the LORD.
18 "Their [1]meat shall be yours; it shall
be yours like the [a]breast of a wave offering and like the right thigh.
19 "[a]All the offerings of the holy *gifts,*
which the sons of Israel offer to the LORD,
I have given to you and your sons and
your daughters with you, as a perpetual
allotment. It is [b]an everlasting covenant
of salt before the LORD to you and your
[1]descendants with you."
20 Then the LORD said to Aaron,
"[a]You shall have no inheritance in their
land nor own any portion among them;
[b]I am your portion and your inheritance
among the sons of Israel.
21 ¶ "To the sons of Levi, behold, I
have given all the [a]tithe in Israel for an
inheritance, in return for their service
which they perform, the service of the
tent of meeting.
22 "[a]The sons of Israel shall not come
near the tent of meeting again, or they
will bear sin and die.
23 "Only the Levites shall perform the
service of the tent of meeting, and they
shall [a]bear their iniquity; it shall be a
perpetual statute throughout your generations, and among the sons of Israel
[b]they shall have no inheritance.
24 "For the tithe of the sons of Israel,
which they offer as an offering to the
LORD, I have given to the Levites for an
inheritance; therefore I have said concerning them, '[a]They shall have no inheritance among the sons of Israel.' "
25 ¶ Then the LORD spoke to Moses,
saying,
26 "Moreover, you shall speak to the
Levites and say to them, 'When you take
from the sons of Israel [a]the tithe which
I have given you from them for your inheritance, then you shall present an offering from it to the LORD, a [b]tithe of the
tithe.
27 'Your offering shall be reckoned to
you as the grain from the threshing floor
or the full produce from the wine vat.
28 'So you shall also present an offering
to the LORD from your tithes, which you
receive from the sons of Israel; and from
it you shall give the LORD'S offering to
Aaron the priest.
29 'Out of all your gifts you shall
present every offering due to the LORD,
from all the [1]best of them, [2]the sacred
part from them.'
30 "You shall say to them, 'When you
have [1]offered from it the best of it, then
the rest shall be reckoned to the Levites
as the product of the threshing floor, and
as the product of the wine vat.
31 'You may eat it anywhere, you and
your households, for it is your compensa-
tion in return for your service in the tent
of meeting.
32 'You will bear no sin by reason of it
when you have [1]offered the [2]best of it.
But you shall not [a]profane the sacred
gifts of the sons of Israel, or you
will die.' "

Ordinance of the Red Heifer

19 Then the LORD spoke to Moses
and Aaron, saying,
2 "This is the statute of the law which
the LORD has commanded, saying, 'Speak
to the sons of Israel that they bring you an
[a]unblemished red heifer in which is no
defect *and* [b]on which a yoke has never
[1]been placed.
3 'You shall give it to [a]Eleazar the
priest, and it shall [b]be brought outside
the camp and be slaughtered in his presence.
4 'Next Eleazar the priest shall take
some of its blood with his finger and
[a]sprinkle some of its blood toward the
front of the tent of meeting seven times.
5 'Then the heifer shall be burned in
his sight; [a]its hide and its flesh and its
blood, with its refuse, shall be burned.
6 'The priest shall take [a]cedar wood
and hyssop and scarlet *material* and cast
it into the midst of the [1]burning heifer.
7 'The priest [a]shall then wash his
clothes and bathe his [1]body in water,
and afterward come into the camp, but
the priest shall be unclean until evening.
8 'The one who burns it shall also
wash his clothes in water and bathe his
[1]body in water, and shall be unclean until evening.
9 'Now a man who is clean shall gather up the ashes of the heifer and deposit
them outside the camp in a clean place,
and [1]the congregation of the sons of Israel shall keep it as [a]water to remove impurity; it is [2]purification from sin.
10 'The one who gathers the ashes of
the heifer [a]shall wash his clothes and be
unclean until evening; and it shall be a
perpetual statute to the sons of Israel and
to the alien who sojourns among them.
11 ¶ '[a]The one who touches the
corpse of any [1]person shall be unclean
for seven days.
12 'That one shall [a]purify himself from
uncleanness with [1]the water on the third
day and on the seventh day, *and then* he
will be clean; but if he does not purify
himself on the third day and on the seventh day, he will not be clean.
13 '[a]Anyone who touches a corpse,
the [1]body of a man who has died, and
does not purify himself, [b]defiles the
[2]tabernacle of the LORD; and that person

18 [1]Lit *flesh* [a]Lev 7:31
19 [1]Lit *seed* [a]Num 18:11 [b]2 Chr 13:5
20 [a]Deut 10:9; 12:12; 14:27,29 [b]Deut 18:2; Josh 13:33; Ezek 44:28
21 [a]Lev 27:30-33; Deut 14:22-29
22 [a]Num 1:51
23 [a]Num 18:1 [b]Num 18:20
24 [a]Deut 10:9
26 [a]Num 18:21 [b]Neh 10:38
29 [1]Lit *fat* [2]Lit *its*
30 [1]Lit *lifted*
32 [1]Lit *lifted* [2]Lit *fat* [a]Lev 22:15,16
19:2 [1]Lit *come up* [a]Lev 22:20-25 [b]Deut 21:3
3 [a]Num 3:4 [b]Lev 4:11,12,21; Num 19:9
4 [a]Lev 4:6,17; 16:14
5 [a]Ex 29:14; Lev 4:11,12
6 [1]Lit *burning of the heifer* [a]Lev 14:4
7 [1]Lit *flesh* [a]Lev 16:26,28; 22:6
8 [1]Lit *flesh*
9 [1]Lit *it shall be to the congregation... Israel, for a guarding as water of impurity* [2]Or *a sin offering* [a]Num 8:7; 31:23
10 [a]Num 19:7
11 [1]Lit *soul of man* [a]Lev 21:1, 11; Num 5:2; 6:6; Acts 21:26, 27
12 [1]Lit *it* [a]Num 19:19; 31:19
13 [1]Lit *soul* [2]Lit *dwelling place* [a]Lev 7:21; 22:3-7 [b]Lev 15:31; 20:3; Num 19:20

shall be cut off from Israel. Because the
water for impurity was not [3c]sprinkled
on him, he shall be unclean; his uncleanness is still on him.
14 ¶ 'This is the law when a man dies
in a tent: everyone who comes into the
tent and everyone who is in the tent shall
be unclean for seven days.
15 'Every open vessel, which has no
covering [1]tied down on it, shall be unclean.
16 '[a]Also, anyone who in the open
field touches one who has been slain with
a sword or who has died *naturally,* or a
human bone or a grave, shall be unclean
for seven days.
17 'Then for the unclean *person* they
shall take some of the [1]ashes of the
[2]burnt [3a]purification from sin and
[4]flowing water shall be [5]added to them
in a vessel.
18 'A clean person shall take hyssop
and dip *it* in the water, and sprinkle *it* on
the tent and on all the furnishings and on
the persons who were there, and on the
one who touched the bone or the one
slain or the one dying *naturally* or the
grave.
19 'Then the clean *person* [a]shall sprinkle on the unclean on the third day and
on the seventh day; and on the seventh
day he shall purify him from uncleanness,
and he shall wash his clothes and bathe
himself in water and shall be clean by
evening.
20 ¶ 'But the man who is unclean and
does not purify himself from uncleanness, that person shall be cut off from the
midst of the assembly, because he has
[a]defiled the sanctuary of the LORD; the
water for impurity has not been sprinkled
on him, he is unclean.
21 'So it shall be a perpetual statute for
them. And he [a]who sprinkles the water
for impurity shall wash his clothes, and
he who touches the water for impurity
shall be unclean until evening.
22 '[a]Furthermore, anything that the
unclean *person* touches shall be unclean;
and the person who touches *it* shall be
unclean until evening.' "

Death of Miriam

20 Then the sons of Israel, the whole
congregation, came to the [a]wil-
derness of Zin in the first month; and the
people stayed at Kadesh. Now Miriam
died there and was buried there.
2 ¶ [a]There was no water for the congregation, [b]and they assembled themselves against Moses and Aaron.
3 [a]The people thus contended with
Moses and spoke, saying, "[b]If only we
had perished [c]when our brothers perished before the LORD!
4 "[a]Why then have you brought the
LORD'S assembly into this wilderness, for
us and our beasts to die [1]here?
5 "Why have you made us come up
from Egypt, to bring us in to this wretched place? [a]It is not a place of [1]grain
or figs or vines or pomegranates, nor is
there water to drink."
6 Then Moses and Aaron came in
from the presence of the assembly to the
doorway of the tent of meeting and [a]fell
on their faces. Then the glory of the LORD
appeared to them;
7 and the LORD spoke to Moses, saying,

The Water of Meribah

8 "Take [a]the rod; and you and your
brother Aaron assemble the congregation
and speak to the rock before their eyes,
that it may yield its water. You shall thus
bring forth water for them out of the rock
and let the congregation and their beasts
drink."
9 ¶ So Moses took the rod [a]from before the LORD, just as He had commanded
him;
10 and Moses and Aaron gathered the
assembly before the rock. And he said to
them, "[a]Listen now, you rebels; shall
we bring forth water for you out of this
rock?"
11 Then Moses lifted up his hand and
struck the rock twice with his rod; and
[a]water came forth abundantly, and the
congregation and their beasts drank.
12 But the LORD said to Moses and Aaron, "[a]Because you have not believed Me,
to treat Me as holy in the sight of the sons
of Israel, therefore you shall not bring this
assembly into the land which I have giv-
en them."
13 Those *were* the waters of [1a]Meri-
bah, [2]because the sons of Israel contended with the LORD, and He proved Himself
holy among them.
14 ¶ From Kadesh Moses then sent
messengers to [a]the king of Edom: "Thus
your brother Israel has said, 'You [b]know
all the hardship that has befallen us;
15 that our fathers went down to
Egypt, and we stayed in Egypt a long
time, and the Egyptians treated us and
our fathers badly.
16 'But [a]when we cried out to the
LORD, He heard our voice and sent [b]an
angel and brought us out from Egypt; now
behold, we are at Kadesh, a town on the
edge of your territory.
17 'Please [a]let us pass through your
land. We will not pass through field or
through vineyard; we will not even drink

13 [3]Or *thrown* [c]Num 19:19
15 [1]Lit *cord*
16 [a]Num 31:19
17 [1]Lit *dust* [2]Lit *burning of the* [3]Or *sin offering* [4]Lit *living* [5]Lit *put* [a]Num 19:9
19 [a]Ezek 36:25; Heb 10:22
20 [a]Num 19:13
21 [a]Num 19:7
22 [a]Lev 5:2,3; 7:21; 22:5,6
20:1 [a]Num 13:21; 27:14; 33:36
2 [a]Ex 17:1 [b]Num 16:19,42
3 [a]Ex 17:2 [b]Num 14:2,3 [c]Num 16:31-35
4 [1]Lit *there* [a]Ex 17:3
5 [1]Lit *seed* [a]Num 16:14
6 [a]Num 14:5
8 [a]Ex 4:17,20; 17:5,6
9 [a]Num 17:10
10 [a]Ps 106:33
11 [a]Ps 78:16; Is 48:21; 1 Cor 10:4
12 [a]Num 20:24; 27:14; Deut 1:37; 3:26,27
13 [1]I.e. contention [2]Or *where* [a]Ex 17:7; Ps 95:8
14 [a]Gen 36:31-39; Deut 2:4 [b]Josh 2:9,10; 9:9,10,24
16 [a]Ex 2:23; 3:7 [b]Ex 14:19
17 [a]Num 21:22

water from a well. We will go along the
king's highway, not turning to the right
or left, until we pass through your territory.'"
18 ¶ [a]Edom, however, said to him,
"You shall not pass through [1]us, or I will
come out with the sword against you."
19 Again, the sons of Israel said to
him, "We will go up by the highway, and
if I and [a]my livestock do drink any of
your water, [b]then I will [1]pay its price.
Let me only pass through on my feet,
[2]nothing *else.*"
20 But he said, "[a]You shall not pass
through." And Edom came out against
him with a heavy [1]force and with a
strong hand.
21 [a]Thus Edom refused to allow Israel
to pass through his territory; [b]so Israel
turned away from him.
22 ¶ Now when they set out from
[a]Kadesh, the sons of Israel, the whole
congregation, came to Mount Hor.

Death of Aaron

23 Then the LORD spoke to Moses and
Aaron at [a]Mount Hor by the border of
the land of Edom, saying,
24 "Aaron will be [a]gathered to his people; for he shall not enter the land which
I have given to the sons of Israel, because
[b]you rebelled against My [1]command at
the waters of Meribah.
25 "Take Aaron and his son [a]Eleazar
and bring them up to Mount Hor;
26 and strip Aaron of his garments and
put them on his son Eleazar. So Aaron
will be [a]gathered *to his people,* and will
die there."
27 So Moses did just as the LORD had
commanded, and they went up to Mount
Hor in the sight of all the congregation.
28 After Moses had stripped Aaron of
his garments and [a]put them on his son
Eleazar, [b]Aaron died there on the mountain top. Then Moses and Eleazar came
down from the mountain.
29 When all the congregation saw that
Aaron had died, all the house of Israel
wept for Aaron thirty [a]days.

Arad Conquered

21 When the Canaanite, the king of
[a]Arad, who lived in the [1]Negev,
heard that Israel was coming by the way
of [2]Atharim, then he fought against Israel and took some of them captive.
2 So [a]Israel made a vow to the LORD
and said, "If You will indeed deliver this
people into my hand, then I will [1]utterly
destroy their cities."
3 The LORD heard the voice of Israel
and delivered up the Canaanites; then
they [1]utterly destroyed them and their
cities. Thus the name of the place was
called [2a]Hormah.
4 ¶ Then they set out from Mount
Hor by the way of the [1]Red Sea, to [a]go
around the land of Edom; and the [2]peo-
ple became impatient because of the journey.
5 The people spoke against God and
Moses, "[a]Why have you brought us up
out of Egypt to die in the wilderness? For
there is no [1]food and no water, and
[2b]we loathe this miserable food."

The Bronze Serpent

6 [a]The LORD sent fiery serpents
among the people and [b]they bit the people, so that [c]many people of Israel died.
7 [a]So the people came to Moses and
said, "We have sinned, because we have
spoken against the LORD and you; [b]inter-
cede with the LORD, that He may remove
the serpents from us." And Moses interceded for the people.
8 Then the LORD said to Moses,
"[1]Make a [a]fiery *serpent,* and set it on a
standard; and it shall come about, that
everyone who is bitten, when he looks at
it, he will live."
9 And Moses made a [a]bronze serpent and set it on the standard; and it
came about, that if a serpent bit any man,
when he looked to the bronze serpent, he
lived.
10 ¶ [a]Now the sons of Israel moved
out and camped in Oboth.
11 They journeyed from Oboth and
camped at Iyeabarim, in the wilderness
which is opposite Moab, to the [1]east.
12 [a]From there they set out and
camped in [1]Wadi Zered.
13 From there they journeyed and
camped on the other side of the Arnon,
which is in the wilderness that comes out
of the border of the Amorites, [a]for the
Arnon is the border of Moab, between
Moab and the Amorites.
14 Therefore it is said in the Book of
the Wars of the LORD,
"Waheb in Suphah,
And the wadis of the Arnon,
15 And the slope of the wadis
That extends to the site of [a]Ar,
And leans to the border of
Moab."
16 ¶ [a]From there *they continued* to
[1]Beer, that is the well where the LORD
said to Moses, "Assemble the people, that
I may give them water."
17 ¶ [a]Then Israel sang this song:
"Spring up, O well! Sing to it!
18 "The well, which the leaders
sank,
Which the nobles of the people
dug,

---

18 [1]Lit *me* [a]Num 24:18
19 [1]Lit *give* [2]Or *no great thing* [a]Ex 12:38 [b]Deut 2:6,28
20 [1]Lit *people* [a]Judg 11:17
21 [a]Judg 11:17 [b]Deut 2:8
22 [a]Num 20:1, 14
23 [a]Num 33:37
24 [1]Lit *mouth* [a]Gen 25:8 [b]Num 20:5,10
25 [a]Num 3:4
26 [a]Num 20:24
28 [a]Ex 29:29 [b]Num 33:38; Deut 10:6; 32:50
29 [a]Gen 1:5; 50:3,10; Deut 34:8
21:1 [1]I.e. South country [2]Or *the spies* [a]Num 33:40; Josh 12:14; Judg 1:16
2 [1]Lit *devote to destruction* [a]Gen 28:20; Judg 11:30
3 [1]Lit *devoted to destruction* [2]I.e. a devoted thing; or Destruction [a]Num 14:45
4 [1]Lit *Sea of Reeds* [2]Lit *soul of the people was short* [a]Deut 2:8
5 [1]Lit *bread* [2]Lit *our soul loathes* [a]Num 14:2,3 [b]Num 11:6
6 [a]Deut 8:15 [b]Jer 8:17 [c]1 Cor 10:9
7 [a]Num 11:2; Ps 78:34; Is 26:16; Hos 5:15 [b]Ex 8:8; 1 Sam 12:19; Acts 8:24
8 [1]Lit *Make for yourself* [a]Is 14:29; 30:6; John 3:14
9 [a]2 Kin 18:4; John 3:14,15
10 [a]Num 33:43, 44
11 [1]Lit *sunrise*
12 [1]I.e. a dry ravine except during rainy season [a]Num 33:45
13 [a]Num 22:36; Judg 11:18
15 [a]Num 21:28; Deut 2:9,18,29
16 [1]I.e. a well [a]Num 33:46-49
17 [a]Ex 15:1; Ps 105:2

With the scepter *and* with their
staffs."
And from the wilderness *they continued*
to Mattanah,
19 and from Mattanah to Nahaliel, and
from Nahaliel to Bamoth,
20 and from Bamoth to the valley that
is in the land of Moab, at the top of Pisgah
which overlooks the [1]wasteland.

Two Victories

21 ¶ [a]Then Israel sent messengers to
Sihon, king of the Amorites, saying,
22 "[a]Let me pass through your land.
We will not turn off into field or vineyard;
we will not drink water from wells. We
will go by the king's highway until we
have passed through your border."
23 [a]But Sihon would not permit Israel
to pass through his border. So Sihon gathered all his people and went out against
Israel in the wilderness, and came to [b]Ja-
haz and fought against Israel.
24 Then [a]Israel [1]struck him with the
edge of the sword, and took possession of
his land from the Arnon to the Jabbok, as
far as the sons of Ammon; for the [b]border
of the sons of Ammon *was* [2]Jazer.
25 Israel took all these cities and [a]Is-
rael lived in all the cities of the Amorites,
in Heshbon, and in all her [1]villages.
26 For Heshbon was the city of Sihon,
king of the Amorites, who had fought
against the former king of Moab and had
taken all his land out of his hand, as far as
the Arnon.
27 Therefore those who use proverbs
say,
"Come to Heshbon! Let it be
built!
So let the city of Sihon be
established.
28 "[a]For a fire went forth from
Heshbon,
A flame from the town of Sihon;
It devoured [b]Ar of Moab,
The [1][c]dominant [2]heights of the
Arnon.
29 "[a]Woe to you, O Moab!
You are ruined, O people of
[b]Chemosh!
[c]He has given his sons as
fugitives,
[d]And his daughters into
captivity,
To an Amorite king, Sihon.
30 "But we have cast them down,
Heshbon is ruined as far as
[a]Dibon,
Then we have laid waste even to
Nophah,
Which *reaches* to Medeba."
31 ¶ Thus Israel lived in the land of
the Amorites.

32 Moses sent to spy out [a]Jazer, and
they captured its villages and dispossessed the Amorites who *were* there.
33 ¶ [a]Then they turned and went up
by the way of Bashan, and Og the king of
Bashan went out [1]with all his people, for
battle at [b]Edrei.
34 But the LORD said to Moses, "[a]Do
not fear him, for I have given him into
your hand, and all his people and his
land; and you shall do to him as you did
to Sihon, king of the Amorites, who lived
at Heshbon."
35 So [a]they [1]killed him and his sons
and all his people, until there was no
remnant left him; and they possessed his
land.

Balak Sends for Balaam

22 [a]Then the sons of Israel journeyed, and camped in the plains
of Moab beyond the Jordan *opposite* Jericho.
2 ¶ Now [a]Balak the son of Zippor
saw all that Israel had done to the Amorites.
3 [a]So Moab was in great fear because
of the people, for they were numerous;
and Moab was in dread of the sons of
Israel.
4 Moab said to the elders of [a]Midian,
"Now this [1]horde will lick up all that is
around us, as the ox licks up the grass of
the field." And Balak the son of Zippor
was king of Moab at that time.
5 So he sent messengers to [a]Balaam
the son of Beor, at [b]Pethor, which is near
the [1]River, *in* the land of the sons of his
people, to call him, saying, "Behold, a
people came out of Egypt; behold, they
cover the surface of the land, and they are
living opposite me.
6 "[a]Now, therefore, please come,
[b]curse this people for me since they are
too [1]mighty for me; perhaps I may be
able to [2]defeat them and drive them out
of the land. For I know that he whom you
bless is blessed, and he whom you curse
is cursed."
7 ¶ So the elders of Moab and the
elders of Midian departed with the *fees
for* [a]divination in their hand; and they
came to Balaam and [1]repeated Balak's
words to him.
8 He said to them, "Spend the night
here, and I will bring word back to you as
the LORD may speak to me." And the leaders of Moab stayed with Balaam.
9 Then [a]God came to Balaam and
said, "Who are these men with you?"
10 Balaam said to God, "Balak the son
of Zippor, king of Moab, has sent *word*
to me,
11 'Behold, there is a people who came

20 [1]Or *Jeshimon*
21 [a]Deut 2:26-37; Judg 11:19
22 [a]Num 20:16, 17
23 [a]Num 20:21 [b]Deut 2:32
24 [1]Lit *smote,* so with Gr and Lat [2]M.T. reads *strong* [a]Amos 2:9 [b]Deut 2:37
25 [1]Lit *daughters* [a]Amos 2:10
28 [1]Lit *lords of the* [2]Or *Bamoth* [a]Jer 48:45 [b]Num 21:15 [c]Num 22:41; Is 15:2; 16:12
29 [a]Jer 48:46 [b]Judg 11:24; 1 Kin 11:33; 2 Kin 23:13 [c]Is 15:5 [d]Is 16:2
30 [a]Num 32:3, 34; Jer 48:18,22
32 [a]Num 32:1, 3,35; Jer 48:32
33 [1]Lit *he and* [a]Deut 3:1-7 [b]Josh 13:12
34 [a]Deut 3:2
35 [1]Lit *smote* [a]Deut 3:3,4
22:1 [a]Num 33:48,49
2 [a]Judg 11:25
3 [a]Ex 15:15
4 [1]Lit *assembly* [a]Num 25:15-18; 31:1-3
5 [1]I.e. Euphrates [a]Josh 24:9; 2 Pet 2:15f; Jude 11 [b]Deut 23:4
6 [1]Or *numerous* [2]Lit *smite* [a]Num 22:17; 23:7,8 [b]Num 22:12; 24:9
7 [1]Lit *spoke* [a]Num 23:23; 24:1; Josh 13:22
9 [a]Gen 20:3

out of Egypt and they cover the surface of
the land; now come, curse them for me;
perhaps I may be able to fight against
them and drive them out.' "
12 God said to Balaam, "Do not go
with them; [a]you shall not curse the people, for they [b]are blessed."
13 So Balaam arose in the morning and
said to Balak's leaders, "Go back to your
land, for the LORD has refused to let me
go with you."
14 The leaders of Moab arose and
went to Balak and said, "Balaam refused
to come with us."
15 ¶ Then Balak again sent leaders,
more numerous and more distinguished
than [1]the former.
16 They came to Balaam and said to
him, "Thus says Balak the son of Zippor,
'Let nothing, I beg you, hinder you from
coming to me;
17 for I will indeed honor you richly,
and I will do whatever you say to me.
[a]Please come then, curse this people
for me.' "
18 Balaam replied to the servants of
Balak, "[a]Though Balak were to give me
his house full of silver and gold, I could
not do anything, either small or great,
contrary to the [1]command of the LORD
my God.
19 "Now please, you also stay here tonight, and I will find out what else the
LORD will speak to me."
20 God came to Balaam at night and
said to him, "If the men have come to call
you, rise up *and* go with them; but [a]only
the word which I speak to you shall
you do."
21 ¶ [a]So Balaam arose in the morning, and saddled his donkey and went
with the leaders of Moab.

The Angel and Balaam

22 But God was angry because he was
going, [a]and the angel of the LORD took
his stand in the way as an adversary
against him. Now he was riding on his
donkey and his two servants were with
him.
23 When the donkey saw the angel of
the LORD standing in the way with his
drawn sword in his hand, the donkey
turned off from the way and went into the
field; but Balaam struck the donkey to
turn her back into the way.
24 Then the angel of the LORD stood in
a narrow path of the vineyards, *with* a
wall on this side and a wall on that side.
25 When the donkey saw the angel of
the LORD, she pressed herself to the wall
and pressed Balaam's foot against the
wall, so he struck her again.
26 The angel of the LORD went further,
and stood in a narrow place where there
was no way to turn to the right hand or
the left.
27 When the donkey saw the angel of
the LORD, she lay down under Balaam; so
[a]Balaam was angry and struck the donkey with his stick.
28 And [a]the LORD opened the mouth
of the donkey, and she said to Balaam,
"What have I done to you, that you have
struck me these three times?"
29 Then Balaam said to the donkey,
"Because you have made a mockery of
me! If there had been a sword in my
hand, [a]I would have killed you by now."
30 The donkey said to Balaam, "Am I
not your donkey on which you have ridden all your life to this day? Have I ever
been accustomed to do so to you?" And
he said, "No."
31 ¶ Then the LORD opened the eyes
of Balaam, and he saw [a]the angel of the
LORD standing in the way with his drawn
sword in his hand; and he bowed [1]all the
way to the ground.
32 The angel of the LORD said to him,
"Why have you struck your donkey these
three times? Behold, I have come out
as an adversary, because your way was
[1a]contrary to me.
33 "But the donkey saw me and turned
aside from me these three times. If she
had not turned aside from me, I would
surely have killed you just now, and let
her live."
34 Balaam said to the angel of the
LORD, "[a]I have sinned, for I did not know
that you were standing in the way against
me. Now then, if it is displeasing to you,
I will turn back."
35 But the angel of the LORD said to
Balaam, "Go with the men, but [a]you
shall speak only the word which I [1]tell
you." So Balaam went along with the
leaders of Balak.
36 ¶ When Balak heard that Balaam
was coming, he went out to meet him at
the city of Moab, which is on the Arnon
border, [1]at the extreme end of the border.
37 Then Balak said to Balaam, "Did I
not urgently send to you to call you? Why
did you not come to me? Am I really unable to honor you?"
38 So Balaam said to Balak, "Behold, I
have come now to you! [a]Am I able to
speak anything at all? The word that God
puts in my mouth, that I shall speak."
39 And Balaam went with Balak, and
they came to Kiriath-huzoth.
40 Balak sacrificed oxen and sheep,
and sent *some* to Balaam and the leaders
who were with him.
41 ¶ Then it came about in the morn-

12 [a]Num 23:8; 24:9 [b]Gen 12:2; 22:17
15 [1]Lit *these*
17 [a]Num 22:6
18 [1]Lit *mouth* [a]Num 22:38; 24:13; 1 Kin 22:14; 2 Chr 18:13
20 [a]Num 22:35; 23:5,12,16,26; 24:13
21 [a]2 Pet 2:15
22 [a]Ex 23:20
27 [a]James 1:19
28 [a]2 Pet 2:16
29 [a]Prov 12:10; Matt 15:19
31 [1]Lit *and prostrated himself to his face* [a]Josh 5:13-15
32 [1]Lit *reckless* [a]2 Pet 2:15
34 [a]Num 14:40
35 [1]Or *speak to* [a]Num 22:20
36 [1]Lit *which is at*
38 [a]Num 22:18

ing that Balak took Balaam and brought
him up to [1][a]the high places of Baal, and
he saw from there [2]a [b]portion of the
people.

The Prophecies of Balaam

23 Then Balaam said to Balak, "Build
seven altars for me here, and prepare seven bulls and seven rams for me
here."
2 Balak did just as Balaam had spoken, and Balak and Balaam offered up a
bull and a ram on each altar.
3 Then Balaam said to Balak, "Stand
beside your burnt offering, and I will go;
perhaps the LORD will come to meet me,
and whatever He shows me I will tell
you." So he went to a bare hill.
4 ¶ Now God met Balaam, and he
said to Him, "I have set up the seven
altars, and I have offered up a bull and a
ram on each altar."
5 Then the LORD [a]put a word in Balaam's mouth and said, "Return to Balak,
and you shall speak thus."
6 So he returned to him, and behold,
he was standing beside his burnt offering,
he and all the leaders of Moab.
7 He took up his [1]discourse and said,
"From [a]Aram Balak has
brought me,
Moab's king from the mountains
of the East,
'[b]Come curse Jacob for me,
And come, denounce Israel!'
8 "[a]How shall I curse whom God
has not cursed?
And how can I denounce whom
the LORD has not
denounced?
9 "As I see him from the top of the
rocks,
And I look at him from the hills;
[a]Behold, a people *who* dwells
apart,
And will not be reckoned among
the nations.
10 "[a]Who can count the dust of
Jacob,
Or number the fourth part of
Israel?
[b]Let [1]me die the death of the
upright,
[c]And let my end be like his!"
11 ¶ Then Balak said to Balaam,
"What have you done to me? [a]I took you
to curse my enemies, but behold, you
have actually blessed them!"
12 He replied, "Must I not be careful
to speak [a]what the LORD puts in my
mouth?"
13 ¶ Then Balak said to him, "Please
come with me to another place from
where you may see them, although you

41 [1]Or *Bamoth-baal* [2]Lit *the end of the camp* [a]Num 21:28 [b]Num 23:13
23:5 [a]Num 22:20; Deut 18:18; Jer 1:9
7 [1]Lit *parable* [a]Num 22:5; Deut 23:4 [b]Num 22:6
8 [a]Num 22:12
9 [a]Deut 32:8; 33:28
10 [1]Lit *my soul* [a]Gen 13:16; 28:14 [b]Is 57:1 [c]Ps 37:37
11 [a]Neh 13:2
12 [a]Num 22:20
16 [a]Num 22:20
18 [1]Lit *parable*
19 [a]1 Sam 15:29 [b]Is 40:8; 55:11
20 [a]Gen 12:2; 22:17; Num 22:12 [b]Is 43:13
21 [1]Or *iniquity* [a]Num 14:18,19, 34; Ps 32:2,5 [b]Deut 9:24; 32:5; Jer 50:20 [c]Ex 3:12; Deut 31:23 [d]Deut 33:5; Ps 89:15-18
22 [a]Num 24:8 [b]Deut 33:17
23 [a]Num 22:7; 24:1; Josh 13:22
24 [a]Gen 49:9; Nah 2:11,12

will only see the extreme end of them
and will not see all of them; and curse
them for me from there."
14 So he took him to the field of Zo-
phim, to the top of Pisgah, and built sev-
en altars and offered a bull and a ram on
each altar.
15 And he said to Balak, "Stand here
beside your burnt offering while I myself
meet *the LORD* over there."
16 Then the LORD met Balaam and
[a]put a word in his mouth and said, "Return to Balak, and thus you shall speak."
17 He came to him, and behold, he
was standing beside his burnt offering,
and the leaders of Moab with him. And
Balak said to him, "What has the LORD
spoken?"
18 Then he took up his [1]discourse and
said,
"Arise, O Balak, and hear;
Give ear to me, O son of Zippor!
19 "[a]God is not a man, that He
should lie,
Nor a son of man, that He
should repent;
[b]Has He said, and will He not
do it?
Or has He spoken, and will He
not make it good?
20 "Behold, I have received *a*
command to bless;
[a]When He has blessed, then [b]I
cannot revoke it.
21 "[a]He has not observed
[1]misfortune in Jacob;
[b]Nor has He seen trouble in
Israel;
[c]The LORD his God is with him,
[d]And the shout of a king is
among them.
22 "[a]God brings them out of Egypt,
He is for them like the [b]horns of
the wild ox.
23 "[a]For there is no omen against
Jacob,
Nor is there any divination
against Israel;
At the proper time it shall be
said to Jacob
And to Israel, what God has
done!
24 "[a]Behold, a people rises like a
lioness,
And as a lion it lifts itself;
It will not lie down until it
devours the prey,
And drinks the blood of the
slain."
25 ¶ Then Balak said to Balaam, "Do
not curse them at all nor bless them
at all!"
26 But Balaam replied to Balak, "Did

I not tell you, '[1a]Whatever the LORD
speaks, that I must do'?"
27 ¶ Then Balak said to Balaam,
"Please come, I will take you to another
place; perhaps it will be [1]agreeable with
God that you curse them for me from
there."
28 So Balak took Balaam to the top of
Peor which overlooks the [1]wasteland.
29 Balaam said to Balak, "Build seven
altars for me here and prepare seven bulls
and seven rams for me here."
30 Balak did just as Balaam had said,
and offered up a bull and a ram on *each*
altar.

The Prophecy from Peor

24 When Balaam saw that it
[1]pleased the LORD to bless Israel,
he did not go as at other times to [2]seek
[a]omens but he set his face toward the
[b]wilderness.
2 And Balaam lifted up his eyes and
saw Israel [1]camping tribe by tribe; and
[a]the Spirit of God came upon him.
3 He took up his [1]discourse and said,

"[a]The oracle of Balaam the son of
Beor,
And the oracle of the man whose
eye is opened;
4 The oracle of him who [a]hears
the [1]words of God,
Who sees the [b]vision of [2]the
Almighty,
Falling down, yet having his eyes
uncovered,
5 How fair are your tents, O Jacob,
Your dwellings, O Israel!
6 "Like [1]valleys that stretch out,
Like gardens beside the river,
Like [a]aloes planted by the LORD,
Like [b]cedars beside the waters.
7 "Water will flow from his buckets,
And his seed *will be* by many
waters,
And his king shall be higher than
[a]Agag,
[b]And his kingdom shall be
exalted.
8 "[a]God brings him out of Egypt,
He is for him like the horns of
the wild ox.
[b]He will devour the nations *who
are* his adversaries,
And will crush their bones in
pieces,
And shatter *them* with his
[c]arrows.
9 "[a]He [1]couches, he lies down as
a lion,
And as a [2]lion, who [3]dares
rouse him?
[b]Blessed is everyone who
blesses you,
And cursed is everyone who
curses you."

10 ¶ Then Balak's anger burned
against Balaam, and he struck his [1]hands
together; and Balak said to Balaam, "I
called you to curse my enemies, but behold, you have persisted in blessing them
these three times!
11 "Therefore, [1]flee to your place now.
I said I would honor you greatly, but behold, the LORD has held you back from
honor."
12 Balaam said to Balak, "[a]Did I not
tell your messengers whom you had sent
to me, saying,
13 'Though Balak were to give me his
house full of silver and gold, I could not
do anything contrary to the [1]command of
the LORD, either good or bad, [a]of my own
[2]accord. [b]What the LORD speaks, that I
will speak'?
14 "And now, behold, [a]I am going to
my people; come, *and* I will advise you
what this people will do to your people in
the [1]days to come."
15 ¶ He took up his discourse and
said,

"[a]The oracle of Balaam the son of
Beor,
And the oracle of the man whose
eye is opened,
16 The oracle of him who hears the
[1]words of God,
And knows the knowledge of the
[2]Most High,
Who sees the vision of [3]the
Almighty,
Falling down, yet having his eyes
uncovered.
17 "I see him, but not now;
I behold him, but not near;
A star shall come forth from
Jacob,
[a]A scepter shall rise from Israel,
[b]And shall crush through the
[1]forehead of Moab,
And [2]tear down all the sons of
[3]Sheth.
18 "[a]Edom shall be a possession,
[b]Seir, its enemies, also will be a
possession,
While Israel performs valiantly.
19 "One from Jacob shall have
dominion,
And will destroy the remnant
from the city."

20 ¶ And he looked at Amalek and
took up his discourse and said,

"Amalek was the first of the
nations,
[a]But his end *shall be*
[1]destruction."

21 ¶ And he looked at the [a]Kenite,
and took up his discourse and said,

26 [1]Lit *saying, Whatever* [a]Num 22:18
27 [1]Lit *right in the sight of God*
28 [1]Or *Jeshimon*
24:1 [1]Lit *was good in the eyes of* [2]Lit *encounter* [a]Num 22:7; 23:23 [b]Num 23:28
2 [1]Lit *dwelling* [a]Num 11:26; 1 Sam 19:20; Rev 1:10
3 [1]Lit *parable,* and so throughout the ch [a]Num 24:15,16
4 [1]Lit *sayings* [2]Heb *Shaddai* [a]Num 22:20 [b]Gen 15:1; Num 12:6
6 [1]Or possibly *palm trees* [a]Ps 45:8 [b]Ps 1:3
7 [a]Num 24:20; 1 Sam 15:8 [b]Ps 145:11-13
8 [a]Num 23:22 [b]Num 23:24; Ps 2:9 [c]Ps 45:5
9 [1]Lit *bows down* [2]Or *lioness* [3]Lit *shall* [a]Gen 49:9; Num 23:24 [b]Gen 12:3; 27:29
10 [1]Lit *palms*
11 [1]Lit *flee for yourself*
12 [a]Num 22:18
13 [1]Lit *mouth* [2]Lit *heart* [a]Num 16:28 [b]Num 22:20
14 [1]Lit *end of the days* [a]Num 31:8,16; Josh 13:22
15 [a]Num 24:3,4
16 [1]Lit *sayings* [2]Heb *Elyon* [3]Heb *Shaddai*
17 [1]Lit *corners* [2]Another reading is *the crown of the head of* [3]I.e. tumult [a]Gen 49:10 [b]Num 21:29; Is 15:1-16:14
18 [a]Gen 27:29; Amos 9:11,12 [b]Gen 32:3
20 [1]Lit *to destroying* [a]Num 24:24
21 [a]Gen 15:19

"Your dwelling place is enduring,
And your nest is set in the cliff.
22 "Nevertheless Kain will be
consumed;
How long will [a]Asshur [1]keep
you captive?"
23 ¶ Then he took up his discourse
and said,
"Alas, who can live except God
has ordained it?
24 "But ships *shall come* from the
coast of [a]Kittim,
And they shall afflict Asshur and
will afflict [b]Eber;
[c]So they also *will come* to
destruction."
25 ¶ Then Balaam arose and departed
and returned to [a]his place, and Balak also
went his way.

The Sin of Peor

25 While Israel remained at
[a]Shittim, the people began [b]to
play the harlot with the daughters of
Moab.
2 For [a]they invited the people to the
sacrifices of their gods, and the people ate
and bowed down to their gods.
3 So [a]Israel joined themselves to
[1]Baal of Peor, and the LORD was angry
against Israel.
4 The LORD said to Moses, "Take all
the leaders of the people and execute
them [1]in broad daylight before the LORD,
[a]so that the fierce anger of the LORD may
turn away from Israel."
5 So Moses said to the judges of Israel, "Each of you [a]slay his men who have
joined themselves to [1]Baal of Peor."
6 ¶ Then behold, one of the sons of
Israel came and brought to his [1]relatives
a [a]Midianite woman, in the sight of Moses and in the sight of all the congregation
of the sons of Israel, [b]while they were
weeping at the doorway of the tent of
meeting.
7 [a]When Phinehas the son of Eleazar, the son of Aaron the priest, saw it, he
arose from the midst of the congregation
and took a spear in his hand,
8 and he went after the man of Israel
into the [1]tent and pierced both of them
through, the man of Israel and the woman, through the [2]body. [a]So the plague
on the sons of Israel was checked.
9 [a]Those who died by the plague
were 24,000.

The Zeal of Phinehas

10 ¶ Then the LORD spoke to Moses,
saying,
11 "[a]Phinehas the son of Eleazar, the
son of Aaron the priest, has turned away
My wrath from the sons of Israel in that
he was jealous with My jealousy among
them, so that I did not destroy the sons of
Israel [b]in My jealousy.
12 "Therefore say, '[a]Behold, I give him
My [b]covenant of peace;
13 and it shall be for him and his
[1]descendants after him, a covenant of a
[a]perpetual priesthood, because he was
jealous for his God and [b]made atonement for the sons of Israel.' "
14 ¶ Now the name of the [1]slain man
of Israel who was [1]slain with the Midianite woman, was Zimri the son of Salu, a
leader of a father's household among the
Simeonites.
15 The name of the Midianite woman
who was [1]slain was [a]Cozbi the daughter
of [b]Zur, [2]who was head of the people of
a father's household in Midian.
16 ¶ Then the LORD spoke to Moses,
saying,
17 "[a]Be hostile to the Midianites and
strike them;
18 for they have been hostile to you
with their tricks, with which they have
deceived you in the affair of Peor and in
the affair of Cozbi, the daughter of the
leader of Midian, their sister who was
slain on the day of the plague because of
Peor."

Census of a New Generation

26 [1]Then it came about after the
[a]plague, [2]that the LORD spoke to
Moses and to Eleazar the son of Aaron the
priest, saying,
2 "[a]Take a [1]census of all the congregation of the sons of Israel from twenty
years old and upward, by their fathers'
households, whoever is able to go out to
war in Israel."
3 So Moses and Eleazar the priest
spoke with them [a]in the plains of Moab
by the Jordan at Jericho, saying,
4 "*Take a census of the people* from
twenty years old and upward, as the LORD
has commanded Moses."
¶ Now the sons of Israel who came out
of the land of Egypt *were:*
5 ¶ Reuben, Israel's firstborn, the
sons of Reuben: *of* Hanoch, the family of
the Hanochites; of Pallu, the family of the
Palluites;
6 of Hezron, the family of the Hezronites; of Carmi, the family of the Car-
mites.
7 These are the families of the Reubenites, and those who were numbered
of them were [a]43,730.
8 The son of Pallu: Eliab.
9 The sons of Eliab: Nemuel and Dathan and Abiram. These are the Dathan
and Abiram who were [a]called by the
congregation, who contended against

---

22 [1]Lit *take* [a]Gen 10:21,22
24 [a]Gen 10:4; Ezek 27:6 [b]Gen 10:21 [c]Num 24:20
25 [a]Num 24:14
25:1 [a]Num 33:49; Josh 2:1 [b]Num 31:16; 1 Cor 10:8; Rev 2:14
2 [a]Ex 34:15; Deut 32:38
3 [1]Or *Baal-peor* [a]Ps 106:28,29; Hos 9:10
4 [1]Lit *in front of the sun* [a]Deut 13:17
5 [1]Or *Baal-peor* [a]Ex 32:27
6 [1]Lit *brothers* [a]Num 22:4 [b]Joel 2:17
7 [a]Ps 106:30
8 [1]Or *inner rooms* [2]Or *belly* [a]Num 16:46-48
9 [a]Num 14:37; 16:48-50; 31:16
11 [a]Ps 106:30 [b]Ex 20:5
12 [a]Ps 106:30, 31 [b]Is 54:10; Ezek 34:25; 37:26
13 [1]Lit *seed* [a]Ex 29:9 [b]Num 16:46
14 [1]Lit *smitten*
15 [1]Lit *smitten* [2]Lit *he* [a]Num 25:18 [b]Num 31:8
17 [a]Num 25:1; 22:4; 31:1-3
26:1 [1]Ch 25:19 in Heb [2]Ch 26:1 in Heb [a]Num 25:9
2 [1]Lit *sum* [a]Ex 30:11-16; 38:25, 26; Num 1:2
3 [a]Num 22:1; 33:48; 35:1
7 [a]Num 1:21
9 [a]Num 1:16; 16:2

Moses and against Aaron in the company
of Korah, when they contended against
the LORD,
10 and [a]the earth opened its mouth
and swallowed them up along with Korah, when that company died, [b]when the
fire devoured 250 men, so that they became a [1]warning.
11 [a]The sons of Korah, however, did
not die.
12 ¶ The sons of Simeon according to
their families: of [1]Nemuel, the family of
the Nemuelites; of Jamin, the family of
the Jaminites; of [2]Jachin, the family
of the Jachinites;
13 of [1]Zerah, the family of the Zerahites; of Shaul, the family of the Shaul-
ites.
14 These are the families of the Simeonites, [a]22,200.
15 ¶ The sons of Gad according to
their families: of [1]Zephon, the family of
the Zephonites; of Haggi, the family of
the Haggites; of Shuni, the family of the
Shunites;
16 of [1]Ozni, the family of the Oznites;
of Eri, the family of the Erites;
17 of [1]Arod, the family of the Aro-
dites; of Areli, the family of the Arelites.
18 These are the families of the sons of
Gad according to those who were numbered of them, [a]40,500.
19 ¶ The [a]sons of Judah *were* Er and
Onan, but Er and Onan died in the land
of Canaan.
20 The [a]sons of Judah according to
their families were: of Shelah, the family
of the Shelanites; of Perez, the family of
the Perezites; of Zerah, the family of the
Zerahites.
21 The sons of Perez were: of Hezron,
the family of the Hezronites; of Hamul,
the family of the Hamulites.
22 These are the families of Judah according to those who were numbered of
them, [a]76,500.
23 ¶ The [a]sons of Issachar according
to their families: *of* Tola, the family of the
Tolaites; of [1]Puvah, the family of the Pu-
nites;
24 of [1]Jashub, the family of the Ja-
shubites; of Shimron, the family of the
Shimronites.
25 These are the families of Issachar
according to those who were numbered
of them, [a]64,300.
26 ¶ The [a]sons of Zebulun according
to their families: of Sered, the family of
the Seredites; of Elon, the family of the
Elonites; of Jahleel, the family of the Jah-
leelites.
27 These are the families of the Zebu-
lunites according to those who were
numbered of them, [a]60,500.
28 ¶ The [a]sons of Joseph according to
their families: Manasseh and Ephraim.
29 The sons of Manasseh: of Machir,
the family of the Machirites; and [a]Ma-
chir [1]became the father of Gilead: of Gilead, the family of the Gileadites.
30 These are the sons of Gilead: *of*
[1]Iezer, the family of the [a]Iezerites; of
Helek, the family of the Helekites;
31 and *of* Asriel, the family of the Asri-
elites; and *of* Shechem, the family of the
Shechemites;
32 and *of* Shemida, the family of the
Shemidaites; and *of* Hepher, the family of
the Hepherites.
33 Now Zelophehad the son of Hepher
had no sons, but only daughters; and
[a]the names of the daughters of Zelophehad were Mahlah, Noah, Hoglah, Milcah
and Tirzah.
34 These are the families of Manasseh;
and those who were numbered of them
were [a]52,700.
35 ¶ These are the sons of Ephraim according to their families: of Shuthelah,
the family of the Shuthelahites; of [1]Be-
cher, the family of the Becherites; of Tahan, the family of the Tahanites.
36 These are the sons of Shuthelah: of
Eran, the family of the Eranites.
37 These are the families of the sons of
Ephraim according to those who were
numbered of them, [a]32,500. These are
the sons of Joseph according to their families.
38 ¶ The sons of Benjamin according
to their families: of Bela, the family of the
Belaites; of Ashbel, the family of the Ash-
belites; of [1]Ahiram, the family of the Ahi-
ramites;
39 of [1]Shephupham, the family of the
Shuphamites; of [2]Hupham, the family of
the Huphamites.
40 The sons of Bela were [1]Ard and
Naaman: *of Ard,* the family of the Ardites;
of Naaman, the family of the Naamites.
41 These are the sons of Benjamin according to their families; and those who
were numbered of them were [a]45,600.
42 ¶ These are the sons of Dan according to their families: of [1]Shuham, the
family of the Shuhamites. These are the
families of Dan according to their families.
43 All the families of the Shuhamites,
according to those who were numbered
of them, were [a]64,400.
44 ¶ The [a]sons of Asher according to
their families: of Imnah, the family of the
Imnites; of Ishvi, the family of the Ish-
vites; of Beriah, the family of the Beriites.
45 Of the sons of Beriah: of Heber, the
family of the Heberites; of Malchiel, the
family of the Malchielites.

10 [1]Lit *sign* [a]Num 16:32 [b]Num 16:35,38
11 [a]Num 16:27, 33; Deut 24:16
12 [1]In Gen 46:10 and Ex 6:15, *Jemuel* [2]In 1 Chr 4:24, *Jarib*
13 [1]In Gen 46:10, *Zohar*
14 [a]Num 1:23
15 [1]In Gen 46:16, *Ziphion*
16 [1]In Gen 46:16, *Ezbon*
17 [1]In Gen 46:16, *Arodi*
18 [a]Num 1:25
19 [a]Gen 38:2; 46:12
20 [a]Gen 49:8; 1 Chr 2:3; Rev 7:5
22 [a]Num 1:27
23 [1]In Gen 46:13, *Puvvah*; in 1 Chr 7:1, *Puah* [a]Gen 46:13; 1 Chr 7:1
24 [1]In Gen 46:13, *Iob*
25 [a]Num 1:29
26 [a]Gen 46:14
27 [a]Num 1:31
28 [a]Gen 46:20; Deut 33:16f
29 [1]Lit *begot* [a]Josh 17:1; 1 Chr 7:14f
30 [1]In Josh 17:2, *Abiezer* [a]Judg 6:11,24,34
33 [a]Num 27:1
34 [a]Num 1:35
35 [1]In 1 Chr 7:20, *Bered*
37 [a]Num 1:33
38 [1]In Gen 46:21, *Ehi*; in 1 Chr 8:1, *Aharah*
39 [1]In Gen 46:21, *Muppim*; in 1 Chr 7:12, *Shuppim* [2]In Gen 46:21, *Muppim* and *Huppim*
40 [1]In 1 Chr 8:3, *Addar*
41 [a]Num 1:37
42 [1]In Gen 46:23, *Hushim*
43 [a]Num 1:39
44 [a]Gen 46:17; 1 Chr 7:30

46 The name of the daughter of Asher *was* Serah.

47 These are the families of the sons of Asher according to those who were numbered of them, [a]53,400.

48 ¶ The [a]sons of Naphtali according to their families: of Jahzeel, the family of the Jahzeelites; of Guni, the family of the Gunites;

49 of Jezer, the family of the Jezerites; of [a]Shillem, the family of the Shillemites.

50 These are the families of Naphtali according to their families; and those who were numbered of them were [a]45,400.

51 ¶ These are those who were numbered of the sons of Israel, [a]601,730.

52 ¶ Then the LORD spoke to Moses, saying,

53 "[1]Among these the land shall be divided for an inheritance according to the number of names.

54 "[a]To the larger *group* you shall increase their inheritance, and to the smaller *group* you shall diminish their inheritance; each shall be given their inheritance according to those who were numbered of them.

55 "But the land shall be [a]divided by lot. They shall [1]receive their inheritance according to the names of the tribes of their fathers.

56 "According to the selection by lot, their inheritance shall be divided between the larger and the smaller *groups.*"

57 ¶ [a]These are those who were numbered of the Levites according to their families: of Gershon, the family of the Gershonites; of Kohath, the family of the Kohathites; of Merari, the family of the Merarites.

58 These are the families of Levi: the family of the Libnites, the family of the Hebronites, the family of the Mahlites, the family of the Mushites, the family of the Korahites. [a]Kohath [1]became the father of Amram.

59 The name of Amram's wife [a]was Jochebed, the daughter of Levi, who was born to Levi in Egypt; and she bore to Amram: Aaron and Moses and their sister Miriam.

60 [a]To Aaron were born Nadab and Abihu, Eleazar and Ithamar.

61 [a]But Nadab and Abihu died when they offered strange fire before the LORD.

62 Those who were numbered of them were [a]23,000, every male from a month old and upward, for [b]they were not numbered among the sons of Israel [c]since no inheritance was given to them among the sons of Israel.

63 ¶ These are those who were numbered by Moses and Eleazar the priest, who numbered the sons of Israel in the plains of Moab by the Jordan at Jericho.

64 [a]But among these there was not a man of those who were numbered by Moses and Aaron the priest, who numbered the sons of Israel in the wilderness of Sinai.

65 For the LORD had said [1]of them, "[a]They shall surely die in the wilderness." And not a man was left of them, [b]except Caleb the son of Jephunneh and Joshua the son of Nun.

A Law of Inheritance

27 Then [a]the daughters of Zelophehad, the son of Hepher, the son of Gilead, the son of Machir, the son of Manasseh, of the families of Manasseh the son of Joseph, came near; and these are [b]the names of his daughters: Mahlah, Noah and Hoglah and Milcah and Tirzah.

2 They stood before Moses and before Eleazar the priest and before the leaders and all the congregation, at the doorway of the tent of meeting, saying,

3 "Our father [a]died in the wilderness, yet he was not among the company of those who gathered themselves together against the LORD in the company of Korah; but he died in his own sin, and [b]he had no sons.

4 "Why should the name of our father be withdrawn from among his family because he had no son? Give us a possession among our father's brothers."

5 [a]So Moses brought their case before the LORD.

6 ¶ Then the LORD spoke to Moses, saying,

7 "[a]The daughters of Zelophehad are right in *their* statements. You shall surely give them a hereditary possession among their father's brothers, and you shall transfer the inheritance of their father to them.

8 "Further, you shall speak to the sons of Israel, saying, 'If a man dies and has no son, then you shall transfer his inheritance to his daughter.

9 'If he has no daughter, then you shall give his inheritance to his brothers.

10 'If he has no brothers, then you shall give his inheritance to his father's brothers.

11 'If his father has no brothers, then you shall give his inheritance to his nearest relative in his own family, and he shall possess it; and it shall be a [a]statutory ordinance to the sons of Israel, just as the LORD commanded Moses.' "

12 ¶ [a]Then the LORD said to Moses, "Go up to this [b]mountain of Abarim, and see the land which I have given to the sons of Israel.

47 [a]Num 1:41
48 [a]Gen 46:24; 1 Chr 7:13
49 [a]1 Chr 7:13
50 [a]Num 1:43
51 [a]Ex 12:37; 38:26; Num 1:46; 11:21
53 [1]Lit *To*
54 [a]Num 33:54
55 [1]Lit *inherit according to* [a]Num 33:54; 34:13
57 [a]Gen 46:11; Ex 6:16; 1 Chr 6:1,16
58 [1]Lit *begot* [a]Ex 6:20
59 [a]Ex 2:1,2; 6:20
60 [a]Num 3:2
61 [a]Lev 10:1,2; Num 3:4
62 [a]Num 3:39 [b]Num 1:47 [c]Num 18:23,24
64 [a]Num 14:29-35; Deut 2:14-16; Heb 3:17
65 [1]Or *to* [a]Num 14:26-35; Ps 90:3-10; 1 Cor 10:5 [b]Deut 1:36; Josh 14:6-10
27:1 [a]Num 26:33; 36:1 [b]Num 26:33
3 [a]Num 26:64,65 [b]Num 26:33
5 [a]Num 9:8; 27:21
7 [a]Num 36:2; Josh 17:4
11 [a]Num 35:29
12 [a]Deut 3:23-27; 32:48-52 [b]Num 33:47,48

13 "When you have seen it, you too [a]will be gathered to your people, [b]as Aaron your brother [1]was;

14 for in the wilderness of Zin, during the strife of the congregation, [a]you rebelled against My [1]command [2]to treat Me as holy before their eyes at the water." (These are the waters of Meribah of Kadesh in the wilderness of Zin.)

Joshua to Succeed Moses

15 ¶ Then Moses spoke to the LORD, saying,

16 "[a]May the LORD, the God of the spirits of all flesh, appoint a man over the congregation,

17 who [a]will go out [1]and come in before them, and who will lead them out and [2]bring them in, so that the congregation of the LORD will not be [b]like sheep which have no shepherd."

18 So the LORD said to Moses, "[1]Take Joshua the son of Nun, a man [a]in whom is the Spirit, and [b]lay your hand on him;

19 and have him stand before Eleazar the priest and before all the congregation, and [a]commission him in their sight.

20 "You shall put some of your [1]authority on him, in order that all the congregation of the sons of Israel may obey *him*.

21 "Moreover, he shall stand before Eleazar the priest, who shall inquire for him [a]by the judgment of the Urim before the LORD. At his [1]command they shall go out and at his [1]command they shall come in, *both* he and the sons of Israel with him, even all the congregation."

22 Moses did just as the LORD commanded him; and he took Joshua and set him before Eleazar the priest and before all the congregation.

23 Then he laid his hands on him and [a]commissioned him, just as the LORD had spoken [1]through Moses.

Laws for Offerings

28 Then the LORD spoke to Moses, saying,

2 "Command the sons of Israel and say to them, 'You shall [1]be careful to present My offering, My [a]food for My offerings by fire, of a soothing aroma to Me, at their appointed time.'

3 "[a]You shall say to them, 'This is the offering by fire which you shall offer to the LORD: two male lambs one year old without defect *as* a continual burnt offering every day.

4 'You shall offer the one lamb in the morning and the other lamb you shall offer [1]at twilight;

5 also [a]a tenth of an ephah of fine flour for a [b]grain offering, mixed with a fourth of a hin of beaten oil.

6 'It is a continual burnt offering which was ordained in Mount Sinai as a soothing aroma, an offering by fire to the LORD.

7 'Then the drink offering with it *shall be* a fourth of a hin for each lamb, [a]in the holy place you shall pour out a drink offering of strong drink to the LORD.

8 'The other lamb you shall offer [1]at twilight; as the grain offering of the morning and as its drink offering, you shall offer it, an offering by fire, a soothing aroma to the LORD.

9 ¶ 'Then on the sabbath day two male lambs one year old without defect, and two-tenths *of an* [1]*ephah* of fine flour mixed with oil as a grain offering, and its drink offering:

10 '*This is* the burnt offering of every sabbath in addition to the [a]continual burnt offering and its drink offering.

11 ¶ 'Then [a]at the beginning of each of your months you shall present a burnt offering to the LORD: two [1]bulls and one ram, seven male lambs one year old without defect;

12 [a]and three-tenths *of an* [1]*ephah* of fine flour mixed with oil for a grain offering, for each bull; and two-tenths of fine flour mixed with oil for a grain offering, for the one ram;

13 and a tenth *of an* [1]*ephah* of fine flour mixed with oil for a grain offering for each lamb, for a burnt offering of a soothing aroma, an offering by fire to the LORD.

14 'Their drink offerings shall be half a hin of wine for a bull and a third of a hin for the ram and a fourth of a hin for a lamb; this is the burnt offering of each month throughout the months of the year.

15 'And one male goat for a sin offering to the LORD; it shall be offered with its drink offering in addition to the [a]continual burnt offering.

16 ¶ '[a]Then on the fourteenth day of the first month shall be the LORD'S Passover.

17 '[a]On the fifteenth day of this month *shall be* a [b]feast, unleavened bread *shall be* eaten for seven days.

18 'On the [a]first day *shall be* a holy convocation; you shall do no laborious work.

19 'You shall present an offering by fire, a burnt offering to the LORD: two [1]bulls and one ram and seven male lambs one year old, [a]having them without defect.

20 'For their grain offering, you shall offer fine flour mixed with oil: three-tenths *of an* [1]*ephah* for a bull and two-tenths for the ram.

13 [1]Lit *was gathered* [a]Num 31:2 [b]Num 20:24,28; Deut 10:6
14 [1]Lit *mouth* [2]Lit *for My sanctity* [a]Num 20:12; Deut 32:51; Ps 106:32
16 [a]Num 16:22
17 [1]Lit *before them and who will* [2]Lit *who will bring* [a]Deut 31:2; 2 Chr 1:10 [b]1 Kin 22:17; Ezek 34:5; Matt 9:36; Mark 6:34
18 [1]Lit *Take for yourself* [a]Num 11:25-29; Deut 34:9 [b]Num 27:23
19 [a]Deut 3:28; 31:3,7,8,23
20 [1]Lit *majesty*
21 [1]Lit *mouth* [a]Ex 28:30; 1 Sam 28:6
23 [1]Lit *by the hand of* [a]Deut 31:23
28:2 [1]Lit *watch* [a]Lev 3:11
3 [a]Ex 29:38-42
4 [1]Lit *between the two evenings*
5 [a]Ex 16:36; Num 15:4 [b]Lev 2:1
7 [a]Ex 29:42
8 [1]Lit *between the two evenings*
9 [1]I.e. Approx one bu
10 [a]Num 28:3
11 [1]Lit *bulls of the herd* [a]Num 10:10; Ezek 46:6,7
12 [1]I.e. Approx one bu [a]Num 15:4-12
13 [1]I.e. Approx one bu
15 [a]Num 28:3
16 [a]Ex 12:1-20; Lev 23:5-8; Deut 16:1-8
17 [a]Lev 23:6 [b]Ex 23:15; 34:18; Deut 16:3-8
18 [a]Lev 23:7
19 [1]Or *bulls of the herd* [a]Deut 15:21
20 [1]I.e. Approx one bu

21 'A tenth *of an* [1]*ephah* you shall offer for [2]each of the seven lambs;
22 and one male goat for a [a]sin offering to make atonement for you.
23 'You shall present these besides
[a]the burnt offering of the morning,
which is for a continual burnt offering.
24 'After this manner you shall present
daily, for seven days, [a]the food of the
offering by fire, of a soothing aroma to the
LORD; it shall be presented with its drink
offering in addition to the [b]continual
burnt offering.
25 'On the seventh day you shall have
a holy convocation; [a]you shall do no
laborious work.
26 ¶ 'Also on [a]the day of the first
fruits, when you present a new grain offering to the LORD in your *Feast of* Weeks,
you shall have a holy convocation; [b]you
shall do no laborious work.
27 'You shall offer a burnt offering for a
soothing aroma to the LORD: two young
bulls, one ram, seven male lambs one
year old;
28 and their grain offering, fine flour
mixed with oil: three-tenths *of an*
[1]*ephah* for each bull, two-tenths for the
one ram,
29 a tenth for [1]each of the seven
lambs;
30 *also* one male goat to make atonement for you.
31 '[a]Besides the continual burnt offering and its grain offering, you shall
present *them* with their drink offerings.
They shall be [1]without defect.

Offerings of the Seventh Month

29 '[a]Now in the seventh month, on
the first day of the month, you
shall also have a holy convocation; [b]you
shall do no laborious work. It will be to
you a day for blowing trumpets.
2 'You shall offer a burnt offering as a
soothing aroma to the LORD: one [1]bull,
one ram, *and* seven male lambs one year
old without defect;
3 also their grain offering, fine flour
mixed with oil: three-tenths *of an*
[1]*ephah* for the bull, two-tenths for the
ram,
4 and one-tenth for [1]each of the sev-
en lambs.
5 '*Offer* one male goat for a sin offering, to make atonement for you,
6 [a]besides the burnt offering of the
new moon and its grain offering, and the
[b]continual burnt offering and its grain
offering, and their drink offerings, according to their ordinance, for a soothing
aroma, an offering by fire to the LORD.
7 ¶ 'Then on [a]the tenth day of this
seventh month you shall have a holy convocation, and you shall humble yourselves; you shall not do any work.
8 'You shall present a burnt offering to
the LORD *as* a soothing aroma: one bull,
one ram, seven male lambs one year old,
[a]having them without defect;
9 and their grain offering, fine flour
mixed with oil: three-tenths *of an*
[1]*ephah* for the bull, two-tenths for the
one ram,
10 a tenth for each of the seven lambs;
11 one male goat for a sin offering, besides [a]the sin offering of atonement and
[b]the continual burnt offering and its
grain offering, and their drink offerings.
12 ¶ 'Then on [a]the fifteenth day of
the seventh month you shall have a holy
convocation; you [b]shall do no laborious
work, and you shall observe a feast to the
LORD for seven days.
13 'You shall present a burnt offering,
an offering by fire as a soothing aroma to
the LORD: thirteen bulls, two rams, fourteen male lambs one year old, which are
without defect;
14 and their grain offering, fine flour
mixed with oil: three-tenths *of an*
[1]*ephah* for [2]each of the thirteen bulls,
two-tenths for [3]each of the two rams,
15 and a tenth for each of the fourteen
lambs;
16 and one male goat for a sin offering,
[a]besides the continual burnt offering, its
grain offering and its drink offering.
17 ¶ 'Then on [a]the second day:
twelve bulls, two rams, fourteen male
lambs one year old without defect;
18 and their grain offering and their
drink offerings for the bulls, for the rams
and for the lambs, by their number [a]ac-
cording to the ordinance;
19 and one male goat for a sin offering,
[a]besides the continual burnt offering and
its grain offering, and their drink offerings.
20 ¶ 'Then on the third day: eleven
bulls, two rams, fourteen male lambs one
year old without defect;
21 and their grain offering and their
drink offerings for the bulls, for the rams
and for the lambs, by their number according to the ordinance;
22 and one male goat for a sin offering,
besides the continual burnt offering and
its grain offering and its drink offering.
23 ¶ 'Then on the fourth day: ten
bulls, two rams, fourteen male lambs one
year old without defect;
24 their grain offering and their drink
offerings for the bulls, for the rams and
for the lambs, by their number according
to the ordinance;
25 and one male goat for a sin offering,

21 [1]I.e. Approx one bu [2]Lit *each lamb*
22 [a]Lev 16:18; Rom 8:3; Gal 4:4f
23 [a]Num 28:3
24 [a]Lev 3:11 [b]Num 28:3
25 [a]Num 28:18
26 [a]Ex 23:16; 34:22; Lev 23:15-21; Deut 16:9-12 [b]Num 28:18
28 [1]I.e. Approx one bu
29 [1]Lit *each lamb*
31 [1]Lit *without defect to you* [a]Num 28:3
29:1 [a]Ex 23:16; 34:22; Lev 23:23-25 [b]Num 28:26
2 [1]Or *bull of a herd,* and so throughout the ch
3 [1]I.e. Approx one bu
4 [1]Lit *each lamb,* and so throughout the ch
6 [a]Num 28:27 [b]Num 28:3
7 [a]Lev 16:29-34; 23:26-32
8 [a]Lev 22:20; Deut 15:21; 17:1
9 [1]I.e. Approx one bu
11 [a]Lev 16:3,5 [b]Num 28:3
12 [a]Lev 23:33-35; Deut 16:13-15 [b]Num 29:1
14 [1]I.e. Approx one bu [2]Lit *each bull* [3]Lit *each ram*
16 [a]Num 28:3
17 [a]Lev 23:36
18 [a]Lev 2:1-16
19 [a]Num 28:8

besides the continual burnt offering, its grain offering and its drink offering.

26 ¶ ‘Then on the fifth day: nine bulls, two rams, fourteen male lambs one year old [a]without defect;

27 and their grain offering and their drink offerings for the bulls, for the rams and for the lambs, by their number according to the ordinance;

28 and one male goat for a sin offering, besides the continual burnt offering and its grain offering and its drink offering.

29 ¶ ‘Then on the sixth day: eight bulls, two rams, fourteen male lambs one year old without defect;

30 and their grain offering and their drink offerings for the bulls, for the rams and for the lambs, by their number according to the ordinance;

31 and one male goat for a sin offering, besides the continual burnt offering, its grain offering and its drink offerings.

32 ¶ ‘Then on the seventh day: seven bulls, two rams, fourteen male lambs one year old without defect;

33 and their grain offering and their drink offerings for the bulls, for the rams and for the lambs, by their number according to the ordinance;

34 and one male goat for a sin offering, besides the continual burnt offering, its grain offering and its drink offering.

35 ¶ ‘[a]On the eighth day you shall have a solemn assembly; you shall do no laborious work.

36 ‘But you shall present a burnt offering, an offering by fire, as a soothing aroma to the LORD: one bull, one ram, seven male lambs one year old without defect;

37 their grain offering and their drink offerings for the bull, for the ram and for the lambs, by their number according to the ordinance;

38 and one male goat for a sin offering, besides the continual burnt offering and its grain offering and its drink offering.

39 ¶ ‘You shall present these to the LORD at your [a]appointed times, besides your [1]votive offerings and your freewill offerings, for your burnt offerings and for your grain offerings and for your drink offerings and for your peace offerings.’ ”

40 [1]Moses spoke to the sons of Israel in accordance with all that the LORD had commanded Moses.

The Law of Vows

30 Then Moses spoke to [a]the heads of the tribes of the sons of Israel, saying, “This is the word which the LORD has commanded.

2 “[a]If a man makes a vow to the LORD, or takes an oath to bind himself with a binding obligation, he shall not violate his word; he shall do according to all that proceeds out of his mouth.

3 ¶ “Also if a woman makes a vow to the LORD, and binds herself by an obligation in her father’s house in her youth,

4 and her father hears her vow and her obligation by which she has bound herself, and her father [1]says nothing to her, then all her vows shall stand and every obligation by which she has bound herself shall stand.

5 “But if her father should forbid her on the day he hears *of it,* none of her vows or her obligations by which she has bound herself shall stand; and the LORD will forgive her because her father had forbidden her.

6 ¶ “However, if she should [1]marry while [2]under her vows or the rash statement of her lips by which she has bound herself,

7 and her husband hears of it and says nothing to her on the day he hears *it,* then her vows shall stand and her obligations by which she has bound herself shall stand.

8 “But if on the day her husband hears *of it,* he forbids her, then he shall annul her vow which [1]she is under and the rash statement of her lips by which she has bound herself; and the LORD will forgive her.

9 ¶ “But the vow of a widow or of a divorced woman, everything by which she has bound herself, shall stand against her.

10 “However, if she vowed in her husband’s house, or bound herself by an obligation with an oath,

11 and her husband heard *it,* but said nothing to her *and* did not forbid her, then all her vows shall stand and every obligation by which she bound herself shall stand.

12 “But if her husband indeed annuls them on the day he hears *them,* then whatever proceeds out of her lips concerning her vows or concerning the obligation of herself shall not stand; her husband has annulled them, and the LORD will forgive her.

13 ¶ “Every vow and every binding oath to humble herself, her husband may confirm it or her husband may annul it.

14 “But if her husband indeed says nothing to her from day to day, then he confirms all her vows or all her obligations which are on her; he has confirmed them, because he said nothing to her on the day he heard them.

15 “But if he indeed annuls them after he has heard them, then he shall bear her guilt.”

16 ¶ These are the statutes which the

26 [a]Heb 7:26
35 [a]Lev 23:36
39 [1]Lit *vows* [a]Lev 23:2
40 [1]Ch 30:1 in Heb
30:1 [a]Num 1:4, 16; 7:2
2 [a]Deut 23:21-23; Matt 5:33
4 [1]Lit *is silent to her,* and so throughout the ch
6 [1]Lit *be to a husband* [2]Lit *her vows are on her*
8 [1]Lit *is on her*

LORD commanded Moses, *as* between a
man and his wife, *and as* between a father and his daughter, *while she is* in her
youth in her father's house.

The Slaughter of Midian

31 Then the LORD spoke to Moses,
saying,
2 "[a]Take full vengeance for the sons
of Israel on the Midianites; afterward you
will be [b]gathered to your people."
3 Moses spoke to the people, saying,
"Arm men from among you for the war,
that they may [1]go against Midian to execute [a]the LORD's vengeance on Midian.
4 "A thousand from each tribe of all
the tribes of Israel you shall send to the
war."
5 So there were [1]furnished from the
thousands of Israel, a thousand from each
tribe, twelve thousand armed for war.
6 Moses sent them, a thousand from
each tribe, to the war, and Phinehas the
son of Eleazar the priest, to the war with
them, [a]and the holy vessels and [b]the
trumpets for the alarm in his hand.
7 So they made war against Midian,
just as the LORD had commanded Moses,
and [a]they killed every male.
8 They killed the kings of Midian
along with the *rest of* their slain: [a]Evi
and Rekem and [b]Zur and Hur and Reba,
the five kings of Midian; they also killed
[c]Balaam the son of Beor with the sword.
9 The sons of Israel captured the
women of Midian and their little ones;
and all their cattle and all their flocks and
all their goods they plundered.
10 Then they burned all their cities
where they lived and all their camps with
fire.
11 [a]They took all the spoil and all the
prey, both of man and of beast.
12 They brought the captives and the
prey and the spoil to Moses, and to Eleazar the priest and to the congregation of
the sons of Israel, to the camp at the
plains of Moab, which are by the Jordan
opposite Jericho.
13 ¶ Moses and Eleazar the priest and
all the leaders of the congregation went
out to meet them outside the camp.
14 Moses was angry with the officers
of the army, the captains of thousands
and the captains of hundreds, who had
come from service in the war.
15 And Moses said to them, "Have you
[1]spared [a]all the women?
16 "[a]Behold, these [1]caused the sons of
Israel, through the [2]counsel of [b]Balaam,
to [3]trespass against the LORD in the matter of Peor, so the plague was among the
congregation of the LORD.
17 "[a]Now therefore, kill every male
among the little ones, and kill every
woman who has known man [1]inti-
mately.
18 "But all the [1]girls who have not
known man [2]intimately, [3]spare for yourselves.
19 "[a]And you, camp outside the camp
seven days; whoever has killed any person and whoever has touched any slain,
purify yourselves, you and your captives,
on the third day and on the seventh day.
20 "You shall purify for yourselves every garment and every article of [1]leather
and all the work of goats' *hair,* and all
articles of wood."
21 ¶ Then Eleazar the priest said to
the men of war who had gone to battle,
"This is the statute of the law which the
LORD has commanded Moses:
22 only the gold and the silver, the
bronze, the iron, the tin and the lead,
23 everything that can stand the fire,
you shall pass through the fire, and it
shall be clean, but it shall be purified with
[a]water for impurity. But whatever cannot stand the fire you shall pass through
the water.
24 "And you shall wash your clothes on
the seventh day and be clean, and afterward you may enter the camp."

Division of the Booty

25 ¶ Then the LORD spoke to Moses,
saying,
26 "You and Eleazar the priest and the
heads of the fathers' *households* of the
congregation take a count of the booty
[1]that was captured, both of man and of
animal;
27 and [a]divide the booty between the
warriors who went out to battle and all
the congregation.
28 "[a]Levy a tax for the LORD from the
men of war who went out to battle, one
[1]in five hundred of the persons and of
the cattle and of the donkeys and of the
sheep;
29 take it from their half and give it to
Eleazar the priest, as an [1]offering to the
LORD.
30 "From the sons of Israel's half, you
shall take one drawn out of every fifty of
the persons, of the cattle, of the donkeys
and of the sheep, from all the animals,
and give them to the Levites who [a]keep
charge of the tabernacle of the LORD."
31 Moses and Eleazar the priest did
just as the LORD had commanded Moses.
32 ¶ Now the booty that remained
from the spoil which the [1]men of war
had plundered was 675,000 sheep,
33 and 72,000 cattle,
34 and 61,000 donkeys,
35 and of human beings, of the women

31:2 [a]Num 25:1,16,17 [b]Num 20:24,26; 27:13
3 [1]Lit *be* [a]Lev 26:25
5 [1]Lit *delivered*
6 [a]Num 14:44 [b]Num 10:8,9
7 [a]Deut 20:13; Judg 21:11; 1 Kin 11:15,16
8 [a]Josh 13:21 [b]Num 25:15 [c]Num 31:16; Josh 13:22
11 [a]Deut 20:14
15 [1]Lit *let...live* [a]Deut 20:14
16 [1]Lit *were to* [2]Lit *word* [3]Possibly *defect from the Lord* [a]Num 25:1-9 [b]Num 31:8
17 [1]Lit *by lying with a man* [a]Deut 7:2; 20:16-18
18 [1]Lit *female children* [2]Lit *by lying with a man* [3]Lit *keep alive*
19 [a]Num 19:11-22
20 [1]Or *skin*
23 [a]Num 19:9, 17
26 [1]Lit *of captives*
27 [a]Josh 22:8
28 [1]Lit *soul from* [a]Num 18:21-30
29 [1]Lit *heave offering,* and so throughout the ch
30 [a]Num 3:7,8, 25,26,31,36,37; 18:3,4
32 [1]Lit *people*

who had not known man [1]intimately, all
the persons were 32,000.
36 ¶ The half, the portion of those
who went out to war, was *as follows:* the
number of sheep was 337,500,
37 and the LORD'S levy of the sheep
was 675;
38 and the cattle were 36,000, from
which the LORD'S levy was 72;
39 and the donkeys were 30,500,
from which the LORD'S levy was 61;
40 and the human beings were
16,000, from whom the LORD'S levy was
32 persons.
41 Moses gave the levy *which was* the
LORD'S offering to Eleazar the priest, just
[a]as the LORD had commanded Moses.
42 ¶ As for the sons of Israel's half,
which Moses [1]separated from the men
who had gone to war—
43 now the congregation's half was
337,500 sheep,
44 and 36,000 cattle,
45 and 30,500 donkeys,
46 and the human beings were
16,000—
47 and from the sons of Israel's half,
Moses took one drawn out of every fifty,
both of man and of animals, and gave
them to the Levites, who kept charge of
the tabernacle of the LORD, just as the
LORD had commanded Moses.
48 ¶ Then the officers who were over
the thousands of the army, the captains of
thousands and the captains of hundreds,
approached Moses,
49 and they said to Moses, "Your servants have taken a census of men of war
who are in our charge, and no man of us
is missing.
50 "So we have brought as an offering
to the LORD what each man found, articles of gold, armlets and bracelets, signet
rings, earrings and necklaces, [a]to make
atonement for ourselves before the
LORD."
51 Moses and Eleazar the priest took
the gold from them, all kinds of wrought
articles.
52 All the gold of the offering which
they offered up to the LORD, from the
captains of thousands and the captains of
hundreds, was 16,750 shekels.
53 [a]The men of war had taken booty,
every man for himself.
54 So Moses and Eleazar the priest
took the gold from the captains of thousands and of hundreds, and brought it to
the tent of meeting as [a]a memorial for
the sons of Israel before the LORD.

Reuben and Gad Settle in Gilead

32 Now the sons of Reuben and the
sons of Gad had an [a]exceedingly
large number of livestock. So when they
saw the land of [b]Jazer and the land of
Gilead, that [1]it was indeed a place suitable for livestock,
2 the sons of Gad and the sons of Reuben came and spoke to Moses and to Eleazar the priest and to the leaders of the
congregation, saying,
3 "[a]Ataroth, Dibon, Jazer, Nimrah,
Heshbon, Elealeh, Sebam, Nebo and
Beon,
4 the land [a]which the LORD [1]con-
quered before the congregation of Israel,
is a land for livestock, and your servants
have livestock."
5 They said, "If we have found favor
in your sight, let this land be given to
your servants as a possession; do not take
us across the Jordan."
6 ¶ But Moses said to the sons of Gad
and to the sons of Reuben, "Shall your
brothers go to war while you yourselves
sit here?
7 "[a]Now why are you [1]discouraging
the sons of Israel from crossing over into
the land which the LORD has given them?
8 "[1]This is what your fathers did
when I sent them from [a]Kadesh-barnea
to see the land.
9 "For when they went up to [a]the
[1]valley of Eshcol and saw the land, they
[2]discouraged the sons of Israel so that
they did not go into the land which the
LORD had given them.
10 "So [a]the LORD'S anger burned in
that day, and He swore, saying,
11 '[a]None of the men who came up
from Egypt, from twenty years old and
upward, shall see the land which I swore
to Abraham, to Isaac and to Jacob; for
they did not follow Me fully,
12 except Caleb the son of Jephunneh
the Kenizzite and Joshua the son of Nun,
[a]for they have followed the LORD fully.'
13 "[a]So the LORD'S anger burned
against Israel, and He made them wander
in the wilderness forty years, until the
entire generation of those who had done
evil in the sight of the LORD was destroyed.
14 "Now behold, you have risen up in
your fathers' place, a brood of sinful men,
to add still more to the burning [a]anger of
the LORD against Israel.
15 "For if you [a]turn away from following Him, He will once more abandon
them in the wilderness, and you will destroy all these people."
16 ¶ Then they came near to him and
said, "We will build here sheepfolds for
our livestock and cities for our little ones;
17 [a]but we ourselves will be armed
ready *to go* before the sons of Israel, until
we have brought them to their place,

35 [1]Lit *by lying with a man*
41 [a]Num 5:9, 10; 18:19
42 [1]Or *divided*
50 [a]Ex 30:12-16
53 [a]Num 31:32; Deut 20:14
54 [a]Ex 30:16
32:1 [1]Lit *behold, the place, a place for* [a]Ex 12:38 [b]Num 21:32
3 [a]Num 32:34-38
4 [1]Lit *smote* [a]Num 21:34
7 [1]Lit *restraining the hearts of* [a]Num 13:27-14:4
8 [1]Lit *Thus your fathers* [a]Num 13:3,26; Deut 1:19-25
9 [1]Or *wadi* [2]Lit *restrained the hearts of* [a]Num 13:24; Deut 1:24
10 [a]Num 14:11f; Deut 1:34
11 [a]Num 14:28-30
12 [a]Deut 1:36; Josh 14:8f
13 [a]Num 14:33-35
14 [a]Deut 1:34f
15 [a]Deut 30:17, 18; 2 Chr 7:19, 20
17 [a]Josh 4:12, 13

while our little ones live in the fortified
cities because of the inhabitants of the
land.
18 "[a]We will not return to our homes
until every one of the sons of Israel has
possessed his inheritance.
19 "For we will not have an inheritance
with them on the other side of the Jordan
and beyond, because our inheritance has
fallen to us [a]on this side of the Jordan
toward the east."
20 ¶ [a]So Moses said to them, "If you
will do [1]this, if you will arm yourselves
before the LORD for the war,
21 and all of you armed men cross over
the Jordan before the LORD until He has
driven His enemies out from before Him,
22 [a]and the land is subdued before
the LORD, then afterward you shall return
and be free of obligation toward the LORD
and toward Israel, and this land shall be
yours for a possession before the LORD.
23 "But if you will not do so, behold,
you have sinned against the LORD, and be
sure [a]your sin will find you out.
24 "Build yourselves cities for your little ones, and sheepfolds for your sheep,
and [a]do [1]what you have promised."
25 ¶ The sons of Gad and the sons of
Reuben spoke to Moses, saying, "Your
servants will do just as my lord commands.
26 "[a]Our little ones, our wives, our
livestock and all our cattle shall [1]remain
there in the cities of Gilead;
27 while your servants, everyone who
is armed for war, will [a]cross over in the
presence of the LORD to battle, just as my
lord says."
28 ¶ So Moses gave command concerning them to Eleazar the priest, and to
Joshua the son of Nun, and to the heads
of the fathers' *households* of the tribes of
the sons of Israel.
29 Moses said to them, "If the sons of
Gad and the sons of Reuben, everyone
who is armed for battle, will cross with
you over the Jordan in the presence of the
LORD, and the land is subdued before you,
then you shall give them the land of Gilead for a possession;
30 but if they will not cross over with
you armed, they shall have possessions
among you in the land of Canaan."
31 The sons of Gad and the sons of
Reuben answered, saying, "As the LORD
has said to your servants, so we will do.
32 "We ourselves will cross over armed
in the presence of the LORD into the land
of Canaan, and the possession of our inheritance *shall remain* with us across the
Jordan."
33 ¶ [a]So Moses gave to them, to the
sons of Gad and to the sons of Reuben and
to the half-tribe of Joseph's son Manasseh, the kingdom of Sihon, king of the
Amorites and the kingdom of Og, the
king of Bashan, the land with its cities
with *their* [1]territories, the cities of the
surrounding land.
34 The sons of Gad built Dibon and
Ataroth and [a]Aroer,
35 and Atroth-shophan and Jazer and
Jogbehah,
36 and [a]Beth-nimrah and Beth-haran
as fortified cities, and sheepfolds for
sheep.
37 The sons of Reuben built Heshbon
and Elealeh and Kiriathaim,
38 and [a]Nebo and Baal-meon—*their*
names being changed—and Sibmah, and
they gave *other* names to the cities which
they built.
39 The sons of [a]Machir the son of Manasseh went to Gilead and took it, and
dispossessed the Amorites who were
in it.
40 So Moses gave [a]Gilead to Machir
the son of Manasseh, and he lived in it.
41 Jair the son of Manasseh went and
took its [1]towns, and called them
[2a]Havvoth-jair.
42 Nobah went and took Kenath and
its villages, and called it Nobah after [a]his
own name.

Review of the Journey from Egypt to Jordan

33 These are the journeys of the sons
of Israel, by which they came out
from the land of Egypt by their armies,
under [a]the [1]leadership of Moses and
Aaron.
2 Moses recorded their starting
places according to their journeys by the
[1]command of the LORD, and these are
their journeys according to their starting
places.
3 [a]They journeyed from Rameses in
the first month, on the fifteenth day of
the first month; on the [1]next day after
the Passover the sons of Israel [b]started
out [2]boldly in the sight of all the Egyptians,
4 while the Egyptians were burying
all their firstborn whom the LORD had
struck down among them. The LORD had
also executed judgments [a]on their gods.
5 ¶ Then [a]the sons of Israel journeyed from Rameses and camped in Succoth.
6 [a]They journeyed from Succoth and
camped in Etham, which is on the edge
of the wilderness.
7 [a]They journeyed from Etham and
turned back to Pi-hahiroth, which faces

18 [a]Josh 22:1-4
19 [a]Josh 12:1; 13:8
20 [1]Lit *this thing* [a]Deut 3:18
22 [a]Deut 3:20
23 [a]Gen 4:7; 44:16; Is 59:12
24 [1]Lit *that which has come out of your mouth* [a]Num 30:2
26 [1]Lit *be* [a]Josh 1:14
27 [a]Josh 4:12
33 [1]Lit *borders* [a]Deut 3:8-17; Josh 12:1-6
34 [a]Deut 2:36
36 [a]Num 32:3
38 [a]Is 46:1
39 [a]Gen 50:23
40 [a]Deut 3:12, 13,15; Josh 17:1
41 [1]Lit *tent villages* [2]I.e. the towns of Jair [a]Deut 3:14; Judg 10:4
42 [a]2 Sam 18:18; Ps 49:11
33:1 [1]Lit *hand* [a]Ps 77:20; 105:26; Mic 6:4
2 [1]Lit *mouth*
3 [1]Lit *morrow* [2]Lit *with a high hand* [a]Ex 12:37 [b]Ex 14:8
4 [a]Ex 12:12
5 [a]Ex 12:37
6 [a]Ex 13:20
7 [a]Ex 14:1,2

Baal-zephon, and they camped before
Migdol.
8 [a]They journeyed [1]from before Ha-
hiroth and passed through the midst of
the sea into the wilderness; and [b]they
went three days' journey in the wilderness of Etham and camped at Marah.
9 [a]They journeyed from Marah and
came to Elim; and in Elim there were
twelve springs of water and seventy palm
trees, and they camped there.
10 They journeyed from Elim and
camped by the [1]Red Sea.
11 They journeyed from the [1]Red Sea
and camped in [a]the wilderness of Sin.
12 They journeyed from the wilderness of Sin and camped at Dophkah.
13 They journeyed from Dophkah and
camped at Alush.
14 They journeyed from Alush and
camped [a]at Rephidim; now it was there
that the people had no water to drink.
15 They journeyed from Rephidim and
camped in [a]the wilderness of Sinai.
16 They journeyed from the wilderness of Sinai and camped at [a]Kibroth-
hattaavah.
17 ¶ They journeyed from Kibroth-
hattaavah and camped at [a]Hazeroth.
18 They journeyed from Hazeroth and
camped at Rithmah.
19 They journeyed from Rithmah and
camped at Rimmon-perez.
20 They journeyed from Rimmon-
perez and camped at [a]Libnah.
21 They journeyed from Libnah and
camped at Rissah.
22 They journeyed from Rissah and
camped in Kehelathah.
23 They journeyed from Kehelathah
and camped at Mount Shepher.
24 They journeyed from Mount Shepher and camped at Haradah.
25 They journeyed from Haradah and
camped at Makheloth.
26 They journeyed from Makheloth
and camped at Tahath.
27 They journeyed from Tahath and
camped at Terah.
28 They journeyed from Terah and
camped at Mithkah.
29 They journeyed from Mithkah and
camped at Hashmonah.
30 They journeyed from Hashmonah
and camped at [a]Moseroth.
31 They journeyed from Moseroth and
camped at Bene-jaakan.
32 They journeyed from [a]Bene-jaakan
and camped at Hor-haggidgad.
33 They journeyed from Hor-
haggidgad and camped at [a]Jotbathah.
34 They journeyed from Jotbathah and
camped at Abronah.
35 They journeyed from Abronah and
camped at [a]Ezion-geber.
36 They journeyed from Ezion-geber
and camped in the wilderness of [a]Zin,
that is, Kadesh.
37 They journeyed from Kadesh and
camped at [a]Mount Hor, [b]at the edge of
the land of Edom.
38 ¶ [a]Then Aaron the priest went up
to Mount Hor at the [1]command of the
LORD, and died there in the fortieth year
after the sons of Israel had come from the
land of Egypt, on the first *day* in the fifth
month.
39 Aaron was one hundred twenty-
three years old when he died on
Mount Hor.
40 ¶ Now the Canaanite, the king of
[a]Arad [1]who lived in the [2]Negev in the
land of Canaan, heard of the coming of
the sons of Israel.
41 ¶ Then they journeyed from Mount
Hor and camped at Zalmonah.
42 They journeyed from Zalmonah and
camped at Punon.
43 They journeyed from Punon and
camped at [a]Oboth.
44 They journeyed from Oboth and
camped at Iye-abarim, at the border of
Moab.
45 They journeyed from Iyim and
camped at Dibon-gad.
46 They journeyed from Dibon-gad
and camped at Almon-diblathaim.
47 They journeyed from Almon-
diblathaim and camped in the mountains
of [a]Abarim, before Nebo.
48 They journeyed from the mountains of Abarim and [a]camped in the
plains of Moab by the Jordan *opposite*
Jericho.
49 They camped by the Jordan, from
Beth-jeshimoth as far as [a]Abel-shittim in
the plains of Moab.

Law of Possessing the Land

50 ¶ Then the LORD spoke to Moses in
the plains of Moab by the Jordan *opposite*
Jericho, saying,
51 "Speak to the sons of Israel and say
to them, '[a]When you cross over the Jordan into the land of Canaan,
52 then you shall drive out all the inhabitants of the land from before you, and
[a]destroy all their figured stones, and destroy all their molten images and demolish all their high places;
53 [a]and you shall take possession of
the land and live in it, for I have given the
land to you to possess it.
54 '[a]You shall inherit the land by lot
according to your families; to the larger
you shall give more inheritance, and to
the smaller you shall give less inheri-

8 [1]Many mss read *from Pi-hahiroth* [a]Ex 14:22 [b]Ex 15:22,23
9 [a]Ex 15:27
10 [1]Lit *Sea of Reeds*
11 [1]Lit *Sea of Reeds* [a]Ex 16:1
14 [a]Ex 17:1
15 [a]Ex 19:1
16 [a]Num 11:34
17 [a]Num 11:35
20 [a]Deut 1:1
30 [a]Deut 10:6
32 [a]Gen 36:27; Deut 10:6; 1 Chr 1:42
33 [a]Deut 10:7
35 [a]Deut 2:8
36 [a]Num 20:1
37 [a]Num 20:22 [b]Num 20:16
38 [1]Lit *mouth* [a]Num 20:28; Deut 10:6
40 [1]Lit *and he* [2]I.e. South country [a]Num 21:1
43 [a]Num 21:10, 11
47 [a]Num 27:12
48 [a]Num 22:1
49 [a]Num 25:1
51 [a]Josh 3:17
52 [a]Ex 23:24; Lev 26:1; Deut 7:5; 12:3,30; Ps 106:34-36
53 [a]Deut 11:31; 17:14; Josh 21:43
54 [a]Num 26:53-56

tance. Wherever the lot falls to anyone, that shall be his. You shall inherit according to the tribes of your fathers.

55 'But if you do not drive out the inhabitants of the land from before you, then it shall come about that those whom you let remain of them *will become* [a]as pricks in your eyes and as thorns in your sides, and they will trouble you in the land in which you live.

56 'And as I plan to do to them, so I will do to you.' "

Instruction for Apportioning Canaan

34 Then the LORD spoke to Moses, saying,

2 "Command the sons of Israel and say to them, 'When you enter [a]the land of Canaan, this is the land that shall fall to you as an inheritance, *even the* land of Canaan according to its borders.

3 '[a]Your southern [1]sector shall [2]extend from the wilderness of Zin along the side of Edom, and your southern border shall [2]extend from the end of the Salt Sea [b]eastward.

4 'Then your border shall turn *direction* from the south to the ascent of Akrabbim and [1]continue to Zin, and its [2]termination shall be to the south of [a]Kadesh-barnea; and it shall [3]reach Hazaraddar and [1]continue to Azmon.

5 'The border shall turn *direction* from Azmon to the brook of Egypt, and its termination shall be at [a]the sea.

6 ¶ 'As for the western border, you shall have the Great Sea, that is, *its* [1]coastline; this shall be your west border.

7 ¶ '[a]And this shall be your north border: you shall draw your *border* line from the Great Sea to Mount Hor.

8 'You shall draw a line from Mount Hor to [a]the [1]Lebo-hamath, and the termination of the border shall be at Zedad;

9 and the border shall proceed to Ziphron, and its termination shall be at Hazar-enan. This shall be your north border.

10 ¶ 'For your eastern border you shall also draw a line from Hazar-enan to Shepham,

11 and the border shall go down from Shepham to [a]Riblah on the east side of Ain; and the border shall go down and reach to the [1]slope on the east side of the Sea of [b]Chinnereth.

12 'And the border shall go down to the Jordan and its termination shall be at the Salt Sea. This shall be your land according to its borders all around.' "

13 ¶ So Moses commanded the sons of Israel, saying, "[a]This is the land that you are to apportion by lot among you as a possession, which the LORD has commanded to give to the nine and a half tribes.

14 "[a]For the tribe of the sons of Reuben have received *theirs* according to their fathers' households, and the tribe of the sons of Gad according to their fathers' households, and the half-tribe of Manasseh have received their possession.

15 "The two and a half tribes have received their possession across the Jordan opposite Jericho, eastward toward the sunrising."

16 ¶ Then the LORD spoke to Moses, saying,

17 "[a]These are the names of the men who shall apportion the land to you for inheritance: Eleazar the priest and Joshua the son of Nun.

18 "You shall take one leader of every tribe to apportion the land for inheritance.

19 "These are the names of the men: of the tribe of [a]Judah, [b]Caleb the son of Jephunneh.

20 "Of the tribe of the sons of [a]Simeon, Samuel the son of Ammihud.

21 "Of the tribe of [a]Benjamin, Elidad the son of Chislon.

22 "Of the tribe of the sons of Dan a leader, Bukki the son of Jogli.

23 "Of the sons of Joseph: of the tribe of the sons of Manasseh a leader, Hanniel the son of Ephod.

24 "Of the tribe of the sons of Ephraim a leader, Kemuel the son of Shiphtan.

25 "Of the tribe of the sons of Zebulun a leader, Elizaphan the son of Parnach.

26 "Of the tribe of the sons of Issachar a leader, Paltiel the son of Azzan.

27 "Of the tribe of the sons of Asher a leader, Ahihud the son of Shelomi.

28 "Of the tribe of the sons of Naphtali a leader, Pedahel the son of Ammihud."

29 These are those whom the LORD commanded to apportion the inheritance to the sons of Israel in the land of Canaan.

Cities for the Levites

35 [a]Now the LORD spoke to Moses in the plains of Moab by the Jordan *opposite* Jericho, saying,

2 "Command the sons of Israel that they give to the Levites from the inheritance of their possession cities to live in; and you shall give to the Levites pasture lands around the cities.

3 "The cities shall be theirs to live in; and their pasture lands shall be for their cattle and for their herds and for all their beasts.

4 ¶ "The pasture lands of the cities

---

55 [a]Josh 23:13

34:2 [a]Gen 17:8; Ps 78:54,55; 105:11

3 [1]Lit *side* [2]Lit *be* [a]Josh 15:1-3 [b]Josh 15:5

4 [1]Lit *pass along* [2]Lit *goings out*, and so throughout the ch [3]Lit *go forth to* [a]Num 32:8

5 [a]Josh 15:4

6 [1]Lit *border*

7 [a]Ezek 47:15-17

8 [1]Or *entrance of Hamath* [a]Josh 13:5

11 [1]Lit *shoulder* [a]2 Kin 23:33 [b]Deut 3:17; Josh 13:27

13 [a]Gen 15:18; Num 26:52-56; Deut 11:24; Josh 14:1-5

14 [a]Num 32:33

17 [a]Josh 14:1,2

19 [a]Gen 29:35; Deut 33:7; Ps 60:7 [b]Num 13:6, 30; 26:65; Deut 1:36

20 [a]Gen 29:33; 49:5; Ezek 48:24

21 [a]Gen 49:27; Deut 33:12; Ps 68:27

35:1 [a]Lev 25:32-34

which you shall give to the Levites *shall extend* from the wall of the city [1]outward a thousand cubits around.
5 "You shall also measure outside the city on the east side two thousand cubits, and on the south side two thousand cubits, and on the west side two thousand cubits, and on the north side two thousand cubits, with the city in the center. This shall become theirs as pasture lands for the cities.

Cities of Refuge

6 "The cities which you shall give to the Levites *shall be* the [a]six cities of refuge, which you shall give for the manslayer to flee to; and in addition to them you shall give forty-two cities.
7 "All the cities which you shall give to the Levites *shall be* [a]forty-eight cities, [1]together with their pasture lands.
8 "[a]As for the cities which you shall give from the possession of the sons of Israel, you shall take more from the larger and you shall take less from the smaller; each shall give some of his cities to the Levites in proportion to his possession which he inherits."
9 ¶ Then the LORD spoke to Moses, saying,
10 "[a]Speak to the sons of Israel and say to them, 'When you cross the Jordan into the land of Canaan,
11 [a]then you shall select for yourselves cities to be your [b]cities of refuge, that the manslayer who has [1]killed any person [c]unintentionally may flee there.
12 '[a]The cities shall be to you as a refuge from the avenger, so that the manslayer will not die until he stands before the congregation for [1]trial.
13 'The cities which you are to give shall be your six cities of refuge.
14 'You [a]shall give three cities across the Jordan and three cities [1]in the land of Canaan; they are to be cities of refuge.
15 'These six cities shall be for refuge for the sons of Israel, and for the alien and for the sojourner among them; that anyone who [1]kills a person [a]unintentionally may flee there.
16 ¶ '[a]But if he struck him down with an iron object, so that he died, he is a murderer; the murderer shall surely be put to death.
17 'If he struck him down with a stone in the hand, by which he will die, and *as a result* he died, he is a murderer; the murderer [a]shall surely be put to death.
18 'Or if he struck him with a wooden object in the hand, by which he might

4 [1]Lit *and outward*
6 [a]Josh 20:7-9
7 [1]Lit *them* [a]Josh 21:41
8 [a]Lev 25:32-34; Num 26:54; 33:54; Josh 21:1-42
10 [a]Josh 20:1-9
11 [1]Lit *smote* [a]Deut 19:1-13 [b]Josh 20:2f [c]Ex 21:13; Lev 4:2f, 22f; Num 35:22-25
12 [1]Lit *judgment* [a]Deut 19:4-6; Josh 20:2,3
14 [1]Lit *you shall give in* [a]Deut 4:41
15 [1]Lit *smites* [a]Num 35:11
16 [a]Ex 21:12, 14; Lev 24:17
17 [a]Num 35:31

The Cities of Refuge

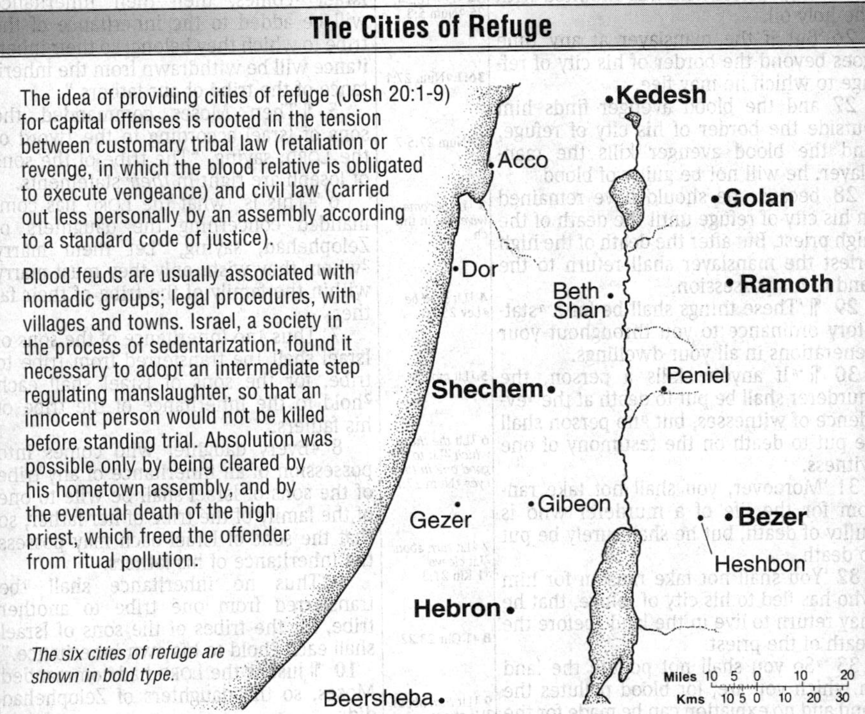

The idea of providing cities of refuge (Josh 20:1-9) for capital offenses is rooted in the tension between customary tribal law (retaliation or revenge, in which the blood relative is obligated to execute vengeance) and civil law (carried out less personally by an assembly according to a standard code of justice).

Blood feuds are usually associated with nomadic groups; legal procedures, with villages and towns. Israel, a society in the process of sedentarization, found it necessary to adopt an intermediate step regulating manslaughter, so that an innocent person would not be killed before standing trial. Absolution was possible only by being cleared by his hometown assembly, and by the eventual death of the high priest, which freed the offender from ritual pollution.

The six cities of refuge are shown in bold type.

die, and *as a result* he died, he is a murderer; the murderer shall surely be put to
death.
19 'The blood avenger himself shall put
the murderer to death; he shall put him
to death when he meets him.
20 '[a]If he pushed him of hatred, or
threw something at him [b]lying in wait
and *as a result* he died,
21 or if he struck him down with his
hand in enmity, and *as a result* he died,
the one who struck him shall surely be
put to death, he is a murderer; the blood
avenger shall put the murderer to death
when he meets him.
22 ¶ '[a]But if he pushed him suddenly
without enmity, or threw something at
him without lying in wait,
23 or with any [1]deadly object of stone,
and without seeing it dropped on him so
that he died, while he was not his enemy
nor seeking his injury,
24 then [a]the congregation shall judge
between the slayer and the blood avenger
according to these ordinances.
25 'The congregation shall deliver the
manslayer from the hand of the blood
avenger, and the congregation shall restore him to his city of refuge to which he
fled; and he shall live in it until the death
of the high priest who was anointed with
the holy oil.
26 'But if the manslayer at any time
goes beyond the border of his city of refuge to which he may flee,
27 and the blood avenger finds him
outside the border of his city of refuge,
and the blood avenger kills the manslayer, he will not be guilty of blood
28 because he should have remained
in his city of refuge until the death of the
high priest. But after the death of the high
priest the manslayer shall return to the
land of his possession.
29 ¶ 'These things shall be for a [a]stat-
utory ordinance to you throughout your
generations in all your dwellings.
30 ¶ '[a]If anyone kills a person, the
murderer shall be put to death at the [1]ev-
idence of witnesses, but [b]no person shall
be put to death on the testimony of one
witness.
31 'Moreover, you shall not take ransom for the life of a murderer who is
guilty of death, but he shall surely be put
to death.
32 'You shall not take ransom for him
who has fled to his city of refuge, that he
may return to live in the land [1]before the
death of the priest.
33 '[a]So you shall not pollute the land
in which you are; for blood pollutes the
land and no expiation can be made for the
land for the blood that is shed on it, except [b]by the blood of him who shed it.
34 'You shall not [a]defile the land in
which you live, in the midst of which [b]I
dwell; for I the LORD am dwelling in the
midst of the sons of Israel.' "

Inheritance by Marriage

36 [a]And the heads of the fathers'
households of the family of the
sons of Gilead, the son of Machir, the son
of Manasseh, of the families of the sons of
Joseph, came near and spoke before Moses and before the leaders, the heads of
the fathers' *households* of the sons of Israel,
2 and they said, "The LORD commanded my lord to give the land by lot to
the sons of Israel as an inheritance, and
my lord [a]was commanded by the LORD to
give the inheritance of Zelophehad our
brother to his daughters.
3 "But if they [1]marry one of the sons
of the *other* tribes of the sons of Israel,
their inheritance will be withdrawn from
the inheritance of our fathers and will be
added to the inheritance of the tribe to
which they belong; thus it will be withdrawn from our allotted inheritance.
4 "When the [a]jubilee of the sons of
Israel [1]comes, then their inheritance
will be added to the inheritance of the
tribe to which they belong; so their inheritance will be withdrawn from the inheritance of the tribe of our fathers."
5 ¶ Then Moses commanded the
sons of Israel according to the [1]word of
the LORD, saying, "The tribe of the sons
of Joseph are right in *their* statements.
6 "[a]This is [1]what the LORD has commanded concerning the daughters of
Zelophehad, saying, 'Let them marry
[2]whom they wish; only they must marry
within the family of the tribe of their father.'
7 "Thus [a]no inheritance of the sons of
Israel shall [1]be transferred from tribe to
tribe, for the sons of Israel shall each
[2]hold to the inheritance of the tribe of
his fathers.
8 "[a]Every daughter who comes into
possession of an inheritance of any tribe
of the sons of Israel shall be wife to one
of the family of the tribe of her father, so
that the sons of Israel each may possess
the inheritance of his fathers.
9 "Thus no inheritance shall [1]be
transferred from one tribe to another
tribe, for the tribes of the sons of Israel
shall each [2]hold to his own inheritance."
10 ¶ Just as the LORD had commanded
Moses, so the daughters of Zelophehad
did:

20 [a]Gen 4:8; 2 Sam 3:27; 20:10 [b]Ex 21:14; Deut 19:11
22 [a]Num 35:11
23 [1]Lit *by which he may die*
24 [a]Josh 20:6
29 [a]Num 27:11
30 [1]Lit *mouth* [a]Num 35:16 [b]Deut 17:6; 19:15; Matt 18:16; John 7:51; 8:17,18
32 [1]Or *until*
33 [a]Deut 21:7, 8; Ps 106:38 [b]Gen 9:6
34 [a]Lev 18:24, 25 [b]Num 5:3
36:1 [a]Num 27:1
2 [a]Num 27:5-7
3 [1]Lit *become wives to,* in this ch
4 [1]Lit *shall be* [a]Lev 25:10
5 [1]Lit *mouth*
6 [1]Lit *the thing which* [2]Lit *to the good one in their eyes* [a]Num 27:7
7 [1]Lit *turn about* [2]Lit *cleave* [a]1 Kin 21:3
8 [a]1 Chr 23:22
9 [1]Lit *turn about* [2]Lit *cleave*

11 [a]Mahlah, Tirzah, Hoglah, Milcah
and Noah, the daughters of Zelophehad
married their uncles' sons.
12 They married *those* from the families of the sons of Manasseh the son of
Joseph, and their inheritance [1]remained
with the tribe of the family of their father.
13 ¶ [a]These are the commandments
and the ordinances which the LORD commanded to the sons of Israel through Moses in the plains of Moab by the Jordan
opposite Jericho.

11 [a]Num 26:33
12 [1]Lit *was*
13 [a]Lev 26:46; 27:34; Num 22:1

Deuteronomy

Title and Background

The word "Deuteronomy" means "repetition of the law." After forty years the Israelites were about to enter Canaan. But before they did, Moses wanted to remind them of their history, all that God had done for them, and the laws they had to continue to obey as God's chosen people.

Author and Date of Writing

The book itself testifies that, for the most part, Moses wrote it (1:5; 31:9,22,24) as other Old Testament books agree (1 Kings 2:3; 8:53; 2 Kings 14:6; 18:12). Jesus bears the same testimony (Matthew 19:7–8; Mark 10:3–5; John 5:45–47), and so do other New Testament writers (Acts 3:22–23; 7:37–38; Romans 10:19). Moreover, Jesus quotes Deuteronomy as authoritative (Matthew 4:4,7,10). The book was written shortly before Moses' death in about 1406 B.C.

Theme and Message

Moses reminded the people of God's goodness to them—how God was with them throughout their journey and gave them the land of Canaan. He also summarized God's laws, including the Ten Commandments. One subject that pervades the whole book is the love relationship of the Lord to His people and that of the people to the Lord as their sovereign God.

Outline

I. Preamble (1:1–5)
II. Historical Prologue (1:6—4:43)
III. Stipulations of the Covenant (4:44—26:19)
  A. Primary Demands (4:44—11:32)
  B. Supplementary Requirements (12:1—26:19)
IV. Ratification, and Curses and Blessings (27:1—30:20)
V. Succession Under the Covenant (31:1—34:12)

Israel's History after the Exodus

1 These are the words which Moses
spoke to all Israel [a]across the Jordan
in the wilderness, in the [b]Arabah opposite [1]Suph, between Paran and Tophel
and Laban and Hazeroth and Dizahab.
2 It is eleven days' *journey* from [a]Ho-
reb by the way of Mount [b]Seir to
[c]Kadesh-barnea.
3 In the [a]fortieth year, on the first
day of the eleventh month, Moses spoke
to the children of Israel, [b]according to all
that the LORD had commanded him *to
give* to them,
4 after he had [1a]defeated Sihon the
king of the Amorites, who lived in Heshbon, and [b]Og the king of Bashan, who
lived in [c]Ashtaroth [2]and Edrei.
5 Across the Jordan in the land of
Moab, Moses undertook to expound this
law, saying,
6 ¶ "The LORD our God [a]spoke to us
at Horeb, saying, 'You have [1]stayed long
enough at this mountain.
7 'Turn and set your journey, and go
to [a]the hill country of the Amorites, and
to all their neighbors in the Arabah, in
the hill country and in the lowland and in
[b]the [1]Negev and by the seacoast, the
land of the Canaanites, and Lebanon, as
far as the great river, the river Euphrates.
8 'See, I have placed the land before
you; go in and possess the land which the
LORD [a]swore to give to your fathers, to
Abraham, to Isaac, and to Jacob, to them
and their [1]descendants after them.'
9 ¶ "I spoke to you at that time, saying, '[a]I am not able to bear *the burden* of
you alone.
10 'The LORD your God has [a]multi-
plied you, and behold, you are this day
like the stars of heaven in number.
11 'May the LORD, the God of your fathers, increase you a thousand-fold more
than you are and bless you, [a]just as He
has [1]promised you!
12 'How can I alone bear the load and
burden of you and your strife?
13 '[1a]Choose wise and discerning and
experienced men from your tribes, and I
will appoint them as your heads.'

1:1 [1]Perhaps Red Sea [a]Deut 4:46 [b]Deut 2:8
2 [a]Ex 3:1 [b]Gen 32:3 [c]Num 13:26; Deut 9:23
3 [a]Num 33:38 [b]Deut 4:1
4 [1]Lit *smitten* [2]So with ancient versions; M.T. omits *and* [a]Num 21:21-26; Deut 2:26-35; Josh 13:10; Neh 9:22 [b]Num 21:33-35; Josh 13:12 [c]Josh 12:4
6 [1]Lit *dwelt* [a]Num 10:11-13
7 [1]I.e. South country [a]Gen 15:18; Deut 11:24; Josh 10:40 [b]Gen 12:9
8 [1]Lit *seed* [a]Gen 12:7; Ex 33:1; Num 14:23; Heb 6:13
9 [a]Ex 18:18; Num 11:14
10 [a]Gen 15:5; Ex 32:13; Deut 7:7
11 [1]Lit *spoken to* [a]Deut 1:8
13 [1]Lit *Give for yourselves* [a]Ex 18:21

14 "You answered me and said, 'The thing which you have said to do is good.'

15 "So I took the heads of your tribes, wise and experienced men, and [1]appointed them heads over you, leaders of thousands and [2]of hundreds, [2]of fifties and [2]of tens, and officers for your tribes.

16 ¶ "Then I charged your judges at that time, saying, 'Hear *the cases* between your [1]fellow countrymen, and [a]judge righteously between a man and his [2]fellow countryman, or the alien who is with him.

17 '[a]You shall not show partiality in judgment; you shall hear the small and the great alike. You shall [b]not fear [1]man, for the judgment is God's. [c]The case that is too hard for you, you shall bring to me, and I will hear it.'

18 "[a]I commanded you at that time all the things that you should do.

19 ¶ "Then we set out from [a]Horeb, and went through all that [b]great and terrible wilderness which you saw on the way to the [c]hill country of the Amorites, just as the LORD our God had commanded us; and we came to [a]Kadesh-barnea.

20 "I said to you, 'You have come to the hill country of the Amorites which the LORD our God is about to give us.

21 'See, the LORD your God has placed the land before you; go up, take possession, as the LORD, the God of your fathers, has spoken to you. [a]Do not fear or be dismayed.'

22 ¶ "[a]Then all of you approached me and said, 'Let us send men before us, that they may search out the land for us, and bring back to us word of the way by which we should go up and the cities which we shall enter.'

23 "The thing pleased me and I took twelve of your men, one man for each tribe.

24 "[a]They turned and went up into the hill country, and came to the valley of Eshcol and spied it out.

25 "Then they took *some* of the fruit of the land in their hands and brought it down to us; and they brought us back a report and said, 'It is a good land which the LORD our God is about to give us.'

26 ¶ "[a]Yet you were not willing to go up, but [b]rebelled against the [1]command of the LORD your God;

27 and [a]you grumbled in your tents and said, 'Because the LORD hates us, He has brought us out of the land of Egypt to deliver us into the hand of the Amorites to destroy us.

28 'Where can we go up? Our brethren have made our hearts melt, saying, "The people are bigger and taller than we; the cities are large and fortified to heaven. And besides, we saw [a]the sons of the Anakim there." '

29 "Then I said to you, 'Do not be shocked, nor fear them.

30 'The LORD your God who goes before you will [a]Himself fight on your behalf, [1]just as He did for you in Egypt before your eyes,

31 and in the wilderness where you saw how [a]the LORD your God carried you, just as a man carries his son, in all the way which you have walked until you came to this place.'

32 "But [1a]for all this, you did not trust the LORD your God,

33 [a]who goes before you on *your* way, [b]to seek out a place for you to encamp, in fire by night and cloud by day, to show you the way in which you should go.

34 ¶ "Then the LORD heard the sound of your words, and He was angry and [a]took an oath, saying,

35 '[a]Not one of these men, this evil generation, shall see the good land which I swore to give your fathers,

36 except Caleb the son of Jephunneh; he shall see it, and [a]to him and to his sons I will give the land on which he has set foot, because he has followed the LORD fully.'

37 "[a]The LORD was angry with me also on your account, saying, '[b]Not even you shall enter there.

38 'Joshua the son of Nun, who stands before you, [a]he shall enter there; encourage him, for [b]he will cause Israel to inherit it.

39 'Moreover, [a]your little ones who you said would become a prey, and your sons, who this day have [b]no knowledge of good or evil, shall enter there, and I will give it to them and they shall possess it.

40 'But as for you, [a]turn around and set out for the wilderness by the way to the [1]Red Sea.'

41 ¶ "[a]Then you said to me, 'We have sinned against the LORD; we will indeed go up and fight, just as the LORD our God commanded us.' And every man of you girded on his weapons of war, and regarded it as easy to go up into the hill country.

42 "[a]And the LORD said to me, 'Say to them, "Do not go up nor fight, for I am not among you; otherwise you will be [1]defeated before your enemies." '

43 "So I spoke to you, but you would not listen. Instead [a]you rebelled against the [1]command of the LORD, and acted presumptuously and went up into the hill country.

44 "[a]The Amorites who [1]lived in that hill country came out against you and

---

15 [1]Lit *gave* [2]Lit *leaders of*
16 [1]Lit *brothers* [2]Lit *brother* [a]Deut 16:18; John 7:24
17 [1]Lit *because of man* [a]Deut 10:17; 16:19; 24:17; 2 Chr 19:5,6; Prov 24:23-26; Acts 10:34; James 2:1,9 [b]Prov 29:25 [c]Ex 18:22,26
18 [a]Ex 18:20
19 [a]Deut 1:2 [b]Deut 2:7; 8:15; 32:10; Jer 2:6 [c]Deut 1:7
21 [a]Josh 1:6,9
22 [a]Num 13:1-3
24 [a]Num 13:21-25
26 [1]Lit *mouth* [a]Num 14:1-4 [b]Deut 9:23
27 [a]Deut 9:28; Ps 106:25
28 [a]Num 13:28, 33; Deut 9:2
30 [1]Lit *according to all that* [a]Ex 14:14; Deut 3:22; 20:4; Neh 4:20
31 [a]Deut 32:10-12; Is 46:3,4; 63:9; Hos 11:3; Acts 13:18
32 [1]Lit *in this matter* [a]Num 14:11; Ps 106:24; Heb 3:19; 4:2; Jude 5
33 [a]Ex 13:21; Num 9:15-23; Neh 9:12; Ps 78:14 [b]Num 10:33
34 [a]Num 14:28-30; Heb 3:18
35 [a]Ps 95:11; 106:26; Ezek 20:15; 1 Cor 10:5; Heb 3:14-19
36 [a]Num 14:24; Josh 14:9
37 [a]Num 20:12; Deut 3:26; 4:21 [b]Num 27:13,18
38 [a]Num 14:30 [b]Num 34:17; Deut 3:28; 31:7; Josh 11:23
39 [a]Num 14:3, 31 [b]Is 7:15,16
40 [1]Lit *Sea of Reeds* [a]Num 14:25
41 [a]Num 14:40
42 [1]Lit *smitten* [a]Num 14:41-43
43 [1]Lit *mouth* [a]Num 14:40
44 [1]Lit *dwelt* [a]Num 14:45

chased you [b]as bees do, and crushed you
from Seir to Hormah.
45 "Then you returned and wept before
the LORD; but the [a]LORD did not listen to
your voice nor give ear to you.
46 "So you remained in [a]Kadesh many
days, [1]the days that you spent *there.*

Wanderings in the Wilderness

2 "[a]Then we turned and set out for
the wilderness by the way to the
[1]Red Sea, as the LORD spoke to me, and
circled [b]Mount Seir for many days.
2 "And the LORD spoke to me, saying,
3 'You have circled this mountain
long enough. *Now* turn north,
4 [a]and command the people, saying,
"You will pass through the [b]territory of
your brothers the sons of Esau who live
in Seir; and [c]they will be afraid of you. So
be very careful;
5 do not [1]provoke them, for I will
not give you any of their land, even *as
little as* a [2]footstep [a]because I have giv-
en Mount Seir to Esau as a possession.
6 "You shall buy food from them with
money so that you may eat, and you shall
also purchase water from them with
money so that you may drink.
7 "For the LORD your God has blessed
you in all [1]that you have done; He has
known your [2]wanderings through this
[a]great wilderness. These [b]forty years
the LORD your God has been with you;
you have not lacked a thing."'
8 ¶ "So we passed beyond our brothers the sons of Esau, who live in Seir,
away from the [a]Arabah road, away from
Elath and [b]from Ezion-geber. And we
turned and passed through by the way of
the wilderness of Moab.
9 "Then the LORD said to me, 'Do not
harass Moab, nor provoke them to war,
for I will not give you any of [1]their land
as a possession, because I have given [a]Ar
to [b]the sons of Lot as a possession.
10 (The [a]Emim lived there formerly, a
people as great, numerous, and tall as the
Anakim.
11 Like the Anakim, they are also regarded as [a]Rephaim, but the Moabites
call them Emim.
12 [a]The Horites formerly lived in Seir,
but the sons of Esau dispossessed them
and destroyed them from before them
and settled in their place, [b]just as Israel
did to the land of [1]their possession
which the LORD gave to them.)
13 'Now arise and cross over the
[1]brook Zered yourselves.' So we crossed
over the [1]brook Zered.
14 "Now the [1]time that it took for us
to come from Kadesh-barnea until we
crossed over the [2]brook Zered was
[a]thirty-eight years, until [b]all the generation of the men of war perished from
within the camp, as [c]the LORD had
sworn to them.
15 "[a]Moreover the hand of the LORD
was against them, to destroy them from
within the camp until they all perished.
16 ¶ "So it came about when [a]all the
men of war had finally perished from
among the people,
17 that the LORD spoke to me, saying,
18 'Today you shall cross over [a]Ar, the
border of Moab.
19 'When you come opposite the
[a]sons of Ammon, do not harass them nor
provoke them, for I will not give you any
of the land of the sons of Ammon as a
possession, because I have given it to
[b]the sons of Lot as a possession.'
20 (It is also regarded as the land of the
[a]Rephaim, *for* Rephaim formerly lived in
it, but the Ammonites call them Zamzum-
min,
21 a people as great, numerous, and
tall as the Anakim, but the LORD destroyed them before them. And they dispossessed them and settled in their place,
22 just as He did for the sons of Esau,
who [a]live in Seir, when He destroyed
[b]the Horites from before them; they dispossessed them and settled in their place
even to this day.
23 And the [a]Avvim, who lived in villages as far as Gaza, the [1b]Caphtorim
who came from [2c]Caphtor, destroyed
them and lived in their place.)
24 'Arise, set out, and pass through the
[1a]valley of Arnon. Look! I have given
Sihon the Amorite, king of Heshbon, and
his land into your hand; begin to take
possession and contend with him in battle.
25 'This day I will begin to put [a]the
dread and fear of you [1]upon the peoples
[2]everywhere under the heavens, who,
when they hear the report of you, [b]will
tremble and be in anguish because
of you.'
26 ¶ "[a]So I sent messengers from the
wilderness of Kedemoth to Sihon king of
Heshbon with words of peace, saying,
27 'Let me pass through your land, I
will [1]travel only on the highway; I will
not turn aside to the right or to the left.
28 'You will sell me food for money so
that I may eat, and give me water for
money so that I may drink, [a]only let me
pass through on [1]foot,
29 just as the sons of Esau who live in
Seir and the Moabites who live in [a]Ar
did for me, until I cross over the Jordan
into the land which the LORD our God is
giving to us.'
30 "But [a]Sihon king of Heshbon was

44 [b]Ps 118:12
45 [a]Job 27:8,9; Ps 66:18; John 9:31
46 [1]Lit *as the days* [a]Num 20:1, 22; Deut 2:7,14; Judg 11:17
2:1 [1]Lit *Sea of Reeds* [a]Num 21:4 [b]Deut 1:2
4 [a]Num 20:14-21 [b]Gen 36:8 [c]Ex 15:15, 16
5 [1]Or *engage in strife with* [2]Lit *treading of a sole of a foot* [a]Gen 36:8; Josh 24:4
7 [1]Lit *the work of your hand* [2]Lit *goings* [a]Deut 1:19 [b]Num 14:33,34; 32:13; Deut 2:14
8 [a]Deut 1:1 [b]Num 33:35; 1 Kin 9:26
9 [1]Lit *his* [a]Num 21:15,28; Deut 2:18,29 [b]Gen 19:36,37
10 [a]Gen 14:5
11 [a]Gen 14:5; Deut 2:20
12 [1]Lit *his* [a]Gen 36:20; Deut 2:22 [b]Num 21:25,35
13 [1]Or *wadi*
14 [1]Lit *days in which we went* [2]Or *wadi* [a]Deut 2:7 [b]Num 14:29-35; 26:64, 65; Ps 106:26; 1 Cor 10:5 [c]Deut 1:34,35
15 [a]Jude 5
16 [a]Deut 2:14
18 [a]Deut 2:9
19 [a]Gen 19:38 [b]Deut 2:9
20 [a]Deut 2:11
22 [a]Gen 36:8; Deut 2:5 [b]Deut 2:12
23 [1]I.e. Philistines [2]I.e. Crete [a]Josh 13:3 [b]Gen 10:14; 1 Chr 1:12 [c]Jer 47:4; Amos 9:7
24 [1]Or *wadi* [a]Num 21:13,14; Judg 11:18
25 [1]Lit *in front of* [2]Lit *under all the heavens* [a]Ex 23:27; Deut 11:25; Josh 2:9 [b]Ex 15:14-16
26 [a]Num 21:21-32; Deut 1:4; Judg 11:19-21
27 [1]Lit *go by the way*
28 [1]Lit *my feet* [a]Num 20:19
29 [a]Deut 2:9
30 [a]Num 21:23

not willing for us to pass [1]through his
land; for the [b]LORD your God hardened
his spirit and made his heart obstinate, in
order to deliver him into your hand, as *he*
is today.
31 "The LORD said to me, 'See, I have
begun to deliver Sihon and his land [1]over
to you. Begin to [2]occupy, that you may
possess his land.'
32 ¶ "Then Sihon [1]with all his people
came out to meet us in battle at Jahaz.
33 "[a]The LORD our God delivered him
[1]over to us, and we [2b]defeated him
with his sons and all his people.
34 "So we captured all his cities at that
time and [1a]utterly destroyed [2]the men,
women and children of every city. We
left no survivor.
35 "We took [a]only the animals as our
booty and the spoil of the cities which we
had captured.
36 "From [a]Aroer which is on the edge
of the [1]valley of Arnon and *from* the city
which is in the [1]valley, even to Gilead,
there was no city that was too high for us;
the LORD our God delivered all [2]over
to us.
37 "[a]Only you did not go near to the
land of the sons of Ammon, all along the
[1]river [b]Jabbok and the cities of the hill
country, and wherever the LORD our God
had commanded us.

Conquests Recounted

3 "[a]Then we turned and went up the
road to Bashan, and Og, king of Bashan, [1]with all his people came out to
meet us in battle at Edrei.
2 "But the LORD said to me, 'Do not
fear him, for I have delivered him and all
his people and his land into your hand;
and you shall do to him just as you did to
Sihon king of the Amorites, who lived at
Heshbon.'
3 "So the LORD our God delivered Og
also, king of Bashan, with all his people
into our hand, and we smote [1]them until
no survivor was [2]left.
4 "We captured all his cities at that
time; there was not a city which we did
not take from them: sixty cities, all the
region of [a]Argob, the kingdom of Og in
Bashan.
5 "All these were cities fortified with
high walls, gates and bars, besides a great
many [1]unwalled towns.
6 "We [1]utterly destroyed them, as we
did to [a]Sihon king of Heshbon, [2b]utter-
ly destroying [3]the men, women and children of every city.
7 "[a]But all the animals and the spoil of
the cities we took as our booty.
8 ¶ "[a]Thus we took the land at that
time from the hand of the two kings of
the Amorites who were beyond the Jordan, from the [1]valley of Arnon to Mount
Hermon
9 (Sidonians [a]call Hermon [b]Sirion,
and the Amorites call it [c]Senir):
10 all the cities of the plateau and all
Gilead and [a]all Bashan, as far as Salecah
and Edrei, cities of the kingdom of Og in
Bashan.
11 (For only Og king of Bashan was left
of the remnant of the [a]Rephaim. Behold,
his [1]bedstead was an iron [1]bedstead; it
is in [b]Rabbah of the sons of Ammon. Its
length was nine cubits and its width four
cubits [2]by ordinary cubit.)
12 ¶ "So we took possession of this
land at that time. From [a]Aroer, which is
by the [1]valley of Arnon, and half the hill
country of [b]Gilead and its cities I gave to
the Reubenites and to the Gadites.
13 "The rest of Gilead and all Bashan,
the kingdom of Og, I gave to the half-tribe
of Manasseh, all the region of Argob (concerning all Bashan, it is called the land of
Rephaim.
14 [a]Jair the son of Manasseh took all
the region of Argob as far as the border of
the Geshurites and the Maacathites, and
called [1]it, *that is,* Bashan, after his own
name, [2]Havvoth-jair, *as it is* to this day.)
15 "[a]To Machir I gave Gilead.
16 "To the Reubenites and to the Gadites I gave from Gilead even as far as the
[1]valley of Arnon, the middle of the [1]val-
ley [2]as a border and as far as the [1]river
[a]Jabbok, the border of the sons of Ammon;
17 the Arabah also, with the Jordan
[1]as *a* border, from [2a]Chinnereth [b]even
as far as the sea of the Arabah, [c]the Salt
Sea, [3]at the foot of the slopes of Pisgah on
the east.
18 ¶ "Then I commanded you at that
time, saying, '[a]The LORD your God has
given you this land to possess it; [b]all you
valiant men shall cross over armed before
your brothers, the sons of Israel.
19 '[a]But your wives and your little
ones and your livestock (I know that you
have [b]much livestock) shall remain in
your cities which I have given you,
20 [a]until the LORD gives rest to your
fellow countrymen as to you, and they
also possess the land which the LORD
your God will give them beyond the Jordan. [b]Then you may return every man to
his possession which I have given you.'
21 "I commanded Joshua at that time,
saying, 'Your eyes have seen all that the
LORD your God has done to these two
kings; so the LORD shall do to all the kingdoms into which you are about to cross.
22 'Do not fear them, for the LORD your
God [a]is the one fighting for you.'

30 [1]Lit *by him* [b]Ex 4:21; Josh 11:20
31 [1]Lit *before you* [2]Lit *possess*
32 [1]Lit *he and*
33 [1]Lit *before us* [2]Lit *smote* [a]Ex 23:31; Deut 7:2 [b]Deut 29:7
34 [1]Or *put under the ban* [2]Lit *every city of man...* [a]Deut 3:6; 7:2
35 [a]Deut 3:7
36 [1]Or *wadi* [2]Lit *before us* [a]Deut 3:12; 4:48; Josh 12:2; 13:9
37 [1]Or *wadi* [a]Deut 2:19 [b]Gen 32:22; Num 21:24; Deut 3:16
3:1 [1]Lit *he and* [a]Num 21:33-35
3 [1]Lit *him* [2]Lit *left to him*
4 [a]Deut 3:13,14; 1 Kin 4:13
5 [1]Or *rural*
6 [1]Or *put them under the ban* [2]Or *putting under the ban* [3]Lit *every city of men...* [a]Deut 1:4 [b]Deut 2:34
7 [a]Deut 2:35
8 [1]Or *wadi* [a]Num 32:33; Josh 12:1-7; 13:8-12
9 [a]Deut 4:48; Josh 11:17; Ps 42:6; 133:3 [b]Ps 29:6 [c]1 Chr 5:23
10 [a]Josh 13:11
11 [1]Or *couch* [2]Lit *by a man's forearm* [a]Gen 14:5; Deut 2:11, 20 [b]2 Sam 11:1; 12:26; Jer 49:2
12 [1]Or *wadi* [a]Deut 2:36 [b]Num 32:32-38; Josh 13:8-13
14 [1]Lit *them* [2]I.e. the towns of Jair [a]Num 32:41; 1 Chr 2:22
15 [a]Num 32:39, 40
16 [1]Or *wadi* [2]Lit *and* [a]Num 21:24; Deut 2:37
17 [1]Lit *and* [2]I.e. the Sea of Galilee [3]Lit *under* [a]Num 34:11; Josh 13:27 [b]Josh 12:3 [c]Gen 14:3; Josh 3:16
18 [a]Josh 1:13 [b]Num 32:20; Josh 4:12,13
19 [a]Josh 1:14 [b]Ex 12:38
20 [a]Josh 1:15 [b]Josh 22:4
22 [a]Ex 14:14; Deut 1:30; 20:4; Neh 4:20

23 ¶ "I also pleaded with the LORD at
that time, saying,
24 'O Lord [1]GOD, You have begun to
show Your servant [a]Your greatness and
Your strong hand; for what [b]god is there
in heaven or on earth who can do such
works and mighty acts as Yours?
25 'Let me, I pray, cross over and see
the [a]fair land that is beyond the Jordan,
[1]that good hill country and Lebanon.'
26 "But [a]the LORD was angry with me
on your account, and would not listen to
me; and the LORD said to me, '[1]Enough!
Speak to Me no more of this matter.
27 'Go up to the top of [a]Pisgah and lift
up your eyes to the west and north and
south and east, and see *it* with your eyes,
[b]for you shall not cross over this Jordan.
28 '[a]But charge Joshua and encourage
him and strengthen him, [b]for he shall go
across [1]at the head of this people, and he
will give them as an inheritance the land
which you will see.'
29 "So we remained in the valley opposite [a]Beth-peor.

Israel Urged to Obey God's Law

4 "Now, O Israel, listen to the statutes
and the judgments which [a]I am
teaching you to perform, so that [b]you
may live and go in and take possession of
the land which the LORD, the God of your
fathers, is giving you.
2 "[a]You shall not add to the word
which [b]I am commanding you, nor take
away from it, that you may keep the commandments of the LORD your God which
I command you.
3 "[a]Your eyes have seen what the
LORD has done in the case of Baal-peor,
for all the men who followed Baal-peor,
the LORD your God has destroyed [1]them
from among you.
4 "But you who held fast to the LORD
your God are alive today, every one of
you.
5 ¶ "See, I have taught you statutes
and judgments [a]just as the LORD my God
commanded me, that you should do thus
in the land where you are entering to
possess it.
6 "So keep and do *them*, [a]for that is
your wisdom and your understanding in
the sight of the peoples who will hear all
these statutes and say, 'Surely this great
nation is a wise and understanding people.'
7 "For [a]what great nation is there that
has a god [b]so near to it as is the LORD our
God [c]whenever we call on Him?
8 "Or what great nation is there that
has [a]statutes and judgments as righteous
as this whole law which I am setting before you today?

24 [1]Heb *YHWH*, usually rendered *LORD* [a]Deut 11:2 [b]Ex 8:10; 15:11; 2 Sam 7:22; Ps 71:19; 86:8
25 [1]Lit *this* [a]Deut 4:22
26 [1]Lit *Enough for you* [a]Deut 1:37
27 [a]Num 23:14; 27:12 [b]Deut 1:37
28 [1]Lit *before this people* [a]Num 27:18; Deut 31:3,7,8,23 [b]Deut 1:38
29 [a]Num 25:1-3; Deut 4:46; 34:6
4:1 [a]Deut 1:3 [b]Lev 18:5; Deut 5:33; 8:1; 16:20; 30:16,19; Ezek 20:11; Rom 10:5
2 [a]Deut 12:32; Prov 30:6; Rev 22:18 [b]Deut 4:5, 14,40
3 [1]Lit *him* [a]Num 25:1-9
5 [a]Lev 26:46; 27:34
6 [a]Deut 30:19, 20; 32:46,47; Job 28:28; Ps 19:7; 111:10; Prov 1:7; 2 Tim 3:15
7 [a]Deut 4:32-34; 2 Sam 7:23 [b]Ps 34:17,18; 145:18; 148:14; Is 55:6 [c]Ps 34:18; 85:9
8 [a]Ps 89:14; 97:2; 119:144, 160,172
9 [a]Deut 4:23; 6:12; 8:11,14, 19; Prov 4:23; 23:19 [b]Deut 6:2; 12:1; 16:3 [c]Gen 18:19; Deut 4:10; 6:7,20-25; 11:19; 32:46; Ps 78:5,6; Prov 22:6; Eph 6:4
10 [1]Or *reverence* [a]Deut 14:23; 17:19; 31:12,13 [b]Deut 4:9
11 [a]Ex 19:18; Heb 12:18,19
13 [1]Lit *Words* [a]Ex 34:28; Deut 10:4 [b]Ex 31:18; 34:1,28
15 [a]Josh 23:11 [b]Is 40:18
16 [a]Deut 4:25; 9:12; 31:29 [b]Ex 20:4; Lev 26:1; Deut 5:8,9; 27:15; Rom 1:23
17 [a]Rom 1:23
19 [a]Gen 2:1; Deut 17:3; 2 Kin 17:16; 21:3 [b]Deut 13:5,10; Job 31:26-28
20 [a]1 Kin 8:51; Jer 11:4 [b]Ex 19:5; Deut 7:6; 14:2; 26:18; Titus 2:14; 1 Pet 2:9
21 [a]Num 20:12; Deut 1:37
22 [a]Num 27:13, 14

9 ¶ "Only [a]give heed to yourself and
keep your soul diligently, so that you do
not forget the things which your eyes
have seen and they do not depart from
your heart [b]all the days of your life; but
[c]make them known to your sons and
your grandsons.
10 "*Remember* the day you stood before
the LORD your God at Horeb, when the
LORD said to me, 'Assemble the people to
Me, that I may let them hear My words
[a]so they may learn to [1]fear Me all the
days they live on the earth, and that they
may [b]teach their children.'
11 "You came near and stood at the foot
of the mountain, [a]and the mountain
burned with fire to the *very* heart of the
heavens: darkness, cloud and thick
gloom.
12 "Then the LORD spoke to you from
the midst of the fire; you heard the sound
of words, but you saw no form—only a
voice.
13 "So He declared to you His covenant
which He commanded you to perform,
that is, [a]the Ten [1]Commandments; and
[b]He wrote them on two tablets of stone.
14 "The LORD commanded me at that
time to teach you statutes and judgments,
that you might perform them in the land
where you are going over to possess it.
15 ¶ "So [a]watch yourselves carefully,
since you did not see any [b]form on the
day the LORD spoke to you at Horeb from
the midst of the fire,
16 so that you do not [a]act corruptly
and [b]make a graven image for yourselves
in the form of any figure, the likeness of
male or female,
17 the likeness of any animal that is on
the earth, the likeness of [a]any winged
bird that flies in the sky,
18 the likeness of anything that creeps
on the ground, the likeness of any fish
that is in the water below the earth.
19 "And *beware* not to lift up your eyes
to heaven and see the sun and the moon
and the stars, [a]all the host of heaven,
[b]and be drawn away and worship them
and serve them, those which the LORD
your God has allotted to all the peoples
under the whole heaven.
20 "But the LORD has taken you and
brought you out of [a]the iron furnace,
from Egypt, to [b]be a people for His own
possession, as today.
21 ¶ "[a]Now the LORD was angry with
me on your account, and swore that I
would not cross the Jordan, and that I
would not enter the good land which the
LORD your God is giving you as an inheritance.
22 "For [a]I will die in this land, I shall

not cross the Jordan, but you shall cross
and take possession of this [b]good land.
23 "So watch yourselves, [a]that you do
not forget the covenant of the LORD your
God which He made with you, and
[b]make for yourselves a graven image in
the form of anything *against* which the
LORD your God has commanded you.
24 "For the LORD your God is a [a]con-
suming fire, a [b]jealous God.
25 ¶ "When you [1]become the father
of children and children's children and
have remained long in the land, and [a]act
corruptly, and [b]make an [2]idol in the
form of anything, and [c]do that which is
evil in the sight of the LORD your God *so
as* to provoke Him to anger,
26 I [a]call heaven and earth to witness
against you today, that you will [b]surely
perish quickly from the land where you
are going over the Jordan to possess it.
You shall not [1]live long on it, but will be
utterly destroyed.
27 "The LORD will [a]scatter you among
the peoples, and you will be left few in
number among the nations where the
LORD drives you.
28 "[a]There you will serve gods, the
work of man's hands, [b]wood and stone,
[c]which neither see nor hear nor eat nor
smell.
29 "[a]But from there you will seek the
LORD your God, and you will find *Him* if
you search for Him [b]with all your heart
and all your soul.
30 "When you [a]are in distress and all
these things have come upon you, [b]in
the latter days [c]you will return to the
LORD your God and listen to His voice.
31 "For the LORD your God is a [a]com-
passionate God; [b]He will not fail you nor
[c]destroy you nor [d]forget the covenant
with your fathers which He swore to
them.
32 ¶ "Indeed, [a]ask now concerning
the former days which were before you,
since the [b]day that God created [1]man on
the earth, and *inquire* [c]from one end of
the heavens to the other. [d]Has *anything*
been done like this great thing, or has
anything been heard like it?
33 "[a]Has *any* people heard the voice of
God speaking from the midst of the fire,
as you have heard *it*, and survived?
34 "[a]Or has a god tried to go to take for
himself a nation from within *another* nation [b]by trials, by signs and wonders and
by war and [c]by a mighty hand and by an
outstretched arm and by great terrors,
[1]as the LORD your God did for you in
Egypt before your eyes?
35 "To you it was shown that you might
know that the LORD, He is God; [a]there is
no other besides Him.

22 [b]Deut 3:25
23 [a]Deut 4:9 [b]Deut 4:16
24 [a]Ex 24:17; Deut 9:3; Is 30:27; Heb 12:29 [b]Deut 5:9
25 [1]Lit *beget* [2]Or *a graven image* [a]Deut 4:16 [b]Deut 4:23 [c]2 Kin 17:17
26 [1]Lit *prolong your days* [a]Deut 30:19; Is 1:2; Mic 6:2 [b]Deut 7:4
27 [a]Lev 26:33; Deut 28:64; Neh 1:8
28 [a]Deut 28:36; Jer 16:13 [b]Deut 29:17 [c]Ps 115:4-8; Is 44:12-20
29 [a]Deut 30:1-3; 2 Chr 15:4; Is 55:6; Jer 29:13 [b]Deut 6:5
30 [a]Ps 18:6 [b]Deut 31:29; Jer 23:20; Hos 3:5; Heb 1:2 [c]Jer 4:1
31 [a]Ex 34:6; 2 Chr 30:9; Neh 9:31; Ps 103:8; Jon 4:2 [b]Deut 31:6; Josh 1:5; 1 Chr 28:20; Heb 13:5 [c]Jer 30:11 [d]Lev 26:45
32 [1]Or *Adam* [a]Deut 32:7; Job 8:8 [b]Gen 1:27; Is 45:12 [c]Deut 28:64; Matt 24:31 [d]Deut 4:7; 2 Sam 7:23
33 [a]Ex 20:22; Deut 5:24
34 [1]Lit *according to all that* [a]Ex 14:30; Deut 33:29 [b]Deut 7:19 [c]Deut 5:15; Ps 136:12
35 [a]Ex 8:10; Deut 4:39; 1 Sam 2:2; Is 43:10-12; Mark 12:32
36 [a]Ex 19:9; Deut 4:33; Neh 9:13; Heb 12:25 [b]Deut 8:5
37 [1]Lit *And instead, because* [2]Lit *his seed* [3]Lit *with His presence* [a]Deut 7:7 [b]Ex 33:14; Is 63:9
38 [a]Num 32:4
39 [a]Deut 4:35; Josh 2:11
40 [1]Lit *commanding* [2]Lit *prolong your days* [a]Lev 22:31; Deut 4:2; Ps 105:45 [b]Deut 4:1 [c]Ex 23:26; Deut 32:47
41 [1]Lit *sunrise* [a]Num 35:6; Deut 19:2-13; Josh 20:7-9
43 [a]Josh 20:8
46 [1]Lit *smote* [a]Deut 3:29 [b]Num 21:21-25
47 [1]Lit *sunrise* [a]Deut 1:4
48 [1]Or *wadi* [a]Deut 2:36 [b]Deut 3:9; Ps 133:3
49 [1]Lit *under*

36 "[a]Out of the heavens He let you
hear His voice [b]to discipline you; and on
earth He let you see His great fire, and
you heard His words from the midst of
the fire.
37 "[1a]Because He loved your fathers,
therefore He chose [2]their descendants
after them. And He [3b]personally
brought you from Egypt by His great
power,
38 driving out from before you nations
greater and mightier than you, to bring
you in *and* [a]to give you their land for an
inheritance, as it is today.
39 "Know therefore today, and take it
to your heart, that [a]the LORD, He is God
in heaven above and on the earth below;
there is no other.
40 "[a]So you shall keep His statutes and
His commandments which I am [1]giving
you today, that [b]it may go well with you
and with your children after you, and
[c]that you may [2]live long on the land
which the LORD your God is giving you
for all time."
41 ¶ [a]Then Moses set apart three cities across the Jordan to the [1]east,
42 that a manslayer might flee there,
who unintentionally slew his neighbor
without having enmity toward him in
time past; and by fleeing to one of these
cities he might live:
43 [a]Bezer in the wilderness on the
plateau for the Reubenites, and Ramoth
in Gilead for the Gadites, and Golan in
Bashan for the Manassites.
44 ¶ Now this is the law which Moses
set before the sons of Israel;
45 these are the testimonies and the
statutes and the ordinances which Moses
spoke to the sons of Israel, when they
came out from Egypt,
46 across the Jordan, in the valley [a]op-
posite Beth-peor, in the land of [b]Sihon
king of the Amorites who lived at Heshbon, whom Moses and the sons of Israel
[1]defeated when they came out from
Egypt.
47 They took possession of his land
and the land of [a]Og king of Bashan, the
two kings of the Amorites, *who were*
across the Jordan to the [1]east,
48 from [a]Aroer, which is on the edge
of the [1]valley of Arnon, even as far as
[b]Mount Sion (that is, Hermon),
49 with all the Arabah across the Jordan to the east, even as far as the sea of
the Arabah, [1]at the foot of the slopes of
Pisgah.

The Ten Commandments Repeated

5 Then Moses summoned all Israel and
said to them:
¶ "Hear, O Israel, the statutes and the

ordinances which I am speaking today in
your [1]hearing, that you may learn them
and observe [2]them carefully.
2 "The LORD our God made [a]a covenant with us at Horeb.
3 "[a]The LORD did not make this covenant with our fathers, but with us, *with*
all those of [1]us alive here today.
4 "The LORD spoke to you [a]face to face
at the mountain [b]from the midst of the
fire,
5 *while* [a]I was standing between the
LORD and you at that time, to declare to
you the word of the LORD; [b]for you were
afraid because of the fire and did not go
up the mountain. [1]He said,
6 ¶ '[a]I am the LORD your God who
brought you out of the land of Egypt, out
of the house of [1]slavery.
7 ¶ '[a]You shall have no other gods
[1]before Me.
8 ¶ '[a]You shall not make for yourself
[1]an idol, *or* any likeness *of* what is in
heaven above [2]or on the earth beneath
[2]or in the water under the earth.
9 'You shall not worship them or
serve them; for I, the LORD your God, am
a jealous God, [a]visiting the iniquity of
the fathers on the children, and on the
third and the fourth *generations* of those
who hate Me,
10 but [a]showing lovingkindness to
thousands, to those who love Me and
keep My commandments.
11 ¶ '[a]You shall not take the name of
the LORD your God in vain, for the LORD
will not [1]leave him unpunished who
takes His name in vain.
12 ¶ '[a]Observe the sabbath day to
keep it holy, as the LORD your God commanded you.
13 'Six days you shall labor and do all
your work,
14 but [a]the seventh day is a sabbath of
the LORD your God; *in it* you shall not do
any work, you or your son or your daughter or your male servant or your female
servant or your ox or your donkey or any
of your cattle or your sojourner who
[1]stays with you, so that your male servant and your female servant may rest as
well as you.
15 '[a]You shall remember that you
were a slave in the land of Egypt, and the
LORD your God brought you out of there
by a mighty hand and by an outstretched
arm; therefore the LORD your God commanded you to observe the sabbath day.
16 ¶ '[a]Honor your father and your
mother, as the LORD your God has commanded you, [b]that your days may be prolonged and that it may go well with you
on the land which the LORD your God
gives you.

17 ¶ '[a]You shall not murder.
18 ¶ '[a]You shall not commit adultery.
19 ¶ '[a]You shall not steal.
20 ¶ '[a]You shall not bear false witness
against your neighbor.
21 ¶ '[a]You shall not covet your neighbor's wife, and you shall not desire your
neighbor's house, his field or his male
servant or his female servant, his ox or
his donkey or anything that belongs to
your neighbor.'

Moses Interceded

22 ¶ "These words the LORD spoke to
all your assembly at the mountain from
the midst of the fire, *of* the cloud and *of*
the thick gloom, with a great voice, and
He added no more. [a]He wrote them on
two tablets of stone and gave them to me.
23 "And when you heard the voice
from the midst of the darkness, while the
mountain was burning with fire, you
came near to me, all the heads of your
tribes and your elders.
24 "You said, 'Behold, the LORD our
God has shown us His glory and His greatness, and we have heard His voice from
the midst of the fire; we have seen today
that God speaks with man, yet he lives.
25 '[a]Now then why should we die? For
this great fire will consume us; if we hear
the voice of the LORD our God any longer,
then we will die.
26 'For [a]who is there of all flesh who
has heard the voice of the living God
speaking from the midst of the fire, as we
have, and lived?
27 '[1]Go near and hear all that the LORD
our God says; then speak to us all that the
LORD our God speaks to you, and we will
hear and do *it.*'
28 ¶ "The LORD heard the voice of
your words when you spoke to me, [a]and
the LORD said to me, 'I have heard the
voice of the words of this people which
they have spoken to you. They have done
well in all that they have spoken.
29 '[a]Oh that they had such a heart in
them, that they would fear Me and [b]keep
all My commandments always, that [c]it
may be well with them and with their
sons forever!
30 'Go, say to them, "Return to your
tents."
31 '[a]But as for you, stand here by Me,
that I may speak to you all the commandments and the statutes and the judgments
which you shall teach them, that they
may observe *them* in the land which I
give them to possess.'
32 "So you shall observe to do just as
the LORD your God has commanded you;
[a]you shall not turn aside to the right or
to the left.

5:1 [1]Lit *ears* [2]Lit *to do them*
2 [a]Ex 19:5; Mal 4:4
3 [1]Lit *us ourselves* [a]Jer 31:32; Heb 8:9
4 [a]Num 14:14; Deut 34:10 [b]Deut 4:33
5 [1]Lit *saying* [a]Gal 3:19 [b]Ex 19:16,21-24; 20:18; Heb 12:18-21
6 [1]Lit *slaves* [a]Ex 20:2-17; Lev 26:1; Deut 6:4; Ps 81:10
7 [1]Or *besides* [a]Ex 20:3
8 [1]Or *a graven image* [2]Lit *or what is* [a]Ex 20:4-6; Lev 26:1; Deut 4:15-18; 27:15; Ps 97:7
9 [a]Ex 34:7; Num 14:18; Deut 7:10
10 [a]Num 14:18; Deut 7:9; Jer 32:18
11 [1]Or *hold him guiltless* [a]Ex 20:7; Lev 19:12; Deut 6:13; 10:20; Matt 5:33
12 [a]Ex 16:23-30; 20:8-11; 31:13f; Mark 2:27f
14 [1]Lit *is in your gates* [a]Gen 2:2; Heb 4:4
15 [a]Ex 20:11
16 [a]Ex 20:12; Lev 19:3; Deut 27:16; Matt 15:4; 19:19; Mark 7:10; 10:19; Luke 18:20; Eph 6:2, 3; Col 3:20 [b]Deut 4:40
17 [a]Gen 9:6; Ex 20:13; Lev 24:17; Matt 5:21f; 19:18; Mark 10:19; Rom 13:9; James 2:11
18 [a]Ex 20:14; Lev 20:10; Matt 5:27f; 19:18; Mark 10:19; Luke 18:20; Rom 13:9; James 2:11
19 [a]Ex 20:15; Lev 19:11
20 [a]Ex 20:16; 23:1; Matt 19:18
21 [a]Ex 20:17; Rom 7:7; 13:9
22 [a]Ex 24:12; 31:18; Deut 4:13
25 [a]Ex 20:18, 19; Deut 18:16
26 [a]Deut 4:33
27 [1]Lit *Go yourself*
28 [a]Deut 18:17
29 [a]Ps 81:13; Is 48:18 [b]Deut 11:1 [c]Deut 5:16, 33
31 [a]Ex 24:12
32 [a]Deut 17:20; 28:14; Josh 1:7; 23:6; Prov 4:27

33 “[a]You shall walk in all the way
which the LORD your God has commanded you, [b]that you may live and that it
may be well with you, and that you may
prolong *your* days in the land which you
will possess.

Obey God and Prosper

6 “Now this is the commandment, the
statutes and the judgments which
the LORD your God has commanded *me* to
teach you, that you might do *them* in the
land where you are going over to possess it,
2 so that you and your son and your
grandson might [a]fear the LORD your God,
to keep all His statutes and His commandments which I command you, [b]all the
days of your life, and that your days may
be prolonged.
3 “O Israel, you should listen and [1]be
careful to do *it,* that [a]it may be well with
you and that you may multiply greatly,
just as the LORD, the God of your fathers,
has promised you, *in* [b]a land flowing
with milk and honey.
4 ¶ “[a]Hear, O Israel! The LORD is
our God, the [b]LORD is one!
5 “[a]You shall love the LORD your God
[b]with all your heart and with all your
soul and with all your might.
6 “[a]These words, which I am commanding you today, shall be on your
heart.
7 [a]You shall teach them diligently to
your sons and shall talk of them when you
sit in your house and when you walk by
the way and when you lie down and
when you rise up.
8 “[a]You shall bind them as a sign on
your hand and they shall be as [1]frontals
[2]on your forehead.
9 “[a]You shall write them on the doorposts of your house and on your gates.
10 ¶ “Then it shall come about when
the LORD your God brings you into the
land which He swore to your fathers,
Abraham, Isaac and Jacob, to give you,
[a]great and splendid cities which you did
not build,
11 and houses full of all good things
which you did not fill, and hewn cisterns
which you did not dig, vineyards and olive trees which you did not plant, and
[a]you eat and are satisfied,
12 then watch yourself, that [a]you do
not forget the LORD who brought you
from the land of Egypt, out of the house
of [1]slavery.
13 “[a]You shall [1]fear *only* the LORD
your God; and you shall [2]worship Him
and [b]swear by His name.
14 “[a]You shall not follow other gods,
any of the gods of the peoples who surround you,
15 for the LORD your God in the midst
of you is a [a]jealous God; otherwise the
anger of the LORD your God will be kindled against you, and He will [1]wipe you
off the face of the earth.
16 ¶ “[a]You shall not put the LORD
your God to the test, [b]as you tested *Him*
at Massah.
17 “[a]You should diligently keep the
commandments of the LORD your God,
and His testimonies and His statutes
which He has commanded you.
18 “You shall do what is right and good
in the sight of the LORD, that [a]it may be
well with you and that you may go in and
possess the good land which the LORD
swore to *give* your fathers,
19 by driving out all your enemies
from before you, as the LORD has spoken.
20 ¶ “[a]When your son asks you in
time to come, saying, ‘What *do* the testimonies and the statutes and the judgments *mean* which the LORD our God
commanded you?’
21 then you shall say to your son, ‘We
were slaves to Pharaoh in Egypt, and the
LORD brought us from Egypt with a
mighty hand.
22 ‘Moreover, the LORD showed great
and distressing signs and wonders before
our eyes against Egypt, Pharaoh and all
his household;
23 He brought us out from there in
order to bring us in, to give us the land
which He had sworn to our fathers.’
24 “So the LORD commanded us to observe all these statutes, [a]to fear the LORD
our God for our good always and [b]for our
survival, as *it is* today.
25 “[a]It will be righteousness for us if
we [1]are careful to observe all this commandment before the LORD our God, just
as He commanded us.

Warnings

7 “[a]When the LORD your God brings
you into the land where you are entering to possess it, and clears away many
nations before you, the Hittites and the
Girgashites and the Amorites and the Canaanites and the Perizzites and the Hivites and the Jebusites, [b]seven nations
greater and stronger than you,
2 and when the LORD your God delivers them before you and you [1]defeat
them, [a]then you shall [2]utterly destroy
them. [b]You shall make no covenant with
them [c]and show no favor to them.
3 “Furthermore, [a]you shall not intermarry with them; you shall not give your
[1]daughters to [2]their sons, nor shall you
take [3]their daughters for your [4]sons.

33 [a]Deut 10:12; Jer 7:23; Luke 1:6 [b]Deut 4:1, 40; 12:25,28; 22:7; Eph 6:3

6:2 [a]Ex 20:20; Deut 10:12; Ps 111:10; 128:1; Eccl 12:13 [b]Deut 4:9

3 [1]Lit *keep* [a]Deut 5:33 [b]Ex 3:8,17

4 [a]Matt 22:37; Mark 12:29,30; Luke 10:27 [b]Deut 4:35,39; John 10:30; 1 Cor 8:4; Eph 4:6

5 [a]Matt 22:37; Mark 12:30; Luke 10:27 [b]Deut 4:29; 10:12

6 [a]Deut 11:18

7 [a]Deut 4:9; 11:19; Eph 6:4

8 [1]Or *frontlet bands* [2]Lit *between your eyes* [a]Ex 12:14; 13:9, 16; Deut 11:18; Prov 3:3; 6:21; 7:3

9 [a]Deut 11:20

10 [a]Deut 9:1; 19:1; Josh 24:13; Ps 105:44

11 [a]Deut 8:10; 11:15; 14:29

12 [1]Lit *slaves* [a]Deut 4:9

13 [1]Or *reverence* [2]Or *serve* [a]Deut 13:4; Matt 4:10; Luke 4:8 [b]Deut 5:11; 10:20; Ps 63:11; Matt 5:33

14 [a]Jer 25:6

15 [1]Lit *destroy* [a]Deut 4:24; 5:9

16 [a]Matt 4:7; Luke 4:12 [b]Ex 17:7

17 [a]Deut 11:22; Ps 119:4

18 [a]Deut 4:40

20 [a]Ex 13:8,14

24 [a]Deut 10:12; Jer 32:39 [b]Ps 41:2; Luke 10:28

25 [1]Lit *keep* [a]Deut 24:13; Rom 10:3

7:1 [a]Deut 20:16-18 [b]Acts 13:19

2 [1]Lit *smite* [2]Lit *surely devote to the ban* [a]Num 31:17; Josh 11:11 [b]Ex 23:32 [c]Deut 7:16; 13:8

3 [1]Lit *daughter* [2]Lit *his son* [3]Lit *his daughter* [4]Lit *son* [a]Ex 34:15, 16; Josh 23:12; Ezra 9:2

4 "For [1]they will turn your [2]sons away from [3]following Me to serve other gods; then the anger of the LORD will be kindled against you and [a]He will quickly destroy you.

5 "But thus you shall do to them: [a]you shall tear down their altars, and smash their *sacred* pillars, and hew down their [1]Asherim, and burn their graven images with fire.

6 "For you are [a]a holy people to the LORD your God; the LORD your God has chosen you to be [b]a people for His [1]own possession out of all the peoples who are on the face of the [2]earth.

7 ¶ "[a]The LORD did not set His love on you nor choose you because you were more in number than any of the peoples, for you were the fewest of all peoples,

8 but because the LORD loved you and kept the [a]oath which He swore to your forefathers, [b]the LORD brought you out by a mighty hand and redeemed you from the house of [1]slavery, from the hand of Pharaoh king of Egypt.

9 "Know therefore that the LORD your God, [a]He is God, [b]the faithful God, [c]who keeps [1]His covenant and [1]His lovingkindness to a thousandth generation with those who [d]love Him and keep His commandments;

10 but [a]repays those who hate Him to [1]their faces, to destroy [2]them; He will not delay [3]with him who hates Him, He will repay him to his face.

11 "Therefore, you shall keep the commandment and the statutes and the judgments which I am commanding you today, to do them.

Promises of God

12 ¶ "[a]Then it shall come about, because you listen to these judgments and keep and do them, that the LORD your God will keep with you [1]His covenant and [1]His lovingkindness which He swore to your forefathers.

13 "He will [a]love you and bless you and [b]multiply you; He will also bless the fruit of your womb and the fruit of your ground, your grain and your new wine and your oil, the increase of your herd and the young of your flock, [1]in the land which He swore to your forefathers to give you.

14 "You shall be blessed above all peoples; there will be no male or female [a]barren among you or among your cattle.

15 "[a]The LORD will remove from you all sickness; and He will not put on you any of the harmful diseases of Egypt which you have known, but He will lay them on all who hate you.

16 "You shall consume all the peoples whom the LORD your God will deliver to you; [a]your eye shall not pity them, nor shall you serve their gods, for that *would be* [b]a snare to you.

17 ¶ "If you should say in your heart, 'These nations are greater than I; how can I [a]dispossess them?'

18 you shall not be afraid of them; you shall well [a]remember what the LORD your God did to Pharaoh and to all Egypt:

19 [a]the great trials which your eyes saw and the signs and the wonders and the mighty hand and the outstretched arm by which the LORD your God brought you out. So shall the LORD your God do to all the peoples of whom you are afraid.

20 "Moreover, the LORD your God will send [a]the hornet against them, until those who are left and hide themselves from you perish.

21 "You shall not dread [1]them, for [a]the LORD your God is in your midst, [b]a great and awesome God.

22 "[a]The LORD your God will clear away these nations before you little by little; you will not be able to put an end to them quickly, for the [1]wild beasts would grow too numerous for you.

23 "[a]But the LORD your God will deliver them before you, and will [1]throw them into great confusion until they are destroyed.

24 "[a]He will deliver their kings into your hand so that you will make their name perish from under heaven; [b]no man will be able to stand before you until you have destroyed them.

25 "The graven images of their gods you are to [a]burn with fire; you shall [b]not covet the silver or the gold that is on them, nor take it for yourselves, or you will be [c]snared by it, for it is an [d]abomination to the LORD your God.

26 "You shall not bring an abomination into your house, and like it come under the [a]ban; you shall utterly detest it and you shall utterly abhor it, for it is something banned.

God's Gracious Dealings

8 "All the commandments that I am commanding you today you shall be careful to do, that you [a]may live and multiply, and go in and possess the land which the LORD swore *to give* to your forefathers.

2 "[a]You shall remember all the way which the LORD your God has [b]led you in the wilderness these forty years, that He might humble you, [c]testing you, to know what was in your heart, whether you would keep His commandments or not.

3 "He humbled you and let you be hungry, and fed you with manna which

---

4 [1]Lit *he* [2]Lit *son* [3]Lit *after* [a]Deut 4:26

5 [1]I.e. wooden symbols of a female deity [a]Ex 23:24; 34:13; Deut 12:3

6 [1]Or *special treasure* [2]Lit *ground* [a]Ex 19:6; Deut 14:2,21; Ps 50:5; Jer 2:3 [b]Ex 19:5; Deut 4:20; 14:2; 26:18; Ps 135:4; Titus 2:14; 1 Pet 2:9

7 [a]Deut 4:37

8 [1]Lit *slaves* [a]Ex 32:13 [b]Ex 13:3

9 [1]Lit *the* [a]Deut 4:35,39 [b]Is 49:7; 1 Cor 1:9; 1 Thess 5:24; 2 Tim 2:13 [c]Ex 20:6; Dan 9:4 [d]Deut 5:10

10 [1]Lit *his face* [2]Lit *him* [3]Lit *to* [a]Is 59:18; Nah 1:2

12 [1]Lit *the* [a]Lev 26:3-13; Deut 28:1-14

13 [1]Lit *on the ground* [a]Ps 146:8; Prov 15:9; John 14:21 [b]Lev 26:9; Deut 13:17; 30:5

14 [a]Ex 23:26

15 [a]Ex 15:26

16 [a]Deut 7:2 [b]Ex 23:33; Judg 8:27; Ps 106:36

17 [a]Num 33:53

18 [a]Ps 105:5

19 [a]Deut 4:34

20 [a]Ex 23:28; Josh 24:12

21 [1]Lit *from before them* [a]Ex 29:45; Josh 3:10 [b]Deut 10:17; Neh 1:5; 9:32

22 [1]Lit *beasts of the field* [a]Ex 23:29,30

23 [1]Lit *confuse them with* [a]Ex 23:27; Josh 10:10

24 [a]Josh 6:2; 10:23-25 [b]Deut 11:25; Josh 1:5; 10:8; 23:9

25 [a]Ex 32:20; Deut 12:3; 1 Chr 14:12 [b]Ex 20:17 [c]Deut 7:16; Judg 8:27 [d]Deut 17:1

26 [a]Lev 27:28f

8:1 [a]Deut 4:1

2 [a]Deut 8:16 [b]Ps 136:16; Amos 2:10 [c]Ex 15:25; 20:20; 2 Chr 32:31

you did not know, nor did your fathers
know, that He might make you [1]under-
stand that [a]man does not live by bread
alone, but man lives by everything that
proceeds out of the mouth of the LORD.
4 "[a]Your clothing did not wear out on
you, nor did your foot swell these forty
years.
5 "[a]Thus you are to know in your
heart that the LORD your God was disciplining you just as a man disciplines his
son.
6 "Therefore, you shall keep the commandments of the LORD your God, to
walk in His ways and to [1]fear Him.
7 "For [a]the LORD your God is bringing
you into a good land, a land of brooks of
water, of fountains and springs, flowing
forth in valleys and hills;
8 a land of wheat and barley, of vines
and fig trees and pomegranates, a land of
olive oil and honey;
9 a land where you will eat food without scarcity, in which you will not lack
anything; a land whose stones are iron,
and out of whose hills you can dig copper.
10 "When [a]you have eaten and are satisfied, you shall bless the LORD your God
for the good land which He has given
you.
11 ¶ "[1]Beware that you do not [a]for-
get the LORD your God by not keeping His
commandments and His ordinances and
His statutes which I am commanding you
today;
12 otherwise, [a]when you have eaten
and are satisfied, and have built good
houses and lived *in them,*
13 and when your herds and your
flocks multiply, and your silver and gold
multiply, and all that you have multiplies,
14 then your heart will become
proud and you will [a]forget the LORD
your God who brought you out from the
land of Egypt, out of the house of [2]slav-
ery.
15 "He led you through [a]the great and
terrible wilderness, *with its* [b]fiery serpents and scorpions and thirsty ground
where there was no water; He [c]brought
water for you out of the rock of flint.
16 "In the wilderness He fed you manna [a]which your fathers did not know,
that He might humble you and that He
might [b]test you, to do good for you [1]in
the end.
17 "Otherwise, [a]you may say in your
heart, 'My power and the strength of my
hand made me this wealth.'
18 "But you shall remember the LORD
your God, for [a]it is He who is giving you
power to make wealth, that He may confirm His covenant which He swore to
your fathers, as *it is* this day.

3 [1]Lit *know* [a]Matt 4:4; Luke 4:4
4 [a]Deut 29:5; Neh 9:21
5 [a]Deut 4:36; 2 Sam 7:14; Prov 3:12; Heb 12:6; Rev 3:19
6 [1]Or *reverence*
7 [a]Deut 11:9-12; Jer 2:7
10 [a]Deut 6:11
11 [1]Lit *Take heed to yourself* [a]Deut 4:9
12 [a]Prov 30:9; Hos 13:6
14 [1]Lit *lifted up* [2]Lit *slaves* [a]Deut 8:11; Ps 106:21
15 [a]Deut 1:19; Jer 2:6 [b]Num 21:6 [c]Ex 17:6; Num 20:11; Deut 32:13; Ps 78:15; 114:8
16 [1]Lit *at your end* [a]Ex 16:15 [b]Deut 8:2
17 [a]Deut 9:4
18 [a]Prov 10:22; Hos 2:8
19 [a]Deut 4:26; 30:18
20 [a]Ezek 5:5-17
9:1 [1]Lit *and fortified* [a]Deut 4:38; 7:1; 11:23 [b]Deut 1:28
2 [a]Num 13:22, 28,33; Josh 11:21,22
3 [a]Deut 31:3; Josh 3:11 [b]Deut 4:24; Heb 12:29 [c]Ex 23:31; Deut 7:24
4 [1]Lit *you saying* [a]Deut 8:17; 9:7, 24; 31:27 [b]Lev 18:3,24-30; Deut 12:31; 18:9-14
5 [1]Lit *word* [a]Titus 3:5 [b]Gen 12:7; 13:15; 15:7; 17:8; 26:4; 28:13
6 [1]Or *stiff-necked* [a]Deut 9:13; 10:16; 31:27
7 [a]Ex 14:10f; Num 14:22
8 [a]Ex 32:7-10; Ps 106:19
9 [a]Ex 24:18; 34:28; Deut 8:3; 9:18

19 "It shall come about if you ever forget the LORD your God and go after other
gods and serve them and worship them,
[a]I testify against you today that you will
surely perish.
20 "Like the nations that the LORD
makes to perish before you, so [a]you shall
perish; because you would not listen to
the voice of the LORD your God.

Israel Provoked God

9 "Hear, O Israel! You are crossing
over the Jordan today to go in to dispossess [a]nations greater and mightier
than you, great cities [1b]fortified to
heaven,
2 a people great and tall, the sons
of the Anakim, whom you know and of
whom you have heard *it said,* '[a]Who can
stand before the sons of Anak?'
3 "Know therefore today that [a]it is
the LORD your God who is crossing over
before you as [b]a consuming fire. He will
destroy them and He will subdue them
before you, so that [c]you may drive them
out and destroy them quickly, just as the
LORD has spoken to you.
4 ¶ "[a]Do not say in your heart when
the LORD your God has driven them out
before [1]you, 'Because of my righteousness the LORD has brought me in to possess this land,' but *it is* [b]because of the
wickedness of these nations *that* the
LORD is dispossessing them before you.
5 "It is [a]not for your righteousness or
for the uprightness of your heart that you
are going to possess their land, but *it is*
because of the wickedness of these nations *that* the LORD your God is driving
them out before you, in order to confirm
[b]the [1]oath which the LORD swore to
your fathers, to Abraham, Isaac and Jacob.
6 ¶ "Know, then, *it is* not because of
your righteousness *that* the LORD your
God is giving you this good land to possess, for you are [a]a [1]stubborn people.
7 "Remember, do not forget how you
provoked the LORD your God to wrath in
the wilderness; [a]from the day that you
left the land of Egypt until you arrived
at this place, you have been rebellious
against the LORD.
8 "Even [a]at Horeb you provoked the
LORD to wrath, and the LORD was so angry
with you that He would have destroyed
you.
9 "When I went up to the mountain to
receive the tablets of stone, the tablets of
the covenant which the LORD had made
with you, then I remained on the mountain forty days and nights; [a]I neither ate
bread nor drank water.
10 "The LORD gave me the two tablets

of stone [a]written by the finger of God;
and on them *were* all the words which
the LORD had spoken with you at the
mountain from the midst of the fire on
the day of the assembly.
11 "It came about [a]at the end of forty
days and nights that the LORD gave me
the two tablets of stone, the tablets of the
covenant.
12 "[a]Then the LORD said to me, 'Arise,
go down from here quickly, for your people whom you brought out of Egypt have
acted corruptly. They have [b]quickly
turned aside from the way which I commanded them; they have made a molten
image for themselves.'
13 "The [a]LORD spoke further to me,
saying, 'I have seen this people, and indeed, it is a [1b]stubborn people.
14 '[a]Let Me alone, that I may destroy
them and [b]blot out their name from under heaven; and I will make of you a nation mightier and greater than they.'
15 ¶ "[a]So I turned and came down
from the mountain while the mountain
was burning with fire, and the two tablets
of the covenant were in my two hands.
16 "And I saw that you had indeed
sinned against the LORD your God. You
had made for yourselves a molten calf;
you had turned aside quickly from the
way which the LORD had commanded
you.
17 "I took hold of the two tablets and
threw them from my hands and smashed
them before your eyes.
18 "[a]I fell down before the LORD, [b]as
at the first, forty days and nights; [c]I neither ate bread nor drank water, [d]because
of all your sin which you had committed
in doing what was evil in the sight of the
LORD to provoke Him to anger.
19 "For [a]I was afraid of the anger and
hot displeasure with which the LORD was
wrathful against you in order to destroy
you, [b]but the LORD listened to me that
time also.
20 "The LORD was angry enough with
Aaron to destroy him; so I also prayed for
Aaron at the same time.
21 "[a]I took your [1]sinful *thing,* the calf
which you had made, and burned it with
fire and crushed it, grinding it very small
until it was as fine as dust; and I threw its
dust into the brook that came down from
the mountain.
22 ¶ "Again at [a]Taberah and at [b]Mas-
sah and at [c]Kibroth-hattaavah you provoked the LORD to wrath.
23 "When the LORD sent you from
[a]Kadesh-barnea, saying, '[b]Go up and
possess the land which I have given you,'
then you rebelled against the [1]command

10 [a]Deut 4:13
11 [a]Deut 9:9
12 [a]Ex 32:7,8 [b]Judg 2:17
13 [1]Or *stiff-necked* [a]Ex 32:9 [b]Deut 10:16; 31:27; 2 Kin 17:14
14 [a]Ex 32:10 [b]Ps 9:5; 109:13
15 [a]Ex 32:15-19
18 [a]Ex 34:28 [b]Deut 10:10 [c]Deut 9:9 [d]Ex 34:9
19 [a]Ex 32:10f; Heb 12:21 [b]Ex 34:10; Deut 10:10
21 [1]Lit *sin* [a]Ex 32:20
22 [a]Num 11:3 [b]Ex 17:7 [c]Num 11:34
23 [1]Lit *mouth* [a]Deut 1:2 [b]Deut 1:21 [c]Deut 1:26; Ps 106:24
24 [a]Deut 9:7; 31:27
25 [1]Lit *fell down* [a]Deut 9:18
26 [a]Ex 32:11-13; 1 Sam 7:9; Jer 15:1
28 [1]Lit *spoken to* [a]Ex 32:12; Num 14:16
29 [a]Deut 4:20; 1 Kin 8:51; Neh 1:10; Ps 106:40 [b]Deut 4:34
10:1 [a]Ex 34:1 [b]Ex 25:10
2 [a]Deut 4:13 [b]Ex 25:16
3 [a]Ex 25:5; 37:1-9 [b]Ex 34:4
4 [1]Lit *Words* [a]Ex 34:28; Deut 4:13 [b]Ex 20:1 [c]Deut 9:10; 18:16
5 [a]Ex 34:29 [b]Ex 40:20 [c]1 Kin 8:9
6 [1]Or *the wells of the sons of Jaakan* [a]Num 33:30,31 [b]Num 20:25-28; 33:38
7 [a]Num 33:33, 34
8 [a]Num 3:6; 18:1-7; Deut 31:9

of the LORD your God; [c]you neither believed Him nor listened to His voice.
24 "[a]You have been rebellious against
the LORD from the day I knew you.
25 ¶ "[a]So I fell down before the LORD
the forty days and nights, which I [1]did
because the LORD had said He would destroy you.
26 "[a]I prayed to the LORD and said,
'O Lord GOD, do not destroy Your people,
even Your inheritance, whom You have
redeemed through Your greatness, whom
You have brought out of Egypt with a
mighty hand.
27 'Remember Your servants, Abraham, Isaac, and Jacob; do not look at the
stubbornness of this people or at their
wickedness or their sin.
28 'Otherwise the land from which
You brought us may say, "[a]Because the
LORD was not able to bring them into the
land which He had [1]promised them and
because He hated them He has brought
them out to slay them in the wilderness."
29 'Yet they are Your people, even
[a]Your inheritance, whom You have
brought out by Your [b]great power and
Your outstretched arm.'

The Tablets Rewritten

10 "At that time the LORD said to me,
'[a]Cut out for yourself two tablets
of stone like the former ones, and come
up to Me on the mountain, and [b]make an
ark of wood for yourself.
2 '[a]I will write on the tablets the
words that were on the former tablets
which you shattered, and [b]you shall put
them in the ark.'
3 "So [a]I made an ark of acacia wood
and [b]cut out two tablets of stone like the
former ones, and went up on the mountain with the two tablets in my hand.
4 "He wrote on the tablets, like the
former writing, [a]the Ten [1]Command-
ments [b]which the LORD had spoken to
you on the mountain from the midst of
the fire [c]on the day of the assembly; and
the LORD gave them to me.
5 "Then I turned and [a]came down
from the mountain and [b]put the tablets
in the ark which I had made; [c]and there
they are, as the LORD commanded me."
6 ¶ (Now the sons of Israel set out
from [1]Beeroth [a]Bene-jaakan to Mose-
rah. [b]There Aaron died and there he was
buried and Eleazar his son ministered as
priest in his place.
7 [a]From there they set out to Gudgodah, and from Gudgodah to Jotbathah, a
land of brooks of water.
8 [a]At that time the LORD set apart
the tribe of Levi to carry the ark of the
covenant of the LORD, to stand before the

LORD [b]to serve Him and to bless in His
name until this day.
9 [a]Therefore, Levi does not have a
portion or inheritance with his brothers;
the LORD is his inheritance, just as the
LORD your God spoke to him.)
10 ¶ "[a]I, moreover, stayed on the
mountain forty days and forty nights like
the first time, and the LORD listened to
me that time also; the LORD was not willing to destroy you.
11 "Then the LORD said to me, 'Arise,
proceed on your journey ahead of the
people, that they may go in and possess
the land which I swore to their fathers to
give them.'
12 ¶ "[a]Now, Israel, what does the
LORD your God require from you, but to
[1]fear the LORD your God, to walk in all
His ways and [b]love Him, and to serve the
LORD your God with [c]all your heart and
with all your soul,
13 *and* to keep the LORD'S commandments and His statutes which I am commanding you today for your good?
14 "Behold, [a]to the LORD your God belong heaven and the [1]highest heavens,
[b]the earth and all that is in it.
15 "[a]Yet on your fathers did the LORD
set His affection to love them, and He
chose their [1]descendants after them,
even you above all peoples, as *it is* this
day.
16 "[a]So circumcise [1]your heart, and
[b]stiffen your neck no longer.
17 "[a]For the LORD your God is the God
of gods and the [b]Lord of lords, the great,
the mighty, and the awesome God [c]who
does not show partiality nor [d]take a
bribe.
18 "He executes justice for [a]the orphan and the widow, and shows His love
for the alien by giving him food and clothing.
19 "[a]So show your love for the alien,
for you were aliens in the land of Egypt.
20 "You shall fear the LORD your God;
you shall serve Him and [a]cling to Him,
and [b]you shall swear by His name.
21 "He is [a]your praise and He is your
God, who has done these great and awesome things for you which your eyes have
seen.
22 "[a]Your fathers went down to Egypt
seventy persons *in all,* [b]and now the
LORD your God has made you as numerous as the stars of heaven.

Rewards of Obedience

11 "You shall therefore [a]love the
LORD your God, and always
[b]keep His charge, His statutes, His ordinances, and His commandments.
2 "Know this day [a]that I *am* not
speaking with your sons who have not
known and who have not seen the [1]disci-
pline of the LORD your God—His greatness, His mighty hand and His outstretched arm,
3 and [a]His signs and His works
which He did in the midst of Egypt to
Pharaoh the king of Egypt and to all his
land;
4 and what He did to Egypt's army, to
its horses and its chariots, [a]when He
made the water of the [1]Red Sea to [2]en-
gulf them while they were pursuing you,
and the LORD [3]completely destroyed
them;
5 and what He did to you in the wilderness until you came to this place;
6 and [a]what He did to Dathan and
Abiram, the sons of Eliab, the son of Reuben, when the earth opened its mouth
and swallowed them, their households,
their tents, and [b]every living thing that
[1]followed them, among all Israel—
7 but your own eyes have seen all the
great work of the LORD which He did.
8 ¶ "You shall therefore keep every
commandment which I am commanding
you today, [a]so that you may be strong
and go in and possess the land into which
you are about to cross to possess it;
9 [a]so that you may prolong *your* days
on the land which the LORD swore to your
fathers to give to them and to their
[1]descendants, [b]a land flowing with milk
and honey.
10 "For the land, into which you are
entering to possess it, is not like the land
of Egypt from which you came, where
you used to sow your seed and water it
with your [1]foot like a vegetable garden.
11 "But [a]the land into which you are
about to cross to possess it, a land of hills
and valleys, drinks water from the rain of
heaven,
12 a land for which the LORD your God
cares; [a]the eyes of the LORD your God are
always on it, from the [1]beginning even to
the end of the year.
13 ¶ "It shall come about, [a]if you listen obediently to my commandments
which I am commanding you today, [b]to
love the LORD your God and to serve Him
[c]with all your heart and all your soul,
14 that [1a]He will give the rain for
your land in its season, the [2b]early and
[3]late rain, that you may gather in your
grain and your new wine and your oil.
15 "[1a]He will give grass in your fields
for your cattle, and [b]you will eat and be
satisfied.
16 "[1a]Beware that your hearts are not
deceived, and that you do not turn away
and serve other gods and worship them.
17 "Or [a]the anger of the LORD will be

8 [b]Deut 17:12; 18:5; 21:5
9 [a]Num 18:20, 24; Deut 18:1,2; Ezek 44:28
10 [a]Ex 34:28; Deut 9:18
12 [1]Or *reverence* [a]Mic 6:8 [b]Deut 6:5; Matt 22:37; 1 Tim 1:5 [c]Deut 4:29
14 [1]Lit *heaven of heavens* [a]1 Kin 8:27; Neh 9:6; Ps 68:33; 115:16 [b]Ps 24:1
15 [1]Lit *seed* [a]Deut 4:37
16 [1]Lit *the foreskin of your heart* [a]Lev 26:41; Jer 4:4 [b]Deut 9:6
17 [a]Josh 22:22; Ps 136:2; Dan 2:47; 1 Tim 6:15; Rev 19:16 [b]Rev 17:14 [c]Deut 1:17; Acts 10:34; Rom 2:11; Gal 2:6; Eph 6:9 [d]Deut 16:19
18 [a]Ex 22:22-24; Ps 68:5; 146:9
19 [a]Lev 19:34; Ezek 47:22,23
20 [a]Deut 11:22; 13:4 [b]Deut 5:11; 6:13; Ps 63:11
21 [a]Ps 109:1; 148:14; Jer 17:14
22 [a]Gen 46:27 [b]Gen 15:5; 22:17; Deut 1:10
11:1 [a]Deut 6:5; 10:12 [b]Lev 18:30; 22:9
2 [1]Or *instruction* [a]Deut 4:34
3 [a]Ex 7:8-21
4 [1]Lit *Sea of Reeds* [2]Lit *flow over their faces* [3]Lit *to this day* [a]Ex 14:28; Deut 1:40; 2:1
6 [1]Lit *was at their feet* [a]Num 16:1-35; Ps 106:16-18 [b]Num 26:10,11
8 [a]Deut 31:6,7, 23; Josh 1:6,7
9 [1]Lit *seed* [a]Deut 4:40; 5:16,33; 6:2; Prov 10:27 [b]Ex 3:8
10 [1]I.e. probably a treadmill
11 [a]Deut 8:7
12 [1]Lit *beginning of the year* [a]1 Kin 9:3
13 [a]Lev 26:3; Deut 7:12 [b]Deut 11:1 [c]Deut 4:29
14 [1]So some ancient versions; M.T. reads *I* [2]I.e. autumn [3]I.e. spring [a]Lev 26:4; Deut 28:12 [b]Joel 2:23; James 5:7
15 [1]So some ancient versions; M.T. reads *I* [a]Ps 104:14 [b]Deut 6:11
16 [1]Lit *Watch yourselves* [a]Job 31:27
17 [a]Deut 6:15; 9:19

kindled against you, and He will [b]shut up
the heavens [c]so that there will be no rain
and the ground will not yield its fruit; and
[d]you will perish quickly from the good
land which the LORD is giving you.
18 ¶ "[a]You shall therefore [1]impress
these words of mine on your heart and on
your soul; and you shall bind them as a
sign on your hand, and they shall be as
[2]frontals [3]on your forehead.
19 "[a]You shall teach them to your sons,
talking of them when you sit in your
house and when you walk along the road
and when you lie down and when you
rise up.
20 "[a]You shall write them on the doorposts of your house and on your gates,
21 so that [a]your days and the days of
your sons may be multiplied on the land
which the LORD swore to your fathers to
give them, as [1b]long as the heavens *remain* above the earth.
22 "For if you are [a]careful to keep all
this commandment which I am commanding you to do, [b]to love the LORD
your God, to walk in all His ways and
[c]hold fast to Him,
23 then the LORD will [a]drive out all
these nations from before you, and you
will [b]dispossess nations greater and
mightier than you.
24 "[a]Every place on which the sole of
your foot treads shall be yours; [b]your border will be from the wilderness to Lebanon, *and* from the river, the river Euphrates, as far as [1]the western sea.
25 "[a]No man will be able to stand before you; the LORD your God will lay the
dread of you and the fear of you on all the
land on which you set foot, as He has
spoken to you.
26 ¶ "[a]See, I am setting before you
today a blessing and a curse:
27 the [a]blessing, if you listen to the
commandments of the LORD your God,
which I am commanding you today;
28 and the [a]curse, if you do not listen
to the commandments of the LORD your
God, but turn aside from the way which
I am commanding you today, [1]by following other gods which you have not
known.
29 ¶ "It shall come about, when the
LORD your God brings you into the land
where you are entering to possess it,
[a]that you shall place the blessing on
Mount Gerizim and the curse on Mount
Ebal.
30 "Are they not across the Jordan,
west of the way toward the sunset, in the
land of the Canaanites who live in the
Arabah, opposite [a]Gilgal, beside [b]the
[1]oaks of Moreh?
31 "For you are about to cross the Jordan to go in to possess the land which the
LORD your God is giving you, and [a]you
shall possess it and live in it,
32 and you shall be careful to do all the
statutes and the judgments which I am
setting before you today.

Laws of the Sanctuary

12 "These are the statutes and the
judgments which you shall carefully observe in the land which the LORD,
the God of your fathers, has given you to
possess [1a]as long as you live on the
[2]earth.
2 "You shall utterly destroy all the
places where the nations whom you shall
dispossess serve their gods, on the [a]high
mountains and on the hills and under every green tree.
3 "[a]You shall tear down their altars
and smash their *sacred* pillars and burn
their [1]Asherim with fire, and you shall
cut down the engraved images of their
gods and [b]obliterate their name from
that place.
4 "You shall not act like this toward
the LORD your God.
5 "[a]But you shall seek *the LORD* at the
place which the LORD your God will
choose from all your tribes, to establish
His name there for His dwelling, and
there you shall come.
6 "There you shall bring your burnt
offerings, your sacrifices, [a]your tithes,
the [1]contribution of your hand, your votive offerings, your freewill offerings, and
the firstborn of your herd and of your
flock.
7 "There also you and your households shall eat before the LORD your God,
and [a]rejoice in all [1]your undertakings in
which the LORD your God has blessed
you.
8 ¶ "You shall not do at all what we
are doing here today, every man *doing*
whatever is right in his own eyes;
9 for you have not as yet come to
[a]the resting place and the [b]inheritance
which the LORD your God is giving you.
10 "When you cross the Jordan and live
in the land which the LORD your God is
giving you to inherit, and [a]He gives you
rest from all your enemies around *you* so
that you live in security,
11 [a]then it shall come about that the
place in which the LORD your God will
choose for His name to dwell, there you
shall bring all that I command you: your
burnt offerings and your sacrifices,
your tithes and the [1]contribution of
your hand, and all your choice votive offerings which you will vow to the LORD.
12 "And you shall [a]rejoice before the
LORD your God, you and your sons and

17 [b]1 Kin 8:35; 2 Chr 6:26; 7:13 [c]Deut 28:24 [d]Deut 4:26
18 [1]Lit *put* [2]Lit *frontlet bands* [3]Lit *between your eyes* [a]Ex 13:9,16; Deut 6:8
19 [a]Deut 4:9, 10; 6:7; Prov 22:6
20 [a]Deut 6:9
21 [1]Lit *the days of the heavens* [a]Prov 3:2; 4:10; 9:11 [b]Ps 72:5
22 [a]Deut 6:17 [b]Deut 11:1 [c]Deut 10:20
23 [a]Deut 4:38 [b]Deut 9:1
24 [1]I.e. the Mediterranean [a]Josh 1:3; 14:9 [b]Gen 15:18; Ex 23:31; Deut 1:7, 8
25 [a]Ex 23:27; Deut 7:24
26 [a]Deut 30:1, 19
27 [a]Deut 28:1-14
28 [1]Lit *to follow* [a]Deut 28:15-68
29 [a]Deut 27:12; Josh 8:33
30 [1]Lit *terebinths* [a]Josh 4:19 [b]Gen 12:6
31 [a]Deut 17:14; Josh 21:43
12:1 [1]Lit *all the days* [2]Lit *ground* [a]Deut 4:9,10; 1 Kin 8:40
2 [a]2 Kin 16:4; 17:10,11
3 [1]I.e. wooden symbols of a female deity [a]Num 33:52; Deut 7:5; Judg 2:2 [b]Ex 23:13; Ps 16:4; Zech 13:2
5 [a]Ex 20:24; Deut 12:11,13; 2 Chr 7:12; Ps 78:68
6 [1]Or *heave offering* [a]Deut 14:22
7 [1]Lit *the putting forth of your hand* [a]Lev 23:40; Deut 12:12,18; 14:26; 28:47; Eccl 3:12, 13; 5:18-20
9 [a]Deut 3:20; 25:19; Ps 95:11 [b]Deut 4:21
10 [a]Josh 11:23
11 [1]Or *heave offering* [a]Deut 12:5; 15:20; 16:2; 17:8; 18:6
12 [a]Deut 12:7

daughters, your male and female servants, and the [b]Levite who is within
your gates, since [c]he has no portion or
inheritance with you.
13 ¶ "[a]Be careful that you do not offer
your burnt offerings in every *cultic* place
you see,
14 but in the place which the LORD
chooses in one of your tribes, there you
shall offer your burnt offerings, and there
you shall do all that I command you.
15 ¶ "[a]However, you may slaughter
and eat meat within any of your gates,
[1]whatever you desire, according to the
blessing of the LORD your God which He
has given you; the unclean and the clean
may eat of it, as of [b]the gazelle and the
deer.
16 "[a]Only you shall not eat the blood;
[b]you are to pour it out on the ground like
water.
17 "[a]You are not allowed to eat within
your gates the tithe of your grain or new
wine or oil, or the firstborn of your herd
or flock, or any of your votive offerings
which you vow, or your freewill offerings, or the [1]contribution of your hand.
18 "But [a]you shall eat them before the
LORD your God in [b]the place which the
LORD your God will choose, you and your
son and daughter, and your male and female servants, and the [c]Levite who is
within your gates; and you shall [d]rejoice
before the LORD your God in all [1]your
undertakings.
19 "[a]Be careful that you do not forsake
the Levite [1]as long as you live in your
land.
20 ¶ "When the LORD your God extends your border [a]as He has promised
you, and you say, 'I will eat meat,' because [1]you desire to eat meat, *then* you
may eat meat, [2]whatever you desire.
21 "If the place which the LORD your
God chooses to put His name is too far
from you, then you may slaughter of your
herd and flock which the LORD has given
you, as I have commanded you; and you
may eat within your gates [1]whatever you
desire.
22 "Just as a gazelle or a deer is eaten,
so you will eat it; the unclean and the
clean alike may eat of it.
23 "Only be sure [a]not to eat the blood,
for the blood is the [1]life, and you shall
not eat the [1]life with the flesh.
24 "You shall not eat it; you shall pour
it out on the ground like water.
25 "You shall not eat it, so that [a]it may
be well with you and your sons after you,
for [b]you will be doing what is right in the
sight of the LORD.
26 "[a]Only your holy things which you
may have and your votive offerings, you
shall take and go to the place which the
LORD chooses.
27 "And [a]you shall offer your burnt offerings, the flesh and the blood, on the
altar of the LORD your God; and the blood
of your sacrifices shall be poured out on
the altar of the LORD your God, and [b]you
shall eat the flesh.
28 ¶ "Be careful to listen to all these
words which I command you, so that [a]it
may be well with you and your sons after
you forever, for you will be doing what is
good and right in the sight of the LORD
your God.
29 ¶ "When [a]the LORD your God cuts
off before you the nations which you are
going in to dispossess, and you dispossess
them and dwell in their land,
30 beware that you are not ensnared
[1]to follow them, after they are destroyed
before you, and that you do not inquire
after their gods, saying, 'How do these
nations serve their gods, that I also may
do likewise?'
31 "[a]You shall not behave thus toward
the LORD your God, for every abominable
act which the LORD hates they have done
for their gods; for [b]they even burn their
sons and daughters in the fire to their
gods.
32 ¶ "[1a]Whatever I command you,
you shall be careful to do; [b]you shall not
add to nor take away from it.

Shun Idolatry

13 "[a]If a prophet or a dreamer of
dreams arises among you and
gives you a sign or a wonder,
2 and the sign or the wonder comes
true, concerning which he spoke to you,
saying, '[a]Let us go after other gods
(whom you have not known) and let us
serve them,'
3 you shall not listen to the words of
that prophet or that dreamer of dreams;
for the LORD your God is [a]testing you to
find out if [b]you love the LORD your God
with all your heart and with all your soul.
4 "[a]You shall follow the LORD your
God and fear Him; and you shall keep His
commandments, listen to His voice, serve
Him, and [b]cling to Him.
5 "But that prophet or that dreamer of
dreams shall be [a]put to death, because
he has [1]counseled [2]rebellion against the
LORD your God who brought you from the
land of Egypt and redeemed you from
the house of [3]slavery, [b]to seduce you
from the way in which the LORD your God
commanded you to walk. [c]So you shall
purge the evil from among you.
6 ¶ "[a]If your brother, your mother's
son, or your son or daughter, or the wife
[1]you cherish, or your friend who is as

12 [b]Deut 12:18, 19; 26:11-13 [c]Deut 10:9; 14:29
13 [a]Deut 12:5, 11
15 [1]Lit *in every desire of your soul* [a]Deut 12:20-23 [b]Deut 12:22; 14:5; 15:22
16 [a]Gen 9:4; Lev 7:26; 17:10-12; 1 Sam 14:33f; Acts 15:20,29 [b]Deut 15:23
17 [1]Lit *heave offering* [a]Deut 12:26
18 [1]Lit *the putting forth of your hand* [a]Deut 14:23 [b]Deut 12:5 [c]Deut 12:12 [d]Deut 12:7; Eccl 3:12f; 5:18-20
19 [1]Lit *all your days upon your land* [a]Deut 14:27
20 [1]Lit *your soul desires* [2]Lit *in every desire of your soul* [a]Gen 15:18; Deut 11:24; 19:8
21 [1]Lit *in every desire of your soul*
23 [1]Lit *soul* [a]Gen 9:4; Lev 17:10-14; Deut 12:16
25 [a]Deut 4:40; Is 3:10 [b]Ex 15:26; 1 Kin 11:38
26 [a]Num 5:9f; 18:19; Deut 12:17
27 [a]Lev 1:9,13 [b]Lev 3:1-17
28 [a]Deut 4:40; Eccl 8:12
29 [a]Josh 23:4
30 [1]Lit *after them*
31 [a]Deut 9:5 [b]Lev 18:21; Deut 18:10; Ps 106:37; Jer 32:35
32 [1]Lit *Everything that* [a]Deut 4:2; Josh 1:7 [b]Prov 30:6; Rev 22:18
13:1 [a]Matt 24:24; Mark 13:22; 2 Thess 2:9
2 [a]Deut 13:6,13
3 [a]Ex 20:20; Deut 8:2,16; 1 Cor 11:19 [b]Deut 6:5
4 [a]2 Kin 23:3; 2 Chr 34:31; 2 John 6 [b]Deut 10:20
5 [1]Lit *spoken* [2]Lit *turning aside* [3]Lit *slaves* [a]Deut 13:9,15; 17:5; 1 Kin 18:40 [b]Deut 4:19; 13:10 [c]1 Cor 5:13
6 [1]Lit *of your bosom* [a]Deut 17:2-7; 29:18

your own soul, entice you secretly, saying, '[b]Let us go and serve other gods' (whom neither you nor your fathers have known,

7 of the gods of the peoples who are around you, near you or far from you, from one end of the earth to the other end),

8 [a]you shall not yield to him or listen to him; [b]and your eye shall not pity him, nor shall you spare or conceal him.

9 "[a]But you shall surely kill him; [b]your hand shall be first against him to put him to death, and afterwards the hand of all the people.

10 "So you shall stone him [1]to death because he has sought [a]to seduce you from the LORD your God who brought you out from the land of Egypt, out of the house of [2]slavery.

11 "Then [a]all Israel will hear and be afraid, and will never again do such a wicked thing among you.

12 ¶ "If you hear in one of your cities, which the LORD your God is giving you to live in, *anyone* saying *that*

13 some worthless men have gone out from among you and have seduced the inhabitants of their city, saying, '[a]Let us go and serve other gods' (whom you have not known),

14 then you shall investigate and search out and inquire thoroughly. If it is true *and* the matter established that this abomination has been done among you,

15 [a]you shall surely strike the inhabitants of that city with the edge of the sword, [1]utterly destroying it and all that is in it and its cattle with the edge of the sword.

16 "[a]Then you shall gather all its booty into the middle of its open square and burn the city and all its booty with fire as a whole burnt offering to the LORD your God; and it shall be a [1b]ruin forever. It shall never be rebuilt.

17 "Nothing from that which is put under the ban shall cling to your hand, in order that the LORD may turn from [a]His burning anger and [b]show mercy to you, and have compassion on you and [c]make you increase, just [d]as He has sworn to your fathers,

18 [1]if you will listen to the voice of the LORD your God, [2]keeping all His commandments which I am commanding you today, [3]and doing what is right in the sight of the LORD your God.

Clean and Unclean Animals

14 "You are [a]the sons of the LORD your God; [b]you shall not cut yourselves nor [1]shave your forehead for the sake of the dead.

2 "For you are [a]a holy people to the LORD your God, and the LORD has chosen you to be a [b]people for His [1]own possession out of all the peoples who are on the face of the earth.

3 ¶ "[a]You shall not eat any detestable thing.

4 "[a]These are the animals which you may eat: the ox, the sheep, the goat,

5 [1]the deer, the gazelle, the roebuck, the wild goat, the ibex, the antelope and the mountain sheep.

6 "Any animal that divides the hoof and has the hoof split in [1]two *and* [2]chews the cud, among the animals, that you may eat.

7 "Nevertheless, you are not to eat of these among those which [1]chew the cud, or among those that divide the hoof in [2]two: the camel and the [3]rabbit and the [4]shaphan, for though they [1]chew the cud, they do not divide the hoof; they are unclean for you.

8 "The pig, because it divides the hoof but *does* not *chew* the cud, it is unclean for you. You shall not eat any of their flesh nor touch their carcasses.

9 ¶ "These you may eat of all that are in water: anything that has fins and scales you may eat,

10 but anything that does not have fins and scales you shall not eat; it is unclean for you.

11 ¶ "You may eat any clean bird.

12 "But [a]these are the ones which you shall not eat: the [1]eagle and the vulture and the [2]buzzard,

13 and the red kite, the falcon, and the kite in their kinds,

14 and every raven in its kind,

15 and the ostrich, the owl, the sea gull, and the hawk in their kinds,

16 the little owl, the [1]great owl, the white owl,

17 the pelican, the carrion vulture, the cormorant,

18 the stork, and the heron in their kinds, and the hoopoe and the bat.

19 "And all the [1]teeming life with wings are unclean to you; they shall not be eaten.

20 "You may eat any clean bird.

21 ¶ "[a]You shall not eat anything which dies *of itself.* You may give it to the alien who is in your [1]town, so that he may eat it, or you may sell it to a foreigner, for you are [b]a holy people to the LORD your God. [c]You shall not boil a young goat in its mother's milk.

22 ¶ "You [a]shall surely tithe all the produce from [1]what you sow, which comes out of the field every year.

23 "You shall eat in the presence of the LORD your God, [a]at the place where He

---

6 [b]Deut 13:2
8 [a]Prov 1:10 [b]Deut 7:2
9 [a]Deut 13:5 [b]Lev 24:14; Deut 17:7
10 [1]Lit *with stones so that he dies* [2]Lit *slaves* [a]Deut 13:5
11 [a]Deut 19:20
13 [a]Deut 13:2
15 [1]Or *putting it under the ban* [a]Deut 13:5
16 [1]Lit *mound* [a]Deut 7:25,26 [b]Josh 8:28; Is 17:1; 25:2; Jer 49:2
17 [a]Ex 32:12; Num 25:4 [b]Deut 30:3 [c]Deut 7:13 [d]Gen 22:17; 26:4,24; 28:14
18 [1]Or *for* [2]Lit *to keep* [3]Lit *to do*
14:1 [1]Lit *make a baldness between your eyes* [a]Rom 8:16; 9:8, 26; Gal 3:26; 1 John 3:1 [b]Lev 19:28; 21:5; Jer 16:6; 41:5
2 [1]Or *special treasure* [a]Lev 20:26; Deut 7:6; Rom 12:1 [b]Ex 19:5; Deut 4:20; 26:18; Titus 2:14; 1 Pet 2:9
3 [a]Ezek 4:14
4 [a]Lev 11:2-45; Acts 10:14
5 [1]Exact identification of these animals is uncertain
6 [1]Lit *two hoofs* [2]Lit *brings up*
7 [1]Lit *brings up* [2]Lit *a cleaving* [3]Or *hare* [4]A small, shy, furry animal *(Hyrax syriacus)* found in the peninsula of the Sinai, northern Israel, and the region round the Dead Sea; KJV *coney,* orig NASB *rock-badger*
12 [1]Or *vulture* [2]Or *black vulture* [a]Lev 11:13
16 [1]Or *great horned owl*
19 [1]I.e. flying insects
21 [1]Lit *gates* [a]Lev 17:15; 22:8; Ezek 4:14; 44:31 [b]Deut 14:2 [c]Ex 23:19; 34:26
22 [1]Lit *your seed* [a]Lev 27:30; Deut 12:6,17; Neh 10:37
23 [a]Deut 12:5

chooses to establish His name, the tithe of your grain, your new wine, your oil, and the firstborn of your herd and your flock, so that you may [b]learn to fear the LORD your God always.

24 "If the [1]distance is so great for you that you are not able to [2]bring *the tithe,* since the place where the LORD your God chooses [a]to set His name is too far away from you when the LORD your God blesses you,

25 then you shall [1]exchange *it* for money, and bind the money in your hand and go to the place which the LORD your God chooses.

26 "You may spend the money for whatever your [1]heart desires: for oxen, or sheep, or wine, or strong drink, or whatever your [1]heart [2]desires; and [a]there you shall eat in the presence of the LORD your God and rejoice, you and your household.

27 "Also you shall not neglect [a]the Levite who is in your [1]town, [b]for he has no portion or inheritance among you.

28 ¶ "[a]At the end of every third year you shall bring out all the tithe of your produce in that year, and shall deposit *it* in your [1]town.

29 "The Levite, [a]because he has no portion or inheritance among you, and [b]the alien, the [1]orphan and the widow who are in your [2]town, shall come and [c]eat and be satisfied, in order that [d]the LORD your God may bless you in all the work of your hand which you do.

The Sabbatic Year

15 "[a]At the end of *every* seven years you shall [1]grant a remission *of debts.*

2 "This is the manner of remission: every creditor shall release what he has loaned to his neighbor; he shall not exact it of his neighbor and his brother, because the LORD'S remission has been proclaimed.

3 "[a]From a foreigner you may exact *it,* but your hand shall release whatever of yours is with your brother.

4 "However, there will be no poor among you, since [a]the LORD will surely bless you in the land which the LORD your God is giving you as an inheritance to possess,

5 if only you listen obediently to the voice of the LORD your God, to observe carefully all this commandment which I am commanding you today.

6 "[a]For the LORD your God will bless you as He has promised you, and you will lend to many nations, but you will not borrow; and you will rule over many nations, but they will not rule over you.

7 ¶ "If there is [a]a poor man with you, one of your brothers, in any of your [1]towns in your land which the LORD your God is giving you, [b]you shall not harden your heart, nor close your hand from your poor brother;

8 but [a]you shall freely open your hand to him, and shall generously lend him sufficient for his need *in* whatever he lacks.

9 "Beware that there is no base [1]thought in your heart, saying, '[a]The seventh year, the year of remission, is near,' and [b]your eye is hostile toward your poor brother, and you give him nothing; then he [c]may cry to the LORD against you, and it will be a sin in you.

10 "You shall generously give to him, and your heart shall not be grieved when you give to him, because [a]for this thing the LORD your God will bless you in all your work and in all [1]your undertakings.

11 "[a]For the poor will never cease *to be* [1]in the land; therefore I command you, saying, 'You shall freely open your hand to your brother, to your needy and poor in your land.'

12 ¶ "[a]If your [1]kinsman, a Hebrew man or woman, is sold to you, then he shall serve you six years, but in the seventh year you shall set him [2]free.

13 "When you set him [1]free, you shall not send him away empty-handed.

14 "You shall furnish him liberally from your flock and from your threshing floor and from your wine vat; you shall give to him as the LORD your God has blessed you.

15 "You shall remember that you were a slave in the land of Egypt, and the LORD your God redeemed you; therefore I command you [1]this today.

16 "It shall come about [a]if he says to you, 'I will not go out from you,' because he loves you and your household, since he fares well with you;

17 then you shall take an awl and pierce it through his ear into the door, and he shall be your servant forever. Also you shall do likewise to your maidservant.

18 ¶ "It shall not seem hard to you when you set him [1]free, for he has given you six years *with* [2]double the service of a hired man; so the LORD your God will bless you in whatever you do.

19 ¶ "[a]You shall consecrate to the LORD your God all the firstborn males that are born of your herd and of your flock; you shall not work with the firstborn of your herd, nor shear the firstborn of your flock.

20 "[a]You and your household shall eat

23 [b]Deut 4:10; Ps 2:11; 111:10; 147:11; Is 8:13; Jer 32:38-40

24 [1]Lit *way* [2]Lit *carry* it [a]Deut 12:5,21

25 [1]Lit *give in money*

26 [1]Lit *soul* [2]Lit *asks of you* [a]Deut 12:7

27 [1]Lit *gates* [a]Deut 12:12 [b]Num 18:20; Deut 10:9; 18:12

28 [1]Lit *gates* [a]Deut 26:12

29 [1]Or *fatherless* [2]Lit *gates* [a]Deut 10:9 [b]Deut 16:11,14; 24:19-21; 26:12; Ps 94:6; Is 1:17 [c]Deut 6:11 [d]Deut 15:10; Mal 3:10

15:1 [1]Lit *make a release* [a]Deut 31:10

3 [a]Deut 23:20

4 [a]Deut 28:8

6 [a]Deut 28:12, 13

7 [1]Lit *gates* [a]Lev 25:35; Deut 15:11 [b]1 John 3:17

8 [a]Matt 5:42; Luke 6:34; Gal 2:10

9 [1]Lit *word* [a]Deut 15:1 [b]Matt 20:15 [c]Ex 22:23; Deut 24:15; Job 34:28; Ps 12:5; James 5:4

10 [1]Lit *the putting forth of your hand* [a]Deut 14:29; Ps 41:1; Prov 22:9

11 [1]Lit *in the midst of* [a]Matt 26:11; Mark 14:7; John 12:8

12 [1]Lit *brother* [2]Lit *free from you* [a]Ex 21:2-6; Lev 25:39-43; Jer 34:14

13 [1]Lit *free from you*

15 [1]Lit *this thing*

16 [a]Ex 21:5,6

18 [1]Lit *free from you* [2]Lit *double the amount*

19 [a]Ex 13:2,12

20 [a]Lev 7:15-18; Deut 12:5; 14:23

it every year before the LORD your God in
the place which the LORD chooses.
21 "[a]But if it has any [1]defect, *such as*
lameness or blindness, *or* any serious
[1]defect, you shall not sacrifice it to the
LORD your God.
22 "You shall eat it within your gates;
[a]the unclean and the clean alike *may eat*
it, as [a]a gazelle or a deer.
23 "Only [a]you shall not eat its blood;
you are to pour it out on the ground like
water.

The Feasts of Passover, of Weeks, and of Booths

16 "Observe [a]the month of Abib
and [1b]celebrate the Passover to
the LORD your God, for in the month of
Abib the LORD your God brought you out
of Egypt by night.
2 "You shall sacrifice the Passover to
the LORD your God from the flock and
the herd, in the place where the LORD
chooses to establish His name.
3 "[a]You shall not eat leavened bread
with it; seven days you shall eat with it
unleavened bread, the bread of affliction
(for you came out of the land of Egypt in
haste), so that you may remember [b]all
the days of your life the day when you
came out of the land of Egypt.
4 "For seven days no leaven shall be
seen with you in all your territory, and
[a]none of the flesh which you sacrifice on
the evening of the first day shall remain
overnight until morning.
5 "You are not allowed to sacrifice the
Passover in any of your [1]towns which
the LORD your God is giving you;
6 but [a]at the place where the LORD
your God chooses to establish His name,
you shall sacrifice the Passover in the evening at sunset, at the time that you came
out of Egypt.
7 "You shall [a]cook and eat *it* in the
place which the LORD your God chooses.
In the morning you are to return to your
tents.
8 "Six days you shall eat unleavened
bread, and [a]on the seventh day there
shall be [b]a solemn assembly to the LORD
your God; you shall do no work *on it.*
9 ¶ "[a]You shall count seven weeks
for yourself; you shall begin to count sev-
en weeks from the time you begin to put
the sickle to the standing grain.
10 "Then you shall [1]celebrate the Feast
of Weeks to the LORD your God with a
tribute of a freewill offering of your hand,
which you shall give just as the LORD your
God blesses you;
11 and you shall [a]rejoice before the
LORD your God, you and your son and
your daughter and your male and female
servants and [b]the Levite who is in your
[1]town, and [c]the stranger and the [2]or-
phan and the widow who are in your
midst, in the place where the LORD your
God chooses to establish His name.
12 "[a]You shall remember that you
were a slave in Egypt, and you shall be
careful to observe these statutes.
13 ¶ "[a]You shall [1]celebrate the Feast
of Booths seven days after you have gathered in from your threshing floor and
your wine vat;
14 and you shall [a]rejoice in your feast,
you and your son and your daughter and
your male and female servants and the
Levite and the stranger and the [1]orphan
and the widow who are in your [2]towns.
15 "Seven days you shall celebrate a
feast to the LORD your God in the place
which the LORD chooses, because the
LORD your God will bless you in all your
produce and in all the work of your
hands, so that you will be altogether joyful.
16 ¶ "[a]Three times in a year all your
males shall appear before the LORD your
God in the place which He chooses, at
the Feast of Unleavened Bread and at the
Feast of Weeks and at the Feast of Booths,
and [b]they shall not appear before the
LORD empty-handed.
17 "Every man [1]shall give as he is able,
according to the blessing of the LORD your
God which He has given you.
18 ¶ "You shall appoint for yourself
judges and officers in all your [1]towns
which the LORD your God is giving you,
according to your tribes, and they shall
judge the people with righteous judgment.
19 "[a]You shall not distort justice; [b]you
shall not [1]be partial, and [c]you shall not
take a bribe, for a bribe blinds the eyes of
the wise and perverts the words of the
righteous.
20 "Justice, *and only* justice, you shall
pursue, that [a]you may live and possess
the land which the LORD your God is giving you.
21 ¶ "[a]You shall not plant for yourself
an [1]Asherah of any kind of tree beside
the altar of the LORD your God, which you
shall make for yourself.
22 "[a]You shall not set up for yourself a
sacred pillar which the LORD your God
hates.

Administration of Justice

17 "[a]You shall not sacrifice to the
LORD your God an ox or a sheep
which has a blemish *or* any [1]defect, for
that is a detestable thing to the LORD your
God.

---

21 [1]Lit *blemish* [a]Lev 22:19-25; Deut 17:1
22 [a]Deut 12:15, 16,22
23 [a]Gen 9:4; Lev 7:26; 17:10; 19:26; Deut 12:16,23
16:1 [1]Lit *perform* [a]Ex 12:2 [b]Num 28:16
3 [a]Ex 12:8,15, 19,39; 13:3; 34:18 [b]Deut 4:9
4 [a]Ex 12:8,10; 34:25
5 [1]Lit *gates*
6 [a]Deut 12:5
7 [a]Ex 12:8; 2 Chr 35:13
8 [a]Num 28:25 [b]Ex 12:16; 13:6; Lev 23:8,36
9 [a]Ex 23:16; 34:22; Lev 23:15; Num 28:26
10 [1]Lit *perform*
11 [1]Lit *gates* [2]Or *fatherless* [a]Deut 12:7 [b]Deut 12:12 [c]Deut 14:29
12 [a]Deut 15:15
13 [1]Lit *perform* [a]Lev 23:34-43
14 [1]Or *fatherless* [2]Lit *gates* [a]Deut 16:11
16 [a]Ex 23:14-17; 34:23, 24 [b]Ex 34:20
17 [1]Lit *according to the gift of his hand*
18 [1]Lit *gates*
19 [1]Lit *regard persons* [a]Ex 23:2; Lev 19:15; Deut 1:17; 10:17 [b]Prov 24:23 [c]Ex 23:8; Prov 17:23; Eccl 7:7
20 [a]Deut 4:1
21 [1]I.e. wooden symbol of a female deity [a]Deut 7:5; 2 Kin 17:16; 21:3; 2 Chr 33:3
22 [a]Lev 26:1
17:1 [1]Lit *evil thing* [a]Deut 15:21

2 ¶ "[a]If there is found in your midst,
in any of your [1]towns, which the LORD
your God is giving you, a man or a woman
who does what is evil in the sight of the
LORD your God, by transgressing His covenant,
3 and has gone and [a]served other
gods and worshiped them, [b]or the sun or
the moon or any of the heavenly host,
[c]which I have not commanded,
4 and if it is told you and you have
heard of it, then you shall inquire thoroughly. Behold, if it is true and the thing
certain that this detestable thing has been
done in Israel,
5 then you shall bring out that man or
that woman who has done this evil deed
to your gates, *that is,* the man or the
woman, and [a]you shall stone them to
[1]death.
6 "[a]On the [1]evidence of two witnesses or three witnesses, he who is to
die shall be put to death; he shall not be
put to death on the [1]evidence of one
witness.
7 "[a]The hand of the witnesses shall
be first against him to put him to death,
and afterward the hand of all the people.
[b]So you shall purge the evil from your
midst.
8 ¶ "[a]If any case is too difficult for
you to decide, between [1]one kind of
homicide or another, between [2]one kind
of lawsuit or another, and between [3]one
kind of assault or another, being cases of
dispute in your [4]courts, then you shall
arise and go up to [b]the place which the
LORD your God chooses.
9 "So you shall come to [a]the Levitical
priest or the judge who is *in office* in
those days, and you shall inquire *of them*
and they will declare to you the verdict in
the case.
10 "You shall do according to the
[1]terms of the verdict which they declare
to you from that place which the LORD
chooses; and you shall be careful to observe according to all that they teach you.
11 "[a]According to the [1]terms of the
law which they teach you, and according
to the verdict which they tell you, you
shall do; you shall not turn aside from the
word which they declare to you, to the
right or the left.
12 "The man who acts [a]presumptuous-
ly by not listening to the priest who
stands there to serve the LORD your God,
nor to the judge, that man shall die; thus
you shall purge the evil from Israel.
13 "Then all the people will hear and be
afraid, and will not act [a]presumptuously
again.
14 ¶ "When you enter the land which
the LORD your God gives you, and you
[a]possess it and live in it, and you say, '[b]I
will set a king over me like all the nations
who are around me,'
15 you shall surely set a king over you
whom the LORD your God chooses, *one*
[a]from among your [1]countrymen you
shall set as king over yourselves; you may
not put a foreigner over yourselves who
is not your [1]countryman.
16 "[a]Moreover, he shall not multiply
horses for himself, nor shall he [b]cause
the people to return to Egypt to multiply
horses, since [c]the LORD has said to you,
'You shall never again return that way.'
17 "[a]He shall not multiply wives for
himself, [1]or else his heart will turn away;
nor shall he greatly increase silver and
gold for himself.
18 ¶ "Now it shall come about when
he sits on the throne of his kingdom, he
shall write for himself a copy of this law
on a scroll [1a]in the presence of the Levitical priests.
19 "It shall be with him and he shall
read it [a]all the days of his life, that he
may learn to fear the LORD his God, [1]by
carefully observing all the words of this
law and these statutes,
20 that his heart may not be lifted up
above his [1]countrymen [a]and that he
may not turn aside from the commandment, to the right or the left, so that he
and his sons may continue long in his
kingdom in the midst of Israel.

Portion of the Levites

18 "[a]The Levitical priests, the
whole tribe of Levi, shall have no
portion or inheritance with Israel; they
shall eat the LORD'S offerings by fire and
His [1]portion.
2 "[a]They shall have no inheritance
among their [1]countrymen; the LORD is
their inheritance, as He [2]promised them.
3 ¶ "[a]Now this shall be the priests'
due from the people, from those who offer a sacrifice, either an ox or a sheep, of
which they shall give to the priest the
shoulder and the two cheeks and the
stomach.
4 "You shall give him the [a]first fruits
of your grain, your new wine, and your
oil, and the first shearing of your sheep.
5 "[a]For the LORD your God has chosen him and his sons from all your tribes,
to [b]stand [1]and serve in the name of the
LORD forever.
6 ¶ "Now if a Levite comes from any
of your [1]towns throughout Israel where
he [a]resides, and comes [2]whenever he
desires to the place which the LORD
chooses,
7 then he shall serve in the name of

2 [1]Lit *gates* [a]Deut 13:6-11
3 [a]Ex 22:20 [b]Job 31:26-28 [c]Jer 7:22
5 [1]Lit *death with stones* [a]Lev 24:14; Josh 7:25
6 [1]Lit *mouth* [a]Num 35:30; Deut 19:15; Matt 18:16; John 8:17; 2 Cor 13:1; 1 Tim 5:19; Heb 10:28
7 [a]Lev 24:14; Deut 13:9 [b]1 Cor 5:13
8 [1]Lit *blood to blood* [2]Lit *judgment to judgment* [3]Lit *stroke to stroke* [4]Lit *gates* [a]2 Chr 19:10; Hag 2:11 [b]Deut 12:5; Ps 122:5
9 [a]Deut 19:17
10 [1]Lit *mouth*
11 [1]Lit *mouth* [a]Deut 25:1
12 [a]Num 15:30; Deut 1:43; 17:13; 18:20; Hos 4:4
13 [a]Deut 17:12
14 [a]Deut 11:31; Josh 21:43 [b]1 Sam 8:5,19, 20; 10:19
15 [1]Lit *brother(s)* [a]Jer 30:21
16 [a]1 Kin 4:26; 10:26-29; Ps 20:7 [b]Is 31:1; Ezek 17:15 [c]Ex 13:17,18; Hos 11:5
17 [1]Lit *nor* [a]2 Sam 5:13; 12:11; 1 Kin 11:3,4
18 [1]Lit *from before* [a]Deut 31:24-26
19 [1]Lit *to keep to do them* [a]Deut 4:9,10; Josh 1:8
20 [1]Lit *brothers* [a]Deut 5:32; 1 Kin 15:5
18:1 [1]Or *inheritance* [a]Deut 10:9; 1 Cor 9:13
2 [1]Lit *brothers* [2]Lit *spoke to* [a]Num 18:20
3 [a]Lev 7:32-34; Num 18:11,12
4 [a]Num 18:12
5 [1]Lit *to* [a]Ex 29:9 [b]Deut 10:8
6 [1]Lit *gates* [2]Lit *with all the desire of his soul* [a]Num 35:2,3

the LORD his God, like all his fellow Levites who stand there before the LORD.
8 "[a]They shall eat [1]equal portions,
except *what they receive* from the sale of
their fathers' *estates.*

Spiritism Forbidden

9 ¶ "When you enter the land which
the LORD your God gives you, you shall
not learn to [1a]imitate the detestable
things of those nations.
10 "There shall not be found among
you anyone [a]who makes his son or his
daughter pass through the fire, one who
uses divination, one [b]who practices
witchcraft, or one who interprets omens,
or a sorcerer,
11 or one who casts a spell, [a]or a medium, or a spiritist, or one who calls up
the dead.
12 "For whoever does these things is
detestable to the LORD; and [a]because of
these detestable things the LORD your
God will drive them out before you.
13 "[a]You shall be [1]blameless before
the LORD your God.
14 "For those nations, which you shall
dispossess, listen to those who [a]practice
witchcraft and to diviners, but as for you,
the LORD your God has not allowed you *to*
do so.
15 ¶ "[a]The LORD your God will raise
up for you a prophet like me from among
you, from your [1]countrymen, you shall
listen to him.
16 "This is [a]according to all that you
asked of the LORD your God in Horeb on
the day of the assembly, saying, 'Let me
not hear again the voice of the LORD my
God, let me not see this great fire anymore, or I will die.'
17 "[a]The LORD said to me, 'They have
[1]spoken well.
18 'I will raise up a prophet from
among their [1]countrymen like you, and
[a]I will put My words in his mouth, and
[b]he shall speak to them all that I command him.
19 '[a]It shall come about that whoever
will not listen to My words which he shall
speak in My name, I Myself will require
it of him.
20 'But the prophet who speaks a word
[a]presumptuously in My name which I
have not commanded him to speak, or
[b]which he speaks in the name of other
gods, [1]that prophet shall die.'
21 "[1]You may say in your heart, 'How
will we know the word which the LORD
has not spoken?'
22 "[a]When a prophet speaks in the
name of the LORD, if the thing does not
come about or come true, that is the
thing which the LORD has not spoken.
The prophet has spoken it [b]presumptu-
ously; you shall not be afraid of him.

Cities of Refuge

19 "[a]When the LORD your God cuts
off the nations, whose land the
LORD your God gives you, and you dispossess them and settle in their cities and in
their houses,
2 [a]you shall set aside three cities for
yourself in the midst of your land, which
the LORD your God gives you to [1]possess.
3 "You shall prepare the [1]roads for
yourself, and divide into three parts the
territory of your land which the LORD
your God will give you as a possession,
[2]so that any manslayer may flee there.
4 ¶ "[a]Now this is the case of the
manslayer who may flee there and live:
when he [1]kills his friend [2]unintentional-
ly, [3]not hating him previously—
5 as when *a man* goes into the forest
with his friend to cut wood, and his hand
[1]swings the axe to cut down the tree,
and the iron *head* slips off the [2]handle
and [3]strikes his friend so that he dies—
he may flee to one of these cities and live;
6 otherwise the avenger of blood
might pursue the manslayer [1]in the heat
of his anger, and overtake him, because
the way is long, and [2]take his life, though
he was not deserving of death, since he
had not hated him previously.
7 "Therefore, I command you, saying,
'You shall set aside three cities for yourself.'
8 ¶ "If the LORD your God [a]enlarges
your territory, just as He has sworn to
your fathers, and gives you all the land
which He [1]promised to give your fathers—
9 if you [1]carefully observe all this
commandment which I command you today, [a]to love the LORD your God, and
to walk in His ways always—[b]then you
shall add three more cities for yourself,
besides these three.
10 "So innocent blood will not be shed
in the midst of your land which the LORD
your God gives you as an inheritance, and
[a]bloodguiltiness be on you.
11 ¶ "But [a]if there is a man who hates
his neighbor and lies in wait for him and
rises up against him and strikes [1]him so
that he dies, and he flees to one of these
cities,
12 then the elders of his city shall send
and take him from there and deliver him
into the hand of the avenger of blood,
that he may die.
13 "[1a]You shall not pity him, but [b]you
shall purge the blood of the innocent
from Israel, that it may go well with you.

8 [1]Lit *portion like portion* [a]Lev 27:30-33; Num 18:21-24; 2 Chr 31:4; Neh 12:44
9 [1]Lit *do according to* [a]Deut 9:5
10 [a]Deut 12:31 [b]Ex 22:18; Lev 19:26,31; 20:6; Jer 27:9,10; Mal 3:5
11 [a]Lev 19:31
12 [a]Lev 18:24
13 [1]Lit *complete, perfect*; or *having integrity* [a]Gen 6:9; 17:1; Matt 5:48
14 [a]2 Kin 21:6
15 [1]Lit *brothers* [a]Matt 21:11; Luke 2:25-34; 7:16; 24:19; John 1:21,25; 4:19; Acts 3:22; 7:37
16 [a]Ex 20:18, 19; Deut 5:23-27
17 [1]Lit *done well what they have spoken* [a]Deut 5:28
18 [1]Lit *brothers* [a]Is 51:16; John 17:8 [b]John 4:25; 8:28; 12:49,50
19 [a]Acts 3:23; Heb 12:25
20 [1]Lit *and that* [a]Deut 13:5; 17:12 [b]Deut 13:1,2; Jer 14:14; Zech 13:3
21 [1]Lit *if you say*
22 [a]Jer 28:9 [b]Deut 18:20
19:1 [a]Deut 6:10,11
2 [1]Lit *possess it* [a]Deut 4:41; Josh 20:2
3 [1]Lit *road* [2]Lit *and it shall be for every manslayer to flee there*
4 [1]Lit *smites* [2]Lit *without knowledge* [3]Lit *and he was not hating him previously* [a]Num 35:9-34
5 [1]Lit *is thrust with* [2]Lit *wood* [3]Lit *finds*
6 [1]Lit *while his heart is hot* [2]Lit *smite him in the soul*
8 [1]Lit *spoke* [a]Gen 15:18
9 [1]Lit *keep...to do it* [a]Deut 6:5 [b]Josh 20:7
10 [a]Num 35:33; Deut 21:1-9
11 [1]Lit *him in the soul* [a]Ex 21:12; Num 35:16; 1 John 3:15
13 [1]Lit *Your eye* [a]Deut 7:2 [b]1 Kin 2:31

Laws of Landmark and Testimony

14 ¶ "[a]You shall not move your neighbor's boundary mark, which the ancestors have set, in your inheritance which you will inherit in the land that the LORD your God gives you to [1]possess.

15 ¶ "[a]A single witness shall not rise up against a man on account of any iniquity or any sin [1]which he has committed; on the [2]evidence of two or three witnesses a matter shall be confirmed.

16 "[a]If a malicious witness rises up against a man to [1]accuse him of [2]wrongdoing,

17 then both the men who have the dispute shall stand [a]before the LORD, before the priests and the judges who will be *in office* in those days.

18 "The judges [a]shall investigate thoroughly, and if the witness is a false witness *and* he has [1]accused his brother falsely,

19 then [a]you shall do to him just as he had intended to do to his brother. Thus you shall purge the evil from among you.

20 "[a]The rest will hear and be afraid, and will never again do such an evil thing among you.

21 "Thus [1a]you shall not show pity: [b]life for life, [c]eye for eye, tooth for tooth, hand for hand, foot for foot.

Laws of Warfare

20 "When you go out to battle against your enemies and see [a]horses and chariots *and* people more numerous than you, [b]do not be afraid of them; for the LORD your God, who brought you up from the land of Egypt, is with you.

2 "When you are approaching the battle, the priest shall come near and speak to the people.

3 "He shall say to them, 'Hear, O Israel, you are approaching the battle against your enemies today. Do not be fainthearted. [a]Do not be afraid, or panic, or tremble before them,

4 for the LORD your God [a]is the one who goes with you, to fight for you against your enemies, to save you.'

5 "The officers also shall speak to the people, saying, 'Who is the man that has built a new house and has not [a]dedicated it? Let him depart and return to his house, otherwise he might die in the battle and another man would dedicate it.

6 'Who is the man that has planted a vineyard and has not [1]begun to use its fruit? Let him depart and return to his house, otherwise he might die in the battle and another man [1]would begin to use its fruit.

7 '[a]And who is the man that is engaged to a woman and has not [1]married her? Let him depart and return to his house, otherwise he might die in the battle and another man [2]would marry her.'

8 "Then the officers shall speak further to the people and say, '[a]Who is the man that is afraid and fainthearted? Let him depart and return to his house, so that [1]he might not make his brothers' hearts melt like his heart.'

9 "When the officers have finished speaking to the people, they shall appoint commanders of armies at the head of the people.

10 ¶ "When you approach a city to fight against it, you shall [1]offer it terms of peace.

11 "If it [1]agrees to make peace with you and opens to you, then all the people who are found in it shall become your [a]forced labor and shall serve you.

12 "However, if it does not make peace with you, but makes war against you, then you shall besiege it.

13 "When the LORD your God gives it into your hand, [a]you shall strike all the [1]men in it with the edge of the sword.

14 "Only the women and the children and [a]the animals and all that is in the city, all its spoil, you shall take as booty for yourself; and you shall [1]use the spoil of your enemies which the LORD your God has given you.

15 "Thus you shall do to all the cities that are very far from you, which are not of the cities of these nations [1]nearby.

16 "[a]Only in the cities of these peoples that the LORD your God is giving you as an inheritance, you shall not leave alive anything that breathes.

17 "But you shall [1]utterly destroy them, the Hittite and the Amorite, the Canaanite and the Perizzite, the Hivite and the Jebusite, as the LORD your God has commanded you,

18 so that they may not teach you to do [a]according to all their detestable things which they have done for their gods, so that you would [b]sin against the LORD your God.

19 ¶ "When you besiege a city a long time, to make war against it in order to capture it, you shall not destroy its trees by swinging an axe against them; for you may eat from them, and you shall not cut them down. [1]For is the tree of the field a man, that it should [2]be besieged by you?

20 "Only the trees which you know [1]are not fruit trees you shall destroy and cut down, that you may construct siegeworks against the city that is making war with you until it falls.

---

14 [1]Lit *possess it* [a]Deut 27:17; Job 24:2; Prov 22:28; Hos 5:10

15 [1]Lit *in any sin, which he sins* [2]Lit *mouth of two witnesses, or by the mouth of three* [a]Num 35:30; Deut 17:6; Matt 18:16; John 8:17; 2 Cor 13:1; 1 Tim 5:19; Heb 10:28

16 [1]Lit *testify against* [2]Lit *turning aside* [a]Ex 23:1; Ps 27:12

17 [a]Deut 17:9

18 [1]Lit *testified against* [a]Deut 25:1

19 [a]Prov 19:5

20 [a]Deut 17:13; 21:21

21 [1]Lit *your eye* [a]Deut 19:13 [b]Ex 21:23; Lev 24:20 [c]Matt 5:38

20:1 [a]Deut 3:22; 7:18; 31:6, 8; Ps 20:7; Is 31:1 [b]2 Chr 32:7,8; Ps 23:4; Is 41:10

3 [a]Deut 20:1; Josh 23:10

4 [a]Deut 1:30; 3:22; Josh 23:10

5 [a]Neh 12:27

6 [1]Lit *treat(ed) it as common*

7 [1]Lit *taken* [2]Lit *take* [a]Deut 24:5

8 [1]So with Gr and other ancient versions [a]Judg 7:3

10 [1]Lit *call to it for peace*

11 [1]Lit *answers peace* [a]1 Kin 9:21

13 [1]Lit *males* [a]Num 31:7

14 [1]Lit *eat* [a]Josh 8:2

15 [1]Lit *here*

16 [a]Ex 23:31-33; Num 21:2,3; Deut 7:1-5; Josh 11:14

17 [1]Or *put them under the ban*

18 [a]Ex 34:12-16; Deut 7:4; 9:5; 12:30, 31 [b]Ex 23:33; 2 Kin 21:3-15; Ps 106:34-41

19 [1]Read as interrogative with ancient versions [2]Lit *come before you in the siege*

20 [1]Lit *they are not trees for food*

Expiation of a Crime

21 "If a slain person is found lying
in the open country in the land
which the LORD your God gives you to
[1]possess, *and* it is not known who has
struck him,
2 then your elders and your judges
shall go out and measure *the distance* to
the cities which are around the slain one.
3 "It shall be that the city which is
nearest to the slain man, that is, the elders of that city, shall take a heifer of the
herd, which has not been worked and
which has not pulled in a yoke;
4 and the elders of that city shall
bring the heifer down to a valley with
running water, which has not been
plowed or sown, and shall break the heifer's neck there in the valley.
5 "Then [a]the priests, the sons of Levi,
shall come near, for the LORD your God
has chosen them to serve Him and to
bless in the name of the LORD; and every
dispute and every [1]assault [2]shall be settled by them.
6 "All the elders of that city [1]which
is nearest to the slain man shall [a]wash
their hands over the heifer whose neck
was broken in the valley;
7 and they shall answer and say, 'Our
hands did not shed this blood, nor did our
eyes see *it.*
8 '[1]Forgive Your people Israel whom
You have redeemed, O LORD, and do not
place the guilt of [a]innocent blood in the
midst of Your people Israel.' And the
bloodguiltiness shall be [2]forgiven them.
9 "[a]So you shall remove the guilt of
innocent blood from your midst, when
you do what is right in the eyes of the
LORD.

Domestic Relations

10 ¶ "When you go out to battle
against your enemies, and [a]the LORD
your God delivers them into your hands
and you take them away captive,
11 and see among the captives a beautiful woman, and have a desire for her
and would take her as a wife for yourself,
12 then you shall bring her home to
your house, and she shall [a]shave her
head and [1]trim her nails.
13 "She shall also [1]remove the clothes
of her captivity and shall remain in your
house, and [a]mourn her father and mother a full month; and after that you may go
in to her and be her husband and she
shall be your wife.
14 "It shall be, if you are not pleased
with her, then you shall let her go [1]wher-
ever she wishes; but you shall certainly
not sell her for money, you shall not
[2]mistreat her, because you have [a]hum-
bled her.
15 ¶ "If a man has two wives, the one
loved and [a]the other [1]unloved, and *both*
the loved and the [1]unloved have borne
him sons, if the firstborn son belongs to
the [1]unloved,
16 then it shall be in the day he [1]wills
what he has to his sons, he cannot make
the son of the loved the firstborn before
the son of the [2]unloved, who is the firstborn.
17 "But he shall acknowledge the firstborn, the son of the [1]unloved, by giving
him a double portion of all that [2]he has,
for he is the [a]beginning of his strength;
[b]to him belongs the right of the firstborn.
18 ¶ "If any man has a stubborn and
rebellious son who will [a]not obey his
father or his mother, and when they chastise him, he will not even listen to them,
19 then his father and mother shall
seize him, and bring him out to the elders
of his city [1]at the gateway of his hometown.
20 "They shall say to the elders of his
city, 'This son of ours is stubborn and
rebellious, he will not obey us, he is a
glutton and a drunkard.'
21 "[a]Then all the men of his city shall
stone him to death; so [b]you shall remove
the evil from your midst, and [c]all Israel
will hear *of it* and fear.
22 ¶ "If a man has committed a sin
[a]worthy of death and he is put to death,
and you hang him on a tree,
23 [a]his corpse shall not hang all night
on the tree, but you shall surely bury him
on the same day (for [b]he who is hanged
is [1]accursed of God), so that you [c]do not
defile your land which the LORD your God
gives you as an inheritance.

Sundry Laws

22 "[a]You shall not see your [1]coun-
tryman's ox or his sheep straying
away, and [2]pay no attention to them; you
shall certainly bring them back to your
countryman.
2 "If your countryman is not near you,
or if you do not know him, then you shall
bring it home to your house, and it shall
remain with you until your countryman
looks for it; then you shall restore it to
him.
3 "Thus you shall do with his donkey,
and you shall do the same with his garment, and you shall do likewise with anything lost by your countryman, which he
has lost and you have found. You are not
allowed to [1]neglect *them.*
4 "You shall not see your countryman's donkey or his ox fallen down on
the way, and [1]pay no attention to them;

21:1 [1]Lit *possess it*
5 [1]Lit *stroke* [2]Lit *shall be according to their mouth* [a]Deut 17:9-11; 19:17; 1 Chr 23:13
6 [1]Lit *who are* [a]Matt 27:24
8 [1]Lit *Cover over, atone for* [2]Lit *covered over, atoned for* [a]Num 35:33,34; Jon 1:14
9 [a]Deut 19:13
10 [a]Josh 21:44
12 [1]Lit *do* [a]Lev 14:8,9; Num 6:9
13 [1]Lit *remove from her* [a]Ps 45:10
14 [1]Lit *according to her soul* [2]Or *enslave* [a]Gen 34:2
15 [1]Lit *hated* [a]Gen 29:33
16 [1]Lit *makes to inherit* [2]Lit *hated*
17 [1]Lit *hated* [2]Lit *is found with him* [a]Gen 49:3 [b]Gen 25:31
18 [a]Ex 20:12; Lev 19:3; Prov 1:8; Eph 6:1-3
19 [1]Lit *and to the gate of his place*
21 [a]Lev 20:2, 27; 24:14-23; Num 15:25,36 [b]Deut 19:19 [c]Deut 13:11
22 [a]Deut 22:26; Matt 26:66; Mark 14:64; Acts 23:29
23 [1]Lit *the curse of God* [a]Josh 8:29; 10:26,27; John 19:31 [b]Gal 3:13 [c]Lev 18:25; Num 35:34
22:1 [1]Lit *brother,* and so through v 4 [2]Lit *hide yourself from them* [a]Ex 23:4,5; Prov 27:10; Zech 7:9
3 [1]Lit *hide yourself*
4 [1]Lit *hide yourself from them*

you shall certainly help him to raise *them* up.

5 ¶ "A woman shall not wear man's clothing, nor shall a man put on a woman's clothing; for whoever does these things is an abomination to the LORD your God.

6 ¶ "If you happen to come upon a bird's nest along the way, in any tree or on the ground, with young ones or eggs, and the mother sitting on the young or on the eggs, [a]you shall not take the mother with the young;

7 you shall certainly let the mother go, but the young you may take for yourself, [a]in order that it may be well with you and that you may prolong your days.

8 ¶ "When you build a new house, you shall make a parapet for your roof, so that you will not bring bloodguilt on your house if anyone falls from it.

9 ¶ "[a]You shall not sow your vineyard with two kinds of seed, or [1]all the produce of the seed which you have sown and the increase of the vineyard will become defiled.

10 ¶ "[a]You shall not plow with an ox and a donkey together.

11 ¶ "[a]You shall not wear a material mixed of wool and linen together.

12 ¶ "[a]You shall make yourself tassels on the four corners of your garment with which you cover yourself.

Laws on Morality

13 ¶ "[a]If any man takes a wife and goes in to her and *then* [1]turns against her,

14 and charges her with shameful deeds and [1]publicly defames her, and says, 'I took this woman, *but* when I came near her, I did not find her a virgin,'

15 then the girl's father and her mother shall take and bring out the *evidence* of the girl's virginity to the elders of the city at the gate.

16 "The girl's father shall say to the elders, 'I gave my daughter to this man for a wife, but he [1]turned against her;

17 and behold, he has charged her with shameful deeds, saying, "I did not find your daughter a virgin." But [1]this is the evidence of my daughter's virginity.' And they shall spread the garment before the elders of the city.

18 "So [a]the elders of that city shall take the man and chastise him,

19 and they shall fine him a hundred *shekels* of silver and give it to the girl's father, because he [1]publicly defamed a virgin of Israel. And she shall remain his wife; he cannot [2]divorce her all his days.

20 ¶ "But if this [1a]charge is true, that the girl was not found a virgin,

21 then they shall bring out the girl to the doorway of her father's house, and the men of her city shall stone her [1]to death because she has [a]committed an act of folly in Israel by playing the harlot in her father's house; thus [b]you shall purge the evil from among you.

22 ¶ "[a]If a man is found lying with a married woman, then both of them shall die, the man who lay with the woman, and the woman; thus you shall purge the evil from Israel.

23 ¶ "[a]If there is a girl who is a virgin engaged to a man, and *another* man finds her in the city and lies with her,

24 then you shall bring them both out to the gate of that city and you shall stone them [1]to death; the girl, because she did not cry out in the city, and the man, because he has violated his neighbor's wife. Thus you shall purge the evil from among you.

25 ¶ "But if in the field the man finds the girl who is engaged, and the man forces her and lies with her, then only the man who lies with her shall die.

26 "But you shall do nothing to the girl; there is no sin in the girl worthy of death, for just as a man rises against his neighbor and murders him, so is this case.

27 "When he found her in the field, the engaged girl cried out, but there was no one to save her.

28 ¶ "[a]If a man finds a girl who is a virgin, who is not engaged, and seizes her and lies with her and they are discovered,

29 then the man who lay with her shall give to the girl's father fifty *shekels* of silver, and she shall become his wife because he has violated her; he cannot divorce her all his days.

30 ¶ "[1a]A man shall not take his father's wife so that he will not uncover his father's skirt.

Persons Excluded from the Assembly

23 "[a]No one who is [1]emasculated or has his male organ cut off shall enter the assembly of the LORD.

2 "No one of illegitimate birth shall enter the assembly of the LORD; none of his *descendants*, even to the tenth generation, shall enter the assembly of the LORD.

3 "[a]No Ammonite or Moabite shall enter the assembly of the LORD; none of their *descendants*, even to the tenth generation, shall ever enter the assembly of the LORD,

4 [a]because they did not meet you with [1]food and water on the way when you came out of Egypt, and because they

---

6 [a]Lev 22:28

7 [a]Deut 4:40

9 [1]Lit *the fullness* [a]Lev 19:19

10 [a]2 Cor 6:14-16

11 [a]Lev 19:19

12 [a]Num 15:37-41; Matt 23:5

13 [1]Lit *hates her* [a]Gen 29:21; Deut 24:1; Judg 15:1

14 [1]Lit *causes an evil name to go out against her*

16 [1]Lit *hated her*

17 [1]Lit *these are*

18 [a]Ex 18:21; Deut 1:9-18

19 [1]Lit *caused an evil name to go out against a virgin* [2]Lit *send her away*

20 [1]Lit *matter* [a]Deut 17:4

21 [1]Lit *with stones so that she dies* [a]Gen 34:7; Lev 19:29; 21:9; Deut 23:17,18; Judg 20:5-10; 2 Sam 13:12,13 [b]Deut 13:5; 17:7; 19:19

22 [a]Lev 20:10; Ezek 16:38; Matt 5:27,28; John 8:5; 1 Cor 6:9; Heb 13:4

23 [a]Lev 19:20-22; Matt 1:18,19

24 [1]Lit *with stones so that they die*

28 [a]Ex 22:16

30 [1]Ch 23:1 in Heb [a]Lev 18:8; 20:11; Deut 27:20; 1 Cor 5:1

23:1 [1]Lit *wounded by crushing of testicles* [a]Lev 21:20; 22:24

3 [a]Neh 13:1,2

4 [1]Lit *bread* [a]Neh 13:2

Major Social Concerns in the Covenant

1. Personhood	Everyone's person is to be secure (Ex 20:13; Deut 5:17; Ex 21:16-21,26-31; Lev 19:14; Deut 24:7; 27:18).
2. False Accusation	Everyone is to be secure against slander and false accusation (Ex 20:16; Deut 5:20; Ex 23:1-3; Lev 19:16; Deut 19:15-21).
3. Woman	No woman is to be taken advantage of within her subordinate status in society (Ex 21:7-11,20,26-32; 22:16-17; Deut 21:10-14; 22:13-30; 24:1-5).
4. Punishment	Punishment for wrongdoing shall not be excessive so that the culprit is dehumanized (Deut 25:1-5).
5. Dignity	Every Israelite's dignity and right to be God's freedman and servant are to be honored and safeguarded (Ex 21:2,5-6; Lev 25; Deut 15:12-18).
6. Inheritance	Every Israelite's inheritance in the promised land is to be secure (Lev 25; Num 27:5-7; 36:1-9; Deut 25:5-10).
7. Property	Everyone's property is to be secure (Ex 20:15; Deut 5:19; Ex 21:33-36; 22:1-15; 23:4-5; Lev 19:35-36; Deut 22:1-4; 25:13-15).
8. Fruit of Labor	Everyone is to receive the fruit of his labors (Lev 19:13; Deut 24:14; 25:4).
9. Fruit of the Ground	Everyone is to share the fruit of the ground (Ex 23:10-11; Lev 19:9-10; 23:22; 25:3-55; Deut 14:28-29; 24:19-21).
10. Rest on Sabbath	Everyone, down to the humblest servant and the resident alien, is to share in the weekly rest of God's Sabbath (Ex 20:8-11; Deut 5:12-15; Ex 23:12).
11. Marriage	The marriage relationship is to be kept inviolate (Ex 20:14; Deut 5:18; see also Lev 18:6-23; 20:10-21; Deut 22:13-30).
12. Exploitation	No one, however disabled, impoverished or powerless, is to be oppressed or exploited (Ex 22:21-27; Lev 19:14,33-34; 25:35-36; Deut 23:19; 24:6,12-15,17; 27:18).
13. Fair Trial	Everyone is to have free access to the courts and is to be afforded a fair trial (Ex 23:6,8; Lev 19:15; Deut 1:17; 10:17-18; 16:18-20; 17:8-13; 19:15-21).
14. Social Order	Every person's God-given place in the social order is to be honored (Ex 20:12; Deut 5:16; Ex 21:15,17; 22:28; Lev 19:3,32; 20:9; Deut 17:8-13; 21:15-21; 27:16).
15. Law	No one shall be above the law, not even the king (Deut 17:18-20).
16. Animals	Concern for the welfare of other creatures is to be extended to the animal world (Ex 23:5,11; Lev 25:7; Deut 22:4,6-7; 25:4).

hired against you [b]Balaam the son of
Beor from Pethor of [2]Mesopotamia, to
curse you.
5 "Nevertheless, the LORD your God
was not willing to listen to Balaam, but
the LORD your God [a]turned the curse
into a blessing for you because the LORD
your God [b]loves you.
6 "[a]You shall never seek their peace
or their prosperity all your days.
7 ¶ "You shall not detest an Edomite,
for [a]he is your brother; you shall not detest an Egyptian, [b]because you were an
alien in his land.
8 "The sons of the third generation
who are born to them may enter the assembly of the LORD.
9 ¶ "When you go out as [1]an army
against your enemies, you shall keep
yourself from every evil thing.
10 ¶ "[a]If there is among you any man
who is unclean because of a nocturnal
emission, then he must go outside the
camp; he may not [1]reenter the camp.
11 "But it shall be when evening approaches, he shall bathe himself with water, and at sundown he may [1]reenter the
camp.
12 ¶ "You shall also have a place outside the camp and go out there,
13 and you shall have a [1]spade among
your tools, and it shall be when you sit
down outside, you shall dig with it and
shall turn [2]to cover up your excrement.
14 "Since [a]the LORD your God walks in
the midst of your camp to deliver you and
to [1]defeat your enemies before you,
therefore your camp must be [b]holy; and
He must not see [2]anything indecent
among you [3]or He will turn away from
you.
15 ¶ "[a]You shall not hand over to his
master a slave who has [1]escaped from
his master to you.
16 "He shall live with you in your
midst, in the place which he shall choose
in one of your [1]towns where it pleases
him; [a]you shall not mistreat him.
17 ¶ "[a]None of the daughters of Israel
shall be a cult prostitute, [b]nor shall any
of the sons of Israel be a cult prostitute.
18 "You shall not bring the hire of a
harlot or the wages of a [1a]dog into the
house of the LORD your God for any votive
offering, for both of these are an abomination to the LORD your God.
19 ¶ "[a]You shall not charge interest to
your [1]countrymen: interest on money,
food, *or* anything that may be loaned at
interest.
20 "[a]You may charge interest to a foreigner, but to your [1]countrymen you
shall not charge interest, so that [b]the
LORD your God may bless you in all [2]that

4 [2]Heb *Aram-naharaim* [b]Num 22:5; Josh 24:9; 2 Pet 2:15; Jude 11
5 [a]Prov 26:2 [b]Deut 4:37
6 [a]Ezra 9:12
7 [a]Gen 25:24-26; Obad 10 [b]Ex 22:21; Lev 19:34; Deut 10:19
9 [1]Or *a camp*
10 [1]Lit *come to the midst of* [a]Lev 15:16
11 [1]Lit *come to the midst of*
13 [1]Lit *peg* [2]Lit *and*
14 [1]Lit *give* [2]Lit *nakedness of anything* [3]Lit *and* [a]Lev 26:12 [b]Ex 3:5
15 [1]Lit *delivered himself* [a]1 Sam 30:15
16 [1]Lit *gates* [a]Ex 22:21; Prov 22:22
17 [a]Lev 19:29; Deut 22:21 [b]Gen 19:5; 2 Kin 23:7
18 [1]I.e. male prostitute, sodomite [a]Lev 18:22
19 [1]Lit *brother* [a]Ex 22:25; Lev 25:35-37; Neh 5:2-7; Ps 15:5
20 [1]Lit *brother* [2]Lit *the putting forth of your hand* [3]Lit *possess it* [a]Deut 28:12 [b]Deut 15:10
21 [1]Lit *for* [a]Num 30:1; Job 22:27; Ps 61:8; Eccl 5:4; Matt 5:33
23 [1]Lit *spoken with your mouth*
24 [1]Lit *according to your satisfaction of your soul* [2]Or *vessel*
25 [a]Matt 12:1; Mark 2:23; Luke 6:1
24:1 [1]Lit *if* [a]Num 5:12; Deut 22:13-21 [b]Matt 5:31; Mark 10:4
3 [1]Lit *hates her*
4 [a]Jer 3:1
5 [a]Deut 20:7 [b]Prov 5:18
7 [1]Lit *found stealing* [2]Lit *brothers* [a]Ex 21:16
8 [1]Lit *a mark or stroke* [a]Lev 13:1-14

you undertake in the land which you are
about to enter to [3]possess.
21 ¶ "[a]When you make a vow to the
LORD your God, you shall not delay to pay
it, for it would be sin in you, [1]and the
LORD your God will surely require it of
you.
22 "However, if you refrain from vow-
ing, it would not be sin in you.
23 "You shall be careful to perform
what goes out from your lips, just as you
have voluntarily vowed to the LORD your
God, what you have [1]promised.
24 ¶ "When you enter your neighbor's
vineyard, then you may eat grapes [1]until
you are fully satisfied, but you shall not
put any in your [2]basket.
25 ¶ "[a]When you enter your neighbor's standing grain, then you may pluck
the heads with your hand, but you shall
not wield a sickle in your neighbor's
standing grain.

Law of Divorce

24 "When a man takes a wife and
marries her, and it happens [1]that
she finds no favor in his eyes because he
has found some [a]indecency in her, and
[b]he writes her a certificate of divorce
and puts *it* in her hand and sends her out
from his house,
2 and she leaves his house and goes
and becomes another man's *wife,*
3 and if the latter husband [1]turns
against her and writes her a certificate of
divorce and puts *it* in her hand and sends
her out of his house, or if the latter husband dies who took her to be his wife,
4 *then* her [a]former husband who
sent her away is not allowed to take her
again to be his wife, since she has been
defiled; for that is an abomination before
the LORD, and you shall not bring sin on
the land which the LORD your God gives
you as an inheritance.
5 ¶ "[a]When a man takes a new wife,
he shall not go out with the army nor be
charged with any duty; he shall be free at
home one year and shall [b]give happiness
to his wife whom he has taken.

Sundry Laws

6 ¶ "No one shall take a handmill or
an upper millstone in pledge, for he
would be taking a life in pledge.
7 ¶ "[a]If a man is [1]caught kidnapping
any of his [2]countrymen of the sons of
Israel, and he deals with him violently or
sells him, then that thief shall die; so you
shall purge the evil from among you.
8 ¶ "[a]Be careful against [1]an infection of leprosy, that you diligently observe and do according to all that the
Levitical priests teach you; as I have

commanded them, so you shall be careful
to do.
9 "Remember what the LORD your
God did [a]to Miriam on the way as you
came out of Egypt.
10 ¶ "[a]When you make your neighbor a loan of any sort, you shall not enter
his house to take his pledge.
11 "You shall remain outside, and the
man to whom you make the loan shall
bring the pledge out to you.
12 "If he is a poor man, you shall not
sleep with his pledge.
13 "[a]When the sun goes down you
shall surely return the pledge to him, that
he may sleep in his cloak and bless you;
and [b]it will be righteousness for you before the LORD your God.
14 ¶ "[a]You shall not oppress a hired
servant *who is* poor and needy, whether
he is one of your [1]countrymen or one of
your aliens who is in your land in your
[2]towns.
15 "[a]You shall give him his wages on
his day [1]before the sun sets, for he is
poor and sets his [2]heart on it; so that [b]he
will not cry against you to the LORD and
it become sin in you.
16 ¶ "[a]Fathers shall not be put to
death [1]for *their* sons, nor shall sons be
put to death [1]for *their* fathers; everyone
shall be put to death for his own sin.
17 ¶ "[a]You shall not pervert the justice [1]due an alien *or* [2]an orphan, nor
[b]take a widow's garment in pledge.
18 "But you shall remember that you
were a slave in Egypt, and that the LORD
your God redeemed you from there;
therefore I am commanding you to do
this thing.
19 ¶ "[a]When you reap your harvest in
your field and have forgotten a sheaf in
the field, you shall not go back to get it;
it shall be [b]for the alien, for the [1]orphan,
and for the widow, in order that the LORD
your God [c]may bless you in all the work
of your hands.
20 "[a]When you beat your olive tree,
you shall not go over the boughs [1]again;
it shall be [b]for the alien, for the [2]orphan,
and for the widow.
21 ¶ "When you gather the grapes of
your vineyard, you shall not [1]go over it
again; it shall be for the alien, for the
[2]orphan, and for the widow.
22 "You shall remember that you were
a slave in the land of Egypt; therefore I am
commanding you to do this thing.

Sundry Laws

25 "[a]If there is a dispute between
men and they go to [1]court, and
[2]the judges decide their case, [b]and they
justify the righteous and condemn the
wicked,
2 then it shall be if the wicked man
[1a]deserves to be beaten, the judge shall
then make him lie down and be beaten in
his presence with the number of stripes
according to his [2]guilt.
3 "[a]He may beat him forty times *but*
no more, so that he does not beat him
with many more stripes than these and
your brother is not [b]degraded in your
eyes.
4 ¶ "[a]You shall not muzzle the ox
while he is threshing.
5 ¶ "When brothers live together and
one of them dies and has no son, the wife
of the deceased shall not be *married* outside *the family* to a strange man. [a]Her
husband's brother shall go in to her and
take her to himself as wife and perform
the duty of a husband's brother to her.
6 "It shall be that the firstborn whom
she bears shall [1]assume the name of his
dead brother, so that [a]his name will not
be blotted out from Israel.
7 "[a]But if the man does not desire to
take his brother's wife, then his brother's
wife shall go up to the gate to the elders
and say, 'My husband's brother refuses to
establish a name for his brother in Israel;
he is not willing to perform the duty of a
husband's brother to me.'
8 "Then the elders of his city shall
summon him and speak to him. And *if*
he persists and says, 'I do not desire to
take her,'
9 [a]then his brother's wife shall come
to him in the sight of the elders, and pull
his sandal off his foot and [b]spit in his
face; and she shall [1]declare, 'Thus it is
done to the man who does not build up
his brother's house.'
10 "In Israel his name shall be called,
'The house of him whose sandal is removed.'
11 ¶ "If *two* men, a man and his
[1]countryman, are struggling together,
and the wife of one comes near to deliver
her husband from the hand of the one
who is striking him, and puts out her
hand and seizes his genitals,
12 then you shall cut off her [1]hand;
[2a]you shall not show pity.
13 ¶ "[a]You shall not have in your bag
[1]differing weights, a large and a small.
14 "You shall not have in your house
[1]differing measures, a large and a small.
15 "You shall have a full and just
weight; you shall have a full and just
[1]measure, [a]that your days may be prolonged in the [2]land which the LORD your
God gives you.
16 "For [a]everyone who does these

9 [a]Num 12:10
10 [a]Ex 22:26,27
13 [a]Ex 22:26 [b]Deut 6:25; Ps 106:31; Dan 4:27
14 [1]Lit *brothers* [2]Lit *gates* [a]Lev 19:13; 25:35-43; Deut 15:7-18; Prov 14:31; Amos 4:1; 1 Tim 5:18
15 [1]Lit *that the sun shall not go down on it* [2]Lit *soul* [a]Lev 19:13; Jer 22:13; James 5:4 [b]Ex 22:23; Deut 15:9; Job 35:9; James 5:4
16 [1]Or *with* [a]2 Kin 14:6; 2 Chr 25:4; Jer 31:29,30; Ezek 18:20
17 [1]Lit *of* [2]Or *the fatherless* [a]Ex 23:9; Lev 19:33; Deut 1:17; 10:17; 16:19; 27:19 [b]Ex 22:22
19 [1]Or *fatherless* [a]Lev 19:9, 10; 23:22 [b]Deut 14:29 [c]Prov 19:17
20 [1]Lit *after yourself* [2]Or *fatherless* [a]Lev 19:10 [b]Deut 24:19
21 [1]Lit *glean it after yourself* [2]Or *fatherless*
25:1 [1]Lit *the judgment* [2]Lit *they judge them* [a]Deut 17:8-13; 19:17 [b]Deut 1:16,17
2 [1]Lit *is a son of beating* [2]Or *wickedness* [a]Prov 19:29; Luke 12:48
3 [a]2 Cor 11:24 [b]Job 18:3
4 [a]Prov 12:10; 1 Cor 9:9; 1 Tim 5:18
5 [a]Matt 22:24; Mark 12:19; Luke 20:28
6 [1]Lit *stand on* [a]Ruth 4:5,10
7 [a]Ruth 4:5,6
9 [1]Lit *answer and say* [a]Ruth 4:7,8 [b]Num 12:14
11 [1]Lit *brother*
12 [1]Lit *palm* [2]Lit *your eye* [a]Deut 7:2; 19:13
13 [1]Lit *a stone and a stone* [a]Lev 19:35-37; Prov 11:1; 20:23; Ezek 45:10; Mic 6:11
14 [1]Lit *an ephah and an ephah*
15 [1]Lit *ephah* [2]Lit *ground* [a]Ex 20:12
16 [a]Prov 11:1

things, everyone who acts unjustly is an
abomination to the LORD your God.
17 ¶ "[a]Remember what Amalek did
to you along the way when you came out
from Egypt,
18 how he met you along the way and
attacked among you all the stragglers at
your rear when you were faint and weary; and he [a]did not [1]fear God.
19 "Therefore it shall come about when
the LORD your God has given you [a]rest
from all your surrounding enemies, in the
land which the LORD your God gives you
as an inheritance to [1]possess, you shall
blot out the memory of Amalek from under heaven; you must not forget.

Offering First Fruits

26 "Then it shall be, when you enter
the land which the LORD your
God gives you as an inheritance, and you
possess it and live in it,
2 that you shall take some of [a]the
first of all the produce of the ground
which you bring in from your land that
the LORD your God gives you, and you
shall put *it* in a basket and [b]go to the
place where the LORD your God chooses
to establish His name.
3 "You shall go to the priest who is in
office at that time and say to him, 'I declare this day to the LORD [1]my God that
I have entered the land which the LORD
swore to our fathers to give us.'
4 "Then the priest shall take the basket from your hand and set it down before the altar of the LORD your God.
5 "You shall answer and say before the
LORD your God, '[a]My father was a [1]wan-
dering Aramean, and he went down to
Egypt and [2]sojourned there, [b]few in
number; but there he became a [c]great,
mighty and populous nation.
6 'And the [a]Egyptians treated us
harshly and afflicted us, and imposed
hard labor on us.
7 'Then [a]we cried to the LORD, the
God of our fathers, and the LORD heard
our voice and saw our affliction and our
toil and our oppression;
8 [a]and the LORD brought us out of
Egypt with a mighty hand and an outstretched arm and with great terror and
with signs and wonders;
9 and He has brought us to this place
and has given us this land, [a]a land flowing with milk and honey.
10 'Now behold, I have brought the
first of the produce of the ground [a]which
You, O LORD have given me.' And you
shall set it down before the LORD your
God, and worship before the LORD your
God;
11 and you and [a]the Levite and the
alien who is among you shall [b]rejoice in
all the good which the LORD your God has
given you and your household.
12 ¶ "[a]When you have finished [1]pay-
ing all the tithe of your increase in the
third year, the year of tithing, then you
shall give it to the Levite, to the stranger,
to the [2]orphan and to the widow, that
they may eat in your [3]towns and be satisfied.
13 "You shall say before the LORD your
God, 'I have removed the sacred *portion*
from *my* house, and also have given it to
the Levite and the alien, the [1]orphan and
the widow, according to all Your commandments which You have commanded
me; [a]I have not transgressed or forgotten
any of Your commandments.
14 'I have not eaten of it [1]while
mourning, nor have I removed any of it
while I was unclean, nor offered any of it
to the dead. I have listened to the voice
of the LORD my God; I have done according to all that You have commanded me.
15 '[a]Look down from Your holy habitation, from heaven, and bless Your people
Israel, and the ground which You have
given us, [b]a land flowing with milk and
honey, as You swore to our fathers.'
16 ¶ "This day the LORD your God
commands you to do these statutes and
ordinances. You shall therefore be careful
to do them [a]with all your heart and with
all your soul.
17 "[a]You have today declared the LORD
to be your God, and [1]that you would
walk in His ways and keep His statutes,
His commandments and His ordinances,
and listen to His voice.
18 "The LORD has today declared you to
be [a]His people, a treasured possession,
as He promised you, and [1]that you
should keep all His commandments;
19 and [1]that He will [a]set you high
above all nations which He has made, for
praise, fame, and honor; and that you
shall be [b]a consecrated people to the
LORD your God, as He has spoken."

The Curses of Mount Ebal

27 Then Moses and the elders of Israel charged the people, saying,
"Keep all the commandments which I
command you today.
2 "[a]So it shall be on the day when you
cross the Jordan to the land which the
LORD your God gives you, that you shall
set up for yourself large stones and coat
them with lime
3 and write on them all the words of
this law, when you cross over, so that you
may enter the land which the LORD your
God gives you, [a]a land flowing with milk

17 [a]Ex 17:8-16
18 [1]Or *reverence* [a]Ps 36:1; Rom 3:18
19 [1]Lit *possess it* [a]Deut 12:9
26:2 [a]Ex 22:29; 23:16,19; Num 18:13; Prov 3:9 [b]Deut 12:5
3 [1]So with Gr; Heb *your*
5 [1]Or *perishing* [2]Or *lived as an alien* [a]Gen 43:1-14 [b]Gen 46:27 [c]Deut 1:10; 10:22
6 [a]Ex 1:8-11
7 [a]Ex 2:23-25; 3:9
8 [a]Deut 4:34; 34:11,12
9 [a]Ex 3:8,17
10 [a]Deut 8:18; Prov 10:22
11 [a]Deut 12:12 [b]Deut 12:7; 16:11; Eccl 3:12, 13; 5:18-20
12 [1]Lit *tithing* [2]Or *fatherless* [3]Lit *gates* [a]Lev 27:30; Num 18:24; Deut 14:28,29; Heb 7:5,9,10
13 [1]Or *fatherless* [a]Ps 119:141,153, 176
14 [1]Lit *while in my*
15 [a]Ps 80:14; Is 63:15; Zech 2:13 [b]Deut 26:9
16 [a]Deut 4:29
17 [1]Lit *to walk in* [a]Ps 48:14
18 [1]Lit *to keep all* [a]Ex 6:7; 19:5; Deut 4:20; 7:6; 14:2; 28:9; 29:13; Titus 2:14; 1 Pet 2:9
19 [1]Lit *to set you* [a]Deut 4:7,8; 28:1,13 [b]Ex 19:6; Deut 7:6; Is 62:12; Jer 2:3; 1 Pet 2:9
27:2 [a]Josh 8:30-32
3 [a]Deut 26:9

and honey, as the LORD, the God of your fathers, [1]promised you.

4 "So it shall be when you cross the Jordan, you shall set up [a]on Mount Ebal, these stones, [1]as I am commanding you today, and you shall coat them with lime.

5 "Moreover, you shall build there an altar to the LORD your God, an altar of stones; you [a]shall not [1]wield an iron *tool* on them.

6 "You shall build the altar of the LORD your God of [1]uncut stones, and you shall offer on it burnt offerings to the LORD your God;

7 and you shall sacrifice peace offerings and eat there, and [a]rejoice before the LORD your God.

8 "You shall write on the [1]stones all the words of this law very distinctly."

9 ¶ Then Moses and the Levitical priests spoke to all Israel, saying, "Be silent and listen, O Israel! This day you have become a people for the LORD your God.

10 "You shall therefore [1]obey the LORD your God, and do His commandments and His statutes which I command you today."

11 ¶ Moses also charged the people on that day, saying,

12 "When you cross the Jordan, these shall stand on [a]Mount Gerizim to bless the people: [b]Simeon, Levi, Judah, Issachar, Joseph, and Benjamin.

13 "For the curse, these shall stand on Mount Ebal: Reuben, Gad, Asher, Zebulun, Dan, and Naphtali.

14 "The Levites shall then answer and say to all the men of Israel with a loud voice,

15 ¶ 'Cursed is the man who makes [1a]an idol or a molten image, an abomination to the LORD, the work of the hands of the craftsman, and sets *it* up in secret.' And [b]all the people shall answer and say, 'Amen.'

16 ¶ '[a]Cursed is he who dishonors his father or mother.' And all the people shall say, 'Amen.'

17 ¶ '[a]Cursed is he who moves his neighbor's boundary mark.' And all the people shall say, 'Amen.'

18 ¶ '[a]Cursed is he who misleads a blind *person* on the road.' And all the people shall say, 'Amen.'

19 ¶ '[a]Cursed is he who distorts the justice due an alien, [1]orphan, and widow.' And all the people shall say, 'Amen.'

20 ¶ '[a]Cursed is he who lies with his father's wife, because he has uncovered his father's skirt.' And all the people shall say, 'Amen.'

21 ¶ '[a]Cursed is he who lies with any animal.' And all the people shall say, 'Amen.'

22 ¶ '[a]Cursed is he who lies with his sister, the daughter of his father or of his mother.' And all the people shall say, 'Amen.'

23 ¶ '[a]Cursed is he who lies with his mother-in-law.' And all the people shall say, 'Amen.'

24 ¶ '[a]Cursed is he who strikes his neighbor in secret.' And all the people shall say, 'Amen.'

25 ¶ '[a]Cursed is he who accepts a bribe to strike down an innocent person.' And all the people shall say, 'Amen.'

26 ¶ '[a]Cursed is he who does not confirm the words of this law by doing them.' And all the people shall say, 'Amen.'

Blessings at Gerizim

28 "[a]Now it shall be, if you diligently [1]obey the LORD your God, being careful to do all His commandments which I command you today, the LORD your God [b]will set you high above all the nations of the earth.

2 "All these blessings will come upon you and [a]overtake you if you [1]obey the LORD your God:

3 ¶ "Blessed *shall* you *be* in the city, and blessed *shall* you *be* [a]in the [1]country.

4 ¶ "Blessed *shall be* the [1]offspring of your [2]body and the [1]produce of your ground and the [1]offspring of your beasts, the increase of your herd and the young of your flock.

5 ¶ "Blessed *shall be* your basket and your kneading bowl.

6 ¶ "Blessed *shall* you *be* [a]when you come in, and blessed *shall* you *be* when you go out.

7 ¶ "The LORD shall cause your enemies who rise up against you to be [1]defeated before you; they will come out against you one way and will flee before you seven ways.

8 "The LORD will command the blessing upon you in your barns and in [a]all that you put your hand to, and He will bless you in the land which the LORD your God gives you.

9 "[a]The LORD will establish you as a holy people to Himself, as He swore to you, if you keep the commandments of the LORD your God and walk in His ways.

10 "So all the peoples of the earth will see that [1a]you are called by the name of the LORD, and they will be afraid of you.

11 "[a]The LORD will make you abound in prosperity, in the [1]offspring of your [2]body and in the [1]offspring of your beast and in the [1]produce of your ground, in

3 [1]Lit *spoke to*
4 [1]Lit *which* [a]Deut 11:29; Josh 8:30
5 [1]Lit *lift up* [a]Ex 20:25; Josh 8:31
6 [1]Lit *whole*
7 [a]Deut 26:11
8 [1]I.e. stones coated with lime, cf v 4
10 [1]Lit *listen to the voice of*
12 [a]Deut 11:29 [b]Josh 8:33-35
15 [1]Or *a graven image* [a]Ex 20:4, 23; 34:17; Lev 19:4; 26:1; Deut 4:16,23; 5:8; Is 44:9 [b]1 Cor 14:16
16 [a]Ex 20:12; 21:17; Lev 19:3; 20:9; Deut 5:16; Ezek 22:7
17 [a]Deut 19:14; Prov 22:28
18 [a]Lev 19:14
19 [1]Or *fatherless* [a]Ex 22:21; 23:9; Lev 19:33; Deut 10:18; 24:17
20 [a]Lev 18:8; 20:11; Deut 22:30; 1 Cor 5:1
21 [a]Ex 22:19; Lev 18:23; 20:15
22 [a]Lev 18:9; 20:17
23 [a]Lev 20:14
24 [a]Ex 21:12; Lev 24:17; Num 35:30,31
25 [a]Ex 23:7; Deut 10:17; Ps 15:5; Ezek 22:12
26 [a]Ps 119:21; Jer 11:3; Gal 3:10
28:1 [1]Lit *listen to the voice of* [a]Ex 15:26; 23:22-27; Lev 26:3-13; Deut 7:12-26; 11:13 [b]Deut 28:13; 26:19; 1 Chr 14:2
2 [1]Lit *listen to the voice of* [a]Zech 1:6
3 [1]Or *field* [a]Gen 39:5
4 [1]Lit *fruit* [2]Lit *womb*
6 [a]Ps 121:8
7 [1]Lit *smitten*
8 [a]Deut 15:10
9 [a]Ex 19:5
10 [1]Lit *the name of the LORD is called upon you* [a]2 Chr 7:14
11 [1]Lit *fruit* [2]Or *womb* [a]Deut 28:4; Prov 10:22

the land which the LORD swore to your
fathers to give you.
12 "The LORD will open for you His
good storehouse, the heavens, to give
rain to your land in its season and to bless
all the work of your hand; and [a]you shall
lend to many nations, but you shall not
borrow.
13 "[a]The LORD will make you the head
and not the tail, and you only will be
above, and you will not be underneath, if
you listen to the commandments of the
LORD your God, which I charge you today, to [1]observe *them* carefully,
14 and [a]do not turn aside from any of
the words which I command you today,
to the right or to the left, to go after other
gods to serve them.

Consequences of Disobedience

15 ¶ "[a]But it shall come about, if you
do not [1]obey the LORD your God, to observe to do all His commandments and
His statutes with which I charge you today, that all these curses will come upon
you and overtake you:
16 ¶ "[a]Cursed *shall* you *be* in the city,
and cursed *shall* you *be* in the [1]country.
17 ¶ "[a]Cursed *shall be* your basket
and your kneading bowl.
18 ¶ "[a]Cursed *shall be* the [1]offspring
of your [2]body and the [1]produce of your
ground, the increase of your herd and the
young of your flock.
19 ¶ "[a]Cursed *shall* you *be* when you
come in, and cursed *shall* you *be* when
you go out.
20 ¶ "[a]The LORD will send upon you
curses, confusion, and [b]rebuke, in all
[1]you undertake to do, until you are destroyed and until [c]you perish quickly, on
account of the evil of your deeds, because
you have forsaken Me.
21 "[a]The LORD will make the pestilence cling to you until He has consumed
you from the land where you are entering
to possess it.
22 "[a]The LORD will smite you with consumption and with fever and with inflam-
mation and with fiery heat and with [1]the
sword and [b]with blight and with mildew, and they will pursue you until [c]you
perish.
23 "[1]The heaven which is over your
head shall be bronze, and the earth
which is under you, iron.
24 "[a]The LORD will make the rain of
your land powder and dust; from heaven
it shall come down on you until you are
destroyed.
25 ¶ "[a]The LORD shall cause you to be
[1]defeated before your enemies; you will
go out one way against them, but you will
flee seven ways before them, and you
will [b]be *an example of* terror to all the
kingdoms of the earth.
26 "[a]Your carcasses will be food to all
birds of the sky and to the beasts of the
earth, and there will be no one to frighten
them away.
27 ¶ "[a]The LORD will smite you with
the boils of Egypt and with [b]tumors and
with the scab and with the itch, from
which you cannot be healed.
28 "The LORD will smite you with madness and with blindness and with bewilderment of heart;
29 and you will [1a]grope at noon, as
the blind man gropes in darkness, and
you will not prosper in your ways; but
you shall only be oppressed and robbed
continually, with none to save you.
30 "[a]You shall betroth a wife, but another man will violate her; [b]you shall
build a house, but you will not live in it;
you shall plant a vineyard, but you will
not [1]use its fruit.
31 "Your ox shall be slaughtered before
your eyes, but you will not eat of it; your
donkey shall be torn away from you, and
will not be restored to you; your sheep
shall be given to your enemies, and you
will have none to save you.
32 "[a]Your sons and your daughters
shall be given to another people, while
your eyes look on and yearn for them
continually; but there will be nothing
[1]you can do.
33 "[a]A people whom you do not know
shall eat up the produce of your ground
and all your labors, and you will never be
anything but oppressed and crushed continually.
34 "You shall be driven mad by the
sight of [1]what you see.
35 "[a]The LORD will strike you on the
knees and legs with sore boils, from
which you cannot be healed, from the
sole of your foot to the crown of your
head.
36 "[a]The LORD will bring you and your
king, whom you set over you, to a nation
which neither you nor your fathers have
known, and there you shall serve other
gods, [b]wood and stone.
37 "[a]You shall become a horror, a proverb, and a taunt among all the people
where the LORD drives you.
38 ¶ "[a]You shall bring out much seed
to the field but you will gather in little, for
[b]the locust will consume it.
39 "[a]You shall plant and cultivate vineyards, but you will neither drink of the
wine nor gather *the grapes,* for the worm
will devour them.
40 "[a]You shall have olive trees
throughout your territory but you will not

12 [a]Deut 23:20
13 [1]Lit *keep and do* [a]Deut 28:1, 44
14 [a]Deut 5:32; Josh 1:7
15 [1]Lit *listen to the voice of* [a]Lev 26:14-43; Josh 23:15; Dan 9:11
16 [1]Or *field* [a]Deut 28:3
17 [a]Deut 28:5
18 [1]Lit *fruit* [2]Or *womb* [a]Deut 28:4
19 [a]Deut 28:6
20 [1]Lit *the putting forth of your hand which you do* [a]Deut 28:8; Mal 2:2 [b]Ps 80:16; Is 51:20; 66:15 [c]Deut 4:26
21 [a]Lev 26:25; Num 14:12; Jer 24:10; Amos 4:10
22 [1]Another reading is *drought* [a]Lev 26:16 [b]Amos 4:9 [c]Deut 4:26
23 [1]Lit *Your*
24 [a]Deut 11:17; 28:12
25 [1]Lit *smitten* [a]Deut 28:7; Is 30:17 [b]2 Chr 29:8; Jer 15:4; 24:9; Ezek 23:46
26 [a]Jer 7:33; 16:4; 19:7; 34:20
27 [a]Ex 9:9; Deut 7:15; 28:60,61 [b]1 Sam 5:6
29 [1]Lit *be groping* [a]Ex 10:21
30 [1]Lit *begin it* [a]Job 31:10; Jer 8:10 [b]Amos 5:11
32 [1]Lit *in the power of your hand* [a]Deut 28:41
33 [a]Jer 5:15,17
34 [1]Lit *your eyes which you*
35 [a]Deut 28:27
36 [a]2 Kin 17:4, 6; 24:12,14; 25:7,11; 2 Chr 36:1-21; Jer 39:1-9 [b]Deut 4:28; Jer 16:13
37 [a]1 Kin 9:7,8; Jer 19:8; 24:9; 25:9; 29:18
38 [a]Is 5:10; Mic 6:15; Hag 1:6 [b]Ex 10:4; Joel 1:4
39 [a]Is 5:10; 17:10,11
40 [a]Jer 11:16; Mic 6:15

anoint yourself with the oil, for your olives will drop off.
41 "[a]You shall [1]have sons and daughters but they will not be yours, for they
will go into captivity.
42 "[a]The cricket shall possess all your
trees and the produce of your ground.
43 "[a]The alien who is among you shall
rise above you higher and higher, but you
will go down lower and lower.
44 "[a]He shall lend to you, but you will
not lend to him; [b]he shall be the head,
and you will be the tail.
45 ¶ "So all these curses shall come on
you and pursue you and overtake you
[a]until you are destroyed, because you
would not [1]obey the LORD your God by
keeping His commandments and His statutes which He commanded you.
46 "They shall become [a]a sign and a
wonder on you and your [1]descendants
forever.
47 ¶ "[a]Because you did not serve the
LORD your God with joy and a glad heart,
for the abundance of all things;
48 therefore you shall serve your enemies whom the LORD will send against
you, [a]in hunger, in thirst, in nakedness,
and in the lack of all things; and He [b]will
put an iron yoke on your neck until He
has destroyed you.
49 ¶ "[a]The LORD will bring a nation
against you from afar, from the end of the
earth, [b]as the eagle swoops down, a nation whose language you shall not understand,
50 a nation of fierce countenance who
will [a]have no respect for the old, nor
show favor to the young.
51 "Moreover, it shall eat the [1]off-
spring of your herd and the produce of
your ground until you are destroyed, who
also leaves you no grain, new wine, or oil,
nor the increase of your herd or the
young of your flock until they have
caused you to perish.
52 "[a]It shall besiege you in all your
[1]towns until your high and fortified walls
in which you trusted come down
throughout your land, and it shall besiege
you in all your [1]towns throughout your
land which the LORD your God has given
you.
53 "[a]Then you shall eat the [1]offspring
of your own body, the flesh of your sons
and of your daughters whom the LORD
your God has given you, during the siege
and the distress by which your enemy
will [2]oppress you.
54 "The man who is [1]refined and very
delicate among you [2]shall be hostile toward his brother and toward the wife
[3]he cherishes and toward the rest of his
children who remain,
55 so that he will not give *even* one
of them any of the flesh of his children
which he will eat, since he has nothing
else left, during the siege and the distress
by which your enemy will [1]oppress you
in all your [2]towns.
56 "[a]The [1]refined and delicate woman
among you, who would not venture to set
the sole of her foot on the ground for
delicateness and [2]refinement, [3]shall be
hostile toward the husband [4]she cherishes and toward her son and daughter,
57 and toward her afterbirth which issues from between her [1]legs and toward
her children whom she bears; for [a]she
will eat them secretly for lack of anything
else, during the siege and the distress by
which your enemy will [2]oppress you in
your [3]towns.
58 ¶ "If you are not careful to observe
all the words of this law which are written in this book, to [1a]fear this honored
and awesome [b]name, [2]the LORD your
God,
59 then the LORD will bring extraordinary plagues on you and [1]your descendants, even [2]severe and lasting plagues,
and miserable and chronic sicknesses.
60 "[a]He will bring back on you all the
diseases of Egypt of which you were
afraid, and they will cling to you.
61 "Also every sickness and every
plague which, not written in the book of
this law, the LORD will bring on you [a]un-
til you are destroyed.
62 "Then you shall be left few in number, [a]whereas you were as numerous as
the stars of heaven, because you did not
[1]obey the LORD your God.
63 "It shall come about that as the LORD
[a]delighted over you to prosper you, and
multiply you, so the LORD will [b]delight
over you to make you perish and destroy
you; and you will be [c]torn from the land
where you are entering to possess it.
64 "Moreover, the LORD will [a]scatter
you among all peoples, from one end of
the earth to the other end of the earth;
and there you shall [b]serve other gods,
wood and stone, which you or your fathers have not known.
65 "[a]Among those nations you shall
find no rest, and there will be no resting
place for the sole of your foot; but there
[b]the LORD will give you a trembling
heart, failing of eyes, and despair of soul.
66 "So your life shall [1]hang in doubt
before you; and you will be in dread night
and day, and shall have no assurance of
your life.
67 "[a]In the morning you shall say,
'Would that it were evening!' And at evening you shall say, 'Would that it were
morning!' because of the dread of your

41 [1]Lit *beget* [a]Deut 28:32
42 [a]Deut 28:38
43 [a]Deut 28:13
44 [a]Deut 28:12 [b]Deut 28:13
45 [1]Lit *listen to the voice of* [a]Deut 4:25,26
46 [1]Lit *seed* [a]Num 26:10; Is 8:18; Ezek 5:15; 14:8
47 [a]Deut 12:7; Neh 9:35-37
48 [a]Lam 4:4-6 [b]Jer 28:13,14
49 [a]Is 5:26-30; 7:18-20; Jer 5:15; 6:22,23 [b]Jer 48:40; 49:22; Lam 4:19; Hos 8:1
50 [a]Is 47:6
51 [1]Lit *fruit*
52 [1]Lit *gates* [a]Jer 10:17,18; Zeph 1:15,16
53 [1]Lit *fruit* [2]Or *distress* [a]Lev 26:29; 2 Kin 6:28,29; Jer 19:9; Lam 2:20; 4:10
54 [1]Lit *tender* [2]Lit *his eye shall be evil toward* [3]Lit *of his bosom*
55 [1]Or *distress* [2]Lit *gates*
56 [1]Lit *tender* [2]Lit *tenderness* [3]Lit *her eye shall be evil toward* [4]Lit *of her bosom* [a]Lam 4:10
57 [1]Lit *feet* [2]Or *distress* [3]Lit *gates* [a]2 Kin 6:28,29; Lam 4:10
58 [1]Or *reverence* [2]Heb *YHWH* [a]Ps 99:3; Mal 1:14 [b]Is 42:8
59 [1]Lit *plague on your seed* [2]Lit *great*
60 [a]Deut 28:27
61 [a]Deut 4:25, 26
62 [1]Lit *listen to the voice of* [a]Deut 1:10; Neh 9:23
63 [a]Jer 32:41 [b]Prov 1:26 [c]Jer 12:14; 45:4
64 [a]Lev 26:33; Deut 4:27; Neh 1:8 [b]Deut 4:28; 29:26; 32:17
65 [a]Lam 1:3 [b]Lev 26:36
66 [1]Lit *be hung for you in front*
67 [a]Job 7:4

heart which you dread, and for the sight of your eyes which you will see.

68 “The LORD will bring you back to Egypt in ships, by the way about which I spoke to you, ‘You will never see it again!’ And there you will offer yourselves for sale to your enemies as male and female slaves, but there will be no buyer.”

The Covenant in Moab

29 [a]These are the words of the covenant which the LORD commanded Moses to make with the sons of Israel in the land of Moab, besides the [b]covenant which He had made with them at Horeb.

2 ¶ [1]And Moses summoned all Israel and said to them, “You have seen all that the LORD did before your eyes in the land of Egypt to Pharaoh and all his servants and all his land;

3 [a]the great trials which your eyes have seen, those great signs and wonders.

4 “Yet to this day [a]the LORD has not given you a heart to know, nor eyes to see, nor ears to hear.

5 “I have led you forty years in the wilderness; [a]your clothes have not worn out on you, and your sandal has not worn out on your foot.

6 “[a]You have not eaten bread, nor have you drunk wine or strong drink, in order that you might know that I am the LORD your God.

7 “[a]When you [1]reached this place, Sihon the king of Heshbon and Og the king of Bashan came out to meet us for battle, but we [2]defeated them;

8 and we took their land and [a]gave it as an inheritance to the Reubenites, the Gadites, and the half-tribe of the Manassites.

9 “[a]So keep the words of this covenant to do them, [b]that you may prosper in all that you do.

10 ¶ “You stand today, all of you, before the LORD your God: your chiefs, your tribes, your elders and your officers, *even* all the men of Israel,

11 your little ones, your wives, and the alien who is within your camps, from [a]the one who chops your wood to the one who draws your water,

12 that you may enter into the covenant with the LORD your God, and into His oath which the LORD your God is making with you today,

13 in order that He may establish you today as His people and that [a]He may be your God, just as He spoke to you and as He swore to your fathers, to Abraham, Isaac, and Jacob.

14 ¶ “Now not with you alone am I [a]making this covenant and this oath,

15 [a]but both with those who stand here with us today in the presence of the LORD our God and with those who are not with us here today

16 (for you know how we lived in the land of Egypt, and how we came through the midst of the nations through which you passed;

17 moreover, you have seen their abominations and their idols *of* [a]wood, stone, silver, and gold, which *they had* with them);

18 [a]so that there will not be among you a man or woman, or family or tribe, whose heart turns away today from the LORD our God, to go and serve the gods of those nations; that there will not be among you [b]a root bearing poisonous fruit and wormwood.

19 “It shall be when he hears the words of this curse, that he will [1]boast, saying, ‘I have peace though I walk in the stubbornness of my heart in order [2]to destroy the watered *land* with the dry.’

20 “The LORD shall never be willing to forgive him, but rather the anger of the LORD and [a]His jealousy will [1b]burn against that man, and every curse which is written in this book will [2]rest on him, and the LORD will [c]blot out his name from under heaven.

21 “Then the LORD will single him out for [1]adversity from all the tribes of Israel, according to all the curses of the covenant [a]which are written in this book of the law.

22 ¶ “Now the generation to come, your sons who rise up after you and [a]the foreigner who comes from a distant land, when they see the plagues of the land and the diseases with which the LORD has [1]afflicted it, will say,

23 ‘All its land is [a]brimstone and salt, [b]a burning waste, [1]unsown and unproductive, and no grass grows in it, like the overthrow of [c]Sodom and Gomorrah, Admah and Zeboiim, which the LORD overthrew in His anger and in His wrath.’

24 “All the nations will say, ‘[a]Why has the LORD done thus to this land? Why this great [1]outburst of anger?’

25 “Then *men* will say, ‘[a]Because they forsook the covenant of the LORD, the God of their fathers, which He made with them when He brought them out of the land of Egypt.

26 ‘They went and served other gods and worshiped them, gods whom they have not known and whom He had not [1]allotted to them.

27 ‘Therefore, the anger of the LORD burned against that land, [a]to bring upon

29:1 [a]Lev 26:46; 27:34 [b]Deut 5:2,3
2 [1]Ch 29:1 in Heb
3 [a]Deut 4:34; 7:19
4 [a]Is 6:9,10; Ezek 12:2; Matt 13:14; Acts 28:26,27; Rom 11:8
5 [a]Deut 8:4
6 [a]Deut 8:3
7 [1]Lit *came to* [2]Lit *smote* [a]Num 21:21-24,33,35; Deut 2:26-3:17
8 [a]Num 32:32, 33; Deut 3:12,13
9 [a]Deut 4:6; 1 Kin 2:3 [b]Josh 1:7
11 [a]Josh 9:21, 23,27
13 [a]Gen 17:7; Ex 6:7
14 [a]Jer 31:31; Heb 8:7,8
15 [a]Acts 2:39
17 [a]Ex 20:23; Deut 4:28; 28:36
18 [a]Deut 13:6 [b]Deut 32:32; Heb 12:15
19 [1]Lit *bless himself in his heart* [2]I.e. to destroy everything
20 [1]Lit *smoke* [2]Lit *lie down* [a]Ps 79:5; Ezek 23:25 [b]Ps 74:1; 80:4 [c]Ex 32:33; Deut 9:14; 2 Kin 14:27
21 [1]Lit *evil* [a]Deut 30:10
22 [1]Lit *made it sick* [a]Jer 19:8; 49:17; 50:13
23 [1]Lit *it is not sown and does not cause to sprout* [a]Gen 19:24; Is 34:9; Jer 17:6; Zeph 2:9 [b]Is 1:7; 64:11 [c]Jude 7
24 [1]Lit *heat* [a]1 Kin 9:8; Jer 22:8
25 [a]2 Kin 17:9-23; 2 Chr 36:13-21
26 [1]Lit *portioned*
27 [a]Dan 9:11

it every curse which is written in this
book;
28 and [a]the LORD uprooted them from
their land in anger and in fury and in
great wrath, and cast them into another
land, as *it is* this day.'
29 ¶ "[a]The secret things belong to the
LORD our God, but [b]the things revealed
belong to us and to our sons forever, that
we may observe all the words of this law.

Restoration Promised

30 "So it shall be when all of these
things have come upon you, [a]the
blessing and the curse which I have set
before you, and you [1]call *them* to mind
[b]in all nations where the LORD your God
has banished you,
2 and you [a]return to the LORD your
God and [1]obey Him [b]with all your heart
and soul according to all that I command
you today, you and your sons,
3 then the LORD your God will [a]re-
store [1]you from captivity, and have compassion on you, and [b]will gather you
again from all the peoples where the
LORD your God has [c]scattered you.
4 "If your outcasts are at the ends of
the [1]earth, [a]from there the LORD your
God will gather you, and from there He
will [2]bring you back.
5 "[a]The LORD your God will bring you
into the land which your fathers possessed, and you shall possess it; and He
will prosper you and [b]multiply you more
than your fathers.
6 ¶ "Moreover [a]the LORD your God
will circumcise your heart and the heart
of your [1]descendants, [b]to love the LORD
your God with all your heart and with all
your soul, so that you may live.
7 "[a]The LORD your God will [1]inflict
all these curses on your enemies and on
those who hate you, who persecuted you.
8 "And you shall again [1]obey the
LORD, and observe all His commandments which I command you today.
9 "[a]Then the LORD your God will
[1]prosper you abundantly in all the work
of your hand, in the [2]offspring of your
[3]body and in the [2]offspring of your cattle
and in the [2]produce of your ground, for
[b]the LORD will again rejoice over you for
good, just as He rejoiced over your fathers;
10 [1]if you [2]obey the LORD your God
to keep His commandments and His statutes which [a]are written in this book of
the law, [1]if you turn to the LORD your
God [b]with all your heart and soul.
11 ¶ "For this commandment which I
command you today is not too difficult for
you, nor is it [1]out of reach.
12 "It is not in heaven, [1]that you
should say, '[a]Who will go up to heaven
for us to get it for us and make us hear it,
that we may observe it?'
13 "Nor is it beyond the sea, [1]that you
should say, 'Who will cross the sea for us
to get it for us and make us hear it, that
we may observe it?'
14 "But the word is very near you, in
your mouth and in your heart, that you
may observe it.

Choose Life

15 ¶ "See, [a]I have set before you today life and [1]prosperity, and death and
[2]adversity;
16 in that I command you today [a]to
love the LORD your God, to walk in His
ways and to keep His commandments
and His statutes and His judgments, that
you [b]may live and multiply, and that the
LORD your God may bless you in the land
where you are entering to possess it.
17 "But if your heart turns away and
you will not obey, but are drawn away
and worship other gods and serve them,
18 I declare to you today that [a]you
shall surely perish. You will not prolong
your days in the land where you are crossing the Jordan to enter [1]and possess it.
19 "[a]I call heaven and earth to witness
against you today, that I have set before
you life and death, [b]the blessing and the
curse. So choose life in order that you
may live, you and your [1]descendants,
20 [a]by loving the LORD your God, by
obeying His voice, and [b]by holding fast
to Him; [c]for [1]this is your life and the
length of your days, [2]that you may live in
[d]the land which the LORD swore to your
fathers, to Abraham, Isaac, and Jacob, to
give them."

Moses' Last Counsel

31 So Moses went and spoke these
words to all Israel.
2 And he said to them, "I am [a]a hundred and twenty years old today; [b]I am
no longer able to come and go, and the
LORD has said to me, '[c]You shall not cross
this Jordan.'
3 "[a]It is the LORD your God who will
cross ahead of you; He will destroy these
nations before you, and you shall dispossess them. [b]Joshua is the one who will
cross ahead of you, just as the LORD has
spoken.
4 "The LORD will do to them just as He
did to Sihon and Og, the kings of the
Amorites, and to their land, when He destroyed them.
5 "[a]The LORD will deliver them up before you, and you shall do to them according to all the commandments which I
have commanded you.

28 [a]2 Chr 7:20; Ps 52:5; Prov 2:22; Ezek 19:12,13

29 [a]Acts 1:7 [b]John 5:39; Acts 17:11; 2 Tim 3:16

30:1 [1]Lit *cause them to return to your heart* [a]Deut 11:26; 30:15,19 [b]Lev 26:40-45; Deut 28:64; 29:28; 1 Kin 8:47

2 [1]Lit *listen to His voice* [a]Deut 4:29,30; Neh 1:9 [b]Deut 4:29

3 [1]Lit *your captivity* [a]Gen 28:15; 48:21; Ps 126:1,4; Jer 29:14 [b]Ps 147:2; Jer 32:37; Ezek 34:13 [c]Deut 4:27

4 [1]Lit *sky* [2]Lit *take you* [a]Neh 1:9; Is 43:6; 48:20; 62:11

5 [a]Jer 29:14; 30:3 [b]Deut 7:13; 13:17

6 [1]Lit *seed* [a]Deut 10:16 [b]Deut 6:5

7 [1]Lit *put* [a]Deut 7:15

8 [1]Lit *listen to the voice of*

9 [1]Lit *make you have excess for good* [2]Lit *fruit* [3]Lit *womb* [a]Jer 31:27,28 [b]Jer 32:41

10 [1]Or *for you will* [2]Lit *listen to the voice of* [a]Deut 29:21 [b]Deut 4:29

11 [1]Lit *far off*

12 [1]Lit *to say* [a]Rom 10:6-8

13 [1]Lit *to say*

15 [1]Lit *good* [2]Lit *evil* [a]Deut 11:26

16 [a]Deut 6:5 [b]Deut 4:1; 30:19

18 [1]Lit *to* [a]Deut 4:26; 8:19

19 [1]Lit *seed* [a]Deut 4:26 [b]Deut 30:1

20 [1]Lit *that* [2]Lit *to dwell* [a]Deut 6:5 [b]Deut 10:20 [c]Deut 4:1; 32:47; Acts 17:25,28 [d]Gen 12:7; 17:1-8

31:2 [a]Deut 34:7 [b]Num 27:17; 1 Kin 3:7 [c]Deut 1:37; 3:27

3 [a]Deut 9:3 [b]Num 27:18

5 [a]Deut 7:2

6 "[a]Be strong and courageous, [b]do not be afraid or tremble at them, for [c]the LORD your God is the one who goes with you. [d]He will not fail you or forsake you."

7 ¶ Then Moses called to Joshua and said to him in the sight of all Israel, "[a]Be strong and courageous, for you shall go with this people into the land which the LORD has sworn to their fathers to give them, and you shall give it to them as an inheritance.

8 "[a]The LORD is the one who goes ahead of you; He will be with you. [b]He will not fail you or forsake you. Do not fear or be dismayed."

9 ¶ So Moses wrote this law and gave it to the priests, the sons of Levi [a]who carried the ark of the covenant of the LORD, and to all the elders of Israel.

10 Then Moses commanded them, saying, "At the end of *every* seven years, at the time of [a]the year of remission of debts, at the [b]Feast of Booths,

11 when all Israel comes [a]to appear before the LORD your God at [b]the place which He will choose, [c]you shall read this law in front of all Israel in their hearing.

12 "Assemble the people, the men and the women and children and [1]the alien who is in your [2]town, so that they may hear and [a]learn and fear the LORD your God, and be careful to observe all the words of this law.

13 "Their children, who have not known, will hear and learn to fear the LORD your God, as long as you live on the land [1]which you are about to cross the Jordan to [2]possess."

Israel Will Fall Away

14 ¶ Then the LORD said to Moses, "Behold, [1a]the time for you to die is near; call Joshua, and present yourselves at the tent of meeting, that I may commission him." [b]So Moses and Joshua went and presented themselves at the tent of meeting.

15 [a]The LORD appeared in the tent in a pillar of cloud, and the pillar of cloud stood at the doorway of the tent.

16 The LORD said to Moses, "Behold, [a]you are about to lie down with your fathers; and [b]this people will arise and play the harlot with the strange gods of the land, into the midst of which they are going, and [c]will forsake Me and break My covenant which I have made with them.

17 "[a]Then My anger will be kindled against them in that day, and [b]I will forsake them and [c]hide My face from them, and they will be consumed, and many evils and troubles will come upon them; so that they will say in that day, '[d]Is it not because our God is not among us that these evils have come upon us?'

18 "But I will surely hide My face in that day because of all the evil which they will do, for they will turn to other gods.

19 ¶ "Now therefore, [a]write this song for yourselves, and teach it to the sons of Israel; put it [1]on their lips, so that this song may be a witness for Me against the sons of Israel.

20 "[a]For when I bring them into the land flowing with milk and honey, which I swore to their fathers, and they have eaten and are satisfied and [b]become [1]prosperous, then they will turn to other gods and serve them, and spurn Me and break My covenant.

21 "Then it shall come about, [a]when many evils and troubles have come upon them, that this song will testify before them as a witness (for it shall not be forgotten from the [1]lips of their descendants); for [b]I know their intent which they are [2]developing today, before I have brought them into the land which I swore."

22 [a]So Moses wrote this song the same day, and taught it to the sons of Israel.

Joshua Is Commissioned

23 ¶ [a]Then He commissioned Joshua the son of Nun, and said, "[b]Be strong and courageous, for you shall bring the sons of Israel into the land which I swore to them, and [c]I will be with you."

24 ¶ It came about, when Moses finished writing the words of this law in a book until they were complete,

25 that Moses commanded the Levites [a]who carried the ark of the covenant of the LORD, saying,

26 "Take this book of the law and place it beside the ark of the covenant of the LORD your God, that it may [1]remain there as a witness against you.

27 "For I know [a]your rebellion and [b]your [1]stubbornness; behold, while I am still alive with you today, you have been rebellious against the LORD; how much more, then, after my death?

28 "Assemble to me all the elders of your tribes and your officers, that I may speak these words in their hearing and [a]call the heavens and the earth to witness against them.

29 "For I know that after my death you will [a]act corruptly and turn from the way which I have commanded you; and evil will befall you in the latter days, for you will do that which is evil in the sight of the LORD, provoking Him to anger with the work of your hands."

6 [a]Josh 10:25; 1 Chr 22:13 [b]Deut 1:29; 7:18; 20:1 [c]Deut 20:4 [d]Josh 1:5; Heb 13:5
7 [a]Deut 1:38; 3:28
8 [a]Ex 13:21; 33:14 [b]Deut 31:6; Josh 1:5; Heb 13:5
9 [a]Num 4:5,6, 15; Deut 10:8; 31:25,26; Josh 3:3
10 [a]Deut 15:1,2 [b]Lev 23:34; Deut 16:13
11 [a]Deut 16:16 [b]Deut 12:5 [c]Josh 8:34; 2 Kin 23:2
12 [1]Lit *your alien* [2]Lit *gates* [a]Deut 4:10
13 [1]Lit *where* [2]Lit *possess it*
14 [1]Lit *your days to die are* [a]Num 27:12,13; Deut 4:22; 32:50 [b]Ex 33:9-11
15 [a]Ex 33:9
16 [a]Gen 15:15 [b]Ex 34:15; Deut 4:25-28; Judg 2:11,12,17 [c]Judg 10:6; 1 Kin 18:18; 19:10; Jer 2:13
17 [a]Judg 2:14; 6:13 [b]2 Chr 15:2; 24:20 [c]Ps 104:29; Is 8:17 [d]Num 14:42
19 [1]Lit *in their mouths* [a]Deut 31:22
20 [1]Lit *fat* [a]Deut 6:10-12; 8:10,19; 11:16, 17 [b]Deut 32:15-17
21 [1]Lit *mouth of its seed* [2]Lit *making* [a]Lev 26:41; Deut 4:30 [b]1 Chr 28:9; John 2:24,25
22 [a]Deut 31:19
23 [a]Num 27:23; Deut 31:7 [b]Josh 1:6 [c]Ex 3:12
25 [a]Deut 31:9
26 [1]Lit *be*
27 [1]Lit *stiff neck* [a]Deut 9:7, 24 [b]Ex 32:9; Deut 9:6,13
28 [a]Deut 4:26; 30:19; 32:1
29 [a]Judg 2:19

30 ¶ Then Moses spoke in the hearing
of all the assembly of Israel the words of
this song, until they were complete:

The Song of Moses

32 "[a]Give ear, O heavens, and let
me speak;
And let the earth hear the words
of my mouth.
2 "[a]Let my teaching drop as the
rain,
My speech distill as the dew,
[b]As the droplets on the fresh
grass
And as the showers on the herb.
3 "[a]For I proclaim the name of the
LORD;
[b]Ascribe greatness to our God!
4 "[a]The Rock! His work is perfect,
[b]For all His ways are [1]just;
[c]A God of faithfulness and
without injustice,
Righteous and upright is He.
5 "[1a]They have acted corruptly
toward Him,
They are not His children,
because of their defect;
[b]*But are* a perverse and crooked
generation.
6 "Do you thus [a]repay the LORD,
[b]O foolish and unwise people?
[c]Is not He your Father who has
bought you?
[d]He has made you and
established you.
7 "Remember the days of old,
Consider the years of all
generations.
[a]Ask your father, and he will
inform you,
Your elders, and they will tell
you.
8 "[a]When the Most High gave the
nations their inheritance,
When He separated the sons
of [1]man,
He set the boundaries of the
peoples
[b]According to the number of the
sons of Israel.
9 "[a]For the LORD's portion is His
people;
Jacob is the allotment of His
inheritance.
10 "[a]He found him in a desert land,
And in the howling waste of a
wilderness;
He encircled him, He cared for
him,
He guarded him as [b]the pupil of
His eye.
11 "[a]Like an eagle that stirs up its
nest,
That hovers over its young,
[b]He spread His wings and
caught them,
He carried them on His pinions.
12 "[a]The LORD alone guided him,
[b]And there was no foreign god
with him.
13 "[a]He made him ride on the high
places of the earth,
And he ate the produce of the
field;
[b]And He made him suck honey
from the rock,
And [c]oil from the flinty rock,
14 Curds of cows, and milk of the
flock,
With fat of lambs,
And rams, the breed of Bashan,
and goats,
[a]With the finest of the wheat—
And of the [b]blood of grapes you
drank wine.

15 ¶ "[a]But [1]Jeshurun grew fat and
kicked—
You are grown fat, thick, and
sleek—
[b]Then he forsook God [c]who
made him,
And scorned [d]the Rock of his
salvation.
16 "[a]They made Him jealous with
strange *gods;*
[b]With abominations they
provoked Him to anger.
17 "[a]They sacrificed to demons who
were not God,
[b]To gods whom they have not
known,
[c]New *gods* who came lately,
Whom your fathers did not
dread.
18 "You neglected [a]the Rock who
begot you,
[b]And forgot the God who gave
you birth.
19 ¶ "[a]The LORD saw *this,* and
spurned *them*
[b]Because of the provocation of
His sons and daughters.
20 "Then He said, 'I will hide My
face from them,
[a]I will see what their end
shall be;
[b]For they are a perverse
generation,
[c]Sons in whom is no
faithfulness.
21 '[a]They have made Me jealous
with *what* is not God;
They have provoked Me to anger
with their [1b]idols.
[c]So I will make them jealous
with *those who* are not a
people;

32:1 [a]Deut 4:26; Ps 50:4; Is 1:2; Jer 6:19
2 [a]Is 55:10,11 [b]Ps 72:6
3 [a]Ex 33:19; 34:5,6 [b]Deut 3:24; 5:24
4 [1]Or *judgment* [a]Deut 32:15,18, 30; 2 Sam 22:31 [b]Gen 18:25; Dan 4:37 [c]Deut 7:9
5 [1]Lit *It has* [a]Deut 4:25; 31:29 [b]Matt 17:17
6 [a]Ps 116:12 [b]Deut 32:28 [c]Deut 1:31; Ps 74:2; Is 63:16 [d]Deut 32:15
7 [a]Ex 12:26; Ps 78:5-8
8 [1]Or *Adam* [a]Acts 17:26 [b]Num 23:9; Deut 33:28
9 [a]1 Sam 10:1; 1 Kin 8:51,53; Jer 10:16
10 [a]Deut 1:19 [b]Ps 17:8; Prov 7:2; Zech 2:8
11 [a]Ex 19:4; Deut 33:12 [b]Ps 18:10-18
12 [a]Deut 4:35, 39 [b]Deut 32:39; Is 43:12
13 [a]Is 58:14 [b]Deut 8:8; Ps 81:16 [c]Job 29:6
14 [a]Ps 81:16; 147:14 [b]Gen 49:11
15 [1]I.e. Israel [a]Deut 31:20 [b]Judg 10:6 [c]Deut 32:6 [d]Deut 32:4; Ps 89:26
16 [a]Ps 78:58 [b]Ps 106:29
17 [a]Lev 17:7; 1 Cor 10:20 [b]Deut 28:64 [c]Judg 5:8
18 [a]Deut 32:4 [b]Ps 106:21
19 [a]Lev 26:30; Ps 106:40 [b]Jer 44:21-23
20 [a]Deut 31:29 [b]Deut 32:5 [c]Deut 9:23
21 [1]Lit *vanities* [a]Deut 32:16; 1 Cor 10:22 [b]Deut 32:17; 1 Kin 16:13,26 [c]Rom 10:19

I will provoke them to anger
with a foolish nation,
22 [a]For a fire is kindled in My
anger,
And burns to the lowest part of
[1]Sheol,
[b]And consumes the earth with
its yield,
And sets on fire the foundations
of the mountains.

23 ¶ '[a]I will heap misfortunes on
them;
[b]I will use My arrows on them.
24 '[a]*They will be* wasted by famine,
and consumed by [1]plague
[b]And bitter destruction;
[c]And the teeth of beasts I will
send upon them,
[d]With the venom of crawling
things of the dust.
25 '[a]Outside the sword will bereave,
And inside terror—
[b]Both young man and virgin,
The nursling with the man of
gray hair.
26 'I would have said, "[a]I will cut
them to pieces,
[b]I will remove the memory of
them from men,"
27 Had I not feared the provocation
by the enemy,
That their adversaries would
misjudge,
That they would say, "[a]Our
hand is [1]triumphant,
And the LORD has not done all
this." '

28 ¶ "[a]For they are a nation
[1]lacking in counsel,
And there is no understanding in
them.
29 "[a]Would that they were wise,
that they understood this,
[b]That they would discern their
[1]future!
30 "[a]How could one chase a
thousand,
And two put ten thousand to
flight,
Unless their [b]Rock had sold
them,
And the LORD had given
them up?
31 "Indeed their rock is not like our
Rock,
[a]Even our enemies [1]themselves
judge this.
32 "For their vine is from the vine of
Sodom,
And from the fields of Gomorrah;
Their grapes are grapes of
[a]poison,
Their clusters, bitter.
33 "Their wine is the venom of
[1]serpents,
And the [2]deadly poison of
cobras.

34 ¶ '[a]Is it not laid up in store
with Me,
Sealed up in My treasuries?
35 '[a]Vengeance is Mine, and
retribution,
[b]In due time their foot will slip;
[c]For the day of their calamity is
near,
And the impending things are
hastening upon them.'
36 "[a]For the LORD will vindicate His
people,
[b]And will have compassion on
His servants,
When He sees that *their*
[1]strength is gone,
And there is none *remaining,*
bond or free.
37 "And He will say, '[a]Where are
their gods,
The rock in which they sought
refuge?
38 '[a]Who ate the fat of their
sacrifices,
And drank the wine of their
drink offering?
[b]Let them rise up and help you,
Let them be your hiding place!
39 '[a]See now that I, I am He,
[b]And there is no god
besides Me;
[c]It is I who put to death and
give life.
[d]I have wounded and it is I who
heal,
[e]And there is no one who can
deliver from My hand.
40 'Indeed, [a]I lift up My hand to
heaven,
And say, as I live forever,
41 [a]If I sharpen My [1]flashing
sword,
And My hand takes hold on
justice,
[b]I will render vengeance on My
adversaries,
And I will repay those who
hate Me.
42 '[a]I will make My arrows drunk
with blood,
[b]And My sword will devour
flesh,
With the blood of the slain and
the captives,
From the long-haired [1]leaders of
the enemy.'
43 "[a]Rejoice, O nations, *with* His
people;

22 [1]I.e. the nether world [a]Num 16:33-35; Ps 18:7,8; Lam 4:11 [b]Lev 26:20
23 [a]Deut 29:21 [b]Ps 18:14; 45:5
24 [1]Lit *burning heat* [a]Deut 28:22,48 [b]Ps 91:6 [c]Lev 26:22 [d]Amos 5:18,19
25 [a]Lam 1:20; Ezek 7:15 [b]2 Chr 36:17; Lam 2:21
26 [a]Deut 4:27; 28:64 [b]Deut 9:14
27 [1]Lit *high* [a]Num 15:30
28 [1]Lit *perishing* [a]Deut 32:6
29 [1]Or *latter end* [a]Deut 5:29 [b]Deut 31:29
30 [a]Lev 26:7,8 [b]Deut 32:4; Ps 44:12
31 [1]Lit *are judges* [a]Ex 14:25
32 [a]Deut 29:18
33 [1]Lit *dragons* [2]Lit *cruel*
34 [a]Job 14:17; Jer 44:21
35 [a]Ps 94:1; Rom 12:19; Heb 10:30 [b]Jer 23:12 [c]Ezek 7:5-10
36 [1]Lit *hand* [a]Ps 135:14; Heb 10:30 [b]Lev 26:43-45; Deut 30:1-3
37 [a]Judg 10:14; Jer 2:28
38 [a]Num 25:1,2 [b]Jer 11:12
39 [a]Is 41:4; 43:10 [b]Deut 32:12; Is 45:5 [c]1 Sam 2:6; Ps 68:20 [d]Ps 51:8 [e]Ps 50:22
40 [a]Ezek 20:5,6; 21:4,5
41 [1]Or *lightning* [a]Is 34:6-8 [b]Jer 50:28-32
42 [1]Lit *head* [a]Deut 32:23 [b]Jer 12:12; 46:10,14
43 [a]Rom 15:10

[b]For He will avenge the blood of
His servants,
[c]And will render vengeance on
His adversaries,
[d]And will atone for His land *and*
His people."
44 ¶ Then Moses came and spoke all
the words of this song in the hearing of
the people, he, with [1a]Joshua the son
of Nun.
45 When Moses had finished speaking
all these words to all Israel,
46 he said to them, "[a]Take to your
heart all the words with which I am
warning you today, which you shall command [b]your sons to observe [1]carefully,
even all the words of this law.
47 "For it is not an idle word for you;
indeed [a]it is your life. And [b]by this word
you will prolong your days in the land,
[1]which you are about to cross the Jordan
to [2]possess."
48 ¶ [a]The LORD spoke to Moses that
very same day, saying,
49 "[a]Go up to this mountain of the Abarim, Mount Nebo, which is in the land
of Moab [1]opposite Jericho, and look at
the land of Canaan, which I am giving to
the sons of Israel for a possession.
50 "Then die on the mountain where
you ascend, and be [a]gathered to your
people, as Aaron your brother died on
Mount Hor and was gathered to his people,
51 [a]because you broke faith with Me
in the midst of the sons of Israel at the
waters of Meribah-kadesh, in the [b]wil-
derness of Zin, because you did not treat
Me as holy in the midst of the sons of
Israel.
52 "[a]For you shall see the land at a
distance, but [b]you shall not go there, into
the land which I am giving the sons of
Israel."

The Blessing of Moses

33 Now this is the blessing with
which Moses [a]the man of God
blessed the sons of Israel before his
death.
2 He said,
"[a]The LORD came from Sinai,
[b]And [1]dawned on them from
Seir;
[c]He shone forth from Mount
Paran,
And He came from [d]the [2]midst
of ten thousand holy ones;
[e]At His right hand there was
[3]flashing lightning for them.
3 "[a]Indeed, He loves [1]the people;
[b]All [2]Your holy ones are in
Your hand,
[c]And they [3]followed in Your
steps;
Everyone receives of Your words.
4 "[a]Moses charged us with a law,
[b]A possession for the assembly
of Jacob.
5 "[a]And He was king in Jeshurun,
When the heads of the people
were gathered,
The tribes of Israel together.

6 ¶ "[a]May Reuben live and not
die,
Nor his men be few."

7 ¶ [a]And this regarding Judah; so
he said,
"Hear, O LORD, the voice of
Judah,
And bring him to his people.
With his hands he contended for
[1]them,
And may You be a help against
his adversaries."

8 ¶ Of Levi he said,
"*Let* Your [a]Thummim and Your
Urim *belong* to [1]Your
[b]godly man,
[c]Whom You proved at Massah,
With whom You contended at
the waters of Meribah;
9 [a]Who said of his father and his
mother,
'I did not consider them';
And he did not acknowledge his
brothers,
Nor did he regard his own sons,
For [b]they observed Your word,
And kept Your covenant.
10 "[a]They shall teach Your
ordinances to Jacob,
And Your law to Israel.
[b]They shall put incense
[1]before You,
And [c]whole burnt offerings on
Your altar.
11 "O LORD, bless his substance,
And accept the work of his
hands;
Shatter the loins of those who
rise up against him,
And those who hate him, so that
they will not rise *again.*"

12 ¶ Of Benjamin he said,
"[a]May the beloved of the LORD
dwell in security by Him,
[b]Who shields him all the day,
[c]And he dwells between His
shoulders."
13 ¶ Of Joseph he said,
"[a]Blessed of the LORD *be* his
land,

43 [b]2 Kin 9:7; Rev 6:10; 19:2 [c]Is 1:24,25 [d]Ps 65:3; 79:9; 85:1
44 [1]Lit *Hoshea* [a]Num 13:8,16
46 [1]Lit *to do* [a]Ezek 40:4; 44:5 [b]Deut 4:9
47 [1]Lit *where* [2]Lit *possess it* [a]Deut 8:3; 30:20 [b]Deut 4:40; 33:25
48 [a]Num 27:12
49 [1]Lit *which is opposite* [a]Num 27:12-14; Deut 3:27
50 [a]Gen 25:8
51 [a]Num 20:12 [b]Num 27:14
52 [a]Deut 34:1-3 [b]Deut 1:37; 3:27
33:1 [a]Josh 14:6
2 [1]Lit *rose to* [2]Lit *myriads of holiness* [3]Or *a fiery law* [a]Ex 19:18,20; Ps 68:8,17 [b]Judg 5:4 [c]Num 10:12; Hab 3:3 [d]Dan 7:10; Acts 7:53 [e]Ex 23:20-22
3 [1]Lit *peoples* [2]Lit *His* [3]Or *lie down at Your feet* [a]Deut 4:37; Mal 1:2 [b]Deut 7:6; 14:2 [c]Deut 6:1-9; Luke 10:39
4 [a]Deut 4:2; John 7:19 [b]Ps 119:111
5 [a]Num 23:21
6 [a]Gen 49:3,4
7 [1]Lit *him* [a]Gen 49:8-12
8 [1]Lit *him* [a]Ex 28:30; Lev 8:8 [b]Ps 106:16 [c]Ex 17:7; Num 20:13,24; Deut 6:16
9 [a]Ex 32:27-29 [b]Mal 2:5
10 [1]Lit *in Your nostrils* [a]Lev 10:11; Deut 31:9-13 [b]Lev 16:12,13 [c]Ps 51:19
12 [a]Deut 4:37f; 12:10 [b]Deut 32:11 [c]Ex 28:12
13 [a]Gen 27:27, 28; 49:22-26

With the choice things of
heaven, with the dew,
And from the deep lying
beneath,
14 And with the choice yield of the
sun,
And with the choice produce of
the months.
15 "And with the [1]best things of
[a]the ancient mountains,
And with the choice things of
the everlasting hills,
16 And with the choice things of
the earth and its fullness,
And the favor [a]of Him who
dwelt in the bush.
Let it come to the head of
Joseph,
And to the crown of the head of
the one distinguished among
his brothers.
17 "As the firstborn of his ox,
majesty is his,
And his horns are the horns of
[a]the wild ox;
With them he will [b]push the
peoples,
All [1]at once, *to* the ends of the
earth.
And those are the ten thousands
of Ephraim,
And those are the thousands of
Manasseh."

18 ¶ [a]Of Zebulun he said,
"Rejoice, Zebulun, in your going
forth,
And, Issachar, in your tents.
19 "[a]They will call peoples *to* the
mountain;
There they will offer [b]righteous
sacrifices;
For they will [1]draw out [c]the
abundance of the seas,
And the hidden treasures of the
sand."

20 ¶ [a]Of Gad he said,
"Blessed is the one who
enlarges Gad;
He lies down [b]as a [1]lion,
And tears the arm, also the
crown of the head.
21 "[a]Then he [1]provided the first
part for himself,
[b]For there the ruler's portion
was [2]reserved;
[c]And he came *with* the leaders
of the people;
[d]He executed the justice of the
LORD,
And His ordinances with Israel."

22 ¶ [a]Of Dan he said,
"Dan is [b]a lion's whelp,
That leaps forth from Bashan."

23 ¶ Of Naphtali he said,
"[a]O Naphtali, satisfied with favor,
And full of the blessing of the
LORD,
Take possession of the sea and
the south."

24 ¶ [a]Of Asher he said,
"More blessed than sons is Asher;
May he be favored by his
brothers,
[b]And may he dip his foot in oil.
25 "[a]Your locks will be iron and
bronze,
[b]And according to your days, so
will your leisurely walk be.

26 ¶ "[a]There is none like the God
of [1]Jeshurun,
[b]Who rides the heavens [2]to
your help,
And through the skies in His
majesty.
27 "[a]The eternal God is a [1]dwelling
place,
[b]And underneath are the
everlasting arms;
[c]And He drove out the enemy
from before you,
[d]And said, 'Destroy!'
28 "[a]So Israel dwells in security,
[b]The fountain of Jacob secluded,
[c]In a land of grain and new
wine;
[d]His heavens also drop down
dew.
29 "[a]Blessed are you, O Israel;
[b]Who is like you, a people saved
by the LORD,
[c]Who is the shield of your help
[d]And the sword of your majesty!
[e]So your enemies will cringe
before you,
[f]And you will tread upon their
high places."

The Death of Moses

34 [a]Now Moses went up from the
plains of Moab to Mount Nebo, to
the top of Pisgah, which is opposite Jericho. And the LORD [b]showed him all the
land, Gilead as far as Dan,
2 and all Naphtali and the land of
Ephraim and Manasseh, and all the land
of Judah as far as the [1a]western sea,
3 and the [1]Negev and the plain in
the valley of Jericho, [a]the city of palm
trees, as far as Zoar.
4 Then the LORD said to him, "This is
the land which [a]I swore to Abraham,

15 [1]Or *chief* [a]Hab 3:6
16 [a]Ex 2:2-6; 3:2,4
17 [1]Or *together* [a]Num 23:22 [b]1 Kin 22:11; Ps 44:5
18 [a]Gen 49:13-15
19 [1]Lit *suck* [a]Ex 15:17; Ps 2:6; Is 2:3 [b]Ps 4:5; 51:19 [c]Is 60:5
20 [1]Or *lioness* [a]Gen 49:19 [b]Gen 49:9
21 [1]Lit *saw* [2]Or *covered up* [a]Num 32:1-5 [b]Num 34:14 [c]Josh 4:12 [d]Josh 22:1-3
22 [a]Gen 49:16 [b]Ezek 19:2,3
23 [a]Gen 49:21
24 [a]Gen 49:20 [b]Job 29:6
25 [a]Ps 147:13 [b]Deut 4:40; 32:47
26 [1]I.e. Israel [2]Lit *in* [a]Ex 15:11; Deut 4:35; Ps 86:8; Jer 10:6 [b]Deut 10:14; Ps 68:33, 34; 104:3; Hab 3:8
27 [1]Or *refuge* [a]Ps 90:1,2 [b]Gen 49:24 [c]Ex 34:11; Josh 24:18 [d]Deut 7:2
28 [a]Deut 33:12; Jer 23:6 [b]Num 23:9; Deut 32:8 [c]Gen 27:28,37 [d]Deut 33:13
29 [a]Ps 1:1; 32:1,2 [b]Deut 4:32; 2 Sam 7:23 [c]Gen 15:1; Ps 33:20; 115:9-11 [d]Ps 68:34 [e]Ps 66:3 [f]Num 33:52
34:1 [a]Deut 32:49 [b]Deut 32:52
2 [1]I.e. Mediterranean Sea [a]Deut 11:24
3 [1]I.e. South country [a]Judg 1:16; 3:13; 2 Chr 28:15
4 [a]Gen 12:7; 26:3; 28:13

Isaac, and Jacob, saying, 'I will give it to
your [1]descendants'; I have let you see *it*
with your eyes, but you shall not go over
there."
5 So Moses [a]the servant of the LORD
[b]died there in the land of Moab, according to the [1]word of the LORD.
6 And He buried him in the valley in
the land of Moab, [a]opposite Beth-peor;
but [b]no man knows his burial place to
this day.
7 Although Moses was [a]one hundred and twenty years old when he died,
[b]his eye was not dim, nor his vigor
abated.
8 So the sons of Israel wept for Moses
in the plains of Moab thirty days; then the
days of weeping *and* mourning for Moses
came to an end.
9 ¶ Now Joshua the son of Nun was
[a]filled with the spirit of wisdom, for Moses had laid his hands on him; and the
sons of Israel listened to him and did as
the LORD had commanded Moses.
10 Since that time [a]no prophet has
risen in Israel like Moses, whom [b]the
LORD knew face to face,
11 for all the signs and wonders which
the LORD sent him to perform in the land
of Egypt against Pharaoh, all his servants,
and all his land,
12 and for all the mighty [1]power and
for all the great terror which Moses performed in the sight of all Israel.

4 [1]Lit *seed*
5 [1]Lit *mouth* [a]Num 12:7; Josh 1:1,2 [b]Deut 32:50
6 [a]Deut 3:29; 4:46 [b]Jude 9
7 [a]Deut 31:2 [b]Gen 27:1; 48:10
9 [a]Num 27:18, 23; Is 11:2
10 [a]Deut 18:15, 18 [b]Ex 33:11; Num 12:8; Deut 5:4
12 [1]Lit *hand*

Joshua

Title and Background

This book is named after its leading character, Joshua, whom God named as Israel's leader before Moses' death. Where Deuteronomy ends the book of Joshua begins, with the tribes still camped on the east side of the Jordan River.

Author and Date of Writing

The earliest Jewish traditions (Talmud) claim that Joshua wrote his own book except for the final section about his funeral, which is assigned to Eleazar son of Aaron. Others think that Samuel may have shaped or compiled the materials of the book. However, we have no sure knowledge of who the author was. The book of Joshua was written sometime before 1000 B.C.

Theme and Message

The theme of the book is the establishment of Israel in the promised land. With God's help the people crossed the Jordan River and took possession of all the main areas of Canaan. Toward the end of the book Joshua reminded the people of God's covenant promises to them and instructed them to keep on loving and obeying God.

Outline

I. Preparation for Possession of Canaan (1:1—5:12)
II. The Conquest of Canaan (5:13—12:24)
III. The Division of Land by Tribes (13:1—21:45)
IV. Farewell and Death of Joshua (22:1—24:33)

God's Charge to Joshua

1 Now it came about after the death of
Moses the servant of the LORD, that
the LORD spoke to Joshua the son of Nun,
Moses' [1]servant, saying,
2 "Moses [a]My servant is dead; now
therefore arise, [b]cross this Jordan, you
and all this people, to the land which I am
giving to them, to the sons of Israel.
3 "[a]Every place on which the sole of
your foot treads, I have given it to you,
just as I spoke to Moses.
4 "[a]From the wilderness and this Lebanon, even as far as the great river, the
river Euphrates, all the land of the Hittites, and as far as the Great Sea toward
the setting of the sun will be your territory.
5 "[a]No man will *be able to* stand before you all the days of your life. Just as I
have been with Moses, I will be with you;
[b]I will not fail you or forsake you.
6 "[a]Be strong and courageous, for you
shall give this people possession of the
land which I swore to their fathers to give
them.
7 "Only be strong and very courageous; [1a]be careful to do according to all
the law which Moses My servant commanded you; do not turn from it to the
right or to the left, so that you may [2]have
success wherever you go.
8 "[a]This book of the law shall not depart from your mouth, but you shall meditate on it day and night, so that you may
[1]be careful to do according to all that is
written in it; [b]for then you will make
your way prosperous, and then you will
[2]have success.
9 "Have I not commanded you? [a]Be
strong and courageous! [b]Do not tremble
or be dismayed, for the LORD your God is
with you wherever you go."

Joshua Assumes Command

10 ¶ Then Joshua commanded the officers of the people, saying,
11 "Pass through the midst of the camp
and command the people, saying, 'Prepare provisions for yourselves, for within
[a]three days you are to cross this Jordan,
to go in to possess the land which the
LORD your God is giving you, to possess it.' "
12 ¶ [a]To the Reubenites and to the
Gadites and to the half-tribe of Manasseh,
Joshua [1]said,
13 "Remember the word which Moses
the servant of the LORD commanded you,

1:1 [1]Or *minister*
2 [a]Num 12:7; Deut 34:5 [b]Josh 1:11
3 [a]Deut 11:24
4 [a]Gen 15:18; Num 34:3
5 [a]Deut 7:24 [b]Deut 31:6,7; Heb 13:5
6 [a]Deut 31:6,7, 23
7 [1]Lit *observe* [2]Or *act wisely* [a]Deut 5:32
8 [1]Lit *observe* [2]Or *act wisely* [a]Deut 31:24; Josh 8:34 [b]Deut 29:9; Ps 1:1-3
9 [a]Josh 1:7 [b]Deut 31:8
11 [a]Josh 3:2
12 [1]Lit *said, saying* [a]Num 32:20-22

saying, '[a]The LORD your God gives you rest and will give you this land.'

14 "Your wives, your little ones, and your cattle shall remain in the land which Moses gave you beyond the Jordan, but you shall cross before your brothers in battle array, all your valiant warriors, and shall help them,

15 until the LORD gives your brothers rest, as *He gives* you, and they also possess the land which the LORD your God is giving them. [a]Then you shall return to [1]your own land, and possess [2]that which Moses [b]the servant of the LORD gave you beyond the Jordan toward the sunrise."

16 ¶ They answered Joshua, saying, "All that you have commanded us we will do, and wherever you send us we will go.

17 "Just as we obeyed Moses in all things, so we will obey you; only [a]may the LORD your God be with you as He was with Moses.

18 "Anyone who rebels against your [1]command and does not obey your words in all that you command him, shall be put to death; only be strong and courageous."

Rahab Shelters Spies

2 Then Joshua the son of Nun sent two men as spies secretly from [a]Shittim, saying, "Go, view the land, especially Jericho." So they went and came into the house of [b]a harlot whose name was Rahab, and [1]lodged there.

2 It was told the king of Jericho, saying, "Behold, men from the sons of Israel have come here tonight to search out the land."

3 And the king of Jericho sent *word* to Rahab, saying, "Bring out the men who have come to you, who have entered your house, for they have come to search out all the land."

4 But the [a]woman had taken the two men and hidden them, and she said, "Yes, the men came to me, but I did not know where they were from.

5 "It came about when *it was time* to shut the gate at dark, that the men went out; I do not know where the men went. Pursue them quickly, for you will overtake them."

6 But [a]she had brought them up to the roof and hidden them in the stalks of flax which she had laid in order on the roof.

7 So the men pursued them on the road to the Jordan to the fords; and as soon as those who were pursuing them had gone out, they shut the gate.

8 ¶ Now before they lay down, [1]she came up to them on the roof,

9 and said to the men, "[a]I know that the LORD has given you the land, and that the [b]terror of you has fallen on us, and that all the inhabitants of the land have [1]melted away before you.

10 "[a]For we have heard how the LORD dried up the water of the [1]Red Sea before you when you came out of Egypt, and [b]what you did to the two kings of the Amorites who were beyond the Jordan, to Sihon and Og, whom you [2]utterly destroyed.

11 "When we heard *it,* [a]our hearts melted and no [1]courage remained in any man any longer because of you; for the [b]LORD your God, He is God in heaven above and on earth beneath.

12 "Now therefore, please swear to me by the LORD, since I have dealt kindly with you, that you also will deal kindly with my father's household, and give me a [a]pledge of [1]truth,

13 and [1]spare my father and my mother and my brothers and my sisters, with all who belong to them, and deliver our [2]lives from death."

14 So the men said to her, "Our [1]life [2]for yours if you do not tell this business of ours; and it shall come about when the LORD gives us the land that we will [a]deal kindly and [3]faithfully with you."

The Promise to Rahab

15 ¶ Then she let them down by a rope through the window, for her house was on the city wall, so that she was living on the wall.

16 She said to them, "[a]Go to the hill country, so that the pursuers will not happen upon you, and hide yourselves there for three days until the pursuers return. Then afterward you may go on your way."

17 The men said to her, "[a]We *shall be* free from this oath [1]to you which you have made us swear,

18 [1]unless, when we come into the land, you tie this cord of scarlet thread in the window through which you let us down, and [a]gather to yourself into the house your father and your mother and your brothers and all your father's household.

19 "It shall come about that anyone who goes out of the doors of your house into the street, his blood *shall be* on his own head, and we *shall be* free; but anyone who is with you in the house, [a]his blood *shall be* on our head if a hand is *laid* on him.

20 "But if you tell this business of ours, then we shall be free from the oath which you have made us swear."

21 She said, "According to your

---

13 [a]Deut 3:18-20
15 [1]Lit *the land of your possession* [2]Lit *it* [a]Josh 22:4 [b]Josh 1:1
17 [a]Josh 1:5,9
18 [1]Lit *mouth*
2:1 [1]Lit *lay down* [a]Num 25:1; Josh 3:1 [b]Heb 11:31; James 2:25
4 [a]2 Sam 17:19
6 [a]James 2:25
8 [1]Lit *then she*
9 [1]Or *become demoralized* [a]Num 20:24; Josh 9:24 [b]Ex 23:27; Deut 2:25; Josh 9:9,10
10 [1]Lit *Sea of Reeds* [2]Or *put under the ban* [a]Ex 14:21; Num 23:22; 24:8 [b]Num 21:21-35
11 [1]Lit *spirit arose* [a]Josh 5:1; 7:5; Ps 22:14; Is 13:7; 19:1 [b]Deut 4:39
12 [1]Or *faithfulness* [a]Josh 2:18, 19
13 [1]Lit *let live* [2]Lit *souls*
14 [1]Lit *soul* [2]Lit *instead of you to die* [3]Or *truly* [a]Gen 24:49
16 [a]James 2:25
17 [1]Lit *of yours* [a]Gen 24:8
18 [1]Lit *behold* [a]Josh 2:12
19 [a]Matt 27:25

words, so be it." So she sent them away,
and they departed; and she tied the scarlet cord in the window.
22 ¶ They departed and came to the
hill country, and remained there for three
days until the pursuers returned. Now
the pursuers had sought *them* [1]all along
the road, but had not found *them.*
23 Then the two men returned and
came down from the hill country and
crossed over and came to Joshua the son
of Nun, and they related to him all that
had happened to them.
24 They said to Joshua, "Surely the
LORD has given all the land into our
hands; moreover, [a]all the inhabitants of
the land have [1]melted away before us."

Israel Crosses the Jordan

3 Then Joshua rose early in the morning; and he and all the sons of Israel
set out from [a]Shittim and came to the
Jordan, and they lodged there before they
crossed.
2 [a]At the end of three days the officers went through the midst of the camp;
3 and they commanded the people,
saying, "When you see the [a]ark of the
covenant of the LORD your God with the
Levitical priests carrying it, then you shall
set out from your place and go after it.
4 "However, there shall be between
you and it a distance of about 2,000 [1]cu-
bits by measure. Do not come near it, that
you may know the way by which you
shall go, for you have not passed this way
before."
5 ¶ Then Joshua said to the people,
"[a]Consecrate yourselves, for tomorrow
the LORD will do wonders among you."
6 And Joshua spoke to the priests,
saying, "Take up the ark of the covenant
and cross over ahead of the people." So
they took up the ark of the covenant and
went ahead of the people.
7 ¶ Now the LORD said to Joshua,
"This day I will begin to [a]exalt you in the
sight of all Israel, that they may know that
just as I have been with Moses, I will be
with you.
8 "You shall, moreover, command the
priests who are carrying the ark of the
covenant, saying, 'When you come to the
edge of the waters of the Jordan, you shall
stand *still* in the Jordan.' "
9 Then Joshua said to the sons of Israel, "Come here, and hear the words of
the LORD your God."
10 Joshua said, "By this you shall know
that [a]the living God is among you, and
that He will assuredly [b]dispossess from
before you the Canaanite, the Hittite, the
Hivite, the Perizzite, the Girgashite, the
Amorite, and the Jebusite.

22 [1]Lit *through all the road*
24 [1]Or *become demoralized* [a]Josh 2:9
3:1 [a]Josh 2:1
2 [a]Josh 1:11
3 [a]Deut 31:9
4 [1]I.e. One cubit equals approx 18 in.
5 [a]Ex 19:10,11; Josh 7:13
7 [a]Josh 4:14
10 [a]Deut 5:26; 1 Thess 1:9 [b]Ex 33:2; Deut 7:1
11 [a]Job 41:11; Ps 24:1; Zech 6:5
12 [a]Josh 4:2
13 [1]Lit *going* [2]Lit *and they will* [a]Ex 15:8
14 [a]Ps 132:8; Acts 7:44f
15 [a]1 Chr 12:15; Jer 12:5; 49:19
16 [1]Lit *going* [a]Ps 66:6; 74:15; 114:3,5 [b]Josh 3:13 [c]Deut 1:1
17 [a]Ex 14:21, 22,29
4:1 [a]Deut 27:2; Josh 3:17
2 [a]Josh 3:12
3 [a]Josh 4:20
5 [1]Lit *Cross before the ark*
6 [1]Lit *That this may be* [2]Lit *tomorrow* [a]Ex 12:26; 13:14; Josh 4:21

11 "Behold, the ark of the covenant of
[a]the Lord of all the earth is crossing over
ahead of you into the Jordan.
12 "Now then, [a]take for yourselves
twelve men from the tribes of Israel, one
man for each tribe.
13 "It shall come about when the soles
of the feet of the priests who carry the ark
of the LORD, the Lord of all the earth, rest
in the waters of the Jordan, the waters of
the Jordan will be cut off, *and* the waters
which are [1]flowing down from above
[2]will [a]stand in one heap."
14 ¶ So when the people set out from
their tents to cross the Jordan with the
priests carrying [a]the ark of the covenant
before the people,
15 and when those who carried the
ark came into the Jordan, and the feet of
the priests carrying the ark were dipped
in the edge of the water (for the [a]Jordan
overflows all its banks all the days of harvest),
16 [a]the waters which were [1]flowing
down from above stood *and* rose up in
[b]one heap, a great distance away at
Adam, the city that is beside Zarethan;
and those which were [1]flowing down toward the sea of the [c]Arabah, the Salt Sea,
were completely cut off. So the people
crossed opposite Jericho.
17 And the priests who carried the ark
of the covenant of the LORD stood firm
[a]on dry ground in the middle of the
Jordan while all Israel crossed on dry
ground, until all the nation had finished
crossing the Jordan.

Memorial Stones from Jordan

4 Now when all the nation had finished crossing the [a]Jordan, the LORD
spoke to Joshua, saying,
2 "[a]Take for yourselves twelve men
from the people, one man from each
tribe,
3 and command them, saying, 'Take
up for yourselves twelve stones from here
out of the middle of the Jordan, from the
place where the priests' feet are standing
firm, and carry them over with you and
lay them down in [a]the lodging place
where you will lodge tonight.' "
4 So Joshua called the twelve men
whom he had appointed from the sons of
Israel, one man from each tribe;
5 and Joshua said to them, "[1]Cross
again to the ark of the LORD your God into
the middle of the Jordan, and each of you
take up a stone on his shoulder, according to the number of the tribes of the sons
of Israel.
6 "[1]Let this be a sign among you, so
that [a]when your children ask [2]later, saying, 'What do these stones mean to you?'

7 then you shall say to them, 'Because the [a]waters of the Jordan were cut off before the ark of the covenant of the LORD; when it crossed the Jordan, the waters of the Jordan were cut off.' So these stones shall become a [b]memorial to the sons of Israel forever."

8 ¶ Thus the sons of Israel did as Joshua commanded, and took up twelve stones from the middle of the Jordan, just as the LORD spoke to Joshua, according to the number of the tribes of the sons of Israel; and they carried them over with them to [a]the lodging place and put them down there.

9 Then Joshua set up twelve [a]stones in the middle of the Jordan at the place where the feet of the priests who carried the ark of the covenant were standing, and they are there to this day.

10 For the priests who carried the ark were standing in the middle of the Jordan until everything was completed that the LORD had commanded Joshua to speak to the people, according to all that Moses had commanded Joshua. And the people hurried and crossed;

11 and when all the people had finished crossing, the ark of the LORD and the priests crossed before the people.

12 [a]The sons of Reuben and the sons of Gad and the half-tribe of Manasseh crossed over in battle array before the sons of Israel, just as Moses had spoken to them;

13 about 40,000 equipped for war, crossed for battle before the LORD to the desert plains of Jericho.

14 ¶ [a]On that day the LORD exalted Joshua in the sight of all Israel; so that they [1]revered him, just as they had [1]revered Moses all the days of his life.

15 ¶ Now the LORD said to [1]Joshua,

16 "Command the priests who carry [a]the ark of the testimony that they come up from the Jordan."

17 So Joshua commanded the priests, saying, "Come up from the Jordan."

18 It came about when the priests who carried the ark of the covenant of the LORD had come up from the middle of the Jordan, and the soles of the priests' feet were [1]lifted up to the dry ground, that the waters of the Jordan returned to their place, and went over all its banks as before.

19 ¶ Now the people came up from the Jordan on the [a]tenth of the first month and camped at Gilgal on the eastern edge of Jericho.

20 [1a]Those twelve stones which they had taken from the Jordan, Joshua set up [b]at Gilgal.

21 He said to the sons of [1]Israel, "When your children ask their fathers in time to come, saying, 'What are these stones?'

22 then you shall inform your children, saying, 'Israel crossed this Jordan on [a]dry ground.'

23 "For the LORD your God dried up the waters of the Jordan before you until you had crossed, just as the LORD your God had done to the [1]Red Sea, [a]which He dried up before us until we had crossed;

24 that [a]all the peoples of the earth may know that the [b]hand of the LORD is mighty, so that you may [1c]fear the LORD your God [2]forever."

Israel Is Circumcised

5 Now it came about when all the kings of the Amorites who *were* beyond the Jordan to the west, and all the kings of the [a]Canaanites who *were* by the sea, [b]heard how the LORD had dried up the waters of the Jordan before the sons of Israel until [1]they had crossed, that their hearts melted, and there was no spirit in them any longer because of the sons of Israel.

2 ¶ At that time the LORD said to Joshua, "Make for yourself [a]flint knives and circumcise again the sons of Israel the second time."

3 So Joshua made himself flint knives and circumcised the sons of Israel at [1]Gibeath-haaraloth.

4 This is the reason why Joshua circumcised them: [a]all the people who came out of Egypt who were males, all the men of war, died in the wilderness along the way after they came out of Egypt.

5 For all the people who came out were circumcised, but all the people who were born in the wilderness along the way as they came out of Egypt had not been circumcised.

6 For the sons of Israel walked [a]forty years in the wilderness, until all the nation, *that is,* the men of war who came out of Egypt, [1]perished because they did not listen to the voice of the LORD, [b]to whom the LORD had sworn that He would not let them see the land which the LORD had sworn to their fathers to give us, a land flowing with milk and honey.

7 Their children whom He raised up in their place, Joshua [1]circumcised; for they were uncircumcised, because they had not circumcised them along the way.

8 ¶ Now when they had finished circumcising all the nation, they remained in their places in the camp until they were [1]healed.

9 Then the LORD said to Joshua, "Today I have rolled away [a]the reproach of

---

7 [a]Josh 3:13 [b]Ex 12:14; Num 16:40

8 [a]Josh 4:20

9 [a]Gen 28:18; Josh 24:26f; 1 Sam 7:12

12 [a]Num 32:17

14 [1]Or *feared* [a]Josh 3:7

15 [1]Lit *Joshua, saying*

16 [a]Ex 25:16

18 [1]Lit *drawn out*

19 [a]Deut 1:3

20 [1]Lit *these* [a]Josh 4:8 [b]Josh 4:3,8

21 [1]Lit *Israel, saying,*

22 [a]Josh 3:17

23 [1]Lit *Sea of Reeds* [a]Ex 14:21

24 [1]Or *reverence* [2]Lit *all the days* [a]1 Kin 8:42; 2 Kin 19:19; Ps 106:8 [b]Ex 15:16; 1 Chr 29:12; Ps 89:13 [c]Ex 14:31; Ps 76:7f; Jer 10:7

5:1 [1]Other mss read *we* [a]Num 13:29 [b]Josh 2:10,11

2 [a]Ex 4:25

3 [1]I.e. the hill of the foreskins

4 [a]Deut 2:14

6 [1]Lit *were finished* [a]Deut 2:7, 14 [b]Num 14:29-35; 26:63-65

7 [1]Lit *circumcised them*

8 [1]Lit *revived*

9 [a]Zeph 2:8

Egypt from you." So the name of that place is called [1]Gilgal to this day.

10 ¶ While the sons of Israel camped at Gilgal [a]they observed the Passover on the evening of the [b]fourteenth day of the month on the desert plains of Jericho.

11 On the [1]day after the Passover, on [2]that very day, they ate some of the produce of the land, unleavened cakes and parched *grain.*

12 [a]The manna ceased on the [1]day after they had eaten some of the produce of the land, so that the sons of Israel no longer had manna, but they ate some of the yield of the land of Canaan during that year.

13 ¶ Now it came about when Joshua was by Jericho, that he lifted up his eyes and looked, and behold, [a]a man was standing opposite him with his sword drawn in his hand, and Joshua went to him and said to him, "Are you for us or for our adversaries?"

14 He said, "No; rather I indeed come now *as* captain of the host of the LORD." And Joshua [a]fell on his face to the earth, and bowed down, and said to him, "What has my lord to say to his servant?"

15 The captain of the LORD'S host said to Joshua, "[a]Remove your sandals from your feet, for the place where you are standing is holy." And Joshua did so.

The Conquest of Jericho

6 Now Jericho was tightly shut because of the sons of Israel; no one went out and no one came in.

2 The LORD said to Joshua, "See, I have given Jericho into your hand, with [a]its king *and* the valiant warriors.

3 "You shall march around the city, all the men of war circling the city once. You shall do so for six days.

4 "Also seven priests shall carry seven [a]trumpets of rams' horns before the ark; then on the seventh day you shall march around the city seven times, and the priests shall blow the trumpets.

5 "It shall be that when they make a long blast with the ram's horn, and when you hear the sound of the trumpet, all the people shall shout with a great shout; and the wall of the city will fall down [1]flat, and the people will go up every man [2]straight ahead."

6 ¶ So Joshua the son of Nun called the priests and said to them, "Take up the ark of the covenant, and let seven priests carry seven trumpets of rams' horns before the ark of the LORD."

7 Then [1]he said to the people, "Go forward, and march around the city, and let the armed men go on before the ark of the LORD."

8 And it was *so,* that when Joshua had spoken to the people, the seven priests carrying the seven trumpets of rams' horns before the LORD went forward and blew the trumpets; and the ark of the covenant of the LORD followed them.

9 The armed men went before the priests who blew the trumpets, and [a]the rear guard came after the ark, while they continued to blow the trumpets.

10 But Joshua commanded the people, saying, "You shall not shout nor let your voice be heard nor let a word proceed out of your mouth, until the day I tell you, 'Shout!' Then you shall shout!"

11 So he had the ark of the LORD [1]taken around the city, circling *it* once; then they came into the camp and spent the night in the camp.

12 ¶ Now Joshua rose early in the morning, and the priests took up the ark of the LORD.

13 [a]The seven priests carrying the seven trumpets of rams' horns before the ark of the LORD went on continually, and blew the trumpets; and the armed men went before them and [b]the rear guard came after the ark of the LORD, while they continued to blow the trumpets.

14 Thus the second day they marched around the city once and returned to the camp; they did so for six days.

15 ¶ Then on the seventh day they rose early at the dawning of the day and marched around the city in the same manner seven times; only on that day they marched around the city seven times.

16 At the seventh time, when the priests blew the trumpets, Joshua said to the people, "[a]Shout! For the LORD has given you the city.

17 "The city shall be [a]under the ban, it and all that is in it belongs to the LORD; only Rahab the harlot [1]and all who are with her in the house shall live, because she hid the messengers whom we sent.

18 "But as for you, only keep yourselves from the things under the ban, so that you do not [1]covet *them* and [a]take some of the things under the ban, and make the camp of Israel accursed and bring trouble on it.

19 "[a]But all the silver and gold and articles of bronze and iron are holy to the LORD; they shall go into the treasury of the LORD."

20 So the people shouted, and [1]*priests* blew the trumpets; and when the people heard the sound of the trumpet, the people shouted with a great shout and the [a]wall fell down [2]flat, so that the people went up into the city,

9 [1]I.e. rolling
10 [a]Ex 12:18 [b]Josh 4:19
11 [1]Lit *morrow* [2]Lit *this*
12 [1]Lit *morrow* [a]Ex 16:35
13 [a]Gen 18:1,2; 32:24,30; Num 22:31
14 [a]Gen 17:3
15 [a]Ex 3:5
6:2 [a]Deut 7:24
4 [a]Lev 25:9
5 [1]Lit *in its place* [2]Lit *before himself*
7 [1]Or *they*
9 [a]Josh 6:13; Is 52:12
11 [1]Lit *to go around*
13 [a]Josh 6:4 [b]Josh 6:9
16 [a]2 Chr 13:14f
17 [1]Lit *she and all* [a]Lev 27:28; Deut 20:17
18 [1]Lit *devote* [a]Josh 7:1
19 [a]Num 31:11, 12,21-23
20 [1]Or *they* [2]Lit *in its place* [a]Heb 11:30

every man straight [3]ahead, and they took
the city.
21 [a]They [1]utterly destroyed everything in the city, both man and woman,
young and old, and ox and sheep and
donkey, with the edge of the sword.
22 ¶ Joshua said to the two men who
had spied out the land, "[a]Go into the
harlot's house and bring the woman and
all she has out of there, as you have
sworn to her."
23 So the young men who were spies
went in and [a]brought out Rahab and her
father and her mother and her brothers
and all she had; they also brought out all
her relatives and placed them outside the
camp of Israel.
24 [a]They burned the city with fire,
and all that was in it. Only the silver and
gold, and articles of bronze and iron, they
put into the treasury of the [1]house of the
LORD.
25 However, [a]Rahab the harlot and
her father's household and all she had,
Joshua [1]spared; and she has lived in the
midst of Israel to this day, for [b]she hid
the messengers whom Joshua sent to spy
out Jericho.
26 ¶ Then Joshua made them take an
oath at that time, saying, "[a]Cursed before the LORD is the man who rises up and
builds this city Jericho; with *the loss of*
his firstborn he shall lay its foundation,
and with *the loss of* his youngest son he
shall set up its gates."
27 So [a]the LORD was with Joshua, and
his [b]fame was in all the land.

Israel Is Defeated at Ai

7 [a]But the sons of Israel acted unfaithfully in regard to the things under the
ban, for Achan, the son of Carmi, the son
of Zabdi, the son of Zerah, from the tribe
of Judah, took some of the things under
the ban, therefore the anger of the LORD
burned against the sons of Israel.
2 ¶ Now Joshua sent men from Jericho to Ai, which is near [a]Beth-aven, east
of Bethel, and said to them, "[1]Go up and
spy out the land." So the men went up
and spied out Ai.
3 They returned to Joshua and said to
him, "Do not let all the people go up; *only*
about two or three thousand men need go
up [1]to Ai; do not make all the people toil
up there, for they are few."
4 So about three thousand men from
the people went up there, but [a]they fled
[1]from the men of Ai.
5 The men of Ai struck down about
thirty-six of their men, and pursued them
[1]from the gate as far as Shebarim and
struck them down on the descent, so the
[a]hearts of the people melted and became
as water.
6 ¶ Then Joshua [a]tore his clothes
and fell to the earth on his face before the
ark of the LORD until the evening, *both* he
and the elders of Israel; and [b]they put
dust on their heads.
7 Joshua said, "Alas, O Lord [1]GOD,
why did You ever bring this people over
the Jordan, *only* to deliver us into the
hand of the Amorites, to destroy us? If
only we had been willing [2]to dwell beyond the Jordan!
8 "O Lord, what can I say since Israel
has turned *their* [1]back before their enemies?
9 "[a]For the Canaanites and all the inhabitants of the land will hear of it, and
they will surround us and cut off our
name from the earth. And what will You
do for Your great name?"
10 ¶ So the LORD said to Joshua, "Rise
up! Why is it that you have fallen on your
face?
11 "Israel has sinned, and [a]they have
also transgressed My covenant which I
commanded them. And they have even
taken some of the things under the ban
and have both stolen and deceived. Moreover, they have also put *them* among
their own things.
12 "Therefore the [a]sons of Israel cannot stand before their enemies; they turn
their [1]backs before their enemies, for
they have become accursed. I will not be
with you anymore unless you destroy the
things under the ban from your midst.
13 "Rise up! [a]Consecrate the people
and say, 'Consecrate yourselves for tomorrow, for thus the LORD, the God of
Israel, has said, "[b]There are things under
the ban in your midst, O Israel. You cannot stand before your enemies until you
have removed the things under the ban
from your midst."
14 'In the morning then you shall come
near by your tribes. And it shall be that
the tribe which [a]the LORD takes *by lot*
shall come near by families, and the family which the LORD takes shall come near
by households, and the household which
the LORD takes shall come near man by
man.
15 '[a]It shall be that the one who is
taken with the things under the ban shall
be burned with fire, he and all that belongs to him, because he has transgressed
the covenant of the LORD, and because he
[b]has committed a disgraceful thing in Israel.' "

The Sin of Achan

16 ¶ So Joshua arose early in the morn-

---

20 [3]Lit *before himself*
21 [1]Or *put under the ban* [a]Deut 20:16
22 [a]Josh 2:12-19
23 [a]Heb 11:31
24 [1]I.e. tabernacle [a]Deut 20:16-18
25 [1]Lit *let live* [a]Heb 11:31 [b]Josh 2:6
26 [a]1 Kin 16:34
27 [a]Gen 39:2; Judg 1:19 [b]Josh 9:1,3
7:1 [a]Josh 6:17-19
2 [1]Lit *saying, Go* [a]Josh 18:12; 1 Sam 13:5; 14:23
3 [1]Lit *and smite*
4 [1]Lit *before* [a]Lev 26:17; Deut 28:25
5 [1]Or *before* [a]Lev 26:36; Josh 2:11; Ezek 21:7; Nah 2:10
6 [a]Job 2:12 [b]Job 42:6; Lam 2:10; Rev 18:19
7 [1]Heb *YHWH,* usually rendered LORD [2]Lit *and had dwelt*
8 [1]Lit *neck*
9 [a]Ex 32:12; Deut 9:28
11 [a]Josh 6:18, 19
12 [1]Lit *necks* [a]Num 14:39,45; Judg 2:14
13 [a]Josh 3:5 [b]Josh 6:18
14 [a]Prov 16:33
15 [a]1 Sam 14:38f [b]Gen 34:7; Judg 20:6

ing and brought Israel near by [1]tribes,
and the tribe of Judah was taken.
17 He brought the family of Judah
near, and he took the family of the Zerahites;
and he brought the family of the
Zerahites near man by man, and Zabdi
was taken.
18 He brought his household near
man by man; and [a]Achan, son of Carmi,
son of Zabdi, son of Zerah, from the tribe
of Judah, was taken.
19 Then Joshua said to Achan, "My
son, I implore you, [a]give glory to the
LORD, the God of Israel, and give praise to
Him; and tell me now what you have
done. Do not hide it from me."
20 So Achan answered Joshua and
said, "Truly, I have sinned against the
LORD, the God of Israel, and [1]this is what
I did:
21 when I saw among the spoil a beautiful
mantle from Shinar and two hundred
shekels of silver and a bar of gold fifty
shekels in weight, then I [a]coveted them
and took them; and behold, they are concealed
in the earth inside my tent with
the silver underneath it."
22 ¶ So Joshua sent messengers, and
they ran to the tent; and behold, it was
concealed in his tent with the silver underneath
it.
23 They took them from inside the
tent and brought them to Joshua and to all
the sons of Israel, and they poured them
out before the LORD.
24 Then Joshua and all Israel with
him, took Achan the son of Zerah, the
silver, the mantle, the bar of gold, his
sons, his daughters, his [1]oxen, his donkeys,
his sheep, his tent and all that belonged
to him; and they brought them up
to [a]the valley of [2]Achor.
25 Joshua said, "Why have you [a]troubled
us? The LORD will trouble you this
day." And all Israel stoned [1]them with
stones; and they burned them with fire
[2]after they had stoned them with stones.
26 They raised over him a great heap
of stones that stands to this day, and the
LORD turned from the fierceness of His
anger. Therefore the name of that place
has been called [a]the valley of [1]Achor to
this day.

The Conquest of Ai

8 Now the LORD said to Joshua, "[a]Do
not fear or be dismayed. Take all the
people of war with you and arise, go up
to Ai; see, [b]I have given into your hand
the king of Ai, his people, his city, and his
land.
2 "You shall do to Ai and its king just
as you did to Jericho and its king; you
shall [a]take only its spoil and its cattle as
plunder for yourselves. [1]Set an ambush
for the city behind it."
3 ¶ So Joshua rose with all the people
of war to go up to Ai; and Joshua chose
30,000 men, valiant warriors, and sent
them out at night.
4 He commanded them, saying, "See,
you are [a]going to ambush the city from
behind [1]it. Do not go very far from the
city, but all of you be ready.
5 "Then I and all the people who are
with me will approach the city. And
when they come out to meet us as at the
first, [a]we will flee before them.
6 "They will come out after us until
we have drawn them away from the city,
for they will say, '*They* are fleeing before
us as at the first.' So we will flee before
them.
7 "And you shall rise from *your* ambush
and take possession of the city, for
the LORD your God will deliver it into
your hand.
8 "Then it will be when you have
seized the city, that you shall set the city
on fire. You shall do *it* [a]according to the
word of the LORD. See, I have commanded
you."
9 So Joshua sent them away, and they
went to the place of ambush and remained
between Bethel and Ai, on the
west side of Ai; but Joshua spent that
night among the people.
10 ¶ Now Joshua [a]rose early in the
morning and mustered the people, and
he went up with the elders of Israel before
the people to Ai.
11 Then all the people of war who
were with him went up and drew near
and arrived in front of the city, and
camped on the north side of Ai. Now
there was a valley between him and Ai.
12 And he took about 5,000 men and
set them in ambush between [a]Bethel
and Ai, on the west side of the [1]city.
13 So they stationed the people, all the
army that was on the north side of the
city, and its rear guard on the west side
of the city, and Joshua spent that night in
the midst of the valley.
14 It came about when the king of Ai
saw *it,* that the men of the city hurried
and rose up early and went out to meet
Israel in battle, he and all his people at
the appointed place before the desert
plain. But he did not know that *there was*
an ambush against him behind the city.
15 Joshua and all Israel pretended to
be beaten before them, and fled [a]by the
way of the wilderness.
16 And all the people who were in the
city were called together to pursue them,
and they pursued Joshua and [a]were
drawn away from the city.

16 [1]Lit *its tribes*
18 [a]Num 32:23; Acts 5:1-10
19 [a]1 Sam 6:5; 2 Chr 30:22; Jer 13:16; John 9:24
20 [1]Lit *thus and thus I did*
21 [a]Eph 5:5; 1 Tim 6:10
24 [1]Or *cattle* [2]I.e. trouble [a]Josh 15:7
25 [1]Lit *him* [2]Lit *and they stoned* [a]Josh 6:18
26 [1]I.e. trouble [a]Is 65:10; Hos 2:15
8:1 [a]Josh 1:9; 10:8 [b]Josh 6:2
2 [1]Lit *Set for yourself* [a]Deut 20:14; Josh 8:27
4 [1]Lit *the city* [a]Judg 20:29
5 [a]Judg 20:32
8 [a]Deut 20:16-18; Josh 8:2
10 [a]Gen 22:3
12 [1]I.e. Ai [a]Gen 12:8; 28:19; Judg 1:22
15 [a]Josh 15:61; 16:1; 18:12
16 [a]Judg 20:31

17 So not a man was left in Ai or Bethel who had not gone out after Israel, and they left the city [1]unguarded and pursued Israel.

18 ¶ Then the LORD said to Joshua, "[a]Stretch out the javelin that is in your hand toward Ai, for I will give it into your hand." So Joshua stretched out the javelin that was in his hand toward the city.

19 The *men in* ambush rose quickly from their place, and when he had stretched out his hand, they ran and entered the city and captured it, and they quickly set the city on fire.

20 When the men of Ai turned [1]back and looked, behold, the smoke of the city ascended to the sky, and they had no place to flee this way or that, for the people who had been fleeing to the wilderness turned against the pursuers.

21 When Joshua and all Israel saw that the *men in* ambush had captured the city and that the smoke of the city ascended, they turned back and [1]slew the men of Ai.

22 [1]The others came out from the city to encounter them, so that they were *trapped* in the midst of Israel, [2]some on this side and some on that side; and they [3]slew them until [a]no one was left [4]of those who survived or escaped.

23 But they took alive the king of Ai and brought him to Joshua.

24 ¶ Now when Israel had finished killing all the inhabitants of Ai in the field in the wilderness where they pursued them, and all of them were fallen by the edge of the sword until they were destroyed, then all Israel returned to Ai and struck it with the edge of the sword.

25 [a]All who fell that day, both men and women, were 12,000—all the [1]people of Ai.

26 For Joshua [a]did not withdraw his hand with which he stretched out the javelin until he had [1]utterly destroyed all the inhabitants of Ai.

27 [a]Israel took only the cattle and the spoil of that city as plunder for themselves, according to the word of the LORD which He had commanded Joshua.

28 So Joshua burned Ai and made it [a]a heap forever, a desolation until this day.

29 [a]He hanged the king of Ai on a tree until evening; and at sunset Joshua gave command and they took his body down from the tree and threw it at the entrance of the city gate, and raised over it a great heap of stones *that stands* to this day.

30 ¶ Then Joshua built an altar to the LORD, the God of Israel, in [a]Mount Ebal,

31 just as Moses the servant of the LORD had commanded the sons of Israel, as it is written in the book of the law of Moses, [a]an altar of uncut stones on which no man had wielded an iron *tool;* and they offered burnt offerings on it to the LORD, and sacrificed peace offerings.

32 He [a]wrote there on the stones a copy of the law of Moses, which [1]he had written, in the presence of the sons of Israel.

33 [a]All Israel with their elders and officers and their judges were standing on both sides of the ark before the Levitical priests who carried the ark of the covenant of the LORD, the stranger as well as the native. Half of them *stood* in front of [b]Mount Gerizim and half of them in front of Mount Ebal, just as Moses the servant of the LORD had given command at first to bless the people of Israel.

34 Then afterward he read all the words of the law, the blessing and the curse, according to all that is written in [a]the book of the law.

35 There was not a word of all that Moses had commanded which Joshua did not read before all the assembly of Israel [a]with the women and the little ones and the strangers who were [1]living among them.

Guile of the Gibeonites

9 Now it came about when [a]all the kings who were beyond the Jordan, in the hill country and in the lowland and on all the [b]coast of the Great Sea toward Lebanon, [c]the Hittite and the Amorite, the Canaanite, the Perizzite, the Hivite and the Jebusite, heard of it,

2 that they gathered themselves together with [1a]one accord to fight with Joshua and with Israel.

3 ¶ When the inhabitants of [a]Gibeon heard what Joshua had done to Jericho and to Ai,

4 they also acted craftily and [1]set out as envoys, and took worn-out sacks on their donkeys, and wineskins worn-out and torn and [2]mended,

5 and worn-out and patched sandals on their feet, and worn-out clothes on themselves; and all the bread of their provision was dry *and* had become crumbled.

6 They went to Joshua to the [a]camp at Gilgal and said to him and to the men of Israel, "We have come from a far country; now therefore, make a covenant with us."

7 The men of Israel said to the [a]Hivites, "Perhaps you are living [1]within our land; [b]how then shall we make a covenant with you?"

8 But they said to Joshua, "[a]We are your servants." Then Joshua said to them,

---

17 [1]Lit *open*
18 [a]Ex 14:16; 17:9-13; Josh 8:26
20 [1]Lit *behind them*
21 [1]Lit *smote*
22 [1]Lit *These came* [2]Lit *these...those* [3]Lit *smote* [4]Lit *for it* [a]Josh 8:8
25 [1]Lit *men* [a]Deut 20:16-18
26 [1]Or *put under the ban* [a]Ex 17:11,12
27 [a]Josh 8:2
28 [a]Deut 13:16
29 [a]Deut 21:22, 23
30 [a]Deut 27:2-8
31 [a]Ex 20:25
32 [1]I.e. Moses [a]Deut 27:2,3,8
33 [a]Deut 27:11-14 [b]Deut 11:29
34 [a]Josh 1:8
35 [1]Lit *walking* [a]Ex 12:38; Deut 31:12; Zech 8:23
9:1 [a]Num 13:29; Josh 3:10 [b]Num 34:6 [c]Ex 3:17; 23:23
2 [1]Lit *one mouth* [a]Ps 83:3, 5
3 [a]Josh 9:17,22; 10:2; 21:17
4 [1]Lit *went and traveled as envoys* [2]Lit *tied up*
6 [a]Josh 5:10
7 [1]Lit *among us* [a]Josh 9:1; 11:19 [b]Ex 23:32; Deut 7:2
8 [a]Deut 20:11; 2 Kin 10:5

"Who are you and where do you come
from?"
9 They said to him, "Your servants
have come from [a]a very far country because of the [1]fame of the LORD your God;
for [b]we have heard the report of Him and
all that He did in Egypt,
10 and all that He did to the two kings
of the Amorites who were beyond the
Jordan, to Sihon king of Heshbon and to
Og king of Bashan who was at Ashtaroth.
11 "So our elders and all the inhabitants
of our country spoke to us, saying, 'Take
provisions in your hand for the journey,
and go to meet them and say to them,
"[a]We are your servants; now then, make
a covenant with us." '
12 "This our bread *was* warm *when* we
took it for our provisions out of our
houses on the day that we left to come to
you; but now behold, it is dry and has
become crumbled.
13 "These wineskins which we filled
were new, and behold, they are torn; and
these our clothes and our sandals are
worn out because of the very long journey."
14 So the men *of Israel* took some of
their provisions, and [a]did not ask for the
[1]counsel of the LORD.
15 [a]Joshua made peace with them
and made a covenant with them, to let
them live; and the leaders of the congregation swore *an oath* to them.
16 ¶ It came about at the end of three
days after they had made a covenant with
them, that they heard that they were
neighbors and that they were living
[1]within their land.
17 Then the sons of Israel set out and
came to their cities on the third day. Now
their cities *were* [a]Gibeon and Chephirah
and Beeroth and Kiriath-jearim.
18 The sons of Israel did not strike
them because the leaders of the congregation had sworn to them by the LORD the
God of Israel. And the whole congregation grumbled against the leaders.
19 But all the leaders said to the whole
congregation, "We have sworn to them
by the LORD, the God of Israel, and now
we cannot touch them.
20 "This we will do to them, even let
them live, so that wrath will not be upon
us for the oath which we swore to them."
21 The leaders said to them, "Let them
live." So they became [a]hewers of wood
and drawers of water for the whole congregation, just as the leaders had spoken
to them.
22 ¶ Then Joshua called for them and
spoke to them, saying, "Why have you
deceived us, saying, 'We are very far from
you,' [a]when you are living [1]within our
land?
23 "Now therefore, you are [a]cursed,
and [1]you shall never cease being slaves,
both hewers of wood and drawers of water for the house of my God."
24 So they answered Joshua and said,
"[a]Because it was certainly told your servants that the LORD your God had commanded His servant Moses to give you all
the land, and to destroy all the inhabitants of the land before you; therefore we
feared greatly for our lives because of
you, and have done this thing.
25 "Now behold, [a]we are in your
hands; do as it seems good and right in
your sight to do to us."
26 Thus he did to them, and delivered
them from the hands of the sons of Israel,
and they did not kill them.
27 But Joshua made them that day
hewers of wood and drawers of water for
the congregation and for the altar of the
LORD, to this day, [a]in the place which He
would choose.

Five Kings Attack Gibeon

10 Now it came about when Adoni-
zedek king of Jerusalem heard
that Joshua had captured Ai, and had [1]ut-
terly destroyed it (just [a]as he had done to
Jericho and its king, so he had done to Ai
and its king), and that the inhabitants of
Gibeon had [b]made peace with Israel and
were [2]within their land,
2 that [1]he [a]feared greatly, because
Gibeon *was* a great city, like one of the
royal cities, and because it was greater
than Ai, and all its men *were* mighty.
3 Therefore Adoni-zedek king of Jerusalem sent *word* [a]to Hoham king of
Hebron and to Piram king of Jarmuth and
to Japhia king of Lachish and to Debir
king of Eglon, saying,
4 "Come up to me and help me, and
let us [1]attack Gibeon, for it has [a]made
peace with Joshua and with the sons of
Israel."
5 So the five kings of [a]the Amorites,
the king of Jerusalem, the king of Hebron,
the king of Jarmuth, the king of Lachish,
and the king of Eglon, gathered together
and went up, they with all their armies,
and camped by Gibeon and fought
against it.
6 ¶ Then the men of Gibeon sent
word to Joshua to the camp at Gilgal, saying, "Do not [1]abandon your servants;
come up to us quickly and save us and
help us, for all the kings of the Amorites
that live in the hill country have assembled against us."
7 So Joshua went up from Gilgal, he

9 [1]Or *name* [a]Josh 9:16,17 [b]Josh 2:9; 9:24
11 [a]Josh 9:8
14 [1]Lit *mouth* [a]Num 27:21
15 [a]Ex 23:32
16 [1]Lit *among them*
17 [a]Josh 18:25
21 [a]Deut 29:11
22 [1]Lit *among us* [a]Josh 9:16
23 [1]Lit *a servant shall not be cut off from you* [a]Gen 9:25
24 [a]Josh 9:9
25 [a]Gen 16:6
27 [a]Deut 12:5
10:1 [1]Or *put under the ban* [2]Lit *among them* [a]Josh 8:21f [b]Josh 9:15
2 [1]Lit *they* [a]Ex 15:14-16
3 [a]Josh 10:23
4 [1]Lit *smite* [a]Josh 9:15
5 [a]Num 13:29
6 [1]Lit *slacken your hands from*

and [a]all the people of war with him and all the valiant warriors.

8 The LORD said to Joshua, "[a]Do not fear them, for I have given them into your hands; not [1]one of them shall stand before you."

9 So Joshua came upon them suddenly [1]by marching all night from Gilgal.

10 [a]And the LORD confounded them before Israel, and He [1]slew them with a great slaughter at Gibeon, and pursued them by the way of the ascent of Beth-horon and struck them as far as Azekah and Makkedah.

11 As they fled from before Israel, *while* they were at the descent of Beth-horon, [a]the LORD threw large stones from heaven on them as far as Azekah, and they died; *there were* more who died [1]from the hailstones than those whom the sons of Israel killed with the sword.

12 ¶ Then Joshua spoke to the LORD in the day when the LORD delivered up the Amorites before the sons of Israel, and he said in the sight of Israel,

"O [a]sun, stand still at Gibeon,
And O moon in the valley of Aijalon."

13 [a]So the sun stood still, and the moon stopped,
Until the nation avenged themselves of their enemies.

Is it not written in [b]the book of Jashar? And [c]the sun stopped in the middle of the sky and did not hasten to go *down* for about a whole day.

14 There was no day like that before it or after it, when the LORD listened to the voice of a man; for [a]the LORD fought for Israel.

15 ¶ Then Joshua and all Israel with him returned to the camp to Gilgal.

Victory at Makkedah

16 ¶ Now these [a]five kings had fled and hidden themselves in the cave at Makkedah.

17 It was told Joshua, saying, "The five kings have been found hidden in the cave at Makkedah."

18 Joshua said, "Roll large stones against the mouth of the cave, and assign men by it to guard them,

19 but do not stay *there* yourselves; pursue your enemies and [1]attack them in the rear. Do not allow them to enter their cities, for the LORD your God has delivered them into your hand."

20 It came about when Joshua and the sons of Israel had finished [1]slaying them with a very great slaughter, [a]until they were destroyed, and the survivors *who* remained of them [2]had entered the fortified cities,

21 that all the people returned to the camp to Joshua at Makkedah in peace. No one [1]uttered a word against any of the sons of Israel.

22 ¶ Then Joshua said, "Open the mouth of the cave and bring these five kings out to me from the cave."

23 They did so, and [a]brought these five kings out to him from the cave: the king of Jerusalem, the king of Hebron, the king of Jarmuth, the king of Lachish, *and* the king of Eglon.

24 When they brought these kings out to Joshua, Joshua called for all the men of Israel, and said to the chiefs of the men of war who had gone with him, "Come near, [a]put your feet on the necks of these kings." So they came near and put their feet on their necks.

25 Joshua then said to them, "[a]Do not fear or be dismayed! Be strong and courageous, for thus the LORD will do to all your enemies with whom you fight."

26 So afterward Joshua struck them and put them to death, and he [a]hanged them on five trees; and they hung on the trees until evening.

27 It came about at [1]sunset that Joshua gave a command, and [a]they took them down from the trees and threw them into the cave where they had hidden themselves, and put large stones over the mouth of the cave, to this very day.

28 ¶ Now Joshua captured Makkedah on that day, and struck it and its king with the edge of the sword; [a]he [1]utterly destroyed [2]it and every [3]person who was in it. He left no survivor. Thus he did to the king of Makkedah [b]just as he had done to the king of Jericho.

Joshua's Conquest of Southern Palestine

29 ¶ Then Joshua and all Israel with him passed on from Makkedah to [a]Libnah, and fought against Libnah.

30 The LORD gave it also with its king into the hands of Israel, and he struck it and every person who *was* in it with the edge of the sword. He left no survivor in it. Thus he did to its king just as he had done to the king of Jericho.

31 ¶ And Joshua and all Israel with him passed on from Libnah to Lachish, and they camped by it and fought against it.

32 The LORD gave Lachish into the hands of Israel; and he captured it on the second day, and struck it and every person who *was* in it with the edge of the sword, according to all that he had done to Libnah.

33 ¶ Then Horam king of [a]Gezer

7 [a]Josh 8:1
8 [1]Lit *a man* [a]Josh 1:5,9
9 [1]Lit *he went up*
10 [1]Lit *struck* [a]Deut 7:23
11 [1]Lit *with* [a]Ps 18:12f; Is 28:2
12 [a]Hab 3:11
13 [a]Hab 3:11 [b]2 Sam 1:18 [c]Is 38:8
14 [a]Ex 14:14; Deut 1:30; Josh 10:42
16 [a]Josh 10:5
19 [1]Lit *smite their tail*
20 [1]Lit *striking* [2]Lit *and had* [a]Deut 20:16
21 [1]Lit *sharpened his tongue*
23 [a]Deut 7:24
24 [a]Mal 4:3
25 [a]Josh 10:8
26 [a]Josh 8:29
27 [1]Lit *the time of the going of the sun* [a]Deut 21:22,23
28 [1]Or *put under the ban* [2]Some mss read *them* [3]Lit *soul,* and so throughout the ch [a]Deut 20:16 [b]Josh 6:21
29 [a]Josh 15:42; 21:13
33 [a]Josh 16:3, 10; Judg 1:29; 1 Kin 9:16f

came up to help Lachish, and Joshua [1]de-
feated him and his people until he had
left him no survivor.
34 ¶ And Joshua and all Israel with
him passed on from Lachish to Eglon, and
they camped by it and fought against it.
35 They captured it on that day and
struck it with the edge of the sword; and
he [1]utterly destroyed that day every person who *was* in it, according to all that he
had done to Lachish.
36 ¶ Then Joshua and all Israel with
him went up from Eglon to [a]Hebron, and
they fought against it.
37 They captured it and struck it and
its king and all its cities and all the persons who *were* in it with the edge of the
sword. He left no survivor, according to
all that he had done to Eglon. And he
[1]utterly destroyed it and every person
who *was* in it.
38 ¶ Then Joshua and all Israel with
him returned to [a]Debir, and they fought
against it.
39 He captured it and its king and all
its cities, and they struck them with the
edge of the sword, and [1]utterly destroyed every person *who was* in it. He
left no survivor. Just as he had done to
Hebron, so he did to Debir and its king,
as he had also done to Libnah and its
king.
40 ¶ Thus Joshua struck all the land,
[a]the hill country and the [1]Negev and the
lowland and the slopes and [b]all their
kings. He left no survivor, but [c]he [2]ut-
terly destroyed all who breathed, just as
the LORD, the God of Israel, had commanded.
41 Joshua struck them from Kadesh-
barnea even as far as Gaza, and all the
country of [a]Goshen even as far as Gibeon.
42 Joshua captured all these kings and
their lands at one time, because [a]the
LORD, the God of Israel, fought for Israel.
43 So Joshua and all Israel with him
returned to the camp at Gilgal.

Northern Palestine Taken

11 Then it came about, when Jabin
king of [a]Hazor heard *of it,* that he
sent to Jobab king of Madon and to the
king of Shimron and to the king of Achshaph,
2 and to the kings who were of the
north in the hill country, and in the [a]Ara-
bah—south of [1]Chinneroth and in the
lowland and on the [2]heights of Dor on
the west—
3 to the Canaanite on the east and on
the west, and the Amorite and the Hittite
and the Perizzite and the Jebusite in the
hill country, and [a]the Hivite [1]at the foot
of [b]Hermon in the land of [c]Mizpeh.
4 They came out, they and all their
armies with them, [a]*as* many people as
the sand that is on the seashore, with
very many horses and chariots.
5 So all of these kings having agreed
to meet, came and encamped together at
the waters of Merom, to fight against Israel.
6 ¶ Then the LORD said to Joshua,
"[a]Do not be afraid because of them, for
tomorrow at this time I will deliver all of
them slain before Israel; you shall [b]ham-
string their horses and burn their chariots
with fire."
7 So Joshua and all the people of war
with him came upon them suddenly by
the waters of Merom, and attacked them.
8 The LORD delivered them into the
hand of Israel, so that they [1]defeated
them, and pursued them as far as Great
Sidon and [a]Misrephoth-maim and the
valley of [b]Mizpeh to the east; and they
struck them until no survivor was left to
them.
9 Joshua did to them as the LORD had
told him; he [a]hamstrung their horses
and burned their chariots with fire.
10 ¶ Then Joshua turned back at that
time, and captured [a]Hazor and struck its
king with the sword; for Hazor formerly
was the head of all these kingdoms.
11 [a]They struck every person who
was in it with the edge of the sword,
[1]utterly destroying *them;* there was no
one left who breathed. And he burned
Hazor with fire.
12 Joshua captured all the cities of
these kings, and all their kings, and he
struck them with the edge of the sword,
and utterly destroyed them; just [a]as Moses the servant of the LORD had commanded.
13 However, Israel did not burn any
cities that stood on their mounds, except
Hazor alone, *which* Joshua burned.
14 [a]All the spoil of these cities and the
cattle, the sons of Israel took as their
plunder; but they struck every man with
the edge of the sword, until they had
destroyed them. They left no one who
breathed.
15 Just as the LORD had commanded
Moses his servant, so Moses commanded
Joshua, and so Joshua did; he left nothing
undone of all that the LORD had commanded Moses.
16 ¶ Thus Joshua took all that land:
[a]the hill country and all the [1]Negev, all
that land of Goshen, the lowland, [b]the
Arabah, the hill country of Israel and its
lowland
17 from [a]Mount Halak, that rises to-

33 [1]Lit *smote*
35 [1]Or *put under the ban*
36 [a]Num 13:22; Judg 1:10,20; 2 Sam 5:1,3,5, 13; 2 Chr 11:10
37 [1]Or *put it under the ban*
38 [a]Josh 15:15; Judg 1:11; 1 Chr 6:58
39 [1]Or *put it under the ban*
40 [1]I.e. South country [2]Or *put it under the ban* [a]Deut 1:7 [b]Deut 7:24 [c]Deut 20:16
41 [a]Josh 11:16; 15:51
42 [a]Josh 10:14
11:1 [a]Josh 11:10
2 [1]I.e. Sea of Galilee [2]Or *Naphoth-dor* [a]Josh 12:3; 13:27
3 [1]Lit *under* [a]Deut 7:1; Judg 3:3,5; 1 Kin 9:20 [b]Josh 11:17; 13:5,11 [c]Josh 15:38; 18:26
4 [a]Judg 7:12
6 [a]Josh 10:8 [b]2 Sam 8:4
8 [1]Lit *smote* [a]Josh 13:6 [b]Josh 11:3
9 [a]Josh 11:6
10 [a]Josh 11:1
11 [1]Or *putting them under the ban,* and so throughout the ch [a]Deut 20:16
12 [a]Num 33:50-52; Deut 7:2; 20:16f
14 [a]Num 31:11, 12
16 [1]I.e. South country [a]Josh 10:40,41 [b]Josh 11:2
17 [a]Josh 12:7

ward Seir, even as far as Baal-gad in the valley of Lebanon [1]at the foot of Mount Hermon. And he captured [b]all their kings and struck them down and put them to death.

18 Joshua waged war a long time with all these kings.

19 There was not a city which made peace with the sons of Israel except [a]the Hivites living in Gibeon; they took them all in battle.

20 [a]For it was of the LORD to [1]harden their hearts, to meet Israel in battle in order that he might [b]utterly destroy them, that they might [2]receive no mercy, but that he might destroy them, just as the LORD had commanded Moses.

21 ¶ Then Joshua came at that time and cut off [a]the Anakim from the hill country, from Hebron, from Debir, from Anab and from all the hill country of Judah and from all the hill country of Israel. Joshua utterly destroyed them with their cities.

22 There were no Anakim left in the land of the sons of Israel; only in Gaza, in [a]Gath, and in [b]Ashdod some remained.

23 So Joshua took the whole land, according to all that the LORD had spoken to Moses, and [a]Joshua gave it for an inheritance to Israel according to their divisions by their tribes. [b]Thus the land had rest from war.

Kings Defeated by Israel

12 Now these are the [a]kings of the land whom the sons of Israel [1]defeated, and whose land they possessed beyond the Jordan toward the sunrise, from the valley of the Arnon as far as Mount Hermon, and all the Arabah to the east:

2 Sihon king of the Amorites, who lived in Heshbon, *and* ruled [a]from Aroer, which is on the edge of the valley of the Arnon, both the middle of the valley and half of Gilead, even as far as the brook Jabbok, the border of the sons of Ammon;

3 and the [a]Arabah as far as the Sea of [1]Chinneroth toward the east, and as far as the sea of the Arabah, *even* the Salt Sea, eastward [2]toward [b]Beth-jeshimoth, and on the south, [3]at the foot of the slopes of Pisgah;

4 and the territory of Og king of Bashan, one of [a]the remnant of Rephaim, who lived at [b]Ashtaroth and at Edrei,

5 and ruled over Mount Hermon and [a]Salecah and all Bashan, as far as [b]the border of the Geshurites and the Maacathites, and half of Gilead, *as far as* the border of Sihon king of Heshbon.

6 Moses the servant of the LORD and the sons of Israel [1]defeated them; and [a]Moses the servant of the LORD gave it to the Reubenites and the Gadites and the half-tribe of Manasseh as a possession.

7 ¶ Now these are the kings of the land whom Joshua and the sons of Israel [1]defeated beyond the Jordan toward the west, from Baal-gad in the valley of Lebanon even as far as [a]Mount Halak, which rises toward Seir; and Joshua gave it to the tribes of Israel as a possession according to their divisions,

8 in [a]the hill country, in the lowland, in the Arabah, on the slopes, and in the wilderness, and in the [1]Negev; the Hittite, the Amorite and the Canaanite, the Perizzite, the Hivite and the Jebusite:

9 the [a]king of Jericho, one; the [b]king of Ai, which is beside Bethel, one;

10 the [a]king of Jerusalem, one; the king of Hebron, one;

11 the king of Jarmuth, one; the king of Lachish, one;

12 the king of Eglon, one; the king of Gezer, one;

13 the king of Debir, one; the king of Geder, one;

14 the king of Hormah, one; the king of [a]Arad, one;

15 the king of Libnah, one; the king of Adullam, one;

16 the king of Makkedah, one; the king of Bethel, one;

17 the king of Tappuah, one; the [a]king of Hepher, one;

18 the king of [a]Aphek, one; the king of Lasharon, one;

19 the king of Madon, one; the king of Hazor, one;

20 the king of Shimron-meron, one; the king of Achshaph, one;

21 the king of Taanach, one; the king of Megiddo, one;

22 the king of [a]Kedesh, one; the king of Jokneam in Carmel, one;

23 the king of Dor in the [1]heights of Dor, one; the king of [a]Goiim in Gilgal, one;

24 the king of Tirzah, one: [a]in all, thirty-one kings.

Canaan Divided among the Tribes

13 Now [a]Joshua was old *and* advanced in years when the LORD said to him, "You are old *and* advanced in years, and very much of the land remains to be possessed.

2 "This is the land that remains: all the regions *of* the Philistines and all *those of* the [a]Geshurites;

3 from the Shihor which is [1]east of Egypt, even as far as the border of Ekron to the north (it is counted as Canaanite); the [a]five lords of the Philistines: the Ga-

---

17 [1]Lit *under* [b]Deut 7:24

19 [a]Josh 9:3,7

20 [1]Lit *make strong* [2]Lit *have* [a]Ex 14:17 [b]Deut 7:16

21 [a]Num 13:33; Deut 9:2

22 [a]1 Sam 17:4; 1 Kin 2:39; 1 Chr 8:13 [b]Josh 15:46f; 1 Sam 5:1; Is 20:1

23 [a]Deut 1:38 [b]Deut 12:9,10; 25:19; Heb 4:8

12:1 [1]Lit *smote* [a]Num 32:33; Deut 3:8-17

2 [a]Deut 2:36

3 [1]I.e. Galilee [2]Lit *the way of* [3]Lit *under* [a]Josh 11:2 [b]Josh 13:20

4 [a]Deut 3:11 [b]Deut 1:4

5 [a]Deut 3:10; Josh 13:11; 1 Chr 5:11 [b]Deut 3:14; 1 Sam 27:8

6 [1]Lit *smote* [a]Num 32:33; Deut 3:12

7 [1]Lit *smote* [a]Josh 11:17

8 [1]I.e. South country [a]Josh 11:16

9 [a]Josh 6:2 [b]Josh 8:29

10 [a]Josh 10:23

14 [a]Num 21:1

17 [a]1 Kin 4:10

18 [a]Josh 13:4; 2 Kin 13:17

22 [a]Josh 19:37; 20:7; 21:32

23 [1]Or *Naphath-dor* [a]Gen 14:1

24 [a]Deut 7:24

13:1 [a]Josh 14:10

2 [a]Josh 13:11; 1 Sam 27:8

3 [1]Lit *on the face of* [a]1 Sam 6:4,16

zite, the Ashdodite, the Ashkelonite, the Gittite, the Ekronite; and the Avvite

4 [1]to the south, all the land of the Canaanite, and Mearah that belongs to the Sidonians, as far as [a]Aphek, to the border of the [b]Amorite;

5 and the land of the [a]Gebalite, and all of Lebanon, toward the [1]east, [b]from Baal-gad below Mount Hermon as far as [2]Lebo-hamath.

6 "All the inhabitants of the hill country from Lebanon as far as [a]Misrephoth-maim, all the Sidonians, I will [1]drive them out from before the sons of Israel; [b]only allot it to Israel for an inheritance as I have commanded you.

7 "Now therefore, apportion this land for an inheritance to the nine tribes and the half-tribe of Manasseh."

8 ¶ With [1]the other half-tribe, the Reubenites and the Gadites received their inheritance which Moses gave them [a]beyond the Jordan to the east, just as Moses the servant of the LORD gave to them;

9 from Aroer, which is on the edge of the valley of the Arnon, with the city which is in the middle of the valley, and all the plain of Medeba, as far as Dibon;

10 and all the cities of Sihon king of the Amorites, who reigned in Heshbon, as far as the border of the sons of Ammon;

11 and [a]Gilead, and the [1]territory of the Geshurites and Maacathites, and all Mount Hermon, and all Bashan as far as Salecah;

12 all the kingdom of [a]Og in Bashan, who reigned in Ashtaroth and in Edrei (he alone was left of the remnant of the Rephaim); for Moses [b]struck them and dispossessed them.

13 But the sons of Israel did not dispossess the Geshurites or the Maacathites; for Geshur and Maacath live among Israel until this day.

14 [a]Only to the tribe of Levi he did not give an inheritance; the offerings by fire to the LORD, the God of Israel, are [1]their inheritance, as He spoke to him.

15 ¶ So Moses gave *an inheritance* to the tribe of the sons of Reuben according to their families.

16 Their [1]territory was [a]from Aroer, which is on the edge of the valley of the Arnon, with the city which is in the middle of the valley and all the plain by Medeba;

17 Heshbon, and all its cities which are on the plain: Dibon and Bamoth-baal and Beth-baal-meon,

18 and [a]Jahaz and Kedemoth and Mephaath,

19 and [a]Kiriathaim and Sibmah and Zereth-shahar on the hill of the valley,

20 and Beth-peor and the slopes of Pisgah and Beth-jeshimoth,

21 even all the cities of the plain and all the kingdom of Sihon king of the Amorites who reigned in Heshbon, whom Moses struck with the chiefs of Midian, [a]Evi and Rekem and Zur and Hur and Reba, the princes of Sihon, who lived in the land.

22 The sons of Israel also killed [a]Balaam the son of Beor, the diviner, with the sword among *the rest of* their slain.

23 The border of the sons of Reuben was the [1]Jordan. This was the inheritance of the sons of Reuben according to their families, the cities and their villages.

24 ¶ Moses also gave *an inheritance* to the tribe of Gad, to the sons of Gad, according to their families.

25 Their territory was [a]Jazer, and all the cities of Gilead, and half the land of the sons of Ammon, as far as Aroer which is before Rabbah;

26 and from Heshbon as far as Ramath-mizpeh and Betonim, and from Mahanaim as far as the border of [1]Debir;

27 and in the valley, Beth-haram and Beth-nimrah and Succoth and Zaphon, the rest of the kingdom of Sihon king of Heshbon, with the Jordan [1]as a border, as far as the *lower* end of the Sea of [2a]Chinnereth beyond the Jordan to the east.

28 This is the inheritance of the sons of Gad according to their families, the cities and their villages.

29 ¶ Moses also gave *an inheritance* to the half-tribe of Manasseh; and it was for the half-tribe of the sons of Manasseh according to their families.

30 Their territory was from Mahanaim, all Bashan, all the kingdom of Og king of Bashan, and all [a]the [1]towns of Jair, which are in Bashan, sixty cities;

31 also half of Gilead, with [a]Ashtaroth and Edrei, the cities of the kingdom of Og in Bashan, *were* for the sons of Machir the son of Manasseh, for half of the sons of Machir according to their families.

32 ¶ These are *the territories* which Moses apportioned for an inheritance in the plains of Moab, beyond the Jordan at Jericho to the east.

33 But [a]to the tribe of Levi, Moses did not give an inheritance; the LORD, the God of Israel, is their inheritance, as He had [1]promised to them.

Caleb's Request

14 Now these are *the territories* which the sons of Israel inherited in the land of Canaan, which [a]Eleazar the priest, and Joshua the son of Nun, and

4 [1]Or *from the Teman* [a]Josh 12:18; 19:30; 1 Sam 4:1; 1 Kin 20:26,30 [b]Ezek 16:3; Amos 2:10

5 [1]Lit *sunrise* [2]Or *the entrance of Hamath* [a]1 Kin 5:18 [b]Josh 12:7

6 [1]Or *dispossess* [a]Josh 11:8 [b]Num 33:54

8 [1]Lit *it, the* [a]Josh 12:1-6

11 [1]Or *border* [a]Gen 37:25; Num 32:29; Josh 13:25; 17:5f

12 [a]Deut 3:11 [b]Num 21:24

14 [1]Lit *his* [a]Deut 18:1,2

16 [1]Or *border* [a]Josh 13:9

18 [a]Num 21:23; Judg 11:20; Is 15:4; Jer 48:34

19 [a]Num 32:37; Jer 48:1,23; Ezek 25:9

21 [a]Num 31:8

22 [a]Num 31:8

23 [1]Lit *Jordan and border*

25 [a]Num 21:32; Josh 21:39; 2 Sam 24:5; 1 Chr 6:81; 26:31; Is 16:8f; Jer 48:32

26 [1]Or *Lidebir*

27 [1]Lit *and border* [2]I.e. Galilee [a]Num 34:11; Deut 3:17

30 [1]Lit *tent villages* [a]Num 32:41

31 [a]Josh 9:10; 12:4; 13:12; Judg 10:6; 1 Sam 7:3f; 12:10; 1 Chr 6:71

33 [1]Lit *spoken to* [a]Deut 18:1f; Josh 13:14

14:1 [a]Num 34:16-29

the heads of the [1]households of the
tribes of the sons of Israel apportioned to
them for an inheritance,
2 by the [a]lot of their inheritance, as
the LORD commanded [1]through Moses,
for the nine tribes and the half-tribe.
3 For [a]Moses had given the inheritance of the two tribes and the half-tribe
beyond the Jordan; but [b]he did not give
an inheritance to the Levites among
them.
4 For the sons of Joseph were two
tribes, [a]Manasseh and Ephraim, and
they did not give a portion to the Levites
in the land, except cities to live in, with
their pasture lands for their livestock and
for their property.
5 Thus the sons of Israel did just [a]as
the LORD had commanded Moses, and
they divided the land.
6 ¶ Then the sons of Judah drew near
to Joshua in Gilgal, and [a]Caleb the son
of Jephunneh the Kenizzite said to him,
"You know the word which the LORD
spoke to Moses the man of God concerning [1]you and me in Kadesh-barnea.
7 "I was forty years old when [a]Moses
the servant of the LORD sent me from
Kadesh-barnea to spy out the land, and I
brought word back to him as *it was* in my
heart.
8 "Nevertheless my brethren who
went up with me made the heart of the
people [1]melt with fear; but [a]I followed
the LORD my God fully.
9 "So Moses swore on that day, saying,
'Surely [a]the land on which your foot has
trodden will be an inheritance to you and
to your children forever, because you
have followed the LORD my God fully.'
10 "Now behold, the LORD has let me
live, just as He spoke, these forty-five
years, from the time that the LORD spoke
this word to Moses, when Israel walked
in the wilderness; and now behold, I am
eighty-five years old today.
11 "[a]I am still as strong today as I was
in the day Moses sent me; as my strength
was then, so my strength is now, for war
and for [b]going out and coming in.
12 "Now then, give me this hill country
about which the LORD spoke on that day,
for you heard on that day that [a]Anakim
were there, with great fortified cities;
perhaps the LORD will be with me, and I
will [1]drive them out as the LORD has spoken."
13 ¶ So Joshua [a]blessed him and
[b]gave Hebron to Caleb the son of Jephunneh for an inheritance.
14 Therefore, Hebron became the inheritance of Caleb the son of Jephunneh
the Kenizzite until this day, because he
followed the LORD God of Israel fully.
15 Now the name of Hebron was formerly [1]Kiriath-arba; *for Arba* was the
greatest man among the Anakim. [a]Then
the land had rest from war.

Territory of Judah

15 Now [a]the lot for the tribe of the
sons of Judah according to their
families [1]reached the [b]border of Edom,
southward to the [c]wilderness of Zin at
the extreme south.
2 Their south border was from the
lower end of the Salt Sea, from the bay
that turns to the south.
3 Then it proceeded southward to
the ascent of Akrabbim and continued to
Zin, then went up by the south of Kadesh-
barnea and continued to Hezron, and
went up to Addar and turned about to
Karka.
4 It [a]continued to Azmon and proceeded to the [1b]brook of Egypt, and the
[2]border ended at the sea. This shall be
your south border.
5 The [a]east border *was* the Salt Sea,
as far as the [1]mouth of the Jordan. And
the [b]border of the north side was from
the bay of the sea at the [1]mouth of the
Jordan.
6 Then the border went up to Beth-
hoglah, and continued on the north of
Beth-arabah, and the border went up to
the stone of Bohan the son of Reuben.
7 The border went up to Debir from
[a]the valley of Achor, and turned northward toward Gilgal which is opposite the
ascent of Adummim, which is on the
south of the valley; and the border continued to the waters of En-shemesh and [1]it
ended at En-rogel.
8 Then the border went up the valley
of Ben-hinnom to the slope of the [a]Jebu-
site on the south (that is, Jerusalem); and
the border went up to the top of the
mountain which is before the valley of
Hinnom to the west, which is at the end
of the valley of Rephaim toward the
north.
9 From the top of the mountain the
border curved to the spring of the waters
of Nephtoah and proceeded to the cities
of Mount Ephron, then the border curved
to [a]Baalah (that is, [b]Kiriath-jearim).
10 The border turned about from Baalah westward to Mount Seir, and continued to the slope of Mount Jearim on the
north (that is, Chesalon), and went down
to Beth-shemesh and continued through
[a]Timnah.
11 The border proceeded to the side
of Ekron northward. Then the border
curved to Shikkeron and continued to
Mount Baalah and proceeded to Jabneel,
and the [1]border ended at the sea.

1 [1]Lit *fathers'*
2 [1]Lit *by the hand of* [a]Num 26:55; 33:54; 34:13
3 [a]Num 32:33 [b]Josh 13:14
4 [a]Gen 41:51f; 46:20; 48:1,5; Num 26:28; 2 Chr 30:1
5 [a]Num 35:1f; Josh 21:2
6 [1]Lit *me and concerning you* [a]Num 13:6,30; 14:6,24,30
7 [a]Num 13:1-31
8 [1]Lit *become demoralized* [a]Num 14:24; Deut 1:36
9 [a]Deut 1:36
11 [a]Deut 34:7 [b]Deut 31:2
12 [1]Or *dispossess* [a]Num 13:33
13 [a]Josh 22:6 [b]Judg 1:20; 1 Chr 6:55f
15 [1]I.e. the city of Arba [a]Josh 11:23
15:1 [1]Lit *was to* [a]Num 34:3,4 [b]Num 20:16 [c]Deut 32:51
4 [1]Or *wadi* [2]Lit *goings out of the border were* [a]Num 34:5 [b]Gen 15:18; 1 Kin 8:65
5 [1]Lit *end* [a]Num 34:3,10-12 [b]Josh 18:15-19
7 [1]Lit *the goings out of it were* [a]Josh 7:24
8 [a]Josh 15:63
9 [a]1 Chr 13:6 [b]Judg 18:12
10 [a]Gen 38:13; Judg 14:1
11 [1]Lit *goings out...were*

12 The west border *was* [a]at the Great
Sea, even *its* [1]coastline. This is the border around the sons of Judah according to
their families.
13 ¶ Now [a]he gave to Caleb the son of
Jephunneh a portion [b]among the sons of
Judah, according to the [1]command of the
LORD to Joshua, *namely,* [2]Kiriath-arba,
Arba being the father of Anak (that is,
Hebron).
14 [a]Caleb [1]drove out from there the
three [b]sons of Anak: Sheshai and Ahiman and Talmai, the children of Anak.
15 Then [a]he went up from there
against the inhabitants of Debir; now the
name of Debir formerly was Kiriath-
sepher.
16 And Caleb said, "The one who [1]at-
tacks Kiriath-sepher and captures it, [2]I
will give him Achsah my daughter as a
wife."
17 [a]Othniel the son of Kenaz, the
brother of Caleb, captured it; so he gave
him Achsah his daughter as a wife.
18 [a]It came about that when she came
to him, she persuaded him to ask her
father for a field. So she alighted from the
donkey, and Caleb said to her, "What do
you want?"
19 Then she said, "Give me a blessing;
since you have given me the land of the
[1]Negev, give me also springs of water."
So he gave her the upper springs and the
lower springs.
20 ¶ This is the inheritance of the
tribe of the sons of Judah according to
their families.
21 ¶ Now the cities at the extremity of
the tribe of the sons of Judah toward the
border of Edom in the south were Kabzeel and [a]Eder and Jagur,
22 and Kinah and Dimonah and Ada-
dah,
23 and Kedesh and Hazor and Ithnan,
24 Ziph and Telem and Bealoth,
25 and Hazor-hadattah and Kerioth-
hezron (that is, Hazor),
26 Amam and Shema and Moladah,
27 and Hazar-gaddah and Heshmon
and Beth-pelet,
28 and Hazar-shual and [a]Beersheba
and Biziothiah,
29 Baalah and Iim and Ezem,
30 and Eltolad and Chesil and Hormah,
31 and [a]Ziklag and Madmannah and
Sansannah,
32 and Lebaoth and Shilhim and Ain
and Rimmon; in all, twenty-nine cities
with their villages.
33 ¶ In the lowland: [a]Eshtaol and Zorah and Ashnah,
34 and Zanoah and En-gannim, Tappuah and Enam,
35 Jarmuth and [a]Adullam, Socoh and
Azekah,
36 and Shaaraim and Adithaim and
Gederah and Gederothaim; fourteen cities with their villages.
37 ¶ Zenan and Hadashah and Migdal-
gad,
38 and Dilean and Mizpeh and Joktheel,
39 [a]Lachish and Bozkath and Eglon,
40 and Cabbon and Lahmas and Chit-
lish,
41 and Gederoth, Beth-dagon and Naamah and Makkedah; sixteen cities with
their villages.
42 ¶ Libnah and Ether and Ashan,
43 and Iphtah and Ashnah and Nezib,
44 and Keilah and Achzib and Mareshah; nine cities with their villages.
45 ¶ Ekron, with its towns and its villages;
46 from Ekron even to the sea, all that
were by the [1]side of Ashdod, with their
villages.
47 ¶ Ashdod, its towns and its villages;
Gaza, its towns and its villages; as far as
[a]the [1]brook of Egypt and the Great Sea,
even *its* [2]coastline.
48 ¶ In the hill country: Shamir and
Jattir and Socoh,
49 and Dannah and Kiriath-sannah
(that is, Debir),
50 and Anab and Eshtemoh and Anim,
51 and Goshen and Holon and Giloh;
eleven cities with their villages.
52 ¶ Arab and Dumah and Eshan,
53 and Janum and Beth-tappuah and
Aphekah,
54 and Humtah and Kiriath-arba (that
is, Hebron), and Zior; nine cities with
their villages.
55 ¶ Maon, Carmel and Ziph and Juttah,
56 and Jezreel and Jokdeam and Zanoah,
57 Kain, Gibeah and Timnah; ten cities with their villages.
58 ¶ Halhul, Beth-zur and Gedor,
59 and Maarath and Beth-anoth and
Eltekon; six cities with their villages.
60 ¶ Kiriath-baal (that is, Kiriath-
jearim), and Rabbah; two cities with their
villages.
61 ¶ In the wilderness: Beth-arabah,
Middin and Secacah,
62 and Nibshan and the City of Salt
and Engedi; six cities with their villages.
63 ¶ Now as for the [a]Jebusites, the inhabitants of Jerusalem, the sons of Judah
could not [1]drive them out; so the Jebusites live with the sons of Judah at Jerusalem until this day.

12 [1]Lit *border* [a]Num 34:6
13 [1]Lit *mouth* [2]I.e. the city of Arba [a]Josh 14:13-15 [b]Num 13:6
14 [1]Or *dispossessed* [a]Josh 11:21,22 [b]Num 13:33; Deut 9:2
15 [a]Josh 10:38
16 [1]Lit *smites* [2]Lit *and I*
17 [a]Judg 1:13; 3:9
18 [a]Judg 1:14
19 [1]I.e. South country
21 [a]Gen 35:21
28 [a]Gen 21:31
31 [a]1 Sam 27:6; 30:1
33 [a]Judg 13:25; 16:31
35 [a]1 Sam 22:1
39 [a]Josh 10:3; 2 Kin 14:19
46 [1]Lit *hand*
47 [1]Or *wadi* [2]Lit *border* [a]Josh 15:4
63 [1]Or *dispossess them* [a]Judg 1:21; 2 Sam 5:6; 1 Chr 11:4

Territory of Ephraim

16 Then the lot for the sons of Joseph went from the Jordan at Jericho to the waters of Jericho on the east into [a]the wilderness, going up from Jericho through the hill country to Bethel.

2 It went from Bethel to Luz, and [a]continued to the border of the Archites at Ataroth.

3 It went down westward to the territory of the Japhletites, as far as the territory of lower [a]Beth-horon even to [b]Gezer, and [1]it ended at the sea.

4 ¶ The [a]sons of Joseph, Manasseh and Ephraim, received their inheritance.

5 Now *this* was the territory of the sons of Ephraim according to their families: the border of their inheritance eastward was [a]Ataroth-addar, as far as upper Beth-horon.

6 Then the border went westward at [a]Michmethath on the north, and the border turned about eastward to Taanath-shiloh and continued *beyond* it to the east of Janoah.

7 It went down from Janoah to Ataroth and to [a]Naarah, then reached Jericho and came out at the Jordan.

8 From [a]Tappuah the border continued westward to the [1]brook of Kanah, and [2]it ended at the sea. This is the inheritance of the tribe of the sons of Ephraim according to their families,

9 *together* with the cities which were set apart for the sons of Ephraim in the midst of the inheritance of the sons of Manasseh, all the cities with their villages.

10 [a]But they did not [1]drive out the Canaanites who lived in Gezer, so [b]the Canaanites live in the midst of Ephraim to this day, and they became forced laborers.

Territory of Manasseh

17 Now *this* was the lot for the tribe of [a]Manasseh, for he was the firstborn of Joseph. To Machir the firstborn of Manasseh, the father of Gilead, [1]were allotted Gilead and Bashan, because he was a man of war.

2 So *the lot* was *made* for the rest of the sons of Manasseh according to their families: for the sons of Abiezer and for the sons of Helek and for the sons of Asriel and for the sons of Shechem and for the sons of Hepher and for the sons of Shemida; these *were* the male [1]descendants of Manasseh the son of Joseph according to their families.

3 ¶ However, [a]Zelophehad, the son of Hepher, the son of Gilead, the son of Machir, the son of Manasseh, had no sons, only daughters; and these are the names of his daughters: Mahlah and Noah, Hoglah, Milcah and Tirzah.

4 They came near before Eleazar the priest and before Joshua the son of Nun and before the leaders, saying, "The LORD commanded Moses to give us an inheritance among our brothers." So [a]according to the [1]command of the LORD he gave them an inheritance among their father's brothers.

5 Thus there fell ten portions to Manasseh, besides the land of Gilead and Bashan, which is beyond the Jordan,

6 because the daughters of Manasseh received an inheritance among his sons. And the [a]land of Gilead belonged to the rest of the sons of Manasseh.

7 ¶ The border of Manasseh [1]ran from Asher to Michmethath which was east of Shechem; then the border went [2]southward to the inhabitants of En-tappuah.

8 The land of Tappuah belonged to Manasseh, but [a]Tappuah on the border of Manasseh *belonged* to the sons of Ephraim.

9 The [a]border went down to the [1]brook of Kanah, southward of the [1]brook (these cities *belonged* to Ephraim among the cities of Manasseh), and the border of Manasseh *was* on the north side of the [1]brook and [2]it ended at the sea.

10 The south side *belonged* to Ephraim and the north side to Manasseh, and the sea was [1]their border; and they reached to Asher on the north and to Issachar on the east.

11 In Issachar and in Asher, [a]Manasseh had Beth-shean and its towns and Ibleam and its towns, and the inhabitants of Dor and its towns, and the inhabitants of En-dor and its towns, and the inhabitants of Taanach and its towns, and the inhabitants of Megiddo and its towns, the third is [b]Napheth.

12 [a]But the sons of Manasseh could not take possession of these cities, because the Canaanites persisted in living in that land.

13 It came about when the sons of Israel became strong, [a]they put the Canaanites to forced labor, but they did not [1]drive them out completely.

14 ¶ Then the [a]sons of Joseph spoke to Joshua, saying, "Why have you given me only one lot and one portion for an inheritance, since I am a numerous people whom the LORD has thus far blessed?"

15 Joshua said to them, "If you are a numerous people, go [1]up to the forest and [2]clear a place for yourself there in the land of the Perizzites and of the Reph-

16:1 [a]Josh 8:15; 18:12
2 [a]Josh 18:13
3 [1]Lit *the goings out of it were* [a]Josh 18:13; 1 Kin 9:17 [b]Josh 10:33
4 [a]Josh 17:14
5 [a]Josh 18:13
6 [a]Josh 17:7
7 [a]1 Chr 7:28
8 [1]Or *wadi* [2]Lit *the goings out of it were* [a]Josh 17:8
10 [1]Or *dispossess* [a]Judg 1:29; 1 Kin 9:16 [b]Josh 17:12,13
17:1 [1]Lit *and there was to him* [a]Gen 41:51; 46:20; 48:17f
2 [1]Lit *sons*
3 [a]Num 26:33; 27:1-7
4 [1]Lit *mouth* [a]Num 27:5-7
6 [a]Josh 13:30,31
7 [1]Lit *was* [2]Lit *to the right hand*
8 [a]Josh 16:8
9 [1]Or *wadi* [2]Lit *goings out of it were* [a]Josh 16:8f
10 [1]Lit *its*
11 [a]1 Chr 7:29 [b]Josh 11:2; 12:23
12 [a]Judg 1:27
13 [1]Or *dispossess* [a]Josh 16:10
14 [a]Num 13:7
15 [1]Lit *up for yourself* [2]Lit *cut down*

aim, since the hill country of Ephraim is too narrow for you."

16 The sons of Joseph said, "The hill country is not enough for us, and all the Canaanites who live in the valley land have [a]chariots of iron, both those who are in Beth-shean and its towns and those who are in the valley of Jezreel."

17 Joshua spoke to the house of Joseph, to Ephraim and Manasseh, saying, "You are a numerous people and have great power; you shall not have one lot *only,*

18 but the hill country shall be yours. For though it is a forest, you shall [1]clear it, and to its [2]farthest borders it shall be yours; for you shall [3]drive out the Canaanites, even though they have [a]chariots of iron *and* though they are strong."

Rest of the Land Divided

18 Then the whole congregation of the sons of Israel assembled themselves at [a]Shiloh, and set up the tent of meeting there; and the land was subdued before them.

2 ¶ There remained among the sons of Israel seven tribes who had not divided their inheritance.

3 So Joshua said to the sons of Israel, "[a]How long will you put off entering to take possession of the land which the LORD, the God of your fathers, has given you?

4 "Provide for yourselves three men from [1]each tribe that I may send them, and that they may arise and walk through the land and write a description of it according to their inheritance; then they shall [2]return to me.

5 "They shall divide it into seven portions; [a]Judah shall stay in its territory on the south, and the house of Joseph shall stay in their territory on the north.

6 "You shall describe the land in seven divisions, and bring *the description* here to me. [a]I will cast lots for you here before the LORD our God.

7 "For [a]the Levites have no portion among you, because the priesthood of the LORD is [1]their inheritance. Gad and Reuben and the half-tribe of Manasseh also have received their inheritance eastward beyond the Jordan, which Moses the servant of the LORD gave them."

8 ¶ Then the men arose and went, and Joshua commanded those who went to describe the land, saying, "Go and walk through the land and describe it, and return to me; then I will cast lots for you here before the LORD in [a]Shiloh."

9 So the men went and passed through the land, and described it by cities in seven divisions in a book; and they came to Joshua to the camp at Shiloh.

10 And [a]Joshua cast lots for them in Shiloh before the LORD, and there Joshua divided the land to the sons of Israel according to their divisions.

The Territory of Benjamin

11 ¶ Now the lot of the tribe of the sons of Benjamin came up according to their families, and the territory of their lot [1]lay between the sons of Judah and the sons of Joseph.

12 [a]Their border on the north side was from the Jordan, then the border went up to the side of Jericho on the north, and went up through the hill country westward, and [1]it ended at the wilderness of Beth-aven.

13 From there the border continued to [a]Luz, to the side of Luz (that is, Bethel) southward; and the border went down to Ataroth-addar, near the hill which *lies* on the south of [b]lower Beth-horon.

14 The border extended *from there* and turned round on the west side southward, from the hill which *lies* before Beth-horon southward; and [1]it ended at Kiriath-baal (that is, Kiriath-jearim), a city of the sons of Judah. This *was* the west side.

15 Then the [a]south side *was* from the edge of Kiriath-jearim, and the border went westward and went to the fountain of the waters of Nephtoah.

16 The border went down to the edge of the hill which is in the [a]valley of Ben-hinnom, which is in the valley of Rephaim northward; and it went down to the valley of Hinnom, to the slope of the Jebusite southward, and went down to En-rogel.

17 It extended northward and went to En-shemesh and went to Geliloth, which is opposite the ascent of Adummim, and it went down to the [a]stone of Bohan the son of Reuben.

18 It continued to the side in front of the Arabah northward and went down to the Arabah.

19 The border continued to the side of Beth-hoglah northward; and the [1]border ended at the north bay of the Salt Sea, at the south end of the Jordan. This *was* the south border.

20 Moreover, the Jordan was its border on the east side. This *was* the inheritance of the sons of Benjamin, according to their families *and* according to its borders all around.

21 ¶ Now the cities of the tribe of the sons of Benjamin according to their families were Jericho and Beth-hoglah and Emek-keziz,

16 [a]Josh 17:18; Judg 1:19; 4:3, 13
18 [1]Lit *cut it down* [2]Lit *goings out* [3]Or *dispossess* [a]Josh 17:16
18:1 [a]Judg 21:19; Jer 7:12; 26:6,9
3 [a]Judg 18:9
4 [1]Lit *the* [2]Lit *come*
5 [a]Josh 15:1
6 [a]Josh 14:2
7 [1]Lit *his* [a]Num 18:7,20; Josh 13:33
8 [a]Josh 18:1
10 [a]Num 34:16-29; Josh 19:51
11 [1]Lit *went out*
12 [1]Lit *the goings out of it were* [a]Josh 16:1
13 [a]Gen 28:19; Judg 1:23 [b]Josh 16:3
14 [1]Lit *the goings out of it were*
15 [a]Josh 15:5-9
16 [a]2 Kin 23:10
17 [a]Josh 15:6
19 [1]Lit *goings out of the border were*

22 and Beth-arabah and Zemaraim and
Bethel,
23 and Avvim and Parah and Ophrah,
24 and Chephar-ammoni and Ophni
and [a]Geba; twelve cities with their villages.
25 Gibeon and Ramah and Beeroth,
26 and Mizpeh and Chephirah and
Mozah,
27 and Rekem and Irpeel and Taralah,
28 and [a]Zelah, Haeleph and the Jebusite (that is, Jerusalem), Gibeah, Kiriath;
fourteen cities with their villages. This is
the inheritance of the [b]sons of Benjamin
according to their families.

Territory of Simeon

19 Then the second lot [1]fell to Simeon, to the tribe of the sons of Simeon according to their families, and their
inheritance was in the midst of the inheritance of the sons of Judah.
2 So they had as their inheritance Beersheba or [1]Sheba and Moladah,
3 and Hazar-shual and Balah and
Ezem,
4 and Eltolad and Bethul and Hormah,
5 and Ziklag and Beth-marcaboth and
Hazar-susah,
6 and Beth-lebaoth and Sharuhen;
thirteen cities with their villages;
7 Ain, Rimmon and Ether and Ashan;
four cities with their villages;
8 and all the villages which *were*
around these cities as far as Baalath-beer,
Ramah of the [1]Negev. This *was* the inheritance of the tribe of the sons of Simeon according to their families.
9 The inheritance of the sons of Simeon *was taken* from the portion of the
sons of Judah, for the share of the sons of
Judah was too large for them; so the sons
of Simeon received *an* inheritance in the
midst of [1]Judah's inheritance.

Territory of Zebulun

10 ¶ Now the third lot came up for the
sons of Zebulun according to their families. And the territory of their inheritance
was as far as Sarid.
11 Then their border went up to the
west and to Maralah, it then [1]touched
Dabbesheth and reached to the [2]brook
that is before Jokneam.
12 Then it turned from Sarid to the
east toward the sunrise as far as the border of Chisloth-tabor, and it proceeded to
Daberath and [1]up to Japhia.
13 From there it continued eastward
toward the sunrise to Gath-hepher, to
Eth-kazin, and it proceeded to Rimmon
[1]which stretches to Neah.
14 The border circled around it on the

24 [a]Ezra 2:26; Is 10:29
28 [a]2 Sam 21:14 [b]Num 26:38
19:1 [1]Lit *came out*
2 [1]In Josh 15:26, *Shema*
8 [1]I.e. South country
9 [1]Lit *their*
11 [1]Or *reached to* [2]Or *wadi*
12 [1]Lit *went up*
13 [1]Or *and is marked off*
14 [1]Lit *the goings out of it were*
17 [1]Lit *came out*
18 [a]1 Sam 28:4; 2 Kin 4:8
22 [1]Lit *the goings out of their border were* [a]Judg 4:6; Ps 89:12
24 [1]Lit *came out*
27 [1]Lit *sunrise* [2]Lit *from the left hand* [a]1 Kin 9:13
28 [a]Gen 10:19; Judg 1:31; Acts 27:3
29 [1]Lit *the goings out of it were* [a]Judg 1:31
32 [1]Lit *came out*

north to Hannathon, and [1]it ended at the
valley of Iphtahel.
15 *Included* also *were* Kattah and Nahalal and Shimron and Idalah and Bethlehem; twelve cities with their villages.
16 This *was* the inheritance of the
sons of Zebulun according to their families, these cities with their villages.

Territory of Issachar

17 ¶ The fourth lot [1]fell to Issachar, to
the sons of Issachar according to their
families.
18 Their territory was to Jezreel and
included Chesulloth and [a]Shunem,
19 and Hapharaim and Shion and Ana-
harath,
20 and Rabbith and Kishion and Ebez,
21 and Remeth and En-gannim and
En-haddah and Beth-pazzez.
22 The border reached to [a]Tabor and
Shahazumah and Beth-shemesh, and
[1]their border ended at the Jordan; sixteen cities with their villages.
23 This *was* the inheritance of the
tribe of the sons of Issachar according to
their families, the cities with their villages.

Territory of Asher

24 ¶ Now the fifth lot [1]fell to the tribe
of the sons of Asher according to their
families.
25 Their territory was Helkath and
Hali and Beten and Achshaph,
26 and Allammelech and Amad and
Mishal; and it reached to Carmel on the
west and to Shihor-libnath.
27 It turned toward the [1]east to Beth-
dagon and reached to Zebulun, and to the
valley of Iphtahel northward to Beth-
emek and Neiel; then it proceeded on
[2]north to [a]Cabul,
28 and Ebron and Rehob and Hammon
and Kanah, as far as Great [a]Sidon.
29 The border turned to Ramah and to
the fortified city of Tyre; then the border
turned to Hosah, and [1]it ended at the sea
by the region of [a]Achzib.
30 *Included* also *were* Ummah, and
Aphek and Rehob; twenty-two cities with
their villages.
31 This *was* the inheritance of the
tribe of the sons of Asher according to
their families, these cities with their villages.

Territory of Naphtali

32 ¶ The sixth lot [1]fell to the sons of
Naphtali; to the sons of Naphtali according to their families.
33 Their border was from Heleph,
from the oak in Zaanannim and Adami-

nekeb and Jabneel, as far as Lakkum, and
[1]it ended at the Jordan.
34 Then the border turned westward
to Aznoth-tabor and proceeded from
there to Hukkok; and it reached to Zebulun on the south and [1]touched Asher on
the west, and to Judah at the Jordan toward the [2]east.
35 The fortified cities *were* Ziddim,
Zer and [a]Hammath, Rakkath and [b]Chin-
nereth,
36 and Adamah and Ramah and Hazor,
37 and Kedesh and Edrei and En-
hazor,
38 and Yiron and Migdal-el, Horem
and Beth-anath and Beth-shemesh; nineteen cities with their villages.
39 This *was* the inheritance of the
tribe of the sons of Naphtali according to
their families, the cities with their villages.

Territory of Dan

40 ¶ The seventh lot [1]fell to the tribe
of the sons of Dan according to their families.
41 The territory of their inheritance
was Zorah and Eshtaol and Ir-shemesh,
42 and Shaalabbin and Aijalon and Ith-
lah,
43 and Elon and Timnah and Ekron,
44 and Eltekeh and Gibbethon and Baalath,
45 and Jehud and Bene-berak and
Gath-rimmon,
46 and Me-jarkon and Rakkon, with
the territory over against [1]Joppa.
47 The territory of the [a]sons of Dan
proceeded [1]beyond them; for the sons of
Dan went up and fought with Leshem
and captured it. Then they struck it with
the edge of the sword and possessed it
and [2]settled in it; and they called [3b]Le-
shem Dan after the name of Dan their
father.
48 This *was* the inheritance of the
tribe of the sons of Dan according to their
families, these cities with their villages.
49 ¶ When they finished apportioning
the land for inheritance by its borders,
the sons of Israel gave an inheritance in
their midst to Joshua the son of Nun.
50 In accordance with the [1]command
of the LORD they gave him the city for
which he asked, [a]Timnath-serah in the
hill country of Ephraim. So he built the
city and [2]settled in it.
51 ¶ [a]These are the inheritances
which Eleazar the priest, and Joshua the
son of Nun, and the heads of the [1]house-
holds of the tribes of the sons of Israel
distributed by lot in Shiloh before the
LORD at the doorway of the tent of meeting. So they finished dividing the land.

Six Cities of Refuge

20 Then the LORD spoke to Joshua,
saying,
2 "Speak to the sons of Israel, saying,
'[1]Designate [a]the cities of refuge, of
which I spoke to you [2]through Moses,
3 that the manslayer who [1]kills any
person unintentionally, without premedi-
tation, may flee there, and they shall become your refuge from the avenger of
blood.
4 'He shall flee to one of these cities,
and shall stand at the entrance of the
[a]gate of the city and state his case in the
hearing of the elders of that city; and they
shall [1]take him into the city to them and
give him a place, so that he may dwell
among them.
5 'Now [a]if the avenger of blood pursues him, then they shall not deliver the
manslayer into his hand, because he
struck his neighbor without premedita-
tion and did not hate him beforehand.
6 'He shall dwell in that city [a]until he
stands before the congregation for judgment, until the death of the one who is
high priest in those days. Then the manslayer shall [1]return to his own city and to
his own house, to the city from which he
fled.' "
7 ¶ So they [1]set apart [a]Kedesh in
[2]Galilee in the hill country of Naphtali
and Shechem in the hill country of Ephraim, and Kiriath-arba (that is, Hebron) in
[b]the hill country of Judah.
8 Beyond the Jordan east of Jericho,
they [1]designated Bezer in the wilderness
on the plain from the tribe of Reuben,
and Ramoth in Gilead from the tribe of
Gad, and Golan in Bashan from the tribe
of Manasseh.
9 [a]These were the appointed cities
for all the sons of Israel and for the stranger who sojourns among them, that whoever [1]kills any person unintentionally
may flee there, and not die by the hand
of the avenger of blood until he stands
before the congregation.

Forty-eight Cities of the Levites

21 Then the heads of [1]households of
[a]the Levites approached Eleazar
the priest, and Joshua the son of Nun, and
the heads of [1]households of the tribes of
the sons of Israel.
2 They spoke to them at Shiloh in the
land of Canaan, saying, "[a]The LORD commanded [1]through Moses to give us cities
to live in, with their pasture lands for our
cattle."
3 So the sons of Israel gave the Levites from their inheritance these cities

33 [1]Lit *the goings out of it were*
34 [1]Or *reached to* [2]Lit *sunrise*
35 [a]Gen 10:18; 1 Kin 8:65 [b]Deut 3:17
40 [1]Lit *came out*
46 [1]Heb *Japho*
47 [1]Lit *from* [2]Lit *dwelt* [3]I.e. Laish [a]Judg 18:1 [b]Judg 18:29
50 [1]Lit *mouth* [2]Lit *dwelt* [a]Num 13:8; Josh 24:30
51 [1]Lit *fathers* [a]Josh 18:10
20:2 [1]Lit *Set for yourselves* [2]Lit *by the hand of* [a]Num 35:6-34; Deut 4:41-43; 19:2ff
3 [1]Lit *smites*
4 [1]Lit *gather* [a]Ruth 4:1; Job 5:4; Jer 38:7
5 [a]Num 35:12
6 [1]Lit *return and come* [a]Num 35:12
7 [1]Lit *sanctified* [2]Heb *Galil* [a]Josh 21:32; 1 Chr 6:76 [b]Josh 21:11; Luke 1:39
8 [1]Lit *set*
9 [1]Lit *smites* [a]Num 35:13ff
21:1 [1]Lit *fathers* [a]Num 35:1-8
2 [1]Lit *by the hand of* [a]Num 35:2

with their pasture lands, according to the
[1]command of the LORD.
4 Then the lot came out for the families of the Kohathites. And the sons of
Aaron the priest, who were of the Levites, [1]received thirteen cities by lot
from the tribe of Judah and from the tribe
of the Simeonites and from the tribe of
Benjamin.
5 ¶ The rest of the sons of Kohath
[1]received ten cities by lot from the families of the tribe of Ephraim and from the
tribe of Dan and from the half-tribe of
Manasseh.
6 ¶ The sons of Gershon [1]received
thirteen cities by lot from the families of
the tribe of Issachar and from the tribe of
Asher and from the tribe of Naphtali and
from the half-tribe of Manasseh in Bashan.
7 ¶ The sons of Merari according to
their families [1]received twelve cities
from the tribe of Reuben and from the
tribe of Gad and from the tribe of Zebulun.
8 ¶ Now the [a]sons of Israel gave by
lot to the Levites these cities with their
pasture lands, as the LORD had commanded [1]through Moses.
9 ¶ They gave these cities which are
here mentioned by name from the tribe
of the sons of Judah and from the tribe of
the sons of Simeon;
10 and they were for the sons of Aaron, one of the families of the Kohathites,
of the sons of Levi, for the lot was theirs
first.
11 Thus [a]they gave them Kiriath-
arba, *Arba being* the [b]father of Anak (that
is, Hebron), in the hill country of Judah,
with its surrounding pasture lands.
12 But the fields of the city and its villages they gave to Caleb the son of Jephunneh as his possession.
13 ¶ So [a]to the sons of Aaron the
priest they gave [b]Hebron, the city of refuge for the manslayer, with its pasture
lands, and [c]Libnah with its pasture
lands,
14 and [a]Jattir with its pasture lands
and [b]Eshtemoa with its pasture lands,
15 and [1]Holon with its pasture lands
and [a]Debir with its pasture lands,
16 and [1]Ain with its pasture lands and
[a]Juttah with its pasture lands *and* [b]Beth-
shemesh with its pasture lands; nine cities from these two tribes.
17 From the tribe of Benjamin, [a]Gibe-
on with its pasture lands, [b]Geba with its
pasture lands,
18 Anathoth with its pasture lands and
[1]Almon with its pasture lands; four cities.
19 All the cities of the sons of Aaron,
the priests, were thirteen cities with
their pasture lands.
20 ¶ Then the cities from the tribe of
Ephraim were allotted to the [a]families of
the sons of Kohath, the Levites, *even to*
the rest of the sons of Kohath.
21 They gave them [a]Shechem, the
city of refuge for the manslayer, with
its pasture lands, in the hill country of
Ephraim, and Gezer with its pasture
lands,
22 and Kibzaim with its pasture lands
and Beth-horon with its pasture lands;
four cities.
23 From the tribe of Dan, Elteke with
its pasture lands, Gibbethon with its pasture lands,
24 Aijalon with its pasture lands,
Gath-rimmon with its pasture lands; four
cities.
25 From the half-tribe of Manasseh,
they allotted Taanach with its pasture
lands and Gath-rimmon with its pasture
lands; two cities.
26 All the cities with their pasture
lands for the families of the rest of the
sons of Kohath were ten.
27 ¶ [a]To the sons of Gershon, one of
the families of the Levites, from the half-
tribe of Manasseh, *they gave* Golan in Bashan, the city of refuge for the manslayer,
with its pasture lands, and Be-eshterah
with its pasture lands; two cities.
28 From the tribe of Issachar, *they
gave* Kishion with its pasture lands, Daberath with its pasture lands,
29 Jarmuth with its pasture lands, En-
gannim with its pasture lands; four cities.
30 From the tribe of Asher, *they gave*
Mishal with its pasture lands, Abdon with
its pasture lands,
31 Helkath with its pasture lands and
Rehob with its pasture lands; four cities.
32 From the tribe of Naphtali, *they
gave* [a]Kedesh in Galilee, the city of refuge for the manslayer, with its pasture
lands and Hammoth-dor with its pasture
lands and Kartan with its pasture lands;
three cities.
33 All the cities of the Gershonites according to their families were thirteen
cities with their pasture lands.
34 ¶ To the families of [a]the sons of
Merari, the rest of the Levites, *they gave*
from the tribe of Zebulun, Jokneam with
its pasture lands and Kartah with its pasture lands.
35 Dimnah with its pasture lands, Nahalal with its pasture lands; four cities.
36 From the tribe of Reuben, *they gave*
[a]Bezer with its pasture lands and Jahaz
with its pasture lands,
37 Kedemoth with its pasture lands

3 [1]Lit *mouth*
4 [1]Lit *had*
5 [1]Lit *had*
6 [1]Lit *had*
7 [1]Lit *had*
8 [1]Lit *by the hand of* [a]Gen 49:5ff
11 [a]1 Chr 6:55 [b]Josh 14:15; 15:13
13 [a]1 Chr 6:57 [b]Josh 15:54 [c]Josh 15:42
14 [a]Josh 15:48 [b]Josh 15:50
15 [1]In 1 Chr 6:58, *Hilen* [a]Josh 15:49
16 [1]In 1 Chr 6:59, *Ashan* [a]Josh 15:55 [b]Josh 15:10
17 [a]Josh 18:25 [b]Josh 18:24
18 [1]In 1 Chr 6:60, *Allemeth*
20 [a]1 Chr 6:66
21 [a]Josh 20:7
27 [a]1 Chr 6:71
32 [a]Josh 20:7
34 [a]1 Chr 6:77
36 [a]Deut 4:43; Josh 20:8

and Mephaath with its pasture lands; four
cities.
38 From the tribe of Gad, *they gave*
[a]Ramoth in Gilead, the city of refuge for
the manslayer, with its pasture lands and
[b]Mahanaim with its pasture lands,
39 Heshbon with its pasture lands, Jazer with its pasture lands; four cities in
all.
40 All *these were* the cities of the sons
of Merari according to their families, the
rest of the families of the Levites; and
their lot was twelve cities.
41 ¶ [a]All the cities of the Levites in
the midst of the possession of the sons of
Israel were forty-eight cities with their
pasture lands.
42 These cities each had its surrounding pasture lands; thus *it was* with all
these cities.
43 ¶ [a]So the LORD gave Israel all the
land which He had sworn to give to their
fathers, and [b]they possessed it and lived
in it.
44 And the LORD [a]gave them rest on
every side, according to all that He had
sworn to their fathers, and [b]no one of all
their enemies stood before them; [c]the
LORD gave all their enemies into their
hand.
45 [a]Not [1]one of the good promises
which the LORD had [2]made to the house
of Israel failed; all came to pass.

Tribes beyond Jordan Return

22 [a]Then Joshua summoned the
Reubenites and the Gadites and
the half-tribe of Manasseh,
2 and said to them, "You have kept
all that Moses the servant of the LORD
commanded you, [a]and have listened to
my voice in all that I commanded you.
3 "You have not forsaken your brothers these many days to this day, but have
kept the charge of the commandment of
the LORD your God.
4 "And now [a]the LORD your God has
given rest to your brothers, as He spoke
to them; therefore turn now and go to
your tents, to the land of your possession,
which Moses the servant of the LORD
gave you beyond the Jordan.
5 "Only be very careful to observe the
commandment and the law which Moses
the servant of the LORD commanded you,
to [a]love the LORD your God and walk
in all His ways and keep His commandments and hold fast to Him and serve
Him [b]with all your heart and with all
your soul."
6 So Joshua [a]blessed them and sent
them away, and they went to their tents.
7 ¶ Now [a]to the one half-tribe of Manasseh Moses had given *a possession* in
Bashan, but [b]to the other half Joshua
gave *a possession* among their brothers
westward beyond the Jordan. So when
Joshua sent them away to their tents, he
blessed them,
8 and said to [1]them, "Return to your
tents with great riches and with very
much livestock, with silver, gold, bronze,
iron, and with very many clothes; [a]di-
vide the spoil of your enemies with your
brothers."
9 The sons of Reuben and the sons of
Gad and the half-tribe of Manasseh returned *home* and departed from the sons
of Israel at Shiloh which is in the land of
Canaan, to go to the [a]land of Gilead, to
the land of their possession which they
had possessed, according to the [1]com-
mand of the LORD [2]through Moses.

The Offensive Altar

10 ¶ When they came to the region of
the Jordan which is in the land of Canaan,
the sons of Reuben and the sons of Gad
and the half-tribe of Manasseh built an
altar there by the Jordan, a large altar in
appearance.
11 And the sons of Israel heard *it*
[1]said, "Behold, the sons of Reuben and
the sons of Gad and the half-tribe of Manasseh have [a]built an altar at the [2]fron-
tier of the land of Canaan, in the region
of the Jordan, on the side *belonging to* the
sons of Israel."
12 When the sons of Israel heard *of it,*
the whole congregation of the sons of Israel gathered themselves at [a]Shiloh to go
up against them in war.
13 ¶ Then the sons of Israel sent to the
sons of Reuben and to the sons of Gad and
to the half-tribe of Manasseh, into the
land of Gilead, [a]Phinehas the son of Eleazar the priest,
14 and with him ten chiefs, one chief
for each father's household from each of
the tribes of Israel; and [a]each one of
them *was* the head of his father's household among the [1]thousands of Israel.
15 They came to the sons of Reuben
and to the sons of Gad and to the half-
tribe of Manasseh, to the land of Gilead,
and they spoke with them saying,
16 "Thus says the whole congregation
of the LORD, 'What is this unfaithful act
which you have committed against the
God of Israel, turning away from following the LORD this day, by [a]building yourselves an altar, to rebel against the LORD
this day?
17 'Is not [a]the iniquity of Peor
[1]enough for us, from which we have not
cleansed ourselves to this day, although a
plague came on the congregation of the
LORD,

38 [a]Deut 4:43; 1 Kin 4:13 [b]Gen 32:2; 2 Sam 2:8
41 [a]Num 35:7
43 [a]Deut 34:4 [b]Num 33:53; Deut 11:31; 17:14
44 [a]Josh 1:13; 23:1 [b]Deut 7:24 [c]Ex 23:31
45 [1]Lit *a word from every good word* [2]Lit *spoken* [a]Josh 23:14; 1 Kin 8:56
22:1 [a]Num 32:20-22
2 [a]Josh 1:12-18
4 [a]Num 32:18; Deut 3:20
5 [a]Deut 5:10 [b]Deut 4:29
6 [a]Gen 47:7; Josh 14:13; 2 Sam 6:18; Luke 24:50
7 [a]Num 32:33 [b]Josh 17:1-13
8 [1]Lit *them, saying, "Return* [a]Num 31:27; 1 Sam 30:16
9 [1]Lit *mouth* [2]Lit *by the hand of* [a]Num 32:1, 26,29
11 [1]Lit *saying* [2]Lit *front* [a]Deut 12:5; Josh 22:19
12 [a]Josh 18:1
13 [a]Num 25:7, 11; 31:6
14 [1]Or *families* [a]Num 1:4
16 [a]Josh 22:11
17 [1]Lit *little for us* [a]Num 25:1-9

18 that you must turn away this day from following the LORD? If you rebel against the LORD today, [a]He will be angry with the whole congregation of Israel tomorrow.

19 'If, however, the land of your possession is unclean, then [1]cross into the land of the possession of the LORD, where the LORD'S tabernacle [2]stands, and take possession among us. Only do not rebel against the LORD, or rebel against us by [a]building an altar for yourselves, besides the altar of the LORD our God.

20 'Did not [a]Achan the son of Zerah act unfaithfully in the things under the ban, and wrath fall on all the congregation of Israel? And that man did not perish alone in his iniquity.' "

21 ¶ Then the sons of Reuben and the sons of Gad and the half-tribe of Manasseh answered and spoke to the heads of the [1]families of Israel.

22 "The [a]Mighty One, God, the LORD, the Mighty One, God, the LORD! [b]He knows, and may Israel itself know. If *it was* in rebellion, or if in an unfaithful act against the LORD do not save us this day!

23 "If we have built us an altar to turn away from following the LORD, or if to [a]offer a burnt offering or grain offering on it, or if to offer sacrifices of peace offerings on it, may the LORD Himself require it.

24 "But truly we have done this out of concern, [1]for a reason, saying, 'In time to come your sons may say to our [2]sons, "What have you to do with the LORD, the God of Israel?

25 "For the LORD has made the Jordan a border between us and you, *you* sons of Reuben and sons of Gad; you have no portion in the LORD." So your sons may make our sons stop fearing the LORD.'

26 ¶ "Therefore we said, 'Let us [1]build an altar, not for burnt offering or for sacrifice;

27 rather it shall be [a]a witness between us and you and between our generations after us, that we are to [b]perform the service of the LORD before Him with our burnt offerings, and with our sacrifices and with our peace offerings, so that your sons will not say to our sons in time to come, "You have no portion in the LORD." '

28 "Therefore we said, 'It shall also come about if they say *this* to us or to our generations in time to come, then we shall say, "See the copy of the altar of the LORD which our fathers made, not for burnt offering or for sacrifice; rather it is a witness between us and you." '

29 "Far be it from us that we should rebel against the LORD and turn away from following the LORD this day, by [a]building an altar for burnt offering, for grain offering or for sacrifice, besides the altar of the LORD our God which is before His [1]tabernacle."

30 ¶ So when Phinehas the priest and the leaders of the congregation, even the heads of the [1]families of Israel who *were* with him, heard the words which the sons of Reuben and the sons of Gad and the sons of Manasseh spoke, it pleased them.

31 And Phinehas the son of Eleazar the priest said to the sons of Reuben and to the sons of Gad and to the sons of Manasseh, "Today we know that the [a]LORD is in our midst, because you have not committed this unfaithful act against the LORD; now you have delivered the sons of Israel from the hand of the LORD."

32 ¶ Then Phinehas the son of Eleazar the priest and the leaders returned from the sons of Reuben and from the sons of Gad, from the land of Gilead to the land of Canaan, to the sons of Israel, and brought back word to them.

33 The word pleased the sons of Israel, and the sons of Israel [a]blessed God; and they did not speak of going up against them in war to destroy the land in which the sons of Reuben and the sons of Gad were living.

34 The sons of Reuben and the sons of Gad [a]called the altar *Witness;* "For," *they said,* "it is a witness between us that the LORD is God."

Joshua's Farewell Address

23 Now it came about after many days, when the LORD had given [a]rest to Israel from all their enemies [1]on every side, and Joshua was old, advanced in years,

2 that [a]Joshua called for all Israel, for their elders and their heads and their judges and their officers, and said to them, "I am old, advanced in years.

3 "And you have seen all that the LORD your God has done to all these nations because of you, for [a]the LORD your God is He who has been fighting for you.

4 "See, [a]I have apportioned to you these nations which remain as an inheritance for your tribes, with all the nations which I have cut off, from the Jordan even to the Great Sea toward the setting of the sun.

5 "The LORD your God, He will thrust them out from before you and [1a]drive them from before you; and [b]you will possess their land, just as the LORD your God [2]promised you.

6 "[a]Be very firm, then, to keep and do all that is written in the book of the law

---

18 [a]Num 16:22
19 [1]Lit *cross for yourselves* [2]Lit *abides* [a]Josh 22:11
20 [a]Josh 7:1-26
21 [1]Lit *thousands*
22 [a]Deut 10:17 [b]1 Kin 8:39; Job 10:7; Ps 44:21
23 [a]Deut 12:11
24 [1]Lit *from* [2]Lit *sons, saying*
26 [1]Lit *prepare to build for ourselves*
27 [a]Gen 31:48; Josh 24:27 [b]Deut 12:6,11, 26f
29 [1]Lit *dwelling place* [a]Deut 12:13f
30 [1]Lit *thousands*
31 [a]Ex 25:8; Lev 26:11f; 2 Chr 15:2
33 [a]1 Chr 29:20; Dan 2:19; Luke 2:28
34 [a]Gen 31:47-49
23:1 [1]Lit *from round about* [a]Josh 21:44
2 [a]Josh 24:1
3 [a]Deut 1:30
4 [a]Ex 23:30
5 [1]Or *dispossess* [2]Lit *spoke to* [a]Ex 23:20 [b]Num 33:53
6 [a]Deut 5:32; Josh 1:7

of Moses, so that you may not turn aside
from it to the right hand or to the left,
7 so that you will not [1]associate with
these nations, these which remain
among you, or [a]mention the name of
their gods, or [b]make *anyone* swear *by*
them, or [c]serve them, or bow down to
them.
8 "But you are to cling to the LORD
your God, as you have done to this day.
9 "[a]For the LORD has [1]driven out
great and strong nations from before you;
and as for you, [b]no man has stood before
you to this day.
10 "[a]One of your men puts to flight a
thousand, for the LORD your God is [b]He
who fights for you, just as He [1]promised
you.
11 "So take diligent heed to yourselves
to love the LORD your God.
12 "For if you ever go back and [a]cling
to the rest of these nations, these which
remain among you, and [b]intermarry
with them, so that you [1]associate with
them and they with you,
13 know with certainty that the LORD
your God will not continue to [1]drive
these nations out from before you; but
they will be a [a]snare and a trap to you,
and a whip on your sides and thorns in
your eyes, until you perish from off this
good land which the LORD your God has
given you.
14 ¶ "Now behold, today [a]I am going
the way of all the earth, and you know in
all your hearts and in all your souls that
[b]not one word of all the good words
which the LORD your God spoke concerning you has failed; all have [1]been fulfilled
for you, not [2]one of them has failed.
15 "It shall come about that just as all
the good words which the LORD your God
spoke to you have come upon you, so
[a]the LORD will bring upon you all the
threats, until He has destroyed you from
off this good land which the LORD your
God has given you.
16 "[a]When you transgress the covenant of the LORD your God, which He
commanded you, and go and serve other
gods and bow down to them, then the
anger of the LORD will burn against you,
and you will perish quickly from off the
good land which He has given you."

Joshua Reviews Israel's History

24 Then [a]Joshua gathered all the
tribes of Israel to Shechem, and
called for the elders of Israel and for their
heads and their judges and their officers;
and they presented themselves before
God.
2 Joshua said to all the people, "Thus
says the LORD, the God of Israel, 'From
ancient times your fathers lived beyond
the [1]River, *namely,* [a]Terah, the father of
Abraham and the father of Nahor, and
they served other gods.
3 'Then [a]I took your father Abraham
from beyond the [1]River, and led him
through all the land of Canaan, and [b]mul-
tiplied his [2]descendants and gave him
[c]Isaac.
4 'To Isaac I gave [a]Jacob and Esau,
and [b]to Esau I gave Mount Seir to possess
it; but [c]Jacob and his sons went down to
Egypt.
5 'Then [a]I sent Moses and Aaron, and
I plagued Egypt [1]by what I did in its
midst; and afterward I brought you out.
6 'I brought your fathers out of Egypt,
and [a]you came to the sea; and Egypt
pursued your fathers with chariots and
horsemen to the [1]Red Sea.
7 'But when they cried out to the
LORD, He put darkness between you and
the Egyptians, and brought the sea upon
them and covered them; and your own
eyes saw what I did in Egypt. And [a]you
lived in the wilderness for a long time.
8 'Then [a]I brought you into the land
of the Amorites who lived beyond the
Jordan, and they fought with you; and I
gave them into your hand, and you took
possession of their land when I destroyed
them before you.
9 'Then [a]Balak the son of Zippor,
king of Moab, arose and fought against
Israel, and he sent and summoned Balaam the son of Beor to curse you.
10 'But I [a]was not willing to listen to
Balaam. So he had to bless you, and I
delivered you from his hand.
11 '[a]You crossed the Jordan and came
to Jericho; and the citizens of Jericho
fought against you, *and* [b]the Amorite and
the Perizzite and the Canaanite and the
Hittite and the Girgashite, the Hivite and
the Jebusite. Thus [c]I gave them into your
hand.
12 'Then I [a]sent the hornet before you
and it [1]drove out the two kings of the
Amorites from before you, *but* [b]not by
your sword or your bow.
13 '[a]I gave you a land on which you
had not labored, and cities which you had
not built, and you have lived in them; you
are eating of vineyards and olive groves
which you did not plant.'

"We Will Serve the LORD"

14 ¶ "Now, therefore, [1a]fear the
LORD and serve Him in sincerity and
[2]truth; and put away the gods which
your fathers served beyond the [3]River
and in Egypt, and serve the LORD.
15 "If it is disagreeable in your sight to
serve the LORD, choose for yourselves to-

7 [1]Lit *go among* [a]Ex 23:13; Ps 16:4 [b]Deut 6:13; 10:20 [c]Ex 20:5
9 [1]Or *dispossessed* [a]Ex 23:23,30 [b]Deut 7:24
10 [1]Lit *spoke to* [a]Lev 26:8; Deut 28:7; 32:20 [b]Deut 3:22; Josh 23:3
12 [1]Lit *go among* [a]Ex 34:15,16; Ps 106:34,35 [b]Deut 7:3,4; Ezra 9:2; Neh 13:25
13 [1]Or *dispossess* [a]Ex 23:33; 34:12; Deut 7:16
14 [1]Lit *come* [2]Lit *one word* [a]1 Kin 2:2 [b]Josh 21:45
15 [a]Lev 26:14-33; Deut 28:15
16 [a]Deut 4:25, 26
24:1 [a]Josh 23:2
2 [1]I.e. Euphrates [a]Gen 11:27-32
3 [1]I.e. Euphrates [2]Lit *seed* [a]Gen 12:1; 24:7 [b]Gen 15:5 [c]Gen 21:3
4 [a]Gen 25:25,26 [b]Gen 36:8; Deut 2:5 [c]Gen 46:6,7
5 [1]Lit *according to* [a]Ex 4:14-17
6 [1]Lit *Sea of Reeds* [a]Ex 14:2-31
7 [a]Deut 1:46; 2:14
8 [a]Num 21:21-32
9 [a]Num 22:2-6
10 [a]Deut 23:5
11 [a]Josh 3:14-17 [b]Ex 23:23,28; Deut 7:1 [c]Ex 23:31
12 [1]Lit *drove them out* [a]Ex 23:28; Deut 7:20 [b]Ps 44:3
13 [a]Deut 6:10, 11
14 [1]Or *reverence* [2]Or *faithfulness* [3]I.e. Euphrates [a]Deut 10:12; 18:13; 1 Sam 12:24

day whom you will serve: whether the gods which your fathers served which were beyond the River, or [a]the gods of the Amorites in whose land you are living; but as for me and my house, we will serve the LORD."

16 ¶ The people answered and said, "Far be it from us that we should forsake the LORD to serve other gods;

17 for the LORD our God is He who brought us and our fathers up out of the land of Egypt, from the house of [1]bondage, and who did these great signs in our sight and preserved us through all the way in which we went and among all the peoples through whose midst we passed.

18 "The LORD drove out from before us all the peoples, even the Amorites who lived in the land. We also will serve the LORD, for He is our God."

19 ¶ Then Joshua said to the people, "You will not be able to serve the LORD, [a]for He is a holy God. He is [b]a jealous God; [c]He will not forgive your transgression or your sins.

20 "[a]If you forsake the LORD and serve foreign gods, then He will turn and do you harm and consume you after He has done good to you."

21 The people said to Joshua, "No, but we will serve the LORD."

22 Joshua said to the people, "You are witnesses against yourselves that [a]you have chosen for yourselves the LORD, to serve Him." And they said, "We are witnesses."

23 "Now therefore, put away the foreign gods which are in your midst, and [a]incline your hearts to the LORD, the God of Israel."

24 [a]The people said to Joshua, "We will serve the LORD our God and we will [1]obey His voice."

25 [a]So Joshua made a covenant with the people that day, and made for them a statute and an ordinance in Shechem.

26 And Joshua [a]wrote these words in the book of the law of God; and he took a large stone and set it up there under the oak that was by the sanctuary of the LORD.

27 Joshua said to all the people, "Behold, [a]this stone shall be for a witness against us, for it has heard all the words of the LORD which He spoke [1]to us; thus it shall be for a witness against you, so that you do not deny your God."

28 Then Joshua dismissed the people, each to his inheritance.

Joshua's Death and Burial

29 ¶ It came about after these things that Joshua the son of Nun, the servant of the LORD, died, being one hundred and ten years old.

30 And they buried him in the territory of his inheritance in [a]Timnath-serah, which is in the hill country of Ephraim, on the north of Mount Gaash.

31 ¶ [a]Israel served the LORD all the days of Joshua and all the days of the elders who [1]survived Joshua, and had known all the deeds of the LORD which He had done for Israel.

32 ¶ Now [a]they buried the bones of Joseph, which the sons of Israel brought up from Egypt, at Shechem, in the piece of ground [b]which Jacob had bought from the sons of Hamor the father of Shechem for one hundred [1]pieces of money; and they became the inheritance of Joseph's sons.

33 And Eleazar the son of Aaron died; and they buried him [1]at Gibeah of [a]Phinehas his son, which was given him in the hill country of Ephraim.

---

15 [a]Judg 6:10
17 [1]Lit *bondmen*
19 [a]Lev 19:2; 20:7,26 [b]Ex 20:5; 34:14 [c]Ex 23:21
20 [a]Deut 4:25, 26
22 [a]Ps 119:173
23 [a]1 Kin 8:57, 58; Ps 119:36; 141:4
24 [1]Lit *listen to* [a]Ex 19:8; 24:3, 7; Deut 5:27
25 [a]Ex 24:8
26 [a]Deut 31:24
27 [1]Lit *with* [a]Josh 22:27,34
30 [a]Josh 19:50
31 [1]Lit *prolonged days after* [a]Judg 2:6f
32 [1]Heb *qesitah* [a]Gen 50:24,25; Ex 13:19 [b]Gen 33:19; John 4:5; Acts 7:15f
33 [1]Or *on the hill* [a]Josh 22:13

Judges

Title and Background

The title describes the type of leaders Israel had from the time of the elders who outlived Joshua until the time of the monarchy. Their principal purpose for having these leaders is best expressed in 2:16: "Then the LORD raised up judges who delivered them from the hands of those who plundered them." The book tells of Israel's history for the period between the death of Joshua and the ministry of Samuel.

Author and Date of Writing

According to the tradition, Samuel wrote the book, but actual authorship is uncertain. It is possible that Samuel assembled some of the accounts from the period of the judges and that some of the prophets had a hand in shaping and editing the material (see 1 Chronicles 29:29). The date of composition was undoubtedly sometime after 1000 B.C.

Theme and Message

On the one hand, the book of Judges is an account of frequent apostasy, provoking divine chastening. On the other hand, it tells of urgent appeals to God in times of crisis, moving the Lord to raise up leaders (judges) through whom He throws off foreign oppressors and restores the land to peace. It is a number of accounts of recurring cycles (apostasy, oppression, distress and deliverance). Judges reveals an age when "there was no king in Israel; everyone did what was right in his own eyes" (21:25).

Outline

I. Introduction: Incomplete Conquest and Apostasy (1:1—3:6)
  A. First Episode (1:1—2:5)
  B. Second Episode (2:6—3:6)
II. Oppression by Nations and Deliverance by Judges (3:7—16:31)
III. Epilogue: Religious and Moral Disorder (17:1—21:25)
  A. First Episode (17:1—18:31)
  B. Second Episode (19:1—21:25)

Jerusalem Is Captured

1 Now it came about after the death of
Joshua that the sons of Israel [a]in-
quired of the LORD, saying, "Who shall go
up first for us [b]against the Canaanites, to
fight against them?"
2 The LORD said, "[a]Judah shall go up;
behold, I have given the land into his
hand."
3 Then Judah said to Simeon his
brother, "Come up with me into [1]the
territory allotted me, that we may fight
against the Canaanites; and [2]I in turn
will go with you into [3]the territory allotted you." So Simeon went with him.
4 Judah went up, and [a]the LORD gave
the Canaanites and the Perizzites into
their hands, and they [1]defeated ten thousand men at Bezek.
5 They found Adoni-bezek in Bezek
and fought against him, and they [1]defeat-
ed the Canaanites and the Perizzites.
6 But Adoni-bezek fled; and they pursued him and caught him and cut off his
[1]thumbs and big toes.
7 Adoni-bezek said, "Seventy kings
with their thumbs and their big toes cut
off used to gather up *scraps* under my
table; [a]as I have done, so God has repaid
me." So they brought him to Jerusalem
and he died there.
8 ¶ Then the sons of Judah fought
against [a]Jerusalem and captured it and
struck it with the edge of the sword and
set the city on fire.
9 Afterward the sons of Judah went
down to fight against the Canaanites living in the hill country and in the [1]Negev
and in the lowland.
10 [a]So Judah went against the Canaanites who lived in Hebron (now the
name of Hebron formerly *was* Kiriath-
arba); and they struck Sheshai and Ahiman and Talmai.

1:1 [a]Num 27:21 [b]Judg 1:27; 2:21-23; 3:1-6
2 [a]Gen 49:8
3 [1]Lit *my lot* [2]Lit *I, even I* [3]Lit *your lot*
4 [1]Lit *smote them* [a]Ps 44:2; 78:55
5 [1]Lit *smote*
6 [1]Lit *thumbs of his hands and his feet*
7 [a]Lev 24:19
8 [a]Josh 15:63; Judg 1:21
9 [1]I.e. South country
10 [a]Josh 15:13-19

Capture of Other Cities

11 ¶ Then [a]from there he went
against the inhabitants of Debir (now the
name of Debir formerly *was* Kiriath-
sepher).
12 And Caleb said, "The one who attacks Kiriath-sepher and captures it, I will
even give him my daughter Achsah for a
wife."
13 [a]Othniel the son of Kenaz, Caleb's
younger brother, captured it; so he gave
him his daughter Achsah for a wife.
14 Then [a]it came about when she
came *to him,* that she persuaded him to
ask her father for a field. Then she alighted from [1]her donkey, and Caleb said to
her, "What [2]do you want?"
15 She said to him, "Give me a blessing, since you have given me the land of
the [1]Negev, give me also springs of water." So Caleb gave her the upper springs
and the lower springs.
16 ¶ The [1]descendants of [a]the Kenite, Moses' father-in-law, went up from
the [b]city of palms with the sons of Judah,
to the wilderness of Judah which is in the
south of [c]Arad; and they went and lived
with the people.
17 Then Judah went with Simeon his
brother, and they struck the Canaanites
living in Zephath, and utterly destroyed
it. So the name of the city was called
[a]Hormah.
18 And Judah took [a]Gaza with its territory and Ashkelon with its territory and
Ekron with its territory.
19 Now the LORD was with Judah, and
they took possession of the hill country;
but they could not [1]drive out the inhabitants of the valley because they had [a]iron
chariots.
20 Then they gave Hebron to Caleb,
[a]as Moses had [1]promised; and he drove
out from there [b]the three sons of Anak.
21 [a]But the sons of Benjamin did not
drive out the [b]Jebusites who lived in Jerusalem; so the Jebusites have lived with
the sons of Benjamin in Jerusalem to this
day.
22 ¶ Likewise the house of Joseph
went up against Bethel, and the LORD was
with them.
23 The house of Joseph spied out Bethel ([a]now the name of the city was formerly Luz).
24 The spies saw a man coming out of
the city and they said to him, "Please
show us the entrance to the city and [a]we
will treat you kindly."
25 So he showed them the entrance to
the city, and they struck the city with the
edge of the sword, [a]but they let the man
and all his family go free.

11 [a]Josh 15:15
13 [a]Judg 3:9
14 [1]Lit *the* [2]Lit *for yourself* [a]Josh 15:18
15 [1]I.e. South country
16 [1]Lit *sons* [a]Num 10:29-32; Judg 4:11 [b]Deut 34:3; Judg 3:13 [c]Num 21:1
17 [a]Num 21:3
18 [a]Josh 11:22
19 [1]Or *dispossess* [a]Josh 17:16; Judg 4:3,13
20 [1]Lit *spoken* [a]Josh 14:9 [b]Josh 15:14; Judg 1:10
21 [a]Josh 15:63; Judg 1:8 [b]1 Chr 11:4
23 [a]Gen 28:19
24 [a]Josh 2:12
25 [a]Josh 6:25
26 [1]Lit *it*
27 [a]Josh 17:12 [b]Judg 1:1
29 [a]Josh 16:10
30 [1]Perhaps same as *Nahalal*
34 [1]Lit *pressed*
35 [1]Lit *dwelling* [2]Lit *hand* [3]Lit *was heavy*
36 [a]Josh 15:3
2:1 [a]Judg 6:11; 13:2-21 [b]Judg 2:5 [c]Ex 20:2 [d]Gen 17:7,8; Lev 26:42,44; Deut 7:9
2 [1]Lit *listened to My voice* [a]Ex 23:32; Deut 7:2-5 [b]Ex 34:12, 13
3 [a]Josh 23:13

26 The man went into the land of the
Hittites and built a city and named it Luz
[1]which is its name to this day.

Places Not Conquered

27 ¶ [a]But Manasseh did not take possession of Beth-shean and its villages, or
Taanach and its villages, or the inhabitants of Dor and its villages, or the inhabitants of Ibleam and its villages, or the
inhabitants of Megiddo and its villages; so
[b]the Canaanites persisted in living in
that land.
28 It came about when Israel became
strong, that they put the Canaanites to
forced labor, but they did not drive them
out completely.
29 ¶ [a]Ephraim did not drive out the
Canaanites who were living in Gezer;
so the Canaanites lived in Gezer among
them.
30 ¶ Zebulun did not drive out the inhabitants of Kitron, or the inhabitants of
[1]Nahalol; so the Canaanites lived among
them and became subject to forced labor.
31 ¶ Asher did not drive out the inhabitants of Acco, or the inhabitants of Sidon,
or of Ahlab, or of Achzib, or of Helbah, or
of Aphik, or of Rehob.
32 So the Asherites lived among the
Canaanites, the inhabitants of the land;
for they did not drive them out.
33 ¶ Naphtali did not drive out the inhabitants of Beth-shemesh, or the inhabitants of Beth-anath, but lived among the
Canaanites, the inhabitants of the land;
and the inhabitants of Beth-shemesh and
Beth-anath became forced labor for them.
34 ¶ Then the Amorites [1]forced the
sons of Dan into the hill country, for they
did not allow them to come down to the
valley;
35 yet the Amorites persisted in [1]liv-
ing in Mount Heres, in Aijalon and in
Shaalbim; but when the [2]power of the
house of Joseph [3]grew strong, they became forced labor.
36 The border of the Amorites ran
from the [a]ascent of Akrabbim, from Sela
and upward.

Israel Rebuked

2 Now [a]the angel of the LORD came up
from Gilgal to [b]Bochim. And he said,
"[c]I brought you up out of Egypt and led
you into the land which I have sworn to
your fathers; and I said, '[d]I will never
break My covenant with you,
2 and as for you, [a]you shall make no
covenant with the inhabitants of this
land; [b]you shall tear down their altars.'
But you have not [1]obeyed Me; what is
this you have done?
3 "Therefore I also said, '[a]I will not

drive them out before you; but they will
[1]become [b]*as thorns* in your sides and
their gods will be a snare to you.' "
4 When the angel of the LORD spoke
these words to all the sons of Israel, the
people lifted up their voices and wept.
5 So they named that place [1]Bochim;
and there they sacrificed to the LORD.

Joshua Dies

6 ¶ [a]When Joshua had dismissed the
people, the sons of Israel went each to his
inheritance to possess the land.
7 The people served the LORD all the
days of Joshua, and all the days of the
elders who [1]survived Joshua, who had
seen all the great work of the LORD which
He had done for Israel.
8 Then Joshua the son of Nun, the
servant of the LORD, died at the age of one
hundred and ten.
9 And they buried him in the territory of [a]his inheritance in Timnath-heres,
in the hill country of Ephraim, north of
Mount Gaash.
10 All that generation also were gathered to their fathers; and there arose another generation after them who [a]did
not know the LORD, nor yet the work
which He had done for Israel.

Israel Serves Baals

11 ¶ Then the sons of Israel did [a]evil
in the sight of the LORD and [1]served the
[b]Baals,
12 and [a]they forsook the LORD, the
God of their fathers, who had brought
them out of the land of Egypt, and followed other gods from *among* the gods of
the peoples who were around them, and
bowed themselves down to them; thus
they provoked the LORD to anger.
13 So they forsook the LORD and
[a]served Baal and the Ashtaroth.
14 [a]The anger of the LORD burned
against Israel, and He gave them into
the hands of plunderers who plundered
them; and [b]He sold them into the hands
of their enemies around *them,* so that
they could no longer stand before their
enemies.
15 Wherever they went, the hand of
the LORD was against them for evil, as the
LORD had spoken and [a]as the LORD had
sworn to them, so that they were severely distressed.
16 ¶ [a]Then the LORD raised up judges
[1]who delivered them from the hands of
those who plundered them.
17 Yet they did not listen to their
judges, for they played the harlot after
other gods and bowed themselves down
to them. They turned aside quickly from
the way [a]in which their fathers had
walked in obeying the commandments of
the LORD; they did not do as *their fathers.*
18 When the LORD raised up judges for
them, [a]the LORD was with the judge and
delivered them from the hand of their
enemies all the days of the judge; for the
LORD was [b]moved to pity by their groaning because of those who oppressed and
afflicted them.
19 But it came about when the judge
died, that they would turn back and act
more corruptly than their fathers, in following other gods to serve them and bow
down to them; they did not abandon their
practices or their stubborn ways.
20 [a]So the anger of the LORD burned
against Israel, and He said, "Because this
nation has transgressed My covenant
which I commanded their fathers and has
not listened to My voice,
21 [a]I also will no longer drive out before them any of the nations which Joshua left when he died,
22 in order to [a]test Israel by them,
whether they will keep the way of the
LORD to walk in it as their fathers [1]did, or
not."
23 So the LORD allowed those nations
to remain, not driving them out quickly;
and He did not give them into the hand
of Joshua.

Idolatry Leads to Servitude

3 [a]Now these are the nations which
the LORD left, to test Israel by them
(*that is,* all who had not [1]experienced
any of the wars of Canaan;
2 only in order that the generations
of the sons of Israel might [1]be taught
war, [2]those who had not [3]experienced
it formerly).
3 *These nations are:* the five lords of
the Philistines and all the Canaanites and
the Sidonians and [a]the Hivites who lived
in Mount Lebanon, from Mount Baal-
hermon as far as [1]Lebo-hamath.
4 They were for [1a]testing Israel, to
find out if they would [2]obey the commandments of the LORD, which He had
commanded their fathers [3]through Moses.
5 [a]The sons of Israel lived among the
Canaanites, the Hittites, the Amorites,
the Perizzites, the Hivites, and the Jebusites;
6 and [a]they took their daughters for
themselves as wives, and gave their own
daughters to their sons, and served their
gods.
7 ¶ The sons of Israel did [a]what was
evil in the sight of the LORD, and [b]forgot
the LORD their God and [c]served the Baals
and the [1]Asheroth.
8 Then the anger of the LORD was

3 [1]Some ancient mss read *be adversaries, and* [b]Num 33:55
5 [1]I.e. weepers
6 [a]Josh 24:28-31
7 [1]Lit *prolonged days after*
9 [a]Josh 19:49f
10 [a]Ex 5:2; 1 Sam 2:12
11 [1]Or *worshiped* [a]Judg 3:7, 12; 4:1; 6:1 [b]Judg 6:25; 8:33; 10:6
12 [a]Deut 31:16
13 [a]Judg 10:6
14 [a]Deut 31:17; Ps 106:40-42 [b]Deut 28:25; 32:30
15 [a]Lev 26:14-39; Deut 28:15-68
16 [1]Lit *and they* [a]Ps 106:43-45
17 [a]Judg 2:7
18 [a]Josh 1:5 [b]Deut 32:36; Ps 106:44
20 [a]Judg 2:14
21 [a]Josh 23:4,5, 13
22 [1]Lit *kept* [a]Deut 8:2; 13:3
3:1 [1]Lit *known* [a]Judg 1:1; 2:21, 22
2 [1]Lit *know, to teach them* [2]Lit *only* [3]Lit *known*
3 [1]Or *the entrance of Hamath* [a]Josh 9:7; 11:19
4 [1]Lit *testing by them* [2]Lit *hear* [3]Lit *by the hand of* [a]Deut 8:2
5 [a]Ps 106:35
6 [a]Ex 34:15,16; Deut 7:3,4; Josh 23:12
7 [1]I.e. wooden symbol of a female deity [a]Judg 2:11 [b]Deut 4:9 [c]Judg 2:13

kindled against Israel, so that He sold
them into the hands of Cushan-
rishathaim king of [1]Mesopotamia; and
the sons of Israel served Cushan-
rishathaim eight years.

The First Judge Delivers Israel

9 When the sons of Israel cried to the
LORD, the LORD raised up a deliverer for
the sons of Israel to deliver them, [a]Oth-
niel the son of Kenaz, Caleb's younger
brother.
10 [a]The Spirit of the LORD came upon
him, and he judged Israel. When he went
out to war, the LORD gave Cushan-
rishathaim king of [1]Mesopotamia into
his hand, so that [2]he prevailed over
Cushan-rishathaim.
11 Then the land had rest forty years.
And Othniel the son of Kenaz died.
12 ¶ Now the sons of Israel again [a]did
evil in the sight of the LORD. So [b]the
LORD strengthened Eglon the king of
Moab against Israel, because they had
done evil in the sight of the LORD.
13 And he gathered to himself the
sons of Ammon and Amalek; and he went
and [1]defeated Israel, and they possessed
[a]the city of the palm trees.
14 The sons of Israel served Eglon the
king of Moab eighteen years.

Ehud Delivers from Moab

15 ¶ But when the sons of Israel
[a]cried to the LORD, the LORD raised up a
deliverer for them, Ehud the son of Gera,
the Benjamite, a left-handed man. And
the sons of Israel sent tribute by [1]him to
Eglon the king of Moab.
16 Ehud made himself a sword which
had two edges, a cubit in length, and he
bound it on his right thigh under his
cloak.
17 He presented the tribute to Eglon
king of Moab. Now Eglon was a very fat
man.
18 It came about when he had finished
presenting the tribute, that he sent away
the people who had carried the tribute.
19 But he himself turned back from
the idols which were at Gilgal, and said,
"I have a secret message for you,
O king." And he said, "Keep silence."
And all who attended him left him.
20 Ehud came to him while he was
sitting alone in his cool roof chamber.
And Ehud said, "I have a message from
God for you." And he arose from his seat.
21 Ehud stretched out his left hand,
took the sword from his right thigh and
thrust it into his belly.
22 The handle also went in after the
blade, and the fat closed over the blade,

8 [1]Heb *Aram-naharaim*
9 [a]Judg 1:13
10 [1]Heb *Aram* [2]Lit *his hand was strong* [a]Num 11:25-29; 24:2
12 [a]Judg 2:11 [b]Judg 2:14
13 [1]Lit *smote* [a]Deut 34:3; Judg 1:16
15 [1]Lit *his hand* [a]Ps 78:34
24 [1]Lit *covering his feet* [a]1 Sam 24:3
25 [1]Lit *were ashamed* [2]Lit *earth*
27 [a]Judg 6:34; 1 Sam 13:3
28 [a]Judg 7:24; 12:5
31 [a]Judg 5:6
4:1 [a]Judg 2:19
2 [a]Josh 11:1,10 [b]Judg 4:13,16
3 [a]Judg 1:19
4 [1]Lit *woman prophetess*
5 [1]Or *live* [a]Gen 35:8

for he did not draw the sword out of his
belly; and the refuse came out.
23 Then Ehud went out into the ves-
tibule and shut the doors of the roof
chamber behind him, and locked *them.*
24 ¶ When he had gone out, his servants came and looked, and behold, the
doors of the roof chamber were locked;
and they said, "[a]He is only [1]relieving
himself in the cool room."
25 They waited until they [1]became
anxious; but behold, he did not open the
doors of the roof chamber. Therefore
they took the key and opened them, and
behold, their master had fallen to the
[2]floor dead.
26 ¶ Now Ehud escaped while they
were delaying, and he passed by the idols
and escaped to Seirah.
27 It came about when he had arrived,
that [a]he blew the trumpet in the hill
country of Ephraim; and the sons of Israel
went down with him from the hill country, and he *was* in front of them.
28 He said to them, "Pursue *them,* for
the LORD has given your enemies the Moabites into your hands." So they went
down after him and seized [a]the fords of
the Jordan opposite Moab, and did not
allow anyone to cross.
29 They struck down at that time
about ten thousand Moabites, all robust
and valiant men; and no one escaped.
30 So Moab was subdued that day under the hand of Israel. And the land was
undisturbed for eighty years.

Shamgar Delivers from Philistines

31 ¶ After him came [a]Shamgar the
son of Anath, who struck down six hundred Philistines with an oxgoad; and he
also saved Israel.

Deborah and Barak Deliver from Canaanites

4 Then [a]the sons of Israel again did
evil in the sight of the LORD, after
Ehud died.
2 And the LORD sold them into the
hand of [a]Jabin king of Canaan, who
reigned in Hazor; and the commander
of his army was Sisera, who lived in
[b]Harosheth-hagoyim.
3 The sons of Israel cried to the LORD;
for he had nine hundred [a]iron chariots,
and he oppressed the sons of Israel severely for twenty years.
4 ¶ Now Deborah, a [1]prophetess, the
wife of Lappidoth, was judging Israel at
that time.
5 She used to [1]sit under the [a]palm
tree of Deborah between Ramah and
Bethel in the hill country of Ephraim; and

the sons of Israel came up to her for judgment.
6 Now she sent and summoned [a]Bar-
ak the son of Abinoam from Kedesh-
naphtali, and said to him, "[1]Behold, the
LORD, the God of Israel, has commanded,
'Go and march to Mount Tabor, and take
with you ten thousand men from the sons
of Naphtali and from the sons of Zebulun.
7 'I will draw out to you Sisera, the
commander of Jabin's army, with his
chariots and his [1]many *troops* to the river Kishon, and [a]I will give him into your
hand.' "
8 Then Barak said to her, "If you will
go with me, then I will go; but if you will
not go with me, I will not go."
9 She said, "I will surely go with you;
nevertheless, the honor shall not be
yours on the journey that you are about to
take, [a]for the LORD will sell Sisera into
the hands of a woman." Then Deborah
arose and went with Barak to Kedesh.
10 Barak called [a]Zebulun and Naphtali together to Kedesh, and ten thousand
men went up [1b]with him; Deborah also
went up with him.
11 ¶ Now Heber [a]the Kenite had separated himself from the Kenites, from the
sons of Hobab the father-in-law of Moses,
and had pitched his tent as far away as
the [1]oak in [b]Zaanannim, which is near
Kedesh.
12 ¶ Then they told Sisera that Barak
the son of Abinoam had gone up to
Mount Tabor.
13 Sisera called together all his chariots, [a]nine hundred iron chariots, and all
the people who *were* with him, from
[b]Harosheth-hagoyim to the river Kishon.
14 Deborah said to Barak, "Arise! For
this is the day in which the LORD has
given Sisera into your hands; [1]behold,
[a]the LORD has gone out before you." So
Barak went down from Mount Tabor with
ten thousand men following him.
15 [a]The LORD [1]routed Sisera and all
his chariots and all *his* army with the
edge of the sword before Barak; and Sisera alighted from *his* chariot and fled
away on foot.
16 But Barak pursued the chariots and
the army as far as Harosheth-hagoyim,
and all the army of Sisera fell by the edge
of the sword; [a]not even one was left.
17 ¶ Now Sisera fled away on foot to
the tent of Jael the wife of Heber the
Kenite, for *there was* peace between Jabin the king of Hazor and the house of
Heber the Kenite.
18 Jael went out to meet Sisera, and
said to him, "Turn aside, my master, turn
aside to me! Do not be afraid." And he
turned aside to her into the tent, and she
covered him with a [1]rug.
19 [a]He said to her, "Please give me a
little water to drink, for I am thirsty." So
she opened a [1]bottle of milk and gave
him a drink; then she covered him.
20 He said to her, "Stand in the doorway of the tent, and it shall be if anyone
comes and inquires of you, and says, 'Is
there anyone here?' that you shall
say, 'No.' "
21 But Jael, Heber's wife, [a]took a tent
peg and [1]seized a hammer in her hand,
and went secretly to him and drove the
peg into his temple, and it went through
into the ground; for he was sound asleep
and exhausted. So he died.
22 And behold, as Barak pursued Sisera, Jael came out to meet him and said
to him, "Come, and I will show you the
man whom you are seeking." And he entered [1]with her, and behold Sisera was
lying dead with the tent peg in his temple.
23 ¶ So [a]God subdued on that day Jabin the king of Canaan before the sons of
Israel.
24 The hand of the sons of Israel
pressed heavier and heavier upon Jabin
the king of Canaan, until they had [1]de-
stroyed Jabin the king of Canaan.

The Song of Deborah and Barak

5 [a]Then Deborah and Barak the son of
Abinoam sang on that day, saying,
2 "[a]That [1]the leaders led in Israel,
That [b]the people volunteered,
Bless the LORD!
3 "Hear, O kings; give ear, O rulers!
[a]I—to the LORD, I will sing,
I will sing praise to the LORD,
the God of Israel.
4 "[a]LORD, when You went out from
Seir,
When You marched from the
field of Edom,
[b]The earth quaked, the heavens
also dripped,
Even the clouds dripped water.
5 "[a]The mountains [1]quaked at the
presence of the LORD,
[b]This Sinai, at the presence of
the LORD, the God of Israel.
6 ¶ "In the days of [a]Shamgar the
son of Anath,
In the days of [b]Jael, the
highways [1]were deserted,
And travelers [2]went by
[3]roundabout ways.
7 "The peasantry ceased, they
ceased in Israel,
Until I, Deborah, arose,
Until I arose, a mother in Israel.

6 [1]Or *Has not... commanded...?* [a]Heb 11:32
7 [1]Lit *multitude* [a]Ps 83:9
9 [a]Judg 4:21
10 [1]Lit *at his feet* [a]Judg 5:18 [b]Judg 4:14; 5:15
11 [1]Or *terebinth* [a]Judg 1:16 [b]Josh 19:33
13 [a]Judg 4:3 [b]Judg 4:2
14 [1]Or *has not the LORD gone...?* [a]Deut 9:3; 2 Sam 5:24; Ps 68:7
15 [1]Lit *confused* [a]Deut 7:23; Josh 10:10
16 [a]Ex 14:28; Ps 83:9
18 [1]Or *blanket*
19 [1]I.e. skin container [a]Judg 5:24-27
21 [1]Lit *placed* [a]Judg 5:26
22 [1]Lit *to*
23 [a]Neh 9:24; Ps 18:47
24 [1]Lit *cut off*
5:1 [a]Ex 15:1
2 [1]Or *locks hung loose in* [a]Judg 5:9 [b]Ps 110:3
3 [a]Ps 27:6
4 [a]Deut 33:2; Ps 68:7 [b]Ps 68:8,9
5 [1]Lit *flowed* [a]Ex 19:18 [b]Ps 68:8
6 [1]Lit *had ceased* [2]Lit *walked* [3]Lit *twisted* [a]Judg 3:31 [b]Judg 4:17

8 "[a]New gods were chosen;
Then war *was* in the gates.
Not a shield or a spear was seen
Among forty thousand in Israel.
9 "My heart *goes out* to [a]the
commanders of Israel,
The volunteers among the
people;
Bless the LORD!
10 "[a]You who ride on [1]white
donkeys,
You who sit on *rich* carpets,
And you who travel on the
road—[2]sing!
11 "At the sound of those who divide
flocks among [a]the watering
places,
There they shall recount [b]the
righteous deeds of the LORD,
The righteous deeds for His
[1]peasantry in Israel.
Then the people of the LORD
went down [c]to the gates.

12 ¶ "[a]Awake, awake, Deborah;
Awake, awake, [1]sing a song!
Arise, Barak, and [b]take away
your captives, O son of
Abinoam.
13 "Then survivors came down to
the nobles;
The people of the LORD came
down to me as warriors.
14 "From Ephraim those whose root
is [a]in Amalek *came down,*
Following you, Benjamin, with
your peoples;
From Machir commanders came
down,
And from Zebulun those who
wield the staff of [1]office.
15 "And the [1]princes of Issachar
were with Deborah;
As *was* Issachar, so *was* Barak;
Into the valley they rushed [a]at
his [2]heels;
Among the divisions of Reuben
There were great resolves of
heart.
16 "Why did you sit among [a]the
[1]sheepfolds,
To hear the piping for the flocks?
Among the divisions of Reuben
There were great searchings of
heart.
17 "[a]Gilead [1]remained across the
Jordan;
And why did Dan stay in ships?
Asher sat at the seashore,
And [1]remained by its landings.
18 "[a]Zebulun *was* a people who
despised their lives *even* to
death,
And Naphtali also, on the high
places of the field.

19 ¶ "[a]The kings came *and* fought;
Then fought the kings of Canaan
[b]At Taanach near the waters of
Megiddo;
[c]They took no plunder in silver.
20 "[a]The stars fought from heaven,
From their courses they fought
against Sisera.
21 "The torrent of Kishon swept
them away,
The ancient torrent, the torrent
Kishon.
[a]O my soul, march on with
strength.
22 "[a]Then the horses' hoofs beat
From the dashing, the dashing of
his [1]valiant steeds.
23 'Curse Meroz,' said the angel of
the LORD,
'Utterly curse its inhabitants;
[a]Because they did not come to
the help of the LORD,
To the help of the LORD against
the warriors.'

24 ¶ "[a]Most blessed of women is
Jael,
The wife of Heber the Kenite;
Most blessed is she of women in
the tent.
25 "He asked for water *and* she gave
him milk;
In a magnificent bowl she
brought him curds.
26 "She reached out her hand for the
tent peg,
And her right hand for the
workmen's hammer.
Then she struck Sisera, she
smashed his head;
And she shattered and pierced
his temple.
27 "Between her feet he bowed, he
fell, he lay;
Between her feet he bowed, he
fell;
Where he bowed, there he fell
[1]dead.

28 ¶ "Out of the window she looked
and lamented,
The mother of Sisera through the
[1]lattice,
'Why does his chariot delay in
coming?
Why do the [2]hoofbeats of his
chariots tarry?'
29 "Her wise princesses would
answer her,
Indeed she repeats her words to
herself,

8 [a]Deut 32:17
9 [a]Judg 5:2
10 [1]Or *tawny* [2]Or *declare it* [a]Judg 10:4; 12:14
11 [1]Or *rural dwellers* [a]Gen 24:11; 29:2,3 [b]1 Sam 12:7; Mic 6:5 [c]Judg 5:8
12 [1]Or *utter* [a]Ps 57:8 [b]Ps 68:18; Eph 4:8
14 [1]Lit *the scribe* [a]Judg 12:15
15 [1]So with ancient versions; Heb *My princes* [2]Lit *feet* [a]Judg 4:10
16 [1]Or *saddlebags* [a]Num 32:1, 2,24,36
17 [1]Or *dwelt* [a]Josh 22:9
18 [a]Judg 4:6,10
19 [a]Josh 11:1-5; Judg 4:13 [b]Judg 1:27 [c]Judg 5:30
20 [a]Josh 10:12-14
21 [a]Ex 15:2; Ps 44:5
22 [1]Lit *mighty ones* [a]Job 39:19-25
23 [a]Judg 5:13
24 [a]Judg 4:19-21
27 [1]Lit *devastated*
28 [1]Or *window* [2]Lit *steps*

30 '[a]Are they not finding, are they
not dividing the spoil?
A maiden, two maidens for every
warrior;
To Sisera a spoil of dyed work,
A spoil of dyed work
embroidered,
Dyed work of double embroidery
on the [1]neck of the
spoiler?'
31 "[a]Thus let all Your enemies
perish, O LORD;
[b]But let those who love Him be
like the rising of the sun in
its might."
And the land was undisturbed for forty
years.

Israel Oppressed by Midian

6 Then the sons of Israel [a]did what
was evil in the sight of the LORD; and
the LORD gave them into the hands of
[b]Midian seven years.
2 The [1]power of Midian prevailed
against Israel. Because of Midian the sons
of Israel made for themselves [a]the dens
which were in the mountains and the
caves and the strongholds.
3 For it was when Israel had sown,
that the Midianites would come up with
the Amalekites and the sons of the east
and [1]go against them.
4 So they would camp against them
and [a]destroy the produce of the earth
[1]as far as Gaza, and [b]leave no sustenance in Israel as well as no sheep, ox, or
donkey.
5 For they would come up with their
livestock and their tents, they would
come in [a]like locusts for number, both
they and their camels were innumerable;
and they came into the land to devastate it.
6 So Israel was brought [a]very low because of Midian, and the sons of Israel
cried to the LORD.
7 ¶ Now it came about when the
sons of Israel cried to the LORD on account of Midian,
8 that the LORD sent a prophet to the
sons of Israel, and [a]he said to them,
"Thus says the LORD, the God of Israel, 'It
was I who brought you up from Egypt and
brought you out from the house of [1]slav-
ery.
9 'I delivered you from the hands of
the Egyptians and from the hands of all
your oppressors, and dispossessed them
before you and gave you their land,
10 and I said to you, "I am the LORD
your God; you [a]shall not fear the gods of
the Amorites in whose land you live. But
you have not [1]obeyed Me." ' "

Gideon Is Visited

11 ¶ Then [a]the angel of the LORD
came and sat under the [1]oak that was in
Ophrah, which belonged to Joash the
[b]Abiezrite as his son [c]Gideon was beating out wheat in the wine press in order
to save *it* from the Midianites.
12 The angel of the LORD appeared to
him and said to him, "The LORD is with
you, O valiant warrior."
13 Then Gideon said to him, "O my
lord, if the LORD is with us, why then has
all this happened to us? And where are all
His miracles which our fathers told us
about, saying, 'Did not the LORD bring us
up from Egypt?' But [a]now the LORD has
abandoned us and given us into the hand
of Midian."
14 The LORD [1]looked at him and said,
"[a]Go in this your strength and deliver
Israel from the hand of Midian. Have I
not sent you?"
15 [a]He said to Him, "O Lord, [1]how
shall I deliver Israel? Behold, my family is
the least in [b]Manasseh, and I am the
youngest in my father's house."
16 [a]But the LORD said to him, "Surely
I will be with you, and you shall [1]defeat
Midian as one man."
17 So [1]Gideon said to Him, "If now I
have found favor in Your sight, then show
me [a]a sign that it is You who speak
with me.
18 "Please do not depart from here, until I come *back* to You, and bring out my
offering and lay it before You." And He
said, "I will remain until you return."
19 ¶ Then Gideon went in and [a]pre-
pared a young goat and unleavened bread
from an [1]ephah of flour; he put the meat
in a basket [2]and the broth in a pot, and
brought *them* out to him under the [3]oak
and presented *them*.
20 The angel of God said to him, "Take
the meat and the unleavened bread and
lay them on this rock, and pour out the
broth." And he did so.
21 Then the angel of the LORD put out
the end of the staff that was in his hand
and touched the meat and the unleavened bread; and [a]fire sprang up from the
rock and consumed the meat and the unleavened bread. Then the angel of the
LORD [1]vanished from his sight.
22 [a]When Gideon saw that he was
the angel of the LORD, [1]he said, "Alas,
O Lord [2]GOD! For now I have seen the
angel of the LORD face to face."
23 The LORD said to him, "Peace to
you, do not fear; you shall not die."
24 Then Gideon built an altar there to
the LORD and named it [1]The LORD is

30 [1]Lit *necks of the spoil* [a]Ex 15:9
31 [a]Ps 68:2; 92:9 [b]Ps 19:4-6; 89:36,37
6:1 [a]Judg 2:11 [b]Num 22:4; 25:15-18; 31:1-3
2 [1]Lit *hand* [a]1 Sam 13:6; Heb 11:38
3 [1]Lit *go up*
4 [1]Lit *until your coming to* [a]Lev 26:16 [b]Deut 28:31
5 [a]Judg 7:12; 8:10
6 [a]Deut 28:43
8 [1]Lit *slaves* [a]Judg 2:1,2
10 [1]Lit *listened to My voice* [a]2 Kin 17:35; Jer 10:2
11 [1]Or *terebinth* [a]Judg 2:1; 6:14; 13:3 [b]Josh 17:2; Judg 6:15 [c]Heb 11:32
13 [a]Judg 6:1; Ps 44:9
14 [1]Or *turned toward* [a]Heb 11:32-34
15 [1]Lit *with what* [a]Ex 3:11 [b]Judg 6:11
16 [1]Lit *smite* [a]Ex 3:12; Josh 1:5
17 [1]Lit *he* [a]Judg 6:37; Is 38:7,8
19 [1]I.e. Approx one bu [2]Lit *and he put* [3]Or *terebinth* [a]Gen 18:6-8
21 [1]Or *departed* [a]Lev 9:24
22 [1]Lit *Gideon* [2]Heb *YHWH,* usually rendered *LORD* [a]Gen 32:30; Ex 33:20; Judg 13:21,22
24 [1]Heb *Yahweh-shalom*

Peace. To this day it is still [a]in Ophrah of
the Abiezrites.
25 ¶ Now on the same night the LORD
said to him, "Take your father's bull [1]and
a second bull seven years old, and pull
down the altar of Baal which belongs to
your father, and cut down the [2a]Ashe-
rah that is beside it;
26 and build an altar to the LORD your
God on the top of this stronghold in an
orderly manner, and take a second bull
and offer a burnt offering with the wood
of the Asherah which you shall cut
down."
27 Then Gideon took ten men of his
servants and did as the LORD had spoken
to him; and because he was too afraid of
his father's household and the men of the
city to do it by day, he did it by night.

The Altar of Baal Destroyed

28 ¶ When the men of the city arose
early in the morning, behold, the altar of
Baal was torn down, and the Asherah
which was beside it was cut down, and
the second bull was offered on the altar
which had been built.
29 They said to one another, "Who did
this thing?" And when they searched
about and inquired, they said, "Gideon
the son of Joash did this thing."
30 Then the men of the city said to
Joash, "Bring out your son, that he may
die, for he has torn down the altar of Baal,
and indeed, he has cut down the Asherah
which was beside it."
31 But Joash said to all who stood
against him, "Will you contend for Baal,
or will you deliver him? Whoever will
[1]plead for him shall be put to death by
morning. If he is a god, let him contend
for himself, because someone has torn
down his altar."
32 Therefore on that day he named
him [a]Jerubbaal, that is to say, "Let Baal
contend against him," because he had
torn down his altar.
33 ¶ Then all the Midianites and the
Amalekites and the sons of the east assembled themselves; and they crossed
over and camped in [a]the valley of Jezreel.
34 So [a]the Spirit of the LORD [1]came
upon Gideon; and he [b]blew a trumpet,
and the Abiezrites were called together
to follow him.
35 He sent messengers throughout
Manasseh, and they also were called together to follow him; and he sent messengers to Asher, [a]Zebulun, and Naphtali,
and [b]they came up to meet them.

Sign of the Fleece

36 ¶ Then Gideon said to God, "[a]If
You will deliver Israel [1]through me, as
You have spoken,
37 behold, I will put a fleece of wool
on the threshing floor. If there is dew on
the fleece only, and it is dry on all the
ground, then I will know that You will
deliver Israel [1]through me, as You have
spoken."
38 And it was so. When he arose early
the next morning and squeezed the
fleece, he drained the dew from the
fleece, a bowl full of water.
39 Then Gideon said to God, "[a]Do not
let Your anger burn against me that I may
speak once more; please let me make a
test once more with the fleece, let it now
be dry only on the fleece, and let there be
dew on all the ground."
40 God did so that night; for it was dry
only on the fleece, and dew was on all the
ground.

Gideon's 300 Chosen Men

7 Then [a]Jerubbaal (that is, Gideon)
and all the people who were with
him, rose early and camped beside [1]the
spring of Harod; and the camp of Midian
was on the north side of [2]them by the
hill of [b]Moreh in the valley.
2 ¶ The LORD said to Gideon, "The
people who are with you are too many for
Me to give Midian into their hands, [a]for
Israel [1]would become boastful, saying,
'My own [2]power has delivered me.'
3 "Now therefore [1]come, proclaim in
the hearing of the people, saying, '[a]Who-
ever is afraid and trembling, let him return and depart from Mount Gilead.' " So
22,000 people returned, but 10,000 remained.
4 ¶ [a]Then the LORD said to Gideon,
"The people are still too many; bring
them down to the water and I will test
them for you there. Therefore it shall be
that he of whom I say to you, 'This one
shall go with you,' he shall go with you;
but everyone of whom I say to you, 'This
one shall not go with you,' he shall
not go."
5 So he brought the people down to
the water. And the LORD said to Gideon,
"You shall separate everyone who laps
the water with his tongue as a dog laps,
as well as everyone who kneels to drink."
6 Now the number of those who
lapped, putting their hand to their
mouth, was 300 men; but all the rest of
the people kneeled to drink water.
7 The LORD said to Gideon, "I will
deliver you [a]with the 300 men who
lapped and will give the Midianites into
your hands; so let all the *other* people go,
each man to his [1]home."
8 So [1]the 300 men took the people's

24 [a]Judg 8:32
25 [1]Or *even* [2]I.e. wooden symbol of a female deity, also vv 26, 28, 30 [a]Ex 34:13
31 [1]Or *contend*
32 [a]Judg 7:1
33 [a]Josh 17:16
34 [1]Lit *clothed* [a]Judg 3:10 [b]Judg 3:27
35 [a]Judg 4:6,10; 5:18 [b]Judg 7:3
36 [1]Lit *by my hand* [a]Judg 6:14, 16,17
37 [1]Lit *by my hand*
39 [a]Gen 18:32
7:1 [1]Or *En-Harod* [2]Lit *him* [a]Judg 6:32 [b]Gen 12:6; Deut 11:30
2 [1]Lit *glorify itself against me* [2]Lit *hand* [a]Deut 8:17,18
3 [1]Or *please* [a]Deut 20:8
4 [a]1 Sam 14:6
7 [1]Lit *place* [a]1 Sam 14:6
8 [1]Lit *they*

provisions and their trumpets into their
hands. And [2]Gideon sent all the *other*
men of Israel, each to his tent, but retained the 300 men; and the camp of
Midian was below him in the valley.
9 ¶ Now the same night it came
about that the LORD said to him, "Arise,
go down against the camp, [a]for I have
given it into your hands.
10 "But if you are afraid to go down, go
with Purah your servant down to the
camp,
11 and you will hear what they say;
and [a]afterward your hands will be
strengthened that you may go down
against the camp." So he went with Purah his servant down to the [1]outposts of
the army that was in the camp.
12 Now the Midianites and the Amalekites and all the sons of the east were
lying in the valley [a]as numerous as locusts; and their camels were without
number, [b]as numerous as the sand on
the seashore.
13 When Gideon came, behold, a man
was relating a dream to his friend. And he
said, "Behold, I [1]had a dream; [2]a loaf of
barley bread was tumbling into the camp
of Midian, and it came to the tent and
struck it so that it fell, and turned it [3]up-
side down so that the tent lay flat."
14 His friend replied, "This is nothing
less than the sword of Gideon the son of
Joash, a man of Israel; God has given Midian and all the camp [a]into his hand."
15 ¶ When Gideon heard the account
of the dream and its interpretation, he
bowed in worship. He returned to the
camp of Israel and said, "Arise, for the
LORD has given the camp of Midian into
your hands."
16 He divided the 300 men into three
[1]companies, and he put trumpets and
empty pitchers into the hands of all of
them, with torches inside the pitchers.
17 He said to them, "Look at me and
do likewise. And behold, when I come to
the outskirts of the camp, [1]do as I do.
18 "When I and all who are with me
blow the trumpet, then you also blow the
trumpets all around the camp and say,
'For the LORD and for Gideon.' "

Confusion of the Enemy

19 ¶ So Gideon and the hundred men
who were with him came to the outskirts
of the camp at the beginning of the middle watch, when they had just posted the
watch; and they blew the trumpets and
smashed the pitchers that were in their
hands.
20 When the three [1]companies blew
the trumpets and broke the pitchers, they
held the torches in their left hands and
the trumpets in their right hands for
blowing, and cried, "A sword for the
LORD and for Gideon!"
21 Each stood in his place around the
camp; and [a]all the [1]army ran, crying out
as they fled.
22 When they blew 300 trumpets, the
[a]LORD set the sword of one against another even throughout the whole [1]army;
and the [1]army fled as far as Beth-shittah
toward Zererah, as far as the edge of
[b]Abel-meholah, by Tabbath.
23 The men of Israel were summoned
from [a]Naphtali and Asher and all Manasseh, and they pursued Midian.
24 ¶ Gideon sent messengers throughout all the hill country of Ephraim, saying, "Come down [1]against Midian and
[a]take the waters before them, as far as
Beth-barah and the Jordan." So all the
men of Ephraim were summoned and
they took the waters as far as Beth-barah
and the Jordan.
25 They captured the two leaders of
Midian, [a]Oreb and Zeeb, and they killed
Oreb at the rock of Oreb, and they killed
Zeeb at the wine press of Zeeb, while
they pursued Midian; and they brought
the heads of Oreb and Zeeb to Gideon
[b]from across the Jordan.

Zebah and Zalmunna Routed

8 Then the men of Ephraim said to
him, "[a]What is this thing you have
done to us, not calling us when you went
to fight against Midian?" And they contended with him vigorously.
2 But he said to them, "What have I
done now in comparison with you? Is not
the gleaning *of the grapes* of Ephraim better than the vintage of Abiezer?
3 "God has given the leaders of Midian, Oreb and Zeeb into your hands; and
what was I able to do in comparison with
you?" Then their [1]anger toward him subsided when he said [2]that.
4 ¶ Then Gideon and the 300 men
who were with him came [a]to the Jordan
and crossed over, weary yet pursuing.
5 He said to the men of [a]Succoth,
"Please give loaves of bread to the people
who are following me, for they are weary,
and I am pursuing Zebah and Zalmunna,
the kings of Midian."
6 The leaders of Succoth said,
"[1a]Are the hands of Zebah and Zalmunna already in your hands, that we should
give bread to your army?"
7 Gideon said, "[1]All right, [a]when
the LORD has given Zebah and Zalmunna
into my hand, then I will [2]thrash your
[3]bodies with the thorns of the wilderness and with briers."
8 He went up from there to [1a]Penu-

8 [2]Lit *he*
9 [a]Josh 2:24; 10:8; 11:6
11 [1]Lit *extremity of the battle array* [a]Judg 7:15; 1 Sam 14:9,10
12 [a]Judg 6:5; 8:10 [b]Josh 11:4
13 [1]Lit *dreamed* [2]Lit *and behold, a loaf* [3]Lit *upwards*
14 [a]Josh 2:9
16 [1]Lit *heads*
17 [1]Lit *it shall come about that just as I do, so you shall do*
20 [1]Lit *heads*
21 [1]Or *camp* [a]2 Kin 7:7
22 [1]Or *camp* [a]1 Sam 14:20 [b]1 Kin 4:12; 19:16
23 [a]Judg 6:35
24 [1]Lit *to meet* [a]Judg 3:28
25 [a]Ps 83:11; Is 10:26 [b]Judg 8:4
8:1 [a]Judg 12:1
3 [1]Lit *spirit* [2]Lit *this thing*
4 [a]Judg 7:25
5 [a]Gen 33:17
6 [1]Lit *Is the palm* [a]Judg 8:15
7 [1]Lit *For thus* [2]Or *trample* [3]Lit *flesh* [a]Judg 7:15
8 [1]In Gen 32:30, *Peniel* [a]Gen 32:31

el and spoke similarly to them; and the
men of Penuel answered him just as the
men of Succoth had answered.
9 So he spoke also to the men of Penuel, saying, "When I return safely, [a]I
will tear down this tower."
10 ¶ Now Zebah and Zalmunna were
in Karkor, and their [1]armies with them,
about 15,000 men, all who were left of
the entire [2]army of the sons of the east;
[a]for the fallen were 120,000 [3]swords-
men.
11 Gideon went up by the way of
those who lived in tents on the east of
Nobah and Jogbehah, and [1]attacked the
camp when the camp was [2]unsuspect-
ing.
12 When Zebah and Zalmunna fled, he
pursued them and captured the two kings
of Midian, Zebah and Zalmunna, and
routed the whole [1]army.
13 ¶ Then Gideon the son of Joash returned from the battle [1]by the ascent of
Heres.
14 And he captured a youth [1]from
Succoth and questioned him. Then *the
youth* wrote down for him the princes
of Succoth and its elders, seventy-seven
men.
15 He came to the men of Succoth and
said, "Behold Zebah and Zalmunna, concerning whom you taunted me, saying,
'[1a]Are the hands of Zebah and Zalmunna already in your hand, that we should
give bread to your men who are weary?' "
16 He took the elders of the city, and
thorns of the wilderness and briers, and
he [1]disciplined the men of Succoth with
them.
17 [a]He tore down the tower of Penuel
and killed the men of the city.
18 ¶ Then he said to Zebah and Zalmunna, "What kind of men *were* they
whom you killed at Tabor?" And they
said, "They were like you, each one [1]re-
sembling the son of a king."
19 He said, "They *were* my brothers,
the sons of my mother. *As* the LORD lives,
if only you had let them live, I would not
kill you."
20 So he said to Jether his firstborn,
"Rise, kill them." But the youth did not
draw his sword, for he was afraid, because he was still a youth.
21 Then Zebah and Zalmunna said,
"Rise up yourself, and fall on us; for as the
man, so is his strength." [a]So Gideon
arose and killed Zebah and Zalmunna,
and [b]took the crescent ornaments which
were on their camels' necks.
22 ¶ Then the men of Israel said to
Gideon, "Rule over us, both you and your
son, also your son's son, for you have
delivered us from the hand of Midian."
23 But Gideon said to them, "I will not
rule over you, nor shall my son rule over
you; [a]the LORD shall rule over you."
24 Yet Gideon said to them, "I would
[1]request of you, that each of you give me
[2]an earring from his spoil." (For they had
gold earrings, because they were [a]Ishma-
elites.)
25 They said, "We will surely give
them." So they spread out a garment, and
every one of them threw an earring there
from his spoil.
26 The weight of the gold earrings that
he requested was 1,700 *shekels* of gold,
besides the crescent ornaments and the
pendants and the purple robes which
were on the kings of Midian, and besides
the neck bands that *were* on their camels'
necks.
27 Gideon made it into [a]an ephod,
and placed it in his city, Ophrah, and all
Israel played the harlot with it there, so
that it became a snare to Gideon and his
household.

Forty Years of Peace

28 So Midian was subdued before the
sons of Israel, and they did not lift up
their heads anymore. And the land was
undisturbed for forty years in the days of
Gideon.
29 ¶ Then [a]Jerubbaal the son of Joash
went and lived in his own house.
30 Now Gideon had [a]seventy sons
who [1]were his direct descendants, for he
had many wives.
31 His concubine who was in Shechem also bore him a son, and he
[1]named him Abimelech.
32 And Gideon the son of Joash died at
a ripe old age and was buried in the tomb
of his father Joash, in Ophrah of the Abiezrites.
33 ¶ Then it came about, as soon as
Gideon was dead, [a]that the sons of Israel
again played the harlot with the Baals,
and made [b]Baal-berith their god.
34 Thus the sons of Israel [a]did not
remember the LORD their God, who had
delivered them from the hands of all their
enemies on every side;
35 [a]nor did they show kindness to the
household of Jerubbaal (*that is,* Gideon)
in accord with all the good that he had
done to Israel.

Abimelech's Conspiracy

9 And [a]Abimelech the son of Jerubbaal went to Shechem to his moth-
er's [1]relatives, and spoke to them and to
the whole clan of the household of his
mother's father, saying,
2 "Speak, now, in the hearing of all
the leaders of Shechem, 'Which is better

9 [a]Judg 8:17
10 [1]Or *camps* [2]Or *camp* [3]Lit *men who drew sword* [a]Judg 6:5; 7:12; Is 9:4
11 [1]Lit *smote* [2]Or *secure*
12 [1]Or *camp*
13 [1]Or *from*
14 [1]Lit *of the men of*
15 [1]Lit *Is the palm* [a]Judg 8:6
16 [1]Lit *made the men...to know*
17 [a]Judg 8:9
18 [1]Lit *like the form of the sons*
21 [a]Ps 83:11 [b]Judg 8:26
23 [a]1 Sam 8:7; 10:19; 12:12; Ps 10:16
24 [1]Lit *request a request* [2]Or *a nose ring* [a]Gen 25:13-16
27 [a]Ex 28:6-35; Judg 17:5; 18:14-20
29 [a]Judg 7:1
30 [1]Lit *came from his loins* [a]Judg 9:2,5
31 [1]Lit *appointed his name*
33 [a]Judg 2:11, 12 [b]Judg 9:4,27, 46
34 [a]Deut 4:9; Judg 3:7
35 [a]Judg 9:16-18
9:1 [1]Lit *brothers* [a]Judg 8:31,35

for you, that [a]seventy men, all the sons of Jerubbaal, rule over you, or that one man rule over you?' Also, remember that I am [b]your bone and your flesh."

3 And his mother's [1]relatives spoke all these words on his behalf in the hearing of all the leaders of Shechem; and [2]they were inclined to follow Abimelech, for they said, "He is [a]our [3]relative."

4 They gave him seventy *pieces* of silver from the house of [a]Baal-berith with which Abimelech hired worthless and reckless fellows, and they followed him.

5 Then he went to his father's house at Ophrah and [a]killed his brothers the sons of Jerubbaal, [b]seventy men, on one stone. But Jotham the youngest son of Jerubbaal was left, for he hid himself.

6 All the men of Shechem and all [1]Beth-millo assembled together, and they went and made Abimelech king, by the [2]oak of the pillar which was in Shechem.

7 ¶ Now when they told Jotham, he went and stood on the top of [a]Mount Gerizim, and lifted his voice and called out. Thus he said to them, "Listen to me, O men of Shechem, that God may listen to you.

8 "Once the trees went forth to anoint a king over them, and they said to the olive tree, 'Reign over us!'

9 "But the olive tree said to them, 'Shall I leave my fatness with [1]which God and men are honored, and go to wave over the trees?'

10 "Then the trees said to the fig tree, 'You come, reign over us!'

11 "But the fig tree said to them, 'Shall I leave my sweetness and my good [1]fruit, and go to wave over the trees?'

12 "Then the trees said to the vine, 'You come, reign over us!'

13 "But the vine said to them, 'Shall I leave my new wine, which cheers God and men, and go to wave over the trees?'

14 "Finally all the trees said to the bramble, 'You come, reign over us!'

15 "The bramble said to the trees, 'If in [1]truth you are anointing me as king over you, come and take refuge in my shade; but if not, may fire come out from the bramble and consume the cedars of Lebanon.'

16 ¶ "Now therefore, if you have dealt in [1]truth and integrity in making Abimelech king, and if you have dealt well with [a]Jerubbaal and his house, and [2]have dealt with him [3]as he deserved—

17 for my father fought for you and [1]risked his life and delivered you from the hand of Midian;

18 but you have risen against my father's house today and have killed [a]his sons, seventy men, on one stone, and have made Abimelech, [b]the son of his maidservant, king over the men of Shechem, because he is your [1]relative—

19 if then you have dealt in [1]truth and integrity with Jerubbaal and his house this day, rejoice in Abimelech, and let him also rejoice in you.

20 "But if not, let fire come out from Abimelech and consume the men of Shechem and [1]Beth-millo; and let fire come out from the men of Shechem and from [1]Beth-millo, and consume Abimelech."

21 Then Jotham escaped and fled, and went to Beer and remained there because of Abimelech his brother.

Shechem and Abimelech Fall

22 ¶ Now Abimelech ruled over Israel three years.

23 [a]Then God sent an evil spirit between Abimelech and the men of Shechem; and the men of Shechem [b]dealt treacherously with Abimelech,

24 [a]so that the violence [1]done to the seventy sons of Jerubbaal might come, and [b]their blood might be laid on Abimelech their brother, who killed them, and on the men of Shechem, who strengthened his hands to kill his brothers.

25 The men of Shechem set [1]men in ambush against him on the tops of the mountains, and they robbed all who might pass by them along the road; and it was told to Abimelech.

26 ¶ Now Gaal the son of Ebed came with his [1]relatives, and crossed over into Shechem; and the men of Shechem put their trust in him.

27 They went out into the field and gathered *the grapes of* their vineyards and trod *them*, and held a [1]festival; and they went into the house of [a]their god, and ate and drank and cursed Abimelech.

28 Then Gaal the son of Ebed said, "Who is Abimelech, and who is Shechem, that we should serve him? Is he not the son of Jerubbaal, and *is* Zebul *not* his [1]lieutenant? Serve the men of [a]Hamor the father of Shechem; but why should we serve him?

29 "[1a]Would, therefore, that this people were under my authority! Then I would remove Abimelech." And he said to Abimelech, "Increase your army and come out."

30 ¶ When Zebul the ruler of the city heard the words of Gaal the son of Ebed, his anger burned.

31 He sent messengers to Abimelech [1]deceitfully, saying, "Behold, Gaal the son of Ebed and his [2]relatives have come

2 [a]Judg 8:30; 9:5,18 [b]Gen 29:14
3 [1]Lit *brothers* [2]Lit *their hearts inclined after* [3]Lit *brother* [a]Gen 29:15
4 [a]Judg 8:33
5 [a]2 Kin 11:1,2 [b]Judg 8:30; 9:2, 18
6 [1]Or *the house of Millo* [2]Or *terebinth*
7 [a]Deut 11:29, 30
9 [1]Lit *which by me*
11 [1]Or *produce*
15 [1]Or *sincerity*
16 [1]Or *sincerity* [2]Lit *if you have* [3]Lit *according to the dealing of his hands* [a]Judg 8:35
17 [1]Lit *cast his soul in front*
18 [1]Lit *brother* [a]Judg 8:30; 9:2,5 [b]Judg 8:31
19 [1]Or *sincerity*
20 [1]Or *the house of Millo*
23 [a]1 Sam 16:14; Is 19:2, 14 [b]Is 33:1
24 [1]Lit *of the seventy* [a]Deut 27:25; Judg 9:56,57 [b]Num 35:33
25 [1]Lit *liers-in-wait for*
26 [1]Lit *brothers*
27 [1]Lit *rejoicing* [a]Judg 8:33; 9:46
28 [1]Lit *overseer* [a]Gen 34:2
29 [1]Lit *And who will give this people into my hand* [a]2 Sam 15:4
31 [1]Or *in Tormah* [2]Lit *brothers*

to Shechem; and behold, they are [3]stirring up the city against you.

32 "Now therefore, arise by night, you and the people who are with you, and lie in wait in the field.

33 "In the morning, as soon as the sun is up, you shall rise early and rush upon the city; and behold, when he and the people who are with him come out against you, you shall [a]do to them [1]whatever you can."

34 ¶ So Abimelech and all the people who *were* with him arose by night and lay in wait against Shechem in four [1]companies.

35 Now Gaal the son of Ebed went out and stood in the entrance of the city gate; and Abimelech and the people who *were* with him arose from the ambush.

36 When Gaal saw the people, he said to Zebul, "[1]Look, people are coming down from the tops of the mountains." But Zebul said to him, "You are seeing the shadow of the mountains as *if they were* men."

37 Gaal spoke again and said, "Behold, people are coming down from [a]the [1]highest part of the land, and one [2]company comes by the way of [3]the diviners' [4]oak."

38 Then Zebul said to him, "Where is your [1]boasting now with which you said, 'Who is Abimelech that we should serve him?' Is this not the people whom you despised? Go out now and fight with them!"

39 So Gaal went out before the leaders of Shechem and fought with Abimelech.

40 Abimelech chased him, and he fled before him; and many fell wounded up to the entrance of the gate.

41 Then Abimelech remained at Arumah, but Zebul drove out Gaal and his [1]relatives so that they could not remain in Shechem.

42 ¶ Now it came about the next day, that the people went out to the field, and it was told to Abimelech.

43 So he took [1]his people and divided them into three [2]companies, and lay in wait in the field; when he looked and [3]saw the people coming out from the city, he arose against them and [4]slew them.

44 Then Abimelech and the [1]company who was with him dashed forward and stood in the entrance of the city gate; the other two [2]companies then dashed against all who *were* in the field and [3]slew them.

45 Abimelech fought against the city all that day, and he captured the city and killed the people who *were* in it; then he [a]razed the city and sowed it with salt.

46 ¶ When all the leaders of the tower of Shechem heard of *it,* they entered the inner chamber of the [1]temple of [a]El-berith.

47 It was told Abimelech that all the leaders of the tower of Shechem were gathered together.

48 So Abimelech went up to Mount [a]Zalmon, he and all the people who *were* with him; and Abimelech took [1]an axe in his hand and cut down a branch from the trees, and lifted it and laid *it* on his shoulder. Then he said to the people who *were* with him, "What you have seen me do, hurry *and* do [2]likewise."

49 All the people also cut down each one his branch and followed Abimelech, and put *them* on the inner chamber and set the inner chamber on fire over those *inside,* so that all the men of the tower of Shechem also died, about a thousand men and women.

50 ¶ Then Abimelech went to Thebez, and he camped against Thebez and captured it.

51 But there was a strong tower in the center of the city, and all the men and women with all the leaders of the city fled there and shut themselves in; and they went up on the roof of the tower.

52 So Abimelech came to the tower and fought against it, and approached the entrance of the tower to burn it with fire.

53 But [a]a certain woman threw an upper millstone on Abimelech's head, crushing his skull.

54 Then [a]he called quickly to the young man, his armor bearer, and said to him, "Draw your sword and kill me, so that it will not be said of me, 'A woman slew him.'" So [1]the young man pierced him through, and he died.

55 When the men of Israel saw that Abimelech was dead, each departed to his [1]home.

56 Thus [a]God repaid the wickedness of Abimelech, which he had done to his father in killing his seventy brothers.

57 Also God returned all the wickedness of the men of Shechem on their heads, and the curse of Jotham the son of Jerubbaal came [1]upon them.

Oppression of Philistines and Ammonites

10 Now after Abimelech died, Tola the son of Puah, the son of Dodo, a man of Issachar, [a]arose to save Israel; and he lived in Shamir in the hill country of Ephraim.

2 He judged Israel twenty-three years. Then he died and was buried in Shamir.

31 [3]Lit *besieging*
33 [1]Lit *as your hand can find* [a]1 Sam 10:7
34 [1]Lit *heads*
36 [1]Lit *Behold*
37 [1]Or *center* [2]Lit *head* [3]Heb *Elommeonenim* [4]Or *terebinth* [a]Ezek 38:12
38 [1]Lit *mouth*
41 [1]Lit *brothers*
43 [1]Lit *the* [2]Lit *heads* [3]Lit *behold* [4]Lit *smote*
44 [1]Singular with Gr; Heb plural, *heads* [2]Lit *heads* [3]Lit *smote*
45 [a]2 Kin 3:25
46 [1]Lit *house* [a]Judg 8:33
48 [1]Lit *the axes* [2]Lit *like me* [a]Ps 68:14
53 [a]2 Sam 11:21
54 [1]Lit *his* [a]1 Sam 31:4
55 [1]Lit *place*
56 [a]Gen 9:5,6; Ps 94:23
57 [1]Lit *to*
10:1 [a]Judg 2:16

3 ¶ After him, Jair the Gileadite arose
and judged Israel twenty-two years.
4 He had thirty sons who rode on
thirty donkeys, and they had thirty cities
[1]in the land of Gilead [a]that are called
[2]Havvoth-jair to this day.
5 And Jair died and was buried in Ka-
mon.
6 ¶ Then the sons of Israel again did
evil in the sight of the LORD, [a]served the
Baals and the Ashtaroth, the gods of
Aram, the gods of Sidon, the gods of
Moab, [b]the gods of the sons of Ammon,
and the gods of the Philistines; thus
[c]they forsook the LORD and did not serve
Him.
7 The anger of the LORD burned
against Israel, and He [a]sold them into the
hands of the Philistines and into the
hands of the sons of Ammon.
8 They [1]afflicted and crushed the
sons of Israel [2]that year; for eighteen
years they *afflicted* all the sons of Israel
who were beyond the Jordan [3]in Gilead
in the land of the Amorites.
9 The sons of Ammon crossed the Jordan to fight also against Judah, Benjamin,
and the house of Ephraim, so that Israel
was greatly distressed.
10 ¶ Then the [a]sons of Israel cried out
to the LORD, saying, "We have sinned
against You, for indeed, we have forsaken
our God and served the Baals."
11 The LORD said to the sons of Israel,
"*Did I* not *deliver you* [a]from the Egyptians, [b]the Amorites, [c]the sons of Ammon, and the Philistines?
12 "Also when the Sidonians, the Amalekites and the Maonites [a]oppressed you,
you cried out to Me, and I delivered you
from their hands.
13 "Yet [a]you have forsaken Me and
served other gods; therefore I will no
longer deliver you.
14 "[a]Go and cry out to the gods which
you have chosen; let them deliver you in
the time of your distress."
15 The sons of Israel said to the LORD,
"We have sinned, [a]do to us whatever
seems good to You; only please deliver us
this day."
16 [a]So they put away the foreign gods
from among them and served the LORD;
and [1][b]He could bear the misery of Israel
no longer.
17 ¶ Then the sons of Ammon were
summoned and they camped in Gilead.
And the sons of Israel gathered together
and camped in [a]Mizpah.
18 The people, the leaders of Gilead,
said to one another, "Who is the man
who will begin to fight against the sons of
Ammon? He shall become head over all
the inhabitants of Gilead."

4 [1]Lit *which are in* [2]I.e. the towns of Jair [a]Num 32:41
6 [a]Judg 2:13 [b]Judg 11:24 [c]Deut 31:16,17; 32:15
7 [a]1 Sam 12:9
8 [1]Lit *shattered* [2]Lit *in that* [3]Lit *which is in*
10 [a]1 Sam 12:10
11 [a]Judg 2:12 [b]Num 21:21-25 [c]Judg 3:13
12 [a]Ps 106:42
13 [a]Jer 2:13
14 [a]Deut 32:37
15 [a]1 Sam 3:18
16 [1]Lit *His soul was short with the misery* [a]Josh 24:23 [b]Deut 32:36
17 [a]Judg 11:29
11:1 [1]Or *mighty man of valor* [2]Lit *begat* [a]Heb 11:32
3 [1]Lit *to* [a]2 Sam 10:6,8
4 [a]Judg 10:9,17
7 [a]Gen 26:27
8 [a]Judg 10:18
9 [1]Lit *before*
10 [1]Lit *hearer* [2]Lit *according to your word* [a]Gen 31:50; Jer 29:23; 42:5; Mic 1:2
11 [a]Judg 10:17; 11:29; 20:1; 1 Sam 10:17
13 [a]Num 21:24 [b]Gen 32:22

Jephthah the Ninth Judge

11 Now [a]Jephthah the Gileadite was
a [1]valiant warrior, but he was the
son of a harlot. And Gilead [2]was the father of Jephthah.
2 Gilead's wife bore him sons; and
when his wife's sons grew up, they drove
Jephthah out and said to him, "You shall
not have an inheritance in our father's
house, for you are the son of another
woman."
3 So Jephthah fled from his brothers
and lived in the land of [a]Tob; and worthless fellows gathered themselves [1]about
Jephthah, and they went out with him.
4 ¶ It came about after a while that
[a]the sons of Ammon fought against Israel.
5 When the sons of Ammon fought
against Israel, the elders of Gilead went
to get Jephthah from the land of Tob;
6 and they said to Jephthah, "Come
and be our chief that we may fight against
the sons of Ammon."
7 Then Jephthah said to the elders of
Gilead, "[a]Did you not hate me and drive
me from my father's house? So why have
you come to me now when you are in
trouble?"
8 The elders of Gilead said to Jephthah, "For this reason we have now returned to you, that you may go with us
and fight with the sons of Ammon and
[a]become head over all the inhabitants of
Gilead."
9 So Jephthah said to the elders of
Gilead, "If you take me back to fight
against the sons of Ammon and the LORD
gives them up [1]to me, will I become your
head?"
10 The elders of Gilead said to Jephthah, "[a]The LORD is [1]witness between
us; surely we will do [2]as you have said."
11 Then Jephthah went with the elders of Gilead, and the people made him
head and chief over them; and Jephthah
spoke all his words before the LORD at
[a]Mizpah.
12 ¶ Now Jephthah sent messengers
to the king of the sons of Ammon, saying,
"What is between you and me, that you
have come to me to fight against my
land?"
13 The king of the sons of Ammon said
to the messengers of Jephthah, "Because
Israel [a]took away my land when they
came up from Egypt, from the Arnon as
far as the [b]Jabbok and the Jordan; therefore, return them peaceably now."
14 But Jephthah sent messengers
again to the king of the sons of Ammon,
15 and they said to him, "Thus says
Jephthah, 'Israel did not take away the

land of Moab nor the land of the sons of Ammon.

16 'For when they came up from Egypt, and Israel [a]went through the wilderness to the [1]Red Sea and [b]came to Kadesh,

17 then Israel [a]sent messengers to the king of Edom, saying, "Please let us pass through your land," but the king of Edom would not listen. [b]And they also sent to the king of Moab, but he would not consent. So Israel remained at Kadesh.

18 'Then they went through the wilderness and [a]around the land of Edom and the land of Moab, and came to the east side of the land of Moab, and they camped beyond the Arnon; but they [b]did not enter the territory of Moab, for the Arnon *was* the border of Moab.

19 'And Israel sent [a]messengers to Sihon king of the Amorites, the king of Heshbon, and Israel said to him, "Please let us pass through your land to our place."

20 'But Sihon did not trust Israel to pass through his territory; so Sihon gathered all his people and camped in Jahaz and fought with Israel.

21 'The LORD, the God of Israel, gave Sihon and all his people into the hand of Israel, and they [1a]defeated them; so Israel possessed all the land of the Amorites, the inhabitants of that country.

22 '[a]So they possessed all the territory of the Amorites, from the Arnon as far as the Jabbok, and from the wilderness as far as the Jordan.

23 'Since now the LORD, the God of Israel, drove out the Amorites from before His people Israel, are you then to possess it?

24 'Do you not possess what [a]Chemosh your god gives you to possess? So whatever the LORD our God has driven out before us, we will possess it.

25 'Now are you any better than [a]Balak the son of Zippor, king of Moab? Did he ever strive with Israel, or did he ever fight against them?

26 '[a]While Israel lived in Heshbon and its villages, and in Aroer and its villages, and in all the cities that are on the banks of the Arnon, three hundred years, why did you not recover them within that time?

27 'I therefore have not sinned against you, but you are doing me wrong by making war against me; [a]may the LORD, the Judge, judge today between the sons of Israel and the sons of Ammon.' "

28 But the king of the sons of Ammon [1]disregarded the message which Jephthah sent him.

16 [1]Lit *Sea of Reeds* [a]Num 14:25; Deut 1:40 [b]Num 20:1,4-21

17 [a]Num 20:14-21 [b]Josh 24:9

18 [a]Num 21:4; Deut 2:8 [b]Deut 2:9,18,19

19 [a]Num 21:21-32; Deut 2:26-36

21 [1]Lit *smote* [a]Num 21:24; Deut 2:32-34

22 [a]Deut 2:36, 37

24 [a]Num 21:29; 1 Kin 11:7

25 [a]Num 22:2; Josh 24:9; Mic 6:5

26 [a]Num 21:25, 26; Deut 2:36

27 [a]Gen 16:5; 18:25; 31:53; 1 Sam 24:12,15

28 [1]Lit *did not listen to the words*

29 [a]Judg 3:10

33 [1]Lit *even until you are coming to* [a]Ezek 27:17

34 [a]Judg 10:17; 11:11 [b]Ex 15:20; 1 Sam 18:6; Jer 31:4

35 [1]Lit *opened my mouth* [a]Num 30:2; Eccl 5:4,5

36 [1]Lit *opened your mouth* [2]Lit *according to what has proceeded from your mouth* [a]Num 30:2

37 [1]Lit *go and go down on* [a]Gen 30:23; Luke 1:25

39 [1]Lit *knew no man*

40 [1]Lit *recount*; ancient versions, *lament*

12:1 [1]Or *northward* [a]Judg 8:1

Jephthah's Tragic Vow

29 ¶ Now [a]the Spirit of the LORD came upon Jephthah, so that he passed through Gilead and Manasseh; then he passed through Mizpah of Gilead, and from Mizpah of Gilead he went on to the sons of Ammon.

30 Jephthah made a vow to the LORD and said, "If You will indeed give the sons of Ammon into my hand,

31 then it shall be that whatever comes out of the doors of my house to meet me when I return in peace from the sons of Ammon, it shall be the LORD'S, and I will offer it up as a burnt offering."

32 So Jephthah crossed over to the sons of Ammon to fight against them; and the LORD gave them into his hand.

33 He struck them with a very great slaughter from Aroer [1]to the entrance of [a]Minnith, twenty cities, and as far as Abel-keramim. So the sons of Ammon were subdued before the sons of Israel.

34 ¶ When Jephthah came to his house at [a]Mizpah, behold, his daughter was coming out to meet him [b]with tambourines and with dancing. Now she was his one *and* only child; besides her he had no son or daughter.

35 When he saw her, he tore his clothes and said, "Alas, my daughter! You have brought me very low, and you are among those who trouble me; for I have [1]given my word to the LORD, and [a]I cannot take *it* back."

36 So she said to him, "My father, you have [1]given your word to the LORD; [a]do to me [2]as you have said, since the LORD has avenged you of your enemies, the sons of Ammon."

37 She said to her father, "Let this thing be done for me; let me alone two months, that I may [1]go to the mountains and weep because of [a]my virginity, I and my companions."

38 Then he said, "Go." So he sent her away for two months; and she left with her companions, and wept on the mountains because of her virginity.

39 At the end of two months she returned to her father, who did to her according to the vow which he had made; and she [1]had no relations with a man. Thus it became a custom in Israel,

40 that the daughters of Israel went yearly to [1]commemorate the daughter of Jephthah the Gileadite four days in the year.

Jephthah and His Successors

12 Then the men of Ephraim were summoned, and they crossed [1]to Zaphon and [a]said to Jephthah, "Why did

you cross over to fight against the sons of
Ammon without calling us to go with
you? We will burn your house down on
you."
2 Jephthah said to them, "I and my
people were at great strife with the sons
of Ammon; when I called you, you did not
deliver me from their hand.
3 "When I saw that you would not deliver *me*, I [1][a]took my life in my hands
and crossed over against the sons of Ammon, and the LORD gave them into my
hand. Why then have you come up to me
this day to fight against me?"
4 Then Jephthah gathered all the
men of Gilead and fought Ephraim; and
the men of Gilead [1]defeated Ephraim,
because they said, "You are fugitives of
Ephraim, O Gileadites, in the midst of
Ephraim *and* in the midst of Manasseh."
5 The Gileadites [a]captured the fords
of the Jordan opposite Ephraim. And it
happened when *any of* the fugitives of
Ephraim said, "Let me cross over," the
men of Gilead would say to him, "Are you
an Ephraimite?" If he said, "No,"
6 then they would say to him, "Say
now, 'Shibboleth.' " But he said, "Sibboleth," for he could not [1]pronounce it correctly. Then they seized him and slew
him at the fords of the Jordan. Thus there
fell at that time 42,000 of Ephraim.
7 ¶ Jephthah judged Israel six years.
Then Jephthah the Gileadite died and
was buried in *one of* the cities of Gilead.
8 ¶ Now Ibzan of Bethlehem judged
Israel after him.
9 He had thirty sons, and thirty
daughters *whom* he [1]gave in marriage
outside *the family*, and he brought in thirty daughters from outside for his sons.
And he judged Israel seven years.
10 Then Ibzan died and was buried in
Bethlehem.
11 ¶ Now Elon the Zebulunite judged
Israel after him; and he judged Israel ten
years.
12 Then Elon the Zebulunite died and
was buried at Aijalon in the land of Zebulun.
13 ¶ Now Abdon the son of Hillel the
Pirathonite judged Israel after him.
14 He had forty sons and thirty grandsons who rode on seventy donkeys; and
he judged Israel eight years.
15 Then Abdon the son of Hillel the
Pirathonite died and was buried at Pira-
thon in the land of Ephraim, in the hill
country of the Amalekites.

Philistines Oppress Again

13 Now the sons of Israel [a]again did
evil in the sight of the LORD, so
that the LORD gave them into the hands
of the Philistines forty years.
2 ¶ There was a certain man of [a]Zo-
rah, of the family of the Danites, whose
name was Manoah; and his wife was barren and had borne no *children*.
3 [a]Then the angel of the LORD appeared to the woman and said to her,
"Behold now, you are barren and have
borne no *children*, but you shall conceive
and give birth to a son.
4 "Now therefore, be careful [a]not to
drink wine or strong drink, nor eat any
unclean thing.
5 "[a]For behold, you shall conceive
and give birth to a son, and no razor shall
come upon his head, for the boy shall be
a [b]Nazirite to God from the womb; and
he shall begin to deliver Israel from the
hands of the Philistines."
6 Then the woman came and told her
husband, saying, "[a]A man of God came
to me and his appearance was like the
appearance of the angel of God, very awesome. And I did not ask him where he
came from, nor did he tell me his name.
7 "But he said to me, 'Behold, you
shall conceive and give birth to a son, and
now you shall not drink wine or strong
drink nor eat any unclean thing, for the
boy shall be a Nazirite to God from the
womb to the day of his death.' "
8 ¶ Then Manoah entreated the LORD
and said, "O Lord, please let [a]the man of
God whom You have sent come to us
again that he may teach us what to do for
the boy who is to be born."
9 God listened to the voice of Manoah; and [a]the angel of God came again to
the woman as she was sitting in the field,
but Manoah her husband was not with
her.
10 So the woman ran quickly and told
her [1]husband, "Behold, [a]the man who
[2]came the *other* day has appeared
to me."
11 Then Manoah arose and followed
his wife, and when he came to the man
he said to him, "Are you [a]the man who
spoke to the woman?" And he said,
"I am."
12 Manoah said, "Now when your
words come *to pass*, what shall be the
boy's mode of life and his vocation?"
13 So [a]the angel of the LORD said to
Manoah, "[b]Let the woman pay attention
[1]to all that I said.
14 "She should not eat anything that
comes from the [a]vine nor drink wine or
strong drink, nor eat any unclean thing;
let her observe all that I commanded."
15 ¶ Then Manoah said to [a]the angel
of the LORD, "Please let us detain you so

3 [1]Lit *put my soul in my palm* [a]1 Sam 19:5; 28:21; Job 13:14
4 [1]Lit *smote*
5 [a]Judg 3:28
6 [1]Lit *speak so*
9 [1]Lit *sent outside*
13:1 [a]Judg 2:11
2 [a]Josh 19:41
3 [a]Judg 6:11,14; 13:6,8,10,11; Luke 1:11-13
4 [a]Num 6:2,3; Luke 1:15
5 [a]Luke 1:15 [b]Num 6:2-5
6 [a]Judg 6:11; 13:8,10,11
8 [a]Judg 13:3,7
9 [a]Judg 13:8
10 [1]Lit *husband, and said to him* [2]Lit *came to me* [a]Judg 13:9
11 [a]Judg 13:8
13 [1]Lit *from* [a]Judg 13:11 [b]Judg 13:4
14 [a]Num 6:4
15 [a]Judg 13:3

that we may prepare a young goat for you."

16 The angel of the LORD said to Manoah, "Though you detain me, [a]I will not eat your [1]food, but if you prepare a burnt offering, *then* offer it to the LORD." For Manoah did not know that he was the angel of the LORD.

17 Manoah said to the angel of the LORD, "[a]What is your name, so that when your words come *to pass,* we may honor you?"

18 But the angel of the LORD said to him, "Why do you ask my name, seeing it is [1a]wonderful?"

19 So [a]Manoah took the young goat with the grain offering and offered it on the rock to the LORD, and He performed wonders while Manoah and his wife looked on.

20 For it came about when the flame went up from the altar toward heaven, that the angel of the LORD ascended in the flame of the altar. When Manoah and his wife saw *this,* they [a]fell on their faces to the ground.

21 ¶ Now the angel of the LORD did not appear to Manoah or his wife again. [a]Then Manoah knew that he was the angel of the LORD.

22 So Manoah said to his wife, "[a]We will surely die, for we have seen God."

23 But his wife said to him, "If the LORD had desired to kill us, He would not have accepted a burnt offering and a grain offering from our hands, nor would He have [a]shown us all these things, nor would He have let us hear *things* like this at this time."

24 ¶ Then the woman gave birth to a son and named him Samson; and the [a]child grew up and the LORD blessed him.

25 And [a]the Spirit of the LORD began to stir him in [1b]Mahaneh-dan, between Zorah and Eshtaol.

Samson's Marriage

14 Then Samson went down to Timnah and saw a woman in Timnah, *one* of the daughters of the Philistines.

2 So he came [1]back and told his father and [2]mother, "I saw a woman in Timnah, *one* of the daughters of the Philistines; now therefore, get her for me as a wife."

3 Then his father and his mother said to him, "Is there no woman among the daughters of your [1a]relatives, or among all [2]our people, that you go to [b]take a wife from the uncircumcised Philistines?" But Samson said to his father, "Get her for me, for she [3]looks good to me."

4 However, his father and mother did not know that [a]it was of the LORD, for He was seeking an occasion against the Philistines. Now at that time the Philistines were ruling over Israel.

5 ¶ Then Samson went down to Timnah with his father and mother, and came as far as the vineyards of Timnah; and behold, a young lion *came* roaring toward him.

6 [a]The Spirit of the LORD [1]came upon him mightily, so that [b]he tore him as one tears a young goat though he had nothing in his hand; but he did not tell his father or mother what he had done.

7 So he went down and talked to the woman; and she [1]looked good to Samson.

8 When he returned later to take her, he turned aside to look at the carcass of the lion; and behold, a swarm of bees and honey were in the body of the lion.

9 So he scraped [1]the honey into his [2]hands and went on, eating as he went. When he came to his father and mother, he gave *some* to them and they ate *it;* but he did not tell them that he had scraped the honey out of the body of the lion.

10 ¶ Then his father went down to the woman; and Samson made a feast there, for the young men customarily did this.

11 When they saw him, they brought thirty companions to be with him.

Samson's Riddle

12 Then Samson said to them, "Let me now [a]propound a riddle to you; if you will indeed tell it to me within the seven days of the feast, and find it out, then I will give you thirty linen wraps and thirty [b]changes of clothes.

13 "But if you are unable to tell me, then you shall give me thirty linen wraps and thirty changes of clothes." And they said to him, "Propound your riddle, that we may hear it."

14 So he said to them,

"Out of the eater came something
to eat,
And out of the strong came
something sweet."

But they could not tell the riddle in three days.

15 ¶ Then it came about on the [1]fourth day that they said to Samson's wife, "[a]Entice your husband, so that he will tell us the riddle, [b]or we will burn you and your father's house with fire. Have you invited us to impoverish us? Is this not *so?*"

16 Samson's wife wept before him and said, "[a]You only hate me, and you do not love me; you have propounded a riddle to the sons of my people, and have not told

16 [1]Lit *bread* [a]Judg 6:20
17 [a]Gen 32:29
18 [1]I.e. incomprehensible [a]Is 9:6
19 [a]Judg 6:20, 21
20 [a]Lev 9:24; 1 Chr 21:16; Ezek 1:28; Matt 17:6
21 [a]Judg 13:16
22 [a]Gen 32:30; Deut 5:26; Judg 6:22
23 [a]Ps 25:14
24 [a]1 Sam 3:19; Luke 1:80
25 [1]I.e. the camp of Dan [a]Judg 3:10 [b]Judg 18:11,12
14:2 [1]Lit *up* [2]Lit *mother, saying,*
3 [1]Lit *brothers* [2]Lit *my* [3]Lit *is right in my eyes* [a]Gen 24:3,4 [b]Ex 34:16; Deut 7:3
4 [a]Josh 11:20
6 [1]Lit *rushed upon* [a]Judg 3:10 [b]1 Sam 17:34-36
7 [1]Lit *was right in Samson's eyes*
9 [1]Lit *it* [2]Lit *palms*
12 [a]Ezek 17:2 [b]Gen 45:22; 2 Kin 5:22
15 [1]So with some ancient versions; Heb *seventh* [a]Judg 16:5 [b]Judg 15:6
16 [a]Judg 16:15

it to me." And he said to her, "Behold, I
have not told *it* to my father or mother;
so should I tell you?"
17 However she wept before him sev-
en days while their feast lasted. And on
the seventh day he told her because she
pressed him so hard. She then told the
riddle to the sons of her people.
18 So the men of the city said to him
on the seventh day before the sun went
down,

"What is sweeter than honey?
And what is stronger than a
lion?"

And he said to them,

"If you had not plowed with my
heifer,
You would not have found out
my riddle."

19 Then [a]the Spirit of the LORD
[1]came upon him mightily, and he went
down to Ashkelon and killed thirty of
them and took their spoil and gave the
changes *of clothes* to those who told the
riddle. And his anger burned, and he
went up to his father's house.
20 But Samson's wife was [a]*given* to
his companion who had been his
[1]friend.

Samson Burns Philistine Crops

15 But after a while, in the time of
wheat harvest, Samson visited his
wife [a]with a young goat, and said, "I will
go in to my wife in *her* room." But her
father did not let him enter.
2 Her father said, "I really thought
that you hated her intensely; so I [a]gave
her to your companion. Is not her younger sister [1]more beautiful than she?
Please let her be yours [2]instead."
3 Samson then said to them, "This
time I shall be blameless in regard to the
Philistines when I do them harm."
4 Samson went and caught three
hundred foxes, and took torches, and
turned *the foxes* tail to tail and put one
torch in the middle between two tails.
5 When he had set fire to the torches,
he released [1]the foxes into the standing
grain of the Philistines, thus burning up
both the shocks and the standing grain,
along with the vineyards *and* groves.
6 Then the Philistines said, "Who did
this?" And they said, "Samson, the son-
in-law of the Timnite, because [1]he took
his wife and gave her to his companion."
So the Philistines came up and [a]burned
her and her father with fire.
7 Samson said to them, "Since you
act like this, I will surely take revenge on
you, but after that I will quit."
8 He struck them [1]ruthlessly with a
great slaughter; and he went down and
lived in the cleft of the rock of Etam.
9 ¶ Then the Philistines went up and
camped in Judah, and spread out in Lehi.
10 The men of Judah said, "Why have
you come up against us?" And they said,
"We have come up to bind Samson in
order to do to him as he did to us."
11 Then 3,000 men of Judah went
down to the cleft of the rock of Etam and
said to Samson, "Do you not know [a]that
the Philistines are rulers over us? What
then is this that you have done to us?"
And he said to them, "As they did to me,
so I have done to them."
12 They said to him, "We have come
down to bind you so that we may give you
into the hands of the Philistines." And
Samson said to them, "Swear to me that
you will not [1]kill me."
13 So they said to [1]him, "No, but we
will bind you fast and give you into their
hands; yet surely we will not kill you."
Then they bound him with two new
ropes and brought him up from the rock.
14 ¶ When he came to Lehi, the Philistines shouted as they met him. And [a]the
Spirit of the LORD [1]came upon him
mightily so that the ropes that were on
his arms were as flax that is burned with
fire, and his bonds [2]dropped from his
hands.
15 He found a fresh jawbone of a donkey, so he [1]reached out and took it and
[2]killed [a]a thousand men with it.
16 Then Samson said,

"With the jawbone of a donkey,
[1]Heaps upon heaps,
With the jawbone of a donkey
I have [2]killed a thousand men."

17 When he had finished speaking, he
threw the jawbone from his hand; and he
named that place [1]Ramath-lehi.
18 Then he became very thirsty, and
he [a]called to the LORD and said, "You
have given this great deliverance by the
hand of Your servant, and now [1]shall I
die of thirst [2]and fall into the hands of
the uncircumcised?"
19 But God split the hollow place that
is in Lehi so that water came out of it.
When he drank, [a]his [1]strength returned
and he revived. Therefore he named it
[2]En-hakkore, which is in Lehi to this
day.
20 So [a]he judged Israel twenty years
in [b]the days of the Philistines.

Samson's Weakness

16 Now Samson went to [a]Gaza and
saw a harlot there, and went in to
her.
2 *When it was told* to the Gazites,
saying, "Samson has come here," they

19 [1]Lit *rushed upon* [a]Judg 3:10; 13:25
20 [1]Or *best man* [a]Judg 15:2
15:1 [a]Gen 38:17
2 [1]Lit *better* [2]Lit *instead of her* [a]Judg 14:20
5 [1]Lit *them*
6 [1]I.e. the Timnite [a]Judg 14:15
8 [1]Lit *leg on thigh*
11 [a]Lev 26:25; Deut 28:43f; Judg 13:1; 14:4; Ps 106:40-42
12 [1]Lit *fall upon me yourselves*
13 [1]Lit *him, saying*
14 [1]Lit *rushed upon* [2]Lit *were melted* [a]Judg 14:19; 1 Sam 11:6
15 [1]Lit *stretched out his hand* [2]Lit *smote* [a]Lev 26:8; Josh 23:10
16 [1]Lit *Heap, two heaps*; Heb is same root as donkey [2]Lit *smitten*
17 [1]I.e. the high place of the jawbone
18 [1]Or *I shall... uncircumcised* [2]Or *or* [a]Judg 16:28
19 [1]Lit *spirit* [2]I.e. the spring of him who called [a]Is 40:29
20 [a]Judg 16:31; Heb 11:32 [b]Judg 13:1
16:1 [a]Josh 15:47

[a]surrounded *the place* and lay in wait for
him all night at the gate of the city. And
they kept silent all night, saying, "*Let us
wait* until the morning light, then we will
kill him."
3 Now Samson lay until midnight,
and at midnight he arose and took hold of
the doors of the city gate and the two
posts and pulled them up along with the
bars; then he put them on his shoulders
and carried them up to the top of the
mountain which is opposite Hebron.
4 ¶ After this it came about that he
loved a woman in the valley of Sorek,
whose name was Delilah.
5 The [a]lords of the Philistines came
up to her and said to her, "[b]Entice him,
and see where his great strength *lies* and
[1]how we may overpower him that we
may bind him to afflict him. Then we will
each give you eleven hundred *pieces* of
silver."
6 So Delilah said to Samson, "Please
tell me where your great strength is and
[1]how you may be bound to afflict you."
7 Samson said to her, "If they bind
me with seven fresh cords that have not
been dried, then I will become weak and
be like any *other* man."
8 Then the lords of the Philistines
brought up to her seven fresh cords that
had not been dried, and she bound him
with them.
9 Now she had *men* lying in wait in
an inner room. And she said to him, "The
Philistines are upon you, Samson!" But
he snapped the cords as a string of tow
snaps when it [1]touches fire. So his
strength was not discovered.
10 ¶ Then Delilah said to Samson,
"Behold, you have deceived me and told
me lies; now please tell me [1]how you
may be bound."
11 He said to her, "If they bind me
tightly with new ropes [1]which have not
been used, then I will become weak and
be like any *other* man."
12 So Delilah took new ropes and
bound him with them and said to him,
"The Philistines are upon you, Samson!"
For the *men* were lying in wait in the
inner room. But he snapped [1]the ropes
from his arms like a thread.
13 ¶ Then Delilah said to Samson, "Up
to now you have deceived me and told
me lies; tell me [1]how you may be
bound." And he said to her, "If you
weave the seven locks of my [2]hair with
the web [3][and fasten it with a pin, then
I will become weak and be like any other
man."
14 So while he slept, Delilah took the
seven locks of his [1]hair and wove them
into the web]. And she fastened *it* with
the pin and said to him, "The Philistines
are upon you, Samson!" But he awoke
from his sleep and pulled out the pin of
the loom and the web.

Delilah Extracts His Secret

15 ¶ Then she said to him, "[a]How can
you say, 'I love you,' when your heart
is not with me? You have deceived me
these three times and have not told me
where your great strength is."
16 It came about when she pressed
him daily with her words and urged him,
that his soul was [1]annoyed to death.
17 So he told her all *that was* in his
heart and said to her, "A razor has never
come on my head, for I have been a
[a]Nazirite to God from my mother's
womb. If I am shaved, then my strength
will leave me and I will become weak and
be like any *other* man."
18 ¶ When Delilah saw that he had
told her all *that was* in his heart, she sent
and called the lords of the Philistines, saying, "Come up once more, for he has told
me all *that is* in his heart." Then the lords
of the Philistines came up to her and
brought the money in their hands.
19 She made him sleep on her knees,
and called for a man and had him shave
off the seven locks of his [1]hair. Then she
began to afflict him, and his strength left
him.
20 She said, "The Philistines are upon
you, Samson!" And he awoke from his
sleep and said, "I will go out as at other
times and shake myself free." But he did
not know that [a]the LORD had departed
from him.
21 Then the Philistines seized him and
gouged out his eyes; and they brought
him down to Gaza and bound him with
bronze chains, and he was a grinder in
the prison.
22 However, the hair of his head began to grow again after it was shaved off.
23 ¶ Now the lords of the Philistines
assembled to offer a great sacrifice to
[a]Dagon their god, and to rejoice, for they
said,

"Our god has given Samson our
enemy into our hands."

24 When the people saw him, [a]they
praised their god, for they said,

"Our god has given our enemy
into our hands,
Even the destroyer of our
country,
Who has slain many of us."

25 It so happened when [1]they were in
high spirits, that they said, "Call for Samson, that he may amuse us." So they
called for Samson from the prison, and he

---

2 [a]1 Sam 23:26; Ps 118:10-12
5 [1]Lit *by what* [a]Josh 13:3 [b]Judg 14:15
6 [1]Lit *by what*
9 [1]Lit *smells*
10 [1]Lit *by what*
11 [1]Lit *with which work has not been done*
12 [1]Lit *them*
13 [1]Lit *by what* [2]Lit *head* [3]The passage in brackets is found in Gr but not in any Heb mss
14 [1]Lit *head*
15 [a]Judg 14:16
16 [1]Lit *impatient to the point of*
17 [a]Num 6:2,5; Judg 13:5
19 [1]Lit *head*
20 [a]Num 14:42, 43; Josh 7:12; 1 Sam 16:14
23 [a]1 Sam 5:2
24 [a]1 Sam 31:9; 1 Chr 10:9; Ps 97:7
25 [1]Lit *their heart was pleasant*

[2]entertained them. And they made him
stand between the pillars.
26 Then Samson said to the boy who
was holding his hand, "Let me feel the
pillars on which the house rests, that I
may lean against them."
27 Now the house was full of men and
women, and all the lords of the Philistines were there. And about 3,000 men
and women were on the roof looking on
while Samson was amusing *them.*

Samson Is Avenged

28 ¶ [a]Then Samson called to the LORD
and said, "O Lord [1]GOD, please remember me and please strengthen me just this
time, O God, that I may at once [b]be
avenged of the Philistines for my two
eyes."
29 Samson grasped the two middle pillars on which the house rested, and
braced himself against them, the one
with his right hand and the other with his
left.
30 And Samson said, "Let me die with
the Philistines!" And he bent with [1]all
his might so that the house fell on the
lords and all the people who were in it.
So the dead whom he killed at his death
were more than those whom he killed in
his life.
31 Then his brothers and all his father's household came down, took him,
brought him up and buried him between
Zorah and Eshtaol in the tomb of Manoah
his father. [a]Thus he had judged Israel
twenty years.

Micah's Idolatry

17 Now there was a man of the hill
country of Ephraim whose name
was Micah.
2 He said to his mother, "The eleven
hundred *pieces* of silver which were tak-
en from you, about which you uttered a
curse [1]in my hearing, behold, the silver
is with me; I took it." And his mother
said, "Blessed be my son by the LORD."
3 He then returned the eleven hundred *pieces* of silver to his mother, and
his mother said, "I wholly dedicate the
silver from my hand to the LORD for my
son [a]to make a graven image and a molten image; now therefore, I will return
[1]them to you."
4 So when he returned the silver to
his mother, his mother took two hundred
pieces of silver and gave them to the silversmith who made [1]them into a graven
image and a molten image, and [2]they
were in the house of Micah.
5 And the man Micah had a
[1a]shrine and he made an [b]ephod and
[2c]household idols and [3]consecrated
one of his sons, [d]that he might become
his priest.
6 In those days [a]there was no king in
Israel; [b]every man did what was right in
his own eyes.
7 ¶ Now there was a young man from
[a]Bethlehem in Judah, of the family of
Judah, who was a Levite; and he was
[1]staying there.
8 Then the man departed from the
city, from Bethlehem in Judah, to [1]stay
wherever he might find *a place;* and as he
made his journey, he came to the [a]hill
country of Ephraim to the house of Micah.
9 Micah said to him, "Where do you
come from?" And he said to him, "I am a
Levite from Bethlehem in Judah, and I am
going to [1]stay wherever I may find *a
place.*"
10 Micah then said to him, "Dwell
with me and be [a]a father and a priest to
me, and I will give you ten *pieces* of silver
a year, a suit of clothes, and your mainte-
nance." So the Levite went *in.*
11 The Levite agreed to live with the
man, and the young man became to him
like one of his sons.
12 So Micah [1]consecrated the Levite,
and the young man [a]became his priest
and [2]lived in the house of Micah.
13 Then Micah said, "Now I know that
the LORD will prosper me, seeing I have
a Levite as priest."

Danites Seek Territory

18 [a]In those days there was no king
of Israel; and [b]in those days the
tribe of the Danites was seeking an inheritance for themselves to live in, for until
that day [1]an inheritance had not [2]been
allotted to them as a possession among
the tribes of Israel.
2 So the sons of Dan sent from their
family five men out of their whole number, [1]valiant men from [a]Zorah and Eshtaol, to spy out the land and to search it;
and they said to them, "Go, search the
land." And they came to [b]the hill country
of Ephraim, to the house of Micah, and
lodged there.
3 When they were near the house of
Micah, they recognized the voice of the
young man, the Levite; and they turned
aside there and said to him, "Who
brought you here? And what are you doing in this *place?* And what do you have
here?"
4 He said to them, "Thus and so has
Micah done to me, and he has hired me
and [a]I have become his priest."
5 They said to him, "Inquire of God,
please, that we may know whether our

25 [2]Lit *made sport before them*
28 [1]Heb *YHWH,* usually rendered LORD [a]Judg 15:18 [b]Jer 15:15
30 [1]Lit *strength*
31 [a]Judg 15:20
17:2 [1]Lit *and also spoke it in my ears*
3 [1]Lit *it* [a]Ex 20:4,23; 34:17
4 [1]Lit *it* [2]Lit *it was*
5 [1]Lit *house of gods* [2]Heb *teraphim* [3]Lit *filled the hand of* [a]Judg 18:24 [b]Judg 8:27; 18:14 [c]Gen 31:19 [d]Num 3:10
6 [a]Judg 18:1; 19:1 [b]Deut 12:8; Judg 21:25
7 [1]Or *sojourning* [a]Judg 19:1; Ruth 1:1,2; Mic 5:2; Matt 2:1
8 [1]Or *sojourn* [a]Josh 24:33
9 [1]Or *sojourn*
10 [a]Judg 18:19
12 [1]Lit *filled the hand of* [2]Lit *was* [a]Num 16:10; 18:1-7
18:1 [1]Lit *it* [2]Lit *fallen* [a]Judg 17:6; 19:1 [b]Josh 19:40-48
2 [1]Lit *men, sons of valor* [a]Judg 13:25 [b]Judg 17:1
4 [a]Judg 17:12

way on which we are going will be prosperous."
6 The priest said to them, "Go in
peace; your way in which you are going
[1]has the LORD'S approval."
7 ¶ Then the five men departed and
came to [a]Laish and saw the people who
were in it living in security, after the
manner of the Sidonians, quiet and secure; for there was no [1]ruler humiliating
them for anything in the land, and they
were far from the Sidonians and had no
dealings with anyone.
8 When they came back to their
brothers at Zorah and Eshtaol, their
brothers said to them, "What *do* you *re-*
port?"
9 They said, "Arise, and let us go up
against them; for we have seen the land,
and behold, it is very good. And will you
[1]sit still? Do not delay to go, to enter, to
possess the land.
10 "When you enter, you will come to
a secure people with a spacious land; for
God has given it into your hand, [a]a place
where there is no lack of anything that is
on the earth."
11 ¶ Then from the family of the Danites, from Zorah and from Eshtaol, six
hundred men armed with weapons of
war set out.
12 They went up and camped at
Kiriath-jearim in Judah. Therefore they
called that place [1a]Mahaneh-dan to this
day; behold, it is [2]west of Kiriath-jearim.
13 They passed from there to the hill
country of Ephraim and came to the
house of Micah.

Danites Take Micah's Idols

14 ¶ Then the five men who went to
spy out the country of Laish said to their
kinsmen, "Do you know that there are in
these houses [a]an ephod and [1]household
idols and a graven image and a molten
image? Now therefore, consider what
you should do."
15 They turned aside there and came
to the house of the young man, the Levite, to the house of Micah, and asked
him of his welfare.
16 The six hundred men armed with
their weapons of war, who were of the
sons of Dan, stood by the entrance of the
gate.
17 Now the five men who went to spy
out the land went up *and* entered there,
and took [a]the graven image and the
ephod and [1]household idols and the molten image, while the priest stood by the
entrance of the gate with the six hundred
men armed with weapons of war.
18 When these went into Micah's
house and took the graven image, the
ephod and [1]household idols and the molten image, the priest said to them, "What
are you doing?"
19 They said to him, "Be silent, [a]put
your hand over your mouth and come
with us, and be to us [b]a father and a
priest. Is it better for you to be a priest to
the house of one man, or to be priest to
a tribe and a family in Israel?"
20 The priest's heart was glad, and he
took the ephod and [1]household idols and
the graven image and went among the
people.
21 ¶ Then they turned and departed,
and put the little ones and the livestock
and the valuables in front of them.
22 When they had gone some distance
from the house of Micah, the men who
were in the houses near Micah's house
assembled and overtook the sons of Dan.
23 They cried to the sons of Dan, who
turned [1]around and said to Micah,
"What is *the matter* with you, that you
have assembled together?"
24 He said, "You have taken away my
gods which I made, and the priest, and
have gone away, and what do I have besides? So how can you say to me, 'What
is *the matter* with you?' "
25 The sons of Dan said to him, "Do
not let your voice be heard among us, or
else [1]fierce men will fall upon you and
you will [2]lose your life, with the lives of
your household."
26 So the sons of Dan went on their
way; and when Micah saw that they were
too strong for him, he turned and went
back to his house.
27 ¶ Then they took what Micah had
made and the priest who had belonged to
him, and came to [a]Laish, to a people
quiet and secure, and struck them with
the edge of the sword; and they burned
the city with fire.
28 And there was no one to deliver
them, because it was far from Sidon and
they had no dealings with anyone, and it
was in the valley which is near [a]Beth-
rehob. And they rebuilt the city and lived
in it.
29 [a]They called the name of the city
Dan, after the name of Dan their father
who was born in Israel; however, the
name of the city formerly was Laish.
30 The sons of Dan set up for themselves [a]the graven image; and Jonathan,
the son of [b]Gershom, the son of [1]Manas-
seh, [a]he and his sons were priests to the
tribe of the Danites until the day of the
captivity of the land.
31 So they set up for themselves Micah's graven image which he had made,
all the time that the [a]house of God was
at Shiloh.

6 [1]Lit *is before the LORD*
7 [1]Lit *possessor of restraint* [a]Josh 19:47; Judg 18:29
9 [1]Lit *be*
10 [a]Deut 8:9
12 [1]I.e. the camp of Dan [2]Lit *behind* [a]Judg 13:25
14 [1]Heb *teraphim* [a]Judg 17:5
17 [1]Heb *teraphim* [a]Gen 31:19,30; Is 41:29; Mic 5:13
18 [1]Heb *teraphim*
19 [a]Job 21:5; 29:9; 40:4 [b]Judg 17:10
20 [1]Heb *teraphim*
23 [1]Lit *their faces*
25 [1]Lit *bitter of soul* [2]Lit *gather*
27 [a]Josh 19:47; Judg 18:7
28 [a]2 Sam 10:6
29 [a]Josh 19:47
30 [1]Some ancient versions read *Moses* [a]Judg 17:3,5 [b]Ex 2:22; 18:3
31 [a]Josh 18:1

A Levite's Concubine Degraded

19 Now it came about in those days,
when [a]there was no king in Isra-
el, that there was a certain Levite [1]stay-
ing in the remote part of the hill country
of Ephraim, who took a concubine for
himself from Bethlehem in Judah.
2 But his concubine played the harlot
against him, and she went away from him
to her father's house in Bethlehem in Judah, and was there for a period of four
months.
3 Then her husband arose and went
after her to [a]speak [1]tenderly to her in
order to bring her back, [2]taking with him
his servant and a pair of donkeys. So she
brought him into her father's house, and
when the girl's father saw him, he was
glad to meet him.
4 His father-in-law, the girl's father,
detained him; and he remained with him
three days. So they ate and drank and
lodged there.
5 Now on the fourth day they got up
early in the morning, and he [1]prepared
to go; and the girl's father said to his son-
in-law, "[a]Sustain [2]yourself with a piece
of bread, and afterward you may go."
6 So both of them sat down and ate
and drank together; and the girl's father
said to the man, "Please be willing to
spend the night, and [a]let your heart be
merry."
7 Then the man arose to go, but his
father-in-law urged him so that he spent
the night there again.
8 On the fifth day he arose to go early
in the morning, and the girl's father said,
"Please sustain [1]yourself, and wait until
[2]afternoon"; so both of them ate.
9 When the man arose to go along
with his concubine and servant, his
father-in-law, the girl's father, said to
him, "Behold now, the day has drawn
[1]to a close; please spend the night. Lo,
the day is [2]coming to an end; spend the
night here that your heart may be merry.
Then tomorrow you may arise early for
your journey so that you may go [3]home."
10 ¶ But the man was not willing to
spend the night, so he arose and departed
and came to *a place* opposite [a]Jebus (that
is, Jerusalem). And there were with him
a pair of saddled donkeys; his concubine
also was with him.
11 When they *were* near Jebus, the
day was almost gone; and [a]the servant
said to his master, "Please come, and let
us turn aside into this city of the Jebusites
and spend the night in it."
12 However, his master said to him,
"We will not turn aside into the city of
foreigners who are not of the sons of Israel; but we will go on as far as Gibeah."
13 He said to his servant, "Come and
let us approach one of these places; and
we will spend the night in Gibeah or Ramah."
14 So they passed along and went their
way, and the sun set on them near Gibeah which belongs to Benjamin.
15 They turned aside there in order to
enter *and* lodge in Gibeah. When [1]they
entered, [1]they sat down in the open
square of the city, for no one took them
into *his* house to spend the night.
16 ¶ Then behold, an old man was
coming out of the field from his work at
evening. Now the man was from [a]the
hill country of Ephraim, and he was
[1]staying in Gibeah, but the men of the
place [b]were Benjamites.
17 And he lifted up his eyes and saw
the traveler in the open square of the city;
and the old man said, "Where are you
going, and where do you come from?"
18 He said to him, "We are passing
from Bethlehem in Judah to the remote
part of the hill country of Ephraim, *for* I
am from there, and I went to Bethlehem
in Judah. But I am *now* going to [1]my
house, and no man will take me into his
house.
19 "Yet there is both straw and fodder
for our donkeys, and also bread and wine
for me, [1]your maidservant, and [a]the
young man who is with your servants;
there is no lack of anything."
20 The old man said, "[a]Peace to you.
Only let me *take care of* all your needs;
however, do not spend the night in the
open square."
21 [a]So he took him into his house
and gave the donkeys fodder, and they
washed their feet and ate and drank.
22 ¶ While they were [1]celebrating,
behold, [a]the men of the city, certain
[2b]worthless fellows, surrounded the
house, pounding the door; and they
spoke to the owner of the house, the old
man, saying, "Bring out the man who
came into your house that we may have
[3]relations with him."
23 Then the man, the owner of the
house, went out to them and said to
them, "No, my fellows, please do not act
so wickedly; since this man has come into
my house, [a]do not commit this act of
folly.
24 "[a]Here is my virgin daughter and
his concubine. Please let me bring them
out that you may ravish them and do to
them [1]whatever you wish. But do not
commit such an act of folly against this
man."
25 But the men would not listen to
him. So the man seized his concubine

19:1 [1]Or *sojourning* [a]Judg 18:1
3 [1]Lit *to her heart* [2]Lit *and* [a]Gen 34:3; 50:21
5 [1]Lit *arose* [2]Lit *your heart* [a]Gen 18:5; Judg 19:8
6 [a]Judg 16:25; 19:9,22; Ruth 3:7; 1 Kin 21:7; Esth 1:10
8 [1]Lit *your heart* [2]Lit *the day declines*
9 [1]Lit *toward evening* [2]Lit *declining* [3]Lit *to your tent*
10 [a]1 Chr 11:4, 5
11 [a]Judg 19:19
15 [1]So with Gr; M.T. *he*
16 [1]Or *sojourning* [a]Judg 19:1 [b]Judg 19:14
18 [1]Heb *the house of the* LORD, cf v 29
19 [1]I.e. my concubine [a]Judg 19:11
20 [a]Gen 43:23; Judg 6:23
21 [a]Gen 24:32, 33
22 [1]Lit *making their hearts merry* [2]Lit *sons of Belial* [3]Lit *intercourse* [a]Gen 19:4,5; Ezek 16:46-48 [b]Deut 13:13; 1 Sam 2:12; 1 Kin 21:10; 2 Cor 6:15
23 [a]Gen 34:7; Deut 22:21; Judg 20:6; 2 Sam 13:12
24 [1]Lit *the good in your eyes* [a]Gen 19:8

and brought *her* out to them; and they raped her and abused her all night until morning, then let her go at the approach of dawn.

26 [1]As the day began to dawn, the woman came and fell down at the doorway of the man's house where her master was, until *full* daylight.

27 ¶ When her master arose in the morning and opened the doors of the house and went out to go on his way, then behold, his concubine was lying at the doorway of the house with her hands on the threshold.

28 He said to her, "Get up and let us go," [a]but there was no answer. Then he placed her on the donkey; and the man arose and went to his [1]home.

29 When he entered his house, he took a knife and laid hold of his concubine and [a]cut her in twelve pieces, limb by limb, and sent her throughout the territory of Israel.

30 All who saw *it* said, "Nothing like this has *ever* happened or been seen from the day when the sons of Israel came up from the land of Egypt to this day. Consider it, [a]take counsel and speak up!"

Resolve to Punish the Guilty

20 Then all the sons of Israel from Dan to Beersheba, including the land of Gilead, came out, and the congregation assembled as one man to the LORD at [a]Mizpah.

2 The [1]chiefs of all the people, *even* of all the tribes of Israel, took their stand in the assembly of the people of God, 400,000 foot [2]soldiers [a]who drew the sword.

3 (Now the sons of Benjamin heard that the sons of Israel had gone up to Mizpah.) And the sons of Israel said, "Tell *us,* how did this wickedness take place?"

4 So the Levite, the husband of the woman who was murdered, answered and said, "I came with my concubine to spend the night at Gibeah which belongs to Benjamin.

5 "But the [a]men of Gibeah rose up against me and surrounded the house at night because of me. They intended to kill me; instead, they [b]ravished my concubine so that she died.

6 "And I [a]took hold of my concubine and cut her in pieces and sent her throughout the land of Israel's inheritance; for [b]they have committed a lewd and disgraceful act in Israel.

7 "Behold, all you sons of Israel, [a]give your advice and counsel here."

8 ¶ Then all the people arose as one man, saying, "Not one of us will go to his tent, nor will any of us return to his house.

9 "But now this is the thing which we will do to Gibeah; *we will go up* against it by lot.

10 "And we will take 10 men out of 100 throughout the tribes of Israel, and 100 out of 1,000, and 1,000 out of 10,000 to [1]supply food for the people, that when they come to [2]Gibeah of Benjamin, they may [3]punish *them* for all the disgraceful acts that they have committed in Israel."

11 Thus all the men of Israel were gathered against the city, united as one man.

12 ¶ Then the tribes of Israel sent men through the entire [1]tribe of Benjamin, saying, "What is this wickedness that has taken place among you?

13 "Now then, deliver up the men, the [1a]worthless fellows in Gibeah, that we may put them to death and [b]remove *this* wickedness from Israel." But the sons of Benjamin would not listen to the voice of their brothers, the sons of Israel.

14 The sons of Benjamin gathered from the cities to Gibeah, to go out to battle against the sons of Israel.

15 From the cities on that day the [a]sons of Benjamin were [1]numbered, 26,000 men who draw the sword, besides the inhabitants of Gibeah who were [1]numbered, 700 choice men.

16 Out of all these people 700 [a]choice men were left-handed; each one could sling a stone at a hair and not miss.

17 ¶ Then the men of Israel besides Benjamin were [1]numbered, 400,000 men who draw the sword; all these were men of war.

Civil War, Benjamin Defeated

18 ¶ Now the sons of Israel arose, went up to Bethel, and [a]inquired of God and said, "Who shall go up first for us to battle against the sons of Benjamin?" Then the LORD said, "Judah *shall go up* first."

19 ¶ So the sons of Israel arose in the morning and camped against Gibeah.

20 The men of Israel went out to battle against Benjamin, and the men of Israel arrayed for battle against them at Gibeah.

21 Then the sons of Benjamin came out of Gibeah and [1a]felled to the ground on that day 22,000 men of Israel.

22 But the people, the men of Israel, encouraged themselves and arrayed for battle again in the place where they had arrayed themselves the first day.

23 [a]The sons of Israel went up and wept before the LORD until evening, and [b]inquired of the LORD, saying, "Shall we

19:26 [1]Lit *At the turning of the morning*
28 [1]Lit *place* [a]Judg 20:5
29 [a]1 Sam 11:7
30 [a]Judg 20:7; Prov 13:10
20:1 [a]1 Sam 7:5
2 [1]Lit *cornerstones* [2]Lit *men* [a]Judg 8:10
5 [a]Judg 19:22 [b]Judg 19:25f
6 [a]Judg 19:29 [b]Gen 34:7; Josh 7:15
7 [a]Judg 19:30
10 [1]Lit *take* [2]Heb *Geba* [3]Lit *do*
12 [1]Lit *tribes*
13 [1]Lit *sons of Belial* [a]2 Cor 6:15 [b]Deut 13:5; 17:12; 1 Cor 5:13
15 [1]Or *mustered* [a]Num 1:36,37; 2:23; 26:41
16 [a]Judg 3:15; 1 Chr 12:2
17 [1]Or *mustered*
18 [a]Num 27:21; Judg 20:23,27
21 [1]Lit *destroyed* [a]Judg 20:25
23 [a]Josh 7:6,7 [b]Judg 20:18

again draw near for battle against the
sons of my brother Benjamin?" And the
LORD said, "Go up against him."
24 ¶ Then the sons of Israel [1]came
against the sons of Benjamin the second
day.
25 Benjamin went out [1]against them
from Gibeah the second day and [2]felled
to the ground again 18,000 men of the
sons of Israel; all these drew the sword.
26 Then [a]all the sons of Israel and all
the people went up and came to Bethel
and wept; thus they remained there before the LORD and fasted that day until
evening. And they offered burnt offerings
and peace offerings before the LORD.
27 The sons of Israel [a]inquired of the
LORD (for the ark of the covenant of God
was there in those days,
28 and Phinehas the son of Eleazar,
Aaron's son, stood before it to *minister* in
those days), saying, "Shall I yet again go
out to battle against the sons of my brother Benjamin, or shall I cease?" And the
LORD said, "Go up, [a]for tomorrow I will
deliver them into your hand."
29 ¶ [a]So Israel set men in ambush
around Gibeah.
30 The sons of Israel went up against
the sons of Benjamin on the third day and
arrayed themselves against Gibeah as at
other times.
31 [a]The sons of Benjamin went out
[1]against the people and were drawn
away from the city, and they began to
strike [2]and kill some of the people as
at other times, on the highways, one of
which goes up to Bethel and the other to
Gibeah, *and* in the field, about thirty men
of Israel.
32 The sons of Benjamin said, "They
are struck down before us, as at the first."
But the sons of Israel said, "Let us flee
that we may draw them away from the
city to the highways."
33 Then all the men of Israel arose
from their place and arrayed themselves
at Baal-tamar; [a]and the men of Israel in
ambush broke out of their place, even out
of Maareh-geba.
34 When ten thousand choice men
from all Israel came against Gibeah, the
battle became [1]fierce; [a]but [2]Benjamin
did not know that [3]disaster was [4]close
to them.
35 And the LORD struck Benjamin before Israel, so that the sons of Israel destroyed 25,100 men of Benjamin that
day, all [1]who draw the sword.
36 ¶ So the sons of Benjamin saw that
they were [1]defeated. [a]When the men of
Israel gave [2]ground to Benjamin because
they relied on the men in ambush whom
they had set against Gibeah,
37 [a]the men in ambush hurried and
rushed against Gibeah; the men in ambush also deployed and struck all the city
with the edge of the sword.
38 Now the appointed sign between
the men of Israel and the men in ambush
was [a]that they would make a great cloud
of smoke rise from the city.
39 Then the men of Israel turned in
the battle, and Benjamin began to strike
[1]and kill about thirty men of Israel, [a]for
they said, "Surely they are [2]defeated before us, as in the first battle."
40 But when the cloud began to rise
from the city in a column of smoke, Benjamin looked [a]behind them; and behold,
the whole city was going up *in smoke* to
heaven.
41 Then the men of Israel turned, and
the men of Benjamin were terrified; for
they saw that [1a]disaster was [2]close to
them.
42 Therefore, they turned their backs
before the men of Israel [a]toward the direction of the wilderness, but the battle
overtook them while those who came out
of the cities destroyed them in the midst
of them.
43 [a]They surrounded Benjamin, pursued them without rest *and* trod them
down opposite Gibeah toward the [1]east.
44 Thus 18,000 men of Benjamin fell;
all these were valiant warriors.
45 [1]The rest turned and fled toward
the wilderness to the rock of [a]Rimmon,
but they [2]caught 5,000 of them on the
highways and overtook them [3]at Gidom
and [4]killed 2,000 of them.
46 So all of Benjamin who fell that day
were 25,000 men who draw the sword;
all these were valiant warriors.
47 But 600 men turned and fled toward the wilderness to the rock of Rimmon, and they remained at the rock of
Rimmon four months.
48 The men of Israel then turned back
against the sons of Benjamin and struck
them with the edge of the sword, both
the entire city with the cattle and all that
they found; they also set on fire all the
cities which they found.

Mourning Lost Tribe

21 Now the men of Israel [a]had
sworn in Mizpah, saying, "None
of us shall give his daughter to Benjamin
[1]in marriage."
2 [a]So the people came to Bethel and
sat there before God until evening, and
lifted up their voices and wept [1]bitterly.
3 They said, "Why, O LORD, God of
Israel, has this come about in Israel, so
that one tribe should be *missing* today in
Israel?"

24 [1]Lit *approached*
25 [1]Lit *to meet* [2]Lit *destroyed*
26 [a]Judg 20:23; 21:2
27 [a]Judg 20:18
28 [a]Judg 7:9
29 [a]Josh 8:4
31 [1]Lit *to meet* [2]Lit *slain ones* [a]Josh 8:16
33 [a]Josh 8:19
34 [1]Lit *heavy* [2]Lit *they* [3]Lit *evil* [4]Lit *touching* [a]Josh 8:14; Job 21:13
35 [1]Lit *these*
36 [1]Lit *smitten* [2]Lit *place* [a]Josh 8:15
37 [a]Josh 8:19
38 [a]Josh 8:20
39 [1]Lit *slain ones* [2]Lit *smitten* [a]Judg 20:32
40 [a]Josh 8:20
41 [1]Lit *evil* [2]Lit *touching* [a]Prov 5:22; 11:5,6; 29:6
42 [a]Josh 8:15, 24
43 [1]Lit *sunrise* [a]Hos 9:9; 10:9
45 [1]So with Gr; Heb *And they* [2]Lit *gleaned* [3]Lit *as far as* [4]Lit *smote* [a]Judg 21:13
21:1 [1]Lit *for a wife* [a]Judg 21:7, 18
2 [1]Lit *with great weeping* [a]Judg 20:26

4 It came about the next day that the people arose early and built [a]an altar there and offered burnt offerings and peace offerings.

5 ¶ Then the sons of Israel said, “Who is there among all the tribes of Israel who did not come up in the assembly to the LORD?” For [1]they had taken a great oath concerning him [a]who did not come up to the LORD at Mizpah, saying, “He shall surely be put to death.”

6 And the sons of Israel were sorry for their brother Benjamin and said, “One tribe is cut off from Israel today.

7 “What shall we do for wives for those who are left, since we have [a]sworn by the LORD not to give them any of our daughters in marriage?”

Provision for Their Survival

8 ¶ And they said, “What one is there of the tribes of Israel who did not come up to the LORD at Mizpah?” And behold, no one had come to the camp from Jabesh-gilead to the assembly.

9 For when the people were [1]numbered, behold, not one of the inhabitants of Jabesh-gilead was there.

10 And the congregation sent 12,000 of the valiant warriors there, and commanded them, saying, “Go and [a]strike the inhabitants of Jabesh-gilead with the edge of the sword, with the women and the little ones.

11 “This is the thing that you shall do: you [a]shall utterly destroy every man and every woman who has [1]lain with a man.”

12 And they found among the inhabitants of Jabesh-gilead 400 young virgins who had not known a man by lying with [1]him; and they brought them to the camp at Shiloh, which is in the land of Canaan.

13 ¶ Then the whole congregation sent *word* and spoke to the sons of Benjamin who were [a]at the rock of Rimmon, and [b]proclaimed peace to them.

14 Benjamin returned at that time, and they gave them the women whom they had kept alive from the women of Jabesh-gilead; yet they [1]were not enough for them.

15 And the people were sorry for Benjamin because the LORD had made a breach in the tribes of Israel.

16 ¶ Then the elders of the congregation said, “What shall we do for wives for those who are left, since the women are destroyed out of Benjamin?”

17 They said, “*There must be* an inheritance for the survivors of Benjamin, so that a tribe will not be blotted out from Israel.

18 “But we cannot give them wives of our daughters.” For the sons of Israel [a]had sworn, saying, “Cursed is he who gives a wife to Benjamin.”

19 ¶ So they said, “Behold, there is a feast of the LORD from year to year in [a]Shiloh, which is on the north side of Bethel, on the east side of the highway that goes up from Bethel to Shechem, and on the south side of Lebonah.”

20 And they commanded the sons of Benjamin, saying, “Go and lie in wait in the vineyards,

21 and watch; and behold, if the daughters of Shiloh come out to [1a]take part in the dances, then you shall come out of the vineyards and each of you shall catch his wife from the daughters of Shiloh, and go to the land of Benjamin.

22 “It shall come about, when their fathers or their brothers come to complain to us, that we shall say to them, ‘Give them to us voluntarily, because we did not take for each man *of Benjamin* [1]a wife in battle, [2a]nor did you give *them* to them, *else* you would now be guilty.’ ”

23 The sons of Benjamin did so, and took wives according to their number from those who danced, whom they carried away. And they went and returned to their inheritance and [a]rebuilt the cities and lived in them.

24 The sons of Israel departed from there at that time, every man to his tribe and family, and each one of them went out from there to his inheritance.

25 ¶ [a]In those days there was no king in Israel; everyone did what was right in his own eyes.

---

4 [a]Deut 12:5; 2 Sam 24:25
5 [1]Lit *there was a great oath* [a]Judg 5:23
7 [a]Judg 21:1
9 [1]Or *mustered*
10 [a]Num 31:17; Judg 5:23; 1 Sam 11:7
11 [1]Lit *known lying with* [a]Num 31:17
12 [1]Lit *a male*
13 [a]Judg 20:47 [b]Deut 20:10
14 [1]Lit *did not find it so*
18 [a]Judg 21:1
19 [a]Josh 18:1; Judg 18:31; 1 Sam 1:3
21 [1]Lit *dance* [a]Ex 15:20; Judg 11:34
22 [1]Lit *his* [2]Lit *because* [a]Judg 21:1,18
23 [a]Judg 20:48
25 [a]Judg 17:6; 18:1; 19:1

Ruth

Title and Background

This book is named after the leading character whose story is told here. Ruth was the great-grandmother of David and an ancestress of Jesus (Matthew 1:1,5). The story is set in the time of the judges and reflects a temporary time of peace between Israel and Moab. It gives a series of intimate glances into the private lives of the members of an Israelite family and presents a delightful account of a remnant of true faith and piety during this period.

Author and Date of Writing

The author is unknown, although Jewish tradition points to Samuel. This is unlikely because the mention of David (4:17,22) implies a later date. The literary style of Hebrew used suggests it was written during the monarchy, probably sometime after 1000 B.C.

Theme and Message

Redemption is a key concept throughout the book; the Hebrew word in its various forms occurs twenty-three times. The word shows how God is working out His plan for salvation. The book of Ruth also illustrates love and devotion—self-giving love that fulfills God's law, and God's love in blessing the lives of His children.

Outline

I. Introduction: Naomi Emptied (1:1–5)
II. Naomi Returns From Moab (1:6–22)
III. Ruth and Boaz Meet in the Harvest Fields (2:1–23)
IV. Ruth Goes to Boaz at the Threshing Floor (3:1–18)
V. Boaz Arranges to Marry Ruth (4:1–12)
VI. Conclusion: Naomi Filled (4:13–17)
VII. Epilogue: Genealogy of David (4:18–22)

Naomi Widowed

1 Now it came about in the days
[a]when the judges [1]governed, that
there was [b]a famine in the land. And a
certain man [c]of Bethlehem in Judah
went to sojourn in the land of Moab
[2]with his wife and his two sons.
2 The name of the man *was* Elimelech, and the name of his wife, Naomi;
and the names of his two sons *were* Mahlon and Chilion, Ephrathites of Bethlehem in Judah. Now they [a]entered the
land of Moab and remained there.
3 Then Elimelech, Naomi's husband,
died; and she was left with her two sons.
4 They took for themselves Moabite
women *as* wives; the name of the one
was Orpah and the name of the other
Ruth. And they lived there about ten
years.
5 Then [1]both Mahlon and Chilion
also died, and the woman was bereft of
her two children and her husband.
6 ¶Then she arose with her
daughters-in-law that she might return
from the land of Moab, for she had heard
in the land of Moab that the LORD had
[a]visited His people in [b]giving them food.
7 So she departed from the place
where she was, and her two daughters-
in-law with her; and they went on the
way to return to the land of Judah.
8 And Naomi said to her two
daughters-in-law, "Go, return each of
you to her mother's house. [a]May the
LORD deal kindly with you as you have
dealt with the dead and with me.
9 "May the LORD grant that you may
find rest, each in the house of her husband." Then she kissed them, and they
lifted up their voices and wept.
10 And they said to her, "*No,* but we
will surely return with you to your people."
11 But Naomi said, "Return, my
daughters. Why should you go with me?
Have I yet sons in my womb, that [a]they
may be your husbands?
12 "Return, my daughters! Go, for I am
too old to have a husband. If I said I have

1:1 [1]Or *judged* [2]Lit *he, and* [a]Judg 2:16-18 [b]Gen 12:10; 26:1; 2 Kin 8:1 [c]Judg 17:8; Mic 5:2
2 [a]Judg 3:30
5 [1]Lit *both of them*
6 [a]Ex 4:31; Jer 29:10; Zeph 2:7 [b]Ps 132:15; Matt 6:11
8 [a]2 Tim 1:16
11 [a]Gen 38:11; Deut 25:5

hope, if I should even have a husband
tonight and also bear sons,
13 would you therefore wait until they
were grown? Would you therefore refrain
from marrying? No, my daughters; for it
is [1]harder for me than for you, for [a]the
hand of the LORD has gone forth
against me."

Ruth's Loyalty

14 And they lifted up their voices and
wept again; and Orpah kissed her
mother-in-law, but Ruth clung to her.
15 ¶ Then she said, "Behold, your
sister-in-law has gone back to her people
and her [a]gods; return after your sister-in-
law."
16 But Ruth said, "Do not urge me to
leave you *or* turn back from following
you; for where you go, I will go, and
where you lodge, I will lodge. Your people *shall be* my people, and your God, my
God.
17 "Where you die, I will die, and there
I will be buried. Thus may [a]the LORD do
to me, and worse, if *anything but* death
parts you and me."
18 When [a]she saw that she was determined to go with her, she [1]said no more
to her.
19 ¶ So they both went until they
came to Bethlehem. And when they had
come to Bethlehem, [a]all the city was
stirred because of them, and [1]the wom-
en said, "Is this Naomi?"
20 She said to them, "Do not call me
[1]Naomi; call me [2]Mara, for [3a]the Almighty has dealt very bitterly with me.
21 "I went out full, but [a]the LORD has
brought me back empty. Why do you call
me Naomi, since the LORD has witnessed
against me and [1]the Almighty has afflicted me?"
22 ¶ So Naomi returned, and with her
Ruth the Moabitess, her daughter-in-law,
who returned from the land of Moab.
And they came to Bethlehem at [a]the beginning of barley harvest.

Ruth Gleans in Boaz' Field

2 Now Naomi had [1]a kinsman of her
husband, a [2]man of great wealth, of
the family of [a]Elimelech, whose name
was Boaz.
2 And Ruth the Moabitess said to Naomi, "Please let me go to the field and
[a]glean among the ears of grain after one
in whose sight I may find favor." And she
said to her, "Go, my daughter."
3 So she departed and went and
gleaned in the field after the reapers; and
[1]she happened to come to the portion of
the field belonging to Boaz, who was of
the family of Elimelech.
4 Now behold, Boaz came from Bethlehem and said to the reapers, "[a]May the
LORD be with you." And they said to him,
"May the LORD bless you."
5 Then Boaz said to his servant who
was [1]in charge of the reapers, "Whose
young woman is this?"
6 The servant [1]in charge of the reapers replied, "She is the young Moabite
woman who returned with Naomi from
the land of Moab.
7 "And she said, 'Please let me glean
and gather after the reapers among the
sheaves.' Thus she came and has remained from the morning until now; she
has been sitting in the house for a little
while."
8 ¶ Then Boaz said to Ruth, "[1]Listen
carefully, my daughter. Do not go to glean
in another field; furthermore, do not go
on from this one, but stay here with my
maids.
9 "Let your eyes be on the field which
they reap, and go after them. Indeed, I
have commanded the servants not to
touch you. When you are thirsty, go to
the [1]water jars and drink from what the
servants draw."
10 Then she [a]fell on her face, bowing
to the ground and said to him, "Why have
I found favor in your sight that you should
take notice of me, since I am a foreigner?"
11 Boaz replied to her, "All that you
have done for your mother-in-law after
the death of your husband has been fully
reported to me, and how you left your
father and your mother and the land of
your birth, and came to a people that you
did not previously know.
12 "[a]May the LORD reward your work,
and your wages be full from the LORD, the
God of Israel, [b]under whose wings you
have come to seek refuge."
13 Then she said, "I have found favor
in your sight, my lord, for you have comforted me and indeed have spoken [1]kind-
ly to your maidservant, though I am not
like one of your maidservants."
14 ¶ At mealtime Boaz said to her,
"[1]Come here, that you may eat of the
bread and dip your piece of bread in the
vinegar." So she sat beside the reapers;
and he [2]served her roasted grain, and
she ate and was satisfied [a]and had some
left.
15 When she rose to glean, Boaz commanded his servants, saying, "Let her
glean even among the sheaves, and do
not insult her.
16 "Also you shall purposely pull out for
her *some grain* from the bundles and
leave *it* that she may glean, and do not
rebuke her."

13 [1]Lit *more bitter* [a]Judg 2:15; Job 19:21; Ps 32:4
15 [a]Josh 24:15; Judg 11:24
17 [a]1 Sam 3:17; 2 Kin 6:31
18 [1]Lit *ceased to speak* [a]Acts 21:14
19 [1]Lit *they* [a]Matt 21:10
20 [1]I.e. pleasant [2]I.e. bitter [3]Heb *Shaddai* [a]Ex 6:3; Job 6:4
21 [1]Heb *Shaddai* [a]Job 1:21
22 [a]Ex 9:31; Lev 23:10,11
2:1 [1]Or *an acquaintance* [2]Or *mighty, valiant man* [a]Ruth 1:2
2 [a]Lev 19:9,10; 23:22; Deut 24:19; Ruth 2:7
3 [1]Lit *her chance chanced upon*
4 [a]Judg 6:12; Ps 129:8; Luke 1:28; 2 Thess 3:16
5 [1]Lit *appointed over*
6 [1]Lit *who was appointed over*
8 [1]Lit *Have you not heard*
9 [1]Lit *vessels*
10 [a]1 Sam 25:23
12 [a]1 Sam 24:19 [b]Ruth 1:16; Ps 17:8; 36:7; 57:1; 61:4; 63:7; 91:4
13 [1]Lit *to the heart of your*
14 [1]Lit *Draw near* [2]Lit *held out to* [a]Ruth 2:18

17 ¶ So she gleaned in the field until
evening. Then she beat out what she had
gleaned, and it was about an ephah of
barley.
18 She took *it* up and went into the
city, and her mother-in-law saw what she
had gleaned. She also took *it* out and
[a]gave [1]Naomi what she had left after
[2]she was satisfied.
19 Her mother-in-law then said to her,
"Where did you glean today and where
did you work? May he who [a]took notice
of you be blessed." So she told her
mother-in-law with whom she had
worked and said, "The name of the man
with whom I worked today is Boaz."
20 Naomi said to her daughter-in-law,
"[a]May he be blessed of the LORD who
has not withdrawn his kindness to the
living and to the dead." Again Naomi said
to her, "The man is [1]our relative, he is
one of our [2]closest relatives."
21 Then Ruth the Moabitess said,
"[1]Furthermore, he said to me, 'You
should stay close to my servants until
they have finished all my harvest.' "
22 Naomi said to Ruth her daughter-
in-law, "It is good, my daughter, that you
go out with his maids, so that *others* do
not fall upon you in another field."
23 So she stayed close by the maids of
Boaz in order to glean until [a]the end of
the barley harvest and the wheat harvest.
And she lived with her mother-in-law.

Boaz Will Redeem Ruth

3 Then Naomi her mother-in-law said
to her, "My daughter, shall I not seek
[1]security for you, that it may be well
with you?
2 "Now is not Boaz [a]our [1]kinsman,
with whose maids you were? Behold, he
winnows barley at the threshing floor tonight.
3 "Wash yourself therefore, and
anoint yourself and put on your *best*
clothes, and go down to the threshing
floor; *but* do not make yourself known to
the man until he has finished eating and
drinking.
4 "It shall be when he lies down, that
you shall [1]notice the place where he lies,
and you shall go and uncover his feet and
lie down; then he will tell you what you
shall do."
5 She said to her, "[a]All that you say
I will do."
6 ¶ So she went down to the threshing floor and did according to all that her
mother-in-law had commanded her.
7 When Boaz had eaten and drunk
and [a]his heart was merry, he went to lie
down at the end of the heap of grain; and
she came secretly, and uncovered his feet
and lay down.
8 It happened in the middle of the
night that the man was startled and
[1]bent forward; and behold, a woman was
lying at his feet.
9 He said, "Who are you?" And she
answered, "I am Ruth your maid. So
spread your covering over your maid, for
you are a [1]close relative."
10 Then he said, "[a]May you be
blessed of the LORD, my daughter. You
have shown your last kindness to be better than the first by not going after young
men, whether poor or rich.
11 "Now, my daughter, do not fear. I
will do for you whatever you [1]ask, for all
my people in the [2]city know that you are
[a]a woman of excellence.
12 "Now it is true I am a [1]close relative; however, there is a [1]relative closer
than I.
13 "Remain this night, and when morning comes, [a]if he will [1]redeem you,
good; let him redeem you. But if he does
not wish to [1]redeem you, then I will redeem you, [b]as the LORD lives. Lie down
until morning."
14 ¶ So she lay at his feet until morning and rose before one could recognize
another; and he said, "[a]Let it not be
known that the woman came to the
threshing floor."
15 Again he said, "Give me the cloak
that is on you and hold it." So she held it,
and he measured six *measures* of barley
and laid *it* on her. Then [1]she went into
the city.
16 When she came to her mother-in-
law, she said, "[1]How did it go, my daughter?" And she told her all that the man
had done for her.
17 She said, "These six *measures* of
barley he gave to me, for he said, 'Do
not go to your mother-in-law empty-
handed.' "
18 Then she said, "Wait, my daughter,
until you know how the matter [1]turns
out; for the man will not rest until he has
[2]settled it today."

The Marriage of Ruth

4 Now Boaz went up to the gate and
sat down there, and behold, [a]the
[1]close relative of whom Boaz spoke was
passing by, so he said, "Turn aside,
[2]friend, sit down here." And he turned
aside and sat down.
2 He took ten men of the [a]elders of
the city and said, "Sit down here." So
they sat down.
3 Then he said to the [1]closest relative, "Naomi, who has come back from
the land of Moab, has to sell the piece

18 [1]Lit *her* [2]Lit *her satiety* [a]Ruth 2:14
19 [a]Ps 41:1
20 [1]Lit *near to us* [2]Lit *redeemers* [a]2 Sam 2:5
21 [1]Lit *Also that*
23 [a]Deut 16:9
3:1 [1]Lit *rest*
2 [1]Or *acquaintance* [a]Deut 25:5-10
4 [1]Lit *know*
5 [a]Eph 6:1; Col 3:20
7 [a]Judg 19:6,9; 2 Sam 13:28; 1 Kin 21:7; Esth 1:10
8 [1]Lit *twisted himself*
9 [1]Or *redeemer*
10 [a]Ruth 2:20
11 [1]Lit *say* [2]Lit *gate* [a]Prov 12:4; 31:10
12 [1]Or *redeemer*
13 [1]Or *act as close relative to* [a]Deut 25:5; Matt 22:24 [b]Judg 8:19; Jer 4:2; 12:16
14 [a]Rom 14:16; 2 Cor 8:21
15 [1]So with many mss; M.T. *he*
16 [1]Lit *Who are you?*
18 [1]Lit *falls* [2]Lit *finished the matter*
4:1 [1]Or *redeemer* [2]Lit *a certain one* [a]Ruth 3:12
2 [a]1 Kin 21:8; Prov 31:23
3 [1]Lit *redeemer*

of land [a]which belonged to our brother Elimelech.

4 "So I thought to [1]inform you, saying, '[a]Buy *it* before those who are sitting *here,* and before the elders of my people. If you will redeem *it,* redeem *it;* but if [2]not, tell me that I may know; for [b]there is no one but you to redeem *it,* and I am after you.' " And he said, "I will redeem *it.*"

5 Then Boaz said, "On the day you buy the field from the hand of Naomi, you must also acquire Ruth the Moabitess, the widow of the deceased, in order [a]to raise up the name of the deceased on his inheritance."

6 [a]The [1]closest relative said, "I cannot redeem *it* for myself, because I would [2]jeopardize my own inheritance. Redeem *it* for yourself; you *may have* my right of redemption, for I cannot redeem *it.*"

7 ¶ Now this was [a]*the custom* in former times in Israel concerning the redemption and the exchange *of land* to confirm any matter: a man removed his sandal and gave it to another; and this was the *manner of* attestation in Israel.

8 So the [1]closest relative said to Boaz, "Buy *it* for yourself." And he removed his sandal.

9 Then Boaz said to the elders and all the people, "You are witnesses today that I have bought from the hand of Naomi all that belonged to Elimelech and all that belonged to Chilion and Mahlon.

10 "Moreover, I have acquired Ruth the Moabitess, the widow of Mahlon, to be my wife in order to raise up the name of the deceased on his inheritance, so [a]that the name of the deceased will not be cut off from his brothers or from the [1]court of his *birth* place; you are witnesses today."

11 All the people who were in the [1]court, and the elders, said, "*We are* witnesses. May the LORD make the woman who is coming into your home [a]like Rachel and Leah, both of whom built the house of Israel; and may you achieve [2]wealth in Ephrathah and [3]become famous in Bethlehem.

12 "Moreover, may your house be like the house of [a]Perez whom Tamar bore to Judah, through the [1]offspring which the LORD will give you by this young woman."

13 ¶ So Boaz took Ruth, and she became his wife, and he went in to her. And [a]the LORD [1]enabled her to conceive, and she gave birth to a son.

14 Then the [a]women said to Naomi, "Blessed is the LORD who has not left you without a [1]redeemer today, and may his name [2]become famous in Israel.

15 "May he also be to you a restorer of life and a sustainer of your old age; for your daughter-in-law, who loves you [1][a]and is better to you than seven sons, has given birth to him."

The Line of David Began Here

16 Then Naomi took the child [1]and laid him in her lap, and became his nurse.

17 The neighbor women gave him a name, saying, "A son has been born to Naomi!" So they named him Obed. He is the father of Jesse, the father of David.

18 ¶ Now these are the generations of Perez: [a]to Perez [1]was born Hezron,

19 and to Hezron was born Ram, and to Ram, Amminadab,

20 and to Amminadab was born Nahshon, and to Nahshon, Salmon,

21 and to Salmon was born Boaz, and to Boaz, Obed,

22 and to Obed was born Jesse, and to Jesse, David.

3 [a]Lev 25:25

4 [1]Lit *uncover your ear* [2]Lit *no one will redeem* [a]Jer 32:7f [b]Lev 25:25

5 [a]Gen 38:8; Deut 25:5f; Matt 22:24

6 [1]Lit *redeemer* [2]Lit *ruin* [a]Lev 25:25

7 [a]Deut 25:8-10

8 [1]Lit *redeemer*

10 [1]Lit *gate* [a]Deut 25:6

11 [1]Lit *gate* [2]Or *power* [3]Lit *call the name in* [a]Gen 29:25-30

12 [1]Lit *seed* [a]Gen 38:29; 46:12; Ruth 4:18

13 [1]Lit *gave her conception* [a]Gen 29:31; 33:5

14 [1]Or *closest relative* [2]Lit *be called in* [a]Luke 1:58

15 [1]Lit *who* [a]Ruth 1:16,17; 2:11,12

16 [1]I.e. as her own

18 [1]Lit *begot,* and so through v 22 [a]Matt 1:3-6

1 Samuel

Title and Background

1 and 2 Samuel are named after the individual whom God used to establish kingship in Israel. These two books were originally one book, but it was divided into two parts by the translators of the *Septuagint* (the Greek translation of the Old Testament). The book of 1 Samuel records the lives of Samuel and Saul, and much of the life of David.

Author and Date of Writing

Who the author was is uncertain because the book itself gives no indication as to his identity. The author probably wrote shortly after the division of the kingdom that followed upon the death of Solomon in 930 B.C.

Theme and Message

1 Samuel portrays the establishment of kingship in Israel. When the people demanded a king, Samuel, by God's leading, anointed Saul to be the first king of Israel. But Saul was disobedient to God, and God rejected him as king. Then Samuel secretly anointed David to take Saul's place. The struggles between Saul and David make up the rest of the book. The weaknesses and sins of these men are shown, as well as the goodness of Samuel and David and their obedience to God.

Outline

I. Background for the Establishment of Kingship in Israel (1:1—7:17)
II. Establishment of Kingship in Israel (8:1—12:25)
III. Failure of Saul's Kingship (13:1—15:35)
IV. David and Saul (16:1—30:31)
V. Death of Saul (31:1–13)

Elkanah and His Wives

1 Now there was a certain man from
[a]Ramathaim-zophim from the [b]hill
country of Ephraim, and his name was
[c]Elkanah the son of Jeroham, the son of
Elihu, the son of Tohu, the son of Zuph,
an Ephraimite.
2 He had [a]two wives: the name of
one was [b]Hannah and the name of the
other Peninnah; and Peninnah had children, but Hannah had no children.
3 ¶ Now this man would go up from
his city [a]yearly [b]to worship and to sacrifice to the LORD of hosts in [c]Shiloh. And
the two sons of Eli, Hophni and Phinehas,
were priests to the LORD there.
4 When the day came that Elkanah
sacrificed, he [a]would give portions to Peninnah his wife and to all her sons and
her daughters;
5 but to Hannah he would give a double portion, for he loved Hannah, [a]but
the LORD had closed her womb.
6 Her rival, however, [a]would provoke her bitterly to irritate her, because
the LORD had closed her womb.

1:1 [a]1 Sam 1:19 [b]Josh 17:17,18; 24:33 [c]1 Chr 6:22-28,33-38
2 [a]Deut 21:15-17 [b]Luke 2:36
3 [a]Ex 34:23; 1 Sam 1:21; Luke 2:41 [b]Ex 23:14; Deut 12:5-7; 16:16 [c]Josh 18:1
4 [a]Deut 12:17, 18
5 [a]Gen 16:1; 30:1
6 [a]Job 24:21
8 [a]Ruth 4:15
9 [a]1 Sam 3:3
10 [1]Lit *bitter of soul*
11 [1]Lit *seed of men* [a]Num 30:6-11 [b]Gen 29:32 [c]Num 6:5; Judg 13:5
12 [1]Lit *multiplied*
13 [a]Gen 24:42-45

7 It happened year after year, as often
as she went up to the house of the LORD,
she would provoke her; so she wept and
would not eat.
8 Then Elkanah her husband said to
her, "Hannah, why do you weep and why
do you not eat and why is your heart sad?
[a]Am I not better to you than ten sons?"
9 ¶ Then Hannah rose after eating
and drinking in Shiloh. Now Eli the priest
was sitting on the seat by the doorpost of
[a]the temple of the LORD.
10 She, [1]greatly distressed, prayed to
the LORD and wept bitterly.
11 She [a]made a vow and said,
"O LORD of hosts, if You will indeed
[b]look on the affliction of Your maidservant and remember me, and not forget
Your maidservant, but will give Your
maidservant a [1]son, then I will give him
to the LORD all the days of his life, and [c]a
razor shall never come on his head."
12 ¶ Now it came about, as she [1]con-
tinued praying before the LORD, that Eli
was watching her mouth.
13 As for Hannah, [a]she was speaking
in her heart, only her lips were moving,

but her voice was not heard. So Eli thought she was drunk.

14 Then Eli said to her, "[a]How long will you make yourself drunk? Put away your wine from you."

15 But Hannah replied, "No, my lord, I am a woman [1]oppressed in spirit; I have drunk neither wine nor strong drink, but I [a]have poured out my soul before the LORD.

16 "Do not [1]consider your maidservant as a worthless woman, for I have spoken until now out of my great concern and [2]provocation."

17 Then Eli answered and said, "[a]Go in peace; and may the God of Israel [b]grant your petition that you have asked of Him."

18 She said, "[a]Let your maidservant find favor in your sight." So the woman went her way and ate, and [b]her face was no longer *sad.*

Samuel Is Born to Hannah

19 ¶ Then they arose early in the morning and worshiped before the LORD, and returned again to their house in [a]Ramah. And Elkanah [1]had relations with Hannah his wife, and [b]the LORD remembered her.

20 It came about [1]in due time, after Hannah had conceived, that she gave birth to a son; and she named him Samuel, *saying,* "[a]Because I have asked him of the LORD."

21 ¶ Then the man Elkanah [a]went up with all his household to offer to the LORD the yearly sacrifice and *pay* his vow.

22 But Hannah did not go up, for she said to her husband, "*I will not go up* until the child is weaned; then I will [a]bring him, that he may appear before the LORD and [b]stay there forever."

23 [a]Elkanah her husband said to her, "Do what seems best [1]to you. Remain until you have weaned him; only [b]may the LORD confirm His word." So the woman remained and nursed her son until she weaned him.

24 Now when she had weaned him, [a]she took him up with her, with a three-year-old bull and one ephah of flour and a jug of wine, and brought him to [b]the house of the LORD in Shiloh, although the child was young.

25 Then [a]they slaughtered the bull, and [b]brought the boy to Eli.

26 She said, "Oh, my lord! [a]As your soul lives, my lord, I am the woman who stood here beside you, praying to the LORD.

27 "[a]For this boy I prayed, and the LORD has given me my petition which I asked of Him.

28 "[a]So I have also [1]dedicated him to the LORD; as long as he lives he is [1]dedicated to the LORD." And [b]he worshiped the LORD there.

Hannah's Song of Thanksgiving

2 Then Hannah [a]prayed and said,
"My heart exults in the LORD;
[b]My [1]horn is exalted in the LORD,
My mouth [2]speaks boldly against my enemies,
Because [c]I rejoice in Your salvation.

2 "[a]There is no one holy like the LORD,
Indeed, [b]there is no one besides You,
[c]Nor is there any rock like our God.

3 "[1]Boast no more so very proudly,
[a]Do not let arrogance come out of your mouth;
[b]For the LORD is a God of knowledge,
[c]And with Him actions are weighed.

4 "[a]The bows of the mighty are shattered,
[b]But the feeble gird on strength.

5 "Those who were full hire themselves out for bread,
But those who were hungry cease *to hunger.*
[a]Even the barren gives birth to seven,
But [b]she who has many children languishes.

6 "[a]The LORD kills and makes alive;
[b]He brings down to [1]Sheol and raises up.

7 "[a]The LORD makes poor and rich;
[b]He brings low, He also exalts.

8 "[a]He raises the poor from the dust,
[b]He lifts the needy from the ash heap
[c]To make them sit with nobles,
And inherit a seat of honor;
[d]For the pillars of the earth are the LORD's,
And He set the world on them.

9 "[a]He keeps the feet of His godly ones,
[b]But the wicked ones are silenced in darkness;
[c]For not by might shall a man prevail.

10 "[a]Those who contend with the LORD will be shattered;
[b]Against them He will thunder in the heavens,
[c]The LORD will judge the ends of the earth;

14 [a]Acts 2:4
15 [1]Lit *severe* [a]Job 30:16; Ps 42:4; Lam 2:19
16 [1]Lit *give* [2]Lit *my provocation*
17 [a]Judg 18:6; 1 Sam 25:35; 2 Kin 5:19; Mark 5:34; Luke 7:50 [b]Ps 20:3-5
18 [a]Gen 33:15; Ruth 2:13 [b]Rom 15:13
19 [1]Lit *knew* [a]1 Sam 1:1 [b]Gen 21:1
20 [1]Lit *at the circuit of the days* [a]Gen 41:51; Ex 2:10; Matt 1:21
21 [a]Deut 12:11; 1 Sam 1:3
22 [a]Luke 2:22 [b]1 Sam 1:11
23 [1]Lit *in your eyes* [a]Num 30:7 [b]1 Sam 1:17
24 [a]Num 15:9; Deut 12:5 [b]Josh 18:1; 1 Sam 4:3
25 [a]Lev 1:5 [b]Luke 2:22
26 [a]2 Kin 2:2
27 [a]1 Sam 1:11-13; Ps 6:9
28 [1]Lit *lent* [a]1 Sam 1:11 [b]Gen 24:26
2:1 [1]I.e. strength [2]Lit *is enlarged* [a]1 Sam 2:1-10; Luke 1:46-55 [b]Deut 33:17; Job 16:15; Ps 75:10 [c]Ps 9:14; Is 12:2
2 [a]Ex 15:11; Lev 19:2; Ps 86:8 [b]2 Sam 22:32 [c]Deut 32:30
3 [1]Lit *Talk much* [a]Prov 8:13 [b]1 Sam 16:7; 1 Kin 8:39 [c]Prov 16:2
4 [a]Ps 37:15 [b]Ps 18:39; Heb 11:32-34
5 [a]Ruth 4:15; Ps 113:9 [b]Jer 15:9
6 [1]I.e. the nether world [a]Deut 32:39; 2 Kin 5:7; Rev 1:18 [b]Is 26:19
7 [a]Deut 8:17 [b]Job 5:11; Ps 75:7; James 4:10
8 [a]Job 42:10-12; Ps 75:7 [b]2 Sam 7:8; Dan 2:48; James 2:5 [c]Job 36:7; Ps 113:8 [d]Job 38:4-6; Ps 75:3
9 [a]Ps 91:11; Prov 3:26; 1 Pet 1:5 [b]Matt 8:12 [c]Ps 33:16
10 [a]Ex 15:6; Ps 2:9 [b]1 Sam 7:10; 2 Sam 22:14; Ps 18:13 [c]Ps 96:13; Matt 25:31

[d]And He will give strength to
His king,
[e]And will exalt the [1]horn of His
anointed."

11 ¶ Then Elkanah went to his home at [a]Ramah. [b]But the boy ministered to the LORD before Eli the priest.

The Sin of Eli's Sons

12 ¶ Now the sons of Eli were [1a]worthless men; they did not know the LORD

13 [a]and the custom of the priests with the people. When any man was offering a sacrifice, the priest's servant would come while the meat was boiling, with a three-pronged fork in his hand.

14 Then he would thrust it into the pan, or kettle, or caldron, or pot; all that the fork brought up the priest would take for himself. Thus they did in Shiloh to all the Israelites who came there.

15 Also, before [a]they burned the fat, the priest's servant would come and say to the man who was sacrificing, "Give the priest meat for roasting, as he will not take boiled meat from you, only raw."

16 If the man said to him, "They must surely [1]burn the fat [2]first, and then take as much as [3]you desire," then he would say, "No, but you shall give *it to me* now; and if not, I will take it by force."

17 Thus the sin of the young men was very great before the LORD, for the men [a]despised the offering of the LORD.

Samuel before the LORD as a Boy

18 ¶ Now [a]Samuel was ministering before the LORD, *as* a boy [1b]wearing a linen ephod.

19 And his mother would make him a little [a]robe and bring it to him from year to year when she would come up with her husband to offer [b]the yearly sacrifice.

20 Then Eli would [a]bless Elkanah and his wife and say, "May the LORD give you [1]children from this woman in place of [2]the one she [b]dedicated to the LORD." And they went to their own [3]home.

21 ¶ [a]The LORD visited Hannah; and she conceived and gave birth to three sons and two daughters. And [b]the boy Samuel grew before the LORD.

Eli Rebukes His Sons

22 ¶ Now Eli was very old; and he heard [a]all that his sons were doing to all Israel, and how they lay with [b]the women who served at the doorway of the tent of meeting.

23 He said to them, "Why do you do such things, the evil things that I hear from all these people?

24 "No, my sons; for the report is not good [a]which I hear [1]the LORD's people circulating.

25 "If one man sins against another, [a]God will mediate for him; but [b]if a man sins against the LORD, who can intercede for him?" But they would not listen to the voice of their father, for the [c]LORD desired to put them to death.

26 ¶ Now the boy [a]Samuel [1]was growing in stature and in favor both with the LORD and with men.

27 ¶ Then [a]a man of God came to Eli and said to him, "Thus says the LORD, '[b]Did I *not* indeed reveal Myself to the house of your father when they were in Egypt *in bondage* to Pharaoh's house?

28 '[a]Did I *not* choose them from all the tribes of Israel to be My priests, to go up to My altar, to burn incense, to carry an ephod before Me; and did I *not* [b]give to the house of your father all the fire *offerings* of the sons of Israel?

29 'Why do you [a]kick at My sacrifice and at My offering [b]which I have commanded *in My* [c]dwelling, and [d]honor your sons above Me, by making yourselves fat with the [1]choicest of every offering of My people Israel?'

30 "Therefore the LORD God of Israel declares, '[a]I did indeed say that your house and the house of your father should walk before Me forever'; but now the LORD declares, 'Far be it from Me—for [b]those who honor Me I will honor, and those [c]who despise Me will be lightly esteemed.

31 'Behold, [a]the days are coming when I will break your [1]strength and the [1]strength of your father's house so that there will not be an old man in your house.

32 'You will see [a]the distress of *My* dwelling, in *spite of* all the good that [1]I do for Israel; and an [b]old man will not be in your house forever.

33 'Yet I will not cut off every man of yours from My altar [1]so that your eyes will fail *from weeping* and your soul grieve, and all the increase of your house will die [2]in the prime of life.

34 'This will be [a]the sign to you which will come concerning your two sons, Hophni and Phinehas: [b]on the same day both of them will die.

35 'But [a]I will raise up for Myself a faithful priest who will do according to what is in My heart and in My soul; and [b]I will build him an enduring house, and he will walk before [c]My anointed always.

36 'Everyone who is left in your house will come and bow down to him for a [1]piece of silver or a loaf of bread and say, "Please [2]assign me to one of the priest's

---

10 [1]I.e. strength [d]Ps 21:1,7 [e]Ps 89:24
11 [a]1 Sam 1:1, 19 [b]1 Sam 1:28; 2:18; 3:1
12 [1]Lit *sons of Belial* [a]Jer 2:8; 9:3,6; 2 Cor 6:15
13 [a]Lev 7:29-34
15 [a]Lev 3:3-5, 16
16 [1]Lit *offer up in smoke* [2]Lit *like the day* [3]Lit *your soul*
17 [a]Mal 2:7-9
18 [1]Lit *girded with* [a]1 Sam 2:11; 3:1 [b]1 Sam 2:28; 22:18; 2 Sam 6:14; 1 Chr 15:27
19 [a]Ex 28:31 [b]1 Sam 1:3,21
20 [1]Lit *seed* [2]Lit *the one asked for which was lent* [3]Lit *place* [a]Luke 2:34 [b]1 Sam 1:11,27, 28
21 [a]Gen 21:1 [b]Judg 13:24; 1 Sam 2:26; 3:19-21; Luke 1:80; 2:40
22 [a]1 Sam 2:13-17 [b]Ex 38:8
24 [1]Or *making the LORD's people transgress* [a]1 Kin 15:26
25 [a]Deut 1:17 [b]Num 15:30; 1 Sam 3:14; Heb 10:26,27 [c]Josh 11:20
26 [1]Lit *was going on both great and good* [a]1 Sam 2:21; Luke 2:52
27 [a]Deut 33:1; Judg 13:6 [b]Ex 4:14-16; 12:1,43
28 [a]Ex 28:1-4; 30:7,8; Lev 8:7,8 [b]Lev 7:35,36
29 [1]Or *first* [a]1 Sam 2:13-17 [b]Deut 12:5-9 [c]Ps 26:8 [d]Matt 10:37
30 [a]Ex 29:9; Num 25:13 [b]Ps 50:23 [c]Mal 2:9
31 [1]Or *arm* [a]1 Sam 4:11-18; 22:17-20
32 [1]Lit *He does* [a]1 Kin 2:26,27 [b]Zech 8:4
33 [1]Lit *to waste away your eyes and to grieve your soul* [2]Lit *as men*
34 [a]1 Sam 10:7-9; 1 Kin 13:3 [b]1 Sam 4:11,17
35 [a]1 Sam 3:1; 7:9; 9:12,13 [b]1 Sam 8:3-5; 25:28; 2 Sam 7:11,27; 1 Kin 11:38 [c]1 Sam 10:9,10; 12:3; 16:13
36 [1]Or *payment* [2]Lit *attach*

offices so that I may eat a piece of bread." ' "

The Prophetic Call to Samuel

3 Now [a]the boy Samuel was ministering to the LORD before Eli. And [b]word from the LORD was rare in those days, [1]visions were infrequent.

2 ¶ It happened at that time as Eli was lying down in his place (now [a]his eyesight had begun to grow dim *and* he could not see *well*),

3 and [a]the lamp of God had not yet gone out, and Samuel was lying down in the temple of the LORD where the ark of God *was*,

4 that the LORD called Samuel; and he said, "[a]Here I am."

5 Then he ran to Eli and said, "Here I am, for you called me." But he said, "I did not call, lie down again." So he went and lay down.

6 The LORD called yet again, "Samuel!" So Samuel arose and went to Eli and said, "Here I am, for you called me." But he [1]answered, "I did not call, my son, lie down again."

7 [a]Now Samuel did not yet know the LORD, nor had the word of the LORD yet been revealed to him.

8 So the LORD called Samuel again for the third time. And he arose and went to Eli and said, "Here I am, for you called me." Then Eli discerned that the LORD was calling the boy.

9 And Eli said to Samuel, "Go lie down, and it shall be if He calls you, that you shall say, 'Speak, LORD, for Your servant is listening.' " So Samuel went and lay down in his place.

10 ¶ Then the LORD came and stood and called as at other times, "Samuel! Samuel!" And Samuel said, "Speak, for Your servant is listening."

11 The LORD said to Samuel, "Behold, [a]I am about to do a thing in Israel at which both ears of everyone who hears it will tingle.

12 "In that day [a]I will carry out against Eli all that I have spoken concerning his house, from beginning to end.

13 "For [a]I have told him that I am about to judge his house forever for [b]the iniquity which he knew, because [c]his sons brought a curse on themselves and [d]he did not rebuke them.

14 "Therefore I have sworn to the house of Eli that [a]the iniquity of Eli's house shall not be atoned for by sacrifice or offering forever."

15 ¶ So Samuel lay down until morning. Then he [a]opened the doors of the house of the LORD. But Samuel was afraid to tell [b]the vision to Eli.

16 Then Eli called Samuel and said, "Samuel, my son." And he said, "Here I am."

17 He said, "What is the word that He spoke to you? Please do not hide it from me. [a]May God do so to you, and more also, if you hide anything from me of all the words that He spoke to you."

18 So Samuel told him everything and hid nothing from him. And he said, "[a]It is the LORD; let Him do what seems good to Him."

19 ¶ Thus [a]Samuel grew and [b]the LORD was with him and [c]let none of his words [1]fail.

20 All Israel [a]from Dan even to Beersheba knew that Samuel was confirmed as a prophet of the LORD.

21 And [a]the LORD appeared again at Shiloh, [b]because the LORD revealed Himself to Samuel at Shiloh by the word of the LORD.

Philistines Take the Ark in Victory

4 Thus the word of Samuel came to all Israel. Now Israel went out to meet the Philistines in battle and camped beside [a]Ebenezer while the Philistines camped in [b]Aphek.

2 The Philistines drew up in battle array to meet Israel. When the battle spread, Israel was [1]defeated before the Philistines who killed about four thousand men on the battlefield.

3 When the people came into the camp, the elders of Israel said, "[a]Why has the LORD defeated us today before the Philistines? [b]Let us take to ourselves from Shiloh the ark of the covenant of the LORD, that [1]it may come among us and deliver us from the power of our enemies."

4 So the people sent to Shiloh, and from there they carried the ark of the covenant of the LORD of hosts [a]who sits *above* the cherubim; and the two sons of Eli, Hophni and Phinehas, *were* there with the ark of the covenant of God.

5 ¶ As the ark of the covenant of the LORD came into the camp, [a]all Israel shouted with a great shout, so that the earth resounded.

6 When the Philistines heard the noise of the shout, they said, "What *does* the noise of this great shout in the camp of the Hebrews *mean?*" Then they understood that the ark of the LORD had come into the camp.

7 The Philistines were afraid, for they said, "God has come into the camp." And they said, "[a]Woe to us! For nothing like this has happened before.

8 "Woe to us! Who shall deliver us from the hand of these mighty gods?

3:1 [1]Lit *no vision spread abroad* [a]1 Sam 2:11,18 [b]Ps 74:9; Ezek 7:26; Amos 8:11,12
2 [a]Gen 27:1; 48:10; 1 Sam 4:15
3 [a]Ex 25:31-37; Lev 24:2,3
4 [a]Is 6:8
6 [1]Lit *said*
7 [a]Acts 19:2; 1 Cor 13:11
11 [a]2 Kin 21:12; Jer 19:3
12 [a]1 Sam 2:27-36
13 [a]1 Sam 2:29-31 [b]1 Sam 2:22 [c]1 Sam 2:12,17,22 [d]Deut 17:12; 21:18
14 [a]Lev 15:31; Is 22:14
15 [a]1 Chr 15:23 [b]1 Sam 3:10
17 [a]2 Sam 3:35
18 [a]Ex 34:5-7; Lev 10:3; Job 2:10; Is 39:8
19 [1]Lit *fall to the ground* [a]1 Sam 2:21 [b]Gen 21:22; 28:15; 39:2 [c]1 Sam 9:6
20 [a]Judg 20:1
21 [a]Gen 12:7 [b]1 Sam 3:10
4:1 [a]1 Sam 7:12 [b]Josh 12:18; 1 Sam 29:1
2 [1]Lit *smitten*
3 [1]Or *he* [a]Josh 7:7,8 [b]Num 10:35; Josh 6:6
4 [a]Ex 25:22; 2 Sam 6:2; Ps 80:1
5 [a]Josh 6:5,20
7 [a]Ex 15:14

These are the gods who smote the Egyptians with all *kinds of* plagues in the wilderness.

9 “[a]Take courage and be men, O Philistines, or you will become slaves to the Hebrews, [b]as they have been slaves to you; therefore, be men and fight.”

10 ¶ So the Philistines fought and [a]Israel was [1]defeated, and [b]every man fled to his tent; and the slaughter was very great, for there fell of Israel thirty thousand foot soldiers.

11 And the ark of God was taken; and [a]the two sons of Eli, Hophni and Phinehas, died.

12 ¶ Now a man of Benjamin ran from the battle line and came to Shiloh the same day with [a]his clothes torn and [1]dust on his head.

13 When he came, behold, [a]Eli was sitting on *his* seat [1]by the road eagerly watching, because his heart was trembling for the ark of God. So the man came to tell *it* in the city, and all the city cried out.

14 When Eli heard the noise of the outcry, he said, “What *does* the noise of this commotion *mean?*” Then the man came hurriedly and told Eli.

15 Now Eli was ninety-eight years old, and [a]his eyes were set so that he could not see.

16 The man said to Eli, “I am the one who came from the battle line. Indeed, I escaped from the battle line today.” And he said, “[a]How did things go, my son?”

17 Then the one who brought the news replied, “Israel has fled before the Philistines and there has also been a great slaughter among the people, and your two sons also, Hophni and Phinehas, are dead, and the ark of God has been taken.”

18 When he mentioned the ark of God, [1a]Eli fell off the seat backward beside the gate, and his neck was broken and he died, for [2]he was old and heavy. Thus he judged Israel forty years.

19 ¶ Now his daughter-in-law, Phinehas's wife, was pregnant and about to give birth; and when she heard the news that the ark of God was taken and that her father-in-law and her husband had died, she kneeled down and gave birth, for her pains came upon her.

20 And about the time of her death the women who stood by her said to her, “[a]Do not be afraid, for you have given birth to a son.” But she did not answer or pay attention.

21 And she called the boy [1]Ichabod, saying, “[a]The glory has departed from Israel,” because [b]the ark of God was taken and because of her father-in-law and her husband.

22 She said, “The glory has departed from Israel, for the ark of God was taken.”

Capture of the Ark Provokes God

5 Now the Philistines took the ark of God and [a]brought it from Ebenezer to [b]Ashdod.

2 Then the Philistines took the ark of God and brought it to [a]the house of Dagon and set it by Dagon.

3 When the Ashdodites arose early the next morning, behold, [a]Dagon had fallen on his face to the ground before the ark of the LORD. So they took Dagon and [b]set him in his place again.

4 But when they arose early the next morning, behold, [a]Dagon had fallen on his face to the ground before the ark of the LORD. And the head of Dagon and both the palms of his hands *were* cut off on the threshold; [1]only the trunk of Dagon was left to him.

5 Therefore neither the priests of Dagon nor all who enter Dagon's house [a]tread on the threshold of Dagon in Ashdod to this day.

6 ¶ Now [a]the hand of the LORD was heavy on the Ashdodites, and [b]He ravaged them and smote them with [c]tumors, both Ashdod and its territories.

7 When the men of Ashdod saw that it was so, they said, “The ark of the God of Israel must not remain with us, for His hand is severe on us and on Dagon our god.”

8 So they sent and [a]gathered all the lords of the Philistines to them and said, “What shall we do with the ark of the God of Israel?” And they said, “Let the ark of the God of Israel be brought around to Gath.” And they brought the ark of the God of Israel *around.*

9 After they had brought it around, [a]the hand of the LORD was against the city with very great confusion; and He smote the men of the city, both young and old, so that [b]tumors broke out on them.

10 So they sent the ark of God to Ekron. And as the ark of God came to Ekron the Ekronites cried out, saying, “They have brought the ark of the God of Israel around to [1]us, to kill [1]us and [2]our people.”

11 They [a]sent therefore and gathered all the lords of the Philistines and said, “Send away the ark of the God of Israel, and let it return to its own place, so that it will not kill [1]us and [2]our people.” For there was a deadly confusion throughout

9 [a]1 Cor 16:13 [b]Judg 13:1; 1 Sam 14:21

10 [1]Lit *smitten* [a]Deut 28:15,25; 1 Sam 4:2 [b]2 Sam 18:17; 19:8; 2 Kin 14:12; 2 Chr 25:22

11 [a]1 Sam 2:34; Ps 78:56-64

12 [1]Lit *ground* [a]Josh 7:6; 2 Sam 1:2; 15:32; Neh 9:1; Job 2:12

13 [1]Gr version reads *beside the gate watching the road* [a]1 Sam 1:9; 4:18

15 [a]1 Sam 3:2; 1 Kin 14:4

16 [a]2 Sam 1:4

18 [1]Lit *he* [2]Lit *the man* [a]1 Sam 4:13

20 [a]Gen 35:16-19

21 [1]I.e. No glory [a]Ps 26:8; Jer 2:11 [b]1 Sam 4:11

5:1 [a]1 Sam 4:1; 7:12 [b]Josh 13:3

2 [a]Judg 16:23-30; 1 Chr 10:8-10

3 [a]Is 19:1; 46:1, 2 [b]Is 46:7

4 [1]So with ancient versions; Heb *only Dagon* [a]Ezek 6:4,6; Mic 1:7

5 [a]Zeph 1:9

6 [a]Ex 9:3; 1 Sam 5:7,11; Ps 32:4; 145:20; 147:6; Acts 13:11 [b]1 Sam 6:5 [c]Deut 28:27; Ps 78:66

8 [a]1 Sam 5:11; 29:6-11

9 [a]Deut 2:15; 1 Sam 5:11; 7:13; 12:15 [b]1 Sam 5:6

10 [1]Lit *me* [2]Lit *my*

11 [1]Lit *me* [2]Lit *my* [a]1 Sam 5:8

the city; [b]the hand of God was very
heavy there.
12 And the men who did not die were
smitten with tumors and [a]the cry of the
city went up to heaven.

The Ark Returned to Israel

6 Now the ark of the LORD had been in
the [1]country of the Philistines seven
months.
2 And [a]the Philistines called for the
priests and the diviners, saying, "What
shall we do with the ark of the LORD? Tell
us [1]how we shall send it to its place."
3 They said, "If you send away the
ark of the God of Israel, [a]do not send it
empty; but you shall surely [b]return to
Him a guilt offering. Then you will be
healed and it will be known to you why
His hand is not removed from you."
4 Then they said, "What shall be the
guilt offering which we shall return to
Him?" And they said, "Five golden [a]tu-
mors and five golden mice [b]*according to*
the number of the lords of the Philistines,
for one plague was on all of [1]you and on
your lords.
5 "So you shall make likenesses of
your tumors and likenesses of your mice
that ravage the land, and [a]you shall give
glory to the God of Israel; perhaps [b]He
will ease His hand from you, [c]your gods,
and your land.
6 "Why then do you harden your
hearts [a]as the Egyptians and Pharaoh
hardened their hearts? When He had severely dealt with them, [b]did they not
allow [1]the people to go, and they departed?
7 "Now therefore, take and [a]prepare
a new cart and two milch cows on which
there [b]has never been a yoke; and hitch
the cows to the cart and take their calves
home, away from them.
8 "Take the ark of the LORD and place
it on the cart; and put [a]the articles of
gold which you return to Him as [b]a guilt
offering in a box by its side. Then send it
away that it may go.
9 "Watch, if it goes up by the way of
its own territory to [a]Beth-shemesh, then
He has done us this great evil. But if not,
then [b]we will know that it was not His
hand that struck us; it happened to us by
chance."
10 ¶ Then the men did so, and took
two milch cows and hitched them to the
cart, and shut up their calves at home.
11 They put the ark of the LORD on the
cart, and the box with the golden mice
and the likenesses of their tumors.
12 And the cows took the straight way
in the [1]direction of [a]Beth-shemesh;
they went along [b]the highway, lowing as
they went, and did not turn aside to the
right or to the left. And the lords of the
Philistines followed them to the border of
Beth-shemesh.
13 ¶ Now *the people of* Beth-shemesh
were reaping their wheat harvest in the
valley, and they raised their eyes and saw
the ark and were glad to see *it.*
14 The cart came into the field of Joshua the Beth-shemite and stood there
where there *was* a large stone; and they
split the wood of the cart and [a]offered
the cows as a burnt offering to the LORD.
15 [a]The Levites took down the ark of
the LORD and the box that was with it, in
which were the articles of gold, and put
them on the large stone; and the men of
Beth-shemesh offered burnt offerings and
sacrificed sacrifices that day to the LORD.
16 When the [a]five lords of the Philistines saw it, they returned to Ekron that
day.
17 ¶ [a]These are the golden tumors
which the Philistines returned for a guilt
offering to the LORD: one for Ashdod, one
for Gaza, one for Ashkelon, one for Gath,
one for Ekron;
18 and the golden mice, *according* to
the number of all the cities of the Philistines belonging to the five lords, [a]both of
fortified cities and of country villages.
[b]The large [1]stone on which they set the
ark of the LORD *is a witness* to this day in
the field of Joshua the Beth-shemite.
19 ¶ [a]He struck down some of the
men of Beth-shemesh because they had
looked into the ark of the LORD. He struck
down of all the people, 50,070 men, and
the people mourned because the LORD
had struck the people with a great slaughter.
20 The men of Beth-shemesh said,
"[a]Who is able to stand before the LORD,
this holy God? And to whom shall He go
up from us?"
21 So they sent messengers to the inhabitants of [a]Kiriath-jearim, saying,
"The Philistines have brought back the
ark of the LORD; come down and take it
up to you."

Deliverance from the Philistines

7 And the men of Kiriath-jearim came
and took the ark of the LORD and
[a]brought it into the house of Abinadab
on the hill, and consecrated Eleazar his
son to keep the ark of the LORD.
2 From the day that the ark remained
at Kiriath-jearim, the time was long, for it
was twenty years; and all the house of
Israel lamented after the LORD.
3 ¶ Then Samuel spoke to all the
house of Israel, saying, "[a]If you return to
the LORD with all your heart, [b]remove

5:11 [b]1 Sam 5:6,9
12 [a]Ex 12:30; Is 15:3
6:1 [1]Lit *field*
2 [1]Or *with what* [a]Gen 41:8; Ex 7:11; Is 2:6
3 [a]Ex 23:15; Deut 16:16 [b]Lev 5:15,16
4 [1]Lit *them* [a]1 Sam 5:6,9,12; 6:17 [b]Josh 13:3; Judg 3:3; 1 Sam 6:17,18
5 [a]Josh 7:19; 1 Chr 16:28,29; Is 42:12; Jer 13:16; John 9:24; Rev 14:7 [b]1 Sam 5:6,11 [c]1 Sam 5:3,4,7
6 [1]Lit *them* [a]Ex 7:13; 8:15,32; 9:34; 14:17 [b]Ex 12:31
7 [a]2 Sam 6:3 [b]Num 19:2; Deut 21:3,4
8 [a]1 Sam 6:4,5 [b]1 Sam 6:3
9 [a]Josh 15:10; 21:16 [b]1 Sam 6:3
12 [1]Lit *way* [a]1 Sam 6:9 [b]Num 20:19
14 [a]2 Sam 24:22; 1 Kin 19:21
15 [a]Josh 3:3
16 [a]Josh 13:3; Judg 3:3
17 [a]1 Sam 6:4
18 [1]So some mss and versions; Heb *Abel* [a]Deut 3:5 [b]1 Sam 6:14,15
19 [a]Ex 19:21; Num 4:5,15,20; 2 Sam 6:7
20 [a]Lev 11:44, 45; 2 Sam 6:9; Mal 3:2; Rev 6:17
21 [a]Josh 9:17; 15:9,60; 1 Chr 13:5,6
7:1 [a]2 Sam 6:3, 4
3 [a]1 Kin 8:48; Is 55:7; Hos 6:1; Joel 2:12-14 [b]Gen 35:2; Josh 24:14,23; Judg 10:16

the foreign gods and the [c]Ashtaroth from
among you and [d]direct your hearts to the
LORD and [e]serve Him alone; and He will
deliver you from the hand of the Philistines."
4 So the sons of Israel removed the
Baals and the Ashtaroth and served the
LORD alone.
5 ¶ Then Samuel said, "Gather all Israel to [a]Mizpah and [b]I will pray to the
LORD for you."
6 They gathered to Mizpah, and drew
water and [a]poured it out before the
LORD, and [b]fasted on that day and said
there, "[c]We have sinned against the
LORD." And Samuel judged the sons of
Israel at Mizpah.
7 ¶ Now when the Philistines heard
that the sons of Israel had gathered to
Mizpah, the lords of the Philistines went
up against Israel. And when the sons of
Israel heard it, [a]they were afraid of the
Philistines.
8 Then the sons of Israel said to Samuel, "[a]Do not cease to cry to the LORD
our God for us, that He may save us from
the hand of the Philistines."
9 Samuel took [a]a suckling lamb and
offered it for a whole burnt offering to the
LORD; and Samuel cried to the LORD for
Israel and [b]the LORD answered him.
10 Now Samuel was offering up the
burnt offering, and the Philistines drew
near to battle against Israel. But [a]the
LORD thundered with a great [1]thunder
on that day against the Philistines and
[b]confused them, so that they were
[2]routed before Israel.
11 The men of Israel went out of Mizpah and pursued the Philistines, and
struck them down as far as below Beth-
car.
12 ¶ Then Samuel [a]took a stone and
set it between Mizpah and Shen, and
named it [1]Ebenezer, saying, "Thus far
the LORD has helped us."
13 [a]So the Philistines were subdued
and [b]they did not come anymore within
the border of Israel. And the hand of the
LORD was against the Philistines all the
days of Samuel.
14 The cities which the Philistines had
taken from Israel were restored to Israel,
from Ekron even to Gath; and Israel delivered their territory from the hand of the
Philistines. So there was peace between
Israel and [a]the Amorites.

Samuel's Ministry

15 ¶ Now Samuel [a]judged Israel all
the days of his life.
16 He used to go annually on circuit to
[a]Bethel and [b]Gilgal and [c]Mizpah, and
he judged Israel in all these places.

3 [c]Judg 2:13; 1 Sam 31:10 [d]Deut 13:4; 2 Chr 19:3 [e]Deut 6:13; 10:20; 13:4; Josh 24:14; Matt 4:10; Luke 4:8
5 [a]Judg 10:17; 20:1 [b]1 Sam 8:6; 12:17-19
6 [a]1 Sam 1:15; Ps 62:8; Lam 2:19 [b]Lev 16:29; Neh 9:1 [c]Judg 10:10; 1 Kin 8:47; Ps 106:6
7 [a]1 Sam 13:6; 17:11
8 [a]1 Sam 12:19-24; Is 37:4
9 [a]Lev 22:27 [b]Ps 99:6; Jer 15:1
10 [1]Lit *voice* [2]Lit *smitten* [a]1 Sam 2:10; 2 Sam 22:14,15; Ps 29:3,4 [b]Josh 10:10; Ps 18:14
12 [1]I.e. The stone of help [a]Gen 35:14; Josh 4:9; 24:26
13 [a]Judg 13:1-15 [b]1 Sam 13:5
14 [a]Num 13:29; Josh 10:5-10
15 [a]1 Sam 7:6
16 [a]Gen 28:19; 35:6 [b]Josh 5:9, 10 [c]1 Sam 7:5
17 [a]1 Sam 1:1, 19; 2:11 [b]Judg 21:4
8:1 [a]Deut 16:18,19
2 [a]Gen 22:19; 1 Kin 19:3; Amos 5:5
3 [a]Ex 23:6,8; Deut 16:19
4 [a]1 Sam 7:17
5 [a]Deut 17:14, 15
6 [1]Or *evil* [a]1 Sam 12:17 [b]1 Sam 15:11
7 [a]Ex 16:8; 1 Sam 10:19
9 [1]Lit *testify to* [2]Lit *custom* [a]Ezek 3:18 [b]1 Sam 8:11-18; 10:25
10 [a]1 Sam 8:4
11 [1]Lit *custom* [a]Deut 17:14-20; 1 Sam 10:25 [b]1 Sam 14:52 [c]2 Sam 15:1
12 [1]Lit *plow his plowing* [a]Num 31:14; 1 Sam 22:7
14 [a]1 Kin 21:7; Ezek 46:18

17 Then his return *was* to [a]Ramah, for
his house *was* there, and there he judged
Israel; and he [b]built there an altar to the
LORD.

Israel Demands a King

8 And it came about when Samuel was
old that [a]he appointed his sons
judges over Israel.
2 Now the name of his firstborn was
Joel, and the name of his second, Abijah;
they were judging in [a]Beersheba.
3 His sons, however, did not walk in
his ways, but turned aside after dishonest
gain and [a]took bribes and perverted justice.
4 ¶ Then all the elders of Israel gathered together and came to Samuel at [a]Ra-
mah;
5 and they said to him, "Behold, you
have grown old, and your sons do not
walk in your ways. Now [a]appoint a king
for us to judge us like all the nations."
6 But the thing was [1a]displeasing in
the sight of Samuel when they said, "Give
us a king to judge us." And [b]Samuel
prayed to the LORD.
7 The LORD said to Samuel, "Listen to
the voice of the people in regard to all
that they say to you, for [a]they have not
rejected you, but they have rejected Me
from being king over them.
8 "Like all the deeds which they have
done since the day that I brought them up
from Egypt even to this day—in that they
have forsaken Me and served other
gods—so they are doing to you also.
9 "Now then, listen to their voice;
[a]however, you shall solemnly [1]warn
them and tell them of [b]the [2]procedure
of the king who will reign over them."

Warning concerning a King

10 ¶ So Samuel spoke all the words of
the LORD to [a]the people who had asked
of him a king.
11 He said, "[a]This will be the [1]proce-
dure of the king who will reign over you:
[b]he will take your sons and place *them*
for himself in his chariots and among his
horsemen and [c]they will run before his
chariots.
12 "[a]He will appoint for himself commanders of thousands and of fifties, and
some to [1]do his plowing and to reap his
harvest and to make his weapons of war
and equipment for his chariots.
13 "He will also take your daughters for
perfumers and cooks and bakers.
14 "[a]He will take the best of your fields
and your vineyards and your olive groves
and give *them* to his servants.
15 "He will take a tenth of your seed

and of your vineyards and give to his officers and to his servants.
16 "He will also take your male servants
and your female servants and your best
young men and your donkeys and [1]use
them for his work.
17 "He will take a tenth of your flocks,
and you yourselves will become his servants.
18 "Then [a]you will cry out in that day
because of your king whom you have chosen for yourselves, but [b]the LORD will not
answer you in that day."
19 ¶ Nevertheless, the people [a]re-
fused to listen to the voice of Samuel, and
they said, "No, but there shall be a king
over us,
20 [a]that we also may be like all the
nations, that our king may judge us and
go out before us and fight our battles."
21 Now after Samuel had heard all the
words of the people, [a]he repeated them
in the LORD'S hearing.
22 The LORD said to Samuel, "[a]Listen
to their voice and [1]appoint them a king."
So Samuel said to the men of Israel, "Go
every man to his city."

Saul's Search

9 Now there was a man of Benjamin
whose name was [a]Kish the son of
Abiel, the son of Zeror, the son of Beco-
rath, the son of Aphiah, the son of a Benjamite, a mighty man of [1]valor.
2 He had a son whose name was Saul,
a [a]choice and handsome *man*, and there
was not a more handsome person than he
among the sons of Israel; [b]from his shoulders and up he was taller than any of the
people.
3 ¶ Now the donkeys of Kish, Saul's
father, were lost. So Kish said to his son
Saul, "Take now with you one of the servants, and arise, go search for the donkeys."
4 He passed through [a]the hill country of Ephraim and passed through the
land of [b]Shalishah, but they did not find
them. Then they passed through the land
of [c]Shaalim, but *they were* not *there*.
Then he passed through the land of the
Benjamites, but they did not find *them*.
5 ¶ When they came to the land of
[a]Zuph, Saul said to his servant who was
with him, "Come, and let us return, [b]or
else my father will cease *to be concerned*
about the donkeys and will become anxious for us."
6 He said to him, "Behold now, there
is [a]a man of God in this city, and the man
is held in honor; [b]all that he says surely
comes true. Now let us go there, [c]per-
haps he can tell us about our journey on
which we have set out."

16 [1]Lit *make*
18 [a]Is 8:21 [b]Prov 1:25-28; Is 1:15; Mic 3:4
19 [a]Is 66:4; Jer 44:16
20 [a]1 Sam 8:5
21 [a]Judg 11:11
22 [1]Lit *cause a king to reign for them* [a]1 Sam 8:7
9:1 [1]Or *wealth or influence* [a]1 Sam 14:51; 1 Chr 8:33; 9:36-39
2 [a]1 Sam 10:24 [b]1 Sam 10:23
4 [a]Josh 24:33 [b]2 Kin 4:42 [c]Josh 19:42
5 [a]1 Sam 1:1 [b]1 Sam 10:2
6 [a]Deut 33:1; 1 Kin 13:1; 2 Kin 5:8 [b]1 Sam 3:19 [c]Gen 24:42
7 [a]1 Kin 14:3; 2 Kin 5:15; 8:8, 9; Ezek 13:19
8 [a]1 Sam 9:6
9 [a]2 Sam 24:11; 2 Kin 17:13; 1 Chr 9:22; 26:28; 29:29; Is 30:10; Amos 7:12
11 [a]Gen 24:11, 15; 29:8,9; Ex 2:16
12 [1]Or *behold* [a]Gen 31:54; Num 28:11-15; 1 Kin 3:2 [b]1 Sam 7:17; 10:5
13 [a]Luke 9:16; John 6:11
15 [1]Lit *uncovered the ear* [a]1 Sam 15:1; Acts 13:21
16 [a]1 Sam 10:1 [b]Ex 3:7,9
17 [1]Lit *answered* [a]1 Sam 16:12
20 [a]1 Sam 9:3

7 Then Saul said to his servant, "But
behold, if we go, what shall we bring the
man? For the bread is gone from our sack
and there is [a]no present to bring to the
man of God. What do we have?"
8 The servant answered Saul again
and said, "Behold, I have in my hand a
fourth of a shekel of silver; I will give *it*
to the man of God and he will [a]tell us our
way."
9 (Formerly in Israel, when a man
went to inquire of God, he used to say,
"Come, and let us go to the seer"; for *he
who is called* a prophet now was formerly
called [a]a seer.)
10 Then Saul said to his servant, "Well
said; come, let us go." So they went to the
city where the man of God was.
11 ¶ As they went up the slope to the
city, [a]they found young women going
out to draw water and said to them, "Is
the seer here?"
12 They answered them and said, "He
is; [1]see, *he is* ahead of you. Hurry now,
for he has come into the city today, for
[a]the people have a sacrifice on [b]the high
place today.
13 "As soon as you enter the city you
will find him before he goes up to the
high place to eat, for the people will not
eat until he comes, because [a]he must
bless the sacrifice; afterward those who
are invited will eat. Now therefore, go up
for you will find him at once."
14 So they went up to the city. As they
came into the city, behold, Samuel was
coming out toward them to go up to the
high place.

God's Choice for King

15 ¶ Now a day before Saul's coming,
[a]the LORD had [1]revealed *this* to Samuel
saying,
16 "About this time tomorrow I will
send you a man from the land of Benjamin, and [a]you shall anoint him to be
prince over My people Israel; and he will
deliver My people from the hand of the
Philistines. For [b]I have regarded My people, because their cry has come to Me."
17 When Samuel saw Saul, the LORD
[1]said to him, "[a]Behold, the man of
whom I spoke to you! This one shall rule
over My people."
18 Then Saul approached Samuel in
the gate and said, "Please tell me where
the seer's house is."
19 Samuel answered Saul and said, "I
am the seer. Go up before me to the high
place, for you shall eat with me today;
and in the morning I will let you go, and
will tell you all that is on your mind.
20 "[a]As for your donkeys which were
lost three days ago, do not set your mind

on them, for they have been found. And
[b]for whom is all that is desirable in Israel? Is it not for you and for all your father's household?"
21 Saul replied, "[a]Am I not a Benjamite, of [b]the smallest of the tribes of
Israel, and my family the least of all the
families of the [1]tribe of Benjamin? Why
then do you speak to me in this way?"
22 ¶ Then Samuel took Saul and his
servant and brought them into the hall
and gave them a place at the head of
those who were invited, who were about
thirty men.
23 Samuel said to the cook, "[1]Bring
the portion that I gave you, concerning
which I said to you, 'Set it [2]aside.'"
24 Then the cook [a]took up the leg
with what was on it and set *it* before Saul.
And *Samuel* said, "Here is what has been
reserved! Set *it* before you *and* eat, because it has been kept for you until the
appointed time, [1]since I said I have invited the people." So Saul ate with Samuel
that day.
25 ¶ When they came down from the
high place into the city, *Samuel* spoke
with Saul [a]on the [1]roof.
26 And they arose early; and at daybreak Samuel called to Saul on the roof,
saying, "Get up, that I may send you
away." So Saul arose, and both he and
Samuel went out into the street.
27 As they were going down to the
edge of the city, Samuel said to Saul, "Say
to the servant that he might go ahead of
us and pass on, but you remain standing
now, that I may proclaim the word of God
to you."

Saul among Prophets

10 Then [a]Samuel took the flask of
oil, poured it on his head, [b]kissed
him and said, "Has not [c]the LORD anointed you a ruler over [d]His inheritance?
2 "When you go from me today, then
you will find two men close to [a]Rachel's
tomb in the territory of Benjamin at Zel-
zah; and they will say to you, '[b]The donkeys which you went to look for have
been found. Now behold, your father has
[1]ceased to be concerned about the donkeys and is anxious for you, saying,
"What shall I do about my son?"'
3 "Then you will go on further from
there, and you will come as far as the
[1a]oak of Tabor, and there three men going up [b]to God at Bethel will meet you,
one carrying three young goats, another
carrying three loaves of bread, and another carrying a jug of wine;
4 and they will greet you and give
you two *loaves* of bread, which you will
accept from their hand.
5 "Afterward you will come to [1a]the
hill of God where the Philistine garrison
is; and it shall be as soon as you have
come there to the city, that you will meet
[b]a group of prophets coming down from
the high place with harp, tambourine,
flute, and a lyre before them, and [c]they
will be prophesying.
6 "Then [a]the Spirit of the LORD will
come upon you mightily, and [b]you shall
prophesy with them and be changed into
another man.
7 "It shall be when these signs come
to you, [a]do for yourself what [1]the occasion requires, for [b]God is with you.
8 "And [a]you shall go down before me
to Gilgal; and behold, I will come down
to you to offer burnt offerings and
[b]sacrifice peace offerings. [c]You shall wait
seven days until I come to you and show
you what you should do."
9 ¶ Then it happened when he
turned his back to leave Samuel, God
[a]changed [1]his heart; and all those signs
came about on that day.
10 [a]When they came to [1]the hill
there, behold, a group of prophets met
him; and the Spirit of God came upon
him mightily, so that he prophesied
among them.
11 It came about, when all who knew
him previously saw that he prophesied
now with the prophets, that the people
said to one another, "What has happened
to the son of Kish? [a]Is Saul also among
the prophets?"
12 A man there said, "Now, who is
their father?" Therefore it became a proverb: "[a]Is Saul also among the prophets?"
13 When he had finished prophesying,
he came to the high place.
14 ¶ Now [a]Saul's uncle said to him
and his servant, "Where did you go?"
And he said, "[b]To look for the donkeys.
When we saw that they could not be
found, we went to Samuel."
15 Saul's uncle said, "Please tell me
what Samuel said to you."
16 So Saul said to his uncle, "[a]He told
us plainly that the donkeys had been
found." But he did not tell him about the
matter of the kingdom which Samuel had
mentioned.

Saul Publicly Chosen King

17 ¶ Thereafter Samuel called the
[a]people together to the LORD at Mizpah;
18 and he said to the sons of Israel,
"[a]Thus says the LORD, the God of Israel,
'I brought Israel up from Egypt, and I delivered you from the hand of the Egyptians and from the [1]power of all the kingdoms that were oppressing you.'
19 "But you [a]have today rejected your

20 [b]1 Sam 8:5; 12:13
21 [1]So some ancient versions; Heb *tribes* [a]1 Sam 15:17 [b]Judg 20:46-48
23 [1]Lit *Give* [2]Lit *with you*
24 [1]Lit *saying* [a]Ex 29:22,27; Lev 7:32,33; Num 18:18
25 [1]Gr adds *and they spread a bed for Saul on the roof and he slept* [a]Deut 22:8; Luke 5:19; Acts 10:9
10:1 [a]Ex 30:23-33; 1 Sam 16:13; 2 Kin 9:3, 6 [b]Ps 2:12 [c]1 Sam 16:13; 26:9; 2 Sam 1:14 [d]Deut 32:9; Ps 78:71
2 [1]Lit *abandoned the matter of* [a]Gen 35:16-20; 48:7 [b]1 Sam 9:3-5
3 [1]Or *terebinth* [a]Gen 35:8 [b]Gen 28:19; 35:1,3,7
5 [1]Or *Gibeath-haelohim* [a]1 Sam 13:2,3 [b]1 Sam 19:20; 2 Kin 2:3, 5,15 [c]2 Kin 3:15; 1 Chr 25:1-6; 1 Cor 14:1
6 [a]Num 11:25, 29; Judg 14:6 [b]1 Sam 10:10; 19:23,24
7 [1]Lit *your hand finds* [a]Eccl 9:10 [b]Josh 1:5; Judg 6:12; Heb 13:5
8 [a]1 Sam 11:14; 13:8 [b]1 Sam 11:15 [c]1 Sam 13:8
9 [1]Lit *for him another heart* [a]1 Sam 10:6
10 [1]Or *Gibeath* [a]1 Sam 10:5,6; 19:20
11 [a]1 Sam 19:24; Amos 7:14,15; Matt 13:54-57; John 7:15
12 [a]1 Sam 19:23,24
14 [a]1 Sam 14:50 [b]1 Sam 9:3-6
16 [a]1 Sam 9:20
17 [a]Judg 20:1; 1 Sam 7:5
18 [1]Lit *hand* [a]Judg 6:8,9
19 [a]1 Sam 8:6, 7; 12:12

God, who delivers you from all your calamities and your distresses; yet you have [1]said, 'No, but set a king over us!' Now therefore, [b]present yourselves before the LORD by your tribes and by your clans."

20 ¶ Thus Samuel brought all the tribes of Israel near, and the tribe of Benjamin was taken by lot.

21 Then he brought the tribe of Benjamin near by its families, and the Matrite family was taken. And Saul the son of Kish was taken; but when they looked for him, he could not be found.

22 Therefore [a]they inquired further of the LORD, "Has the man come here yet?" So the LORD said, "Behold, he is hiding himself by the baggage."

23 So they ran and took him from there, and when he stood among the people, [a]he was taller than any of the people from his shoulders upward.

24 Samuel said to all the people, "Do you see him [a]whom the LORD has chosen? Surely there is no one like him among all the people." So all the people shouted and said, "[1b]*Long* live the king!"

25 ¶ Then Samuel told the people [a]the ordinances of the kingdom, and wrote *them* in the book and [b]placed *it* before the LORD. And Samuel sent all the people away, each one to his house.

26 Saul also went [a]to his house at Gibeah; and the valiant *men* whose hearts God had touched went with him.

27 But certain [1a]worthless men said, "How can this one deliver us?" And they despised him and [b]did not bring him any present. But he kept silent.

Saul Defeats the Ammonites

11 Now [a]Nahash the Ammonite came up and [1]besieged [b]Jabesh-gilead; and all the men of Jabesh said to Nahash, "Make [c]a covenant with us and we will serve you."

2 But Nahash the Ammonite said to them, "I will make *it* with you on this condition, [a]that I will gouge out the right eye of every one of you, thus I will make it [b]a reproach on all Israel."

3 [a]The elders of Jabesh said to him, "Let us alone for seven days, that we may send messengers throughout the territory of Israel. Then, if there is no one to deliver us, we will come out to you."

4 Then the messengers came [a]to Gibeah of Saul and spoke these words in the hearing of the people, and all the people [b]lifted up their voices and wept.

5 ¶ Now behold, Saul was coming from the field [a]behind the oxen, and [1]he said, "What is *the matter* with the people that they weep?" So they related to him the words of the men of Jabesh.

6 Then [a]the Spirit of God came upon Saul mightily when he heard these words, and [1]he became very angry.

7 He took a yoke of oxen and [a]cut them in pieces, and sent *them* throughout the territory of Israel by the hand of messengers, saying, "[b]Whoever does not come out after Saul and after Samuel, so shall it be done to his oxen." Then the dread of the LORD fell on the people, and they came out [c]as one man.

8 He [1]numbered them in [a]Bezek; and the [b]sons of Israel were 300,000, and the men of Judah 30,000.

9 They said to the messengers who had come, "Thus you shall say to the men of Jabesh-gilead, 'Tomorrow, by the time the sun is hot, you will have deliverance.' " So the messengers went and told the men of Jabesh; and they were glad.

10 Then the men of Jabesh said, "[a]Tomorrow we will come out to you, and you may do to us whatever seems good [1]to you."

11 The next morning Saul put the people [a]in three companies; and they came into the midst of the camp at the morning watch and struck down the Ammonites until the heat of the day. Those who survived were scattered, so that no two of them were left together.

12 ¶ Then the people said to Samuel, "[a]Who is he that said, 'Shall Saul reign over us?' [1b]Bring the men, that we may put them to death."

13 But Saul said, "[a]Not a man shall be put to death this day, for today [b]the LORD has accomplished deliverance in Israel."

14 ¶ Then Samuel said to the people, "Come and let us go to [a]Gilgal and [b]renew the kingdom there."

15 So all the people went to Gilgal, and there they made Saul king [a]before the LORD in Gilgal. There they also [b]offered sacrifices of peace offerings before the LORD; and there Saul and all the men of Israel rejoiced greatly.

Samuel Addresses Israel

12 Then Samuel said to all Israel, "Behold, [a]I have listened to your voice in all that you said to me and I [b]have [1]appointed a king over you.

2 "Now, [a]here is the king walking before you, but [b]I am old and gray, and behold [c]my sons are with you. And [d]I have walked before you from my youth even to this day.

3 "Here I am; bear witness against me before the LORD and [a]His anointed. [b]Whose ox have I taken, or whose donkey have I taken, or whom have I de-

---

19 [1]So with several mss and versions; M.T. *said to Him* [b]Josh 7:14-18; 24:1; Prov 16:33
22 [a]1 Sam 23:2, 4
23 [a]1 Sam 9:2
24 [1]Lit *May the king live* [a]Deut 17:15; 2 Sam 21:6 [b]1 Kin 1:25,34,39
25 [a]Deut 17:14-20; 1 Sam 8:11-18 [b]Deut 31:26
26 [a]1 Sam 11:4; 15:34
27 [1]Lit *sons of Belial,* cf 2 Cor 6:15 [a]Deut 13:13; 1 Sam 25:17 [b]1 Kin 10:25; 2 Chr 17:5
11:1 [1]Lit *camped against* [a]1 Sam 12:12 [b]Judg 21:8; 1 Sam 31:11 [c]Gen 26:28; 1 Kin 20:34; Job 41:4; Ezek 17:13
2 [a]Num 16:14 [b]1 Sam 17:26; Ps 44:13
3 [a]1 Sam 8:4
4 [a]1 Sam 10:26; 15:34 [b]Gen 27:38; Judg 2:4; 20:23,26; 21:2; 1 Sam 30:4
5 [1]Lit *Saul* [a]1 Kin 19:19
6 [1]Lit *his anger burned exceedingly* [a]Judg 3:10; 6:34; 11:29; 13:25; 14:6; 1 Sam 10:10; 16:13
7 [a]Judg 19:29 [b]Judg 21:5,8 [c]Judg 20:1
8 [1]Lit *mustered* [a]Judg 1:5 [b]Judg 20:2
10 [1]Lit *in your sight* [a]1 Sam 11:3
11 [a]Judg 7:16, 20
12 [1]Lit *Give* [a]1 Sam 10:27 [b]Luke 19:27
13 [a]1 Sam 10:27; 2 Sam 19:22 [b]Ex 14:13,30; 1 Sam 19:5
14 [a]1 Sam 7:16; 10:8 [b]1 Sam 10:25
15 [a]1 Sam 10:17 [b]1 Sam 10:8
12:1 [1]Lit *made* [a]1 Sam 8:7,9,22 [b]1 Sam 10:24; 11:14,15
2 [a]1 Sam 8:20 [b]1 Sam 8:1,5 [c]1 Sam 8:3,5 [d]1 Sam 3:10,19, 20
3 [a]1 Sam 10:1; 24:6; 2 Sam 1:14 [b]Ex 20:17; Num 16:15; Acts 20:33

frauded? Whom have I oppressed, or
[c]from whose hand have I taken a bribe to
blind my eyes with it? I will restore *it* to
you."
4 They said, "You have not defrauded
us or oppressed us or taken anything from
any man's hand."
5 He said to them, "The LORD is witness against you, and His anointed is witness this day that [a]you have found nothing [b]in my hand." And they said, "*He is*
witness."
6 ¶ Then Samuel said to the people,
"It is the LORD who [1a]appointed Moses
and Aaron and who brought your fathers
up from the land of Egypt.
7 "So now, take your stand, [a]that I
may plead with you before the LORD concerning all the righteous acts of the LORD
which He did for you and your fathers.
8 "[a]When Jacob went into Egypt and
[b]your fathers cried out to the LORD, then
[c]the LORD sent Moses and Aaron [1d]who
brought your fathers out of Egypt and settled them in this place.
9 "But [a]they forgot the LORD their
God, so [b]He sold them into the hand of
Sisera, captain of the army of Hazor, and
[c]into the hand of the Philistines and
[d]into the hand of the king of Moab,
and they fought against them.
10 "[a]They cried out to the LORD and
said, 'We have sinned because we have
forsaken the LORD and have served [b]the
Baals and the Ashtaroth; but [c]now deliver us from the hands of our enemies, and
we will serve You.'
11 "Then the LORD sent [a]Jerubbaal and
[1b]Bedan and [c]Jephthah and [d]Samuel,
and delivered you from the hands of your
enemies all around, so that you lived in
security.

The King Confirmed

12 "When you saw [a]that Nahash the
king of the sons of Ammon came against
you, you said to me, '[b]No, but a king
shall reign over us,' [c]although the LORD
your God *was* your king.
13 "Now therefore, [a]here is the king
whom you have chosen, [b]whom you
have asked for, and behold, the LORD has
set a king over you.
14 "[a]If you will fear the LORD and serve
Him, and listen to His voice and not rebel
against the [1]command of the LORD, then
both you and also the king who reigns
over you will follow the LORD your God.
15 "[a]If you will not listen to the voice
of the LORD, but rebel against the [1]com-
mand of the LORD, then [b]the hand of the
LORD will be against you, [c]*as it was*
against your fathers.
16 "Even now, [a]take your stand and
see this great thing which the LORD will
do before your eyes.
17 "[a]Is it not the wheat harvest today?
[b]I will call to the LORD, that He may send
[1]thunder and rain. Then you will know
and see that [c]your wickedness is great
which you have done in the sight of the
LORD by asking for yourselves a king."
18 So Samuel called to the LORD, and
the LORD sent [1]thunder and rain that
day; and [a]all the people greatly feared
the LORD and Samuel.
19 ¶ Then all the people said to Samuel, "[a]Pray for your servants to the LORD
your God, so that we may not die, for we
have added to all our sins [b]*this* evil by
asking for ourselves a king."
20 Samuel said to the people, "Do not
fear. You have committed all this evil, yet
[a]do not turn aside from following the
LORD, but serve the LORD with all your
heart.
21 "You must not turn aside, for *then*
you would go after [a]futile things which
can not profit or deliver, because they are
futile.
22 "For [a]the LORD will not abandon His
people [b]on account of His great name,
because the LORD [c]has been pleased to
make you a people for Himself.
23 "Moreover, as for me, [a]far be it
from me that I should sin against the
LORD by ceasing to pray for you; but [b]I
will instruct you in the good and right
way.
24 "[a]Only [1]fear the LORD and serve
Him in truth with all your heart; for consider [b]what great things He has done for
you.
25 "[a]But if you still do wickedly, [b]both
you and your king [c]will be swept away."

War with the Philistines

13 Saul was *thirty* years old when he
began to reign, and he reigned
forty two years over Israel.
2 ¶ Now Saul chose for himself 3,000
men of Israel, of which 2,000 were with
Saul in [a]Michmash and in the hill country of Bethel, while 1,000 were with Jonathan at [b]Gibeah of Benjamin. But he
sent away the rest of the people, each to
his tent.
3 Jonathan smote [a]the garrison of
the Philistines that was in [b]Geba, and
the Philistines heard of *it*. Then Saul
[c]blew the trumpet throughout the land,
saying, "Let the Hebrews hear."
4 All Israel heard [1]the news that Saul
had smitten the garrison of the Philistines, and also that Israel [a]had become
odious to the Philistines. The people
were then summoned [2]to Saul at Gilgal.
5 ¶ Now the Philistines assembled to

3 [c]Ex 23:8; Deut 16:19
5 [a]Acts 23:9; 24:20 [b]Ex 22:4
6 [1]Lit *made* [a]Ex 6:26; Mic 6:4
7 [a]Ezek 20:35; Mic 6:1-5
8 [1]Lit *and they brought* [a]Gen 46:5,6 [b]Ex 2:23-25 [c]Ex 3:10; 4:14-16 [d]1 Sam 10:18
9 [a]Deut 32:18; Judg 3:7 [b]Judg 4:2 [c]Judg 3:31; 10:7; 13:1 [d]Judg 3:12-30
10 [a]Judg 10:10 [b]Judg 2:13; 3:7 [c]Judg 10:15,16
11 [1]Gr and Syr read *Barak* [a]Judg 6:31,32; 7:1 [b]Judg 4:6; 11:1 [c]Judg 11:29 [d]1 Sam 3:20
12 [a]1 Sam 11:1, 2 [b]1 Sam 8:6,19 [c]Judg 8:23; 1 Sam 8:7
13 [a]1 Sam 10:24 [b]1 Sam 8:5; 12:17,19; Hos 13:11
14 [1]Lit *mouth* [a]Josh 24:14
15 [1]Lit *mouth* [a]Lev 26:14,15; Josh 24:20; Is 1:20 [b]1 Sam 5:9 [c]1 Sam 12:9
16 [a]Ex 14:13,31
17 [1]Lit *sounds* [a]Prov 26:1 [b]1 Sam 7:9,10; James 5:16ff [c]1 Sam 8:7
18 [1]Lit *sounds* [a]Ex 14:31
19 [a]Ex 9:28; 1 Sam 12:23; Jer 15:1; 1 John 5:16 [b]1 Sam 12:17,20
20 [a]Deut 11:16
21 [a]Deut 11:16; Is 41:29; Hab 2:18
22 [a]Deut 31:6; 1 Kin 6:13 [b]Ex 32:12; Num 14:13; Josh 7:9; Ps 106:8; Jer 14:21 [c]Deut 7:6-11; 1 Pet 2:9
23 [a]Rom 1:9; 1 Cor 9:16; Col 1:9; 1 Thess 3:10; 2 Tim 1:3 [b]1 Kin 8:36; Ps 34:11; Prov 4:11
24 [1]Or *reverence* [a]Eccl 12:13 [b]Deut 10:21; Is 5:12
25 [a]Is 1:20; 3:11 [b]Josh 24:20 [c]1 Sam 31:1-5; Hos 10:3
13:2 [a]1 Sam 13:5; 14:31 [b]1 Sam 10:26
3 [a]1 Sam 10:5 [b]1 Sam 13:16; 14:5 [c]Judg 3:27; 6:34
4 [1]Lit *saying* [2]Lit *after* [a]Gen 34:30; Ex 5:21; 2 Sam 10:6

fight with Israel, 30,000 chariots and 6,000 horsemen, and [a]people like the sand which is on the seashore in abundance; and they came up and camped in Michmash, east of [b]Beth-aven.

6 When the men of Israel saw that they were in a strait (for the people were hard-pressed), then [a]the people hid themselves in caves, in thickets, in cliffs, in cellars, and in pits.

7 Also *some of* the Hebrews crossed the Jordan into the land of [a]Gad and Gilead. But as for Saul, he *was* still in Gilgal, and all the people followed him trembling.

8 ¶ Now [a]he waited seven days, according to the appointed time set by Samuel, but Samuel did not come to Gilgal; and the people were scattering from him.

9 So Saul said, "Bring to me the burnt offering and the peace offerings." And [a]he offered the burnt offering.

10 As soon as he finished offering the burnt offering, behold, Samuel came; and [a]Saul went out to meet him *and* to [1]greet him.

11 But Samuel said, "What have you done?" And Saul said, "Because I saw that the people were scattering from me, and that you did not come within the appointed days, and that [a]the Philistines were assembling at Michmash,

12 therefore I said, 'Now the Philistines will come down against me at Gilgal, and I have not asked the favor of the LORD.' So I forced myself and offered the burnt offering."

13 Samuel said to Saul, "[a]You have acted foolishly; [b]you have not kept the commandment of the LORD your God, which He commanded you, for now the LORD would have established your kingdom [1]over Israel [c]forever.

14 "But [a]now your kingdom shall not endure. [b]The LORD has sought out for Himself a man after His own heart, and the LORD has appointed him as ruler over His people, because you have not kept what the LORD commanded you."

15 ¶ Then Samuel arose and went up from Gilgal to [a]Gibeah of Benjamin. And Saul [1]numbered the people who were present with him, [b]about six hundred men.

16 Now Saul and his son Jonathan and the people who were present with them were staying in [a]Geba of Benjamin while the Philistines camped at Michmash.

17 And [a]the [1]raiders came from the camp of the Philistines in three [2]companies: one [3]company turned [4]toward [b]Ophrah, to the land of Shual,

18 and another [1]company turned [2]toward [a]Beth-horon, and another [1]company turned [2]toward the border which overlooks the valley of [b]Zeboim toward the wilderness.

19 ¶ Now [a]no blacksmith could be found in all the land of Israel, for the Philistines said, "Otherwise the Hebrews will make [1b]swords or spears."

20 So all Israel went down to the Philistines, each to sharpen his plowshare, his mattock, his axe, and his hoe.

21 The charge was [1]two-thirds of a shekel for the plowshares, the mattocks, the forks, and the axes, and to fix the hoes.

22 So it came about on the day of battle that [a]neither sword nor spear was found in the hands of any of the people who *were* with Saul and Jonathan, but they were found with Saul and his son Jonathan.

23 And [a]the garrison of the Philistines went out to [b]the pass of Michmash.

Jonathan's Victory

14 Now the day came that Jonathan, the son of Saul, said to the young man who was carrying his armor, "Come and let us cross over to the Philistines' garrison that is on the other side." But he did not tell his father.

2 Saul was staying in the outskirts of [a]Gibeah under the pomegranate tree which is in [b]Migron. And the people who *were* with him *were* [c]about six hundred men,

3 and Ahijah, the [a]son of Ahitub, [b]Ichabod's brother, the son of Phinehas, the son of Eli, the priest of the LORD at [c]Shiloh, [d]was [1]wearing an ephod. And the people did not know that Jonathan had gone.

4 [a]Between the passes by which Jonathan sought to cross over to the Philistines' garrison, there was a sharp crag on the one side and a sharp crag on the other side, and the name of the one was Bozez, and the name of the other Seneh.

5 The one crag rose on the north opposite Michmash, and the other on the south opposite Geba.

6 ¶ Then Jonathan said to the young man who was carrying his armor, "Come and let us cross over to the garrison of [a]these uncircumcised; perhaps the LORD will work for us, for [b]the LORD is not restrained to save by many or by few."

7 His armor bearer said to him, "Do all that is in your heart; turn yourself, *and* here I am with you according to your [1]desire."

8 Then Jonathan said, "[a]Behold, we will cross over to the men and reveal ourselves to them.

9 "If they [1]say to us, 'Wait until we

---

5 [a]Josh 11:4 [b]Josh 18:12; 1 Sam 14:23
6 [a]Judg 6:2
7 [a]Num 32:33
8 [a]1 Sam 10:8
9 [a]Deut 12:5-14; 2 Sam 24:25; 1 Kin 3:4
10 [1]Lit *bless* [a]1 Sam 15:13
11 [a]1 Sam 13:2, 5,16,23
13 [1]Lit *to* [a]2 Chr 16:9 [b]1 Sam 15:11, 22,28 [c]1 Sam 1:22
14 [a]1 Sam 15:28 [b]Acts 7:46; 13:22
15 [1]Lit *mustered* [a]1 Sam 13:2 [b]1 Sam 13:2,6,7; 14:2
16 [a]1 Sam 13:2, 3
17 [1]Lit *destroyers* [2]Lit *heads* [3]Lit *head* [4]Lit *toward the direction of* [a]1 Sam 14:15 [b]Josh 18:23
18 [1]Lit *head* [2]Lit *the direction of* [a]Josh 16:3; 18:13,14 [b]Neh 11:34
19 [1]Lit *sword or spear* [a]Judg 5:8; 2 Kin 24:14; Jer 24:1; 29:2 [b]Judg 5:8
21 [1]Heb *pim*
22 [a]Judg 5:8
23 [a]1 Sam 14:1; 2 Sam 23:14 [b]1 Sam 14:4,5; Is 10:28
14:2 [a]1 Sam 13:15,16 [b]Is 10:28 [c]1 Sam 13:15
3 [1]Lit *carrying* [a]1 Sam 22:9-12, 20 [b]1 Sam 4:21 [c]1 Sam 1:3 [d]1 Sam 2:28
4 [a]1 Sam 13:23
6 [a]1 Sam 17:26, 36; Jer 9:25,26 [b]Judg 7:4,7; 1 Sam 17:46,47; Ps 115:3; 135:6; Zech 4:6; Matt 19:26
7 [1]Lit *heart*
8 [a]Judg 7:9-14
9 [1]Lit *say thus*

come to you'; then we will stand in our
place and not go up to them.
10 "But if they [1]say, 'Come up to us,'
then we will go up, for the LORD has giv-
en them into our hands; and [a]this shall
be the sign to us."
11 When both of them revealed themselves to the garrison of the Philistines,
the Philistines said, "Behold, [a]Hebrews
are coming out of the holes where they
have hidden themselves."
12 So the men of the garrison [1]hailed
Jonathan and his armor bearer and said,
"Come up to us and [a]we will tell you
something." And Jonathan said to his armor bearer, "Come up after me, for [b]the
LORD has given them into the hands of
Israel."
13 Then Jonathan climbed up on his
hands and feet, with his armor bearer
behind him; and they fell before Jonathan, and his armor bearer put some to
death after him.
14 That first slaughter which Jonathan
and his armor bearer made was about
twenty men within about half a furrow in
an acre of land.
15 And there was a trembling in the
camp, in the field, and among all the people. Even the garrison and [a]the raiders
trembled, and [b]the earth quaked so
[c]that it became a [1]great trembling.
16 ¶ Now Saul's watchmen in Gibeah
of Benjamin looked, and behold, the multitude melted away; and they went here
and *there.*
17 Saul said to the people who *were*
with him, "[1]Number now and see who
has gone from us." And when they had
[1]numbered, behold, Jonathan and his armor bearer were not *there.*
18 Then Saul said to Ahijah, "[a]Bring
the ark of God here." For the ark of God
was at that time with the sons of Israel.
19 [a]While Saul talked to the priest,
the commotion in the camp of the Philistines continued and increased; so Saul
said to the priest, "Withdraw your hand."
20 Then Saul and all the people who
were with him rallied and came to the
battle; and behold, [a]every man's sword
was against his fellow, *and there was* very
great confusion.
21 Now the Hebrews *who* were with
the Philistines previously, who went up
with them all around in the camp, even
[a]they also *turned* to be with the Israelites who *were* with Saul and Jonathan.
22 When all the [a]men of Israel who
had hidden themselves in the hill country
of Ephraim heard that the Philistines had
fled, even they also pursued them closely
in the battle.
23 So [a]the LORD delivered Israel that
day, and the battle [1]spread beyond
[b]Beth-aven.

Saul's Foolish Order

24 ¶ Now the men of Israel were hard-
pressed on that day, for Saul had [a]put the
people under oath, saying, "Cursed be
the man who eats food [1]before evening,
and until I have avenged myself on my
enemies." So none of the people tasted
food.
25 All *the people of* the land entered
the forest, and there was honey on the
ground.
26 When the people entered the forest, behold, [a]*there was* a flow of honey;
but no man put his hand to his mouth, for
the people feared the oath.
27 But Jonathan had not heard when
his father put the people under oath;
therefore, [a]he put out the end of the staff
that *was* in his hand and dipped it in the
honeycomb, and put his hand to his
mouth, and [b]his eyes brightened.
28 Then one of the people said, "Your
father strictly put the people under oath,
saying, 'Cursed be the man who eats food
today.'" And the people were weary.
29 Then Jonathan said, "[a]My father
has troubled the land. See now, how my
eyes have brightened because I tasted a
little of this honey.
30 "How much more, if only the people
had eaten freely today of the spoil of their
enemies which they found! For now the
slaughter among the Philistines has not
been great."
31 ¶ They struck among the Philistines that day from [a]Michmash to [b]Aija-
lon. And the people were very weary.
32 [a]The people [1]rushed greedily
upon the spoil, and took sheep and oxen
and calves, and slew *them* on the ground;
and the people ate *them* [b]with the blood.
33 Then they told Saul, saying, "Behold, the people are [a]sinning against the
LORD by eating with the blood." And he
said, "You have acted treacherously; roll
a great stone to me today."
34 Saul said, "Disperse yourselves
among the people and say to them, 'Each
one of you bring me his ox or his sheep,
and slaughter *it* here and eat; and do not
sin against the LORD by eating with the
blood.'" So all the people that night
brought each one his ox [1]with him and
slaughtered *it* there.
35 And [a]Saul built an altar to the
LORD; it was the first altar that he built to
the LORD.
36 ¶ Then Saul said, "Let us go down
after the Philistines by night and take
spoil among them until the morning
light, and let us not leave a man of them."

---

10 [1]Lit *say thus* [a]Gen 24:14; Judg 6:36
11 [a]1 Sam 13:6; 14:22
12 [1]Lit *answered* [a]1 Sam 17:43,44 [b]2 Sam 5:24
15 [1]Lit *trembling of God* [a]1 Sam 13:17,18 [b]1 Sam 7:10 [c]Gen 35:5; 2 Kin 7:6
17 [1]Lit *muster(ed)*
18 [a]1 Sam 23:9; 30:7
19 [a]Num 27:21
20 [a]Judg 7:22; 2 Chr 20:23
21 [a]1 Sam 29:4
22 [a]1 Sam 13:6
23 [1]Lit *passed over* [a]Ex 14:30; 1 Sam 10:19; 14:23; 1 Chr 11:14; 2 Chr 32:22; Ps 44:7 [b]1 Sam 13:5
24 [1]Lit *until* [a]Josh 6:26
26 [a]Matt 3:4
27 [a]1 Sam 14:43 [b]1 Sam 30:12
29 [a]Josh 7:25; 1 Kin 18:18
31 [a]1 Sam 14:5 [b]Josh 10:12
32 [1]Lit *did with regard to the spoil* [a]1 Sam 15:19 [b]Gen 9:4; Lev 3:17; 17:10-14; 19:26; Deut 12:16,23; Acts 15:20
33 [a]Lev 7:26, 27; 19:26; Deut 12:16,23-25; 15:23
34 [1]Lit *in his hand*
35 [a]1 Sam 7:12, 17; 2 Sam 24:25; James 4:8

And they said, "Do whatever seems good [1]to you." So [a]the priest said, "Let us draw near to God here."

37 Saul [a]inquired of God, "Shall I go down after the Philistines? Will You give them into the hand of Israel?" But [b]He did not answer him on that day.

38 Saul said, "[a]Draw near here, all you [1]chiefs of the people, and investigate and see how this sin has happened today.

39 "For [a]as the LORD lives, who delivers Israel, though it is in Jonathan my son, he shall surely die." But not one of all the people answered him.

40 Then he said to all Israel, "You shall be on one side and I and Jonathan my son will be on the other side." And the people said to Saul, "Do what seems good [1]to you."

41 Therefore, Saul said to the LORD, the God of Israel, "[a]Give a perfect *lot.*" And Jonathan and Saul were taken, but the people escaped.

42 Saul said, "Cast *lots* between me and Jonathan my son." And Jonathan was taken.

43 ¶ Then Saul said to Jonathan, "[a]Tell me what you have done." So Jonathan told him and said, "[b]I indeed tasted a little honey with the end of the staff that was in my hand. Here I am, I must die!"

44 Saul said, "[a]May God do [1]this *to me* and more also, for [b]you shall surely die, Jonathan."

45 But the people said to Saul, "Must Jonathan die, who has [1]brought about this great deliverance in Israel? Far from it! As the LORD lives, [a]not one hair of his head shall fall to the ground, for [b]he has worked with God this day." So the people [2]rescued Jonathan and he did not die.

46 Then Saul went up from [1]pursuing the Philistines, and the Philistines went to their own place.

Constant Warfare

47 ¶ Now when Saul had taken the kingdom over Israel, he fought against all his enemies on every side, against Moab, [a]the sons of Ammon, Edom, [b]the kings of Zobah, and [c]the Philistines; and wherever he turned, he [1]inflicted punishment.

48 He acted valiantly and [1a]defeated the Amalekites, and delivered Israel from the hands of [2]those who plundered them.

49 ¶ Now [a]the sons of Saul were Jonathan and Ishvi and Malchi-shua; and the names of his two daughters *were these:* the name of the firstborn [b]Merab and the name of the younger [c]Michal.

50 The name of Saul's wife was Ahinoam the daughter of Ahimaaz. And [a]the name of the captain of his army was Abner the son of Ner, Saul's uncle.

51 [a]Kish *was* the father of Saul, and Ner the father of Abner *was* the son of Abiel.

52 ¶ Now the war against the Philistines was severe all the days of Saul; and when Saul saw any mighty man or any valiant man, he [1a]attached him to [2]his staff.

Saul's Disobedience

15 Then Samuel said to Saul, "[a]The LORD sent me to anoint you as king over His people, over Israel; now therefore, listen to the [1]words of the LORD.

2 "Thus says the LORD of hosts, 'I will [1]punish Amalek [a]*for* what he did to Israel, how he set himself against him on the way while he was coming up from Egypt.

3 'Now go and strike Amalek and [a]utterly destroy all that he has, and do not spare him; but [b]put to death both man and woman, child and infant, ox and sheep, camel and donkey.' "

4 ¶ Then Saul summoned the people and [1]numbered them in [a]Telaim, 200,000 foot soldiers and 10,000 men of Judah.

5 Saul came to the city of Amalek and set an ambush in the valley.

6 Saul said to [a]the Kenites, "Go, depart, go down from among the Amalekites, so that I do not destroy you with them; for [b]you showed kindness to all the sons of Israel when they came up from Egypt." So the Kenites departed from among the Amalekites.

7 So [a]Saul [1]defeated the Amalekites, from [b]Havilah as you go to [c]Shur, which is [2]east of Egypt.

8 He captured [a]Agag the king of the Amalekites alive, and [b]utterly destroyed all the people with the edge of the sword.

9 But Saul and the people [a]spared Agag and the best of the sheep, the oxen, the fatlings, the lambs, and all that was good, and were not willing to destroy them utterly; but everything despised and worthless, that they utterly destroyed.

Samuel Rebukes Saul

10 ¶ Then the word of the LORD came to Samuel, saying,

11 "[a]I regret that I have made Saul king, for [b]he has turned back from [1]following Me and has not carried out My commands." And Samuel was distressed and [c]cried out to the LORD all night.

12 Samuel rose early in the morning to meet Saul; and it was told Samuel, saying, "Saul came to [a]Carmel, and behold, he

36 [1]Lit *in your eyes* [a]1 Sam 14:3,18,19
37 [a]1 Sam 10:22 [b]1 Sam 28:6
38 [1]Lit *corners* [a]Josh 7:11,12; 1 Sam 10:19,20
39 [a]1 Sam 14:24,44; 2 Sam 12:5
40 [1]Lit *in your eyes*
41 [a]Acts 1:24
43 [a]Josh 7:19 [b]1 Sam 14:27
44 [1]Lit *thus* [a]Ruth 1:17; 1 Sam 25:22 [b]1 Sam 14:39
45 [1]Lit *worked* [2]Lit *ransomed* [a]2 Sam 14:11; 1 Kin 1:52; Luke 21:18; Acts 27:34 [b]2 Cor 6:1
46 [1]Lit *after*
47 [1]Or *condemned* [a]1 Sam 11:1-13 [b]2 Sam 8:3-10 [c]1 Sam 14:52
48 [1]Lit *smote* [2]Lit *its plunderers* [a]1 Sam 15:3, 7
49 [a]1 Sam 31:2; 1 Chr 8:33; 10:2 [b]1 Sam 18:17-19 [c]1 Sam 18:20, 27; 19:12; 2 Sam 6:20-23
50 [a]2 Sam 2:8
51 [a]1 Sam 9:1, 21
52 [1]Lit *gathered* [2]Lit *himself* [a]1 Sam 8:11
15:1 [1]Lit *sound of the words* [a]1 Sam 9:16; 10:1
2 [1]Or *visit* [a]Ex 17:8-16; Num 24:20; Deut 25:17-19
3 [a]Num 24:20; Deut 20:16-18; Josh 6:17-21 [b]1 Sam 22:19
4 [1]Lit *mustered* [a]Josh 15:24
6 [a]Num 24:21; Judg 1:16; 4:11 [b]Ex 18:9,10; Num 10:29-32
7 [1]Lit *smote* [2]Lit *before* [a]1 Sam 14:48 [b]Gen 25:18 [c]Gen 16:7; Ex 15:22; 1 Sam 27:8
8 [a]Num 24:7; 1 Sam 15:20; Esth 3:1 [b]1 Sam 27:8,9; 30:1; 2 Sam 8:12
9 [a]1 Sam 15:3, 15,19
11 [1]Lit *after* [a]Gen 6:6,7; Ex 32:14; 1 Sam 15:35; 2 Sam 24:16 [b]Josh 22:16; 1 Sam 13:13; 1 Kin 9:6, 7 [c]Ex 32:11-13; Luke 6:12
12 [a]Josh 15:55; 1 Sam 25:2

set up a monument for himself, then
turned and proceeded on [1]down to [b]Gil-
gal."
13 Samuel came to Saul, and Saul said
to him, "[a]Blessed are you of the LORD! I
have carried out the command of the
LORD."
14 But Samuel said, "[a]What then is
this [1]bleating of the sheep in my ears,
and the [1]lowing of the oxen which I
hear?"
15 Saul said, "They have brought them
from the Amalekites, for [a]the people
spared the best of the sheep and oxen, to
sacrifice to the LORD your God; but the
rest we have utterly destroyed."
16 Then Samuel said to Saul, "Wait,
and let me tell you what the LORD said
to me last night." And he said to him,
"Speak!"
17 ¶ Samuel said, "Is it not true,
[a]though you were little in your own
eyes, you were *made* the head of the
tribes of Israel? And the LORD anointed
you king over Israel,
18 and the LORD sent you on a [1]mis-
sion, and said, '[a]Go and utterly destroy
the sinners, the Amalekites, and fight
against them until they are exterminated.'
19 "Why then did you not obey the
voice of the LORD, [a]but rushed upon the
spoil and did what was evil in the sight of
the LORD?"
20 ¶ Then Saul said to Samuel, "[a]I did
obey the voice of the LORD, and went on
the [1]mission on which the LORD sent
me, and have brought back Agag the king
of Amalek, and have utterly destroyed the
Amalekites.
21 "But [a]the people took *some* of the
spoil, sheep and oxen, the choicest of the
things devoted to destruction, to sacrifice
to the LORD your God at Gilgal."
22 Samuel said,
"[a]Has the LORD as much delight
in burnt offerings and
sacrifices
As in obeying the voice of the
LORD?
Behold, [b]to obey is better than
sacrifice,
And to heed than the fat of
rams.
23 "For rebellion is as the sin of
[a]divination,
And insubordination is as
[b]iniquity and idolatry.
Because you have rejected the
word of the LORD,
[c]He has also rejected you from
being king."
24 ¶ Then Saul said to Samuel, "[a]I
have sinned; [b]I have indeed transgressed
the [1]command of the LORD and your
words, because I feared the people and
listened to their voice.
25 "Now therefore, [a]please pardon my
sin and return with me, that I may worship the LORD."
26 But Samuel said to Saul, "I will not
return with you; for [a]you have rejected
the word of the LORD, and the LORD has
rejected you from being king over Israel."
27 As Samuel turned to go, [a]*Saul*
seized the edge of his robe, and it tore.
28 So Samuel said to him, "[a]The LORD
has torn the kingdom of Israel from you
today and has given it to your neighbor,
who is better than you.
29 "Also the [1a]Glory of Israel [b]will
not lie or change His mind; for He is not
a man that He should change His mind."
30 Then he said, "I have sinned; [a]*but*
please honor me now before the elders of
my people and before Israel, and go back
with me, [b]that I may worship the LORD
your God."
31 So Samuel went back following
Saul, and Saul worshiped the LORD.
32 ¶ Then Samuel said, "Bring me
Agag, the king of the Amalekites." And
Agag came to him [1]cheerfully. And Agag
said, "Surely the bitterness of death is
past."
33 But Samuel said, "[a]As your sword
has made women childless, so shall your
mother be childless among women." And
Samuel hewed Agag to pieces before the
LORD at Gilgal.
34 ¶ Then Samuel went to [a]Ramah,
but Saul went up to his house at [b]Gibeah
of Saul.
35 [a]Samuel did not see Saul again until the day of his death; for Samuel
[b]grieved over Saul. And the LORD regretted that He had made Saul king over Israel.

Samuel Goes to Bethlehem

16 Now the LORD said to Samuel,
"[a]How long will you grieve over
Saul, since [b]I have rejected him from being king over Israel? [c]Fill your horn with
oil and go; I will send you to [d]Jesse the
Bethlehemite, for I have [e]selected a king
for Myself among his sons."
2 But Samuel said, "How can I go?
When Saul hears *of it,* he will kill me."
And the LORD said, "[a]Take a heifer with
you and say, 'I have come to sacrifice to
the LORD.'
3 "You shall invite Jesse to the sacrifice, and [a]I will show you what you shall
do; and [b]you shall anoint for Me the one
whom I [1]designate to you."
4 So Samuel did what the LORD said,
and came to [a]Bethlehem. And the elders

12 [1]Lit *and went down* [b]1 Sam 13:12,15
13 [a]Gen 14:19; Judg 17:2; Ruth 3:10; 2 Sam 2:5
14 [1]Lit *sound* [a]Ex 32:21-24
15 [a]Gen 3:12, 13; Ex 32:22,23; 1 Sam 15:9,21
17 [a]1 Sam 9:21; 10:22
18 [1]Lit *way* [a]1 Sam 15:3
19 [a]1 Sam 14:32
20 [1]Lit *way* [a]1 Sam 15:13
21 [a]Ex 32:22, 23; 1 Sam 15:15
22 [a]Ps 40:6-8; 51:16,17; Is 1:11-15; Mic 6:6-8; Heb 10:6-9 [b]Jer 7:22, 23; Hos 6:6; Matt 12:7; Mark 12:33
23 [a]Deut 18:10 [b]Gen 31:19,34 [c]1 Sam 13:14
24 [1]Lit *mouth* [a]Num 22:34; 2 Sam 12:13; Ps 51:4 [b]Prov 29:25; Is 51:12, 13
25 [a]Ex 10:17
26 [a]1 Sam 13:14; 16:1
27 [a]1 Kin 11:30,31
28 [a]1 Sam 28:17,18; 1 Kin 11:31
29 [1]Or *Eminence* [a]1 Chr 29:11 [b]Num 23:19; Ezek 24:14; Titus 1:2
30 [a]John 5:44; 12:43 [b]Is 29:13
32 [1]Or *in bonds*
33 [a]Gen 9:6; Judg 1:7; Matt 7:2
34 [a]1 Sam 7:17 [b]1 Sam 11:4
35 [a]1 Sam 19:24 [b]1 Sam 16:1
16:1 [a]1 Sam 15:35 [b]1 Sam 13:13,14; 15:23 [c]1 Sam 9:16; 10:1; 2 Kin 9:1 [d]Ruth 4:17-22 [e]Ps 78:70,71; Acts 13:22
2 [a]1 Sam 20:29
3 [1]Lit *say to you* [a]Ex 4:15; Acts 9:6 [b]Deut 17:14, 15; 1 Sam 9:16
4 [a]Gen 48:7; Luke 2:4

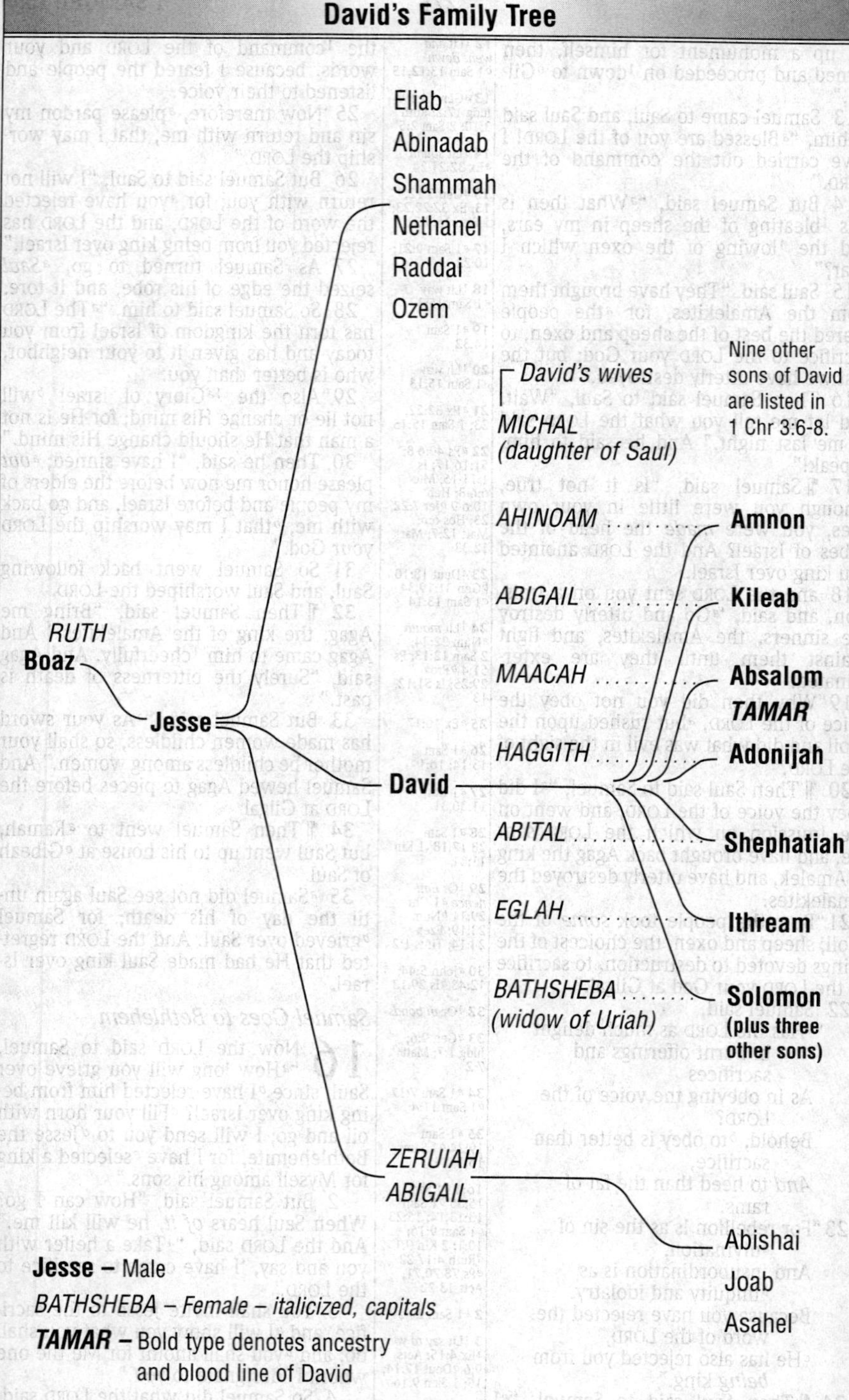

David's Family Tree
Eliab
Abinadab
Shammah
Nethanel
Raddai
Ozem
David's wives
Nine other sons of David are listed in 1 Chr 3:6-8.
MICHAL (daughter of Saul)
AHINOAM
Amnon
ABIGAIL
Kileab
MAACAH
Absalom
TAMAR
HAGGITH
Adonijah
RUTH
Boaz
Jesse
David
ABITAL
Shephatiah
EGLAH
Ithream
BATHSHEBA (widow of Uriah)
Solomon (plus three other sons)
ZERUIAH
ABIGAIL
Abishai
Joab
Asahel
Jesse – Male
BATHSHEBA – Female – italicized, capitals
TAMAR – Bold type denotes ancestry and blood line of David

of the city came trembling to meet him
and said, "[b]Do you come in peace?"
5 He said, "In peace; I have come to
sacrifice to the LORD. [a]Consecrate yourselves and come with me to the sacrifice." He also consecrated Jesse and his
sons and invited them to the sacrifice.
6 ¶ When they entered, he looked at
[a]Eliab and thought, "Surely the LORD's
anointed is before Him."
7 But the LORD said to Samuel, "Do
not look at his appearance or at the height
of his stature, because I have rejected
him; for [1]God *sees* not as man sees, for
man looks at the outward appearance,
[a]but the LORD looks at the heart."
8 Then Jesse called [a]Abinadab and
made him pass before Samuel. And he
said, "The LORD has not chosen this one
either."
9 Next Jesse made [1a]Shammah pass
by. And he said, "The LORD has not chosen this one either."
10 Thus Jesse made seven of his sons
pass before Samuel. But Samuel said to
Jesse, "The LORD has not chosen these."
11 And Samuel said to Jesse, "Are
these all the children?" And he said,
"[a]There remains yet the youngest, and
behold, he is tending the sheep." Then
Samuel said to Jesse, "Send and [1]bring
him; for we will not sit down until he
comes here."

David Anointed

12 So he sent and brought him in.
Now he was ruddy, with [a]beautiful eyes
and a handsome appearance. And the
LORD said, "[b]Arise, anoint him; for this
is he."
13 Then Samuel took the horn of oil
and [a]anointed him in the midst of his
brothers; and [b]the Spirit of the LORD
came mightily upon David from that day
forward. And Samuel arose and went to
Ramah.
14 ¶ [a]Now the Spirit of the LORD departed from Saul, and [b]an evil spirit from
the LORD terrorized him.
15 Saul's servants then said to him,
"Behold now, an evil spirit from God is
terrorizing you.
16 "Let our lord now command your
servants who are before you. Let them
seek a man who is a skillful player on the
harp; and it shall come about when the
evil spirit from God is on you, that [a]he
shall play *the harp* with his hand, and you
will be well."
17 So Saul said to his servants, "Provide for me now a man who can play well
and bring *him* to me."
18 Then one of the young men said,
"Behold, I have seen a son of Jesse the
Bethlehemite who is a skillful musician,
[a]a mighty man of valor, a warrior, one
prudent in speech, and a handsome man;
and [b]the LORD is with him."
19 So Saul sent messengers to Jesse
and said, "Send me your son David who
is with the flock."
20 Jesse [a]took a donkey *loaded with*
bread and a jug of wine and a young goat,
and sent *them* to Saul by David his son.
21 Then David came to Saul and [1a]at-
tended him; and [2]Saul loved him greatly,
and he became his armor bearer.
22 Saul sent to Jesse, saying, "Let David now stand before me, for he has
found favor in my sight."
23 So it came about whenever [a]the
evil spirit from God came to Saul, David
would take the harp and play *it* with his
hand; and Saul would be refreshed and be
well, and the evil spirit would depart
from him.

Goliath's Challenge

17 Now [a]the Philistines gathered
their armies for battle; and they
were gathered at Socoh which belongs to
Judah, and they camped between [b]Socoh
and [c]Azekah, in [d]Ephes-dammim.
2 Saul and the men of Israel were
gathered and camped in [a]the valley of
Elah, and drew up in battle array to encounter the Philistines.
3 The Philistines stood on the mountain on one side while Israel stood on the
mountain on the other side, with the valley between them.
4 Then a champion came out from
the armies of the Philistines named [a]Go-
liath, from [b]Gath, whose height was six
[1]cubits and a span.
5 *He had* a bronze helmet on his
head, and he was clothed with scale-
armor [1]which weighed five thousand
shekels of bronze.
6 *He* also *had* bronze [1]greaves on his
legs and a [a]bronze javelin *slung* between
his shoulders.
7 [a]The shaft of his spear was like a
weaver's beam, and the head of his spear
weighed six hundred shekels of iron;
[b]his shield-carrier also walked before
him.
8 He stood and shouted to the ranks
of Israel and said to them, "Why do you
come out to draw up in battle array? Am
I not the Philistine and you [a]servants of
Saul? Choose a man for yourselves and let
him come down to me.
9 "[a]If he is able to fight with me and
[1]kill me, then we will become your servants; but if I prevail against him and
[1]kill him, then you shall become our servants and serve us."

4 [b]1 Kin 2:13; 2 Kin 9:22; 1 Chr 12:17
5 [a]Gen 35:2; Ex 19:10
6 [a]1 Sam 17:13
7 [1]So with Gr; Heb He does *not see what man sees* [a]1 Sam 2:3; 1 Kin 8:39; 1 Chr 28:9; Luke 16:15
8 [a]1 Sam 17:13
9 [1]In 2 Sam 13:3, *Shimeah*; in 1 Chr 2:13, *Shimea* [a]1 Sam 17:13
11 [1]Lit *take* [a]1 Sam 17:12; 2 Sam 13:3
12 [a]Gen 39:6; Ex 2:2; Acts 7:20 [b]1 Sam 9:17
13 [a]1 Sam 10:1 [b]Num 27:18; 1 Sam 10:6
14 [a]Judg 16:20; 1 Sam 11:6 [b]Judg 9:23; 1 Sam 16:15; 1 Kin 22:19-22
16 [a]1 Sam 18:10; 2 Kin 3:15
18 [a]1 Sam 17:32-36 [b]1 Sam 3:19
20 [a]1 Sam 10:4; Prov 18:16
21 [1]Lit *stood before him* [2]Lit *he* [a]Gen 41:46; Prov 22:29
23 [a]1 Sam 16:14-16
17:1 [a]1 Sam 13:5 [b]Josh 15:35; 2 Chr 28:18 [c]Josh 10:10 [d]1 Chr 11:13
2 [a]1 Sam 21:9
4 [1]I.e. One cubit equals approx 18 in. [a]2 Sam 21:19 [b]Josh 11:22
5 [1]Lit *and the weight of the armor* was
6 [1]Or *shin guards* [a]1 Sam 17:45
7 [a]2 Sam 21:19; 1 Chr 11:23 [b]1 Sam 17:41
8 [a]1 Sam 8:17
9 [1]Lit *smite* [a]2 Sam 2:12-16

10 Again the Philistine said, "[a]I defy the ranks of Israel this day; give me a man that we may fight together."

11 When Saul and all Israel heard these words of the Philistine, they were dismayed and greatly afraid.

12 ¶ Now David was [a]the son of [1]the [b]Ephrathite of Bethlehem in Judah, whose name was Jesse, and [c]he had eight sons. And [2]Jesse was old in the days of Saul, advanced *in years* among men.

13 The three older sons of Jesse had [1]gone after Saul to the battle. And [a]the names of his three sons who went to the battle were Eliab the firstborn, and the second to him Abinadab, and the third Shammah.

14 [a]David was the youngest. Now the three oldest followed Saul,

15 [a]but David went back and forth from Saul [b]to tend his father's flock at Bethlehem.

16 The Philistine came [1]forward morning and evening for forty days and took his stand.

17 ¶ Then Jesse said to David his son, "[a]Take now for your brothers an ephah of this roasted grain and these ten loaves and run to the camp to your brothers.

18 "[a]Bring also these ten cuts of cheese to the commander of *their* thousand, [b]and look into the welfare of your brothers, and bring back [1]news of them.

19 "For Saul and they and all the men of Israel are in the valley of Elah, fighting with the Philistines."

David Accepts the Challenge

20 ¶ So David arose early in the morning and left the flock with a keeper and took *the supplies* and went as Jesse had commanded him. And he came to the [a]circle of the camp while the army was going out in battle array shouting the war cry.

21 Israel and the Philistines drew up in battle array, army against army.

22 Then David left his [a]baggage in the [1]care of the baggage keeper, and ran to the battle line and entered in order to greet his brothers.

23 As he was talking with them, behold, the champion, the Philistine from Gath named Goliath, was coming up from the army of the Philistines, and he spoke [a]these same words; and David heard *them*.

24 ¶ When all the men of Israel saw the man, they fled from him and were greatly afraid.

25 The men of Israel said, "Have you seen this man who is coming up? Surely he is coming up to defy Israel. And it will be that the king will enrich the man who kills him with great riches and [a]will give him his daughter and make his father's house [1]free in Israel."

26 ¶ Then David spoke to the men who were standing by him, saying, "What will be done for the man who kills this Philistine and takes away [a]the reproach from Israel? For who is this [b]uncircumcised Philistine, that he should [c]taunt the armies of [d]the living God?"

27 The people [1]answered him in accord with this word, saying, "[a]Thus it will be done for the man who kills him."

28 ¶ Now Eliab his oldest brother heard when he spoke to the men; and [a]Eliab's anger burned against David and he said, "Why have you come down? And with whom have you left those few sheep in the wilderness? I know your insolence and the wickedness of your heart; for you have come down in order to see the battle."

29 But David said, "What have I done now? Was it not just a [1]question?"

30 Then he turned [1]away from him to another and [a]said the same thing; and the people answered the same thing as [2]before.

David Kills Goliath

31 ¶ When the words which David spoke were heard, they told *them* [1]to Saul, and he sent for him.

32 David said to Saul, "[a]Let no man's heart fail on account of him; [b]your servant will go and fight with this Philistine."

33 Then Saul said to David, "[a]You are not able to go against this Philistine to fight with him; for you are *but* a youth while he has been a warrior from his youth."

34 But David said to Saul, "Your servant was tending his father's sheep. When a lion or a bear came and took a lamb from the flock,

35 I went out after him and [1]attacked him, and [a]rescued *it* from his mouth; and when he rose up against me, I seized *him* by his beard and [1]struck him and killed him.

36 "Your servant has [1]killed both the lion and the bear; and this uncircumcised Philistine will be like one of them, since he has taunted the armies of the living God."

37 And David said, "[a]The LORD who delivered me from the paw of the lion and from the paw of the bear, He will deliver me from the hand of this Philistine." And Saul said to David, "[b]Go, and may the LORD be with you."

38 Then Saul clothed David with his

---

10 [a]1 Sam 17:26,36,45; 2 Sam 21:21

12 [1]Lit *this* [2]Lit *the man* [a]Ruth 4:22; 1 Sam 16:18 [b]Gen 35:19 [c]1 Sam 16:10,11; 1 Chr 2:13-15

13 [1]Lit *gone; they went* [a]1 Sam 16:6,8,9

14 [a]1 Sam 16:11

15 [a]1 Sam 16:21-23 [b]1 Sam 16:11,19

16 [1]Lit *near*

17 [a]1 Sam 25:18

18 [1]Lit *their pledge* [a]1 Sam 16:20 [b]Gen 37:13,14

20 [a]1 Sam 26:5, 7

22 [1]Lit *hand* [a]Judg 18:21; Is 10:28

23 [a]1 Sam 17:8-10

25 [1]I.e. free from taxes and public service [a]Josh 15:16

26 [a]1 Sam 11:2 [b]1 Sam 14:6; 17:36; Jer 9:25, 26 [c]1 Sam 17:10 [d]Deut 5:26; 2 Kin 19:4; Jer 10:10

27 [1]Lit *said to* [a]1 Sam 17:25

28 [a]Gen 37:4, 8-36; Prov 18:19; Matt 10:36

29 [1]Lit *word*

30 [1]Lit *from beside him* [2]Lit *the former word* [a]1 Sam 17:26,27

31 [1]Lit *before*

32 [a]Deut 20:1-4 [b]1 Sam 16:18

33 [a]Num 13:31

35 [1]Lit *smote* [a]Amos 3:12

36 [1]Lit *smitten*

37 [a]2 Cor 1:10; 2 Tim 4:17,18 [b]1 Sam 20:13; 1 Chr 22:11,16

garments and put a bronze helmet on his head, and he clothed him with armor.

39 David girded his sword over his armor and tried to walk, for he had not tested *them.* So David said to Saul, "I cannot go with these, for I have not tested *them.*" And David took them [1]off.

40 He took his stick in his hand and chose for himself five smooth stones from the brook, and put them in the shepherd's bag which he had, even in *his* pouch, and [a]his sling was in his hand; and he approached the Philistine.

41 ¶ Then the Philistine came on and approached David, with the shield-bearer in front of him.

42 When the Philistine looked and saw David, [a]he disdained him; for he was *but* a youth, and [b]ruddy, with a handsome appearance.

43 The Philistine said to David, "[a]Am I a dog, that you come to me with sticks?" And [b]the Philistine cursed David by his gods.

44 The Philistine also said to David, "Come to me, and I will give your flesh [a]to the birds of the sky and the beasts of the field."

45 Then David said to the Philistine, "You come to me with a sword, a spear, and a javelin, [a]but I come to you in the name of the LORD of hosts, the God of the armies of Israel, whom you have taunted.

46 "This day the LORD will deliver you up into my hands, and I will strike you down and remove your head from you. And I will give the [a]dead bodies of the army of the Philistines this day to the birds of the sky and the wild beasts of the earth, [b]that all the earth may know that there is a God in Israel,

47 and that all this assembly may know that [a]the LORD does not deliver by sword or by spear; [b]for the battle is the LORD'S and He will give you into our hands."

48 ¶ Then it happened when the Philistine rose and came and drew near to meet David, that [a]David ran quickly toward the battle line to meet the Philistine.

49 And David put his hand into his bag and took from it a stone and slung *it,* and struck the Philistine on his forehead. And the stone sank into his forehead, so that he fell on his face to the ground.

50 ¶ Thus David prevailed over the Philistine with a sling and a stone, and he struck the Philistine and killed him; but there was no sword in David's hand.

51 Then David ran and stood over the Philistine and [a]took his sword and drew it out of its sheath and killed him, and cut off his head with it. [b]When the Philistines saw that their champion was dead, they fled.

52 The men of Israel and Judah arose and shouted and pursued the Philistines [1]as far as the valley, and to the gates of [a]Ekron. And the slain Philistines [2]lay along the way to [b]Shaaraim, even to Gath and Ekron.

53 The sons of Israel returned from chasing the Philistines and plundered their camps.

54 Then David took the Philistine's head and brought it to Jerusalem, but he put his weapons in his tent.

55 ¶ Now when Saul saw David going out against the Philistine, he said to Abner the commander of the army, "Abner, whose son is [a]this young man?" And Abner said, "By your life, O king, I do not know."

56 The king said, "You inquire whose son the youth is."

57 So when David returned from killing the Philistine, Abner took him and [a]brought him before Saul with the Philistine's head in his hand.

58 Saul said to him, "Whose son are you, young man?" And David answered, "[a]*I am* the son of your servant Jesse the Bethlehemite."

Jonathan and David

18 Now it came about when he had finished speaking to Saul, that [a]the soul of Jonathan was knit to the soul of David, and [b]Jonathan loved him as himself.

2 Saul took him that day and [a]did not let him return to his father's house.

3 Then [a]Jonathan made a covenant with David because he loved him as himself.

4 [a]Jonathan stripped himself of the robe that was on him and gave it to David, with his armor, including his sword and his bow and his belt.

5 So David went out wherever Saul sent him, *and* [1]prospered; and Saul set him over the men of war. And it was pleasing in the sight of all the people and also in the sight of Saul's servants.

6 ¶ It happened as they were coming, when David returned from killing the Philistine, that [a]the women came out of all the cities of Israel, singing and dancing, to meet King Saul, with tambourines, with joy and with [1]musical instruments.

7 The women [a]sang as they [1]played, and said,

"[b]Saul has slain his thousands,
[c]And David his ten thousands."

8 Then Saul became very angry, for this saying [1]displeased him; and he said, "They have ascribed to David ten thou-

---

39 [1]Lit *off from himself*
40 [a]Judg 20:16
42 [a]Ps 123:4; Prov 16:18 [b]1 Sam 16:12
43 [a]1 Sam 24:14; 2 Sam 3:8; 2 Kin 8:13 [b]1 Kin 20:10
44 [a]1 Sam 17:46
45 [a]2 Sam 22:35; 2 Chr 32:8; Ps 124:8; Heb 11:32-34
46 [a]Deut 28:26 [b]Josh 4:24; 1 Kin 8:43; 18:36; 2 Kin 19:19; Is 37:20
47 [a]1 Sam 14:6; 2 Chr 14:11; 20:15; Ps 44:6; Hos 1:7; Zech 4:6 [b]2 Chr 20:15
48 [a]Ps 27:3
51 [a]1 Sam 21:9; 2 Sam 23:21 [b]Heb 11:34
52 [1]Lit *until your coming to* [2]Lit *fell* [a]Josh 15:11 [b]Josh 15:36
55 [a]1 Sam 16:12,21,22
57 [a]1 Sam 17:54
58 [a]1 Sam 17:12
18:1 [a]Gen 44:30 [b]Deut 13:6; 1 Sam 20:17; 2 Sam 1:26
2 [a]1 Sam 17:15
3 [a]1 Sam 20:8-17
4 [a]Gen 41:42; 1 Sam 17:38; Esth 6:8
5 [1]Or *acted wisely*
6 [1]I.e. triangles; or three-stringed instruments [a]Ex 15:20,21; Judg 11:34; Ps 68:25; 149:3
7 [1]Or *danced* [a]Ex 15:21; 1 Sam 21:11; 29:5 [b]1 Sam 21:11 [c]2 Sam 18:3
8 [1]Lit *was evil in his eyes*

sands, but to me they have ascribed thousands. Now [a]what more can he have but
the kingdom?"
9 Saul looked at David with suspicion
from that day on.

Saul Turns against David

10 ¶ Now it came about on the next
day that [a]an evil spirit from God came
mightily upon Saul, and [b]he raved in the
midst of the house, while David was playing *the harp* with his hand, [1c]as usual;
and [2d]a spear *was* in Saul's hand.
11 [a]Saul hurled the spear for he
thought, "I will [1]pin David to the wall."
But David [2]escaped from his presence
twice.
12 ¶ Now [a]Saul was afraid of David,
[b]for the LORD was with him but [c]had
departed from Saul.
13 Therefore Saul removed him from
[1]his presence and appointed him as his
commander of a thousand; and [a]he went
out and came in before the people.
14 David was [1]prospering in all his
ways for [a]the LORD *was* with him.
15 When Saul saw that he was [1]pros-
pering greatly, he dreaded him.
16 But [a]all Israel and Judah loved David, and he went out and came in before
them.
17 ¶ Then Saul said to David, "[a]Here
is my older daughter Merab; I will give
her to you as a wife, only be a valiant man
for me and fight [b]the LORD's battles." For
Saul thought, "My hand shall not be
against him, but [c]let the hand of the Philistines be against him."
18 But David said to Saul, "[a]Who am
I, and what is my life *or* my father's family
in Israel, that I should be the king's son-
in-law?"
19 So it came about at the time when
Merab, Saul's daughter, should have
been given to David, that she was given
to [a]Adriel [b]the Meholathite for a wife.

David Marries Saul's Daughter

20 ¶ Now [a]Michal, Saul's daughter,
loved David. When they told Saul, the
thing was agreeable [1]to him.
21 Saul thought, "I will give her to him
that she may become a snare to him, and
[a]that the hand of the Philistines may be
against him." Therefore Saul said to David, "[b]For a second time you may be my
son-in-law today."
22 Then Saul commanded his servants, "Speak to David secretly, saying,
'Behold, the king delights in you, and all
his servants love you; now therefore, become the king's son-in-law.' "
23 So Saul's servants spoke these
words [1]to David. But David said, "Is it
trivial in your sight to become the king's
son-in-law, [a]since I am a poor man and
lightly esteemed?"
24 The servants of Saul reported to
him [1]according to these words *which*
David spoke.
25 Saul then said, "Thus you shall
say to David, 'The king does not desire
any [a]dowry except a hundred foreskins
of the Philistines, [b]to take vengeance
on the king's enemies.' " Now [c]Saul
planned to make David fall by the hand
of the Philistines.
26 When his servants told David these
words, [1]it pleased David to become the
king's son-in-law. [2a]Before the days had
expired
27 David rose up and went, [a]he and
his men, and struck down two hundred
men among the Philistines. Then [b]David
brought their foreskins, and they gave
them in full number to the king, that he
might become the king's son-in-law. So
Saul gave him Michal his daughter for a
wife.
28 When Saul saw and knew that the
LORD was with David, and *that* Michal,
Saul's daughter, loved him,
29 then Saul was even more afraid of
David. Thus Saul was David's enemy continually.
30 ¶ Then the commanders of the Philistines [a]went out *to battle,* and it happened as often as they went out, that David [b]behaved himself more wisely than
all the servants of Saul. So his name was
highly esteemed.

David Protected from Saul

19 Now Saul told Jonathan his son
and all his servants [a]to put David
to death. But [b]Jonathan, Saul's son,
greatly delighted in David.
2 So Jonathan told David saying,
"Saul my father is seeking to put you to
death. Now therefore, please be on guard
in the morning, and stay in a secret place
and hide yourself.
3 "I will go out and stand beside my
father in the field where you are, and I
will speak with my father about you; [a]if
I [1]find out anything, then I will tell you."
4 Then Jonathan [a]spoke well of David to Saul his father and said to him,
"[b]Do not let the king sin against his
servant David, since he has not sinned
against you, and since his deeds *have*
been very [1]beneficial to you.
5 "For [a]he took his life in his hand
and struck the Philistine, and [b]the LORD
brought about a great deliverance for all
Israel; you saw *it* and rejoiced. [c]Why
then will you sin against innocent blood

8 [a]1 Sam 15:28

10 [1]Lit *day by day* [2]Lit *the* [a]1 Sam 16:14 [b]1 Sam 19:23,24 [c]1 Sam 16:23 [d]1 Sam 19:9

11 [1]Lit *strike David and the wall* [2]Lit *turned about* [a]1 Sam 19:10; 20:33

12 [a]1 Sam 18:15,29 [b]1 Sam 16:13,18 [c]1 Sam 16:14; 28:15

13 [1]Lit *with him* [a]Num 27:17; 1 Sam 18:16; 2 Sam 5:2

14 [1]Or *acting wisely* [a]Gen 39:2,3,23; Josh 6:27; 1 Sam 16:18

15 [1]Or *acting very wisely*

16 [a]1 Sam 18:5

17 [a]1 Sam 17:25 [b]Num 21:14; 1 Sam 17:36,47; 25:28 [c]1 Sam 18:21,25

18 [a]1 Sam 9:21; 18:23; 2 Sam 7:18

19 [a]2 Sam 21:8 [b]Judg 7:22; 1 Kin 19:16

20 [1]Lit *in his sight* [a]1 Sam 18:28

21 [a]1 Sam 18:17 [b]1 Sam 18:26

23 [1]Lit *in the ears of* [a]Gen 29:20; 34:12

24 [1]Lit *by saying according*

25 [a]Gen 34:12; Ex 22:17 [b]1 Sam 14:24 [c]1 Sam 18:17

26 [1]Lit *it was agreeable in the sight of* [2]Lit *And the days had not expired* [a]1 Sam 18:21

27 [a]1 Sam 18:17 [b]2 Sam 3:14

30 [a]2 Sam 11:1 [b]1 Sam 18:5

19:1 [a]1 Sam 18:8,9 [b]1 Sam 18:1-3

3 [1]Lit *see* [a]1 Sam 20:9,13

4 [1]Lit *good* [a]1 Sam 20:32; Prov 31:8,9 [b]Gen 42:22; Prov 17:13; Jer 18:20

5 [a]Judg 9:17; 1 Sam 17:49,50; 28:21; Ps 119:109 [b]1 Sam 11:13; 1 Chr 11:14 [c]Deut 19:10-13; 1 Sam 20:32; Ps 94:21; Matt 27:4

by putting David to death without a
cause?"
6 Saul listened to the voice of Jonathan, and Saul vowed, "As the LORD lives,
he shall not be put to death."
7 Then Jonathan called David, and
Jonathan told him all these words. And
Jonathan brought David to Saul, and he
was in his presence as [a]formerly.
8 ¶ When there was war again, David
went out and fought with the Philistines
and [1]defeated them with great slaughter,
so that they fled before him.
9 Now there was [a]an evil spirit from
the LORD on Saul as he was sitting in his
house [b]with his spear in his hand, [c]and
David was playing *the harp* with *his*
hand.
10 [a]Saul tried to [1]pin David to the
wall with the spear, but he slipped away
out of Saul's presence, so that he [2]stuck
the spear into the wall. And David fled
and escaped that night.
11 ¶ Then [a]Saul sent messengers to
David's house to watch him, in order to
put him to death in the morning. But Michal, David's wife, told him, saying, "If
you do not save your life tonight, tomorrow you will be put to death."
12 [a]So Michal let David down
through a window, and he went out and
fled and escaped.
13 Michal took [a]the [1]household idol
and laid *it* on the bed, and put a quilt of
goats' *hair* at its head, and covered *it* with
clothes.
14 When Saul sent messengers to take
David, she said, "[a]He is sick."
15 Then Saul sent messengers to see
David, saying, "Bring him up to me on
[1]his bed, that I may put him to death."
16 When the messengers entered, behold, the [1]household idol *was* on the bed
with the quilt of goats' *hair* at its head.
17 So Saul said to Michal, "Why have
you deceived me like this and let my enemy go, so that he has escaped?" And Michal said to Saul, "He said to me, 'Let me
go! [a]Why should I put you to death?' "
18 ¶ Now David fled and escaped and
came [a]to Samuel at Ramah, and told him
all that Saul had done to him. And he and
Samuel went and stayed in [b]Naioth.
19 It was told Saul, saying, "Behold,
David is at Naioth in Ramah."
20 Then [a]Saul sent messengers to
take David, but when they saw [b]the company of the prophets prophesying, with
Samuel standing *and* presiding over
them, the Spirit of God came upon the
messengers of Saul; and [c]they also
prophesied.
21 When it was told Saul, he sent other messengers, and they also prophesied.
So Saul sent messengers again the third
time, and they also prophesied.
22 Then he himself went to Ramah
and came as far as the large well that is in
Secu; and he asked and said, "Where are
Samuel and David?" And *someone* said,
"Behold, they are at Naioth in Ramah."
23 He [1]proceeded there to Naioth in
Ramah; and [a]the Spirit of God came
upon him also, so that he went along
prophesying continually until he came to
Naioth in Ramah.
24 He also stripped off his clothes, and
he too prophesied before Samuel and
[1]lay down [2a]naked all that day and all
that night. Therefore they say, "[b]Is Saul
also among the prophets?"

David and Jonathan Covenant

20 Then David fled from Naioth in
Ramah, and came and [a]said [1]to
Jonathan, "What have I done? What is my
iniquity? And what is my sin before your
father, that he is seeking my life?"
2 He said to him, "Far from it, you
shall not die. Behold, my father does
nothing either great or small [1]without
disclosing it to me. So why should my
father hide this thing from me? It is
not so!"
3 Yet David [a]vowed again, [1]saying,
"Your father knows well that I have found
favor in your sight, and he has said, 'Do
not let Jonathan know this, or he will be
grieved.' But truly [b]as the LORD lives and
as your soul lives, there is [2]hardly a step
between me and death."
4 Then Jonathan said to David,
"Whatever [1]you say, I will do for you."
5 So David said to Jonathan, "Behold,
tomorrow is [a]the new moon, and I ought
[b]to sit down to eat with the king. But let
me go, [c]that I may hide myself in the
field until the third evening.
6 "If your father misses me at all, then
say, 'David earnestly asked *leave* of me to
run to [a]Bethlehem his city, because it is
[b]the yearly sacrifice there for the whole
family.'
7 "If he [1]says, 'It is good,' your servant *will be* safe; but if he is very angry,
[a]know that he has decided on evil.
8 "Therefore deal kindly with your
servant, for [a]you have brought your servant into a covenant of the LORD with
you. But [b]if there is iniquity in me, put
me to death yourself; for why then should
you bring me to your father?"
9 Jonathan said, "Far be it from you!
For if I should indeed learn that evil has
been decided by my father to come upon
you, then would I not tell you about it?"
10 Then David said to Jonathan, "Who

7 [a]1 Sam 16:21; 18:2,10,13

8 [1]Lit *smote*

9 [a]1 Sam 16:14; 18:10,11 [b]1 Sam 18:10 [c]1 Sam 16:16

10 [1]Lit *strike David and the wall* [2]Lit *struck* [a]1 Sam 18:11; 20:33; Prov 1:16

11 [a]Judg 16:2; Ps 59: title

12 [a]Josh 2:15; Acts 9:25; 2 Cor 11:33

13 [1]Heb *teraphim* [a]Gen 31:19; Judg 18:14,17

14 [a]Josh 2:5

15 [1]Lit *the*

16 [1]Heb *teraphim*

17 [a]2 Sam 2:22

18 [a]1 Sam 7:17 [b]1 Sam 19:22,23

20 [a]1 Sam 19:11,14; John 7:32 [b]1 Sam 10:5,6,10 [c]Num 11:25; Joel 2:28

23 [1]Lit *went* [a]1 Sam 10:10

24 [1]Lit *fell* [2]I.e. without outward garments [a]2 Sam 6:20; Is 20:2; Mic 1:8 [b]1 Sam 10:10-12

20:1 [1]Lit *before* [a]1 Sam 24:9

2 [1]Lit *and he does not uncover my ear*

3 [1]Lit *and said* [2]Lit *about* [a]Deut 6:13 [b]1 Sam 25:26; 2 Kin 2:6

4 [1]Lit *your soul says*

5 [a]Num 10:10; 28:11-15; Amos 8:5 [b]1 Sam 20:24,27 [c]1 Sam 19:2

6 [a]1 Sam 17:58 [b]Deut 12:5; 1 Sam 9:12

7 [1]Lit *says thus* [a]1 Sam 25:17

8 [a]1 Sam 18:3; 23:18 [b]2 Sam 14:32

will tell me [1]if your father answers you harshly?"

11 Jonathan said to David, "Come, and let us go out into the field." So both of them went out to the field.

12 ¶ Then Jonathan said to David, "The LORD, the God of Israel, *be witness!* When I have sounded out my father about this time tomorrow, *or* the third day, behold, if there is good *feeling* toward David, shall I not then send to you and [1]make it known to you?

13 "If it please my father *to do* you harm, [a]may the LORD do so to Jonathan and more also, if I do not [1]make it known to you and send you away, that you may go in safety. And [b]may the LORD be with you as He has been with my father.

14 "If I am still alive, will you not show me the lovingkindness of the LORD, that I may not die?

15 "[a]You shall not cut off your lovingkindness from my house forever, not even when the LORD cuts off every one of the enemies of David from the face of the earth."

16 So Jonathan made a *covenant* with the house of David, *saying,* "[a]May the LORD require *it* at the hands of David's enemies."

17 Jonathan made David vow again because of his love for him, because [a]he loved him as he loved his own life.

18 ¶ Then Jonathan said to him, "[a]Tomorrow is the new moon, and you will be missed because your seat will be empty.

19 "When you have stayed for three days, you shall go down quickly and come to the place where you hid yourself on that eventful day, and you shall remain by the stone Ezel.

20 "I will shoot three arrows to the side, as though I shot at a target.

21 "And behold, I will send the lad, *saying,* 'Go, find the arrows.' If I specifically say to the lad, 'Behold, the arrows are on this side of you, get them,' then come; for there is safety for you and [1]no harm, as the LORD lives.

22 "But if I [1]say to the youth, '[a]Behold, the arrows are beyond you,' go, for the LORD has sent you away.

23 "[a]As for the [1]agreement of which you and I have spoken, behold, [b]the LORD is between you and me forever."

24 ¶ So David hid in the field; and when the new moon came, the king sat down to eat food.

25 The king sat on his seat as usual, the seat by the wall; then Jonathan rose up and Abner sat down by Saul's side, but [a]David's place was empty.

26 Nevertheless Saul did not speak anything that day, for he thought, "It is an accident, [a]he is not clean, surely *he is* not clean."

27 It came about the next day, the second *day* of the new moon, that David's place was empty; so Saul said to Jonathan his son, "Why has the son of Jesse not come to the meal, either yesterday or today?"

28 Jonathan then answered Saul, "[a]David earnestly asked leave of me *to go* to Bethlehem,

29 for he said, 'Please [1]let me go, since our family has a sacrifice in the city, and my brother has commanded me to attend. And now, if I have found favor in your sight, please let me get away that I may see my brothers.' For this reason he has not come to the king's table."

Saul Is Angry with Jonathan

30 ¶ Then Saul's anger burned against Jonathan and he said to him, "You son of a perverse, rebellious woman! Do I not know that you are choosing the son of Jesse to your own shame and to the shame of your mother's nakedness?

31 "For [1]as long as the son of Jesse lives on the earth, neither you nor your kingdom will be established. Therefore now, send and bring him to me, for [a]he [2]must surely die."

32 But Jonathan answered Saul his father and said to him, "[a]Why should he be put to death? What has he done?"

33 Then [a]Saul hurled his spear at him to strike him down; [b]so Jonathan knew that his father had decided to put David to death.

34 Then Jonathan arose from the table in fierce anger, and did not eat food on the second day of the new moon, for he was grieved over David because his father had dishonored him.

35 ¶ Now it came about in the morning that Jonathan went out into the field for the appointment with David, and a little lad *was* with him.

36 He said to his lad, "[a]Run, find now the arrows which I am about to shoot." As the lad was running, he shot [1]an arrow past him.

37 When the lad reached the place of the arrow which Jonathan had shot, Jonathan called after the lad and said, "[a]Is not the arrow beyond you?"

38 And Jonathan called after the lad, "Hurry, be quick, do not stay!" And Jonathan's lad picked up the arrow and came to his master.

39 But the lad was not aware of anything; only Jonathan and David knew about the matter.

40 Then Jonathan gave his weapons to

10 [1]Lit *or what*
12 [1]Lit *uncover your ear*
13 [1]Lit *uncover your ear* [a]Ruth 1:17; 1 Sam 3:17 [b]Josh 1:5; 1 Sam 17:37; 18:12; 1 Chr 22:11,16
15 [a]2 Sam 9:1,3
16 [a]Deut 23:21; 1 Sam 25:22
17 [a]1 Sam 18:1
18 [a]1 Sam 20:5, 25
21 [1]Lit *there is nothing*
22 [1]Lit *say thus* [a]1 Sam 20:37
23 [1]Lit *word* [a]1 Sam 20:14,15 [b]Gen 31:49,53; 1 Sam 20:42
25 [a]1 Sam 20:18
26 [a]Lev 7:20, 21; 15:5; 1 Sam 16:5
28 [a]1 Sam 20:6
29 [1]Lit *send me away*
31 [1]Lit *all the days which* [2]Lit *is a son of death* [a]2 Sam 12:5
32 [a]Gen 31:36; 1 Sam 19:5; Prov 31:9; Matt 27:23
33 [a]1 Sam 18:11; 19:10 [b]1 Sam 20:7
36 [1]Lit *the* [a]1 Sam 20:20,21
37 [a]1 Sam 20:22

his lad and said to him, "Go, bring *them*
to the city."
41 When the lad was gone, David rose
from the south side and fell on his face to
the ground, and [a]bowed three times.
And they kissed each other and wept together, but [b]David *wept* the more.
42 Jonathan said to David, "[a]Go in
safety, inasmuch as we have sworn to
each other in the name of the LORD, saying, '[b]The LORD will be between me and
you, and between my [1]descendants and
your [1]descendants forever.'" [2]Then he
rose and departed, while Jonathan went
into the city.

David Takes Consecrated Bread

21 Then David came to [a]Nob to
Ahimelech the priest; and Ahimelech [b]came trembling to meet David and
said to him, "Why are you alone and no
one with you?"
2 David said to Ahimelech the priest,
"The king has commissioned me with a
matter and has said to me, '[a]Let no one
know anything about the matter on
which I am sending you and with which
I have commissioned you; and I have directed the young men to a certain place.'
3 "Now therefore, what [1]do you have
on hand? Give [2]me five loaves of bread,
or whatever can be found."
4 The priest answered David and
said, "There is no ordinary bread [1]on
hand, but there is [a]consecrated bread; if
only the young men have [b]kept themselves from women."
5 David answered the priest and said
to him, "[a]Surely women have been kept
from us as previously when I set out and
the [b]vessels of the young men were holy,
though it was an ordinary journey; how
much more then today will [1]their vessels
be holy?"
6 So [a]the priest gave him consecrated *bread;* for there was no bread there
but the [b]bread of the Presence which
was removed from before the LORD, in
order to put hot bread *in its place* when
it was taken away.
7 ¶ Now one of the servants of Saul
was there that day, detained before the
LORD; and his name was [a]Doeg the
Edomite, the [b]chief of Saul's shepherds.
8 ¶ David said to Ahimelech, "Now is
there not a spear or a sword [1]on hand?
For I brought neither my sword nor my
weapons [2]with me, because the king's
matter was urgent."
9 Then the priest said, "[a]The sword
of Goliath the Philistine, whom you
[1]killed [b]in the valley of Elah, behold, it
is wrapped in a cloth behind the ephod;
if you would take it for yourself, take *it.*
For there is no other except it here." And
David said, "There is none like it; give it
to me."
10 ¶ Then David arose and fled that
day from Saul, and went to [a]Achish king
of Gath.
11 But the [a]servants of Achish said to
him, "Is this not David the king of the
land? [b]Did they not sing of this one as
they danced, saying,
'Saul has slain his thousands,
And David his ten thousands'?"
12 David [a]took these words [1]to heart
and greatly feared Achish king of Gath.
13 So he [a]disguised his sanity before
them, and acted insanely in their hands,
and scribbled on the doors of the gate,
and let his saliva run down into his beard.
14 Then Achish said to his servants,
"Behold, you see the man behaving as a
madman. Why do you bring him to me?
15 "Do I lack madmen, that you have
brought this one to act the madman in my
presence? Shall this one come into my
house?"

The Priests Slain at Nob

22 So David departed from there and
[a]escaped to [b]the cave of Adullam; and when his brothers and all his
father's household heard *of it,* they went
down there to him.
2 Everyone who was in distress, and
everyone who [1]was in debt, and everyone who was [2]discontented gathered to
him; and he became captain over them.
Now there were [a]about four hundred
men with him.
3 ¶ And David went from there to
Mizpah of Moab; and he said to the king
of Moab, "Please let my father and my
mother come *and stay* with you until I
know what God will do for me."
4 Then he left them with the king of
Moab; and they stayed with him all the
time that David was in the stronghold.
5 [a]The prophet Gad said to David,
"Do not stay in the stronghold; depart,
and go into the land of Judah." So David
departed and went into the forest of He-
reth.
6 ¶ Then Saul heard that David and
the men who were with him had been
discovered. Now [a]Saul was sitting in
Gibeah, under the tamarisk tree on the
height with his spear in his hand, and all
his servants were standing around him.
7 Saul said to his servants who stood
around him, "Hear now, O Benjamites!
Will the son of Jesse also give to all of you
fields and vineyards? [a]Will he make you
all commanders of thousands and commanders of hundreds?
8 "For all of you have conspired

---

41 [a]Gen 42:6 [b]1 Sam 18:3
42 [1]Lit *seed* [2]Ch 21:1 in Heb [a]1 Sam 20:22 [b]1 Sam 20:15, 16,23
21:1 [a]1 Sam 22:19; Neh 11:32; Is 10:32 [b]1 Sam 16:4
2 [a]Ps 141:3
3 [1]Lit *is under your hand?* [2]Lit *in my hand*
4 [1]Lit *under my hand* [a]Ex 25:30; Lev 24:5-9; Matt 12:4 [b]Ex 19:15
5 [1]Lit *it* be holy *in the vessel* [a]Ex 19:14,15 [b]1 Thess 4:4
6 [a]Matt 12:3,4; Luke 6:3,4 [b]Lev 24:5-9
7 [a]1 Sam 14:47; 22:9; Ps 52: title [b]1 Chr 27:29,31
8 [1]Lit *under your hand* [2]Lit *in my hand*
9 [1]Lit *smote* [a]1 Sam 17:51,54 [b]1 Sam 17:2
10 [a]Ps 34: title
11 [a]Ps 56: title [b]1 Sam 18:7; 29:5
12 [1]Lit *in his* [a]Luke 2:19
13 [a]Ps 34: title
22:1 [a]Ps 57: title [b]Josh 12:15; 15:35; 2 Sam 23:13; Ps 142: title
2 [1]Lit *had a creditor* [2]Lit *bitter of soul* [a]1 Sam 23:13; 25:13
5 [a]2 Sam 24:11; 1 Chr 21:9; 29:29; 2 Chr 29:25
6 [a]Judg 4:5; 1 Sam 14:2
7 [a]1 Sam 8:12; 1 Chr 12:16-18

against me so that there is no one who
[1]discloses to me [a]when my son makes *a*
covenant with the son of Jesse, and there
is none of you [b]who is sorry for me or
[1]discloses to me that my son has stirred
up my servant against me to lie in ambush, as *it is* this day."
9 Then [a]Doeg the Edomite, who was
[1]standing by the servants of Saul, said,
"[b]I saw the son of Jesse coming to Nob,
to [c]Ahimelech the son of Ahitub.
10 "[a]He inquired of the LORD for him,
[b]gave him provisions, and [c]gave him the
sword of Goliath the Philistine."
11 ¶ Then the king sent someone to
summon Ahimelech the priest, the son of
Ahitub, and all his father's household,
the priests who were in Nob; and all of
them came to the king.
12 Saul said, "Listen now, son of Ahitub." And he [1]answered, "Here I am, my
lord."
13 Saul then said to him, "Why have
you and the son of Jesse conspired against
me, in that you have given him bread and
a sword and have inquired of God for
him, so that he would rise up against me
[a]by lying in ambush as *it is* this day?"
14 ¶ [a]Then Ahimelech answered the
king and said, "And who among all your
servants is as faithful as David, even the
king's son-in-law, who [1]is captain over
your guard, and is honored in your
house?
15 "Did I *just* begin [a]to inquire of God
for him today? Far be it from me! [b]Do not
let the king impute anything to his servant *or* to any of the household of my
father, for your servant knows nothing
[1]at all of this whole affair."
16 But the king said, "You shall surely
die, Ahimelech, you and all your father's
household!"
17 And [a]the king said to the [1]guards
who were attending him, "Turn around
and put the priests of the LORD to death,
because their hand also is with David and
because they knew that he was fleeing
and did not [2]reveal it to me." But the
[b]servants of the king were not willing
to put forth their hands to [3]attack the
priests of the LORD.
18 Then the king said to Doeg, "You
turn around and [1]attack the priests."
And Doeg the Edomite turned around
and [2]attacked the priests, and [a]he killed
that day eighty-five men [b]who wore the
linen ephod.
19 And [a]he struck Nob the city of the
priests with the edge of the sword, both
men and women, children and infants;
also oxen, donkeys, and sheep *he struck*
with the edge of the sword.
20 ¶ But [a]one son of Ahimelech the
son of Ahitub, named Abiathar, [b]escaped
and fled after David.
21 Abiathar told David that Saul had
killed the priests of the LORD.
22 Then David said to Abiathar, "I
knew on that day, when [a]Doeg the
Edomite was there, that he would surely
tell Saul. I have brought about *the death*
of every person in your father's household.
23 "Stay with me; do not be afraid, for
[a]he who seeks my life seeks your life, for
you are [1]safe with me."

David Delivers Keilah

23 Then they told David, saying,
"Behold, the Philistines are fighting against [a]Keilah and are plundering
the threshing floors."
2 So David [a]inquired of the LORD,
saying, "Shall I go and [1]attack these Philistines?" And the LORD said to David,
"Go and [1]attack the Philistines and deliver Keilah."
3 But David's men said to him, "Behold, we are afraid here in Judah. How
much more then if we go to Keilah
against the ranks of the Philistines?"
4 Then David inquired of the LORD
once more. And the LORD answered him
and said, "Arise, go down to Keilah, for
[a]I will give the Philistines into your
hand."
5 So David and his men went to Keilah and fought with the Philistines; and
he led away their livestock and struck
them with a great slaughter. Thus David
delivered the inhabitants of Keilah.
6 ¶ Now it came about, when Abiathar the son of Ahimelech [a]fled to David
at Keilah, *that* he came down *with* an
ephod in his hand.
7 When it was told Saul that David
had come to Keilah, Saul said, "God has
[1]delivered him into my hand, for he shut
himself in by entering a city with double
gates and bars."
8 So Saul summoned all the people
for war, to go down to Keilah to besiege
David and his men.
9 Now David knew that Saul was
plotting evil against him; so he said to
[a]Abiathar the priest, "[b]Bring the ephod
here."
10 Then David said, "O LORD God of
Israel, Your servant has heard for certain
that Saul is seeking to come to Keilah to
destroy the city on my account.
11 "Will the men of Keilah surrender
me into his hand? Will Saul come down
just as Your servant has heard? O LORD
God of Israel, I pray, tell Your servant."
And the LORD said, "He will come down."
12 Then David said, "Will the men of

8 [1]Lit *uncovers my ear* [a]1 Sam 18:3; 20:16 [b]1 Sam 23:21
9 [1]Or *set over* [a]Ps 52: title [b]1 Sam 21:1 [c]1 Sam 14:3; 21:1
10 [a]Num 27:21; 1 Sam 10:22 [b]1 Sam 21:6 [c]1 Sam 21:9
12 [1]Lit *said*
13 [a]1 Sam 22:8
14 [1]So with Gr; Heb *turns aside to* [a]1 Sam 19:4, 5; 20:32
15 [1]Lit *small or great* [a]2 Sam 5:19,23 [b]2 Sam 19:18,19
17 [1]Lit *runners* [2]Lit *uncover my ear* [3]Lit *fall upon* [a]2 Kin 10:25 [b]Ex 1:17
18 [1]Lit *smite* [2]Lit *smote* [a]1 Sam 2:31 [b]1 Sam 2:18
19 [a]1 Sam 15:3
20 [a]1 Sam 23:6, 9; 30:7; 1 Kin 2:26,27 [b]1 Sam 23:6
22 [a]1 Sam 21:7
23 [1]Lit *a charge* [a]1 Kin 2:26
23:1 [a]Josh 15:44; Neh 3:17, 18
2 [1]Lit *smite* [a]1 Sam 23:4,6, 9-12; 2 Sam 5:19,23
4 [a]Josh 8:7; Judg 7:7
6 [a]1 Sam 22:20
7 [1]Lit *alienated*
9 [a]1 Sam 22:20 [b]1 Sam 23:6; 30:7

Keilah surrender me and my men into
the hand of Saul?" And the LORD said,
"[a]They will surrender you."
13 Then David and his men, [a]about
six hundred, arose and departed from Keilah, and they went [b]wherever they
could go. When it was told Saul that David had escaped from Keilah, he [1]gave up
the pursuit.
14 David stayed in the wilderness in
the strongholds, and remained in the hill
country in the wilderness of [a]Ziph. And
Saul sought him every day, but [b]God did
not deliver him into his hand.

Saul Pursues David

15 ¶ Now David [1]became aware that
Saul had come out to seek his life while
David was in the wilderness of Ziph at
Horesh.
16 And Jonathan, Saul's son, arose and
went to David at Horesh, and [1a]encour-
aged him in God.
17 Thus he said to him, "[a]Do not be
afraid, because the hand of Saul my father
will not find you, and you will be king
over Israel and I will be next to you; and
[b]Saul my father knows that also."
18 So [a]the two of them made a covenant before the LORD; and David stayed
at Horesh while Jonathan went to his
house.
19 ¶ Then [a]Ziphites came up to Saul
at Gibeah, saying, "Is David not hiding
with us in the strongholds at Horesh, on
[b]the hill of Hachilah, which is on the
[1]south of [2]Jeshimon?
20 "Now then, O king, come down according to all the desire of your soul to
[1]do so; and [a]our part *shall be* to surrender him into the king's hand."
21 Saul said, "May you be blessed of
the LORD, [a]for you have had compassion
on me.
22 "Go now, make more sure, and investigate and see his place where his
[1]haunt is, *and* who has seen him there;
for I am told that he is very cunning.
23 "So look, and learn about all the hiding places where he hides himself and
return to me with certainty, and I will go
with you; and if he is in the land, I will
search him out among all the thousands
of Judah."
24 ¶ Then they arose and went to Ziph
before Saul. Now David and his men
were in the wilderness of [a]Maon, in the
Arabah to the [1]south of [2]Jeshimon.
25 When Saul and his men went to
seek *him,* they told David, and he came
down to the rock and stayed in the wilderness of Maon. And when Saul heard
it, he pursued David in the wilderness of
Maon.
26 Saul went on one side of the mountain, and David and his men on the other
side of the mountain; and David was hur-
rying to get away from Saul, for Saul and
his men [a]were surrounding David and
his men to seize them.
27 But a messenger came to Saul, saying, "Hurry and come, for the Philistines
have made a raid on the land."
28 So Saul returned from pursuing David and went to meet the Philistines;
therefore they called that place [1]the
Rock of Escape.
29 [1]David went up from there and
stayed in the strongholds of [a]Engedi.

David Spares Saul's Life

24 Now [a]when Saul returned from
pursuing the Philistines, [b]he was
told, saying, "Behold, David is in the wilderness of Engedi."
2 Then [a]Saul took three thousand
chosen men from all Israel and went to
seek David and his men in front of the
Rocks of the Wild Goats.
3 He came to the sheepfolds on the
way, where there *was* a cave; and Saul
[a]went in to [1]relieve himself. Now [b]Da-
vid and his men were sitting in the inner
recesses of the cave.
4 The men of David said to him, "Behold, [a]*this is* the day of which the LORD
said to you, 'Behold; [b]I am about to give
your enemy into your hand, and you shall
do to him as it seems good [1]to you.'"
Then David arose and cut off the edge of
Saul's robe secretly.
5 It came about afterward that [a]Da-
vid's [1]conscience bothered him because
he had cut off the edge of Saul's *robe.*
6 So he said to his men, "[a]Far be
it from me because of the LORD that I
should do this thing to my lord, the
LORD's anointed, to stretch out my hand
against him, since he is the LORD's
anointed."
7 David [1]persuaded his men with
these words and did not allow them to
rise up against Saul. And Saul arose, [2]left
the cave, and went on *his* way.
8 ¶ Now afterward David arose and
went out of the cave and called after Saul,
saying, "My lord the king!" And when
Saul looked behind him, [a]David bowed
with his face to the ground and prostrated
himself.
9 David said to Saul, "Why do you
listen to the words of men, saying, 'Behold, David seeks [1]to harm you'?
10 "[a]Behold, this day your eyes have
seen that the LORD had given you today
into my hand in the cave, and [b]some said
to kill you, but *my eye* had pity on you;
and I said, 'I will not stretch out my hand

12 [a]Judg 15:10-13; 1 Sam 23:20
13 [1]Lit *ceased going out* [a]1 Sam 22:2; 25:13 [b]2 Sam 15:20
14 [a]Josh 15:55; 2 Chr 11:8 [b]Ps 32:7
15 [1]Lit *saw*
16 [1]Lit *strengthened his hand* [a]1 Sam 30:6; Neh 2:18
17 [a]Ps 27:1,3; 118:6; Is 54:17; Heb 13:6 [b]1 Sam 20:31; 24:20
18 [a]1 Sam 18:3; 20:12-17,42; 2 Sam 9:1; 21:7
19 [1]Lit *right side* [2]Or *the desert* [a]1 Sam 26:1; Ps 54: title [b]1 Sam 26:3
20 [1]Lit *come down* [a]1 Sam 23:12
21 [a]1 Sam 22:8
22 [1]Lit *foot*
24 [1]Lit *right side* [2]Or *the desert* [a]Josh 15:55; 1 Sam 25:2
26 [a]Ps 17:9
28 [1]Heb *Sela-hammahlekoth*
29 [1]Ch 24:1 in Heb [a]Josh 15:62; 2 Chr 20:2
24:1 [a]1 Sam 23:28,29 [b]1 Sam 23:19
2 [a]1 Sam 26:2
3 [1]Lit *cover his feet* [a]Judg 3:24 [b]Ps 57: title; 142: title
4 [1]Lit *in your sight* [a]1 Sam 23:17; 25:28-30 [b]1 Sam 26:8,11
5 [1]Lit *heart struck* [a]2 Sam 24:10
6 [a]1 Sam 26:11
7 [1]Lit *tore apart* [2]Lit *from*
8 [a]1 Sam 25:23, 24; 1 Kin 1:31
9 [1]Lit *your hurt*
10 [a]Ps 7:3,4 [b]1 Sam 24:4

against my lord, for he is the LORD'S
anointed.'
11 "Now, [a]my father, see! Indeed, see
the edge of your robe in my hand! For in
that I cut off the edge of your robe and did
not kill you, know and perceive that there
is no evil or [1]rebellion in my hands, and
I have not sinned against you, though you
[b]are lying in wait for my life to take it.
12 "[a]May the LORD judge between
[1]you and me, and may the LORD avenge
me on you; but my hand shall not be
against you.
13 "As the proverb of the ancients says,
'[a]Out of the wicked comes forth wickedness'; but my hand shall not be against
you.
14 "After whom has the king of Israel
come out? Whom are you pursuing? [a]A
dead dog, [b]a single flea?
15 "[a]The LORD therefore be judge and
decide between [1]you and me; and may
He see and [b]plead my cause and [2]deliver
me from your hand."
16 ¶ When David had finished speaking these words to Saul, Saul said, "[a]Is
this your voice, my son David?" Then
Saul lifted up his voice and wept.
17 [a]He said to David, "You are more
righteous than I; for [b]you have dealt well
with me, while I have dealt wickedly
with you.
18 "You have declared today that you
have done good to me, that [a]the LORD
delivered me into your hand and *yet* you
did not kill me.
19 "For if a man [a]finds his enemy, will
he let him go away [1]safely? May the
LORD therefore reward you with good in
return for what you have done to me this
day.
20 "Now, behold, [a]I know that you will
surely be king, and that [b]the kingdom of
Israel will be established in your hand.
21 "So now [a]swear to me by the LORD
that you will not cut off my [1]descendants
after me and that you will not destroy my
name from my father's household."
22 David swore to Saul. And Saul went
to his home, but David and his men went
up to [a]the stronghold.

Samuel's Death

25 [a]Then Samuel died; and all Israel
gathered together and [b]mourned
for him, and [c]buried him at his house in
Ramah. And David arose and went down
to the [d]wilderness of Paran.

Nabal and Abigail

2 ¶ Now *there was* a man in [a]Maon
whose business was in [b]Carmel; and the
man was very [1]rich, and he had three
thousand sheep and a thousand goats.
And it came about while [c]he was shearing his sheep in Carmel
3 (now the man's name was Nabal,
and his [a]wife's name was Abigail. And
the woman was [1]intelligent and beautiful in appearance, but the man was harsh
and evil in *his* dealings, and he was [b]a
Calebite),
4 that David heard in the wilderness
that Nabal was shearing his sheep.
5 So David sent ten young men; and
David said to the young men, "Go up to
Carmel, [1]visit Nabal and greet him in my
name;
6 and thus you shall say, '[1]Have a
long life, [a]peace be to you, and peace be
to your house, and peace be to all that you
have.
7 'Now I have heard [a]that you have
shearers; now your shepherds have been
with us and we have not insulted them,
[b]nor have they missed anything all the
days they were in Carmel.
8 'Ask your young men and they will
tell you. Therefore let *my* young men find
favor in your eyes, for we have come on
[a]a [1]festive day. Please give whatever
you find at hand to your servants and to
your son David.' "
9 ¶ When David's young men came,
they spoke to Nabal according to all these
words in David's name; then they waited.
10 But Nabal answered David's servants and said, "[a]Who is David? And
who is the son of Jesse? There are many
servants today who are each breaking
away from his master.
11 "Shall I then [a]take my bread and my
water and my meat that I have slaughtered for my shearers, and give it to men
[1]whose origin I do not know?"
12 So David's young men retraced
their way and went back; and they came
and told him according to all these words.
13 David said to his men, "Each *of you*
gird on his sword." So each man girded
on his sword. And David also girded on
his sword, and about [a]four hundred men
went up behind David while two hundred [b]stayed with the baggage.
14 ¶ But one of the young men told
Abigail, Nabal's wife, saying, "Behold,
David sent messengers from the wilderness to [1a]greet our master, and he
scorned them.
15 "Yet the men were very good to us,
and we were not [a]insulted, nor did we
miss anything [1]as long as we went about
with them, while we were in the fields.
16 "[a]They were a wall to us both by
night and by day, all the time we were
with them tending the sheep.
17 "Now therefore, know and [1]consid-
er what you should do, for evil is plotted

11 [1]Lit *transgression* [a]2 Kin 5:13 [b]1 Sam 23:14,23; 26:20
12 [1]Lit *me and you* [a]Gen 16:5; 31:53; Judg 11:27; 1 Sam 26:10,23
13 [a]Matt 7:16-20
14 [a]2 Sam 9:8 [b]1 Sam 26:20
15 [1]Lit *me and you* [2]Lit *vindicate* [a]1 Sam 24:12 [b]Ps 35:1; 43:1; 119:154; Mic 7:9
16 [a]1 Sam 26:17
17 [a]1 Sam 26:21 [b]Matt 5:44
18 [a]1 Sam 26:23
19 [1]Lit *on a good road* [a]1 Sam 23:17
20 [a]1 Sam 23:17 [b]1 Sam 13:14
21 [1]Lit *seed* [a]Gen 21:23; 1 Sam 20:14-17; 2 Sam 21:6-8
22 [a]1 Sam 23:29
25:1 [a]1 Sam 28:3 [b]Num 20:29; Deut 34:8 [c]2 Kin 21:18; 2 Chr 33:20 [d]Gen 21:21; Num 10:12; 13:3
2 [1]Lit *great* [a]1 Sam 23:24 [b]Josh 15:55 [c]Gen 38:13; 2 Sam 13:23
3 [1]Lit *of good understanding* [a]Prov 31:10 [b]Josh 15:13; 1 Sam 30:14
5 [1]Lit *go into*
6 [1]Lit *To life* [a]1 Chr 12:18; Ps 122:7; Luke 10:5
7 [a]2 Sam 13:23, 24 [b]1 Sam 25:15,21
8 [1]Lit *good* [a]Neh 8:10-12; Esth 9:19,22
10 [a]Judg 9:28
11 [1]Lit *from where they are* [a]Judg 8:6,15
13 [a]1 Sam 23:13 [b]1 Sam 30:24
14 [1]Lit *bless* [a]1 Sam 13:10; 15:13
15 [1]Lit *all the days* [a]1 Sam 25:7,21
16 [a]Ex 14:22; Job 1:10
17 [1]Lit *see*

against our master and against all his household; and he is such a [2]worthless man that no one can speak to him."

Abigail Intercedes

18 ¶ Then Abigail hurried and [a]took two hundred *loaves* of bread and two jugs of wine and five sheep already prepared and five measures of roasted grain and a hundred clusters of raisins and two hundred cakes of figs, and loaded *them* on donkeys.

19 She said to her young men, "[a]Go on before me; behold, I am coming after you." But she did not tell her husband Nabal.

20 It came about as she was riding on her donkey and coming down by the hidden part of the mountain, that behold, David and his men were coming down toward her; so she met them.

21 Now David had said, "Surely in vain I have guarded all that this *man* has in the wilderness, so that nothing was missed of all that belonged to him; and he has [a]returned me evil for good.

22 "[a]May God do so to the enemies of David, and more also, [b]if by morning I leave *as much as* one [1]male of any who belong to him."

23 ¶ When Abigail saw David, she hurried and dismounted from her donkey, and fell on her face before David [a]and bowed herself to the ground.

24 She fell at his feet and said, "On me [1]alone, my lord, be the blame. And please let your maidservant speak [2]to you, and listen to the words of your maidservant.

25 "Please do not let my lord [1]pay attention to this [2]worthless man, Nabal, for as his name is, so is he. [3]Nabal is his name and folly is with him; but I your maidservant did not see the young men of my lord whom you sent.

26 ¶ "Now therefore, my lord, as the LORD lives, and as your soul lives, since the LORD has restrained you from [1]shedding blood, and [a]from [2]avenging yourself by your own hand, now then [b]let your enemies and those who seek evil against my lord, be as Nabal.

27 "Now let [a]this [1]gift which your maidservant has brought to my lord be given to the young men who [2]accompany my lord.

28 "Please forgive [a]the transgression of your maidservant; for [b]the LORD will certainly make for my lord an enduring house, because my lord is [c]fighting the battles of the LORD, and [d]evil will not be found in you all your days.

29 "Should anyone rise up to pursue you and to seek your [1]life, then the [1]life of my lord shall be bound in the bundle of the living with the LORD your God; but the [1]lives of your enemies [a]He will sling out [2]as from the hollow of a sling.

30 "And when the LORD does for my lord according to all the good that He has spoken concerning you, and [a]appoints you ruler over Israel,

31 this will not [1]cause grief or a troubled heart to my lord, both by having shed blood without cause and by my lord having [2]avenged himself. [a]When the LORD deals well with my lord, then remember your maidservant."

32 ¶ Then David said to Abigail, "[a]Blessed be the LORD God of Israel, who sent you this day to meet me,

33 and blessed be your discernment, and blessed be you, [a]who have kept me this day from [1]bloodshed and from [2]avenging myself by my own hand.

34 "Nevertheless, as the LORD God of Israel lives, [a]who has restrained me from harming you, unless you had come quickly to meet me, surely there would not have been left to Nabal until the morning light *as much as* one [1]male."

35 So David received from her hand what she had brought him and said to her, "[a]Go up to your house in peace. See, I have listened to [1]you and [2b]granted your request."

36 ¶ Then Abigail came to Nabal, and behold, he was holding [a]a feast in his house, like the feast of a king. And Nabal's heart was merry within him, [b]for he was very drunk; so [c]she did not tell him anything [1]at all until the morning light.

37 But in the morning, when the wine had gone out of Nabal, his wife told him these things, and his heart died within him so that he became *as* a stone.

38 About ten days later, [a]the LORD struck Nabal and he died.

David Marries Abigail

39 ¶ When David heard that Nabal was dead, he said, "Blessed be the LORD, who has [a]pleaded the cause of my reproach from the hand of Nabal and [b]has kept back His servant from evil. The LORD has also returned the evildoing of Nabal on his own head." Then David sent [1c]a proposal to Abigail, to take her as his wife.

40 When the servants of David came to Abigail at Carmel, they spoke to her, saying, "David has sent us to you to take you as his wife."

41 She arose [a]and bowed with her face to the ground and said, "Behold, your maidservant is a maid [b]to wash the feet of my lord's servants."

17 [2]Lit *son of Belial*
18 [a]2 Sam 16:1; 1 Chr 12:40
19 [a]Gen 32:16, 20
21 [a]Ps 109:5; Prov 17:13
22 [1]Lit *who urinates against the wall* [a]1 Sam 3:17; 20:13 [b]1 Kin 14:10
23 [a]1 Sam 20:41
24 [1]Lit *even me* [2]Lit *in your ears*
25 [1]Lit *set his heart to* [2]Lit *man of Belial* [3]I.e. Fool
26 [1]Lit *coming in with blood* [2]Lit *saving* [a]Heb 10:30 [b]2 Sam 18:32
27 [1]Lit *blessing* [2]Lit *walk at the feet of* [a]Gen 33:11; 1 Sam 30:26
28 [a]1 Sam 25:24 [b]1 Sam 22:14; 2 Sam 7:11,16 [c]1 Sam 18:17 [d]1 Sam 24:11; Ps 7:3
29 [1]Lit *soul* [2]Lit *in the midst* [a]Jer 10:18
30 [a]1 Sam 13:14
31 [1]Lit *become staggering to you or a stumbling of the heart* [2]Lit *saved* [a]Gen 40:14; 1 Sam 25:30
32 [a]Ex 18:10; 1 Kin 1:48; Ps 41:13; 72:18; 106:48; Luke 1:68
33 [1]Lit *coming in with blood* [2]Lit *saving* [a]1 Sam 25:26
34 [1]Lit *who urinates against the wall* [a]1 Sam 25:26
35 [1]Lit *your voice* [2]Lit *lifted up your face* [a]1 Sam 20:42; 2 Kin 5:19 [b]Gen 19:21
36 [1]Lit *small or large* [a]2 Sam 13:28 [b]Prov 20:1; Is 5:11; Hos 4:11 [c]1 Sam 25:19
38 [a]1 Sam 26:10; 2 Sam 6:7; Ps 104:29
39 [1]Lit *and spoke* [a]1 Sam 24:15; Prov 22:23 [b]1 Sam 25:26,34 [c]Song 8:8
41 [a]1 Sam 25:23 [b]Mark 1:7

42 Then [a]Abigail quickly arose, and
rode on a donkey, with her five maidens
who [1]attended her; and she followed the
messengers of David and became his
wife.
43 ¶ David had also taken Ahinoam
of [a]Jezreel, and [b]they both became his
wives.
44 ¶ Now Saul had given [a]Michal his
daughter, David's wife, to Palti the son of
Laish, who was from [b]Gallim.

David Again Spares Saul

26 Then the Ziphites came to Saul at
Gibeah, saying, "[a]Is not David
hiding on the hill of Hachilah, *which is*
before [1]Jeshimon?"
2 So Saul arose and went down to the
wilderness of Ziph, having with him
[a]three thousand chosen men of Israel,
to search for David in the wilderness of
Ziph.
3 Saul camped in the hill of Hachilah,
which is before [1]Jeshimon, [a]beside the
road, and David was staying in the wilderness. When [b]he saw that Saul came
after him into the wilderness,
4 David sent out spies, and he knew
that Saul was definitely coming.
5 David then arose and came to the
place where Saul had camped. And David
saw the place where Saul lay, and [a]Ab-
ner the son of Ner, the commander of his
army; and Saul was lying in the circle of
the camp, and the people were camped
around him.
6 ¶ Then David said to Ahimelech
[a]the Hittite and to [b]Abishai the son of
Zeruiah, Joab's brother, saying, "Who
[c]will go down with me to Saul in the
camp?" And Abishai said, "I will go down
with you."
7 So David and Abishai came to the
people by night, and behold, Saul lay
sleeping inside the circle of the camp
with his spear stuck in the ground at his
head; and Abner and the people were
lying around him.
8 Then Abishai said to David, "Today
God has delivered your enemy into your
hand; now therefore, please let me strike
him with the spear [1]to the ground with
one stroke, and I will not [2]strike him the
second time."
9 But David said to Abishai, "Do not
destroy him, for [a]who can stretch out his
hand against the LORD's anointed and be
without guilt?"
10 David also said, "As the LORD lives,
[a]surely the LORD will strike him, or [b]his
day will come that he dies, or [c]he will go
down into battle and perish.
11 "[a]The LORD forbid that I should
stretch out my hand against the LORD's
anointed; but now please take the spear
that is at his head and the jug of water,
and let us go."
12 So David took the spear and the jug
of water from *beside* Saul's head, and
they went away, but no one saw or knew
it, nor did any awake, for they were all
asleep, because [a]a sound sleep from the
LORD had fallen on them.
13 ¶ Then David crossed over to the
other side and stood on top of the mountain at a distance *with* a large area between them.
14 David called to the people and to
Abner the son of Ner, saying, "Will you
not answer, Abner?" Then Abner replied,
"Who are you who calls to the king?"
15 So David said to Abner, "Are you
not a man? And who is like you in Israel?
Why then have you not guarded your lord
the king? For one of the people came to
destroy the king your lord.
16 "This thing that you have done is
not good. As the LORD lives, *all* of you
[1a]must surely die, because you did not
guard your lord, the LORD's anointed.
And now, see where the king's spear is
and the jug of water that was at his head."
17 ¶ Then Saul recognized David's
voice and said, "[a]Is this your voice, my
son David?" And David said, "It is my
voice, my lord the king."
18 He also said, "[a]Why then is my
lord pursuing his servant? For what have
I done? Or what evil is in my hand?
19 "Now therefore, please let my lord
the king listen to the words of his servant.
If [a]the LORD has stirred you up against
me, [b]let Him [1]accept an offering; but [c]if
it is [2]men, cursed are they before the
LORD, for [d]they have driven me out today
so that I would have no attachment with
the inheritance of the LORD, saying, 'Go,
serve other gods.'
20 "Now then, do not let my blood fall
to the ground away from the presence of
the LORD; for the king of Israel has come
out to search for [a]a single flea, just as one
hunts a partridge in the mountains."
21 ¶ Then Saul said, "[a]I have sinned.
Return, my son David, for I will not harm
you again because my life was precious in
your sight this day. Behold, I have played
the fool and have committed a serious
error."
22 David replied, "Behold the spear of
the king! Now let one of the young men
come over and take it.
23 "[a]The LORD will repay each man *for*
his righteousness and his faithfulness; for
the LORD delivered you into *my* hand today, but [b]I refused to stretch out my
hand against the LORD's anointed.
24 "Now behold, as your life was

42 [1]Lit *walked at her feet* [a]Gen 24:61-67
43 [a]Josh 15:56 [b]1 Sam 27:3; 30:5
44 [a]1 Sam 18:27; 2 Sam 3:14 [b]Is 10:30
26:1 [1]Or *the desert* [a]1 Sam 23:19; Ps 54: title
2 [a]1 Sam 13:2; 24:2
3 [1]Or *the desert* [a]1 Sam 24:3 [b]1 Sam 23:15
5 [a]1 Sam 14:50, 51; 17:55
6 [a]Gen 23:3; 26:34; Josh 3:10; 1 Kin 10:29; 2 Kin 7:6 [b]1 Chr 2:16 [c]Judg 7:10, 11
8 [1]Lit *even into* [2]Lit *repeat with respect to him*
9 [a]1 Sam 24:6,7; 2 Sam 1:14,16
10 [a]Deut 32:35; 1 Sam 25:26,38; Rom 12:19; Heb 10:30 [b]Gen 47:29; Deut 31:14; Ps 37:13 [c]1 Sam 31:6
11 [a]1 Sam 24:6, 12; Rom 12:17, 19; 1 Pet 3:9
12 [a]Gen 2:21; 15:12; Is 29:10
16 [1]Lit *are surely sons of death* [a]1 Sam 20:31
17 [a]1 Sam 24:16
18 [a]1 Sam 24:9, 11-14
19 [1]Lit *smell* [2]Lit *sons of men* [a]2 Sam 16:11 [b]Gen 8:21 [c]1 Sam 24:9 [d]Josh 22:25-27
20 [a]1 Sam 24:14
21 [a]Ex 9:27; 1 Sam 15:24,30; 24:17
23 [a]1 Sam 24:19; Ps 7:8; 18:20; 62:12 [b]1 Sam 24:12

[a]highly valued in my sight this day, so
may my life be highly valued in the sight
of the LORD, and may He [b]deliver me
from all distress."
25 Then Saul said to David, "[a]Blessed
are you, my son David; you will both accomplish much and surely prevail." So
[b]David went on his way, and Saul returned to his place.

David Flees to the Philistines

27 Then David said [1]to himself,
"Now I will perish one day by the
hand of Saul. [a]There is nothing better for
me than [2]to escape into the land of the
Philistines. Saul then will despair of
searching for me anymore in all the territory of Israel, and I will escape from his
hand."
2 So David arose and crossed over, he
and [a]the six hundred men who were
with him, to [b]Achish the son of Maoch,
king of Gath.
3 And David lived with Achish at
Gath, he and his men, [a]each with his
household, *even* David with [b]his two
wives, Ahinoam the Jezreelitess, and Abigail the Carmelitess, Nabal's [1]widow.
4 Now it was told Saul that David had
fled to Gath, so he no longer searched for
him.
5 ¶ Then David said to Achish, "If
now I have found favor in your sight, let
them give me a place in one of the cities
in the country, that I may live there; for
why should your servant live in the royal
city with you?"
6 So Achish gave him Ziklag that day;
therefore [a]Ziklag has belonged to the
kings of Judah to this day.
7 The number of days that David
lived in the country of the Philistines was
[a]a year and four months.
8 ¶ Now David and his men went up
and raided [a]the Geshurites and the Gir-
zites and [b]the Amalekites; for they were
the inhabitants of the land from ancient
times, as you come to [c]Shur even as far
as the land of Egypt.
9 David [1]attacked the land and did
not leave a man or a woman alive, and he
[a]took away the sheep, the cattle, the
donkeys, the camels, and the clothing.
Then he returned and came to Achish.
10 Now Achish said, "Where have you
[a]made a raid today?" And David said,
"Against the [1]Negev of Judah and against
the [1]Negev of [b]the Jerahmeelites and
against the [1]Negev of [c]the Kenites."
11 David did not leave a man or a
woman alive to bring to Gath, saying,
"Otherwise they will tell about us, saying, 'So has David done and so *has been*
his practice all the time he has lived in
the country of the Philistines.'"
12 So Achish believed David, saying,
"He has surely made himself odious
among his people Israel; therefore he will
become my servant forever."

Saul and the Spirit Medium

28 Now it came about in those days
that [a]the Philistines gathered
their armed camps for war, to fight
against Israel. And Achish said to David,
"Know assuredly that you will go out
with me in the camp, you and your men."
2 David said to Achish, "Very well,
you shall know what your servant can
do." So Achish said to David, "Very well,
I will make you [1]my bodyguard [a]for
life."
3 ¶ Now [a]Samuel was dead, and all
Israel had lamented him and buried him
[b]in Ramah, his own city. And Saul had
removed from the land those who [c]were
mediums and spiritists.
4 So the Philistines gathered together
and came and camped [a]in Shunem; and
Saul gathered all Israel together and they
camped in [b]Gilboa.
5 When Saul saw the camp of the Philistines, he was afraid and his heart trembled greatly.
6 [a]When Saul inquired of the LORD,
[b]the LORD did not answer him, either by
[c]dreams or by [d]Urim or by prophets.
7 Then Saul said to his servants,
"Seek for me a woman who is a medium,
that I may go to her and inquire of her."
And his servants said to him, "Behold,
[a]there is a woman who is a medium at
[b]En-dor."
8 ¶ Then Saul [a]disguised himself by
putting on other clothes, and went, he
and two men with him, and they came to
the woman by night; and he said, "[b]Con-
jure up for me, please, and [c]bring up for
me whom I shall [1]name to you."
9 But the woman said to him, "Behold, you know [a]what Saul has done,
how he has cut off those who are mediums and spiritists from the land. Why are
you then laying a snare for my life to
bring about my death?"
10 Saul vowed to her by the LORD, saying, "As the LORD lives, no punishment
shall come upon you for this thing."
11 Then the woman said, "Whom
shall I bring up for you?" And he said,
"Bring up Samuel for me."
12 When the woman saw Samuel, she
cried out with a loud voice; and the woman spoke to Saul, saying, "Why have you
deceived me? For you are Saul."
13 The king said to her, "Do not be
afraid; but what do you see?" And the

24 [a]1 Sam 18:30 [b]Ps 54:7
25 [a]1 Sam 24:19 [b]1 Sam 24:22
27:1 [1]Lit *in his heart* [2]Lit *that I should surely escape* [a]1 Sam 26:19
2 [a]1 Sam 25:13 [b]1 Sam 21:10; 1 Kin 2:39
3 [1]Lit *wife* [a]1 Sam 30:3; 2 Sam 2:3 [b]1 Sam 25:42,43
6 [a]Josh 15:31; 19:5; Neh 11:28
7 [a]1 Sam 29:3
8 [a]Josh 13:2,13 [b]Ex 17:8; 1 Sam 15:7,8 [c]Ex 15:22
9 [1]Lit *smote* [a]1 Sam 15:3; Job 1:3
10 [1]I.e. South country [a]1 Sam 23:27 [b]1 Sam 30:29; 1 Chr 2:9,25 [c]Judg 1:16; 4:11
28:1 [a]1 Sam 29:1
2 [1]Lit *keeper of my head* [a]1 Sam 1:22,28
3 [a]1 Sam 25:1 [b]1 Sam 7:17 [c]Lev 19:31; 20:27; Deut 18:10; 1 Sam 15:23
4 [a]Josh 19:18; 1 Sam 28:4; 1 Kin 1:3; 2 Kin 4:8 [b]1 Sam 31:1
6 [a]1 Chr 10:13, 14 [b]1 Sam 14:37; Prov 1:24-31 [c]Num 12:6; Joel 2:28 [d]Ex 28:30; Num 27:21
7 [a]Acts 16:16 [b]Josh 17:11; Ps 83:10
8 [1]Lit *say* [a]2 Chr 18:29; 35:22 [b]1 Chr 10:13; Is 8:19 [c]Deut 18:10,11
9 [a]1 Sam 28:3

woman said to Saul, "I see a [1]divine being coming up out of the earth."
14 He said to her, "What is his form?"
And she said, "An old man is coming up,
and [a]he is wrapped with a robe." And
Saul knew that it was Samuel, and [b]he
bowed with his face to the ground and
did homage.
15 ¶ Then Samuel said to Saul, "Why
have you disturbed me by bringing me
up?" And Saul answered, "I am greatly
distressed; for the Philistines are waging
war against me, and [a]God has departed
from me and [b]no longer answers me,
either through prophets or by dreams;
therefore I have called you, that you may
make known to me what I should do."
16 Samuel said, "Why then do you ask
me, since the LORD has departed from
you and has become your adversary?
17 "The LORD has done [1]accordingly
[a]as He spoke through me; for the LORD
has torn the kingdom out of your hand
and given it to your neighbor, to David.
18 "As [a]you did not [1]obey the LORD
and did not execute His fierce wrath on
Amalek, so the LORD has done this thing
to you this day.
19 "Moreover the LORD will also give
over Israel along with you into the hands
of the Philistines, therefore tomorrow
[a]you and your sons will be with me. Indeed the LORD will give over the army of
Israel into the hands of the Philistines!"
20 ¶ Then Saul immediately fell full
length upon the ground and was very
afraid because of the words of Samuel;
also there was no strength in him, for he
had eaten no [1]food all day and all night.
21 The woman came to Saul and saw
that he was terrified, and said to him,
"Behold, your maidservant has [1]obeyed
you, and [a]I have [2]taken my life in my
hand and have listened to your words
which you spoke to me.
22 "So now also, please listen to the
voice of your maidservant, and let me set
a piece of bread before you that *you may*
eat and have strength when you go on
your way."
23 But he refused and said, "[a]I will
not eat." [b]However, his servants together with the woman urged him, and he
listened to [1]them. So he arose from the
ground and sat on [c]the bed.
24 The woman had a [a]fattened calf in
the house, and she quickly slaughtered
it; and she [b]took flour, kneaded it and
baked unleavened bread from it.
25 She brought *it* before Saul and his
servants, and they ate. Then they arose
and went away that night.

13 [1]Or *god*
14 [a]1 Sam 15:27 [b]1 Sam 24:8
15 [a]1 Sam 16:14; 18:12 [b]1 Sam 28:6
17 [1]Lit *for himself* [a]1 Sam 15:28
18 [1]Lit *listen to the voice of* [a]1 Sam 15:20, 26; 1 Kin 20:42
19 [a]1 Sam 31:2; Job 3:17-19
20 [1]Lit *bread*
21 [1]Lit *listened to your voice* [2]Lit *put* [a]Judg 12:3; 1 Sam 19:5; Job 13:14
23 [1]Lit *their voices* [a]1 Kin 21:4 [b]2 Kin 5:13 [c]Esth 1:6; Ezek 23:41
24 [a]Gen 18:7; Luke 15:23,27, 30 [b]Gen 18:6
29:1 [a]1 Sam 28:1 [b]Josh 12:18; 19:30; 1 Sam 4:1; 1 Kin 20:30 [c]1 Kin 21:1; 2 Kin 9:30
2 [a]1 Sam 28:1,2
3 [1]Lit *fell* [a]1 Sam 27:7 [b]1 Sam 27:1-6; 1 Chr 12:19,20; Dan 6:5
4 [1]Lit *those* [a]1 Sam 27:6 [b]1 Sam 14:21
5 [a]1 Sam 18:7; 21:11
6 [a]2 Sam 3:25; 2 Kin 19:27; Is 37:28 [b]1 Sam 27:8-12; 29:3
8 [a]1 Sam 27:10-12
9 [a]2 Sam 14:17, 20; 19:27 [b]1 Sam 29:4
10 [a]1 Chr 12:19,22

The Philistines Mistrust David

29 Now [a]the Philistines gathered together all their armies to [b]Aphek,
while the Israelites were camping by the
spring which is in [c]Jezreel.
2 And the lords of the Philistines
were proceeding on by hundreds and by
thousands, and [a]David and his men were
proceeding on in the rear with Achish.
3 Then the commanders of the Philistines said, "What *are* these Hebrews *do-*
ing here?" And Achish said to the commanders of the Philistines, "Is this not
David, the servant of Saul the king of Israel, [a]who has been with me these days, or
rather these years, and [b]I have found no
fault in him from the day he [1]deserted *to*
me to this day?"
4 But the commanders of the Philistines were angry with him, and the commanders of the Philistines said to him,
"Make the man go back, that he may return [a]to his place where you have assigned him, and do not let him go down
to battle with us, [b]or in the battle he may
become an adversary to us. For with what
could this *man* make himself acceptable
to his lord? *Would it* not *be* with the
heads of [1]these men?
5 "Is this not David, [a]of whom they
sing in the dances, saying,
'Saul has slain his thousands,
And David his ten thousands'?"
6 ¶ Then Achish called David and
said to him, "*As* the LORD lives, you *have*
been upright, and [a]your going out and
your coming in with me in the army are
pleasing in my sight; [b]for I have not
found evil in you from the day of your
coming to me to this day. Nevertheless,
you are not pleasing in the sight of the
lords.
7 "Now therefore return and go in
peace, that you may not displease the
lords of the Philistines."
8 David said to Achish, "[a]But what
have I done? And what have you found in
your servant from the day when I came
before you to this day, that I may not go
and fight against the enemies of my lord
the king?"
9 But Achish replied to David, "I
know that you are pleasing in my sight,
[a]like an angel of God; nevertheless [b]the
commanders of the Philistines have said,
'He must not go up with us to the battle.'
10 "Now then arise early in the morning [a]with the servants of your lord who
have come with you, and as soon as
you have arisen early in the morning
and have light, depart."
11 So David arose early, he and his
men, to depart in the morning to return

to the land of the Philistines. And the Philistines went up to Jezreel.

David's Victory over the Amalekites

30 Then it happened when David and his men came to [a]Ziklag on the third day, that [b]the Amalekites had made a raid on the [1]Negev and on [c]Ziklag, and had [2]overthrown Ziklag and burned it with fire;

2 and they took captive the women *and all* who were in it, both small and great, [1a]without killing anyone, and carried *them* off and went their way.

3 When David and his men came to the city, behold, it was burned with fire, and their wives and their sons and their daughters had been taken captive.

4 Then David and the people who were with him [a]lifted their voices and wept until there was no strength in them to weep.

5 Now [a]David's two wives had been taken captive, Ahinoam the Jezreelitess and Abigail the [1]widow of Nabal the Carmelite.

6 Moreover David was greatly distressed because [a]the people spoke of stoning him, for all the people were [1]embittered, each one because of his sons and his daughters. But [b]David strengthened himself in the LORD his God.

7 ¶ Then [a]David said to [b]Abiathar the priest, the son of Ahimelech, "Please bring me the ephod." So Abiathar brought the ephod to David.

8 [a]David inquired of the LORD, saying, "[b]Shall I pursue this band? Shall I overtake them?" And He said to him, "Pursue, for you will surely overtake them, [c]and you will surely rescue *all*."

9 So David went, [a]he and the six hundred men who were with him, and came to the brook Besor, *where* those left behind remained.

10 But David pursued, he and four hundred men, for [a]two hundred who were too exhausted to cross the brook Besor remained *behind*.

11 ¶ Now they found an Egyptian in the field and brought him to David, and gave him bread and he ate, and they provided him water to drink.

12 They gave him a piece of fig cake and two clusters of raisins, and he ate; [a]then his spirit [1]revived. For he had not eaten bread or drunk water for three days and three nights.

13 David said to him, "To whom do you belong? And where are you from?" And he said, "I am a young man of Egypt, a servant of an Amalekite; and my master left me behind when I fell sick three days ago.

14 "We made a raid on [a]the [1]Negev of the Cherethites, and on that which belongs to Judah, and on [b]the [1]Negev of Caleb, and [c]we burned Ziklag with fire."

15 Then David said to him, "Will you bring me down to this band?" And he said, "Swear to me by God that you will not kill me or deliver me into the hands of my master, and I will bring you down to this band."

16 ¶ When he had brought him down, behold, they were [1]spread over all the land, [a]eating and drinking and [2]dancing because of [b]all the great spoil that they had taken from the land of the Philistines and from the land of Judah.

17 David [1]slaughtered them [a]from the twilight [2]until the evening of [3]the next day; and not a man of them escaped, except four hundred young men who rode on [b]camels and fled.

18 So David [a]recovered all that the Amalekites had taken, and [1]rescued his two wives.

19 But nothing of theirs was missing, whether small or great, sons or daughters, spoil or anything that they had taken for themselves; [a]David brought *it* all back.

20 So David had [1]captured all the sheep and the cattle *which the people* drove ahead of [2]the *other* livestock, and they said, "[a]This is David's spoil."

The Spoils Are Divided

21 ¶ When [a]David came to the two hundred men who were too exhausted to follow David, who had also been left at the brook Besor, and they went out to meet David and to meet the people who were with him, then David approached the people and greeted them.

22 Then all the wicked and worthless men among those who went with David said, "Because they did not go with [1]us, we will not give them any of the spoil that we have recovered, except to every man his wife and his children, that they may lead *them* away and depart."

23 Then David said, "You must not do so, my brothers, with what the LORD has given us, who has kept us and delivered into our hand the band that came against us.

24 "And who will listen to you in this matter? For [a]as his share is who goes down to the battle, so shall his share be who stays by the baggage; they shall share alike."

25 So it has been from that day forward, that he made it a statute and an ordinance for Israel to this day.

26 ¶ Now when David came to Ziklag, he sent *some* of the spoil to the elders of

30:1 [1]I.e. South country [2]Lit *smote* [a]1 Sam 29:4,11 [b]1 Sam 15:7; 27:8-10 [c]1 Sam 27:6,8

2 [1]Lit *they did not kill* [a]1 Sam 27:11

4 [a]Num 14:1

5 [1]Lit *wife* [a]1 Sam 25:42, 43; 2 Sam 2:2

6 [1]Lit *bitter in soul* [a]Ex 17:4; John 8:59 [b]1 Sam 23:16; Ps 18:2; 27:14; 31:24; 71:4,5; Rom 4:20

7 [a]1 Sam 23:6,9 [b]1 Sam 22:20-23

8 [a]1 Sam 23:2,4; Ps 50:15; 91:15 [b]Ex 15:9 [c]1 Sam 30:18

9 [a]1 Sam 27:2

10 [a]1 Sam 30:9, 21

12 [1]Lit *returned to him* [a]Judg 15:19

14 [1]I.e. South country [a]1 Sam 30:1,16; 2 Sam 8:18; 1 Kin 1:38, 44; Ezek 25:16; Zeph 2:5 [b]Josh 14:13; 15:13; 21:12 [c]1 Sam 30:1

16 [1]Lit *left* [2]Lit *keeping a pilgrim-feast* [a]Luke 12:19; 17:27f [b]1 Sam 30:14

17 [1]Lit *smote* [2]Lit *even until* [3]Lit *their* [a]1 Sam 11:11 [b]Judg 7:12; 1 Sam 15:3

18 [1]Lit *David rescued* [a]Gen 14:16

19 [a]1 Sam 30:8

20 [1]Lit *taken* [2]Lit *those livestock* [a]1 Sam 30:26-31

21 [a]1 Sam 30:10

22 [1]Lit *me*

24 [a]Num 31:27; Josh 22:8

Judah, to his friends, saying, "Behold, [a]a [1]gift for you from the spoil of [b]the enemies of the LORD:

27 to those who were in [a]Bethel, and to those who were in [b]Ramoth of the [1]Negev, and to those who were in [c]Jattir,

28 and to those who were in [a]Aroer, and to those who were in Siphmoth, and to those who were in [b]Eshtemoa,

29 and to those who were in Racal, and to those who were in the cities of [a]the Jerahmeelites, and to those who were in the cities of [b]the Kenites,

30 and to those who were in [a]Hormah, and to those who were in [b]Borashan, and to those who were in Athach,

31 and to those who were in [a]Hebron, and to all the places where David himself and his men were accustomed to [b]go."

Saul and His Sons Slain

31 [a]Now the Philistines were fighting against Israel, and the men of Israel fled from before the Philistines and fell slain [b]on Mount Gilboa.

2 The Philistines overtook Saul and his sons; and the Philistines [1]killed [a]Jonathan and Abinadab and Malchi-shua the sons of Saul.

3 [a]The battle went heavily against Saul, and the archers [1]hit him; and he was badly wounded by the archers.

4 [a]Then Saul said to his armor bearer, "Draw your sword and pierce me through with it, otherwise [b]these uncircumcised will come and pierce me through and make sport of me." But his armor bearer would not, for he was greatly afraid. [c]So Saul took his sword and fell on it.

5 When his armor bearer saw that Saul was dead, he also fell on his sword and died with him.

6 Thus Saul died with his three sons, his armor bearer, and all his men on that day together.

7 ¶ When the men of Israel who were on the other side of the valley, with those who were beyond the Jordan, saw that the men of Israel had fled and that Saul and his sons were dead, they abandoned the cities and fled; then the Philistines came and lived in them.

8 ¶ It came about on the [1]next day when the Philistines came to strip the slain, that they found Saul and his three sons fallen on Mount Gilboa.

9 They cut off his head and stripped off his weapons, and sent *them* [1]throughout the land of the Philistines, [a]to carry the good news [b]to the house of their idols and to the people.

10 They put his weapons in the [1]temple of [a]Ashtaroth, and [b]they fastened his body to the wall of [c]Beth-shan.

11 Now when [a]the inhabitants of Jabesh-gilead heard [1]what the Philistines had done to Saul,

12 [a]all the valiant men rose and walked all night, and took the body of Saul and the bodies of his sons from the wall of Beth-shan, and they came to Jabesh and [b]burned them there.

13 They took their bones and [a]buried them under [b]the tamarisk tree at Jabesh, and [c]fasted seven days.

26 [1]Lit *blessing* [a]1 Sam 25:27 [b]1 Sam 18:17; 25:28
27 [1]I.e. South country [a]Gen 12:8; Josh 7:2; 8:9; 16:1 [b]Josh 19:8 [c]Josh 15:48; 21:14
28 [a]Josh 13:16; 1 Chr 11:44 [b]Josh 15:50
29 [a]1 Sam 27:10 [b]Judg 1:16; 1 Sam 15:6
30 [a]Num 14:45; 21:3; Josh 12:14; 15:30; 19:4; Judg 1:17 [b]Josh 15:42; 19:7
31 [a]Num 13:22; Josh 14:13-15; 21:11-13; 2 Sam 2:1 [b]1 Sam 23:22
31:1 [a]1 Chr 10:1-12 [b]1 Sam 28:4
2 [1]Lit *smote* [a]1 Chr 8:33f
3 [1]Lit *found* [a]2 Sam 1:6
4 [a]Judg 9:54; 1 Chr 10:4 [b]Judg 14:3; 1 Sam 14:6; 17:26,36 [c]2 Sam 1:6,10
8 [1]Lit *morrow*
9 [1]Lit *into...around* [a]2 Sam 1:20 [b]Judg 16:23,24
10 [1]Lit *house* [a]Judg 2:13; 1 Sam 7:3 [b]1 Sam 31:12; 2 Sam 21:12 [c]Josh 17:11
11 [1]Lit *about him what* [a]1 Sam 11:1-13
12 [a]2 Sam 2:4-7 [b]2 Chr 16:14
13 [a]2 Sam 21:12-14 [b]1 Sam 22:6 [c]2 Sam 1:12

2 Samuel

Title and Background

1 and 2 Samuel were originally one book (see Introduction to 1 Samuel).

Author and Date of Writing

See Introduction to 1 Samuel.

Theme and Message

2 Samuel depicts David as a true (though imperfect) representative of the ideal theocratic king. Under David's rule the Lord caused the nation to prosper and to defeat its enemies. In chapter 7 we read of the Lord's promise that David's dynasty would endure forever and of the establishment of the Davidic covenant.

Outline

I. David Becomes King Over Judah (1:1—4:12)
II. David Becomes King Over All Israel (5:1–5)
III. David's Kingship in Its Accomplishments and Glory (5:6—9:13)
IV. David's Kingship in Its Weaknesses and Failures (10:1—20:26)
V. Final Reflections on David's Reign (21:1—24:25)

David Learns of Saul's Death

1 Now it came about after [a]the death
of Saul, when David had returned
from [b]the slaughter of the Amalekites,
that David remained two days in Ziklag.
2 On the third day, behold, [a]a man
came out of the camp from Saul, [b]with
his clothes torn and [1]dust on his head.
And it came about when he came to David that [c]he fell to the ground and prostrated himself.
3 Then David said to him, "From
where do you come?" And he said to him,
"I have escaped from the camp of Israel."
4 David said to him, "[a]How did
things go? Please tell me." And he said,
"The people have fled from the battle,
and also many of the people have fallen
and are dead; and Saul and Jonathan his
son are dead also."
5 So David said to the young man
who told him, "How do you know that
Saul and his son Jonathan are dead?"
6 The young man who told him said,
"By chance I happened to be on [a]Mount
Gilboa, and behold, [b]Saul was leaning on
his spear. And behold, the chariots and
the horsemen pursued him closely.
7 "When he looked behind him, he
saw me and called to me. And I said,
'Here I am.'
8 "He said to me, 'Who are you?' And
I [1]answered him, '[a]I am an Amalekite.'
9 "Then he said to me, 'Please stand
beside me and kill me, for agony has
seized me because my [1]life still lingers
in me.'
10 "So I stood beside him [a]and killed
him, because I knew that he could not
live after he had fallen. And [b]I took the
crown which *was* on his head and the
bracelet which *was* on his arm, and I
have brought them here to my lord."
11 ¶ Then [a]David took hold of his
clothes and tore them, and *so* also *did* all
the men who *were* with him.
12 They mourned and wept and [a]fasted until evening for Saul and his son Jonathan and for the people of the LORD and
the house of Israel, because they had fallen by the sword.
13 David said to the young man who
told him, "Where are you from?" And he
[1]answered, "[a]I am the son of an alien,
an Amalekite."
14 Then David said to him, "How is it
you were not afraid [a]to stretch out your
hand to destroy the LORD's anointed?"
15 And David called one of the young
men and said, "Go, [1]cut him down." [a]So
he struck him and he died.
16 David said to him, "[a]Your blood is
on your head, for [b]your mouth has testified against you, saying, 'I have killed the
LORD'S anointed.' "

1:1 [a]1 Sam 31:6 [b]1 Sam 30:1,17, 26
2 [1]Lit *ground* [a]2 Sam 4:10 [b]1 Sam 4:12 [c]1 Sam 25:23
4 [a]1 Sam 4:16
6 [a]1 Sam 28:4; 31:1-6; 1 Chr 10:4-10 [b]1 Sam 31:2-4
8 [1]Lit *said to* [a]1 Sam 15:3; 30:1,13,17
9 [1]Lit *whole life is still in me*
10 [a]Judg 9:54 [b]2 Kin 11:12
11 [a]Gen 37:29, 34; Josh 7:6; 2 Chr 34:27; Ezra 9:3
12 [a]2 Sam 3:35
13 [1]Lit *said* [a]2 Sam 1:8
14 [a]1 Sam 24:6; 26:9,11,16
15 [1]Lit *fall upon him* [a]2 Sam 4:10,12
16 [a]1 Sam 26:9; 2 Sam 3:28,29; 1 Kin 2:32 [b]2 Sam 1:10; Luke 19:22

David's Dirge for Saul and Jonathan

17 ¶ Then David [a]chanted with this lament over Saul and Jonathan his son,

18 and he told *them* to teach the sons of Judah *the song of* the bow; behold, it is written in [a]the book of Jashar.

19 "[1]Your beauty, O Israel, is slain
on your high places!
[a]How have the mighty fallen!
20 "[a]Tell *it* not in Gath,
Proclaim it not in the streets of
Ashkelon,
Or [b]the daughters of the
Philistines will rejoice,
The daughters of [c]the
uncircumcised will exult.
21 "[a]O mountains of Gilboa,
[b]Let not dew or rain be on you,
nor fields of offerings;
For there the shield of the
mighty was defiled,
The shield of Saul, not [c]anointed
with oil.
22 "[a]From the blood of the slain,
from the fat of the mighty,
[b]The bow of Jonathan did not
turn back,
And the sword of Saul did not
return empty.
23 "Saul and Jonathan, beloved and
pleasant in their life,
And in their death they were not
parted;
[a]They were swifter than eagles,
[b]They were stronger than lions.
24 "O daughters of Israel, weep over
Saul,
Who clothed you luxuriously in
scarlet,
Who put ornaments of gold on
your apparel.
25 "[a]How have the mighty fallen in
the midst of the battle!
Jonathan is slain on your high
places.
26 "I am distressed for you, my
brother Jonathan;
You have been very pleasant
to me.
[a]Your love to me was more
wonderful
Than the love of women.
27 "[a]How have the mighty fallen,
And [b]the weapons of war
perished!"

David Made King over Judah

2 Then it came about afterwards that [a]David inquired of the LORD, saying, "Shall I go up to one of the cities of Judah?" And the LORD said to him, "Go up." So David said, "Where shall I go up?" And He said, "[b]To Hebron."

2 So David went up there, and [a]his two wives also, Ahinoam the Jezreelitess and Abigail the [1]widow of Nabal the Carmelite.

3 And [a]David brought up his men who *were* with him, each with his household; and they lived in the cities of Hebron.

4 Then the men of Judah came and there [a]anointed David king over the house of Judah.

¶ And they told David, saying, "It was [b]the men of Jabesh-gilead who buried Saul."

5 David sent messengers to the men of Jabesh-gilead, and said to them, "[a]May you be blessed of the LORD because you have [1]shown this kindness to Saul your lord, and have buried him.

6 "Now [a]may the LORD [1]show lovingkindness and truth to you; and I also will [1]show this goodness to you, because you have done this thing.

7 "Now therefore, let your hands be strong and be [1]valiant; for Saul your lord is dead, and also the house of Judah has anointed me king over them."

Ish-bosheth Made King over Israel

8 ¶ But [a]Abner the son of Ner, commander of Saul's army, had taken [1]Ish-bosheth the son of Saul and brought him over to [b]Mahanaim.

9 He made him king over [a]Gilead, over the [b]Ashurites, over [c]Jezreel, over Ephraim, and over Benjamin, even over all Israel.

10 Ish-bosheth, Saul's son, was forty years old when he became king over Israel, and he was king for two years. The house of Judah, however, followed David.

11 [a]The [1]time that David was king in Hebron over the house of Judah was seven years and six months.

Civil War

12 ¶ Now Abner the son of Ner, went out from Mahanaim to [a]Gibeon with the servants of Ish-bosheth the son of Saul.

13 And [a]Joab the son of Zeruiah and the servants of David went out and met [1]them by the pool of Gibeon; and they sat down, [2]one on the one side of the pool and [2]the other on the other side of the pool.

14 Then Abner said to Joab, "Now let the young men arise and [1a]hold a contest before us." And Joab said, "Let them arise."

15 So they arose and went over by count, twelve for Benjamin and Ish-bosheth the son of Saul, and twelve of the servants of David.

16 Each one of them seized his [1]oppo-

---

17 [a]2 Chr 35:25
18 [a]Josh 10:13
19 [1]Lit *The* [a]2 Sam 1:25,27
20 [a]1 Sam 31:8-13; Mic 1:10 [b]Ex 15:20, 21; 1 Sam 18:6 [c]1 Sam 14:6
21 [a]1 Sam 31:1 [b]Ezek 31:15 [c]Is 21:5
22 [a]Deut 32:42; Is 34:6 [b]1 Sam 18:4
23 [a]Jer 4:13 [b]Judg 14:18
25 [a]2 Sam 1:19, 27
26 [a]1 Sam 18:1-4
27 [a]2 Sam 1:19, 25 [b]Is 13:5
2:1 [a]1 Sam 23:2,4,9-12 [b]Josh 14:13; 1 Sam 30:31
2 [1]Lit *wife* [a]1 Sam 25:42,43
3 [a]1 Sam 30:9; 1 Chr 12:1
4 [a]1 Sam 16:13; 2 Sam 5:3,5 [b]1 Sam 31:11-13
5 [1]Lit *done* [a]1 Sam 23:21; Ps 115:15
6 [1]Lit *do* [a]Ex 34:6; 2 Tim 1:16
7 [1]Lit *sons of valor*
8 [1]I.e. man of shame; cf 1 Chr 8:33, *Eshbaal* [a]1 Sam 14:50 [b]Gen 32:2; 2 Sam 17:24
9 [a]Josh 22:9 [b]Judg 1:32 [c]1 Sam 29:1
11 [1]Lit *number of days* [a]2 Sam 5:5
12 [a]Josh 10:12; 18:25
13 [1]Lit *them together* [2]Lit *these* [a]2 Sam 8:16; 1 Chr 2:16; 11:6
14 [1]Lit *make sport* [a]2 Sam 2:16,17
16 [1]Lit *fellow*

nent by the head and *thrust* his sword in
his [2]opponent's side; so they fell down
together. Therefore that place was called
[3]Helkath-hazzurim, which is in Gibeon.
17 That day the battle was very severe,
and [a]Abner and the men of Israel were
beaten before the servants of David.
18 ¶ Now [a]the three sons of Zeruiah
were there, Joab and Abishai and Asahel;
and Asahel *was* [b]*as* [1]swift-footed as one
of the gazelles which is in the field.
19 Asahel pursued Abner and did not
[1]turn to the right or to the left from following Abner.
20 Then Abner looked behind him and
said, "Is that you, Asahel?" And he answered, "It is I."
21 So Abner said to him, "[1]Turn to
your right or to your left, and take hold of
one of the young men for yourself, and
take for yourself his spoil." But Asahel
was not willing to turn aside from following him.
22 Abner repeated again to Asahel,
"Turn [1]aside from following me. Why
should I strike you to the ground? [a]How
then could I lift up my face to your brother Joab?"
23 However, he refused to turn aside;
therefore Abner struck him in the belly
with the butt end of the spear, so that the
spear came out at his back. And he fell
there and died on the spot. And it came
about that all who came to the place
where [a]Asahel had fallen and died, stood
still.
24 ¶ But Joab and Abishai pursued Abner, and when the sun was going down,
they came to the hill of Ammah, which is
in front of Giah by the way of the wilderness of Gibeon.
25 The sons of Benjamin gathered together behind Abner and became one
band, and they stood on the top of a certain hill.
26 Then Abner called to Joab and said,
"Shall the sword devour forever? Do you
not know that it will be bitter in the end?
How long will you [1]refrain from telling
the people to turn back from following
their brothers?"
27 Joab said, "As God lives, if you had
not spoken, surely then the people would
have gone away in the morning, each
from following his brother."
28 So Joab blew the trumpet; and all
the people halted and pursued Israel no
longer, [a]nor did they continue to fight
anymore.
29 Abner and his men then went
through the Arabah all that night; so they
crossed the Jordan, walked all morning,
and came to [a]Mahanaim.
30 ¶ Then Joab returned from following Abner; when he had gathered all the
people together, [1]nineteen of David's
servants besides Asahel were missing.
31 But the servants of David had
struck down many of Benjamin and Abner's men, *so that* three hundred and sixty men died.
32 And they took up Asahel and buried
him [a]in his father's tomb which was in
Bethlehem. Then Joab and his men went
all night until the day [1]dawned at Hebron.

The House of David Strengthened

3 Now [a]there was a long war between
the house of Saul and the house of
David; and David grew steadily stronger,
but the house of Saul grew weaker continually.
2 ¶ [a]Sons were born to David at Hebron: his firstborn was Amnon, by
[b]Ahinoam the Jezreelitess;
3 and his second, Chileab, by Abigail
the [1]widow of Nabal the Carmelite; and
the third, Absalom the son of [a]Maacah,
the daughter of Talmai, king of [b]Geshur;
4 and the fourth, [a]Adonijah the son
of Haggith; and the fifth, Shephatiah the
son of Abital;
5 and the sixth, Ithream, by David's
wife Eglah. These were born to David at
Hebron.

Abner Joins David

6 ¶ It came about while there was
war between the house of Saul and the
house of David that [a]Abner was making
himself strong in the house of Saul.
7 Now Saul had a concubine whose
name was [a]Rizpah, the daughter of Aiah;
and [1]Ish-bosheth said to Abner, "Why
have you gone in to my father's concubine?"
8 Then Abner was very angry over
the words of Ish-bosheth and said, "[a]Am
I a dog's head that belongs to Judah? Today I show kindness to the house of Saul
your father, to his brothers and to his
friends, and have not delivered you into
the hands of David; and yet today you
charge me with a guilt concerning the
woman.
9 "[a]May God do so to Abner, and
more also, if [b]as the LORD has sworn to
David, I do not accomplish this for him,
10 [a]to transfer the kingdom from the
house of Saul and to establish the throne
of David over Israel and over Judah,
[b]from Dan even to Beersheba."
11 And he could no longer answer Abner a word, because he was afraid of him.
12 ¶ Then Abner sent messengers to
David in his place, saying, "Whose is the
land? Make your covenant with me, and

16 [2]Lit *fellow's* [3]I.e. the field of sword-edges
17 [a]2 Sam 3:1
18 [1]Lit *light in his feet* [a]1 Chr 2:16 [b]1 Chr 12:8; Hab 3:19
19 [1]Lit *turn to go to*
21 [1]Lit *Turn for yourself*
22 [1]Lit *aside for yourself* [a]2 Sam 3:27
23 [a]2 Sam 20:12
26 [1]Lit *not tell the people*
28 [a]2 Sam 3:1
29 [a]2 Sam 2:8
30 [1]Lit *nineteen men*
32 [1]Lit *lighted on them* [a]Gen 47:29,30; Judg 8:32
3:1 [a]1 Kin 14:30; Ps 46:9
2 [a]1 Chr 3:1-3 [b]1 Sam 25:42,43
3 [1]Lit *wife* [a]1 Sam 27:8; 1 Chr 3:2 [b]2 Sam 14:32; 15:8
4 [a]1 Kin 1:5
6 [a]2 Sam 2:8,9
7 [1]So some ancient mss and versions; M.T. *he* [a]2 Sam 21:8-11
8 [a]1 Sam 24:14; 2 Sam 9:8
9 [a]1 Kin 19:2 [b]1 Sam 15:28
10 [a]1 Sam 15:28 [b]1 Sam 3:20

behold, my hand shall be with you to bring all Israel over to you."

13 He said, "Good! I will make a covenant with you, but I demand one thing of you, [1]namely, [a]you shall not see my face unless you [b]first bring Michal, Saul's daughter, when you come to see [2]me."

14 So David sent messengers to Ish-bosheth, Saul's son, saying, "Give me my wife Michal, to whom I was betrothed [a]for a hundred foreskins of the Philistines."

15 Ish-bosheth sent and took her from *her* husband, from [1]Paltiel the son of Laish.

16 But her husband went with her, weeping as he went, and followed her as far as [a]Bahurim. Then Abner said to him, "Go, return." So he returned.

17 ¶ Now Abner had [1]consultation with [a]the elders of Israel, saying, "In times past you were seeking for David to be king over you.

18 "Now then, do *it!* For the LORD has spoken of David, saying, '[a]By the hand of My servant David [1]I will save My people Israel from the hand of the Philistines and from the hand of all their enemies.' "

19 Abner also spoke in the hearing of Benjamin; and in addition Abner went to speak in the hearing of David in Hebron all that seemed good to Israel and to [a]the whole house of Benjamin.

20 ¶ Then Abner and twenty men with him came to David at Hebron. And David made a feast for Abner and the men who were with him.

21 Abner said to David, "Let me arise and go and [a]gather all Israel to my lord the king, that they may make a covenant with you, and that [b]you may be king over all that your soul desires." So David sent Abner away, and he went in peace.

22 ¶ And behold, [a]the servants of David and Joab came from a raid and brought much spoil with them; but Abner was not with David in Hebron, for he had sent him away, and he had gone in peace.

23 When Joab and all the army that was with him arrived, they told Joab, saying, "Abner the son of Ner came to the king, and he has sent him away, and he has gone in peace."

24 Then Joab came to the king and said, "What have you done? Behold, Abner came to you; why then have you sent him away and he is already gone?

25 "You know Abner the son of Ner, that he came to deceive you and to learn of [a]your going out and coming in and to find out all that you are doing."

Joab Murders Abner

26 ¶ When Joab came out from David, he sent messengers after Abner, and they brought him back from the well of Sirah; but David did not know *it.*

27 So when Abner returned to Hebron, Joab took him aside into the middle of the gate to speak with him privately, and there [a]he struck him in the belly so that he died on account of the blood of Asahel his brother.

28 Afterward when David heard it, he said, "I and my kingdom are innocent before the LORD forever of the blood of Abner the son of Ner.

29 "[a]May it [1]fall on the head of Joab and on all his father's house; and may there not fail from the house of Joab [b]one who has a discharge, or who is a leper, or who takes hold of a distaff, or who falls by the sword, or who lacks bread."

30 So Joab and Abishai his brother killed Abner [a]because he had put their brother Asahel to death in the battle at Gibeon.

David Mourns Abner

31 ¶ Then David said to Joab and to all the people who were with him, "[a]Tear your clothes and gird on sackcloth and lament before Abner." And King David walked behind the bier.

32 Thus they buried Abner in Hebron; and the king lifted up his voice and wept at [a]the grave of Abner, and all the people wept.

33 [a]The king chanted a *lament* for Abner and said,

"Should Abner die as a fool dies?
34 "Your hands were not bound, nor
your feet put in fetters;
As one falls before the [1]wicked,
you have fallen."

And all the people wept again over him.

35 Then all the people came [a]to [1]persuade David to eat bread while it was still day; but David vowed, saying, "[b]May God do so to me, and more also, if I taste bread or anything else [c]before the sun goes down."

36 Now all the people took note *of it,* and it [1]pleased them, just as everything the king did [2]pleased all the people.

37 So all the people and all Israel understood that day that it had not been *the will* of the king to put Abner the son of Ner to death.

38 Then the king said to his servants, "Do you not know that a prince and a great man has fallen this day in Israel?

39 "I am [a]weak today, though anointed king; and these men [b]the sons of Zeruiah are too difficult for me. [c]May the LORD repay the evildoer according to his evil."

---

13 [1]Lit *saying* [2]Lit *my face* [a]Gen 43:3 [b]1 Sam 18:20; 19:11
14 [a]1 Sam 18:25,27
15 [1]In 1 Sam 25:44, *Palti*
16 [a]2 Sam 16:5; 19:16
17 [1]Lit *a word* [a]1 Sam 8:4
18 [1]So many ancient mss and versions; M.T. *he* [a]1 Sam 9:16; 15:28
19 [a]1 Sam 10:20,21; 1 Chr 12:29
21 [a]2 Sam 3:10, 12 [b]1 Kin 11:37
22 [a]1 Sam 27:8
25 [a]Deut 28:6; 1 Sam 29:6; Is 37:28
27 [a]2 Sam 2:23; 20:9,10; 1 Kin 2:5
29 [1]Lit *whirl* [a]Deut 21:6-9; 1 Kin 2:31-33 [b]Lev 13:46
30 [a]2 Sam 2:23
31 [a]Gen 37:34; Judg 11:35
32 [a]Job 31:28, 29; Prov 24:17
33 [a]2 Sam 1:17; 2 Chr 35:25
34 [1]Lit *sons of wickedness*
35 [1]Lit *cause* [a]2 Sam 12:17 [b]1 Sam 3:17 [c]2 Sam 1:12
36 [1]Lit *was good in their eyes* [2]Lit *was good in the eyes of all*
39 [a]1 Chr 29:1; 2 Chr 13:7 [b]2 Sam 19:5-7 [c]1 Kin 2:32-34

Ish-bosheth Murdered

4 Now when [1]Ish-bosheth, Saul's son,
heard that [a]Abner had died in Hebron, [2b]he lost courage, and all Israel
was disturbed.
2 Saul's son *had* two men who were
commanders of bands: the name of the
one was Baanah and the name of the other Rechab, sons of Rimmon the Beeroth-
ite, of the sons of Benjamin (for [a]Beeroth
is also considered [b]*part* of Benjamin,
3 and the Beerothites fled to [a]Gitta-
im and have been aliens there until
this day).
4 ¶ Now [a]Jonathan, Saul's son, had a
son crippled in his feet. He was five years
old when the [b]report of Saul and Jonathan came from Jezreel, and his nurse
took him up and fled. And it happened
that in her hurry to flee, he fell and became lame. And his name was [1c]Me-
phibosheth.
5 ¶ So the sons of Rimmon the Bee-
rothite, Rechab and Baanah, departed
and came to the house of [a]Ish-bosheth in
the heat of the day while he was taking
his midday rest.
6 [1]They came to the middle of the
house as [2]if to get wheat, and [a]they
struck him in the belly; and Rechab and
Baanah his brother escaped.
7 Now when they came into the
house, as he was lying on his bed in his
bedroom, they struck him and killed him
and beheaded him. And they took his
head and [1a]traveled by way of the Arabah all night.
8 Then they brought the head of Ish-
bosheth to David at Hebron and said to
the king, "Behold, the head of Ish-
bosheth [a]the son of Saul, your enemy,
who sought your life; thus the LORD has
given my lord the king vengeance this
day on Saul and his [1]descendants."
9 ¶ David answered Rechab and Baanah his brother, sons of Rimmon the Bee-
rothite, and said to them, "As the LORD
lives, [a]who has redeemed my life from
all distress,
10 [a]when one told me, saying, 'Behold, Saul is dead,' and [1]thought he was
bringing good news, I seized him and
killed him in Ziklag, which was the reward I gave him for *his* news.
11 "How much more, when wicked
men have killed a righteous man in his
own house on his bed, shall I not now
[a]require his blood from your hand and
[1]destroy you from the earth?"
12 Then [a]David commanded the
young men, and they killed them and cut
off their hands and feet and hung them up
beside the pool in Hebron. But they took
the head of Ish-bosheth [b]and buried it in
the grave of Abner in Hebron.

David King over All Israel

5 [a]Then all the tribes of Israel came to
David at Hebron and [1]said, "Behold,
we are [b]your bone and your flesh.
2 "Previously, when Saul was king
over us, [a]you were the one who led Israel out and in. And the LORD said to you,
'[b]You will shepherd My people Israel,
and you will be [c]a ruler over Israel.' "
3 So all the elders of Israel came to
the king at Hebron, and King David
[a]made a covenant with them before the
LORD at Hebron; then [b]they anointed David king over Israel.
4 David was [a]thirty years old when
he became king, *and* [b]he reigned forty
years.
5 At Hebron [a]he reigned over Judah
seven years and six months, and in Jerusalem he reigned thirty-three years over
all Israel and Judah.
6 ¶ [a]Now the king and his men went
to [b]Jerusalem against the Jebusites, the
inhabitants of the land, and they said to
[1]David, "You shall not come in here, but
the blind and lame will turn you away";
[2]thinking, "David cannot enter here."
7 Nevertheless, David captured the
stronghold of Zion, that is [a]the city of
David.
8 David said on that day, "Whoever
would strike the Jebusites, let him reach
the lame and the blind, who are hated by
David's soul, through the water tunnel."
Therefore they say, "The blind or the
lame shall not come into the house."
9 So David lived in the stronghold
and called it [a]the city of David. And David built all around from the [1b]Millo and
inward.
10 [a]David became greater and greater, for the LORD God of hosts was with
him.
11 ¶ [a]Then Hiram king of Tyre sent
messengers to David with cedar trees and
carpenters and stonemasons; and [b]they
built a house for David.
12 And David realized that the LORD
had established him as king over Israel,
and that He had exalted his kingdom for
the sake of His people Israel.
13 ¶ Meanwhile [a]David took more
concubines and wives from Jerusalem, after he came from Hebron; and more sons
and daughters were born to David.
14 Now [a]these are the names of those
who were born to him in Jerusalem:
Shammua, Shobab, Nathan, Solomon,
15 Ibhar, Elishua, Nepheg, Japhia,
16 Elishama, Eliada and Eliphelet.

4:1 [1]So some ancient mss; M.T. *he* [2]Lit *his hands dropped* [a]2 Sam 3:27 [b]Ezra 4:4
2 [a]Josh 9:17 [b]Josh 18:25
3 [a]Neh 11:33
4 [1]I.e. Merib-baal [a]2 Sam 9:3, 6 [b]1 Sam 31:1-4 [c]1 Chr 8:34; 9:40
5 [a]2 Sam 2:8
6 [1]Lit *And here* [2]Lit *takers of wheat* [a]2 Sam 2:23
7 [1]Lit *went* [a]2 Sam 2:29
8 [1]Lit *seed* [a]1 Sam 24:4; 25:29
9 [a]Gen 48:16; 1 Kin 1:29; Ps 31:7
10 [1]Lit *he was as a bearer of good news in his own eyes* [a]2 Sam 1:2,4,15
11 [1]Lit *burn* [a]Gen 9:5; Ps 9:12
12 [a]2 Sam 1:15 [b]2 Sam 3:32
5:1 [1]Lit *said, saying* [a]1 Chr 11:1-3 [b]2 Sam 19:13
2 [a]1 Sam 18:5, 13,16 [b]Gen 49:24; 2 Sam 7:7 [c]1 Sam 25:30
3 [a]2 Sam 3:21 [b]1 Sam 16:13; 2 Sam 2:4
4 [a]Gen 41:46; Num 4:3; Luke 3:23 [b]1 Kin 2:11; 1 Chr 26:31
5 [a]2 Sam 2:11; 1 Chr 3:4; 29:27
6 [1]Lit *David, saying* [2]Lit *saying* [a]1 Chr 11:4-9 [b]Josh 15:63; 18:28; Judg 1:21
7 [a]2 Sam 6:12, 16; 1 Kin 2:10; 9:24
9 [1]I.e. citadel [a]2 Sam 5:7 [b]1 Kin 9:15,24
10 [a]2 Sam 3:1
11 [a]1 Kin 5:1, 10,18; 1 Chr 14:1 [b]Ps 30: title
13 [a]Deut 17:17; 1 Chr 3:9
14 [a]1 Chr 3:5-8

War with the Philistines

17 ¶ When the Philistines heard that
they had anointed David king over Israel,
[a]all the Philistines went up to seek out
David; and when David heard *of it,* he
went down to the [b]stronghold.
18 Now the Philistines came and
spread themselves out in [a]the valley of
Rephaim.
19 Then [a]David inquired of the LORD,
saying, "Shall I go up against the Philistines? Will You give them into my hand?"
And [b]the LORD said to David, "Go up, for
I will certainly give the Philistines into
your hand."
20 So David came to [a]Baal-perazim
and [1]defeated them there; and he said,
"The LORD has broken through my enemies before me like the breakthrough of
waters." Therefore he named that place
[2]Baal-perazim.
21 They abandoned their idols there,
so [a]David and his men carried them
away.
22 ¶ Now [a]the Philistines came up
once again and spread themselves out in
the valley of Rephaim.
23 When [a]David inquired of the
LORD, He said, "You shall not go *directly*
up; circle around behind them and come
at them in front of the [1]balsam trees.
24 "It shall be, when [a]you hear the
sound of marching in the tops of the [1]bal-
sam trees, then you shall act promptly,
for then [b]the LORD will have gone out
before you to strike the army of the Philistines."
25 Then David did so, just as the LORD
had commanded him, and struck down
the Philistines from [1a]Geba [2]as far as
[b]Gezer.

Peril in Moving the Ark

6 [a]Now David again gathered all the
chosen men of Israel, thirty thousand.
2 And David arose and went with all
the people who were with him to
[1a]Baale-judah, to bring up from there
the ark of God which is called by the
[b]Name, the very name of the LORD of
hosts who [c]is [2]enthroned *above* the
cherubim.
3 They [1]placed the ark of God on [a]a
new cart that they might bring it from the
house of Abinadab which was on the hill;
and Uzzah and Ahio, the sons of Abinadab, were leading the new cart.
4 So [a]they brought it with the ark of
God from the house of Abinadab, which
was on the hill; and Ahio was walking
ahead of the ark.
5 Meanwhile, David and all the
house of Israel [a]were celebrating before
the LORD [b]with all kinds of *instruments
made of* [1]fir wood, and with lyres, harps,
tambourines, castanets and cymbals.
6 ¶ But when they came to the
[a]threshing floor of Nacon, Uzzah
[b]reached out toward the ark of God and
took hold of it, for the oxen nearly upset *it.*
7 And the anger of the LORD burned
against Uzzah, and [a]God struck him
down there for [1]his irreverence; and he
died there by the ark of God.
8 David became angry because [1]of
the LORD'S outburst against Uzzah, and
that place is called [2]Perez-uzzah to this
day.
9 So [a]David was afraid of the LORD
that day; and he said, "How can the ark
of the LORD come to me?"
10 And David was unwilling to move
the ark of the LORD into the city of David
with him; but David took it aside to the
house of [a]Obed-edom the Gittite.
11 Thus the ark of the LORD remained
in the house of Obed-edom the Gittite
three months, and the LORD [a]blessed
Obed-edom and all his household.

The Ark Is Brought to Jerusalem

12 ¶ Now it was told King David, saying, "The LORD has blessed the house of
Obed-edom and all that belongs to him,
on account of the ark of God." [a]David
went and brought up the ark of God from
the house of Obed-edom into [b]the city of
David with gladness.
13 And so it was, that when the [a]bear-
ers of the ark of the LORD had gone six
paces, he sacrificed an [b]ox and a fatling.
14 And [a]David was dancing before
the LORD with all *his* might, and David
was [1b]wearing a linen ephod.
15 So David and all the house of Israel
were bringing up the ark of the LORD with
shouting and the sound of the trumpet.
16 ¶ Then it happened *as* the ark of
the LORD came into the city of David that
[a]Michal the daughter of Saul looked out
of the window and saw King David leaping and dancing before the LORD; and she
despised him in her heart.
17 ¶ So they brought in the ark of the
LORD and set it [a]in its place inside the
tent which David had pitched for it; and
[b]David offered burnt offerings and peace
offerings before the LORD.
18 When David had finished offering
the burnt offering and the peace offering,
[a]he blessed the people in the name of
the LORD of hosts.
19 Further, he distributed to all the
people, to all the multitude of Israel, both
to men and women, a cake of bread and

17 [a]1 Sam 29:1 [b]2 Sam 23:14; 1 Chr 11:16
18 [a]Gen 14:5; Josh 15:8; 17:15; 18:16
19 [a]1 Sam 23:2 [b]2 Sam 2:1
20 [1]Lit *David smote* [2]I.e. the master of breakthrough [a]1 Chr 14:11; Is 28:21
21 [a]1 Chr 14:12
22 [a]2 Sam 5:18
23 [1]Or *baka-shrubs* [a]2 Sam 5:19
24 [1]Or *baka-shrubs* [a]2 Kin 7:6 [b]Judg 4:14
25 [1]In 1 Chr 14:16, *Gibeon* [2]Lit *until you are coming to* [a]Is 28:21 [b]Josh 12:12; 21:21
6:1 [a]1 Chr 13:5-14
2 [1]I.e. Kiriath-jearim [2]Lit *sitting* [a]Josh 15:9, 10; 1 Sam 7:1 [b]Lev 24:16 [c]Ex 25:22
3 [1]Lit *caused to ride* [a]Num 7:4-9; 1 Sam 6:7
4 [a]1 Sam 7:1; 1 Chr 13:7
5 [1]Or *cypress* [a]1 Sam 18:6,7 [b]1 Chr 13:8
6 [a]1 Chr 13:9 [b]Num 4:15,19, 20
7 [1]Lit *the* [a]1 Sam 6:19
8 [1]Lit *the LORD broke through a breakthrough* [2]I.e. the breakthrough of Uzzah
9 [a]Ps 119:120; Luke 5:8
10 [a]1 Chr 26:4-8
11 [a]Gen 30:27; 39:5
12 [a]1 Chr 15:25-16:3 [b]1 Kin 8:1
13 [a]Num 4:15; Josh 3:3; 1 Chr 15:2,15 [b]1 Kin 8:5
14 [1]Lit *girded with* [a]Ex 15:20, 21; Judg 11:34 [b]Ex 19:6; 1 Sam 2:18,28
16 [a]2 Sam 3:14
17 [a]1 Chr 15:1; 2 Chr 1:4 [b]1 Kin 8:62-65
18 [a]1 Kin 8:14, 15

one of dates and one of raisins to each
one. Then all the people departed each to
his house.
20 ¶ But when David returned to bless
his household, Michal the daughter of
Saul came out to meet David and said,
"How the king of Israel distinguished
himself today! [a]He uncovered himself today in the eyes of his servants' maids as
one of the [b]foolish ones shamelessly uncovers himself!"
21 So David said to Michal, "[a]*It was*
before the LORD, who chose me above
your father and above all his house, to
appoint me ruler over the people of the
LORD, over Israel; therefore I will celebrate before the LORD.
22 "I will be more lightly esteemed
than this and will be humble in my own
eyes, but with the maids of whom you
have spoken, with them I will be distinguished."
23 Michal the daughter of Saul had no
child to the day of her death.

David Plans to Build a Temple

7 [a]Now it came about when the king
lived in his house, and the LORD had
given him rest on every side from all his
enemies,
2 that the king said to [a]Nathan the
prophet, "See now, I dwell in [b]a house of
cedar, but the ark of God [c]dwells within
tent curtains."
3 Nathan said to the king, "[a]Go, do
all that is in your mind, for the LORD is
with you."
4 ¶ But in the same night the word of
the LORD came to Nathan, saying,
5 "Go and say to My servant David,
'Thus says the LORD, "[a]Are you the one
who should build Me a house to dwell in?
6 "For [a]I have not dwelt in a house
since the day I brought up the sons of
Israel from Egypt, even to this day; but I
have been moving about [b]in a tent, even
in a [1]tabernacle.
7 "[a]Wherever I have gone with all the
sons of Israel, did I speak a word with one
of the tribes of Israel, [b]which I commanded to shepherd My people Israel,
saying, 'Why have you not built Me a
house of cedar?' " '

God's Covenant with David

8 "Now therefore, thus you shall say to
My servant David, 'Thus says the LORD of
hosts, "[a]I took you from the pasture,
from following the sheep, [b]to be ruler
over My people Israel.
9 "[a]I have been with you wherever
you have gone and [b]have cut off all your
enemies from before you; and I will make
you a great name, like the names of the
great men who are on the earth.
10 "I will also appoint a place for My
people Israel and [a]will plant them, that
they may live in their own place and not
be disturbed again, [b]nor will the [1]wick-
ed afflict them any more as formerly,
11 even [a]from the day that I commanded judges to be over My people Israel; and [b]I will give you rest from all your
enemies. The LORD also declares to you
that [c]the LORD will make a house for you.
12 "[a]When your days are complete and
you [b]lie down with your fathers, [c]I will
raise up your [1]descendant after you, who
will come forth from [2]you, and I will
establish his kingdom.
13 "[a]He shall build a house for My
name, and [b]I will establish the throne of
his kingdom forever.
14 "[a]I will be a father to him and he
will be a son to Me; [b]when he commits
iniquity, I will correct him with the rod
of men and the strokes of the sons of men,
15 but My lovingkindness shall not depart from him, [a]as I took *it* away from
Saul, whom I removed from before you.
16 "[a]Your house and your kingdom
shall endure before [1]Me forever; your
throne shall be established forever." ' "
17 In accordance with all these words
and all this vision, so Nathan spoke to
David.

David's Prayer

18 ¶ Then David the king went in and
sat before the LORD, and he said, "[a]Who
am I, O Lord [1]GOD, and what is my
house, that You have brought me
this far?
19 "And yet this was insignificant in
Your eyes, O Lord GOD, [a]for You have
spoken also of the house of Your servant
concerning the distant future. And [b]this
is the [1]custom of man, O Lord GOD.
20 "Again what more can David say to
You? For [a]You know Your servant,
O Lord GOD!
21 "[a]For the sake of Your word, and
according to Your own heart, You have
done all this greatness to let Your servant
know.
22 "For this reason [a]You are great,
O Lord GOD; for [b]there is none like You,
and there is no God besides You, [c]ac-
cording to all that we have heard with our
ears.
23 "And [a]what one nation on the earth
is like Your people Israel, whom God
went to redeem for Himself as a people
and to make a name for Himself, and [b]to
do a great thing for You and awesome
things for Your land, before [c]Your people
whom [d]You have redeemed for Yourself

20 [a]2 Sam 6:14, 16; Eccl 7:17 [b]Judg 9:4
21 [a]1 Sam 13:14; 15:28
7:1 [a]1 Chr 17:1-27
2 [a]2 Sam 7:17; 12:1; 1 Kin 1:22; 1 Chr 29:29; 2 Chr 9:29 [b]2 Sam 5:11 [c]Ex 26:1
3 [a]1 Kin 8:17, 18; 1 Chr 22:7
5 [a]1 Kin 5:3,4; 8:19
6 [1]Lit *dwelling place* [a]Josh 18:1; 1 Kin 8:16 [b]Ex 40:18,34
7 [a]Lev 26:11,12 [b]2 Sam 5:2
8 [a]1 Sam 16:11, 12; Ps 78:70,71 [b]2 Sam 6:21
9 [a]1 Sam 5:10 [b]Ps 18:37-42
10 [1]Lit *sons of wickedness* [a]Ex 15:17; Is 5:2,7 [b]Ps 89:22,23; Is 60:18
11 [a]Judg 2:14-16; 1 Sam 12:9-11 [b]2 Sam 7:1 [c]1 Sam 25:28; 2 Sam 7:27
12 [1]Lit *seed* [2]Lit *your bowels* [a]1 Kin 2:1 [b]Deut 31:16; Acts 13:36 [c]1 Kin 8:20; Ps 132:11
13 [a]1 Kin 6:12; 8:19 [b]Is 9:7; 49:8
14 [a]Ps 89:26, 27; 2 Cor 6:18; Heb 1:5 [b]1 Kin 11:34; Ps 89:30-33
15 [a]1 Sam 15:23; 16:14
16 [1]So with Gr and some ancient mss; M.T. *you* [a]2 Sam 7:13; Ps 89:36,37
18 [1]Heb *YHWH,* usually rendered *LORD,* and so through out the ch [a]Ex 3:11; 1 Sam 18:18
19 [1]Or *law* [a]2 Sam 7:11-16; 1 Chr 17:17 [b]Is 55:8,9
20 [a]1 Sam 16:7; John 21:17
21 [a]1 Chr 17:19; Eph 4:32
22 [a]Deut 3:24; Ps 48:1; 86:10 [b]Ex 15:11; 1 Sam 2:2 [c]Ex 10:2; Ps 44:1
23 [a]Deut 4:32-38 [b]Deut 10:21 [c]Deut 15:15 [d]Deut 9:26

from Egypt, *from* nations and their gods?
24 "For [a]You have established for Yourself Your people Israel as Your own people forever, and [b]You, O LORD, have become their God.
25 "Now therefore, O LORD God, the
word that You have spoken concerning
Your servant and his house, confirm *it*
forever, and do as You have spoken,
26 [a]that Your name may be magnified
forever, by saying, 'The LORD of hosts is
God over Israel'; and may the house of
Your servant David be established before You.
27 "For You, O LORD of hosts, the God
of Israel, have [1]made a revelation to Your
servant, saying, '[a]I will build you a
house'; therefore Your servant has found
[2]courage to pray this prayer to You.
28 "Now, O Lord GOD, You are God,
and [a]Your words are truth, and You have
[1]promised this good thing to Your servant.
29 "Now therefore, may it please You to
bless the house of Your servant, that it
may continue forever before You. For
You, O Lord GOD, have spoken; and
[a]with Your blessing may the house of
Your servant be blessed forever."

David's Triumphs

8 [a]Now after this it came about that
David [1]defeated the Philistines and
subdued them; and David took [2]control
of the chief city from the hand of the
Philistines.
2 ¶ [a]He [1]defeated [b]Moab, and measured them with the line, making them
lie down on the ground; and he measured
two lines to put to death and one full line
to keep alive. And [c]the Moabites became
servants to David, [d]bringing tribute.
3 ¶ Then David [1]defeated [a]Hadade-
zer, the son of Rehob king of Zobah, as
[b]he went to restore his [2]rule at the
[3]River.
4 David captured from him 1,700
horsemen and 20,000 foot soldiers; and
David [a]hamstrung the chariot horses,
but reserved *enough* of them for 100
chariots.
5 When [a]the Arameans of Damascus
came to help Hadadezer, king of Zobah,
David [1]killed 22,000 Arameans.
6 Then David put garrisons among
the Arameans of Damascus, and [a]the Arameans became servants to David, bringing tribute. And [b]the LORD helped David
wherever he went.
7 David took the shields of gold
which were [1]carried by the servants of
Hadadezer and brought them to Jerusalem.
8 From [1]Betah and from [a]Berothai,
cities of Hadadezer, King David took a
very large amount of bronze.
9 ¶ Now when Toi king of [a]Hamath
heard that David had [1]defeated all the
army of Hadadezer,
10 Toi sent [1]Joram his son to King David to [2]greet him and bless him, because
he had fought against Hadadezer and
[3]defeated him; for Hadadezer [4]had been
at war with Toi. And [5]*Joram* brought
with him articles of silver, of gold and of
bronze.
11 King David also [a]dedicated these
to the LORD, with the silver and gold that
he had dedicated from all the nations
which he had subdued:
12 from [1]Aram and [a]Moab and [b]the
sons of Ammon and [c]the Philistines and
[d]Amalek, and from the spoil of Hadadezer, son of Rehob, king of Zobah.
13 ¶ So [a]David made a name *for himself* when he returned from [1]killing
18,000 [2]Arameans in [b]the Valley of Salt.
14 He put garrisons in Edom. In all
Edom he put garrisons, and [a]all the
Edomites became servants to David. And
[b]the LORD helped David wherever he
went.
15 ¶ So David reigned over all Israel;
and David [1]administered justice and
righteousness for all his people.
16 [a]Joab the son of Zeruiah *was* over
the army, and [b]Jehoshaphat the son of
Ahilud *was* [c]recorder.
17 [a]Zadok the son of Ahitub and
Ahimelech the son of Abiathar *were*
[b]priests, and Seraiah *was* [c]secretary.
18 [a]Benaiah the son of Jehoiada [1]was
over the [b]Cherethites and the Pelethites;
and David's sons were [2c]chief ministers.

David's Kindness to Mephibosheth

9 Then David said, "Is there yet [1]any-
one left of the house of Saul, [a]that I
may show him kindness for Jonathan's
sake?"
2 Now there was a servant of the
house of Saul whose name was Ziba, and
they called him to David; and the king
said to him, "Are you [a]Ziba?" And he
said, "*I am* your servant."
3 The king said, "Is there not yet anyone of the house of Saul to whom I may
show the [a]kindness of God?" And Ziba
said to the king, "[b]There is still a son of
Jonathan who is crippled in both feet."
4 So the king said to him, "Where is
he?" And Ziba said to the king, "Behold,
he is [a]in the house of Machir the son of
Ammiel in Lo-debar."
5 Then King David sent and brought
him from the house of Machir the son of
Ammiel, from Lo-debar.

24 [a]Deut 32:6 [b]Gen 17:7,8; Ex 6:7
26 [a]Ps 72:18, 19; Matt 6:9
27 [1]Lit *uncovered the ear of* [2]Lit *his heart* [a]2 Sam 7:13
28 [1]Or *spoken* [a]Ex 34:6; John 17:17
29 [a]Num 6:24-26
8:1 [1]Lit *smote* [2]Lit *the bridle of the mother city* [a]1 Chr 18
2 [1]Lit *smote* [a]Num 24:17 [b]1 Sam 22:3,4 [c]2 Sam 8:6; 1 Kin 4:21 [d]2 Kin 3:4; 17:3
3 [1]Lit *smote* [2]Lit *hand* [3]I.e. Euphrates [a]1 Sam 14:47; 2 Sam 10:16,19 [b]2 Sam 10:15-19
4 [a]Josh 11:6,9
5 [1]Lit *smote* [a]1 Kin 11:23-25
6 [a]2 Sam 8:2 [b]2 Sam 3:18
7 [1]Lit *on*
8 [1]In 1 Chr 18:8, *Tibhath* [a]Ezek 47:16
9 [1]Lit *smitten* [a]1 Kin 8:65; 2 Chr 8:4
10 [1]In 1 Chr 18:10, *Hadoram* [2]Lit *ask him of his welfare* [3]Lit *smitten* [4]Lit *was a man of wars* [5]Lit *there were in his hand*
11 [a]1 Kin 7:51
12 [1]Some mss read *Edom* [a]2 Sam 8:2 [b]2 Sam 10:14 [c]2 Sam 5:17-25 [d]1 Sam 27:8; 30:17-20
13 [1]Lit *smiting* [2]Some mss read *Edom* [a]2 Sam 7:9 [b]2 Kin 14:7
14 [a]Gen 27:37-40; Num 24:17,18 [b]2 Sam 8:6
15 [1]Lit *was doing*
16 [a]1 Chr 11:6 [b]1 Kin 4:3 [c]2 Kin 18:18,37
17 [a]1 Chr 6:4-8 [b]1 Chr 16:39,40 [c]2 Kin 18:18
18 [1]Lit *and the Cherethites* [2]Lit *priests* [a]1 Kin 4:4 [b]1 Sam 30:14; 2 Sam 15:18; 20:7,23; 1 Kin 1:38,44 [c]1 Chr 18:17
9:1 [1]Lit *he who is* [a]1 Sam 20:14-17,42
2 [a]2 Sam 16:1-4; 19:17,29
3 [a]1 Sam 20:14 [b]2 Sam 4:4
4 [a]2 Sam 17:27-29

6 [a]Mephibosheth, the son of Jonathan the son of Saul, came to David and [b]fell on his face and prostrated himself. And David said, "Mephibosheth." And he said, "Here is your servant!"

7 David said to him, "Do not fear, for [a]I will surely show kindness to you for the sake of your father Jonathan, and [b]will restore to you all the [1]land of your [2]grandfather Saul; and [c]you shall [3]eat at my table regularly."

8 Again he prostrated himself and said, "What is your servant, that you should regard [a]a dead dog like me?"

9 ¶ Then the king called Saul's servant Ziba and said to him, "[a]All that belonged to Saul and to all his house I have given to your master's [1]grandson.

10 "You and your sons and your servants shall cultivate the land for him, and you shall bring in *the produce* so that your master's grandson may have food; nevertheless [a]Mephibosheth your master's grandson [b]shall [1]eat at my table regularly." Now Ziba had fifteen sons and twenty servants.

11 Then Ziba said to the king, "According [a]to all that my lord the king commands his servant so your servant will do." So Mephibosheth ate at [1]David's table as one of the king's sons.

12 Mephibosheth had a young son whose name was Mica. And all who lived in the house of Ziba were servants to Mephibosheth.

13 So Mephibosheth lived in Jerusalem, for [a]he ate at the king's table regularly. Now [b]he was lame in both feet.

Ammon and Aram Defeated

10 [a]Now it happened afterwards that [b]the king of the Ammonites died, and Hanun his son became king in his place.

2 Then David said, "I will show kindness to Hanun the son of [a]Nahash, just as his father showed kindness to me." So David sent [1]some of his servants to console him concerning his father. But when David's servants came to the land of the Ammonites,

3 the princes of the Ammonites said to Hanun their lord, "[1]Do you think that David is honoring your father because he has sent consolers to you? [a]Has David not sent his servants to you in order to search the city, to spy it out and overthrow it?"

4 So Hanun took David's servants and [a]shaved off half of their beards, and [b]cut off their garments in the middle as far as their hips, and sent them away.

5 When they told *it* to David, he sent to meet them, for the men were greatly humiliated. And the king said, "[1]Stay at Jericho until your beards grow, and *then* return."

6 ¶ Now when the sons of Ammon saw that [a]they had become odious to David, the sons of Ammon sent and [b]hired the Arameans of [c]Beth-rehob and the [d]Arameans of Zobah, 20,000 foot soldiers, and the king of [e]Maacah with 1,000 men, and the men of Tob with 12,000 men.

7 When David heard *of it,* he sent Joab and all the army, the mighty men.

8 The sons of Ammon came out and drew up in battle array [a]at the entrance of the [1]city, while the Arameans of Zobah and of Rehob and the men of [b]Tob and Maacah *were* by themselves in the field.

9 ¶ Now when Joab saw that [1]the battle was set against him in front and in the rear, he selected from all the choice men of Israel, and arrayed *them* against the Arameans.

10 But the remainder of the people he placed in the hand of Abishai his brother, and he arrayed *them* against the sons of Ammon.

11 He said, "If the Arameans are too strong for me, then you shall help me, but if the sons of Ammon are too strong for you, then I will come to help you.

12 "[a]Be strong, and let us show ourselves courageous for the sake of our people and for the cities of our God; and [b]may the LORD do what is good in His sight."

13 So Joab and the people who were with him drew near to the battle against the Arameans, and [a]they fled before him.

14 When the sons of Ammon saw that the Arameans fled, they *also* fled before Abishai and entered the city. [a]Then Joab returned from *fighting* against the sons of Ammon and came to Jerusalem.

15 ¶ When the Arameans saw that they had been [1]defeated by Israel, they gathered themselves together.

16 [a]And Hadadezer sent and brought out the Arameans who were beyond the [1]River, and they came to Helam; and [b]Shobach the commander of the army of Hadadezer [2]led them.

17 Now when it was told David, he gathered all Israel together and crossed the Jordan, and came to Helam. And the Arameans arrayed themselves to meet David and fought against him.

18 But the Arameans fled before Israel, and David killed [a]700 charioteers of the Arameans and 40,000 horsemen and

6 [a]2 Sam 16:4; 19:24-30 [b]1 Sam 25:23

7 [1]Lit *field* [2]Lit *father* [3]Lit *eat bread* [a]2 Sam 9:1,3 [b]2 Sam 12:8 [c]2 Sam 19:28; 1 Kin 2:7; 2 Kin 25:29

8 [a]2 Sam 16:9; 24:14

9 [1]Lit *son* [a]2 Sam 16:4; 19:29

10 [1]Lit *eat bread* [a]2 Sam 9:7,11,13 [b]2 Sam 19:28; 1 Kin 2:7

11 [1]Lit *my* [a]2 Sam 16:1-4; 19:24-30

13 [a]2 Sam 9:7, 11 [b]2 Sam 9:3

10:1 [a]1 Chr 19:1-19 [b]1 Sam 11:1

2 [1]Lit *by the hand of* [a]1 Sam 11:1

3 [1]Lit *In your eyes is David honoring* [a]Gen 42:9,16

4 [a]Is 15:2; Jer 41:5 [b]Is 20:4

5 [1]Lit *Return to*

6 [a]Gen 34:30; 1 Sam 27:12 [b]2 Sam 8:3,5; 2 Kin 7:6 [c]Judg 18:28 [d]2 Sam 8:3 [e]Deut 3:14

8 [1]Lit *gate* [a]1 Chr 19:9 [b]Judg 11:3,5

9 [1]Lit *the faces of the battle were against*

12 [a]Deut 31:6; Josh 1:6; 1 Cor 16:13 [b]1 Sam 3:18

13 [a]1 Kin 20:13-21

14 [a]2 Sam 11:1

15 [1]Lit *smitten before*

16 [1]I.e. Euphrates [2]Lit *before* [a]2 Sam 8:3-8 [b]1 Chr 19:16

18 [a]1 Chr 19:18

struck down Shobach the commander of their army, and he died there.

19 When all the kings, servants of Hadadezer, saw that they were [1]defeated by Israel, [a]they made peace with Israel and served them. So the Arameans feared to help the sons of Ammon anymore.

Bathsheba, David's Great Sin

11 [a]Then it happened [1b]in the spring, at the time when kings go out *to battle,* that David sent Joab and his servants with him and all Israel, and they destroyed the sons of Ammon and [c]besieged Rabbah. But David stayed at Jerusalem.

2 ¶ Now when evening came David arose from his bed and walked around on [a]the roof of the king's house, and from the roof he saw a woman bathing; and the woman was very beautiful in appearance.

3 So David sent and inquired about the woman. And one said, "Is this not [a]Bathsheba, the daughter of Eliam, the wife of [b]Uriah the Hittite?"

4 David sent messengers and took her, and when she came to him, [a]he lay with her; [b]and when she had purified herself from her uncleanness, she returned to her house.

5 The woman conceived; and she sent and told David, and said, "[a]I am pregnant."

6 ¶ Then David sent to Joab, *saying,* "Send me Uriah the Hittite." So Joab sent Uriah to David.

7 When Uriah came to him, [a]David asked concerning the welfare of Joab and [1]the people and the state of the war.

8 Then David said to Uriah, "Go down to your house, and [a]wash your feet." And Uriah went out of the king's house, and a present from the king [1]was sent out after him.

9 But Uriah slept [a]at the door of the king's house with all the servants of his lord, and did not go down to his house.

10 Now when they told David, saying, "Uriah did not go down to his house," David said to Uriah, "Have you not come from a journey? Why did you not go down to your house?"

11 Uriah said to David, "[a]The ark and Israel and Judah are staying in [1]temporary shelters, and my lord Joab and [b]the servants of my lord are camping in the open field. Shall I then go to my house to eat and to drink and to lie with my wife? By your life and the life of your soul, I will not do this thing."

12 Then David said to Uriah, "[a]Stay here today also, and tomorrow I will let you go." So Uriah remained in Jerusalem that day and the [1]next.

13 Now David called him, and he ate and drank before him, and he [a]made him drunk; and in the evening he went out to lie on his bed [b]with his lord's servants, but he did not go down to his house.

14 ¶ Now in the morning David [a]wrote a letter to Joab and sent *it* by the hand of Uriah.

15 [a]He had written in the letter, saying, "[1]Place Uriah in the front line of the [2]fiercest battle and withdraw from him, [b]so that he may be struck down and die."

16 So it was as Joab kept watch on the city, that he put Uriah at the place where he knew there *were* valiant men.

17 The men of the city went out and fought against Joab, and some of the people among David's servants fell; and [a]Uriah the Hittite also died.

18 Then Joab sent and reported to David all the events of the war.

19 He charged the messenger, saying, "When you have finished telling all the events of the war to the king,

20 and if it happens that the king's wrath rises and he says to you, 'Why did you go so near to the city to fight? Did you not know that they would shoot from the wall?

21 'Who [a]struck down Abimelech the son of Jerubbesheth? Did not a woman throw an upper millstone on him from the wall so that he died at Thebez? Why did you go so near the wall?'—then you shall say, 'Your servant Uriah the Hittite is dead also.' "

22 ¶ So the messenger departed and came and reported to David all that Joab had sent him *to tell.*

23 The messenger said to David, "The men prevailed against us and came out against us in the field, but we [1]pressed them as far as the entrance of the gate.

24 "Moreover, the archers shot at your servants from the wall; so some of the king's servants are dead, and your servant Uriah the Hittite is also dead."

25 Then David said to the messenger, "Thus you shall say to Joab, 'Do not let this thing [1]displease you, for the sword devours one as well as another; make your battle against the city stronger and overthrow it'; and *so* encourage him."

26 ¶ Now when the wife of Uriah heard that Uriah her husband was dead, [a]she mourned for her husband.

27 When the *time of* mourning was over, David sent and [1]brought her to his house and [a]she became his wife; then she bore him a son. But [b]the thing that David had done was evil in the sight of the LORD.

19 [1]Lit *smitten before* [a]2 Sam 8:6

11:1 [1]Lit *at the return of the year* [a]1 Chr 20:1 [b]2 Sam 10:14; 1 Kin 20:22,26 [c]2 Sam 12:26-29; Jer 49:2,3; Amos 1:14

2 [a]Deut 22:8; 1 Sam 9:25; Matt 24:17; Acts 10:9

3 [a]1 Chr 3:5 [b]2 Sam 23:39

4 [a]Ps 51: title; James 1:14,15 [b]Lev 12:2-5; 15:18-28; 18:19

5 [a]Lev 20:10; Deut 22:22

7 [1]Lit *welfare of* [a]Gen 37:14; 1 Sam 17:22

8 [1]Lit *went out* [a]Gen 43:24; Luke 7:44

9 [a]1 Kin 14:27, 28

11 [1]Or *booths* [a]2 Sam 7:2,6 [b]2 Sam 20:6

12 [1]Lit *morrow* [a]Job 20:12-14

13 [a]Prov 20:1; 23:29-35 [b]2 Sam 11:9

14 [a]1 Kin 21:8-10

15 [1]Lit *Give* [2]Lit *strong* [a]Eccl 8:11; Jer 17:9 [b]2 Sam 12:9

17 [a]2 Sam 11:21

21 [a]Judg 9:50-54

23 [1]Lit *were upon*

25 [1]Lit *be evil in your sight*

26 [a]Gen 50:10; Deut 34:8; 1 Sam 31:13

27 [1]Lit *gathered* [a]2 Sam 12:9 [b]Ps 51:4,5

Nathan Rebukes David

12 Then the LORD sent [a]Nathan to
David. And [b]he came to him and
[1]said,
"There were two men in one city,
the one rich and the other
poor.
2 "The rich man had a great many
flocks and herds.
3 "But the poor man had nothing
except [a]one little ewe lamb
Which he bought and nourished;
And it grew up together with
him and his children.
It would eat of his [1]bread and
drink of his cup and lie in
his bosom,
And was like a daughter to him.
4 "Now a traveler came to the rich
man,
And he [1]was unwilling to take
from his own flock or his
own herd,
To prepare for the wayfarer who
had come to him;
Rather he took the poor man's
ewe lamb and prepared it
for the man who had come
to him."
5 Then David's anger burned greatly
against the man, and he said to Nathan,
"As the LORD lives, surely the man who
has done this [1a]deserves to die.
6 "He must make restitution for the
lamb [a]fourfold, because he did this thing
and had no compassion."
7 ¶ Nathan then said to David,
"[a]You are the man! Thus says the LORD
God of Israel, '[b]It is I who anointed you
king over Israel and it is I who delivered
you from the hand of Saul.
8 'I also gave you [a]your master's
house and your master's wives into your
[1]care, and I gave you the house of Israel
and Judah; and if *that had been* too little,
I would have added to you many more
things like these!
9 'Why [a]have you despised the word
of the LORD by doing evil in His sight?
[b]You have struck down Uriah the Hittite
with the sword, [c]have taken his wife to
be your wife, and have killed him with
the sword of the sons of Ammon.
10 'Now therefore, [a]the sword shall
never depart from your house, because
you have despised Me and have taken the
wife of Uriah the Hittite to be your wife.'
11 "Thus says the LORD, 'Behold, I will
raise up evil against you from your own
household; [a]I will even take your wives
before your eyes and give *them* to your
companion, and he will lie with your
wives in [1]broad daylight.
12 'Indeed [a]you did it secretly, but [b]I
will do this thing before all Israel, and
[1]under the sun.' "
13 Then David said to Nathan, "[a]I
have sinned against the LORD." And Nathan said to David, "The LORD also has
[1b]taken away your sin; you shall not die.
14 "However, because by this deed you
have [a]given occasion to the enemies of
the LORD to blaspheme, the child also that
is born to you shall surely die."
15 So Nathan went to his house.

Loss of a Child

¶ Then the LORD struck the child that
Uriah's [1]widow bore to David, so that he
was *very* sick.
16 David therefore inquired of God for
the child; and David [a]fasted and went
and [b]lay all night on the ground.
17 [a]The elders of his household stood
beside him in order to raise him up from
the ground, but he was unwilling and
would not eat food with them.
18 Then it happened on the seventh
day that the child died. And the servants
of David were afraid to tell him that the
child was dead, for they said, "Behold,
while the child was *still* alive, we spoke
to him and he did not listen to our voice.
How then can we tell him that the child
is dead, since he might do *himself* harm!"
19 But when David saw that his servants were whispering together, David
perceived that the child was dead; so David said to his servants, "Is the child
dead?" And they said, "He is dead."
20 So David arose from the ground,
[a]washed, anointed *himself,* and changed
his clothes; and he came into the house
of the LORD and [b]worshiped. Then he
came to his own house, and when he
requested, they set food before him and
he ate.
21 ¶ Then his servants said to him,
"What is this thing that you have done?
[1]While the child was alive, you fasted
and wept; but when the child died, you
arose and ate food."
22 He said, "While the child was *still*
alive, [a]I fasted and wept; for I said,
'[b]Who knows, the LORD may be gracious
to me, that the child may live.'
23 "But now he has died; why should
I fast? Can I bring him back again? [a]I
will go to him, but [b]he will not return
to me."

Solomon Born

24 ¶ Then David comforted his wife
Bathsheba, and went in to her and lay
with her; and she gave birth to a son, and
[1a]he named him Solomon. Now the
LORD loved him

12:1 [1]Lit *said to him* [a]2 Sam 7:2, 4,17 [b]Ps 51: title
3 [1]Lit *morsel* [a]2 Sam 11:3
4 [1]Lit *spared*
5 [1]Lit *is a son of death* [a]1 Sam 26:16
6 [a]Ex 22:1; Luke 19:8
7 [a]1 Kin 20:42 [b]1 Sam 16:13
8 [1]Lit *bosom* [a]2 Sam 9:7
9 [a]1 Sam 15:23, 26 [b]2 Sam 11:14-17 [c]2 Sam 11:27
10 [a]2 Sam 13:28; 18:14; 1 Kin 2:25
11 [1]Lit *the sight of this sun* [a]Deut 28:30; 2 Sam 16:21,22
12 [1]Lit *before* [a]2 Sam 11:4-15 [b]2 Sam 16:22
13 [1]Lit *caused your sin to pass away* [a]1 Sam 15:24,30; 2 Sam 24:10; Luke 18:13 [b]Lev 20:10; 24:17; Prov 28:13; Mic 7:18
14 [a]Is 52:5; Rom 2:24
15 [1]Lit *wife*
16 [a]Neh 1:4 [b]2 Sam 13:31
17 [a]Gen 24:2
20 [a]Ruth 3:3; Matt 6:17 [b]Ps 95:6-8; 103:1, 8-17; Prov 3:7
21 [1]Lit *On account of*
22 [a]Is 38:1-3 [b]Jon 3:9
23 [a]Gen 37:35 [b]Job 7:8-10
24 [1]Some mss read *she* [a]1 Chr 22:9; Matt 1:6

25 and sent *word* through Nathan the prophet, and he named him [1]Jedidiah for the LORD'S sake.

War Again

26 ¶ [a]Now Joab fought against [b]Rabbah of the sons of Ammon and captured the royal city.

27 Joab sent messengers to David and said, "I have fought against Rabbah, I have even captured the city of waters.

28 "Now therefore, gather the rest of the people together and camp against the city and capture it, or I will capture the city myself and it will be named after me."

29 So David gathered all the people and went to Rabbah, fought against it and captured it.

30 Then [a]he took the crown of [1]their king from his head; and its weight *was* a talent of gold, and *in it* [2]*was* a precious stone; and it was *placed* on David's head. And he brought out the spoil of the city in great amounts.

31 He also brought out the people who were in it, and [a]set *them* under saws, sharp iron instruments, and iron axes, and made them pass through the brickkiln. And thus he did to all the cities of the sons of Ammon. Then David and all the people returned *to* Jerusalem.

Amnon and Tamar

13 Now it was after this that [a]Absalom the son of David had a beautiful sister whose name was [b]Tamar, and [c]Amnon the son of David loved her.

2 Amnon was so frustrated because of his sister Tamar that he made himself ill, for she was a virgin, and it seemed [1]hard to Amnon to do anything to her.

3 But Amnon had a friend whose name was Jonadab, the son of [1a]Shimeah, David's brother; and Jonadab was a very shrewd man.

4 He said to him, "O son of the king, why are you so depressed morning after morning? Will you not tell me?" Then Amnon said to him, "I am in love with Tamar, the sister of my brother Absalom."

5 Jonadab then said to him, "Lie down on your bed and pretend to be ill; when your father comes to see you, say to him, 'Please let my sister Tamar come and give me *some* food to eat, and let her prepare the food in my sight, that I may see *it* and eat from her hand.'"

6 So Amnon lay down and pretended to be ill; when the king came to see him, Amnon said to the king, "Please let my sister Tamar come and [a]make me a couple of cakes in my sight, that I may eat from her hand."

7 ¶ Then David sent to the house for Tamar, saying, "Go now to your brother Amnon's house, and prepare food for him."

8 So Tamar went to her brother Amnon's house, and he was lying down. And she took dough, kneaded *it,* made cakes in his sight, and baked the cakes.

9 She took the pan and [1]dished *them* out before him, but he refused to eat. And Amnon said, "[a]Have everyone go out from me." So everyone went out from him.

10 Then Amnon said to Tamar, "Bring the food into the [1]bedroom, that I may eat from your hand." So Tamar took the cakes which she had made and brought them into the bedroom to her brother Amnon.

11 When she brought *them* to him to eat, he [a]took hold of her and said to her, "Come, lie with me, my sister."

12 But she answered him, "No, my brother, do not violate me, for [a]such a thing is not done in Israel; do not do this [b]disgraceful thing!

13 "As for me, where could I [1]get rid of my reproach? And as for you, you will be like one of the [2]fools in Israel. Now therefore, please speak to the king, for [a]he will not withhold me from you."

14 However, he would not listen to [1]her; since he was stronger than she, he [a]violated her and lay with her.

15 ¶ Then Amnon hated her with a very great hatred; for the hatred with which he hated her was greater than the love with which he had loved her. And Amnon said to her, "Get up, go away!"

16 But she said to him, "No, because this wrong in sending me away is greater than the other that you have done to me!" Yet he would not listen to her.

17 Then he called his young man who attended him and said, "Now throw this woman out of my *presence,* and lock the door behind her."

18 Now she had on [a]a [1]long-sleeved garment; for in this manner the virgin daughters of the king dressed themselves in robes. Then his attendant took her out and locked the door behind her.

19 [a]Tamar put [1]ashes on her head and [b]tore her [2]long-sleeved garment which *was* on her; and [c]she put her hand on her head and went away, crying aloud as she went.

20 ¶ Then Absalom her brother said to her, "Has Amnon your brother been with you? But now keep silent, my sister, he is your brother; do not take this matter to

25 [1]I.e. beloved of the LORD

26 [a]1 Chr 20:1-3 [b]Deut 3:11

30 [1]Or *Malcam;* cf Zeph 1:5 [2]Or were *precious stones* [a]1 Chr 20:2

31 [a]1 Chr 20:3; Heb 11:37

13:1 [a]2 Sam 3:2,3; 1 Chr 3:2 [b]1 Chr 3:9 [c]2 Sam 3:2

2 [1]Lit *hard in Amnon's eyes*

3 [1]In 1 Sam 16:9, *Shammah;* in 1 Chr 2:13, *Shimea* [a]1 Sam 16:9

6 [a]Gen 18:6

9 [1]Lit *poured* [a]Gen 45:1

10 [1]Or *inner room*

11 [a]Gen 39:12

12 [a]Lev 20:17 [b]Judg 19:23; 20:6

13 [1]Lit *cause to go* [2]Or *disgraceful ones* [a]Gen 20:12

14 [1]Lit *her voice* [a]Lev 18:9; Deut 22:25; 27:22; 2 Sam 12:11

18 [1]Lit *a varicolored tunic* [a]Gen 37:3,23

19 [1]Or *dust* [2]Lit *varicolored tunic* [a]1 Sam 4:12; Esth 4:1 [b]Gen 37:29; 2 Sam 1:11 [c]Jer 2:37

heart." So Tamar remained and was desolate in her brother Absalom's house.
21 Now when King David heard of all
these matters, he was very angry.
22 But Absalom did not speak to Amnon [a]either good or bad; for [b]Absalom
hated Amnon because he had violated his
sister Tamar.
23 ¶ Now it came about after two full
years that Absalom [a]had sheepshearers
in Baal-hazor, which is near Ephraim,
and Absalom invited all the king's sons.

Absalom Avenges Tamar

24 Absalom came to the king and said,
"Behold now, your servant has sheepshearers; please let the king and his servants go with your servant."
25 But the king said to Absalom, "No,
my son, we should not all go, for we will
be burdensome to you." Although he
[1]urged him, he would not go, but blessed
him.
26 Then [a]Absalom said, "If not,
please let my brother Amnon go with us."
And the king said to him, "Why should
he go with you?"
27 But when Absalom [1]urged him, he
let Amnon and all the king's sons go with
him.
28 ¶ Absalom commanded his servants, saying, "See now, [a]when Amnon's heart is merry with wine, and
when I say to you, 'Strike Amnon,' then
put him to death. Do not fear; have not I
myself commanded you? Be courageous
and be [1]valiant."
29 The servants of Absalom did to Amnon just as Absalom had commanded.
Then all the king's sons arose and each
mounted [a]his mule and fled.
30 ¶ Now it was while they were on
the way that the report came to David,
saying, "Absalom has struck down all the
king's sons, and not one of them is left."
31 Then the king arose, [a]tore his
clothes and [b]lay on the ground; and all
his servants were standing by with
clothes torn.
32 [a]Jonadab, the son of Shimeah, David's brother, [1]responded, "Do not let
my lord [2]suppose they have put to death
all the young men, the king's sons, for
Amnon alone is dead; because by the [3]in-
tent of Absalom this has been determined
since the day that he violated his sister
Tamar.
33 "Now therefore, do not let my lord
the king [a]take the report to [1]heart,
namely, 'all the king's sons are dead,' for
only Amnon is dead."
34 ¶ Now [a]Absalom had fled. And
[b]the young man who was the watchman
raised his eyes and looked, and behold,
many people were coming from the road
behind him by the side of the mountain.
35 Jonadab said to the king, "Behold,
the king's sons have come; according to
your servant's word, so it happened."
36 As soon as he had finished speaking, behold, the king's sons came and lifted their voices and wept; and also the
king and all his servants wept [1]very bitterly.
37 ¶ Now [a]Absalom fled and went to
[b]Talmai the son of Ammihud, the king of
[c]Geshur. And *David* mourned for his son
every day.
38 [a]So Absalom had fled and gone to
Geshur, and was there three years.
39 *The heart of* King David longed to
go out to Absalom; for [a]he was comforted concerning Amnon, since he was
dead.

The Woman of Tekoa

14 Now Joab the son of Zeruiah perceived that [a]the king's heart *was*
inclined toward Absalom.
2 So Joab sent to [a]Tekoa and
[1]brought a wise woman from there and
said to her, "Please pretend to be a
mourner, and put on mourning garments
now, and do not [b]anoint yourself with
oil, but be like a woman who has been
mourning for the dead many days;
3 then go to the king and speak to
him in this manner." So Joab put [a]the
words in her mouth.
4 ¶ Now when the woman of Tekoa
[1]spoke to the king, she fell on her face to
the ground and [a]prostrated herself and
said, "[b]Help, O king."
5 The king said to her, "What is your
trouble?" And she [1]answered, "Truly I
am a widow, for my husband is dead.
6 "Your maidservant had two sons,
but the two of them struggled together in
the field, and there was no [1]one to separate them, so one struck the other and
killed him.
7 "Now behold, [a]the whole family has
risen against your maidservant, and they
say, 'Hand over the one who struck his
brother, that we may put him to death for
the life of his brother whom he killed,
[b]and destroy the heir also.' Thus they
will extinguish my coal which is left, so
as to [1]leave my husband neither name nor
remnant on the face of the earth."
8 ¶ Then the king said to the woman,
"Go to your house, and I will give orders
concerning you."
9 The woman of Tekoa said to the
king, "O my lord, the king, [a]the iniquity
is on me and my father's house, but [b]the
king and his throne are guiltless."
10 So the king said, "Whoever speaks

22 [a]Gen 31:24 [b]Lev 19:17; 1 John 2:9,11; 3:10,12,15
23 [a]1 Sam 25:7
25 [1]Lit *broke through*
26 [a]2 Sam 3:27; 11:13-15
27 [1]Lit *broke through*
28 [1]Lit *sons of valor* [a]Judg 19:6, 9,22; 1 Sam 25:36-38
29 [a]2 Sam 18:9; 1 Kin 1:33,38
31 [a]2 Sam 1:11 [b]2 Sam 12:16
32 [1]Lit *answered and said* [2]Lit *say* [3]Lit *mouth* [a]2 Sam 13:3-5
33 [1]Lit *his heart* [a]2 Sam 19:19
34 [a]2 Sam 13:37,38 [b]2 Sam 18:24
36 [1]Lit *with a very great weeping*
37 [a]2 Sam 13:34 [b]2 Sam 3:3 [c]2 Sam 14:23,32
38 [a]2 Sam 13:34
39 [a]2 Sam 12:19-23
14:1 [a]2 Sam 13:39
2 [1]Lit *took* [a]2 Sam 23:26; 2 Chr 11:6; Amos 1:1 [b]2 Sam 12:20
3 [a]2 Sam 14:19
4 [1]Many mss and ancient versions read *came* [a]1 Sam 25:23 [b]2 Kin 6:26-28
5 [1]Lit *said*
6 [1]Lit *deliverer between*
7 [1]Lit *set* [a]Num 35:19; Deut 19:12,13 [b]Matt 21:38
9 [a]Gen 43:9; 1 Sam 25:24 [b]1 Kin 2:33

to you, bring him to me, and he will not touch you anymore."

11 Then she said, "Please let the king remember the LORD your God, [a]*so that* the avenger of blood will not continue to destroy, otherwise they will destroy my son." And he said, "[b]As the LORD lives, not one hair of your son shall fall to the ground."

12 ¶ Then the woman said, "Please let your maidservant speak a word to my lord the king." And he said, "Speak."

13 The woman said, "[a]Why then have you planned such a thing against the people of God? For in speaking this word the king is as one who is guilty, *in that* the king does not bring back [b]his banished one.

14 "For [a]we will surely die and are [b]like water spilled on the ground which cannot be gathered up again. Yet God does not take away life, but plans [1]ways so that [c]the banished one will not be cast out from him.

15 "Now [1]the reason I have come to speak this word to my lord the king is that the people have made me afraid; so your maidservant said, 'Let me now speak to the king, perhaps the king will perform the [2]request of his maidservant.

16 'For the king will hear [1]and deliver his maidservant from the [2]hand of the man who would destroy [3]both me and my son from [a]the inheritance of God.'

17 "Then your maidservant said, 'Please let the word of my lord the king be [1]comforting, for as [a]the angel of God, so is my lord the king to discern good and evil. And may the LORD your God be with you.' "

18 ¶ Then the king answered and said to the woman, "Please do not hide anything from me that I am about to ask you." And the woman said, "Let my lord the king please speak."

19 So the king said, "Is the hand of Joab with you in all this?" And the woman replied, "As your soul lives, my lord the king, no one can turn to the right or to the left from anything that my lord the king has spoken. Indeed, it was [a]your servant Joab who commanded me, and it was he who put all these words in the mouth of your maidservant;

20 in order to change the appearance of things your servant Joab has done this thing. But my lord is wise, [a]like the wisdom of the angel of God, to know all that is in the earth."

Absalom Is Recalled

21 ¶ Then the king said to Joab, "Behold now, [a]I will surely do this thing; go therefore, bring back the young man Absalom."

22 Joab fell on his face to the ground, prostrated himself and blessed the king; then Joab said, "Today your servant knows that I have found favor in your sight, O my lord, the king, in that the king has performed the [1]request of his servant."

23 So Joab arose and went to [a]Geshur and brought Absalom to Jerusalem.

24 However the king said, "Let him turn to [a]his own house, and let him not see my face." So Absalom turned to his own house and did not see the king's face.

25 ¶ Now in all Israel was no one as handsome as Absalom, so highly praised; [a]from the sole of his foot to the crown of his head there was no defect in him.

26 When he [a]cut the hair of his head (and it was at the end of every year that he cut *it,* for it was heavy on him so he cut it), he weighed the hair of his head at 200 shekels by the king's weight.

27 [a]To Absalom there were born three sons, and one daughter whose name was [b]Tamar; she was a woman of beautiful appearance.

28 ¶ Now Absalom lived two full years in Jerusalem, [a]and did not see the king's face.

29 Then Absalom sent for Joab, to send him to the king, but he would not come to him. So he sent again a second time, but he would not come.

30 Therefore he said to his servants, "See, [a]Joab's [1]field is next to mine, and he has barley there; go and set it on fire." So Absalom's servants set the [1]field on fire.

31 Then Joab arose, came to Absalom at his house and said to him, "Why have your servants set my [1]field on fire?"

32 Absalom [1]answered Joab, "Behold, I sent for you, saying, 'Come here, that I may send you to the king, to say, "Why have I come from Geshur? It would be better for me still to be there." ' Now therefore, let me see the king's face, [a]and if there is iniquity in me, let him put me to death."

33 So when Joab came to the king and told him, he called for Absalom. Thus he came to the king and prostrated himself on his face to the ground before the king, and [a]the king kissed Absalom.

Absalom's Conspiracy

15 Now it came about after this that [a]Absalom provided for himself a chariot and horses and fifty men as runners before him.

2 Absalom used to rise early and

11 [a]Num 35:19, 21; Deut 19:4-10 [b]1 Sam 14:45; 1 Kin 1:52; Matt 10:30
13 [a]2 Sam 12:7; 1 Kin 20:40-42 [b]2 Sam 13:37,38
14 [1]Lit *devices* [a]Job 30:23; 34:15; Heb 9:27 [b]Ps 58:7 [c]Num 35:15,25,28
15 [1]Lit *that* [2]Lit *word*
16 [1]Lit *to* [2]Lit *palm* [3]Lit *together* [a]Deut 32:9; 1 Sam 26:19
17 [1]Lit *for rest* [a]1 Sam 29:9; 2 Sam 14:20; 19:27
19 [a]2 Sam 14:3
20 [a]2 Sam 14:17; 19:27
21 [a]2 Sam 14:11
22 [1]Lit *word*
23 [a]Deut 3:14; 2 Sam 13:37,38
24 [a]2 Sam 13:20
25 [a]Deut 28:35; Job 2:7; Is 1:6
26 [a]Ezek 44:20
27 [a]2 Sam 18:18 [b]2 Sam 13:1
28 [a]2 Sam 14:24
30 [1]Lit *portion* [a]Judg 15:3-5
31 [1]Lit *portion*
32 [1]Lit *said to* [a]1 Sam 20:8; Prov 28:13
33 [a]Gen 33:4; Luke 15:20
15:1 [a]1 Kin 1:5

[a]stand beside the way to the gate; and
when any man had a suit to come to the
king for judgment, Absalom would call to
him and say, "From what city are you?"
And he would say, "Your servant is from
one of the tribes of Israel."
3 Then Absalom would say to him,
"See, [a]your [1]claims are good and right,
but no man listens to you on the part of
the king."
4 Moreover, Absalom would say,
"[a]Oh that one would appoint me judge
in the land, then every man who has any
suit or cause could come to me and I
would give him justice."
5 And when a man came near to prostrate himself before him, he would put
out his hand and take hold of him and
[a]kiss him.
6 In this manner Absalom dealt with
all Israel who came to the king for judgment; [a]so Absalom stole away the hearts
of the men of Israel.
7 ¶ Now it came about at the end
of [1]forty years that Absalom said to the
king, "Please let me go and pay my vow
which I have vowed to the LORD, in [a]He-
bron.
8 "For your servant [a]vowed a vow
while I was living at Geshur in Aram,
saying, '[b]If the LORD shall indeed bring
me back to Jerusalem, then I will serve
the LORD.'"
9 The king said to him, "Go in
peace." So he arose and went to Hebron.
10 But Absalom sent spies throughout
all the tribes of Israel, saying, "As soon as
you hear the sound of the trumpet, then
you shall say, '[a]Absalom is king in Hebron.'"
11 Then two hundred men went with
Absalom from Jerusalem, [a]who were invited and [b]went [1]innocently, and they
did not know anything.
12 And Absalom sent for [a]Ahithophel
the Gilonite, David's counselor, from his
city [b]Giloh, while he was offering the
sacrifices. And the conspiracy was strong,
for [c]the people increased continually
with Absalom.

David Flees Jerusalem

13 ¶ Then a messenger came to David,
saying, "[a]The hearts of the men of Israel
are [1]with Absalom."
14 David said to all his servants who
were with him at Jerusalem, "[a]Arise and
let us flee, for *otherwise* none of us will
escape from Absalom. Go in haste, or he
will overtake us quickly and bring down
calamity on us and strike the city with the
edge of the sword."
15 Then the king's servants said to the
king, "Behold, your servants *are ready to*
do whatever my lord the king chooses."
16 So the king went out and all his
household [1]with him. But [a]the king left
ten concubines to keep the house.
17 The king went out and all the people [1]with him, and they stopped at the
last house.
18 Now all his servants passed on beside him, [a]all the Cherethites, all the Pelethites and all the Gittites, [b]six hundred
men who had come [1]with him from
Gath, passed on before the king.
19 ¶ Then the king said to [a]Ittai the
Gittite, "Why will you also go with us?
Return and remain with the king, for you
are a foreigner and also an exile; *return* to
your own place.
20 "You came *only* yesterday, and shall
I today make you wander with us, while
[a]I go where I will? Return and take back
your brothers; [b]mercy and [1]truth be
with you."
21 But Ittai answered the king and
said, "As the LORD lives, and as my lord
the king lives, surely [a]wherever my lord
the king may be, whether for death or for
life, there also your servant will be."
22 Therefore David said to Ittai, "Go
and pass over." So Ittai the Gittite passed
over with all his men and all the little
ones who *were* with him.
23 While all the country was weeping
with a loud voice, all the people passed
over. The king also passed over [a]the
brook Kidron, and all the people passed
over toward [b]the way of the wilderness.
24 ¶ Now behold, [a]Zadok also *came,*
and all the Levites with him [b]carrying
the ark of the covenant of God. And they
set down the ark of God, and [c]Abiathar
came up until all the people had finished
passing from the city.
25 The king said to Zadok, "Return the
ark of God to the city. If I find favor in the
sight of the LORD, then [a]He will bring me
back again and show me both it and [b]His
habitation.
26 "But if He should say thus, '[a]I have
no delight in you,' behold, here I am, [b]let
Him do to me as seems good [1]to Him."
27 The king said also to Zadok the
priest, "Are you *not* [a]a seer? Return to
the city in peace and your [b]two sons with
you, your son Ahimaaz and Jonathan the
son of Abiathar.
28 "See, I am going to wait [a]at the
fords of the wilderness until word comes
from you to inform me."
29 Therefore Zadok and Abiathar returned the ark of God to Jerusalem and
remained there.
30 ¶ And David went up the ascent of
the *Mount of* Olives, and wept as he
went, and [a]his head was covered and he

2 [a]Ruth 4:1; 2 Sam 19:8
3 [1]Lit *words* [a]Prov 12:2
4 [a]Judg 9:29
5 [a]2 Sam 14:33; 20:9
6 [a]Rom 16:18
7 [1]Some ancient versions render *four* [a]2 Sam 3:2, 3
8 [a]2 Sam 13:37, 38 [b]Gen 28:20, 21
10 [a]1 Kin 1:34; 2 Kin 9:13
11 [1]Lit *in their integrity* [a]1 Sam 9:13 [b]1 Sam 22:15
12 [a]2 Sam 15:31 [b]Josh 15:51 [c]Ps 3:1
13 [1]Lit *after* [a]Judg 9:3; 2 Sam 15:6
14 [a]2 Sam 12:11; Ps 3: title
16 [1]Lit *at his feet* [a]2 Sam 16:21,22
17 [1]Lit *at his feet*
18 [1]Lit *at his feet* [a]2 Sam 8:18 [b]1 Sam 23:13; 25:13; 30:1,9
19 [a]2 Sam 18:2
20 [1]Or *faithfulness* [a]1 Sam 23:13 [b]2 Sam 2:6
21 [a]Ruth 1:16, 17; Prov 17:17
23 [a]1 Kin 15:13; 2 Chr 29:16 [b]2 Sam 15:28; 16:2
24 [a]2 Sam 8:17; 20:25 [b]Num 4:15; 1 Sam 4:4, 5 [c]1 Sam 22:20
25 [a]Ps 43:3 [b]Ex 15:13; Jer 25:30
26 [1]Lit *in His sight* [a]2 Sam 11:27; 1 Chr 21:7 [b]1 Sam 3:18
27 [a]1 Sam 9:6-9 [b]2 Sam 17:17
28 [a]Josh 5:10; 2 Sam 17:16
30 [a]Esth 6:12; Ezek 24:17,23

walked [b]barefoot. Then all the people
who were with him each covered his
head and went up weeping as they went.
31 Now someone told David, saying,
"[a]Ahithophel is among the conspirators
with Absalom." And David said,
"O LORD, I pray, [b]make the counsel of
Ahithophel foolishness."
32 ¶ It happened as David was coming
to the summit, where God was worshiped, that behold, Hushai the [a]Archite
met him with his [1]coat torn and [2]dust
on his head.
33 David said to him, "If you pass over
with me, then you will be [a]a burden
to me.
34 "But if you return to the city, and
[a]say to Absalom, 'I will be your servant,
O king; as I have been your father's servant in time past, so I will now be your
servant,' then you can thwart the counsel
of Ahithophel for me.
35 "Are not Zadok and Abiathar the
priests with you there? So it shall be that
[a]whatever you hear from the king's
house, you shall report to Zadok and Abiathar the priests.
36 "Behold [a]their two sons are with
them there, Ahimaaz, Zadok's son and
Jonathan, Abiathar's son; and [b]by them
you shall send me everything that you
hear."
37 So Hushai, [a]David's friend, came
into the city, and [b]Absalom came into
Jerusalem.

Ziba, a False Servant

16 Now when David had passed [a]a
little beyond the summit, behold,
[b]Ziba the servant of Mephibosheth met
him [c]with a couple of saddled donkeys,
and on them *were* two hundred loaves of
bread, a hundred clusters of raisins, a
hundred summer fruits, and a jug of
wine.
2 The king said to Ziba, "Why do you
have these?" And Ziba said, "[a]The donkeys are for the king's household to ride,
and the bread and summer fruit for the
young men to eat, and the wine, [b]for
whoever is faint in the wilderness to
drink."
3 Then the king said, "And where is
[a]your master's son?" And [b]Ziba said to
the king, "Behold, he is staying in Jerusalem, for he said, 'Today the house of Israel will restore the kingdom of my father
to me.' "
4 So the king said to Ziba, "Behold,
all that belongs to Mephibosheth is
yours." And Ziba said, "I prostrate myself; let me find favor in your sight, O my
lord, the king!"

David Is Cursed

5 ¶ When King David came to [a]Ba-
hurim, behold, there came out from there
a man of the family of the house of Saul
[b]whose name was Shimei, the son of
Gera; he came out [c]cursing continually
as he came.
6 He threw stones at David and at all
the servants of King David; and all the
people and all the mighty men were at his
right hand and at his left.
7 Thus Shimei said when he cursed,
"Get out, get out, [a]you man of bloodshed, and worthless fellow!
8 "[a]The LORD has returned upon you
all [b]the bloodshed of the house of Saul, in
whose place you have reigned; and the
LORD has given the kingdom into the
hand of your son Absalom. And behold,
you are *taken* in your own evil, for you
are a man of bloodshed!"
9 ¶ Then [a]Abishai the son of Zeruiah
said to the king, "Why should [b]this dead
dog [c]curse my lord the king? Let me go
over now and [1]cut off his head."
10 But the king said, "[a]What have I to
do with you, O sons of Zeruiah? [b]If he
curses, and if the LORD has told him,
'Curse David,' [c]then who shall say, 'Why
have you done so?' "
11 Then David said to Abishai and to
all his servants, "Behold, [a]my son who
came out from [1]me seeks my life; how
much more now this Benjamite? Let him
alone and let him curse, [b]for the LORD
has told him.
12 "Perhaps the LORD will look on my
affliction and [1a]return good to me instead of his cursing this day."
13 So David and his men went on the
way; and Shimei went along on the hill-
side parallel with him and as he went he
cursed and cast stones and threw dust at
him.
14 The king and all the people who
were with him arrived weary and he refreshed himself there.

Absalom Enters Jerusalem

15 ¶ [a]Then Absalom and all the people, the men of Israel, entered Jerusalem,
and Ahithophel with him.
16 Now it came about when [a]Hushai
the Archite, David's friend, came to Absalom, that [b]Hushai said to Absalom,
"[c]*Long* live the king! *Long* live the king!"
17 Absalom said to Hushai, "Is this
your [1]loyalty to your friend? [a]Why did
you not go with your friend?"
18 Then Hushai said to Absalom, "No!
For whom the LORD, this people, and all
the men of Israel have chosen, his I will
be, and with him I will remain.

---

30 [b]Is 20:2-4
31 [a]2 Sam 15:12 [b]2 Sam 16:23; 17:14,23
32 [1]Or *tunic* [2]Lit *ground* [a]Josh 16:2
33 [a]2 Sam 19:35
34 [a]2 Sam 16:19
35 [a]2 Sam 17:15,16
36 [a]2 Sam 15:27 [b]2 Sam 17:17
37 [a]2 Sam 16:16; 1 Chr 27:33 [b]2 Sam 16:15
16:1 [a]2 Sam 15:32 [b]2 Sam 9:2-13 [c]1 Sam 25:18
2 [a]Judg 10:4 [b]2 Sam 17:29
3 [a]2 Sam 9:9,10 [b]2 Sam 19:26,27
5 [a]2 Sam 3:16; 17:18 [b]2 Sam 19:16-23; 1 Kin 2:8,9,44 [c]Ex 22:28; 1 Sam 17:43
7 [a]2 Sam 12:9
8 [a]2 Sam 21:1-9 [b]2 Sam 1:16; 3:28,29; 4:11,12
9 [1]Lit *take off* [a]1 Sam 26:8; 2 Sam 19:21; Luke 9:54 [b]2 Sam 9:8 [c]Ex 22:28
10 [a]2 Sam 3:39; 19:22 [b]John 18:11 [c]Rom 9:20
11 [1]Lit *my body* [a]2 Sam 12:11 [b]Gen 45:5; 1 Sam 26:19
12 [1]Lit *the LORD will return* [a]Deut 23:5; Rom 8:28
15 [a]2 Sam 15:12,37
16 [a]2 Sam 15:37 [b]2 Sam 15:34 [c]1 Sam 10:24; 2 Kin 11:12
17 [1]Or *kindness* [a]2 Sam 19:25

19 "Besides, [a]whom should I serve?
Should I not *serve* in the presence of his
son? As I have served in your father's
presence, so I will be in your presence."
20 ¶ Then Absalom said to Ahithophel, "Give your advice. What shall
we do?"
21 Ahithophel said to Absalom, "[a]Go
in to your father's concubines, whom he
has left to keep the house; then all Israel
will hear that you have made yourself odious to your father. The hands of all who
are with you will also be strengthened."
22 So they pitched a tent for Absalom
on the roof, [a]and Absalom went in to his
father's concubines [b]in the sight of all
Israel.
23 [a]The advice of Ahithophel, which
he [1]gave in those days, *was* as if one
inquired of the word of God; [b]so was all
the advice of Ahithophel *regarded* by
both David and Absalom.

Hushai's Counsel

17 Furthermore, Ahithophel said to
Absalom, "Please let me choose
12,000 men that I may arise and pursue
David tonight.
2 "[a]I will come upon him while he is
weary and [1]exhausted and terrify him, so
that all the people who are with him will
flee. Then [b]I will strike down the king
alone,
3 and I will bring back all the people
to you. [1]The return of everyone depends
on the man you seek; *then* all the people
will be at [a]peace."
4 So the [1]plan pleased Absalom and
all the elders of Israel.
5 ¶ Then Absalom said, "Now call
[a]Hushai the Archite also, and let us hear
what [1]he has to say."
6 When Hushai had come to Absalom, Absalom said to [1]him, "Ahithophel
has spoken [2]thus. Shall we [3]carry out
his plan? If not, you speak."
7 So Hushai said to Absalom, "[a]This
time the advice that Ahithophel has [1]giv-
en is not good."
8 Moreover, Hushai said, "You know
your father and his men, that they are
mighty men and they are [1]fierce, [a]like a
bear robbed of her cubs in the field. And
your father is an [2]expert in warfare, and
will not spend the night with the people.
9 "Behold, he has now hidden himself
in one of the [1]caves or in another place;
and it will be [2]when he falls on them at
the first attack, that whoever hears *it* will
say, 'There has been a slaughter among
the people who follow Absalom.'
10 "And even the one who is valiant,
whose heart is like the heart of a lion,
will completely [1]lose heart; for all Israel knows that your father is a mighty man
and those who are with him are valiant
men.
11 "But I counsel that all Israel be surely gathered to you, [a]from Dan even to
Beersheba, [b]as the sand that is by the sea
in abundance, and that [1]you personally
go into battle.
12 "So we shall come to him in one of
the places where he can be found, and we
will [1]fall on him [a]as the dew falls on the
ground; and of him and of all the men
who are with him, not even one will be
left.
13 "If he withdraws into a city, then all
Israel shall bring ropes to that city, and
we will [a]drag it into the [1]valley until not
even a small stone is found there."
14 Then Absalom and all the men of
Israel said, "The counsel of Hushai the
Archite is better than the counsel of
Ahithophel." For [a]the LORD had ordained to thwart the good counsel of
Ahithophel, so that the LORD might bring
calamity on Absalom.

Hushai's Warning Saves David

15 ¶ Then [a]Hushai said to Zadok and
to Abiathar the priests, "[1]This is what
Ahithophel counseled Absalom and the
elders of Israel, and [1]this is what I have
counseled.
16 "Now therefore, send quickly and
tell David, saying, '[a]Do not spend the
night at the fords of the wilderness, but
by all means cross over, or else the king
and all the people who are with him will
be [1]destroyed.' "
17 [a]Now Jonathan and Ahimaaz were
staying at [b]En-rogel, and a maidservant
would go and tell them, and they would
go and tell King David, for they could not
be seen entering the city.
18 But a lad did see them and told Absalom; so the two of them departed quickly and came to the house of a man [a]in
Bahurim, who had a well in his courtyard, and they went down [1]into it.
19 And [a]the woman [1]took a covering
and spread it over the well's mouth and
scattered grain on it, so that nothing was
known.
20 Then Absalom's servants came to
the woman at the house and said,
"Where are Ahimaaz and Jonathan?" And
[a]the woman said to them, "They have
crossed the brook of water." And when
they searched and could not find *them,*
they returned to Jerusalem.
21 ¶ It came about after they had departed that they came up out of the well
and went and told King David; and they
said to David, "[a]Arise and cross over the

19 [a]2 Sam 15:34
21 [a]2 Sam 15:16; 20:3
22 [a]2 Sam 15:16; 20:3 [b]2 Sam 12:11,12
23 [1]Lit *advised* [a]2 Sam 17:14,23 [b]2 Sam 15:12
17:2 [1]Lit *slack of hands* [a]2 Sam 16:14 [b]1 Kin 22:31
3 [1]Lit *Like the return of the whole is the man whom you seek* [a]Jer 6:14
4 [1]Lit *word was pleasing in the sight of*
5 [1]Lit *is in his mouth—even he* [a]2 Sam 15:32-34
6 [1]Lit *him, saying* [2]Lit *according to this word* [3]Lit *do his word*
7 [1]Lit *advised* [a]2 Sam 16:21
8 [1]Lit *bitter of soul* [2]Lit *man of war* [a]Hos 13:8
9 [1]Lit *pits* [2]Lit *according to a falling among them*
10 [1]Lit *melt* [a]Josh 2:9-11
11 [1]Lit *your face go* [a]1 Sam 3:20 [b]Gen 22:17; 1 Sam 13:5
12 [1]Lit *settle down* [a]Ps 110:3; Mic 5:7
13 [1]Or *wadi* [a]Mic 1:6
14 [a]2 Sam 15:31,34; Ps 9:15,16
15 [1]Lit *Thus and thus* [a]2 Sam 15:35,36
16 [1]Lit *swallowed up* [a]2 Sam 15:28
17 [a]2 Sam 15:27,36 [b]Josh 15:7; 18:16
18 [1]Lit *there* [a]2 Sam 3:16; 16:5
19 [1]Lit *took and spread the covering* [a]Josh 2:4-6
20 [a]Lev 19:11; Josh 2:3-5; 1 Sam 19:12-17
21 [a]2 Sam 17:15,16

water quickly for thus Ahithophel has
counseled against you."
22 Then David and all the people who
were with him arose and crossed the Jordan; and by [1]dawn not even one remained who had not crossed the Jordan.
23 ¶ Now when Ahithophel saw that
his counsel was not [1]followed, he [2]sad-
dled *his* donkey and arose and went to his
home, to [a]his city, and [3b]set his house
in order, and [c]strangled himself; thus he
died and was buried in the grave of his
father.
24 ¶ Then David came to [a]Mahanaim.
And Absalom crossed the Jordan, he and
all the men of Israel with him.
25 Absalom set [a]Amasa over the army
in place of Joab. Now Amasa was the son
of a man whose name was [1]Ithra the
Israelite, who went in to Abigail the
daughter of [b]Nahash, sister of Zeruiah,
Joab's mother.
26 And Israel and Absalom camped in
the land of Gilead.
27 ¶ Now when David had come to
Mahanaim, Shobi [a]the son of Nahash
from [b]Rabbah of the sons of Ammon,
[c]Machir the son of Ammiel from Lo-
debar, and [d]Barzillai the Gileadite from
Rogelim,
28 brought [a]beds, basins, pottery,
wheat, barley, flour, parched *grain*,
beans, lentils, parched *seeds*,
29 honey, curds, sheep, and cheese of
the herd, for David and for the people
who *were* with him, [a]to eat; for they
said, "The people are hungry and weary
and thirsty in the wilderness."

Absalom Slain

18 Then David [1]numbered the people who were with him and [a]set
over them commanders of thousands and
commanders of hundreds.
2 David sent the people out, [a]one
third under the [1]command of Joab, one
third under the [1]command of Abishai
the son of Zeruiah, Joab's brother, and
one third under the [1]command of [b]Ittai
the Gittite. And the king said to the people, "I myself will surely go out with you
also."
3 But the people said, "[a]You should
not go out; for if we indeed flee, they will
not care about us; even if half of us die,
they will not care about us. But [1]you are
worth ten thousand of us; therefore now
it is better that you *be ready* to help us
from the city."
4 Then the king said to them, "Whatever seems best to you I will do." So [a]the
king stood beside the gate, and all the
people went out by hundreds and thousands.
5 The king charged Joab and Abishai
and Ittai, saying, "*Deal* gently for my sake
with the young man Absalom." And [a]all
the people heard when the king charged
all the commanders concerning Absalom.
6 ¶ Then the people went out into
the field against Israel, and the battle took
place in [a]the forest of Ephraim.
7 The people of Israel were [1]defeat-
ed there before the servants of David, and
the slaughter there that day was great,
20,000 men.
8 For the battle there was spread over
the whole countryside, and the forest devoured more people that day than the
sword devoured.
9 ¶ Now Absalom happened to meet
the servants of David. For Absalom was
riding on *his* mule, and the mule went
under the thick branches of a great oak.
And [a]his head caught fast in the oak, so
he was [1]left hanging between heaven
and earth, while the mule that was under
him kept going.
10 When a certain man saw *it,* he told
Joab and said, "Behold, I saw Absalom
hanging in an oak."
11 Then Joab said to the man who had
told him, "Now behold, you saw *him!*
Why then did you not strike him there to
the ground? And I would have given you
ten *pieces* of silver and a belt."
12 The man said to Joab, "Even if I
should receive a thousand *pieces of* silver
in my hand, I would not put out my hand
against the king's son; for [a]in our hearing
the king charged you and Abishai and Ittai, saying, '[1]Protect for me the young
man Absalom!'
13 "Otherwise, if I had dealt treacherously against his life (and [a]there is nothing hidden from the king), then you yourself would have stood aloof."
14 Then Joab said, "I will not [1]waste
time here with you." [a]So he took three
spears in his hand and thrust them
through the heart of Absalom while he
was yet alive in the [2]midst of the oak.
15 And ten young men who carried
Joab's armor gathered around and struck
Absalom and killed him.
16 ¶ Then [a]Joab blew the trumpet,
and the people returned from pursuing
Israel, for Joab restrained the people.
17 They took Absalom and cast him
into [1]a deep pit in the forest and [a]erect-
ed over him a very great heap of stones.
And [b]all Israel fled, each to his tent.
18 Now Absalom in his lifetime had
taken and [a]set up for himself a pillar
which is in [b]the King's Valley, for he
said, "[c]I have no son [1]to preserve my
name." So he named the pillar after his

22 [1]Lit *the light of the morning*
23 [1]Lit *done* [2]Lit *bound* [3]Lit *gave charge to* [a]2 Sam 15:12 [b]2 Kin 20:1 [c]Matt 27:5
24 [a]Gen 32:2, 10; 2 Sam 2:8
25 [1]In 1 Chr 2:17, *Jether the Ishmaelite* [a]2 Sam 19:13; 20:9-12; 1 Kin 2:5,32 [b]1 Chr 2:16
27 [a]1 Sam 11:1; 2 Sam 10:1,2 [b]2 Sam 12:26,29 [c]2 Sam 9:4 [d]2 Sam 19:31-39; 1 Kin 2:7
28 [a]Prov 11:25; Matt 5:7
29 [a]2 Sam 16:2, 14; Prov 21:26; Eccl 11:1; Rom 12:13
18:1 [1]Lit *mustered* [a]Ex 18:25; Num 31:14; 1 Sam 22:7
2 [1]Lit *hand* [a]Judg 7:16; 1 Sam 11:11 [b]2 Sam 15:19-22
3 [1]So with some ancient versions; M.T. *for now there are ten thousand like us* [a]2 Sam 21:17
4 [a]2 Sam 18:24
5 [a]2 Sam 18:12
6 [a]Josh 17:15, 18; 2 Sam 17:26
7 [1]Lit *smitten*
9 [1]Lit *placed* [a]2 Sam 14:26
12 [1]So with some mss and the ancient versions; M.T. *Take care whoever you are of* [a]2 Sam 18:5
13 [a]2 Sam 14:19,20
14 [1]Lit *tarry thus* [2]Lit *heart* [a]2 Sam 14:30
16 [a]2 Sam 2:28; 20:22
17 [1]Lit *the great* [a]Deut 21:20,21; Josh 7:26; 8:29 [b]2 Sam 19:8; 20:1,22
18 [1]Lit *for the sake of remembering* [a]1 Sam 15:12 [b]Gen 14:17 [c]2 Sam 14:27

own name, and it is called Absalom's Monument to this day.

David Is Grief-stricken

19 ¶ Then [a]Ahimaaz the son of Zadok said, "Please let me run and bring the king news [b]that the LORD has [1]freed him from the hand of his enemies."

20 But Joab said to him, "You are not the man to carry news this day, but you shall carry news another day; however, you shall carry no news today because the king's son is dead."

21 Then Joab said to the Cushite, "Go, tell the king what you have seen." So the Cushite bowed to Joab and ran.

22 Now Ahimaaz the son of Zadok said once more to Joab, "But whatever happens, please let me also run after the Cushite." And Joab said, "Why would you run, my son, since [a]you will have no reward for going?"

23 "But whatever happens," *he said,* "I will run." So he said to him, "Run." Then Ahimaaz ran by way of the plain and passed up the Cushite.

24 ¶ Now [a]David was sitting between the two gates; and [b]the watchman went up to the roof of the gate by the wall, and raised his eyes and looked, and behold, a man running by himself.

25 The watchman called and told the king. And the king said, "If he is by himself there is good news in his mouth." And he came nearer and nearer.

26 Then the watchman saw another man running; and the watchman called to the gatekeeper and said, "Behold, *another* man running by himself." And the king said, "This one also is bringing good news."

27 The watchman said, "I [1]think the running of the first one [a]is like the running of Ahimaaz the son of Zadok." And the king said, "[b]This is a good man and comes with good news."

28 ¶ Ahimaaz called and said to the king, "[1]All is well." And [a]he prostrated himself before the king with his face to the ground. And he said, "[b]Blessed is the LORD your God, who has delivered up the men who lifted their hands against my lord the king."

29 The king said, "[a]Is it well with the young man Absalom?" And Ahimaaz answered, "When Joab sent the king's servant, and your servant, I saw a great tumult, but [b]I did not know what *it was.*"

30 Then the king said, "Turn aside and stand here." So he turned aside and stood still.

31 ¶ Behold, the Cushite arrived, and the Cushite said, "Let my lord the king receive good news, for [a]the LORD has [1]freed you this day from the hand of all those who rose up against you."

32 Then the king said to the Cushite, "[a]Is it well with the young man Absalom?" And the Cushite answered, "[b]Let the enemies of my lord the king, and all who rise up against you for evil, be as that young man!"

33 ¶ [1]The king was deeply moved and went up to the chamber over the gate and wept. And thus he said as he walked, "[a]O my son Absalom, my son, my son Absalom! [b]Would I had died instead of you, O Absalom, my son, my son!"

Joab Reproves David's Lament

19 Then it was told Joab, "Behold, [a]the king is weeping and mourns for Absalom."

2 The [1]victory that day was turned to mourning for all the people, for the people heard *it* said that day, "The king is grieved for his son."

3 So the people went by stealth into the city that day, as people who are humiliated steal away when they flee in battle.

4 The king [a]covered his face and [1]cried out with a loud voice, "[b]O my son Absalom, O Absalom, my son, my son!"

5 Then Joab came into the house to the king and said, "Today you have covered with shame the faces of all your servants, who today have saved your life and the lives of your sons and daughters, the lives of your wives, and the lives of your concubines,

6 by loving those who hate you, and by hating those who love you. For you have shown today that [1]princes and servants are nothing to you; for I know this day that if Absalom were alive and all of us were dead today, then [2]you would be pleased.

7 "Now therefore arise, go out and speak [1]kindly to your servants, for I swear by the LORD, if you do not go out, surely [a]not a man will pass the night with you, and this will be worse for you than all the evil that has come upon you from your youth until now."

David Restored as King

8 So the king arose and sat in the gate. When they told all the people, saying, "Behold, the king is [a]sitting in the gate," then all the people came before the king.

¶ Now [b]Israel had fled, each to his tent.

9 All the people were quarreling throughout all the tribes of Israel, saying, "[a]The king delivered us from the [1]hand

19 [1]Lit *vindicated* [a]2 Sam 15:36 [b]2 Sam 18:31
22 [a]2 Sam 18:29
24 [a]2 Sam 19:8 [b]2 Sam 13:34; 2 Kin 9:17
27 [1]Lit *see* [a]2 Kin 9:20 [b]1 Kin 1:42
28 [1]Lit *Peace* [a]1 Sam 25:23; 2 Sam 14:4 [b]1 Sam 17:46
29 [a]2 Sam 20:9; 2 Kin 4:26 [b]2 Sam 18:22
31 [1]Lit *vindicated* [a]Judg 5:31; 2 Sam 18:19
32 [a]2 Sam 18:29 [b]1 Sam 25:26
33 [1]Ch 19:1 in Heb [a]2 Sam 19:4 [b]Ex 32:32; Rom 9:3
19:1 [a]2 Sam 18:5,14
2 [1]Lit *salvation*
4 [1]Lit *the king cried* [a]2 Sam 15:30 [b]2 Sam 18:33
6 [1]Or *commanders* [2]Lit *it would be right in your eyes*
7 [1]Lit *to the heart* [a]Prov 14:28
8 [a]2 Sam 15:2; 18:24 [b]2 Sam 18:17
9 [1]Lit *palm* [a]2 Sam 8:1-14

of our enemies and [b]saved us from the
[2]hand of the Philistines, but now [c]he
has fled out of the land from Absalom.
10 "However, Absalom, whom we
anointed over us, has died in battle. Now
then, why are you silent about bringing
the king back?"
11 ¶ Then King David sent to [a]Zadok
and Abiathar the priests, saying, "Speak
to the elders of Judah, saying, 'Why are
you the last to bring the king back to his
house, since the word of all Israel has
come to the king, *even* to his house?
12 'You are my brothers; [a]you are my
bone and my flesh. Why then should you
be the last to bring back the king?'
13 "Say to [a]Amasa, 'Are you not my
bone and my flesh? [b]May God do so to
me, and more also, if you will not be
[c]commander of the army before me continually [d]in place of Joab.'"
14 Thus he turned the hearts of all the
men of Judah [a]as one man, so that they
sent *word* to the king, *saying*, "Return,
you and all your servants."
15 The king then returned and came
as far as the Jordan. And Judah came to
[a]Gilgal in order to go to meet the king,
to bring the king across the Jordan.
16 ¶ Then [a]Shimei the son of Gera,
the Benjamite who was from Bahurim,
hurried and came down with the men of
Judah to meet King David.
17 There were a thousand men of Benjamin with him, with [a]Ziba the servant
of the house of Saul, and his fifteen sons
and his twenty servants with him; and
they rushed to the Jordan before the king.
18 Then they kept crossing the ford to
bring over the king's household, and to
do what was good in his sight. And Shimei the son of Gera fell down before the
king as he was about to cross the Jordan.
19 So he said to the king, "[a]Let not
my lord consider me guilty, nor remember what your servant did wrong on the
day when my lord the king came out from
Jerusalem, so that the king would [1]take
it to heart.
20 "For your servant knows that I have
sinned; therefore behold, I have come today, [a]the first of all the house of Joseph
to go down to meet my lord the king."
21 But Abishai the son of Zeruiah said,
"[a]Should not Shimei be put to death
for this, [b]because he cursed the LORD's
anointed?"
22 David then said, "[a]What have I to
do with you, O sons of Zeruiah, that you
should this day be an adversary to me?
[b]Should any man be put to death in Israel
today? For do I not know that I am king
over Israel today?"
23 The king said to Shimei, "[a]You
shall not die." Thus the king swore to
him.
24 ¶ Then [a]Mephibosheth the [1]son
of Saul came down to meet the king; and
[b]he had neither [2]cared for his feet, nor
[2]trimmed his mustache, nor [c]washed
his clothes, from the day the king departed until the day he came *home* in peace.
25 It was when he came from Jerusalem to meet the king, that the king said
to him, "[a]Why did you not go with me,
Mephibosheth?"
26 So he answered, "O my lord, the
king, my servant deceived me; for your
servant said, 'I will saddle a donkey for
myself that I may ride on it and go with
the king,' [a]because your servant is lame.
27 "Moreover, [a]he has slandered your
servant to my lord the king; but my lord
the king is [b]like the angel of God, therefore do what is good in your sight.
28 "For [a]all my father's household was
nothing but dead men before my lord the
king; [b]yet you set your servant among
those who ate at your own table. What
right do I have yet that I should [1]com-
plain anymore to the king?"
29 So the king said to him, "Why do
you still speak of your affairs? I have [1]de-
cided, 'You and Ziba shall divide the
land.'"
30 Mephibosheth said to the king,
"Let him even take it all, since my lord
the king has come safely to his own
house."
31 ¶ Now [a]Barzillai the Gileadite had
come down from Rogelim; and he went
on to the Jordan with the king to [1]escort
him over the Jordan.
32 Now Barzillai was very old, being
eighty years old; and he had [1a]sustained
the king while he stayed at Mahanaim,
for he was a very great man.
33 The king said to Barzillai, "You
cross over with me and I will [1]sustain
you in Jerusalem with me."
34 But Barzillai said to the king,
"[a]How long [1]have I yet to live, that I
should go up with the king to Jerusalem?
35 "I am [1]now [a]eighty years old. Can
I distinguish between good and bad? Or
can your servant taste what I eat or what
I drink? Or can I hear anymore [b]the
voice of singing men and women? [c]Why
then should your servant be an added
burden to my lord the king?
36 "Your servant would merely cross
over the Jordan with the king. Why
should the king compensate me *with* this
reward?
37 "Please let your servant return, that
I may die in my own city near the grave
of my father and my mother. However,
here is your servant [a]Chimham, let him

9 [2]Lit *palm* [b]2 Sam 5:20; 8:1 [c]2 Sam 15:14
11 [a]2 Sam 15:29
12 [a]2 Sam 5:1
13 [a]2 Sam 17:25 [b]1 Kin 19:2 [c]2 Sam 8:16 [d]2 Sam 3:27-39; 19:5-7
14 [a]Judg 20:1
15 [a]Josh 5:9; 1 Sam 11:14,15
16 [a]2 Sam 16:5-13; 1 Kin 2:8
17 [a]2 Sam 16:1-4; 19:26,27
19 [1]Lit *set* [a]1 Sam 22:15; 2 Sam 16:6-8
20 [a]2 Sam 16:5
21 [a]2 Sam 16:7, 8 [b]Ex 22:28
22 [a]2 Sam 3:39; 16:9,10 [b]1 Sam 11:13
23 [a]1 Kin 2:8
24 [1]I.e. grandson [2]Lit *done* [a]2 Sam 9:6-10 [b]2 Sam 12:20 [c]Ex 19:10
25 [a]2 Sam 16:17
26 [a]2 Sam 9:3
27 [a]2 Sam 16:3, 4 [b]2 Sam 14:17, 20
28 [1]Lit *cry out* [a]2 Sam 21:6-9 [b]2 Sam 9:7,10, 13
29 [1]Lit *said*
31 [1]Lit *send* [a]2 Sam 17:27-29; 1 Kin 2:7
32 [1]Or *provided food for* [a]2 Sam 17:27-29
33 [1]Or *provide food for*
34 [1]Lit *are the days of the years of my life* [a]Gen 47:8
35 [1]Lit *today* [a]Ps 90:10 [b]Eccl 2:8; Is 5:11,12 [c]2 Sam 15:33
37 [a]2 Sam 19:40; 1 Kin 2:7; Jer 41:17

cross over with my lord the king, and do for him what is good in your sight."

38 The king answered, "Chimham shall cross over with me, and I will do for him what is good in your sight; and whatever you [1]require of me, I will do for you."

39 All the people crossed over the Jordan and the king crossed too. The king then [a]kissed Barzillai and blessed him, and he returned to his place.

40 ¶ Now the king went on to Gilgal, and Chimham went on with him; and all the people of Judah and also [a]half the people of Israel [1]accompanied the king.

41 And behold, all the men of Israel came to the king and said to the king, "[a]Why had our brothers [b]the men of Judah stolen you away, and brought the king and his household and all David's men with him over the Jordan?"

42 Then all the men of Judah answered the men of Israel, "Because [a]the king is a close relative to [1]us. Why then [2]are you angry about this matter? Have we eaten at all at the king's *expense,* or has [3]anything been taken for us?"

43 But the men of Israel answered the men of Judah and said, "[1a]We have ten parts in the king, therefore [1]we also have more *claim* on David than you. Why then did you treat us with contempt? Was it not [1]our advice first to bring back [1]our king?" Yet the words of the men of Judah were harsher than the words of the men of Israel.

Sheba's Revolt

20 Now [a]a worthless fellow happened to be there whose name was Sheba, the son of [b]Bichri, a Benjamite; and he blew the trumpet and said,

"[c]We have no portion in David,
Nor do we have inheritance in
[d]the son of Jesse;
[e]Every man to his tents,
O Israel!"

2 So all the men of Israel [1]withdrew from following David *and* followed Sheba the son of Bichri; but the men of Judah [2]remained steadfast to their king, from the Jordan even to Jerusalem.

3 ¶ Then David came to his house at Jerusalem, and [a]the king took the ten women, the concubines whom he had left to keep the house, and placed them under guard and provided them with sustenance, but did not go in to them. So they were shut up until the day of their death, living as widows.

4 ¶ Then the king said to [a]Amasa, "Call out the men of Judah for me within three days, and be present here yourself."

5 So Amasa went to call out *the men* of Judah, but he [a]delayed longer than the set time which he had appointed him.

6 And David said to [a]Abishai, "Now Sheba the son of Bichri will do us more harm than Absalom; [b]take your lord's servants and pursue him, so that he does not find for himself fortified cities and escape from our sight."

7 So Joab's men went out after him, [a]along with the Cherethites and the Pelethites and all the mighty men; and they went out from Jerusalem to pursue Sheba the son of Bichri.

8 When they were at the large stone which is in [a]Gibeon, Amasa came [1]to meet them. Now Joab was [2]dressed in his military attire, and over it was a belt with a sword in its sheath fastened at his waist; and as he went forward, it fell out.

9 Joab said to Amasa, "Is it well with you, my brother?" And [a]Joab took Amasa by the beard with his right hand to kiss him.

Amasa Murdered

10 But Amasa was not on guard against the sword which was in Joab's hand so [a]he struck him in the belly with it and poured out his inward parts on the ground, and did not *strike* him again, and he died. Then Joab and Abishai his brother pursued Sheba the son of Bichri.

11 Now there stood by him one of Joab's young men, and said, "Whoever favors Joab and whoever is for David, [a]*let him* follow Joab."

12 But Amasa lay wallowing in *his* blood in the middle of the highway. And when the man saw that all the people stood still, he [1]removed Amasa from the highway into the field and threw a garment over him when he saw that everyone who came by him stood still.

Revolt Put Down

13 As soon as he was removed from the highway, all the men passed on after Joab to pursue Sheba the son of Bichri.

14 ¶ Now he went through all the tribes of Israel to Abel, even Beth-maacah, and all the Berites; and they were gathered together and also went after him.

15 They came and besieged him in [a]Abel Beth-maacah, and [b]they [1]cast up a siege ramp against the city, and it stood by the rampart; and all the people who were with Joab were wreaking destruction in order to topple the wall.

16 Then [a]a wise woman called from the city, "Hear, hear! Please tell Joab, 'Come here that I may speak with you.' "

17 So he approached her, and the woman said, "Are you Joab?" And he an-

38 [1]Lit *choose*
39 [a]Gen 31:55; Ruth 1:14; 2 Sam 14:33
40 [1]Lit *crossed over with* [a]2 Sam 19:9,10
41 [a]Judg 8:1; 12:1 [b]2 Sam 19:11,12
42 [1]Lit *me* [2]Lit *is it hot to you* [3]Or *a gift* [a]2 Sam 19:12
43 [1]Singular in Heb [a]2 Sam 5:1; 1 Kin 11:30,31
20:1 [a]2 Sam 16:7 [b]Gen 46:21 [c]2 Sam 19:43; 1 Kin 12:16 [d]1 Sam 22:7-9 [e]1 Sam 13:2; 2 Sam 18:17; 2 Chr 10:16
2 [1]Lit *went up* [2]Lit *clung to*
3 [a]2 Sam 15:16; 16:21,22
4 [a]2 Sam 17:25; 19:13
5 [a]1 Sam 13:8
6 [a]2 Sam 21:17 [b]2 Sam 11:11; 1 Kin 1:33
7 [a]2 Sam 8:18; 1 Kin 1:38
8 [1]Lit *before* [2]Lit *girded with military garment as clothing* [a]2 Sam 2:13; 3:30
9 [a]Matt 26:49
10 [a]2 Sam 2:23; 3:27; 1 Kin 2:5
11 [a]2 Sam 20:13
12 [1]Lit *caused to turn*
15 [1]Lit *poured out* [a]1 Kin 15:20; 2 Kin 15:29 [b]2 Kin 19:32; Ezek 4:2
16 [a]2 Sam 14:2

swered, "I am." Then she said to him,
"Listen to the words of your maidservant." And he answered, "I am listening."
18 Then she spoke, saying, "Formerly
they used to say, 'They will surely ask
advice at Abel,' and thus they ended *the*
dispute.
19 "I am of those who are peaceable
and faithful in Israel. [a]You are seeking to
destroy a city, even a mother in Israel.
Why would you swallow up [b]the inheritance of the LORD?"
20 Joab replied, "Far be it, far be it
from me that I should swallow up or destroy!
21 "Such is not the case. But a man
from [a]the hill country of Ephraim, [b]She-
ba the son of Bichri by name, has lifted up
his hand against King David. Only hand
him over, and I will depart from the city."
And the woman said to Joab, "Behold, his
head will be thrown to you over the
wall."
22 Then the woman [a]wisely came to
all the people. And they cut off the head
of Sheba the son of Bichri and threw it to
Joab. So [b]he blew the trumpet, and they
were dispersed from the city, each to his
tent. Joab also returned to the king at
Jerusalem.
23 ¶ [a]Now Joab was over the whole
army of Israel, and Benaiah the son of
Jehoiada was over the Cherethites and
the Pelethites;
24 and Adoram was over the forced
labor, and [a]Jehoshaphat the son of Ahilud was the recorder;
25 and Sheva was scribe, and Zadok
and [a]Abiathar were priests;
26 and Ira the Jairite was also a priest
to David.

Gibeonite Revenge

21 Now there was [a]a famine in the
days of David for three years, year
after year; and [b]David sought the presence of the LORD. And the LORD said, "It
is for Saul and his bloody house, because
he put the Gibeonites to death."
2 So the king called the Gibeonites
and spoke to them (now the Gibeonites
were not of the sons of Israel but of the
remnant of the Amorites, and [a]the sons
of Israel [1]made a covenant with them,
but Saul had sought to [2]kill them in his
zeal for the sons of Israel and Judah).
3 Thus David said to the Gibeonites,
"What should I do for you? And how can
I make atonement that you may bless
[a]the inheritance of the LORD?"
4 Then the Gibeonites said to him,
"[a]We have no *concern* of silver or gold
with Saul or his house, nor is it for us to
put any man to death in Israel." And he
said, "I will do for you whatever you say."
5 So they said to the king, "[a]The
man who consumed us and who planned
[1]to exterminate us from remaining within any border of Israel,
6 let seven men from his sons be giv-
en to us, and we will [1]hang them [a]be-
fore the LORD in Gibeah of Saul, [b]the
chosen of the LORD." And the king said,
"I will give *them.*"
7 ¶ But the king spared [a]Mephibo-
sheth, the son of Jonathan the son of Saul,
[b]because of the oath of the LORD which
was between them, between David and
Saul's son Jonathan.
8 So the king took the two sons of
[a]Rizpah the daughter of Aiah, Armoni
and Mephibosheth whom she had borne
to Saul, and the five sons of [1b]Merab the
daughter of Saul, whom she had borne to
Adriel the son of Barzillai the [c]Mehola-
thite.
9 Then he gave them into the hands
of the Gibeonites, and they [1]hanged
them in the mountain before the LORD, so
that the seven of them fell together; and
they were put to death in the first days of
harvest at [a]the beginning of barley harvest.
10 ¶ [a]And Rizpah the daughter of
Aiah took sackcloth and spread it for herself on the rock, from the beginning of
harvest until [1]it rained on them from the
sky; and [b]she [2]allowed neither the birds
of the sky to rest on them by day nor the
beasts of the field by night.
11 When it was told David what Rizpah the daughter of Aiah, the concubine
of Saul, had done,
12 then David went and took [a]the
bones of Saul and the bones of Jonathan
his son from the men of Jabesh-gilead,
who had stolen them from the open
square of [b]Beth-shan, [c]where the Philistines had hanged them on the day [d]the
Philistines struck down Saul in Gilboa.
13 He brought up the bones of Saul
and the bones of Jonathan his son from
there, and they gathered the bones of
those who had been [1]hanged.
14 They buried the bones of Saul and
Jonathan his son in the country of Benjamin in [a]Zela, in the grave of Kish his
father; thus they did all that the king commanded, and after that [b]God was moved
by prayer for the land.
15 ¶ Now when [a]the Philistines were
at war again with Israel, David went
down and his servants with him; and as
they fought against the Philistines, David
became weary.
16 Then Ishbi-benob, who was
[a]among the descendants of the [1]giant,

19 [a]Deut 20:10 [b]1 Sam 26:19; 2 Sam 14:16; 21:3
21 [a]Josh 24:33 [b]2 Sam 20:2
22 [a]2 Sam 20:16; Eccl 9:13-16 [b]2 Sam 20:1
23 [a]2 Sam 8:16-18; 1 Kin 4:3-6
24 [a]1 Kin 4:3
25 [a]1 Kin 4:4
21:1 [a]Gen 12:10; 26:1; 42:5 [b]Num 27:21
2 [1]Lit *had sworn to* [2]Lit *smite* [a]Josh 9:3,15-20
3 [a]1 Sam 26:19; 2 Sam 20:19
4 [a]Num 35:31, 32
5 [1]Lit *against us that we should be exterminated* [a]2 Sam 21:1
6 [1]Lit *expose them* [a]Num 25:4 [b]1 Sam 10:24
7 [a]2 Sam 4:4; 9:10 [b]1 Sam 18:3; 20:12-17; 23:18; 2 Sam 9:1-7
8 [1]So Gr and Heb mss [a]2 Sam 3:7 [b]1 Sam 18:19 [c]1 Kin 19:16
9 [1]Lit *exposed them* [a]Ex 9:31, 32
10 [1]Lit *water was poured* [2]Lit *gave* [a]Deut 21:23 [b]1 Sam 17:44,46
12 [a]1 Sam 31:11-13 [b]Josh 17:11 [c]1 Sam 31:10 [d]1 Sam 31:3,4
13 [1]Lit *exposed*
14 [a]Josh 18:28 [b]Josh 7:26; 2 Sam 24:25
15 [a]2 Sam 5:17-25
16 [1]Heb *Raphah* [a]Num 13:22,28; Josh 15:14; 2 Sam 21:18-22

the weight of whose spear was three hundred *shekels* of bronze in weight, [2]was girded with a new *sword,* and he [3]intended to kill David.

17 But [a]Abishai the son of Zeruiah helped him, and struck the Philistine and killed him. Then the men of David swore to him, saying, "[b]You shall not go out again with us to battle, so that you do not extinguish [c]the lamp of Israel."

18 ¶ [a]Now it came about after this that there was war again with the Philistines at Gob; then [b]Sibbecai the Hushathite struck down Saph, who was among the descendants of the [1]giant.

19 There was war with the Philistines again at Gob, and Elhanan the son of Jaare-oregim the Bethlehemite [1]killed [2]Goliath the Gittite, [a]the shaft of whose spear was like a weaver's beam.

20 There was war at Gath again, where there was a man of *great* stature who had six fingers on each hand and six toes on each foot, twenty-four in number; and he also had been born [a]to the [1]giant.

21 When he defied Israel, Jonathan the son of Shimei, David's brother, struck him down.

22 [a]These four were born to the [1]giant in Gath, and they fell by the hand of David and by the hand of his servants.

David's Psalm of Deliverance

22 [a]And David spoke [b]the words of this song to the LORD in the day that the LORD delivered him from the [1]hand of all his enemies and from the [1]hand of Saul.

2 He said,
"[a]The LORD is my [1]rock and my
fortress and my deliverer;
3 [1a]My God, my rock, in whom I
take refuge,
My [b]shield and [c]the horn of my
salvation, my stronghold and
[d]my refuge;
My savior, You save me from
violence.
4 "I call upon the LORD, [a]who is
worthy to be praised,
And I am saved from my
enemies.
5 "For [a]the waves of death
encompassed me;
[b]The torrents of [1]destruction
[2]overwhelmed me;
6 [a]The cords of [1]Sheol
surrounded me;
The snares of death
confronted me.
7 "[a]In my distress I called upon the
LORD,
Yes, I [1]cried to my God;
And from His temple He heard
my voice,
And my cry for help *came* into
His ears.
8 "Then [a]the earth shook and
quaked,
[b]The foundations of heaven
were trembling
And were shaken, because He
was angry.
9 "Smoke went up [1]out of His
nostrils,
[a]Fire from His mouth devoured;
[b]Coals were kindled by it.
10 "He bowed the heavens also, and
came down
With [a]thick darkness under His
feet.
11 "[a]And He rode on a cherub and
flew;
And He [1]appeared on [b]the
wings of the wind.
12 "[a]And He made darkness
[1]canopies around Him,
A mass of waters, thick clouds of
the sky.
13 "From the brightness before Him
[a]Coals of fire were kindled.
14 "[a]The LORD thundered from
heaven,
And the Most High uttered His
voice.
15 "[a]And He sent out arrows, and
scattered them,
Lightning, and [1]routed them.
16 "Then the channels of the sea
appeared,
The foundations of the world
were [1]laid bare
By the rebuke of the LORD,
[a]At the blast of the breath of
His nostrils.
17 "[a]He sent from on high, He
took me;
[b]He drew me out of many
waters.
18 "He delivered me from my strong
enemy,
From those who hated me, for
they were too strong for me.
19 "They confronted me in the day
of my calamity,
[a]But the LORD was my support.
20 "[a]He also brought me forth into a
broad place;
He rescued me, [b]because He
delighted in me.
21 "[a]The LORD has rewarded me
according to my
righteousness;
[b]According to the cleanness of
my hands He has
recompensed me.

16 [2]Lit *and he was* [3]Lit *said*
17 [a]2 Sam 20:6-10 [b]2 Sam 18:3 [c]2 Sam 22:29; 1 Kin 11:36
18 [1]Heb *Raphah* [a]1 Chr 20:4-8 [b]1 Chr 11:29; 27:11
19 [1]Lit *smote* [2]In 1 Chr 20:5, *Lahmi, the brother of Goliath* [a]1 Sam 17:7
20 [1]Heb *Raphah* [a]2 Sam 21:16,18
22 [1]Heb *Raphah* [a]1 Chr 20:8
22:1 [1]Lit *palm* [a]Ps 18:2-50 [b]Ex 15:1; Deut 31:30
2 [1]Lit *crag* [a]1 Sam 23:25; 24:2; Ps 31:3; 71:3
3 [1]Lit *God of my rock* [a]Deut 32:4, 37; 1 Sam 2:2 [b]Gen 15:1; Deut 33:29 [c]Luke 1:69 [d]Ps 9:9
4 [a]Ps 48:1; 96:4
5 [1]Heb *Belial* [2]Or *terrified* [a]Ps 93:4; Jon 2:3 [b]Ps 69:14,15
6 [1]I.e. the nether world [a]Ps 116:3
7 [1]Or *called* [a]Ps 116:4; 120:1
8 [a]Judg 5:4; Ps 97:4 [b]Job 26:11
9 [1]Or *in His wrath* [a]Ps 97:3; Heb 12:29 [b]2 Sam 22:13
10 [a]Ex 19:16; 1 Kin 8:12; Ps 97:2; Nah 1:3
11 [1]Many mss read *sped* [a]2 Sam 6:2 [b]Ps 104:3
12 [1]Or *pavilions* [a]Job 36:29
13 [a]2 Sam 22:9
14 [a]Job 37:2-5; Ps 29:3
15 [1]Lit *confused* [a]Deut 32:23; Josh 10:10; 1 Sam 7:10
16 [1]Or *uncovered* [a]Ex 15:8; Nah 1:4
17 [a]Ps 144:7 [b]Ex 2:10
19 [a]Ps 23:4
20 [a]Ps 31:8; 118:5 [b]2 Sam 15:26
21 [a]1 Sam 26:23; 1 Kin 8:32 [b]Ps 24:4

22 "[a]For I have kept the ways of the
LORD,
And have not acted wickedly
against my God.
23 "[a]For all His ordinances *were*
before me,
And *as for* His statutes, I did not
depart from [1]them.
24 "[a]I was also [1]blameless toward
Him,
And I kept myself from my
iniquity.
25 "[a]Therefore the LORD has
recompensed me according
to my righteousness,
According to my cleanness
before His eyes.
26 "[a]With the [1]kind You show
Yourself [1]kind,
With the [2]blameless You show
Yourself [2]blameless;
27 [a]With the pure You show
Yourself pure,
[b]And with the perverted You
show Yourself [1]astute.
28 "[a]And You save an afflicted
people;
[b]But Your eyes are on the
haughty *whom* You abase.
29 "[a]For You are my lamp, O LORD;
And the LORD illumines my
darkness.
30 "[a]For by You I can [1]run upon a
troop;
By my God I can leap over a
wall.
31 "[a]As for God, His way is
[1]blameless;
[b]The word of the LORD is tested;
[c]He is a shield to all who take
refuge in Him.
32 "[a]For who is God, besides the
LORD?
[b]And who is a rock, besides our
God?
33 "[a]God is my strong fortress;
And He [1]sets the [2]blameless in
[3]His way.
34 "[a]He makes [1]my feet like hinds'
feet,
[b]And sets me on my high
places.
35 "[a]He trains my hands for battle,
[b]So that my arms can bend a
bow of bronze.
36 "You have also given me [a]the
shield of Your salvation,
And Your [1]help makes me great.
37 "[a]You enlarge my steps
under me,
And my [1]feet have not slipped.
38 "I pursued my enemies and
[a]destroyed them,
And I did not turn back until
they were consumed.
39 "And I have devoured them and
shattered them, so that they
did not rise;
And [a]they fell under my feet.
40 "For You have girded me with
strength for battle;
You have [1]subdued under me
[a]those who rose up
against me.
41 "You have also [a]made my
enemies turn *their* backs
to me,
And I [1]destroyed those who
hated me.
42 "[a]They looked, but there was
none to save;
[b]*Even* to the LORD, but He did
not answer them.
43 "[a]Then I pulverized them as the
dust of the earth;
[b]I crushed *and* stamped them as
the mire of the streets.
44 "[a]You have also delivered me
from the contentions of my
people;
[b]You have kept me as head of
the nations;
[c]A people whom I have not
known serve me.
45 "[a]Foreigners pretend obedience
to me;
As soon as they hear, they
obey me.
46 "Foreigners [1]lose heart,
[a]And [2]come trembling out of
their [3]fortresses.
47 "The LORD lives, and blessed be
my rock;
And exalted be [1a]God, the rock
of my salvation,
48 [a]The God who executes
vengeance for me,
[b]And brings down peoples
under me,
49 Who also brings me out from my
enemies;
You even lift me above [a]those
who rise up against me;
[b]You rescue me from the violent
man.
50 "[a]Therefore I will give thanks to
You, O LORD, among the
nations,
And I will sing praises to Your
name.
51 "[a]*He* is a tower of [1]deliverance
to His king,
And [b]shows lovingkindness to
His anointed,
[c]To David and his [2]descendants
forever."

22 [a]Gen 18:19; Ps 128:1; Prov 8:32
23 [1]Lit *it* [a]Deut 6:6-9; Ps 119:30
24 [1]Lit *complete*; or *having integrity* [a]Gen 6:9; Eph 1:4; Col 1:21
25 [a]2 Sam 22:21
26 [1]Or *loyal* [2]Lit *complete*; or *having integrity* [a]Matt 5:7
27 [1]Lit *twisted* [a]Matt 5:8; 1 John 3:3 [b]Lev 26:23; Rom 1:28
28 [a]Ex 3:7; Ps 72:12 [b]Is 2:11
29 [a]2 Sam 21:17; 1 Kin 11:36; Ps 27:1
30 [1]Or *crush a troop* [a]2 Sam 5:6-8
31 [1]Lit *complete*; or *having integrity* [a]Deut 32:4; Matt 5:48 [b]Ps 12:6; Prov 30:5 [c]2 Sam 22:3; Ps 84:9
32 [a]1 Sam 2:2 [b]2 Sam 22:2
33 [1]Or *sets free* [2]Lit *complete*; or *having integrity* [3]Another reading is *my* [a]2 Sam 22:2; Ps 31:3
34 [1]Another reading is *His* [a]2 Sam 2:18; Hab 3:19 [b]Deut 32:13
35 [a]Ps 144:1 [b]Job 20:24
36 [1]Lit *answering* [a]Eph 6:16
37 [1]Lit *ankles* [a]2 Sam 22:20; Prov 4:12
38 [a]Ex 15:9
39 [a]Mal 4:3
40 [1]Lit *caused to bow down* [a]Ps 44:5
41 [1]Or *silenced* [a]Ex 23:27; Josh 10:24
42 [a]Is 17:7 [b]1 Sam 28:6; Is 1:15
43 [a]2 Kin 13:7 [b]Is 10:6; Mic 7:10
44 [a]2 Sam 3:1 [b]2 Sam 8:1-14 [c]Is 55:5
45 [a]Ps 66:3
46 [1]Lit *languish* [2]Lit *gird themselves* [3]Lit *fastnesses* [a]1 Sam 14:11; Mic 7:17
47 [1]Lit *the God of the rock* [a]2 Sam 22:3; Ps 89:26
48 [a]1 Sam 24:12; 2 Sam 4:8; Ps 94:1 [b]Ps 144:2
49 [a]Ps 44:5 [b]Ps 140:1
50 [a]Rom 15:9
51 [1]I.e. victories; lit *salvation* [2]Lit *seed* [a]Ps 144:10 [b]Ps 89:24 [c]2 Sam 7:12-16

David's Last Song

23 Now these are the last words of David.
David the son of Jesse declares,
[a]The man who was raised on
high declares,
[b]The anointed of the God of
Jacob,
And the sweet psalmist of Israel,
2 "[a]The Spirit of the LORD spoke
by me,
And His word was on my
tongue.
3 "The God of Israel said,
[a]The Rock of Israel spoke to me,
'[b]He who rules over men
righteously,
[c]Who rules in the fear of God,
4 [a]Is as the light of the morning
when the sun rises,
A morning without clouds,
When the tender grass *springs*
out of the earth,
Through sunshine after rain.'
5 "Truly is not my house so with
God?
For [a]He has made an everlasting
covenant with me,
Ordered in all things, and
secured;
For all my salvation and all *my*
desire,
Will He not indeed make *it*
grow?
6 "[a]But the worthless, every one of
them will be thrust away
like thorns,
Because they cannot be taken in
hand;
7 But the man who touches them
Must be [1]armed with iron and
the shaft of a spear,
And [a]they will be completely
burned with fire in *their*
[2]place."

His Mighty Men

8 ¶ [a]These are the names of the
mighty men whom David had: Josheb-
basshebeth a Tahchemonite, chief of the
[1]captains, he was *called* Adino the Ez-
nite, because of eight hundred slain *by*
him at one time;
9 and after him was Eleazar the son
of [a]Dodo the [b]Ahohite, one of the three
mighty men with David when they [1]de-
fied the Philistines who were gathered
there to battle and the men of Israel had
[2]withdrawn.
10 [a]He arose and struck the Philistines until his hand was weary and
[1]clung to the sword, and [b]the LORD
brought about a great [2]victory that day;
and the people returned after him only to
strip *the slain.*
11 ¶ Now after him was Shammah the
son of Agee a [a]Hararite. And the Philistines were gathered [1]into a troop where
there was a plot of ground full of lentils,
and the people fled from the Philistines.
12 But he took his stand in the midst
of the plot, defended it and struck the
Philistines; and [a]the LORD brought about
a great [1]victory.
13 ¶ Then three of the thirty chief
men went down and came to David in the
harvest time to the [a]cave of Adullam,
while the troop of the Philistines was
camping in [b]the valley of Rephaim.
14 David was then [a]in the stronghold,
while the garrison of the Philistines was
then in Bethlehem.
15 [a]David had a craving and said, "Oh
that someone would give me water to
drink from the well of Bethlehem which
is by the gate!"
16 [a]So the three mighty men broke
through the camp of the Philistines, and
drew water from the well of Bethlehem
which was by the gate, and took *it* and
brought *it* to David. Nevertheless he
would not drink it, but [b]poured it out to
the LORD;
17 and he said, "Be it far from me,
O LORD, that I should do this. [a]*Shall I*
drink the blood of the men who went in
jeopardy of their lives?" Therefore he
would not drink it. These things the three
mighty men did.
18 ¶ [a]Abishai, the brother of Joab, the
son of Zeruiah, was [b]chief of the [1]thirty.
And he swung his spear against three
hundred [2]and killed *them,* and had a
name as well as the three.
19 He was most honored of the thirty,
therefore he became their commander;
however, he did not attain to the three.
20 ¶ Then [a]Benaiah the son of Jehoiada, the son of a valiant man of [b]Kabzeel,
who had done mighty deeds, [1]killed the
[2]two *sons of* Ariel of Moab. He also went
down and killed a lion in the middle of a
pit on a snowy day.
21 He [1]killed an Egyptian, [2]an im-
pressive man. Now the Egyptian *had* a
spear in his hand, but he went down to
him with a club and snatched the spear
from the Egyptian's hand and killed him
with his own spear.
22 These *things* [a]Benaiah the son of
Jehoiada did, and had a name as well as
the three mighty men.
23 He was honored among the thirty,
but he did not attain to the three. And
David appointed him over his guard.
24 ¶ [a]Asahel the brother of Joab was

23:1 [a]2 Sam 7:8,9; Ps 78:70, 71 [b]1 Sam 16:12,13; Ps 89:20
2 [a]Matt 22:43; 2 Pet 1:21
3 [a]2 Sam 22:2,3, 32 [b]Ps 72:1-3; Is 11:1-5 [c]2 Chr 19:7,9
4 [a]Judg 5:31; Ps 72:6
5 [a]2 Sam 7:12-16; Ps 89:29; Is 55:3
6 [a]Matt 13:41
7 [1]Lit *filled* [2]Lit *sitting* [a]Matt 3:10; 13:30; Heb 6:8
8 [1]Or *three* [a]1 Chr 11:11-47
9 [1]Lit *reproached* [2]Lit *gone up* [a]1 Chr 27:4 [b]1 Chr 8:4
10 [1]Lit *his hand clung* [2]Lit *salvation* [a]1 Chr 11:13 [b]1 Sam 11:13; 19:5
11 [1]Possibly at Lehi [a]2 Sam 23:33
12 [1]Lit *salvation* [a]2 Sam 23:10
13 [a]1 Sam 22:1 [b]2 Sam 5:18
14 [a]1 Sam 22:4, 5
15 [a]1 Chr 11:17
16 [a]1 Chr 11:18 [b]Gen 35:14
17 [a]Lev 17:10
18 [1]So two Heb mss and Syriac; M.T. *three* [2]Lit *slain ones* [a]2 Sam 10:10, 14; 18:2 [b]1 Chr 11:20,21
20 [1]Lit *smote* [2]Or *two lion-like heroes* [a]2 Sam 8:18; 20:23 [b]Josh 15:21
21 [1]Lit *smote* [2]Lit *a man of appearance*
22 [a]2 Sam 23:20
24 [a]2 Sam 2:18; 1 Chr 27:7

among the thirty; Elhanan the son of Dodo of Bethlehem,

25 [a]Shammah the [b]Harodite, Elika the Harodite,

26 Helez the Paltite, Ira the son of Ikkesh the [a]Tekoite,

27 Abiezer the [a]Anathothite, Mebunnai the Hushathite,

28 Zalmon the Ahohite, Maharai the [a]Netophathite,

29 [a]Heleb the son of Baanah the Netophathite, Ittai the son of Ribai of [b]Gibeah of the sons of Benjamin,

30 Benaiah a [a]Pirathonite, Hiddai of the brooks of [b]Gaash,

31 Abi-albon the Arbathite, Azmaveth the [a]Barhumite,

32 Eliahba the [a]Shaalbonite, the sons of Jashen, Jonathan,

33 [a]Shammah the Hararite, Ahiam the son of Sharar the Ararite,

34 Eliphelet the son of Ahasbai, the son of [a]the Maacathite, [b]Eliam the son of [c]Ahithophel the Gilonite,

35 [a]Hezro the [b]Carmelite, Paarai the Arbite,

36 Igal the son of Nathan of [a]Zobah, Bani the Gadite,

37 Zelek the Ammonite, Naharai the [a]Beerothite, armor bearers of Joab the son of Zeruiah,

38 Ira the [a]Ithrite, Gareb the Ithrite,

39 [a]Uriah the Hittite; thirty-seven in all.

The Census Taken

24 [a]Now [b]again the anger of the LORD burned against Israel, and it incited David against them to say, "[c]Go, number Israel and Judah."

2 The king said to Joab the commander of the army who was with him, "Go about now through all the tribes of Israel, [a]from Dan to Beersheba, and [1]register the people, that I may know the number of the people."

3 But Joab said to the king, "[a]Now may the LORD your God add to the people a hundred times as many as they are, while the eyes of my lord the king *still* see; but why does my lord the king delight in this thing?"

4 Nevertheless, the king's word prevailed against Joab and against the commanders of the army. So Joab and the commanders of the army went out from the presence of the king to [1]register the people of Israel.

5 They crossed the Jordan and camped in [a]Aroer, on the right side of the city that is in the middle of the valley of Gad and toward [b]Jazer.

6 Then they came to Gilead and to [1]the land of Tahtim-hodshi, and they came to Dan-jaan and around to [a]Sidon,

7 and came to the [a]fortress of Tyre and to all the cities of the [b]Hivites and of the Canaanites, and they went out to the south of Judah, *to* [c]Beersheba.

8 So when they had gone about through the whole land, they came to Jerusalem at the end of nine months and twenty days.

9 And Joab gave [a]the number of the [1]registration of the people to the king; and there were in Israel [b]eight hundred thousand valiant men who drew the sword, and the men of Judah were five hundred thousand men.

10 ¶ Now [a]David's heart [1]troubled him after he had numbered the people. So David said to the LORD, "[b]I have sinned greatly in what I have done. But now, O LORD, please [2]take away the iniquity of Your servant, for [c]I have acted very foolishly."

11 When David arose in the morning, the word of the LORD came to [a]the prophet Gad, David's [b]seer, saying,

12 "Go and speak to David, 'Thus the LORD says, "I am offering you three things; choose for yourself one of them, which I will do to you." ' "

13 So Gad came to David and told him, and said to him, "Shall [a]seven years of famine come to you in your land? Or will you flee three months before your foes while they pursue you? Or shall there be three days' pestilence in your land? Now consider and see what answer I shall return to Him who sent me."

14 Then David said to Gad, "I am in great distress. Let us now fall into the hand of the LORD [a]for His mercies are great, but do not let me fall into the hand of man."

Pestilence Sent

15 ¶ So [a]the LORD [1]sent a pestilence upon Israel from the morning until the appointed time, and seventy thousand men of the people [b]from Dan to Beersheba died.

16 [a]When the angel stretched out his hand toward Jerusalem to destroy it, [b]the LORD relented from the calamity and said to the angel who destroyed the people, "It is enough! Now relax your hand!" And the angel of the LORD was by the threshing floor of Araunah the Jebusite.

17 Then David spoke to the LORD when he saw the angel who was striking down the people, and said, "Behold, [a]it is I who have sinned, and it is I who have done wrong; but [b]these sheep, what have they done? Please let Your hand be against me and against my father's house."

25 [a]1 Chr 11:27 [b]Judg 7:1
26 [a]2 Sam 14:2
27 [a]Josh 21:18
28 [a]2 Kin 25:23
29 [a]1 Chr 11:30 [b]Josh 18:28
30 [a]Judg 12:13, 15 [b]Josh 24:30
31 [a]2 Sam 3:16
32 [a]Josh 19:42
33 [a]2 Sam 23:11
34 [a]2 Sam 10:6, 8; 20:14 [b]2 Sam 11:3 [c]2 Sam 15:12
35 [a]1 Chr 11:37 [b]Josh 15:55
36 [a]2 Sam 8:3
37 [a]2 Sam 4:2
38 [a]1 Chr 2:53
39 [a]2 Sam 11:3, 6
24:1 [a]1 Chr 21:1 [b]2 Sam 21:1,2 [c]1 Chr 27:23,24
2 [1]Lit *muster* [a]Judg 20:1; 2 Sam 3:10
3 [a]Deut 1:11
4 [1]Lit *muster*
5 [a]Deut 2:36; Josh 13:9,16 [b]Num 21:32; 32:35
6 [1]Or *Kadesh in the land of the Hittite* [a]Josh 19:28; Judg 1:31
7 [a]Josh 19:29 [b]Josh 11:3; Judg 3:3 [c]Gen 21:22-33
9 [1]Lit *muster* [a]Num 1:44-46 [b]1 Chr 21:5
10 [1]Lit *smote* [2]Lit *cause to pass away* [a]1 Sam 24:5 [b]2 Sam 12:13 [c]1 Sam 13:13; 2 Chr 16:9
11 [a]1 Sam 22:5; 1 Chr 29:29 [b]1 Sam 9:9
13 [a]1 Chr 21:12; Ezek 14:21
14 [a]Ps 51:1; 130:4,7
15 [1]Lit *gave* [a]1 Chr 21:14; 27:24 [b]2 Sam 24:2
16 [a]Ex 12:23; 2 Kin 19:35; Acts 12:23 [b]Ex 32:14; 1 Sam 15:11
17 [a]2 Sam 24:10 [b]2 Sam 7:8; Ps 74:1

David Builds an Altar

18 ¶ So Gad came to David that day
and said to him, "[a]Go up, erect an altar
to the LORD on the threshing floor of
[1]Araunah the Jebusite."
19 David went up according to the
word of Gad, just as the LORD had commanded.
20 Araunah looked down and saw the
king and his servants crossing over toward him; and Araunah went out and
bowed his face to the ground before the
king.
21 Then Araunah said, "Why has my
lord the king come to his servant?" And
David said, "To buy the threshing floor
from you, in order to build an altar to the
LORD, [a]that the plague may be held back
from the people."
22 Araunah said to David, "Let my
lord the king take and offer up what
is good in his sight. Look, [a]the oxen
for the burnt offering, the threshing
sledges and the yokes of the oxen for
the wood.
23 "Everything, O king, Araunah gives
to the king." And Araunah said to the
king, "May the LORD your God [a]accept
you."
24 However, the king said to Araunah,
"No, but I will surely buy *it* from you for
a price, for [a]I will not offer burnt offerings to the LORD my God [1]which cost me
nothing." So [b]David bought the threshing floor and the oxen for fifty shekels of
silver.
25 David built there an altar to the
LORD and offered burnt offerings and
peace offerings. [a]Thus the LORD was
moved by prayer for the land, and the
plague was held back from Israel.

18 [1]In 2 Chr 3:1, *Ornan* [a]1 Chr 21:18
21 [a]Num 16:44-50
22 [a]1 Sam 6:14; 1 Kin 19:21
23 [a]Ezek 20:40, 41
24 [1]Lit *gratuitously* [a]Mal 1:13,14 [b]1 Chr 21:24,25
25 [a]2 Sam 21:14

1 Kings

Title and Background

1 and 2 Kings (like 1,2 Samuel and 1,2 Chronicles) are actually one literary work, called in Hebrew tradition simply "Kings." Together Samuel and Kings relate the whole history of the monarchy, from its rise under the ministry of Samuel to its destruction at the hands of the Babylonians. Beginning with Solomon's reign, 1 Kings records the history of Israel through the divided kingdom to the death of Ahab.

Author and Date of Writing

There is little conclusive evidence as to the author of 1,2 Kings. Whoever the author may have been, it is clear that he was familiar with the book of Deuteronomy—as were many of Israel's prophets. The book was probably written subsequent to Jehoiachin's release from prison (562 B.C.) and prior to the end of the Babylonian exile in 538.

Theme and Message

No explicit statement of purpose or theme is found in 1 or 2 Kings. In general, they described the history of the kings of Israel and Judah in the light of God's covenants. The author was primarily concerned with Israel's faithfulness to the covenants, so he recorded the activities of each ruler as to his/her obedience to the covenant. Obedience to God brought peace and prosperity; disobedience and idol worship resulted in war and disaster.

Outline

I. Solomon's Reign (1:1—12:24)
II. Israel and Judah From Jeroboam/Rehoboam to Ahab/Asa (12:25—16:34)
III. Elijah and King Ahab (17:1—22:40)
IV. Jehoshaphat King of Judah (22:41–50)
V. Ahaziah King of Israel (22:51–53)

David in Old Age

1 Now King David was old, advanced
in age; and they covered him with
clothes, but he could not keep warm.
2 So his servants said to him, "Let
them seek a young virgin for my lord the
king, and let her [1]attend the king and
become his nurse; and let her lie in your
bosom, that my lord the king may keep
warm."
3 So they searched for a beautiful girl
throughout all the territory of Israel, and
found Abishag the [a]Shunammite, and
brought her to the king.
4 The girl was very beautiful; and she
became the king's nurse and served him,
but the king did not [1]cohabit with her.
5 ¶ Now [a]Adonijah the son of Haggith exalted himself, saying, "I will be
king." So [b]he prepared for himself chariots and horsemen with fifty men to run
before him.
6 His father had never [1]crossed him
at any time by asking, "Why have you
done so?" And he was also a very handsome man, and [2a]he was born after Absalom.
7 [1]He had conferred with [a]Joab the
son of Zeruiah and with [b]Abiathar the
priest; and following [c]Adonijah they
helped him.
8 But [a]Zadok the priest, [b]Benaiah
the son of Jehoiada, [c]Nathan the prophet, [d]Shimei, Rei, and [e]the mighty men
who belonged to David, were not with
Adonijah.
9 ¶ Adonijah sacrificed sheep and
oxen and fatlings by the [1]stone of Zohe-
leth, which is beside [a]En-rogel; and he
invited all his brothers, the king's sons,
and all the men of Judah, the king's servants.
10 But he did not invite Nathan the
prophet, Benaiah, the mighty men, and
[a]Solomon his brother.

Nathan and Bathsheba

11 ¶ Then Nathan spoke to [a]Bathshe-
ba the mother of Solomon, saying, "Have
you not heard that Adonijah the son of

1:2 [1]Lit *stand before*
3 [a]Josh 19:18; 1 Sam 28:4
4 [1]Lit *know her*
5 [a]2 Sam 3:4 [b]2 Sam 15:1
6 [1]Lit *pained him* [2]Lit *she gave him birth* [a]2 Sam 3:3,4
7 [1]Lit *his words were* [a]1 Chr 11:6 [b]1 Sam 22:20,23; 2 Sam 20:25 [c]1 Kin 2:22
8 [a]2 Sam 20:25; 1 Chr 16:39 [b]2 Sam 8:18 [c]2 Sam 12:1 [d]1 Kin 4:18 [e]2 Sam 23:8-39
9 [1]Or *Gliding* or *Serpent Stone* [a]Josh 15:7; 18:16; 2 Sam 17:17
10 [a]2 Sam 12:24
11 [a]2 Sam 12:24

Haggith has become king, and David our lord does not know *it?*

12 "So now come, please let me [a]give you counsel and save your life and the life of your son Solomon.

13 "Go [1]at once to King David and say to him, 'Have you not, my lord, O king, sworn to your maidservant, saying, "[a]Surely Solomon your son shall be king after me, and he shall sit on my throne"? Why then has Adonijah become king?'

14 "Behold, while you are still there speaking with the king, I will come in after you and confirm your words."

15 ¶ So Bathsheba went in to the king in the bedroom. Now [a]the king was very old, and Abishag the Shunammite was ministering to the king.

16 Then Bathsheba bowed and prostrated herself [1]before the king. And the king said, "What [2]do you wish?"

17 She said to him, "My lord, you swore to your maidservant by the LORD your God, *saying,* '[a]Surely your son Solomon shall be king after me and he shall sit on my throne.'

18 "Now, behold, Adonijah is king; and now, my lord the king, you do not know *it.*

19 "[a]He has sacrificed oxen and fatlings and sheep in abundance, and has invited all the sons of the king and Abiathar the priest and Joab the commander of the army, but he has not invited Solomon your servant.

20 "As for you now, my lord the king, the eyes of all Israel are on you, to tell them who shall sit on the throne of my lord the king after him.

21 "Otherwise it will come about, [a]as soon as my lord the king sleeps with his fathers, that I and my son Solomon will be considered [1]offenders."

22 ¶ Behold, while she was still speaking with the king, Nathan the prophet came in.

23 They told the king, saying, "Here is Nathan the prophet." And when he came in before the king, he prostrated himself [1]before the king with his face to the ground.

24 Then Nathan said, "My lord the king, have you said, 'Adonijah shall be king after me, and he shall sit on my throne'?

25 "[a]For he has gone down today and has sacrificed oxen and fatlings and sheep in abundance, and has invited all the king's sons and the commanders of the army and Abiathar the priest, and behold, they are eating and drinking before him; and they say, '[b]*Long* live King Adonijah!'

26 "[a]But me, *even* me your servant, and Zadok the priest and Benaiah the son of Jehoiada and your servant Solomon, he has not invited.

27 "Has this thing been done by my lord the king, and you have not shown to your [1]servants who should sit on the throne of my lord the king after him?"

28 ¶ Then King David said, "Call Bathsheba to me." And she came into the king's presence and stood before the king.

29 The king vowed and said, "[a]As the LORD lives, who has redeemed my life from all distress,

30 surely as [a]I vowed to you by the LORD the God of Israel, saying, 'Your son Solomon shall be king after me, and he shall sit on my throne in my place'; I will indeed do so this day."

31 Then Bathsheba bowed with her face to the ground, and prostrated herself [1]before the king and said, "[a]May my lord King David live forever."

32 ¶ Then King David said, "Call to me [a]Zadok the priest, Nathan the prophet, and Benaiah the son of Jehoiada." And they came into the king's presence.

33 The king said to them, "Take with you [a]the servants of your lord, and have my son Solomon ride on my own mule, and bring him down to [b]Gihon.

34 "Let Zadok the priest and Nathan the prophet [a]anoint him there as king over Israel, and [b]blow the trumpet and say, '[c]*Long* live King Solomon!'

35 "Then you shall come up after him, and he shall come and sit on my throne and be king in my place; for I have appointed him to be ruler over Israel and Judah."

36 Benaiah the son of Jehoiada answered the king and said, "Amen! Thus may the LORD, the God of my lord the king, say.

37 "[a]As the LORD has been with my lord the king, so may He be with Solomon, and [b]make his throne greater than the throne of my lord King David!"

Solomon Anointed King

38 ¶ So [a]Zadok the priest, Nathan the prophet, Benaiah the son of Jehoiada, [b]the Cherethites, and the Pelethites went down and had Solomon ride on King David's mule, and brought him to [c]Gihon.

39 Zadok the priest then [a]took the horn of oil from the tent and [b]anointed Solomon. Then they [c]blew the trumpet, and all the people said, "[d]*Long* live King Solomon!"

40 All the people went up after him, and the people [1]were playing on flutes and rejoicing with great joy, so that the earth [2]shook at their noise.

12 [a]Prov 15:22
13 [1]Lit *and enter* [a]1 Kin 1:30; 1 Chr 22:9-13
15 [a]1 Kin 1:1
16 [1]Lit *to* [2]Lit *to you*
17 [a]1 Kin 1:13
19 [a]1 Kin 1:9
21 [1]Lit *sinners* [a]Deut 31:16; 2 Sam 7:12; 1 Kin 2:10
23 [1]Lit *to*
25 [a]1 Kin 1:9 [b]1 Sam 10:24
26 [a]1 Kin 1:8, 10
27 [1]Some mss read *servant*
29 [a]2 Sam 4:9
30 [a]1 Kin 1:13, 17
31 [1]Lit *to* [a]Dan 2:4; 3:9
32 [a]1 Kin 1:8
33 [a]2 Sam 20:6, 7 [b]2 Chr 32:30; 33:14
34 [a]1 Sam 10:1; 16:3,12; 2 Sam 5:3; 1 Kin 19:16; 2 Kin 9:3 [b]2 Sam 15:10 [c]1 Kin 1:25
37 [a]Josh 1:5,17; 1 Sam 20:13 [b]1 Kin 1:47
38 [a]1 Kin 1:8 [b]2 Sam 8:18 [c]1 Kin 1:33
39 [a]Ex 30:23-32; Ps 89:20 [b]1 Chr 29:22 [c]1 Kin 1:34 [d]1 Sam 10:24
40 [1]Lit *fluting* [2]Lit *was split*

41 ¶ Now Adonijah and all the guests who *were* with him heard *it* as they finished eating. When Joab heard the sound of the trumpet, he said, "Why [1]is the city making such an uproar?"

42 While he was still speaking, behold, [a]Jonathan the son of Abiathar the priest came. Then Adonijah said, "Come in, for [b]you are a valiant man and bring good news."

43 But Jonathan replied to Adonijah, "No! Our lord King David has made Solomon king.

44 "The king has also sent with him Zadok the priest, Nathan the prophet, Benaiah the son of Jehoiada, the Cherethites, and the Pelethites; and they have made him ride on the king's mule.

45 "Zadok the priest and Nathan the prophet have anointed him king in Gihon, and they have come up from there rejoicing, [a]so that the city is in an uproar. This is the noise which you have heard.

46 "Besides, [a]Solomon has even taken his seat on the throne of the kingdom.

47 "Moreover, the king's servants came to bless our lord King David, saying, 'May [a]your God make the name of Solomon better than your name and his throne greater than your throne!' And [b]the king bowed himself on the bed.

48 "The king has also said thus, 'Blessed be the LORD, the God of Israel, who [a]has granted one to sit on my throne today while my own eyes see *it*.' "

49 ¶ Then all the guests of Adonijah were terrified; and they arose and each went on his way.

50 And Adonijah was afraid of Solomon, and he arose, went and [a]took hold of the horns of the altar.

51 Now it was told Solomon, saying, "Behold, Adonijah is afraid of King Solomon, for behold, he has taken hold of the horns of the altar, saying, 'Let King Solomon swear to me today that he will not put his servant to death with the sword.' "

52 Solomon said, "If he is a worthy man, [a]not one of his hairs will fall to the ground; but if wickedness is found in him, he will die."

53 So King Solomon sent, and they brought him down from the altar. And he came and prostrated himself [1]before King Solomon, and Solomon said to him, "Go to your house."

David's Charge to Solomon

2 As David's [1a]time to die drew near, he charged Solomon his son, saying,

2 "[a]I am going the way of all the earth. [b]Be strong, therefore, and [1]show yourself a man.

3 "Keep the charge of the LORD your God, to walk in His ways, to keep His statutes, His commandments, His ordinances, and His testimonies, [a]according to what is written in the Law of Moses, that [b]you may succeed in all that you do and wherever you turn,

4 so that [a]the LORD may carry out His promise which He spoke concerning me, saying, '[b]If your sons are careful of their way, [c]to walk before Me in [1]truth with all their heart and with all their soul, [2d]you shall not lack a man on the throne of Israel.'

5 ¶ "Now you also know what Joab the [a]son of Zeruiah did to me, what he did to the two commanders of the armies of Israel, to [b]Abner the son of Ner, and to [c]Amasa the son of Jether, whom he killed; he also [1]shed the blood of war in peace. And he put the blood of war on his belt [2]about his waist, and on his sandals [3]on his feet.

6 "[a]So act according to your wisdom, and do not let his gray hair go down to [1]Sheol in peace.

7 "But [a]show kindness to the sons of Barzillai the Gileadite, and [b]let them be among those who eat at your table; [c]for they [1]assisted me when I fled from Absalom your brother.

8 "Behold, [a]there is with you Shimei the son of Gera the Benjamite, of Bahurim; now it was he who cursed me with a [1]violent curse on the day I went to Mahanaim. But when [b]he came down to me at the Jordan, I swore to him by the LORD, saying, 'I will not put you to death with the sword.'

9 "Now therefore, do not let him go unpunished, [a]for you are a wise man; and you will know what you ought to do to him, and you will bring his gray hair down to [1]Sheol with blood."

Death of David

10 ¶ Then [a]David slept with his fathers and was buried in [b]the city of David.

11 [a]The days that David reigned over Israel *were* forty years: [b]seven years he reigned in Hebron and thirty-three years he reigned in Jerusalem.

12 And [a]Solomon sat on the throne of David his father, and his kingdom was firmly established.

13 ¶ Now Adonijah the son of Haggith came to Bathsheba the mother of Solomon. And she said, "[a]Do you come peacefully?" And he said, "Peacefully."

14 Then he said, "I have something *to say* to you." And she said, "Speak."

41 [1]Lit *is the sound of the city an uproar*

42 [a]2 Sam 15:27,36; 17:17 [b]2 Sam 18:27

45 [a]1 Kin 1:40

46 [a]1 Chr 29:23

47 [a]1 Kin 1:37 [b]Gen 47:31

48 [a]2 Sam 7:12; 1 Kin 3:6

50 [a]Ex 27:2; 30:10; 1 Kin 2:28

52 [a]1 Sam 14:45; 2 Sam 14:11; Acts 27:34

53 [1]Lit *to*

2:1 [1]Lit *days* [a]Gen 47:29; Deut 31:14

2 [1]Lit *become a man* [a]Josh 23:14 [b]Deut 31:7,23; Josh 1:6,7

3 [a]Deut 17:18-20 [b]1 Chr 22:12,13

4 [1]Or *faithfulness* [2]Lit *there shall not be cast off to you a man from before Me* [a]2 Sam 7:25 [b]Ps 132:12 [c]2 Kin 20:3 [d]2 Sam 7:12,13; 1 Kin 8:25; 9:5

5 [1]Lit *made* [2]Lit *that was about* [3]Lit *that were on* [a]2 Sam 2:13,18 [b]2 Sam 3:27; 1 Kin 2:32 [c]2 Sam 20:10

6 [1]I.e. the nether world [a]1 Kin 2:9

7 [1]Lit *came near to* [a]2 Sam 19:31-38 [b]2 Sam 9:7,10 [c]2 Sam 17:27-29

8 [1]Or *grievous* [a]2 Sam 16:5-8 [b]2 Sam 19:18-23

9 [1]I.e. the nether world [a]1 Kin 2:6

10 [a]Acts 2:29; 13:36 [b]2 Sam 5:7; 1 Kin 3:1

11 [a]2 Sam 5:4, 5; 1 Chr 3:4; 29:26,27 [b]2 Sam 5:5

12 [a]1 Chr 29:23; 2 Chr 1:1

13 [a]1 Sam 16:4

15 So he said, "You know that [a]the
kingdom was mine and [b]that all Israel
[1]expected me to be king; [c]however, the
kingdom has turned about and become
my brother's, [d]for it was his from the
LORD.
16 "Now I am making one request of
you; do not [1]refuse me." And she said to
him, "Speak."
17 Then he said, "Please speak to Solomon the king, for he will not [1]refuse you,
that he may give me [a]Abishag the Shunammite as a wife."
18 Bathsheba said, "Very well; I will
speak to the king for you."

Adonijah Executed

19 ¶ So Bathsheba went to King Solomon to speak to him for Adonijah. And
the king arose to meet her, bowed before
her, and sat on his throne; then he [a]had
a throne set for the king's mother, and
[b]she sat on his right.
20 Then she said, "I am making one
small request of you; [a]do not [1]refuse
me." And the king said to her, "Ask, my
mother, for I will not [2]refuse you."
21 So she said, "[a]Let Abishag the Shunammite be given to Adonijah your
brother as a wife."
22 King Solomon answered and said to
his mother, "And why are you asking Abishag the Shunammite for Adonijah? [a]Ask
for him also the kingdom—[b]for he is my
older brother—even for him, for [c]Abia-
thar the priest, and for Joab the son of
Zeruiah!"
23 Then King Solomon swore by the
LORD, saying, "May God do so to me and
more also, if Adonijah has [a]not spoken
this word against his own [1]life.
24 "Now therefore, as the LORD lives,
who has established me and set me on
the throne of David my father and [a]who
has made me a house as He promised,
surely Adonijah shall be put to death today."
25 So King Solomon [a]sent Benaiah
the son of Jehoiada; and he fell upon him
so that he died.
26 ¶ Then to Abiathar the priest the
king said, "[a]Go to Anathoth to your own
field, [b]for you [1]deserve to die; but I will
not put you to death at this time, because
[c]you carried the ark of the Lord [2]GOD
before my father David, and because
[d]you were afflicted in everything with
which my father was afflicted."
27 So Solomon dismissed Abiathar
from being priest to the LORD, in order to
fulfill [a]the word of the LORD, which He
had spoken concerning the house of Eli in
Shiloh.

Joab Executed

28 ¶ Now the news came to Joab, [a]for
Joab had followed Adonijah, [b]although
he had not followed Absalom. And Joab
fled to the tent of the LORD and [c]took
hold of the horns of the altar.
29 It was told King Solomon that Joab
had fled to the tent of the LORD, and behold, he is beside the altar. Then Solomon [a]sent Benaiah the son of Jehoiada,
saying, "[b]Go, fall upon him."
30 So Benaiah came to the tent of the
LORD and said to him, "Thus the king has
said, 'Come out.'" But he said, "No, for
I will die here." And Benaiah brought the
king word again, saying, "Thus spoke
Joab, and thus he answered me."
31 The king said to him, "[a]Do as he
has spoken and fall upon him and bury
him, [b]that you may remove from me and
from my father's house the blood which
Joab shed without cause.
32 "[a]The LORD will return his blood on
his own head, [b]because he fell upon two
men more righteous and better than he
and killed them with the sword, while
my father David did not know *it:* [c]Abner
the son of Ner, commander of the army
of Israel, and [d]Amasa the son of Jether,
commander of the army of Judah.
33 "[a]So shall their blood return on the
head of Joab and on the head of his
[1]descendants forever; but to David and
his [1]descendants and his house and his
throne, may there be peace from the
LORD forever."
34 Then [a]Benaiah the son of Jehoiada
went up and fell upon him and put him to
death, and he was buried at his own
house [b]in the wilderness.
35 [a]The king appointed Benaiah the
son of Jehoiada over the army in his
place, and the king appointed [b]Zadok the
priest [c]in the place of Abiathar.

Shimei Executed

36 ¶ Now the king sent and called for
[a]Shimei and said to him, "Build for yourself a house in Jerusalem and live there,
and do not go out from there to any place.
37 "For on the day you go out and
[a]cross over the [1]brook Kidron, you will
know for certain that you shall surely die;
[b]your blood shall be on your own head."
38 Shimei then said to the king, "The
word is good. As my lord the king has
said, so your servant will do." So Shimei
lived in Jerusalem many days.
39 ¶ But it came about at the end of
three years, that two of the servants of
Shimei ran away [a]to Achish son of Maacah, king of Gath. And they told Shimei,

15 [1]Lit *set their faces on me* [a]2 Sam 3:3,4; 1 Kin 2:22 [b]1 Kin 1:5-25 [c]1 Kin 1:38-50 [d]1 Chr 22:9,10; 28:5-7
16 [1]Lit *turn away my face*
17 [1]Lit *turn away your face* [a]1 Kin 1:3,4
19 [a]1 Kin 15:13 [b]Ps 45:9
20 [1]Lit *turn away my face* [2]Lit *turn away your face* [a]1 Kin 2:16
21 [a]1 Kin 1:3,4
22 [a]2 Sam 12:8 [b]1 Kin 1:6; 2:15; 1 Chr 3:2,5 [c]1 Kin 1:7
23 [1]Lit *soul* [a]Ruth 1:17
24 [a]2 Sam 7:11, 13; 1 Chr 22:10
25 [a]2 Sam 8:18
26 [1]Lit *are a man of death* [2]Heb *YHWH,* usually rendered LORD [a]Josh 21:18; Jer 1:1 [b]1 Sam 26:16 [c]1 Sam 23:6; 2 Sam 15:24-29 [d]1 Sam 22:20-23; 23:8,9
27 [a]1 Sam 2:27-36
28 [a]1 Kin 1:7 [b]2 Sam 17:25; 18:2 [c]1 Kin 1:50
29 [a]1 Kin 2:25 [b]Ex 21:14
31 [a]Ex 21:14 [b]Num 35:33; Deut 19:13; 21:8,9
32 [a]Gen 9:6; Judg 9:24,57; Ps 7:16 [b]2 Chr 21:13,14 [c]2 Sam 3:27 [d]2 Sam 20:9,10
33 [1]Lit *seed* [a]2 Sam 3:29
34 [a]1 Kin 2:25 [b]Josh 15:61; Matt 3:1
35 [a]1 Kin 4:4 [b]1 Chr 6:53; 24:3; 29:22 [c]1 Kin 2:27
36 [a]2 Sam 16:5; 1 Kin 2:8
37 [1]Or *wadi* [a]2 Sam 15:23; 2 Kin 23:6; John 18:1 [b]Josh 2:19; 2 Sam 1:16; Ezek 18:13
39 [a]1 Sam 27:2

saying, “Behold, your servants are in
Gath.”
40 Then Shimei arose and saddled his
donkey, and went to Gath to Achish to
look for his servants. And Shimei went
and brought his servants from Gath.
41 It was told Solomon that Shimei
had gone from Jerusalem to Gath, and
had returned.
42 So the king sent and called for
Shimei and said to him, “Did I not make
you swear by the LORD and solemnly
warn you, saying, ‘You will know for certain that on the day you depart and go
anywhere, you shall surely die’? And you
said to me, ‘The word which I have heard
is good.’
43 “Why then have you not kept the
oath of the LORD, and the command
which I [1]have laid on you?”
44 The king also said to Shimei, “[a]You
know all the evil which [1]you acknowledge in your heart, which you did to my
father David; therefore [b]the LORD shall
return your evil on your own head.
45 “But King Solomon shall be blessed,
and [a]the throne of David shall be established before the LORD forever.”
46 [a]So the king commanded Benaiah
the son of Jehoiada, and he went out and
fell upon him so that he died.
¶ [b]Thus the kingdom was established
in the hands of Solomon.

Solomon’s Rule Consolidated

3 Then [a]Solomon [1]formed a marriage
alliance with Pharaoh king of Egypt,
and took Pharaoh’s daughter [b]and
brought her to the city of David [c]until he
had finished building his own house and
the house of the LORD and [d]the wall
around Jerusalem.
2 [a]The people were still sacrificing
on the high places, because there was no
house built for the name of the LORD until
those days.
3 ¶ Now [a]Solomon loved the LORD,
[b]walking in the statutes of his father David, except he sacrificed and burned incense on the high places.
4 [a]The king went to [b]Gibeon to sacrifice there, [c]for that was the great high
place; Solomon offered a thousand burnt
offerings on that altar.
5 [a]In Gibeon the LORD appeared to
Solomon [b]in a dream at night; and God
said, “[c]Ask what *you wish* me to give
you.”

Solomon’s Prayer

6 Then Solomon said, “[a]You have
shown great lovingkindness to Your servant David my father, [b]according as he
walked before You in [1]truth and righteousness and uprightness of heart toward You; and [c]You have [2]reserved for
him this great lovingkindness, that You
have given him a son to sit on his throne,
as *it is* this day.
7 “Now, O LORD my God, [a]You have
made Your servant king in place of my
father David, yet [b]I am but a little child;
[c]I do not know how to go out or come in.
8 “[a]Your servant is in the midst of
Your people which You have chosen, [b]a
great people who are too many to be
numbered or counted.
9 “So [a]give Your servant [1]an understanding heart to judge Your people [b]to
discern between good and evil. For who
is able to judge this [2]great people of
Yours?”

God’s Answer

10 ¶ [1]It was pleasing in the sight of
the Lord that Solomon had asked this
thing.
11 God said to him, “Because you have
asked this thing and have [a]not asked for
yourself [1]long life, nor have asked riches
for yourself, nor have you asked for the
life of your enemies, but have asked for
yourself [2]discernment to understand justice,
12 behold, [a]I have done according to
your words. Behold, [b]I have given you a
wise and discerning heart, so that there
has been no one like you before you, nor
shall one like you arise after you.
13 “[a]I have also given you what you
have not asked, both [b]riches and honor,
so that there will not be any among the
kings like you all your days.
14 “[a]If you walk in My ways, keeping
My statutes and commandments, as your
father David walked, then I will [b]prolong
your days.”
15 ¶ Then [a]Solomon awoke, and behold, it was a dream. And he came to
Jerusalem and stood before the ark of the
covenant of the Lord, and offered burnt
offerings and made peace offerings, and
[b]made a feast for all his servants.

Solomon Wisely Judges

16 ¶ Then two women who were harlots came to the king and stood before
him.
17 The one woman said, “Oh, my lord,
[1]this woman and I live in the same
house; and I gave birth to a child while
she *was* in the house.
18 “It happened on the third day after I
gave birth, that this woman also gave
birth to a child, and we were together.
There was no stranger with us in the
house, only the two of us in the house.

---

43 [1]Lit *commanded*
44 [1]Lit *your heart acknowledges* [a]2 Sam 16:5-13 [b]1 Sam 25:39; 2 Kin 11:1,12-16; Ps 7:16
45 [a]2 Sam 7:13; Prov 25:5
46 [a]1 Kin 2:25, 34 [b]1 Kin 2:12; 2 Chr 1:1
3:1 [1]Lit *made himself a son-in-law of Pharaoh* [a]1 Kin 7:8; 9:16, 24; 2 Chr 8:11 [b]1 Kin 9:24 [c]1 Kin 7:1; 9:10 [d]1 Kin 9:15
2 [a]Lev 17:3-5; Deut 12:2,13,14; 1 Kin 22:43
3 [a]Deut 6:5; 10:12,13; 11:13; 30:16; Ps 31:23; 145:20; 1 Cor 8:3 [b]1 Kin 2:3; 9:4; 11:4,6,38
4 [a]2 Chr 1:3 [b]Josh 18:21-25 [c]1 Chr 16:39; 21:29
5 [a]1 Kin 9:2; 11:9 [b]Num 12:6; Matt 1:20; 2:13 [c]John 15:7
6 [1]Or *faithfulness* [2]Lit *kept* [a]2 Sam 7:8-17; 2 Chr 1:8 [b]1 Kin 9:4 [c]1 Kin 1:48
7 [a]1 Chr 22:9-13 [b]1 Chr 29:1; Jer 1:6,7 [c]Num 27:17
8 [a]Ex 19:6; Deut 7:6 [b]Gen 15:5; 22:17
9 [1]Lit *a hearing* [2]Lit *heavy* [a]2 Chr 1:10; Ps 72:1,2; Prov 2:3-9; James 1:5 [b]2 Sam 14:17; Heb 5:14
10 [1]Lit *the thing*
11 [1]Lit *many days* [2]Lit *hearing* [a]James 4:3
12 [a]1 John 5:14, 15 [b]1 Kin 4:29-31; 5:12; 10:23,24; Eccl 1:16
13 [a]1 Kin 4:21-24; 10:23, 27; Matt 6:33; Eph 3:20 [b]Prov 3:16
14 [a]1 Kin 3:6 [b]Ps 91:16; Prov 3:2
15 [a]Gen 41:7 [b]1 Kin 8:65
17 [1]Lit *I and this woman*

19 "This woman's son died in the night, because she lay on it.

20 "So she arose in the middle of the night and took my son from beside me while your maidservant slept, and laid him in her bosom, and laid her dead son in my bosom.

21 "When I rose in the morning to nurse my son, behold, he was dead; but when I looked at him carefully in the morning, behold, he was not my son, whom I had borne."

22 Then the other woman said, "No! For the living one is my son, and the dead one is your son." But [1]the first woman said, "No! For the dead one is your son, and the living one is my son." Thus they spoke before the king.

23 ¶ Then the king said, "[1]The one says, 'This is my son who is living, and your son is the dead one'; and [1]the other says, 'No! For your son is the dead one, and my son is the living one.' "

24 The king said, "Get me a sword." So they brought a sword before the king.

25 The king said, "Divide the living child in two, and give half to the one and half to the other."

26 Then the woman whose child *was* the living one spoke to the king, for [1a]she was deeply stirred over her son and said, "Oh, my lord, give her the living child, and by no means kill him." But the other said, "He shall be neither mine nor yours; divide *him!*"

27 Then the king said, "Give [1]the first woman the living child, and by no means kill him. She is his mother."

28 When all Israel heard of the judgment which the king had [1]handed down, they feared the king, for [a]they saw that the wisdom of God was in him to [2]administer justice.

Solomon's Officials

4 Now King Solomon was king over all Israel.

2 These were his officials: Azariah the son of Zadok *was* [a]the priest;

3 Elihoreph and Ahijah, the sons of Shisha *were* secretaries; [a]Jehoshaphat the son of Ahilud *was* the recorder;

4 and [a]Benaiah the son of Jehoiada *was* over the army; and Zadok and [b]Abiathar *were* priests;

5 and Azariah the son of Nathan *was* over [a]the deputies; and Zabud the son of Nathan, a priest, *was* the king's friend;

6 and Ahishar was over the household; and Adoniram the son of Abda *was* over the men subject to forced labor.

7 ¶ Solomon had twelve deputies over all Israel, who [1]provided for the

22 [1]Lit *this one was saying*

23 [1]Lit *this one*

26 [1]Lit *her compassion grew warm* [a]Gen 43:30; Is 49:15; Jer 31:20; Hos 11:8

27 [1]Lit *her the living child*

28 [1]Lit *judged* [2]Lit *do* [a]1 Kin 3:9,11,12; Dan 1:17; Col 2:2,3

4:2 [a]1 Chr 6:10

3 [a]2 Sam 8:16

4 [a]1 Kin 2:35 [b]1 Kin 2:27

5 [a]1 Kin 4:7

7 [1]Lit *nourished* [2]Lit *nourish*

8 [a]Josh 24:33

9 [a]Judg 1:35 [b]Josh 21:16

10 [a]Josh 15:35 [b]Josh 12:17

11 [1]Or *Naphoth-dor* [a]Josh 11:1,2

12 [a]Judg 5:19 [b]Josh 17:11 [c]Josh 3:16 [d]1 Kin 19:16 [e]1 Chr 6:68

13 [a]1 Kin 22:3-15 [b]Num 32:41 [c]Deut 3:4

14 [a]Josh 13:26

15 [a]2 Sam 15:27

16 [1]Or *in Aloth* [a]2 Sam 15:32

18 [a]1 Kin 1:8

19 [a]Deut 3:8-10

20 [1]Lit *sea* [a]Gen 22:17; 32:12; 1 Kin 3:8

21 [1]Ch 5:1 in Heb [2]I.e. Euphrates [a]2 Chr 9:26 [b]Gen 15:18; Josh 1:4 [c]2 Sam 8:2,6

22 [1]Lit *bread* [2]I.e. One kor equals approx 10 bu

23 [1]Lit *oxen of the pasture*

24 [1]Lit *beyond* [2]I.e. Euphrates [a]Judg 1:18 [b]Ps 72:11 [c]1 Chr 22:9

25 [a]Jer 23:6; Mic 4:4; Zech 3:10

king and his household; each man had to [2]provide for a month in the year.

8 These are their names: Ben-hur, in the [a]hill country of Ephraim;

9 Ben-deker in Makaz and [a]Shaalbim and [b]Beth-shemesh and Elonbeth-hanan;

10 Ben-hesed, in Arubboth ([a]Socoh *was* his and all the land of [b]Hepher);

11 Ben-abinadab, *in* all [1]the [a]height of Dor (Taphath the daughter of Solomon was his wife);

12 Baana the son of Ahilud, *in* [a]Taanach and Megiddo, and all [b]Beth-shean which is beside [c]Zarethan below Jezreel, from Beth-shean to [d]Abel-meholah as far as the other side of [e]Jokmeam;

13 Ben-geber, in [a]Ramoth-gilead ([b]the towns of Jair, the son of Manasseh, which are in Gilead were his: [c]the region of Argob, which is in Bashan, sixty great cities with walls and bronze bars *were* his);

14 Ahinadab the son of Iddo, *in* [a]Mahanaim;

15 [a]Ahimaaz, in Naphtali (he also married Basemath the daughter of Solomon);

16 Baana the son of [a]Hushai, in Asher and [1]Bealoth;

17 Jehoshaphat the son of Paruah, in Issachar;

18 [a]Shimei the son of Ela, in Benjamin;

19 Geber the son of Uri, in the land of Gilead, [a]the country of Sihon king of the Amorites and of Og king of Bashan; and *he was* the only deputy who *was* in the land.

Solomon's Power, Wealth and Wisdom

20 ¶ [a]Judah and Israel *were* as numerous as the sand that is on the [1]seashore in abundance; *they* were eating and drinking and rejoicing.

21 ¶ [1a]Now Solomon ruled over all the kingdoms [b]from the [2]River *to* the land of the Philistines and to the border of Egypt; [c]*they* brought tribute and served Solomon all the days of his life.

22 ¶ Solomon's [1]provision for one day was thirty [2]kors of fine flour and sixty [2]kors of meal,

23 ten fat oxen, twenty [1]pasture-fed oxen, a hundred sheep besides deer, gazelles, roebucks, and fattened fowl.

24 For he had dominion over everything [1]west of the [2]River, from Tiphsah even to [a]Gaza, [b]over all the kings [1]west of the [2]River; and [c]he had peace on all sides around about him.

25 [a]So Judah and Israel lived in safety,

every man under his vine and his fig tree,
[b]from Dan even to Beersheba, all the
days of Solomon.
26 [a]Solomon had [1]40,000 stalls of
horses for his chariots, and 12,000 horsemen.
27 Those deputies [1]provided for King
Solomon and all who came to King Solomon's table, each in his month; they left
nothing lacking.
28 They also brought barley and straw
for the horses and [a]swift steeds to the
place where it should be, each according
to his charge.
29 ¶ Now [a]God gave Solomon wisdom and very great discernment and
breadth of [1]mind, [b]like the sand that is
on the seashore.
30 Solomon's wisdom surpassed the
wisdom of all [a]the sons of the east and
[b]all the wisdom of Egypt.
31 For [a]he was wiser than all men,
than [b]Ethan the Ezrahite, Heman, [c]Cal-
col and [1]Darda, the sons of Mahol; and
his [2]fame was *known* in all the surrounding nations.
32 [a]He also spoke 3,000 proverbs,
and his songs were 1,005.
33 He spoke of trees, from the cedar
that is in Lebanon even to the hyssop that
grows on the wall; he spoke also of animals and birds and creeping things and
fish.
34 [1]Men [a]came from all peoples to
hear the wisdom of Solomon, from all the
kings of the earth who had heard of his
wisdom.

Alliance with King Hiram

5 [a]Now Hiram king of Tyre sent his
servants to Solomon, when he heard
that they had anointed him king in place
of his father, for [b]Hiram had [1]always
been a friend of David.
2 Then [a]Solomon sent *word* to Hiram, saying,
3 "You know that [a]David my father
was unable to build a house for the name
of the LORD his God because of the wars
which surrounded him, until the LORD
put them under the soles of his feet.
4 "But now [a]the LORD my God has
given me rest on every side; there is neither adversary nor [1]misfortune.
5 "Behold, [a]I [1]intend to build a house
for the name of the LORD my God, as the
LORD spoke to David my father, saying,
'Your son, whom I will set on your throne
in your place, he will build the house for
My name.'
6 "Now therefore, command that they
cut for me [a]cedars from Lebanon, and
my servants will be with your servants;
and I will give you wages for your servants according to all that you say, for you
know that there is no one among us who
knows how to cut timber like the Sidonians."
7 ¶ When Hiram heard the words of
Solomon, he rejoiced greatly and said,
"Blessed be the LORD today, who has giv-
en to David a wise son over this great
people."
8 So Hiram sent *word* to Solomon,
saying, "I have heard *the message* which
you have sent me; I will do [1]what you
desire concerning the cedar and cypress
timber.
9 "My servants will bring *them* down
from Lebanon to the sea; and I will make
them into rafts *to go* by sea [a]to the place
where you [1]direct me, and I will have
them broken up there, and you shall carry
them away. Then [b]you shall accomplish
my desire by giving food to my household."
10 So [1]Hiram [2]gave Solomon [3]as
much as he desired of the cedar and cypress timber.
11 [a]Solomon then gave Hiram 20,000
[1]kors of wheat as food for his household,
and twenty [1]kors of beaten oil; thus Solomon would give Hiram year by year.
12 [a]The LORD gave wisdom to Solomon, just as He [1]promised him; and
there was peace between Hiram and Solomon, and the two of them made a covenant.

Conscription of Laborers

13 ¶ Now [a]King Solomon [1]levied
forced laborers from all Israel; and the
forced laborers [2]numbered 30,000 men.
14 He sent them to Lebanon, 10,000 a
month in relays; they were in Lebanon a
month *and* two months at home. And
[a]Adoniram *was* over the forced laborers.
15 Now [a]Solomon had 70,000
[1]transporters, and 80,000 hewers *of
stone* in the mountains,
16 [a]besides Solomon's 3,300 chief
deputies who *were* over the [1]project *and*
who ruled over the people who were doing the work.
17 Then [a]the king commanded, and
they quarried great stones, costly stones,
to lay the foundation of the house with
cut stones.
18 So Solomon's builders and [1]Hi-
ram's builders and [a]the Gebalites [2]cut
them, and prepared the timbers and the
stones to build the house.

The Building of the Temple

6 [a]Now it came about in the four hundred and eightieth year after the sons
of Israel came out of the land of Egypt, in
the fourth year of Solomon's reign over

25 [b]1 Sam 3:20
26 [1]One ms reads *4000*, cf 2 Chr 9:25 [a]1 Kin 10:26; 2 Chr 1:14
27 [1]Or *nourished*
28 [a]Esth 8:10, 14; Mic 1:13
29 [1]Lit *heart* [a]1 Kin 3:12 [b]1 Kin 4:20
30 [a]Gen 29:1; Judg 6:33 [b]Is 19:11; Acts 7:22
31 [1]In 1 Chr 2:6, *Dara* [2]Lit *name* [a]1 Kin 3:12 [b]1 Chr 15:19; Ps 89: title [c]1 Chr 2:6
32 [a]Prov 1:1; 10:1; 25:1; Eccl 12:9; Song 1:1
34 [1]Lit *they* [a]1 Kin 10:1; 2 Chr 9:23
5:1 [1]Lit *all the day* [a]2 Chr 2:3 [b]2 Sam 5:11; 1 Chr 14:1
2 [a]2 Chr 2:3
3 [a]2 Sam 7:5; 1 Chr 28:2,3
4 [1]Lit *evil occurrence* [a]1 Kin 4:24; 1 Chr 22:9
5 [1]Lit *say* [a]2 Sam 7:12,13; 1 Chr 17:12; 22:10; 28:6; 2 Chr 2:4
6 [a]2 Chr 2:8
8 [1]Lit *all your pleasure*
9 [1]Lit *send* [a]2 Chr 2:16 [b]Ezra 3:7; Ezek 27:17
10 [1]Heb *Hirom* [2]Lit *was giving* [3]Lit *all his desire*
11 [1]I.e. One kor equals approx 10 bu [a]2 Chr 2:10
12 [1]Lit *spoke to* [a]1 Kin 3:12
13 [1]Lit *raised up* [2]Lit *was* [a]1 Kin 4:6; 9:15
14 [a]1 Kin 4:6; 12:18
15 [1]Or *burden bearers* [a]1 Kin 9:20-22; 2 Chr 2:17,18
16 [1]Lit *work* [a]1 Kin 9:23
17 [a]1 Kin 6:7; 1 Chr 22:2
18 [1]Heb *Hirom's* [2]Or *chiseled* [a]Josh 13:5; Ezek 27:9
6:1 [a]2 Chr 3:1,2

Israel, in the month of Ziv which is the second month, that he [1]began to build the house of the LORD.

2 As for the house which King Solomon built for the LORD, its length *was* sixty [1]cubits and its width twenty *cubits* and its height thirty cubits.

3 The porch in front of the nave of the house *was* twenty cubits [1]in length, [2]corresponding to the width of the house, *and* its [3]depth along the front of the house *was* ten cubits.

4 Also for the house [a]he made windows with *artistic* frames.

5 [a]Against the wall of the house he built stories encompassing the walls of the house around both the nave and the [b]inner sanctuary; thus he made [c]side chambers all around.

6 The lowest story *was* five cubits wide, and the middle *was* six cubits wide, and the third *was* seven cubits wide; for on the outside he [1]made offsets *in the wall* of the house all around in order that *the beams* would not [2]be inserted in the walls of the house.

7 ¶ [a]The house, while it was being built, was built of stone [1]prepared at the quarry, and there was neither hammer nor axe nor any iron tool heard in the house while it was being built.

8 ¶ The doorway for the [1]lowest side chamber *was* on the right side of the house; and they would go up by winding stairs to the middle *story,* and from the middle to the third.

9 So [a]he built the house and finished it; and he covered the house with beams and [1]planks of cedar.

10 He also built the stories against the whole house, each five [1]cubits high; and they [2]were fastened to the house with timbers of cedar.

11 ¶ Now the word of the LORD came to Solomon saying,

12 "*Concerning* this house which you are building, [a]if you will walk in My statutes and execute My ordinances and keep all My commandments by walking in them, then I will carry out My word with you which I spoke to David your father.

13 "[a]I will dwell among the sons of Israel, and [b]will not forsake My people Israel."

14 ¶ [a]So Solomon built the house and finished it.

15 Then he [a]built the walls of the house on the inside with boards of cedar; from the floor of the house to the [1]ceiling he overlaid *the walls* on the inside with wood, and he overlaid the floor of the house with boards of cypress.

16 [a]He built twenty cubits on the rear part of the house with boards of cedar from the floor to the [1]ceiling; he built *them* for it on the inside as an inner sanctuary, *even* as [b]the most holy place.

17 The house, that is, the nave in front of *the inner sanctuary,* was forty [1]cubits *long.*

18 There was cedar on the house within, carved *in the shape* of [a]gourds and open flowers; all was cedar, there was no stone seen.

19 Then he prepared an inner sanctuary within the house in order to place there the ark of the covenant of the LORD.

20 [1]The inner sanctuary *was* twenty cubits in length, twenty cubits in width, and twenty cubits in height, and he overlaid it with pure gold. He also overlaid the altar with cedar.

21 So Solomon overlaid the inside of the house with pure gold. And he drew chains of gold across the front of the inner sanctuary, and he overlaid it with gold.

22 He overlaid the whole house with gold, until all the house was finished. Also [a]the whole altar which was by the inner sanctuary he overlaid with gold.

23 ¶ [a]Also in the inner sanctuary he made two cherubim of olive wood, each ten cubits high.

24 Five cubits *was* the one wing of the cherub and five cubits the other wing of the cherub; from the end of one wing to the end of the other wing *were* ten cubits.

25 The other cherub *was* ten cubits; both the cherubim were of the same measure and the same form.

26 The height of the one cherub *was* ten cubits, and so *was* the other cherub.

27 He placed the cherubim in the midst of the inner house, and [a]the wings of the cherubim were spread out, so that the wing of the one was touching the *one* wall, and the wing of the other cherub was touching the other wall. So their wings were touching each other in the center of the house.

28 He also overlaid the cherubim with gold.

29 ¶ Then he carved all the walls of the house round about with carved engravings of cherubim, palm trees, and open flowers, inner and outer *sanctuaries.*

30 He overlaid the floor of the house with gold, inner and outer *sanctuaries.*

31 ¶ For the entrance of the inner sanctuary he made doors of olive wood, the lintel *and* five-sided doorposts.

32 So *he made* two doors of olive wood, and he carved on them carvings of cherubim, palm trees, and open flowers,

1 [1]Lit *built*
2 [1]I.e. One cubit equals approx 18 in.
3 [1]Lit *in its length* [2]Lit *on the face of* [3]Lit *width*
4 [a]Ezek 40:16; 41:16
5 [a]Ezek 41:6 [b]1 Kin 6:16,19, 20 [c]Ezek 41:5
6 [1]Lit *gave* [2]Lit *take hold*
7 [1]Lit *finished* [a]Ex 20:25; Deut 27:5,6
8 [1]So with Gr and versions; M.T. *middle*
9 [1]Lit *rows* [a]1 Kin 6:14,38
10 [1]I.e. One cubit equals approx 18 in. [2]Lit *took hold*
12 [a]2 Sam 7:5-16; 1 Kin 9:4
13 [a]Ex 25:8; 29:45; Lev 26:11 [b]Deut 31:6; Josh 1:5; Heb 13:5
14 [a]1 Kin 6:9, 38
15 [1]Lit *walls of ceiling* [a]1 Kin 7:7
16 [1]Lit *walls* [a]2 Chr 3:8 [b]Ex 26:33,34; Lev 16:2; 1 Kin 8:6; Heb 9:3
17 [1]I.e. One cubit equals approx 18 in.
18 [a]1 Kin 7:24
20 [1]Lit *before*
22 [a]Ex 30:1,3,6
23 [a]Ex 37:7-9; 2 Chr 3:10-12
27 [a]Ex 25:20; 37:9; 1 Kin 8:7

and overlaid them with gold; and he spread the gold on the cherubim and on the palm trees.

33 ¶ So also he made for the entrance of the nave four-sided doorposts of olive wood

34 and [a]two doors of cypress wood; the two leaves of the one door turned on pivots, and the two [1]leaves of the other door turned on pivots.

35 He carved *on it* cherubim, palm trees, and open flowers; and he overlaid *them* with gold evenly applied on the engraved work.

36 [a]He built the inner court with three rows of cut stone and a row of cedar beams.

37 ¶ [a]In the fourth year the foundation of the house of the LORD was laid, in the month of Ziv.

38 In the eleventh year, in the month of Bul, which is the eighth month, the house was finished throughout all its parts and according to all its plans. So he was seven years in building it.

Solomon's Palace

7 Now [a]Solomon was building his own house thirteen years, and he finished all his house.

2 [a]He built the house of the forest of Lebanon; its length was 100 [1]cubits and its width 50 cubits and its height 30 cubits, on four rows of cedar pillars with cedar beams on the pillars.

3 It was paneled with cedar above the side chambers which were on the 45 pillars, 15 in each row.

4 *There were artistic window* frames in three rows, and window was opposite window in three ranks.

5 All the doorways and doorposts *had* squared *artistic* frames, and window was opposite window in three ranks.

6 ¶ Then he made [a]the hall of pillars; its length was 50 cubits and its width 30 cubits, and a porch *was* in front of them and pillars and a [b]threshold in front of them.

7 ¶ He made the hall of the [a]throne where he was to judge, the hall of judgment, and [b]it was paneled with cedar from floor to floor.

8 ¶ His house where he was to live, the other court inward from the hall, was of the same workmanship. [a]He also made a house like this hall for Pharaoh's daughter, [b]whom Solomon had married.

9 ¶ All these were of costly stones, of stone cut according to measure, sawed with saws, inside and outside; even from the foundation to the coping, and so on the outside to the great court.

10 ¶ The foundation was of costly stones, *even* large stones, stones of ten cubits and stones of eight cubits.

11 And above were costly stones, stone cut according to measure, and cedar.

12 So [a]the great court all around *had* three rows of cut stone and a row of cedar beams even as the inner court of the house of the LORD, and [b]the porch of the house.

Hiram's Work in the Temple

13 ¶ Now [a]King Solomon sent and brought Hiram from Tyre.

14 [a]He was a widow's son from the tribe of Naphtali, and his father was a man of Tyre, a worker in bronze; and [b]he was filled with wisdom and understanding and skill for doing any work in bronze. So he came to King Solomon and [c]performed all his work.

15 ¶ He fashioned [a]the two pillars of bronze; [b]eighteen cubits was the height of one pillar, and a line of twelve cubits [1]measured the circumference of both.

16 He also made two capitals of molten bronze to set on the tops of the pillars; the height of the one capital was five [1]cubits and the height of the other capital was five cubits.

17 *There were* nets of network and twisted threads of chainwork for the capitals which were on the top of the pillars; seven for the one capital and seven for the other capital.

18 So he made the pillars, and two rows around on the one network to cover the capitals which were on the top of the pomegranates; and so he did for the other capital.

19 The capitals which *were* on the top of the pillars in the porch were of lily design, four cubits.

20 *There were* capitals on the two pillars, even above *and* close to the [1]rounded projection which was beside the network; and [a]the pomegranates *numbered* two hundred in rows around [2]both capitals.

21 [a]Thus he set up the pillars at the [b]porch of the nave; and he set up the right pillar and named it [1]Jachin, and he set up the left pillar and named it [2]Boaz.

22 On the top of the pillars was lily design. So the work of the pillars was finished.

23 ¶ [a]Now he made the sea of [b]cast *metal* ten cubits from brim to brim, circular in form, and its height was five cubits, and [1]thirty cubits in circumference.

24 Under its brim [a]gourds went around encircling it ten to a cubit, [b]completely surrounding the sea; the gourds were in two rows, cast [1]with the rest.

34 [1]So with Gr; M.T. *curtains* [a]Ezek 41:23-25
36 [a]1 Kin 7:12; Jer 36:10
37 [a]1 Kin 6:1
7:1 [a]1 Kin 3:1; 9:10; 2 Chr 8:1
2 [1]I.e. One cubit equals approx 18 in. [a]1 Kin 10:17, 21; 2 Chr 9:16
6 [a]1 Kin 7:12 [b]Ezek 41:25,26
7 [a]Ps 122:5; Prov 20:8 [b]1 Kin 6:15,16
8 [a]1 Kin 9:24; 2 Chr 8:11 [b]1 Kin 3:1
12 [a]1 Kin 6:36 [b]1 Kin 7:6
13 [a]2 Chr 2:13, 14; 4:11
14 [a]2 Chr 2:14 [b]Ex 28:3; 31:3-5; 35:31; 36:1 [c]2 Chr 4:11-16
15 [1]Lit *went around the other pillar* [a]2 Kin 25:17; 2 Chr 3:15; 4:12; Jer 52:21 [b]1 Kin 7:41
16 [1]I.e. One cubit equals approx 18 in.
20 [1]Lit *belly* [2]Lit *on the other capital* [a]1 Kin 7:42; 2 Chr 3:16; 4:13; Jer 52:23
21 [1]I.e. he shall establish [2]I.e. in it is strength [a]2 Chr 3:17 [b]1 Kin 6:3
23 [1]Lit *a line of 30 cubits went around it* [a]2 Chr 4:2 [b]2 Kin 16:17; 25:13
24 [1]Lit *in its casting* [a]1 Kin 6:18 [b]2 Chr 4:3

25 [a]It stood on twelve oxen, three facing north, three facing west, three facing south, and three facing east; and the sea *was set* on top of them, and all their rear parts *turned* inward.

26 It was a handbreadth thick, and its brim was made like the brim of a cup, *as* a lily blossom; it could hold two thousand baths.

27 ¶ Then [a]he made the ten stands of bronze; the length of each stand was four cubits and its width four cubits and its height three cubits.

28 This was the design of the stands: they had borders, even borders between the [1]frames,

29 and on the borders which were between the [1]frames *were* lions, oxen and cherubim; and on the [1]frames there *was* a pedestal above, and beneath the lions and oxen *were* wreaths of hanging work.

30 Now each stand had four bronze wheels with bronze axles, and its four feet had supports; beneath the basin *were* cast supports with wreaths at each side.

31 Its opening inside the crown at the top *was* a cubit, and its opening *was* round like the design of a pedestal, a cubit and a half; and also on its opening *there were* engravings, and their borders were square, not round.

32 The four wheels *were* underneath the borders, and the axles of the wheels *were* on the stand. And the height of a wheel *was* a cubit and a half.

33 The workmanship of the wheels *was* like the workmanship of a chariot wheel. Their axles, their rims, their spokes, and their hubs *were* all cast.

34 Now *there were* four supports at the four corners of each stand; its supports *were* part of the stand itself.

35 On the top of the stand *there was* a circular form half a [1]cubit high, and on the top of the stand its [2]stays and its borders *were* part of it.

36 He engraved on the plates of its stays and on its borders, cherubim, lions and palm trees, according to the clear space on each, with wreaths *all* around.

37 [a]He made the ten stands like this: all of them had one casting, one measure and one form.

38 ¶ [a]He made ten basins of bronze, one basin held forty baths; each basin *was* four cubits, *and* on each of the ten stands *was* one basin.

39 Then he set the stands, five on the right side of the house and five on the left side of the house; and he set the sea *of cast metal* on the right side of the house eastward toward the south.

40 ¶ Now Hiram made the basins and the shovels and the bowls. So Hiram finished doing all the work which he performed for King Solomon *in* the house of the LORD:

41 the two pillars and the *two* bowls of the capitals which *were* on the top of the [a]two pillars, and the two networks to cover the two bowls of the capitals which *were* on the top of the pillars;

42 and the [a]four hundred pomegranates for the two networks, two rows of pomegranates for each network to cover the two bowls of the capitals which *were* on the tops of the pillars;

43 and the ten stands with the ten basins on the stands;

44 and [a]the one sea and the twelve oxen under the sea;

45 and [a]the pails and the shovels and the bowls; even all these utensils which Hiram made for King Solomon *in* the house of the LORD *were* of polished bronze.

46 [a]In the plain of the Jordan the king cast them, in the clay ground between [b]Succoth and [c]Zarethan.

47 Solomon left all the utensils *unweighed,* because *they were* too many; [a]the weight of the bronze could not be ascertained.

48 ¶ Solomon made all the furniture which *was in* the house of the LORD: [a]the golden altar and the golden table on which *was* the [b]bread of the Presence;

49 and the lampstands, five on the right side and five on the left, in front of the inner sanctuary, of pure gold; and [a]the flowers and the lamps and the tongs, of gold;

50 and the cups and the snuffers and the bowls and the spoons and the [a]firepans, of pure gold; and the hinges both for the doors of the inner house, the most holy place, *and* for the doors of the house, *that is,* of the nave, of gold.

51 ¶ [a]Thus all the work that King Solomon performed *in* the house of the LORD was finished. And [b]Solomon brought in the things dedicated by his father David, the silver and the gold and the utensils, *and* he put them in the treasuries of the house of the LORD.

The Ark Brought into the Temple

8 [a]Then Solomon assembled the elders of Israel and all [b]the heads of the tribes, the leaders of the fathers' *households* of the sons of Israel, to King Solomon in Jerusalem, [c]to bring up the ark of the covenant of the LORD from [d]the city of David, which is Zion.

2 All the men of Israel assembled themselves to King Solomon at [a]the feast, in the month Ethanim, which is the seventh month.

25 [a]2 Chr 4:4,5; Jer 52:20
27 [a]1 Kin 7:38; 2 Kin 25:13; 2 Chr 4:14
28 [1]Or *crossbars*
29 [1]Or *crossbars*
35 [1]I.e. One cubit equals approx 18 in. [2]Lit *hands*
37 [a]2 Chr 4:14
38 [a]Ex 30:18; 2 Chr 4:6
41 [a]1 Kin 7:17, 18
42 [a]1 Kin 7:20
44 [a]1 Kin 7:23, 25
45 [a]Ex 27:3; 2 Chr 4:16
46 [a]2 Chr 4:17 [b]Gen 33:17; Josh 13:27 [c]Josh 3:16
47 [a]1 Chr 22:3, 14
48 [a]Ex 30:1-3; 37:10-29; 2 Chr 4:8 [b]Ex 25:30
49 [a]Ex 25:31-38
50 [a]Ex 27:3; 2 Kin 25:15
51 [a]2 Chr 5:1 [b]2 Sam 8:11; 1 Chr 18:11; 2 Chr 5:1
8:1 [a]2 Chr 5:2-10 [b]Num 1:4; 7:2 [c]2 Sam 6:12-17; 1 Chr 15:25-29 [d]2 Sam 5:7
2 [a]Lev 23:34; 1 Kin 8:65; 2 Chr 7:8-10

3 Then all the elders of Israel came, and [a]the priests took up the ark.

4 They brought up the ark of the LORD and [a]the tent of meeting and all the holy utensils, which were in the tent, and the priests and the Levites brought them up.

5 And King Solomon and all the congregation of Israel, who were assembled to him, [a]were with him before the ark, sacrificing [1]so many sheep and oxen they could not be counted or numbered.

6 Then [a]the priests brought the ark of the covenant of the LORD [b]to its place, into the inner sanctuary of the house, to the most holy place, [c]under the wings of the cherubim.

7 For the cherubim spread *their* wings over the place of the ark, and the cherubim made a covering over the ark and its poles from above.

8 But [a]the poles were so long that the ends of the poles could be seen from the holy place before the inner sanctuary, but they could not be seen outside; they are there to this day.

9 [a]There was nothing in the ark except the two tablets of stone which Moses put there at Horeb, where [b]the LORD made a covenant with the sons of Israel, when they came out of the land of Egypt.

10 It happened that when the priests came from the holy place, [a]the cloud filled the house of the LORD,

11 so that the priests could not stand to minister because of the cloud, for the glory of the LORD filled the house of the LORD.

Solomon Addresses the People

12 ¶ [a]Then Solomon said,

"The LORD has said that [b]He
would dwell in the thick
cloud.

13 "[a]I have surely built You a lofty
house,
[b]A place for Your dwelling
forever."

14 ¶ Then the king [1]faced about and [a]blessed all the assembly of Israel, while all the assembly of Israel was standing.

15 He said, "[a]Blessed be the LORD, the God of Israel, [b]who spoke with His mouth to my father David and has fulfilled *it* with His hand, saying,

16 '[a]Since the day that I brought My people Israel from Egypt, I did not choose a city out of all the tribes of Israel *in which* to build a house that [b]My name might be there, but [c]I chose David to be over My people Israel.'

17 "[a]Now it was [1]in the heart of my father David to build a house for the name of the LORD, the God of Israel.

18 "But the LORD said to my father David, 'Because it was [1]in your heart to build a house for My name, you did well that it was [1]in your heart.

19 '[a]Nevertheless you shall not build the house, but your son who [1]will be born to you, he will build the house for My name.'

20 "Now the LORD has fulfilled His word which He spoke; for [a]I have risen in place of my father David and sit on the throne of Israel, as the LORD [1]promised, and have built the house for the name of the LORD, the God of Israel.

21 "There I have set a place for the ark, [a]in which is the covenant of the LORD, which He made with our fathers when He brought them from the land of Egypt."

The Prayer of Dedication

22 ¶ Then [a]Solomon stood before the altar of the LORD in the presence of all the assembly of Israel and [b]spread out his hands toward heaven.

23 He said, "O LORD, the God of Israel, [a]there is no God like You in heaven above or on earth beneath, [b]keeping covenant and *showing* lovingkindness to Your servants who walk before You with all their heart,

24 who have kept with Your servant, my father David, that which You have [1]promised him; indeed, You have spoken with Your mouth and have fulfilled it with Your hand as it is this day.

25 "Now therefore, O LORD, the God of Israel, keep with Your servant David my father that which You have [1]promised him, saying, '[2][a]You shall not lack a man to sit on the throne of Israel, if only your sons take heed to their way to walk before Me as you have walked.'

26 "Now therefore, O God of Israel, let Your word, I pray, be confirmed [a]which You have spoken to Your servant, my father David.

27 ¶ "But will God indeed dwell on the earth? Behold, [a]heaven and the [1]highest heaven cannot contain You, how much less this house which I have built!

28 "Yet have regard to the [a]prayer of Your servant and to his supplication, O LORD my God, to listen to the cry and to the prayer which Your servant prays before You today;

29 [a]that Your eyes may be open toward this house night and day, toward [b]the place of which You have said, 'My name shall be there,' to listen to the prayer which Your servant shall pray toward this place.

30 "[a]Listen to the supplication of Your servant and of Your people Israel, [b]when

3 [a]Num 7:9; Deut 31:9; Josh 3:3,6
4 [a]1 Kin 3:4; 2 Chr 1:3
5 [1]Lit *sheep and oxen...numbered for multitude* [a]2 Sam 6:13; 2 Chr 1:6
6 [a]1 Kin 8:3 [b]1 Kin 6:19 [c]1 Kin 6:27
8 [a]Ex 25:13-15; 37:4,5
9 [a]Ex 25:16,21; Deut 10:2-5; Heb 9:4 [b]Ex 24:7,8; 40:20; Deut 4:13
10 [a]Ex 40:34, 35; 2 Chr 7:1,2
12 [a]2 Chr 6:1 [b]Lev 16:2; Ps 18:11; 97:2
13 [a]2 Sam 7:13 [b]Ex 15:17; Ps 132:14
14 [1]Lit *turned his face about* [a]2 Sam 6:18; 1 Kin 8:55
15 [a]1 Chr 29:10,20; Neh 9:5; Luke 1:68 [b]2 Sam 7:12,13; 1 Chr 22:10
16 [a]2 Sam 7:4, 5; 1 Chr 17:3-10; 2 Chr 6:5 [b]Deut 12:5, 11 [c]1 Sam 16:1; 2 Sam 7:8
17 [1]Lit *with* [a]2 Sam 7:2,3; 1 Chr 17:1,2
18 [1]Lit *with*
19 [1]Lit *will come forth from your loins* [a]2 Sam 7:5,12, 13; 1 Kin 5:3,5; 1 Chr 17:11,12; 22:8-10
20 [1]Lit *spoke* [a]1 Chr 28:5,6
21 [a]Deut 31:26; 1 Kin 8:9
22 [a]1 Kin 8:54; 2 Chr 6:12 [b]Ex 9:33; Ezra 9:5
23 [a]1 Sam 2:2; 2 Sam 7:22 [b]Deut 7:9; Neh 1:5; 9:32; Dan 9:4
24 [1]Lit *spoken to*
25 [1]Lit *spoken to* [2]Lit *There shall not be cut off to you a man from before Me* [a]1 Kin 2:4
26 [a]2 Sam 7:25
27 [1]Lit *heaven of heavens* [a]2 Chr 2:6; Ps 139:7-16; Is 66:1; Jer 23:24; Acts 7:49
28 [a]Phil 4:6
29 [a]2 Chr 7:15; Neh 1:6 [b]Deut 12:11
30 [a]Neh 1:6 [b]Dan 6:10

they pray toward this place; hear in heav-
en Your dwelling place; hear and [c]for-
give.
31 ¶ "[a]If a man sins against his neighbor and is made to take an oath, and he
comes *and* takes an oath before Your altar
in this house,
32 then hear in heaven and act and
judge Your servants, [a]condemning the
wicked by bringing his way on his own
head and justifying the righteous by giving him according to his righteousness.
33 ¶ "[a]When Your people Israel are
[1]defeated before an enemy, because they
have sinned against You, [b]if they turn to
You again and confess Your name and
pray and make supplication to You in this
house,
34 then hear in heaven, and forgive
the sin of Your people Israel, and bring
them back to the land which You gave to
their fathers.
35 ¶ "[a]When the heavens are shut up
and there is no rain, because they have
sinned against You, and they pray toward
this place and confess Your name and
turn from their sin when You afflict them,
36 then hear in heaven and forgive the
sin of Your servants and of Your people
Israel, [a]indeed, teach them the good way
in which they should walk. And [b]send
rain on Your land, which You have given
Your people for an inheritance.
37 ¶ "[a]If there is famine in the land,
if there is pestilence, if there is blight *or*
mildew, locust *or* grasshopper, if their enemy besieges them in the land of their
[1]cities, whatever plague, whatever sickness *there is,*
38 whatever prayer or supplication is
made by any man *or* by all Your people
Israel, [1]each knowing the [2]affliction of
his own heart, and spreading his [3]hands
toward this house;
39 then hear in heaven Your dwelling
place, and forgive and act and render to
each according to all his ways, [a]whose
heart You know, for [b]You alone know
the hearts of all the sons of men,
40 that they may [1]fear You all the days
that they live [2]in the land which You
have given to our fathers.
41 ¶ "Also concerning the foreigner
who is not of Your people Israel, when he
comes from a far country for Your name's
sake
42 (for they will hear of Your great
name [a]and Your mighty hand, and of
Your outstretched arm); when he comes
and prays toward this house,
43 hear in heaven Your dwelling
place, and do according to all for which
the foreigner calls to You, in order [a]that
all the peoples of the earth may know
Your name, to [1]fear You, as *do* Your people Israel, and that they may know that
[2]this house which I have built is called
by Your name.
44 ¶ "When Your people go out to battle against [1]their enemy, by whatever
way You shall send them, and [a]they pray
to the LORD [2]toward the city which You
have chosen and the house which I have
built for Your name,
45 then hear in heaven their prayer
and their supplication, and maintain their
[1]cause.
46 ¶ "When they sin against You (for
[a]there is no man who does not sin) and
You are angry with them and deliver
them to an enemy, so that [1]they take
them away captive [b]to the land of the
enemy, far off or near;
47 [a]if they [1]take thought in the land
where they have been taken captive, and
repent and make supplication to You in
the land of those who have taken them
captive, saying, '[b]We have sinned and
have committed iniquity, we have acted
wickedly';
48 [a]if they return to You with all their
heart and with all their soul in the land of
their enemies who have taken them captive, and [b]pray to You toward their land
which You have given to their fathers,
the city which You have chosen, and the
house which I have built for Your name;
49 then hear their prayer and their
supplication in heaven Your dwelling
place, and maintain their [1]cause,
50 and forgive Your people who have
sinned against You and all their transgressions which they have transgressed
against You, and [a]make them *objects of*
compassion before those who have taken
them captive, that they may have compassion on them
51 ([a]for they are Your people and
Your inheritance which You have
brought forth from Egypt, [b]from the
midst of the iron furnace),
52 [a]that Your eyes may be open to the
supplication of Your servant and to the
supplication of Your people Israel, to listen to them whenever they call to You.
53 "For You have separated them from
all the peoples of the earth as Your inheritance, [a]as You spoke through Moses
Your servant, when You brought our fathers forth from Egypt, O Lord [1]GOD."

Solomon's Benediction

54 ¶ [a]When Solomon had finished
praying this entire prayer and supplication to the LORD, [b]he arose from before
the altar of the LORD, from kneeling on
his knees with his [1]hands spread toward
heaven.

30 [c]Ex 34:6,7; Ps 85:2; Dan 9:9; 1 John 1:9
31 [a]Ex 22:8-11
32 [a]Deut 25:1
33 [1]Lit *smitten* [a]Lev 26:17,25; Deut 28:25,48 [b]Lev 26:40-42
35 [a]Lev 26:19; Deut 11:16,17; 2 Sam 24:10-13
36 [a]1 Sam 12:23; Ps 5:8; 25:4,5; 27:11; 86:11; 119:133; Jer 6:16 [b]1 Kin 18:1,41-45; Jer 14:22
37 [1]Lit *gates* [a]Lev 26:16,25, 26; Deut 28:21-23,38-42
38 [1]Lit *who shall know each* [2]Lit *plague* [3]Lit *palms*
39 [a]1 Sam 2:3; 16:7 [b]1 Chr 28:9; Ps 11:4; Jer 17:10; John 2:24,25; Acts 1:24
40 [1]Or *revere* [2]Lit *on the face of the land*
42 [a]Ex 13:3; Deut 3:24
43 [1]Or *reverence* [2]Lit *Your name is called upon this house which I have built* [a]Josh 4:23, 24; 1 Sam 17:46; Ps 67:2
44 [1]Lit *his* [2]Lit *in the way of* [a]2 Chr 14:11
45 [1]Lit *right* or *justice*
46 [1]Lit *their captors take them captive* [a]Ps 130:3,4; 143:2; Prov 20:9; Eccl 7:20; Rom 3:23; 1 John 1:8-10 [b]Lev 26:34-39; 2 Kin 17:6,18; 25:21
47 [1]Lit *return to their heart* [a]Lev 26:40-42; Neh 9:2 [b]Ezra 9:6,7; Neh 1:6; Ps 106:6; Dan 9:5
48 [a]Deut 4:29; 1 Sam 7:3,4; Neh 1:9 [b]Dan 6:10; Jon 2:4
49 [1]Lit *judgment*
50 [a]2 Chr 30:9; Ps 106:46; Acts 7:10
51 [a]Ex 32:11, 12; Deut 9:26-29 [b]Deut 4:20; Jer 11:4
52 [a]1 Kin 8:29
53 [1]Heb *YHWH,* usually rendered LORD [a]Ex 19:5,6; Deut 9:26-29
54 [1]Lit *palms* [a]2 Chr 7:1 [b]2 Chr 6:13

55 And he stood and [a]blessed all the
assembly of Israel with a loud voice, saying:
56 ¶ "Blessed be the LORD, who has
given rest to His people Israel, [a]according to all that He [1]promised; [b]not one
word has [2]failed of all His good [3]promise, which He [1]promised through Moses
His servant.
57 "May the LORD our God be with us,
as He was with our fathers; [a]may He not
leave us or forsake us,
58 that [a]He may incline our hearts to
Himself, to walk in all His ways and to
keep His commandments and His statutes and His ordinances, which He commanded our fathers.
59 "And may these words of mine, with
which I have made supplication before
the LORD, be near to the LORD our God
day and night, that He may maintain the
[1]cause of His servant and the [1]cause of
His people Israel, [2]as each day requires,
60 so [a]that all the peoples of the earth
may know that [b]the LORD is God; there
is no one else.
61 "[a]Let your heart therefore be
[1]wholly devoted to the LORD our God, to
walk in His statutes and to keep His commandments, as at this day."

Dedicatory Sacrifices

62 ¶ [a]Now the king and all Israel with
him [b]offered sacrifice before the LORD.
63 Solomon offered for the sacrifice of
peace offerings, which he offered to the
LORD, 22,000 oxen and 120,000 sheep.
[a]So the king and all the sons of Israel
dedicated the house of the LORD.
64 On the same day the king consecrated the middle of the court that *was*
before the house of the LORD, because
there he [1]offered the burnt offering and
the grain offering and the fat of the peace
offerings; for [a]the bronze altar that *was*
before the LORD *was* too small to hold the
burnt offering and the grain offering and
the fat of the peace offerings.
65 ¶ So [a]Solomon observed the feast
at that time, and all Israel with him, a
great assembly [b]from the entrance of Hamath [c]to the brook of Egypt, before the
LORD our God, for seven days and seven
more days, *even* fourteen days.
66 On the eighth day he sent the people away and they blessed the king. Then
they went to their tents joyful and glad of
heart for all the goodness that the LORD
had [1]shown to David His servant and to
Israel His people.

God's Promise and Warning

9 [a]Now it came about when Solomon
had finished building the house of
the LORD, and [b]the king's house, and
[c]all [1]that Solomon desired to do,
2 that [a]the LORD appeared to Solomon a second time, as He had appeared
to him at Gibeon.
3 The LORD said to him, "[a]I have
heard your prayer and your supplication,
which you have made before Me; I have
consecrated this house which you have
built [b]by putting My name there forever,
and [c]My eyes and My heart will be there
perpetually.
4 "As for you, [a]if you will walk before
Me as your father David walked, in integrity of heart and uprightness, doing according to all that I have commanded you
and will keep My statutes and My ordinances,
5 then [a]I will establish the throne of
your kingdom over Israel forever, just as
I [1]promised to your father David, saying,
'[2]You shall not lack a man on the throne
of Israel.'
6 ¶ "[a]But if you or your sons indeed
turn away from following Me, and do not
keep My commandments and My statutes
which I have set before you, and go and
serve other gods and worship them,
7 [a]then I will cut off Israel from the
land which I have given them, and [b]the
house which I have consecrated for My
name, I will [1]cast out of My sight. So
[c]Israel will become a proverb and a byword among all peoples.
8 "And this house will become [1a]a
heap of ruins; everyone who passes by
will be astonished and hiss and say,
'[b]Why has the LORD done thus to this
land and to this house?'
9 "And they will say, '[a]Because they
forsook the LORD their God, who brought
their fathers out of the land of Egypt, and
adopted other gods and worshiped them
and served them, therefore the LORD has
brought all this adversity on them.' "

Cities Given to Hiram

10 ¶ [a]It came about [b]at the end of
twenty years in which Solomon had built
the two houses, the house of the LORD
and the king's house
11 (Hiram king of Tyre had supplied
Solomon with cedar and cypress timber
and gold according to all his desire), then
King Solomon gave Hiram twenty cities
in the land of Galilee.
12 So Hiram came out from Tyre to see
the cities which Solomon had given him,
and they [1]did not please him.
13 He said, "What are these cities
which you have given me, my brother?"
So [1]they were called the land of [2a]Cabul to this day.

55 [a]Num 6:23-26; 2 Sam 6:18; 1 Kin 8:14
56 [1]Lit *spoke* [2]Lit *fallen* [3]Lit *word* [a]Deut 12:10 [b]Josh 21:45
57 [a]Deut 31:6; Josh 1:5; 1 Sam 12:22; Rom 8:31; Heb 13:5
58 [a]Ps 119:36; Jer 31:33
59 [1]Lit *judgment* [2]Lit *the thing of a day in its day*
60 [a]Josh 4:24; 1 Sam 17:46; 1 Kin 8:43; 2 Kin 19:19 [b]Deut 4:35; 1 Kin 18:39; Jer 10:10-12
61 [1]Lit *complete with* [a]Deut 18:13; 1 Kin 11:4; 2 Kin 20:3
62 [a]2 Chr 7:4-10 [b]2 Sam 6:17-19; Ezra 6:16
63 [a]Ezra 6:15-18; Neh 12:27
64 [1]Lit *made* [a]2 Chr 4:1
65 [a]Lev 23:34-42; 1 Kin 8:2 [b]Num 34:8; Josh 13:5; Judg 3:3; 2 Kin 14:25 [c]Gen 15:18; Ex 23:31; Num 34:5; Josh 13:3
66 [1]Lit *done*
9:1 [1]Lit *Solomon's desire which he was pleased to do* [a]2 Chr 7:11 [b]1 Kin 7:1 [c]2 Chr 8:6
2 [a]1 Kin 3:5; 2 Chr 1:7
3 [a]2 Kin 20:5; Ps 10:17 [b]1 Kin 8:29 [c]Deut 11:12; 2 Chr 6:40
4 [a]1 Kin 3:6; 2 Kin 20:3; Ps 128:1
5 [1]Lit *spoke* [2]Lit *There shall not be cut off to you a man* [a]2 Sam 7:12; 1 Kin 2:4; 1 Chr 22:10
6 [a]2 Sam 7:14-16; 1 Chr 28:9; Ps 89:30ff
7 [1]Lit *send* [a]Lev 18:24-29; Deut 4:26; 2 Kin 17:23 [b]Jer 7:4-14 [c]Deut 28:37; Ps 44:14; Jer 24:9
8 [1]Heb *high* [a]2 Kin 25:9; 2 Chr 36:19 [b]Deut 29:24-26; 2 Chr 7:21; Jer 22:8
9 [a]Deut 29:25-28; Jer 2:10-13
10 [a]2 Chr 8:1 [b]1 Kin 6:37
12 [1]Lit *were not right in his sight*
13 [1]Lit *he called them* [2]I.e. as good as nothing [a]Josh 19:27

14 [a]And Hiram sent to the king 120 talents of gold.

15 ¶ Now this is the account of the forced labor which King Solomon [a]levied to build the house of the LORD, his own house, the [1b]Millo, the wall of Jerusalem, [c]Hazor, [d]Megiddo, and [e]Gezer.

16 *For* Pharaoh king of Egypt had gone up and captured Gezer and burned it with fire, and killed the [a]Canaanites who lived in the city, and had [b]given it *as* a dowry to his daughter, Solomon's wife.

17 So Solomon rebuilt Gezer and the lower [a]Beth-horon

18 and [a]Baalath and Tamar in the wilderness, in the land *of Judah,*

19 and all the storage cities which Solomon had, even [a]the cities for [1]his chariots and the cities for [1b]his horsemen, and [2c]all that it pleased Solomon to build in Jerusalem, in Lebanon, and in all the land [3]under his rule.

20 *As for* all the people who were left of the Amorites, the Hittites, the Perizzites, the Hivites and the Jebusites, who were not of the sons of Israel,

21 [a]their descendants who were left after them in the land [b]whom the sons of Israel were unable to destroy utterly, [c]from them Solomon levied [d]forced laborers, even to this day.

22 But Solomon [a]did not make slaves of the sons of Israel; for they were men of war, his servants, his princes, his captains, his chariot commanders, and his horsemen.

23 ¶ These *were* the [1a]chief officers who *were* over Solomon's work, five hundred and fifty, [b]who ruled over the people doing the work.

24 ¶ As soon as [a]Pharaoh's daughter came up from the city of David to her house which *Solomon* had built for her, [b]then he built the Millo.

25 ¶ Now [a]three times in a year Solomon offered burnt offerings and peace offerings on the altar which he built to the LORD, burning incense with them *on the altar* which *was* before the LORD. So he finished the house.

26 ¶ King Solomon also built a [a]fleet of ships in [b]Ezion-geber, which is near Eloth on the shore of the [1]Red Sea, in the land of Edom.

27 [a]And Hiram sent his servants with the fleet, sailors who knew the sea, along with the servants of Solomon.

28 They went to [a]Ophir and took four hundred and twenty talents of gold from there, and brought *it* to King Solomon.

The Queen of Sheba

10 [a]Now when the [a]queen of [b]Sheba heard about the fame of Solomon concerning the name of the LORD, she came [c]to test him with difficult questions.

2 So she came to Jerusalem with a very large retinue, with camels [a]carrying spices and very much gold and precious stones. When she came to Solomon, she spoke with him about all that was in her heart.

3 Solomon [1]answered all her questions; nothing was hidden from the king which he did not [2]explain to her.

4 When the queen of Sheba perceived all the wisdom of Solomon, the house that he had built,

5 the food of his table, the seating of his servants, the attendance of his waiters and their attire, his cupbearers, and [1]his stairway by which he went up to the house of the LORD, there was no more spirit in her.

6 Then she said to the king, "It was a true report which I heard in my own land about your words and your wisdom.

7 "Nevertheless I did not believe the [1]reports, until I came and my eyes had seen it. And behold, the half was not told me. You exceed *in* wisdom and prosperity the report which I heard.

8 "How [a]blessed are your men, how blessed are these your servants who stand before you continually *and* hear your wisdom.

9 "[a]Blessed be the LORD your God who delighted in you to set you on the throne of Israel; [b]because the LORD loved Israel forever, therefore He made you king, [c]to do justice and righteousness."

10 [a]She gave the king a hundred and twenty talents of gold, and a very great *amount* of spices and precious stones. Never again did such abundance of spices come in as that which the queen of Sheba gave King Solomon.

11 ¶ [a]Also the ships of Hiram, which brought gold from Ophir, brought in from Ophir a very great *number of* almug trees and precious stones.

12 [a]The king made of the almug trees supports for the house of the LORD and for the king's house, also lyres and harps for the singers; such almug trees have not come in *again* nor have they been seen to this day.

13 ¶ King Solomon gave to the queen of Sheba all her desire which she requested, besides what he gave her according to [1]his royal bounty. Then she turned and went to her own land [2]together with her servants.

Wealth, Splendor and Wisdom

14 ¶ [a]Now the weight of gold which

---

14 [a]1 Kin 9:11
15 [1]I.e. citadel [a]1 Kin 5:13 [b]2 Sam 5:9; 1 Kin 9:24 [c]Josh 11:1; 19:36 [d]Josh 17:11 [e]Judg 1:29
16 [a]Josh 16:10 [b]1 Kin 3:1; 7:8
17 [a]Josh 10:10; 16:3; 21:22; 2 Chr 8:5
18 [a]Josh 19:44
19 [1]Lit *the* [2]Lit *the desire of Solomon which he desired to build in Jerusalem* [3]Lit *of* [a]1 Kin 10:26; 2 Chr 1:14 [b]1 Kin 4:26 [c]1 Kin 9:1
21 [a]Judg 1:21-29; 3:1 [b]Josh 15:63; 17:12,13 [c]Judg 1:28,35 [d]Gen 9:25,26; Ezra 2:55,58
22 [a]Lev 25:39
23 [1]Or *officers of the deputies* [a]2 Chr 8:10 [b]1 Kin 5:16
24 [a]1 Kin 3:1; 7:8 [b]2 Sam 5:9; 1 Kin 9:15; 11:27; 2 Chr 32:5
25 [a]Ex 23:14-17; Deut 16:16
26 [1]Lit *Sea of Reeds* [a]1 Kin 22:48 [b]Num 33:35; Deut 2:8; 1 Kin 22:48
27 [a]1 Kin 5:6,9; 10:11
28 [a]1 Chr 29:4; 2 Chr 8:18
10:1 [a]2 Chr 9:1; Matt 12:42; Luke 11:31 [b]Gen 10:7,28; Ps 72:10,15 [c]Judg 14:12-14; Ps 49:4
2 [a]1 Kin 10:10
3 [1]Lit *told her all her words* [2]Lit *tell her*
5 [1]Or *his burnt offering which he offered*
7 [1]Lit *words*
8 [a]Prov 8:34
9 [a]1 Kin 5:7 [b]1 Chr 17:22; 2 Chr 2:11 [c]2 Sam 8:15; 23:3; Ps 72:2
10 [a]1 Kin 10:2
11 [a]1 Kin 9:27, 28; Job 22:24
12 [a]2 Chr 9:11
13 [1]Lit *the hand of King Solomon* [2]Lit *she and*
14 [a]2 Chr 9:13-28

came in to Solomon in one year was 666
talents of gold,
15 besides *that* from the traders and
the [1]wares of the merchants and all the
kings of the [a]Arabs and the governors of
the country.
16 [a]King Solomon made 200 large
shields of beaten gold, [1]using 600 *shekels of* gold on each large shield.
17 *He made* [a]300 shields of beaten
gold, [1]using three minas of gold on each
shield, and [b]the king put them in the
house of the forest of Lebanon.
18 Moreover, the king made a great
throne of [a]ivory and overlaid it with refined gold.
19 *There were* six steps to the throne
and a round top to the throne at its rear,
and [1]arms [2]on each side of the seat, and
two lions standing beside the [1]arms.
20 Twelve lions were standing there
on the six steps on the one side and on
the other; nothing like *it* was made for
any other kingdom.
21 All King Solomon's drinking vessels
were of gold, and all the vessels of the
house of the forest of Lebanon *were* of
pure gold. None was of silver; it was not
considered [1]valuable in the days of Solomon.
22 For [a]the king had at sea the ships
of Tarshish with the ships of Hiram; once
every three years the ships of Tarshish
came bringing gold and silver, ivory and
apes and peacocks.
23 ¶ [a]So King Solomon became greater than all the kings of the earth in riches
and in wisdom.
24 All the earth was seeking the presence of Solomon, [a]to hear his wisdom
which God had put in his heart.
25 [a]They brought every man his gift,
articles of silver and gold, garments,
weapons, spices, horses, and mules, so
much year by year.
26 ¶ [a]Now Solomon gathered chariots
and horsemen; and he had 1,400 chariots
and 12,000 horsemen, and he [1]stationed
them in the [b]chariot cities and with the
king in Jerusalem.
27 [a]The king made silver *as common*
as stones in Jerusalem, and he made cedars as plentiful as sycamore trees that
are in the [1]lowland.
28 [a]Also Solomon's import of horses
was from Egypt and Kue, *and* the king's
merchants procured *them* from Kue for a
price.
29 A chariot [1]was imported from
Egypt for 600 *shekels* of silver, and a
horse for 150; and [2]by the same means
they exported them [a]to all the kings of
the Hittites and to the kings of the Arameans.

Solomon Turns from God

11
Now [a]King Solomon loved many
foreign women along with the
daughter of Pharaoh: Moabite, Ammonite, Edomite, Sidonian, and Hittite
women,
2 from the nations concerning which
the LORD had said to the sons of Israel,
"[a]You shall not [1]associate with them,
nor shall they [1]associate with you, *for*
they will surely turn your heart away
after their gods." Solomon held fast to
these in love.
3 [a]He had seven hundred wives,
princesses, and three hundred concubines, and his wives turned his heart
away.
4 For when Solomon was old, his
wives turned his heart away after other
gods; and [a]his heart was not [1]wholly
devoted to the LORD his God, as the heart
of David his father *had been.*
5 For Solomon went after [a]Ashtoreth
the goddess of the Sidonians and after
[1b]Milcom the detestable idol of the Ammonites.
6 Solomon did what was evil in the
sight of the LORD, and did not follow the
LORD fully, as David his father *had done.*
7 Then Solomon built a high place for
[a]Chemosh the detestable idol of Moab,
on the mountain which is [1]east of Jerusalem, and for [b]Molech the detestable idol
of the sons of Ammon.
8 Thus also he did for all his foreign
wives, who burned incense and sacrificed to their gods.
9 ¶ Now [a]the LORD was angry with
Solomon [b]because his heart was turned
away from the LORD, the God of Israel,
[c]who had appeared to him twice,
10 and [a]had commanded him concerning this thing, that he should not go
after other gods; but he did not observe
what the LORD had commanded.
11 So the LORD said to Solomon, "Because [1]you have done this, and you have
not kept My covenant and My statutes,
which I have commanded you, [a]I will
surely tear the kingdom from you, and
will give it to your servant.
12 "Nevertheless I will not do it in your
days for the sake of your father David, *but*
I will tear it out of the hand of your son.
13 "However, [a]I will not tear away all
the kingdom, *but* [b]I will give one tribe to
your son for the sake of My servant David
and [c]for the sake of Jerusalem which I
have chosen."

God Raises Adversaries

14 ¶ Then the LORD raised up an ad-

15 [1]Or *traffic* [a]2 Chr 9:14
16 [1]Lit *he brought up* [a]1 Kin 14:26-28; 2 Chr 12:9,10
17 [1]Lit *he brought up* [a]1 Kin 14:26 [b]1 Kin 7:2
18 [a]1 Kin 10:22; 2 Chr 9:17; Ps 45:8
19 [1]Lit *hands* [2]Lit *on this side and on this at the place of the seat*
21 [1]Lit *anything*
22 [a]1 Kin 9:26-28; 22:48; 2 Chr 20:36
23 [a]1 Kin 3:12, 13; 4:30
24 [a]1 Kin 3:9, 12,28
25 [a]Ps 68:29
26 [1]So with ancient versions; Heb *led* [a]1 Kin 4:26; 2 Chr 1:14-17; 9:25 [b]1 Kin 9:19
27 [1]Heb *Shephelah* [a]Deut 17:17; 2 Chr 1:15
28 [a]Deut 17:16; 2 Chr 1:16; 9:28
29 [1]Lit *came up and went out from* [2]Lit *in like manner by their hand* [a]2 Kin 7:6, 7
11:1 [a]Deut 17:17; Neh 13:23-27
2 [1]Lit *go among* [a]Ex 23:31-33; 34:12-16; Deut 7:3
3 [a]2 Sam 5:13-16
4 [1]Lit *complete with* [a]1 Kin 9:4
5 [1]In Jer 49:1, 3, *Malcam* [a]Judg 2:13; 10:6; 1 Sam 7:3,4 [b]1 Kin 11:7
7 [1]Lit *before* [a]Num 21:29; Judg 11:24; 2 Kin 23:13 [b]Lev 20:2-5; 2 Kin 23:10; Acts 7:43
9 [a]Ps 90:7 [b]1 Kin 11:2,4 [c]1 Kin 3:5; 9:2
10 [a]1 Kin 6:12; 9:6,7
11 [1]Lit *this is with you* [a]1 Sam 2:30; 1 Kin 11:29-31; 12:15, 16,20; 2 Kin 17:15,21
13 [a]2 Sam 7:15; 1 Chr 17:13; Ps 89:33 [b]1 Kin 11:32,36; 12:20 [c]1 Kin 8:29

versary to Solomon, Hadad the Edomite;
he was of the [1]royal line in Edom.
15 For it came about, [a]when David
was in Edom, and Joab the commander of
the army had gone up to bury the slain,
and had [b]struck down every male in
Edom
16 (for Joab and all Israel stayed there
six months, until he had cut off every
male in Edom),
17 that Hadad fled [1]to Egypt, he and
certain Edomites of his father's servants
with him, while Hadad *was* a young boy.
18 They arose from Midian and came
to [a]Paran; and they took men with them
from Paran and came to Egypt, to Pharaoh
king of Egypt, who gave him a house and
assigned him food and gave him land.
19 Now Hadad found great favor [1]be-
fore Pharaoh, so that he gave him in marriage the sister of his own wife, the sister
of Tahpenes the queen.
20 The sister of Tahpenes bore his son
Genubath, whom Tahpenes weaned in
Pharaoh's house; and Genubath was in
Pharaoh's house among the sons of Pharaoh.
21 But [a]when Hadad heard in Egypt
that David slept with his fathers and that
Joab the commander of the army was
dead, Hadad said to Pharaoh, "Send me
away, that I may go to my own country."
22 Then Pharaoh said to him, "But
what have you lacked with me, that behold, you are seeking to go to your own
country?" And he answered, "Nothing;
nevertheless you must surely [1]let
me go."
23 ¶ [a]God also raised up *another* adversary to him, Rezon the son of Eliada,
who had fled from his lord [b]Hadadezer
king of Zobah.
24 He gathered men to himself and became leader of a marauding band, [a]after
David slew them of *Zobah;* and they went
to Damascus and stayed [1]there, and
reigned in Damascus.
25 So he was an adversary to Israel all
the days of Solomon, along with the evil
that Hadad *did;* and he abhorred Israel
and reigned over Aram.
26 ¶ Then [a]Jeroboam the son of Nebat, an Ephraimite of Zeredah, Solomon's
servant, whose mother's name was Zeru-
ah, a widow, [b]also [1]rebelled against the
king.
27 Now this was the reason why he
[1]rebelled against the king: [a]Solomon
built the [2]Millo, *and* closed up the
breach of the city of his father David.
28 Now the man Jeroboam was a valiant warrior, and when [a]Solomon saw
that the young man was [1]industrious, he
appointed him over all the [2]forced labor
of the house of Joseph.
29 It came about at that time, when
Jeroboam went out of Jerusalem, that
[a]the prophet Ahijah the Shilonite found
him on the road. Now [1]Ahijah had
clothed himself with a new cloak; and
both of them were alone in the field.
30 Then [a]Ahijah took hold of the new
cloak which was on him and tore it into
twelve pieces.
31 He said to Jeroboam, "Take for
yourself ten pieces; for thus says the
LORD, the God of Israel, 'Behold, [a]I will
tear the kingdom out of the hand of Solomon and give you ten tribes
32 ([a]but he will have one tribe, for the
sake of My servant David and for the sake
of Jerusalem, [b]the city which I have chosen from all the tribes of Israel),
33 because they have forsaken Me,
and [a]have worshiped Ashtoreth the goddess of the Sidonians, [b]Chemosh the god
of Moab, and Milcom the god of the sons
of Ammon; and they have not walked in
My ways, doing what is right in My sight
and *observing* My statutes and My ordinances, as his father David *did.*
34 'Nevertheless I will not take the
whole kingdom out of his hand, but I will
make him [1]ruler all the days of his life,
for the sake of My servant David whom I
chose, who observed My commandments
and My statutes;
35 but [a]I will take the kingdom from
his son's hand and give it to you, *even* ten
tribes.
36 'But [a]to his son I will give one tribe,
[b]that My servant David may have a lamp
always before Me in Jerusalem, [a]the city
where I have chosen for Myself to put My
name.
37 'I will take you, and you shall reign
over whatever [1]you desire, and you shall
be king over Israel.
38 'Then it will be, that if you listen to
all that I command you and walk in My
ways, and do what is right in My sight by
observing My statutes and My commandments, as My servant David did, then [a]I
will be with you and [b]build you an enduring house as I built for David, and I
will give Israel to you.
39 'Thus I will afflict the [1]descendants
of David for this, but not always.' "
40 Solomon sought therefore to put
Jeroboam to death; but Jeroboam arose
and fled to Egypt to [a]Shishak king of
Egypt, and he was in Egypt until the
death of Solomon.

The Death of Solomon

41 ¶ [a]Now the rest of the acts of Solomon and whatever he did, and his wis-

14 [1]Lit *king's seed*
15 [a]2 Sam 8:14; 1 Chr 18:12,13 [b]Deut 20:13
17 [1]Lit *to go into*
18 [a]Num 10:12; Deut 1:1
19 [1]Lit *in the sight of*
21 [a]1 Kin 2:10
22 [1]Lit *send me away*
23 [a]1 Kin 11:14 [b]2 Sam 8:3; 10:16
24 [1]Lit *in it* [a]2 Sam 10:8,18
26 [1]Lit *lifted up a hand* [a]1 Kin 11:11,28; 12:2, 20; 2 Chr 13:6 [b]2 Sam 20:21
27 [1]Lit *lifted up a hand* [2]I.e. citadel [a]1 Kin 9:15, 24
28 [1]Lit *a doer of work* [2]Lit *burden* [a]Prov 22:29
29 [1]Lit *he* [a]1 Kin 12:15; 14:2; 2 Chr 9:29
30 [a]1 Sam 15:27,28
31 [a]1 Kin 11:11,12
32 [a]1 Kin 11:13; 12:21 [b]1 Kin 11:13; 14:21
33 [a]1 Sam 7:3; 1 Kin 11:5-8 [b]Num 21:29; Jer 48:7,13
34 [1]Or *prince*
35 [a]1 Kin 11:12; 12:16,17
36 [a]1 Kin 11:13 [b]1 Kin 15:4; 2 Kin 8:19; Ps 132:17
37 [1]Lit *your soul desires*
38 [a]Deut 31:8; Josh 1:5 [b]2 Sam 7:11,27
39 [1]Lit *seed*
40 [a]1 Kin 14:25; 2 Chr 12:2-9
41 [a]2 Chr 9:29

dom, are they not written in the book of the acts of Solomon?

42 Thus [a]the time that Solomon reigned in Jerusalem over all Israel was forty years.

43 And Solomon [a]slept with his fathers and was buried in the city of his father David, and his son [b]Rehoboam reigned in his place.

King Rehoboam Acts Foolishly

12 [a]Then Rehoboam went to Shechem, for all Israel had come to [b]Shechem to make him king.

2 Now [a]when Jeroboam the son of Nebat heard *of it,* [1]he was living in Egypt (for he was yet in Egypt, where he had fled from the presence of King Solomon).

3 Then they sent and called him, and Jeroboam and all the assembly of Israel came and spoke to Rehoboam, saying,

4 "[a]Your father made our yoke hard; now therefore lighten the hard service of your father and his heavy yoke which he put on us, and we will serve you."

5 Then he said to them, "[a]Depart [1]for three days, then return to me." So the people departed.

6 ¶ King Rehoboam [a]consulted with the elders who had [1]served his father Solomon while he was still alive, saying, "How do you counsel *me* to answer this people?"

7 Then they spoke to him, saying, "[a]If you will be a servant to this people today, and will serve them and [1]grant them their petition, and speak good words to them, then they will be your servants forever."

8 But he forsook the counsel of the elders which they had given him, and consulted with the young men who grew up with him [1]and served him.

9 So he said to them, "What counsel do you give that we may answer this people who have spoken to me, saying, 'Lighten the yoke which your father put on us'?"

10 The young men who grew up with him spoke to him, saying, "Thus you shall say to this people who spoke to you, saying, 'Your father made our yoke heavy, now you make it lighter for us!' But you shall speak to them, 'My little finger is thicker than my father's loins!

11 'Whereas my father loaded you with a heavy yoke, I will add to your yoke; my father disciplined you with whips, but I will discipline you with scorpions.' "

12 ¶ Then Jeroboam and all the people came to Rehoboam on the third day as the king had [1]directed, saying, "[a]Return to me on the third day."

13 The king answered the people harshly, for he forsook the advice of the elders which they had [1]given him,

14 and he spoke to them according to the advice of the young men, saying, "[a]My father made your yoke heavy, but I will add to your yoke; my father disciplined you with whips, but I will discipline you with scorpions."

15 So the king did not listen to the people; [a]for it was a turn *of events* from the LORD, [b]that He might establish His word, which the LORD spoke through Ahijah the Shilonite to Jeroboam the son of Nebat.

The Kingdom Divided Jeroboam Rules Israel

16 ¶ When all Israel *saw* that the king did not listen to them, the people answered the king, saying,

"What portion do we have in
David?
We have no inheritance in the
son of Jesse;
[a]To your tents, O Israel!
Now look after your own house,
David!"

So Israel departed to their tents.

17 But [a]as for the sons of Israel who lived in the cities of Judah, Rehoboam reigned over them.

18 Then King Rehoboam sent [a]Adoram, who was over the forced labor, and all Israel stoned him [1]to death. And King Rehoboam made haste to mount his chariot to flee to Jerusalem.

19 [a]So Israel has been in rebellion against the house of David to this day.

20 ¶ It came about when all Israel heard that Jeroboam had returned, that they sent and called him to the assembly and made him king over all Israel. [a]None but the tribe of Judah followed the house of David.

21 ¶ [a]Now when Rehoboam had come to Jerusalem, he assembled all the house of Judah and the tribe of Benjamin, 180,000 chosen men who were warriors, to fight against the house of Israel to restore the kingdom to Rehoboam the son of Solomon.

22 But the word of God came to [a]Shemaiah the man of God, saying,

23 "Speak to Rehoboam the son of Solomon, king of Judah, and to all the house of Judah and Benjamin and to the [a]rest of the people, saying,

24 'Thus says the LORD, "You must not go up and fight against your [1]relatives the sons of Israel; return every man to his house, [a]for this thing has come from Me." ' " So they listened to the word of

---

42 [a]2 Chr 9:30
43 [a]1 Kin 2:10; 2 Chr 9:31 [b]1 Kin 14:21; Matt 1:7
12:1 [a]2 Chr 10:1 [b]Judg 9:6
2 [1]Lit *Jeroboam* [a]1 Kin 11:26,40
4 [a]1 Sam 8:11-18; 1 Kin 4:7,21-25; 9:15
5 [1]Lit *yet three* [a]1 Kin 12:12
6 [1]Lit *stood before* [a]1 Kin 4:1-6; Job 12:12; 32:7
7 [1]Lit *answer them* [a]2 Chr 10:7; Prov 15:1
8 [1]Lit *who stood before*
12 [1]Lit *spoken* [a]1 Kin 12:5
13 [1]Lit *advised*
14 [a]Ex 1:13,14; 5:5-9,16-18
15 [a]Deut 2:30; Judg 14:4; 1 Kin 12:24; 2 Chr 10:15 [b]1 Kin 11:11,31
16 [a]2 Sam 20:1
17 [a]1 Kin 11:13,36
18 [1]Lit *with stones that he died* [a]2 Sam 20:24; 1 Kin 4:6; 5:14
19 [a]2 Kin 17:21
20 [a]1 Kin 11:13,32,36
21 [a]2 Chr 11:1
22 [a]2 Chr 11:2; 12:5-7
23 [a]1 Kin 12:17
24 [1]Lit *brothers* [a]1 Kin 12:15

the LORD, and returned and went *their*
way according to the word of the LORD.

Jeroboam's Idolatry

25 ¶ Then [a]Jeroboam built Shechem
in the hill country of Ephraim, and lived
[1]there. And he went out from there and
built [b]Penuel.
26 Jeroboam said in his heart, "Now
the kingdom will return to the house of
David.
27 "[a]If this people go up to offer sacrifices in the house of the LORD at Jerusalem, then the heart of this people will
return to their lord, *even* to Rehoboam
king of Judah; and they will kill me and
return to Rehoboam king of Judah."
28 So the king [1]consulted, and [a]made
two golden [b]calves, and he said to them,
"It is too much for you to go up to Jerusalem; [c]behold your gods, O Israel, that
brought you up from the land of Egypt."
29 He set [a]one in [b]Bethel, and the
other he put in [c]Dan.
30 Now [a]this thing became a sin, for
the people went *to worship* before the
one as far as Dan.
31 And [a]he made houses on high
places, and [b]made priests from among
[1]all the people who were not of the sons
of Levi.
32 Jeroboam [1]instituted a feast in the
eighth month on the fifteenth day of the
month, [a]like the feast which is in Judah,
and he [2]went up to the altar; thus he did
in Bethel, sacrificing to the calves which
he had made. And he stationed in Bethel
[b]the priests of the high places which he
had made.
33 Then he [1]went up to the altar
which he had made in Bethel on the fifteenth day in the eighth month, even in
the month which he had [2a]devised [3]in
his own heart; and he [2]instituted a feast
for the sons of Israel and [1]went up to the
altar [b]to burn [4]incense.

Jeroboam Warned, Stricken

13 Now behold, there came [a]a man
of God from Judah to Bethel by
the word of the LORD, while Jeroboam
was standing by the altar [b]to burn incense.
2 [a]He cried against the altar by the
word of the LORD, and said, "O altar, altar, thus says the LORD, 'Behold, a son
shall be born to the house of David, [b]Josi-
ah by name; and on you he shall sacrifice
the priests of the high places who burn
incense on you, and human bones shall
be burned on you.' "
3 Then he gave a [1]sign the same day,
saying, "[a]This is the [1]sign which the
LORD has spoken, 'Behold, the altar shall
be split apart and the [2]ashes which are
on it shall be poured out.' "
4 Now when the king heard the saying of the man of God, which he cried
against the altar in Bethel, Jeroboam
stretched out his hand from the altar, saying, "Seize him." But his hand which he
stretched out against him dried up, so
that he could not draw it back to himself.
5 The altar also was split apart and
the [1]ashes were poured out from the altar, according to the [2]sign which the
man of God had given by the word of the
LORD.
6 The king said to the man of God,
"Please [1a]entreat the LORD your God,
and pray for me, that my hand may be
restored to me." So [b]the man of God
[2]entreated the LORD, and the king's hand
was restored to him, and it became as it
was before.
7 Then the king said to the man of
God, "Come home with me and refresh
yourself, and [a]I will give you a reward."
8 But the man of God said to the king,
"[a]If you were to give me half your house
I would not go with you, nor would I eat
bread or drink water in this place.
9 "For so [1]it was commanded me by
the word of the LORD, saying, 'You shall
eat no bread, nor drink water, nor return
by the way which you came.' "
10 So he went another way and did
not return by the way which he came to
Bethel.

The Disobedient Prophet

11 ¶ Now [a]an old prophet was living
in Bethel; and his [1]sons came and told
him all the deeds which the man of God
had done that day in Bethel; the words
which he had spoken to the king, these
also they related to their father.
12 Their father said to them, "[1]Which
way did he go?" Now his sons [2]had seen
the way which the man of God who came
from Judah had gone.
13 Then he said to his sons, "Saddle
the donkey for me." So they saddled the
donkey for him and he rode away on it.
14 So he went after the man of God
and found him sitting under [1]an oak; and
he said to him, "Are you the man of God
who came from Judah?" And he said,
"I am."
15 Then he said to him, "Come home
with me and eat bread."
16 He said, "[a]I cannot return with
you, nor go with you, nor will I eat bread
or drink water with you in this place.
17 "For a command *came* to me [a]by
the word of the LORD, 'You shall eat no
bread, nor drink water there; do not return by going the way which you came.' "

25 [1]Lit *in it* [a]Gen 12:6; Judg 9:45-49 [b]Gen 32:30,31; Judg 8:8,17

27 [a]Deut 12:5-7,14

28 [1]Lit *took counsel* [a]2 Kin 10:29; 17:16; Hos 8:4-7 [b]Hos 10:5 [c]Ex 32:4,8

29 [a]Hos 10:5 [b]Gen 28:19 [c]Judg 18:26-31

30 [a]1 Kin 13:34; 2 Kin 17:21

31 [1]Or *extremities of* [a]1 Kin 13:32 [b]1 Kin 13:33; 2 Kin 17:32; 2 Chr 11:15; 13:9

32 [1]Lit *made* [2]Or *offered upon* [a]Lev 23:33,34; Num 29:12; 1 Kin 8:2,5 [b]Amos 7:10-13

33 [1]Or *offered upon* [2]Lit *made* [3]Lit *from* [4]Or *sacrifices* [a]Num 15:39 [b]1 Kin 13:1

13:1 [a]1 Kin 12:22; 2 Kin 23:17 [b]1 Kin 12:33

2 [a]1 Kin 13:32 [b]2 Kin 23:15,16

3 [1]Lit *wonder* [2]Lit *ashes of fat* [a]Ex 4:1-5; Judg 6:17; Is 38:7; John 2:18; 1 Cor 1:22

5 [1]Lit *ashes of fat* [2]Lit *wonder*

6 [1]Lit *soften the face of* [2]Lit *softened the face of* [a]Ex 8:8,28; 9:28; 10:17; Acts 8:24; James 5:16 [b]Luke 6:27, 28

7 [a]1 Sam 9:7,8; 2 Kin 5:15

8 [a]Num 22:18; 24:13; 1 Kin 13:16,17

9 [1]Lit *he commanded me*

11 [1]Lit *son* [a]1 Kin 13:25; 2 Kin 23:18

12 [1]Lit *Where is the way he went* [2]Some ancient versions read *showed him*

14 [1]Or a *terebinth*

16 [a]1 Kin 13:8, 9

17 [a]1 Kin 20:35

18 He said to him, "[a]I also am a prophet like you, and [b]an angel spoke to me by the word of the LORD, saying, 'Bring him back with you to your house, that he may eat bread and drink water.' " *But* [c]he lied to him.

19 So he went back with him, and ate bread in his house and drank water.

20 ¶ Now it came about, as they were sitting down at the table, that the word of the LORD came to the prophet who had brought him back;

21 and he cried to the man of God who came from Judah, saying, "Thus says the LORD, 'Because you have [1]disobeyed the [2]command of the LORD, and have not observed the commandment which the LORD your God commanded you,

22 but have returned and eaten bread and drunk water in the place of which He said to you, "Eat no bread and drink no water"; your body shall not come to the grave of your fathers.' "

23 It came about after he had eaten bread and after he had drunk, that he saddled the donkey for him, for the prophet whom he had brought back.

24 Now when he had gone, [a]a lion met him on the way and killed him, and his body was thrown on the road, with the donkey standing beside it; the lion also was standing beside the body.

25 And behold, men passed by and saw the body thrown on the road, and the lion standing beside the body; so they came and told *it* in the city where [a]the old prophet lived.

26 ¶ Now when the prophet who brought him back from the way heard *it,* he said, "It is the man of God, who [1]disobeyed the [2]command of the LORD; therefore the LORD has given him to the lion, which has torn him and killed him, according to the word of the LORD which He spoke to him."

27 Then he spoke to his sons, saying, "Saddle the donkey for me." And they saddled *it.*

28 He went and found his body thrown on the road with the donkey and the lion standing beside the body; the lion had not eaten the body nor torn the donkey.

29 So the prophet took up the body of the man of God and laid it on the donkey and brought it back, and he came to the city of the old prophet to mourn and to bury him.

30 He laid his body in his own grave, and they mourned over him, *saying,* "[a]Alas, my brother!"

31 After he had buried him, he spoke to his sons, saying, "When I die, bury me in the grave in which the man of God is buried; [a]lay my bones beside his bones.

32 "[a]For the thing shall surely come to pass which he cried by the word of the LORD against the altar in Bethel and [b]against all the houses of the high places which are in the cities of [c]Samaria."

33 ¶ After this event Jeroboam did not return from his evil way, but [a]again he made priests of the high places from among [1]all the people; [b]any who would, he ordained, to be priests of the high places.

34 [1a]This event became sin to the house of Jeroboam, [b]even to blot *it* out and destroy *it* from off the face of the earth.

Ahijah Prophesies against the King

14 At that time Abijah the son of Jeroboam became sick.

2 Jeroboam said to his wife, "Arise now, and [a]disguise yourself so that they will not know that you are the wife of Jeroboam, and go to [b]Shiloh; behold, Ahijah the prophet is there, who [c]spoke concerning me *that I would be* king over this people.

3 "[a]Take ten loaves with you, *some* cakes and a jar of honey, and go to him. He will tell you what will happen to the boy."

4 ¶ Jeroboam's wife did so, and arose and went to [a]Shiloh, and came to the house of [b]Ahijah. Now Ahijah could not see, [c]for his eyes were [1]dim because of his age.

5 Now the LORD had said to Ahijah, "Behold, the wife of Jeroboam is coming to [1]inquire of you concerning her son, for he is sick. You shall say thus and thus to her, for it will be when she arrives that [a]she will pretend to be another woman."

6 ¶ When Ahijah heard the sound of her feet coming in the doorway, he said, "Come in, wife of Jeroboam, why do you pretend to be another woman? For I am sent to you *with* a harsh *message.*

7 "Go, say to Jeroboam, 'Thus says the LORD God of Israel, "[a]Because I exalted you from among the people and made you leader over My people Israel,

8 and [a]tore the kingdom away from the house of David and gave it to you—[b]yet you have not been like My servant David, who kept My commandments and who followed Me with all his heart, [c]to do only that which was right in My sight;

9 you also have done more evil than all who were before you, and [a]have gone and made for yourself other gods and [b]molten images to provoke Me to anger, and have [c]cast Me behind your back—

10 therefore behold, I am bringing calamity on the house of Jeroboam, and

---

18 [a]Matt 7:15; 1 John 4:1 [b]Gal 1:8 [c]Prov 12:19, 22; 19:5; Jer 29:31,32; Ezek 13:8,9; 1 Tim 4:1,2

21 [1]Lit *rebelled against* [2]Lit *mouth*

24 [a]1 Kin 20:36

25 [a]1 Kin 13:11

26 [1]Lit *rebelled against* [2]Lit *mouth*

30 [a]Jer 22:18

31 [a]Ruth 1:17; 2 Kin 23:17,18

32 [a]1 Kin 13:2 [b]Lev 26:30; 1 Kin 12:31 [c]1 Kin 16:24; John 4:5; Acts 8:14

33 [1]Or *extremities of* [a]1 Kin 12:31,32 [b]Judg 17:5

34 [1]Lit *by this thing he became* [a]1 Kin 12:30; 2 Kin 17:21 [b]1 Kin 14:10; 15:29,30

14:2 [a]1 Sam 28:8; 2 Sam 14:2; 2 Chr 18:29 [b]Josh 18:1 [c]1 Kin 11:29-31

3 [a]1 Sam 9:7,8; 1 Kin 13:7; 2 Kin 4:42

4 [1]Lit *set* [a]1 Kin 14:2 [b]1 Kin 11:29 [c]1 Sam 3:2; 4:15

5 [1]Lit *seek a word from* [a]2 Sam 14:2

7 [a]2 Sam 12:7; 1 Kin 11:28-31; 16:2

8 [a]1 Kin 11:31 [b]1 Kin 11:33,38 [c]1 Kin 15:5

9 [a]1 Kin 12:28; 2 Chr 11:15 [b]Ex 34:17 [c]Neh 9:26; Ps 50:17; Ezek 23:35

[a]will cut off from Jeroboam [1]every male
person, [b]both bond and free in Israel,
and I [c]will make a clean sweep of the
house of Jeroboam, as one sweeps away
dung until it is all gone.
11 "[a]Anyone belonging to Jeroboam
who dies in the city the dogs will eat. And
he who dies in the field the birds of the
heavens will eat; for the LORD has spoken *it.*" '
12 "Now you, arise, go to your house.
[a]When your feet enter the city the child
will die.
13 "All Israel shall mourn for him and
bury him, for [1]he alone of Jeroboam's
family will come to the grave, because in
him [a]something good was found toward
the LORD God of Israel in the house of
Jeroboam.
14 "Moreover, [a]the LORD will raise up
for Himself a king over Israel who will cut
off the house of Jeroboam this day [1]and
from now on.
15 ¶ "For the LORD will strike Israel, as
a reed is shaken in the water; and [a]He
will uproot Israel from [b]this good land
which He gave to their fathers, and [c]will
scatter them beyond the *Euphrates* River,
[d]because they have made their
[1]Asherim, provoking the LORD to anger.
16 "He will give up Israel [a]on account
of the sins of Jeroboam, which he [1]com-
mitted and with which he made Israel to
sin."
17 ¶ Then Jeroboam's wife arose and
departed and came to [a]Tirzah. [b]As she
was entering the threshold of the house,
the child died.
18 [a]All Israel buried him and
mourned for him, according to the word
of the LORD which He spoke through His
servant Ahijah the prophet.
19 ¶ Now the rest of the acts of Jeroboam, [a]how he made war and how he
reigned, behold, they are written in the
Book of the Chronicles of the Kings of
Israel.
20 The time that Jeroboam reigned
was twenty-two years; and he slept with
his fathers, and Nadab his son reigned in
his place.

Rehoboam Misleads Judah

21 ¶ [a]Now Rehoboam the son of Solomon reigned in Judah. Rehoboam was
forty-one years old when he became
king, and he reigned seventeen years in
Jerusalem, [b]the city which the LORD had
chosen from all the tribes of Israel to put
His name there. And his mother's name
was Naamah the Ammonitess.
22 [a]Judah did evil in the sight of the
LORD, and they [b]provoked Him to jealousy more than all that their fathers had
done, with [1]the sins which they [2]com-
mitted.
23 For they also built for themselves
[a]high places and *sacred* [b]pillars and
[1c]Asherim on every high hill and [d]be-
neath every luxuriant tree.
24 There were also [a]male cult prostitutes in the land. They did according to
all the abominations of the nations which
the LORD dispossessed before the sons of
Israel.
25 ¶ [a]Now it happened in the fifth
year of King Rehoboam, that Shishak the
king of Egypt came up against Jerusalem.
26 He took away the treasures of the
house of the LORD and the treasures of
the king's house, and [a]he took everything, [1b]even taking all the shields of
gold which Solomon had made.
27 So King Rehoboam made shields of
bronze in their place, and [a]committed
them to the [1]care of the commanders of
the [2]guard who guarded the doorway of
the king's house.
28 Then it happened as often as the
king entered the house of the LORD, that
the [1]guards would carry them and would
bring them back into the [1]guards' room.
29 ¶ [a]Now the rest of the acts of Rehoboam and all that he did, are they not
written in the Book of the Chronicles of
the Kings of Judah?
30 [a]There was war between Rehoboam and Jeroboam continually.
31 And Rehoboam slept with his fathers and was buried with his fathers
in the city of David; and [a]his mother's
name was Naamah the Ammonitess. And
Abijam his son became king in his place.

Abijam Reigns over Judah

15 [a]Now in the eighteenth year of
King Jeroboam, the son of Nebat,
Abijam became king over Judah.
2 He reigned three years in Jerusalem; and his mother's name was [1a]Maa-
cah the daughter of [2b]Abishalom.
3 He walked in all the sins of his
father which he had committed before
him; and [a]his heart was not [1]wholly devoted to the LORD his God, like the heart
of his father David.
4 But for David's sake the LORD his
God gave him a [a]lamp in Jerusalem, to
raise up his son after him and to establish
Jerusalem;
5 [a]because David did what was right
in the sight of the LORD, and had not
turned aside from anything that He commanded him all the days of his life, [b]ex-
cept in the case of Uriah the Hittite.
6 [a]There was war between Rehoboam and Jeroboam all the days of his life.
7 ¶ Now [a]the rest of the acts of Abi-

10 [1]Lit *him who urinates against the wall* [a]1 Kin 21:21; 2 Kin 9:8 [b]Deut 32:36; 2 Kin 14:26 [c]1 Kin 15:29
11 [a]1 Kin 16:4
12 [a]1 Kin 14:17
13 [1]Lit *the one* [a]2 Chr 19:3
14 [1]Lit *and what even now?* [a]1 Kin 15:27-29
15 [1]I.e. wooden symbols of a female deity [a]Deut 29:28; 2 Kin 17:6; Ps 52:5 [b]Josh 23:15 [c]2 Kin 15:29 [d]Ex 34:13; Deut 12:3
16 [1]Lit *sinned* [a]1 Kin 12:30
17 [a]1 Kin 15:21; Song 6:4 [b]1 Kin 14:12
18 [a]1 Kin 14:13
19 [a]1 Kin 14:30; 2 Chr 13:2-20
21 [a]2 Chr 12:13 [b]1 Kin 11:32
22 [1]Lit *their* [2]Lit *sinned* [a]2 Chr 12:1 [b]Deut 32:21; Ps 78:58; 1 Cor 10:22
23 [1]I.e. wooden symbols of a female deity [a]Deut 12:2; Ezek 16:24 [b]Deut 16:22 [c]1 Kin 14:15 [d]2 Kin 17:10; Is 57:5; Jer 2:20
24 [a]Gen 19:5; Deut 23:17; 1 Kin 15:12; 2 Kin 23:7
25 [a]1 Kin 11:40; 2 Chr 12:2
26 [1]Lit *and he took away* [a]1 Kin 15:18; 2 Chr 12:9 [b]1 Kin 10:17; 2 Chr 9:15
27 [1]Lit *hand* [2]Lit *runner* [a]1 Sam 8:11
28 [1]Lit *runners*
29 [a]2 Chr 12:15
30 [a]1 Kin 12:21
31 [a]1 Kin 14:21
15:1 [a]2 Chr 13:1
2 [1]In 2 Chr 13:2, *Micaiah, the daughter of Uriel* [2]In 2 Chr 11:20, *Absalom* [a]2 Chr 13:2 [b]2 Chr 11:21
3 [1]Lit *complete with* [a]1 Kin 11:4; Ps 119:80
4 [a]2 Sam 21:17; 1 Kin 11:36; 2 Chr 21:7
5 [a]1 Kin 9:4; Luke 1:6 [b]2 Sam 11:3f
6 [a]1 Kin 14:30; 2 Chr 12:15-13:20
7 [a]2 Chr 13:2

Rulers of Israel and Judah

SCRIPTURE	KINGS	SYNCHRONISM OR CORRELATION	LENGTH OF REIGN	HISTORICAL DATA	DATES
1. 1 Kin 12:1-24	***Rehoboam***		*17 years*		*930-913*
1 Kin 14:21-31	*(Judah)*				
2. 1 Kin 12:25–14:20	**Jeroboam I**		22 years		930-909
	(Israel)				
3. 1 Kin 15:1-8	***Abijah***	*18th of Jeroboam*	*3 years*		*913-910*
	(Judah)				
4. 1 Kin 15:9-24	***Asa***	*20th of Jeroboam*	*41 years*		*910-869*
	(Judah)				
5. 1 Kin 15:25-31	**Nadab**	2nd of Asa	2 years		909-908
	(Israel)				
6. 1 Kin 15:32–16:7	**Baasha**	3rd of Asa	24 years		908-886
	(Israel)				
7. 1 Kin 16:8-14	**Elah**	26th of Asa	2 years		886-885
	(Israel)				
8. 1 Kin 16:15-20	**Zimri**	27th of Asa	7 days		885
	(Israel)				
9. 1 Kin 16:21-22	**Tibni**			Overlap with Omri	885-880
	(Israel)				
10. 1 Kin 16:23-28	**Omri**	27th of Asa		Made king by the people	885
	(Israel)			Overlap with Tibni	885-880
			12 years	Official reign = 11 actual years	885-874
		31st of Asa		Beginning of sole reign	880
11. 1 Kin 16:29–22:40	**Ahab**	38th of Asa	22 years	Official reign = 21 actual years	874-853
	(Israel)				
12. 1 Kin 22:41-50	***Jehoshaphat***			*Co-regency with Asa*	*872-869*
	(Judah)		*25 years*	*Official reign*	*872-848*
		4th of Ahab		*Beginning of sole reign*	*869*
				Has Jehoram as regent	*853-848*
13. 1 Kin 22:51–	**Ahaziah**	17th of Jehoshaphat	2 years	Official reign = 1 yr. actual reign	853-852
2 Kin 1:18	(Israel)				
14. 2 Kin 1:17	**Joram**	2nd of Jehoram			852
2 Kin 3:1–8:15	(Israel)	18th of Jehoshaphat	12 years	Official reign = 11 actual years	852-841
15. 2 Kin 8:16-24	***Jehoram***	*5th of Joram*		*Beginning of sole reign*	*848*
	(Judah)		*8 years*	*Official reign = 7 actual years*	*848-841*
16. 2 Kin 8:25-29	***Ahaziah***	*12th of Joram*	*1 year*	*Nonaccession-year reckoning*	*841*
2 Kin 9:29	*(Judah)*	*11th of Joram*		*Accession-year reckoning*	*841*
17. 2 Kin 9:30–10:36	**Jehu**		28 years		841-814
	(Israel)				
18. 2 Kin 11	***Athaliah***		*7 years*		*841-835*
	(Judah)				
19. 2 Kin 12	***Joash***	*7th of Jehu*	*40 years*		*835-796*
	(Judah)				
20. 2 Kin 13:1-9	**Jehoahaz**	23rd of Joash	17 years		814-798
	(Israel)				
21. 2 Kin 13:10-25	**Jehoash**	37th of Joash	16 years		798-782
	(Israel)				

Rulers of Israel and Judah

SCRIPTURE	KINGS	SYNCHRONISM OR CORRELATION	LENGTH OF REIGN	HISTORICAL DATA	DATES
***22.** 2 Kin 14:1-22*	***Amaziah***	*2nd of Jehoash*	*29 years*		*796-767*
	(Judah)			*Overlap with Azariah*	*792-767*
23. 2 Kin 14:23-29	**Jeroboam II**			Co-regency with Jehoash	793-782
	(Israel)		41 years	Total reign	793-753
		15th of Amaziah		Beginning of sole reign	782
***24.** 2 Kin 15:1-7*	***Azariah***			*Overlap with Amaziah*	*792-767*
	(Judah)		*52 years*	*Total reign*	*792-740*
		27th of Jeroboam		*Beginning of sole reign*	*767*
25. 2 Kin 15:8-12	**Zechariah**	38th of Azariah	6 months		753
	(Israel)				
26. 2 Kin 15:13-15	**Shallum**	39th of Azariah	1 month		752
	(Israel)				
27. 2 Kin 15:16-22	**Menahem**	39th of Azariah	10 years	Ruled in Samaria	752-742
	(Israel)				
28. 2 Kin 15:23-26	**Pekahiah**	50th of Azariah	2 years		742-740
	(Israel)				
29. 2 Kin 15:27-31	**Pekah**			In Gilead; overlapping years	752-740
	(Israel)		20 years	Total reign	752-732
		52nd of Azariah		Beginning of sole reign	740
***30.** 2 Kin 15:32-38*	***Jotham***			*Co-regency with Azariah*	*750-740*
2 Kin 15:30	*(Judah)*		*16 years*	*Official reign*	*750-735*
				Reign to his 20th year	*750-732*
		2nd of Pekah		*Beginning of co-regency*	*750*
***31.** 2 Kin 16*	***Ahaz***			*Total reign*	*735-715*
	(Judah)	*17th of Pekah*			*735*
			16 years	*From 20th of Jotham*	*732-715*
32. 2 Kin 15:30	**Hoshea**			20th of Jotham	732
2 Kin 17	(Israel)	12th of Ahaz*	9 years		732-722
***33.** 2 Kin 18:1–20:21*	***Hezekiah***	*3rd of Hoshea**	*29 years*		*715-686*
	(Judah)				
***34.** 2 Kin 21:1-18*	***Manasseh***			*Co-regency with Hezekiah*	*697-686*
	(Judah)		*55 years*	*Total reign*	*697-642*
***35.** 2 Kin 21:19-26*	***Amon***		*2 years*		*642-640*
	(Judah)				
***36.** 2 Kin 22:1–23:30*	***Josiah***		*31 years*		*640-609*
	(Judah)				
***37.** 2 Kin 23:31-33*	***Jehoahaz***		*3 months*		*609*
	(Judah)				
***38.** 2 Kin 23:34–24:7*	***Jehoiakim***		*11 years*		*609-598*
	(Judah)				
***39.** 2 Kin 24:8-17*	***Jehoiachin***		*3 months*		*598-597*
	(Judah)				
***40.** 2 Kin 24:18–25:26*	***Zedekiah***		*11 years*		*597-586*
	(Judah)				

*These data arise when the reign of Hoshea is thrown 12 years in advance of its historical position.

*Italics denote kings of **Judah**.* Non-italic type denotes kings of **Israel**.

jam and all that he did, are they not written in the Book of the Chronicles of the Kings of Judah? [b]And there was war between Abijam and Jeroboam.

Asa Succeeds Abijam

8 [a]And Abijam slept with his fathers and they buried him in the city of David; and Asa his son became king in his place.

9 ¶ So in the twentieth year of Jeroboam the king of Israel, Asa began to reign as king of Judah.

10 He reigned forty-one years in Jerusalem; and [a]his mother's name was Maacah the daughter of Abishalom.

11 [a]Asa did what was right in the sight of the LORD, like David his father.

12 [a]He also put away the male cult prostitutes from the land and [b]removed all the idols which his fathers had made.

13 [1a]He also removed Maacah his mother from *being* queen mother, because she had made a horrid image [2]as an Asherah; and Asa cut down her horrid image and [b]burned *it* at the brook Kidron.

14 [a]But the high places were not taken away; nevertheless [b]the heart of Asa was [1]wholly devoted to the LORD all his days.

15 [a]He brought into the house of the LORD the dedicated things of his father and his own dedicated things: silver and gold and utensils.

16 ¶ [a]Now there was war between Asa and Baasha king of Israel all their days.

17 [a]Baasha king of Israel went up against Judah and [1b]fortified Ramah [c]in order to prevent *anyone* from going out or coming in to Asa king of Judah.

18 Then [a]Asa took all the silver and the gold which were left in the treasuries of the house of the LORD and the treasuries of the king's house, and delivered them into the hand of his servants. And [b]King Asa sent them to Ben-hadad the son of Tabrimmon, the son of Hezion, king of Aram, who lived in [c]Damascus, saying,

19 "*Let there be* a [a]treaty between [1]you and me, *as* between my father and your father. Behold, I have sent you a present of silver and gold; go, break your treaty with Baasha king of Israel so that he will withdraw from me."

20 So Ben-hadad listened to King Asa and sent the commanders of his armies against the cities of Israel, and [1]conquered [a]Ijon, [b]Dan, [c]Abel-beth-maacah and all [d]Chinneroth, besides all the land of Naphtali.

21 When Baasha heard *of it*, [a]he ceased [1]fortifying Ramah and remained in [b]Tirzah.

22 Then King Asa made a proclamation to all Judah—none was exempt—and they carried away the stones of Ramah and its timber with which Baasha had built. And King Asa built with them [a]Geba of Benjamin and Mizpah.

Jehoshaphat Succeeds Asa

23 ¶ [a]Now the rest of all the acts of Asa and all his might and all that he did and the cities which he built, are they not written in the Book of the Chronicles of the Kings of Judah? But in the time of his old age he was diseased in his feet.

24 And Asa slept with his fathers and was buried with his fathers in the city of David his father; and [a]Jehoshaphat his son reigned in his place.

Nadab, then Baasha, Rules over Israel

25 ¶ Now [a]Nadab the son of Jeroboam became king over Israel in the second year of Asa king of Judah, and he reigned over Israel two years.

26 He did evil in the sight of the LORD, and [a]walked in the way of his father and [b]in his sin which he made Israel sin.

27 Then [a]Baasha the son of Ahijah of the house of Issachar conspired against him, and Baasha struck him down at [b]Gibbethon, which belonged to the Philistines, while Nadab and all Israel were laying siege to Gibbethon.

28 ¶ So Baasha killed him in the third year of Asa king of Judah and reigned in his place.

29 It came about as soon as he was king, he struck down all the household of Jeroboam. He did not leave to Jeroboam [1]any persons alive, until he had destroyed them, [a]according to the word of the LORD, which He spoke by His servant Ahijah the Shilonite,

30 *and* because of the sins of Jeroboam which he sinned, and [a]which he made Israel sin, because of his provocation with which he provoked the LORD God of Israel to anger.

31 ¶ [a]Now the rest of the acts of Nadab and all that he did, are they not written in the Book of the Chronicles of the Kings of Israel?

War with Judah

32 [a]There was war between Asa and Baasha king of Israel all their days.

33 ¶ In the third year of Asa king of Judah, Baasha the son of Ahijah became king over all Israel at Tirzah, *and reigned* twenty-four years.

34 He did evil in the sight of the LORD,

---

7 [b]2 Chr 13:3-20
8 [a]2 Chr 14:1
10 [a]1 Kin 15:2
11 [a]2 Chr 14:2
12 [a]Deut 23:17; 1 Kin 14:24; 22:46 [b]1 Kin 11:7,8; 14:23; 2 Chr 14:2-5
13 [1]Lit *also Maacah his mother and he removed her* [2]Or *for Asherah* [a]2 Chr 15:16-18 [b]Ex 32:20
14 [1]Lit *complete with* [a]1 Kin 22:43; 2 Kin 12:3 [b]1 Kin 8:61; 15:3
15 [a]1 Kin 7:51
16 [a]1 Kin 15:32
17 [1]Lit *built* [a]2 Chr 16:1-6 [b]Josh 18:25; 1 Kin 15:21,22 [c]1 Kin 12:26-29
18 [a]1 Kin 14:26; 15:15 [b]2 Kin 12:17,18; 2 Chr 16:2 [c]Gen 14:15; 1 Kin 11:23,24
19 [1]Lit *me and you* [a]2 Chr 16:7
20 [1]Lit *smote* [a]2 Kin 15:29 [b]Judg 18:29; 1 Kin 12:29 [c]2 Sam 20:15; 2 Kin 15:29 [d]Josh 11:2; 12:3
21 [1]Lit *building* [a]1 Kin 15:17 [b]1 Kin 14:17; 16:15-18
22 [a]Josh 18:24; 21:17
23 [a]2 Chr 16:11-14
24 [a]1 Kin 22:41-44; 2 Chr 17:1; Matt 1:8
25 [a]1 Kin 14:20
26 [a]1 Kin 12:28-33; 13:33, 34 [b]1 Kin 14:16; 15:30,34
27 [a]1 Kin 14:14 [b]Josh 19:44; 21:23; 1 Kin 16:15
29 [1]Lit *any breath* [a]1 Kin 14:9-16
30 [a]1 Kin 15:26
31 [a]1 Kin 14:19
32 [a]1 Kin 15:16

and [a]walked in the way of Jeroboam and in his sin which he made Israel sin.

Prophecy against Baasha

16 Now the word of the LORD came to [a]Jehu the son of [b]Hanani against Baasha, saying,

2 "Inasmuch as I [a]exalted you from the dust and made you leader over My people Israel, and [b]you have walked in the way of Jeroboam and have made My people Israel sin, provoking Me to anger with their sins,

3 behold, [a]I will consume [b]Baasha and his house, and [c]I will make your house like the house of Jeroboam the son of Nebat.

4 "[a]Anyone of Baasha who dies in the city the dogs will eat, and anyone of his who dies in the field the birds of the heavens will eat."

5 ¶ [a]Now the rest of the acts of Baasha and what he did and his might, are they not written in the Book of the Chronicles of the Kings of Israel?

The Israelite Kings

6 And Baasha slept with his fathers and was buried in [a]Tirzah, and Elah his son became king in his place.

7 Moreover, the word of the LORD through [a]the prophet Jehu the son of Hanani also came against Baasha and his household, both because of all the evil which he did in the sight of the LORD, provoking Him to anger with [b]the work of his hands, in being like the house of Jeroboam, and because [c]he struck [1]it.

8 ¶ In the twenty-sixth year of Asa king of Judah, Elah the son of Baasha became king over Israel at Tirzah, *and reigned* two years.

9 His servant [a]Zimri, commander of half his chariots, conspired against him. Now he *was* at Tirzah drinking himself drunk in the house of Arza, [b]who *was* over the household at Tirzah.

10 Then Zimri went in and struck him and put him to death in the twenty-seventh year of Asa king of Judah, and became king in his place.

11 It came about when he became king, as soon as he sat on his throne, that [a]he [1]killed all the household of Baasha; he did not leave [2]a single male, neither of his [3]relatives nor of his friends.

12 ¶ Thus Zimri destroyed all the household of Baasha, [a]according to the word of the LORD, which He spoke against Baasha through [b]Jehu the prophet,

13 for all the sins of Baasha and the sins of Elah his son, which they sinned and which they made Israel sin, [a]provoking the LORD God of Israel to anger with their [1]idols.

14 [a]Now the rest of the acts of Elah and all that he did, are they not written in the Book of the Chronicles of the Kings of Israel?

15 ¶ In the twenty-seventh year of Asa king of Judah, Zimri reigned seven days at Tirzah. Now the people were camped against [a]Gibbethon, which belonged to the Philistines.

16 The people who were camped heard [1]it said, "Zimri has conspired and has also struck down the king." Therefore all Israel made Omri, the commander of the army, king over Israel that day in the camp.

17 Then Omri and all Israel with him went up from Gibbethon and besieged Tirzah.

18 When Zimri saw that the city was taken, he went into the citadel of the king's house and burned the king's house over him with fire, and [a]died,

19 because of his sins which he sinned, doing evil in the sight of the LORD, [a]walking in the way of Jeroboam, and in his sin which he did, making Israel sin.

20 [a]Now the rest of the acts of Zimri and his conspiracy which he [1]carried out, are they not written in the Book of the Chronicles of the Kings of Israel?

21 ¶ Then the people of Israel were divided into two parts: half of the people followed Tibni the son of Ginath, to make him king; the *other* half followed Omri.

22 But the people who followed Omri prevailed over the people who followed Tibni the son of Ginath. And Tibni died and Omri became king.

23 In the thirty-first year of Asa king of Judah, Omri became king over Israel *and reigned* twelve years; he reigned six years at [a]Tirzah.

24 He bought the hill [1]Samaria from Shemer for two talents of silver; and he built on the hill, and named the city which he built [1a]Samaria, after the name of Shemer, the owner of the hill.

25 ¶ [a]Omri did evil in the sight of the LORD, and [b]acted more wickedly than all who *were* before him.

26 For he [a]walked in all the way of Jeroboam the son of Nebat and in his sins which he made Israel sin, provoking the LORD God of Israel with their [1]idols.

27 Now the rest of the acts of Omri which he did and his might which he [1]showed, are they not written in the Book of the Chronicles of the Kings of Israel?

28 So Omri slept with his fathers and

34 [a]1 Kin 15:26

16:1 [a]1 Kin 16:7; 2 Chr 19:2; 20:34 [b]2 Chr 16:7-10

2 [a]1 Sam 2:8; 1 Kin 14:7 [b]1 Kin 15:34

3 [a]1 Kin 14:10; 21:21 [b]1 Kin 16:11 [c]1 Kin 15:29

4 [a]1 Kin 14:11; 21:24

5 [a]1 Kin 14:19; 15:31

6 [a]1 Kin 14:17; 15:21

7 [1]Or *him* [a]1 Kin 16:1 [b]Ps 115:4; Is 2:8 [c]1 Kin 14:14; 15:27,29

9 [a]2 Kin 9:30-33 [b]Gen 24:2; 39:4; 1 Kin 18:3

11 [1]Lit *smote* [2]Lit *him who urinates against the wall* [3]Lit *redeemers* [a]1 Kin 15:29; 16:3

12 [a]1 Kin 16:3 [b]2 Chr 19:2; 20:34

13 [1]Lit *vanities* [a]Deut 32:21; 1 Kin 15:30

14 [a]1 Kin 16:5

15 [a]1 Kin 15:27

16 [1]Lit *saying*

18 [a]1 Sam 31:4, 5; 2 Sam 17:23

19 [a]1 Kin 12:28; 14:16; 15:26

20 [1]Lit *conspired* [a]1 Kin 16:5,14,27

23 [a]1 Kin 15:21

24 [1]Heb *Shomeron* [a]1 Kin 16:28,29,32

25 [a]Mic 6:16 [b]1 Kin 14:9; 16:30-33

26 [1]Lit *vanities* [a]1 Kin 16:19

27 [1]Lit *did*

was buried in Samaria; and Ahab his son became king in his place.

29 ¶ Now Ahab the son of Omri became king over Israel in the thirty-eighth year of Asa king of Judah, and Ahab the son of Omri reigned over Israel in Samaria twenty-two years.

30 Ahab the son of Omri did evil in the sight of the LORD [a]more than all who were before him.

31 ¶ It came about, as though it had been a trivial thing for him to walk in the sins of Jeroboam the son of Nebat, that [a]he married Jezebel the daughter of Ethbaal king of the [b]Sidonians, and went to serve Baal and worshiped him.

32 So he erected an altar for Baal in [a]the house of Baal which he built in Samaria.

33 Ahab also made [a]the [1]Asherah. Thus [b]Ahab did more to provoke the LORD God of Israel than all the kings of Israel who were before him.

34 [a]In his days Hiel the Bethelite built Jericho; he laid its foundations with the *loss of* Abiram his firstborn, and set up its gates with the *loss of* his youngest son Segub, according to the word of the LORD, which He spoke by Joshua the son of Nun.

Elijah Predicts Drought

17 Now Elijah the Tishbite, who was of [1a]the settlers of Gilead, said to Ahab, "[b]As the LORD, the God of Israel lives, before whom I stand, surely [c]there shall be neither dew nor rain these years, except by my word."

2 The word of the LORD came to him, saying,

3 "Go away from here and turn eastward, and hide yourself by the brook Cherith, which is [1]east of the Jordan.

4 "It shall be that you will drink of the brook, and [a]I have commanded the ravens to provide for you there."

5 So he went and did according to the word of the LORD, for he went and lived by the brook Cherith, which is [1]east of the Jordan.

6 The ravens brought him bread and meat in the morning and bread and meat in the evening, and he would drink from the brook.

7 It happened after a while that the brook dried up, because there was no rain in the land.

8 ¶ Then the word of the LORD came to him, saying,

9 "Arise, go to [a]Zarephath, which belongs to Sidon, and stay there; behold, [b]I have commanded a widow there to provide for you."

10 So he arose and went to Zarephath, and when he came to the gate of the city, behold, a widow was there gathering sticks; and [a]he called to her and said, "Please get me a little water in a [1]jar, that I may drink."

11 As she was going to get *it*, he called to her and said, "Please bring me a piece of bread in your hand."

12 But she said, "[a]As the LORD your God lives, [b]I have no [1]bread, only a handful of flour in the [2]bowl and a little oil in the jar; and behold, I am gathering [3]a few sticks that I may go in and prepare for me and my son, that we may eat it and [c]die."

13 Then Elijah said to her, "Do not fear; go, do as you have said, but make me a little bread cake from [1]it first and bring *it* out to me, and afterward you may make *one* for yourself and for your son.

14 "For thus says the LORD God of Israel, 'The [1]bowl of flour shall not be exhausted, nor shall the jar of oil [2]be empty, until the day that the LORD sends rain on the face of the earth.' "

15 So she went and did according to the word of Elijah, and she and he and her household ate for *many* days.

16 The [1]bowl of flour was not exhausted nor did the jar of oil [2]become empty, according to the word of the LORD which He spoke through Elijah.

Elijah Raises the Widow's Son

17 ¶ Now it came about after these things that the son of the woman, the mistress of the house, became sick; and his sickness was so severe that there was no breath left in him.

18 So she said to Elijah, "[a]What do I have to do with you, O [b]man of God? [1]You have come to me to bring my iniquity to remembrance and to put my son to death!"

19 He said to her, "Give me your son." Then he took him from her bosom and carried him up to the upper room where he was living, and laid him on his own bed.

20 He called to the LORD and said, "O LORD my God, have You also brought calamity to the widow with whom I am [1]staying, by causing her son to die?"

21 [a]Then he stretched himself upon the child three times, and called to the LORD and said, "O LORD my God, I pray You, let this child's life return [1]to him."

22 The LORD heard the voice of Elijah, [a]and the life of the child returned [1]to him and he revived.

23 Elijah took the child and brought him down from the upper room into the house and gave him to his mother; and Elijah said, "See, your son is alive."

---

30 [a]1 Kin 14:9; 16:25

31 [a]Deut 7:1-5 [b]Judg 18:7; 1 Kin 11:1-5; 2 Kin 10:18; 17:16

32 [a]2 Kin 10:21,26,27

33 [1]I.e. wooden symbol of a female deity [a]2 Kin 13:6 [b]1 Kin 14:9; 16:29,30; 21:25

34 [a]Josh 6:26

17:1 [1]Or *Tishbe in Gilead* [a]Judg 12:4 [b]1 Kin 18:10; 22:14; 2 Kin 3:14; 5:20 [c]1 Kin 18:1; Luke 4:25; James 5:17

3 [1]Lit *before*

4 [a]1 Kin 17:9

5 [1]Lit *before*

9 [a]Obad 20; Luke 4:26 [b]1 Kin 17:4

10 [1]Or *vessel* [a]Gen 24:17; John 4:7

12 [1]Lit *cake* [2]Lit *pitcher* [3]Lit *two* [a]1 Kin 17:1 [b]2 Kin 4:2-7 [c]Gen 21:15,16

13 [1]Lit *there*

14 [1]Lit *pitcher* [2]Lit *lack*

16 [1]Lit *pitcher* [2]Lit *lack*

18 [1]Or *Have you come...death?* [a]2 Sam 16:10; 2 Kin 3:13; Luke 4:34; John 2:4 [b]1 Kin 12:22

20 [1]Lit *sojourning*

21 [1]Lit *upon his inward part* [a]2 Kin 4:34,35; Acts 20:10

22 [1]Lit *upon his inward part* [a]Luke 7:14; Heb 11:35

24 Then the woman said to Elijah, "[a]Now I know that you are a man of God and that the word of the LORD in your mouth is truth."

Obadiah Meets Elijah

18 Now it happened [a]*after* many days that the word of the LORD came to Elijah in the third year, saying, "Go, show yourself to Ahab, and [b]I will send rain on the face of the earth."

2 So Elijah went to show himself to Ahab. Now the famine *was* severe in Samaria.

3 Ahab called Obadiah [a]who *was* over the household. (Now Obadiah [1b]feared the LORD greatly;

4 for [a]when Jezebel [1]destroyed the prophets of the LORD, Obadiah took a hundred prophets and hid them by fifties in a cave, and [b]provided them with bread and water.)

5 Then Ahab said to Obadiah, "Go through the land to all the springs of water and to all the valleys; perhaps we will find grass and keep the horses and mules alive, and not [1]have to kill some of the cattle."

6 So they divided the land between them to [1]survey it; Ahab went one way by himself and Obadiah went another way by himself.

7 ¶ Now as Obadiah was on the way, behold, Elijah [1]met him, [a]and he recognized him and fell on his face and said, "Is this you, Elijah my master?"

8 He said to him, "It is I. Go, say to your master, 'Behold, Elijah *is here.*' "

9 He said, "What [1]sin have I committed, that you are giving your servant into the hand of Ahab to put me to death?

10 "[a]As the LORD your God lives, there is no nation or kingdom where my master has not sent to search for you; and when they said, 'He is not *here,*' he made the kingdom or nation swear that they could not find you.

11 "And now you are saying, 'Go, say to your master, "Behold, Elijah *is here.*" '

12 "It will come about when I leave you [a]that the Spirit of the LORD will carry you where I do not know; so when I come and tell Ahab and he cannot find you, he will kill me, although *I* your servant have [1]feared the LORD from my youth.

13 "[a]Has it not been told to my master what I did when Jezebel killed the prophets of the LORD, that I hid [1]a hundred prophets of the LORD by fifties in a cave, and provided them with bread and water?

14 "And now you are saying, 'Go, say to your master, "Behold, Elijah *is here*" '; he will then kill me."

15 Elijah said, "[a]As the LORD of hosts lives, before whom I stand, I will surely show myself to him today."

16 So Obadiah went to meet Ahab and told him; and Ahab went to meet Elijah.

17 ¶ When Ahab saw Elijah, [a]Ahab said to him, "Is this you, you troubler of Israel?"

18 He said, "I have not troubled Israel, but you and your father's house *have,* because [a]you have forsaken the commandments of the LORD and [b]you have followed the Baals.

19 "Now then send *and* gather to me all Israel at [a]Mount Carmel, [b]*together* with 450 prophets of Baal and 400 prophets of [c]the Asherah, who eat at Jezebel's table."

God or Baal on Mount Carmel

20 ¶ So Ahab sent *a message* among all the sons of Israel and brought the prophets together at Mount Carmel.

21 Elijah came near to all the people and said, "[a]How long *will* you [1]hesitate between two opinions? [b]If the LORD is God, follow Him; but if Baal, follow him." But the people did not answer him a word.

22 Then Elijah said to the people, "I [a]alone am left a prophet of the LORD, but Baal's prophets are [b]450 men.

23 "Now let them give us two oxen; and let them choose one ox for themselves and cut it up, and place it on the wood, but put no fire *under it;* and I will prepare the other ox and lay it on the wood, and I will not put a fire *under it.*

24 "Then you call on the name of your god, and I will call on the name of the LORD, and [a]the God who answers by fire, He is God." And all the people said, "[1]That is a good idea."

25 ¶ So Elijah said to the prophets of Baal, "Choose one ox for yourselves and prepare it first for you are many, and call on the name of your god, but put no fire *under it.*"

26 Then they took the ox which [1]was given them and they prepared it and called on the name of Baal from morning until noon saying, "O Baal, answer us." But there was [a]no voice and no one answered. And they [2]leaped about the altar which [3]they made.

27 It came about at noon, that Elijah mocked them and said, "Call out with a loud voice, for he is a god; either he is occupied or gone aside, or is on a journey, or perhaps he is asleep and needs to be awakened."

28 So they cried with a loud voice and [a]cut themselves according to their cus-

24 [a]John 2:11; 3:2; 16:30

18:1 [a]1 Kin 17:1; Luke 4:25; James 5:17 [b]Deut 28:12

3 [1]Or *revered* [a]1 Kin 16:9 [b]Neh 7:2; Job 28:28

4 [1]Lit *cut off* [a]1 Kin 18:13 [b]Matt 10:40-42

5 [1]Lit *cut off*

6 [1]Lit *pass through*

7 [1]Lit *to meet* [a]2 Kin 1:6-8

9 [1]Lit *have I sinned*

10 [a]1 Kin 17:1

12 [1]Or *revered* [a]2 Kin 2:16; Ezek 3:12,14; Acts 8:39

13 [1]Lit *a hundred men of the prophets* [a]1 Kin 18:4

15 [a]1 Kin 17:1

17 [a]Josh 7:25; 1 Kin 21:20

18 [a]1 Kin 9:9; 2 Chr 15:2 [b]1 Kin 16:31; 21:25,26

19 [a]Josh 19:26; 2 Kin 2:25 [b]1 Kin 18:22 [c]1 Kin 16:33

21 [1]Lit *limp on the two divided opinions* [a]2 Kin 17:41; Matt 6:24 [b]Josh 24:15

22 [a]1 Kin 19:10,14 [b]1 Kin 18:19

24 [1]Lit *The matter is good* [a]1 Kin 18:38

26 [1]Lit *he gave* [2]Lit *limped;* i.e. a type of ceremonial dance [3]So some mss and the ancient versions; M.T. *he* [a]Ps 115:4,5; Jer 10:5

28 [a]Lev 19:28; Deut 14:1

tom with swords and lances until the blood gushed out on them.

29 When midday was past, they [1]raved [a]until the time of the offering of the *evening* sacrifice; but there was no voice, no one answered, and no [2]one paid attention.

30 ¶ Then Elijah said to all the people, "Come near to me." So all the people came near to him. And [a]he repaired the altar of the LORD which had been torn down.

31 Elijah took twelve stones according to the number of the tribes of the sons of Jacob, to whom the word of the LORD had come, saying, "[a]Israel shall be your name."

32 So with the stones he built an altar in [a]the name of the LORD, and he made a trench around the altar, large enough to hold two [1]measures of seed.

33 [a]Then he arranged the wood and cut the ox in pieces and laid *it* on the wood.

34 And he said, "Fill four pitchers with water and pour *it* on the burnt offering and on the wood." And he said, "Do it a second time," and they did it a second time. And he said, "Do it a third time," and they did it a third time.

35 The water flowed around the altar and he also filled the trench with water.

Elijah's Prayer

36 [a]At the time of the offering of the *evening* sacrifice, Elijah the prophet came near and said, "[b]O LORD, the God of Abraham, Isaac and Israel, today let it be known that [c]You are God in Israel and that I am Your servant and [d]I have done all these things at Your word.

37 "Answer me, O LORD, answer me, that this people may know that You, O LORD, are God, and *that* You have turned their heart back again."

38 Then the [a]fire of the LORD fell and consumed the burnt offering and the wood and the stones and the dust, and licked up the water that was in the trench.

39 When all the people saw it, they fell on their faces; and they said, "[a]The LORD, He is God; the LORD, He is God."

40 Then Elijah said to them, "Seize the prophets of Baal; do not let one of them escape." So they seized them; and Elijah brought them down to [a]the brook Kishon, [b]and slew them there.

41 ¶ Now Elijah said to Ahab, "Go up, eat and drink; for there is the sound of the roar of a *heavy* shower."

42 So Ahab went up to eat and drink. But Elijah went up to the top of [a]Carmel; and he [b]crouched down on the earth and put his face between his knees.

43 He said to his servant, "Go up now, look toward the sea." So he went up and looked and said, "There is nothing." And he said, "Go back" seven times.

44 It came about at the seventh *time,* that he said, "Behold, [a]a cloud as small as a man's hand is coming up from the sea." And he said, "Go up, say to Ahab, '[1]Prepare *your chariot* and go down, so that the *heavy* shower does not stop you.' "

45 In a little while the sky grew black with clouds and wind, and there was a heavy shower. And Ahab rode and went to [a]Jezreel.

46 Then [a]the hand of the LORD was on Elijah, and [b]he girded up his loins and [1]outran Ahab [2]to Jezreel.

Elijah Flees from Jezebel

19 Now Ahab told Jezebel all that Elijah had done, and [1a]how he had killed all the prophets with the sword.

2 Then Jezebel sent a messenger to Elijah, saying, "[a]So may the gods do to me and even more, if I do not make your [1]life as the [1]life of one of them by tomorrow about this time."

3 And he [1]was afraid and arose and ran for his [2]life and came to [a]Beersheba, which belongs to Judah, and left his servant there.

4 But he himself went a day's journey into the wilderness, and came and sat down under a [1]juniper tree; and [a]he requested for himself that he might die, and said, "It is enough; now, O LORD, take my [2]life, for I am not better than my fathers."

5 He lay down and slept under a [1]juniper tree; and behold, there was [a]an angel touching him, and he said to him, "Arise, eat."

6 Then he looked and behold, there was at his head a bread cake *baked on* hot stones, and a jar of water. So he ate and drank and lay down again.

7 The angel of the LORD came again a second time and touched him and said, "Arise, eat, because the journey is too great for you."

8 So he arose and ate and drank, and went in the strength of that food [a]forty days and forty nights to [b]Horeb, the mountain of God.

Elijah at Horeb

9 ¶ Then he came there to a cave and lodged there; and behold, [a]the word of the LORD *came* to him, and He said to him, "What are you doing here, Elijah?"

10 He said, "[a]I have been very zealous for the LORD, the God of hosts; for the

---

29 [1]Lit *prophesied* [2]Lit *attentiveness* [a]Ex 29:39,41

30 [a]1 Kin 19:10,14; 2 Chr 33:16

31 [a]Gen 32:28; 35:10; 2 Kin 17:34

32 [1]Heb *seahs;* i.e. one seah equals approx 11 qts [a]Col 3:17

33 [a]Gen 22:9; Lev 1:7,8

36 [a]1 Kin 18:29 [b]Gen 28:13; Ex 3:6; 4:5; Matt 22:32 [c]1 Kin 8:43 [d]Num 16:28-32

38 [a]Gen 15:17; Lev 9:24; 10:1,2; Judg 6:21; 2 Kin 1:12; 1 Chr 21:26; 2 Chr 7:1; Job 1:16

39 [a]1 Kin 18:21,24

40 [a]Judg 4:7; 5:21 [b]Deut 13:5; 18:20; 2 Kin 10:24,25

42 [a]1 Kin 18:19,20 [b]James 5:18

44 [1]Lit *Tie, harness* [a]Luke 12:54

45 [a]Josh 17:16; Judg 6:33

46 [1]Lit *ran before* [2]Lit *until you are coming to* [a]2 Kin 3:15; Is 8:11; Ezek 3:14 [b]2 Kin 4:29; Jer 1:17; 1 Pet 1:13

19:1 [1]Lit *all about how* [a]1 Kin 18:40

2 [1]Lit *soul* [a]Ruth 1:17; 1 Kin 20:10; 2 Kin 6:31

3 [1]Reading of many mss; Heb text may read *saw* [2]Lit *soul* [a]Gen 21:31

4 [1]Or *broom-tree* [2]Lit *soul* [a]Num 11:15; Jer 20:14-18; Jon 4:3,8

5 [1]Or *broom-tree* [a]Gen 28:12

8 [a]Ex 24:18; 34:28; Deut 9:9-11,18; Matt 4:2 [b]Ex 3:1; 4:27

9 [a]Ex 33:21,22

10 [a]Ex 20:5; 34:14

sons of Israel have forsaken Your covenant, [b]torn down Your altars and killed
Your prophets with the sword. And [c]I
alone am left; and they seek my life, to
take it away."
11 ¶ So He said, "[a]Go forth and stand
on the mountain before the LORD." And
behold, the LORD was passing by! And [b]a
great and strong wind was rending the
mountains and breaking in pieces the
rocks before the LORD; *but* the LORD *was*
not in the wind. And after the wind an
earthquake, *but* the LORD *was* not in the
earthquake.
12 After the earthquake a fire, *but* the
LORD *was* not in the fire; and after the fire
[a]a sound of a gentle blowing.
13 When Elijah heard *it,* [a]he wrapped
his face in his mantle and went out and
stood in the entrance of the cave. And
behold, [b]a voice *came* to him and said,
"What are you doing here, Elijah?"
14 Then he said, "[a]I have been very
zealous for the LORD, the God of hosts; for
the sons of Israel have forsaken Your covenant, torn down Your altars and killed
Your prophets with the sword. And I
alone am left; and they seek my life, to
take it away."
15 ¶ The LORD said to him, "Go, return on your way to the wilderness of
Damascus, and when you have arrived,
[a]you shall anoint Hazael king over Aram;
16 and [a]Jehu the son of Nimshi you
shall anoint king over Israel; and [b]Elisha
the son of Shaphat of Abel-meholah you
shall anoint as prophet in your place.
17 "It shall come about, the [a]one who
escapes from the sword of Hazael, Jehu
[b]shall put to death, and the one who
escapes from the sword of Jehu, Elisha
shall put to death.
18 "[a]Yet I will leave 7,000 in Israel, all
the knees that have not bowed to Baal
and every mouth that has not [b]kissed
him."
19 ¶ So he departed from there and
found Elisha the son of Shaphat, while he
was plowing with twelve pairs *of oxen*
before him, and he with the twelfth. And
Elijah passed over to him and threw [a]his
mantle on him.
20 He left the oxen and ran after Elijah
and said, "Please [a]let me kiss my father
and my mother, then I will follow you."
And he said to him, "Go back again, for
what have I done to you?"
21 So he returned from following him,
and took the pair of oxen and sacrificed
them and [a]boiled their flesh with the
implements of the oxen, and gave *it* to
the people and they ate. Then he arose
and followed Elijah and ministered to
him.

War with Aram

20 Now [a]Ben-hadad king of Aram
gathered all his army, [b]and there
were thirty-two kings with him, and
horses and chariots. And he went up and
[c]besieged Samaria and fought against it.
2 Then he sent messengers to the
city to Ahab king of Israel and said to him,
"Thus says Ben-hadad,
3 'Your silver and your gold are mine;
your most beautiful wives and children
are also mine.' "
4 The king of Israel replied, "It is according to your word, my lord, O king; I
am yours, and all that I have."
5 Then the messengers returned and
said, "Thus says [1]Ben-hadad, 'Surely, I
sent to you saying, "You shall give me
your silver and your gold and your wives
and your children,"
6 but about this time tomorrow I will
send my servants to you, and they will
search your house and the houses of your
servants; and [1]whatever is desirable in
your eyes, they will [2]take in their hand
and carry away.' "
7 ¶ Then the king of Israel called all
the elders of the land and said, "Please
observe and [a]see how this man is looking for trouble; for he sent to me for my
wives and my children and my silver and
my gold, and I did not refuse him."
8 All the elders and all the people
said to him, "Do not listen or consent."
9 So he said to the messengers of
Ben-hadad, "Tell my lord the king, 'All
that you sent for to your servant at the
first I will do, but this thing I cannot
do.' " And the messengers departed and
brought him word again.
10 Ben-hadad sent to him and said,
"May [a]the gods do so to me and more
also, if the dust of Samaria will suffice for
handfuls for all the people who [1]fol-
low me."
11 Then the king of Israel replied,
"Tell *him,* '[a]Let not him who girds on *his*
armor boast like him who takes *it* off.' "
12 When *Ben-hadad* heard this message, as [a]he was drinking [1]with the
kings in the [2]temporary shelters, he said
to his servants, "Station *yourselves.*" So
they stationed *themselves* against the
city.

Ahab Victorious

13 ¶ Now behold, a prophet approached Ahab king of Israel and said,
"Thus says the LORD, 'Have you seen all
this great multitude? Behold, [a]I will deliver them into your hand today, and
[b]you shall know that I am the LORD.' "
14 Ahab said, "By whom?" So he said,

10 [b]Rom 11:3,4 [c]1 Kin 18:22
11 [a]Ex 19:20; 24:12,18 [b]Ezek 1:4
12 [a]Job 4:16; Zech 4:6
13 [a]Ex 3:6 [b]1 Kin 19:9
14 [a]1 Kin 19:10
15 [a]2 Kin 8:8-15
16 [a]2 Kin 9:1-10 [b]1 Kin 19:19-21; 2 Kin 2:9,15
17 [a]2 Kin 8:12; 13:3,22 [b]2 Kin 9:14-10:25
18 [a]Rom 11:4 [b]Hos 13:2
19 [a]1 Sam 28:14; 2 Kin 2:8, 13,14
20 [a]Matt 8:21, 22; Luke 9:61, 62; Acts 20:37
21 [a]2 Sam 24:22
20:1 [a]1 Kin 15:18,20; 2 Kin 6:24 [b]1 Kin 22:31 [c]1 Kin 16:24; 2 Kin 6:24
5 [1]Lit *Ben-hadad, saying*
6 [1]Lit *all the desire of your eyes* [2]Lit *put*
7 [a]2 Kin 5:7
10 [1]Lit *are at my feet* [a]1 Kin 19:2; 2 Kin 6:31
11 [a]Prov 27:1
12 [1]Lit *he and* [2]Or *booths* [a]1 Kin 16:9; Prov 31:4,5
13 [a]1 Kin 20:28 [b]1 Kin 18:36

"Thus says the LORD, 'By the young men of the rulers of the provinces.' " Then he said, "Who shall [1]begin the battle?" And he [2]answered, "You."

15 Then he mustered the young men of the rulers of the provinces, and there were 232; and after them he mustered all the people, *even* all the sons of Israel, 7,000.

16 ¶ They went out at noon, while [a]Ben-hadad was drinking himself drunk in the [1]temporary shelters [2]with the thirty-two kings who helped him.

17 The young men of the rulers of the provinces went out first; and Ben-hadad sent out and they told him, saying, "Men have come out from Samaria."

18 [a]Then he said, "If they have come out for peace, take them alive; or if they have come out for war, take them alive."

19 ¶ So these went out from the city, the young men of the rulers of the provinces, and the army which followed them.

20 They [1]killed each his man; and the Arameans fled and Israel pursued them, and Ben-hadad king of Aram escaped on a horse with horsemen.

21 The king of Israel went out and [1]struck the horses and chariots, and [1]killed the Arameans with a great slaughter.

22 ¶ Then [a]the prophet came near to the king of Israel and said to him, "Go, strengthen yourself and observe and see what you have to do; for [b]at the turn of the year the king of Aram will come up against you."

23 ¶ Now the servants of the king of Aram said to him, "[a]Their gods are gods of the mountains, therefore they were stronger than we; but rather let us fight against them in the plain, *and* surely we will be stronger than they.

24 "Do this thing: remove the kings, each from his place, and put captains in their place,

25 and [1]muster an army like the army that you have lost, horse for horse, and chariot for chariot. Then we will fight against them in the plain, and surely we will be stronger than they." And he listened to their voice and did so.

Another Aramean War

26 ¶ [a]At the turn of the year, Ben-hadad mustered the Arameans and went up to [b]Aphek to fight against Israel.

27 The sons of Israel were mustered and were provisioned and went to meet them; and the sons of Israel camped before them like two little flocks of goats, [a]but the Arameans filled the country.

28 Then [a]a man of God came near and spoke to the king of Israel and said, "Thus says the LORD, 'Because the Arameans have said, "[b]The LORD is a god of *the* mountains, but He is not a god of *the* valleys," therefore [c]I will give all this great multitude into your hand, and you shall know that I am the LORD.' "

29 So they camped one over against the other seven days. And on the seventh day the battle was joined, and the sons of Israel [1]killed *of* the Arameans 100,000 foot soldiers in one day.

30 But the rest fled to [a]Aphek into the city, and the wall fell on 27,000 men who were left. And Ben-hadad fled and came into the city [b]into an inner chamber.

31 ¶ [a]His servants said to him, "Behold now, we have heard that the kings of the house of Israel are merciful kings, please let us [b]put sackcloth on our loins and ropes on our heads, and go out to the king of Israel; perhaps he will save your [1]life."

32 So [a]they girded sackcloth on their loins and *put* ropes on their heads, and came to the king of Israel and said, "[b]Your servant Ben-hadad says, 'Please let me live.' " And he said, "Is he still alive? He is my brother."

33 Now the men [1]took this as an omen, and quickly [2]catching his word said, "Your brother Ben-hadad." Then he said, "Go, bring him." Then Ben-hadad came out to him, and he [3]took him up into the chariot.

34 *Ben-hadad* said to him, "[a]The cities which my father took from your father I will restore, and you shall make streets for yourself in Damascus, as my father made in Samaria." *Ahab said,* "And I will let you go with this covenant." So he made a covenant with him and let him go.

35 ¶ Now a certain man of [a]the sons of the prophets said to [1]another [b]by the word of the LORD, "Please strike me." But the man refused to strike him.

36 Then he said to him, "Because you have not listened to the voice of the LORD, behold, as soon as you have departed from me, [a]a lion will [1]kill you." And as soon as he had departed from him a lion found him and [2]killed him.

37 Then he found another man and said, "Please [1]strike me." And the man [2]struck him, [3]wounding him.

38 So the prophet departed and waited for the king by the way, and [a]disguised himself with a bandage over his eyes.

39 As the king passed by, he cried to the king and said, "Your servant went out into the midst of the battle; and behold, a man turned aside and brought a man to me and said, 'Guard this man; if for any

14 [1]Lit *bind* [2]Lit *said*
16 [1]Or *booths* [2]Lit *he and the 32 kings* [a]1 Kin 16:9; 20:12; Prov 20:1
18 [a]2 Kin 14:8-12
20 [1]Lit *smote*
21 [1]Lit *smote*
22 [a]1 Kin 20:13 [b]2 Sam 11:1; 1 Kin 20:26
23 [a]1 Kin 14:23; Jer 16:19-21; Rom 1:21-23
25 [1]Lit *number*
26 [a]1 Kin 20:22 [b]2 Kin 13:17
27 [a]Judg 6:3-5; 1 Sam 13:5-8
28 [a]1 Kin 17:18 [b]1 Kin 20:23 [c]1 Kin 20:13
29 [1]Lit *smote*
30 [a]1 Kin 20:26 [b]1 Kin 22:25; 2 Chr 18:24
31 [1]Lit *soul* [a]1 Kin 20:23-26 [b]Gen 37:34; 2 Sam 3:31
32 [a]1 Kin 20:31 [b]1 Kin 20:3-6
33 [1]Lit *divined* [2]Lit *caught from him* [3]Lit *caused him to come up*
34 [a]1 Kin 15:20
35 [1]Lit *his neighbor* [a]2 Kin 2:3-7 [b]1 Kin 13:17,18
36 [1]Lit *smite* [2]Lit *smote* [a]1 Kin 13:24
37 [1]Lit *smite* [2]Lit *smote* [3]Lit *striking and wounding*
38 [a]1 Kin 14:2

reason he is missing, [a]then your life shall
be for his life, or else you shall pay a
talent of silver.'
40 "While your servant was busy here
and there, he was gone." And the king of
Israel said to him, "So shall your judgment be; you yourself have decided *it.*"
41 Then he hastily took the bandage
away from his eyes, and the king of Israel
recognized him that he was of the prophets.
42 He said to him, "Thus says the
LORD, 'Because you have let go out of *your*
hand the man whom I had devoted to
destruction, therefore [a]your [1]life shall
go for his [1]life, and your people for his
people.' "
43 So [a]the king of Israel went to his
house sullen and vexed, and came to Samaria.

Ahab Covets Naboth's Vineyard

21 Now it came about after these
things that Naboth the Jezreelite
had a vineyard which *was* in [a]Jezreel beside the palace of Ahab king of Samaria.
2 Ahab spoke to Naboth, saying,
"[a]Give me your vineyard, that I may
have it for a vegetable garden because it
is close beside my house, and I will give
you a better vineyard than it in its place;
if [1]you like, I will give you the price of
[2]it in money."
3 But Naboth said to Ahab, "The
LORD forbid me [a]that I should give you
the inheritance of my fathers."
4 [a]So Ahab came into his house sullen and vexed because of the word which
Naboth the Jezreelite had spoken to him;
for he said, "I will not give you the inheritance of my fathers." And he lay down on
his bed and turned away his face and ate
no [1]food.
5 ¶ But Jezebel his wife came to him
and said to him, "How is it that your spirit
is so sullen that you are not eating
[1]food?"
6 So he said to her, "Because I spoke
to Naboth the Jezreelite and said to him,
'Give me your vineyard for money; or
else, if it pleases you, I will give you a
vineyard in its place.' But he said, 'I will
not give you my vineyard.' "
7 Jezebel his wife said to him, "[a]Do
you now [1]reign over Israel? Arise, eat
bread, and let your heart be joyful; I will
give you the vineyard of Naboth the Jezreelite."
8 ¶ [a]So she wrote letters in Ahab's
name and sealed them with his seal, and
sent letters to [b]the elders and to the nobles who were living with Naboth in his
city.
9 Now she wrote in the letters, say-

39 [a]2 Kin 10:24
42 [1]Lit *soul* [a]1 Kin 20:39
43 [a]1 Kin 21:4
21:1 [a]Judg 6:33; 1 Kin 18:45,46
2 [1]Lit *it is good in your eyes* [2]Lit *this* [a]1 Sam 8:14
3 [a]Lev 25:23; Num 36:7; Ezek 46:18
4 [1]Lit *bread* [a]1 Kin 20:43
5 [1]Lit *bread*
7 [1]Lit *exercise kingship* [a]1 Sam 8:14
8 [a]Esth 3:12; 8:8,10 [b]1 Kin 20:7
10 [1]Lit *so that he dies* [a]1 Sam 2:12; 2 Sam 20:1 [b]Ex 22:28; Lev 24:15,16; Acts 6:11 [c]Lev 24:14
12 [a]Is 58:4
13 [1]Lit *with stones so that he died* [a]2 Kin 9:26; 2 Chr 24:21; Acts 7:58,59; Heb 11:37
18 [a]1 Kin 16:29
19 [a]2 Sam 12:9 [b]1 Kin 22:38; 2 Kin 9:26
20 [1]Lit *said* [a]1 Kin 18:17 [b]1 Kin 21:25; 2 Kin 17:17; Rom 7:14
21 [a]1 Kin 14:10; 2 Kin 9:8
22 [a]1 Kin 15:29 [b]1 Kin 16:3,11 [c]1 Kin 12:30; 13:34; 14:16

ing, "Proclaim a fast and seat Naboth at
the head of the people;
10 and seat two [a]worthless men before him, and let them testify against him,
saying, '[b]You cursed God and the king.'
Then take him out and [c]stone him [1]to
death."

Jezebel's Plot

11 ¶ So the men of his city, the elders
and the nobles who lived in his city, did
as Jezebel had sent *word* to them, just as
it was written in the letters which she
had sent them.
12 They [a]proclaimed a fast and seated
Naboth at the head of the people.
13 Then the two worthless men came
in and sat before him; and the worthless
men testified against him, even against
Naboth, before the people, saying, "Naboth cursed God and the king." [a]So they
took him outside the city and stoned him
[1]to death with stones.
14 Then they sent *word* to Jezebel,
saying, "Naboth has been stoned and is
dead."
15 ¶ When Jezebel heard that Naboth
had been stoned and was dead, Jezebel
said to Ahab, "Arise, take possession of
the vineyard of Naboth, the Jezreelite,
which he refused to give you for money;
for Naboth is not alive, but dead."
16 When Ahab heard that Naboth was
dead, Ahab arose to go down to the vineyard of Naboth the Jezreelite, to take possession of it.
17 ¶ Then the word of the LORD came
to Elijah the Tishbite, saying,
18 "Arise, go down to meet Ahab king
of Israel, [a]who is in Samaria; behold, he
is in the vineyard of Naboth where he has
gone down to take possession of it.
19 "You shall speak to him, saying,
'Thus says the LORD, "[a]Have you murdered and also taken possession?" ' And
you shall speak to him, saying, 'Thus says
the LORD, "[b]In the place where the dogs
licked up the blood of Naboth the dogs
will lick up your blood, even yours." ' "
20 ¶ Ahab said to Elijah, "[a]Have you
found me, O my enemy?" And he [1]an-
swered, "I have found *you,* [b]because you
have sold yourself to do evil in the sight
of the LORD.
21 "Behold, I will bring evil upon you,
and [a]will utterly sweep you away, and
will cut off from Ahab every male, both
bond and free in Israel;
22 and [a]I will make your house [b]like
the house of Jeroboam the son of Nebat,
and like the house of Baasha the son of
Ahijah, because of the provocation with
which you have provoked *Me* to anger,
and *because* you [c]have made Israel sin.

23 "Of Jezebel also has the LORD spoken, saying, '[a]The dogs will eat Jezebel
in the [1]district of Jezreel.'
24 "[a]The one belonging to Ahab, who
dies in the city, the dogs will eat, and the
one who dies in the field the birds of
heaven will eat."
25 ¶ [a]Surely there was no one like
Ahab who sold himself to do evil in the
sight of the LORD, [1]because Jezebel his
wife incited him.
26 [a]He acted very abominably in following idols, [b]according to all that the
Amorites had done, whom the LORD cast
out before the sons of Israel.
27 ¶ It came about when Ahab heard
these words, that [a]he tore his clothes
and put [1]on sackcloth and fasted, and he
lay in sackcloth and went about [2]de-
spondently.
28 Then the word of the LORD came to
Elijah the Tishbite, saying,
29 "Do you see how Ahab has humbled
himself before Me? Because he has humbled himself before Me, I will not bring
the evil in his days, *but* I will bring the
evil upon his house [a]in his son's days."

Ahab's Third Campaign against Aram

22 Three [1]years passed without war
between Aram and Israel.
2 [a]In the third year [b]Jehoshaphat
the king of Judah came down to the king
of Israel.
3 Now the king of Israel said to his
servants, "Do you know that [a]Ramoth-
gilead belongs to us, and we [1]are still
doing nothing to take it out of the hand of
the king of Aram?"
4 And he said to Jehoshaphat, "Will
you go with me to battle at Ramoth-
gilead?" And Jehoshaphat said to the king
of Israel, "[a]I am as you are, my people as
your people, my horses as your horses."
5 ¶ Moreover, Jehoshaphat said to
the king of Israel, "Please inquire [1]first
for the word of the LORD."
6 Then [a]the king of Israel gathered
the prophets together, about four hundred men, and said to them, "Shall I go
against Ramoth-gilead to battle or shall I
refrain?" And they said, "Go up, for the
Lord will give *it* into the hand of the
king."
7 But [a]Jehoshaphat said, "Is there
not yet a prophet of the LORD here that
we may inquire of him?"
8 The king of Israel said to Jehoshaphat, "There is yet one man by whom we
may inquire of the LORD, but I hate him,
because he does not prophesy good concerning me, but evil. *He is* Micaiah son of
Imlah." But Jehoshaphat said, "Let not
the king say so."
9 Then the king of Israel called an
officer and said, "[1]Bring quickly Micaiah
son of Imlah."
10 Now the king of Israel and Jehoshaphat king of Judah were sitting each on
his throne, arrayed in *their* robes, at the
threshing floor at the entrance of the gate
of Samaria; and [a]all the prophets were
prophesying before them.
11 Then Zedekiah the son of Chenaanah made [a]horns of iron for himself and
said, "Thus says the LORD, '[b]With these
you will gore the Arameans until they are
consumed.' "
12 All the prophets were prophesying
thus, saying, "Go up to Ramoth-gilead
and prosper, for the LORD will give *it* into
the hand of the king."

Micaiah Predicts Defeat

13 ¶ Then the messenger who went to
summon Micaiah spoke to him saying,
"Behold now, the words of the prophets
are uniformly favorable to the king.
Please let your word be like the word of
one of them, and speak favorably."
14 But Micaiah said, "[a]As the LORD
lives, what [b]the LORD says to me, that I
shall speak."
15 ¶ When he came to the king, the
king said to him, "Micaiah, shall we go to
Ramoth-gilead to battle, or shall we refrain?" And he [1]answered him, "[a]Go up
and succeed, and the LORD will give *it*
into the hand of the king."
16 Then the king said to him, "How
many times must I adjure you to speak to
me nothing but the truth in the name of
the LORD?"
17 So he said,
"I saw all Israel
Scattered on the mountains,
[a]Like sheep which have no
shepherd.
And the LORD said, 'These have
no master.
Let each of them return to his
house in peace.' "
18 Then the king of Israel said to Jehoshaphat, "[a]Did I not tell you that he
would not prophesy good concerning me,
but evil?"
19 ¶ [1]Micaiah said, "Therefore, hear
the word of the LORD. [a]I saw the LORD
sitting on His throne, and [b]all the host of
heaven standing by Him on His right and
on His left.
20 "The LORD said, 'Who will entice
Ahab to go up and fall at Ramoth-gilead?'
And one said this while another said that.
21 "Then a spirit came forward and

21:23 [1]Lit *portion;* some mss read *rampart* [a]2 Kin 9:10,30-37
24 [a]1 Kin 14:11; 16:4
25 [1]Or *whom Jezebel his wife incited* [a]1 Kin 16:30-33; 21:20
26 [a]1 Kin 15:12; 2 Kin 17:12 [b]Gen 15:16; Lev 18:25-30; 2 Kin 21:11
27 [1]Lit *sackcloth on his flesh* [2]Or *softly* [a]Gen 37:34; 2 Sam 3:31; 2 Kin 6:30
29 [a]2 Kin 9:25-37
22:1 [1]Lit *they sat for three years*
2 [a]2 Chr 18:2 [b]1 Kin 15:24
3 [1]Lit *are silent so as not* [a]Deut 4:43; Josh 21:38; 1 Kin 4:13
4 [a]2 Kin 3:7
5 [1]Lit *as the day*
6 [a]1 Kin 18:19
7 [a]2 Kin 3:11
9 [1]Lit *Hasten Micaiah*
10 [a]1 Kin 22:6
11 [a]Zech 1:18-21 [b]Deut 33:17
14 [a]1 Kin 18:10,15 [b]Num 22:18; 24:13
15 [1]Lit *said to* [a]1 Kin 22:12
17 [a]Num 27:17; 1 Kin 22:34-36; 2 Chr 18:16; Matt 9:36; Mark 6:34
18 [a]1 Kin 22:8
19 [1]Lit *he* [a]Is 6:1; Ezek 1:26-28; Dan 7:9,10 [b]Job 1:6; 2:1; Ps 103:20, 21; Dan 7:10; Matt 18:10; Heb 1:7,14

stood before the LORD and said, 'I will entice him.'

22 "The LORD said to him, 'How?' And he said, 'I will go out and [a]be a deceiving spirit in the mouth of all his prophets.' Then He said, 'You are to entice *him* and also prevail. Go and do so.'

23 "Now therefore, behold, [a]the LORD has put a deceiving spirit in the mouth of all these your prophets; and the LORD has proclaimed disaster against you."

24 ¶ Then [a]Zedekiah the son of Chenaanah came near and struck Micaiah on the cheek and said, "[b]How did the Spirit of the LORD pass from me to speak to you?"

25 Micaiah said, "Behold, you shall see on that day when you [a]enter an inner room to hide yourself."

26 Then the king of Israel said, "Take Micaiah and return him to Amon the governor of the city and to Joash the king's son;

27 and say, 'Thus says the king, "[a]Put this man in prison and feed him [1]sparingly with bread and water until I return safely." ' "

28 Micaiah said, "[a]If you indeed return safely the LORD has not spoken by me." And he said, "[b]Listen, all you people."

Defeat and Death of Ahab

29 ¶ So [a]the king of Israel and Jehoshaphat king of Judah went up against Ramoth-gilead.

30 The king of Israel said to Jehoshaphat, "[a]I will disguise myself and go into the battle, but you put on your robes." So the king of Israel disguised himself and went into the battle.

31 Now [a]the king of Aram had commanded the thirty-two captains of his chariots, saying, "Do not fight with small or great, but with the king of Israel alone."

32 So when the captains of the chariots saw Jehoshaphat, they said, "Surely it is the king of Israel," and they turned aside to fight against him, and Jehoshaphat cried out.

33 When the captains of the chariots saw that it was not the king of Israel, they turned back from pursuing him.

34 ¶ Now a certain man drew his bow at random and struck the king of Israel [1]in a joint of the armor. So he said to the driver of his chariot, "Turn [2]around and take me out of the [3]fight; [a]for I am severely wounded."

35 The battle [1]raged that day, and the king was propped up in his chariot in front of the Arameans, and died at evening, and the blood from the wound ran into the bottom of the chariot.

36 [a]Then a cry passed throughout the army close to sunset, saying, "Every man to his city and every man to his [1]country."

37 ¶ So the king died and was brought to Samaria, and they buried the king in Samaria.

38 They washed the chariot by the pool of Samaria, and the dogs licked up his blood (now the harlots bathed themselves *there*), [a]according to the word of the LORD which He spoke.

39 Now the rest of the acts of Ahab and all that he did and [a]the ivory house which he built and all the cities which he built, are they not written in the Book of the Chronicles of the Kings of Israel?

40 So Ahab slept with his fathers, and Ahaziah his son became king in his place.

The New Rulers

41 ¶ [a]Now Jehoshaphat the son of Asa became king over Judah in the fourth year of Ahab king of Israel.

42 Jehoshaphat was thirty-five years old when he became king, and he reigned twenty-five years in Jerusalem. And his mother's name was Azubah the daughter of Shilhi.

43 [a]He walked in all the way of Asa his father; he did not turn aside from it, doing right in the sight of the LORD. [b]However, the high places were not taken away; the people still sacrificed and burnt incense on the high places.

44 [a]Jehoshaphat also made peace with the king of Israel.

45 ¶ Now the rest of the acts of Jehoshaphat, and his might which he showed and how he warred, are they not written [a]in the Book of the Chronicles of the Kings of Judah?

46 The remnant of [a]the sodomites who remained in the days of his father Asa, he [1]expelled from the land.

47 ¶ Now [a]there was no king in Edom; a deputy was king.

48 Jehoshaphat made [a]ships of Tarshish to go to [b]Ophir for gold, but [c]they did not go for the ships were broken at [d]Ezion-geber.

49 Then Ahaziah the son of Ahab said to Jehoshaphat, "Let my servants go with your servants in the ships." But Jehoshaphat was not willing.

50 [a]And Jehoshaphat slept with his fathers and was buried with his fathers in the city of his father David, and Jehoram his son became king in his place.

51 ¶ Ahaziah the son of Ahab [a]became king over Israel in Samaria in the

22 [a]Judg 9:23; 1 Sam 16:14; 18:10; 19:9; Ezek 14:9; 2 Thess 2:11
23 [a]Ezek 14:9
24 [a]1 Kin 22:11; Matt 5:39; Acts 23:2, 3 [b]2 Chr 18:23
25 [a]1 Kin 20:30
27 [1]Lit *with bread of affliction and water of affliction* [a]2 Chr 16:10; 18:25-27
28 [a]Deut 18:22 [b]Mic 1:2
29 [a]1 Kin 22:3, 4
30 [a]2 Chr 35:22
31 [a]1 Kin 20:1, 16,24; 2 Chr 18:30
34 [1]Lit *between the scale-armor and the breastplate* [2]Lit *your hand* [3]Lit *camp* [a]2 Chr 35:23
35 [1]Lit *went up*
36 [1]Lit *land* [a]2 Kin 14:12
38 [a]1 Kin 21:19
39 [a]Amos 3:15
41 [a]2 Chr 20:31
43 [a]2 Chr 17:3 [b]1 Kin 15:14; 2 Kin 12:3
44 [a]1 Kin 22:2; 2 Kin 8:16,18; 2 Chr 19:2
45 [a]2 Chr 20:34
46 [1]Lit *consumed* [a]Gen 19:5; Deut 23:17; 1 Kin 14:24; 15:12; Jude 7
47 [a]2 Sam 8:14; 2 Kin 3:9
48 [a]1 Kin 10:22; 2 Chr 20:36 [b]1 Kin 9:28 [c]2 Chr 20:37 [d]1 Kin 9:26
50 [a]2 Chr 21:1
51 [a]1 Kin 22:40

seventeenth year of Jehoshaphat king of
Judah, and he reigned two years over Israel.
52 He did evil in the sight of the LORD
and [a]walked in the way of his father and
in the way of his mother and in the way
of Jeroboam the son of Nebat, who
caused Israel to sin.
53 [a]So he served Baal and worshiped
him and provoked the LORD God of Israel
to anger, according to all that his father
had done.

52 [a]1 Kin 15:26; 21:25
53 [a]Judg 2:11; 1 Kin 16:30-32

2 Kings

Title and Background

See Introduction to 1 Kings.

Author and Date of Writing

See Introduction to 1 Kings.

Theme and Message

2 Kings continues the stories of the great prophets Elijah and Elisha. It also tells the history of the northern and southern kingdoms until they were both finally conquered. In both kingdoms God's prophets continually warned the people that God would punish them if they did not repent of their sins.

Outline

I. Elijah and Elisha (1:1—8:15)
II. Israel and Judah From Joram/Jehoram to Israel's Exile (8:16—17:41)
III. Judah From Hezekiah to the Babylonian Exile (18:1—25:30)

Ahaziah's Messengers Meet Elijah

1 Now [a]Moab rebelled against Israel
after the death of Ahab.
2 And Ahaziah fell through the lattice
in his upper chamber which *was* in Samaria, and became ill. So he sent messengers and said to them, "Go, [a]inquire of
Baal-zebub, the god of Ekron, [b]whether
I will recover from this sickness."
3 But the angel of the LORD said to
[a]Elijah the Tishbite, "Arise, go up to
meet the messengers of the king of Samaria and say to them, 'Is it because
there is no God in Israel *that* you are
going to inquire of [b]Baal-zebub, the god
of Ekron?'
4 "Now therefore thus says the LORD,
'[1a]You shall not come down from the
bed where you have gone up, but you
shall surely die.' " Then Elijah departed.
5 ¶ When the messengers returned
to him he said to them, "[1]Why have you
returned?"
6 They said to him, "A man came up
to meet us and said to us, 'Go, return to
the king who sent you and say to him,
"Thus says the LORD, 'Is it because there
is no God in Israel *that* you are sending
[a]to inquire of Baal-zebub, the god of Ekron? Therefore [1]you shall not come
down from the bed where you have gone
up, but shall surely die.' " ' "
7 He said to them, "What kind of
man was he who came up to meet you
and spoke these words to you?"
8 They [1]answered him, "[a]*He was* a
hairy man with a leather girdle [2]bound
about his loins." And he said, "It is Elijah
the Tishbite."
9 ¶ Then *the king* [a]sent to him a captain of fifty with his fifty. And he went up
to him, and behold, he was sitting on
the top of the hill. And he said to him,
"O man of God, the king says, 'Come
down.' "
10 Elijah replied to the captain of fifty,
"If I am a man of God, [a]let fire come
down from heaven and consume you and
your fifty." [b]Then fire came down from
heaven and consumed him and his fifty.
11 ¶ So he again sent to him another
captain of fifty with his fifty. And he said
to him, "O man of God, thus says the
king, 'Come down quickly.' "
12 Elijah replied to them, "If I am a
man of God, let fire come down from
heaven and consume you and your fifty."
Then the fire of God came down from
heaven and consumed him and his fifty.
13 ¶ So he [a]again sent the captain of
a third fifty with his fifty. When the third
captain of fifty went up, he came and
bowed down on his knees before Elijah,
and begged him and said to him, "O man
of God, please let my life and the lives of
these fifty servants of yours be precious in
your sight.
14 "Behold fire came down from heav-
en and consumed the first two captains of
fifty with their fifties; but now let my
[1]life be precious in your sight."

1:1 [a]2 Sam 8:2; 2 Kin 3:5
2 [a]2 Kin 1:3,6, 16; Matt 10:25; Mark 3:22 [b]2 Kin 8:7-10
3 [a]1 Kin 17:1; 21:17 [b]2 Kin 1:2
4 [1]Lit *The bed where you went up, you shall not come down from it* [a]2 Kin 1:6,16
5 [1]Lit *What is this that you have returned?*
6 [1]V 4, note 1 [a]2 Kin 1:2
8 [1]Lit *said* [2]Or *girt* [a]Zech 13:4; Matt 3:4; Mark 1:6
9 [a]2 Kin 6:13,14
10 [a]1 Kin 18:36-38; Luke 9:54 [b]Job 1:16
13 [a]Is 1:5; Jer 5:3
14 [1]Lit *soul*

15 [a]The angel of the LORD said to Elijah, "Go down with him; [b]do not be afraid of him." So he arose and went down with him to the king.

16 Then he said to him, "Thus says the LORD, 'Because you have sent messengers [a]to inquire of Baal-zebub, the god of Ekron—is it because there is no God in Israel to inquire of His word?—therefore [1]you shall not come down from the bed where you have gone up, but shall surely die.' "

Jehoram Reigns over Israel

17 ¶ So Ahaziah died according to the word of the LORD which Elijah had spoken. And because he had no son, Jehoram became king in his place [a]in the second year of Jehoram the son of Jehoshaphat, king of Judah.

18 Now the rest of the acts of Ahaziah which he did, are they not written in the Book of the Chronicles of the Kings of Israel?

Elijah Taken to Heaven

2 And it came about when the LORD was about to [a]take up Elijah by a [1]whirlwind to heaven, that Elijah went with [b]Elisha from [c]Gilgal.

2 Elijah said to Elisha, "[a]Stay here please, for the LORD has sent me as far as [b]Bethel." But Elisha said, "[c]As the LORD lives and as you yourself live, I will not leave you." So they went down to Bethel.

3 Then [a]the sons of the prophets who *were at* Bethel came out to Elisha and said to him, "Do you know that the LORD will take away your master from over [1]you today?" And he said, "Yes, I know; be still."

4 ¶ Elijah said to him, "Elisha, please [a]stay here, for the LORD has sent me to [b]Jericho." But he said, "[a]As the LORD lives, and as you yourself live, I will not leave you." So they came to Jericho.

5 [a]The sons of the prophets who *were* at Jericho approached Elisha and said to him, "[a]Do you know that the LORD will take away your master from over [1]you today?" And he [2]answered, "Yes, I know; be still."

6 Then Elijah said to him, "Please [a]stay here, for the LORD has sent me to [b]the Jordan." And he said, "As the LORD lives, and as you yourself live, I will not leave you." So the two of them went on.

7 ¶ Now [a]fifty men of the sons of the prophets went and stood opposite *them* at a distance, while the two of them stood by the Jordan.

8 Elijah [a]took his mantle and folded it together and [b]struck the waters, and they were divided here and there, so that the two of them crossed over on dry ground.

9 ¶ When they had crossed over, Elijah said to Elisha, "Ask what I shall do for you before I am taken from you." And Elisha said, "Please, let a [a]double portion of your spirit be upon me."

10 He said, "You have asked a hard thing. *Nevertheless,* if you [a]see me when I am taken from you, it shall be so for you; but if not, it shall not be *so.*"

11 As they were going along and talking, behold, *there appeared* [a]a chariot of fire and horses of fire which separated the two of them. And Elijah went up by a [1]whirlwind to heaven.

12 Elisha saw *it* and cried out, "[a]My father, my father, the [1]chariots of Israel and its horsemen!" And he saw [2]Elijah no more. Then [b]he took hold of his own clothes and tore them in two pieces.

13 He also took up the mantle of Elijah that fell from him and returned and stood by the bank of the Jordan.

14 He took the mantle of Elijah that fell from him and struck the waters and said, "Where is the LORD, the God of Elijah?" And when he also had [a]struck the waters, they were divided here and there; and Elisha crossed over.

Elisha Succeeds Elijah

15 ¶ Now when [a]the sons of the prophets who *were* at Jericho opposite *him* saw him, they said, "The spirit of Elijah rests on Elisha." And they came to meet him and bowed themselves to the ground before him.

16 They said to him, "Behold now, there are with your servants fifty strong men, please let them go and search for your master; perhaps [a]the Spirit of the LORD has taken him up and cast him on some mountain or into some valley." And he said, "You shall not send."

17 But when [a]they urged him until he was ashamed, he said, "Send." They sent therefore fifty men; and they searched three days but did not find him.

18 They returned to him while he was staying at Jericho; and he said to them, "Did I not say to you, 'Do not go'?"

19 ¶ Then the men of the city said to Elisha, "Behold now, the situation of this city is pleasant, as my lord sees; but the water is bad and the land [1]is unfruitful."

20 He said, "Bring me a new jar, and put salt [1]in it." So they brought *it* to him.

21 He went out to the spring of water and [a]threw salt [1]in it and said, "Thus says the LORD, 'I have [2]purified these waters; there shall not be from there death or [3]unfruitfulness any longer.' "

22 So the waters have been [1]purified

---

15 [a]2 Kin 1:3 [b]Is 51:12; Jer 1:17; Ezek 2:6
16 [1]V 4, note 1 [a]2 Kin 1:3
17 [a]2 Kin 3:1; 8:16
2:1 [1]Or *windstorm* [a]Gen 5:24; Heb 11:5 [b]1 Kin 19:16-21 [c]Josh 4:19
2 [a]Ruth 1:15 [b]1 Kin 12:28,29 [c]1 Sam 1:26; 2 Kin 2:4,6
3 [1]Lit *your head* [a]2 Kin 4:1,38; 5:22
4 [a]2 Kin 2:2 [b]Josh 6:26
5 [1]Lit *your head* [2]Lit *said* [a]2 Kin 2:3
6 [a]2 Kin 2:2 [b]Josh 3:8,15-17
7 [a]2 Kin 2:15,16
8 [a]1 Kin 19:13, 19 [b]Ex 14:21, 22; 2 Kin 2:14
9 [a]Num 11:17-25; Deut 21:17
10 [a]Acts 1:10
11 [1]Or *windstorm* [a]2 Kin 6:17
12 [1]Lit *chariot* [2]Lit *him* [a]2 Kin 13:14 [b]Gen 37:34; Job 1:20
14 [a]2 Kin 2:8
15 [a]2 Kin 2:7
16 [a]1 Kin 18:12; Acts 8:39
17 [a]2 Kin 8:11
19 [1]Lit *causes barrenness*
20 [1]Lit *there*
21 [1]Lit *there* [2]Lit *healed* [3]Lit *barrenness* [a]Ex 15:25,26; 2 Kin 4:41; 6:6
22 [1]Lit *healed*

to this day, according to the word of Elisha which he spoke.
23 ¶ Then he went up from there to
Bethel; and as he was going up by the
way, young lads came out from the city
and [a]mocked him and said to him, "Go
up, you baldhead; go up, you baldhead!"
24 When he looked behind him and
saw them, he [a]cursed them in the name
of the LORD. Then two female bears came
out of the woods and tore up forty-two
lads of [1]their number.
25 He went from there to [a]Mount
Carmel, and from there he returned to
Samaria.

Jehoram Meets Moab Rebellion

3 Now Jehoram the son of Ahab became king over Israel at Samaria [a]in
the eighteenth year of Jehoshaphat king
of Judah, and reigned twelve years.
2 He did evil in the sight of the LORD,
though not like his father and his mother;
for [a]he put away the *sacred* pillar of Baal
[b]which his father had made.
3 Nevertheless, [a]he clung to the sins
of Jeroboam the son of Nebat, [b]which he
made Israel sin; he did not depart from
them.
4 ¶ Now Mesha king of Moab was a
sheep breeder, and [a]used to pay the king
of Israel 100,000 lambs and the wool of
100,000 rams.
5 But [a]when Ahab died, the king of
Moab rebelled against the king of Israel.
6 And King Jehoram went out of Samaria [1]at that time and mustered all Israel.
7 Then he went and sent *word* to Jehoshaphat the king of Judah, saying, "The
king of Moab has rebelled against me.
Will you go with me to fight against
Moab?" And he said, "I will go up; [a]I am
as you are, my people as your people, my
horses as your horses."
8 He said, "Which way shall we go
up?" And he [1]answered, "The way of the
wilderness of Edom."
9 ¶ So [a]the king of Israel went with
[b]the king of Judah and [c]the king of
Edom; and they made a circuit of seven
days' journey, and there was no water for
the army or for the cattle that followed
them.
10 Then the king of Israel said, "Alas!
For the LORD has called these three kings
to give them into the hand of Moab."
11 But Jehoshaphat said, "[a]Is there
not a prophet of the LORD here, that we
may inquire of the LORD by him?" And
one of the king of Israel's servants answered and said, "[b]Elisha the son of Shaphat is here, [c]who used to pour water on
the hands of Elijah."
12 Jehoshaphat said, "The word of the
LORD is with him." So the king of Israel
and Jehoshaphat and the king of Edom
went down to him.
13 ¶ Now Elisha said to the king of
Israel, "What do I have to do with you?
[a]Go to the prophets of your father and to
the prophets of your mother." And the
king of Israel said to him, "No, for the
LORD has called these three kings *together* to give them into the hand of Moab."
14 Elisha said, "[a]As the LORD of hosts
lives, before whom I stand, were it not
that I regard the presence of Jehoshaphat
the king of Judah, I would not look at you
nor see you.
15 "But now [a]bring me a minstrel."
And it came about, when the minstrel
played, that [b]the hand of the LORD came
upon him.
16 He said, "Thus says the LORD,
'Make this valley full of trenches.'
17 "For thus says the LORD, 'You shall
not see wind nor shall you see rain; yet
that valley [a]shall be filled with water, so
that you shall drink, both you and your
cattle and your beasts.
18 'This is but a [a]slight thing in the
sight of the LORD; He will also give the
Moabites into your hand.
19 '[a]Then you shall strike every fortified city and every choice city, and fell
every good tree and stop all springs of
water, and mar every good piece of land
with stones.' "
20 It happened in the morning [a]about
the time of offering the sacrifice, that behold, water came by the way of Edom,
and the country was filled with water.
21 ¶ Now all the Moabites heard that
the kings had come up to fight against
them. And all who were able to [1]put on
armor and older were summoned and
stood on the border.
22 They rose early in the morning, and
the sun shone on the water, and the Moabites saw the water opposite *them* as red
as blood.
23 Then they said, "This is blood; the
kings have surely fought together, and
they have slain one another. Now therefore, Moab, to the spoil!"
24 But when they came to the camp of
Israel, the Israelites arose and struck the
Moabites, so that they fled before them;
and they went forward [1]into the land,
[2]slaughtering the Moabites.
25 [a]Thus they destroyed the cities;
and each one threw a stone on every
piece of good land and filled it. So they
stopped all the springs of water and felled
all the good trees, until in [b]Kir-hareseth
only they left its stones; however, the
slingers went about *it* and struck it.

23 [a]2 Chr 36:16; Ps 31:17, 18
24 [1]Lit *them* [a]Neh 13:25-27
25 [a]1 Kin 18:19,20; 2 Kin 4:25
3:1 [a]2 Kin 1:17
2 [a]Ex 23:24; 2 Kin 10:18, 26-28 [b]1 Kin 16:31,32
3 [a]1 Kin 12:28-32 [b]1 Kin 14:9,16
4 [a]2 Sam 8:2; Is 16:1,2
5 [a]2 Kin 1:1
6 [1]Lit *in that day*
7 [a]1 Kin 22:4
8 [1]Lit *said*
9 [a]2 Kin 3:1 [b]2 Kin 3:7 [c]1 Kin 22:47
11 [a]1 Kin 22:7 [b]2 Kin 2:25 [c]1 Kin 19:21; John 13:4,5,13, 14
13 [a]1 Kin 18:19; 22:6-11, 22-25
14 [a]1 Kin 17:1; 2 Kin 5:16
15 [a]1 Sam 16:23; 1 Chr 25:1 [b]1 Kin 18:46; Ezek 1:3
17 [a]Ps 107:35
18 [a]Jer 32:17, 27; Mark 10:27; Luke 1:37
19 [a]2 Kin 3:25
20 [a]Ex 29:39,40
21 [1]Lit *gird themselves with a belt*
24 [1]Lit *into it* [2]Lit *smiting*
25 [a]2 Kin 3:19 [b]Is 16:7; Jer 48:31,36

26 When the king of Moab saw that
the battle was too fierce for him, he took
with him 700 men who drew swords, to
break through to the king of Edom; but
they could not.
27 Then he took his oldest son who
was to reign in his place, and [a]offered
him as a burnt offering on the wall. And
there came great wrath against Israel, and
they departed from him and returned to
their own land.

The Widow's Oil

4 Now a certain woman of the wives of
[a]the sons of the prophets cried out
to [1]Elisha, "Your servant my husband is
dead, and you know that your servant
feared the LORD; and [b]the creditor has
come to take my two children to be his
slaves."
2 Elisha said to her, "What shall I do
for you? Tell me, what do you have in the
house?" And she said, "Your maidservant
has nothing in the house except [a]a jar of
oil."
3 Then he said, "Go, borrow vessels
at large for yourself from all your neighbors, *even* empty vessels; do not get a
few.
4 "And you shall go in and shut the
door behind you and your sons, and pour
out into all these vessels, and you shall set
aside what is full."
5 So she went from him and shut the
door behind her and her sons; they were
bringing *the vessels* to her and she
poured.
6 When [a]the vessels were full, she
said to her son, "Bring me another vessel." And he said to her, "There is not
one vessel more." And the oil stopped.
7 Then she came and told [a]the man
of God. And he said, "Go, sell the oil and
pay your debt, and you *and* your sons can
live on the rest."

The Shunammite Woman

8 ¶ Now there came a day when Elisha passed over to [a]Shunem, where
there was a [1]prominent woman, and she
persuaded him to eat [2]food. And so it
was, as often as he passed by, he turned
in there to eat [2]food.
9 She said to her husband, "Behold
now, I perceive that this is a holy [a]man
of God passing by us continually.
10 "Please, let us [a]make a little walled
upper chamber and let us set a bed for
him there, and a table and a chair and
a lampstand; and it shall be, when he
comes to us, *that* he can turn in there."
11 ¶ [1]One day he came there and
turned in to the upper chamber and
[2]rested.

27 [a]Amos 2:1; Mic 6:7

4:1 [1]Lit *Elisha, saying* [a]2 Kin 2:3 [b]Lev 25:39-41, 48; 1 Sam 22:2; Neh 5:2-5

2 [a]1 Kin 17:12

6 [a]Matt 14:20

7 [a]1 Kin 12:22

8 [1]Lit *great* [2]Lit *bread* [a]Josh 19:18

9 [a]2 Kin 4:7

10 [a]Matt 10:41, 42; 25:40; Rom 12:13

11 [1]Lit *Now a day came that* [2]Lit *lay there*

12 [a]2 Kin 4:29-31; 5:20-27; 8:4,5

13 [1]Lit *fearful* [2]Lit *fear* [3]Lit *said*

14 [1]Lit *said*

16 [1]Lit *when the time revives* [a]Gen 18:14 [b]2 Kin 4:28

17 [1]Lit *when the time revived*

20 [1]Lit *knees*

21 [a]2 Kin 4:32 [b]2 Kin 4:7

23 [a]Num 10:10; 28:11; 1 Chr 23:31

24 [1]Lit *riding*

25 [1]Lit *this Shunammite* [a]2 Kin 2:25

26 [1]Lit *said*

27 [1]Lit *bitter* [a]2 Kin 4:25

12 Then he said to [a]Gehazi his servant, "Call this Shunammite." And when
he had called her, she stood before him.
13 He said to him, "Say now to her,
'Behold, you have been [1]careful for us
with all this [2]care; what can I do for you?
Would you be spoken for to the king or to
the captain of the army?' " And she [3]an-
swered, "I live among my own people."
14 So he said, "What then is to be
done for her?" And Gehazi [1]answered,
"Truly she has no son and her husband is
old."
15 He said, "Call her." When he had
called her, she stood in the doorway.
16 Then he said, "[a]At this season
[1]next year you will embrace a son." And
she said, "No, my lord, O man of God,
[b]do not lie to your maidservant."
17 ¶ The woman conceived and bore a
son at that season [1]the next year, as Elisha had said to her.

The Shunammite's Son

18 ¶ When the child was grown, the
day came that he went out to his father to
the reapers.
19 He said to his father, "My head, my
head." And he said to his servant, "Carry
him to his mother."
20 When he had taken him and
brought him to his mother, he sat on her
[1]lap until noon, and *then* died.
21 She went up and [a]laid him on the
bed of [b]the man of God, and shut *the
door* behind him and went out.
22 Then she called to her husband and
said, "Please send me one of the servants
and one of the donkeys, that I may run to
the man of God and return."
23 He said, "Why will you go to him
today? It is neither [a]new moon nor sabbath." And she said, "*It will be* well."
24 Then she saddled a donkey and said
to her servant, "Drive and go forward; do
not slow down [1]the pace for me unless I
tell you."
25 So she went and came to the man
of God to [a]Mount Carmel.
¶ When the man of God saw her at a
distance, he said to Gehazi his servant,
"Behold, [1]there is the Shunammite.
26 "Please run now to meet her and say
to her, 'Is it well with you? Is it well with
your husband? Is it well with the child?' "
And she [1]answered, "It is well."
27 When she came to the man of God
[a]to the hill, she caught hold of his feet.
And Gehazi came near to push her away;
but the man of God said, "Let her alone,
for her soul is [1]troubled within her; and
the LORD has hidden it from me and has
not told me."
28 Then she said, "Did I ask for a son

from my lord? Did I not say, '[a]Do not
deceive me'?"
29 ¶ Then he said to Gehazi, "[a]Gird
up your loins and [b]take my staff in your
hand, and go your way; if you meet any
man, do not [c]salute him, and if anyone
salutes you, do not answer him; and [d]lay
my staff on the lad's face."
30 The mother of the lad said, "[a]As
the LORD lives and as you yourself live, I
will not leave you." And he arose and
followed her.
31 Then Gehazi passed on before
them and laid the staff on the lad's face,
but there was no sound or [1]response. So
he returned to meet him and told [2]him,
"The lad [a]has not awakened."
32 ¶ When Elisha came into the
house, behold the lad was dead and laid
on his bed.
33 So he entered and [a]shut the door
behind them both and prayed to the
LORD.
34 And [a]he went up and lay on the
child, and put his mouth on his mouth
and his eyes on his eyes and his hands on
his hands, and he stretched himself on
him; and the flesh of the child became
warm.
35 Then he returned and walked in
the house once back and forth, and went
up and [a]stretched himself on him; and
the lad sneezed seven times and the lad
opened his eyes.
36 He called Gehazi and said, "Call
this Shunammite." So he called her. And
when she came in to him, he said, "Take
up your son."
37 Then she went in and fell at his feet
and bowed herself to the ground, and
[a]she took up her son and went out.

The Poisonous Stew

38 ¶ When Elisha returned to [a]Gilgal,
there was [b]a famine in the land. [1]As
[c]the sons of the prophets [d]were sitting
before him, he said to his servant, "[e]Put
on the large pot and boil stew for the sons
of the prophets."
39 Then one went out into the field to
gather herbs, and found a wild vine and
gathered from it his lap full of wild
gourds, and came and sliced them into
the pot of stew, for they did not know
what they were.
40 So they poured *it* out for the men to
eat. And as they were eating of the stew,
they cried out and said, "O man of God,
there is [a]death in the pot." And they
were unable to eat.
41 But he said, "Now bring meal."
[a]He threw it into the pot and said, "Pour
it out for the people that they may eat."
Then there was no harm in the pot.

28 [a]2 Kin 4:16
29 [a]1 Kin 18:46; 2 Kin 9:1 [b]Ex 4:17; 2 Kin 2:14 [c]Luke 10:4 [d]Ex 7:19,20; 14:16
30 [a]2 Kin 2:2,4
31 [1]Lit *attentiveness* [2]Lit *him, saying* [a]John 11:11
33 [a]2 Kin 4:4; Matt 6:6; Luke 8:51
34 [a]1 Kin 17:21-23
35 [a]1 Kin 17:21
37 [a]Heb 11:35
38 [1]Lit *And* [a]2 Kin 2:1 [b]2 Kin 8:1 [c]2 Kin 2:3 [d]Luke 10:39; Acts 22:3 [e]Ezek 11:3,7,11; 24:3
40 [a]Ex 10:17
41 [a]Ex 15:25; 2 Kin 2:21
42 [a]Matt 14:16-21; 15:32-38
43 [a]Luke 9:13; John 6:9
44 [a]Matt 14:20; 15:37; John 6:13
5:1 [1]Lit *before* [a]Luke 4:27
2 [1]Lit *was before* [a]2 Kin 6:23; 13:20
3 [1]Lit *before*
4 [1]Lit *He*
5 [1]Lit *enter* [a]1 Sam 9:7; 2 Kin 4:42 [b]Judg 14:12; 2 Kin 5:22,23
7 [1]Lit *an occasion* [a]Gen 37:29 [b]Gen 30:2; 1 Sam 2:6 [c]1 Kin 20:7; Luke 11:54
8 [a]1 Kin 12:22
10 [a]John 9:7

42 ¶ Now a man came from Baal-
shalishah, and brought the man of God
bread of the first fruits, twenty loaves of
barley and fresh ears of grain in his sack.
And he said, "[a]Give *them* to the people
that they may eat."
43 His attendant said, "What, [a]will I
set this before a hundred men?" But he
said, "Give *them* to the people that they
may eat, for thus says the LORD, 'They
shall eat and have *some* left over.' "
44 So he set *it* before them, and they
ate and [a]had *some* left over, according to
the word of the LORD.

Naaman Is Healed

5 Now [a]Naaman, captain of the army
of the king of Aram, was a great man
[1]with his master, and highly respected,
because by him the LORD had given victory to Aram. The man was also a valiant
warrior, *but he was* a leper.
2 Now the Arameans had gone out
[a]in bands and had taken captive a little
girl from the land of Israel; and she
[1]waited on Naaman's wife.
3 She said to her mistress, "I wish
that my master were [1]with the prophet
who is in Samaria! Then he would cure
him of his leprosy."
4 [1]Naaman went in and told his master, saying, "Thus and thus spoke the girl
who is from the land of Israel."
5 Then the king of Aram said, "Go
[1]now, and I will send a letter to the king
of Israel." He departed and [a]took with
him ten talents of silver and six thousand
shekels of gold and ten [b]changes of
clothes.
6 ¶ He brought the letter to the king
of Israel, saying, "And now as this letter
comes to you, behold, I have sent Naaman my servant to you, that you may cure
him of his leprosy."
7 When the king of Israel read the
letter, [a]he tore his clothes and said,
"[b]Am I God, to kill and to make alive,
that this man is sending *word* to me to
cure a man of his leprosy? But [c]consider
now, and see how he is seeking [1]a quarrel against me."
8 ¶ It happened when Elisha [a]the
man of God heard that the king of Israel
had torn his clothes, that he sent *word* to
the king, saying, "Why have you torn
your clothes? Now let him come to me,
and he shall know that there is a prophet
in Israel."
9 So Naaman came with his horses
and his chariots and stood at the doorway
of the house of Elisha.
10 Elisha sent a messenger to him, saying, "[a]Go and wash in the Jordan seven

times, and your flesh will be restored to
you and *you will* be clean."
11 But Naaman was furious and went
away and said, "Behold, I [1]thought, 'He
will surely come out to me and stand and
call on the name of the LORD his God, and
wave his hand over the place and cure
the leper.'
12 "Are not [1]Abanah and Pharpar, the
rivers of Damascus, better than all the
waters of Israel? Could I not wash in
them and be clean?" So he turned and
[a]went away in a rage.
13 [a]Then his servants came near and
spoke to him and said, "[b]My father, had
the prophet told you *to do some* great
thing, would you not have done *it?* How
much more *then,* when he says to you,
'Wash, and be clean'?"
14 So he went down and dipped *himself* seven times in the Jordan, according
to the word of the man of God; and [a]his
flesh was restored like the flesh of a little
child and [b]he was clean.

Gehazi's Greed

15 ¶ When he returned to the man of
God [1]with all his company, and came
and stood before him, he said, "Behold
now, [a]I know that there is no God in all
the earth, but in Israel; so please [b]take a
[2]present from your servant now."
16 But he said, "[a]As the LORD lives,
before whom I stand, [b]I will take nothing." And he urged him to take *it,* but he
refused.
17 Naaman said, "If not, please let
your servant at least be given two mules'
load of [a]earth; for your servant will no
longer offer burnt offering nor will he sacrifice to other gods, but to the LORD.
18 "In this matter may the LORD pardon
your servant: when my master goes into
the house of Rimmon to worship there,
and [a]he leans on my hand and I bow
myself in the house of Rimmon, when I
bow myself in the house of Rimmon, the
LORD pardon your servant in this matter."
19 He said to him, "[a]Go in peace." So
he departed from him some distance.
20 ¶ But [a]Gehazi, the servant of Elisha the man of God, [1]thought, "Behold,
my master has spared this Naaman the
Aramean, [2]by not receiving from his
hands what he brought. [b]As the LORD
lives, I will run after him and take something from him."
21 So Gehazi pursued Naaman. When
Naaman saw one running after him, he
came down from the chariot to meet him
and said, "Is all well?"
22 He said, "[a]All is well. My master
has sent me, saying, 'Behold, just now
two young men of the sons of the prophets have come to me from [b]the hill country of Ephraim. Please give them a talent
of silver and [c]two changes of clothes.' "
23 Naaman said, "[a]Be pleased to take
two talents." And he urged him, and
bound two talents of silver in two bags
with two changes of clothes and gave
them to two of his servants; and they
carried *them* before him.
24 When he came to the [1]hill, he took
them from their hand and [a]deposited
them in the house, and he sent the men
away, and they departed.
25 But he went in and stood before his
master. And Elisha said to him, "Where
have you been, Gehazi?" And he said,
"[a]Your servant went nowhere."
26 ¶ Then he said to him, "Did not my
heart go *with you,* when the man turned
from his chariot to meet you? [a]Is it a time
to receive money and to receive clothes
and olive groves and vineyards and sheep
and oxen and male and female servants?
27 "Therefore, the leprosy of Naaman
shall cling to you and to your [1]descen-
dants forever." So he went out from his
presence [a]a leper *as white* as snow.

The Axe Head Recovered

6 Now [a]the sons of the prophets said
to Elisha, "Behold now, the place
before you where we are living is too
limited for us.
2 "Please let us go to the Jordan and
each of us take from there a beam, and let
us make a place there for ourselves where
we may live." So he said, "Go."
3 Then one said, "Please be willing
to go with your servants." And he [1]an-
swered, "I shall go."
4 So he went with them; and when
they came to the Jordan, they cut down
trees.
5 But as one was felling a beam, [1]the
axe head fell into the water; and he cried
out and said, "Alas, my master! For it was
borrowed."
6 Then the man of God said, "Where
did it fall?" And when he showed him the
place, [a]he cut off a stick and threw *it* in
there, and made the iron float.
7 He said, "Take it up for yourself."
So he put out his hand and took it.

The Arameans Plot to Capture Elisha

8 ¶ Now the king of Aram was warring against Israel; and he [1]counseled
with his servants saying, "In such and
such a place shall be my camp."
9 [a]The man of God sent *word* to the
king of Israel saying, "Beware that you do

11 [1]Lit *said*
12 [1]Another reading is *Amanah* [a]Prov 14:17; 16:32; 19:11
13 [a]1 Sam 28:23 [b]2 Kin 2:12; 6:21; 8:9
14 [a]2 Kin 5:10; Job 33:25 [b]Luke 4:27; 5:13
15 [1]Lit *he and* [2]Lit *blessing* [a]Josh 2:11; 1 Sam 17:46,47; 2 Kin 5:8 [b]1 Sam 25:27
16 [a]2 Kin 3:14 [b]Gen 14:22,23; 2 Kin 5:20,26
17 [a]Ex 20:24
18 [a]2 Kin 7:2, 17
19 [a]Ex 4:18; 1 Sam 1:17; Mark 5:34
20 [1]Lit *said* [2]Lit *from* [a]2 Kin 4:12,31,36 [b]Ex 20:7; 2 Kin 6:31
22 [a]2 Kin 4:26 [b]Josh 24:33 [c]2 Kin 5:5
23 [a]2 Kin 6:3
24 [1]Lit *Ophel* [a]Josh 7:1,11,12, 21; 1 Kin 21:16
25 [a]2 Kin 5:22
26 [a]2 Kin 5:16
27 [1]Lit *seed* [a]Ex 4:6; Num 12:10
6:1 [a]2 Kin 2:3
3 [1]Lit *said*
5 [1]Lit *as for the iron, it fell*
6 [a]Ex 15:25; 2 Kin 2:21; 4:41
8 [1]Lit *took counsel*
9 [a]2 Kin 4:1,7; 6:12

not pass this place, for the Arameans are
coming down there."
10 The king of Israel sent to the place
about which the man of God had told
him; thus he warned him, so that he
guarded himself there, [1]more than once
or twice.
11 ¶ Now the heart of the king of
Aram was enraged over this thing; and
he called his servants and said to them,
"Will you tell me which of us is for the
king of Israel?"
12 One of his servants said, "No, my
lord, O king; but Elisha, the prophet who
is in Israel, tells the king of Israel the
words that you speak in your bedroom."
13 So he said, "Go and see where he
is, that I may send and take him." And it
was told him, saying, "Behold, he is in
[a]Dothan."
14 He sent horses and chariots and a
great army there, and they came by night
and surrounded the city.
15 ¶ Now when the attendant of the
man of God had risen early and gone out,
behold, an army with horses and chariots
was circling the city. And his servant said
to him, "Alas, my master! [1]What shall
we do?"
16 So he [1]answered, "[a]Do not fear,
for [b]those who are with us are more than
those who are with them."
17 Then Elisha prayed and said,
"[a]O LORD, I pray, open his eyes that he
may see." And the LORD opened the servant's eyes and he saw; and behold, the
mountain was full of [b]horses and chariots of fire all around Elisha.
18 When they came down to him, Elisha prayed to the LORD and said, "Strike
this [1]people with blindness, I pray." So
He [a]struck them with blindness according to the word of Elisha.
19 Then Elisha said to them, "This is
not the way, nor is this the city; follow
me and I will bring you to the man whom
you seek." And he brought them to Samaria.
20 ¶ When they had come into Samaria, Elisha said, "O [a]LORD, open the eyes
of these *men,* that they may see." So the
LORD opened their eyes and they saw;
and behold, they were in the midst of
Samaria.
21 Then the king of Israel when he
saw them, said to Elisha, "[a]My father,
shall I [1]kill them? Shall I [1]kill them?"
22 He [1]answered, "You shall not [2]kill
them. Would you [2a]kill those you have
taken captive with your sword and with
your bow? [b]Set bread and water before
them, that they may eat and drink and go
to their master."
23 So he prepared a great feast for
them; and when they had eaten and
drunk he sent them away, and they went
to their master. And [a]the marauding
bands of Arameans did not come again
into the land of Israel.

The Siege of Samaria—Cannibalism

24 ¶ Now it came about after this, that
[a]Ben-hadad king of Aram gathered all his
army and went up and besieged Samaria.
25 There was a great [a]famine in Samaria; and behold, they besieged it, until
a donkey's head was sold for eighty *shekels* of silver, and a fourth of a [1]kab of
dove's dung for five *shekels* of silver.
26 As the king of Israel was passing by
on the wall a woman cried out to him,
saying, "Help, my lord, O king!"
27 He said, "[1]If the LORD does not
help you, from where shall I help you?
From the threshing floor, or from the
wine press?"
28 And the king said to her, "[a]What
[1]is the matter with you?" And she [2]an-
swered, "This woman said to me, 'Give
your son that we may eat him today, and
we will eat my son tomorrow.'
29 "[a]So we boiled my son and ate him;
and I said to her on the next day, 'Give
your son, that we may eat him'; but she
has hidden her son."
30 When the king heard the words of
the woman, [a]he tore his clothes—now
he was passing by on the wall—and the
people looked, and behold, he had sackcloth [1]beneath on his [2]body.
31 Then he said, "May [a]God do so to
me and more also, if the head of Elisha
the son of Shaphat [1]remains on him today."
32 ¶ Now Elisha was sitting in his
house, and [a]the elders were sitting with
him. And *the king* sent a man from his
presence; but before the messenger came
to him, he said to the elders, "Do you
[b]see how this son of a murderer has sent
to take away my head? Look, when the
messenger comes, shut the door and
[1]hold the door shut against him. Is not
the sound of his master's feet behind
him?"
33 While he was still talking with
them, behold, the messenger came down
to him and he said, "[a]Behold, this evil is
from the LORD; why should I wait for the
LORD any longer?"

Elisha Promises Food

7 Then Elisha said, "Listen to the word
of the LORD; thus says the LORD,
'[a]Tomorrow about this time a [1]measure
of fine flour will be *sold* for a shekel, and
two measures of barley for a shekel, in
the gate of Samaria.' "

10 [1]Lit *not once or twice*
13 [a]Gen 37:17
15 [1]Lit *How*
16 [1]Lit *said* [a]Ex 14:13 [b]2 Chr 32:7,8; Rom 8:31
17 [a]2 Kin 6:20 [b]2 Kin 2:11; Ps 68:17; Zech 6:1-7
18 [1]Lit *nation* [a]Gen 19:11
20 [a]2 Kin 6:17
21 [1]Lit *smite* [a]2 Kin 2:12; 5:13; 8:9
22 [1]Lit *said* [2]Lit *smite* [a]Deut 20:11-16; 2 Chr 28:8-15 [b]Rom 12:20
23 [a]2 Kin 5:2; 24:2
24 [a]1 Kin 20:1
25 [1]I.e. One kab equals approx 2 qts [a]Lev 26:26
27 [1]Lit *No, let the LORD help you*
28 [1]Lit *to you* [2]Lit *said* [a]Judg 18:23
29 [a]Lev 26:27-29; Deut 28:52,53,57; Lam 4:10
30 [1]Lit *within* [2]Lit *flesh* [a]1 Kin 21:27
31 [1]Lit *stands* [a]Ruth 1:17; 1 Kin 19:2
32 [1]Lit *press him with the door* [a]Ezek 8:1; 14:1; 20:1 [b]1 Kin 18:4,13, 14; 21:10,13
33 [a]Is 8:21
7:1 [1]Heb *seah* [a]2 Kin 7:18

2 [a]The royal officer on whose hand the king was leaning answered the man of God and said, "Behold, [b]if the LORD should make windows in heaven, could this thing be?" Then he said, "Behold, you will see it with your own eyes, but you will not eat [1]of it."

Four Lepers Relate Arameans' Flight

3 ¶ Now there were four [a]leprous men at the entrance of the gate; and they said to one another, "Why do we sit here until we die?

4 "If we say, 'We will enter the city,' then the famine is in the city and we will die there; and if we sit here, we die also. Now therefore come, and let us [1]go over to [a]the camp of the Arameans. If they spare us, we will live; and if they kill us, we will but die."

5 They arose at twilight to go to the camp of the Arameans; when they came to the outskirts of the camp of the Arameans, behold, there was no one there.

6 For [a]the Lord had caused the army of the Arameans to hear a sound of chariots and a sound of horses, *even* the sound of a great army, so that they said to one another, "Behold, the king of Israel has hired against us [b]the kings of the Hittites and [c]the kings of the Egyptians, to come upon us."

7 Therefore they [a]arose and fled in the twilight, and left their tents and their horses and their donkeys, *even* the camp just as it was, and fled for their life.

8 When these lepers came to the outskirts of the camp, they entered one tent and ate and drank, and [a]carried from there silver and gold and clothes, and went and hid *them;* and they returned and entered another tent and carried from there *also,* and went and hid *them.*

9 ¶ Then they said to one another, "We are not doing right. This day is a day of good news, but we are keeping silent; if we wait until morning light, punishment will [1]overtake us. Now therefore come, let us go and tell the king's household."

10 So they came and called to the gatekeepers of the city, and they told them, saying, "We came to the camp of the Arameans, and behold, there was no one there, nor the voice of man, only the horses tied and the donkeys tied, and the tents just as they were."

11 The gatekeepers called and told *it* within the king's household.

12 Then the king arose in the night and said to his servants, "I will now tell you what the Arameans have done to us. They know that [a]we are hungry; therefore they have gone from the camp [b]to hide themselves in the field, saying, 'When they come out of the city, we will capture them alive and get into the city.' "

13 One of his servants said, "Please, let some *men* take five of the horses which remain, which are left [1]in the city. Behold, they *will be in any case* like all the multitude of Israel who are left in it; behold, they *will be in any case* like all the multitude of Israel who have already perished, so let us send and see."

14 They took therefore two chariots with horses, and the king sent after the army of the Arameans, saying, "Go and see."

The Promise Fulfilled

15 They went after them to the Jordan, and behold, all the way was full of clothes and equipment which the Arameans had thrown away in their haste. Then the messengers returned and told the king.

16 ¶ So the people went out and plundered the camp of the Arameans. Then a [1]measure of fine flour *was sold* for a shekel and two [1]measures of barley for a shekel, [a]according to the word of the LORD.

17 Now the king appointed [a]the royal officer on whose hand he leaned [1]to have charge of the gate; but the people trampled on him at the gate, and he died just as the man of God had said, [b]who spoke when the king came down to him.

18 It happened just as the man of God had spoken to the king, saying, "[a]Two [1]measures of barley for a shekel and a [1]measure of fine flour for a shekel, will be *sold* tomorrow about this time at the gate of Samaria."

19 Then the royal officer answered the man of God and said, "Now behold, [a]if the LORD should make windows in heaven, could such a thing be?" And he said, "Behold, you will see it with your own eyes, but you will not eat [1]of it."

20 And so it happened to him, for the people trampled on him at the gate and he died.

Jehoram Restores the Shunammite's Land

8 Now [a]Elisha spoke to the woman whose son he had restored to life saying, "Arise and go [1]with your household, and sojourn wherever you can sojourn; for the [b]LORD has called for a famine, and [c]it will even come on the land for seven years."

2 So the woman arose and did accord

2 [1]Lit *from there* [a]2 Kin 5:18; 7:17,19 [b]Gen 7:11; Mal 3:10

3 [a]Lev 13:45,46; Num 5:2-4; 12:10-14

4 [1]Lit *fall* [a]2 Kin 6:24

6 [a]2 Sam 5:24 [b]1 Kin 10:29 [c]2 Chr 12:2,3; Is 31:1; 36:9

7 [a]Ps 48:4-6; Prov 28:1

8 [a]Josh 7:21

9 [1]Lit *find*

12 [a]2 Kin 6:25-29 [b]Josh 8:4-12

13 [1]Lit *in it*

16 [1]Heb *seah;* i.e. one seah equals approx 11 qts [a]2 Kin 7:1

17 [1]Lit *over the gate* [a]2 Kin 7:2 [b]2 Kin 6:32

18 [1]Heb *seah;* i.e. one seah equals approx 11 qts [a]2 Kin 7:1

19 [1]Lit *from there* [a]2 Kin 7:2

8:1 [1]Lit *you and your* [a]2 Kin 4:18,31-35 [b]Ps 105:16; Hag 1:11 [c]Gen 41:27,54

ing to the word of the man of God, and
she went with her household and sojourned in the land of the Philistines sev-
en years.
3 At the end of seven years, the woman returned from the land of the Philistines; and she went out to [1]appeal to the
king for her house and for her field.
4 Now the king was talking with
[a]Gehazi, the servant of the man of God,
saying, "Please relate to me all the great
things that Elisha has done."
5 As he was relating to the king
[a]how he had restored to life the one who
was dead, behold, the woman whose son
he had restored to life [1]appealed to the
king for her house and for her field. And
Gehazi said, "My lord, O king, this is the
woman and this is her son, whom Elisha
restored to life."
6 When the king asked the woman,
she related *it* to him. So the king appointed for her a certain officer, saying, "Restore all that was hers and all the produce
of the field from the day that she left the
land even until now."

Elisha Predicts Evil from Hazael

7 ¶ Then Elisha came to [a]Damascus.
Now [b]Ben-hadad king of Aram was sick,
and it was told him, saying, "[c]The man
of God has come here."
8 The king said to [a]Hazael, "[b]Take a
gift in your hand and go to meet the man
of God, and [c]inquire of the LORD by him,
saying, 'Will I recover from this sickness?' "
9 So Hazael went to meet him and
took a gift in his hand, even every kind of
good thing of Damascus, forty camels'
loads; and he came and stood before him
and said, "[a]Your son Ben-hadad king of
Aram has sent me to you, saying, 'Will I
recover from this sickness?' "
10 Then Elisha said to him, "[a]Go, say
to him, 'You will surely recover,' but the
[b]LORD has shown me that he will certainly die."
11 He [1]fixed his gaze steadily *on him*
[a]until he was ashamed, and [b]the man of
God wept.
12 Hazael said, "Why does my lord
weep?" Then he [1]answered, "Because
[a]I know the evil that you will do to the
sons of Israel: their strongholds you will
set on fire, and their young men you will
kill with the sword, and their little ones
you [b]will dash in pieces, and their wom-
en with child you will rip up."
13 Then Hazael said, "But what is your
servant, [a]*who is but* a dog, that he should
do this great thing?" And Elisha [1]an-
swered, "[b]The LORD has shown me that
you will be king over Aram."
14 So he departed from Elisha and
returned to his master, who said to
him, "What did Elisha say to you?" And
he [1]answered, "He told me that [a]you
would surely recover."
15 On the following day, he took the
cover and dipped it in water and spread
it on his face, [a]so that he died. And Hazael became king in his place.

Another Jehoram Reigns in Judah

16 ¶ Now in the fifth year of [a]Joram
the son of Ahab king of Israel, Jehoshaphat being then the king of Judah, Jehoram the son of Jehoshaphat king of Judah
became king.
17 He was [a]thirty-two years old when
he became king, and he reigned eight
years in Jerusalem.
18 He walked in the way of the kings
of Israel, just as the house of Ahab had
done, for [a]the daughter of Ahab became
his wife; and he did evil in the sight of the
LORD.
19 However, the LORD was not willing
to destroy Judah, for the sake of David His
servant, [a]since He had [1]promised him
to give a [2]lamp to him through his sons
always.
20 ¶ In his days [a]Edom revolted from
under the hand of Judah, and made a king
over themselves.
21 Then Joram crossed over to Zair,
and all his chariots with him. And he
arose by night and struck the Edomites
who had surrounded him and the captains of the chariots; [a]but *his* [1]army fled
to their tents.
22 [a]So Edom revolted [1]against Judah
to this day. Then [b]Libnah revolted at the
same time.
23 The rest of the acts of Joram and all
that he did, are they not written in the
Book of the Chronicles of the Kings of
Judah?

Ahaziah Succeeds Jehoram in Judah

24 So Joram slept with his fathers and
[a]was buried with his fathers in the city
of David; and [b]Ahaziah his son became
king in his place.
25 ¶ [a]In the twelfth year of Joram the
son of Ahab king of Israel, Ahaziah the
son of Jehoram king of Judah began to
reign.
26 [a]Ahaziah *was* twenty-two years
old when he became king, and he reigned
one year in Jerusalem. And his mother's
name *was* Athaliah the granddaughter of
Omri king of Israel.
27 [a]He walked in the way of the
house of Ahab and did evil in the sight of
the LORD, like the house of Ahab *had*

3 [1]Lit *cry out*
4 [a]2 Kin 4:12; 5:20-27
5 [1]Lit *cried out* [a]2 Kin 4:35
7 [a]1 Kin 11:24 [b]2 Kin 6:24 [c]2 Kin 5:20
8 [a]1 Kin 19:15, 17 [b]1 Kin 14:3 [c]2 Kin 1:2
9 [a]2 Kin 5:13
10 [a]2 Kin 8:14 [b]2 Kin 8:15
11 [1]Lit *made his face stand fast and he set* [a]2 Kin 2:17 [b]Luke 19:41
12 [1]Lit *said* [a]2 Kin 10:32,33; 12:17; 13:3,7 [b]2 Kin 15:16; Nah 3:10
13 [1]Lit *said* [a]1 Sam 17:43; 2 Sam 9:8 [b]1 Kin 19:15
14 [1]Lit *said* [a]2 Kin 8:10
15 [a]2 Kin 8:10
16 [a]2 Kin 1:17; 3:1
17 [a]2 Chr 21:5-10
18 [a]2 Kin 8:27
19 [1]Lit *said* [2]I.e. descendant on the throne [a]2 Sam 7:12-15; 1 Kin 11:36
20 [a]1 Kin 22:47; 2 Kin 3:9, 26,27; 8:22
21 [1]Lit *the people* [a]2 Sam 18:17; 19:8
22 [1]Lit *from under the hand of* [a]Gen 27:40 [b]Josh 21:13; 2 Kin 19:8
24 [a]2 Chr 21:20 [b]2 Chr 21:1,7
25 [a]2 Chr 22:1-6
26 [a]2 Chr 22:2
27 [a]2 Chr 22:3

done, because he was a son-in-law of the
house of Ahab.
28 ¶ Then he went with Joram the son
of Ahab to war against [a]Hazael king of
Aram at [b]Ramoth-gilead, and the Arameans [1]wounded Joram.
29 So [a]King Joram returned to be
healed in Jezreel of the wounds which
the Arameans had [1]inflicted on him at
[b]Ramah when he fought against Hazael
king of Aram. Then [c]Ahaziah the son of
Jehoram king of Judah went down to see
Joram the son of Ahab in Jezreel because
he was sick.

Jehu Reigns over Israel

9 Now Elisha the prophet called one of
[a]the sons of the prophets and said to
him, "[b]Gird up your loins, and [c]take
this flask of oil in your hand and go to
[d]Ramoth-gilead.
2 "When you arrive there, [1]search
out [a]Jehu the son of Jehoshaphat the son
of Nimshi, and go in and [2b]bid him arise
from among his brothers, and bring him
to an inner room.
3 "Then take the flask of oil and pour
it on his head and say, 'Thus says the
LORD, "[a]I have anointed you king over
Israel." ' Then open the door and flee and
do not wait."
4 ¶ So [a]the young man, the servant
of the prophet, went to Ramoth-gilead.
5 When he came, behold, the captains of the army were sitting, and he
said, "I have a word for you, O captain."
And Jehu said, "[1]For which *one* of us?"
And he said, "For you, O captain."
6 He arose and went into the house,
and he poured the oil on his head and
said to him, "Thus says the LORD, the God
of Israel, '[a]I have anointed you king over
the people of the LORD, *even* over Israel.
7 'You shall strike the house of Ahab
your master, [a]that I may avenge [b]the
blood of My servants the prophets, and
the blood of all the servants of the LORD,
[c]at the hand of Jezebel.
8 'For the whole house of Ahab shall
perish, and [a]I will cut off from Ahab [b]ev-
ery male person [c]both bond and free in
Israel.
9 '[a]I will make the house of Ahab like
the house of Jeroboam the son of Nebat,
and [b]like the house of Baasha the son of
Ahijah.
10 '[a]The dogs shall eat Jezebel in the
territory of Jezreel, and none shall bury
her.' " Then he opened the door and fled.
11 ¶ Now Jehu came out to the servants of his master, and one said to him,
"[a]Is all well? Why did this [b]mad fellow
come to you?" And he said to them, "You
know *very well* the man and his talk."
12 They said, "It is a lie, tell us now."
And he said, "Thus and thus he said to
me, 'Thus says the LORD, "I have anointed you king over Israel." ' "
13 Then [a]they hurried and each man
took his garment and placed it under him
on the bare steps, and [b]blew the trumpet, saying, "Jehu is king!"

Jehoram (Joram) Is Assassinated

14 ¶ So Jehu the son of Jehoshaphat
the son of Nimshi conspired against Joram. [a]Now Joram [1]with all Israel was
[2]defending Ramoth-gilead against Hazael
king of Aram,
15 but [a]King [1]Joram had returned to
Jezreel to be healed of the wounds which
the Arameans had [2]inflicted on him
when he fought with Hazael king of
Aram. So Jehu said, "If this is your mind,
then let no one escape *or* [3]leave the city
to go tell *it* in Jezreel."
16 Then Jehu rode in a chariot and
went to Jezreel, for Joram was lying
there. [a]Ahaziah king of Judah had come
down to see Joram.
17 ¶ Now the watchman was standing
on the tower in Jezreel and he saw the
[1]company of Jehu as he came, and said,
"I see a [1]company." And Joram said,
"Take a horseman and send him to meet
them and let him say, 'Is it peace?' "
18 So a horseman went to meet him
and said, "Thus says the king, 'Is it
peace?' " And Jehu said, "[a]What have
you to do with peace? Turn behind me."
And the watchman [1]reported, "The messenger came to them, but he did not return."
19 Then he sent out a second horseman, who came to them and said, "Thus
says the king, 'Is it peace?' " And Jehu
[1]answered, "What have you to do with
peace? Turn behind me."
20 The watchman [1]reported, "He
came even to them, and he did not return; and [a]the driving is like the driving
of [b]Jehu the son of Nimshi, for he drives
furiously."
21 ¶ Then [1]Joram said, "[2]Get ready."
And they made his chariot ready. [1a]Jo-
ram king of Israel and Ahaziah king of
Judah went out, each in his chariot, and
they went out to meet Jehu and found
him in the [3b]property of Naboth the Jezreelite.
22 When [1]Joram saw Jehu, he said,
"Is it peace, Jehu?" And he [2]answered,
"What peace, [a]so long as the harlotries of
your mother Jezebel and her witchcrafts
are so many?"
23 So [1]Joram [2]reined about and fled
and said to Ahaziah, "[a]*There is* treachery, O Ahaziah!"

---

28 [1]Lit *smote* [a]2 Kin 8:15 [b]1 Kin 22:3,29
29 [1]Lit *struck* [a]2 Kin 9:15 [b]2 Kin 8:28; 2 Chr 22:5,6 [c]2 Kin 9:16
9:1 [a]2 Kin 2:3 [b]2 Kin 4:29 [c]1 Sam 10:1; 16:1; 1 Kin 1:39 [d]2 Kin 8:28,29
2 [1]Lit *and look there for* [2]Lit *cause him to* [a]1 Kin 19:16,17; 2 Kin 9:14,20 [b]2 Kin 9:5,11
3 [a]2 Chr 22:7
4 [a]2 Kin 9:1
5 [1]Lit *To whom of us all?*
6 [a]1 Sam 2:7,8; 1 Kin 19:16; 2 Kin 9:3; 2 Chr 22:7
7 [a]Deut 32:35, 43 [b]1 Kin 18:4; 21:15,21,25 [c]2 Kin 9:32-37
8 [a]1 Kin 21:21; 2 Kin 10:17 [b]1 Sam 25:22 [c]Deut 32:36; 2 Kin 14:26
9 [a]1 Kin 14:10, 11; 15:29 [b]1 Kin 16:3-5,11,12
10 [a]1 Kin 21:23; 2 Kin 9:35,36
11 [a]2 Kin 9:17, 19,22 [b]Jer 29:26; Hos 9:7; Mark 3:21
13 [a]Matt 21:7,8; Mark 11:7,8 [b]2 Sam 15:10; 1 Kin 1:34,39
14 [1]Lit *he and* [2]Lit *keeping* [a]1 Kin 22:3; 2 Kin 8:28
15 [1]Heb *Jehoram* [2]Lit *struck* [3]Lit *go out from* [a]2 Kin 8:29
16 [a]2 Kin 8:29
17 [1]Lit *multitude*
18 [1]Lit *told, saying* [a]2 Kin 9:19, 22
19 [1]Lit *said*
20 [1]Lit *told, saying* [a]2 Sam 18:27 [b]1 Kin 19:17
21 [1]Heb *Jehoram* [2]Lit *Yoke the chariot* [3]Lit *portion* [a]2 Chr 22:7 [b]1 Kin 21:1-7,15-19; 2 Kin 9:26
22 [1]Heb *Jehoram* [2]Lit *said* [a]1 Kin 16:30-33; 18:19; 2 Chr 21:13
23 [1]Heb *Jehoram* [2]Lit *turned his hands* [a]2 Kin 11:14

24 And [a]Jehu [1]drew his bow with his
full strength and [2]shot [3]Joram between
his arms; and the arrow went [4]through
his heart and he sank in his chariot.
25 Then *Jehu* said to Bidkar his officer,
"Take *him* up and [a]cast him into the
[1]property of the field of Naboth the Jezreelite, for I remember when [2]you and I
were riding together after Ahab his father, that the [b]LORD laid this [c]oracle
against him:
26 'Surely [a]I have seen yesterday the
blood of Naboth and the blood of his
sons,' says the LORD, 'and [b]I will repay
you in this [1]property,' says the LORD.
Now then, take and cast him into the
[1]property, according to the word of the
LORD."

Jehu Assassinates Ahaziah

27 ¶ [a]When Ahaziah the king of Judah saw *this,* he fled by the way of the
garden house. And Jehu pursued him and
said, "[1]Shoot him too, in the chariot." *So
they shot him* at the ascent of Gur, which
is at [b]Ibleam. But he fled to Megiddo and
died there.
28 [a]Then his servants carried him in
a chariot to Jerusalem and buried him in
his grave with his fathers in the city of
David.
29 ¶ Now in [a]the eleventh year of Joram, the son of Ahab, Ahaziah became
king over Judah.
30 ¶ When Jehu came to Jezreel, Jezebel heard *of it,* and [a]she painted her eyes
and adorned her head and looked out the
window.
31 As Jehu entered the gate, she said,
"[a]Is it [1]well, Zimri, [2]your master's murderer?"
32 Then he lifted up his face to the
window and said, "Who is on my side?
Who?" And two or three officials looked
down at him.

Jezebel Is Slain

33 He said, "Throw her down." So
they threw her down, and some of her
blood was sprinkled on the wall and on
the horses, and he trampled her under
foot.
34 When he came in, he ate and
drank; and he said, "See now to [a]this
cursed woman and bury her, for [b]she is
a king's daughter."
35 They went to bury her, but they
found nothing more of her than the skull
and the feet and the palms of her hands.
36 Therefore they returned and told
him. And he said, "This is the word of the
LORD, which He spoke by His servant Elijah the Tishbite, saying, '[a]In the [1]prop-
erty of Jezreel the dogs shall eat the flesh
of Jezebel;
37 and [a]the corpse of Jezebel will be
as dung on the face of the field in the
[1]property of Jezreel, so they cannot say,
"This is Jezebel." ' "

Judgment upon Ahab's House

10 Now Ahab had seventy sons in
[a]Samaria. And Jehu wrote letters
and sent *them* to Samaria, to the rulers of
Jezreel, the elders, and to the guardians
of *the children of* Ahab, saying,
2 "Now, [a]when this letter comes to
you, since your master's sons are with
you, [1]as well as the chariots and horses
and a fortified city and the weapons,
3 select the best and [1]fittest of your
master's sons, and set *him* on his father's
throne, and fight for your master's
house."
4 But they feared greatly and said,
"Behold, [a]the two kings did not stand
before him; how then can we stand?"
5 And the one who *was* over the
household, and he who *was* over the city,
the elders, and the guardians of *the children,* sent *word* to Jehu, saying, "[a]We
are your servants, all that you say to us we
will do, we will not make any man king;
do what is good in your sight."
6 Then he wrote a letter to them a
second time saying, "If you are on my
side, and you will listen to my voice, take
the heads of the men, your master's sons,
and come to me at Jezreel tomorrow
about this time." Now the king's sons,
seventy persons, *were* with the great
men of the city, *who* were rearing them.
7 When the letter came to them, they
took the king's sons and [a]slaughtered
them, seventy persons, and put their
heads in baskets, and sent *them* to him at
Jezreel.
8 When the messenger came and told
him, saying, "They have brought the
heads of the king's sons," he said, "Put
them in two heaps at the entrance of the
gate until morning."
9 Now in the morning he went out
and stood and said to all the people, "You
are [1]innocent; behold, [a]I conspired
against my master and killed him, but
[b]who [2]killed all these?
10 "Know then that [a]there shall fall
to the earth nothing of the word of the
LORD, which the LORD spoke concerning
the house of Ahab, for the LORD has done
[b]what He spoke [1]through His servant
Elijah."
11 So Jehu [1]killed all who remained of
the house of Ahab in [a]Jezreel, and all his
great men and his acquaintances and his

24 [1]Lit *filled his hand with the bow* [2]Lit *smote* [3]Heb *Jehoram* [4]Lit *out at* [a]1 Kin 22:34
25 [1]Lit *portion* [2]Lit *I and you* [a]1 Kin 21:1 [b]1 Kin 21:19, 24-29 [c]Is 13:1
26 [1]Lit *portion* [a]1 Kin 21:13,19 [b]2 Kin 9:21,25
27 [1]Lit *smite* [a]2 Chr 22:7,9 [b]Josh 17:11; Judg 1:27
28 [a]2 Kin 23:30
29 [a]2 Kin 8:25
30 [a]Jer 4:30; Ezek 23:40
31 [1]Lit *peace* [2]Lit *his* [a]1 Kin 16:9-20; 2 Kin 9:18-22
34 [a]1 Kin 21:25 [b]1 Kin 16:31
36 [1]Lit *portion* [a]1 Kin 21:23
37 [1]Lit *portion* [a]Jer 8:1-3
10:1 [a]1 Kin 16:24-29
2 [1]Lit *and with you the* [a]2 Kin 5:6
3 [1]Lit *most upright*
4 [a]2 Kin 9:24,27
5 [a]Josh 9:8,11; 1 Kin 20:4,32; 2 Kin 18:14
7 [a]Judg 9:5; 2 Kin 11:1
9 [1]Lit *just* [2]Lit *smote* [a]2 Kin 9:14-24 [b]2 Kin 10:6
10 [1]Lit *by the hand of* [a]2 Kin 9:7-10 [b]1 Kin 21:19-29
11 [1]Lit *smote* [a]Hos 1:4

priests, until he left him without a survivor.
12 ¶ Then he arose and departed and
went to Samaria. On the way while he
was at [1]Beth-eked of the shepherds,
13 [a]Jehu [1]met the [2]relatives of Ahaziah king of Judah and said, "Who are
you?" And they [3]answered, "We are the
[2]relatives of Ahaziah; and we have come
down [4]to greet the sons of the king and
the sons of the queen mother."
14 He said, "Take them alive." So they
took them alive and killed them at the pit
of Beth-eked, forty-two men; and he left
none of them.
15 ¶ Now when he had departed from
there, he [1]met [a]Jehonadab the son of
[b]Rechab *coming* to meet him; and he
[2]greeted him and said to him, "Is your
heart right, as my heart is with your
heart?" And Jehonadab [3]answered, "It
is." *Jehu said,* "If it is, [c]give *me* your
hand." And he gave him his hand, and he
took him up to him into the chariot.
16 He said, "Come with me and [a]see
my zeal for the LORD." So [1]he made him
ride in his chariot.
17 When he came to Samaria, [a]he
[1]killed all who remained to Ahab in Samaria, until he had destroyed him, [b]ac-
cording to the word of the LORD which
He spoke to Elijah.

Jehu Destroys Baal Worshipers

18 ¶ Then Jehu gathered all the people
and said to them, "[a]Ahab served Baal a
little; Jehu will serve him much.
19 "Now, [a]summon all the prophets of
Baal, all his worshipers and all his priests;
let no one be missing, for I have a great
sacrifice for Baal; whoever is missing
shall not live." But Jehu did it in [1]cun-
ning, so that he might destroy the worshipers of Baal.
20 And Jehu said, "[a]Sanctify a solemn
assembly for Baal." And [b]they proclaimed *it.*
21 Then Jehu sent [1]throughout Israel
and all the worshipers of Baal came, so
that there was not a man left who did not
come. And when they went into [a]the
house of Baal, the house of Baal was filled
from one end to the other.
22 He said to the one who *was* [1]in
charge of the wardrobe, "Bring out garments for all the worshipers of Baal." So
he brought out garments for them.
23 Jehu went into the house of Baal
with Jehonadab the son of Rechab; and he
said to the worshipers of Baal, "Search
and see that there is here with you none
of the servants of the LORD, but only the
worshipers of Baal."
24 Then they went in to offer sacrifices and burnt offerings.
¶ Now Jehu had stationed for himself
eighty men outside, and he had said,
"[a]The one who permits any of the men
whom I bring into your hands to escape
[1]shall give up his life in exchange."
25 ¶ Then it came about, as soon as he
had finished offering the burnt offering,
that Jehu said to the [1a]guard and to the
royal officers, "[b]Go in, [2]kill them; let
none come out." And they [3]killed them
with the edge of the sword; and the
[1]guard and the royal officers threw *them*
out, and went to the [4]inner room of the
house of Baal.
26 They brought out the *sacred* [a]pil-
lars of the house of Baal and burned
them.
27 They also broke down the *sacred*
pillar of Baal and broke down the house
of Baal, and [a]made it a latrine to this day.
28 ¶ Thus Jehu eradicated Baal out of
Israel.
29 However, [a]*as for* the sins of Jeroboam the son of Nebat, which he made
Israel sin, from these Jehu did not depart,
even the [b]golden calves that *were* at
Bethel and that *were* at Dan.
30 The LORD said to Jehu, "Because
you have done well in executing what is
right in My eyes, *and* have done to the
house of Ahab according to all that *was* in
My heart, [a]your sons of the fourth generation shall sit on the throne of Israel."
31 But Jehu [1a]was not careful to walk
in the law of the LORD, the God of Israel,
with all his heart; [b]he did not depart
from the sins of Jeroboam, which he
made Israel sin.
32 ¶ In those days the [a]LORD began to
cut off *portions* [1]from Israel; and [b]Haza-
el [2]defeated them throughout the territory of Israel:
33 from the Jordan eastward, all the
land of Gilead, the Gadites and the Reubenites and the Manassites, from [a]Aroer,
which is by the valley of the Arnon, even
[b]Gilead and Bashan.

Jehoahaz Succeeds Jehu

34 Now the rest of the acts of Jehu and
all that he did and all his might, are they
not written in the Book of the Chronicles
of the Kings of Israel?
35 And Jehu slept with his fathers, and
they buried him in Samaria. And Jehoahaz his son became king in his place.
36 Now the [1]time which Jehu reigned
over Israel in Samaria *was* twenty-eight
years.

12 [1]I.e. house of binding
13 [1]Lit *found* [2]Lit *brothers* [3]Lit *said* [4]Lit *about the welfare of* [a]2 Kin 8:24,29; 2 Chr 21:17; 22:8
15 [1]Lit *found* [2]Lit *blessed* [3]Lit *said* [a]Jer 35:6-19 [b]1 Chr 2:55 [c]Ezra 10:19; Ezek 17:18
16 [1]Lit *they* [a]1 Kin 19:10
17 [1]Lit *smote* [a]2 Kin 9:8 [b]2 Kin 10:10
18 [a]1 Kin 16:31,32
19 [1]Lit *insidiousness* [a]1 Kin 18:19; 22:6
20 [a]Joel 1:14 [b]Ex 32:4-6
21 [1]Lit *in all* [a]1 Kin 16:32; 2 Kin 11:18
22 [1]Lit *over the*
24 [1]Lit *his soul for his soul* [a]1 Kin 20:30-42
25 [1]Lit *runners* [2]Lit *smite* [3]Lit *smote* [4]Lit *city* [a]1 Sam 22:17 [b]1 Kin 18:40
26 [a]1 Kin 14:23; 2 Kin 3:2
27 [a]Ezra 6:11; Dan 2:5; 3:29
29 [a]1 Kin 12:28-30; 13:33, 34 [b]1 Kin 12:29
30 [a]2 Kin 15:12
31 [1]Lit *did not watch* [a]Prov 4:23 [b]2 Kin 10:29
32 [1]Lit *in* [2]Lit *smote* [a]2 Kin 13:25; 14:25 [b]1 Kin 19:17; 2 Kin 8:12; 13:22
33 [a]Deut 2:36 [b]Amos 1:3-5
36 [1]Lit *days*

Athaliah Queen of Judah

11 [a]When Athaliah the mother of
Ahaziah saw that her son was
dead, she rose and destroyed all the royal
[1]offspring.
2 But Jehosheba, the daughter of
King Joram, sister of Ahaziah, [a]took Joash the son of Ahaziah and stole him from
among the king's sons who were being
put to death, and placed him and his
nurse in the bedroom. So they hid him
from Athaliah, and he was not put to
death.
3 So he was hidden with her in the
house of the LORD six years, while Athaliah was reigning over the land.
4 ¶ [a]Now in the seventh year Jehoiada sent and brought the captains of hundreds of [b]the Carites and of the [1]guard,
and brought them to him in the house of
the LORD. Then he made a covenant with
them and put them under oath in the
house of the LORD, and showed them the
king's son.
5 He commanded them, saying,
"This is the thing that you shall do: [a]one
third of you, who come in on the sabbath
and keep watch over the king's house
6 (one third also *shall be* at the gate
Sur, and one third at the gate behind the
[1]guards), [2]shall keep watch over the
house for defense.
7 "Two parts of you, *even* all who go
out on the sabbath, shall also keep watch
over the house of the LORD for the king.
8 "Then you shall surround the king,
each with his weapons in his hand;
and whoever comes within the ranks
shall be put to death. And [a]be with the
king when he goes out and when he
comes in."
9 ¶ So the captains of hundreds [a]did
according to all that Jehoiada the priest
commanded. And each one of them took
his men who were to come in on the
sabbath, with those who were to go out
on the sabbath, and came to Jehoiada the
priest.
10 [a]The priest gave to the captains of
hundreds the spears and shields that *had
been* King David's, which *were* in the
house of the LORD.
11 The [1]guards stood each with his
weapons in his hand, from the right
[2]side of the house to the left [2]side of the
house, by the altar and by the house,
around the king.
12 Then he brought the king's son out
and [a]put the crown on him and *gave him*
[b]the testimony; and they made him king
and anointed him, and they clapped their
hands and said, "[c]*Long* live the king!"
13 ¶ [a]When Athaliah heard the noise

11:1 [1]Lit *seed* [a]2 Chr 22:10-12
2 [a]2 Kin 11:21; 12:1
4 [1]Lit *runners* [a]2 Chr 23:1-21 [b]2 Sam 20:23; 2 Kin 11:19
5 [a]1 Chr 9:25
6 [1]Lit *runners* [2]Lit *and shall*
8 [a]Num 27:16, 17
9 [a]2 Chr 23:8
10 [a]2 Sam 8:7; 1 Chr 18:7
11 [1]Lit *runners* [2]Lit *shoulder*
12 [a]2 Sam 1:10 [b]Ex 25:16; 31:18 [c]1 Sam 10:24
13 [a]2 Chr 23:12
14 [1]Lit *trumpets* [a]2 Kin 23:3; 2 Chr 34:31 [b]1 Kin 1:39,40 [c]Gen 37:29; 44:13 [d]2 Kin 9:23
15 [1]Lit *from within*
16 [1]Lit *placed hands to her* [a]Gen 9:6; Lev 24:17
17 [a]Josh 24:25; 2 Chr 15:12-14; 34:31 [b]1 Sam 10:25; 2 Sam 5:3
18 [1]Lit *offices* [a]2 Kin 10:26,27 [b]Deut 12:2,3 [c]1 Kin 18:40
19 [1]Lit *runners* [a]2 Kin 11:4 [b]2 Kin 11:6
20 [a]Prov 11:10
21 [1]Ch 12:1 in Heb [a]2 Chr 24:1-14
12:1 [a]2 Chr 24:1
3 [a]2 Kin 14:4; 15:35
4 [a]2 Kin 22:4 [b]Ex 30:13-16; 35:5,22,29; 1 Chr 29:3-9

of the guard *and of* the people, she came
to the people in the house of the LORD.
14 She looked and behold, the king
was standing [a]by the pillar, according to
the custom, with the captains and the
[1]trumpeters beside the king; and [b]all
the people of the land rejoiced and blew
trumpets. Then Athaliah [c]tore her
clothes and cried, "[d]Treason! Treason!"
15 And Jehoiada the priest commanded the captains of hundreds who were
appointed over the army and said to
them, "Bring her out [1]between the
ranks, and whoever follows her put to
death with the sword." For the priest
said, "Let her not be put to death in the
house of the LORD."
16 So they [1]seized her, and when she
arrived at the horses' entrance of the
king's house, she was [a]put to death
there.
17 ¶ Then [a]Jehoiada made a covenant
between the LORD and the king and the
people, that they would be the LORD's
people, also [b]between the king and
the people.
18 All the people of the land went to
[a]the house of Baal, and tore it down;
[b]his altars and his images they broke in
pieces thoroughly, and [c]killed Mattan
the priest of Baal before the altars. And
the priest appointed [1]officers over the
house of the LORD.
19 He took the captains of hundreds
and the [a]Carites and the [1]guards and all
the people of the land; and they brought
the king down from the house of the
LORD, and came by the way of [b]the gate
of the [1]guards to the king's house. And
he sat on the throne of the kings.
20 So [a]all the people of the land rejoiced and the city was quiet. For they
had put Athaliah to death with the sword
at the king's house.
21 ¶ [1a]Jehoash was seven years old
when he became king.

Joash (Jehoash) Reigns over Judah

12 In the seventh year of Jehu, [a]Je-
hoash became king, and he
reigned forty years in Jerusalem; and his
mother's name was Zibiah of Beersheba.
2 Jehoash did right in the sight of the
LORD all his days in which Jehoiada the
priest instructed him.
3 Only [a]the high places were not
taken away; the people still sacrificed and
burned incense on the high places.

The Temple to Be Repaired

4 ¶ Then Jehoash said to the priests,
"All the money of the sacred things
[a]which is brought into the house of the
LORD, in current money, *both* [b]the mon-

ey of each man's assessment *and* all the
money [1]which any man's heart prompts
him to bring into the house of the LORD,
5 let the priests take it for themselves, each from his acquaintance; and
they shall repair the [1]damages of the
house wherever any damage may be
found."
6 ¶ But it came about that in the
twenty-third year of King Jehoash [a]the
priests had not repaired the damages of
the house.
7 Then King Jehoash called for Jehoiada the priest, and for the *other* priests
and said to them, "Why do you not repair
the damages of the house? Now therefore
take no *more* money from your acquaintances, but pay it for the damages of the
house."
8 So the priests agreed that they
would take no *more* money from the people, nor repair the damages of the house.
9 ¶ But [a]Jehoiada the priest took a
chest and bored a hole in its lid and put
it beside the altar, on the right side as one
comes into the house of the LORD; and
the priests who guarded the threshold
put in it all the money which was brought
into the house of the LORD.
10 When they saw that there was
much money in the chest, [a]the king's
scribe and the high priest came up and
tied *it* in bags and counted the money
which was found in the house of the
LORD.
11 They gave the money which was
weighed out into the hands of those who
did the work, who had the oversight of
the house of the LORD; and they [1]paid it
out to the carpenters and the builders
who worked on the house of the LORD;
12 and [a]to the masons and the stonecutters, and for buying timber and hewn
stone to repair the damages to the house
of the LORD, and for all that was [1]laid out
for the house to repair it.
13 But [a]there were not made for the
house of the LORD [b]silver cups, snuffers,
bowls, trumpets, any vessels of gold, or
vessels of silver from the money which
was brought into the house of the LORD;
14 for they gave that to those who did
the work, and with it they repaired the
house of the LORD.
15 Moreover, [a]they did not require an
accounting from the men into whose
hand they gave the money to pay to those
who did the work, for they dealt faithfully.
16 The [a]money from the guilt offerings and [b]the money from the sin offerings was not brought into the house of
the LORD; [c]it was for the priests.
17 ¶ Then [a]Hazael king of Aram went
up and fought against Gath and captured
it, and [b]Hazael set his face to go up to
Jerusalem.
18 [a]Jehoash king of Judah took all the
sacred things that Jehoshaphat and Jehoram and Ahaziah, his fathers, kings of
Judah, had dedicated, and [b]his own sacred things and all the gold that was
found among the treasuries of the house
of the LORD and of the king's house, and
sent *them* to Hazael king of Aram. Then
he went away from Jerusalem.

Joash (Jehoash) Succeeded by Amaziah in Judah

19 ¶ Now the rest of the acts of Joash
and all that he did, are they not written
in the Book of the Chronicles of the Kings
of Judah?
20 [a]His servants arose and made a
conspiracy and [b]struck down Joash at
[c]the house of Millo *as he was* going
down to Silla.
21 For Jozacar the son of Shimeath and
Jehozabad the son of [a]Shomer, his servants, struck *him* and he died; and they
buried him with his fathers in the city of
David, and [b]Amaziah his son became
king in his place.

Kings of Israel: Jehoahaz and Jehoash

13 In the twenty-third year of Joash
the son of Ahaziah, king of Judah,
Jehoahaz the son of Jehu became king
over Israel at Samaria, *and he reigned*
seventeen years.
2 He did evil in the sight of the LORD,
and followed the sins of Jeroboam the son
of Nebat, [a]with which he made Israel
sin; he did not turn from them.
3 [a]So the anger of the LORD was kindled against Israel, and He gave them
continually into the hand of [b]Hazael king
of Aram, and into the hand of [c]Ben-
hadad the son of Hazael.
4 Then [a]Jehoahaz entreated the favor of the LORD, and the LORD listened to
him; for [b]He saw the oppression of Israel, how the king of Aram oppressed them.
5 The LORD gave Israel a [1a]deliver-
er, so that they [2]escaped from under the
hand of the Arameans; and the sons of
Israel lived in their tents as formerly.
6 Nevertheless they did not turn
away from the sins of the house of Jeroboam, [a]with which he made Israel sin, but
walked in [1]them; and [b]the Asherah also
remained standing in Samaria.
7 For he left to Jehoahaz of the [1]army
not more than fifty horsemen and ten
chariots and 10,000 footmen, for the

4 [1]Lit *which it comes into...to bring*
5 [1]Lit *breaches*, and so through v 12
6 [a]2 Chr 24:5
9 [a]Mark 12:41; Luke 21:1
10 [a]2 Sam 8:17; 2 Kin 19:2; 22:3, 4,12
11 [1]Lit *brought*
12 [1]Lit *went out* [a]2 Kin 22:5,6
13 [a]2 Chr 24:14 [b]1 Kin 7:48,50
15 [a]2 Kin 22:7; 1 Cor 4:2; 2 Cor 8:20
16 [a]Lev 5:15-18 [b]Lev 4:24,29 [c]Lev 7:7; Num 18:19
17 [a]1 Kin 19:17; 2 Kin 8:12; 10:32,33 [b]2 Chr 24:23,24
18 [a]1 Kin 14:26; 15:18; 2 Kin 16:8; 18:15,16 [b]2 Kin 12:4
20 [a]2 Chr 24:25-27 [b]2 Kin 14:5 [c]Judg 9:6; 2 Sam 5:9; 1 Kin 11:27
21 [a]2 Chr 24:26 [b]2 Kin 14:1
13:2 [a]1 Kin 12:26-33
3 [a]Judg 2:14 [b]2 Kin 12:17 [c]2 Kin 13:24,25
4 [a]Num 21:7-9 [b]Ex 3:7,9; 2 Kin 14:26
5 [1]Or *savior* [2]Lit *went out* [a]2 Kin 13:25; 14:25,27; Neh 9:27
6 [1]Lit *it* [a]2 Kin 13:2 [b]1 Kin 16:33
7 [1]Lit *people*

king of Aram had destroyed them and
[a]made them like the dust at threshing.
8 Now the rest of the acts of Jehoahaz, and all that he did and his might,
are they not written in the Book of the
Chronicles of the Kings of Israel?
9 And Jehoahaz slept with his fathers, and they buried him in Samaria;
and Joash his son became king in his
place.
10 ¶ In the thirty-seventh year of Joash king of Judah, Jehoash the son of Jehoahaz became king over Israel in Samaria, *and reigned* sixteen years.
11 He did evil in the sight of the LORD;
he did not turn away from all the sins of
Jeroboam the son of Nebat, with which
he made Israel sin, but he walked in
[1]them.
12 [a]Now the rest of the acts of Joash
and all that he did and his might with
which he fought against Amaziah king of
Judah, are they not written in the Book of
the Chronicles of the Kings of Israel?
13 So Joash slept with his fathers, and
Jeroboam sat on his throne; and Joash
was buried in Samaria with the kings of
Israel.

Death of Elisha

14 ¶ When Elisha [1]became sick with
the illness of which he was to die, Joash
the king of Israel came down to him and
wept over [2]him and said, "[a]My father,
my father, the chariots of Israel and its
horsemen!"
15 Elisha said to him, "Take a bow and
arrows." So he [1]took a bow and arrows.
16 Then he said to the king of Israel,
"Put your hand on the bow." And he put
his hand *on it,* then Elisha laid his hands
on the king's hands.
17 He said, "Open the window toward
the east," and he opened *it.* Then Elisha
said, "Shoot!" And he shot. And he said,
"The LORD'S arrow of victory, even the
arrow of victory over Aram; for you will
[1]defeat the Arameans at [a]Aphek until
you have [2]destroyed *them.*"
18 Then he said, "Take the arrows,"
and he took them. And he said to the king
of Israel, "Strike the ground," and he
struck *it* three times and [1]stopped.
19 So [a]the man of God was angry with
him and said, "You should have struck
five or six times, then you would have
struck Aram until you would have [1]de-
stroyed *it.* But now you shall strike Aram
[b]*only* three times."
20 ¶ Elisha died, and they buried him.
Now [a]the bands of the Moabites would
invade the land in the spring of the year.
21 As they were burying a man, behold, they saw a marauding band; and
they cast the man into the grave of Elisha.
And when the man [1]touched the bones
of Elisha he [a]revived and stood up on his
feet.
22 ¶ Now [a]Hazael king of Aram had
oppressed Israel all the days of Jehoahaz.
23 But the [a]LORD was gracious to
them and [b]had compassion on them and
turned to them because of [c]His covenant
with Abraham, Isaac, and Jacob, and
would not destroy them or cast them
from His presence until now.
24 ¶ When Hazael king of Aram died,
Ben-hadad his son became king in his
place.
25 Then [a]Jehoash the son of Jehoahaz
took again from the hand of Ben-hadad
the son of Hazael the cities which he had
taken in war from the hand of Jehoahaz
his father. [b]Three times Joash [1]defeated
him and recovered the cities of Israel.

Amaziah Reigns over Judah

14 [a]In the second year of Joash son
of Joahaz king of Israel, [b]Amaziah
the son of Joash king of Judah became
king.
2 He was twenty-five years old when
he became king, and he reigned twenty-
nine years in Jerusalem. And his mother's
name was Jehoaddin of Jerusalem.
3 He did right in the sight of the
LORD, yet not like David his father; he did
according to all that Joash his father had
done.
4 Only [a]the high places were not
taken away; [b]the people still sacrificed
and burned incense on the high places.
5 Now it came about, as soon as the
kingdom was firmly in his hand, that he
[1a]killed his servants who had slain the
king his father.
6 But the sons of the [1]slayers he did
not put to death, according to what is
written in the book of the Law of Moses,
as the LORD commanded, saying, "[a]The
fathers shall not be put to death for the
sons, nor the sons be put to death for the
fathers; but [b]each shall be put to death
for his own sin."
7 ¶ He [1]killed *of* Edom in [a]the Valley of Salt 10,000 and took [b]Sela by war,
and named it [c]Joktheel to this day.
8 ¶ [a]Then Amaziah sent messengers
to Jehoash, the son of Jehoahaz son of
Jehu, king of Israel, saying, "[b]Come, let
us face each other."
9 Jehoash king of Israel sent to Amaziah king of Judah, saying, "[a]The thorn
bush which was in Lebanon sent to the
cedar which was in Lebanon, saying,
'Give your daughter to my son in marriage.' But there passed by a wild beast

7 [a]Amos 1:3
11 [1]Lit *it*
12 [a]2 Kin 13:14-19; 14:8-15
14 [1]Lit *was sick with his sickness* [2]Lit *his face* [a]2 Kin 2:12
15 [1]Lit *took to himself*
17 [1]Lit *smite* [2]Lit *made an end of* [a]1 Kin 20:26
18 [1]Lit *stood*
19 [1]Lit *made an end of* [a]2 Kin 5:20 [b]2 Kin 13:25
20 [a]2 Kin 3:7; 24:2
21 [1]Lit *went and touched* [a]Matt 27:52
22 [a]2 Kin 8:12, 13
23 [a]2 Kin 14:27 [b]1 Kin 8:28 [c]Gen 13:16,17; 17:2-5
25 [1]Lit *smote* [a]2 Kin 10:32,33; 14:25 [b]2 Kin 13:18,19
14:1 [a]2 Chr 25:1 [b]2 Kin 13:10
4 [a]2 Kin 12:3 [b]2 Kin 16:4
5 [1]Lit *smote* [a]2 Kin 12:20
6 [1]Lit *smiters* [a]Deut 24:16 [b]Jer 31:30; Ezek 18:4,20
7 [1]Lit *smote* [a]2 Sam 8:13; 1 Chr 18:12; 2 Chr 25:11 [b]Is 16:1 [c]Josh 15:38
8 [a]2 Chr 25:17-24 [b]2 Sam 2:14-17
9 [a]Judg 9:8-15

that was in Lebanon, and trampled the thorn bush.

10 “[a]You have indeed [1]defeated Edom, and [b]your heart has [2]become proud. Enjoy your glory and stay at home; for why should you provoke trouble so that you, even you, would fall, and Judah with you?”

11 ¶ But Amaziah would not listen. So Jehoash king of Israel went up; and he and Amaziah king of Judah faced each other at [a]Beth-shemesh, which belongs to Judah.

12 Judah was defeated [1]by Israel, and [a]they fled each to his tent.

13 Then Jehoash king of Israel captured Amaziah king of Judah, the son of Jehoash the son of Ahaziah, at Beth-shemesh, and came to Jerusalem and tore down the wall of Jerusalem from [a]the Gate of Ephraim to [b]the Corner Gate, 400 [1]cubits.

14 [a]He took all the gold and silver and all the utensils which were found in the house of the LORD, and in the treasuries of the king's house, the hostages also, and returned to Samaria.

Jeroboam II Succeeds Jehoash in Israel

15 ¶ [a]Now the rest of the acts of Jehoash which he did, and his might and how he fought with Amaziah king of Judah, are they not written in the Book of the Chronicles of the Kings of Israel?

16 So Jehoash slept with his fathers and was buried in Samaria with the kings of Israel; and Jeroboam his son became king in his place.

Azariah (Uzziah) Succeeds Amaziah in Judah

17 ¶ [a]Amaziah the son of Joash king of Judah lived fifteen years after the death of Jehoash son of Jehoahaz king of Israel.

18 Now the rest of the acts of Amaziah, are they not written in the Book of the Chronicles of the Kings of Judah?

19 They conspired against him in Jerusalem, and he fled to [a]Lachish; but they sent after him to Lachish and killed him there.

20 Then they brought him on horses and he was buried at Jerusalem with his fathers in the city of David.

21 All the people of Judah took [1]Azariah, who *was* sixteen years old, and made him king in the place of his father Amaziah.

22 [a]He built Elath and restored it to Judah after the king slept with his fathers.

23 ¶ In the fifteenth year of Amaziah the son of Joash king of Judah, Jeroboam the son of Joash king of Israel became king in Samaria, *and reigned* forty-one years.

24 He did evil in the sight of the LORD; he did not depart from all the sins of Jeroboam the son of Nebat, which he made Israel sin.

25 [a]He restored the border of Israel from [b]the entrance of Hamath as far as [c]the Sea of the Arabah, according to the word of the LORD, the God of Israel, which He spoke [1]through His servant [d]Jonah the son of Amittai, the prophet, who was of [e]Gath-hepher.

26 For the [a]LORD saw the affliction of Israel, *which was* very bitter; for [b]there was neither bond nor free, nor was there any helper for Israel.

27 The [a]LORD did not say that He would blot out the name of Israel from under heaven, but He saved them by the hand of Jeroboam the son of Joash.

Zechariah Reigns over Israel

28 ¶ Now the rest of the acts of Jeroboam and all that he did and his might, how he fought and how he recovered for Israel, [a]Damascus and [b]Hamath, *which had belonged* to Judah, are they not written in the Book of the Chronicles of the Kings of Israel?

29 And Jeroboam slept with his fathers, even with the kings of Israel, and Zechariah his son became king in his place.

Series of Kings: Azariah (Uzziah) over Judah

15 [a]In the twenty-seventh year of Jeroboam king of Israel, Azariah son of Amaziah king of Judah became king.

2 He was [a]sixteen years old when he became king, and he reigned fifty-two years in Jerusalem; and his mother's name was [1]Jecoliah of Jerusalem.

3 He did right in the sight of the LORD, according to all that his father Amaziah had done.

4 Only [a]the high places were not taken away; the people still sacrificed and burned incense on the high places.

5 [a]The LORD struck the king, so that he was a leper to the day of his death. And he [b]lived in a separate house, [1]while Jotham the king's son was over the household, judging the people of the land.

6 Now the rest of the acts of Azariah and all that he did, are they not written in the Book of the Chronicles of the Kings of Judah?

7 And Azariah slept with his fathers,

---

10 [1]Lit *smitten* [2]Lit *lifted you up* [a]2 Kin 14:7 [b]Deut 8:14; 2 Chr 26:16

11 [a]Josh 19:38

12 [1]Lit *before* [a]2 Sam 18:17

13 [1]I.e. One cubit equals approx 18 in. [a]Neh 8:16; 12:39 [b]2 Chr 25:23

14 [a]1 Kin 14:26; 2 Kin 12:18

15 [a]2 Kin 13:12,13

17 [a]2 Chr 25:25-28

19 [a]Josh 10:31; 2 Kin 18:14,17

21 [1]In 2 Chr 26:1, *Uzziah*

22 [a]1 Kin 9:26; 2 Kin 16:6; 2 Chr 8:17

25 [1]Lit *by* [a]2 Kin 10:32; 13:25 [b]1 Kin 8:65 [c]Deut 3:17 [d]Jon 1:1; Matt 12:39,40 [e]Josh 19:13

26 [a]2 Kin 13:4 [b]Deut 32:36

27 [a]2 Kin 13:23

28 [a]1 Kin 11:24 [b]2 Chr 8:3

15:1 [a]2 Kin 14:17

2 [1]In 2 Chr 26:3, *Jechiliah* [a]2 Chr 26:3,4

4 [a]2 Kin 12:3

5 [1]Lit *and* [a]2 Chr 26:21-23 [b]Lev 13:46; Num 12:14

and they buried him with his fathers in the city of David, and Jotham his son became king in his place.

Zechariah over Israel

8 ¶ [a]In the thirty-eighth year of Azariah king of Judah, Zechariah the son of Jeroboam became king over Israel in Samaria *for* six months.

9 He did evil in the sight of the LORD, as his fathers had done; he did not depart from the sins of Jeroboam the son of Nebat, which he made Israel sin.

10 Then Shallum the son of Jabesh conspired against him and [a]struck him before the people and [1]killed him, and reigned in his place.

11 Now the rest of the acts of Zechariah, behold they are written in the Book of the Chronicles of the Kings of Israel.

12 This is [a]the word of the LORD which He spoke to Jehu, saying, "Your sons to the fourth generation shall sit on the throne of Israel." And so it was.

13 ¶ Shallum son of Jabesh became king in the [a]thirty-ninth year of Uzziah king of Judah, and he reigned one month in [b]Samaria.

14 Then Menahem son of Gadi went up from [a]Tirzah and came to Samaria, and struck Shallum son of Jabesh in Samaria, and killed him and became king in his place.

15 Now the rest of the acts of Shallum and his conspiracy which he made, behold they are written in the Book of the Chronicles of the Kings of Israel.

16 Then Menahem struck Tiphsah and all who were in it and its borders from Tirzah, because they did not open *to him;* therefore he struck *it* and ripped up [a]all its women who were with child.

Menahem over Israel

17 ¶ In the [a]thirty-ninth year of Azariah king of Judah, Menahem son of Gadi became king over Israel *and reigned* ten years in Samaria.

18 He did evil in the sight of the LORD; he did not depart all his days from the sins of Jeroboam the son of Nebat, which he made Israel sin.

19 ¶ [a]Pul, king of Assyria, came against the land, and Menahem gave Pul a thousand talents of silver so that his hand might be with him to [b]strengthen the kingdom [1]under his rule.

20 Then Menahem exacted the money from Israel, even from all the mighty men of wealth, from each man fifty shekels of silver to pay the king of Assyria. So the king of Assyria returned and did not remain there in the land.

21 Now the rest of the acts of Menahem and all that he did, are they not written in the Book of the Chronicles of the Kings of Israel?

22 And Menahem slept with his fathers, and Pekahiah his son became king in his place.

Pekahiah over Israel

23 ¶ In [a]the fiftieth year of Azariah king of Judah, Pekahiah son of Menahem became king over Israel in Samaria, *and reigned* two years.

24 He did evil in the sight of the LORD; he did not depart from the sins of Jeroboam son of Nebat, which he made Israel sin.

25 Then Pekah son of Remaliah, his officer, conspired against him and struck him in Samaria, in [a]the castle of the king's house with Argob and Arieh; and with him were fifty men of the Gileadites, and he killed him and became king in his place.

26 Now the rest of the acts of Pekahiah and all that he did, behold they are written in the Book of the Chronicles of the Kings of Israel.

Pekah over Israel

27 ¶ In [a]the fifty-second year of Azariah king of Judah, [b]Pekah son of Remaliah became king over Israel in Samaria, *and reigned* twenty years.

28 He did evil in the sight of the LORD; he did not depart from the sins of Jeroboam son of Nebat, which he made Israel sin.

29 ¶ In the days of Pekah king of Israel, [1a]Tiglath-pileser king of Assyria came and [2]captured Ijon and Abel-beth-maacah and Janoah and Kedesh and Hazor and Gilead and Galilee, all the land of Naphtali; and [b]he carried them captive to Assyria.

30 And Hoshea the son of Elah made a conspiracy against Pekah the son of Remaliah, and struck him and put him to death and became king in his place, in the twentieth year of Jotham the son of Uzziah.

31 Now the rest of the acts of Pekah and all that he did, behold, they are written in the Book of the Chronicles of the Kings of Israel.

Jotham over Judah

32 ¶ In the second year of Pekah the son of Remaliah king of Israel, Jotham the son of [1]Uzziah king of Judah became king.

33 [a]He was twenty-five years old when he became king, and he reigned sixteen years in Jerusalem; and his moth-

8 [a]2 Kin 15:1
10 [1]Lit *smote* [a]Amos 7:9
12 [a]2 Kin 10:30
13 [a]2 Kin 15:1, 8 [b]1 Kin 16:24
14 [a]1 Kin 14:17
16 [a]2 Kin 8:12; Hos 13:16
17 [a]2 Kin 15:1, 8,13
19 [1]Lit *in his hand* [a]1 Chr 5:25,26 [b]2 Kin 14:5
23 [a]2 Kin 15:1, 8,13,17
25 [a]1 Kin 16:18
27 [a]2 Kin 15:23 [b]2 Chr 28:6; Is 7:1
29 [1]In 1 Chr 5:6, 26, *Tilgath-pilneser* [2]Lit *took* [a]2 Kin 15:19 [b]2 Kin 17:6
32 [1]I.e. Azariah
33 [a]2 Chr 27:1

er's name *was* Jerusha the daughter of Zadok.

34 [a]He did what was right in the sight of the LORD; he did according to all that his father Uzziah had done.

35 Only [a]the high places were not taken away; the people still sacrificed and burned incense on the high places. [b]He built the upper gate of the house of the LORD.

36 Now the rest of the acts of Jotham and all that he did, are they not written in the Book of the Chronicles of the Kings of Judah?

37 In those days [a]the LORD began to send Rezin king of Aram and Pekah the son of Remaliah against Judah.

38 And Jotham slept with his fathers, and he was buried with his fathers in the city of David his father; and Ahaz his son became king in his place.

Ahaz Reigns over Judah

16 In the seventeenth year of Pekah the son of Remaliah, [a]Ahaz the son of Jotham, king of Judah, became king.

2 [a]Ahaz *was* twenty years old when he became king, and he reigned sixteen years in Jerusalem; and he did not do what was right in the sight of the LORD his God, as his father David *had done.*

3 But he walked in the way of the kings of Israel, [a]and even made his son pass through the fire, [b]according to the abominations of the nations whom the LORD had [1]driven out from before the sons of Israel.

4 He [a]sacrificed and burned incense on the high places and on the hills and under every green tree.

5 ¶ Then [a]Rezin king of Aram and Pekah son of Remaliah, king of Israel, came up to Jerusalem to *wage* war; and they besieged Ahaz, [b]but could not [1]overcome him.

6 At that time Rezin king of Aram recovered [a]Elath for Aram, and cleared the Judeans out of [1]Elath entirely; and the [2]Arameans came to Elath and have lived there to this day.

Ahaz Seeks Help of Aram

7 ¶ [a]So Ahaz sent messengers to [b]Tiglath-pileser king of Assyria, saying, "I am your servant and your son; come up and deliver me from the [1]hand of the king of Aram and from the [1]hand of the king of Israel, who are rising up against me."

8 [a]Ahaz took the silver and gold that was found in the house of the LORD and in the treasuries of the king's house, and sent a present to the king of Assyria.

9 [a]So the king of Assyria listened to him; and the king of Assyria went up against Damascus and [b]captured it, and carried *the people of* it away into exile to [c]Kir, and put Rezin to death.

Damascus Falls

10 ¶ Now King Ahaz went to Damascus to meet [a]Tiglath-pileser king of Assyria, and saw the altar which *was* at Damascus; and King Ahaz sent to [b]Urijah the priest the [1]pattern of the altar and its model, according to all its workmanship.

11 So Urijah the priest built an altar; according to all that King Ahaz had sent from Damascus, thus Urijah the priest made *it,* [1]before the coming of King Ahaz from Damascus.

12 When the king came from Damascus, the king saw the altar; then [a]the king approached the altar and [1]went up to it,

13 and [1]burned his burnt offering and his meal offering, and poured his drink offering and sprinkled the blood of his peace offerings on the altar.

14 [a]The bronze altar, which *was* before the LORD, [1]he brought from the front of the house, from between [b]*his* altar and the house of the LORD, and he put it on the north side of *his* altar.

15 Then King Ahaz [1]commanded Urijah the priest, saying, "Upon the great altar [2]burn [a]the morning burnt offering and the evening meal offering and the king's burnt offering and his meal offering, with the burnt offering of all the people of the land and their meal offering and their drink offerings; and sprinkle on it all the blood of the burnt offering and all the blood of the sacrifice. But [b]the bronze altar shall be for me to inquire *by.*"

16 So Urijah the priest did according to all that King Ahaz commanded.

17 ¶ Then King Ahaz [a]cut off the borders of the stands, and removed the laver from them; he also [b]took down the sea from the bronze oxen which were under it and put it on a pavement of stone.

18 The covered way for the sabbath which they had built in the house, and the outer entry of the king, he removed from the house of the LORD because of the king of Assyria.

Hezekiah Reigns over Judah

19 Now the rest of the acts of Ahaz which he did, are they not written [a]in the Book of the Chronicles of the Kings of Judah?

20 So [a]Ahaz slept with his fathers, and [b]was buried with his fathers in the city of David; and his son Hezekiah reigned in his place.

34 [a]2 Kin 15:3, 4; 2 Chr 26:4,5
35 [a]2 Kin 12:3 [b]2 Chr 23:20; 27:3
37 [a]2 Kin 16:5; Is 7:1
16:1 [a]2 Chr 28:1
2 [a]2 Chr 28:1-4
3 [1]Or *dispossessed* [a]Lev 18:21; 2 Kin 17:17; 21:6 [b]Deut 12:31; 2 Kin 21:2,11
4 [a]Deut 12:2; 2 Kin 14:4
5 [1]Lit *fight* [a]2 Kin 15:37; Is 7:1 [b]2 Chr 28:5, 6
6 [1]Heb *Eloth* [2]So with some ancient versions; Heb *Edomites* [a]2 Kin 14:22; 2 Chr 26:2
7 [1]Lit *palm* [a]2 Chr 28:16 [b]2 Kin 15:29
8 [a]2 Kin 12:17, 18; 18:15
9 [a]2 Chr 28:21 [b]Amos 1:3-5 [c]Is 22:6; Amos 9:7
10 [1]Lit *likeness* [a]2 Kin 15:29 [b]Is 8:2
11 [1]Lit *until*
12 [1]Or *offered on it* [a]2 Chr 26:16,19
13 [1]Lit *offered in smoke*
14 [1]Lit *he also* [a]Ex 27:1,2; 40:6,29; 2 Chr 4:1 [b]2 Kin 16:11
15 [1]Lit *commanded him, Urijah* [2]Lit *offer in smoke* [a]Ex 29:39-41 [b]2 Kin 16:14
17 [a]1 Kin 7:27, 28,38 [b]1 Kin 7:23,25
19 [a]2 Chr 28:26
20 [a]Is 14:28 [b]2 Chr 28:27

Hoshea Reigns over Israel

17 In the twelfth year of Ahaz king of Judah, [a]Hoshea the son of Elah became king over Israel in Samaria, *and reigned* nine years.

2 He did evil in the sight of the LORD, only not as the kings of Israel who were before him.

3 [a]Shalmaneser king of Assyria came up [b]against him, and Hoshea became his servant and paid him tribute.

4 But the king of Assyria found conspiracy in Hoshea, who had sent messengers to So king of Egypt and had offered no tribute to the king of Assyria, as *he had done* year by year; so the king of Assyria shut him up and bound him in prison.

5 ¶ Then the king of Assyria invaded the whole land and went up to [a]Samaria and besieged it three years.

Israel Captive

6 In the ninth year of Hoshea, [a]the king of Assyria captured Samaria and [b]carried Israel away into exile to Assyria, and [c]settled them in Halah and Habor, *on* the river of [d]Gozan, and [e]in the cities of the Medes.

Why Israel Fell

7 ¶ Now [a]*this* came about because the sons of Israel had sinned against the LORD their God, [b]who had brought them up from the land of Egypt from under the hand of Pharaoh, king of Egypt, [c]and they had [1]feared other gods

8 and [a]walked in the [1]customs of the nations whom the LORD had driven out before the sons of Israel, and *in the customs* [b]of the kings of Israel which they had [2]introduced.

9 The sons of Israel [1]did things secretly which were not right against the LORD their God. Moreover, they built for themselves high places in all their towns, from [a]watchtower to fortified city.

10 [a]They set for themselves *sacred* pillars and [1b]Asherim on every high hill and under every green tree,

11 and there they burned incense on all the high places as the nations *did* which the LORD had carried away to exile before them; and they did evil things provoking the LORD.

12 They served idols, [a]concerning which the LORD had said to them, "You shall not do this thing."

13 Yet the [a]LORD warned Israel and Judah [b]through all His prophets *and* [c]every seer, saying, "[d]Turn from your evil ways and keep My commandments, My statutes according to all the law which I commanded your fathers, and which I sent to you through My servants the prophets."

14 However, they did not listen, but [a]stiffened their neck [1]like their fathers, who did not believe in the LORD their God.

15 [a]They rejected His statutes and [b]His covenant which He made with their fathers and His warnings with which He warned them. And [c]they followed vanity and [d]became vain, and *went* after the nations which surrounded them, concerning which the [e]LORD had commanded them not to do like them.

16 They forsook all the commandments of the LORD their God and made for themselves molten images, *even* [a]two calves, and [b]made an [1]Asherah and [c]worshiped all the host of heaven and [d]served Baal.

17 Then [a]they made their sons and their daughters pass through the fire, and [b]practiced divination and enchantments, and [c]sold themselves to do evil in the sight of the LORD, provoking Him.

18 So the LORD was very angry with Israel and [a]removed them from His [1]sight; [b]none was left except the tribe of Judah.

19 ¶ Also [a]Judah did not keep the commandments of the LORD their God, but [b]walked in the [1]customs [2]which Israel had [3]introduced.

20 The LORD rejected all the [1]descendants of Israel and afflicted them and [a]gave them into the hand of plunderers, until He had cast them [2]out of His sight.

21 ¶ When [a]He had torn Israel from the house of David, [b]they made Jeroboam the son of Nebat king. Then [c]Jeroboam drove Israel away from following the LORD and made them [1]commit a great sin.

22 The sons of Israel walked in all the sins of Jeroboam which he did; they did not depart from them

23 [a]until the LORD removed Israel from His sight, [b]as He spoke through all His servants the prophets. [a]So Israel was carried away into exile from their own land to Assyria until this day.

Cities of Israel Filled with Strangers

24 ¶ [a]The king of Assyria brought *men* from Babylon and from Cuthah and from [1b]Avva and from [c]Hamath and Sephar-vaim, and settled *them* in the cities of Samaria in place of the sons of Israel. So they possessed Samaria and lived in its cities.

25 At the beginning of their living there, they [a]did not fear the LORD; there-

---

17:1 [a]2 Kin 15:30

3 [a]Hos 10:14 [b]2 Kin 18:9-12

5 [a]Hos 13:16

6 [a]Hos 13:16 [b]Deut 28:64; 29:27,28 [c]2 Kin 18:11; 1 Chr 5:26 [d]Is 37:12 [e]Is 13:17; 21:2

7 [1]Lit *revered,* and so throughout the ch [a]Josh 23:16 [b]Ex 14:15-30 [c]Judg 6:10

8 [1]Lit *statutes* [2]Lit *made* [a]Lev 18:3; Deut 18:9 [b]2 Kin 16:3; 17:19

9 [1]Or *uttered words which* [a]2 Kin 18:8

10 [1]I.e. wooden symbols of a female deity [a]Ex 34:12-14 [b]1 Kin 14:23; Mic 5:14

12 [a]Ex 20:4

13 [a]Neh 9:29, 30 [b]2 Kin 17:23 [c]1 Sam 9:9 [d]Jer 7:3-7; 18:11; Ezek 18:31

14 [1]Lit *like the neck of* [a]Ex 32:9; 33:3; Acts 7:51

15 [a]Jer 8:9 [b]Ex 24:6-8; Deut 29:25 [c]Deut 32:21 [d]Jer 2:5; Rom 1:21-23 [e]Deut 12:30,31

16 [1]I.e. a wooden symbol of a female deity [a]1 Kin 12:28 [b]1 Kin 14:15,23 [c]Deut 4:19; 2 Kin 21:3 [d]1 Kin 16:31

17 [a]2 Kin 16:3 [b]Lev 19:26; Deut 18:10-12 [c]1 Kin 21:20

18 [1]Lit *face* [a]2 Kin 17:6 [b]1 Kin 11:13,32, 36

19 [1]Lit *statutes* [2]Lit *of Israel which they* [3]Lit *made* [a]1 Kin 14:22,23 [b]2 Kin 16:3

20 [1]Lit *seed* [2]Lit *from His face* [a]2 Kin 15:29

21 [1]Lit *sin* [a]1 Kin 11:11,31 [b]1 Kin 12:20 [c]1 Kin 12:28-33

23 [a]2 Kin 17:6 [b]2 Kin 17:13

24 [1]In 2 Kin 18:34, *Ivvah* [a]Ezra 4:2,10 [b]2 Kin 18:34 [c]1 Kin 8:65

25 [a]2 Kin 17:32-41

fore the LORD sent lions among them
which killed some of them.
26 So they spoke to the king of Assyria,
saying, "The nations whom you have carried away into exile in the cities of Samaria do not know the custom of the god
of the land; so he has sent lions among
them, and behold, they kill them because
they do not know the custom of the god
of the land."
27 ¶ Then the king of Assyria commanded, saying, "Take there one of the
priests whom you carried away into [1]ex-
ile and let [2]him go and live there; and let
him teach them the custom of the god of
the land."
28 So one of the priests whom they
had carried away into exile from Samaria
came and lived at Bethel, and taught
them how they should fear the LORD.
29 ¶ But every nation still made gods
of its own and put them [a]in the houses
of the high places which the people of
Samaria had made, every nation in their
cities in which they lived.
30 [a]The men of Babylon made
Succoth-benoth, the men of Cuth made
Nergal, the men of Hamath made
Ashima,
31 and the Avvites made Nibhaz and
Tartak; and [a]the Sepharvites burned
their children in the fire to [b]Adramme-
lech and Anammelech the gods of [c]Seph-
arvaim.
32 [a]They also feared the LORD and
[1b]appointed from among themselves
priests of the high places, who acted for
them in the houses of the high places.
33 They feared the LORD and served
their own gods according to the custom of
the nations from among whom they had
been carried away into exile.
34 ¶ To this day they do according to
the earlier customs: they do not fear the
LORD, nor do they [1]follow their statutes
or their ordinances or the law, or the
commandments which the LORD commanded the sons of Jacob, [a]whom He
named Israel;
35 with whom the LORD made a covenant and commanded them, saying,
"[a]You shall not fear other gods, nor
[b]bow down yourselves to them nor
[c]serve them nor sacrifice to them.
36 "But the LORD, [a]who brought you
up from the land of Egypt with great power and with [b]an outstretched arm, [c]Him
you shall fear, and to Him you shall bow
yourselves down, and to Him you shall
sacrifice.
37 "The statutes and the ordinances
and the law and the commandment
which He wrote for you, [a]you shall observe to do forever; and you shall not fear
other gods.
38 "The covenant that I have made
with you, [a]you shall not forget, nor shall
you fear other gods.
39 "But the LORD your God you shall
fear; and He will deliver you from the
hand of all your enemies."
40 However, they did not listen, but
they did according to their earlier custom.
41 [a]So while these nations feared the
LORD, they also served their [1]idols; their
children likewise and their grandchildren, as their fathers did, so they do to
this day.

Hezekiah Reigns over Judah

18 Now it came about [a]in the third
year of Hoshea, the son of Elah
king of Israel, that [b]Hezekiah the son of
Ahaz king of Judah became king.
2 He was [a]twenty-five years old
when he became king, and he reigned
twenty-nine years in Jerusalem; and his
mother's name was Abi the daughter of
Zechariah.
3 [a]He did right in the sight of the
LORD, according to all that his father David had done.
4 [a]He removed the high places and
broke down the *sacred* pillars and cut
down the [1]Asherah. He also broke in
pieces [b]the bronze serpent that Moses
had made, for until those days the sons of
Israel burned incense to it; and it was
called [2]Nehushtan.
5 [a]He trusted in the LORD, the God
of Israel; [b]so that after him there was
none like him among all the kings of Judah, nor *among those* who were before
him.
6 For he [a]clung to the LORD; he did
not depart from following Him, but kept
His commandments, which the LORD had
commanded Moses.

Hezekiah Victorious

7 [a]And the LORD was with him;
wherever he went he prospered. And
[b]he rebelled against the king of Assyria
and did not serve him.
8 [a]He [1]defeated the Philistines as
far as Gaza and its territory, from [b]watch-
tower to fortified city.
9 ¶ Now in the fourth year of King
Hezekiah, which was the seventh year of
Hoshea son of Elah king of Israel, [a]Shal-
maneser king of Assyria came up against
Samaria and besieged it.
10 At the end of three years they captured it; in the sixth year of Hezekiah,
which was [a]the ninth year of Hoshea
king of Israel, Samaria was captured.

27 [1]Lit *exile from there* [2]Lit *them*
29 [a]1 Kin 12:31; 13:32
30 [a]2 Kin 17:24
31 [a]2 Kin 17:17 [b]2 Kin 19:37 [c]2 Kin 17:24
32 [1]Lit *made for themselves from among* [a]Zeph 1:5 [b]1 Kin 12:31
34 [1]Lit *do according to* [a]Gen 32:28; 35:10
35 [a]Judg 6:10 [b]Ex 20:5 [c]Deut 5:9
36 [a]Ex 14:15-30 [b]Ex 6:6; 9:15 [c]Lev 19:32; Deut 6:13
37 [a]Deut 5:32
38 [a]Deut 4:23; 6:12
41 [1]Or *graven images* [a]Zeph 1:5; Matt 6:24
18:1 [a]2 Kin 16:2; 17:1 [b]2 Chr 28:27
2 [a]2 Chr 29:1,2
3 [a]2 Kin 20:3; 2 Chr 31:20
4 [1]I.e. a wooden symbol of a female deity [2]I.e. a piece of bronze [a]2 Kin 18:22; 2 Chr 31:1 [b]Num 21:8,9
5 [a]2 Kin 19:10 [b]2 Kin 23:25
6 [a]Deut 10:20; Josh 23:8
7 [a]Gen 39:2,3; 1 Sam 18:14 [b]2 Kin 16:7
8 [1]Lit *smote* [a]2 Chr 28:18; Is 14:29 [b]2 Kin 17:9
9 [a]2 Kin 17:3-7
10 [a]2 Kin 17:6

11 Then the king of Assyria carried Israel away into exile to Assyria, and put them in [a]Halah and on the Habor, the river of Gozan, and in the cities of the Medes,

12 because they [a]did not obey the voice of the LORD their God, but transgressed His covenant, *even* all that Moses the servant of the LORD commanded; they would neither listen nor do *it.*

Invasion of Judah

13 ¶ [a]Now in the fourteenth year of King Hezekiah, Sennacherib king of Assyria came up against all the fortified cities of Judah and seized them.

14 Then Hezekiah king of Judah sent to the king of Assyria at Lachish, saying, "[a]I have done wrong. [1]Withdraw from me; whatever you [2]impose on me I will bear." So the king of Assyria [3]required of Hezekiah king of Judah three hundred talents of silver and thirty talents of gold.

15 [a]Hezekiah gave *him* all the silver which was found in the house of the LORD, and in the treasuries of the king's house.

16 At that time Hezekiah cut off *the gold from* the doors of the temple of the LORD, and *from* the doorposts which Hezekiah king of Judah had overlaid, and gave it to the king of Assyria.

17 ¶ Then the king of Assyria sent [a]Tartan and Rab-saris and Rabshakeh from Lachish to King Hezekiah with a large army to Jerusalem. So they went up and came to Jerusalem. And when they went up, they came and stood by the [b]conduit of the upper pool, which is on the highway of the [1]fuller's field.

18 When they called to the king, [a]Eliakim the son of Hilkiah, who was over the household, and [b]Shebnah the scribe and Joah the son of Asaph the recorder, came out to them.

19 ¶ Then Rabshakeh said to them, "Say now to Hezekiah, 'Thus says the great king, the king of Assyria, "[a]What is this confidence that you [1]have?

20 "You say (but *they are* [1]only empty words), '*I have* counsel and strength for the war.' Now on whom do you rely, [a]that you have rebelled against me?

21 "Now behold, you [1a]rely on the staff of this crushed reed, *even* on Egypt; on which if a man leans, it will go into his [2]hand and pierce it. So is Pharaoh king of Egypt to all who rely on him.

22 "But if you say to me, 'We trust in the LORD our God,' is it not He whose high places and [a]whose altars Hezekiah has taken away, and has said to Judah and to Jerusalem, 'You shall worship before this altar in Jerusalem'?

23 "Now therefore, [1]come, make a bargain with my master the king of Assyria, and I will give you two thousand horses, if you are able on your part to set riders on them.

24 "How then can you [1]repulse one [2]official of the least of my master's servants, and [3]rely on Egypt for chariots and for horsemen?

25 "Have I now come up [1]without the LORD's approval against this place to destroy it? The LORD said to me, 'Go up against this land and destroy it.' " ' "

26 ¶ Then Eliakim the son of Hilkiah, and Shebnah and Joah, said to Rabshakeh, "Speak now to your servants in Aramaic, for we [1]understand *it;* and do not speak with us in [2a]Judean in the hearing of the people who are on the wall."

27 But Rabshakeh said to them, "Has my master sent me only to your master and to you to speak these words, *and* not to the men who sit on the wall, *doomed* to eat their own dung and drink their own urine with you?"

28 ¶ Then Rabshakeh stood and cried with a loud voice in Judean, [1]saying, "Hear the word of the great king, the king of Assyria.

29 "Thus says the king, '[a]Do not let Hezekiah deceive you, for he will not be able to deliver you from [1]my hand;

30 nor let Hezekiah make you trust in the LORD, saying, "The LORD will surely deliver us, and this city will not be given into the hand of the king of Assyria."

31 'Do not listen to Hezekiah, for thus says the king of Assyria, "[1]Make your peace with me and come out to me, and eat [a]each of his vine and each of his fig tree and drink each of the waters of his own cistern,

32 until I come and take you away [a]to a land like your own land, a land of grain and new wine, a land of bread and vineyards, a land of olive trees and honey, that you may live and not die." But do not listen to Hezekiah when he misleads you, saying, "The LORD will deliver us."

33 '[a]Has any one of the gods of the nations delivered his land from the hand of the king of Assyria?

34 '[a]Where are the gods of Hamath and [b]Arpad? Where are the gods of Sepharvaim, Hena and [1c]Ivvah? Have they delivered Samaria from my hand?

35 'Who among all the gods of the lands [1]have delivered their land from my hand, [a]that the LORD should deliver Jerusalem from my hand?' "

36 ¶ But the people were silent and answered him not a word, for the king's

11 [a]1 Chr 5:26
12 [a]1 Kin 9:6; Dan 9:6,10
13 [a]2 Chr 32:1; Is 36:1-39:8
14 [1]Lit *Return* [2]Lit *give* [3]Lit *put on* [a]2 Kin 18:7
15 [a]1 Kin 15:18,19; 2 Kin 12:18; 16:8
17 [1]I.e. launderer's [a]Is 20:1 [b]2 Kin 20:20; Is 7:3
18 [a]2 Kin 19:2; Is 22:20 [b]Is 22:15
19 [1]Lit *trust* [a]2 Chr 32:10
20 [1]Lit *a word of the lips* [a]2 Kin 18:7
21 [1]Lit *rely for yourself* [2]Lit *palm* [a]Is 30:2,3, 7; Ezek 29:6,7
22 [a]2 Kin 18:4; 2 Chr 31:1
23 [1]Lit *please exchange pledges*
24 [1]Lit *turn away the face of* [2]Or *governor* [3]Lit *rely for yourself*
25 [1]Lit *without the LORD*
26 [1]Lit *hear* [2]I.e. Hebrew [a]Ezra 4:7; Dan 2:4
28 [1]Lit *and spoke, saying,*
29 [1]Heb *his* [a]2 Chr 32:15
31 [1]Lit *Make with me a blessing* [a]1 Kin 4:20, 25
32 [a]Deut 8:7-9; 11:12
33 [a]2 Kin 19:12; Is 10:10, 11
34 [1]In 2 Kin 17:24, *Avva* [a]2 Kin 19:13 [b]Is 10:9 [c]2 Kin 17:24
35 [1]Lit *who have* [a]Ps 2:1-3; 59:7

commandment was, "Do not answer
him."
37 Then [a]Eliakim the son of Hilkiah,
who was over the household, and Shebna
the scribe and Joah the son of Asaph, the
recorder, came to Hezekiah [b]with their
clothes torn and told him the words of
Rabshakeh.

Isaiah Encourages Hezekiah

19 [a]And when King Hezekiah heard
it, he [b]tore his clothes, [c]covered
himself with sackcloth and entered the
house of the LORD.
2 Then he sent Eliakim who was over
the household with Shebna the scribe
and the elders of the priests, [a]covered
with sackcloth, to [b]Isaiah the prophet
the son of Amoz.
3 They said to him, "Thus says Hezekiah, 'This day is a day of distress, rebuke,
and rejection; for children have come to
birth and there is no strength to *deliver.*
4 '[a]Perhaps the LORD your God will
hear all the words of Rabshakeh, whom
his master the king of Assyria has sent
[b]to reproach the living God, and will rebuke the words which the LORD your God
has heard. Therefore, offer a prayer for
[c]the remnant that is left.' "
5 So the servants of King Hezekiah
came to Isaiah.
6 Isaiah said to them, "Thus you shall
say to your master, 'Thus says the LORD,
"Do not be afraid because of the words
that you have heard, with which the
[a]servants of the king of Assyria [b]have
blasphemed Me.
7 "Behold, I will put a spirit in him so
that [a]he will hear a rumor and return to
his own land. And [b]I will make him fall
by the sword in his own land." ' "

Sennacherib Defies God

8 ¶ Then Rabshakeh returned and
found the king of Assyria fighting against
[a]Libnah, for he had heard that [1]the king
had left [b]Lachish.
9 When he heard *them* say concerning Tirhakah king of [1]Cush, "Behold, he
has come out to fight against you," he
sent messengers again to Hezekiah saying,
10 "Thus you shall say to Hezekiah king
of [1]Judah, 'Do not [a]let your God in
whom you trust deceive you saying, "[b]Je-
rusalem will not be given into the hand of
the king of Assyria."
11 'Behold, you have heard what the
kings of Assyria have done to all the
lands, destroying them completely. So
will you be [1]spared?
12 '[a]Did the gods of [1]those nations
which my fathers destroyed deliver them,

37 [a]2 Kin 18:26 [b]2 Kin 6:30

19:1 [a]2 Chr 32:20-22; Is 37:1 [b]2 Kin 18:37 [c]1 Kin 21:27

2 [a]2 Sam 3:31 [b]Is 1:1; 2:1

4 [a]Josh 14:12; 2 Sam 16:12 [b]2 Kin 18:35 [c]Is 1:9

6 [a]2 Kin 18:17 [b]2 Kin 18:22-25

7 [a]2 Kin 7:6 [b]2 Kin 19:37

8 [1]Lit *he* [a]Josh 10:29 [b]2 Kin 18:14

9 [1]Or *Ethiopia*

10 [1]Lit *Judah, saying,* [a]2 Kin 18:5 [b]2 Kin 18:30

11 [1]Lit *delivered*

12 [1]Lit *the* [a]2 Kin 18:33 [b]2 Kin 17:6 [c]Gen 11:31 [d]Is 37:12

13 [a]2 Kin 18:34

14 [1]Lit *letters...read them* [2]Lit *Hezekiah spread* [a]Is 37:14

15 [1]Lit *seated* [a]Ex 25:22; Is 37:14 [b]2 Kin 5:15

16 [a]Ps 31:2; Is 37:17 [b]1 Kin 8:29; 2 Chr 6:40 [c]2 Kin 19:4

18 [a]Is 44:9-20; Acts 17:29

19 [a]1 Kin 8:42, 43 [b]2 Kin 19:15

20 [a]2 Kin 20:5

21 [a]Jer 14:17; Lam 2:13 [b]Ps 109:25; Matt 27:39

22 [1]Lit *on high* [a]2 Kin 19:4 [b]2 Kin 19:6 [c]Is 5:24; 30:11-15

23 [a]2 Kin 18:17

even [b]Gozan and [c]Haran and Rezeph
and [d]the sons of Eden who *were* in Telassar?
13 '[a]Where is the king of Hamath, the
king of Arpad, the king of the city of Sepharvaim, and *of* Hena and Ivvah?' "

Hezekiah's Prayer

14 ¶ Then [a]Hezekiah took the [1]letter
from the hand of the messengers and
read it, and he went up to the house of
the LORD and [2]spread it out before the
LORD.
15 Hezekiah prayed before the LORD
and said, "O LORD, the God of Israel,
[a]who are [1]enthroned *above* the cherubim, [b]You are the God, You alone, of
all the kingdoms of the earth. You have
made heaven and earth.
16 "[a]Incline Your ear, O LORD, and
hear; [b]open Your eyes, O LORD, and see;
and listen to the words of Sennacherib,
which he has sent [c]to reproach the living
God.
17 "Truly, O LORD, the kings of Assyria
have devastated the nations and their
lands
18 and have cast their gods into the
fire, [a]for they were not gods but the
work of men's hands, wood and stone. So
they have destroyed them.
19 "Now, O LORD our God, I pray, deliver us from his hand [a]that all the kingdoms of the earth may know that You
alone, O [b]LORD, are God."

God's Answer through Isaiah

20 ¶ Then Isaiah the son of Amoz sent
to Hezekiah saying, "Thus says the LORD,
the God of Israel, 'Because you have
prayed to Me about Sennacherib king of
Assyria, [a]I have heard *you.*'
21 "This is the word that the LORD has
spoken against him:
'She has despised you and
mocked you,
[a]The virgin daughter of Zion;
She [b]has shaken *her* head
behind you,
The daughter of Jerusalem!
22 'Whom have you [a]reproached
and [b]blasphemed?
And against whom have you
raised *your* voice,
And [1]haughtily lifted up your
eyes?
Against the [c]Holy One of Israel!
23 '[a]Through your messengers you
have reproached the Lord,
And you have said, "With my
many chariots
I came up to the heights of the
mountains,

To the remotest parts of
Lebanon;
And I [1]cut down its tall cedars
and its choice cypresses.
And I [1]entered its farthest
lodging place, its [b]thickest
forest.
24 "I dug *wells* and drank foreign
waters,
And with the sole of my feet I
[1a]dried up
All the rivers of [2]Egypt."
25 ¶ '[a]Have you not heard?
Long ago I did it;
From ancient times I planned it.
[b]Now I have brought it to pass,
That you should turn fortified
cities into ruinous heaps.
26 'Therefore their inhabitants were
short of strength,
They were dismayed and put to
shame;
They were [a]as the vegetation of
the field and as the green
herb,
As grass on the housetops is
scorched before it is
grown up.
27 'But [a]I know your sitting down,
And your going out and your
coming in,
And your raging against Me.
28 'Because of your raging
against Me,
And because your [1]arrogance
has come up to My ears,
Therefore I [a]will put My hook
in your nose,
And My bridle in your lips,
And [b]I will turn you back by the
way which you came.
29 ¶ 'Then this shall be [a]the sign for
you: [1]you will eat this year what grows of
itself, in the second year what springs
from the same, and in the third year sow,
reap, plant vineyards, and eat their fruit.
30 '[a]The surviving remnant of the
house of Judah will again take root downward and bear fruit upward.
31 'For out of Jerusalem will go forth a
remnant, and [a]out of Mount Zion [1]survi-
vors. [b]The zeal of [2]the LORD will perform this.
32 ¶ 'Therefore thus says the LORD
concerning the king of Assyria, "[a]He will
not come to this city or shoot an arrow
there; and he will not come before it
with a shield or throw up a siege ramp
against it.
33 "[a]By the way that he came, by the
same he will return, and he shall not
come to this city," ' declares the LORD.
34 '[a]For I will defend this city to save

23 [1]So with some ancient versions; M.T. *will cut...will enter* [b]2 Chr 26:10; Is 10:18
24 [1]So with some ancient versions; M.T. *will dry up* [2]Lit *the besieged place* [a]Is 19:6
25 [a]Is 45:7 [b]Is 10:5
26 [a]Ps 129:6
27 [a]Ps 139:1
28 [1]Lit *complacency* [a]Ezek 19:9; 29:4 [b]2 Kin 19:33,36
29 [1]Lit *eating* [a]Ex 3:12; 2 Kin 20:8,9
30 [a]2 Kin 19:4; 2 Chr 32:22,23
31 [1]Lit *those who escape* [2]Some ancient mss read *the LORD of hosts* [a]Is 10:20 [b]Is 9:7
32 [a]Is 8:7-10
33 [a]2 Kin 19:28
34 [a]2 Kin 20:6; Is 31:5 [b]1 Kin 11:12,13
35 [1]Lit *they* [2]Lit *dead bodies* [a]2 Sam 24:16; 2 Chr 32:21
36 [a]2 Kin 19:7, 28,33 [b]Jon 1:2
37 [1]Some ancient mss read *Adrammelech and Sharezer his sons smote him* [a]2 Kin 19:17,31 [b]Gen 8:4; Jer 51:27 [c]Ezra 4:2
20:1 [1]Lit *sick to the point of death* [a]2 Chr 32:24; Is 38:1-22 [b]2 Sam 17:23
3 [1]Lit *great weeping* [a]Neh 5:19; 13:14,22, 31 [b]2 Kin 18:3-6 [c]2 Sam 12:21,22
5 [a]1 Sam 9:16; 10:1 [b]2 Kin 19:20 [c]Ps 39:12
6 [1]Lit *days* [a]2 Kin 19:34
9 [a]Is 38:7
10 [1]Lit *said*
11 [a]Josh 10:12-14; Is 38:8

it for My own sake and [b]for My servant
David's sake.' "
35 ¶ [a]Then it happened that night
that the angel of the LORD went out and
struck 185,000 in the camp of the Assyrians; and when [1]men rose early in the
morning, behold, all of them were [2]dead.
36 So [a]Sennacherib king of Assyria
departed and returned *home,* and lived at
[b]Nineveh.
37 It came about as he was worshiping
in the house of Nisroch his god, that
[1a]Adrammelech and Sharezer killed
him with the sword; and they escaped
into [b]the land of Ararat. And [c]Esarhad-
don his son became king in his place.

Hezekiah's Illness and Recovery

20 [a]In those days Hezekiah became
[1]mortally ill. And Isaiah the
prophet the son of Amoz came to him and
said to him, "Thus says the LORD, '[b]Set
your house in order, for you shall die and
not live.' "
2 Then he turned his face to the wall
and prayed to the LORD, saying,
3 "[a]Remember now, O LORD, I beseech You, [b]how I have walked before
You in truth and with a whole heart and
have done what is good in Your sight."
And [c]Hezekiah wept [1]bitterly.
4 Before Isaiah had gone out of the
middle court, the word of the LORD came
to him, saying,
5 "Return and say to [a]Hezekiah the
leader of My people, 'Thus says the LORD,
the God of your father David, "[b]I have
heard your prayer, [c]I have seen your
tears; behold, I will heal you. On the
third day you shall go up to the house of
the LORD.
6 "I will add fifteen years to your [1]life,
and I will deliver you and this city from
the hand of the king of Assyria; and [a]I
will defend this city for My own sake and
for My servant David's sake." ' "
7 Then Isaiah said, "Take a cake of
figs." And they took and laid *it* on the
boil, and he recovered.
8 ¶ Now Hezekiah said to Isaiah,
"What will be the sign that the LORD will
heal me, and that I shall go up to the
house of the LORD the third day?"
9 Isaiah said, "[a]This shall be the sign
to you from the LORD, that the LORD will
do the thing that He has spoken: shall the
shadow go forward ten steps or go back
ten steps?"
10 So Hezekiah [1]answered, "It is easy
for the shadow to decline ten steps; no,
but let the shadow turn backward ten
steps."
11 Isaiah the prophet cried to the
LORD, and [a]He brought the shadow on

the [1]stairway back ten steps by which it
had gone down on the [1]stairway of Ahaz.

Hezekiah Shows Babylon His Treasures

12 ¶ [a]At that time [1]Berodach-baladan
a son of Baladan, king of Babylon, sent
letters and a present to Hezekiah, for he
heard that Hezekiah had been sick.
13 Hezekiah listened to them, and
showed them [a]all his treasure house, the
silver and the gold and the spices and the
precious oil and the house of his armor
and all that was found in his treasuries.
There was nothing in his house nor in all
his dominion that Hezekiah did not show
them.
14 Then Isaiah the prophet came to
King Hezekiah and said to him, "What
did these men say, and from where have
they come to you?" And Hezekiah said,
"They have come from a far country,
from Babylon."
15 He said, "What have they seen in
your house?" So Hezekiah [1]answered,
"They have seen all that is in my house;
there is nothing among my treasuries that
I have not shown them."
16 ¶ Then Isaiah said to Hezekiah,
"Hear the word of the LORD.
17 'Behold, the days are coming when
[a]all that is in your house, and all that
your fathers have laid up in store to this
day will be carried to Babylon; nothing
shall be left,' says the LORD.
18 'Some [a]of your sons who shall issue
from you, whom you will beget, will be
taken away; and they will become [b]offi-
cials in the palace of the king of Babylon.' "
19 Then Hezekiah said to Isaiah, "The
word of the LORD which you have spoken
is [a]good." For he [1]thought, "Is it not so,
if there will be peace and truth in my
days?"
20 ¶ [a]Now the rest of the acts of Hezekiah and all his might, and how he
[b]made the pool and the conduit and
brought water into the city, are they not
written in the Book of the Chronicles of
the Kings of Judah?
21 [a]So Hezekiah slept with his fathers, and Manasseh his son became king
in his place.

Manasseh Succeeds Hezekiah

21 [a]Manasseh was twelve years old
when he became king, and he
reigned fifty-five years in Jerusalem; and
his mother's name was Hephzibah.
2 [a]He did evil in the sight of the
LORD, [b]according to the abominations of
the nations whom the LORD dispossessed
before the sons of Israel.
3 For [a]he rebuilt the high places
which Hezekiah his father had destroyed;
and [b]he erected altars for Baal and made
an [1]Asherah, as Ahab king of Israel had
done, and [c]worshiped all the host of
heaven and served them.
4 [a]He built altars in the house of the
LORD, of which the LORD had said, "[b]In
Jerusalem I will put My name."
5 For he built altars for [a]all the host
of heaven in [b]the two courts of the house
of the LORD.
6 [a]He made his son pass through the
fire, [b]practiced witchcraft and used divination, and dealt with mediums and spiritists. He did much evil in the sight of the
LORD provoking *Him to anger.*
7 Then [a]he set the carved image of
Asherah that he had made, in the house
of which the LORD said to David and to
his son Solomon, "[b]In this house and in
Jerusalem, which I have chosen from all
the tribes of Israel, I will put My name
forever.
8 "And I [a]will not make the feet of
Israel wander anymore from the land
which I gave their fathers, if only they
will observe to do according to all that I
have commanded them, and according to
all the law that My servant Moses commanded them."
9 But they did not listen, and Manasseh [a]seduced them to do evil more than
the nations whom the LORD destroyed before the sons of Israel.

The King's Idolatries Rebuked

10 ¶ Now the LORD spoke through His
servants the prophets, saying,
11 "[a]Because Manasseh king of Judah
has done these abominations, [b]having
done wickedly more than all the Amorites did who *were* before him, and [c]has
also made Judah sin [d]with his idols;
12 therefore thus says the LORD, the
God of Israel, 'Behold, I am bringing *such*
calamity on Jerusalem and Judah, that
whoever hears of it, [a]both his ears will
tingle.
13 '[a]I will stretch over Jerusalem the
line of Samaria and the plummet of the
house of Ahab, and I will wipe Jerusalem
as one wipes a dish, wiping it and turning
it upside down.
14 'I will abandon the remnant of My
inheritance and deliver them into the
hand of their enemies, and they will become as plunder and spoil to all their enemies;
15 because they have done evil in My
sight, and have been provoking Me to

---

11 [1]Lit *steps*

12 [1]Many mss and ancient versions read *Merodach-baladan*; cf Is 39:1 [a]2 Chr 32:31; Is 39:1-8

13 [a]2 Chr 32:27

15 [1]Lit *said*

17 [a]2 Kin 24:13; 25:13-15; 2 Chr 36:10; Jer 52:17-19

18 [a]2 Kin 24:12; 2 Chr 33:11 [b]Dan 1:3-7

19 [1]Lit *said* [a]1 Sam 3:18

20 [a]2 Chr 32:32 [b]Neh 3:16

21 [a]2 Chr 32:33

21:1 [a]2 Chr 33:1-9

2 [a]Jer 15:4 [b]2 Kin 16:3

3 [1]I.e. a wooden symbol of a female deity [a]2 Kin 18:4 [b]1 Kin 16:31-33 [c]Deut 17:2-5; 2 Kin 17:16; 23:5

4 [a]2 Kin 16:10-16 [b]2 Sam 7:13; 1 Kin 8:29

5 [a]2 Kin 23:4,5 [b]1 Kin 7:12; 2 Kin 23:12

6 [a]Lev 18:21; 2 Kin 16:3; 17:17 [b]Lev 19:26,31; Deut 18:10-14

7 [a]Deut 16:21; 2 Kin 23:6 [b]1 Kin 8:29; 9:3; 2 Chr 7:12,16

8 [a]2 Sam 7:10; 2 Kin 18:11,12

9 [a]Prov 29:12

11 [a]2 Kin 21:2; 24:3,4 [b]Gen 15:16; 1 Kin 21:26 [c]2 Kin 21:16 [d]2 Kin 21:21

12 [a]1 Sam 3:11; Jer 19:3

13 [a]Is 34:11; Amos 7:7,8

anger since the day their fathers came
from Egypt, even to this day.' "
16 ¶ [a]Moreover, Manasseh shed very
much innocent blood until he had filled
Jerusalem from one end to another; besides his sin [b]with which he made Judah
sin, in doing evil in the sight of the LORD.
17 [a]Now the rest of the acts of Manasseh and all that he did and his sin which
he [1]committed, are they not written in
the Book of the Chronicles of the Kings of
Judah?
18 [a]And Manasseh slept with his fathers and was buried in the garden of his
own house, [b]in the garden of Uzza, and
Amon his son became king in his place.

Amon Succeeds Manasseh

19 ¶ [a]Amon was twenty-two years
old when he became king, and he reigned
two years in Jerusalem; and his mother's
name *was* Meshullemeth the daughter of
Haruz of Jotbah.
20 He did evil in the sight of the LORD,
[a]as Manasseh his father had done.
21 For he walked in all the way that
his father had walked, and served the
idols that his father had served and worshiped them.
22 So [a]he forsook the LORD, the God
of his fathers, and did not walk in the way
of the LORD.
23 [a]The servants of Amon conspired
against him and killed the king in his own
house.
24 Then [a]the people of the land
[1]killed all those who had conspired
against King Amon, and the people of the
land made Josiah his son king in his place.
25 Now the rest of the acts of Amon
which he did, are they not written in the
Book of the Chronicles of the Kings of
Judah?
26 He was buried in his grave [a]in the
garden of Uzza, and Josiah his son became king in his place.

Josiah Succeeds Amon

22 [a]Josiah was eight years old when
he became king, and he reigned
thirty-one years in Jerusalem; and his
mother's name *was* Jedidah the daughter
of Adaiah of [b]Bozkath.
2 He did right in the sight of the LORD
and walked in all the way of his father
David, nor did he [a]turn aside to the right
or to the left.
3 ¶ Now [a]in the eighteenth year of
King Josiah, the king sent Shaphan, the
son of Azaliah the son of Meshullam the
scribe, to the house of the LORD saying,
4 "[a]Go up to Hilkiah the high priest
that he may [1]count the money brought
in to the house of the LORD which the
doorkeepers have gathered from the people.
5 "[a]Let them deliver it into the hand
of the workmen who have the oversight
of the house of the LORD, and let them
give it to the workmen who are in the
house of the LORD to repair the [1]damages
of the house,
6 to the carpenters and the builders
and the masons and for buying timber
and hewn stone to repair the house.
7 "Only [a]no accounting shall be made
with them for the money delivered into
their hands, for they deal faithfully."

The Lost Book

8 ¶ Then Hilkiah the high priest said
to Shaphan the scribe, "[a]I have found
the book of the law in the house of the
LORD." And Hilkiah gave the book to Shaphan who read it.
9 Shaphan the scribe came to the
king and brought back word to the king
and said, "Your servants have emptied
out the money that was found in the
house, and have delivered it into the
hand of the workmen who have the oversight of the house of the LORD."
10 Moreover, Shaphan the scribe told
the king saying, "Hilkiah the priest has
given me a book." And Shaphan read it in
the presence of the king.
11 ¶ When the king heard the words
of the book of the law, [a]he tore his
clothes.
12 Then the king commanded Hilkiah
the priest, [a]Ahikam the son of Shaphan,
[1b]Achbor the son of Micaiah, Shaphan
the scribe, and Asaiah the king's servant
saying,
13 "Go, inquire of the LORD for me and
the people and all Judah concerning the
words of this book that has been found,
for [a]great is the wrath of the LORD that
burns against us, because our fathers
have not listened to the words of this
book, to do according to all that is written
concerning us."

Huldah Predicts

14 ¶ So Hilkiah the priest, Ahikam,
Achbor, Shaphan, and Asaiah went to
Huldah the prophetess, the wife of Shallum the son of [1a]Tikvah, the son of Harhas, keeper of the wardrobe (now she
lived in Jerusalem in the [b]Second Quarter); and they spoke to her.
15 She said to them, "Thus says the
LORD God of Israel, 'Tell the man who
sent you to me,
16 thus says the LORD, "Behold, I
[a]bring evil on this place and on its inhabitants, *even* all the words of the book
which the king of Judah has read.

16 [a]2 Kin 24:4 [b]2 Kin 21:11
17 [1]Lit *sinned* [a]2 Chr 33:11-19
18 [a]2 Chr 33:20 [b]2 Kin 21:26
19 [a]2 Chr 33:21-23
20 [a]2 Kin 21:2-6,11,16
22 [a]2 Kin 22:17; 1 Chr 28:9
23 [a]2 Kin 12:20; 14:19
24 [1]Lit *smote* [a]2 Kin 14:5
26 [a]2 Kin 21:18
22:1 [a]2 Chr 34:1 [b]Josh 15:39
2 [a]Deut 5:32; Josh 1:7
3 [a]2 Chr 34:8
4 [1]Or *total* [a]2 Kin 12:4,9,10
5 [1]Lit *breach* [a]2 Kin 12:11-14
7 [a]2 Kin 12:15; 1 Cor 4:2
8 [a]Deut 31:24-26; 2 Chr 34:14,15
11 [a]Gen 37:34; Josh 7:6
12 [1]In 2 Chr 34:20, *Abdon, son of Micah* [a]2 Kin 25:22; Jer 26:24 [b]2 Chr 34:20
13 [a]Deut 29:23-28; 31:17, 18
14 [1]In 2 Chr 34:22, *Tokhath, son of Hasrah* [a]2 Chr 34:22 [b]Zeph 1:10
16 [a]Deut 29:27; Dan 9:11-14

17 "[a]Because they have forsaken Me
and have burned incense to other gods
that they might provoke Me to anger with
all the work of their hands, therefore My
wrath burns against this place, and it
shall not be quenched." '
18 "But to [a]the king of Judah who sent
you to inquire of the LORD thus shall you
say to him, 'Thus says the LORD God of
Israel, "*Regarding* the words which you
have heard,
19 [a]because your heart was tender
and [b]you humbled yourself before the
LORD when you heard what I spoke
against this place and against its inhabitants that they should become [c]a desolation and a [d]curse, and you have [e]torn
your clothes and wept before Me, I truly
have heard you," declares the LORD.
20 "Therefore, behold, I will gather you
to your fathers, and [a]you will be gathered to your grave in peace, and your eyes
will not see all the evil which I will bring
on this place." ' " So they brought back
word to the king.

Josiah's Covenant

23 [a]Then the king sent, and they
gathered to him all the elders of
Judah and of Jerusalem.
2 The king went up to the house of
the LORD and all the men of Judah and all
the inhabitants of Jerusalem with him,
and the priests and the prophets and all
the people, both small and great; and [a]he
read in their hearing all the words of the
book of the covenant [b]which was found
in the house of the LORD.
3 [a]The king stood by the pillar and
made a covenant before the LORD, [b]to
walk after the LORD, and to keep His commandments and His testimonies and His
statutes with all *his* heart and all *his* soul,
to carry out the words of this covenant
that were written in this book. And all
the people [1]entered into the covenant.

Reforms under Josiah

4 ¶ Then the king commanded Hilki-
ah the high priest and [a]the priests of the
second order and the [1]doorkeepers, [b]to
bring out of the temple of the LORD all
the vessels that were made for Baal, for
[2]Asherah, and for all the host of heaven;
and [c]he burned them outside Jerusalem
in the fields of the Kidron, and carried
their ashes to Bethel.
5 He did away with the idolatrous
priests whom the kings of Judah had appointed to burn incense in the high
places in the cities of Judah and in the
surrounding area of Jerusalem, also those
who burned incense to Baal, to the sun
and to the moon and to the constellations
and to all the [a]host of heaven.
6 He brought out the Asherah from
the house of the LORD outside Jerusalem
to the brook Kidron, and burned it at the
brook Kidron, and [a]ground *it* to dust, and
[b]threw its dust on the graves of the
[1]common people.
7 He also broke down the houses of
the [a]*male* cult prostitutes which *were* in
the house of the LORD, where [b]the wom-
en were weaving [1]hangings for the Asherah.
8 Then he brought all the priests
from the cities of Judah, and defiled the
high places where the priests had burned
incense, from [a]Geba to Beersheba; and
he broke down the high places of the
gates which *were* at the entrance of the
gate of Joshua the governor of the city,
which *were* on one's left at the city gate.
9 Nevertheless [a]the priests of the
high places did not go up to the altar of
the LORD in Jerusalem, but they ate unleavened bread among their brothers.
10 [a]He also defiled [1]Topheth, which
is in the valley of the son of Hinnom,
[b]that no man might make his son or his
daughter pass through the fire for [c]Mo-
lech.
11 He did away with the horses which
the kings of Judah had given to the [a]sun,
at the entrance of the house of the LORD,
by the chamber of Nathan-melech the official, which *was* in the precincts; and he
burned the chariots of the sun with fire.
12 [a]The altars which *were* on the
roof, the upper chamber of Ahaz, which
the kings of Judah had made, and [b]the
altars which Manasseh had made in the
two courts of the house of the LORD, the
king broke down; and he [1]smashed them
there and [c]threw their dust into the
brook Kidron.
13 The high places which *were* before
Jerusalem, which *were* on the right of
[a]the mount of destruction which Solomon the king of Israel had built for [b]Ash-
toreth the abomination of the Sidonians,
and for [c]Chemosh the abomination of
Moab, and for Milcom the abomination of
the sons of Ammon, the king defiled.
14 [a]He broke in pieces the *sacred* pillars and cut down the Asherim and
[b]filled their places with human bones.
15 ¶ Furthermore, [a]the altar that *was*
at Bethel *and* the [b]high place which Jeroboam the son of Nebat, who made Israel
sin, had made, even that altar and the
high place he broke down. Then he
[1c]demolished its stones, ground them to
dust, and burned the Asherah.
16 Now when Josiah turned, he saw
the graves that *were* there on the moun-

17 [a]Deut 29:25, 26; 2 Kin 21:22
18 [a]2 Chr 34:26
19 [a]1 Sam 24:5; Ps 51:17 [b]Ex 10:3; 1 Kin 21:29 [c]Lev 26:31 [d]Jer 26:6 [e]2 Kin 22:11
20 [a]2 Kin 23:30
23:1 [a]2 Chr 34:29-32
2 [a]Deut 31:10-13 [b]2 Kin 22:8
3 [1]Lit *took a stand in* [a]2 Kin 11:14,17 [b]Deut 13:4
4 [1]Lit *keepers of the threshold* [2]I.e. a wooden symbol of a female deity, and so throughout the ch [a]2 Kin 25:18; Jer 52:24 [b]2 Kin 21:3,7; 2 Chr 33:3 [c]2 Kin 23:15
5 [a]2 Kin 21:3
6 [1]Lit *sons of the people* [a]2 Kin 23:15 [b]2 Chr 34:4
7 [1]Or *tents*; lit *houses* [a]1 Kin 14:24; 15:12 [b]Ex 35:25,26; Ezek 16:16
8 [a]Josh 21:17; 1 Kin 15:22
9 [a]Ezek 44:10-14
10 [1]I.e. place of burning [a]Is 30:33; Jer 7:31, 32; 19:4-6 [b]Lev 18:21 [c]1 Kin 11:7
11 [a]Deut 4:19; Job 31:26; Ezek 8:16
12 [1]Or *ran from there* [a]Jer 19:13; Zeph 1:5 [b]2 Kin 21:5; 2 Chr 33:5 [c]2 Kin 23:4,6
13 [a]1 Kin 11:7 [b]1 Kin 11:5 [c]Num 21:29
14 [a]Deut 7:5,25 [b]2 Kin 23:16
15 [1]So the Gr; Heb *burned the high place* [a]1 Kin 13:1 [b]1 Kin 12:28-33 [c]2 Kin 23:6

tain, and he sent and took the bones from
the graves and burned *them* on the altar
and defiled it [a]according to the word of
the LORD which the man of God proclaimed, who proclaimed these things.
17 Then he said, "What is this monument that I see?" And the men of the city
told him, "[a]It is the grave of the man
of God who came from Judah and proclaimed these things which you have
done against the altar of Bethel."
18 He said, "Let him alone; let no one
disturb his bones." So they [1]left his
bones undisturbed [a]with the bones of
the prophet who came from Samaria.
19 Josiah also removed all the houses
of the high places which *were* [a]in the
cities of Samaria, which the kings of Israel had made provoking [1]the LORD; and
he did to them [2]just as he had done in
Bethel.
20 All the priests of the high places
who *were* there [a]he slaughtered on the
altars and burned human bones on them;
then he returned to Jerusalem.

Passover Reinstituted

21 ¶ Then the king commanded all the
people saying, "[a]Celebrate the Passover
to the LORD your God [b]as it is written in
this book of the covenant."
22 [a]Surely such a Passover had not
been celebrated from the days of the
judges who judged Israel, nor in all the
days of the kings of Israel and of the kings
of Judah.
23 But in the eighteenth year of King
Josiah, this Passover was observed to the
LORD in Jerusalem.
24 ¶ Moreover, Josiah [1]removed [a]the
mediums and the spiritists and the [b]tera-
phim and [c]the idols and all the abominations that were seen in the land of Judah
and in Jerusalem, [d]that he might [2]con-
firm the words of the law which were
written [e]in the book that Hilkiah the
priest found in the house of the LORD.
25 Before him there was no king [a]like
him who turned to the LORD with all his
heart and with all his soul and with all his
might, according to all the law of Moses;
nor did any like him arise after him.
26 ¶ However, the LORD did not turn
from the fierceness of His great wrath
with which His anger burned against Judah, [a]because of all the provocations
with which Manasseh had provoked
Him.
27 The LORD said, "I will remove Judah also from My sight, [a]as I have removed Israel. And [b]I will cast off Jerusalem, this city which I have chosen, and
the [1]temple of which I said, 'My name
shall be there.' "

16 [a]1 Kin 13:2
17 [a]1 Kin 13:1, 30,31
18 [1]Lit *let his bones escape with* [a]1 Kin 13:11,31
19 [1]So with ancient versions [2]Lit *according to all the acts* [a]2 Chr 34:6,7
20 [a]2 Kin 10:25; 11:18
21 [a]2 Chr 35:1-17 [b]Num 9:2-4; Deut 16:2-8
22 [a]2 Chr 35:18,19
24 [1]Lit *consumed* [2]Or *perform* [a]Lev 19:31; 2 Kin 21:6 [b]Gen 31:19 mg [c]2 Kin 21:11,21 [d]Deut 18:10-22 [e]2 Kin 22:8
25 [a]2 Kin 18:5
26 [a]2 Kin 21:11-13; Jer 15:4
27 [1]Lit *house* [a]2 Kin 18:11 [b]2 Kin 21:13,14
29 [a]2 Chr 35:20-24 [b]Jer 46:2 [c]Judg 5:19
30 [1]Lit *him, dead* [a]2 Kin 9:28 [b]2 Chr 36:1-4
31 [a]1 Chr 3:15; Jer 22:11 [b]2 Kin 24:18
32 [a]2 Kin 21:2-7
33 [a]2 Kin 23:29 [b]2 Kin 25:6 [c]1 Kin 8:65
34 [1]So with Gr; Heb *he came* [a]1 Chr 3:15 [b]2 Kin 24:17; 2 Chr 36:4 [c]Jer 22:11,12; Ezek 19:3,4
35 [1]Lit *mouth* [a]2 Kin 23:33
36 [a]2 Chr 36:5; Jer 22:18,19; 26:1
37 [a]2 Kin 23:32
24:1 [a]2 Chr 36:6; Jer 25:1; Dan 1:1,2
2 [a]Jer 35:11f [b]2 Kin 6:23

Jehoahaz Succeeds Josiah

28 ¶ Now the rest of the acts of Josiah
and all that he did, are they not written
in the Book of the Chronicles of the Kings
of Judah?
29 [a]In his days [b]Pharaoh Neco king of
Egypt went up to the king of Assyria to
the river Euphrates. And King Josiah
went to meet him, and when *Pharaoh
Neco* saw him he killed him at [c]Me-
giddo.
30 [a]His servants drove [1]his body in a
chariot from Megiddo, and brought him
to Jerusalem and buried him in his own
tomb. [b]Then the people of the land took
Jehoahaz the son of Josiah and anointed
him and made him king in place of his
father.
31 ¶ [a]Jehoahaz was twenty-three
years old when he became king, and he
reigned three months in Jerusalem; and
his mother's name was [b]Hamutal the
daughter of Jeremiah of Libnah.
32 He did evil in the sight of the LORD,
[a]according to all that his fathers had
done.
33 [a]Pharaoh Neco imprisoned him at
[b]Riblah in the land of [c]Hamath, that he
might not reign in Jerusalem; and he imposed on the land a fine of one hundred
talents of silver and a talent of gold.

Jehoiakim Made King by Pharaoh

34 Pharaoh Neco made [a]Eliakim the
son of Josiah king in the place of Josiah
his father, and [b]changed his name to Jehoiakim. But he took Jehoahaz away and
[1c]brought *him* to Egypt, and he died
there.
35 So Jehoiakim [a]gave the silver and
gold to Pharaoh, but he taxed the land in
order to give the money at the [1]com-
mand of Pharaoh. He exacted the silver
and gold from the people of the land, each
according to his valuation, to give it to
Pharaoh Neco.
36 ¶ [a]Jehoiakim was twenty-five
years old when he became king, and he
reigned eleven years in Jerusalem; and
his mother's name *was* Zebidah the
daughter of Pedaiah of Rumah.
37 He did evil in the sight of the LORD,
[a]according to all that his fathers had
done.

Babylon Controls Jehoiakim

24 [a]In his days Nebuchadnezzar
king of Babylon came up, and Jehoiakim became his servant *for* three
years; then he turned and rebelled
against him.
2 The LORD sent against him [a]bands
of Chaldeans, [b]bands of Arameans,

[c]bands of Moabites, and bands of Ammonites. So He sent them against Judah
to destroy it, [d]according to the word of
the LORD which He had spoken through
His servants the prophets.
3 [a]Surely at the [1]command of the
LORD it came upon Judah, to remove
them from His sight [b]because of the sins
of Manasseh, according to all that he had
done,
4 and [a]also for the innocent blood
which he shed, for he filled Jerusalem
with innocent blood; and the LORD would
not forgive.
5 Now the rest of the acts of Jehoiakim and all that he did, are they not written in the Book of the Chronicles of the
Kings of Judah?

Jehoiachin Reigns

6 So [a]Jehoiakim slept with his fathers, and Jehoiachin his son became
king in his place.
7 [a]The king of Egypt did not come
out of his land again, [b]for the king of
Babylon had taken all that belonged to
the king of Egypt from [c]the brook of
Egypt to the river Euphrates.
8 ¶ [a]Jehoiachin was [b]eighteen years
old when he became king, and he reigned
three months in Jerusalem; and his mother's name *was* Nehushta the daughter of
Elnathan of Jerusalem.
9 He did evil in the sight of the LORD,
[a]according to all that his father had done.

Deportation to Babylon

10 ¶ At that time the servants of Nebuchadnezzar king of Babylon went up to
Jerusalem, and the city came under siege.
11 And Nebuchadnezzar the king of
Babylon came to the city, while his servants were besieging it.
12 [a]Jehoiachin the king of Judah went
out to the king of Babylon, he and his
mother and his servants and his captains
and his officials. So [b]the king of Babylon
took him captive in the eighth year of his
reign.
13 [a]He carried out from there all the
treasures of the house of the LORD, and
the treasures of the king's house, and
[b]cut in pieces all the vessels of gold
[c]which Solomon king of Israel had made
in the temple of the LORD, just as the
LORD had said.
14 Then [a]he led away into exile all
Jerusalem and all the captains and all the
mighty men of valor, [b]ten thousand captives, and [c]all the craftsmen and the
smiths. None remained [d]except the
poorest people of the land.
15 ¶ So [a]he led Jehoiachin away into
exile to Babylon; also the king's mother
and the king's wives and his officials and
the leading men of the land, he led away
into exile from Jerusalem to Babylon.
16 All the men of valor, [a]seven thousand, and the craftsmen and the smiths,
one thousand, all strong and fit for war,
and these the king of Babylon brought
into exile to Babylon.

Zedekiah Made King

17 [a]Then the king of Babylon made
[1]his uncle Mattaniah king in his place,
and changed his name to Zedekiah.
18 ¶ [a]Zedekiah was twenty-one years
old when he became king, and he reigned
eleven years in Jerusalem; and his mother's name was [b]Hamutal the daughter of
Jeremiah of Libnah.
19 He did evil in the sight of the LORD,
[a]according to all that Jehoiakim had
done.
20 For [a]through the anger of the LORD
this came about in Jerusalem and Judah
until He cast them out from His presence.
And [b]Zedekiah rebelled against the king
of Babylon.

Nebuchadnezzar Besieges Jerusalem

25 [a]Now in the ninth year of his
reign, on the tenth day of the
tenth month, [b]Nebuchadnezzar king of
Babylon came, he and all his army,
against Jerusalem, camped against it and
[c]built a siege wall all around [1]it.
2 So the city was under siege until
the eleventh year of King Zedekiah.
3 On the ninth day of the *fourth*
month [a]the famine was so severe in the
city that there was no food for the people
of the land.
4 [a]Then the city was broken into,
and all the men of war *fled* by night by
way of the gate between the two walls
beside [b]the king's garden, though the
Chaldeans were all around the city. And
[1]they went by way of the Arabah.
5 But the army of the Chaldeans pursued the king and overtook him in the
plains of Jericho and all his army was scattered from him.
6 Then [a]they captured the king and
[b]brought him to the king of Babylon at
[c]Riblah, and [1]he passed sentence on
him.
7 [a]They slaughtered the sons of Zedekiah before his eyes, then [b]put out the
eyes of Zedekiah and bound him with
bronze fetters and brought him to Babylon.

Jerusalem Burned and Plundered

8 ¶ [a]Now on the seventh day of the
[b]fifth month, which was the nineteenth
year of King Nebuchadnezzar, king of

---

2 [c]2 Kin 13:20 [d]2 Kin 23:27
3 [1]Lit *mouth* [a]2 Kin 18:25 [b]2 Kin 23:26
4 [a]2 Kin 21:16
6 [a]Jer 22:18,19
7 [a]Jer 37:5-7 [b]Jer 46:2 [c]Gen 15:18
8 [a]1 Chr 3:16 [b]2 Chr 36:9
9 [a]2 Kin 21:2-7
12 [a]Jer 22:24-30; 24:1; 29:1,2 [b]2 Chr 36:10
13 [a]2 Kin 20:17; Is 39:6 [b]2 Kin 25:13-15 [c]1 Kin 7:48-50
14 [a]Jer 24:1 [b]2 Kin 24:16; Jer 52:28 [c]Jer 24:1; 29:2 [d]2 Kin 25:12
15 [a]2 Chr 36:10; Jer 22:24-28; Ezek 17:12
16 [a]2 Kin 24:14
17 [1]I.e. Jehoiachin's uncle [a]2 Chr 36:10-13; Jer 37:1
18 [a]Jer 27:1; 28:1; 52:1 [b]2 Kin 23:31
19 [a]2 Kin 23:37
20 [a]Deut 4:24; 29:27; 2 Kin 23:26 [b]2 Chr 36:13; Ezek 17:15
25:1 [1]Lit *against it* [a]2 Chr 36:17-20; Jer 39:1-7 [b]Jer 21:2; 34:1,2; Ezek 24:2 [c]Ezek 21:22
3 [a]2 Kin 6:24, 25; Lam 4:9,10
4 [1]So some ancient mss and versions; M.T. *he* [a]Ezek 33:21 [b]Neh 3:15
6 [1]Lit *they spoke judgment with him* [a]Jer 34:21,22 [b]Jer 32:4 [c]2 Kin 23:33
7 [a]Jer 39:6,7 [b]Ezek 12:13
8 [a]Jer 52:12 [b]Jer 39:8-12

Babylon, Nebuzaradan the captain of the
guard, a servant of the king of Babylon,
came to Jerusalem.
9 [a]He burned the house of the LORD,
[b]the king's house, and all the houses
of Jerusalem; even every great house he
burned with fire.
10 So all the army of the Chaldeans
who *were with* the captain of the guard
[a]broke down the walls around Jerusalem.
11 Then [a]the rest of the people who
were left in the city and the deserters
who had deserted to the king of Babylon
and the rest of the people, Nebuzaradan
the captain of the guard carried away into
exile.
12 But the captain of the guard left
some of [a]the poorest of the land to be
vinedressers and plowmen.
13 ¶ [a]Now the bronze pillars which
were in the house of the LORD, and the
stands and [b]the bronze sea which were
in the house of the LORD, the Chaldeans
broke in pieces and carried the [1]bronze
to Babylon.
14 [a]They took away the pots, the
shovels, the snuffers, the spoons, and all
the bronze vessels which were used in
temple service.
15 The captain of the guard also took
away the firepans and the basins, what
was fine gold and what was fine silver.
16 The two pillars, the one sea, and
the stands which Solomon had made for
the house of the LORD—[a]the bronze of
all these vessels was beyond weight.
17 [a]The height of the one pillar was
eighteen [1]cubits, and a bronze capital
was on it; the height of the capital was
three [1]cubits, with a network and pomegranates on the capital all around, all of
bronze. And the second pillar was like
these with network.
18 ¶ Then the captain of the guard
took [a]Seraiah the chief priest and [b]Zeph-
aniah the second priest, with the three
officers of the temple.
19 From the city he took one official
who was overseer of the men of war, and
five [1]of the king's advisers who were
found in the city; and the [2]scribe of the
captain of the army who mustered the
people of the land; and sixty men of
the people of the land who were found in
the city.
20 Nebuzaradan the captain of the
guard took them and brought them to the
king of Babylon at [a]Riblah.
21 Then the king of Babylon struck
them down and put them to death at Riblah in the land of Hamath. [a]So Judah was
led away into exile from its land.

Gedaliah Made Governor

22 ¶ Now *as for* the people who were
left in the land of Judah, whom Nebuchadnezzar king of Babylon had left, he
appointed [a]Gedaliah the son of Ahikam,
the son of Shaphan over them.
23 [a]When all the captains of the
forces, they and *their* men, heard that the
king of Babylon had appointed Gedaliah
governor, they came to Gedaliah to [b]Miz-
pah, namely, Ishmael the son of Nethaniah, and Johanan the son of Kareah, and
Seraiah the son of Tanhumeth the Netophathite, and Jaazaniah the son of the
Maacathite, they and their men.
24 Gedaliah swore to them and their
men and said to them, "Do not be afraid
of the servants of the Chaldeans; live in
the land and serve the king of Babylon,
and it will be well with you."
25 ¶ [a]But it came about in the seventh month, that Ishmael the son of
Nethaniah, the son of Elishama, of the
royal [1]family, came [2]with ten men and
struck Gedaliah down so that he died
along with the Jews and the Chaldeans
who were with him at Mizpah.
26 [a]Then all the people, both small
and great, and the captains of the forces
arose and went to Egypt; for they were
afraid of the Chaldeans.
27 ¶ [a]Now it came about in the thirty-
seventh year of [b]the exile of Jehoiachin
king of Judah, in the twelfth month, on
the twenty-seventh *day* of the month,
that Evil-merodach king of Babylon, in
the year that he became king, [1c]released
Jehoiachin king of Judah from prison;
28 and he [a]spoke kindly to him and
set his throne above the throne of the
kings who *were* with him in Babylon.
29 [1]Jehoiachin changed his prison
clothes and [2a]had his meals in [3]the
king's presence regularly all the days of
his life;
30 and for his [a]allowance, a regular
allowance was given him by the king, a
portion for each day, all the days of his
life.

---

9 [a]1 Kin 9:8; 2 Chr 36:19; Ps 74:3-7 [b]Amos 2:5
10 [a]2 Kin 14:13; Neh 1:3
11 [a]2 Chr 36:20
12 [a]2 Kin 24:14; Jer 40:7
13 [1]Lit *bronze of them* [a]1 Kin 7:15-22; 2 Kin 20:17; 2 Chr 3:15-17; 36:18 [b]1 Kin 7:23-26; 2 Chr 4:2-4
14 [a]Ex 27:3; 1 Kin 7:47-50; 2 Chr 4:16
16 [a]1 Kin 7:47
17 [1]I.e. One cubit equals approx 18 in. [a]1 Kin 7:15-22
18 [1]Lit *keepers of the door* [a]1 Chr 6:14; Ezra 7:1 [b]Jer 21:1; 29:25,29
19 [1]Lit *men of those seeing the king's face* [2]Or *scribe, a captain* [a]Esth 1:14
20 [a]2 Kin 23:33
21 [a]Deut 28:64; 2 Kin 23:27
22 [a]Jer 39:14; 40:7-9
23 [a]Jer 40:7-9 [b]Josh 18:26
25 [1]Lit *seed* [2]Lit *and ten men with him* [a]Jer 41:1,2
26 [a]Jer 43:4-7
27 [1]Lit *lifted up the head of* [a]Jer 52:31-34 [b]2 Kin 24:12,15 [c]Gen 40:13,20
28 [a]Dan 2:37; 5:18,19
29 [1]Lit *he* [2]Lit *ate bread* [3]Lit *his presence* [a]2 Sam 9:7
30 [a]Neh 11:23; 12:47

1 Chronicles

Title and Background

The Hebrew title can be translated "the events (or annals) of the days (or years)." The *Septuagint* (the Greek translation of the Old Testament) translators dubbed the book "the things omitted," indicating that they regarded it as a supplement to Samuel and Kings.

Author and Date of Writing

According to ancient Jewish tradition, Ezra wrote Chronicles, but this cannot be established with certainty. A growing consensus dates Chronicles in the latter half of the fifth century B.C., thus possibly within Ezra's lifetime. It must be acknowledged that the author, if not Ezra, at least shared many basic concerns with that reforming priest.

Theme and Message

Chronicles was written for the exiles who had returned to Israel after the Babylonian captivity, to remind them that they were still God's chosen people. The burning issue was the question of continuity with the past: Is God still interested in us? Are His covenants still in force? Now that we have no Davidic king and are subject to Persia, do God's promises to David still have meaning for us?

Outline

I. Genealogies: From Creation to Restoration (1:1—9:44)
II. The Reign of David (10:1—29:30)

Genealogy from Adam

1 [a]Adam, Seth, Enosh,
2 Kenan, Mahalalel, Jared,
3 Enoch, Methuselah, Lamech,
4 Noah, Shem, Ham and Japheth.
5 ¶ [a]The sons of Japheth *were* Gomer, Magog, Madai, Javan, Tubal, Meshech and Tiras.
6 The sons of Gomer *were* Ashkenaz,
[1]Diphath, and Togarmah.
7 The sons of Javan *were* Elishah,
Tarshish, Kittim and [1]Rodanim.
8 ¶ The sons of Ham *were* Cush, Mizraim, Put, and Canaan.
9 The sons of Cush *were* Seba, Havilah, Sabta, Raama and Sabteca; and the
sons of Raamah *were* Sheba and Dedan.
10 Cush [1]became the father of Nimrod; he began to be a mighty one in the
earth.
11 ¶ [a]Mizraim became the father of
the people of Lud, Anam, Lehab, Naph-
tuh,
12 Pathrus, Casluh, from which the
[1]Philistines came, and Caphtor.
13 ¶ Canaan became the father of Sidon, his firstborn, Heth,
14 and the Jebusites, the Amorites, the
Girgashites,
15 the Hivites, the Arkites, the Sinites,

1:1 [a]Gen 4:25-5:32
5 [a]Gen 10:2-4
6 [1]In Gen 10:3, *Riphath*
7 [1]In Gen 10:4, *Dodanim*
10 [1]Lit *begot,* and so through-out the ch
11 [a]Gen 10:13-18
12 [1]Or *people of Pelisht*
17 [1]In Gen 10:23, *Mash* [a]Gen 10:22-29
22 [1]In Gen 10:28, *Obal*
24 [a]Gen 11:10-26; Luke 3:34-36
29 [a]Gen 25:13-16

16 the Arvadites, the Zemarites and
the Hamathites.
17 ¶ [a]The sons of Shem *were* Elam,
Asshur, Arpachshad, Lud, Aram, Uz, Hul,
Gether and [1]Meshech.
18 Arpachshad became the father of
Shelah and Shelah became the father of
Eber.
19 Two sons were born to Eber, the
name of the one was Peleg, for in his days
the earth was divided, and his brother's
name was Joktan.
20 Joktan became the father of Almodad, Sheleph, Hazarmaveth, Jerah,
21 Hadoram, Uzal, Diklah,
22 [1]Ebal, Abimael, Sheba,
23 Ophir, Havilah and Jobab; all these
were the sons of Joktan.
24 ¶ [a]Shem, Arpachshad, Shelah,
25 Eber, Peleg, Reu,
26 Serug, Nahor, Terah,
27 Abram, that is Abraham.

Descendants of Abraham

28 ¶ The sons of Abraham *were* Isaac
and Ishmael.
29 [a]These are their genealogies: the
firstborn of Ishmael *was* Nebaioth, then
Kedar, Adbeel, Mibsam,
30 Mishma, Dumah, Massa, Hadad,
Tema,

31 Jetur, Naphish and Kedemah; these
were the sons of Ishmael.
32 [a]The sons of Keturah, Abraham's
concubine, *whom* she bore, *were* Zimran,
Jokshan, Medan, Midian, Ishbak and Shuah. And the sons of Jokshan *were* Sheba
and Dedan.
33 The sons of Midian were Ephah,
Epher, Hanoch, Abida and Eldaah. All
these were the sons of Keturah.
34 ¶ [a]Abraham became the father of
Isaac. The sons of Isaac *were* [b]Esau and
Israel.
35 [a]The sons of Esau *were* Eliphaz,
Reuel, Jeush, Jalam and Korah.
36 The sons of Eliphaz *were* Teman,
Omar, [1]Zephi, Gatam, Kenaz, Timna and
Amalek.
37 The sons of Reuel *were* Nahath, Zerah, Shammah and Mizzah.
38 [a]The sons of Seir *were* Lotan, Shobal, Zibeon, Anah, Dishon, Ezer and Dishan.
39 The sons of Lotan *were* Hori and
[1]Homam; and Lotan's sister *was* Timna.
40 The sons of Shobal *were* [1]Alian,
Manahath, Ebal, [2]Shephi and Onam.
And the sons of Zibeon *were* Aiah and
Anah.
41 The [1]son of Anah *was* Dishon. And
the sons of Dishon *were* [2]Hamran, Eshban, Ithran and Cheran.
42 The sons of Ezer *were* Bilhan, Zaavan and [1]Jaakan. The sons of Dishan
were Uz and Aran.
43 ¶ [a]Now these are the kings who
reigned in the land of Edom before any
king of the sons of Israel reigned. Bela
was the son of Beor, and the name of his
city was Dinhabah.
44 When Bela died, Jobab the son of
Zerah of [a]Bozrah became king in his
place.
45 When Jobab died, Husham of the
land of [a]the Temanites became king in
his place.
46 When Husham died, Hadad the son
of Bedad, who [1]defeated Midian in the
field of Moab, became king in his place;
and the name of his city *was* Avith.
47 When Hadad died, Samlah of Masrekah became king in his place.
48 When Samlah died, Shaul of Reho-
both by the River became king in his
place.
49 When Shaul died, Baal-hanan the
son of Achbor became king in his place.
50 When Baal-hanan died, [1]Hadad became king in his place; and the name of
his city was [2]Pai, and his wife's name
was Mehetabel, the daughter of Matred,
the daughter of Mezahab.
51 Then Hadad died.

¶ Now the chiefs of Edom were: chief
Timna, chief [1]Aliah, chief Jetheth,
52 chief Oholibamah, chief Elah, chief
Pinon,
53 chief Kenaz, chief Teman, chief
Mibzar,
54 chief Magdiel, chief Iram. These
were the chiefs of Edom.

Genealogy: Twelve Sons of Jacob (Israel)

2 [a]These are the sons of Israel: Reuben, Simeon, Levi, Judah, Issachar,
Zebulun,
2 Dan, Joseph, Benjamin, Naphtali,
Gad and Asher.
3 ¶ [a]The sons of Judah *were* Er,
Onan and Shelah; *these* three were born
to him by Bath-shua the Canaanitess.
And Er, Judah's firstborn, was wicked in
the sight of the LORD, so He put him to
death.
4 [a]Tamar his daughter-in-law bore
him Perez and Zerah. Judah had five sons
in all.
5 ¶ The sons of Perez *were* Hezron
and Hamul.
6 The sons of Zerah *were* [1]Zimri,
Ethan, Heman, Calcol and [2]Dara; five of
them in all.
7 The [1]son of Carmi *was* [2a]Achar,
the troubler of Israel, who violated the
ban.
8 The [1]son of Ethan *was* Azariah.

Genealogy of David

9 ¶ Now the sons of Hezron, who
were born to him *were* Jerahmeel, Ram
and Chelubai.
10 Ram [1]became the father of Amminadab, and Amminadab became the father of Nahshon, leader of the sons of
Judah;
11 Nahshon became the father of Salma, Salma became the father of Boaz,
12 Boaz became the father of Obed,
and Obed became the father of Jesse;
13 and Jesse became the father of Eliab
his firstborn, then Abinadab the second,
[1]Shimea the third,
14 Nethanel the fourth, Raddai the
fifth,
15 Ozem the sixth, David the seventh;
16 and their sisters *were* Zeruiah and
Abigail. And the three sons of Zeruiah
were [1]Abshai, Joab and Asahel.
17 Abigail bore Amasa, and the father
of Amasa was [1]Jether the Ishmaelite.
18 ¶ Now Caleb the son of Hezron had
sons by Azubah *his* wife, and by Jerioth;
and these were her sons: Jesher, Shobab,
and Ardon.

32 [a]Gen 25:1-4
34 [a]1 Chr 1:28 [b]Gen 25:25,26; 32:28
35 [a]Gen 36:4-10
36 [1]In Gen 36:11, *Zepho*
38 [a]Gen 36:20-28
39 [1]In Gen 36:22, *Hemam*
40 [1]In Gen 36:23, *Alvan* [2]In Gen 36:23, *Shepho*
41 [1]Lit *sons* [2]In Gen 36:26, *Hemdan*
42 [1]Or *Akan*, as in Gen 36:27
43 [a]Gen 36:31-43
44 [a]Is 34:6
45 [a]Job 2:11
46 [1]Lit *smote*
50 [1]In Gen 36:39, *Hadar* [2]In Gen 36:39, *Pau*
51 [1]In Gen 36:40, *Alvah*
2:1 [a]Gen 35:22-26; 46:8-25
3 [a]Gen 38:2-10
4 [a]Gen 38:13-30
6 [1]In Josh 7:1, *Zabdi* [2]In 1 Kin 4:31, *Darda*
7 [1]Lit *sons* [2]In Josh 7:18, *Achan* [a]Josh 7:1
8 [1]Lit *sons*
10 [1]Lit *begot*, and so throughout the ch
13 [1]In 1 Sam 16:9, *Shammah*; in 2 Sam 13:3, *Shimeah*
16 [1]In 2 Sam 2:18, *Abishai*
17 [1]In 2 Sam 17:25, *Ithra the Israelite*

19 When Azubah died, Caleb married
Ephrath, who bore him Hur.
20 Hur became the father of Uri, and
Uri became the father of Bezalel.
21 ¶ Afterward Hezron went in to the
daughter of Machir the father of Gilead,
whom he married when he was sixty
years old; and she bore him Segub.
22 Segub became the father of Jair,
who had twenty-three cities in the land
of Gilead.
23 But Geshur and Aram took [1]the
towns of Jair from them, with Kenath and
its villages, *even* sixty cities. All these
were the sons of Machir, the father of
Gilead.
24 After the death of Hezron in Caleb-
ephrathah, Abijah, Hezron's wife, bore
him Ashhur the father of Tekoa.
25 ¶ Now the sons of Jerahmeel the
firstborn of Hezron *were* Ram the firstborn, then Bunah, Oren, Ozem *and* Ahijah.
26 Jerahmeel had another wife, whose
name was Atarah; she was the mother of
Onam.
27 The sons of Ram, the firstborn of
Jerahmeel, were Maaz, Jamin and Eker.
28 The sons of Onam were Shammai
and Jada. And the sons of Shammai *were*
Nadab and Abishur.
29 The name of Abishur's wife *was*
Abihail, and she bore him Ahban and Mo-
lid.
30 The sons of Nadab *were* Seled and
Appaim, and Seled died without sons.
31 The [1]son of Appaim *was* Ishi. And
the [1]son of Ishi *was* Sheshan. And the
[1]son of Sheshan *was* Ahlai.
32 The sons of Jada the brother of
Shammai *were* Jether and Jonathan, and
Jether died without sons.
33 The sons of Jonathan *were* Peleth
and Zaza. These were the sons of Jerahmeel.
34 Now Sheshan had no sons, only
daughters. And Sheshan had an Egyptian
servant whose name was Jarha.
35 Sheshan gave his daughter to Jarha
his servant in marriage, and she bore him
Attai.
36 Attai became the father of Nathan,
and Nathan became the father of Zabad,
37 and Zabad became the father of
Ephlal, and Ephlal became the father of
Obed,
38 and Obed became the father of
Jehu, and Jehu became the father of Azariah,
39 and Azariah became the father of
Helez, and Helez became the father of
Eleasah,
40 and Eleasah became the father of
Sismai, and Sismai became the father of
Shallum,
41 and Shallum became the father of
Jekamiah, and Jekamiah became the father of Elishama.
42 ¶ Now the sons of Caleb, the brother of Jerahmeel, *were* Mesha his firstborn, who was the father of Ziph; and
[1]his son was Mareshah, the father of Hebron.
43 The sons of Hebron *were* Korah and
Tappuah and Rekem and Shema.
44 Shema became the father of Ra-
ham, the father of Jorkeam; and Rekem
became the father of Shammai.
45 The son of Shammai was Maon,
and Maon *was* the father of Bethzur.
46 Ephah, Caleb's concubine, bore Haran, Moza and Gazez; and Haran became
the father of Gazez.
47 The sons of Jahdai *were* Regem, Jotham, Geshan, Pelet, Ephah and Shaaph.
48 Maacah, Caleb's concubine, bore
Sheber and Tirhanah.
49 She also bore Shaaph the father of
Madmannah, Sheva the father of Mach-
bena and the father of Gibea; and the
daughter of Caleb *was* Achsah.
50 These were the sons of Caleb.
¶ The [1]sons of Hur, the firstborn of
Ephrathah, *were* Shobal the father of
Kiriath-jearim,
51 Salma the father of Bethlehem *and*
Hareph the father of Beth-gader.
52 Shobal the father of Kiriath-jearim
had sons: Haroeh, half of the Manahathites,
53 and the families of Kiriath-jearim:
the Ithrites, the Puthites, the Shumath-
ites and the Mishraites; from these came
the Zorathites and the Eshtaolites.
54 The sons of Salma *were* Bethlehem
and the Netophathites, Atroth-beth-joab
and half of the Manahathites, the Zorites.
55 The families of scribes who lived at
Jabez *were* the Tirathites, the Shimeath-
ites *and* the Sucathites. Those are the Kenites who came from Hammath, the father of the house of Rechab.

Family of David

3 [a]Now these were the sons of David
who were born to him in Hebron:
the firstborn *was* Amnon, by Ahinoam
the Jezreelitess; the second *was* Daniel,
by Abigail the Carmelitess;
2 the third *was* Absalom the son of
Maacah, the daughter of Talmai king of
Geshur; the fourth *was* Adonijah the son
of Haggith;
3 the fifth *was* Shephatiah, by Abital;
the sixth *was* Ithream, by his wife Eglah.
4 Six were born to him in Hebron,
and [a]there he reigned seven years and

23 [1]Or *Havvoth-jair*
31 [1]Lit *sons*
42 [1]Lit *the sons of*
50 [1]Lit *son*
3:1 [a]2 Sam 3:2-5
4 [a]2 Sam 2:11; 5:4,5; 1 Kin 2:11; 1 Chr 29:27

six months. And in Jerusalem he reigned thirty-three years.

5 [a]These were born to him in Jerusalem: Shimea, Shobab, Nathan and [b]Solomon, four, by [c]Bath-shua the daughter of Ammiel;

6 and Ibhar, Elishama, Eliphelet,

7 Nogah, Nepheg and Japhia,

8 Elishama, Eliada and Eliphelet, nine.

9 All *these were* the sons of David, besides the sons of the concubines; and [a]Tamar *was* their sister.

10 ¶ Now Solomon's son *was* Rehoboam, Abijah *was* his son, Asa his son, Jehoshaphat his son,

11 Joram his son, Ahaziah his son, Joash his son,

12 Amaziah his son, Azariah his son, Jotham his son,

13 Ahaz his son, Hezekiah his son, Manasseh his son,

14 Amon his son, Josiah his son.

15 The sons of Josiah *were* Johanan the firstborn, and the second *was* Jehoiakim, the third Zedekiah, the fourth Shallum.

16 The sons of Jehoiakim *were* Jeconiah his son, Zedekiah his son.

17 The sons of Jeconiah, the prisoner, *were* Shealtiel his son,

18 and Malchiram, Pedaiah, Shenazzar, Jekamiah, Hoshama and Nedabiah.

19 The sons of Pedaiah *were* Zerubbabel and Shimei. And the [1]sons of Zerubbabel *were* Meshullam and Hananiah, and Shelomith *was* their sister;

20 and Hashubah, Ohel, Berechiah, Hasadiah and Jushab-hesed, five.

21 The [1]sons of Hananiah *were* Pelatiah and Jeshaiah, the sons of Rephaiah, the sons of Arnan, the sons of Obadiah, the sons of Shecaniah.

22 The [1]descendants of Shecaniah *were* Shemaiah, and the sons of Shemaiah: Hattush, Igal, Bariah, Neariah and Shaphat, six.

23 The [1]sons of Neariah *were* Elioenai, Hizkiah and Azrikam, three.

24 The sons of Elioenai *were* Hodaviah, Eliashib, Pelaiah, Akkub, Johanan, Delaiah and Anani, seven.

Line of Hur, Asher

4 [a]The sons of Judah *were* Perez, Hezron, Carmi, Hur and Shobal.

2 Reaiah the son of Shobal [1]became the father of Jahath, and Jahath became the father of Ahumai and Lahad. These *were* the families of the Zorathites.

3 These *were* the [1]sons of Etam: Jezreel, Ishma and Idbash; and the name of their sister *was* Hazzelelponi.

4 Penuel *was* the father of Gedor, and Ezer the father of Hushah. These *were* the sons of Hur, the firstborn of Ephrathah, the father of Bethlehem.

5 Ashhur, the father of Tekoa, had two wives, Helah and Naarah.

6 Naarah bore him Ahuzzam, Hepher, Temeni and Haahashtari. These were the sons of Naarah.

7 The sons of Helah *were* Zereth, [1]Izhar and Ethnan.

8 Koz became the father of Anub and Zobebah, and the families of Aharhel the son of Harum.

9 Jabez was more honorable than his brothers, and his mother named him Jabez saying, "Because I bore *him* with pain."

10 Now Jabez called on the God of Israel, saying, "Oh that You would bless me indeed and enlarge my border, and that Your hand might be with me, and that You would keep *me* from harm that *it* may not pain me!" And God granted him what he requested.

11 ¶ Chelub the brother of Shuhah became the father of Mehir, who was the father of Eshton.

12 Eshton became the father of Bethrapha and Paseah, and Tehinnah the father of [1]Ir-nahash. These are the men of Recah.

13 ¶ Now the sons of Kenaz *were* Othniel and Seraiah. And the sons of Othniel *were* Hathath and Meonothai.

14 Meonothai became the father of Ophrah, and Seraiah became the father of Joab the father of [1]Ge-harashim, for they were craftsmen.

15 The sons of Caleb the son of Jephunneh *were* Iru, Elah and Naam; and the [1]son of Elah *was* [2]Kenaz.

16 The sons of Jehallelel *were* Ziph and Ziphah, Tiria and Asarel.

17 The [1]sons of Ezrah *were* Jether, Mered, Epher and Jalon. ([2]And these are the sons of Bithia the daughter of Pharaoh, whom Mered took) and she conceived *and bore* Miriam, Shammai and Ishbah the father of Eshtemoa.

18 His Jewish wife bore Jered the father of Gedor, and Heber the father of Soco, and Jekuthiel the father of Zanoah.

19 The sons of the wife of Hodiah, the sister of Naham, *were* the [1]fathers of Keilah the Garmite and Eshtemoa the Maacathite.

20 The sons of Shimon *were* Amnon and Rinnah, Benhanan and Tilon. And the sons of Ishi *were* Zoheth and Benzoheth.

21 The sons of Shelah the son of Judah *were* Er the father of Lecah and Laadah the father of Mareshah, and the families of the house of the linen workers at Beth-ashbea;

5 [a]2 Sam 5:14-16; 1 Chr 14:4-7 [b]2 Sam 12:24,25 [c]2 Sam 11:3
9 [a]2 Sam 13:1
19 [1]Lit *son*
21 [1]Lit *son*
22 [1]Lit *sons*
23 [1]Lit *son*
4:1 [a]1 Chr 2:3
2 [1]Lit *begot,* and so throughout the ch
3 [1]So with some ancient versions; Heb *father*
7 [1]Another reading is *Zohar*
12 [1]Or *the city of Nahash*
14 [1]Or *valley of craftsmen*
15 [1]Lit *sons* [2]Lit *and Kenaz*
17 [1]Lit *son* [2]In the Heb the words in ( ) are at the end of v. 18
19 [1]Lit *father*

22 and Jokim, the men of Cozeba, Joash, Saraph, who ruled in Moab, and Jashubi-lehem. And the [1]records are ancient.

23 These were the potters and the inhabitants of Netaim and Gederah; they lived there with the king for his work.

Descendants of Simeon

24 ¶ The sons of Simeon *were* [1]Nemuel and Jamin, [2]Jarib, [3]Zerah, Shaul;

25 Shallum his son, Mibsam his son, Mishma his son.

26 The sons of Mishma *were* Hammuel his son, Zaccur his son, Shimei his son.

27 Now Shimei had sixteen sons and six daughters; but his brothers did not have many sons, nor did all their family multiply like the sons of Judah.

28 They lived at Beersheba, Moladah and Hazar-shual,

29 at Bilhah, Ezem, Tolad,

30 Bethuel, Hormah, Ziklag,

31 Beth-marcaboth, Hazar-susim, Beth-biri and Shaaraim. These *were* their cities until the reign of David.

32 Their villages *were* Etam, Ain, Rimmon, Tochen and Ashan, five cities;

33 and all their villages that *were* around the same cities as far as [1]Baal. These *were* their settlements, and they have their genealogy.

34 ¶ Meshobab and Jamlech and Joshah the son of Amaziah,

35 and Joel and Jehu the son of Joshibiah, the son of Seraiah, the son of Asiel,

36 and Elioenai, Jaakobah, Jeshohaiah, Asaiah, Adiel, Jesimiel, Benaiah,

37 Ziza the son of Shiphi, the son of Allon, the son of Jedaiah, the son of Shimri, the son of Shemaiah;

38 these mentioned by name *were* leaders in their families; and their fathers' houses increased greatly.

39 They went to the entrance of Gedor, even to the east side of the valley, to seek pasture for their flocks.

40 They found rich and good pasture, and [a]the land was broad and quiet and peaceful; for those who lived there formerly *were* Hamites.

41 [a]These, recorded by name, came in the days of Hezekiah king of Judah, and [1]attacked their tents and the Meunites who were found there, and destroyed them utterly to this day, and lived in their place, because there was pasture there for their flocks.

42 From them, from the sons of Simeon, five hundred men went to [a]Mount Seir, with Pelatiah, Neariah, Rephaiah and Uzziel, the sons of Ishi, as their leaders.

43 [a]They [1]destroyed the remnant of the Amalekites who escaped, and have lived there to this day.

Genealogy from Reuben

5 Now the sons of Reuben the firstborn of Israel (for [a]he was the firstborn, but because [b]he defiled his father's bed, [c]his birthright was given to the sons of Joseph the son of Israel; so that he is not enrolled in the genealogy according to the birthright.

2 [a]Though Judah prevailed over his brothers, and [b]from him *came* the leader, yet the birthright belonged to Joseph),

3 [a]the sons of Reuben the firstborn of Israel *were* Hanoch and Pallu, Hezron and Carmi.

4 The sons of Joel *were* Shemaiah his son, Gog his son, [a]Shimei his son,

5 Micah his son, Reaiah his son, Baal his son,

6 Beerah his son, whom [1]Tilgath-pilneser king of Assyria carried away into exile; he was leader of the Reubenites.

7 His [1]kinsmen by their families, [a]in the genealogy of their generations, *were* Jeiel the chief, then Zechariah

8 and Bela the son of Azaz, the son of Shema, the son of Joel, who lived in [a]Aroer, even to Nebo and Baal-meon.

9 To the east he settled as far as the entrance of the wilderness from the river Euphrates, [a]because their cattle had increased in the land of Gilead.

10 In the days of Saul [a]they made war with the Hagrites, who fell by their hand, so that they [1]occupied their tents throughout [2]all the land east of Gilead.

11 ¶ Now the sons of Gad lived opposite them in the land of [a]Bashan as far as [b]Salecah.

12 Joel *was* the chief and Shapham the second, then Janai and Shaphat in Bashan.

13 Their [1]kinsmen of their fathers' households *were* Michael, Meshullam, Sheba, Jorai, Jacan, Zia and Eber, seven.

14 These *were* the sons of Abihail, the son of Huri, the son of Jaroah, the son of Gilead, the son of Michael, the son of Jeshishai, the son of Jahdo, the son of Buz;

15 Ahi the son of Abdiel, the son of Guni, *was* head of their fathers' households.

16 They lived in Gilead, in Bashan and in its towns, and in all the pasture lands of [a]Sharon, as far as their [1]borders.

17 All of these were enrolled in the genealogies in the days of [a]Jotham king of Judah and in the days of [b]Jeroboam king of Israel.

18 ¶ The sons of Reuben and the Gadites and the half-tribe of Manasseh, *con-*

22 [1]Lit *words*
24 [1]In Gen 46:10 and Ex 6:15, *Jemuel* [2]In Num 26:12, *Jachin* [3]In Gen 46:10 and Ex 6:15, *Zohar*
33 [1]In Josh 19:8, *Baalath*
40 [a]Judg 18:7-10
41 [1]Lit *smote* [a]1 Chr 4:33-38
42 [a]Gen 36:8,9
43 [1]Lit *smote* [a]1 Sam 15:7,8; 30:17
5:1 [a]Gen 29:32; 1 Chr 2:1 [b]Gen 35:22; 49:4 [c]Gen 48:15-22
2 [a]Gen 49:8-10; Ps 60:7; 108:8 [b]Mic 5:2; Matt 2:6
3 [a]Gen 46:9; Ex 6:14; Num 26:5-9
4 [a]1 Chr 5:8
6 [1]In 2 Kin 15:29, *Tiglath-pileser*
7 [1]Lit *brothers* [a]1 Chr 5:17
8 [a]Num 32:34; Josh 12:2
9 [a]Josh 22:8,9
10 [1]Lit *dwelt in* [2]Lit *all the face of the east* [a]1 Chr 5:18-21
11 [a]Josh 13:11 [b]Deut 3:10
13 [1]Lit *brother*
16 [1]Lit *goings out* [a]1 Chr 27:29; Song 2:1; Is 35:2; 65:10
17 [a]2 Kin 15:5, 32 [b]2 Kin 14:16, 28

sisting of valiant men, men who bore
shield and sword and shot with bow and
were skillful in battle, *were* 44,760, who
[a]went to war.
19 They made war against [a]the Hagrites, [b]Jetur, Naphish and Nodab.
20 They were helped against them,
and the Hagrites and all who *were* with
them were given into their hand; for
[a]they cried out to God in the battle, and
He answered their prayers because [b]they
trusted in Him.
21 They took away their cattle: their
50,000 camels, 250,000 sheep, 2,000
donkeys; and 100,000 [1]men.
22 For many fell slain, because [a]the
war *was* of God. And [b]they settled in
their place until the [c]exile.
23 ¶ Now the sons of the half-tribe of
Manasseh lived in the land; from Bashan
to Baal-hermon and [a]Senir and Mount
Hermon they were numerous.
24 These were the heads of their fathers' households, even Epher, Ishi, Eliel,
Azriel, Jeremiah, Hodaviah and Jahdiel,
mighty men of valor, famous men, heads
of their fathers' households.
25 ¶ But they [a]acted treacherously
against the God of their fathers and
[b]played the harlot [c]after the gods of the
peoples of the land, whom God had destroyed before them.
26 So the God of Israel stirred up the
spirit of [a]Pul, king of Assyria, even the
spirit of [1]Tilgath-pilneser king of Assyria,
and he [b]carried them away into exile,
namely the Reubenites, the Gadites and
the half-tribe of Manasseh, and brought
them to Halah, Habor, Hara and to the
river of Gozan, to this day.

Genealogy: The Priestly Line

6 [1a]The sons of Levi *were* [2]Gershon,
Kohath and Merari.
2 The sons of Kohath *were* Amram,
Izhar, Hebron and Uzziel.
3 The children of Amram *were* Aaron, Moses and Miriam. And the sons of
Aaron *were* Nadab, Abihu, Eleazar and
Ithamar.
4 Eleazar [1]became the father of
Phinehas, *and* Phinehas became the father of Abishua,
5 and Abishua became the father of
Bukki, and Bukki became the father of
Uzzi,
6 and Uzzi became the father of Zerahiah, and Zerahiah became the father of
Meraioth,
7 Meraioth became the father of Amariah, and Amariah became the father of
Ahitub,
8 and [a]Ahitub became the father of
Zadok, and Zadok [b]became the father of
Ahimaaz,
9 and Ahimaaz became the father of
Azariah, and Azariah became the father
of Johanan,
10 and Johanan became the father of
Azariah ([a]it was he who served as the
priest in the house [b]which Solomon built
in Jerusalem),
11 and [a]Azariah became the father of
Amariah, and Amariah became the father
of Ahitub,
12 and Ahitub became the father of
Zadok, and Zadok became the father of
[1]Shallum,
13 and Shallum became the father
of Hilkiah, and Hilkiah became the father
of Azariah,
14 and Azariah became the father of
[a]Seraiah, and Seraiah became the father
of Jehozadak;
15 and Jehozadak went *along* when
the LORD carried Judah and Jerusalem
away into exile [1]by Nebuchadnezzar.
16 ¶ [1a]The sons of Levi *were* [2]Ger-
shom, Kohath and Merari.
17 These are the names of the sons of
Gershom: Libni and Shimei.
18 The sons of Kohath *were* Amram,
Izhar, Hebron and Uzziel.
19 The sons of [a]Merari *were* Mahli
and Mushi. And these are the families of
the Levites according to their fathers'
households.
20 Of Gershom: Libni his son, Jahath
his son, Zimmah his son,
21 Joah his son, Iddo his son, Zerah his
son, Jeatherai his son.
22 The sons of Kohath *were* Amminadab his son, Korah his son, Assir his son,
23 Elkanah his son, Ebiasaph his son
and Assir his son,
24 Tahath his son, Uriel his son, Uzziah his son and Shaul his son.
25 The sons of Elkanah *were* Amasai
and Ahimoth.
26 *As for* Elkanah, the sons of Elkanah
were Zophai his son and Nahath his son,
27 Eliab his son, Jeroham his son, Elkanah his son.
28 The sons of Samuel *were* [a]Joel the
firstborn, and Abijah the second.
29 The sons of Merari *were* Mahli, Libni his son, Shimei his son, Uzzah his son,
30 Shimea his son, Haggiah his son,
Asaiah his son.
31 ¶ [a]Now these are those whom David appointed over the service of song in
the house of the LORD, [b]after the ark rested *there.*
32 They ministered with song before
the tabernacle of the tent of meeting, until Solomon had built the house of the

18 [a]Num 1:3
19 [a]1 Chr 5:10 [b]Gen 25:15; 1 Chr 1:31
20 [a]2 Chr 14:11-13 [b]Ps 9:10; 20:7,8; 22:4,5
21 [1]Lit *souls of men*
22 [a]Josh 23:10; 2 Chr 32:8; Rom 8:31 [b]1 Chr 4:41 [c]2 Kin 15:29; 17:6
23 [a]Deut 3:9
25 [a]Deut 32:15-18 [b]Ex 34:15 [c]2 Kin 17:7
26 [1]In 2 Kin 15:29, *Tiglath-pileser* [a]2 Kin 15:19,29; 2 Chr 28:20 [b]2 Kin 17:6
6:1 [1]Ch 5:27 in Heb [2]In v 16, *Gershom* [a]Gen 46:11; Ex 6:16-25
4 [1]Lit *begot*, and so throughout the ch
8 [a]2 Sam 8:17 [b]2 Sam 15:27
10 [a]2 Chr 26:17 [b]1 Kin 6:1; 2 Chr 3:1
11 [a]Ezra 7:3
12 [1]In ch 9:11, *Meshullam*
14 [a]Neh 11:11
15 [1]Lit *by the hand of*
16 [1]Ch 6:1 in Heb [2]In v 1, *Gershon* [a]Gen 46:11; Ex 6:16
19 [a]Num 3:33; 1 Chr 23:21
28 [a]1 Sam 8:2; 1 Chr 6:33
31 [a]1 Chr 15:16-22,27; 16:4-6 [b]2 Sam 6:17; 1 Kin 8:4; 1 Chr 15:25-16:1

LORD in Jerusalem; and they [1]served in
their office according to their order.
33 These are those who [1]served with
their sons: From the sons of the Kohathites *were* Heman the singer, the son of
Joel, the son of Samuel,
34 the son of Elkanah, the son of Jeroham, the son of Eliel, the son of Toah,
35 the son of Zuph, the son of Elkanah,
the son of Mahath, the son of Amasai,
36 the son of Elkanah, the son of Joel,
the son of Azariah, the son of Zephaniah,
37 the son of Tahath, the son of Assir,
the son of Ebiasaph, the son of Korah,
38 the son of Izhar, the son of Kohath,
the son of Levi, the son of Israel.
39 *Heman's* brother Asaph stood at his
right hand, even Asaph the son of Berechiah, the son of Shimea,
40 the son of Michael, the son of Baa-
seiah, the son of Malchijah,
41 the son of Ethni, the son of Zerah,
the son of Adaiah,
42 the son of Ethan, the son of Zimmah, the son of Shimei,
43 the son of Jahath, the son of Gershom, the son of Levi.
44 On the left hand *were* their [1]kins-
men the sons of Merari: Ethan the son of
Kishi, the son of Abdi, the son of Malluch,
45 the son of Hashabiah, the son of
Amaziah, the son of Hilkiah,
46 the son of Amzi, the son of Bani,
the son of Shemer,
47 the son of Mahli, the son of Mushi,
the son of Merari, the son of Levi.
48 Their [1]kinsmen the Levites were
[2]appointed for all the service of the tabernacle of the house of God.
49 ¶ But Aaron and his sons [1a]offered
on the altar of burnt offering and [b]on the
altar of incense, for all the work of the
most holy place, and [c]to make atonement for Israel, according to all that Moses the servant of God had commanded.
50 [a]These are the sons of Aaron: Eleazar his son, Phinehas his son, Abishua his
son,
51 Bukki his son, Uzzi his son, Zerahiah his son,
52 Meraioth his son, Amariah his son,
Ahitub his son,
53 Zadok his son, Ahimaaz his son.
54 ¶ Now these are their settlements
according to their camps within their borders. To the sons of Aaron of the families
of the Kohathites (for theirs was the
[a]*first* lot),
55 to them they gave [a]Hebron in the
land of Judah and its pasture lands
around it;
56 [a]but the fields of the city and its
villages, they gave to Caleb the son of
Jephunneh.
57 [a]To the sons of Aaron they gave
the *following* cities of refuge: Hebron,
Libnah also with its pasture lands, Jattir,
Eshtemoa with its pasture lands,
58 [1]Hilen with its pasture lands, Debir with its pasture lands,
59 [1]Ashan with its pasture lands and
Beth-shemesh with its pasture lands;
60 and from the tribe of Benjamin:
Geba with its pasture lands, [1]Allemeth
with its pasture lands, and Anathoth with
its pasture lands. All their cities throughout their families were thirteen cities.
61 ¶ [a]Then to the rest of the sons of
Kohath *were given* by lot, from the family
of the tribe, from the half-tribe, the half
of Manasseh, ten cities.
62 To the sons of Gershom, according
to their families, *were given* from the
tribe of Issachar and from the tribe of
Asher, the tribe of Naphtali, and the tribe
of Manasseh, thirteen cities in Bashan.
63 [a]To the sons of Merari *were given*
by lot, according to their families, from
the tribe of Reuben, the tribe of Gad and
the tribe of Zebulun, twelve cities.
64 [a]So the sons of Israel gave to the
Levites the cities with their pasture
lands.
65 They gave by lot from the tribe of
the sons of Judah, the tribe of the sons of
Simeon and the tribe of the sons of Benjamin, [a]these cities which are mentioned
by name.
66 ¶ [a]Now some of the families of the
sons of Kohath had cities of their territory
from the tribe of Ephraim.
67 They gave to them the *following*
cities of refuge: Shechem in the hill country of Ephraim with its pasture lands, Gezer also with its pasture lands,
68 Jokmeam with its pasture lands,
Beth-horon with its pasture lands,
69 Aijalon with its pasture lands and
Gath-rimmon with its pasture lands;
70 and from the half-tribe of Manasseh: Aner with its pasture lands and Bile-
am with its pasture lands, for the rest of
the family of the sons of Kohath.
71 ¶ To the sons of Gershom *were giv-
en,* from the family of the half-tribe of
Manasseh: Golan in Bashan with its pasture lands and Ashtaroth with its pasture
lands;
72 and from the tribe of Issachar: Kedesh with its pasture lands, Daberath
with its pasture lands
73 and Ramoth with its pasture lands,
Anem with its pasture lands;
74 and from the tribe of Asher: Mashal
with its pasture lands, Abdon with its pasture lands,

32 [1]Lit *stood over*
33 [1]Lit *stood*
44 [1]Lit *brothers*
48 [1]Lit *brothers* [2]Lit *given*
49 [1]Lit *offered up in smoke* [a]Ex 27:1-8 [b]Ex 30:1-7 [c]Ex 30:10-16
50 [a]1 Chr 6:4-8; Ezra 7:5
54 [a]Josh 21:4, 10
55 [a]Josh 14:13; 21:11f
56 [a]Josh 15:13
57 [a]Josh 21:13, 19
58 [1]In Josh 21:15, *Holon*
59 [1]In Josh 21:16, *Ain*
60 [1]In Josh 21:18, *Almon*
61 [a]Josh 21:5; 1 Chr 6:66-70
63 [a]Josh 21:7, 34-40
64 [a]Num 35:1-8; Josh 21:3,41,42
65 [a]1 Chr 6:57-60
66 [a]Josh 21:20-26

75 Hukok with its pasture lands and
Rehob with its pasture lands;
76 and from the tribe of Naphtali: Kedesh in Galilee with its pasture lands,
Hammon with its pasture lands and Kiriathaim with its pasture lands.
77 ¶ To the rest of *the Levites,* the
sons of Merari, *were given,* from the tribe
of Zebulun: Rimmono with its pasture
lands, Tabor with its pasture lands;
78 and beyond the Jordan at Jericho,
on the east side of the Jordan, *were given
them,* from the tribe of Reuben: Bezer in
the wilderness with its pasture lands, Jah-
zah with its pasture lands,
79 Kedemoth with its pasture lands
and Mephaath with its pasture lands;
80 and from the tribe of Gad: Ramoth
in Gilead with its pasture lands, Mahanaim with its pasture lands,
81 Heshbon with its pasture lands and
Jazer with its pasture lands.

Genealogy from Issachar

7 Now the sons of Issachar *were* four:
Tola, [1]Puah, [2]Jashub and Shimron.
2 The sons of Tola *were* Uzzi, Rephaiah, Jeriel, Jahmai, Ibsam and Samuel,
heads of their fathers' households. *The
sons* of Tola *were* mighty men of valor in
their generations; [a]their number in the
days of David was 22,600.
3 The [1]son of Uzzi *was* Izrahiah. And
the sons of Izrahiah *were* Michael, Obadiah, Joel, Isshiah; all five of them *were*
[a]chief men.
4 With them by their generations according to their fathers' households were
36,000 [1]troops of the army for war, for
they had many wives and sons.
5 Their [1]relatives among all the families of Issachar *were* mighty men of valor,
enrolled by genealogy, in all 87,000.

Descendants of Benjamin

6 ¶ [a]*The sons of* Benjamin *were*
three: Bela and Becher and Jediael.
7 The sons of Bela were five: Ezbon,
Uzzi, Uzziel, Jerimoth and Iri. They *were*
heads of fathers' households, mighty men
of valor, and were 22,034 enrolled by
genealogy.
8 The sons of Becher *were* Zemirah,
Joash, Eliezer, Elioenai, Omri, Jeremoth,
Abijah, Anathoth and Alemeth. All these
were the sons of Becher.
9 They were enrolled by genealogy,
according to their generations, heads of
their fathers' households, 20,200 mighty
men of valor.
10 The [1]son of Jediael *was* Bilhan.
And the sons of Bilhan *were* Jeush, Benjamin, Ehud, Chenaanah, Zethan, Tarshish
and Ahishahar.
11 All these *were* sons of Jediael, according to the heads of their fathers'
households, 17,200 mighty men of valor,
who were [1]ready to go out with the army
to war.
12 [1]Shuppim and [2]Huppim *were* the
sons of [3]Ir; Hushim *was* the [4]son of
[5]Aher.

Sons of Naphtali

13 ¶ The sons of Naphtali *were* [1]Jahzi-
el, Guni, Jezer, and [2]Shallum, the sons of
Bilhah.

Descendants of Manasseh

14 ¶ The sons of Manasseh *were* Asriel, whom his Aramean concubine bore;
she bore Machir the father of Gilead.
15 Machir took a wife for Huppim and
Shuppim, [1]whose sister's name was Maacah. And the name of the second was
Zelophehad, and Zelophehad had daughters.
16 Maacah the wife of Machir bore a
son, and she named him Peresh; and the
name of his brother *was* Sheresh, and his
sons *were* Ulam and Rakem.
17 The [1]son of Ulam *was* Bedan.
These *were* the sons of Gilead the son of
Machir, the son of Manasseh.
18 His sister Hammolecheth bore Ish-
hod and [1]Abiezer and Mahlah.
19 The sons of Shemida were Ahian
and Shechem and Likhi and Aniam.

Descendants of Ephraim

20 ¶ [a]The sons of Ephraim *were* Shuthelah and [1]Bered his son, Tahath his
son, Eleadah his son, Tahath his son,
21 Zabad his son, Shuthelah his son,
and Ezer and Elead whom the men of
Gath who were born in the land killed,
because they came down to take their
livestock.
22 Their father Ephraim [a]mourned
many days, and his relatives [b]came to
comfort him.
23 Then he went in to his wife, and
she conceived and bore a son, and he
named him [1]Beriah, because misfortune
had come upon his house.
24 His daughter was Sheerah, [a]who
built lower and upper Beth-horon, also
Uzzen-sheerah.
25 Rephah was his son *along* with Re-
sheph, Telah his son, Tahan his son,
26 Ladan his son, Ammihud his son,
Elishama his son,
27 [1]Non his son and [a]Joshua his son.
28 ¶ [a]Their possessions and settlements *were* Bethel with its towns, and to
the east [1]Naaran, and to the west Gezer
with its towns, and Shechem with its
towns as far as [2]Ayyah with its towns,

7:1 [1]In Gen 46:13, *Puvah;* in Num 26:23, *Puvah* [2]In Gen 46:13, *Iob*
2 [a]2 Sam 24:1-9
3 [1]Lit *sons* [a]1 Chr 5:24
4 [1]Or *bands*
5 [1]Lit *brothers,* and so throughout the ch
6 [a]1 Chr 8:1-40
10 [1]Lit *sons*
11 [1]Lit *going out*
12 [1]In Num 26:39, *Shephupham* [2]In Num 26:39, *Hupham* [3]In v 7, *Iri* [4]Lit *sons* [5]In Num 26:38, *Ahiram*
13 [1]In Gen 46:24, *Jahzeel* [2]In Gen 46:24 and Num 26:49, *Shillem*
15 [1]Lit *and his*
17 [1]Lit *sons*
18 [1]In Num 26:30, *Iezer*
20 [1]In Num 26:35, *Becher* [a]Num 26:35,36
22 [a]Gen 37:34 [b]Job 2:11; John 11:19
23 [1]I.e. on misfortune
24 [a]Josh 16:3,5; 2 Chr 8:5
27 [1]In Ex 33:11, *Nun* [a]Ex 17:9-14; 24:13
28 [1]In Josh 16:7, *Naarah* [2]Many mss read *Azzah* [a]Josh 16:2

29 and along the borders of the sons of Manasseh, Beth-shean with its towns, Taanach with its towns, Megiddo with its towns, Dor with its towns. In these lived the [a]sons of Joseph the son of Israel.

Descendants of Asher

30 ¶ [a]The sons of Asher *were* Imnah, Ishvah, Ishvi and Beriah, and Serah their sister.

31 The sons of Beriah *were* Heber and Malchiel, who was the father of Birzaith.

32 Heber [1]became the father of Japhlet, [2]Shomer and Hotham, and Shua their sister.

33 The sons of Japhlet *were* Pasach, Bimhal and Ashvath. These were the sons of Japhlet.

34 The sons of [1]Shemer *were* Ahi and Rohgah, Jehubbah and Aram.

35 The [1]sons of his brother Helem *were* Zophah, Imna, Shelesh and Amal.

36 The sons of Zophah *were* Suah, Harnepher, Shual, Beri and Imrah,

37 Bezer, Hod, Shamma, Shilshah, Ithran and Beera.

38 The sons of Jether *were* Jephunneh, Pispa and Ara.

39 The sons of Ulla *were* Arah, Hanniel and Rizia.

40 All these *were* the sons of Asher, heads of the fathers' houses, choice and mighty men of valor, heads of the princes. And the number of them enrolled by genealogy for service in war was 26,000 men.

Genealogy from Benjamin

8 And [a]Benjamin [1]became the father of Bela his firstborn, Ashbel the second, [b]Aharah the third,

2 Nohah the fourth and Rapha the fifth.

3 Bela had sons: [1]Addar, Gera, Abihud,

4 Abishua, Naaman, Ahoah,

5 Gera, Shephuphan and Huram.

6 These are the sons of Ehud: these are the heads of fathers' *households* of the inhabitants of Geba, and they carried them into exile to Manahath,

7 namely, Naaman, Ahijah and Gera—he carried them into exile; and he became the father of Uzza and Ahihud.

8 Shaharaim became the father of children in the [1]country of Moab after he had [2]sent away Hushim and Baara his wives.

9 By Hodesh his wife he became the father of Jobab, Zibia, Mesha, Malcam,

10 Jeuz, Sachia, Mirmah. These were his sons, heads of fathers' *households.*

11 By Hushim he became the father of Abitub and Elpaal.

29 [a]Judg 1:22-29
30 [a]Gen 46:17; Num 26:44-46
32 [1]Lit *begot* [2]In v 34, *Shemer*
34 [1]In v 32, *Shomer*
35 [1]Lit *son*
8:1 [1]Lit *begot,* and so throughout the ch [a]Gen 46:21; 1 Chr 7:6-12 [b]1 Chr 7:12
3 [1]In Gen 46:21 and Num 26:40, *Ard*
8 [1]Lit *field* [2]Lit *sent them away*
14 [1]Or *his brothers*
21 [1]In v 13, *Shema*
28 [1]Lit *these*
29 [a]1 Chr 9:35-38
31 [1]In ch 9:37, *Zechariah*
32 [1]In ch 9:38, *Shimeam* [2]Lit *brothers*
33 [1]1 Sam 14:49, *Ishvi* [2]In 2 Sam 2:8, *Ish-bosheth* [a]1 Chr 9:39-44
34 [1]In 2 Sam 4:4, *Mephibosheth*
35 [1]In 9:41, *Tahrea*
36 [1]In 9:42, *Jarah*
37 [1]In 9:43, *Rephaiah*

12 The sons of Elpaal *were* Eber, Misham, and Shemed, who built Ono and Lod, with its towns;

13 and Beriah and Shema, who were heads of fathers' *households* of the inhabitants of Aijalon, who put to flight the inhabitants of Gath;

14 and [1]Ahio, Shashak and Jeremoth.

15 Zebadiah, Arad, Eder,

16 Michael, Ishpah and Joha *were* the sons of Beriah.

17 Zebadiah, Meshullam, Hizki, Heber,

18 Ishmerai, Izliah and Jobab *were* the sons of Elpaal.

19 Jakim, Zichri, Zabdi,

20 Elienai, Zillethai, Eliel,

21 Adaiah, Beraiah and Shimrath *were* the sons of [1]Shimei.

22 Ishpan, Eber, Eliel,

23 Abdon, Zichri, Hanan,

24 Hananiah, Elam, Anthothijah,

25 Iphdeiah and Penuel *were* the sons of Shashak.

26 Shamsherai, Shehariah, Athaliah,

27 Jaareshiah, Elijah and Zichri *were* the sons of Jeroham.

28 These were heads of the fathers' *households* according to their generations, chief men [1]who lived in Jerusalem.

29 ¶ [a]Now in Gibeon, *Jeiel,* the father of Gibeon lived, and his wife's name was Maacah;

30 and his firstborn son *was* Abdon, then Zur, Kish, Baal, Nadab,

31 Gedor, Ahio and [1]Zecher.

32 Mikloth became the father of [1]Shimeah. And they also lived with their [2]relatives in Jerusalem opposite their *other* [2]relatives.

Genealogy from King Saul

33 [a]Ner became the father of Kish, and Kish became the father of Saul, and Saul became the father of Jonathan, Malchi-shua, [1]Abinadab and [2]Eshbaal.

34 The son of Jonathan *was* [1]Merib-baal, and Merib-baal became the father of Micah.

35 The sons of Micah *were* Pithon, Melech, [1]Tarea and Ahaz.

36 Ahaz became the father of [1]Jehoaddah, and Jehoaddah became the father of Alemeth, Azmaveth and Zimri; and Zimri became the father of Moza.

37 Moza became the father of Binea; [1]Raphah *was* his son, Eleasah his son, Azel his son.

38 Azel had six sons, and these *were* their names: Azrikam, Bocheru, Ishmael, Sheariah, Obadiah and Hanan. All these *were* the sons of Azel.

39 The sons of Eshek his brother *were*

Ulam his firstborn, Jeush the second and
Eliphelet the third.
40 The sons of Ulam were mighty men
of valor, archers, and had many sons and
grandsons, 150 *of them.* All these *were* of
the sons of Benjamin.

People of Jerusalem

9 So all Israel was enrolled by genealogies; and behold, they are written in
the Book of the Kings of Israel. And [a]Ju-
dah was carried away into exile to Babylon for their unfaithfulness.
2 ¶ [a]Now the first who lived in their
possessions in their cities *were* Israel, the
priests, the Levites and [b]the [1]temple
servants.
3 Some of the sons of Judah, of the
sons of Benjamin and of the sons of
Ephraim and Manasseh lived in [a]Jerusa-
lem:
4 Uthai the son of Ammihud, the son
of Omri, the son of Imri, the son of Bani,
from the sons of Perez the [a]son of Judah.
5 From the Shilonites *were* Asaiah
the firstborn and his sons.
6 From the sons of Zerah *were* Jeuel
and their [1]relatives, 690 *of them.*
7 From the sons of Benjamin *were*
Sallu the son of Meshullam, the son of
Hodaviah, the son of Hassenuah,
8 and Ibneiah the son of Jeroham,
and Elah the son of Uzzi, the son of Mi-
chri, and Meshullam the son of Shephatiah, the son of Reuel, the son of Ibnijah;
9 and their relatives according to
their generations, [a]956. All these *were*
heads of fathers' *households* according to
their fathers' houses.
10 ¶ [a]From the priests *were* Jedaiah,
Jehoiarib, Jachin,
11 and [1]Azariah the son of Hilkiah,
the son of Meshullam, the son of Zadok,
the son of Meraioth, the son of Ahitub,
[a]the chief officer of the house of God;
12 and Adaiah the son of Jeroham, the
son of Pashhur, the son of Malchijah, and
Maasai the son of Adiel, the son of Jahze-
rah, the son of Meshullam, the son of
Meshillemith, the son of Immer;
13 and their relatives, heads of their
fathers' households, 1,760 very able men
for the work of the service of the house
of God.
14 ¶ [a]Of the Levites *were* Shemaiah
the son of Hasshub, the son of Azrikam,
the son of Hashabiah, of the sons of Merari;
15 and Bakbakkar, Heresh and Galal
and Mattaniah the son of Mica, the son of
[1]Zichri, the son of Asaph,
16 and [1]Obadiah the son of [2]Shema-
iah, the son of Galal, the son of Jeduthun,
and Berechiah the son of Asa, the son of
Elkanah, who lived in the villages of the
Netophathites.
17 ¶ Now the gatekeepers *were* [1]Shal-
lum and Akkub and Talmon and Ahiman
and their relatives (Shallum the chief
18 *being stationed* until now at [a]the
king's gate to the east). These *were* the
gatekeepers for the camp of the sons of
Levi.
19 Shallum the son of Kore, the son of
[1]Ebiasaph, the son of Korah, and his relatives of his father's house, the Korahites,
were over the work of the service, keepers of the thresholds of the tent; and their
fathers had been over the camp of the
LORD, keepers of the entrance.
20 [a]Phinehas the son of Eleazar was
ruler over them previously, *and* the LORD
was with him.
21 [a]Zechariah the son of Meshelemiah was gatekeeper of the entrance of the
tent of meeting.
22 All these who were chosen to be
gatekeepers at the thresholds were 212.
These were enrolled by genealogy in
their villages, [a]whom David and Samuel
the seer appointed [b]in their office of
trust.
23 So they and their sons [1]had charge
of the gates of the house of the LORD,
even the house of the tent, as guards.
24 The gatekeepers were [1]on the four
sides, to the east, west, north and south.
25 Their relatives in their villages
[a]*were* to come in every seven days from
time to time *to be* with [1]them;
26 for the four chief gatekeepers who
were Levites, were in an office of trust,
and were over the chambers and over the
treasuries in the house of God.
27 They spent the night around the
house of God, [a]because the watch was
[1]committed to them; and they *were* [2]in
charge of opening *it* morning by morning.
28 ¶ Now some of them [1]had charge
of the utensils of service, for [2]they counted them when they brought them in and
when they took them out.
29 Some of them also were appointed
over the furniture and over all the utensils of the sanctuary and [a]over the fine
flour and the wine and the oil and the
frankincense and the spices.
30 Some of [a]the sons of the priests
prepared the mixing of the spices.
31 Mattithiah, one of the Levites, who
was the firstborn of Shallum the Korahite,
had [a]the [1]responsibility over the things
which were baked in pans.
32 Some of their relatives of the sons
of the Kohathites [a]*were* over the showbread to prepare it every sabbath.
33 ¶ Now these are [a]the singers,
heads of fathers' *households* of the Le-

9:1 [a]1 Chr 5:25, 26
2 [1]Heb *Nethinim* [a]Ezra 2:70; Neh 7:73; 11:3-22 [b]Ezra 2:43,58; 8:20
3 [a]Neh 11:1
4 [a]Gen 46:12; Num 26:20
6 [1]Lit *brothers,* and so throughout the ch
9 [a]Neh 11:8
10 [a]Neh 11:10-14
11 [1]In Neh 11:11, *Seraiah* [a]Jer 20:1
14 [a]Neh 11:15-19
15 [1]In Neh 11:17, *Zabdi*
16 [1]In Neh 11:17, *Abda* [2]In Neh 11:17, *Shammua*
17 [1]In v 21, *Meshelemiah*; in 26:14, *Shelemiah*; in Neh 12:25, *Meshullam*
18 [a]Ezek 44:1; 46:1,2
19 [1]In Ex 6:24, *Abiasaph*
20 [a]Num 25:7-13
21 [a]1 Chr 26:2, 14
22 [a]1 Chr 26:1 [b]2 Chr 31:15,18
23 [1]Lit were *over the gates*
24 [1]Lit *to the four winds*
25 [1]Lit *these* [a]2 Kin 11:5,7; 2 Chr 23:8
27 [1]Lit *on them* [2]Lit *over the opening* [a]1 Chr 23:30-32
28 [1]Lit *were over the* [2]Lit *by count they brought them in and by count they took them out*
29 [a]1 Chr 23:29
30 [a]Ex 30:23-25
31 [1]Lit *office of trust* [a]1 Chr 9:22
32 [a]Lev 24:5-8
33 [a]1 Chr 6:31-47; 25:1

vites, *who lived* in the chambers *of the*
temple free *from other service;* for they
were [1]engaged [b]in their work day and
night.
34 These were heads of fathers' *house-*
holds of the Levites according to their
generations, chief men, [1]who lived in
Jerusalem.

Ancestry and Descendants of Saul

35 ¶ [a]In Gibeon Jeiel the father of
Gibeon lived, and his wife's name was
Maacah,
36 and his firstborn son *was* Abdon,
then Zur, Kish, Baal, Ner, Nadab,
37 Gedor, Ahio, Zechariah and Mikloth.
38 Mikloth became the father of Shimeam. And they also lived with their relatives in Jerusalem opposite their *other*
relatives.
39 [a]Ner became the father of Kish,
and Kish became the father of Saul, and
Saul became the father of Jonathan,
Malchi-shua, Abinadab and Eshbaal.
40 The son of Jonathan *was* Merib-
baal; and Merib-baal became the father of
Micah.
41 The sons of Micah *were* Pithon,
Melech, Tahrea [a]*and Ahaz.*
42 Ahaz became the father of Jarah,
and Jarah became the father of Alemeth,
Azmaveth and Zimri; and Zimri became
the father of Moza,
43 and Moza became the father of Binea and Rephaiah his son, Eleasah his son,
Azel his son.
44 Azel had six sons whose names are
these: Azrikam, Bocheru and Ishmael and
Sheariah and Obadiah and Hanan. These
were the sons of Azel.

Defeat and Death of Saul and His Sons

10 [a]Now the Philistines fought
against Israel; and the men of Israel fled before the Philistines and fell slain
on Mount Gilboa.
2 The Philistines closely pursued
Saul and his sons, and the Philistines
struck down Jonathan, [1a]Abinadab and
Malchi-shua, the sons of Saul.
3 The battle became heavy against
Saul, and the archers [1]overtook him; and
he was wounded by the archers.
4 Then Saul said to his armor bearer,
"Draw your sword and thrust me through
with it, otherwise these uncircumcised
will come and abuse me." But his armor
bearer would not, for he was greatly
afraid. [a]Therefore Saul took his sword
and fell on it.
5 When his armor bearer saw that
Saul was dead, he likewise fell on his
sword and died.
6 [a]Thus Saul died with his three
sons, and all *those* of his house died together.
7 ¶ When all the men of Israel who
were in the valley saw that they had fled,
and that Saul and his sons were dead,
they forsook their cities and fled; and the
Philistines came and lived in them.
8 ¶ It came about the next day, when
the Philistines came to strip the slain,
that they found Saul and his sons fallen
on Mount Gilboa.
9 [a]So they stripped him and took his
head and his armor and sent *messengers*
around the land of the Philistines to carry
the good news to their idols and to the
people.
10 They put his armor in the house of
their gods and fastened his head in the
house of Dagon.

Jabesh-gilead's Tribute to Saul

11 When all Jabesh-gilead heard all
that the Philistines had done to Saul,
12 [a]all the valiant men arose and took
away the body of Saul and the bodies of
his sons and brought them to Jabesh, and
they buried their bones under the oak in
Jabesh, and fasted seven days.
13 ¶ [a]So Saul died for his trespass
which he committed against the LORD,
because of the word of the LORD which he
did not keep; and also [b]because he asked
counsel of a medium, making inquiry
of it,
14 and did not inquire of the LORD.
Therefore He killed him and [a]turned the
kingdom to David the son of Jesse.

David Made King over All Israel

11 [a]Then all Israel gathered to David at Hebron [1]and said, "Behold, we are your bone and your flesh.
2 "In times past, even when Saul was
king, you *were* the one who led out and
brought in Israel; and the LORD your God
said to you, '[a]You shall shepherd My
people Israel, and you shall be prince
over My people Israel.' "
3 So all the elders of Israel came to
the king at Hebron, and David made a
covenant with them in Hebron before the
LORD; and [a]they anointed David king
over Israel, [b]according to the word of the
LORD through Samuel.

Jerusalem, Capital City

4 ¶ Then David and all Israel went to
Jerusalem ([a]that is, Jebus); and the Jebusites, the inhabitants of the land, *were*
there.
5 The inhabitants of Jebus said to Da-

33 [1]Lit *over them in the work* [b]Ps 134:1
34 [1]Lit *these*
35 [a]1 Chr 8:29-32
39 [a]1 Chr 8:33-38
41 [a]1 Chr 8:35-37
10:1 [a]1 Sam 31:1-13
2 [1]In 1 Sam 14:49, *Ishvi* [a]1 Sam 31:2
3 [1]Lit *found him*
4 [a]1 Sam 31:4
6 [a]1 Sam 31:6
9 [a]1 Sam 31:9
12 [a]1 Sam 31:12f
13 [a]1 Sam 13:13,14; 15:23 [b]Lev 19:31; 20:6; 1 Sam 28:7
14 [a]1 Sam 15:28; 1 Chr 12:23
11:1 [1]Lit *saying* [a]2 Sam 5:1,3, 6-10
2 [a]2 Sam 5:2; 7:7
3 [a]2 Sam 2:4; 5:3,5 [b]1 Sam 16:1,3,12,13
4 [a]Josh 15:8,63; Judg 1:21

vid, "You shall not enter here." Nevertheless David captured the stronghold of
Zion (that is, the city of David).
6 Now David had said, "Whoever
strikes down a Jebusite first shall be chief
and commander." [a]Joab the son of Zeruiah went up first, so he became chief.
7 Then David dwelt in the stronghold; therefore it was called the city of
David.
8 He [1]built the city all around, from
the [2]Millo even to the surrounding area;
and Joab [3]repaired the rest of the city.
9 [a]David became greater and greater, for the LORD of hosts *was* with him.

David's Mighty Men

10 ¶ [a]Now these are the heads of the
mighty men whom David had, who gave
him strong support in his kingdom, together with all Israel, to make him king,
[b]according to the word of the LORD concerning Israel.
11 These *constitute* the list of the
mighty men whom David had: [a]Jashobe-
am, the son of a Hachmonite, [b]the chief
of the thirty; he lifted up his spear against
three hundred [1]whom he killed at one
time.
12 ¶ After him was Eleazar the son of
[a]Dodo, the Ahohite, who *was* [1]one of
the three mighty men.
13 He was with David at [1]Pasdammim
[a]when the Philistines were gathered together there to battle, and there was a
plot of ground full of barley; and the people fled before the Philistines.
14 They took their stand in the midst
of the plot and defended it, and struck
down the Philistines; and the LORD saved
them by a great [1]victory.
15 ¶ Now three of the thirty chief men
went down to the rock to David, into the
cave of Adullam, while [a]the army of the
Philistines was camping in the valley of
Rephaim.
16 David was then in the stronghold,
while [a]the garrison of the Philistines *was*
then in Bethlehem.
17 David had a craving and said, "Oh
that someone would give me water to
drink from the well of Bethlehem, which
is by the gate!"
18 So the three broke through the
camp of the Philistines and drew water
from the well of Bethlehem which *was* by
the gate, and took *it* and brought *it* to
David; nevertheless David would not
drink it, but poured it out to the LORD;
19 and he said, "Be it far from me before my God that I should do this. Shall I
drink the blood of these men *who went*
[1]at the risk of their lives? For at the risk
of their lives they brought it." Therefore
he would not drink it. These things the
three mighty men did.
20 ¶ As for [1]Abshai the brother of
Joab, he was chief of the [2]thirty, and he
swung his spear against three hundred
[3]and killed them; and he had a name as
well as the [2]thirty.
21 Of the three in the second *rank* he
was the most honored and became their
commander; however, he did not attain
to the *first* three.
22 ¶ [a]Benaiah the son of Jehoiada, the
son of a valiant man of Kabzeel, mighty in
deeds, struck down the [1]two *sons of*
Ariel of Moab. He also went down and
[2]killed a lion inside a pit on a snowy day.
23 He [1]killed an Egyptian, a man of
great stature five [2]cubits tall. Now in the
Egyptian's hand *was* [a]a spear like a weaver's beam, but he went down to him with
a club and snatched the spear from the
Egyptian's hand and [1]killed him with his
own spear.
24 These *things* Benaiah the son of Jehoiada did, and had a name as well as the
three mighty men.
25 Behold, he was honored among the
thirty, but he did not attain to the three;
and David appointed him over his guard.
26 ¶ Now the mighty men of the armies *were* Asahel the brother of Joab, Elhanan the son of Dodo of Bethlehem,
27 [1]Shammoth the Harorite, Helez
the [2]Pelonite,
28 Ira the son of Ikkesh the Tekoite,
Abiezer the Anathothite,
29 [1]Sibbecai the Hushathite, [2]Ilai the
Ahohite,
30 Maharai the Netophathite, [1]Heled
the son of Baanah the Netophathite,
31 Ithai the son of Ribai of Gibeah of
the sons of Benjamin, Benaiah the Pirathonite,
32 [1]Hurai of the brooks of Gaash,
[2]Abiel the Arbathite,
33 Azmaveth the Baharumite, Eliahba
the Shaalbonite,
34 the sons of [1]Hashem the Gizonite,
Jonathan the son of Shagee the Hararite,
35 Ahiam the son of [1]Sacar the Hararite, [2]Eliphal the son of Ur,
36 Hepher the Mecherathite, Ahijah
the Pelonite,
37 Hezro the Carmelite, [1]Naarai the
son of Ezbai,
38 Joel the brother of Nathan, Mibhar
the son of Hagri,
39 Zelek the Ammonite, Naharai the
Berothite, the armor bearer of Joab the
son of Zeruiah,
40 Ira the Ithrite, Gareb the Ithrite,
41 Uriah the Hittite, Zabad the son of
Ahlai,
42 Adina the son of Shiza the Reuben-

6 [a]2 Sam 8:16
8 [1]Or *fortified* [2]I.e. citadel [3]Lit *revived*
9 [a]2 Sam 3:1
10 [a]2 Sam 23:8-39 [b]1 Chr 11:3
11 [1]Lit *slain ones* [a]2 Sam 23:8 [b]1 Chr 12:18
12 [1]Lit *among* [a]1 Chr 27:4
13 [1]In 1 Sam 17:1, *Ephesdammim* [a]2 Sam 23:11,12
14 [1]Or *salvation*
15 [a]1 Chr 14:9
16 [a]1 Sam 10:5
19 [1]Lit *with their souls*
20 [1]In 2 Sam 23:18, *Abishai* [2]So Syriac; M.T. *three* [3]Lit *slain ones*
22 [1]Or *two lion-like heroes* of [2]Lit *smote* [a]2 Sam 8:18
23 [1]Lit *smote* [2]I.e. One cubit equals approx 18 in. [a]1 Sam 17:7
27 [1]In 2 Sam 23:25, *Shammah the Harodite* [2]In 2 Sam 23:26, *Paltite*
29 [1]In 2 Sam 23:27, *Mebunnai* [2]In 2 Sam 23:28, *Zalmon*
30 [1]In 2 Sam 23:29, *Heleb*
32 [1]In 2 Sam 23:30, *Hiddai* [2]In 2 Sam 23:31, *Abi-albon*
34 [1]In 2 Sam 23:32, *Jashen*
35 [1]In 2 Sam 23:33, *Sharar* [2]In 2 Sam 23:34, *Eliphelet the son of Ahasbai*
37 [1]In 2 Sam 23:35, *Paarai the Arbite*

ite, a chief of the Reubenites, and thirty
with him,
43 Hanan the son of Maacah and Joshaphat the Mithnite,
44 Uzzia the Ashterathite, Shama and
Jeiel the sons of Hotham the Aroerite,
45 Jediael the son of Shimri and Joha
his brother, the Tizite,
46 Eliel the Mahavite and Jeribai and
Joshaviah, the sons of Elnaam, and Ith-
mah the Moabite,
47 Eliel and Obed and Jaasiel the Me-
zobaite.

David's Supporters in Ziklag

12 [a]Now these are the ones who
came to David at Ziklag, while he
was still restricted because of Saul the son
of Kish; and they were among the mighty
men who helped *him* in war.
2 They were equipped with bows,
[a]using both the right hand and the left *to*
sling stones and *to shoot* arrows from the
bow; [b]*they were* Saul's kinsmen from
Benjamin.
3 The chief was Ahiezer, then Joash,
the sons of Shemaah the Gibeathite; and
Jeziel and Pelet, the sons of Azmaveth,
and Beracah and Jehu the Anathothite,
4 and Ishmaiah the Gibeonite, a
mighty man among the thirty, and over
the thirty. [1]Then Jeremiah, Jahaziel, Johanan, Jozabad the Gederathite,
5 [1]Eluzai, Jerimoth, Bealiah, Shemariah, Shephatiah the Haruphite,
6 Elkanah, Isshiah, Azarel, Joezer, Jashobeam, the Korahites,
7 and Joelah and Zebadiah, the sons
of Jeroham of Gedor.
8 ¶ From the Gadites there [1]came
over to David in the stronghold in the
wilderness, mighty men of valor, men
trained for war, who could handle shield
and spear, and whose faces were like the
faces of lions, and [a]*they were* as swift as
the gazelles on the mountains.
9 Ezer *was* the first, Obadiah the second, Eliab the third,
10 Mishmannah the fourth, Jeremiah
the fifth,
11 Attai the sixth, Eliel the seventh,
12 Johanan the eighth, Elzabad the
ninth,
13 Jeremiah the tenth, Machbannai
the eleventh.
14 These of the sons of Gad were
[1]captains of the army; [a]he who was least
was equal to a hundred and the greatest
to a thousand.
15 [a]These are the ones who crossed
the Jordan in the first month when it was
overflowing all its banks and they put to
flight all those in the valleys, both to the
east and to the west.

16 ¶ Then some of the sons of Benjamin and Judah came to the stronghold to
David.
17 David went out to meet them, and
said to them, "If you come peacefully to
me to help me, my heart shall be united
with you; but if to betray me to my adversaries, since there is no [1]wrong in my
hands, may the God of our fathers look on
it and decide."
18 Then [a]the Spirit [1]came upon
[b]Amasai, who was the chief of the thirty,
and he said,

"*We* are yours, O David,
And with you, O son of Jesse!
[c]Peace, peace to you,
And peace to him who helps
you;
Indeed, your God helps you!"

Then David received them and made
them [2]captains of the band.
19 ¶ [a]From Manasseh also some defected to David when he was about to go
to battle with the Philistines against Saul.
But they did not help them, for the lords
of the Philistines after consultation sent
him away, saying, "At *the cost of* our
heads he may defect to his master Saul."
20 As he went to Ziklag there defected
to him from Manasseh: Adnah, Jozabad,
Jediael, Michael, Jozabad, Elihu and Zillethai, [1]captains of thousands who belonged to Manasseh.
21 They helped David against [a]the
band of raiders, for they were all mighty
men of valor, and were captains in the
army.
22 For day by day *men* came to David
to help him, until there was a great army
[a]like the army of God.

Supporters Gathered at Hebron

23 ¶ Now these are the numbers of
the [1]divisions equipped for war, [a]who
came to David at Hebron, [b]to turn the
kingdom of Saul to him, [c]according to
the [2]word of the LORD.
24 The sons of Judah who bore shield
and spear *were* 6,800, equipped for war.
25 Of the sons of Simeon, mighty men
of valor for war, 7,100.
26 Of the sons of Levi 4,600.
27 Now Jehoiada was the leader of *the*
house of Aaron, and with him were
3,700,
28 also [a]Zadok, a young man mighty
of valor, and of his father's house twenty-
two captains.
29 Of the sons of Benjamin, [a]Saul's
kinsmen, 3,000; for until now [b]the
greatest part of them had kept their allegiance to the house of Saul.
30 Of the sons of Ephraim 20,800,

12:1 [a]1 Sam 27:2-6
2 [a]Judg 3:15; 20:16 [b]1 Chr 12:29
4 [1]In Heb the beginning of v 5, making 41 vv in ch
5 [1]V 6 in Heb
8 [1]Lit *separated themselves* [a]2 Sam 2:18
14 [1]Or *chiefs* [a]Deut 32:30
15 [a]Josh 3:15; 4:18
17 [1]Lit *violence*
18 [1]Lit *clothed* [2]Or *chiefs* [a]Judg 3:10; 6:34 [b]1 Chr 2:17 [c]1 Sam 25:5,6
19 [a]1 Sam 29:2-9
20 [1]Or *chiefs*
21 [a]1 Sam 30:1
22 [a]Gen 32:2; Josh 5:13-15
23 [1]Lit *heads* [2]Lit *mouth* [a]2 Sam 2:3,4 [b]1 Chr 10:14 [c]1 Chr 11:10
28 [a]2 Sam 8:17; 1 Chr 6:8,53
29 [a]1 Chr 12:2 [b]2 Sam 2:8,9

mighty men of valor, famous men in their
fathers' households.
31 Of the half-tribe of Manasseh
18,000, who were designated by name to
come and make David king.
32 Of the sons of Issachar, [a]men who
understood the times, with knowledge of
what Israel should do, their chiefs *were*
two hundred; and all their kinsmen *were*
at their command.
33 Of Zebulun, there were 50,000
who went out in the army, who could
draw up in battle formation with all kinds
of weapons of war and helped *David*
[1]with [a]an undivided heart.
34 Of Naphtali *there were* 1,000 captains, and with them 37,000 with shield
and spear.
35 Of the Danites who could draw up
in battle formation, *there were* 28,600.
36 Of Asher *there were* 40,000 who
went out in the army to draw up in battle
formation.
37 From the other side of the Jordan,
of the Reubenites and the Gadites and of
the half-tribe of Manasseh, *there were*
120,000 with all *kinds* of weapons of war
for the battle.
38 ¶ All these, being men of war who
could draw up in battle formation, came
to Hebron with [a]a perfect heart to make
David king over all Israel; and all the rest
also of Israel were of one mind to make
David king.
39 They were there with David three
days, eating and drinking, for their kinsmen had prepared for them.
40 Moreover those who were near to
them, *even* as far as Issachar and Zebulun
and Naphtali, [a]brought food on donkeys,
camels, mules and on oxen, great quantities of flour cakes, fig cakes and bunches
of raisins, wine, oil, oxen and sheep.
There was joy indeed in Israel.

Peril in Transporting the Ark

13 Then David consulted with the
captains of the thousands and the
hundreds, even with every leader.
2 David said to all the assembly of
Israel, "If it seems good to you, and if it
is from the LORD our God, let us send
everywhere to our kinsmen who remain
in all the land of Israel, also to the priests
and Levites who are with them in their
cities with pasture lands, that they may
meet with us;
3 and let us bring back the ark of our
God to us, [a]for we did not seek it in the
days of Saul."
4 Then all the assembly said that they
would do so, for the thing was right in the
eyes of all the people.
5 ¶ [a]So David assembled all Israel together, from the Shihor of Egypt even to
the entrance of Hamath, [b]to bring the
ark of God from Kiriath-jearim.
6 [a]David and all Israel went up to
[b]Baalah, *that is,* to Kiriath-jearim, which
belongs to Judah, to bring up from there
the ark of God, the LORD [c]who is enthroned *above* the cherubim, where His
name is called.
7 They [1]carried the ark of God on a
new cart from [a]the house of Abinadab,
and Uzza and Ahio drove the cart.
8 David and all Israel were celebrating before God with all *their* might,
[a]even with songs and with lyres, harps,
tambourines, cymbals and with trumpets.
9 ¶ When they came to [a]the threshing floor of Chidon, Uzza put out his hand
to hold the ark, because the oxen nearly
upset *it.*
10 The anger of the LORD burned
against Uzza, so He struck him down
[a]because he put out his hand to the ark;
[b]and he died there before God.
11 Then David became angry because
[1]of the LORD's outburst against Uzza; and
he called that place [2]Perez-uzza to this
day.
12 David was afraid of God that day,
saying, "How can I bring the ark of God
home to me?"
13 So David did not take the ark with
him to the city of David, but took it aside
[a]to the house of Obed-edom the Gittite.
14 Thus the ark of God remained with
the family of Obed-edom in his house
three months; and [a]the LORD blessed the
family of Obed-edom with all that he had.

David's Family Enlarged

14 [a]Now Hiram king of Tyre sent
messengers to David with cedar
trees, masons and carpenters, to build a
house for him.
2 And David realized that the LORD
had established him as king over Israel,
and that his kingdom was highly exalted,
for the sake of His people Israel.
3 ¶ Then David took more wives at
Jerusalem, and David [1]became the father
of more sons and daughters.
4 [a]These are the names of the children [1]born *to him* in Jerusalem: Shammua, Shobab, Nathan, Solomon,
5 Ibhar, Elishua, Elpelet,
6 Nogah, Nepheg, Japhia,
7 Elishama, Beeliada and Eliphelet.

Philistines Defeated

8 ¶ When the Philistines heard that
David had been anointed king over all
Israel, all the Philistines went up in
search of David; and David heard of it and
went out against them.

32 [a]Esth 1:13
33 [1]Lit *not of double heart* [a]Ps 12:2
38 [a]2 Sam 5:1-3; 1 Chr 12:33
40 [a]1 Sam 25:18
13:3 [a]1 Sam 7:1,2
5 [a]2 Sam 6:1; 1 Kin 8:65; 1 Chr 15:3 [b]1 Sam 6:21; 7:1
6 [a]2 Sam 6:2-11 [b]Josh 15:9 [c]Ex 25:22; 2 Kin 19:15
7 [1]Lit *caused to ride* [a]1 Sam 7:1
8 [a]1 Chr 15:16
9 [a]2 Sam 6:6
10 [a]1 Chr 15:13,15 [b]Lev 10:2
11 [1]Lit *the LORD had broken through a break-through* [2]I.e. the breakthrough of Uzza
13 [a]1 Chr 15:25
14 [a]1 Chr 26:4, 5
14:1 [a]2 Sam 5:11
3 [1]Lit *begot*
4 [1]Lit *were to* [a]1 Chr 3:5-8

9 Now the Philistines had come and
[a]made a raid in the valley of Rephaim.
10 David inquired of God, saying,
"Shall I go up against the Philistines? And
will You give them into my hand?" Then
the LORD said to him, "Go up, for I will
give them into your hand."
11 So they came up to Baal-perazim,
and David [1]defeated them there; and David said, "God has broken through my
enemies by my hand, like the breakthrough of waters." Therefore they
named that place [2]Baal-perazim.
12 They abandoned their gods there;
so David gave the order and they were
burned with fire.
13 ¶ The Philistines made [a]yet another raid in the valley.
14 David inquired again of God, and
God said to him, "You shall not go up
after them; circle around [1]behind them
and come at them in front of the [2]balsam
trees.
15 "It shall be when you hear the sound
of marching in the tops of the balsam
trees, then you shall go out to battle, for
God will have gone out before you to
strike the army of the Philistines."
16 David did just as God had commanded him, and they struck down the
army of the Philistines from [1]Gibeon
even as far as Gezer.
17 Then the fame of David went out
into all the lands; and [a]the LORD brought
the fear of him on all the nations.

Plans to Move the Ark to Jerusalem

15 Now *David* built houses for himself in the city of David; and he
prepared a place for the ark of God and
[a]pitched a tent for it.
2 Then David said, "[a]No one is to
carry the ark of God but the Levites; for
the LORD chose them to carry the ark of
God and to minister to Him forever."
3 And [a]David assembled all Israel at
Jerusalem to bring up the ark of the LORD
[b]to its place which he had prepared
for it.
4 David gathered together the sons of
Aaron and [a]the Levites:
5 of the sons of Kohath, Uriel the
chief, and 120 of his [1]relatives;
6 of the sons of Merari, Asaiah
the chief, and 220 of his relatives;
7 of the sons of Gershom, Joel the
chief, and 130 of his relatives;
8 of the sons of Elizaphan, Shemaiah
the chief, and 200 of his relatives;
9 of the sons of Hebron, Eliel the
chief, and 80 of his relatives;
10 of the sons of Uzziel, Amminadab
the chief, and 112 of his relatives.
11 ¶ Then David called for [a]Zadok
and [b]Abiathar the priests, and for the
Levites, for Uriel, Asaiah, Joel, Shemaiah,
Eliel and Amminadab,
12 and said to them, "You are the
heads of the fathers' *households* of the
Levites; [a]consecrate yourselves both you
and your relatives, that you may bring up
the ark of the LORD God of Israel [b]to *the
place* that I have prepared for it.
13 "[a]Because you did not *carry it* at the
first, the LORD our God made an outburst
on us, for we did not seek Him according
to the ordinance."
14 [a]So the priests and the Levites consecrated themselves to bring up the ark of
the LORD God of Israel.
15 The sons of [a]the Levites carried
the ark of God on their shoulders with
the poles thereon, as Moses had commanded according to the word of the
LORD.
16 ¶ Then David spoke to the chiefs of
the Levites [a]to appoint their relatives
the singers, with instruments of music,
harps, lyres, loud-sounding cymbals, to
raise sounds of joy.
17 So [a]the Levites appointed Heman
the son of Joel, and from his relatives,
Asaph the son of Berechiah; and from the
sons of Merari their relatives, Ethan the
son of Kushaiah,
18 and with them their relatives of the
second rank, Zechariah, [1]Ben, Jaaziel,
Shemiramoth, Jehiel, Unni, Eliab, Benaiah, Maaseiah, Mattithiah, Eliphelehu,
Mikneiah, Obed-edom and Jeiel, the
gatekeepers.
19 So the singers, Heman, Asaph and
Ethan *were appointed* to sound aloud
cymbals of bronze;
20 and Zechariah, Aziel, Shemiramoth, Jehiel, Unni, Eliab, Maaseiah and
Benaiah, with [1]harps *tuned* to [a]alamoth;
21 and Mattithiah, Eliphelehu, Mikneiah, Obed-edom, Jeiel and Azaziah, to
lead with [1]lyres tuned to [a]the sheminith.
22 Chenaniah, chief of the Levites,
was *in charge of* the singing; he gave instruction in singing because he was skillful.
23 Berechiah and Elkanah were gatekeepers for the ark.
24 Shebaniah, Joshaphat, Nethanel,
Amasai, Zechariah, Benaiah and Eliezer,
the priests, [a]blew the trumpets before
the ark of God. Obed-edom and Jehiah
also *were* gatekeepers for the ark.
25 ¶ [a]So *it was* David, with the elders
of Israel and the captains over thousands,
who went to bring up the ark of the covenant of the LORD from [b]the house of
Obed-edom with joy.
26 Because God was helping the Le-

---

9 [a]1 Chr 11:15; 14:13
11 [1]Lit *smote* [2]I.e. the master of breakthrough
13 [a]1 Chr 14:9
14 [1]Lit *from upon* [2]Or *baka shrubs*
16 [1]In 2 Sam 5:25, *Geba*
17 [a]Ex 15:14-16; Deut 2:25
15:1 [a]1 Chr 15:3; 16:1; 17:1-5
2 [a]Num 4:15; Deut 10:8
3 [a]1 Kin 8:1; 1 Chr 13:5 [b]Ex 40:20f; 2 Sam 6:12,17; 1 Chr 15:1,12
4 [a]1 Chr 6:16-30; 12:26
5 [1]Lit *brothers*; i.e. fellow tribesmen, and so throughout the ch
11 [a]1 Chr 12:28 [b]1 Sam 22:20-23; 1 Kin 2:26,35
12 [a]Ex 19:14, 15; 2 Chr 35:6 [b]1 Chr 15:1,3
13 [a]2 Sam 6:3; 1 Chr 13:7
14 [a]1 Chr 15:12
15 [a]Ex 25:14; Num 4:5f
16 [a]1 Chr 13:8; 25:1
17 [a]1 Chr 25:1
18 [1]Omitted in Gr and many mss
20 [1]Or *harps of maiden-like tone* [a]Ps 46: title
21 [1]Or *octave harps* [a]Ps 6: title
24 [a]1 Chr 15:28; 16:6
25 [a]2 Sam 6:12, 15 [b]1 Chr 13:13

vites who were carrying the ark of the covenant of the LORD, they sacrificed [a]seven bulls and seven rams.

27 Now David was clothed with a robe of fine linen with all the Levites who were carrying the ark, and the singers and Chenaniah the leader of the singing *with* the singers. [a]David also wore an ephod of linen.

28 Thus all Israel brought up the ark of the covenant of the LORD with shouting, and with sound of the horn, with trumpets, with loud-sounding cymbals, with harps and lyres.

29 ¶ It happened when the ark of the covenant of the LORD came to the city of David, that [a]Michal the daughter of Saul looked out of the window and saw King David leaping and celebrating; and she despised him in her heart.

A Tent for the Ark

16 And they brought in the ark of God and [a]placed it inside the tent which David had pitched for it, and they offered burnt offerings and peace offerings before God.

2 When David had finished offering the burnt offering and the peace offerings, he blessed the people in the name of the LORD.

3 He distributed to everyone of Israel, both man and woman, to everyone a loaf of bread and a portion *of meat* and a raisin cake.

4 ¶ He appointed some of the Levites *as* ministers before the ark of the LORD, even to celebrate and to thank and praise the LORD God of Israel:

5 Asaph the chief, and second to him Zechariah, *then* [1]Jeiel, Shemiramoth, Jehiel, Mattithiah, Eliab, Benaiah, Obed-edom and Jeiel, with musical instruments, harps, lyres; also Asaph *played* loud-sounding cymbals,

6 and Benaiah and Jahaziel the priests *blew* trumpets continually before the ark of the covenant of God.

7 ¶ Then on that day David [a]first assigned [1]Asaph and his [2]relatives to give thanks to the LORD.

Psalm of Thanksgiving

8 [a]Oh give thanks to the LORD,
call upon His name;
[b]Make known His deeds among
the peoples.
9 Sing to Him, sing praises to Him;
[1]Speak of all His [2]wonders.
10 [1]Glory in His holy name;
Let the heart of those who seek
the LORD be glad.
11 [a]Seek the LORD and His
strength;
Seek His face continually.
12 [a]Remember His wonderful deeds
which He has done,
[b]His marvels and the judgments
from His mouth,
13 O seed of Israel His servant,
Sons of Jacob, His chosen ones!
14 He is the LORD our God;
[a]His judgments are in all the
earth.
15 Remember His covenant forever,
The word which He commanded
to a thousand generations,
16 [a]*The covenant* which He made
with Abraham,
And His oath to Isaac.
17 [a]He also confirmed it to Jacob
for a statute,
To Israel as an everlasting
covenant,
18 Saying, "[a]To you I will give the
land of Canaan,
As the portion of your
inheritance."
19 [a]When they were only a few in
number,
Very few, and strangers in it,
20 And they wandered about from
nation to nation,
And from *one* kingdom to
another people,
21 He permitted no man to oppress
them,
And [a]He reproved kings for
their sakes, *saying,*
22 "Do not touch My anointed ones,
And [a]do My prophets no harm."
23 [a]Sing to the LORD, all the earth;
Proclaim good tidings of His
salvation from day to day.
24 Tell of His glory among the
nations,
His wonderful deeds among all
the peoples.
25 For [a]great is the LORD, and
greatly to be praised;
He also is [b]to be feared above
all gods.
26 For all the gods of the peoples
are [1a]idols,
[b]But the LORD made the
heavens.
27 Splendor and majesty are before
Him,
Strength and joy are in His place.
28 Ascribe to the LORD, O families
of the peoples,
Ascribe to the LORD glory and
strength.
29 Ascribe to the LORD the glory
due His name;
Bring an [1]offering, and come
before Him;

---

26 [a]Num 23:1-4,29
27 [a]2 Sam 6:14
29 [a]2 Sam 3:13f; 6:16
16:1 [a]1 Chr 15:1
5 [1]In 1 Chr 15:18, *Jaaziel*
7 [1]Lit *by the hand of Asaph* [2]Lit *brothers* [a]2 Sam 22:1; 23:1
8 [a]1 Chr 16:8-36; Ps 105:1-15 [b]1 Kin 8:43; 2 Kin 19:19
9 [1]Or *Meditate on* [2]I.e. wonderful acts
10 [1]Or *Boast*
11 [a]Ps 24:6
12 [a]Ps 103:2 [b]Ps 78:43-68
14 [a]Ps 48:10
16 [a]Gen 12:7; 17:2; 22:16-18; 26:3
17 [a]Gen 35:11, 12
18 [a]Gen 13:15
19 [a]Gen 34:30; Deut 7:7
21 [a]Gen 12:17; 20:3; Ex 7:15-18
22 [a]Gen 20:7
23 [a]Ps 96:1-13
25 [a]Ps 144:3-6 [b]Ps 89:7
26 [1]Or *non-existent things* [a]Lev 19:4 [b]Ps 102:25
29 [1]Or *a grain offering*

[a]Worship the LORD in [2]holy
array.
30 Tremble before Him, all the
earth;
Indeed, the world is firmly
established, it will not be
moved.
31 [a]Let the heavens be glad, and
let the earth rejoice;
And let them say among the
nations, "[b]The LORD
reigns."
32 [a]Let the sea [1]roar, and [2]all it
contains;
Let the field exult, and all that is
in it.
33 Then the trees of the forest will
sing for joy before the LORD;
For He is coming to judge the
earth.
34 [a]O give thanks to the LORD, for
He is good;
For His lovingkindness is
everlasting.
35 [a]Then say, "Save us, O God of
our salvation,
And gather us and deliver us
from the nations,
To give thanks to Your holy
name,
And [1]glory in Your praise."
36 [a]Blessed be the LORD, the God
of Israel,
From everlasting even to
everlasting.
Then all the people [b]said, "Amen," and
praised the LORD.

Worship before the Ark

37 ¶ So he left Asaph and his [1]rela-
tives there [a]before the ark of the covenant of the LORD to minister before the
ark continually, [b]as every day's work required;
38 and [a]Obed-edom with [1]his 68 relatives; Obed-edom, also the son of Jeduthun, and [b]Hosah as gatekeepers.
39 *He left* [a]Zadok the priest and his
[1]relatives the priests [b]before the [2]taber-
nacle of the LORD in the high place which
was at Gibeon,
40 to offer burnt offerings to the LORD
on the altar of burnt offering continually
morning and evening, [a]even according
to all that is written in the law of the
LORD, which He commanded Israel.
41 With them *were* [a]Heman and Jeduthun, and [b]the rest who were chosen,
who were designated by name, to [c]give
thanks to the LORD, because His lovingkindness is everlasting.
42 And with them *were* Heman and
Jeduthun *with* trumpets and cymbals for
those who should sound aloud, and *with*

29 [2]Or *the splendor of holiness* [a]Ps 29:2
31 [a]Is 44:23; 49:13 [b]Ps 93:1; 96:10
32 [1]Or *thunder* [2]Lit *its fullness* [a]Ps 98:7
34 [a]2 Chr 5:13; 7:3; Ezra 3:11; Ps 106:1; 136:1; Jer 33:11
35 [1]Lit *boast* [a]Ps 106:47,48
36 [a]1 Kin 8:15, 56; Ps 72:18 [b]Deut 27:15; Neh 8:6
37 [1]Lit *brothers* [a]1 Chr 16:4,5 [b]2 Chr 8:14; Ezra 3:4
38 [1]Lit *their brothers, 68* [a]1 Chr 13:14 [b]1 Chr 26:10
39 [1]Lit *brothers* [2]Lit *dwelling place* [a]1 Chr 15:11 [b]1 Kin 3:4
40 [a]Ex 29:38-42; Num 28:3,4
41 [a]1 Chr 6:33 [b]1 Chr 25:1-6 [c]2 Chr 5:13
42 [a]1 Chr 25:7; 2 Chr 7:6; 29:27
43 [a]2 Sam 6:19
17:1 [a]2 Sam 7:1-29
4 [a]1 Chr 28:2,3
5 [1]Lit *been* [a]Ex 40:2,3; 2 Sam 7:6
6 [a]2 Sam 7:7
9 [1]Lit *sons of wickedness*
11 [1]Lit *seed*
13 [a]2 Cor 6:18; Heb 1:5 [b]1 Chr 10:14

instruments *for* [a]the songs of God, and
the sons of Jeduthun for the gate.
43 ¶ [a]Then all the people departed
each to his house, and David returned to
bless his household.

God's Covenant with David

17 [a]And it came about, when David
dwelt in his house, that David
said to Nathan the prophet, "Behold, I am
dwelling in a house of cedar, but the ark
of the covenant of the LORD is under curtains."
2 Then Nathan said to David, "Do all
that is in your heart, for God is with you."
3 ¶ It came about the same night that
the word of God came to Nathan, saying,
4 "Go and tell David My servant,
'Thus says the LORD, "[a]You shall not
build a house for Me to dwell in;
5 for I have not dwelt in a house
since the day that I brought up Israel to
this day, [a]but I have [1]gone from tent to
tent and from *one* dwelling place *to another.*
6 "In all places where I have walked
with all Israel, have I spoken a word
[a]with any of the judges of Israel, whom
I commanded to shepherd My people,
saying, 'Why have you not built for Me a
house of cedar?' " '
7 "Now, therefore, thus shall you say
to My servant David, 'Thus says the LORD
of hosts, "I took you from the pasture,
from following the sheep, to be leader
over My people Israel.
8 "I have been with you wherever you
have gone, and have cut off all your enemies from before you; and I will make
you a name like the name of the great
ones who are in the earth.
9 "I will appoint a place for My people
Israel, and will plant them, so that they
may dwell in their own place and not be
moved again; and the [1]wicked will not
waste them anymore as formerly,
10 even from the day that I commanded judges *to be* over My people Israel.
And I will subdue all your enemies.
¶ Moreover, I tell you that the LORD
will build a house for you.
11 "When your days are fulfilled that
you must go *to be* with your fathers, that
I will set up *one of* your [1]descendants
after you, who will be of your sons; and
I will establish his kingdom.
12 "He shall build for Me a house, and
I will establish his throne forever.
13 "[a]I will be his father and he shall be
My son; and I will not take My lovingkindness away from him, [b]as I took it
from him who was before you.
14 "But I will settle him in My house

and in My kingdom forever, and his throne shall be established forever." ' "

15 According to all these words and according to all this vision, so Nathan spoke to David.

David's Prayer in Response

16 ¶ Then David the king went in and sat before the LORD and said, "[a]Who am I, O LORD God, and what is my house that You have brought me this far?

17 "This was a small thing in Your eyes, O God; but You have spoken of Your servant's house for a great while to come, and have regarded me according to the standard of a man of high degree, O LORD God.

18 "What more can David still *say* to You concerning the honor *bestowed* on Your servant? For You know Your servant.

19 "O LORD, [a]for Your servant's sake, and according to Your own heart, You have wrought all this greatness, to make known all these great things.

20 "O LORD, there is none like You, nor is there any God besides You, according to all that we have heard with our ears.

21 "And what one nation in the earth is like Your people Israel, whom God went to redeem for Himself *as* a people, to make You a name by great and terrible things, in driving out nations from before Your people, whom You redeemed out of Egypt?

22 "[a]For Your people Israel You made Your own people forever, and You, O LORD, became their God.

23 ¶ "Now, O LORD, let the word that You have spoken concerning Your servant and concerning his house be established forever, and do as You have spoken.

24 "Let Your name be established and magnified forever, saying, 'The LORD of hosts is the God of Israel, *even* a God to Israel; and the house of David Your servant is established before You.'

25 "For You, O my God, have revealed to Your servant that You will build for him a house; therefore Your servant has found *courage* to pray before You.

26 "Now, O LORD, You are God, and have [1]promised this good thing to Your servant.

27 "And now it has pleased You to bless the house of Your servant, that it may [1]continue forever before You; for You, O LORD, have blessed, and it is blessed forever."

David's Kingdom Strengthened

18 Now after this [a]it came about that David [1]defeated the Philistines and subdued them and took Gath and its towns from the hand of the Philistines.

2 He defeated Moab, and the Moabites became servants to David, bringing tribute.

3 ¶ David also defeated Hadadezer king of Zobah *as far as* Hamath, as he went to establish his [1]rule to the Euphrates River.

4 David took from him 1,000 chariots and 7,000 horsemen and 20,000 foot soldiers, and David hamstrung all the chariot horses, but reserved *enough* of them for 100 chariots.

5 ¶ When the Arameans of [1]Damascus came to help Hadadezer king [a]of Zobah, David [2]killed 22,000 men of the Arameans.

6 Then David put *garrisons* among the Arameans of [1]Damascus; and the Arameans became servants to David, bringing tribute. And the LORD helped David wherever he went.

7 David took the shields of gold which were [1]carried by the servants of Hadadezer and brought them to Jerusalem.

8 Also from [1]Tibhath and from Cun, cities of Hadadezer, David took a very large amount of bronze, with which [a]Solomon made the bronze sea and the pillars and the bronze utensils.

9 ¶ Now when [1]Tou king of Hamath heard that David had [2]defeated all the army of Hadadezer king of Zobah,

10 he sent [1]Hadoram his son to King David to [2]greet him and to bless him, because he had fought against Hadadezer and had [3]defeated him; for Hadadezer had been at war with Tou. And *Hadoram brought* all kinds of articles of gold and silver and bronze.

11 King David also dedicated these to the LORD with the silver and the gold which he had carried away from all the nations: from Edom, Moab, the sons of Ammon, the Philistines, and from Amalek.

12 ¶ Moreover Abishai the son of Zeruiah [1]defeated 18,000 Edomites in the Valley of Salt.

13 Then he put garrisons in Edom, and all the Edomites became servants to David. And the LORD helped David wherever he went.

14 ¶ So David reigned over all Israel; and he [1]administered justice and righteousness for all his people.

15 [a]Joab the son of Zeruiah *was* over the army, and Jehoshaphat the son of Ahilud *was* recorder;

16 and Zadok the son of Ahitub and

16 [a]2 Sam 7:18
19 [a]2 Sam 7:21; Is 37:35
22 [a]Ex 19:5,6
26 [1]Lit *said*
27 [1]Lit *be*
18:1 [1]Lit *smote,* and so in vv 1-3 [a]2 Sam 8:1-18
3 [1]Lit *hand*
5 [1]Heb *Darmeseq* [2]Lit *smote* [a]1 Chr 19:6
6 [1]Heb *Darmeseq*
7 [1]Lit *on*
8 [1]In 2 Sam 8:8, *Betah* [a]1 Kin 7:40-47; 2 Chr 4:11-18
9 [1]In 2 Sam 8:9, *Toi* [2]Lit *smitten*
10 [1]In 2 Sam 8:10, *Joram* [2]Lit *ask him of his welfare* [3]Lit *smitten*
12 [1]Lit *smote*
14 [1]Lit *was doing*
15 [a]1 Chr 11:6

Abimelech the son of Abiathar *were*
priests, and Shavsha *was* secretary;
17 and Benaiah the son of Jehoiada
was over the Cherethites and the Pelethites, and the sons of David *were* chiefs
at the king's side.

David's Messengers Abused

19 [a]Now it came about after this,
that Nahash the king of the sons
of Ammon died, and his son became king
in his place.
2 Then David said, "I will show kindness to Hanun the son of Nahash, because his father showed kindness to me."
So David sent messengers to console him
concerning his father. And David's servants came into the land of the sons of
Ammon to Hanun to console him.
3 But the princes of the sons of Ammon said to Hanun, "[1]Do you think that
David is honoring your father, in that he
has sent comforters to you? Have not his
servants come to you to search and to
overthrow and to spy out the land?"
4 So Hanun took David's servants
and shaved them and cut off their garments in the middle as far as their hips,
and sent them away.
5 Then *certain persons* went and told
David about the men. And he sent to
meet them, for the men were greatly humiliated. And the king said, "[1]Stay at Jericho until your beards grow, and *then*
return."
6 ¶ When the sons of Ammon saw
that they had made themselves odious to
David, Hanun and the sons of Ammon
sent 1,000 talents of silver to hire for
themselves chariots and horsemen from
Mesopotamia, from Aram-maacah and
[a]from Zobah.
7 So they hired for themselves
32,000 chariots, and the king of Maacah
and his people, who came and camped
before [a]Medeba. And the sons of Ammon gathered together from their cities
and came to battle.
8 When David heard *of it,* he sent
Joab and all the army, the mighty men.
9 The sons of Ammon came out and
drew up in battle array at the entrance of
the city, and the kings who had come
were by themselves in the field.

Ammon and Aram Defeated

10 ¶ Now when Joab saw that the
[1]battle was set against him in front and
in the rear, he selected from all the
choice men of Israel and they arrayed
themselves against the Arameans.
11 But the remainder of the people he
placed in the hand of [1]Abshai his brother; and they arrayed themselves against
the sons of Ammon.
12 He said, "If the Arameans are too
strong for me, then you shall help me; but
if the sons of Ammon are too strong for
you, then I will help you.
13 "Be strong, and let us show ourselves courageous for the sake of our people and for the cities of our God; and may
the LORD do what is good in His sight."
14 So Joab and the people who were
with him drew near to the battle against
the Arameans, and they fled before him.
15 When the sons of Ammon saw that
the Arameans fled, they also fled before
Abshai his brother and entered the city.
Then Joab came to Jerusalem.
16 ¶ When the Arameans saw that
they had been [1]defeated by Israel, they
sent messengers and brought out the Arameans who were beyond the [2]River,
with Shophach the commander of the
army of Hadadezer [3]leading them.
17 When it was told David, he gathered all Israel together and crossed the
Jordan, and came upon them and drew up
in formation against them. And when David drew up in battle array against the
Arameans, they fought against him.
18 The Arameans fled before Israel,
and David killed of the Arameans 7,000
charioteers and 40,000 foot soldiers, and
put to death Shophach the commander of
the army.
19 So when the servants of Hadadezer
saw that they were [1]defeated by Israel,
they made peace with David and served
him. Thus the Arameans were not willing
to help the sons of Ammon anymore.

War with Philistine Giants

20 [a]Then it happened [1]in the
spring, at the time when kings go
out *to battle,* that Joab led out the army
and ravaged the land of the sons of Ammon, and came and besieged Rabbah. But
David stayed at Jerusalem. And [b]Joab
struck Rabbah and overthrew it.
2 [a]David took the crown of [1]their
king from his head, and he found it to
weigh a talent of gold, and there was a
precious stone in it; and it was placed on
David's head. And he brought out the
spoil of the city, a very great amount.
3 He brought out the people who
were in it, [a]and cut *them* with saws and
with sharp instruments and with axes.
And thus David did to all the cities of the
sons of Ammon. Then David and all the
people returned *to* Jerusalem.
4 ¶ [a]Now it came about after this,
that war [1]broke out at [2]Gezer with the
Philistines; then Sibbecai the Hushathite

19:1 [a]2 Sam 10:1-19
3 [1]Lit *In your eyes is David honoring your father because*
5 [1]Lit *Return to*
6 [a]1 Chr 18:5,9
7 [a]Num 21:30; Josh 13:9,16
10 [1]Lit *the face of the battle*
11 [1]In 2 Sam 10:10, *Abishai*
16 [1]Lit *smitten before* [2]I.e. Euphrates [3]Lit *before*
19 [1]Lit *smitten before*
20:1 [1]Lit *at the return of the year* [a]2 Sam 11:1 [b]2 Sam 12:26
2 [1]In Zeph 1:5, *Malcam* [a]2 Sam 12:30,31
3 [a]2 Sam 12:31
4 [1]Lit *stood up* [2]In 2 Sam 21:18, *Gob* [a]2 Sam 21:18-22

[3]killed Sippai, one of the descendants of
the [4]giants, and they were subdued.
5 And there was war with the Philistines again, and Elhanan the son of [a]Jair
[1]killed Lahmi the brother of Goliath the
Gittite, the [b]shaft of whose spear *was*
like a weaver's beam.
6 Again there was war at Gath,
where there was a man of *great* stature
who had twenty-four fingers and toes, six
fingers on each hand and six *toes on each*
foot; and he also was descended from the
giants.
7 When he taunted Israel, Jonathan
the son of Shimea, David's brother,
[1]killed him.
8 These were descended from the
giants in Gath, and they fell by the hand
of David and by the hand of his servants.

Census Brings Pestilence

21 [a]Then Satan stood up against Israel and moved David to number
Israel.
2 So David said to Joab and to the
princes of the people, "[a]Go, number Israel from Beersheba even to Dan, and
bring me *word* that I may know their
number."
3 Joab said, "[a]May the LORD add to
His people a hundred times as many as
they are! But, my lord the king, are they
not all my lord's servants? Why does my
lord seek this thing? Why should he be a
cause of guilt to Israel?"
4 Nevertheless, the king's word prevailed against Joab. Therefore, Joab departed and went throughout all Israel,
and came to Jerusalem.
5 Joab gave the number of the [1]cen-
sus of *all* the people to David. And [a]all
Israel were 1,100,000 men who drew
the sword; and Judah *was* 470,000 men
who drew the sword.
6 [a]But he did not [1]number Levi and
Benjamin among them, for the king's
[2]command was abhorrent to Joab.
7 ¶ [1]God was displeased with this
thing, so He struck Israel.
8 David said to God, "I have sinned
greatly, in that I have done this thing.
[a]But now, please take away the iniquity
of Your servant, for I have done very foolishly."
9 ¶ The LORD spoke to [a]Gad, David's
[b]seer, saying,
10 "Go and speak to David, saying,
'Thus says the LORD, "I [1]offer you three
things; choose for yourself one of them,
which I will do to you." ' "
11 So Gad came to David and said to
him, "Thus says the LORD, 'Take for yourself
12 [a]either three years of famine, or
three months to be swept away before
your foes, while the sword of your enemies overtakes *you,* or else three days of
the sword of the LORD, even pestilence in
the land, and the angel of the LORD destroying throughout all the territory of Israel.' Now, therefore, consider what answer I shall return to Him who sent me."
13 David said to Gad, "I am in great
distress; please let me fall into the hand
of the LORD, [a]for His mercies are very
great. But do not let me fall into the hand
of man."
14 ¶ [a]So the LORD [1]sent a pestilence
on Israel; 70,000 men of Israel fell.
15 And God sent an angel to Jerusalem
to destroy it; but as he was about to destroy *it,* the LORD saw and [a]was sorry
over the calamity, and said to the destroying angel, "It is enough; now relax your
hand." And the angel of the LORD was
standing by the threshing floor of [1]Ornan
the Jebusite.
16 Then David lifted up his eyes and
saw the angel of the LORD standing between earth and heaven, with his drawn
sword in his hand stretched out over Jerusalem. Then David and the elders,
[a]covered with sackcloth, fell on their
faces.
17 David said to God, "Is it not I who
[1]commanded to count the people? Indeed, I am the one who has sinned and
done very wickedly, [a]but these sheep,
what have they done? O LORD my
God, please let Your hand be against
me and my father's household, but not
against Your people that they should be
plagued."

David's Altar

18 ¶ [a]Then the angel of the LORD
[1]commanded Gad to say to David, that
David should go up and build an altar to
the LORD on the threshing floor of Ornan
the Jebusite.
19 So David went up at the word of
Gad, which he spoke in the name of the
LORD.
20 Now Ornan turned back and saw
the angel, and his four sons *who were*
with him hid themselves. And Ornan was
threshing wheat.
21 As David came to Ornan, Ornan
looked and saw David, and went out from
the threshing floor and prostrated himself
[1]before David with his face to the
ground.
22 Then David said to Ornan, "Give
me the [1]site of *this* threshing floor, that
I may build on it an altar to the LORD; for
the full price you shall give it to me, that
the plague may be restrained from the
people."

4 [3]Lit *smote* [4]Heb *Raphah,* and so in vv 6, 8
5 [1]Lit *smote* [a]2 Sam 21:19 [b]1 Sam 17:7; 1 Chr 11:23
7 [1]Lit *smote*
21:1 [a]2 Sam 24:1-25
2 [a]1 Chr 27:23, 24
3 [a]Deut 1:11
5 [1]Lit *muster* [a]2 Sam 24:9
6 [1]Lit *muster* [2]Lit *word* [a]1 Chr 27:24
7 [1]Lit *it was evil in the sight of God*
8 [a]2 Sam 12:13
9 [a]2 Sam 24:11; 1 Chr 29:29 [b]1 Sam 9:9
10 [1]Lit *stretch out to*
12 [a]2 Sam 24:13
13 [a]Ps 51:1; 130:4,7
14 [1]Lit *gave* [a]1 Chr 27:24
15 [1]In 2 Sam 24:16, *Araunah* [a]Ex 32:14; 1 Sam 15:11; Jon 3:10
16 [a]1 Kin 21:27
17 [1]Lit *said* [a]2 Sam 7:8; Ps 74:1
18 [1]Lit *said to* [a]2 Chr 3:1
21 [1]Lit *to*
22 [1]Lit *place*

23 Ornan said to David, "Take *it* for
yourself; and let my lord the king do what
is good in his sight. See, I will give the
oxen for burnt offerings and the threshing sledges for wood and the wheat for
the grain offering; I will give *it* all."
24 But King David said to Ornan, "No,
but I will surely buy *it* for the full price;
for I will not take what is yours for the
LORD, or offer a burnt offering [1]which
costs me nothing."
25 So [a]David gave Ornan 600 shekels
of gold by weight for the [1]site.
26 Then David built an altar to the
LORD there and offered burnt offerings
and peace offerings. And he called to the
LORD and [a]He answered him with fire
from heaven on the altar of burnt offering.
27 The LORD commanded the angel,
and he put his sword back in its sheath.
28 ¶ At that time, when David saw
that the LORD had answered him on the
threshing floor of Ornan the Jebusite, he
offered sacrifice there.
29 [a]For the tabernacle of the LORD,
which Moses had made in the wilderness, and the altar of burnt offering *were*
in the high place at Gibeon at that time.
30 But David could not go before it to
inquire of God, for he was terrified by the
sword of the angel of the LORD.

David Prepares for Temple Building

22 Then David said, "[a]This is the
house of the LORD God, and this
is the altar of burnt offering for Israel."
2 ¶ So David [1]gave orders to gather
[a]the foreigners who were in the land of
Israel, and [b]he set stonecutters to hew
out stones to build the house of God.
3 David [a]prepared large quantities of
iron [1]to make the nails for the doors of
the gates and for the clamps, and more
[b]bronze than could be weighed;
4 and timbers of cedar logs beyond
number, for [a]the Sidonians and Tyrians
brought large quantities of cedar timber
to David.
5 David said, "My son [a]Solomon is
young and inexperienced, and the house
that is to be built for the LORD shall be
exceedingly magnificent, famous and
glorious throughout all lands. *Therefore*
now I will make preparation for it." So
David made ample preparations before his
death.

Solomon Charged with the Task

6 ¶ Then [a]he called for his son Solomon, and charged him to build a house
for the LORD God of Israel.
7 David said to Solomon, "[a]My son,
[1]I had intended to build a house to the
name of the LORD my God.
8 "But the word of the LORD came to
me, saying, '[a]You have shed much blood
and have [1]waged great wars; you shall
not build a house to My name, because
you have shed *so* much blood on the
earth before Me.
9 'Behold, a son will be born to you,
who shall be a man of rest; and [a]I will
give him rest from all his enemies on
every side; for [b]his name shall be [1]Solo-
mon, and I will give peace and quiet to
Israel in his days.
10 '[a]He shall build a house for My
name, and he shall be My son and I will
be his father; and I will establish the
throne of his kingdom over Israel forever.'
11 "Now, my son, [a]the LORD be with
you that you may be successful, and build
the house of the LORD your God just as He
has spoken concerning you.
12 "[a]Only the LORD give you discretion
and understanding, and give you charge
over Israel, so that you may [b]keep the
law of the LORD your God.
13 "[a]Then you will prosper, if you are
careful to observe the statutes and the
ordinances which the LORD commanded
Moses concerning Israel. [b]Be strong and
courageous, do not fear nor be dismayed.
14 "Now behold, [1]with great pains I
have prepared for the house of the LORD
[a]100,000 talents of gold and 1,000,000
talents of silver, and [b]bronze and iron
beyond weight, for [2]they are in great
quantity; also timber and stone I have
prepared, and you may add to them.
15 "Moreover, there are many workmen with you, stonecutters and masons
of stone and carpenters, and all men who
are skillful in every kind of work.
16 "Of the gold, the silver and the
bronze and the iron there is no limit.
Arise and work, and may [a]the LORD be
with you."
17 ¶ [a]David also commanded all the
leaders of Israel to help his son Solomon,
saying,
18 "Is not the LORD your God with you?
And [a]has He not given you rest on every
side? For He has given the inhabitants of
the land into my hand, and the land is
subdued before the LORD and before His
people.
19 "Now [a]set your heart and your soul
to seek the LORD your God; arise, therefore, and build the sanctuary of the LORD
God, [b]so that you may bring the ark of
the covenant of the LORD and the holy
vessels of God into the house that is to be
built [c]for the name of the LORD."

24 [1]Lit *gratuitously*
25 [1]Lit *place* [a]2 Sam 24:24
26 [a]Lev 9:24; Judg 6:21
29 [a]1 Kin 3:4; 1 Chr 16:39
22:1 [a]1 Chr 21:18-28; 2 Chr 3:1
2 [1]Lit *said to* [a]1 Kin 9:20,21; 2 Chr 2:17 [b]1 Kin 5:17,18
3 [1]Lit *for* [a]1 Chr 29:2,7 [b]1 Chr 22:14
4 [a]1 Kin 5:6-10
5 [a]1 Kin 3:7; 1 Chr 29:1
6 [a]1 Kin 2:1
7 [1]Lit *as for me, it was in my heart* [a]2 Sam 7:2,3; 1 Chr 17:1
8 [1]Lit *made* [a]1 Chr 28:3
9 [1]I.e. peaceful [a]1 Kin 4:20,25 [b]2 Sam 12:24,25
10 [a]2 Sam 7:13, 14; 1 Chr 17:12
11 [a]1 Chr 22:16
12 [a]1 Kin 3:9-12; 2 Chr 1:10 [b]1 Kin 2:3
13 [a]1 Chr 28:7 [b]Josh 1:6-9
14 [1]Lit *in my affliction* [2]Lit *it is* [a]1 Chr 29:4 [b]1 Chr 22:3
16 [a]1 Chr 22:11
17 [a]1 Chr 28:1-6
18 [a]1 Chr 22:9; 23:25
19 [a]1 Chr 28:9 [b]1 Kin 8:6,21; 2 Chr 5:7 [c]1 Chr 22:7

Solomon Reigns

23 [a]Now when David [1]reached old age, [b]he made his son Solomon king over Israel.

2 And he gathered together all the leaders of Israel with the priests and the Levites.

Offices of the Levites

3 [a]The Levites were numbered from thirty years old and upward, and [b]their number by [1]census of men was 38,000.

4 Of these, 24,000 were [a]to oversee the work of the house of the LORD; and 6,000 *were* [b]officers and judges,

5 and 4,000 *were* gatekeepers, and [a]4,000 *were* praising the LORD with the instruments which [1]David made for giving praise.

6 David divided them into divisions [a]according to the sons of Levi: Gershon, Kohath, and Merari.

Gershonites

7 ¶ Of the Gershonites *were* [1]Ladan and Shimei.

8 The sons of Ladan *were* Jehiel the first and Zetham and Joel, three.

9 The sons of Shimei *were* Shelomoth and Haziel and Haran, three. These were the heads of the fathers' *households* of Ladan.

10 The sons of Shimei *were* Jahath, [1]Zina, Jeush and Beriah. These four *were* the sons of Shimei.

11 Jahath was the first and Zizah the second; but Jeush and Beriah did not have many sons, so they became a father's household, one [1]class.

Kohathites

12 ¶ The sons of Kohath were four: Amram, Izhar, Hebron and Uzziel.

13 [a]The sons of Amram were Aaron and Moses. And [b]Aaron was set apart to sanctify him as most holy, he and his sons forever, [c]to burn incense before the LORD, to minister to Him and to bless in His name forever.

14 But *as for* [a]Moses the man of God, his sons were named among the tribe of Levi.

15 The sons of Moses *were* Gershom and Eliezer.

16 The [1]son of Gershom *was* [2]Shebuel the chief.

17 The [1]son of Eliezer was Rehabiah the chief; and Eliezer had no other sons, but the sons of Rehabiah were very many.

18 The [1]son of Izhar was [2]Shelomith the chief.

19 The sons of Hebron *were* Jeriah the first, Amariah the second, Jahaziel the third and Jekameam the fourth.

20 The sons of Uzziel *were* Micah the first and Isshiah the second.

Merarites

21 ¶ The sons of Merari were Mahli and Mushi. The sons of Mahli *were* Eleazar and Kish.

22 Eleazar died and had no sons, but daughters only, so their brothers, the sons of Kish, took them *as wives.*

23 The sons of Mushi *were* three: Mahli, Eder and Jeremoth.

Duties Revised

24 ¶ [a]These were the sons of Levi according to their fathers' households, *even* the heads of the fathers' *households* of those of them who were [1]counted, in the number of names by their [2]census, doing the work for the service of the house of the LORD, [b]from twenty years old and upward.

25 For David said, "The LORD God of Israel [a]has given rest to His people, and He dwells in Jerusalem forever.

26 "Also, [a]the Levites will no longer need to carry the tabernacle and all its utensils for its service."

27 For by the last words of David the sons of Levi *were* numbered from twenty years old and upward.

28 For their office is [1]to assist the sons of Aaron with the service of the house of the LORD, in the courts and in the chambers and in the purifying of all holy things, even the work of the service of the house of God,

29 [a]and with the showbread, and [b]the fine flour for a grain offering, and unleavened wafers, or [c]*what is baked in* the pan or [d]what is well-mixed, and [e]all measures of volume and size.

30 They are to stand every morning to thank and to praise the LORD, and likewise at evening,

31 and to offer all burnt offerings to the LORD, [a]on the sabbaths, the new moons and [b]the fixed festivals in the number *set* by the ordinance concerning them, continually before the LORD.

32 Thus [a]they are to keep charge of the tent of meeting, and charge of the holy place, and [b]charge of the sons of Aaron their [1]relatives, for the service of the house of the LORD.

Divisions of Levites

24 Now the divisions of the [1]descendants of Aaron *were these:* [a]the sons of Aaron *were* Nadab, Abihu, Eleazar and Ithamar.

2 [a]But Nadab and Abihu died before

23:1 [1]Lit *became old and sated with days* [a]1 Chr 29:28 [b]1 Kin 1:1-40; 2:12; 1 Chr 28:5; 29:22

3 [1]Lit *their heads* [a]Num 4:3-49 [b]Num 4:48; 1 Chr 23:24

4 [a]Ezra 3:8,9 [b]1 Chr 26:29

5 [1]Lit *I made* [a]1 Chr 15:16

6 [a]1 Chr 6:1

7 [1]In Ex 6:17, *Libni*

10 [1]In v 11, *Zizah*

11 [1]Lit *mustering*

13 [a]Ex 6:20 [b]Ex 28:1 [c]Ex 30:6-10

14 [a]Deut 33:1; Ps 90: title

16 [1]Lit *sons* [2]In ch 24:20, *Shubael*

17 [1]Lit *sons...were*

18 [1]Lit *sons* [2]In ch 24:22, *Shelomoth*

24 [1]Lit *mustered* [2]Lit *heads* [a]Num 10:17,21 [b]1 Chr 23:3

25 [a]1 Chr 22:18

26 [a]Num 4:5, 15; 7:9; Deut 10:8

28 [1]Lit *at the hand of*

29 [a]Lev 24:5-9 [b]Lev 6:20 [c]1 Chr 9:31 [d]Lev 6:21 [e]Lev 19:35,36

31 [a]Is 1:13,14 [b]Lev 23:2-4

32 [1]Lit *brothers* [a]Num 1:53; 1 Chr 9:27 [b]Num 3:6-9,38

24:1 [1]Lit *sons* [a]Ex 6:23

2 [a]Lev 10:2

their father and had no [1]sons. So Eleazar
and Ithamar served as priests.
3 David, with [a]Zadok of the sons of
Eleazar and Ahimelech of the sons of Ithamar, divided them according to their offices [1]for their ministry.
4 Since more chief men were found
from the [1]descendants of Eleazar than
the [1]descendants of Ithamar, they divided them thus: *there were* sixteen heads of
fathers' households of the [1]descendants
of Eleazar and eight of the [1]descendants
of Ithamar, according to their fathers'
households.
5 [a]Thus they were divided by lot, the
one as the other; for they were officers of
the sanctuary and officers of God, both
from the [1]descendants of Eleazar and the
[1]descendants of Ithamar.
6 Shemaiah, the son of Nethanel the
scribe, from the Levites, recorded them
in the presence of the king, the princes,
Zadok the priest, [a]Ahimelech the son of
Abiathar, and the heads of the fathers'
households of the priests and of the Levites; one father's household taken for
Eleazar and one taken for Ithamar.
7 ¶ Now the first lot came out for Jehoiarib, the second for Jedaiah,
8 the third for Harim, the fourth for
Seorim,
9 the fifth for Malchijah, the sixth for
Mijamin,
10 the seventh for Hakkoz, the eighth
for [a]Abijah,
11 the ninth for Jeshua, the tenth for
Shecaniah,
12 the eleventh for Eliashib, the
twelfth for Jakim,
13 the thirteenth for Huppah, the fourteenth for Jeshebeab,
14 the fifteenth for Bilgah, the sixteenth for Immer,
15 the seventeenth for Hezir, the eighteenth for Happizzez,
16 the nineteenth for Pethahiah,
the twentieth for Jehezkel,
17 the twenty-first for Jachin, the
twenty-second for Gamul,
18 the twenty-third for Delaiah, the
twenty-fourth for Maaziah.
19 [a]These were their offices for their
ministry when *they* came in to the house
of the LORD according to the ordinance
given to them through Aaron their father,
just as the LORD God of Israel had commanded him.
20 ¶ Now for the rest of the sons of
Levi: of the sons of Amram, [1]Shubael; of
the sons of Shubael, Jehdeiah.
21 Of Rehabiah: of the sons of Rehabiah, Isshiah the first.
22 Of the Izharites, [1]Shelomoth; of
the sons of Shelomoth, Jahath.
23 The sons [a]*of Hebron:* Jeriah *the
first,* Amariah the second, Jahaziel the
third, Jekameam the fourth.
24 *Of* the sons of Uzziel, Micah; of the
sons of Micah, Shamir.
25 The brother of Micah, Isshiah; of
the sons of Isshiah, Zechariah.
26 The sons of Merari, Mahli and Mushi; the sons of Jaaziah, Beno.
27 The sons of Merari: by Jaaziah *were*
Beno, Shoham, Zaccur and Ibri.
28 By Mahli: Eleazar, who had no
sons.
29 By Kish: the sons of Kish, Jerahmeel.
30 The sons of Mushi: Mahli, Eder and
Jerimoth. These *were* the sons of the Levites according to their fathers' households.
31 [a]These also cast lots just as their
[1]relatives the sons of Aaron in the presence of David the king, [b]Zadok, Ahimelech, and the heads of the fathers'
households of the priests and of the
Levites—the head of fathers' *households*
as well as those of his younger brother.

Number and Services of Musicians

25 Moreover, David and the commanders of the army set apart for
the service *some* of the sons of [a]Asaph
and of Heman and of Jeduthun, who *were*
to [b]prophesy with lyres, [c]harps and
cymbals; and the number of [1]those who
performed their service was:
2 Of the sons of Asaph: Zaccur, Joseph, Nethaniah and [1]Asharelah; the
sons of Asaph *were* under the [2]direction
of Asaph, who prophesied under the [2]di-
rection of the king.
3 [a]Of Jeduthun, the sons of Jeduthun: Gedaliah, [1]Zeri, Jeshaiah, [2]Shim-
ei, Hashabiah and Mattithiah, six, under
the [3]direction of their father Jeduthun
with the harp, who prophesied in giving
thanks and praising the LORD.
4 Of Heman, the sons of Heman: Bukkiah, Mattaniah, [1]Uzziel, [2]Shebuel and
Jerimoth, Hananiah, Hanani, Eliathah,
Giddalti and Romamti-ezer, Joshbeka-
shah, Mallothi, Hothir, Mahazioth.
5 All these *were* the sons of Heman
[a]the king's seer to [1]exalt him according
to the words of God, for God gave fourteen sons and three daughters to Heman.
6 All these were under the [1]direc-
tion of their father to sing in the house
of the LORD, [a]with cymbals, harps and
lyres, for the service of the house of God.
[b]Asaph, Jeduthun and Heman *were* under the [1]direction of the king.
7 Their number who were trained in
singing to the LORD, with their [1]rela-
tives, all who were skillful, *was* [a]288.

2 [1]Or *children*
3 [1]Lit *in their service* [a]1 Chr 6:8
4 [1]Lit *sons*
5 [1]Lit *sons* [a]1 Chr 24:31
6 [a]1 Chr 18:16
10 [a]Neh 12:4; Luke 1:5
19 [a]1 Chr 9:25
20 [1]In 23:16, *Shebuel*
22 [1]In 23:18, *Shelomith*
23 [a]1 Chr 23:19
31 [1]Lit *brothers* [a]1 Chr 24:5,6 [b]1 Chr 24:6
25:1 [1]Lit *workmen according to their service* [a]1 Chr 6:33,39 [b]2 Kin 3:15 [c]1 Chr 15:16
2 [1]In v 14, *Jesharelah* [2]Lit *hand*(s)
3 [1]In v 11, *Izri* [2]So with mss and ancient versions, cf v 17 [3]Lit *hands* [a]1 Chr 16:41,42
4 [1]In v 18, *Azarel* [2]In v 20, *Shubael*
5 [1]Lit *lift up the horn* [a]2 Sam 24:11; 1 Chr 21:9
6 [1]Lit *hands* [a]1 Chr 15:16 [b]1 Chr 15:19
7 [1]Lit *brothers,* and so throughout the ch [a]1 Chr 23:5

Divisions of Musicians

8 [a]They cast lots for their duties, all
alike, the small as well as the great, the
teacher *as well* as the pupil.
9 ¶ Now the first lot came out for
Asaph to Joseph, the second for Gedaliah,
he with his relatives and sons *were*
twelve;
10 the third to Zaccur, his sons and his
relatives, twelve;
11 the fourth to [1]Izri, his sons and his
relatives, twelve;
12 the fifth to Nethaniah, his sons and
his relatives, twelve;
13 the sixth to Bukkiah, his sons and
his relatives, twelve;
14 the seventh to [1]Jesharelah, his
sons and his relatives, twelve;
15 the eighth to Jeshaiah, his sons and
his relatives, twelve;
16 the ninth to Mattaniah, his sons
and his relatives, twelve;
17 the tenth to Shimei, his sons and
his relatives, twelve;
18 the eleventh to Azarel, his sons and
his relatives, twelve;
19 the twelfth to Hashabiah, his sons
and his relatives, twelve;
20 for the thirteenth, Shubael, his sons
and his relatives, twelve;
21 for the fourteenth, Mattithiah, his
sons and his relatives, twelve;
22 for the fifteenth to Jeremoth, his
sons and his relatives, twelve;
23 for the sixteenth to Hananiah,
his sons and his relatives, twelve;
24 for the seventeenth to Joshbeka-
shah, his sons and his relatives, twelve;
25 for the eighteenth to Hanani, his
sons and his relatives, twelve;
26 for the nineteenth to Mallothi,
his sons and his relatives, twelve;
27 for the twentieth to Eliathah, his
sons and his relatives, twelve;
28 for the twenty-first to Hothir, his
sons and his relatives, twelve;
29 for the twenty-second to Giddalti,
his sons and his relatives, twelve;
30 for the twenty-third to Mahazioth,
his sons and his relatives, twelve;
31 for the twenty-fourth to Romamti-
ezer, his sons and his relatives, twelve.

Divisions of the Gatekeepers

26 For the divisions of the gatekeepers *there were* of the Korahites,
[1]Meshelemiah the son of Kore, of the
sons of [2]Asaph.
2 Meshelemiah had sons: Zechariah
the firstborn, Jediael the second, Zebadiah the third, Jathniel the fourth,
3 Elam the fifth, Johanan the sixth,
Eliehoenai the seventh.
4 [a]Obed-edom had sons: Shemaiah
the firstborn, Jehozabad the second, Joah
the third, Sacar the fourth, Nethanel the
fifth,
5 Ammiel the sixth, Issachar the seventh *and* Peullethai the eighth; God had
indeed blessed him.
6 Also to his son Shemaiah sons were
born who ruled over the house of their
father, for they were mighty men of valor.
7 The sons of Shemaiah *were* Othni,
Rephael, Obed and Elzabad, whose brothers, Elihu and Semachiah, were valiant
men.
8 All these *were* of the sons of Obed-
edom; they and their sons and their [1]rel-
atives *were* able men with strength for
the service, 62 from Obed-edom.
9 Meshelemiah had sons and relatives, 18 valiant men.
10 Also [a]Hosah, *one* of the sons of
Merari had sons: Shimri the first (although he was not the firstborn, his father made him first),
11 Hilkiah the second, Tebaliah the
third, Zechariah the fourth; all the sons
and relatives of Hosah *were* 13.
12 ¶ To these divisions of the gatekeepers, the chief men, *were given* duties
like their relatives to minister in the
house of the LORD.
13 [a]They cast lots, the small and the
great alike, according to their fathers'
households, for every gate.
14 The lot to the east fell to [1]Shelemi-
ah. Then they cast lots *for* his son Zechariah, a counselor with insight, and his lot
came out to the north.
15 For Obed-edom *it fell* to the south,
and to his sons went the storehouse.
16 For Shuppim and Hosah *it was* to
the west, by the gate of Shallecheth, on
the ascending highway. Guard corre-
sponded to guard.
17 On the east there were six Levites,
on the north four daily, on the south four
daily, and at the storehouse two by two.
18 At the [1a]Parbar on the west *there
were* four at the highway and two at the
Parbar.
19 These were the divisions of the
gatekeepers of the sons of Korah and of
the sons of Merari.

Keepers of the Treasure

20 ¶ [1]The Levites, their relatives,
[2]had [a]charge of the treasures of the
house of God and of the treasures of the
dedicated gifts.
21 The sons of Ladan, the sons of the
Gershonites belonging to Ladan, *namely,*
the Jehielites, *were* the heads of the fathers' *households,* belonging to Ladan
the Gershonite.

8 [a]1 Chr 26:13
11 [1]In v 3, *Zeri*
14 [1]In v 2, *Asherelah*
26:1 [1]In v 14, *Shelemiah* [2]In 9:19, *Ebiasaph*
4 [a]2 Sam 6:11; 1 Chr 13:14
8 [1]Lit *brothers,* and so throughout the ch
10 [a]1 Chr 16:38
13 [a]1 Chr 24:5, 31; 25:8
14 [1]In 9:17, *Shallum*
18 [1]Possibly *court or colonnade* [a]2 Kin 23:11
20 [1]So Gr; Heb *As for the Levites, Ahijah had* [2]Lit *were over* [a]1 Chr 26:22,24, 26; 28:12; Ezra 2:69

22 ¶ The sons of Jehieli, Zetham and Joel his brother, [1]had charge of the treasures of the house of the LORD.

23 As for the Amramites, the Izharites, the Hebronites and the Uzzielites,

24 Shebuel the son of Gershom, the son of Moses, was officer over the treasures.

25 His relatives by Eliezer *were* Rehabiah his son, Jeshaiah his son, Joram his son, Zichri his son and Shelomoth his son.

26 This Shelomoth and his relatives [1]had charge of all the treasures of the dedicated gifts [a]which King David and the heads of the fathers' *households,* the commanders of thousands and hundreds, and the commanders of the army, had dedicated.

27 They dedicated [1]part of the spoil won in battles to repair the house of the LORD.

28 And all that Samuel the seer had dedicated and Saul the son of Kish, Abner the son of Ner and Joab the son of Zeruiah, everyone who had dedicated *anything, all of this* was [1]in the care of [2]Shelomoth and his relatives.

Outside Duties

29 ¶ As for the Izharites, Chenaniah and his sons [a]were *assigned* to outside duties for Israel, as [b]officers and judges.

30 As for the Hebronites, [a]Hashabiah and his relatives, 1,700 capable men, had charge of the affairs of Israel [1]west of the Jordan, for all the work of the LORD and the service of the king.

31 As for the Hebronites, [a]Jerijah the chief [1](these Hebronites were investigated according to their genealogies and fathers' *households,* in the fortieth year of David's reign, and men of outstanding capability were found among them at [b]Jazer of Gilead)

32 and his relatives, capable men, *were* 2,700 in number, heads of fathers' *households.* And King David made them overseers of the Reubenites, the Gadites and the half-tribe of the Manassites [a]concerning [1]all the affairs of God and of the king.

Commanders of the Army

27 Now *this is* the enumeration of the sons of Israel, the heads of fathers' *households,* the commanders of thousands and of hundreds, and their officers who served the king in all the affairs of the divisions which came in and went out month by month throughout all the months of the year, each division *numbering* 24,000:

2 ¶ Jashobeam the son of Zabdiel [1][a]had charge of the first division for the first month; and in his division *were* 24,000.

3 *He was* from the sons of Perez, *and was* chief of all the commanders of the army for the first month.

4 Dodai the Ahohite and his division had charge of the division for the second month, Mikloth *being* the chief officer; and in his division *were* 24,000.

5 The third commander of the army for the third month *was* Benaiah, the son of Jehoiada the priest, *as* chief; and in his division *were* 24,000.

6 This Benaiah *was* the mighty man of the thirty, and had charge of thirty; and over his division was Ammizabad his son.

7 The fourth for the fourth month *was* Asahel the brother of Joab, and Zebadiah his son after him; and in his division *were* 24,000.

8 The fifth for the fifth month *was* the commander Shamhuth the Izrahite; and in his division *were* 24,000.

9 The sixth for the sixth month *was* Ira the son of Ikkesh the Tekoite; and in his division *were* 24,000.

10 The seventh for the seventh month *was* Helez the Pelonite of the sons of Ephraim; and in his division *were* 24,000.

11 The eighth for the eighth month *was* Sibbecai the Hushathite of the Zerahites; and in his division *were* 24,000.

12 The ninth for the ninth month *was* Abiezer the Anathothite of the Benjamites; and in his division *were* 24,000.

13 The tenth for the tenth month *was* Maharai the Netophathite of the Zerahites; and in his division *were* 24,000.

14 The eleventh for the eleventh month *was* Benaiah the Pirathonite of the sons of Ephraim; and in his division *were* 24,000.

15 The twelfth for the twelfth month *was* Heldai the Netophathite of Othniel; and in his division *were* 24,000.

Chief Officers of the Tribes

16 ¶ Now in charge of the tribes of Israel: chief officer for the Reubenites was Eliezer the son of Zichri; for the Simeonites, Shephatiah the son of Maacah;

17 for Levi, Hashabiah the son of Kemuel; for Aaron, Zadok;

18 for Judah, Elihu, *one* of David's brothers; for Issachar, Omri the son of Michael;

19 for Zebulun, Ishmaiah the son of Obadiah; for Naphtali, Jeremoth the son of Azriel;

20 for the sons of Ephraim, Hoshea the son of Azaziah; for the half-tribe of Manasseh, Joel the son of Pedaiah;

---

22 [1]Lit *were over*

26 [1]Lit *were over* [a]2 Sam 8:11

27 [1]Heb *from the battles and from the spoil*

28 [1]Lit *under the hand* [2]Heb *Shelomith*

29 [a]Neh 11:16 [b]1 Chr 23:4

30 [1]Lit *beyond the Jordan westward* [a]1 Chr 27:17

31 [1]Heb *according to the Hebronites... father's households* [a]1 Chr 23:19 [b]1 Chr 6:81

32 [1]Lit *every matter of God and matter of the king* [a]2 Chr 19:11

27:2 [1]Lit *was over,* and so throughout the ch [a]2 Sam 23:8-30; 1 Chr 11:11-31

21 for the half-tribe of Manasseh in Gilead, Iddo the son of Zechariah; for Benjamin, Jaasiel the son of Abner;

22 for Dan, Azarel the son of Jeroham. [a]These *were* the princes of the tribes of Israel.

23 But David did not [1]count those twenty years of age and under, [a]because the LORD had said He would multiply Israel [b]as the stars of heaven.

24 Joab the son of Zeruiah had begun to count *them,* but did not finish; and because of [a]this, wrath came upon Israel, and the number was not included in the account of the chronicles of King David.

Various Overseers

25 ¶ Now Azmaveth the son of Adiel had charge of the king's storehouses. And Jonathan the son of Uzziah had charge of the storehouses in the country, in the cities, in the villages and in the towers.

26 Ezri the son of Chelub had charge of the [1]agricultural workers who tilled the soil.

27 Shimei the Ramathite had charge of the vineyards; and Zabdi the Shiphmite had charge of the [1]produce of the vineyards *stored* in the wine cellars.

28 Baal-hanan the Gederite had charge of the olive and [a]sycamore trees in the [1]Shephelah; and Joash had charge of the stores of oil.

29 Shitrai the Sharonite had charge of the cattle which were grazing in [a]Sharon; and Shaphat the son of Adlai had charge of the cattle in the valleys.

30 Obil the Ishmaelite had charge of the camels; and Jehdeiah the Meronothite had charge of the donkeys.

31 Jaziz the [a]Hagrite had charge of the flocks. All these were [1]overseers of the property which belonged to King David.

Counselors

32 ¶ Also Jonathan, David's uncle, *was* a counselor, a man of understanding, and a scribe; and Jehiel the son of Hachmoni [1]tutored the king's sons.

33 [a]Ahithophel *was* counselor to the king; and [b]Hushai the Archite *was* the king's friend.

34 Jehoiada the son of [a]Benaiah, and [b]Abiathar [1]succeeded Ahithophel; and Joab was the [c]commander of the king's army.

David's Address about the Temple

28 Now [a]David assembled at Jerusalem all the officials of Israel, the princes of the tribes, and the commanders of the divisions that served the king, and the commanders of thousands, and the commanders of hundreds, and the overseers of all the property and livestock belonging to the king and his sons, with the officials and [b]the mighty men, even all the valiant men.

2 Then King David rose to his feet and said, "Listen to me, my brethren and my people; I [a]*had* [1]intended to build a [2]permanent home for the ark of the covenant of the LORD and for [b]the footstool of our God. So I had made preparations to build *it.*

3 "But God said to me, '[a]You shall not build a house for My name because you are a man of war and have shed blood.'

4 "Yet, the LORD, the God of Israel, [a]chose me from all the house of my father to be king over Israel [b]forever. For [c]He has chosen Judah to be a leader; and [d]in the house of Judah, my father's house, and among the sons of my father He took pleasure in me to make *me* king over all Israel.

5 "[a]Of all my sons (for the LORD has given me many sons), [b]He has chosen my son Solomon to sit on the throne of the kingdom of the LORD over Israel.

6 "He said to me, 'Your son [a]Solomon is the one who shall build My house and My courts; for I have chosen him to be a son to Me, and I will be a father to him.

7 'I will establish his kingdom forever [a]if he resolutely performs My commandments and My ordinances, as [1]is done now.'

8 "So now, in the sight of all Israel, the assembly of the LORD, and in the hearing of our God, observe and seek after all the commandments of the LORD your God so that you may possess the good land and bequeath *it* to your sons after you forever.

9 ¶ "As for you, my son Solomon, know the God of your father, and [a]serve Him with [1]a whole heart and a willing [2]mind; [b]for the LORD searches all hearts, and understands every intent of the thoughts. [c]If you seek Him, He will let you find Him; but if you forsake Him, He will reject you forever.

10 "Consider now, for the LORD has chosen you to build a house for the sanctuary; [a]be courageous and act."

11 ¶ Then David gave to his son Solomon [a]the plan of [b]the porch *of the temple,* its buildings, its storehouses, its upper rooms, its inner rooms and [c]the room for the mercy seat;

12 and the plan of all that he had in [1]mind, for the courts of the house of the LORD, and for all the surrounding rooms, for [a]the storehouses of the house of God and for the storehouses of the dedicated things;

13 also for [a]the divisions of the priests and [b]the Levites and for all the work of

---

22 [a]1 Chr 28:1
23 [1]Lit *take their number from* [a]1 Chr 21:2-5 [b]Gen 15:5; 22:17; 26:4
24 [a]2 Sam 24:12-15; 1 Chr 21:1-7
26 [1]Lit *doers of the work of the field for the tilling of...*
27 [1]Lit *what was in the vineyards of the storehouses of wine*
28 [1]Or *lowlands* [a]1 Kin 10:27; 2 Chr 1:15
29 [a]1 Chr 5:16
31 [1]Or *rulers* [a]1 Chr 5:10
32 [1]Lit *was with*
33 [a]2 Sam 15:12 [b]2 Sam 15:32,37
34 [1]Lit *after* [a]1 Chr 27:5 [b]1 Kin 1:7 [c]1 Chr 11:6
28:1 [a]1 Chr 23:2; 27:1-31 [b]1 Chr 11:10-47
2 [1]Lit *in my heart* [2]Lit *house of rest* [a]1 Chr 17:1,2 [b]Ps 132:7; Is 66:1
3 [a]1 Chr 22:8
4 [a]1 Sam 16:6-13 [b]1 Chr 17:23,27 [c]Gen 49:8-10; 1 Chr 5:2 [d]1 Sam 16:1
5 [a]1 Chr 3:1-9; 14:3-7 [b]1 Chr 22:9,10
6 [a]2 Sam 7:13, 14
7 [1]Lit *at this day* [a]1 Chr 22:13
9 [1]Or *the same* [2]Lit *soul* [a]1 Kin 8:61; 1 Chr 29:17-19 [b]1 Sam 16:7 [c]2 Chr 15:2; Jer 29:13
10 [a]1 Chr 22:13
11 [a]Ex 25:40; 1 Chr 28:12,19 [b]1 Kin 6:3 [c]Ex 25:17-22
12 [1]Lit *the spirit with him* [a]1 Chr 26:20,28
13 [a]1 Chr 24:1 [b]1 Chr 23:6

the service of the house of the LORD and
for all the utensils of service in the house
of the LORD;
14 for the golden *utensils*, the weight
of gold for all utensils for every kind of
service; for the silver utensils, the weight
of silver for all utensils for every kind of
service;
15 and the weight *of gold* for the
[a]golden lampstands and their golden
lamps, with the weight of each lampstand
and its lamps; and *the weight of silver* for
the silver lampstands, with the weight of
each lampstand and its lamps according
to the use of each lampstand;
16 and the gold by weight for the tables of showbread, for each table; and
silver for the silver tables;
17 and the forks, the basins, and the
pitchers of pure gold; and for the golden
bowls with the weight for each bowl; and
for the silver bowls with the weight for
each bowl;
18 and for [a]the altar of incense refined gold by weight; and gold for the
model of the chariot, *even* [b]the cherubim that spread out *their wings* and covered the ark of the covenant of the LORD.
19 ¶ "All *this*," *said David*, "the LORD
made me understand in writing by His
hand upon me, [a]all the [1]details of this
pattern."
20 ¶ Then David said to his son Solomon, "[a]Be strong and courageous, and
act; do not fear nor be dismayed, for the
LORD God, my God, is with you. [b]He will
not fail you nor forsake you until all the
work for the service of the house of the
LORD is finished.
21 "Now behold, [a]*there are* the divisions of the priests and the Levites for all
the service of the house of God, and [b]ev-
ery willing man of any skill will be with
you in all the work for all kinds of service.
The officials also and all the people will
be entirely at your command."

Offerings for the Temple

29 Then King David said to the entire assembly, "My son Solomon,
whom alone God has chosen, [a]is still
young and inexperienced and the work is
great; for [b]the [1]temple is not for man,
but for the LORD God.
2 "Now [a]with all my ability I have
provided for the house of my God the
gold for the *things of* gold, and the silver
for the *things of* silver, and the bronze for
the *things of* bronze, the iron for the
things of iron, and wood for the *things of*
wood, onyx stones and inlaid *stones*,
stones of antimony and stones of various
colors, and all kinds of precious stones
and alabaster in abundance.
3 "Moreover, in my delight in the
house of my God, the treasure I have of
gold and silver, I give to the house of my
God, over and above all that I have already provided for the holy [1]temple,
4 *namely*, [a]3,000 talents of gold, of
[b]the gold of Ophir, and 7,000 talents of
refined silver, to overlay the walls of the
[1]buildings;
5 of gold for the *things of* gold and of
silver for the *things of* silver, that is, for
all the work [1]done by the craftsmen.
Who then is willing [2]to consecrate himself this day to the LORD?"
6 ¶ Then [a]the rulers of the fathers'
households, and the princes of the tribes
of Israel, and the commanders of thousands and of hundreds, with [b]the overseers over the king's work, offered willingly;
7 and for the service for the house of
God they gave 5,000 talents and 10,000
[a]darics of gold, and 10,000 talents of
silver, and 18,000 talents of brass, and
100,000 talents of iron.
8 [1]Whoever possessed *precious*
stones gave them to the treasury of the
house of the LORD, [2]in care of [a]Jehiel the
Gershonite.
9 Then the people rejoiced because
they had offered so willingly, for they
made their offering to the LORD [a]with a
whole heart, and King David also rejoiced
greatly.

David's Prayer

10 ¶ So David blessed the LORD in the
sight of all the assembly; and David said,
"Blessed are You, O LORD God of Israel
our father, forever and ever.
11 "[a]Yours, O LORD, is the greatness
and the power and the glory and the victory and the majesty, indeed everything
that is in the heavens and the earth;
Yours is the dominion, O LORD, and You
exalt Yourself as head over all.
12 "[a]Both riches and honor *come* from
You, and You rule over all, and [b]in Your
hand is power and might; and it lies in
Your hand to make great and to strength-
en everyone.
13 "Now therefore, our God, we thank
You, and praise Your glorious name.
14 ¶ "But who am I and who are my
people that we should [1]be able to offer as
generously as this? For all things come
from You, and from Your hand we have
given You.
15 "For [a]we are sojourners before You,
and tenants, as all our fathers were; [b]our
days on the earth are like a shadow, and
there is no hope.
16 "O LORD our God, all this abundance
that we have provided to build You a

---

15 [a]Ex 25:31-39
18 [a]Ex 30:1-10 [b]Ex 25:18-22
19 [1]Lit *works* [a]1 Chr 28:11,12
20 [a]1 Chr 22:13 [b]Josh 1:5; Heb 13:5
21 [a]1 Chr 28:13 [b]Ex 35:25-35; 36:1,2
29:1 [1]Lit *palace* [a]1 Chr 22:5 [b]1 Chr 29:19
2 [a]1 Chr 22:3-5
3 [1]Lit *house*
4 [1]Lit *houses* [a]1 Chr 22:14 [b]1 Kin 9:28
5 [1]Lit *by the hand of the craftsmen* [2]Lit *to fill his hand*
6 [a]1 Chr 27:1; 28:1 [b]1 Chr 27:25-31
7 [a]Ezra 2:69; Neh 7:70
8 [1]Lit *those with whom were found* [2]Lit *under the hand of* [a]1 Chr 23:8
9 [a]1 Kin 8:61; 2 Cor 9:7
11 [a]Matt 6:13; Rev 5:13
12 [a]2 Chr 1:12 [b]2 Chr 20:6
14 [1]Lit *retain strength*
15 [a]Lev 25:23 [b]Job 14:2,10-12

house for Your holy name, it is from Your hand, and all is Yours.

17 "Since I know, O my God, that [a]You try the heart and [b]delight in uprightness, I, in the integrity of my heart, have willingly offered all these *things;* so now with joy I have seen Your people, who are present here, make *their* offerings willingly to You.

18 "O LORD, the God of Abraham, Isaac and Israel, our fathers, preserve this forever in the [1]intentions of the heart of Your people, and direct their heart to You;

19 and [a]give to my son Solomon a perfect heart to keep Your commandments, Your testimonies and Your statutes, and to do *them* all, and [b]to build the [1]temple, for which I have made provision."

20 ¶ Then David said to all the assembly, "Now bless the LORD your God." And [a]all the assembly blessed the LORD, the God of their fathers, and [b]bowed low and did homage to the LORD and to the king.

Sacrifices

21 On the next day [a]they [1]made sacrifices to the LORD and offered burnt offerings to the LORD, 1,000 bulls, 1,000 rams *and* 1,000 lambs, with their drink offerings and sacrifices in abundance for all Israel.

22 So they ate and drank that day before the LORD with great gladness.

Solomon Again Made King

¶ And they made Solomon the son of David king [a]a second time, and they [b]anointed *him* as ruler for the LORD and Zadok as priest.

23 Then [a]Solomon sat on the throne of the LORD as king instead of David his father; and he prospered, and all Israel obeyed him.

24 All the officials, the mighty men, and also all the sons of King David [1]pledged allegiance to King Solomon.

25 [a]The LORD highly exalted Solomon in the sight of all Israel, and [b]bestowed on him royal majesty which had not been on any king before him in Israel.

26 ¶ Now [a]David the son of Jesse reigned over all Israel.

27 [a]The period which he reigned over Israel *was* forty years; he reigned in Hebron seven years and [1]in Jerusalem thirty-three *years.*

Death of David

28 Then he died in [a]a [1]ripe old age, [b]full of days, riches and honor; and his son Solomon reigned in his place.

29 Now the acts of King David, from first to last, are written in the chronicles of [a]Samuel the seer, in the chronicles of [b]Nathan the prophet and in the chronicles of [c]Gad the seer,

30 with all his reign, his power, and the circumstances which came on him, on Israel, and on all the kingdoms of the lands.

---

17 [a]1 Chr 28:9 [b]Ps 15:2
18 [1]Lit *intent of the thoughts of the heart*
19 [1]Lit *palace* [a]1 Chr 28:9; Ps 72:1 [b]1 Chr 29:1,2
20 [a]Josh 22:33 [b]Ex 4:31
21 [1]Lit *sacrificed* [a]1 Kin 8:62,63
22 [a]1 Chr 23:1 [b]1 Kin 1:33-39
23 [a]1 Kin 2:12
24 [1]Lit *put a hand under Solomon*
25 [a]2 Chr 1:1 [b]1 Kin 3:13; 2 Chr 1:12
26 [a]1 Chr 18:14
27 [1]Lit *he reigned in* [a]2 Sam 5:4,5; 1 Kin 2:11; 1 Chr 3:4
28 [1]Lit *good* [a]Gen 15:15; Acts 13:36 [b]1 Chr 23:1
29 [a]1 Sam 9:9 [b]2 Sam 7:2-4; 12:1-7 [c]1 Sam 22:5

2 Chronicles

Title and Background

See Introduction to 1 Chronicles.

Author and Date of Writing

See Introduction to 1 Chronicles.

Theme and Message

2 Chronicles continues the history of David's royal line. This book, like 1 Chronicles, shows that the people's relationship to God was most important. When the author wrote about the kings, he measured them on the basis of their faithfulness to God. The reigns of evil kings are reported by the author briefly, while the reigns of good kings are described in more detail.

Outline

I. The Reign of Solomon (1:1—9:31)
II. The Kings of Judah (10:1—36:14)
III. The Destruction of Jerusalem (36:15–23)

Solomon Worships at Gibeon

1 Now [a]Solomon the son of David established himself securely over his
kingdom, and the LORD his God *was* with
him and [b]exalted him greatly.
2 ¶ Solomon spoke to all Israel, [a]to
the commanders of thousands and of
hundreds and to the judges and to every
leader in all Israel, the heads of the fathers' *households.*
3 Then Solomon and all the assembly
with him went to [a]the high place which
was at Gibeon, [b]for God's tent of meeting was there, which Moses the servant
of the LORD had made in the wilderness.
4 However, David had brought up
[a]the ark of God from Kiriath-jearim [1]to
[b]the place he had prepared for it, for he
had pitched a tent for it in Jerusalem.
5 Now [a]the bronze altar, which Bezalel the son of Uri, the son of Hur, had
made, [1]was there before the tabernacle
of the LORD, and Solomon and the assembly sought it out.
6 Solomon went up there before the
LORD to the bronze altar which *was* at the
tent of meeting, and [a]offered a thousand
burnt offerings on it.
7 ¶ [a]In that night God appeared to
Solomon and said to him, "Ask what I
shall give you."

Solomon's Prayer for Wisdom

8 Solomon said to God, "You have
dealt with my father David with great lovingkindness, and [a]have made me king in
his place.
9 "Now, O LORD God, [a]Your [1]prom-
ise to my father David is fulfilled, for You
have made me king over [b]a people as
numerous as the dust of the earth.
10 "[a]Give me now wisdom and knowledge, [b]that I may go out and come in
before this people, for who can rule this
great people of Yours?"
11 [a]God said to Solomon, "Because
[1]you had this in mind, and did not ask for
riches, wealth or honor, or the life of
those who hate you, nor have you even
asked for long life, but you have asked for
yourself wisdom and knowledge that you
may rule My people over whom I have
made you king,
12 wisdom and knowledge have been
granted to you. And [a]I will give you
riches and wealth and honor, [1]such as
none of the kings who were before you
has possessed nor those who will [2]come
after you."
13 [a]So Solomon went [1]from the high
place which was at Gibeon, from the tent
of meeting, to Jerusalem, and he reigned
over Israel.

Solomon's Wealth

14 ¶ [a]Solomon amassed chariots and
horsemen. [b]He had 1,400 chariots and
12,000 horsemen, and he stationed them
in [c]the chariot cities and with the king at
Jerusalem.
15 [a]The king made [b]silver and gold as

1:1 [a]1 Kin 2:12, 46 [b]1 Chr 29:25
2 [a]1 Chr 28:1
3 [a]1 Kin 3:4 [b]Ex 36:8
4 [1]Lit *where David had prepared for it* [a]1 Chr 15:25-28 [b]2 Chr 6:2
5 [1]Lit *he put* [a]Ex 31:9; 38:1-7
6 [a]1 Kin 3:4
7 [a]1 Kin 3:5-14
8 [a]1 Chr 28:5
9 [1]Lit *word* [a]2 Sam 7:12-16 [b]Gen 13:16; 22:17; 28:14
10 [a]1 Kin 3:9 [b]Num 27:17; 2 Sam 5:2
11 [1]Lit *this was in your heart* [a]1 Kin 3:11
12 [1]Lit *which was not so to the kings who were before you* [2]Lit *be* [a]1 Chr 29:25; 2 Chr 9:22
13 [1]Lit *to* [a]2 Chr 1:3
14 [a]1 Kin 10:26-29 [b]1 Kin 4:26 [c]1 Kin 9:19
15 [a]1 Kin 10:27 [b]Deut 17:17

plentiful in Jerusalem as stones, and he
made cedars as plentiful as sycamores in
the [1]lowland.
16 Solomon's [a]horses were imported
from Egypt and from Kue; the king's traders procured them from Kue for a price.
17 They [1]imported chariots from
Egypt for 600 *shekels* of silver apiece and
horses for 150 apiece, and [2]by the same
means they [3]exported them to all the
kings of the Hittites and the kings of
Aram.

Solomon Will Build a Temple and Palace

2 [1a]Now Solomon [2]decided to build a
house for the name of the LORD and
a [3]royal palace for himself.
2 [1]So [a]Solomon [2]assigned 70,000
men to carry loads and 80,000 men to
quarry *stone* in the mountains and 3,600
to supervise them.
3 ¶ [a]Then Solomon sent *word* to
[1]Huram the king of Tyre, saying, "[b]As
you dealt with David my father and sent
him cedars to build him a house to dwell
in, so do for me.
4 "Behold, I am about to build a house
for the name of the LORD my God, dedicating it to Him, [a]to burn fragrant incense before Him and *to set out* [b]the
showbread continually, and to offer
[c]burnt offerings morning and evening,
[d]on sabbaths and on new moons and on
the appointed feasts of the LORD our God,
this *being required* forever in Israel.
5 "The house which I am about to
build *will be* great, for [a]greater is our
God than all the gods.
6 "But [a]who is able to build a house
for Him, for the heavens and the highest
heavens cannot contain Him? So who am
I, that I should build a house for Him,
except to [1]burn *incense* before Him?
7 "Now [a]send me a skilled man to
work in gold, silver, brass and iron, and
in purple, crimson and violet *fabrics,* and
who knows how to make engravings, to
work with the skilled men [1b]whom I
have in Judah and Jerusalem, whom David my father provided.
8 "[a]Send me also cedar, cypress and
algum timber from Lebanon, for I know
that your servants know how to cut timber of Lebanon; and indeed [b]my servants
will work with your servants,
9 to prepare timber in abundance for
me, for the house which I am about to
build *will be* great and wonderful.
10 "Now behold, [a]I will give to your
servants, the woodsmen who cut the timber, 20,000 [1]kors of crushed wheat and
20,000 [1]kors of barley, and 20,000
baths of wine and 20,000 baths of oil."

Huram to Assist

11 ¶ Then Huram, king of Tyre, [1]an-
swered in a letter sent to Solomon: "[a]Be-
cause the LORD loves His people, He has
made you king over them."
12 Then Huram [1]continued, "Blessed
be [a]the LORD, the God of Israel, who has
made heaven and earth, who has given
King David a wise son, [2]endowed with
discretion and understanding, [b]who will
build a house for the LORD and a [3]royal
palace for himself.
13 ¶ "Now I am sending Huram-abi, a
skilled man, [1]endowed with understanding,
14 [a]the son of a [1]Danite woman and
[2]a Tyrian father, who knows how to
work in gold, silver, bronze, iron, stone
and wood, *and* in purple, violet, linen
and crimson fabrics, and *who knows how*
to make all kinds of engravings and to
[3]execute any design which may be assigned to him, *to work* with your skilled
men and with [4]those of my lord David
your father.
15 "Now then, let my lord send to his
servants wheat and barley, oil and wine,
of [a]which he has spoken.
16 "[a]We will cut whatever timber you
need from Lebanon and bring it to you on
rafts by sea to Joppa, so that you may
carry it up to Jerusalem."
17 ¶ Solomon numbered all the aliens
who *were* in the land of Israel, [a]follow-
ing the [1]census which his father David
had [2]taken; and 153,600 were found.
18 [a]He appointed 70,000 of them to
carry loads and 80,000 to quarry *stones*
in the mountains and 3,600 supervisors
to make the people work.

The Temple Construction in Jerusalem

3 [a]Then Solomon began to build the
house of the LORD in Jerusalem on
Mount Moriah, where *the LORD* had appeared to his father David, at the place
that David had prepared [b]on the threshing floor of [1]Ornan the Jebusite.
2 He began to build on the second
day in the second month [1]of the fourth
year of his reign.

Dimensions and Materials of the Temple

3 Now these are the [1]foundations
which [a]Solomon laid for building the
house of God. The length in [2]cubits, according to the old standard *was* sixty cubits, and the width twenty cubits.

15 [1]Heb *shephelah*
16 [a]Deut 17:16
17 [1]Lit *brought up and brought out* [2]Lit *and in like manner by their hand* [3]Lit *brought out*
2:1 [1]Ch 1:18 in Heb [2]Lit *said* [3]Lit *house for his royalty* [a]1 Kin 5:5
2 [1]Ch 2:1 in Heb [2]Lit *numbered* [a]1 Kin 5:15,16; 2 Chr 2:18
3 [1]In 1 Kin 5:18, *Hiram* [a]1 Kin 5:2-11 [b]1 Chr 14:1
4 [a]Ex 30:7 Ex 25:30 [c]Ex 29:38-42 [d]Num 28:9,10
5 [a]Ex 15:11; 1 Chr 16:25
6 [1]Lit *offer up in smoke* [a]1 Kin 8:27; 2 Chr 6:18
7 [1]Lit *who are with me* [a]Ex 31:3-5; 2 Chr 2:13,14 [b]1 Chr 22:15
8 [a]1 Kin 5:6 [b]2 Chr 9:10,11
10 [1]I.e. One kor equals approx 10 bu [a]1 Kin 5:11
11 [1]Lit *said...and he sent* [a]1 Kin 10:9; 2 Chr 9:8
12 [1]Lit *said* [2]Lit *knowing discretion* [3]Lit *house for his royalty* [a]Ps 33:6; 102:25 [b]2 Chr 2:1
13 [1]Lit *knowing understanding*
14 [1]Lit *a woman of the daughters of Dan* [2]Lit *whose father is a Tyrian man* [3]Lit *devise any device* [4]Lit *skilled men* [a]1 Kin 7:14
15 [a]2 Chr 2:10
16 [a]1 Kin 5:8,9
17 [1]Lit *numbering* [2]Lit *numbered of them* [a]1 Chr 22:2
18 [a]2 Chr 2:2
3:1 [1]In 2 Sam 24:18, *Araunah* [a]1 Kin 6:1 [b]1 Chr 21:18
2 [1]Lit *in*
3 [1]Lit *founding of Solomon to build* [2]I.e. One cubit equals approx 18 in. [a]1 Kin 6:2

4 The porch which was in front of the house [a]was as long as the width of the house, twenty cubits, and the height 120; and inside he overlaid it with pure gold.

5 He overlaid [a]the [1]main room with cypress wood and overlaid it with fine gold, and [2]ornamented it with palm trees and chains.

6 Further, he [1]adorned the house with precious stones; and the gold was gold from [2]Parvaim.

7 [a]He also overlaid the house with gold—the beams, the thresholds and its walls and its doors; and he [b]carved cherubim on the walls.

8 ¶ Now he made [a]the [1]room of the holy of holies: its length across the width of the house *was* twenty cubits, and its width *was* twenty cubits; and he overlaid it with fine gold, *amounting* to 600 talents.

9 The weight of the nails was fifty shekels of gold. He also overlaid [a]the upper rooms with gold.

10 ¶ [a]Then he made two [1]sculptured cherubim in the room of the holy of holies and overlaid them with gold.

11 The wingspan of the cherubim *was* twenty cubits; the wing of one, of five cubits, touched the wall of the house, and *its* other wing, of five cubits, touched the wing of the other cherub.

12 The wing of the other cherub, of five cubits, touched the wall of the house; and *its* other wing of five cubits was attached to the wing of the [1]first cherub.

13 The wings of these cherubim extended twenty cubits, and they stood on their feet [1]facing the *main* room.

14 [a]He made the veil of violet, purple, crimson and fine linen, and he worked cherubim on it.

15 ¶ [a]He also made two pillars for the front of the house, thirty-five cubits [1]high, and the capital on the top of each *was* five cubits.

16 He made chains in the inner sanctuary and placed *them* on the tops of the pillars; and he made one hundred pomegranates and placed *them* on the chains.

17 [a]He erected the pillars in front of the temple, one on the right and the other on the left, and named the one on the right Jachin and the one on the left Boaz.

Furnishings of the Temple

4 Then [a]he made a bronze altar, twenty cubits in length and twenty cubits in width and ten cubits in height.

2 [a]Also he made the cast *metal* sea, ten cubits from brim to brim, circular in form, and its height *was* five cubits and [1]its circumference thirty cubits.

3 Now figures like oxen *were* under it *and* all around it, ten cubits, entirely encircling the sea. The oxen *were* in two rows, cast [1]in one piece.

4 It stood on twelve oxen, three facing the north, three facing west, three facing south and three facing east; and the sea *was set* on top of them and all their hindquarters turned inwards.

5 It was a handbreadth thick, and its brim was made like the brim of a cup, *like* a lily blossom; it [a]could hold 3,000 baths.

6 [a]He also made ten basins in which to wash, and he set five on the right side and five on the left [1]to rinse things for the burnt offering; but the sea *was* for the priests to wash in.

7 ¶ Then [a]he made the ten golden lampstands in the way prescribed for them and he set them in the temple, five on the right side and five on the left.

8 He also made [a]ten tables and placed them in the temple, five on the right side and five on the left. And he made one hundred golden bowls.

9 Then he made [a]the court of the priests and [b]the great court and doors for the court, and overlaid their doors with bronze.

10 [a]He set the sea on the right [1]side *of the house* toward the southeast.

11 ¶ [a]Huram also made the pails, the shovels and the bowls. So Huram finished doing the work which he performed for King Solomon in the house of God:

12 the two pillars, the bowls and the two capitals on top of the pillars, and the two networks to cover the two bowls of the capitals which were on top of the pillars,

13 and [a]the four hundred pomegranates for the two networks, two rows of pomegranates for each network to cover the two bowls of the capitals which were on the pillars.

14 [a]He also made the stands and he made the basins on the stands,

15 *and* the one sea with the twelve oxen under it.

16 The pails, the shovels, the forks and all its utensils, [a]Huram-abi made of polished bronze for King Solomon for the house of the LORD.

17 On the plain of the Jordan the king cast them in the clay ground between Succoth and Zeredah.

18 [a]Thus Solomon made all these utensils in great quantities, for the weight of the bronze could not be found out.

19 ¶ Solomon also made all the things that *were* in the house of God: even the golden altar, [a]the tables with the bread of the Presence on them,

20 the lampstands with their lamps of

4 [a]1 Kin 6:3
5 [1]Lit *great house* [2]Lit *put on it palm trees* [a]1 Kin 6:17
6 [1]Lit *overlaid...for beauty* [2]Or *country of gold*
7 [a]1 Kin 6:20-22 [b]1 Kin 6:29-35
8 [1]Lit *house* [a]Ex 26:33; 1 Kin 6:16
9 [a]1 Chr 28:11
10 [1]Lit *cherubim of sculptured work* [a]Ex 25:18-20; 1 Kin 6:23-28
12 [1]Lit *other*
13 [1]Lit *and their faces to*
14 [a]Ex 26:31
15 [1]Lit *long* [a]1 Kin 7:15-20
17 [a]1 Kin 7:21
4:1 [a]Ex 27:1,2; 2 Kin 16:14
2 [1]Lit *a line of 30 cubits encircling it round about* [a]1 Kin 7:23-26
3 [1]Lit *in its casting*
5 [a]1 Kin 7:26
6 [1]Lit *in which to* [a]Ex 30:17-21; 1 Kin 7:38,40
7 [a]Ex 25:31-40; 1 Kin 7:49
8 [a]1 Kin 7:48
9 [a]1 Kin 6:36 [b]2 Kin 21:5
10 [1]Lit *shoulder* [a]1 Kin 7:39
11 [a]1 Kin 7:40-51
13 [a]1 Kin 7:20
14 [a]1 Kin 7:27-43
16 [a]1 Kin 7:14; 2 Chr 2:13
18 [a]1 Kin 7:47
19 [a]2 Chr 4:8

pure gold, [a]to burn in front of the inner sanctuary in the way prescribed;

21 the flowers, the lamps, and the tongs of gold, of purest gold;

22 and the snuffers, the bowls, the spoons and the firepans of pure gold; and the entrance of the house, its inner doors for the holy of holies and the doors of the house, *that is,* of the nave, of gold.

The Ark Is Brought into the Temple

5 [a]Thus all the work that Solomon performed for the house of the LORD was finished. And Solomon brought in the [1b]things that David his father had dedicated, even the silver and the gold and all the utensils, *and* put *them* in the treasuries of the house of God.

2 ¶ [a]Then Solomon assembled to Jerusalem the elders of Israel and all the heads of the tribes, the leaders of the fathers' *households* of the sons of Israel, [b]to bring up the ark of the covenant of the LORD out of the city of David, which is Zion.

3 [a]All the men of Israel assembled themselves to the king at [b]the feast, that is *in* the seventh month.

4 Then all the elders of Israel came, and [a]the Levites took up the ark.

5 They brought up the ark and the tent of meeting and all the holy utensils which *were* in the tent; the Levitical priests brought them up.

6 And King Solomon and all the congregation of Israel who were assembled with him before the ark, were sacrificing [1]so many sheep and oxen that they could not be counted or numbered.

7 Then the priests brought the ark of the covenant of the LORD to its place, into the inner sanctuary of the house, to the holy of holies, under the wings of the cherubim.

8 For the cherubim spread their wings over the place of the ark, so that the cherubim made a covering over the ark and its [1]poles.

9 The poles were so long that [a]the ends of the poles of the ark could be seen in front of the inner sanctuary, but they could not be seen outside; and [1]they are there to this day.

10 [a]There was nothing in the ark except the two tablets which Moses put *there* at Horeb, where the LORD made a covenant with the sons of Israel, when they came out of Egypt.

The Glory of God Fills the Temple

11 ¶ When the priests came forth from the holy place (for all the priests who were present had sanctified themselves, without regard [a]to divisions),

20 [a]Ex 25:31-37; 2 Chr 5:7

5:1 [1]Lit *dedicated things of David,* [a]1 Kin 7:51 [b]2 Sam 8:11; 1 Chr 18:11

2 [a]1 Kin 8:1-9 [b]2 Sam 6:12-15; 1 Chr 15:25-28; 2 Chr 1:4

3 [a]1 Kin 8:2 [b]2 Chr 7:8-10

4 [a]Josh 3:6; 2 Chr 5:7

6 [1]Lit *sheep...numbered for multitude*

8 [1]Lit *poles above*

9 [1]Lit *it is* [a]1 Kin 8:8,9

10 [a]Deut 10:2-5; Heb 9:4

11 [a]1 Chr 24:1-5

12 [a]1 Chr 25:1-4 [b]1 Chr 13:8; 15:16,24 [c]2 Chr 7:6

13 [a]1 Chr 16:42 [b]1 Chr 16:34; 2 Chr 7:3; Ezra 3:11; Ps 100:5; Jer 33:11

14 [a]Ex 40:35; 1 Kin 8:11

6:1 [a]1 Kin 8:12-50

3 [1]Lit *turned his face about*

6 [a]2 Chr 12:13 [b]1 Chr 28:4

7 [1]Lit *with* [a]1 Kin 5:3; 1 Chr 28:2

8 [1]Lit *with*

9 [1]Lit *will come forth from your loins*

10 [1]Lit *spoke*

12 and all the Levitical singers, [a]Asaph, Heman, Jeduthun, and their sons and kinsmen, clothed in fine linen, [b]with cymbals, harps and lyres, standing east of the altar, and with them one hundred and twenty priests [c]blowing trumpets

13 in unison when the trumpeters and the singers were to make themselves heard with one voice to praise and to glorify the LORD, and when they lifted up their voice [a]accompanied by trumpets and cymbals and instruments of music, and when they praised the LORD *saying,* "[b]*He* indeed is good for His lovingkindness is everlasting," then the house, the house of the LORD, was filled with a cloud,

14 so that the priests could not stand to minister because of the cloud, for [a]the glory of the LORD filled the house of God.

Solomon's Dedication

6 [a]Then Solomon said,
"The LORD has said that He
would dwell in the thick
cloud.
2 "I have built You a lofty house,
And a place for Your dwelling
forever."

3 ¶ Then the king [1]faced about and blessed all the assembly of Israel, while all the assembly of Israel was standing.

4 He said, "Blessed be the LORD, the God of Israel, who spoke with His mouth to my father David and has fulfilled *it* with His hands, saying,

5 'Since the day that I brought My people from the land of Egypt, I did not choose a city out of all the tribes of Israel *in which* to build a house that My name might be there, nor did I choose any man for a leader over My people Israel;

6 but [a]I have chosen Jerusalem that My name might be there, and I [b]have chosen David to be over My people Israel.'

7 "[a]Now it was [1]in the heart of my father David to build a house for the name of the LORD, the God of Israel.

8 "But the LORD said to my father David, 'Because it was [1]in your heart to build a house for My name, you did well that it was [1]in your heart.

9 'Nevertheless you shall not build the house, but your son who [1]will be born to you, he shall build the house for My name.'

10 "Now the LORD has fulfilled His word which He spoke; for I have risen in the place of my father David and sit on the throne of Israel, as the LORD [1]promised, and have built the house for the name of the LORD, the God of Israel.

11 "There I have set the ark [a]in which
is the covenant of the LORD, which He
made with the sons of Israel."

Solomon's Prayer of Dedication

12 ¶ Then he stood before the altar of
the LORD in the presence of all the assembly of Israel and spread out his hands.
13 [a]Now Solomon had made a bronze
platform, five cubits long, five cubits
wide and three cubits high, and had set it
in the midst of the court; and he stood on
it, [b]knelt on his knees in the presence of
all the assembly of Israel and spread out
his hands toward heaven.
14 He said, "O LORD, the God of Israel, [a]there is no god like You in heaven or
on earth, [b]keeping covenant and *showing* lovingkindness to Your servants who
walk before You with all their heart;
15 [a]who has kept with Your servant
David, my father, that which You have
[1]promised him; indeed You have spoken
with Your mouth and have fulfilled it
with Your hand, as it is this day.
16 "Now therefore, O LORD, the God of
Israel, keep with Your servant David, my
father, that which You have [1]promised
him, saying, '[2][a]You shall not lack a man
to sit on the throne of Israel, if only your
sons take heed to their way, to walk in
My law as you have walked before Me.'
17 "Now therefore, O LORD, the God of
Israel, let Your word be confirmed which
You have spoken to Your servant David.
18 ¶ "But [a]will God indeed dwell
with mankind on the earth? Behold,
[b]heaven and the [1]highest heaven cannot contain You; how much less this
house which I have built.
19 "Yet have regard to the prayer of
Your servant and to his supplication,
O LORD my God, to listen to the cry and
to the prayer which Your servant prays
before You;
20 that Your [a]eye may be open toward
this house day and night, toward [b]the
place of which You have said that *You
would* put Your name there, to listen to
the prayer which Your servant shall pray
toward this place.
21 "Listen to the supplications of Your
servant and of Your people Israel when
they pray toward this place; hear from
Your dwelling place, from heaven; [a]hear
and forgive.
22 ¶ "If a man sins against his neighbor and is made to take an oath, and he
comes *and* takes an oath before Your altar
in this house,
23 then hear from heaven and act and
judge Your servants, [1][a]punishing the
wicked by bringing his way on his own
head and justifying the righteous by giving him according to his righteousness.
24 ¶ "If Your people Israel [1]are defeated before an enemy because [a]they
have sinned against You, and they return
to You and confess Your name, and pray
and make supplication before You in this
house,
25 then hear from heaven and forgive
the sin of Your people Israel, and bring
them back to the land which You have
given to them and to their fathers.
26 ¶ "When the [a]heavens are shut up
and there is no rain because they have
sinned against You, and they pray toward
this place and confess Your name, and
turn from their sin when You afflict them;
27 then hear in heaven and forgive the
sin of Your servants and Your people Israel, indeed, [a]teach them the good way in
which they should walk. And send rain
on Your land which You have given to
Your people for an inheritance.
28 ¶ "If there is [a]famine in the land,
if there is pestilence, if there is blight or
mildew, if there is locust or grasshopper,
if their enemies besiege them in the land
of their [1]cities, whatever plague or whatever sickness *there is,*
29 whatever prayer or supplication is
made by any man or by all Your people
Israel, [1]each knowing his own affliction
and his own pain, and spreading his
hands toward this house,
30 then hear from heaven Your dwelling place, and forgive, and render to each
according to all his ways, whose heart
You know [a]for You alone know the
hearts of the sons of men,
31 that they may [1]fear You, to walk in
Your ways [2]as long as they live in the
land which You have given to our fathers.
32 ¶ "Also concerning [a]the foreigner
who is not from Your people Israel, when
he comes from a far country for Your
great name's sake and Your mighty hand
and Your outstretched arm, when they
come and pray toward this house,
33 then hear from heaven, from Your
dwelling place, and do according to all for
which the foreigner calls to You, in order
that all the peoples of the earth may know
Your name, and [1]fear You as *do* Your
people Israel, and that they may know
that [2]this house which I have built is
[a]called by Your name.
34 ¶ "When Your people go out to battle against their enemies, by whatever
way You shall send them, and they pray
to You toward this city which You have
chosen and the house which I have built
for Your name,
35 then hear from heaven their prayer

11 [a]2 Chr 5:7, 10
13 [a]Neh 8:4 [b]1 Kin 8:54
14 [a]Ex 15:11; Deut 3:24 [b]Deut 7:9
15 [1]Lit *spoken to* [a]1 Chr 22:9, 10
16 [1]Lit *spoken to* [2]Lit *There shall not be cut off to you a man from before Me* [a]1 Kin 2:4; 2 Chr 7:18
18 [1]Lit *heaven of heavens* [a]Ps 113:5,6 [b]2 Chr 2:6; Is 66:1; Acts 7:49
20 [a]Ps 33:18; 34:15 [b]Deut 12:11
21 [a]Is 43:25; 44:22; Mic 7:18
23 [1]Lit *returning* [a]Is 3:11; Rom 2:8,9
24 [1]Lit *smitten* [a]Ps 51:4
26 [a]1 Kin 17:1
27 [a]Ps 94:12
28 [1]Lit *gates* [a]2 Chr 20:9
29 [1]Lit *whoever shall know*
30 [a]1 Sam 16:7; 1 Chr 28:9
31 [1]Or *reverence* [2]Lit *all the days that they live on the face of the land*
32 [a]Is 56:3-8
33 [1]Or *reverence* [2]Lit *Your name is called upon this house* [a]2 Chr 7:14

and their supplication, and maintain their cause.

36 ¶ "When they sin against You ([a]for there is no man who does not sin) and You are angry with them and deliver them to an enemy, so that [1]they take them away captive to a land far off or near,

37 if they [1]take thought in the land where they are taken captive, and repent and make supplication to You in the land of their captivity, saying, 'We have sinned, we have committed iniquity and have acted wickedly';

38 [a]if they return to You with all their heart and with all their soul in the land of their captivity, where they have been taken captive, and pray toward their land which You have given to their fathers and the city which You have chosen, and toward the house which I have built for Your name,

39 then hear from heaven, from Your dwelling place, their prayer and supplications, and maintain their cause and forgive Your people who have sinned against You.

40 ¶ "Now, O my God, I pray, [a]let Your eyes be open and [b]Your ears attentive to the prayer *offered* in this place.

41 ¶ "[a]Now therefore arise, O LORD God, to Your resting place, You and the ark of Your might; let Your priests, O LORD God, be clothed with salvation and let Your godly ones rejoice in what is good.

42 ¶ "O LORD God, do not turn away the face of Your anointed; [a]remember *Your* lovingkindness to Your servant David."

The Shekinah Glory

7 [a]Now when Solomon had finished praying, [b]fire came down from heaven and consumed the burnt offering and the sacrifices, and the glory of the LORD filled the house.

2 [a]The priests could not enter into the house of the LORD because the glory of the LORD filled the LORD's house.

3 All the sons of Israel, seeing the fire come down and the glory of the LORD upon the house, bowed down on the pavement with their faces to the ground, and they worshiped and gave praise to the LORD, *saying,* "[a]Truly He is good, truly His lovingkindness is everlasting."

Sacrifices Offered

4 ¶ [a]Then the king and all the people offered sacrifice before the LORD.

5 King Solomon offered a sacrifice of 22,000 oxen and 120,000 sheep. Thus the king and all the people dedicated the house of God.

6 The priests stood at their posts, and [a]the Levites also, with the instruments of music to the LORD, which King David had made for giving praise to the LORD—"for His lovingkindness is everlasting"—whenever [1]he gave praise by their [2]means, while [b]the priests on the other side blew trumpets; and all Israel was standing.

7 ¶ [a]Then Solomon consecrated the middle of the court that *was* before the house of the LORD, for there he offered the burnt offerings and the fat of the peace offerings because the bronze altar which Solomon had made was not able to contain the burnt offering, the grain offering and the fat.

The Feast of Dedication

8 ¶ So [a]Solomon observed the feast at that time for seven days, and all Israel with him, a very great assembly *who came* from the entrance of Hamath to the [b]brook of Egypt.

9 On the eighth day they held [a]a solemn assembly, for the dedication of the altar they observed seven days and the feast seven days.

10 Then on the twenty-third day of the seventh month he sent the people to their tents, rejoicing and happy of heart because of the goodness that the LORD had shown to David and to Solomon and to His people Israel.

God's Promise and Warning

11 ¶ [a]Thus Solomon finished the house of the LORD and the king's palace, and successfully completed all that [1]he had planned on doing in the house of the LORD and in his palace.

12 ¶ Then the LORD appeared to Solomon at night and said to him, "I have heard your prayer and [a]have chosen this place for Myself as a house of sacrifice.

13 "[a]If I shut up the heavens so that there is no rain, or if I command the locust to devour the land, or if I send pestilence among My people,

14 [a]and My people [1]who are called by My name humble themselves and pray and seek My face and turn from their wicked ways, then I will hear from heaven, will forgive their sin and will heal their land.

15 "[a]Now My eyes will be open and My ears attentive to the [1]prayer *offered* in this place.

16 "For [a]now I have chosen and consecrated this house that My name may be there forever, and My eyes and My heart will be there perpetually.

36 [1]Lit *their captors take them captive* [a]Job 15:14-16; James 3:2; 1 John 1:8-10
37 [1]Lit *return to their heart*
38 [a]Jer 29:12,13
40 [a]2 Chr 7:15; Neh 1:6,11 [b]Ps 17:1
41 [a]Ps 132:8,9
42 [a]Ps 89:24, 28; 132:10-12; Is 55:3
7:1 [a]1 Kin 8:54 [b]Lev 9:23f; 1 Kin 18:24,38
2 [a]2 Chr 5:14
3 [a]2 Chr 5:13; 20:21
4 [a]1 Kin 8:62,63
6 [1]Lit *David* [2]Lit *hand* [a]1 Chr 15:16-21 [b]2 Chr 5:12
7 [a]1 Kin 8:64-66
8 [a]1 Kin 8:65 [b]Gen 15:18
9 [a]Lev 23:36
11 [1]Lit *came upon the heart of Solomon to do* [a]1 Kin 9:1-9
12 [a]Deut 12:5, 11
13 [a]2 Chr 6:26-28
14 [1]Lit *over whom My name is called* [a]2 Chr 6:37-39; James 4:10
15 [1]Lit *prayer of this place* [a]2 Chr 6:20,40
16 [a]2 Chr 7:12

17 "As for you, if you walk before Me as
your father David walked, even to do according to all that I have commanded
you, and will keep My statutes and My
ordinances,
18 then I will establish your royal
throne as I covenanted with your father
David, saying, '[1][a]You shall not lack a
man *to be* ruler in Israel.'
19 ¶ "[a]But if you turn away and forsake My statutes and My commandments
which I have set before you, and go and
serve other gods and worship them,
20 [a]then I will uproot you from My
land which I have given [1]you, and this
house which I have consecrated for My
name I will cast out of My sight and I will
make it [b]a proverb and a byword among
all peoples.
21 "As for this house, which was exalted, everyone who passes by it will be
astonished and say, '[a]Why has the LORD
done thus to this land and to this house?'
22 "And they will say, 'Because [a]they
forsook the LORD, the God of their fathers
who brought them from the land of
Egypt, and they adopted other gods and
worshiped them and served them; therefore He has brought all this adversity on
them.' "

Solomon's Activities and Accomplishments

8 [a]Now it came about at the end of the
twenty years in which Solomon had
built the house of the LORD and his own
house
2 that he built the cities which Huram had given to [1]him, and settled the
sons of Israel there.
3 ¶ Then Solomon went to Hamath-
zobah and captured it.
4 He built Tadmor in the wilderness
and all the storage cities which he had
built in Hamath.
5 He also built upper [a]Beth-horon
and lower Beth-horon, [b]fortified cities
with walls, gates and bars;
6 and Baalath and all the storage cities that Solomon had, and all the cities for
[1]his chariots and cities for [1]his horsemen, and all that it pleased Solomon to
build in Jerusalem, in Lebanon, and in all
the land [2]under his rule.
7 ¶ [a]All of the people who were left
of the Hittites, the Amorites, the Perizzites, the Hivites and the Jebusites, who
were not of Israel,
8 *namely,* from their descendants
who were left after them in the land
whom the sons of Israel had not destroyed, [a]them Solomon raised as forced
laborers to this day.

9 But Solomon did not make slaves
for his work from the sons of Israel; they
were men of war, his chief captains and
commanders of his chariots and his
horsemen.
10 These were the chief [1]officers of
King Solomon, two hundred and fifty
who ruled over the people.
11 ¶ [a]Then Solomon brought Pharaoh's daughter up from the city of David
to the house which he had built for her,
for he said, "My wife shall not dwell in
the house of David king of Israel, because
[1]the places are holy where the ark of the
LORD has entered."
12 ¶ Then Solomon offered burnt offerings to the LORD on [a]the altar of the
LORD which he had built before the
porch;
13 and [a]*did so* according to the daily
rule, offering *them* up [b]according to the
commandment of Moses, for [c]the sabbaths, [d]the new moons and the [e]three
annual feasts—the Feast of Unleavened
Bread, the Feast of Weeks and the Feast
of Booths.
14 ¶ Now according to the ordinance
of his father David, he appointed [a]the
divisions of the priests for their service,
and [b]the Levites for their duties of praise
and ministering before the priests according to the daily rule, and [c]the gatekeepers by their divisions at every gate; for
[d]David the man of God had so commanded.
15 And they did not depart from the
commandment of the king to the priests
and Levites in any manner or concerning
the storehouses.
16 ¶ Thus all the work of Solomon was
carried out [1]from the day of the foundation of the house of the LORD, and until it
was finished. So the house of the LORD
was completed.
17 ¶ Then Solomon went to [a]Ezion-
geber and to [b]Eloth on the seashore in
the land of Edom.
18 And Huram by his servants sent
him ships and servants who knew the
sea; and they went with Solomon's servants to Ophir, and [a]took from there four
hundred and fifty talents of gold and
brought them to King Solomon.

Visit of the Queen of Sheba

9 [a]Now when the queen of Sheba
heard of the fame of Solomon, she
came to Jerusalem to test Solomon with
difficult questions. She had a very large
retinue, with camels carrying spices and
a large amount of gold and precious
stones; and when she came to Solomon,
she spoke with him about all that was on
her heart.

18 [1]Lit *There shall not be cut off to you a man* [a]1 Kin 2:4; 2 Chr 6:16
19 [a]Lev 26:14, 33; Deut 28:15
20 [1]Ancient versions and Heb read *them* [a]Deut 29:28; 1 Kin 14:15 [b]Deut 28:37
21 [a]Deut 29:24-27
22 [a]Judg 2:13
8:1 [a]1 Kin 9:10-28
2 [1]Lit *Solomon*
5 [a]1 Chr 7:24 [b]2 Chr 14:7
6 [1]Lit *the* [2]Lit *of*
7 [a]Gen 15:18-21; 1 Kin 9:20
8 [a]1 Kin 4:6; 9:21
10 [1]Or *deputies*
11 [1]Lit *they are* [a]1 Kin 3:1; 7:8
12 [a]2 Chr 4:1
13 [a]Ex 29:38-42 [b]Num 28:3 [c]Num 28:9,10 [d]Num 28:11 [e]Ex 23:14-17; 34:22, 23; Deut 16:16
14 [a]1 Chr 24:1 [b]1 Chr 25:1 [c]1 Chr 26:1 [d]Neh 12:24,36
16 [1]So ancient versions; M.T. *as far as*
17 [a]1 Kin 9:26 [b]2 Kin 14:22
18 [a]2 Chr 9:10, 13
9:1 [a]1 Kin 10:1-13; Matt 12:42; Luke 11:31

2 Solomon [1]answered all her questions; nothing was hidden from Solomon which he did not [2]explain to her.

3 When the queen of Sheba had seen the wisdom of Solomon, the house which he had built,

4 the food at his table, the seating of his servants, the attendance of his ministers and their attire, his cupbearers and their attire, and [1]his stairway by which he went up to the house of the LORD, she was breathless.

5 Then she said to the king, "It was a true report which I heard in my own land about your words and your wisdom.

6 "Nevertheless I did not believe their reports until I came and my eyes had seen it. And behold, the half of the greatness of your wisdom was not told me. You surpass the report that I heard.

7 "How [1]blessed are your men, how [1]blessed are these your servants who stand before you continually and hear your wisdom.

8 "Blessed be the LORD your God who delighted in you, [a]setting you on His throne as king for the LORD your God; [b]because your God loved Israel establishing them forever, therefore He made you king over them, to do justice and righteousness."

9 Then she gave the king one hundred and twenty talents of gold and a very great *amount of* spices and precious stones; there had never been spice like that which the queen of Sheba gave to King Solomon.

10 ¶ The servants of Huram and the servants of Solomon [a]who brought gold from Ophir, also brought algum trees and precious stones.

11 From the algum trees the king made steps for the house of the LORD and for the king's palace, and lyres and harps for the singers; and none like that was seen before in the land of Judah.

12 ¶ King Solomon gave to the queen of Sheba all her desire which she requested besides *a return for* what she had brought to the king. Then she turned and went to her own land with her servants.

Solomon's Wealth and Power

13 ¶ [a]Now the weight of gold which came to Solomon in one year was 666 talents of gold,

14 besides that which the traders and merchants brought; and all [a]the kings of Arabia and the governors of the country brought gold and silver to Solomon.

15 King Solomon made 200 large shields of beaten gold, [1]using 600 *shekels of* beaten gold on each large shield.

16 *He made* 300 shields of beaten gold, [1]using three hundred shekels of gold on each shield, and the king put them in the house of the forest of Lebanon.

17 ¶ Moreover, the king made a great throne of ivory and overlaid it with pure gold.

18 *There were* six steps to the throne and a footstool in gold attached to the throne, and [1]arms [2]on each side of the seat, and two lions standing beside the [1]arms.

19 Twelve lions were standing there on the six steps on the one side and on the other; nothing like *it* was made for any *other* kingdom.

20 All King Solomon's drinking vessels *were* of gold, and all the vessels of the house of the forest of Lebanon *were* of pure gold; silver was not considered [1]valuable in the days of Solomon.

21 [a]For the king had ships which went to Tarshish with the servants of Huram; once every three years the ships of Tarshish came bringing gold and silver, ivory and apes and peacocks.

22 ¶ [a]So King Solomon became greater than all the kings of the earth in riches and wisdom.

23 And all the kings of the earth were seeking the presence of Solomon, to hear his wisdom which God had put in his heart.

24 [a]They brought every man his gift, articles of silver and gold, garments, weapons, spices, horses and mules, so much year by year.

25 ¶ Now Solomon had [a]4,000 stalls for horses and chariots and 12,000 horsemen, and he stationed them in the chariot cities and with the king in Jerusalem.

26 [a]He was the ruler over all the kings from the Euphrates River even to the land of the Philistines, and as far as the border of Egypt.

27 [a]The king made silver *as common* as stones in Jerusalem, and he made cedars as plentiful as sycamore trees that are in the [1]lowland.

28 [a]And they were bringing horses for Solomon from Egypt and from all countries.

29 ¶ [a]Now the rest of the acts of Solomon, from first to last, [b]are they not written in the [1]records of Nathan the prophet, and in the prophecy of Ahijah the Shilonite, and in the visions of [2]Iddo the seer concerning Jeroboam the son of Nebat?

30 [a]Solomon reigned forty years in Jerusalem over all Israel.

Death of Solomon

31 And Solomon slept with his fathers

2 [1]Lit *told her all her words* [2]Lit *tell*
4 [1]Or *his burnt offering which he offered*
7 [1]Or *happy*
8 [a]1 Chr 28:5; 29:23 [b]Deut 7:8; 2 Chr 2:11
10 [a]1 Kin 10:11; 2 Chr 8:18
13 [a]1 Kin 10:14-28
14 [a]Ps 68:29; 72:10
15 [1]Lit *he brought up*
16 [1]Lit *he brought up*
18 [1]Lit *hands* [2]Lit *on this side and on this at the place of the seat*
20 [1]Lit *anything*
21 [a]2 Chr 20:36,37
22 [a]1 Kin 3:13; 2 Chr 1:12
24 [a]Ps 72:10
25 [a]Deut 17:16; 1 Kin 4:26; 10:26; 2 Chr 1:14
26 [a]Gen 15:18; 1 Kin 4:21,24
27 [1]Heb *shephelah* [a]2 Chr 1:15-17
28 [a]2 Chr 1:16
29 [1]Lit *words* [2]Heb *Jedo* [a]1 Kin 11:41-43 [b]1 Chr 29:29
30 [a]1 Kin 11:42,43

and was buried in [a]the city of his father David; and his son Rehoboam reigned in his place.

Rehoboam's Reign of Folly

10 [a]Then Rehoboam went to Shechem, for all Israel had come to Shechem to make him king.

2 When Jeroboam the son of Nebat heard *of it* (for [a]he was in Egypt where he had fled from the presence of King Solomon), Jeroboam returned from Egypt.

3 So they sent and summoned him. When Jeroboam and all Israel came, they spoke to Rehoboam, saying,

4 "Your father made our [a]yoke hard; now therefore lighten the hard service of your father and his heavy yoke which he put on us, and we will serve you."

5 He said to them, "Return to me again in three days." So the people departed.

6 ¶ Then King Rehoboam [a]consulted with the elders who had [1]served his father Solomon while he was still alive, saying, "How do you counsel *me* to answer this people?"

7 They spoke to him, saying, "If you will be kind to this people and please them and [a]speak good words to them, then they will be your servants forever."

8 But he [a]forsook the counsel of the elders which they had given him, and consulted with the young men who grew up with him [1]and served him.

9 So he said to them, "What counsel do you give that we may answer this people, who have spoken to me, saying, 'Lighten the yoke which your father put on us'?"

10 The young men who grew up with him spoke to him, saying, "Thus you shall say to the people who spoke to you, saying, 'Your father made our yoke heavy, but you make it lighter for us.' Thus you shall say to them, 'My little finger is thicker than my father's loins!

11 'Whereas my father loaded you with a heavy yoke, I will add to your yoke; my father disciplined you with whips, but I *will discipline you* with scorpions.' "

12 ¶ So Jeroboam and all the people came to Rehoboam on the third day as the king had [1]directed, saying, "Return to me on the third day."

13 The king answered them harshly, and King Rehoboam forsook the counsel of the elders.

14 He spoke to them according to the advice of the young men, saying, "[1]My father made your yoke heavy, but I will add to it; my father disciplined you with whips, but I *will discipline you* with scorpions."

15 So the king did not listen to the people, [a]for it was a turn *of events* from God [b]that the LORD might establish His word, which He spoke through Ahijah the Shilonite to Jeroboam the son of Nebat.

16 ¶ When all Israel *saw* that the king did not listen to them the people answered the king, saying,

"[a]What portion do we have in
David?
We have no inheritance in the
son of Jesse.
Every man to your tents,
O Israel;
Now look after your own house,
David."

[b]So all Israel departed to their tents.

17 But as for the sons of Israel who lived in the cities of Judah, Rehoboam reigned over them.

18 Then King Rehoboam sent Hadoram, who was [a]over the forced labor, and the sons of Israel stoned him [1]to death. And King Rehoboam made haste to mount his chariot to flee to Jerusalem.

19 So [a]Israel has been in rebellion against the house of David to this day.

Rehoboam Reigns over Judah and Builds Cities

11 [a]Now when Rehoboam had come to Jerusalem, he assembled the house of Judah and Benjamin, 180,000 chosen men who were warriors, to fight against Israel to restore the kingdom to Rehoboam.

2 But the word of the LORD came to [a]Shemaiah the man of God, saying,

3 "Speak to Rehoboam the son of Solomon, king of Judah, and to all Israel in Judah and Benjamin, saying,

4 'Thus says the LORD, "You shall not go up or fight against [a]your [1]relatives; return every man to his house, [b]for this thing is from Me." ' " So they listened to the words of the LORD and returned from going against Jeroboam.

5 ¶ Rehoboam lived in Jerusalem and [a]built cities for defense in Judah.

6 Thus he built Bethlehem, Etam, Tekoa,

7 Beth-zur, Soco, Adullam,

8 Gath, Mareshah, Ziph,

9 Adoraim, Lachish, Azekah,

10 Zorah, Aijalon and Hebron, which are fortified cities in Judah and in Benjamin.

11 He also strengthened the fortresses and put officers in them and stores of food, oil and wine.

31 [a]1 Kin 2:10
10:1 [a]1 Kin 12:1-20
2 [a]1 Kin 11:40
4 [a]1 Kin 5:13-16
6 [1]Lit *stood before* [a]Job 8:8,9; 32:7
7 [a]Prov 15:1
8 [1]Lit *who stood before* [a]2 Sam 17:14; Prov 13:20
12 [1]Lit *spoken*
14 [1]Many mss read *I have made*
15 [a]2 Chr 25:16-20 [b]1 Kin 11:29-39
16 [a]2 Sam 20:1 [b]2 Chr 10:19
18 [1]Lit *with stones that he died* [a]1 Kin 4:6; 5:14
19 [a]1 Kin 12:19
11:1 [a]1 Kin 12:21-24
2 [a]2 Chr 12:5-7, 15
4 [1]Lit *brothers* [a]2 Chr 28:8-11 [b]2 Chr 10:15
5 [a]2 Chr 8:2-6; 11:23

12 *He put* shields and spears in every
city and strengthened them greatly. So he
held Judah and Benjamin.
13 ¶ Moreover, the priests and the Levites who were in all Israel stood with
him from all their districts.

Jeroboam Appoints False Priests

14 For [a]the Levites left their pasture
lands and their property and came to Judah and Jerusalem, for [b]Jeroboam and
his sons had excluded them from serving
as priests to the LORD.
15 [a]He set up priests of his own for
the high places, for the satyrs and for the
calves which he had made.
16 [a]Those from all the tribes of Israel
who set their hearts on seeking the LORD
God of Israel [1]followed them to Jerusalem, to sacrifice to the LORD God of their
fathers.
17 [a]They strengthened the kingdom
of Judah and supported Rehoboam the
son of Solomon for three years, for they
walked in the way of David and Solomon
for three years.

Rehoboam's Family

18 ¶ Then Rehoboam took as a wife
Mahalath the daughter of Jerimoth the
son of David *and of* Abihail the daughter
of [a]Eliab the son of Jesse,
19 and she bore him sons: Jeush,
Shemariah and Zaham.
20 After her he took [a]Maacah the
daughter of [1]Absalom, and she bore him
Abijah, Attai, Ziza and Shelomith.
21 Rehoboam loved Maacah the
daughter of Absalom more than all his
other wives and concubines. For [a]he had
taken eighteen wives and sixty concubines and fathered twenty-eight sons and
sixty daughters.
22 [a]Rehoboam appointed Abijah the
son of Maacah as head and leader among
his brothers, for he *intended* to make him
king.
23 He acted wisely and distributed
[1]some of his sons through all the territories of Judah and Benjamin to all the fortified cities, and he gave them food in
abundance. And he sought many wives
for them.

Shishak of Egypt Invades Judah

12 [a]When the kingdom of Rehoboam was established and strong,
[b]he and all Israel with him forsook the
law of the LORD.
2 [a]And it came about in King Rehoboam's fifth year, because they had been
unfaithful to the LORD, that [b]Shishak
king of Egypt came up against Jerusalem
3 with 1,200 chariots and 60,000
horsemen. And the people who came
with him from Egypt were without number: [a]the Lubim, the Sukkiim and the
Ethiopians.
4 He captured [a]the fortified cities of
Judah and came as far as Jerusalem.
5 Then [a]Shemaiah the prophet came
to Rehoboam and the princes of Judah
who had gathered at Jerusalem because
of Shishak, and he said to them, "Thus
says the LORD, '[b]You have forsaken Me,
so I also have forsaken you [1]to Shishak.' "
6 So the princes of Israel and the king
humbled themselves and said, "The
[a]LORD is righteous."
7 ¶ When the LORD saw that they
humbled themselves, the word of the
LORD came to Shemaiah, saying, "[a]They
have humbled themselves *so* I will not
destroy them, but I will grant them some
measure of deliverance, and [b]My wrath
shall not be poured out on Jerusalem by
means of Shishak.
8 "But they will become his slaves so
[a]that they may learn *the difference between* My service and the service of the
kingdoms of the countries."

Plunder Impoverishes Judah

9 ¶ [a]So Shishak king of Egypt came
up against Jerusalem, and took the treasures of the house of the LORD and the
treasures of the king's palace. He took
everything; [b]he even took the golden
shields which Solomon had made.
10 Then King Rehoboam made shields
of bronze in their place and committed
them to the [1]care of the commanders of
the [2]guard who guarded the door of the
king's house.
11 As often as the king entered the
house of the LORD, the [1]guards came and
carried them and *then* brought them back
into the [1]guards' room.
12 And [a]when he humbled himself,
the anger of the LORD turned away from
him, so as not to destroy *him* completely;
and also conditions [b]were good in Judah.
13 ¶ [a]So King Rehoboam strengthened himself in Jerusalem and reigned.
Now Rehoboam was forty-one years old
when he began to reign, and he reigned
seventeen years in Jerusalem, the city
which the LORD had chosen from all the
tribes of Israel, to put His name there.
And his mother's name was Naamah the
Ammonitess.
14 He did evil [a]because he did not set
his heart to seek the LORD.
15 ¶ [a]Now the acts of Rehoboam,
from first to last, are they not written in
the [1]records of [b]Shemaiah the prophet
and of [c]Iddo the seer, according to gene-

---

14 [a]Num 35:2-5 [b]1 Kin 12:28-33; 2 Chr 13:9
15 [a]1 Kin 12:31; 13:33
16 [1]Lit *came after* [a]2 Chr 15:9
17 [a]2 Chr 12:1
18 [a]1 Sam 16:6
20 [1]In 1 Kin 15:2, *Abishalom* [a]1 Kin 15:2; 2 Chr 13:2
21 [a]Deut 17:17
22 [a]Deut 21:15-17
23 [1]Lit *from all*
12:1 [a]2 Chr 11:17; 12:13 [b]2 Chr 26:13-16
2 [a]1 Kin 14:25 [b]1 Kin 11:40
3 [a]2 Chr 16:8; Nah 3:9
4 [a]2 Chr 11:5-12
5 [1]Lit *in the hand of* [a]2 Chr 11:2 [b]Deut 28:15; 2 Chr 15:2
6 [a]Ex 9:27; Dan 9:14
7 [a]1 Kin 21:29 [b]2 Chr 34:25-27; Ps 78:38
8 [a]Deut 28:47, 48
9 [a]1 Kin 14:26-28 [b]1 Kin 10:16,17; 2 Chr 9:15,16
10 [1]Lit *hands* [2]Lit *runners*
11 [1]Lit *runners*
12 [a]2 Chr 12:6, 7 [b]2 Chr 19:3
13 [a]1 Kin 14:21
14 [a]2 Chr 19:3
15 [1]Lit *words* [a]1 Kin 14:29 [b]2 Chr 12:5 [c]2 Chr 9:29

alogical enrollment? And *there were* wars
between Rehoboam and Jeroboam continually.
16 And Rehoboam slept with his fathers and was buried in the city of David;
and his son [a]Abijah became king in his
place.

Abijah Succeeds Rehoboam

13 [a]In the eighteenth year of King
Jeroboam, Abijah became king
over Judah.
2 He reigned three years in Jerusalem; and his mother's name was Micaiah
the daughter of Uriel of Gibeah.
¶ [a]Now there was war between Abijah
and Jeroboam.
3 Abijah began the battle with an
army of valiant warriors, 400,000 chosen
men, while Jeroboam drew up in battle
formation against him with 800,000 chosen men *who were* valiant warriors.

Civil War

4 ¶ Then Abijah stood on Mount
[a]Zemaraim, which is in the hill country
of Ephraim, and said, "Listen to me, Jeroboam and all Israel:
5 "Do you not know that [a]the LORD
God of Israel gave the rule over Israel
forever to David [1]and his sons by [b]a
covenant of salt?
6 "Yet [a]Jeroboam the son of Nebat,
the servant of Solomon the son of David,
rose up and rebelled against his [1]master,
7 and worthless men gathered about
him, scoundrels, who proved too strong
for Rehoboam, the son of Solomon, when
[1a]he was young and timid and could not
hold his own against them.
8 ¶ "So now you intend to resist the
kingdom of the LORD [1]through the sons
of David, [2]being a great multitude and
having with you [a]the golden calves
which Jeroboam made for gods for you.
9 "[a]Have you not driven out the
priests of the LORD, the sons of Aaron and
the Levites, and made for yourselves
priests like the peoples of *other* lands?
Whoever comes [b]to consecrate himself
with a young bull and seven rams, even
he may become a priest of *what are* [c]no
gods.
10 "But as for us, the LORD is our God,
and we have not forsaken Him; and the
sons of Aaron are ministering to the LORD
as priests, and the Levites [1]attend to
their work.
11 "Every morning and evening [a]they
[1]burn to the LORD burnt offerings and
fragrant incense, and [b]the showbread is
set on the clean table, and the golden
lampstand with its lamps is *ready* to light
every evening; for we keep the charge of
the LORD our God, but you have forsaken
Him.
12 "Now behold, God is with us at *our*
head and [a]His priests with the signal
trumpets to sound the alarm against you.
O sons of Israel, do not fight against the
LORD God of your fathers, for you will not
succeed."
13 ¶ But Jeroboam [a]had set an ambush to come from the rear, so that *Israel*
was in front of Judah and the ambush was
behind them.
14 When Judah turned around, behold, [1]they were attacked both front and
rear; so [a]they cried to the LORD, and the
priests blew the trumpets.
15 Then the men of Judah raised a war
cry, and when the men of Judah raised
the war cry, then it was that God [1a]rout-
ed Jeroboam and all Israel before Abijah
and Judah.
16 When the sons of Israel fled before
Judah, [a]God gave them into their hand.
17 Abijah and his people defeated
them with a great slaughter, so that
500,000 chosen men of Israel fell slain.
18 Thus the sons of Israel were subdued at that time, and the sons of Judah
[1]conquered [a]because they trusted in the
LORD, the God of their fathers.
19 Abijah pursued Jeroboam and captured from him *several* cities, Bethel with
its villages, Jeshanah with its villages and
[1]Ephron with its villages.

Death of Jeroboam

20 Jeroboam did not again recover
strength in the days of Abijah; and the
[a]LORD struck him and [b]he died.
21 ¶ But Abijah became powerful; and
took fourteen wives to himself, and became the father of twenty-two sons and
sixteen daughters.
22 Now the rest of the acts of Abijah,
and his ways and his words are written in
[a]the [1]treatise of [b]the prophet Iddo.

Asa Succeeds Abijah in Judah

14 [a]So Abijah slept with his fathers,
and they buried him in the city of
David, and his son Asa became king in his
place. The land was undisturbed for ten
years during his days.
2 ¶ [1]Asa did good and right in the
sight of the LORD his God,
3 for he removed [a]the foreign altars
and [b]high places, tore down the *sacred*
pillars, cut down the [1c]Asherim,
4 and commanded Judah to seek the
LORD God of their fathers and to observe
the law and the commandment.
5 He also removed the high places
and the [a]incense altars from all the cities

16 [a]2 Chr 11:20
13:1 [a]1 Kin 15:1,2
2 [a]1 Kin 15:7
4 [a]Josh 18:22
5 [1]Lit *to him and to his sons* [a]2 Sam 7:12-16 [b]Lev 2:13; Num 18:19
6 [1]Or *lord* [a]1 Kin 11:26
7 [1]Lit *Rehoboam* [a]2 Chr 12:13
8 [1]Lit *in the hands of* [2]Lit *and you are a* [a]1 Kin 12:28; 2 Chr 11:15
9 [a]2 Chr 11:14, 15 [b]Ex 29:29-33 [c]Jer 2:11; 5:7
10 [1]Lit *in the work*
11 [1]Lit *offer up in smoke* [a]Ex 29:38; 2 Chr 2:4 [b]Ex 25:30-39; Lev 24:5-9
12 [a]Num 10:8,9
13 [a]Josh 8:4-9
14 [1]Lit *the battle was before and behind them* [a]2 Chr 14:11
15 [1]Lit *smote* [a]2 Chr 14:12
16 [a]2 Chr 16:8
18 [1]Lit *were strong* [a]2 Chr 14:11
19 [1]Another reading is *Ephrain*
20 [a]1 Sam 25:38 [b]1 Kin 14:20
22 [1]Heb *midrash* [a]2 Chr 24:27 [b]2 Chr 9:29
14:1 [a]1 Kin 15:8
2 [1]Ch 14:1 in Heb
3 [1]I.e. wooden symbols of a female deity [a]Deut 7:5 [b]1 Kin 15:12-14 [c]Ex 34:13
5 [a]2 Chr 34:4,7

of Judah. And the kingdom was undisturbed under him.
6 [a]He built fortified cities in Judah,
since the land was undisturbed, and
[1]there was no one at war with him during those years, [b]because the LORD had
given him rest.
7 For he said to Judah, "[a]Let us build
these cities and surround *them* with walls
and towers, gates and bars. The land is
still [1]ours because we have sought the
LORD our God; we have sought Him, and
He has given us rest on every side." So
they built and prospered.
8 Now Asa had an army of [a]300,000
from Judah, bearing large shields and
spears, and 280,000 from Benjamin,
bearing shields and wielding bows; all of
them were valiant warriors.
9 ¶ Now Zerah the Ethiopian [a]came
out against them with an army of a million men and 300 chariots, and he came
to [b]Mareshah.
10 So Asa went out [1]to meet him, and
they drew up in battle formation in the
valley of Zephathah at Mareshah.
11 Then Asa [a]called to the LORD his
God and said, "LORD, there is no one besides You to help *in the battle* between
the powerful and those who have no
strength; so help us, O LORD our God,
[b]for we trust in You, and in Your name
have come against this multitude.
O LORD, You are our God; let not man
prevail against You."
12 So [a]the LORD [1]routed the Ethiopians before Asa and before Judah, and the
Ethiopians fled.
13 Asa and the people who *were* with
him pursued them as far as [a]Gerar; and
so many Ethiopians fell that [1]they could
not recover, for they were shattered before the LORD and before His army. And
they carried away very much plunder.
14 They [1]destroyed all the cities
around Gerar, [a]for the dread of the LORD
had fallen on them; and they despoiled all
the cities, for there was much plunder in
them.
15 They also struck down [1]those who
owned livestock, and they carried away
large numbers of sheep and camels. Then
they returned to Jerusalem.

The Prophet Azariah Warns Asa

15 Now [a]the Spirit of God came on
Azariah the son of Oded,
2 and he went out [1]to meet Asa and
said to him, "Listen to me, Asa, and all
Judah and Benjamin: [a]the LORD is with
you when you are with Him. And [b]if you
seek Him, He will let you find Him; but
if you forsake Him, He will forsake you.
3 "[a]For many days Israel was without
the true God and without [b]a teaching
priest and without law.
4 "But [a]in their distress they turned
to the LORD God of Israel, and they sought
Him, and He let them find Him.
5 "[a]In those times there was no peace
to him who went out or to him who came
in, for many disturbances [1]afflicted all
the inhabitants of the lands.
6 "[a]Nation was crushed by nation,
and city by city, for God troubled them
with every kind of distress.
7 "But you, [a]be strong and do not
[1]lose courage, for there is [b]reward for
your work."

Asa's Reforms

8 ¶ Now when Asa heard these
words and the [1]prophecy which Azariah
the son of Oded the prophet spoke, he
took courage and removed the abominable idols from all the land of Judah and
Benjamin and from [a]the cities which he
had captured in the hill country of Ephraim. [b]He then restored the altar of the
LORD which was in front of the porch of
the LORD.
9 He gathered all Judah and Benjamin
and those from Ephraim, Manasseh and
Simeon [a]who resided with them, for
many defected to him from Israel when
they saw that the LORD his God was with
him.
10 So they assembled at Jerusalem in
the third month of the fifteenth year of
Asa's reign.
11 [a]They sacrificed to the LORD that
day 700 oxen and 7,000 sheep from the
spoil they had brought.
12 [a]They entered into the covenant to
seek the LORD God of their fathers with
all their heart and soul;
13 and whoever would not seek the
LORD God of Israel [a]should be put to
death, whether small or great, man or
woman.
14 Moreover, they made an oath to the
LORD with a loud voice, with shouting,
with trumpets and with horns.
15 All Judah rejoiced concerning the
oath, for they had sworn with their whole
heart and had sought Him [1]earnestly,
and He let them find Him. So [a]the LORD
gave them rest on every side.
16 ¶ [a]He also removed Maacah, the
mother of King Asa, from the *position of*
queen mother, because she had made a
horrid image [1]as [b]an Asherah, and [c]Asa
cut down her horrid image, crushed *it*
and burned *it* at the brook Kidron.
17 But the high places were not removed from Israel; nevertheless Asa's
heart was blameless all his days.
18 He brought into the house of God

6 [1]Lit *there was not with him war* [a]2 Chr 11:5 [b]2 Chr 15:15

7 [1]Lit *before us* [a]2 Chr 8:5

8 [a]2 Chr 13:3

9 [a]2 Chr 12:2,3; 16:8 [b]2 Chr 11:8

10 [1]Lit *before him*

11 [a]2 Chr 13:14 [b]2 Chr 13:18

12 [1]Lit *struck* [a]2 Chr 13:15

13 [1]Or *there was none left alive* [a]Gen 10:19

14 [1]Lit *smote* [a]2 Chr 17:10

15 [1]Lit *tents of livestock*

15:1 [a]2 Chr 20:14; 24:20

2 [1]Lit *before Asa* [a]2 Chr 20:17 [b]2 Chr 15:4,15

3 [a]1 Kin 12:28-33 [b]Lev 10:8-11; 2 Chr 17:9

4 [a]Deut 4:29

5 [1]Lit *were on* [a]Judg 5:6

6 [a]Matt 24:7

7 [1]Lit *let your hands drop* [a]Josh 1:7,9 [b]Ps 58:11

8 [1]With several ancient versions; Heb *the prophecy, Oded the prophet* [a]2 Chr 13:19 [b]2 Chr 4:1; 8:12

9 [a]2 Chr 11:16

11 [a]2 Chr 14:13-15

12 [a]2 Chr 23:16

13 [a]Ex 22:20; Deut 13:6-9

15 [1]Lit *with their whole desire* [a]2 Chr 14:7

16 [1]Or for *Asherah* [a]1 Kin 15:13-15 [b]Ex 34:13 [c]2 Chr 14:2-5

the dedicated things of his father and his
own dedicated things: silver and gold and
utensils.
19 And there was no more war until
the thirty-fifth year of Asa's reign.

Asa Wars against Baasha

16 In the thirty-sixth year of Asa's
reign [a]Baasha king of Israel came
up against Judah and [1]fortified Ramah in
order to prevent *anyone* from going out
or coming in to Asa king of Judah.
2 Then Asa brought out silver and
gold from the treasuries of the house of
the LORD and the king's house, and sent
them to Ben-hadad king of Aram, who
lived in Damascus, saying,
3 "*Let there be* a treaty between [1]you
and me, *as* between my father and your
father. Behold, I have sent you silver and
gold; go, break your treaty with Baasha
king of Israel so that he will withdraw
from me."
4 So Ben-hadad listened to King Asa
and sent the commanders of his armies
against the cities of Israel, and they [1]con-
quered Ijon, Dan, Abel-maim and all
[a]the [2]store cities of Naphtali.
5 When Baasha heard *of it,* he ceased
[1]fortifying Ramah and stopped his work.
6 Then King Asa brought all Judah,
and they carried away the stones of Ramah and its timber with which Baasha
had been building, and with them he
[1]fortified Geba and Mizpah.

Asa Imprisons the Prophet

7 ¶ At that time [a]Hanani the seer
came to Asa king of Judah and said to
him, "[b]Because you have relied on the
king of Aram and have not relied on the
LORD your God, therefore the army of
the king of Aram has escaped out of your
hand.
8 "Were not [a]the Ethiopians and the
Lubim [b]an immense army with very
many chariots and horsemen? Yet [c]be-
cause you relied on the LORD, He delivered them into your hand.
9 "For [a]the eyes of the LORD move to
and fro throughout the earth that He may
strongly support those [b]whose heart is
completely His. You have acted foolishly
in this. Indeed, from now on you will
surely have wars."
10 Then Asa was angry with the seer
and put him in [1]prison, for he was enraged at him for this. And Asa oppressed
some of the people at the same time.
11 ¶ [a]Now, the acts of Asa from first
to last, behold, they are written in the
Book of the Kings of Judah and Israel.
12 In the thirty-ninth year of his reign
Asa became diseased in his feet. His disease was severe, yet even in his disease
he [a]did not seek the LORD, but the physicians.
13 So Asa slept with his fathers, [1]hav-
ing died in the forty-first year of his reign.
14 They buried him in his own tomb
which he had cut out for himself in the
city of David, and they laid him in the
resting place which he had filled [a]with
spices of various kinds blended by the
perfumers' art; and [b]they made a very
great fire for him.

Jehoshaphat Succeeds Asa

17 [a]Jehoshaphat his son then became king in his place, and made
his position over Israel firm.
2 He placed troops in all [a]the fortified cities of Judah, and set garrisons in
the land of Judah and in the cities of
Ephraim [b]which Asa his father had captured.

His Good Reign

3 The LORD was with Jehoshaphat because he [1]followed the example of his
father David's earlier days and did not
seek the Baals,
4 but sought the God of his father,
[1]followed His commandments, [a]and did
not act as Israel did.
5 So the LORD established the kingdom in his [1]control, and all Judah
brought tribute to Jehoshaphat, and [a]he
had great riches and honor.
6 [1]He took great pride in the ways of
the LORD and again [a]removed the high
places and the Asherim from Judah.
7 ¶ Then in the third year of his reign
he sent his officials, Ben-hail, Obadiah,
Zechariah, Nethanel and Micaiah, [a]to
teach in the cities of Judah;
8 and with them [a]the Levites, Shemaiah, Nethaniah, Zebadiah, Asahel,
Shemiramoth, Jehonathan, Adonijah, Tobijah and Tobadonijah, the Levites; and
with them Elishama and Jehoram, the
priests.
9 They taught in Judah, *having* [a]the
book of the law of the LORD with them;
and they went throughout all the cities of
Judah and taught among the people.
10 ¶ Now [a]the dread of the LORD was
on all the kingdoms of the lands which
were around Judah, so that they did not
make war against Jehoshaphat.
11 Some of the Philistines [a]brought
gifts and silver as tribute to Jehoshaphat;
the Arabians also brought him flocks,
7,700 rams and 7,700 male goats.
12 So Jehoshaphat grew greater and
greater, and he built fortresses and store
cities in Judah.
13 He had large supplies in the cities

16:1 [1]Lit *built* [a]1 Kin 15:17-22
3 [1]Lit *me and you*
4 [1]Lit *smote* [2]Lit *storage places of the cities* [a]Ex 1:11
5 [1]Lit *building*
6 [1]Lit *built*
7 [a]1 Kin 16:1; 2 Chr 19:2 [b]2 Chr 14:11; 32:7,8
8 [a]2 Chr 14:9 [b]2 Chr 12:3 [c]2 Chr 13:16,18
9 [a]Prov 15:3; Jer 16:17; Zech 4:10 [b]2 Chr 15:17
10 [1]Lit *the house of the stocks*
11 [a]1 Kin 15:23,24
12 [a]Jer 17:5
13 [1]Lit *and*
14 [a]Gen 50:2; John 19:39,40 [b]2 Chr 21:19
17:1 [a]1 Kin 15:24
2 [a]2 Chr 11:5 [b]2 Chr 15:8
3 [1]Lit *walked in the earlier ways of his father*
4 [1]Lit *walked in* [a]1 Kin 12:28
5 [1]Lit *hand* [a]2 Chr 18:1
6 [1]Lit *his heart was high* [a]2 Chr 15:17
7 [a]2 Chr 15:3; 35:3
8 [a]2 Chr 19:8
9 [a]Deut 6:4-9
10 [a]2 Chr 14:14
11 [a]2 Chr 9:14; 26:8

of Judah, and warriors, valiant men, in
Jerusalem.
14 This was their muster according to
their fathers' households: of Judah, commanders of thousands, Adnah *was* the
commander, and with him 300,000 valiant warriors;
15 and next to him *was* Johanan the
commander, and with him 280,000;
16 and next to him Amasiah the son of
Zichri, [a]who volunteered for the LORD,
and with him 200,000 valiant warriors;
17 and of Benjamin, Eliada a valiant
warrior, and with him 200,000 armed
with bow and shield;
18 and next to him Jehozabad, and
with him 180,000 equipped for war.
19 These are they who served the
king, apart from [a]those whom the king
put in the fortified cities through all Judah.

Jehoshaphat Allies with Ahab

18 Now [a]Jehoshaphat had great
riches and honor; and he allied
himself by marriage with Ahab.
2 [a]Some years later he went down to
visit Ahab at Samaria. And Ahab slaughtered many sheep and oxen for him and
the people who were with him, and induced him to go up against Ramoth-
gilead.
3 Ahab king of Israel said to Jehoshaphat king of Judah, "Will you go with me
against Ramoth-gilead?" And he said to
him, "I am as you are, and my people as
your people, and *we will be* with you in
the battle."
4 ¶ Moreover, Jehoshaphat said to
the king of Israel, "Please inquire [1]first
for the word of the LORD."
5 Then the king of Israel assembled
the prophets, four hundred men, and said
to them, "Shall we go against Ramoth-
gilead to battle, or shall I refrain?" And
they said, "Go up, for God will give *it* into
the hand of the king."
6 But Jehoshaphat said, "Is there not
yet a prophet of the LORD here that we
may inquire of him?"
7 The king of Israel said to Jehoshaphat, "There is yet one man by whom we
may inquire of the LORD, but I hate him,
for he never prophesies good concerning
me but always evil. He is Micaiah, son of
Imla." But Jehoshaphat said, "Let not the
king say so."

Ahab's False Prophets Assure Victory

8 Then the king of Israel called an
officer and said, "[1]Bring quickly Micaiah, Imla's son."

16 [a]Judg 5:2,9; 1 Chr 29:9
19 [a]2 Chr 17:2
18:1 [a]2 Chr 17:5
2 [a]1 Kin 22:2-35
4 [1]Lit *as the day*
8 [1]Lit *Hasten*
9 [a]Ruth 4:1
13 [a]Num 22:18-20,35
16 [a]Num 27:17; 1 Kin 22:17; Ezek 34:5; 35:4-8; Matt 9:36; Mark 6:34
18 [a]Is 6:1-5; Dan 7:9,10
20 [a]Job 1:6; 2 Thess 2:9
21 [a]John 8:44

9 Now the king of Israel and Jehoshaphat the king of Judah were sitting each
on his throne, arrayed in *their* robes, and
they were sitting [a]at the threshing floor
at the entrance of the gate of Samaria; and
all the prophets were prophesying before
them.
10 Zedekiah the son of Chenaanah
made horns of iron for himself and said,
"Thus says the LORD, 'With these you
shall gore the Arameans until they are
consumed.' "
11 All the prophets were prophesying
thus, saying, "Go up to Ramoth-gilead
and succeed, for the LORD will give *it* into
the hand of the king."

Micaiah Brings Word from God

12 ¶ Then the messenger who went to
summon Micaiah spoke to him saying,
"Behold, the words of the prophets are
uniformly favorable to the king. So please
let your word be like one of them and
speak favorably."
13 But Micaiah said, "As the LORD
lives, [a]what my God says, that I will
speak."
14 ¶ When he came to the king, the
king said to him, "Micaiah, shall we go
to Ramoth-gilead to battle, or shall I refrain?" He said, "Go up and succeed, for
they will be given into your hand."
15 Then the king said to him, "How
many times must I adjure you to speak to
me nothing but the truth in the name of
the LORD?"
16 So he said,
"I saw all Israel
Scattered on the mountains,
[a]Like sheep which have no
shepherd;
And the LORD said,
'These have no master.
Let each of them return to his
house in peace.' "
17 Then the king of Israel said to Jehoshaphat, "Did I not tell you that he
would not prophesy good concerning me,
but evil?"
18 ¶ Micaiah said, "Therefore, hear
the word of the LORD. [a]I saw the LORD
sitting on His throne, and all the host of
heaven standing on His right and on His
left.
19 "The LORD said, 'Who will entice
Ahab king of Israel to go up and fall at
Ramoth-gilead?' And one said this while
another said that.
20 "Then a [a]spirit came forward and
stood before the LORD and said, 'I will
entice him.' And the LORD said to
him, 'How?'
21 "He said, 'I will go and be [a]a deceiving spirit in the mouth of all his proph-

ets.' Then He said, 'You are to entice *him*
and prevail also. Go and do so.'
22 "Now therefore, behold, [a]the LORD
has put a deceiving spirit in the mouth of
these your prophets, for the LORD has proclaimed disaster against you."
23 ¶ Then Zedekiah the son of
Chenaanah came near and [a]struck Micaiah on the cheek and said, "[1]How did the
Spirit of the LORD pass from me to speak
to you?"
24 Micaiah said, "Behold, you will see
on that day when you enter an inner
room to hide yourself."
25 Then the king of Israel said,
"[a]Take Micaiah and return him to Amon
[b]the governor of the city and to Joash the
king's son;
26 and say, 'Thus says the king, "[a]Put
this *man* in prison and feed him [1]spar-
ingly with bread and water until I return
safely." '"
27 Micaiah said, "If you indeed return
safely, the LORD has not spoken by me."
And he said, "[a]Listen, all you people."

Ahab's Defeat and Death

28 ¶ So the king of Israel and Jehoshaphat king of Judah went up against
Ramoth-gilead.
29 The king of Israel said to Jehoshaphat, "I will disguise myself and go into
battle, but you put on your robes." So the
king of Israel disguised himself, and they
went into battle.
30 Now the king of Aram had commanded the captains of his chariots, saying, "Do not fight with small or great, but
with the king of Israel alone."
31 So when the captains of the chariots saw Jehoshaphat, they said, "It is the
king of Israel," and they turned aside to
fight against him. But Jehoshaphat [a]cried
out, and the LORD helped him, and God
diverted them from him.
32 When the captains of the chariots
saw that it was not the king of Israel, they
turned back from pursuing him.
33 A certain man drew his bow at random and struck the king of Israel [1]in a
joint of the armor. So he said to the driver
of the chariot, "Turn [2]around and take
me out of the [3]fight, for I am severely
wounded."
34 The battle raged that day, and the
king of Israel propped himself up in his
chariot in front of the Arameans until the
evening; and at sunset he died.

Jehu Rebukes Jehoshaphat

19 Then Jehoshaphat the king of Judah returned in safety to his
house in Jerusalem.
2 [a]Jehu the son of Hanani the seer
went out to meet him and said to King
Jehoshaphat, "[b]Should you help the
wicked and love those who hate the LORD
and [1c]so *bring* wrath on yourself from
the LORD?
3 "But [1a]there is *some* good in you,
for [b]you have removed the [2]Asheroth
from the land and you [c]have set your
heart to seek God."
4 ¶ So Jehoshaphat lived in Jerusalem
and went out again among the people
from Beersheba to the hill country of
Ephraim and [a]brought them back to the
LORD, the God of their fathers.

Reforms Instituted

5 He appointed [a]judges in the land
in all the fortified cities of Judah, city by
city.
6 He said to the judges, "Consider
what you are doing, for [a]you do not judge
for man but for the LORD who is with you
[1]when you render judgment.
7 "Now then let the fear of the LORD
be upon you; [1]be very careful what you
do, for [2]the LORD our God will [a]have no
part in unrighteousness [b]or partiality or
the taking of a bribe."
8 ¶ In Jerusalem also Jehoshaphat appointed some [a]of the Levites and priests,
and some of the heads of the fathers'
households of Israel, for the judgment of
the LORD and to judge [1]disputes among
the inhabitants of Jerusalem.
9 Then he charged them saying,
"Thus you shall do in the fear of the LORD,
faithfully and wholeheartedly.
10 "[a]Whenever any dispute comes to
you from your brethren who live in their
cities, between blood and blood, between
law and commandment, statutes and ordinances, you shall warn them so that
they may not be guilty before the LORD,
and [b]wrath may *not* come on you and
your brethren. Thus you shall do and you
will not be guilty.
11 "Behold, Amariah the chief priest
will be over you in [1a]all that pertains to
the LORD, and Zebadiah the son of Ishmael, the ruler of the house of Judah, in [1]all
that pertains to the king. Also the Levites
shall be officers before you. [2b]Act resolutely, and the LORD be with the upright."

Judah Invaded

20 Now it came about after this that
the sons of Moab and the sons
of Ammon, together with some of the
[1a]Meunites, came to make war against
Jehoshaphat.
2 Then some came and reported to
Jehoshaphat, saying, "A great multitude
is coming against you from beyond the

22 [a]Is 19:14; Ezek 14:9
23 [1]Lit *Which way* [a]Jer 20:2; Mark 14:65; Acts 23:2
25 [a]2 Chr 18:8 [b]2 Chr 34:8
26 [1]Lit *with bread of affliction and water of affliction* [a]2 Chr 16:10
27 [a]Mic 1:2
31 [a]2 Chr 13:14,15
33 [1]Lit *between the scale-armor and the breastplate* [2]Lit *your hand* [3]Lit *camp*
19:2 [1]Lit *by this* [a]1 Kin 16:1; 2 Chr 20:34 [b]2 Chr 18:1,3 [c]2 Chr 24:18
3 [1]Lit *good things are found* [2]I.e. wooden pillars [a]2 Chr 12:12 [b]2 Chr 17:6 [c]2 Chr 12:14
4 [a]2 Chr 15:8-13
5 [a]Deut 16:18-20
6 [1]Lit *in the word of judgment* [a]Lev 19:15; Deut 1:17
7 [1]Lit *be careful and do* [2]Lit *there is not with the LORD our God* [a]Gen 18:25; Deut 32:4 [b]Deut 10:17,18
8 [1]So the versions; Heb reads *disputes. And they returned to Jerusalem,* or *And they lived in Jerusalem* [a]2 Chr 17:8,9
10 [a]Deut 17:8 [b]2 Chr 19:2
11 [1]Lit *every matter of* [2]Lit *Be strong and do* [a]2 Chr 19:8 [b]1 Chr 28:20
20:1 [1]So with Gr; Heb *Ammonites* [a]1 Chr 4:41; 2 Chr 26:7

sea, out of [1]Aram and behold, they are in
[a]Hazazon-tamar (that is Engedi)."
3 Jehoshaphat was afraid and
[1a]turned his attention to seek the LORD,
and [b]proclaimed a fast throughout all Judah.
4 So Judah gathered together to
[a]seek help from the LORD; they even
came from all the cities of Judah to seek
the LORD.

Jehoshaphat's Prayer

5 ¶ Then Jehoshaphat stood in the assembly of Judah and Jerusalem, in the
house of the LORD before the new court,
6 and he said, "O LORD, the God of
our fathers, [a]are You not God in the
heavens? And [b]are You not ruler over all
the kingdoms of the nations? Power and
might are in Your hand so that no one can
stand against You.
7 "Did You not, O our God, drive out
the inhabitants of this land before Your
people Israel and [a]give it to the descendants of [b]Abraham Your friend forever?
8 "They have lived in it, and have built
You a sanctuary there for Your name, saying,
9 '[a]Should evil come upon us, the
sword, *or* judgment, or pestilence, or
famine, we will stand before this house
and before You (for [b]Your name is in this
house) and cry to You in our distress, and
You will hear and deliver *us.*'
10 "Now behold, [a]the sons of Ammon
and Moab and [1]Mount Seir, [b]whom You
did not let Israel invade when they came
out of the land of Egypt (they turned aside
from them and did not destroy them),
11 see *how* they are rewarding us by
[a]coming to drive us out from Your possession which You have given us as an
inheritance.
12 "O our God, [a]will You not judge
them? For we are powerless before this
great multitude who are coming against
us; nor do we know what to do, but [b]our
eyes are on You."
13 ¶ All Judah was standing before the
LORD, with their infants, their wives and
their children.

Jahaziel Answers the Prayer

14 Then in the midst of the assembly
[a]the Spirit of the LORD came upon Jahaziel the son of Zechariah, the son of Benaiah, the son of Jeiel, the son of Mattaniah,
the Levite of the sons of Asaph;
15 and he said, "Listen, all Judah and
the inhabitants of Jerusalem and King Jehoshaphat: thus says the LORD to you,
[a]Do not fear or be dismayed because of
this great multitude, for [b]the battle is not
yours but God's.
16 'Tomorrow go down against them.
Behold, they will come up by the ascent
of Ziz, and you will find them at the end
of the valley in front of the wilderness of
Jeruel.
17 'You *need* not fight in this *battle;*
station yourselves, [a]stand and see the
salvation of the LORD on your behalf,
O Judah and Jerusalem.' Do not fear or be
dismayed; tomorrow go out to face them,
[b]for the LORD is with you."
18 ¶ Jehoshaphat [a]bowed his head
with *his* face to the ground, and all Judah
and the inhabitants of Jerusalem fell
down before the LORD, worshiping the
LORD.
19 The Levites, from the sons of the
Kohathites and of the sons of the Korahites, stood up to praise the LORD God of
Israel, with a very loud voice.

Enemies Destroy Themselves

20 ¶ They rose early in the morning
and went out to the wilderness of Tekoa;
and when they went out, Jehoshaphat
stood and said, "Listen to me, O Judah
and inhabitants of Jerusalem, [a]put your
trust in the LORD your God and you will
be established. Put your trust in His
prophets and succeed."
21 When he had consulted with the
people, he appointed those who sang to
the LORD and those who [a]praised *Him* in
holy attire, as they went out before the
army and said, "[b]Give thanks to the
LORD, for His lovingkindness is everlasting."
22 When they began singing and praising, the LORD [a]set ambushes against the
sons of [b]Ammon, Moab and Mount Seir,
who had come against Judah; so they
were [1]routed.
23 For the sons of Ammon and Moab
rose up against the inhabitants of Mount
Seir destroying *them* completely; and
when they had finished with the inhabitants of Seir, [a]they helped to destroy one
another.
24 ¶ When Judah came to the lookout
of the wilderness, they looked toward the
multitude, and behold, they *were* corpses
lying on the ground, and no one had escaped.
25 When Jehoshaphat and his people
came to take their spoil, they found much
among them, *including* goods, [1]gar-
ments and valuable things which they
took for themselves, more than they
could carry. And they were three days
taking the spoil because there was so
much.

Triumphant Return to Jerusalem

26 Then on the fourth day they assem-

---

2 [1]Another reading is *Edom* [a]Gen 14:7
3 [1]Lit *set his face* [a]2 Chr 19:3 [b]1 Sam 7:6; Ezra 8:21
4 [a]Joel 1:14
6 [a]Deut 4:39 [b]1 Chr 29:11
7 [a]Is 41:8 [b]James 2:23
9 [a]2 Chr 6:28-30 [b]2 Chr 6:20
10 [1]I.e. Edom [a]2 Chr 20:1,22 [b]Num 20:17-21
11 [a]Ps 83:12
12 [a]Judg 11:27 [b]Ps 25:15; 121:1,2
14 [a]2 Chr 15:1; 24:20
15 [a]Ex 14:13; Deut 20:1-4; 2 Chr 32:7,8 [b]1 Sam 17:47
17 [a]Ex 14:13 [b]2 Chr 15:2
18 [a]Ex 4:31
20 [a]Is 7:9
21 [a]1 Chr 16:29; Ps 29:2 [b]1 Chr 16:34
22 [1]Lit *struck down* [a]2 Chr 13:13 [b]2 Chr 20:10
23 [a]Judg 7:22; 1 Sam 14:20
25 [1]So several ancient mss; others read *corpses*

bled in the valley of Beracah, for there
they blessed the LORD. Therefore they
have named that place "The Valley of
[1]Beracah" until today.
27 Every man of Judah and Jerusalem
returned with Jehoshaphat at their head,
returning to Jerusalem with joy, [a]for the
LORD had made them to rejoice over their
enemies.
28 They came to Jerusalem with harps,
lyres and trumpets to the house of the
LORD.
29 And [a]the dread of God was on all
the kingdoms of the lands when they
heard that the LORD had fought against
the enemies of Israel.
30 So the kingdom of Jehoshaphat was
at peace, [a]for his God gave him rest on
all sides.
31 ¶ [a]Now Jehoshaphat reigned over
Judah. He *was* thirty-five years old when
he became king, and he reigned in Jerusalem twenty-five years. And his mother's
name *was* Azubah the daughter of Shilhi.
32 He walked in the way of his father
Asa and did not depart from it, doing
right in the sight of the LORD.
33 [a]The high places, however, were
not removed; [b]the people had not yet
directed their hearts to the God of their
fathers.
34 ¶ Now the rest of the acts of Jehoshaphat, first [1]to last, behold, they are
written in the annals of [a]Jehu the son of
Hanani, which is [2]recorded in the Book
of the Kings of Israel.

Alliance Displeases God

35 ¶ [a]After this Jehoshaphat king of
Judah allied himself with Ahaziah king of
Israel. He acted wickedly [1]in so doing.
36 So he allied himself with him to
make ships to go [a]to Tarshish, and they
made the ships in Ezion-geber.
37 Then Eliezer the son of Dodavahu
of Mareshah prophesied against Jehoshaphat saying, "Because you have allied
yourself with Ahaziah, the LORD has destroyed your works." So the ships were
broken and could not go to Tarshish.

Jehoram Succeeds Jehoshaphat in Judah

21 [a]Then Jehoshaphat slept with his
fathers and was buried with his
fathers in the city of David, and Jehoram
his son became king in his place.
2 He had brothers, the sons of Jehoshaphat: Azariah, Jehiel, Zechariah,
[1]Azaryahu, Michael and Shephatiah. All
these *were* the sons of Jehoshaphat king
[a]of Israel.
3 Their father gave them many gifts
of silver, gold and precious things, [a]with
fortified cities in Judah, but he gave the
kingdom to Jehoram because he was the
firstborn.
4 ¶ Now when Jehoram had [1]taken
over the kingdom of his father and made
himself [2]secure, he [a]killed all his brothers with the sword, and some of the rulers of Israel also.
5 [a]Jehoram *was* thirty-two years old
when he became king, and he reigned
eight years in Jerusalem.
6 [a]He walked in the way of the kings
of Israel, just as the house of Ahab did
([b]for Ahab's daughter was his wife), and
he did evil in the sight of the LORD.
7 Yet the LORD was not willing to destroy the house of David because of the
covenant which He had made with David, [a]and since He had promised to give
a lamp to him and his sons forever.

Revolt against Judah

8 ¶ In his days [a]Edom revolted
[1]against the rule of Judah and set up a
king over themselves.
9 Then Jehoram crossed over with
his commanders and all his chariots with
him. And he arose by night and struck
down the Edomites who were surrounding him and the commanders of the chariots.
10 So Edom revolted [1]against Judah to
this day. Then Libnah revolted at the
same time [2]against his rule, because he
had forsaken the LORD God of his fathers.
11 Moreover, [a]he made high places in
the mountains of Judah, and caused the
inhabitants of Jerusalem [b]to play the harlot and led Judah astray.
12 ¶ Then a letter came to him from
Elijah the prophet saying, "Thus says the
LORD God of your father David, 'Because
[a]you have not walked in the ways of Jehoshaphat your father [b]and the ways of
Asa king of Judah,
13 but [a]have walked in the way of the
kings of Israel, and have caused Judah
and the inhabitants of Jerusalem to play
the harlot [b]as the house of Ahab played
the harlot, and you [c]have also killed your
brothers, [1]your own family, who were
better than you,
14 behold, the LORD is going to strike
your people, your sons, your wives and all
your possessions with a great [1]calamity;
15 and [a]you will suffer [1]severe sickness, a disease of your bowels, until your
bowels come out because of the sickness,
day by day.'"
16 ¶ Then [a]the LORD stirred up
against Jehoram the spirit of the Philistines and [b]the Arabs who [1]bordered the
Ethiopians;

26 [1]I.e. blessing
27 [a]Neh 12:43
29 [a]2 Chr 14:14; 17:10
30 [a]2 Chr 14:6, 7; 15:15
31 [a]1 Kin 22:41-43
33 [a]2 Chr 17:6 [b]2 Chr 19:3
34 [1]Lit *and* [2]Lit *taken up* [a]2 Chr 19:2
35 [1]Lit *to do* [a]1 Kin 22:48,49
36 [a]2 Chr 9:21
21:1 [a]1 Kin 22:50
2 [1]Or *Azariah* [a]2 Chr 12:6; 23:2
3 [a]2 Chr 11:5
4 [1]Lit *risen up* [2]Lit *strong* [a]Gen 4:8; Judg 9:5
5 [a]2 Kin 8:17-22
6 [a]1 Kin 12:28-30 [b]2 Chr 18:1
7 [a]2 Sam 7:12-17; 1 Kin 11:13,36
8 [1]Lit *from under the hand of* [a]2 Chr 20:22,23; 21:10
10 [1]Lit *from under the hand of* [2]Lit *from under his hand*
11 [a]1 Kin 11:7 [b]Lev 20:5
12 [a]2 Chr 17:3, 4 [b]2 Chr 14:2-5
13 [1]Lit *your father's house* [a]2 Chr 21:6 [b]1 Kin 16:31-33 [c]2 Chr 21:4
14 [1]Lit *blow*
15 [1]Lit *in many sicknesses* [a]2 Chr 21:18,19
16 [1]Lit *were at the hand of* [a]2 Chr 33:11 [b]2 Chr 17:11; 22:1

17 and they came against Judah and invaded it, and carried away all the possessions found in the king's house together with his sons and his wives, so that no son was left to him except [1a]Jehoahaz, the youngest of his sons.

18 ¶ So after all this the LORD smote him [a]in his bowels with an incurable sickness.

19 Now it came about in the course of time, at the end of two years, that his bowels came out because of his sickness and he died in great pain. And his people made no fire for him like [a]the fire for his fathers.

20 He was thirty-two years old when he became king, and he reigned in Jerusalem eight years; and he departed [1a]with no one's regret, and they buried him in the city of David, [b]but not in the tombs of the kings.

Ahaziah Succeeds Jehoram in Judah

22 [a]Then the inhabitants of Jerusalem made [1]Ahaziah, his youngest son, king in his place, for the band of men who came with [b]the Arabs to the camp had slain all the older *sons.* So Ahaziah the son of Jehoram king of Judah began to reign.

2 Ahaziah *was* [1]twenty-two years old when he became king, and he reigned one year in Jerusalem. And his mother's name was Athaliah, the [2]granddaughter of Omri.

3 He also walked in the ways of the house of Ahab, for his mother was his counselor to do wickedly.

4 He did evil in the sight of the LORD like the house of Ahab, for they were his counselors after the death of his father, to [a]his destruction.

Ahaziah Allies with Jehoram of Israel

5 He also walked according to their counsel, and went with Jehoram the son of Ahab king of Israel to wage war against Hazael king of Aram at Ramoth-gilead. But the [1a]Arameans [2]wounded [3]Joram.

6 So he returned to be healed in Jezreel of the wounds [1]which they had inflicted on him at Ramah, when he fought against Hazael king of Aram. And [2]Ahaziah, the son of Jehoram king of Judah, went down to see Jehoram the son of Ahab in Jezreel, because he was sick.

7 ¶ Now [a]the destruction of Ahaziah was from God, in that [1]he went to Joram. For when he came, [b]he went out with Jehoram against Jehu the son of Nimshi, [c]whom the LORD had anointed to cut off the house of Ahab.

Jehu Murders Princes of Judah

8 [a]It came about when Jehu was executing judgment on the house of Ahab, he found the princes of Judah and the sons of Ahaziah's brothers ministering to Ahaziah, and slew them.

9 [a]He also sought Ahaziah, and they caught him while he was hiding in Samaria; they brought him to Jehu, put him to death [b]and buried him. For they said, "He is the son of Jehoshaphat, [c]who sought the LORD with all his heart." So there was no one of the house of Ahaziah to retain the power of the kingdom.

10 ¶ [a]Now when Athaliah the mother of Ahaziah saw that her son was dead, she rose and destroyed all the royal [1]offspring of the house of Judah.

11 But Jehoshabeath the king's daughter took Joash the son of Ahaziah, and stole him from among the king's sons who were being put to death, and placed him and his nurse in the bedroom. So Jehoshabeath, the daughter of King Jehoram, the wife of Jehoiada the priest (for she was the sister of Ahaziah), hid him from Athaliah so that she would not put him to death.

12 He was hidden with them in the house of God six years while Athaliah reigned over the land.

Jehoiada Sets Joash on the Throne of Judah

23 [a]Now in the seventh year Jehoiada strengthened himself, and took captains of hundreds: Azariah the son of Jeroham, Ishmael the son of Johanan, Azariah the son of Obed, Maaseiah the son of Adaiah, and Elishaphat the son of Zichri, *and they entered* into a covenant with him.

2 They went throughout Judah and gathered the Levites from all the cities of Judah, and the heads of the fathers' *households* of [a]Israel, and they came to Jerusalem.

3 Then all the assembly made a covenant with the king in the house of God. And [1]Jehoiada said to them, "Behold, the king's son shall reign, [a]as the LORD has spoken concerning the sons of David.

4 "This is the thing which you shall do: one third of you, of the priests and Levites [a]who come in on the sabbath, *shall be* gatekeepers,

5 and one third *shall be* at the king's house, and a third at the Gate of the Foundation; and all the people *shall be* in the courts of the house of the LORD.

6 "But let no one enter the house of the LORD except the priests and [a]the ministering Levites; they may enter, for

17 [1]In 2 Chr 22:1, *Ahaziah* [a]2 Chr 25:23
18 [a]2 Chr 21:15
19 [a]2 Chr 16:14
20 [1]Lit *without desire* [a]Jer 22:18,28 [b]2 Chr 24:25; 28:27
22:1 [1]In 2 Chr 21:17, *Jehoahaz* [a]2 Kin 8:24-29 [b]2 Chr 21:16
2 [1]So some versions and 2 Kin 8:26; Heb *42 years* [2]Lit *daughter*
4 [a]Prov 13:20
5 [1]Heb *archers* [2]Lit *smote* [3]I.e. Jehoram [a]2 Kin 8:28
6 [1]Lit *with which...smitten* [2]So with 2 Kin 8:29; Heb *Azariah*
7 [1]Lit *to go* [a]2 Chr 10:15 [b]2 Kin 9:21 [c]2 Kin 9:6,7
8 [a]2 Kin 10:11-14
9 [a]2 Kin 9:27 [b]2 Kin 9:28 [c]2 Chr 17:4
10 [1]Lit *seed* [a]2 Kin 11:1-3
23:1 [a]2 Kin 11:4-20
2 [a]2 Chr 11:13-17; 21:2
3 [1]Lit *he* [a]2 Sam 7:12; 2 Chr 21:7
4 [a]1 Chr 9:25
6 [a]1 Chr 23:28-32

they are holy. And let all the people keep the charge of the LORD.

7 "The Levites will surround the king, each man with his weapons in his hand; and whoever enters the house, let him be killed. Thus be with the king when he comes in and when he goes out."

8 ¶ So the Levites and all Judah did according to all that Jehoiada the priest commanded. And each one of them took his men who were to come in on the sabbath, with those who were to go out on the sabbath, for Jehoiada the priest did not dismiss *any of* [a]the divisions.

9 Then Jehoiada the priest gave to the captains of hundreds the spears and the large and small shields which had been King David's, which were in the house of God.

10 He stationed all the people, each man with his weapon in his hand, from the right [1]side of the house to the left [1]side of the house, by the altar and by the house, around the king.

11 Then they brought out the king's son and put the crown on him, and *gave him* [a]the testimony and made him king. And Jehoiada and his sons anointed him and said, "[b]*Long* live the king!"

Athaliah Murdered

12 ¶ When Athaliah heard the noise of the people running and praising the king, she came into the house of the LORD to the people.

13 She looked, and behold, the king was standing by his pillar at the entrance, and the captains and the [1]trumpeters *were* beside the king. And all the people of the land rejoiced and blew trumpets, the singers with *their* musical instruments [2]leading the praise. Then Athaliah tore her clothes and said, "Treason! Treason!"

14 Jehoiada the priest brought out the captains of hundreds who were appointed over the army and said to them, "Bring her out [1]between the ranks; and whoever follows her, put to death with the sword." For the priest said, "Let her not be put to death in the house of the LORD."

15 So they [1]seized her, and when she arrived at the entrance of [a]the Horse Gate of the king's house, they [b]put her to death there.

Reforms Carried Out

16 ¶ Then [a]Jehoiada made a covenant between himself and all the people and the king, that they would be the LORD'S people.

17 And all the people went to the house of Baal and tore it down, and they broke in pieces his altars and his images, and [a]killed Mattan the priest of Baal before the altars.

18 Moreover, Jehoiada placed the offices of the house of the LORD under the [1]authority of [a]the Levitical priests, [b]whom David had assigned over the house of the LORD, to offer the burnt offerings of the LORD, as it is written in the law of Moses—[c]with rejoicing and singing according to the [2]order of David.

19 He stationed [a]the gatekeepers of the house of the LORD, so that no one would enter *who was* in any way unclean.

20 [a]He took the captains of hundreds, the nobles, the rulers of the people and all the people of the land, and brought the king down from the house of the LORD, and came through the upper gate to the king's house. And they placed the king upon the royal throne.

21 So [a]all of the people of the land rejoiced and the city was quiet. For they had put Athaliah to death with the sword.

Young Joash Influenced by Jehoiada

24 [a]Joash *was* seven years old when he became king, and he reigned forty years in Jerusalem; and his mother's name *was* Zibiah from Beersheba.

2 [a]Joash did what was right in the sight of the LORD all the days of Jehoiada the priest.

3 Jehoiada took two wives for him, and he became the father of sons and daughters.

Faithless Priests

4 ¶ Now it came about after this that Joash [1]decided [a]to restore the house of the LORD.

5 He gathered the priests and Levites and said to them, "Go out to the cities of Judah and collect money from all [a]Israel to [1]repair the house of your God [2]annually, and you shall do the matter quickly." But the Levites did not act quickly.

6 So the king summoned Jehoiada the chief *priest* and said to him, "Why have you not required the Levites to bring in from Judah and from Jerusalem [a]the levy *fixed by* Moses the servant of the LORD on the congregation of Israel [b]for the tent of the testimony?"

7 For [a]the sons of the wicked Athaliah had broken into the house of God and even [1]used the holy things of the house of the LORD for the Baals.

Temple Repaired

8 ¶ So the king commanded, and [a]they made a chest and set it outside by the gate of the house of the LORD.

9 [a]They made a proclamation in Ju-

---

8 [a]1 Chr 24:1
10 [1]Lit *shoulder*
11 [a]Ex 25:16,21 [b]1 Sam 10:24
13 [1]Lit *trumpets* [2]Lit *and leading for praising*
14 [1]Lit *from within*
15 [1]Lit *placed hands to her* [a]Neh 3:28; Jer 31:40 [b]2 Chr 22:10
16 [a]2 Kin 11:17
17 [a]Deut 13:6-9; 1 Kin 18:40
18 [1]Lit *hand* [2]Lit *hands of* [a]2 Chr 5:5 [b]1 Chr 23:6, 25-31 [c]1 Chr 25:1
19 [a]1 Chr 9:22
20 [a]2 Kin 11:19
21 [a]2 Kin 11:20
24:1 [a]2 Kin 11:21; 12:1-15
2 [a]2 Chr 26:4,5
4 [1]Lit *was with a heart* [a]2 Chr 24:7
5 [1]Lit *to strengthen* [2]Lit *from year to year* [a]2 Chr 21:2
6 [a]Ex 30:12-16 [b]Num 1:50
7 [1]Lit *made* [a]2 Chr 21:17
8 [a]2 Kin 12:9
9 [a]2 Chr 36:22

dah and Jerusalem to bring to the LORD [b]the levy *fixed by* Moses the servant of God on Israel in the wilderness.

10 All the officers and all the people rejoiced and brought in their levies and [1]dropped *them* into the chest until they had finished.

11 It came about whenever the chest was brought in to the king's officer by the Levites, and when [a]they saw that there was much money, then the king's scribe and the chief priest's officer would come, empty the chest, take it, and return it to its place. Thus they did daily and collected much money.

12 The king and Jehoiada gave it to those who did the work of the service of the house of the LORD; and they hired masons and carpenters to restore the house of the LORD, and also workers in iron and bronze to [1]repair the house of the LORD.

13 So the workmen labored, and the repair work progressed in their hands, and they [1]restored the house of God [2]according to its specifications and strengthened it.

14 When they had finished, they brought the rest of the money before the king and Jehoiada; and it was made into utensils for the house of the LORD, utensils for the service and the burnt offering, and pans and utensils of gold and silver. And they offered burnt offerings in the house of the LORD continually all the days of Jehoiada.

15 ¶ Now when Jehoiada [1]reached a ripe old age he died; he was one hundred and thirty years old at his death.

16 They buried him [a]in the city of David among the kings, because he had done well in [b]Israel and [1]to God and His house.

17 ¶ But after the death of Jehoiada the officials of Judah came and bowed down to the king, and the king listened to them.

18 They abandoned [a]the house of the LORD, the God of their fathers, and [b]served the [1]Asherim and the idols; so [c]wrath came upon Judah and Jerusalem for this their guilt.

19 Yet [a]He sent prophets to them to bring them back to the LORD; though they testified against them, they would not listen.

Joash Murders Son of Jehoiada

20 ¶ [a]Then the Spirit of God [1]came on Zechariah the son of Jehoiada the priest; and he stood above the people and said to them, "Thus God has said, '[b]Why do you transgress the commandments of the LORD and do not prosper? [c]Because you have forsaken the LORD, He has also forsaken you.' "

21 So [a]they conspired against him and at the command of the king they stoned him [1]to death in the court of the house of the LORD.

22 Thus Joash the king did not remember the kindness which his father Jehoiada had shown him, but he murdered his son. And as he died he said, "May [a]the LORD see and [1]avenge!"

Aram Invades and Defeats Judah

23 ¶ Now it happened at the turn of the year that [a]the army of the Arameans came up against him; and they came to Judah and Jerusalem, destroyed all the officials of the people from among the people, and sent all their spoil to the king of Damascus.

24 Indeed the army of the Arameans came with a small number of men; yet [a]the LORD delivered a very great army into their hands, [b]because they had forsaken the LORD, the God of their fathers. Thus they executed judgment on Joash.

25 ¶ [a]When they had departed from him (for they left him very sick), his own servants conspired against him because of the blood of the [1]son of Jehoiada the priest, and murdered him on his bed. So he died, and they buried him in the city of David, but they did not bury him in the tombs of the kings.

26 Now these are those who conspired against him: Zabad the son of Shimeath the Ammonitess, and Jehozabad the son of Shimrith the Moabitess.

27 As to his sons and the many [1]oracles against him and [a]the [2]rebuilding of the house of God, behold, they are written in the [3b]treatise of the Book of the Kings. Then Amaziah his son became king in his place.

Amaziah Succeeds Joash in Judah

25 [a]Amaziah was twenty-five years old when he became king, and he reigned twenty-nine years in Jerusalem. And his mother's name was Jehoaddan of Jerusalem.

2 He did right in the sight of the LORD, [a]yet not with a whole heart.

3 Now [a]it came about as soon as the kingdom was [1]firmly in his grasp, that he killed his servants who had slain his father the king.

4 However, he did not put their children to death, but *did* as it is written in the law in the book of Moses, which the LORD commanded, saying, "[a]Fathers shall not be put to death for sons, nor sons be put to death for fathers, but each shall be put to death for his own sin."

9 [b]2 Chr 24:6
10 [1]Lit *threw*
11 [a]2 Kin 12:10
12 [1]Lit *to strengthen*
13 [1]Lit *set up* [2]Lit *upon its proportion*
15 [1]Lit *became old and satisfied with days*
16 [1]Lit *with* [a]2 Chr 21:20 [b]2 Chr 21:2
18 [1]I.e. wooden symbols of a female deity [a]2 Chr 24:4 [b]Ex 34:12-14 [c]Josh 22:20
19 [a]Jer 7:25
20 [1]Lit *clothed* [a]2 Chr 20:14 [b]Num 14:41 [c]2 Chr 15:2
21 [1]Lit *with stones* [a]Neh 9:26; Matt 23:34,35
22 [1]Lit *seek*, or *require* [a]Gen 9:5
23 [a]2 Kin 12:17
24 [a]2 Chr 16:7, 8 [b]2 Chr 24:20
25 [1]So some ancient versions; Heb *sons* [a]2 Kin 12:20,21
27 [1]Or *burdens upon* [2]Lit *founding* [3]Heb *midrash* [a]2 Chr 24:12 [b]2 Chr 13:22
25:1 [a]2 Kin 14:1-6
2 [a]2 Chr 25:14
3 [1]Lit *firm upon him* [a]2 Kin 14:5
4 [a]Deut 24:16

Amaziah Defeats Edomites

5 ¶ Moreover, Amaziah assembled Judah and appointed them according to *their* fathers' households under commanders of thousands and commanders of hundreds throughout Judah and Benjamin; and he [1]took a census of those [a]from twenty years old and upward and found them to be [b]300,000 choice men, *able* to go to war *and* handle spear and shield.

6 He hired also 100,000 valiant warriors out of Israel for one hundred talents of silver.

7 But [a]a man of God came to him saying, "O king, do not let the army of Israel go with you, for the LORD is not with Israel *nor with* any of the sons of Ephraim.

8 "But if you do go, do *it,* be strong for the battle; *yet* God will [1]bring you down before the enemy, [a]for God has power to help and to [1]bring down."

9 Amaziah said to the man of God, "But what *shall we* do for the hundred talents which I have given to the troops of Israel?" And the man of God answered, "[a]The LORD has much more to give you than this."

10 Then Amaziah [1]dismissed them, the troops which came to him from Ephraim, to go home; so their anger burned against Judah and they returned [2]home in fierce anger.

11 ¶ Now Amaziah strengthened himself and led his people forth, and went to [a]the Valley of Salt and struck down 10,000 of the sons of Seir.

12 The sons of Judah also captured 10,000 alive and brought them to the top of the cliff and threw them down from the top of the cliff, so that they were all dashed to pieces.

13 But the [1]troops whom Amaziah sent back from going with him to battle, raided the cities of Judah, from Samaria to Beth-horon, and struck down 3,000 of them and plundered much spoil.

Amaziah Rebuked for Idolatry

14 ¶ Now after Amaziah came from slaughtering the Edomites, [a]he brought the gods of the sons of Seir, set them up as his gods, bowed down before them and burned incense to them.

15 Then the anger of the LORD burned against Amaziah, and He sent him a prophet who said to him, "Why have you sought the gods of the people [a]who have not delivered their own people from your hand?"

16 As he was talking with him, [1]the king said to him, "Have we appointed you a royal counselor? Stop! Why should you be struck down?" Then the prophet stopped and said, "I know that God has planned to destroy you, because you have done this and have not listened to my counsel."

Amaziah Defeated by Joash of Israel

17 ¶ [a]Then Amaziah king of Judah took counsel and sent to Joash the son of Jehoahaz the son of Jehu, the king of Israel, saying, "Come, let us face each other."

18 Joash the king of Israel sent to Amaziah king of Judah, saying, "[a]The thorn bush which was in Lebanon sent to the cedar which was in Lebanon, saying, 'Give your daughter to my son in marriage.' But there passed by a wild beast that was in Lebanon and trampled the thorn bush.

19 "You said, 'Behold, you have [1]defeated Edom.' And [a]your heart has [2]become proud in boasting. Now stay at home; for why should you provoke trouble so that you, even you, would fall and Judah with you?"

20 ¶ But Amaziah would not listen, for it was from God, that He might deliver them into the hand *of Joash* because they had sought the gods of Edom.

21 So Joash king of Israel went up, and he and Amaziah king of Judah faced each other at Beth-shemesh, which belonged to Judah.

22 Judah was defeated [1]by Israel, and they fled each to his tent.

23 Then Joash king of Israel captured Amaziah king of Judah, the son of Joash the son of [a]Jehoahaz, at Beth-shemesh, and brought him to Jerusalem and tore down the wall of Jerusalem from the Gate of Ephraim to the Corner Gate, 400 [1]cubits.

24 *He took* all the gold and silver and all the utensils which were found in the house of God with [a]Obed-edom, and the treasures of the king's house, the hostages also, and returned to Samaria.

25 ¶ [a]And Amaziah, the son of Joash king of Judah, lived fifteen years after the death of Joash, son of Jehoahaz, king of Israel.

26 Now the rest of the acts of Amaziah, from first to last, behold, are they not written in the Book of the Kings of Judah and Israel?

27 From the time that Amaziah turned away from following the LORD they conspired against him in Jerusalem, and he fled to Lachish; but they sent after him to Lachish and killed him there.

28 Then they brought him on horses and buried him with his fathers in the city of Judah.

5 [1]Lit *mustered* [a]Num 1:3 [b]2 Chr 26:13
7 [a]2 Kin 4:9
8 [1]Lit *cause to stumble* [a]2 Chr 14:11; 20:6
9 [a]Deut 8:18; Prov 10:22
10 [1]Lit *separated* [2]Lit *to their own place*
11 [a]2 Kin 14:7
13 [1]Lit *sons of the troops*
14 [a]2 Chr 28:23
15 [a]2 Chr 25:11,12
16 [1]Lit *he*
17 [a]2 Kin 14:8-14
18 [a]Judg 9:8-15
19 [1]Lit *smitten* [2]Lit *lifted you up to boast* [a]2 Chr 26:16; 32:25
22 [1]Lit *before*
23 [1]I.e. One cubit equals approx 18 in. [a]2 Chr 21:17; 22:1
24 [a]1 Chr 26:15
25 [a]2 Kin 14:17-22

Uzziah Succeeds Amaziah in Judah

26 And all the people of Judah took [1]Uzziah, who *was* sixteen years old, and made him king in the place of his father Amaziah.

2 He built Eloth and restored it to Judah after the king slept with his fathers.

3 Uzziah was [a]sixteen years old when he became king, and he reigned fifty-two years in Jerusalem; and his mother's name was [1]Jechiliah of Jerusalem.

4 He did right in the sight of the LORD according to all that his father Amaziah had done.

5 [a]He continued to seek God in the days of Zechariah, [b]who had understanding [1]through the vision of God; and [2c]as long as he sought the LORD, God prospered him.

Uzziah Succeeds in War

6 ¶ Now he went out and [a]warred against the Philistines, and broke down the wall of Gath and the wall of Jabneh and the wall of Ashdod; and he built cities in *the area of* Ashdod and among the Philistines.

7 [a]God helped him against the Philistines, and against the Arabians who lived in Gur-baal, and the Meunites.

8 The Ammonites also gave [a]tribute to Uzziah, and his [1]fame extended to the border of Egypt, for he became very strong.

9 Moreover, Uzziah built towers in Jerusalem at [a]the Corner Gate and at the [b]Valley Gate and at the corner buttress and fortified them.

10 He built towers in the wilderness and [a]hewed many cisterns, for he had much livestock, both in the [1]lowland and in the plain. *He also had* plowmen and vinedressers in the hill country and the fertile fields, for he loved the soil.

11 Moreover, Uzziah had an army ready for battle, which [1]entered combat by divisions according to the number of their muster, [2]prepared by Jeiel the scribe and Maaseiah the official, under the direction of Hananiah, one of the king's officers.

12 The total number of the heads of the [1]households, of valiant warriors, was 2,600.

13 Under their direction was an [1]elite army of [a]307,500, who could wage war with great power, to help the king against the enemy.

14 Moreover, Uzziah prepared [1]for all the army shields, spears, helmets, body armor, bows and sling stones.

15 In Jerusalem he made engines *of war* invented by skillful men to be on the towers and on the corners for the purpose of shooting arrows and great stones. Hence his [1]fame spread afar, for he was marvelously helped until he *was* strong.

Pride Is Uzziah's Undoing

16 ¶ But [a]when he became strong, his heart was so [1]proud that he acted corruptly, and he was unfaithful to the LORD his God, for [b]he entered the temple of the LORD to burn incense on the altar of incense.

17 Then [a]Azariah the priest entered after him and with him eighty priests of the LORD, valiant men.

18 [a]They opposed Uzziah the king and said to him, "[b]It is not for you, Uzziah, to burn incense to the LORD, [c]but for the priests, the sons of Aaron who are consecrated to burn incense. Get out of the sanctuary, for you have been unfaithful and will have no honor from the LORD God."

19 But Uzziah, with a censer in his hand for burning incense, was enraged; and while he was enraged with the priests, [a]the leprosy broke out on his forehead before the priests in the house of the LORD, beside the altar of incense.

20 Azariah the chief priest and all the priests looked at him, and behold, he *was* leprous on his forehead; and they hurried him out of there, and he himself also hastened to get out because the LORD had smitten him.

21 [a]King Uzziah was a leper to the day of his death; and he lived in [b]a separate house, being a leper, for he was cut off from the house of the LORD. And Jotham his son *was* over the king's house judging the people of the land.

22 ¶ Now the rest of the acts of Uzziah, first to last, the prophet [a]Isaiah, the son of Amoz, has written.

23 So Uzziah slept with his fathers, and they buried him with his fathers [a]in the field of the grave which belonged to the kings, for they said, "He is a leper." And Jotham his son became king in his place.

Jotham Succeeds Uzziah in Judah

27 [a]Jotham was twenty-five years old when he became king, and he reigned sixteen years in Jerusalem. And his mother's name was Jerushah the daughter of Zadok.

2 He did right in the sight of the LORD, according to all that his father Uzziah had done; [a]however he did not enter the temple of the LORD. But the people continued acting corruptly.

3 He built the upper gate of the house

26:1 [1]In 2 Kin 14:21, *Azariah*
3 [1]In 2 Kin 15:2, *Jecoliah* [a]2 Kin 15:2,3
5 [1]Many mss read *in the fear of God* [2]Lit *in the days of his seeking* [a]2 Chr 24:2 [b]Dan 1:17 [c]2 Chr 15:2
6 [a]Is 14:29
7 [a]2 Chr 21:16
8 [1]Lit *name went to the entering of Egypt* [a]2 Chr 17:11
9 [a]2 Chr 25:23 [b]Neh 2:13,15; 3:13
10 [1]Heb *shephelah* [a]Gen 26:18-21
11 [1]Lit *goes out to* [2]Lit *by the hand of*
12 [1]Lit *fathers*
13 [1]Lit *powerful* [a]2 Chr 25:5
14 [1]Lit *for them, for all*
15 [1]Lit *name*
16 [1]Lit *lifted up* [a]Deut 32:15; 2 Chr 25:19 [b]1 Kin 13:1-4
17 [a]1 Chr 6:10
18 [a]2 Chr 19:2 [b]Num 3:10; 16:39,40 [c]Ex 30:7,8
19 [a]2 Kin 5:25-27
21 [a]2 Kin 15:5-7 [b]Lev 13:46
22 [a]Is 1:1
23 [a]2 Chr 21:20; 28:27; Is 6:1
27:1 [a]2 Kin 15:33-35
2 [a]2 Chr 26:16

of the LORD, and he built extensively the wall of [a]Ophel.

4 Moreover, he built [a]cities in the hill country of Judah, and he built fortresses and towers on the wooded *hills.*

5 He fought also with the king of the Ammonites and prevailed over them so that the Ammonites gave him during that year one hundred talents of silver, ten thousand [1]kors of wheat and ten thousand of barley. The Ammonites also paid him this *amount* in the second and in the third year.

6 [a]So Jotham became mighty because he ordered his ways before the LORD his God.

7 [a]Now the rest of the acts of Jotham, even all his wars and his acts, behold, they are written in the Book of the Kings of Israel and Judah.

8 He was [a]twenty-five years old when he became king, and he reigned sixteen years in Jerusalem.

9 And Jotham slept with his fathers, and they buried him in the city of David; and Ahaz his son became king in his place.

Ahaz Succeeds Jotham in Judah

28 [a]Ahaz *was* twenty years old when he became king, and he reigned sixteen years in Jerusalem; and [b]he did not do right in the sight of the LORD as David his father *had done.*

2 [a]But he walked in the ways of the kings of Israel; he also [b]made molten images for the Baals.

3 Moreover, [a]he burned incense in the valley of Ben-hinnom and [b]burned his sons in fire, [c]according to the abominations of the nations whom the LORD had driven out before the sons of Israel.

4 He sacrificed and [a]burned incense on the high places, on the hills and under every green tree.

Judah Is Invaded

5 ¶ Wherefore, [a]the LORD his God delivered him into the hand of the king of Aram; and they [1]defeated him and carried away from him a great number of captives and brought *them* to Damascus. And he was also delivered into the hand of the king of Israel, who [2]inflicted him with heavy casualties.

6 For [a]Pekah the son of Remaliah slew in Judah 120,000 in one day, all valiant men, because they had forsaken the LORD God of their fathers.

7 And Zichri, a mighty man of Ephraim, slew Maaseiah the king's son and Azrikam the ruler of the house and Elkanah the second to the king.

8 ¶ [a]The sons of Israel carried away captive of [b]their brethren 200,000 women, sons and daughters; and they [1]took also a great deal of spoil from them, and brought the spoil to Samaria.

9 But a prophet of the LORD was there, whose name *was* Oded; and [a]he went out to meet the army which came to Samaria and said to them, "Behold, because the LORD, the God of your fathers, [b]was angry with Judah, He has delivered them into your hand, and you have slain them in a rage [c]*which* has even reached heaven.

10 "Now you are proposing to [a]subjugate for yourselves the people of Judah and Jerusalem for male and female slaves. Surely, *do* you not *have* transgressions of your own against the LORD your God?

11 "Now therefore, listen to me and return the captives [a]whom you captured from your brothers, [b]for the burning anger of the LORD is against you."

12 Then some of the heads of the sons of Ephraim—Azariah the son of Johanan, Berechiah the son of Meshillemoth, Jehizkiah the son of Shallum, and Amasa the son of Hadlai—arose against those who were coming from the battle,

13 and said to them, "You must not bring the captives in here, for you are proposing *to bring* upon us guilt against the LORD adding to our sins and our guilt; for our guilt is great so that *His* burning anger is against Israel."

14 So the armed men left the captives and the spoil before the officers and all the assembly.

15 Then [a]the men who were designated by name arose, took the captives, and they clothed all their naked ones from the spoil; and they gave them clothes and sandals, fed them and [b]gave them drink, anointed them *with oil,* led all their feeble ones on donkeys, and brought them to Jericho, [c]the city of palm trees, to their brothers; then they returned to Samaria.

Compromise with Assyria

16 ¶ [a]At that time King Ahaz sent to the [1]kings of Assyria for help.

17 [a]For again the Edomites had come and attacked Judah and carried away captives.

18 [a]The Philistines also had invaded the cities of the [1]lowland and of the Negev of Judah, and had taken Beth-shemesh, Aijalon, Gederoth, and Soco with its villages, Timnah with its villages, and Gimzo with its villages, and they settled there.

19 For the LORD humbled Judah because of Ahaz king of [a]Israel, for he had

---

3 [a]2 Chr 33:14; Neh 3:26
4 [a]2 Chr 11:5
5 [1]I.e. One kor equals approx 10 bu
6 [a]2 Chr 26:5
7 [a]2 Kin 15:36
8 [a]2 Chr 27:1
28:1 [a]2 Kin 16:2-4 [b]2 Chr 27:2
2 [a]2 Chr 22:3 [b]Ex 34:17
3 [a]Josh 15:8 [b]Lev 18:21; 2 Chr 33:6 [c]2 Chr 33:2
4 [a]2 Chr 28:25
5 [1]Lit *smote* [2]Lit *smote him with a great smiting* [a]2 Kin 16:5; 2 Chr 24:24; Is 7:1
6 [a]2 Kin 16:5
8 [1]Lit *plundered* [a]Deut 28:25,41 [b]2 Chr 11:4
9 [a]2 Chr 25:15 [b]Is 47:6 [c]Ezra 9:6; Rev 18:5
10 [a]Lev 25:39
11 [a]2 Chr 28:8 [b]James 2:13
15 [a]2 Chr 28:12 [b]2 Kin 6:22; Prov 25:21,22 [c]Deut 34:3
16 [1]Ancient versions read *king* [a]2 Kin 16:7
17 [a]Obad 10,14
18 [1]Heb *shephelah* [a]Ezek 16:57
19 [a]2 Chr 21:2

brought about a lack of restraint in Judah
and was very unfaithful to the LORD.
20 So [a]Tilgath-pilneser king of Assyria
came against him and afflicted him instead of strengthening him.
21 [a]Although Ahaz took a portion out
of the house of the LORD and out of the
palace of the king and of the princes, and
gave *it* to the king of Assyria, it did not
help him.
22 ¶ Now in the time of his distress
this same King Ahaz [a]became yet more
unfaithful to the LORD.
23 [a]For he sacrificed to the gods of
Damascus which had [1]defeated him, and
said, "[b]Because the gods of the kings
of Aram helped them, I will sacrifice to
them that they may help me." But they
became the [2]downfall of him and all Israel.
24 Moreover, when Ahaz gathered together the utensils of the house of God,
he [a]cut the utensils of the house of God
in pieces; and he [b]closed the doors of the
house of the LORD and [c]made altars for
himself in every corner of Jerusalem.
25 In every city of Judah he made high
places to burn incense to other gods, and
provoked the LORD, the God of his fathers, to anger.
26 [a]Now the rest of his acts and all his
ways, from first to last, behold, they are
written in the Book of the Kings of Judah
and Israel.
27 [a]So Ahaz slept with his fathers,
and they buried him in the city, in Jerusalem, for they did not bring him into the
tombs of the kings of [b]Israel; and Hezekiah his son reigned in his place.

Hezekiah Succeeds Ahaz in Judah

29 [a]Hezekiah became king *when he*
was twenty-five years old; and he
reigned twenty-nine years in Jerusalem.
And his mother's name *was* Abijah, the
daughter of Zechariah.
2 [a]He did right in the sight of the
LORD, according to all that his father David had done.
3 ¶ In the first year of his reign, in
the first month, he [a]opened the doors of
the house of the LORD and repaired them.
4 He brought in the priests and the
Levites and gathered them into the
square on the east.

Reforms Begun

5 Then he said to them, "Listen to
me, O Levites. [a]Consecrate yourselves
now, and consecrate the house of the
LORD, the God of your fathers, and carry
the uncleanness out from the holy place.
6 "For our fathers have been unfaithful and have done evil in the sight of the
LORD our God, and have forsaken Him
and [a]turned their faces away from the
dwelling place of the LORD, and have
[1]turned *their* backs.
7 "They have also [a]shut the doors of
the porch and put out the lamps, and
have not burned incense or offered burnt
offerings in the holy place to the God of
Israel.
8 "Therefore [a]the wrath of the LORD
was against Judah and Jerusalem, and He
has made them an object of terror, of horror, and of [b]hissing, as you see with your
own eyes.
9 "For behold, [a]our fathers have fall-
en by the sword, and our sons and our
daughters and our wives are in captivity
for this.
10 "Now it is in my heart [a]to make a
covenant with the LORD God of Israel,
that His burning anger may turn away
from us.
11 "My sons, do not be negligent now,
for [a]the LORD has chosen you to stand
before Him, to minister to Him, and to be
His ministers and burn incense."
12 ¶ Then the Levites arose: [a]Ma-
hath, the son of Amasai and Joel the son
of Azariah, from the sons of [b]the Kohathites; and from the sons of Merari, Kish
the son of Abdi and Azariah the son of
Jehallelel; and from the Gershonites, Joah
the son of Zimmah and Eden the son of
Joah;
13 and from the sons of Elizaphan,
Shimri and [1]Jeiel; and from the sons of
Asaph, Zechariah and Mattaniah;
14 and from the sons of Heman, [1]Jehi-
el and Shimei; and from the sons of Jeduthun, Shemaiah and Uzziel.
15 They assembled their brothers,
[a]consecrated themselves, and went in
[b]to cleanse the house of the LORD, according to the commandment of the king
[c]by the words of the LORD.
16 So the priests went in to the inner
part of the house of the LORD to cleanse
it, and every unclean thing which they
found in the temple of the LORD they
brought out to the court of the house of
the LORD. Then the Levites received *it* to
carry out to [a]the Kidron [1]valley.
17 Now they began [1]the consecration
[a]on the first *day* of the first month, and
on the eighth day of the month they entered the porch of the LORD. Then they
consecrated the house of the LORD in
eight days, and finished on the sixteenth
day of the first month.
18 Then they went in to King Hezekiah and said, "We have cleansed the
whole house of the LORD, the altar of
burnt offering with all of its utensils, and

20 [a]1 Chr 5:26
21 [a]2 Kin 16:8, 9
22 [a]Is 1:5; Jer 5:3; Rev 16:11
23 [1]Lit *smitten* [2]Lit *stumbling* [a]2 Chr 25:14 [b]Jer 44:17,18
24 [a]2 Kin 16:17 [b]2 Chr 29:7 [c]2 Chr 30:14; 33:3-5
26 [a]2 Kin 16:19,20
27 [a]2 Kin 16:20; 2 Chr 24:25; Is 14:28 [b]2 Chr 21:2
29:1 [a]2 Kin 18:1-3
2 [a]2 Chr 28:1; 34:2
3 [a]2 Chr 28:24; 29:7
5 [a]2 Chr 29:15, 34; 35:6
6 [1]Lit *given* [a]Ezek 8:16
7 [a]2 Chr 28:24
8 [a]2 Chr 24:20 [b]Jer 25:9,18
9 [a]2 Chr 28:5-8, 17
10 [a]2 Chr 23:16
11 [a]Num 3:6; 8:6
12 [a]2 Chr 31:13 [b]Num 3:19,20
13 [1]Or *Jeuel*
14 [1]Or *Jehuel*, 1 Chr 15:18, 20
15 [a]2 Chr 29:5 [b]1 Chr 23:28 [c]2 Chr 30:12
16 [1]Or *wadi* [a]2 Chr 15:16
17 [1]Lit *to consecrate* [a]2 Chr 29:3

the table of showbread with all of its
utensils.
19 "Moreover, [a]all the utensils which
King Ahaz had discarded during his reign
in his unfaithfulness, we have prepared
and consecrated; and behold, they are before the altar of the LORD."

Hezekiah Restores Temple Worship

20 ¶ Then King Hezekiah arose early
and assembled the princes of the city and
went up to the house of the LORD.
21 They brought seven bulls, seven
rams, seven lambs and seven male goats
[a]for a sin offering for the kingdom, the
sanctuary, and Judah. And he ordered the
priests, the sons of Aaron, to offer *them*
on the altar of the LORD.
22 So they slaughtered the bulls, and
the priests took the blood and sprinkled it
on the altar. They also slaughtered the
rams and sprinkled the blood on the altar;
they slaughtered the lambs also and
[a]sprinkled the blood on the altar.
23 Then they brought the male goats
of the sin offering before the king and the
assembly, and [a]they laid their hands on
them.
24 The priests slaughtered them and
purged the altar with their blood [a]to
atone for all Israel, for the king ordered
the burnt offering and the sin offering for
all Israel.
25 ¶ [a]He then stationed the Levites in
the house of the LORD with cymbals, with
harps and with lyres, [b]according to the
command of David and of [c]Gad the
king's seer, and of [d]Nathan the prophet;
for the command was from the LORD
through His prophets.
26 The Levites stood with [a]the *musical* instruments of David, and [b]the
priests with the trumpets.
27 Then Hezekiah gave the order to
offer the burnt offering on the altar.
When the burnt offering began, [a]the
song to the LORD also began with the
trumpets, [1]*accompanied* by the instruments of David, king of Israel.
28 While the whole assembly worshiped, the singers also sang and the
trumpets sounded; all this *continued* until the burnt offering was finished.
29 ¶ Now at the completion of the
burnt offerings, [a]the king and all who
were present with him bowed down and
worshiped.
30 Moreover, King Hezekiah and the
officials ordered the Levites to sing
praises to the LORD with the words of
David and Asaph the seer. [a]So they sang
praises with joy, and bowed down and
worshiped.
31 ¶ Then Hezekiah said, "[a]Now *that*
you have [1]consecrated yourselves to the
LORD, come near and bring sacrifices and
thank offerings to the house of the LORD."
And the assembly brought sacrifices and
thank offerings, and [b]all those who were
[2]willing *brought* burnt offerings.
32 The number of the burnt offerings
which the assembly brought was 70
bulls, 100 rams, and 200 lambs; all these
were for a burnt offering to the LORD.
33 The consecrated things were 600
bulls and 3,000 sheep.
34 But the priests were too few, so
that they were unable to skin all the
burnt offerings; [a]therefore their brothers
the Levites helped them until the work
was completed and until the *other* priests
had consecrated themselves. For [b]the Levites were more [1]conscientious to consecrate themselves than the priests.
35 There *were* also [1a]many burnt offerings with [b]the fat of the peace offerings and with [c]the libations for the burnt
offerings. Thus the service of the house of
the LORD was established *again.*
36 Then Hezekiah and all the people
rejoiced over what God had prepared for
the people, because the thing came about
suddenly.

All Israel Invited to the Passover

30 Now Hezekiah sent to all Israel
and Judah and wrote letters also
to Ephraim and Manasseh, that they
should come to the house of the LORD at
Jerusalem to [1]celebrate the Passover to
the LORD God of Israel.
2 For the king and his princes and all
the assembly in Jerusalem had decided
[a]to celebrate the Passover in the second
month,
3 since they could not celebrate it
[a]at that time, because the priests had
not consecrated themselves in sufficient
numbers, nor had the people been gathered to Jerusalem.
4 Thus the thing was right in the
sight of the king and [1]all the assembly.
5 So they established a decree to cir-
culate a [1]proclamation throughout all Israel [a]from Beersheba even to Dan, that
they should come to celebrate the Passover to the LORD God of Israel at Jerusalem. For they had not celebrated *it* in
great numbers as it was [2]prescribed.
6 [a]The [1]couriers went throughout
all Israel and Judah with the letters from
the hand of the king and his princes, even
according to the command of the king,
saying, "O sons of Israel, return to the
LORD God of Abraham, Isaac and Israel,
that He may return to those of you who
escaped *and* are left from [b]the [2]hand of
the kings of Assyria.

19 [a]2 Chr 28:24
21 [a]Lev 4:3-14
22 [a]Lev 4:18
23 [a]Lev 4:15
24 [a]Lev 4:26
25 [a]1 Chr 25:6 [b]2 Chr 8:14 [c]2 Sam 24:11 [d]2 Sam 7:2
26 [a]1 Chr 23:5 [b]2 Chr 5:12
27 [1]Lit *and according to the authority of the instruments* [a]2 Chr 23:18
29 [a]2 Chr 20:18
30 [a]Ps 100:1; 106:12
31 [1]Lit *filled your hands* [2]Lit *willing of heart* [a]2 Chr 13:9 [b]Ex 35:5,22
34 [1]Lit *upright of heart* [a]2 Chr 35:11 [b]2 Chr 30:3
35 [1]Lit *the burnt offerings to an abundance* [a]2 Chr 29:32 [b]Lev 3:16 [c]Num 15:5-10
30:1 [1]Lit *do,* so in vv 2, 3, 5, 13, 21, 23
2 [a]Num 9:10, 11; 2 Chr 30:13, 15
3 [a]2 Chr 29:17, 34
4 [1]Lit *in the sight of all*
5 [1]Lit *voice* [2]Lit *written* [a]Judg 20:1
6 [1]Lit *runners* [2]Lit *palm* [a]Esth 8:14; Job 9:25; Jer 51:31 [b]2 Chr 28:20

7 “[a]Do not be like your fathers and your brothers, who were unfaithful to the LORD God of their fathers, so that [b]He made them a horror, as you see.

8 “Now do not [a]stiffen your neck like your fathers, but [1]yield to the LORD and enter His sanctuary which He has consecrated forever, and serve the LORD your God, [b]that His burning anger may turn away from you.

9 “For [a]if you return to the LORD, your brothers and your sons *will find* compassion before those who led them captive and will return to this land. [b]For the LORD your God is gracious and compassionate, and will not turn *His* face away from you if you return to Him.”

10 ¶ So the [1]couriers passed from city to city through the country of Ephraim and Manasseh, and as far as Zebulun, but [a]they laughed them to scorn and mocked them.

11 Nevertheless [a]some men of Asher, Manasseh and Zebulun humbled themselves and came to Jerusalem.

12 The [a]hand of God was also on Judah to give them one heart to do what the king and the princes commanded by the word of the LORD.

Passover Reinstituted

13 ¶ Now many people were gathered at Jerusalem to celebrate the Feast of Unleavened Bread [a]in the second month, a very large assembly.

14 They arose and removed the altars which *were* in Jerusalem; they also [a]removed all the incense altars and [b]cast *them* into the brook Kidron.

15 Then [a]they slaughtered the Passover *lambs* on the fourteenth of the second month. And [b]the priests and Levites were ashamed of themselves, and consecrated themselves and brought burnt offerings to the house of the LORD.

16 [a]They stood at their stations after their custom, according to the law of Moses the man of God; the priests sprinkled the blood *which they received* from the hand of the Levites.

17 For *there were* many in the assembly who had not consecrated themselves; therefore, [a]the Levites *were* over the slaughter of the Passover *lambs* for everyone who *was* unclean, in order to consecrate *them* to the LORD.

18 For a multitude of the people, [a]*even* many from Ephraim and Manasseh, Issachar and Zebulun, had not purified themselves, [b]yet they ate the Passover [c]otherwise than [1]prescribed. For Hezekiah prayed for them, saying, “May the good LORD pardon

19 [a]everyone who prepares his heart to seek God, the LORD God of his fathers, though not according to the purification *rules* of the sanctuary.”

20 So the LORD heard Hezekiah and [a]healed the people.

21 The sons of Israel present in Jerusalem [a]celebrated the Feast of Unleavened Bread *for* seven days with great joy, and the Levites and the priests praised the LORD day after day with loud instruments to the LORD.

22 Then Hezekiah [a]spoke [1]encouragingly to all the Levites who showed good insight *in the things* of the LORD. So they ate for the appointed seven days, sacrificing peace offerings and [b]giving thanks to the LORD God of their fathers.

23 ¶ Then the whole assembly [a]decided to celebrate *the feast* another seven days, so they celebrated the seven days with joy.

24 For [a]Hezekiah king of Judah had contributed to the assembly 1,000 bulls and 7,000 sheep, and the princes had contributed to the assembly 1,000 bulls and 10,000 sheep; and [b]a large number of priests consecrated themselves.

25 All the assembly of Judah rejoiced, with the priests and the Levites and [a]all the assembly that came from Israel, both the sojourners who came from the land of Israel and those living in Judah.

26 So there was great joy in Jerusalem, because there was nothing like this in Jerusalem [a]since the days of Solomon the son of David, king of Israel.

27 Then [a]the Levitical priests arose and [b]blessed the people; and their voice was heard and their prayer came to [c]His holy dwelling place, to heaven.

Idols Are Destroyed

31 Now when all this was finished, all Israel who were present went out to the cities of Judah, [a]broke the pillars in pieces, cut down the [1]Asherim and pulled down the high places and the altars throughout all Judah and Benjamin, as well as in Ephraim and Manasseh, [2]until they had destroyed them all. Then all the sons of Israel returned to their cities, each to his possession.

2 ¶ And Hezekiah appointed [a]the divisions of the priests and the Levites by their divisions, each according to his service, *both* the priests and the Levites, [b]for burnt offerings and for peace offerings, to minister and to give thanks and to praise in the gates of the camp of the LORD.

Reforms Continued

3 *He* also *appointed* [a]the king's portion of his goods for the burnt offerings,

---

7 [a]Ezek 20:13 [b]2 Chr 29:8

8 [1]Lit *give a hand* [a]Ex 32:9 [b]2 Chr 29:10

9 [a]Deut 30:2 [b]Ex 34:6,7; Mic 7:18

10 [1]Lit *runners* [a]2 Chr 36:16

11 [a]2 Chr 30:18,21,25

12 [a]2 Cor 3:5; Phil 2:13; Heb 13:20,21

13 [a]2 Chr 30:2

14 [a]2 Chr 28:24 [b]2 Chr 29:16

15 [a]2 Chr 30:2, 3 [b]2 Chr 29:34

16 [a]2 Chr 35:10,15

17 [a]2 Chr 29:34

18 [1]Lit *written* [a]2 Chr 30:11,25 [b]Num 9:10 [c]Ex 12:43-49

19 [a]2 Chr 19:3

20 [a]James 5:16

21 [a]Ex 12:15; 13:6

22 [1]Lit *to the heart of* [a]2 Chr 32:6 [b]Ezra 10:11

23 [a]1 Kin 8:65

24 [a]2 Chr 35:7, 8 [b]2 Chr 29:34; 30:3

25 [a]2 Chr 30:11,18

26 [a]2 Chr 7:8-10

27 [a]2 Chr 23:18 [b]Num 6:23 [c]Deut 26:15; Ps 68:5

31:1 [1]I.e. wooden symbols of a female deity [2]Lit *even to completion* [a]2 Kin 18:4

2 [a]1 Chr 24:1 [b]1 Chr 23:28-31

3 [a]2 Chr 35:7

namely, for the morning and evening burnt offerings, and the burnt offerings for the sabbaths and for the new moons and for the fixed festivals, [b]as it is written in the law of the LORD.

4 Also he [1]commanded the people who lived in Jerusalem to give [a]the portion due to the priests and the Levites, that they might devote themselves to [b]the law of the LORD.

5 As soon as the [1]order spread, the sons of Israel provided in abundance the first fruits of grain, new wine, oil, honey and of all the produce of the field; and they brought in abundantly [a]the tithe of all.

6 The sons of Israel and Judah who lived in the cities of Judah also brought in the tithe of oxen and sheep, and [a]the tithe of [1]sacred gifts which were consecrated to the LORD their God, and placed *them* in heaps.

7 In the third month they began to [1]make the heaps, and finished *them* by the seventh month.

8 When Hezekiah and the rulers came and saw the heaps, they blessed the LORD and [a]His people Israel.

9 Then Hezekiah questioned the priests and the Levites concerning the heaps.

10 Azariah the chief priest [a]of the house of Zadok said to [1]him, "[b]Since the contributions began to be brought into the house of the LORD, we have had enough to eat with plenty left over, for the LORD has blessed His people, and this great quantity is left over."

11 ¶ Then Hezekiah commanded *them* to prepare [a]rooms in the house of the LORD, and they prepared *them.*

12 They faithfully brought in the contributions and the tithes and the consecrated things; and Conaniah the Levite *was* the officer in charge [a]of them and his brother Shimei *was* second.

13 Jehiel, Azaziah, Nahath, Asahel, Jerimoth, Jozabad, Eliel, Ismachiah, Mahath and Benaiah *were* overseers [1]under the authority of Conaniah and Shimei his brother by the appointment of King Hezekiah, and [a]Azariah *was* the *chief* officer of the house of God.

14 Kore the son of Imnah the Levite, the keeper of the eastern *gate, was* over the freewill offerings of God, to apportion the contributions for the LORD and the most holy things.

15 [1]Under his authority *were* [a]Eden, Miniamin, Jeshua, Shemaiah, Amariah and Shecaniah in [b]the cities of the priests, to distribute faithfully *their portions* to their brothers by divisions, whether great or small,

16 without regard to their genealogical enrollment, to the males from [1a]thirty years old and upward—everyone who entered the house of the LORD [b]for his daily obligations—for their work in their duties according to their divisions;

17 as well as the priests who were enrolled genealogically according to their fathers' households, and the Levites [a]from twenty years old and upwards, by their duties *and* their divisions.

18 The genealogical enrollment *included* [1]all their little children, their wives, their sons and their daughters, for the whole assembly, for they consecrated themselves [2]faithfully in holiness.

19 Also for the sons of Aaron the priests *who were* in [a]the pasture lands of their cities, or in each and every city, [b]*there were* men who were designated by name to distribute portions to every male among the priests and to everyone genealogically enrolled among the Levites.

20 ¶ Thus Hezekiah did throughout all Judah; and [a]he did what *was* good, right and true before the LORD his God.

21 Every work which he began in the service of the house of God in law and in commandment, seeking his God, he did with all his heart and [a]prospered.

Sennacherib Invades Judah

32 After these [1]acts of faithfulness [a]Sennacherib king of Assyria came and invaded Judah and besieged the fortified cities, and [2]thought to break into them for himself.

2 Now when Hezekiah saw that Sennacherib had come and that [1]he intended to make war on Jerusalem,

3 he decided with his officers and his warriors to cut off the *supply of* water from the springs which *were* outside the city, and they helped him.

4 So many people assembled [a]and stopped up all the springs and [b]the stream which flowed [1]through the region, saying, "Why should the kings of Assyria come and find abundant water?"

5 And he took courage and [a]rebuilt all the wall that had been broken down and [1]erected towers on it, and *built* [b]another outside wall and strengthened the [c]Millo *in* the city of David, and made weapons and shields in great number.

6 He appointed military officers over the people and gathered them to him in the square at the city gate, and [a]spoke [1]encouragingly to them, saying,

7 "[a]Be strong and courageous, do not fear or be dismayed because of the king of Assyria nor because of all the horde that

3 [b]Num 28:1-29:40
4 [1]Lit *said to* [a]Num 18:8 [b]Mal 2:7
5 [1]Lit *word* [a]Neh 13:12
6 [1]Lit *consecrated things* [a]Lev 27:30; Deut 14:28
7 [1]Lit *found*
8 [a]Deut 33:29; Ps 33:12; 144:15
10 [1]Lit *him, and he said* [a]1 Chr 6:8,9 [b]Mal 3:10
11 [a]1 Kin 6:5,8
12 [a]2 Chr 35:9
13 [1]Lit *from the hand of* [a]2 Chr 31:10
15 [1]Lit *under his hand* [a]2 Chr 29:12 [b]Josh 21:9-19
16 [1]Heb *three* [a]1 Chr 23:3 [b]Ezra 3:4
17 [a]1 Chr 23:24
18 [1]Lit *with all* [2]Lit *in their faithfulness*
19 [a]Lev 25:34; Num 35:2-5 [b]2 Chr 31:12-15
20 [a]2 Kin 20:3; 22:2
21 [a]Deut 29:9; Prov 3:9,10
32:1 [1]Lit *things and this faithfulness* [2]Lit *said* [a]2 Kin 18:13-19, 37; Is 36:1-37:38
2 [1]Lit *his face for war against*
4 [1]Lit *in the midst of the land* [a]2 Kin 20:20 [b]2 Chr 32:30
5 [1]Lit *raised on the towers* [a]2 Chr 25:23 [b]2 Kin 25:4 [c]1 Kin 9:24
6 [1]Lit *upon their hearts* [a]2 Chr 30:22
7 [a]1 Chr 22:13

is with him; [b]for the one with us is greater than the one with him.

8 "With him is *only* [a]an arm of flesh, but [b]with us is the LORD our God to help us and to fight our battles." And the people relied on the words of Hezekiah king of Judah.

Sennacherib Undermines Hezekiah

9 ¶ After this [a]Sennacherib king of Assyria sent his servants to Jerusalem while he *was* [1]besieging Lachish with all his forces with him, against Hezekiah king of Judah and against all Judah who *were* at Jerusalem, saying,

10 "Thus says Sennacherib king of Assyria, 'On what are you trusting that you are remaining in Jerusalem under siege?

11 'Is not Hezekiah misleading you to give yourselves over to die by hunger and by thirst, saying, "The LORD our God will deliver us from the [1]hand of the king of Assyria"?

12 '[a]Has not the same Hezekiah taken away His high places and His altars, and said to Judah and [1]Jerusalem, "You shall worship before one altar, and on it you shall [2]burn incense"?

13 'Do you not know what I and my fathers have done to all the peoples of the lands? [a]Were the gods of the nations of the lands able at all to deliver their land from my hand?

14 '[a]Who *was there* among all the gods of those nations which my fathers utterly destroyed who could deliver his people out of my hand, that your God should be able to deliver you from my hand?

15 'Now therefore, do not let Hezekiah deceive you or mislead you like this, and do not believe him, for [a]no god of any nation or kingdom was able to deliver his people from my hand or from the hand of my fathers. How much less will your God deliver you from my hand?' "

16 ¶ His servants spoke further against the LORD God and against His servant Hezekiah.

17 He also wrote letters to insult the LORD God of Israel, and to speak against Him, saying, "[a]As the gods of the nations of the lands [1]have not delivered their people from my hand, so the God of Hezekiah will not deliver His people from my hand."

18 [a]They called this out with a loud voice in the language of Judah to the people of Jerusalem who were on the wall, to frighten and terrify them, so that they might take the city.

19 They spoke [1]of the God of Jerusalem as of [a]the gods of the peoples of the earth, the work of men's hands.

Hezekiah's Prayer Is Answered

20 ¶ But King Hezekiah and Isaiah the prophet, the son of Amoz, prayed about this and cried out to heaven.

21 And the LORD sent an angel who destroyed every mighty warrior, commander and officer in the camp of the king of Assyria. So he returned [1]in shame to his own land. And when he had entered the temple of his god, some of his own children killed him there with the sword.

22 So the LORD [a]saved Hezekiah and the inhabitants of Jerusalem from the hand of Sennacherib the king of Assyria and from the hand of all *others,* and [1]guided them on every side.

23 And [a]many were bringing gifts to the LORD at Jerusalem and choice presents to Hezekiah king of Judah, so that [b]he was exalted in the sight of all nations thereafter.

24 ¶ [a]In those days Hezekiah became [1]mortally ill; and he prayed to the LORD, and [2]the LORD spoke to him and gave him a sign.

25 But Hezekiah gave no return for the benefit [1]he received, [a]because his heart was [2]proud; [b]therefore wrath came on him and on Judah and Jerusalem.

26 However, [a]Hezekiah [1]humbled the pride of his heart, both he and the inhabitants of Jerusalem, so that the wrath of the LORD did not come on them in the days of Hezekiah.

27 ¶ Now Hezekiah had immense riches and honor; and he made for himself treasuries for silver, gold, precious stones, spices, shields and all kinds of valuable articles,

28 storehouses also for the produce of grain, wine and oil, pens for all kinds of cattle and [1]sheepfolds for the flocks.

29 He made cities for himself and acquired flocks and herds in abundance, for [a]God had given him very great [1]wealth.

30 It was Hezekiah who [a]stopped the upper outlet of the waters of [b]Gihon and directed them to the west side of the city of David. And Hezekiah prospered in all that he did.

31 Even *in the matter of* [a]the envoys of the rulers of Babylon, who sent to him to inquire of [b]the wonder that had happened in the land, God left him *alone only* [c]to test him, that He might know all that was in his heart.

32 ¶ Now the rest of the acts of Hezekiah and his deeds of devotion, behold, they are written in the vision of Isaiah the prophet, the son of Amoz, in the Book of the Kings of Judah and Israel.

33 So Hezekiah slept with his fathers,

7 [b]2 Kin 6:16
8 [a]Jer 17:5 [b]2 Chr 20:17
9 [1]Lit *against* [a]2 Kin 18:17
11 [1]Lit *palm*
12 [1]Lit *Jerusalem, saying,* [2]Lit *offer up in smoke* [a]2 Chr 31:1
13 [a]2 Kin 18:33-35
14 [a]Is 10:9-11
15 [a]Ex 5:2; Is 36:18-20; Dan 3:15
17 [1]Lit *who have* [a]2 Chr 32:14
18 [a]2 Kin 18:28
19 [1]Lit *to* [a]Ps 115:4-8
21 [1]Lit *in shame of face*
22 [1]Another reading is *gave them rest* [a]Is 31:5
23 [a]2 Sam 8:10 [b]2 Chr 1:1
24 [1]Lit *sick to the point of death* [2]Lit *He* [a]2 Kin 20:1-11; Is 38:1-8
25 [1]Lit *to him* [2]Lit *high* [a]2 Chr 26:16; 32:31 [b]2 Chr 24:18
26 [1]Lit *humbled himself in* [a]Jer 26:18,19
28 [1]So ancient versions; Heb *flocks for the sheepfolds*
29 [1]Lit *possessions, property* [a]1 Chr 29:12
30 [a]2 Kin 20:20 [b]1 Kin 1:33
31 [a]2 Kin 20:12; Is 39:1 [b]2 Chr 32:24; Is 38:7,8 [c]Deut 8:16

and they buried him in the [1]upper section of the tombs of the sons of David; and all Judah and the inhabitants of Jerusalem [a]honored him at his death. And his son Manasseh became king in his place.

Manasseh Succeeds Hezekiah in Judah

33 [a]Manasseh was twelve years old when he became king, and he reigned fifty-five years in Jerusalem.

2 [a]He did evil in the sight of the LORD according to the abominations of the nations whom the LORD dispossessed before the sons of Israel.

3 For [a]he rebuilt the high places which Hezekiah his father had broken down; [b]he also erected altars for the Baals and made [1]Asherim, and worshiped all the host of heaven and served them.

4 [a]He built altars in the house of the LORD of which the LORD had said, "My name shall be [b]in Jerusalem forever."

5 For he built altars for all the host of heaven in [a]the two courts of the house of the LORD.

6 [a]He made his sons pass through the fire in the valley of Ben-hinnom; and he practiced witchcraft, used divination, practiced sorcery and [b]dealt with mediums and spiritists. He did much evil in the sight of the LORD, provoking Him *to anger.*

7 Then he put [a]the carved image of the idol which he had made in the house of God, of which God had said to David and to Solomon his son, "[b]In this house and in Jerusalem, which I have chosen from all the tribes of Israel, I will put My name forever;

8 and I will not again remove the foot of Israel from the land [a]which I have appointed for your fathers, if only they will observe to do all that I have commanded them according to all the law, the statutes and the ordinances *given* through Moses."

9 Thus Manasseh misled Judah and the inhabitants of Jerusalem to do more evil than the nations whom the LORD destroyed before the sons of Israel.

Manasseh's Idolatry Rebuked

10 ¶ The LORD spoke to Manasseh and his people, but [a]they paid no attention.

11 [a]Therefore the LORD brought the commanders of the army of the king of Assyria against them, and they captured Manasseh with [1]hooks, [b]bound him with bronze *chains* and took him to Babylon.

12 When [a]he was in distress, he entreated the LORD his God and [b]humbled himself greatly before the God of his fathers.

13 When he prayed to Him, [a]He was moved by his entreaty and heard his supplication, and brought him again to Jerusalem to his kingdom. Then Manasseh [b]knew that the LORD *was* God.

14 ¶ Now after this he built the outer wall of the city of David on the west side of [a]Gihon, in the valley, even to the entrance of the [b]Fish Gate; and he encircled the [c]Ophel *with it* and made it very high. Then he put army commanders in all the fortified cities of Judah.

15 He also [a]removed the foreign gods and the idol from the house of the LORD, as well as all the altars which he had built on the mountain of the house of the LORD and in Jerusalem, and he threw *them* outside the city.

16 He set up the altar of the LORD and sacrificed [a]peace offerings and thank offerings on it; and he ordered Judah to serve the LORD God of Israel.

17 Nevertheless [a]the people still sacrificed in the high places, *although* only to the LORD their God.

18 ¶ Now the rest of the acts of Manasseh even [a]his prayer to his God, and the words of [b]the seers who spoke to him in the name of the LORD God of Israel, behold, they are among the records of the kings of [c]Israel.

19 His prayer also and [a]*how God* was entreated by him, and all his sin, his unfaithfulness, and [b]the sites on which he built high places and erected the Asherim and the carved images, before he humbled himself, behold, they are written in the records of the [1]Hozai.

20 So Manasseh slept with his fathers, and they buried him in his own house. And Amon his son became king in his place.

Amon Becomes King in Judah

21 ¶ [a]Amon *was* twenty-two years old when he became king, and he reigned two years in Jerusalem.

22 He did evil in the sight of the LORD as Manasseh his father [a]had done, and Amon sacrificed to all [b]the carved images which his father Manasseh had made, and he served them.

23 Moreover, he did not humble himself before the LORD [a]as his father Manasseh had [1]done, but Amon multiplied guilt.

24 Finally [a]his servants conspired against him and put him to death in his own house.

25 But the people of the land [1]killed all the conspirators against King Amon

---

33 [1]Or *ascent to* [a]Ps 112:6; Prov 10:7

33:1 [a]2 Kin 21:1-9

2 [a]2 Chr 28:3; Jer 15:4

3 [1]I.e. wooden symbols of a female deity [a]2 Chr 31:1 [b]Deut 16:21; 2 Kin 23:5,6

4 [a]2 Chr 28:24 [b]2 Sam 7:13; 2 Chr 7:16

5 [a]2 Chr 4:9

6 [a]2 Chr 28:3 [b]Lev 19:31; 20:27

7 [a]2 Chr 33:15 [b]1 Kin 9:3-5; 2 Chr 7:16; 33:4

8 [a]2 Sam 7:10

10 [a]Neh 9:29; Jer 25:4

11 [1]I.e. thongs put through the nose [a]Deut 28:36 [b]2 Chr 36:6

12 [a]Ps 118:5; 120:1; 130:1,2 [b]2 Chr 32:26

13 [a]1 Chr 5:20; Ezra 8:23 [b]Dan 4:32

14 [a]1 Kin 1:33 [b]Neh 3:3 [c]2 Chr 27:3

15 [a]2 Chr 33:3-7

16 [a]Lev 7:11-18

17 [a]2 Chr 32:12

18 [a]2 Chr 33:12,13 [b]2 Chr 33:10 [c]2 Chr 21:2

19 [1]Gr reads *seers* [a]2 Chr 33:13 [b]2 Chr 33:3

21 [a]2 Kin 21:19-24

22 [a]2 Chr 33:2-7 [b]2 Chr 34:3,4

23 [1]Lit *humbled himself* [a]2 Chr 33:12,19

24 [a]2 Chr 25:27

25 [1]Lit *smote*

and the people of the land made Josiah
his son king in his place.

Josiah Succeeds Amon in Judah

34 [a]Josiah *was* eight years old when
he became king, and he reigned
thirty-one years in Jerusalem.
2 [a]He did right in the sight of the
LORD, and walked in the ways of his father David and did not turn aside to the
right or to the left.
3 For in the eighth year of his reign
while he was still a youth, he began to
[a]seek the God of his father David; and in
the twelfth year he began [b]to purge Judah and Jerusalem of the high places, the
Asherim, the carved images and the molten images.
4 They tore down the altars of the
Baals in his presence, and [a]the incense
altars that were high above them he
chopped down; also the Asherim, the
carved images and the molten images he
broke in pieces and [b]ground to powder
and scattered *it* on the graves of those
who had sacrificed to them.
5 Then [a]he burned the bones of the
priests on their altars and purged Judah
and Jerusalem.
6 [a]In the cities of Manasseh, Ephraim, Simeon, even as far as Naphtali, in
their surrounding ruins,
7 he also tore down the altars and
[a]beat the Asherim and the carved images
into powder, and chopped down all the
incense altars throughout the land of Israel. Then he returned to Jerusalem.

Josiah Repairs the Temple

8 ¶ [a]Now in the eighteenth year of
his reign, when he had purged the land
and the house, he sent Shaphan the son
of Azaliah, and Maaseiah [b]an official of
the city, and Joah the son of Joahaz the
recorder, to repair the house of the LORD
his God.
9 They came to [a]Hilkiah the high
priest and delivered the money that was
brought into the house of God, which the
Levites, the [1]doorkeepers, had collected
[2]from [b]Manasseh and Ephraim, and
from all the remnant of Israel, and from
all Judah and Benjamin and the inhabitants of Jerusalem.
10 Then they gave *it* into the hands of
the workmen who had the oversight of
the house of the LORD, and the workmen
who were working in the house of the
LORD [1]used it to restore and repair the
house.
11 They in turn gave *it* to the carpenters and to the builders to buy quarried
stone and timber for couplings and to

34:1 [a]2 Kin 22:1,2; Jer 1:2; 3:6
2 [a]2 Chr 29:2
3 [a]2 Chr 15:2; Prov 8:17 [b]1 Kin 13:2; 2 Chr 33:22
4 [a]2 Kin 23:4,5, 11 [b]Ex 32:20
5 [a]1 Kin 13:2; 2 Kin 23:20
6 [a]2 Kin 23:15, 19
7 [a]2 Chr 31:1
8 [a]2 Kin 22:3-20 [b]2 Chr 18:25
9 [1]Lit *guardians of the threshold* [2]Lit *from the hand of* [a]2 Chr 35:8 [b]2 Chr 30:10,18
10 [1]Lit *gave*
11 [a]2 Chr 33:4-7
12 [a]2 Kin 12:15 [b]1 Chr 25:1
13 [a]Neh 4:10
14 [a]2 Chr 34:9
16 [1]Lit *returned* [2]Lit *given into the hand of*
19 [a]Deut 28:3-68 [b]Josh 7:6
20 [1]In 2 Kin 22:12, *Achbor, son of Micaiah*
21 [a]2 Chr 29:8
22 [1]So with Gr [2]In 2 Kin 22:14 *Tikvah, son of Harhas*

make beams for the houses [a]which the
kings of Judah had let go to ruin.
12 [a]The men did the work faithfully
with foremen over them to supervise: Jahath and Obadiah, the Levites of the sons
of Merari, Zechariah and Meshullam of
the sons of the Kohathites, and [b]the Levites, all who were skillful with musical
instruments.
13 *They were* also over [a]the burden
bearers, and supervised all the workmen
from job to job; and *some* of the Levites
were scribes and officials and gatekeepers.

Hilkiah Discovers Lost Book of the Law

14 ¶ When they were bringing out the
money which had been brought into the
house of the LORD, [a]Hilkiah the priest
found the book of the law of the LORD
given by Moses.
15 Hilkiah responded and said to Shaphan the scribe, "I have found the book
of the law in the house of the LORD." And
Hilkiah gave the book to Shaphan.
16 Then Shaphan brought the book to
the king and [1]reported further word to
the king, saying, "Everything that was
[2]entrusted to your servants they are doing.
17 "They have also emptied out the
money which was found in the house of
the LORD, and have delivered it into the
hands of the supervisors and the workmen."
18 Moreover, Shaphan the scribe told
the king saying, "Hilkiah the priest gave
me a book." And Shaphan read from it in
the presence of the king.
19 ¶ When the king heard [a]the words
of the law, [b]he tore his clothes.
20 Then the king commanded Hilkiah,
Ahikam the son of Shaphan, [1]Abdon the
son of Micah, Shaphan the scribe, and
Asaiah the king's servant, saying,
21 "Go, inquire of the LORD for me and
for those who are left in Israel and in
Judah, concerning the words of the book
which has been found; for [a]great is the
wrath of the LORD which is poured out on
us because our fathers have not observed
the word of the LORD, to do according to
all that is written in this book."

Huldah, the Prophetess, Speaks

22 ¶ So Hilkiah and *those* whom the
king [1]had told went to Huldah the prophetess, the wife of Shallum the son of
[2]Tokhath, the son of Hasrah, the keeper
of the wardrobe (now she lived in Jerusalem in the Second Quarter); and they
spoke to her regarding this.

23 She said to them, “Thus says the
LORD, the God of Israel, ‘Tell the man
who sent you to Me,
24 thus says the LORD, “Behold, [a]I am
bringing evil on this place and on its inhabitants, *even* all [b]the curses written in
the book which they have read in the
presence of the king of Judah.
25 “[a]Because they have forsaken Me
and have burned incense to other gods,
that they might provoke Me to anger with
all the works of their hands; therefore My
wrath will be poured out on this place
and it shall not be quenched.” ’
26 “But to the king of Judah who sent
you to inquire of the LORD, thus you will
say to him, ‘Thus says the LORD God of
Israel *regarding* the words which you
have heard,
27 “[a]Because your heart was tender
and you humbled yourself before God
when you heard His words against this
place and against its inhabitants, and *because* you humbled yourself before Me,
tore your clothes and wept before Me, I
truly have heard you,” declares the LORD.
28 “Behold, I will gather you to your
fathers and you shall be gathered to your
grave in peace, so your eyes will not see
all the evil which I will bring on this place
and on its inhabitants.” ’ ” And they
brought back word to the king.
29 ¶ [a]Then the king sent and gathered all the elders of Judah and Jerusalem.
30 The king went up to the house of
the LORD and [a]all the men of Judah, the
inhabitants of Jerusalem, the priests, the
Levites and all the people, from the greatest to the least; and he read in their hearing all the words of the book of the covenant which was found in the house of
the LORD.

Josiah’s Good Reign

31 Then the king [a]stood in his place
and [b]made a covenant before the LORD to
walk after the LORD, and to keep His commandments and His testimonies and His
statutes with all his heart and with all his
soul, to perform the words of the covenant written in this book.
32 Moreover, he made all who were
present in Jerusalem and Benjamin to
stand *with him.* So the inhabitants of Jerusalem did according to the covenant of
God, the God of their fathers.
33 Josiah [a]removed all the abominations from all the lands belonging to the
sons of Israel, and made all who were
present in Israel to serve the LORD their
God. Throughout his [1]lifetime they did
not turn from following the LORD God of
their fathers.

24 [a]2 Chr 36:14-20 [b]Deut 28:15-68
25 [a]2 Chr 33:3
27 [a]2 Kin 22:19; 2 Chr 12:7; 32:26
29 [a]2 Kin 23:1-3
30 [a]Neh 8:1-3
31 [a]2 Kin 11:14; 23:3; 2 Chr 30:16 [b]2 Chr 23:16; 29:10
33 [1]Lit *days* [a]2 Chr 34:3-7
35:1 [a]2 Kin 23:21 [b]Ex 12:6; Num 9:3
2 [a]2 Chr 29:11
3 [a]2 Chr 17:8,9; Neh 8:7 [b]1 Chr 23:26
4 [a]1 Chr 9:10-13 [b]2 Chr 8:14
5 [1]Lit *sons of the people,* and so throughout the ch [a]Ezra 6:18
6 [a]2 Chr 35:1 [b]2 Chr 29:5
8 [a]2 Chr 31:13
9 [a]2 Chr 31:12
10 [a]2 Chr 35:5
11 [1]I.e. the Levites [2]So with Gr [a]2 Chr 35:1,6 [b]2 Chr 29:22 [c]2 Chr 29:34
13 [a]Ex 12:8,9

The Passover Observed Again

35 Then Josiah [a]celebrated the Passover to the LORD in Jerusalem,
and [b]they slaughtered the Passover *animals* on the fourteenth *day* of the first
month.
2 He set the priests in their offices
and [a]encouraged them in the service of
the house of the LORD.
3 He also said to [a]the Levites who
taught all Israel *and* who were holy to the
LORD, “Put the holy ark in the house
which Solomon the son of David king of
Israel built; [b]it will be a burden on *your*
shoulders no longer. Now serve the LORD
your God and His people Israel.
4 “[a]Prepare *yourselves* by your fathers’ households in your divisions, according to the writing of David king of
Israel and [b]according to the writing of
his son Solomon.
5 “Moreover, [a]stand in the holy place
according to the sections of the fathers’
households of your brethren the [1]lay
people, and according to the Levites, by
division of a father’s household.
6 “Now [a]slaughter the Passover *animals,* [b]sanctify yourselves and prepare
for your brethren to do according to the
word of the LORD by Moses.”
7 ¶ Josiah contributed to the lay people, to all who were present, flocks of
lambs and young goats, all for the Passover offerings, numbering 30,000 plus
3,000 bulls; these were from the king’s
possessions.
8 His officers also contributed a freewill offering to the people, the priests and
the Levites. Hilkiah and Zechariah and
Jehiel, [a]the officials of the house of God,
gave to the priests for the Passover offerings 2,600 *from the flocks* and 300 bulls.
9 [a]Conaniah also, and Shemaiah and
Nethanel, his brothers, and Hashabiah
and Jeiel and Jozabad, the officers of the
Levites, contributed to the Levites for the
Passover offerings 5,000 *from the flocks*
and 500 bulls.
10 ¶ So the service was prepared, and
[a]the priests stood at their stations and
the Levites by their divisions according to
the king’s command.
11 [1a]They slaughtered the Passover
animals, and while [b]the priests sprinkled
[2]the blood *received* from their hand,
[c]the Levites skinned *them.*
12 Then they removed the burnt offerings that *they* might give them to the sections of the fathers’ households of the lay
people to present to the LORD, as it is
written in the book of Moses. *They did*
this also with the bulls.
13 So [a]they roasted the Passover *ani-*

mals on the fire according to the ordinance, and they boiled [b]the holy things
in pots, in kettles, in pans, and carried
them speedily to all the lay people.
14 Afterwards they prepared for themselves and for the priests, because the
priests, the sons of Aaron, *were* offering
the burnt offerings and the fat until night;
therefore the Levites prepared for themselves and for the priests, the sons of
Aaron.
15 The singers, the sons of Asaph,
were also at their stations [a]according to
the command of David, Asaph, Heman,
and Jeduthun the king's seer; and [b]the
gatekeepers at each gate did not have to
depart from their service, because the Levites their brethren prepared for them.
16 ¶ So all the service of the LORD was
prepared on that day to celebrate the
Passover, and to offer burnt offerings on
the altar of the LORD according to the
command of King Josiah.
17 Thus [a]the sons of Israel who were
present celebrated the Passover at that
time, and the Feast of Unleavened Bread
seven days.
18 [a]There had not been celebrated a
Passover like it in Israel since the days of
Samuel the prophet; nor had any of the
kings of Israel celebrated such a Passover
as Josiah did with the priests, the Levites,
all Judah and Israel who were present,
and the inhabitants of Jerusalem.
19 In the eighteenth year of Josiah's
reign this Passover was celebrated.

Josiah Dies in Battle

20 ¶ [a]After all this, when Josiah had
set the [1]temple in order, Neco king of
Egypt came up to make war at [b]Carche-
mish on the Euphrates, and Josiah went
out to engage him.
21 But [1]Neco sent messengers to him,
saying, "[a]What have we to do with each
other, O King of Judah? *I am* not *coming*
against you today but against the house
with which I am at war, and God has
ordered me to hurry. Stop for your own
sake from *interfering with* God who is
with me, so that He will not destroy you."
22 However, Josiah would not turn
[1]away from him, but [a]disguised himself
in order to make war with him; nor did
he listen to the words of Neco [b]from the
mouth of God, but came to make war on
the plain of [c]Megiddo.
23 The archers shot King Josiah, and
the king said to his servants, "Take me
away, for I am badly wounded."
24 So his servants took him out of the
chariot and carried him in the second
chariot which he had, and brought him to
Jerusalem [1]where he died and was buried in the tombs of his fathers. [a]All Judah
and Jerusalem mourned for Josiah.
25 Then [a]Jeremiah chanted a lament
for Josiah. And all the male and female
singers speak about Josiah in their lamentations to this day. And they made them
an ordinance in Israel; behold, they are
also written in the Lamentations.
26 Now the rest of the acts of Josiah
and his deeds of devotion as written in
the law of the LORD,
27 and his acts, first to last, behold,
they are written in the Book of the Kings
of Israel and Judah.

Jehoahaz, Jehoiakim, then Jehoiachin Rule

36 [a]Then the people of the land took
[1b]Joahaz the son of Josiah, and
made him king in place of his father in
Jerusalem.
2 Joahaz was twenty-three years old
when he became king, and he reigned
three months in Jerusalem.
3 Then the king of Egypt deposed
him at Jerusalem, and imposed on the
land a fine of one hundred talents of silver and one talent of gold.
4 The king of Egypt made Eliakim his
brother king over Judah and Jerusalem,
and changed his name to Jehoiakim. But
[a]Neco took Joahaz his brother and
brought him to Egypt.
5 ¶ [a]Jehoiakim was twenty-five
years old when he became king, and he
reigned eleven years in Jerusalem; and he
did evil in the sight of the LORD his God.
6 Nebuchadnezzar king of Babylon
came up [a]against him and [b]bound him
with bronze *chains* to take him to Babylon.
7 [a]Nebuchadnezzar also brought
some of the articles of the house of the
LORD to Babylon and put them in his temple at Babylon.
8 [a]Now the rest of the acts of Jehoiakim and [1]the abominations which he
did, and what was found against him, behold, they are written in the Book of the
Kings of Israel and Judah. And Jehoiachin
his son became king in his place.
9 ¶ [a]Jehoiachin was eight years old
when he became king, and he reigned
three months and ten days in Jerusalem,
and he did evil in the sight of the LORD.

Captivity in Babylon Begun

10 [a]At the turn of the year King Nebuchadnezzar sent and brought him to Babylon with the valuable articles of the
house of the LORD, and he made his kinsman [b]Zedekiah king over Judah and Jerusalem.

---

13 [b]Lev 6:28
15 [a]1 Chr 25:1 [b]1 Chr 26:12-19
17 [a]Ex 12:1-20; 2 Chr 30:21
18 [a]2 Kin 23:21; 2 Chr 30:5
20 [1]Lit *house* [a]2 Kin 23:29,30 [b]Is 10:9; Jer 46:2
21 [1]Lit *he* [a]2 Chr 25:19
22 [1]Lit *his face* [a]2 Chr 18:29 [b]2 Chr 35:21 [c]Judg 5:19
24 [1]Lit *and* [a]Zech 12:11
25 [a]Jer 22:10; Lam 4:20
36:1 [1]I.e. short form of Jehoahaz [a]2 Kin 23:30-34 [b]Jer 22:11
4 [a]Jer 22:10-12
5 [a]2 Kin 23:36, 37; Jer 22:13-19; 26:1; 35:1
6 [a]2 Kin 24:1; Jer 25:1-9 [b]2 Chr 33:11
7 [a]2 Kin 24:13
8 [1]Lit *his* [a]2 Kin 24:5
9 [a]2 Kin 24:8-17
10 [a]2 Sam 11:1; Jer 22:25; 24:1; 29:1; Ezek 17:12 [b]Jer 37:1

Zedekiah Rules in Judah

11 ¶ [a]Zedekiah was twenty-one years
old when he became king, and he reigned
eleven years in Jerusalem.
12 He did evil in the sight of the LORD
his God; [a]he did not humble himself
[b]before Jeremiah the prophet [1]who
spoke for the LORD.
13 [a]He also rebelled against King
Nebuchadnezzar who had made him
swear *allegiance* by God. But [b]he stiffened his neck and hardened his heart
against turning to the LORD God of Israel.
14 Furthermore, all the officials of the
priests and the people were very unfaithful *following* all the abominations of the
nations; and they defiled the house of the
LORD which He had sanctified in Jerusalem.
15 ¶ The LORD, the God of their fathers, [a]sent *word* to them again and
again by His messengers, because He had
compassion on His people and on His
dwelling place;
16 but they *continually* [a]mocked the
messengers of God, [b]despised His words
and scoffed at His prophets, [c]until the
wrath of the LORD arose against His people, until there was no remedy.
17 [a]Therefore He brought up against
them the king of the Chaldeans who slew
their young men with the sword in the
house of their sanctuary, and had no compassion on young man or virgin, old man
or infirm; He gave *them* all into his hand.
18 [a]All the articles of the house of
God, great and small, and the treasures of
the house of the LORD, and the treasures
of the king and of his officers, he brought
them all to Babylon.
19 Then [a]they burned the house of
God and broke down the wall of Jerusalem, and burned all its fortified buildings
with fire and destroyed all its valuable
articles.
20 Those who had escaped from the
sword he [a]carried away to Babylon; and
[b]they were servants to him and to his
sons until the rule of the kingdom of Persia,
21 [a]to fulfill the word of the LORD by
the mouth of Jeremiah, until [b]the land
had enjoyed its sabbaths. [c]All the days of
its desolation it kept sabbath [1d]until seventy years were complete.

Cyrus Permits Return

22 ¶ [a]Now in the first year of Cyrus
king of Persia—in order to fulfill the
word of the LORD [b]by the mouth of Jeremiah—the LORD [c]stirred up the spirit of
Cyrus king of Persia, so that he sent a
proclamation throughout his kingdom,
and also *put it* in writing, saying,
23 "Thus says Cyrus king of Persia, 'The
LORD, the God of heaven, has given me all
the kingdoms of the earth, and He has
appointed me to build Him a house in
Jerusalem, which is in Judah. Whoever
there is among you of all His people, may
the LORD his God be with him, and let
him go up!' "

11 [a]2 Kin 24:18-20; Jer 27:1; 28:1; 52:1
12 [1]Lit *from the mouth of the LORD* [a]2 Chr 33:23 [b]Jer 21:3-7
13 [a]Jer 52:3; Ezek 17:15 [b]2 Chr 30:8
15 [a]Jer 7:13; 25:3
16 [a]2 Chr 30:10; Jer 5:12, 13 [b]Prov 1:24-32 [c]Ezra 5:12
17 [a]2 Kin 25:1-7; Jer 21:1-10
18 [a]2 Chr 36:7, 10
19 [a]1 Kin 9:8; 2 Kin 25:9; Jer 52:13
20 [a]2 Kin 25:11 [b]Jer 27:7
21 [1]Lit *to fulfill seventy years* [a]Jer 29:10 [b]Lev 26:34 [c]Lev 25:4 [d]Jer 25:11
22 [a]Ezra 1:1-3 [b]Jer 25:12; 29:10 [c]Is 44:28

Ezra

Title and Background

The books of Ezra and Nehemiah were one in the earliest Hebrew manuscripts. Origen (A.D. 185–253) is the first writer known to distinguish between two books, which he called I Ezra and II Ezra. Although they were regarded as one book, the caption to Nehemiah 1:1 indicates they were two separate compositions.

Author and Date of Writing

Many scholars have assumed that the author/compiler of Ezra-Nehemiah was also the author of 1,2 Chronicles. This viewpoint is based on certain characteristics common to both. The verses at the end of Chronicles and at the beginning of Ezra are virtually identical, and both of these books exhibit a fondness for lists. But there are also striking differences, so the name of the author cannot be known for certain. Ezra can be dated about 440 B.C.

Theme and Message

Ezra tells about the return of the Jews from exile in Babylon and also of the rebuilding of the temple. The people completed and dedicated the temple in 516 B.C. after being delayed for eighteen years by their enemies from the north. A decree from Darius in 520 B.C. allowed them to finish. Ezra taught the people the law and reformed their religious life so the other nations around them could see they were God's chosen nation.

Outline

I. The First Exiles Return to the Land of Judah (1:1—2:70)
II. The Temple Is Rebuilt (3:1—6:22)
III. Ezra's Return and Ministry (7:1—10:44)

Cyrus's Proclamation

1 [a]Now in the first year of Cyrus king
of Persia, in order to fulfill the word
of the LORD by the mouth of Jeremiah, the
LORD stirred up the spirit of Cyrus king of
Persia, so that he [b]sent a proclamation
throughout all his kingdom, and also *put*
it in writing, saying:
2 ¶ "Thus says Cyrus king of Persia, 'The LORD, the God of heaven, has
given me all the kingdoms of the earth
and [a]He has appointed me to build
Him a house in Jerusalem, which is in
Judah.
3 'Whoever there is among you of all
His people, may his God be with him! Let
him go up to Jerusalem which is in Judah
and rebuild the house of the LORD, the
God of Israel; [a]He is the God who is in
Jerusalem.
4 'Every survivor, at whatever place
he may [1]live, let the men of [2]that place
support him with silver and gold, with
goods and cattle, together with a freewill
offering for the house of God which is in
Jerusalem.' "

1:1 [a]2 Chr 36:22; Jer 25:12; 29:10 [b]Ezra 5:13
2 [a]Is 44:28; 45:1,12,13
3 [a]1 Kin 8:23; 18:39; Is 37:16; Dan 6:26
4 [1]Or *reside as an alien* [2]Lit *his*
5 [a]Ezra 1:1,2
6 [1]Lit *strengthened their hands* [a]Neh 6:9; Is 35:3
7 [a]Ezra 5:14; 6:5 [b]2 Kin 24:13; 2 Chr 36:7
8 [a]Ezra 5:14
9 [1]Heb obscure; other possible meanings are *knives, censers* [a]Ezra 8:27

Holy Vessels Restored

5 ¶ Then the heads of fathers' *house-*
holds of Judah and Benjamin and the
priests and the Levites arose, [a]even everyone whose spirit God had stirred to go
up and rebuild the house of the LORD
which is in Jerusalem.
6 All those about them [1a]encour-
aged them with articles of silver, with
gold, with goods, with cattle and with
valuables, aside from all that was given as
a freewill offering.
7 [a]Also King Cyrus brought out the
articles of the house of the LORD, [b]which
Nebuchadnezzar had carried away from
Jerusalem and put in the house of his
gods;
8 and Cyrus, king of Persia, had them
brought out by the hand of Mithredath
the treasurer, and he counted them out to
[a]Sheshbazzar, the prince of Judah.
9 Now this *was* their number: 30
[a]gold dishes, 1,000 silver dishes, 29
[1]duplicates;
10 30 gold bowls, 410 silver bowls of
a second *kind and* 1,000 other articles.

11 All the articles of gold and silver *numbered* 5,400. Sheshbazzar brought them all up with the exiles who went up from Babylon to Jerusalem.

Number of Those Returning

2 [a]Now these are the [1]people of the province who came up out of the captivity of the exiles whom Nebuchadnezzar the king of Babylon had carried away to Babylon, and returned to Jerusalem and Judah, each to his city.
2 [1]These came with Zerubbabel, Jeshua, Nehemiah, [2]Seraiah, [3]Reelaiah, Mordecai, Bilshan, [4]Mispar, Bigvai, [5]Rehum *and* Baanah.
¶ The number of the men of the people of Israel:
3 the sons of Parosh, 2,172;
4 the sons of Shephatiah, 372;
5 the sons of [a]Arah, 775;
6 the sons of [a]Pahath-moab of the sons of Jeshua *and* Joab, 2,812;
7 the sons of Elam, 1,254;
8 the sons of Zattu, 945;
9 the sons of Zaccai, 760;
10 the sons of [1]Bani, 642;
11 the sons of Bebai, 623;
12 the sons of Azgad, 1,222;
13 the sons of [a]Adonikam, 666;
14 the sons of Bigvai, 2,056;
15 the sons of Adin, 454;
16 the sons of Ater of Hezekiah, 98;
17 the sons of Bezai, 323;
18 the sons of [1]Jorah, 112;
19 the sons of Hashum, 223;
20 the sons of [1]Gibbar, 95;
21 the [1]men of [a]Bethlehem, 123;
22 the men of Netophah, 56;
23 the men of Anathoth, 128;
24 the sons of [1]Azmaveth, 42;
25 the sons of [1]Kiriath-arim, Chephirah and Beeroth, 743;
26 the sons of [a]Ramah and Geba, 621;
27 the men of Michmas, 122;
28 the men of Bethel and Ai, 223;
29 the sons of Nebo, 52;
30 the sons of Magbish, 156;
31 the sons of the other Elam, 1,254;
32 the sons of Harim, 320;
33 the sons of Lod, Hadid and Ono, 725;
34 the [1]men of [a]Jericho, 345;
35 the sons of Senaah, 3,630.

Priests Returning

36 ¶ [a]The priests: the sons of Jedaiah of the house of Jeshua, 973;
37 the sons of [a]Immer, 1,052;
38 [a]the sons of Pashhur, 1,247;
39 the sons of [a]Harim, 1,017.

Levites Returning

40 ¶ The Levites: the sons of Jeshua and Kadmiel, of the sons of [1]Hodaviah, 74.
41 The singers: the sons of Asaph, 128.
42 The sons of the gatekeepers: the sons of Shallum, the sons of Ater, the sons of Talmon, the sons of Akkub, the sons of Hatita, the sons of Shobai, in all 139.
43 ¶ The [a]temple servants: the sons of Ziha, the sons of Hasupha, the sons of Tabbaoth,
44 the sons of Keros, the sons of [1]Siaha, the sons of Padon,
45 the sons of Lebanah, the sons of Hagabah, the sons of Akkub,
46 the sons of Hagab, the sons of Shalmai, the sons of Hanan,
47 the sons of Giddel, the sons of Gahar, the sons of Reaiah,
48 the sons of Rezin, the sons of Nekoda, the sons of Gazzam,
49 the sons of Uzza, the sons of Paseah, the sons of Besai,
50 the sons of Asnah, the sons of Meunim, the sons of [1]Nephisim,
51 the sons of Bakbuk, the sons of Hakupha, the sons of Harhur,
52 the sons of [1]Bazluth, the sons of Mehida, the sons of Harsha,
53 the sons of Barkos, the sons of Sisera, the sons of Temah,
54 the sons of Neziah, the sons of Hatipha.
55 ¶ The sons of [a]Solomon's servants: the sons of Sotai, the sons of [1]Hassophereth, the sons of [2]Peruda,
56 the sons of Jaalah, the sons of Darkon, the sons of Giddel,
57 the sons of Shephatiah, the sons of Hattil, the sons of Pochereth-hazzebaim, the sons of [1]Ami.
58 ¶ All the [a]temple servants and the sons of [b]Solomon's servants were 392.
59 ¶ Now these are those who came up from Tel-melah, Tel-harsha, Cherub, [1]Addan *and* Immer, but they were not able to [2]give evidence of their fathers' households and their [3]descendants, whether they were of Israel:
60 the sons of Delaiah, the sons of Tobiah, the sons of Nekoda, 652.

Priests Removed

61 Of the sons of the priests: the sons of [1]Habaiah, the sons of Hakkoz, the sons of [a]Barzillai, who took a wife from the daughters of Barzillai the Gileadite, and he was called by their name.
62 These searched *among* their ancestral registration, but they could not be located; [a]therefore they were considered unclean *and excluded* from the priesthood.

2:1 [1]Lit *sons* [a]2 Kin 24:14-16; 25:11; 2 Chr 36:20; Neh 7:6-73
2 [1]Lit *who* [2]In Neh 7:7, *Azariah* [3]In Neh 7:7, *Raamiah* [4]In Neh 7:7, *Mispereth* [5]In Neh 7:7, *Nehum*
5 [a]Neh 7:10
6 [a]Neh 7:11
10 [1]In Neh 7:15, *Binnui*
13 [a]Ezra 8:13
18 [1]In Neh 7:24, *Hariph*
20 [1]In Neh 7:25, *Gibeon*
21 [1]Lit *sons* [a]Gen 35:19; Matt 2:6
24 [1]In Neh 7:28, *Beth-azmaveth*
25 [1]In Neh 7:29, *Kiriath-jearim*
26 [a]Josh 18:25
34 [1]Lit *sons* [a]1 Kin 16:34; 2 Chr 28:15
36 [a]1 Chr 24:7-18
37 [a]1 Chr 24:14
38 [a]1 Chr 9:12
39 [a]1 Chr 24:8
40 [1]In Ezra 3:9, *Judah*; in Neh 7:43, *Hodevah*
43 [a]1 Chr 9:2
44 [1]In Neh 7:47, *Sia*
50 [1]In Neh 7:52, *Nephushesim*
52 [1]In Neh 7:54, *Bazlith*
55 [1]In Neh 7:57, *Sophereth* [2]In Neh 7:57, *Perida* [a]1 Kin 9:21
57 [1]In Neh 7:59, *Amon*
58 [a]1 Chr 9:2 [b]1 Kin 9:21
59 [1]In Neh 7:61, *Addon* [2]Lit *tell* [3]Lit *seed*
61 [1]In Neh 7:63, *Hobaiah* [a]2 Sam 17:27; 1 Kin 2:7
62 [a]Num 16:39, 40

63 The [1]governor said to them [a]that
they should not eat from the most holy
things until a priest stood up with [b]Urim
and Thummim.
64 ¶ The whole assembly [1]numbered
42,360,
65 besides their male and female servants [1]who numbered 7,337; and they
had 200 [a]singing men and women.
66 Their horses were 736; their
mules, 245;
67 their camels, 435; *their* donkeys,
6,720.
68 ¶ Some of the heads of fathers'
households, when they arrived at the
house of the LORD which is in Jerusalem,
offered willingly for the house of God to
[1]restore it on its foundation.
69 According to their ability they gave
[a]to the treasury for the work 61,000 gold
drachmas and 5,000 silver minas and
100 priestly [1]garments.
70 ¶ [a]Now the priests and the Levites, some of the people, the singers, the
gatekeepers and the temple servants
lived in their cities, and all Israel in their
cities.

Altar and Sacrifices Restored

3 Now when the seventh month came,
and [a]the sons of Israel *were* in the
cities, the people gathered together as
one man to Jerusalem.
2 Then [a]Jeshua the son of Jozadak
and his brothers the priests, and [b]Zerub-
babel the son [c]of Shealtiel and his brothers arose and [d]built the altar of the God
of Israel to offer burnt offerings on it, [e]as
it is written in the law of Moses, the man
of God.
3 So they set up the altar on its foundation, for [1a]they were terrified because
of the peoples of the lands; and they [b]of-
fered burnt offerings on it to the LORD,
burnt offerings morning and evening.
4 They celebrated the [a]Feast of
Booths, [b]as it is written, and *offered*
the fixed number of burnt offerings daily, [c]according to the ordinance, as each
day required;
5 and afterward *there was* a [a]contin-
ual burnt offering, also [b]for the new
moons and [c]for all the fixed festivals of
the LORD that were consecrated, and
from everyone who offered a freewill offering to the LORD.
6 From the first day of the seventh
month they began to offer burnt offerings
to the LORD, but the foundation of the
temple of the LORD had not been laid.
7 Then they gave money to the masons and carpenters, and [a]food, drink
and oil to the Sidonians and to the Tyrians, [b]to bring cedar wood from Lebanon
to the sea at [c]Joppa, according to the
permission they had [1]from [d]Cyrus king
of Persia.

Temple Restoration Begun

8 ¶ Now in the second year of their
coming to the house of God at Jerusalem
in the second month, [a]Zerubbabel the
son of Shealtiel and Jeshua the son of Jozadak and the rest of their brothers the
priests and the Levites, and all who came
from the captivity to Jerusalem, began *the*
work and [b]appointed the Levites from
twenty years and older to oversee the
work of the house of the LORD.
9 Then [a]Jeshua *with* his sons and
brothers stood united *with* Kadmiel and
his sons, the sons of [1]Judah *and* the sons
of Henadad *with* their sons and brothers
the Levites, to oversee the workmen in
the temple of God.
10 ¶ Now when the builders had [a]laid
the foundation of the temple of the LORD,
[1]the priests stood in their apparel with
trumpets, and the Levites, the sons of
Asaph, with cymbals, to praise the LORD
[b]according to the [2]directions of King David of Israel.
11 [a]They sang, praising and giving
thanks to the LORD, *saying,* "[b]For He is
good, for His lovingkindness is upon Israel forever." And all the people shouted
with a great shout when they praised the
LORD because the foundation of the house
of the LORD was laid.
12 Yet many of the priests and Levites
and heads of fathers' *households,* [a]the
old men who had seen the first [1]temple,
wept with a loud voice when the foundation of this house was laid before their
eyes, while many shouted aloud for joy,
13 so that the people could not distinguish the sound of the shout of joy from
the sound of the weeping of the people,
for the people shouted with a loud shout,
and the sound was heard far away.

Adversaries Hinder the Work

4 Now when [a]the enemies of Judah
and Benjamin heard that [b]the people of the exile were building a temple to
the LORD God of Israel,
2 they approached Zerubbabel and
the heads of fathers' *households,* and said
to them, "Let us build with you, for we,
like you, seek your God; [a]and we have
been sacrificing to Him since the days
of [b]Esarhaddon king of Assyria, who
brought us up here."
3 But Zerubbabel and Jeshua and the
rest of the heads of fathers' *households* of
Israel said to them, "[a]You have nothing
in common with us in building a house to
our God; but we ourselves will together

63 [1]Heb *Tirshatha,* a Persian title [a]Lev 2:3 [b]Ex 28:30; Num 27:21
64 [1]Lit *together was*
65 [1]Lit *they were* [a]2 Chr 35:25
68 [1]Lit *establish*
69 [1]Or *tunics* [a]Ezra 8:25-34
70 [a]1 Chr 9:2; Neh 11:3
3:1 [a]Neh 7:73
2 [a]Neh 12:1 [b]Ezra 2:2; Hag 1:1 [c]1 Chr 3:17 [d]Ex 27:1 [e]Deut 12:5
3 [1]Lit *terror* was *upon them* [a]Ezra 4:4 [b]Num 28:2
4 [1]Or *Tabernacles* [2]Lit *by number* [a]Neh 8:14; Zech 14:16 [b]Ex 23:16 [c]Num 29:12
5 [a]Ex 29:38; Num 28:3 [b]Num 28:11 [c]Num 29:39
7 [1]Lit *of* [a]2 Chr 2:10; Acts 12:20 [b]2 Chr 2:16 [c]Acts 9:36 [d]Ezra 1:2
8 [a]Ezra 3:2 [b]1 Chr 23:4
9 [1]In Ezra 2:40, *Hodaviah* [a]Ezra 2:40
10 [1]So with the Gr and some mss; M.T. *they set the priests* [2]Lit *hands* [a]Zech 4:6-10 [b]1 Chr 6:31
11 [a]2 Chr 7:3; Neh 12:24 [b]1 Chr 16:34; 2 Chr 5:13; Ps 100:5; Jer 33:11
12 [1]Lit *house* [a]Hag 2:3
4:1 [a]Ezra 4:7-10 [b]Ezra 1:11
2 [a]2 Kin 17:32 [b]2 Kin 19:37
3 [a]Neh 2:20

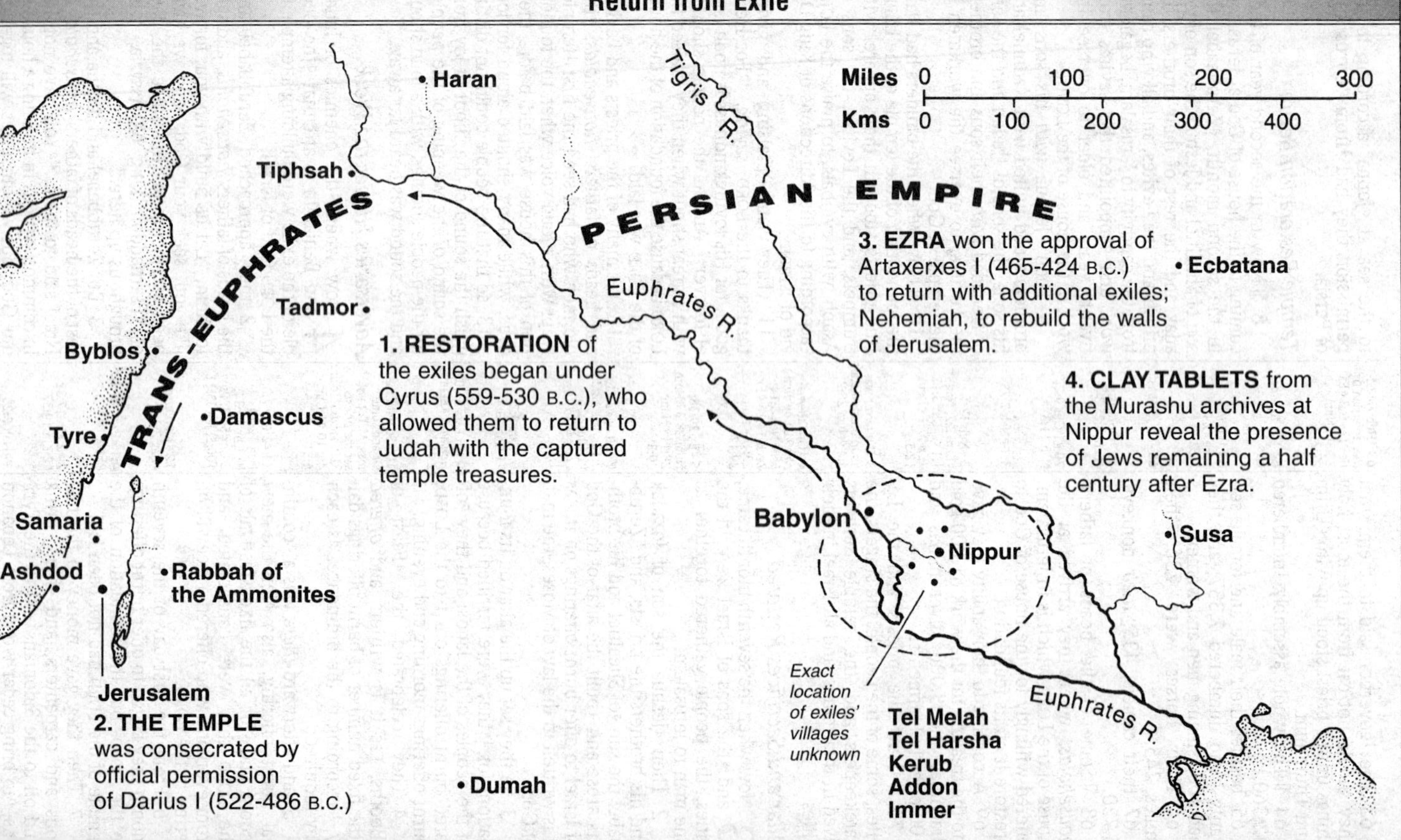

Return from Exile
Miles 0 100 200 300
Kms 0 100 200 300 400
PERSIAN EMPIRE
TRANS-EUPHRATES
Haran
Tiphsah
Tigris R.
Euphrates R.
Tadmor
Byblos
Tyre
Damascus
Samaria
Ashdod
Jerusalem
Rabbah of the Ammonites
Dumah
Babylon
Nippur
Susa
Ecbatana
1. RESTORATION of the exiles began under Cyrus (559-530 B.C.), who allowed them to return to Judah with the captured temple treasures.
2. THE TEMPLE was consecrated by official permission of Darius I (522-486 B.C.)
3. EZRA won the approval of Artaxerxes I (465-424 B.C.) to return with additional exiles; Nehemiah, to rebuild the walls of Jerusalem.
4. CLAY TABLETS from the Murashu archives at Nippur reveal the presence of Jews remaining a half century after Ezra.
Exact location of exiles' villages unknown
Tel Melah
Tel Harsha
Kerub
Addon
Immer
Euphrates R.

build to the LORD God of Israel, [b]as King Cyrus, the king of Persia has commanded us."

4 ¶ Then [a]the people of the land [1]discouraged the people of Judah, and frightened them from building,

5 and hired counselors against them to frustrate their counsel all the days of Cyrus king of Persia, even until the reign of Darius king of Persia.

6 ¶ Now in the reign of [1a]Ahasuerus, in the beginning of his reign, they wrote an accusation against the inhabitants of Judah and Jerusalem.

7 ¶ And in the days of [1]Artaxerxes, Bishlam, Mithredath, Tabeel and the rest of his colleagues wrote to Artaxerxes king of Persia; and the [2]text of the letter was written in Aramaic and translated [a]*from* Aramaic.

The Letter to King Artaxerxes

8 [1]Rehum the commander and Shimshai the scribe wrote a letter against Jerusalem to King Artaxerxes, as follows—

9 then *wrote* Rehum the commander and Shimshai the scribe and [a]the rest of their colleagues, the judges and [b]the lesser governors, the officials, the secretaries, the men of Erech, the Babylonians, the men of Susa, that is, the Elamites,

10 and the rest of the nations which the great and honorable [1]Osnappar deported and settled in the city of Samaria, and in the rest of the region beyond the [2]River. [a]Now

11 this is the copy of the letter which they sent to him:

¶ "To King Artaxerxes: Your servants, the men in the region beyond the River, and now

12 let it be known to the king that the Jews who came up from you have come to us at Jerusalem; they are rebuilding [a]the rebellious and evil city and [b]are finishing the walls and repairing the foundations.

13 "Now let it be known to the king, that if that city is rebuilt and the walls are finished, [a]they will not pay tribute, custom or toll, and it will damage the revenue of the kings.

14 "Now because we [1]are in the service of the palace, and it is not fitting for us to see the king's dishonor, therefore we have sent and informed the king,

15 so that a search may be made in the record books of your fathers. And you will discover in the record books and learn that that city is a rebellious city and damaging to kings and provinces, and that they have incited revolt within it in past days; therefore that city was laid waste.

16 "We inform the king that if that city is rebuilt and the walls finished, as a result you will have no possession in *the province* beyond the River."

The King Replies and Work Stops

17 ¶ *Then* the king sent an answer to Rehum the commander, to Shimshai the scribe, and to the rest of their colleagues who live in Samaria and in the rest of *the provinces* beyond the River: "Peace. And now

18 the document which you sent to us has been [1a]translated and read before me.

19 "A decree has been [1]issued by me, and a search has been made and it has been discovered that that city has risen up against the kings in past days, that rebellion and revolt have been perpetrated in it,

20 [a]that mighty kings have [1]ruled over Jerusalem, governing all *the provinces* [b]beyond the River, and that [c]tribute, custom and toll were paid to them.

21 "So, now issue a decree to make these men stop *work,* that this city may not be rebuilt until a decree is issued by me.

22 "Beware of being negligent in carrying out this *matter;* why should damage increase to the detriment of the kings?"

23 ¶ Then as soon as the copy of King Artaxerxes' document was read before Rehum and Shimshai the scribe and their colleagues, they went in haste to Jerusalem to the Jews and stopped them by force of arms.

24 ¶ Then work on the house of God in Jerusalem ceased, and it was stopped until the second year of the reign of Darius king of Persia.

Temple Work Resumed

5 When the prophets, [a]Haggai the prophet and [b]Zechariah the son of Iddo, prophesied to the Jews who were in Judah and Jerusalem in the name of the God of Israel, who was over them,

2 then [a]Zerubbabel the son of Shealtiel and Jeshua the son of Jozadak arose and began to rebuild the house of God which is in Jerusalem; and [b]the prophets of God were with them supporting them.

3 ¶ At that time [a]Tattenai, the governor of *the province* beyond the [1]River, and Shethar-bozenai and their colleagues came to them and spoke to them thus, "[b]Who issued you a decree to rebuild this [2]temple and to finish this structure?"

4 [a]Then we told them accordingly what the names of the men were who were reconstructing this building.

---

3 [b]Ezra 1:1,2

4 [1]Lit *weakened the hands of* [a]Ezra 3:3

6 [1]Or *Xerxes;* Heb *Ahashverosh* [a]Esth 1:1; Dan 9:1

7 [1]Heb *Artahshashta* [2]Lit *writing* [a]2 Kin 18:26; Dan 2:4

8 [1]Ch 4:8-6:18 is in Aram

9 [a]2 Kin 17:24 [b]Ezra 5:6; 6:6

10 [1]I.e. probably Ashurbanipal [2]I.e. Euphrates River, and so throughout the ch [a]Ezra 4:11, 17; 7:12

12 [a]2 Chr 36:13 [b]Ezra 5:3,9

13 [a]Ezra 4:20; 7:24

14 [1]Lit *eat the salt*

18 [1]Lit *plainly read before* [a]Neh 8:8

19 [1]Lit *put* forth

20 [1]Lit *been* [a]1 Kin 4:21; 1 Chr 18:3 [b]Gen 15:18; Josh 1:4 [c]Ezra 4:13; 7:24

5:1 [a]Hag 1:1 [b]Zech 1:1

2 [a]Ezra 3:2; Hag 1:12; Zech 4:6-9 [b]Ezra 6:14; Hag 2:4; Zech 3:1

3 [1]I.e. Euphrates River, and so throughout the ch [2]Lit *house,* and so in vv 9, 11, 12 [a]Ezra 6:6,13 [b]Ezra 1:3; 5:9

4 [a]Ezra 5:10

5 But [a]the eye of their God was on
the elders of the Jews, and they did not
stop them until a report could come to
Darius, and then a written reply be returned concerning it.

Adversaries Write to Darius

6 ¶ *This is* the copy of the letter
which [a]Tattenai, the governor of *the*
province beyond the River, and Shethar-
bozenai and his colleagues [b]the officials,
who were beyond the River, sent to Darius the king.
7 They sent a report to him in which
it was written thus: "To Darius the king,
all peace.
8 "Let it be known to the king that we
have gone to the province of Judah, to the
house of the great God, which is being
built with huge stones, and [1]beams are
being laid in the walls; and this work is
going on with great care and is succeeding in their hands.
9 "Then we asked those elders and
said to them thus, 'Who issued you a decree to rebuild this temple and to finish
this structure?'
10 "We also asked them their names so
as to inform you, and that we might write
down the names of the men who were at
their head.
11 "Thus they [1]answered us, saying,
'We are the servants of the God of heaven
and earth and are rebuilding the temple
that was built many years ago, [a]which a
great king of Israel built and finished.
12 'But [a]because our fathers had provoked the God of heaven to wrath, [b]He
gave them into the hand of Nebuchadnezzar king of Babylon, the Chaldean, *who*
destroyed this temple and deported the
people to Babylon.
13 'However, [a]in the first year of Cyrus king of Babylon, King Cyrus [b]issued
a decree to rebuild this house of God.
14 'Also [a]the gold and silver utensils of
the house of God which Nebuchadnezzar
had taken from the temple [1]in Jerusalem, and brought them to the temple of
Babylon, these King Cyrus took from the
temple of Babylon and they were given
to one [b]whose name was Sheshbazzar,
whom he had appointed governor.
15 'He said to him, "Take these utensils, go *and* deposit them in the temple
[1]in Jerusalem and let the house of God
be rebuilt in its place."
16 'Then that Sheshbazzar came *and*
[a]laid the foundations of the house of God
[1]in Jerusalem; and from then until now
it has been under construction and it is
[b]not *yet* completed.'
17 "Now if it pleases the king, [a]let a
search be conducted in the king's treasure house, which is there in Babylon, if
it be that a decree was issued by King
Cyrus to rebuild this house of God at Jerusalem; and let the king send to us his
decision concerning this *matter.*"

Darius Finds Cyrus's Decree

6 Then King Darius issued a decree,
and [a]search was made in the [1]ar-
chives, where the treasures were stored
in Babylon.
2 In [1]Ecbatana in the fortress, which
is [a]in the province of Media, a scroll was
found and there was written in it as follows: "Memorandum—
3 "[a]In the first year of King Cyrus,
Cyrus the king issued a decree: '*Concern-*
ing the house of God at Jerusalem, let the
[1]temple, the place where sacrifices are
offered, be rebuilt and let its foundations
be [2]retained, its height being 60 cubits
and its width 60 cubits;
4 [a]with three layers of huge stones
and [1]one layer of timbers. And let the
cost be paid from the [2]royal treasury.
5 'Also let [a]the gold and silver utensils of the house of God, which Nebuchadnezzar took from the temple in
Jerusalem and brought to Babylon, be
returned and [1]brought to their places in
the temple in Jerusalem; and you shall
put *them* in the house of God.'
6 ¶ "Now *therefore,* [a]Tattenai, governor of *the province* beyond the [1]River,
Shethar-bozenai and [2]your colleagues,
the officials of *the provinces* beyond the
[1]River, [3]keep away from there.
7 "Leave this work on the house of
God alone; let the governor of the Jews
and the elders of the Jews rebuild this
house of God on its site.
8 "Moreover, [a]I issue a decree concerning what you are to do for these elders of Judah in the rebuilding of this
house of God: the full cost is to be paid to
these people from the royal treasury out
of the taxes of *the provinces* beyond the
River, and that without delay.
9 "Whatever is needed, both young
bulls, rams, and lambs for a burnt offering
to the God of heaven, and wheat, salt,
wine and anointing oil, as the priests in
Jerusalem request, *it* is to be given to
them daily without fail,
10 that they may offer [1]acceptable
sacrifices to the God of heaven and [a]pray
for the life of the king and his sons.
11 "And I issued a decree that [a]any
man who violates this edict, a timber
shall be drawn from his house and he
shall be impaled on it and [b]his house
shall be made a refuse heap on account of
this.
12 "May the God who [a]has caused His

---

5 [a]Ezra 7:6,28
6 [a]Ezra 5:3 [b]Ezra 4:9
8 [1]Lit *timber is*
11 [1]Lit *returned us the word* [a]1 Kin 6:1,38
12 [a]2 Chr 36:16,17 [b]2 Kin 25:8-11; Jer 52:12-15
13 [a]Ezra 1:1 [b]Ezra 1:1-4
14 [1]Lit *that was in* [a]Ezra 1:7; 6:5; Dan 5:2 [b]Ezra 1:8; 5:16
15 [1]Lit *that is in*
16 [1]Lit *that is in* [a]Ezra 3:8,10 [b]Ezra 6:15
17 [a]Ezra 6:1,2
6:1 [1]Lit *house of the books* [a]Ezra 5:17
2 [1]Aram *Achmetha* [a]2 Kin 17:6
3 [1]Lit *house* [2]Or *fixed, laid* [a]Ezra 1:1; 5:13
4 [1]So Gr; Aram *a layer of new timber* [2]Lit *king's house* [a]1 Kin 6:36
5 [1]Lit *go* [a]Ezra 1:7; 5:14
6 [1]I.e. Euphrates River, and so throughout the ch [2]Aram *their* [3]Lit *be distant* [a]Ezra 5:3; 6:13
8 [a]Ezra 6:4; 7:14-22
10 [1]Lit *pleasing;* or *sweet-smelling sacrifices* [a]Ezra 7:23; Jer 29:7; 1 Tim 2:1,2
11 [a]Ezra 7:26 [b]Dan 2:5; 3:29
12 [a]Deut 12:5, 11; 1 Kin 9:3

name to dwell there overthrow any king or people who [1]attempts to change *it,* so as to destroy this house of God in Jerusalem. I, Darius, have issued *this* decree, let *it* be carried out with all diligence!”

The Temple Completed and Dedicated

13 ¶ Then [a]Tattenai, the governor of *the province* beyond the River, Shethar-bozenai and their colleagues carried out *the decree* with all diligence, just as King Darius had sent.

14 And [a]the elders of the Jews [1]were successful in building through the prophesying of Haggai the prophet and Zechariah the son of Iddo. And [2]they finished building according to the command of the God of Israel and the decree [b]of Cyrus, [c]Darius, and [d]Artaxerxes king of Persia.

15 This [1]temple was completed [2]on the third day of the [a]month Adar; it was the sixth year of the reign of King Darius.

16 ¶ And the sons of Israel, the priests, the Levites and the rest of the [1]exiles, [a]celebrated the dedication of this house of God with joy.

17 They offered for the dedication of this temple of God 100 bulls, 200 rams, 400 lambs, and as a sin offering for all Israel [a]12 male goats, corresponding to the number of the tribes of Israel.

18 Then they appointed the priests to [a]their divisions and the Levites in [b]their orders for the service of God [1]in Jerusalem, [c]as it is written in the book of Moses.

The Passover Observed

19 ¶ [a]The exiles observed the Passover on [b]the fourteenth of the first month.

20 [a]For the priests and the Levites had purified themselves together; all of them were pure. Then [b]they slaughtered the Passover *lamb* for all the exiles, both for their brothers the priests and for themselves.

21 The sons of Israel who returned from exile and [a]all those who had separated themselves from [b]the impurity of the nations of the land to *join* them, to seek the LORD God of Israel, ate *the Passover.*

22 And [a]they observed the Feast of Unleavened Bread seven days with joy, for the LORD had caused them to rejoice, and [b]had turned the heart of [c]the king of Assyria toward them to [1]encourage them in the work of the house of God, the God of Israel.

Ezra Journeys from Babylon to Jerusalem

7 [a]Now after these things, in the reign of [b]Artaxerxes king of Persia, *there went up* Ezra son of Seraiah, son of Azariah, son of Hilkiah,

2 son of Shallum, son of Zadok, son of Ahitub,

3 son of Amariah, son of Azariah, son of Meraioth,

4 son of Zerahiah, son of Uzzi, son of Bukki,

5 son of Abishua, son of Phinehas, son of Eleazar, son of Aaron the chief priest.

6 This Ezra went up from Babylon, and he was a [a]scribe skilled in the law of Moses, which the LORD God of Israel had given; and the king granted him all [1]he requested [b]because the hand of the LORD his God *was* upon him.

7 [a]Some of the sons of Israel and some of the priests, the Levites, the singers, the gatekeepers and the temple servants went up to Jerusalem in the seventh year of King Artaxerxes.

8 ¶ He came to Jerusalem in the fifth month, which was in the seventh year of the king.

9 For on the first of the first month [1]he began to go up from Babylon; and on the first of the fifth month he came to Jerusalem, [a]because the good hand of his God *was* upon him.

10 For Ezra had set his heart to [1]study the law of the LORD and to practice *it,* and [a]to teach *His* statutes and ordinances in Israel.

King's Decree on Behalf of Ezra

11 ¶ Now this is the copy of the decree which King Artaxerxes gave to Ezra the priest, the scribe, [1]learned in the words of the commandments of the LORD and His statutes to Israel:

12 “[1]Artaxerxes, [a]king of kings, to Ezra the priest, the scribe of the law of the God of heaven, perfect *peace.* And now

13 [a]I have issued a decree that any of the people of Israel and their priests and the Levites in my kingdom who are willing to go to Jerusalem, may go with you.

14 “Forasmuch as you are sent [1]by the king and his [a]seven counselors to inquire concerning Judah and Jerusalem according to the law of your God which is in your hand,

15 and to bring the silver and gold, which the king and his counselors have freely offered to the God of Israel, [a]whose dwelling is in Jerusalem,

16 with [a]all the silver and gold which

12 [1]Lit *sends his hand*
13 [a]Ezra 6:6
14 [1]Lit *were building and succeeding* [2]Lit *built and finished* [a]Ezra 5:1,2 [b]Ezra 1:1; 5:13 [c]Ezra 4:24; 6:12 [d]Ezra 7:1
15 [1]Lit *house* [2]Lit *until* [a]Esth 3:7
16 [1]Lit *sons of the captivity* [a]1 Kin 8:63; 2 Chr 7:5
17 [a]Ezra 8:35
18 [1]Lit *which is in* [a]1 Chr 24:1; 2 Chr 35:5 [b]1 Chr 23:6 [c]Num 3:6; 8:9
19 [a]Ezra 1:11 [b]Ex 12:6
20 [a]2 Chr 29:34; 30:15 [b]2 Chr 35:11
21 [a]Neh 9:2; 10:28 [b]Ezra 9:11
22 [1]Lit *strengthen their hands* [a]Ex 12:15 [b]Ezra 7:27; Prov 21:1 [c]Ezra 1:1; 6:1
7:1 [a]1 Chr 6:4-14 [b]Ezra 7:12,21; Neh 2:1
6 [1]Lit *his request* [a]Ezra 7:11,12,21 [b]Ezra 7:9,28; 8:22
7 [a]Ezra 8:1-20
9 [1]Lit *was the foundation* [a]Ezra 7:6; Neh 2:8
10 [1]Lit *seek* [a]Deut 33:10; Ezra 7:25; Neh 8:1
11 [1]Lit *the scribe of*
12 [1]Ch 7:12-26 is in Aram [a]Ezek 26:7; Dan 2:37
13 [a]Ezra 6:1
14 [1]Lit *from before* [a]Ezra 7:15, 28; 8:25
15 [a]2 Chr 6:2; Ezra 6:12; Ps 135:21
16 [a]Ezra 8:25

you find in the whole province of Babylon, along [b]with the freewill offering of the people and of the priests, who [c]offered willingly for the house of their God which is in Jerusalem;

17 with this money, therefore, you shall diligently buy bulls, rams and lambs, [a]with their grain offerings and their drink offerings and [b]offer them on the altar of the house of your God which is in Jerusalem.

18 "Whatever seems good to you and to your brothers to do with the rest of the silver and gold, you may do according to the will of your God.

19 "Also the utensils which are given to you for the service of the house of your God, deliver in full before the God of Jerusalem.

20 "The rest of the needs for the house of your God, for which you may have occasion to provide, [a]provide *for it* from the royal treasury.

21 ¶ "I, even I, King Artaxerxes, issue a decree to all the treasurers who are *in the provinces* beyond the [1]River, that whatever Ezra the priest, [a]the scribe of the law of the God of heaven, may require of you, it shall be done diligently,

22 *even* up to 100 talents of silver, 100 [1]kors of wheat, 100 baths of wine, 100 baths of oil, and salt [2]as needed.

23 "Whatever is [1]commanded by the God of heaven, let it be done with zeal for the house of the God of heaven, [a]so that there will not be wrath against the kingdom of the king and his sons.

24 "We also inform you that [a]it is not allowed to [1]impose tax, tribute or toll [b]*on* any of the priests, Levites, singers, doorkeepers, Nethinim or servants of this house of God.

25 ¶ "You, Ezra, according to the wisdom of your God which is in your hand, [a]appoint magistrates and judges that they may judge all the people who are in *the province* beyond the River, *even* all those who know the laws of your God; and you may [b]teach anyone who is ignorant *of them.*

26 "[a]Whoever will not observe the law of your God and the law of the king, let judgment be executed upon him strictly, whether for death or for [1]banishment or for confiscation of goods or for imprisonment."

The King's Kindness

27 ¶ Blessed be the LORD, the God of our fathers, [a]who has put *such a thing* as this in the king's heart, to adorn the house of the LORD which is in Jerusalem,

28 and [a]has extended lovingkindness to me before the king and his counselors and before all the king's mighty princes. Thus I was strengthened according to [b]the hand of the LORD my God upon me, and I gathered [1]leading men from Israel to go up with me.

People Who Went with Ezra

8 Now these are the heads of their fathers' *households* and the genealogical enrollment of those who went up with me from Babylon in the reign of King Artaxerxes:

2 of the sons of Phinehas, Gershom; of the sons of Ithamar, Daniel; of the sons of David, [a]Hattush;

3 of the sons of Shecaniah *who was* of the sons of [a]Parosh, Zechariah and with him 150 males *who were in* the genealogical list;

4 of the sons of Pahath-moab, Eliehoenai the son of Zerahiah and 200 males with him;

5 of the sons of Zattu, Shecaniah, the son of Jahaziel and 300 males with him;

6 and of the sons of [a]Adin, Ebed the son of Jonathan and 50 males with him;

7 and of the sons of Elam, Jeshaiah the son of Athaliah and 70 males with him;

8 and of the sons of Shephatiah, Zebadiah the son of Michael and 80 males with him;

9 of the sons of Joab, Obadiah the son of Jehiel and 218 males with him;

10 and of the sons of Bani, Shelomith, the son of Josiphiah and 160 males with him;

11 and of the sons of Bebai, Zechariah the son of Bebai and 28 males with him;

12 and of the sons of Azgad, Johanan the son of Hakkatan and 110 males with him;

13 and of the sons of Adonikam, the last ones, these being their names, Eliphelet, Jeuel and Shemaiah, and 60 males with them;

14 and of the sons of Bigvai, Uthai and [1]Zabbud, and 70 males with [2]them.

Ezra Sends for Levites

15 ¶ Now I assembled them at [a]the river that runs to Ahava, where we camped for three days; and when I observed the people and the priests, I [b]did not find any Levites there.

16 So I sent for Eliezer, Ariel, Shemaiah, Elnathan, Jarib, Elnathan, Nathan, Zechariah and Meshullam, [1]leading men, and for Joiarib and Elnathan, teachers.

17 I sent them to Iddo the [1]leading man at the place Casiphia; and I [2]told them what to say to [3]Iddo *and* his brothers, [a]the temple servants at the place

16 [b]Ezra 1:4,6 [c]1 Chr 29:6

17 [a]Num 15:4-13 [b]Deut 12:5-11

20 [a]Ezra 6:4

21 [1]I.e. Euphrates River, and so throughout the ch [a]Ezra 7:6

22 [1]I.e. One kor equals approx ten bu [2]Lit *without prescription*

23 [1]Lit *from the decree of* [a]Ezra 6:10

24 [1]Lit *throw on them* [a]Ezra 4:13, 20 [b]Ezra 7:7

25 [a]Ex 18:21; Deut 16:18 [b]Ezra 7:10; Mal 2:7; Col 1:28

26 [1]Lit *rooting out* [a]Ezra 6:11, 12

27 [a]Ezra 6:22

28 [1]Lit *heads* [a]Ezra 9:9 [b]Ezra 5:5

8:2 [a]1 Chr 3:22

3 [a]Ezra 2:3

6 [a]Ezra 2:15; Neh 7:20; 10:16

14 [1]Or *Zakkur* [2]Or *him*

15 [a]Ezra 8:21, 31 [b]Ezra 7:7; 8:2

16 [1]Lit *heads*

17 [1]Lit *head* [2]Lit *put words in their mouth to say* [3]So Gr; Heb *Iddo his brother* [a]Ezra 2:43

Casiphia, *that is,* to bring ministers to us
for the house of our God.
18 [a]According to the good hand of our
God upon us they brought us a [b]man of
insight of the sons of Mahli, the son of
Levi, the son of Israel, namely Sherebiah,
and his sons and brothers, 18 men;
19 and Hashabiah and [1]Jeshaiah of
the sons of Merari, with his brothers and
their sons, 20 men;
20 and 220 of [a]the temple servants,
whom David and the princes had given
for the service of the Levites, all of them
designated by name.

Protection of God Invoked

21 ¶ Then I proclaimed [a]a fast there
at [b]the river of Ahava, that we might
[c]humble ourselves before our God to
seek from Him a [1]safe journey for us, our
little ones, and all our possessions.
22 For I was ashamed to request from
the king troops and horsemen to [1]protect
us from the enemy on the way, because
we had said to the king, "[a]The hand of
our God is [2]favorably disposed to all
those who seek Him, but [b]His power and
His anger are against all those who [c]for-
sake Him."
23 So we fasted and sought our God
concerning this *matter,* and He [1a]lis-
tened to our entreaty.
24 ¶ Then I set apart twelve of the
leading priests, [a]Sherebiah, Hashabiah,
and with them ten of their brothers;
25 and I [a]weighed out to them [b]the
silver, the gold and the utensils, the offering for the house of our God which the
king and [c]his counselors and his princes
and all Israel present *there* had offered.
26 [a]Thus I weighed into their hands
650 talents of silver, and silver utensils
worth 100 talents, *and* 100 gold talents,
27 and 20 gold bowls *worth* 1,000 dar-
ics, and two utensils of fine shiny bronze,
precious as gold.
28 Then I said to them, "[a]You are holy
to the LORD, and the [b]utensils are holy;
and the silver and the gold are a freewill
offering to the LORD God of your fathers.
29 "Watch and keep *them* [a]until you
weigh *them* before the leading priests,
the Levites and the heads of the fathers'
households of Israel at Jerusalem, *in* the
chambers of the house of the LORD."
30 So the priests and the Levites [a]ac-
cepted the weighed out silver and gold
and the utensils, to bring *them* to Jerusalem to the house of our God.
31 ¶ Then we journeyed from [a]the
river Ahava on [b]the twelfth of the first
month to go to Jerusalem; and [c]the hand
of our God was over us, and He delivered
us from the hand of the enemy and the
ambushes by the way.
32 [a]Thus we came to Jerusalem and
remained there three days.

Treasure Placed in the Temple

33 On the fourth day the silver and the
gold and the utensils [a]were weighed out
in the house of our God into the hand of
[b]Meremoth the son of Uriah the priest,
and with him *was* Eleazar the son of Phinehas; and with them *were* the Levites,
Jozabad the son of Jeshua and Noadiah
the son of Binnui.
34 Everything *was* numbered and
weighed, and all the weight was recorded
at that time.
35 ¶ [a]The exiles who had come from
the captivity offered burnt offerings to the
God of Israel: [b]12 bulls for all Israel, 96
rams, 77 lambs, 12 male goats for a sin
offering, all as a burnt offering to the
LORD.
36 Then [a]they delivered the king's
edicts to [b]the king's satraps and to the
governors *in the provinces* beyond the
[1]River, and they supported the people
and the house of God.

Mixed Marriages

9 Now when these things had been
completed, the princes approached
me, saying, "The people of Israel and the
priests and the Levites have not [a]separat-
ed themselves from the peoples of the
lands, [b]according to their abominations,
those of the Canaanites, the Hittites, the
Perizzites, the Jebusites, the Ammonites,
the Moabites, the Egyptians and the Amorites.
2 "For [a]they have taken some of their
daughters *as wives* for themselves and for
their sons, so that [b]the holy [1]race has
[c]intermingled with the peoples of the
lands; indeed, the hands of the princes
and the rulers have been foremost in this
unfaithfulness."
3 When I heard about this matter, I
[a]tore my garment and my robe, and
pulled some of the hair from my head and
my beard, and [b]sat down appalled.
4 Then [a]everyone who trembled at
the words of the God of Israel on account
of the unfaithfulness of the exiles gathered to me, and I sat appalled until [b]the
evening offering.

Prayer of Confession

5 ¶ But at the evening offering I arose
from my [1]humiliation, even with my garment and my robe torn, and I fell on my
knees and [a]stretched out my [2]hands to
the LORD my God;
6 and I said, "O my God, I am

---

18 [a]Ezra 7:6,28 [b]2 Chr 30:22
19 [1]So Gr; Heb *with him Jeshaiah*
20 [a]Ezra 2:43; 7:7
21 [1]Lit *straight way* [a]1 Sam 7:6; 2 Chr 20:3 [b]Ezra 8:15,31 [c]Lev 16:29; 23:29; Is 58:3,5
22 [1]Lit *help* [2]Lit *upon all...for good* [a]Ezra 7:6, 9,28 [b]Josh 22:16 [c]2 Chr 15:2
23 [1]Lit *was entreated by us* [a]1 Chr 5:20; 2 Chr 33:13
24 [a]Ezra 8:18, 19
25 [a]Ezra 8:33 [b]Ezra 7:15,16 [c]Ezra 7:14
26 [a]Ezra 1:9-11
28 [a]Lev 21:6-8 [b]Lev 22:2,3
29 [a]Ezra 8:33, 34
30 [a]Ezra 1:9
31 [a]Ezra 8:15, 21 [b]Ezra 7:9 [c]Ezra 8:22
32 [a]Neh 2:11
33 [a]Ezra 8:30 [b]Neh 3:4,21
35 [a]Ezra 2:1 [b]Ezra 6:17
36 [1]I.e. Euphrates River [a]Ezra 7:21-24 [b]Ezra 4:7; 5:6
9:1 [a]Ezra 6:21; Neh 9:2 [b]Lev 18:24-30
2 [1]Lit *seed* [a]Deut 7:3; Ezra 10:2,18 [b]Ex 22:31; Deut 14:2; 2 Cor 6:14 [c]Neh 13:3
3 [a]2 Kin 18:37 [b]Neh 1:4
4 [a]Ezra 10:3; Is 66:2 [b]Ex 29:39
5 [1]Or *fasting* [2]Lit *palms* [a]Ex 9:29

ashamed and embarrassed to lift up my
face to You, my God, for our iniquities
have [1]risen above our heads and our
[a]guilt has grown even to the heavens.
7 "[a]Since the days of our fathers to
this day we *have been* in great guilt, and
on account of our iniquities we, our kings
and our priests have been given into the
hand of the kings of the lands, to the
sword, to captivity and to plunder and to
[1b]open shame, as *it is* this day.
8 "But now for a brief moment grace
has been *shown* from the LORD our God,
[a]to leave us an escaped remnant and to
give us a [b]peg in His holy place, that our
God may [c]enlighten our eyes and grant
us a little reviving in our bondage.
9 "[a]For we are slaves; yet in our bondage our God has not forsaken us, but [b]has
extended lovingkindness to us in the
sight of the kings of Persia, to give us
reviving to raise up the house of our God,
to restore its ruins and to give us a wall
in Judah and Jerusalem.
10 ¶ "Now, our God, what shall we
say after this? For we have forsaken Your
commandments,
11 which You have commanded by
Your servants the prophets, saying, 'The
land which you are entering to possess is
an unclean land with the uncleanness of
the peoples of the lands, with their abominations which have filled it from end to
end *and* [a]with their impurity.
12 'So now do not [a]give your daughters to their sons nor take their daughters
to your sons, and [b]never seek their peace
or their prosperity, that you may be
strong and eat the good *things* of the land
and [c]leave *it* as an inheritance to your
sons forever.'
13 "After all that has come upon us for
our evil deeds and [a]our great guilt, since
You our God have requited *us* less than
our iniquities *deserve,* and have given us
[b]an escaped remnant as this,
14 [a]shall we again break Your commandments and intermarry with the peoples [1]who commit these abominations?
[b]Would You not be angry with us [2]to the
point of destruction, until there is no
remnant nor any who escape?
15 "O LORD God of Israel, [a]You are
righteous, for we have been left an escaped remnant, as *it is* this day; behold,
we are before You in [b]our guilt, for [c]no
one can stand before You because of
this."

Reconciliation with God

10 Now [a]while Ezra was praying
and making confession, weeping
and prostrating himself [b]before the
house of God, a very large assembly,
men, women and children, gathered to
him from Israel; for the people wept bitterly.
2 Shecaniah the son of Jehiel, one of
the sons of Elam, said to Ezra, "[a]We have
been unfaithful to our God and have
[1]married foreign women from the peoples of the land; yet now there is hope for
Israel in spite of this.
3 "So now [a]let us make a covenant
with our God to put away all the wives
and [1b]their children, according to the
counsel of [2]my lord and of [c]those who
tremble at the commandment of our God;
and let it be done [d]according to the law.
4 "Arise! For *this* matter is [1]your responsibility, but we will be with you; [a]be
courageous and act."
5 ¶ Then Ezra rose and [a]made the
leading priests, the Levites and all Israel,
take oath that they would do according to
this [1]proposal; so they took the oath.
6 Then Ezra [a]rose from before the
house of God and went into the chamber
of Jehohanan the son of Eliashib. Although he went there, [b]he did not eat
bread nor drink water, for he was mourning over the unfaithfulness of the exiles.
7 They made a proclamation throughout Judah and Jerusalem to all the exiles,
that they should assemble at Jerusalem,
8 and that whoever would not come
within three days, according to the counsel of the leaders and the elders, all his
possessions should be forfeited and he
himself excluded from the assembly of
the exiles.
9 ¶ So all the men of Judah and Benjamin assembled at Jerusalem within the
three days. It was the ninth month on the
twentieth of the month, and all the people sat in the open square *before* the
house of God, [a]trembling because of this
matter and the heavy rain.
10 Then Ezra the priest stood up and
said to them, "You have been unfaithful
and have married foreign wives adding to
the guilt of Israel.
11 "Now therefore, [a]make confession
to the LORD God of your fathers and [b]do
His will; and [c]separate yourselves from
the peoples of the land and from the foreign wives."
12 Then all the assembly replied with
a loud voice, "That's right! As you have
said, so it is [1]our duty to do.
13 "But there are many people; it is the
rainy season and we are not able to stand
in the open. Nor *can* the task *be done* in
one or two days, for we have transgressed
greatly in this matter.
14 "Let our leaders [1]represent the
whole assembly and let all those in our
cities who have married foreign wives

6 [1]Lit *multiplied over the head* [a]2 Chr 28:9; Ezra 9:13,15; Rev 18:5
7 [1]Lit *shame of faces* [a]2 Chr 29:6; Ps 106:6 [b]Dan 9:7
8 [a]Ezra 9:13-15 [b]Is 22:23 [c]Ps 13:3
9 [a]Neh 9:36 [b]Ezra 7:28
11 [a]Ezra 6:21
12 [a]Ex 34:15, 16; Deut 7:3; Ezra 9:2 [b]Deut 23:6 [c]Prov 13:22
13 [a]Ezra 9:6,7 [b]Ezra 9:8
14 [1]Lit *of these abominations* [2]Lit *to destroy* [a]Ezra 9:2 [b]Deut 9:8,14
15 [a]Neh 9:33; Dan 9:7 [b]Ezra 9:6 [c]Job 9:2; Ps 130:3
10:1 [a]Dan 9:4, 20 [b]2 Chr 20:9
2 [1]Lit *given dwelling to* [a]Ezra 9:2; Neh 13:27
3 [1]Lit *that which is born of them* [2]Or *the Lord* [a]2 Chr 34:31 [b]Ezra 10:44 [c]Ezra 9:4 [d]Deut 7:2,3
4 [1]Lit *upon you* [a]1 Chr 28:10
5 [1]Lit *word, thing* [a]Neh 5:12; 13:25
6 [a]Ezra 10:1 [b]Deut 9:18
9 [a]1 Sam 12:18; Ezra 9:4; 10:3
11 [a]Lev 26:40; Prov 28:13 [b]Rom 12:2 [c]Ezra 10:3
12 [1]Lit *upon us*
14 [1]Lit *stand for*

come at appointed times, together with the elders and judges of each city, until the [a]fierce anger of our God on account of this matter is turned away from us."

15 Only Jonathan the son of Asahel and Jahzeiah the son of Tikvah [1]opposed this, with Meshullam and Shabbethai the Levite supporting them.

16 ¶ But the exiles did so. And [1]Ezra the priest selected men *who were* heads of fathers' *households* for *each of* their father's households, all of them by name. So they [2]convened on the first day of the tenth month to investigate the matter.

17 They finished *investigating* all the men who had married foreign wives by the first day of the first month.

List of Offenders

18 ¶ Among the sons of the priests who had married foreign wives were found of the sons of [a]Jeshua the son of Jozadak, and his brothers: Maaseiah, Eliezer, Jarib and Gedaliah.

19 They [1]pledged to put away their wives, and being guilty, [a]*they offered* a ram of the flock for their offense.

20 Of the sons of Immer *there were* Hanani and Zebadiah;

21 and of the sons of Harim: Maaseiah, Elijah, Shemaiah, Jehiel and Uzziah;

22 and of the sons of Pashhur: Elioenai, Maaseiah, Ishmael, Nethanel, Jozabad and Elasah.

23 ¶ Of Levites *there were* Jozabad, Shimei, Kelaiah (that is, Kelita), Pethahiah, Judah and Eliezer.

24 ¶ Of the singers *there was* Eliashib; and of the gatekeepers: Shallum, Telem and Uri.

25 ¶ Of Israel, of the sons of [a]Parosh *there were* Ramiah, Izziah, Malchijah, Mijamin, Eleazar, Malchijah and Benaiah;

26 and of the sons of Elam: Mattaniah, Zechariah, Jehiel, Abdi, Jeremoth and Elijah;

27 and of the sons of [a]Zattu: Elioenai, Eliashib, Mattaniah, Jeremoth, Zabad and Aziza;

28 and of the sons of Bebai: Jehohanan, Hananiah, Zabbai *and* Athlai;

29 and of the sons of Bani: Meshullam, Malluch and Adaiah, Jashub, Sheal *and* Jeremoth;

30 and of the sons of Pahath-moab: Adna, Chelal, Benaiah, Maaseiah, Mattaniah, Bezalel, Binnui and Manasseh;

31 and *of* the sons of Harim: Eliezer, Isshijah, [a]Malchijah, Shemaiah, Shimeon,

32 Benjamin, Malluch *and* Shemariah;

33 of the sons of Hashum: Mattenai, Mattattah, Zabad, Eliphelet, Jeremai, Manasseh *and* Shimei;

34 of the sons of Bani: Maadai, Amram, Uel,

35 Benaiah, Bedeiah, Cheluhi,

36 Vaniah, Meremoth, Eliashib,

37 Mattaniah, Mattenai, Jaasu,

38 Bani, Binnui, Shimei,

39 Shelemiah, Nathan, Adaiah,

40 Machnadebai, Shashai, Sharai,

41 Azarel, Shelemiah, Shemariah,

42 Shallum, Amariah *and* Joseph.

43 Of the sons of [a]Nebo *there were* Jeiel, Mattithiah, Zabad, Zebina, Jaddai, Joel *and* Benaiah.

44 All these had married [a]foreign wives, and some of them had wives *by whom* they had children.

---

14 [a]2 Kin 23:26; 2 Chr 28:11-13; 29:10; 30:8
15 [1]Lit *stood against*
16 [1]Heb reads *there were set apart Ezra the priest, men...* [2]Lit *sat*
18 [a]Ezra 5:2; Hag 1:1,12; 2:4; Zech 3:1; 6:11
19 [1]Lit *gave their hand* [a]Lev 5:15; 6:6
25 [a]Ezra 2:3; 8:3; Neh 7:8
27 [a]Ezra 2:8; Neh 7:13
31 [a]Neh 3:11
43 [a]Num 32:38; Ezra 2:29
44 [a]1 Kin 11:1-3; Ezra 10:3

Nehemiah

Title and Background

See Introduction to Ezra.

Author and Date of Writing

See Introduction to Ezra. Nehemiah can be dated about 430 B.C.

Theme and Message

Nehemiah continues the history of the Jews upon their return from exile in Babylon. Nehemiah went to Jerusalem in 445 B.C. and led the people in repairing the walls. With Ezra, he provided leadership for the people. A recurring theme of this book is the description of the importance of prayer to Nehemiah.

Outline

I. Nehemiah Rebuilds the Walls (1:1—7:3)
II. Change Under Ezra (7:4—10:39)
III. Nehemiah's Plans (11:1—13:31)

Nehemiah's Grief for the Exiles

1 The words of [a]Nehemiah the son of Hacaliah.

¶ Now it happened in [b]the month Chislev, [c]*in* the twentieth year, while I was in [d]Susa the [1]capitol,

2 that [a]Hanani, one of my brothers, and [1]some men from Judah came; and I asked them concerning the Jews who had escaped *and* had survived the captivity, and about Jerusalem.

3 They said to me, "The remnant there in the [a]province who survived the captivity are in great distress and [b]reproach, and [b]the wall of Jerusalem is broken down and [c]its gates are burned with fire."

4 ¶ When I heard these words, [a]I sat down and wept and mourned for days; and I was fasting and praying before [b]the God of heaven.

5 I said, "I beseech You, O LORD God of heaven, [a]the great and awesome God, [b]who preserves the covenant and lovingkindness for those who love Him and keep His commandments,

6 [a]let Your ear now be attentive and Your eyes open to hear the prayer of Your servant which I am praying before You now, day and night, on behalf of the sons of Israel Your servants, [b]confessing the sins of the sons of Israel which we have sinned against You; [c]I and my father's house have sinned.

7 "[a]We have acted very corruptly against You and have not kept the commandments, nor the statutes, nor the ordinances [b]which You commanded Your servant Moses.

8 "Remember the word which You commanded Your servant Moses, saying, '[a]If you are unfaithful I will scatter you among the peoples;

9 [a]but *if* you return to Me and keep My commandments and do them, though those of you who have been scattered were in the most remote part of the heavens, I [b]will gather them from there and will bring them [c]to the place where I have chosen to cause My name to dwell.'

10 "[a]They are Your servants and Your people whom You redeemed by Your great power and by Your strong hand.

11 "O Lord, I beseech You, [a]may Your ear be attentive to the prayer of Your servant and the prayer of Your servants who delight to [1]revere Your name, and make Your servant successful today and grant him compassion before this man."

¶ Now I was the [b]cupbearer to the king.

Nehemiah's Prayer Answered

2 And it came about in the month Nisan, [a]in the twentieth year of King [b]Artaxerxes, that wine *was* before him, and [c]I took up the wine and gave it to the king. Now I had not been sad in his presence.

2 So the king said to me, "Why is your face sad though you are not sick?

1:1 [1]Or *palace* or *citadel* [a]Neh 10:1 [b]Zech 7:1 [c]Neh 2:1 [d]Esth 1:2; Dan 8:2
2 [1]Lit *he and some* [a]Neh 7:2
3 [a]Neh 7:6 [b]Neh 2:17 [c]Neh 2:3
4 [a]Ezra 9:3; 10:1 [b]Neh 2:4
5 [a]Neh 4:14; 9:32; Dan 9:4 [b]Ex 20:6; Ps 89:2,3
6 [a]Dan 9:17 [b]Ezra 10:1; Dan 9:20 [c]2 Chr 29:6
7 [a]Dan 9:5 [b]Deut 28:14
8 [a]Lev 26:33
9 [a]Deut 30:2,3 [b]Deut 30:4 [c]Deut 12:5
10 [a]Ex 32:11; Deut 9:29
11 [1]Or *fear* [a]Neh 1:6 [b]Gen 40:21; Neh 2:1
2:1 [a]Neh 1:1 [b]Ezra 7:1 [c]Neh 1:11

[a]This is nothing but sadness of heart."
Then I was very much afraid.
3 I said to the king, "[a]Let the king
live forever. Why should my face not be
sad [b]when the city, the place of my fathers' tombs, lies desolate and its gates
have been consumed by fire?"
4 Then the king said to me, "What
would you request?" [a]So I prayed to the
God of heaven.
5 I said to the king, "If it please the
king, and if your servant has found favor
before you, send me to Judah, to the
city of my fathers' tombs, that I may rebuild it."
6 Then the king said to me, the
queen sitting beside him, "How long will
your journey be, and when will you return?" So it pleased the king to send me,
and [a]I gave him a definite time.
7 And I said to the king, "If it please
the king, let letters be given me [a]for the
governors *of the provinces* beyond the
River, that they may allow me to pass
through until I come to Judah,
8 and a letter to Asaph the keeper of
the king's [a]forest, that he may give me
timber to make beams for the gates of
[b]the fortress which is by the [1]temple,
for the wall of the city and for the house
to which I will go." And the king granted
them to me because [c]the good hand of
my God *was* on me.
9 ¶ Then I came to [a]the governors *of
the provinces* beyond the River and gave
them the king's letters. Now [b]the king
had sent with me officers of the army and
horsemen.
10 When [a]Sanballat the Horonite and
Tobiah the Ammonite [1]official heard
about it, it was very displeasing to them
that someone had come to seek the welfare of the sons of Israel.

Nehemiah Inspects Jerusalem's Walls

11 ¶ So I [a]came to Jerusalem and was
there three days.
12 And I arose in the night, I and a few
men with me. I did not tell anyone what
my God was putting into my [1]mind to do
for Jerusalem and there was no animal
with me except the animal on which I
was riding.
13 So I went out at night by [a]the Valley Gate in the direction of the Dragon's
Well and *on* to the [1]Refuse Gate, inspect-
ing the walls of Jerusalem [b]which were
broken down and its [c]gates which were
consumed by fire.
14 Then I passed on to [a]the Fountain
Gate and [b]the King's Pool, but there was
no place for [1]my mount to pass.
15 So I went up at night by the [a]ra-
vine and inspected the wall. Then I entered the Valley Gate again and returned.
16 The officials did not know where I
had gone or what I had done; nor had I as
yet told the Jews, the priests, the nobles,
the officials or the rest who did the work.
17 ¶ Then I said to them, "You see the
bad situation we are in, that [a]Jerusalem
is desolate and its gates burned by fire.
Come, let us rebuild the wall of Jerusalem
so that we will no longer be a reproach."
18 I told them how the hand of my
God had been favorable to me and also
about the king's words which he had spoken to me. Then they said, "Let us arise
and build." [a]So they put their hands to
the good *work.*
19 But when Sanballat the Horonite
and Tobiah the Ammonite [1]official, and
[a]Geshem the Arab heard *it,* [b]they
mocked us and despised us and said,
"What is this thing you are doing? [a]Are
you rebelling against the king?"
20 So I answered them and said to
them, "[a]The God of heaven will give us
success; therefore we His servants will
arise and build, [b]but you have no portion, right or memorial in Jerusalem."

Builders of the Walls

3 Then [a]Eliashib the high priest arose
with his brothers the priests and
built [b]the Sheep Gate; they consecrated
it and [c]hung its doors. They consecrated
[1]the wall to [d]the Tower of the Hundred
and [e]the Tower of Hananel.
2 Next to him [a]the men of Jericho
built, and next to [1]them Zaccur the son
of Imri built.
3 ¶ Now the sons of Hassenaah built
[a]the Fish Gate; they laid its beams and
hung its doors with its bolts and bars.
4 Next to them Meremoth the son of
Uriah the son of Hakkoz made repairs.
And next to him Meshullam the son of
Berechiah the son of Meshezabel made
repairs. And next to [1]him Zadok the son
of Baana *also* made repairs.
5 Moreover, next to [1]him the Tekoites made repairs, but their nobles did not
[2]support the work of their masters.
6 ¶ Joiada the son of Paseah and Meshullam the son of Besodeiah repaired
[a]the Old Gate; they laid its beams and
hung its doors with its bolts and its bars.
7 Next to them Melatiah the Gibeonite and Jadon the Meronothite, the men
of Gibeon and of Mizpah, [1]also made repairs for the official seat of the [a]governor
of the province beyond the River.
8 Next to him Uzziel the son of Har-
haiah of the [a]goldsmiths made repairs.
And next to him Hananiah, one of the

2 [a]Prov 15:13
3 [a]Dan 2:4 [b]2 Kin 25:8-10; 2 Chr 36:19; Neh 1:3; Jer 52:12-14
4 [a]Neh 1:4
6 [a]Neh 13:6
7 [a]Ezra 7:21; 8:36
8 [1]Lit *house* [a]Eccl 2:5,6 [b]Neh 7:2 [c]Ezra 7:6; Neh 2:18
9 [a]Neh 2:7 [b]Ezra 8:22
10 [1]Lit *servant* [a]Neh 2:19; 4:1
11 [a]Ezra 8:32
12 [1]Lit *heart*
13 [1]Lit *Gate of Ash-heaps* [a]Neh 3:13 [b]Neh 1:3 [c]Neh 2:3,17
14 [1]Lit *the animal under me* [a]Neh 3:15 [b]2 Kin 20:20
15 [a]John 18:1
17 [a]Neh 1:3
18 [a]2 Sam 2:7
19 [1]Lit *servant* [a]Neh 6:6 [b]Neh 4:1
20 [a]Ezra 4:3 [b]Neh 2:4; Acts 8:21
3:1 [1]Lit *it* [a]Neh 3:20; 13:28 [b]Neh 3:32; 12:39 [c]Neh 6:1; 7:1 [d]Neh 12:39 [e]Jer 31:38
2 [1]Lit *him* [a]Neh 7:36
3 [a]Neh 12:39
4 [1]Lit *them*
5 [1]Lit *them* [2]Lit *bring their neck to*
6 [a]Neh 12:39
7 [1]Or *which was under the jurisdiction of the governor* of the province *beyond the River, also made repairs* [a]Neh 2:7
8 [a]Neh 3:31,32

perfumers, made repairs, and they restored Jerusalem as far as [b]the Broad
Wall.
9 Next to them Rephaiah the son of
Hur, [a]the official of half the district of
Jerusalem, made repairs.
10 Next to them Jedaiah the son of Ha-
rumaph made repairs opposite his house.
And next to him Hattush the son of Hashabneiah made repairs.
11 Malchijah the son of Harim and
Hasshub the son of Pahath-moab repaired
another section and [a]the Tower of Furnaces.
12 Next to him Shallum the son of Hallohesh, [a]the official of half the district
of Jerusalem, made repairs, he and his
daughters.
13 ¶ Hanun and the inhabitants of Zanoah repaired [a]the Valley Gate. They
built it and hung its doors with its bolts
and its bars, and a thousand cubits of the
wall to the [1]Refuse Gate.
14 ¶ Malchijah the son of Rechab, the
official of the district of [a]Beth-
haccherem repaired the [1b]Refuse Gate.
He built it and hung its doors with its
bolts and its bars.
15 ¶ Shallum the son of Col-hozeh,
the official of the district of Mizpah, [a]re-
paired the Fountain Gate. He built it, covered it and hung its doors with its bolts
and its bars, and the wall of the Pool of
Shelah at [b]the king's garden as far as
[c]the steps that descend from the city of
David.
16 After him Nehemiah the son of Azbuk, [a]official of half the district of Beth-
zur, made repairs as far as *a point* opposite the tombs of David, and as far as [b]the
artificial pool and the house of the mighty
men.
17 After him the Levites carried out
repairs *under* Rehum the son of Bani.
Next to him Hashabiah, the official of half
the district of Keilah, carried out repairs
for his district.
18 After him their brothers carried out
repairs *under* Bavvai the son of Henadad,
official of *the other* half of the district of
Keilah.
19 Next to him Ezer the son of Jeshua,
[a]the official of Mizpah, repaired [1]anoth-
er section in front of the ascent of the
armory [b]at the Angle.
20 After him Baruch the son of Zabbai
zealously repaired another section, from
the Angle to the doorway of the house of
[a]Eliashib the high priest.
21 After him Meremoth the son of Uriah the son of Hakkoz repaired another
section, from the doorway of Eliashib's
house even as far as the end of [1]his
house.
22 After him the priests, [a]the men of
the [1]valley, carried out repairs.
23 After [1]them Benjamin and Hasshub carried out repairs in front of their
house. After [1]them Azariah the son of
Maaseiah, son of Ananiah, carried out repairs beside his house.
24 After him Binnui the son of Henadad repaired another section, from the
house of Azariah as far as [a]the Angle and
as far as the corner.
25 Palal the son of Uzai *made repairs*
in front of the Angle and the tower projecting from the upper house of the king,
which is by [a]the court of the guard. After
him Pedaiah the son of Parosh *made repairs.*
26 [a]The temple servants living in
[b]Ophel *made repairs* as far as the front of
[c]the Water Gate toward the east and the
projecting tower.
27 After [1]them [a]the Tekoites repaired another section in front of the
great projecting tower and as far as the
wall of Ophel.
28 ¶ Above [a]the Horse Gate the
priests carried out repairs, each in front
of his house.
29 After [1]them Zadok the son of Immer carried out repairs in front of his
house. And after him Shemaiah the son of
Shecaniah, the keeper of the East Gate,
carried out repairs.
30 After him Hananiah the son of Shelemiah, and Hanun the sixth son of Za-
laph, repaired another section. After him
Meshullam the son of Berechiah carried
out repairs in front of his own [1]quarters.
31 After him Malchijah, [1]one of [a]the
goldsmiths, carried out repairs as far as
the house of the temple servants and of
the merchants, in front of the [2]Inspec-
tion Gate and as far as the upper room of
the corner.
32 Between the upper room of the corner and [a]the Sheep Gate the goldsmiths
and the merchants carried out repairs.

Work Is Ridiculed

4 [1]Now it came about that when
[a]Sanballat heard that we were rebuilding the wall, he became furious and
very angry and mocked the Jews.
2 He spoke in the presence of his
brothers and [a]the [1]wealthy *men* of Samaria and said, "What are these feeble
Jews doing? Are they going to restore *it*
for themselves? Can they offer sacrifices?
Can they finish in a day? Can they revive
the stones from the [2b]dusty rubble even
the burned ones?"
3 Now Tobiah the Ammonite *was*
near him and he said, "Even what they
are building—[a]if a fox should [1]jump on

8 [b]Neh 12:38
9 [a]Neh 3:12,17
11 [a]Neh 12:38
12 [a]Neh 3:9
13 [1]Lit *Gate of Ash-heaps* [a]Neh 2:13
14 [1]Lit *Gate of Ash-heaps* [a]Jer 6:1 [b]Neh 2:13
15 [a]Neh 2:17 [b]2 Kin 25:4 [c]Neh 12:37
16 [a]Neh 3:9,12, 17 [b]2 Kin 20:20; Is 7:3
19 [1]Lit *a second measure,* and so in vv 20, 21, 24, 30 [a]Neh 3:15 [b]2 Chr 26:9
20 [a]Neh 3:1
21 [1]Lit *Eliashib's*
22 [1]Lit *circle;* i.e. lower Jordan valley [a]Neh 12:28
23 [1]Lit *him*
24 [a]Neh 3:19
25 [a]Jer 32:2
26 [a]Neh 7:46 [b]Neh 11:21 [c]Neh 8:1
27 [1]Lit *him* [a]Neh 3:5
28 [a]2 Kin 11:16; 2 Chr 23:15; Jer 31:40
29 [1]Lit *him*
30 [1]Or *cell*
31 [1]Lit *son of* [2]Or *Mustering* [a]Neh 3:8,32
32 [a]Neh 3:1; 12:39
4:1 [1]Ch 3:33 in Heb [a]Neh 2:10
2 [1]Or *army* [2]Lit *heaps of dust* [a]Ezra 4:9,10 [b]Neh 4:10
3 [1]Lit *go up* [a]Lam 5:18

it, he would break their stone wall down!"

4 ¶ [a]Hear, O our God, how we are despised! [b]Return their reproach on their own heads and give them up for plunder in a land of captivity.

5 Do not [1a]forgive their iniquity and let not their sin be blotted out before You, for they have [2]demoralized the builders.

6 ¶ So we built the wall and the whole wall was joined together to half its *height,* for the people had a [1]mind to work.

7 ¶ [1]Now when Sanballat, Tobiah, the Arabs, the Ammonites and the Ashdodites heard that the [2]repair of the walls of Jerusalem went on, *and* that the breaches began to be closed, they were very angry.

8 All of them [a]conspired together to come *and* fight against Jerusalem and to cause a disturbance in it.

Discouragement Overcome

9 But we prayed to our God, and because of them we [a]set up a guard against them day and night.

10 ¶ Thus [1]in Judah it was said,
"The strength of the burden
bearers is failing,
Yet there is much [2]rubbish;
And we ourselves are unable
To rebuild the wall."

11 Our enemies said, "They will not know or see until we come among them, kill them and put a stop to the work."

12 When the Jews who lived near them came and told us ten times, "[1]They will come up against us from every place where you may turn,"

13 then I stationed *men* in the lowest parts of the space behind the wall, the [1]exposed places, and I [a]stationed the people in families with their swords, spears and bows.

14 When I saw *their fear,* I rose and spoke to the nobles, the officials and the rest of the people: "[a]Do not be afraid of them; remember the Lord who is great and awesome, and [b]fight for your brothers, your sons, your daughters, your wives and your houses."

15 ¶ When our enemies heard that it was known to us, and that [a]God had frustrated their plan, then all of us returned to the wall, each one to his work.

16 From that day on, half of my servants carried on the work while half of them held the spears, the shields, the bows and the breastplates; and the captains *were* behind the whole house of Judah.

17 Those who were rebuilding the wall and those who carried burdens took *their* load with one hand doing the work and the other holding a weapon.

18 As for the builders, each *wore* his sword girded at his side as he built, while [1]the trumpeter *stood* near me.

19 I said to the nobles, the officials and the rest of the people, "The work is great and extensive, and we are separated on the wall far from one another.

20 "At whatever place you hear the sound of the trumpet, [1]rally to us there. [a]Our God will fight for us."

21 ¶ So we carried on the work with half of them holding spears from [1]dawn until the stars [2]appeared.

22 At that time I also said to the people, "Let each man with his servant spend the night within Jerusalem so that they may be a guard for us by night and a laborer by day."

23 So neither I, my brothers, my servants, nor the men of the guard who followed me, none of us removed our clothes, each *took* his weapon *even to* the water.

Usury Abolished

5 Now [a]there was a great outcry of the people and of their wives against their [b]Jewish brothers.

2 For there were those who said, "We, our sons and our daughters are many; therefore let us [a]get grain that we may eat and live."

3 There were others who said, "We are mortgaging our fields, our vineyards and our houses that we might get grain because of the famine."

4 Also there were those who said, "We have borrowed money [a]for the king's tax *on* our fields and our vineyards.

5 "Now [a]our flesh is like the flesh of our brothers, our children like their children. Yet behold, [b]we are forcing our sons and our daughters to be slaves, and some of our daughters are forced into bondage *already,* and [1]we are helpless because our fields and vineyards belong to others."

6 ¶ Then I was very [a]angry when I had heard their outcry and these words.

7 I consulted with myself and contended with the nobles and the rulers and said to them, "[a]You are exacting usury, each from his brother!" Therefore, I held a great assembly against them.

8 I said to them, "We according to our ability [a]have [1]redeemed our Jewish brothers who were sold to the nations; now would you even sell your brothers that they may be sold to us?" Then they were silent and could not find a word *to say.*

9 Again I said, "The thing which you

4 [a]Ps 123:3,4 [b]Ps 79:12
5 [1]Lit *cover* [2]Lit *offended against* [a]Ps 69:27,28; Jer 18:23
6 [1]Lit *heart*
7 [1]Ch 4:1 in Heb [2]Lit *healing*
8 [a]Ps 83:3
9 [a]Neh 4:11
10 [1]Lit *Judah said* [2]Lit *dust*
12 [1]So Gr; Heb omits *they...up*
13 [1]Lit *bare* [a]Neh 4:17,18
14 [a]Num 14:9; Deut 1:29,30 [b]2 Sam 10:12
15 [a]2 Sam 17:14
18 [1]Lit *he who sounded the trumpet*
20 [1]Lit *assemble yourselves* [a]Ex 14:14; Deut 1:30
21 [1]Lit *rising of the dawn* [2]Lit *came out*
5:1 [a]Lev 25:35 [b]Deut 15:7
2 [a]Hag 1:6
4 [a]Ezra 4:13; 7:24
5 [1]Lit *there is not the power in our hands* [a]Gen 37:27 [b]Lev 25:39
6 [a]Ex 11:8
7 [a]Ex 22:25; Lev 25:36; Deut 23:19,20
8 [1]Lit *bought* [a]Lev 25:48

are doing is not good; should you not
walk in the fear of our God because of
[a]the reproach of the nations, our enemies?
10 "And likewise I, my brothers and my
servants are lending them money and
grain. Please, let us leave off this usury.
11 "Please, give back to them this very
day their fields, their vineyards, their olive groves and their houses, also the hundredth *part* of the money and of the grain,
the new wine and the oil that you are
exacting from them."
12 Then they said, "We [a]will give *it*
back and [b]will require nothing from
them; we will do exactly as you say." So
I called the priests and [c]took an oath
from them that they would do according
to this [1]promise.
13 I [a]also shook out the [1]front of my
garment and said, "Thus may God shake
out every man from his house and from
his possessions who does not fulfill this
[2]promise; even thus may he be shaken
out and emptied." And [b]all the assembly
said, "Amen!" And they praised the
LORD. Then the people did according to
this [2]promise.

Nehemiah's Example

14 ¶ Moreover, from the day that I
was appointed to be their governor in the
land of Judah, from [a]the twentieth year
to the [b]thirty-second year of King Artaxerxes, *for* twelve years, neither I nor my
[1]kinsmen have eaten the governor's food
allowance.
15 But the former governors who were
before me [1]laid burdens on the people
and took from them bread and wine besides forty shekels of silver; even their
servants domineered the people. But I
did not do so [a]because of the fear of God.
16 I also [1]applied myself to the work
on this wall; we did not buy any land, and
all my servants were gathered there for
the work.
17 Moreover, [a]*there were* at my table
one hundred and fifty Jews and officials,
besides those who came to us from the
nations that were around us.
18 Now [a]that which was prepared for
each day was one ox *and* six choice
sheep, also birds were prepared for me;
and once in ten days all sorts of wine
were furnished in abundance. Yet for all
this [b]I did not demand the governor's
food *allowance,* because the servitude
was heavy on this people.
19 [a]Remember me, O my God, for
good, *according to* all that I have done for
this people.

The Enemy's Plot

6 Now when it was reported to Sanballat, Tobiah, to Geshem the Arab and
to the rest of our enemies that I had rebuilt the wall, and *that* no breach remained in it, [a]although at that time I had
not set up the doors in the gates,
2 then Sanballat and Geshem sent *a*
message to me, saying, "Come, let us
meet together at [1]Chephirim in the plain
of [a]Ono." But they were planning to
[2]harm me.
3 So I sent messengers to them, saying, "I am doing a great work and I cannot
come down. Why should the work stop
while I leave it and come down to you?"
4 They sent *messages* to me four
times in this manner, and I answered
them in the same way.
5 Then Sanballat sent his servant to
me in the same manner a fifth time with
an open letter in his hand.
6 In it was written, "It is reported
among the nations, and [1]Gashmu says,
that [a]you and the Jews are planning to
rebel; therefore you are rebuilding the
wall. And you are to be their king, according to these reports.
7 "You have also appointed prophets
to proclaim in Jerusalem concerning
[1]you, 'A king is in Judah!' And now it
will be reported to the king according to
these reports. So come now, let us take
counsel together."
8 Then I sent *a message* to him saying, "Such things as you are saying have
not been done, but you are [a]inventing
them [1]in your own mind."
9 For all of them were *trying* to fright-
en us, [1]thinking, "[2]They will become
discouraged with the work and it will not
be done." But now, [a]*O God,* strengthen
my hands.
10 ¶ When I entered the house of Shemaiah the son of Delaiah, son of Mehetabel, [a]who was [1]confined at home, he
said, "Let us meet together in the house
of God, within the temple, and let us
close the doors of the temple, for they are
coming to kill you, and they are coming
to kill you at night."
11 But I said, "[a]Should a man like me
flee? And could one such as I go into the
temple [1]to save his life? I will not go in."
12 Then I perceived [1]that surely God
had not sent him, but he uttered *his*
prophecy against me because Tobiah and
Sanballat had hired him.
13 He was hired for this reason, [a]that
I might become frightened and act accordingly and sin, so that they might have
an evil report in order that they could
reproach me.

9 [a]Neh 4:4
12 [1]Lit *word* [a]2 Chr 28:15 [b]Neh 10:31 [c]Ezra 10:5
13 [1]Lit *bosom* [2]Lit *word* [a]Acts 18:6 [b]Neh 8:6
14 [1]Lit *brothers* [a]Neh 1:1 [b]Neh 13:6
15 [1]Lit *made heavy* [a]Neh 5:9; Job 31:23
16 [1]Or *held fast*
17 [a]1 Kin 18:19
18 [a]1 Kin 4:22, 23 [b]2 Thess 3:8
19 [a]Neh 13:14, 22,31
6:1 [a]Neh 3:1,3
2 [1]Another reading is, one of *the villages* [2]Lit *do evil to me* [a]1 Chr 8:12
6 [1]In v 1 and elsewhere, *Geshem* [a]Neh 2:19
7 [1]Lit *you, saying*
8 [1]Lit *from your heart* [a]Job 13:4; Ps 52:2
9 [1]Lit *saying,* [2]Lit *Their hands will drop from* [a]Ps 138:3
10 [1]Lit *shut up* [a]Jer 36:5
11 [1]Lit *and live* [a]Prov 28:1
12 [1]Lit *and behold God*
13 [a]Neh 6:6

14 [a]Remember, O my God, Tobiah
and Sanballat according to these works of
theirs, and also Noadiah [b]the prophetess
and the rest of the prophets who were
trying to frighten me.

The Wall Is Finished

15 ¶ So [a]the wall was completed on
the twenty-fifth of *the month* Elul, in
fifty-two days.
16 [a]When all our enemies heard *of it,*
and all the nations surrounding us saw *it,*
they [1]lost their confidence; for [b]they
recognized that this work had been accomplished [2]with the help of our God.
17 Also in those days many letters
went from the nobles of Judah to Tobiah,
and Tobiah's *letters* came to them.
18 For many in Judah were bound by
oath to him because he was the son-in-
law of Shecaniah the son of Arah, and his
son Jehohanan had married the daughter
of Meshullam the son of Berechiah.
19 Moreover, they were speaking
about his good deeds in my presence and
reported my words to him. Then Tobiah
sent letters to frighten me.

Census of First Returned Exiles

7 Now when [a]the wall was rebuilt and
I had set up the doors, and the gatekeepers and the singers and the Levites
were appointed,
2 then I put [a]Hanani my brother,
and [b]Hananiah the commander of [c]the
fortress, in charge of Jerusalem, for he
was [d]a faithful man and feared God more
than many.
3 Then I said to them, "Do not let the
gates of Jerusalem be opened until the
sun is hot, and while they are standing
guard, let them shut and bolt the doors.
Also appoint guards from the inhabitants
of Jerusalem, each at his post, and each in
front of his own house."
4 Now the city was large and spacious, but the people in it were few and
the houses were not built.
5 ¶ [a]Then my God put it into my
heart to assemble the nobles, the officials
and the people to be enrolled by genealogies. Then I found the book of the genealogy of those who came up first [1]in which
I found the following record:
6 ¶ [a]These are the [1]people of the
province who came up from the captivity
of the exiles whom Nebuchadnezzar the
king of Babylon had carried away, and
who returned to Jerusalem and Judah,
each to his city,
7 who came with Zerubbabel, Jeshua, Nehemiah, [1]Azariah, [2]Raamiah, Na-
hamani, Mordecai, Bilshan, [3]Mispereth,
Bigvai, [4]Nehum, Baanah.

¶ The number of men of the people of
Israel:
8 the sons of Parosh, 2,172;
9 the sons of Shephatiah, 372;
10 the sons of Arah, 652;
11 the sons of Pahath-moab of the sons
of Jeshua and Joab, 2,818;
12 the sons of Elam, 1,254;
13 the sons of Zattu, 845;
14 the sons of Zaccai, 760;
15 the sons of [1]Binnui, 648;
16 the sons of Bebai, 628;
17 the sons of Azgad, 2,322;
18 the sons of Adonikam, 667;
19 the sons of Bigvai, 2,067;
20 the sons of Adin, 655;
21 the sons of Ater, of Hezekiah, 98;
22 the sons of Hashum, 328;
23 the sons of Bezai, 324;
24 the sons of [1]Hariph, 112;
25 the sons of [1]Gibeon, 95;
26 the men of Bethlehem and Netophah, 188;
27 the men of Anathoth, 128;
28 the men of [1]Beth-azmaveth, 42;
29 the men of [1]Kiriath-jearim, Chephirah and Beeroth, 743;
30 the men of Ramah and Geba, 621;
31 the men of Michmas, 122;
32 the men of Bethel and Ai, 123;
33 the men of the other Nebo, 52;
34 the sons of the other Elam, 1,254;
35 the sons of Harim, 320;
36 the [1]men of Jericho, 345;
37 the sons of Lod, Hadid and
Ono, 721;
38 the sons of Senaah, 3,930.
39 ¶ The priests: the sons of Jedaiah of
the house of Jeshua, 973;
40 the sons of Immer, 1,052;
41 the sons of Pashhur, 1,247;
42 the sons of Harim, 1,017.
43 ¶ The Levites: the sons of Jeshua, of
Kadmiel, of the sons of [1]Hodevah, 74.
44 The singers: the sons of
Asaph, 148.
45 The gatekeepers: the sons of Shallum, the sons of Ater, the sons of Talmon,
the sons of Akkub, the sons of Hatita, the
sons of Shobai, 138.
46 ¶ The temple servants: the sons of
Ziha, the sons of Hasupha, the sons of
Tabbaoth,
47 the sons of Keros, the sons of [1]Sia,
the sons of Padon,
48 the sons of Lebana, the sons of Hag-
aba, the sons of Shalmai,
49 the sons of Hanan, the sons of Giddel, the sons of Gahar,
50 the sons of Reaiah, the sons of Rezin, the sons of Nekoda,
51 the sons of Gazzam, the sons of
Uzza, the sons of Paseah,

14 [a]Neh 13:29 [b]Ezek 13:17 [2]Lit

15 [a]Neh 4:1,2

16 [1]Lit *fell exceedingly in their own eyes* [2]Lit *from our God* [a]Neh 2:10; 4:1,7 [b]Ex 14:25

7:1 [a]Neh 6:1,15

2 [a]Neh 1:2 [b]Neh 10:23 [c]Neh 2:8 [d]Neh 13:13

5 [1]Lit *and I found written in it* [a]Prov 2:6; 3:6

6 [1]Lit *sons* [a]Ezra 2:1-70

7 [1]In Ezra 2:2, *Seraiah* [2]In Ezra 2:2, *Reelaiah* [3]In Ezra 2:2, *Mispar* [4]In Ezra 2:2, *Rehum*

15 [1]In Ezra 2:10, *Bani*

24 [1]In Ezra 2:18, *Jorah*

25 [1]In Ezra 2:20, *Gibbar*

28 [1]In Ezra 2:24, *Azmaveth*

29 [1]In Ezra 2:25, *Kiriath-arim*

36 [1]Lit *sons*

43 [1]In Ezra 2:40, *Hodaviah*

47 [1]In Ezra 2:44, *Siaha*

52 the sons of Besai, the sons of Meunim, the sons of [1]Nephushesim,
53 the sons of Bakbuk, the sons of Hakupha, the sons of Harhur,
54 the sons of [1]Bazlith, the sons of
Mehida, the sons of Harsha,
55 the sons of Barkos, the sons of Sisera, the sons of Temah,
56 the sons of Neziah, the sons of Hatipha.
57 ¶ The sons of Solomon's servants:
the sons of Sotai, the sons of [1]Sophereth,
the sons of [2]Perida,
58 the sons of Jaala, the sons of Darkon, the sons of Giddel,
59 the sons of Shephatiah, the sons of
Hattil, the sons of Pochereth-hazzebaim,
the sons of [1]Amon.
60 ¶ All the temple servants and the
sons of Solomon's servants *were* 392.
61 ¶ These *were* they who came up
from Tel-melah, Tel-harsha, Cherub,
[1]Addon and Immer; but they could not
show their fathers' houses or their
[2]descendants, whether they were of Israel:
62 the sons of Delaiah, the sons of Tobiah, the sons of Nekoda, 642.
63 Of the priests: the sons of [1]Hoba-
iah, the sons of Hakkoz, the sons of Barzillai, who took a wife of the daughters of
Barzillai, the Gileadite, and was named
after them.
64 These searched *among* their ancestral registration, but it could not be located; therefore they were considered unclean *and excluded* from the priesthood.
65 [a]The [1]governor said to them that
they should not eat from the most holy
things until a priest arose with [b]Urim
and Thummim.

Total of People and Gifts

66 ¶ The whole assembly together *was*
42,360,
67 besides their male and their female
servants, [1]of whom *there were* 7,337;
and they had 245 male and female singers.
68 [1a]Their horses were 736; their
mules, 245;
69 *their* camels, 435; *their* donkeys,
6,720.
70 ¶ Some from among the heads of
fathers' *households* gave to the work.
The [1a]governor gave to the treasury
1,000 gold drachmas, 50 basins, 530
priests' garments.
71 Some of the heads of fathers'
households gave into the treasury of the
work 20,000 gold drachmas and 2,200
silver minas.
72 That which the rest of the people
gave was 20,000 gold drachmas and
2,000 silver minas and 67 priests' garments.
73 ¶ Now [a]the priests, the Levites,
the gatekeepers, the singers, some of the
people, the temple servants and all Israel,
lived in their cities.
¶ [b]And when the seventh month
came, the sons of Israel *were* in their cities.

Ezra Reads the Law

8 And all the people gathered as one
man at the square which was in front
of [a]the Water Gate, and they [1]asked
[b]Ezra the scribe to bring [c]the book of
the law of Moses which the LORD had
[2]given to Israel.
2 Then [a]Ezra the priest brought the
law before the assembly of men, women
and all who *could* listen with understanding, on [b]the first day of the seventh
month.
3 He read from it before the square
which was in front of [a]the Water Gate
from [1]early morning until midday, in the
presence of men and women, those who
could understand; and all the people
were attentive to the book of the law.
4 Ezra the scribe stood at a wooden
podium which they had made for the purpose. And beside him stood Mattithiah,
Shema, Anaiah, Uriah, Hilkiah, and Maaseiah on his right hand; and Pedaiah,
Mishael, Malchijah, Hashum, Hashbad-
danah, Zechariah *and* Meshullam on his
left hand.
5 Ezra opened [a]the book in the sight
of all the people for he was standing
above all the people; and when he
opened it, all the people [b]stood up.
6 Then Ezra blessed the LORD the
great God. And all the people answered,
"[a]Amen, Amen!" while lifting up their
hands; then [b]they bowed low and worshiped the LORD with *their* faces to the
ground.
7 Also Jeshua, Bani, Sherebiah, Jamin, Akkub, Shabbethai, Hodiah, Maaseiah, Kelita, Azariah, Jozabad, Hanan, Pelaiah, the Levites, explained the law to
the people while the people *remained* in
their place.
8 They read from the book, from the
law of God, [1]translating to give the sense
so that they understood the reading.

"This Day Is Holy"

9 ¶ Then Nehemiah, who was the
[1a]governor, and Ezra [b]the priest *and*
scribe, and the Levites who taught the
people said to all the people, "[c]This day
is holy to the LORD your God; [d]do not
mourn or weep." For all the people were

52 [1]In Ezra 2:50, *Nephisim*
54 [1]In Ezra 2:52, *Bazluth*
57 [1]In Ezra 2:55, *Hassophereth* [2]In Ezra 2:55, *Peruda*
59 [1]In Ezra 2:57, *Ami*
61 [1]In Ezra 2:59, *Addan* [2]Lit *seed*
63 [1]In Ezra 2:61, *Habaiah*
65 [1]Heb *Tirshatha,* a Persian title [a]Neh 8:9; 10:1 [b]Ex 28:30; Deut 33:8
67 [1]Lit *these*
68 [1]So with some ancient mss and Gr [a]Ezra 2:66
70 [1]Heb *Tirshatha,* a Persian title [a]Neh 7:65; 8:9
73 [a]1 Chr 9:2 [b]Ezra 3:1
8:1 [1]Lit *said to* [2]Lit *commanded* [a]Neh 3:26 [b]Ezra 7:6 [c]2 Chr 34:15
2 [a]Deut 31:9-11; Neh 8:9 [b]Lev 23:24
3 [1]Lit *the light* [a]Neh 8:1
5 [a]Neh 8:3 [b]Judg 3:20; 1 Kin 8:12-14
6 [a]Neh 5:13 [b]Ex 4:31
8 [1]Or *explaining*
9 [1]Heb *Tirshatha,* a Persian title [a]Neh 7:65,70 [b]Neh 12:26 [c]Neh 8:2 [d]Deut 12:7,12

weeping when they heard the words of the law.

10 Then he said to them, "Go, eat of the fat, drink of the sweet, and [a]send portions to him who has nothing prepared; for this day is holy to our Lord. Do not be grieved, for the joy of the LORD is your strength."

11 So the Levites calmed all the people, saying, "Be still, for the day is holy; do not be grieved."

12 All the people went away to eat, to drink, [a]to send portions and to [1]celebrate a great festival, [b]because they understood the words which had been made known to them.

Feast of Booths Restored

13 ¶ Then on the second day the heads of fathers' *households* of all the people, the priests and the Levites were gathered to Ezra the scribe that they might gain insight into the words of the law.

14 They found written in the law how the LORD had commanded through Moses that the sons of Israel [a]should live in booths during the feast of the seventh month.

15 [1a]So they proclaimed and circulated a proclamation in all their cities and [b]in Jerusalem, saying, "[c]Go out to the hills, and bring olive branches and [2]wild olive branches, myrtle branches, palm branches and branches of *other* leafy trees, to make booths, as it is written."

16 So the people went out and brought *them* and made booths for themselves, each [a]on his roof, and in their courts and in the courts of the house of God, and in the square at [b]the Water Gate and in the square at [c]the Gate of Ephraim.

17 The entire assembly of those who had returned from the captivity made booths and lived in [1]them. The sons of Israel [a]had indeed not done so from the days of Joshua the son of Nun to that day. And [b]there was great rejoicing.

18 [a]He read from the book of the law of God daily, from the first day to the last day. And they [b]celebrated the feast seven days, and on [c]the eighth day *there was* a solemn assembly according to the ordinance.

The People Confess Their Sin

9 Now on the twenty-fourth day of [a]this month the sons of Israel assembled [b]with fasting, in sackcloth and with [c]dirt upon them.

2 The [1a]descendants of Israel separated themselves from all foreigners, and stood and [b]confessed their sins and the iniquities of their fathers.

3 While [a]they stood in their place, they read from the book of the law of the LORD their God for a fourth of the day; and for *another* fourth they confessed and worshiped the LORD their God.

4 [a]Now on the Levites' platform stood Jeshua, Bani, Kadmiel, Shebaniah, Bunni, Sherebiah, Bani *and* Chenani, and they cried with a loud voice to the LORD their God.

5 ¶ Then the Levites, Jeshua, Kadmiel, Bani, Hashabneiah, Sherebiah, Hodiah, Shebaniah *and* Pethahiah, said, "Arise, bless the LORD your God forever and ever!

O may Your glorious name be
blessed
And exalted above all blessing
and praise!

6 "[a]You alone are the LORD.
[b]You have made the heavens,
The heaven of heavens with all
their host,
The earth and all that is on it,
The seas and all that is in them.
[c]You give life to all of them
And the heavenly host bows
down before You.

7 "You are the LORD God,
[a]Who chose Abram
And brought him out from [b]Ur
of the Chaldees,
And [c]gave him the name
Abraham.

8 "You found [a]his heart faithful
before You,
And made a covenant with him
To give *him* the land of the
Canaanite,
Of the Hittite and the Amorite,
Of the Perizzite, the Jebusite and
the Girgashite—
To give *it* to his [1]descendants.
And You [b]have fulfilled Your
promise,
For You are righteous.

9 ¶ "[a]You saw the affliction of our
fathers in Egypt,
And [b]heard their cry by the
[1]Red Sea.

10 "Then You performed [a]signs and
wonders against Pharaoh,
Against all his servants and all
the people of his land;
For You knew that [b]they acted
arrogantly toward them,
And [c]made a name for Yourself
as *it is* this day.

11 "[a]You divided the sea before
them,
So they passed through the midst
of the sea on dry ground;

---

10 [a]Deut 26:11-13

12 [1]Lit *make a great rejoicing* [a]Neh 8:10 [b]Neh 8:7,8

14 [a]Lev 23:34, 40,42

15 [1]Lit *And that they will cause to be heard* [2]Lit *oil tree,* species unknown [a]Lev 23:4 [b]Deut 16:16 [c]Lev 23:40

16 [a]Jer 32:29 [b]Neh 8:1 [c]2 Kin 14:13; Neh 12:39

17 [1]Lit *the booths* [a]2 Chr 7:8; 8:13 [b]2 Chr 30:21

18 [a]Deut 31:11 [b]Lev 23:36 [c]Num 29:35

9:1 [a]Neh 8:2 [b]Ezra 8:23 [c]1 Sam 4:12

2 [1]Lit *seed* [a]Ezra 10:11; Neh 13:3 [b]Prov 28:13; Jer 3:13

3 [a]Neh 8:4

4 [a]Neh 8:7

6 [a]Deut 6:4; 2 Kin 19:15 [b]Gen 1:1 [c]Col 1:16f

7 [a]Gen 12:1 [b]Gen 11:31 [c]Gen 17:5

8 [1]Lit *seed* [a]Gen 15:6,18-21 [b]Josh 21:43-45

9 [1]Lit *Sea of Reeds* [a]Ex 3:7 [b]Ex 14:10-14,31

10 [a]Ex 7:8-12:32 [b]Ex 5:2 [c]Ex 9:16

11 [a]Ex 14:21

And [b]their pursuers You hurled
into the depths,
Like a stone into [1]raging waters.
12 "And with a pillar of cloud [a]You
led them by day,
And with a pillar of fire by night
To light for them the way
In which they were to go.
13 "Then [a]You came down on
Mount Sinai,
And [b]spoke with them from
heaven;
You gave them [c]just ordinances
and true laws,
Good statutes and
commandments.
14 "So You made known to them
[a]Your holy sabbath,
And laid down for them
commandments, statutes and
law,
Through Your servant Moses.
15 "You [a]provided bread from
heaven for them for their
hunger,
You [b]brought forth water from a
rock for them for their
thirst,
And You [c]told them to enter in
order to possess
The land which You [1]swore to
give them.

16 ¶ "But they, our fathers, [a]acted
arrogantly;
They [1b]became stubborn and
would not listen to Your
commandments.
17 "They refused to listen,
And [a]did not remember Your
wondrous deeds which You
had performed among them;
So they became stubborn and
[b]appointed a leader to
return to their slavery [1]in
Egypt.
But You are a God [c]of
forgiveness,
Gracious and compassionate,
Slow to anger and abounding in
lovingkindness;
And You did not forsake them.
18 "Even when they [a]made for
themselves
A calf of molten metal
And said, 'This is your God
Who brought you up from
Egypt,'
And committed great
[1]blasphemies,
19 [a]You, in Your great compassion,
Did not forsake them in the
wilderness;
[b]The pillar of cloud did not
leave them by day,
To guide them on their way,
Nor the pillar of fire by night, to
light for them the way in
which they were to go.
20 "[a]You gave Your good Spirit to
instruct them,
Your manna You did not
withhold from their mouth,
And You gave them water for
their thirst.
21 "Indeed, [a]forty years You
provided for them in the
wilderness *and* they were
not in want;
Their clothes did not wear out,
nor did their feet swell.
22 "You also gave them kingdoms
and peoples,
And allotted *them* to them as a
[1]boundary.
[a]They took possession of the
land of Sihon [2]the king of
Heshbon
And the land of Og the king of
Bashan.
23 "You made their sons numerous
as [a]the stars of heaven,
And You brought them into the
land
Which You had told their fathers
to enter and possess.
24 "[a]So their sons entered and
possessed the land.
And [b]You subdued before them
the inhabitants of the land,
the Canaanites,
And You gave them into their
hand, with their kings and
the peoples of the land,
To do with them [1]as they
desired.
25 "[a]They captured fortified cities
and a [1b]fertile land.
They took possession of [c]houses
full of every good thing,
Hewn cisterns, vineyards, olive
groves,
Fruit trees in abundance.
So they ate, were filled and
[d]grew fat,
And [e]reveled in Your great
goodness.

26 ¶ "[a]But they became disobedient
and rebelled against You,
And [b]cast Your law behind their
backs
And [c]killed Your prophets who
had [d]admonished them
So that they might return to You,
And [e]they committed great
[1]blasphemies.

---

11 [1]Lit *strong, mighty* [b]Ex 15:1, 5,10
12 [a]Ex 13:21,22
13 [a]Ex 19:11, 18-20 [b]Ex 20:1 [c]Ps 19:7-9
14 [a]Ex 16:23; 20:8
15 [1]Lit *lifted up Your hand* [a]Ex 16:4,14,15 [b]Ex 17:6; Num 20:7-13 [c]Deut 1:8,21
16 [1]Lit *stiffened their neck*; so also v 17 [a]Neh 9:10 [b]Deut 1:26-33; 31:27; Neh 9:29
17 [1]So Gr and some Heb mss; Heb reads *in their rebellion* [a]Ps 78:11,42-55 [b]Num 14:4 [c]Ex 34:6,7; Num 14:18
18 [1]Lit *acts of contempt* [a]Ex 32:4-8,31
19 [a]Deut 8:2-4; Neh 9:27,31 [b]Neh 9:12
20 [a]Num 11:17; Neh 9:30; Is 63:11-14
21 [a]Deut 2:7
22 [1]Lit *side, corner* [2]So the Gr and the Latin; Heb reads *and the land of the king of Heshbon* [a]Num 21:21-35
23 [a]Gen 15:5; 22:17
24 [1]Lit *according to their desire* [a]Josh 11:23; 21:43 [b]Josh 18:1
25 [1]Lit *fat* [a]Deut 3:5 [b]Num 13:27 [c]Deut 6:11 [d]Deut 32:15 [e]1 Kin 8:66
26 [1]Lit *acts of contempt* [a]Judg 2:11 [b]1 Kin 14:9 [c]2 Chr 36:16 [d]Neh 9:30 [e]Neh 9:18

27 "Therefore You [a]delivered them
into the hand of their
oppressors who oppressed
them,
But when they cried to You [b]in
the time of their distress,
You heard from heaven, and
according to Your great
compassion
You [c]gave them deliverers who
delivered them from the
hand of their oppressors.
28 "But [a]as soon as they had rest,
they did evil again
before You;
Therefore You abandoned them
to the hand of their
enemies, so that they ruled
over them.
When they cried again to You,
You heard from heaven,
And [b]many times You rescued
them according to Your
compassion,
29 And [a]admonished them in order
to turn them back to Your
law.
Yet [b]they acted arrogantly and
did not listen to Your
commandments but sinned
against Your ordinances,
By [c]which if a man observes
them he shall live.
And they [1d]turned a stubborn
shoulder and stiffened their
neck, and would not listen.
30 "[a]However, You bore with them
for many years,
And [b]admonished them by
[c]Your Spirit through Your
prophets,
Yet they would not give ear.
Therefore You gave them into
the hand of the peoples of
the lands.
31 "Nevertheless, in Your great
compassion You [a]did not
make an end of them or
forsake them,
For You are [b]a gracious and
compassionate God.

32 ¶ "Now therefore, our God, [a]the
great, the mighty, and the
awesome God, who keeps
covenant and
lovingkindness,
Do not let all the hardship seem
insignificant before You,
Which has come upon us, our
kings, our princes, our
priests, our prophets, our
fathers and on all Your
people,

27 [a]Judg 2:14 [b]Deut 4:29 [c]Judg 2:16
28 [a]Judg 3:11 [b]Ps 106:43
29 [1]Lit *gave* [a]Neh 9:26,30 [b]Neh 9:10,16 [c]Lev 18:5 [d]Zech 7:11
30 [a]Ps 95:10; Acts 13:18 [b]2 Kin 17:13-18; 2 Chr 36:15,16; Neh 9:26,29 [c]Neh 9:20
31 [a]Jer 4:27 [b]Neh 9:17
32 [a]Neh 1:5 [b]2 Kin 15:19,29; 2 Kin 17:3-6; Ezra 4:2,10
33 [a]Gen 18:25; Jer 12:1
34 [1]Lit *testimonies* [2]Or *witnessed*
35 [a]Deut 28:47 [b]Neh 9:25
36 [a]Deut 28:48
37 [a]Deut 28:33
38 [1]Ch 10:1 in Heb [a]Neh 10:29 [b]Neh 10:1
10:1 [1]Ch 10:2 in Heb [2]Heb *Tirshatha,* a Persian title [a]Neh 9:38

[b]From the days of the kings of
Assyria to this day.
33 "However, [a]You are just in all
that has come upon us;
For You have dealt faithfully, but
we have acted wickedly.
34 "For our kings, our leaders, our
priests and our fathers have
not kept Your law
Or paid attention to Your
commandments and Your
[1]admonitions with which
You have [2]admonished
them.
35 "But [a]they, in their own
kingdom,
[b]With Your great goodness
which You gave them,
With the broad and rich land
which You set before them,
Did not serve You or turn from
their evil deeds.
36 "Behold, [a]we are slaves today,
And as to the land which You
gave to our fathers to eat of
its fruit and its bounty,
Behold, we are slaves in it.
37 "[a]Its abundant produce is for the
kings
Whom You have set over us
because of our sins;
They also rule over our bodies
And over our cattle as they
please,
So we are in great distress.

A Covenant Results

38 ¶ "[1]Now because of all this
[a]We are making an agreement
in writing;
And on the [b]sealed document
are the names of our
leaders, our Levites *and* our
priests."

Signers of the Document

10 [1]Now on the [a]sealed document
were the names of: Nehemiah the
[2]governor, the son of Hacaliah, and Zedekiah,
2 Seraiah, Azariah, Jeremiah,
3 Pashhur, Amariah, Malchijah,
4 Hattush, Shebaniah, Malluch,
5 Harim, Meremoth, Obadiah,
6 Daniel, Ginnethon, Baruch,
7 Meshullam, Abijah, Mijamin,
8 Maaziah, Bilgai, Shemaiah. These
were the priests.
9 And the Levites: Jeshua the son of
Azaniah, Binnui of the sons of Henadad,
Kadmiel;
10 also their brothers Shebaniah, Hodiah, Kelita, Pelaiah, Hanan,
11 Mica, Rehob, Hashabiah,

12 Zaccur, Sherebiah, Shebaniah,
13 Hodiah, Bani, Beninu.
14 The leaders of the people: Parosh,
Pahath-moab, Elam, Zattu, Bani,
15 Bunni, Azgad, Bebai,
16 Adonijah, Bigvai, Adin,
17 Ater, Hezekiah, Azzur,
18 Hodiah, Hashum, Bezai,
19 Hariph, Anathoth, Nebai,
20 Magpiash, Meshullam, Hezir,
21 Meshezabel, Zadok, Jaddua,
22 Pelatiah, Hanan, Anaiah,
23 Hoshea, Hananiah, Hasshub,
24 Hallohesh, Pilha, Shobek,
25 Rehum, Hashabnah, Maaseiah,
26 Ahiah, Hanan, Anan,
27 Malluch, Harim, Baanah.

Obligations of the Document

28 ¶ Now [a]the rest of the people, the
priests, the Levites, the gatekeepers, the
singers, the temple servants and [b]all
those who had separated themselves
from the peoples of the lands to the law
of God, their wives, their sons and their
daughters, all those who had knowledge
and understanding,
29 are joining with their [1]kinsmen,
their nobles, and are [2a]taking on themselves a curse and an oath to walk in
God's law, which was given through Moses, God's servant, and to keep and to
observe all the commandments of [3]GOD
our Lord, and His ordinances and His statutes;
30 and [a]that we will not give our
daughters to the peoples of the land or
take their daughters for our sons.
31 As [a]for the peoples of the land who
bring wares or any grain on the sabbath
day to sell, we will not buy from them on
the sabbath or a holy day; and we will
forego *the crops* the [b]seventh year and
the [c]exaction of every debt.
32 ¶ We also [1]placed ourselves under
obligation to contribute yearly [a]one third
of a shekel for the service of the house of
our God:
33 for the [a]showbread, for the continual grain offering, for the continual burnt
offering, the sabbaths, the new moon, for
the appointed times, for the holy things
and for the sin offerings to make atonement for Israel, and all the work of the
house of our God.
34 ¶ Likewise [a]we cast lots [b]for the
supply of wood *among* the priests, the
Levites and the people so that they might
bring it to the house of our God, according to our fathers' households, at fixed
times annually, to burn on the altar of the
LORD our God, as it is written in the law;
35 and that they might bring the first
fruits of our ground and [a]the first fruits
of all the fruit of every tree to the house
of the LORD annually,
36 and [a]bring to the house of our God
the firstborn of our sons and of our cattle,
and the firstborn of our herds and our
flocks as it is written in the law, for the
priests who are ministering in the house
of our God.
37 [a]We will also bring the first of our
[1]dough, our contributions, the fruit of
every tree, the new wine and the oil [b]to
the priests at the chambers of the house
of our God, and the [c]tithe of our ground
to the Levites, for the Levites are they
who receive the tithes in all the rural
towns.
38 [a]The priest, the son of Aaron, shall
be with the Levites when the Levites receive tithes, and the Levites shall bring
up the tenth of the tithes to the house of
our God, to the chambers of [b]the storehouse.
39 For the sons of Israel and the sons
of Levi shall bring the [a]contribution of
the grain, the new wine and the oil to the
chambers; there are the utensils of the
sanctuary, the priests who are ministering, the gatekeepers and the singers.
Thus [b]we will not [1]neglect the house of
our God.

Time Passes
Heads of Provinces

11 Now [a]the leaders of the people
lived in Jerusalem, but the rest of
the people [b]cast lots to bring one out of
ten to live in Jerusalem, [c]the holy city,
while nine-tenths *remained* in the *other*
cities.
2 And the people blessed all the men
who [a]volunteered to live in Jerusalem.
3 ¶ [a]Now these are the heads of the
provinces who lived in Jerusalem, but in
the cities of Judah [b]each lived on his own
property in their cities—the [1]Israelites,
the priests, the Levites, the [2c]temple
servants and the [3d]descendants of Solomon's servants.
4 Some of the sons of Judah and some
of the sons of Benjamin lived in Jerusalem. From the sons of Judah: Athaiah the
son of Uzziah, the son of Zechariah, the
son of Amariah, the son of Shephatiah,
the son of Mahalalel, of the sons of Perez;
5 and Maaseiah the son of Baruch,
the son of Col-hozeh, the son of Hazaiah,
the son of Adaiah, the son of Joiarib, the
son of Zechariah, the son of the Shilonite.
6 All the sons of Perez who lived in
Jerusalem were 468 able men.
7 ¶ Now these are the sons of Benjamin: Sallu the son of Meshullam, the son
of Joed, the son of Pedaiah, the son of

28 [a]Ezra 2:36-58 [b]Neh 9:2
29 [1]Lit *brothers* [2]Lit *entering into a* [3]Heb *YHWH,* usually rendered *LORD* [a]Neh 5:12
30 [a]Ex 34:16; Deut 7:3
31 [a]Neh 13:15-22 [b]Ex 23:10,11; Lev 25:1-7 [c]Deut 15:1,2
32 [1]Lit *imposed commandments on us* [a]Ex 30:11-16; Matt 17:24
33 [a]Lev 24:5,6; 2 Chr 2:4
34 [a]Neh 11:1 [b]Neh 13:31
35 [a]Ex 23:19; 34:26; Deut 26:2
36 [a]Ex 13:2
37 [1]Or *coarse meal* [a]Lev 23:17 [b]Neh 13:5,9 [c]Lev 27:30; Num 18:21
38 [a]Num 18:26 [b]Neh 13:12,13
39 [1]Lit *forsake* [a]Deut 12:6 [b]Neh 13:10,11
11:1 [a]Neh 7:4 [b]Neh 10:34 [c]Neh 11:18; Is 48:2
2 [a]Judg 5:9
3 [1]Lit *Israel* [2]Heb *Nethinim* [3]Lit *sons* [a]1 Chr 9:2-34 [b]Neh 7:73; 11:20 [c]Ezra 2:43 [d]Neh 7:57

Kolaiah, the son of Maaseiah, the son of Ithiel, the son of Jeshaiah;

8 and after him Gabbai *and* Sallai, 928.

9 Joel the son of Zichri was their overseer, and Judah the son of Hassenuah was second [1]in command of the city.

10 ¶ From the priests: Jedaiah the son of Joiarib, Jachin,

11 Seraiah the son of Hilkiah, the son of Meshullam, the son of Zadok, the son of Meraioth, the son of Ahitub, the leader of the house of God,

12 and their [1]kinsmen who performed the work of the [2]temple, 822; and Adaiah the son of Jeroham, the son of Pelaliah, the son of Amzi, the son of Zechariah, the son of Pashhur, the son of Malchijah,

13 and his kinsmen, heads of fathers' *households,* 242; and Amashsai the son of Azarel, the son of Ahzai, the son of Meshillemoth, the son of Immer,

14 and their brothers, valiant warriors, 128. And their overseer was Zabdiel, the son of [1]Haggedolim.

15 ¶ Now from the Levites: Shemaiah the son of Hasshub, the son of Azrikam, the son of Hashabiah, the son of Bunni;

16 and Shabbethai and Jozabad, from the [1]leaders of the Levites, who were [2]in charge of [a]the outside work of the house of God;

17 and Mattaniah the son of Mica, the son of [1]Zabdi, the son of Asaph, who was the [2]leader in beginning the thanksgiving at prayer, and Bakbukiah, the second among his brethren; and [3]Abda the son of [4]Shammua, the son of Galal, the son of Jeduthun.

18 All the Levites in [a]the holy city *were* 284.

19 ¶ Also the gatekeepers, Akkub, Talmon and their brethren who kept watch at the gates, *were* 172.

Outside Jerusalem

20 The rest of Israel, of the priests *and* of the Levites, *were* in all the cities of Judah, each [a]on his own inheritance.

21 But [a]the temple servants were living in Ophel, and Ziha and Gishpa were [1]in charge of the temple servants.

22 ¶ Now [a]the overseer of the Levites in Jerusalem was Uzzi the son of Bani, the son of Hashabiah, the son of Mattaniah, the son of Mica, from the sons of Asaph, who were the singers for the [1]service of the house of God.

23 [a]For *there was* a commandment from the king concerning them and a firm regulation for the song leaders [b]day by day.

24 Pethahiah the son of Meshezabel, of the sons [a]of Zerah the son of Judah, was the [b]king's [1]representative in all matters concerning the people.

25 ¶ Now as for the villages with their fields, some of the sons of Judah lived in [a]Kiriath-arba and its [1]towns, in [b]Dibon and its [1]towns, and in Jekabzeel and its villages,

26 and in Jeshua, in Moladah and Beth-pelet,

27 and in Hazar-shual, in Beersheba and its towns,

28 and in Ziklag, in Meconah and in its towns,

29 and in En-rimmon, in Zorah and in Jarmuth,

30 Zanoah, Adullam, and their villages, Lachish and its fields, Azekah and its towns. So they encamped from Beersheba as far as the valley of Hinnom.

31 The sons of Benjamin also *lived* from Geba *onward,* at Michmash and Aija, at Bethel and its towns,

32 at Anathoth, Nob, Ananiah,

33 Hazor, Ramah, Gittaim,

34 Hadid, Zeboim, Neballat,

35 Lod and Ono, the valley of craftsmen.

36 From the Levites, *some* divisions in Judah belonged to Benjamin.

Priests and Levites Who Returned to Jerusalem with Zerubbabel

12 Now these are [a]the priests and the Levites who came up with Zerubbabel the son of Shealtiel, and Jeshua: Seraiah, Jeremiah, Ezra,

2 Amariah, Malluch, Hattush,

3 Shecaniah, Rehum, Meremoth,

4 Iddo, Ginnethoi, Abijah,

5 Mijamin, Maadiah, Bilgah,

6 Shemaiah and Joiarib, Jedaiah,

7 Sallu, Amok, Hilkiah and Jedaiah. These were the heads of the priests and their [1]kinsmen in the days of Jeshua.

8 ¶ The Levites *were* Jeshua, Binnui, Kadmiel, Sherebiah, Judah, *and* Mattaniah *who was* [1]in charge of the songs of thanksgiving, he and his brothers.

9 Also Bakbukiah and Unni, their brothers, stood opposite them [a]in *their* service divisions.

10 Jeshua [1]became the father of Joiakim, and Joiakim [1]became the father of Eliashib, and Eliashib [1]became the father of Joiada,

11 and Joiada became the father of Jonathan, and Jonathan became the father of Jaddua.

12 ¶ Now in the days of Joiakim, the priests, the heads of fathers' *households* were: of Seraiah, Meraiah; of Jeremiah, Hananiah;

9 [1]Lit *over*

12 [1]Lit *brothers,* and so throughout the ch [2]Lit *house*

14 [1]Or *the great ones*

16 [1]Lit *heads* [2]Lit *over* [a]1 Chr 26:29

17 [1]In 1 Chr 9:15, *Zichri* [2]Lit *head* [3]In 1 Chr 9:16, *Obadiah* [4]In 1 Chr 9:16, *Shemaiah*

18 [a]Neh 11:1

20 [a]Neh 11:3

21 [1]Lit *over* [a]Neh 3:26

22 [1]Or *work* [a]Neh 11:9,14

23 [a]Ezra 6:8; 7:20 [b]Neh 12:47

24 [1]Lit *hand* [a]Gen 38:30 [b]1 Chr 18:17

25 [1]Lit *daughters,* and so throughout the ch [a]Josh 14:15 [b]Josh 13:9,17

12:1 [a]Ezra 2:1; 7:7

7 [1]Lit *brothers*

8 [1]Lit *over*

9 [a]Neh 12:24

10 [1]Lit *begot,* and so in vv 11, 12

13 of Ezra, Meshullam; of Amariah, Jehohanan;
14 of [1]Malluchi, Jonathan; of Shebaniah, Joseph;
15 of Harim, Adna; of Meraioth, Helkai;
16 of Iddo, Zechariah; of Ginnethon, Meshullam;
17 of Abijah, Zichri; of Miniamin, of Moadiah, Piltai;
18 of Bilgah, Shammua; of Shemaiah, Jehonathan;
19 of Joiarib, Mattenai; of Jedaiah, Uzzi;
20 of Sallai, Kallai; of Amok, Eber;
21 of Hilkiah, Hashabiah; of Jedaiah, Nethanel.

The Chief Levites

22 ¶ As for the Levites, the heads of
fathers' *households* were registered in
the days of Eliashib, Joiada, and Johanan
and Jaddua; so *were* the priests in the
reign of Darius the Persian.
23 The sons of Levi, the heads of fathers' *households,* were registered in the
Book of the Chronicles up to the days of
Johanan the son of Eliashib.
24 The heads of the Levites *were*
Hashabiah, Sherebiah and Jeshua the son
of Kadmiel, with their brothers opposite
them, [a]to praise *and* give thanks, [1]as
prescribed by David the man of God, [b]di-
vision corresponding to division.
25 Mattaniah, Bakbukiah, Obadiah,
Meshullam, Talmon *and* Akkub *were*
gatekeepers keeping watch at [a]the storehouses of the gates.
26 These *served* in the days of Joiakim
the son of Jeshua, the son of Jozadak, and
in the days of [a]Nehemiah the governor
and of Ezra the priest *and* scribe.

Dedication of the Wall

27 ¶ Now at the dedication of the wall
of Jerusalem they sought out the Levites
from all their places, to bring them to
Jerusalem so that they might celebrate
the dedication with gladness, with hymns
of thanksgiving and with songs [a]*to the*
accompaniment of cymbals, harps and
lyres.
28 So the sons of the singers were assembled from the district around Jerusalem, and from [a]the villages of the Netophathites,
29 from Beth-gilgal and from *their*
fields in Geba and Azmaveth, for the singers had built themselves villages around
Jerusalem.
30 The priests and the Levites [a]puri-
fied themselves; they also purified the
people, the gates and the wall.

Procedures for the Temple

31 ¶ Then I had the leaders of Judah
come up on top of the wall, and I appointed two great [1]choirs, [2a]the first proceeding to the right on top of the wall
toward [b]the Refuse Gate.
32 Hoshaiah and half of the leaders of
Judah followed them,
33 with Azariah, Ezra, Meshullam,
34 Judah, Benjamin, Shemaiah, Jeremiah,
35 and some of the sons of the priests
with trumpets; *and* Zechariah the son of
Jonathan, the son of Shemaiah, the son of
Mattaniah, the son of Micaiah, the son
of Zaccur, the son of Asaph,
36 and his [1]kinsmen, Shemaiah, Azarel, Milalai, Gilalai, Maai, Nethanel, Judah *and* Hanani, [a]with the musical instruments of David the man of God. And
Ezra the scribe went before them.
37 At [a]the Fountain Gate they went
directly up [b]the steps of the city of David
by the stairway of the wall above the
house of David to [c]the Water Gate on the
east.
38 ¶ [a]The second [1]choir proceeded
to the [2]left, while I followed them with
half of the people on the wall, [b]above the
Tower of Furnaces, to [c]the Broad Wall,
39 and above [a]the Gate of Ephraim,
by [b]the Old Gate, by the [c]Fish Gate,
[d]the Tower of Hananel and the Tower of
the Hundred, as far as the Sheep Gate;
and they stopped at [e]the Gate of the
Guard.
40 Then the two choirs took their
stand in the house of God. So did I and
half of the officials with me;
41 and the priests, Eliakim, Maaseiah,
Miniamin, Micaiah, Elioenai, Zechariah
and Hananiah, with the trumpets;
42 and Maaseiah, Shemaiah, Eleazar,
Uzzi, Jehohanan, Malchijah, Elam and
Ezer. And the singers [1]sang, with Jezra-
hiah *their* leader,
43 and on that day they offered great
sacrifices and rejoiced because [a]God had
given them great joy, even the women
and children rejoiced, so that the joy of
Jerusalem was heard from afar.
44 ¶ On that day [a]men were also appointed over the chambers for the stores,
the contributions, the first fruits and the
tithes, to gather into them from the fields
of the cities the portions required by the
law for the priests and Levites; for Judah
rejoiced over the priests and Levites who
[1]served.
45 For they performed the [1]worship
of their God and the service of purification, together with the singers and the
gatekeepers [a]in accordance with the

14 [1]In Neh 12:2, *Malluch*
24 [1]Lit *in the commandment of* [a]Neh 11:17 [b]Neh 12:9
25 [a]1 Chr 26:15
26 [a]Neh 8:9
27 [a]1 Chr 15:16,28
28 [a]1 Chr 9:16
30 [a]Neh 13:22, 30
31 [1]Lit *thanksgiving choirs* [2]Heb *and processions to the right* [a]Neh 12:38 [b]Neh 2:13
36 [1]Lit *brothers* [a]Neh 12:24
37 [a]Neh 2:14 [b]Neh 3:15 [c]Neh 3:26
38 [1]Lit *thanksgiving choir* [2]Lit *front* [a]Neh 12:31 [b]Neh 3:11 [c]Neh 3:8
39 [a]Neh 8:16 [b]Neh 3:6 [c]Neh 3:3 [d]Neh 3:1 [e]Neh 3:25
42 [1]Lit *caused their voices to be heard*
43 [a]Ps 9:2; 92:4
44 [1]Lit *stood* [a]Neh 13:4,5,12, 13
45 [1]Lit *service* [a]1 Chr 25:1

command of David *and* of his son Solomon.
46 For in the days of David and
[a]Asaph, in ancient times, *there were*
[1][b]leaders of the singers, songs of praise
and hymns of thanksgiving to God.
47 So all Israel in the days of Zerubbabel and Nehemiah gave the portions due
the singers and the gatekeepers [a]as each
day required, and [b]set apart the consecrated *portion* for the Levites, and the
Levites set apart the consecrated *portion*
for the sons of Aaron.

Foreigners Excluded

13 On that day [a]they read aloud
from the book of Moses in the
hearing of the people; and there was
found written in it that [b]no Ammonite or
Moabite should ever enter the assembly
of God,
2 because they did not meet the sons
of Israel with bread and water, but
[a]hired Balaam against them to curse
them. However, [b]our God turned the
curse into a blessing.
3 So when they heard the law, [a]they
excluded [b]all foreigners from Israel.

Tobiah Expelled and the Temple Cleansed

4 ¶ Now prior to this, Eliashib the
priest, [a]who was appointed over the
chambers of the house of our God, being
[1]related to [b]Tobiah,
5 had prepared a large [1]room for
him, where formerly they put the grain
offerings, the frankincense, the utensils
and the tithes of grain, wine and oil [a]pre-
scribed for the Levites, the singers and
the gatekeepers, and the [2]contributions
for the priests.
6 But during all this *time* I was not in
Jerusalem, for in [a]the thirty-second year
of [b]Artaxerxes king of Babylon I had
gone to the king. After some time, however, I asked leave from the king,
7 and I came to Jerusalem and
[1]learned about the evil that Eliashib had
done for Tobiah, [a]by preparing a [2]room
for him in the courts of the house of God.
8 It was very displeasing to me, so I
[a]threw all of Tobiah's household goods
out of the room.
9 Then I gave an order and [a]they
cleansed the rooms; and I returned there
the utensils of the house of God with the
grain offerings and the frankincense.

Tithes Restored

10 ¶ I also [1]discovered that [a]the portions of the Levites had not been given
them, so that the Levites and the singers
who performed the service had [2]gone
away, [b]each to his own field.
11 So I [1][a]reprimanded the officials
and said, "[b]Why is the house of God forsaken?" Then I gathered them together
and restored them to their posts.
12 All Judah then brought [a]the tithe
of the grain, wine and oil into the storehouses.
13 In charge of the storehouses I appointed Shelemiah the priest, Zadok the
scribe, and Pedaiah of the Levites, and in
addition to them was Hanan the son of
Zaccur, the son of Mattaniah; for [a]they
were considered reliable, and it was
[1]their task to distribute to their [2]kins-
men.
14 [a]Remember me for this, O my
God, and do not blot out my loyal deeds
which I have performed for the house of
my God and its services.

Sabbath Restored

15 ¶ In those days I saw in Judah some
who were treading wine presses [a]on the
sabbath, and bringing in sacks of grain
and loading *them* on donkeys, as well as
wine, grapes, figs and all kinds of loads,
[b]and they brought *them* into Jerusalem
on the sabbath day. So [c]I admonished
them on the day they sold food.
16 Also men of Tyre were living
[1]there *who* imported fish and all kinds of
merchandise, and sold *them* to the sons
of Judah on the sabbath, even in Jerusalem.
17 Then [a]I [1]reprimanded the nobles
of Judah and said to them, "What is this
evil thing you are doing, [2]by profaning
the sabbath day?
18 "[a]Did not your fathers do the same,
so that our God brought on us and on this
city all this trouble? Yet you are adding to
the wrath on Israel by profaning the sabbath."
19 ¶ [a]It came about that just as it
grew dark at the gates of Jerusalem before
the sabbath, I commanded that the doors
should be shut [1]and that they should not
open them until after the sabbath. Then
I stationed some of my servants at the
gates *so that* no load would enter on the
sabbath day.
20 Once or twice the traders and merchants of every kind of merchandise
spent the night outside Jerusalem.
21 Then [a]I [1]warned them and said to
them, "Why do you spend the night in
front of the wall? If you do so again, I will
[2]use force against you." From that time
on they did not come on the sabbath.
22 And I commanded the Levites that

46 [1]Lit *heads* [a]2 Chr 29:30 [b]1 Chr 9:33
47 [a]Neh 11:23 [b]Num 18:21
13:1 [a]Neh 9:3 [b]Deut 23:3-5; Neh 13:23
2 [a]Num 22:3-11 [b]Deut 23:5
3 [a]Neh 9:2; 10:28 [b]Ex 12:38
4 [1]Lit *close to* [a]Neh 12:44 [b]Neh 2:10; 6:1, 17,18
5 [1]Or *chamber* [2]Lit *heave offerings* [a]Num 18:21
6 [a]Neh 5:14 [b]Ezra 6:22
7 [1]Or *understood* [2]Or *chamber,* and so in vv 8, 9 [a]Neh 13:5
8 [a]John 2:13-16
9 [a]2 Chr 29:5, 15,16
10 [1]Or *knew* [2]Lit *fled* [a]Deut 12:19; Neh 10:37 [b]Neh 12:28,29
11 [1]Or *contended with* [a]Neh 13:17,25 [b]Neh 10:39
12 [a]Neh 10:37; 12:44; Mal 3:10
13 [1]Lit *on them to* [2]Lit *brothers* [a]Neh 7:2
14 [a]Neh 5:19; 13:22,31
15 [a]Ex 20:8; 34:21; Deut 5:12-14; Jer 17:22 [b]Neh 10:31; Jer 17:21 [c]Neh 9:29; 13:21
16 [1]Lit *in it*
17 [1]Or *contended with* [2]Lit *and* [a]Neh 13:11,25
18 [a]Ezra 9:13; Jer 17:21
19 [1]Lit *and commanded* [a]Lev 23:32
21 [1]Lit *witnessed against* [2]Lit *send a hand against* [a]Neh 13:15

[a]they should purify themselves and come as gatekeepers to sanctify the sabbath day. *For* this also [b]remember me, O my God, and have compassion on me according to the greatness of Your lovingkindness.

Mixed Marriages Forbidden

23 ¶ In those days I also saw that the
Jews had [1a]married women from [b]Ashdod, [c]Ammon *and* Moab.
24 As for their children, half spoke in
the language of Ashdod, and none of them was able to speak the language of Judah, but [1]the language of his own people.
25 So [a]I contended with them and
cursed them and [b]struck some of them and pulled out their hair, and [c]made them swear by God, "You shall not give your daughters to their sons, nor take of their daughters for your sons or for yourselves.
26 "[a]Did not Solomon king of Israel sin
regarding these things? [b]Yet among the many nations there was no king like him, and [c]he was loved by his God, and God made him king over all Israel; nevertheless the foreign women caused even him to sin.
27 "[1]Do we then hear about you that
you have committed all this great evil [a]by acting unfaithfully against our God by [2]marrying foreign women?"
28 Even one of the sons of Joiada, the
son of Eliashib the high priest, was a son-in-law of [a]Sanballat the Horonite, so I drove him away from me.
29 [a]Remember them, O my God,
[1]because they have defiled the priesthood and the [b]covenant of the priesthood and the Levites.
30 ¶ [a]Thus I purified them from
everything foreign and appointed duties for the priests and the Levites, each in his task,
31 and *I arranged* [a]for the supply of
wood at appointed times and for the first fruits. [b]Remember me, O my God, for good.

22 [a]1 Chr 15:12; Neh 12:30 [b]Neh 13:14, 31
23 [1]Lit *given dwelling to* [a]Ex 34:11-16; Deut 7:1-5; Ezra 9:2; Neh 10:30 [b]Neh 4:7 [c]Ezra 9:1; Neh 13:1
24 [1]Lit *according to the tongue of people and people*
25 [a]Neh 13:11, 17 [b]Deut 25:2 [c]Neh 10:29,30
26 [a]1 Kin 11:1 [b]1 Kin 3:13; 2 Chr 1:12 [c]2 Sam 12:24,25
27 [1]Or *Is it reported* [2]Lit *giving dwelling to* [a]Ezra 10:2; Neh 13:23
28 [a]Neh 2:10, 19; 4:1
29 [1]Lit *for the defilings of* [a]Neh 6:14 [b]Num 25:13
30 [a]Neh 10:30
31 [a]Neh 10:34 [b]Neh 13:14,22

Esther

Title and Background

This book has the name of its leading character, a beautiful Jewish girl whom King Ahasuerus of Persia chose to be his queen. The setting is in Susa, the Persian capital during Ahasuerus's rule (486–465 B.C.).

Author and Date of Writing

We do not know who wrote the book, but it is clear that the author was a Jew, both from the purpose of the book in accounting for the origin of a Jewish festival and from the Jewish nationalism that permeates the story. Many things point to the fact that he was a resident of a Persian city. The earliest date for the book would be shortly after the events narrated, that is, around 460 B.C.; the latest date would be before the Persian empire fell to Greece in 331.

Theme and Message

The central purpose of the author was to record the institution of the annual festival of Purim and to keep alive for later generations the memory of the great deliverance of the Jewish people during the reign of Ahasuerus. Although the name of God does not appear in the book, His care for His chosen people is clearly shown. Feasting is a prominent theme in Esther (see Outline).

Outline

I. The Feast of Ahasuerus (1:1—2:18)
II. The Feasts of Esther (2:19—7:10)
III. The Feasts of Purim (8:1—10:3)

The Banquets of the King

1 Now it took place in the days of [a]Ahasuerus, the Ahasuerus who reigned [b]from India to [1]Ethiopia over [c]127 provinces,

2 in those days as King Ahasuerus [a]sat on his royal throne which *was* at the citadel in [b]Susa,

3 in the third year of his reign [a]he gave a banquet for all his princes and attendants, the army *officers* of Persia and Media, the nobles and the princes of his provinces being in his presence.

4 [1]And he displayed the riches of his royal glory and the splendor of his great majesty for many days, 180 days.

5 ¶ When these days were completed, the king gave a banquet lasting seven days for all the people who were present at the citadel in Susa, from the greatest to the least, in the court of [a]the garden of the king's palace.

6 *There were hangings of* fine white and violet linen held by cords of fine purple linen on silver rings and marble columns, *and* [a]couches of gold and silver on a mosaic pavement of porphyry, marble, mother-of-pearl and precious stones.

7 Drinks were served in golden vessels of various kinds, and the royal wine was plentiful [a]according to the king's [1]bounty.

8 The drinking was *done* according to the law, there was no compulsion, for so the king had given orders to each official of his household that he should do according to the desires of each person.

9 Queen Vashti also gave a banquet for the women in the [1]palace which belonged to King Ahasuerus.

Queen Vashti's Refusal

10 ¶ On the seventh day, when the heart of the king was [a]merry with wine, he commanded Mehuman, Biztha, Harbona, Bigtha, Abagtha, Zethar and Carkas, the seven eunuchs who served in the presence of King Ahasuerus,

11 to bring Queen Vashti before the king with *her* royal [a]crown in order to display her beauty to the people and the princes, for she was beautiful.

12 But Queen Vashti refused to come at the king's command delivered by the eunuchs. Then the king became very angry and his wrath burned within him.

13 ¶ Then the king said to [a]the wise men [b]who understood the times—for it

1:1 [1]Lit *Cush* [a]Ezra 4:6; Dan 9:1 [b]Esth 8:9 [c]Esth 9:30
2 [a]1 Kin 1:46 [b]Neh 1:1; Dan 8:2
3 [a]Esth 2:18
4 [1]Lit *When*
5 [a]Esth 7:7,8
6 [a]Ezek 23:41; Amos 6:4
7 [1]Lit *hand* [a]Esth 2:18
9 [1]Lit *royal house*
10 [a]Judg 16:25
11 [a]Esth 2:17; 6:8
13 [a]Jer 10:7; Dan 2:2 [b]1 Chr 12:32

was the custom of the king so *to speak* before all who knew law and justice

14 and were close to him: Carshena, Shethar, Admatha, Tarshish, Meres, Marsena and Memucan, the seven princes of Persia and Media [a]who [1]had access to the king's presence and sat in the first place in the kingdom—

15 "According to law, what is to be done with Queen Vashti, because she did not [1]obey the command of King Ahasuerus *delivered* by the eunuchs?"

16 In the presence of the king and the princes, Memucan said, "Queen Vashti has wronged not only the king but *also* all the princes and all the peoples who are in all the provinces of King Ahasuerus.

17 "For the queen's conduct will [1]become known to all the women causing them [2]to look with contempt on their husbands by saying, 'King Ahasuerus commanded Queen Vashti to be brought in to his presence, but she did not come.'

18 "This day the ladies of Persia and Media who have heard of the queen's conduct will speak in *the same way* to all the king's princes, and there will be plenty of contempt and anger.

19 "If it pleases the king, let a royal [1]edict be issued by him and let it be written in the laws of Persia and Media so [a]that it cannot [2]be repealed, that Vashti may no longer come into the presence of King Ahasuerus, and let the king give her royal position to [3]another who is more worthy than she.

20 "When the king's edict which he will make is heard throughout all his kingdom, [1]great as it is, then [a]all women will give honor to their husbands, great and small."

21 ¶ *This* word pleased the king and the princes, and the king did [1]as Memucan proposed.

22 So he sent letters to all the king's provinces, [a]to each province according to its script and to every people according to their language, that every man should [b]be the master in his own house and the one who speaks in the language of his own people.

Vashti's Successor Sought

2 After these things [a]when the anger of King Ahasuerus had subsided, he remembered Vashti and what she had done and [b]what had been decreed against her.

2 Then the king's attendants, who served him, said, "[a]Let beautiful young virgins be sought for the king.

3 "Let the king appoint overseers in [a]all the provinces of his kingdom that they may gather every beautiful young virgin to the citadel of Susa, to the harem, into the custody of [b]Hegai, the king's eunuch, who is in charge of the women; and [c]let their cosmetics be given *them.*

4 "Then let the young lady who pleases the king be queen in place of Vashti." And the matter pleased the king, and he did accordingly.

5 ¶ *Now* there was at the citadel in Susa a Jew whose name was [a]Mordecai, the son of Jair, the son of Shimei, the son of Kish, a Benjamite,

6 [a]who had been taken into exile from Jerusalem with the captives who had been exiled with Jeconiah king of Judah, whom Nebuchadnezzar the king of Babylon had exiled.

7 He was bringing up Hadassah, that is [a]Esther, his uncle's daughter, for she had no father or mother. Now the young lady was beautiful of form and [1]face, and when her father and her mother died, Mordecai took her as his own daughter.

Esther Finds Favor

8 ¶ So it came about when the command and decree of the king were heard and [a]many young ladies were gathered to the citadel of Susa into the custody of [b]Hegai, that Esther was taken to the king's [1]palace into the custody of Hegai, who was in charge of the women.

9 Now the young lady pleased him and found favor with him. So he quickly provided her with her [a]cosmetics and [1]food, gave her seven choice maids from the king's palace and transferred her and her maids to the best place in the harem.

10 [a]Esther did not make known her people or her kindred, for Mordecai had instructed her that she should not make *them* known.

11 Every day Mordecai walked back and forth in front of the court of the harem to learn how Esther was and how she fared.

12 ¶ Now when the turn of each young lady came to go in to King Ahasuerus, after the end of her twelve months under the regulations for the women—for the days of their beautification were completed as follows: six months with oil of myrrh and six months with spices and the cosmetics for women—

13 the young lady would go in to the king in this way: anything that she [1]desired was given her to take with her from the harem to the king's palace.

14 In the evening she would go in and in the morning she would return to the second harem, to the [1]custody of Shaashgaz, the king's eunuch who was in charge of the concubines. She would not again go in to the king unless the king delighted

14 [1]Lit *saw the face of the king* [a]2 Kin 25:19; Matt 18:10
15 [1]Lit *do*
17 [1]Lit *go forth* [2]Lit *to despise... in their eyes*
19 [1]Lit *word go forth from* [2]Lit *pass away* [3]Lit *her neighbor* [a]Esth 8:8; Dan 6:8
20 [1]Lit *for great is it* [a]Eph 5:22; Col 3:18
21 [1]Lit *accrding to the word of*
22 [a]Esth 3:12; 8:9 [b]Eph 5:22-24
2:1 [a]Esth 7:10 [b]Esth 1:19,20
2 [a]1 Kin 1:2
3 [a]Esth 1:1,2 [b]Esth 2:8,15 [c]Esth 2:9,12
5 [a]Esth 3:2
6 [a]2 Kin 24:14, 15; 2 Chr 36:10
7 [1]Lit *good of appearance* [a]Esth 2:15
8 [1]Lit *house* [a]Esth 2:3 [b]Esth 2:3,15
9 [1]Lit *portions* [a]Esth 2:3,12
10 [a]Esth 2:20
13 [1]Lit *said*
14 [1]Lit *hand*

in her and she was summoned by name.
15 ¶ Now when the turn of Esther,
[a]the daughter of Abihail the uncle of
Mordecai who had taken her as his
daughter, came to go in to the king, she
did not request anything except what
[b]Hegai, the king's eunuch who was in
charge of the women, [1]advised. And Esther found favor in the eyes of all who
saw her.
16 So Esther was taken to King
Ahasuerus to his royal palace in the tenth
month which is the month Tebeth, in the
seventh year of his reign.

Esther Becomes Queen

17 ¶ The king loved Esther more than
all the women, and she found favor and
kindness with him more than all the virgins, so that [a]he set the royal crown on
her head and made her queen instead of
Vashti.
18 Then [a]the king gave a great banquet, Esther's banquet, for all his princes
and his servants; he also made a holiday
for the provinces and gave gifts [b]accord-
ing to the king's bounty.
19 ¶ [a]When the virgins were gathered together the second time, then Mordecai [b]was sitting at the king's gate.
20 [a]Esther had not yet made known
her kindred or her people, even as Mordecai had commanded her; for Esther did
[1]what Mordecai told her as she had done
[b]when under his care.

Mordecai Saves the King

21 In those days, while Mordecai was
sitting at the king's gate, [a]Bigthan and
Teresh, two of the king's officials from
those who guarded the door, became angry and sought to [1]lay hands on King
Ahasuerus.
22 But the [1]plot became known to
Mordecai and [a]he told Queen Esther,
and Esther [2]informed the king in Mordecai's name.
23 Now when the plot was investigated and found *to be so,* they were both
hanged on a [1]gallows; and it was written
in [a]the Book of the Chronicles in the
king's presence.

Haman's Plot against the Jews

3 After these events King Ahasuerus
[a]promoted Haman, the son of Hammedatha [b]the Agagite, and [a]advanced
him and [1]established his authority over
all the princes who *were* with him.
2 All the king's servants who were at
the king's gate bowed down [1]and paid
homage to Haman; for so the king had
commanded concerning him. But [a]Mor-
decai neither bowed down nor paid homage.
3 Then the king's servants who were
at [a]the king's gate said to Mordecai,
"[b]Why are you transgressing the king's
command?"
4 Now it was when they had spoken
daily to him and he would not listen to
them, that they told Haman to see whether Mordecai's reason would stand; for he
had told them that he was a Jew.
5 When Haman saw that [a]Mordecai
neither bowed down nor paid homage to
him, Haman was filled with rage.
6 But he [1]disdained to [2]lay hands
on Mordecai alone, for they had told
him *who* the people of Mordecai *were;*
therefore Haman [a]sought to destroy all
the Jews, the people of Mordecai, who
were throughout the whole kingdom of
Ahasuerus.
7 ¶ In the first month, which is the
month Nisan, in the twelfth year of King
Ahasuerus, [1]Pur, that is the lot, was
[a]cast before Haman from day to day and
from month *to month,* [2]until the twelfth
month, that is [b]the month Adar.
8 Then Haman said to King Ahasuerus, "There is a certain people scattered
and dispersed among the peoples in all
the provinces of your kingdom; [a]their
laws are different from *those* of all *other*
people and they do not observe the king's
laws, so it is not in the king's interest to
let them remain.
9 "If it is pleasing to the king, let it be
[1]decreed that they be destroyed, and I
will pay ten thousand talents of silver into
the hands of those who carry on the
king's business, to put into the king's
treasuries."
10 Then [a]the king took his signet ring
from his hand and gave it to Haman, the
son of Hammedatha [b]the Agagite, [c]the
enemy of the Jews.
11 The king said to Haman, "The silver is [1]yours, and the people *also,* to do
with them as you please."
12 ¶ [a]Then the king's scribes were
summoned on the thirteenth day of the
first month, and it was written just as
Haman commanded to [b]the king's satraps, to the governors who were over
each province and to the princes of each
people, each province according to its
script, each people according to its language, being written [c]in the name of
King Ahasuerus and sealed with the
king's signet ring.
13 Letters were sent by [a]couriers to
all the king's provinces [b]to destroy, to
kill and to annihilate all the Jews, both
young and old, women and children, [c]in
one day, the thirteenth *day* of the twelfth

---

15 [1]Lit *said* [a]Esth 2:7; 9:29 [b]Esth 2:3,8
17 [a]Esth 1:11
18 [a]Esth 1:3 [b]Esth 1:7
19 [a]Esth 2:3,4 [b]Esth 2:21; 3:2
20 [1]Lit *the word of Mordecai* [a]Esth 2:10 [b]Esth 2:7
21 [1]Lit *send a hand against* [a]Esth 6:2
22 [1]Lit *matter,* so also v 23 [2]Lit *told* [a]Esth 6:1,2
23 [1]Lit *tree* [a]Esth 10:2
3:1 [1]Lit *set his seat* [a]Esth 5:11 [b]Esth 3:10; 8:3
2 [1]Lit *and prostrated themselves before* [a]Esth 2:19; 5:9
3 [a]Esth 2:19 [b]Esth 3:2
5 [a]Esth 5:9
6 [1]Lit *despised in his eyes* [2]Lit *send a hand against* [a]Ps 83:4
7 [1]Lit *he cast Pur...before* [2]Gr *and the lot fell on the thirteenth day of* [a]Esth 9:24-26 [b]Ezra 6:15
8 [a]Ezra 4:12-15; Acts 16:20,21
9 [1]Lit *written*
10 [a]Gen 41:42; Esth 8:2 [b]Esth 3:1 [c]Esth 7:6
11 [1]Lit *given to you*
12 [a]Esth 8:9 [b]Ezra 8:36 [c]1 Kin 21:8; Esth 8:8,10
13 [a]2 Chr 30:6; Esth 8:10,14 [b]Esth 7:4 [c]Esth 8:12

month, which is the month Adar, and to [d]seize their possessions as plunder.

14 [a]A copy of the edict to be [1]issued as law in every province was published to all the peoples so that they should be ready for this day.

15 The couriers went out impelled by the king's command while the decree was [1]issued at the citadel in Susa; and while the king and Haman sat down to drink, [a]the city of Susa was in confusion.

Esther Learns of Haman's Plot

4 When Mordecai learned [a]all that had been done, [1]he tore his clothes, put on sackcloth and ashes, and went out into the midst of the city and wailed loudly and bitterly.

2 He went as far as the king's gate, for no one was to enter the king's gate clothed in sackcloth.

3 In each and every province where the command and decree of the king came, there was great mourning among the Jews, with [a]fasting, weeping and wailing; and many lay on sackcloth and ashes.

4 ¶ Then Esther's maidens and her eunuchs came and told her, and the queen writhed in great anguish. And she sent garments to clothe Mordecai that he might remove his sackcloth from him, but he did not accept *them.*

5 Then Esther summoned Hathach from the king's eunuchs, whom [1]the king had appointed to attend her, and ordered him *to go* to Mordecai to learn what this *was* and why it *was.*

6 So Hathach went out to Mordecai to the city square in front of the king's gate.

7 Mordecai told him all that had happened to him, and [a]the exact amount of money that Haman had promised to pay to the king's treasuries for the destruction of the Jews.

8 He also gave him [a]a copy of the text of the edict which had been issued in Susa for their destruction, that he might show Esther and inform her, and to order her to go in to the king to implore his favor and to plead with him for her people.

9 ¶ Hathach came back and related Mordecai's words to Esther.

10 Then Esther spoke to Hathach and ordered him *to reply* to Mordecai:

11 "All the king's servants and the people of the king's provinces know that for any man or woman who [a]comes to the king to the inner court who is not summoned, [b]he has but one law, that he be put to death, unless the king holds out [c]to him the golden scepter so that he may live. And I have not been summoned to come to the king for these thirty days."

12 They related Esther's words to Mordecai.

13 ¶ Then Mordecai told *them* to reply to Esther, "Do not imagine that you in the king's palace can escape any more than all the Jews.

14 "For if you remain silent at this time, relief and [a]deliverance will arise for the Jews from another place and you and your father's house will perish. And who knows whether you have not attained royalty for such a time as this?"

Esther Plans to Intercede

15 Then Esther told *them* to reply to Mordecai,

16 "Go, assemble all the Jews who are found in Susa, and fast for me; [a]do not eat or drink for [b]three days, night or day. I and my maidens also will fast in the same way. And thus I will go in to the king, which is not according to the law; and if I perish, I perish."

17 So Mordecai went away and did just as Esther had commanded him.

Esther Plans a Banquet

5 Now it came about [a]on the third day that Esther put on her royal robes and stood [b]in the inner court of the king's palace in front of the king's [1]rooms, and the king was sitting on his royal throne in the [2]throne room, opposite the entrance to the palace.

2 When the king saw Esther the queen standing in the court, [a]she obtained favor in his sight; and [b]the king extended to Esther the golden scepter which *was* in his hand. So Esther came near and touched the top of the scepter.

3 Then the king said to her, "What is *troubling* you, Queen Esther? And what is your request? [a]Even to half of the kingdom it shall be given to you."

4 Esther said, "If it pleases the king, may the king and Haman come this day to the banquet that I have prepared for him."

5 ¶ Then the king said, "[a]Bring Haman quickly that we may do [1]as Esther desires." So the king and Haman came to the banquet which Esther had prepared.

6 [1]As they drank their wine at the banquet, [a]the king said to Esther, "[b]What is your petition, for it shall be granted to you. And what is your request? Even to half of the kingdom it shall be done."

7 So Esther replied, "My petition and my request is:

8 [a]if I have found favor in the sight of the king, and if it pleases the king to grant

---

13 [d]Esth 8:11; 9:10

14 [1]Lit *given* [a]Esth 8:13,14

15 [1]Lit *given* [a]Esth 8:15

4:1 [1]Lit *Mordecai* [a]2 Sam 1:11; Esth 3:8-10; Jon 3:5,6

3 [a]Esth 4:16

5 [1]Lit *he*

7 [a]Esth 3:9

8 [a]Esth 3:14

11 [a]Esth 5:1; 6:4 [b]Dan 2:9 [c]Esth 5:2; 8:4

14 [a]Lev 26:42; 2 Kin 13:5

16 [a]Joel 1:14; 2:12 [b]Esth 5:1

5:1 [1]Lit *house* [2]Lit *royal house* [a]Esth 4:16 [b]Esth 4:11; 6:4

2 [a]Esth 2:9 [b]Esth 4:11; 8:4

3 [a]Esth 7:2; Mark 6:23

5 [1]Lit *the word of Esther* [a]Esth 6:14

6 [1]Lit *at the banquet of wine* [a]Esth 7:2 [b]Esth 5:3

8 [a]Esth 7:3; 8:5

my petition and do [1]what I request, may the king and Haman come to [b]the banquet which I will prepare for them, and tomorrow I will do [2]as the king says."

Haman's Pride

9 ¶ Then Haman went out that day glad and pleased of heart; but when Haman saw Mordecai [a]in the king's gate and [b]that he did not stand up or [1]tremble before him, Haman was filled with anger against Mordecai.

10 Haman controlled himself, however, went to his house and [1]sent for his friends and his wife [a]Zeresh.

11 Then Haman recounted to them the glory of his riches, and the [1a]number of his sons, and every *instance* where the king had magnified him and how he had [2b]promoted him above the princes and servants of the king.

12 Haman also said, "Even Esther the queen let no one but me come with the king to the banquet which she had prepared; and [a]tomorrow also I am [1]invited by her with the king.

13 "Yet all of this [1]does not satisfy me every time I see Mordecai the Jew sitting at [a]the king's gate."

14 Then Zeresh his wife and all his friends said to him, "[a]Have a [1]gallows fifty cubits high made and in the morning ask the king to have Mordecai hanged on it; then go joyfully with the king to the banquet." And the [2]advice pleased Haman, so he had the gallows made.

The King Plans to Honor Mordecai

6 During that night [1]the king [a]could not sleep so he gave an order to bring [b]the book of records, the chronicles, and they were read before the king.

2 It was found written what [a]Mordecai had reported concerning Bigthana and Teresh, two of the king's eunuchs who were doorkeepers, that they had sought to lay hands on King Ahasuerus.

3 The king said, "What honor or dignity has been bestowed on Mordecai for this?" Then the king's servants who attended him said, "Nothing has been done for him."

4 So the king said, "Who is in the court?" Now Haman had just [a]entered the outer court of the king's palace in order to speak to the king about [b]hanging Mordecai on the gallows which he had prepared for him.

5 The king's servants said to him, "Behold, Haman is standing in the court." And the king said, "Let him come in."

6 So Haman came in and the king said to him, "What is to be done for the man [a]whom the king desires to honor?" And Haman said [1]to himself, "Whom would the king desire to honor more than me?"

7 Then Haman said to the king, "For the man whom the king desires to honor,

8 let them bring a royal robe which the king has worn, and [a]the horse on which the king has ridden, and on whose head [b]a royal crown has been placed;

9 and let the robe and the horse be handed over to one of the king's most noble princes and let them array the man whom the king desires to honor and lead him on horseback through the city square, [a]and proclaim before him, 'Thus it shall be done to the man whom the king desires to honor.' "

Haman Must Honor Mordecai

10 ¶ Then the king said to Haman, "Take quickly the robes and the horse as you have said, and do so for Mordecai the Jew, who is sitting at the king's gate; do not fall short in anything of all that you have said."

11 So Haman took the robe and the horse, and arrayed Mordecai, and led him *on horseback* through the city square, and proclaimed before him, "Thus it shall be done to the man whom the king desires to honor."

12 ¶ Then Mordecai returned to the king's gate. But Haman hurried home, mourning, [a]with *his* head covered.

13 Haman recounted [a]to Zeresh his wife and all his friends everything that had happened to him. Then his wise men and Zeresh his wife said to him, "If Mordecai, before whom you have begun to fall, is [1]of Jewish origin, you will not overcome him, but will surely fall before him."

14 ¶ While they were still talking with him, the king's eunuchs arrived and hastily [a]brought Haman to the banquet which Esther had prepared.

Esther's Plea

7 Now the king and Haman came to drink *wine* with Esther the queen.

2 And the king said to Esther on the second day also [1]as they drank their wine at the banquet, "[a]What is your petition, Queen Esther? It shall be granted you. And what is your request? [b]Even to half of the kingdom it shall be done."

3 Then Queen Esther replied, "[a]If I have found favor in your sight, O king, and if it pleases the king, let my life be given me as my petition, and my people as my request;

4 for [a]we have been sold, I and my people, to be destroyed, [b]to be killed and

8 [1]Lit *my request* [2]Lit *according to the word of the king* [b]Esth 6:14
9 [1]Or *move for* [a]Esth 2:19 [b]Esth 3:5
10 [1]Lit *sent and brought* [a]Esth 6:13
11 [1]Lit *multitude* [2]Lit *lifted* [a]Esth 9:7-10 [b]Esth 3:1
12 [1]Lit *summoned to her* [a]Esth 5:8
13 [1]Lit *is not suitable to me* [a]Esth 5:9
14 [1]Lit *tree* [2]Lit *thing* [a]Esth 6:4; 7:9,10
6:1 [1]Lit *the king's sleep fled* [a]Dan 6:18 [b]Esth 2:23; 10:2
2 [a]Esth 2:21,22
4 [a]Esth 4:11 [b]Esth 5:14
6 [1]Lit *in his heart* [a]Esth 6:7, 9,11
8 [a]1 Kin 1:33 [b]Esth 1:11; 2:17
9 [a]Gen 41:43
12 [a]2 Sam 15:30
13 [1]Lit *from the seed of the Jews* [a]Esth 5:10
14 [a]Esth 5:8
7:2 [1]Lit *at the banquet of wine* [a]Esth 5:6; 9:12 [b]Esth 5:3
3 [a]Esth 5:8; 8:5
4 [a]Esth 3:9 [b]Esth 3:13

to be annihilated. Now if we had only been sold as slaves, men and women, I would have remained silent, for the [1]trouble would not be commensurate with the [2]annoyance to the king."

5 Then King Ahasuerus [1]asked Queen Esther, "Who is he, and where is he, [2]who would presume to do thus?"

6 Esther said, "[a]A foe and an enemy is this wicked Haman!" Then Haman became terrified before the king and queen.

Haman Is Hanged

7 The king arose [a]in his anger from [1]drinking wine *and went* into [b]the palace garden; but Haman stayed to beg for his life from Queen Esther, for he saw that harm had been determined against him by the king.

8 Now when the king returned from the palace garden into the [1]place where they were drinking wine, Haman was falling on [a]the couch where Esther was. Then the king said, "Will he even assault the queen with me in the house?" As the word went out of the king's mouth, they covered Haman's face.

9 Then Harbonah, one of the eunuchs who *were* before the king said, "Behold indeed, [a]the gallows standing at Haman's house fifty cubits high, which Haman made for Mordecai [b]who spoke good on behalf of the king!" And the king said, "Hang him on it."

10 [a]So they hanged Haman on the [1]gallows which he had prepared for Mordecai, [b]and the king's anger subsided.

Mordecai Promoted

8 On that day King Ahasuerus gave the house of Haman, [a]the enemy of the Jews, to Queen Esther; and Mordecai came before the king, for Esther had disclosed [b]what he was to her.

2 [a]The king took off his signet ring which he had taken away from Haman, and gave it to Mordecai. And Esther set Mordecai over the house of Haman.

3 ¶ Then Esther spoke again to the king, fell at his feet, wept and implored him to avert the evil *scheme* of Haman the Agagite and his plot which he had devised against the Jews.

4 [a]The king extended the golden scepter to Esther. So Esther arose and stood before the king.

5 Then she said, "[a]If it pleases the king and if I have found favor before him and the matter *seems* proper to the king and I am pleasing in his sight, let it be written to revoke the [b]letters devised by Haman, the son of Hammedatha the Agagite, which he wrote to destroy the Jews who are in all the king's provinces.

6 "For [a]how can I endure to see the calamity which will befall my people, and how can I endure to see the destruction of my kindred?"

7 So King Ahasuerus said to Queen Esther and to Mordecai the Jew, "Behold, [a]I have given the house of Haman to Esther, and him they have hanged on the gallows because he had stretched out his hands against the Jews.

The King's Decree Avenges the Jews

8 "Now you write to the Jews [1]as you see fit, in the king's name, and [a]seal *it* with the king's signet ring; for a decree which is written in the name of the king and sealed with the king's signet ring [b]may not be revoked."

9 ¶ [a]So the king's scribes were called at that time in the third month (that is, the month Sivan), on the twenty-third [1]day; and it was written according to all that Mordecai commanded to the Jews, the satraps, the governors and the princes of the provinces which *extended* [b]from India to [2]Ethiopia, 127 provinces, to [c]every province according to its script, and to every people according to their language as well as to the Jews according to their script and their language.

10 He wrote in the name of King Ahasuerus, and sealed it with the king's signet ring, and sent letters by couriers on [a]horses, riding on steeds sired by the royal stud.

11 [1]In them the king granted the Jews who were in each and every city *the right* [a]to assemble and to defend their lives, [b]to destroy, to kill and to annihilate the entire army of any people or province which might attack them, including children and women, and [c]to plunder their spoil,

12 on [a]one day in all the provinces of King Ahasuerus, the thirteenth *day* of the twelfth month (that is, the month Adar).

13 [a]A copy of the edict to be [1]issued as law in each and every province was published to all the peoples, so that the Jews would be ready for this day to avenge themselves on their enemies.

14 The couriers, hastened and impelled by the king's command, went out, riding on the royal steeds; and the decree was given out at the citadel in Susa.

15 ¶ Then Mordecai went out from the presence of the king [a]in royal robes of [1]blue and white, with a large crown of gold and [b]a garment of fine linen and purple; and [c]the city of Susa shouted and rejoiced.

4 [1]Or *enemy could not compensate for the loss* [2]Or *damage*
5 [1]Lit *said and said to* [2]Lit *whose heart has been filled*
6 [a]Esth 3:10
7 [1]Lit *the banquet of wine* [a]Esth 1:12 [b]Esth 1:5
8 [1]Lit *house of the banquet of wine* [a]Esth 1:6
9 [a]Esth 5:14 [b]Esth 2:22
10 [1]Lit *tree* [a]Ps 7:16; 94:23 [b]Esth 7:7,8
8:1 [a]Esth 7:6 [b]Esth 2:7,15
2 [a]Esth 3:10
4 [a]Esth 4:11; 5:2
5 [a]Esth 5:8; 7:3 [b]Esth 3:13
6 [a]Esth 7:4; 9:1
7 [a]Esth 8:1
8 [1]Lit *according to the good in your eyes* [a]Esth 3:12; 8:10 [b]Esth 1:19
9 [1]Lit *in it* [2]Lit *Cush* [a]Esth 3:12 [b]Esth 1:1 [c]Esth 1:22; 3:12
10 [a]1 Kin 4:28
11 [1]Lit *Which* [a]Esth 9:2 [b]Esth 3:13 [c]Esth 9:10
12 [a]Esth 3:13; 9:1
13 [1]Lit *given* [a]Esth 3:14
15 [1]Or *violet* [a]Esth 5:11 [b]Gen 41:42 [c]Esth 3:15

16 For the Jews there was [a]light and gladness and joy and honor.

17 In each and every province and in each and every city, wherever the king's commandment and his decree arrived, there was gladness and joy for the Jews, a feast and a [1a]holiday. And [b]many among the peoples of the land became Jews, for the dread of the Jews had fallen on them.

The Jews Destroy Their Enemies

9 Now [a]in the twelfth month (that is, the month Adar), on [b]the thirteenth [1]day [c]when the king's command and edict [2]were about to be executed, on the day when the enemies of the Jews hoped to gain the mastery over them, it was turned to the contrary so that the Jews themselves gained the mastery over those who hated them.

2 [a]The Jews assembled in their cities throughout all the provinces of King Ahasuerus to lay hands on those who sought their harm; and no one could stand before them, [b]for the dread of them had fallen on all the peoples.

3 Even all the princes of the provinces, [a]the satraps, the governors and those who were doing the king's business [1]assisted the Jews, because the dread of Mordecai had fallen on them.

4 Indeed, Mordecai was great in the king's house, and his fame spread throughout all the provinces; for the man Mordecai [a]became greater and greater.

5 Thus [a]the Jews struck all their enemies with [1]the sword, killing and destroying; and they did what they pleased to those who hated them.

6 At the citadel in Susa the Jews killed and destroyed five hundred men,

7 and Parshandatha, Dalphon, Aspatha,

8 Poratha, Adalia, Aridatha,

9 Parmashta, Arisai, Aridai and Vaizatha,

10 [a]the ten sons of Haman the son of Hammedatha, the Jews' enemy; but [b]they did not lay their hands on the plunder.

11 ¶ On that day the number of those who were killed at the citadel in Susa [1]was reported to the king.

12 The king said to Queen Esther, "The Jews have killed and destroyed five hundred men and the ten sons of Haman at the citadel in Susa. What then have they done in the rest of the king's provinces! [a]Now what is your petition? It shall even be granted you. And what is your further request? It shall also be done."

13 Then said Esther, "If it pleases the king, [a]let tomorrow also be granted to the Jews who are in Susa to do according to the edict of today; and let Haman's ten sons be hanged on the gallows."

14 So the king commanded that it should be done so; and an edict was issued in Susa, and Haman's ten sons were hanged.

15 The Jews who were in Susa assembled also on the fourteenth day of the month Adar and killed [a]three hundred men in Susa, but [b]they did not lay their hands on the plunder.

16 ¶ Now [a]the rest of the Jews who *were* in the king's provinces [b]assembled, to defend their lives and [1]rid themselves of their enemies, and kill 75,000 of those who hated them; but they did not lay their hands on the plunder.

17 *This was done* on [a]the thirteenth day of the month Adar, and [b]on the fourteenth [1]day they rested and made it a day of feasting and rejoicing.

18 ¶ But the Jews who were in Susa [a]assembled on the thirteenth and [b]the fourteenth [1]of the same month, and they rested on the fifteenth [1]day and made it a day of feasting and rejoicing.

19 Therefore the Jews of the rural areas, who live in [a]the rural towns, make the fourteenth day of the month Adar *a* [1b]holiday for rejoicing and feasting and [c]sending portions *of food* to one another.

The Feast of Purim Instituted

20 ¶ Then Mordecai recorded these events, and he sent letters to all the Jews who were in all the provinces of King Ahasuerus, both near and far,

21 obliging them to celebrate the fourteenth day of the month Adar, and the fifteenth day [1]of the same month, annually,

22 because on those days the Jews [1]rid themselves of their enemies, and *it was a* month which was [a]turned for them from sorrow into gladness and from mourning into a [2]holiday; that they should make them days of feasting and rejoicing and [b]sending portions *of food* to one another and gifts to the poor.

23 ¶ Thus the Jews undertook what they had started to do, and what Mordecai had written to them.

24 For Haman the son of Hammedatha, the Agagite, the adversary of all the Jews, had schemed against the Jews to destroy them and [a]had cast Pur, that is the lot, to disturb them and destroy them.

25 But [a]when it came [1]to the king's attention, he commanded by letter [b]that

16 [a]Ps 97:11; 112:4
17 [1]Lit *good day* [a]Esth 9:19 [b]Esth 9:27
9:1 [1]Lit *day in it* [2]Lit *drew near* [a]Esth 8:12 [b]Esth 9:17 [c]Esth 3:13
2 [a]Esth 8:11; 9:15-18 [b]Esth 8:17
3 [1]Lit *lifted up* [a]Ezra 8:36
4 [a]2 Sam 3:1; 1 Chr 11:9
5 [1]Lit *the stroke of* [a]Esth 3:13
10 [a]Esth 5:11 [b]Esth 8:11
11 [1]Lit *came*
12 [a]Esth 5:6; 7:2
13 [a]Esth 8:11; 9:15
15 [a]Esth 9:12 [b]Esth 9:10
16 [1]Lit *have rest from* [a]Esth 9:2 [b]Lev 26:7,8; Esth 8:11
17 [1]Lit *in it* [a]Esth 9:1 [b]Esth 9:21
18 [1]Lit *in it* [a]Esth 8:11; 9:2 [b]Esth 9:21
19 [1]Lit *rejoicing and feasting and a good day and sending* [a]Deut 3:5; Zech 2:4 [b]Esth 9:22 [c]Neh 8:10
21 [1]Lit *in it*
22 [1]Lit *had rest from* [2]Lit *good day* [a]Ps 30:11 [b]Neh 8:12
24 [a]Esth 3:7
25 [1]Lit *before the king, he* [a]Esth 7:4-10 [b]Esth 3:6-15

his wicked scheme which he had [2]de-
vised against the Jews, [c]should return on
his own head and that he and his sons
should be hanged on the [3]gallows.
26 Therefore they called these days
Purim after the name of Pur. [1]And [a]be-
cause of the instructions in this letter,
both what they had seen in this regard
and what had happened to them,
27 the Jews established and [1]made a
custom for themselves and for their
[2]descendants and for [a]all those who allied themselves with them, so that [3]they
would not fail [b]to celebrate these two
days according to their [4]regulation and
according to their appointed time annually.
28 So these days were to be remembered and celebrated throughout every
generation, every family, every province
and every city; and these days of Purim
were not to [1]fail from among the Jews, or
their memory [2]fade from their [3]descen-
dants.
29 ¶ Then Queen Esther, [a]daughter
of Abihail, with Mordecai the Jew, wrote
with full authority to confirm [b]this second letter about Purim.
30 He sent letters to all the Jews, [a]to
the 127 provinces of the kingdom of
Ahasuerus, *namely,* words of peace and
truth,
31 to establish these days of Purim at
their appointed times, just as Mordecai
the Jew and Queen Esther had established for them, and just as they had
established for themselves and for their
[1]descendants with [2]instructions [a]for
their times of fasting and their lamentations.
32 The command of Esther established
these [1]customs for [a]Purim, and it was
written in the book.

Mordecai's Greatness

10 Now King Ahasuerus laid a tribute on the land and on the [a]coast-
lands of the sea.
2 And all the [1]accomplishments of
his authority and strength, and the full
account of the greatness of Mordecai [a]to
which the king [2]advanced him, are they
not written in [b]the Book of the Chronicles of the Kings of Media and Persia?
3 For Mordecai the Jew was [a]second
only to King Ahasuerus, and great among
the Jews and in favor with his many kinsmen, [b]one who sought the good of his
people and one who spoke for the welfare
of his whole nation.

25 [2]Lit *schemed* [3]Lit *tree* [c]Ps 7:16
26 [1]Lit *Therefore because of all the words* [a]Esth 9:20
27 [1]Lit *received* [2]Lit *seed* [3]Lit *it should not pass away* [4]Lit *writing* [a]Esth 8:17 [b]Esth 9:20,21
28 [1]Lit *pass away* [2]Lit *end* [3]Lit *seed*
29 [a]Esth 2:15 [b]Esth 9:20,21
30 [a]Esth 1:1
31 [1]Lit *seed* [2]Lit *words* [a]Esth 4:3
32 [1]Lit *words* [a]Esth 9:26
10:1 [a]Is 11:11; 24:15
2 [1]Lit *doings* [2]Lit *made him great* [a]Esth 8:15; 9:4 [b]Esth 2:23
3 [a]Gen 41:43,44 [b]Neh 2:10

Job

Title and Background

The book of Job is named for its main character, a righteous man who was very rich. Even after losing everything he owned and suffering from a terrible sickness, Job still confessed his trust in God.

Author and Date of Writing

Although most of the book consists of the words of Job and his counselors, Job himself was not the author. We can be sure the author was an Israelite who probably had access to oral and/or written sources from which he composed the book.

Two dates are involved: (1) the date of the man Job and his historical setting, and (2) the date of the inspired writer of the book. The latter could be dated anytime from the reign of Solomon to the exile. The date of the actual events described in this book was most likely between 2000 and 1000 B.C., and probably late in that millennium.

Theme and Message

The book provides a profound statement on the justice of God in light of human suffering. How can the justice of an almighty God be defended in the face of evil, especially human suffering, and even more particularly, the suffering of the innocent? The suffering of the righteous must be seen in the light of the cosmic struggle between God and Satan.

Outline

I. Prologue (1:1—2:13)
II. Dialogue—Dispute: Job and His Friends (3:1—27:23)
III. Interlude on Wisdom (28:1–28)
IV. Monologues: Job, Elihu and God (29:1—42:6)
V. Epilogue (42:7–17)

Job's Character and Wealth

1 There was a man in the [a]land of Uz
whose name was [b]Job; and that man
was [c]blameless, upright, [d]fearing God
and [e]turning away from evil.
2 [a]Seven sons and three daughters
were born to him.
3 [a]His possessions also were 7,000
sheep, 3,000 camels, 500 yoke of oxen,
500 female donkeys, and very many servants; and that man was [b]the greatest of
all the [1]men of the east.
4 His sons used to go and hold a feast
in the house of each one on his day, and
they would send and invite their three
sisters to eat and drink with them.
5 When the days of feasting had completed their cycle, Job would send and
consecrate them, rising up early in the
morning and offering [a]burnt offerings *according to* the number of them all; for Job
said, "[b]Perhaps my sons have sinned and
[c]cursed God in their hearts." Thus Job
did continually.
6 ¶ [a]Now there was a day when the
[b]sons of God came to present themselves
before the LORD, and [1]Satan also came
among them.
7 The LORD said to Satan, "From
where do you come?" Then Satan answered the LORD and said, "[a]From roam-
ing about on the earth and walking
around on it."
8 The LORD said to Satan, "Have you
[1]considered [a]My servant Job? For there
is no one like him on the earth, [b]a blameless and upright man, [2]fearing God and
turning away from evil."
9 Then [a]Satan answered the [1]LORD,
"Does Job fear God for nothing?
10 "[a]Have You not made a hedge about
him and his house and all that he has, on
every side? [b]You have blessed the work
of his hands, and his [c]possessions have
increased in the land.
11 "[a]But put forth Your hand now and
[b]touch all that he has; he will surely
curse You to Your face."
12 Then the LORD said to Satan, "Behold, all that he has is in your [1]power,
only do not put forth your hand on him."

1:1 [a]Jer 25:20; Lam 4:21 [b]Ezek 14:14,20; James 5:11 [c]Gen 6:9; 17:1; Deut 18:13 [d]Gen 22:12; 42:18; Ex 18:21; Prov 8:13 [e]Job 28:28
2 [a]Job 42:13
3 [1]Lit *sons* [a]Job 42:12 [b]Job 29:25
5 [a]Gen 8:20; Job 42:8 [b]Job 8:4 [c]1 Kin 21:10,13
6 [1]I.e. the adversary, and so throughout chs 1 and 2 [a]Job 2:1 [b]Job 38:7
7 [a]1 Pet 5:8
8 [1]Lit *set your heart to* [2]Or *revering* [a]Num 12:7; Josh 1:2,7; Job 42:7,8 [b]Job 1:1
9 [1]Lit *LORD and said* [a]Rev 12:9f
10 [a]Job 29:2-6; Ps 34:7 [b]Job 31:25 [c]Job 1:3; 31:25
11 [a]Job 2:5 [b]Job 19:21
12 [1]Lit *hand*

So Satan departed from the presence of
the LORD.

Satan Allowed to Test Job

13 ¶ Now on the day when his sons
and his daughters were eating and drinking wine in their oldest brother's house,
14 a messenger came to Job and said,
"The oxen were plowing and the [1]don-
keys feeding beside them,
15 and [1]the [a]Sabeans [2]attacked and
took them. They also [3]slew the servants
with the edge of the sword, and [4]I alone
have escaped to tell you."
16 While he was still speaking, another also came and said, "[a]The fire of God
fell from heaven and burned up the sheep
and the servants and consumed them,
and I alone have escaped to tell you."
17 While he was still speaking, another also came and said, "The [a]Chaldeans
formed three bands and made a raid on
the camels and took them and [1]slew the
servants with the edge of the sword, and
I alone have escaped to tell you."
18 While he was still speaking, another also came and said, "Your sons and
your daughters were eating and drinking
wine in their oldest brother's house,
19 and behold, a great wind came from
across the wilderness and struck the four
corners of the house, and it fell on the
young people and they died, and I alone
have escaped to tell you."
20 ¶ Then Job arose and [a]tore his
robe and shaved his head, and he fell to
the ground and worshiped.
21 He said,
"[a]Naked I came from my
mother's womb,
And naked I shall return there.
The [b]LORD gave and the LORD
has taken away.
Blessed be the name of the
LORD."
22 ¶ [a]Through all this Job did not sin
nor did he [1]blame God.

Job Loses His Health

2 [a]Again there was a day when the
sons of God came to present themselves before the LORD, and Satan also
came among them to present himself before the LORD.
2 The LORD said to Satan, "Where
have you come from?" Then Satan answered the LORD and said, "From roam-
ing about on the earth and walking
around on it."
3 The LORD said to Satan, "Have you
[1]considered My servant Job? For there is
no one like him on the earth, a blameless
and upright man [2]fearing God and turning away from evil. And he still [a]holds
fast his integrity, although you incited Me
against him to [3]ruin him without cause."
4 Satan answered the LORD and said,
"Skin for skin! Yes, all that a man has he
will give for his life.
5 "[a]However, put forth Your hand
now, and [b]touch his bone and his flesh;
he will curse You to Your face."
6 So the LORD said to Satan, "Behold,
he is in your [1]power, only spare his life."
7 ¶ Then Satan went out from the
presence of the LORD and smote Job with
[a]sore boils from the sole of his foot to the
crown of his head.
8 And he took a potsherd to scrape
himself while [a]he was sitting among the
ashes.
9 ¶ Then his wife said to him, "Do
you still hold fast your integrity? Curse
God and die!"
10 But he said to her, "You speak as
one of the foolish women speaks. [a]Shall
we indeed accept good from God and not
accept adversity?" [b]In all this Job did not
sin with his lips.
11 ¶ Now when Job's three friends
heard of all this adversity that had come
upon him, they came each one from his
own place, Eliphaz the [a]Temanite, Bildad the [b]Shuhite and Zophar the Naamathite; and they made an appointment together to come to [c]sympathize with him
and comfort him.
12 When they lifted up their eyes at a
distance and did not recognize him, they
raised their voices and wept. And each of
them [a]tore his robe and they [b]threw
dust over their heads toward the sky.
13 [a]Then they sat down on the
ground with him for seven days and sev-
en nights with no one speaking a word to
him, for they saw that *his* pain was very
great.

Job's Lament

3 Afterward Job opened his mouth and
cursed [1]the day of his *birth.*
2 And Job [1]said,
3 "[a]Let the day perish on which I
was to be born,
And the night *which* said, 'A
[1]boy is conceived.'
4 "May that day be darkness;
Let not God above care for it,
Nor light shine on it.
5 "Let [a]darkness and black gloom
claim it;
Let a cloud settle on it;
Let the blackness of the day
terrify it.
6 "*As for* that night, let darkness
seize it;
Let it not rejoice among the days
of the year;

14 [1]Lit *female donkeys*

15 [1]Lit *Sheba* [2]Lit *fell upon* [3]Lit *smote* [4]Lit *only I alone,* and so also vv 16, 17,19 [a]Gen 10:7; Job 6:19

16 [a]Gen 19:24; Lev 10:2; Num 11:1-3

17 [1]Lit *smote* [a]Gen 11:28,31

20 [a]Gen 37:29, 34; Josh 7:6

21 [a]Eccl 5:15 [b]1 Sam 2:7,8; Job 2:10

22 [1]Lit *ascribe unseemliness to* [a]Job 2:10

2:1 [a]Job 1:6-8

3 [1]Lit *set your heart to* [2]Or *reveering* [3]Lit *swallow him up* [a]Job 27:5,6

5 [a]Job 1:11 [b]Job 19:20

6 [1]Lit *hand*

7 [a]Deut 28:35; Job 7:5; 13:28; 30:17,18,30

8 [a]Job 42:6; Jer 6:26; Ezek 27:30; Jon 3:6

10 [a]Job 1:21 [b]Job 1:22; Ps 39:1; James 1:12

11 [a]Gen 36:11; Job 6:19; Jer 49:7 [b]Gen 25:2 [c]Job 42:11; Rom 12:15

12 [a]Job 1:20 [b]Josh 7:6; Neh 9:1; Lam 2:10; Ezek 27:30

13 [a]Gen 50:10; Ezek 3:15

3:1 [1]Lit *his day*

2 [1]Lit *answered and said*

3 [1]Lit *man-child* [a]Jer 20:14-18

5 [a]Jer 13:16

Let it not come into the number
of the months.
7 "Behold, let that night be barren;
Let no joyful shout enter it.
8 "Let those curse it who curse the
day,
Who are [1]prepared to [a]rouse
Leviathan.
9 "Let the stars of its twilight be
darkened;
Let it wait for light but have
none,
And let it not see the [1]breaking
dawn;
10 Because it did not shut the
opening of my *mother's*
womb,
Or hide trouble from my eyes.

11 ¶ "[a]Why did I not die [1]at birth,
Come forth from the womb and
expire?
12 "Why did the knees receive me,
And why the breasts, that I
should suck?
13 "For now I [a]would have lain
down and been quiet;
I would have slept then, I would
have been at rest,
14 With [a]kings and *with*
[b]counselors of the earth,
Who rebuilt [c]ruins for
themselves;
15 Or with [a]princes [b]who had
gold,
Who were filling their houses
with silver.
16 "Or like a miscarriage which is
[1]discarded, I would not be,
As infants that never saw light.
17 "There the wicked cease from
raging,
And there the [1]weary are at
[a]rest.
18 "The prisoners are at ease
together;
They do not hear the voice of
the taskmaster.
19 "The small and the great are
there,
And the slave is free from his
master.

20 ¶ "Why is [a]light given to him
who suffers,
And life to the bitter of soul,
21 Who [1a]long for death, but there
is none,
And dig for it more than for
[b]hidden treasures,
22 Who rejoice greatly,
And exult when they find the
grave?
23 "*Why is light given* to a man
[a]whose way is hidden,
And whom [b]God has hedged in?
24 "For [a]my groaning comes at the
sight of my food,
And [b]my cries pour out like
water.
25 "For [1a]what I fear comes
upon me,
And what I dread befalls me.
26 "I [a]am not at ease, nor am I
quiet,
And I am not at rest, but turmoil
comes."

Eliphaz: Innocent Do Not Suffer

4 Then Eliphaz the Temanite [1]answered,
2 "If one ventures a word with you,
will you become impatient?
But [a]who can refrain [1]from
speaking?
3 "Behold [a]you have admonished
many,
And you have strengthened weak
hands.
4 "Your words have [1]helped the
tottering to stand,
And you have strengthened
[2]feeble knees.
5 "But now it has come to you, and
you [a]are impatient;
It [b]touches you, and you are
dismayed.
6 "Is not your [1a]fear *of God* [b]your
confidence,
And the integrity of your ways
your hope?

7 ¶ "Remember now, [a]who *ever*
perished being innocent?
Or where were the upright
destroyed?
8 "According to what I have seen,
[a]those who plow iniquity
And those who sow trouble
harvest it.
9 "By [a]the breath of God they
perish,
And [b]by the [1]blast of His anger
they come to an end.
10 "The [a]roaring of the lion and the
voice of the *fierce* lion,
And the teeth of the young lions
are broken.
11 "The [a]lion perishes for lack of
prey,
And the [b]whelps of the lioness
are scattered.

12 ¶ "Now a word [a]was brought to
me stealthily,
And my ear received a [b]whisper
of it.
13 "Amid disquieting [a]thoughts from
the visions of the night,
When deep sleep falls on men,

8 [1]Or *skillful* [a]Job 41:1,25
9 [1]Lit *eyelids*
11 [1]Lit *from the womb* [a]Job 10:18,19
13 [a]Job 3:13-19; 7:8-10,21; 10:21,22; 14:10-15,20-22; 16:22; 17:13-16; 19:25-27; 21:13, 23-26; 24:19,20; 26:5,6; 34:22
14 [a]Job 12:18 [b]Job 12:17 [c]Job 15:28; Is 58:12
15 [a]Job 12:21 [b]Job 27:16,17
16 [1]Lit *hidden*
17 [1]Lit *weary of strength* [a]Job 17:16
20 [a]Jer 20:18
21 [1]Lit *wait* [a]Rev 9:6 [b]Prov 2:4
23 [a]Job 19:6,8, 12 [b]Job 19:8; Ps 88:8; Lam 3:7
24 [a]Job 6:7; 33:20 [b]Job 30:16; Ps 42:4
25 [1]Lit *the fear I fear and* [a]Job 9:28; 30:15
26 [a]Job 7:13,14
4:1 [1]Lit *answered and said*
2 [1]Lit *in words* [a]Job 32:18-20
3 [a]Job 4:3,4; 29:15,16,21,25
4 [1]Lit *caused* [2]Lit *bowing*
5 [a]Job 6:14 [b]Job 19:21
6 [1]Or *reverence* [a]Job 1:1 [b]Prov 3:26
7 [a]Job 8:20; 36:6,7; Ps 37:25
8 [a]Job 15:31,35; Prov 22:8; Hos 10:13; Gal 6:7
9 [1]Lit *wind* [a]Job 15:30; Is 11:4; 30:33; 2 Thess 2:8 [b]Job 40:11-13
10 [a]Job 5:15; Ps 58:6
11 [a]Job 29:17; Ps 34:10 [b]Job 5:4; 20:10; 27:14
12 [a]Job 4:12-17; 33:15-18 [b]Job 26:14
13 [a]Job 33:15

14 Dread came upon me, and
trembling,
And made [1]all my bones shake.
15 "Then a [1]spirit passed by my
face;
The hair of my flesh bristled up.
16 "It stood still, but I could not
discern its appearance;
A form *was* before my eyes;
There was silence, then I heard a
voice:
17 'Can [a]mankind be just [1]before
God?
Can a man be pure [1]before his
[b]Maker?
18 '[a]He puts no trust even in His
servants;
And against His angels He
charges error.
19 'How much more those who
dwell in [a]houses of clay,
Whose [b]foundation is in the
dust,
Who are crushed before the
moth!
20 '[a]Between morning and evening
they are broken in pieces;
Unobserved, they [b]perish
forever.
21 'Is not their [a]tent-cord plucked
up within them?
They die, yet [b]without wisdom.'

God Is Just

5 "Call now, is there anyone who
will answer you?
And to which of the [a]holy ones
will you turn?
2 "For [a]anger slays the foolish man,
And jealousy kills the simple.
3 "I have seen the [a]foolish taking
root,
And I [b]cursed his abode
immediately.
4 "His [a]sons are far from safety,
They are even [1]oppressed in the
gate,
And there is no deliverer.
5 "[1]His harvest the hungry devour
And take it to a *place of* thorns,
And the [2a]schemer is eager for
their wealth.
6 "For [a]affliction does not come
from the dust,
Nor does trouble sprout from the
ground,
7 For [a]man is born for trouble,
As sparks fly upward.
8 ¶ "But as for me, I would [a]seek
God,
And I would place my cause
before God;
9 Who [a]does great and
unsearchable things,
[1]Wonders without number.
10 "He [a]gives rain on the earth
And sends water on the fields,
11 So that [a]He sets on high those
who are lowly,
And those who mourn are lifted
to safety.
12 "He [a]frustrates the plotting of the
shrewd,
So that their hands cannot attain
success.
13 "He [a]captures the wise by their
own shrewdness,
And the advice of the cunning is
quickly thwarted.
14 "By day they [a]meet with
darkness,
And grope at noon as in the
night.
15 "But He saves from [a]the sword of
their mouth,
And [b]the poor from the hand of
the mighty.
16 "So the helpless has hope,
And [a]unrighteousness must shut
its mouth.

17 ¶ "Behold, how [a]happy is the
man whom God reproves,
So do not despise the [b]discipline
of [1]the Almighty.
18 "For [a]He inflicts pain, and [1]gives
relief;
He wounds, and His hands *also*
heal.
19 "[1]From six troubles [a]He will
deliver you,
Even in seven [b]evil will not
touch you.
20 "In [a]famine He will redeem you
from death,
And [b]in war from the power of
the sword.
21 "You will be [a]hidden from the
scourge of the tongue,
[b]And you will not be afraid of
violence when it comes.
22 "You will [a]laugh at violence and
famine,
[b]And you will not be afraid of
[1]wild beasts.
23 "For you will be in league with
the stones of the field,
And [a]the beasts of the field will
be at peace with you.
24 "You will know that your [a]tent is
secure,
For you will visit your abode and
fear no loss.
25 "You will know also that your
[1a]descendants will be
many,

14 [1]Lit *the multitude of*
15 [1]Or *breath passed over*
17 [1]Lit *from* [a]Job 9:2; 25:4 [b]Job 31:15; 32:22; 35:10; 36:3
18 [a]Job 15:15
19 [a]Job 10:9; 33:6 [b]Gen 2:7; 3:19; Job 22:16
20 [a]Job 14:2 [b]Job 14:20; 20:7
21 [a]Job 8:22 [b]Job 18:21; 36:12
5:1 [a]Job 15:15
2 [a]Prov 12:16; 27:3
3 [a]Jer 12:2 [b]Job 24:18; 31:30
4 [1]Lit *crushed* [a]Job 4:11
5 [1]Lit *Whose* [2]Ancient versions read *thirsty* [a]Job 18:8-10; 22:10
6 [a]Job 15:35
7 [a]Job 14:1
8 [a]Job 13:2,3; Ps 50:15
9 [1]Or *Miracles* [a]Job 9:10; 37:14,16; 42:3
10 [a]Job 36:27-29; 37:6-11; 38:26
11 [a]Job 22:29; 36:7
12 [a]Ps 33:10
13 [a]Job 37:24; 1 Cor 3:19
14 [a]Job 12:25; 15:30; 18:18; 20:26; 24:13
15 [a]Job 4:10,11; Ps 35:10 [b]Job 29:17; 34:28; 36:6,15; 38:15
16 [a]Ps 107:42
17 [1]Heb *Shaddai,* and so throughout ch 6 [a]Ps 94:12 [b]Job 36:15,16; Prov 3:11; Heb 12:5-11; James 1:12
18 [1]Lit *binds* [a]Deut 32:39; 1 Sam 2:6; Is 30:26; Hos 6:1
19 [1]Lit *In* [a]Ps 34:19 [b]Ps 91:10
20 [a]Ps 33:19; 37:19 [b]Ps 144:10
21 [a]Job 5:15; Ps 31:20 [b]Ps 91:5,6
22 [1]Lit *beasts of the earth* [a]Job 8:21 [b]Ps 91:13; Ezek 34:25; Hos 2:18
23 [a]Is 11:6-9; 65:25
24 [a]Job 8:6
25 [1]Lit *seed* [a]Ps 112:2

And [b]your offspring as the grass
of the earth.
26 "You will [a]come to the grave in
full vigor,
Like the stacking of grain in its
season.
27 "Behold this; we have investigated
it, *and* so it is.
Hear it, and know for yourself."

Job's Friends Are No Help

6 Then Job [1]answered,
2 "[a]Oh that my grief were
actually weighed
And laid in the balances together
with my calamity!
3 "For then it would be [a]heavier
than the sand of the seas;
Therefore my words have been
rash.
4 "For the [a]arrows of the Almighty
are within me,
[1]Their [b]poison my spirit drinks;
The [c]terrors of God are arrayed
against me.
5 "Does the [a]wild donkey bray over
his grass,
Or does the ox low over his
fodder?
6 "Can something tasteless be eaten
without salt,
Or is there any taste in the
[1]white of an egg?
7 "My soul [a]refuses to touch *them;*
They are like loathsome food
to me.

8 ¶ "Oh that my request might
come to pass,
And that God would grant my
longing!
9 "Would that God were [a]willing to
crush me,
That He would loose His hand
and cut me off!
10 "But it is still my consolation,
And I rejoice in unsparing pain,
That I [a]have not [1]denied the
words of the Holy One.
11 "What is my strength, that I
should wait?
And what is my end, that I
should [1a]endure?
12 "Is my strength the strength of
stones,
Or is my flesh bronze?
13 "Is it that my [a]help is not
within me,
And that [1b]deliverance is driven
from me?

14 ¶ "For the [a]despairing man
there should be kindness
from his friend;
So that he does not [b]forsake the
[1]fear of the Almighty.
15 "My brothers have acted
[a]deceitfully like a [1]wadi,
Like the torrents of [1]wadis
which vanish,
16 Which are turbid because of ice
And into which the snow
[1]melts.
17 "When [a]they become waterless,
they [1]are silent,
When it is hot, they vanish from
their place.
18 "The [1]paths of their course wind
along,
They go up into nothing and
perish.
19 "The caravans of [a]Tema looked,
The travelers of [b]Sheba hoped
for them.
20 "They [a]were [1]disappointed for
they had trusted,
They came there and were
confounded.
21 "Indeed, you have now become
such,
[a]You see a terror and are afraid.
22 "Have I said, 'Give me
something,'
Or, 'Offer a bribe for me from
your wealth,'
23 Or, 'Deliver me from the hand of
the adversary,'
Or, 'Redeem me from the hand
of the tyrants'?

24 ¶ "Teach me, and [a]I will be
silent;
And show me how I have erred.
25 "How painful are honest words!
But what does your argument
prove?
26 "Do you intend to reprove *my*
words,
When the [a]words of one in
despair belong to the wind?
27 "You would even [a]cast *lots* for
[b]the orphans
And [c]barter over your friend.
28 "Now please look at me,
And *see* if I [a]lie to your face.
29 "Desist now, let there be no
injustice;
Even desist, [a]my righteousness
is yet in it.
30 "Is there injustice on my tongue?
Cannot [a]my palate discern
[1]calamities?

Job's Life Seems Futile

7 "[1]Is not man [a]forced to labor on
earth,
And *are not* his days like the
days of [b]a hired man?

25 [b]Is 44:3,4; 48:19
26 [a]Job 42:17
6:1 [1]Lit *answered and said*
2 [a]Job 31:6
3 [a]Job 23:2
4 [1]Lit *Whose* [a]Job 16:13; Ps 38:2 [b]Job 20:16; 21:20 [c]Job 30:15
5 [a]Job 39:5-8
6 [1]Heb *hallamuth,* meaning uncertain. Perhaps the juice of a plant
7 [a]Job 3:24; 33:20
9 [a]Num 11:15; 1 Kin 19:4; Job 7:16; 9:21; 10:1
10 [1]Lit *hidden* [a]Job 22:22; 23:11,12
11 [1]Lit *prolong my soul* [a]Job 21:4
13 [1]So ancient versions [a]Job 26:2 [b]Job 26:3
14 [1]Or *reverence* [a]Job 4:5 [b]Job 1:5; 15:4
15 [1]Or *brooks* [a]Jer 15:18
16 [1]Lit *hides itself*
17 [1]Or *cease* [a]Job 24:19
18 [1]Or *caravans turn from their course, they go up into the waste and perish*
19 [a]Gen 25:15; Is 21:14; Jer 25:23 [b]Job 1:15
20 [1]Lit *ashamed* [a]Jer 14:3
21 [a]Ps 38:11
24 [a]Ps 39:1
26 [a]Job 8:2; 15:2; 16:3
27 [a]Joel 3:3; Nah 3:10 [b]Job 22:9; 24:3,9 [c]2 Pet 2:3
28 [a]Job 27:4; 33:3; 36:4
29 [a]Job 13:18; 19:6; 23:10; 27:5,6; 34:5; 42:1-6
30 [1]Or *words* [a]Job 12:11
7:1 [1]Lit *Has not man compulsory labor* [a]Job 5:7; 10:17; 14:1,14 [b]Job 14:6

2 "As a slave who pants for the shade,
And as a hired man who eagerly waits for his wages,
3 So am I allotted months of vanity,
And [a]nights of trouble are appointed me.
4 "When I [a]lie down I say,
'When shall I arise?'
But the night continues,
And I am [1]continually tossing until dawn.
5 "My [a]flesh is clothed with worms and a crust of dirt,
My skin hardens and runs.
6 "My days are [a]swifter than a weaver's shuttle,
And come to an end [b]without hope.

7 ¶ "Remember that my life [a]is *but* breath;
My eye will [b]not again see good.
8 "The [a]eye of him who sees me will behold me no longer;
Your eyes *will be* on me, but [b]I will not be.
9 "When a [a]cloud vanishes, it is gone,
So [b]he who goes down to [c]Sheol does not come up.
10 "He will not return again to his house,
Nor will [a]his place know him anymore.

11 ¶ "Therefore [a]I will not restrain my mouth;
I will speak in the anguish of my spirit,
I will complain in the bitterness of my soul.
12 "Am I the sea, or [a]the sea monster,
That You set a guard over me?
13 "If I say, '[a]My bed will comfort me,
My couch will [1]ease my complaint,'
14 Then You frighten me with dreams
And terrify me by visions;
15 So that my soul would choose suffocation,
Death rather than my [1]pains.
16 "I [1a]waste away; I will not live forever.
Leave me alone, [b]for my days are *but* a breath.
17 "[a]What is man that You magnify him,
And that You [1]are concerned about him,
18 That [a]You examine him every morning
And try him every moment?
19 "[1a]Will You never turn Your gaze away from me,
Nor let me alone until I swallow my spittle?
20 "[a]Have I sinned? What have I done to You,
O [b]watcher of men?
Why have You set me as Your target,
So that I am a burden to myself?
21 "Why then [a]do You not pardon my transgression
And take away my iniquity?
For now I will [b]lie down in the dust;
And You will seek me, [c]but I will not be."

Bildad Says God Rewards the Good

8 Then Bildad the Shuhite [1]answered,
2 "How long will you say these things,
And the [a]words of your mouth be a mighty wind?
3 "Does [a]God pervert justice?
Or does [1]the Almighty pervert what is right?
4 "[a]If your sons sinned against Him,
Then He delivered them into the [1]power of their transgression.
5 "If you would [a]seek God
And implore the compassion of [1]the Almighty,
6 If you are pure and upright,
Surely now [a]He would rouse Himself for you
And restore your righteous [1b]estate.
7 "Though your beginning was insignificant,
Yet your [a]end will increase greatly.

8 ¶ "Please [a]inquire of past generations,
And consider the things searched out by their fathers.
9 "For we are *only* of yesterday and know nothing,
Because [a]our days on earth are as a shadow.
10 "Will they not teach you *and* tell you,
And bring forth words from their minds?

11 ¶ "Can the papyrus grow up without a marsh?
Can the rushes grow without water?

---

3 [a]Job 16:7
4 [1]Lit *sated with* [a]Deut 28:67; Job 7:13,14
5 [a]Job 2:7; 17:14
6 [a]Job 9:25 [b]Job 13:15; 14:19; 17:15,16; 19:10
7 [a]Job 7:16; Ps 78:39; James 4:14 [b]Job 9:25
8 [a]Job 8:18; 20:9 [b]Job 7:21
9 [a]Job 30:15 [b]Job 3:13-19 [c]2 Sam 12:23; Job 11:8; 14:13; 17:13,16
10 [a]Job 8:18; 20:9; 27:21,23
11 [a]Job 10:1; 21:4; 23:2; Ps 40:9
12 [a]Ezek 32:2,3
13 [1]Lit *bear* [a]Job 7:4; Ps 6:6
15 [1]Lit *bones*
16 [1]Or *loathe* [a]Job 6:9; 9:21; 10:1 [b]Job 7:7
17 [1]Lit *set Your heart on* [a]Job 22:2; Ps 8:4; 144:3; Heb 2:6
18 [a]Job 14:3
19 [1]Lit *How long will You not* [a]Job 9:18; 10:20; 14:6
20 [a]Job 35:3,6 [b]Ps 36:6
21 [a]Job 9:28; 10:14 [b]Job 10:9 [c]Job 7:8
8:1 [1]Lit *answered and said*
2 [a]Job 6:26
3 [1]Heb *Shaddai* [a]Gen 18:25; Deut 32:4; 2 Chr 19:7; Job 34:10, 12; 36:23; 37:23; Rom 3:5
4 [1]Lit *hand* [a]Job 1:5,18,19
5 [1]Heb *Shaddai* [a]Job 5:17-27
6 [1]Lit *place* [a]Job 22:27; 34:28; Ps 7:6 [b]Job 5:24
7 [a]Job 42:12
8 [a]Deut 4:32; 32:7; Job 15:18; 20:4
9 [a]Job 14:2

12 "While it is still green *and* not cut
down,
Yet it withers before any *other*
[1]plant.
13 "So are the paths of [a]all who
forget God;
And the [b]hope of the godless
will perish,
14 Whose confidence is fragile,
And whose trust a
[a]spider's [1]web.
15 "He [1]trusts in his [a]house, but it
does not stand;
He holds fast to it, but it does
not endure.
16 "He [1a]thrives before the sun,
And his [b]shoots spread out over
his garden.
17 "His roots wrap around a rock
pile,
He [1]grasps a house of stones.
18 "If he is [1]removed from [a]his
place,
Then it will deny him, *saying,*
'[b]I never saw you.'
19 "Behold, [a]this is the joy of His
way;
And out of the dust others will
spring.
20 "Lo, [a]God will not reject *a man
of* integrity,
Nor [b]will He [1]support the
evildoers.
21 "He will yet fill [a]your mouth
with laughter
And your lips with shouting.
22 "Those who hate you will be
[a]clothed with shame,
And the [b]tent of the wicked will
be no longer."

Job Says There Is No Arbitrator between God and Man

9 Then Job [1]answered,
2 "In truth I know that this is so;
But how can a [a]man be in the
right [1]before God?
3 "If one wished to [a]dispute with
Him,
He could not answer Him once
in a thousand *times.*
4 "[a]Wise in heart and [b]mighty in
strength,
Who has [1c]defied Him
[2]without harm?
5 "[a]*It is God* who removes the
mountains, they know
not *how,*
When He overturns them in His
anger;
6 Who [a]shakes the earth out of its
place,
And its [b]pillars tremble;
7 Who commands the [a]sun [1]not
to shine,
And sets a seal upon the stars;
8 Who alone [a]stretches out the
heavens
And [1b]tramples down the waves
of the sea;
9 Who makes the [a]Bear, Orion
and the Pleiades,
And the [b]chambers of the south;
10 Who [a]does great things,
[1]unfathomable,
And wondrous works without
number.
11 "Were He to pass by me, [a]I
would not see Him;
Were He to move past *me,* I
would not perceive Him.
12 "Were He to snatch away, who
could [a]restrain Him?
Who could say to Him, '[b]What
are You doing?'
13 ¶ "God will not turn back His
anger;
Beneath Him crouch the helpers
of [a]Rahab.
14 "How then can [a]I [1]answer Him,
And choose my words [2]before
Him?
15 "For [a]though I were right, I could
not [1]answer;
I would have to [b]implore the
mercy of my judge.
16 "If I called and He answered me,
I could not believe that He was
listening to my voice.
17 "For He [a]bruises me with a
tempest
And multiplies my wounds
without cause.
18 "He will [a]not allow me to get my
breath,
But saturates me with
[b]bitterness.
19 "If *it is a matter* of power,
[a]behold, *He is* the
strong one!
And if *it is a matter* of justice,
who can summon [1]Him?
20 "[a]Though I am righteous, my
mouth will [b]condemn me;
Though I am guiltless, He will
declare me guilty.
21 "I am [a]guiltless;
I do not take notice of myself;
I [b]despise my life.
22 "It is *all* one; therefore I say,
'He [a]destroys the guiltless and
the wicked.'
23 "If the scourge kills suddenly,
He [a]mocks the despair of the
innocent.

12 [1]Lit *reed*
13 [a]Ps 9:17 [b]Job 11:20; 13:16; 15:34; 20:5; 27:8
14 [1]Lit *house* [a]Is 59:5,6
15 [1]Lit *leans on* [a]Job 8:22; 27:18; Ps 49:11
16 [1]Lit *is lush* [a]Ps 37:35; Jer 11:16 [b]Ps 80:11
17 [1]Heb *sees*
18 [1]Lit *swallowed up* [a]Job 7:10 [b]Job 7:8
19 [a]Job 20:5
20 [1]Lit *strengthen the hand of* [a]Job 4:7 [b]Job 21:30
21 [a]Job 5:22; Ps 126:1,2
22 [a]Ps 132:18 [b]Job 8:15; 15:34; 18:14; 21:28
9:1 [1]Lit *answered and said*
2 [1]Lit *with* [a]Job 4:17; 25:4
3 [a]Job 10:2; 13:19; 23:6; 40:2
4 [1]Lit *stiffened his neck against* [2]Lit *and remained safe* [a]Job 11:6; 12:13; 28:23; 38:36,37 [b]Job 9:19; 23:6 [c]2 Chr 13:12; Prov 29:1
5 [a]Job 9:5-10; 26:6-14; 41:11
6 [a]Is 2:19,21; 13:13; Hag 2:6 [b]Ps 75:3
7 [1]Lit *and it does not shine* [a]Is 13:10; Ezek 32:7,8
8 [1]Lit *treads upon the heights of* [a]Gen 1:1; Job 37:18; Ps 104:2; Is 40:22 [b]Job 38:16; Ps 77:19
9 [a]Job 38:31,32; Amos 5:8 [b]Job 37:9
10 [1]Lit *until there is no searching out* [a]Job 5:9
11 [a]Job 23:8,9; 35:14
12 [a]Job 10:7; 11:10 [b]Is 45:9
13 [a]Job 26:12; Ps 89:10; Is 30:7; 51:9
14 [1]Or *plead my case* [2]Lit *with* [a]Job 9:3,32
15 [1]Or *plead my case* [a]Job 9:20, 21; 10:15 [b]Job 8:5
17 [a]Job 16:12, 14; 30:22
18 [a]Job 7:19; 10:20 [b]Job 13:26; 27:2
19 [1]So with Gr; Heb *me* [a]Job 9:4
20 [a]Job 9:15 [b]Job 9:29; 15:6
21 [a]Job 1:1; 12:4; 13:18 [b]Job 7:16
22 [a]Job 10:7,8
23 [a]Job 24:12

24 "The earth [a]is given into the
hand of the wicked;
He [b]covers the faces of its
judges.
If *it is* not *He,* then who is it?
25 ¶ "Now [a]my days are swifter
than a runner;
They flee away, [b]they see no
good.
26 "They slip by like [a]reed boats,
Like an [b]eagle that swoops on
[1]its prey.
27 "Though I say, 'I will forget [a]my
complaint,
I will leave off my *sad*
countenance and be
cheerful,'
28 I am [a]afraid of all my pains,
I know that [b]You will not
acquit me.
29 "I am accounted [a]wicked,
Why then should I toil in vain?
30 "If I should [a]wash myself with
snow
And cleanse [b]my hands with
lye,
31 Yet You would plunge me into
the pit,
And my own clothes would
abhor me.
32 "For [a]*He is* not a man as I am
that [b]I may answer Him,
That we may go to [1]court
together.
33 "There is no [a]umpire
between us,
Who may lay his hand upon us
both.
34 "Let Him [a]remove His rod
from me,
And let not dread of Him
terrify me.
35 "*Then* I [a]would speak and not
fear Him;
But I am not like that in myself.

Job Despairs of God's Dealings

10 "[a]I loathe my own life;
I will give full vent to [b]my
complaint;
[1]I will speak in the bitterness of
my soul.
2 "I will say to God, '[a]Do not
condemn me;
Let me know why You contend
with me.
3 'Is it [1]right for You indeed to
[a]oppress,
To reject [b]the labor of Your
hands,
And [2]to look favorably on [c]the
schemes of the wicked?

24 [a]Job 10:3; 12:6; 16:11 [b]Job 12:17
25 [a]Job 7:6 [b]Job 7:7
26 [1]Lit *food* [a]Is 18:2 [b]Job 39:29; Hab 1:8
27 [a]Job 7:11
28 [a]Job 3:25 [b]Job 7:21; 10:14
29 [a]Job 10:2; Ps 37:33
30 [a]Jer 2:22 [b]Job 31:7
32 [1]Lit *judgment* [a]Eccl 6:10 [b]Job 9:3; Rom 9:20
33 [a]1 Sam 2:25; Job 9:19; Is 1:18
34 [a]Job 13:21
35 [a]Job 13:22
10:1 [1]Lit *My soul loathes* [a]Job 7:16 [b]Job 7:11
2 [a]Job 9:29
3 [1]Lit *good* [2]Lit *You shine forth* [a]Job 9:22-24; 16:11; 19:6; 27:2 [b]Job 10:8; 14:15; Ps 138:8; Is 64:8 [c]Job 21:16; 22:18
4 [a]1 Sam 16:7; Job 28:24; 34:21
5 [a]Job 36:26
6 [a]Job 14:16
7 [a]Job 9:21; 13:18 [b]Job 9:12; 23:13; 27:22
8 [1]Lit *together round about* [a]Job 10:3; Ps 119:73 [b]Job 9:22
9 [a]Job 4:19; 33:6 [b]Job 7:21
12 [a]Job 33:4
13 [a]Job 23:13
14 [a]Job 7:20 [b]Job 7:21; 9:28
15 [1]Lit *see* [a]Job 10:7; Is 3:11 [b]Job 6:29
16 [a]Is 38:13; Lam 3:10; Hos 13:7 [b]Job 5:9
17 [1]Lit *Changes and warfare are with me* [a]Ruth 1:21; Job 16:8 [b]Job 7:1
18 [a]Job 3:11-13
20 [a]Job 14:1

4 'Have You eyes of flesh?
Or do You [a]see as a man sees?
5 'Are Your days as the days of a
mortal,
Or [a]Your years as man's years,
6 That [a]You should seek for my
guilt
And search after my sin?
7 'According to Your knowledge [a]I
am indeed not guilty,
Yet there is [b]no deliverance
from Your hand.
8 ¶ '[a]Your hands fashioned and
made me [1]altogether,
[b]And would You destroy me?
9 'Remember now, that You have
made me as [a]clay;
And would You [b]turn me into
dust again?
10 'Did You not pour me out like
milk
And curdle me like cheese;
11 Clothe me with skin and flesh,
And knit me together with bones
and sinews?
12 'You have [a]granted me life and
lovingkindness;
And Your care has preserved my
spirit.
13 'Yet [a]these things You have
concealed in Your heart;
I know that this is within You:
14 If I sin, then You would [a]take
note of me,
And [b]would not acquit me of
my guilt.
15 'If [a]I am wicked, woe to me!
And [b]if I am righteous, I dare
not lift up my head.
I am sated with disgrace and
[1]conscious of my misery.
16 'Should *my head* be lifted up,
[a]You would hunt me like a
lion;
And again You would show Your
[b]power against me.
17 'You renew [a]Your witnesses
against me
And increase Your anger
toward me;
[1b]Hardship after hardship is
with me.
18 ¶ '[a]Why then have You brought
me out of the womb?
Would that I had died and no
eye had seen me!
19 'I should have been as though I
had not been,
Carried from womb to tomb.'
20 "Would He not let [a]my few days
alone?

[1b]Withdraw from me that I may
have a little cheer
21 Before I go—[a]and I shall not
return—
[b]To the land of darkness and
[c]deep shadow,
22 The land of utter gloom as
darkness *itself,*
Of deep shadow without order,
And which shines as the
darkness."

Zophar Rebukes Job

11 Then Zophar the Naamathite
[1]answered,
2 "Shall a multitude of words go
unanswered,
And a [a]talkative man be
acquitted?
3 "Shall your boasts silence men?
And shall you [a]scoff and none
rebuke?
4 "For [a]you have said, 'My
teaching is pure,
And [b]I am innocent in your
eyes.'
5 "But would that God might speak,
And open His lips against you,
6 And show you the secrets of
wisdom!
For sound wisdom [1a]has two
sides.
Know then that God [2]forgets a
part of [b]your iniquity.

7 ¶ "[a]Can you discover the depths
of God?
Can you discover the limits of
the Almighty?
8 "*They are* [a]high as [1]the heavens,
what can you do?
Deeper than [2b]Sheol, what can
you know?
9 "Its measure is longer than the
earth
And broader than the sea.
10 "If He passes by or shuts up,
Or calls an assembly, [a]who can
restrain Him?
11 "For [a]He knows false men,
And He [b]sees iniquity [1]without
investigating.
12 "[1a]An idiot will become
intelligent
When the [2]foal of a [b]wild
donkey is born a man.

13 ¶ "[a]If you would [b]direct your
heart right
And [c]spread out your hand to
Him,
14 If iniquity is in your hand, [a]put
it far away,
And do not let wickedness dwell
in your tents;
15 "Then, indeed, you could [a]lift up
your face without *moral*
defect,
And you would be steadfast and
[b]not fear.
16 "For you would [a]forget *your*
trouble,
As [b]waters that have passed by,
you would remember *it.*
17 "Your [1]life would be [2a]brighter
than noonday;
Darkness would be like the
morning.
18 "Then you would trust, because
there is hope;
And you would look around and
rest securely.
19 "You would [a]lie down and none
would disturb *you,*
And many would [b]entreat your
[1]favor.
20 "But the [a]eyes of the wicked will
fail,
And [1]there will [b]be no escape
for them;
And their [c]hope is [2d]to breathe
their last."

Job Chides His Accusers

12 Then Job [1]responded,
2 "Truly then [a]you are the
people,
And with you wisdom will die!
3 "But [a]I have intelligence as well
as you;
I am not inferior to you.
And [1]who does not know such
things as these?
4 "I am a [a]joke to [1]my friends,
The one who called on God and
He answered him;
The just *and* [b]blameless *man* is
a joke.
5 "[1]He who is at ease holds
calamity in contempt,
As prepared for those whose feet
slip.
6 "The [a]tents of the destroyers
prosper,
And those who provoke God
[b]are secure,
[1]Whom God brings [c]into their
power.

7 ¶ "But now ask the beasts, and
let them teach you;
And the birds of the heavens,
and let them tell you.
8 "Or speak to the earth, and let it
teach you;

20 [1]Lit *Put* [b]Job 7:16,19
21 [a]2 Sam 12:23; Job 3:13-19; 16:22 [b]Ps 88:12 [c]Job 10:22; 34:22; 38:17; Ps 23:4
11:1 [1]Lit *answered and said*
2 [a]Job 8:2; 15:2; 18:2
3 [a]Job 17:2; 21:3
4 [a]Job 6:10 [b]Job 10:7
6 [1]Lit *is double* [2]Lit *causes to be forgotten for you* [a]Job 9:4 [b]Job 15:5; 22:5
7 [a]Job 33:12,13; 36:26; 37:5,23; Rom 11:33
8 [1]Lit *the heights of heaven* [2]I.e. the nether world [a]Job 22:12; 35:5 [b]Job 26:6; 38:17
10 [a]Job 9:12
11 [1]Or *even He does not consider* [a]Job 34:21-23 [b]Job 24:23; 28:24; 31:4
12 [1]Lit *A hollow man* [2]Lit *donkey* [a]Ps 39:5,11; 62:9; 144:4; Eccl 1:2; 11:10 [b]Job 39:5
13 [a]Job 5:17-27; 11:13-20 [b]1 Sam 7:3; Ps 78:8 [c]Job 22:27; Ps 88:9; 143:6
14 [a]Job 22:23
15 [a]Job 22:26 [b]Ps 27:3; 46:2
16 [a]Is 65:16 [b]Job 22:11
17 [1]Lit *duration of life* [2]Lit *above noonday* [a]Job 22:26
19 [1]Lit *face* [a]Lev 26:6; Is 17:2; Mic 4:4; Zeph 3:13 [b]Is 45:14
20 [1]Lit *escape has perished from them* [2]Lit *the expiring of the soul* [a]Deut 28:65; Job 17:5 [b]Job 27:22; 34:22 [c]Job 8:13 [d]Job 6:9
12:1 [1]Lit *answered and said*
2 [a]Job 17:10
3 [1]Lit *with whom is there not like these?* [a]Job 13:2
4 [1]Lit *his* [a]Job 17:6; 30:1,9,10; 34:7 [b]Job 6:29
5 [1]Lit *Contempt for calamity is the thought of him who is at ease*
6 [1]*Or He who brings God into his hand* [a]Job 9:24; 21:7-9 [b]Job 24:23 [c]Job 22:18

And let the fish of the sea
declare to you.
9 "Who among all these does not
know
That [a]the hand of the LORD has
done this,
10 [a]In whose hand is the life of
every living thing,
And [b]the breath of all mankind?
11 "Does not [a]the ear test words,
As the palate [1]tastes its food?
12 "Wisdom is with [a]aged men,
With [1]long life is understanding.

Job Speaks of the Power of God

13 ¶ "With Him are [a]wisdom and
[a]might;
To Him belong counsel and
[b]understanding.
14 "Behold, He [a]tears down, and it
cannot be rebuilt;
He [1b]imprisons a man, and
[2]there can be no release.
15 "Behold, He [a]restrains the
waters, and they dry up;
And He [b]sends them out, and
they [1]inundate the earth.
16 "With Him are strength and
sound wisdom,
The [a]misled and the misleader
belong to Him.
17 "He makes [a]counselors walk
[1]barefoot
And makes fools of [b]judges.
18 "He [a]loosens the [1]bond of kings
And binds their loins with a
girdle.
19 "He makes priests walk [1]barefoot
And overthrows [a]the secure
ones.
20 "He deprives the trusted ones of
speech
And [a]takes away the
discernment of the elders.
21 "He [a]pours contempt on nobles
And [b]loosens the belt of the
strong.
22 "He [a]reveals mysteries from the
darkness
And brings the deep darkness
into light.
23 "He [a]makes the nations great,
then destroys them;
He [1]enlarges the nations, then
leads them away.
24 "He [a]deprives of intelligence the
chiefs of the earth's people
And makes them wander in a
pathless waste.
25 "They [a]grope in darkness with no
light,
And He makes them [b]stagger
like a drunken man.

Job Says His Friends' Proverbs Are Ashes

13 "[a]Behold, my eye has seen all
this,
My ear has heard and
understood it.
2 "[a]What you know I also know;
I am not inferior to you.
3 ¶ "But [a]I would speak to [1]the
Almighty,
And I desire to [b]argue with
God.
4 "But you [a]smear with lies;
You are all [b]worthless
physicians.
5 "O that you would [a]be
completely silent,
And that it would become your
wisdom!
6 "Please hear my argument
And listen to the contentions of
my lips.
7 "Will you [a]speak what is unjust
for God,
And speak what is deceitful for
Him?
8 "Will you [a]show partiality for
Him?
Will you contend for God?
9 "Will it be well when He
examines you?
Or [a]will you deceive Him as one
deceives a man?
10 "He will surely reprove you
If you secretly [a]show partiality.
11 "Will not [a]His [1]majesty terrify
you,
And the dread of Him fall
on you?
12 "Your memorable sayings are
proverbs of ashes,
Your defenses are defenses of
clay.

Job Is Sure He Will Be Vindicated

13 ¶ "[a]Be silent before me so that I
may speak;
Then let come on me what may.
14 "Why should I take my flesh in
my teeth
And [a]put my life in my [1]hands?
15 "[a]Though He slay me,
I will hope in Him.
Nevertheless I [b]will argue my
ways [1]before Him.
16 "This also will be my [a]salvation,
For [b]a godless man may not
come before His presence.
17 "Listen carefully to my speech,
And let my declaration *fill* your
ears.

9 [a]Is 41:20
10 [a]Acts 17:28 [b]Job 27:3; 33:4
11 [1]Lit *tastes food for itself* [a]Job 34:3
12 [1]Lit *length of days* [a]Job 15:10; 32:7
13 [a]Job 9:4 [b]Job 11:6; 26:12; 32:8; 36:5; 38:36
14 [1]Lit *shuts against* [2]Lit *it is not opened* [a]Job 19:10; Is 25:2 [b]Job 37:7
15 [1]Lit *overturn* [a]Deut 11:17; 1 Kin 8:35; 17:1 [b]Gen 7:11-24
16 [a]Job 13:7,9
17 [1]Or *stripped* [a]Job 3:14 [b]Job 9:24
18 [1]Or *discipline* [a]Ps 116:16
19 [1]Or *stripped* [a]Job 24:22; 34:24-28; 35:9
20 [a]Job 17:4; 32:9
21 [a]Job 34:19; Ps 107:40 [b]Job 12:18
22 [a]Dan 2:22; 1 Cor 4:5
23 [1]Or *spreads out* [a]Is 9:3; 26:15
24 [a]Job 12:20
25 [a]Job 5:14 [b]Is 24:20
13:1 [a]Job 12:9
2 [a]Job 12:3
3 [1]Heb *Shaddai* [a]Job 13:22; 23:4 [b]Job 13:15
4 [a]Ps 119:69 [b]Jer 23:32
5 [a]Job 13:13; 21:5; Prov 17:28
7 [a]Job 27:4
8 [a]Lev 19:15; Prov 24:23
9 [a]Job 12:16
10 [a]Job 13:8; 32:21; 34:19
11 [1]Lit *exaltation* [a]Job 31:23
13 [a]Job 13:5
14 [1]Lit *palm* [a]Ps 119:109
15 [1]Lit *to His face* [a]Job 7:6 [b]Job 27:5
16 [a]Job 23:7; Is 12:1,2 [b]Job 34:21-23

18 "Behold now, I have [a]prepared
my case;
I know that [b]I will be
vindicated.
19 "[a]Who will contend with me?
For then I would be silent
and [b]die.

20 ¶ "Only two things do not do
to me,
Then I will not hide from Your
face:
21 [a]Remove Your [1]hand from me,
And let not the dread of You
terrify me.
22 "Then call, and [a]I will answer;
Or let me speak, then reply
to me.
23 "[a]How many are my iniquities
and sins?
Make known to me my
[1]rebellion and my sin.
24 "Why do You [a]hide Your face
And consider me [b]Your enemy?
25 "Will You cause a [a]driven leaf to
tremble?
Or will You pursue the dry
[b]chaff?
26 "For You write [a]bitter things
against me
And [b]make me to inherit the
iniquities of my youth.
27 "You [a]put my feet in the stocks
And watch all my paths;
You [1]set a limit for the soles of
my feet,
28 While [1]I am decaying like a
[a]rotten thing,
Like a garment that is
moth-eaten.

Job Speaks of the Finality of Death

14 "[a]Man, who is born of woman,
Is [1]short-lived and [b]full of
turmoil.
2 "[a]Like a flower he comes forth
and withers.
He also flees like [b]a shadow and
does not remain.
3 "You also [a]open Your eyes
on him
And [b]bring [1]him into judgment
with Yourself.
4 "[a]Who can make the clean out of
the unclean?
No one!
5 "Since his days are determined,
The [a]number of his months is
with You;
And his limits You have [1]set so
that he cannot pass.
6 "[a]Turn Your gaze from him that
he may [1]rest,
Until he [2]fulfills his day like a
hired man.

7 ¶ "For there is hope for a tree,
When it is cut down, that it will
sprout again,
And its shoots will not [1]fail.
8 "Though its roots grow old in the
ground
And its stump dies in the dry
soil,
9 At the scent of water it will
flourish
And put forth sprigs like a plant.
10 "But [a]man dies and lies prostrate.
Man [b]expires, and where is he?
11 "*As* [a]water [1]evaporates from the
sea,
And a river becomes parched
and dried up,
12 So [a]man lies down and does not
rise.
Until the heavens are no longer,
[1]He will not awake nor be
aroused out of [2]his sleep.

13 ¶ "Oh that You would hide me
in [1]Sheol,
That You would conceal me
[a]until Your wrath returns
to You,
That You would set a limit for
me and remember me!
14 "If a man dies, will he live *again?*
All the days of my struggle I will
wait
Until my change comes.
15 "You will call, and I will
answer You;
You will long for [a]the work of
Your hands.
16 "For now You [a]number my steps,
You do not [b]observe my sin.
17 "My transgression is [a]sealed up
in a bag,
And You [1]wrap up my iniquity.

18 ¶ "But the falling mountain
[1]crumbles away,
And the rock moves from its
place;
19 Water wears away stones,
Its torrents wash away the dust
of the earth;
So You [a]destroy man's hope.
20 "You forever overpower him and
he [a]departs;
You change his appearance and
send him away.
21 "His sons achieve honor, but [a]he
does not know *it;*
Or they become insignificant, but
he does not perceive it.
22 "But his [1]body pains him,

18 [a]Job 23:4 [b]Job 9:21; 10:7; 12:4
19 [a]Is 50:8 [b]Job 7:21; 10:8
21 [1]Lit *palm* [a]Job 9:34; Ps 39:10
22 [a]Job 9:16; 14:15
23 [1]Or *transgression* [a]Job 7:21
24 [a]Ps 13:1; 44:24; 88:14; Is 8:17 [b]Job 19:11; 33:10; Lam 2:5
25 [a]Lev 26:36 [b]Job 21:18
26 [a]Job 9:18 [b]Ps 25:7
27 [1]Lit *carve for* [a]Job 33:11
28 [1]Lit *he is* [a]Job 2:7
14:1 [1]Lit *short of days* [a]Job 5:7 [b]Eccl 2:23
2 [a]Ps 90:5,6; 103:15; Is 40:6, 7; James 1:10; 1 Pet 1:24 [b]Job 8:9
3 [1]So with some ancient versions; M.T. *me* [a]Ps 8:4; 144:3 [b]Ps 143:2
4 [a]Job 15:14; 25:4; Ps 51:5
5 [1]Lit *made* [a]Job 21:21
6 [1]Lit *cease* [2]Lit *makes acceptable* [a]Job 7:19; Ps 39:13
7 [1]Or *cease*
10 [a]Job 3:13; 14:10-15 [b]Job 13:9
11 [1]Lit *disappears* [a]Is 19:5
12 [1]Lit *They* [2]Lit *their* [a]Job 3:13
13 [1]I.e. the nether world [a]Is 26:20
15 [a]Job 10:3
16 [a]Job 31:4; 34:21; Ps 139:1-3; Prov 5:21 [b]Job 10:6
17 [1]Lit *plaster;* or *glue together* [a]Deut 32:32-34
18 [1]Lit *withers*
19 [a]Job 7:6
20 [a]Job 4:20; 20:7
21 [a]Eccl 9:5
22 [1]Lit *flesh*

And he mourns only for
himself."

Eliphaz Says Job Presumes Much

15 Then Eliphaz the Temanite [1]responded,
2 "Should a wise man answer with
windy knowledge
[a]And fill [1]himself with the east
wind?
3 "Should he argue with useless
talk,
Or with words which are not
profitable?
4 "Indeed, you do away with
[1]reverence
And hinder meditation before
God.
5 "For [a]your guilt teaches your
mouth,
And you choose the language of
[b]the crafty.
6 "Your [a]own mouth condemns
you, and not I;
And your own lips testify
against you.
7 ¶ "Were you the first man to be
born,
Or [a]were you brought forth
before the hills?
8 "Do you hear the [a]secret counsel
of God,
And limit wisdom to yourself?
9 "[a]What do you know that we do
not know?
What do you understand that
[1]we do not?
10 "Both the [a]gray-haired and the
aged are among us,
Older than your father.
11 "Are [a]the consolations of God too
small for you,
Even the [b]word *spoken* gently
with you?
12 "Why does your [a]heart carry you
away?
And why do your eyes flash,
13 That you should turn your spirit
against God
And allow *such* words to go out
of your mouth?
14 "What is man, that [a]he should be
pure,
Or [b]he who is born of a woman,
that he should be righteous?
15 "Behold, He puts no trust in His
[a]holy ones,
And the [b]heavens are not pure
in His sight;
16 How much less one who is
[a]detestable and corrupt,
Man, who [b]drinks iniquity like
water!

What Eliphaz Has Seen of Life

17 ¶ "I will tell you, listen to me;
And what I have seen I will also
declare;
18 What wise men have told,
And have not concealed from
[a]their fathers,
19 To whom alone the land was
given,
And no alien passed among
them.
20 "The wicked man writhes [a]in
pain all *his* days,
And [1]numbered are the years
[b]stored up for the ruthless.
21 "[1]Sounds of [a]terror are in his
ears;
[b]While at peace the destroyer
comes upon him.
22 "He does not believe that he will
[a]return from darkness,
And he is destined for [b]the
sword.
23 "He wanders about for food,
saying, 'Where is it?'
He knows that a day of
[a]darkness is [1]at hand.
24 "Distress and anguish terrify him,
They overpower him like a king
ready for the attack,
25 Because he has stretched out his
hand against God
And conducts himself
[a]arrogantly against [1]the
Almighty.
26 "He rushes [1]headlong at Him
With [2]his massive shield.
27 "For he has [a]covered his face
with his fat
And made his thighs heavy with
flesh.
28 "He has [a]lived in desolate cities,
In houses no one would inhabit,
Which are destined to become
[1]ruins.
29 "He [a]will not become rich, nor
will his wealth endure;
And his grain will not bend
down to the ground.
30 "He will [a]not [1]escape from
darkness;
The [b]flame will wither his
shoots,
And by [c]the breath of His
mouth he will go away.
31 "Let him not [a]trust in emptiness,
deceiving himself;
For emptiness will be his
[1]reward.
32 "It will be accomplished [a]before
his time,
And his palm [b]branch will not
be green.

15:1 [1]Lit *answered and said*

2 [1]Lit *his belly* [a]Job 6:26

4 [1]Lit *fear*

5 [a]Job 22:5 [b]Job 5:12,13

6 [a]Job 18:7

7 [a]Job 38:4,21; Prov 8:25

8 [a]Job 29:4; Rom 11:34; 1 Cor 2:11

9 [1]Lit *is not within us?* [a]Job 12:3; 13:2

10 [a]Job 12:12; 32:6,7

11 [a]Job 5:17-19; 36:15,16 [b]Job 6:10; 23:12

12 [a]Job 11:13; 36:13

14 [a]Job 14:4; Prov 20:9; Eccl 7:20 [b]Job 25:4

15 [a]Job 5:1 [b]Job 25:5

16 [a]Ps 14:1 [b]Job 34:7; Prov 19:28

18 [a]Job 8:8; 20:4

20 [1]Lit *the number of years are* [a]Job 15:24 [b]Job 24:1; 27:13

21 [1]Lit *A sound of terrors is* [a]Job 15:24; 18:11; 20:25; 24:17; 27:20 [b]Job 20:21; 1 Thess 5:3

22 [a]Job 15:30 [b]Job 19:29; 27:14; 33:18; 36:12

23 [1]Lit *ready at his hand* [a]Job 15:22,30

25 [1]Heb *Shaddai* [a]Job 36:9

26 [1]Lit *with a stiff neck* [2]Lit *the thick-bossed shields*

27 [a]Ps 73:7; 119:70

28 [1]Or *heaps* [a]Job 3:14; Is 5:8, 9

29 [a]Job 27:16, 17

30 [1]Lit *turn aside* [a]Job 5:14; 15:22 [b]Job 15:34; 20:26; 22:20; 31:12 [c]Job 4:9

31 [1]Lit *exchange* [a]Job 35:13; Is 59:4

32 [a]Job 22:16; Eccl 7:17 [b]Job 18:16

33 "He will drop off his unripe grape
like the vine,
And will [a]cast off his flower like
the olive tree.
34 "For the company of [a]the godless
is barren,
And fire consumes [b]the tents of
[1]the corrupt.
35 "They [a]conceive [1]mischief and
bring forth iniquity,
And their [2]mind prepares
deception."

Job Says Friends Are Sorry Comforters

16 Then Job [1]answered,
2 "I have heard many such
things;
[1a]Sorry comforters are you all.
3 "Is there *no* limit to [a]windy
words?
Or what plagues you that you
answer?
4 "I too could speak like you,
If [1]I were in your place.
I could compose words
against you
And [a]shake my head at you.
5 "I could strengthen you with my
mouth,
And the solace of my lips could
lessen *your pain.*

Job Says God Shattered Him

6 ¶ "If I speak, [a]my pain is not
lessened,
And if I hold back, what has
left me?
7 "But now He has [a]exhausted me;
You have laid [b]waste all my
company.
8 "You have shriveled me up,
[a]It has become a witness;
And my [b]leanness rises up
against me,
It testifies to my face.
9 "His anger has [a]torn me and
[1]hunted me down,
He has [b]gnashed at me with His
teeth;
My [c]adversary [2]glares at me.
10 "They have [a]gaped at me with
their mouth,
They have [1b]slapped me on the
cheek with contempt;
They have [c]massed themselves
against me.
11 "God hands me over to ruffians
And tosses me into the hands of
the wicked.
12 "I was at ease, but [a]He
shattered me,
And He has grasped me by the
neck and shaken me to
pieces;
He has also set me up as His
[b]target.
13 "His [a]arrows surround me.
Without mercy He splits my
kidneys open;
He pours out [b]my gall on the
ground.
14 "He [a]breaks through me with
breach after breach;
He [b]runs at me like a warrior.
15 "I have sewed [a]sackcloth over my
skin
And [b]thrust my horn in the
dust.
16 "My face is flushed from
[a]weeping,
[b]And deep darkness is on my
eyelids,
17 Although there is no [a]violence
in my hands,
And [b]my prayer is pure.

18 ¶ "O earth, do not cover my
blood,
And let there be no *resting* place
for my cry.
19 "Even now, behold, [a]my witness
is in heaven,
And my [1]advocate is [b]on high.
20 "My friends are my scoffers;
[a]My eye [1]weeps to God.
21 "O that a man might plead with
God
As a man with his neighbor!
22 "For when a few years are past,
I shall go the way [a]of no return.

Job Says He Has Become a Byword

17 "My spirit is broken, my days
are extinguished,
The [1a]grave is *ready* for me.
2 "[a]Surely mockers are with me,
And my eye [1]gazes on their
provocation.

3 ¶ "Lay down, now, a pledge [a]for
me with Yourself;
Who is there that will [1]be my
guarantor?
4 "For You have [1a]kept their heart
from understanding,
Therefore You will not exalt
them.
5 "He who [a]informs against friends
for a share *of the spoil,*
The [b]eyes of his children also
will languish.

6 ¶ "But He has made me a
[a]byword of the people,
And I am [1]one at whom men
[b]spit.

---

33 [a]Job 14:2
34 [1]Lit *a bribe* [a]Job 8:13 [b]Job 8:22
35 [1]Or *pain* [2]Lit *belly* [a]Ps 7:14; Is 59:4
16:1 [1]Lit *answered and said*
2 [1]Lit *Comforters of trouble* [a]Job 13:4; 21:34
3 [a]Job 6:26
4 [1]Lit *your soul were in place of my soul* [a]Ps 22:7; 109:25; Zeph 2:15; Matt 27:39
6 [a]Job 9:27,28
7 [a]Job 7:3 [b]Job 16:20; 19:13-15
8 [a]Job 10:17 [b]Job 19:20; Ps 109:24
9 [1]Lit *borne a grudge against me* [2]Lit *sharpens his eyes* [a]Job 19:11; Hos 6:1 [b]Ps 35:16; Lam 2:16; Acts 7:54 [c]Job 13:24; 33:10
10 [1]Lit *struck* [a]Ps 22:13 [b]Is 50:6; Lam 3:30; Acts 23:2 [c]Job 30:12; Ps 35:15
12 [a]Job 9:17 [b]Job 7:20; Lam 3:12
13 [a]Job 6:4; 19:12; 25:3 [b]Job 20:25
14 [a]Job 9:17 [b]Joel 2:7
15 [a]Gen 37:34; Ps 69:11 [b]Ps 7:5
16 [a]Job 16:20 [b]Job 24:17
17 [a]Is 59:6; Jon 3:8 [b]Job 27:4
19 [1]Or *witness* [a]Gen 31:50; Job 19:25-27; Rom 1:9; Phil 1:8; 1 Thess 2:5 [b]Job 31:2
20 [1]Or *drips* [a]Job 17:7
22 [a]Job 3:13
17:1 [1]Lit *graves* [a]Ps 88:3,4
2 [1]Lit *lodges* [a]Job 12:4; 17:6
3 [1]Lit *strike hands with me* [a]Ps 119:122; Is 38:14
4 [1]Lit *hidden* [a]Job 12:20
5 [a]Lev 19:13,16 [b]Job 11:20
6 [1]Lit *a spitting to the faces* [a]Job 17:2 [b]Job 30:10

7 "My eye has also grown [a]dim
because of grief,
And all my [b]members are as a
shadow.
8 "The upright will be appalled at
this,
And the [a]innocent will stir up
himself against the godless.
9 "Nevertheless [a]the righteous will
hold to his way,
And [b]he who has clean hands
will grow stronger and
stronger.
10 "But come again all of [1]you now,
For I [a]do not find a wise man
among you.
11 "My [a]days are past, my plans are
torn apart,
Even the wishes of my heart.
12 "They make night into day,
saying,
'The light is near,' in the
presence of darkness.
13 "If I look for [a]Sheol as my home,
I [1]make my bed in the darkness;
14 If I call to the [a]pit, 'You are my
father';
To the [b]worm, 'my mother and
my sister';
15 Where now is [a]my hope?
And who regards my hope?
16 "[1]Will it go down with me to
Sheol?
Shall we together [a]go down into
the dust?"

Bildad Speaks of the Wicked

18 Then Bildad the Shuhite [1]responded,
2 "How long will you hunt for
words?
Show understanding and then
we can talk.
3 "Why are we [a]regarded as beasts,
As stupid in your eyes?
4 "O [1]you who tear yourself in
your anger—
For your sake is the earth to be
abandoned,
Or the rock to be moved from its
place?

5 ¶ "Indeed, the [a]light of the
wicked goes out,
And the [1]flame of his fire gives
no light.
6 "The light in his tent is
[a]darkened,
And his lamp goes out above
him.
7 "His [1]vigorous stride is
shortened,
And his [a]own scheme brings
him down.
8 "For he is [a]thrown into the net
by his own feet,
And he steps on the webbing.
9 "A snare seizes *him* by the heel,
And a trap snaps shut on him.
10 "A noose for him is hidden in the
ground,
And a trap for him on the path.
11 "All around [a]terrors frighten him,
And [b]harry him at every step.
12 "His strength is [a]famished,
And calamity is ready at his side.
13 "[1]His skin is devoured by disease,
The firstborn of death [a]devours
his [2]limbs.
14 "He is [a]torn from [1]the security
of his tent,
And [2]they march him before the
king of [b]terrors.
15 "[1]There dwells in his tent
nothing of his;
[a]Brimstone is scattered on his
habitation.
16 "His [a]roots are dried below,
And his [b]branch is cut off
above.
17 "[a]Memory of him perishes from
the earth,
And he has no name abroad.
18 "[1]He is driven from light [a]into
darkness,
And [b]chased from the inhabited
world.
19 "He has no [a]offspring or posterity
among his people,
Nor any survivor where he
sojourned.
20 "Those [1]in the west are appalled
at [a]his [2]fate,
And those [3]in the east are
seized with horror.
21 "Surely such are the [a]dwellings
of the wicked,
And this is the place of him who
does not know God."

Job Feels Insulted

19 Then Job [1]responded,
2 "How long will you
torment [1]me
And crush me with words?
3 "These ten times you have
insulted me;
You are not ashamed to
wrong me.
4 "Even if I have truly erred,
My error lodges with me.
5 "If indeed you [a]vaunt yourselves
against me
And prove my disgrace to me,
6 Know then that [a]God has
wronged me
And has closed [b]His net
around me.

7 [a]Job 16:16 [b]Job 16:8
8 [a]Job 22:19
9 [a]Prov 4:18 [b]Job 22:30; 31:7
10 [1]With some ancient mss and versions; M.T. *them* [a]Job 12:2
11 [a]Job 7:6
13 [1]Lit *spread out* [a]Job 3:13
14 [a]Job 7:5; 13:28; 30:30 [b]Job 21:26; 25:6
15 [a]Job 7:6
16 [1]So the Gr; Heb possibly *Let my limbs sink down to Sheol, since there is rest in the dust for all* [a]Job 3:17; 21:33
18:1 [1]Lit *answered and said*
3 [a]Ps 73:22
4 [1]Lit *he...tears himself...his*
5 [1]Lit *spark* [a]Job 21:17; Prov 13:9; 20:20; 24:20
6 [a]Job 12:25
7 [1]Lit *steps of his strength* [a]Job 15:6
8 [a]Job 22:10; Ps 9:15; 35:8; Is 24:17,18
11 [a]Job 15:21 [b]Job 18:18; 20:8
12 [a]Is 8:21
13 [1]Heb *It eats parts of his skin* [2]Or *parts* [a]Zech 14:12
14 [1]Lit *his tent his trust* [2]Or *you or she shall march* [a]Job 8:22; 18:6 [b]Job 15:21
15 [1]A suggested reading is *Fire dwells in his tent* [a]Ps 11:6
16 [a]Is 5:24; Hos 9:16; Amos 2:9; Mal 4:1 [b]Job 15:30,32
17 [a]Job 24:20; Ps 34:16; Prov 10:7
18 [1]Lit *They drive him...And chase him* [a]Job 5:14; Is 8:22 [b]Job 20:8; 27:21-23
19 [a]Job 27:14, 15; Is 14:22
20 [1]Lit *who come after* [2]Lit *day* [3]Lit *who have gone before* [a]Ps 37:13; Jer 50:27; Obad 12
21 [a]Job 21:28
19:1 [1]Lit *answered and said*
2 [1]Lit *my soul*
5 [a]Ps 35:26; 38:16; 55:12,13
6 [a]Job 16:11; 27:2 [b]Job 18:8-10; Ps 66:11; Lam 1:13

Everything Is against Him

7 ¶ "Behold, [a]I cry, 'Violence!' but
I get no answer;
I shout for help, but there is no
justice.
8 "He has [a]walled up my way so
that I cannot pass,
And He has put [b]darkness on
my paths.
9 "He has [a]stripped my honor
from me
And removed the [b]crown from
my head.
10 "He [a]breaks me down on every
side, and I am gone;
And He has uprooted my [b]hope
[c]like a tree.
11 "He has also [a]kindled His anger
against me
And [b]considered me as His
enemy.
12 "His [a]troops come together,
And [b]build up their [1]way
against me
And camp around my tent.

13 ¶ "He has [a]removed my
brothers far from me,
And my [b]acquaintances are
completely estranged
from me.
14 "My relatives have failed,
And my [a]intimate friends have
forgotten me.
15 "Those who live in my house and
my maids consider me a
stranger.
I am a foreigner in their sight.
16 "I call to my servant, but he does
not answer;
I have to implore him with my
mouth.
17 "My breath is [1]offensive to my
wife,
And I am loathsome to my own
brothers.
18 "Even young children despise me;
I rise up and they speak
against me.
19 "All [1]my [a]associates abhor me,
And those I love have turned
against me.
20 "My [a]bone clings to my skin and
my flesh,
And I have escaped *only* by the
skin of my teeth.
21 "Pity me, pity me, O you my
friends,
For the [a]hand of God has
struck me.
22 "Why do you [a]persecute me as
God *does,*
And are not satisfied with my
flesh?

Job Says, "My Redeemer Lives"

23 ¶ "Oh that my words were
written!
Oh that they were [a]inscribed in
a book!
24 "That with an iron stylus and lead
They were engraved in the rock
forever!
25 "As for me, I know that [a]my
[1]Redeemer lives,
And [2]at the last He will take His
stand on the [3]earth.
26 "Even after my skin [1]is
destroyed,
Yet from my flesh I shall [a]see
God;
27 Whom I [1]myself shall behold,
And whom my eyes will see and
not another.
My [2]heart [a]faints [3]within me!
28 "If you say, 'How shall we
[a]persecute him?'
And '[1]What pretext for a case
against him can we find?'
29 "*Then* be afraid of [a]the sword for
yourselves,
For wrath *brings* the punishment
of the sword,
So that you may know [b]there is
judgment."

Zophar Says, "The Triumph of the Wicked Is Short"

20 Then Zophar the Naamathite
[1]answered,
2 "Therefore my disquieting
thoughts make me
[1]respond,
Even because of my [2]inward
agitation.
3 "I listened to [a]the reproof which
insults me,
And the spirit of my
understanding makes me
answer.
4 "Do you know this from [a]of old,
From the establishment of man
on earth,
5 That the [a]triumphing of the
wicked is short,
And [b]the joy of the godless
momentary?
6 "Though his loftiness [1a]reaches
the heavens,
And his head touches the clouds,
7 He [a]perishes forever like his
refuse;
Those who have seen him [b]will
say, 'Where is he?'
8 "He flies away like a [a]dream, and
they cannot find him;
Even like a vision of the night he
is [b]chased away.

7 [a]Job 9:24; 30:20,24; Hab 1:2
8 [a]Job 3:23; Lam 3:7,9 [b]Job 30:26
9 [a]Job 12:17,19; Ps 89:44 [b]Job 16:15; Ps 89:39; Lam 5:16
10 [a]Job 12:14 [b]Job 7:6 [c]Job 24:20
11 [a]Job 16:9 [b]Job 13:24; 33:10
12 [1]I.e. siege-work [a]Job 16:13 [b]Job 30:12
13 [a]Job 16:7; Ps 69:8 [b]Job 16:20; Ps 88:8,18
14 [a]Job 19:19
17 [1]Lit *strange*
19 [1]Lit *the men of my council* [a]Ps 38:11; 55:12,13
20 [a]Job 16:8; 33:21; Ps 102:5; Lam 4:8
21 [a]Job 1:11; Ps 38:2
22 [a]Job 13:24, 25; 16:11; 19:6; Ps 69:26
23 [a]Is 30:8; Jer 36:2
25 [1]Or *Vindicator, defender*; lit *kinsman* [2]Or *as the Last* [3]Lit *dust* [a]Job 16:19; Ps 78:35; Prov 23:11; Is 43:14; Jer 50:34
26 [1]Lit *which they have cut off* [a]Ps 17:15; Matt 5:8; 1 Cor 13:12; 1 John 3:2
27 [1]Or *on my side* [2]Lit *kidneys* [3]Lit *in my loins* [a]Ps 73:26
28 [1]Or *the root of the matter is found in him* [a]Job 19:22
29 [a]Job 15:22 [b]Job 22:4; Ps 1:5; 9:7; Eccl 12:14
20:1 [1]Lit *answered and said*
2 [1]Lit *return* [2]Lit *haste within me*
3 [a]Job 19:3
4 [a]Job 8:8
5 [a]Job 8:12,13; Ps 37:35,36 [b]Job 8:13
6 [1]Lit *goes up to* [a]Is 14:13,14; Obad 3,4
7 [a]Job 4:20; 14:20 [b]Job 7:10; 8:18
8 [a]Ps 73:20; 90:5 [b]Job 18:18; 27:21-23

9 "The [a]eye which saw him sees
him no longer,
And [b]his place no longer
beholds him.
10 "His [a]sons [1]favor the poor,
And his hands [b]give back his
wealth.
11 "His [a]bones are full of his
youthful vigor,
But it lies down with him [1]in
the dust.
12 ¶ "Though [a]evil is sweet in his
mouth
And he hides it under his
tongue,
13 *Though* he [1]desires it and will
not let it go,
But holds it [a]in his [2]mouth,
14 *Yet* his food in his stomach is
changed
To the [1]venom of cobras within
him.
15 "He swallows riches,
But will [a]vomit them up;
God will expel them from his
belly.
16 "He sucks [a]the poison of cobras;
The viper's tongue slays him.
17 "He does not look at [a]the
streams,
The rivers flowing with honey
and curds.
18 "He [a]returns what he has
attained
And cannot swallow *it;*
As to the riches of his trading,
He cannot even enjoy *them.*
19 "For he has [a]oppressed *and*
forsaken the poor;
He has seized a house which he
has not built.
20 ¶ "Because he knew no quiet
[1]within him,
He does [a]not retain anything he
desires.
21 "Nothing remains [1]for him to
devour,
Therefore [a]his prosperity does
not endure.
22 "In the fullness of his plenty he
will be cramped;
The [a]hand of everyone who
suffers will come *against*
him.
23 "When he [a]fills his belly,
God will send His fierce anger
on him
And will [b]rain *it* on him [1]while
he is eating.
24 "He may [a]flee from the iron
weapon,
But the bronze bow will pierce
him.
25 "It is drawn forth and comes out
of his back,
Even the glittering point from
[a]his gall.
[b]Terrors come upon him,
26 Complete [a]darkness is held in
reserve for his treasures,
And unfanned [b]fire will devour
him;
It will consume the survivor in
his tent.
27 "The [a]heavens will reveal his
iniquity,
And the earth will rise up
against him.
28 "The [a]increase of his house will
depart;
His possessions will flow away
[b]in the day of His anger.
29 "This is the wicked man's
[a]portion from God,
Even the heritage decreed to him
by God."

Job Says God Will Deal with the Wicked

21 Then Job [1]answered,
2 "Listen carefully to my
speech,
And let this be your *way of*
consolation.
3 "Bear with me that I may speak;
Then after I have spoken, you
may [a]mock.
4 "As for me, is [a]my complaint
[1]to man?
And [b]why should [2]I not be
impatient?
5 "Look at me, and be astonished,
And [a]put *your* hand over *your*
mouth.
6 "Even when I remember, I am
disturbed,
And [a]horror takes hold of my
flesh.
7 "Why [a]do the wicked *still* live,
Continue on, also become very
[b]powerful?
8 "Their [1a]descendants are
established with them in
their sight,
And their offspring before their
eyes,
9 Their houses [a]are safe from fear,
And the rod of God is not on
them.
10 "His ox mates [1]without fail;
His cow calves and does not
abort.
11 "They send forth their little ones
like the flock,
And their children skip about.

---

9 [a]Job 7:8; 8:18 [b]Job 7:10
10 [1]Or *seek the favor of* [a]Job 5:4; 27:14 [b]Job 20:18; 27:16,17
11 [1]Lit *on* [a]Job 21:23,24
12 [a]Job 15:16
13 [1]Lit *has compassion on* [2]Lit *palate* [a]Num 11:18-20,33; Job 20:23
14 [1]Lit *gall*
15 [a]Job 20:10, 20,21
16 [a]Deut 32:24, 33
17 [a]Deut 32:13, 14; Job 29:6
18 [a]Job 20:10, 15
19 [a]Job 24:2-4; 35:9
20 [1]Lit *in his belly* [a]Eccl 5:13-15
21 [1]Or *of what he devours* [a]Job 15:29
22 [a]Job 5:5
23 [1]Or *as his food* [a]Job 20:13, 14 [b]Num 11:18-20,33; Ps 78:30,31
24 [a]Is 24:18; Amos 5:19
25 [a]Job 16:13 [b]Job 18:11,14
26 [a]Job 18:18 [b]Job 15:30; Ps 21:9
27 [a]Deut 31:28; Is 26:21
28 [a]Deut 28:31 [b]Job 20:15; 21:30
29 [a]Job 27:13; 31:2,3
21:1 [1]Lit *answered and said*
3 [a]Job 11:3; 17:2
4 [1]Or *against* [2]Lit *my spirit* [a]Job 7:11 [b]Job 6:11
5 [a]Judg 18:19; Job 13:5; 29:9; 40:4
6 [a]Ps 55:5
7 [a]Job 9:24; Ps 73:3; Jer 12:1; Hab 1:13 [b]Job 12:19
8 [1]Lit *seed* [a]Ps 17:14
9 [a]Job 12:6
10 [1]Lit *and does not fail*

12 "They [1]sing to the timbrel and harp
And rejoice at the sound of the flute.
13 "They [a]spend their days in prosperity,
And [1]suddenly they go down to [2]Sheol.
14 "They say to God, '[a]Depart from us!
We do not even desire the knowledge of Your ways.
15 '[1]Who is [2]the Almighty, that we should serve Him,
And [a]what would we gain if we entreat Him?'
16 "Behold, their prosperity is not in their hand;
The [a]counsel of the wicked is far from me.

17 ¶ "How often is [a]the lamp of the wicked put out,
Or does their [b]calamity fall on them?
Does [1]God apportion destruction in His anger?
18 "Are they as [a]straw before the wind,
And like [b]chaff which the storm carries away?
19 "*You say,* '[a]God stores away [1]a man's iniquity for his sons.'
Let [2]God repay him so that he may know *it.*
20 "Let his [a]own eyes see his decay,
And let him [b]drink of the wrath of [1]the Almighty.
21 "For what does he care for his household [1]after him,
When the number of his months is cut off?
22 "Can anyone [a]teach God knowledge,
In that He [b]judges those on high?
23 "One [a]dies in his full strength,
Being wholly at ease and [1]satisfied;
24 His [1]sides are filled out with fat,
And the [a]marrow of his bones is moist,
25 While another dies with a bitter soul,
Never even [1]tasting *anything* good.
26 "Together they [a]lie down in the dust,
And [b]worms cover them.

27 ¶ "Behold, I know your thoughts,
And the plans by which you would wrong me.
28 "For you say, 'Where is the house of [a]the nobleman,
And where is the [b]tent, the dwelling places of the wicked?'
29 "Have you not asked wayfaring men,
And do you not recognize their [1]witness?
30 "For the [a]wicked is reserved for the day of calamity;
They will be led forth at [b]the day of fury.
31 "Who will [1]confront him with his actions,
And who will repay him for what he has done?
32 "While he is carried to the grave,
Men will keep watch over *his* tomb.
33 "The [a]clods of the valley will [1]gently cover him;
Moreover, [b]all men will [2]follow after him,
While countless ones *go* before him.
34 "How then will you vainly [a]comfort me,
For your answers remain *full of* [1]falsehood?"

Eliphaz Accuses and Exhorts Job

22

Then Eliphaz the Temanite [1]responded,
2 "Can a vigorous [a]man be of use to God,
Or a wise man be useful to himself?
3 "Is there any pleasure to [1]the Almighty if you are righteous,
Or profit if you make your ways perfect?
4 "Is it because of your [1]reverence that He reproves you,
That He [a]enters into judgment against you?
5 "Is not [a]your wickedness great,
And your iniquities without end?
6 "For you have [a]taken pledges of your brothers without cause,
And [b]stripped [1]men naked.
7 "To the weary you have [a]given no water to drink,
And from the hungry you have [b]withheld bread.
8 "But the earth [a]belongs to the [b]mighty man,
And [c]the honorable man dwells in it.
9 "You have sent [a]widows away empty,
And the [1]strength of the [b]orphans has been crushed.
10 "Therefore [a]snares surround you,
And sudden [b]dread terrifies you,

12 [1]Lit *lifted up the voice*
13 [1]So with most versions; M.T. *are shattered by Sheol* [2]I.e. the nether world [a]Job 21:23; 36:11
14 [a]Job 22:17
15 [1]Lit *What* [2]Heb *Shaddai* [a]Job 22:17; 34:9
16 [a]Job 22:18
17 [1]Lit *He* [a]Job 18:5,6 [b]Job 31:2,3
18 [a]Job 13:25; Ps 83:13 [b]Ps 1:4; 35:5; Is 17:13; Hos 13:3
19 [1]Lit *his* [2]Lit *Him* [a]Ex 20:5; Jer 31:29; Ezek 18:2
20 [1]Heb *Shaddai* [a]Num 14:28-32; Jer 31:30; Ezek 18:4 [b]Ps 60:3; Is 51:17; Jer 25:15; Rev 14:10
21 [1]I.e. after he dies
22 [a]Job 35:11; 36:22; Is 40:14; Rom 11:34 [b]Job 4:18; 15:15; Ps 82:1
23 [1]Or *quiet* [a]Job 20:11; 21:13
24 [1]So with Syr; Heb uncertain. Some render as, *his pails are full of milk* [a]Prov 3:8
25 [1]Lit *eating*
26 [a]Job 3:13; 20:11; Eccl 9:2 [b]Job 24:20; Is 14:11
28 [a]Job 1:3; 31:37 [b]Job 8:22; 18:21
29 [1]Lit *signs*
30 [a]Job 20:29; Prov 16:4; 2 Pet 2:9 [b]Job 21:17, 20; 40:11
31 [1]Lit *declare his way to his face*
33 [1]Lit *be sweet to him* [2]Lit *draw* [a]Job 3:22; 17:16 [b]Job 3:19; 24:24
34 [1]Or *faithlessness* [a]Job 16:2
22:1 [1]Lit *answered and said*
2 [a]Job 35:7; Luke 17:10
3 [1]Heb *Shaddai*
4 [1]Or *fear* [a]Job 14:3; 19:29
5 [a]Job 11:6; 15:5
6 [1]Lit *clothing of the naked* [a]Ex 22:26; Deut 24:6,17; Job 24:3,9; Ezek 18:16 [b]Job 31:19,20
7 [a]Job 31:16,17 [b]Job 31:31
8 [a]Job 9:24 [b]Job 12:19 [c]Is 3:3; 9:15
9 [1]Lit *arms* [a]Job 24:3,21; 29:13; 31:16,18 [b]Job 6:27
10 [a]Job 18:8 [b]Job 15:21

11 Or [a]darkness, so that you cannot
see,
And an [b]abundance of water
covers you.

12 ¶ "Is not God [a]*in* the height of
heaven?
Look also at the [1]distant stars,
how high they are!
13 "You say, '[a]What does God
know?
Can He judge through the thick
darkness?
14 '[a]Clouds are a hiding place for
Him, so that He cannot see;
And He walks on the [1]vault of
heaven.'
15 "Will you keep to the ancient
path
Which [a]wicked men have trod,
16 Who were snatched away
[a]before their time,
Whose [b]foundations were
[1]washed away by a river?
17 "They [a]said to God, 'Depart
from us!'
And 'What can [1]the Almighty do
to them?'
18 "Yet He [a]filled their houses with
good *things;*
But [b]the counsel of the wicked
is far from me.
19 "The [a]righteous see and are glad,
And the innocent mock them,
20 *Saying,* 'Truly our adversaries are
cut off,
And their [1]abundance [a]the fire
has consumed.'

21 ¶ "[1a]Yield now and be at peace
with Him;
Thereby good will come to you.
22 "Please receive [1a]instruction
from His mouth
And establish His words in your
heart.
23 "If you [a]return to [1]the Almighty,
you will be [2]restored;
If you [b]remove unrighteousness
far from your tent,
24 And [a]place *your* [1]gold in the
dust,
And *the gold of* Ophir among
the stones of the brooks,
25 Then [1]the Almighty will be your
[2]gold
And choice silver to you.
26 "For then you will [a]delight in
[1]the Almighty
And lift up your face to God.
27 "You will [a]pray to Him, and [b]He
will hear you;
And you will pay your vows.
28 "You will also decree a thing, and
it will be established for
you;
And [a]light will shine on your
ways.
29 "When [1]you are cast down, you
will speak with [2]confidence,
And the [3a]humble person He
will save.
30 "He will deliver one who is not
innocent,
And he will be [a]delivered
through the cleanness of
your hands."

Job Says He Longs for God

23 Then Job [1]replied,
2 "Even today my [a]complaint
is rebellion;
[1]His hand is [b]heavy despite my
groaning.
3 "Oh that I knew where I might
find Him,
That I might come to His seat!
4 "I would [a]present *my* case before
Him
And fill my mouth with
arguments.
5 "I would learn the words *which*
He would [1]answer,
And perceive what He would say
to me.
6 "Would He contend with me by
[a]the greatness of *His*
power?
No, surely He would pay
attention to me.
7 "There the upright would [a]reason
with Him;
And I [1]would be [b]delivered
forever from my Judge.

8 ¶ "Behold, I go forward but He is
not *there,*
And backward, but I [a]cannot
perceive Him;
9 When He acts on the left, I
cannot behold *Him;*
He turns on the right, I cannot
see Him.
10 "But He knows the [1]way I take;
When He has [a]tried me, I shall
come forth as gold.
11 "My foot has [a]held fast to His
path;
I have kept His way and not
turned aside.
12 "I have not departed from the
command of His lips;
I have treasured the [a]words of
His mouth [1]more than my
[2]necessary food.
13 "But He is unique and who can
turn Him?

11 [a]Job 5:14 [b]Job 38:34; Ps 69:2; 124:5; Lam 3:54
12 [1]Lit *head, top-most* [a]Job 11:7-9
13 [a]Ps 10:11; 59:7; 64:5; 94:7; Is 29:15; Ezek 8:12
14 [1]Lit *circle* [a]Job 26:9
15 [a]Job 34:36
16 [1]Lit *poured out* [a]Job 15:32; 21:13,18 [b]Job 14:19; Ps 90:5; Is 28:2; Matt 7:26,27
17 [1]Heb *Shaddai* [a]Job 21:14,15
18 [a]Job 12:6 [b]Job 21:16
19 [a]Ps 52:6; 58:10; 107:42
20 [1]Or *excess* [a]Job 15:30
21 [1]Or *Know intimately* [a]Ps 34:10
22 [1]Or *law* [a]Job 6:10; 23:12; Prov 2:6
23 [1]Heb *Shaddai* [2]Lit *built up* [a]Job 8:5; 11:13; Is 19:22; 31:6; Zech 1:3 [b]Job 11:14
24 [1]Lit *ore* [a]Job 31:24,25
25 [1]Heb *Shaddai* [2]Lit *ore*
26 [1]Heb *Shaddai* [a]Job 27:10; Ps 37:4; Is 58:14
27 [a]Job 11:13; 33:26; Is 58:9 [b]Job 34:28
28 [a]Job 11:17; Ps 112:4
29 [1]Lit *they cast* you *down* [2]Lit *pride* [3]Lit *lowly of eyes* [a]Job 5:11; 36:7; Matt 23:12; James 4:6; 1 Pet 5:5
30 [a]Job 42:7,8; Ps 18:20; 24:3,4
23:1 [1]Lit *answered and said*
2 [1]So with Gr and Syr; M.T. *My* [a]Job 7:11 [b]Job 6:2,3; Ps 32:4
4 [a]Job 13:18
5 [1]Lit *answer me*
6 [a]Job 9:4
7 [1]Or *bring forth my justice forever* [a]Job 13:3 [b]Job 13:16; 23:10
8 [a]Job 9:11; 35:14
10 [1]Lit *way with me* [a]Job 7:18; Ps 7:9; 11:5; 66:10; Zech 13:9; 1 Pet 1:7
11 [a]Job 31:7; Ps 17:5; 44:18
12 [1]Or with some versions, *in my breast* [2]Lit *prescribed portion* [a]Job 6:10; 22:22

And *what* His soul desires, that
He does.
14 "For He performs what is
appointed for me,
And many such *decrees* are with
Him.
15 "Therefore, I would be dismayed
at His presence;
When I consider, I am terrified
of Him.
16 "*It is* God *who* has made my
[a]heart faint,
And the Almighty *who* has
dismayed me,
17 But I [a]am not silenced by the
darkness,
Nor [b]deep gloom *which*
covers me.

Job Says God Seems to Ignore Wrongs

24 "[a]Why are [1]times not stored
up by the Almighty,
And why do those who know
Him not see [b]His days?
2 "[1]Some [a]remove the landmarks;
They seize and [2]devour flocks.
3 "They drive away the donkeys of
the [a]orphans;
They take the [b]widow's ox for a
pledge.
4 "They push [a]the needy aside
from the road;
The [b]poor of the land are made
to hide themselves
altogether.
5 "Behold, as [a]wild donkeys in the
wilderness
They [b]go forth seeking food in
their activity,
As [1]bread for *their* children in
the desert.
6 "They harvest their fodder in the
field
And glean the vineyard of the
wicked.
7 "[a]They spend the night naked,
without clothing,
And have no covering against the
cold.
8 "They are wet with the mountain
rains
And hug the rock for want of a
shelter.
9 "[1]Others snatch the [a]orphan
from the breast,
And against the poor they take a
pledge.
10 "They cause *the poor* to go about
naked without clothing,
And they take away the sheaves
from the hungry.
11 "Within the walls they produce
oil;
They tread wine presses but
thirst.
12 "From the city men groan,
And the souls of the wounded
cry out;
Yet God [a]does not pay attention
to folly.

13 ¶ "[1]Others have been with
those who rebel against the
light;
They do not want to know its
ways
Nor abide in its paths.
14 "The murderer [a]arises at dawn;
He [b]kills the poor and the
needy,
And at night he is as a thief.
15 "The eye of the [a]adulterer waits
for the twilight,
Saying, 'No eye will see me.'
And he [1]disguises his face.
16 "In the dark they [a]dig into
houses,
They [b]shut themselves up by
day;
They do not know the light.
17 "For the morning is the same to
him as thick darkness,
For he is familiar with the
[a]terrors of thick darkness.

18 ¶ "They are [1a]insignificant on
the surface of the water;
Their portion is [b]cursed on the
earth.
They do not turn [2]toward the
[c]vineyards.
19 "Drought and heat [1a]consume
the snow waters,
So does [2b]Sheol *those who*
have sinned.
20 "A [1a]mother will forget him;
The [b]worm feeds sweetly till he
is [c]no longer remembered.
And wickedness will be broken
[d]like a tree.
21 "He wrongs the [1]barren woman
And does no good for [a]the
widow.
22 "But He drags off the valiant by
[a]His power;
He rises, but [b]no one has
assurance of life.
23 "He provides them [a]with
security, and they are
supported;
And His [b]eyes are on their
ways.
24 "They are exalted a [a]little while,
then they are gone;

16 [a]Deut 20:3; Job 27:2; Jer 51:46
17 [a]Job 10:18, 19 [b]Job 19:8
24:1 [1]I.e. times of judgment [a]Acts 1:7 [b]Is 2:12; Jer 46:10; Obad 15; Zeph 1:7
2 [1]Lit *They* [2]Or *pasture* [a]Deut 19:14; 27:17; Prov 23:10
3 [a]Job 6:27 [b]Deut 24:17; Job 22:9
4 [a]Job 24:14; 29:16; 30:25; 31:19 [b]Job 29:12; Ps 41:1; Prov 14:31; 28:28; Amos 8:4
5 [1]Lit *his bread* [a]Job 39:5-8 [b]Ps 104:23
7 [a]Ex 22:26; Job 22:6
9 [1]Lit *They* [a]Job 6:27
12 [a]Job 9:23,24
13 [1]Lit *They*
14 [a]Mic 2:1 [b]Ps 10:8
15 [1]Or *puts a covering on his face* [a]Prov 7:9
16 [a]Ex 22:2; Matt 6:19 [b]John 3:20
17 [a]Job 15:21
18 [1]Or *light* or *swift* [2]Lit *to the path of* [a]Job 22:11,16; 27:20 [b]Job 5:3 [c]Job 24:6,11
19 [1]Lit *seize* [2]I.e. nether world [a]Job 6:16, 17 [b]Job 21:13
20 [1]Lit *womb* [a]Is 49:15 [b]Job 21:26 [c]Job 18:17; Ps 34:16; Prov 10:7 [d]Job 19:10; Dan 4:14
21 [1]Lit *barren who does not bear* [a]Job 22:9
22 [a]Job 9:4 [b]Job 18:20
23 [a]Job 12:6 [b]Job 10:4; 11:11
24 [a]Ps 37:10

Moreover, they are [b]brought low
and like everything
gathered up;
Even like the heads of grain they
are cut off.
25 "Now if it is not so, [a]who can
prove me a liar,
And make my speech
worthless?"

Bildad Says Man Is Inferior

25 Then Bildad the Shuhite [1]answered,
2 "[a]Dominion and awe [1]belong to
Him
Who establishes peace in [b]His
heights.
3 "Is there any number to [a]His
troops?
And upon whom does His light
not rise?
4 "How then can a man be [a]just
with God?
Or how can he be [b]clean who is
born of woman?
5 "If even [a]the moon has no
brightness
And the [b]stars are not pure in
His sight,
6 How much less [a]man, *that*
[b]maggot,
And the son of man, *that*
worm!"

Job Rebukes Bildad

26 Then Job [1]responded,
2 "What a help you are to
[1a]the weak!
How you have saved the arm
[b]without strength!
3 "What counsel you have given to
one without wisdom!
What helpful insight you have
abundantly [1]provided!
4 "To whom have you uttered
words?
And whose [1]spirit was
expressed through you?

The Greatness of God

5 ¶ "The [1a]departed spirits
tremble
Under the waters and their
inhabitants.
6 "Naked is [1a]Sheol before Him,
And [2b]Abaddon has no
covering.
7 "He [a]stretches out the north over
empty space
And hangs the earth on nothing.
8 "He [a]wraps up the waters in His
clouds,
And the cloud does not burst
under them.
9 "He [1a]obscures the face of the
[2]full moon
And spreads His cloud over it.
10 "He has inscribed a [a]circle on the
surface of the waters
At the [b]boundary of light and
darkness.
11 "The pillars of heaven tremble
And are amazed at His rebuke.
12 "He [a]quieted the sea with His
power,
And by His [b]understanding He
shattered [c]Rahab.
13 "By His breath the [a]heavens are
[1]cleared;
His hand has pierced [b]the
fleeing serpent.
14 "Behold, these are the fringes of
His ways;
And how faint [a]a word we hear
of Him!
But His mighty [b]thunder, who
can understand?"

Job Affirms His Righteousness

27 Then Job [1]continued his [a]discourse and said,
2 "As God lives, [a]who has taken
away my right,
And the Almighty, [b]who has
embittered my soul,
3 For as long as [1]life is in me,
And the [2a]breath of God is in
my nostrils,
4 My lips certainly will not speak
unjustly,
Nor will [a]my tongue mutter
deceit.
5 "Far be it from me that I should
declare you right;
Till I die [a]I will not put away
my integrity from me.
6 "I [a]hold fast my righteousness
and will not let it go.
My heart does not reproach any
of my days.

The State of the Godless

7 ¶ "May my enemy be as the
wicked
And [1]my opponent as the
unjust.
8 "For what is [a]the hope of the
godless [1]when he is cut off,
When God requires [b]his [2]life?
9 "Will God [a]hear his cry
When [b]distress comes
upon him?
10 "Will he take [a]delight in the
Almighty?
Will he call on God at all times?
11 "I will instruct you in the [1]power
of God;

24 [b]Job 14:21
25 [a]Job 6:28; 27:4
25:1 [1]Lit *answered and said*
2 [1]Lit *are with Him* [a]Job 9:4; 36:5,22; 37:23; 42:2 [b]Job 16:19; 31:2
3 [a]Job 16:13
4 [a]Job 4:17; 9:2 [b]Job 14:4
5 [a]Job 31:26 [b]Job 15:15
6 [a]Job 7:17 [b]Job 17:14
26:1 [1]Lit *responded and said*
2 [1]Lit *no power* [a]Job 6:11,12 [b]Ps 71:9
3 [1]Lit *made known*
4 [1]Lit *breath has gone forth*
5 [1]Or *shades;* Heb *Rephaim* [a]Job 3:13; Ps 88:10
6 [1]I.e. the nether world [2]I.e. place of destruction [a]Job 9:5-10; 26:6-14; 38:17; 41:11 [b]Job 28:22; 31:12
7 [a]Job 9:8
8 [a]Job 37:11; Prov 30:4
9 [1]Lit *covers* [2]Or *throne* [a]Job 22:14; Ps 97:2; 105:39
10 [a]Job 38:1-11; Prov 8:29 [b]Job 38:19,20,24
12 [a]Is 51:15; Jer 31:35 [b]Job 12:13 [c]Job 9:13
13 [1]Lit *made beautiful* [a]Job 9:8 [b]Is 27:1
14 [a]Job 4:12 [b]Job 36:29; 37:4,5
27:1 [1]Or *again took up* [a]Job 13:12; 29:1
2 [a]Job 16:11; 34:5 [b]Job 9:18
3 [1]Lit *breath* [2]Or *spirit* [a]Job 32:8; 33:4
4 [a]Job 6:28; 33:3
5 [a]Job 6:29
6 [a]Job 2:3; 13:18
7 [1]Lit *he who rises up against me*
8 [1]Or *though he gains* [2]Lit *soul* [a]Job 8:13; 11:20 [b]Job 12:10
9 [a]Job 35:12,13; Ps 18:41; Prov 1:28; Is 1:15; Jer 14:12; Mic 3:4 [b]Prov 1:27
10 [a]Job 22:26, 27; Ps 37:4; Is 58:14
11 [1]Lit *hand*

What is with the Almighty I will
not conceal.
12 “Behold, all of you have seen *it;*
Why then do you [1]act foolishly?
13 ¶ “This is [a]the portion of a
wicked man from God,
And the inheritance *which*
[b]tyrants receive from the
Almighty.
14 “Though his sons are many,
[1]they are destined [a]for the
sword;
And his [b]descendants will not
be satisfied with bread.
15 “His survivors will be buried
because of the plague,
And [1]their [a]widows will not be
able to weep.
16 “Though he piles up silver like
dust
And prepares garments as
plentiful as the clay,
17 He may prepare *it,* [a]but the just
will wear *it*
And the innocent will divide the
silver.
18 “He has built his [a]house like the
[1]spider’s web,
Or as a hut *which* the watchman
has made.
19 “He lies down rich, but never
[1]again;
He opens his eyes, and [a]it is no
longer.
20 “[a]Terrors overtake him like a
flood;
A tempest steals him away [b]in
the night.
21 “The east [a]wind carries him
away, and he is gone,
For it whirls him [b]away from his
place.
22 “For it will hurl at him [a]without
sparing;
He will surely try to [b]flee from
its [1]power.
23 “*Men* will clap their hands at him
And will [a]hiss him from his
place.

Job Tells of Earth’s Treasures

28 “Surely there is a [1]mine for
silver
And a place [2]where they refine
gold.
2 “Iron is taken from the dust,
And copper is smelted from rock.
3 “*Man* puts an end to darkness,
And [a]to the farthest limit he
searches out
The rock in gloom and deep
shadow.

12 [1]Or *speak vanity*
13 [a]Job 20:29 [b]Job 15:20
14 [1]Lit *the sword is for them* [a]Job 15:22; 18:19 [b]Job 20:10
15 [1]So ancient versions; Heb *his* [a]Ps 78:64
17 [a]Job 20:18-21
18 [1]So ancient versions; Heb *moth* [a]Job 8:15; 18:14
19 [1]So ancient versions; Heb *will be gathered* [a]Job 7:8,21; 20:7
20 [a]Job 15:21 [b]Job 20:8; 34:20
21 [a]Job 21:18 [b]Job 7:10
22 [1]Lit *hand* [a]Jer 13:14; Ezek 5:11; 24:14 [b]Job 11:20
23 [a]Job 18:18; 20:8
28:1 [1]Or *source* [2]Lit *for gold they refine*
3 [a]Eccl 1:13
4 [1]Lit *breaks open* [2]Lit *sojourning*
6 [1]Or *place*
8 [1]Lit *sons of pride*
9 [1]Lit *roots*
11 [1]Lit *weeping*
12 [a]Job 28:23, 28; Eccl 7:24
13 [a]Matt 13:44-46
15 [a]Prov 3:13, 14; 8:10,11; 16:16
17 [a]Prov 8:10; 16:16
18 [a]Prov 8:11
19 [a]Prov 8:19
20 [a]Job 28:23, 28

4 “He [1]sinks a shaft far from
[2]habitation,
Forgotten by the foot;
They hang and swing to and fro
far from men.
5 “The earth, from it comes food,
And underneath it is turned up
as fire.
6 “Its rocks are the [1]source of
sapphires,
And its dust *contains* gold.
7 “The path no bird of prey knows,
Nor has the falcon’s eye caught
sight of it.
8 “The [1]proud beasts have not
trodden it,
Nor has the *fierce* lion passed
over it.
9 “He puts his hand on the flint;
He overturns the mountains at
the [1]base.
10 “He hews out channels through
the rocks,
And his eye sees anything
precious.
11 “He dams up the streams from
[1]flowing,
And what is hidden he brings
out to the light.

The Search for Wisdom Is Harder

12 ¶ “But [a]where can wisdom be
found?
And where is the place of
understanding?
13 “[a]Man does not know its value,
Nor is it found in the land of the
living.
14 “The deep says, ‘It is not in me’;
And the sea says, ‘It is not
with me.’
15 “[a]Pure gold cannot be given in
exchange for it,
Nor can silver be weighed as its
price.
16 “It cannot be valued in the gold of
Ophir,
In precious onyx, or sapphire.
17 “[a]Gold or glass cannot equal it,
Nor can it be exchanged for
articles of fine gold.
18 “Coral and crystal are not to be
mentioned;
And the acquisition of [a]wisdom
is above *that of* pearls.
19 “The topaz of Ethiopia cannot
equal it,
Nor can it be valued in [a]pure
gold.
20 “[a]Where then does wisdom come
from?
And where is the place of
understanding?

21 "Thus it is hidden from the eyes
of all living
And concealed from the birds of
the sky.
22 "[1a]Abaddon and Death say,
'With our ears we have heard a
report of it.'

23 ¶ "[a]God understands its way,
And He knows its place.
24 "For He [a]looks to the ends of the
earth
And sees everything under the
heavens.
25 "When He imparted [a]weight to
the wind
And [b]meted out the waters by
measure,
26 When He set a [a]limit for the
rain
And a course for the
[b]thunderbolt,
27 Then He saw it and declared it;
He established it and also
searched it out.
28 "And to man He said, 'Behold,
the [a]fear of the Lord, that is
wisdom;
And to depart from evil is
understanding.' "

Job's Past Was Glorious

29 And Job again took up his [a]discourse and said,
2 "Oh that I were as in months
gone by,
As in the days when God
[a]watched over me;
3 When [a]His lamp shone over my
head,
And [b]by His light I walked
through darkness;
4 As I was in [1]the prime of my
days,
When the [2a]friendship of God
was over my tent;
5 When [1]the Almighty was yet
with me,
And my children were
around me;
6 When my steps were bathed in
[a]butter,
And the [b]rock poured out for
me streams of oil!
7 "When I went out to [a]the gate of
the city,
When I [1]took my seat in the
square,
8 The young men saw me and hid
themselves,
And the old men arose *and*
stood.
9 "The princes [a]stopped talking
And [b]put *their* hands on their
mouths;
10 The voice of the nobles was
[1a]hushed,
And their [b]tongue stuck to their
palate.
11 "For when [a]the ear heard, it
called me blessed,
And when the eye saw, it gave
witness of me,
12 Because I delivered [a]the poor
who cried for help,
And the [b]orphan who had no
helper.
13 "The blessing of the one [a]ready
to perish came upon me,
And I made the [b]widow's heart
sing for joy.
14 "I [a]put on righteousness, and it
clothed me;
My justice was like a robe and a
turban.
15 "I was [a]eyes to the blind
And feet to the lame.
16 "I was a father to [a]the needy,
And I investigated the case
which I did not know.
17 "I [a]broke the jaws of the wicked
And snatched the prey from his
teeth.
18 "Then I [1]thought, 'I shall die [2]in
my nest,
And I shall multiply *my* days as
the sand.
19 'My [a]root is spread out to the
waters,
And [b]dew lies all night on my
branch.
20 'My glory is *ever* new with me,
And my [a]bow is renewed in my
hand.'

21 ¶ "To me [a]they listened and
waited,
And kept silent for my counsel.
22 "After my words they did not
[a]speak again,
And [b]my speech dropped on
them.
23 "They waited for me as for the
rain,
And opened their mouth as for
the spring rain.
24 "I smiled on them when they did
not believe,
And the light of my face they did
not cast down.
25 "I chose a way for them and sat
as [a]chief,
And dwelt as a king among the
troops,
As one who [b]comforted the
mourners.

22 [1]I.e. Destruction [a]Job 26:6; Prov 8:32-36
23 [a]Job 9:4; Prov 8:22-36
24 [a]Ps 11:4; 33:13,14; 66:7; Prov 15:3
25 [a]Ps 135:7 [b]Job 12:15; 38:8-11
26 [a]Job 37:6,11, 12; 38:26-28 [b]Job 37:3; 38:25
28 [a]Ps 111:10; Prov 1:7; 9:10; Eccl 12:13
29:1 [a]Num 23:7; 24:3; Job 13:12; 27:1
2 [a]Jer 31:28
3 [a]Job 18:6 [b]Job 11:17
4 [1]Lit *the days of my autumn* [2]Lit *counsel* [a]Job 15:8; Ps 25:14; Prov 3:32
5 [1]Heb *Shaddai*
6 [a]Deut 32:14; Job 20:17 [b]Deut 32:13; Ps 81:16
7 [1]Lit *set up* [a]Job 31:21
9 [a]Job 29:21 [b]Job 21:5
10 [1]Lit *hidden* [a]Job 29:22 [b]Ps 137:6
11 [a]Job 4:3,4
12 [a]Job 24:4,9; 34:28; Ps 72:12; Prov 21:13 [b]Job 31:17,21
13 [a]Job 31:19 [b]Job 22:9
14 [a]Job 27:5,6; Ps 132:9; Is 59:17; 61:10; Eph 6:14
15 [a]Num 10:31
16 [a]Job 24:4; Prov 29:7
17 [a]Ps 3:7
18 [1]Lit *said* [2]Lit *with*
19 [a]Jer 17:8 [b]Hos 14:5
20 [a]Gen 49:24; Ps 18:34
21 [a]Job 4:3; 29:9
22 [a]Job 29:10 [b]Deut 32:2
25 [a]Job 1:3; 31:37 [b]Job 4:4; 16:5

Job's Present State Is Humiliating

30 "But now those younger than I
[a]mock me,
Whose fathers I disdained to put
with the dogs of my flock.
2 "Indeed, what *good was* the
strength of their hands
to me?
Vigor had perished from them.
3 "From want and famine they are
gaunt
Who gnaw the dry ground by
night in waste and
desolation,
4 Who pluck [1]mallow by the
bushes,
And whose food is the root of
the broom shrub.
5 "They are driven from the
community;
They shout against them as
against a thief,
6 So that they dwell in dreadful
[1]valleys,
In holes of the earth and of the
rocks.
7 "Among the bushes they [1]cry
out;
Under the nettles they are
gathered together.
8 "[1]Fools, even [2]those without a
name,
They were scourged from the
land.
9 ¶ "And now I have become their
[1a]taunt,
I have even become a [b]byword
to them.
10 "They abhor me *and* stand aloof
from me,
And they do not [1]refrain from
[a]spitting at my face.
11 "Because [1]He has loosed [2]His
[3]bowstring and
[a]afflicted me,
They have cast off [b]the bridle
before me.
12 "On the right hand their [1]brood
arises;
They [a]thrust aside my feet [b]and
build up against me their
ways of destruction.
13 "They [a]break up my path,
They profit [1]from my
destruction;
No one restrains them.
14 "As *through* a wide breach they
come,
[1]Amid the tempest they roll on.
15 "[a]Terrors are turned against me;
They pursue my [1]honor as the
wind,
And my [2]prosperity has passed
away [b]like a cloud.
16 ¶ "And now [a]my soul is poured
out [1]within me;
Days of affliction have seized me.
17 "At night it pierces [a]my bones
[1]within me,
And my gnawing *pains* take no
rest.
18 "By a great force my garment is
[a]distorted;
It binds me about as the collar of
my coat.
19 "He has cast me into the [a]mire,
And I have become like dust and
ashes.
20 "I [a]cry out to You for help, but
You do not answer me;
I stand up, and You turn Your
attention against me.
21 "You have [1]become cruel to me;
With the might of Your hand
You [a]persecute me.
22 "You [a]lift me up to the wind *and*
cause me to ride;
And You dissolve me in a storm.
23 "For I know that You [a]will bring
me to death
And to the [b]house of meeting
for all living.

24 ¶ "Yet does not one in a heap of
ruins stretch out *his* hand,
Or in his disaster therefore [a]cry
out for help?
25 "Have I not [a]wept for the [1]one
whose life is hard?
Was not my soul grieved for
[b]the needy?
26 "When I [a]expected good, then
evil came;
When I waited for light, [b]then
darkness came.
27 "[1]I am seething [a]within and
cannot relax;
Days of affliction confront me.
28 "I go about [1a]mourning without
comfort;
I stand up in the assembly *and*
[b]cry out for help.
29 "I have become a brother to
[a]jackals
And a companion of ostriches.
30 "My [a]skin turns black [1]on me,
And my [b]bones burn with
[2]fever.
31 "Therefore my [a]harp [1]is turned
to mourning,
And my flute to the sound of
those who weep.

Job Asserts His Integrity

31 "I have made a covenant with
my [a]eyes;

30:1 [a]Job 12:4
4 [1]I.e. plant of the salt marshes
6 [1]Or *wadis*
7 [1]Or *bray*
8 [1]Lit *Sons of fools* [2]Lit *sons*
9 [1]Lit *song* [a]Job 12:4 [b]Job 17:6; Ps 69:11; Lam 3:14,63
10 [1]Lit *withhold spit from my face* [a]Num 12:14; Deut 25:9; Job 17:6; Is 50:6; Matt 26:67
11 [1]Or *they* [2]Some mss read *my* [3]Or *cord* [a]Ruth 1:21; Ps 88:7 [b]Ps 32:9
12 [1]Possibly *sprout* or *offspring* [a]Ps 140:4,5 [b]Job 19:12
13 [1]Lit *for* [a]Is 3:12
14 [1]Lit *Under*
15 [1]Or *nobility* [2]Or *welfare* [a]Job 3:25; 31:23; Ps 55:3-5 [b]Job 7:9; Hos 13:3
16 [1]Lit *upon* [a]1 Sam 1:15; Job 3:24; Ps 22:14; 42:4; Is 53:12
17 [1]Lit *from upon* [a]Job 30:30
18 [a]Job 2:7
19 [a]Ps 69:2,14
20 [a]Job 19:7
21 [1]Lit *turned to be* [a]Job 10:3; 16:9,14; 19:6,22
22 [a]Job 9:17; 27:21
23 [a]Job 9:22; 10:8 [b]Job 3:19; Eccl 12:5
24 [a]Job 19:7
25 [1]Lit *hard of day* [a]Ps 35:13, 14; Rom 12:15 [b]Job 24:4
26 [a]Job 3:25,26; Jer 8:15 [b]Job 19:8
27 [1]Lit *My inward parts are boiling* [a]Lam 2:11
28 [1]Or *blackened, but not by the heat of the sun* [a]Job 30:31; Ps 38:6; 42:9; 43:2 [b]Job 19:7
29 [a]Ps 44:19; Mic 1:8
30 [1]Lit *from upon* [2]Lit *heat* [a]Job 2:7 [b]Ps 102:3
31 [1]Lit *becomes* [a]Is 24:8
31:1 [a]Matt 5:28

How then could I gaze at a
virgin?
2 "And what is [a]the portion of God
from above
Or the heritage of the Almighty
from on high?
3 "Is it not [a]calamity to the unjust
And disaster to [b]those who
work iniquity?
4 "Does He not [a]see my ways
And [b]number all my steps?

5 ¶ "If I have [a]walked with
falsehood,
And my foot has hastened after
deceit,
6 Let Him [a]weigh me with
[1]accurate scales,
And let God know [b]my integrity.
7 "If my step has [a]turned from the
way,
Or my heart [1]followed my eyes,
Or if any [b]spot has stuck to my
hands,
8 Let me [a]sow and another eat,
And let my [1b]crops be
uprooted.

9 ¶ "If my heart has been [a]enticed
by a woman,
Or I have lurked at my
neighbor's doorway,
10 May my wife [a]grind for another,
And let [b]others [1]kneel down
over her.
11 "For that would be a [a]lustful
crime;
Moreover, it would be [b]an
iniquity *punishable by*
judges.
12 "For it would be [a]fire that
consumes to [1b]Abaddon,
And would [c]uproot all my
[2]increase.

13 ¶ "If I have [a]despised the claim
of my male or female slaves
When they filed a complaint
against me,
14 What then could I do when God
arises?
And when He calls me to
account, what will I answer
Him?
15 "Did not [a]He who made me in
the womb make him,
And the same one fashion us in
the womb?

16 ¶ "If I have kept [a]the poor from
their desire,
Or have caused the eyes of [b]the
widow to fail,
17 Or have [a]eaten my morsel
alone,
And [b]the orphan has not
[1]shared it
18 (But from my youth he grew up
with me as with a father,
And from [1]infancy I guided her),
19 If I have seen anyone perish [a]for
lack of clothing,
Or that [b]the needy had no
covering,
20 If his loins have not
[1]thanked me,
And if he has not been warmed
with the fleece of my sheep,
21 If I have lifted up my hand
against [a]the orphan,
Because I saw [1]I had support
[b]in the gate,
22 Let my shoulder fall from the
[1]socket,
And my [a]arm be broken off [2]at
the elbow.
23 "For [a]calamity from God is a
terror to me,
And because of [b]His [1]majesty I
can do nothing.

24 ¶ "If I have put my confidence *in*
[a]gold,
And called fine gold my trust,
25 If I have [a]gloated because my
wealth was great,
And because my hand had
secured *so* much;
26 If I have [a]looked at the [1]sun
when it shone
Or the moon going in splendor,
27 And my heart became secretly
enticed,
And my hand [1]threw a kiss from
my mouth,
28 That too would have been [a]an
iniquity *calling for*
[1]judgment,
For I would have [b]denied God
above.

29 ¶ "Have I [a]rejoiced at the
extinction of my enemy,
Or [1]exulted when evil
befell him?
30 "[1]No, [a]I have not [2]allowed my
mouth to sin
By asking for his life in [b]a curse.
31 "Have the men of my tent not
said,
'Who can [1]find one who has not
been [a]satisfied with his
meat'?
32 "The alien has not lodged outside,
For I have opened my doors to
the [1]traveler.
33 "Have I [a]covered my
transgressions like [1]Adam,
By hiding my iniquity in my
bosom,

2 [a]Job 20:29
3 [a]Job 18:12; 21:30 [b]Job 34:22
4 [a]2 Chr 16:9; Job 24:23; 28:24; 34:21; 36:7; Prov 5:21; 15:3 [b]Job 14:16; 31:37
5 [a]Job 15:31; Mic 2:11
6 [1]Lit *just* [a]Job 6:2,3 [b]Job 23:10; 27:5,6
7 [1]Lit *walked after* [a]Job 23:11 [b]Job 9:30
8 [1]Or *offspring* [a]Lev 26:16; Job 20:18; Mic 6:15 [b]Job 31:12
9 [a]Job 24:15; 31:1
10 [1]I.e. sexual relations [a]Is 47:2 [b]Deut 28:30; Jer 8:10
11 [a]Lev 20:10; Deut 22:24 [b]Job 31:28
12 [1]I.e. place of destruction [2]Or *yield* [a]Job 15:30 [b]Job 26:6 [c]Job 20:28; 31:8
13 [a]Deut 24:14, 15
15 [a]Job 10:3
16 [a]Job 5:16; 20:19 [b]Ex 22:22-24; Job 22:9
17 [1]Lit *eaten from it* [a]Job 22:7 [b]Job 29:12
18 [1]Lit *my mother's womb*
19 [a]Job 22:6; 29:13 [b]Job 24:4
20 [1]Lit *blessed*
21 [1]Lit *my help* [a]Job 29:12; 31:17 [b]Job 29:7
22 [1]Lit *shoulder*, or *back* [2]Lit *from the bone of the upper arm* [a]Job 38:15
23 [1]Lit *exaltation* [a]Job 31:3 [b]Job 13:11
24 [a]Job 22:24; Mark 10:23-25
25 [a]Job 1:3,10; Ps 62:10
26 [1]Lit *light* [a]Deut 4:19; 17:3; Ezek 8:16
27 [1]Lit *kissed my mouth*
28 [1]Lit *judges* [a]Deut 17:2-7; Job 31:11 [b]Josh 24:27; Is 59:13
29 [1]Lit *lifted myself up* [a]Prov 17:5; 24:17; Obad 12
30 [1]Lit *And* [2]Lit *given my palate* [a]Ps 7:4 [b]Job 5:3
31 [1]Lit *give* [a]Job 22:7
32 [1]M.T. *way*
33 [1]Or *mankind* [a]Gen 3:10; Prov 28:13

34 Because I [a]feared the great
multitude,
And the contempt of families
terrified me,
And kept silent and did not go
out of doors?
35 "Oh that I had one to hear me!
Behold, here is my [1]signature;
[a]Let the Almighty answer me!
And the indictment which my
[b]adversary has written,
36 Surely I would carry it on my
shoulder,
I would bind it to myself like a
crown.
37 "I would declare to Him [a]the
number of my steps;
Like [b]a prince I would approach
Him.

38 ¶ "If my [a]land cries out
against me,
And its furrows weep together;
39 If I have [a]eaten its [1]fruit
without money,
Or have [b]caused [2]its owners to
lose their lives,
40 Let [a]briars [1]grow instead of
wheat,
And stinkweed instead of
barley."
The words of Job are ended.

Elihu in Anger Rebukes Job

32 Then these three men ceased answering Job, because he was
righteous in his own eyes.
2 But the anger of Elihu the son of
Barachel the [a]Buzite, of the family of
Ram burned; against Job his anger burned
because he justified himself [1c]before
God.
3 And his anger burned against his
three friends because they had found no
answer, and yet had condemned Job.
4 Now Elihu had waited [1]to speak
to Job because they were years older
than he.
5 And when Elihu saw that there was
no answer in the mouth of the three men
his anger burned.
6 ¶ So Elihu the son of Barachel the
Buzite [1]spoke out and said,
"I am young in years and you
are [a]old;
Therefore I was shy and afraid to
tell you [2]what I think.
7 "I [1]thought [2a]age should speak,
And [3]increased years should
teach wisdom.
8 "But it is a spirit in man,
And the [a]breath of the Almighty
gives them [b]understanding.

34 [a]Ex 23:2
35 [1]Lit *mark* [a]Job 19:7; 30:20,24,28; 35:14 [b]Job 27:7
37 [a]Job 31:4 [b]Job 1:3; 29:25
38 [a]Job 24:2
39 [1]Lit *strength* [2]Lit *the soul of its owners to expire* [a]Job 24:6, 10-12; James 5:4 [b]1 Kin 21:19
40 [1]Lit *come forth* [a]Job 32:13; Is 5:6
32:1 [a]Job 10:7; 13:18; 27:5,6; 31:6
2 [1]Or *more than* [a]Gen 22:21 [b]Job 27:5,6 [c]Job 30:21
4 [1]Lit *for Job with words*; or possibly *while they were speaking with Job*
6 [1]Lit *answered* [2]Lit *my knowledge* [a]Job 15:10
7 [1]Lit *said* [2]Lit *days* [3]Lit *many* [a]Job 8:8,9
8 [a]Job 33:4 [b]Job 38:36
9 [1]Or *nobles* [a]Job 32:7
10 [1]Or *said* [2]Lit *my knowledge*
11 [1]Lit *searched out words*
12 [1]Lit *Behold*
13 [1]Lit *drive away* [a]Jer 9:23
14 [1]Lit *words*
15 [1]Lit *moved away from*
16 [1]Lit *stand*
21 [a]Lev 19:15; Job 13:8,10; 34:19
33:1 [a]Job 13:6
2 [1]Lit *palate*
3 [a]Job 6:28; 27:4; 36:4
4 [a]Gen 2:7; Job 10:3; 32:8

9 "The [1]abundant *in years* may not
be wise,
Nor may [a]elders understand
justice.
10 "So I [1]say, 'Listen to me,
I too will tell [2]what I think.'
11 ¶ "Behold, I waited for your
words,
I listened to your reasonings,
While you [1]pondered what to
say.
12 "I even paid close attention to
you;
[1]Indeed, there was no one who
refuted Job,
Not one of you who answered
his words.
13 "Do not say,
'[a]We have found wisdom;
God will [1]rout him, not man.'
14 "For he has not arranged *his*
words against me,
Nor will I reply to him with your
[1]arguments.
15 ¶ "They are dismayed, they no
longer answer;
Words have [1]failed them.
16 "Shall I wait, because they do not
speak,
Because they [1]stop *and* no
longer answer?
17 "I too will answer my share,
I also will tell my opinion.
18 "For I am full of words;
The spirit within me
constrains me.
19 "Behold, my belly is like unvented
wine,
Like new wineskins it is about to
burst.
20 "Let me speak that I may get
relief;
Let me open my lips and answer.
21 "Let me now [a]be partial to no
one,
Nor flatter *any* man.
22 "For I do not know how to flatter,
Else my Maker would soon take
me away.

Elihu Claims to Speak for God

33 "However now, Job, please
[a]hear my speech,
And listen to all my words.
2 "Behold now, I open my mouth,
My tongue in my [1]mouth
speaks.
3 "My words are *from* the
uprightness of my heart,
And my lips speak [a]knowledge
sincerely.
4 "The [a]Spirit of God has
made me,

And the [b]breath of [1]the
Almighty gives me life.
5 "[a]Refute me if you can;
Array yourselves before me, take
your stand.
6 "Behold, I belong to God like you;
I too have been [1]formed out of
the [a]clay.
7 "Behold, [a]no fear of me should
terrify you,
Nor should my pressure weigh
heavily on you.

8 ¶ "Surely you have spoken in my
hearing,
And I have heard the sound of
your words:
9 'I am [a]pure, [b]without
transgression;
I am innocent and there [c]is no
guilt in me.
10 'Behold, He [1]invents pretexts
against me;
He [a]counts me as His enemy.
11 'He [a]puts my feet in the stocks;
He watches all my paths.'
12 "Behold, let me [1]tell you, [a]you
are not right in this,
For God is greater than man.

13 ¶ "Why do you [a]complain
against Him
That He does not give an
account of all His doings?
14 "Indeed [a]God speaks once,
Or twice, *yet* no one notices it.
15 "In a [a]dream, a vision of the
night,
When sound sleep falls on men,
While they slumber in their
beds,
16 Then [a]He opens the ears of
men,
And seals their instruction,
17 That He may turn man aside
from his conduct,
And [1]keep man from pride;
18 He [a]keeps back his soul from
the pit,
And his life from [1]passing over
[b]into Sheol.

19 ¶ "[1]Man is also chastened with
[a]pain on his bed,
And with unceasing complaint in
his bones;
20 So that his life [a]loathes bread,
And his soul favorite food.
21 "His [a]flesh wastes away from
sight,
And his [b]bones which were not
seen stick out.
22 "Then [a]his soul draws near to
the pit,

4 [1]Heb *Shaddai* [b]Job 27:3
5 [a]Job 33:32
6 [1]Lit *cut out of* [a]Job 4:19
7 [a]Job 13:21
9 [a]Job 9:21; 10:7; 13:18; 16:17 [b]Job 7:21; 13:23; 14:17 [c]Job 10:14
10 [1]Lit *finds* [a]Job 13:24
11 [a]Job 13:27
12 [1]Lit *answer* [a]Eccl 7:20
13 [a]Job 40:2; Is 45:9
14 [a]Job 33:29; 40:5; Ps 62:11
15 [a]Job 4:12-17; 33:15-18
16 [a]Job 36:10, 15
17 [1]Lit *hide*
18 [1]M.T. *perishing by the sword* [a]Job 33:22,24, 28,30 [b]Job 15:22
19 [1]Lit *He* [a]Job 30:17
20 [a]Job 3:24; 6:7; Ps 107:18
21 [a]Job 16:8 [b]Job 19:20; Ps 22:17; 102:5
22 [a]Job 33:18, 28
23 [1]Lit *his uprightness* [a]Gen 40:8
24 [a]Job 33:18, 28; Is 38:17 [b]Job 36:18; Ps 49:7
26 [a]Job 22:27; 34:28; Ps 50:14, 15 [b]Job 22:26
27 [a]2 Sam 12:13; Luke 15:21 [b]Rom 6:21
28 [a]Job 22:28
29 [1]Lit *twice, three times* [a]Eph 1:11; Phil 2:13
30 [a]Job 33:18; Zech 9:11
32 [1]Lit *there are words*
33 [a]Ps 34:11
34:3 [a]Job 12:11
5 [a]Job 13:18; 33:9 [b]Job 27:2
6 [1]Or *Although I am right I am accounted a liar*

And his life to those who bring
death.
23 ¶ "If there is an angel *as*
[a]mediator for him,
One out of a thousand,
To remind a man what is [1]right
for him,
24 Then let him be gracious to him,
and say,
'Deliver him from [a]going down
to the pit,
I have found a [b]ransom';
25 Let his flesh become fresher than
in youth,
Let him return to the days of his
youthful vigor;
26 Then he will [a]pray to God, and
He will accept him,
That [b]he may see His face with
joy,
And He may restore His
righteousness to man.
27 "He will sing to men and say,
'I [a]have sinned and perverted
what is right,
And it is not [b]proper for me.
28 'He has redeemed my soul from
going to the pit,
And my life shall [a]see the light.'

29 ¶ "Behold, God does [a]all these
[1]oftentimes with men,
30 To [a]bring back his soul from the
pit,
That he may be enlightened with
the light of life.
31 "Pay attention, O Job, listen
to me;
Keep silent, and let me speak.
32 "*Then* if [1]you have anything to
say, answer me;
Speak, for I desire to justify you.
33 "If not, [a]listen to me;
Keep silent, and I will teach you
wisdom."

Elihu Vindicates God's Justice

34 Then Elihu continued and said,
2 "Hear my words, you wise
men,
And listen to me, you who
know.
3 "For [a]the ear tests words
As the palate tastes food.
4 "Let us choose for ourselves what
is right;
Let us know among ourselves
what is good.
5 "For Job has said, '[a]I am
righteous,
But [b]God has taken away my
right;
6 [1]Should I lie concerning my
right?

My [2a]wound is incurable,
though I am without transgression.'
7 "What man is like Job,
Who [a]drinks up derision like water,
8 Who goes [a]in company with the workers of iniquity,
And walks with wicked men?
9 "For he has said, '[a]It profits a man nothing
When he [1]is pleased with God.'

10 ¶ "Therefore, listen to me, you men of understanding.
Far be it from God to [a]do wickedness,
And from the Almighty to do wrong.
11 "For He pays a man according to [a]his work,
And makes [1]him find it according to his way.
12 "Surely, [a]God will not act wickedly,
And the Almighty will not pervert justice.
13 "Who [a]gave Him authority over the earth?
And who [b]has laid *on Him* the whole world?
14 "If He should [1]determine to do so,
If He should [a]gather to Himself His spirit and His breath,
15 All [a]flesh would perish together,
And man would [b]return to dust.

16 ¶ "But if *you have* understanding, hear this;
Listen to the sound of my words.
17 "Shall [a]one who hates justice rule?
And [b]will you condemn the righteous mighty One,
18 Who says to a king, 'Worthless one,'
To nobles, 'Wicked ones';
19 Who shows no [a]partiality to princes
Nor regards the rich above the poor,
For they all are the [b]work of His hands?
20 "In a moment they die, and [a]at midnight
People are shaken and pass away,
And [b]the mighty are taken away without a hand.

21 ¶ "For [a]His eyes are upon the ways of a man,
And He sees all his steps.
22 "There is [a]no darkness or deep shadow
Where the workers of iniquity may hide themselves.
23 "For He does not [a]*need to* consider a man further,
That he should go before God in judgment.
24 "He breaks in pieces [a]mighty men without inquiry,
And sets others in their place.
25 "Therefore He [a]knows their works,
And [b]He overthrows *them* in the night,
And they are crushed.
26 "He [a]strikes them like the wicked
[1]In a public place,
27 Because they [a]turned aside from following Him,
And [b]had no regard for any of His ways;
28 So that they caused [a]the cry of the poor to come to Him,
And that He might [b]hear the cry of the afflicted—
29 When He keeps quiet, who then can condemn?
And when He hides His face, who then can behold Him,
That is, in regard to both nation and man?—
30 So that [a]godless men would not rule
Nor be snares of the people.

31 ¶ "For has anyone said to God,
'I have borne *chastisement;*
I will not offend *anymore;*
32 Teach me what I do not see;
If I have [a]done iniquity,
I will not do it again'?
33 "Shall He [a]recompense on your terms, because you have rejected *it?*
For you must choose, and not I;
Therefore declare what you know.
34 "Men of understanding will say to me,
And a wise man who hears me,
35 'Job [a]speaks without knowledge,
And his words are without wisdom.
36 'Job ought to be tried [1]to the limit,
Because he answers [a]like wicked men.
37 'For he adds [a]rebellion to his sin;

6 [2]Lit *arrow* [a]Job 6:4
7 [a]Job 15:16
8 [a]Job 22:15
9 [1]Or *takes delight in God* [a]Job 21:15; 35:3; Ps 50:18
10 [a]Gen 18:25; Deut 32:4; Job 8:3; 34:12; Rom 9:14
11 [1]Lit *a man* [a]Job 34:25; Ps 62:12; Prov 24:12; Jer 32:19; Ezek 33:20; Matt 16:27; Rom 2:6; 2 Cor 5:10; Rev 22:12
12 [a]Job 34:10
13 [a]Job 38:4 [b]Job 38:5
14 [1]Lit *set His mind on Himself* [a]Job 12:10; Ps 104:29; Eccl 12:7
15 [a]Gen 7:21; Job 9:22 [b]Gen 3:19; Job 10:9
17 [a]2 Sam 23:3; Job 34:30 [b]Job 40:8
19 [a]Lev 19:15; Deut 10:17; 2 Chr 19:7; Acts 10:34; Rom 2:11; Gal 2:6; Eph 6:9; Col 3:25; 1 Pet 1:17 [b]Job 10:3
20 [a]Ex 12:29; Job 34:25; 36:20 [b]Job 12:19
21 [a]Job 24:23; 31:4; Prov 5:21; 15:3; Jer 16:17
22 [a]Ps 139:11, 12; Amos 9:2,3
23 [a]Job 11:11
24 [a]Job 12:19
25 [a]Job 34:11 [b]Job 34:20
26 [1]Lit *In the place of the ones seeing* [a]Ps 9:5; 11:5
27 [a]1 Sam 15:11 [b]Job 21:14
28 [a]Job 35:9; James 5:4 [b]Ex 22:23; Job 22:27
30 [a]Job 5:15; 20:5; 34:17; Prov 29:2-12
32 [a]Job 33:27
33 [a]Job 41:11
35 [a]Job 35:16; 38:2
36 [1]Or *to the end* [a]Job 22:15
37 [a]Job 23:2

He [b]claps his hands among us,
And multiplies his words against
God.' "

Elihu Sharply Reproves Job

35 Then Elihu continued and said,
2 "Do you think this is
according to [a]justice?
Do you say, 'My righteousness is
more than God's'?
3 "For you say, '[a]What advantage
will it be to [1]You?
[b]What profit will I have, more
than if I had sinned?'
4 "I will answer you,
And your friends with you.
5 "[a]Look at the heavens and see;
And behold [b]the clouds—they
are higher than you.
6 "If you have sinned, [a]what do
you accomplish against Him?
And if your transgressions are
many, what do you do to
Him?
7 "If you are righteous, [a]what do
you give to Him,
Or what does He receive from
your hand?
8 "Your wickedness is for a man
like yourself,
And your righteousness is for a
son of man.

9 ¶ "Because of the [a]multitude of
oppressions they cry out;
They cry for help because of the
arm [b]of the mighty.
10 "But [a]no one says, 'Where is God
my Maker,
Who [b]gives songs in the night,
11 Who [a]teaches us more than the
beasts of the earth
And makes us wiser than the
birds of the heavens?'
12 "There [a]they cry out, but He
does not answer
Because of the pride of evil
men.
13 "Surely [a]God will not listen to
[1]an empty *cry,*
Nor will the Almighty regard it.
14 "How much less when [a]you say
you do not behold Him,
The [b]case is before Him, and
you must wait for Him!
15 "And now, because He has not
visited *in* His anger,
Nor has He acknowledged
[1]transgression well,
16 So Job opens his mouth
[1]emptily;
He multiplies words [a]without
knowledge."

Elihu Speaks of God's Dealings with Men

36 Then Elihu continued and said,
2 "Wait for me a little, and I
will show you
That there [1]is yet more to be
said in God's behalf.
3 "I will fetch my knowledge from
afar,
And I will ascribe [a]righteousness
to my Maker.
4 "For truly [a]my words are not
false;
One who is [b]perfect in
knowledge is with you.
5 "Behold, God is mighty but does
not [a]despise *any;*
He is [b]mighty in strength of
understanding.
6 "He does not [a]keep the wicked
alive,
But gives justice to [b]the
afflicted.
7 "He does not [a]withdraw His eyes
from the righteous;
But [b]with kings on the throne
He has seated them forever, and
they are exalted.
8 "And if they are bound in fetters,
And are caught in the cords of
[a]affliction,
9 Then He declares to them their
work
And their transgressions, that
they have [a]magnified
themselves.
10 "[a]He opens their ear to
instruction,
And [b]commands that they
return from evil.
11 "If they hear and serve *Him,*
They will [a]end their days in
prosperity
And their years in [b]pleasures.
12 "But if they do not hear, they
shall [1]perish [a]by the sword
And they will [b]die without
knowledge.
13 "But the godless in heart lay up
anger;
They do not cry for help when
He binds them.
14 "[1]They die in youth,
And their life *perishes* among
the [a]cult prostitutes.
15 "He delivers the afflicted in
[1]their [a]affliction,
And [b]opens their ear [2]in *time
of* oppression.
16 "Then indeed, He [a]enticed you
from the mouth of distress,
Instead of it, a broad place with
no constraint;

37 [b]Job 27:23
35:2 [a]Job 27:2
3 [1]Or *you* [a]Job 34:9 [b]Job 9:30, 31
5 [a]Gen 15:5; Ps 8:3 [b]Job 22:12
6 [a]Job 7:20; Prov 8:36; Jer 7:19
7 [a]Job 22:2,3; Prov 9:12; Luke 17:10; Rom 11:35
9 [a]Ex 2:23 [b]Job 12:19
10 [a]Job 21:14; 27:10; 36:13; Is 51:13 [b]Job 8:21; Ps 42:8; 77:6; 149:5; Acts 16:25
11 [a]Job 36:22; Ps 94:12; Jer 32:33
12 [a]Prov 1:28
13 [1]Or *false-hood* [a]Job 27:9; Prov 15:29; Is 1:15; Jer 11:11; Mic 3:4
14 [a]Job 9:11; 23:8,9 [b]Job 31:35
15 [1]Or *arro-gance*
16 [1]Lit *vainly* [a]Job 34:35; 38:2
36:2 [1]Lit *are yet words for God*
3 [a]Job 8:3; 37:23
4 [a]Job 33:3 [b]Job 37:16
5 [a]Ps 22:24; 69:33; 102:17 [b]Job 12:13
6 [a]Job 8:22; 34:26 [b]Job 5:15
7 [a]Ps 33:18; 34:15 [b]Job 5:11; Ps 113:8
8 [a]Job 36:15,21
9 [a]Job 15:25
10 [a]Job 33:16; 36:15 [b]2 Kin 17:13; Job 36:21; Jon 3:8
11 [a]1 Tim 4:8 [b]Ps 16:11
12 [1]Lit *pass away* [a]Job 15:22 [b]Job 4:21
14 [1]Or *Their soul dies* [a]Deut 23:17
15 [1]Lit *his* [2]Or *in adversity* [a]Job 36:8,21 [b]Job 36:10
16 [a]Hos 2:14

And that which was set on your
table was full of [1]fatness.

17 ¶ "But you were full of
[a]judgment on the wicked;
Judgment and justice take hold
of you.
18 "*Beware* that [a]wrath does not
entice you to scoffing;
And do not let the greatness of
the [b]ransom turn you aside.
19 "Will your [1]riches keep you from
distress,
Or all the forces of *your*
strength?
20 "Do not long for [a]the night,
When people [1]vanish in their
place.
21 "Be careful, do [a]not turn to evil,
For you have preferred this to
[b]affliction.
22 "Behold, God is exalted in His
power;
Who is a [a]teacher like Him?
23 "Who has appointed Him His
way,
And who has said, '[a]You have
done wrong'?

24 ¶ "Remember that you should
[a]exalt His work,
Of which men have [b]sung.
25 "All men have seen it;
Man beholds from afar.
26 "Behold, God is [a]exalted, and
[b]we do not know *Him;*
The [c]number of His years is
unsearchable.
27 "For [a]He draws up the drops of
water,
They distill rain from [1]the
[2]mist,
28 Which the clouds pour down,
They drip upon man abundantly.
29 "Can anyone understand the
[a]spreading of the clouds,
The [b]thundering of His
[1]pavilion?
30 "Behold, He spreads His
[1]lightning about Him,
And He covers the depths of the
sea.
31 "For by these He [a]judges peoples;
He [b]gives food in abundance.
32 "He covers *His* hands with the
[1]lightning,
And [a]commands it to strike the
mark.
33 "Its [a]noise declares [1]His
presence;
The cattle also, concerning what
is coming up.

Elihu Says God Is Back of the Storm

37 "At this also my heart trembles,
And leaps from its place.
2 "Listen closely to the [a]thunder of
His voice,
And the rumbling that goes out
from His mouth.
3 "Under the whole heaven He lets
it loose,
And His [1]lightning to the [a]ends
of the earth.
4 "After it, a voice roars;
He thunders with His majestic
voice,
And He does not restrain [1]the
lightnings when His voice is
heard.
5 "God [a]thunders with His voice
wondrously,
Doing [b]great things which we
cannot comprehend.
6 "For to [a]the snow He says, 'Fall
on the earth,'
And to the [1b]downpour and the
rain, 'Be strong.'
7 "He [a]seals the hand of every
man,
That [b]all men may know His
work.
8 "Then the beast goes into its [a]lair
And remains in its [1]den.
9 "Out of the [1a]south comes the
storm,
And out of the [2]north the cold.
10 "From the breath of God [a]ice is
made,
And the expanse of the waters is
frozen.
11 "Also with moisture He [a]loads
the thick cloud;
He [b]disperses [c]the cloud of His
[1]lightning.
12 "It changes direction, turning
around by His guidance,
That [1]it may do whatever He
[a]commands [2]it
On the [b]face of the inhabited
earth.
13 "Whether for [1a]correction, or for
[b]His world,
Or for [c]lovingkindness, He
causes it to [2]happen.

14 ¶ "Listen to this, O Job,
Stand and consider the wonders
of God.
15 "Do you know how God
establishes them,
And makes the [1]lightning of His
cloud to shine?
16 "Do you know about the layers of
the thick clouds,

16 [1]Or *rich food*
17 [a]Job 22:5,10, 11
18 [a]Jon 4:4,9 [b]Job 33:24
19 [1]Or *cry*
20 [1]Lit *go up* [a]Job 34:20,25
21 [a]Job 36:10; Ps 31:6; 66:18 [b]Job 36:8,15; Heb 11:25
22 [a]Job 35:11
23 [a]Deut 32:4; Job 8:3
24 [a]Ps 92:5; Rev 15:3 [b]Ex 15:1; Judg 5:1; 1 Chr 16:9; Ps 59:16; 138:5
26 [a]Job 11:7-9; 37:23 [b]1 Cor 13:12 [c]Job 10:5; Ps 90:2; 102:24, 27; Heb 1:12
27 [1]Lit *its* [2]Or *flood* [a]Job 5:10; 36:26-29; 37:6, 11; 38:28; Ps 147:8
29 [1]Lit *booth* [a]Job 37:11,16 [b]Job 26:14
30 [1]Lit *light*
31 [a]Job 37:13 [b]Ps 104:27; 136:25; Acts 14:17
32 [1]Lit *light* [a]Job 37:11,12,15
33 [1]Lit *concerning Him* [a]Job 37:2
37:2 [a]Job 36:33; 37:4,5; Ps 29:3-9
3 [1]Lit *light* [a]Job 28:24; 37:11,12; 38:13
4 [1]Lit *them*
5 [a]Job 26:14 [b]Job 5:9; 37:14, 16,23
6 [1]Lit *shower of rain and shower of rains* [a]Job 38:22 [b]Job 36:27
7 [a]Job 12:14 [b]Ps 111:2
8 [1]Lit *dens* [a]Job 38:40; Ps 104:21,22
9 [1]Lit *chamber* [2]Lit *scattering winds* [a]Job 9:9
10 [a]Job 38:29; Ps 147:17
11 [1]Lit *light* [a]Job 36:27 [b]Job 36:29 [c]Job 37:15
12 [1]Lit *they* [2]Lit *them* [a]Job 36:32; Ps 148:8 [b]Is 14:21; 27:6
13 [1]Lit *the rod* [2]Lit *be found* [a]Ex 9:18,23; 1 Sam 12:18,19 [b]Job 38:26,27 [c]1 Kin 18:41-46
15 [1]Lit *light*

The [a]wonders of one [b]perfect
in knowledge,
17 You whose garments are hot,
When the land is still because of
the south wind?
18 "Can you, with Him, [a]spread out
the skies,
Strong as a molten mirror?
19 "Teach us what we shall say to
Him;
We [a]cannot arrange *our case*
because of darkness.
20 "Shall it be told Him that I would
speak?
[1]Or should a man say that he
would be swallowed up?

21 ¶ "Now [1]men do not see the
light which is bright in the
skies;
But the wind has passed and
cleared them.
22 "Out of the north comes golden
splendor;
Around God is awesome majesty.
23 "The Almighty—[a]we cannot find
Him;
He is [b]exalted in power
And [c]He will not do violence
[d]to justice and abundant
righteousness.
24 "Therefore men [a]fear Him;
He does not [b]regard any who
are wise of heart."

God Speaks Now to Job

38 Then the LORD [a]answered Job
out of the whirlwind and said,
2 "Who is this that [a]darkens
counsel
By words without knowledge?
3 "Now [a]gird up your loins like a
man,
And [b]I will ask you, and you
instruct Me!
4 "Where were you [a]when I laid
the foundation of the earth?
Tell *Me,* if you [1]have
understanding,
5 Who set its [a]measurements?
Since you know.
Or who stretched the line on it?
6 "On what [a]were its bases sunk?
Or who laid its cornerstone,
7 When the morning stars sang
together
And all the [a]sons of God
shouted for joy?

8 ¶ "Or *who* [a]enclosed the sea
with doors
When, bursting forth, it went out
from the womb;
9 When I made a cloud its garment
And thick darkness its swaddling
band,
10 And I [1a]placed boundaries on it
And set a bolt and doors,
11 And I said, 'Thus far you shall
come, but no farther;
And here shall your proud waves
stop'?

God's Mighty Power

12 ¶ "Have you [1]ever in your life
commanded the morning,
And caused the dawn to know
its place,
13 That it might take hold of [a]the
ends of the earth,
And [b]the wicked be shaken out
of it?
14 "It is changed like clay *under* the
seal;
And they stand forth like a
garment.
15 "[a]From the wicked their light is
withheld,
And the [b]uplifted arm is broken.

16 ¶ "Have you entered into [a]the
springs of the sea
Or walked [1]in the recesses of
the deep?
17 "Have the gates of death been
revealed to you,
Or have you seen the gates of
[a]deep darkness?
18 "Have you understood the
[1]expanse of [a]the earth?
Tell *Me,* if you know all this.

19 ¶ "Where is the way to the
dwelling of light?
And darkness, where is its place,
20 That you may take it to [a]its
territory
And that you may discern the
paths to its [1]home?
21 "You know, for [a]you were born
then,
And the number of your days is
great!
22 "Have you entered the
storehouses [a]of the snow,
Or have you seen the
storehouses of the [b]hail,
23 Which I have reserved for the
time of distress,
For the day of war and battle?
24 "Where is the way that [a]the light
is divided,
Or the east wind scattered on
the earth?

25 ¶ "Who has cleft a channel for
the flood,
Or a way for the thunderbolt,

---

16 [a]Job 37:5,14, 23 [b]Job 36:4
18 [a]Job 9:8; Ps 104:2; Is 44:24; 45:12; Jer 10:12; Zech 12:1
19 [a]Job 9:14; Rom 8:26
20 [1]Or *If a man speak, surely he shall be swallowed up*
21 [1]Lit *they*
23 [a]Job 11:7,8; Rom 11:33; 1 Tim 6:16 [b]Job 9:4; 36:5 [c]Is 63:9; Lam 3:33; Ezek 18:23,32; 33:11 [d]Job 8:3
24 [a]Matt 10:28 [b]Job 5:13; Matt 11:25; 1 Cor 1:26
38:1 [a]Job 40:6
2 [a]Job 35:16; 42:3
3 [a]Job 40:7 [b]Job 42:4
4 [1]Lit *know understanding* [a]Job 15:7; Ps 104:5; Prov 8:29; 30:4
5 [a]Prov 8:29; Is 40:12
6 [a]Job 26:7
7 [a]Job 1:6
8 [a]Gen 1:9; Ps 104:6-9; Prov 8:29; Jer 5:22
10 [1]Lit *broke My decree on it* [a]Gen 1:9; Ps 33:7; 104:9; Prov 8:29; Jer 5:22
12 [1]Lit *from your days*
13 [a]Job 28:24; 37:3 [b]Job 34:25, 26; 36:6
15 [a]Job 5:14 [b]Num 15:30; Ps 10:15; 37:17
16 [1]Or *in search of* [a]Gen 7:11; 8:2; Prov 8:24, 28
17 [a]Job 10:21; 26:6; 34:22
18 [1]Or *width* [a]Job 28:24
20 [1]Lit *house* [a]Job 26:10
21 [a]Job 15:7
22 [a]Job 37:6 [b]Ex 9:18; Josh 10:11; Is 30:30; Ezek 13:11,13; Rev 16:21
24 [a]Job 26:10

26 To bring [a]rain on a land without
[1]people,
On a desert without a man in it,
27 To [a]satisfy the waste and
desolate land
And to make the [1]seeds of grass
to sprout?
28 "Has [a]the rain a father?
Or who has begotten the drops
of dew?
29 "From whose womb has come
the [a]ice?
And the frost of heaven, who has
given it birth?
30 "Water [1]becomes hard like stone,
And the surface of the deep is
imprisoned.

31 ¶ "Can you bind the chains of
the [a]Pleiades,
Or loose the cords of Orion?
32 "Can you lead forth a
[1]constellation in its season,
And guide the Bear with her
[2]satellites?
33 "Do you know the [a]ordinances of
the heavens,
Or fix their rule over the earth?

34 ¶ "Can you lift up your voice to
the clouds,
So that an [a]abundance of water
will cover you?
35 "Can you [a]send forth lightnings
that they may go
And say to you, 'Here we are'?
36 "Who has [a]put wisdom in the
innermost being
Or given [b]understanding to the
[1]mind?
37 "Who can count the clouds by
wisdom,
Or [a]tip the water jars of the
heavens,
38 When the dust hardens into a
mass
And the clods stick together?

39 ¶ "Can you hunt the [a]prey for
the lion,
Or satisfy the appetite of the
young lions,
40 When they [a]crouch in *their*
dens
And lie in wait in *their* lair?
41 "Who prepares for [a]the raven its
nourishment
When its young cry to God
And wander about without food?

God Speaks of Nature and Its Beings

39 "Do you know the time the
[1a]mountain goats give
birth?
Do you observe the calving of
the [b]deer?
2 "Can you count the months they
fulfill,
Or do you know the time they
give birth?
3 "They kneel down, they bring
forth their young,
They get rid of their labor pains.
4 "Their offspring become strong,
they grow up in the open
field;
They leave and do not return to
them.

5 ¶ "Who sent out the [a]wild
donkey free?
And who loosed the bonds of the
swift donkey,
6 To whom I gave [a]the wilderness
for a home
And the salt land for his dwelling
place?
7 "He scorns the tumult of the city,
The shoutings of the driver he
does not hear.
8 "He explores the mountains for
his pasture
And searches after every green
thing.
9 "Will the [a]wild ox consent to
serve you,
Or will he spend the night at
your manger?
10 "Can you bind the wild ox in a
furrow with [1]ropes,
Or will he harrow the valleys
after you?
11 "Will you trust him because his
strength is great
And leave your labor to him?
12 "Will you have faith in him that
he will return your [1]grain
And gather *it from* your
threshing floor?

13 ¶ "The ostriches' wings flap
joyously
With the pinion and plumage of
[1]love,
14 For she abandons her eggs to the
earth
And warms them in the dust,
15 And she forgets that a foot may
crush [1]them,
Or that a wild beast may trample
[1]them.
16 "She treats her young [a]cruelly, as
if *they* were not hers;
Though her labor be in vain, *she*
is [1]unconcerned;
17 Because God has made her forget
wisdom,
And has not given her a share of
understanding.

---

26 [1]Lit *man* [a]Job 36:27
27 [1]Or *growth* [a]Ps 104:13,14; 107:35
28 [a]Job 36:27, 28; Ps 147:8; Jer 14:22
29 [a]Job 37:10; Ps 147:17
30 [1]Lit *hides itself*
31 [a]Job 9:9; Amos 5:8
32 [1]Heb *Mazzaroth* [2]Lit *sons*
33 [a]Ps 148:6; Jer 31:35,36
34 [a]Job 22:11; 36:27,28; 38:37
35 [a]Job 36:32; 37:3
36 [1]Or *rooster* [a]Job 9:4; Ps 51:6; Eccl 2:26 [b]Job 32:8
37 [a]Job 38:34
39 [a]Ps 104:21
40 [a]Job 37:8
41 [a]Ps 147:9; Matt 6:26; Luke 12:24
39:1 [1]Lit *goats of the rock* [a]Deut 14:5; 1 Sam 24:2; Ps 104:18 [b]Ps 29:9
5 [a]Job 6:5; 11:12; 24:5; Ps 104:11
6 [a]Job 24:5; Jer 2:24; Hos 8:9
9 [a]Num 23:22; Deut 33:17; Ps 22:21; 29:6; 92:10; Is 34:7
10 [1]Lit *his rope*
12 [1]Lit *seed*
13 [1]Or *a stork*
15 [1]Lit *it*
16 [1]Lit *without fear* [a]Lam 4:3

18 "When she lifts herself [1]on high,
She laughs at the horse and his rider.
19 ¶ "Do you give the horse *his* might?
Do you clothe his neck with a mane?
20 "Do you make him [a]leap like the locust?
His majestic [b]snorting is terrible.
21 "[1]He paws in the valley, and rejoices in *his* strength;
He [a]goes out to meet the weapons.
22 "He laughs at fear and is not dismayed;
And he does not turn back from the sword.
23 "The quiver rattles against him,
The flashing spear and javelin.
24 "With shaking and rage he [1]races over the ground,
And he does not stand still at the voice of the trumpet.
25 "As often as the trumpet *sounds* he says, 'Aha!'
And he scents the battle from afar,
And the thunder of the captains and the war cry.
26 ¶ "Is it by your understanding that the hawk soars,
Stretching his wings toward the south?
27 "Is it at your [1]command that the eagle mounts up
And makes [a]his nest on high?
28 "On the cliff he dwells and lodges,
Upon the rocky crag, an inaccessible place.
29 "From there he [a]spies out food;
His eyes see *it* from afar.
30 "His young ones also suck up blood;
And [a]where the slain are, there is he."

Job: What Can I Say?

40 Then the LORD said to Job,
2 "Will the faultfinder [a]contend with the Almighty?
Let him who [b]reproves God answer it."
3 ¶ Then Job answered the LORD and said,
4 "Behold, I am insignificant; what can I reply to You?
I [a]lay my hand on my mouth.
5 "Once I have spoken, and [a]I will not answer;
Even twice, and I will add nothing more."

God Questions Job

6 ¶ Then the [a]LORD answered Job out of the storm and said,
7 "Now [a]gird up your loins like a man;
I will [b]ask you, and you instruct Me.
8 "Will you really [a]annul My judgment?
Will you [b]condemn Me [c]that you may be justified?
9 "Or do you have an arm like God,
And can you [a]thunder with a voice like His?
10 ¶ "[a]Adorn yourself with eminence and dignity,
And clothe yourself with honor and majesty.
11 "Pour out [a]the overflowings of your anger,
And look on everyone who is [b]proud, and make him low.
12 "Look on everyone who is proud, *and* [a]humble him,
And [b]tread down the wicked [1]where they stand.
13 "[a]Hide them in the dust together;
Bind [1]them in the hidden *place.*
14 "Then I will also [1]confess to you,
That your own right hand can save you.

God's Power Shown in Creatures

15 ¶ "Behold now, [1]Behemoth, which [a]I made [2]as well as you;
He eats grass like an ox.
16 "Behold now, his strength in his loins
And his power in the muscles of his belly.
17 "He bends his tail like a cedar;
The sinews of his thighs are knit together.
18 "His bones are tubes of bronze;
His [1]limbs are like bars of iron.
19 ¶ "He is the [a]first of the ways of God;
Let his [b]maker bring near his sword.
20 "Surely the mountains [a]bring him food,
And all the beasts of the field [b]play there.
21 "Under the lotus plants he lies down,
In the covert of the reeds and the marsh.
22 "The lotus plants cover him with [1]shade;

18 [1]Or *to flee*
20 [a]Joel 2:5 [b]Jer 8:16
21 [1]Lit *They paw* [a]Jer 8:6
24 [1]Or *swallows up*
27 [1]Lit *mouth* [a]Jer 49:16; Obad 4
29 [a]Job 9:26
30 [a]Matt 24:28; Luke 17:37
40:2 [a]Job 9:3; 10:2; 33:13; Is 45:9 [b]Job 13:3; 23:4; 31:35
4 [a]Job 21:5; 29:9
5 [a]Job 9:3,15
6 [a]Job 38:1
7 [a]Job 38:3 [b]Job 38:3; 42:4
8 [a]Rom 3:4 [b]Job 10:3,7; 16:11; 19:6; 27:2 [c]Job 13:18; 27:6
9 [a]Job 37:5; Ps 29:3
10 [a]Ps 93:1; 104:1
11 [a]Is 42:25; Nah 1:6,8 [b]Is 2:12; Dan 4:37
12 [1]Lit *under them* [a]1 Sam 2:7; Is 2:12; 13:11; Dan 4:37 [b]Is 63:3
13 [1]Or *their faces* [a]Is 2:10-12
14 [1]Or *praise you*
15 [1]Or *the hippopotamus* [2]Lit *with* [a]Job 40:19
18 [1]Lit *bones*
19 [a]Job 41:33 [b]Job 40:15
20 [a]Ps 104:14 [b]Ps 104:26
22 [1]Lit *his shade*

The willows of the brook
surround him.
23 "If a river [1]rages, he is not
alarmed;
He is confident, though the
[a]Jordan rushes to his
mouth.
24 "Can anyone capture him [1]when
he is on watch,
With [2]barbs can anyone pierce
his nose?

God's Power Shown in Creatures

41 "[1]Can you draw out
[2a]Leviathan with a
fishhook?
Or press down his tongue with a
cord?
2 "Can you [a]put a [1]rope in his
nose
Or pierce his jaw with a [2]hook?
3 "Will he make many supplications
to you,
Or will he speak to you soft
words?
4 "Will he make a covenant
with you?
Will you take him for a servant
forever?
5 "Will you play with him as with a
bird,
Or will you bind him for your
maidens?
6 "Will the [1]traders bargain
over him?
Will they divide him among the
merchants?
7 "Can you fill his skin with
harpoons,
Or his head with fishing spears?
8 "Lay your hand on him;
Remember the battle; [1]you will
not do it again!
9 "[1]Behold, [2]your expectation is
false;
Will [3]you be laid low even at
the sight of him?
10 "No one is so fierce that he dares
to [a]arouse him;
Who then is he that can stand
before Me?
11 "Who has [1a]given to Me that I
should repay *him?*
Whatever is [b]under the whole
heaven is Mine.

12 ¶ "I will not keep silence
concerning his limbs,
Or his mighty strength, or his
[1]orderly frame.
13 "Who can [1]strip off his outer
armor?
Who can come within his double
[2]mail?
14 "Who can open the doors of his
face?
Around his teeth there is terror.
15 "*His* [1]strong scales are *his* pride,
Shut up *as with* a tight seal.
16 "One is so near to another
That no air can come between
them.
17 "They are joined one to another;
They clasp each other and
cannot be separated.
18 "His sneezes flash forth light,
And his eyes are like the
[a]eyelids of the morning.
19 "Out of his mouth go burning
torches;
Sparks of fire leap forth.
20 "Out of his nostrils smoke goes
forth
As *from* a boiling pot and
burning rushes.
21 "His breath kindles coals,
And a flame goes forth from his
mouth.
22 "In his neck lodges strength,
And dismay leaps before him.
23 "The folds of his flesh are joined
together,
Firm on him and immovable.
24 "His heart is as hard as a stone,
Even as hard as a lower
millstone.
25 "When he raises himself up, the
[1]mighty fear;
Because of the crashing they are
bewildered.
26 "The sword that reaches him
cannot avail,
Nor the spear, the dart or the
javelin.
27 "He regards iron as straw,
Bronze as rotten wood.
28 "The [1]arrow cannot make him
flee;
Slingstones are turned into
stubble for him.
29 "Clubs are regarded as stubble;
He laughs at the rattling of the
javelin.
30 "His underparts are *like* sharp
potsherds;
He [1]spreads out *like* a threshing
sledge on the mire.
31 "He makes the depths boil like a
pot;
He makes the sea like a jar of
ointment.
32 "Behind him he makes a wake to
shine;
One would think the deep to be
gray-haired.
33 "[a]Nothing on [1]earth is like him,
One made without fear.

---

23 [1]Or *oppresses* [a]Gen 13:10
24 [1]Lit *in his eyes* [2]Lit *snares*
41:1 [1]Ch 40:25 in Heb [2]Or *the crocodile* [a]Job 3:8; Ps 74:14; 104:26; Is 27:1
2 [1]Lit *rope of rushes* [2]Or *thorn* or *ring* [a]2 Kin 19:28; Is 37:29
6 [1]Lit *partners*
8 [1]Lit *do not add*
9 [1]Ch 41:1 in Heb [2]Lit *his* [3]Lit *he*
10 [a]Job 3:8
11 [1]Lit *anticipated* [a]Rom 11:35 [b]Ex 19:5; Deut 10:14; Job 9:5-10; 26:6-14; 28:24; Ps 24:1; 50:12; 1 Cor 10:26
12 [1]Or *graceful*
13 [1]Lit *uncover the face of his garment* [2]So Gr; Heb *bridle*
15 [1]Lit *rows of shields*
18 [a]Job 3:9
25 [1]Or *gods*
28 [1]Lit *son of the bow*
30 [1]Or *moves across*
33 [1]Lit *dust* [a]Job 40:19

34 "[1]He looks on everything that is high;
He is king over all the [a]sons of pride."

Job's Confession

42 Then Job answered the LORD and said,
2 "I know that [a]You can do all things,
And that no purpose of Yours can be thwarted.
3 'Who is this that [a]hides counsel without knowledge?'
"Therefore I have declared that which I did not understand,
Things [b]too wonderful for me, which I did not know."
4 'Hear, now, and I will speak;
I will [a]ask You, and You instruct me.'
5 "I have [a]heard of You by the hearing of the ear;
But now my [b]eye sees You;
6 Therefore I retract,
And I repent in dust and ashes."

God Displeased with Job's Friends

7 ¶ It came about after the LORD had
spoken these words to Job, that the LORD
said to Eliphaz the Temanite, "My wrath
is kindled against you and against your
two friends, because you have not spoken
of Me what is right [a]as My servant Job
has.
8 "Now therefore, take for yourselves
[a]seven bulls and seven rams, and go to
My servant Job, and offer up a [b]burnt
offering for yourselves, and My servant
Job will [c]pray for you. [d]For I will [1]ac-
cept him so that I may not do with you
according to your folly, because you have
not spoken of Me what is right, as My
servant Job has."
9 So Eliphaz the Temanite and Bildad
the Shuhite *and* Zophar the Naamathite
went and did as the LORD told them; and
the LORD [1]accepted Job.

God Restores Job's Fortunes

10 ¶ The LORD [a]restored the fortunes
of Job when he prayed for his friends, and
the LORD increased all that Job had twofold.
11 Then all his [a]brothers and all his
sisters and all who had known him before
came to him, and they ate bread with him
in his house; and they [b]consoled him and
comforted him for all the adversities that
the LORD had brought on him. And each
one gave him one [1]piece of money, and
each a ring of gold.
12 [a]The LORD blessed the latter *days*
of Job more than his beginning; [b]and he
had 14,000 sheep and 6,000 camels and
1,000 yoke of oxen and 1,000 female
donkeys.
13 [a]He had seven sons and three
daughters.
14 He named the first Jemimah, and
the second Keziah, and the third Keren-
happuch.
15 In all the land no women were
found so fair as Job's daughters; and their
father gave them inheritance among their
brothers.
16 After this, Job lived 140 years, and
saw his sons and his grandsons, four generations.
17 [a]And Job died, an old man and full
of days.

34 [1]Ch 41:26 in Heb [a]Job 28:8
42:2 [a]Gen 18:14; Matt 19:26
3 [a]Job 38:2 [b]Ps 40:5; 131:1; 139:6
4 [a]Job 38:3; 40:7
5 [a]Job 26:14; Rom 10:17 [b]Is 6:5; Eph 1:17,18
7 [a]Job 40:3-5; 42:1-6
8 [1]Lit *lift up his face* [a]Num 23:1 [b]Job 1:5 [c]Gen 20:17; James 5:16; 1 John 5:16 [d]Job 22:30
9 [1]Lit *lifted up the face of*
10 [a]Deut 30:3; Job 1:2,3; Ps 14:7; 85:1-3; 126:1-6
11 [1]Heb *qesitah* [a]Job 19:13 [b]Job 2:11
12 [a]Job 1:10; 8:7; James 5:11 [b]Job 1:3
13 [a]Job 1:2
17 [a]Gen 15:15; 25:8; Job 5:26

Psalms

Title and Background

The names "Psalms" and "Psalter" come from the *Septuagint* (the Greek translation of the Old Testament). Both originally referred to stringed instruments (e.g., harp, lyre, lute), then to songs sung with their accompaniment. The traditional Hebrew title means "praises," even though many of the psalms are prayers.

Author and Date of Writing

Of the 150 psalms, 100 of them are thought to be written by the following authors: David—73; Asaph—12; Sons of Korah—10; Moses—1; Heman the Ezrahite—1; Ethan the Ezrahite—1; and two by Solomon. The rest of the psalms have no recorded author. The final collection and arrangement of the Psalter was the work of postexilic temple personnel, completed probably in the third century B.C. By the first century A.D. it could be referred to as the "book of Psalms" (Luke 20:42; Acts 1:20).

Theme and Message

The Psalter is not a book of catechism or doctrine. It is rather for the most part a book of prayer and praise. It speaks to God in prayer and of God in praise and in professions of faith and trust. At the core of the theology of the Psalter is the conviction that the gravitational center of life, but also of history and the whole creation, is God. He is the great King over all, and the One to whom all things are subject.

Outline

Book I:	Psalms 1—41
Book II:	Psalms 42—72
Book III:	Psalms 73—89
Book IV:	Psalms 90—106
Book V:	Psalms 107—150

The following expressions occur often in the Psalms:

Selah	May mean *Pause, Crescendo* or *Musical Interlude*
Maskil	Possibly *Contemplative,* or *Didactic,* or *Skillful Psalm*
Mikhtam	Possibly *Epigrammatic Poem,* or *Atonement Psalm*
Sheol	The nether world

BOOK 1

Psalm 1

The Righteous and the Wicked Contrasted.

1 ¶ How blessed is the man who
[a]does not walk in the
[b]counsel of the wicked,
Nor stand in the [1c]path of
sinners,
Nor [d]sit in the seat of scoffers!
2 But his [a]delight is [b]in the law
of the LORD,
And in His law he meditates
[c]day and [d]night.
3 He will be like [a]a tree *firmly*
planted by [1]streams of
water,
Which yields its fruit in its
season
And its [2]leaf does not wither;
And [3]in whatever he does, [b]he
prospers.
4 ¶ The wicked are not so,
But they are like [a]chaff which
the wind drives away.
5 Therefore [a]the wicked will not
stand in the [b]judgment,

1:1 [1]Or *way* [a]Prov 4:14 [b]Ps 5:9,10; 10:2-11; 36:1-4 [c]Ps 17:4; 119:104 [d]Ps 26:4,5; Jer 15:17

2 [a]Ps 119:14,16, 35 [b]Josh 1:8 [c]Ps 25:5 [d]Ps 63:5,6

3 [1]Or *canals* [2]Or *foliage* [3]Or *all that he does prospers* [a]Ps 92:12-14; Jer 17:8; Ezek 19:10 [b]Gen 39:2,3,23; Ps 128:2

4 [a]Job 21:18; Ps 35:5; Is 17:13

5 [a]Ps 5:5 [b]Ps 9:7,8,16

Nor sinners in [c]the assembly of
the righteous.
6 For the LORD [1a]knows the way
of the righteous,
But the way of [b]the wicked will
perish.

Psalm 2

The Reign of the LORD's Anointed.

1 ¶ Why are [a]the [1]nations in an
uproar
And the peoples [b]devising a vain
thing?
2 The [a]kings of the earth take
their stand
And the rulers take counsel
together
[b]Against the LORD and against
His [1c]Anointed, saying,
3 "Let us [a]tear their fetters apart
And cast away their cords
from us!"

4 ¶ He who [1]sits in the heavens
[a]laughs,
The Lord [b]scoffs at them.
5 Then He will speak to them in
His [a]anger
And [b]terrify them in His fury,
saying,
6 "But as for Me, I have [1]installed
[a]My King
Upon Zion, [b]My holy
mountain."

7 ¶ "I will surely tell of the
[1]decree of the LORD:
He said to Me, 'You are
[a]My Son,
Today I have begotten You.
8 'Ask of Me, and [a]I will surely
give [b]the [1]nations as Your
inheritance,
And the *very* [c]ends of the earth
as Your possession.
9 'You shall [1a]break them with a
[2]rod of iron,
You shall [b]shatter them like
[3]earthenware.'"

10 ¶ Now therefore, O kings,
[a]show discernment;
Take warning, O [1]judges of the
earth.
11 [1]Worship the LORD with
[2a]reverence
And rejoice with [b]trembling.
12 [1]Do homage to [a]the Son, that
He not become angry, and
you perish *in* the way,
For [b]His wrath may [2]soon be
kindled.
How blessed are all who [c]take
refuge in Him!

Psalm 3

Morning Prayer of Trust in God.

A Psalm of David, when [+]he fled
from Absalom his son.

1 ¶ O LORD, how [a]my adversaries
have increased!
Many are rising up against me.
2 Many are saying [1]of my soul,
"There is no [2a]deliverance for
him in God." [3]Selah.
3 ¶ But You, O LORD, are [a]a shield
about me,
My [b]glory, and the One who
[c]lifts my head.
4 I was crying to the LORD with
my voice,
And He [a]answered me from
[b]His holy [1]mountain. Selah.
5 [1]I [a]lay down and slept;
I awoke, for the LORD
sustains me.
6 I will [a]not be afraid of ten
thousands of people
Who have [b]set themselves
against me round about.
7 ¶ [a]Arise, O LORD; [b]save me,
O my God!
For You [1]have [c]smitten all my
enemies on the [2]cheek;
You [3]have [d]shattered the teeth
of the wicked.
8 [1a]Salvation belongs to the LORD;
Your [b]blessing [2]*be* upon Your
people! Selah.

Psalm 4

Evening Prayer of Trust in God.

[+]For the choir director; on stringed
instruments. A Psalm of David.

1 ¶ [a]Answer me when [b]I call,
O God [1]of my
righteousness!
You have [2c]relieved me in my
distress;
Be [d]gracious to me and [e]hear
my prayer.

2 ¶ O sons of men, how long will
[a]my [1]honor become [b]a
reproach?
How long will you love [c]what is
worthless and aim at
[d]deception? [2]Selah.
3 But know that the LORD has
[1a]set apart the [b]godly man
for Himself;
The LORD [c]hears when I call to
Him.

5 [c]Ps 89:5
6 [1]Or *approves* or *has regard to* [a]Ps 37:18; Nah 1:7; John 10:14; 2 Tim 2:19 [b]Ps 9:5
2:1 [1]Or *Gentiles* [a]Ps 46:6; Acts 4:25 [b]Ps 21:11
2 [1]Or *Messiah* [a]Ps 48:4-6 [b]Ps 74:18 [c]John 1:41
3 [a]Jer 5:5
4 [1]Or *is enthroned* [a]Ps 37:13 [b]Ps 59:8
5 [a]Ps 21:8 [b]Ps 78:49
6 [1]Or *consecrated* [a]Ps 45:6 [b]Ps 48:1
7 [1]Or *decree: The LORD said to Me* [a]Acts 13:33; Heb 1:5
8 [1]Or *Gentiles* [a]Ps 21:1 [b]Ps 22:27 [c]Ps 67:7
9 [1]Another reading is *rule* [2]Or *scepter* or *staff* [3]Lit *potter's ware* [a]Ps 89:23; Rev 2:26 [b]Ps 28:5
10 [1]Or *leaders* [a]Prov 8:15
11 [1]Or *Serve* [2]Or *fear* [a]Ps 5:7 [b]Ps 119:119
12 [1]Lit *Kiss;* some ancient versions read *Do homage purely,* or, *Lay hold of instruction* [2]Or *quickly, suddenly, easily* [a]Ps 2:7 [b]Rev 6:16 [c]Ps 5:11
3:1 [+]2 Sam 15:13-17,29 [a]2 Sam 15:12; Ps 69:4
2 [1]Or *to* [2]Or *salvation* [3]*Selah* may mean: *Pause, Crescendo* or *Musical interlude* [a]Ps 22:7
3 [a]Ps 5:12 [b]Ps 62:7 [c]Ps 9:13
4 [1]Or *hill* [a]Ps 4:3 [b]Ps 2:6
5 [1]Or *As for me, I* [a]Lev 26:6; Ps 4:8; Prov 3:24
6 [a]Ps 23:4 [b]Ps 118:10-13
7 [1]Or *smite* [2]Or *jaw* [3]Or *shatter* [a]Ps 7:6 [b]Ps 6:4 [c]Job 16:10 [d]Ps 57:4
8 [1]Or *Deliverance* [2]Or *is* [a]Ps 28:8; Is 43:11 [b]Ps 29:11
4:1 [+]I.e. Belonging to the choir director's anthology [1]I.e. who maintains my right [2]Lit *made room for* [a]Ps 3:4 [b]Ps 18:6 [c]Ps 18:18 [d]Ps 25:16 [e]Ps 17:6
2 [1]Or *glory* [2]*Selah* may mean: *Pause, Crescendo* or *Musical interlude* [a]Ps 3:3 [b]Ps 69:7-10 [c]Ps 12:2 [d]Ps 31:18
3 [1]Another reading is *dealt wonderfully with* [a]Ps 135:4 [b]Ps 31:23 [c]Ps 6:8

4 ¶ [1a]Tremble, [2b]and do not sin;
[3c]Meditate in your heart upon
your bed, and be still. Selah.
5 Offer [1]the [a]sacrifices of
righteousness,
And [b]trust in the LORD.

6 ¶ Many are saying, "[a]Who will
show us *any* good?"
[b]Lift up the light of Your
countenance upon us,
O LORD!
7 You have put [a]gladness in my
heart,
More than when their grain and
new wine abound.
8 In peace I will [1]both [a]lie down
and sleep,
For You alone, O LORD, make me
to [b]dwell in safety.

Psalm 5

Prayer for Protection from the Wicked.

For the choir director; for +flute accompaniment. A Psalm of David.

1 ¶ [a]Give ear to my words,
O LORD,
Consider my [1b]groaning.
2 Heed [a]the sound of my cry for
help, [b]my King and my
God,
For to You I pray.
3 In the morning, O LORD, [1]You
will hear my voice;
In the [a]morning I will order *my*
[2]*prayer* to You and *eagerly*
[b]watch.

4 ¶ For You are not a God [a]who
takes pleasure in
wickedness;
[b]No evil [1]dwells with You.
5 The [a]boastful shall not [b]stand
before Your eyes;
You [c]hate all who do iniquity.
6 You [a]destroy those who speak
falsehood;
The LORD abhors [b]the man of
bloodshed and deceit.
7 But as for me, [a]by Your
abundant lovingkindness I
will enter Your house,
[1]At Your holy temple I will
[b]bow in [c]reverence
for You.

8 ¶ O LORD, [a]lead me [b]in Your
righteousness [c]because of
[1]my foes;
Make Your way [2]straight
before me.
9 There is [a]nothing [1]reliable in
[2]what they say;
Their [b]inward part is destruction
itself.
Their [c]throat is an open grave;
They [3]flatter with their tongue.
10 Hold them guilty, O God;
[a]By their own devices let them
fall!
In the multitude of their
transgressions [b]thrust them
out,
For they are [c]rebellious
against You.

11 ¶ But let all who [a]take refuge in
You [b]be glad,
Let them ever sing for joy;
And [1]may You [c]shelter them,
That those who [d]love Your
name may exult in You.
12 For it is You who [a]blesses the
righteous man, O LORD,
You [b]surround him with favor as
with a shield.

Psalm 6

Prayer for Mercy in Time of Trouble.

For the choir director; with stringed instruments, +upon an eight-string lyre. A Psalm of David.

1 ¶ O LORD, [a]do not rebuke me in
Your anger,
Nor chasten me in Your wrath.
2 Be gracious to me, O LORD, for I
am [a]pining away;
[b]Heal me, O LORD, for [c]my
bones are dismayed.
3 And my [a]soul is greatly
dismayed;
But You, O LORD—[b]how long?

4 ¶ Return, O LORD, [a]rescue my
[1]soul;
Save me because of Your
lovingkindness.
5 For [a]there is no [1]mention of
You in death;
In [2]Sheol who will give You
thanks?

6 ¶ I am [a]weary with my sighing;
Every night I make my bed
swim,
I dissolve my couch with [b]my
tears.
7 My [a]eye has wasted away with
grief;
It has become old because of all
my adversaries.

8 ¶ [a]Depart from me, all you who
do iniquity,
For the LORD [b]has heard the
voice of my weeping.

4 [1]I.e. with anger or fear [2]Or *but* [3]Lit *Speak* [a]Ps 99:1 [b]Ps 119:11; Eph 4:26 [c]Ps 77:6
5 [1]Or *righteous sacrifices* [a]Deut 33:19; Ps 51:19 [b]Ps 37:3,5; 62:8
6 [a]Job 7:7; 9:25 [b]Num 6:26; Ps 80:3,7,19
7 [a]Ps 97:11,12; Is 9:3; Acts 14:17
8 [1]Or *at the same time* [a]Job 11:19; Ps 3:5 [b]Lev 25:18; Deut 12:10; Ps 16:9
5:1 +Heb *Nehiloth* [1]Or *meditation* [a]Ps 54:2 [b]Ps 104:34
2 [a]Ps 140:6 [b]Ps 84:3
3 [1]Or *May You hear* [2]Or sacrifice [a]Ps 88:13 [b]Ps 130:5
4 [1]Lit *sojourns* [a]Ps 11:5; 34:16 [b]Ps 92:15
5 [a]Ps 73:3; 75:4 [b]Ps 1:5 [c]Ps 11:5; 45:7
6 [a]Ps 52:4,5 [b]Ps 55:23
7 [1]Or *Toward* [a]Ps 69:13 [b]Ps 138:2 [c]Ps 115:11,13
8 [1]Or *those who lie in wait for me* [2]Or *smooth* [a]Ps 31:3 [b]Ps 31:1 [c]Ps 27:11
9 [1]Or *true* [2]Lit *his mouth* [3]Or *make their tongue smooth* [a]Ps 52:3 [b]Ps 7:14 [c]Rom 3:13
10 [a]Ps 9:16 [b]Ps 36:12 [c]Ps 107:10,11
11 [1]Or *You shelter* [a]Ps 2:12 [b]Ps 33:1; 64:10 [c]Ps 12:7 [d]Ps 69:36
12 [a]Ps 29:11 [b]Ps 32:7,10
6:1 +Or *according to a lower octave* (Heb *Sheminith*) [a]Ps 38:1; 118:18
2 [a]Ps 102:4,11 [b]Ps 41:4; 147:3; Hos 6:1 [c]Ps 22:14; 31:10
3 [a]Ps 88:3; John 12:27 [b]Ps 90:13
4 [1]Or *life* [a]Ps 17:13
5 [1]Or *remembrance* [2]I.e. the nether world [a]Ps 30:9; 88:10-12; 115:17; Eccl 9:10; Is 38:18
6 [a]Ps 69:3 [b]Ps 42:3
7 [a]Job 17:7; Ps 31:9; 38:10
8 [a]Ps 119:115; Matt 7:23; Luke 13:27 [b]Ps 3:4; 28:6

9 The LORD [a]has heard my
supplication,
The LORD [b]receives my prayer.
10 All my enemies will [a]be
ashamed and greatly
dismayed;
They shall [1]turn back, they will
[b]suddenly be ashamed.

Psalm 7

The LORD Implored to Defend the Psalmist against the Wicked.

A +Shiggaion of David, which he sang to the LORD •concerning Cush, a Benjamite.

1 ¶ O LORD my God, [a]in You I
have taken refuge;
Save me from all those who
pursue me, and
[b]deliver me,
2 Or he will tear [1]my soul [a]like a
lion,
[2]Dragging me away, while there
is none to deliver.

3 ¶ O LORD my God, if I have done
this,
If there is [a]injustice in my
hands,
4 If I have [a]rewarded evil to [1]my
friend,
Or have [b]plundered [2]him who
without cause was my
adversary,
5 Let the enemy pursue [1]my soul
and overtake [2]*it;*
And let him trample my life
down to the ground
And lay my glory in the dust.
[3]Selah.

6 ¶ [a]Arise, O LORD, in Your anger;
[b]Lift up Yourself against [c]the
rage of my adversaries,
And [d]arouse Yourself [1]for me;
You have appointed
judgment.
7 Let the assembly of the [a]peoples
encompass You,
And over [1]them return on high.
8 The LORD [a]judges the peoples;
[1b]Vindicate me, O LORD,
according to my
righteousness and my
integrity that is in me.
9 O let [a]the evil of the wicked
come to an end, but
[b]establish the righteous;
For the righteous God [c]tries the
hearts and [1]minds.
10 My [a]shield is [1]with God,
Who [b]saves the upright in heart.
11 God is a [a]righteous judge,
And a God who has [b]indignation
every day.

12 ¶ If [1]a man [a]does not repent,
He will [b]sharpen His sword;
He has [c]bent His bow and
[2]made it ready.
13 He has also prepared [1]for
Himself deadly weapons;
He makes His [a]arrows fiery
shafts.
14 Behold, he travails with
wickedness,
And he [a]conceives mischief and
brings forth falsehood.
15 He has dug a pit and hollowed it
out,
And has [a]fallen into the hole
which he made.
16 His [a]mischief will return upon
his own head,
And his [b]violence will descend
upon [1]his own pate.

17 ¶ I will give thanks to the LORD
[a]according to His
righteousness
And will [b]sing praise to the
name of the LORD Most
High.

Psalm 8

The LORD's Glory and Man's Dignity.

For the choir director; on the Gittith.
A Psalm of David.

1 ¶ O LORD, our Lord,
How majestic is Your name in all
the earth,
Who have [1a]displayed Your
splendor above the heavens!
2 [a]From the mouth of infants and
nursing babes You have
established [1b]strength
Because of Your adversaries,
To make [c]the enemy and the
revengeful cease.
3 ¶ When I [1a]consider [b]Your
heavens, the work of Your
fingers,
The [c]moon and the stars, which
You have [2]ordained;
4 [a]What is man that You [1]take
thought of him,
And the son of man that You
care for him?
5 Yet You have made him a [a]little
lower than [1]God,
And [b]You crown him with
[c]glory and majesty!
6 You make him to [a]rule over the
works of Your hands;
You have [b]put all things under
his feet,
7 All sheep and oxen,
And also the [1]beasts of the field,

9 [a]Ps 116:1 [b]Ps 66:19
10 [1]Or *again be ashamed suddenly* [a]Ps 71:13 [b]Ps 73:19
7:1 +I.e. Dithyrambic rhythm; or wild passionate song •Or *concerning the words of* [a]Ps 31:1 [b]Ps 31:15
2 [1]Or *me* [2]Or *Rending it in pieces, while* [a]Ps 57:4; Is 38:13
3 [a]1 Sam 24:11
4 [1]Lit *him who was at peace with me* [2]Or *my adversary without cause* [a]Ps 109:4 [b]1 Sam 24:7
5 [1]Or *me* [2]Or me [3]*Selah* may mean: *Pause, Crescendo* or *Musical interlude*
6 [1]One ancient version reads *O my God* [a]Ps 3:7 [b]Ps 94:2 [c]Ps 138:7 [d]Ps 35:23
7 [1]Lit *it* [a]Ps 22:27
8 [1]Lit *Judge* [a]Ps 96:13 [b]Ps 18:20
9 [1]Lit *kidneys,* figurative for inner man [a]Ps 34:21 [b]Ps 37:23 [c]Ps 11:4; Jer 11:20; Rev 2:23
10 [1]Lit *upon* [a]Ps 18:2 [b]Ps 97:10
11 [a]Ps 50:6 [b]Ps 90:9
12 [1]Lit *he* [2]Lit *fixed it* [a]Ps 58:5 [b]Deut 32:41 [c]Ps 64:7
13 [1]Or *His deadly weapons* [a]Ps 18:14
14 [a]Job 15:35; Is 59:4; James 1:15
15 [a]Job 4:8; Ps 57:6
16 [1]I.e. the crown of his own head [a]Esth 9:25; Ps 140:9 [b]Ps 140:11
17 [a]Ps 71:15 [b]Ps 9:2
8:1 [1]Or *set* [a]Ps 57:5
2 [1]Or *a bulwark* [a]Matt 21:16; 1 Cor 1:27 [b]Ps 29:1 [c]Ps 44:16
3 [1]Or *see* [2]Or *appointed, fixed* [a]Ps 111:2 [b]Ps 89:11 [c]Ps 136:9
4 [1]Or *remember him* [a]Job 7:17; Ps 144:3; Heb 2:6-8
5 [1]Or *the angels;* Heb *Elohim* [a]Gen 1:26; Ps 82:6 [b]Ps 103:4 [c]Ps 21:5
6 [a]Gen 1:26 [b]1 Cor 15:27; Eph 1:22; Heb 2:8
7 [1]Or *animals*

8 The birds of the heavens and the fish of the sea,
Whatever passes through the paths of the seas.

9 ¶ [a]O LORD, our Lord,
How majestic is Your name in all the earth!

Psalm 9

A Psalm of Thanksgiving for God's Justice.

For the choir director; on +Muth-labben. A Psalm of David.

1 ¶ I will give thanks to the LORD with all [a]my heart;
I will [b]tell of all Your [1]wonders.
2 I will be glad and [a]exult in You;
I will [b]sing praise to Your name, O [c]Most High.

3 ¶ When my enemies turn back,
They stumble and [a]perish before You.
4 For You have [a]maintained [1]my just cause;
You have sat on the throne [2b]judging righteously.
5 You have [a]rebuked the nations,
You have destroyed the wicked;
You have [b]blotted out their name forever and ever.
6 [1]The enemy has come to an end in perpetual ruins,
And You have uprooted the cities;
The very [a]memory of them has perished.

7 ¶ But the [a]LORD [1]abides forever;
He has established His [b]throne for judgment,
8 And He will [a]judge the world in righteousness;
He will execute judgment for the peoples with equity.
9 [1]The LORD also will be a [a]stronghold for the oppressed,
A stronghold in times of trouble;
10 And [1]those who [a]know Your name will put their trust in You,
For You, O LORD, have not [b]forsaken those who seek You.

11 ¶ Sing praises to the LORD, who [a]dwells in Zion;
[b]Declare among the peoples His deeds.
12 For [a]He who [1]requires blood remembers them;
He does not forget [b]the cry of the afflicted.
13 Be gracious to me, O LORD;
See my affliction from those [a]who hate me,
You who [b]lift me up from the gates of death,
14 That I may tell of [a]all Your praises,
That in the gates of the daughter of Zion
I may [b]rejoice in Your [1]salvation.
15 The nations have sunk down [a]in the pit which they have made;
In the [b]net which they hid, their own foot has been caught.
16 The LORD has [a]made Himself known;
He has [b]executed judgment.
In the work of his own hands the wicked is snared.
[1]Higgaion [2]Selah.

17 ¶ The wicked will [1a]return to [2]Sheol,
Even all the nations who [b]forget God.
18 For the [a]needy will not always be forgotten,
Nor the [b]hope of the afflicted perish forever.
19 [a]Arise, O LORD, do not let man prevail;
Let the nations be [b]judged before You.
20 Put them [a]in fear, O LORD;
Let the nations know that they are [b]but men. Selah.

Psalm 10

A Prayer for the Overthrow of the Wicked.

1 ¶ Why [a]do You stand afar off, O LORD?
Why [b]do You hide [1]*Yourself* in times of trouble?
2 In [a]pride the wicked [1]hotly pursue the afflicted;
[2]Let them be [b]caught in the plots which they have devised.

3 ¶ For the wicked [a]boasts of his [b]heart's desire,
And [1]the greedy man curses *and* [c]spurns the LORD.
4 The wicked, in the haughtiness of his countenance, [a]does not seek *Him.*
All his [1]thoughts are, "[b]There is no God."

9 [a]Ps 8:1
9:1 +I.e. "Death to the Son" [1]Or *miracles* [a]Ps 86:12 [b]Ps 26:7
2 [a]Ps 5:11; 104:34 [b]Ps 66:2, 4 [c]Ps 83:18; 92:1
3 [a]Ps 27:2
4 [1]Lit *my right and my cause* [2]Or *a righteous Judge* [a]Ps 140:12 [b]Ps 50:6
5 [a]Ps 119:21 [b]Ps 69:28; Prov 10:7
6 [1]Or *O enemy, desolations are finished forever; And their cities You have plucked up* [a]Ps 34:16
7 [1]Or *sits* as king [a]Ps 10:16 [b]Ps 89:14
8 [a]Ps 96:13; 98:9
9 [1]Or *Let the LORD also be* [a]Ps 32:7; 59:9,16,17
10 [1]Or *let those...name put* [a]Ps 91:14 [b]Ps 37:28; 94:14
11 [a]Ps 76:2 [b]Ps 105:1; 107:22
12 [1]I.e. avenges bloodshed [a]Gen 9:5; Ps 72:14 [b]Ps 9:18
13 [a]Ps 38:19 [b]Ps 30:3; 86:13
14 [1]Or *deliverance* [a]Ps 106:2 [b]Ps 13:5; 20:5; 35:9; 51:12
15 [a]Ps 7:15,16 [b]Ps 57:6
16 [1]Perhaps, resounding music or meditation [2]*Selah* may mean: *Pause, Crescendo* or *Musical interlude* [a]Ex 7:5 [b]Ps 9:4
17 [1]Or *turn* [2]I.e. the nether world [a]Ps 49:14 [b]Job 8:13; Ps 50:22
18 [a]Ps 9:12; 12:5 [b]Ps 62:5; 71:5; Prov 23:18
19 [a]Num 10:35 [b]Ps 9:5
20 [a]Ps 14:5 [b]Ps 62:9
10:1 [1]Or Your eyes [a]Ps 22:1 [b]Ps 13:1; 55:1
2 [1]Lit *burn* [2]Or *They will be caught* [a]Ps 73:6, 8 [b]Ps 7:16; 9:16
3 [1]Or *blesses the greedy man* [a]Ps 49:6; 94:3,4 [b]Ps 112:10 [c]Ps 10:13
4 [1]Or *plots* [a]Ps 10:13; 36:2 [b]Ps 14:1; 36:1

5 ¶ His ways [1a]prosper at all times;
Your judgments are on high, [b]out of his sight;
As for all his adversaries, he snorts at them.
6 He says to himself, "[a]I will not be moved;
[1]Throughout all generations [b]I will not be in adversity."
7 His [a]mouth is full of curses and deceit and [b]oppression;
[c]Under his tongue is mischief and wickedness.
8 He sits in the [a]lurking places of the villages;
In the hiding places he [b]kills the innocent;
His eyes [1]stealthily watch for the [2c]unfortunate.
9 He lurks in a hiding place as [a]a lion in his [1]lair;
He [b]lurks to catch [c]the afflicted;
He catches the afflicted when he draws him into his [d]net.
10 He [1]crouches, he [2]bows down,
And the [3]unfortunate fall [4]by his mighty ones.
11 He [a]says to himself, "God has forgotten;
He has hidden His face; He will never see it."

12 ¶ Arise, O LORD; O God, [a]lift up Your hand.
[b]Do not forget the afflicted.
13 Why has the wicked [a]spurned God?
He has said to himself, "You will not require *it*."
14 You have seen *it*, for You have beheld [a]mischief and vexation to [1]take it into Your hand.
The [2b]unfortunate commits *himself* to You;
You have been the [c]helper of the orphan.
15 [a]Break the arm of the wicked and the evildoer,
[1b]Seek out his wickedness until You find none.

16 ¶ The LORD is [a]King forever and ever;
[b]Nations have perished from His land.
17 O LORD, You have heard the [a]desire of the [1]humble;
You will [b]strengthen their heart,
[c]You will incline Your ear
18 To [1]vindicate the [a]orphan and the [b]oppressed,
So that man who is of the earth will no longer cause [c]terror.

Psalm 11

The LORD a Refuge and Defense.

For the choir director. *A Psalm* of David.

1 ¶ In the LORD I [a]take refuge;
How can you say to my soul,
"Flee *as* a bird to your [b]mountain;
2 For, behold, the wicked [a]bend the bow,
They [1b]make ready their arrow upon the string
To [c]shoot in darkness at the upright in heart.
3 If the [a]foundations are destroyed,
What can the righteous do?"

4 ¶ The LORD is in His [a]holy temple; the [1]LORD'S [b]throne is in heaven;
His [c]eyes behold, His eyelids test the sons of men.
5 The LORD [a]tests the righteous and [b]the wicked,
And the one who loves violence His soul hates.
6 Upon the wicked He will [a]rain [1]snares;
[b]Fire and brimstone and [c]burning wind will be the portion of [d]their cup.
7 For the LORD is [a]righteous, [b]He loves [1]righteousness;
The upright will [c]behold His face.

Psalm 12

God, a Helper against the Treacherous.

For the choir director; [+]upon an eight-stringed lyre. A Psalm of David.

1 ¶ Help, LORD, for [a]the godly man ceases to be,
For the faithful disappear from among the sons of men.
2 They [a]speak [1]falsehood to one another;
With [b]flattering [2]lips and with a double heart they speak.
3 May the LORD cut off all flattering lips,
The tongue that [a]speaks great things;
4 Who [a]have said, "With our tongue we will prevail;
Our lips are [1]our own; who is lord over us?"

5 [1]Lit *are strong* [a]Ps 52:7 [b]Ps 28:5
6 [1]Lit *To* [a]Ps 49:11; Eccl 8:11 [b]Rev 18:7
7 [a]Rom 3:14 [b]Ps 73:8 [c]Job 20:12; Ps 140:3
8 [1]Lit *lie in wait* [2]Or *poor* [a]Ps 11:2 [b]Ps 94:6 [c]Ps 72:12
9 [1]Or *thicket* [a]Ps 17:12 [b]Ps 59:3; Mic 7:2 [c]Ps 10:2 [d]Ps 140:5
10 [1]Or *is crushed* [2]Or *is bowed down* [3]Or *poor* [4]Or *into his claws*
11 [a]Ps 10:4
12 [a]Ps 17:7; Mic 5:9 [b]Ps 9:12
13 [a]Ps 10:3
14 [1]Lit *put, give* [2]Or *poor* [a]Ps 10:7 [b]Ps 22:11 [c]Ps 68:5
15 [1]Or *May You seek* [a]Ps 37:17 [b]Ps 140:11
16 [a]Ps 29:10 [b]Deut 8:20
17 [1]Or *afflicted* [a]Ps 9:18 [b]1 Chr 29:18 [c]Ps 34:15
18 [1]Lit *judge* [a]Ps 146:9 [b]Ps 9:9; 74:21 [c]Is 29:20
11:1 [a]Ps 2:12 [b]Ps 121:1
2 [1]Or *fixed* [a]Ps 7:12; 37:14 [b]Ps 64:3 [c]Ps 64:4
3 [a]Ps 82:5; 87:1; 119:152
4 [1]Lit *LORD*, His throne [a]Ps 18:6; Mic 1:2; Hab 2:20 [b]Ps 103:19; Is 66:1; Matt 5:34; Rev 4:2 [c]Ps 33:18; 34:15,16
5 [a]Gen 22:1; Ps 34:19; James 1:12 [b]Ps 5:5
6 [1]Or *coals of fire* [a]Ps 18:13,14 [b]Gen 19:24; Ezek 38:22 [c]Jer 4:11,12 [d]Ps 75:8
7 [1]Or *righteous deeds* [a]Ps 7:9,11 [b]Ps 33:5; 45:7 [c]Ps 16:11; 17:15
12:1 [+]Or *according to a lower octave* (Heb *Sheminith*) [a]Is 57:1; Mic 7:2
2 [1]Or *emptiness* [2]Lit *lip* [a]Ps 10:7; 41:6 [b]Ps 28:3; 55:21; Jer 9:8; Rom 16:18
3 [a]Dan 7:8; Rev 13:5
4 [1]Lit *with us* [a]Ps 73:8,9

5 "Because of the [a]devastation of
the afflicted, because of the
groaning of the needy,
Now [b]I will arise," says the
LORD; "I will [c]set him in
the safety for which he
longs."
6 ¶ The [a]words of the LORD are
pure words;
As silver [b]tried in a furnace on
the earth, refined seven
times.
7 You, O LORD, will keep them;
You will [a]preserve him from this
generation forever.
8 The [a]wicked strut about on
every side
When [1b]vileness is exalted
among the sons of men.

Psalm 13

Prayer for Help in Trouble.

For the choir director. A Psalm of David.

1 ¶ How long, O LORD? Will You
[a]forget me forever?
How long [b]will You hide Your
face from me?
2 How long shall I [a]take counsel
in my soul,
Having [b]sorrow in my heart all
the day?
How long will my enemy be
exalted over me?

3 ¶ [a]Consider *and* answer me,
O LORD my God;
[b]Enlighten my eyes, or I will
[c]sleep the *sleep of* death,
4 And my enemy will [a]say, "I
have overcome him,"
And [b]my adversaries will rejoice
when I am shaken.
5 ¶ But I have [a]trusted in Your
lovingkindness;
My heart shall [b]rejoice in Your
salvation.
6 I will [a]sing to the LORD,
Because He has [b]dealt
bountifully with me.

Psalm 14

Folly and Wickedness of Men.

For the choir director. *A Psalm* of David.

1 ¶ The fool has [a]said in his heart,
"There is no God."
They are corrupt, they have
committed abominable
[1]deeds;
There is [b]no one who does
good.
2 The LORD has [a]looked down
from heaven upon the sons
of men
To see if there are any who
[1b]understand,
Who [c]seek after God.
3 They have all [a]turned aside,
together they have become
corrupt;
There is [b]no one who does
good, not even one.

4 ¶ Do all the workers of
wickedness [a]not know,
Who [b]eat up my people *as* they
eat bread,
And [c]do not call upon the
Lord?
5 There they are in great dread,
For God is with the [a]righteous
generation.
6 You would put to shame the
counsel of the afflicted,
But the LORD is his [a]refuge.

7 ¶ Oh, that [a]the salvation of
Israel [1]would come out of
Zion!
When the LORD [2b]restores His
captive people,
Jacob will rejoice, Israel will be
glad.

Psalm 15

Description of a Citizen of Zion.

A Psalm of David.

1 ¶ O LORD, who may [1]abide [a]in
Your tent?
Who may dwell on Your [b]holy
hill?
2 He who [a]walks with integrity,
and works righteousness,
And [b]speaks truth in his heart.
3 He [a]does not slander [1]with his
tongue,
Nor [b]does evil to his neighbor,
Nor [c]takes up a reproach against
his friend;
4 In [1]whose eyes a reprobate is
despised,
But [2]who [a]honors those who
fear the LORD;
He [b]swears to his own hurt and
does not change;
5 He [a]does not put out his money
[1]at interest,
Nor [b]does he take a bribe
against the innocent.
[c]He who does these things will
never be shaken.

---

5 [a]Ps 9:9; 10:18 [b]Is 33:10 [c]Ps 34:6; 35:10
6 [a]2 Sam 22:31; Ps 18:30; 19:8, 10; 119:140 [b]Prov 30:5
7 [a]Ps 37:28; 97:10
8 [1]Or *worthlessness* [a]Ps 55:10, 11 [b]Is 32:5
13:1 [a]Ps 44:24 [b]Job 13:24; Ps 89:46
2 [a]Ps 42:4 [b]Ps 42:9
3 [a]Ps 5:1 [b]1 Sam 14:29; Ezra 9:8; Job 33:30; Ps 18:28 [c]Jer 51:39
4 [a]Ps 12:4 [b]Ps 25:2; 38:16
5 [a]Ps 52:8 [b]Ps 9:14
6 [a]Ps 96:1,2 [b]Ps 116:7; 119:17; 142:7
14:1 [1]Lit *doings* [a]Ps 10:4; 53:1 [b]Ps 14:1-3; 130:3; Rom 3:10-12
2 [1]Or *act wisely* [a]Ps 33:13,14; 102:19 [b]Ps 92:6 [c]1 Chr 22:19
3 [a]Ps 58:3 [b]Ps 143:2
4 [a]Ps 82:5 [b]Ps 27:2; Jer 10:25; Mic 3:3 [c]Ps 79:6; Is 64:7
5 [a]Ps 73:15; 112:2
6 [a]Ps 9:9; 40:17; 46:1; 142:5
7 [1]Lit *would be* [2]Or *restores the fortunes of His people* [a]Ps 53:6 [b]Ps 85:1,2
15:1 [1]Lit *sojourn* [a]Ps 27:5,6; 61:4 [b]Ps 24:3
2 [a]Ps 24:4; Is 33:15 [b]Zech 8:16; Eph 4:25
3 [1]Lit *according to* [a]Ps 50:20 [b]Ps 28:3 [c]Ex 23:1
4 [1]Lit *his* [2]Lit *he* [a]Acts 28:10 [b]Judg 11:35
5 [1]I.e. to a fellow Israelite [a]Ex 22:25; Lev 25:36; Deut 23:20; Ezek 18:8 [b]Ex 23:8; Deut 16:19 [c]2 Pet 1:10

Psalm 16

The LORD *the Psalmist's Portion in Life and Deliverer in Death.*

A [+]Mikhtam of David.

1 ¶ [a]Preserve me, O God, for [b]I
take refuge in You.
2 [1]I said to the LORD, "You are
[2]my Lord;
I [a]have no good besides You."
3 As for the [1a]saints who are in
the earth,
[2]They are the majestic ones [b]in
whom is all my delight.
4 The [1a]sorrows of those who
have [2]bartered for another
god will be multiplied;
I shall not pour out their drink
offerings of [b]blood,
Nor will I [c]take their names
upon my lips.

5 ¶ The LORD is the [a]portion of
my inheritance and
my [b]cup;
You support my [c]lot.
6 The [a]lines have fallen to me in
pleasant places;
Indeed, my heritage is [b]beautiful
to me.

7 ¶ I will bless the LORD who has
[a]counseled me;
Indeed, my [1b]mind instructs me
in the night.
8 [a]I have [b]set the LORD
continually before me;
Because He is [c]at my right
hand, [d]I will not be shaken.
9 Therefore [a]my heart is glad and
[b]my glory rejoices;
My flesh also will [c]dwell
securely.
10 For You [a]will not abandon my
soul to [1]Sheol;
Nor will You [2b]allow Your
[3]Holy One to [4]undergo
decay.
11 You will make known to me
[a]the path of life;
In [b]Your presence is fullness of
joy;
In Your right hand there are
[c]pleasures forever.

Psalm 17

Prayer for Protection against Oppressors.

A Prayer of David.

1 ¶ Hear a [a]just cause, O LORD,
[b]give heed to my cry;
[c]Give ear to my prayer, which is
not from [d]deceitful lips.
2 Let [a]my [1]judgment come forth
from Your presence;
Let Your eyes look with [b]equity.
3 You have [a]tried my heart;
You have visited *me* by night;
You have [b]tested me and [c]You
find [1]nothing;
I have [d]purposed that my mouth
will not transgress.
4 As for the deeds of men, [a]by the
word of Your lips
I have kept from the [b]paths of
the violent.
5 My [a]steps have held fast to Your
[1]paths.
My [b]feet have not slipped.

6 ¶ I have [a]called upon You, for
You will answer me, O God;
[b]Incline Your ear to me, hear
my speech.
7 [a]Wondrously show Your
lovingkindness,
O [b]Savior of those who take
refuge [1]at Your right hand
From those who rise up *against
them.*
8 Keep me as [1]the [a]apple of the
eye;
Hide me [b]in the shadow of Your
wings
9 From the [a]wicked who
despoil me,
My [b]deadly enemies who
surround me.
10 They have [a]closed their
[1]unfeeling *heart,*
With their mouth they [b]speak
proudly.
11 They have now [a]surrounded us
in our steps;
They set their eyes [b]to cast *us*
down to the ground.
12 He is [a]like a lion that is eager to
tear,
And as a young lion [b]lurking in
hiding places.

13 ¶ [a]Arise, O LORD, confront him,
[b]bring him low;
[c]Deliver my soul from the
wicked with [d]Your sword,
14 From men with [a]Your hand,
O LORD,
From men [1]of the world,
[b]whose portion is in *this*
life,
And whose belly You [c]fill with
Your treasure;
They are satisfied with children,
And leave their abundance to
their babes.

16:1 [+]Possibly *Epigrammatic Poem* or *Atonement Psalm* [a]Ps 17:8 [b]Ps 7:1
2 [1]Or O my soul, *you said* [2]Or *the Lord* [a]Ps 73:25
3 [1]Lit *holy ones;* i.e. the godly [2]Lit *And the majestic ones...delight* [a]Ps 101:6 [b]Ps 119:63
4 [1]I.e. sorrows due to idolatry [2]Or *hastened to* [a]Ps 32:10 [b]Ps 106:37 [c]Ex 23:13; Josh 23:7
5 [a]Ps 73:26; Lam 3:24 [b]Ps 23:5 [c]Ps 125:3 mg
6 [a]Ps 78:55 [b]Jer 3:19
7 [1]Lit *kidneys,* figurative for inner man [a]Ps 73:24 [b]Ps 77:6
8 [a]Ps 16:8-11; Acts 2:25-28 [b]Ps 27:8 [c]Ps 73:23 [d]Ps 112:6
9 [a]Ps 4:7 [b]Ps 30:12 [c]Ps 4:8
10 [1]I.e. the nether world [2]Lit *give* [3]Or *godly one* [4]Or *see corruption* or *the pit* [a]Ps 49:15 [b]Acts 13:35
11 [a]Ps 139:24; Matt 7:14 [b]Ps 21:6 [c]Job 36:11; Ps 36:7
17:1 [a]Ps 9:4 [b]Ps 61:1 [c]Ps 88:2 [d]Is 29:13
2 [1]I.e. vindication [a]Ps 103:6 [b]Ps 98:9
3 [1]Or *no evil device in me; My mouth* [a]Ps 26:1 [b]Job 23:10; Ps 66:10; Zech 13:9; 1 Pet 1:7 [c]Jer 50:20 [d]Ps 39:1
4 [a]Ps 119:9 [b]Ps 10:5-11
5 [1]Lit *tracks* [a]Job 23:11; Ps 44:18 [b]Ps 18:36
6 [a]Ps 86:7 [b]Ps 88:2
7 [1]Or *from those who rise up...at Your right hand* [a]Ps 31:21 [b]Ps 20:6
8 [1]Lit *the pupil, the daughter of the eye* [a]Deut 32:10; Zech 2:8 [b]Ruth 2:12; Ps 36:7
9 [a]Ps 31:20 [b]Ps 27:12
10 [1]Lit *fat* [a]Job 15:27; Ps 73:7 [b]1 Sam 2:3; Ps 31:18
11 [a]Ps 88:17 [b]Ps 37:14
12 [a]Ps 7:2 [b]Ps 10:9
13 [a]Ps 3:7 [b]Ps 55:23 [c]Ps 22:20 [d]Ps 7:12
14 [1]Or *whose portion in life is of the world* [a]Ps 17:7 [b]Ps 73:3-7; Luke 16:25 [c]Ps 49:6

15 As for me, I shall [a]behold Your face in righteousness;
[b]I will be satisfied [1]with Your [c]likeness when I awake.

Psalm 18

The LORD Praised for Giving Deliverance.

For the choir director. *A Psalm* of David the servant of the LORD, +who spoke to the LORD the words of this song in the day that the LORD delivered him from the hand of all his enemies and from the hand of Saul. And he said,

1 ¶ "I love You, O LORD, [a]my strength."
2 The LORD is [a]my [1]rock and [b]my fortress and my [c]deliverer,
My God, my rock, in whom I take refuge;
My [d]shield and the [e]horn of my salvation, my [f]stronghold.
3 I call upon the LORD, who is [a]worthy to be praised,
And I am [b]saved from my enemies.
4 ¶ The [a]cords of death encompassed me,
And the [b]torrents of [1]ungodliness [2]terrified me.
5 The [a]cords of [1]Sheol surrounded me;
The snares of death confronted me.
6 In my [a]distress I called upon the LORD,
And cried to my God for help;
He heard my voice [b]out of His temple,
And my [c]cry for help before Him came into His ears.
7 ¶ Then the [a]earth shook and quaked;
And the [b]foundations of the mountains were trembling
And were shaken, because He was angry.
8 Smoke went up [1]out of His nostrils,
And [a]fire from His mouth devoured;
Coals were kindled by it.
9 He [a]bowed the heavens also, and came down
With thick [b]darkness under His feet.
10 He rode upon a [a]cherub and flew;
And He sped upon the [b]wings of the wind.
11 He made [a]darkness His hiding place, [b]His [1]canopy around Him,
Darkness of waters, thick clouds of the skies.
12 From the [a]brightness before Him passed His thick clouds,
Hailstones and [b]coals of fire.
13 The LORD also [a]thundered in the heavens,
And the Most High uttered His voice,
Hailstones and coals of fire.
14 He [a]sent out His arrows, and scattered them,
And lightning flashes in abundance, and [1]routed them.
15 Then the [a]channels of water appeared,
And the foundations of the world were [1]laid bare
At Your [b]rebuke, O LORD,
At the blast of the [c]breath of Your nostrils.
16 ¶ He [a]sent from on high, He took me;
He drew me out of [b]many waters.
17 He [a]delivered me from my strong enemy,
And from those who hated me, for they were [b]too mighty for me.
18 They confronted me in [a]the day of my calamity,
But [b]the LORD was my stay.
19 He brought me forth also into a [a]broad place;
He rescued me, because [b]He delighted in me.
20 ¶ The LORD has [a]rewarded me according to my righteousness;
According to the [b]cleanness of my hands He has recompensed me.
21 For I have [a]kept the ways of the LORD,
And have [b]not wickedly departed from my God.
22 For all [a]His ordinances were before me,
And I did not put away His [b]statutes from me.
23 I was also [1][a]blameless with Him,
And I [b]kept myself from my iniquity.
24 Therefore the LORD has [a]recompensed me according to my righteousness,

15 [1]Or *with* beholding [a]Ps 11:7; 16:11; 140:13; 1 John 3:2 [b]Ps 4:6,7 [c]Num 12:8
18:1 +2 Sam 22:1-51 [a]Ps 59:17
2 [1]Or *crag* [a]Deut 32:18; 1 Sam 2:2; Ps 18:31,46; 28:1; 31:3; 42:9; 71:3; 78:15 [b]Ps 144:2 [c]Ps 19:14 [d]Ps 28:7; 33:20; 59:11; 84:9,11; Prov 30:5 [e]Ps 75:10 [f]Ps 59:9
3 [a]Ps 48:1; 96:4; 145:3 [b]Ps 34:6
4 [1]Or *destruction;* Heb *Belial* [2]Or *were assailing* or *terrifying* [a]Ps 116:3 [b]Ps 69:2; 124:3,4
5 [1]I.e. the nether world [a]Ps 116:3
6 [a]Ps 50:15; 120:1 [b]Ps 3:4 [c]Ps 34:15
7 [a]Judg 5:4; Ps 68:7,8; Is 13:13; Hag 2:6 [b]Ps 114:4,6
8 [1]Or *in His wrath* [a]Ps 50:3
9 [a]Ps 144:5 [b]Ps 97:2
10 [a]Ps 80:1; 99:1 [b]Ps 104:3
11 [1]Or *pavilion* [a]Deut 4:11 [b]Ps 97:2
12 [a]Ps 104:2 [b]Ps 97:3; 140:10; Hab 3:4
13 [a]Ps 29:3; 104:7
14 [1]Lit *confused* [a]Ps 144:6; Hab 3:11
15 [1]Or *uncovered* [a]Ps 106:9 [b]Ps 76:6 [c]Ps 18:8
16 [a]Ps 144:7 [b]Ps 32:6
17 [a]Ps 59:1 [b]Ps 35:10; 142:6
18 [a]Ps 59:16 [b]Ps 16:8
19 [a]Ps 4:1; 31:8; 118:5 [b]Ps 37:23; 41:11
20 [a]1 Sam 24:19; Job 33:26; Ps 7:8 [b]Job 22:30; Ps 24:4
21 [a]Ps 37:34; 119:33; Prov 8:32 [b]2 Chr 34:33; Ps 119:102
22 [a]Ps 119:30 [b]Ps 119:83
23 [1]Lit *complete;* or *having integrity;* or *perfect* [a]Ps 18:32 [b]Ps 19:12,13; 25:11; 66:18
24 [a]1 Sam 26:23; Ps 18:20

According to the cleanness of my
hands in His eyes.

25 ¶ With [a]the kind You show
Yourself kind;
With the [1]blameless [b]You show
Yourself blameless;
26 With the pure You show Yourself
[a]pure,
And with the crooked [b]You
show Yourself [1]astute.
27 For You [a]save an afflicted
people,
But [b]haughty eyes You abase.
28 For You [a]light my lamp;
The LORD my God [b]illumines my
darkness.
29 For by You I can [1a]run upon a
troop;
And by my God I can [b]leap over
a wall.

30 ¶ As for God, His way is
[1a]blameless;
The [b]word of the LORD is tried;
He is a [c]shield to all who take
refuge in Him.
31 For [a]who is God, but the LORD?
And who is a [b]rock, except our
God,
32 The God who [a]girds me with
strength
And [1]makes my way
[2b]blameless?
33 He [a]makes my feet like hinds'
feet,
And [b]sets me upon my high
places.
34 He [a]trains my hands for battle,
So that my arms can [b]bend a
bow of bronze.
35 You have also given me [a]the
shield of Your salvation,
And Your [b]right hand
upholds me;
And [c]Your [1]gentleness makes
me great.
36 You [a]enlarge my steps
under me,
And my [1b]feet have not
slipped.

37 ¶ I [a]pursued my enemies and
overtook them,
And I did not turn back [b]until
they were consumed.
38 I shattered them, so that they
were [a]not able to rise;
They fell [b]under my feet.
39 For You have [a]girded me with
strength for battle;
You have [1b]subdued under me
those who rose up
against me.
40 You have also made my enemies
[a]turn their backs to me,
And I [1b]destroyed those who
hated me.
41 They cried for help, but there
was [a]none to save,
Even to the LORD, but [b]He did
not answer them.
42 Then I beat them fine as the
[a]dust before the wind;
I emptied them out as the mire
of the streets.

43 ¶ You have delivered me from
the [a]contentions of the
people;
You have placed me as [b]head of
the nations;
A [c]people whom I have not
known serve me.
44 As soon as they hear, they
obey me;
Foreigners [1a]submit to me.
45 Foreigners [a]fade away,
And [b]come trembling out of
their [1]fortresses.

46 ¶ The LORD [a]lives, and blessed
be [b]my rock;
And exalted be [c]the God of my
salvation,
47 The God who [a]executes
vengeance for me,
And [b]subdues peoples
under me.
48 He [a]delivers me from my
enemies;
Surely You [b]lift me above those
who rise up against me;
You rescue me from the [c]violent
man.
49 Therefore I will [a]give thanks to
You among the nations,
O LORD,
And I will [b]sing praises to Your
name.
50 He gives great [1a]deliverance to
His king,
And shows lovingkindness to
[b]His anointed,
To David and [c]his [2]descendants
forever.

Psalm 19

The Works and the Word of God.

For the choir director. A Psalm of David.

1 ¶ The [a]heavens are telling of the
glory of God;
And their [b]expanse is declaring
the work of His hands.
2 Day to [a]day pours forth
speech,

25 [1]V 23, note 1 [a]1 Kin 8:32; Ps 62:12; Matt 5:7 [b]Ps 18:30
26 [1]Lit *twisted* [a]Job 25:5; Hab 1:13 [b]Lev 26:23, 24,27,28; Prov 3:34
27 [a]Ps 72:12 [b]Ps 101:5; Prov 6:17
28 [a]1 Kin 15:4; Job 18:6; Ps 132:17 [b]Ps 27:1
29 [1]Or *crush a troop* [a]Ps 118:10-12 [b]Ps 18:33; 40:2
30 [1]V 23, note 1 [a]Deut 32:4; Ps 19:7; 145:17; Rev 15:3 [b]Ps 12:6 [c]Ps 17:7; 91:4
31 [a]Deut 32:39; 1 Sam 2:2; Ps 86:8-10; Is 45:5 [b]Deut 32:31; Ps 18:2; 62:2
32 [1]Or *has made* [2]Lit *complete;* or *having integrity* [a]Ps 18:39; Is 45:5 [b]Ps 18:23
33 [a]Hab 3:19 [b]Deut 32:13
34 [a]Ps 144:1 [b]Job 29:20
35 [1]Or *condescension* [a]Ps 33:20 [b]Ps 63:8; 119:117 [c]Ps 138:6
36 [1]Lit *ankles* [a]Ps 18:33 [b]Ps 66:9; Prov 4:12
37 [a]Ps 44:5 [b]Ps 37:20
38 [a]Ps 36:12 [b]Ps 47:3
39 [1]Lit *caused to bow down* [a]Ps 18:32 [b]Ps 18:47
40 [1]Or *silenced* [a]Ps 21:12 [b]Ps 94:23
41 [a]Ps 50:22 [b]Job 27:9; Prov 1:28
42 [a]Ps 83:13
43 [a]2 Sam 3:1; 19:9; Ps 35:1 [b]2 Sam 8:1-18; Ps 89:27 [c]Is 55:5
44 [1]Lit *deceive me;* i.e. give feigned obedience [a]Ps 66:3
45 [1]Lit *fastnesses* [a]Ps 37:2 [b]Mic 7:17
46 [a]Job 19:25 [b]Ps 18:2 [c]Ps 51:14
47 [a]Ps 94:1 [b]Ps 18:43; 47:3; 144:2
48 [a]Ps 3:7 [b]Ps 27:6; 59:1 [c]Ps 11:5
49 [a]Rom 15:9 [b]Ps 108:1
50 [1]I.e. victories; lit *salvations* [2]Lit *seed* [a]Ps 21:1; 144:10 [b]Ps 28:8 [c]Ps 89:4
19:1 [a]Ps 8:1; 50:6; Rom 1:19, 20 [b]Gen 1:6,7
2 [a]Ps 74:16

And [b]night to night reveals
knowledge.
3 There is no speech, nor are
there words;
Their voice is not heard.
4 Their [1a]line has gone out
through all the earth,
And their utterances to the end
of the world.
In them He has [b]placed a tent
for the sun,
5 Which is as a bridegroom coming
out of his chamber;
It rejoices as a strong man to run
his course.
6 Its [a]rising is from [1]one end of
the heavens,
And its circuit to the [2]other end
of them;
And there is nothing hidden
from its heat.

7 ¶ [a]The law of the LORD is
[1b]perfect, [c]restoring the
soul;
The testimony of the LORD is
[d]sure, making [e]wise the
simple.
8 The precepts of the LORD are
[a]right, [b]rejoicing the heart;
The commandment of the LORD
is [c]pure, [d]enlightening the
eyes.
9 The fear of the LORD is clean,
enduring forever;
The judgments of the LORD are
[a]true; they are [b]righteous
altogether.
10 They are more desirable than
[a]gold, yes, than much fine
gold;
[b]Sweeter also than honey and
the drippings of the
honeycomb.
11 Moreover, by them [a]Your
servant is warned;
In keeping them there is great
[b]reward.
12 Who can [a]discern *his* errors?
[b]Acquit me of [c]hidden
faults.
13 Also keep back Your servant
[a]from presumptuous
sins;
Let them not [b]rule over me;
Then I will be [1c]blameless,
And I shall be acquitted of
[d]great transgression.
14 Let the words of my mouth and
[a]the meditation of my heart
Be acceptable in Your sight,
O LORD, [b]my rock and my
[c]Redeemer.

Psalm 20

Prayer for Victory over Enemies.

For the choir director. A Psalm of David.

1 ¶ May the LORD answer you [a]in
the day of trouble!
May the [b]name of the [c]God of
Jacob set you *securely* on
high!
2 May He send you help [a]from
the sanctuary
And [b]support you from Zion!
3 May He [a]remember all your
meal offerings
And [b]find your burnt offering
[1]acceptable! [2]Selah.

4 ¶ May He grant you your
[a]heart's desire
And [b]fulfill all your [1]counsel!
5 [1]We will [a]sing for joy over your
[2]victory,
And in the name of our God we
will [b]set up our banners.
May the LORD [c]fulfill all your
petitions.
6 ¶ Now [a]I know that the LORD
saves His anointed;
He will [b]answer him from His
holy heaven
With the [1c]saving strength of
His right hand.
7 Some [1]*boast* in chariots and
some in [a]horses,
But [b]we [2]will boast in the
name of the LORD, our God.
8 They have [a]bowed down and
fallen,
But we have [b]risen and stood
upright.
9 [1a]Save, O LORD;
May the [b]King answer us in the
day we call.

Psalm 21

Praise for Deliverance.

For the choir director. A Psalm of David.

1 ¶ O LORD, in Your strength the
king will [a]be glad,
And in Your [1]salvation how
greatly he will rejoice!
2 You have [a]given him his heart's
desire,
And You have not withheld the
request of his lips. [1]Selah.
3 For You [a]meet him with the
blessings of good things;
You set a [b]crown of fine gold on
his head.
4 He asked life of You,
You [a]gave it to him,

2 [b]Ps 139:12
4 [1]Another reading is *sound* [a]Rom 10:18 [b]Ps 104:2
6 [1]Lit *the* [2]Lit *the ends* [a]Ps 113:3; Eccl 1:5
7 [1]I.e. blameless [a]Ps 111:7 [b]Ps 119:160 [c]Ps 23:3 [d]Ps 93:5 [e]Ps 119:98-100
8 [a]Ps 119:128 [b]Ps 119:14 [c]Ps 12:6 [d]Ps 36:9
9 [a]Ps 119:142 [b]Ps 119:138
10 [a]Ps 119:72, 127 [b]Ps 119:103
11 [a]Ps 17:4 [b]Ps 24:5,6; Prov 29:18
12 [a]Ps 40:12; 139:6 [b]Ps 51:1,2 [c]Ps 90:8; 139:23,24
13 [1]Lit *complete* [a]Num 15:30 [b]Ps 119:133 [c]Ps 18:32 [d]Ps 25:11
14 [a]Ps 104:34 [b]Ps 18:2 [c]Ps 31:5; Is 47:4
20:1 [a]Ps 50:15 [b]Ps 91:14 [c]Ps 46:7,11
2 [a]Ps 3:4 [b]Ps 110:2
3 [1]Lit *fat* [2]*Selah* may mean: *Pause, Crescendo* or *Musical interlude* [a]Acts 10:4 [b]Ps 51:19
4 [1]Or *purpose* [a]Ps 21:2 [b]Ps 145:19
5 [1]Or *Let us sing* [2]Or *salvation* [a]Ps 9:14 [b]Ps 60:4 [c]1 Sam 1:17
6 [1]Or *mighty deeds of the victory of His right hand* [a]Ps 41:11 [b]Is 58:9 [c]Ps 28:8
7 [1]Or praise *chariots,* or trust, or are strong *through* [2]Lit *make mention of;* or *praise the name* [a]Ps 33:17 [b]2 Chr 32:8
8 [a]Is 2:11,17 [b]Ps 37:24; Mic 7:8
9 [1]Or *O LORD, save the king; answer us* [a]Ps 3:7 [b]Ps 17:6
21:1 [1]Or *victory* [a]Ps 59:16,17
2 [1]*Selah* may mean: *Pause, Crescendo* or *Musical interlude* [a]Ps 20:4; 37:4
3 [a]Ps 59:10 [b]2 Sam 12:30
4 [a]Ps 61:6; 133:3

[b]Length of days forever and
ever.
5 His [a]glory is great through Your
[1]salvation,
[b]Splendor and majesty You place
upon him.
6 For You make him [1]most
[a]blessed forever;
You make him joyful [b]with
gladness in Your presence.

7 ¶ For the king [a]trusts in the
LORD,
And through the lovingkindness
of the Most High [b]he will
not be shaken.
8 Your hand will [a]find out all your
enemies;
Your right hand will find out
those who hate you.
9 You will make them [a]as a fiery
oven in the time [1]of your
anger;
The LORD will [b]swallow them up
in His wrath,
And [c]fire will devour them.
10 Their [1]offspring You will destroy
from the earth,
And their [2a]descendants from
among the sons of men.
11 Though they [1a]intended evil
against You
And [b]devised a plot,
They will not succeed.
12 For You will [a]make them turn
their back;
You will [1]aim [b]with Your
bowstrings at their faces.
13 Be exalted, O LORD, in Your
strength;
We will [a]sing and praise Your
power.

Psalm 22

A Cry of Anguish and a Song of Praise.

For the choir director; upon +Aijeleth Hashshahar. A Psalm of David.

1 ¶ [a]My God, my God, why have
You forsaken me?
[1b]Far from my deliverance are
the words of my
[2c]groaning.
2 O my God, I [a]cry by day, but
You do not answer;
And by night, but [1]I have no
rest.
3 Yet [a]You are holy,
O You who [1]are enthroned upon
[b]the praises of Israel.
4 In You our fathers [a]trusted;
They trusted and You [b]delivered
them.
5 To You they cried out and were
delivered;
[a]In You they trusted and were
not [1]disappointed.

6 ¶ But I am a [a]worm and not a
man,
A [b]reproach of men and
[c]despised by the people.
7 All who see me [1a]sneer at me;
They [2]separate with the lip,
they [b]wag the head, *saying,*
8 "[1]Commit *yourself* to the LORD;
[a]let Him deliver him;
Let Him rescue him, because He
delights in him."

9 ¶ Yet You are He who [a]brought
me forth from the womb;
You made me trust *when* upon
my mother's breasts.
10 Upon You I was cast [a]from
[1]birth;
You have been my God from my
mother's womb.

11 ¶ [a]Be not far from me, for
[1]trouble is near;
For there is [b]none to help.
12 Many [a]bulls have
surrounded me;
Strong *bulls* of [b]Bashan have
encircled me.
13 They [a]open wide their mouth
at me,
As a ravening and a roaring
[b]lion.
14 I am [a]poured out like water,
And all my [b]bones are out of
joint;
My [c]heart is like wax;
It is melted within [1]me.
15 My [a]strength is dried up like a
potsherd,
And [b]my tongue cleaves to my
jaws;
And You [c]lay me [1]in the dust of
death.
16 For [a]dogs have surrounded me;
[1]A band of evildoers has
encompassed me;
[2]They [b]pierced my hands and
my feet.
17 I can count all my bones.
[a]They look, they stare at me;
18 They [a]divide my garments
among them,
And for my clothing they cast
lots.

19 ¶ But You, O LORD, [a]be not far
off;
O You my help, [b]hasten to my
assistance.

4 [b]Ps 91:16
5 [1]Or *victory* [a]Ps 9:14 [b]Ps 8:5
6 [1]Lit *blessings* [a]1 Chr 17:27 [b]Ps 43:4
7 [a]Ps 125:1 [b]Ps 112:6
8 [a]Is 10:10
9 [1]Or *of your presence* [a]Mal 4:1 [b]Lam 2:2 [c]Ps 50:3
10 [1]Lit *fruit* [2]Lit *seed* [a]Ps 37:28
11 [1]Lit *stretched out* [a]Ps 2:1-3 [b]Ps 10:2
12 [1]Lit *make ready* [a]Ps 18:40 [b]Ps 7:12
13 [a]Ps 59:16
22:1 +Lit *the hind of the morning* [1]Or Why are You so *far from helping me,* and from *the words of my groaning?* [2]Lit *roaring* [a]Matt 27:46; Mark 15:34 [b]Ps 10:1 [c]Job 3:24; Ps 6:6
2 [1]Lit *there is no silence for me* [a]Ps 42:3
3 [1]Or *inhabit the praises* [a]Ps 99:9 [b]Deut 10:21; Ps 148:14
4 [a]Ps 78:53 [b]Ps 107:6
5 [1]Or *ashamed* [a]Is 49:23
6 [a]Job 25:6; Is 41:14 [b]Ps 31:11 [c]Is 49:7
7 [1]Or *mock me* [2]I.e. make mouths at me [a]Ps 79:4; Is 53:3; Luke 23:35 [b]Matt 27:39; Mark 15:29
8 [1]Lit *Roll;* another reading is *He committed* himself [a]Ps 91:14; Matt 27:43
9 [a]Ps 71:5
10 [1]Lit a *womb* [a]Is 46:3
11 [1]Or *distress* [a]Ps 71:12 [b]2 Kin 14:26; Ps 72:12; Is 63:5
12 [a]Ps 22:21 [b]Deut 32:14; Amos 4:1
13 [a]Job 16:10; Ps 35:21; Lam 2:16 [b]Ps 10:9
14 [1]Lit *my inward parts* [a]Job 30:16 [b]Ps 31:10; Dan 5:6 [c]Josh 7:5; Job 23:16; Ps 73:26; Nah 2:10
15 [1]Lit *to* [a]Ps 38:10 [b]John 19:28 [c]Ps 104:29
16 [1]Or *An assembly* [2]Another reading is *Like a lion, my...* [a]Ps 59:6 [b]Matt 27:35; John 20:25
17 [a]Luke 23:27
18 [a]Matt 27:35; Mark 15:24; Luke 23:34; John 19:24
19 [a]Ps 22:11 [b]Ps 70:5

20 Deliver my [1]soul from [a]the
sword,
My [b]only *life* from the [2]power
of the dog.
21 Save me from the [a]lion's mouth;
From the horns of the [b]wild
oxen You [c]answer me.

22 ¶ I will [a]tell of Your name to my
brethren;
In the midst of the assembly I
will praise You.
23 [a]You who fear the LORD, praise
Him;
All you [1]descendants of Jacob,
[b]glorify Him,
And [c]stand in awe of Him, all
you [1]descendants of Israel.
24 For He has [a]not despised nor
abhorred the affliction of the
afflicted;
Nor has He [b]hidden His face
from him;
But [c]when he cried to Him for
help, He heard.

25 ¶ From You *comes* [a]my praise in
the great assembly;
I shall [b]pay my vows before
those who fear Him.
26 The [1]afflicted will eat and [a]be
satisfied;
Those who seek Him will
[b]praise the LORD.
Let your [c]heart live forever!
27 All the [a]ends of the earth will
remember and turn to the
LORD,
And all the [b]families of the
nations will worship
before [1]You.
28 For the [a]kingdom is the LORD'S
And He [b]rules over the nations.
29 All the [1a]prosperous of the
earth will eat and worship,
All those who [b]go down to the
dust will bow before Him,
Even he who [2c]cannot keep his
soul alive.
30 [1a]Posterity will serve Him;
It will be told of the Lord to
[b]the *coming* generation.
31 They will come and [a]will
declare His righteousness
To a people [b]who will be born,
that He has performed *it*.

Psalm 23

The LORD, the Psalmist's Shepherd.

A Psalm of David.

1 ¶ The LORD is my [a]shepherd,
I [1]shall [b]not want.
2 He makes me lie down in
[a]green pastures;
He [b]leads me beside [1c]quiet
waters.
3 He [a]restores my soul;
He [b]guides me in the [1c]paths
of righteousness
For His name's sake.

4 ¶ Even though I [a]walk through
the [1]valley of the shadow of
death,
I [b]fear no [2]evil, for [c]You are
with me;
Your [d]rod and Your staff, they
comfort me.
5 You [a]prepare a table before me
in the presence of my
enemies;
You [1]have [b]anointed my head
with oil;
My [c]cup overflows.
6 [1]Surely [a]goodness and
lovingkindness will follow
me all the days of my life,
And I will [2b]dwell in the house
of the LORD [3]forever.

Psalm 24

The King of Glory Entering Zion.

A Psalm of David.

1 ¶ The [a]earth is the LORD'S, and
[1]all it contains,
The [b]world, and those who
dwell in it.
2 For He has [a]founded it upon the
seas
And established it upon the
rivers.
3 Who may [a]ascend into the [b]hill
of the LORD?
And who may stand in His holy
[c]place?
4 He who has [a]clean hands and a
[b]pure heart,
Who has not [c]lifted up his soul
[1]to falsehood
And has not [d]sworn deceitfully.
5 He shall receive a [a]blessing from
the LORD
And [1b]righteousness from the
God of his salvation.
6 [1]This is the generation of those
who [a]seek Him,
Who seek Your face—*even* Jacob.
[2]Selah.

7 ¶ [a]Lift up your heads, O gates,
And be lifted up, O [1]ancient
doors,
That the King of [b]glory may
come in!
8 Who is the King of glory?

20 [1]Or *life* [2]Lit *paw* [a]Ps 37:14 [b]Ps 35:17
21 [a]Ps 22:13 [b]Ps 22:12 [c]Ps 34:4
22 [a]Ps 40:10; Heb 2:12
23 [1]Lit *seed* [a]Ps 135:19 [b]Ps 86:12 [c]Ps 33:8
24 [a]Ps 69:33 [b]Ps 27:9 [c]Ps 31:22; Heb 5:7
25 [a]Ps 35:18 [b]Ps 61:8; Eccl 5:4
26 [1]Or *poor* [a]Ps 107:9 [b]Ps 40:16 [c]Ps 69:32
27 [1]Some versions read *Him* [a]Ps 2:8 [b]Ps 86:9
28 [a]Ps 47:7; Obad 21; Zech 14:9; Matt 6:13 [b]Ps 47:8
29 [1]Lit *fat ones* [2]Or *did not* [a]Ps 17:10; Hab 1:16 [b]Ps 28:1; Is 26:19 [c]Ps 89:48
30 [1]Lit *A seed* [a]Ps 102:28 [b]Ps 102:18
31 [a]Ps 40:9 [b]Ps 78:6
23:1 [1]Or *do* [a]Ps 78:52; Is 40:11; Jer 31:10; Ezek 34:11-13; John 10:11; 1 Pet 2:25 [b]Ps 34:9; Phil 4:19
2 [1]Lit *waters of rest* [a]Ps 65:11-13; Ezek 34:14 [b]Rev 7:17 [c]Ps 36:8
3 [1]Lit *tracks* [a]Ps 19:7 [b]Ps 5:8 [c]Ps 85:13; Prov 4:11
4 [1]Or *valley of deep darkness* [2]Or *harm* [a]Job 10:21; Ps 107:14 [b]Ps 3:6 [c]Ps 16:8; Is 43:2 [d]Mic 7:14
5 [1]Or *anoint* [a]Ps 78:19 [b]Ps 92:10; Luke 7:46 [c]Ps 16:5
6 [1]Or *Only* [2]Another reading is *return to* [3]Lit *for length of days* [a]Ps 25:7 [b]Ps 27:4-6
24:1 [1]Lit *its fullness* [a]1 Cor 10:26 [b]Ps 89:11
2 [a]Ps 104:3
3 [a]Ps 15:1 [b]Ps 2:6 [c]Ps 65:4
4 [1]Or *in vain* [a]Job 17:9; Ps 22:30 [b]Ps 51:10; Matt 5:8 [c]Ezek 18:15 [d]Ps 15:4
5 [1]I.e. as vindicated [a]Ps 115:13 [b]Ps 36:10
6 [1]Or *Such* [2]*Selah* may mean: *Pause, Crescendo* or *Musical interlude* [a]Ps 27:4
7 [1]Lit *everlasting* [a]Ps 118:20; Is 26:2 [b]Ps 29:2; Acts 7:2; 1 Cor 2:8

The LORD [a]strong and mighty,
The LORD [b]mighty in battle.
9 Lift up your heads, O gates,
And lift *them* up, O [1]ancient doors,
That the King of [a]glory may come in!
10 Who is this King of glory?
The LORD of [a]hosts,
He is the King of glory. Selah.

Psalm 25

Prayer for Protection, Guidance and Pardon.

A Psalm of David.

1 ¶ To You, O LORD, I [a]lift up my soul.
2 O my God, in You [a]I trust,
Do not let me [b]be ashamed;
Do not let my [c]enemies exult over me.
3 Indeed, [a]none of those who wait for You will be ashamed;
[1]Those who [b]deal treacherously without cause will be ashamed.

4 ¶ [a]Make me know Your ways, O LORD;
Teach me Your paths.
5 Lead me in [a]Your truth and teach me,
For You are the [b]God of my salvation;
For You I [c]wait all the day.
6 [a]Remember, O LORD, Your compassion and Your lovingkindnesses,
For they have been [1b]from of old.
7 Do not remember the [a]sins of my youth or my transgressions;
[b]According to Your lovingkindness remember me,
For Your [c]goodness' sake, O LORD.

8 ¶ [a]Good and [b]upright is the LORD;
Therefore He [c]instructs sinners in the way.
9 He [a]leads the [1]humble in justice,
And He [b]teaches the [1]humble His way.
10 All the paths of the LORD are [a]lovingkindness and truth
To [b]those who keep His covenant and His testimonies.
11 For [a]Your name's sake, O LORD,
[b]Pardon my iniquity, for it is great.

12 ¶ Who is the man who [a]fears the LORD?
He will [b]instruct him in the way he should choose.
13 His soul will [a]abide in [1]prosperity,
And his [2]descendants will [b]inherit the [3]land.
14 The [1a]secret of the LORD is for those who fear Him,
[2]And He will [b]make them know His covenant.
15 My [a]eyes are continually toward the LORD,
For He will [1b]pluck my feet out of the net.

16 ¶ [a]Turn to me and be gracious to me,
For I am [b]lonely and afflicted.
17 [1]The [a]troubles of my heart are enlarged;
Bring me [b]out of my distresses.
18 [a]Look upon my affliction and my [1]trouble,
And [b]forgive all my sins.
19 Look upon my enemies, for they [a]are many,
And they [b]hate me with violent hatred.
20 [a]Guard my soul and deliver me;
Do not let me [b]be ashamed, for I take refuge in You.
21 Let [a]integrity and uprightness preserve me,
For [b]I wait for You.
22 [a]Redeem Israel, O God,
Out of all his troubles.

Psalm 26

Protestation of Integrity and Prayer for Protection.

A Psalm of David.

1 ¶ [1a]Vindicate me, O LORD, for I have [b]walked in my integrity,
And I have [c]trusted in the LORD [2d]without wavering.
2 [a]Examine me, O LORD, and try me;
[b]Test my [1]mind and my heart.
3 For Your [a]lovingkindness is before my eyes,
And I have [b]walked in Your [1]truth.
4 I do not [a]sit with [1]deceitful men,
Nor will I go with [2b]pretenders.
5 I [a]hate the assembly of evildoers,

8 [a]Deut 4:34; Ps 96:7 [b]Ex 15:3; Ps 76:3-6
9 [1]Lit *everlasting* [a]Ps 26:8
10 [a]Gen 32:2; Josh 5:14; 2 Sam 5:10; Neh 9:6
25:1 [a]Ps 86:4
2 [a]Ps 31:1 [b]Ps 25:20 [c]Ps 13:4
3 [1]Or *Let those...be ashamed* [a]Ps 37:9; Is 49:23 [b]Ps 119:158; Is 21:2; Hab 1:13
4 [a]Ex 33:13; Ps 27:11
5 [a]Ps 25:10 [b]Ps 79:9 [c]Ps 40:1
6 [1]Or *everlasting* [a]Ps 98:3 [b]Ps 103:17
7 [a]Job 13:26 [b]Ps 51:1 [c]Ps 31:19
8 [a]Ps 86:5 [b]Ps 92:15 [c]Ps 32:8
9 [1]Or *afflicted* [a]Ps 23:3 [b]Ps 27:11
10 [a]Ps 40:11 [b]Ps 103:18
11 [a]Ps 31:3 [b]Ex 34:9
12 [a]Ps 31:19 [b]Ps 25:8
13 [1]Lit *good* [2]Lit *seed* [3]Or *earth* [a]Prov 1:33; Jer 23:6 [b]Ps 37:11; Matt 5:5
14 [1]Or *counsel* or *intimacy* [2]Or *And His covenant, to make them know it* [a]Prov 3:32; John 7:17 [b]Gen 17:1
15 [1]Lit *bring out* [a]Ps 123:2 [b]Ps 31:4
16 [a]Ps 69:16 [b]Ps 143:4
17 [1]Some commentators read *Relieve the troubles of my heart* [a]Ps 40:12 [b]Ps 107:6
18 [1]Lit *toil* [a]2 Sam 16:12; Ps 31:7 [b]Ps 103:3
19 [a]Ps 3:1 [b]Ps 9:13
20 [a]Ps 86:2 [b]Ps 25:2
21 [a]Ps 41:12 [b]Ps 25:3
22 [a]Ps 130:8
26:1 [1]Lit *Judge* [2]Lit *I do not slide* [a]Ps 7:8 [b]2 Kin 20:3; Prov 20:7 [c]Ps 13:5 [d]Heb 10:23
2 [1]Lit *kidneys,* figurative for inner man [a]Ps 17:3 [b]Ps 7:9
3 [1]Or *faithfulness* [a]Ps 48:9 [b]2 Kin 20:3; Ps 86:11
4 [1]Or *worthless men;* lit *men of falsehood* [2]Or *dissemblers, hypocrites* [a]Ps 1:1 [b]Ps 28:3
5 [a]Ps 31:6

And I will not sit with the wicked.
6 I shall [a]wash my hands in innocence,
And I will go about [b]Your altar, O LORD,
7 That I may proclaim with the voice of [a]thanksgiving
And declare all Your [1]wonders.
8 ¶ O LORD, I [a]love the habitation of Your house
And the place [1]where Your [b]glory dwells.
9 [a]Do not [1]take my soul away *along* with sinners,
Nor my life with [b]men of bloodshed,
10 In whose hands is a [a]wicked scheme,
And whose right hand is full of [b]bribes.
11 But as for me, I shall [a]walk in my integrity;
[b]Redeem me, and be gracious to me.
12 [a]My foot stands on a [b]level place;
In the [c]congregations I shall bless the LORD.

Psalm 27

A Psalm of Fearless Trust in God.

A Psalm of David.

1 ¶ The LORD is my [a]light and my [b]salvation;
Whom shall I fear?
The LORD is the [1c]defense of my life;
[d]Whom shall I dread?
2 When evildoers came upon me to [a]devour my flesh,
My adversaries and my enemies, they [b]stumbled and fell.
3 Though a [a]host encamp against me,
My heart will not fear;
Though war arise against me,
In *spite of* this I [1]shall be [b]confident.

4 ¶ [a]One thing I have asked from the LORD, that I shall seek:
That I may [b]dwell in the house of the LORD all the days of my life,
To behold [c]the [1]beauty of the LORD
And to [2d]meditate in His temple.
5 For in the [a]day of trouble He will [b]conceal me in His [1]tabernacle;
In the secret place of His tent He will [c]hide me;
He will [d]lift me up on a rock.
6 And now [a]my head will be lifted up above my enemies around me,
And I will offer in His tent [b]sacrifices [1]with shouts of joy;
I will [c]sing, yes, I will sing praises to the LORD.

7 ¶ [a]Hear, O LORD, when I cry with my voice,
And be gracious to me and [b]answer me.
8 *When You said,* "[a]Seek My face," my heart said to You,
"Your face, O LORD, [b]I shall seek."
9 [a]Do not hide Your face from me,
Do not turn Your servant away in [b]anger;
You have been [c]my help;
[d]Do not abandon me nor [e]forsake me,
O God of my salvation!
10 [1]For my father and [a]my mother have forsaken me,
But [b]the LORD will take me up.

11 ¶ [a]Teach me Your way, O LORD,
And lead me in a [b]level path
Because of [1]my foes.
12 Do not deliver me over to the [1a]desire of my adversaries,
For [b]false witnesses have risen against me,
And such as [c]breathe out violence.
13 [1]*I would have despaired* unless I had believed that I would see the [a]goodness of the LORD
In the [b]land of the living.
14 [a]Wait for the LORD;
Be [b]strong and let your heart take courage;
Yes, wait for the LORD.

Psalm 28

A Prayer for Help, and Praise for Its Answer.

A Psalm of David.

1 ¶ To You, O LORD, I call;
My [a]rock, do not be deaf to me,
For if You [b]are silent to me,
I will become like those who [c]go down to the pit.
2 Hear the [a]voice of my supplications when I cry to You for help,

---

6 [a]Ps 73:13 [b]Ps 43:3,4
7 [1]Or *miracles* [a]Ps 9:1
8 [1]Lit *of the tabernacle of Your glory* [a]Ps 27:4 [b]Ps 24:7
9 [1]Lit *gather* [a]Ps 28:3 [b]Ps 139:19
10 [a]Ps 37:7 [b]Ps 15:5
11 [a]Ps 26:1 [b]Ps 44:26; 69:18
12 [a]Ps 40:2 [b]Ps 27:11 [c]Ps 22:22
27:1 [1]Or *refuge* [a]Ps 18:28; Is 60:20; Mic 7:8 [b]Ex 15:2; Ps 62:7; 118:14; Is 33:2; Jon 2:9 [c]Ps 28:8 [d]Ps 118:6
2 [a]Ps 14:4 [b]Ps 9:3
3 [1]Lit *am confident* [a]Ps 3:6 [b]Job 4:6
4 [1]Lit *delightfulness* [2]Lit *inquire* [a]Ps 26:8 [b]Ps 23:6 [c]Ps 90:17 [d]Ps 18:6
5 [1]Or *shelter* [a]Ps 50:15 [b]Ps 31:20 [c]Ps 17:8 [d]Ps 40:2
6 [1]Lit *of shouts* [a]Ps 3:3 [b]Ps 107:22 [c]Ps 13:6
7 [a]Ps 4:3; 61:1 [b]Ps 13:3
8 [a]Ps 105:4; Amos 5:6 [b]Ps 34:4
9 [a]Ps 69:17 [b]Ps 6:1 [c]Ps 40:17 [d]Ps 94:14 [e]Ps 37:28
10 [1]Or *If my father...forsake me, Then the LORD* [a]Is 49:15 [b]Is 40:11
11 [1]Or *those who lie in wait for me* [a]Ps 25:4; 86:11 [b]Ps 5:8; 26:12
12 [1]Lit *soul* [a]Ps 41:2 [b]Deut 19:18; Ps 35:11; Matt 26:60 [c]Acts 9:1
13 [1]Or *Surely I believed* [a]Ps 31:19 [b]Job 28:13; Ps 52:5; 116:9; 142:5; Is 38:11; Jer 11:19; Ezek 26:20
14 [a]Ps 25:3; 37:34; 40:1; 62:5; 130:5; Prov 20:22; Is 25:9 [b]Ps 31:24
28:1 [a]Ps 18:2 [b]Ps 35:22; 39:12; 83:1 [c]Ps 88:4; 143:7; Prov 1:12
2 [a]Ps 140:6

When I [b]lift up my hands
[c]toward [1]Your holy
[d]sanctuary.
3 [a]Do not drag me away with the
wicked
And with those who work
iniquity,
Who [b]speak peace with their
neighbors,
While evil is in their hearts.
4 Requite them [a]according to their
work and according to the
evil of their practices;
Requite them according to the
deeds of their hands;
Repay them their [1]recompense.
5 Because they [a]do not regard the
works of the LORD
Nor the deeds of His hands,
He will tear them down and not
build them up.

6 ¶ Blessed be the LORD,
Because He [a]has heard the voice
of my supplication.
7 The LORD is my [a]strength and
my [b]shield;
My heart [c]trusts in Him, and I
am helped;
Therefore [d]my heart exults,
And with [e]my song I shall thank
Him.
8 The LORD is [1]their [a]strength,
And He is a [2b]saving defense to
His anointed.
9 [a]Save Your people and bless
[b]Your inheritance;
Be their [c]shepherd also, and
[d]carry them forever.

Psalm 29

The Voice of the LORD in the Storm.

A Psalm of David.

1 ¶ [a]Ascribe to the LORD, O [1]sons
of the mighty,
Ascribe to the LORD glory and
strength.
2 Ascribe to the LORD the glory
[1]due to His name;
Worship the LORD [a]in [2]holy
array.

3 ¶ The [a]voice of the LORD is
upon the waters;
The God of glory [b]thunders,
The LORD is over [1c]many
waters.
4 The voice of the LORD is
[a]powerful,
The voice of the LORD is
majestic.
5 The voice of the LORD breaks the
cedars;
Yes, the LORD breaks in pieces
[a]the cedars of Lebanon.
6 He makes Lebanon [a]skip like a
calf,
And [b]Sirion like a young
wild ox.
7 The voice of the LORD hews out
[1]flames of fire.
8 The voice of the LORD [1]shakes
the wilderness;
The LORD shakes the wilderness
of [a]Kadesh.
9 The voice of the LORD makes
[a]the deer to calve
And strips the forests bare;
And [b]in His temple everything
says, "Glory!"

10 ¶ The LORD sat *as King* at the
[a]flood;
Yes, the LORD sits as [b]King
forever.
11 [1]The LORD will give [a]strength
to His people;
[2]The LORD will bless His people
with [b]peace.

Psalm 30

Thanksgiving for Deliverance from Death.

A Psalm; a Song at the Dedication
of the House. *A Psalm* of David.

1 ¶ I will [a]extol You, O LORD, for
You have [b]lifted me up,
And have not let my [c]enemies
rejoice over me.
2 O LORD my God,
I [a]cried to You for help, and You
[b]healed me.
3 O LORD, You have [a]brought up
my soul from [1]Sheol;
You have kept me alive, [2]that I
would not [b]go down to the
pit.
4 [a]Sing praise to the LORD, you
[b]His godly ones,
And [c]give thanks to His holy
[1d]name.
5 For [a]His anger is but for a
moment,
His [b]favor is for a lifetime;
Weeping may [c]last for the night,
But a shout of joy *comes* in the
morning.

6 ¶ Now as for me, I said in my
prosperity,
"I will [a]never be moved."
7 O LORD, by Your favor You have
made my mountain to stand
strong;

2 [1]Lit *the innermost place of Your sanctuary* [b]Ps 134:2; 141:2; Lam 2:19; 1 Tim 2:8 [c]Ps 5:7; 138:2 [d]1 Kin 6:5
3 [a]Ps 26:9 [b]Ps 12:2; 55:21; 62:4; Jer 9:8
4 [1]Or *dealings* [a]Ps 62:12; 2 Tim 4:14; Rev 18:6; 22:12
5 [a]Is 5:12
6 [a]Ps 28:2
7 [a]Ps 18:2; 59:17 [b]Ps 3:3 [c]Ps 13:5; 112:7 [d]Ps 16:9 [e]Ps 40:3; 69:30
8 [1]A few mss and ancient versions read *the strength of His people* [2]Or *refuge of salvation* [a]Ps 20:6; 89:17 [b]Ps 27:1; 140:7
9 [a]Ps 106:47 [b]Deut 9:29; 32:9; 1 Kin 8:51; Ps 33:12; 106:40 [c]Ps 80:1 [d]Deut 1:31; Is 40:11; 46:3; 63:9
29:1 [1]Or *sons of gods* [a]1 Chr 16:28,29; Ps 96:7-9
2 [1]Lit *of His name* [2]Or *the majesty of holiness* [a]2 Chr 20:21; Ps 110:3
3 [1]Or *great* [a]Ps 104:7 [b]Job 37:4, 5; Ps 18:13 [c]Ps 18:16; 107:23
4 [a]Ps 68:33
5 [a]Judg 9:15; 1 Kin 5:6; Ps 104:16; Is 2:13; 14:8
6 [a]Ps 114:4,6 [b]Deut 3:9
7 [1]I.e. lightning
8 [1]Or *causes...to whirl* [a]Num 13:26
9 [a]Job 39:1 [b]Ps 26:8
10 [a]Gen 6:17 [b]Ps 10:16
11 [1]Or *May the LORD give* [2]Or *May the LORD bless* [a]Ps 28:8; 68:35; Is 40:29 [b]Ps 37:11; 72:3
30:1 [a]Ps 118:28; 145:1 [b]Ps 3:3 [c]Ps 25:2; 35:19,24
2 [a]Ps 88:13 [b]Ps 6:2; 103:3; Is 53:5
3 [1]I.e. the nether world [2]Some mss read *from among those who go down* [a]Ps 86:13 [b]Ps 28:1
4 [1]Lit *memorial* [a]Ps 149:1 [b]Ps 50:5 [c]Ps 97:12 [d]Ex 3:15; Ps 135:13; Hos 12:5
5 [a]Ps 103:9; Is 26:20; 54:7,8 [b]Ps 118:1 [c]Ps 126:5; 2 Cor 4:17
6 [a]Ps 10:6; 62:2,6

You [a]hid Your face, I was dismayed.
8 To You, O LORD, I called,
And to the Lord I made supplication:
9 "What profit is there in my blood, if I [a]go down to the pit?
Will the [b]dust praise You? Will it declare Your faithfulness?

10 ¶ "[a]Hear, O LORD, and be gracious to me;
O LORD, be my [b]helper."
11 You have turned for me [a]my mourning into dancing;
You have [b]loosed my sackcloth and girded me with [c]gladness,
12 That *my* [1a]soul may sing praise to You and not be silent.
O LORD my God, I will [b]give thanks to You forever.

Psalm 31

A Psalm of Complaint and of Praise.

For the choir director. A Psalm of David.

1 ¶ [a]In You, O LORD, I have taken refuge;
Let me never [b]be ashamed;
[c]In Your righteousness deliver me.
2 [a]Incline Your ear to me, rescue me quickly;
Be to me a [b]rock of [1]strength,
A stronghold to save me.
3 For You are my [1]rock and [a]my fortress;
For [b]Your name's sake You will lead me and guide me.
4 You will [a]pull me out of the net which they have secretly laid for me,
For You are my [b]strength.
5 [a]Into Your hand I commit my spirit;
You have [b]ransomed me, O LORD, [c]God of [1]truth.
6 ¶ I hate those who [a]regard [1]vain idols,
But I [b]trust in the LORD.
7 I will [a]rejoice and be glad in Your lovingkindness,
Because You have [b]seen my affliction;
You have known the troubles of my soul,
8 And You have not [a]given me over into the hand of the enemy;
You have set my feet in a large place.

9 ¶ Be gracious to me, O LORD, for [a]I am in distress;
My [b]eye is wasted away from grief, [c]my soul and my body *also.*
10 For my life is spent with [a]sorrow
And my years with sighing;
My [b]strength has failed because of my iniquity,
And [c]my [1]body has wasted away.
11 Because of all my adversaries, I have become a [a]reproach,
Especially to my [b]neighbors,
And an object of dread to my acquaintances;
Those who see me in the street flee from me.
12 I am [a]forgotten as a dead man, out of mind;
I am like a broken vessel.
13 For I have heard the [1a]slander of many,
[b]Terror is on every side;
While they [c]took counsel together against me,
They [d]schemed to take away my life.

14 ¶ But as for me, I trust in You, O LORD,
I say, "[a]You are my God."
15 My [a]times are in Your hand;
[b]Deliver me from the hand of my enemies and from those who persecute me.
16 Make Your [a]face to shine upon Your servant;
[b]Save me in Your lovingkindness.
17 Let me not be [a]put to shame, O LORD, for I call upon You;
Let the [b]wicked be put to shame, let them [c]be silent in [1]Sheol.
18 Let the [a]lying lips be mute,
Which [b]speak arrogantly against the righteous
With pride and contempt.

19 ¶ How great is Your [a]goodness,
Which You have stored up for those who fear You,
Which You have wrought for those who [b]take refuge in You,
[c]Before the sons of men!
20 You hide them in the [a]secret place of Your presence from the [b]conspiracies of man;
You keep them secretly in a [1]shelter from the [c]strife of tongues.
21 [a]Blessed be the LORD,

7 [a]Deut 31:17; Ps 104:29; 143:7
9 [a]Ps 28:1 [b]Ps 6:5
10 [a]Ps 4:1; 27:7 [b]Ps 27:9; 54:4
11 [a]Eccl 3:4; Jer 31:4,13 [b]Is 20:2 [c]Ps 4:7
12 [1]Lit *glory* [a]Ps 16:9; 57:8; 108:1 [b]Ps 44:8
31:1 [a]Ps 31:1-3; 71:1-3 [b]Ps 25:2 [c]Ps 143:1
2 [1]Or *refuge, protection* [a]Ps 17:6; 71:2; 86:1; 102:2 [b]Ps 18:2; 71:3
3 [1]Or *crag* [a]Ps 18:2 [b]Ps 23:3; 25:11
4 [a]Ps 25:15 [b]Ps 46:1
5 [1]Or *faithfulness* [a]Luke 23:46; Acts 7:59 [b]Ps 55:18; 71:23 [c]Deut 32:4; Ps 71:22
6 [1]Lit *empty vanities* [a]Jon 2:8 [b]Ps 52:8
7 [a]Ps 90:14 [b]Ps 10:14
8 [a]Deut 32:30; Ps 37:33
9 [a]Ps 66:14; 69:17 [b]Ps 6:7 [c]Ps 63:1
10 [1]Or *bones, substance* [a]Ps 13:2 [b]Ps 39:11 [c]Ps 32:3; 38:3; 102:3
11 [a]Ps 69:19 [b]Job 19:13; Ps 38:11; 88:8,18
12 [a]Ps 88:5
13 [1]Lit *whispering* [a]Ps 50:20; Jer 20:10 [b]Lam 2:22 [c]Ps 62:4; Matt 27:1 [d]Ps 41:7
14 [a]Ps 140:6
15 [a]Job 14:5; 24:1 [b]Ps 143:9
16 [a]Num 6:25; Ps 4:6; 80:3 [b]Ps 6:4
17 [1]I.e. the nether world [a]Ps 25:2,20 [b]Ps 25:3 [c]1 Sam 2:9; Ps 94:17; 115:17
18 [a]Ps 109:2; 120:2 [b]1 Sam 2:3; Ps 94:4; Jude 15
19 [a]Ps 65:4; 145:7; Is 64:4; Rom 2:4; 11:22 [b]Ps 5:11 [c]Ps 23:5
20 [1]Or *pavilion* [a]Ps 27:5 [b]Ps 37:12 [c]Job 5:21; Ps 31:13
21 [a]Ps 28:6

For He has made [b]marvelous His lovingkindness to me in a besieged [c]city.
22 As for me, [a]I said in my alarm,
"I am [b]cut off from before Your eyes";
Nevertheless You [c]heard the voice of my supplications
When I cried to You.

23 ¶ O love the LORD, all you [a]His godly ones!
The LORD [b]preserves the faithful
And fully [c]recompenses the proud doer.
24 [a]Be strong and let your heart take courage,
All you who [1]hope in the LORD.

Psalm 32

Blessedness of Forgiveness and of Trust in God.

A Psalm of David. A +Maskil.

1 ¶ [a]How blessed is he whose transgression is forgiven,
Whose sin is covered!
2 How blessed is the man to whom the LORD [a]does not impute iniquity,
And in whose spirit there is [b]no deceit!

3 ¶ When [a]I kept silent *about my sin,* [b]my [1]body wasted away
Through my [2c]groaning all day long.
4 For day and night [a]Your hand was heavy upon me;
My [1b]vitality was drained away *as* with the fever heat of summer. [2]Selah.
5 I [a]acknowledged my sin to You,
And my iniquity I [b]did not hide;
I said, "[c]I will confess my transgressions to the LORD";
And You [d]forgave the [1]guilt of my sin. Selah.
6 Therefore, let everyone who is godly pray to You [1a]in a time when You may be found;
Surely [b]in a flood of great waters they will not reach him.
7 You are [a]my hiding place; You [b]preserve me from trouble;
You surround me with [1c]songs of deliverance. Selah.

8 ¶ I will [a]instruct you and teach you in the way which you should go;
I will counsel you [b]with My eye upon you.

21 [b]Ps 17:7 [c]1 Sam 23:7; Ps 87:5
22 [a]Ps 116:11 [b]Ps 88:5; Is 38:11; Lam 3:54 [c]Ps 18:6
23 [a]Ps 30:4 [b]Ps 145:20; Rev 2:10 [c]Deut 32:41; Ps 94:2
24 [1]Or *wait for* [a]Ps 27:14
32:1 +Possibly *Contemplative,* or *Didactic,* or *Skillful Psalm* [a]Ps 85:2; Rom 4:7
2 [a]2 Cor 5:19 [b]John 1:47
3 [1]Or *bones, substance* [2]Lit *roaring* [a]Ps 39:2 [b]Ps 31:10 [c]Ps 38:8
4 [1]Lit *life juices were turned into the drought of summer* [2]*Selah* may mean: *Pause, Crescendo* or *Musical interlude* [a]1 Sam 5:6; Job 23:2; Ps 38:2 [b]Ps 22:15
5 [1]Or *iniquity* [a]Lev 26:40 [b]Job 31:33 [c]Ps 38:18; Prov 28:13; 1 John 1:9 [d]Ps 103:12
6 [1]Lit *in a time of finding out* [a]Ps 69:13; Is 55:6 [b]Ps 46:1-3; Is 43:2
7 [1]Or *shouts* [a]Ps 9:9 [b]Ps 121:7 [c]Ex 15:1; Judg 5:1; Ps 40:3
8 [a]Ps 25:8 [b]Ps 33:18
9 [a]Prov 26:3
10 [a]Ps 16:4; Prov 13:21; Rom 2:9 [b]Ps 5:11; Prov 16:20
11 [a]Ps 64:10 [b]Ps 7:10
33:1 [a]Ps 32:11; Phil 3:1 [b]Ps 92:1
2 [a]Ps 71:22 [b]Ps 144:9
3 [a]Ps 40:3; Is 42:10; Rev 5:9 [b]Ps 98:4
4 [a]Ps 19:8 [b]Ps 119:90
5 [a]Ps 11:7 [b]Ps 119:64
6 [a]Gen 1:6; Ps 148:5; Heb 11:3 [b]Ps 104:30 [c]Gen 2:1
7 [1]Some versions read *in a water skin;* i.e. container [a]Ex 15:8; Josh 3:16; Ps 78:13
8 [a]Ps 67:7 [b]Ps 96:9
9 [1]Or *stood forth* [a]Gen 1:3; Ps 148:5
10 [a]Ps 2:1-3; Is 8:10
11 [a]Job 23:12; Prov 19:21 [b]Ps 40:5; Is 55:8

9 Do not be [a]as the horse or as the mule which have no understanding,
Whose trappings include bit and bridle to hold them in check,
Otherwise they will not come near to you.
10 Many are the [a]sorrows of the wicked,
But [b]he who trusts in the LORD, lovingkindness shall surround him.
11 Be [a]glad in the LORD and rejoice, you righteous ones;
And shout for joy, all you who are [b]upright in heart.

Psalm 33

Praise to the Creator and Preserver.

1 ¶ [a]Sing for joy in the LORD, O you righteous ones;
Praise is [b]becoming to the upright.
2 Give thanks to the LORD with the [a]lyre;
Sing praises to Him with a [b]harp of ten strings.
3 Sing to Him a [a]new song;
Play skillfully with [b]a shout of joy.
4 For the word of the LORD [a]is upright,
And all His work is *done* [b]in faithfulness.
5 He [a]loves righteousness and justice;
The [b]earth is full of the lovingkindness of the LORD.

6 ¶ By the [a]word of the LORD the heavens were made,
And [b]by the breath of His mouth [c]all their host.
7 He gathers the [a]waters of the sea together [1]as a heap;
He lays up the deeps in storehouses.
8 Let [a]all the earth fear the LORD;
Let all the inhabitants of the world [b]stand in awe of Him.
9 For [a]He spoke, and it was done;
He commanded, and it [1]stood fast.
10 The LORD [a]nullifies the counsel of the nations;
He frustrates the plans of the peoples.
11 The [a]counsel of the LORD stands forever,
The [b]plans of His heart from generation to generation.

12 Blessed is the [a]nation whose
God is the LORD,
The people whom He has
[b]chosen for His own
inheritance.

13 ¶ The LORD [a]looks from heaven;
He [b]sees all the sons of men;
14 From [a]His dwelling place He
looks out
On all the inhabitants of the
earth,
15 He who [a]fashions [1]the hearts of
them all,
He who [b]understands all their
works.
16 [a]The king is not saved by a
mighty army;
A warrior is not delivered by
great strength.
17 A [a]horse is a false hope for
victory;
Nor does it deliver anyone by its
great strength.

18 ¶ Behold, [a]the eye of the LORD
is on those who fear Him,
On those who [1b]hope for His
lovingkindness,
19 To [a]deliver their soul from
death
And to keep them alive [b]in
famine.
20 Our soul [a]waits for the LORD;
He is our [b]help and our shield.
21 For our [a]heart rejoices in Him,
Because we trust in His holy
name.
22 Let Your lovingkindness, O LORD,
be upon us,
According as we have [1]hoped
in You.

Psalm 34

The LORD, a Provider and Deliverer.

A Psalm of David when he [+]feigned madness before [•]Abimelech, who drove him away and he departed.

1 ¶ I will [a]bless the LORD at all
times;
His [b]praise shall continually be
in my mouth.
2 My soul will [a]make its boast in
the LORD;
The [b]humble will hear it and
rejoice.
3 O [a]magnify the LORD with me,
And let us [b]exalt His name
together.

4 ¶ I [a]sought the LORD, and He
answered me,
And [b]delivered me from all my
fears.
5 They [a]looked to Him and were
radiant,
And their faces will [b]never be
ashamed.
6 This [1]poor man cried, and [a]the
LORD heard him
And saved him out of all his
troubles.
7 The [a]angel of the LORD encamps
around those who fear Him,
And rescues them.

8 ¶ O [a]taste and see that the LORD
is good;
How [b]blessed is the man who
takes refuge in Him!
9 O fear the LORD, you [a]His
saints;
For to those who fear Him there
is [b]no want.
10 The young lions do lack and
suffer hunger;
But they who seek the LORD
shall [a]not be in want of any
good thing.
11 [a]Come, you children, listen
to me;
[b]I will teach you [c]the fear of
the LORD.
12 [a]Who is the man who desires
life
And loves *length of* days that he
may [b]see good?
13 Keep [a]your tongue from evil
And your lips from speaking
[b]deceit.
14 [a]Depart from evil and do good;
Seek peace and [b]pursue it.

15 ¶ The [a]eyes of the LORD are
toward the righteous
And His ears are *open* to their
cry.
16 The [a]face of the LORD is against
evildoers,
To [b]cut off the memory of them
from the earth.
17 *The righteous* [a]cry, and the
LORD hears
And delivers them out of all
their troubles.
18 The LORD [a]is near to the
[b]brokenhearted
And saves those who are
[1c]crushed in spirit.

19 ¶ [a]Many are the [b]afflictions of
the righteous,
But the LORD [c]delivers him out
of them all.
20 He keeps all his bones,
[a]Not one of them is broken.
21 [a]Evil shall slay the wicked;

---

12 [a]Ps 144:15 [b]Ex 19:5; Deut 7:6; Ps 28:9
13 [a]Job 28:24; Ps 14:2 [b]Ps 11:4
14 [a]1 Kin 8:39; Ps 102:19
15 [1]Or *their heart together* [a]Job 10:8; Ps 119:73 [b]2 Chr 16:9; Job 34:21; Jer 32:19
16 [a]Ps 44:6
17 [a]Ps 20:7; Prov 21:31
18 [1]Or *wait* [a]Job 36:7; Ps 32:8; 1 Pet 3:12 [b]Ps 32:10
19 [a]Ps 56:13; Acts 12:11 [b]Job 5:20; Ps 37:19
20 [a]Ps 62:1; Is 8:17 [b]Ps 115:9
21 [a]Ps 13:5; Zech 10:7; John 16:22
22 [1]Or *waited for*
34:1 [+]Or *changed his behavior* [•]Possibly a title of King Achish of Gath, see 1 Sam 21:10-15 [a]Eph 5:20; 1 Thess 5:18 [b]Ps 71:6
2 [a]Ps 44:8; Jer 9:24; 1 Cor 1:31 [b]Ps 69:32
3 [a]Ps 35:27; Luke 1:46 [b]Ps 18:46
4 [a]2 Chr 15:2; Ps 9:10; Matt 7:7 [b]Ps 34:6
5 [a]Ps 36:9; Is 60:5 [b]Ps 25:3
6 [1]Or *afflicted* [a]Ps 34:4
7 [a]Ps 91:11; Dan 6:22
8 [a]Ps 119:103; Heb 6:5; 1 Pet 2:3 [b]Ps 2:12
9 [a]Ps 31:23 [b]Ps 23:1
10 [a]Ps 84:11
11 [a]Ps 66:16 [b]Ps 32:8 [c]Ps 111:10
12 [a]Ps 34:12-16; 1 Pet 3:10-12 [b]Eccl 3:13
13 [a]Ps 141:3; Prov 13:3; James 1:26 [b]1 Pet 2:22
14 [a]Ps 37:27; Is 1:16 [b]Rom 14:19; Heb 12:14
15 [a]Job 36:7; Ps 33:18
16 [a]Lev 17:10; Jer 44:11; Amos 9:4 [b]Job 18:17; Ps 9:6; Prov 10:7
17 [a]Ps 34:6
18 [1]Or *contrite* [a]Ps 145:18 [b]Ps 147:3; Is 61:1 [c]Ps 51:17; Is 57:15
19 [a]Prov 24:16 [b]Ps 71:20; 2 Tim 3:11f [c]Ps 34:4
20 [a]John 19:33
21 [a]Ps 94:23; Prov 24:16

And those who hate the
righteous will be
[1]condemned.
22 The LORD [a]redeems the soul of
His servants,
And none of those who [b]take
refuge in Him will be
[1]condemned.

Psalm 35

Prayer for Rescue from Enemies.

A Psalm of David.

1 ¶ Contend, O LORD, with those
who [a]contend with me;
Fight against those who [b]fight
against me.
2 Take hold of [1a]buckler and
shield
And rise up for [b]my help.
3 Draw also the spear and [1]the
battle-axe to meet those
who pursue me;
Say to my soul, "I am [a]your
salvation."
4 Let those be [a]ashamed and
dishonored who seek my
[1]life;
Let those be [b]turned back and
humiliated who devise evil
against me.
5 Let them be [a]like chaff before
the wind,
With the angel of the LORD
driving *them* on.
6 Let their way be dark and
[a]slippery,
With the angel of the LORD
pursuing them.
7 For [a]without cause they [b]hid
their net for me;
Without cause they dug a [1]pit
for my soul.
8 Let [a]destruction come upon him
unawares,
And [b]let the net which he hid
catch himself;
Into that very [c]destruction let
him fall.

9 ¶ And my soul shall [a]rejoice in
the LORD;
It shall [b]exult in His salvation.
10 All my [a]bones will say, "LORD,
[b]who is like You,
Who delivers the afflicted from
him [c]who is too strong for
him,
And [d]the afflicted and the needy
from him who robs him?"
11 [a]Malicious witnesses rise up;
They ask me of things that I do
not know.
12 They [a]repay me evil for good,
To the bereavement of my soul.
13 But as for me, [a]when they were
sick, my [b]clothing was
sackcloth;
I [c]humbled my soul with fasting,
And my [d]prayer kept returning
to my bosom.
14 I went about as though it were
my friend or brother;
I [a]bowed down [1]mourning, as
one who sorrows for a
mother.
15 But [a]at my [1]stumbling they
rejoiced and gathered
themselves together;
The [2b]smiters whom I did not
know gathered together
against me,
They [3c]slandered me without
ceasing.
16 Like godless jesters at a feast,
They [a]gnashed at me with their
teeth.

17 ¶ Lord, [a]how long will You
look on?
Rescue my soul [b]from their
ravages,
My [c]only *life* from the lions.
18 I will [a]give You thanks in the
great congregation;
I will [b]praise You among a
mighty throng.
19 [a]Do not let those who are
wrongfully [b]my enemies
rejoice over me;
Nor let those [c]who hate me
without cause [1d]wink
maliciously.
20 For they do not speak peace,
But they devise [a]deceitful words
against those who are quiet
in the land.
21 They [a]opened their mouth wide
against me;
They said, "[b]Aha, aha, our eyes
have seen it!"

22 ¶ [a]You have seen it, O LORD,
[b]do not keep silent;
O Lord, [c]do not be far from me.
23 [a]Stir up Yourself, and awake to
my right
And to my cause, my God and
my Lord.
24 [a]Judge me, O LORD my God,
according to Your
righteousness,
And [b]do not let them rejoice
over me.
25 Do not let them say in their
heart, "[a]Aha, our desire!"
Do not let them say, "We have
[b]swallowed him up!"

21 [1]Or *held guilty*
22 [1]V 21, note 1 [a]1 Kin 1:29; Ps 71:23 [b]Ps 37:40
35:1 [a]Ps 18:43; Is 49:25 [b]Ps 56:2
2 [1]I.e. small shield [a]Ps 91:4 [b]Ps 44:26
3 [1]Or *close up the path against those* [a]Ps 62:2
4 [1]Or *soul* [a]Ps 70:2 [b]Ps 40:14; 129:5
5 [a]Job 21:18; Ps 83:13; Is 29:5
6 [a]Ps 73:18; Jer 23:12
7 [1]*Pit* has been transposed from line above [a]Ps 69:4; 109:3; 140:5 [b]Ps 9:15
8 [a]Ps 55:23; Is 47:11; 1 Thess 5:3 [b]Ps 9:15 [c]Ps 73:18
9 [a]Is 61:10 [b]Ps 9:14; 13:5; Luke 1:47
10 [a]Ps 51:8 [b]Ex 15:11; Ps 86:8; Mic 7:18 [c]Ps 18:17 [d]Ps 37:14; 109:16
11 [a]Ps 27:12
12 [a]Ps 38:20; 109:5; Jer 18:20; John 10:32
13 [a]Job 30:25 [b]Ps 69:11 [c]Ps 69:10 [d]Matt 10:13; Luke 10:6
14 [1]Or *dressed in black* [a]Ps 38:6
15 [1]Or *limping* [2]Or *smitten ones* [3]Lit *tore* [a]Obad 12 [b]Job 30:1,8, 12 [c]Ps 7:2
16 [a]Job 16:9; Ps 37:12; Lam 2:16
17 [a]Ps 13:1; Hab 1:13 [b]Ps 35:7 [c]Ps 22:20, 21
18 [a]Ps 22:22 [b]Ps 22:25
19 [1]Or *wink the eye* [a]Ps 13:4; 30:1; 38:16 [b]Ps 38:19; 69:4 [c]John 15:25 [d]Prov 6:13; 10:10
20 [a]Ps 55:21; Jer 9:8; Mic 6:12
21 [a]Job 16:10; Ps 22:13 [b]Ps 40:15; 70:3
22 [a]Ex 3:7; Ps 10:14 [b]Ps 28:1 [c]Ps 10:1; 22:11; 38:21; 71:12
23 [a]Ps 7:6; 44:23; 59:4; 80:2
24 [a]Ps 9:4; 26:1; 43:1 [b]Ps 35:19
25 [a]Ps 35:21 [b]Ps 56:1; 124:3; Prov 1:12; Lam 2:16

26 Let [a]those be ashamed and
humiliated altogether who
rejoice at my distress;
Let those be [b]clothed with
shame and dishonor who
[c]magnify themselves
over me.
27 ¶ Let them [a]shout for joy and
rejoice, who favor [b]my
vindication;
And [c]let them say continually,
"The LORD be magnified,
Who [d]delights in the prosperity
of His servant."
28 And [a]my tongue shall declare
Your righteousness
And Your praise all day long.

Psalm 36

Wickedness of Men and Lovingkindness of God.

For the choir director. *A Psalm* of David the servant of the LORD.

1 ¶ Transgression speaks to the
ungodly within [1]his heart;
There is [a]no fear of God before
his eyes.
2 For [1]it [a]flatters him in his *own*
eyes
Concerning the discovery of his
iniquity *and* the hatred *of it.*
3 The [a]words of his mouth are
wickedness and deceit;
He has [b]ceased to [1]be wise *and*
to do good.
4 He [a]plans wickedness upon his
bed;
He sets himself on a [b]path that
is not good;
He [c]does not despise evil.
5 ¶ Your [a]lovingkindness, O LORD,
[1]extends to the heavens,
Your faithfulness *reaches* to the
skies.
6 Your [a]righteousness is like the
[1]mountains of God;
Your [b]judgments are *like* a great
deep.
O LORD, You [c]preserve man and
beast.
7 How [a]precious is Your
lovingkindness, O God!
And the children of men [b]take
refuge in the shadow of
Your wings.
8 They [a]drink their fill of the
[1]abundance of Your house;
And You give them to drink of
the [b]river of Your delights.
9 For with You is the [a]fountain of
life;
In Your light we see light.
10 ¶ O continue Your
lovingkindness to [a]those
who know You,
And Your [b]righteousness to the
upright in heart.
11 Let not the foot of pride come
upon me,
And let not the hand of the
wicked drive me away.
12 There the doers of iniquity have
fallen;
They have been thrust down and
[a]cannot rise.

Psalm 37

Security of Those Who Trust in the LORD, and Insecurity of the Wicked.

A Psalm of David.

1 ¶ [a]Do not fret because of
evildoers,
Be not [b]envious toward
wrongdoers.
2 For they will [a]wither quickly
like the grass
And [b]fade like the green herb.
3 [a]Trust in the LORD and do
good;
[b]Dwell in the land and
[1c]cultivate faithfulness.
4 [a]Delight yourself in the LORD;
And He will [b]give you the
desires of your heart.
5 [a]Commit your way to the LORD,
Trust also in Him, and He will
do it.
6 He will bring forth [a]your
righteousness as the light
And your judgment [b]as the
noonday.
7 ¶ [1]Rest in the LORD and [a]wait
[2]patiently for Him;
[b]Do not fret because of him
who [c]prospers in his way,
Because of the man who carries
out wicked schemes.
8 Cease from anger and [a]forsake
wrath;
Do not fret; *it leads* only to
evildoing.
9 For [a]evildoers will be cut off,
But those who wait for the LORD,
they will [b]inherit the land.
10 Yet [a]a little while and the
wicked man will be no
more;
And you will look carefully for
[b]his place and he will not
be *there.*
11 But [a]the humble will inherit the
land

26 [a]Ps 40:14 [b]Ps 109:29 [c]Job 19:5; Ps 38:16
27 [a]Ps 32:11 [b]Ps 9:4 [c]Ps 40:16; 70:4 [d]Ps 147:11; 149:4
28 [a]Ps 51:14; 71:15,24
36:1 [1]Another reading is *my heart* [a]Rom 3:18
2 [1]Or *he flatters himself* [a]Deut 29:19; Ps 10:11; 49:18
3 [1]Or *understand to do good* [a]Ps 10:7; 12:2 [b]Ps 94:8; Jer 4:22
4 [a]Prov 4:16; Mic 2:1 [b]Is 65:2 [c]Ps 52:3; Rom 12:9
5 [1]Lit *is in* [a]Ps 57:10; 103:11; 108:4
6 [1]Or *mighty mountains* [a]Ps 71:19 [b]Job 11:8; Ps 77:19; Rom 11:33 [c]Neh 9:6; Ps 104:14,15; 145:16
7 [a]Ps 40:5; 139:17 [b]Ruth 2:12; Ps 17:8; 57:1; 91:4
8 [1]Lit *fatness* [a]Ps 63:5; 65:4; Is 25:6; Jer 31:12-14 [b]Job 20:17; Ps 46:4; Rev 22:1
9 [a]Jer 2:13
10 [a]Jer 22:16 [b]Ps 24:5
12 [a]Ps 140:10; Is 26:14
37:1 [a]Prov 23:17; 24:19 [b]Ps 73:3; Prov 3:31
2 [a]Job 14:2; Ps 90:6; 92:7; James 1:11 [b]Ps 129:6
3 [1]Or *feed securely* or *feed on His faithfulness* [a]Ps 62:8 [b]Deut 30:20 [c]Is 40:11; Ezek 34:13,14
4 [a]Job 22:26; Ps 94:19; Is 58:14 [b]Ps 21:2; 145:19; Matt 7:7,8
5 [a]Ps 55:22; Prov 16:3; 1 Pet 5:7
6 [a]Ps 97:11; Is 58:8,10; Mic 7:9 [b]Job 11:17
7 [1]Or *Be still* [2]Or *longingly* [a]Ps 40:1; 62:5; Lam 3:26 [b]Ps 37:1,8 [c]Jer 12:1
8 [a]Eph 4:31; Col 3:8
9 [a]Ps 37:2,22 [b]Ps 25:13; Prov 2:21; Is 57:13; 60:21; Matt 5:5
10 [a]Job 24:24 [b]Job 7:10; Ps 37:35,36
11 [a]Matt 5:5

And will delight themselves in
[b]abundant prosperity.

12 ¶ The wicked [a]plots against the
righteous
And [b]gnashes at him with his
teeth.
13 The Lord [a]laughs at him,
For He sees [b]his day is coming.
14 The wicked have drawn the
sword and [a]bent their bow
To cast down the [b]afflicted and
the needy,
To [c]slay those who are upright
in conduct.
15 Their sword will enter their own
heart,
And their [a]bows will be broken.

16 ¶ [a]Better is the little of the
righteous
Than the abundance of many
wicked.
17 For the [a]arms of the wicked will
be broken,
But the LORD [b]sustains the
righteous.
18 The LORD [a]knows the days of
the [1]blameless,
And their [b]inheritance will be
forever.
19 They will not be ashamed in the
time of evil,
And [a]in the days of famine they
will have abundance.
20 But the [a]wicked will perish;
And the enemies of the LORD
will be like the [1]glory of the
pastures,
They vanish—[b]like smoke they
vanish away.
21 The wicked borrows and does
not pay back,
But the righteous [a]is gracious
and gives.
22 For [a]those blessed by Him will
[b]inherit the land,
But those [c]cursed by Him will
be cut off.

23 ¶ [a]The steps of a man are
established by the LORD,
And He [b]delights in his way.
24 When [a]he falls, he will not be
hurled headlong,
Because [b]the LORD is the One
[1]who holds his hand.
25 I have been young and now I am
old,
Yet [a]I have not seen the
righteous forsaken
Or [b]his [1]descendants begging
bread.
26 All day long [a]he is gracious and
lends,

11 [b]Ps 72:7
12 [a]Ps 31:13 [b]Ps 35:16
13 [a]Ps 2:4 [b]1 Sam 26:10; Job 18:20
14 [a]Ps 11:2; Lam 2:4 [b]Ps 35:10 [c]Ps 11:2
15 [a]1 Sam 2:4; Ps 46:9
16 [a]Prov 15:16
17 [a]Job 38:15; Ps 10:15; Ezek 30:21 [b]Ps 71:6
18 [1]Lit *complete; or perfect* [a]Ps 1:6 [b]Ps 37:27
19 [a]Job 5:20; Ps 33:19
20 [1]I.e. flowers [a]Ps 73:27 [b]Ps 68:2
21 [a]Ps 112:5
22 [a]Prov 3:33 [b]Ps 37:9 [c]Job 5:3
23 [a]1 Sam 2:9; Ps 40:2 [b]Ps 147:11
24 [1]Or *who sustains him with His hand* [a]Ps 145:14; Prov 24:16; Mic 7:8 [b]Ps 147:6
25 [1]Lit *seed* [a]Ps 37:28; Is 41:17; Heb 13:5 [b]Ps 109:10
26 [1]Lit *seed* [a]Deut 15:8; Ps 37:21 [b]Ps 147:13
27 [1]Or *And dwell forever* [a]Ps 34:14 [b]Ps 37:18
28 [1]Lit *judgment* [2]Lit *seed* [a]Ps 11:7 [b]Ps 37:25 [c]Ps 31:23 [d]Ps 21:10; Prov 2:22; Is 14:20
29 [a]Ps 37:9; Prov 2:21 [b]Ps 37:18
30 [a]Ps 49:3; Prov 10:13 [b]Ps 101:1
31 [a]Deut 6:6; Ps 40:8; Is 51:7; Jer 31:33 [b]Ps 26:1
32 [a]Ps 10:8 [b]Ps 37:14
33 [a]Ps 31:8; 2 Pet 2:9 [b]Ps 34:22
34 [a]Ps 27:14 [b]Ps 52:5
35 [1]Lit *native;* Heb obscure [a]Job 5:3; Jer 12:2 [b]Job 8:16
36 [1]Ancient versions read *I passed by* [a]Job 20:5; Ps 37:10
37 [1]Lit *complete; or perfect* [2]Lit *an end* [a]Ps 37:18 [b]Ps 7:10 [c]Is 57:1
38 [1]Lit *end* [a]Ps 1:4-6 [b]Ps 37:9
39 [a]Ps 3:8 [b]Ps 9:9
40 [a]Ps 54:4 [b]Ps 22:4; Is 31:5; Dan 3:17 [c]1 Chr 5:20; Ps 34:22

And [b]his [1]descendants are a
blessing.

27 ¶ [a]Depart from evil and do
good,
[1]So you will abide [b]forever.
28 For the LORD [a]loves [1]justice
And [b]does not forsake His godly
ones;
They are [c]preserved forever,
But the [2d]descendants of the
wicked will be cut off.
29 The righteous will [a]inherit the
land
And [b]dwell in it forever.
30 The mouth of the righteous
[a]utters wisdom,
And his tongue [b]speaks justice.
31 The [a]law of his God is in his
heart;
His [b]steps do not slip.
32 The [a]wicked spies upon the
righteous
And [b]seeks to kill him.
33 The LORD will [a]not leave him in
his hand
Or [b]let him be condemned
when he is judged.
34 [a]Wait for the LORD and keep His
way,
And He will exalt you to inherit
the land;
When the [b]wicked are cut off,
you will see it.

35 ¶ I have [a]seen a wicked,
violent man
Spreading himself like a
[b]luxuriant [1]tree in its
native soil.
36 Then [1]he passed away, and lo,
he [a]was no more;
I sought for him, but he could
not be found.
37 Mark the [1a]blameless man, and
behold the [b]upright;
For the man of peace will have a
[2c]posterity.
38 But transgressors will be
altogether [a]destroyed;
The [1]posterity of the wicked
will be [b]cut off.
39 But the [a]salvation of the
righteous is from the LORD;
He is their strength [b]in time of
trouble.
40 [a]The LORD helps them and
delivers them;
He [b]delivers them from the
wicked and saves them,
Because they [c]take refuge in
Him.

Psalm 38

Prayer of a Suffering Penitent.

A Psalm of David, for a memorial.

1 ¶ O LORD, [a]rebuke me not in
Your wrath,
And chasten me not in Your
burning anger.
2 For Your [a]arrows have sunk
deep into me,
And [b]Your hand has pressed
down on me.
3 There is [a]no soundness in my
flesh [b]because of Your
indignation;
There is no health [c]in my bones
because of my sin.
4 For my [a]iniquities are gone over
my head;
As a heavy burden they weigh
too much for me.
5 My [1]wounds grow foul *and*
fester
Because of [a]my folly.
6 I am bent over and [a]greatly
bowed down;
I [b]go mourning all day long.
7 For my loins are filled with
[a]burning,
And there is [b]no soundness in
my flesh.
8 I am [a]benumbed and [1]badly
crushed;
I [2b]groan because of the
[3]agitation of my heart.

9 ¶ Lord, all [a]my desire is
[1]before You;
And my [b]sighing is not hidden
from You.
10 My heart throbs, [a]my strength
fails me;
And the [b]light of my eyes, even
[1]that [2]has gone from me.
11 My [1a]loved ones and my friends
stand aloof from my plague;
And my kinsmen [b]stand afar off.
12 Those who [a]seek my life [b]lay
snares *for me;*
And those who [c]seek to injure
me have [1]threatened
destruction,
And they [d]devise treachery all
day long.

13 ¶ But I, like a deaf man, do not
hear;
And *I am* like a [a]mute man who
does not open his mouth.
14 Yes, I am like a man who does
not hear,
And in whose mouth are no
arguments.
15 For [a]I [1]hope in You, O LORD;
You [b]will answer, O Lord my
God.
16 For I said, "May they not rejoice
over me,
Who, when my foot slips,
[a]would magnify themselves
against me."
17 For I am [a]ready to fall,
And [b]my [1]sorrow is continually
before me.
18 For I [1a]confess my iniquity;
I am full of [b]anxiety because of
my sin.
19 But my [a]enemies are vigorous
and [1]strong,
And many are those who [b]hate
me wrongfully.
20 And those who [a]repay evil for
good,
They [b]oppose me, because I
follow what is good.
21 Do not forsake me, O LORD;
O my God, [a]do not be far
from me!
22 Make [a]haste to help me,
O Lord, [b]my salvation!

Psalm 39

The Vanity of Life.

For the choir director, for +Jeduthun.
A Psalm of David.

1 ¶ I said, "I will [a]guard my ways
That I [b]may not sin with my
tongue;
I will guard [c]my mouth as with
a muzzle
While the wicked are in my
presence."
2 I was [a]mute [1]and silent,
I [2]refrained *even* from good,
And my [3]sorrow grew worse.
3 My [a]heart was hot within me,
While I was musing the fire
burned;
Then I spoke with my tongue:
4 "LORD, make me to know
[a]my end
And what is the extent of my
days;
Let me know how [b]transient
I am.
5 "Behold, You have made [a]my
days *as* handbreadths,
And my [b]lifetime as nothing in
Your sight;
Surely every man [1]at his best is
[2]a mere [c]breath. [3]Selah.
6 "Surely every man [a]walks about
as [1]a phantom;
Surely they make an [b]uproar for
nothing;
He [c]amasses *riches* and does not
know who will gather them.

38:1 [a]Ps 6:1
2 [a]Job 6:4 [b]Ps 32:4
3 [a]Is 1:6 [b]Ps 102:10 [c]Job 33:19; Ps 6:2; 31:10
4 [a]Ezra 9:6; Ps 40:12
5 [1]Or *stripes* [a]Ps 69:5
6 [a]Ps 35:14 [b]Job 30:28; Ps 42:9; 43:2
7 [a]Ps 102:3 [b]Ps 38:3
8 [1]Or *greatly* [2]Lit *roar* [3]Lit *growling* [a]Lam 1:13,20f; 2:11; 5:17 [b]Job 3:24; Ps 22:1; 32:3
9 [1]Or known *to You* [a]Ps 10:17 [b]Ps 6:6; 102:5
10 [1]Lit *they have* [2]Lit *is not with me* [a]Ps 31:10 [b]Ps 6:7; 69:3; 88:9
11 [1]Or *lovers* [a]Ps 31:11; 88:18 [b]Luke 23:49
12 [1]Lit *spoken* [a]Ps 54:3 [b]Ps 140:5 [c]Ps 35:4 [d]Ps 35:20
13 [a]Ps 39:2,9
15 [1]Or *wait for* [a]Ps 39:7 [b]Ps 17:6
16 [a]Ps 35:26
17 [1]Lit *pain* [a]Ps 35:15 [b]Ps 13:2
18 [1]Or *declare* [a]Ps 32:5 [b]2 Cor 7:9,10
19 [1]Or *numerous* [a]Ps 18:17 [b]Ps 35:19
20 [a]Ps 35:12 [b]Ps 109:5; 1 John 3:12
21 [a]Ps 22:19; 35:22
22 [a]Ps 40:13,17 [b]Ps 27:1
39:1 +1 Chr 16:41 [a]1 Kin 2:4; 2 Kin 10:31; Ps 119:9 [b]Job 2:10; Ps 34:13; James 3:5-12 [c]Ps 141:3; James 3:2
2 [1]Lit *with silence* [2]Lit *kept silence* [3]Lit *pain* [a]Ps 38:13
3 [a]Ps 32:4; Jer 20:9; Luke 24:32
4 [a]Job 6:11; Ps 90:12; 119:84 [b]Ps 78:39; 103:14
5 [1]Lit *standing firm* [2]Or *altogether vanity* [3]*Selah* may mean: *Pause, Crescendo* or *Musical interlude* [a]Ps 89:47 [b]Ps 144:4 [c]Job 14:2; Ps 62:9; Eccl 6:12
6 [1]Lit *an image* [a]1 Cor 7:31; James 1:10,11; 1 Pet 1:24 [b]Ps 127:2; Eccl 5:17 [c]Ps 49:10; Eccl 2:26; 5:14; Luke 12:20

7 ¶ "And now, Lord, for what do I
wait?
My [a]hope is in You.
8 "[a]Deliver me from all my
transgressions;
Make me not the [b]reproach of
the foolish.
9 "I have become [a]mute, I do not
open my mouth,
Because it is [b]You who have
done *it.*
10 "[a]Remove Your plague from me;
Because of [b]the opposition of
Your hand I am [1]perishing.
11 "With [a]reproofs You chasten a
man for iniquity;
You [b]consume as a moth what is
precious to him;
Surely [c]every man is a mere
breath. Selah.
12 ¶ "[a]Hear my prayer, O LORD,
and give ear to my cry;
Do not be silent [b]at my tears;
For I am [c]a stranger with You,
A [d]sojourner like all my fathers.
13 "[a]Turn Your gaze away from me,
that I may [1]smile *again*
Before I depart and am no
more."

Psalm 40

God Sustains His Servant.

For the choir director. A Psalm of David.

1 ¶ I [a]waited [1]patiently for the
LORD;
And He inclined to me and
[b]heard my cry.
2 He brought me up out of the
[a]pit of destruction, out of
the [1]miry clay,
And [b]He set my feet upon a
rock [c]making my footsteps
firm.
3 He put a [a]new song in my
mouth, a song of praise to
our God;
Many will [b]see and fear
And will trust in the LORD.
4 ¶ How [a]blessed is the man who
has made the LORD his trust,
And [b]has not [1]turned to the
proud, nor to those who
[c]lapse into falsehood.
5 Many, O LORD my God, are [a]the
wonders which You have
done,
And Your [b]thoughts toward us;
There is none to compare
with You.
If I would declare and speak of
them,
They [c]would be too numerous
to count.
6 ¶ [1a]Sacrifice and meal offering
You have not desired;
My ears You have [2]opened;
Burnt offering and sin offering
You have not required.
7 Then I said, "Behold, I come;
In the scroll of the book it is
[1]written of me.
8 [a]I delight to do Your will, O my
God;
[b]Your Law is within my heart."
9 ¶ I have [a]proclaimed glad tidings
of righteousness in the great
congregation;
Behold, I will [b]not restrain my
lips,
O LORD, [c]You know.
10 I have [a]not hidden Your
righteousness within my
heart;
I have [b]spoken of Your
faithfulness and Your
salvation;
I have not concealed Your
lovingkindness and Your
truth from the great
congregation.
11 ¶ You, O LORD, will not withhold
Your compassion from me;
[1]Your [a]lovingkindness and Your
truth will continually
preserve me.
12 For evils beyond number have
[a]surrounded me;
My [b]iniquities have overtaken
me, so that I am not able to
see;
They are [c]more numerous than
the hairs of my head,
And my [d]heart has [1]failed me.
13 ¶ [a]Be pleased, O LORD, to
deliver me;
Make [b]haste, O LORD, to
help me.
14 Let those be [a]ashamed and
humiliated together
Who [b]seek my [1]life to
destroy it;
Let those be turned back and
dishonored
Who delight [2]in my hurt.
15 Let those [a]be [1]appalled because
of their shame
Who [b]say to me, "Aha, aha!"
16 [a]Let all who seek You rejoice
and be glad in You;
Let those who love Your
salvation [b]say continually,
"The LORD be magnified!"
17 Since [a]I am afflicted and needy,

7 [a]Ps 38:15
8 [a]Ps 51:9,14; 79:9 [b]Ps 44:13; 79:4; 119:22
9 [a]Ps 39:2 [b]2 Sam 16:10; Job 2:10
10 [1]Or *wasting away* [a]Job 9:34; 13:21 [b]Ps 32:4
11 [a]Ezek 5:15; 2 Pet 2:16 [b]Job 13:28; Ps 90:7; Is 50:9 [c]Ps 39:5
12 [a]Ps 102:1; 143:1 [b]2 Kin 20:5; Ps 56:8 [c]Lev 25:23; 1 Chr 29:15; Ps 119:19; Heb 11:13; 1 Pet 2:11 [d]Gen 47:9
13 [1]Or *become cheerful* [a]Job 7:19; 10:20,21; 14:6; Ps 102:24
40:1 [1]Or *intently* [a]Ps 25:5; 27:14; 37:7 [b]Ps 34:15
2 [1]Lit *mud of the mire* [a]Ps 69:2,14; Jer 38:6 [b]Ps 27:5 [c]Ps 37:23
3 [a]Ps 32:7; 33:3 [b]Ps 52:6; 64:9
4 [1]Lit *regard* [a]Ps 34:8; 84:12 [b]Job 37:24 [c]Ps 125:5
5 [a]Job 5:9; Ps 136:4 [b]Ps 139:17; Is 55:8 [c]Ps 71:15; 139:18
6 [1]I.e. Blood sacrifice [2]Lit *dug;* or possibly *pierced* [a]1 Sam 15:22; Ps 51:16; Is 1:11; Jer 6:20; 7:22,23; Amos 5:22; Mic 6:6-8; Heb 10:5-7
7 [1]Or *prescribed for*
8 [a]John 4:34 [b]Ps 37:31; Jer 31:33; 2 Cor 3:3
9 [a]Ps 22:22,25 [b]Ps 119:13 [c]Josh 22:22; Ps 139:4
10 [a]Acts 20:20, 27 [b]Ps 89:1
11 [1]Or *May...preserve* [a]Ps 43:3; 57:3; 61:7; Prov 20:28
12 [1]Lit *forsaken* [a]Ps 18:5; 116:3 [b]Ps 38:4; 65:3 [c]Ps 69:4 [d]Ps 73:26
13 [a]Ps 70:1 [b]Ps 22:19; 71:12
14 [1]Or *soul* [2]Or *to injure me* [a]Ps 35:4,26; 70:2; 71:13 [b]Ps 63:9
15 [1]Or *desolated* [a]Ps 70:3 [b]Ps 35:21; 70:3
16 [a]Ps 70:4 [b]Ps 35:27
17 [a]Ps 70:5; 86:1; 109:22

[1][b]Let the Lord be mindful
of me.
You are my help and my
deliverer;
Do not delay, O my God.

Psalm 41

The Psalmist in Sickness Complains of Enemies and False Friends.

For the choir director. A Psalm of David.

1 ¶ How blessed is he who
[a]considers the [1]helpless;
The LORD will deliver him [b]in a
day of [2]trouble.
2 The LORD will [a]protect him and
keep him alive,
And he shall [1]be called [b]blessed
upon the earth;
And [c]do not give him over to
the desire of his enemies.
3 The LORD will sustain him upon
his sickbed;
In his illness, You [1]restore him
to health.

4 ¶ As for me, I said, "O LORD, be
gracious to me;
[a]Heal my soul, for [b]I have
sinned against You."
5 My enemies [a]speak evil
against me,
"When will he die, and his name
perish?"
6 And [1]when he comes to see *me,*
he [a]speaks [2]falsehood;
His heart gathers wickedness to
itself;
When he goes outside, he
tells it.
7 All who hate me whisper
together against me;
Against me they [a]devise my
hurt, *saying,*
8 "A wicked thing is poured out
[1]upon him,
That when he lies down, he will
[a]not rise up again."
9 Even my [a]close friend in whom
I trusted,
Who ate my bread,
Has lifted up his heel against me.

10 ¶ But You, O LORD, be gracious
to me and [a]raise me up,
That I may repay them.
11 By this I know that [a]You are
pleased with me,
Because [b]my enemy does not
shout in triumph over me.
12 As for me, [a]You uphold me in
my integrity,
And You set me [b]in Your
presence forever.

13 ¶ [a]Blessed be the LORD, the God
of Israel,
From everlasting to everlasting.
Amen and Amen.

BOOK 2

Psalm 42

Thirsting for God in Trouble and Exile.

For the choir director. A +Maskil
of the sons of Korah.

1 ¶ As the deer [1]pants for the
water brooks,
So my soul [1a]pants for You,
O God.
2 My soul [a]thirsts for God, for the
[b]living God;
When shall I come and
[1c]appear before God?
3 My [a]tears have been my food
day and night,
While *they* [b]say to me all day
long, "Where is your God?"
4 These things I remember and I
[a]pour out my soul
within me.
For I [b]used to go along with the
throng *and* [1]lead them in
procession to the house of
God,
With the voice of [c]joy and
thanksgiving, a multitude
keeping festival.

5 ¶ [a]Why are you [1b]in despair,
O my soul?
And *why* have you become
[c]disturbed within me?
[2d]Hope in God, for I shall
[3]again praise [4]Him
For the [5e]help of His presence.
6 O my God, my soul is [1]in
despair within me;
Therefore I [a]remember You
from [b]the land of the Jordan
And the [2]peaks of [c]Hermon,
from Mount Mizar.
7 Deep calls to deep at the sound
of Your waterfalls;
All Your [a]breakers and Your
waves have rolled over me.
8 The LORD will [a]command His
lovingkindness in the
daytime;
And His song will be with me
[b]in the night,
A prayer to [c]the God of my life.

9 ¶ I will say to God [a]my rock,
"Why have You
forgotten me?

17 [1]Or *The Lord is mindful* [b]Ps 40:5; 1 Pet 5:7
41:1 [1]Or *poor* [2]Or *evil* [a]Ps 82:3,4; Prov 14:21 [b]Ps 27:5; 37:19
2 [1]Or *be blessed* [a]Ps 37:28 [b]Ps 37:22 [c]Ps 27:12
3 [1]Lit *turn all his bed*
4 [a]Ps 6:2; 103:3; 147:3 [b]Ps 51:4
5 [a]Ps 38:12
6 [1]Or *if he* [2]Or *emptiness* [a]Ps 12:2; 62:4; Prov 26:24-26
7 [a]Ps 56:5
8 [1]Or *within* [a]Ps 71:10,11
9 [a]2 Sam 15:12; Job 19:13,19; Ps 55:12,13,20; Jer 20:10; Mic 7:5; Matt 26:23; Luke 22:21; John 13:18
10 [a]Ps 3:3
11 [a]Ps 37:23; 147:11 [b]Ps 25:2
12 [a]Ps 18:32; 37:17; 63:8 [b]Job 36:7; Ps 21:6
13 [a]Ps 72:18, 19; 89:52; 106:48; 150:6
42:1 +Possibly *Contemplative,* or *Didactic,* or *Skillful Psalm* [1]Lit *longs for* [a]Ps 119:131
2 [1]Some mss read *see the face of God* [a]Ps 63:1; 84:2; 143:6 [b]Josh 3:10; Ps 84:2; Jer 10:10; Dan 6:26; Matt 26:63; Rom 9:26; 1 Thess 1:9 [c]Ex 23:17; Ps 43:4; 84:7
3 [a]Ps 80:5; 102:9 [b]Ps 79:10; 115:2; Joel 2:17; Mic 7:10
4 [1]Or *move slowly with them* [a]1 Sam 1:15; Job 30:16; Ps 62:8; Lam 2:19 [b]Ps 55:14; 122:1; Is 30:29 [c]Ps 100:4
5 [1]Or *sunk down* [2]Or *Wait for* [3]Or *still* [4]Some ancient versions read *Him, the help of my countenance and my God* [5]Or *saving acts of* [a]Ps 42:11; 43:5 [b]Ps 38:6; Matt 26:38 [c]Ps 77:3 [d]Ps 71:14; Lam 3:24 [e]Ps 44:3
6 [1]Or *sunk down* [2]Lit *Hermons* [a]Ps 61:2 [b]2 Sam 17:22 [c]Deut 3:8
7 [a]Ps 69:1,2; 88:7; Jon 2:3
8 [a]Ps 57:3; 133:3 [b]Job 35:10; Ps 16:7; 63:6; 77:6; 149:5 [c]Eccl 5:18; 8:15
9 [a]Ps 18:2

Why do I go [b]mourning
[1]because of the [c]oppression of the enemy?"
10 As a shattering of my bones, my adversaries revile me,
While they [a]say to me all day long, "Where is your God?"
11 [a]Why are you [1]in despair, O my soul?
And why have you become disturbed within me?
[2]Hope in God, for I shall yet praise Him,
The [3]help of my countenance and my God.

Psalm 43

Prayer for Deliverance.

1 ¶ [a]Vindicate me, O God, and [b]plead my case against an ungodly nation;
[1]O deliver me from [c]the deceitful and unjust man!
2 For You are the [a]God of my strength; why have You [b]rejected me?
Why do I go [c]mourning
[1]because of the oppression of the enemy?

3 ¶ O send out Your [a]light and Your truth, let them lead me;
Let them bring me to Your [b]holy hill
And to Your [c]dwelling places.
4 Then I will go to [a]the altar of God,
To God [1]my exceeding [b]joy;
And upon the [c]lyre I shall praise You, O God, my God.

5 ¶ [a]Why are you [1]in despair, O my soul?
And why are you disturbed within me?
[2]Hope in God, for I shall [3]again praise Him,
The [4]help of my countenance and my God.

Psalm 44

Former Deliverances and Present Troubles.

For the choir director. A [+]Maskil of the sons of Korah.

1 ¶ O God, we have heard with our ears,
Our [a]fathers have told us
The [b]work that You did in their days,
In the [c]days of old.

2 You with Your own hand [a]drove out the nations;
Then You [b]planted them;
You [c]afflicted the peoples,
Then You [d]spread them abroad.
3 For by their own sword they [a]did not possess the land,
And their own arm did not save them,
But Your right hand and Your [b]arm and the [c]light of Your presence,
For You [d]favored them.

4 ¶ You are [a]my King, O God;
[b]Command [1]victories for Jacob.
5 Through You we will [a]push back our adversaries;
Through Your name we will [b]trample down those who rise up against us.
6 For I will [a]not trust in my bow,
Nor will my sword save me.
7 But You [a]have saved us from our adversaries,
And You have [b]put to shame those who hate us.
8 In God we have [a]boasted all day long,
And we will [b]give thanks to Your name forever. [1]Selah.

9 ¶ Yet You [a]have rejected *us* and brought us to [b]dishonor,
And [c]do not go out with our armies.
10 You cause us to [a]turn back from the adversary;
And those who hate us [b]have taken spoil for themselves.
11 You give us as [a]sheep [1]to be eaten
And have [b]scattered us among the nations.
12 You [a]sell Your people [1]cheaply,
And have not [2]profited by their sale.
13 You make us a [a]reproach to our neighbors,
A scoffing and a [b]derision to those around us.
14 You make us [a]a byword among the nations,
A [1b]laughingstock among the peoples.
15 All day long my dishonor is before me
And [1]my [a]humiliation has overwhelmed me,
16 Because of the voice of him who [a]reproaches and reviles,

9 [1]Or *while the enemy oppresses* [b]Ps 38:6 [c]Ps 17:9
10 [a]Ps 42:3; Joel 2:17
11 [1]Or *sunk down* [2]Or *Wait for* [3]Or *saving acts of* [a]Ps 42:5
43:1 [1]Or *May You* [a]Ps 26:1 [b]1 Sam 24:15; Ps 35:1 [c]Ps 5:6
2 [1]Or *while the enemy oppresses* [a]Ps 18:1 [b]Ps 44:9 [c]Ps 42:9
3 [a]Ps 36:9 [b]Ps 2:6 [c]Ps 84:1
4 [1]Lit *the gladness of my joy* [a]Ps 26:6 [b]Ps 21:6 [c]Ps 33:2
5 [1]Or *sunk down* [2]Or *Wait for* [3]Or *still* [4]Or *saving acts of* [a]Ps 42:5
44:1 [+]Possibly *Contemplative,* or *Didactic,* or *Skillful Psalm* [a]Ex 12:26; Deut 6:20; Judg 6:13; Ps 78:3 [b]Ps 78:12 [c]Deut 32:7; Ps 77:5; Is 51:9
2 [a]Josh 3:10; Neh 9:24; Ps 78:55 [b]Ex 15:17; 2 Sam 7:10; Jer 24:6; Amos 9:15 [c]Ps 135:10-12 [d]Ps 80:9-11; Zech 2:6
3 [a]Deut 8:17; Josh 24:12 [b]Ps 77:15 [c]Ps 4:6 [d]Deut 4:37; Ps 106:4
4 [1]Lit *salvation* [a]Ps 74:12 [b]Ps 42:8
5 [a]Deut 33:17; Ps 60:12; Dan 8:4 [b]Ps 108:13; Zech 10:5
6 [a]1 Sam 17:47; Ps 33:16; Hos 1:7
7 [a]Ps 136:24 [b]Ps 53:5
8 [1]*Selah* may mean: *Pause, Crescendo* or *Musical interlude* [a]Ps 34:2 [b]Ps 30:12
9 [a]Ps 43:2 [b]Ps 69:19 [c]Ps 60:10
10 [a]Lev 26:17; Josh 7:8; Ps 89:43 [b]Ps 89:41
11 [1]Lit *for food* [a]Ps 44:22; Rom 8:36 [b]Lev 26:33; Deut 4:27; Ps 106:27; Ezek 20:23
12 [1]Lit *for no wealth* [2]Or *set a high price on them* [a]Deut 32:30; Judg 2:14; Is 52:3; Jer 15:13
13 [a]Deut 28:37; Ps 79:4 [b]Ps 80:6; Ezek 23:32
14 [1]Lit *shaking of the head* [a]Job 17:6; Ps 69:11; Jer 24:9 [b]2 Kin 19:21; Ps 109:25
15 [1]Lit *the shame of my face has covered me* [a]2 Chr 32:21; Ps 69:7
16 [a]Ps 74:10

Because of the presence of the
[b]enemy and the avenger.
17 ¶ All this has come upon us, but
we have [a]not forgotten You,
And we have not [b]dealt falsely
with Your covenant.
18 Our heart has not [a]turned
back,
And our steps [b]have not
deviated from Your way,
19 Yet You have [a]crushed us in a
place of [b]jackals
And covered us with [c]the
shadow of death.
20 ¶ If we had [a]forgotten the name
of our God
Or extended our [1]hands to [b]a
strange god,
21 Would not God [a]find this out?
For He knows the secrets of the
heart.
22 But [a]for Your sake we are killed
all day long;
We are considered as [b]sheep to
be slaughtered.
23 [a]Arouse Yourself, why [b]do You
sleep, O Lord?
Awake, [c]do not reject us
forever.
24 Why do You [a]hide Your face
And [b]forget our affliction and
our oppression?
25 For our [a]soul has sunk down
into the dust;
Our body cleaves to the earth.
26 [a]Rise up, be our help,
And [b]redeem us for the sake of
Your lovingkindness.

Psalm 45

A Song Celebrating the King's Marriage.

For the choir director; according to the +Shoshannim. A •Maskil of the sons of Korah. A Song of Love.

1 ¶ My heart [1]overflows with a
good theme;
I [2]address my [3]verses to the
[4]King;
My tongue is the pen of [a]a
ready writer.
2 You are fairer than the sons of
men;
[a]Grace is poured [1]upon Your
lips;
Therefore God has [b]blessed You
forever.
3 ¶ Gird [a]Your sword on *Your*
thigh, O [1b]Mighty One,
In Your splendor and Your
majesty!
4 And in Your majesty ride on
victoriously,
For the cause of truth and
[a]meekness *and*
righteousness;
Let Your [b]right hand teach You
[1]awesome things.
5 Your [a]arrows are sharp;
The [b]peoples fall under You;
Your arrows are [c]in the heart of
the King's enemies.
6 ¶ [a]Your throne, O God, is
forever and ever;
A scepter of [b]uprightness is the
scepter of Your kingdom.
7 You have [a]loved righteousness
and hated wickedness;
Therefore God, Your God, has
[b]anointed You
With the oil of joy above Your
fellows.
8 All Your garments are *fragrant
with* [a]myrrh and aloes *and*
cassia;
Out of ivory palaces [b]stringed
instruments have made You
glad.
9 Kings' daughters are among
[a]Your noble ladies;
At Your [b]right hand stands the
queen in [c]gold from Ophir.
10 ¶ Listen, O daughter, give
attention and incline
your ear:
[a]Forget your people and your
father's house;
11 Then the King will desire your
beauty.
Because He is your [a]Lord, [b]bow
down to Him.
12 The daughter of [a]Tyre *will come*
with a gift;
The [b]rich among the people will
seek your favor.
13 ¶ The King's daughter is all
glorious within;
Her clothing is [a]interwoven
with gold.
14 She will be [a]led to the King [b]in
embroidered work;
The [c]virgins, her companions
who follow her,
Will be brought to You.
15 They will be led forth with
gladness and rejoicing;
They will enter into the King's
palace.
16 ¶ In place of your fathers will be
your sons;
You shall make them princes in
all the earth.

16 [b]Ps 8:2

17 [a]Ps 78:7; 119:61,83,109, 141,153,176 [b]Ps 78:57

18 [a]Ps 78:57 [b]Job 23:11; Ps 119:51,157

19 [a]Ps 51:8; 94:5 [b]Job 30:29; Is 13:22; Jer 9:11 [c]Job 3:5; Ps 23:4

20 [1]Lit *palms* [a]Ps 78:11 [b]Deut 6:14; Ps 81:9

21 [a]Ps 139:1,2; Jer 17:10

22 [a]Rom 8:36 [b]Is 53:7; Jer 12:3

23 [a]Ps 7:6 [b]Ps 78:65 [c]Ps 77:7

24 [a]Job 13:24; Ps 88:14 [b]Ps 42:9; Lam 5:20

25 [a]Ps 119:25

26 [a]Ps 35:2 [b]Ps 6:4; 25:22

45:1 +Or possibly *Lilies* •Possibly *Contemplative*, or *Didactic*, or *Skillful Psalm* [1]Lit *is astir* [2]Lit *am saying* [3]Lit *works* [4]Probably refers to Solomon as a type of Christ [a]Ezra 7:6

2 [1]Or *through* [a]Luke 4:22 [b]Ps 21:6

3 [1]Or *warrior* [a]Heb 4:12; Rev 1:16 [b]Is 9:6

4 [1]Or *fearful* [a]Zeph 2:3 [b]Ps 21:8

5 [a]Ps 18:14; 120:4; Is 5:28; 7:13 [b]Ps 92:9 [c]2 Sam 18:14

6 [a]Ps 93:2; Heb 1:8,9 [b]Ps 98:9

7 [a]Ps 11:7; 33:5 [b]Ps 2:2

8 [a]Song 4:14; John 19:39 [b]Ps 150:4

9 [a]Song 6:8 [b]1 Kin 2:19 [c]1 Kin 9:28; Is 13:12

10 [a]Deut 21:13; Ruth 1:16,17

11 [a]Gen 18:12; 1 Pet 3:6 [b]Eph 5:33

12 [a]Ps 87:4 [b]Ps 22:29; 68:29; 72:10,11; Is 49:23

13 [a]Ex 39:2,3

14 [a]Song 1:4 [b]Judg 5:30; Ezek 16:10 [c]Ps 45:9

17 I will cause [a]Your name to be
remembered in all
generations;
Therefore the peoples [b]will give
You thanks forever and ever.

Psalm 46

God the Refuge of His People.

For the choir director. *A Psalm* of the sons of Korah, +set to Alamoth. A Song.

1 ¶ God is our [a]refuge and
strength,
[1]A very [b]present help [c]in
[2]trouble.
2 Therefore we will [a]not fear,
though [b]the earth should
change
And though [c]the mountains slip
into the heart of the [1]sea;
3 Though its [a]waters roar *and*
foam,
Though the mountains quake at
its swelling pride. [1]Selah.

4 ¶ There is a [a]river whose
streams make glad the [b]city
of God,
The holy [c]dwelling places of the
Most High.
5 God is [a]in the midst of her, she
will not be moved;
God will [b]help her [1]when
morning dawns.
6 The [1]nations [a]made an uproar,
the kingdoms tottered;
He [2b]raised His voice, the earth
[c]melted.
7 The LORD of hosts [a]is with
us;
The God of Jacob is [b]our
stronghold. Selah.

8 ¶ Come, [a]behold the works of
the LORD,
[1]Who has wrought [b]desolations
in the earth.
9 He [a]makes wars to cease to the
end of the earth;
He [b]breaks the bow and cuts
the spear in two;
He [c]burns the chariots with fire.
10 "[1]Cease *striving* and [a]know that
I am God;
I will be [b]exalted among the
[2]nations, I will be exalted
in the earth."
11 The LORD of hosts is with
us;
The God of Jacob is our
stronghold. Selah.

17 [a]Mal 1:11 [b]Ps 138:4
46:1 +Possibly *for soprano voices* [1]Or *Abundantly available for help* [2]Or *tight places* [a]Ps 14:6 [b]Deut 4:7; Ps 145:18 [c]Ps 9:9
2 [1]Lit *seas* [a]Ps 23:4 [b]Ps 82:5 [c]Ps 18:7
3 [1]*Selah* may mean: *Pause, Crescendo* or *Musical interlude* [a]Ps 93:3; Jer 5:22
4 [a]Ps 36:8; Is 8:6; Rev 22:1 [b]Ps 48:1; Is 60:14; Rev 3:12 [c]Ps 43:3
5 [1]Lit *at the turning of the morning* [a]Deut 23:14; Is 12:6; Ezek 43:7; Hos 11:9; Joel 2:27; Zech 2:5 [b]Ps 37:40; Is 41:14; Luke 1:54
6 [1]Or *Gentiles* [2]Lit *gave forth* [a]Ps 2:1 [b]Ps 18:13; Jer 25:30; Joel 2:11; Amos 1:2 [c]Amos 9:5; Mic 1:4; Nah 1:5
7 [a]Num 14:9; 2 Chr 13:12 [b]Ps 9:9
8 [1]Or *Which He has wrought as desolations* [a]Ps 66:5 [b]Is 61:4; Jer 51:43
9 [a]Is 2:4; Mic 4:3 [b]1 Sam 2:4; Ps 76:3 [c]Is 9:5; Ezek 39:9
10 [1]Or *Let go, relax* [2]Or *Gentiles* [a]Ps 100:3 [b]Is 2:11
47:1 [1]Or *a ringing cry* [a]Ps 98:8 [b]Ps 106:47
2 [a]Deut 7:21; Neh 1:5; Ps 66:3 [b]Mal 1:14
3 [a]Ps 18:47
4 [1]*Selah* may mean: *Pause, Crescendo* or *Musical interlude* [a]1 Pet 1:4 [b]Amos 6:8; Nah 2:2
5 [1]Or *amid* [a]Ps 68:18 [b]Ps 98:6
6 [a]Ps 68:4 [b]Ps 89:18
7 [1]Heb *Maskil* [a]Zech 14:9 [b]1 Cor 14:15
8 [1]Or *has taken His seat* [a]1 Chr 16:31; Ps 22:28 [b]Ps 97:2
9 [1]Or *nobles* [2]Lit *has greatly exalted Himself* [a]Ps 72:11; Is 49:7 [b]Rom 4:11 [c]Ps 89:18 [d]Ps 97:9
48:1 [a]1 Chr 16:25; Ps 96:4 [b]Ps 46:4 [c]Ps 2:6; Is 2:3; Mic 4:1; Zech 8:3
2 [a]Ps 50:2 [b]Lam 2:15 [c]Matt 5:35
3 [a]Ps 46:7
4 [a]2 Sam 10:6-19

Psalm 47

God the King of the Earth.

For the choir director.
A Psalm of the sons of Korah.

1 ¶ O [a]clap your hands, all
peoples;
[b]Shout to God with the voice
of [1]joy.
2 For the LORD Most High is to be
[a]feared,
A [b]great King over all the earth.
3 He [a]subdues peoples under us
And nations under our feet.
4 He chooses our [a]inheritance
for us,
The [b]glory of Jacob whom He
loves. [1]Selah.

5 ¶ God has [a]ascended [1]with a
shout,
The LORD, [1]with the [b]sound of
a trumpet.
6 [a]Sing praises to God, sing
praises;
Sing praises to [b]our King, sing
praises.
7 For God is the [a]King of all the
earth;
Sing praises [b]with a [1]skillful
psalm.
8 God [a]reigns over the nations,
God [1]sits on [b]His holy throne.
9 The [1a]princes of the people
have assembled themselves
as the [b]people of the God of
Abraham,
For the [c]shields of the earth
belong to God;
He [2]is [d]highly exalted.

Psalm 48

The Beauty and Glory of Zion.

A Song; a Psalm of the sons of Korah.

1 ¶ [a]Great is the LORD, and greatly
to be praised,
In the [b]city of our God, His
[c]holy mountain.
2 [a]Beautiful in elevation, [b]the joy
of the whole earth,
Is Mount Zion *in* the far north,
The [c]city of the great King.
3 God, in her palaces,
Has made Himself known as a
[a]stronghold.

4 ¶ For, lo, the [a]kings assembled
themselves,
They passed by together.
5 They saw *it,* then they were
amazed;

They were [a]terrified, they [1]fled
in alarm.
6 [1]Panic seized them there,
Anguish, as of [a]a woman in
childbirth.
7 With the [a]east wind
You [b]break the [c]ships of
Tarshish.
8 As we have heard, so have we
seen
In the city of the LORD of hosts,
in the city of our God;
God will [a]establish her forever.
[1]Selah.

9 ¶ We have thought on [a]Your
lovingkindness, O God,
In the midst of Your temple.
10 As is Your [a]name, O God,
So is Your [b]praise to the ends of
the earth;
Your [c]right hand is full of
righteousness.
11 Let Mount [a]Zion be glad,
Let the [a]daughters of Judah
rejoice
Because of Your judgments.
12 Walk about Zion and go around
her;
Count her [a]towers;
13 Consider her [a]ramparts;
Go through her palaces,
That you may [b]tell *it* to the next
generation.
14 For [1]such is God,
Our God forever and ever;
He will [a]guide us [2]until death.

Psalm 49

The Folly of Trusting in Riches.

For the choir director.
A Psalm of the sons of Korah.

1 ¶ [a]Hear this, all peoples;
Give ear, all [b]inhabitants of the
world,
2 Both [a]low and high,
Rich and poor together.
3 My mouth will [a]speak wisdom,
And the meditation of my heart
will be [b]understanding.
4 I will incline my ear to [a]a
proverb;
[b]I will [1]express my [c]riddle on
the harp.

5 ¶ Why should I [a]fear in days of
adversity,
When the iniquity of my [1]foes
surrounds me,
6 Even those who [a]trust in their
wealth
And boast in the abundance of
their riches?
7 No man can by any means
[a]redeem *his* brother
Or give to God a [b]ransom
for him—
8 For [a]the redemption of [1]his
soul is costly,
And he should cease *trying*
forever—
9 That he should [a]live on
eternally,
That he should not [1][b]undergo
decay.

10 ¶ For he sees *that even* [a]wise
men die;
The [b]stupid and the senseless
alike perish
And [c]leave their wealth to
others.
11 Their [1][a]inner thought is *that*
their houses [b]are forever
And their dwelling places to all
generations;
They have [c]called their lands
after their own names.
12 But [a]man in *his* [1]pomp will not
endure;
He is like the [2]beasts that
[3]perish.

13 ¶ This is the [a]way of those who
are foolish,
And of those after them who
[b]approve their words.
[1]Selah.
14 As sheep they are appointed [a]for
[1]Sheol;
Death shall be their shepherd;
And the [b]upright shall rule over
them in the morning,
And their form shall be for
[1]Sheol [c]to consume
[2]So that they have no
habitation.
15 But God will [a]redeem my soul
from the [1]power of [2]Sheol,
For [b]He will receive me. Selah.

16 ¶ Do not be afraid [a]when a man
becomes rich,
When the [1]glory of his house is
increased;
17 For when he dies he will [a]carry
nothing away;
His [1]glory will not descend after
him.
18 Though while he lives he
[a]congratulates [1]himself—
And though *men* praise you
when you do well for
yourself—
19 [1]He shall [a]go to the generation
of his fathers;
They will never see [b]the light.

5 [1]Lit *were hurried away* [a]Ex 15:15
6 [1]Lit *Trembling* [a]Is 13:8
7 [a]Jer 18:17 [b]1 Kin 22:48 [c]1 Kin 10:22; Ezek 27:25
8 [1]*Selah* may mean: *Pause, Crescendo* or *Musical interlude* [a]Ps 87:5
9 [a]Ps 26:3
10 [a]Deut 28:58; Josh 7:9; Mal 1:11 [b]Ps 65:1 [c]Is 41:10
11 [a]Ps 97:8
12 [a]Neh 3:1
13 [a]Ps 122:7 [b]Ps 78:5-7
14 [1]Lit *this* [2]Lit *upon;* some mss and the Gr read *forever* [a]Ps 23:4; Is 58:11
49:1 [a]Ps 78:1; Is 1:2; Mic 1:2 [b]Ps 33:8
2 [a]Ps 62:9
3 [a]Ps 37:30 [b]Ps 119:130
4 [1]Lit *open up* [a]Ps 78:2 [b]2 Kin 3:15 [c]Num 12:8
5 [1]Lit *supplanters* [a]Ps 23:4
6 [a]Job 31:24; Ps 52:7; Prov 11:28; Mark 10:24
7 [a]Matt 25:8 [b]Job 36:18
8 [1]Lit *their* [a]Matt 16:26
9 [1]Or *see corruption* or *the pit* [a]Ps 22:29 [b]Ps 16:10
10 [a]Eccl 2:16 [b]Ps 92:6 [c]Ps 39:6; Eccl 2:18; Luke 12:20
11 [1]Some versions read *graves are their houses* [a]Ps 64:6 [b]Ps 10:6 [c]Gen 4:17; Deut 3:14
12 [1]Lit *honor* [2]Or *animals* [3]Lit *are destroyed* [a]Ps 49:20
13 [1]*Selah* may mean: *Pause, Crescendo* or *Musical interlude* [a]Jer 17:11 [b]Ps 49:18
14 [1]I.e. the nether world [2]Lit *Away from his habitation* [a]Ps 9:17 [b]Dan 7:18; Mal 4:3; 1 Cor 6:2; Rev 2:26 [c]Job 24:19
15 [1]Lit *hand* [2]I.e. the nether world [a]Ps 16:10; Hos 13:14 [b]Gen 5:24; Ps 16:11
16 [1]Or *wealth* [a]Ps 37:7
17 [1]Or *wealth* [a]Ps 17:14; 1 Tim 6:7
18 [1]Lit *his soul* [a]Deut 29:19; Ps 10:3; Luke 12:19
19 [1]Lit *You;* or *It* [a]Gen 15:15 [b]Job 33:30; Ps 56:13

20 [a]Man in *his* [1]pomp, yet without understanding,
Is [b]like the [2]beasts that [3]perish.

Psalm 50

God the Judge of the Righteous and the Wicked.

A Psalm of +Asaph.

1 ¶ [a]The Mighty One, God, the LORD, has spoken,
And summoned the earth [b]from the rising of the sun to its setting.
2 Out of Zion, [a]the perfection of beauty,
God [b]has shone forth.
3 May our God [a]come and not keep silence;
[b]Fire devours before Him,
And it is very [c]tempestuous around Him.
4 He [a]summons the heavens above,
And the earth, to judge His people:
5 "Gather My [a]godly ones to Me,
Those who have made a [b]covenant with Me by [c]sacrifice."
6 And the [a]heavens declare His righteousness,
For [b]God Himself is judge. [1]Selah.
7 ¶ "[a]Hear, O My people, and I will speak;
O Israel, I will testify [1]against you;
I am God, [b]your God.
8 "I do [a]not reprove you for your sacrifices,
And your burnt offerings are continually before Me.
9 "I shall take no [a]young bull out of your house
Nor male goats out of your folds.
10 "For [a]every beast of the forest is Mine,
The cattle on a thousand hills.
11 "I know every [a]bird of the mountains,
And everything that moves in the field is [1]Mine.
12 "If I were hungry I would not tell you,
For the [a]world is Mine, and [1]all it contains.
13 "Shall I eat the flesh of [1a]bulls
Or drink the blood of male goats?
14 "Offer to God [a]a sacrifice of thanksgiving
And [b]pay your vows to the Most High;
15 [a]Call upon Me in the day of trouble;
I shall [b]rescue you, and you will [c]honor Me."

16 ¶ But to the wicked God says,
"What right have you to tell of My statutes
And to take [a]My covenant in your mouth?
17 "For you [a]hate discipline,
And you [b]cast My words behind you.
18 "When you see a thief, you [1a]are pleased with him,
And [2]you [b]associate with adulterers.
19 "You [1a]let your mouth loose in evil
And your [b]tongue frames deceit.
20 "You sit and [a]speak against your brother;
You slander your own mother's son.
21 "These things you have done and [a]I kept silence;
You thought that I was just like you;
I will [b]reprove you and state *the case* in order before your eyes.

22 ¶ "Now consider this, you who [a]forget God,
Or I will [b]tear *you* in pieces, and there will be none to deliver.
23 "He who [a]offers a sacrifice of thanksgiving honors Me;
And to him who [1b]orders *his* way *aright*
I shall [c]show the salvation of God."

Psalm 51

A Contrite Sinner's Prayer for Pardon.

For the choir director. A Psalm of David, when +Nathan the prophet came to him, after he had gone in to Bathsheba.

1 ¶ [a]Be gracious to me, O God, according to Your lovingkindness;
According to the greatness of [b]Your compassion [c]blot out my transgressions.
2 [a]Wash me thoroughly from my iniquity
And [b]cleanse me from my sin.
3 For [1]I [a]know my transgressions,
And my sin is ever before me.

---

20 [1]Lit *honor* [2]Or *animals* [3]Lit *are destroyed* [a]Ps 49:12 [b]Eccl 3:19
50:1 +1 Chr 15:17; 2 Chr 29:30 [a]Josh 22:22 [b]Ps 113:3
2 [a]Ps 48:2; Lam 2:15 [b]Deut 33:2; Ps 80:1
3 [a]Ps 96:13 [b]Lev 10:2; Num 16:35; Ps 97:3; Dan 7:10 [c]Ps 18:12
4 [a]Deut 4:26; Is 1:2
5 [a]Ps 30:4 [b]Ex 24:7; 2 Chr 6:11; Ps 25:10 [c]Ps 50:8
6 [1]*Selah* may mean: *Pause, Crescendo* or *Musical interlude* [a]Ps 89:5 [b]Ps 75:7
7 [1]Or *to* [a]Ps 49:1 [b]Ex 20:2; Ps 48:14
8 [a]Ps 40:6; Is 1:11; Hos 6:6
9 [a]Ps 69:31
10 [a]Ps 104:24
11 [1]Or *in My mind;* lit *with Me* [a]Matt 6:26
12 [1]Lit *its fullness* [a]Ex 19:5; Deut 10:14; Ps 24:1; 1 Cor 10:26
13 [1]Lit *strong ones* [a]Ps 50:9
14 [a]Ps 27:6; Hos 14:2; Rom 12:1; Heb 13:15 [b]Num 30:2; Deut 23:21; Ps 22:25
15 [a]Ps 91:15; Zech 13:9 [b]Ps 81:7 [c]Ps 22:23
16 [a]Is 29:13
17 [a]Prov 5:12; Rom 2:21 [b]1 Kin 14:9; Neh 9:26
18 [1]Some ancient versions read *run together* [2]Lit *your part is with* [a]Rom 1:32 [b]1 Tim 5:22
19 [1]Lit *send* [a]Ps 10:7 [b]Ps 36:3
20 [a]Job 19:18; Matt 10:21
21 [a]Eccl 8:11; Is 42:14 [b]Ps 90:8
22 [a]Job 8:13; Ps 9:17 [b]Ps 7:2
23 [1]Lit *sets* [a]Ps 50:14 [b]Ps 85:13 [c]Ps 91:16
51:1 +2 Sam 12:1 [a]Ps 4:1 [b]Ps 69:16 [c]Ps 51:9; Is 43:25; Acts 3:19; Col 2:14
2 [a]Ps 51:7; Is 1:16; Jer 4:14; Acts 22:16; Rev 1:5 [b]Jer 33:8; Ezek 36:33; Heb 9:14; 1 John 1:7
3 [1]Or *I myself know* [a]Is 59:12

4 [a]Against You, You only, I have
sinned
And done what is [b]evil in Your
sight,
So that [c]You [1]are justified
[2]when You speak
And [3]blameless when You judge.

5 ¶ Behold, I was [a]brought forth
in iniquity,
And in sin my mother
conceived me.
6 Behold, You desire [a]truth in the
[1]innermost being,
And in the hidden part You will
[b]make me know wisdom.
7 [1]Purify me [a]with hyssop, and I
shall be clean;
[2]Wash me, and I shall be
[b]whiter than snow.
8 [1]Make me to hear [a]joy and
gladness,
Let the [b]bones which You have
broken rejoice.
9 [a]Hide Your face from my sins
And blot out all my iniquities.

10 ¶ [a]Create [1]in me a [b]clean
heart, O God,
And renew [2]a [c]steadfast spirit
within me.
11 [a]Do not cast me away from Your
presence
And do not take Your [b]Holy
Spirit from me.
12 Restore to me the [a]joy of Your
salvation
And sustain me with a [b]willing
spirit.
13 *Then* I will [a]teach transgressors
Your ways,
And sinners will [1]be [b]converted
to You.

14 ¶ Deliver me from
[a]bloodguiltiness, O God,
[b]the God of my salvation;
Then my [c]tongue will joyfully
sing of Your righteousness.
15 O Lord, [1a]open my lips,
That my mouth may [b]declare
Your praise.
16 For You [a]do not delight in
sacrifice, otherwise I would
give it;
You are not pleased with burnt
offering.
17 The sacrifices of God are a
[a]broken spirit;
A broken and a contrite heart,
O God, You will not despise.

18 ¶ [a]By Your favor do good to
Zion;
[1b]Build the walls of Jerusalem.
19 Then You will delight in
[1a]righteous sacrifices,
In [b]burnt offering and whole
burnt offering;
Then [2]young bulls will be
offered on Your altar.

Psalm 52

Futility of Boastful Wickedness.

For the choir director. A [+]Maskil of David,
[•]when Doeg the Edomite came and told
Saul and said to him, "David has come
to the house of Ahimelech."

1 ¶ Why do you [a]boast in evil,
O mighty man?
The [b]lovingkindness of God
endures all day long.
2 Your tongue devises
[a]destruction,
Like a [b]sharp razor, [c]O worker
of deceit.
3 You [a]love evil more than good,
[b]Falsehood more than speaking
what is right. [1]Selah.
4 You love all words that devour,
O [a]deceitful tongue.

5 ¶ [1]But God will break you down
forever;
He will snatch you up and [a]tear
you away from *your* tent,
And [b]uproot you from the [c]land
of the living. Selah.
6 The righteous will [a]see and fear,
And will [b]laugh at him, *saying,*
7 "Behold, the man who would not
make God his refuge,
But [a]trusted in the abundance of
his riches
And [b]was strong in [1]his *evil*
desire."

8 ¶ But as for me, I am like a
[a]green olive tree in the
house of God;
I [b]trust in the lovingkindness of
God forever and ever.
9 I will [a]give You thanks forever,
because You have done *it,*
And I will wait on Your name,
[b]for *it is* good, in the
presence of Your godly ones.

Psalm 53

Folly and Wickedness of Men.

For the choir director; according to
[+]Mahalath. A [•]Maskil of David.

1 ¶ [a]The fool has said in his heart,
"There is no God,"
They are corrupt, and have
committed abominable
injustice;

4 [1]Or *may be in the right* [2]Many mss read *in Your words* [3]Lit *pure* [a]Gen 20:6; 2 Sam 12:13; Ps 41:4 [b]Luke 15:21 [c]Rom 3:4
5 [a]Job 14:4; Ps 58:3; Eph 2:3
6 [1]Or *inward parts* [a]Job 38:36; Ps 15:2 [b]Prov 2:6; Eccl 2:26; James 1:5
7 [1]Or *May You purify...that I may be clean* [2]Or *May You wash* [a]Ex 12:22; Lev 14:4; Num 19:18; Heb 9:19 [b]Is 1:18
8 [1]Or *May You make* [a]Is 35:10; Joel 1:16 [b]Ps 35:10
9 [a]Jer 16:17
10 [1]Lit *for* [2]Or *an upright* [a]Ezek 18:31; Eph 2:10 [b]Ps 24:4; Matt 5:8; Acts 15:9 [c]Ps 78:37
11 [a]2 Kin 13:23; Jer 7:15 [b]Is 63:10
12 [a]Ps 13:5 [b]Ps 110:3
13 [1]Or *turn back* [a]Acts 9:21 [b]Ps 22:27
14 [a]2 Sam 12:9; Ps 26:9 [b]Ps 25:5 [c]Ps 35:28
15 [1]Or *may You open* [a]Ex 4:15 [b]Ps 9:14
16 [a]1 Sam 15:22; Ps 40:6
17 [a]Ps 34:18
18 [1]Or *May You build* [a]Ps 69:35; Is 51:3 [b]Ps 102:16
19 [1]Or *sacrifices of righteousness* [2]Lit *they will offer young bulls* [a]Ps 4:5 [b]Ps 66:13
52:1 [+]Possibly *Contemplative,* or *Didactic,* or *Skillful Psalm* [•]1 Sam 22:9 [a]Ps 94:4 [b]Ps 52:8
2 [a]Ps 5:9 [b]Ps 57:4 [c]Ps 101:7
3 [1]*Selah* may mean: *Pause, Crescendo* or *Musical interlude* [a]Ps 36:4 [b]Ps 58:3; Jer 9:5
4 [a]Ps 120:3
5 [1]Or *Also* [a]Is 22:18 [b]Prov 2:22 [c]Ps 27:13
6 [a]Ps 37:34 [b]Job 22:19
7 [1]Or *his destruction* [a]Ps 49:6 [b]Ps 10:6
8 [a]Ps 92:12; Jer 11:16 [b]Ps 13:5
9 [a]Ps 30:12 [b]Ps 54:6
53:1 [+]I.e. sickness, a sad tone [•]Possibly *Contemplative,* or *Didactic,* or *Skillful Psalm* [a]Ps 10:4

[b]There is no one who does
good.
2 God has looked down from
heaven upon the sons
of men
To see if there is [a]anyone who
[1]understands,
Who [b]seeks after God.
3 [a]Every one of them has turned
aside; together they have
become corrupt;
There is no one who does good,
not even one.

4 ¶ Have the workers of
wickedness [a]no knowledge,
Who eat up My people *as though*
they ate bread
And have not called upon God?
5 There they were in great [1]fear
[a]*where* no [1]fear had been;
For God [b]scattered the bones of
[2]him who encamped against
you;
You [c]put *them* to shame,
because [d]God had rejected
them.
6 Oh, that [a]the salvation of Israel
[1]would come out of Zion!
When God [2]restores His captive
people,
[3]Let Jacob rejoice, let Israel be
glad.

Psalm 54

Prayer for Defense against Enemies.

For the choir director; on stringed instruments. A [+]Maskil of David, [•]when the Ziphites came and said to Saul, "Is not David hiding himself among us?"

1 ¶ Save me, O God, by [a]Your
name,
And [1]vindicate me by [b]Your
power.
2 [a]Hear my prayer, O God;
[b]Give ear to the words of my
mouth.
3 For strangers have [a]risen
against me
And [b]violent men have [c]sought
my [1]life;
They have [d]not set God before
them. [2]Selah.

4 ¶ Behold, [a]God is my helper;
The Lord is [1]the [b]sustainer of
my soul.
5 [1]He will [a]recompense the evil
to [2]my foes;
[3b]Destroy them [c]in Your
[4]faithfulness.

6 ¶ [1a]Willingly I will sacrifice
to You;
I will give [b]thanks to Your
name, O LORD, for it is
good.
7 For [1]He has [a]delivered me from
all [2]trouble,
And my eye has [b]looked *with
satisfaction* upon my
enemies.

Psalm 55

Prayer for the Destruction of the Treacherous.

For the choir director; on stringed instruments. A [+]Maskil of David.

1 ¶ [a]Give ear to my prayer,
O God;
And [b]do not hide Yourself from
my supplication.
2 Give [a]heed to me and
answer me;
I am restless in my [b]complaint
and [1c]am surely distracted,
3 Because of the voice of the
enemy,
Because of the [a]pressure of the
wicked;
For they [b]bring down [1]trouble
upon me
And in anger they [c]bear a
grudge against me.

4 ¶ My [a]heart is in anguish
within me,
And the terrors of [b]death have
fallen upon me.
5 Fear and [a]trembling come
upon me,
And [1b]horror has
overwhelmed me.
6 I said, "Oh, that I had wings like
a dove!
I would fly away and [1a]be at
rest.
7 "Behold, I would wander far
away,
I would [a]lodge in the
wilderness. [1]Selah.
8 "I would hasten to my place of
refuge
From the [a]stormy wind *and*
tempest."

9 ¶ [1]Confuse, O Lord, [a]divide
their tongues,
For I have seen [b]violence and
strife in the city.
10 Day and night they go around
her upon her walls,
And iniquity and mischief are in
her midst.
11 [a]Destruction is in her midst;
[b]Oppression and deceit do not
depart from her [1]streets.

1 [b]Rom 3:10
2 [1]Or *acts wisely* [a]Rom 3:11 [b]2 Chr 15:2
3 [a]Rom 3:12
4 [a]Jer 4:22
5 [1]Or *dread* [2]Or possibly *those* [a]Lev 26:17; Prov 28:1 [b]Ps 141:7; Jer 8:1; Ezek 6:5 [c]Ps 44:7 [d]2 Kin 17:20; Jer 6:30; Lam 5:22
6 [1]Lit *would be* [2]Or *restores the fortunes of His people* [3]Or *Jacob will rejoice, Israel will be glad* [a]Ps 14:7
54:1 [+]Possibly *Contemplative*, or *Didactic*, or *Skillful Psalm* [1]Lit *judge* [•]1 Sam 23:19; 26:1 [a]Ps 20:1 [b]2 Chr 20:6
2 [a]Ps 17:6 [b]Ps 5:1
3 [1]Or *soul* [2]*Selah* may mean: *Pause, Crescendo* or *Musical interlude* [a]Ps 86:14 [b]Ps 18:48 [c]1 Sam 20:1; Ps 40:14 [d]Ps 36:1
4 [1]Lit *as those who sustain* [a]Ps 30:10 [b]Ps 37:17; Is 41:10
5 [1]Lit *The evil will return* [2]Or *those who lie in wait for me* [3]Or *Put to silence* [4]Or *truth* [a]Ps 94:23 [b]Ps 143:12 [c]Ps 89:49; Is 42:3
6 [1]Or *With a freewill offering* [a]Num 15:3; Ps 116:17 [b]Ps 50:14
7 [1]Or *it;* i.e. His name [2]Or *distress* [a]Ps 34:6 [b]Ps 59:10
55:1 [+]Possibly *Contemplative*, or *Didactic*, or *Skillful Psalm* [a]Ps 54:2 [b]Ps 27:9
2 [1]Or *I must moan* [a]Ps 66:19 [b]1 Sam 1:16; Job 9:27; Ps 64:1 [c]Is 38:14; Ezek 7:16
3 [1]Or *wickedness* [a]Ps 17:9 [b]2 Sam 16:7 [c]Ps 71:11
4 [a]Ps 38:8 [b]Ps 18:4
5 [1]Lit *shuddering* [a]Ps 119:120 [b]Job 21:6; Is 21:4; Ezek 7:18
6 [1]Lit *settle down* [a]Job 3:13
7 [1]*Selah* may mean: *Pause, Crescendo* or *Musical interlude* [a]1 Sam 23:14
8 [a]Is 4:6
9 [1]Lit *Swallow up* [a]Gen 11:9 [b]Ps 11:5; Jer 6:7
11 [1]Or *plaza* [a]Ps 5:9 [b]Ps 10:7

12 ¶ For it is [a]not an enemy who
reproaches me,
Then I could bear *it;*
Nor is it one who hates me who
[b]has exalted himself
against me,
Then I could hide myself from
him.
13 But it is you, a man [1]my equal,
My [a]companion and my
[2b]familiar friend;
14 We who had sweet [1]fellowship
together
[a]Walked in the house of God in
the throng.
15 Let [1]death come [a]deceitfully
upon them;
Let them [b]go down alive to
[2]Sheol,
For evil is in their dwelling, in
their midst.

16 ¶ As for me, I shall [a]call upon
God,
And the LORD will save me.
17 [a]Evening and [b]morning and at
[c]noon, I will complain and
murmur,
And He will hear my voice.
18 He will [a]redeem my soul in
peace [1]from the battle
which is against me,
For they are [b]many *who strive*
with me.
19 God will [a]hear and [1]answer
them—
Even the one [b]who [2]sits
enthroned from of old—
Selah.
With whom there [3]is no change,
And who [c]do not fear God.
20 He has put forth his hands
against [a]those who were at
peace with him;
He has [1b]violated his covenant.
21 His [1]speech was [a]smoother
than butter,
But his heart was war;
His words were [a]softer than oil,
Yet they were drawn [b]swords.

22 ¶ [a]Cast [1]your burden upon the
LORD and He will sustain
you;
[b]He will never allow the
righteous to [2c]be shaken.
23 But You, O God, will bring them
down to the [1a]pit of
destruction;
[b]Men of bloodshed and deceit
will [c]not live out half their
days.
But I will [d]trust in You.

12 [a]Ps 41:9 [b]Ps 35:26
13 [1]Lit *according to my valuation* [2]Or *acquaintance* [a]2 Sam 15:12 [b]Job 19:14; Ps 41:9
14 [1]Lit *counsel;* or *intimacy* [a]Ps 42:4
15 [1]Another reading is *desolations be upon them* [2]I.e. the nether world [a]Ps 64:7; Prov 6:15; Is 47:11; 1 Thess 5:3 [b]Num 16:30
16 [a]Ps 57:2
17 [a]Ps 141:2; Dan 6:10; Acts 3:1 [b]Ps 5:3 [c]Acts 10:9
18 [1]Or *so that none may approach me* [a]Ps 103:4 [b]Ps 56:2
19 [1]Or *afflict* [2]Or *abides from* [3]Lit *are no changes* [a]Ps 78:59 [b]Deut 33:27; Ps 90:2 [c]Ps 36:1
20 [1]Lit *profaned* [a]Ps 7:4 [b]Num 30:2; Ps 89:34
21 [1]Lit *mouth* [a]Ps 12:2; Prov 5:3 [b]Ps 57:4
22 [1]Or *what He has given you* [2]Or *totter* [a]Ps 37:5; 1 Pet 5:7 [b]Ps 37:24 [c]Ps 15:5
23 [1]Or *lowest pit* [a]Ps 73:18; Is 38:17; Ezek 28:8 [b]Ps 5:6 [c]Job 15:32; Prov 10:27 [d]Ps 25:2
56:1 +Or *The silent dove of those who are far off,* or, *The dove of the distant terebinths* •Possibly *Epigrammatic Poem,* or *Atonement Psalm* △1 Sam 21:10,11 [1]Or *snapped at* [2]Or *A fighting man* [a]Ps 57:3 [b]Ps 17:9
2 [1]Or *snapped at* [2]Or *many are fighting* [a]Ps 35:25 [b]Ps 35:1
3 [1]Lit *In the day* [2]Or *I am one who puts* [a]Ps 55:4 [b]Ps 11:1
4 [1]Lit *flesh* [a]Ps 56:10 [b]Ps 118:6; Heb 13:6
5 [1]Or *trouble my affairs* [2]Or *purposes* [a]2 Pet 3:16 [b]Ps 41:7
6 [1]Or *stir up strife* [2]Lit *heels* [3]Lit *soul* [a]Ps 59:3; Is 54:15 [b]Ps 17:11 [c]Ps 71:10
7 [1]Or *will they have escape?* [a]Ps 36:12; Prov 19:5; Ezek 17:15; Rom 2:3 [b]Ps 55:23
8 [a]Ps 139:3 [b]2 Kin 20:5; Ps 39:12 [c]Mal 3:16

Psalm 56

Supplication for Deliverance and Grateful Trust in God.

For the choir director; according to +Jonath elem rehokim. A •Mikhtam of David, △when the Philistines seized him in Gath.

1 ¶ Be gracious to me, O God, for
man has [1a]trampled
upon me;
[2]Fighting all day long he
[b]oppresses me.
2 My foes have [1a]trampled upon
me all day long,
For [2]they are many who [b]fight
proudly against me.
3 [1]When I am [a]afraid,
[2]I will [b]put my trust in
You.
4 [a]In God, whose word I
praise,
In God I have put my trust;
I shall not be afraid.
[b]What can *mere* [1]man do
to me?
5 All day long they [1a]distort my
words;
All their [2b]thoughts are against
me for evil.
6 They [1a]attack, they lurk,
They [b]watch my [2]steps,
As they have [c]waited *to take* my
[3]life.
7 Because of wickedness, [1a]cast
them forth,
In anger [b]put down the peoples,
O God!

8 ¶ You [a]have taken account of
my wanderings;
Put my [b]tears in Your bottle.
Are *they* not in [c]Your book?
9 Then my enemies will [a]turn
back [b]in the day when I
call;
This I know, [1]that [c]God is
for me.
10 In God, *whose* word I praise,
In the LORD, *whose* word I
praise,
11 In God I have put my [1]trust, I
shall not be afraid.
What can man do to me?
12 Your [a]vows are *binding* upon
me, O God;
I will render thank offerings
to You.
13 For You have [a]delivered my soul
from death,
[1]Indeed [b]my feet from
stumbling,

9 [1]Or *because* [a]Ps 9:3 [b]Ps 102:2 [c]Ps 41:11; Rom 8:31
11 [1]Or *trust without fear* **12** [a]Ps 50:14 **13** [1]Or *have You not delivered* [a]Ps 33:19 [b]Ps 116:8

So that I may [c]walk before
God
In the [d]light of the [2]living.

Psalm 57

Prayer for Rescue from Persecutors.

For the choir director; *set to* +Al-tashheth.
A •Mikhtam of David, △when he fled
from Saul in the cave.

1 ¶ Be gracious to me, O God, be
gracious to me,
For my soul [a]takes refuge
in You;
And in the [b]shadow of Your
wings I will take refuge
Until destruction [c]passes by.
2 I will cry to God Most High,
To God who [a]accomplishes *all
things* for me.
3 He will [a]send from heaven and
save me;
He reproaches him who
[1b]tramples upon me.
[2]Selah.
God will send forth His
[c]lovingkindness and His
[3]truth.

4 ¶ My soul is among [a]lions;
I must lie among those who
breathe forth fire,
Even the sons of men, whose
[b]teeth are spears and
arrows
And their [c]tongue a sharp
sword.
5 [a]Be exalted above the heavens,
O God;
Let Your glory *be* above all the
earth.
6 They have [1]prepared a [a]net for
my steps;
My soul is [b]bowed down;
They [c]dug a pit before me;
They *themselves* have [d]fallen
into the midst of it. Selah.

7 ¶ [a]My [b]heart is steadfast,
O God, my heart is
steadfast;
I will sing, yes, I will sing
praises!
8 Awake, [a]my glory!
Awake, [b]harp and lyre!
I will awaken the dawn.
9 [a]I will give thanks to You,
O Lord, among the peoples;
I will sing praises to You among
the [1]nations.
10 For Your [a]lovingkindness is
great to the heavens
And Your [1]truth to the
clouds.
11 [a]Be exalted above the heavens,
O God;
Let Your glory *be* above all the
earth.

Psalm 58

Prayer for the Punishment of the Wicked.

For the choir director; *set to* +Al-tashheth.
A •Mikhtam of David.

1 ¶ Do you indeed [1]speak
righteousness, O [2]gods?
Do you [a]judge [3]uprightly,
O sons of men?
2 No, in heart you [a]work
unrighteousness;
On earth you [b]weigh out the
violence of your hands.
3 The wicked are estranged [a]from
the womb;
These who speak lies [b]go astray
from [1]birth.
4 They have venom like the
[a]venom of a serpent;
Like a deaf cobra that stops up
its ear,
5 So that it [a]does not hear the
voice of [1b]charmers,
Or a skillful caster of spells.

6 ¶ O God, [a]shatter their teeth in
their mouth;
Break out the fangs of the young
lions, O LORD.
7 Let them [a]flow away like water
that runs off;
When he [1b]aims his arrows, let
them be as [2]headless shafts.
8 *Let them be* as a snail which
[1]melts away as it goes
along,
Like the [a]miscarriages of a
woman which never see the
sun.
9 Before your [a]pots can feel *the
fire of* thorns
He will [b]sweep them away with
a whirlwind, the [1]green and
the burning alike.

10 ¶ The [a]righteous will rejoice
when he [b]sees the
vengeance;
He will [c]wash his feet in the
blood of the wicked.
11 And men will say, "Surely there
is a [1a]reward for the
righteous;
Surely there is a God who
[b]judges [2]on earth!"

---

13 [2]Or *life* [c]Ps 116:9 [d]Job 33:30

57:1 +Lit *Do Not Destroy* •Possibly *Epigrammatic Poem* or *Atonement Psalm* △1 Sam 22:1; 24:3 [a]Ps 2:12 [b]Ruth 2:12; Ps 17:8 [c]Is 26:20

2 [a]Ps 138:8

3 [1]Or *snaps at* [2]*Selah* may mean: *Pause, Crescendo* or *Musical interlude* [3]Or *faithfulness* [a]Ps 18:16 [b]Ps 56:2 [c]Ps 25:10

4 [a]Ps 35:17 [b]Prov 30:14 [c]Ps 55:21; Prov 12:18

5 [a]Ps 57:11

6 [1]Or *spread* [a]Ps 10:9 [b]Ps 145:14 [c]Ps 7:15 [d]Prov 26:27; Eccl 10:8

7 [a]Ps 57:7-11 [b]Ps 112:7

8 [a]Ps 16:9 [b]Ps 150:3

9 [1]Lit *peoples* [a]Ps 108:3

10 [1]Or *faithfulness* [a]Ps 36:5

11 [a]Ps 57:5

58:1 +Lit *Do Not Destroy* •Possibly *Epigrammatic Poem* or *Atonement Psalm* [1]Another reading is *speak righteousness in silence* [2]Or *mighty ones* or *judges* [3]Or *uprightly the sons of men* [a]Ps 82:2

2 [a]Mal 3:15 [b]Ps 94:20; Is 10:1

3 [1]Lit *the womb* [a]Ps 51:5; Is 48:8 [b]Ps 53:3

4 [a]Deut 32:33; Ps 140:3

5 [1]Or *whisperers* [a]Jer 8:17 [b]Eccl 10:11

6 [a]Job 4:10; Ps 3:7

7 [1]Lit *bends* [2]Lit *though they were cut off* [a]Josh 2:11; Ps 112:10; Is 13:7; Ezek 21:7 [b]Ps 64:3

8 [1]I.e. secretes slime [a]Job 3:16; Eccl 6:3

9 [1]Lit *living* [a]Ps 118:12; Eccl 7:6 [b]Job 27:21; Ps 83:15; Prov 10:25

10 [a]Job 22:19; Ps 32:11 [b]Deut 32:43; Ps 91:8; Jer 11:20 [c]Ps 68:23

11 [1]Lit *fruit* [2]Or *in* [a]Ps 18:20; Is 3:10; Luke 6:23 [b]Ps 9:8

Psalm 59

Prayer for Deliverance from Enemies.

For the choir director; *set to* +Al-tashheth. A •Mikhtam of David, ∆when Saul sent *men* and they watched the house in order to kill him.

1 ¶ [a]Deliver me from my enemies,
O my God;
[1b]Set me *securely* on high away
from those who rise up
against me.
2 Deliver me from [a]those who do
iniquity
And save me from [b]men of
bloodshed.
3 For behold, they [a]have [1]set an
ambush for my [2]life;
[3]Fierce men [4a]launch an attack
against me,
[b]Not for my transgression nor
for my sin, O LORD,
4 [1a]For no guilt of *mine,* they run
and set themselves
against me.
[b]Arouse Yourself to [2]help me,
and see!
5 You, [a]O LORD God of hosts, the
God of Israel,
Awake to [1b]punish all the
nations;
[c]Do not be gracious to any *who
are* treacherous in iniquity.
[2]Selah.
6 They [a]return at evening, they
howl like a [b]dog,
And go around the city.
7 Behold, they [a]belch forth with
their mouth;
[b]Swords are in their lips,
For, *they say,* "[c]Who hears?"
8 But You, O LORD, [a]laugh at
them;
You [b]scoff at all the nations.

9 ¶ *Because of* [1]his [a]strength I
will watch for You,
For God is my [b]stronghold.
10 [1]My God [a]in His lovingkindness
will meet me;
God will let me [b]look
triumphantly upon [2]my foes.
11 Do not slay them, [a]or my people
will forget;
[1b]Scatter them by Your power,
and bring them down,
O Lord, [c]our shield.
12 [1]*On account of* the [a]sin of their
mouth *and* the words of
their lips,
Let them even be [b]caught in
their pride,
And on account of [c]curses and
[2]lies which they utter.
13 [1a]Destroy *them* in wrath,
[1]destroy *them* that they may
be no more;
That *men* may [b]know that God
[2]rules in Jacob
To the ends of the earth. Selah.
14 They [a]return at evening, they
howl like a dog,
And go around the city.
15 They [a]wander about [1]for food
And [2]growl if they are not
satisfied.

16 ¶ But as for me, I shall [a]sing of
Your strength;
Yes, I shall [b]joyfully sing of Your
lovingkindness in the
[c]morning,
For You have been my
[d]stronghold
And a [e]refuge in the day of my
distress.
17 [a]O my strength, I will sing
praises to You;
For God is my [b]stronghold, the
[1]God who shows me
lovingkindness.

Psalm 60

Lament over Defeat in Battle, and Prayer for Help.

For the choir director; according to +Shushan Eduth. A •Mikhtam of David, to teach; ∆when he struggled with Aram-naharaim and with Aram-zobah, and Joab returned, and smote twelve thousand of Edom in the Valley of Salt.

1 ¶ O God, [a]You have rejected us.
You have [1b]broken us;
You have been [c]angry; O,
[d]restore us.
2 You have made the [1a]land
quake, You have split it
open;
[b]Heal its breaches, for it totters.
3 You have [1a]made Your people
experience hardship;
You have given us [2]wine to
[b]drink that makes us
stagger.
4 You have given a [a]banner to
those who fear You,
That it may be displayed because
of the truth. [1]Selah.
5 [a]That Your [b]beloved may be
delivered,
[c]Save with Your right hand, and
answer [1]us!

59:1 +Lit *Do Not Destroy* •Possibly *Epigrammatic Poem* or *Atonement Psalm* ∆1 Sam 19:11 [1]Or *May You put me in an inaccessibly high place* [a]Ps 143:9 [b]Ps 20:1
2 [a]Ps 28:3 [b]Ps 26:9; Prov 29:10
3 [1]Or *lain in wait* [2]Lit *soul* [3]Or *Strong* [4]Or *stir up strife* [a]Ps 56:6 [b]1 Sam 24:11; Ps 7:3
4 [1]Lit *Without guilt* [2]Lit *meet* [a]Ps 35:19 [b]Ps 7:6
5 [1]Lit *visit* [2]*Selah* may mean: *Pause, Crescendo* or *Musical interlude* [a]Ps 69:6 [b]Ps 9:5; Is 26:14 [c]Is 2:9; Jer 18:23
6 [a]Ps 59:14 [b]Ps 22:16
7 [a]Ps 94:4; Prov 15:2 [b]Ps 57:4; Prov 12:18 [c]Job 22:13; Ps 10:11
8 [a]Ps 37:13; Prov 1:26 [b]Ps 2:4
9 [1]Many mss and some ancient versions read *My strength* [a]Ps 18:17 [b]Ps 9:9
10 [1]Many mss and some ancient versions read *The God of my lovingkindness* [2]Lit *those who lie in wait for me* [a]Ps 21:3 [b]Ps 54:7
11 [1]Or *Make them wander* [a]Deut 4:9 [b]Ps 106:27; Is 33:3 [c]Ps 84:9
12 [1]Or *The sin of their mouth is the word of their lips,* [2]Lit *lying* [a]Prov 12:13 [b]Zeph 3:11 [c]Ps 10:7
13 [1]Lit *Bring to an end* [2]Or *is Ruler* [a]Ps 104:35 [b]Ps 83:18
14 [a]Ps 59:6
15 [1]Or *to devour* [2]Another reading is *tarry all night* [a]Job 15:23
16 [a]Ps 21:13 [b]Ps 101:1 [c]Ps 5:3 [d]Ps 59:9 [e]2 Sam 22:3; Ps 46:1
17 [1]Lit *God of my lovingkindness* [a]Ps 59:9 [b]Ps 59:10
60:1 +Lit *The lily of testimony* •Possibly *Epigrammatic Poem* or *Atonement Psalm* ∆2 Sam 8:3,13; 1 Chr 18:3,12 [1]Or *broken out upon us* [a]Ps 44:9 [b]2 Sam 5:20 [c]Ps 79:5 [d]Ps 80:3
2 [1]Or *earth* [a]Ps 18:7 [b]2 Chr 7:14; Is 30:26 **3** [1]Lit *caused Your people to see* [2]Lit *wine of staggering* [a]Ps 66:12 [b]Ps 75:8; Is 51:17; Jer 25:15 **4** [1]*Selah* may mean: *Pause, Crescendo* or *Musical interlude* [a]Ps 20:5; Is 5:26 **5** [1]Some authorities read *me* [a]Ps 60:5-12 [b]Deut 33:12; Ps 127:2; Is 5:1; Jer 11:15 [c]Ps 17:7

6 ¶ God has spoken in His
[1a]holiness:
"I will exult, I will portion out
[b]Shechem and measure out
the valley of [c]Succoth.
7 "[a]Gilead is Mine, and Manasseh
is Mine;
[b]Ephraim also is the [1]helmet of
My head;
Judah is My [2c]scepter.
8 "[a]Moab is My washbowl;
Over [b]Edom I shall throw My
shoe;
Shout loud, O [c]Philistia, because
of Me!"
9 ¶ Who will bring me into the
besieged city?
Who [1]will lead me to Edom?
10 Have not You Yourself, O God,
[a]rejected us?
And [b]will You not go forth with
our armies, O God?
11 O give us help against the
adversary,
For [a]deliverance [1]by man is in
vain.
12 [1]Through God we shall [a]do
valiantly,
And it is He who will [b]tread
down our adversaries.

Psalm 61

Confidence in God's Protection.

For the choir director; on a stringed instrument. *A Psalm* of David.

1 ¶ [a]Hear my cry, O God;
[b]Give heed to my prayer.
2 From the [a]end of the earth I call
to You when my heart is
[b]faint;
Lead me to [c]the rock that is
higher than I.
3 For You have been a [a]refuge
for me,
A [b]tower of strength [1]against
the enemy.
4 Let me [1a]dwell in Your tent
forever;
Let me [b]take refuge in the
shelter of Your wings.
[2]Selah.
5 ¶ For You have heard my [a]vows,
O God;
You have given *me* the
inheritance of those who
[b]fear Your name.
6 You will [1a]prolong the king's
[2]life;
His years will be as many
generations.
7 He will [1]abide [a]before God
forever;

6 [1]Or *sanctuary* [a]Ps 89:35 [b]Gen 12:6; 33:18; Josh 17:7 [c]Gen 33:17; Josh 13:27
7 [1]Lit *protection* [2]Or *lawgiver* [a]Josh 13:31 [b]Deut 33:17 [c]Gen 49:10
8 [a]2 Sam 8:2 [b]2 Sam 8:14 [c]2 Sam 8:1
9 [1]Or *has led*
10 [a]Ps 60:1; 108:11 [b]Josh 7:12; Ps 44:9
11 [1]Lit *of* [a]Ps 146:3
12 [1]Or *In* or *With* [a]Num 24:18; Ps 118:16 [b]Ps 44:5; Is 63:3
61:1 [a]Ps 64:1 [b]Ps 86:6
2 [a]Ps 42:6 [b]Ps 77:3 [c]Ps 18:2; 94:22
3 [1]Lit *from* [a]Ps 62:7 [b]Ps 59:9; Prov 18:10
4 [1]Or *sojourn* [2]*Selah* may mean: *Pause, Crescendo* or *Musical interlude* [a]Ps 23:6; 27:4 [b]Ps 17:8; 91:4
5 [a]Job 22:27; Ps 56:12 [b]Deut 28:58; Neh 1:11; Ps 86:11; 102:15; Is 59:19; Mal 2:5; 4:2
6 [1]Lit *add days to* [2]Lit *days* [a]Ps 21:4
7 [1]Or *sit enthroned* [a]Ps 41:12 [b]Ps 40:11
8 [a]Judg 5:3; Ps 30:4; 33:2; 71:22 [b]Ps 65:1; Is 19:21
62:1 +Cf 1 Chr 16:41; 25:1; Ps 39 and 77 titles [a]Ps 33:20 [b]Ps 37:39
2 [a]Ps 89:26 [b]Ps 59:17; 62:6
3 [a]Is 30:13
4 [1]Lit *his* [2]*Selah* may mean: *Pause, Crescendo* or *Musical interlude* [a]Ps 4:2 [b]Ps 28:3; 55:21
5 [a]Ps 62:1
6 [a]Ps 62:2
7 [a]Ps 85:9; Jer 3:23 [b]Ps 46:1
8 [a]Ps 37:3,5; 52:8; Is 26:4 [b]1 Sam 1:15; Ps 42:4; Lam 2:19
9 [a]Ps 49:2 [b]Job 7:16; Ps 39:5; Is 40:17 [c]Ps 116:11 [d]Is 40:15
10 [1]Lit *become vain in robbery* [a]Is 30:12 [b]Is 61:8; Ezek 22:29; Nah 3:1 [c]Job 31:25; Ps 49:6; 52:7; Mark 10:24; Luke 12:15; 1 Tim 6:10
11 [1]Or *One thing* [2]Or *These two things I have heard* [a]Job 33:14; 40:5

Appoint [b]lovingkindness and
truth that they may preserve
him.
8 So I will [a]sing praise to Your
name forever,
That I may [b]pay my vows day by
day.

Psalm 62

God Alone a Refuge from Treachery and Oppression.

For the choir director; +according to Jeduthun. A Psalm of David.

1 ¶ [a]My soul *waits* in silence for
God only;
From Him [b]is my salvation.
2 He only is my [a]rock and my
salvation,
My [b]stronghold; I shall not be
greatly shaken.
3 ¶ How long will you assail a
man,
That you may murder *him,* all of
you,
Like a [a]leaning wall, like a
tottering fence?
4 They have counseled only to
thrust him down from his
high position;
They [a]delight in falsehood;
They [b]bless with [1]their mouth,
But inwardly they curse. [2]Selah.
5 ¶ My soul, [a]wait in silence for
God only,
For my hope is from Him.
6 He only is [a]my rock and my
salvation,
My stronghold; I shall not be
shaken.
7 On God my [a]salvation and my
glory *rest;*
The rock of my strength, my
[b]refuge is in God.
8 [a]Trust in Him at all times,
O people;
[b]Pour out your heart before
Him;
God is a refuge for us. Selah.
9 ¶ Men of [a]low degree are only
[b]vanity and men of rank are
a [c]lie;
In the [d]balances they go up;
They are together lighter than
breath.
10 [a]Do not trust in oppression
And do not [1]vainly hope in
[b]robbery;
If riches increase, [c]do not set
your heart *upon them.*
11 ¶ [1]Once God has [a]spoken;
[2]Twice I have heard this:

That [b]power belongs to God;
12 And lovingkindness [a]is Yours,
O Lord,
For You [b]recompense a man
according to his work.

Psalm 63

The Thirsting Soul Satisfied in God.

A Psalm of David, [+]when he was
in the wilderness of Judah.

1 ¶ O God, [a]You are my God; I
shall seek You [1]earnestly;
My soul [b]thirsts for You, my
flesh [2]yearns for You,
In a [c]dry and weary land where
there is no water.
2 Thus I have [a]seen You in the
sanctuary,
To see Your power and Your
glory.
3 Because Your [a]lovingkindness is
better than life,
My lips will praise You.
4 So I will bless You [a]as long as I
live;
I will [b]lift up my hands in Your
name.
5 My soul is [a]satisfied as with
[1]marrow and fatness,
And my mouth offers [b]praises
with joyful lips.

6 ¶ When I remember You [a]on
my bed,
I meditate on You in the [b]night
watches,
7 For [a]You have been my help,
And in the [b]shadow of Your
wings I sing for joy.
8 My soul [a]clings [1]to You;
Your [b]right hand upholds me.

9 ¶ But those who [a]seek my [1]life
to destroy it,
Will go into the [2b]depths of the
earth.
10 [1]They will be [2a]delivered over
to the power of the sword;
They will be a [3b]prey for foxes.
11 But the [a]king will rejoice in
God;
Everyone who [b]swears by Him
will glory,
For the [c]mouths of those who
speak lies will be stopped.

Psalm 64

Prayer for Deliverance from Secret Enemies.

For the choir director. A Psalm of David.

1 ¶ Hear my voice, O God, in [a]my
[1]complaint;
[b]Preserve my life from dread of
the enemy.
2 Hide me from the [a]secret
counsel of evildoers,
From the tumult of [b]those who
do iniquity,
3 Who [a]have sharpened their
tongue like a sword.
They [b]aimed bitter speech *as*
their arrow,
4 To [a]shoot [1]from concealment at
the blameless;
Suddenly they shoot at him, and
[b]do not fear.
5 They [1]hold fast to themselves an
evil purpose;
They [2]talk of [a]laying snares
secretly;
They say, "[b]Who can see
them?"
6 They [1]devise injustices, *saying,*
"We are [2]ready with a
well-conceived plot";
For the [3a]inward thought and
the heart of a man are
[4]deep.

7 ¶ But [a]God [1]will shoot at them
with an arrow;
Suddenly [2]they will be
wounded.
8 So [1]they [2]will [a]make him
stumble;
[b]Their own tongue is against
them;
All who see them will [c]shake
the head.
9 Then all men [1]will [a]fear,
And they [2]will [b]declare the
work of God,
And [3]will consider [4]what He
has done.
10 The righteous man will be [a]glad
in the LORD and will [b]take
refuge in Him;
And all the upright in heart will
glory.

Psalm 65

God's Abundant Favor to Earth and Man.

For the choir director. A Psalm of David.
A Song.

1 ¶ There will be silence [1]before
You, *and* praise in Zion,
O God,
And to You the [a]vow will be
performed.
2 O You who hear prayer,
To You [a]all [1]men come.
3 [1a]Iniquities prevail against me;
As for our transgressions, You
[2b]forgive them.

---

11 [b]Ps 59:17; Rev 19:1
12 [a]Ps 86:5 [b]Job 34:11; Ps 28:4; Jer 17:10; Matt 16:27; Rom 2:6; 1 Cor 3:8; Rev 2:23
63:1 [+]1 Sam 22:5; 23:14 [1]Lit *early* [2]Lit *faints* [a]Ps 118:28 [b]Ps 42:2; Matt 5:6 [c]Ps 143:6
2 [a]Ps 27:4
3 [a]Ps 69:16
4 [a]Ps 104:33 [b]Ps 28:2
5 [1]Lit *fat* [a]Ps 36:8 [b]Ps 71:23
6 [a]Ps 4:4 [b]Ps 16:7
7 [a]Ps 27:9 [b]Ps 17:8
8 [1]Lit *after* [a]Num 32:12; Deut 1:36; Hos 6:3 [b]Ps 18:35
9 [1]Lit *soul* [2]Lit *lowest places* [a]Ps 40:14 [b]Ps 55:15
10 [1]Lit *They will pour him out* [2]Lit *poured out by* [3]Lit *portion* [a]Jer 18:21; Ezek 35:5 [b]Lam 5:18
11 [a]Ps 21:1 [b]Deut 6:13; Is 45:23 [c]Job 5:16; Ps 107:42; Rom 3:19
64:1 [1]Or *concern* [a]Ps 55:2 [b]Ps 140:1
2 [a]Ps 56:6 [b]Ps 59:2
3 [a]Ps 140:3 [b]Ps 58:7
4 [1]Lit *in* [a]Ps 10:8 [b]Ps 55:19
5 [1]Lit *make firm* [2]Lit *tell of* [a]Ps 140:5 [b]Job 22:13; Ps 10:11
6 [1]Or *search out* [2]Lit *complete* [3]Or *inward part* [4]Or *unsearchable* [a]Ps 49:11
7 [1]Or *shot* [2]Or *they were wounded;* lit *their wounds occurred* [a]Ps 7:12
8 [1]Or *they make their tongue a stumbling for themselves* [2]Or *made* [a]Ps 9:3 [b]Prov 12:13 [c]Ps 22:7; Jer 18:16; Lam 2:15
9 [1]Or *feared* [2]Or *declared* [3]Or *considered* [4]Lit *His work* [a]Ps 40:3 [b]Jer 51:10
10 [a]Job 22:19; Ps 32:11 [b]Ps 11:1
65:1 [1]Lit *to* [a]Ps 116:18
2 [1]Lit *flesh* [a]Ps 86:9; Is 66:23
3 [1]Lit *Words of iniquities* [2]Lit *cover over, atone for* [a]Ps 38:4 [b]Ps 79:9

4 How [a]blessed is the one whom
You [b]choose and bring near *to You*
To dwell in Your courts.
We will be [c]satisfied with the goodness of Your house,
Your holy temple.

5 ¶ By [a]awesome *deeds* You answer us in righteousness,
O [b]God of our salvation,
You who are the trust of all the [c]ends of the earth and of the farthest [1][d]sea;
6 Who [a]establishes the mountains by His strength,
Being [b]girded with might;
7 Who [a]stills the roaring of the seas,
The roaring of their waves,
And the [b]tumult of the peoples.
8 They who dwell in the [a]ends *of the earth* stand in awe of Your signs;
You make the [1]dawn and the sunset shout for joy.

9 ¶ You visit the earth and [a]cause it to overflow;
You greatly [b]enrich it;
The [1][c]stream of God is full of water;
You prepare their [d]grain, for thus You prepare [2]the earth.
10 You water its furrows abundantly,
You [1]settle its ridges,
You soften it [a]with showers,
You bless its growth.
11 You have crowned the year [1]with Your [2][a]bounty,
And Your [3]paths [b]drip *with* fatness.
12 [a]The pastures of the wilderness drip,
And the [b]hills gird themselves with rejoicing.
13 The meadows are [a]clothed with flocks
And the valleys are [b]covered with grain;
They [c]shout for joy, yes, they sing.

Psalm 66

Praise for God's Mighty Deeds and for His Answer to Prayer.

For the choir director. A Song. A Psalm.

1 ¶ [a]Shout joyfully to God, all the earth;
2 Sing the [a]glory of His name;
Make His [b]praise glorious.
3 Say to God, "How [a]awesome are Your works!
Because of the greatness of Your power Your enemies will [1][b]give feigned obedience to You.
4 "[a]All the earth will worship You,
And will [b]sing praises to You;
They will sing praises to Your name." [1]Selah.

5 ¶ [a]Come and see the works of God,
Who is [b]awesome in *His* deeds toward the sons of men.
6 He [a]turned the sea into dry land;
They passed through [b]the river on foot;
There let us [c]rejoice in Him!
7 He [a]rules by His might forever;
His [b]eyes keep watch on the nations;
Let not the rebellious [c]exalt themselves. Selah.

8 ¶ Bless our God, O peoples,
And [1][a]sound His praise abroad,
9 Who [1][a]keeps us in life
And [b]does not allow our feet to [2]slip.
10 For You have [a]tried us, O God;
You have [b]refined us as silver is refined.
11 You [a]brought us into the net;
You laid an oppressive burden upon our loins.
12 You made men [a]ride over our heads;
We went through [b]fire and through water,
Yet You [c]brought us out into *a place of* abundance.
13 I shall [a]come into Your house with burnt offerings;
I shall [b]pay You my vows,
14 Which my lips uttered
And my mouth spoke when I was [a]in distress.
15 I shall [a]offer to You burnt offerings of fat beasts,
With the smoke of [b]rams;
I shall make *an offering of* [1]bulls with male goats. Selah.

16 ¶ [a]Come *and* hear, all who [1]fear God,
And I will [b]tell of what He has done for my soul.
17 I cried to Him with my mouth,
And [1]He was [a]extolled with my tongue.
18 If I [1][a]regard wickedness in my heart,
The [b]Lord [2]will not [3]hear;

4 [a]Ps 33:12 [b]Ps 4:3 [c]Ps 36:8
5 [1]Or *seas* [a]Ps 45:4 [b]Ps 85:4 [c]Ps 22:27 [d]Ps 107:23
6 [a]Ps 95:4 [b]Ps 93:1
7 [a]Ps 89:9; Matt 8:26 [b]Ps 2:1; Is 17:12
8 [1]Lit *the outgoings of the morning and evening* [a]Ps 2:8; Is 24:16
9 [1]Or *channel* [2]Lit *it* [a]Lev 26:4; Job 5:10; Ps 68:9; Jer 5:24 [b]Ps 104:24 [c]Ps 46:4 [d]Ps 104:14
10 [1]Or *smooth* [a]Deut 32:2; Ps 72:6
11 [1]Lit *of* [2]Or *goodness* [3]I.e. wagon tracks [a]Ps 104:28 [b]Job 36:28; Ps 147:14
12 [a]Job 38:26; Joel 2:22 [b]Ps 98:8; Is 55:12
13 [a]Ps 144:13; Is 30:23 [b]Ps 72:16 [c]Ps 98:8; Is 44:23
66:1 [a]Ps 81:1
2 [a]Ps 79:9; Is 42:8 [b]Is 42:12
3 [1]Lit *deceive* [a]Ps 47:2 [b]Ps 18:44
4 [1]*Selah* may mean: *Pause, Crescendo* or *Musical interlude* [a]Ps 22:27; Zech 14:16 [b]Ps 67:4
5 [a]Ps 46:8 [b]Ps 106:22
6 [a]Ex 14:21; Ps 106:9 [b]Josh 3:16; Ps 114:3 [c]Ps 105:43
7 [a]Ps 145:13 [b]Ps 11:4 [c]Ps 140:8
8 [1]Lit *cause to hear the sound of His praise* [a]Ps 98:4
9 [1]Lit *puts our soul in life* [2]Or *dodder, stumble* [a]Ps 30:3 [b]Ps 121:3
10 [a]Job 23:10; Ps 7:9 [b]Is 48:10; Zech 13:9; Mal 3:3; 1 Pet 1:7
11 [a]Lam 1:13; Ezek 12:13
12 [a]Is 51:23 [b]Ps 78:21; Is 43:2 [c]Ps 18:19
13 [a]Ps 96:8; Jer 17:26 [b]Ps 22:25; Eccl 5:4
14 [a]Ps 18:6
15 [1]Or *cattle* [a]Ps 51:19 [b]Num 6:14
16 [1]Or *revere* [a]Ps 34:11 [b]Ps 71:15
17 [1]Or *praise was under my tongue* [a]Ps 30:1
18 [1]Or *had regarded* [2]Or *would* [3]Or *have heard* [a]Job 36:21; John 9:31 [b]Job 27:9; Ps 18:41; Prov 1:28; Is 1:15; James 4:3

19 But certainly [a]God has heard;
He has given heed to the voice
of my prayer.
20 [a]Blessed be God,
Who [b]has not turned away my
prayer
Nor His lovingkindness from me.

Psalm 67

The Nations Exhorted to Praise God.

For the choir director; with stringed instruments. A Psalm. A Song.

1 ¶ God be gracious to us and
[a]bless us,
And [b]cause His face to shine
[1]upon us— [2]Selah.
2 That [a]Your way may be known
on the earth,
[b]Your salvation among all
nations.
3 Let the [a]peoples praise You,
O God;
Let all the peoples praise You.
4 Let the [a]nations be glad and
sing for joy;
For You will [b]judge the peoples
with uprightness
And [c]guide the nations on the
earth. Selah.
5 Let the [a]peoples praise You,
O God;
Let all the peoples praise You.
6 The [a]earth has yielded its
produce;
God, our God, [b]blesses us.
7 God blesses us,
[1]That [a]all the ends of the earth
may fear Him.

Psalm 68

The God of Sinai and of the Sanctuary.

For the choir director. A Psalm of David. A Song.

1 ¶ [1]Let [a]God arise, [2]let His
enemies be scattered,
And [3]let those who hate Him
flee before Him.
2 As [a]smoke is driven away, *so*
drive *them* away;
As [b]wax melts before the fire,
So let the [c]wicked perish before
God.
3 But let the [a]righteous be glad;
let them exult before God;
Yes, let them rejoice with
gladness.
4 Sing to God, [a]sing praises to His
name;
[1b]Lift up *a song* for Him who
[c]rides through the deserts,
Whose [d]name is [2]the LORD, and
exult before Him.
5 ¶ A [a]father of the fatherless and
a [b]judge [1]for the widows,
Is God in His [c]holy habitation.
6 God [1a]makes a home for the
lonely;
He [b]leads out the prisoners into
prosperity,
Only [c]the rebellious dwell in a
parched land.
7 ¶ O God, when You [a]went forth
before Your people,
When You [b]marched through
the wilderness, [1]Selah.
8 The [a]earth quaked;
The [b]heavens also dropped *rain*
at the presence of God;
[1c]Sinai itself *quaked* at the
presence of God, the God of
Israel.
9 You [a]shed abroad a plentiful
rain, O God;
You confirmed Your inheritance
when it was [1]parched.
10 Your creatures settled in it;
You [a]provided in Your goodness
for the poor, O God.
11 ¶ The Lord gives the [1]command;
The [a]women who proclaim the
good tidings are a great
host:
12 "[a]Kings of armies flee, they flee,
And she who remains at home
will [b]divide the spoil!"
13 [1]When you lie down [a]among
the [2]sheepfolds,
You are like the wings of a dove
covered with silver,
And its pinions with glistening
gold.
14 When the Almighty [a]scattered
the kings [1]there,
It was snowing in [b]Zalmon.
15 ¶ A [1a]mountain of God is the
mountain of Bashan;
A mountain *of many* peaks is the
mountain of Bashan.
16 Why do you look with envy,
O mountains with *many*
peaks,
At the mountain which God has
[a]desired for His abode?
Surely [b]the LORD will dwell
there forever.
17 The [a]chariots of God are
[1]myriads, [b]thousands upon
thousands;

19 [a]Ps 18:6
20 [a]Ps 68:35 [b]Ps 22:24
67:1 [1]Lit *with* [2]*Selah* may mean: *Pause, Crescendo* or *Musical interlude* [a]Num 6:25 [b]Ps 4:6
2 [a]Ps 98:2; Acts 18:25; Titus 2:11 [b]Is 52:10
3 [a]Ps 66:4
4 [a]Ps 100:1 [b]Ps 9:8 [c]Ps 47:8
5 [a]Ps 67:3
6 [a]Lev 26:4; Ps 85:12; Ezek 34:27; Zech 8:12 [b]Ps 29:11
7 [1]Or *And let all...earth fear Him* [a]Ps 22:27
68:1 [1]Or *God shall* [2]Or *His enemies shall* [3]Or *those who hate Him shall* [a]Num 10:35; Ps 12:5
2 [a]Ps 37:20; Is 9:18; Hos 13:3 [b]Ps 22:14; Mic 1:4 [c]Ps 9:3
3 [a]Ps 32:11
4 [1]Or *Cast up* a highway [2]Heb YAH [a]Ps 66:2 [b]Is 57:14 [c]Deut 33:26; Ps 18:10; Is 40:3 [d]Ex 6:3; Ps 83:18
5 [1]Lit *of* [a]Ps 10:14 [b]Deut 10:18 [c]Deut 26:15
6 [1]Lit *makes the solitary to dwell in a house* [a]Ps 107:4-7 [b]Ps 69:33; Acts 12:7 [c]Ps 78:17
7 [1]*Selah* may mean: *Pause, Crescendo* or *Musical interlude* [a]Ex 13:21; Ps 78:14; Hab 3:13 [b]Judg 5:4; Ps 78:52
8 [1]Lit *This is Sinai* which [a]Ex 19:18; Judg 5:4; 2 Sam 22:8; Ps 77:18; Jer 10:10 [b]Judg 5:4; Ps 18:9; Is 45:8 [c]Ex 19:18; Judg 5:5
9 [1]Lit *weary* [a]Lev 26:4; Deut 11:11; Job 5:10; Ezek 34:26
10 [a]Ps 65:9
11 [1]Lit *word* [a]Ex 15:20; 1 Sam 18:6
12 [a]Josh 10:16; Judg 5:19; Ps 135:11 [b]Judg 5:30; 1 Sam 30:24
13 [1]Lit *If* [2]Or *cooking stones or saddle bags* [a]Gen 49:14; Judg 5:16
14 [1]Lit *in it* [a]Josh 10:10 [b]Judg 9:48
15 [1]Or *mighty mountain is* [a]Ps 36:6
16 [a]Deut 12:5; Ps 87:1 [b]Ps 132:14
17 [1]Lit *twice ten thousand*
[a]2 Kin 6:17; Hab 3:8 [b]Deut 33:2; Dan 7:10

[2]The Lord is among them *as at*
Sinai, in holiness.
18 You have [a]ascended on high,
You have [b]led captive *Your*
captives;
You have received gifts among
men,
Even *among* the rebellious also,
that [1]the LORD God may
dwell *there.*

19 ¶ Blessed be the Lord, who daily
[a]bears our burden,
[b]The God *who* is our salvation.
Selah.
20 God is to us a [a]God of
deliverances;
And [b]to [1]GOD the Lord belong
escapes [2]from death.
21 Surely God will [a]shatter the
head of His enemies,
The hairy crown of him who
goes on in his guilty deeds.
22 The Lord [1]said, "[a]I will bring
them back from Bashan.
I will bring *them* back from the
depths of the sea;
23 That [1a]your foot may shatter
them in blood,
The tongue of your [b]dogs *may*
have its portion from *your*
enemies."

24 ¶ They have seen [a]Your
[1]procession, O God,
The [1]procession of my God, my
King, [2b]into the sanctuary.
25 The [a]singers went on, the
musicians after *them,*
[1]In the midst of the [b]maidens
beating tambourines.
26 [a]Bless God in the congregations,
Even the LORD, *you who are* of
the [b]fountain of Israel.
27 There is [a]Benjamin, the
[1]youngest, [2]ruling them,
The princes of Judah *in* their
throng,
The princes of [b]Zebulun, the
princes of Naphtali.

28 ¶ [1]Your God has [a]commanded
your strength;
Show Yourself strong, O God,
[b]who have acted [2]on our
behalf.
29 [1]Because of Your temple at
Jerusalem
[a]Kings will bring gifts to You.
30 Rebuke the [a]beasts [1]in the
reeds,
The herd of [b]bulls with the
calves of the peoples,
Trampling under foot the pieces
of silver;
He has [c]scattered the peoples
who delight in war.
31 Envoys will come out of [a]Egypt;
[1b]Ethiopia will quickly stretch
out her hands to God.

32 ¶ Sing to God, O [a]kingdoms of
the earth,
[b]Sing praises to the Lord, Selah.
33 To Him who [a]rides upon the
[1b]highest heavens, which
are from ancient times;
Behold, [c]He [2]speaks forth with
His voice, a [d]mighty voice.
34 [a]Ascribe strength to God;
His majesty is over Israel
And [b]His strength is in the
[1]skies.
35 [1]O God, *You are* [a]awesome
from Your [2]sanctuary.
The God of Israel Himself [b]gives
strength and power to the
people.
[c]Blessed be God!

Psalm 69

A Cry of Distress and Imprecation on Adversaries.

For the choir director; according
to +Shoshannim. *A Psalm* of David.

1 ¶ Save me, O God,
For the [a]waters have
[1]threatened my life.
2 I have sunk in deep [a]mire, and
there is no foothold;
I have come into deep waters,
and a [1b]flood overflows me.
3 I am [a]weary with my crying; my
throat is parched;
My [b]eyes fail while I wait for
my God.
4 Those [a]who hate me without a
cause are more than the
hairs of my head;
Those who would [1]destroy me
[b]are powerful, being
wrongfully my enemies;
[c]What I did not steal, I then
have to restore.

5 ¶ O God, it is You who knows
[a]my folly,
And [b]my wrongs are not hidden
from You.
6 May those who wait for You not
[a]be ashamed through me,
O Lord [1]GOD of hosts;
May those who seek You not be
dishonored through me,
O God of Israel,

17 [2]Another reading is *The Lord came from Sinai into the sanctuary*
18 [1]Heb *YAH* [a]Ps 7:7; Eph 4:8 [b]Judg 5:12
19 [a]Ps 55:22; Is 46:4 [b]Ps 65:5
20 [1]Heb *YHWH,* usually rendered *LORD* [2]I.e. in view of; lit *for* [a]Ps 106:43 [b]Deut 32:39; Ps 49:15
21 [a]Ps 110:6; Hab 3:13
22 [1]Or *says* [a]Num 21:33; Amos 9:1-3
23 [1]Some versions render, you may *bathe your foot in blood* [a]Ps 58:10 [b]1 Kin 21:19; Jer 15:3
24 [1]Lit *goings* [2]Lit *in the sanctuary;* or *in holiness* [a]Ps 77:13 [b]Ps 63:2
25 [1]Or *The maidens in the midst* [a]1 Chr 13:8; Ps 47:6 [b]Ex 15:20; Judg 11:34
26 [a]Ps 22:22 [b]Deut 33:28; Is 48:1
27 [1]Or *smallest* [2]Or *their ruler* [a]Judg 5:14; 1 Sam 9:21 [b]Judg 5:18
28 [1]Some mss read *Command, God* [2]Lit *for us* [a]Ps 29:11 [b]Is 26:12
29 [1]Or *From Your temple* [a]1 Kin 10:10; 2 Chr 32:23; Ps 45:12; Is 18:7
30 [1]Lit *of* [a]Job 40:21; Ezek 29:3 [b]Ps 22:12 [c]Ps 18:14
31 [1]Lit *Cush* [a]Is 19:19 [b]Is 45:14; Zeph 3:10
32 [a]Ps 102:22 [b]Ps 67:4
33 [1]Lit *heaven of heavens of old* [2]Lit *gives forth* [a]Deut 33:26; Ps 18:10 [b]Deut 10:14; 1 Kin 8:27 [c]Ps 46:6 [d]Ps 29:4
34 [1]Lit *clouds* [a]Ps 29:1 [b]Ps 150:1
35 [1]Or *Awesome is God from your sanctuary* [2]Lit *holy places* [a]Deut 7:21; Ps 47:2 [b]Ps 29:11; Is 40:29 [c]Ps 66:20; 2 Cor 1:3
69:1 +Or possibly *Lilies* [1]Lit *come to the soul* [a]Job 22:11; Ps 32:6; Jon 2:5
2 [1]Lit *flowing stream* [a]Ps 40:2 [b]Jon 2:3
3 [a]Ps 6:6 [b]Deut 28:32; Ps 38:10; Is 38:14
4 [1]Or *silence* [a]Ps 35:19; John 15:25 [b]Ps 35:19 [c]Ps 35:11; Jer 15:10 **5** [a]Ps 38:5 [b]Ps 44:21
6 [1]Heb *YHWH,* usually rendered *LORD* [a]2 Sam 12:14

7 Because [a]for Your sake I have
borne reproach;
[b]Dishonor has covered my
face.
8 I have become [a]estranged [1]from
my brothers
And an alien to my mother's
sons.
9 For [a]zeal for Your house has
consumed me,
And [b]the reproaches of those
who reproach You have
fallen on me.
10 When I wept [a]in my soul with
fasting,
It became my reproach.
11 When I made [a]sackcloth my
clothing,
I became [b]a byword to them.
12 Those who [a]sit in the gate talk
about me,
And I *am* the [1b]song of the
drunkards.

13 ¶ But as for me, my prayer is to
You, O LORD, [a]at an
acceptable time;
O God, in the [b]greatness of
Your lovingkindness,
Answer me with [1]Your saving
truth.
14 Deliver me from the [a]mire and
do not let me sink;
May I be [b]delivered from [1]my
foes and from the [2a]deep
waters.
15 May the [1a]flood of water not
overflow me
Nor the deep swallow me up,
Nor the [b]pit shut its mouth
on me.

16 ¶ Answer me, O LORD, for [a]Your
lovingkindness is good;
[b]According to the greatness of
Your compassion, [c]turn
to me,
17 And [a]do not hide Your face from
Your servant,
For I am [b]in distress; answer me
quickly.
18 Oh draw near to my soul *and*
[a]redeem it;
[b]Ransom me because of my
enemies!
19 You know my [a]reproach and my
shame and my dishonor;
All my adversaries are
[1]before You.

20 ¶ Reproach has [a]broken my
heart and I am so sick.
And [b]I looked for sympathy, but
there was none,
And for [c]comforters, but I found
none.
21 They also gave me [1a]gall [2]for
my food
And for my thirst they [b]gave me
vinegar to drink.

22 ¶ May [a]their table before them
become a snare;
And [1b]when they are in peace,
may it become a trap.
23 May their [a]eyes grow dim so
that they cannot see,
And make their [b]loins shake
continually.
24 [a]Pour out Your indignation on
them,
And may Your burning anger
overtake them.
25 May their [1a]camp be desolate;
May none dwell in their tents.
26 For they have [a]persecuted him
whom [b]You Yourself have
smitten,
And they tell of the pain of those
whom [c]You have
[1]wounded.
27 Add [a]iniquity to their iniquity,
And [b]may they not come into
[c]Your righteousness.
28 May they be [a]blotted out of the
[b]book of life
And may they not be
[1c]recorded with the
righteous.

29 ¶ But I am [a]afflicted and in pain;
[1]May Your salvation, O God,
[b]set me *securely* on high.
30 I will [a]praise the name of God
with song
And [b]magnify Him with
[c]thanksgiving.
31 And it will [a]please the LORD
better than an ox
Or a young bull with horns and
hoofs.
32 The [a]humble [1]have seen *it and*
are glad;
You who seek God, [b]let your
heart [2]revive.
33 For [a]the LORD hears the needy
And [b]does not despise His *who*
are prisoners.

34 ¶ Let [a]heaven and earth praise
Him,
The seas and [b]everything that
moves in them.
35 For God will [a]save Zion and
[b]build the cities of Judah,
That they may dwell there and
[c]possess it.

7 [a]Jer 15:15 [b]Ps 44:15; Is 50:6; Jer 51:51
8 [1]Lit *to* [a]Job 19:13-15; Ps 31:11
9 [a]Ps 119:139; John 2:17 [b]Ps 89:41; Rom 15:3
10 [a]Ps 35:13
11 [a]1 Kin 20:31; Ps 35:13 [b]1 Kin 9:7; Job 17:6; Ps 44:14; Jer 24:9
12 [1]Lit *songs* [a]Gen 19:1; Ruth 4:1 [b]Job 30:9
13 [1]Or *the faithfulness of Your salvation* [a]Ps 32:6; Is 49:8; 2 Cor 6:2 [b]Ps 51:1
14 [1]Lit *those who hate me* [2]Lit *deep places of water* [a]Ps 69:2 [b]Ps 144:7
15 [1]Lit *stream* [a]Ps 124:4 [b]Num 16:33; Ps 28:1
16 [a]Ps 63:3 [b]Ps 51:1 [c]Ps 25:16
17 [a]Ps 27:9 [b]Ps 31:9
18 [a]2 Sam 4:9; Ps 26:11 [b]Ps 119:134
19 [1]Or known *to You* [a]Ps 22:6
20 [a]Jer 23:9 [b]Ps 142:4; Is 63:5 [c]Job 16:2
21 [1]Or *poison* [2]Or *in* [a]Deut 29:18 [b]Matt 27:34; Mark 15:23; Luke 23:36; John 19:28-30
22 [1]Lit *for those who are secure* [a]Rom 11:9 [b]1 Thess 5:3
23 [a]Is 6:10 [b]Dan 5:6
24 [a]Ps 79:6; Jer 10:25; Ezek 20:8; Hos 5:10
25 [1]Lit *encampment* [a]Matt 23:38; Luke 13:35; Acts 1:20
26 [1]Lit *pierced* [a]2 Chr 28:9; Zech 1:15 [b]Is 53:4 [c]Ps 109:22
27 [a]Neh 4:5; Ps 109:14; Rom 1:28 [b]Is 26:10 [c]Ps 103:17
28 [1]Lit *written* [a]Ex 32:32; Rev 3:5 [b]Phil 4:3; Rev 13:8 [c]Ps 87:6; Ezek 13:9; Luke 10:20; Heb 12:23
29 [1]Or *Your salvation, O God, will set...* [a]Ps 70:5 [b]Ps 20:1
30 [a]Ps 28:7 [b]Ps 34:3 [c]Ps 50:14
31 [a]Ps 50:13
32 [1]Some mss and ancient versions read *will see* [2]Or *live* [a]Ps 34:2 [b]Ps 22:26
33 [a]Ps 12:5 [b]Ps 68:6
34 [a]Ps 96:11; Is 44:23 [b]Is 55:12
35 [a]Ps 46:5 [b]Ps 147:2; Is 44:26 [c]Obad 17

36 The [1][a]descendants of His servants will inherit it,
And those who love His name [b]will dwell in it.

Psalm 70

Prayer for Help against Persecutors.

For the choir director. *A Psalm* of David; for a memorial.

1 ¶ [a]O God, *hasten* to deliver me;
O LORD, hasten to my help!
2 [a]Let those be ashamed and humiliated
Who seek my [1]life;
Let those be turned back and dishonored
Who delight [2]in my hurt.
3 [a]Let those be [1]turned back because of their shame
Who say, "Aha, aha!"

4 ¶ Let all who seek You rejoice and be glad in You;
And let those who love Your salvation say continually,
"Let God be magnified."
5 But [a]I am afflicted and needy;
[b]Hasten to me, O God!
You are my help and my deliverer;
O LORD, do not delay.

Psalm 71

Prayer of an Old Man for Deliverance.

1 ¶ [a]In You, O LORD, I have taken refuge;
Let me never be ashamed.
2 [a]In Your righteousness deliver me and rescue me;
[b]Incline Your ear to me and save me.
3 [a]Be to me a rock of [b]habitation to which I may continually come;
You have given [c]commandment to save me,
For You are [d]my [1]rock and my fortress.
4 [a]Rescue me, O my God, out of the hand of the wicked,
Out of the [1]grasp of the wrongdoer and ruthless man,
5 For You are my [a]hope;
O Lord [1]GOD, *You are* my [b]confidence from my youth.
6 [1]By You I have been [a]sustained from *my* birth;
You are He who [b]took me from my mother's womb;
My [c]praise is continually [2]of You.

7 ¶ I have become a [a]marvel to many,
For You are [b]my strong refuge.
8 My [a]mouth is filled with Your praise
And with [b]Your glory all day long.
9 Do not cast me off in the [a]time of old age;
Do not forsake me when my strength fails.
10 For my enemies have spoken [1]against me;
And those who [a]watch for my [2]life [b]have consulted together,
11 Saying, "[a]God has forsaken him;
Pursue and seize him, for there is [b]no one to deliver."

12 ¶ O God, [a]do not be far from me;
O my God, [b]hasten to my help!
13 Let those who are adversaries of my soul be [a]ashamed *and* consumed;
Let them be [b]covered with reproach and dishonor, who [c]seek [1]to injure me.
14 But as for me, I will [a]hope continually,
And will [1][b]praise You yet more and more.
15 My [a]mouth shall tell of Your righteousness
And of [b]Your salvation all day long;
For I [c]do not know the [1]sum *of them.*
16 I will come [a]with the mighty deeds of the Lord [1]GOD;
I will [b]make mention of Your righteousness, Yours alone.

17 ¶ O God, You [a]have taught me from my youth,
And I still [b]declare Your wondrous deeds.
18 And even when *I am* [a]old and gray, O God, do not forsake me,
Until I [b]declare Your [1]strength to *this* generation,
Your power to all who are to come.
19 [1]For Your [a]righteousness, O God, *reaches* to the [2]heavens,

36 [1]Lit *seed* [a]Ps 25:13; 102:28 [b]Ps 37:29
70:1 [a]Ps 40:13-17; 70:1-5
2 [1]Or *soul* [2]Or *to injure me* [a]Ps 35:4,26
3 [1]Some mss read *appalled* [a]Ps 40:15
5 [a]Ps 40:17 [b]Ps 141:1
71:1 [a]Ps 25:2,3; 31:1-3; 71:1-3
2 [a]Ps 31:1 [b]Ps 17:6
3 [1]Or *crag* [a]Ps 31:2,3 [b]Deut 33:27; Ps 90:1; 91:9 [c]Ps 7:6; 42:8 [d]Ps 18:2
4 [1]Lit *palm* [a]Ps 140:1,4
5 [1]Heb *YHWH,* usually rendered LORD [a]Ps 39:7; Jer 14:8; 17:7, 13,17; 50:7 [b]Ps 22:9
6 [1]Lit *Upon You I have been supported* [2]Lit *in* [a]Ps 22:10; Is 46:3 [b]Job 10:18; Ps 22:9 [c]Ps 34:1
7 [a]Is 8:18; 1 Cor 4:9 [b]Ps 61:3
8 [a]Ps 35:28; 63:5 [b]Ps 96:6; 104:1
9 [a]Ps 71:18; 92:14; Is 46:4
10 [1]Lit *with reference to* [2]Lit *soul* [a]Ps 56:6 [b]Ps 31:13; 83:3; Matt 27:1
11 [a]Ps 3:2 [b]Ps 7:2
12 [a]Ps 10:1; 22:11; 35:22; 38:21 [b]Ps 38:22; 40:13; 70:1,5
13 [1]Lit *my injury* [a]Ps 35:4,26; 40:14 [b]Ps 109:29 [c]Esth 9:2; Ps 71:24
14 [1]Lit *add upon all Your praise* [a]Ps 130:7 [b]Ps 71:8
15 [1]Lit *numbers* [a]Ps 35:28 [b]Ps 96:2 [c]Ps 40:5
16 [1]Heb *YHWH,* usually rendered LORD [a]Ps 106:2 [b]Ps 51:14
17 [a]Deut 4:5; 6:7 [b]Ps 26:7; 40:5; 119:27
18 [1]Lit *arm* [a]Ps 71:9 [b]Ps 22:31; 78:4,6
19 [1]Or *And* [2]Lit *height* [a]Ps 36:6; 57:10

You who have [b]done great
things;
O God, [c]who is like You?
20 You who have [a]shown [1]me
many troubles and distresses
Will [b]revive [1]me again,
And will bring [1]me up again
[c]from the depths of the
earth.
21 May You increase my [a]greatness
And turn *to* [b]comfort me.

22 ¶ I will also praise You with [1a]a
harp,
Even Your [2]truth, O my God;
To You I will sing praises with
the [b]lyre,
O [c]Holy One of Israel.
23 My lips will [a]shout for joy when
I sing praises to You;
And my [b]soul, which You have
redeemed.
24 My [a]tongue also will utter Your
righteousness all day long;
For they are [b]ashamed, for they
are humiliated who seek
[1]my hurt.

Psalm 72

The Reign of the Righteous King.

A Psalm of Solomon.

1 ¶ Give the king [a]Your
judgments, O God,
And [b]Your righteousness to the
king's son.
2 [1]May [2]he [a]judge Your people
with righteousness
And [3b]Your afflicted with
justice.
3 [1]Let the mountains bring
[2a]peace to the people,
And the hills, in righteousness.
4 [1]May he [a]vindicate the
[2]afflicted of the people,
Save the children of the needy
And crush the oppressor.

5 ¶ [1]Let them fear You [a]while the
sun *endures,*
And [2]as long as the moon,
throughout all generations.
6 [1]May he come down [a]like rain
upon the mown grass,
Like [b]showers that water the
earth.
7 In his days [1]may the [a]righteous
flourish,
And [b]abundance of peace till the
moon is no more.

8 ¶ May he also rule [a]from sea
to sea
And from the River to the ends
of the earth.
9 [1]Let [a]the nomads of the desert
[b]bow before him,
And his enemies [c]lick the dust.
10 [1]Let the kings of [a]Tarshish and
of the [2b]islands bring
presents;
The kings of [c]Sheba and [d]Seba
[e]offer [3]gifts.
11 [1]And let all [a]kings bow down
before him,
All [b]nations serve him.

12 ¶ For he will [a]deliver the needy
when he cries for help,
The [1]afflicted also, and him who
has no helper.
13 He will have [a]compassion on
the poor and needy,
And the [1]lives of the needy he
will save.
14 He will [1a]rescue their [2]life
from oppression and
violence,
And their blood will be
[b]precious in his sight;
15 So may he live, and may the
[a]gold of Sheba be given to
him;
And let [1]them pray for him
continually;
Let [1]them bless him all day
long.

16 ¶ May there be abundance of
grain in the earth on top of
the mountains;
Its fruit will wave like *the cedars*
of [a]Lebanon;
And may those from the city
flourish like [b]vegetation of
the earth.
17 May his [a]name endure forever;
May his name [1]increase [2b]as
long as the sun *shines;*
And let *men* [c]bless themselves
by him;
[d]Let all nations call him blessed.

18 ¶ [a]Blessed be the LORD God, the
God of Israel,
Who alone [b]works wonders.
19 And blessed be His [a]glorious
name forever;
And may the whole [b]earth be
filled with His glory.
[c]Amen, and Amen.

20 ¶ The prayers of David the son
of Jesse are ended.

19 [b]Ps 126:2; Luke 1:49 [c]Deut 3:24; Ps 35:10
20 [1]Another reading is *us* [a]Ps 60:3 [b]Ps 80:18; Hos 6:1 [c]Ps 86:13
21 [a]Ps 18:35 [b]Ps 23:4; Is 12:1
22 [1]Lit *an instrument of a harp* [2]Or *faithfulness* [a]Ps 33:2 [b]Ps 33:2 [c]2 Kin 19:22; Ps 78:41; Is 1:4
23 [a]Ps 5:11 [b]Ps 34:22
24 [1]Or *to injure me* [a]Ps 35:28 [b]Ps 71:13
72:1 [a]1 Kin 3:9; 1 Chr 22:13 [b]Ps 24:5
2 [1]Or *He will judge* [2]Many of the pronouns in this Psalm may be rendered *He* since the typical reference is to the Messiah [3]Or *Your humble* [a]Is 9:7 [b]Ps 82:3
3 [1]Or *The mountains will bring* [2]Or *prosperity* [a]Is 2:4; Mic 4:3; Zech 9:10
4 [1]Or *He will vindicate* [2]Or *humble* [a]Is 11:4
5 [1]Or *They will fear* [2]Lit *before the moon* [a]Ps 72:17
6 [1]Or *He will come down* [a]Deut 32:2; 2 Sam 23:4; Hos 6:3 [b]Ps 65:10
7 [1]Or *the righteous will flourish* [a]Ps 92:12 [b]Is 2:4
8 [a]Ex 23:31; Zech 9:10
9 [1]Or *The nomads...will bow* [a]Ps 74:14; Is 23:13 [b]Ps 22:29 [c]Is 49:23; Mic 7:17
10 [1]Or *The kings...will bring* [2]Or *coastlands* [3]Or *tribute* [a]2 Chr 9:21; Ps 48:7 [b]Ps 97:1; Is 42:4; Zeph 2:11 [c]1 Kin 10:1; Job 6:19; Is 60:6 [d]Gen 10:7; Is 43:3 [e]Ps 45:12
11 [1]Or *All kings will bow down* [a]Ps 138:4; Is 49:23 [b]Ps 86:9
12 [1]Or *humble* [a]Job 29:12; Ps 72:4
13 [1]Lit *souls* [a]Prov 19:17
14 [1]Lit *redeem* [2]Lit *soul* [a]Ps 69:18 [b]1 Sam 26:21; Ps 116:15
15 [1]Lit *him* [a]Is 60:6
16 [a]Ps 104:16 [b]Job 5:25
17 [1]Or *sprout forth* [2]Lit *before the sun* [a]Ex 3:15; Ps 135:13 [b]Ps 89:36 [c]Gen 12:3 [d]Luke 1:48

18 [a]1 Chr 29:10; Ps 41:13 [b]Ex 15:11; Job 5:9; Ps 77:14
19 [a]Neh 9:5; Ps 96:8 [b]Num 14:21 [c]Ps 41:13

BOOK 3

Psalm 73

The End of the Wicked Contrasted with That of the Righteous.

A Psalm of Asaph.

1 ¶ Surely God is [a]good to Israel,
To those who are [b]pure in
heart!
2 But as for me, [a]my feet came
close to stumbling,
My steps [1]had almost slipped.
3 For I was [a]envious of the
[1]arrogant
As I saw the [b]prosperity of the
wicked.
4 For there are no pains in their
death,
And their [1]body is fat.
5 They are [a]not [1]in trouble *as
other* [2]men,
Nor are they [b]plagued [3]like
mankind.
6 Therefore pride is [a]their
necklace;
The [b]garment of violence covers
them.
7 Their eye [1]bulges from [a]fatness;
The imaginations of *their* heart
[2]run riot.
8 They [a]mock and [1]wickedly
speak of oppression;
They [b]speak from on high.
9 They have [a]set their mouth
[1]against the heavens,
And their tongue [2]parades
through the earth.

10 ¶ Therefore [1]his people return
to this place,
And waters of [a]abundance are
[2]drunk by them.
11 They say, "[a]How does God
know?
And is there knowledge [1]with
the Most High?"
12 Behold, [a]these are the wicked;
And always [b]at ease, they have
increased *in* wealth.
13 Surely [a]in vain I have [1]kept my
heart pure
And [b]washed my hands in
innocence;
14 For I have been stricken [a]all day
long
And [1b]chastened every
morning.

15 ¶ If I had said, "I will speak
thus,"
Behold, I would have betrayed
the [a]generation of Your
children.
16 When I [a]pondered to
understand this,
It was [1]troublesome in my sight
17 Until I came into the
[1a]sanctuary of God;
Then I perceived their [b]end.
18 Surely You set them in [a]slippery
places;
You cast them down to
[1b]destruction.
19 How they are [1a]destroyed in a
moment!
They are utterly swept away by
[b]sudden terrors!
20 Like a [a]dream when one
awakes,
O Lord, when [b]aroused, You
will [c]despise their [1]form.

21 ¶ When my [a]heart was
embittered
And I was [b]pierced [1]within,
22 Then I was [a]senseless and
ignorant;
I was *like* [1]a [b]beast
[2]before You.
23 Nevertheless [a]I am continually
with You;
You have taken hold of my right
hand.
24 With Your counsel You will
[a]guide me,
And afterward [b]receive me [1]to
glory.

25 ¶ [a]Whom have I in heaven
but You?
And [1]besides You, I desire
nothing on earth.
26 My [a]flesh and my heart may fail,
But God is the [1]strength of my
heart and my [b]portion
forever.
27 For, behold, [a]those who are far
from You will [b]perish;
You have [1]destroyed all those
who [2c]are unfaithful
to You.
28 But as for me, [a]the nearness of
God is my good;
I have made the Lord [1]GOD my
[b]refuge,
That I may [c]tell of all Your
works.

Psalm 74

An Appeal against the Devastation of the Land by the Enemy.

A [+]Maskil of Asaph.

1 ¶ O God, why have You
[a]rejected *us* forever?

73:1 [a]Ps 86:5 [b]Ps 24:4; Matt 5:8
2 [1]Lit *were caused to slip* [a]Ps 94:18
3 [1]Or *boasters* [a]Ps 37:1; Prov 23:17 [b]Job 21:7; Ps 37:7; Jer 12:1
4 [1]Or *belly*
5 [1]Lit *in the trouble of men* [2]Or *mortals* [3]Lit *with* [a]Job 21:9; Ps 73:12 [b]Ps 73:14
6 [a]Gen 41:42; Prov 1:9 [b]Ps 109:18
7 [1]Lit *goes forth* [2]Lit *overflow* [a]Job 15:27; Ps 17:10; Jer 5:28
8 [1]Or *they speak in wickedness; From on high they speak of oppression* [a]Ps 1:1 [b]Ps 17:10; 2 Pet 2:18; Jude 16
9 [1]Or *in* [2]Lit *walks* [a]Rev 13:6
10 [1]Or *His* [2]Lit *drained out* [a]Ps 23:5
11 [1]Lit *in* [a]Job 22:13
12 [a]Ps 49:6 [b]Jer 49:31; Ezek 23:42
13 [1]Or *cleansed my heart* [a]Job 21:15 [b]Ps 26:6
14 [1]Lit *my chastening* [a]Ps 38:6 [b]Job 33:19; Ps 118:18
15 [a]Ps 14:5
16 [1]Lit *labor, trouble* [a]Eccl 8:17
17 [1]Lit *sanctuaries* [a]Ps 27:4 [b]Ps 37:38
18 [1]Lit *ruins* [a]Ps 35:6 [b]Ps 35:8
19 [1]Lit *become a desolation* [a]Num 16:21; Is 47:11 [b]Job 18:11
20 [1]Or *image* [a]Job 20:8 [b]Ps 78:65 [c]1 Sam 2:30
21 [1]Lit *in my kidneys* [a]Judg 10:16 [b]Acts 2:37
22 [1]Or *an animal* [2]Lit *with You* [a]Ps 49:10 [b]Job 18:3; Ps 49:20; Eccl 3:18
23 [a]Ps 16:8
24 [1]Or *with honor* [a]Ps 32:8; Is 58:11 [b]Gen 5:24; Ps 49:15
25 [1]Or *with* [a]Ps 16:2; Phil 3:8
26 [1]Lit *rock* [a]Ps 38:10 [b]Ps 16:5
27 [1]Or *silenced* [2]Lit *go to a whoring from* [a]Ps 119:155 [b]Ps 37:20 [c]Ex 34:15; Num 15:39; Ps 106:39; Hos 4:12
28 [1]Heb *YHWH*, usually rendered *LORD* [a]Ps 65:4; Heb 10:22; James 4:8 [b]Ps 14:6 [c]Ps 40:5
74:1 [+]Possibly *Contemplative*, or *Didactic*, or *Skillful Psalm* [a]Ps 44:9

Why does Your anger [b]smoke
against the [c]sheep of Your
[1]pasture?
2 Remember Your congregation,
which You have [a]purchased
of old,
Which You have [b]redeemed to
be the [c]tribe of Your
inheritance;
And this Mount [d]Zion, where
You have dwelt.
3 [1]Turn Your footsteps toward the
[a]perpetual ruins;
The enemy [b]has damaged
everything within the
sanctuary.
4 Your adversaries have [a]roared in
the midst of Your meeting
place;
They have set up their [b]own
[1]standards [c]for signs.
5 It seems as if one had lifted up
His [1a]axe in a [2]forest of trees.
6 And now [1]all its [a]carved work
They smash with hatchet and
[2]hammers.
7 They have [1a]burned Your
sanctuary [2]to the ground;
They have [b]defiled the dwelling
place of Your name.
8 They [a]said in their heart, "Let
us [1]completely [2]subdue
them."
They have burned all the
meeting places of God in the
land.
9 We do not see our [a]signs;
There is [b]no longer any prophet,
Nor is there any among us who
knows [c]how long.
10 How long, O God, will the
adversary [a]revile,
And the enemy [b]spurn Your
name forever?
11 Why [a]do You withdraw Your
hand, even Your right hand?
From within Your bosom,
[b]destroy *them!*

12 ¶ Yet God is [a]my king from of
old,
Who works deeds of deliverance
in the midst of the earth.
13 [1]You [a]divided the sea by Your
strength;
[1]You [b]broke the heads of the
[c]sea monsters [2]in the
waters.
14 [1]You crushed the heads of
[2a]Leviathan;
[1]You gave him as food for the
[3]creatures [b]of the
wilderness.
15 [1]You [a]broke open springs and
torrents;
[1]You [b]dried up ever-flowing
streams.
16 Yours is the day, Yours also is
the night;
[1]You have [a]prepared the [2]light
and the sun.
17 [1]You have [a]established all the
boundaries of the earth;
[1]You have [2]made [b]summer and
winter.

18 ¶ Remember this, [1]O LORD, that
the enemy has [a]reviled,
And a [b]foolish people has
spurned Your name.
19 Do not deliver the soul of Your
[a]turtledove to the wild
beast;
[b]Do not forget the life of Your
afflicted forever.
20 Consider the [a]covenant;
For the [b]dark places of the land
are full of the habitations of
violence.
21 Let not the [a]oppressed return
dishonored;
Let the [b]afflicted and needy
praise Your name.

22 ¶ Arise, O God, *and* [a]plead Your
own cause;
Remember [1]how the [b]foolish
man reproaches You all day
long.
23 Do not forget the voice of Your
[a]adversaries,
The [b]uproar of those who rise
against You which ascends
continually.

Psalm 75

God Abases the Proud, but Exalts the Righteous.

For the choir director; *set to* [+]Al-tashheth.
A Psalm of Asaph, a Song.

1 ¶ We [a]give thanks to You,
O God, we give thanks,
For Your name is [b]near;
Men declare [c]Your wondrous
works.
2 "When I select an [a]appointed
time,
It is I who [b]judge with equity.
3 "The [a]earth and all who dwell in
it [1]melt;
It is I who have firmly set its
[b]pillars. [2]Selah.
4 "I said to the boastful, 'Do not
boast,'

1 [1]Or *pasturing* [b]Deut 29:20; Ps 18:8 [c]Ps 79:13
2 [a]Ex 15:16; Deut 32:6 [b]Ex 15:13; Ps 77:15; Is 63:9 [c]Deut 32:9; Is 63:17; Jer 10:16 [d]Ps 9:11
3 [1]Lit *Lift up* [a]Is 61:4 [b]Ps 79:1
4 [1]Lit *signs* [a]Lam 2:7 [b]Num 2:2 [c]Ps 74:9
5 [1]Lit *axes* [2]Lit *thicket* [a]Jer 46:22
6 [1]Lit *altogether* [2]Or *axes* [a]1 Kin 6:18
7 [1]Lit *set on fire* [2]Or *To the ground they...* [a]2 Kin 25:9 [b]Ps 89:39; Lam 2:2
8 [1]Lit *altogether* [2]Or *oppress* [a]Ps 83:4
9 [a]Ps 78:43 [b]1 Sam 3:1; Lam 2:9; Ezek 7:26; Amos 8:11 [c]Ps 6:3
10 [a]Ps 44:16 [b]Lev 24:16
11 [a]Lam 2:3 [b]Ps 59:13
12 [a]Ps 44:4
13 [1]Or *You Yourself* [2]Lit *on* [a]Ex 14:21; Ps 78:13 [b]Is 51:9 [c]Ps 148:7; Jer 51:34
14 [1]Or *You Yourself* [2]Or *sea monster* [3]Lit *people* [a]Job 41:1; Ps 104:26; Is 27:1 [b]Ps 72:9
15 [1]Or *You Yourself* [a]Ex 17:5; Num 20:11; Ps 78:15; Is 48:21 [b]Ex 14:21; Josh 2:10; Ps 114:3
16 [1]Or *You Yourself* [2]Or *luminary* [a]Gen 1:14-18; Ps 104:19
17 [1]Or *You Yourself* [2]Or *formed* [a]Deut 32:8; Acts 17:26 [b]Gen 8:22; Ps 147:16-18
18 [1]Or *that the enemy has reviled the LORD* [a]Ps 74:10 [b]Deut 32:6; Ps 14:1
19 [a]Song 2:14 [b]Ps 9:18
20 [a]Gen 17:7; Ps 106:45 [b]Ps 88:6
21 [a]Ps 103:6 [b]Ps 35:10; Is 41:17
22 [1]Lit *Your reproach from the foolish man* [a]Ps 43:1; Is 3:13; Ezek 20:35 [b]Ps 14:1
23 [a]Ps 74:10 [b]Ps 65:7
75:1 [+]Lit *Do Not Destroy* [a]Ps 79:13 [b]Ps 145:18 [c]Ps 26:7
2 [a]Ps 102:13 [b]Ps 9:8; Is 11:4
3 [1]Or *totter* [2]*Selah* may mean: *Pause, Crescendo* or *Musical interlude* [a]Ps 46:6; Is 24:19 [b]1 Sam 2:8

And to the wicked, '[a]Do not lift
up the horn;
5 Do not lift up your horn on high,
[a]Do not speak with insolent
[1]pride.' "

6 ¶ For not from the east, nor from
the west,
Nor from the [1a]desert *comes*
exaltation;
7 But [a]God is the Judge;
He [b]puts down one and exalts
another.
8 For a [a]cup is in the hand of the
LORD, and the wine foams;
It is [1b]well mixed, and He
pours out of this;
Surely all the wicked of the earth
must drain *and* [c]drink down
its dregs.

9 ¶ But as for me, I will [a]declare
it forever;
I will sing praises to the God of
Jacob.
10 And all the [a]horns of the wicked
[1]He will cut off,
But [b]the horns of the righteous
will be lifted up.

Psalm 76

The Victorious Power of the God of Jacob.

For the choir director; on stringed
instruments. A Psalm of Asaph, a Song.

1 ¶ God is [a]known in Judah;
His name is [b]great in Israel.
2 His [1a]tabernacle is in [b]Salem;
His [c]dwelling place also is in
Zion.
3 There He [a]broke the [1]flaming
arrows,
The shield and the sword and
the [2]weapons of war.
[3]Selah.

4 ¶ You are resplendent,
[1]More majestic than the
mountains of prey.
5 The [a]stouthearted were
plundered,
[1]They sank into sleep;
And none of the [2]warriors could
use his hands.
6 At Your [a]rebuke, O God of
Jacob,
Both [1b]rider and horse were
cast into a dead sleep.
7 You, even You, are [a]to be
feared;
And [b]who may stand in Your
presence when once [1]You
are angry?

8 ¶ You caused judgment to be
heard from heaven;
The earth [a]feared and was still
9 When God [a]arose to judgment,
To save all the humble of the
earth. Selah.
10 For the [1a]wrath of man shall
praise You;
With a remnant of wrath You
will gird Yourself.

11 ¶ [a]Make vows to the LORD your
God and [b]fulfill *them;*
Let all who are around Him
[c]bring gifts to Him who is
to be feared.
12 He will cut off the spirit of
princes;
He is [1a]feared by the kings of
the earth.

Psalm 77

Comfort in Trouble from Recalling God's Mighty Deeds.

For the choir director; [+]according
to Jeduthun. A Psalm of Asaph.

1 ¶ My voice *rises* to God, and I
will [a]cry aloud;
My voice *rises* to God, and He
will hear me.
2 In the [a]day of my trouble I
sought the Lord;
[b]In the night my [c]hand was
stretched out [1]without
weariness;
My soul [d]refused to be
comforted.
3 *When* I remember God, then I
am [a]disturbed;
When I [b]sigh, then [c]my spirit
grows faint. [1]Selah.
4 You have held my eyelids *open;*
I am so troubled that I [a]cannot
speak.
5 I have considered the [a]days of
old,
The years of long ago.
6 I will remember my [a]song in
the night;
I [b]will meditate with my heart,
And my spirit [1]ponders:

7 ¶ Will the Lord [a]reject forever?
And will He [b]never be favorable
again?
8 Has His [a]lovingkindness ceased
forever?
Has *His* [1b]promise come to an
end [2]forever?
9 Has God [a]forgotten to be
gracious,
Or has He in anger [1]withdrawn
His [b]compassion? Selah.
10 Then I said, "[a]It is my [1]grief,

4 [a]Zech 1:21
5 [1]Lit *neck* [a]1 Sam 2:3; Ps 94:4
6 [1]Or *mountainous desert* [a]Ps 3:3
7 [a]Ps 50:6 [b]1 Sam 2:7; Ps 147:6; Dan 2:21
8 [1]Lit *full of mixture* [a]Job 21:20; Ps 11:6; Jer 25:15 [b]Prov 23:30 [c]Obad 16
9 [a]Ps 22:22
10 [1]Heb *I* [a]Ps 101:8; Jer 48:25 [b]1 Sam 2:1; Ps 89:17
76:1 [a]Ps 48:3 [b]Ps 99:3
2 [1]Lit *shelter* [a]Ps 27:5; Lam 2:6 [b]Gen 14:18 [c]Ps 9:11
3 [1]Lit *fiery shafts of the bow* [2]Lit *battle* [3]*Selah* may mean: *Pause, Crescendo* or *Musical interlude* [a]Ps 46:9
4 [1]Or *Majestic from the mountains*
5 [1]Lit *They slumbered their sleep* [2]Lit *men of might have found their hands* [a]Is 10:12
6 [1]Lit *chariot* [a]Ps 80:16 [b]Ex 15:1; Ps 78:53
7 [1]Lit *Your anger is* [a]1 Chr 16:25; Ps 89:7 [b]Ezra 9:15; Ps 130:3; Nah 1:6; Mal 3:2; Rev 6:17
8 [a]1 Chr 16:30; 2 Chr 20:29; Ps 33:8
9 [a]Ps 9:7
10 [1]Lit *wraths* [a]Ex 9:16; Rom 9:17
11 [a]Eccl 5:4-6 [b]Ps 50:14 [c]2 Chr 32:23; Ps 68:29
12 [1]Lit *awesome to* [a]Ps 47:2
77:1 [+]1 Chr 16:41 [a]Ps 3:4
2 [1]Lit *and did not grow numb* [a]Ps 50:15 [b]Ps 63:6; Is 26:9 [c]Job 11:13; Ps 88:9 [d]Gen 37:35
3 [1]*Selah* may mean: *Pause, Crescendo* or *Musical interlude* [a]Ps 42:5 [b]Ps 55:2 [c]Ps 61:2
4 [a]Ps 39:9
5 [a]Deut 32:7; Ps 44:1; Is 51:9
6 [1]Lit *searched* [a]Ps 42:8 [b]Ps 4:4
7 [a]Ps 44:9 [b]Ps 85:1
8 [1]Lit *word* [2]Lit *from generation to generation* [a]Ps 89:49 [b]2 Pet 3:9
9 [1]Lit *shut up* [a]Is 49:15 [b]Ps 25:6
10 [1]Or *infirmity, the years of the right hand of the Most High* [a]Ps 31:22

That the [b]right hand of the Most
High has changed."

11 ¶ I shall remember the [a]deeds of
[1]the LORD;
Surely I will [a]remember Your
wonders of old.
12 I will [a]meditate on all Your
work
And muse on Your deeds.
13 Your way, O God, is [a]holy;
[b]What god is great like our God?
14 You are the [a]God who works
wonders;
You have [b]made known Your
strength among the peoples.
15 You have by Your [1]power
[a]redeemed Your people,
The sons of Jacob and [b]Joseph.
Selah.

16 ¶ The [a]waters saw You, O God;
The waters saw You, they were
in anguish;
The deeps also trembled.
17 The [a]clouds poured out water;
The skies [b]gave forth a sound;
Your [c]arrows [1]flashed here and
there.
18 The [a]sound of Your thunder was
in the whirlwind;
The [b]lightnings lit up the world;
The [c]earth trembled and shook.
19 Your [a]way was in the sea
And Your paths in the mighty
waters,
And Your footprints may not be
known.
20 You [a]led Your people like a flock
By the hand of [b]Moses and
Aaron.

Psalm 78

God's Guidance of His People in Spite of Their Unfaithfulness.

A [+]Maskil of Asaph.

1 ¶ [a]Listen, O my people, to my
[1]instruction;
[b]Incline your ears to the words
of my mouth.
2 I will [a]open my mouth in a
parable;
I will utter [b]dark sayings of old,
3 Which we have heard and
known,
And [a]our fathers have told us.
4 We will [a]not conceal them from
their children,
But [b]tell to the generation to
come the praises of the
LORD,
And His strength and His
[c]wondrous works that He
has done.

5 ¶ For He established a
[a]testimony in Jacob
And appointed a [b]law in Israel,
Which He [c]commanded our
fathers
That they should [1][d]teach them
to their children,
6 [a]That the generation to come
might know, *even* [b]the
children *yet* to be born,
That they may arise and [c]tell
them to their children,
7 That they should put their
confidence in God
And [a]not forget the works of
God,
But [b]keep His commandments,
8 And [a]not be like their fathers,
A [b]stubborn and rebellious
generation,
A generation that [c]did not
[1]prepare its heart
And whose spirit was not
[d]faithful to God.

9 ¶ The sons of Ephraim [1]were
[a]archers equipped with
bows,
Yet [b]they turned back in the day
of battle.
10 They [a]did not keep the covenant
of God
And refused to [b]walk in His
law;
11 They [a]forgot His deeds
And His [1]miracles that He had
shown them.
12 [a]He wrought wonders before
their fathers
In the land of Egypt, in the
[b]field of Zoan.
13 He [a]divided the sea and caused
them to pass through,
And He made the waters stand
[b]up like a heap.
14 Then He led them with the
cloud by [a]day
And all the night with a [b]light
of fire.
15 He [a]split the rocks in the
wilderness
And gave *them* abundant drink
like the ocean depths.
16 He [a]brought forth streams also
from the rock
And caused waters to run down
like rivers.
17 ¶ Yet they still continued to sin
against Him,

10 [b]Ps 44:2
11 [1]Heb *YAH* [a]Ps 105:5
12 [a]Ps 145:5
13 [a]Ps 63:2 [b]Ex 15:11; Ps 71:19
14 [a]Ps 72:18 [b]Ps 106:8
15 [1]Lit *arm* [a]Ex 6:6; Deut 9:29; Ps 74:2 [b]Ps 80:1
16 [a]Ex 14:21; Ps 114:3; Hab 3:8
17 [1]Lit *went* [a]Judg 5:4 [b]Ps 68:33 [c]Ps 18:14
18 [a]Ps 18:13 [b]Ps 97:4 [c]Judg 5:4; Ps 18:7
19 [a]Is 51:10; Hab 3:15
20 [a]Ex 13:21; Ps 78:52; Is 63:11-13 [b]Ex 6:26; Ps 105:26
78:1 [+]Possibly *Contemplative,* or *Didactic,* or *Skillful Psalm* [1]Or *law, teaching* [a]Is 51:4 [b]Is 55:3
2 [a]Ps 49:4; Matt 13:35 [b]Prov 1:6
3 [a]Ps 44:1
4 [a]Ex 12:26; Deut 6:7; Job 15:18; Ps 145:4; Is 38:19; Joel 1:3 [b]Ex 13:8; Ps 22:30 [c]Job 37:16; Ps 26:7
5 [1]Lit *make them known* [a]Ps 19:7; Is 8:20 [b]Ps 147:19 [c]Deut 6:4-9 [d]Deut 4:9
6 [a]Ps 102:18 [b]Ps 22:31 [c]Deut 11:19
7 [a]Deut 4:9 [b]Deut 4:2; Josh 22:5
8 [1]Or *put right* [a]2 Kin 17:14; 2 Chr 30:7; Ezek 20:18 [b]Ex 32:9; Deut 9:7; Judg 2:19; Is 30:9 [c]Job 11:13; Ps 78:37 [d]Ps 51:10
9 [1]Or *being* [a]1 Chr 12:2 [b]Judg 20:39; Ps 78:57
10 [a]Judg 2:20; 1 Kin 11:11; 2 Kin 17:15 [b]Ps 119:1; Jer 32:23
11 [1]Or *wonderful works* [a]Ps 106:13
12 [a]Ex chs 7-12; Ps 106:22 [b]Num 13:22; Ps 78:43; Is 19:11; Ezek 30:14
13 [a]Ex 14:21; Ps 74:13 [b]Ex 15:8; Ps 33:7
14 [a]Ex 13:21; Ps 105:39 [b]Ex 14:24
15 [a]Ex 17:6; Num 20:11; Ps 105:41; Is 48:21; 1 Cor 10:4
16 [a]Num 20:8

To [a]rebel against the Most High
in the desert.
18 And in their heart they [a]put
God to the test
By asking [b]food according to
their desire.
19 Then they spoke against God;
They said, "[a]Can God prepare a
table in the wilderness?
20 "Behold, He [a]struck the rock so
that waters gushed out,
And streams were overflowing;
Can He give bread also?
Will He provide [1b]meat for His
people?"

21 ¶ Therefore the LORD heard and
[1]was [a]full of wrath;
And a fire was kindled against
Jacob
And anger also mounted against
Israel,
22 Because they [a]did not believe in
God
And did not trust in His
salvation.
23 Yet He commanded the clouds
above
And [a]opened the doors of
heaven;
24 He [a]rained down manna upon
them to eat
And gave them [1b]food from
heaven.
25 Man did eat the bread of
[1]angels;
He sent them [2]food [3a]in
abundance.
26 He [a]caused the east wind to
blow in the heavens
And by His [1]power He directed
the south wind.
27 When He rained [1]meat upon
them like the dust,
Even [a]winged fowl like the sand
of the seas,
28 Then He let *them* fall in the
midst of [1]their camp,
Round about their dwellings.
29 So they [a]ate and were well
filled,
And their desire He gave to
them.
30 [1]Before they had satisfied their
desire,
[a]While their food was in their
mouths,
31 The [a]anger of God rose against
them
And killed [1]some of their
[b]stoutest ones,
And [2]subdued the choice men
of Israel.

32 In spite of all this they [a]still
sinned
And [b]did not believe in His
wonderful works.
33 So He brought [a]their days to an
end in [1]futility
And their years in sudden
terror.

34 ¶ When He killed them, then
they [a]sought Him,
And returned and searched
[b]diligently for God;
35 And they remembered that God
was their [a]rock,
And the Most High God their
[b]Redeemer.
36 But they [a]deceived Him with
their mouth
And [b]lied to Him with their
tongue.
37 For their heart was not
[a]steadfast toward Him,
Nor were they faithful in His
covenant.
38 But He, being [a]compassionate,
[1b]forgave *their* iniquity and
did not destroy *them;*
And often He [2c]restrained His
anger
And did not arouse all His
wrath.
39 Thus [a]He remembered that they
were but [b]flesh,
A [1c]wind that passes and does
not return.

40 ¶ How often they [a]rebelled
against Him in the
wilderness
And [b]grieved Him in the
[c]desert!
41 Again and again they [1a]tempted
God,
And pained the [b]Holy One of
Israel.
42 They [a]did not remember [b]His
[1]power,
The day when He [c]redeemed
them from the adversary,
43 When He performed His [a]signs
in Egypt
And His [b]marvels in the field of
Zoan,
44 And [a]turned their rivers to
blood,
And their streams, they could
not drink.
45 He sent among them swarms of
[a]flies which devoured them,
And [b]frogs which destroyed
them.
46 He gave also their crops to the
[a]grasshopper

17 [a]Deut 9:22; Is 63:10; Heb 3:16
18 [a]Ex 17:6; Deut 6:16; Ps 78:41; 1 Cor 10:9 [b]Num 11:4
19 [a]Ex 16:3; Num 11:4; Ps 23:5
20 [1]Lit *flesh* [a]Num 20:11; Ps 78:15 [b]Num 11:18
21 [1]Or *became infuriated* [a]Num 11:1
22 [a]Deut 1:32; Heb 3:18
23 [a]Gen 7:11; Mal 3:10
24 [1]Lit *grain* [a]Ex 16:4 [b]Ps 105:40; John 6:31
25 [1]Lit *mighty ones* [2]Or *provision* [3]Lit *to satiation* [a]Ex 16:3
26 [1]Or *strength* [a]Num 11:31
27 [1]Lit *flesh* [a]Ex 16:13; Ps 105:40
28 [1]Lit *His*
29 [a]Num 11:19
30 [1]Lit *They were not estranged from* [a]Num 11:33
31 [1]Lit *among their fat ones* [2]Lit *caused to bow down* [a]Num 11:33; Job 20:23 [b]Is 10:16
32 [a]Num chs 14 [b]Num 14:11; Ps 78:11
33 [1]Lit *vanity, a mere breath* [a]Num 14:29
34 [a]Num 21:7; Hos 5:15 [b]Ps 63:1
35 [a]Deut 32:4 [b]Ex 15:13; Deut 9:26; Ps 74:2; Is 41:14
36 [a]Ex 24:7; Ezek 33:31 [b]Ex 32:7; Is 57:11
37 [a]Ps 51:10; Acts 8:21
38 [1]Lit *covered over, atoned for* [2]Lit *turned away* [a]Ex 34:6 [b]Num 14:18-20 [c]Is 48:9
39 [1]Or *breath* [a]Job 10:9; Ps 103:14 [b]Gen 6:3 [c]Job 7:7; Ps 103:14; James 4:14
40 [a]Ps 95:8; Heb 3:16 [b]Ps 95:10; Is 63:10; Eph 4:30 [c]Ps 106:14
41 [1]Or *put God to the test* [a]Num 14:22 [b]2 Kin 19:22; Ps 89:18
42 [1]Lit *hand* [a]Judg 8:34 [b]Ps 44:3 [c]Ps 106:10
43 [a]Ps 105:27 [b]Ex 4:21
44 [a]Ex 7:20; Ps 105:29
45 [a]Ex 8:24; Ps 105:31 [b]Ex 8:6; Ps 105:30
46 [a]1 Kin 8:37; Ps 105:34

And the product of their labor to
the [b]locust.
47 He [1]destroyed their vines with
[a]hailstones
And their sycamore trees with
frost.
48 He gave over their [a]cattle also
to the hailstones
And their herds to bolts of
lightning.
49 He [a]sent upon them His burning
anger,
Fury and indignation and
trouble,
[1]A band of destroying angels.
50 He leveled a path for His anger;
He did not spare their soul from
death,
But [a]gave over their life to the
plague,
51 And [a]smote all the firstborn in
Egypt,
The [b]first *issue* of their virility
in the tents of [c]Ham.
52 But He [a]led forth His own
people like sheep
And guided them in the
wilderness [b]like a flock;
53 He led them [a]safely, so that they
did not fear;
But [b]the sea engulfed their
enemies.

54 ¶ So [a]He brought them to His
holy [1]land,
To this [2b]hill country [c]which
His right hand had gained.
55 He also [a]drove out the nations
before them
And [b]apportioned them for an
inheritance by measurement,
And made the tribes of Israel
dwell in their tents.
56 Yet they [1a]tempted and
[b]rebelled against the Most
High God
And did not keep His
testimonies,
57 But turned back and [a]acted
treacherously like their
fathers;
They [b]turned aside like a
treacherous bow.
58 For they [a]provoked Him with
their [b]high places
And [c]aroused His jealousy with
their [d]graven images.
59 When God heard, He [1]was filled
with [a]wrath
And greatly [b]abhorred Israel;
60 So that He [a]abandoned the
[b]dwelling place at Shiloh,
The tent [1]which He had pitched
among men,

46 [b]Ex 10:14
47 [1]Lit *was killing* [a]Ex 9:23-25; Ps 105:32
48 [a]Ex 9:19
49 [1]Lit *A deputation of angels of evil* [a]Ex 15:7
50 [a]Ex 12:29
51 [a]Ex 12:29; Ps 105:36 [b]Gen 49:3 [c]Ps 105:23
52 [a]Ex 15:22 [b]Ps 77:20
53 [a]Ex 14:19 [b]Ex 14:27; Ps 106:11
54 [1]Lit *border, territory* [2]Or *mountain* [a]Ex 15:17 [b]Ps 68:16; Is 11:9 [c]Ps 44:3
55 [a]Josh 11:16-23; Ps 44:2 [b]Josh 13:7; Ps 105:11
56 [1]Or *put to the test* [a]Ps 78:18 [b]Judg 2:11-13; Ps 78:40
57 [a]Ezek 20:27 [b]Hos 7:16
58 [a]Deut 4:25; Judg 2:12; 1 Kin 14:9; Is 65:3 [b]Lev 26:30; 1 Kin 3:2; 2 Kin 16:4; Jer 17:3 [c]Deut 32:16; 1 Kin 14:22 [d]Ex 20:4; Lev 26:1; Deut 4:25
59 [1]Or *became infuriated* [a]Deut 1:34; Ps 106:40 [b]Lev 26:30; Deut 32:19; Amos 6:8
60 [1]Some ancient versions read *where He dwelt* [a]1 Sam 4:11; Ps 78:67; Jer 7:12 [b]Josh 18:1
61 [a]Ps 63:2 [b]1 Sam 4:17
62 [1]Or *became infuriated* [a]Judg 20:21; 1 Sam 4:10
63 [1]Or *their* [a]Num 11:1; Is 26:11; Jer 48:45 [b]Jer 7:34; Lam 2:21
64 [1]Or *their* [a]1 Sam 4:17 [b]Job 27:15; Ezek 24:23
65 [1]Or *sobered up from* [a]Ps 44:23 [b]Is 42:13
66 [1]Lit *smote* [a]1 Sam 5:6
67 [a]Ps 78:60
68 [a]Ps 87:2
69 [a]1 Kin 6:1-38
70 [a]1 Sam 16:11
71 [1]Lit *following* [2]Lit *ewes which gave suck, He...* [a]2 Sam 7:8; Is 40:11 [b]Gen 33:13 [c]2 Sam 5:2; 1 Chr 11:2; Ps 28:9 [d]1 Sam 10:1
72 [a]1 Kin 9:4
79:1 [1]Lit *come into* [a]Lam 1:10 [b]Ps 74:2 [c]Ps 74:3 [d]2 Kin 25:9; 2 Chr 36:17-19; Jer 26:18; Mic 3:12

61 And gave up His [a]strength to
captivity
And His glory [b]into the hand of
the adversary.
62 He also [a]delivered His people to
the sword,
And [1]was filled with wrath at
His inheritance.
63 [a]Fire devoured [1]His young
men,
And [1]His [b]virgins had no
wedding songs.
64 [1]His [a]priests fell by the sword,
And [1]His [b]widows could not
weep.

65 ¶ Then the Lord [a]awoke as *if*
from sleep,
Like a [b]warrior [1]overcome by
wine.
66 He [1a]drove His adversaries
backward;
He put on them an everlasting
reproach.
67 He also [a]rejected the tent of
Joseph,
And did not choose the tribe of
Ephraim,
68 But chose the tribe of Judah,
Mount [a]Zion which He loved.
69 And He [a]built His sanctuary like
the heights,
Like the earth which He has
founded forever.
70 He also [a]chose David His
servant
And took him from the
sheepfolds;
71 From [1a]the care of the [2]ewes
[b]with suckling lambs He
brought him
To [c]shepherd Jacob His people,
And Israel [d]His inheritance.
72 So he shepherded them
according to the [a]integrity
of his heart,
And guided them with his skillful
hands.

Psalm 79

A Lament over the Destruction of Jerusalem, and Prayer for Help.

A Psalm of Asaph.

1 ¶ O God, the [a]nations have
[1]invaded [b]Your inheritance;
They have defiled Your [c]holy
temple;
They have [d]laid Jerusalem in
ruins.

2 They have given the [a]dead
bodies of Your servants for
food to the birds of the
heavens,
The flesh of Your godly ones to
the beasts of the earth.
3 They have poured out their
blood like water round about
Jerusalem;
And there was [a]no one to bury
them.
4 We have become a [a]reproach to
our neighbors,
A scoffing and derision to those
around us.
5 [a]How long, O LORD? Will You
be angry forever?
Will Your [b]jealousy [c]burn like
fire?
6 [a]Pour out Your wrath upon the
nations which [b]do not
know You,
And upon the kingdoms which
[c]do not call upon Your
name.
7 For they have [a]devoured Jacob
And [b]laid waste his [1]habitation.

8 ¶ [a]Do not remember [1]the
iniquities of *our* forefathers
against us;
Let Your compassion come
quickly to [b]meet us,
For we are [c]brought very low.
9 [a]Help us, O God of our
salvation, for the glory of
[b]Your name;
And deliver us and [1c]forgive
our sins [d]for Your name's
sake.
10 [a]Why should the nations say,
"Where is their God?"
Let there be known among the
nations in our sight,
[b]Vengeance for the blood of
Your servants which has
been shed.
11 Let [a]the groaning of the prisoner
come before You;
According to the greatness of
Your [1]power preserve
[2]those who are [a]doomed to
die.
12 And return to our neighbors
[a]sevenfold [b]into their
bosom
[1]The [c]reproach with which
they have reproached You,
O Lord.
13 So we Your people and the
[a]sheep of Your [1]pasture
Will [b]give thanks to You forever;
To all generations we will [c]tell
of Your praise.

Psalm 80

God Implored to Rescue His People from Their Calamities.

For the choir director; *set to*
+El Shoshannim; •Eduth.
A Psalm of Asaph.

1 ¶ Oh, give ear, [a]Shepherd of
Israel,
You who lead [b]Joseph like a
flock;
You who [c]are enthroned *above*
the cherubim, shine forth!
2 Before [a]Ephraim and Benjamin
and Manasseh, [b]stir up Your
power
And come to save us!
3 O God, [a]restore us
And [b]cause Your face to shine
upon us, [1]and we will be
saved.

4 ¶ O [a]LORD God *of* hosts,
[b]How long will You [1]be angry
with the prayer of Your
people?
5 You have fed them with the
[a]bread of tears,
And You have made them to
drink tears in [1]large
measure.
6 You make us [1]an object of
contention [a]to our
neighbors,
And our enemies laugh among
themselves.
7 O God *of* hosts, restore us
And cause Your face to shine
upon us, [1]and we will be
saved.

8 ¶ You removed a [a]vine from
Egypt;
You [b]drove out the [1]nations and
[c]planted it.
9 You [a]cleared *the ground*
before it,
And it [b]took deep root and filled
the land.
10 The mountains were covered
with its shadow,
And [1]the cedars of God with its
[a]boughs.
11 It was sending out its branches
[a]to the sea
And its shoots to the River.
12 Why have You [a]broken down its
[1]hedges,
So that all who pass *that* way
pick its *fruit?*
13 A boar from the forest [a]eats it
away
And whatever moves in the field
feeds on it.

2 [a]Deut 28:26; Jer 7:33
3 [a]Jer 14:16
4 [a]Ps 44:13; Dan 9:16
5 [a]Ps 13:1 [b]Deut 29:20; Ezek 36:5 [c]Ps 89:46; Zeph 3:8
6 [a]Ps 69:24; Jer 10:25; Ezek 21:31; Zeph 3:8 [b]1 Thess 4:5; 2 Thess 1:8 [c]Ps 14:4
7 [1]Lit *pasture* [a]Ps 53:4 [b]2 Chr 36:19; Jer 39:8
8 [1]Or our *former iniquities* [a]Ps 106:6; Is 64:9 [b]Ps 21:3 [c]Deut 28:43; Ps 116:6; Is 26:5
9 [1]Lit *cover over, atone for* [a]2 Chr 14:11 [b]Ps 31:3 [c]Ps 25:11 [d]Jer 14:7
10 [a]Ps 42:10 [b]Ps 94:1
11 [1]Lit *arm* [2]Lit *the children of death* [a]Ps 102:20
12 [1]Lit *Their* [a]Gen 4:15; Lev 26:21; Ps 12:6; Prov 6:31; Is 30:26 [b]Ps 35:13; Is 65:6; Jer 32:18; Luke 6:38 [c]Ps 74:10
13 [1]Or *pasturing* [a]Ps 74:1 [b]Ps 44:8 [c]Ps 89:1; Is 43:21
80:1 +Possibly *to the Lilies* •Lit *A testimony* [a]Ps 23:1 [b]Ps 77:15; Amos 5:15 [c]Ex 25:22; 1 Sam 4:4; 2 Sam 6:2; Ps 99:1
2 [a]Num 2:18-24 [b]Ps 35:23
3 [1]Or *that we may* [a]Ps 60:1; Lam 5:21 [b]Num 6:25; Ps 4:6
4 [1]Lit *smoke against* [a]Ps 59:5 [b]Ps 79:5
5 [1]Lit *a third part of a* [a]Ps 42:3; Is 30:20
6 [1]Lit *a strife to* [a]Ps 44:13
7 [1]Or *that we may*
8 [1]Or *Gentiles* [a]Ps 80:15; Is 5:1; Jer 2:21; Ezek 17:6 [b]Josh 13:6; 2 Chr 20:7; Ps 44:2; Acts 7:45 [c]Jer 11:17; Ezek 17:23; Amos 9:15
9 [a]Ex 23:28; Josh 24:12; Is 5:2 [b]Hos 14:5
10 [1]Or *its boughs are like the cedars of God* [a]Gen 49:22
11 [a]Ps 72:8
12 [1]Or *walls, fences* [a]Ps 89:40; Is 5:5
13 [a]Jer 5:6

14 ¶ O God *of* hosts, [a]turn again
now, we beseech You;
[b]Look down from heaven and
see, and take care of this
vine,
15 Even the [1a]shoot which Your
right hand has planted,
And on the [2]son whom You
have [3]strengthened for
Yourself.
16 It is [a]burned with fire, it is cut
down;
They perish at the [b]rebuke of
Your countenance.
17 Let [a]Your hand be upon the
man of Your right hand,
Upon the son of man whom You
[b]made strong for Yourself.
18 Then we shall not [a]turn back
from You;
[b]Revive us, and we will call
upon Your name.
19 O LORD God of hosts,
[a]restore us;
Cause Your face to shine *upon*
us, [1]and we will be saved.

Psalm 81

God's Goodness and Israel's Waywardness.

For the choir director; [+]on the Gittith.
A Psalm of Asaph.

1 ¶ [a]Sing for joy to God our
[b]strength;
Shout [c]joyfully to the [d]God of
Jacob.
2 Raise a song, strike [a]the timbrel,
The sweet sounding [b]lyre with
the [c]harp.
3 Blow the trumpet at the [a]new
moon,
At the full moon, on our [b]feast
day.
4 For it is a statute for Israel,
An ordinance of the God of
Jacob.
5 He established it for a testimony
in Joseph
When he [1a]went throughout
the land of Egypt.
I heard a [b]language that I did
not know:

6 ¶ "I [1a]relieved his shoulder of
the burden,
His hands were freed from the
[2]basket.
7 "You [a]called in trouble and I
rescued you;
I [b]answered you in the hiding
place of thunder;
I proved you at the [c]waters of
Meribah. [1]Selah.
8 "[a]Hear, O My people, and I will
[1]admonish you;
O Israel, if you [b]would listen
to Me!
9 "Let there be no [a]strange god
among you;
Nor shall you worship any
foreign god.
10 "[a]I, the LORD, am your God,
Who brought you up from the
land of Egypt;
[b]Open your mouth wide and I
will [c]fill it.

11 ¶ "But My people [a]did not listen
to My voice,
And Israel did not [1]obey Me.
12 "So I [a]gave [1]them over to the
stubbornness of their heart,
To walk in their own devices.
13 "Oh that My people [a]would listen
to Me,
That Israel would [b]walk in My
ways!
14 "I would quickly [a]subdue their
enemies
And [b]turn My hand against their
adversaries.
15 "[a]Those who hate the LORD
would [b]pretend obedience
to Him,
And their time *of punishment*
would be forever.
16 "[1]But I would feed you with the
[2a]finest of the wheat,
And with [b]honey from the rock
I would satisfy you."

Psalm 82

Unjust Judgments Rebuked.

A Psalm of Asaph.

1 ¶ God takes His [a]stand in [1]His
own congregation;
He [b]judges in the midst of the
[2c]rulers.
2 How long will you [a]judge
unjustly
And [b]show partiality to the
wicked? [1]Selah.
3 [a]Vindicate the weak and
fatherless;
Do justice to the afflicted and
destitute.
4 [a]Rescue the weak and needy;
Deliver *them* out of the hand of
the wicked.

5 ¶ They [a]do not know nor do
they understand;
They [b]walk about in darkness;
All the [c]foundations of the earth
are shaken.
6 [1]I [a]said, "You are gods,

14 [a]Ps 90:13 [b]Ps 102:19; Is 63:15
15 [1]Or *root* [2]Or figuratively: *branch* [3]Or *secured* [a]Ps 80:8
16 [a]2 Chr 36:19; Ps 74:8; Jer 52:13 [b]Ps 39:11
17 [a]Ps 89:21 [b]Ps 80:15
18 [a]Is 50:5 [b]Ps 71:20
19 [1]Or *that we may* [a]Ps 80:3
81:1 [+]Or *according to* [a]Ps 51:14 [b]Ps 46:1 [c]Ps 66:1 [d]Ps 84:8
2 [a]Ex 15:20; Ps 149:3 [b]Ps 92:3 [c]Ps 108:2
3 [a]Num 10:10 [b]Lev 23:24
5 [1]Lit *went out over* [a]Ex 11:4 [b]Deut 28:49; Ps 114:1; Jer 5:15
6 [1]Lit *removed his shoulder from* [2]Or *brick load* [a]Is 9:4
7 [1]*Selah* may mean: *Pause, Crescendo* or *Musical interlude* [a]Ex 2:23; Ps 50:15 [b]Ex 19:19 [c]Ex 17:6; Num 20:13; Ps 95:8
8 [1]Or *bear witness against* [a]Ps 50:7 [b]Ps 95:7
9 [a]Ex 20:3; Deut 5:7; Ps 44:20; Is 43:12
10 [a]Ex 20:2; Deut 5:6 [b]Job 29:23 [c]Ps 37:4
11 [1]Lit *yield to* [a]Deut 32:15; Ps 106:25
12 [1]Lit *him* [a]Job 8:4; Acts 7:42; Rom 1:24
13 [a]Deut 5:29; Ps 81:8; Is 48:18 [b]Ps 128:1; Is 42:24; Jer 7:23
14 [a]Ps 18:47 [b]Amos 1:8
15 [a]Rom 1:30 [b]Ps 18:44
16 [1]Lit *He would feed him* [2]Lit *fat* [a]Deut 32:14; Ps 147:14 [b]Deut 32:13
82:1 [1]Lit *the congregation of God* [2]Lit *gods* [a]Is 3:13 [b]2 Chr 19:6; Ps 58:11 [c]Ex 21:6
2 [1]*Selah* may mean: *Pause, Crescendo* or *Musical interlude* [a]Ps 58:1 [b]Deut 1:17; Prov 18:5
3 [a]Deut 24:17; Ps 10:18; Is 11:4; Jer 22:16
4 [a]Job 29:12
5 [a]Ps 14:4; Jer 4:22; Mic 3:1 [b]Prov 2:13; Is 59:9; Jer 23:12 [c]Ps 11:3
6 [1]Lit *I, on my part* [a]Ps 82:1; John 10:34

And all of you are [b]sons of the Most High.
7 "Nevertheless [a]you will die like men
And fall like *any* [b]one of the princes."
8 [a]Arise, O God, [b]judge the earth!
For it is You who [c]possesses all the nations.

Psalm 83

God Implored to Confound His Enemies.

A Song, a Psalm of Asaph.

1 ¶ O God, [a]do not remain quiet;
[b]Do not be silent and, O God, do not be still.
2 For behold, Your enemies [a]make an uproar,
And [b]those who hate You have [1c]exalted themselves.
3 They [a]make shrewd plans against Your people,
And [1]conspire together against [b]Your [2]treasured ones.
4 They have said, "Come, and [a]let us wipe them out [1]as a nation,
That the [b]name of Israel be remembered no more."
5 For they have [1a]conspired together with one mind;
Against You they make a covenant:
6 The tents of [a]Edom and the [b]Ishmaelites,
[c]Moab and the [d]Hagrites;
7 [a]Gebal and [b]Ammon and [c]Amalek,
[d]Philistia with the inhabitants of [e]Tyre;
8 [a]Assyria also has joined with them;
They have become [1]a help to the [b]children of Lot.
[2]Selah.

9 ¶ Deal with them [a]as with Midian,
As [b]with Sisera *and* Jabin at the torrent of Kishon,
10 Who were destroyed at En-dor,
Who [a]became as dung for the ground.
11 Make their nobles like [a]Oreb and Zeeb
And all their princes like [b]Zebah and Zalmunna,
12 Who said, "[a]Let us possess for ourselves
The [b]pastures of God."

13 ¶ O my God, make them like the [1a]whirling dust,
Like [b]chaff before the wind.
14 Like [a]fire that burns the forest
And like a flame that [b]sets the mountains on fire,
15 So pursue them [a]with Your tempest
And terrify them with Your storm.
16 [a]Fill their faces with dishonor,
That they may seek Your name, O LORD.
17 Let them be [a]ashamed and dismayed forever,
And let them be humiliated and perish,
18 That they may [a]know that [b]You alone, whose name is the LORD,
Are the [c]Most High over all the earth.

Psalm 84

Longing for the Temple Worship.

For the choir director; +on the Gittith. A Psalm of the sons of Korah.

1 ¶ How lovely are Your [a]dwelling places,
O LORD of hosts!
2 My [a]soul longed and even yearned for the courts of the LORD;
My heart and my flesh sing for joy to the [b]living God.
3 The bird also has found a house,
And the swallow a nest for herself, where she may lay her young,
Even Your [a]altars, O LORD of hosts,
[b]My King and my God.
4 How [a]blessed are those who dwell in Your house!
They are [b]ever praising You.
[1]Selah.

5 ¶ How blessed is the man whose [a]strength is in You,
In [1]whose heart are the [b]highways *to Zion!*
6 Passing through the valley of [1]Baca they make it a [2]spring;
The [a]early rain also covers it with blessings.
7 They [a]go from strength to strength,
[1]*Every one of them* [b]appears before God in Zion.

8 ¶ O [a]LORD God of hosts, hear my prayer;

6 [b]Ps 89:26 **7** [a]Job 21:32; Ps 49:12; Ezek 31:14 [b]Ps 83:11 **8** [a]Ps 12:5 [b]Ps 58:11 [c]Ps 2:8; Rev 11:15
83:1 [a]Ps 28:1 [b]Ps 109:1 **2** [1]Lit *lifted up the head* [a]Ps 2:1; Is 17:12 [b]Ps 81:15 [c]Judg 8:28; Zech 1:21 **3** [1]Or *consult* [2]Or *hidden ones* [a]Ps 64:2; Is 29:15 [b]Ps 27:5 **4** [1]Lit *from* [a]Esth 3:6; Ps 74:8; Jer 48:2 [b]Ps 41:5; Jer 11:19 **5** [1]Or *consulted* [a]Ps 2:2; Dan 6:7 **6** [a]2 Chr 20:10; Ps 137:7 [b]Gen 25:12-16 [c]2 Chr 20:10 [d]1 Chr 5:10 **7** [a]Josh 13:5; Ezek 27:9 [b]2 Chr 20:10 [c]1 Sam 15:2 [d]1 Sam 4:1 [e]Ezek 27:3; Amos 1:9 **8** [1]Lit *an arm* [2]*Selah* may mean: *Pause, Crescendo* or *Musical interlude* [a]2 Kin 15:19 [b]Deut 2:9 **9** [a]Judg 7:1-24 [b]Judg 4:7 **10** [a]Zeph 1:17 **11** [a]Judg 7:25 [b]Judg 8:12 **12** [a]2 Chr 20:11 [b]Ps 132:13 **13** [1]Or *tumble-weed* [a]Is 17:13 [b]Job 21:18; Ps 35:5; Is 40:24; Jer 13:24 **14** [a]Is 9:18 [b]Ex 19:18; Deut 32:22 **15** [a]Job 9:17; Ps 58:9 **16** [a]Job 10:15; Ps 109:29 **17** [a]Ps 35:4 **18** [a]Ps 59:13 [b]Ps 86:10; Is 45:21 [c]Ps 9:2
84:1 +Or *according to* [a]Ps 43:3 **2** [a]Ps 42:1 [b]Ps 42:2 **3** [a]Ps 43:4 [b]Ps 5:2 **4** [1]*Selah* may mean: *Pause, Crescendo* or *Musical interlude* [a]Ps 65:4 [b]Ps 42:5 **5** [1]Lit *their* [a]Ps 81:1 [b]Ps 86:11; Jer 31:6 **6** [1]Probably, *Weeping;* or *Balsam trees* [2]Or *place of springs* [a]Ps 107:35; Joel 2:23 **7** [1]Some ancient versions read *The God of gods will be seen in Zion* [a]Prov 4:18; Is 40:31; John 1:16; 2 Cor 3:18 [b]Ex 34:23; Deut 16:16; Ps 42:2 **8** [a]Ps 59:5

Give ear, O [b]God of Jacob! Selah.
9 Behold our [a]shield, O God,
And look upon the face of [b]Your anointed.
10 For [a]a day in Your courts is better than a thousand *outside.*
I would rather stand at the threshold of the house of my God
Than dwell in the tents of wickedness.
11 For the LORD God is [a]a sun and [b]shield;
The LORD gives grace and [c]glory;
[d]No good thing does He withhold [1]from those who walk [2]uprightly.
12 O LORD of hosts,
How [a]blessed is the man who trusts in You!

Psalm 85

Prayer for God's Mercy upon the Nation.

For the choir director. A Psalm of the sons of Korah.

1 ¶ O LORD, You showed [a]favor to Your land;
You [1b]restored the captivity of Jacob.
2 You [a]forgave the iniquity of Your people;
You [b]covered all their sin. [1]Selah.
3 You [a]withdrew all Your fury;
You [b]turned away from Your burning anger.
4 ¶ [a]Restore us, O God of our salvation,
And [b]cause Your indignation toward us to cease.
5 Will [a]You be angry with us forever?
Will You prolong Your anger to [1]all generations?
6 Will You not Yourself [1a]revive us again,
That Your people may [b]rejoice in You?
7 Show us Your lovingkindness, O LORD,
And [a]grant us Your salvation.
8 ¶ [1]I will hear what God the LORD will say;
For He will [a]speak peace to His people, [2]to His godly ones;
But let them not [b]turn back to [3]folly.
9 Surely [a]His salvation is near to those who [1]fear Him,
That [b]glory may dwell in our land.
10 [a]Lovingkindness and [1]truth have met together;
[b]Righteousness and peace have kissed each other.
11 [1]Truth [a]springs from the earth,
And righteousness looks down from heaven.
12 Indeed, [a]the LORD will give what is good,
And our [b]land will yield its produce.
13 [a]Righteousness will go before Him
And will make His footsteps into a way.

Psalm 86

A Psalm of Supplication and Trust.

A Prayer of David.

1 ¶ [a]Incline Your ear, O LORD, *and* answer me;
For I am [b]afflicted and needy.
2 [a]Preserve my [1]soul, for I am a [b]godly man;
O You my God, save Your servant who [c]trusts in You.
3 Be [a]gracious to me, O Lord,
For [b]to You I cry all day long.
4 Make glad the soul of Your servant,
For to You, O Lord, [a]I lift up my soul.
5 For You, Lord, are [a]good, and [b]ready to forgive,
And [c]abundant in lovingkindness to all who call upon You.
6 [a]Give ear, O LORD, to my prayer;
And give heed to the voice of my supplications!
7 In [a]the day of my trouble I shall call upon You,
For [b]You will answer me.
8 There is [a]no one like You among the gods, O Lord,
Nor are there any works [b]like Yours.
9 [a]All nations whom You have made shall come and worship before You, O Lord,
And they shall glorify Your name.
10 For You are [a]great and [b]do [1]wondrous deeds;
You alone [c]are God.
11 ¶ [a]Teach me Your way, O LORD;
I will walk in Your truth;
[b]Unite my heart to fear Your name.

---

8 [b]Ps 81:1
9 [a]Gen 15:1; Ps 3:3 [b]1 Sam 16:6; 2 Sam 19:21; Ps 2:2
10 [a]Ps 27:4
11 [1]Lit *with regard to* [2]Lit *with integrity* [a]Is 60:19; Mal 4:2; Rev 21:23 [b]Gen 15:1 [c]Ps 85:9 [d]Ps 34:9
12 [a]Ps 2:12
85:1 [1]Or *restore the fortunes* [a]Ps 77:7 [b]Ezra 1:11; Ps 14:7; Jer 30:18; Ezek 39:25; Hos 6:11; Joel 3:1
2 [1]*Selah* may mean: *Pause, Crescendo* or *Musical interlude* [a]Num 14:19; 1 Kin 8:34; Ps 78:38; Jer 31:34 [b]Ps 32:1
3 [a]Ps 78:38 [b]Ex 32:12; Deut 13:17; Ps 106:23; Jon 3:9
4 [a]Ps 80:3 [b]Dan 9:16
5 [1]Lit *generation and generation* [a]Ps 74:1
6 [1]Or *bring to life* [a]Ps 71:20 [b]Ps 33:1
7 [a]Ps 106:4
8 [1]Or *Let me hear* [2]Lit *even to* [3]Or *stupidity* [a]Ps 29:11; Hag 2:9; Zech 9:10 [b]Ps 78:57; 2 Pet 2:21
9 [1]Or *reverence* [a]Ps 34:18; Is 46:13 [b]Ps 84:11; Hag 2:7; Zech 2:5; John 1:14
10 [1]Or *faithfulness* [a]Ps 25:10; Prov 3:3 [b]Ps 72:3; Is 32:17
11 [1]Or *Faithfulness* [a]Is 45:8
12 [a]Ps 84:11; James 1:17 [b]Lev 26:4; Ps 67:6; Ezek 34:27; Zech 8:12
13 [a]Ps 89:14
86:1 [a]Ps 17:6 [b]Ps 40:17
2 [1]Or *life* [a]Ps 25:20 [b]Ps 4:3 [c]Ps 25:2
3 [a]Ps 4:1 [b]Ps 25:5
4 [a]Ps 25:1
5 [a]Ps 25:8 [b]Ps 130:4 [c]Ex 34:6; Neh 9:17; Ps 103:8; Joel 2:13; Jon 4:2
6 [a]Ps 55:1
7 [a]Ps 50:15 [b]Ps 17:6
8 [a]Ex 15:11; 2 Sam 7:22; 1 Kin 8:23; Ps 89:6; Jer 10:6 [b]Deut 3:24
9 [a]Ps 22:27; Is 66:23; Rev 15:4
10 [1]Or *miracles* [a]Ps 77:13 [b]Ex 15:11; Ps 72:18 [c]Deut 6:4; Ps 83:18; Is 37:16; Mark 12:29; 1 Cor 8:4
11 [a]Ps 25:5 [b]Jer 32:39

12 I will [a]give thanks to You,
O Lord my God, with all my heart,
And will glorify Your name forever.
13 For Your lovingkindness toward me is great,
And You have [a]delivered my soul from the [1]depths of [2]Sheol.

14 ¶ O God, arrogant men have [a]risen up against me,
And [1]a band of violent men have sought my [2]life,
And they have not set You before them.
15 But You, O Lord, are a God [a]merciful and gracious,
Slow to anger and abundant in lovingkindness and [1]truth.
16 [a]Turn to me, and be gracious to me;
Oh [b]grant Your strength to Your servant,
And save the [c]son of Your handmaid.
17 [a]Show me a sign for good,
That those who hate me may [b]see *it* and be ashamed,
Because You, O LORD, [c]have helped me and comforted me.

Psalm 87

The Privileges of Citizenship in Zion.

A Psalm of the sons of Korah. A Song.

1 ¶ His [a]foundation is in the holy mountains.
2 The LORD [a]loves the gates of Zion
More than all the *other* dwelling places of Jacob.
3 [a]Glorious things are spoken of you,
O [b]city of God. [1]Selah.
4 "I shall mention [1a]Rahab and Babylon [2]among those who know Me;
Behold, Philistia and [b]Tyre with [3c]Ethiopia:
'This one was born there.' "
5 But of Zion it shall be said, "This one and that one were born in her";
And the Most High Himself will [a]establish her.
6 The LORD will count when He [a]registers the peoples,
"This one was born there." Selah.
7 Then those who [a]sing as well as those who [1b]play the flutes *shall say,*
"All my [c]springs *of joy* are in you."

Psalm 88

A Petition to Be Saved from Death.

A Song. A Psalm of the sons of Korah. For the choir director; according to Mahalath Leannoth. A +Maskil of Heman •the Ezrahite.

1 ¶ O LORD, the [a]God of my salvation,
I have [b]cried out by day and in the night before You.
2 Let my prayer [a]come before You;
[b]Incline Your ear to my cry!
3 For my [a]soul has [1]had enough troubles,
And [b]my life has drawn near to [2]Sheol.
4 I am reckoned among those who [a]go down to the pit;
I have become like a man [b]without strength,
5 [1]Forsaken [a]among the dead,
Like the slain who lie in the grave,
Whom You remember no more,
And they are [b]cut off from Your hand.
6 You have put me in [a]the lowest pit,
In [b]dark places, in the [c]depths.
7 Your wrath [a]has rested upon me,
And You have afflicted me with [b]all Your waves. [1]Selah.
8 You have removed [a]my acquaintances far from me;
You have made me an [1b]object of loathing to them;
I am [c]shut up and cannot go out.
9 My [a]eye has wasted away because of affliction;
I have [b]called upon You every day, O LORD;
I have [c]spread out my [1]hands to You.
10 ¶ Will You perform wonders for the dead?
Will [a]the [1]departed spirits rise *and* praise You? Selah.
11 Will Your lovingkindness be declared in the grave,
Your faithfulness in [1]Abaddon?
12 Will Your wonders be made known in the [a]darkness?
And Your [1]righteousness in the land of forgetfulness?

12 [a]Ps 111:1
13 [1]Lit *lowest Sheol* [2]I.e. the nether world [a]Ps 30:3
14 [1]Or *an assembly* [2]Lit *soul* [a]Ps 54:3
15 [1]Or *faithfulness* [a]Ps 86:5
16 [a]Ps 25:16 [b]Ps 68:35 [c]Ps 116:16
17 [a]Judg 6:17; Ps 119:122 [b]Ps 112:10 [c]Ps 118:13
87:1 [a]Ps 78:69; Is 28:16
2 [a]Ps 78:67,68
3 [1]*Selah* may mean: *Pause, Crescendo* or *Musical interlude* [a]Is 60:1 [b]Ps 46:4; 48:8
4 [1]I.e. Egypt [2]Or *as* [3]Lit *Cush* [a]Job 9:13; Ps 89:10; Is 19:23-25 [b]Ps 45:12 [c]Ps 68:31
5 [a]Ps 48:8
6 [a]Ps 69:28; Is 4:3; Ezek 13:9
7 [1]Or *dance* [a]Ps 68:25; 149:3 [b]2 Sam 6:14; Ps 30:11 [c]Ps 36:9
88:1 +Possibly *Contemplative,* or *Didactic,* or *Skillful Psalm* •1 Kin 4:31; 1 Chr 2:6; Ps 89: title [a]Ps 24:5; 27:9 [b]Ps 22:2; 86:3; Luke 18:7
2 [a]Ps 18:6 [b]Ps 31:2; 86:1
3 [1]Or *been satisfied with* [2]I.e. the nether world [a]Ps 107:26 [b]Ps 107:18; 116:3
4 [a]Ps 28:1; 143:7 [b]Job 29:12; Ps 22:11
5 [1]Lit *A freed one among the dead* [a]Ps 31:12 [b]Ps 31:22; Is 53:8
6 [a]Ps 86:13; Lam 3:55 [b]Ps 143:3 [c]Ps 69:15
7 [1]*Selah* may mean: *Pause, Crescendo* or *Musical interlude* [a]Ps 32:4; 39:10 [b]Ps 42:7
8 [1]Lit *abomination to them* [a]Job 19:13,19; Ps 31:11; 142:4 [b]Job 30:10 [c]Ps 142:7; Jer 32:2; 36:5
9 [1]Lit *palms* [a]Ps 6:7; 31:9 [b]Ps 22:2; 86:3 [c]Job 11:13; Ps 143:6
10 [1]Or *ghosts, shades* [a]Ps 6:5; 30:9
11 [1]I.e. place of destruction
12 [1]I.e. faithfulness to His gracious promises [a]Job 10:21; Ps 88:6

13 ¶ But I, O LORD, have cried out
[a]to You for help,
And [b]in the morning my prayer
comes before You.
14 O LORD, why [a]do You reject my
soul?
Why do You [b]hide Your face
from me?
15 I was afflicted and [a]about to die
from my youth on;
I suffer [b]Your terrors; I am
[1]overcome.
16 Your [a]burning anger has passed
over me;
Your terrors have
[1b]destroyed me.
17 They have [a]surrounded me
[b]like water all day long;
They have [c]encompassed me
altogether.
18 You have removed [a]lover and
friend far from me;
My acquaintances are *in*
darkness.

Psalm 89

The LORD's Covenant with David, and Israel's Afflictions.

A [+]Maskil of [•]Ethan [Δ]the Ezrahite.

1 ¶ I will [a]sing of the
lovingkindness of the LORD
forever;
To all generations I will [b]make
known Your [c]faithfulness
with my mouth.
2 For I have said,
"[a]Lovingkindness will be
built up forever;
In the heavens You will establish
Your [b]faithfulness."
3 "I have made a covenant with
[a]My chosen;
I have [b]sworn to David My
servant,
4 I will establish your [a]seed
forever
And build up your [b]throne to all
generations." [1]Selah.

5 ¶ The [a]heavens will praise Your
wonders, O LORD;
Your faithfulness also [b]in the
assembly of the [c]holy ones.
6 For [a]who in the skies is
comparable to the LORD?
Who among the [1b]sons of the
mighty is like the LORD,
7 A God [a]greatly feared in the
council of the [b]holy ones,
And [c]awesome above all those
who are around Him?
8 O LORD God of hosts, [a]who is
like You, O mighty [1]LORD?
Your faithfulness also
surrounds You.
9 You rule the swelling of the sea;
When its waves rise, You [a]still
them.
10 You Yourself crushed [1a]Rahab
like one who is slain;
You [b]scattered Your enemies
with [2]Your mighty arm.

11 ¶ The [a]heavens are Yours, the
earth also is Yours;
The [b]world and [1]all it contains,
You have founded them.
12 The [a]north and the south, You
have created them;
[b]Tabor and [c]Hermon [d]shout for
joy at Your name.
13 You have [1]a strong arm;
Your hand is mighty, Your [a]right
hand is exalted.
14 [a]Righteousness and justice are
the foundation of Your
throne;
[b]Lovingkindness and [1]truth go
before You.
15 How blessed are the people who
know the [1a]joyful sound!
O LORD, they walk in the [b]light
of Your countenance.
16 In [a]Your name they rejoice all
the day,
And by Your righteousness they
are exalted.
17 For You are the glory of [a]their
strength,
And by Your favor [1]our [b]horn is
exalted.
18 For our [a]shield belongs to the
LORD,
[1]And our king to the [b]Holy One
of Israel.

19 ¶ [1]Once You spoke in vision to
Your godly [2]ones,
And said, "I have [3]given help to
one who is [a]mighty;
I have exalted one [b]chosen from
the people.
20 "I have [a]found David My servant;
With My holy [b]oil I have
anointed him,
21 With whom [a]My hand will be
established;
My arm also will [b]strengthen
him.
22 "The enemy will not [1]deceive
him,
Nor the [2a]son of wickedness
afflict him.
23 "But I shall [a]crush his adversaries
before him,

13 [a]Ps 30:2 [b]Ps 5:3
14 [a]Ps 43:2 [b]Job 13:24; Ps 13:1
15 [1]Or *embarrassed* [a]Prov 24:11 [b]Job 6:4
16 [1]Or *silenced* [a]2 Chr 28:11; Is 13:13; Lam 1:12 [b]Lam 3:54; Ezek 37:11
17 [a]Ps 118:10-12 [b]Ps 124:4 [c]Ps 17:11
18 [a]Job 19:13; Ps 88:8
89:1 [+]Possibly *Contemplative,* or *Didactic,* or *Skillful Psalm* [•]1 Kin 4:31 [Δ]Ps 88: title [a]Ps 59:16 [b]Ps 40:10 [c]Ps 36:5; Is 25:1; Lam 3:23
2 [a]Ps 103:17 [b]Ps 36:5
3 [a]1 Kin 8:16 [b]Ps 132:11
4 [1]*Selah* may mean: *Pause, Crescendo* or *Musical interlude* [a]2 Sam 7:16 [b]2 Sam 7:13; Is 9:7; Luke 1:33
5 [a]Ps 19:1 [b]Ps 149:1 [c]Job 5:1
6 [1]Or *sons of gods* [a]Ps 86:8 [b]Ps 29:1
7 [a]Ps 47:2 [b]Ps 89:5 [c]Ps 96:4
8 [1]Heb *YAH* [a]Ps 35:10
9 [a]Ps 65:7
10 [1]I.e. Egypt [2]Lit *the arm of Your might* [a]Ps 87:4; Is 30:7 [b]Ps 18:14
11 [1]Lit *its fullness* [a]Gen 1:1; 1 Chr 29:11; Ps 96:5 [b]Ps 24:1
12 [a]Job 26:7 [b]Josh 19:22; Judg 4:6; Jer 46:18 [c]Deut 3:8; Josh 11:17; Ps 133:3; Song 4:8 [d]Ps 98:8
13 [1]Lit *an arm with strength* [a]Ps 98:1
14 [1]Or *faithfulness* [a]Ps 97:2 [b]Ps 85:13
15 [1]Or *blast of the trumpet, shout of joy* [a]Lev 23:24; Num 10:10; Ps 98:6 [b]Ps 4:6
16 [a]Ps 105:3
17 [1]Another reading is *You exalt our horn* [a]Ps 28:8 [b]Ps 75:10
18 [1]Or *Even to the Holy One of Israel our King* [a]Ps 47:9 [b]Ps 71:22
19 [1]Or *At that time* [2]Some mss read *one* [3]Lit *placed help upon* [a]2 Sam 17:10 [b]1 Kin 11:34; Ps 78:70
20 [a]1 Sam 13:14; Acts 13:22 [b]1 Sam 16:13
21 [a]Ps 18:35 [b]Ps 18:32
22 [1]Or *exact usury from him* [2]Or *wicked man* [a]2 Sam 7:10; Ps 125:3
23 [a]2 Sam 7:9; Ps 18:40

And strike those who hate him.
24 "My [a]faithfulness and My lovingkindness will be with him,
And in My name his [b]horn will be exalted.
25 "I shall also set his hand [a]on the sea
And his right hand on the rivers.
26 "He will cry to Me, 'You are [a]my Father,
My God, and the [b]rock of my salvation.'
27 "I also shall make him *My* [a]firstborn,
The [b]highest of the kings of the earth.
28 "My [a]lovingkindness I will keep for him forever,
And My [b]covenant shall be confirmed to him.
29 "So I will establish his [1a]descendants forever
And his [b]throne [c]as the days of heaven.

30 ¶ "If his sons [a]forsake My law
And do not walk in My judgments,
31 If they [1]violate My statutes
And do not keep My commandments,
32 Then I will punish their transgression with the [a]rod
And their iniquity with stripes.
33 "But I will not break off [a]My lovingkindness from him,
Nor deal falsely in My faithfulness.
34 "My [a]covenant I will not [1]violate,
Nor will I [b]alter [2]the utterance of My lips.
35 "[1]Once I have [a]sworn by My holiness;
I will not lie to David.
36 "His [1a]descendants shall endure forever
And his [b]throne [c]as the sun before Me.
37 "It shall be established forever [a]like the moon,
And the [b]witness in the sky is faithful." [1]Selah.

38 ¶ But You have [a]cast off and [b]*rejected*,
You have been full of wrath [1]against Your [c]anointed.
39 You have [a]spurned the covenant of Your servant;
You have [b]profaned [c]his crown [1]in the dust.
40 You have [a]broken down all his walls;
You have [b]brought his strongholds to ruin.
41 [a]All who pass along the way plunder him;
He has become a [b]reproach to his neighbors.
42 You have [a]exalted the right hand of his adversaries;
You have [b]made all his enemies rejoice.
43 You also turn back the edge of his sword
And have [a]not made him stand in battle.
44 You have made his [1a]splendor to cease
And cast his throne to the ground.
45 You have [a]shortened the days of his youth;
You have [b]covered him with shame. Selah.

46 ¶ [a]How long, O LORD?
Will You hide Yourself forever?
Will Your [b]wrath burn like fire?
47 [a]Remember [1]what my span of life is;
For what [b]vanity [2]You have created all the sons of men!
48 What man can live and not [a]see death?
Can he [b]deliver his soul from the [1]power of [2]Sheol? Selah.

49 ¶ Where are Your former lovingkindnesses, O Lord,
Which You [a]swore to David in Your faithfulness?
50 Remember, O Lord, the [a]reproach of Your servants;
[1]How I bear in my bosom *the reproach of* all the many peoples,
51 With which [a]Your enemies have reproached, O LORD,
With which they have reproached the footsteps of [b]Your anointed.

52 ¶ [a]Blessed be the LORD forever!
Amen and Amen.

BOOK 4

Psalm 90

God's Eternity and Man's Transitoriness.

A Prayer of +Moses, the man of God.

1 ¶ Lord, You have been our [1a]dwelling place in all generations.

24 aPs 89:1 bPs 132:17
25 aPs 72:8
26 a2 Sam 7:14; 1 Chr 22:10; Jer 3:19 b2 Sam 22:47; Ps 95:1
27 aEx 4:22; Ps 2:7; Jer 31:9; Col 1:15 bNum 24:7; Ps 72:11; Rev 19:16
28 aPs 89:33 bPs 89:3
29 1Lit *seed* aPs 18:50 b1 Kin 2:4; Ps 89:4; Is 9:7; Jer 33:17 cDeut 11:21
30 a2 Sam 7:14; Ps 119:53
31 1Lit *profane*
32 aJob 9:34
33 a2 Sam 7:15
34 1Lit *profane* 2Lit *that which goes forth* aDeut 7:9; Jer 33:20 bNum 23:19
35 1Or *One thing* aPs 60:6; Amos 4:2
36 1Lit *seed* aPs 89:29; Luke 1:33 bPs 72:5 cPs 72:17
37 1*Selah* may mean: *Pause, Crescendo* or *Musical interlude* aPs 72:5 bJob 16:19
38 1Lit *with* aPs 44:9 bDeut 32:19; 1 Chr 28:9 cPs 20:6
39 1Lit *to the ground* aPs 78:59; Lam 2:7 bPs 74:7 cLam 5:16
40 aPs 80:12 bLam 2:2
41 aPs 80:12 bPs 44:13
42 aPs 13:2 bPs 80:6
43 aPs 44:10
44 1Lit *clearness, luster* aEzek 28:7
45 aPs 102:23 bPs 44:15
46 aPs 13:1 bPs 79:5
47 1Lit *of what duration I am* 2Or *have You...men?* aJob 7:7 bPs 39:5; Eccl 1:2
48 1Lit *hand* 2I.e. the nether world aPs 22:29 bPs 49:15
49 a2 Sam 7:15; Jer 30:9; Ezek 34:23
50 1Lit *My bearing in my bosom* aPs 69:9
51 aPs 74:10 bPs 89:38
52 aPs 41:13
90:1 +Deut 33:1 1Or *hiding place;* some ancient mss read *place of refuge* aDeut 33:27; Ps 71:3; Ezek 11:16

2 Before [a]the mountains were
born
[1]Or You [b]gave birth to the
earth and the world,
Even [c]from everlasting to
everlasting, You are God.

3 ¶ You [a]turn man back into dust
And say, "Return, O children of
men."
4 For [a]a thousand years in Your
sight
Are like [b]yesterday when it
passes by,
[1]Or *as* a [c]watch in the night.
5 You [a]have [1]swept them away
like a flood, they [2][b]fall
asleep;
In the morning they are like
[c]grass which [3]sprouts
anew.
6 In the morning it [a]flourishes
and [1]sprouts anew;
Toward evening it [b]fades and
[c]withers away.

7 ¶ For we have been [a]consumed
by Your anger
And by Your wrath we have
been [1]dismayed.
8 You have [a]placed our iniquities
before You,
Our [b]secret *sins* in the light of
Your presence.
9 For [a]all our days have declined
in Your fury;
We have finished our years like a
[1]sigh.
10 As for the days of our [1]life,
[2]they contain seventy years,
Or if due to strength, [a]eighty
years,
Yet their pride is *but* [b]labor and
sorrow;
For soon it is gone and we [c]fly
away.
11 Who [1]understands the [a]power
of Your anger
And Your fury, according to the
[b]fear [2]that is due You?
12 So [a]teach us to number our
days,
That we may [1][b]present to You a
heart of wisdom.

13 ¶ Do [a]return, O LORD; [b]how
long *will it be?*
And [1]be [c]sorry for Your
servants.
14 O [a]satisfy us in the morning
with Your lovingkindness,
That we may [b]sing for joy and
be glad all our days.
15 [a]Make us glad [1]according to the
days You have afflicted us,
And the [b]years we have seen
[2]evil.
16 Let Your [a]work appear to Your
servants
And Your [b]majesty [1]to their
children.
17 Let the [a]favor of the Lord our
God be upon us;
And [1][b]confirm for us the work
of our hands;
Yes, [1]confirm the work of our
hands.

Psalm 91

Security of the One Who Trusts in the LORD.

1 ¶ He who dwells in the [a]shelter
of the Most High
Will abide in the [b]shadow of the
Almighty.
2 I will say to the LORD, "My
[a]refuge and my [b]fortress,
My God, in whom I [c]trust!"
3 For it is He who delivers you
from the [a]snare of the
trapper
And from the deadly [b]pestilence.
4 He will [a]cover you with His
pinions,
And [b]under His wings you may
seek refuge;
His [c]faithfulness is a [d]shield
and bulwark.

5 ¶ You [a]will not be afraid of the
[b]terror by night,
Or of the [c]arrow that flies by
day;
6 Of the [a]pestilence that [1]stalks
in darkness,
Or of the [b]destruction that lays
waste at noon.
7 A thousand may fall at your side
And ten thousand at your right
hand,
But [a]it shall not approach you.
8 You will only look on with your
eyes
And [a]see the recompense of the
wicked.
9 [1]For you have made the LORD,
[a]my refuge,
Even the Most High, [b]your
dwelling place.
10 [a]No evil will befall you,
Nor will any plague come near
your [1]tent.

11 ¶ For He will give [a]His angels
charge concerning you,
To guard you in all your ways.

---

2 [1]Or *And* [a]Job 15:7; Prov 8:25 [b]Gen 1:1; Ps 102:25 [c]Ps 93:2; Jer 10:10
3 [a]Gen 3:19; Job 34:14; Ps 104:29
4 [1]Or *And* [a]2 Pet 3:8 [b]Ps 39:5 [c]Ex 14:24; Judg 7:19
5 [1]Or *flooded* [2]Lit *become asleep* [3]Or *passes away* [a]Job 22:16 [b]Job 14:12; Ps 76:5 [c]Ps 103:15; Is 40:6
6 [1]Or *passes away* [a]Job 14:2 [b]Ps 92:7; Matt 6:30 [c]James 1:11
7 [1]Or *terrified* [a]Ps 39:11
8 [a]Ps 50:21; Jer 16:17 [b]Ps 19:12; Eccl 12:14
9 [1]Or *whisper* [a]Ps 78:33
10 [1]Lit *years* [2]Lit *in them are* [a]2 Kin 19:35 [b]Eccl 12:2-7; Jer 20:18 [c]Job 20:8; Ps 78:39
11 [1]Or *knows* [2]Lit *of You* [a]Ps 76:7 [b]Neh 5:9
12 [1]Or *gain, bring in* [a]Deut 32:29; Ps 39:4 [b]Prov 2:1-6
13 [1]Or *repent in regard to* [a]Ps 6:4 [b]Ps 6:3 [c]Ex 32:12; Deut 32:36; Ps 106:45; Amos 7:3; Jon 3:9
14 [a]Ps 36:8; Jer 31:14 [b]Ps 31:7
15 [1]Or *as many days as* [2]Or *trouble* [a]Ps 86:4 [b]Deut 2:14-16; Ps 31:10
16 [1]Or *upon* [a]Deut 32:4; Ps 44:1; Hab 3:2 [b]1 Kin 8:11; Is 6:3
17 [1]Or *give permanence to* [a]Ps 27:4 [b]Ps 37:23; Is 26:12; 1 Cor 3:7
91:1 [a]Ps 27:5 [b]Ps 17:8; Is 25:4
2 [a]Ps 14:6 [b]Ps 18:2; Jer 16:19 [c]Ps 25:2
3 [a]Ps 124:7; Prov 6:5 [b]1 Kin 8:37; 2 Chr 20:9; Ps 91:6
4 [a]Is 51:16 [b]Ps 17:8 [c]Ps 40:11 [d]Ps 35:2
5 [a]Job 5:19-23; Ps 23:4 [b]Song 3:8 [c]Ps 64:4
6 [1]Or *walks* [a]2 Kin 19:35; Ps 91:10 [b]Job 5:22
7 [a]Gen 7:23; Josh 14:10
8 [a]Ps 37:34
9 [1]Or *For You O LORD are my Refuge; You have made the Most High your dwelling place* [a]Ps 91:2 [b]Ps 90:1
10 [1]Or *dwelling* [a]Prov 12:21
11 [a]Ps 34:7; Matt 4:6; Luke 4:10; Heb 1:14

12 They will [a]bear you up in their hands,
That you do not strike your foot against a stone.
13 You will [a]tread upon the lion and cobra,
The young lion and the [1]serpent you will trample down.

14 ¶ "[a]Because he has loved Me, therefore I will deliver him;
I will [b]set him *securely* on high, because he has [c]known My name.
15 "He will [a]call upon Me, and I will answer him;
I will be with him in [1]trouble;
I will rescue him and [b]honor him.
16 "With [1]a [a]long life I will satisfy him
And [2b]let him see My salvation."

Psalm 92

Praise for the LORD's Goodness.

A Psalm, a Song for the Sabbath day.

1 ¶ It is [a]good to give thanks to the LORD
And to [b]sing praises to Your name, O Most High;
2 To [a]declare Your lovingkindness in the morning
And Your [b]faithfulness [1]by night,
3 [1]With the [a]ten-stringed lute and [1]with the [a]harp,
[1]With resounding music [2]upon the [a]lyre.
4 For You, O LORD, have made me glad by [1]what You [a]have done,
I will [b]sing for joy at the [c]works of Your hands.

5 ¶ How [a]great are Your works, O LORD!
Your [1b]thoughts are very [c]deep.
6 A [a]senseless man has no knowledge,
Nor does a [a]stupid man understand this:
7 That when the wicked [a]sprouted up like grass
And all [b]who did iniquity flourished,
It *was only* that they might be [c]destroyed forevermore.
8 But You, O LORD, are [a]on high forever.
9 For, behold, Your enemies, O LORD,
For, behold, [a]Your enemies will perish;
All who do iniquity will be [b]scattered.

10 ¶ But You have exalted my [a]horn like *that of* the wild ox;
I have [1]been [b]anointed with fresh oil.
11 And my eye has [a]looked *exultantly* upon [1]my foes,
My ears hear of the evildoers who rise up against me.
12 The [a]righteous man will [1]flourish like the palm tree,
He will grow like a [b]cedar in Lebanon.
13 [a]Planted in the house of the LORD,
They will flourish [b]in the courts of our God.
14 They will still [1a]yield fruit in old age;
They shall be [2]full of sap and very green,
15 To [1]declare that [a]the LORD is upright;
He is my [b]rock, and there is [c]no unrighteousness in Him.

Psalm 93

The Majesty of the LORD.

1 ¶ [a]The LORD [1]reigns, He is [b]clothed with majesty;
The LORD has [c]clothed and girded Himself with strength;
Indeed, the [d]world is firmly established, it will not be moved.
2 Your [a]throne is established from of old;
You [b]are from everlasting.

3 ¶ The [a]floods have lifted up, O LORD,
The floods have lifted up their voice,
The floods lift up their pounding waves.
4 More than the sounds of many waters,
Than the mighty breakers of the sea,
The LORD [a]on high is mighty.
5 Your [a]testimonies are fully confirmed;
[b]Holiness befits Your house,
O LORD, [1]forevermore.

---

12 [a]Matt 4:6; Luke 4:11
13 [1]Or *dragon* [a]Judg 14:6; Dan 6:22; Luke 10:19
14 [a]Ps 145:20 [b]Ps 59:1 [c]Ps 9:10
15 [1]Or *distress* [a]Job 12:4; Ps 50:15 [b]1 Sam 2:30; John 12:26
16 [1]Lit *length of days* [2]Or *cause him to feast his eyes on* [a]Deut 6:2; Ps 21:4; Prov 3:1,2 [b]Ps 50:23
92:1 [a]Ps 147:1 [b]Ps 135:3
2 [1]Lit *nights* [a]Ps 59:16 [b]Ps 89:1
3 [1]Lit *Upon* [2]Lit *by means of* [a]1 Sam 10:5; 1 Chr 13:8; Neh 12:27; Ps 33:2
4 [1]Lit *Your working* [a]Ps 40:5; 90:16 [b]Ps 106:47 [c]Ps 8:6; 111:7; 143:5
5 [1]Or *purposes* [a]Ps 40:5; 111:2; Rev 15:3 [b]Ps 33:11; 40:5; 139:17 [c]Ps 36:6; Rom 11:33
6 [a]Ps 49:10; 73:22; 94:8
7 [a]Job 12:6; Ps 90:5 [b]Ps 94:4 [c]Ps 37:38
8 [a]Ps 83:18; 93:4; 113:5
9 [a]Ps 37:20 [b]Ps 68:1; 89:10
10 [1]Or *become moist* [a]Ps 75:10; 89:17; 112:9 [b]Ps 23:5; 45:7
11 [1]Or *those who lie in wait for me* [a]Ps 54:7; 91:8
12 [1]Lit *sprout* [a]Num 24:6; Ps 1:3; 52:8; 72:7; Jer 17:8; Hos 14:5,6 [b]Ps 104:16; Ezek 31:3
13 [a]Ps 80:15; Is 60:21 [b]Ps 100:4; 116:19
14 [1]Or *thrive in* [2]Lit *fat and* [a]Prov 11:30; Is 37:31; John 15:2; James 3:18
15 [1]Or *show forth* [a]Job 34:10; Ps 25:8 [b]Deut 32:4; Ps 18:2; 94:22 [c]Rom 9:14
93:1 [1]Or *has assumed kingship* [a]Ps 96:10; 97:1; 99:1 [b]Ps 104:1 [c]Ps 65:6; Is 51:9 [d]Ps 96:10
2 [a]Ps 45:6; Lam 5:19 [b]Ps 90:2
3 [a]Ps 96:11; 98:7,8
4 [a]Ps 65:7; 89:6,9; 92:8
5 [1]Lit *for length of days* [a]Ps 19:7 [b]Ps 29:2; 96:9; 1 Cor 3:17

Psalm 94

The LORD Implored to Avenge His People.

1 ¶ O LORD, God of [1a]vengeance,
God of [1]vengeance, [2b]shine forth!
2 [a]Rise up, O [b]Judge of the earth,
Render recompense [c]to the proud.
3 How long shall the wicked, O LORD,
How long shall the [a]wicked exult?
4 They pour forth *words,* they [a]speak arrogantly;
All who do wickedness [b]vaunt themselves.
5 They [a]crush Your people, O LORD,
And [b]afflict Your heritage.
6 They [a]slay the widow and the [1]stranger
And murder the orphans.
7 [a]They have said, "[1]The LORD does not see,
Nor does the God of Jacob pay heed."

8 ¶ Pay heed, you [a]senseless among the people;
And when will you understand, [a]stupid ones?
9 He who [a]planted the ear, [1]does He not hear?
He who formed the eye, [1]does He not see?
10 He who [1a]chastens the nations, will He not rebuke,
Even He who [b]teaches man knowledge?
11 The LORD [a]knows the thoughts of man,
[1]That they are a *mere* breath.

12 ¶ Blessed is the man whom [a]You chasten, O [1]LORD,
And [b]whom You teach out of Your law;
13 That You may grant him [a]relief from the [b]days of adversity,
Until [c]a pit is dug for the wicked.
14 For [a]the LORD will not abandon His people,
Nor will He [b]forsake His inheritance.
15 For [1a]judgment [2]will again be righteous,
And all the upright in heart [3]will follow it.
16 Who will [a]stand up for me against evildoers?
Who will take his stand for me [b]against those who do wickedness?

17 ¶ If [a]the LORD had not been my help,
My soul would soon have dwelt in *the abode of* silence.
18 If I should say, "[a]My foot has slipped,"
Your lovingkindness, O LORD, will hold me up.
19 When my anxious thoughts [1]multiply within me,
Your [a]consolations delight my soul.
20 Can a [1a]throne of destruction be allied with You,
One [b]which devises [2]mischief by decree?
21 They [a]band themselves together against the [1]life of the righteous
And [b]condemn [2]the innocent to death.
22 But the LORD has been my [a]stronghold,
And my God the [b]rock of my refuge.
23 He has [a]brought back their wickedness upon them
And will [1b]destroy them in their evil;
The LORD our God will [1]destroy them.

Psalm 95

Praise to the LORD, and Warning against Unbelief.

1 ¶ O come, let us [a]sing for joy to the LORD,
Let us shout joyfully to [b]the rock of our salvation.
2 Let us [a]come before His presence [b]with [1]thanksgiving,
Let us shout joyfully to Him [c]with [2]psalms.
3 For the LORD is a [a]great God
And a great King [b]above all gods,
4 In whose hand are the [a]depths of the earth,
The peaks of the mountains are His also.
5 [1]The sea is His, for it was He [a]who made it,
And His hands formed the dry land.

6 ¶ Come, let us [a]worship and bow down,
Let us [b]kneel before the LORD our [c]Maker.

94:1 [1]Or *avenging acts* [2]Or *has shone forth* [a]Deut 32:35; Is 35:4; Nah 1:2; Rom 12:19 [b]Ps 50:2; 80:1
2 [a]Ps 7:6 [b]Gen 18:25 [c]Ps 31:23
3 [a]Job 20:5
4 [a]Ps 31:18; 75:5 [b]Ps 10:3; 52:1
5 [a]Is 3:15 [b]Ps 79:1
6 [1]Or *sojourner* [a]Is 10:2
7 [1]Heb YAH [a]Job 22:13; Ps 10:11
8 [a]Ps 92:6
9 [1]Or *can* [a]Ex 4:11; Prov 20:12
10 [1]Or *instructs* [a]Ps 44:2 [b]Job 35:11; Is 28:26
11 [1]Or *For* [a]Job 11:11; 1 Cor 3:20
12 [1]Heb YAH [a]Deut 8:5; Job 5:17; Ps 119:71; Prov 3:11,12; Heb 12:5,6 [b]Ps 119:171
13 [a]Job 34:29; Hab 3:16 [b]Ps 49:5 [c]Ps 9:15; 55:23
14 [a]1 Sam 12:22; Lam 3:31; Rom 11:2 [b]Ps 37:28
15 [1]I.e. administration of justice [2]Lit *will return to righteousness* [3]Lit *will be after it* [a]Ps 97:2; Is 42:3; Mic 7:9
16 [a]Num 10:35; Is 28:21; 33:10 [b]Ps 17:13; 59:2
17 [a]Ps 124:1,2
18 [a]Ps 38:16; 73:2
19 [1]Or *are many* [a]Is 57:18; 66:13
20 [1]Or *tribunal* [2]Or *trouble, misfortune* [a]Amos 6:3 [b]Ps 50:16; 58:2
21 [1]Or *soul* [2]Lit *innocent blood* [a]Ps 56:6; 59:3 [b]Ex 23:7; Ps 106:38; Prov 17:15; Matt 27:4
22 [a]Ps 9:9; 59:9 [b]Ps 18:2; 71:7
23 [1]Or *silence* [a]Ps 7:16; 140:9, 11 [b]Gen 19:15
95:1 [a]Ps 66:1; 81:1 [b]Ps 89:26
2 [1]Or *a song of thanksgiving* [2]Or *songs* (with instrumental accompaniment) [a]Mic 6:6 [b]Ps 100:4; 147:7; Jon 2:9 [c]Ps 81:2; Eph 5:19; James 5:13
3 [a]Ps 48:1; 135:5; 145:3 [b]Ps 96:4; 97:9
4 [a]Ps 135:6
5 [1]Lit *Who has the sea* [a]Gen 1:9,10; Ps 146:6; Jon 1:9
6 [a]Ps 96:9; 99:5,9 [b]2 Chr 6:13; Dan 6:10; Phil 2:10 [c]Ps 100:3; 149:2; Is 17:7; Hos 8:14

7 For He is our God,
And [a]we are the people of His [1b]pasture and the sheep of His hand.
[c]Today, [2]if you would hear His voice,
8 Do not harden your hearts, as at [1a]Meribah,
As in the day of [2b]Massah in the wilderness,
9 "When your fathers [a]tested Me,
They tried Me, though they had seen My work.
10 "For [a]forty years I loathed *that* generation,
And said they are a people who err in their heart,
And they do not know My ways.
11 "Therefore I [a]swore in My anger,
Truly they shall not enter into My [b]rest."

Psalm 96

A Call to Worship the LORD the Righteous Judge.

1 ¶ [a]Sing to the LORD a [b]new song;
Sing to the LORD, all the earth.
2 Sing to the LORD, bless His name;
[a]Proclaim good tidings of His salvation from day to day.
3 Tell of [a]His glory among the nations,
His wonderful deeds among all the peoples.
4 For [a]great is the LORD and [b]greatly to be praised;
He is to be [c]feared [d]above all gods.
5 For [a]all the gods of the peoples are [1]idols,
But [b]the LORD made the heavens.
6 [a]Splendor and majesty are before Him,
Strength and beauty are in His sanctuary.

7 ¶ [1]Ascribe to the LORD, O [a]families of the peoples,
[1b]Ascribe to the LORD glory and strength.
8 [1]Ascribe to the LORD the [a]glory of His name;
Bring an [2b]offering and come into His courts.
9 [a]Worship the LORD in [1]holy attire;
[b]Tremble before Him, all the earth.
10 Say among the nations, "[a]The LORD reigns;

7 [1]Lit *pasturing* [2]Or *O that you would obey* [a]Ps 79:13 [b]Ps 74:1 [c]Heb 3:7-11
8 [1]Or *place of strife* [2]Or *temptation* [a]Ex 17:2-7; Num 20:13 [b]Ex 17:7; Deut 6:16
9 [a]Num 14:22; Ps 78:18; 1 Cor 10:9
10 [a]Acts 7:36; Heb 3:10
11 [a]Num 14:23; Deut 1:35; Heb 4:3 [b]Deut 12:9
96:1 [a]1 Chr 16:23-33 [b]Ps 40:3
2 [a]Ps 71:15
3 [a]Ps 145:12
4 [a]Ps 48:1 [b]Ps 18:3 [c]Ps 89:7 [d]Ps 95:3
5 [1]Or *non-existent things* [a]1 Chr 16:26; Jer 10:11 [b]Ps 115:15; Is 42:5
6 [a]Ps 104:1
7 [1]Lit *Give* [a]Ps 22:27 [b]1 Chr 16:28; Ps 29:1
8 [1]Lit *Give* [2]Or *meal offering* [a]Ps 79:9 [b]Ps 45:12
9 [1]Or *the splendor of holiness* [a]1 Chr 16:29; 2 Chr 20:21; Ps 29:2 [b]Ps 33:8
10 [1]Or *uprightness* [a]Ps 93:1 [b]Ps 9:8
11 [1]Or *thunder* [2]Lit *its fullness* [a]Ps 69:34; Is 49:13 [b]Ps 97:1 [c]Ps 98:7
12 [a]Ps 65:13; Is 35:1 [b]Is 44:23
13 [a]Ps 98:9 [b]Rev 19:11
97:1 [1]Or *has assumed Kingship* [2]Or *coastlands* [a]Ps 96:10 [b]Ps 96:11 [c]Is 42:10
2 [a]Ex 19:9; Deut 4:11; 1 Kin 8:12; Ps 18:11 [b]Ps 89:14
3 [a]Ps 18:8; Dan 7:10; Hab 3:5 [b]Mal 4:1; Heb 12:29
4 [a]Ex 19:16; Ps 77:18 [b]Ps 96:9
5 [a]Ps 46:6; Amos 9:5; Mic 1:4; Nah 1:5 [b]Josh 3:11
6 [a]Ps 19:1 [b]Ps 98:2; Is 6:3
7 [1]Or *All the gods have worshiped Him* [2]Or *supernatural powers* [a]Ps 78:58; Is 42:17; Jer 10:14 [b]Ps 106:36; Jer 50:2; Hab 2:18 [c]Heb 1:6
8 [1]Or possibly *hears and is glad* [a]Ps 48:11; Zeph 3:14
9 [1]Or *supernatural powers* [a]Ps 83:18 [b]Ex 18:11; Ps 95:3
10 [a]Ps 34:14; Prov 8:13; Amos 5:15; Rom 12:9

Indeed, the [a]world is firmly established, it will not be moved;
He will [b]judge the peoples with [1]equity."

11 ¶ Let the [a]heavens be glad, and let the [b]earth rejoice;
Let [c]the sea [1]roar, and [2]all it contains;
12 Let the [a]field exult, and all that is in it.
Then all the [b]trees of the forest will sing for joy
13 Before the LORD, [a]for He is coming,
For He is coming to judge the earth.
[b]He will judge the world in righteousness
And the peoples in His faithfulness.

Psalm 97

The LORD's Power and Dominion.

1 ¶ [a]The LORD [1]reigns, let the [b]earth rejoice;
Let the many [2c]islands be glad.
2 [a]Clouds and thick darkness surround Him;
[b]Righteousness and justice are the foundation of His throne.
3 [a]Fire goes before Him
And [b]burns up His adversaries round about.
4 His [a]lightnings lit up the world;
The earth saw and [b]trembled.
5 The mountains [a]melted like wax at the presence of the LORD,
At the presence of the [b]Lord of the whole earth.
6 The [a]heavens declare His righteousness,
And [b]all the peoples have seen His glory.

7 ¶ Let all those be ashamed who serve [a]graven images,
Who boast themselves of [b]idols;
[1c]Worship Him, all you [2]gods.
8 Zion [1]heard *this* and [a]was glad,
And the daughters of Judah have rejoiced
Because of Your judgments, O LORD.
9 For You are the LORD [a]Most High over all the earth;
You are exalted far [b]above all [1]gods.

10 ¶ [a]Hate evil, you who love the LORD,

Who [b]preserves the souls of His
godly ones;
He [c]delivers them from the
hand of the wicked.
11 [a]Light is sown *like seed* for the
righteous
And [b]gladness for the upright in
heart.
12 Be [a]glad in the LORD, you
righteous ones,
And [b]give thanks [1]to His holy
name.

Psalm 98

A Call to Praise the LORD for His Righteousness.

A Psalm.

1 ¶ O sing to the LORD a [a]new
song,
For He has done [b]wonderful
things,
His [c]right hand and His [d]holy
arm have [1]gained the
victory for Him.
2 [a]The LORD has made known His
salvation;
He has [b]revealed His
[1]righteousness in the sight
of the nations.
3 He has [a]remembered His
lovingkindness and His
faithfulness to the house of
Israel;
[b]All the ends of the earth have
seen the salvation of our
God.
4 ¶ [a]Shout joyfully to the LORD, all
the earth;
[b]Break forth and sing for joy and
sing praises.
5 Sing praises to the LORD with the
[a]lyre,
With the lyre and the [1b]sound
of melody.
6 With [a]trumpets and the sound
of the horn
[b]Shout joyfully before [c]the
King, the LORD.
7 ¶ Let the [a]sea roar and [1]all it
contains,
The [b]world and those who dwell
in it.
8 Let the [a]rivers clap their hands,
Let the [b]mountains sing together
for joy
9 Before the LORD, for He is
coming to [a]judge the earth;
He will judge the world with
righteousness
And [b]the peoples with [1]equity.

Psalm 99

Praise to the LORD for His Fidelity to Israel.

1 ¶ [a]The LORD reigns, let the
peoples tremble;
He [1b]is enthroned *above* the
cherubim, let the earth
shake!
2 The LORD [1]is [a]great in Zion,
And He is [b]exalted above all the
peoples.
3 Let them praise Your [a]great and
awesome name;
[b]Holy is [1]He.
4 The [1]strength of the King
[a]loves [2]justice;
You have established [3b]equity;
You have [c]executed [2]justice and
righteousness in Jacob.
5 [1a]Exalt the LORD our God
And [b]worship at His footstool;
[c]Holy is He.
6 ¶ [a]Moses and Aaron were
among His [b]priests,
And [a]Samuel was among those
who [c]called on His name;
They [d]called upon the LORD and
He answered them.
7 He [a]spoke to them in the pillar
of cloud;
They [b]kept His testimonies
And the statute that He gave
them.
8 O LORD our God, You [a]answered
them;
You were a [b]forgiving God to
them,
And *yet* an [c]avenger of their *evil*
deeds.
9 Exalt the LORD our God
And worship at His holy hill,
For holy is the LORD our God.

Psalm 100

All Men Exhorted to Praise God.

A Psalm for +Thanksgiving.

1 ¶ [a]Shout joyfully to the LORD, all
the earth.
2 [a]Serve the LORD with gladness;
[b]Come before Him with joyful
singing.
3 Know that [a]the LORD [1]Himself
is God;
It is He who has [b]made us, and
[2]not we ourselves;
We are [c]His people and the
sheep of His pasture.

4 ¶ Enter His gates [a]with
[1]thanksgiving
And His courts with praise.

10 [b]Ps 31:23; Prov 2:8 [c]Ps 37:40; Jer 15:21; Dan 3:28
11 [a]Job 22:28; Ps 112:4; Prov 4:18 [b]Ps 64:10
12 [1]Lit *for the memory of His holiness* [a]Ps 32:11 [b]Ps 30:4
98:1 [1]Or *accomplished salvation* [a]Ps 33:3 [b]Ps 40:5 [c]Ex 15:6 [d]Is 52:10
2 [1]I.e. faithfulness to His gracious promises [a]Is 52:10 [b]Is 62:2; Rom 3:25
3 [a]Luke 1:54 [b]Ps 22:27
4 [a]Ps 100:1 [b]Is 44:23
5 [1]Or *voice of song* (accompanied by music) [a]Ps 92:3 [b]Is 51:3
6 [a]Num 10:10; 2 Chr 15:14 [b]Ps 66:1 [c]Ps 47:7
7 [1]Lit *its fullness* [a]Ps 96:11 [b]Ps 24:1
8 [a]Ps 93:3; Is 55:12 [b]Ps 65:12
9 [1]Or *uprightness* [a]Ps 96:13 [b]Ps 96:10
99:1 [1]Lit *sits* [a]Ps 97:1 [b]Ex 25:22; 1 Sam 4:4; Ps 80:1
2 [1]Or *in Zion is great* [a]Ps 48:1; Is 12:6 [b]Ps 97:9
3 [1]Or *it* [a]Deut 28:58; Ps 76:1 [b]Lev 19:2; Josh 24:19; 1 Sam 2:2; Ps 22:3; Is 6:3
4 [1]Or *You have established in equity the strength of the King who loves justice* [2]Or *judgment* [3]Or *uprightness* [a]Ps 11:7 [b]Ps 17:2 [c]Ps 103:6; Jer 23:5
5 [1]The verb is plural [a]Ps 34:3 [b]Ps 132:7 [c]Ps 99:3
6 [a]Jer 15:1 [b]Ex 24:6-8; Lev 8:1-30 [c]1 Sam 7:9; Ps 22:4 [d]Ex 15:25
7 [a]Ex 33:9; Num 12:5 [b]Ps 105:28
8 [a]Ps 106:44 [b]Num 14:20; Ps 78:38 [c]Ex 32:28; Num 20:12; Ps 95:11
100:1 +Or *thank offering* [a]Ps 95:1
2 [a]Deut 12:11 [b]Ps 95:2
3 [1]Or *He* [2]Some mss read *His we are* [a]Deut 4:35; 1 Kin 18:39; Ps 46:10 [b]Job 10:3; Ps 95:6 [c]Ps 74:1; Is 40:11; Ezek 34:30
4 [1]Or *a thank offering* [a]Ps 95:2

Give thanks to Him, [b]bless His
name.
5 For [a]the LORD is good;
[b]His lovingkindness is
everlasting
And His [c]faithfulness to all
generations.

Psalm 101

The Psalmist's Profession of Uprightness.

A Psalm of David.

1 ¶ I will [a]sing of lovingkindness
and [1]justice,
To You, O LORD, I will sing
praises.
2 I will [1a]give heed to the
[2]blameless way.
When will You come to me?
I will walk within my house in
the [3b]integrity of my heart.
3 I will set no [a]worthless thing
before my eyes;
I hate the [1]work of those who
[b]fall away;
It shall not fasten its grip on me.
4 A [a]perverse heart shall depart
from me;
I will know no evil.
5 Whoever secretly [a]slanders his
neighbor, him I will
[1]destroy;
No one who has a [b]haughty look
and an arrogant heart will I
endure.

6 ¶ My eyes shall be upon the
faithful of the land, that they
may dwell with me;
He who walks in a [1a]blameless
way is the one who will
minister to me.
7 He who [a]practices deceit shall
not dwell within my house;
He who speaks falsehood [b]shall
not [1]maintain his position
before me.
8 [a]Every morning I will [1b]destroy
all the wicked of the land,
So as to [c]cut off from the [d]city
of the LORD all those who do
iniquity.

Psalm 102

Prayer of an Afflicted Man for Mercy on Himself and on Zion.

A Prayer of the Afflicted when he is faint
and +pours out his complaint
before the LORD.

1 ¶ [a]Hear my prayer, O LORD!
And let my cry for help [b]come
to You.
2 [a]Do not hide Your face from me
in the day of my distress;
[b]Incline Your ear to me;
In the day when I call [a]answer
me quickly.
3 For my days [a]have been
[1]consumed in smoke,
And my [b]bones have been
scorched like a hearth.
4 My heart [a]has been smitten like
[1]grass and has [b]withered
away,
Indeed, I [c]forget to eat my
bread.
5 Because of the [1]loudness of my
groaning
My [a]bones [2]cling to my flesh.
6 I [1]resemble a [a]pelican of the
wilderness;
I have become like an owl of the
waste places.
7 I [a]lie awake,
I have become like a lonely bird
on a housetop.

8 ¶ My enemies [a]have reproached
me all day long;
Those who [1b]deride me [2]have
used my *name* as a [c]curse.
9 For I have eaten ashes like bread
And [a]mingled my drink with
weeping
10 [a]Because of Your indignation
and Your wrath,
For You have [b]lifted me up and
cast me away.
11 My days are like a [1a]lengthened
shadow,
And [2]I [b]wither away like
[3]grass.

12 ¶ But You, O LORD, [1a]abide
forever,
And Your [2b]name to all
generations.
13 You will [a]arise *and* have
[b]compassion on Zion;
For [c]it is time to be gracious to
her,
For the [d]appointed time has
come.
14 Surely Your servants [1]find
pleasure in her stones
And feel pity for her dust.
15 [1]So the [2a]nations will fear the
name of the LORD
And [b]all the kings of the earth
Your glory.
16 For the LORD has [a]built up Zion;
He has [b]appeared in His glory.
17 He has [a]regarded the prayer of
the [1]destitute
And has not despised their
prayer.

4 [b]Ps 96:2
5 [a]1 Chr 16:34; 2 Chr 5:13; Ezra 3:11; Ps 25:8; Jer 33:11; Nah 1:7 [b]Ps 136:1 [c]Ps 119:90
101:1 [1]Or *judgment* [a]Ps 51:14
2 [1]Or *behave prudently in* [2]Or *way of integrity* [3]Or *blamelessness* [a]1 Sam 18:5 [b]1 Kin 9:4
3 [1]Or *practice of apostasy* [a]Deut 15:9 [b]Josh 23:6; Ps 40:4
4 [a]Prov 11:20
5 [1]Or *silence* [a]Ps 50:20; Jer 9:4 [b]Ps 10:4; Prov 6:17
6 [1]Or *way of integrity* [a]Ps 119:1
7 [1]Lit *be established before my eyes* [a]Ps 43:1 [b]Ps 52:4
8 [1]Or *silence* [a]Jer 21:12 [b]Ps 75:10 [c]Ps 118:10-12 [d]Ps 46:4
102:1 +Ps 142:2 [a]Ps 39:12 [b]Ex 2:23; 1 Sam 9:16
2 [a]Ps 69:17 [b]Ps 31:2
3 [1]Or *finished* [a]Ps 37:20; James 4:14 [b]Job 30:30; Lam 1:13
4 [1]Lit *herbage* [a]Ps 90:5 [b]Ps 37:2; Is 40:7 [c]1 Sam 1:7; 2 Sam 12:17; Ezra 10:6; Job 33:20
5 [1]Lit *voice* [2]Lit *have cleaved* [a]Job 19:20; Lam 4:8
6 [1]Lit *have become similar to* [a]Is 34:11; Zeph 2:14
7 [a]Ps 77:4
8 [1]Or *made a fool of* [2]Lit *have sworn by me* [a]Ps 31:11 [b]Acts 26:11 [c]2 Sam 16:5; Is 65:15; Jer 29:22
9 [a]Ps 42:3
10 [a]Ps 38:3 [b]Job 27:21
11 [1]Lit *stretched out* [2]Or *as for me, I* [3]Lit *herbage* [a]Job 14:2; Ps 109:23 [b]Ps 102:4
12 [1]Or *sit enthroned* [2]Lit *memorial* [a]Ps 9:7; Lam 5:19 [b]Ex 3:15; Ps 135:13
13 [a]Ps 12:5 [b]Is 60:10; Zech 1:12 [c]Ps 119:126 [d]Ps 75:2; Dan 8:19
14 [1]Or *have found*
15 [1]Or *And* [2]Or *Gentiles, heathen* [a]1 Kin 8:43; Ps 67:7 [b]Ps 138:4
16 [a]Ps 147:2 [b]Is 60:1
17 [1]Or *naked* [a]Neh 1:6; Ps 22:24

18 ¶ [1]This will be [a]written for the
[b]generation to come,
[2]That [c]a people yet to be
created [3]may praise [4]the
LORD.
19 For He [a]looked down from His
holy height;
[b]From heaven the LORD gazed
[1]upon the earth,
20 To hear the [a]groaning of the
prisoner,
To [b]set free [1]those who were
doomed to death,
21 That *men* may [a]tell of the name
of the LORD in Zion
And His praise in Jerusalem,
22 When [a]the peoples are gathered
together,
And the kingdoms, to serve the
LORD.

23 ¶ He has weakened my strength
in the way;
He has [a]shortened my days.
24 I say, "O my God, [a]do not take
me away in the [1]midst of
my days,
Your [b]years are throughout all
generations.
25 "Of old You [a]founded the earth,
And the [b]heavens are the work
of Your hands.
26 "[1]Even they will [a]perish, but
You endure;
And all of them will wear out
like a garment;
Like clothing You will change
them and they will be
changed.
27 "But You are [1a]the same,
And Your years will not come to
an end.
28 "The [a]children of Your servants
will continue,
And their [1b]descendants will be
established before You."

Psalm 103

Praise for the LORD's Mercies.

A Psalm of David.

1 ¶ [a]Bless the LORD, O my soul,
And all that is within me, *bless*
His [b]holy name.
2 Bless the LORD, O my soul,
And [a]forget none of His
benefits;
3 Who [a]pardons all your
iniquities,
Who [b]heals all your diseases;
4 Who [a]redeems your life from
the pit,
Who [b]crowns you with
lovingkindness and
compassion;
5 Who [a]satisfies your [1]years with
good things,
So that your youth is [b]renewed
like the eagle.

6 ¶ The LORD [a]performs
[1]righteous deeds
And judgments for all who are
[b]oppressed.
7 He [a]made known His ways to
Moses,
His [b]acts to the sons of Israel.
8 The LORD is [a]compassionate and
gracious,
[b]Slow to anger and abounding in
lovingkindness.
9 He [a]will not always strive
with us,
Nor will He [b]keep *His anger*
forever.
10 He has [a]not dealt with us
according to our sins,
Nor rewarded us according to
our iniquities.
11 For as high [a]as the heavens are
above the earth,
So great is His lovingkindness
toward those who [1]fear
Him.
12 As far as the east is from the
west,
So far has He [a]removed our
transgressions from us.
13 Just [a]as a father has compassion
on *his* children,
So the LORD has compassion on
those who [1]fear Him.
14 For [a]He Himself knows [1]our
frame;
He [b]is mindful that we are *but*
[c]dust.

15 ¶ As for man, his days are [a]like
grass;
As a [b]flower of the field, so he
flourishes.
16 When the [a]wind has passed
over it, it is no more,
And its [b]place acknowledges it
no longer.
17 But the [a]lovingkindness of the
LORD is from everlasting to
everlasting on those who
[1]fear Him,
And His [2]righteousness [b]to
children's children,
18 To [a]those who keep His
covenant
And remember His precepts to
do them.

---

18 [1]Or *Let this be written* [2]Or *And* [3]Or *will* [4]Heb YAH [a]Deut 31:19; Rom 15:4; 1 Cor 10:11 [b]Ps 22:30 [c]Ps 22:31
19 [1]Lit *toward* [a]Deut 26:15; Ps 14:2 [b]Ps 33:13
20 [1]Lit *the sons of death* [a]Ps 79:11 [b]Ps 146:7
21 [a]Ps 22:22
22 [a]Ps 22:27; Is 49:22; Zech 8:20-23
23 [a]Ps 39:5
24 [1]Lit *half* [a]Ps 39:13; Is 38:10 [b]Job 36:26; Ps 90:2; Hab 1:12
25 [a]Gen 1:1; Neh 9:6; Heb 1:10-12 [b]Ps 96:5
26 [1]Lit *They themselves* [a]Is 34:4; Matt 24:35; 2 Pet 3:10; Rev 20:11
27 [1]Lit *He* [a]Is 41:4; Mal 3:6; James 1:17
28 [1]Lit *seed* [a]Ps 69:36 [b]Ps 89:4
103:1 [a]Ps 104:1 [b]Ps 33:21; Ezek 36:21
2 [a]Deut 6:12
3 [a]Ex 34:7; Ps 86:5; Is 43:25 [b]Ex 15:26; Ps 30:2; Jer 30:17
4 [a]Ps 49:15 [b]Ps 5:12
5 [1]Or *desire* [a]Ps 107:9 [b]Is 40:31
6 [1]Or *deeds of vindication* [a]Ps 99:4 [b]Ps 12:5
7 [a]Ex 33:13; Ps 99:7 [b]Ps 78:11
8 [a]Ex 34:6; Num 14:18; Neh 9:17; Ps 86:15; Jon 4:2; James 5:11 [b]Ps 145:8; Joel 2:13; Nah 1:3
9 [a]Ps 30:5; Is 57:16 [b]Jer 3:5; Mic 7:18
10 [a]Ezra 9:13; Lam 3:22
11 [1]Or *revere* [a]Ps 36:5
12 [a]2 Sam 12:13; Is 38:17; Zech 3:9; Heb 9:26
13 [1]Or *revere* [a]Mal 3:17
14 [1]I.e. what we are made of [a]Is 29:16 [b]Ps 78:39 [c]Gen 3:19; Eccl 12:7
15 [a]Ps 90:5; Is 40:6; 1 Pet 1:24 [b]Job 14:2; James 1:10
16 [a]Is 40:7 [b]Job 7:10
17 [1]Or *revere* [2]I.e. faithfulness to His gracious promises [a]Ps 25:6 [b]Ex 20:6; Deut 5:10; Ps 105:8
18 [a]Deut 7:9; Ps 25:10

19 ¶ The LORD has established His
[a]throne in the heavens,
And His [1][b]sovereignty rules
over [2]all.
20 Bless the LORD, you [a]His angels,
[b]Mighty in strength, who
[c]perform His word,
[d]Obeying the voice of His word!
21 Bless the LORD, all you [a]His
hosts,
You [b]who serve Him, doing His
will.
22 Bless the LORD, [a]all you works
of His,
In all places of His dominion;
Bless the LORD, O my soul!

Psalm 104

The LORD's Care over All His Works.

1 ¶ [a]Bless the LORD, O my soul!
O LORD my God, You are very
great;
You are [b]clothed with splendor
and majesty,
2 Covering Yourself with [a]light as
with a cloak,
[b]Stretching out heaven like a
tent curtain.
3 [1]He [a]lays the beams of His
upper chambers in the
waters;
[1]He makes the [b]clouds His
chariot;
[1]He walks upon the [c]wings of
the wind;
4 [1]He makes [2a]the winds His
messengers,
[3]Flaming [b]fire His ministers.
5 ¶ He [a]established the earth
upon its foundations,
So that it will not [1]totter forever
and ever.
6 You [a]covered it with the deep
as with a garment;
The waters were standing above
the mountains.
7 At Your [a]rebuke they fled,
At the [b]sound of Your thunder
they hurried away.
8 The mountains rose; the valleys
sank down
To the [a]place which You
established for them.
9 You set a [a]boundary that they
may not pass over,
So that they will not return to
cover the earth.
10 ¶ [1]He sends forth [a]springs in
the valleys;
They flow between the
mountains;

11 They [a]give drink to every beast
of the field;
The [b]wild donkeys quench their
thirst.
12 [1]Beside them the birds of the
heavens [a]dwell;
They [2]lift up *their* voices among
the branches.
13 [1]He [a]waters the mountains
from His upper chambers;
[b]The earth is satisfied with the
fruit of His works.

14 ¶ [1]He causes the [a]grass to grow
for the [2]cattle,
And [b]vegetation for the [3]labor
of man,
So that [4]he may bring forth
[5]food [c]from the earth,
15 And [a]wine which makes man's
heart glad,
[b]So that he may make *his* face
glisten with oil,
And [1]food which [c]sustains
man's heart.
16 The trees of the LORD [1]drink
their fill,
The cedars of Lebanon which He
planted,
17 Where the [a]birds build their
nests,
And the [b]stork, whose home is
the [1]fir trees.

18 ¶ The high mountains are for the
[a]wild goats;
The [b]cliffs are a refuge for the
[1c]shephanim.
19 He made the moon [a]for the
seasons;
The [b]sun knows the place of its
setting.
20 You [a]appoint darkness and it
becomes night,
In which all the [b]beasts of the
forest [1]prowl about.
21 The [a]young lions roar after their
prey
[1]And [b]seek their food from
God.
22 *When* the sun rises they
withdraw
And lie down in their [a]dens.
23 Man goes forth to [a]his work
And to his labor until evening.

24 ¶ O LORD, how [a]many are Your
works!
[1]In [b]wisdom You have made
them all;
The [c]earth is full of Your
[2]possessions.

19 [1]Or *kingdom* [2]I.e. the universe [a]Ps 11:4 [b]Ps 47:2; Dan 4:17
20 [a]Ps 148:2 [b]Ps 29:1 [c]Matt 6:10 [d]Ps 91:11; Heb 1:14
21 [a]1 Kin 22:19; Neh 9:6; Ps 148:2; Luke 2:13 [b]Ps 104:4
22 [a]Ps 145:10
104:1 [a]Ps 103:22 [b]Ps 93:1
2 [a]Dan 7:9 [b]Is 40:22
3 [1]Lit *The one who* [a]Amos 9:6 [b]Is 19:1 [c]Ps 18:10
4 [1]Lit *Who* [2]Or *His angels, spirits* [3]Or *His ministers flames of fire* [a]Ps 148:8; Heb 1:7 [b]2 Kin 2:11
5 [1]Or *move out of place* [a]Job 38:4; Ps 24:2
6 [a]Gen 1:2
7 [a]Ps 18:15; Is 50:2 [b]Ps 29:3
8 [a]Ps 33:7
9 [a]Job 38:10; Jer 5:22
10 [1]Lit *The one who sends* [a]Ps 107:35; Is 41:18
11 [a]Ps 104:13 [b]Job 39:5
12 [1]Or *Over, Above* [2]Lit *give forth* [a]Matt 8:20
13 [1]Lit *Who* [a]Ps 65:9 [b]Jer 10:13
14 [1]Lit *Who* [2]Or *beasts* [3]Or *cultivation by* or *service of* [4]Or *He* [5]Lit *bread* [a]Job 38:27; Ps 147:8 [b]Gen 1:29 [c]Job 28:5
15 [1]Lit *bread* [a]Judg 9:13; Prov 31:6; Eccl 10:19 [b]Ps 23:5; Luke 7:46 [c]Gen 18:5; Judg 19:5
16 [1]Lit *are satisfied*
17 [1]Or *cypress* [a]Ps 104:12 [b]Lev 11:19
18 [1]Small, shy, furry animals *(Hyrax syriacus)* found in the peninsula of the Sinai, northern Israel, and the region round the Dead Sea; KJV *coney,* orig NASB *rock badgers* [a]Job 39:1 [b]Prov 30:26 [c]Lev 11:5
19 [a]Gen 1:14 [b]Ps 19:6
20 [1]Lit *creep* [a]Ps 74:16; Is 45:7 [b]Ps 50:10; Is 56:9; Mic 5:8
21 [1]Lit *And to seek* [a]Job 38:39 [b]Ps 145:15; Joel 1:20
22 [a]Job 37:8
23 [a]Gen 3:19
24 [1]Or *With* [2]Or *creatures* [a]Ps 40:5 [b]Ps 136:5; Prov 3:19; Jer 10:12 [c]Ps 65:9

25 [1]There is the [a]sea, great and
[2]broad,
In which are swarms without
number,
Animals both small and great.
26 There the [a]ships move along,
And [1b]Leviathan, which You
have formed to sport in it.

27 ¶ They all [a]wait for You
To [b]give them their food in
[1]due season.
28 You give to them, they gather
it up;
You [a]open Your hand, they are
satisfied with good.
29 You [a]hide Your face, they are
dismayed;
You [b]take away their [1]spirit,
they expire
And [c]return to their dust.
30 You send forth Your [1a]Spirit,
they are created;
And You renew the face of the
ground.

31 ¶ Let the [a]glory of the LORD
endure forever;
Let the LORD [b]be glad in His
works;
32 [1]He [a]looks at the earth, and it
[b]trembles;
He [c]touches the mountains, and
they smoke.
33 [1]I will sing to the LORD [2a]as
long as I live;
[1]I will [b]sing praise to my God
[3]while I have my being.
34 Let my [a]meditation be pleasing
to Him;
As for me, I shall [b]be glad in
the LORD.
35 Let sinners be [a]consumed from
the earth
And let the [b]wicked be no
more.
[c]Bless the LORD, O my soul.
[1d]Praise [2]the LORD!

Psalm 105

The LORD's Wonderful Works in Behalf of Israel.

1 ¶ Oh [a]give thanks to the LORD,
[b]call upon His name;
[c]Make known His deeds among
the peoples.
2 Sing to Him, [a]sing praises to
Him;
[1b]Speak of all His [2]wonders.
3 [1]Glory in His holy name;
Let the [a]heart of those who seek
the LORD be glad.
4 Seek the LORD and [a]His
strength;
[b]Seek His face continually.
5 Remember His [1a]wonders
which He has done,
His marvels and the [b]judgments
[2]uttered by His mouth,
6 O seed of [a]Abraham, His
servant,
O sons of [b]Jacob, His [c]chosen
ones!
7 He is the LORD our God;
His [a]judgments are in all the
earth.

8 ¶ He has [a]remembered His
covenant forever,
The word which He commanded
to a [b]thousand generations,
9 *The* [a]*covenant* which He made
with Abraham,
And His [b]oath to Isaac.
10 Then He [a]confirmed it to Jacob
for a statute,
To Israel as an everlasting
covenant,
11 Saying, "[a]To you I will give the
land of Canaan
As the [1b]portion of your
inheritance,"
12 When they were only a [a]few
men in number,
Very few, and [b]strangers in it.
13 And they wandered about from
nation to nation,
From *one* kingdom to another
people.
14 He [a]permitted no man to
oppress them,
And He [b]reproved kings for
their sakes:
15 "[a]Do not touch My anointed
ones,
And do My prophets no harm."

16 ¶ And He [a]called for a famine
upon the land;
He [b]broke the whole staff of
bread.
17 He [a]sent a man before them,
Joseph, *who* was [b]sold as a
slave.
18 They afflicted his [a]feet with
fetters,
[1]He himself was laid in irons;
19 Until the time that his [a]word
came to pass,
The word of the LORD [1b]tested
him.
20 The [a]king sent and released
him,
The ruler of peoples, and set him
free.
21 He [a]made him lord of his house
And ruler over all his
possessions,

25 [1]Or *This* [2]Or *broad of dimensions* (lit *hands*) [a]Ps 8:8
26 [1]Or *a sea monster* [a]Ps 107:23; Ezek 27:9 [b]Job 41:1; Ps 74:14; Is 27:1
27 [1]Lit *its appointed time* [a]Ps 145:15 [b]Job 36:31; Ps 136:25
28 [a]Ps 145:16
29 [1]Or *breath* [a]Deut 31:17; Ps 30:7 [b]Job 34:14; Ps 146:4; Eccl 12:7 [c]Gen 3:19; Job 10:9; Ps 90:3
30 [1]Or *breath* [a]Job 33:4; Ezek 37:9
31 [a]Ps 86:12 [b]Gen 1:31
32 [1]Lit *The one who* [a]Judg 5:5; Ps 97:4 [b]Hab 3:10 [c]Ex 19:18; Ps 144:5
33 [1]Or *Let me sing* [2]Lit *in my lifetime* [3]Lit *while I still am* [a]Ps 63:4 [b]Ps 146:2
34 [a]Ps 19:14 [b]Ps 9:2
35 [1]Or *Hallelujah!* [2]Heb *YAH* [a]Ps 59:13 [b]Ps 37:10 [c]Ps 104:1 [d]Ps 105:45
105:1 [a]1 Chr 16:8-22; Ps 106:1; Is 12:4 [b]Ps 99:6 [c]Ps 145:12
2 [1]Or *Meditate on* [2]I.e. wonderful acts [a]Ps 96:1 [b]Ps 77:12
3 [1]Or *Boast* [a]Ps 33:21
4 [a]Ps 63:2 [b]Ps 27:8
5 [1]I.e. wonderful acts [2]Lit *of His mouth* [a]Ps 40:5 [b]Ps 119:13
6 [a]Ps 105:42 [b]Ps 135:4 [c]1 Chr 16:13; Ps 106:5
7 [a]Is 26:9
8 [a]Ps 105:42; Luke 1:72 [b]Deut 7:9
9 [a]Gen 12:7; Gal 3:17 [b]Gen 26:3
10 [a]Gen 28:13-15
11 [1]Lit *measuring line* [a]Gen 13:15 [b]Josh 23:4; Ps 78:55
12 [a]Gen 34:30; Deut 7:7 [b]Gen 23:4; Heb 11:9
14 [a]Gen 20:7 [b]Gen 12:17
15 [a]Gen 26:11
16 [a]Gen 41:54 [b]Lev 26:26; Is 3:1; Ezek 4:16
17 [a]Gen 45:5 [b]Gen 37:28; Acts 7:9
18 [1]Lit *His soul came into* [a]Gen 39:20
19 [1]Or *refined* [a]Gen 40:20 [b]Ps 66:10
20 [a]Gen 41:14
21 [a]Gen 41:40-44

22 To [1]imprison his princes [2a]at will,
That he might teach his elders wisdom.
23 [a]Israel also came into Egypt;
Thus Jacob [b]sojourned in the land of Ham.
24 And He [a]caused His people to be very fruitful,
And made them stronger than their adversaries.

25 ¶ He [a]turned their heart to hate His people,
To [b]deal craftily with His servants.
26 He [a]sent Moses His servant,
And [b]Aaron, whom He had chosen.
27 They [1a]performed His wondrous acts among them,
And miracles in the land of Ham.
28 He [a]sent darkness and made *it* dark;
And they did not [b]rebel against His words.
29 He [a]turned their waters into blood
And caused their fish to die.
30 Their land swarmed with [a]frogs
Even in the [b]chambers of their kings.
31 He spoke, and there came a [a]swarm of flies
And [b]gnats in all their territory.
32 He [1]gave them [a]hail for rain,
And flaming fire in their land.
33 He [a]struck down their vines also and their fig trees,
And shattered the trees of their territory.
34 He spoke, and [a]locusts came,
And young locusts, even without number,
35 And ate up all vegetation in their land,
And ate up the fruit of their ground.
36 He also [a]struck down all the firstborn in their land,
The [b]first fruits of all their vigor.

37 ¶ Then He brought them out with [a]silver and gold,
And among His tribes there was not one who stumbled.
38 Egypt was [a]glad when they departed,
For the [b]dread of them had fallen upon them.
39 He spread a [a]cloud for a [1]covering,
And [b]fire to illumine by night.
40 [1]They [a]asked, and He brought [b]quail,
And satisfied them with the [2c]bread of heaven.
41 He opened the [1]rock and [a]water flowed out;
[2]It ran in the dry places *like* a river.
42 For He [a]remembered His holy word
With Abraham His servant;
43 And He brought forth His people with joy,
His chosen ones with a joyful [a]shout.
44 He [a]gave them also the lands of the [1]nations,
That they [b]might take possession of *the fruit of* the peoples' labor,
45 So that they might [a]keep His statutes
And observe His laws,
[1]Praise [2]the LORD!

Psalm 106

Israel's Rebelliousness and the LORD's Deliverances.

1 ¶ [1]Praise [2]the LORD!
Oh [a]give thanks to the LORD, for He [b]is good;
For [c]His lovingkindness is everlasting.
2 Who can speak of the [a]mighty deeds of the LORD,
Or can show forth all His praise?
3 How blessed are those who keep [1]justice,
[2]Who [a]practice righteousness at all times!

4 ¶ Remember me, O LORD, in *Your* [a]favor [1]toward Your people;
Visit me with Your salvation,
5 That I may see the [a]prosperity of Your chosen ones,
That I may [b]rejoice in the gladness of Your nation,
That I may [c]glory with Your [1]inheritance.

6 ¶ [a]We have sinned [1b]like our fathers,
We have committed iniquity, we have behaved wickedly.
7 Our fathers in Egypt did not understand Your [1]wonders;
They [a]did not remember [2]Your abundant kindnesses,
But [b]rebelled by the sea, at the [3]Red Sea.
8 Nevertheless He saved them [a]for the sake of His name,
That He might [b]make His power known.

22 [1]Lit *bind* [2]Lit *at his* [a]Gen 41:44
23 [a]Gen 46:6; Acts 7:15 [b]Acts 13:17
24 [a]Ex 1:7
25 [a]Ex 1:8 [b]Ex 1:10; Acts 7:19
26 [a]Ex 3:10 [b]Ex 4:14; Num 16:5
27 [1]Lit *set the words of His signs* [a]Ps 78:43-51
28 [a]Ex 10:21 [b]Ps 99:7
29 [a]Ex 7:20
30 [a]Ex 8:6 [b]Ex 8:3
31 [a]Ex 8:21 [b]Ex 8:16
32 [1]Or *made their rain hail* [a]Ex 9:23-25
33 [a]Ps 78:47
34 [a]Ex 10:12-15
36 [a]Ex 12:29; Ps 135:8 [b]Gen 49:3
37 [a]Ex 12:35
38 [a]Ex 12:33 [b]Ex 15:16
39 [1]Or *curtain* [a]Ex 13:21; Neh 9:12; Ps 78:14; Is 4:5 [b]Ex 40:38
40 [1]Or *One* [2]Or *food* [a]Ex 16:12; Ps 78:18 [b]Ex 16:13; Num 11:31; Ps 78:27 [c]Ex 16:15; Neh 9:15; Ps 78:24; John 6:31
41 [1]Or *boulder* [2]Lit *They went* [a]Ex 17:6; Num 20:11; Ps 78:15; Is 48:21; 1 Cor 10:4
42 [a]Gen 15:13; Ps 105:8
43 [a]Ex 15:1; Ps 106:12
44 [1]Or *Gentiles* [a]Josh 11:16-23; Ps 78:55 [b]Deut 6:10
45 [1]Or *Hallelujah!* [2]Heb *YAH* [a]Deut 4:1
106:1 [1]Or *Hallelujah!* [2]Heb *YAH* [a]Ps 105:1; Jer 33:11 [b]2 Chr 5:13; Ezra 3:11; Ps 100:5 [c]1 Chr 16:34
2 [a]Ps 145:4
3 [1]Or *judgment* [2]Many Heb mss read *The one who performs* [a]Ps 15:2
4 [1]Lit *of* [a]Ps 44:3
5 [1]I.e. people [a]Ps 1:3 [b]Ps 118:15 [c]Ps 105:3
6 [1]Lit *with* [a]1 Kin 8:47; Ezra 9:7; Neh 1:7; Jer 3:25; Dan 9:5 [b]2 Chr 30:7; Neh 9:2; Ps 78:8; Zech 1:4
7 [1]I.e. wonderful acts [2]Lit *the multitude of Your lovingkindnesses* [3]Lit *Sea of Reeds* [a]Judg 3:7; Ps 78:11 [b]Ex 14:11; Ps 78:17
8 [a]Ezek 20:9 [b]Ex 9:16

9 Thus He [a]rebuked the [1]Red Sea
and it [b]dried up,
And He [c]led them through the
deeps, as through the
wilderness.
10 So He [a]saved them from the
[1]hand of the one who hated
them,
And [b]redeemed them from the
[1]hand of the enemy.
11 [a]The waters covered their
adversaries;
Not one of them was left.
12 Then they [a]believed His words;
They [b]sang His praise.

13 ¶ They quickly [a]forgot His
works;
They [b]did not wait for His
counsel,
14 But [a]craved intensely in the
wilderness,
And [1b]tempted God in the
desert.
15 So He [a]gave them their request,
But [b]sent a [1]wasting disease
among them.

16 ¶ When they became [a]envious
of Moses in the camp,
And of Aaron, the holy one of
the LORD,
17 The [a]earth opened and
swallowed up Dathan,
And engulfed the [1]company of
Abiram.
18 And a [a]fire blazed up in their
[1]company;
The flame consumed the wicked.

19 ¶ They [a]made a calf in Horeb
And worshiped a molten image.
20 Thus they [a]exchanged their
glory
For the image of an ox that eats
grass.
21 They [a]forgot God their Savior,
Who had done [b]great things in
Egypt,
22 [1a]Wonders in the land of Ham
And awesome things by the
[2]Red Sea.
23 Therefore [a]He said that He
would destroy them,
Had not [b]Moses His chosen one
stood in the breach before
Him,
To turn away His wrath from
destroying *them.*
24 Then they [a]despised the
[b]pleasant land;
They [c]did not believe in His
word,
25 But [a]grumbled in their tents;
They did not listen to the voice
of the LORD.
26 Therefore He [1a]swore to them
That He would cast them down
in the wilderness,
27 And that He would [a]cast their
seed among the nations
And [b]scatter them in the lands.

28 ¶ They [a]joined themselves also
to [1]Baal-peor,
And ate [b]sacrifices offered to the
dead.
29 Thus they [a]provoked *Him* to
anger with their deeds,
And the plague broke out among
them.
30 Then Phinehas [a]stood up and
interposed,
And so the [b]plague was stayed.
31 And it was [a]reckoned to him for
righteousness,
To all generations forever.

32 ¶ They also [a]provoked *Him* to
wrath at the waters of
[1]Meribah,
So that it [b]went hard with
Moses on their account;
33 Because they [a]were rebellious
against [1]His Spirit,
He spoke rashly with his lips.

34 ¶ They [a]did not destroy the
peoples,
As [b]the LORD commanded them,
35 But [a]they mingled with the
nations
And learned their [1]practices,
36 And [a]served their idols,
[b]Which became a snare to them.
37 They even [a]sacrificed their sons
and their daughters to the
[b]demons,
38 And shed [a]innocent blood,
The blood of their [b]sons and
their daughters,
Whom they sacrificed to the
idols of Canaan;
And the land was [c]polluted with
the blood.
39 Thus they became [a]unclean in
their [1]practices,
And [b]played the harlot in their
deeds.

40 ¶ Therefore the [a]anger of the
LORD was kindled against
His people
And He [b]abhorred His
[1c]inheritance.
41 Then [a]He gave them into the
hand of the [1]nations,

9 [1]Lit *Sea of Reeds* [a]Ps 18:15; Is 50:2; Nah 1:4 [b]Ex 14:21; Is 51:10 [c]Is 63:11-13
10 [1]Or *power* [a]Ex 14:30 [b]Ps 78:42
11 [a]Ex 14:27; Ps 78:53
12 [a]Ex 14:31 [b]Ex 15:1-21; Ps 105:43
13 [a]Ex 15:24 [b]Ps 107:11
14 [1]Or *put God to the test* [a]Num 11:4; Ps 78:18; 1 Cor 10:6 [b]Ex 17:2; 1 Cor 10:9
15 [1]Or *leanness into their soul* [a]Num 11:31; Ps 78:29 [b]Is 10:16
16 [a]Num 16:1-3
17 [1]Or *assembly, band* [a]Num 16:32; Deut 11:6
18 [1]Or *assembly, band* [a]Num 16:35
19 [a]Ex 32:4; Deut 9:8; Acts 7:41
20 [a]Jer 2:11; Rom 1:23
21 [a]Ps 78:11 [b]Deut 10:21
22 [1]I.e. Wonderful acts [2]Lit *Sea of Reeds* [a]Ps 105:27
23 [a]Ex 32:10; Deut 9:14; Ezek 20:8 [b]Ex 32:11-14; Deut 9:25-29
24 [a]Num 14:31 [b]Deut 8:7; Jer 3:19; Ezek 20:6 [c]Deut 1:32; Heb 3:19
25 [a]Num 14:2; Deut 1:27
26 [1]Lit *lifted up His hand* [a]Num 14:28-35; Ps 95:11; Ezek 20:15; Heb 3:11
27 [a]Deut 4:27 [b]Lev 26:33; Ps 44:11
28 [1]Or *Baal of Peor* [a]Num 25:3; Deut 4:3; Hos 9:10 [b]Num 25:2
29 [a]Num 25:4
30 [a]Num 25:7 [b]Num 25:8
31 [a]Gen 15:6; Num 25:11-13
32 [1]Lit *strife* [a]Num 20:2-13; Ps 81:7 [b]Num 20:12
33 [1]Or *his spirit* [a]Num 20:3; Ps 78:40
34 [a]Judg 1:21 [b]Deut 7:2
35 [1]Lit *works* [a]Judg 3:5
36 [a]Judg 2:12 [b]Deut 7:16
37 [a]Deut 12:31; 2 Kin 16:3; Ezek 16:20; 1 Cor 10:20 [b]Lev 17:7
38 [a]Ps 94:21 [b]Deut 18:10 [c]Num 35:33; Is 24:5; Jer 3:1
39 [1]Lit *works* [a]Lev 18:24; Ezek 20:18 [b]Lev 17:7; Num 15:39; Judg 2:17; Hos 4:12
40 [1]I.e. people [a]Judg 2:14; Ps 78:59 [b]Lev 26:30; Deut 32:19 [c]Deut 9:29
41 [1]Or *Gentiles* [a]Judg 2:14; Neh 9:27

And those who hated them ruled over them.
42 Their enemies also [a]oppressed them,
And they were subdued under their [1]power.
43 Many times He would [a]deliver them;
They, however, were rebellious in their [b]counsel,
And *so* [c]sank down in their iniquity.

44 ¶ Nevertheless He looked upon their distress
When He [a]heard their cry;
45 And He [a]remembered His covenant for their sake,
And [1][b]relented [c]according to the greatness of His lovingkindness.
46 He also made them [a]*objects* of compassion
In the presence of all their captors.

47 ¶ [a]Save us, O LORD our God,
And [b]gather us from among the nations,
To give thanks to Your holy name
And [1][c]glory in Your praise.
48 [a]Blessed be the LORD, the God of Israel,
From everlasting even to everlasting.
And let all the people say, "Amen."
[1]Praise [2]the LORD!

BOOK 5

Psalm 107

The LORD Delivers Men from Manifold Troubles.

1 ¶ Oh [a]give thanks to the LORD, for [b]He is good,
For His lovingkindness is everlasting.
2 Let [a]the redeemed of the LORD say *so,*
Whom He has [b]redeemed from the hand of the adversary
3 And [a]gathered from the lands,
From the east and from the west,
From the north and from the [1]south.

4 ¶ They [a]wandered in the wilderness in a [1]desert region;
They did not find a way to [2]an inhabited [b]city.
5 *They were* hungry [1]and thirsty;
Their [a]soul fainted within them.
6 Then they [a]cried out to the LORD in their trouble;
He delivered them out of their distresses.
7 He led them also by a [1][a]straight way,
To go to [2][b]an inhabited city.
8 [a]Let them give thanks to the LORD for His lovingkindness,
And for His [1]wonders to the sons of men!
9 For He has [a]satisfied the [1]thirsty soul,
And the [b]hungry soul He has filled with what is good.

10 ¶ There were those who [a]dwelt in darkness and in the shadow of death,
[b]Prisoners in [1]misery and [2]chains,
11 Because they had [a]rebelled against the words of God
And [b]spurned the [c]counsel of the Most High.
12 Therefore He humbled their heart with labor;
They stumbled and there was [a]none to help.
13 Then they [a]cried out to the LORD in their trouble;
He saved them out of their distresses.
14 He [a]brought them out of darkness and the shadow of death
And [b]broke their bands apart.
15 [a]Let them give thanks to the LORD for His lovingkindness,
And for His [1]wonders to the sons of men!
16 For He has [a]shattered gates of bronze
And cut bars of iron asunder.

17 ¶ Fools, because of [1]their rebellious way,
And [a]because of their iniquities, were afflicted.
18 Their [a]soul abhorred all kinds of food,
And they [b]drew near to the [c]gates of death.
19 Then they cried out to the LORD in their trouble;
He saved them out of their distresses.
20 He [a]sent His word and [b]healed them,
And [c]delivered *them* from their [1]destructions.
21 [a]Let them give thanks to the LORD for His lovingkindness,

42 [1]Lit *hand* [a]Judg 4:3
43 [a]Judg 2:16-18 [b]Ps 81:12 [c]Judg 6:6
44 [a]Judg 3:9
45 [1]Lit *was sorry* [a]Lev 26:42; Ps 105:8 [b]Judg 2:18 [c]Ps 69:16
46 [a]1 Kin 8:50; 2 Chr 30:9; Ezra 9:9; Neh 1:11; Jer 42:12
47 [1]Lit *boast* [a]1 Chr 16:35 [b]Ps 147:2 [c]Ps 47:1
48 [1]Or *Hallelujah!* [2]Heb *YAH* [a]Ps 41:13
107:1 [a]1 Chr 16:34; Ps 106:1; Jer 33:11 [b]2 Chr 5:13; Ezra 3:11; Ps 100:5
2 [a]Is 35:9 [b]Ps 78:42
3 [1]Lit *sea* [a]Deut 30:3; Neh 1:9; Ps 106:47; Is 11:12; Ezek 11:17
4 [1]Lit *waste* [2]Or *a habitable city;* lit *a city of habitation* [a]Num 14:33; Deut 2:7; Josh 5:6 [b]Ps 107:7
5 [1]Lit *also* [a]Ps 77:3
6 [a]Ps 50:15
7 [1]Or *level* [2]Or *a habitable city;* lit *a city of habitation* [a]Ezra 8:21; Ps 5:8; Jer 31:9 [b]Ps 107:4
8 [1]I.e. wonderful acts [a]Ps 107:15
9 [1]Or *parched* [a]Ps 22:26 [b]Ps 146:7; Matt 5:6; Luke 1:53
10 [1]Lit *affliction* [2]Lit *irons* [a]Ps 143:3; Is 42:7; Mic 7:8; Luke 1:79 [b]Job 36:8; Ps 102:20
11 [a]Ps 78:40; Lam 3:42 [b]Num 15:31; 2 Chr 36:16; Prov 1:25; Is 5:24 [c]Ps 73:24
12 [a]Ps 22:11
13 [a]Ps 107:6
14 [a]Ps 86:13 [b]Ps 116:16; Jer 2:20; Nah 1:13; Luke 13:16; Acts 12:7
15 [1]I.e. wonderful acts [a]Ps 107:8
16 [a]Is 45:1
17 [1]Lit *the way of their transgression* [a]Is 65:6; Jer 30:14; Lam 3:39; Ezek 24:23
18 [a]Job 33:20; Ps 102:4 [b]Job 33:22; Ps 88:3 [c]Job 38:17; Ps 9:13
20 [1]Or *pits* [a]Ps 147:15; Matt 8:8 [b]2 Kin 20:5; Ps 30:2 [c]Job 33:28; Ps 30:3
21 [a]Ps 107:8

And for His [1]wonders to the
sons of men!
22 Let them also offer [a]sacrifices of
thanksgiving,
And [b]tell of His works with
joyful singing.

23 ¶ Those who [a]go down to the
sea in ships,
Who do business on great
waters;
24 They have seen the works of the
LORD,
And His [1]wonders in the deep.
25 For He [a]spoke and raised up a
[b]stormy wind,
Which [c]lifted up the waves [1]of
the sea.
26 They rose up to the heavens,
they went down to the
depths;
Their soul [a]melted away in *their*
misery.
27 They reeled and [a]staggered like
a drunken man,
And [1]were at their wits' end.
28 Then they cried to the LORD in
their trouble,
And He brought them out of
their distresses.
29 He [a]caused the storm to be still,
So that the waves [1]of the sea
were hushed.
30 Then they were glad because
they were quiet,
So He guided them to their
desired haven.
31 [a]Let them give thanks to the
LORD for His lovingkindness,
And for His [1b]wonders to the
sons of men!
32 Let them [a]extol Him also [b]in
the congregation of the
people,
And [c]praise Him at the seat of
the elders.

33 ¶ He [1a]changes rivers into a
[2]wilderness
And springs of water into a
thirsty ground;
34 A [a]fruitful land into a [b]salt
waste,
Because of the wickedness of
those who dwell in it.
35 He [1a]changes a [2]wilderness
into a pool of water
And a dry land into springs of
water;
36 And there He makes the hungry
to dwell,
So that they may establish [1a]an
inhabited city,
37 And sow fields and [a]plant
vineyards,
And [1]gather a fruitful harvest.
38 Also He blesses them and they
[a]multiply greatly,
And He [b]does not let their cattle
decrease.

39 ¶ When they are [a]diminished
and [b]bowed down
Through oppression, misery and
sorrow,
40 He [a]pours contempt upon
[1]princes
And [b]makes them wander [c]in a
pathless waste.
41 But He [a]sets the needy
[1]securely on high away
from affliction,
And [b]makes *his* families like a
flock.
42 The [a]upright see it and are glad;
But all [b]unrighteousness shuts
its mouth.
43 Who is [a]wise? Let him give
heed to these things,
And consider the
[b]lovingkindnesses of the
LORD.

Psalm 108

God Praised and Supplicated to Give Victory.

A Song, a Psalm of David.

1 ¶ [a]My heart is steadfast, O God;
I will sing, I will sing praises,
even with my [1]soul.
2 Awake, harp and lyre;
I will awaken the dawn!
3 I will give thanks to You,
O LORD, among the peoples,
And I will sing praises to You
among the nations.
4 For Your [a]lovingkindness is
great [b]above the heavens,
And Your truth *reaches* to the
skies.
5 [a]Be exalted, O God, above the
heavens,
And Your glory above all the
earth.
6 [a]That Your beloved may be
delivered,
Save with Your right hand, and
answer me!

7 ¶ God has spoken in His
[1]holiness:
"I will exult, I will portion out
Shechem
And measure out the valley of
Succoth.
8 "Gilead is Mine, Manasseh is
Mine;

21 [1]I.e. wonderful acts
22 [a]Lev 7:12; Ps 50:14; 116:17 [b]Ps 9:11; 73:28; 118:17
23 [a]Is 42:10; Jon 1:3
24 [1]I.e. wonderful acts
25 [1]Lit *of it* [a]Ps 105:31,34 [b]Ps 148:8; Jon 1:4 [c]Ps 93:3,4
26 [a]Ps 22:14; 119:28
27 [1]Lit *all their wisdom was swallowed up* [a]Job 12:25; Is 24:20
29 [1]Lit *of it* [a]Ps 65:7; 89:9; Matt 8:26; Luke 8:24
31 [1]I.e. wonderful acts [a]Ps 107:8,15,21 [b]Ps 78:4; 111:4
32 [a]Ps 34:3; 99:5; Is 25:1 [b]Ps 22:22,25 [c]Ps 35:18
33 [1]Or *turns* [2]Or *desert* [a]1 Kin 17:1,7; Ps 74:15; Is 42:15; 50:2
34 [a]Gen 13:10; 14:3; 19:24,25; Deut 29:23 [b]Job 39:6; Jer 17:6
35 [1]Or *turns* [2]Or *desert* [a]Ps 105:41; 114:8; Is 35:6,7; 41:18
36 [1]Or *a habitable city; lit a city of habitation* [a]Ps 107:4,7
37 [1]Lit *acquire fruits of yield* [a]2 Kin 19:29; Is 65:21; Amos 9:14
38 [a]Gen 12:2; 17:20; Ex 1:7; Deut 1:10 [b]Deut 7:14
39 [a]2 Kin 10:32; Ezek 5:11; 29:15 [b]Ps 38:6; 44:25; 57:6
40 [1]Or *nobles* [a]Job 12:21 [b]Job 12:24 [c]Deut 32:10
41 [1]Lit *in an inaccessibly high place* [a]1 Sam 2:8; Ps 59:1; 113:7,8 [b]Job 21:11; Ps 78:52; 113:9
42 [a]Job 22:19; Ps 52:6 [b]Job 5:16; Ps 63:11; Rom 3:19
43 [a]Ps 64:9; Jer 9:12; Hos 14:9 [b]Ps 107:1
108:1 [1]Lit *glory* [a]Ps 57:7-11; 108:1-5
4 [a]Num 14:18; Deut 7:9; Ps 36:5; 100:5; Mic 7:18-20 [b]Ps 113:4
5 [a]Ps 57:5
6 [a]Ps 60:5-12; 108:6-13
7 [1]Or *sanctuary*

Ephraim also is the [1]helmet of My head;
[a]Judah is My [2]scepter.
9 "Moab is My washbowl;
Over Edom I shall throw My shoe;
Over Philistia I will shout aloud."

10 ¶ [a]Who will bring me into the besieged city?
Who [1]will lead me to Edom?
11 Have not You Yourself, O God, [a]rejected us?
And will You not go forth with our armies, O God?
12 Oh give us help against the adversary,
For [a]deliverance [1]by man is in vain.
13 [1]Through God we will do valiantly,
And [a]it is He who shall tread down our adversaries.

Psalm 109

Vengeance Invoked upon Adversaries.

For the choir director. A Psalm of David.

1 ¶ O [a]God of my praise,
[b]Do not be silent!
2 For they have opened the [1]wicked and [a]deceitful mouth against me;
They have spoken [2]against me with a [b]lying tongue.
3 They have also surrounded me with words of hatred,
And fought against me [a]without cause.
4 In return [a]for my love they act as my accusers;
But [b]I am *in* prayer.
5 Thus they have [1a]repaid me evil for good
And [b]hatred for my love.

6 ¶ Appoint a wicked man over him,
And let an [1a]accuser stand at his right hand.
7 When he is judged, let him [a]come forth guilty,
And let his [b]prayer become sin.
8 Let [a]his days be few;
Let [b]another take his office.
9 Let his [a]children be fatherless
And his [b]wife a widow.
10 Let his [a]children wander about and beg;
And let them [b]seek *sustenance* [1]far from their ruined homes.
11 Let [a]the creditor [1]seize all that he has,
And let [b]strangers plunder the product of his labor.
12 Let there be none to [1a]extend lovingkindness to him,
Nor [b]any to be gracious to his fatherless children.
13 Let his [a]posterity be [1]cut off;
In a following generation let their [b]name be blotted out.

14 ¶ Let [a]the iniquity of his fathers be remembered [1]before the LORD,
And do not let the sin of his mother be [b]blotted out.
15 Let [a]them be before the LORD continually,
That He may [b]cut off their memory from the earth;
16 Because he did not remember to show lovingkindness,
But persecuted the [a]afflicted and needy man,
And the [b]despondent in heart, to [c]put *them* to death.
17 He also loved cursing, so [a]it came to him;
And he did not delight in blessing, so it was far from him.
18 But he [a]clothed himself with cursing as with his garment,
And it [b]entered into [1]his body like water
And like oil into his bones.
19 Let it be to him as [a]a garment with which he covers himself,
And for a belt with which he constantly [b]girds himself.
20 [1]Let this be the [a]reward of my accusers from the LORD,
And of those who [b]speak evil against my soul.

21 ¶ But You, O [1]GOD, the Lord, deal *kindly* with me [a]for Your name's sake;
Because [b]Your lovingkindness is good, deliver me;
22 For [a]I am afflicted and needy,
And [1]my heart is [b]wounded within me.
23 I am passing [a]like a shadow when it lengthens;
I am shaken off [b]like the locust.
24 My [a]knees [1]are weak from [b]fasting,
And my flesh has grown lean, without fatness.
25 I also have become a [a]reproach to them;

8 [1]Lit *protection* [2]Or *lawgiver* [a]Gen 49:10
10 [1]Or *has led* [a]Ps 60:9
11 [a]Ps 44:9
12 [1]Lit *of* [a]Is 30:3
13 [1]Or *In* or *With* [a]Is 60:12
109:1 [a]Deut 10:21 [b]Ps 28:1
2 [1]Lit *wicked mouth and the deceitful* [2]Lit *with* [a]Ps 10:7 [b]Ps 120:2
3 [a]Ps 35:7; John 15:25
4 [a]Ps 38:20 [b]Ps 69:13
5 [1]Lit *laid upon me* [a]Ps 35:12 [b]John 7:7
6 [1]Or *adversary, Satan* [a]Zech 3:1
7 [a]Ps 1:5 [b]Prov 28:9
8 [a]Ps 55:23 [b]Acts 1:20
9 [a]Ex 22:24 [b]Jer 18:21
10 [1]Or *out of their desolate places* [a]Gen 4:12; Job 30:5-8; Ps 59:15 [b]Ps 37:25
11 [1]Lit *ensnare, strike at* [a]Neh 5:7; Job 5:5 [b]Is 1:7; Lam 5:2; Ezek 7:21
12 [1]Lit *continue* [a]Ezra 7:28 [b]Job 5:4; Is 9:17
13 [1]Lit *for cutting off* [a]Job 18:19; Ps 21:10 [b]Ps 9:5; Prov 10:7
14 [1]Lit *to* [a]Ex 20:5; Num 14:18; Is 65:6; Jer 32:18 [b]Neh 4:5; Jer 18:23
15 [a]Ps 90:8; Jer 16:17 [b]Job 18:17; Ps 34:16
16 [a]Ps 37:14 [b]Ps 34:18 [c]Ps 37:32
17 [a]Prov 14:14; Ezek 35:9; Matt 7:2
18 [1]Lit *his inward parts* [a]Ps 73:6; Ezek 7:27 [b]Num 5:22
19 [a]Ps 73:6; Ezek 7:27 [b]2 Sam 22:40; Ps 30:11; Is 11:5
20 [1]Lit *This is* [a]Ps 54:5; Is 3:11; 2 Tim 4:14 [b]Ps 41:5
21 [1]Heb *YHWH*, usually rendered *LORD* [a]Ps 23:3; Ezek 36:22 [b]Ps 69:16
22 [1]Lit *one has pierced my heart within me* [a]Ps 40:17 [b]Job 24:12; Ps 143:4; Prov 18:14
23 [a]Ps 102:11 [b]Ex 10:19; Job 39:20
24 [1]Or *totter* [a]Heb 12:12 [b]Ps 35:13
25 [a]Ps 22:6

When they see me, they [b]wag
their head.
26 ¶ [a]Help me, O LORD my God;
Save me according to Your
lovingkindness.
27 [1]And let them [a]know that this
is Your hand;
You, LORD, have done it.
28 [a]Let them curse, but You bless;
When they arise, they shall be
ashamed,
But Your [b]servant shall be glad.
29 [1]Let [a]my accusers be clothed
with dishonor,
And [2]let them [b]cover
themselves with their own
shame as with a robe.

30 ¶ With my mouth I will give
thanks abundantly to the
LORD;
And in the midst of many [a]I will
praise Him.
31 For He stands [a]at the right hand
of the needy,
To save him from those who
[b]judge his soul.

Psalm 110

The LORD Gives Dominion to the King.

A Psalm of David.

1 ¶ [a]The LORD says to my Lord:
"[b]Sit at My right hand
Until I make [c]Your enemies a
footstool for Your feet."
2 The LORD will stretch forth Your
strong [a]scepter from Zion,
saying,
"[b]Rule in the midst of Your
enemies."
3 Your [a]people [1]will volunteer
freely in the day of Your
[2]power;
[b]In [3]holy array, from the womb
of the dawn,
[4]Your youth are to You *as*
the [c]dew.

4 ¶ [a]The LORD has sworn and will
[b]not [1]change His mind,
"You are a [c]priest forever
According to the order of
Melchizedek."
5 The Lord is [a]at Your right hand;
He [1]will [b]shatter kings in the
[c]day of His wrath.
6 He will [a]judge among the
nations,
He [1]will fill *them* with
[b]corpses,
He [2]will [c]shatter the [3]chief
men over a broad country.
7 He will [a]drink from the brook
by the wayside;
Therefore He will [b]lift up *His*
head.

Psalm 111

The LORD Praised for His Goodness.

1 ¶ [1]Praise [2]the LORD!
I [a]will give thanks to the LORD
with all *my* heart,
In the [b]company of the upright
and in the assembly.
2 [a]Great are the works of the
LORD;
They are [1b]studied by all who
delight in them.
3 [1a]Splendid and majestic is His
work,
And [b]His righteousness endures
forever.
4 He has made His [1]wonders [2]to
be remembered;
The LORD is [a]gracious and
compassionate.
5 He has [a]given [1]food to those
who [2]fear Him;
He will [b]remember His covenant
forever.
6 He has made known to His
people the power of His
works,
In giving them the heritage of
the nations.

7 ¶ The works of His hands are
[1a]truth and justice;
All His precepts [b]are [2]sure.
8 They are [a]upheld forever and
ever;
They are performed in [1b]truth
and uprightness.
9 He has sent [a]redemption to His
people;
He has [1]ordained His covenant
forever;
[b]Holy and [2]awesome is His
name.
10 The [1a]fear of the LORD is the
beginning of wisdom;
A [b]good understanding have all
those who [2]do *His*
commandments;
His [c]praise endures forever.

Psalm 112

Prosperity of the One Who Fears the LORD.

1 ¶ [1]Praise [2]the LORD!

25 [b]Ps 22:7; Jer 18:16; Lam 2:15; Matt 27:39; Mark 15:29
26 [a]Ps 119:86
27 [1]Or *That they may know* [a]Job 37:7
28 [a]2 Sam 16:11 [b]Is 65:14
29 [1]Or *My accusers will be* [2]Or *they will cover* [a]Job 8:22; Ps 132:18 [b]Job 8:22; Ps 35:26
30 [a]Ps 22:22
31 [a]Ps 16:8 [b]Ps 37:33
110:1 [a]Matt 22:44; Mark 12:36; Luke 20:42; Acts 2:34; Heb 1:13 [b]Matt 26:64; Eph 1:20; Col 3:1; Heb 1:3 [c]1 Cor 15:25; Eph 1:22
2 [a]Ps 45:6; Jer 48:17; Ezek 19:14 [b]Ps 2:9; Dan 7:13
3 [1]Lit *will be freewill offerings* [2]Or *army* [3]Or *the splendor of holiness* [4]Or *The dew of Your youth is Yours* [a]Judg 5:2; Neh 11:2 [b]1 Chr 16:29; Ps 96:9 [c]2 Sam 17:12; Mic 5:7
4 [1]Lit *be sorry* [a]Heb 7:21 [b]Num 23:19 [c]Zech 6:13; Heb 5:6
5 [1]Or *has shattered* [a]Ps 16:8 [b]Ps 68:14 [c]Ps 2:5; Rom 2:5; Rev 6:17
6 [1]Or *has filled* [2]Or *has shattered* [3]Lit *head over* [a]Is 2:4; Joel 3:12; Mic 4:3 [b]Is 66:24 [c]Ps 68:21
7 [a]Judg 7:5 [b]Ps 27:6
111:1 [1]Or *Hallelujah! I will* [2]Heb YAH [a]Ps 35:18 [b]Ps 89:7
2 [1]Lit *sought out* [a]Ps 92:5 [b]Ps 143:5
3 [1]Lit *Splendor and majesty* [a]Ps 96:6 [b]Ps 112:3
4 [1]I.e. wonderful acts [2]Lit *a memorial* [a]Ps 86:5
5 [1]Lit *prey* [2]Or *revere* [a]Matt 6:31-33 [b]Ps 105:8
7 [1]Or *faithfulness* [2]Or *trustworthy* [a]Rev 15:3 [b]Ps 19:7
8 [1]Or *faithfulness* [a]Ps 119:160; Is 40:8; Matt 5:18 [b]Ps 19:9
9 [1]Lit *commanded* [2]I.e. inspiring reverence [a]Luke 1:68 [b]Ps 99:3; Luke 1:49
10 [1]Or *reverence for* [2]Lit *do them* [a]Job 28:28; Prov 1:7; Eccl 12:13 [b]Ps 119:98; Prov 3:4 [c]Ps 145:2
112:1 [1]Or *Hallelujah! Blessed* [2]Heb YAH

How [a]blessed is the man who
[3]fears the LORD,
Who greatly [b]delights in His
commandments.
2 His [1a]descendants will be
mighty [2]on earth;
The generation of the [b]upright
will be blessed.
3 [a]Wealth and riches are in his
house,
And his righteousness endures
forever.
4 Light arises in the darkness [a]for
the upright;
He is [b]gracious and
compassionate and
righteous.
5 It is well with the man who [a]is
gracious and lends;
He will [1]maintain his cause in
judgment.
6 For he will [a]never be shaken;
The [b]righteous will be
[1]remembered forever.

7 ¶ He will not fear [a]evil tidings;
His [b]heart is steadfast, [c]trusting
in the LORD.
8 His [a]heart is upheld, he [b]will
not fear,
Until he [c]looks *with satisfaction*
on his adversaries.
9 [1]He [a]has given freely to the
poor,
His righteousness endures
forever;
His [b]horn will be exalted in
honor.

10 ¶ The [a]wicked will see it and be
[1]vexed,
He will [b]gnash his teeth and
[c]melt away;
The [d]desire of the wicked will
perish.

Psalm 113

The LORD Exalts the Humble.

1 ¶ [1]Praise [2]the LORD!
[a]Praise, O [b]servants of the
LORD,
Praise the name of the LORD.
2 [a]Blessed be the name of the
LORD
From this time forth and forever.
3 [a]From the rising of the sun to
its setting
The [b]name of the LORD is to be
praised.
4 The LORD is [a]high above all
nations;
His [b]glory is above the heavens.
5 ¶ [a]Who is like the LORD our
God,
Who [b]is enthroned on high,
6 Who [1a]humbles Himself to
behold
The things that are in heaven
and in the earth?
7 He [a]raises the poor from the
dust
And lifts the needy from the ash
heap,
8 To make *them* [a]sit with
[1]princes,
With the [1]princes of His people.
9 He [a]makes the barren woman
abide in the house
As a joyful mother of children.
[1]Praise [2]the LORD!

Psalm 114

God's Deliverance of Israel from Egypt.

1 ¶ When Israel went forth [a]from
Egypt,
The house of Jacob from a people
of [b]strange language,
2 Judah became [a]His sanctuary,
Israel, [b]His dominion.

3 ¶ The [a]sea looked and fled;
The [b]Jordan turned back.
4 The mountains [a]skipped like
rams,
The hills, like lambs.
5 What [a]ails you, O sea, that you
flee?
O Jordan, that you turn back?
6 O mountains, that you skip like
rams?
O hills, like lambs?

7 ¶ [a]Tremble, O earth, before the
Lord,
Before the God of Jacob,
8 Who [a]turned the rock into a
[b]pool of water,
The [c]flint into a fountain of
water.

Psalm 115

Heathen Idols Contrasted with the LORD.

1 ¶ [a]Not to us, O LORD, not to us,
But [b]to Your name give glory
Because of Your lovingkindness,
because of Your [1]truth.
2 [a]Why should the nations say,
"[b]Where, now, is their God?"
3 But our [a]God is in the heavens;
He [b]does whatever He pleases.
4 Their [a]idols are silver and gold,
The [b]work of man's hands.

1 [3]Or *reveres* [a]Ps 128:1 [b]Ps 1:2
2 [1]Lit *seed* [2]Or *in the land* [a]Ps 102:28 [b]Ps 128:4
3 [a]Prov 3:16; Matt 6:33
4 [a]Job 11:17; Ps 97:11 [b]Ps 37:26
5 [1]Or *conduct his affairs with justice* [a]Ps 37:21
6 [1]Lit *for an eternal remembrance* [a]Ps 15:5 [b]Prov 10:7
7 [a]Prov 1:33 [b]Ps 57:7 [c]Ps 56:4
8 [a]Heb 13:9 [b]Ps 27:1; Prov 1:33; Is 12:2 [c]Ps 54:7
9 [1]Lit *He has scattered, he has given to...* [a]2 Cor 9:9 [b]Ps 75:10
10 [1]Or *angry* [a]Ps 86:17 [b]Ps 35:16; Matt 8:12; Luke 13:28 [c]Ps 58:7 [d]Job 8:13; Prov 10:28
113:1 [1]Or *Hallelujah! Praise* [2]Heb YAH [a]Ps 135:1 [b]Ps 34:22
2 [a]Ps 145:21; Dan 2:20
3 [a]Ps 50:1; Is 59:19; Mal 1:11 [b]Ps 18:3
4 [a]Ps 97:9 [b]Ps 8:1
5 [a]Ex 15:11; Ps 35:10 [b]Ps 103:19
6 [1]Or *looks far below in the heavens and on the earth?* [a]Ps 11:4; Is 57:15
7 [a]1 Sam 2:8; Ps 107:41
8 [1]Or *nobles* [a]Job 36:7
9 [1]Or *Hallelujah!* [2]Heb YAH [a]1 Sam 2:5; Ps 68:6; Is 54:1
114:1 [a]Ex 12:51 [b]Ps 81:5
2 [a]Ex 15:17; Ps 78:68 [b]Ex 19:6
3 [a]Ex 14:21; Ps 77:16 [b]Josh 3:13
4 [a]Ex 19:18; Judg 5:5; Ps 18:7; Hab 3:6
5 [a]Hab 3:8
7 [a]Ps 96:9
8 [a]Ex 17:6; Num 20:11; Ps 78:15 [b]Ps 107:35 [c]Deut 8:15
115:1 [1]Or *faithfulness* [a]Is 48:11; Ezek 36:22 [b]Ps 29:2
2 [a]Ps 79:10 [b]Ps 42:3
3 [a]Ps 103:19 [b]Ps 135:6; Dan 4:35
4 [a]Ps 115:4-8; Jer 10:4 [b]Deut 4:28; 2 Kin 19:18; Is 37:19; Jer 10:3

5 They have mouths, but they
[a]cannot speak;
They have eyes, but they cannot
see;
6 They have ears, but they cannot
hear;
They have noses, but they
cannot smell;
7 [1]They have hands, but they
cannot feel;
[2]They have feet, but they cannot
walk;
They cannot make a sound with
their throat.
8 [a]Those who make them [1]will
become like them,
Everyone who trusts in them.

9 ¶ O [a]Israel, [b]trust in the LORD;
He is their [c]help and their
shield.
10 O house of [a]Aaron, trust in the
LORD;
He is their help and their shield.
11 You who [1a]fear the LORD, trust
in the LORD;
He is their help and their shield.
12 The LORD [a]has been mindful of
us; He will bless *us;*
He will bless the house of Israel;
He will bless the house of Aaron.
13 He will [a]bless those who [1]fear
the LORD,
[b]The small together with the
great.
14 May the LORD [a]give you
increase,
You and your children.
15 May you be blessed of the LORD,
[a]Maker of heaven and earth.

16 ¶ The heavens are [a]the heavens
of the LORD,
But [b]the earth He has given to
the sons of men.
17 The [a]dead do not praise [1]the
LORD,
Nor *do* any who go down into
[b]silence;
18 But as for us, we will [a]bless
[1]the LORD
From this time forth and forever.
[2]Praise [1]the LORD!

Psalm 116

Thanksgiving for Deliverance from Death.

1 ¶ [a]I love the LORD, because He
[b]hears
My voice *and* my supplications.
2 Because He has [a]inclined His
ear to me,
Therefore I shall call *upon Him*
as long as I live.
3 The [a]cords of death
encompassed me
And the [1]terrors of [2]Sheol
[3]came upon me;
I found distress and sorrow.
4 Then [a]I called upon the name of
the LORD:
"O LORD, I beseech You, [1b]save
my life!"

5 ¶ [a]Gracious is the LORD, and
[b]righteous;
Yes, our God is [c]compassionate.
6 The LORD preserves [a]the simple;
I was [b]brought low, and He
saved me.
7 Return to your [a]rest, O my soul,
For the LORD has [b]dealt
bountifully with you.
8 For You have [a]rescued my soul
from death,
My eyes from tears,
My feet from stumbling.
9 I shall walk before the LORD
In the [1a]land of the living.
10 I [a]believed when I said,
"I am [b]greatly afflicted."
11 I [a]said in my alarm,
"[b]All men are liars."

12 ¶ What shall I [a]render to the
LORD
For all His [b]benefits
[1]toward me?
13 I shall lift up the [a]cup of
salvation
And [b]call upon the name of the
LORD.
14 I shall [a]pay my vows to the
LORD,
Oh *may it be* [b]in the presence
of all His people.
15 [a]Precious in the sight of the
LORD
Is the death of His godly ones.
16 O LORD, [1]surely I am [a]Your
servant,
I am Your servant, the [b]son of
Your handmaid,
You have [c]loosed my bonds.
17 To You I shall offer [a]a sacrifice
of thanksgiving,
And [b]call upon the name of the
LORD.
18 I shall [a]pay my vows to the
LORD,
Oh *may it be* in the presence of
all His people,
19 In the [a]courts of the LORD'S
house,
In the midst of you,
O [b]Jerusalem.
[1]Praise [2]the LORD!

5 [a]Jer 10:5
7 [1]Lit *Their hands* [2]Lit *Their feet*
8 [1]Or *are like them* [a]Ps 135:18; Is 44:9-11
9 [a]Ps 118:2; 135:19 [b]Ps 37:3; 62:8 [c]Ps 33:20
10 [a]Ps 118:3; 135:19
11 [1]Or *revere* [a]Ps 22:23; 103:11; 135:20
12 [a]Ps 98:3
13 [1]Or *revere* [a]Ps 103:11; 112:1; 128:1 [b]Rev 11:18; 19:5
14 [a]Deut 1:11
15 [a]Gen 1:1; Neh 9:6; Ps 96:5; 102:25; 121:2; 124:8; 134:3; 146:6; Acts 14:15; Rev 14:7
16 [a]Ps 89:11 [b]Ps 8:6
17 [1]Heb *YAH* [a]Ps 6:5; 88:10-12; Is 38:18 [b]Ps 31:17
18 [1]Heb *YAH* [2]Or *Hallelujah!* [a]Ps 113:2; Dan 2:20
116:1 [a]Ps 18:1 [b]Ps 6:8; 66:19; Is 37:17; Dan 9:18
2 [a]Ps 17:6; 31:2; 40:1
3 [1]Lit *straits* [2]I.e. the nether world [3]Lit *found me* [a]Ps 18:4,5
4 [1]Or *deliver my soul* [a]Ps 18:6; 118:5 [b]Ps 17:13; 22:20
5 [a]Ps 86:15; 103:8 [b]Ezra 9:15; Neh 9:8; Ps 119:137; 145:17; Jer 12:1; Dan 9:14 [c]Ex 34:6
6 [a]Ps 19:7; Prov 1:4 [b]Ps 79:8; 142:6
7 [a]Jer 6:16; Matt 11:29 [b]Ps 13:6; 142:7
8 [a]Ps 49:15; 56:13; 86:13
9 [1]Lit *lands* [a]Ps 27:13
10 [a]2 Cor 4:13 [b]Ps 88:7
11 [a]Ps 31:22 [b]Ps 62:9; Rom 3:4
12 [1]Lit *upon* [a]2 Chr 32:25; 1 Thess 3:9 [b]Ps 103:2
13 [a]Ps 16:5 [b]Ps 80:18; 105:1
14 [a]Ps 50:14; 116:18 [b]Ps 22:25
15 [a]Ps 72:14
16 [1]Or *because* [a]Ps 86:16; 119:125; 143:12 [b]Ps 86:16 [c]Ps 107:14
17 [a]Lev 7:12; Ps 50:14 [b]Ps 116:13
18 [a]Ps 116:14
19 [1]Or *Hallelujah!* [2]Heb *YAH* [a]Ps 92:13; 96:8; 135:2 [b]Ps 102:21

Psalm 117

A Psalm of Praise.

1 ¶ [a]Praise the LORD, all nations;
Laud Him, all peoples!
2 For His [a]lovingkindness [1]is great toward us,
And the [2b]truth of the LORD is everlasting.
[3]Praise [4]the LORD!

Psalm 118

Thanksgiving for the LORD's Saving Goodness.

1 ¶ [a]Give thanks to the LORD, for [b]He is good;
For His lovingkindness is everlasting.
2 Oh let [a]Israel say,
"His lovingkindness is everlasting."
3 Oh let the [a]house of Aaron say,
"His lovingkindness is everlasting."
4 Oh let those [a]who [1]fear the LORD say,
"His lovingkindness is everlasting."

5 ¶ From *my* [a]distress I called upon [1]the LORD;
[1]The LORD answered me *and* [b]*set me* in a large place.
6 The LORD is [a]for me; I will [b]not fear;
[c]What can man do to me?
7 The LORD is for me [a]among those who help me;
Therefore I will [b]look *with satisfaction* on those who hate me.
8 It is [a]better to take refuge in the LORD
Than to trust in man.
9 It is [a]better to take refuge in the LORD
Than to trust in princes.

10 ¶ All nations [a]surrounded me;
In the name of the LORD I will surely [b]cut them off.
11 They [a]surrounded me, yes, they surrounded me;
In the name of the LORD I will surely cut them off.
12 They surrounded me [a]like bees;
They were extinguished as a [b]fire of thorns;
In the name of the LORD I will surely cut them off.
13 You [a]pushed me violently so that I [1]was falling,
But the LORD [b]helped me.
14 [1a]The LORD is my strength and song,
And He has become [b]my salvation.
15 ¶ The sound of [a]joyful shouting and salvation is in the tents of the righteous;
The [b]right hand of the LORD does valiantly.
16 The [a]right hand of the LORD is exalted;
The right hand of the LORD does valiantly.
17 I [a]will not die, but live,
And [b]tell of the works of [1]the LORD.
18 [1]The LORD has [a]disciplined me severely,
But He has [b]not given me over to death.

19 ¶ [a]Open to me the gates of righteousness;
I shall enter through them, I shall give thanks to [1]the LORD.
20 This is the gate of the LORD;
The [a]righteous will enter through it.
21 I shall give thanks to You, for You have [a]answered me,
And You have [b]become my salvation.

22 ¶ The [a]stone which the builders rejected
Has become the chief corner *stone*.
23 This is [1]the LORD'S doing;
It is marvelous in our eyes.
24 This is the day which the LORD has made;
Let us [a]rejoice and be glad in it.
25 O LORD, [a]do save, we beseech You;
O LORD, we beseech You, do send [b]prosperity!
26 [a]Blessed is the one who comes in the name of the LORD;
We have [b]blessed you from the house of the LORD.
27 [a]The LORD is God, and He has given us [b]light;
Bind the festival sacrifice with cords [1]to the [c]horns of the altar.
28 [a]You are my God, and I give thanks to You;
You are my God, [b]I extol You.
29 [a]Give thanks to the LORD, for He is good;
For His lovingkindness is everlasting.

117:1 [a]Rom 15:11
2 [1]Lit *prevails over us* [2]Or *faithfulness* [3]Or *Hallelujah!* [4]Heb *YAH* [a]Ps 103:11 [b]Ps 100:5; 146:6
118:1 [a]1 Chr 16:8,34; Ps 106:1; 107:1; Jer 33:11 [b]2 Chr 5:13; 7:3; Ezra 3:11; Ps 100:5; 136:1-26
2 [a]Ps 115:9
3 [a]Ps 115:10
4 [1]Or *revere* [a]Ps 115:11
5 [1]Heb *YAH* [a]Ps 18:6; 86:7; 120:1 [b]Ps 18:19
6 [a]Job 19:27; Ps 56:9; Heb 13:6 [b]Ps 23:4; 27:1 [c]Ps 56:4,11
7 [a]Ps 54:4 [b]Ps 54:7; 59:10
8 [a]2 Chr 32:7,8; Ps 40:4; 108:12; Is 31:1,3; 57:13; Jer 17:5
9 [a]Ps 146:3
10 [a]Ps 3:6; 88:17 [b]Ps 18:40
11 [a]Ps 88:17
12 [a]Deut 1:44 [b]Ps 58:9; Nah 1:10
13 [1]Or *fell* [a]Ps 140:4 [b]Ps 86:17
14 [1]Heb *YAH* [a]Ex 15:2; Is 12:2 [b]Ps 27:1
15 [a]Ps 68:3 [b]Ex 15:6; Ps 89:13; Luke 1:51
16 [a]Ex 15:6; Ps 89:13
17 [1]Heb *YAH* [a]Ps 6:5; 116:8,9; Hab 1:12 [b]Ps 73:28; 107:22
18 [1]Heb *YAH* [a]Ps 73:14; Jer 31:18; 1 Cor 11:32; 2 Cor 6:9 [b]Ps 86:13
19 [1]Heb *YAH* [a]Is 26:2
20 [a]Ps 15:1,2; 24:3-6; 140:13; Is 35:8; Rev 22:14
21 [a]Ps 116:1; 118:5 [b]Ps 118:14
22 [a]Matt 21:42; Mark 12:10,11; Luke 20:17; Acts 4:11; Eph 2:20; 1 Pet 2:7
23 [1]Lit *from the LORD*
24 [a]Ps 31:7
25 [a]Ps 106:47 [b]Ps 122:6,7
26 [a]Matt 21:9; 23:39; Mark 11:9; Luke 13:35; 19:38; John 12:13 [b]Ps 129:8
27 [1]Lit *unto* [a]1 Kin 18:39 [b]Esth 8:16; Ps 18:28; 27:1; 1 Pet 2:9 [c]Ex 27:2
28 [a]Ps 63:1; 140:6 [b]Ex 15:2; Is 25:1
29 [a]Ps 118:1

Psalm 119

Meditations and Prayers Relating to the Law of God.

א Aleph.

1 ¶ How blessed are those whose
way is [1a]blameless,
Who [b]walk in the law of the
LORD.
2 How blessed are those who
[a]observe His testimonies,
Who [b]seek Him [c]with all *their*
heart.
3 They also [a]do no
unrighteousness;
They walk in His ways.
4 You have [1a]ordained Your
precepts,
[2]That we should keep *them*
diligently.
5 Oh that my [a]ways may be
established
To [b]keep Your statutes!
6 Then I [a]shall not be ashamed
When I look [1]upon all Your
commandments.
7 I shall [a]give thanks to You with
uprightness of heart,
When I learn Your righteous
judgments.
8 I shall keep Your statutes;
Do not [a]forsake me utterly!

ב Beth.

9 ¶ How can a young man keep his
way pure?
By [a]keeping *it* according to Your
word.
10 With [a]all my heart I have
sought You;
Do not let me [b]wander from
Your commandments.
11 Your word I have [a]treasured in
my heart,
That I may not sin against You.
12 Blessed are You, O LORD;
[a]Teach me Your statutes.
13 With my lips I have [a]told of
All the [b]ordinances of Your
mouth.
14 I have [a]rejoiced in the way of
Your testimonies,
[1]As much as in all riches.
15 I will [a]meditate on Your
precepts
And [1]regard [b]Your ways.
16 I shall [1a]delight in Your
statutes;
I shall [b]not forget Your word.

ג Gimel.

17 ¶ [a]Deal bountifully with Your
servant,
That I may live and keep Your
word.
18 Open my eyes, that I may behold
Wonderful things from Your law.
19 I am a [a]stranger in the earth;
Do not hide Your
commandments from me.
20 My soul is crushed [1a]with
longing
After Your ordinances at all
times.
21 You [a]rebuke the arrogant, [1]the
[b]cursed,
Who [c]wander from Your
commandments.
22 [a]Take away reproach and
contempt from me,
For I [b]observe Your testimonies.
23 Even though [a]princes sit *and*
talk against me,
Your servant [b]meditates on Your
statutes.
24 Your testimonies also are my
[a]delight;
They are [1]my counselors.

ד Daleth.

25 ¶ My [a]soul cleaves to the dust;
[b]Revive me [c]according to Your
word.
26 I have told of my ways, and You
have answered me;
[a]Teach me Your statutes.
27 Make me understand the way of
Your precepts,
So I will [a]meditate on Your
wonders.
28 My [a]soul [1]weeps because of
grief;
[b]Strengthen me according to
Your word.
29 Remove the false way from me,
And graciously grant me Your
law.
30 I have chosen the faithful way;
I have [1]placed Your ordinances
before me.
31 I [a]cling to Your testimonies;
O LORD, do not put me to
shame!
32 I shall run the way of Your
commandments,
For You will [a]enlarge my heart.

ה He.

33 ¶ [a]Teach me, O LORD, the way
of Your statutes,
And I shall observe it to the end.
34 [a]Give me understanding, that I
may [b]observe Your law
And keep it [c]with all *my* heart.
35 Make me walk in the [a]path of
Your commandments,
For I [b]delight in it.

119:1 [1]Lit *complete;* or *having integrity* [a]Ps 101:2; Prov 11:20 [b]Ps 128:1; Ezek 11:20; Mic 4:2
2 [a]Ps 25:10 [b]Deut 4:29; Ps 119:10 [c]Deut 6:5
3 [a]1 John 3:9
4 [1]Lit *commanded* [2]Lit *To keep* [a]Deut 4:13; Neh 9:13
5 [a]Ps 40:2; Prov 4:26 [b]Deut 12:1; 2 Chr 7:17
6 [1]Lit *to* [a]Job 22:26; Ps 119:80
7 [a]Ps 119:62
8 [a]Ps 38:21
9 [a]1 Kin 2:4; 2 Chr 6:16
10 [a]2 Chr 15:15; Ps 119:2 [b]Ps 119:21
11 [a]Ps 37:31; Luke 2:19
12 [a]Ps 119:26
13 [a]Ps 40:9 [b]Ps 119:72
14 [1]Lit *As over all* [a]Ps 119:111
15 [1]Or *look upon* [a]Ps 1:2 [b]Ps 25:4; Is 58:2
16 [1]Lit *delight myself* [a]Ps 1:2 [b]Ps 119:93
17 [a]Ps 13:6
19 [a]Gen 47:9; Lev 25:23; 1 Chr 29:15; Ps 39:12; Heb 11:13
20 [1]Lit *for* [a]Ps 42:1
21 [1]Or *Cursed are those who wander...* [a]Ps 68:30 [b]Deut 27:26; Ps 37:22 [c]Ps 119:10
22 [a]Ps 39:8 [b]Ps 119:2
23 [a]Ps 119:161 [b]Ps 119:15
24 [1]Lit *the men of my counsel* [a]Ps 119:16
25 [a]Ps 44:25 [b]Ps 119:37 [c]Ps 119:65
26 [a]Ps 25:4
27 [a]Ps 105:2
28 [1]Lit *drops* [a]Ps 22:14 [b]Ps 20:2; 1 Pet 5:10
30 [1]Or *accounted Your ordinances worthy*
31 [a]Deut 11:22
32 [a]1 Kin 4:29; Is 60:5; 2 Cor 6:11
33 [a]Ps 119:5
34 [a]Ps 119:27 [b]1 Chr 22:12; Ezek 44:24 [c]Ps 119:2
35 [a]Ps 25:4; Is 40:14 [b]Ps 112:1

36 [a]Incline my heart to Your
testimonies
And not to [b]*dishonest* gain.
37 Turn away my [a]eyes from
looking at vanity,
And [b]revive me in Your ways.
38 [a]Establish Your [1]word to Your
servant,
[2]As that which produces
reverence for You.
39 [a]Turn away my reproach which
I dread,
For Your ordinances are good.
40 Behold, I [a]long for Your
precepts;
Revive me through Your
righteousness.

ו Vav.

41 ¶ May Your [a]lovingkindnesses
also come to me, O LORD,
Your salvation [b]according to
Your [1]word;
42 So I will have an [a]answer for
him who [b]reproaches me,
For I trust in Your word.
43 And do not take the word of
truth utterly out of my
mouth,
For I [1a]wait for Your
ordinances.
44 So I will [a]keep Your law
continually,
Forever and ever.
45 And I will [a]walk [1]at liberty,
For I [b]seek Your precepts.
46 I will also speak of Your
testimonies [a]before kings
And shall not be ashamed.
47 I shall [1a]delight in Your
commandments,
Which I [b]love.
48 And I shall lift up my hands to
Your commandments,
Which I [a]love;
And I will [b]meditate on Your
statutes.

ז Zayin.

49 ¶ Remember the word to Your
servant,
[1]In which You have made me
hope.
50 This is my [a]comfort in my
affliction,
That Your word has
[1]revived me.
51 The arrogant [a]utterly deride me,
Yet I do not [b]turn aside from
Your law.
52 I have [a]remembered Your
ordinances from [1]of old,
O LORD,
And comfort myself.

36 [a]1 Kin 8:58 [b]Ezek 33:31; Mark 7:21; Luke 12:15; Heb 13:5
37 [a]Is 33:15 [b]Ps 71:20
38 [1]Or *promise* [2]Lit *Which is for the fear of You* [a]2 Sam 7:25
39 [a]Ps 119:22
40 [a]Ps 119:20
41 [1]Or *promise* [a]Ps 119:77 [b]Ps 119:58
42 [a]Prov 27:11 [b]Ps 102:8
43 [1]Or *hope in* [a]Ps 119:49
44 [a]Ps 119:33
45 [1]Lit *in a wide place* [a]Prov 4:12 [b]Ps 119:94
46 [a]Matt 10:18; Acts 26:1
47 [1]Lit *delight myself* [a]Ps 119:16 [b]Ps 119:97
48 [a]Ps 119:97 [b]Ps 119:15
49 [1]Lit *On*
50 [1]Or *preserved me alive* [a]Job 6:10; Rom 15:4
51 [a]Job 30:1; Jer 20:7 [b]Job 23:11; Ps 44:18
52 [1]Or *everlasting* [a]Ps 103:18
53 [a]Ex 32:19; Ezra 9:3; Neh 13:25; Ps 119:158 [b]Ps 89:30
54 [a]Gen 47:9; Ps 119:19
55 [a]Ps 63:6 [b]Ps 42:8; Is 26:9; Acts 16:25
56 [1]Or *Because* [a]Ps 119:22
57 [1]Lit *said that I would keep* [a]Ps 16:5; Lam 3:24 [b]Deut 33:9
58 [1]Or *promise* [a]1 Kin 13:6 [b]Ps 119:2 [c]Ps 41:4 [d]Ps 119:41
59 [a]Mark 14:72; Luke 15:17
61 [a]Job 36:8; Ps 140:5 [b]Ps 119:83
62 [a]Ps 119:55 [b]Ps 119:7
63 [1]Or *revere* [a]Ps 101:6
64 [a]Ps 33:5 [b]Ps 119:12
66 [1]Or *judgment* [a]Phil 1:9
67 [a]Ps 119:71; Jer 31:18; Heb 12:5-11
68 [a]Ps 86:5; Matt 19:17 [b]Deut 8:16; Ps 125:4 [c]Ps 119:12
69 [1]Lit *besmear me with lies* [a]Job 13:4; Ps 109:2 [b]Ps 119:56
70 [1]Lit *gross like fat* [a]Deut 32:15; Job 15:27; Ps 17:10; Is 6:10; Jer 5:28; Acts 28:27 [b]Ps 119:16
71 [a]Ps 119:67

53 Burning [a]indignation has seized
me because of the wicked,
Who [b]forsake Your law.
54 Your statutes are my songs
In the house of my [a]pilgrimage.
55 O LORD, I [a]remember Your
name [b]in the night,
And keep Your law.
56 This has become mine,
[1]That I [a]observe Your precepts.

ח Heth.

57 ¶ The LORD is my [a]portion;
I have [1]promised to [b]keep Your
words.
58 I [a]sought Your favor [b]with all
my heart;
[c]Be gracious to me [d]according
to Your [1]word.
59 I [a]considered my ways
And turned my feet to Your
testimonies.
60 I hastened and did not delay
To keep Your commandments.
61 The [a]cords of the wicked have
encircled me,
But I have [b]not forgotten Your
law.
62 At [a]midnight I shall rise to give
thanks to You
Because of Your [b]righteous
ordinances.
63 I am a [a]companion of all those
who [1]fear You,
And of those who keep Your
precepts.
64 [a]The earth is full of Your
lovingkindness, O LORD;
[b]Teach me Your statutes.

ט Teth.

65 ¶ You have dealt well with Your
servant,
O LORD, according to Your word.
66 Teach me good [1a]discernment
and knowledge,
For I believe in Your
commandments.
67 [a]Before I was afflicted I went
astray,
But now I keep Your word.
68 You are [a]good and [b]do good;
[c]Teach me Your statutes.
69 The arrogant [1]have [a]forged a lie
against me;
With all *my* heart I will [b]observe
Your precepts.
70 Their heart is [1a]covered with
fat,
But I [b]delight in Your law.
71 It is [a]good for me that I was
afflicted,
That I may learn Your statutes.

72 The [a]law of Your mouth is
better to me
Than thousands of gold and
silver *pieces.*

י Yodh.

73 ¶ [a]Your hands made me and
[1]fashioned me;
[b]Give me understanding, that I
may learn Your
commandments.
74 May those who [1]fear You [a]see
me and be glad,
Because I [2b]wait for Your word.
75 I know, O LORD, that Your
judgments are [a]righteous,
And that [b]in faithfulness You
have afflicted me.
76 O may Your lovingkindness
[1]comfort me,
According to Your [2]word to
Your servant.
77 May [a]Your compassion come to
me that I may live,
For Your law is my [b]delight.
78 May [a]the arrogant be ashamed,
for they subvert me [b]with a
lie;
But I shall [c]meditate on Your
precepts.
79 May those who [1]fear You turn
to me,
Even those who know Your
testimonies.
80 May my heart be [1a]blameless in
Your statutes,
So that I will not [b]be ashamed.

כ Kaph.

81 ¶ My [a]soul languishes for Your
salvation;
I [1b]wait for Your word.
82 My [a]eyes fail *with longing* for
Your [1]word,
[2]While I say, "When will You
comfort me?"
83 Though I have [a]become like a
wineskin in the smoke,
I do [b]not forget Your statutes.
84 How many are the [a]days of Your
servant?
When will You [b]execute
judgment on those who
persecute me?
85 The arrogant have [a]dug pits
for me,
Men who are not [1]in accord
with Your law.
86 All Your commandments are
[a]faithful;
They have [b]persecuted me with
a lie; [c]help me!
87 They almost destroyed me [1]on
earth,
But as for me, I [a]did not forsake
Your precepts.
88 Revive me according to Your
lovingkindness,
So that I may keep the testimony
of Your mouth.

ל Lamedh.

89 ¶ [a]Forever, O LORD,
Your word [1]is settled in heaven.
90 Your [a]faithfulness *continues*
[1]throughout all generations;
You [b]established the earth, and
it [c]stands.
91 They stand this day according to
Your [a]ordinances,
For [b]all things are Your servants.
92 If Your law had not been my
[a]delight,
Then I would have perished [b]in
my affliction.
93 I will [a]never forget Your
precepts,
For by them You have
[1b]revived me.
94 I am Yours, [a]save me;
For I have [b]sought Your
precepts.
95 The wicked [a]wait for me to
destroy me;
I shall diligently consider Your
testimonies.
96 I have seen [1]a limit to all
perfection;
Your commandment is
exceedingly broad.

מ Mem.

97 ¶ O how I [a]love Your law!
It is my [b]meditation all the day.
98 Your [a]commandments make me
wiser than my enemies,
For they are ever [1]mine.
99 I have more insight than all my
teachers,
For Your testimonies are my
[a]meditation.
100 I understand [a]more than the
aged,
Because I have [b]observed Your
precepts.
101 I have [a]restrained my feet from
every evil way,
That I may keep Your word.
102 I have not [a]turned aside from
Your ordinances,
For You Yourself have taught me.
103 How [a]sweet are Your [1]words to
my [2]taste!
Yes, sweeter than honey to my
mouth!
104 From Your precepts I [a]get
understanding;

72 [a]Ps 19:10; 119:127; Prov 8:10,11,19
73 [1]Lit *established* [a]Job 10:8; 31:15; Ps 100:3; 138:8; 139:15, 16 [b]Ps 119:34
74 [1]Or *revere* [2]Or *hope in* [a]Ps 34:2; 35:27; 107:42 [b]Ps 119:43
75 [a]Ps 119:138 [b]Heb 12:10
76 [1]Lit *be for my comfort* [2]Or *promise*
77 [a]Ps 119:41 [b]Ps 119:16
78 [a]Jer 50:32 [b]Ps 119:86 [c]Ps 119:15
79 [1]Or *revere*
80 [1]Lit *complete;* or *having integrity* [a]Ps 119:1 [b]Ps 119:46
81 [1]Or *hope in* [a]Ps 84:2 [b]Ps 119:43
82 [1]Or *promise* [2]Lit *Saying* [a]Ps 69:3; 119:123; Is 38:14; Lam 2:11
83 [a]Job 30:30 [b]Ps 119:61
84 [a]Ps 39:4 [b]Rev 6:10
85 [1]Lit *according to Your law* [a]Ps 7:15; 35:7; 57:6; Jer 18:22
86 [a]Ps 119:138 [b]Ps 35:19; 119:78,161 [c]Ps 109:26
87 [1]Lit *in the earth* [a]Is 58:2
89 [1]Lit *stands firm* [a]Ps 89:2; 119:160; Is 40:8; Matt 24:35; 1 Pet 1:25
90 [1]Lit *to* [a]Ps 36:5; 89:1,2 [b]Ps 148:6 [c]Eccl 1:4
91 [a]Jer 31:35; 33:25 [b]Ps 104:2-4
92 [a]Ps 119:16 [b]Ps 119:50
93 [1]Or *kept me alive* [a]Ps 119:16, 83 [b]Ps 119:25
94 [a]Ps 119:146 [b]Ps 119:45
95 [a]Ps 40:14; Is 32:7
96 [1]Lit *an end of*
97 [a]Ps 119:47, 48,127,163,165 [b]Ps 1:2; 119:15
98 [1]Or *with me* [a]Deut 4:6; Ps 119:130
99 [a]Ps 119:15
100 [a]Job 32:7-9 [b]Ps 119:22,56
101 [a]Prov 1:15
102 [a]Deut 17:20; Josh 23:6; 1 Kin 15:5
103 [1]Or *promises* [2]Lit *palate* [a]Ps 19:10; Prov 8:11; 24:13,14
104 [a]Ps 119:130

Therefore I [b]hate every false
way.

ℵ Nun.

105 ¶ Your word is a [a]lamp to my
feet
And a light to my path.
106 I have [a]sworn and I will
confirm it,
That I will keep Your righteous
ordinances.
107 I am exceedingly [a]afflicted;
[1b]Revive me, O LORD, according
to Your word.
108 O accept the [a]freewill offerings
of my mouth, O LORD,
And [b]teach me Your ordinances.
109 My [1a]life is continually [2]in my
hand,
Yet I do not [b]forget Your law.
110 The wicked have [a]laid a snare
for me,
Yet I have not [b]gone astray from
Your precepts.
111 I have [a]inherited Your
testimonies forever,
For they are the [b]joy of my
heart.
112 I have [a]inclined my heart to
perform Your statutes
Forever, *even* [b]to the end.

ס Samekh.

113 ¶ I hate those who are
[a]double-minded,
But I love Your [b]law.
114 You are my [a]hiding place and
my [b]shield;
I [1c]wait for Your word.
115 [a]Depart from me, evildoers,
That I may [b]observe the
commandments of my God.
116 [a]Sustain me according to Your
[1]word, that I may live;
And [b]do not let me be
[2]ashamed of my hope.
117 Uphold me that I may be [a]safe,
That I may [b]have regard for
Your statutes continually.
118 You have [1]rejected all those
[a]who wander from Your
statutes,
For their deceitfulness is
[2]useless.
119 You have [1]removed all the
wicked of the earth *like*
[a]dross;
Therefore I [b]love Your
testimonies.
120 My flesh [1a]trembles for fear
of You,
And I am [b]afraid of Your
judgments.

ע Ayin.

121 ¶ I have [a]done justice and
righteousness;
Do not leave me to my
oppressors.
122 Be [a]surety for Your servant for
good;
Do not let the arrogant
[b]oppress me.
123 My [a]eyes fail *with longing* for
Your salvation
And for Your righteous [1]word.
124 Deal with Your servant
[a]according to Your
lovingkindness
And [b]teach me Your statutes.
125 [a]I am Your servant; [b]give me
understanding,
That I may know Your
testimonies.
126 It is time for the LORD to [a]act,
For they have broken Your law.
127 Therefore I [a]love Your
commandments
Above gold, yes, above fine gold.
128 Therefore I esteem right all *Your*
[a]precepts concerning
everything,
I [b]hate every false way.

פ Pe.

129 ¶ Your testimonies are
[a]wonderful;
Therefore my soul [b]observes
them.
130 The [a]unfolding of Your words
gives light;
It gives [b]understanding to the
simple.
131 I [a]opened my mouth wide and
[b]panted,
For I [c]longed for Your
commandments.
132 [a]Turn to me and be gracious
to me,
After Your manner [1]with those
who love Your name.
133 Establish my [a]footsteps in Your
[1]word,
And do not let any iniquity
[b]have dominion over me.
134 [a]Redeem me from the
oppression of man,
That I may keep Your precepts.
135 [a]Make Your face shine upon
Your servant,
And [b]teach me Your statutes.
136 My eyes [1]shed [a]streams of
water,
Because they [b]do not keep Your
law.

104 [b]Ps 119:128
105 [a]Prov 6:23
106 [a]Neh 10:29
107 [1]Or *Keep me alive* [a]Ps 119:25 [b]Ps 119:25
108 [a]Hos 14:2; Heb 13:15 [b]Ps 119:12
109 [1]Lit *soul* [2]I.e. in danger [a]Judg 12:3; Job 13:14 [b]Ps 119:16
110 [a]Ps 91:3 [b]Ps 119:10
111 [a]Deut 33:4 [b]Ps 119:14
112 [a]Ps 119:36 [b]Ps 119:33
113 [a]1 Kin 18:21; James 1:8 [b]Ps 119:47
114 [1]Or *hope in* [a]Ps 31:20 [b]Ps 84:9 [c]Ps 119:74
115 [a]Ps 6:8; Matt 7:23 [b]Ps 119:22
116 [1]Or *promise* [2]Lit *put to shame because of* [a]Ps 37:17 [b]Ps 25:2; Rom 5:5; Phil 1:20
117 [a]Ps 12:5; Prov 29:25 [b]Ps 119:6
118 [1]Lit *made light of* [2]Lit *falsehood* [a]Ps 119:10
119 [1]Lit *caused to cease* [a]Is 1:22; Ezek 22:18 [b]Ps 119:47
120 [1]Lit *bristles up from* [a]Job 4:14; Hab 3:16 [b]Ps 119:161
121 [a]2 Sam 8:15; Job 29:14
122 [a]Job 17:3; Heb 7:22 [b]Ps 119:134
123 [1]Or *promise* [a]Ps 119:82
124 [a]Ps 51:1 [b]Ps 119:12
125 [a]Ps 116:16 [b]Ps 119:27
126 [a]Jer 18:23; Ezek 31:11
127 [a]Ps 19:10
128 [a]Ps 19:8 [b]Ps 119:104
129 [a]Ps 119:18 [b]Ps 119:22
130 [a]Prov 6:23 [b]Ps 19:7
131 [a]Job 29:23; Ps 81:10 [b]Ps 42:1 [c]Ps 119:20
132 [1]Lit *to* [a]Ps 25:16
133 [1]Or *promise* [a]Ps 17:5 [b]Ps 19:13; Rom 6:12
134 [a]Ps 119:84; Luke 1:74
135 [a]Num 6:25; Ps 4:6 [b]Ps 119:12
136 [1]Lit *run down* [a]Jer 9:1; Lam 3:48 [b]Ps 119:158

צ Tsadhe.

137 ¶ [a]Righteous are You, O LORD,
And upright are Your judgments.
138 You have commanded Your testimonies in [a]righteousness
And exceeding [b]faithfulness.
139 My [a]zeal has [1]consumed me,
Because my adversaries have forgotten Your words.
140 Your [1a]word is very [2]pure,
Therefore Your servant [b]loves it.
141 I am small and [a]despised,
Yet I do not [b]forget Your precepts.
142 Your righteousness is an everlasting righteousness,
And [a]Your law is truth.
143 Trouble and anguish have [1]come upon me,
Yet Your commandments are my [a]delight.
144 Your [a]testimonies are righteous forever;
[b]Give me understanding that I may live.

ק Qoph.

145 ¶ I cried [a]with all my heart; answer me, O LORD!
I will [b]observe Your statutes.
146 I cried to You; [a]save me
And I shall keep Your testimonies.
147 I [1a]rise before dawn and cry for help;
I [2]wait for Your words.
148 My eyes anticipate the [a]night watches,
That I may [b]meditate on Your [1]word.
149 Hear my voice [a]according to Your lovingkindness;
[b]Revive me, O LORD, according to Your ordinances.
150 Those who follow after wickedness draw near;
They are far from Your law.
151 You are [a]near, O LORD,
And all Your commandments are [b]truth.
152 Of old I have [a]known from Your testimonies
That You have founded them [b]forever.

ר Resh.

153 ¶ [a]Look upon my [b]affliction and rescue me,
For I do not [c]forget Your law.
154 [a]Plead my cause and [b]redeem me;
Revive me according to Your [1]word.
155 Salvation is [a]far from the wicked,
For they [b]do not seek Your statutes.
156 [1a]Great are Your mercies, O LORD;
Revive me according to Your ordinances.
157 Many are my [a]persecutors and my adversaries,
Yet I do not [b]turn aside from Your testimonies.
158 I behold the [a]treacherous and [b]loathe *them,*
Because they do not keep Your [1]word.
159 Consider how I [a]love Your precepts;
[b]Revive me, O LORD, according to Your lovingkindness.
160 The [a]sum of Your word is [b]truth,
And every one of Your righteous ordinances [c]is everlasting.

ש Shin.

161 ¶ [a]Princes persecute me without cause,
But my heart [b]stands in awe of Your words.
162 I [a]rejoice at Your [1]word,
As one who [b]finds great spoil.
163 I [a]hate and despise falsehood,
But I [b]love Your law.
164 Seven times a day I praise You,
Because of Your [a]righteous ordinances.
165 Those who love Your law have [a]great peace,
And [1b]nothing causes them to stumble.
166 I [a]hope for Your salvation, O LORD,
And do Your commandments.
167 My [a]soul keeps Your testimonies,
And I [b]love them exceedingly.
168 I [a]keep Your precepts and Your testimonies,
For all my [b]ways are before You.

ת Tav.

169 ¶ Let my [a]cry [1]come before You, O LORD;
[b]Give me understanding [c]according to Your word.
170 Let my [a]supplication come before You;
[b]Deliver me according to Your [1]word.
171 Let my [a]lips utter praise,

137 [a]Ezra 9:15; Neh 9:33; Ps 116:5; Jer 12:1; Lam 1:18; Dan 9:7
138 [a]Ps 19:7-9 [b]Ps 119:86
139 [1]Lit *put an end to* [a]Ps 69:9; John 2:17
140 [1]Or *promise* [2]Lit *refined* [a]Ps 12:6 [b]Ps 119:47
141 [a]Ps 22:6 [b]Ps 119:61
142 [a]Ps 19:9
143 [1]Lit *found me* [a]Ps 119:24
144 [a]Ps 19:9 [b]Ps 119:27
145 [a]Ps 119:10 [b]Ps 119:22
146 [a]Ps 3:7
147 [1]Lit *anticipate the dawn* [2]Or *hope in* [a]Ps 5:3
148 [1]Or *promise* [a]Ps 63:6 [b]Ps 119:15
149 [a]Ps 119:124 [b]Ps 119:25
151 [a]Ps 34:18; Is 50:8 [b]Ps 119:142
152 [a]Ps 119:125 [b]Ps 119:89; Luke 21:33
153 [a]Lam 5:1 [b]Ps 119:50 [c]Ps 119:16; Prov 3:1; Hos 4:6
154 [1]Or *promise* [a]1 Sam 24:15; Ps 35:1; Mic 7:9 [b]Ps 119:134
155 [a]Job 5:4 [b]Ps 119:45
156 [1]Or *Many* [a]2 Sam 24:14
157 [a]Ps 7:1 [b]Ps 119:51
158 [1]Or *promise* [a]Is 21:2 [b]Ps 139:21
159 [a]Ps 119:47 [b]Ps 119:25
160 [a]Ps 139:17 [b]Ps 119:142 [c]Ps 119:89
161 [a]1 Sam 24:11; Ps 119:23 [b]Ps 119:120
162 [1]Or *promise* [a]Ps 119:14 [b]1 Sam 30:16; Is 9:3
163 [a]Ps 31:6; Prov 13:5 [b]Ps 119:47
164 [a]Ps 119:7
165 [1]Lit *they have no stumbling block* [a]Ps 37:11; Prov 3:2; Is 26:3 [b]Prov 3:23; Is 63:13; 1 John 2:10
166 [a]Gen 49:18; Ps 119:81
167 [a]Ps 119:129 [b]Ps 119:47
168 [a]Ps 119:22 [b]Job 24:23; Ps 139:3; Prov 5:21
169 [1]Lit *come near before* [a]Job 16:18; Ps 18:6 [b]Ps 119:27 [c]Ps 119:65
170 [1]Or *promise* [a]Ps 28:2 [b]Ps 22:20
171 [a]Ps 51:15

For You [b]teach me Your
statutes.
172 Let my [a]tongue sing of Your
[1]word,
For all Your [b]commandments are
righteousness.
173 Let Your [a]hand be [1]ready to
help me,
For I have [b]chosen Your
precepts.
174 I [a]long for Your salvation,
O LORD,
And Your law is my [b]delight.
175 Let my [a]soul live that it may
praise You,
And let Your ordinances
help me.
176 I have [a]gone astray like a lost
sheep; seek Your servant,
For I do [b]not forget Your
commandments.

Psalm 120

Prayer for Deliverance from the Treacherous.

A Song of +Ascents.

1 ¶ [a]In my trouble I cried to the
LORD,
And He answered me.
2 Deliver my soul, O LORD, from
[a]lying lips,
From a [b]deceitful tongue.
3 What shall be given to you, and
what more shall be done to
you,
You [a]deceitful tongue?
4 [a]Sharp arrows of the warrior,
With the *burning* [b]coals of the
broom tree.

5 ¶ Woe is me, for I sojourn in
[a]Meshech,
For I dwell among the [b]tents of
[c]Kedar!
6 Too long has my soul had its
dwelling
With those who [a]hate peace.
7 I [a]am *for* peace, but when I
speak,
They are [b]for war.

Psalm 121

The LORD the Keeper of Israel.

A Song of Ascents.

1 ¶ I will [a]lift up my eyes to [b]the
mountains;
From where shall my help
come?
2 My [a]help *comes* from the LORD,
Who [b]made heaven and earth.

171 [b]Ps 94:12; 119:12; Is 2:3; Mic 4:2
172 [1]Or *promise* [a]Ps 51:14 [b]Ps 119:138
173 [1]Lit *to help me* [a]Ps 37:24; 73:23 [b]Josh 24:22; Luke 10:42
174 [a]Ps 119:166 [b]Ps 119:16,24
175 [a]Is 55:3
176 [a]Is 53:6; Jer 50:6; Matt 18:12; Luke 15:4 [b]Ps 119:16
120:1 +Ex 34:24; 1 Kin 12:27 [a]Ps 18:6; 66:14; 102:2; Jon 2:2
2 [a]Ps 109:2; Prov 12:22 [b]Ps 52:4; Zeph 3:13
3 [a]Ps 52:4; Zeph 3:13
4 [a]Ps 45:5; Prov 25:18; Is 5:28 [b]Ps 140:10
5 [a]Gen 10:2; 1 Chr 1:5; Ezek 27:13; 38:2,3; 39:1 [b]Song 1:5 [c]Gen 25:13; Is 21:16; 60:7; Jer 2:10; 49:28; Ezek 27:21
6 [a]Ps 35:20
7 [a]Ps 109:4 [b]Ps 55:21
121:1 [a]Ps 123:1; Is 40:26 [b]Ps 87:1
2 [a]Ps 124:8 [b]Ps 115:15
3 [a]1 Sam 2:9; Ps 66:9 [b]Ps 41:2; 127:1; Is 27:3
5 [a]Ps 91:4 [b]Ps 16:8; 91:1; Is 25:4
6 [a]Ps 91:5; Is 49:10; Jon 4:8; Rev 7:16
7 [1]Or *keep* [a]Ps 41:2; 91:10-12
8 [1]Or *keep* [a]Deut 28:6 [b]Ps 113:2; 115:18
122:1 [a]Ps 42:4; Is 2:3; Mic 4:2; Zech 8:21
2 [a]Ps 9:14; 87:2; 116:19; Jer 7:2
3 [a]Ps 48:13; 147:2 [b]2 Sam 5:9; Neh 4:6
4 [1]Heb YAH [2]Or *A testimony* [a]Ex 23:17; Deut 16:16; Ps 84:5
5 [a]Deut 17:8; 2 Chr 19:8; Ps 89:29
6 [a]Ps 29:11; Jer 29:7 [b]Ps 102:14
7 [a]Ps 51:18; Is 62:6 [b]Ps 48:3, 13; Jer 17:27
8 [a]Ps 133:1 [b]1 Sam 25:6; John 20:19
9 [a]Neh 2:10; Esth 10:3

3 He will not [a]allow your foot to
slip;
He who [b]keeps you will not
slumber.
4 Behold, He who keeps Israel
Will neither slumber nor
sleep.

5 ¶ The LORD is your [a]keeper;
The LORD is your [b]shade on
your right hand.
6 The [a]sun will not smite you by
day,
Nor the moon by night.
7 The LORD will [1a]protect you
from all evil;
He will keep your soul.
8 The LORD will [1a]guard your
going out and your
coming in
[b]From this time forth and
forever.

Psalm 122

Prayer for the Peace of Jerusalem.

A Song of Ascents, of David.

1 ¶ I was glad when they said
to me,
"Let us [a]go to the house of the
LORD."
2 Our feet are standing
Within your [a]gates, O Jerusalem,
3 Jerusalem, that is [a]built
As a city that is [b]compact
together;
4 To which the tribes [a]go up,
even the tribes of [1]the
LORD—
[2]An ordinance for Israel—
To give thanks to the name of
the LORD.
5 For there [a]thrones were set for
judgment,
The thrones of the house of
David.

6 ¶ Pray for the [a]peace of
Jerusalem:
"May they prosper who [b]love
you.
7 "May peace be within your
[a]walls,
And prosperity within your
[b]palaces."
8 For the sake of my [a]brothers
and my friends,
I will now say, "[b]May peace be
within you."
9 For the sake of the house of the
LORD our God,
I will [a]seek your good.

Psalm 123

Prayer for the LORD*'s Help.*

A Song of Ascents.

1 ¶ To You I [a]lift up my eyes,
O You who [b]are enthroned in the heavens!
2 Behold, as the eyes of [a]servants *look* to the hand of their master,
As the eyes of a maid to the hand of her mistress,
So our [b]eyes *look* to the LORD our God,
Until He is gracious to us.

3 ¶ [a]Be gracious to us, O LORD, be gracious to us,
For we are greatly filled [b]with contempt.
4 Our soul is greatly filled
With the [a]scoffing of [b]those who are at ease,
And with the [c]contempt of the proud.

Psalm 124

Praise for Rescue from Enemies.

A Song of Ascents, of David.

1 ¶ "[a]Had it not been the LORD who was on our side,"
[b]Let Israel now say,
2 "Had it not been the LORD who was on our side
When men rose up against us,
3 Then they would have [a]swallowed us alive,
When their [b]anger was kindled against us;
4 Then the [a]waters would have engulfed us,
The stream would have [1]swept over our soul;
5 Then the [a]raging waters would have [1]swept over our soul."

6 ¶ Blessed be the LORD,
Who has not given us [1]to be [a]torn by their teeth.
7 Our soul has [a]escaped [b]as a bird out of the [c]snare of the trapper;
The snare is broken and we have escaped.
8 Our [a]help is in the name of the LORD,
Who [b]made heaven and earth.

Psalm 125

The LORD *Surrounds His People.*

A Song of Ascents.

1 ¶ Those who trust in the LORD
Are as Mount Zion, which [a]cannot be moved but [b]abides forever.
2 As the mountains surround Jerusalem,
So [a]the LORD surrounds His people
[b]From this time forth and forever.
3 For the [a]scepter of wickedness shall not rest upon the [1]land of the righteous,
So that the righteous [b]will not put forth their hands to do wrong.

4 ¶ [a]Do good, O LORD, to those who are good
And to those who are [b]upright in their hearts.
5 But as for those who [a]turn aside to their [b]crooked ways,
The LORD will lead them away with the [c]doers of iniquity.
[d]Peace be upon Israel.

Psalm 126

Thanksgiving for Return from Captivity.

A Song of Ascents.

1 ¶ When the LORD [a]brought back [1]the captive ones of Zion,
We were [b]like those who dream.
2 Then our [a]mouth was filled with laughter
And our [b]tongue with joyful shouting;
Then they said among the nations,
"The LORD has [c]done great things for them."
3 The LORD has done great things for us;
We are [a]glad.

4 ¶ Restore our captivity, O LORD,
As the [1a]streams in the [2]South.
5 Those who sow in [a]tears shall reap with [b]joyful shouting.
6 He who goes to and fro weeping, carrying *his* bag of seed,
Shall indeed come again with a shout of joy, bringing his sheaves *with him.*

123:1 [a]Ps 121:1; 141:8 [b]Ps 2:4; 11:4
2 [a]Prov 27:18; Mal 1:6 [b]Ps 25:15
3 [a]Ps 4:1; 51:1 [b]Neh 4:4; Ps 119:22
4 [a]Neh 2:19; Ps 79:4 [b]Job 12:5; Is 32:9,11; Amos 6:1 [c]Neh 4:4; Ps 119:22
124:1 [a]Ps 94:17 [b]Ps 129:1
3 [a]Num 16:30; Ps 35:25; 56:1; 57:3; Prov 1:12 [b]Gen 39:19; Ps 138:7
4 [1]Or *passed over* [a]Job 22:11; Ps 18:16; 32:6; 69:2; 144:7
5 [1]Or *passed over* [a]Job 38:11
6 [1]Lit *as a prey to* [a]Ps 27:2; Prov 30:14
7 [a]Ps 141:10; 2 Cor 11:33; Heb 11:34 [b]Prov 6:5 [c]Ps 91:3; Hos 9:8
8 [a]Ps 121:2 [b]Gen 1:1; Ps 134:3
125:1 [a]Ps 46:5 [b]Ps 61:7; Eccl 1:4
2 [a]Zech 2:5 [b]Ps 121:8
3 [1]Lit *lot* [a]Ps 89:22; Prov 22:8; Is 14:5 [b]1 Sam 24:10; Ps 55:20; Acts 12:1
4 [a]Ps 119:68 [b]Ps 7:10; 11:2; 32:11; 36:10; 94:15
5 [a]Job 23:11; Ps 40:4; 101:3 [b]Prov 2:15; Is 59:8 [c]Ps 92:7; 94:4 [d]Ps 128:6; Gal 6:16
126:1 [1]Or *those who returned to* [a]Ps 85:1; Jer 29:14; Hos 6:11 [b]Acts 12:9
2 [a]Job 8:21 [b]Ps 51:14; Is 35:6 [c]1 Sam 12:24; Ps 71:19; Luke 1:49
3 [a]Is 25:9; Zeph 3:14
4 [1]Lit *stream-beds* [2]Heb *Negev* [a]Is 35:6; 43:19
5 [a]Ps 80:5; Jer 31:9,16; Lam 1:2 [b]Is 35:10; 51:11; 61:7; Gal 6:9

Psalm 127

Prosperity Comes from the L*ORD.*

A Song of Ascents, of Solomon.

1 ¶ Unless the LORD [a]builds the house,
They labor in vain who build it;
Unless the LORD [b]guards the city,
The watchman keeps awake in vain.
2 It is vain for you to rise up early,
To [1]retire late,
To [a]eat the bread of [2]painful labors;
For He gives to His [b]beloved [c]*even in his* sleep.

3 ¶ Behold, [a]children are a [1]gift of the LORD,
The [b]fruit of the womb is a reward.
4 Like arrows in the hand of a [a]warrior,
So are the children of one's youth.
5 How [a]blessed is the man whose quiver is full of them;
[b]They will not be ashamed
When they [c]speak with their enemies [d]in the gate.

Psalm 128

Blessedness of the Fear of the L*ORD.*

A Song of Ascents.

1 ¶ [a]How blessed is everyone who fears the LORD,
Who [b]walks in His ways.
2 When you shall [a]eat of the [1b]fruit of your hands,
You will be happy and [c]it will be well with you.
3 Your wife shall be like a [a]fruitful vine
[1]Within your house,
Your children like [b]olive plants
Around your table.
4 Behold, for thus shall the man be blessed
Who fears the LORD.

5 ¶ [a]The LORD bless you [b]from Zion,
And may you see the prosperity of Jerusalem all the days of your life.
6 Indeed, may you see your [a]children's children.
[b]Peace be upon Israel!

Psalm 129

Prayer for the Overthrow of Zion's Enemies.

A Song of Ascents.

1 ¶ "[1]Many times they have [2a]persecuted me from my [b]youth up,"
[c]Let Israel now say,
2 "[1]Many times they have [2]persecuted me from my youth up;
Yet they have [a]not prevailed against me.
3 "The plowers plowed upon my back;
They lengthened their furrows."
4 The LORD [a]is righteous;
He has cut in two the [b]cords of the wicked.

5 ¶ May all who [a]hate Zion
Be [b]put to shame and turned backward;
6 Let them be like [a]grass upon the housetops,
Which withers before it [1]grows up;
7 With which the reaper does not fill his [1]hand,
Or the binder of sheaves his [a]bosom;
8 Nor do those who pass by say,
"The [a]blessing of the LORD be upon you;
We bless you in the name of the LORD."

Psalm 130

Hope in the L*ORD's Forgiving Love.*

A Song of Ascents.

1 ¶ Out of the [a]depths I have cried to You, O LORD.
2 Lord, [a]hear my voice!
Let [b]Your ears be attentive
To the [c]voice of my supplications.
3 If You, [1]LORD, should mark iniquities,
O Lord, who could [a]stand?
4 But there is [a]forgiveness with You,
That You may be [b]feared.

5 ¶ I wait for the LORD, my [a]soul does wait,
And [1b]in His word do I hope.
6 My soul *waits* for the Lord
More than the watchmen [a]for the morning;
Indeed, more than the watchmen for the morning.
7 O Israel, [a]hope in the LORD;

127:1 [a]Ps 78:69 [b]Ps 121:4
2 [1]Lit *delay sitting* [2]Lit *toils* [a]Gen 3:17,19 [b]Ps 60:5 [c]Job 11:18,19; Prov 3:24; Eccl 5:12
3 [1]Or *heritage* [a]Gen 33:5; 48:4; Josh 24:3,4; Ps 113:9 [b]Deut 7:13; 28:4; Is 13:18
4 [a]Ps 112:2; 120:4
5 [a]Ps 128:2,3 [b]Prov 27:11 [c]Is 29:21; Amos 5:12 [d]Gen 34:20
128:1 [a]Ps 112:1; 119:1 [b]Ps 119:3
2 [1]Lit *labor* [a]Is 3:10 [b]Ps 109:11; Hag 2:17 [c]Eccl 8:12; Eph 6:3
3 [1]Lit *In the innermost parts of* [a]Ezek 19:10 [b]Ps 52:8; 144:12
5 [a]Ps 134:3 [b]Ps 20:2; 135:21
6 [a]Gen 48:11; 50:23; Job 42:16; Ps 103:17; Prov 17:6 [b]Ps 125:5
129:1 [1]Lit *Much* [2]Lit *showed hostility toward* [a]Ex 1:11; Judg 3:8; Ps 88:15 [b]Is 47:12; Jer 2:2; 22:21; Ezek 16:22; Hos 2:15; 11:1 [c]Ps 124:1
2 [1]Lit *Much* [2]Lit *showed hostility toward* [a]Jer 1:19; 15:20; 20:11; Matt 16:18; 2 Cor 4:8,9
4 [a]Ps 119:137 [b]Ps 140:5
5 [a]Mic 4:11 [b]Ps 70:3; 71:13
6 [1]Lit *draws out* [a]2 Kin 19:26; Ps 37:2; Is 37:27
7 [1]Lit *palm* [a]Ps 79:12
8 [a]Ruth 2:4; Ps 118:26
130:1 [a]Ps 42:7; 69:2; Lam 3:55
2 [a]Ps 64:1; 119:149 [b]2 Chr 6:40; Neh 1:6,11 [c]Ps 28:2; 140:6
3 [1]Heb YAH [a]Ps 76:7; 143:2; Nah 1:6; Mal 3:2; Rev 6:17
4 [a]Ex 34:7; Neh 9:17; Ps 86:5; Is 55:7; Dan 9:9 [b]1 Kin 8:39,40; Jer 33:8,9
5 [1]Lit *for* [a]Ps 27:14; 33:20; 40:1; 62:1,5; Is 8:17; 26:8 [b]Ps 119:74,81
6 [a]Ps 63:6; 119:147
7 [a]Ps 131:3

For with the LORD there is
[b]lovingkindness,
And with Him is [c]abundant
redemption.
8 And He will [a]redeem Israel
From all his iniquities.

Psalm 131

Childlike Trust in the LORD.

A Song of Ascents, of David.

1 ¶ O LORD, my heart is not
[a]proud, nor my eyes
[1b]haughty;
Nor do I [2]involve myself in
[c]great matters,
Or in things [d]too [3]difficult
for me.
2 Surely I have [a]composed and
quieted my soul;
Like a weaned [b]child *rests*
[1]against his mother,
My soul is like a weaned child
[1]within me.
3 O Israel, [a]hope in the LORD
[b]From this time forth and
forever.

Psalm 132

Prayer for the LORD'S Blessing upon the Sanctuary.

A Song of Ascents.

1 ¶ Remember, O LORD, on David's
behalf,
All [a]his affliction;
2 How he swore to the LORD
And vowed to [a]the Mighty One
of Jacob,
3 "Surely I will not [1]enter [a]my
house,
Nor [2]lie on my bed;
4 I will not [a]give sleep to my eyes
Or slumber to my eyelids,
5 Until I find a [a]place for the
LORD,
[1]A dwelling place for [b]the
Mighty One of Jacob."
6 ¶ Behold, we heard of it in
[a]Ephrathah,
We found it in the [b]field of
[1]Jaar.
7 Let us go into His [1a]dwelling
place;
Let us [b]worship at His
[c]footstool.
8 [a]Arise, O LORD, to Your [b]resting
place,
You and the ark of Your
[c]strength.
9 Let Your priests be [a]clothed
with righteousness,

7 [b]Ps 86:5; 103:4 [c]Ps 111:9; Rom 3:24; Eph 1:7
8 [a]Ps 103:3,4; Luke 1:68; Titus 2:14
131:1 [1]Or *lofty* [2]Lit *go after, walk* [3]Or *marvelous* [a]2 Sam 22:28; Ps 101:5; Is 2:12; Zeph 3:11 [b]Prov 30:13; Is 5:15 [c]Jer 45:5; Rom 12:16 [d]Job 42:3; Ps 139:6
2 [1]Or *upon* [a]Ps 62:1 [b]Matt 18:3; 1 Cor 14:20
3 [a]Ps 130:7 [b]Ps 113:2
132:1 [a]Gen 49:24; 2 Sam 16:12
2 [a]Gen 49:24; Is 49:26; 60:16
3 [1]Lit *come into the tabernacle of* [2]Lit *go up into the couch of* [a]Job 21:28
4 [a]Prov 6:4
5 [1]Lit *Dwelling places* [a]1 Kin 8:17; 1 Chr 22:7; Ps 26:8; Acts 7:46 [b]Ps 132:2
6 [1]Or *the wood* [a]Gen 35:19; 1 Sam 17:12 [b]1 Sam 7:1
7 [1]Lit *dwelling places* [a]Ps 43:3 [b]Ps 5:7; 99:5 [c]1 Chr 28:2
8 [a]Num 10:35; 2 Chr 6:41; Ps 68:1 [b]Ps 132:14 [c]Ps 78:61
9 [a]Job 29:14 [b]Ps 30:4; 132:16; 149:5
10 [a]Ps 2:2; 132:17
11 [a]Ps 89:3,35 [b]2 Sam 7:12-16; 1 Chr 17:11-14; 2 Chr 6:16; Ps 89:4; Acts 2:30
12 [a]Luke 1:32; Acts 2:30
13 [a]Ps 48:1,2; 78:68 [b]Ps 68:16
14 [a]Ps 132:8 [b]Ps 68:16; Matt 23:21
15 [a]Ps 147:14 [b]Ps 107:9
16 [a]2 Chr 6:41; Ps 132:9
17 [a]Ezek 29:21; Luke 1:69 [b]1 Kin 11:36; 15:4; 2 Kin 8:19; 2 Chr 21:7; Ps 18:28
18 [a]Job 8:22; Ps 35:26; 109:29 [b]Ps 21:3
133:1 [a]Gen 13:8; Heb 13:1
2 [a]Ex 29:7; 30:25,30; Lev 8:12 [b]Ex 28:33; 39:24
3 [a]Prov 19:12; Hos 14:5; Mic 5:7 [b]Deut 3:9; 4:48 [c]Ps 48:2; 74:2; 78:68 [d]Lev 25:21; Deut 28:8; Ps 42:8 [e]Ps 21:4

And let Your [b]godly ones sing
for joy.
10 ¶ For the sake of David Your
servant,
Do not turn away the face of
Your [a]anointed.
11 The LORD has [a]sworn to David
A truth from which He will not
turn back:
"[b]Of the fruit of your body I will
set upon your throne.
12 "If your sons will keep My
covenant
And My testimony which I will
teach them,
Their sons also shall [a]sit upon
your throne forever."
13 ¶ For the LORD has [a]chosen
Zion;
He has [b]desired it for His
habitation.
14 "This is My [a]resting place
forever;
Here I will [b]dwell, for I have
desired it.
15 "I will abundantly [a]bless her
provision;
I will [b]satisfy her needy with
bread.
16 "Her [a]priests also I will clothe
with salvation,
And her [a]godly ones will sing
aloud for joy.
17 "There I will cause the [a]horn of
David to spring forth;
I have prepared a [b]lamp for
Mine anointed.
18 "His enemies I will [a]clothe with
shame,
But upon himself his [b]crown
shall shine."

Psalm 133

The Excellency of Brotherly Unity.

A Song of Ascents, of David.

1 ¶ Behold, how good and how
pleasant it is
For [a]brothers to dwell together
in unity!
2 It is like the precious [a]oil upon
the head,
Coming down upon the beard,
Even Aaron's beard,
Coming down upon the [b]edge of
his robes.
3 It is like the [a]dew of [b]Hermon
Coming down upon the
[c]mountains of Zion;
For there the LORD [d]commanded
the blessing—[e]life forever.

Psalm 134

Greetings of Night Watchers.

A Song of Ascents.

1 ¶ Behold, [a]bless the LORD, all
[b]servants of the LORD,
Who [1c]serve [d]by night in the
house of the LORD!
2 [a]Lift up your hands to the
[b]sanctuary
And bless the LORD.
3 May the LORD [a]bless you from
Zion,
He who [b]made heaven and
earth.

Psalm 135

Praise the LORD's Wonderful Works. Vanity of Idols.

1 ¶ [1a]Praise [2]the LORD!
Praise the name of the LORD;
Praise *Him*, O [b]servants of the
LORD,
2 You who stand in the house of
the LORD,
In the [a]courts of the house of
our God!
3 [1]Praise [2]the LORD, for [a]the
LORD is good;
[b]Sing praises to His name, [c]for
it is lovely.
4 For [1]the LORD has [a]chosen
Jacob for Himself,
Israel for His [2b]own possession.

5 ¶ For I know that [a]the LORD is
great
And that our Lord is [b]above all
gods.
6 [a]Whatever the LORD pleases, He
does,
In heaven and in earth, in the
seas and in all deeps.
7 [1]He [a]causes the [2]vapors to
ascend from the ends of the
earth;
Who [b]makes lightnings for the
rain,
Who [a]brings forth the wind
from His treasuries.

8 ¶ [1]He [a]smote the firstborn of
Egypt,
[2]Both of man and beast.
9 [1]He sent [a]signs and wonders
into your midst, O Egypt,
Upon [b]Pharaoh and all his
servants.
10 [1a]He [b]smote many nations
And slew mighty kings,
11 [a]Sihon, king of the Amorites,
And [b]Og, king of Bashan,
And [c]all the kingdoms of
Canaan;
12 And He [a]gave their land as a
heritage,
A heritage to Israel His people.
13 Your [a]name, O LORD, is
everlasting,
Your [1]remembrance, O LORD,
[2]throughout all generations.
14 For the LORD will [a]judge His
people
And [b]will have compassion on
His servants.
15 The [a]idols of the nations are *but*
silver and gold,
The work of man's hands.
16 They have mouths, but they do
not speak;
They have eyes, but they do not
see;
17 They have ears, but they do not
hear,
Nor is there any breath at all in
their mouths.
18 Those who make them will be
like them,
Yes, everyone who trusts in
them.

19 ¶ O house of [a]Israel, bless the
LORD;
O house of Aaron, bless the
LORD;
20 O house of Levi, bless the LORD;
You [a]who [1]revere the LORD,
bless the LORD.
21 Blessed be the LORD [a]from Zion,
Who [b]dwells in Jerusalem.
[1]Praise [2]the LORD!

Psalm 136

Thanks for the LORD's Goodness to Israel.

1 ¶ [a]Give thanks to the LORD, for
[b]He is good,
For [c]His lovingkindness is
everlasting.
2 Give thanks to the [a]God of gods,
For His lovingkindness is
everlasting.
3 Give thanks to the [a]Lord of
lords,
For His lovingkindness is
everlasting.
4 To Him who [a]alone does great
[1]wonders,
For His lovingkindness is
everlasting;
5 To Him who [a]made the heavens
[1b]with skill,
For His lovingkindness is
everlasting;

134:1 [1]Lit *stand* [a]Ps 103:21 [b]Ps 135:1,2 [c]Deut 10:8; 1 Chr 23:30; 2 Chr 29:11 [d]1 Chr 9:33
2 [a]Ps 28:2; 1 Tim 2:8 [b]Ps 63:2
3 [a]Ps 128:5 [b]Ps 124:8
135:1 [1]Or *Hallelujah!* [2]Heb YAH [a]Ps 113:1 [b]Ps 134:1
2 [a]Ps 92:13; 116:19
3 [1]Or *Hallelujah!* [2]Heb YAH [a]Ps 100:5; 119:68 [b]Ps 68:4 [c]Ps 147:1
4 [1]Heb YAH [2]Or *special treasure* [a]Deut 7:6; 10:15; Ps 105:6 [b]Ex 19:5; Mal 3:17; Titus 2:14; 1 Pet 2:9
5 [a]Ps 48:1; 95:3; 145:3 [b]Ps 97:9
6 [a]Ps 115:3
7 [1]Lit *The one who* [2]I.e. clouds [a]Jer 10:13; 51:16 [b]Job 28:25,26; 38:25, 26; Zech 10:1
8 [1]Lit *The one who* [2]Lit *From man to beast* [a]Ex 12:12; Ps 78:51; 105:36
9 [1]Lit *The one who* [a]Ex 7:10; Deut 6:22; Ps 78:43 [b]Ps 136:15
10 [1]Lit *The one who* [a]Num 21:24; Ps 135:10-12; 136:17-21 [b]Ps 44:2
11 [a]Num 21:21-26; Deut 29:7 [b]Num 21:33-35 [c]Josh 12:7-24
12 [a]Deut 29:8; Ps 78:55; 136:21,22
13 [1]Or *memorial* [2]Lit *to* [a]Ex 3:15; Ps 102:12
14 [a]Deut 32:36; Ps 50:4 [b]Ps 90:13; 106:46
15 [a]Ps 115:4-8; 135:15-18
19 [a]Ps 115:9
20 [1]Lit *fear* [a]Ps 118:4
21 [1]Or *Hallelujah!* [2]Heb YAH [a]Ps 128:5; 134:3 [b]Ps 132:14
136:1 [a]1 Chr 16:34; Ps 106:1; 107:1; 118:1; Jer 33:11 [b]2 Chr 5:13; 7:3; Ezra 3:11; Ps 100:5 [c]1 Chr 16:41; 2 Chr 20:21; Ps 118:1-4
2 [a]Deut 10:17
3 [a]Deut 10:17
4 [1]I.e. wonderful acts [a]Deut 6:22; Job 9:10; Ps 72:18
5 [1]Lit *with understanding* [a]Gen 1:1 [b]Ps 104:24; Prov 3:19; Jer 10:12; 51:15

6 To Him who [a]spread out the
earth above the waters,
For His lovingkindness is
everlasting;
7 To Him who [a]made *the* great
lights,
For His lovingkindness is
everlasting:
8 The [a]sun to rule [1]by day,
For His lovingkindness is
everlasting,
9 The [a]moon and stars to rule [1]by
night,
For His lovingkindness is
everlasting.

10 ¶ To Him who [a]smote [1]the
Egyptians in their firstborn,
For His lovingkindness is
everlasting,
11 And [a]brought Israel out from
their midst,
For His lovingkindness is
everlasting,
12 With a [a]strong hand and an
[b]outstretched arm,
For His lovingkindness is
everlasting.
13 To Him who [a]divided the [1]Red
Sea [2]asunder,
For His lovingkindness is
everlasting,
14 And [a]made Israel pass through
the midst of it,
For His lovingkindness is
everlasting;
15 But [a]He [1]overthrew Pharaoh
and his army in the
[2]Red Sea,
For His lovingkindness is
everlasting.
16 To Him who [a]led His people
through the wilderness,
For His lovingkindness is
everlasting;
17 To Him who [a]smote great kings,
For His lovingkindness is
everlasting,
18 And [a]slew [1]mighty kings,
For His lovingkindness is
everlasting:
19 [a]Sihon, king of the Amorites,
For His lovingkindness is
everlasting,
20 And [a]Og, king of Bashan,
For His lovingkindness is
everlasting,
21 And [a]gave their land as a
heritage,
For His lovingkindness is
everlasting,
22 Even a heritage to Israel His
[a]servant,

6 [a]Gen 1:2; Ps 24:2; Is 42:5; Jer 10:12
7 [a]Gen 1:14-18; Ps 74:16
8 [1]Or *over the* [a]Gen 1:16
9 [1]Or *over the* [a]Gen 1:16
10 [1]Lit *Egypt* [a]Ex 12:29; Ps 78:51
11 [a]Ex 12:51; Ps 105:43
12 [a]Ex 6:1; 1 Kin 8:42; Neh 1:10; Ps 44:3; Jer 32:21 [b]Ex 6:6; Deut 4:34; 2 Kin 17:36; 2 Chr 6:32; Jer 32:17
13 [1]Lit *Sea of Reeds* [2]Lit *in parts* [a]Ex 14:21; Ps 66:6
14 [a]Ex 14:22; Ps 106:9
15 [1]Lit *shook off* [2]Lit *Sea of Reeds* [a]Ex 14:27; Ps 78:53
16 [a]Ex 13:18; Deut 8:15; Ps 78:52
17 [a]Ps 135:10-12
18 [1]Lit *majestic* [a]Deut 29:7
19 [a]Num 21:21-24
20 [a]Num 21:33-35
21 [a]Josh 12:1
22 [a]Ps 105:6; Is 41:8
23 [a]Ps 9:12
24 [a]Judg 6:9; Neh 9:28; Ps 107:2
25 [a]Ps 104:27
26 [a]Gen 24:3; 2 Chr 36:23; Ezra 1:2; Neh 1:4
137:1 [a]Ezek 1:1 [b]Neh 1:4
2 [1]Or *poplars* [2]Lit *lyres* [a]Lev 23:40; Is 44:4 [b]Job 30:31; Is 24:8; Ezek 26:13
3 [1]Lit *asked* [2]Lit *words of song* [a]Ps 80:6 [b]Is 49:17
4 [a]2 Chr 29:27; Neh 12:46
5 [1]I.e. become lame [a]Is 65:11
6 [1]Lit *cause to ascend* [a]Job 29:10; Ps 22:15; Ezek 3:26 [b]Neh 2:3
7 [a]Ps 83:4-8; Is 34:5; Jer 49:7-22; Lam 4:21; Ezek 25:12-14; Amos 1:11; Obad 10-14 [b]Ps 74:7; Hab 3:13
8 [1]Or *devastator* [2]Lit *your recompense* [a]Is 13:1-22; Jer 25:12 [b]Jer 50:15; Rev 18:6
9 [a]2 Kin 8:12; Is 13:16; Hos 13:16; Nah 3:10

For His lovingkindness is
everlasting.

23 ¶ Who [a]remembered us in our
low estate,
For His lovingkindness is
everlasting,
24 And has [a]rescued us from our
adversaries,
For His lovingkindness is
everlasting;
25 Who [a]gives food to all flesh,
For His lovingkindness is
everlasting.
26 Give thanks to the [a]God of
heaven,
For His lovingkindness is
everlasting.

Psalm 137

An Experience of the Captivity.

1 ¶ By the [a]rivers of Babylon,
There we sat down and [b]wept,
When we remembered Zion.
2 Upon the [1a]willows in the
midst of it
We [b]hung our [2]harps.
3 For there our captors
[1a]demanded of us [2]songs,
And [b]our tormentors mirth,
saying,
"Sing us one of the songs of
Zion."

4 ¶ How can we sing [a]the LORD'S
song
In a foreign land?
5 If I [a]forget you, O Jerusalem,
May my right hand [1]forget *her
skill.*
6 May my [a]tongue cling to the
roof of my mouth
If I do not remember you,
If I do not [1b]exalt Jerusalem
Above my chief joy.

7 ¶ Remember, O LORD, against
the sons of [a]Edom
The day of Jerusalem,
Who said, "Raze it, raze it
[b]To its very foundation."
8 O daughter of Babylon, you
[1a]devastated one,
How blessed will be the one
who [b]repays you
With [2]the recompense with
which you have repaid us.
9 How blessed will be the one
who seizes and [a]dashes
your little ones
Against the rock.

Psalm 138

Thanksgiving for the LORD's Favor.

A Psalm of David.

1 ¶ [a]I will give You thanks with
all my heart;
I will sing praises to You before
the [b]gods.
2 I will bow down [a]toward Your
holy temple
And [b]give thanks to Your name
for Your lovingkindness and
Your [1]truth;
For You have [c]magnified Your
[2]word [3]according to all
Your name.
3 On the day I [a]called, You
answered me;
You made me bold with
[b]strength in my soul.

4 ¶ [a]All the kings of the earth will
give thanks to You, O LORD,
When they have heard the words
of Your mouth.
5 And they will [a]sing of the ways
of the LORD,
For [b]great is the glory of the
LORD.
6 For [a]though the LORD is exalted,
Yet He [b]regards the lowly,
But the [c]haughty He knows
from afar.

7 ¶ Though I [a]walk in the midst
of trouble, You will
[1b]revive me;
You will [c]stretch forth Your
hand against the wrath of
my enemies,
And Your right hand will
[d]save me.
8 The LORD will [a]accomplish what
concerns me;
Your [b]lovingkindness, O LORD, is
everlasting;
[c]Do not forsake the [d]works of
Your hands.

Psalm 139

God's Omnipresence and Omniscience.

For the choir director. A Psalm of David.

1 ¶ O LORD, You have [a]searched
me and known *me.*
2 You [a]know [1]when I sit down
and [2]when I rise up;
You [b]understand my thought
from afar.
3 You [1a]scrutinize my [2]path and
my lying down,
And are intimately acquainted
with all my ways.

138:1 [a]Ps 111:1 [b]Ps 95:3; 96:4; 97:7
2 [1]Or *faithfulness* [2]Or *promise* [3]Or *together with* [a]1 Kin 8:29; Ps 5:7; 28:2 [b]Ps 140:13 [c]Is 42:21
3 [a]Ps 118:5 [b]Ps 28:7; 46:1
4 [a]Ps 72:11; 102:15
5 [a]Ps 145:7 [b]Ps 21:5
6 [a]Ps 113:4-7 [b]Prov 3:34; Is 57:15; Luke 1:48; James 4:6; 1 Pet 5:5 [c]Ps 40:4; 101:5
7 [1]Or *keep me alive* [a]Ps 23:4; 143:11 [b]Ezra 9:8,9; Ps 71:20; Is 57:15 [c]Ex 7:5; 15:12; Is 5:25; Jer 51:25; Ezek 6:14; 25:13 [d]Ps 20:6; 60:5
8 [a]Ps 57:2; Phil 1:6 [b]Ps 136:1 [c]Job 10:8; Ps 27:9; 71:9; 119:8 [d]Job 10:3; 14:15; Ps 100:3
139:1 [a]Ps 17:3; 44:21; Jer 12:3
2 [1]Lit *my sitting* [2]Lit *my rising* [a]2 Kin 19:27 [b]Ps 94:11; Is 66:18; Matt 9:4
3 [1]Lit *winnow* [2]Or *journeying* [a]Job 14:16; 31:4
4 [1]Lit *For there is not* [a]Heb 4:13
5 [a]Ps 34:7; 125:2 [b]Job 9:33
6 [a]Rom 11:33 [b]Job 42:3
7 [a]Jer 23:24
8 [1]I.e. the nether world [a]Amos 9:2-4 [b]Job 26:6; Prov 15:11
10 [a]Ps 23:2,3
11 [1]Lit *bruise;* some commentators read *cover* [a]Job 22:13
12 [1]Lit *from* [a]Job 34:22; Dan 2:22 [b]1 John 1:5
13 [1]Lit *kidneys* [a]Ps 119:73; Is 44:24 [b]Job 10:11
14 [1]Some ancient versions read *You are fearfully wonderful* [a]Ps 40:5
15 [1]Lit *bones were* [a]Job 10:8-10; Eccl 11:5 [b]Ps 63:9
16 [a]Job 10:8-10; Eccl 11:5 [b]Ps 56:8 [c]Job 14:5
17 [a]Ps 40:5; 92:5

4 [1]Even before there is a word on
my tongue,
Behold, O LORD, You [a]know it
all.
5 You have [a]enclosed me behind
and before,
And [b]laid Your hand upon me.
6 *Such* [a]knowledge is [b]too
wonderful for me;
It is *too* high, I cannot attain
to it.

7 ¶ [a]Where can I go from Your
Spirit?
Or where can I flee from Your
presence?
8 [a]If I ascend to heaven, You are
there;
If I make my bed in [1]Sheol,
behold, [b]You are there.
9 If I take the wings of the dawn,
If I dwell in the remotest part of
the sea,
10 Even there Your hand will
[a]lead me,
And Your right hand will lay
hold of me.
11 If I say, "Surely the [a]darkness
will [1]overwhelm me,
And the light around me will be
night,"
12 Even the [a]darkness is not dark
[1]to You,
And the night is as bright as the
day.
[b]Darkness and light are alike
to You.

13 ¶ For You [a]formed my [1]inward
parts;
You [b]wove me in my mother's
womb.
14 I will give thanks to You, for [1]I
am fearfully and wonderfully
made;
[a]Wonderful are Your works,
And my soul knows it very well.
15 My [1a]frame was not hidden
from You,
When I was made in secret,
And skillfully wrought in the
[b]depths of the earth;
16 Your [a]eyes have seen my
unformed substance;
And in [b]Your book were all
written
The [c]days that were ordained
for me,
When as yet there was not one
of them.

17 ¶ How precious also are Your
[a]thoughts to me, O God!
How vast is the sum of them!

18 If I should count them, they
would [a]outnumber the
sand.
When [b]I awake, I am still
with You.

19 ¶ O that You would [a]slay the
wicked, O God;
[b]Depart from me, therefore,
[c]men of bloodshed.
20 For they [a]speak [1]against You
wickedly,
And Your enemies [2b]take *Your
name* in vain.
21 Do I not [a]hate those who hate
You, O LORD?
And do I not [b]loathe those who
rise up against You?
22 I hate them with the utmost
hatred;
They have become my enemies.

23 ¶ [a]Search me, O God, and know
my heart;
[b]Try me and know my anxious
thoughts;
24 And see if there be any
[1a]hurtful way in me,
And [b]lead me in the
[c]everlasting way.

Psalm 140

Prayer for Protection against the Wicked.

For the choir director. A Psalm of David.

1 ¶ [a]Rescue me, O LORD, from evil
men;
Preserve me from [b]violent men
2 Who [a]devise evil things in *their*
hearts;
They [b]continually stir up wars.
3 They [a]sharpen their tongues as
a serpent;
[b]Poison of a viper is under their
lips. [1]Selah.

4 ¶ [a]Keep me, O LORD, from the
hands of the wicked;
[b]Preserve me from violent men
Who have [1]purposed to [2c]trip
up my feet.
5 The proud have [a]hidden a trap
for me, and cords;
They have spread a [b]net by the
[1]wayside;
They have set [c]snares for me.
Selah.

6 ¶ I [a]said to the LORD, "You are
my God;
[b]Give ear, O LORD, to the
[c]voice of my supplications.
7 "O [1]GOD the Lord, [a]the strength
of my salvation,
You have [b]covered my head in
the day of [2]battle.
8 "Do not grant, O LORD, the
[a]desires of the wicked;
Do not promote [b]his *evil* device,
that they *not* be exalted.
Selah.

9 ¶ "As for the head of those who
surround me,
May the [a]mischief of their lips
cover them.
10 "May [a]burning coals fall upon
them;
May they be [b]cast into the fire,
Into [1]deep pits from which they
[c]cannot rise.
11 "May a [1]slanderer not be
established in the earth;
[a]May evil hunt the violent man
[2]speedily."

12 ¶ I know that the LORD will
[a]maintain the cause of the
afflicted
And [b]justice for the poor.
13 Surely the [a]righteous will give
thanks to Your name;
The [b]upright will dwell in Your
presence.

Psalm 141

An Evening Prayer for Sanctification and Protection.

A Psalm of David.

1 ¶ O LORD, I call upon You;
[a]hasten to me!
[b]Give ear to my voice when I
call to You!
2 May my prayer be [1]counted as
[a]incense before You;
The [b]lifting up of my hands as
the [c]evening offering.
3 Set a [a]guard, O LORD, [1]over my
mouth;
Keep watch over the [b]door of
my lips.
4 [a]Do not incline my heart to any
evil thing,
To practice deeds [1]of
wickedness
With men who [b]do iniquity;
And [c]do not let me eat of their
delicacies.

5 ¶ Let the [a]righteous smite me
[1]in kindness and
reprove me;
It is [b]oil upon the head;
Do not let my head refuse
it,
[2]For still my prayer [c]is [3]against
their wicked deeds.

18 [a]Ps 40:5 [b]Ps 3:5
19 [a]Is 11:4 [b]Ps 6:8 [c]Ps 5:6
20 [1]Or *of* [2]Some mss read *lift themselves up* against You [a]Jude 15 [b]Ex 20:7; Deut 5:11
21 [a]2 Chr 19:2; Ps 26:5 [b]Ps 119:158
23 [a]Job 31:6; Ps 26:2 [b]Ps 7:9; Prov 17:3; Jer 11:20; 1 Thess 2:4
24 [1]Lit *way of pain* [a]Ps 146:9; Prov 15:9; Jer 25:5 [b]Ps 5:8 [c]Ps 16:11
140:1 [a]Ps 17:13 [b]Ps 18:48
2 [a]Ps 7:14; Prov 6:14; Is 59:4; Hos 7:15 [b]Ps 56:6
3 [1]*Selah* may mean: *Pause, Crescendo* or *Musical interlude* [a]Ps 57:4 [b]Ps 58:4; Rom 3:13; James 3:8
4 [1]Or *devised* [2]Lit *push violently* [a]Ps 71:4 [b]Ps 140:1 [c]Ps 36:11
5 [1]Lit *track* [a]Job 18:9; Ps 35:7 [b]Ps 31:4; Lam 1:13 [c]Ps 141:9; Is 8:14; Amos 3:5
6 [a]Ps 16:2 [b]Ps 143:1 [c]Ps 116:1
7 [1]Heb *YHWH,* usually rendered LORD [2]Lit *weapons* [a]Ps 28:8 [b]Ps 144:10
8 [a]Ps 112:10 [b]Esth 9:25; Ps 10:2
9 [a]Ps 7:16; Prov 18:7
10 [1]Lit *watery* [a]Ps 11:6 [b]Ps 21:9; Matt 3:10 [c]Ps 36:12
11 [1]Lit *man of tongue* [2]Lit *thrust upon thrust* [a]Ps 34:21
12 [a]1 Kin 8:45; Ps 9:4 [b]Ps 12:5
13 [a]Ps 97:12 [b]Ps 11:7
141:1 [a]Ps 22:19 [b]Ps 5:1
2 [1]Lit *fixed* [a]Ex 30:8; Luke 1:10; Rev 5:8 [b]1 Tim 2:8 [c]Ex 29:39; 1 Kin 18:29; Dan 9:21
3 [1]Lit *to* [a]Ps 34:13; Prov 13:3 [b]Mic 7:5
4 [1]Lit *in* [a]Ps 119:36 [b]Is 32:6; Hos 6:8; Mal 3:15 [c]Prov 23:6
5 [1]Or *lovingly* [2]Lit *And my prayer* [3]Or *in spite of their calamities* [a]Prov 9:8; Eccl 7:5; Gal 6:1 [b]Ps 23:5 [c]Ps 35:14

6 Their judges are [a]thrown down
by the sides of the rock,
And they hear my words, for
they are pleasant.
7 As when one [a]plows and breaks
open the earth,
Our [b]bones have been scattered
at the [c]mouth of [1]Sheol.

8 ¶ For my [a]eyes are toward You,
O [1]GOD, the Lord;
In You I [b]take refuge; [c]do not
[2]leave me defenseless.
9 Keep me from the [1a]jaws of the
trap which they have set
for me,
And from the [b]snares of those
who do iniquity.
10 Let the wicked [a]fall into their
own nets,
While I pass by [1b]safely.

Psalm 142

Prayer for Help in Trouble.

+Maskil of David, when he was
•in the cave. A Prayer.

1 ¶ I [a]cry aloud with my voice to
the LORD;
I [b]make supplication with my
voice to the LORD.
2 I [a]pour out my complaint before
Him;
I declare my [b]trouble before
Him.
3 When [a]my spirit [1]was
overwhelmed within me,
You knew my path.
In the way where I walk
They have [b]hidden a trap
for me.
4 Look to the right and see;
For there is [a]no one who
regards me;
[1]There is no [b]escape for me;
[c]No one cares for my soul.

5 ¶ I cried out to You, O LORD;
I said, "You are [a]my refuge,
My [b]portion in the [c]land of the
living.
6 "[a]Give heed to my cry,
For I am [b]brought very low;
Deliver me from my persecutors,
For they are too [c]strong for me.
7 "[a]Bring my soul out of prison,
So that I may give thanks to
Your name;
The righteous will surround
me,
For You will [b]deal bountifully
with me."

Psalm 143

Prayer for Deliverance and Guidance.

A Psalm of David.

1 ¶ Hear my prayer, O LORD,
[a]Give ear to my supplications!
Answer me in Your
[b]faithfulness, in Your
[c]righteousness!
2 And [a]do not enter into judgment
with Your servant,
For in Your sight [b]no man living
is righteous.
3 For the enemy has persecuted
my soul;
He has crushed my life [a]to the
ground;
He [b]has made me dwell in dark
places, like those who have
long been dead.
4 Therefore [a]my spirit [1]is
overwhelmed within me;
My heart is [2b]appalled
within me.

5 ¶ I [a]remember the days of old;
I [b]meditate on all Your doings;
I [c]muse on the work of Your
hands.
6 I [a]stretch out my hands to You;
My [b]soul *longs* for You, as a
[1]parched land. [2]Selah.

7 ¶ [a]Answer me quickly, O LORD,
my [b]spirit fails;
[c]Do not hide Your face
from me,
Or I will become like [d]those
who go down to the pit.
8 Let me hear Your
[a]lovingkindness [b]in the
morning;
For I trust [c]in You;
Teach me the [d]way in which I
should walk;
For to You I [e]lift up my soul.
9 [a]Deliver me, O LORD, from my
enemies;
[1]I take refuge in You.

10 ¶ [a]Teach me to do Your will,
For You are my God;
Let [b]Your good Spirit [c]lead me
on level [1]ground.
11 [a]For the sake of Your name,
O LORD, [b]revive me.
[c]In Your righteousness bring my
soul out of trouble.
12 And in Your lovingkindness,
[1a]cut off my enemies
And [b]destroy all those who
afflict my soul,
For [c]I am Your servant.

6 [a]2 Chr 25:12
7 [1]I.e. the nether world [a]Ps 129:3 [b]Ps 53:5 [c]Num 16:32,33; Ps 88:3-5
8 [1]Heb *YHWH,* usually rendered LORD [2]Lit *pour out my soul* [a]Ps 25:15; 123:2 [b]Ps 2:12; 11:1 [c]Ps 27:9
9 [1]Lit *hands of the trap* [a]Ps 38:12; 64:5; 91:3; 119:110 [b]Ps 140:5
10 [1]Lit *altogether* [a]Ps 7:15; 35:8; 57:6 [b]Ps 124:7
142:1 +Possibly *Contemplative,* or *Didactic,* or *Skillful Psalm* •1 Sam 22:1; 24:3 [a]Ps 77:1 [b]Ps 30:8
2 [a]Ps 102: title [b]Ps 77:2
3 [1]Lit *fainted* [a]Ps 77:3; 143:4 [b]Ps 140:5
4 [1]Lit *Escape has perished from me* [a]Ps 31:11; 88:8,18 [b]Job 11:20; Jer 25:35 [c]Jer 30:17
5 [a]Ps 91:2,9 [b]Ps 16:5; 73:26 [c]Ps 27:13
6 [a]Ps 17:1 [b]Ps 79:8; 116:6 [c]Ps 18:17
7 [a]Ps 143:11; 146:7 [b]Ps 13:6
143:1 [a]Ps 140:6 [b]Ps 89:1,2 [c]Ps 71:2
2 [a]Job 14:3; 22:4 [b]1 Kin 8:46; Job 4:17; 9:2; 25:4; Ps 130:3; Eccl 7:20; Rom 3:10,20; Gal 2:16
3 [a]Ps 44:25 [b]Ps 88:6; Lam 3:6
4 [1]Lit *faints* [2]Or *desolate* [a]Ps 77:3; 142:3 [b]Lam 3:11
5 [a]Ps 77:5,10,11 [b]Ps 77:12 [c]Ps 105:2
6 [1]Lit *weary* [2]*Selah* may mean: *Pause, Crescendo* or *Musical interlude* [a]Job 11:13; Ps 88:9 [b]Ps 42:2; 63:1
7 [a]Ps 69:17 [b]Ps 73:26; 84:2; Jer 8:18; Lam 1:22 [c]Ps 27:9; 69:17; 102:2 [d]Ps 28:1; 88:4
8 [a]Ps 90:14 [b]Ps 46:5 [c]Ps 25:2 [d]Ps 27:11; 32:8; 86:11 [e]Ps 25:1; 86:4
9 [1]Lit *To You have I hidden* [a]Ps 31:15; 59:1
10 [1]Lit *land* [a]Ps 25:4,5; 119:12 [b]Neh 9:20 [c]Ps 23:3
11 [a]Ps 25:11 [b]Ps 119:25 [c]Ps 31:1; 71:2
12 [1]Or *silence* [a]Ps 54:5 [b]Ps 52:5 [c]Ps 116:16

Psalm 144

Prayer for Rescue and Prosperity.

A Psalm of David.

1 ¶ Blessed be the LORD, [a]my rock,
Who [b]trains my hands for war,
And my fingers for battle;
2 My lovingkindness and [a]my fortress,
My [b]stronghold and my deliverer,
My [c]shield and He in whom I take refuge,
Who [d]subdues [1]my people under me.
3 O LORD, [a]what is man, that You take knowledge of him?
Or the son of man, that You think of him?
4 [a]Man is like a mere breath;
His [b]days are like a passing shadow.

5 ¶ [a]Bow Your heavens, O LORD, and [b]come down;
[c]Touch the mountains, that they may smoke.
6 Flash forth [a]lightning and scatter them;
Send out Your [b]arrows and confuse them.
7 Stretch forth Your hand [a]from on high;
Rescue me and [b]deliver me out of great waters,
Out of the hand of [c]aliens
8 Whose mouths [a]speak deceit,
And whose [b]right hand is a right hand of falsehood.

9 ¶ I will sing a [a]new song to You, O God;
Upon a [b]harp of ten strings I will sing praises to You,
10 Who [a]gives salvation to kings,
Who [b]rescues David His servant from the evil sword.
11 Rescue me and deliver me out of the hand of [a]aliens,
Whose mouth [b]speaks deceit
And whose [c]right hand is a right hand of falsehood.

12 ¶ Let our sons in their youth be as [a]grown-up plants,
And our daughters as [b]corner pillars [1]fashioned as for a palace;
13 Let our [a]garners be full, furnishing every kind of produce,
And our flocks bring forth thousands and ten thousands in our [1]fields;
14 Let our [a]cattle [1]bear
Without [2b]mishap and without [3c]loss,
Let there be no [d]outcry in our streets!
15 How blessed are the people who are so situated;
How [a]blessed are the people whose God is the LORD!

Psalm 145

The LORD Extolled for His Goodness.

A Psalm of Praise, of David.

1 ¶ I will [a]extol You, [b]my God, O King,
And I will [c]bless Your name forever and ever.
2 Every day I will bless You,
And I will [a]praise Your name forever and ever.
3 [a]Great is the LORD, and highly to be praised,
And His [b]greatness is unsearchable.
4 One [a]generation shall praise Your works to another,
And shall declare Your mighty acts.
5 On the [a]glorious [1]splendor of Your majesty
And [b]on Your wonderful works, I will meditate.
6 Men shall speak of the [1]power of Your [a]awesome acts,
And I will [b]tell of Your greatness.
7 They shall [1]eagerly utter the memory of Your [a]abundant goodness
And will [b]shout joyfully of Your righteousness.

8 ¶ The LORD is [a]gracious and merciful;
Slow to anger and great in lovingkindness.
9 The LORD is [a]good to all,
And His [b]mercies are over all His works.
10 [a]All Your works shall give thanks to You, O LORD,
And Your [b]godly ones shall bless You.
11 They shall speak of the [a]glory of Your kingdom
And talk of Your power;
12 To [a]make known to the sons of men [1]Your mighty acts
And the [b]glory of the majesty of [1]Your kingdom.
13 Your kingdom is [1]an [a]everlasting kingdom,

144:1 [a]Ps 18:2 [b]2 Sam 22:35; Ps 18:34
2 [1]Another reading is *peoples* [a]Ps 18:2; 91:2 [b]Ps 59:9 [c]Ps 3:3; 28:7; 84:9 [d]Ps 18:39
3 [a]Job 7:17; Ps 8:4; Heb 2:6
4 [a]Ps 39:11 [b]Job 8:9; 14:2; Ps 102:11; 109:23
5 [a]Ps 18:9 [b]Is 64:1 [c]Ps 104:32
6 [a]Ps 18:14 [b]Ps 7:13; 58:7; Hab 3:11; Zech 9:14
7 [a]Ps 18:16 [b]Ps 69:1,14 [c]Ps 18:44; 54:3
8 [a]Ps 12:2; 41:6 [b]Gen 14:22; Deut 32:40; Ps 106:26; Is 44:20
9 [a]Ps 33:3; 40:3 [b]Ps 33:2
10 [a]Ps 18:50 [b]2 Sam 18:7; Ps 140:7
11 [a]Ps 18:44; 54:3 [b]Ps 12:2; 41:6 [c]Gen 14:22; Deut 32:40; Ps 106:26; Is 44:20
12 [1]Lit *cut after the pattern of* [a]Ps 92:12-14; 128:3 [b]Song 4:4; 7:4
13 [1]Lit *outside* [a]Prov 3:9,10
14 [1]Lit *be laden* [2]Lit *bursting forth* [3]Lit *going out* [a]Prov 14:4 [b]2 Kin 25:10,11 [c]Amos 5:3 [d]Is 24:11; Jer 14:2
15 [a]Ps 33:12
145:1 [a]Ps 30:1; 66:17 [b]Ps 5:2 [c]Ps 34:1
2 [a]Ps 71:6
3 [a]Ps 48:1; 86:10; 147:5 [b]Job 5:9; 9:10; 11:7; Is 40:28; Rom 11:33
4 [a]Ps 22:30,31; Is 38:19
5 [1]Or *majesty of Your splendor* [a]Ps 145:12 [b]Ps 119:27
6 [1]Or *strength* [a]Deut 10:21; Ps 66:3; 106:22 [b]Deut 32:3
7 [1]Or *bubble over with* [a]Ps 31:19; Is 63:7 [b]Ps 51:14
8 [a]Ex 34:6; Num 14:18; Ps 86:5,15; 103:8
9 [a]Ps 100:5; 136:1; Jer 33:11; Nah 1:7; Matt 19:17; Mark 10:18 [b]Ps 145:15
10 [a]Ps 19:1; 103:22 [b]Ps 68:26
11 [a]Jer 14:21
12 [1]Lit *His* [a]Ps 105:1 [b]Ps 145:5; Is 2:10,19,21
13 [1]Lit *a kingdom of all ages* [a]Ps 10:16; 29:10; 1 Tim 1:17; 2 Pet 1:11

And Your dominion *endures*
throughout all generations.

14 ¶ The LORD [a]sustains all who
fall
And [b]raises up all who are
bowed down.
15 The eyes of all [1]look to You,
And You [a]give them their food
in due time.
16 You [a]open Your hand
And satisfy the desire of every
living thing.

17 ¶ The LORD is [a]righteous in all
His ways
And kind in all His deeds.
18 The LORD is [a]near to all who
call upon Him,
To all who call upon Him [b]in
truth.
19 He will [a]fulfill the desire of
those who fear Him;
He will also [b]hear their cry and
will save them.
20 The LORD [a]keeps all who love
Him,
But all the [b]wicked He will
destroy.
21 My [a]mouth will speak the praise
of the LORD,
And [b]all flesh will [c]bless His
holy name forever and ever.

Psalm 146

The LORD an Abundant Helper.

1 ¶ [1]Praise [2]the LORD!
[a]Praise the LORD, O my soul!
2 I will praise the LORD [a]while I
live;
I will [b]sing praises to my God
while I have my being.
3 [a]Do not trust in princes,
In [1]mortal [b]man, in whom
there is [c]no salvation.
4 His [a]spirit departs, he [b]returns
to [1]the earth;
In that very day his [c]thoughts
perish.
5 How [a]blessed is he whose help
is the God of Jacob,
Whose [b]hope is in the LORD his
God,
6 Who [a]made heaven and earth,
The [b]sea and all that is in them;
Who [c]keeps [1]faith forever;
7 Who [a]executes justice for the
oppressed;
Who [b]gives food to the hungry.
The LORD [c]sets the prisoners
free.

8 ¶ The LORD [a]opens *the eyes of*
the blind;
The LORD [b]raises up those who
are bowed down;
The LORD [c]loves the righteous;
9 The LORD [1a]protects the
[2]strangers;
He [3b]supports the fatherless and
the widow,
But He [4]thwarts [c]the way of
the wicked.
10 The LORD will [a]reign forever,
Your God, O Zion, to all
generations.
[1]Praise [2]the LORD!

Psalm 147

Praise for Jerusalem's Restoration and Prosperity.

1 ¶ [1]Praise [2]the LORD!
For [a]it is good to sing praises to
our God;
For [3]it is pleasant *and* praise is
[b]becoming.
2 The LORD [a]builds up Jerusalem;
He [b]gathers the outcasts of
Israel.
3 He heals the [a]brokenhearted
And [b]binds up their [1]wounds.
4 He [a]counts the number of the
stars;
He [1b]gives names to all of
them.
5 [a]Great is our Lord and abundant
in strength;
His [b]understanding is [1]infinite.
6 The LORD [1a]supports the
afflicted;
He brings down the wicked to
the ground.

7 ¶ [a]Sing to the LORD with
thanksgiving;
Sing praises to our God on the
lyre,
8 Who [a]covers the heavens with
clouds,
Who [b]provides rain for the
earth,
Who [c]makes grass to [1]grow on
the mountains.
9 He [a]gives to the beast its food,
And to the [b]young ravens which
cry.
10 He does not delight in the
strength of the [a]horse;
He [b]does not take pleasure in
the legs of a man.
11 The LORD [a]favors those who fear
Him,
[b]Those who wait for His
lovingkindness.

12 ¶ Praise the LORD, O Jerusalem!
Praise your God, O Zion!

---

14 [a]Ps 37:24 [b]Ps 146:8
15 [1]Lit *wait;* or *hope for* [a]Ps 104:27
16 [a]Ps 104:28
17 [a]Ps 116:5
18 [a]Deut 4:7; Ps 34:18 [b]John 4:24
19 [a]Ps 21:2 [b]Ps 10:17; Prov 15:29; 1 John 5:14
20 [a]Ps 31:23 [b]Ps 9:5
21 [a]Ps 71:8 [b]Ps 65:2 [c]Ps 145:1
146:1 [1]Or *Hallelujah!* [2]Heb YAH [a]Ps 103:1
2 [a]Ps 63:4 [b]Ps 104:33
3 [1]Lit *a son of a man* [a]Ps 118:9 [b]Ps 118:8; Is 2:22 [c]Ps 60:11
4 [1]Lit *his earth* [a]Ps 104:29 [b]Eccl 12:7 [c]Ps 33:10; 1 Cor 2:6
5 [a]Ps 144:15; Jer 17:7 [b]Ps 71:5
6 [1]Or *truth* [a]Ps 115:15; Rev 14:7 [b]Acts 14:15 [c]Ps 117:2
7 [a]Ps 103:6 [b]Ps 107:9 [c]Ps 68:6; Is 61:1
8 [a]Matt 9:30; John 9:7 [b]Ps 145:14 [c]Ps 11:7
9 [1]Or *keeps* [2]Or *sojourners* [3]Or *relieves* [4]Lit *makes crooked* [a]Ex 22:21; Lev 19:34 [b]Deut 10:18; Ps 68:5 [c]Ps 147:6
10 [1]Or *Hallelujah!* [2]Heb YAH [a]Ex 15:18; Ps 10:16
147:1 [1]Or *Hallelujah!* [2]Heb YAH [3]Or *He is gracious* [a]Ps 92:1 [b]Ps 33:1
2 [a]Ps 51:18 [b]Deut 30:3; Ps 106:47; Is 11:12; Ezek 39:28
3 [1]Lit *sorrows* [a]Ps 34:18; Is 61:1 [b]Job 5:18; Is 30:26; Ezek 34:16
4 [1]Or *calls them all by* their *names* [a]Gen 15:5 [b]Is 40:26
5 [1]Lit *innumerable* [a]Ps 48:1 [b]Is 40:28
6 [1]Or *relieves* [a]Ps 37:24
7 [a]Ps 33:2
8 [1]Lit *spring forth* [a]Job 26:8 [b]Job 5:10; Ps 104:13 [c]Job 38:27; Ps 104:14
9 [a]Ps 104:27 [b]Job 38:41; Matt 6:26
10 [a]Ps 33:17 [b]1 Sam 16:7
11 [a]Ps 149:4 [b]Ps 33:18

13 For He has strengthened the
[a]bars of your gates;
He has [b]blessed your sons
within you.
14 He [a]makes [1]peace in your
borders;
He [b]satisfies you with [c]the
[2]finest of the wheat.
15 He sends forth His [a]command to
the earth;
His [b]word runs very swiftly.
16 He gives [a]snow like wool;
He scatters the [b]frost like ashes.
17 He casts forth His [a]ice as
fragments;
Who can stand before His
[b]cold?
18 He [a]sends forth His word and
melts them;
He [b]causes His wind to blow
and the waters to flow.
19 He [a]declares His words to Jacob,
His [b]statutes and His ordinances
to Israel.
20 He [a]has not dealt thus with any
nation;
And as for His ordinances, they
have [b]not known them.
[1]Praise [2]the LORD!

Psalm 148

The Whole Creation Invoked to Praise the LORD.

1 ¶ [1]Praise [2]the LORD!
Praise the LORD [a]from the
heavens;
Praise Him [b]in the heights!
2 Praise Him, [a]all His angels;
Praise Him, [b]all His hosts!
3 Praise Him, sun and moon;
Praise Him, all stars of light!
4 Praise Him, [1a]highest heavens,
And the [b]waters that are above
the heavens!
5 Let them praise the name of the
LORD,
For [a]He commanded and they
were created.
6 He has also [a]established them
forever and ever;
He has made a [b]decree which
will not pass away.

7 ¶ Praise the LORD from the
earth,
[a]Sea monsters and all [b]deeps;
8 [a]Fire and hail, [b]snow and
[c]clouds;
[d]Stormy wind, [e]fulfilling His
word;
9 [a]Mountains and all hills;
Fruit [b]trees and all cedars;
10 [a]Beasts and all cattle;
[b]Creeping things and winged
fowl;
11 [a]Kings of the earth and all
peoples;
Princes and all judges of the
earth;
12 Both young men and virgins;
Old men and children.

13 ¶ Let them praise the name of
the LORD,
For His [a]name alone is exalted;
His [b]glory is above earth and
heaven.
14 And He has [a]lifted up a horn for
His people,
[b]Praise for all His godly ones;
Even for the sons of Israel, a
people [c]near to Him.
[1]Praise [2]the LORD!

Psalm 149

Israel Invoked to Praise the LORD.

1 ¶ [1]Praise [2]the LORD!
Sing to the LORD a [a]new song,
And His praise [b]in the
congregation of the godly
ones.
2 Let Israel be glad in [a]his Maker;
Let the sons of Zion rejoice in
their [b]King.
3 Let them praise His name with
[a]dancing;
Let them sing praises to Him
with [b]timbrel and lyre.
4 For the LORD [a]takes pleasure in
His people;
He will [b]beautify the afflicted
ones with salvation.

5 ¶ Let the [a]godly ones exult in
glory;
Let them [b]sing for joy on their
beds.
6 *Let* the [a]high praises of God *be*
in their [1]mouth,
And a [b]two-edged [c]sword in
their hand,
7 To [a]execute vengeance on the
nations
And punishment on the peoples,
8 To bind their kings [a]with chains
And their [b]nobles with fetters of
iron,
9 To [a]execute on them the
judgment written;
This is an [b]honor for all His
godly ones.
[1]Praise [2]the LORD!

13 [a]Neh 3:3 [b]Ps 37:26
14 [1]Lit *your borders peace* [2]Lit *fat* [a]Ps 29:11; Is 54:13 [b]Ps 132:15 [c]Deut 32:14; Ps 81:16
15 [a]Job 37:12; Ps 148:5 [b]Ps 104:4
16 [a]Job 37:6; Ps 148:8 [b]Job 38:29
17 [a]Job 37:10 [b]Job 37:9
18 [a]Ps 33:9 [b]Ps 107:25
19 [a]Deut 33:3 [b]Mal 4:4
20 [1]Or *Hallelujah!* [2]Heb YAH [a]Deut 4:7; Rom 3:1 [b]Ps 79:6; Jer 10:25
148:1 [1]Or *Hallelujah!* [2]Heb YAH [a]Ps 69:34 [b]Job 16:19; Ps 102:19; Matt 21:9
2 [a]Ps 103:20 [b]Ps 103:21
4 [1]Lit *heavens of heavens* [a]Deut 10:14; 1 Kin 8:27; Neh 9:6; Ps 68:33 [b]Gen 1:7
5 [a]Gen 1:1; Ps 33:6
6 [a]Ps 89:37; Jer 31:35 [b]Job 38:33
7 [a]Gen 1:21; Ps 74:13 [b]Gen 1:2; Deut 33:13; Hab 3:10
8 [a]Ps 18:12 [b]Ps 147:16 [c]Ps 135:7 [d]Ps 107:25 [e]Job 37:12; Ps 103:20
9 [a]Is 44:23 [b]Is 55:12
10 [a]Is 43:20 [b]Hos 2:18
11 [a]Ps 102:15
13 [a]Is 12:4 [b]Ps 8:1
14 [1]Or *Hallelujah!* [2]Heb YAH [a]1 Sam 2:1; Ps 75:10 [b]Deut 10:21; Ps 109:1; Jer 17:14 [c]Lev 10:3; Eph 2:17
149:1 [1]Or *Hallelujah!* [2]Heb YAH [a]Ps 33:3 [b]Ps 35:18
2 [a]Ps 95:6 [b]Judg 8:23; Ps 47:6; Zech 9:9
3 [a]2 Sam 6:14; Ps 150:4 [b]Ex 15:20; Ps 81:2
4 [a]Job 36:11; Ps 16:11 [b]Ps 132:16; Is 61:3
5 [a]Ps 132:16 [b]Job 35:10; Ps 42:8
6 [1]Lit *throat* [a]Ps 66:17 [b]Heb 4:12 [c]Neh 4:17
7 [a]Ezek 25:17; Mic 5:15
8 [a]Job 36:8 [b]Nah 3:10
9 [1]Or *Hallelujah!* [2]Heb YAH [a]Deut 7:12; Ezek 28:26 [b]Ps 112:9

Psalm 150

A Psalm of Praise.

1 ¶ [1]Praise [2]the LORD!
Praise God in His [a]sanctuary;
Praise Him in His mighty
[3b]expanse.
2 Praise Him for His [a]mighty
deeds;
Praise Him according to His
excellent [b]greatness.
3 ¶ Praise Him with [a]trumpet sound;
Praise Him with [b]harp and
lyre.
4 Praise Him with [a]timbrel and
dancing;
Praise Him with [b]stringed
instruments and [c]pipe.
5 Praise Him with loud [a]cymbals;
Praise Him with resounding
cymbals.
6 Let [a]everything that has breath
praise [1]the LORD.
[2]Praise the [1]LORD!

150:1 [1]Or *Hallelujah!* [2]Heb YAH [3]Or *firmament* [a]Ps 73:17 [b]Ps 19:1 **2** [a]Ps 145:12 [b]Deut 3:24; Ps 145:3 **3** [a]Ps 98:6 [b]Ps 33:2 **4** [a]Ps 149:3 [b]Ps 45:8; Is 38:20 [c]Gen 4:21; Job 21:12 **5** [a]2 Sam 6:5; 1 Chr 13:8; Ezra 3:10; Neh 12:27 **6** [1]Heb YAH [2]Or *Hallelujah!* [a]Ps 103:22

Proverbs

Title and Background

The Hebrew word translated "proverb" is also translated "taunt" (Isaiah 14:4), "discourse" (Numbers 23:7,18) and "parable" (Ezekiel 17:2), so its meaning is considerably broader than the English term. Most proverbs are short, compact statements that express a truth about human behavior. A common feature of the proverbs is the use of figurative language.

Author and Date of Writing

Although the book begins with a title ascribing the proverbs to Solomon, it is clear from later chapters that he was not the only author of the book (see Outline). Since Solomon has a prominent role in the book, most of Proverbs would stem from the tenth century B.C. and Israel's united kingdom.

Theme and Message

According to the prologue (1:1–7), Proverbs was written to give "prudence to the naive, to the youth knowledge and discretion" (1:4), and to make the wise wiser (1:5). Acquiring wisdom and knowing how to avoid the pitfalls of folly will lead to health and success. Although Proverbs is a practical book dealing with the art of living, it bases wisdom solidly on the fear of the Lord (1:7).

Outline

I. Prologue: Purpose and Theme (1:1–7)
II. The Superiority of the Way of Wisdom (1:8—9:18)
III. The Proverbs of Solomon (10:1—22:16)
IV. Sayings of the Wise (22:17—24:34)
V. More Proverbs of Solomon (25:1—29:27)
VI. The Words of Agur and Lemuel (30:1—31:9)
VII. Epilogue: The Excellent Wife (31:10–31)

The Usefulness of Proverbs

1 The [a]proverbs of Solomon [b]the son of David, king of Israel:
2 To know [a]wisdom and instruction,
To discern the sayings of [b]understanding,
3 To [a]receive instruction in wise behavior,
[b]Righteousness, justice and equity;
4 To give [a]prudence to the [1]naive,
To the youth [b]knowledge and discretion,
5 A wise man will hear and [a]increase in learning,
And a [b]man of understanding will acquire wise counsel,
6 To understand a proverb and a figure,
The words of the wise and their [a]riddles.
7 ¶ [a]The fear of the LORD is the beginning of knowledge;
Fools despise wisdom and instruction.

The Enticement of Sinners

8 ¶ [a]Hear, my son, your father's instruction
And [b]do not forsake your mother's teaching;
9 Indeed, they are a [a]graceful wreath to your head
And [1b]ornaments about your neck.
10 My son, if sinners [a]entice you,
[b]Do not consent.
11 If they say, "Come with us,
Let us [a]lie in wait for blood,
Let us [b]ambush the innocent without cause;
12 Let us [a]swallow them alive like Sheol,
Even whole, as those who [b]go down to the pit;
13 We will find all *kinds* of precious wealth,

1:1 [a]1 Kin 4:32; Prov 10:1; 25:1; Eccl 12:9 [b]Eccl 1:1
2 [a]Prov 15:33 [b]Prov 4:1
3 [a]Prov 2:1; 19:20 [b]Prov 2:9
4 [1]Lit *simple ones* [a]Prov 8:5, 12 [b]Prov 2:10, 11; 3:21
5 [a]Prov 9:9 [b]Prov 14:6; Eccl 9:11
6 [a]Num 12:8; Ps 49:4; 78:2; Dan 8:23
7 [a]Job 28:28; Ps 111:10; Prov 9:10; 15:33; Eccl 12:13
8 [a]Prov 4:1 [b]Prov 6:20
9 [1]Lit *necklaces* [a]Prov 4:9 [b]Gen 41:42; Dan 5:29
10 [a]Prov 16:29 [b]Gen 39:7-10; Deut 13:8; Ps 50:18; Eph 5:11
11 [a]Prov 12:6; Jer 5:26 [b]Ps 10:8; Prov 1:18
12 [a]Ps 124:3 [b]Ps 28:1

We will fill our houses with spoil;
14 Throw in your lot [1]with us,
We shall all have one purse,"
15 My son, [a]do not walk in the way with them.
[b]Keep your feet from their path,
16 For [a]their feet run to evil
And they hasten to shed blood.
17 Indeed, it is [1]useless to spread the *baited* net
In the sight of any [2]bird;
18 But they [a]lie in wait for their own blood;
They ambush their own lives.
19 So are the ways of everyone who [a]gains by violence;
It takes away the life of its possessors.

Wisdom Warns

20 ¶ [a]Wisdom shouts in the street,
She [1]lifts her voice in the square;
21 At the head of the noisy *streets* she cries out;
At the entrance of the gates in the city she utters her sayings:
22 "How long, O [1a]naive ones, will you love [2]being simple-minded?
And [b]scoffers delight themselves in scoffing
And fools [c]hate knowledge?
23 "Turn to my reproof,
Behold, I will [a]pour out my spirit on you;
I will make my words known to you.
24 "Because [a]I called and you [b]refused,
I [c]stretched out my hand and no one paid attention;
25 And you [a]neglected all my counsel
And did not [b]want my reproof;
26 I will also [a]laugh at your [b]calamity;
I will mock when your [c]dread comes,
27 When your dread comes like a storm
And your calamity comes like a [a]whirlwind,
When distress and anguish come upon you.
28 "Then they will [a]call on me, but I will not answer;
They will [b]seek me diligently but they will not find me,
29 Because they [a]hated knowledge

14 [1]Lit *in the midst of us*
15 [a]Ps 1:1; Prov 4:14 [b]Ps 119:101
16 [a]Prov 6:17, 18; Is 59:7
17 [1]Lit *in vain* [2]Lit *possessor of wing*
18 [a]Prov 11:19
19 [a]Prov 15:27
20 [1]Lit *gives* [a]Prov 8:1-3; 9:3
22 [1]Lit *simple ones* [2]Or *naivete* [a]Prov 1:4,32; 8:5; 9:4; 22:3 [b]Ps 1:1 [c]Prov 1:29; 5:12
23 [a]Is 32:15; Joel 2:28; John 7:39
24 [a]Is 65:12; 66:4; Jer 7:13 [b]Zech 7:11 [c]Is 65:2; Rom 10:21
25 [a]Ps 107:11; Luke 7:30 [b]Prov 15:10
26 [a]Ps 2:4 [b]Prov 6:15 [c]Prov 10:24
27 [a]Prov 10:25
28 [a]1 Sam 8:18; Job 27:9; 35:12; Ps 18:41; Is 1:15; Jer 11:11; 14:12; Ezek 8:18; Mic 3:4; Zech 7:13; James 4:3 [b]Prov 8:17
29 [a]Job 21:14; Prov 1:22
30 [a]Ps 81:11; Prov 1:25
31 [a]Job 4:8; Prov 5:22,23; 22:8; Is 3:11; Jer 6:19 [b]Prov 14:14
32 [1]Lit *simple ones* [a]Jer 2:19
33 [1]Lit *dwell* [a]Ps 25:12,13; Prov 3:24-26
2:1 [a]Prov 4:10 [b]Prov 3:1
2 [a]Prov 22:17
3 [1]Lit *Give*
4 [a]Prov 3:14 [b]Job 3:21; Matt 13:44
5 [a]Prov 1:7
6 [a]1 Kin 3:12; Job 32:8; James 1:5
7 [a]Ps 84:11; Prov 30:5
8 [a]1 Sam 2:9; Ps 66:9
9 [a]Prov 8:20 [b]Prov 4:18
10 [a]Prov 14:33 [b]Prov 22:18
11 [a]Prov 4:6; 6:22
12 [a]Prov 28:26

And did not choose the fear of the LORD.
30 "They [a]would not accept my counsel,
They spurned all my reproof.
31 "So they shall [a]eat of the fruit of their own way
And be [b]satiated with their own devices.
32 "For the [a]waywardness of the [1]naive will kill them,
And the complacency of fools will destroy them.
33 "But [a]he who listens to me shall [1]live securely
And will be at ease from the dread of evil."

The Pursuit of Wisdom Brings Security

2 My son, if you will [a]receive my words
And [b]treasure my commandments within you,
2 [a]Make your ear attentive to wisdom,
Incline your heart to understanding;
3 For if you cry for discernment,
[1]Lift your voice for understanding;
4 If you seek her as [a]silver
And search for her as for [b]hidden treasures;
5 Then you will discern the [a]fear of the LORD
And discover the knowledge of God.
6 For [a]the LORD gives wisdom;
From His mouth *come* knowledge and understanding.
7 He stores up sound wisdom for the upright;
He is a [a]shield to those who walk in integrity,
8 Guarding the paths of justice,
And He [a]preserves the way of His godly ones.
9 Then you will discern [a]righteousness and justice
And equity *and* every [b]good course.
10 For [a]wisdom will enter your heart
And [b]knowledge will be pleasant to your soul;
11 Discretion will [a]guard you,
Understanding will watch over you,
12 To [a]deliver you from the way of evil,

From the man who speaks
[b]perverse things;
13 From those who [a]leave the
paths of uprightness
To walk in the [b]ways of
darkness;
14 Who [a]delight in doing evil
And rejoice in the perversity of
evil;
15 Whose paths are [a]crooked,
And who are devious in their
ways;
16 To [a]deliver you from the strange
woman,
From the [1b]adulteress who
flatters with her words;
17 That leaves the [a]companion of
her youth
And forgets the [b]covenant of her
God;
18 For [a]her house [1]sinks down to
death
And her tracks *lead* to the
[2]dead;
19 None [a]who go to her return
again,
Nor do they reach the [b]paths of
life.
20 So you will [a]walk in the way of
good men
And keep to the [b]paths of the
righteous.
21 For [a]the upright will [1]live in
the land
And [b]the blameless will remain
in it;
22 But [a]the wicked will be cut off
from the land
And [b]the treacherous will be
[c]uprooted from it.

The Rewards of Wisdom

3 My son, [a]do not forget my
[1]teaching,
But let your heart [b]keep my
commandments;
2 For [a]length of days and years of
life
And peace they will add to you.
3 Do not let [a]kindness and truth
leave you;
[b]Bind them around your neck,
[c]Write them on the tablet of
your heart.
4 So you will [a]find favor and
[b]good [1]repute
In the sight of God and man.
5 [a]Trust in the LORD with all your
heart
And [b]do not lean on your own
understanding.
6 In all your ways [a]acknowledge
Him,
And He will [b]make your paths
straight.
7 [a]Do not be wise in your own
eyes;
[b]Fear the LORD and turn away
from evil.
8 It will be [a]healing to your
[1]body
And [b]refreshment to your bones.
9 [a]Honor the LORD from your
wealth
And from the [b]first of all your
produce;
10 So your [a]barns will be filled
with plenty
And your [b]vats will overflow
with new wine.
11 [a]My son, do not reject the
[1]discipline of the LORD
Or loathe His reproof,
12 For [a]whom the LORD loves He
reproves,
Even [b]as a father *corrects* the
son in whom he delights.

13 ¶ [a]How blessed is the man who
finds wisdom
And the man who gains
understanding.
14 For her [a]profit is better than the
profit of silver
And her gain better than fine
gold.
15 She is [a]more precious than
[1]jewels;
And nothing you desire compares
with her.
16 [1a]Long life is in her right hand;
In her left hand are [b]riches and
honor.
17 Her [a]ways are pleasant ways
And all her paths are [b]peace.
18 She is a [a]tree of life to those
who take hold of her,
And happy are all who hold her
fast.
19 The LORD [a]by wisdom founded
the earth,
By understanding He
[b]established the heavens.
20 By His knowledge the [a]deeps
were broken up
And the [b]skies drip with dew.
21 My son, [a]let them not [1]vanish
from your sight;
Keep sound wisdom and
discretion,
22 So they will be [a]life to your soul
And [b]adornment to your neck.
23 Then you will [a]walk in your
way securely
And your foot will not [b]stumble.

12 [b]Prov 6:12
13 [a]Prov 21:16 [b]Ps 82:5; Prov 4:19; John 3:19
14 [a]Prov 10:23; Jer 11:15
15 [a]Ps 125:5; Prov 21:8
16 [1]Lit *strange woman* [a]Prov 6:24 [b]Prov 23:27
17 [a]Mal 2:14 [b]Gen 2:24
18 [1]Lit *bows down* [2]Lit *departed spirits* [a]Prov 7:27
19 [a]Eccl 7:26 [b]Ps 16:11; Prov 5:6
20 [a]Heb 6:12 [b]Prov 4:18
21 [1]Or *dwell* [a]Ps 37:9; Prov 10:30 [b]Prov 28:10
22 [a]Ps 37:38; Prov 10:30 [b]Prov 11:3 [c]Deut 28:63; Ps 52:5
3:1 [1]Or *law* [a]Ps 119:61; Prov 4:5 [b]Ex 20:6; Deut 30:16
2 [a]Ps 91:16; Prov 3:16
3 [a]2 Sam 15:20; Prov 14:22 [b]Deut 6:8; Prov 1:9 [c]Prov 7:3; Jer 17:1; 2 Cor 3:3
4 [1]Lit *understanding* [a]1 Sam 2:26; Prov 8:35; Luke 2:52 [b]Ps 111:10
5 [a]Ps 37:3; Prov 22:19 [b]Prov 23:4; Jer 9:23
6 [a]1 Chr 28:9; Prov 16:3; Phil 4:6; James 1:5 [b]Is 45:13; Jer 10:23
7 [a]Rom 12:16 [b]Job 1:1; Prov 8:13
8 [1]Lit *navel* [a]Prov 4:22 [b]Job 21:24
9 [a]Is 43:23 [b]Ex 23:19; Deut 26:2; Mal 3:10
10 [a]Deut 28:8 [b]Joel 2:24
11 [1]Or *instruction* [a]Job 5:17; Heb 12:5
12 [a]Rev 3:19 [b]Deut 8:5; Prov 13:24
13 [a]Prov 8:32
14 [a]Job 28:15-19; Prov 8:10
15 [1]Lit *corals* [a]Job 28:18; Prov 8:11
16 [1]Lit *Length of days* [a]Prov 3:2 [b]Prov 8:18
17 [a]Matt 11:29 [b]Ps 119:165; Prov 16:7
18 [a]Gen 2:9; Prov 11:30; Rev 2:7
19 [a]Ps 104:24; Prov 8:27 [b]Prov 8:27
20 [a]Gen 7:11 [b]Deut 33:28; Job 36:28
21 [1]Lit *depart* [a]Prov 4:21
22 [a]Deut 32:47; Prov 4:22 [b]Prov 1:9 **23** [a]Prov 4:12 [b]Ps 91:12; Is 5:27

24 When you [a]lie down, you will
not be afraid;
When you lie down, your sleep
will be sweet.
25 [a]Do not be afraid of sudden fear
Nor of the [1][b]onslaught of the
wicked when it comes;
26 For the LORD will be [1]your
confidence
And will [a]keep your foot from
being caught.

27 ¶ [a]Do not withhold good from
[1]those to whom it is due,
When it is in your power to
do *it.*
28 [a]Do not say to your neighbor,
"Go, and come back,
And tomorrow I will give *it,*"
When you have it with you.
29 [a]Do not devise harm against
your neighbor,
While he lives securely beside
you.
30 [a]Do not contend with a man
without cause,
If he has done you no harm.
31 [a]Do not envy a man of violence
And do not choose any of his
ways.
32 For the [a]devious are an
abomination to the LORD;
But [1]He is [b]intimate with the
upright.
33 The [a]curse of the LORD is on the
house of the wicked,
But He [b]blesses the dwelling of
the righteous.
34 Though [a]He scoffs at the
scoffers,
Yet [b]He gives grace to the
afflicted.
35 [a]The wise will inherit honor,
But fools [1]display dishonor.

A Father's Instruction

4 Hear, *O* sons, the [a]instruction of
a father,
And [b]give attention that you
may [1]gain understanding,
2 For I give you [1]sound [a]teaching;
[b]Do not abandon my
[2]instruction.
3 When I was a son to my father,
[a]Tender and [b]the only son in
the sight of my mother,
4 Then he [a]taught me and said
to me,
"Let your heart [b]hold fast my
words;
[c]Keep my commandments and
live;
5 [a]Acquire wisdom! [b]Acquire
understanding!
Do not forget nor turn away
from the words of my
mouth.
6 "Do not forsake her, and she will
guard you;
[a]Love her, and she will watch
over you.
7 "[a]The [1]beginning of wisdom *is:*
[b]Acquire wisdom;
And with all your acquiring, get
understanding.
8 "[a]Prize her, and she will exalt
you;
She will honor you if you
embrace her.
9 "She will place [a]on your head a
garland of grace;
She will present you with a
crown of beauty."

10 ¶ Hear, my son, and [a]accept my
sayings
And the [b]years of your life will
be many.
11 I have [a]directed you in the way
of wisdom;
I have led you in upright paths.
12 When you walk, your [a]steps will
not be impeded;
And if you run, you [b]will not
stumble.
13 [a]Take hold of instruction; do not
let go.
Guard her, for she is your [b]life.
14 [a]Do not enter the path of the
wicked
And do not proceed in the way
of evil men.
15 Avoid it, do not pass by it;
Turn away from it and pass on.
16 For they [a]cannot sleep unless
they do evil;
And [1]they are robbed of sleep
unless they make *someone*
stumble.
17 For they [a]eat the bread of
wickedness
And drink the wine of violence.
18 But the [a]path of the righteous is
like the [b]light of dawn,
That [c]shines brighter and
brighter until the [d]full day.
19 The [a]way of the wicked is like
darkness;
They do not know over what
they [1][b]stumble.

20 ¶ My son, [a]give attention to my
words;
[b]Incline your ear to my sayings.
21 [a]Do not let them depart from
your sight;
[b]Keep them in the midst of your
heart.

24 [a]Job 11:19; Ps 3:5; Prov 1:33; 6:22
25 [1]Lit *storm* [a]Ps 91:5; 1 Pet 3:14 [b]Job 5:21
26 [1]Or *at your side* [a]1 Sam 2:9
27 [1]Lit *its owners* [a]Rom 13:7; Gal 6:10
28 [a]Lev 19:13; Deut 24:15
29 [a]Prov 6:14; 14:22
30 [a]Prov 26:17; Rom 12:18
31 [a]Ps 37:1; Prov 24:1
32 [1]Lit *His private counsel is* [a]Prov 11:20 [b]Job 29:4; Ps 25:14
33 [a]Lev 26:14, 16; Deut 11:28; Zech 5:3,4; Mal 2:2 [b]Job 8:6; Ps 1:3
34 [a]James 4:6 [b]1 Pet 5:5
35 [1]Lit *raise high* [a]Dan 12:3
4:1 [1]Lit *know* [a]Ps 34:11; Prov 1:8 [b]Prov 1:2; 2:2
2 [1]Lit *good* [2]Or *law* [a]Deut 32:2; Job 11:4 [b]Ps 89:30; 119:87; Prov 3:1
3 [a]1 Chr 22:5; 29:1 [b]Zech 12:10
4 [a]Eph 6:4 [b]Ps 119:168 [c]Prov 7:2
5 [a]Prov 4:7 [b]Prov 16:16
6 [a]2 Thess 2:10
7 [1]Or *the primary thing is wisdom* [a]Prov 8:23 [b]Prov 23:23
8 [a]1 Sam 2:30
9 [a]Prov 1:9
10 [a]Prov 2:1 [b]Prov 3:2
11 [a]1 Sam 12:23
12 [a]Job 18:7; Ps 18:36 [b]Ps 91:11; Prov 3:23
13 [a]Prov 3:18 [b]Prov 3:22; John 6:63
14 [a]Ps 1:1; Prov 1:15
16 [1]Lit *their sleep is robbed* [a]Ps 36:4; Mic 2:1
17 [a]Prov 13:2
18 [a]Is 26:7; Matt 5:14; Phil 2:15 [b]2 Sam 23:4 [c]Dan 12:3 [d]Job 11:17
19 [1]Or *may stumble* [a]Job 18:5,6; Prov 2:13; Is 59:9,10; Jer 23:12; John 12:35 [b]John 11:10
20 [a]Prov 5:1 [b]Prov 2:2
21 [a]Prov 3:21 [b]Prov 7:1,2

22 For they are [a]life to those who
find them
And [b]health to all [1]their body.
23 Watch over your heart with all
diligence,
For [a]from it *flow* the springs of
life.
24 Put away from you a [a]deceitful
mouth
And [b]put devious [1]speech far
from you.
25 Let your eyes look directly ahead
And let your [1]gaze be fixed
straight in front of you.
26 [a]Watch the path of your feet
And all your [b]ways will be
established.
27 [a]Do not turn to the right nor to
the left;
[b]Turn your foot from evil.

Pitfalls of Immorality

5 My son, [a]give attention to my
wisdom,
[b]Incline your ear to my
understanding;
2 That you may [a]observe
discretion
And your [b]lips may reserve
knowledge.
3 For the lips of an [1a]adulteress
[b]drip honey
And [c]smoother than oil is her
[2]speech;
4 But in the end she is [a]bitter as
wormwood,
[b]Sharp as a two-edged sword.
5 Her feet [a]go down to death,
Her steps take hold of Sheol.
6 [1]She does not ponder the [a]path
of life;
Her ways are [b]unstable, she
[c]does not know *it.*

7 ¶ [a]Now then, *my* sons, listen
to me
And [b]do not depart from the
words of my mouth.
8 [a]Keep your way far from her
And do not go near the [b]door of
her house,
9 Or you will give your vigor to
others
And your years to the cruel one;
10 And strangers will be filled with
your strength
And your hard-earned goods *will
go* to the house of an alien;
11 And you groan at your [1]final
end,
When your flesh and your body
are consumed;
12 And you say, "How I have
[a]hated instruction!
And my heart [b]spurned reproof!
13 "I have not listened to the voice
of my [a]teachers,
Nor inclined my ear to my
instructors!
14 "I was almost in utter ruin
In the midst of the assembly and
congregation."

15 ¶ Drink water from your own
cistern
And [1]fresh water from your own
well.
16 Should your [a]springs be
dispersed abroad,
Streams of water in the streets?
17 Let them be yours alone
And not for strangers with you.
18 Let your [a]fountain be blessed,
And [b]rejoice in the [c]wife of
your youth.
19 *As* a loving [a]hind and a graceful
doe,
Let her breasts satisfy you at all
times;
Be [1]exhilarated always with her
love.
20 For why should you, my son, be
exhilarated with an
[1a]adulteress
And embrace the bosom of a
[b]foreigner?
21 For the [a]ways of a man are
before the eyes of the LORD,
And He [b]watches all his paths.
22 His [a]own iniquities will capture
the wicked,
And he will be held with the
cords of his sin.
23 He will [a]die for lack of
instruction,
And in the greatness of his folly
he will go astray.

Parental Counsel

6 My son, if you have become
[a]surety for your neighbor,
Have [1]given a pledge for a
stranger,
2 *If* you have been snared with the
words of your mouth,
Have been caught with the
words of your mouth,
3 Do this then, my son, and
deliver yourself;
Since you have come into the
[1]hand of your neighbor,
Go, humble yourself, and
importune your neighbor.
4 Give no [a]sleep to your eyes,
Nor slumber to your eyelids;
5 Deliver yourself like a gazelle
from *the hunter's* hand

---

22 [1]Lit *his* [a]Prov 3:22 [b]Prov 3:8; 12:18
23 [a]Matt 12:34; 15:18,19; Mark 7:21; Luke 6:45
24 [1]Or *lips* [a]Prov 6:12; 10:32 [b]Prov 19:1
25 [1]Or *eyelids*
26 [a]Prov 5:21; Heb 12:13 [b]Ps 119:5
27 [a]Deut 5:32; 28:14 [b]Prov 1:15; Is 1:16
5:1 [a]Prov 4:20 [b]Prov 22:17
2 [a]Prov 3:21 [b]Mal 2:7
3 [1]Lit *strange woman* [2]Lit *palate* [a]Prov 2:16; 5:20; 7:5; 22:14 [b]Song 4:11 [c]Ps 55:21
4 [a]Eccl 7:26 [b]Ps 57:4; Heb 4:12
5 [a]Prov 7:27
6 [1]Lit *That she not watch* [a]Prov 4:26; 5:21 [b]2 Pet 2:14 [c]Prov 30:20
7 [a]Prov 7:24 [b]Ps 119:102
8 [a]Prov 7:25 [b]Prov 9:14
11 [1]Or *latter*
12 [a]Prov 1:7,22, 29 [b]Prov 1:25; 12:1
13 [a]Prov 1:8
15 [1]Lit *flowing*
16 [a]Prov 5:18; 9:17; Song 4:12, 15
18 [a]Prov 9:17; Song 4:12,15 [b]Eccl 9:9 [c]Mal 2:14
19 [1]Lit *intoxicated* [a]Song 2:9,17; 4:5; 7:3
20 [1]Lit *strange woman* [a]Prov 5:3 [b]Prov 2:16; 6:24; 7:5; 23:27
21 [a]Job 14:16; 31:4; 34:21; Ps 119:168; Prov 15:3; Jer 16:17; 32:19; Hos 7:2; Heb 4:13 [b]Prov 4:26
22 [a]Num 32:23; Ps 7:15; 9:15; 40:12; Prov 1:31,32
23 [a]Job 4:21; 36:12
6:1 [1]Lit *clapped your palms* [a]Prov 11:15; 17:18; 20:16; 22:26; 27:13
3 [1]Lit *palm*
4 [a]Ps 132:4

And like a [a]bird from the hand
of the fowler.
6 ¶ Go to the [a]ant, O [b]sluggard,
Observe her ways and be wise,
7 Which, having [a]no chief,
Officer or ruler,
8 Prepares her food [a]in the
summer
And gathers her provision in the
harvest.
9 How long will you lie down,
O sluggard?
When will you arise from your
sleep?
10 "[a]A little sleep, a little slumber,
A little folding of the hands to
[1]rest"—
11 [a]Your poverty will come in like
a [1]vagabond
And your need like [2]an
armed man.
12 ¶ A [a]worthless person, a wicked
man,
Is the one who walks with a
[b]perverse mouth,
13 Who [a]winks with his eyes, who
[1]signals with his feet,
Who [2]points with his fingers;
14 Who *with* [a]perversity in his
heart continually [b]devises
evil,
Who [1c]spreads strife.
15 Therefore [a]his calamity will
come suddenly;
[b]Instantly he will be broken and
there will be [c]no healing.
16 ¶ There are six things which the
LORD hates,
Yes, seven which are an
abomination [1]to Him:
17 [a]Haughty eyes, a [b]lying tongue,
And hands that [c]shed innocent
blood,
18 A heart that devises [a]wicked
plans,
[b]Feet that run rapidly to evil,
19 A [a]false witness *who* utters lies,
And one who [1b]spreads strife
among brothers.
20 ¶ [a]My son, observe the
commandment of your father
And do not forsake the
[1]teaching of your mother;
21 [a]Bind them continually on your
heart;
Tie them around your neck.
22 When you [a]walk about, [1]they
will guide you;
When you sleep, [1]they will
watch over you;
And when you awake, [1]they will
talk to you.
23 For [a]the commandment is a
lamp and the [1]teaching is
light;
And reproofs for discipline are
the way of life
24 To [a]keep you from the evil
woman,
From the smooth tongue of the
[1]adulteress.
25 [a]Do not desire her beauty in
your heart,
Nor let her capture you with her
[b]eyelids.
26 For [a]on account of a harlot *one
is reduced* to a loaf of bread,
And [1]an adulteress [b]hunts for
the precious life.
27 Can a man [1]take fire in his
bosom
And his clothes not be burned?
28 Or can a man walk on hot coals
And his feet not be scorched?
29 So is the one who [a]goes in to
his neighbor's wife;
Whoever touches her [b]will not
[1]go unpunished.
30 [1]Men do not despise a thief if
he steals
To [a]satisfy [2]himself when he is
hungry;
31 But when he is found, he must
[a]repay sevenfold;
He must give all the [1]substance
of his house.
32 The one who commits adultery
with a woman is [a]lacking
[1]sense;
He who would [b]destroy
[2]himself does it.
33 Wounds and disgrace he will
find,
And his reproach will not be
blotted out.
34 For [a]jealousy [1]enrages a man,
And he will not spare in the
[b]day of vengeance.
35 He will not [1]accept any ransom,
Nor will he be [2]satisfied though
you give many [3]gifts.

The Wiles of the Harlot

7 My son, [a]keep my words
And treasure my commandments
within you.
2 [a]Keep my commandments and
live,
And my [1]teaching [b]as the
[2]apple of your eye.
3 [a]Bind them on your fingers;
[b]Write them on the tablet of
your heart.
4 Say to wisdom, "You are my
sister,"

5 [a]Ps 91:3
6 [a]Prov 30:24 [b]Prov 6:9
7 [a]Prov 30:27
8 [a]Prov 10:5
10 [1]Lit *lie down* [a]Prov 24:33
11 [1]Lit *one who walks* [2]Lit *a man with a shield* [a]Prov 24:34
12 [a]Prov 16:27 [b]Prov 4:24
13 [1]Lit *scrapes* [2]Lit *instructs with* [a]Job 15:12; Ps 35:19; Prov 10:10
14 [1]Lit *sends out* [a]Prov 17:20 [b]Prov 3:29; Mic 2:1 [c]Prov 6:19
15 [a]Prov 24:22 [b]Is 30:13; Jer 19:11 [c]2 Chr 36:16
16 [1]Lit *of His soul*
17 [a]Ps 18:27; Prov 21:4 [b]Ps 31:18; Prov 12:22 [c]Deut 19:10; Prov 28:17; Is 1:15
18 [a]Gen 6:5; Prov 24:2 [b]Prov 1:16; Is 59:7; Rom 3:15
19 [1]Lit *sends out* [a]Ps 27:12; Prov 12:17 [b]Prov 6:14
20 [1]Or *law* [a]Eph 6:1
21 [a]Prov 3:3
22 [1]Lit *she* [a]Prov 3:23
23 [1]Or *law* [a]Ps 19:8
24 [1]Lit *foreign woman* [a]Prov 5:3
25 [a]Matt 5:28 [b]2 Kin 9:30; Jer 4:30; Ezek 23:40
26 [1]Lit *a man's wife* [a]Prov 5:9 [b]Prov 7:23; Ezek 13:18
27 [1]Lit *snatch up*
29 [1]Lit *be innocent* [a]Ezek 18:6 [b]Prov 16:5
30 [1]Lit *They do not*; or *Do not men...?* [2]Lit *his soul* [a]Job 38:39
31 [1]Or *wealth* [a]Ex 22:1-4
32 [1]Lit *heart* [2]Lit *his soul* [a]Prov 7:7 [b]Prov 7:22
34 [1]Lit *is the rage of* [a]Prov 27:4; Song 8:6 [b]Prov 11:4
35 [1]Lit *lift up the face of any* [2]Lit *willing* [3]Or *bribes*
7:1 [a]Prov 2:1
2 [1]Or *law* [2]Lit *pupil* [a]Prov 4:4 [b]Deut 32:10; Ps 17:8; Zech 2:8
3 [a]Deut 6:8; Prov 6:21 [b]Prov 3:3

And call understanding *your* intimate friend;
5 That they may keep you from an [1]adulteress,
From the foreigner who [2]flatters with her words.

6 ¶ For [a]at the window of my house
I looked out [b]through my lattice,
7 And I saw among the [1a]naive,
And discerned among the [2]youths
A young man [b]lacking [3]sense,
8 Passing through the street near [a]her corner;
And he [1]takes the way to [b]her house,
9 In the [a]twilight, in the [1]evening,
In the [2]middle of the night and *in* the darkness.
10 And behold, a woman *comes* to meet him,
[a]Dressed as a harlot and cunning of heart.
11 She is [a]boisterous and rebellious,
Her [b]feet do not remain at home;
12 *She is* now in the streets, now [a]in the squares,
And [b]lurks by every corner.
13 So she seizes him and kisses him
[1]And with a [a]brazen face she says to him:
14 "[1]I was due to offer [a]peace offerings;
Today I have [b]paid my vows.
15 "Therefore I have come out to meet you,
To seek your presence earnestly, and I have found you.
16 "I have spread my couch with [a]coverings,
With colored [b]linens of Egypt.
17 "I have sprinkled my bed
With [a]myrrh, aloes and [b]cinnamon.
18 "Come, let us drink our fill of love until morning;
Let us delight ourselves with caresses.
19 "For [1]my husband is not at home,
He has gone on a long journey;
20 He has taken a [a]bag of money [1]with him,
At the full moon he will come home."
21 With her many persuasions she entices him;
With her [1a]flattering lips she seduces him.
22 Suddenly he follows her
As an ox goes to the slaughter,
Or as [1]*one in* fetters to the discipline of a fool,
23 Until an arrow pierces through his liver;
As a [a]bird hastens to the snare,
So he does not know that it *will cost him* his life.

24 ¶ Now therefore, *my* sons, [a]listen to me,
And pay attention to the words of my mouth.
25 Do not let your heart [a]turn aside to her ways,
Do not stray into her paths.
26 For many are the [1]victims she has cast down,
And [a]numerous are all her slain.
27 Her [a]house is the way to Sheol,
Descending to the chambers of death.

The Commendation of Wisdom

8 Does not [a]wisdom call,
And understanding [1]lift up her voice?
2 On top of [a]the heights beside the way,
Where the paths meet, she takes her stand;
3 Beside the [a]gates, at the opening to the city,
At the entrance of the doors, she cries out:
4 "To you, O men, I call,
And my voice is to the sons of men.
5 "O [1a]naive ones, understand prudence;
And, O [b]fools, understand [2]wisdom.
6 "Listen, for I will speak [a]noble things;
And the opening of my lips *will reveal* [b]right things.
7 "For my [a]mouth will utter truth;
And wickedness is an abomination to my lips.
8 "All the utterances of my mouth are in righteousness;
There is nothing [a]crooked or perverted in them.
9 "They are all [a]straightforward to him who understands,
And right to those who [b]find knowledge.
10 "Take my [a]instruction and not silver,
And knowledge rather than choicest gold.
11 "For wisdom is [a]better than [1]jewels;

5 [1]Lit *strange woman* [2]Lit *is smooth*
6 [a]Judg 5:28 [b]Song 2:9
7 [1]Lit *simple ones* [2]Lit *sons* [3]Lit *heart* [a]Prov 1:22 [b]Prov 6:32; 9:4
8 [1]Lit *steps* [a]Prov 7:12 [b]Prov 7:27
9 [1]Lit *evening of the day* [2]Lit *pupil* (of the eye) [a]Job 24:15
10 [a]Gen 38:14, 15; 1 Tim 2:9
11 [a]Prov 9:13 [b]1 Tim 5:13; Titus 2:5
12 [a]Prov 9:14 [b]Prov 23:28
13 [1]Lit *She makes bold her face and says* [a]Prov 21:29
14 [1]Lit *Sacrifices of peace offerings are with me* [a]Lev 7:11 [b]Lev 7:16
16 [a]Prov 31:22 [b]Is 19:9; Ezek 27:7
17 [a]Ps 45:8 [b]Ex 30:23
19 [1]Lit *the man*
20 [1]Lit *in his hand* [a]Gen 42:35
21 [1]Lit *smooth* [a]Prov 5:3; 6:24
22 [1]Or *as a stag goes into a trap;* so some ancient versions
23 [a]Eccl 9:12
24 [a]Prov 5:7
25 [a]Prov 5:8
26 [1]Lit *mortally wounded* [a]Prov 9:18
27 [a]Prov 2:18; 5:5; 9:18; 1 Cor 6:9,10; Rev 22:15
8:1 [1]Lit *give* [a]Prov 1:20,21; 8:1-3; 9:3; 1 Cor 1:24
2 [a]Prov 9:3,14
3 [a]Job 29:7
5 [1]Lit *simple* [2]Lit *heart* [a]Prov 1:4 [b]Prov 1:22, 32; 3:35
6 [a]Prov 22:20 [b]Prov 23:16
7 [a]Ps 37:30; John 8:14; Rom 15:8
8 [a]Deut 32:5; Prov 2:15; Phil 2:15
9 [a]Prov 14:6 [b]Prov 3:13
10 [a]Prov 3:14, 15; 8:19
11 [1]Lit *corals* [a]Job 28:15,18; Ps 19:10

And [b]all desirable things cannot
compare with her.

12 ¶ "I, wisdom, [a]dwell with
prudence,
And I find [b]knowledge *and*
discretion.
13 "The [a]fear of the LORD is to hate
evil;
[b]Pride and arrogance and [c]the
evil way
And the [d]perverted mouth, I
hate.
14 "[a]Counsel is mine and [b]sound
wisdom;
I am understanding, [c]power is
mine.
15 "By me [a]kings reign,
And rulers decree justice.
16 "By me princes rule, and nobles,
All who judge rightly.
17 "I [a]love those who love me;
And [b]those who diligently seek
me will find me.
18 "[a]Riches and honor are with me,
Enduring [b]wealth and
righteousness.
19 "My fruit is [a]better than gold,
even pure gold,
And my yield *better* than
[b]choicest silver.
20 "I walk in the way of
righteousness,
In the midst of the paths of
justice,
21 To endow those who love me
with wealth,
That I may [a]fill their treasuries.

22 ¶ "The LORD possessed me [a]at
the beginning of His way,
Before His works [1]of old.
23 "From everlasting I was
[1a]established,
From the beginning, [b]from the
earliest times of the earth.
24 "When there were no [a]depths I
was [1]brought forth,
When there were no springs
abounding with water.
25 "[a]Before the mountains were
settled,
Before the hills I was [1]brought
forth;
26 While He had not yet made the
earth and the [1]fields,
Nor the first dust of the world.
27 "When He [a]established the
heavens, I was there,
When [b]He inscribed a circle on
the face of the deep,
28 When He made firm the skies
above,
When the springs of the deep
became [1]fixed,
29 When [a]He set for the sea its
boundary
So that the water would not
transgress His [1]command,
When He marked out [b]the
foundations of the earth;
30 Then [a]I was beside Him, *as* a
master workman;
And I was daily *His* delight,
[1]Rejoicing always before Him,
31 [1]Rejoicing in the world, His
earth,
And *having* [a]my delight in the
sons of men.

32 ¶ "Now therefore, *O* sons,
[a]listen to me,
For [b]blessed are they who keep
my ways.
33 "[a]Heed instruction and be wise,
And do not neglect *it.*
34 "[a]Blessed is the man who listens
to me,
Watching daily at my gates,
Waiting at my doorposts.
35 "For [a]he who finds me finds life
And [b]obtains favor from the
LORD.
36 "But he who [1]sins against me
[a]injures himself;
All those who [b]hate me [c]love
death."

Wisdom's Invitation

9 Wisdom has [a]built her house,
She has hewn out her seven
pillars;
2 She has [1a]prepared her food,
she has [b]mixed her wine;
She has also [c]set her table;
3 She has [a]sent out her maidens,
she [b]calls
From the [c]tops of the heights of
the city:
4 "[a]Whoever is [1]naive, let him
turn in here!"
To him who [b]lacks
[2]understanding she says,
5 "Come, [a]eat of my food
And drink of the wine I have
mixed.
6 "[1]Forsake *your* folly and [a]live,
And [b]proceed in the way of
understanding."

7 ¶ He who [a]corrects a scoffer
gets dishonor for himself,
And he who reproves a wicked
man *gets* [1]insults for
himself.
8 [a]Do not reprove a scoffer, or he
will hate you,
[b]Reprove a wise man and he
will love you.

11 [b]Prov 3:15
12 [a]Prov 8:5 [b]Prov 1:4
13 [a]Prov 3:7 [b]1 Sam 2:3; Prov 16:18; Is 13:11 [c]Prov 15:9 [d]Prov 6:12
14 [a]Prov 1:25; Is 28:29; Jer 32:19 [b]Prov 2:7 [c]Eccl 7:19
15 [a]2 Chr 1:10; Prov 29:4; Dan 2:21; Matt 28:18; Rom 13:1
17 [a]1 Sam 2:30; Prov 4:6; John 14:21 [b]Prov 2:4; John 7:37; James 1:5
18 [a]Prov 3:16 [b]Ps 112:3; Matt 6:33
19 [a]Job 28:15; Prov 3:14 [b]Prov 10:20
21 [a]Prov 24:4
22 [1]Lit *from then* [a]Job 28:26-28; Ps 104:24; Prov 3:19
23 [1]Or *consecrated* [a]John 1:1-3 [b]John 17:5
24 [1]Or *born* [a]Gen 1:2; Ex 15:5; Job 38:16; Prov 3:20
25 [1]Or *born* [a]Job 15:7; Ps 90:2
26 [1]Lit *outside places*
27 [a]Prov 3:19 [b]Job 26:10
28 [1]Lit *strong*
29 [1]Lit *mouth* [a]Job 38:10; Ps 104:9 [b]Job 38:6; Ps 104:5
30 [1]Or *Playing* [a]John 1:2
31 [1]Or *Playing* [a]Ps 16:3; John 13:1
32 [a]Prov 5:7 [b]Ps 119:1; Prov 29:18; Luke 11:28
33 [a]Prov 4:1
34 [a]Prov 3:13
35 [a]Prov 4:22; John 17:3 [b]Prov 3:4
36 [1]Or *misses me* [a]Prov 1:31 [b]Prov 5:12 [c]Prov 21:6
9:1 [a]1 Cor 3:9; Eph 2:20-22; 1 Pet 2:5
2 [1]Lit *slaughtered her slaughter* [a]Matt 22:4 [b]Song 8:2 [c]Luke 14:16
3 [a]Ps 68:11; Matt 22:3 [b]Prov 8:1 [c]Prov 9:14
4 [1]Lit *simple* [2]Lit *heart* [a]Prov 8:5 [b]Prov 6:32
5 [a]Song 5:1; Is 55:1; John 6:27
6 [1]Or *Forsake the simple ones* [a]Prov 8:35 [b]Ezek 11:20
7 [1]Lit *a blemish* [a]Prov 23:9
8 [a]Prov 15:12; Matt 7:6 [b]Ps 141:5; Prov 10:8

9 Give *instruction* to a wise man
and he will be still wiser,
Teach a righteous man and he
will [a]increase *his* learning.
10 The [a]fear of the LORD is the
beginning of wisdom,
And the knowledge of the Holy
One is understanding.
11 For [a]by me your days will be
multiplied,
And years of life will be added to
you.
12 If you are wise, you are wise
[a]for yourself,
And if you [b]scoff, you alone will
bear it.

13 ¶ The [1]woman of folly is
[a]boisterous,
She is [2]naive and [b]knows
nothing.
14 She sits at the doorway of her
house,
On a seat by [a]the high places of
the city,
15 Calling to those who pass by,
Who are making their paths
straight:
16 "[a]Whoever is [1]naive, let him
turn in here,"
And to him who lacks
[2]understanding she says,
17 "Stolen water is sweet;
And [a]bread *eaten* in secret is
pleasant."
18 But he does not know that the
[1]dead are there,
That her guests are in the
[a]depths of Sheol.

Contrast of the Righteous and the Wicked

10 The [a]proverbs of Solomon.
[b]A wise son makes a father
glad,
But [c]a foolish son is a grief to
his mother.
2 [1a]Ill-gotten gains do not profit,
But righteousness delivers from
death.
3 The LORD [a]will not allow the
[1]righteous to hunger,
But He [b]will [2]reject the craving
of the wicked.
4 Poor is he who works with a
negligent hand,
But the [a]hand of the diligent
makes rich.
5 He who gathers in summer is a
son who acts wisely,
But he who sleeps in harvest is a
son who acts shamefully.
6 [a]Blessings are on the head of
the righteous,
But [b]the mouth of the wicked
conceals violence.
7 The [a]memory of the righteous is
blessed,
But [b]the name of the wicked
will rot.
8 The [a]wise of heart will receive
commands,
But [1]a babbling fool will be
[2]ruined.
9 He [a]who walks in integrity
walks securely,
But [b]he who perverts his ways
will be found out.
10 He [a]who winks the eye causes
trouble,
And [1b]a babbling fool will be
[2]ruined.
11 The [a]mouth of the righteous is a
fountain of life,
But [b]the mouth of the wicked
conceals violence.
12 Hatred stirs up strife,
But [a]love covers all
transgressions.
13 On [a]the lips of the discerning,
wisdom is found,
But [b]a rod is for the back of him
who lacks [1]understanding.
14 Wise men [a]store up knowledge,
But with [b]the mouth of the
foolish, ruin is at hand.
15 The [a]rich man's wealth is his
[1]fortress,
The [b]ruin of the poor is their
poverty.
16 The [1a]wages of the righteous is
life,
The income of the wicked,
punishment.
17 He [a]is *on* the path of life who
heeds instruction,
But he who ignores reproof goes
astray.
18 He [a]who conceals hatred *has*
lying lips,
And he who spreads slander is a
fool.
19 When there are [a]many words,
transgression is unavoidable,
But [b]he who restrains his lips is
wise.
20 The tongue of the righteous is *as*
[a]choice silver,
The heart of the wicked is *worth*
little.
21 The [a]lips of the righteous feed
many,
But fools [b]die for lack of
[1]understanding.
22 It is the [a]blessing of the LORD
that makes rich,
And He adds no sorrow to it.

9 [a]Prov 1:5
10 [a]Job 28:28; Ps 111:10; Prov 1:7
11 [a]Prov 3:16; 10:27
12 [a]Job 22:2; Prov 14:14 [b]Prov 19:29
13 [1]Or *foolish woman* [2]Lit *simple* [a]Prov 7:11 [b]Prov 5:6
14 [a]Prov 9:3
16 [1]Lit *simple* [2]Lit *heart* [a]Prov 9:4
17 [a]Prov 20:17
18 [1]Lit *departed spirits* [a]Prov 7:27
10:1 [a]Prov 1:1 [b]Prov 15:20; 29:3 [c]Prov 17:25; 29:15
2 [1]Lit *Treasures of wickedness* [a]Ps 49:7; Prov 11:4; 21:6; Ezek 7:19; Luke 12:19,20
3 [1]Lit *soul of the righteous* [2]Lit *thrust away* [a]Ps 34:9,10; 37:25; Prov 28:25; Matt 6:33 [b]Ps 112:10; Prov 28:9
4 [a]Prov 13:4; 21:5
6 [a]Prov 28:20 [b]Prov 10:11; Obad 10
7 [a]Ps 112:6 [b]Ps 9:5,6; 109:13; Eccl 8:10
8 [1]Lit *the foolish of lips* [2]Lit *thrust down* [a]Prov 9:8; Matt 7:24
9 [a]Ps 23:4; Prov 3:23; 28:18; Is 33:15,16 [b]Prov 26:26; Matt 10:26; 1 Tim 5:25
10 [1]Lit *the foolish of lips* [2]Lit *thrust down* [a]Ps 35:19; Prov 6:13 [b]Prov 10:8
11 [a]Ps 37:30; Prov 13:14; 18:4 [b]Prov 10:6
12 [a]Prov 17:9; 1 Cor 13:4-7; James 5:20; 1 Pet 4:8
13 [1]Lit *heart* [a]Prov 10:31 [b]Prov 19:29; 26:3
14 [a]Prov 9:9 [b]Prov 10:8,10; 13:3; 18:7
15 [1]Lit *strong city* [a]Job 31:24; Ps 52:7; Prov 18:11 [b]Prov 19:7
16 [1]Or *work* [a]Prov 11:18,19
17 [a]Prov 6:23
18 [a]Prov 26:24
19 [a]Job 11:2; Prov 18:21; Eccl 5:3 [b]Prov 17:27; James 1:19; 3:2
20 [a]Prov 8:19
21 [1]Lit *heart* [a]Prov 10:11 [b]Prov 5:23; Hos 4:6
22 [a]Gen 24:35; 26:12; Deut 8:18; Prov 8:21

23 Doing wickedness is like [a]sport
to a fool,
And *so is* wisdom to a man of
understanding.
24 What [a]the wicked fears will
come upon him,
But the [b]desire of the righteous
will be granted.
25 When the [a]whirlwind passes,
the wicked is no more,
But the [b]righteous *has* an
everlasting foundation.
26 Like vinegar to the teeth and
smoke to the eyes,
So is the [a]lazy one to those who
send him.
27 The [a]fear of the LORD prolongs
[1]life,
But the [b]years of the wicked
will be shortened.
28 The [a]hope of the righteous is
gladness,
But the [b]expectation of the
wicked perishes.
29 The [a]way of the LORD is a
stronghold to the upright,
But [b]ruin to the workers of
iniquity.
30 The [a]righteous will never be
shaken,
But [b]the wicked will not dwell
in the land.
31 The [a]mouth of the righteous
flows with wisdom,
But the [b]perverted tongue will
be cut out.
32 The lips of the righteous bring
forth [a]what is acceptable,
But the [b]mouth of the wicked
what is perverted.

Contrast the Upright and the Wicked

11 A [a]false balance is an
abomination to the LORD,
But a [b]just weight is His delight.
2 When [a]pride comes, then comes
dishonor,
But with the humble is wisdom.
3 The [a]integrity of the upright will
guide them,
But the [b]crookedness of the
treacherous will destroy
them.
4 [a]Riches do not profit in the day
of wrath,
But [b]righteousness delivers from
death.
5 The [a]righteousness of the
blameless will smooth his
way,
But [b]the wicked will fall by his
own wickedness.
6 The righteousness of the upright
will deliver them,
But the treacherous will [a]be
caught by *their own* greed.
7 When a wicked man dies, *his*
[a]expectation will perish,
And the [b]hope of strong men
perishes.
8 The righteous is delivered from
trouble,
But the wicked [1]takes his place.
9 With *his* [a]mouth the godless
man destroys his neighbor,
But through knowledge the
[b]righteous will be delivered.
10 When it [a]goes well with the
righteous, the city rejoices,
And when the wicked perish,
there is joyful shouting.
11 By the blessing of the upright a
city is exalted,
But by the mouth of the wicked
it is torn down.
12 He who despises his neighbor
lacks [1]sense,
But a man of understanding
keeps silent.
13 He [a]who goes about as a
talebearer reveals secrets,
But he who is [1]trustworthy
[b]conceals a matter.
14 Where there is no [a]guidance the
people fall,
But in abundance of counselors
there is [1]victory.
15 He who is [a]guarantor for a
stranger will surely suffer
for it,
But he who hates [1]being a
guarantor is secure.
16 A [a]gracious woman attains
honor,
And ruthless men attain riches.
17 The [a]merciful man does
[1]himself good,
But the cruel man [2]does himself
harm.
18 The wicked earns deceptive
wages,
But he who [a]sows righteousness
gets a true reward.
19 He who is steadfast in
[a]righteousness *will attain* to
life,
And [b]he who pursues evil *will
bring about* his own death.
20 The perverse in heart are an
abomination to the LORD,
But the [a]blameless in *their*
[1]walk are His [b]delight.
21 [1]Assuredly, the evil man will
not go unpunished,
But the [2]descendants of the
righteous will be delivered.

23 [a]Prov 2:14; 15:21
24 [a]Job 15:21; Prov 1:27; Is 66:4 [b]Ps 145:19; Prov 15:8; Matt 5:6; 1 John 5:14, 15
25 [a]Job 21:18; Ps 58:9; Prov 12:7 [b]Ps 15:5; Prov 12:3; Matt 7:24,25
26 [a]Prov 26:6
27 [1]Lit *days* [a]Prov 3:2; 9:11; 14:27 [b]Job 15:32,33; 22:16; Ps 55:23
28 [a]Prov 11:23 [b]Job 8:13; 11:20; Prov 11:7
29 [a]Prov 13:6 [b]Prov 21:15
30 [a]Ps 37:29; 125:1; Prov 2:21 [b]Prov 2:22
31 [a]Ps 37:30; Prov 10:13 [b]Prov 17:20
32 [a]Eccl 12:10 [b]Prov 2:12; 6:12
11:1 [a]Lev 19:35,36; Deut 25:13-16; Prov 20:10,23; Mic 6:11 [b]Prov 16:11
2 [a]Prov 16:18; 18:12; 29:23
3 [a]Prov 13:6 [b]Prov 19:3; 22:12
4 [a]Prov 10:2; Ezek 7:19; Zeph 1:18 [b]Gen 7:1
5 [a]Prov 3:6 [b]Prov 5:22
6 [a]Ps 7:15,16; 9:15; Eccl 10:8
7 [a]Prov 10:28 [b]Job 8:13,14
8 [1]Lit *enters*
9 [a]Prov 16:29 [b]Prov 11:6
10 [a]Prov 28:12
12 [1]Lit *heart*
13 [1]Lit *faithful of spirit* [a]Lev 19:16; Prov 20:19; 1 Tim 5:13 [b]Prov 19:11
14 [1]Lit *deliverance* [a]Prov 15:22; 20:18; 24:6
15 [1]Lit *those who strike hands* [a]Prov 6:1; 27:13
16 [a]Prov 31:28, 30
17 [1]Lit *good to his own soul* [2]Lit *troubles his flesh* [a]Matt 5:7; 25:34-36
18 [a]Hos 10:12; Gal 6:8,9; James 3:18
19 [a]Prov 10:16; 12:28; 19:23 [b]Prov 21:16; Rom 6:23; James 1:15
20 [1]Lit *way* [a]Ps 119:1; Prov 13:6 [b]1 Chr 29:17
21 [1]Lit *Hand to hand* [2]Lit *seed*

22 *As* a [a]ring of gold in a swine's snout
So is a beautiful woman who lacks [1]discretion.
23 The desire of the righteous is only good,
But the [a]expectation of the wicked is wrath.
24 There is one who scatters, and *yet* increases all the more,
And there is one who withholds what is justly due, *and yet it results* only in want.
25 The [1a]generous man will be [2]prosperous,
And he who [b]waters will himself be watered.
26 He who withholds grain, the [a]people will curse him,
But [b]blessing will be on the head of him who [c]sells *it.*
27 He who diligently seeks good seeks favor,
But [a]he who seeks evil, evil will come to him.
28 He who [a]trusts in his riches will fall,
But [b]the righteous will flourish like the *green* leaf.
29 He who [a]troubles his own house will [b]inherit wind,
And [c]the foolish will be servant to the wisehearted.
30 The fruit of the righteous is [a]a tree of life,
And [b]he who is wise [1]wins souls.
31 If [a]the righteous will be rewarded in the earth,
How much more the wicked and the sinner!

Contrast the Upright and the Wicked

12 Whoever loves [1]discipline loves knowledge,
But he who hates reproof is stupid.
2 A [a]good man will obtain favor from the LORD,
But He will condemn a man [1]who devises evil.
3 A man will [a]not be established by wickedness,
But the root of the [b]righteous will not be moved.
4 An [1a]excellent wife is the crown of her husband,
But she who shames *him* is like [b]rottenness in his bones.
5 The thoughts of the righteous are just,
But the counsels of the wicked are deceitful.
6 The [a]words of the wicked lie in wait for blood,
But the [b]mouth of the upright will deliver them.
7 The [a]wicked are overthrown and are no more,
But the [b]house of the righteous will stand.
8 A man will be praised according to his insight,
But one of perverse [1]mind will be despised.
9 Better is he who is lightly esteemed and has a servant
Than he who honors himself and lacks bread.
10 A [a]righteous man has regard for the life of his animal,
But *even* the compassion of the wicked is cruel.
11 He [a]who tills his land will have plenty of bread,
But he who pursues worthless *things* lacks [1]sense.
12 The [a]wicked man desires the [1]booty of evil men,
But the root of the righteous [b]yields *fruit.*
13 [1]An evil man is ensnared by the transgression of his lips,
But the [a]righteous will escape from trouble.
14 A man will be [a]satisfied with good by the fruit of his [1]words,
And the [b]deeds of a man's hands will return to him.
15 The [a]way of a fool is right in his own eyes,
But a wise man is he who listens to counsel.
16 A [a]fool's anger is known at once,
But a prudent man conceals dishonor.
17 He who [1]speaks truth tells what is right,
But a false witness, deceit.
18 There is one who [a]speaks rashly like the thrusts of a sword,
But the [b]tongue of the wise brings healing.
19 Truthful lips will be established forever,
But a [a]lying tongue is only for a moment.
20 Deceit is in the heart of those who devise evil,
But counselors of peace have joy.
21 [a]No harm befalls the righteous,
But the wicked are filled with trouble.

22 [1]Lit *taste* [a]Gen 24:47
23 [a]Prov 10:28; Rom 2:8,9
25 [1]Lit *soul of blessing* [2]Lit *made fat* [a]Prov 3:9,10; 2 Cor 9:6,7 [b]Matt 5:7
26 [a]Prov 24:24 [b]Job 29:13 [c]Gen 42:6
27 [a]Esth 7:10; Ps 7:15,16; 57:6
28 [a]Ps 49:6; Mark 10:25; 1 Tim 6:17 [b]Ps 1:3; 92:12; Jer 17:8
29 [a]Prov 15:27 [b]Eccl 5:16 [c]Prov 14:19
30 [1]Lit *takes* [a]Prov 3:18 [b]Prov 14:25; Dan 12:3; 1 Cor 9:19-22; James 5:20
31 [a]2 Sam 22:21,25; Prov 13:21; 1 Pet 4:18
12:1 [1]Or *instruction*
2 [1]Lit *of evil devices* [a]Prov 3:4; 8:35
3 [a]Prov 11:5 [b]Prov 10:25
4 [1]Or *virtuous* [a]Prov 31:11; 1 Cor 11:7 [b]Prov 14:30; Hab 3:16
6 [a]Prov 1:11,16 [b]Prov 14:3
7 [a]Job 34:25; Prov 10:25 [b]Matt 7:24-27
8 [1]Lit *heart*
10 [a]Deut 25:4
11 [1]Lit *heart* [a]Prov 28:19
12 [1]Lit *net* [a]Prov 21:10 [b]Prov 11:30
13 [1]Lit *In the transgression of the lips is an evil snare* [a]Prov 11:8; 21:23; 2 Pet 2:9
14 [1]Lit *mouth* [a]Prov 13:2; 15:23; 18:20 [b]Job 34:11; Prov 1:31; 24:12; Is 3:10,11; Hos 4:9
15 [a]Prov 14:12; 16:2; 21:2
16 [a]Prov 14:33; 27:3; 29:11
17 [1]Lit *breathes*
18 [a]Ps 57:4 [b]Prov 4:22; 15:4
19 [a]Ps 52:4,5; Prov 19:9
21 [a]Ps 91:10; 121:7; Prov 1:33; 1 Pet 3:13

22 [a]Lying lips are an abomination
to the LORD,
But those who deal faithfully are
His delight.
23 A [a]prudent man conceals
knowledge,
But the heart of fools proclaims
folly.
24 The hand of the diligent will
rule,
But the [1]slack *hand* will be [a]put
to forced labor.
25 [a]Anxiety in a man's heart
weighs it down,
But a [b]good word makes it glad.
26 The righteous is a guide to his
neighbor,
But the way of the wicked leads
them astray.
27 A [1]lazy man does not [2]roast his
prey,
But the [a]precious possession of
a man *is* diligence.
28 [a]In the way of righteousness is
life,
And in *its* pathway there is no
death.

Contrast the Upright and the Wicked

13 A [a]wise son *accepts his* father's
discipline,
But a [b]scoffer does not listen to
rebuke.
2 From the fruit of a man's mouth
he [1a]enjoys good,
But the [2]desire of the
treacherous is [b]violence.
3 The one who [a]guards his mouth
preserves his life;
The one who [b]opens wide his
lips [1]comes to ruin.
4 The soul of the sluggard craves
and *gets* nothing,
But the soul of the diligent is
made fat.
5 A righteous man [a]hates
falsehood,
But a wicked man [1b]acts
disgustingly and shamefully.
6 Righteousness [a]guards the [1]one
whose way is blameless,
But wickedness subverts the
[2]sinner.
7 There is one who [a]pretends to
be rich, but has nothing;
Another [1]pretends to be [b]poor,
but has great wealth.
8 The ransom of a man's life is his
wealth,
But the poor hears no rebuke.
9 The [a]light of the righteous
[1]rejoices,
But the [b]lamp of the wicked
goes out.
10 Through insolence [1]comes
nothing but strife,
But wisdom is with those who
receive counsel.
11 Wealth *obtained* by [1]fraud
dwindles,
But the one who gathers [2]by
labor increases *it.*
12 Hope deferred makes the heart
sick,
But desire [1]fulfilled is a tree of
life.
13 The one who [a]despises the
word will be [1]in debt to it,
But the one who fears the
commandment will be
[b]rewarded.
14 The [1]teaching of the wise is a
[a]fountain of life,
To turn aside from the [b]snares
of death.
15 [a]Good understanding produces
favor,
But the way of the treacherous is
hard.
16 Every [a]prudent man acts with
knowledge,
But a fool [1]displays folly.
17 A wicked messenger falls into
adversity,
But [a]a faithful envoy *brings*
healing.
18 Poverty and shame *will come* to
him who [a]neglects
[1]discipline,
But he who regards reproof will
be honored.
19 Desire realized is sweet to the
soul,
But it is an abomination to fools
to turn away from evil.
20 [a]He who walks with wise men
will be wise,
But the companion of fools will
suffer harm.
21 [a]Adversity pursues sinners,
But the [b]righteous will be
rewarded with prosperity.
22 A good man [a]leaves an
inheritance to his
[1]children's children,
And the [b]wealth of the sinner is
stored up for the righteous.
23 [a]Abundant food *is in* the fallow
ground of the poor,
But [1]it is swept away by
injustice.
24 He who [a]withholds his [1]rod
hates his son,
But he who loves him
[2b]disciplines him diligently.

22 [a]Rev 22:15
23 [a]Prov 10:14; 11:13; 13:16; 15:2; 29:11
24 [1]Lit *slackness* [a]Gen 49:15; Judg 1:28; 1 Kin 9:21
25 [a]Prov 15:13 [b]Is 50:4
27 [1]Lit *slackness* [2]Or *catch* [a]Prov 10:4; 13:4
28 [a]Deut 30:15f; 32:46f; Jer 21:8
13:1 [a]Prov 10:1; 15:20 [b]Prov 9:7, 8; 15:12
2 [1]Lit *eats* [2]Lit *soul* [a]Prov 12:14 [b]Prov 1:31; Hos 10:13
3 [1]Lit *ruin is his* [a]Prov 18:21; 21:23; James 3:2 [b]Prov 18:7; 20:19
5 [1]Lit *causes a bad odor and causes shame* [a]Col 3:9 [b]Prov 3:35
6 [1]Lit *blamelessness of way* [2]Lit *sin* [a]Prov 11:3
7 [1]Lit *impoverishes himself* [a]Prov 11:24; Luke 12:20,21 [b]Luke 12:33; 2 Cor 6:10; James 2:5
9 [1]I.e. shines brightly [a]Job 29:3; Prov 4:18 [b]Job 18:5; Prov 24:20
10 [1]Lit *gives*
11 [1]Lit *vanity* [2]Or *gradually*; lit *on the hand*
12 [1]Lit *coming*
13 [1]Lit *pledged to it* [a]Num 15:31; 2 Chr 36:16 [b]Prov 13:21
14 [1]Or *law* [a]Prov 10:11; 14:27 [b]Ps 18:5
15 [a]Ps 111:10; Prov 3:4
16 [1]Lit *spreads out* [a]Prov 12:23
17 [a]Prov 25:13
18 [1]Or *instruction* [a]Prov 15:5, 32
20 [a]Prov 2:20; 15:31
21 [a]Ps 32:10; 54:5; Is 47:11 [b]Prov 11:31; 13:13; Is 3:10
22 [1]Lit *sons' sons* [a]Ezra 9:12; Ps 37:25 [b]Job 27:16,17; Prov 28:8; Eccl 2:26
23 [1]Lit *there is what is swept* [a]Prov 12:11
24 [1]I.e. correction or discipline [2]Lit *seeks him diligently with discipline* [a]Prov 19:18; 22:15; 23:13,14; 29:15, 17 [b]Deut 8:5; Prov 3:12; Heb 12:7

25 The [a]righteous [1]has enough to
satisfy his appetite,
But the stomach of the [b]wicked
is in need.

Contrast the Upright and the Wicked

14 The [a]wise woman builds her
house,
But the foolish tears it down
with her own hands.
2 He who [a]walks in his
uprightness fears the LORD,
But he who is [b]devious in his
ways despises Him.
3 In the mouth of the foolish is a
rod [1]for *his* back,
But [a]the lips of the wise will
protect them.
4 Where no oxen are, the manger
is clean,
But much revenue *comes* by the
strength of the ox.
5 A [a]trustworthy witness will not
lie,
But a [b]false witness [1c]utters
lies.
6 A scoffer seeks wisdom and *finds*
none,
But knowledge is easy to one
who has understanding.
7 Leave the [a]presence of a fool,
Or you will not [1]discern [2]words
of knowledge.
8 The wisdom of the sensible is to
understand his way,
But [a]the foolishness of fools is
deceit.
9 Fools mock at [1]sin,
But [a]among the upright there is
[2]good will.
10 The heart knows its own
[a]bitterness,
And a stranger does not share its
joy.
11 The [a]house of the wicked will
be destroyed,
But the tent of the upright will
flourish.
12 There [a]is a way *which seems*
right to a man,
But its [b]end is the way of death.
13 Even in laughter the heart may
be in pain,
And the [a]end of joy may be
grief.
14 The backslider in heart will have
his [a]fill of his own ways,
But a good man will [b]*be
satisfied* [1]with his.
15 The [1]naive believes everything,
But the sensible man considers
his steps.
16 A wise man [1]is cautious and
[a]turns away from evil,
But a fool is arrogant and
careless.
17 A quick-tempered man acts
foolishly,
And a man of evil devices is
hated.
18 The [1]naive inherit foolishness,
But the sensible are crowned
with knowledge.
19 The [a]evil will bow down before
the good,
And the wicked at the gates of
the righteous.
20 The [a]poor is hated even by his
neighbor,
But those who love the rich are
many.
21 He who [a]despises his neighbor
sins,
But [b]happy is he who is gracious
to the [1]poor.
22 Will they not go astray who
[a]devise evil?
But kindness and truth *will be to*
those who devise good.
23 In all labor there is profit,
But [1]mere talk *leads* only to
poverty.
24 The [a]crown of the wise is their
riches,
But the folly of fools is
foolishness.
25 A truthful witness saves lives,
But he who [1a]utters lies is
[2]treacherous.
26 In the [1a]fear of the LORD there
is strong confidence,
And [2]his children will have
refuge.
27 The [1]fear of the LORD is a
fountain of life,
That one may avoid the snares of
death.
28 In a multitude of people is a
king's glory,
But in the dearth of people is a
prince's ruin.
29 He who is [a]slow to anger has
great understanding,
But he who is [1]quick-tempered
exalts folly.
30 A [a]tranquil heart is life to the
body,
But passion is [b]rottenness to the
bones.
31 He [a]who oppresses the poor
taunts [b]his Maker,
But he who is gracious to the
needy honors Him.
32 The wicked is [a]thrust down by
his [1]wrongdoing,

25 [1]Lit *eats to the satisfaction of his soul* [a]Ps 34:10; 103:5; 132:15; Prov 10:3 [b]Prov 13:18; Luke 15:14
14:1 [a]Ruth 4:11; Prov 31:10-27
2 [a]Prov 19:1; 28:6 [b]Prov 2:15
3 [1]Lit *of pride* [a]Prov 12:6
5 [1]Lit *breathes out* [a]Rev 1:5; 3:14 [b]Ex 23:1; Deut 19:16; Prov 6:19; 12:17 [c]Prov 19:5
7 [1]Lit *know* [2]Lit *lips* [a]Prov 23:9
8 [a]1 Cor 3:19
9 [1]Lit *guilt* [2]Or the *favor* of God [a]Prov 3:34; 11:20
10 [a]1 Sam 1:10; Job 21:25
11 [a]Job 8:15
12 [a]Prov 12:15; 16:25 [b]Rom 6:21
13 [a]Eccl 2:1,2
14 [1]Lit *from himself* [a]Prov 1:31; 12:21 [b]Prov 12:14; 18:20
15 [1]Lit *simple*
16 [1]Lit *fears* [a]Job 28:28; Ps 34:14; Prov 3:7; 22:3
18 [1]Lit *simple*
19 [a]1 Sam 2:36; Prov 11:29
20 [a]Prov 19:7
21 [1]Or *afflicted* [a]Prov 11:12 [b]Ps 41:1; Prov 19:17; 28:8
22 [a]Ps 36:4; Prov 3:29; 12:2; Mic 2:1
23 [1]Lit *word of lips*
24 [a]Prov 10:22; 13:8; 21:20
25 [1]Lit *breathes out* [2]Lit *treachery* [a]Prov 14:5
26 [1]Or *reverence* [2]Or *His* [a]Prov 18:10; 19:23; Is 33:6
27 [1]Or *reverence*
29 [1]Lit *short of spirit* [a]Prov 16:32; 19:11; Eccl 7:9; James 1:19
30 [a]Prov 15:13 [b]Prov 12:4; Hab 3:16
31 [a]Prov 17:5; Matt 25:40; 1 John 3:17 [b]Job 31:15; Prov 22:2
32 [1]Or *calamity* [a]Prov 6:15; 24:16

But the [b]righteous has a refuge
when he dies.
33 Wisdom rests in the heart of one
who has understanding,
But in the [1]hearts of fools it is
made known.
34 Righteousness exalts a nation,
But sin is a disgrace to *any*
people.
35 The king's favor is toward a
[a]servant who acts wisely,
But his anger is toward him who
acts shamefully.

Contrast the Upright and the Wicked

15 A [a]gentle answer turns away
wrath,
But a [1b]harsh word stirs up
anger.
2 The [a]tongue of the wise makes
knowledge [1]acceptable,
But the [b]mouth of fools spouts
folly.
3 The [a]eyes of the LORD are in
every place,
Watching the evil and the good.
4 A [1]soothing tongue is a tree of
life,
But perversion in it [2]crushes the
spirit.
5 A fool [1]rejects his father's
discipline,
But he who regards reproof is
sensible.
6 Great wealth is *in* the house of
the [a]righteous,
But trouble is in the income of
the wicked.
7 The lips of the wise spread
knowledge,
But the hearts of fools are not so.
8 The [a]sacrifice of the wicked is
an abomination to the LORD,
But [b]the prayer of the upright is
His delight.
9 The way of the wicked is an
abomination to the LORD,
But He loves one who [a]pursues
righteousness.
10 Grievous punishment is for him
who forsakes the way;
He who hates reproof will die.
11 [1a]Sheol and [2]Abaddon *lie open*
before the LORD,
How much more the [b]hearts
of [3]men!
12 A [a]scoffer does not love one
who reproves him,
He will not go to the wise.
13 A [a]joyful heart makes a
[1]cheerful face,
But [2]when the heart is [b]sad,
the [c]spirit is broken.
14 The [a]mind of the intelligent
seeks knowledge,
But the mouth of fools feeds on
folly.
15 All the days of the afflicted are
bad,
But a [1]cheerful heart *has* a
continual feast.
16 [a]Better is a little with the [1]fear
of the LORD
Than great treasure and turmoil
with it.
17 [a]Better is a [1]dish of [2]vegetables
where love is
Than a [b]fattened ox *served* with
hatred.
18 A [a]hot-tempered man stirs up
strife,
But the [b]slow to anger [c]calms a
dispute.
19 The way of the lazy is as a hedge
of thorns,
But the path of the upright is a
highway.
20 A [a]wise son makes a father glad,
But a foolish man [b]despises his
mother.
21 Folly is joy to him who lacks
[1]sense,
But a man of understanding
[a]walks straight.
22 Without consultation, plans are
frustrated,
But with many counselors they
[1]succeed.
23 A [a]man has joy in an [1]apt
answer,
And how delightful is a timely
[b]word!
24 The [a]path of life *leads* upward
for the wise
That he may keep away from
[1]Sheol below.
25 The LORD will [a]tear down the
house of the proud,
But He will [b]establish the
boundary of the [c]widow.
26 Evil plans are an abomination to
the LORD,
But pleasant words are pure.
27 He who [a]profits illicitly troubles
his own house,
But he who [b]hates bribes will
live.
28 The heart of the righteous
[a]ponders how to answer,
But the [b]mouth of the wicked
pours out evil things.
29 The LORD is [a]far from the
wicked,
But He [b]hears the prayer of the
righteous.

32 [b]Gen 49:18; Ps 16:11; 17:15; 37:37; 73:24; 2 Cor 1:9; 5:8; 2 Tim 4:18
33 [1]Lit *inward part*
35 [a]Matt 24:45, 47; 25:21,23
15:1 [1]Lit *painful* [a]Judg 8:1-3; Prov 15:18; 25:15 [b]1 Sam 25:10-13
2 [1]Lit *good* [a]Prov 15:7 [b]Prov 12:23; 13:16; 15:28
3 [a]2 Chr 16:9; Job 31:4; Jer 16:17; Zech 4:10; Heb 4:13
4 [1]Lit *healing* [2]Lit *is the crushing of the spirit*
5 [1]Or *despises*
6 [a]Prov 8:21
8 [a]Prov 21:27; Eccl 5:1; Is 1:11; Jer 6:20; Mic 6:7 [b]Prov 15:29
9 [a]1 Tim 6:11
11 [1]I.e. the nether world [2]I.e. place of destruction [3]Lit *sons of Adam* [a]Job 26:6; Ps 139:8 [b]1 Sam 16:7; 2 Chr 6:30; Ps 44:21; Acts 1:24
12 [a]Prov 13:1; Amos 5:10
13 [1]Lit *good* [2]Lit *in sadness of heart* [a]Prov 17:22 [b]Prov 12:25 [c]Prov 17:22; 18:14
14 [a]Prov 18:15
15 [1]Lit *good*
16 [1]Or *reverence* [a]Ps 37:16; Prov 16:8; Eccl 4:6; 1 Tim 6:6
17 [1]Or *portion* [2]Or *herbs* [a]Prov 17:1 [b]Matt 22:4; Luke 15:23
18 [a]Prov 16:28; 26:21; 29:22 [b]Prov 14:29 [c]Gen 13:8; Prov 16:14; Eccl 10:4
20 [a]Prov 10:1; 29:3 [b]Prov 30:17
21 [1]Lit *heart* [a]Prov 14:8; Eph 5:15
22 [1]Or *are established*
23 [1]Lit *answer of his mouth* [a]Prov 12:14 [b]Prov 25:11; Is 50:4
24 [1]I.e. the nether world [a]Prov 4:18
25 [a]Prov 12:7; 14:11 [b]Deut 19:14; Prov 23:10 [c]Ps 68:5; 146:9
27 [a]Prov 1:19; 28:25; 1 Tim 6:10 [b]Ex 23:8; Deut 16:19; 1 Sam 12:3; Is 33:15
28 [a]1 Pet 3:15 [b]Prov 10:32; 15:2
29 [a]Ps 18:41; Prov 1:28 [b]Ps 145:18,19

30 [1]Bright eyes gladden the heart;
Good news puts fat on the bones.
31 He whose ear listens to the life-giving reproof
Will dwell among the wise.
32 He who [a]neglects discipline [b]despises himself,
But he who [c]listens to reproof acquires [1]understanding.
33 The [1]fear of the LORD is the instruction for wisdom,
And before honor *comes* humility.

Contrast the Upright and the Wicked

16 The [a]plans of the heart belong to man,
But the answer of the tongue is from the LORD.
2 All the ways of a man are clean in his own sight,
But the [a]LORD weighs the [1]motives.
3 [1a]Commit your works to the LORD
And your plans will be established.
4 The LORD [a]has made everything for [1]its own purpose,
Even the [b]wicked for the day of evil.
5 Everyone who is proud in heart is an abomination to the LORD;
Assuredly, he will not be unpunished.
6 By [a]lovingkindness and truth iniquity is atoned for,
And by the [1b]fear of the LORD one keeps away from evil.
7 When a man's ways are pleasing to the LORD,
He [a]makes even his enemies to be at peace with him.
8 Better is a little with righteousness
Than great income with injustice.
9 The mind of [a]man plans his way,
But [b]the LORD directs his steps.
10 A divine [a]decision is in the lips of the king;
His mouth should not [1]err in judgment.
11 A [a]just balance and scales belong to the LORD;
All the [1]weights of the bag are His [2]concern.
12 It is an abomination for kings to commit wicked acts,
For a [a]throne is established on righteousness.
13 Righteous lips are the delight of kings,
And he who speaks right is loved.
14 The fury of a king is *like* messengers of death,
But a wise man will appease it.
15 In the light of a king's face is life,
And his favor is like a cloud with the [1a]spring rain.
16 How much [a]better it is to get wisdom than gold!
And to get understanding is to be chosen above silver.
17 The [a]highway of the upright is to depart from evil;
He who watches his way preserves his [1]life.
18 [a]Pride *goes* before destruction,
And a haughty spirit before stumbling.
19 It is better to be [a]humble in spirit with the lowly
Than to [b]divide the spoil with the proud.
20 He who gives attention to the word will [a]find good,
And [b]blessed is he who trusts in the LORD.
21 The [a]wise in heart will be called understanding,
And sweetness of [1]speech [b]increases [2]persuasiveness.
22 Understanding is a fountain of life to one who has it,
But the discipline of fools is folly.
23 The [a]heart of the wise instructs his mouth
And adds [1]persuasiveness to his lips.
24 [a]Pleasant words are a honeycomb,
Sweet to the soul and [b]healing to the bones.
25 [a]There is a way *which seems* right to a man,
But its end is the way of death.
26 A worker's appetite works for him,
For his [1]hunger urges him *on.*
27 A [a]worthless man digs up evil,
While [1]his words are like [b]scorching fire.
28 A perverse man spreads strife,
And a slanderer separates intimate friends.
29 A man of violence [a]entices his neighbor
And leads him in a way that is not good.

30 [1]Lit *The light of the eyes gladdens*
32 [1]Lit *heart* [a]Prov 1:7; 8:33 [b]Prov 8:36 [c]Prov 15:5
33 [1]Or *reverence*
16:1 [a]Prov 16:9; 19:21
2 [1]Lit *spirits* [a]1 Sam 16:7; Dan 5:27
3 [1]Lit *Roll* [a]Ps 37:5; 55:22; Prov 3:6; 1 Pet 5:7
4 [1]Or *His* [a]Gen 1:31; Eccl 3:11 [b]Rom 9:22
6 [1]Or *reverence* [a]Dan 4:27; Luke 11:41 [b]Prov 8:13; 14:16
7 [a]Gen 33:4; 2 Chr 17:10
9 [a]Prov 16:1; 19:21 [b]Ps 37:23; Prov 20:24; Jer 10:23
10 [1]Lit *be unfaithful* [a]1 Kin 3:28
11 [1]Lit *stones* [2]Lit *work* [a]Prov 11:1
12 [a]Prov 25:5
15 [1]Lit *latter* [a]Job 29:23
16 [a]Prov 8:10, 19
17 [1]Lit *soul* [a]Is 35:8
18 [a]Prov 11:2; 18:12; Jer 49:16; Obad 3,4
19 [a]Prov 3:34; 29:23; Is 57:15 [b]Ex 15:9; Judg 5:30; Prov 1:13, 14
20 [a]Prov 19:8 [b]Ps 2:12; 34:8; Jer 17:7
21 [1]Lit *lips* [2]Or *learning* [a]Hos 14:9 [b]Prov 16:23
23 [1]Or *learning* [a]Ps 37:30; Prov 15:28; Matt 12:34
24 [a]Ps 19:10; Prov 15:26; 24:13,14 [b]Prov 4:22; 17:22
25 [a]Prov 12:15; 14:12
26 [1]Lit *mouth*
27 [1]Lit *on his lips* [a]Prov 6:12, 14,18 [b]James 3:6
29 [a]Prov 1:10; 12:26

30 He who winks his eyes *does so* to devise perverse things;
He who compresses his lips brings evil to pass.
31 A [a]gray head is a crown of glory;
It [b]is found in the way of righteousness.
32 He who is slow to anger is better than the mighty,
And he who rules his spirit, than he who captures a city.
33 The [a]lot is cast into the lap,
But its every [b]decision is from the LORD.

Contrast the Upright and the Wicked

17 [a]Better is a dry morsel and quietness with it
Than a house full of [1]feasting with strife.
2 A servant who acts wisely will rule over a son who acts shamefully,
And will share in the inheritance among brothers.
3 The [a]refining pot is for silver and the furnace for gold,
But [b]the LORD tests hearts.
4 An [a]evildoer listens to wicked lips;
A [1]liar pays attention to a destructive tongue.
5 He who mocks the [a]poor taunts his Maker;
He who [b]rejoices at calamity will not go unpunished.
6 [a]Grandchildren are the crown of old men,
And the [b]glory of sons is their fathers.
7 [1a]Excellent speech is not fitting for a fool,
Much less are [b]lying lips to a prince.
8 A [a]bribe is a [1]charm in the sight of its owner;
Wherever he turns, he prospers.
9 He who [a]conceals a transgression seeks love,
But he who repeats a matter [b]separates intimate friends.
10 A rebuke goes deeper into one who has understanding
Than a hundred blows into a fool.
11 A rebellious man seeks only evil,
So a cruel messenger will be sent against him.
12 Let a [a]man meet a [b]bear robbed of her cubs,
Rather than a fool in his folly.
13 He who [a]returns evil for good,
[b]Evil will not depart from his house.
14 The beginning of strife is *like* letting out water,
So [a]abandon the quarrel before it breaks out.
15 He who [a]justifies the wicked and he who condemns the righteous,
Both of them alike are an abomination to the LORD.
16 Why is there a price in the hand of a fool to [a]buy wisdom,
When [1]he has no sense?
17 A [a]friend loves at all times,
And a brother is born for adversity.
18 A man lacking in [1]sense [2a]pledges
And becomes guarantor in the presence of his neighbor.
19 He who [a]loves transgression loves strife;
He who [b]raises his door seeks destruction.
20 He who has a crooked [1]mind [a]finds no good,
And he who is [b]perverted in his language falls into evil.
21 He who [a]sires a fool *does so* to his sorrow,
And the father of a fool has no joy.
22 A [a]joyful heart [1]is good medicine,
But a broken spirit [b]dries up the bones.
23 A wicked man receives a [a]bribe from the bosom
To [b]pervert the ways of justice.
24 Wisdom is in the presence of the one who has understanding,
But the [a]eyes of a fool are on the ends of the earth.
25 A [a]foolish son is a grief to his father
And [b]bitterness to her who bore him.
26 It is also not good to [a]fine the righteous,
Nor to strike the noble for *their* uprightness.
27 He who [a]restrains his words [1]has knowledge,
And he who has a [b]cool spirit is a man of understanding.
28 Even a fool, when he [a]keeps silent, is considered wise;
When he closes his lips, he is *considered* prudent.

31 [a]Prov 20:29 [b]Prov 3:1,2
33 [a]Prov 18:18 [b]Prov 29:26
17:1 [1]Lit *sacrifices of strife* [a]Prov 15:17
3 [a]Prov 27:21 [b]1 Chr 29:17; Ps 26:2; Prov 15:11; Jer 17:10; Mal 3:3
4 [1]Lit *falsehood* [a]Prov 14:15
5 [a]Prov 14:31 [b]Job 31:29; Prov 24:17; Obad 12
6 [a]Gen 48:11; Prov 13:22 [b]Ex 20:12; Mal 1:6
7 [1]Lit *A lip of abundance* [a]Prov 24:7 [b]Ps 31:18; Prov 12:22
8 [1]Lit *stone of favor* [a]Prov 21:14; Is 1:23; Amos 5:12
9 [a]Prov 10:12; James 5:20; 1 Pet 4:8 [b]Prov 16:28
12 [a]Prov 29:9 [b]2 Sam 17:8; Hos 13:8
13 [a]Ps 35:12; 109:5; Jer 18:20 [b]2 Sam 12:10; 1 Kin 21:22; Prov 13:21
14 [a]Prov 20:3; 25:8; 1 Thess 4:11
15 [a]Ex 23:7; Prov 18:5; 24:24; Is 5:23
16 [1]Lit *there is no heart* [a]Prov 23:23
17 [a]Ruth 1:16; Prov 18:24
18 [1]Lit *heart* [2]Lit *shakes hands* [a]Prov 6:1; 11:15; 22:26
19 [a]Prov 29:22 [b]Prov 16:18; 29:23
20 [1]Lit *heart* [a]Prov 24:20 [b]James 3:8
21 [a]Prov 10:1; 17:25; 19:13
22 [1]Lit *causes good healing* [a]Prov 15:13 [b]Ps 22:15
23 [a]Prov 17:8 [b]Ex 23:8; Mic 3:11; 7:3
24 [a]Eccl 2:14
25 [a]Prov 19:13 [b]Prov 10:1
26 [a]Prov 17:15; 18:5
27 [1]Lit *knows* [a]Prov 10:19; James 1:19 [b]Prov 14:29
28 [a]Job 13:5

Contrast the Upright and the Wicked

18 He who separates himself seeks *his own* desire,
He [1a]quarrels against all sound wisdom.
2 A fool does not delight in understanding,
But only [a]in revealing his own [1]mind.
3 When a wicked man comes, contempt also comes,
And with dishonor *comes* scorn.
4 The words of a man's mouth are [a]deep waters;
[1]The fountain of wisdom is a bubbling brook.
5 To [a]show partiality to the wicked is not good,
Nor to [b]thrust aside the righteous in judgment.
6 A fool's lips [1]bring strife,
And his mouth calls for [a]blows.
7 A [a]fool's mouth is his ruin,
And his lips are the snare of his soul.
8 The words of a whisperer are like dainty morsels,
And they go down into the [1]innermost parts of the body.
9 He also who is [a]slack in his work
[b]Is brother to him who destroys.
10 The [a]name of the LORD is a [b]strong tower;
The righteous runs into it and [c]is [1]safe.
11 A [a]rich man's wealth is his strong city,
And like a high wall in his own imagination.
12 [a]Before destruction the heart of man is haughty,
But [b]humility *goes* before honor.
13 He who [a]gives an answer before he hears,
It is folly and shame to him.
14 The [a]spirit of a man can endure his sickness,
But *as for* a [b]broken spirit who can bear it?
15 The [1a]mind of the prudent acquires knowledge,
And the [b]ear of the wise seeks knowledge.
16 A man's [a]gift makes room for him
And brings him before great men.
17 The first [1]to plead his case *seems* right,
Until [2]another comes and examines him.
18 The *cast* [a]lot puts an end to strife
And [1]decides between the mighty ones.
19 A brother offended *is harder to be won* than a strong city,
And contentions are like the bars of a citadel.
20 With the [1a]fruit of a man's mouth his stomach will be satisfied;
[b]He will be satisfied *with* the product of his lips.
21 [a]Death and life are in the [1]power of the tongue,
And those who love it will eat its [b]fruit.
22 He who finds a [a]wife finds a good thing
And [b]obtains favor from the LORD.
23 The [a]poor man utters supplications,
But the [b]rich man [c]answers roughly.
24 A man of *too many* friends *comes* to [1]ruin,
But there is [a]a [2]friend who sticks closer than a brother.

On Life and Conduct

19 [a]Better is a poor man who [b]walks in his integrity
Than he who is perverse in [1]speech and is a fool.
2 Also it is not good for a person to be without knowledge,
And he who hurries [1a]his footsteps [2]errs.
3 The [a]foolishness of man ruins his way,
And his heart [b]rages against the LORD.
4 [a]Wealth adds many friends,
But a poor man is separated from his friend.
5 A [a]false witness will not go unpunished,
And he who [1b]tells lies will not escape.
6 [a]Many will seek the favor of a [1]generous man,
And every man is a friend to him who [b]gives gifts.
7 All the brothers of a poor man hate him;
How much more do his [a]friends abandon him!
He [b]pursues *them with* words, *but* they are [1]gone.
8 He who gets [1]wisdom loves his own soul;

18:1 [1]Lit *breaks out* [a]Prov 3:21
2 [1]Lit *heart* [a]Prov 12:23; Eccl 10:3
4 [1]Or *A bubbling brook, a fountain of wisdom* [a]Prov 20:5
5 [a]Lev 19:15; Deut 1:17; Ps 82:2; Prov 17:15 [b]Ex 23:2; Prov 17:26; Mic 3:9
6 [1]Lit *come with* [a]Prov 19:29
7 [a]Ps 64:8; Prov 10:14; Eccl 10:12
8 [1]Lit *chambers of the belly*
9 [a]Prov 10:4 [b]Prov 28:24
10 [1]Lit *set on high* [a]Ex 3:15 [b]2 Sam 22:2; Ps 18:2 [c]Prov 29:25
11 [a]Prov 10:15
12 [a]Prov 11:2 [b]Prov 15:33
13 [a]Prov 20:25; John 7:51
14 [a]Prov 17:22 [b]Prov 15:13
15 [1]Lit *heart* [a]Prov 15:14; Eph 1:17 [b]Prov 15:31
16 [a]Gen 32:20; 1 Sam 25:27
17 [1]Lit *in his plea* [2]Lit *his neighbor*
18 [1]Lit *makes a division* [a]Prov 16:33
20 [1]I.e. speech [a]Prov 12:14 [b]Prov 14:14
21 [1]Lit *hand* [a]Prov 12:13; Matt 12:37 [b]Prov 13:2; Is 3:10; Hos 10:13
22 [a]Gen 2:18; Prov 12:4 [b]Prov 8:35
23 [a]Prov 19:7 [b]James 2:3 [c]1 Kin 12:13; 2 Chr 10:13
24 [1]Lit *be broken in pieces* [2]Or *lover* [a]Prov 17:17; John 15:14
19:1 [1]Lit *his lips* [a]Prov 28:6 [b]Ps 26:11; Prov 14:2
2 [1]Lit *with his feet* [2]Lit *sins* [a]Prov 21:5
3 [a]Prov 11:3 [b]Is 8:21
4 [a]Prov 14:20
5 [1]Lit *breathes* [a]Ex 23:1; Deut 19:16-19; Prov 19:9 [b]Prov 6:19
6 [1]Or *noble* [a]Prov 29:26 [b]Prov 18:16
7 [1]Lit *not* [a]Ps 38:11 [b]Prov 18:23
8 [1]Lit *heart*

He who keeps understanding will [a]find good.
9 A [a]false witness will not go unpunished,
And he who [1]tells lies will perish.
10 Luxury is [a]not fitting for a fool;
Much less for a [b]slave to rule over princes.
11 A man's [a]discretion makes him slow to anger,
And it is his glory [b]to overlook a transgression.
12 The [a]king's wrath is like the roaring of a lion,
But his favor is like [b]dew on the grass.
13 A [a]foolish son is destruction to his father,
And the [b]contentions of a wife are a constant dripping.
14 House and wealth are an [a]inheritance from fathers,
But a prudent wife is from the LORD.
15 [a]Laziness casts into a deep sleep,
And an idle [1]man will suffer hunger.
16 He who [a]keeps the commandment keeps his soul,
But he who [1]is careless of [2]conduct will die.
17 One who [a]is gracious to a poor man lends to the LORD,
And He will repay him for his [1b]good deed.
18 [a]Discipline your son while there is hope,
And do not desire [1]his death.
19 *A man of* great anger will bear the penalty,
For if you rescue *him,* you will only have to do it again.
20 [a]Listen to counsel and accept discipline,
That you may be wise [1]the rest of your days.
21 Many [a]plans are in a man's heart,
But the [b]counsel of the LORD will stand.
22 What is desirable in a man is his [1]kindness,
And *it is* better to be a poor man than a liar.
23 The [1a]fear of the LORD *leads* to life,
So that one may sleep [b]satisfied, [2c]untouched by evil.
24 The [a]sluggard buries his hand [b]in the dish,
But will not even bring it back to his mouth.
25 [a]Strike a scoffer and the [1]naive may become shrewd,
But [b]reprove one who has understanding and he will [2]gain knowledge.
26 He [a]who assaults *his* father *and* drives *his* mother away
Is a shameful and disgraceful son.
27 Cease listening, my son, to discipline,
And you will stray from the words of knowledge.
28 A rascally witness makes a mockery of justice,
And the mouth of the wicked [1a]spreads iniquity.
29 [1]Judgments are prepared for [a]scoffers,
And [b]blows for the back of fools.

On Life and Conduct

20 [a]Wine is a mocker, [b]strong drink a brawler,
And whoever [1]is intoxicated by it is not wise.
2 The terror of a king is like the growling of a lion;
He who provokes him to anger [1a]forfeits his own life.
3 [1a]Keeping away from strife is an honor for a man,
But any fool will [2]quarrel.
4 The [a]sluggard does not plow after the autumn,
So he [1]begs during the harvest and has nothing.
5 A plan in the heart of a man is *like* deep water,
But a man of understanding draws it out.
6 Many a man [a]proclaims his own loyalty,
But who can find a [b]trustworthy man?
7 A righteous man who [a]walks in his integrity—
[b]How blessed are his sons after him.
8 [a]A king who sits on the throne of justice
[1]Disperses all evil with his eyes.
9 [a]Who can say, "I have cleansed my heart,
I am pure from my sin"?
10 [1a]Differing weights and differing measures,
Both of them are abominable to the LORD.
11 It is by his deeds that a lad [1a]distinguishes himself
If his conduct is pure and right.

8 [a]Prov 16:20 **9** [1]Lit *breathes* [a]Prov 19:5; Dan 6:24 **10** [a]Prov 17:7; Eccl 10:6 [b]Prov 30:22 **11** [a]Prov 14:29 [b]Matt 5:44; Eph 4:32; Col 3:13 **12** [a]Prov 16:14 [b]Gen 27:28; Deut 33:28; Ps 133:3; Hos 14:5; Mic 5:7 **13** [a]Prov 17:25 [b]Prov 21:9 **14** [a]2 Cor 12:14 **15** [1]Lit *soul* [a]Prov 6:9 **16** [1]Lit *despises* [2]Lit *ways* [a]Prov 13:13; Luke 10:28 **17** [1]Or *benefits* [a]Deut 15:7; Prov 14:31; Eccl 11:1; Matt 10:42; 2 Cor 9:6-8; Heb 6:10 [b]Prov 12:14; Luke 6:38 **18** [1]Lit *causing him to die* [a]Prov 13:24 **20** [1]Lit *in your latter end* [a]Prov 4:1 **21** [a]Prov 16:1 [b]Ps 33:10; Is 14:26 **22** [1]Or *loyalty* **23** [1]Or *reverence* [2]Lit *not visited* [a]Prov 14:27; 1 Tim 4:8 [b]Ps 25:13 [c]Ps 91:10; Prov 12:21 **24** [a]Prov 26:15 [b]Matt 26:23; Mark 14:20 **25** [1]Lit *simple* [2]Lit *discern* [a]Prov 21:11 [b]Prov 9:8 **26** [a]Prov 28:24 **28** [1]Or *swallows* [a]Job 15:16 **29** [1]Gr *Rods* [a]Ps 1:1; Prov 9:12 [b]Prov 10:13 **20:1** [1]Lit *errs* [a]Gen 9:21; Prov 23:29; Is 28:7; Hos 4:11 [b]Prov 31:4; Is 5:22 **2** [1]Lit *sins against* [a]Num 16:38; 1 Kin 2:23; Prov 8:36; Hab 2:10 **3** [1]Lit *Ceasing* [2]Lit *burst out* [a]Gen 13:7f; Prov 17:14 **4** [1]Lit *asks* [a]Prov 13:4 **6** [a]Prov 25:14; Matt 6:2; Luke 18:11 [b]Ps 12:1; Luke 18:8 **7** [a]Prov 19:1 [b]Ps 37:26 **8** [1]Or *Sifts* [a]Prov 20:26 **9** [a]1 Kin 8:46; 2 Chr 6:36; Job 14:4; Eccl 7:20; Rom 3:9; 1 John 1:8 **10** [1]Lit *A stone and a stone, an ephah and an ephah* [a]Prov 11:1 **11** [1]Or *makes himself known* [a]Matt 7:16

12 The hearing [a]ear and the seeing
eye,
The LORD has made both of
them.
13 [a]Do not love sleep, or you will
become poor;
Open your eyes, *and* you will be
satisfied with [1]food.
14 "Bad, bad," says the buyer,
But when he goes his way, then
he boasts.
15 There is gold, and an abundance
of [1]jewels;
But the lips of knowledge are a
more precious thing.
16 Take his garment when he
becomes surety for a
stranger;
And for foreigners, hold him in
pledge.
17 [a]Bread obtained by falsehood is
sweet to a man,
But afterward his mouth will be
filled with gravel.
18 Prepare [a]plans by consultation,
And [b]make war by wise
guidance.
19 He who [a]goes about as a
slanderer reveals secrets,
Therefore do not associate with
[1b]a gossip.
20 He who [a]curses his father or his
mother,
His [b]lamp will go out in [1]time
of darkness.
21 An inheritance gained hurriedly
at the beginning
Will not be blessed in the end.
22 [a]Do not say, "I will repay evil";
[b]Wait for the LORD, and He will
save you.
23 [1a]Differing weights are an
abomination to the LORD,
And a [2b]false scale is not good.
24 [a]Man's steps are *ordained* by
the LORD,
How then can man understand
his way?
25 It is a trap for a man to say
rashly, "It is holy!"
And [a]after the vows to make
inquiry.
26 A [a]wise king winnows the
wicked,
And [1]drives the [b]*threshing*
wheel over them.
27 The [1a]spirit of man is the lamp
of the LORD,
Searching all the [2]innermost
parts of his being.
28 [1]Loyalty and [a]truth preserve the
king,
And he upholds his throne by
[1]righteousness.
29 The glory of young men is their
strength,
And the [1a]honor of old men is
their gray hair.
30 [a]Stripes that wound scour away
evil,
And strokes *reach* the
[1]innermost parts.

On Life and Conduct

21 The king's heart is *like* channels
of water in the hand of the
LORD;
He [a]turns it wherever He
wishes.
2 [a]Every man's way is right in his
own eyes,
But the LORD [b]weighs the
hearts.
3 To do [a]righteousness and justice
Is desired by the LORD more than
sacrifice.
4 Haughty eyes and a proud heart,
The [a]lamp of the wicked, is sin.
5 The plans of the [a]diligent *lead*
surely to advantage,
But everyone [b]who is hasty
comes surely to poverty.
6 The [a]acquisition of treasures by
a lying tongue
Is a fleeting vapor, the [1]pursuit
of [b]death.
7 The violence of the wicked will
drag them away,
Because they [a]refuse to act with
justice.
8 The way of a guilty man is
[a]crooked,
But as for the pure, his conduct
is upright.
9 It is better to live in a corner of
a roof
Than [1]in a house shared with a
contentious woman.
10 The soul of the wicked desires
evil;
His [a]neighbor finds no favor in
his eyes.
11 When the [a]scoffer is punished,
the [1]naive becomes wise;
But when the wise is instructed,
he receives knowledge.
12 The righteous one considers the
house of the wicked,
Turning the [a]wicked to ruin.
13 He who [a]shuts his ear to the cry
of the poor
Will also cry himself and not be
[b]answered.
14 A [a]gift in secret subdues anger,
And a bribe in the bosom, strong
wrath.
15 The exercise of justice is joy for
the righteous,

12 [a]Ex 4:11; Ps 94:9
13 [1]Lit *bread* [a]Prov 6:9,10; 19:15; 24:33
15 [1]Or *corals*
17 [a]Prov 9:17
18 [a]Prov 11:14; 15:22 [b]Prov 24:6; Luke 14:31
19 [1]Lit *one who opens his lips* [a]Prov 11:13 [b]Prov 13:3
20 [1]Lit *pupil* (of eye) [a]Ex 21:17; Lev 20:9; Prov 30:11; Matt 15:4 [b]Job 18:5; Prov 13:9; 24:20
22 [a]Prov 24:29; Matt 5:39; Rom 12:17,19; 1 Thess 5:15; 1 Pet 3:9 [b]Ps 27:14
23 [1]Lit *A stone and a stone* [2]Lit *balance of deceit* [a]Prov 20:10 [b]Prov 11:1
24 [a]Prov 16:9
25 [a]Eccl 5:4,5
26 [1]Lit *turns* [a]Prov 20:8 [b]Is 28:27
27 [1]Lit *breath* [2]Lit *chambers of the body* [a]1 Cor 2:11
28 [1]Lit *Covenant loyalty* [a]Prov 29:14
29 [1]Or *splendor* [a]Prov 16:31
30 [1]Lit *chambers of the body* [a]Ps 89:32; Prov 22:15; Is 53:5; 1 Pet 2:24
21:1 [a]Ezra 6:22
2 [a]Prov 16:2 [b]Prov 16:2; 24:12; Luke 16:15
3 [a]1 Sam 15:22; Prov 15:8; Is 1:11,16,17; Hos 6:6; Mic 6:7,8
4 [a]Prov 24:20; Luke 11:34
5 [a]Prov 10:4; 13:4 [b]Prov 28:22
6 [1]Lit *seekers* [a]Prov 13:11; 20:21 [b]Prov 8:36
7 [a]Amos 5:7; Mic 3:9
8 [a]Prov 2:15
9 [1]Lit *with a woman of contentions and a house of association*
10 [a]Ps 52:3; Prov 2:14; 14:21
11 [1]Lit *simple* [a]Prov 19:25
12 [a]Prov 14:11
13 [a]Matt 18:30-34; 1 John 3:17 [b]James 2:13
14 [a]Prov 18:16; 19:6

But is [a]terror to the workers of
iniquity.
16 A man who wanders from the
way of understanding
Will [a]rest in the assembly of the
[1]dead.
17 He who [a]loves pleasure *will*
become a poor man;
He who loves wine and oil will
not become rich.
18 The wicked is a [a]ransom for the
righteous,
And the [b]treacherous is in the
place of the upright.
19 [a]It is better to live in a desert
land
Than with a contentious and
vexing woman.
20 There is precious [a]treasure and
oil in the dwelling of the
wise,
But a foolish man [b]swallows
it up.
21 He who [a]pursues righteousness
and loyalty
Finds life, righteousness and
honor.
22 A [a]wise man scales the city of
the mighty
And brings down the
[1]stronghold in which they
trust.
23 He who [a]guards his mouth and
his tongue,
Guards his soul from troubles.
24 "Proud," "Haughty," "[a]Scoffer,"
are his names,
Who acts with [b]insolent pride.
25 The [a]desire of the sluggard puts
him to death,
For his hands refuse to work;
26 All day long he [1]is craving,
While the righteous [a]gives and
does not hold back.
27 The [a]sacrifice of the wicked is
an abomination,
How much more when he brings
it with evil intent!
28 A [a]false witness will perish,
But the man who listens *to the*
truth will speak forever.
29 A wicked man [1a]displays a bold
face,
But as for the [b]upright, he
makes his way sure.
30 There is [a]no wisdom and no
understanding
And no counsel against the LORD.
31 The [a]horse is prepared for the
day of battle,
But [b]victory belongs to the
LORD.

15 [a]Prov 10:29
16 [1]Lit *departed spirits* [a]Ps 49:14
17 [a]Prov 23:21
18 [a]Is 43:3 [b]Prov 11:8
19 [a]Prov 21:9
20 [a]Ps 112:3; Prov 8:21; 22:4 [b]Job 20:15,18
21 [a]Prov 15:9; Matt 5:6; 1 Cor 15:58
22 [1]Lit *strength of trust* [a]2 Sam 5:6-9; Prov 24:5; Eccl 7:19; 9:15, 16
23 [a]Prov 12:13; 13:3; 18:21; James 3:2
24 [a]Ps 1:1; Prov 1:22; 3:34; 24:9; Is 29:20 [b]Is 16:6; Jer 48:29
25 [a]Prov 13:4
26 [1]Lit *desires desire* [a]Ps 37:26; 112:5,9; Matt 5:42; Eph 4:28
27 [a]Prov 15:8; Is 66:3; Jer 6:20; Amos 5:22
28 [a]Prov 19:5,9
29 [1]Lit *makes firm with his face* [a]Eccl 8:1 [b]Ps 119:5; Prov 11:5
30 [a]Jer 9:23; Acts 5:38,39; 1 Cor 3:19,20
31 [a]Ps 20:7; 33:17; Is 31:1 [b]Ps 3:8; Jer 3:23; 1 Cor 15:57
22:1 [a]Prov 10:7; Eccl 7:1
2 [1]Lit *meet together* [a]Job 31:15; Prov 14:31
3 [1]Lit *simple* [a]Prov 14:16; 27:12; Is 26:20
4 [1]Or *reverence*
5 [a]Prov 15:19
6 [1]Lit *according to his way* [a]Eph 6:4
7 [a]Prov 18:23; James 2:6
8 [a]Job 4:8 [b]Ps 125:3
9 [1]Lit *has a good eye* [a]Prov 19:17; 2 Cor 9:6 [b]Luke 14:13
10 [a]Gen 21:9, 10; Prov 18:6; 26:20
11 [1]Lit *has grace on his lips* [a]Ps 24:4; Matt 5:8 [b]Prov 14:35; 16:13
13 [a]Prov 26:13
14 [1]Lit *strange woman* [2]Lit *there* [a]Prov 2:16; 5:3; 7:5; 23:27 [b]Eccl 7:26
15 [a]Prov 13:24; 23:14
16 [1]Lit *much* [a]Eccl 5:8; James 2:13 [b]Prov 28:22

On Life and Conduct

22 A [a]*good* name is to be more
desired than great wealth,
Favor is better than silver and
gold.
2 The rich and the poor [1]have a
common bond,
The LORD is the [a]maker of them
all.
3 The [a]prudent sees the evil and
hides himself,
But the [1]naive go on, and are
punished for it.
4 The reward of humility *and* the
[1]fear of the LORD
Are riches, honor and life.
5 [a]Thorns *and* snares are in the
way of the perverse;
He who guards himself will be
far from them.
6 [a]Train up a child [1]in the way
he should go,
Even when he is old he will not
depart from it.
7 The [a]rich rules over the poor,
And the borrower *becomes* the
lender's slave.
8 He who [a]sows iniquity will reap
vanity,
And the [b]rod of his fury will
perish.
9 He who [1]is [a]generous will be
blessed,
For he [b]gives some of his food
to the poor.
10 [a]Drive out the scoffer, and
contention will go out,
Even strife and dishonor will
cease.
11 He who loves [a]purity of heart
And [1]whose speech is
[b]gracious, the king is his
friend.
12 The eyes of the LORD preserve
knowledge,
But He overthrows the words of
the treacherous man.
13 The [a]sluggard says, "There is a
lion outside;
I will be killed in the streets!"
14 The mouth of [1a]an adulteress is
a deep pit;
He who is [b]cursed of the LORD
will fall [2]into it.
15 Foolishness is bound up in the
heart of a child;
The [a]rod of discipline will
remove it far from him.
16 He [a]who oppresses the poor to
make [1]more for himself
Or who gives to the rich, [b]*will*
only *come to* poverty.

17 ¶ [a]Incline your ear and hear the
words of the wise,
And apply your mind to my
knowledge;
18 For it will be [a]pleasant if you
keep them within you,
[1]That they may be ready on
your lips.
19 So that your [a]trust may be in
the LORD,
I have [1]taught you today, even
you.
20 Have I not written to you
[1a]excellent things
Of counsels and knowledge,
21 To make you [a]know the
[1]certainty of the words of
truth
That you may [2b]correctly
answer him who sent you?

22 ¶ [a]Do not rob the poor because
he is poor,
Or [b]crush the afflicted at the
gate;
23 For the LORD will [a]plead their
case
And [1]take the life of those who
rob them.

24 ¶ Do not associate with a man
given to anger;
Or go with a [a]hot-tempered
man,
25 Or you will [a]learn his ways
And [1]find a snare for yourself.

26 ¶ Do not be among those who
[a]give [1]pledges,
Among those who become
guarantors for debts.
27 If you have nothing with which
to pay,
Why should he [a]take your bed
from under you?

28 ¶ [a]Do not move the ancient
boundary
Which your fathers have set.

29 ¶ Do you see a man skilled in his
work?
He will [a]stand before kings;
He will not stand before obscure
men.

On Life and Conduct

23 When you sit down to dine
with a ruler,
Consider carefully [1]what is
before you,
2 And put a knife to your throat
If you are a [a]man of *great*
appetite.
3 Do not [a]desire his delicacies,
For it is deceptive food.

4 ¶ [a]Do not weary yourself to gain
wealth,
[b]Cease from your
[1]consideration *of it.*
5 [1]When you set your eyes on it,
it is gone.
For [a]*wealth* certainly makes
itself wings
Like an eagle that flies *toward*
the heavens.

6 ¶ [a]Do not eat the bread of [1]a
[b]selfish man,
Or desire his delicacies;
7 For as he [1]thinks within
himself, so he is.
He says to you, "Eat and drink!"
But [a]his heart is not with you.
8 You will [a]vomit up [1]the morsel
you have eaten,
And waste your [2]compliments.

9 ¶ [a]Do not speak in the [1]hearing
of a fool,
For he will [b]despise the wisdom
of your words.

10 ¶ Do not move the ancient
boundary
Or [a]go into the fields of the
fatherless,
11 For their [a]Redeemer is strong;
[b]He will plead their case against
you.
12 Apply your heart to discipline
And your ears to words of
knowledge.

13 ¶ [a]Do not hold back discipline
from the child,
Although you [1]strike him with
the rod, he will not die.
14 You shall [1]strike him with
the rod
And [a]rescue his soul from Sheol.
15 ¶ My son, if your heart is [a]wise,
My own heart also will be glad;
16 And my [1]inmost being will
rejoice
When your lips speak [a]what is
right.

17 ¶ [a]Do not let your heart envy
sinners,
But *live* in the [1b]fear of the
LORD [2]always.
18 Surely there is a [1a]future,
And your [b]hope will not be cut
off.
19 Listen, my son, and [a]be wise,
And [b]direct your heart in the
way.
20 Do not be with [a]heavy drinkers
of wine,
Or with [b]gluttonous eaters of
meat;

17 [a]Prov 5:1
18 [1]Lit *They together* [a]Prov 2:10
19 [1]Lit *made you know* [a]Prov 3:5
20 [1]Or *previous* [a]Prov 8:6
21 [1]Lit *truth* [2]Lit *return to words of truth* [a]Luke 1:3,4 [b]Prov 25:13; 1 Pet 3:15
22 [a]Ex 23:6; Job 31:16; Prov 22:16 [b]Zech 7:10; Mal 3:5
23 [1]Lit *rob the soul* [a]1 Sam 25:39; Ps 12:5; 35:10; 140:12; Prov 23:11; Jer 51:36
24 [a]Prov 29:22
25 [1]Lit *take* [a]1 Cor 15:33
26 [1]Lit *strike hands* [a]Prov 17:18
27 [a]Ex 22:26; Prov 20:16
28 [a]Deut 19:14; 27:17; Job 24:2; Prov 23:10
29 [a]Gen 41:46; 1 Kin 10:8
23:1 [1]Or *who*
2 [a]Prov 23:20
3 [a]Ps 141:4; Prov 23:6; Dan 1:5,8,13,15,16
4 [1]Or *understanding* [a]Prov 15:27; 28:20; Matt 6:19; 1 Tim 6:9; Heb 13:5 [b]Prov 3:5,7
5 [1]Lit *Will your eyes fly upon it and it is not?* [a]Prov 27:24; 1 Tim 6:17
6 [1]Lit *an evil eye* [a]Ps 141:4 [b]Deut 15:9; Prov 28:22
7 [1]Lit *reckons in his soul* [a]Prov 26:24,25
8 [1]Lit *your* [2]Lit *pleasant words* [a]Prov 25:16
9 [1]Lit *ears* [a]Matt 7:6 [b]Prov 1:7
10 [a]Jer 22:3; Zech 7:10
11 [a]Job 19:25; Jer 50:34 [b]Prov 22:23
13 [1]Lit *smite* [a]Prov 13:24; 19:18
14 [1]Lit *smite* [a]1 Cor 5:5
15 [a]Prov 23:24f; 27:11; 29:3
16 [1]Lit *kidneys* [a]Prov 8:6
17 [1]Or *reverence* [2]Lit *all the day* [a]Ps 37:1; Prov 24:1,19 [b]Prov 28:14
18 [1]Lit *latter end* [a]Ps 19:11; 58:11; Prov 24:14 [b]Ps 9:18
19 [a]Prov 6:6 [b]Prov 4:23; 9:6
20 [a]Prov 20:1; 23:29,30; Is 5:22; Matt 24:49; Luke 21:34; Rom 13:13; Eph 5:18 [b]Deut 21:20; Prov 28:7

21 For the [a]heavy drinker and the
glutton will come to poverty,
And [b]drowsiness will clothe *one*
with rags.

22 ¶ [a]Listen to your father who
begot you,
And [b]do not despise your
mother when she is old.
23 [a]Buy truth, and do not sell *it,*
Get wisdom and instruction and
understanding.

24 ¶ The father of the righteous will
greatly rejoice,
And [a]he who sires a wise son
will be glad in him.
25 Let your [a]father and your
mother be glad,
And let her rejoice who gave
birth to you.

26 ¶ [a]Give me your heart, my son,
And let your eyes [1b]delight in
my ways.
27 For a harlot is a [a]deep pit
And an [1b]adulterous woman is
a narrow well.
28 Surely she [a]lurks as a robber,
And increases the [1]faithless
among men.

29 ¶ Who has [a]woe? Who has
sorrow?
Who has contentions? Who has
complaining?
Who has wounds without cause?
Who has redness of eyes?
30 Those who [a]linger long over
wine,
Those who go to [1]taste [b]mixed
wine.
31 Do not look on the wine when it
is red,
When it [1]sparkles in the cup,
When it [a]goes down smoothly;
32 At the last it [a]bites like a
serpent
And stings like a [b]viper.
33 Your eyes will see strange things
And your [1]mind will [a]utter
perverse things.
34 And you will be like one who
lies down in the [1]middle of
the sea,
Or like one who lies down on
the top of a [2]mast.
35 "They [a]struck me, *but* I did not
become [1]ill;
They beat me, *but* I did not
know *it.*
When shall I awake?
I will [b]seek [2]another drink."

Precepts and Warnings

24

Do not be [a]envious of evil
men,
Nor desire to [b]be with them;
2 For their [1]minds devise
[a]violence,
And their lips [b]talk of trouble.

3 ¶ [a]By wisdom a house is built,
And by understanding it is
established;
4 And by knowledge the rooms are
[a]filled
With all precious and pleasant
riches.

5 ¶ A [a]wise man is [1]strong,
And a man of knowledge
[2]increases power.
6 For [a]by wise guidance you will
[1]wage war,
And [b]in abundance of
counselors there is victory.

7 ¶ Wisdom is [a]*too* exalted for a
fool,
He does not open his mouth [b]in
the gate.

8 ¶ One who [a]plans to do evil,
Men will call a [1]schemer.
9 The [a]devising of folly is sin,
And the scoffer is an
abomination to men.

10 ¶ If you [a]are slack in the day of
distress,
Your strength is limited.
11 ¶ [a]Deliver those who are being
taken away to death,
And those who are staggering to
slaughter, Oh hold *them*
back.
12 If you say, "See, we did not
know this,"
Does He not [a]consider *it* [b]who
weighs the hearts?
And [c]does He not know *it* who
[d]keeps your soul?
And will He not [1e]render to
man according to his work?

13 ¶ My son, eat [a]honey, for it is
good,
Yes, the [b]honey from the comb
is sweet to your taste;
14 Know *that* [a]wisdom is thus for
your soul;
If you find *it,* then there will be
a [1b]future,
And your hope will not be
cut off.

15 ¶ [a]Do not lie in wait, O wicked
man, against the dwelling of
the righteous;

21 [a]Prov 21:17 [b]Prov 6:10,11
22 [a]Prov 1:8; Eph 6:1 [b]Prov 15:20; 30:17
23 [a]Prov 4:7; 18:15; Matt 13:44
24 [a]Prov 10:1; 15:20; 29:3
25 [a]Prov 27:11
26 [1]Another reading is *observe* [a]Prov 3:1; 4:4 [b]Ps 1:2; 119:24
27 [1]Lit *strange* [a]Prov 22:14 [b]Prov 5:20
28 [1]Lit *treacherous* [a]Prov 6:26; 7:12; Eccl 7:26
29 [a]Is 5:11,22
30 [1]Or *search out* [a]1 Sam 25:36; Prov 20:1; Is 5:11; 28:7; Eph 5:18 [b]Ps 75:8
31 [1]Lit *gives its eye* [a]Song 7:9
32 [a]Job 20:16; Prov 20:1; Eph 5:18 [b]Ps 91:13; Is 11:8
33 [1]Lit *heart* [a]Prov 2:12
34 [1]Lit *heart* [2]Or *lookout*
35 [1]I.e. from the effect of wounds [2]Lit *it yet again* [a]Prov 27:22; Jer 5:3 [b]Prov 26:11; Is 56:12
24:1 [a]Ps 37:1; Prov 3:31; 23:17; 24:19 [b]Ps 1:1; Prov 1:15
2 [1]Lit *hearts* [a]Is 30:12; Jer 22:17 [b]Job 15:35; Ps 10:7; 38:12
3 [a]Prov 9:1; 14:1
4 [a]Prov 8:21
5 [1]Lit *in strength* [2]Lit *strengthens power* [a]Prov 21:22
6 [1]Lit *make battle for yourself* [a]Prov 20:18 [b]Prov 11:14
7 [a]Ps 10:5; Prov 14:6; 17:16 [b]Job 5:4; Ps 127:5
8 [1]Or *deviser of evil* [a]Prov 6:14; 14:22; Rom 1:30
9 [a]Matt 15:19; Acts 8:22
10 [a]Deut 20:8; Job 4:5; Jer 51:46; Heb 12:3
11 [a]Ps 82:4; Is 58:6,7
12 [1]Lit *bring back* [a]Eccl 5:8 [b]1 Sam 16:7; Prov 21:2 [c]Ps 94:9-11 [d]Ps 121:3-8 [e]Job 34:11; Prov 12:14
13 [a]Ps 19:10; 119:103; Prov 25:16; Song 5:1 [b]Prov 16:24; 27:7; Song 4:11
14 [1]Lit *latter end* [a]Prov 2:10 [b]Prov 23:18
15 [a]Ps 10:9,10

Do not destroy his resting place;
16 For a [a]righteous man falls seven times, and rises again,
But the [b]wicked stumble in *time of* calamity.

17 ¶ [a]Do not rejoice when your enemy falls,
And do not let your heart be glad when he stumbles;
18 Or the LORD will see *it* and [1]be displeased,
And turn His anger away from him.

19 ¶ [a]Do not fret because of evildoers
Or be [b]envious of the wicked;
20 For [a]there will be no [1b]future for the evil man;
The [c]lamp of the wicked will be put out.

21 ¶ My son, [1a]fear the LORD and the king;
Do not associate with those who are given to change,
22 For their [a]calamity will rise suddenly,
And who knows the ruin *that comes* from both of them?

23 ¶ These also are [a]sayings of the wise.
To [1b]show partiality in judgment is not good.
24 He [a]who says to the wicked, "You are righteous,"
[b]Peoples will curse him, nations will abhor him;
25 But [a]to those who rebuke the *wicked* will be delight,
And a good blessing will come upon them.
26 He kisses the lips
Who gives [1]a right answer.

27 ¶ Prepare your work outside
And [a]make it ready for yourself in the field;
Afterwards, then, build your house.

28 ¶ Do not be a [a]witness against your neighbor without cause,
And [b]do not deceive with your lips.
29 [a]Do not say, "Thus I shall do to him as he has done to me;
I will [1]render to the man according to his work."

30 ¶ I passed by the field of the sluggard
And by the vineyard of the man [a]lacking [1]sense,
31 And behold, it was completely [a]overgrown with thistles;
Its surface was covered with [1b]nettles,
And its stone [c]wall was broken down.
32 When I saw, I [1]reflected upon it;
I looked, *and* received instruction.
33 "[a]A little sleep, a little slumber,
A little folding of the hands to rest,"
34 Then your poverty will come *as* [1]a robber
And your want like [2]an armed man.

Similitudes, Instructions

25 These also are [a]proverbs of Solomon which the men of Hezekiah, king of Judah, transcribed.
2 ¶ It is the glory of God to [a]conceal a matter,
But the glory of [b]kings is to search out a matter.
3 *As* the heavens for height and the earth for depth,
So the heart of kings is unsearchable.
4 Take away the [a]dross from the silver,
And there comes out a vessel for the [b]smith;
5 Take away the [a]wicked before the king,
And his [b]throne will be established in righteousness.
6 Do not claim honor in the presence of the king,
And do not stand in the place of great men;
7 For [a]it is better that it be said to you, "Come up here,"
Than for you to be placed lower in the presence of the prince,
Whom your eyes have seen.

8 ¶ Do not go out [a]hastily to [1]argue *your case;*
[2]Otherwise, what will you do in [3]the end,
When your neighbor humiliates you?
9 [1a]Argue your case with your neighbor,
And [b]do not reveal the secret of another,
10 Or he who hears *it* will reproach you,
And the evil report about you will not [1]pass away.

16 [a]Job 5:19; Ps 37:24; Mic 7:8 [b]Prov 6:15; 14:32; 24:22; Jer 18:17
17 [a]Job 31:29; Ps 35:15,19; Prov 17:5; Obad 12
18 [1]Lit *it is evil in His eyes*
19 [a]Ps 37:1 [b]Prov 23:17; 24:1
20 [1]Lit *latter end* [a]Job 15:31 [b]Prov 23:18 [c]Job 18:5,6; 21:17; Prov 13:9; 20:20
21 [1]Or *reverence* [a]Rom 13:1-7; 1 Pet 2:17
22 [a]Prov 24:16
23 [1]Lit *regard the face* [a]Prov 1:6; 22:17 [b]Prov 18:5; 28:21
24 [a]Prov 17:15; Is 5:23 [b]Prov 11:26
25 [a]Prov 28:23
26 [1]Or *an honest*
27 [a]Prov 27:23-27
28 [a]Prov 25:18 [b]Lev 6:2,3; 19:11; Eph 4:25
29 [1]Lit *bring back* [a]Prov 20:22; Matt 5:39; Rom 12:17
30 [1]Lit *heart* [a]Prov 6:32
31 [1]I.e. a kind of weed [a]Gen 3:18 [b]Job 30:7 [c]Is 5:5
32 [1]Lit *set my heart*
33 [a]Prov 6:10
34 [1]Or *a vagabond*; lit *one who walks* [2]Lit *a man with a shield*
25:1 [a]Prov 1:1
2 [a]Deut 29:29; Rom 11:33 [b]Ezra 6:1
4 [a]Prov 26:23; Ezek 22:18 [b]Mal 3:2,3
5 [a]Prov 20:8 [b]Prov 16:12
7 [a]Luke 14:7-11
8 [1]Lit *contend* [2]Lit *Lest* [3]Lit *its* [a]Prov 17:14; Matt 5:25
9 [1]Lit *Contend* [a]Matt 18:15 [b]Prov 11:13
10 [1]Lit *return*

11 ¶ *Like* apples of gold in settings of silver
Is a [a]word spoken in [1]right circumstances.
12 *Like* [1]an [a]earring of gold and an [b]ornament of [c]fine gold
Is a wise reprover to a [d]listening ear.
13 Like the cold of snow in the [1]time of harvest
Is a [a]faithful messenger to those who send him,
For he refreshes the soul of his masters.
14 *Like* [a]clouds and [b]wind without rain
Is a man who boasts [1]of his gifts falsely.
15 By [1a]forbearance a ruler may be persuaded,
And a soft tongue breaks the bone.
16 Have you [a]found honey? Eat *only* [1]what you need,
That you not have it in excess and vomit it.
17 Let your foot rarely be in your neighbor's house,
Or he will become [1]weary of you and hate you.
18 *Like* a club and a [a]sword and a sharp [b]arrow
Is a man who bears [c]false witness against his neighbor.
19 *Like* a bad tooth and [1]an unsteady foot
Is confidence in a [a]faithless man in time of trouble.
20 *Like* one who takes off a garment on a cold day, *or like* vinegar on [1]soda,
Is he who sings songs to [2]a troubled heart.
21 [a]If [1]your enemy is hungry, give him food to eat;
And if he is thirsty, give him water to drink;
22 For you will [1]heap burning coals on his head,
And [a]the LORD will reward you.
23 The north wind brings forth rain,
And a [1a]backbiting tongue, an angry countenance.
24 It is [a]better to live in a corner of the roof
Than [1]in a house shared with a contentious woman.
25 *Like* cold water to a weary soul,
So is [a]good news from a distant land.
26 *Like* a [a]trampled spring and a [1]polluted well
Is a righteous man who gives way before the wicked.
27 It is not good to eat much honey,
Nor is it glory to [a]search out [1]one's own glory.
28 *Like* a [a]city that is broken into *and* without walls
Is a man [b]who has no control over his spirit.

Similitudes, Instructions

26 Like snow in summer and like [a]rain in harvest,
So honor is not [b]fitting for a fool.
2 Like a [a]sparrow in *its* [1]flitting, like a swallow in *its* flying,
So a [b]curse without cause does not [2]alight.
3 A [a]whip is for the horse, a bridle for the donkey,
And a [b]rod for the back of fools.
4 [a]Do not answer a fool according to his folly,
Or you will also be like him.
5 [a]Answer a fool as his folly *deserves,*
That he not be [b]wise in his own eyes.
6 He cuts off *his own* feet *and* drinks violence
Who sends a message by the hand of a fool.
7 *Like* the legs *which* [1]are useless to the lame,
So is a proverb in the mouth of fools.
8 Like [1]one who binds a stone in a sling,
So is he who gives honor to a fool.
9 *Like* a thorn *which* [1]falls into the hand of a drunkard,
So is a proverb in the mouth of fools.
10 [1]*Like* an archer who wounds everyone,
So is he who hires a fool or who hires those who pass by.
11 Like [a]a dog that returns to its vomit
Is a fool who [b]repeats [1]his folly.
12 Do you see a man [a]wise in his own eyes?
[b]There is more hope for a fool than for him.
13 The [a]sluggard says, "There is a lion in the road!
A lion is [1]in the open square!"
14 *As* the door turns on its hinges,
So *does* the [a]sluggard on his bed.
15 The [a]sluggard buries his hand in the dish;

11 [1]Lit *its* [a]Prov 15:23
12 [1]Or *a nose ring* [a]Ex 32:2; Ezek 16:12 [b]2 Sam 1:24 [c]Job 28:17 [d]Prov 15:31
13 [1]Lit *day* [a]Prov 13:17
14 [1]Lit *in a gift of falsehood* [a]Jude 12 [b]Jer 5:13; Mic 2:11
15 [1]Lit *length of anger* [a]Gen 32:4; 1 Sam 25:24; Eccl 10:4
16 [1]Lit *your sufficiency* [a]Judg 14:8; 1 Sam 14:25
17 [1]Lit *surfeited with*
18 [a]Ps 57:4; Prov 12:18 [b]Jer 9:8 [c]Ex 20:16; Prov 24:28
19 [1]Lit *a slipping foot* [a]Job 6:15; Is 36:6
20 [1]I.e. natron [2]Lit *an evil*
21 [1]Lit *one who hates you* [a]Ex 23:4; 2 Kin 6:22; 2 Chr 28:15; Matt 5:44; Rom 12:20
22 [1]Lit *snatch up* [a]2 Sam 16:12; Matt 6:4
23 [1]Lit *tongue of secrecy* [a]Ps 101:5
24 [1]Lit *with a woman of contentions and a house of association* [a]Prov 21:9
25 [a]Prov 15:30
26 [1]Lit *ruined* [a]Ezek 32:2
27 [1]Lit *their* [a]Prov 27:2; Luke 14:11
28 [a]Prov 16:32 [b]2 Chr 32:5; Neh 1:3
26:1 [a]1 Sam 12:17 [b]Prov 17:7
2 [1]Lit *wandering* [2]Lit *come* [a]Prov 27:8; Is 16:2 [b]Num 23:8; Deut 23:5; 2 Sam 16:12
3 [a]Ps 32:9 [b]Prov 10:13
4 [a]Prov 23:9; Is 36:21; Matt 7:6
5 [a]Matt 16:1-4 [b]Prov 3:7; Rom 12:16
7 [1]Lit *hang down from*
8 [1]Lit *the binding of*
9 [1]Lit *goes up*
10 [1]Or *A master* workman *produces all things, But he who hires a fool is* like *one who hires those who pass by*
11 [1]Lit *with his* [a]2 Pet 2:22 [b]Ex 8:15
12 [a]Prov 3:7 [b]Prov 29:20
13 [1]Lit *within* [a]Prov 22:13
14 [a]Prov 6:9
15 [a]Prov 19:24

He is weary of bringing it to his
mouth again.
16 The sluggard is [a]wiser in his
own eyes
Than seven men who can [1]give
a discreet answer.
17 *Like* one who takes a dog by the
ears
Is he who passes by *and*
[1]meddles with [a]strife not
belonging to him.
18 Like a madman who throws
[a]Firebrands, arrows and death,
19 So is the man who [a]deceives his
neighbor,
And says, "[b]Was I not joking?"
20 For lack of wood the fire goes
out,
And where there is no
[a]whisperer, [b]contention
quiets down.
21 *Like* charcoal to hot embers and
wood to fire,
So is a [a]contentious man to
kindle strife.
22 The [a]words of a whisperer are
like dainty morsels,
And they go down into the
[1]innermost parts of the
body.
23 *Like* an earthen [a]vessel overlaid
with silver [b]dross
Are burning lips and a wicked
heart.
24 He who [a]hates disguises *it* with
his lips,
But he lays up [b]deceit in his
[1]heart.
25 When [1]he [a]speaks graciously,
do not believe him,
For there are seven abominations
in his heart.
26 *Though his* hatred [a]covers itself
with guile,
His wickedness will be [b]revealed
before the assembly.
27 He who [a]digs a pit will fall
into it,
And he who rolls a stone, it will
come back on him.
28 A lying tongue hates [1]those it
crushes,
And a [a]flattering mouth works
ruin.

Warnings and Instructions

27 [a]Do not boast about tomorrow,
For you [b]do not know what a
day may bring forth.
2 Let [a]another praise you, and not
your own mouth;
A stranger, and not your own
lips.
3 A stone is heavy and the sand
weighty,
But the provocation of a fool is
heavier than both of them.
4 Wrath is fierce and anger is a
flood,
But [a]who can stand before
jealousy?
5 Better is [a]open rebuke
Than love that is concealed.
6 Faithful are the [a]wounds of a
friend,
But [1]deceitful are the [b]kisses of
an enemy.
7 A sated [1]man [2]loathes honey,
But to a famished [1]man any
bitter thing is sweet.
8 Like a [a]bird that wanders from
her nest,
So is a man who [b]wanders from
his [1]home.
9 [a]Oil and perfume make the
heart glad,
So a [1]man's counsel is sweet to
his friend.
10 Do not forsake your own [a]friend
or [b]your father's friend,
And do not go to your brother's
house in the day of your
calamity;
Better is a neighbor who is near
than a brother far away.
11 [a]Be wise, my son, and make my
heart glad,
That I may [b]reply to him who
reproaches me.
12 A prudent man sees evil *and*
hides himself,
The [1]naive proceed *and* pay the
penalty.
13 [a]Take his garment when he
becomes surety for a
stranger;
And for an [1]adulterous woman
hold him in pledge.
14 [a]He who blesses his friend with
a loud voice early in the
morning,
It will be reckoned a curse to
him.
15 A [a]constant dripping on a day of
steady rain
And a contentious woman are
alike;
16 He who would [1]restrain her
[1]restrains the wind,
And [2]grasps oil with his right
hand.
17 Iron sharpens iron,
So one man sharpens another.
18 He who tends the [a]fig tree will
eat its fruit,
And he who [b]cares for his
master will be honored.

16 [1]Lit *return discreetly* [a]Prov 27:11
17 [1]Lit *infuriates himself* [a]Prov 3:30
18 [a]Is 50:11
19 [a]Prov 24:28 [b]Eph 5:4
20 [a]Prov 16:28 [b]Prov 22:10
21 [a]Prov 15:18; 29:22
22 [1]Lit *chambers of the belly* [a]Prov 18:8
23 [a]Matt 23:27; Luke 11:39 [b]Prov 25:4
24 [1]Lit *inward part* [a]Ps 41:6; Prov 10:18 [b]Prov 12:20
25 [1]Lit *his voice is gracious* [a]Ps 28:3; Prov 26:23; Jer 9:8
26 [a]Matt 23:28 [b]Luke 8:17
27 [a]Esth 7:10; Prov 28:10
28 [1]Lit *its crushed ones* [a]Prov 29:5
27:1 [a]James 4:13-16 [b]Luke 12:19,20; James 4:14
2 [a]Prov 25:27; 2 Cor 10:12,18; 12:11
4 [a]Prov 6:34; 1 John 3:12
5 [a]Prov 28:23; Gal 2:14
6 [1]Or *excessive* [a]Ps 141:5; Prov 20:30 [b]Matt 26:49
7 [1]Lit *soul* [2]Lit *tramples on*
8 [1]Lit *place* [a]Prov 26:2; Is 16:2 [b]Gen 21:14
9 [1]Lit *soul's* [a]Ps 23:5; 141:5
10 [a]Prov 18:24 [b]1 Kin 12:6-8; 2 Chr 10:6-8
11 [a]Prov 10:1; 23:15; 29:3 [b]Ps 119:42
12 [1]Lit *simple*
13 [1]Lit *strange* [a]Prov 20:16
14 [a]Ps 12:2
15 [a]Prov 19:13
16 [1]Lit *hide(s)* [2]Lit *encounters*
18 [a]2 Kin 18:31; Song 8:12; Is 36:16; 1 Cor 3:8; 9:7; 2 Tim 2:6 [b]Luke 12:42-44; 19:17

19 As in water face *reflects* face,
So the heart of man *reflects* man.
20 [1a]Sheol and [2]Abaddon are
[b]never satisfied,
Nor are the [c]eyes of man ever
satisfied.
21 The [a]crucible is for silver and
the furnace for gold,
And each [b]*is tested* by the
praise accorded him.
22 Though you [a]pound a fool in a
mortar with a pestle along
with crushed grain,
Yet his foolishness will not
depart from him.

23 ¶ [a]Know well the [1]condition of
your flocks,
And pay attention to your herds;
24 For riches are not forever,
Nor does a [a]crown *endure* to all
generations.
25 *When* the grass disappears, the
new growth is seen,
And the herbs of the mountains
are [a]gathered in,
26 The lambs *will be* for your
clothing,
And the goats *will bring* the
price of a field,
27 And *there will be* goats' milk
enough for your food,
For the food of your household,
And sustenance for your
maidens.

Warnings and Instructions

28 The wicked [a]flee when no one
is pursuing,
But the righteous are [1]bold as a
lion.
2 By the transgression of a land
[a]many are its princes,
But [b]by a man of understanding
and knowledge, so it
endures.
3 A [a]poor man who oppresses the
lowly
Is *like* a driving rain [1]which
leaves no food.
4 Those who forsake the law
[a]praise the wicked,
But those who keep the law
[b]strive with them.
5 Evil men [a]do not understand
justice,
But those who seek the LORD
[b]understand all things.
6 [a]Better is the poor who walks in
his integrity
Than he who is [1]crooked though
he be rich.
7 He who keeps the law is a
discerning son,
But he who is a companion of
[a]gluttons humiliates his
father.
8 He who increases his wealth by
[a]interest and usury
Gathers it [b]for him who is
gracious to the poor.
9 He who turns away his ear from
listening to the law,
Even his [a]prayer is an
abomination.
10 He who leads the upright astray
in an evil way
Will [a]himself fall into his own
pit,
But the [b]blameless will inherit
good.
11 The rich man is [a]wise in his
own eyes,
But the poor who has
understanding [1]sees through
him.
12 When the [a]righteous triumph,
there is great glory,
But [b]when the wicked rise, men
[1]hide themselves.
13 He who [a]conceals his
transgressions will not
prosper,
But he who [b]confesses and
forsakes *them* will find
compassion.
14 How blessed is the man who
[a]fears always,
But he who [b]hardens his heart
will fall into calamity.
15 *Like* a [a]roaring lion and a
rushing bear
Is a [b]wicked ruler over a poor
people.
16 A [a]leader who is a great
oppressor lacks
understanding,
But he who hates unjust gain
will prolong *his* days.
17 A man who is [a]laden with the
guilt of human blood
Will [1]be a fugitive until death;
let no one support him.
18 He who walks blamelessly will
be delivered,
But he who is [1a]crooked will
fall all at once.
19 [a]He who tills his land will
[b]have plenty of food,
But he who follows empty
pursuits will have poverty in
plenty.
20 A [a]faithful man will abound
with blessings,
But he who [b]makes haste to be
rich will not go unpunished.
21 To [1a]show partiality is not
good,

20 [1]I.e. The nether world [2]I.e. the place of destruction [a]Job 26:6; Prov 15:11 [b]Prov 30:15,16; Hab 2:5 [c]Eccl 1:8; 4:8
21 [a]Prov 17:3 [b]Luke 6:26
22 [a]Prov 23:35; 26:11; Jer 5:3
23 [1]Lit *face* [a]Jer 31:10; Ezek 34:12; John 10:3
24 [a]Job 19:9; Ps 89:39; Jer 13:18; Lam 5:16; Ezek 21:26
25 [a]Is 17:5; Jer 40:10,12
28:1 [1]Lit *confident* [a]Lev 26:17, 36; Ps 53:5
2 [a]1 Kin 16:8-28; 2 Kin 15:8-15 [b]Prov 11:11
3 [1]Lit *and there is no bread* [a]Matt 18:28
4 [a]Ps 49:18; Rom 1:32 [b]1 Kin 18:18; Neh 13:11,15; Matt 3:7; 14:4; Eph 5:11
5 [a]Ps 92:6; Is 6:9; 44:18 [b]Ps 119:100; Prov 2:9; John 7:17; 1 Cor 2:15; 1 John 2:20,27
6 [1]Lit *perverse of two ways* [a]Prov 19:1
7 [a]Prov 23:20
8 [a]Ex 22:25; Lev 25:36 [b]Job 27:17; Prov 13:22; 14:31
9 [a]Ps 66:18; 109:7; Prov 15:8; 21:27
10 [a]Ps 7:15; Prov 26:27 [b]Matt 6:33; Heb 6:12; 1 Pet 3:9
11 [1]Lit *examines him* [a]Prov 3:7; 26:5,12
12 [1]Lit *will be searched for* [a]Prov 11:10; 29:2 [b]Prov 28:28; Eccl 10:5, 6
13 [a]Job 31:33; Ps 32:3 [b]Ps 32:5; 1 John 1:9
14 [a]Prov 23:17 [b]Ps 95:8; Rom 2:5
15 [a]Prov 19:12; 1 Pet 5:8 [b]Ex 1:14; Prov 29:2; Matt 2:16
16 [a]Eccl 10:16; Is 3:12
17 [1]Lit *flee to the pit* [a]Gen 9:6; Ex 21:14
18 [1]Lit *perverse of two ways* [a]Prov 10:27
19 [a]Prov 12:11 [b]Prov 20:13
20 [a]Prov 10:6; Matt 24:45; 25:21 [b]Prov 20:21; 28:22; 1 Tim 6:9
21 [1]Lit *regard the face* [a]Prov 24:23

[b]Because for a piece of bread a
man will transgress.
22 A man with an [a]evil eye
[b]hastens after wealth
And does not know that want
will come upon him.
23 He who [a]rebukes a man will
afterward find *more* favor
Than he who [b]flatters with the
tongue.
24 He who [a]robs his father or his
mother
And says, "It is not a
transgression,"
Is the [b]companion of a man who
destroys.
25 An [1]arrogant man [a]stirs up
strife,
But he who [b]trusts in the LORD
[c]will [2]prosper.
26 He who [a]trusts in his own heart
is a fool,
But he who walks wisely will be
delivered.
27 He who [a]gives to the poor will
never want,
But he who [1]shuts his eyes will
have many curses.
28 When the wicked rise, men hide
themselves;
But when they perish, the
righteous increase.

Warnings and Instructions

29 A man who hardens *his* neck
after [a]much reproof
Will [b]suddenly be broken
[1]beyond remedy.
2 When the [a]righteous [1]increase,
the people rejoice,
But when a wicked man rules,
people groan.
3 A man who [a]loves wisdom
makes his father glad,
But he who [b]keeps company
with harlots wastes *his*
wealth.
4 The [a]king gives stability to the
land by justice,
But a man who takes bribes
overthrows it.
5 A man who [a]flatters his
neighbor
Is spreading a net for his steps.
6 By transgression an evil man is
[a]ensnared,
But the righteous [b]sings and
rejoices.
7 The [a]righteous [1]is concerned
for the rights of the poor,
The wicked does not understand
such [2]concern.
8 Scorners [a]set a city aflame,
But [b]wise men turn away anger.
9 When a wise man has a
controversy with a foolish
man,
[1]The foolish man either rages or
laughs, and there is no rest.
10 Men of [a]bloodshed hate the
blameless,
But the upright [1]are concerned
for his life.
11 A [a]fool [1]always loses his
temper,
But a [b]wise man holds it back.
12 If a [a]ruler pays attention to
falsehood,
All his ministers *become* wicked.
13 The [a]poor man and the
oppressor [1]have this in
common:
The LORD gives [b]light to the
eyes of both.
14 If a [a]king judges the poor with
truth,
His [b]throne will be established
forever.
15 The [a]rod and reproof give
wisdom,
But a child [1]who gets his own
way [b]brings shame to his
mother.
16 When the wicked [1]increase,
transgression increases;
But the [a]righteous will see their
fall.
17 [a]Correct your son, and he will
give you comfort;
He will also [1b]delight your soul.
18 Where there is [a]no [1]vision, the
people [b]are unrestrained,
But [c]happy is he who keeps the
law.
19 A slave will not be instructed by
words *alone;*
For though he understands, there
will be no response.
20 Do you see a man who is [a]hasty
in his words?
There is [b]more hope for a fool
than for him.
21 He who pampers his slave from
childhood
Will in the end find him to be a
son.
22 An [a]angry man stirs up strife,
And a hot-tempered man
abounds in transgression.
23 A man's [a]pride will bring him
low,
But a [b]humble spirit will obtain
honor.
24 He who is a partner with a thief
hates his own life;
He [a]hears the oath but tells
nothing.

21 [b]Ezek 13:19
22 [a]Prov 23:6 [b]Prov 21:5
23 [a]Prov 27:5,6 [b]Prov 29:5
24 [a]Prov 19:26 [b]Prov 18:9
25 [1]Lit *broad soul* [2]Lit *be made fat* [a]Prov 15:18 [b]Prov 29:25; 1 Tim 6:6 [c]Prov 11:25
26 [a]Prov 3:5
27 [1]Lit *hides* [a]Prov 11:24; 19:17
29:1 [1]Lit *and there is no remedy* [a]1 Sam 2:25; 2 Chr 36:16; Prov 1:24-31 [b]Prov 6:15
2 [1]Or *become great* [a]Esth 8:15; Prov 11:10; 28:12
3 [a]Prov 10:1; 15:20; 27:11; 28:7 [b]Prov 5:10; 6:26; Luke 15:30
4 [a]2 Chr 9:8; Prov 8:15; 29:14
5 [a]Ps 5:9
6 [a]Prov 22:5; Eccl 9:12 [b]Ex 15:1
7 [1]Lit *knows the cause* [2]Lit *knowledge* [a]Job 29:16; Ps 41:1; Prov 31:8,9
8 [a]Prov 11:11 [b]Prov 16:14
9 [1]Lit *He*
10 [1]Lit *seek his soul* [a]Gen 4:5-8; 1 John 3:12
11 [1]Lit *sends forth all his spirit* [a]Prov 12:16; 14:33 [b]Prov 19:11
12 [a]1 Kin 12:14
13 [1]Lit *meet together* [a]Prov 22:2 [b]Ezra 9:8; Ps 13:3
14 [a]Ps 72:4; Is 11:4 [b]Prov 16:12; 25:5
15 [1]Lit *left to himself* [a]Prov 13:24; 22:15 [b]Prov 10:1; 17:25
16 [1]Or *become great* [a]Ps 37:34, 36; 58:10; 91:8; 92:11; Prov 21:12
17 [1]Lit *give delight to* [a]Prov 13:24; 29:15 [b]Prov 10:1
18 [1]Or *revelation* [a]1 Sam 3:1; Ps 74:9; Amos 8:11,12 [b]Ex 32:25 [c]Ps 1:1,2; 106:3; 119:2; Prov 8:32; John 13:17
20 [a]James 1:19 [b]Prov 26:12
22 [a]Prov 15:18; 26:21
23 [a]Prov 11:2; 16:18; Dan 4:30, 31; Matt 23:12; James 4:6 [b]Prov 15:33; 18:12; 22:4; Is 66:2; Luke 14:11; 18:14; James 4:10
24 [a]Lev 5:1

25 The [a]fear of man [1]brings a
snare,
But he who [b]trusts in the LORD
will be exalted.
26 [a]Many seek the ruler's [1]favor,
But [b]justice for man *comes* from
the LORD.
27 An [a]unjust man is abominable to
the righteous,
And he who is [b]upright in the
way is abominable to the
wicked.

The Words of Agur

30 The words of Agur the son of Ja-
keh, the [1]oracle.
¶ The man declares to Ithiel, to Ithiel
and Ucal:
2 Surely I am more [a]stupid than
any man,
And I do not have the
understanding of a man.
3 Neither have I learned wisdom,
Nor do I have the [a]knowledge of
the Holy One.
4 Who has [a]ascended into heaven
and descended?
Who has gathered the [b]wind in
His fists?
Who has [c]wrapped the waters
in [1]His garment?
Who has [d]established all the
ends of the earth?
What is His [e]name or His son's
name?
Surely you know!
5 ¶ Every [a]word of God is tested;
He is a [b]shield to those who
take refuge in Him.
6 [a]Do not add to His words
Or He will reprove you, and you
will be proved a liar.
7 ¶ Two things I asked of You,
Do not refuse me before I die:
8 Keep deception and [1]lies far
from me,
Give me neither poverty nor
riches;
Feed me with the [a]food that is
my portion,
9 That I not be [a]full and deny
[b]*You* and say, "Who is the
LORD?"
Or that I not be [c]in want and
steal,
And [d]profane the name of my
God.
10 ¶ Do not slander a slave to his
master,
Or he will [a]curse you and you
will be found guilty.

11 ¶ There is a [1]kind of *man* who
[a]curses his father
And does not bless his mother.
12 There is a [1]kind who is [a]pure
in his own eyes,
Yet is not washed from his
filthiness.
13 There is a [1]kind—oh how [a]lofty
are his eyes!
And his eyelids are raised *in
arrogance.*
14 There is a [1]kind of *man* whose
[a]teeth are *like* swords
And his [b]jaw teeth *like* knives,
To [c]devour the afflicted from
the earth
And the needy from among men.
15 ¶ The leech has two daughters,
"Give," "Give."
There are three things that will
not be satisfied,
Four that will not say, "Enough":
16 [1a]Sheol, and the [b]barren
womb,
Earth that is never satisfied with
water,
And fire that never says,
"Enough."
17 The eye that [a]mocks a father
And [1b]scorns a mother,
The [c]ravens of the valley will
pick it out,
And the young [c]eagles will
eat it.
18 ¶ There are three things which
are too wonderful for me,
Four which I do not understand:
19 The way of an [a]eagle in the sky,
The way of a serpent on a rock,
The way of a ship in the middle
of the sea,
And the way of a man with a
maid.
20 This is the way of an
[a]adulterous woman:
She eats and wipes her mouth,
And says, "I have done no
wrong."
21 ¶ Under three things the earth
quakes,
And under four, it cannot
bear up:
22 Under a [a]slave when he
becomes king,
And a fool when he is satisfied
with food,
23 Under an unloved woman when
she gets a husband,
And a maidservant when she
supplants her mistress.
24 ¶ Four things are small on the
earth,

29:25 [1]Lit *gives* [a]Gen 12:12; 20:2; Luke 12:4; John 12:42,43 [b]Ps 91:1-16; Prov 18:10; 28:25
26 [1]Lit *face* [a]Prov 19:6 [b]Is 49:4; 1 Cor 4:4
27 [a]Ps 6:8; 139:21,22; Prov 12:8 [b]Ps 69:4; Prov 29:10; Matt 10:22; 24:9; John 15:18; 17:14; 1 John 3:13
30:1 [1]Or *burden*
2 [a]Ps 49:10; 73:22; Prov 12:1
3 [a]Prov 9:10
4 [1]Lit *the* [a]Ps 68:18; John 3:13; Eph 4:8 [b]Ex 15:10; Ps 135:7 [c]Job 26:8; 38:8,9 [d]Ps 24:2; Is 45:18 [e]Rev 19:12
5 [a]Ps 12:6; 18:30 [b]Ps 3:3; 84:11; Prov 2:7
6 [a]Deut 4:2; 12:32; Rev 22:18
8 [1]Lit *words of falsehood* [a]Job 23:12; Matt 6:11
9 [a]Deut 8:12; 31:20; Neh 9:25; Hos 13:6 [b]Josh 24:27; Job 31:28 [c]Prov 6:30 [d]Ex 20:7
10 [a]Eccl 7:21
11 [1]Or *generation* [a]Ex 21:17; Prov 20:20
12 [1]Or *generation* [a]Prov 16:2; Is 65:5; Luke 18:11; Titus 1:15,16
13 [1]Or *generation* [a]Prov 6:17; Is 2:11; 5:15
14 [1]Or *generation* [a]Ps 57:4 [b]Job 29:17 [c]Ps 14:4; Amos 8:4
16 [1]I.e. The nether world [a]Prov 27:20 [b]Gen 30:1
17 [1]Lit *despises to obey* [a]Gen 9:22 [b]Prov 15:20 [c]Deut 28:26
19 [a]Deut 28:49; Jer 48:40; 49:22
20 [a]Prov 5:6
22 [a]Prov 19:10; Eccl 10:7

But they are exceedingly wise:
25 The [a]ants are not a strong people,
But they prepare their food in the summer;
26 The [1a]shephanim are not mighty people,
Yet they make their houses in the rocks;
27 The locusts have no king,
Yet all of them go out in [a]ranks;
28 The lizard you may grasp with the hands,
Yet it is in kings' palaces.

29 ¶ There are three things which are stately in *their* march,
Even four which are stately when they walk:
30 The lion *which* is [a]mighty among beasts
And does not [1b]retreat before any,
31 The [1]strutting rooster, the male goat also,
And a king *when his* army is with him.

32 ¶ If you have been foolish in exalting yourself
Or if you have plotted *evil,* [a]*put your* hand on your mouth.
33 For the [1]churning of milk produces butter,
And pressing the nose brings forth blood;
So the [1]churning of [a]anger produces strife.

The Words of Lemuel

31 The words of King Lemuel, the [1]oracle which his mother taught him:
2 ¶ What, O my son?
And what, O [a]son of my womb?
And what, O son of my [b]vows?
3 [a]Do not give your strength to women,
Or your ways to that which [b]destroys kings.
4 It is not for [a]kings, O Lemuel,
It is not for kings to [b]drink wine,
Or for rulers to desire strong drink,
5 For they will drink and forget what is decreed,
And [a]pervert the [1]rights of all the [2]afflicted.
6 Give strong drink to him who is [a]perishing,
And wine to him [1b]whose life is bitter.
7 Let him drink and forget his poverty
And remember his trouble no more.
8 [a]Open your mouth for the mute,
For the [1]rights of all the [2]unfortunate.
9 Open your mouth, [a]judge righteously,
And [1]defend the [b]rights of the afflicted and needy.

Description of a Worthy Woman

10 ¶ An [a]excellent wife, who can find?
For her worth is far [b]above jewels.
11 The heart of her husband trusts in her,
And he will have no lack of gain.
12 She does him good and not evil
All the days of her life.
13 She looks for wool and flax
And works with her [1]hands [2]in delight.
14 She is like [a]merchant ships;
She brings her food from afar.
15 She [a]rises also while it is still night
And [b]gives food to her household
And [1]portions to her maidens.
16 She considers a field and buys it;
From [1]her earnings she plants a vineyard.
17 She [a]girds [1]herself with strength
And makes her arms strong.
18 She senses that her gain is good;
Her lamp does not go out at night.
19 She stretches out her hands to the distaff,
And her [1]hands grasp the spindle.
20 She [1a]extends her hand to the poor,
And she stretches out her hands to the needy.
21 She is not afraid of the snow for her household,
For all her household are [a]clothed with scarlet.
22 She makes [a]coverings for herself;
Her clothing is [b]fine linen and [c]purple.
23 Her husband is known [a]in the gates,
When he sits among the elders of the land.
24 She makes [a]linen garments and sells *them,*
And [1]supplies belts to the [2]tradesmen.

25 [a]Prov 6:6
26 [1]Small, shy, furry animals *(Hyrax syriacus)* found in the peninsula of the Sinai, northern Israel, and the region round the Dead Sea; KJV *coney,* orig NASB *badgers* [a]Lev 11:5; Ps 104:18
27 [a]Joel 2:7
30 [1]Lit *turn back* [a]Judg 14:18; 2 Sam 1:23 [b]Mic 5:8
31 [1]Lit *girt in the loins*
32 [a]Job 21:5; 40:4; Mic 7:16
33 [1]Lit *pressing* [a]Prov 10:12; 29:22
31:1 [1]Or *burden*
2 [a]Is 49:15 [b]1 Sam 1:11
3 [a]Prov 5:9 [b]Deut 17:17; 1 Kin 11:1; Neh 13:26
4 [a]Eccl 10:17 [b]Prov 20:1; Is 5:22; Hos 4:11
5 [1]Lit *judgment* [2]Lit *sons of affliction* [a]Ex 23:6; Deut 16:19; Prov 17:15
6 [1]Lit *bitter of soul* [a]Job 29:13 [b]Job 3:20; Is 38:15
8 [1]Lit *judgment* [2]Lit *sons of passing away* [a]Job 29:12-17; Ps 82
9 [1]Lit *judge the afflicted* [a]Lev 19:15; Deut 1:16 [b]Is 1:17; Jer 22:16
10 [a]Ruth 3:11; Prov 12:4; 19:14 [b]Job 28:18; Prov 8:11
13 [1]Lit *palms* [2]Or *willingly*
14 [a]Ezek 27:25
15 [1]Or *prescribed tasks* [a]Prov 20:13; Rom 12:11 [b]Luke 12:42
16 [1]Lit *the fruit of her palms*
17 [1]Lit *her loins* [a]1 Kin 18:46; 2 Kin 4:29; Job 38:3
19 [1]Lit *palms*
20 [1]Lit *spreads out her palm* [a]Deut 15:11; Job 31:16-20; Prov 22:9; Rom 12:13; Eph 4:28
21 [a]2 Sam 1:24
22 [a]Prov 7:16 [b]Gen 41:42; Rev 19:8,14 [c]Judg 8:26; Luke 16:19
23 [a]Deut 16:18; Ruth 4:1,11
24 [1]Lit *gives* [2]Lit *Canaanite* [a]Judg 14:12

25 Strength and [a]dignity are her
clothing,
And she smiles at the [1]future.
26 She [a]opens her mouth in
wisdom,
And the [1]teaching of kindness is
on her tongue.
27 She looks well to the ways of her
household,
And does not eat the [a]bread of
idleness.
28 Her children rise up and bless
her;
Her husband *also,* and he praises
her, *saying:*
29 "Many daughters have done
nobly,
But you excel them all."
30 Charm is deceitful and beauty is
vain,
But a woman who [1a]fears the
LORD, she shall be praised.
31 Give her the [1]product of her
hands,
And let her works praise her in
the gates.

25 [1]Lit *latter days* [a]1 Tim 2:9, 10
26 [1]Or *law* [a]Prov 10:31
27 [a]Prov 19:15
30 [1]Or *reverences* [a]Ps 112:1; Prov 22:4
31 [1]Lit *fruit*

Ecclesiastes

Title and Background

The writer's title ("Preacher") comes from a Hebrew root word related to "assembly" or "congregation." Perhaps the Preacher also held an office in the assembly. The *Septuagint* word for "Preacher" is *ecclesiastes*, from which most English titles of the book are taken.

Author and Date of Writing

No time period or writer's name is mentioned in the book, but several passages strongly suggest that Solomon is the author. Though some date the book as late as the third century B.C., Solomonic authorship would demand a date of the tenth century B.C.

Theme and Message

Life not centered on God is purposeless and meaningless. Without Him, nothing can satisfy (2:25). With Him, all of life and His other good gifts are to be gratefully received and used and enjoyed to the full (2:26; 11:8). The book contains the philosophical and theological reflections of an old man, most of whose life was meaningless because he himself had not relied on God.

Outline

I. Introduction: Working to Accumulate Things to Achieve Happiness Is Profitless (1:1–11)
II. Life Is to Be Enjoyed as a Gift From God (1:12—11:6)
III. Man Should Begin Enjoying Life in His Youth, Remembering That God Will Judge (11:7—12:7)
IV. Conclusion: Reverently Trust in and Obey God (12:8–14)

The Futility of All Endeavor

1 The words of the [a]Preacher, the son of David, king in Jerusalem.
2 "[1a]Vanity of vanities," says the
Preacher,
"[1]Vanity of vanities! All is
[2]vanity."
3 ¶ [a]What advantage does man
have in all his work
Which he does under the sun?
4 A generation goes and a
generation comes,
But the [a]earth [1]remains forever.
5 Also, [a]the sun rises and the sun
sets;
And [1]hastening to its place it
rises there *again.*
6 [1a]Blowing toward the south,
Then turning toward the north,
The wind continues [2]swirling
along;
And on its circular courses the
wind returns.
7 All the rivers [1]flow into the sea,
Yet the sea is not full.
To the place where the rivers
[1]flow,
There they [1]flow again.
8 All things are wearisome;
Man is not able to tell *it.*
[a]The eye is not satisfied with
seeing,
Nor is the ear filled with
hearing.
9 [a]That which has been is that
which will be,
And that which has been done is
that which will be done.
So there is nothing new under
the sun.
10 Is there anything of which one
might say,
"See this, it is new"?
Already it has existed for ages
Which were before us.
11 There is [a]no remembrance of
[1]earlier things;
And also of the [2]later things
which will occur,
There will be for them no
remembrance
Among those who will come
[2]later *still.*

The Futility of Wisdom

12 ¶ I, the [a]Preacher, have been king
over Israel in Jerusalem.

1:1 [a]Eccl 1:12; 7:27; 12:8-10
2 [1]Or *Futility of futilities* [2]Or *futile* [a]Ps 39:5,6; 62:9; 144:4; Eccl 12:8; Rom 8:20
3 [a]Eccl 2:11; 3:9; 5:16
4 [1]Lit *stands* [a]Ps 104:5; 119:90
5 [1]Lit *panting* [a]Ps 19:6
6 [1]Lit *Going* [2]Lit *turning* [a]Eccl 11:5; John 3:8
7 [1]Lit *go*
8 [a]Prov 27:20; Eccl 4:8
9 [a]Eccl 1:10; 2:12; 3:15; 6:10
11 [1]Lit *first* or *former* [2]Lit *latter* or *after* [a]Eccl 2:16; 9:5
12 [a]Eccl 1:1; 7:27; 12:8-10

13 And I [a]set my [1]mind to seek and
[b]explore by wisdom concerning all that
has been done under heaven. *It* is [2]a
grievous [c]task *which* God has given to
the sons of men to be afflicted with.
14 I have seen all the works which
have been done under the sun, and behold, all is [1a]vanity and striving after
wind.
15 What is [a]crooked cannot be
straightened and what is lacking cannot
be counted.
16 ¶ I [1]said to myself, "Behold, I have
magnified and increased [a]wisdom more
than all who were over Jerusalem before
me; and my [2]mind has observed [3]a
wealth of wisdom and knowledge."
17 And I [a]set my [1]mind to know wisdom and to [b]know madness and folly; I
realized that this also is [c]striving after
wind.
18 Because [a]in much wisdom there is
much grief, and increasing knowledge *results in* increasing pain.

The Futility of Pleasure and Possessions

2 I said [1]to myself, "Come now, I will
test you with [a]pleasure. So [2]enjoy
yourself." And behold, it too was futility.
2 [a]I said of laughter, "It is madness,"
and of pleasure, "What does it accomplish?"
3 I explored with my [1]mind *how* to
[a]stimulate my body with wine while my
[1]mind was guiding *me* wisely, and how
to take hold of [b]folly, until I could see
[c]what good there is for the sons of men
[2]to do under heaven the few [3]years of
their lives.
4 I enlarged my works: I [a]built
houses for myself, I planted [b]vineyards
for myself;
5 I made [a]gardens and [b]parks for
myself and I planted in them all kinds of
fruit trees;
6 I made [a]ponds of water for myself
from which to irrigate a forest of growing
trees.
7 I bought male and female slaves
and I had [1a]homeborn slaves. Also I possessed flocks and [b]herds larger than all
who preceded me in Jerusalem.
8 Also, I collected for myself silver
and [a]gold and the treasure of kings and
provinces. I provided for myself [b]male
and female singers and the pleasures of
men—many concubines.
9 ¶ Then I became [a]great and increased more than all who preceded me
in Jerusalem. My wisdom also stood
by me.
10 [a]All that my eyes desired I did not
refuse them. I did not withhold my heart
from any pleasure, for my heart was
pleased because of all my labor and this
was my [b]reward for all my labor.
11 Thus I considered all my activities
which my hands had done and the labor
which I had [1]exerted, and behold all was
[2a]vanity and striving after wind and
there was [b]no profit under the sun.

Wisdom Excels Folly

12 ¶ So I turned to [a]consider wisdom,
madness and folly; for what *will* the man
do who will come after the king *except*
[b]what has already been done?
13 And I saw that [a]wisdom excels folly as light excels darkness.
14 The wise man's eyes are in his
head, but the [a]fool walks in darkness.
And yet I know that [b]one fate befalls
them both.
15 Then I said [1]to myself, "[a]As is the
fate of the fool, it will also befall me.
[b]Why then have I been extremely wise?"
So [2]I said to myself, "This too is vanity."
16 For there is [a]no [1]lasting remembrance of the wise man *as* with the fool,
inasmuch as *in* the coming days all will be
forgotten. And [b]how the wise man and
the fool alike die!
17 So I [a]hated life, for the work which
had been done under the sun was [1]griev-
ous to me; because everything is futility
and striving after wind.

The Futility of Labor

18 ¶ Thus I hated [a]all the fruit of my
labor for which I had labored under the
sun, for I must [b]leave it to the man who
will come after me.
19 And who knows whether he will be
a wise man or [a]a fool? Yet he will have
[1]control over all the fruit of my labor for
which I have labored by acting wisely under the sun. This too is [b]vanity.
20 Therefore I [1]completely despaired
of all the fruit of my labor for which I had
labored under the sun.
21 When there is a man who has labored with wisdom, knowledge and
[a]skill, then he [b]gives his [1]legacy to one
who has not labored with them. This too
is vanity and a great evil.
22 For what does a man get in [a]all his
labor and in [1]his striving with which he
labors under the sun?
23 Because all his days his task is painful and [a]grievous; even at night his
[1]mind [b]does not rest. This too is vanity.
24 ¶ There is [a]nothing better for a
man *than* to eat and drink and [1]tell himself that his labor is good. This also I have
seen that it is [b]from the hand of God.

13 [1]Lit *heart* [2]Lit *an evil* [a]Eccl 1:17 [b]Eccl 3:10 [c]Eccl 2:23
14 [1]Or *futility* [a]Eccl 2:11
15 [a]Eccl 7:13
16 [1]Lit *spoke with my heart, saying* [2]Lit *heart* [3]Lit *an abundance* [a]1 Kin 3:12; Eccl 2:9
17 [1]Lit *heart* [a]Eccl 1:13 [b]Eccl 2:12 [c]Eccl 1:14
18 [a]Eccl 2:23
2:1 [1]Lit *in my heart* [2]Lit *consider with goodness* [a]Eccl 7:4
2 [a]Prov 14:13; Eccl 7:3
3 [1]Lit *heart* [2]Lit *which they do* [3]Lit *days* [a]Judg 9:13; Ps 104:15; Eccl 10:19 [b]Eccl 7:25 [c]Eccl 2:24
4 [a]1 Kin 7:1-12 [b]Song 8:11
5 [a]Song 4:16 [b]Neh 2:8
6 [a]Neh 2:14
7 [1]Lit *sons of the house* [a]Gen 14:14 [b]1 Kin 4:23
8 [a]1 Kin 9:28 [b]2 Sam 19:35
9 [a]1 Chr 29:25; Eccl 1:16
10 [a]Eccl 6:2 [b]Eccl 3:22
11 [1]Lit *labored to do* [2]Or *futility*, and so throughout the ch [a]Eccl 1:14 [b]Eccl 1:3
12 [a]Eccl 1:17 [b]Eccl 1:9
13 [a]Eccl 7:11
14 [a]1 John 2:11 [b]Ps 49:10; Eccl 3:19
15 [1]Lit *in my heart* [2]Lit *I spoke in my heart* [a]Eccl 2:16 [b]Eccl 6:8
16 [1]Lit *forever* [a]Eccl 1:11 [b]Eccl 2:14
17 [1]Lit *evil* [a]Eccl 4:2
18 [a]Eccl 1:3 [b]Ps 39:6
19 [1]Lit *dominion* [a]1 Kin 12:13 [b]1 Tim 6:10
20 [1]Lit *turned aside my heart to despair*
21 [1]Lit *share* [a]Eccl 4:4 [b]Eccl 2:18
22 [1]Lit *the striving of his heart* [a]Eccl 1:3
23 [1]Lit *heart* [a]Job 5:7; Eccl 1:18 [b]Ps 127:2
24 [1]Lit *cause his soul to see good in his labor* [a]Eccl 2:3; Is 56:12; Luke 12:19; 1 Cor 15:32; 1 Tim 6:17 [b]Eccl 3:13

25 For who can eat and who can have
enjoyment without [1]Him?
26 For to a person who is good in His
sight [a]He has given wisdom and knowledge and joy, while to the sinner He has
given the task of gathering and collecting
so that he may [b]give to one who is good
in God's sight. This too is [c]vanity and
striving after wind.

A Time for Everything

3 There is an appointed time for everything. And there is a [a]time for every
[1]event under heaven—
2 A time to give birth and a [a]time
to die;
A time to plant and a time to
uproot what is planted.
3 A [a]time to kill and a time to
heal;
A time to tear down and a time
to build up.
4 A time to [a]weep and a time to
[b]laugh;
A time to mourn and a time to
[c]dance.
5 A time to throw stones and a
time to gather stones;
A time to embrace and a time to
shun embracing.
6 A time to search and a time to
give up as lost;
A time to keep and a time to
throw away.
7 A time to tear apart and a time
to sew together;
A time to [a]be silent and a time
to speak.
8 A time to love and a time to
[a]hate;
A time for war and a time for
peace.
9 ¶ [a]What profit is there to the
worker from that in which he toils?
10 I have seen the [a]task which God
has given the sons of men with which to
occupy themselves.

God Set Eternity in the Heart of Man

11 He has [a]made everything [1]appro-
priate in its time. He has also set eternity
in their heart, [2]yet so that man [b]will not
find out the work which God has done
from the beginning even to the end.
12 ¶ I know that there is [a]nothing
better for them than to rejoice and to do
good in one's lifetime;
13 moreover, that every man who eats
and drinks sees good in all his labor—it
is the [a]gift of God.
14 I know that everything God does
will remain forever; there is nothing to

25 [1]So Gr; Heb *me*
26 [a]Job 32:8; Prov 2:6 [b]Job 27:16,17; Prov 13:22 [c]Eccl 1:14
3:1 [1]Lit *delight* [a]Eccl 3:17; 8:6
2 [a]Job 14:5; Heb 9:27
3 [a]Gen 9:6; 1 Sam 2:6; Hos 6:1,2
4 [a]Rom 12:15 [b]Ps 126:2 [c]Ex 15:20
7 [a]Amos 5:13
8 [a]Ps 101:3; Prov 13:5
9 [a]Eccl 1:3; 2:11; 5:16
10 [a]Eccl 1:13; 2:26
11 [1]Lit *beautiful* [2]Or *without which man* [a]Gen 1:31 [b]Job 5:9; Eccl 7:23; 8:17; Rom 11:33
12 [a]Eccl 2:24
13 [a]Eccl 2:24; 5:19
14 [1]Or *be in awe before Him* [a]Eccl 5:7; 7:18; 8:12,13; 12:13
15 [a]Eccl 1:9; 6:10
16 [a]Eccl 4:1; 5:8; 8:9
17 [1]Lit *in my heart* [2]Or *delight* [a]Gen 18:25; Ps 96:13; 98:9; Eccl 11:9; Matt 16:27; Rom 2:6-10; 2 Thess 1:6-9 [b]Eccl 3:1; 8:6
18 [1]Lit *in my heart* [a]Ps 49:12, 20; 73:22
19 [1]Lit *and they have one fate* [2]Or *futility* [a]Ps 49:12; Eccl 9:12
20 [a]Gen 3:19; Ps 103:14; Eccl 12:7
21 [a]Eccl 12:7
22 [a]Eccl 2:24 [b]Eccl 2:18; 6:12; 8:7; 10:14
4:1 [a]Job 35:9; Ps 12:5; Eccl 3:16; 5:8; Is 5:7 [b]Jer 16:7; Lam 1:9
2 [a]Job 3:11-26; Eccl 2:17; 7:1
3 [a]Job 3:11-22; Eccl 6:3; Luke 23:29
4 [1]Or *futility,* and so throughout the ch [a]Eccl 2:21 [b]Eccl 1:14
5 [a]Prov 6:10; 24:33 [b]Is 9:20
6 [a]Prov 15:16, 17; 16:8

add to it and there is nothing to take from
it, for God has *so* worked that men should
[1a]fear Him.
15 That [a]which is has been already
and that which will be has already been,
for God seeks what has passed by.
16 ¶ Furthermore, I have seen under
the sun *that* in the place of justice there
is [a]wickedness and in the place of righteousness there is wickedness.
17 I said [1]to myself, "[a]God will judge
both the righteous man and the wicked
man," for a [b]time for every [2]matter and
for every deed is there.
18 I said [1]to myself concerning the
sons of men, "God has surely tested them
in order for them to see that they are but
[a]beasts."
19 [a]For the fate of the sons of men
and the fate of beasts [1]is the same. As
one dies so dies the other; indeed, they
all have the same breath and there is no
advantage for man over beast, for all is
[2]vanity.
20 All go to the same place. All came
from the [a]dust and all return to the dust.
21 Who knows that the [a]breath of
man ascends upward and the breath of
the beast descends downward to the
earth?
22 I have seen that [a]nothing is better
than that man should be happy in his
activities, for that is his lot. For who will
bring him to see [b]what will occur after him?

The Evils of Oppression

4 Then I looked again at all the acts of
[a]oppression which were being done
under the sun. And behold *I saw* the tears
of the oppressed and *that* they had [b]no
one to comfort *them;* and on the side of
their oppressors was power, but they had
no one to comfort *them.*
2 So [a]I congratulated the dead who
are already dead more than the living
who are still living.
3 But [a]better *off* than both of them is
the one who has never existed, who has
never seen the evil activity that is done
under the sun.
4 ¶ I have seen that every labor and
every [a]skill which is done is *the result of*
rivalry between a man and his neighbor.
This too is [1b]vanity and striving after
wind.
5 The fool [a]folds his hands and
[b]consumes his own flesh.
6 One hand full of rest is [a]better
than two fists full of labor and striving
after wind.
7 ¶ Then I looked again at vanity under the sun.
8 There was a certain man without a

[1]dependent, having neither a son nor a brother, yet there was no end to all his labor. Indeed, [a]his eyes were not satisfied with riches *and he never asked,* "And [b]for whom am I laboring and depriving myself of pleasure?" This too is vanity and it is a [c]grievous task.

9 ¶ Two are better than one because they have a good return for their labor.

10 For if [1]either of them falls, the one will lift up his companion. But woe to the one who falls when there is not [2]another to lift him up.

11 Furthermore, if two lie down together they [1]keep warm, but [a]how can one be warm *alone?*

12 And if [1]one can overpower him who is alone, two can resist him. A cord of three *strands* is not quickly torn apart.

13 ¶ A [a]poor yet wise lad is better than an old and foolish king who no longer knows *how* to receive [1]instruction.

14 For he has come [a]out of prison to become king, even though he was born poor in his kingdom.

15 I have seen all the living under the sun throng to the side of the second lad who [1]replaces him.

16 There is no end to all the people, to all who were before them, and even the ones who will come later will not be happy with him, for this too is [a]vanity and striving after wind.

Your Attitude Toward God

5 [1a]Guard your steps as you go to the house of God and draw near to listen rather than to offer the [b]sacrifice of fools; for they do not know they are doing evil.

2 [1]Do not be [a]hasty [2]in word or [3]impulsive in thought to bring up a matter in the presence of God. For God is in heaven and you are on the earth; therefore let your [b]words be few.

3 For the dream comes through much [1]effort and the voice of a [a]fool through many words.

4 ¶ When you [a]make a vow to God, do not be late in paying it; for *He takes* no delight in fools. [b]Pay what you vow!

5 It is [a]better that you should not vow than that you should vow and not pay.

6 Do not let your [1]speech cause [2]you to sin and do not say in the presence of the messenger *of God* that it was a [a]mistake. Why should God be angry on account of your voice and destroy the work of your hands?

7 For in many dreams and in many words there is [1]emptiness. Rather, [2a]fear God.

8 ¶ If you see [a]oppression of the poor and [b]denial of justice and righteousness in the province, do not be [c]shocked at the [1]sight; for one [2]official watches over another [2]official, and there are higher [3]officials over them.

9 After all, a king who cultivates the field is an advantage to the land.

The Folly of Riches

10 ¶ [a]He who loves money will not be satisfied with money, nor he who loves abundance *with its* income. This too is [1]vanity.

11 [a]When good things increase, those who consume them increase. So what is the advantage to their owners except to [1]look on?

12 The sleep of the working man is [a]pleasant, whether he eats little or much; but the [1]full stomach of the rich man does not allow him to sleep.

13 ¶ There is a grievous evil *which* I have seen under the sun: [a]riches being [1]hoarded by their owner to his hurt.

14 When those riches were lost through [1]a bad investment and he had fathered a son, then there was nothing [2]to support him.

15 [a]As he had come naked from his mother's womb, so will he return as he came. He will [b]take nothing from the fruit of his labor that he can carry in his hand.

16 This also is a grievous evil—exactly as a man [1]is born, thus will he [2]die. So [a]what is the advantage to him who [b]toils for the wind?

17 Throughout his life [a]*he* also eats in darkness with [b]great vexation, sickness and anger.

18 ¶ Here is what I have seen to be [a]good and [1]fitting: to eat, to drink and [2]enjoy oneself in all one's labor in which he toils under the sun *during* the few [3]years of his life which God has given him; for this is his [4b]reward.

19 Furthermore, as for every man to whom [a]God has given riches and wealth, He has also [b]empowered him to eat from them and to receive his [1]reward and rejoice in his labor; this is the [c]gift of God.

20 For he will not often [1]consider the [2]years of his life, because [a]God keeps [3]him occupied with the gladness of his heart.

The Futility of Life

6 There is an [a]evil which I have seen under the sun and it is prevalent [1]among men—

2 a man to whom God has [a]given riches and wealth and honor so that his soul [b]lacks nothing of all that he desires; yet God has not empowered him to eat

8 [1]Lit *second* [a]Prov 27:20; Eccl 1:8; 5:10 [b]Eccl 2:21 [c]Eccl 1:13
10 [1]Lit *they fall* [2]Lit *a second*
11 [1]Lit *have warmth* [a]1 Kin 1:1-4
12 [1]Lit *he*
13 [1]Or *warning* [a]Eccl 7:19; 9:15
14 [a]Gen 41:14, 41-43
15 [1]Lit *stands in his stead*
16 [a]Eccl 1:14
5:1 [1]Ch 4:17 in Heb [a]Ex 3:5; 30:18-20; Is 1:12 [b]1 Sam 15:22; Prov 15:8; 21:27
2 [1]Ch 5:1 in Heb [2]Lit *with your mouth* [3]Lit *hurry your heart* [a]Prov 20:25 [b]Prov 10:19; Matt 6:7
3 [1]Lit *task* [a]Job 11:2; Prov 15:2; Eccl 10:14
4 [a]Num 30:2; Ps 50:14; 76:11 [b]Ps 66:13,14
5 [a]Prov 20:25; Acts 5:4
6 [1]Lit *mouth* [2]Lit *your body* [a]Lev 4:2,22; Num 15:25
7 [1]Lit *vanity* [2]Or *revere* [a]Eccl 3:14; 7:18; 8:12, 13; 12:13
8 [1]Lit *delight* [2]Lit *high one* [3]Lit *ones* [a]Eccl 4:1 [b]Ezek 18:18 [c]1 Pet 4:12
10 [1]Or *futility* [a]Eccl 1:8; 2:10, 11; 4:8
11 [1]Lit *see with their eyes* [a]Eccl 2:9
12 [1]Lit *satiety* [a]Prov 3:24
13 [1]Lit *guarded* [a]Eccl 6:2
14 [1]Lit *an evil task* [2]Lit *in his hand*
15 [a]Job 1:21 [b]Ps 49:17; 1 Tim 6:7
16 [1]Lit *comes* [2]Lit *go* [a]Eccl 1:3; 2:11; 3:9 [b]Prov 11:29
17 [a]Ps 127:2 [b]Eccl 2:23
18 [1]Lit *beautiful* [2]Lit *see good* [3]Or *days* [4]Or *share* [a]Eccl 2:24 [b]Eccl 2:10
19 [1]Or *share* [a]2 Chr 1:12; Eccl 6:2 [b]Eccl 6:2 [c]Eccl 3:13
20 [1]Lit *remember* [2]Or *days* [3]So with Gr [a]Ex 23:25
6:1 [1]Lit *upon* [a]Eccl 5:13
2 [a]1 Kin 3:13 [b]Ps 17:14; 73:7; Eccl 2:10

from them, for a foreigner [1]enjoys them. This is [2]vanity and a severe affliction.

3 If a man fathers a hundred *children* and lives many years, however many [1]they be, but his soul is not satisfied with good things and he does not even have a *proper* [a]burial, *then* I say, "Better [b]the miscarriage than he,

4 for it comes in futility and goes into obscurity; and its name is covered in obscurity.

5 "It never sees the sun and it never knows *anything;* [1]it is better off than he.

6 "Even if the *other* man lives a thousand years twice and does not [1]enjoy good things—[a]do not all go to one place?"

7 ¶ [a]All a man's labor is for his mouth and yet the [1]appetite is not [2]satisfied.

8 For [a]what advantage does the wise man have over the fool? What *advantage* does the poor man have, knowing *how* to walk before the living?

9 What the eyes [a]see is better than what the soul [1]desires. This too is [b]futility and a striving after wind.

10 ¶ Whatever [a]exists has already been named, and it is known what man is; for he [b]cannot dispute with him who is stronger than he is.

11 For there are many words which increase futility. What *then* is the advantage to a man?

12 For who knows what is good for a man during *his* lifetime, *during* the few [1]years of his futile life? He will [2]spend them like a shadow. For who can tell a man [a]what will be after him under the sun?

Wisdom and Folly Contrasted

7 A [a]good name is better than a
good ointment,
And the [b]day of *one's* death is
better than the day of one's
birth.
2 It is better to go to a house of
mourning
Than to go to a house of
feasting,
Because [1]that is the [a]end of
every man,
And the living [2b]takes *it* to
[3]heart.
3 [a]Sorrow is better than laughter,
For [b]when a face is sad a heart
may be happy.
4 The [1]mind of the wise is in the
house of mourning,
While the [1]mind of fools is in
the house of pleasure.
5 It is better to [a]listen to the
rebuke of a wise man
Than for one to listen to the
song of fools.
6 For as the [1]crackling of [a]thorn
bushes under a pot,
So is the [b]laughter of the fool;
And this too is futility.
7 For [a]oppression makes a wise
man mad,
And a [b]bribe [1]corrupts the
heart.
8 The [a]end of a matter is better
than its beginning;
[b]Patience of spirit is better than
haughtiness of spirit.
9 Do not be [1a]eager in your heart
to be angry,
For anger resides in the bosom
of fools.
10 Do not say, "Why is it that the
former days were better
than these?"
For it is not from wisdom that
you ask about this.
11 Wisdom along with an
inheritance is good
And an [a]advantage to those who
see the sun.
12 For [a]wisdom is [1]protection *just
as* money is [1]protection,
But the advantage of knowledge
is that [b]wisdom preserves
the lives of its possessors.
13 Consider the [a]work of God,
For who is [b]able to straighten
what He has bent?
14 [a]In the day of prosperity be
happy,
But [b]in the day of adversity
consider—
God has made the one as well as
the other
So that man will [c]not discover
anything *that will be* after
him.

15 ¶ I have seen everything during my [1a]lifetime of futility; there is [b]a righteous man who perishes in his righteousness and there is [c]a wicked man who prolongs *his life* in his wickedness.

16 Do not be excessively [a]righteous and do not [b]be overly wise. Why should you ruin yourself?

17 Do not be excessively wicked and do not be a fool. Why should you [a]die before your time?

18 It is good that you grasp one thing and also not [1]let go of the other; for the one who [a]fears God comes forth with [2]both of them.

19 ¶ [a]Wisdom strengthens a wise man more than ten rulers who are in a city.

20 Indeed, [a]there is not a righteous

2 [1]Lit *eats from them* [2]Or *futility*
3 [1]Lit *the days of his years* [a]Is 14:20; Jer 8:2; 22:19 [b]Job 3:16; Eccl 4:3
5 [1]Lit *more rest has this one than that*
6 [1]Lit *see* [a]Eccl 2:14
7 [1]Lit *soul* [2]Lit *filled* [a]Prov 16:26
8 [a]Eccl 2:15
9 [1]Lit *goes after* [a]Eccl 11:9 [b]Eccl 1:14
10 [a]Eccl 1:9; 3:15 [b]Job 9:32; 40:2; Prov 21:30; Is 45:9
12 [1]Lit *days* [2]Lit *do* [a]Eccl 3:22
7:1 [a]Prov 22:1 [b]Eccl 4:2; 7:8
2 [1]I.e. death [2]Lit *gives* [3]Lit *his heart* [a]Eccl 2:14, 16; 3:19,20; 6:6; 9:2,3 [b]Ps 90:12
3 [a]Eccl 2:2 [b]2 Cor 7:10
4 [1]Lit *heart*
5 [a]Ps 141:5; Prov 6:23; 13:18; 15:31,32; 25:12; Eccl 9:17
6 [1]Lit *voice* [a]Ps 58:9; 118:12 [b]Eccl 2:2
7 [1]Lit *destroys* [a]Eccl 4:1; 5:8 [b]Ex 23:8; Deut 16:19; Prov 17:8,23
8 [a]Eccl 7:1 [b]Prov 14:29; 16:32; Gal 5:22; Eph 4:2
9 [1]Lit *hasty in your spirit* [a]Prov 14:17; James 1:19
11 [a]Prov 8:10, 11; Eccl 2:13
12 [1]Lit *in a shadow* [a]Eccl 7:19; 9:18 [b]Prov 3:18; 8:35
13 [a]Eccl 3:11; 8:17 [b]Eccl 1:15
14 [a]Deut 26:11; Eccl 3:22; 9:7; 11:9 [b]Deut 8:5; Job 2:10 [c]Eccl 3:22
15 [1]Lit *days* [a]Eccl 6:12; 9:9 [b]Eccl 8:14 [c]Eccl 8:12,13
16 [a]Prov 25:16; Phil 3:6 [b]Rom 12:3
17 [a]Job 22:16; Ps 55:23; Prov 10:27
18 [1]Lit *rest your hand* [2]Lit *all* [a]Eccl 3:14; 5:7; 8:12,13; 12:13
19 [a]Eccl 7:12; 9:13-18
20 [a]1 Kin 8:46; 2 Chr 6:36; Ps 143:2; Prov 20:9; Rom 3:23

man on earth who *continually* does good
and who never sins.
21 Also, do not [1]take seriously all
words which are spoken, so that you will
not hear your servant [a]cursing you.
22 For [1]you also have realized that
you likewise have many times cursed others.
23 ¶ I tested all this with wisdom, *and*
I said, "I will be wise," [a]but it was far
from me.
24 What has been is remote and [a]ex-
ceedingly [1]mysterious. [b]Who can discover it?
25 I [1a]directed my [2]mind to know,
to investigate and to seek wisdom and an
explanation, and to know the evil of folly
and the foolishness of madness.
26 And I discovered more [a]bitter than
death the woman whose heart is [b]snares
and nets, whose hands are chains. [c]One
who is pleasing to God will escape from
her, but [d]the sinner will be captured by
her.
27 ¶ "Behold, I have discovered this,"
says the Preacher, "*adding* one thing to
another to find an explanation,
28 which [1]I am still seeking but have
not found. I have found one man among
a thousand, but I have not found a [a]wom-
an among all these.
29 "Behold, I have found only this, that
[a]God made men upright, but they have
sought out many devices."

Obey Rulers

8 Who is like the wise man and who
knows the interpretation of a matter?
A man's wisdom [a]illumines [1]him and
causes his [b]stern face to [2]beam.
2 ¶ I say, "Keep the [1]command of
the king because of the [a]oath [2]before
God.
3 "Do not be in a hurry [1a]to leave
him. Do not join in an evil matter, for he
will do whatever he pleases."
4 Since the word of the king is authoritative, [a]who will say to him, "What
are you doing?"
5 ¶ He who [a]keeps a *royal* command
[b]experiences no [1]trouble, for a wise
heart knows the proper time and procedure.
6 For [a]there is a proper time and procedure for every delight, though a man's
trouble is heavy upon him.
7 If no one [a]knows what will happen, who can tell him when it will happen?
8 [a]No man has authority to restrain
the wind with the wind, or authority over
the day of death; and there is no discharge in the time of war, and [b]evil will
not deliver [1]those who practice it.
9 All this I have seen and applied my
[1]mind to every deed that has been done
under the sun wherein a man has exer-
cised [a]authority over *another* man to his
hurt.
10 ¶ So then, I have seen the wicked
buried, those who used to go in and out
from the holy place, and they are [a]*soon*
forgotten in the city where they did thus.
This too is futility.
11 Because the [a]sentence against an
evil deed is not executed quickly, therefore [b]the hearts of the sons of men
among them are given fully to do evil.
12 Although a sinner does evil a hundred *times* and may [a]lengthen his *life,*
still I know that it will be [b]well for those
who fear God, who fear [1]Him openly.
13 But it will [a]not be well for the evil
man and he will not lengthen his days
like a [b]shadow, because he does not fear
God.
14 ¶ There is futility which is done on
the earth, that is, there are [a]righteous
men to whom it [1]happens according to
the deeds of the wicked. On the other
hand, there are [b]evil men to whom it
[1]happens according to the deeds of the
righteous. I say that this too is futility.
15 So I commended pleasure, for there
is nothing good for [a]a man under the sun
except to eat and to drink and to be merry, and this will stand by him in his [1]toils
throughout the days of his life which God
has given him under the sun.
16 ¶ When I [a]gave my heart to know
wisdom and to see the task which has
been done on the earth (even though one
should [1b]never sleep day or night),
17 and I saw every work of God, *I concluded* that [a]man cannot discover the
work which has been done under the
sun. Even though man should seek labori-
ously, he will not discover; and [b]though
the wise man should say, "I know," he
cannot discover.

Men Are in the Hand of God

9 For I have taken all this to my heart
and explain [1]it that righteous men,
wise men, and their deeds are [a]in the
hand of God. [b]Man does not know
whether *it will be* [c]love or hatred; anything [2]awaits him.
2 ¶ [a]It is the same for all. There is
[b]one fate for the righteous and for the
wicked; for the good, for the clean and for
the unclean; for the man who offers a
sacrifice and for the one who does not
sacrifice. As the good man is, so is the
sinner; as the swearer is, so is the one
who [1]is afraid to swear.
3 This is an evil in all that is done
under the sun, that there is [a]one fate for

21 [1]Lit *give your heart to* [a]Prov 30:10
22 [1]Lit *your heart knows also*
23 [a]Eccl 3:11; 8:17
24 [1]Lit *deep* [a]Rom 11:33 [b]Job 11:7; 37:23; Eccl 8:17
25 [1]Lit *turned about* [2]Lit *heart* [a]Eccl 1:15,17; 10:13
26 [a]Prov 5:4 [b]Prov 7:23 [c]Prov 6:23,24 [d]Prov 22:14
28 [1]Lit *my soul still seeks* [a]1 Kin 11:3
29 [a]Gen 1:27
8:1 [1]Lit *his face* [2]Or *change* [a]Ex 34:29,30 [b]Deut 28:50
2 [1]Lit *mouth* [2]Lit *of* [a]Ex 22:11; 2 Sam 21:7; Ezek 17:18
3 [1]Lit *to go out from his presence* [a]Eccl 10:4
4 [a]Job 9:12; Dan 4:35
5 [1]Lit *evil thing* [a]Eccl 12:13 [b]Prov 12:21
6 [a]Eccl 3:1,17
7 [a]Eccl 3:22; 6:12; 7:14; 9:12
8 [1]Lit *its possessors* [a]Ps 49:7 [b]Eccl 8:13
9 [1]Lit *heart* [a]Eccl 4:1; 5:8; 7:7
10 [a]Eccl 1:11; 2:16; 9:5,15
11 [a]Ex 34:6; Ps 86:15; Rom 2:4; 2 Pet 3:9 [b]Eccl 9:3
12 [1]Lit *before Him* [a]Eccl 7:15 [b]Deut 4:40; 12:25; Ps 37:11; Prov 1:33; Is 3:10
13 [a]Eccl 8:8; Is 3:11 [b]Job 14:2; Eccl 6:12
14 [1]Lit *strikes* [a]Ps 73:14; Eccl 7:15 [b]Job 21:7; Ps 73:3,12; Jer 12:1; Mal 3:15
15 [1]Lit *labor* [a]Eccl 2:24; 3:12,13; 5:18; 9:7
16 [1]Lit *see no sleep in his eyes* [a]Eccl 1:13,14 [b]Eccl 2:23
17 [a]Eccl 3:11 [b]Ps 73:16; Eccl 7:23; Rom 11:33
9:1 [1]Lit *all this* [2]Lit *is before them* [a]Deut 33:3; Job 12:10; Ps 119:109 [b]Eccl 10:14 [c]Eccl 9:6
2 [1]Lit *fears an oath* [a]Job 9:22; Eccl 9:11 [b]Eccl 2:14; 3:19; 6:6; 7:2
3 [a]Eccl 9:2; Jer 17:10

all men. Furthermore, [b]the hearts of the
sons of men are full of evil and [c]insanity
is in their hearts throughout their lives.
Afterwards they *go* to the dead.
4 For whoever is joined with all the
living, there is hope; surely a live dog is
better than a dead lion.
5 For the living know they will die;
but the dead [a]do not know anything, nor
have they any longer a reward, for their
[b]memory is forgotten.
6 Indeed their love, their hate and
their zeal have already perished, and they
will no longer have a [a]share in all that is
done under the sun.
7 ¶ Go *then,* [a]eat your bread in happiness and drink your wine with a cheerful heart; for God has already approved
your works.
8 Let your [a]clothes be white all the
time, and let not [b]oil be lacking on your
head.
9 Enjoy life with the woman whom
you love all the days of your [1a]fleeting
life which He has given to you under the
sun[2]; for this is your [b]reward in life and
in your toil in which you have labored
under the sun.

Whatever Your Hand Finds to Do

10 ¶ Whatever your hand finds to do,
[a]do *it* with *all* your might; for there is no
[b]activity or planning or knowledge or
wisdom in [c]Sheol where you are going.
11 ¶ I again saw under the sun that the
[a]race is not to the swift and the [b]battle
is not to the warriors, and neither is
bread to the wise nor [c]wealth to the discerning nor favor to men of ability; for
time and [d]chance overtake them all.
12 Moreover, man does not [a]know
his time: like fish caught in a treacherous
net and [b]birds trapped in a snare, so the
sons of men are [c]ensnared at an evil time
when it [d]suddenly falls on them.
13 ¶ Also this I came to see as wisdom
under the sun, and [1]it impressed me.
14 There [a]was a small city with few
men in it and a great king came to it,
surrounded it and constructed large
siegeworks against it.
15 But there was found in it a [a]poor
wise man and he [1]delivered the city [b]by
his wisdom. Yet [c]no one remembered
that poor man.
16 So I said, "[a]Wisdom is better than
strength." But the wisdom of the poor
man is despised and his words are not
heeded.
17 The [a]words of the wise heard in
quietness are *better* than the shouting of
a ruler among fools.
18 [a]Wisdom is better than weapons
of war, but [b]one sinner destroys much
good.

A Little Foolishness

10 Dead flies make a [a]perfumer's oil
stink, so a little foolishness is
weightier than wisdom *and* honor.
2 A wise man's heart *directs him* toward the right, but the foolish [a]man's
heart *directs him* toward the left.
3 Even when the fool walks along
the road, his [1]sense is lacking and he
[2a]demonstrates to everyone *that* he is a
fool.
4 If the ruler's [1]temper rises against
you, [a]do not abandon your position, because [b]composure allays great offenses.
5 ¶ There is an evil I have seen under
the sun, like an error which goes forth
from the ruler—
6 [a]folly is set in many exalted places
while rich men sit in humble places.
7 I have seen [a]slaves *riding* [b]on
horses and princes walking like slaves on
the land.
8 ¶ [a]He who digs a pit may fall into
it, and a [b]serpent may bite him who
breaks through a wall.
9 He who quarries stones may be
hurt by them, and he who splits logs may
be endangered by them.
10 If the [1]axe is dull and he does not
sharpen *its* edge, then he must [2]exert
more strength. Wisdom has the advantage of giving success.
11 If the serpent bites [1a]before being
charmed, there is no profit for the
charmer.
12 [a]Words from the mouth of a wise
man are gracious, while the lips of a [b]fool
consume him;
13 the beginning of [1]his talking is folly and the end of [2]it is wicked [a]madness.
14 Yet the [a]fool multiplies words. No
man knows what will happen, and who
can tell him [b]what will come after him?
15 The toil of [1]a fool *so* wearies him
that he does not *even* know how to go to
a city.
16 Woe to you, O land, whose [a]king
is a lad and whose princes [1]feast in the
morning.
17 Blessed are you, O land, whose
king is of nobility and whose princes eat
at the appropriate time—for strength and
not for [a]drunkenness.
18 Through [a]indolence the rafters
sag, and through slackness the house
leaks.
19 *Men* prepare a meal for enjoyment,
and [a]wine makes life merry, and [b]mon-
ey [1]is the answer to everything.
20 Furthermore, [a]in your bedcham-
ber do not [b]curse a king, and in your

3 [b]Eccl 8:11 [c]Eccl 1:17
5 [a]Job 14:21 [b]Ps 88:12; Eccl 1:11; 2:16; 8:10; Is 26:14
6 [a]Eccl 2:10; 3:22
7 [a]Eccl 2:24; 8:15
8 [a]Rev 3:4 [b]Ps 23:5
9 [1]Lit *life of vanity* [2]Heb adds *all the days of your vanity* [a]Eccl 6:12; 7:15 [b]Eccl 2:10
10 [a]Eccl 11:6; Rom 12:11; Col 3:23 [b]Eccl 9:5 [c]Gen 37:35; Job 21:13; Is 38:10
11 [a]Amos 2:14, 15 [b]2 Chr 20:15; Ps 76:5; Zech 4:6 [c]Deut 8:17,18 [d]1 Sam 6:9
12 [a]Eccl 8:7 [b]Prov 7:23 [c]Prov 29:6; Is 24:18; Hos 9:8 [d]Luke 21:34,35
13 [1]Lit *great it was to me*
14 [a]2 Sam 20:16-22
15 [1]Or *might have delivered* [a]Eccl 4:13 [b]2 Sam 20:22 [c]Eccl 2:16; 8:10
16 [a]Prov 21:22; Eccl 7:12,19
17 [a]Eccl 7:5; 10:12
18 [a]Eccl 9:16 [b]Josh 7:1-26; 2 Kin 21:2-17
10:1 [a]Ex 30:25
2 [a]Matt 6:33; Col 3:1
3 [1]Lit *heart* [2]Lit *says* [a]Prov 13:16; 18:2
4 [1]Lit *spirit* [a]Eccl 8:3 [b]1 Sam 25:24-33; Prov 25:15
6 [a]Esth 3:1,5f; Prov 28:12; 29:2
7 [a]Prov 19:10 [b]Esth 6:8-10
8 [a]Ps 7:15; Prov 26:27 [b]Amos 5:19
10 [1]Lit *iron* [2]Lit *strengthen*
11 [1]Lit *without enchantment* [a]Ps 58:4,5; Jer 8:17
12 [a]Prov 10:32; 22:11; Luke 4:22 [b]Prov 10:14; 18:7; Eccl 4:5
13 [1]Lit *the words of his mouth* [2]Lit *his mouth* [a]Eccl 7:25
14 [a]Prov 15:2; Eccl 5:3 [b]Eccl 3:22; 6:12; 7:14; 8:7
15 [1]Lit *fools*
16 [1]Lit *eat* [a]Is 3:4,12
17 [a]Prov 31:4; Is 5:11
18 [a]Prov 24:30-34
19 [1]Lit *answers all* [a]Judg 9:13; Ps 104:15; Eccl 2:3 [b]Eccl 7:12
20 [a]2 Kin 6:12; Luke 12:3 [b]Ex 22:28; Acts 23:5

sleeping rooms do not curse a rich man,
for a bird of the heavens will carry the
sound and the winged creature will make
the matter known.

Cast Your Bread on the Waters

11 [a]Cast your bread on the surface
of the waters, for you [a]will find it
[1]after many days.
2 [a]Divide your portion to seven, or
even to eight, for you do not know what
[b]misfortune may occur on the earth.
3 If the clouds are full, they pour out
rain upon the earth; and whether a tree
falls toward the south or toward the
north, wherever the tree falls, there it
[1]lies.
4 He who watches the wind will not
sow and he who looks at the clouds will
not reap.
5 Just as you do not [a]know [1]the path
of the wind and [b]how bones *are formed*
in the womb of the [2]pregnant woman, so
you do not [c]know the activity of God
who makes all things.
6 ¶ Sow your seed [a]in the morning
and do not [1]be idle in the evening, for
you do not know whether [2]morning or
evening sowing will succeed, or whether
both of them alike will be good.
7 ¶ The light is pleasant, and *it is*
good for the eyes to [a]see the sun.
8 Indeed, if a man should live many
years, let him [a]rejoice in them all, and let
him remember the [b]days of darkness, for
they will be many. Everything that is to
come *will be* futility.
9 ¶ Rejoice, young man, during your
childhood, and let your heart be pleasant
during the days of young manhood. And
follow the [1]impulses of your heart and
the [2a]desires of your eyes. Yet know
that [b]God will bring you to judgment for
all these things.
10 So, remove grief and anger from
your heart and put away [1a]pain from
your body, because childhood and the
prime of life are fleeting.

Remember God in Your Youth

12 [a]Remember also your Creator in
the days of your youth, before the
[b]evil days come and the years draw near
when you will say, "I have no delight in
them";
2 before the [a]sun and the light, the
moon and the stars are darkened, and
clouds return after the rain;
3 in the day that the watchmen of the
house tremble, and mighty men [a]stoop,
the grinding ones stand idle because they
are few, and [b]those who look through
[1]windows grow dim;
4 and the doors on the street are shut
as the [a]sound of the grinding mill is low,
and one will arise at the sound of the
bird, and all the [b]daughters of song will
[1]sing softly.
5 Furthermore, [1]men are afraid of a
high place and of terrors on the road; the
almond tree blossoms, the grasshopper
drags himself along, and the caperberry is
ineffective. For man goes to his eternal
[a]home while [b]mourners go about in the
street.
6 *Remember Him* before the silver
cord is [1]broken and the [a]golden bowl is
crushed, the pitcher by the well is shattered and the wheel at the cistern is
crushed;
7 then the [a]dust will return to the
earth as it was, and the [1b]spirit will return to [c]God who gave it.
8 "[a]Vanity of vanities," says the
Preacher, "all is vanity!"

Purpose of the Preacher

9 ¶ In addition to being a wise man,
the Preacher also taught the people
knowledge; and he pondered, searched
out and arranged [a]many proverbs.
10 The Preacher sought to find [a]de-
lightful words and to write [b]words of
truth correctly.
11 ¶ The [a]words of wise men are like
[b]goads, and masters of *these* collections
are like [1]well-driven [c]nails; they are giv-
en by one Shepherd.
12 But beyond this, my son, be
warned: the [1]writing of [a]many books
is endless, and excessive [b]devotion *to
books* is wearying to the body.
13 ¶ The conclusion, when all has
been heard, *is:* [a]fear God and [b]keep His
commandments, because this *applies to*
[c]every person.
14 For [a]God will bring every act to
judgment, everything which is hidden,
whether it is good or evil.

11:1 [1]Lit *in, within* [a]Deut 15:10; Prov 19:17; Matt 10:42; Gal 6:9; Heb 6:10
2 [a]Ps 112:9; Matt 5:42; Luke 6:30; 1 Tim 6:18 [b]Eccl 11:8
3 [1]Lit *is*
5 [1]Or with many mss *how the spirit* enters *the bones in the womb* [2]Lit *full* [a]John 3:8 [b]Ps 139:13-16 [c]Eccl 1:13
6 [1]Lit *let down your hand* [2]Lit *this or that* [a]Eccl 9:10
7 [a]Eccl 6:5
8 [a]Eccl 9:7 [b]Eccl 12:1
9 [1]Lit *ways* [2]Lit *sights* [a]Num 15:39; Job 31:7; Eccl 2:10 [b]Eccl 3:17; Rom 14:10
10 [1]Lit *evil* [a]2 Cor 7:1; 2 Tim 2:22
12:1 [a]Deut 8:18; Neh 4:14; Ps 63:6 [b]Eccl 11:8
2 [a]Is 5:30; Ezek 32:7; Joel 3:15; Matt 24:29
3 [1]Or *holes* [a]Ps 35:14 [b]Gen 27:1; 1 Sam 3:2
4 [1]Lit *be brought low* [a]Jer 25:10; Rev 18:22 [b]2 Sam 19:35
5 [1]Lit *they* [a]Job 17:13 [b]Gen 50:10; Jer 9:17
6 [1]So with Gr; Heb *removed* [a]Zech 4:2
7 [1]Or *breath* [a]Gen 3:19; Job 34:15; Ps 104:29; Eccl 3:20 [b]Job 34:14; Eccl 3:21; Luke 23:46; Acts 7:59 [c]Num 16:22; Is 57:16; Zech 12:1
8 [a]Eccl 1:2
9 [a]1 Kin 4:32
10 [a]Prov 10:32 [b]Prov 22:20
11 [1]Lit *planted* [a]Prov 1:6; Eccl 7:5 [b]Acts 2:37 [c]Ezra 9:8; Is 22:23
12 [1]Lit *making* [a]1 Kin 4:32 [b]Eccl 1:18
13 [a]Eccl 3:14 [b]Deut 4:2; Eccl 8:5 [c]Deut 10:12; Mic 6:8
14 [a]Eccl 3:17; Matt 10:26; Rom 2:16; 1 Cor 4:5

The Song of Solomon

Title and Background

The title in the Hebrew text is "the Song of Songs, which is Solomon's," meaning either by, for or about Solomon. The phrase "Song of Songs" means the greatest of songs.

Author and Date of Writing

Verse 1 seems to ascribe authorship to Solomon. He is referred to seven times in the book, but whether he was the author remains an open question. Consistency of language, style, tone, perspective and recurring refrains seems to argue for a single author. If Solomon is the author, the Song can be dated in the tenth century B.C.

Theme and Message

In ancient Israel everything human came to expression in words. In the Song, love finds words—inspired words that disclose its exquisite charm and beauty as one of God's choicest gifts. The woman's voice of love in the Song suggests that love and wisdom draw men powerfully with the subtlety and mystery of a woman's allurements. God intends that such love be a normal part of marital life in His good creation.

Outline

I. Courtship (1:1—3:5)
II. Wedding Procession (3:6–11)
III. Expressions of Love (4:1—5:1)
IV. Conflict and Solution (5:2—6:13)
V. More Expressions of Love (7:1—8:4)
VI. Conclusion (8:5–14)

The Young Shulammite Bride and Jerusalem's Daughters

1 The [1]Song of [a]Songs, which is Solomon's.
2 ¶ "[1]May he kiss me with the kisses of his mouth!
For your [a]love is better than wine.
3 "Your [a]oils have a pleasing fragrance,
Your [b]name is *like* [1]purified oil;
Therefore the [2c]maidens love you.
4 "Draw me after you *and* let us run *together!*
The [a]king has brought me into his chambers."

¶ "[1]We will rejoice in you and be glad;
We will [2]extol your [b]love more than wine.
Rightly do they love you."

5 ¶ "[1]I am black but [a]lovely,
O [b]daughters of Jerusalem,
Like the [c]tents of [d]Kedar,
Like the curtains of Solomon.
6 "Do not stare at me because I am [1]swarthy,
For the sun has burned me.
My [a]mother's sons were angry with me;
They made me [b]caretaker of the vineyards,
But I have not taken care of my own vineyard.
7 "Tell me, O you [a]whom my soul loves,
Where do you [b]pasture *your flock,*
Where do you make *it* [c]lie down at noon?
For why should I be like one who [1]veils herself
Beside the flocks of your [d]companions?"

Solomon, the Lover, Speaks

8 ¶ "[1]If you yourself do not know,
[a]Most beautiful among women,
Go forth on the trail of the flock
And pasture your young goats
By the tents of the shepherds.

1:1 [1]Or *Best of the Songs* [a]1 Kin 4:32

2 [1]BRIDE [a]Song 1:4; 4:10

3 [1]Lit *oil which is emptied* (from one vessel to another) [2]Or *virgins* [a]Song 4:10; John 12:3 [b]Eccl 7:1 [c]Ps 45:14

4 [1]CHORUS [2]Lit *mention with praise* [a]Ps 45:14, 15 [b]Song 1:4; 4:10

5 [1]BRIDE [a]Song 2:14; 4:3; 6:4 [b]Song 2:7; 3:5, 10; 5:8,16; 8:4 [c]Ps 120:5 [d]Is 60:7

6 [1]Or *black* [a]Ps 69:8 [b]Song 8:11

7 [1]Some versions read *wanders* [a]Song 3:1-4 [b]Song 2:16; 6:3 [c]Is 13:20; Jer 33:12 [d]Song 8:13

8 [1]BRIDEGROOM [a]Song 5:9; 6:1

9 ¶ "[1]To me, [a]my darling, you are
like
My [b]mare among the chariots of
Pharaoh.
10 "Your [a]cheeks are lovely with
ornaments,
Your neck with strings of
[b]beads."

11 ¶ "[1]We will make for you
ornaments of gold
With beads of silver."

12 ¶ "[1]While the king was at his
[2]table,
My [3a]perfume gave forth its
fragrance.
13 "My beloved is to me a pouch of
[a]myrrh
Which lies all night between my
breasts.
14 "My beloved is to me a cluster of
[a]henna blossoms
In the vineyards of [b]Engedi."

15 ¶ "[1,2a]How beautiful you are,
my darling,
[2]How beautiful you are!
Your [b]eyes are *like* doves."

16 ¶ "[1,2]How handsome you are,
[a]my beloved,
And so pleasant!
Indeed, our couch is luxuriant!
17 "The beams of our houses are
[a]cedars,
Our rafters, [1b]cypresses.

The Bride's Admiration

2 "[1]I am the [2a]rose of [b]Sharon,
The [c]lily of the valleys."

2 ¶ "[1]Like a lily among the thorns,
So is [a]my darling among the
[2]maidens."

3 ¶ "[1]Like an [2a]apple tree among
the trees of the forest,
So is my beloved among the
[3]young men.
In his shade I took great delight
and sat down,
And his [b]fruit was sweet to my
[4]taste.
4 "He has [a]brought me to *his*
[1]banquet hall,
And his [b]banner over me is
love.
5 "Sustain me with [a]raisin cakes,
Refresh me with [1b]apples,
Because [c]I am lovesick.
6 "Let [a]his left hand be under my
head
And [a]his right hand
[b]embrace me."

9 [1]Lit *I have compared you to* [a]Song 1:15; 2:2, 10,13 [b]2 Chr 1:16,17
10 [a]Song 5:13 [b]Gen 24:53; Is 61:10
11 [1]CHORUS
12 [1]BRIDE [2]Or *couch* [3]Lit *nard* [a]Song 4:14; Mark 14:3; John 12:3
13 [a]Ps 45:8; John 19:39
14 [a]Song 4:13 [b]1 Sam 23:29
15 [1]BRIDEGROOM [2]Lit *Behold* [a]Song 1:16; 2:10,13; 4:1,7; 6:4,10 [b]Song 4:1; 5:12
16 [1]BRIDE [2]Lit *Behold* [a]Song 2:3,9,17; 5:2,5, 6,8
17 [1]Or *junipers* [a]1 Kin 6:9,10; Jer 22:14 [b]2 Chr 3:5
2:1 [1]BRIDE [2]Lit *crocus* [a]Is 35:1 [b]Is 33:9; 35:2 [c]Song 5:13; 7:2; Hos 14:5
2 [1]BRIDEGROOM [2]Lit *daughters* [a]Song 1:9
3 [1]BRIDE [2]Or *apricot* [3]Lit *sons* [4]Lit *palate* [a]Song 8:5 [b]Song 4:13, 16; 8:11,12
4 [1]Lit *house of wine* [a]Song 1:4 [b]Ps 20:5
5 [1]Or *apricots* [a]2 Sam 6:19; 1 Chr 16:3; Hos 3:1 [b]Song 7:8 [c]Song 5:8
6 [a]Song 8:3 [b]Prov 4:8
7 [1]BRIDEGROOM [2]Or *it* [a]Song 3:5; 5:8,9; 8:4 [b]Song 1:5 [c]Prov 6:5; Song 2:9,17; 3:5; 8:14 [d]Gen 49:21; Ps 18:33; Hab 3:19
8 [1]BRIDE [a]Song 2:17; Is 52:7
9 [1]Lit *of the stags* [a]Prov 6:5; Song 2:17; 3:5; 8:14 [b]Song 2:17; 8:14 [c]Judg 5:28
10 [a]Song 2:13
12 [1]Or *singing* [a]Gen 15:9; Ps 74:19; Jer 8:7
13 [a]Matt 24:32 [b]Song 7:12
14 [1]BRIDEGROOM [2]Or *crag* [3]Or *cliff* [4]Lit *appearance* [a]Song 5:2; 6:9 [b]Jer 48:28 [c]Song 8:13 [d]Song 1:5
15 [1]CHORUS [2]Or *young* [a]Ezek 13:4; Luke 13:32 [b]Song 2:13
16 [1]BRIDE [a]Song 6:3; 7:10 [b]Song 4:5; 6:2,3
17 [1]Lit *the day blows* [a]Song 4:6 [b]Song 2:9

7 ¶ "[1]I [a]adjure you, O [b]daughters
of Jerusalem,
By the [c]gazelles or by the
[d]hinds of the field,
[a]That you do not arouse or
awaken *my* love
Until [2]she pleases."

8 ¶ "[1]Listen! My beloved!
Behold, he is coming,
Climbing [a]on the mountains,
Leaping on the hills!
9 "My beloved is like a [a]gazelle or
a [b]young [1]stag.
Behold, he is standing behind
our wall,
He is looking through the
windows,
He is peering [c]through the
lattice.

10 ¶ "My beloved responded and
said to me,
'[a]Arise, my darling, my beautiful
one,
And come along.
11 'For behold, the winter is past,
The rain is over *and* gone.
12 'The flowers have *already*
appeared in the land;
The time has arrived for
[1]pruning *the vines,*
And the voice of the [a]turtledove
has been heard in our land.
13 'The [a]fig tree has ripened its figs,
And the [b]vines in blossom have
given forth *their* fragrance.
Arise, my darling, my beautiful
one,
And come along!' "

14 ¶ "[1]O [a]my dove, [b]in the clefts
of the [2]rock,
In the secret place of the steep
[3]pathway,
Let me see your [4]form,
[c]Let me hear your voice;
For your voice is sweet,
And your [4]form is [d]lovely."

15 ¶ "[1a]Catch the foxes for us,
The [2]little foxes that are ruining
the vineyards,
While our [b]vineyards are in
blossom."

16 ¶ "[1a]My beloved is mine, and I
am his;
He [b]pastures *his flock* among
the lilies.
17 "[a]Until [1]the cool of the day
when the shadows flee
away,
Turn, my beloved, and be like a
[b]gazelle

And [1]reposed in *their* [b]setting.
13 "His cheeks are like a [a]bed of
balsam,
Banks of sweet-scented herbs;
His lips are [b]lilies
[c]Dripping with liquid myrrh.
14 "His hands are rods of gold
Set with [a]beryl;
His abdomen is carved ivory
Inlaid with [1b]sapphires.
15 "His legs are pillars of alabaster
Set on pedestals of pure gold;
His appearance is like [a]Lebanon
Choice as the [b]cedars.
16 "His [1a]mouth is *full of*
sweetness.
And he is wholly [b]desirable.
This is my beloved and this is
my friend,
O daughters of Jerusalem."

Mutual Delight in Each Other

6 "[1a]Where has your beloved
gone,
O [b]most beautiful among
women?
Where has your beloved turned,
That we may seek him
with you?"

2 ¶ "[1]My beloved has gone down
to his [a]garden,
To the [b]beds of balsam,
To [c]pasture *his flock* in the
gardens
And gather [d]lilies.
3 "[a]I am my beloved's and my
beloved is mine,
He who [b]pastures *his flock*
among the lilies."

4 ¶ "[1a]You are as beautiful as
[b]Tirzah, my darling,
As [c]lovely as [d]Jerusalem,
As [e]awesome as [2]an army with
banners.
5 "Turn your eyes away from me,
For they have confused me;
[a]Your hair is like a flock of goats
That have descended from
Gilead.
6 "[a]Your teeth are like a flock of
ewes
Which have come up from *their*
washing,
All of which bear twins,
And not one among them has
[1]lost her young.
7 "[a]Your temples are like a slice of
a pomegranate
Behind your veil.
8 "There are sixty [a]queens and
eighty concubines,
And [1b]maidens without
number;
9 *But* [a]my dove, my perfect one,
is [1]unique:
She is her mother's [1]only
daughter;
She is the pure *child* of the one
who bore her.
The [2b]maidens saw her and
called her blessed,
The [c]queens and the concubines
also, and they praised her,
saying,

10 ¶ 'Who is this that [1]grows like
the dawn,
As beautiful as the full [a]moon,
As pure [b]as the sun,
As [c]awesome as [2]an army with
banners?'
11 "I went down to the orchard of
nut trees
To see the blossoms of the
valley,
To see whether [a]the vine had
budded
Or the [b]pomegranates had
bloomed.
12 "Before I was aware, my soul
set me
Over the chariots of [1]my noble
people."

13 ¶ "[1,2]Come back, come back,
O Shulammite;
Come back, come back, that we
may gaze at you!"
¶ "[3]Why should you gaze at the
Shulammite,
As at the [a]dance of [4b]the two
companies?

Admiration by the Bridegroom

7 "[1]How beautiful are your [2]feet
in sandals,
O [3a]prince's daughter!
The curves of your hips are like
[4]jewels,
The work of the hands of an
artist.
2 "Your navel is *like* a round goblet
Which never lacks mixed wine;
Your belly is like a heap of
wheat
Fenced about with lilies.
3 "Your [a]two breasts are like two
fawns,
Twins of a gazelle.
4 "Your [a]neck is like a tower of
ivory,
Your eyes *like* the pools in
[b]Heshbon
By the gate of Bath-rabbim;
Your nose is like the tower of
Lebanon,
Which faces toward Damascus.

12 [1]Lit *sitting upon* [b]Ex 25:7

13 [a]Song 6:2 [b]Song 2:1 [c]Song 5:5

14 [1]Lit *lapis lazuli* [a]Ex 28:20; 39:13; Ezek 1:16; Dan 10:6 [b]Ex 24:10; 28:18; Job 28:16; Is 54:11

15 [a]Song 7:4 [b]1 Kin 4:33; Ps 80:10; Ezek 17:23; 31:8

16 [1]Lit *palate* [a]Song 7:9 [b]2 Sam 1:23

6:1 [1]CHORUS [a]Song 5:6 [b]Song 1:8

2 [1]BRIDE [a]Song 4:16; 5:1 [b]Song 5:13 [c]Song 1:7 [d]Song 2:1; 5:13

3 [a]Song 2:16; 7:10 [b]Song 2:16; 4:5

4 [1]BRIDEGROOM [2]Lit *bannered ones* [a]Song 1:15 [b]1 Kin 14:17 [c]Song 1:5 [d]Ps 48:2; 50:2 [e]Song 6:10

5 [a]Song 4:1

6 [1]Or *miscarried* [a]Song 4:2

7 [a]Song 4:3

8 [1]Or *virgins* [a]1 Kin 11:3 [b]Song 1:3

9 [1]Lit *one* [2]Lit *daughters* [a]Song 2:14; 5:2 [b]Gen 30:13 [c]1 Kin 11:3

10 [1]Lit *looks down* [2]Lit *bannered ones* [a]Job 31:26 [b]Matt 17:2; Rev 1:16 [c]Song 6:4

11 [a]Song 7:12 [b]Song 4:13

12 [1]Another reading is *Amminadib*

13 [1]CHORUS [2]Ch 7:1 in Heb [3]BRIDEGROOM [4]Or *Mahanaim* [a]Judg 21:21 [b]Gen 32:2; 2 Sam 17:24

7:1 [1]Ch 7:2 in Heb [2]Lit *footsteps* [3]Or *nobleman's* [4]Or *ornaments* [a]Ps 45:13

3 [a]Song 4:5

4 [a]Song 4:4 [b]Num 21:26

5 "Your head [1]crowns you like
[a]Carmel,
And the flowing locks of your
head are like purple threads;
The king is captivated by *your*
tresses.
6 "How [a]beautiful and how
delightful you are,
[1]*My* love, with *all* your charms!
7 "[1]Your stature is like a palm tree,
And your breasts are *like its*
clusters.
8 "I said, 'I will climb the palm
tree,
I will take hold of its fruit stalks.'
Oh, may your breasts be like
clusters of the vine,
And the fragrance of your
[1]breath like [2a]apples,
9 And your [1a]mouth like the best
wine!"

¶ "[2]It [b]goes *down* smoothly for
my beloved,
Flowing gently *through* the lips
of those who fall asleep.

The Union of Love

10 ¶ "[a]I am my beloved's,
And his [b]desire is for me.
11 "Come, my beloved, let us go out
into the [1]country,
Let us spend the night in the
villages.
12 "Let us rise early *and go* to the
vineyards;
Let us [a]see whether the vine
has budded
And its blossoms have opened,
And whether the pomegranates
have bloomed.
There I will give you my love.
13 "The [a]mandrakes have given
forth fragrance;
And over our doors are all
[b]choice *fruits*,
Both new and old,
Which I have saved up for you,
my beloved.

The Lovers Speak

8 "Oh that you were like a brother
to me
Who nursed at my mother's
breasts.
If I found you outdoors, I would
kiss you;
No one would despise me,
either.
2 "I would lead you *and* [a]bring you
Into the house of my mother,
who used to instruct me;
I would give you spiced wine to
drink from the juice of my
pomegranates.
3 "Let [a]his left hand be under my
head
And his right hand
embrace me."

4 ¶ "[1a]I want you to swear,
O daughters of Jerusalem,
[2]Do not arouse or awaken *my*
love
Until [3]she pleases."

5 ¶ "[1a]Who is this coming up
from the wilderness
Leaning on her beloved?"

¶ "[2]Beneath the [3b]apple tree I
awakened you;
There your mother was in labor
with you,
There she was in labor *and* gave
you birth.
6 "Put me like a [1]seal over your
heart,
Like a [a]seal on your arm.
For love is as strong as death,
[2b]Jealousy is as severe as Sheol;
Its flashes are flashes of fire,
[3]The *very* flame of the LORD.
7 "Many waters cannot quench
love,
Nor will rivers overflow it;
[a]If a man were to give all the
riches of his house for love,
It would be utterly despised."

8 ¶ "[1]We have a little sister,
And she [a]has no breasts;
What shall we do for our sister
On the day when she is
spoken for?
9 "If she is a wall,
We will build on her a
battlement of silver;
But if she is a door,
We will barricade her with
[a]planks of cedar."

10 ¶ "[1]I was a wall, and [a]my
breasts were like towers;
Then I became in his eyes as
one who finds peace.
11 "Solomon had a [a]vineyard at
Baal-hamon;
He [b]entrusted the vineyard to
[c]caretakers.
Each one was to bring a
[d]thousand *shekels* of silver
for its [e]fruit.

5 [1]Lit *is upon* [a]Is 35:2
6 [1]Or With *love among your delights* [a]Song 1:15,16; 4:10
7 [1]Lit *This stature of yours*
8 [1]Lit *nose* [2]Or *apricots* [a]Song 2:5
9 [1]Lit *palate* [2]BRIDE [a]Song 5:16 [b]Prov 23:31
10 [a]Song 2:16; 6:3 [b]Ps 45:11; Gal 2:20
11 [1]Lit *field*
12 [a]Song 6:11
13 [a]Gen 30:14 [b]Song 2:3; 4:13, 16; Matt 13:52
8:2 [a]Song 3:4
3 [a]Song 2:6
4 [1]BRIDEGROOM [2]Or *Why should you arouse* [3]Or *it* [a]Song 2:7; 3:5
5 [1]CHORUS [2]BRIDE [3]Or *apricot* [a]Song 3:6 [b]Song 2:3
6 [1]Or *signet* [2]Or *Its ardor is as inflexible* [3]Another reading is *A vehement flame* [a]Is 49:16; Jer 22:24; Hag 2:23 [b]Prov 6:34
7 [a]Prov 6:35
8 [1]CHORUS [a]Ezek 16:7
9 [a]1 Kin 6:15
10 [1]BRIDE [a]Ezek 16:7
11 [a]Eccl 2:4 [b]Matt 21:33 [c]Song 1:6 [d]Is 7:23 [e]Song 2:3; 8:12

12 "My very own vineyard is [1]at my
disposal;
The thousand *shekels* are for
you, Solomon,
And two hundred are for those
who take care of its fruit."

13 ¶ "[1]O you who sit in the
gardens,
My [a]companions are listening
for your voice—
[b]Let me hear it!"

14 ¶ "[1,2]Hurry, my beloved,
And be [a]like a gazelle or a
young [3]stag
On the [b]mountains of
spices."

12 [1]Lit *before me*

13 [1]BRIDEGROOM [a]Song 1:7 [b]Song 2:14

14 [1]BRIDE [2]Lit *Flee* [3]Lit *of the stags* [a]Song 2:7, 9,17 [b]Song 4:6

Isaiah

Title and Background

The book is named after the prophet whose message it records. Isaiah wrote during the stormy period marking the expansion of the Assyrian empire and the decline of Israel. He warned Judah that her sin would bring captivity at the hands of Babylon. Although the fall of Jerusalem would not take place until 586 B.C., Isaiah assumes its demise and proceeds to predict the restoration of the people from captivity. The decree of Cyrus would allow the Jews to return home, a deliverance that prefigured the greater salvation from sin through Jesus Christ. Significantly, Isaiah's name means "The LORD saves."

Author and Date of Writing

Isaiah son of Amoz was the greatest of the writing prophets and a contemporary of Amos, Hosea and Micah. Most of the events discussed in chapters 1—39 occurred during Isaiah's ministry, so it is likely they were completed around 700 B.C. He lived until at least 681 and may have written chapters 40—66 during his later years.

Theme and Message

Isaiah unveils the full dimensions of God's judgment and salvation. The awful judgment unleashed on Israel and all who defy God is called "the day of the LORD." The Lord's kingdom on earth, with its righteous Ruler and His righteous subjects, is the goal toward which the book of Isaiah steadily moves. The restored earth and the restored people will then conform to the divine ideal, and all will result in the praise and glory of the Holy One of Israel.

Outline

I. Rebuke and Promise (1:1—6:13)
II. Immanuel and His Kingdom (7:1—12:6)
III. Judgment Against the Nations (13:1—23:18)
IV. Judgment and Promise (24:1—27:13)
V. Six Woes on Israel and Assyria (28:1—33:24)
VI. Judgment and Promise (34:1—35:10)
VII. From the Assyrian Threat to the Babylonian Exile (36:1—39:8)
VIII. Deliverance and Restoration of Israel (40:1—48:22)
IX. The Servant's Ministry and Israel's Restoration (49:1—57:21)
X. Everlasting Deliverance and Judgment (58:1—66:24)

Rebellion of God's People

1 The vision of Isaiah the son of Amoz concerning [a]Judah and Jerusalem, which he saw during the [1]reigns of [b]Uzziah, [c]Jotham, [d]Ahaz *and* [e]Hezekiah, kings of Judah.

2 [a]Listen, O heavens, and hear, O [b]earth;
For the LORD speaks,
"[c]Sons I have reared and brought up,
But they have [d]revolted against Me.
3 "An ox knows its owner,
And a donkey its master's manger,
But Israel [a]does not know,
My people [b]do not understand."

4 ¶ Alas, sinful nation,
People weighed down with iniquity,
[1a]Offspring of evildoers,
Sons who [b]act corruptly!
They have [c]abandoned the LORD,
They have [d]despised the Holy One of Israel,
They have turned away [2]from Him.

5 ¶ Where will you be stricken again,
As you [a]continue in *your* rebellion?
The whole head is [b]sick
And the whole heart is faint.

1:1 [1]Lit *days* [a]Is 2:1; 40:9 [b]2 Kin 15:1-7,13; 2 Chr 26:1-23 [c]2 Kin 15:32-38; 2 Chr 27:1-9 [d]2 Kin 16:1-20; 2 Chr 28:1-27; Is 7:1 [e]2 Kin 18:1-20:21; 2 Chr 29:1-32:33

2 [a]Deut 32:1 [b]Mic 1:2 [c]Jer 3:22 [d]Is 30:1,9; 65:2

3 [a]Jer 9:3,6 [b]Is 44:18

4 [1]Lit *Seed* [2]Lit *backward* [a]Is 14:20 [b]Neh 1:7 [c]Is 1:28 [d]Is 5:24

5 [a]Is 31:6 [b]Is 33:24; Ezek 34:4,16

6 [a]From the sole of the foot even
to the head
There is [b]nothing sound in it,
Only bruises, welts and raw
wounds,
[c]Not pressed out or bandaged,
Nor softened with oil.

7 ¶ Your [a]land is desolate,
Your cities are burned with fire,
Your fields—strangers are
devouring them in your
presence;
It is desolation, as overthrown by
strangers.
8 The daughter of Zion is left like
a shelter in a vineyard,
Like a watchman's hut in a
cucumber field, like a
besieged city.
9 [a]Unless the LORD of hosts
Had left us a few [b]survivors,
We would be like [c]Sodom,
We would be like Gomorrah.

God Has Had Enough

10 ¶ Hear [a]the word of the LORD,
You rulers of [b]Sodom;
Give ear to the instruction of our
God,
You people of Gomorrah.
11 "[a]What are your multiplied
sacrifices to Me?"
Says the LORD.
"I [1]have had enough of burnt
offerings of rams
And the fat of fed cattle;
And I take no pleasure in the
blood of bulls, lambs or
goats.
12 "When you come [a]to appear
before Me,
Who requires [1]of you this
trampling of My courts?
13 "Bring your worthless offerings no
longer,
[a]Incense is an abomination
to Me.
[b]New moon and sabbath, the
[c]calling of assemblies—
I cannot [d]endure iniquity and
the solemn assembly.
14 "I hate your new moon *festivals*
and your [a]appointed feasts,
They have become a burden
to Me;
I am [b]weary of bearing *them.*
15 "So when you [a]spread out your
hands *in prayer,*
[b]I will hide My eyes from you;
Yes, even though you [c]multiply
prayers,
I will not listen.
[d]Your hands are [1]covered with
blood.
16 ¶ "[a]Wash yourselves, [b]make
yourselves clean;
[c]Remove the evil of your deeds
from My sight.
[d]Cease to do evil,
17 Learn to do good;
[a]Seek justice,
Reprove the ruthless,
[1b]Defend the orphan,
Plead for the widow.

"Let Us Reason"

18 ¶ "Come now, and [a]let us
reason together,"
Says the LORD,
"[b]Though your sins are as scarlet,
They will be as white as snow;
Though they are red like
crimson,
They will be like wool.
19 "[a]If you consent and obey,
You will [b]eat the best of the
land;
20 "But if you refuse and rebel,
You will be [a]devoured by the
sword."
Truly, [b]the mouth of the LORD
has spoken.

Zion Corrupted, to be Redeemed

21 ¶ How the faithful city has
become a [a]harlot,
She *who* was full of justice!
Righteousness once lodged in
her,
But now murderers.
22 Your silver has become dross,
Your drink diluted with water.
23 Your [a]rulers are rebels
And companions of thieves;
Everyone [b]loves a bribe
And chases after rewards.
They [c]do not [1]defend the
[2]orphan,
Nor does the widow's plea come
before them.
24 ¶ Therefore the Lord [1]GOD of
hosts,
The [a]Mighty One of Israel,
declares,
"Ah, I will be relieved of My
adversaries
And [b]avenge Myself on My foes.
25 "I will also turn My hand against
you,
And will [a]smelt away your dross
as with lye
And will remove all your alloy.
26 "Then I will restore your [a]judges
as at the first,

6 [a]Job 2:7 [b]Ps 38:3 [c]Jer 8:22
7 [a]Lev 26:33; Jer 44:6
9 [a]Rom 9:29 [b]Is 10:20-22; 11:11, 16; 37:4,31,32; 46:3 [c]Gen 19:24
10 [a]Is 8:20; 28:14 [b]Is 3:9; Ezek 16:49; Rom 9:29; Rev 11:8
11 [1]Or *am sated with* [a]Ps 50:8; Jer 6:20; Amos 5:21,22; Mal 1:10
12 [1]Lit *of your hand* [a]Ex 23:17
13 [a]Is 66:3 [b]1 Chr 23:31 [c]Ex 12:16 [d]Jer 7:9,10
14 [a]Is 29:1,2 [b]Is 7:13; 43:24
15 [1]Lit *full of* [a]1 Kin 8:22; Lam 1:17 [b]Is 8:17; 59:2 [c]Mic 3:4 [d]Is 59:3
16 [a]Ps 26:6 [b]Is 52:11 [c]Is 55:7 [d]Jer 25:5
17 [1]Or *Vindicate the fatherless* [a]Jer 22:3; Zeph 2:3 [b]Ps 82:3
18 [a]Is 41:1,21; 43:26; Mic 6:2 [b]Ps 51:7; Is 43:25; 44:22; Rev 7:14
19 [a]Deut 28:1; 30:15,16 [b]Is 55:2
20 [a]Is 3:25; 65:12 [b]Is 40:5; 58:14; Mic 4:4; Titus 1:2
21 [a]Is 57:3-9; Jer 2:20
23 [1]Or *vindicate* [2]Or *fatherless* [a]Hos 5:10; Mic 7:3 [b]Ex 23:8; Mic 7:3 [c]Is 10:2; Jer 5:28; Ezek 22:7; Zech 7:10
24 [1]Heb *YHWH,* usually rendered *LORD* [a]Ps 132:2; Is 49:26; 60:16 [b]Deut 28:63; Is 35:4; 59:18; 61:2; 63:4
25 [a]Ezek 22:19-22; Mal 3:3
26 [a]Is 60:17

And your counselors as at the
beginning;
After that you will be called the
[b]city of righteousness,
A faithful city."
27 ¶ Zion will be [a]redeemed with
justice
And her [1]repentant ones with
righteousness.
28 But [1]transgressors and sinners
will be [a]crushed together,
And those who forsake the LORD
will come to an end.
29 Surely [1]you will be ashamed of
the [2a]oaks which you have
desired,
And you will be embarrassed at
the [b]gardens which you
have chosen.
30 For you will be like an [1]oak
whose [a]leaf fades away
Or as a garden that has no
water.
31 The strong man will become
tinder,
His work also a spark.
Thus they shall both [a]burn
together
And there will be [b]none to
quench *them*.

God's Universal Reign

2 The word which [a]Isaiah the son of
Amoz saw concerning Judah and Je-
rusalem.
2 ¶ Now it will come about that
[a]In the last days
The [b]mountain of the house of
the LORD
Will be established [1]as the chief
of the mountains,
And will be raised above the
hills;
And [c]all the nations will stream
to it.
3 And many peoples will come and
say,
"Come, let us go up to the
mountain of the LORD,
To the house of the God of
Jacob;
That He may teach us
[1]concerning His ways
And that we may walk in His
paths."
For the [2]law will go forth [a]from
Zion
And the word of the LORD from
Jerusalem.
4 And He will judge between the
nations,
And will [1]render decisions for
many peoples;
And [a]they will hammer their
swords into plowshares and
their spears into pruning
hooks.
[b]Nation will not lift up sword
against nation,
And never again will they
learn war.
5 ¶ Come, [a]house of Jacob, and let
us walk in the [b]light of the
LORD.
6 For You have [a]abandoned Your
people, the house of Jacob,
Because they are filled *with
influences* from the east,
And *they are* soothsayers [b]like
the Philistines,
And they [c]strike *bargains* with
the children of foreigners.
7 Their land has also been filled
with silver and gold
And there is no end to their
treasures;
Their land has also been filled
with [a]horses
And there is no end to their
chariots.
8 Their land has also been [a]filled
with idols;
They worship the [b]work of their
hands,
That which their fingers have
made.
9 So [a]the *common* man has been
humbled
And the man *of importance* has
been abased,
But [b]do not forgive them.
10 [a]Enter the rock and hide in the
dust
[b]From the terror of the LORD
and from the splendor of His
majesty.
11 The [1a]proud look of man will
be abased
And the [b]loftiness of man will
be humbled,
And the LORD alone will be
exalted in that day.

A Day of Reckoning Coming

12 ¶ For the LORD of hosts will have
a day *of reckoning*
Against [a]everyone who is proud
and lofty
And against everyone who is
lifted up,
That he may be abased.
13 And *it will be* against all the
cedars of Lebanon that are
lofty and lifted up,
Against all the [a]oaks of Bashan,
14 Against all the [a]lofty mountains,

26 [b]Is 33:5; 60:14; 62:1,2; Zech 8:3
27 [1]Or *returnees* [a]Is 35:9f; 62:12; 63:4
28 [1]Lit *crushing of transgressors and sinners shall be together* [a]Ps 9:5; Is 66:24; 2 Thess 1:8,9
29 [1]So with some mss; M.T. *they* [2]Or *terebinths* [a]Is 57:5 [b]Is 65:3; 66:17
30 [1]Or *terebinth* [a]Is 64:6
31 [a]Is 5:24; 9:19; 26:11; 33:11-14 [b]Is 66:24; Matt 3:12; Mark 9:43
2:1 [a]Is 1:1
2 [1]Lit *on* [a]Mic 4:1-3 [b]Is 27:13; 66:20 [c]Is 56:7
3 [1]Or *some of* [2]Or *instruction* [a]Is 51:4,5; Luke 24:47
4 [1]Or *reprove many* [a]Is 32:17, 18; Joel 3:10 [b]Is 9:5,7; 11:6-9; Hos 2:18; Zech 9:10
5 [a]Is 58:1 [b]Is 60:1,2,19,20; 1 John 1:5
6 [a]Deut 31:17 [b]2 Kin 1:2 [c]2 Kin 16:7,8; Prov 6:1
7 [a]Deut 17:16; Is 30:16; 31:1; Mic 5:10
8 [a]Is 10:11 [b]Ps 115:4-8; Is 17:8; 37:19; 40:19; 44:17
9 [a]Ps 49:2; 62:9; Is 5:15 [b]Neh 4:5
10 [a]Is 2:19,21; Rev 6:15,16 [b]2 Thess 1:9
11 [1]Lit *eyes of the loftiness of men* [a]Is 5:15; 37:23 [b]Ps 18:27; Is 13:11; 23:9; 2 Cor 10:5
12 [a]Job 40:11, 12; Is 24:4,21; Mal 4:1
13 [a]Zech 11:2
14 [a]Is 40:4

Against all the hills that are
lifted up,
15 Against every [a]high tower,
Against every fortified wall,
16 Against all the [a]ships of Tarshish
And against all the beautiful
craft.
17 The pride of man will be
humbled
And the loftiness of men will be
abased;
And the LORD alone will be
exalted in that day,
18 But the [a]idols will completely
vanish.
19 *Men* will [a]go into caves of the
rocks
And into holes of the [1]ground
Before the terror of the LORD
And the splendor of His majesty,
When He arises [b]to make the
earth tremble.
20 In that day men will [a]cast away
to the moles and the [b]bats
Their idols of silver and their
idols of gold,
Which they made for themselves
to worship,
21 In order to [a]go into the caverns
of the rocks and the clefts of
the cliffs
Before the terror of the LORD and
the splendor of His majesty,
When He arises to make the
earth tremble.
22 [1a]Stop regarding man, whose
breath *of life* is in his
nostrils;
For [2b]why should he be
esteemed?

God Will Remove the Leaders

3 For behold, the Lord [1]GOD of
hosts [a]is going to remove
from Jerusalem and Judah
Both [2]supply and support, the
whole [2]supply of bread
And the whole [2]supply of water;
2 [a]The mighty man and the
warrior,
The judge and the prophet,
The diviner and the elder,
3 The captain of fifty and the
honorable man,
The counselor and the expert
artisan,
And the skillful enchanter.
4 And I will make mere [a]lads
their princes,
And [1]capricious children will
rule over them,
5 And the people will be
[a]oppressed,
Each one by another, and each
one by his [b]neighbor;
The youth will storm against the
elder
And the inferior against the
honorable.
6 When a man [a]lays hold of his
brother in his father's house,
saying,
"You have a cloak, you shall be
our ruler,
And these ruins will be under
your [1]charge,"
7 He will [1]protest on that day,
saying,
"I will not be *your* [2a]healer,
For in my house there is neither
bread nor cloak;
You should not appoint me ruler
of the people."
8 For [a]Jerusalem has stumbled and
Judah has fallen,
Because their [1b]speech and
their actions are against the
LORD,
To [c]rebel against [2]His glorious
presence.
9 [1]The expression of their faces
bears witness against them,
And they display their sin like
[a]Sodom;
They do not *even* conceal *it.*
Woe to [2]them!
For they have [b]brought evil on
themselves.
10 Say to the [a]righteous that *it will*
go well *with them,*
For they will eat the fruit of
their actions.
11 Woe to the wicked! *It will go*
badly *with him,*
For [1a]what he deserves will be
done to him.
12 O My people! Their oppressors
[1]are [a]children,
And women rule over them.
O My people! [b]Those who guide
you lead *you* astray
And confuse the direction of
your paths.

God Will Judge

13 ¶ [a]The LORD arises to contend,
And stands to judge the people.
14 The LORD [a]enters into judgment
with the elders and princes
of His people,
"It is you who have [b]devoured
the vineyard;
The [c]plunder of the poor is in
your houses.
15 "What do you mean by [a]crushing
My people

15 [a]Is 25:12

16 [a]1 Kin 10:22; Is 23:1, 14; 60:9

18 [a]Is 21:9; Mic 1:7

19 [1]Lit *dust* [a]Is 2:10 [b]Ps 18:7; Is 2:21; 13:13; 24:1,19,20; Hag 2:6,7; Heb 12:26

20 [a]Is 30:22; 31:7 [b]Lev 11:19

21 [a]Is 2:19

22 [1]Lit *Cease from man* [2]Lit *in what* [a]Ps 146:3; Jer 17:5 [b]Ps 8:4; 144:3,4; Is 40:15,17; James 4:14

3:1 [1]Heb *YHWH,* usually rendered *LORD* [2]Lit *staff* [a]Lev 26:26; Is 5:13; 9:20; Ezek 4:16

2 [a]2 Kin 24:14; Is 9:14,15; Ezek 17:12,13

4 [1]Lit *arbitrary power will rule* [a]Eccl 10:16

5 [a]Mic 7:3-6 [b]Is 9:19; Jer 9:3-8

6 [1]Lit *hand* [a]Is 4:1

7 [1]Lit *lift up his voice* [2]Lit *binder of wounds* [a]Ezek 34:4; Hos 5:13

8 [1]Lit *tongue* [2]Lit *the eyes of His glory* [a]Is 1:7; 6:11 [b]Ps 73:9-11; Is 9:17; 59:3 [c]Is 65:3

9 [1]Or *Their partiality bears* [2]Lit *their soul* [a]Gen 13:13; Is 1:10-15 [b]Prov 8:36; 15:32; Rom 6:23

10 [a]Deut 28:1-14; Eccl 8:12; Is 54:17

11 [1]Lit *the dealing of his hands* [a]Deut 28:15-68; Is 65:6,7

12 [1]Or *deal severely* [a]Is 3:4 [b]Is 9:16; 28:14,15

13 [a]Is 66:16; Hos 4:1; Mic 6:2

14 [a]Job 22:4; Ps 143:2; Ezek 20:35,36 [b]Ps 14:4; Mic 3:3 [c]Job 24:9,14; Ps 10:9; Prov 30:14; Is 10:1,2; Ezek 18:12; James 2:6

15 [a]Ps 94:5

And grinding the face of the
poor?"
Declares the Lord [1]GOD of hosts.

Judah's Women Denounced

16 ¶ Moreover, the LORD said,
"Because the [a]daughters of
Zion are proud
And walk with [1]heads held high
and seductive eyes,
And go along with mincing steps
And tinkle the bangles on their
feet,
17 Therefore the Lord will afflict the
scalp of the daughters of
Zion with scabs,
And the LORD will make their
foreheads bare."
18 In that day the Lord will take away
the beauty of *their* anklets, headbands,
[a]crescent ornaments,
19 dangling earrings, bracelets, veils,
20 [a]headdresses, ankle chains, sashes,
perfume boxes, amulets,
21 [1]finger rings, [a]nose rings,
22 festal robes, outer tunics, cloaks,
money purses,
23 hand mirrors, undergarments, turbans and veils.
24 Now it will come about that
instead of [1]sweet [a]perfume
there will be putrefaction;
Instead of a belt, a rope;
Instead of [b]well-set hair, a
[c]plucked-out scalp;
Instead of fine clothes, a
[d]donning of sackcloth;
And branding instead of beauty.
25 Your men will [a]fall by the sword
And your [1]mighty ones in battle.
26 And her [1a]gates will lament and
mourn,
And deserted she will [b]sit on
the ground.

A Remnant Prepared

4 For seven women will take hold of
[a]one man in that day, saying, "We
will eat our own bread and wear our own
clothes, only let us be called by your
name; [b]take away our reproach!"
2 ¶ In that day the [a]Branch of the
LORD will be beautiful and glorious, and
the [b]fruit of the earth *will be* the pride
and the adornment of the [c]survivors of
Israel.
3 It will come about that he who is
[a]left in Zion and remains in Jerusalem
will be called [b]holy—everyone who is
[c]recorded for life in Jerusalem.
4 When the Lord has washed away
the filth of the [a]daughters of Zion and
[1]purged the [b]bloodshed of Jerusalem
from her midst, by the [c]spirit of judgment and the [d]spirit of burning,
5 then the LORD will create over the
whole area of Mount Zion and over her
assemblies [a]a cloud by day, even smoke,
and the brightness of a flaming fire by
night; for over all the [b]glory will be a
canopy.
6 There will be a [a]shelter to *give*
shade from the heat by day, and refuge
and [1]protection from the storm and the
rain.

Parable of the Vineyard

5 Let me sing now for my
well-beloved
A song of my beloved concerning
His vineyard.
My well-beloved had a [a]vineyard
on [1]a fertile hill.
2 He dug it all around, removed its
stones,
And planted it with [1]the
[a]choicest vine.
And He built a tower in the
middle of it
And also hewed out a [2]wine vat
in it;
Then He [b]expected *it* to produce
good grapes,
But it produced *only* [3]worthless
ones.
3 ¶ "And now, O inhabitants of
Jerusalem and men of Judah,
[a]Judge between Me and My
vineyard.
4 "[a]What more was there to do for
My vineyard [1]that I have
not done in it?
Why, when I expected *it* to
produce *good* grapes did it
produce [2]worthless ones?
5 "So now let Me tell you what I
am going to do to My
vineyard:
I will [a]remove its hedge and it
will be consumed;
I will [b]break down its wall and
it will become [c]trampled
ground.
6 "I will [a]lay it waste;
It will not be pruned or hoed,
But briars and thorns will
come up.
I will also charge the clouds to
[b]rain no rain on it."
7 ¶ For the [a]vineyard of the LORD
of hosts is the house of
Israel
And the men of Judah His
delightful plant.
Thus He looked for justice, but
behold, [b]bloodshed;

15 [1]Heb *YHWH*, usually rendered LORD

16 [1]Lit *outstretched necks* [a]Song 3:11; Is 3:16-4:1,4; 32:9-15

18 [a]Judg 8:21, 26

20 [a]Ex 39:28

21 [1]Or *signet rings* [a]Gen 24:47; Ezek 16:12

24 [1]Or *balsam oil* [a]Esth 2:12 [b]1 Pet 3:3 [c]Is 22:12; Ezek 27:31; Amos 8:10 [d]Is 15:3; Lam 2:10

25 [1]Lit *strength* [a]Is 1:20; 65:12

26 [1]Lit *entrances* [a]Jer 14:2; Lam 1:4 [b]Lam 2:10

4:1 [a]Is 13:12 [b]Gen 30:23; Is 54:4

2 [a]Is 11:1; 53:2; Jer 23:5; 33:15; Zech 3:8; 6:12 [b]Ps 72:16 [c]Is 10:20; 37:31,32; Joel 2:32; Obad 17

3 [a]Is 28:5; 46:3; Rom 11:4,5 [b]Is 52:1; 62:12 [c]Ex 32:32; Ps 69:28; Luke 10:20

4 [1]Lit *rinsed away* [a]Is 3:16 [b]Is 1:15 [c]Is 28:6 [d]Is 1:31; 9:19; Matt 3:11

5 [a]Ex 13:21,22; 24:16; Num 9:15-23 [b]Is 60:1, 2

6 [1]Lit *a hiding place* [a]Ps 27:5; Is 25:4; 32:1,2

5:1 [1]Lit *a horn, the son of fatness* [a]Ps 80:8; Jer 12:10; Matt 21:33; Mark 12:1; Luke 20:9

2 [1]Lit *a bright red grape* [2]Or *wine press* [3]Or *wild grapes* [a]Jer 2:21 [b]Matt 21:19; Mark 11:13; Luke 13:6

3 [a]Matt 21:40

4 [1]Lit *and I have not done* [2]Or *wild grapes* [a]2 Chr 36:16; Jer 2:5; 7:25,26; Mic 6:3; Matt 23:37

5 [a]Ps 89:40 [b]Ps 80:12 [c]Is 10:6; 28:18; Lam 1:15; Luke 21:24; Rev 11:2

6 [a]2 Chr 36:19-21; Is 7:19-25; 24:1,3; Jer 25:11 [b]1 Kin 8:35; 17:1; Jer 14:1-22

7 [a]Ps 80:8-11 [b]Is 3:14,15; 30:12; 59:13

For righteousness, but behold, a
cry of distress.

Woes for the Wicked

8 ¶ Woe to those who [a]add house
to house *and* join field to
field,
Until there is no more room,
So that you have to live alone in
the midst of the land!
9 In my ears the LORD of hosts *has*
sworn, "Surely, [a]many
houses shall become
[b]desolate,
Even great and fine ones,
without occupants.
10 "For [a]ten acres of vineyard will
yield *only* one [1]bath *of*
wine,
And a [b]homer of seed will yield
but an [2]ephah of grain."
11 Woe to those who rise early in
the morning that they may
pursue [a]strong drink,
Who stay up late in the evening
that wine may inflame them!
12 Their banquets are *accompanied*
by lyre and [a]harp, by
tambourine and flute, and by
wine;
But they [b]do not pay attention
to the deeds of the LORD,
Nor do they consider the work of
His hands.

13 ¶ Therefore My people go into
exile for their [a]lack of
knowledge;
And [1]their [b]honorable men are
famished,
And their multitude is parched
with thirst.
14 Therefore [a]Sheol has enlarged
its [1]throat and opened its
mouth without measure;
And [2]Jerusalem's splendor, her
multitude, her din *of revelry*
and the jubilant within her,
descend *into it.*
15 So the *common* man will be
humbled and the man of
importance abased,
[a]The eyes of the proud also will
be abased.
16 But the [a]LORD of hosts will be
[b]exalted in judgment,
And the holy God will show
Himself [c]holy in
righteousness.
17 [a]Then the lambs will graze as in
their pasture,
And strangers will eat in the
waste places of the
[1]wealthy.

18 ¶ Woe to those who drag
[a]iniquity with the cords of
[1]falsehood,
And sin as if with cart ropes;
19 [a]Who say, "Let Him make
speed, let Him hasten His
work, that we may see *it;*
And let the purpose of the Holy
One of Israel draw near
And come to pass, that we may
know *it!*"
20 Woe to those who [a]call evil
good, and good evil;
Who [1][b]substitute darkness for
light and light for darkness;
Who [1]substitute bitter for sweet
and sweet for bitter!
21 Woe to those who are [a]wise in
their own eyes
And clever in their own sight!
22 [a]Woe to those who are heroes
in drinking wine
And valiant men in mixing
strong drink,
23 [a]Who justify the wicked for a
bribe,
And [b]take away the [1]rights of
the ones who are in the
right!
24 ¶ Therefore, [a]as a tongue of fire
consumes stubble
And dry grass collapses into the
flame,
So their [b]root will become [c]like
rot and their blossom [1]blow
away as dust;
For they have [d]rejected the law
of the LORD of hosts
And despised the word of the
Holy One of Israel.
25 On this account the [a]anger of
the LORD has burned against
His people,
And He has stretched out His
hand against them and
struck them down.
And the [b]mountains quaked,
and their [c]corpses [1]lay like
refuse in the middle of the
streets.
[d]For all this His anger [2]is not
spent,
But His [e]hand is still
stretched out.

26 ¶ He will also lift up a [a]standard
to the [1]distant nation,
And will [b]whistle for it [c]from
the ends of the earth;
And behold, it will [d]come with
speed swiftly.
27 [a]No one in it is weary or
stumbles,
None slumbers or sleeps;

---

8 [a]Jer 22:13-17; Mic 2:2; Hab 2:9-12

9 [a]Is 6:11,12 [b]Matt 23:38

10 [1]I.e. Approx 10 1/2 gal. [2]I.e. Approx one bu [a]Lev 26:26; Is 7:23; Hag 1:6; 2:16 [b]Ezek 45:11

11 [a]Prov 23:29, 30; Eccl 10:16, 17; Is 5:22; 22:13; 28:1,3,7, 8

12 [a]Amos 6:5,6 [b]Job 34:27; Ps 28:5

13 [1]Lit *their glory are men of famine* [a]Is 1:3; 27:11; Hos 4:6 [b]Is 3:3

14 [1]Or *appetite* [2]Lit *her* [a]Prov 30:16; Hab 2:5

15 [a]Is 2:11; 10:33

16 [a]Is 28:17; 30:18; 61:8 [b]Is 2:11,17; 33:5,10 [c]Is 8:13; 29:23; 1 Pet 3:15

17 [1]Lit *the fat* [a]Is 7:25; Mic 2:12; Zeph 2:6

18 [1]Or *worthlessness* [a]Is 59:4-8; Jer 23:10-14

19 [a]Ezek 12:22; 2 Pet 3:4

20 [1]Lit *set* [a]Prov 17:15; Amos 5:7 [b]Job 17:12; Matt 6:22,23; Luke 11:34,35

21 [a]Prov 3:7; Rom 12:16; 1 Cor 3:18-20

22 [a]Prov 23:20; Is 5:11; 56:12; Hab 2:15

23 [1]Lit *righteousness* [a]Ex 23:8; Is 1:23; 10:1,2; Mic 3:11; 7:3 [b]Ps 94:21; James 5:6

24 [1]Lit *ascend* [a]Is 9:18,19; Joel 2:5 [b]Job 18:16 [c]Hos 5:12 [d]Is 8:6; 30:9,12; Acts 13:41

25 [1]Lit *were* [2]Lit *has not turned away* [a]2 Kin 22:13,17; Is 66:15 [b]Ps 18:7; Is 64:3; Jer 4:24; Nah 1:5 [c]2 Kin 9:37; Is 14:19; Jer 16:4 [d]Is 9:12,17,19, 21; 10:4; Jer 4:8; Dan 9:16 [e]Ex 7:19; Is 23:11

26 [1]Lit *nations;* probably Assyria [a]Is 13:2,3 [b]Is 7:18; Zech 10:8 [c]Deut 28:49 [d]Is 13:4,5

27 [a]Joel 2:7,8

Nor is the [b]belt at its waist
undone,
Nor its sandal strap broken.
28 [1a]Its arrows are sharp and all
its bows are bent;
The hoofs of its horses [2]seem
like flint and its *chariot*
[b]wheels like a whirlwind.
29 Its [a]roaring is like a lioness, and
it roars like young lions;
It growls as it [b]seizes the prey
And carries *it* off with [c]no one
to deliver *it.*
30 And it will [a]growl over it in that
day like the roaring of the
sea.
If one [b]looks to the land,
behold, there is darkness
and distress;
Even the light is darkened by its
clouds.

Isaiah's Vision

6 In the year of [a]King Uzziah's death
[b]I saw the Lord sitting on a throne,
lofty and exalted, with the train of His
robe filling the temple.
2 Seraphim stood above Him, [a]each
having six wings: with two he covered
his face, and with two he covered his
feet, and with two he flew.
3 And one called out to another and
said,
"[a]Holy, Holy, Holy, is the LORD of
hosts,
The [1b]whole earth is full of His
glory."
4 And the [1]foundations of the thresholds trembled at the voice of him who
called out, while the [2a]temple was filling with smoke.
5 Then I said,
"[a]Woe is me, for I am ruined!
Because I am a man of [b]unclean
lips,
And I live among a [c]people of
unclean lips;
For my eyes have seen the
[d]King, the LORD of hosts."
6 ¶ Then one of the seraphim flew
to me with a burning coal in his hand,
which he had taken from the [a]altar with
tongs.
7 He [a]touched my mouth *with it* and
said, "Behold, this has touched your lips;
and [b]your iniquity is taken away and
your sin is [1]forgiven."

Isaiah's Commission

8 Then I heard the [a]voice of the
Lord, saying, "Whom shall I send, and
who will go for Us?" Then [b]I said, "Here
am I. Send me!"
9 He said, "Go, and tell this people:
'Keep on [a]listening, but do not
perceive;
Keep on looking, but do not
understand.'
10 "[a]Render the hearts of this
people [1b]insensitive,
Their ears [2]dull,
And their eyes [3]dim,
[c]Otherwise they might see with
their eyes,
Hear with their ears,
Understand with their hearts,
And return and be healed."
11 Then I said, "Lord, [a]how long?"
And He answered,
"Until [b]cities are devastated *and*
without inhabitant,
Houses are without people
And the land is utterly desolate,
12 "The LORD has [a]removed men far
away,
And the [1b]forsaken places are
many in the midst of the
land.
13 "Yet there will be a tenth portion
in it,
And it will again be *subject* to
burning,
Like a terebinth or an [a]oak
Whose stump remains when it is
felled.
The [b]holy seed is its stump."

War against Jerusalem

7 Now it came about in the days of
[a]Ahaz, the son of Jotham, the son of
Uzziah, king of Judah, that [b]Rezin the
king of Aram and [c]Pekah the son of Remaliah, king of Israel, went up to Jerusalem
to *wage* war against it, but [d]could not
[1]conquer it.
2 When it was reported to the
[a]house of David, saying, "The Arameans
[1b]have camped in [c]Ephraim," his heart
and the hearts of his people shook as the
trees of the forest shake [2]with the wind.
3 ¶ Then the LORD said to Isaiah, "Go
out now to meet Ahaz, you and your son
[1]Shear-jashub, at the end of the [a]con-
duit of the upper pool, on the highway to
the [2]fuller's field,
4 and say to him, 'Take care and be
[a]calm, have no [b]fear and [c]do not be
fainthearted because of these two stubs of
smoldering [d]firebrands, on account of
the fierce anger of Rezin and Aram and
the [e]son of Remaliah.
5 'Because [a]Aram, *with* Ephraim and
the son of Remaliah, has planned evil
against you, saying,
6 "Let us go up against Judah and [1]ter-
rorize it, and make for ourselves a breach

27 [b]Job 12:18
28 [1]Lit *Which, its arrows* [2]Lit *are regarded as* [a]Ps 7:12,13; 45:5; Is 13:18 [b]Is 21:1; Jer 4:13
29 [a]Jer 51:38; Zeph 3:3; Zech 11:3 [b]Is 10:6; 49:24,25; Mic 5:8 [c]Is 42:22
30 [a]Is 17:12; Jer 6:23; Luke 21:25 [b]Is 8:22; Jer 4:23-28; Joel 2:10; Luke 21:25,26
6:1 [a]2 Kin 15:7; 2 Chr 26:23; Is 1:1 [b]John 12:41; Rev 4:2,3; 20:11
2 [a]Rev 4:8
3 [1]Lit *fullness of the whole earth is His glory* [a]Rev 4:8 [b]Num 14:21; Ps 72:19
4 [1]Lit *door sockets* [2]Lit *house* [a]Rev 15:8
5 [a]Ex 33:20; Luke 5:8 [b]Ex 6:12,30 [c]Is 59:3; Jer 9:3-8 [d]Jer 51:57
6 [a]Rev 8:3
7 [1]Lit *atoned for* [a]Jer 1:9; Dan 10:16 [b]Is 40:2; 53:5,6,11; 1 John 1:7
8 [a]Ezek 10:5; Acts 9:4 [b]Acts 26:19
9 [a]Is 43:8; Matt 13:14; Mark 4:12; Luke 8:10; John 12:40; Acts 28:26; Rom 11:8
10 [1]Lit *fat* [2]Lit *heavy* [3]Lit *besmeared* [a]Matt 13:15 [b]Deut 31:20; 32:15 [c]Jer 5:21
11 [a]Ps 79:5 [b]Lev 26:31; Is 1:7; 3:8,26
12 [1]Or *forsakenness will be great* [a]Deut 28:64 [b]Jer 4:29
13 [a]Job 14:7 [b]Deut 7:6; Ezra 9:2
7:1 [1]Lit *fight against* [a]2 Kin 16:1; Is 1:1 [b]2 Kin 15:37 [c]2 Kin 15:25; 2 Chr 28:6 [d]Is 7:6,7
2 [1]Lit *has settled down on* [2]Lit *from before* [a]Is 7:13; 22:22 [b]Is 8:12 [c]Is 9:9
3 [1]I.e. a remnant shall return [2]I.e. laundryman's [a]2 Kin 18:17; Is 36:2
4 [a]Ex 14:13; Is 30:15; Lam 3:26 [b]Is 10:24; Matt 24:6 [c]Deut 20:3; 1 Sam 17:32; Is 35:4 [d]Amos 4:11; Zech 3:2 [e]Is 7:1,9
5 [a]Is 7:2
6 [1]Lit *cause it a sickening dread*

in [2]its walls and set up the son of Tabeel as king in the midst of it,"

7 thus says the Lord [1]GOD: "[a]It shall not stand nor shall it come to pass.

8 "For the head of Aram is [a]Damascus and the head of Damascus is Rezin (now within another 65 years Ephraim will be shattered, *so that it is* no longer a people),

9 and the head of Ephraim is Samaria and the head of Samaria is the son of Remaliah. [a]If you will not believe, you surely shall not [1]last." ' "

The Child Immanuel

10 ¶ Then the LORD spoke again to Ahaz, saying,

11 "Ask a [a]sign for yourself from the LORD your God; [1]make *it* deep as Sheol or high as [2]heaven."

12 But Ahaz said, "I will not ask, nor will I test the LORD!"

13 Then he said, "Listen now, O [a]house of David! Is it too slight a thing for you to try the patience of men, that you will [b]try the patience of [c]my God as well?

14 "Therefore the Lord Himself will give you a sign: Behold, [a]a [1]virgin will be with child and bear a son, and she will call His name [2b]Immanuel.

15 "He will eat [a]curds and honey [1]at the time He knows *enough* to refuse evil and choose good.

16 "[a]For before the boy will know *enough* to refuse evil and choose good, [b]the land whose two kings you dread will be forsaken.

Trials to Come for Judah

17 "The LORD will bring on you, on your people, and on your father's house such days as have never come since the day that [a]Ephraim separated from Judah, the [b]king of Assyria."

18 ¶ In that day the LORD will [a]whistle for the fly that is in the [1b]remotest part of the rivers of Egypt and for the bee that is in the land of Assyria.

19 They will all come and settle on the steep [1]ravines, on the [a]ledges of the cliffs, [b]on all the thorn bushes and on all the [2]watering places.

20 ¶ In that day the Lord will [a]shave with a [b]razor, [c]hired from regions beyond [d]the [1]Euphrates (*that is,* with the king of Assyria), the head and the hair of the legs; and it will also remove the beard.

21 ¶ Now in that day a man may keep alive a [a]heifer and a pair of sheep;

22 and because of the abundance of the milk produced he will eat curds, for everyone that is left within the land will eat [a]curds and honey.

23 ¶ And it will come about in that day, [a]that every place where there used to be a thousand vines, *valued* at a thousand *shekels* of silver, will become [b]briars and thorns.

24 *People* will come there with bows and arrows because all the land will be briars and thorns.

25 As for all the hills which used to be cultivated with the hoe, you will not go there for fear of briars and thorns; but they will become a place for [1a]pasturing oxen and for sheep to trample.

Damascus and Samaria Fall

8 Then the LORD said to me, "Take for yourself a large tablet and [a]write on it [1]in ordinary letters: [2b]Swift is the booty, speedy is the prey.

2 "And [1]I will take to Myself faithful witnesses for testimony, [a]Uriah the priest and Zechariah the son of Jeberechiah."

3 So I approached the prophetess, and she conceived and gave birth to a son. Then the LORD said to me, "Name him [1a]Maher-shalal-hash-baz;

4 for [a]before the boy knows how to cry out 'My father' or 'My mother,' the wealth of [b]Damascus and the spoil of Samaria will be carried away before the king of Assyria."

5 ¶ Again the LORD spoke to me further, saying,

6 "Inasmuch as these people have
[a]rejected the gently flowing
waters of Shiloah
And rejoice in [b]Rezin and the
son of Remaliah;
7 "Now therefore, behold, the Lord
is about to bring on them
the [a]strong and abundant
waters of the [1b]Euphrates,
Even the [c]king of Assyria and all
his glory;
And it will [d]rise up over all its
channels and go over all its
banks.
8 "Then [a]it will sweep on into
Judah, it will overflow and
pass through,
It will [b]reach even to the neck;
And the spread of its wings will
[1]fill the breadth of [2]your
land, O [c]Immanuel.

A Believing Remnant

9 ¶ "[a]Be broken, O peoples, and
be [1b]shattered;
And give ear, all remote places of
the earth.

---

6 [2]Lit *it*
7 [1]Heb *YHWH,* usually rendered *LORD* [a]Is 8:10; 28:18; Acts 4:25,26
8 [a]Gen 14:15; Is 17:1-3
9 [1]Or *be established* [a]2 Chr 20:20; Is 5:24; 8:6-8; 30:12-14
11 [1]So with the versions; M.T. *make the request deep or high* [2]Lit *heights* [a]2 Kin 19:29; Is 37:30; 38:7,8; 55:13
13 [a]Is 7:2 [b]Is 1:14; 43:24 [c]Is 25:1
14 [1]Or *maiden* [2]I.e. God is with us [a]Matt 1:23 [b]Is 8:8,10
15 [1]Lit *with respect to his knowing* [a]Is 7:22
16 [a]Is 8:4 [b]Is 8:14; 17:3; Jer 7:15; Hos 5:3,9, 14; Amos 1:3-5
17 [a]1 Kin 12:16 [b]2 Chr 28:20; Is 8:7,8; 10:5,6
18 [1]Or *mouth of the rivers;* i.e. the Nile Delta [a]Is 5:26 [b]Is 13:5
19 [1]Or *wadis* [2]Or *pastures* [a]Is 2:19; Jer 16:16 [b]Is 7:24,25
20 [1]Lit *River* [a]2 Kin 18:13-16; Is 24:1 [b]Ezek 5:1-4 [c]Is 10:5,15 [d]Is 8:7; 11:15; Jer 2:18
21 [a]Is 14:30; 27:10; Jer 39:10
22 [a]Is 8:15
23 [a]Is 5:10; 32:13,14 [b]Is 5:6
25 [1]Lit *sending* [a]Is 5:17
8:1 [1]Lit *with the stylus of man* [2]Heb *Maher-shalal-hash-baz* [a]Is 30:8; Hab 2:2 [b]Is 8:3
2 [1]Another reading is *take for me* [a]2 Kin 16:10,11,15,16
3 [1]I.e. swift is the booty, speedy is the prey [a]Is 8:1
4 [a]Is 7:16 [b]Is 7:8,9
6 [a]Is 1:20; 5:24; 7:9; 30:12 [b]Is 7:1
7 [1]Lit *River* [a]Is 17:12,13 [b]Is 7:20; 11:15 [c]Is 7:17; 10:5 [d]Amos 8:8; 9:5
8 [1]Lit *be the fullness of* [2]Or *Your* [a]Is 10:6 [b]Is 30:28 [c]Is 7:14
9 [1]Or *dismayed* [a]Is 17:12-14 [b]Dan 2:34,35

Gird yourselves, yet be [1]shattered;
Gird yourselves, yet be [1]shattered.
10 "[a]Devise a plan, but it will be thwarted;
State a [1]proposal, but [b]it will not stand,
For [2c]God is with us."

11 ¶ For thus the LORD spoke to me [1]with [a]mighty power and instructed me [b]not to walk in the way of this people, saying,

12 "You are not to say, '*It is a* [a]conspiracy!'
In regard to all that this people call a conspiracy,
And [b]you are not to fear [1]what they fear or be in dread of *it.*
13 "It is the [a]LORD of hosts [b]whom you should regard as holy.
And He shall be your fear,
And He shall be your dread.
14 "Then He shall become a [a]sanctuary;
But to both the houses of Israel, a [b]stone to strike and a rock to stumble over,
And a snare and a [c]trap for the inhabitants of Jerusalem.
15 "Many [a]will stumble over them,
Then they will fall and be broken;
They will even be snared and caught."

16 ¶ [a]Bind up the testimony, [b]seal the [1]law among [c]my disciples.

17 And I will [a]wait for the LORD [b]who is hiding His face from the house of Jacob; I will even look eagerly for Him.

18 [a]Behold, I and the children whom the LORD has given me are for [b]signs and wonders in Israel from the LORD of hosts, who [c]dwells on Mount Zion.

19 ¶ When they say to you, "[a]Consult the mediums and the spiritists who whisper and mutter," should not a people [b]consult their God? *Should they* [c]*consult* the dead on behalf of the living?

20 To the [1a]law and to the testimony! If they do not speak according to this word, it is because [b]they have no dawn.

21 They will pass through [1]the land [a]hard-pressed and famished, and it will turn out that when they are hungry, they will be enraged and curse [2]their king and their God as they face upward.

22 Then they will [a]look to the earth, and behold, distress and darkness, the gloom of anguish; and *they will be* [b]driven away into darkness.

Birth and Reign of the Prince of Peace

9 [1]But there will be no *more* [a]gloom for her who was in anguish; in earlier times He [b]treated the [c]land of Zebulun and the land of Naphtali with contempt, but later on He shall make *it* glorious, by the way of the sea, on the other side of Jordan, Galilee of the [2]Gentiles.

2 [1a]The people who walk in darkness
Will see a great light;
Those who live in a dark land,
The light will shine on them.
3 [a]You shall multiply the nation,
You [b]shall [1]increase [2]their gladness;
They will be glad in Your presence
As with the gladness [3]of harvest,
As [4c]men rejoice when they divide the spoil.
4 For [a]You shall break the yoke of their burden and the staff on their shoulders,
The rod of their [b]oppressor, as [1]at the battle of [c]Midian.
5 For every boot of the booted warrior in the *battle* tumult,
And cloak rolled in blood, will be for burning, fuel for the fire.
6 For a [a]child will be born to us, a [b]son will be given to us;
And the [c]government will [1]rest [d]on His shoulders;
And His name will be called [e]Wonderful Counselor,
[f]Mighty God,
Eternal [g]Father, Prince of [h]Peace.
7 There will be [a]no end to the increase of *His* government or of peace,
On the [b]throne of David and over his kingdom,
To establish it and to uphold it with [c]justice and righteousness
From then on and forevermore.
[d]The zeal of the LORD of hosts will accomplish this.

God's Anger with Israel's Arrogance

8 ¶ The Lord sends a [1]message against Jacob,
And it falls on Israel.
9 And all the people know *it,*
That is, [a]Ephraim and the inhabitants of Samaria,
Asserting in pride and in [b]arrogance of heart:

---

9 [1]Or *dismayed*
10 [1]Lit *word* [2]Heb *Immanu-el* [a]Job 5:12; Is 28:18 [b]Is 7:7 [c]Is 8:8; Rom 8:31
11 [1]Lit *with strength of the hand* [a]Ezek 3:14 [b]Ezek 2:8
12 [1]Lit *their fear* [a]Is 7:2 [b]1 Pet 3:14
13 [a]Is 5:16 [b]Num 20:12
14 [a]Is 4:6; Ezek 11:16 [b]Luke 2:34; Rom 9:33; 1 Pet 2:8 [c]Is 24:17
15 [a]Is 28:13; Luke 20:18; Rom 9:32
16 [1]Or *teaching* [a]Is 8:1 [b]Dan 12:4 [c]Is 50:4
17 [a]Is 25:9; Hab 2:3 [b]Deut 31:17; Is 1:15
18 [a]Heb 2:13 [b]Luke 2:34 [c]Ps 9:11; Zech 8:3
19 [a]Lev 20:6; 2 Kin 21:6; Is 19:3 [b]Is 30:2 [c]1 Sam 28:8-11
20 [1]Or *teaching* [a]Is 1:10; Luke 16:29 [b]Is 8:22; Mic 3:6
21 [1]Lit *it* [2]Or *by their king* [a]Is 9:20
22 [a]Is 5:30; Jer 13:16; Amos 5:18; Zeph 1:14 [b]Is 8:20
9:1 [1]Ch 8:23 in Heb [2]Or *nations* [a]Is 8:22 [b]2 Kin 15:29; 2 Chr 16:4 [c]Matt 4:15
2 [1]Ch 9:1 in Heb [a]Matt 4:16; Luke 1:79; Eph 5:8
3 [1]Another reading is *not increase* [2]Lit *the* [3]Lit *in* [4]Lit *they* [a]Is 26:15 [b]Is 35:10 [c]1 Sam 30:16
4 [1]Lit *in the day of Midian* [a]Is 10:27 [b]Is 14:4 [c]Judg 7:25; Is 10:26
6 [1]Lit *be* [a]Is 7:14; Luke 2:11 [b]John 3:16 [c]Matt 28:18; 1 Cor 15:25 [d]Is 22:22 [e]Is 28:29 [f]Deut 10:17; Neh 9:32; Is 10:21 [g]Is 63:16 [h]Is 26:3
7 [a]Dan 2:44; Luke 1:32 [b]Is 16:5 [c]Is 11:4 [d]Is 37:32
8 [1]Lit *word*
9 [a]Is 7:8 [b]Is 46:12

10 "The bricks have fallen down,
But we will [a]rebuild with
smooth stones;
The sycamores have been cut
down,
But we will replace *them* with
cedars."
11 Therefore the LORD raises against
them adversaries from
[a]Rezin
And spurs their enemies on,
12 The Arameans on the east and
the [a]Philistines on the west;
And they [b]devour Israel with
[1]gaping jaws.
[c]In *spite of* all this, His anger
does not turn away
And His hand is still
stretched out.

13 ¶ Yet the people [a]do not turn
back to Him who struck
them,
Nor do they [b]seek the LORD of
hosts.
14 So the LORD cuts off [a]head and
tail from Israel,
Both palm branch and bulrush
[b]in a single day.
15 The head is [a]the elder and
honorable man,
And the prophet who teaches
[b]falsehood is the tail.
16 [a]For those who guide this
people are leading *them*
astray;
And those who are guided by
them are [1]brought to
confusion.
17 Therefore the Lord does [a]not
take pleasure in their young
men,
[b]Nor does He have pity on their
[1]orphans or their widows;
For every one of them is
[c]godless and an [d]evildoer,
And every [e]mouth is speaking
foolishness.
[f]In *spite of* all this, His anger
does not turn away
And His hand is still
stretched out.

18 ¶ [a]For wickedness burns like a
fire;
It consumes briars and thorns;
It even sets the thickets of the
forest aflame
And they roll upward in a
column of smoke.
19 By the [a]fury of the LORD of
hosts the [b]land is
burned up,
And the [c]people are like fuel for
the fire;
No [d]man spares his brother.
20 [1]They slice off *what is* on the
right hand but *still* are
[a]hungry,
And [2]they eat *what is* on the
left hand but they are not
satisfied;
Each of them eats the [b]flesh of
his own arm.
21 Manasseh *devours* Ephraim, and
Ephraim Manasseh,
[a]*And* together they are against
Judah.
[b]In *spite of* all this, His anger
does not turn away
And His hand is still stretched
out.

Assyria Is God's Instrument

10 Woe to those who [a]enact evil
statutes
And to those who constantly
record [1]unjust decisions,
2 So as [a]to [1]deprive the needy of
justice
And rob the poor of My people
of *their* rights,
So [b]that widows may be their
spoil
And that they may plunder the
[2]orphans.
3 Now [a]what will you do in the
[b]day of punishment,
And in the devastation which
will come [c]from afar?
[d]To whom will you flee for
help?
And where will you leave your
[1]wealth?
4 Nothing *remains* but to crouch
[1]among the [a]captives
Or fall [1]among the [b]slain.
[c]In *spite of* all this, His anger
does not turn away
And His hand is still
stretched out.

5 ¶ Woe to [a]Assyria, the [b]rod of
My anger
And the staff in whose hands is
[c]My indignation,
6 I send it against a [a]godless
nation
And commission it against the
[b]people of My fury
To capture booty and [c]to seize
plunder,
And to [1]trample them down like
[d]mud in the streets.
7 Yet it [a]does not so intend,
Nor does [1]it plan so in its heart,

10 [a]Mal 1:4
11 [a]Is 7:1,8
12 [1]Lit *the whole mouth* [a]2 Chr 28:18 [b]Ps 79:7; Jer 10:25 [c]Is 5:25
13 [a]Jer 5:3; Hos 7:10 [b]Is 31:1; Hos 3:5
14 [a]Is 19:15 [b]Rev 18:8
15 [a]Is 3:2,3 [b]Is 28:15; 59:3,4; Jer 23:14,32; Matt 24:24
16 [1]Or *swallowed up* [a]Is 3:12; Matt 15:14; 23:16,24
17 [1]Or *fatherless* [a]Jer 18:21; Amos 4:10; 8:13 [b]Is 27:11 [c]Is 10:6; 32:6 [d]Is 1:4; 14:20; 31:2 [e]Matt 12:34 [f]Is 5:25
18 [a]Ps 83:14; Is 1:7; Nah 1:10; Mal 4:1
19 [a]Is 10:6; 13:9,13; 42:25 [b]Joel 2:3 [c]Is 1:31; 24:6 [d]Mic 7:2,6
20 [1]Lit *he slices* [2]Lit *he eats* [a]Is 8:21,22 [b]Is 49:26
21 [a]2 Chr 28:6, 8; Is 11:13 [b]Is 5:25
10:1 [1]Lit *mischief* or *misfortune* [a]Ps 94:20; Is 29:21; 59:4, 13
2 [1]Lit *turn aside from* [2]Or *fatherless* [a]Is 5:23 [b]Is 1:23; 3:14,15
3 [1]Lit *glory* [a]Job 31:14 [b]Is 13:6; 26:14,21; 29:6; Jer 9:9; Hos 9:7; Luke 19:44 [c]Is 5:26 [d]Is 20:6; 30:5,7; 31:3
4 [1]Lit *under* [a]Is 24:22 [b]Is 22:2; 34:3; 66:16 [c]Is 5:25
5 [a]Is 7:17; 8:7; 14:24-27; Zeph 2:13-15 [b]Jer 51:20 [c]Is 13:5; 30:30; 34:2; 66:14
6 [1]Lit *make them a trampled place* [a]Is 9:17 [b]Is 9:19 [c]Is 5:29 [d]Is 5:25
7 [1]Lit *its heart so plan* [a]Gen 50:20; Mic 4:11, 12; Acts 2:23,24

But rather it is [2]its purpose to
destroy
And to cut off [3]many nations.
8 For it says, "Are not my princes
[1]all kings?
9 "Is not [a]Calno like [b]Carchemish,
Or [c]Hamath like Arpad,
Or [d]Samaria like [e]Damascus?
10 "As my hand has reached to the
[a]kingdoms of the idols,
Whose graven images *were*
greater than those of
Jerusalem and Samaria,
11 Shall I not [1]do to Jerusalem and
her images
Just as I have done to Samaria
and [a]her idols?"

12 ¶ So it will be that when the Lord has completed all His [a]work on Mount Zion and on Jerusalem, *He will say,* "I will [1]punish the fruit of the arrogant heart of the king of Assyria and [b]the pomp of [2]his haughtiness."

13 For [a]he has said,
"By the power of my hand and by
my wisdom I did *this,*
For I have understanding;
And I [b]removed the boundaries
of the peoples
And plundered their treasures,
And like a mighty man I brought
down [1]*their* inhabitants,
14 And my hand reached to the
riches of the peoples like a
[a]nest,
And as one gathers abandoned
eggs, I gathered all the
earth;
And there was not one that
flapped its wing or opened
its beak or chirped."

15 ¶ Is the [a]axe to [b]boast itself
over the one who chops
with it?
Is the saw to exalt itself over the
one who wields it?
That would be like [c]a [1]club
wielding those who lift it,
Or like [c]a rod lifting *him who* is
not wood.
16 Therefore the Lord, the [1]GOD of
hosts, will send a [a]wasting
disease among his [b]stout
warriors;
And under his [c]glory a fire will
be kindled like a burning
flame.
17 And the [a]light of Israel will
become a fire and his [b]Holy
One a flame,
And it will [c]burn and devour his
thorns and his briars in a
single day.
18 And He will [a]destroy the glory
of his forest and of his
fruitful garden, both soul
and body,
And it will be as when a sick
man wastes away.
19 And the [a]rest of the trees of his
forest will be so small in
number
That a child could write them
down.

A Remnant Will Return

20 ¶ Now in that day the [a]remnant of Israel, and those of the house of Jacob [b]who have escaped, will never again rely on the one who struck them, but will truly [c]rely on the LORD, the Holy One of Israel.

21 A [a]remnant will return, the
remnant of Jacob, to the
[b]mighty God.
22 For [a]though your people,
O Israel, may be like the
sand of the sea,
Only a remnant within them will
return;
A [b]destruction is determined,
overflowing with
righteousness.

23 For a complete destruction, one that is decreed, [a]the Lord [1]GOD of hosts will execute in the midst of the whole land.

24 ¶ Therefore thus says the Lord [1]GOD of hosts, "O My people who dwell in [a]Zion, [b]do not fear the Assyrian [2]who [c]strikes you with the rod and lifts up his staff against you, the way Egypt *did.*

25 "For in a very [a]little while [b]My indignation *against you* will be spent and My anger *will be directed* to their destruction."

26 The LORD of hosts will [a]arouse a scourge against him like the slaughter of [b]Midian at the rock of Oreb; and His [c]staff will be over the sea and He will lift it up [d]the way *He did* in Egypt.

27 So it will be in that day, that [1]his [a]burden will be removed from your shoulders and his yoke from your neck, and the yoke will be broken because [b]of fatness.

28 ¶ He has come against Aiath,
He has passed through [a]Migron;
At [b]Michmash he deposited his
[c]baggage.
29 They have gone through [a]the
pass, *saying,*
"[b]Geba will be our lodging
place."

7 [2]Lit *in its heart* [3]Lit *not a few*
8 [1]Lit *altogether*
9 [a]Gen 10:10; Amos 6:2 [b]2 Chr 35:20 [c]Num 34:8 [d]2 Kin 17:6 [e]2 Kin 16:9
10 [a]2 Kin 19:17,18
11 [1]Lit *do thus* [a]Is 2:8
12 [1]Lit *visit* [2]Lit *haughtiness of his eyes* [a]2 Kin 19:31; Is 28:21, 22; 29:14; 65:7 [b]Is 37:23
13 [1]Or *those who sit* on thrones [a]2 Kin 19:22-24; Is 37:24-27; Ezek 28:4; Dan 4:30 [b]Hab 2:6-11
14 [a]Jer 49:16; Obad 4
15 [1]Lit *staff* [a]Jer 51:20 [b]Is 29:16; 45:9; Rom 9:20, 21 [c]Is 10:5
16 [1]Heb *YHWH,* usually rendered LORD [a]Ps 106:15 [b]Is 17:4 [c]Is 8:7; 10:18
17 [a]Is 30:33; 31:9 [b]Is 37:23 [c]Num 11:1-3; Is 27:4; 33:12; Jer 4:4; 7:20
18 [a]Is 10:33,34
19 [a]Is 21:17
20 [a]Is 1:9; 11:11,16; 46:3 [b]Is 4:2; 37:31, 32 [c]2 Chr 14:11; Is 17:7,8; 50:10
21 [a]Is 7:3 [b]Is 9:6
22 [a]Rom 9:27, 28 [b]Is 28:22; Dan 9:27; Rom 9:28
23 [1]Heb *YHWH,* usually rendered LORD [a]Is 28:22; Dan 9:27; Rom 9:28
24 [1]Heb *YHWH,* usually rendered LORD [2]Lit *he* [a]Ps 87:5,6 [b]Is 7:4; 12:2; 37:6 [c]Ex 5:14-16
25 [a]Is 17:14; Hag 2:6 [b]Is 10:5; 26:20; Dan 11:36
26 [a]Is 37:36-38 [b]Judg 7:25; Is 9:4 [c]Ex 14:16 [d]Ex 14:27
27 [1]I.e. the Assyrian [a]Is 9:4; 14:25 [b]Is 30:23; 55:2
28 [a]1 Sam 14:2 [b]1 Sam 13:2,5 [c]Judg 18:21; 1 Sam 17:22
29 [a]1 Sam 13:23 [b]Josh 21:17; 1 Sam 13:16

[c]Ramah is terrified, and
[d]Gibeah of Saul has fled
away.
30 Cry aloud with your voice,
O daughter of [a]Gallim!
Pay attention, Laishah *and*
[1]wretched [b]Anathoth!
31 Madmenah has fled.
The inhabitants of Gebim have
sought refuge.
32 Yet today he will halt at [a]Nob;
He [b]shakes his fist at the
mountain of the [1c]daughter
of Zion, the hill of
Jerusalem.

33 ¶ Behold, the Lord, the [1]GOD of
hosts, will lop off the boughs
with a terrible crash;
Those also who are [a]tall in
stature will be cut down
And those who are lofty will be
abased.
34 He will cut down the thickets of
the forest with an iron *axe,*
And [a]Lebanon will fall [1]by the
Mighty One.

Righteous Reign of the Branch

11 Then a [a]shoot will spring from
the [b]stem of Jesse,
And a [c]branch from [d]his roots
will bear fruit.
2 The [a]Spirit of the LORD will rest
on Him,
The spirit of [b]wisdom and
understanding,
The spirit of counsel and
[c]strength,
The spirit of knowledge and the
fear of the LORD.
3 And He will delight in the fear of
the LORD,
And He will not judge by what
His eyes [a]see,
Nor make a decision by what His
ears hear;
4 But with [a]righteousness He will
judge the [b]poor,
And decide with fairness for the
[c]afflicted of the earth;
And He will strike the earth with
the [d]rod of His mouth,
And with the [e]breath of His lips
He will slay the wicked.
5 Also [a]righteousness will be the
belt about His loins,
And [b]faithfulness the belt about
His waist.

6 ¶ And the [a]wolf will dwell with
the lamb,
And the leopard will lie down
with the young goat,
And the calf and the young lion
[1]and the fatling together;
And a little boy will lead them.
7 Also the cow and the bear will
graze,
Their young will lie down
together,
And the [a]lion will eat straw like
the ox.
8 The nursing child will play by
the hole of the cobra,
And the weaned child will put
his hand on the viper's den.
9 They will [a]not hurt or destroy in
all My holy mountain,
For the [b]earth will be full of the
knowledge of the LORD
As the waters cover the sea.

10 ¶ Then in that day
The [a]nations will resort to the
[b]root of Jesse,
Who will stand as a [1c]signal for
the peoples;
And His [d]resting place will be
[2]glorious.

The Restored Remnant

11 ¶ Then it will happen on that
day that the Lord
Will again recover the second
time with His hand
The [a]remnant of His people,
who will remain,
From [b]Assyria, [c]Egypt, Pathros,
Cush, [d]Elam, Shinar,
Hamath,
And from the [1e]islands of the
sea.
12 And He will lift up a [a]standard
for the nations
And [b]assemble the banished
ones of Israel,
And will gather the dispersed of
Judah
From the four corners of the
earth.
13 Then the [a]jealousy of Ephraim
will depart,
And those who harass Judah will
be cut off;
Ephraim will not be jealous of
Judah,
And Judah will not harass
Ephraim.
14 They will [a]swoop down on the
slopes of the Philistines on
the [b]west;
Together they will [c]plunder the
sons of the east;
[1]They will possess [d]Edom and
[e]Moab,
And the sons of Ammon will be
[2]subject to them.

---

29 [c]Josh 18:25; 1 Sam 7:17 [d]1 Sam 10:26

30 [1]An ancient version reads *Answer her, O Anathoth* [a]1 Sam 25:44 [b]Josh 21:18; Jer 1:1

32 [1]Another reading is *house of* [a]1 Sam 21:1 [b]Is 19:16; Zech 2:9 [c]Is 1:8; Jer 6:23

33 [1]Heb *YHWH,* usually rendered *LORD* [a]Is 37:24; Ezek 31:3; Amos 2:9

34 [1]Or *as a mighty one* [a]Is 2:13

11:1 [a]Is 4:2 [b]Is 9:7; Acts 13:23 [c]Is 6:13; Jer 23:5; Zech 3:8 [d]Rev 5:5

2 [a]Is 42:1; Matt 3:16; John 1:32 [b]John 16:13; 1 Cor 1:30; Eph 1:17 [c]2 Tim 1:7

3 [a]John 2:25

4 [a]Is 9:7 [b]Ps 72:2; Is 3:14 [c]Is 29:19 [d]Ps 2:9; Is 49:2; Mal 4:6 [e]Job 4:9; Is 30:28; 2 Thess 2:8

5 [a]Eph 6:14 [b]Is 25:1

6 [1]Some versions read *will feed together* [a]Is 65:25

7 [a]Is 65:25

9 [a]Job 5:23; Is 65:25; Ezek 34:25; Hos 2:18 [b]Ps 98:2; Is 45:6; Hab 2:14

10 [1]Or *standard* [2]Lit *glory* [a]Luke 2:32; Acts 11:18 [b]Is 11:1; Rom 15:12 [c]Is 11:12; John 3:14 [d]Is 14:3

11 [1]Or *coastlands* [a]Is 10:20-22 [b]Is 19:23-25; Hos 11:11; Zech 10:10 [c]Is 19:21; Mic 7:12 [d]Gen 10:22 [e]Is 24:15

12 [a]Is 11:10 [b]Is 56:8; Zeph 3:10; Zech 10:6

13 [a]Is 9:21; Jer 3:18; Ezek 37:16; Hos 1:11

14 [1]Lit *Edom and Moab will be the outstretching of their hand* [2]Lit *their obedience* [a]Jer 48:40; Hab 1:8 [b]Is 9:12 [c]Jer 49:28 [d]Is 63:1; Dan 11:41; Joel 3:19; Amos 9:12 [e]Is 16:14

15 And the LORD will [1a]utterly
destroy
The tongue of the [2]Sea of Egypt;
And He will [b]wave His hand
over the [3c]River
With His scorching wind;
And He will strike it into seven
streams
And make *men* walk over
[4]dry-shod.
16 And there will be a [a]highway
from Assyria
For the [b]remnant of His people
who will be left,
Just as there was for Israel
In [c]the day that they came up
out of the land of Egypt.

Thanksgiving Expressed

12 Then you will say on that day,
"[a]I will give thanks to You,
O LORD;
For [b]although You were angry
with me,
Your anger is turned away,
And You comfort me.
2 "Behold, [a]God is my salvation,
I will [b]trust and not be afraid;
For [c]the LORD GOD is my
strength and song,
And He has become my
salvation."
3 Therefore you will joyously
[a]draw water
From the [b]springs of salvation.
4 And in that day you will [a]say,
"[b]Give thanks to the LORD, call
on His name.
[c]Make known His deeds among
the peoples;
[1]Make *them* remember that His
name is exalted."
5 [a]Praise the LORD in song, for He
has done [1]excellent things;
Let this be known throughout
the earth.
6 [a]Cry aloud and shout for joy,
O inhabitant of Zion,
For [b]great in your midst is the
Holy One of Israel.

Prophecies about Babylon

13 The [1a]oracle concerning [b]Babylon which [c]Isaiah the son of
Amoz saw.
2 [a]Lift up a standard on the
[1b]bare hill,
Raise your voice to them,
[c]Wave the hand that they may
[d]enter the doors of the
nobles.
3 I have commanded My
consecrated ones,
I have even called My [a]mighty
warriors,
My proudly exulting ones,
To *execute* My anger.
4 A [a]sound of tumult on the
mountains,
Like that of many people!
A sound of the uproar of
kingdoms,
Of nations gathered together!
The LORD of hosts is mustering
the army for battle.
5 They are coming from a far
country,
From the [1a]farthest horizons,
The LORD and His instruments of
[b]indignation,
To [c]destroy the whole land.

Judgment on the Day of the LORD

6 Wail, for the [a]day of the LORD is
near!
It will come as [b]destruction
from [1]the Almighty.
7 Therefore [a]all hands will fall
limp,
And every man's [b]heart will
melt.
8 They will be [a]terrified,
Pains and anguish will take hold
of *them;*
They will [b]writhe like a woman
in labor,
They will look at one another in
astonishment,
Their faces aflame.
9 Behold, [a]the day of the LORD is
coming,
Cruel, with fury and burning
anger,
To make the land a desolation;
And He will exterminate its
sinners from it.
10 For the [a]stars of heaven and
their constellations
Will not flash forth their light;
The [b]sun will be dark when it
rises
And the moon will not shed its
light.
11 Thus I will [a]punish the world
for its evil
And the [b]wicked for their
iniquity;
I will also put an end to the
[c]arrogance of the proud
And abase the [d]haughtiness of
the [1e]ruthless.
12 I will make mortal man
[1a]scarcer than pure gold
And mankind than the [b]gold of
Ophir.
13 Therefore I will make the
[a]heavens tremble,

15 [1]Another reading is *dry up the tongue* [2]Perhaps the Red Sea [3]I.e. Euphrates [4]Lit *in sandals* [a]Is 43:16 [b]Is 19:16 [c]Is 7:20; Rev 16:12

16 [a]Is 19:23 [b]Is 11:11 [c]Ex 14:26-29

12:1 [a]Ps 9:1; Is 25:1 [b]Ps 30:5; Is 40:1

2 [a]Is 32:2 [b]Is 26:3 [c]Ex 15:2; Ps 118:14

3 [a]John 4:10 [b]Is 41:18; Jer 2:13

4 [1]Or *Proclaim to them that* [a]Is 24:15 [b]Ps 105:1 [c]Ps 145:4

5 [1]Or *gloriously* [a]Ex 15:1; Ps 98:1; Is 24:14

6 [a]Is 52:9; Zeph 3:14 [b]Is 1:24; Zeph 3:15-17; Zech 2:5

13:1 [1]Or *burden of* [a]Is 14:28 [b]Is 13:19; Jer 24:1; Matt 1:11; Rev 14:8 [c]Is 1:1

2 [1]Or *windswept mountain* [a]Is 5:26; Jer 50:2 [b]Jer 51:25 [c]Is 10:32 [d]Is 45:1-3; Jer 51:58

3 [a]Joel 3:11

4 [a]Is 5:30; Joel 3:14

5 [1]Lit *end of heaven* [a]Is 5:26 [b]Is 10:5 [c]Is 24:1

6 [1]Heb *Shaddai* [a]Is 2:12; Ezek 30:3; Amos 5:18; Zeph 1:7 [b]Is 10:25; Joel 1:15

7 [a]Ezek 7:17 [b]Is 19:1; Ezek 21:7; Nah 2:10

8 [a]2 Kin 19:26; Is 21:3; Jer 46:5 [b]Is 26:17; Jer 4:31; John 16:21

9 [a]Is 13:6

10 [a]Is 5:30; Ezek 32:7; Joel 2:10; Matt 24:29; Mark 13:24; Luke 21:25; Rev 6:13 [b]Is 24:23; Ezek 32:7; Acts 2:20; Rev 6:12

11 [1]Or *tyrants, despots* [a]Is 26:21 [b]Is 3:11 [c]Is 2:11; Dan 5:22 [d]Jer 48:29 [e]Is 25:3

12 [1]Lit *more precious* [a]Is 4:1 [b]1 Kin 9:28; Job 28:16; Ps 45:9

13 [a]Is 34:4

And [b]the earth will be shaken
from its place
At the fury of the LORD of hosts
In [c]the day of His burning
anger.
14 And it will be that like a hunted
gazelle,
Or like [a]sheep with none to
gather *them,*
They will each turn to his own
people,
And each one flee to his own
land.
15 Anyone who is found will be
[a]thrust through,
And anyone who is captured will
fall by the sword.
16 Their [a]little ones also will be
dashed to pieces
Before their eyes;
Their houses will be plundered
And their wives ravished.

Babylon Will Fall to the Medes

17 ¶ Behold, I am going to [a]stir up
the Medes against them,
Who will not value silver or
[b]take pleasure in gold.
18 And *their* bows will [1]mow down
the [a]young men,
They will not even have
compassion on the fruit of
the womb,
Nor will their [b]eye pity
[2]children.
19 And [a]Babylon, the [b]beauty of
kingdoms, the glory of the
Chaldeans' pride,
Will be as when God
[c]overthrew Sodom and
Gomorrah.
20 It will [a]never be inhabited or
lived in from generation to
generation;
Nor will the [b]Arab pitch *his* tent
there,
Nor will shepherds make *their*
flocks lie down there.
21 But [a]desert creatures will lie
down there,
And their houses will be full of
[1]owls;
Ostriches also will live there,
and [2]shaggy goats will frolic
there.
22 [1]Hyenas will howl in their
fortified towers
And jackals in their luxurious
[a]palaces.
Her *fateful* time also [2]will soon
come
And her days will not be
prolonged.

13 [b]Ps 18:7; Is 2:19; 24:1,19, 20; Hag 2:6 [c]Lam 1:12
14 [a]1 Kin 22:17; Matt 9:36; Mark 6:34; 1 Pet 2:25
15 [a]Is 14:19; Jer 50:25; 51:3,4
16 [a]Ps 137:8,9; Is 13:18; 14:21; Hos 10:14; Nah 3:10
17 [a]Jer 51:11; Dan 5:28 [b]Prov 6:34,35
18 [1]Lit *dash in pieces* [2]Lit *sons* [a]2 Kin 8:12; 2 Chr 36:17 [b]Ezek 9:5,10
19 [a]Is 21:9; 48:14 [b]Dan 4:30; Rev 18:11-16,19,21 [c]Gen 19:24; Deut 29:23; Jer 49:18; Amos 4:11
20 [a]Is 14:23; 34:10-15; Jer 51:37-43 [b]2 Chr 17:11
21 [1]Or *howling creatures* [2]Or *goat demons* [a]Is 34:11-15; Zeph 2:14; Rev 18:2
22 [1]Or *howling creatures* [2]Lit *is near to come* [a]Is 25:2; 32:14; 34:13
14:1 [a]Ps 102:13; Is 49:13,15; 54:7,8 [b]Is 41:8,9; 44:1; 49:7; Zech 1:17; 2:12 [c]Is 56:3,6; Eph 2:12-19
2 [1]Lit *the captors will become their captives* [a]Is 45:14; 49:23; 54:3 [b]Is 60:10; 61:5; Dan 7:18, 27
3 [a]Ezra 9:8,9; Is 11:10; 40:2; Jer 30:10; 46:27
4 [1]Or *proverb* [2]Amended from the meaningless *medhebah* to *marhebah* [a]Hab 2:6 [b]Is 9:4; 16:4; 49:26; 51:13; 54:14
6 [1]Or *ruled* [a]Is 10:14; 47:6
7 [a]Ps 47:1-3; 98:1-9; 126:1-3
8 [a]Is 55:12; Ezek 31:16
9 [1]Or *shades* (Heb *Repha'im*) [2]Lit *male goats* [a]Is 5:14
10 [a]Ezek 32:21
11 [a]Is 5:14
12 [a]Is 34:4; Luke 10:18; Rev 8:10; 9:1

Israel's Taunt

14 When the LORD will [a]have compassion on Jacob and again
[b]choose Israel, and settle them in their
own land, then [c]strangers will join them
and attach themselves to the house of
Jacob.
2 The peoples will take them along
and bring them to their place, and the
[a]house of Israel will possess them as an
inheritance in the land of the LORD [b]as
male servants and female servants; and
[1]they will take their captors captive and
will rule over their oppressors.
3 ¶ And it will be in the day when the
LORD gives you [a]rest from your pain and
turmoil and harsh service in which you
have been enslaved,
4 that you will [a]take up this [1]taunt
against the king of Babylon, and say,
"How [b]the oppressor has ceased,
And how [2]fury has ceased!
5 "The LORD has broken the staff of
the wicked,
The scepter of rulers
6 [a]Which used to strike the
peoples in fury with
unceasing strokes,
Which [1]subdued the nations in
anger with unrestrained
persecution.
7 "The whole earth is at rest *and* is
quiet;
They [a]break forth into shouts of
joy.
8 "Even the [a]cypress trees rejoice
over you, *and* the cedars of
Lebanon, *saying,*
'Since you were laid low, no *tree*
cutter comes up against us.'
9 "[a]Sheol from beneath is excited
over you to meet you when
you come;
It arouses for you the [1]spirits of
the dead, all the [2]leaders of
the earth;
It raises all the kings of the
nations from their thrones.
10 "[a]They will all respond and say
to you,
'Even you have been made weak
as we,
You have become like us.
11 'Your [a]pomp *and* the music of
your harps
Have been brought down to
Sheol;
Maggots are spread out *as your*
bed beneath you
And worms are your covering.'
12 "How you have [a]fallen from
heaven,

O [1b]star of the morning, son of
the dawn!
You have been cut down to the
earth,
You who have weakened the
nations!
13 "But you said in your heart,
'I will [a]ascend to heaven;
I will [b]raise my throne above
the stars of God,
And I will sit on the mount of
assembly
In the recesses of the north.
14 'I will ascend above the heights
of the clouds;
[a]I will make myself like the
Most High.'
15 "Nevertheless you [a]will be thrust
down to Sheol,
To the recesses of the pit.
16 "Those who see you will gaze at
you,
They will [1]ponder over you,
saying,
'Is this the man who made the
earth tremble,
Who shook kingdoms,
17 Who made the world like a
[a]wilderness
And overthrew its cities,
Who [b]did not [1]allow his
prisoners to *go* home?'
18 "All the kings of the nations lie in
glory,
Each in his own [1]tomb.
19 "But you have been [a]cast out of
your tomb
Like [1]a rejected branch,
[2]Clothed with the slain who are
pierced with a sword,
Who go down to the stones of
the [b]pit
Like a [c]trampled corpse.
20 "You will not be united with
them in burial,
Because you have ruined your
country,
You have slain your people.
May the [a]offspring of evildoers
not be mentioned forever.
21 "Prepare for his sons a place of
slaughter
Because of the [a]iniquity of their
fathers.
They must not arise and take
possession of the earth
And fill the face of the world
with cities."
22 "I will rise up against them," declares the LORD of hosts, "and will cut off
from Babylon [a]name and survivors, [b]off-
spring and posterity," declares the LORD.
23 "I will also make it a possession for
the [a]hedgehog and swamps of water, and
I will sweep it with the broom of [b]de-
struction," declares the LORD of hosts.

Judgment on Assyria

24 The LORD of hosts has sworn saying, "Surely, [a]just as I have intended
so it has happened, and just as I have
planned so it will stand,
25 to [a]break Assyria in My land, and
I will trample him on My mountains.
Then his [b]yoke will be removed from
them and his burden removed from their
shoulder.
26 "This is the [a]plan [1]devised against
the whole earth; and this is the [b]hand
that is stretched out against all the nations.
27 "For [a]the LORD of hosts has
planned, and who can frustrate *it?* And as
for His stretched-out hand, who can turn
it back?"
28 ¶ In the [a]year that King Ahaz died
this [1b]oracle came:

Judgment on Philistia

29 "Do not rejoice, O [a]Philistia, all
of you,
Because the rod that [b]struck you
is broken;
For from the serpent's root a
[c]viper will come out,
And its fruit will be a [d]flying
serpent.
30 "[1]Those who are most [a]helpless
will eat,
And the needy will lie down in
security;
I will [2]destroy your root with
[b]famine,
And it will kill off your survivors.
31 "Wail, O [a]gate; cry, O city;
[1]Melt away, O [b]Philistia, all of
you;
For smoke comes from the
[c]north,
And [d]there is no straggler in his
ranks.
32 "How then will one answer the
[a]messengers of the nation?
That [b]the LORD has founded
Zion,
And [c]the afflicted of His people
will seek refuge in it."

Judgment on Moab

15 The [1]oracle concerning [a]Moab.
Surely in a night [b]Ar of Moab
is devastated *and* ruined;
Surely in a night Kir of Moab is
devastated *and* ruined.
2 They have gone up to the
[1]temple and *to* [a]Dibon,
even to the high places to
weep.

12 [1]Heb *Helel;* i.e. shining one [b]2 Pet 1:19; Rev 2:28; 22:16
13 [a]Ezek 28:2 [b]Dan 5:22,23; 8:10; 2 Thess 2:4
14 [a]Is 47:8; 2 Thess 2:4
15 [a]Ezek 28:8; Matt 11:23; Luke 10:15
16 [1]Lit *show themselves attentive to*
17 [1]Lit *open* [a]Joel 2:3 [b]Is 45:13
18 [1]Lit *house*
19 [1]Lit *an abhorred branch* [2]Or *As the clothing of those who are slain* [a]Is 22:16-18 [b]Jer 41:7,9 [c]Is 5:25
20 [a]Job 18:16, 19; Ps 21:10; 37:28; Is 1:4; 31:2
21 [a]Ex 20:5; Lev 26:39; Is 13:16; Matt 23:35
22 [a]Prov 10:7 [b]Job 18:19; Is 47:9
23 [a]Is 34:11; Zeph 2:14 [b]1 Kin 14:10; Is 13:6
24 [a]Job 23:13; Is 46:11; 55:8,9; Acts 4:28
25 [a]Is 10:12; 30:31; 31:8 [b]Is 9:4; 10:27; Nah 1:13
26 [1]Lit *planned* [a]Is 23:9; Zeph 3:6,8 [b]Ex 15:12
27 [a]2 Chr 20:6; Is 43:13; Dan 4:31,35
28 [1]Or *burden* [a]2 Kin 16:20; 2 Chr 28:27 [b]Is 13:1
29 [a]Is 2:6; 11:14; Jer 47:1-7; Ezek 25:15-17; Joel 3:4-8; Amos 1:6-8; Zeph 2:4-7; Zech 9:5-7 [b]2 Chr 26:6 [c]Is 11:8 [d]Is 30:6
30 [1]Lit *the firstborn of the helpless* [2]Lit *put to death* [a]Is 3:14, 15; 7:21,22; 11:4 [b]Is 8:21; 9:20; 51:19
31 [1]Or *Become demoralized* [a]Is 3:26; 24:12; 45:2 [b]Is 14:29 [c]Jer 1:14 [d]Is 34:16
32 [a]Is 37:9 [b]Ps 87:1,5; 102:16; Is 28:16; 44:28; 54:11 [c]Is 4:6; 25:4; 57:13; Zeph 3:12; Heb 11:10; James 2:5
15:1 [1]Or *burden of* [a]Is 11:14; 25:10; Jer 48:1; Ezek 25:8-11; Amos 2:1-3; Zeph 2:8-11 [b]Num 21:28
2 [1]Lit *house* [a]Jer 48:18,22

Moab wails over Nebo and
Medeba;
Everyone's head is [b]bald *and*
every beard is cut off.
3 In their streets they have girded
themselves with [a]sackcloth;
[b]On their housetops and in their
squares
Everyone is wailing, [1c]dissolved
in tears.
4 [a]Heshbon and Elealeh also cry
out,
Their voice is heard all the way
to Jahaz;
Therefore the [1]armed men of
Moab cry aloud;
His soul trembles within him.
5 My heart cries out for Moab;
His fugitives are as far as [a]Zoar
and Eglath-shelishiyah,
For they go up the [b]ascent of
Luhith weeping;
Surely on the road to Horonaim
they raise a cry of distress
[c]over *their* ruin.
6 For the [a]waters of Nimrim are
[1]desolate.
Surely the grass is withered, the
tender grass [2]died out,
There is [b]no green thing.
7 Therefore the [a]abundance *which*
they have acquired and
stored up
They carry off over the brook of
[1]Arabim.
8 For the cry of distress has gone
around the territory of
Moab,
Its wail *goes* as far as Eglaim and
its wailing even to
Beer-elim.
9 For the waters of Dimon are full
of [1]blood;
Surely I will bring added *woes*
upon Dimon,
A [a]lion upon the fugitives of
Moab and upon the remnant
of the land.

Prophecy of Moab's Devastation

16 [a]Send the *tribute* lamb to the
ruler of the land,
From [1b]Sela by way of the
wilderness to the [c]mountain
of the daughter of Zion.
2 Then, like [1a]fleeing birds *or*
scattered [2]nestlings,
The daughters of [b]Moab will be
at the fords of the [c]Arnon.
3 "[1]Give *us* advice, make a
decision;
[2]Cast your [a]shadow like night
[3]at high noon;
[b]Hide the outcasts, do not
betray the fugitive.
4 "Let the [1]outcasts of Moab stay
with you;
Be a hiding place to them from
the destroyer."
For the extortioner has come to
an end, destruction has
ceased,
[a]Oppressors have completely
disappeared from the land.
5 A [a]throne will even be
established in
lovingkindness,
And a judge will sit on it in
faithfulness in the tent of
[b]David;
Moreover, he will seek justice
And be prompt in righteousness.

6 ¶ [a]We have heard of the pride
of Moab, an excessive pride;
Even of his arrogance, pride, and
fury;
[b]His idle boasts are [1]false.
7 Therefore Moab will wail;
everyone of Moab will wail.
You will moan for the [a]raisin
cakes of [b]Kir-hareseth
As those who are utterly
stricken.
8 For the fields of [a]Heshbon have
[1]withered, the vines of
[b]Sibmah *as well;*
The lords of the nations have
trampled down its choice
clusters
Which reached as far as Jazer
and wandered to the
deserts;
[c]Its tendrils spread themselves
out *and* passed over the sea.
9 Therefore I will [a]weep bitterly
for Jazer, for the vine of
Sibmah;
I will drench you with my tears,
O [b]Heshbon and Elealeh;
For the shouting over your
[c]summer fruits and your
harvest has fallen away.
10 [a]Gladness and joy are taken
away from the fruitful field;
In the [b]vineyards also there will
be no cries of joy or jubilant
shouting,
No [c]treader treads out wine in
the presses,
For I have made the shouting to
cease.
11 Therefore my [1a]heart intones
like a harp for Moab
And my [2]inward feelings for
Kir-hareseth.

2 [b]Lev 21:5; Jer 48:37

3 [1]Lit *going down in weeping* [a]Jon 3:6-8 [b]Jer 48:38 [c]Is 22:4

4 [1]Another reading is *the loins of* [a]Num 21:28; 32:3; Jer 48:34

5 [a]Jer 48:34 [b]Jer 48:5 [c]Is 59:7; Jer 4:20

6 [1]Lit *desolations* [2]Lit *come to an end* [a]Is 19:5-7; Jer 48:34 [b]Joel 1:10-12; 2:3

7 [1]Or *the poplars* [a]Is 30:6; Jer 48:36

9 [1]Heb *dam* (a wordplay) [a]2 Kin 17:25; Jer 50:17

16:1 [1]I.e. Petra in Edom [a]2 Kin 3:4; Ezra 7:17 [b]2 Kin 14:7; Is 42:11 [c]Is 10:32

2 [1]Or *fluttering* [2]Lit *nest* [a]Prov 27:8 [b]Jer 48:20, 46 [c]Num 21:13, 14

3 [1]Lit *Bring* [2]Lit *Set* [3]Lit *in the midst of the noon* [a]Is 25:4; 32:2 [b]1 Kin 18:4

4 [1]So the versions; M.T. *My outcasts, as for Moab* [a]Is 9:4; 14:4; 49:26; 51:13; 54:14

5 [a]Is 9:6,7; 32:1; 55:4; Dan 7:14; Mic 4:7; Luke 1:33 [b]Is 9:7

6 [1]Lit *not so* [a]Jer 48:29; Amos 2:1; Obad 3,4; Zeph 2:8,10 [b]Jer 48:30

7 [a]1 Chr 16:3 [b]2 Kin 3:25; Jer 48:31

8 [1]Or *languished* [a]Is 15:4 [b]Num 32:38 [c]Jer 48:32

9 [a]Jer 48:32 [b]Is 15:4 [c]Jer 40:10, 12; 48:32

10 [a]Is 24:8; Jer 48:33 [b]Judg 9:27; Is 24:7; Amos 5:11,17 [c]Job 24:11; Amos 9:13

11 [1]Lit *entrails murmur* [2]Lit *inward part* [a]Is 15:5; 63:15; Jer 48:36; Hos 11:8; Phil 2:1

12 So it will come about when
Moab [a]presents himself,
When he [b]wearies himself upon
his [c]high place
And comes to his sanctuary to
pray,
That he will not prevail.
13 ¶ This is the word which the LORD
spoke earlier concerning Moab.
14 But now the LORD speaks, saying,
"Within three years, as [1a]a hired man
would count them, the glory of [b]Moab
will be degraded along with all *his* great
population, and *his* remnant will be very
small *and* [2]impotent."

Prophecy about Damascus

17 The [1a]oracle concerning [b]Damascus.
"Behold, Damascus is about to be
[c]removed from being a city
And will become a [d]fallen ruin.
2 "The cities [1]of [a]Aroer are
forsaken;
They will be for [b]flocks [2]to lie
down in,
And there will be [c]no one to
frighten *them*.
3 "The [1a]fortified city will
disappear from Ephraim,
And [2]sovereignty from
Damascus
And the remnant of Aram;
They will be like the [b]glory of
the sons of Israel,"
Declares the LORD of hosts.

4 ¶ Now in that day the [a]glory of
Jacob will [1]fade,
And [b]the fatness of his flesh will
become lean.
5 It will be [a]even like the [1]reaper
gathering the standing grain,
As his arm harvests the ears,
Or it will be like one gleaning
ears of grain
In the [b]valley of Rephaim.
6 Yet [a]gleanings will be left in it
like the [1]shaking of an olive
tree,
Two *or* three olives on the
topmost bough,
Four *or* five on the branches of a
fruitful tree,
Declares the LORD, the God of
Israel.
7 In that day man will [a]have
regard for his Maker
And his eyes will look to the
Holy One of Israel.
8 He will not have regard for the
[a]altars, the work of his
hands,
Nor will he look to that which
his [b]fingers have made,
Even the [1c]Asherim and
[2]incense stands.
9 In that day [1]their strong cities
will be like [2]forsaken places
in the forest,
Or like [3]branches which they
abandoned before the sons
of Israel;
And [4]the land will be a
desolation.
10 For [a]you have forgotten the
[b]God of your salvation
And have not remembered the
[c]rock of your refuge.
Therefore you plant delightful
plants
And set them with vine slips of a
strange *god*.
11 In the day that you plant *it* you
carefully fence *it* in,
And in the [a]morning you bring
your seed to blossom;
But the harvest will [b]*be* a heap
In a day of sickliness and
incurable pain.

12 ¶ Alas, the uproar of many
peoples
[a]Who roar like the roaring of
the seas,
And the rumbling of nations
Who rush on like the [b]rumbling
of mighty waters!
13 The [a]nations rumble on like the
rumbling of many waters,
But He will [b]rebuke them and
they will flee far away,
And be chased [c]like chaff in the
mountains before the wind,
Or like whirling dust before a
gale.
14 At evening time, behold, *there is*
terror!
Before morning [a]they are no
more.
[1]Such *will be* the portion of
those who plunder us
And the lot of those who
pillage us.

Message to Ethiopia

18 Alas, oh land of whirring wings
Which lies beyond the rivers of
[1a]Cush,
2 Which sends envoys by the sea,
Even in [a]papyrus vessels on the
surface of the waters.
Go, swift messengers, to a nation
[1b]tall and smooth,
To a people [c]feared [2]far and
wide,
A powerful and oppressive nation

12 [a]Num 22:39-41; Jer 48:35 [b]1 Kin 18:29 [c]Is 15:2

14 [1]Lit *the years of a hireling* [2]Lit *not mighty* [a]Job 7:1; Is 21:16 [b]Is 25:10; Jer 48:42

17:1 [1]Or *burden of* [a]Is 13:1 [b]Gen 14:15; 2 Kin 16:9; Jer 49:23; Amos 1:3-5; Zech 9:1; Acts 9:2 [c]Is 7:16 [d]Is 25:2; Jer 49:2; Mic 1:6

2 [1]Gr reads *forever and ever* [2]Lit *and they will lie down* [a]Num 32:34 [b]Is 7:21; Ezek 25:5; Zeph 2:6 [c]Mic 4:4

3 [1]Or *fortification* [2]Or *royal power, kingdom* [a]Is 7:8 [b]Is 17:4; Hos 9:11

4 [1]Lit *become thin* [a]Is 10:3 [b]Is 10:16

5 [1]Lit *gathering of the harvest, the standing grain* [a]Is 17:11; Jer 51:33; Joel 3:13; Matt 13:30 [b]2 Sam 5:18

6 [1]Lit *striking* [a]Deut 4:27; Is 24:13; Obad 5

7 [a]Is 10:20; Hos 3:5; Mic 7:7

8 [1]I.e. wooden symbols of a female deity [2]Or *sun pillars* [a]2 Chr 34:7; Is 27:9 [b]Is 2:8 [c]Ex 34:13; Deut 7:5; Mic 5:14

9 [1]I.e. man's [2]Gr reads *the deserted places of the Amorites and the Hivites which they abandoned* [3]Or *the treetop* [4]Lit *it*

10 [a]Is 51:13 [b]Ps 68:19; Is 12:2 [c]Deut 32:4; Is 26:4

11 [a]Ps 90:6 [b]Job 4:8; Hos 8:7

12 [a]Is 5:30; Jer 6:23; Ezek 43:2; Luke 21:25 [b]Ps 18:4

13 [a]Is 33:3 [b]Ps 9:5; Is 41:11 [c]Job 21:18; Ps 1:4; Is 29:5

14 [1]Lit *This* [a]2 Kin 19:35; Is 41:12

18:1 [1]Or *Ethiopia* [a]2 Kin 19:9; Is 20:3-5; Ezek 30:4; Zeph 2:12

2 [1]Lit *drawn out* [2]Lit *from it and beyond* [a]Ex 2:3 [b]Is 18:7 [c]Gen 10:8; 2 Chr 12:2-4

Whose land the rivers divide.
3 [a]All you inhabitants of the world
and dwellers on earth,
As soon as a standard is raised
on the mountains, [b]you will
see *it,*
And as soon as the trumpet is
blown, you will hear *it.*
4 For thus the LORD has told me,
"I will look [1]from My [a]dwelling
place quietly
Like dazzling heat in the
[2b]sunshine,
Like a cloud of [c]dew in the heat
of harvest."
5 For [a]before the harvest, as soon
as the bud [1]blossoms
And the flower becomes a
ripening grape,
Then He will cut off the sprigs
with pruning knives
And remove *and* cut away the
spreading branches.
6 They will be left together for
mountain birds [a]of prey,
And for the beasts of the earth;
And the birds of prey will spend
the summer *feeding* on
them,
And all the beasts of the earth
will spend harvest time on
them.
7 At that time a gift of homage will
be brought to the LORD of
hosts
[1]From a [a]people [2]tall and
smooth,
Even from a people feared [3]far
and wide,
A powerful and oppressive
nation,
Whose land the rivers divide—
To the [b]place of the name of the
LORD of hosts, *even* Mount
Zion.

Message to Egypt

19 The [1a]oracle concerning [b]Egypt.
Behold, the LORD is [c]riding on a
swift cloud and is about to
come to Egypt;
The [d]idols of Egypt will tremble
at His presence,
And the [e]heart of the Egyptians
will melt within them.
2 "So I will incite Egyptians against
Egyptians;
And they will [a]each fight against
his brother and each against
his neighbor,
City against city *and* kingdom
against kingdom.
3 "Then the spirit of the Egyptians
will be demoralized within
them;
And I will confound their
strategy,
So that [a]they will resort to idols
and ghosts of the dead
And to [1]mediums and spiritists.
4 "Moreover, I will deliver the
Egyptians into the hand of a
[a]cruel master,
And a [1]mighty king will rule
over them," declares the
Lord [2]GOD of hosts.
5 ¶ [a]The waters from the sea will
dry up,
And the river will be parched
and dry.
6 The [1a]canals will emit a stench,
The [2b]streams of Egypt will thin
out and dry up;
[c]The reeds and rushes will rot
away.
7 The bulrushes by the [a]Nile, by
the [1]edge of the Nile
And all the sown fields by the
Nile
Will become dry, be driven
away, and be no more.
8 And the [a]fishermen will lament,
And all those who cast a [1]line
into the Nile will mourn,
And those who spread nets on
the waters will [2]pine away.
9 Moreover, the manufacturers of
linen made from combed
flax
And the weavers of white [a]cloth
will be [1]utterly dejected.
10 And [1]the [a]pillars *of Egypt* will
be crushed;
All the hired laborers will be
grieved in soul.
11 ¶ The princes of [1a]Zoan are
mere fools;
The advice of Pharaoh's wisest
advisers has become
[2]stupid.
How can you *men* say to
Pharaoh,
"I am a son of the [b]wise, a son of
ancient kings"?
12 Well then, where are your
wise men?
Please let them tell you,
And let them [1]understand what
the LORD of hosts
Has [a]purposed against Egypt.
13 The princes of [1]Zoan have acted
foolishly,
The princes of [a]Memphis are
deluded;

3 [a]Ps 49:1; Mic 1:2 [b]Is 26:11

4 [1]Lit *in* [2]Lit *light* [a]Is 26:21; Hos 5:15 [b]2 Sam 23:4 [c]Prov 19:12; Is 26:19; Hos 14:5

5 [1]Lit *is finished* [a]Is 17:10,11; Ezek 17:6-10

6 [a]Is 46:11; 56:9; Jer 7:33; Ezek 32:4-6; 39:17-20

7 [1]So with some ancient versions and DSS; M.T. implies *Consisting of a people* [2]Lit *drawn out* [3]Lit *from it and beyond* [a]Ps 68:31; Is 45:14; Zeph 3:10; Acts 8:27-38 [b]Zech 14:16,17

19:1 [1]Or *burden of* [a]Is 13:1 [b]Joel 3:19 [c]Ps 18:9, 10; 104:3; Matt 26:64; Rev 1:7 [d]Ex 12:12; Jer 43:12; 44:8 [e]Josh 2:11; Is 13:7

2 [a]Judg 7:22; 1 Sam 14:20; 2 Chr 20:23; Matt 10:21,36

3 [1]Or *ghosts and spirits* [a]1 Chr 10:13; Is 8:19; Dan 2:2

4 [1]Or *fierce* [2]Heb *YHWH,* usually rendered *LORD* [a]Is 20:4; Jer 46:26; Ezek 29:19

5 [a]Is 50:2; Jer 51:36; Ezek 30:12

6 [1]Lit *rivers* [2]Or *Nile branches;* i.e. the delta [a]Ex 7:18 [b]Is 37:25 [c]Ex 2:3; Job 8:11; Is 15:6

7 [1]Or *mouth* [a]Is 23:3,10

8 [1]Lit *hook* [2]Or *languish* [a]Ezek 47:10; Hab 1:15

9 [1]Lit *ashamed* [a]Prov 7:16; Ezek 27:7

10 [1]Lit *her pillars* or, *her weavers* [a]Ps 11:3

11 [1]Or *Tanis* [2]Or *brutish* [a]Num 13:22; Ps 78:12,43; Is 30:4 [b]Gen 41:38,39; 1 Kin 4:30; Acts 7:22

12 [1]Or *know* [a]Is 14:24; Rom 9:17

13 [1]Or *Tanis* [a]Jer 2:16; 46:14, 19; Ezek 30:13

Those who are the [b]cornerstone
of her tribes
Have [2]led Egypt astray.
14 The LORD has mixed within her
a spirit of [a]distortion;
[b]They have led Egypt astray in
all [1]that it does,
As a [c]drunken man [2]staggers in
his vomit.
15 There will be no work for Egypt
[a]Which *its* head or tail, *its* palm
branch or bulrush, may do.
16 ¶ In that day the Egyptians will become like women, and they will tremble
and be in [a]dread because of the [b]waving
of the hand of the LORD of hosts, which
He is going to wave over them.
17 The land of Judah will become a
[1]terror to Egypt; everyone [2]to whom it
is mentioned will be in dread of it, because of the [a]purpose of the LORD of
hosts which He is purposing against
them.
18 ¶ In that day five cities in the land
of Egypt will be speaking the language of
Canaan and [a]swearing *allegiance* to the
LORD of hosts; one will be called the City
of [1]Destruction.
19 ¶ In that day there will be an [a]altar
to the LORD in the midst of the land of
Egypt, and a [b]pillar to the LORD near its
border.
20 It will become a sign and a witness
to the LORD of hosts in the land of Egypt;
for they will cry to the LORD because of
oppressors, and He will send them a
[a]Savior and a [1b]Champion, and He will
deliver them.
21 Thus the LORD will make Himself
known to Egypt, and the Egyptians will
know the LORD in that day. They will
even worship with [a]sacrifice and offering, and will make a vow to the LORD and
perform it.
22 The LORD will strike Egypt, striking
but [a]healing; so they will [b]return to the
LORD, and He will respond to them and
will heal them.
23 ¶ In that day there will be a [a]high-
way from Egypt to Assyria, and the Assyrians will come into Egypt and the Egyptians into Assyria, and the Egyptians will
[b]worship with the Assyrians.
24 ¶ In that day Israel will be the third
party with Egypt and Assyria, a blessing
in the midst of the earth,
25 whom the LORD of hosts has
blessed, saying, "Blessed is [a]Egypt My
people, and Assyria [b]the work of My
hands, and Israel My inheritance."

Prophecy about Egypt and Ethiopia

20 In the year that the [1a]command-
er came to [b]Ashdod, when Sar-
gon the king of Assyria sent him and he
fought against Ashdod and captured it,
2 at that time the LORD spoke through
[a]Isaiah the son of Amoz, saying, "Go and
loosen the [b]sackcloth from your hips and
take your [c]shoes off your feet." And he
did so, going [d]naked and barefoot.
3 And the LORD said, "Even as My
servant Isaiah has gone naked and barefoot three years as a [1a]sign and token
against Egypt and [2b]Cush,
4 so the [a]king of Assyria will lead
away the captives of Egypt and the exiles
of Cush, [b]young and old, naked and barefoot with buttocks uncovered, to the
[1]shame of Egypt.
5 "Then they will be [a]dismayed and
ashamed because of Cush their hope and
Egypt their [b]boast.
6 "So the inhabitants of this coastland
will say in that day, 'Behold, such is our
hope, where we fled [a]for help to be delivered from the king of Assyria; and we,
[b]how shall we escape?' "

God Commands That Babylon Be Taken

21 The [1a]oracle concerning the
[2b]wilderness of the sea.
As [c]windstorms in the [3]Negev
sweep on,
It comes from the wilderness,
from a terrifying land.
2 A [a]harsh vision has been shown
to me;
The [b]treacherous one *still* deals
treacherously, and the
destroyer *still* destroys.
Go up, [c]Elam, lay siege, Media;
I have made an end of all [1]the
groaning she has caused.
3 For this reason my [a]loins are full
of anguish;
Pains have seized me like the
pains of a [b]woman in labor.
I am so bewildered I cannot
hear, so terrified I cannot
see.
4 My [1]mind reels, [2]horror
overwhelms me;
The twilight I longed for has
been [a]turned for me into
trembling.
5 They [a]set the table, they
[1]spread out the cloth, they
eat, they drink;
"Rise up, captains, oil the
shields,"
6 For thus the Lord says to me,
"Go, station the lookout, let him
[a]report what he sees.
7 "When he sees [a]riders, horsemen
in pairs,

13 [2]Or *have caused Egypt to stagger* [b]Zech 10:4
14 [1]Lit *its work* [2]Or *goes astray* [a]Prov 12:8; Matt 17:17 [b]Is 3:12 [c]Is 28:7
15 [a]Is 9:14
16 [a]2 Cor 5:11; Heb 10:31 [b]Is 11:15
17 [1]Or *cause of shame* [2]Lit *who mentions it will be in dread to it* [a]Is 14:24; Dan 4:35
18 [1]Some ancient mss and versions read *the Sun* [a]Is 45:23
19 [a]Is 56:7 [b]Gen 28:18; Ex 24:4; Josh 22:10
20 [1]Lit *Mighty One* [a]Is 43:3 [b]Is 49:25
21 [a]Is 56:7; Zech 14:16-18
22 [a]Deut 32:39; Is 30:26; Heb 12:11 [b]Is 27:13; Hos 14:1
23 [a]Is 11:16 [b]Is 27:13
25 [a]Is 45:14 [b]Ps 100:3; Is 29:23; Eph 2:10
20:1 [1]Heb *Tartan* [a]2 Kin 18:17 [b]1 Sam 5:1
2 [a]Is 1:1 [b]Zech 13:4; Matt 3:4 [c]Ezek 24:17 [d]1 Sam 19:24; Mic 1:8
3 [1]Or *wonder* [2]Or *Ethiopia*, so in vv 4, 5 [a]Is 8:18 [b]Is 37:9
4 [1]Lit *nakedness* [a]Is 19:4 [b]Is 47:2
5 [a]2 Kin 18:21; Is 30:3-5; Ezek 29:6 [b]Jer 9:23; 1 Cor 3:21
6 [a]Is 10:3; Jer 30:1 [b]Matt 23:33; 1 Thess 5:3; Heb 2:3
21:1 [1]Or *burden of* [2]Or *sandy wastes, sea country* [3]I.e. South country [a]Is 13:1 [b]Is 13:20-22; Jer 51:42 [c]Zech 9:14
2 [1]Lit *her groaning* [a]Ps 60:3 [b]Is 24:16 [c]Is 22:6; Jer 49:34
3 [a]Is 13:8 [b]Ps 48:6; Is 13:8; 1 Thess 5:3
4 [1]Lit *heart has wandered* [2]Lit *shuddering* [a]Deut 28:67
5 [1]Or *spread out the rugs* or possibly *they arranged the seating* [a]Jer 51:39; Dan 5:1-4
6 [a]2 Kin 9:17-20
7 [a]Is 21:9

A train of donkeys, a train of
camels,
Let him pay close attention, very
close attention."
8 Then [1]the lookout called,
"[a]O Lord, I stand continually by
day on the watchtower,
And I am stationed every night
at my guard post.
9 "Now behold, here comes a troop
of riders, horsemen in
pairs."
And one said, "[a]Fallen, fallen is
Babylon;
And all the [b]images of her gods
[1]are shattered on the
ground."
10 O my [a]threshed *people,* and my
[1]afflicted of the threshing
floor!
What I have heard from the
LORD of hosts,
The God of Israel, I make known
to you.

Oracles about Edom and Arabia

11 ¶ The [1]oracle concerning [2a]Edom.
One keeps calling to me from
[b]Seir,
"Watchman, [3]how far gone is the
night?
Watchman, [3]how far gone is the
night?"
12 The watchman says,
"Morning comes but also night.
If you would inquire, inquire;
Come back again."

13 ¶ The [1]oracle about [a]Arabia.
In the thickets of Arabia you
[2]must spend the night,
O caravans of [b]Dedanites.
14 Bring water [1]for the thirsty,
O inhabitants of the land of
[a]Tema,
Meet the fugitive with bread.
15 For they have [a]fled from the
swords,
From the drawn sword, and from
the bent bow
And from the press of battle.
16 ¶ For thus the Lord said to me, "In
a [a]year, as [1]a hired man would count it,
all the splendor of [b]Kedar will terminate;
17 and the [a]remainder of the number
of bowmen, the mighty men of the sons
of Kedar, will be few; for the LORD God of
Israel [b]has spoken."

The Valley of Vision

22 The [1]oracle concerning the [a]valley of vision.
What is the matter with you
now, that you have all gone
up to the [b]housetops?
2 You who were full of noise,
You boisterous town, you
[a]exultant city;
Your slain were [b]not slain with
the sword,
Nor [1]did they die in battle.
3 [a]All your rulers have fled
together,
And have been captured
[1]without the bow;
All of you who were found were
taken captive together,
[2]Though they had fled far away.
4 Therefore I say, "Turn your eyes
away from me,
Let me [a]weep bitterly,
Do not [1]try to comfort me
concerning the destruction
of the daughter of my
people."
5 [a]For the Lord [1]GOD of hosts has
a [b]day of panic,
[c]subjugation and confusion
[d]In the valley of vision,
A breaking down of walls
And a crying [2]to the mountain.
6 [a]Elam took up the quiver
With the chariots, [1]infantry *and*
horsemen;
And [b]Kir uncovered the shield.
7 Then your choicest valleys were
full of chariots,
And the horsemen took up fixed
positions at the gate.
8 And He removed the [1]defense of
Judah.
In that day you [2]depended on
the weapons of the [a]house
of the forest,
9 And you saw that the breaches
In the *wall* of the city of David
were many;
And you [a]collected the waters of
the lower pool.
10 Then you counted the houses of
Jerusalem
And tore down houses to fortify
the wall.
11 And you made a reservoir
[a]between the two walls
For the waters of the [b]old pool.
But you did not [1]depend on Him
who made it,
Nor did you [2]take into
consideration Him who
planned it long ago.

12 ¶ Therefore in that day the Lord
[1]GOD of hosts called *you* to
[a]weeping, to wailing,

8 [1]So DSS; M.T. *he called* like a *lion* [a]Hab 2:1

9 [1]Lit *he has shattered to the earth* [a]Is 13:19; 47:5,9; 48:14; Jer 51:8; Rev 14:8; 18:2 [b]Is 46:1; Jer 50:2; 51:44

10 [1]Lit *son* [a]Jer 51:33; Mic 4:13

11 [1]Or *burden* [2]So the Gr; Heb *Dumah, silence* [3]Lit *what* is the time *of the night?* [a]Gen 25:14 [b]Gen 32:3

13 [1]Or *burden* [2]Or *will spend* [a]Jer 25:23,24; 49:28 [b]Gen 10:7; Ezek 27:15

14 [1]Lit *to meet* [a]Gen 25:15; Job 6:19

15 [a]Is 13:14,15; 17:13

16 [1]Lit *the years of a hireling* [a]Is 16:14 [b]Ps 120:5; Song 1:5; Is 42:11; 60:7; Ezek 27:21

17 [a]Is 10:19 [b]Num 23:19; Zech 1:6

22:1 [1]Or *burden of* [a]Ps 125:2; Jer 21:13; Joel 3:12, 14 [b]Is 15:3

2 [1]Lit *dead in battle* [a]Is 23:7; 32:13 [b]Jer 14:18; Lam 2:20

3 [1]Lit *from a bow* [2]So with ancient versions; Heb *They fled far away* [a]Is 21:15

4 [1]Lit *insist* [a]Is 15:3; Jer 9:1; Luke 19:41

5 [1]Heb *YHWH,* usually rendered LORD [2]Or *against* [a]Lam 1:5; 2:2 [b]Is 37:3 [c]Is 10:6; 63:3 [d]Is 22:1

6 [1]Lit *man* [a]Is 21:2; Jer 49:35 [b]2 Kin 16:9; Amos 1:5; 9:7

8 [1]Lit *screen, covering* [2]Or *looked to, considered* [a]1 Kin 7:2; 10:17

9 [a]2 Kin 20:20; Neh 3:16

11 [1]Or *look to, consider* [2]Lit *see...Him* [a]2 Kin 25:4; Jer 39:4 [b]2 Kin 20:20; 2 Chr 32:3,4

12 [1]Heb *YHWH,* usually rendered LORD [a]Is 32:11; Joel 1:13; 2:17

To [b]shaving the head and to
wearing sackcloth.
13 Instead, there is [a]gaiety and
gladness,
Killing of cattle and slaughtering
of sheep,
Eating of meat and drinking of
wine:
"[b]Let us eat and drink, for
tomorrow we may die."
14 But the LORD of hosts revealed
Himself [1]to me,
"Surely this [a]iniquity [b]shall not
be [2]forgiven you
[c]Until you die," says the Lord
[3]GOD of hosts.

15 ¶ Thus says the Lord [1]GOD of
hosts,
"Come, go to this steward,
To [a]Shebna, who is in charge of
the *royal* household,
16 'What right do you have here,
And whom do you have here,
That you have [a]hewn a tomb for
yourself here,
You who hew a tomb on the
height,
You who carve a resting place for
[1]yourself in the rock?
17 'Behold, the LORD is about to hurl
you headlong, O man.
And He is about to grasp you
firmly
18 *And* roll you tightly like a ball,
To be [a]*cast* into a vast country;
There you will die
And there your splendid chariots
will be,
You shame of your master's
house.'
19 "I will [a]depose you from your
office,
And [1]I will pull you down from
your station.
20 "Then it will come about in that
day,
That I will summon My servant
[a]Eliakim the son of Hilkiah,
21 And I will clothe him with your
tunic
And tie your sash securely about
him.
I will entrust him with your
[1]authority,
And he will become a [a]father to
the inhabitants of Jerusalem
and to the house of Judah.
22 "Then I will set [a]the key of the
[b]house of David on his
shoulder,
When he opens no one will shut,
When he shuts no one will
[c]open.

23 "I will drive him *like* a [a]peg in a
firm place,
And he will become a [b]throne
of glory to his father's
house.
24 "So they will hang on him all the
glory of his father's house, offspring and
[1]issue, all the least of vessels, from bowls
to all the jars.
25 "In that day," declares the LORD of
hosts, "the [a]peg driven in a firm place
will give way; it will even [b]break off and
fall, and the load hanging on it will be cut
off, for the [c]LORD has spoken."

The Fall of Tyre

23 The [1]oracle concerning [a]Tyre.
Wail, O [b]ships of [c]Tarshish,
For *Tyre* is destroyed, without
house *or* [2d]harbor;
It is reported to them from the
land of [3e]Cyprus.
2 [a]Be silent, you inhabitants of the
coastland,
You merchants of Sidon;
[1]Your messengers crossed
the sea
3 And *were* on many waters.
[a]The grain of the [1b]Nile, the
harvest of the River was her
revenue;
And she was the [c]market of
nations.
4 Be ashamed, O [a]Sidon;
For the sea speaks, the
stronghold of the sea, saying,
"I have neither travailed nor
given birth,
I have neither brought up young
men *nor* reared virgins."
5 When the report *reaches* Egypt,
They will be in [a]anguish at the
report of Tyre.
6 Pass over to [a]Tarshish;
Wail, O inhabitants of the
coastland.
7 Is this your [a]jubilant *city*,
Whose origin is from antiquity,
Whose feet used to carry her to
[1]colonize distant places?
8 ¶ Who has planned this against
Tyre, [a]the bestower of
crowns,
Whose merchants were princes,
whose traders were the
honored of the earth?
9 [a]The LORD of hosts has planned
it, to [b]defile the pride of all
beauty,
To despise all the [c]honored of
the earth.

12 [b]Mic 1:16
13 [a]Is 5:11,22; 28:7,8; Luke 17:26-29 [b]Is 56:12; 1 Cor 15:32
14 [1]Lit *in my ears* [2]Lit *atoned for* [3]Heb *YHWH,* usually rendered LORD [a]Is 13:11; 26:21; 30:13; 65:7 [b]1 Sam 3:14; Ezek 24:13 [c]Is 65:20
15 [1]Heb *YHWH,* usually rendered LORD [a]2 Kin 18:18,26,37; Is 36:3,11,22; 37:2
16 [1]Lit *himself* [a]2 Sam 18:18; 2 Chr 16:14; Matt 27:60
18 [a]Job 18:18; Is 17:13
19 [1]So with many ancient versions; Heb *He* [a]Job 40:11,12; Ezek 17:24
20 [a]2 Kin 18:18; Is 36:3, 22; 37:2
21 [1]Lit *rule* [a]Gen 45:8; Job 29:16
22 [a]Rev 3:7 [b]Is 7:2,13 [c]Job 12:14
23 [a]Ezra 9:8; Zech 10:4 [b]1 Sam 2:8; Job 36:7
24 [1]Or perhaps, *leaf*
25 [a]Is 22:23 [b]Esth 9:24,25 [c]Is 46:11; Mic 4:4
23:1 [1]Or *burden of* [2]Lit *entering* [3]Heb *Kittim* [a]Josh 19:29; 1 Kin 5:1; Jer 25:22; 47:4; Ezek 26:1-27:36; Joel 3:4-8; Amos 1:9; Zech 9:2-4 [b]Is 2:16 [c]Gen 10:4; 1 Kin 10:22 [d]Is 24:10 [e]Gen 10:4; Is 23:12; Ezek 27:6
2 [1]So DSS; M.T. *Who passed over the sea, they replenished you* [a]Is 47:5
3 [1]Heb *Shihor* [a]Is 19:7-9 [b]Josh 13:3; 1 Chr 13:5; Jer 2:18 [c]Ezek 27:3-23
4 [a]Gen 10:15, 19; Josh 11:8; Judg 10:6; Jer 25:22; 27:3; 47:4; Ezek 28:21,22
5 [a]Ex 15:14-16; Josh 2:9-11
6 [a]Is 23:1
7 [1]Lit *sojourn afar off* [a]Is 22:2; 32:13
8 [a]Ezek 28:2
9 [a]Is 2:11; 13:11 [b]Job 40:11,12; Dan 4:37 [c]Is 5:13; 9:15

10 [1]Overflow your land like the
Nile, O daughter of
Tarshish,
There is no more [2]restraint.
11 He has [a]stretched His hand out
[b]over the sea,
He has [c]made the kingdoms
tremble;
The LORD has given a command
concerning Canaan to
[d]demolish its strongholds.

12 ¶ He has said, "[a]You shall exult
no more, O crushed virgin
daughter of Sidon.
Arise, pass over to [1b]Cyprus;
even there you will find no
rest."
13 ¶ Behold, the land of the Chaldeans—this is the people *which* was not;
[a]Assyria appointed it for [b]desert creatures—they erected their siege towers,
they stripped its palaces, [c]they made it a
ruin.
14 Wail, O [a]ships of Tarshish,
For your stronghold is destroyed.
15 Now in that day Tyre will be forgotten for [a]seventy years like the days of
one king. At the end of seventy years it
will happen to Tyre as *in* the song of the
harlot:
16 Take *your* harp, walk about the
city,
O forgotten harlot;
Pluck the strings skillfully, sing
many songs,
That you may be remembered.
17 It will come about at [a]the end of
seventy years that the LORD will visit
Tyre. Then she will go back to her harlot's wages and will [b]play the harlot with
all the kingdoms [1]on the face of the
earth.
18 Her [a]gain and her harlot's wages
will be [b]set apart to the LORD; it will not
be stored up or hoarded, but her gain will
become sufficient food and choice attire
for those who dwell in the presence of
the LORD.

Judgment on the Earth

24 Behold, the LORD [a]lays the earth
waste, devastates it, distorts its
surface and scatters its inhabitants.
2 And the people will be like the
priest, the servant like his master, the
maid like her mistress, the buyer like the
seller, the lender like the borrower,
the [a]creditor like the debtor.
3 The earth will be completely laid
waste and completely despoiled, for the
LORD has spoken this word.
4 The [a]earth mourns *and* withers,
the world fades *and* withers, the [b]exalt-
ed of the people of the earth fade away.
5 The earth is also [a]polluted [1]by its
inhabitants, for they transgressed laws,
violated statutes, [b]broke the everlasting
covenant.
6 Therefore, a [a]curse devours the
earth, and those who live in it are held
guilty. Therefore, the [b]inhabitants of the
earth are burned, and few men are left.
7 ¶ The [a]new wine mourns,
The vine decays,
All the merry-hearted sigh.
8 The [a]gaiety of tambourines
ceases,
The noise of revelers stops,
The gaiety of the harp ceases.
9 They do not drink wine with
song;
[a]Strong drink is [b]bitter to those
who drink it.
10 The [a]city of chaos is broken
down;
[b]Every house is shut up so that
none may enter.
11 There is an [a]outcry in the
streets concerning the wine;
[b]All joy [1]turns to gloom.
The gaiety of the earth is
banished.
12 Desolation is left in the city
And the [a]gate is battered to
ruins.
13 For [a]thus it will be in the midst
of the earth among the
peoples,
As the [1]shaking of an olive tree,
As the gleanings when the grape
harvest is over.
14 [a]They raise their voices, they
shout for joy;
They cry out from the [1]west
concerning the majesty of
the LORD.
15 Therefore [a]glorify the LORD in
the [1]east,
The [b]name of the LORD, the God
of Israel,
In the [2c]coastlands of the sea.
16 From the [a]ends of the earth we
hear songs, "[b]Glory to the
Righteous One,"
But I say, "[1c]Woe to me! [1]Woe
to me! Alas for me!
The [d]treacherous deal
treacherously,
And the treacherous deal very
treacherously."
17 [a]Terror and pit and snare
[1]Confront you, O inhabitant of
the earth.
18 Then it will be that he who flees
the [1]report of disaster will
fall into the pit,

10 [1]Lit *Pass over* [2]Perhaps *girdle* or *shipyard*
11 [a]Ex 14:21; Is 14:26 [b]Is 19:5; 50:2 [c]Is 13:13 [d]Is 25:2; Zech 9:3,4
12 [1]Heb *Kittim* [a]Ezek 26:13,14; Rev 18:22 [b]Is 23:1
13 [a]Is 10:5 [b]Is 13:21; 18:6 [c]Is 10:7
14 [a]Is 2:16; Ezek 27:25,26
15 [a]Jer 25:11,22
17 [1]Lit *of the earth on the face of the land* [a]Is 23:15 [b]Ezek 16:25-29; Nah 3:4
18 [a]Ps 72:10, 11; Is 60:5-9; Mic 4:13 [b]Ex 28:36; Zech 14:20
24:1 [a]Is 2:19; 13:13; 24:19,20; 30:32; 33:9
2 [a]Lev 25:36,37; Deut 23:19,20
4 [a]Is 33:9 [b]Is 2:12; 24:21
5 [1]Lit *under* [a]Gen 3:17; Num 35:33; Is 9:17; 10:6 [b]Is 33:8
6 [a]Josh 23:15; Is 34:5; 43:28; Zech 5:3,4 [b]Is 1:31; 5:24; 9:19
7 [a]Is 16:10; Joel 1:10,12
8 [a]Is 5:12,14; Ezek 26:13; Hos 2:11; Rev 18:22
9 [a]Is 5:11,22 [b]Is 5:20
10 [a]Is 34:11 [b]Is 23:1
11 [1]Lit is *darkened* [a]Jer 14:2; 46:12 [b]Is 16:10; 32:13
12 [a]Is 14:31; 45:2
13 [1]Lit *striking* [a]Is 17:6; 27:12
14 [1]Lit *sea* [a]Is 12:6; 48:20; 52:8; 54:1
15 [1]Lit *region of light* [2]Or *islands* [a]Is 25:3 [b]Mal 1:11 [c]Is 11:11; 42:4,10,12; 49:1; 51:5; 60:9; 66:19
16 [1]Lit *Wasting to me!* [a]Is 11:12; 42:10 [b]Is 28:5; 60:21 [c]Lev 26:39 [d]Is 21:2; 33:1; Jer 3:20; 5:11
17 [1]Lit *Are upon you* [a]Jer 48:43; Amos 5:19
18 [1]Lit *sound of terror*

And he who [2]climbs out of the
pit will be caught in the
snare;
For the [a]windows [3]above are
opened, and the
[b]foundations of the earth
shake.
19 [a]The earth is broken asunder,
The earth is [b]split through,
The earth is shaken violently.
20 The earth [a]reels to and fro like
a drunkard
And it totters like a [1]shack,
For its [b]transgression is heavy
upon it,
And it will fall, [c]never to rise
again.
21 So it will happen in that day,
That the LORD will [a]punish the
host of [1]heaven on high,
And the [b]kings of the earth on
earth.
22 They will be gathered together
Like [a]prisoners in the
[1]dungeon,
And will be confined in prison;
And after many days they *will*
[b]*be* punished.
23 Then the [a]moon will be abashed
and the sun ashamed,
For the [b]LORD of hosts will reign
on [c]Mount Zion and in
Jerusalem,
And *His* glory will be before His
elders.

Song of Praise for God's Favor

25 O LORD, You are [a]my God;
I will exalt You, I will give
thanks to Your name;
For You have [b]worked wonders,
[c]Plans *formed* long ago, with
perfect faithfulness.
2 For You have made a city into a
[a]heap,
A [b]fortified city into a ruin;
A [c]palace of strangers is a city
no more,
It will never be rebuilt.
3 Therefore a strong people will
[a]glorify You;
[b]Cities of ruthless nations will
revere You.
4 For You have been a [a]defense
for the helpless,
A defense for the needy in his
distress,
A [b]refuge from the storm, a
shade from the heat;
For the breath of the [c]ruthless
Is like a *rain* storm *against* a
wall.
5 Like heat in drought, You subdue
the [a]uproar of aliens;
Like heat by the shadow of a
cloud, the song of the
ruthless is [1]silenced.
6 ¶ [a]The LORD of hosts will
prepare a [1]lavish banquet
for [b]all peoples on this
mountain;
A banquet of [2]aged wine,
[3]choice pieces with
marrow,
And [4]refined, aged wine.
7 And on this mountain He will
swallow up the [1a]covering
which is over all peoples,
Even the veil which is
[2]stretched over all nations.
8 He will [a]swallow up death for
all time,
And the Lord [1]GOD will [b]wipe
tears away from all faces,
And He will remove the
[c]reproach of His people
from all the earth;
For the LORD has spoken.
9 And it will be said in that day,
"Behold, [a]this is our God for
whom we have [b]waited that
[c]He might save us.
This is the LORD for whom we
have waited;
[d]Let us rejoice and be glad in
His salvation."
10 For the hand of the LORD will
rest on this mountain,
And [a]Moab will be trodden
down in his place
As straw is trodden down in the
water of a manure pile.
11 And he will [a]spread out his
hands in the middle of it
As a swimmer spreads out *his*
hands to swim,
But *the Lord* will [b]lay low his
pride together with the
trickery of his hands.
12 The [a]unassailable fortifications
of your walls He will bring
down,
Lay low *and* cast to the ground,
even to the dust.

Song of Trust in God's Protection

26 [a]In that day this song will be
sung in the land of Judah:
"We have a [b]strong city;
He sets up walls and ramparts
for [1c]security.
2 "Open the [a]gates, that the
[b]righteous nation may
enter,
The one that [1]remains faithful.
3 "The steadfast of mind You will
keep in perfect [a]peace,

18 [2]Lit *goes up from the midst of* [3]Lit *from the height;* i.e. heaven [a]Gen 7:11 [b]Ps 18:7; Is 2:19

19 [a]Is 24:1 [b]Num 16:31; Deut 11:6

20 [1]Or *hut* [a]Is 19:14 [b]Is 1:28 [c]Dan 11:19; Amos 8:14

21 [1]Lit *the height in the height* [a]Is 10:12 [b]Ps 76:12

22 [1]Lit *pit* [a]Is 10:4 [b]Ezek 38:8; Zech 9:11

23 [a]Is 13:10 [b]Is 60:19; Zech 14:6; Rev 21:23 [c]Mic 4:7; Heb 12:22

25:1 [a]Ex 15:2; Ps 118:28; Is 7:13 [b]Ps 40:5 [c]Eph 1:11

2 [a]Is 17:1 [b]Is 17:3 [c]Is 13:22

3 [a]Is 24:15 [b]Is 13:11

4 [a]Is 14:32 [b]Is 4:6 [c]Is 29:5

5 [1]Lit *humbled* [a]Jer 51:54-56

6 [1]Lit *feast of fat things;* i.e. abundance [2]Lit *wine on the lees* [3]Lit *fat pieces* [4]Lit *wine refined on the lees* [a]Is 1:19 [b]Is 2:2-4

7 [1]Lit *face of the covering* [2]Lit *woven* [a]2 Cor 3:15; Eph 4:18

8 [1]Heb *YHWH,* usually rendered *LORD* [a]Hos 13:14; 1 Cor 15:54 [b]Is 30:19; Rev 7:17 [c]Ps 69:9; Is 51:7; Matt 5:11; 1 Pet 4:14

9 [a]Is 35:2 [b]Is 8:17 [c]Is 33:22 [d]Ps 20:5; Is 35:1

10 [a]Is 16:14; Jer 48:1-47; Ezek 25:8-11; Amos 2:1-3; Zeph 2:9

11 [a]Is 5:25 [b]Job 40:11; Is 2:10-12

12 [a]Is 15:1

26:1 [1]Or *salvation* [a]Is 4:2 [b]Is 14:31 [c]Is 60:18

2 [1]Lit *keeps faithfulness* [a]Is 60:11 [b]Is 45:25

3 [a]Is 26:12

Because he trusts in You.
4 "[a]Trust in the LORD forever,
For in [1]GOD the LORD, *we have*
an everlasting [b]Rock.
5 "For He has brought low those
who dwell on high, the
[a]unassailable city;
[b]He lays it low, He lays it low to
the ground, He casts it to
the dust.
6 "[a]The foot will trample it,
The feet of the [b]afflicted, the
steps of the helpless."

7 ¶ The [a]way of the righteous is
smooth;
O Upright One, [b]make the path
of the righteous level.
8 Indeed, *while following* the way
of [a]Your judgments,
O LORD,
We have waited for You eagerly;
[b]Your name, even Your
[c]memory, is the desire of
our souls.
9 [a]At night [1]my soul longs
for You,
Indeed, [2]my spirit within me
[b]seeks You diligently;
For when the earth [3]experiences
Your judgments
The inhabitants of the world
[c]learn righteousness.
10 *Though* the wicked is shown
favor,
He does not [a]learn
righteousness;
He [b]deals unjustly in the land of
uprightness,
And does not perceive the
majesty of the LORD.

11 ¶ O LORD, Your hand is lifted up
yet they [a]do not see it.
[1]They see [b]*Your* zeal for the
people and are put to
shame;
Indeed, [2c]fire will devour Your
enemies.
12 LORD, You will establish [a]peace
for us,
Since You have also performed
for us all our works.
13 O LORD our God, [a]other masters
besides You have ruled us;
But through You alone we
[1b]confess Your name.
14 [a]The dead will not live, the
[1]departed spirits will not
rise;
Therefore You have [b]punished
and destroyed them,
And You have wiped out all
remembrance of them.
15 [a]You have increased the nation,
O LORD,
You have increased the nation,
You are glorified;
You have [b]extended all the
borders of the land.
16 O LORD, they sought You [a]in
distress;
They [1]could only whisper a
prayer,
Your chastening was upon them.
17 [a]As the pregnant woman
approaches *the time* to give
birth,
She writhes *and* cries out in her
labor pains,
Thus were we before You,
O LORD.
18 We were pregnant, we writhed
in labor,
We [a]gave birth, as it seems,
only to wind.
We could not accomplish
deliverance for the earth,
Nor were [b]inhabitants of the
world [1]born.
19 Your [a]dead will live;
[1]Their corpses will rise.
You who lie in the dust, [b]awake
and shout for joy,
For your dew *is as* the dew of
the [2]dawn,
And the earth will [3]give birth to
the [4]departed spirits.

20 ¶ Come, my people, [a]enter into
your rooms
And close your doors behind
you;
Hide for a little [1b]while
Until [c]indignation [2]runs *its*
course.
21 For behold, the LORD is about to
[a]come out from His place
To [b]punish the inhabitants of
the earth for their iniquity;
And the earth will [c]reveal her
bloodshed
And will no longer cover her
slain.

The Deliverance of Israel

27 In that day [a]the LORD will
punish [1b]Leviathan the
fleeing serpent,
With His fierce and great and
mighty sword,
Even [1]Leviathan the twisted
serpent;
And [c]He will kill the dragon
who *lives* in the sea.

2 ¶ In that day,
"A [1a]vineyard of wine, sing of it!
3 "I, the LORD, am its keeper;

4 [1]Heb *YAH,* usually rendered *LORD* [a]Is 12:2; 50:10; 51:5 [b]Is 17:10; 30:29; 44:8
5 [a]Is 25:12 [b]Job 40:11-13
6 [a]Is 28:3 [b]Is 3:14,15; 11:4; 29:19
7 [a]Is 57:2 [b]Ps 25:4,5; 27:11; Is 42:16; 52:12
8 [a]Is 51:4; 56:1 [b]Is 12:4; 24:15; 25:1; 26:13 [c]Ex 3:15
9 [1]Lit *with my soul I long* [2]Lit *with my spirit...I seek* [3]Lit *has* [a]Ps 63:5,6; 77:2; 119:62; Is 50:10; Luke 6:12 [b]Ps 63:1; 78:34; Matt 6:33 [c]Is 55:6; Hos 5:15
10 [a]Is 22:12,13; 32:6,7 [b]Hos 11:7; John 5:37, 38
11 [1]Or *Let them see...and be* [2]Or *let the fire for Your adversaries devour them* [a]Is 44:9,18 [b]Is 9:7; 37:32; 59:17 [c]Is 5:24; 9:18,19; 10:17; 66:15,24; Heb 10:27
12 [a]Is 26:3
13 [1]Or *cause to be remembered* [a]Is 2:8; 10:11 [b]Is 63:7
14 [1]Or *shades* [a]Deut 4:28; Ps 135:17; Is 8:19; Hab 2:19 [b]Is 10:3
15 [a]Is 9:3 [b]Is 33:17; 54:2,3
16 [1]Lit *sound forth a whisper* [a]Is 37:3; Hos 5:15
17 [a]Is 13:8; 21:3; John 16:21
18 [1]Lit *fallen* [a]Is 33:11; 59:4 [b]Ps 17:14
19 [1]So with some ancient versions; Heb *My* [2]Lit *lights* [3]Lit *cause to fall* [4]Or *shades* [a]Is 25:8; Ezek 37:1-14; Dan 12:2; Hos 13:14 [b]Eph 5:14
20 [1]Lit *moment* [2]Lit *passes over* [a]Ex 12:22,23; Ps 91:1,4 [b]Ps 30:5; Is 54:7,8; 2 Cor 4:17 [c]Is 10:5,25; 13:5; 34:2; 66:14
21 [a]Mic 1:3; Jude 14 [b]Is 13:11; 30:12-14; 65:6,7 [c]Job 16:18; Luke 11:50
27:1 [1]Or *sea monster* [a]Is 66:16 [b]Job 3:8; 41:1; Ps 74:14; 104:26 [c]Is 51:9
2 [1]Some mss read *a vineyard of delight* [a]Ps 80:8; Is 5:7; Jer 2:21

[a]I water it every moment.
So that no one will [1]damage it,
I [b]guard it night and day.
4 "I have no wrath.
Should [1]someone give Me
[a]briars *and* thorns in battle,
Then I would step on them, [b]I
would burn them
[2]completely.
5 "Or let him [1a]rely on My
protection,
Let him make peace with Me,
Let him [b]make peace with Me."
6 [1]In the days to come Jacob [a]will
take root,
Israel will [b]blossom and sprout,
And they will fill the [2]whole
world with [c]fruit.

7 ¶ Like the striking of Him who
has struck them, has [a]He
struck them?
Or like the slaughter of His slain,
[1]have they been slain?
8 You contended with them [1]by
banishing them, by [a]driving
them away.
With His fierce wind He has
expelled *them* on the day of
the [b]east wind.
9 Therefore through this Jacob's
iniquity will be [a]forgiven;
And this will be [1]the full price
of the [2b]pardoning of
his sin:
When he makes all the [c]altar
stones like pulverized chalk
stones;
When [3]Asherim and incense
altars will not stand.
10 For the fortified city is [a]isolated,
A [1]homestead forlorn and
forsaken like the desert;
[b]There the calf will graze,
And there it will lie down and
[2]feed on its branches.
11 When its [a]limbs are dry, they
are broken off;
Women come *and* make a fire
with them,
For they are not a people of
[b]discernment,
Therefore [c]their Maker [d]will
not have compassion on
them.
And their Creator will not be
gracious to them.
12 ¶ In that day the LORD [a]will start
His threshing from the flowing stream of
the [b]Euphrates to the brook of Egypt, and
you will be [c]gathered up one by one,
O sons of Israel.
13 It will come about also in that day
that a great [a]trumpet will be blown, and
those who were perishing in the land of
[b]Assyria and who were scattered in the
land of Egypt will come and [c]worship the
LORD in the holy mountain at Jerusalem.

Ephraim's Captivity Predicted

28 Woe to the proud crown of the
[a]drunkards of [b]Ephraim,
And to the fading flower of its
glorious beauty,
Which is at the head of the
[1]fertile valley
Of those who are [2]overcome
with wine!
2 Behold, the Lord has a strong
and [a]mighty *agent;*
As a storm of [b]hail, a tempest of
destruction,
Like a storm of [c]mighty
overflowing waters,
He has cast *it* down to the earth
with *His* hand.
3 The proud crown of the
drunkards of Ephraim is
[a]trodden under foot.
4 And the fading flower of its
glorious beauty,
Which is at the head of the
[1]fertile valley,
Will be like the [a]first-ripe fig
prior to summer,
Which [2]one sees,
And [3]as soon as it is in his
[4]hand,
He swallows it.
5 In that day the [a]LORD of hosts
will become a beautiful
[b]crown
And a glorious diadem to the
remnant of His people;
6 A [a]spirit of justice for him who
sits in judgment,
A [b]strength to those who repel
the [1]onslaught at the gate.
7 And these also [a]reel with wine
and stagger from strong
drink:
[b]The priest and [c]the prophet
reel with strong drink,
They are confused by wine, they
stagger from [d]strong drink;
They reel while [1]having
[e]visions,
They totter *when rendering*
judgment.
8 For all the tables are full of filthy
[a]vomit, without a *single*
clean place.
9 ¶ "To [a]whom would He teach
knowledge,
And to whom would He
interpret the message?
Those *just* [b]weaned from milk?

3 [1]Lit *punish* [a]Is 58:11 [b]1 Sam 2:9; Is 31:5; John 10:28
4 [1]Lit *who* [2]Lit *altogether* [a]2 Sam 23:6; Is 10:17 [b]Is 33:12; Matt 3:12; Heb 6:8
5 [1]Lit *take hold of* [a]Is 12:2 [b]Job 22:21; Is 26:3; Rom 5:1; 2 Cor 5:20
6 [1]Lit *Those coming* [2]Lit *face of* [a]Is 37:31 [b]Is 35:1; Hos 14:5 [c]Is 4:2
7 [1]Lit *he was slain* [a]Is 10:12
8 [1]Some ancient versions read *by exact measure* [a]Is 50:1 [b]Jer 4:11; Ezek 19:12; Hos 13:15
9 [1]Lit *all the fruit* [2]Lit *removing* [3]I.e. wooden symbols of a female deity [a]Is 1:25; Dan 11:35 [b]Rom 11:27 [c]Ex 34:13; Deut 12:3; 2 Kin 10:26; Is 17:8
10 [1]Lit *pasture* [2]Lit *consume* [a]Is 32:13 [b]Is 17:2
11 [a]Is 18:5 [b]Deut 32:28; Is 1:3; Jer 8:7 [c]Deut 32:18; Is 43:1 [d]Is 9:17
12 [a]Is 11:11 [b]Gen 15:18 [c]Deut 30:3; Neh 1:9
13 [a]Lev 25:9; 1 Chr 15:24; Matt 24:31; Rev 11:15 [b]Is 19:24 [c]Is 19:21; Zech 14:16; Heb 12:22
28:1 [1]Lit *valley of fatness* [2]Lit *smitten* [a]Is 28:7; Hos 7:5 [b]Is 9:9
2 [a]Is 8:7 [b]Is 28:17; Ezek 13:11 [c]Is 8:6; Nah 1:8
3 [a]Is 26:6
4 [1]Lit *valley of fatness* [2]Lit *the one seeing sees* [3]Lit *while it is yet* [4]Lit *palm* [a]Hos 9:10; Mic 7:1; Nah 3:12
5 [a]Is 41:16 [b]Is 62:3
6 [1]Lit *battle* [a]1 Kin 3:28; Is 11:2; John 5:30 [b]2 Chr 32:6-8; Is 25:4
7 [1]Lit *seeing* [a]Is 5:11; Hos 4:11 [b]Is 24:2 [c]Is 9:15 [d]Hab 2:15 [e]Is 29:11
8 [a]Jer 48:26
9 [a]Is 2:3 [b]Ps 131:2

Those *just* taken from the breast?
10 "For *He says,*
'[1a]Order on order, order on order,
Line on line, line on line,
A little here, a little there.' "
11 Indeed, He will speak to this people
Through [a]stammering lips and a foreign tongue,
12 He who said to them, "Here is [a]rest, give rest to the weary,"
And, "Here is repose," but they would not listen.
13 So the word of the LORD to them will be,
"[1]Order on order, order on order,
Line on line, line on line,
A little here, a little there,"
That they may go and [a]stumble backward, be broken, snared and taken captive.

Judah Is Warned

14 Therefore, [a]hear the word of the LORD, O [b]scoffers,
Who rule this people who are in Jerusalem,
15 Because you have said, "We have made a [a]covenant with death,
And with [1]Sheol we have made a [2]pact.
[b]The overwhelming [3]scourge will not reach us when it passes by,
For we have made [c]falsehood our refuge and we have [d]concealed ourselves with deception."
16 Therefore thus says the Lord
[1]GOD,
"[a]Behold, I am laying in Zion a stone, a tested [b]stone,
A costly cornerstone *for* the foundation, [2]firmly placed.
He who believes *in it* will not be [3]disturbed.
17 "I will make [a]justice the measuring line
And righteousness the level;
Then [b]hail will sweep away the refuge of lies
And the waters will overflow the secret place.
18 "Your [a]covenant with death will be [1b]canceled,
And your pact with Sheol will not stand;
When the [a]overwhelming scourge passes through,
Then you become its [c]trampling *place.*
19 "As [a]often as it passes through, it will [1]seize you;
For [b]morning after morning it will pass through, *anytime* during the day or night,
And it will be [2]sheer [c]terror to understand [3]what it means."
20 The bed is too short on which to stretch out,
And the [a]blanket is too [1]small to wrap oneself in.
21 For the LORD will rise up as *at* Mount [a]Perazim,
He will be stirred up as in the valley of [b]Gibeon,
To do His [c]task, His [1d]unusual task,
And to work His work, His [2]extraordinary work.
22 And now do not carry on as [a]scoffers,
Or your fetters will be made stronger;
For I have heard from the Lord [1]GOD of hosts
Of decisive [b]destruction on all the earth.

23 ¶ Give ear and hear my voice,
Listen and hear my words.
24 Does the [1]farmer plow [2]continually to plant seed?
Does he *continually* [3]turn and harrow the ground?
25 Does he not level its surface
And sow dill and scatter [a]cummin
And [1]plant [b]wheat in rows,
Barley in its place and rye within its [2]area?
26 For his God instructs and teaches him properly.
27 For dill is not threshed with a [a]threshing sledge,
Nor is the cartwheel [1]driven over cummin;
But dill is beaten out with a rod, and cummin with a club.
28 *Grain for* bread is crushed,
Indeed, he does not continue to thresh it forever.
Because the wheel of *his* cart and his horses *eventually* [1]damage *it,*
He does not thresh it longer.
29 This also comes from the LORD of hosts,
Who has made *His* counsel [a]wonderful and *His* wisdom [b]great.

10 [1]Heb *Sav lasav, sav lasav, Kav lakav, kav lakav, Ze' er sham, ze' er sham* These Hebrew monosyllables, imitating the babbling of a child, mock the prophet's preaching [a]2 Chr 36:15; Neh 9:30
11 [a]Is 33:19; 1 Cor 14:21
12 [a]Is 11:10; Jer 6:16; Matt 11:28
13 [1]V 10, note 1 The LORD responds to their scoffing by imitating their mockery, to represent the unintelligible language of a conqueror [a]Is 8:15; Matt 21:44
14 [a]Is 1:10 [b]Is 29:20
15 [1]I.e. the nether world [2]So some ancient versions; Heb *seer* [3]Or *flood* [a]Is 28:18 [b]Is 8:8; Dan 11:22 [c]Is 9:15; Ezek 13:22 [d]Is 29:15
16 [1]Heb *YHWH,* usually rendered *LORD* [2]Lit *well-laid* [3]Lit *in a hurry* [a]Rom 9:33; 1 Pet 2:6 [b]Ps 118:22; Is 8:14; Matt 21:42; Mark 12:10; Luke 20:17; Acts 4:11; Eph 2:20
17 [a]2 Kin 21:13; Is 5:16; Amos 7:7-9 [b]Is 28:2
18 [1]Lit *covered over* [a]Is 28:15 [b]Is 7:7 [c]Is 28:3; Dan 8:13
19 [1]Lit *take* [2]Lit *only* [3]Lit *the report,* or, *the message* [a]2 Kin 24:2 [b]Is 50:4 [c]Job 6:4; Ps 55:4; Lam 2:22
20 [1]Lit *narrow* [a]Is 59:6
21 [1]Lit *task is strange* [2]Lit *work is alien* [a]2 Sam 5:20; 1 Chr 14:11 [b]Josh 10:10; 2 Sam 5:25; 1 Chr 14:16 [c]Is 10:12 [d]Lam 2:15; Luke 19:41-44
22 [1]Heb *YHWH,* usually rendered *LORD* [a]Is 28:14 [b]Is 10:22
24 [1]Lit *plowman* [2]Lit *all day* [3]Lit *open*
25 [1]Lit *put* [2]Lit *region* [a]Matt 23:23 [b]Ex 9:32
27 [1]Lit *rolled* [a]Amos 1:3
28 [1]Lit *discomfit*
29 [a]Is 9:6 [b]Is 31:2; Rom 11:33

Jerusalem Is Warned

29 Woe, O [1]Ariel, [1]Ariel the city *where* David *once* [a]camped!
Add year to year, [2][b]observe *your* feasts on schedule.
2 I will bring distress to Ariel,
And she will be *a city of* lamenting and [a]mourning;
And she will be like an Ariel to me.
3 I will [a]camp against you [1]encircling *you,*
And I will set siegeworks against you,
And I will raise up battle towers against you.
4 Then you will [a]be brought low;
From the earth you will speak,
And from the dust *where* you are prostrate
Your words *will come.*
Your voice will also be like that of a [1]spirit from the ground,
And your speech will whisper from the dust.

5 ¶ But the multitude of your [1]enemies will become like fine [a]dust,
And the multitude of the [b]ruthless ones like the chaff which [2]blows away;
And it will happen [c]instantly, suddenly.
6 From the LORD of hosts you will be [a]punished with [b]thunder and earthquake and loud noise,
With whirlwind and tempest and the flame of a consuming fire.
7 And the [a]multitude of all the nations who wage war against [1]Ariel,
Even all who wage war against her and her stronghold, and who distress her,
Will be like a dream, a [b]vision of the night.
8 It will be as when a hungry man dreams—
And behold, he is eating;
But when he awakens, his [1]hunger is not satisfied,
Or as when a thirsty man dreams—
And behold, he is drinking,
But when he awakens, behold, he is faint
And his [1]thirst is not quenched.
[a]Thus the multitude of all the nations will be
Who wage war against Mount Zion.

9 ¶ [a]Be delayed and wait,
Blind yourselves and be blind;
They [b]become drunk, but not with wine,
They stagger, but not with strong drink.
10 For the LORD has poured over you a spirit of deep [a]sleep,
He has [b]shut your eyes, the prophets;
And He has covered your heads, the seers.
11 The entire vision will be to you like
the words of a sealed [1][a]book, which
when they give it to the one who [2]is
literate, saying, "Please read this," he
will say, "I cannot, for it is sealed."
12 Then the [1]book will be given to the
one who [2]is illiterate, saying, "Please
read this." And he will say, "I [3]cannot
read."
13 ¶ Then the Lord said,
"Because [a]this people draw near with their [1]words
And honor Me with their [2]lip service,
But they remove their hearts far from Me,
And their [3]reverence for Me [4]consists of [5]tradition learned *by rote,*
14 Therefore behold, I will once again deal [a]marvelously with this people, wondrously marvelous;
And [b]the wisdom of their wise men will perish,
And the discernment of their discerning men will be concealed."

15 ¶ Woe to those who deeply [a]hide their [1]plans from the LORD,
And whose [b]deeds are *done* in a dark place,
And they say, "[c]Who sees us?" or "Who knows us?"
16 You turn *things* around!
Shall the potter be considered [1]as equal with the clay,
That [a]what is made would say to its maker, "He did not make me";
Or what is formed say to him who formed it, "He has no understanding"?

Blessing after Discipline

17 ¶ Is it not yet just a little while
[1]Before Lebanon will be turned into a [a]fertile field,
And the fertile field will be considered as a forest?

29:1 [1]I.e. Lion of God, or Jerusalem [2]Lit *let your feasts run their round* [a]2 Sam 5:9 [b]Is 1:14; 5:12; 22:12,13; 29:9, 13
2 [a]Is 3:26; Lam 2:5
3 [1]Lit *like a circle* [a]Luke 19:43, 44
4 [1]Or *ghost* [a]Is 8:19
5 [1]Lit *strangers* [2]Lit *passes away* [a]Is 17:13; 41:15, 16 [b]Is 13:11; 25:3; 29:20 [c]Is 17:14; 30:13; 47:11; 1 Thess 5:3
6 [a]Is 10:3; 26:14,21 [b]1 Sam 2:10; Matt 24:7; Mark 13:8; Luke 21:11; Rev 11:13,19; 16:18
7 [1]V 1, note 1 [a]Mic 4:11,12; Zech 12:9 [b]Job 20:8; Ps 73:20; Is 17:14
8 [1]Lit *soul* [a]Is 54:17
9 [a]Is 29:1 [b]Is 51:17,21,22; 63:6
10 [a]Ps 69:23; Is 6:9,10; Mic 3:6; Rom 11:8 [b]Is 44:18; 2 Thess 2:9-12
11 [1]Or *scroll* [2]Lit *knows books* [a]Is 8:16; Dan 12:4,9; Matt 13:11
12 [1]Or *scroll* [2]Lit *does not know books* [3]Lit *do not know books*
13 [1]Lit *mouth* [2]Lit *lips* [3]Lit *fear of Me* [4]Lit *is* [5]Lit *commandment of rulers* [a]Ezek 33:31; Matt 15:8,9; Mark 7:6,7
14 [a]Is 6:9,10; 28:21; 65:7; Hab 1:5 [b]Is 44:25; Jer 8:9; 49:7; 1 Cor 1:19
15 [1]Lit *counsel* [a]Ps 10:11,13; Is 28:15; 30:1 [b]Job 22:13; Is 57:12; Ezek 8:12 [c]Ps 94:7; Is 47:10; Mal 2:17
16 [1]Lit *like* [a]Is 45:9; 64:8; Jer 18:1-6; Rom 9:19-21
17 [1]Lit *And* [a]Ps 84:6; 107:33,35; Is 32:15

18 On that day the [a]deaf will hear
[b]words of a book,
And out of *their* gloom and
darkness the [c]eyes of the
blind will see.
19 The [a]afflicted also will increase
their gladness in the LORD,
And the [b]needy of mankind will
rejoice in the Holy One of
Israel.
20 For the [a]ruthless will come to
an end and the [b]scorner
will be finished,
Indeed [c]all who [1]are intent on
doing evil will be cut off;
21 Who [1]cause a person to be
indicted by a word,
And [a]ensnare him who
adjudicates at the gate,
And [2b]defraud the one in the
right with [3]meaningless
arguments.
22 ¶ Therefore thus says the LORD,
who redeemed [a]Abraham, concerning
the house of Jacob:
"Jacob [b]shall not now be
ashamed, nor shall his face
now turn pale;
23 But when [1]he sees his
[a]children, the [b]work of My
hands, in his midst,
They will sanctify My name;
Indeed, they will [c]sanctify the
Holy One of Jacob
And will stand in awe of the God
of Israel.
24 "Those who [a]err in [1]mind will
[b]know [2]the truth,
And those who [3]criticize will
[4c]accept instruction.

Judah Warned against Egyptian Alliance

30 "Woe to the [a]rebellious
children," declares the LORD,
"Who [b]execute a plan, but not
Mine,
And [1c]make an alliance, but not
of My Spirit,
In order to add sin to sin;
2 Who [a]proceed down to Egypt
Without [b]consulting [1]Me,
[c]To take refuge in the safety of
Pharaoh
And to seek shelter in the
shadow of Egypt!
3 "Therefore the safety of Pharaoh
will be [a]your shame
And the shelter in the shadow of
Egypt, your humiliation.
4 "For [a]their princes are at Zoan
And their ambassadors arrive at
Hanes.
5 "Everyone will be [a]ashamed
because of a people who
cannot profit them,
Who are [b]not for help or profit,
but for shame and also for
reproach."

6 ¶ The [1]oracle concerning the
[a]beasts of the [b]Negev.
Through a land of [c]distress and
anguish,
From [2]where *come* lioness and
lion, viper and [d]flying
serpent,
They [e]carry their riches on the
[3]backs of young donkeys
And their treasures on [f]camels'
humps,
To a people who cannot profit
them;
7 Even Egypt, whose [a]help is vain
and empty.
Therefore, I have called [1]her
"[2b]Rahab who has been
exterminated."
8 Now go, [a]write it on a tablet
before them
And inscribe it on a scroll,
That it may [1]serve in the time
to come
[2]As a witness forever.
9 For this is a [a]rebellious people,
[b]false sons,
Sons who [1]refuse to [c]listen
To the [2]instruction of the LORD;
10 Who say to the [a]seers, "You
must not see *visions";*
And to the prophets, "You must
not [b]prophesy to us what is
right,
[c]Speak to us [1]pleasant words,
Prophesy illusions.
11 "Get out of the way, [a]turn aside
from the path,
[1b]Let us hear no more about
the Holy One of Israel."
12 Therefore thus says the Holy One of
Israel,
"[a]Since you have rejected this
word
And have put your trust in
[b]oppression and guile, and
have relied on them,
13 Therefore this [a]iniquity will be
to you
Like a [b]breach about to fall,
A bulge in a high wall,
Whose collapse comes [c]suddenly
in an instant,
14 Whose collapse is like the
smashing of a [a]potter's jar,
[1]So ruthlessly shattered
That a sherd will not be found
among its pieces

18 [a]Is 35:5; Matt 11:5; Mark 7:37 [b]Is 29:11 [c]Ps 119:18; Prov 20:12; Is 32:3
19 [a]Ps 25:9; Is 11:4; Matt 5:5 [b]Is 3:14; Matt 11:5; James 1:9
20 [1]Lit *watch evil* [a]Is 29:5 [b]Is 28:14 [c]Is 59:4; Mic 2:1
21 [1]Lit *bring a person under condemnation* [2]Lit *turn aside* [3]Lit *confusion* [a]Amos 5:10 [b]Is 32:7; Amos 5:12
22 [a]Is 41:8 [b]Is 45:17
23 [1]Or *his children see* [a]Is 49:20-26 [b]Is 26:12; Eph 2:10 [c]Is 5:16
24 [1]Lit *spirit* [2]Lit *understanding* [3]Lit *murmur* [4]Lit *learn* [a]Is 30:21; Heb 5:2 [b]Is 41:20 [c]Is 54:13
30:1 [1]Lit *pour out a drink offering* [a]Is 1:2 [b]Is 29:15 [c]Is 8:11
2 [1]Lit *My mouth* [a]Is 31:1; Jer 43:7 [b]Is 8:19 [c]Is 36:9
3 [a]Is 20:5; Jer 42:18
4 [a]Is 19:11
5 [a]Jer 2:36 [b]Is 10:3
6 [1]Or *burden of* [2]Lit *them* [3]Lit *shoulders* [a]Is 46:1 [b]Gen 12:9 [c]Ex 5:10; Deut 4:20; Is 5:30; Jer 11:4 [d]Deut 8:15; Is 14:29 [e]Is 15:7 [f]1 Kin 10:2
7 [1]Lit *this* one [2]M.T. reads *They are Rahab* (or *arrogance*), *to remain* [a]Is 30:5 [b]Job 9:13; Ps 87:4; Is 51:9
8 [1]Lit *be* [2]So the versions; Heb *Forever and ever* [a]Is 8:1
9 [1]Lit *are not willing* [2]Or *law* [a]Is 30:1 [b]Is 28:15 [c]Is 1:10
10 [1]Lit *smooth things* [a]Is 29:10 [b]Is 5:20; Jer 11:21; Amos 2:12 [c]1 Kin 22:8; Jer 6:14; Ezek 13:7; Rom 16:18; 2 Tim 4:3
11 [1]Lit *Cause to cease from our presence* the [a]Acts 13:8 [b]Job 21:14
12 [a]Is 5:24 [b]Is 3:14
13 [a]Is 26:21 [b]1 Kin 20:30; Ps 62:4; Is 58:12 [c]Is 29:5
14 [1]Lit *Crushed, it will not be spared* [a]Ps 2:9; Jer 19:10

To [2]take fire from a hearth
Or to scoop water from a cistern."
15 For thus the Lord [1]GOD, the Holy
One of Israel, has said,
"In [2]repentance and [a]rest you will be saved,
In [b]quietness and trust is your strength."
But you were not willing,
16 And you said, "No, for we will flee on [a]horses,"
Therefore you shall flee!
"And we will ride on swift *horses*,"
Therefore those who pursue you shall be swift.
17 [a]One thousand *will flee* at the threat of one *man;*
You will flee at the threat of five,
Until you are left as a [1]flag on a mountain top
And as a signal on a hill.

God Is Gracious and Just

18 ¶ Therefore the LORD [1a]longs to be gracious to you,
And therefore He [2]waits on [b]high to have compassion on you.
For the LORD is a [c]God of justice;
How blessed are all those who [3d]long for Him.
19 ¶ [1]O people in Zion, [a]inhabitant
in Jerusalem, you will [b]weep no longer.
He will surely be gracious to you at the
sound of your cry; when He hears it, He
will [c]answer you.
20 Although the Lord has given you
[a]bread of privation and water of oppression, *He,* your Teacher will no longer
[b]hide Himself, but your eyes will behold
your Teacher.
21 Your ears will hear a word behind
you, "[1]This is the [a]way, walk in it,"
whenever you [b]turn to the right or to the
left.
22 And you will defile your graven
[a]images overlaid with silver, and your
molten [a]images plated with gold. You
will scatter them as an impure thing, *and*
say to [1]them, "[b]Be gone!"
23 ¶ Then He will [a]give *you* rain for
[1]the seed which you will sow in the
ground, and bread *from* the yield of the
ground, and it will be [2]rich and [3]plente-
ous; on that day [b]your livestock will
graze in a roomy pasture.
24 Also the oxen and the donkeys
which work the ground will eat salted
fodder, which [1]has been [a]winnowed
with shovel and fork.
25 On every lofty mountain and on
[a]every high hill there will be [1]streams
running with water on the day of the
great [b]slaughter, when the towers fall.
26 [a]The light of the moon will be as
the light of the sun, and the light of the
sun will be seven times *brighter,* like the
light of seven days, on the day [b]the LORD
binds up the [c]fracture of His people and
[d]heals the bruise [1]He has inflicted.
27 ¶ Behold, [a]the name of the LORD comes from a [1]remote place;
[b]Burning is His anger and [2]dense is *His* [3]smoke;
His lips are filled with [c]indignation
And His tongue is like a [d]consuming fire;
28 His [a]breath is like an overflowing torrent,
Which [b]reaches to the neck,
To [c]shake the nations back and forth in a [1]sieve,
And to *put* in the jaws of the peoples [d]the bridle which [2]leads to ruin.
29 You will have [1]songs as in the night when you keep the festival,
And gladness of heart as when one marches to *the sound of* the flute,
To go to the mountain of the LORD, to the Rock of Israel.
30 And the LORD will cause [1]His voice of authority to be heard,
And the [2]descending of His arm to be seen in fierce anger,
And *in* the flame of a consuming fire
In cloudburst, downpour and hailstones.
31 For [a]at the voice of the LORD [b]Assyria will be terrified,
When He strikes with the [c]rod.
32 And every [1]blow of the [2a]rod of punishment,
Which the LORD will lay on him,
Will be with *the music of* [b]tambourines and lyres;
And in battles, [c]brandishing weapons, He will fight them.
33 For [1a]Topheth has long been ready,
Indeed, it has been prepared for the king.
He has made it deep and large,
[2]A pyre of fire with plenty of wood;
The [b]breath of the LORD, like a torrent of [c]brimstone, sets it afire.

14 [2]Lit *snatch up*
15 [1]Heb *YHWH,* usually rendered LORD [2]Lit *returning* [a]Ps 116:7; Is 28:12 [b]Is 7:4
16 [a]Is 2:7
17 [1]Lit *pole* [a]Lev 26:36; Deut 28:25; Josh 23:10; Prov 28:1
18 [1]Lit *waits* [2]Lit *is on high* [3]Lit *wait* [a]Is 42:14; Jon 3:4; 2 Pet 3:9 [b]Is 2:11 [c]Is 5:16 [d]Is 8:17
19 [1]M.T. reads *A people will inhabit Zion, Jerusalem* [a]Is 65:9; Ezek 37:25 [b]Is 25:8 [c]Ps 50:15; Is 58:9; Matt 7:7-11
20 [a]1 Kin 22:27; Ps 80:5 [b]Ps 74:9; Amos 8:11
21 [1]Lit *saying, "This* [a]Ps 25:8; Prov 3:6; Is 35:8 [b]Is 29:24
22 [1]Lit *it "Go out"* [a]Ex 32:2; Judg 17:3; Is 46:6 [b]Matt 4:10
23 [1]Lit *your* [2]Lit *fatness* [3]Lit *fat* [a]Ps 65:9-13 [b]Ps 144:13; Is 32:20; Hos 4:16
24 [1]Lit *one winnows* [a]Matt 3:12; Luke 3:17
25 [1]Lit *canals, streams of water* [a]Is 35:6 [b]Is 34:2
26 [1]Lit *of His blow* [a]Is 24:23; Rev 21:23 [b]Is 61:1 [c]Is 1:6 [d]Deut 32:39; Job 5:18; Is 33:24; Jer 33:6; Hos 6:1
27 [1]Lit *distance* [2]Lit *heaviness* [3]Lit *uplifting* [a]Is 59:19 [b]Is 10:17 [c]Is 10:5 [d]Is 66:15
28 [1]Lit *sifting of the worthless* [2]Lit *misleads* [a]Is 11:4; 2 Thess 2:8 [b]Is 8:8 [c]Amos 9:9 [d]2 Kin 19:28; Is 37:29
29 [1]Lit *the song*
30 [1]Lit *the majesty of His voice* [2]Lit *descent*
31 [a]Is 11:4 [b]Is 10:12 [c]Is 10:26
32 [1]Lit *passing* [2]Lit *staff of foundation* [a]Is 10:24 [b]1 Sam 18:6; Jer 31:4 [c]Ezek 32:10
33 [1]I.e. the place of human sacrifice to Molech [2]Lit *Its pile* [a]2 Kin 23:10; Jer 7:31 [b]Is 11:4 [c]Gen 19:24; Is 34:9

Help Not in Egypt but in God

31 Woe to those who go down to
[a]Egypt for help
And [b]rely on horses,
And trust in chariots because
they are many
And in horsemen because they
are very strong,
But they do not [c]look to the
[d]Holy One of Israel, nor
seek the LORD!
2 Yet He also is [a]wise and will
[b]bring disaster
And does [c]not retract His
words,
But will arise against the house
of [d]evildoers
And against the help of the
[e]workers of iniquity.
3 Now the Egyptians are [a]men
and not God,
And their [b]horses are flesh and
not spirit;
So the LORD will [c]stretch out
His hand,
And [d]he who helps will stumble
And he who is helped will fall,
And all of them will come to an
end together.

4 ¶ For thus says the LORD to me,
"As the [a]lion or the young lion
growls over his prey,
Against which a band of
shepherds is called out,
And he will not be terrified at
their voice nor disturbed at
their noise,
So will the LORD of hosts come
down to wage [b]war on
Mount Zion and on its hill."
5 Like [1]flying [a]birds so the LORD
of hosts will protect
Jerusalem.
He will [b]protect and deliver *it;*
He will pass over and rescue *it.*
6 ¶ [a]Return to Him from whom
[1]you have [b]deeply defected, O sons of
Israel.
7 For in that day every man will [a]cast
away his silver idols and his gold idols,
which your [b]sinful hands have made for
you as [b]a sin.
8 And the [a]Assyrian will fall by a
sword not of man,
And a [b]sword not of man will
devour him.
So he will [1c]not escape the
sword,
And his young men will become
[d]forced laborers.
9 "His [a]rock will pass away because
of panic,

31:1 [a]Is 30:2,7; 36:6 [b]Deut 17:16; Ps 20:7; 33:17; Is 2:7; 30:16 [c]Is 9:13; Dan 9:13; Amos 5:4-8 [d]Is 10:17; 43:15; Hos 11:9; Hab 1:12; 3:3
2 [a]Is 28:29; Rom 16:27 [b]Is 45:7 [c]Num 23:19; Jer 44:29 [d]Is 1:4; 9:17; 14:20 [e]Is 22:14; 32:6
3 [a]Ezek 28:9; 2 Thess 2:4 [b]Is 36:9 [c]Is 9:17; Jer 15:6; Ezek 20:33,34 [d]Is 30:5,7; Matt 15:14
4 [a]Num 24:9; Hos 11:10; Amos 3:8 [b]Is 42:13; Zech 12:8
5 [1]Or *hovering* [a]Deut 32:11; Ps 91:4 [b]Is 37:35; 38:6
6 [1]Lit *they* [a]Is 44:22; 55:7; Jer 3:10,14,22; Ezek 18:31,32 [b]Is 1:2,5
7 [a]Is 2:20; 30:22 [b]1 Kin 12:30
8 [1]Lit *flee* [a]Is 10:12; 14:25; 30:31-33; 37:7, 36-38 [b]Is 66:16 [c]Is 21:15 [d]Gen 49:15; Is 14:2
9 [a]Deut 32:31, 37 [b]Is 5:26; 13:2; 18:3 [c]Is 10:16,17; 30:33; Zech 2:5
32:1 [a]Ps 72:1-4; Is 9:6,7; 11:4,5; Jer 23:5; 33:15; Ezek 37:24; Zech 9:9
2 [1]Lit *canals* [2]Lit *heavy* [3]Lit *an exhausted* [a]Is 4:6; 25:4 [b]Is 35:6; 41:18; 43:19,20
3 [1]Or *turned away* [a]Is 29:18
4 [1]Lit *heart* [2]Lit *knowledge* [a]Is 29:24
5 [a]1 Sam 25:25
6 [1]Or *does* [2]Lit *make empty the hungry soul* [3]Lit *he causes to lack* [a]Prov 19:3; 24:7-9; Is 59:7, 13 [b]Is 9:17; 10:6 [c]Is 3:15; 10:2
7 [1]Lit *words of falsehood* [2]Lit *justly* [a]Jer 5:26-28; Mic 7:3 [b]Is 11:4; 61:1 [c]Is 5:23
8 [a]Prov 11:25
9 [a]Is 47:8; Amos 6:1; Zeph 2:15 [b]Is 28:23
10 [a]Is 5:5,6; 7:23; 24:7

And his princes will be terrified
at the [b]standard,"
Declares the LORD, whose [c]fire
is in Zion and whose
furnace is in Jerusalem.

The Glorious Future

32 Behold, a [a]king will reign
righteously
And princes will rule justly.
2 Each will be like a [a]refuge from
the wind
And a shelter from the storm,
Like [1b]streams of water in a dry
country,
Like the [a]shade of a [2]huge rock
in [3]a parched land.
3 Then [a]the eyes of those who see
will not be [1]blinded,
And the ears of those who hear
will listen.
4 The [1]mind of the [a]hasty will
discern the [2]truth,
And the tongue of the
stammerers will hasten to
speak clearly.
5 No longer will the [a]fool be
called noble,
Or the rogue be spoken of *as*
generous.
6 For a fool speaks nonsense,
And his heart [1a]inclines toward
wickedness:
To practice [b]ungodliness and to
speak error against the
LORD,
To [2c]keep the hungry person
unsatisfied
And [3]to withhold drink from the
thirsty.
7 As for a rogue, his weapons are
evil;
He [a]devises wicked schemes
To [b]destroy *the* afflicted with
[1]slander,
[c]Even though *the* needy one
speaks [2]what is right.
8 But [a]the noble man devises
noble plans;
And by noble plans he stands.
9 ¶ Rise up, you [a]women who are
at ease,
And hear my voice;
[b]Give ear to my word,
You complacent daughters.
10 Within a year and *a few* days
You will be troubled,
O complacent *daughters;*
[a]For the vintage is ended,
And the *fruit* gathering will not
come.
11 Tremble, you *women* who are at
ease;

[a]Be troubled, you complacent
daughters;
[b]Strip, undress and put
sackcloth on *your* waist,
12 [a]Beat your breasts for the
pleasant fields, for the
fruitful vine,
13 [a]For the land of my people *in
which* thorns *and* briars
shall come up;
Yea, for all the joyful houses *and
for* the [b]jubilant city.
14 Because [a]the palace has been
abandoned, the [1]populated
[b]city forsaken.
[2]Hill and watch-tower have
become [c]caves forever,
A delight for [d]wild donkeys, a
pasture for flocks;
15 Until the [a]Spirit is poured out
upon us from on high,
And the wilderness becomes a
[b]fertile field,
And the fertile field is considered
as a forest.
16 Then [a]justice will dwell in the
wilderness
And righteousness will abide in
the fertile field.
17 And the [a]work of righteousness
will be peace,
And the service of righteousness,
[b]quietness and [1]confidence
forever.
18 Then my people will live in a
[a]peaceful habitation,
And in secure dwellings and in
undisturbed [b]resting places;
19 And it will [a]hail when the
[b]forest comes down,
And [c]the city will be utterly laid
low.
20 How [a]blessed will you be, you
who sow beside all waters,
Who [1]let out freely the ox and
the donkey.

The Judgment of God

33 Woe [a]to you, O destroyer,
While you were not destroyed;
And he [b]who is treacherous,
while *others* did not deal
treacherously with him.
As soon as you finish destroying,
[c]you will be destroyed;
As soon as you cease to deal
treacherously, *others* will
[d]deal treacherously with
you.
2 O LORD, [a]be gracious to us; we
have [b]waited for You.
Be [1]their [2c]strength every
morning,
Our salvation also in the [d]time
of distress.
3 At the sound of the tumult
[a]peoples flee;
At the [b]lifting up of Yourself
nations disperse.
4 Your spoil is gathered *as* the
caterpillar gathers;
As locusts rushing about men
rush about on it.
5 The LORD is [a]exalted, for He
dwells on high;
He has [b]filled Zion with justice
and righteousness.
6 And He will be the [1a]stability of
your times,
A [b]wealth of salvation, wisdom
and [c]knowledge;
The [d]fear of the LORD is his
treasure.
7 Behold, their brave men cry in
[1]the streets,
The [2a]ambassadors of peace
weep bitterly.
8 The highways are desolate, [1]the
[a]traveler has ceased,
He has [b]broken the covenant,
he has despised the cities,
He has no regard for man.
9 [a]The land mourns *and* pines
away,
[b]Lebanon is shamed *and*
withers;
[c]Sharon is like a desert plain,
And Bashan and Carmel [1]lose
their foliage.
10 "Now [a]I will arise," says the
LORD,
"Now I will be exalted, now I will
be lifted up.
11 "You have [a]conceived [1]chaff, you
will give birth to stubble;
[2]My [b]breath will consume you
like a fire.
12 "The peoples will be burned to
lime,
[a]Like cut thorns which are
burned in the fire.

13 ¶ "You who are far away, [a]hear
what I have done;
And you who are near,
[1]acknowledge My might."
14 [a]Sinners in Zion are terrified;
[b]Trembling has seized the
godless.
"Who among us can live with
[c]the consuming fire?
Who among us can live with
[1]continual [d]burning?"
15 He who [a]walks righteously and
speaks with sincerity,
He who rejects [1]unjust gain

---

11 [a]Is 22:12 [b]Is 47:2
12 [a]Nah 2:7
13 [a]Is 5:6 [b]Is 22:2
14 [1]Lit *multitude of the* [2]Or *Ophel* [a]Is 13:22 [b]Is 6:11 [c]Is 13:21 [d]Ps 104:11; Jer 14:6
15 [a]Is 11:2; Ezek 39:29; Joel 2:28 [b]Ps 107:35; Is 29:17
16 [a]Is 33:5; Zech 8:3
17 [1]Or *security* [a]Ps 72:2; Is 2:4; Rom 14:17; James 3:18 [b]Is 30:15
18 [a]Is 26:3 [b]Is 11:10; Hos 2:18-23; Zech 2:5
19 [a]Is 28:2 [b]Is 10:18 [c]Is 24:10
20 [1]Lit *send out the foot of the ox* [a]Eccl 11:1; Is 30:23
33:1 [a]Is 10:6 [b]Is 24:16 [c]Is 10:12; Hab 2:8 [d]Jer 25:12-14; Matt 7:2
2 [1]Some versions read *our* [2]Lit *arm* [a]Is 30:18 [b]Is 25:9 [c]Is 40:10 [d]Is 37:3
3 [a]Is 17:13 [b]Is 10:33; Jer 25:30
5 [a]Ps 97:9 [b]Is 1:26
6 [1]Or *faithfulness* [a]Is 33:20 [b]Is 45:17 [c]Is 11:9 [d]2 Kin 18:7; Ps 112:1-3; Is 11:3; Matt 6:33
7 [1]Lit *the outside* [2]Lit *messengers* [a]2 Kin 18:18
8 [1]Lit *he who passes along the way* [a]Is 35:8 [b]Is 24:5
9 [1]Lit *shake off* [a]Is 3:26 [b]Is 2:13 [c]Is 35:2
10 [a]Ps 12:5; Is 2:19
11 [1]Lit *dry grass* [2]So one ancient version; M.T. reads *Your breath will* [a]Ps 7:14; Is 26:18; James 1:15 [b]Is 1:31
12 [a]2 Sam 23:6; Is 10:17
13 [1]Lit *know* [a]Ps 48:10; Is 49:1
14 [1]Lit *everlasting* [a]Is 1:28 [b]Is 32:11 [c]Is 30:27; Heb 12:29 [d]Is 9:18
15 [1]Lit *gain of extortioners* [a]Ps 15:2; Is 58:6-11

And shakes his hands so that
they hold no bribe;
He who stops his ears from
hearing about bloodshed
And [b]shuts his eyes from
looking upon evil;
16 He will dwell on the heights,
[a]His refuge will be the
[1]impregnable rock;
[b]His bread will be given *him,*
His water will be sure.

17 ¶ Your eyes will see [a]the King
in His beauty;
They will behold [b]a far-distant
land.
18 Your heart will meditate on
[a]terror:
"Where is [b]he who counts?
Where is he who weighs?
Where is he who counts the
towers?"
19 You will no longer see a fierce
people,
A people of [1a]unintelligible
speech [2]which no one
comprehends,
Of a stammering tongue [3]which
no one understands.
20 [a]Look upon Zion, the city of our
appointed feasts;
Your eyes will see Jerusalem, an
[b]undisturbed habitation,
[c]A tent which will not be
folded;
Its stakes will never be
pulled up,
Nor any of its cords be torn
apart.
21 But there the majestic *One,* the
LORD, will be for us
A place of [a]rivers *and* wide
canals
On which no boat with oars
will go,
And on which no mighty ship
will pass—
22 For the LORD is our [a]judge,
The LORD is [b]our lawgiver,
The LORD is [c]our king;
[d]He will save us—
23 Your tackle hangs slack;
It cannot hold the base of its
mast firmly,
Nor spread out the sail.
Then the [a]prey of an abundant
spoil will be divided;
[b]The lame will take the plunder.
24 And no resident will say, "I am
[a]sick";
The people who dwell [1]there
will be [b]forgiven *their*
iniquity.

God's Wrath against Nations

34 Draw near, [a]O nations, to hear;
and listen, O peoples!
[b]Let the earth and [1]all it
contains hear, and the world
and all that springs from it.
2 For the LORD'S [a]indignation is
against all the nations,
And *His* wrath against all their
armies;
He has [1b]utterly destroyed
them,
He has given them over to
[c]slaughter.
3 So their slain will be [a]thrown
out,
And their corpses [1]will give off
their [b]stench,
And the mountains will [2]be
drenched with their [c]blood.
4 And [a]all the host of heaven will
[1]wear away,
And the [b]sky will be rolled up
like a scroll;
All their hosts will also wither
away
As a leaf withers from the vine,
Or as *one* withers from the fig
tree.
5 For [a]My sword is satiated in
heaven,
Behold it shall descend for
judgment upon [b]Edom
And upon the people whom I
have [c]devoted to
destruction.
6 The sword of the LORD is filled
with blood,
It is [1]sated with fat, with the
blood of lambs and goats,
With the fat of the kidneys of
rams.
For the LORD has a sacrifice in
[a]Bozrah
And a great slaughter in the land
of [b]Edom.
7 [a]Wild oxen will also [1]fall with
them
And [b]young bulls with strong
ones;
Thus their land will be [c]soaked
with blood,
And their dust [2]become greasy
with fat.
8 For the LORD has a day of
[a]vengeance,
A year of recompense for the
[1]cause of Zion.
9 [1]Its streams will be turned into
pitch,
And its loose earth into
[a]brimstone,

15 [b]Ps 119:37
16 [1]Lit *strong-hold of rock* [a]Is 25:4 [b]Is 49:10
17 [a]Is 6:5; 24:23; 33:21,22 [b]Is 26:15
18 [a]Is 17:14 [b]1 Cor 1:20
19 [1]Lit *deepness of lip* [2]Lit *from hearing* [3]Lit *there is no understanding* [a]Deut 28:49,50; Is 28:11; Jer 5:15
20 [a]Ps 48:12 [b]Ps 46:5; 125:1,2; Is 32:18 [c]Is 54:2
21 [a]Is 41:18; 43:19,20; 48:18; 66:12
22 [a]Is 2:4; 11:4; 16:5; 51:5 [b]Is 1:10; 51:4,7; James 4:12 [c]Ps 89:18; Is 33:17; Zech 9:9 [d]Is 25:9; 35:4; 49:25,26; 60:16
23 [a]2 Kin 7:16 [b]2 Kin 7:8; Is 35:6
24 [1]Lit *in it* [a]Is 30:26; 58:8; Jer 30:17 [b]Is 40:2; 44:22; Jer 50:20; Mic 7:18,19; 1 John 1:7-9
34:1 [1]Lit *its fullness* [a]Ps 49:1; Is 41:1; 43:9 [b]Deut 32:1; Is 1:2
2 [1]Lit *put under the ban* [a]Is 26:20 [b]Is 13:5; 24:1 [c]Is 30:25; 63:6; 65:12
3 [1]Lit *their stench will go up* [2]Lit *dissolve* [a]Is 14:19 [b]Joel 2:20; Amos 4:10 [c]Ezek 14:19; 35:6; 38:22
4 [1]Lit *rot* [a]Is 13:13; 51:6; Ezek 32:7,8; Joel 2:31; Matt 24:29; 2 Pet 3:10 [b]Rev 6:12-14
5 [a]Deut 32:41,42; Jer 46:10; Ezek 21:3-5 [b]Is 63:1; Jer 49:7,8,20; Ezek 25:12-14; 35:1-15; Amos 1:11,12; Obad 1-14; Mal 1:4 [c]Is 24:6; 43:28
6 [1]Lit *made fat* [a]Is 63:1; Jer 49:13 [b]Is 63:1
7 [1]Lit *go down* [2]Lit *made fat* [a]Num 23:22; Ps 22:21 [b]Ps 68:30; Jer 50:27 [c]Is 63:6
8 [1]Or *controversy* [a]Is 13:6; 35:4; 47:3; 61:2; 63:4
9 [1]I.e. Edom's [a]Deut 29:23; Ps 11:6; Is 30:33

And its land will become burning
pitch.
10 It will [a]not be quenched night
or day;
Its [b]smoke will go up forever.
From [c]generation to generation
it will be desolate;
[d]None will pass through it
forever and ever.
11 But [1a]pelican and hedgehog will
possess it,
And [2]owl and raven will dwell
in it;
And He will stretch over it the
[b]line of [3]desolation
And the [4]plumb line of
emptiness.
12 Its nobles—there is [a]no one
there
Whom they may proclaim king—
And all its princes will be
[b]nothing.
13 Thorns will come up in its
[a]fortified towers,
Nettles and thistles in its fortified
cities;
It will also be a haunt of [b]jackals
And an abode of ostriches.
14 The desert [a]creatures will meet
with the [1]wolves,
The [2a]hairy goat also will cry to
its kind;
Yes, the [3]night monster will
settle there
And will find herself a resting
place.
15 The tree snake will make its nest
and lay *eggs* there,
And it will hatch and gather
them under its [1]protection.
Yes, [a]the [2]hawks will be
gathered there,
Every one with its kind.

16 ¶ Seek from the [a]book of the LORD,
and read:
Not one of these will be missing;
None will lack its mate.
For [1b]His mouth has
commanded,
And His Spirit has gathered
them.
17 He has cast the [a]lot for them,
And His hand has divided it to
them by [b]line.
They shall possess it forever;
From [c]generation to generation
they will dwell in it.

Zion's Happy Future

35 The [a]wilderness and the desert
will be glad,
And the [1b]Arabah will rejoice
and blossom;
Like the crocus
2 It will [a]blossom profusely
And [b]rejoice with rejoicing and
shout of joy.
The [c]glory of Lebanon will be
given to it,
The majesty of [d]Carmel and
Sharon.
They will see the [e]glory of the
LORD,
The majesty of our God.
3 [a]Encourage the [1]exhausted, and
strengthen the [2]feeble.
4 Say to those with [a]anxious
heart,
"Take courage, fear not.
Behold, your God will come *with*
[b]vengeance;
The [c]recompense of God will
come,
But He will [d]save you."
5 Then the [a]eyes of the blind will
be opened
And the ears of the deaf will be
unstopped.
6 Then the [a]lame will leap like a
deer,
And the [b]tongue of the mute
will shout for joy.
For waters will break forth in the
[c]wilderness
And streams in the [1]Arabah.
7 The [1]scorched land will become
a pool
And the thirsty ground [a]springs
of water;
In the [b]haunt of jackals, its
resting place,
Grass *becomes* reeds and rushes.
8 [a]A highway will be there, [b]a
roadway,
And it will be called the
Highway of [c]Holiness.
The unclean will not travel on it,
But it *will* be for him who walks
that way,
And [d]fools will not wander
on it.
9 No [a]lion will be there,
Nor will any vicious beast go up
on it;
[1]These will not be found there.
But [b]the redeemed will walk
there,
10 And [a]the ransomed of the LORD
will return
And come with joyful shouting to
Zion,
With everlasting joy upon their
heads.
They will [1]find gladness and joy,
And [b]sorrow and sighing will
flee away.

10 [a]Is 1:31; 66:24 [b]Rev 14:11; 19:3 [c]Is 13:20-22; 24:1; 34:10-15; Mal 1:3,4 [d]Ezek 29:11

11 [1]Or *owl* or *jackdaw* [2]Or *great horned owl* [3]Or *formlessness* [4]Lit *stones of void* [a]Zeph 2:14 [b]2 Kin 21:13; Is 24:10; Lam 2:8

12 [a]Jer 27:20; 39:6 [b]Is 41:11, 12

13 [a]Is 13:22; 25:2; 32:13 [b]Ps 44:19; Jer 9:11; 10:22

14 [1]Or *howling creatures* [2]Or *demon* [3]Heb *Lilith* [a]Is 13:21

15 [1]Lit *shade* [2]Or *kites* [a]Deut 14:13

16 [1]So DSS; M.T. *My* [a]Is 30:8 [b]Is 1:20; 40:5; 58:14

17 [a]Is 17:13,14; Jer 13:25 [b]Is 34:11 [c]Is 34:10

35:1 [1]Or *desert* [a]Is 6:11; 7:21-25; 27:10; 41:18; 55:12,13 [b]Is 41:19; 51:3

2 [a]Is 27:6; 32:15 [b]Is 25:9; 35:10; 55:12,13; 66:10,14 [c]Is 60:13 [d]Song 7:5 [e]Is 25:9

3 [1]Lit *slack hands* [2]Lit *tottering knees* [a]Job 4:3,4; Heb 12:12

4 [a]Is 32:4 [b]Is 1:24; 47:3; 61:2; 63:4 [c]Is 34:8; 59:18 [d]Ps 145:19; Is 33:22; 35:4

5 [a]Is 29:18; 32:3,4; 42:7,16; 50:4; Matt 11:5; John 9:6,7

6 [1]Or *desert* [a]Matt 15:30; John 5:8,9; Acts 3:8 [b]Matt 9:32; Luke 11:14 [c]Is 35:1; 41:18; 43:19; 49:10; 51:3; John 7:38

7 [1]Or *mirage* [a]Is 49:10 [b]Is 13:22; 34:13

8 [a]Is 11:16; 19:23; 40:3; 49:11; 62:10 [b]Is 30:21; 51:10 [c]Is 4:3; 52:1; Matt 7:13,14; 1 Pet 1:15,16 [d]Is 33:8

9 [1]Lit *It* [a]Is 5:29; 30:6 [b]Is 51:10; 62:12; 63:4

10 [1]Lit *overtake* [a]Is 1:27; 51:11 [b]Is 25:8; 30:19; 65:19; Rev 7:17; 21:4

Sennacherib Invades Judah

36 [a]Now in the fourteenth year of
King Hezekiah, [b]Sennacherib
king of Assyria came up against all the
fortified cities of Judah and seized them.
2 And the [a]king of Assyria sent Rabshakeh from Lachish to Jerusalem to King
Hezekiah with a large army. And he stood
by the [b]conduit of the upper pool on the
highway of the [1]fuller's field.
3 Then [a]Eliakim the son of Hilkiah,
who was over the household, and [b]Sheb-
na the scribe, and Joah the son of Asaph,
the recorder, came out to him.
4 ¶ Then [a]Rabshakeh said to them,
"Say now to Hezekiah, 'Thus says the
great king, the king of Assyria, "What is
this confidence that you [1]have?
5 "I say, 'Your counsel and strength for
the war are only [1]empty words.' Now on
whom do you rely, that [a]you have rebelled against me?
6 "Behold, you rely on the [a]staff of
this crushed reed, *even* on Egypt, on
which if a man leans, it will go into his
[1]hand and pierce it. [b]So is Pharaoh king
of Egypt to all who rely on him.
7 "But if you say to me, 'We trust in
the LORD our God,' is it not He [a]whose
high places and whose altars Hezekiah
has taken away and has said to Judah and
to Jerusalem, 'You shall worship before
this altar'?
8 "Now therefore, [1]come make a bargain with my master the king of Assyria,
and I will give you two thousand horses,
if you are able on your part to set riders
on them.
9 "How then can you [1]repulse one
[2]official of the least of my master's servants and [3a]rely on Egypt for chariots
and for horsemen?
10 "Have I now come up [1]without the
LORD'S approval against this land to destroy it? [a]The LORD said to me, 'Go up
against this land and destroy it.' " ' "
11 ¶ Then Eliakim and Shebna and
Joah said to Rabshakeh, "Speak now to
your servants in [a]Aramaic, for we [1]un-
derstand *it;* and do not speak with us in
[2b]Judean in the hearing of the people
who are on the wall."
12 But Rabshakeh said, "Has my master sent me only to your master and to
you to speak these words, *and* not to the
men who sit on the wall, *doomed* to eat
their own dung and drink their own
urine with you?"
13 ¶ Then Rabshakeh stood and
[a]cried with a loud voice in Judean and
said, "Hear the words of the great king,
the king of Assyria.
14 "Thus says the king, 'Do not let Hezekiah [a]deceive you, for he will not be
able to deliver you;
15 nor let Hezekiah make you [a]trust
in the LORD, saying, "The LORD will surely deliver us, this city will not be given
into the hand of the king of Assyria."
16 'Do not listen to Hezekiah,' for thus
says the king of Assyria, '[1]Make your
peace with me and come out to me, and
eat each of his [a]vine and each of his fig
tree and drink each of the [b]waters of his
own cistern,
17 until I come and take you away to
a land like your own land, a land of grain
and new wine, a land of bread and vineyards.
18 '*Beware* that Hezekiah does not mislead you, saying, "[a]The LORD will deliver
us." Has any one of the gods of the nations delivered his land from the hand of
the king of Assyria?
19 'Where are the gods of [a]Hamath
and Arpad? Where are the gods of [a]Seph-
arvaim? And when have they [b]delivered
Samaria from my hand?
20 'Who among all the [a]gods of these
lands have delivered their land from my
hand, that the [b]LORD would deliver Jerusalem from my hand?' "
21 ¶ But they were silent and [a]an-
swered him not a word; for the king's
commandment was, "Do not answer
him."
22 Then [a]Eliakim the son of Hilkiah,
who was over the household, and [b]Sheb-
na the scribe and Joah the son of Asaph,
the recorder, came to Hezekiah with
their clothes torn and told him the words
of Rabshakeh.

Hezekiah Seeks Isaiah's Help

37 And [a]when King Hezekiah heard
it, he tore his clothes, covered
himself with sackcloth and entered the
house of the LORD.
2 Then he sent [a]Eliakim who was
over the household with [b]Shebna the
scribe and the elders of the priests, covered with sackcloth, to [c]Isaiah the
prophet, the son of Amoz.
3 They said to him, "Thus says Hezekiah, 'This day is a [a]day of distress, rebuke and rejection; for [b]children have
come to birth, and there is no strength to
[1]deliver.
4 'Perhaps the LORD your God will
hear the words of Rabshakeh, whom his
master the king of Assyria has sent to
[a]reproach the living God, and will rebuke the words which the LORD your God
has heard. Therefore, offer a prayer for
[b]the remnant that is left.' "
5 ¶ So the servants of King Hezekiah
came to Isaiah.

36:1 [a]2 Kin 18:13 [b]2 Chr 32:1
2 [1]I.e. launderer's [a]2 Kin 18:17-20:11; 2 Chr 32:9-24; Is 36:2-38:8 [b]Is 7:3
3 [a]Is 22:20 [b]Is 22:15
4 [1]Lit *trust* [a]2 Kin 18:19
5 [1]Lit *words of lips* [a]2 Kin 18:7
6 [1]Lit *palm* [a]Ezek 29:6,7 [b]Ps 146:3; Is 30:3,5, 7
7 [a]Deut 12:2-5; 2 Kin 18:4,5
8 [1]Lit *please exchange pledges*
9 [1]Lit *turn away the face of* [2]Or *governor* [3]Lit *rely on for yourself* [a]Is 20:5; 30:2-5,7; 31:3
10 [1]Lit *without the LORD* [a]1 Kin 13:18; 22:6,12
11 [1]Lit *hear* [2]I.e. Hebrew [a]Ezra 4:7; Dan 2:4 [b]Is 36:13
13 [a]2 Chr 32:18
14 [a]Is 37:10
15 [a]Is 36:18,20; 37:10,11
16 [1]Lit *Make with me a blessing* [a]1 Kin 4:25; Mic 4:4; Zech 3:10 [b]Prov 5:15
18 [a]Is 36:15
19 [a]Is 10:9-11; 37:11-13; Jer 49:23 [b]2 Kin 17:6
20 [a]1 Kin 20:23,28 [b]Is 36:15
21 [a]Prov 9:7,8; 26:4
22 [a]Is 22:20; 36:3 [b]Is 22:15
37:1 [a]2 Kin 19:1-37; Is 37:1-38
2 [a]Is 22:20 [b]Is 22:15 [c]Is 1:1; 20:2
3 [1]Lit *give birth* [a]Is 22:5; 26:16; 33:2 [b]Is 26:17, 18; 66:9; Hos 13:13
4 [a]Is 36:13-15, 18,20 [b]Is 1:9; 10:20-22; 37:31, 32; 46:3

6 Isaiah said to them, "Thus you shall say to your master, 'Thus says the LORD, "[a]Do not be afraid because of the words that you have heard, with which the servants of the king of Assyria have blasphemed Me.

7 "Behold, I will put a spirit in him so that he will [a]hear a rumor and [b]return to his own land. And I will make him fall by the sword in his own land." ' "

8 ¶ Then Rabshakeh returned and found the king of Assyria fighting against [a]Libnah, for he had heard that [1]the king had left [b]Lachish.

9 When he [a]heard *them* say concerning Tirhakah king of [1b]Cush, "He has come out to fight against you," and when he heard *it* he sent messengers to Hezekiah, saying,

10 "Thus you shall say to Hezekiah king of [1]Judah, '[a]Do not let your God in whom you trust deceive you, saying, "Jerusalem will not be given into the hand of the king of Assyria."

11 '[a]Behold, you have heard what the kings of Assyria have done to all the lands, destroying them completely. So will you be [1]spared?

12 'Did the gods of [1]those nations which my fathers have destroyed deliver them, *even* [a]Gozan and [b]Haran and Rezeph and the sons of Eden who *were* in Telassar?

13 'Where is the king of Hamath, the king of Arpad, the king of the city of Sepharvaim, *and of* Hena and Ivvah?' "

Hezekiah's Prayer in the Temple

14 ¶ Then Hezekiah took the [1]letter from the hand of the messengers and read it, and he went up to the house of the LORD and [2]spread it out before the LORD.

15 Hezekiah prayed to the LORD saying,

16 "O LORD of hosts, the God of Israel, [a]who is enthroned *above* the cherubim, You are the [b]God, You alone, of all the kingdoms of the earth. [c]You have made heaven and earth.

17 "[a]Incline Your ear, O LORD, and hear; open Your eyes, O LORD, and see; and [b]listen to all the words of Sennacherib, who sent *them* to [c]reproach the living God.

18 "Truly, O LORD, the [a]kings of Assyria have devastated all the countries and their lands,

19 and have cast their gods into the fire, for they were not gods but the [a]work of men's hands, wood and stone. So they have [b]destroyed them.

20 "Now, O LORD our God, [a]deliver us from his hand that [b]all the kingdoms of the earth may know that You alone, LORD, [1]are God."

God Answers through Isaiah

21 ¶ Then [a]Isaiah the son of Amoz sent *word* to Hezekiah, saying, "Thus says the LORD, the God of Israel, 'Because you have prayed to Me about Sennacherib king of Assyria,

22 this is the word that the LORD has spoken against him:

"She has despised you and
mocked you,
The [a]virgin [b]daughter of Zion;
She has [c]shaken *her* head
behind you,
The daughter of Jerusalem!

23 "Whom have you [a]reproached
and blasphemed?
And against whom have you
raised *your* voice
And [1]haughtily [b]lifted up your
eyes?
Against the [c]Holy One of Israel!

24 "Through your servants you have
reproached the Lord,
And you have said, 'With my
many chariots I came up to
the heights of the
mountains,
To the remotest parts of
[a]Lebanon;
And I cut down its tall [b]cedars
and its choice cypresses.
And I will go to its [1]highest
peak, its thickest [c]forest.

25 'I dug *wells* and drank waters,
And [a]with the sole of my feet I
dried up
All the rivers of [1]Egypt.'

26 "[a]Have you not heard?
Long ago I did it,
From ancient times I
[b]planned it.
Now [c]I have brought it to pass,
That [d]you should turn fortified
cities into [e]ruinous heaps.

27 "Therefore their inhabitants were
short of strength,
They were dismayed and put to
shame;
They were *as* the [a]vegetation of
the field and *as* the green
herb,
As [b]grass on the housetops [1]is
scorched before it is
grown up.

28 "But I [a]know your sitting down
And your going out and your
coming in
And your raging against Me.

29 "Because of your raging
against Me

6 [a]Is 7:4; 35:4
7 [a]Is 37:9 [b]Is 37:37,38
8 [1]Lit *he* [a]Num 33:20; Josh 10:29 [b]Josh 10:31,32
9 [1]Or *Ethiopia* [a]Is 37:7 [b]Is 18:1; 20:5
10 [1]Lit *Judah, saying* [a]Is 36:15
11 [1]Lit *delivered* [a]Is 10:9-11; 36:18-20
12 [1]Lit *the* [a]2 Kin 17:6; 18:11 [b]Gen 11:31; 12:1-4; Acts 7:2
14 [1]Lit *letters* [2]Lit *Hezekiah spread*
16 [a]Ex 25:22; 1 Sam 4:4; Ps 80:1; 99:1 [b]Deut 10:17; Ps 86:10; 136:2,3 [c]Is 42:5; 45:12; Jer 10:12
17 [a]2 Chr 6:40; Ps 17:6; Dan 9:18 [b]Ps 74:22 [c]Is 37:4
18 [a]2 Kin 15:29; 16:9; 17:6,24; 1 Chr 5:26
19 [a]Is 2:8; 17:8; 41:24,29 [b]Is 26:14
20 [1]So DSS and 2 Kin 19:19; M.T. omits *God* [a]Is 25:9; 33:22; 35:4 [b]1 Kin 18:36,37; Ps 46:10; Is 37:16; Ezek 36:23
21 [a]Is 37:2
22 [a]Jer 14:17; Lam 2:13 [b]Ps 9:14; Zeph 3:14; Zech 2:10 [c]Job 16:4
23 [1]Lit *on high* [a]Is 37:4 [b]Is 2:11; 5:15,21 [c]Ezek 39:7; Hab 1:12
24 [1]Lit *farthest height* [a]Is 10:33, 34 [b]Is 14:8 [c]Is 10:18
25 [1]Or *the besieged place* [a]Deut 11:10; 1 Kin 20:10
26 [a]Is 40:21,28 [b]Acts 2:23; 4:27, 28; 1 Pet 2:8 [c]Is 46:11 [d]Is 10:6 [e]Is 17:1; 25:2
27 [1]So DSS and 2 Kin 19:26; M.T. as *a plowed field* [a]Is 40:7 [b]Ps 129:6
28 [a]Ps 139:1

And because your [1a]arrogance
has come up to My ears,
Therefore I will put My [b]hook
in your nose
And My [c]bridle in your lips,
And I will turn you back [d]by the
way which you came.
30 ¶ "Then this shall be the sign for
you: [1]you will eat this year what [a]grows
of itself, in the second year what springs
from the same, and in the third year sow,
reap, plant vineyards and eat their fruit.
31 "The [a]surviving [b]remnant of the
house of Judah will again [c]take root
downward and bear fruit upward.
32 "For out of Jerusalem will go forth a
[a]remnant and out of Mount Zion [1]survi-
vors. The [b]zeal of the LORD of hosts will
perform this." '
33 ¶ "Therefore, thus says the LORD
concerning the king of Assyria, 'He will
not come to this city or shoot an arrow
there; and he will not come before it with
a shield, or throw up a [a]siege ramp
against it.
34 '[a]By the way that he came, by the
same he will return, and he will not come
to this city,' declares the LORD.
35 'For I will [a]defend this city to save
it [b]for My own sake and for My servant
David's sake.' "

Assyrians Destroyed

36 ¶ Then the [a]angel of the LORD
went out and struck 185,000 in the camp
of the Assyrians; and when [1]men arose
early in the morning, behold, all of these
were [2]dead.
37 So Sennacherib king of Assyria departed and [1]returned *home* and lived at
[a]Nineveh.
38 It came about as he was worshiping
in the house of Nisroch his god, that
Adrammelech and Sharezer his sons
killed him with the sword; and they escaped into the land of [a]Ararat. And
[b]Esarhaddon his son became king in his
place.

Hezekiah Healed

38 [a]In those days Hezekiah became
[1]mortally ill. And [b]Isaiah the
prophet the son of Amoz came to him and
said to him, "Thus says the LORD, '[c]Set
your house in order, for you shall die and
not live.' "
2 Then Hezekiah turned his face to
the wall and prayed to the LORD,
3 and said, "[a]Remember now,
O LORD, I beseech You, how I have
[b]walked before You in truth and with a
[c]whole heart, and [d]have done what is
good in Your sight." And Hezekiah
[e]wept [1]bitterly.

29 [1]Lit *complacency* [a]Is 10:12 [b]Ezek 29:4; 38:4 [c]Is 30:28 [d]Is 37:34
30 [1]Lit *eating* [a]Lev 25:5,11
31 [a]Is 4:2; 10:20 [b]Is 37:4 [c]Is 27:6
32 [1]Lit *those who escape* [a]Is 37:4 [b]2 Kin 19:31; Is 9:7; 59:17; Joel 2:18; Zech 1:14
33 [a]Jer 6:6; 32:24
34 [a]Is 37:29
35 [a]2 Kin 20:6; Is 31:5; 38:6 [b]Is 43:25; 48:9,11
36 [1]Lit *they* [2]Lit *dead bodies* [a]2 Kin 19:35; Is 10:12,33,34
37 [1]Lit *went and returned* [a]Gen 10:11; Jon 1:2; 3:3; 4:11; Zeph 2:13
38 [a]Gen 8:4; Jer 51:27 [b]Ezra 4:2
38:1 [1]Lit *sick to the point of death* [a]2 Kin 20:1-6,9-11; 2 Chr 32:24; Is 38:1-8 [b]Is 1:1; 37:2 [c]2 Sam 17:23
3 [1]Lit *great weeping* [a]Neh 13:14 [b]2 Kin 18:5,6; Ps 26:3 [c]1 Chr 28:9; 29:19 [d]Deut 6:18 [e]Ps 6:6-8
5 [1]Lit *days* [a]2 Kin 18:2,13
6 [a]Is 31:5; 37:35
7 [a]Judg 6:17,21, 36-40; Is 7:11, 14; 37:30
8 [a]2 Kin 20:9-11 [b]Josh 10:12-14
9 [1]Lit *he lived after his illness*
10 [1]Lit *days* [a]Ps 102:24 [b]Ps 107:18 [c]Job 17:11,15; 2 Cor 1:9
11 [a]Ps 27:13; 116:9
12 [a]2 Cor 5:1,4; 2 Pet 1:13,14 [b]Job 7:6 [c]Heb 1:12 [d]Job 6:9 [e]Job 4:20; Ps 73:14
13 [a]Job 10:16 [b]Ps 51:8; Dan 6:24 [c]Ps 32:4
14 [a]Job 30:29; Ps 102:6 [b]Is 59:11; Ezek 7:16; Nah 2:7 [c]Ps 119:123 [d]Job 17:3; Ps 119:122
15 [1]Targum and DSS read *And what shall I say for He* [a]Ps 39:9 [b]1 Kin 21:27 [c]Job 7:11; 10:1; Is 38:17
16 [a]Ps 119:71, 75

4 ¶ Then the word of the LORD came
to Isaiah, saying,
5 "Go and say to Hezekiah, 'Thus says
the LORD, the God of your father David, "I
have heard your prayer, I have seen your
tears; behold, I will add [a]fifteen years to
your [1]life.
6 "I will [a]deliver you and this city
from the hand of the king of Assyria; and
I will defend this city." '
7 ¶ "This shall be the [a]sign to you
from the LORD, that the LORD will do this
thing that He has spoken:
8 "Behold, I will [a]cause the shadow
on the stairway, which has gone down
with the sun on the stairway of Ahaz, to
go back ten steps." So the [b]sun's *shadow*
went back ten steps on the stairway on
which it had gone down.
9 ¶ A writing of Hezekiah king of Judah after his illness and [1]recovery:
10 I said, "[a]In the middle of my
[1]life
I am to enter the [b]gates of
Sheol;
I am to be [c]deprived of the rest
of my years."
11 I said, "I will not see the LORD,
The LORD [a]in the land of the
living;
I will look on man no more
among the inhabitants of the
world.
12 "Like a shepherd's [a]tent my
dwelling is pulled up and
removed from me;
As a [b]weaver I [c]rolled up my
life.
He [d]cuts me off from the loom;
From [e]day until night You make
an end of me.
13 "I composed *my soul* until
morning.
[a]Like a lion—so He [b]breaks all
my bones,
From [c]day until night You make
an end of me.
14 "[a]Like a swallow, *like* a crane, so
I twitter;
I [b]moan like a dove;
My [c]eyes look wistfully to the
heights;
O Lord, I am oppressed, be my
[d]security.
15 ¶ "[a]What shall I say?
[1]For He has spoken to me, and
He Himself has done it;
I will [b]wander about all my
years because of the
[c]bitterness of my soul.
16 "O Lord, [a]by *these* things *men*
live,

And in all these is the life of my
spirit;
[1][b]O restore me to health and
[c]let me live!
17 "Lo, for *my own* welfare I had
great bitterness;
It is You who has [1][a]kept my
soul from the pit of
[2]nothingness,
For You have [b]cast all my sins
behind Your back.
18 "For [a]Sheol cannot thank You,
Death cannot praise You;
Those who go down [b]to the pit
cannot hope for Your
faithfulness.
19 "It is the [a]living who give thanks
to You, as I do today;
A [b]father tells his sons about
Your faithfulness.
20 "The LORD will surely save me;
So we will [a]play my songs on
stringed instruments
[b]All *the* days of our life [c]at the
house of the LORD."

21 ¶ Now [a]Isaiah had said, "Let them take a cake of figs and apply it to the boil, that he may recover."

22 Then Hezekiah had said, "What is the [a]sign that I shall go up to the house of the LORD?"

Hezekiah Shows His Treasures

39 [a]At that time Merodach-baladan son of Baladan, king of Babylon, sent letters and a present to Hezekiah, for he heard that he had been sick and had recovered.

2 Hezekiah [1]was [a]pleased, and showed them *all* his treasure house, the [b]silver and the gold and the spices and the precious oil and his whole armory and all that was found in his treasuries. There was nothing in his house nor in all his dominion that Hezekiah did not show them.

3 Then Isaiah the [a]prophet came to King Hezekiah and said to him, "What did these men say, and from where have they come to you?" And Hezekiah said, "They have come to me from a far [b]country, from Babylon."

4 He said, "What have they seen in your house?" So Hezekiah [1]answered, "They have seen all that is in my house; there is nothing among my treasures that I have not shown them."

5 ¶ Then Isaiah said to Hezekiah, "Hear the [a]word of the LORD of hosts,

6 'Behold, the days are coming when [a]all that is in your house and all that your fathers have laid up in store to this day will be carried to Babylon; nothing will be left,' says the LORD.

7 'And *some* of your sons who will issue from you, whom you will beget, [a]will be taken away, and [b]they will become officials in the palace of the king of Babylon.'"

8 [a]Then Hezekiah said to Isaiah, "The word of the LORD which you have spoken is good." For he [1]thought, "For there will be peace and truth [b]in my days."

The Greatness of God

40 "[a]Comfort, O comfort My
people," says your God.
2 "[a]Speak [1]kindly to Jerusalem;
And call out to her, that her
[2][b]warfare has ended,
That her [3][c]iniquity has been
removed,
That she has received of the
LORD'S hand
[d]Double for all her sins."

3 ¶ [a]A voice [1]is calling,
"[b]Clear the way for the LORD in
the wilderness;
Make smooth in the desert a
highway for our God.
4 "Let every valley be lifted up,
And every mountain and hill be
made low;
And let the rough ground
become a plain,
And the rugged terrain a broad
valley;
5 [1]Then the [a]glory of the LORD
will be revealed,
And [b]all flesh will see *it*
together;
For the [c]mouth of the LORD has
spoken."
6 A voice says, "Call out."
Then [1]he answered, "What shall
I call out?"
[a]All flesh is grass, and all its
[2]loveliness is like the flower
of the field.
7 The [a]grass withers, the flower
fades,
[1]When the [b]breath of the LORD
blows upon it;
Surely the people are grass.
8 The grass withers, the flower
fades,
But [a]the word of our God stands
forever.

9 ¶ Get yourself up on a [a]high
mountain,
O Zion, bearer of [b]good news,
Lift up your voice mightily,
O Jerusalem, bearer of good
news;
Lift *it* up, do not fear.
Say to the [c]cities of Judah,

16 [1]Lit *You will* [b]Ps 39:13 [c]Ps 119:25
17 [1]So some versions; Heb *loved* [2]Or *destruction* [a]Ps 30:3; 86:13; Jon 2:6 [b]Is 43:25; Jer 31:34; Mic 7:19
18 [a]Ps 6:5; 30:9; 88:11; Eccl 9:10 [b]Num 16:33; Ps 28:1
19 [a]Ps 118:17; 119:175 [b]Deut 6:7; 11:19; Ps 78:5-7
20 [a]Ps 33:1-3; 68:24-26 [b]Ps 104:33; 116:2; 146:2 [c]Ps 116:17-19
21 [a]2 Kin 20:7, 8
22 [a]Is 38:7
39:1 [a]2 Kin 20:12-19; 2 Chr 32:31; Is 39:1-8
2 [1]Lit *rejoiced over them* [a]2 Chr 32:25,31; Job 31:25 [b]2 Kin 18:15,16
3 [a]2 Sam 12:1; 2 Chr 16:7 [b]Deut 28:49; Jer 5:15
4 [1]Lit *said*
5 [a]1 Sam 13:13, 14; 15:16
6 [a]2 Kin 24:13; 25:13-15; Jer 20:5
7 [a]2 Kin 24:10-16; 2 Chr 36:10 [b]Dan 1:1-7
8 [1]Lit *said* [a]2 Chr 32:26 [b]2 Chr 34:28
40:1 [a]Is 12:1; 49:13; 51:3,12; 52:9; 61:2; 66:13; Jer 31:10-14; Zeph 3:14-17; 2 Cor 1:4
2 [1]Lit *to the heart of* [2]Or *hard service* [3]Or *penalty of iniquity accepted as paid off* [a]Is 35:4; Zech 1:13 [b]Is 41:11-13; 49:25; 54:15,17 [c]Is 33:24; 53:5,6,11 [d]Jer 16:18; Zech 9:12; Rev 18:6
3 [1]Or *of one calling out* [a]Matt 3:3; Mark 1:3; Luke 3:4-6; John 1:23 [b]Mal 3:1; 4:5,6
5 [1]Or *In order that the* [a]Is 6:3; Hab 2:14 [b]Is 52:10; Joel 2:28 [c]Is 1:20; 34:16; 58:14
6 [1]Another reading is *I said* [2]Or *constancy* [a]Job 14:2; Ps 102:11; 103:15; 1 Pet 1:24,25
7 [1]Or *Because* [a]Ps 90:5,6; James 1:10,11 [b]Job 4:9; 41:21; Is 11:4; 40:24
8 [a]Is 55:11; 59:21; Matt 5:18
9 [a]Is 52:7 [b]Is 61:1 [c]Is 44:26

"[d]Here is your God!"
10 Behold, the Lord [1]GOD will
come [a]with might,
With His [b]arm ruling for Him.
Behold, His [c]reward is with Him
And His recompense before Him.
11 Like a shepherd He will [a]tend
His flock,
In His arm He will gather the
lambs
And carry *them* in His bosom;
He will gently lead the nursing
ewes.

12 ¶ Who has [a]measured the
[1]waters in the hollow of His
hand,
And marked off the heavens by
the [2]span,
And [3]calculated the dust of the
earth by the measure,
And weighed the mountains in a
balance
And the hills in a pair of scales?
13 [a]Who has [1]directed the Spirit of
the LORD,
Or as His [b]counselor has
informed Him?
14 [a]With whom did He consult and
who [b]gave Him
understanding?
And *who* taught Him in the path
of justice and taught Him
knowledge
And informed Him of the way of
understanding?
15 Behold, the [a]nations are like a
drop from a bucket,
And are regarded as a speck of
[b]dust on the scales;
Behold, He lifts up the [1]islands
like fine dust.
16 Even Lebanon is not enough to
burn,
Nor its [a]beasts enough for a
burnt offering.
17 [a]All the nations are as nothing
before Him,
They are regarded by Him as less
than nothing and
[1]meaningless.

18 ¶ [a]To whom then will you liken
God?
Or what likeness will you
compare with Him?
19 *As for* the [1a]idol, a craftsman
casts it,
A goldsmith [b]plates it with gold,
And a silversmith *fashions* chains
of silver.
20 He who is too impoverished for
such an offering
Selects a [a]tree that does not rot;
He seeks out for himself a skillful
craftsman
To [1]prepare [2]an idol that [b]will
not totter.

21 ¶ [a]Do you not know? Have you
not heard?
Has it not been declared to you
from the beginning?
Have you not understood [b]from
the foundations of the earth?
22 It is He who [1]sits above the
[2a]circle of the earth,
And its inhabitants are like
[b]grasshoppers,
Who [c]stretches out the heavens
like a [d]curtain
And spreads them out like a
[e]tent to dwell in.
23 He *it is* who reduces [a]rulers to
nothing,
Who [b]makes the judges of the
earth [1]meaningless.
24 [1]Scarcely have they been
planted,
[1]Scarcely have they been sown,
[1]Scarcely has their stock taken
root in the earth,
But He merely blows on them,
and they wither,
And the [a]storm carries them
away like stubble.
25 "[a]To whom then will you
liken Me
That I would be *his* equal?" says
the Holy One.
26 [a]Lift up your eyes on high
And see [b]who has created these
stars,
The [c]One who leads forth their
host by number,
He calls them all by name;
Because of the [d]greatness of His
might and the [1]strength of
His power,
[e]Not one *of them* is missing.

27 ¶ [a]Why do you say, O Jacob,
and assert, O Israel,
"My way is [b]hidden from the
LORD,
And the [c]justice due me
[1]escapes the notice of [d]my
God"?
28 [a]Do you not know? Have you
not heard?
The [b]Everlasting God, the LORD,
the Creator of the ends of
the earth
Does not become weary or tired.
His understanding is
[c]inscrutable.
29 He gives strength to the [a]weary,
And to *him who* lacks might He
[b]increases power.

9 [d]Is 25:9; 35:2
10 [1]Heb *YHWH,* usually rendered LORD [a]Is 9:6,7 [b]Is 59:16,18 [c]Is 62:11; Rev 22:12
11 [a]Jer 31:10; Ezek 34:12-14, 23,31; Mic 5:4; John 10:11, 14-16
12 [1]DSS reads *waters of the sea* [2]Or *half cubit;* i.e. 9 in. [3]Lit *contained* or *comprehended* [a]Job 38:8-11; Ps 102:25,26; Is 48:13; Heb 1:10-12
13 [1]Or *measured, marked off* [a]Rom 11:34; 1 Cor 2:16 [b]Is 41:28
14 [a]Job 38:4 [b]Job 21:22; Col 2:3
15 [1]Or *coastlands* [a]Jer 10:10 [b]Is 17:13; 29:5
16 [a]Ps 50:9-11; Mic 6:6,7; Heb 10:5-9
17 [1]Or *void* [a]Is 29:7
18 [a]Ex 8:10; 15:11; 1 Sam 2:2; Is 40:25; 46:5; Mic 7:18; Acts 17:29
19 [1]Or *graven image* [a]Ps 115:4-8; Is 41:7; 44:10; Hab 2:18, 19 [b]Is 2:20; 30:22
20 [1]Or *set up* [2]Or a *graven image* [a]Is 44:14 [b]1 Sam 5:3,4; Is 41:7; 46:7
21 [a]Ps 19:1; 50:6; Is 37:26; Acts 14:17; Rom 1:19 [b]Is 48:13; 51:13
22 [1]Or *is enthroned* [2]Or *vault* [a]Job 22:14; Prov 8:27 [b]Num 13:33 [c]Job 9:8; Is 37:16; 42:5; 44:24 [d]Ps 104:2 [e]Job 36:29; Ps 18:11; 19:4
23 [1]Or *void* [a]Job 12:21; Ps 107:40; Is 34:12 [b]Is 5:21; Jer 25:18-27
24 [1]Or *Not even* [a]Is 17:13; 41:16
25 [a]Is 40:18
26 [1]So DSS and ancient versions; M.T. *strong* [a]Is 51:6 [b]Is 42:5; 48:12,13 [c]Ps 147:4 [d]Ps 89:11-13 [e]Is 34:16; 48:13
27 [1]Lit *passes by my God* [a]Is 49:4,14 [b]Is 54:8 [c]Job 27:2; 34:5; Luke 18:7,8 [d]Is 25:1
28 [a]Is 40:21 [b]Gen 21:33; Ps 90:2 [c]Ps 147:5; Rom 11:33
29 [a]Is 50:4; Jer 31:25 [b]Is 41:10

30 Though [a]youths grow weary and
tired,
And vigorous [b]young men
stumble badly,
31 Yet those who [1]wait for the
LORD
Will [a]gain new strength;
They will [2b]mount up *with*
[3]wings like eagles,
They will run and not get tired,
They will walk and not become
weary.

Israel Encouraged

41 "[a]Coastlands, listen to Me [b]in
silence,
And let the peoples [c]gain new
strength;
[d]Let them come forward, then
let them speak;
[e]Let us come together for
judgment.
2 "[a]Who has aroused one from the
east
Whom He [b]calls in
righteousness to His [1]feet?
He [c]delivers up nations
before him
And subdues kings.
He makes them like [d]dust with
his sword,
As the wind-driven [e]chaff with
his bow.
3 "He pursues them, passing on in
safety,
By a way he had not been
[1]traversing with his feet.
4 "[a]Who has performed and
accomplished *it,*
Calling forth the generations
from the beginning?
'[b]I, the LORD, am the first, and
with the last. [c]I am He.' "

5 ¶ The [a]coastlands have seen and
are afraid;
The [b]ends of the earth tremble;
They have drawn near and have
come.
6 Each one helps his neighbor
And says to his brother, "Be
strong!"
7 So the [a]craftsman encourages
the [b]smelter,
And he who smooths *metal* with
the hammer *encourages* him
who beats the anvil,
Saying of the soldering, "It is
good";
And he fastens it with nails,
[c]*So that* it will not totter.
8 "But you, Israel, [a]My servant,
Jacob whom I have chosen,
Descendant of [b]Abraham My
[c]friend,
9 You whom I have [1a]taken from
the ends of the earth,
And called from its [b]remotest
parts
And said to you, 'You are [c]My
servant,
I have [d]chosen you and not
rejected you.
10 'Do not [a]fear, for I am with you;
Do not anxiously look about you,
for I am your God.
I will strengthen you, surely [b]I
will help you,
Surely I will uphold you with My
righteous [c]right hand.'
11 "Behold, [a]all those who are
angered at you will be
shamed and dishonored;
[b]Those who contend with you
will be as nothing and will
perish.
12 "[a]You will seek those who
quarrel with you, but will
not find them,
Those who war with you will be
as nothing and non-existent.
13 "For I am the LORD your God,
[a]who upholds your right
hand,
Who says to you, '[b]Do not fear,
I will help you.'
14 "Do not fear, you [a]worm Jacob,
you men of Israel;
I will help you," declares the
LORD, "[1]and [b]your
Redeemer is the Holy One
of Israel.
15 "Behold, I have made you a new,
sharp threshing sledge with
double edges;
[a]You will thresh the [b]mountains
and pulverize *them,*
And will make the hills like
chaff.
16 "You will [a]winnow them, and the
wind will carry them away,
And the storm will scatter them;
But you will [b]rejoice in the
LORD,
You will glory in the Holy One of
Israel.

17 ¶ "The [1]afflicted and needy are
seeking [a]water, but there is
none,
And their tongue is parched with
thirst;
I, the LORD, [b]will answer them
Myself,
As the God of Israel I [c]will not
forsake them.

30 [a]Jer 6:11; 9:21 [b]Is 9:17
31 [1]Or *hope in* [2]Or *sprout wings* [3]Or *pinions* [a]Job 17:9; Ps 103:5; 2 Cor 4:8-10,16 [b]Ex 19:4; Deut 32:11; Luke 18:1; 2 Cor 4:1, 16; Gal 6:9; Heb 12:3
41:1 [a]Is 11:11 [b]Hab 2:20; Zech 2:13 [c]Is 40:31 [d]Is 34:1; 48:16 [e]Is 1:18; 43:26; 50:8
2 [1]Lit *foot* [a]Is 41:25; 45:1-3; 46:11 [b]Is 42:6 [c]2 Chr 36:23; Ezra 1:2 [d]2 Sam 22:43 [e]Is 40:24
3 [1]Lit *going*
4 [a]Is 41:26; 44:7; 46:10 [b]Is 43:10; 44:6; Rev 1:8,17; 22:13 [c]Is 43:13; 46:4; 48:12
5 [a]Is 41:1; Ezek 26:15,16 [b]Josh 5:1; Ps 67:7
7 [a]Is 44:12,13 [b]Is 40:19 [c]Is 40:20; 46:7
8 [a]Is 42:19; 43:10; 44:1,2,21 [b]Is 29:22; 51:2; 63:16 [c]2 Chr 20:7; James 2:23
9 [1]Or *taken hold of* [a]Is 11:11 [b]Is 43:5-7 [c]Is 42:1; 44:1 [d]Deut 7:6; 14:2; Ps 135:4
10 [a]Deut 20:1; 31:6; Josh 1:9; Ps 27:1; Is 41:13,14; 43:2, 5; Rom 8:31 [b]Is 41:14; 44:2; 49:8 [c]Ps 89:13, 14
11 [a]Is 45:24 [b]Is 17:13; 29:5,7,8
12 [a]Job 20:7-9; Ps 37:35,36; Is 17:14
13 [a]Is 42:6; 45:1 [b]Is 41:10
14 [1]Or *even your Redeemer, the Holy One* [a]Job 25:6; Ps 22:6 [b]Is 35:10; 43:14; 44:6, 22-24
15 [a]Mic 4:13; Hab 3:12 [b]Is 42:15; 64:1; Jer 9:10; Ezek 33:28
16 [a]Jer 51:2 [b]Is 25:9; 35:10; 51:3; 61:10
17 [1]Or *poor* [a]Is 43:20; 44:3; 49:10; 55:1 [b]Is 30:19; 65:24 [c]Is 42:16; 62:12

18 "I will open [a]rivers on the bare heights
And springs in the midst of the valleys;
I will make [b]the wilderness a pool of water
And the dry land fountains of water.
19 "I will put the cedar in the wilderness,
The acacia and the [a]myrtle and the [1]olive tree;
I will place the [a]juniper in the desert
Together with the box tree and the cypress,
20 That [a]they may see and recognize,
And consider and gain insight as well,
That the [b]hand of the LORD has done this,
And the Holy One of Israel has created it.
21 ¶ "[1]Present your case," the LORD says.
"Bring forward your strong *arguments*,"
The [a]King of Jacob says.
22 [a]Let them bring forth and declare to us what is going to take place;
As for the [b]former *events*, declare what they *were*,
That we may consider them and know their outcome.
Or announce to us what is coming;
23 [a]Declare the things that are going to come afterward,
That we may know that you are gods;
Indeed, [b]do good or evil, that we may anxiously look about us and fear together.
24 Behold, [a]you are of [1]no account,
And [b]your work amounts to nothing;
He who chooses you is an [c]abomination.
25 ¶ "I have aroused [a]one from the north, and he has come;
From the rising of the sun he will call on My name;
And he will come upon rulers as *upon* [b]mortar,
Even as the potter treads clay."
26 Who has [a]declared *this* from the beginning, that we might know?
Or from former times, that we may say, "*He is* right!"?
Surely there was [b]no one who declared,
Surely there was no one who proclaimed,
Surely there was no one who heard your words.
27 "[a]Formerly *I said* to Zion, 'Behold, here they are.'
And to Jerusalem, 'I will give a [b]messenger of good news.'
28 "But [a]when I look, there is no one,
And there is no [b]counselor [1]among them
Who, if I ask, can [c]give an answer.
29 "Behold, all of them are [1]false;
Their [a]works are [b]worthless,
Their molten images are [c]wind and emptiness.

God's Promise Concerning His Servant

42 "[a]Behold, My [b]Servant, whom I [1]uphold;
My [c]chosen one *in whom* My [d]soul delights.
I have put My [e]Spirit upon Him;
He will bring forth [f]justice to the [2]nations.
2 "He will not cry out or raise *His voice*,
Nor make His voice heard in the street.
3 "A bruised reed He will not break
And a dimly burning wick He will not extinguish;
He will faithfully bring forth [a]justice.
4 "He will not be [a]disheartened or crushed
Until He has established justice in the earth;
And the [b]coastlands will wait expectantly for His [1]law."
5 ¶ Thus says God the LORD,
Who [a]created the heavens and [b]stretched them out,
Who spread out the [c]earth and its [1]offspring,
Who [d]gives breath to the people on it
And spirit to those who walk in it,
6 "I am the LORD, I have [a]called you in righteousness,
I will also [b]hold you by the hand and [c]watch over you,
And I will appoint you as a [d]covenant to the people,
As a [e]light to the nations,
7 To [a]open blind eyes,

---

18 [a]Is 30:25; 43:19 [b]Ps 107:35; Is 35:6, 7
19 [1]Or *oleaster* [a]Is 35:1; 55:13; 60:13
20 [a]Is 40:5; 43:10 [b]Job 12:9; Is 66:14
21 [1]Lit *Bring near* [a]Is 44:6
22 [a]Is 44:7; 45:21; 46:10 [b]Is 43:9
23 [a]Is 42:9; 44:7,8; 45:3; John 13:19 [b]Jer 10:5
24 [1]Lit *nothing* [a]Ps 115:8; Is 44:9; 1 Cor 8:4 [b]Is 37:19; 41:29 [c]Prov 3:32; 28:9
25 [a]Is 41:2; Jer 50:3 [b]2 Sam 22:43; Is 10:6; Mic 7:10; Zech 10:5
26 [a]Is 41:22; 44:7; 45:21 [b]Hab 2:18,19
27 [a]Is 48:3-8 [b]Is 40:9; 44:28; 52:7; Nah 1:15
28 [1]Lit *out of those* [a]Is 50:2; 59:16; 63:5 [b]Is 40:13,14 [c]Is 46:7
29 [1]Another reading is *nothing* [a]Is 2:8; 17:8; 41:24 [b]Is 44:9 [c]Jer 5:13
42:1 [1]Or *hold fast* [2]Or *Gentiles* [a]Matt 12:18-21 [b]Is 41:8; 43:10; 49:3-6; 52:13; 53:11; Matt 12:18-21; Phil 2:7 [c]Luke 9:35; 1 Pet 2:4,6 [d]Matt 3:17; 17:5; Mark 1:11; Luke 3:22 [e]Is 11:2; 59:21; 61:1; Matt 3:16; Luke 4:18,19,21 [f]Is 2:4
3 [a]Ps 72:2,4; 96:13
4 [1]Or *instruction* [a]Is 40:28 [b]Is 11:11; 24:15; 42:10,12; 49:1; 51:5; 60:9; 66:19
5 [1]Or *vegetation* [a]Ps 102:25,26; Is 45:18 [b]Ps 104:2; Is 40:22 [c]Ps 24:1,2; 136:6 [d]Job 12:10; 33:4; Is 57:16; Dan 5:23; Acts 17:25
6 [a]Is 41:2; Jer 23:5,6 [b]Is 41:13; 45:1 [c]Is 26:3; 27:3 [d]Is 49:8 [e]Is 49:6; 51:4; 60:1,3; Luke 2:32; Acts 13:47; 26:23
7 [a]Is 29:18; 35:5

To [b]bring out prisoners from the dungeon
And those who dwell in darkness from the prison.
8 "[a]I am the LORD, that is [b]My name;
I will not give My [c]glory to another,
Nor My praise to [1]graven images.
9 "Behold, the [a]former things have come to pass,
Now I declare [b]new things;
Before they spring forth I proclaim *them* to you."

10 ¶ Sing to the LORD a [a]new song,
Sing His praise from the [b]end of the earth!
[c]You who go down to the sea, and [d]all that is in it.
You [e]islands, and those who dwell on them.
11 Let the [a]wilderness and its cities lift up *their voices,*
The settlements where [b]Kedar inhabits.
Let the inhabitants of [c]Sela sing aloud,
Let them shout for joy from the tops of the [d]mountains.
12 Let them [a]give glory to the LORD
And declare His praise in the [b]coastlands.
13 [a]The LORD will go forth like a warrior,
He will arouse *His* [b]zeal like a man of war.
He will utter a shout, yes, He will raise a war cry.
He will [c]prevail against His enemies.

The Blindness of the People

14 ¶ "[a]I have kept silent for a long time,
I have kept still and restrained Myself.
Now like a woman in labor I will groan,
I will both gasp and pant.
15 "I will [a]lay waste the mountains and hills
And wither all their vegetation;
I will [b]make the rivers into coastlands
And dry up the ponds.
16 "I will [a]lead the blind by a way they do not know,
In paths they do not know I will guide them.
I will [b]make darkness into light before them
And [c]rugged places into plains.
These are the things I will do,
And I will [d]not leave them undone."
17 They will be turned back *and* be [a]utterly put to shame,
Who trust in [1]idols,
Who say to molten images,
"You are our gods."

18 ¶ [a]Hear, you deaf!
And look, you blind, that you may see.
19 Who is blind but My [a]servant,
Or so deaf as My [b]messenger whom I send?
Who is so blind as he that is [1c]at peace *with Me,*
Or so blind as the servant of the LORD?
20 [a]You have seen many things, but you do not observe *them;*
Your ears are open, but none hears.
21 The LORD was pleased for His righteousness' sake
To make the law [a]great and glorious.
22 But this is a people plundered and despoiled;
All of them are [a]trapped in [1]caves,
Or are [b]hidden away in prisons;
They have become a prey with none to deliver *them,*
And a spoil, with none to say, "Give *them* back!"

23 ¶ Who among you will give ear to this?
Who will give heed and listen hereafter?
24 Who gave Jacob up for spoil, and Israel to plunderers?
Was it not the LORD, against whom we have sinned,
And in whose ways they [a]were not willing to walk,
And whose law they did not [b]obey?
25 So He poured out on him the heat of His anger
And the [a]fierceness of battle;
And it set him aflame all around,
Yet he did not recognize *it;*
And it burned him, but he [1b]paid no attention.

Israel Redeemed

43 But now, thus says the LORD, your [a]Creator, O Jacob,
And He who [b]formed you, O Israel,
"Do not [c]fear, for I have [d]redeemed you;

7 [b]Is 49:9; 61:1
8 [1]Or *idols* [a]Is 43:3,11,15 [b]Ex 3:15; Ps 83:18 [c]Ex 20:3-5; Is 48:11
9 [a]Is 48:3 [b]Is 43:19; 48:6
10 [a]Ps 33:3; 40:3; 98:1 [b]Is 49:6; 62:11 [c]Ps 65:5; 107:23 [d]Ex 20:11; 1 Chr 16:32; Ps 96:11 [e]Is 42:4
11 [a]Is 32:16; 35:1,6 [b]Is 21:16; 60:7 [c]Is 16:1 [d]Is 52:7; Nah 1:15
12 [a]Is 24:15 [b]Is 42:4
13 [a]Ex 15:3 [b]Is 9:7; 26:11; 37:32; 59:17 [c]Is 66:14-16
14 [a]Ps 50:21; Is 57:11
15 [a]Is 2:12-16; Ezek 38:19,20 [b]Is 44:27; 50:2; Nah 1:4-6
16 [a]Is 29:18; 30:21; 32:3; Jer 31:8,9; Luke 1:78,79 [b]Is 29:18; Eph 5:8 [c]Is 40:4; Luke 3:5 [d]Josh 1:5; Ps 94:14; Is 41:17; Heb 13:5
17 [1]Or *graven images* [a]Ps 97:7; Is 1:29; 44:9,11; 45:16
18 [a]Is 29:18; 35:5
19 [1]Or *the devoted one* [a]Is 41:8 [b]Is 44:26 [c]Is 26:3; 27:5
20 [a]Rom 2:21
21 [a]Is 42:4; 51:4
22 [1]Or *holes* [a]Is 24:18 [b]Is 24:22
24 [a]Is 30:15 [b]Is 48:18; 57:17
25 [1]Lit *did not lay it to heart* [a]Is 5:25; 9:19 [b]Is 29:13; 47:7; 57:1; Hos 7:9
43:1 [a]Is 43:15 [b]Is 43:7,21; 44:2,21,24 [c]Is 43:5 [d]Is 44:22, 23; 48:20

I have [e]called you by name; you
are [f]Mine!
2 "When you [a]pass through the
waters, [b]I will be with you;
And through the rivers, they will
not overflow you.
When you [c]walk through the
fire, you will not be
scorched,
Nor will the flame burn you.
3 "For [a]I am the LORD your God,
The Holy One of Israel, your
[b]Savior;
I have given Egypt as your
ransom,
[1][c]Cush and Seba in your place.
4 "Since you are [a]precious in My
sight,
Since you are [b]honored and I
[c]love you,
I will give *other* men in your
place and *other* peoples in
exchange for your life.
5 "Do not fear, for [a]I am with you;
I will bring [b]your offspring from
the east,
And [c]gather you from the west.
6 "I will say to the [a]north, 'Give
them up!'
And to the south, 'Do not hold
them back.'
Bring My [b]sons from afar
And My daughters from the
[c]ends of the earth,
7 Everyone who is [a]called by My
name,
And whom I have [b]created for
My [c]glory,
[d]Whom I have formed, even
whom I have made."

Israel Is God's Witness

8 ¶ Bring out the people who are
[a]blind, even though they
have eyes,
And the deaf, even though they
have ears.
9 All the nations have [a]gathered
together
So that the peoples may be
assembled.
Who among them can [b]declare
this
And proclaim to us the former
things?
Let them present [c]their
witnesses [d]that they may be
justified,
Or let them hear and say, "It is
true."
10 "You are [a]My witnesses,"
declares the LORD,
"And [b]My servant whom I have
chosen,
So that you may know and
believe Me
And understand that [c]I am He.
[d]Before Me there was no God
formed,
And there will be none after Me.
11 "I, even I, am the LORD,
And there is no [a]savior
[b]besides Me.
12 "It is I who have declared and
saved and proclaimed,
And there was no [a]strange *god*
among you;
So you are My witnesses,"
declares the LORD,
"And I am God.
13 "Even [1][a]from eternity [b]I am He,
And there is [c]none who can
deliver out of My hand;
[d]I act and who can reverse it?"

Babylon to Be Destroyed

14 ¶ Thus says the LORD your [a]Redeemer, the Holy One of Israel,
"For your sake I have sent to
Babylon,
And will bring them all down as
fugitives,
[1]Even the [b]Chaldeans, into the
[c]ships [2]in which they
rejoice.
15 "I am the LORD, your Holy One,
[a]The Creator of Israel, your
[b]King."
16 Thus says the LORD,
Who [a]makes a way through
the sea
And a path through the mighty
waters,
17 Who brings forth the [a]chariot
and the horse,
The army and the mighty man
(They will lie down together *and*
not rise again;
They have been [b]quenched *and*
extinguished like a wick):
18 "[a]Do not call to mind the former
things,
Or ponder things of the past.
19 "Behold, I will do
something [a]new,
Now it will spring forth;
Will you not be aware of it?
I will even [b]make a roadway in
the wilderness,
Rivers in the desert.
20 "The beasts of the field will
glorify Me,
The [a]jackals and the ostriches,
Because I have [b]given waters in
the wilderness
And rivers in the desert,
To give drink to My chosen
people.

1 [e]Gen 32:28; Is 43:7; 45:3,4 [f]Is 43:21
2 [a]Ps 66:12; Is 8:7,8 [b]Deut 31:6,8 [c]Is 29:6; 30:27-29; Dan 3:25,27
3 [1]Or *Ethiopia* [a]Ex 20:2 [b]Is 19:20; 43:11; 45:15,21; 49:26; 60:16; 63:8 [c]Is 20:3-5
4 [a]Ex 19:5,6 [b]Is 49:5 [c]Is 63:9
5 [a]Is 8:10; 43:2 [b]Is 41:8; 49:12; 61:9 [c]Is 49:12
6 [a]Ps 107:3 [b]2 Cor 6:18 [c]Is 45:22
7 [a]Is 56:5; 62:2; James 2:7 [b]Ps 100:3; Is 29:23; Eph 2:10 [c]Is 44:23; 46:13 [d]Is 43:1
8 [a]Is 6:9; 42:19; Ezek 12:2
9 [a]Is 34:1; 41:1 [b]Is 41:22,23,26 [c]Is 44:9 [d]Is 43:26
10 [a]Is 44:8 [b]Is 41:8 [c]Is 41:4 [d]Is 45:5,6
11 [a]Is 43:3; 45:21; Hos 13:4 [b]Is 44:6,8
12 [a]Deut 32:16; Ps 81:9
13 [1]So with Gr; Heb *from the day* [a]Ps 90:2; Is 48:16 [b]Is 41:4 [c]Ps 50:22 [d]Job 9:12; Is 14:27
14 [1]Another reading is *As for the Chaldeans, their rejoicing* is turned *into lamentations* [2]Lit *of their rejoicing* [a]Is 41:14 [b]Is 23:13 [c]Jer 51:13
15 [a]Is 43:1 [b]Is 41:20; 44:6
16 [a]Ex 14:21, 22; Ps 77:19; Is 11:15; 44:27; 50:2; 51:10; 63:11,12
17 [a]Ex 15:19 [b]Ps 118:12; Is 1:31
18 [a]Is 65:17; Jer 23:7
19 [a]Is 42:9; 48:6; 2 Cor 5:17 [b]Ex 17:6; Num 20:11; Deut 8:15; Ps 78:16; Is 35:1,6; 41:18, 19; 49:10; 51:3
20 [a]Is 13:22; 35:7 [b]Is 41:17, 18; 48:21

21 "The people whom [a]I formed for Myself
[b]Will declare My praise.

The Shortcomings of Israel

22 ¶ "Yet you have not called on Me, O Jacob;
But you have become [a]weary of Me, O Israel.
23 "You have [a]not brought to Me the sheep of your burnt offerings,
Nor have you [b]honored Me with your sacrifices.
I have not [c]burdened you with [1]offerings,
Nor wearied you with [d]incense.
24 "You have bought Me not [1a]sweet cane with money,
Nor have you [2]filled Me with the fat of your sacrifices;
Rather you have burdened Me with your sins,
You have [b]wearied Me with your iniquities.

25 ¶ "I, even I, am the one who [a]wipes out your transgressions [b]for My own sake,
And I will [c]not remember your sins.
26 "[1]Put Me in remembrance, [a]let us argue our case together;
State your *cause,* [b]that you may be proved right.
27 "Your [a]first [1]forefather sinned,
And your [2b]spokesmen have [3]transgressed against Me.
28 "So I will [1]pollute the [2]princes of the sanctuary,
And I will consign Jacob to the [a]ban and Israel to [b]revilement.

The Blessings of Israel

44 "But now listen, O Jacob, My [a]servant,
And Israel, whom I have chosen:
2 Thus says the LORD who made you
And [a]formed you from the womb, who [b]will help you,
'[c]Do not fear, O Jacob My servant;
And you [d]Jeshurun whom I have chosen.
3 'For [a]I will pour out water on [1]the thirsty *land*
And streams on the dry ground;
I will [b]pour out My Spirit on your [c]offspring
And My blessing on your descendants;

21 [a]Is 43:1 [b]Ps 102:18; Is 42:12; Luke 1:74; 1 Pet 2:9
22 [a]Mic 6:3; Mal 1:13
23 [1]Or *a meal offering* [a]Amos 5:25 [b]Zech 7:5; Mal 1:6-8 [c]Jer 7:21-26 [d]Ex 30:34; Lev 2:1
24 [1]Or *calamus* [2]Or *saturated* [a]Ex 30:23; Jer 6:20 [b]Ps 95:10; Is 1:14; Ezek 6:9; Mal 2:17
25 [a]Is 44:22; Jer 50:20 [b]Is 37:35; Ezek 36:22 [c]Is 38:17; Jer 31:34
26 [1]Or *Report to Me* [a]Is 1:18 [b]Is 43:9
27 [1]Lit *father* [2]Or *interpreters* [3]Or *rebelled* [a]Is 51:2; Ezek 16:3 [b]Is 9:15; Jer 5:31
28 [1]Or *pierce through* [2]Or *holy princes* [a]Is 24:6; Jer 24:9; Dan 9:11; Zech 8:13 [b]Ps 79:4; Ezek 5:15
44:1 [a]Is 41:8; Jer 30:10
2 [a]Is 44:21 [b]Is 41:10 [c]Is 43:5 [d]Deut 32:15
3 [1]Or *him who is thirsty* [a]Is 41:17; Ezek 34:26; Joel 3:18 [b]Is 32:15; Joel 2:28 [c]Is 61:9
4 [1]Another reading is *like grass among the waters* [a]Lev 23:40; Job 40:22
5 [1]Another reading is *will be called by the name of Jacob* [2]Or *with* [a]Ex 13:9; Neh 9:38
6 [a]Is 41:21 [b]Is 41:14 [c]Is 41:4; Rev 1:8 [d]Is 43:11
7 [1]Lit *From My establishing of* [2]Or *people* [a]Is 41:22
8 [a]Is 42:9 [b]Is 43:10 [c]Deut 4:35; 1 Sam 2:2; Is 45:5; Joel 2:27 [d]Is 17:10
9 [1]Or *an idol* [a]Ps 97:7; Is 42:17
10 [1]Or *a graven image* [a]Is 41:29; Jer 10:5; Hab 2:18; Acts 19:26
11 [a]Ps 97:7; Is 42:17
12 [1]Lit *and fashions* [2]Lit *there is no strength* [a]Is 40:19; Jer 10:3-5; Hab 2:18
13 [a]Is 41:7

4 And they will spring up [1]among the grass
Like [a]poplars by streams of water.'
5 "This one will say, 'I am the LORD'S';
And that one [1]will call on the name of Jacob;
And another will [a]write [2]*on* his hand, 'Belonging to the LORD,'
And will name Israel's name with honor.

6 ¶ "Thus says the LORD, the [a]King of Israel and his [b]Redeemer, the LORD of hosts:
'I am the [c]first and I am the last,
And there is no God [d]besides Me.
7 'Who is like Me? [a]Let him proclaim and declare it;
Yes, let him recount it to Me in order,
[1]From the time that I established the ancient [2]nation.
And let them declare to them the things that are coming
And the events that are going to take place.
8 'Do not tremble and do not be afraid;
[a]Have I not long since announced *it* to you and declared *it?*
And [b]you are My witnesses.
Is there any God [c]besides Me,
Or is there any *other* [d]Rock?
I know of none.' "

The Folly of Idolatry

9 ¶ Those who fashion [1]a graven image are all of them futile, and their precious things are of no profit; even their own witnesses fail to see or know, so that they will be [a]put to shame.

10 Who has fashioned a god or cast [1]an idol to [a]no profit?

11 Behold, all his companions will be [a]put to shame, for the craftsmen themselves are mere men. Let them all assemble themselves, let them stand up, let them tremble, let them together be put to shame.

12 ¶ The [a]man shapes iron into a cutting tool and does his work over the coals, [1]fashioning it with hammers and working it with his strong arm. He also gets hungry and [2]his strength fails; he drinks no water and becomes weary.

13 [a]*Another* shapes wood, he extends a measuring line; he outlines it with red

chalk. He works it with planes and outlines it with a compass, and makes it like the form of a man, like the beauty of [b]man, so that it may sit in a [c]house.

14 Surely he cuts cedars for himself, and takes a [1]cypress or an oak and [2]raises *it* for himself among the trees of the forest. He plants a fir, and the rain makes it grow.

15 Then it becomes *something* for a man to burn, so he takes one of them and warms himself; he also makes a fire to bake bread. He also [a]makes a god and worships it; he makes it a graven image and [b]falls down before it.

16 Half of it he burns in the fire; over *this* half he eats meat as he roasts a roast and is satisfied. He also warms himself and says, "Aha! I am warm, I have seen the fire."

17 But the rest of it he [a]makes into a god, his graven image. He falls down before it and worships; he also [b]prays to it and says, "Deliver me, for you are my god."

18 ¶ They do not [a]know, nor do they understand, for He has [b]smeared over their eyes so that they cannot see and their hearts so that they cannot comprehend.

19 No one [1]recalls, nor is there [a]knowledge or understanding to say, "I have burned half of it in the fire and also have baked bread over its coals. I roast meat and eat *it*. Then [2]I make the rest of it into an [b]abomination, [3]I fall down before a block of wood!"

20 He [1a]feeds on ashes; a [b]deceived heart has turned him aside. And he cannot deliver [2]himself, nor say, "[c]Is there not a lie in my right hand?"

God Forgives and Redeems

21 ¶ "[a]Remember these things,
O Jacob,
And Israel, for you are [b]My
servant;
I have formed you, you are My
servant,
O Israel, you will [c]not be
forgotten by Me.
22 "I have [a]wiped out your
transgressions like a thick
cloud
And your sins like a [1]heavy
mist.
[b]Return to Me, for I have
[c]redeemed you."
23 [a]Shout for joy, O heavens, for
the LORD has done *it!*
Shout joyfully, you lower parts of
the earth;
[b]Break forth into a shout of joy,
you mountains,
O forest, and every tree in it;
For [c]the LORD has redeemed
Jacob
And in Israel He [d]shows forth
His glory.

24 ¶ Thus says the LORD, your [a]Redeemer, and the one who [b]formed you from the womb,
"I, the LORD, am the maker of all
things,
[c]Stretching out the heavens by
Myself
And spreading out the earth [1]all
alone,
25 [a]Causing the [1]omens of
boasters to fail,
[2]Making fools out of diviners,
[b]Causing wise men to draw
back
And [3]turning their knowledge
into foolishness,
26 [a]Confirming the word of His
servant
And [1]performing the purpose of
His messengers.
It is I who says of Jerusalem,
'She shall be inhabited!'
And of the [b]cities of Judah,
'[c]They shall be built.'
And I will raise up her ruins
again.
27 "*It is I* who says to the depth of
the sea, 'Be dried up!'
And I will make your
rivers [a]dry.
28 "*It is I* who says of [a]Cyrus, '*He is*
My shepherd!
And he will perform all My
desire.'
And [1]he declares of Jerusalem,
'[b]She will be built,'
And of the temple, '[2]Your
foundation will be laid.' "

God Uses Cyrus

45

Thus says the LORD to [a]Cyrus His
anointed,
Whom I have taken by the right
[b]hand,
To [c]subdue nations before him
And [1]to [d]loose the loins of
kings;
To open doors before him so that
gates will not be shut:
2 "I will go before you and [a]make
the [1]rough places smooth;
I will [b]shatter the doors of
bronze and cut through their
iron [c]bars.
3 "I will give you the [1a]treasures
of darkness
And hidden wealth of secret
places,

13 [b]Ps 115:5-7 [c]Judg 17:4,5; Ezek 8:10,11
14 [1]Or *holm-oak* [2]Lit *makes strong*
15 [a]Is 44:17 [b]2 Chr 25:14
17 [a]Is 44:15 [b]1 Kin 18:26,28; Is 45:20
18 [a]Is 1:3; Jer 10:8,14 [b]Ps 81:12; Is 6:9,10; 29:10
19 [1]Lit *returns to his heart* [2]Or *shall I make ?* [3]Or *shall I fall...?* [a]Is 5:13; 44:18, 19; 45:20 [b]Deut 27:15; 1 Kin 11:5,7; 2 Kin 23:13,14
20 [1]Or *is a companion of ashes* [2]Lit *his soul* [a]Ps 102:9 [b]Job 15:31; Hos 4:12; Rom 1:21,22; 2 Thess 2:11; 2 Tim 3:13 [c]Is 57:11; 59:3,4, 13; Rom 1:25
21 [a]Is 46:8; Zech 10:9 [b]Is 44:1,2 [c]Is 49:15
22 [1]Or *cloud* [a]Ps 51:1,9; Is 43:25; Acts 3:19 [b]Is 31:6; 55:7 [c]Is 43:1; 48:20; 1 Cor 6:20; 1 Pet 1:18,19
23 [a]Ps 69:34; 96:11,12; Is 42:10; 49:13 [b]Ps 98:7,8; 148:7,9; Is 55:12 [c]Is 43:1 [d]Is 49:3; 61:3
24 [1]Or *who was with Me?* [a]Is 41:14; 43:14 [b]Is 44:2 [c]Is 40:22; 42:5; 45:12,18; 51:13
25 [1]Lit *signs* [2]Lit *He makes* [3]Lit *He turns* [a]Is 47:13 [b]2 Sam 15:31; Job 5:12-14; Ps 33:10; Is 29:14; Jer 51:57; 1 Cor 1:20,27
26 [1]Lit *He performs* [a]Zech 1:6; Matt 5:18 [b]Is 40:9 [c]Jer 32:15, 44
27 [a]Is 42:15; 50:2; Jer 50:38; 51:36
28 [1]Lit *to say* [2]Lit *You will be founded* [a]Is 45:1 [b]2 Chr 36:22,23; Ezra 1:1; Is 14:32; 45:13; 54:11
45:1 [1]Lit *I will loose* [a]Is 44:28 [b]Ps 73:23; Is 41:13; 42:6 [c]Is 41:2,25; Jer 50:3,35; 51:11, 20,24 [d]Job 12:21; Is 45:5
2 [1]Another reading is *mountains* [a]Is 40:4 [b]Ps 107:16 [c]Jer 51:30
3 [1]Or *hoarded treasures* [a]Jer 41:8; 50:37

So that you may know that it
is I,
The LORD, the God of Israel, who
[b]calls you by your name.
4 "For the sake of [a]Jacob My
servant,
And Israel My chosen *one,*
I have also [b]called you by your
name;
I have given you a title of honor
Though you have [c]not
known Me.
5 "I am the LORD, and [a]there is no
other;
[b]Besides Me there is no God.
I will [1c]gird you, though you
have not known Me;
6 That [1a]men may know from the
rising to the setting of
the sun
That there is [b]no one
besides Me.
I am the LORD, and there is no
other,
7 The One [a]forming light and
[b]creating darkness,
Causing [1]well-being and
[c]creating calamity;
I am the LORD who does all
these.

God's Supreme Power

8 ¶ "[a]Drip down, O heavens, from
above,
And let the clouds pour down
righteousness;
Let the [b]earth open up and
salvation bear fruit,
[c]And righteousness spring up
with it.
I, the LORD, have created it.

9 ¶ "Woe to *the one* who
[a]quarrels with his
[1]Maker—
An earthenware vessel [2]among
the vessels of earth!
Will the [b]clay say to the
[1]potter, 'What are you
doing?'
Or the thing you are making *say,*
'He has no hands'?
10 "Woe to him who says to a father,
'What are you begetting?'
Or to a woman, 'To what are
you [1]giving birth?' "

11 ¶ Thus says the [a]LORD, the Holy
One of Israel, and his [1b]Maker:
"[2c]Ask Me about the things to
come [3]concerning My
[d]sons,
And you shall commit to Me
[e]the work of My hands.

12 "It is I who [a]made the earth, and
created man upon it.
I [b]stretched out the heavens
with My hands
And I [1]ordained [c]all their host.
13 "I have aroused him in
[a]righteousness
And I will [b]make all his ways
smooth;
He will [c]build My city and will
let My exiles go [d]free,
Without any payment or
reward," says the LORD of
hosts.

14 ¶ Thus says the LORD,
"The [1]products of [a]Egypt and the
merchandise of [2b]Cush
And the Sabeans, men of stature,
Will [c]come over to you and will
be yours;
They will walk behind you, they
will come over in [d]chains
And will [e]bow down to you;
They will make supplication
to you:
'[3]Surely, [f]God is [4]with you, and
[g]there is none else,
No other God.' "
15 Truly, You are a God who
[a]hides Himself,
O God of Israel, [b]Savior!
16 They will be [a]put to shame and
even humiliated, all of them;
The [b]manufacturers of idols will
go away together in
humiliation.
17 Israel has been saved by the
LORD
With an [a]everlasting salvation;
You [b]will not be put to shame
or humiliated
To all eternity.

18 ¶ For thus says the LORD, who
[a]created the heavens (He is the God
who [b]formed the earth and made it, He
established it *and* did not create it [1]a
[c]waste place, *but* formed it to be [d]in-
habited),
"I am the LORD, and [e]there is
none else.
19 "[a]I have not spoken in secret,
In [1]some dark land;
I did not say to the [2b]offspring
of Jacob,
'[c]Seek Me in [3]a waste place';
I, the LORD, [d]speak
righteousness,
[e]Declaring things that are
upright.
20 ¶ "[a]Gather yourselves and come;

3 [b]Ex 33:12,17; Is 43:1; 49:1
4 [a]Is 41:8,9; 44:1 [b]Is 43:1 [c]Acts 17:23
5 [1]Or *arm* [a]Is 45:6,14,18,21; 46:9 [b]Is 44:6,8 [c]Ps 18:39
6 [1]Lit *they* [a]Ps 102:15; Mal 1:11 [b]Is 45:5
7 [1]Or *peace* [a]Is 42:16 [b]Ps 104:20; 105:28 [c]Is 31:2; 47:11; Amos 3:6
8 [a]Ps 72:6; Hos 10:12; 14:5; Joel 3:18 [b]Ps 85:11 [c]Is 60:21; 61:11
9 [1]Lit *Fashioner* [2]Lit *with* [a]Job 15:25; 40:8,9; Ps 2:2,3; Prov 21:30; Jer 50:24 [b]Is 29:16; 64:8; Jer 18:6; Rom 9:20,21
10 [1]Lit *in labor pains with*
11 [1]Lit *Fashioner* [2]Or *Will you ask* [3]Or *upon* [a]Is 43:15; 48:17; Ezek 39:7 [b]Is 44:2; 54:5 [c]Is 8:19 [d]Jer 31:9 [e]Is 19:25; 29:23; 60:21; 64:8
12 [1]Or *commanded* [a]Is 42:5; 45:18; Jer 27:5 [b]Ps 104:2; Is 42:5; 44:24 [c]Gen 2:1; Neh 9:6
13 [a]Is 41:2 [b]Is 45:2 [c]2 Chr 36:22,23; Is 44:28 [d]Is 52:3
14 [1]Lit *labor* [2]Or *Ethiopia* [3]Or *God is with you alone* [4]Or *in* [a]Ps 68:31; Is 19:21 [b]Is 18:1; 43:3 [c]Is 14:1,2; 49:23; 54:3 [d]Ps 149:8 [e]Is 49:23; 60:14 [f]Jer 16:19; Zech 8:20-23; 1 Cor 14:25 [g]Is 45:5
15 [a]Ps 44:24; Is 1:15; 8:17; 57:17 [b]Is 43:3
16 [a]Is 42:17; 44:9 [b]Is 44:11
17 [a]Is 26:4; 51:6; Rom 11:26 [b]Is 49:23; 50:7; 54:4
18 [1]Or *in vain* [a]Is 42:5 [b]Is 45:12 [c]Gen 1:2 [d]Gen 1:26; Ps 115:16 [e]Is 45:5
19 [1]Lit *a place of a land of darkness* [2]Lit *seed* [3]Or *vain* [a]Is 48:16 [b]Is 45:25; 65:9 [c]2 Chr 15:2; Ps 78:34; Jer 29:13,14 [d]Ps 19:8; Is 45:23; 63:1 [e]Is 43:12; 44:8
20 [a]Is 43:9

Draw near together, you fugitives
of the nations;
[b]They have no knowledge,
Who [c]carry about [1]their
wooden idol
And [d]pray to a god who cannot
save.
21 "[a]Declare and set forth *your case;*
Indeed, let them consult
together.
[b]Who has announced this from
of old?
Who has long since declared it?
Is it not I, the LORD?
And there is [c]no other God
besides Me,
A righteous God and a [d]Savior;
There is none except Me.
22 "[a]Turn to Me and [b]be saved, all
the ends of the earth;
For I am God, and there is no
other.
23 "[a]I have sworn by Myself,
The [b]word has gone forth from
My mouth in righteousness
And will not turn back,
That to Me [c]every knee will
bow, every tongue will
[d]swear *allegiance.*
24 "They will say of Me, 'Only [a]in
the LORD are righteousness
and strength.'
Men will come to Him,
And [b]all who were angry at Him
will be put to shame.
25 "In the LORD all the offspring of
Israel
Will be [a]justified and will
[b]glory."

Babylon's Idols and the True God

46 [a]Bel has bowed down, Nebo
stoops over;
Their images are *consigned* to
the beasts and the cattle.
The things [1]that you carry are
burdensome,
A load for the weary *beast.*
2 They stooped over, they have
bowed down together;
They could not rescue the
burden,
But [1]have themselves [a]gone
into captivity.
3 ¶ "[a]Listen to Me, O house of
Jacob,
And all [b]the remnant of the
house of Israel,
You who have been [c]borne by
Me from [1]birth
And have been carried from the
womb;
4 Even to *your* old age [a]I [1]will be
the same,
And even to *your* [2b]graying
years I will bear *you!*
I have [3]done *it,* and I will
carry *you;*
And I will bear *you* and I will
deliver *you.*
5 ¶ "[a]To whom would you
liken Me
And make Me equal and
compare Me,
That we would be alike?
6 "Those who [a]lavish gold from the
purse
And weigh silver on the scale
Hire a goldsmith, and he makes
it *into* a god;
They [b]bow down, indeed they
worship it.
7 "They [a]lift it upon the shoulder
and carry it;
They set it in its place and it
stands *there.*
[b]It does not move from its place.
Though one may cry to it, it
[c]cannot answer;
It [d]cannot deliver him from his
distress.
8 ¶ "[a]Remember this, and be
[1]assured;
[b]Recall it to [2]mind, you
[c]transgressors.
9 "Remember the [a]former things
long past,
For I am God, and there is [b]no
other;
I am God, and there is [c]no one
like Me,
10 Declaring the end from the
beginning,
And from ancient times things
which have not been done,
Saying, '[a]My purpose will be
established,
And I will accomplish all My
good pleasure';
11 Calling a [a]bird of prey from the
[b]east,
The man of [1]My purpose from a
far country.
Truly I have [c]spoken; truly I will
bring it to pass.
I have planned *it, surely* I will
do it.
12 ¶ "[a]Listen to Me, you
[b]stubborn-minded,
Who are [c]far from
righteousness.
13 "I [a]bring near My righteousness,
it is not far off;
And My salvation will not delay.

20 [1]Lit *the wood of their graven image* [b]Is 44:18,19; 48:5-7 [c]Is 46:1,7; Jer 10:5 [d]Is 44:17; 46:6,7
21 [a]Is 41:23; 43:9 [b]Is 41:26; 44:7; 48:14 [c]Is 45:5 [d]Is 43:3,11
22 [a]Num 21:8, 9; 2 Chr 20:12; Mic 7:7; Zech 12:10 [b]Is 30:15; 49:6,12; 52:10
23 [a]Gen 22:16; Is 62:8; Heb 6:13 [b]Is 55:11 [c]Rom 14:11; Phil 2:10 [d]Deut 6:13; Ps 63:11; Is 19:18; 65:16
24 [a]Jer 33:16 [b]Is 41:11
25 [a]1 Kin 8:32; Is 53:11 [b]Is 41:16; 60:19
46:1 [1]Lit *carried by you* [a]Is 2:18; 21:9; Jer 50:2-4; 51:44
2 [1]Or *their soul has* [a]Judg 18:17, 18,24; 2 Sam 5:21; Jer 43:12, 13; 48:7; Hos 10:5,6
3 [1]Lit *the belly* [a]Is 46:12 [b]Is 10:21,22 [c]Ps 71:6; Is 49:1
4 [1]Lit *I am He* [2]Lit *gray hairs* [3]Or *made* you [a]Is 41:4; 43:13; 48:12 [b]Ps 71:18
5 [a]Is 40:18,25
6 [a]Is 40:19; 41:7; 44:12-17; Jer 10:4 [b]Is 44:15,17
7 [a]Is 45:20; 46:1; Jer 10:5 [b]Is 40:20; 41:7 [c]Is 41:28 [d]Is 45:20
8 [1]Lit *firm* [2]Lit *heart* [a]Is 44:21 [b]Is 44:19 [c]Is 50:1
9 [a]Deut 32:7; Is 42:9; 65:17 [b]Is 45:5,21 [c]Is 41:26,27
10 [a]Ps 33:11; Prov 19:21; Is 14:24; 25:1; 40:8; Acts 5:39
11 [1]Lit *His* [a]Is 18:6 [b]Is 41:2 [c]Num 23:19; Is 14:24; 37:26
12 [a]Is 46:3 [b]Ps 76:5; Is 48:4; Zech 7:11,12; Mal 3:13 [c]Ps 119:150; Is 48:1; Jer 2:5
13 [a]Is 51:5; 61:11; Rom 3:21

And I will grant [b]salvation in
Zion,
And My [c]glory for Israel.

Lament for Babylon

47 "[a]Come down and sit in the
dust,
O [b]virgin [c]daughter of Babylon;
Sit on the ground without a
throne,
O daughter of the Chaldeans!
For you shall no longer be called
[d]tender and delicate.
2 "Take the [a]millstones and [b]grind
meal.
Remove your [c]veil, [d]strip off
the skirt,
Uncover the leg, cross the rivers.
3 "Your [a]nakedness will be
uncovered,
Your shame also will be exposed;
I will [b]take vengeance and will
not [1]spare a man."
4 Our [a]Redeemer, the LORD of
hosts is His name,
The Holy One of Israel.
5 "[a]Sit silently, and go into
[b]darkness,
O daughter of the Chaldeans,
For you will no longer be called
The [c]queen of [d]kingdoms.
6 "I was angry with My people,
I profaned My heritage
And gave them into your hand.
You did not show mercy to
them,
On the [a]aged you made your
yoke very heavy.
7 "Yet you said, 'I will be a [a]queen
forever.'
These things you did not
[b]consider
Nor remember the [c]outcome of
[1]them.
8 ¶ "Now, then, hear this, you
[a]sensual one,
Who [b]dwells securely,
Who says in [1]your heart,
'[c]I am, and there is no one
besides me.
I will [d]not sit as a widow,
Nor know loss of children.'
9 "But these [a]two things will come
on you [b]suddenly in
one day:
Loss of children and widowhood.
They will come on you in full
measure
In spite of your many [c]sorceries,
In spite of the great power of
your spells.
10 "You felt [a]secure in your
wickedness and said,

13 [b]Is 61:3; 62:11; Joel 3:17; 1 Pet 2:6 [c]Is 43:7; 44:23
47:1 [a]Is 3:26; Jer 48:18 [b]Is 23:12; 37:22; Jer 46:11 [c]Ps 137:8; Jer 50:42; 51:33; Zech 2:7 [d]Deut 28:56
2 [a]Ex 11:5; Jer 25:10 [b]Job 31:10; Eccl 12:4; Matt 24:41 [c]Gen 24:65; Is 3:23; 1 Cor 11:5 [d]Is 32:11
3 [1]Lit *meet* [a]Ezek 16:37; Nah 3:5 [b]Is 34:8; 63:4
4 [a]Is 41:14
5 [a]Is 23:2; Jer 8:14; Lam 2:10 [b]Is 13:10 [c]Is 47:7 [d]Is 13:19; Dan 2:37
6 [a]Deut 28:50
7 [1]Lit *it* [a]Is 47:5 [b]Is 42:25; 57:11 [c]Deut 32:29; Jer 5:31; Ezek 7:2,3
8 [1]Lit *her* [a]Is 22:13; 32:9; Jer 50:11 [b]Is 32:9, 11; Zeph 2:15 [c]Is 45:5,6,18; 47:10; Zeph 2:15 [d]Rev 18:7
9 [a]Is 13:16,18; 14:22 [b]Ps 73:19; 1 Thess 5:3; Rev 18:8,10 [c]Is 47:13; Nah 3:4; Rev 18:23
10 [1]Lit *it has* [a]Ps 52:7; 62:10; Is 59:4 [b]Is 29:15; Ezek 8:12; 9:9 [c]Is 5:21; 44:20 [d]Is 47:8
11 [a]Is 57:1 [b]Is 13:6; Jer 51:8, 43; Luke 17:27; 1 Thess 5:3 [c]Is 47:9
12 [a]Is 47:9
13 [a]Jer 51:58,64 [b]Is 8:19; 44:25; 47:9; Dan 2:2,10 [c]Is 47:15
14 [a]Is 5:24; Nah 1:10; Mal 4:1 [b]Is 10:17; Jer 51:30,32,58 [c]Is 44:16
15 [1]Lit *side, region* [a]Rev 18:11 [b]Is 5:29; 43:13; 46:7
48:1 [1]Lit *waters* [a]Is 46:12 [b]Num 24:7; Deut 33:28; Ps 68:26 [c]Deut 6:13; Is 45:23; 65:16 [d]Is 58:2; Jer 4:2
2 [a]Is 52:1; 64:10 [b]Is 10:20; Jer 7:4; 21:2; Mic 3:11; Rom 2:17

'[b]No one sees me,'
Your [c]wisdom and your
knowledge, [1]they have
deluded you;
For you have said in your heart,
'[d]I am, and there is no one
besides me.'
11 "But [a]evil will come on you
Which you will not know how to
charm away;
And disaster will fall on you
For which you cannot atone;
And [b]destruction about which
you do not know
Will come on you [c]suddenly.
12 ¶ "Stand *fast* now in your
[a]spells
And in your many sorceries
With which you have labored
from your youth;
Perhaps you will be able to
profit,
Perhaps you may cause
trembling.
13 "You are [a]wearied with your
many counsels;
Let now the [b]astrologers,
Those who prophesy by the
stars,
Those who predict by the new
moons,
Stand up and [c]save you from
what will come upon you.
14 "Behold, they have become [a]like
stubble,
[b]Fire burns them;
They cannot deliver themselves
from the power of the flame;
There will be [c]no coal to
warm by
Nor a fire to sit before!
15 "So have those become to you
with whom you have
labored,
Who have [a]trafficked with you
from your youth;
Each has wandered in his
own [1]way;
There is [b]none to save you.

Israel's Obstinacy

48 "[a]Hear this, O house of Jacob,
who are named Israel
And who came forth from the
[1][b]loins of Judah,
Who [c]swear by the name of the
LORD
And invoke the God of Israel,
But not in truth nor in
[d]righteousness.
2 "For they call themselves after the
[a]holy city
And [b]lean on the God of Israel;

"You will surely [e]put on all of
them as [1]jewels and bind
them on as a bride.
19 "For [a]your waste and desolate
places and your destroyed
land—
Surely now you will be [b]too
cramped for the inhabitants,
And those who [c]swallowed you
will be far away.
20 "The [a]children of [1]whom you
were bereaved will yet say
in your ears,
'The place is too cramped for me;
Make room for me that I may
live *here*.'
21 "Then you will [a]say in your
heart,
'Who has begotten these for me,
Since I have been bereaved of
my children
And am [b]barren, an [c]exile and
a wanderer?
And who has reared these?
Behold, I was [d]left alone;
[1][e]From where did these
come?' "
22 ¶ Thus says the Lord [1]GOD,
"Behold, I will lift up My hand to
the nations
And set up My [a]standard to the
peoples;
And they will [b]bring your sons
in *their* bosom,
And your daughters will be
carried on *their* shoulders.
23 "[a]Kings will be your guardians,
And their princesses your nurses.
They will [b]bow down to you
with their faces to the earth
And [c]lick the dust of your feet;
And *you* will [d]know that I am
the LORD;
Those who hopefully [e]wait for
Me will [f]not be put to
shame.
24 ¶ "[a]Can the prey be taken from
the mighty man,
Or the captives of [1]a tyrant be
rescued?"
25 Surely, thus says the LORD,
"Even the [a]captives of the mighty
man will be taken away,
And the prey of the tyrant will
be rescued;
For I will contend with the one
who contends with you,
And I will [b]save your sons.
26 "I will feed your [a]oppressors with
their [b]own flesh,
And they will become drunk
with their own blood as
with sweet wine;
And [c]all flesh will know that I,
the LORD, am your [d]Savior
And your [e]Redeemer, the
Mighty One of Jacob."

God Helps His Servant

50 Thus says the LORD,
"Where is the [a]certificate of
divorce
By which I have [b]sent your
mother away?
Or to whom of My creditors did
I [c]sell you?
Behold, you were sold for your
[d]iniquities,
And for your [e]transgressions
your mother [f]was sent
away.
2 "Why was there [a]no man when I
came?
When I called, *why* was there
none to answer?
Is My [b]hand so short that it
cannot ransom?
Or have I no power to deliver?
Behold, I [c]dry up the sea with
My rebuke,
I [d]make the rivers a wilderness;
Their fish stink for lack of water
And die of thirst.
3 "I [a]clothe the heavens with
blackness
And make sackcloth their
covering."
4 ¶ The Lord [1]GOD has given Me
the tongue of [a]disciples,
That I may know how to
[b]sustain the weary one with
a word.
He awakens *Me* [c]morning by
morning,
He awakens My ear to listen as a
disciple.
5 The Lord GOD has [a]opened My
ear;
And I was [b]not disobedient
Nor did I turn back.
6 I [a]gave My back to those who
strike *Me*,
And My cheeks to those who
pluck out the beard;
I did not cover My face from
humiliation and spitting.
7 For the Lord GOD [a]helps Me,
Therefore, I am [b]not disgraced;
Therefore, I have set My face
like [c]flint,
And I know that I will not be
ashamed.
8 He who [a]vindicates Me is near;
Who will contend with Me?
Let us [b]stand up to each other;
Who has a case against Me?

18 [1]Lit *an ornament* [e]Is 52:1; 61:10

19 [a]Is 1:7; 3:8; 5:6; 51:3 [b]Is 54:1,2; Zech 10:10 [c]Ps 56:1,2

20 [1]Lit *your bereavement* [a]Is 54:1-3

21 [1]Lit *These, where are they?* [a]Is 29:23; 54:6,7 [b]Is 27:10; Lam 1:1 [c]Is 5:13 [d]Is 1:8 [e]Is 60:8

22 [1]Heb *YHWH,* usually rendered *LORD* [a]Is 11:10, 12; 18:3; 62:10 [b]Is 14:2; 43:6; 60:4

23 [a]Is 14:1,2; 60:3,10,11 [b]Is 45:14; 60:14 [c]Ps 72:9; Mic 7:17 [d]Is 41:20; 43:10; 60:16 [e]Ps 37:9; Is 25:9; 26:8 [f]Ps 25:3; Is 45:17; Joel 2:27

24 [1]So ancient versions and DSS; M.T. reads *the righteous,* cf v 25 [a]Matt 12:29; Luke 11:21

25 [a]Is 10:6; 14:1,2; Jer 50:33,34 [b]Is 25:9; 33:22; 35:4

26 [a]Is 9:4; 14:4; 16:4; 51:13; 54:14 [b]Is 9:20 [c]Is 45:6; Ezek 39:7 [d]Is 43:3 [e]Is 49:7

50:1 [a]Deut 24:1,3; Jer 3:8 [b]Is 54:6,7 [c]Deut 32:30; 2 Kin 4:1; Neh 5:5 [d]Is 52:3; 59:2 [e]Is 1:28; 43:27 [f]Jer 3:8

2 [a]Is 41:28; 59:16; 66:4 [b]Gen 18:14; Num 11:23; Is 59:1 [c]Ex 14:21; Is 19:5; 43:16; 44:27 [d]Josh 3:16; Is 42:15

3 [a]Is 13:10; Rev 6:12

4 [1]Heb *YHWH,* usually rendered *LORD,* and so throughout the ch [a]Is 8:16; 54:13 [b]Is 57:19; Jer 31:25 [c]Ps 5:3; 88:13; 119:147; 143:8

5 [a]Ps 40:6; Is 35:5 [b]Matt 26:39; John 8:29; 14:31; 15:10; Acts 26:19; Phil 2:8; Heb 5:8; 10:7

6 [a]Matt 26:67; 27:30; Mark 14:65; 15:19; Luke 22:63

7 [a]Is 42:1; 49:8 [b]Is 45:17; 54:4 [c]Ezek 3:8,9

8 [a]Is 45:25; Rom 8:33,34 [b]Is 1:18; 41:1; 43:26

Let him draw near to Me.
9 Behold, [a]the Lord GOD
helps Me;
[b]Who is he who condemns Me?
Behold, [c]they will all wear out
like a garment;
The moth will eat them.
10 Who is among you that fears the
LORD,
That obeys the voice of His
[a]servant,
That [b]walks in darkness and has
no light?
Let him [c]trust in the name of
the LORD and rely on his
God.
11 Behold, all you who [a]kindle a
fire,
Who [1]encircle yourselves with
firebrands,
Walk in the light of your fire
And among the brands you have
set ablaze.
This you will have from My
hand:
You will [b]lie down in torment.

Israel Exhorted

51 "[a]Listen to me, you who
[b]pursue righteousness,
Who seek the LORD:
Look to the [c]rock from which
you were hewn
And to the [1]quarry from which
you were dug.
2 "Look to [a]Abraham your father
And to Sarah who gave birth to
you in pain;
When *he* [b]*was but* one I called
him,
Then I blessed him and
multiplied him."
3 Indeed, [a]the LORD will comfort
Zion;
He will comfort all her [b]waste
places.
And her [c]wilderness He will
make like [d]Eden,
And her desert like the [e]garden
of the LORD;
[f]Joy and gladness will be found
in her,
Thanksgiving and sound of a
melody.
4 ¶ "[a]Pay attention to Me, O My
people,
And give ear to Me, O My
[1]nation;
For a [b]law will go forth
from Me,
And I will [2]set My [c]justice for a
[d]light of the peoples.
5 "My [a]righteousness is near, My
salvation has gone forth,
And My [b]arms will judge the
peoples;
The [c]coastlands will wait
for Me,
And for My [d]arm they will wait
expectantly.
6 "[a]Lift up your eyes to the sky,
Then look to the earth beneath;
For the [b]sky will vanish like
smoke,
And the [b]earth will wear out
like a garment
And its inhabitants will die [1]in
like manner;
But My [c]salvation will be
forever,
And My righteousness will not
[2]wane.
7 "[a]Listen to Me, you who know
righteousness,
A people in whose [b]heart is My
law;
Do not fear the [c]reproach of
man,
Nor be dismayed at their
revilings.
8 "For the [a]moth will eat them like
a garment,
And the [b]grub will eat them like
wool.
But My [c]righteousness will be
forever,
And My salvation to all
generations."
9 ¶ [a]Awake, awake, put on
strength, O arm of the LORD;
Awake as in the [b]days of old,
the generations of long ago.
[c]Was it not You who cut Rahab
in pieces,
Who pierced the [d]dragon?
10 Was it not You who [a]dried up
the sea,
The waters of the great deep;
Who made the depths of the sea
a pathway
For the [b]redeemed to cross
over?
11 So the [a]ransomed of the LORD
will return
And come with joyful shouting to
Zion,
And [b]everlasting joy *will be* on
their heads.
They will obtain gladness and
joy,
And [c]sorrow and sighing will
flee away.
12 ¶ "I, even I, am He who
[a]comforts you.

9 [a]Is 41:10 [b]Is 54:17 [c]Job 13:28; Is 51:8

10 [a]Is 49:2,3; 50:4 [b]Is 9:2; 26:9; Eph 5:8 [c]Is 12:2; 26:4

11 [1]Lit *gird* [a]Prov 26:18; Is 9:18; James 3:6 [b]Is 8:22; 65:13-15; Amos 4:9,10

51:1 [1]Lit *excavation of a pit* [a]Is 46:3; 48:12; 51:7 [b]Ps 94:15; Prov 15:9 [c]Gen 17:15-17

2 [a]Is 29:22; 41:8; 63:16 [b]Gen 12:1; 15:5; Deut 1:10; Ezek 33:24

3 [a]Is 40:1; 49:13 [b]Is 52:9 [c]Is 35:1; 41:19 [d]Gen 2:8; Joel 2:3 [e]Gen 13:10 [f]Is 25:9; 41:16; 65:18; 66:10

4 [1]Or *people* [2]Lit *cause to rest* [a]Ps 50:7; 78:1 [b]Deut 18:18; Is 2:3; Mic 4:2 [c]Is 1:27; 42:4 [d]Is 42:6; 49:6

5 [a]Is 46:13; 54:17 [b]Is 40:10 [c]Is 42:4; 60:9 [d]Is 59:16; 63:5

6 [1]Or *like gnats* [2]Lit *be broken* [a]Is 40:26 [b]Ps 102:25,26; Is 13:13; 34:4; Matt 24:35; Heb 1:10-12; 2 Pet 3:10 [c]Is 45:17; 51:8

7 [a]Is 51:1 [b]Ps 37:31 [c]Is 25:8; 54:4; Matt 5:11; Acts 5:41

8 [a]Is 50:9 [b]Is 14:11; 66:24 [c]Is 51:6

9 [a]Is 51:17; 52:1 [b]Ex 6:6; Deut 4:34 [c]Job 26:12; Ps 89:10; Is 30:7 [d]Ps 74:13; Is 27:1

10 [a]Is 11:15,16; 50:2; 63:11,12 [b]Ex 15:13; Ps 106:10; Is 63:9

11 [a]Is 35:10; Jer 31:11,12 [b]Is 60:19; 61:7 [c]Is 25:8; 60:20; 65:19; Rev 7:17; 21:1,4; 22:3

12 [a]Is 51:3

Who are you that you are afraid
of [b]man who dies
And of the son of man who is
made [c]like grass,
13 That you have [a]forgotten the
LORD your Maker,
Who [b]stretched out the heavens
And laid the foundations of the
earth,
That you [c]fear continually all
day long because of the fury
of the oppressor,
As he makes ready to destroy?
But where is the fury of the
[d]oppressor?
14 "The [1a]exile will soon be set free,
and will not die in the dungeon, [b]nor
will his bread be lacking.
15 "For I am the LORD your God, who
[a]stirs up the sea and its waves roar (the
LORD of hosts is His name).
16 "I have [a]put My words in your
mouth and have [b]covered you with the
shadow of My hand, to [1c]establish the
heavens, to found the earth, and to say to
Zion, 'You are My people.' "
17 ¶ [a]Rouse yourself! Rouse
yourself! Arise, O Jerusalem,
You who have [b]drunk from the
LORD'S hand the cup of His
anger;
The [1]chalice of reeling you have
[2]drained to the dregs.
18 There is [a]none to guide her
among all the sons she has
borne,
Nor is there one to take her by
the hand among all the sons
she has reared.
19 These two things have befallen
you;
Who will mourn for you?
The [a]devastation and
destruction, famine and
sword;
How shall I comfort you?
20 Your sons have fainted,
They [a]lie *helpless* at the head of
every street,
Like an [b]antelope in a net,
Full of the wrath of the LORD,
The [c]rebuke of your God.
21 ¶ Therefore, please hear this, you
[a]afflicted,
Who are [b]drunk, but not with
wine:
22 Thus says your Lord, the LORD,
even your God
Who [a]contends for His people,
"Behold, I have taken out of your
hand the [b]cup of reeling,
The [1]chalice of My anger;
You will never drink it again.
23 "I will [a]put it into the hand of
your tormentors,
Who have said to [1]you, '[b]Lie
down that we may walk
over *you.*'
You have even made your back
like the ground
And like the street for those who
walk over *it.*"

Cheer for Prostrate Zion

52 [a]Awake, awake,
Clothe yourself in your
strength, O Zion;
Clothe yourself in your
[b]beautiful garments,
O Jerusalem, the [c]holy city;
For the uncircumcised and the
[d]unclean
Will no longer come into you.
2 Shake yourself [a]from the dust,
[b]rise up,
O captive Jerusalem;
[c]Loose yourself from the chains
around your neck,
O captive daughter of Zion.
3 ¶ For thus says the LORD, "You
were [a]sold for nothing and you will be
[b]redeemed [c]without money."
4 For thus says the Lord [1]GOD, "My
people [a]went down at the first into Egypt
to reside there; then the Assyrian oppressed them without cause.
5 "Now therefore, what do I have
here," declares the LORD, "seeing that
My people have been taken away without
cause?" *Again* the LORD declares, "Those
who rule over them howl, and My
[a]name is continually blasphemed all day
long.
6 "Therefore My people shall [a]know
My name; therefore in that day I am the
one who is speaking, 'Here I am.' "
7 ¶ How lovely on the mountains
Are the feet of him who brings
[a]good news,
Who announces [1]peace
And brings good news of
[2]happiness,
Who announces salvation,
And says to Zion, "Your [b]God
[3]reigns!"
8 Listen! Your watchmen lift up
their [a]voices,
They shout joyfully together;
For they will see [1]with their
own eyes
When the LORD restores Zion.
9 [a]Break forth, shout joyfully
together,
You [b]waste places of Jerusalem;
For the LORD has comforted His
people,
He has [c]redeemed Jerusalem.

12 [b]Ps 118:6; Is 2:22 [c]Is 40:6,7; 1 Pet 1:24

13 [a]Deut 6:12; 8:11; Is 17:10 [b]Job 9:8; Ps 104:2; Is 40:22; 45:12,18; 48:13 [c]Is 7:4; 10:24 [d]Is 49:26; 54:14

14 [1]Lit *one in chains* [a]Is 48:20; 52:2 [b]Is 33:6; 49:10

15 [a]Ps 107:25; Jer 31:35

16 [1]Lit *plant* [a]Deut 18:18; Is 59:21 [b]Ex 33:22; Is 49:2 [c]Is 66:22

17 [1]Lit *bowl of the cup of reeling* [2]Lit *drunk* [a]Is 51:9; 52:1 [b]Job 21:20; Is 29:9; 63:6; Jer 25:15; Rev 14:10; 16:19

18 [a]Ps 88:18; 142:4; Is 49:21

19 [a]Is 8:21; 9:20; 14:30

20 [a]Is 5:25; Jer 14:16 [b]Deut 14:5 [c]Is 66:15

21 [a]Is 54:11 [b]Is 29:9; 51:17; 63:6

22 [1]Lit *bowl of the cup of* [a]Is 3:12,13; 49:25; Jer 50:34 [b]Is 51:17

23 [1]Lit *your soul* [a]Is 49:26; Jer 25:15-17,26,28; Zech 12:2 [b]Josh 10:24

52:1 [a]Is 51:9,17 [b]Ex 28:2,40; 1 Chr 16:29; Ps 110:3; Is 49:18; 61:3,10; Zech 3:4 [c]Neh 11:1; Is 48:2; 64:10; Zech 14:20,21; Matt 4:5; Rev 21:2-27 [d]Is 35:8

2 [a]Is 29:4 [b]Is 60:1 [c]Is 9:4; 10:27; 14:25; Zech 2:7

3 [a]Ps 44:12; Jer 15:13 [b]Is 1:27; 62:12; 63:4 [c]Is 45:13

4 [1]Heb *YHWH,* usually rendered *LORD* [a]Gen 46:6

5 [a]Ezek 36:20, 23; Rom 2:24

6 [a]Is 49:23

7 [1]Or *well-being* [2]Lit *good* [3]Or *is King* [a]Is 40:9; 61:1; Nah 1:15; Rom 10:15; Eph 6:15 [b]Ps 93:1; Is 24:23

8 [1]Lit *eye to eye* [a]Is 62:6

9 [a]Ps 98:4; Is 44:23 [b]Is 44:26; 51:3; 61:4 [c]Is 43:1; 48:20

10 The LORD has bared His
holy [a]arm
In the sight of all the nations,
[1]That [b]all the ends of the earth
may see
The salvation of our God.

11 ¶ [a]Depart, depart, go out from
there,
[b]Touch nothing unclean;
Go out of the midst of her,
[c]purify yourselves,
You who carry the vessels of the
LORD.

12 But you will not go out in
[a]haste,
Nor will you go [1]as fugitives;
For the [b]LORD will go before
you,
And [c]the God of Israel *will be*
your rear guard.

The Exalted Servant

13 ¶ Behold, My [a]servant will
prosper,
He will be high and lifted up and
[1]greatly [b]exalted.

14 Just as many were astonished at
you, *My people,*
So His [a]appearance was marred
more than any man
And His form more than the
sons of men.

15 Thus He will [a]sprinkle many
nations,
Kings will [b]shut their mouths on
account of Him;
For [c]what had not been told
them they will see,
And what they had not heard
they will understand.

The Suffering Servant

53 [a]Who has believed our
message?
And to whom has the arm of the
LORD been revealed?

2 For He grew up before Him like
a [a]tender [1]shoot,
And like a root out of parched
ground;
He has [b]no *stately* form or
majesty
That we should look upon Him,
Nor appearance that we should
[2]be attracted to Him.

3 He was [a]despised and forsaken
of men,
A man of [1]sorrows and
[b]acquainted with [2]grief;
And like one from whom men
hide their face
He was [c]despised, and we did
not [d]esteem Him.

4 ¶ Surely our [1]griefs He Himself
[a]bore,
And our [2]sorrows He carried;
Yet we ourselves esteemed Him
stricken,
[3]Smitten of [b]God, and afflicted.

5 But He was [1]pierced through for
[a]our transgressions,
He was crushed for [b]our
iniquities;
The [c]chastening for our
[2]well-being *fell* upon Him,
And by [d]His scourging we are
healed.

6 All of us like sheep have gone
astray,
Each of us has turned to his own
way;
But the LORD has caused the
iniquity of us all
To [1]fall on Him.

7 ¶ He was oppressed and He was
afflicted,
Yet He did not [a]open His
mouth;
[b]Like a lamb that is led to
slaughter,
And like a sheep that is silent
before its shearers,
So He did not open His mouth.

8 By oppression and judgment He
was taken away;
And as for His generation, who
considered
That He was cut off out of the
land of the [1]living
[a]For the transgression of my
people, to whom the stroke
was due?

9 His grave was assigned with
wicked men,
Yet He was with a [a]rich man in
His death,
[b]Because He had [c]done no
violence,
Nor was there any deceit in His
mouth.

10 ¶ But the LORD was pleased
To [a]crush Him, [1b]putting *Him*
to grief;
If [2]He would render Himself *as*
a guilt [c]offering,
He will see [d]*His* [3]offspring,
He will prolong *His* days,
And the [4]good [e]pleasure of the
LORD will prosper in His
hand.

11 As a result of the [1]anguish of
His soul,
He will [a]see [2]*it and* be
satisfied;
By His [b]knowledge the
Righteous One,

10 [1]Lit *And...earth will see* [a]Ps 98:1-3; Is 51:9; 66:18, 19 [b]Is 45:22; 48:20

11 [a]Is 48:20; Jer 50:8; Zech 2:6,7; 2 Cor 6:17 [b]Num 19:11,16 [c]Lev 22:2; Is 1:16

12 [1]Lit *in flight* [a]Ex 12:11,33; Deut 16:3 [b]Is 26:7; 42:16; 49:10,11 [c]Ex 14:19,20; Is 58:8

13 [1]Or *very high* [a]Is 42:1; 49:1-7; 53:11 [b]Is 57:15; Phil 2:9

14 [a]Is 53:2,3

15 [a]Num 19:18-21; Ezek 36:25 [b]Job 21:5 [c]Rom 15:21; Eph 3:5

53:1 [a]John 12:38; Rom 10:16

2 [1]Lit *suckling* [2]Lit *desire* [a]Is 11:1 [b]Is 52:14

3 [1]Or *pains* [2]Or *sickness* [a]Ps 22:6; Is 49:7; Luke 18:31-33 [b]Is 53:10 [c]Mark 10:33,34 [d]John 1:10,11

4 [1]Or *sickness* [2]Or *pains* [3]Or *Struck down by* [a]Matt 8:17 [b]John 19:7

5 [1]Or *wounded* [2]Or *peace* [a]Is 53:8; Heb 9:28 [b]Is 53:10; Rom 4:25; 1 Cor 15:3 [c]Deut 11:2; Heb 5:8 [d]1 Pet 2:24, 25

6 [1]Lit *encounter Him*

7 [a]Matt 26:63; 27:12-14; Mark 14:61; 15:5; Luke 23:9; John 19:9 [b]Acts 8:32, 33; Rev 5:6

8 [1]Or *life* [a]Is 53:5,12

9 [a]Matt 27:57-60 [b]Is 42:1-3 [c]1 Pet 2:22

10 [1]Lit *He made Him sick* [2]Lit *His soul* [3]Lit *seed* [4]Or *will of* [a]Is 53:5 [b]Is 53:3,4 [c]Is 53:6, 12; John 1:29 [d]Ps 22:30; Is 54:3; 61:9; 66:22 [e]Is 46:10

11 [1]Or *toilsome labor* [2]Another reading is *light* [a]John 10:14-18 [b]Is 45:25; Rom 5:18,19

My Servant, will justify the
many,
As He will [c]bear their iniquities.
12 Therefore, I will allot Him a
[a]portion with the great,
And He will divide the booty
with the strong;
Because He poured out
[1][b]Himself to death,
And was [c]numbered with the
transgressors;
Yet He Himself [d]bore the sin of
many,
And interceded for the
transgressors.

The Fertility of Zion

54 "[a]Shout for joy, O barren one,
you who have borne no
child;
Break forth into joyful shouting
and cry aloud, you who have
not travailed;
For the sons of the [b]desolate
one *will be* [c]more
numerous
Than the sons of the married
woman," says the LORD.
2 "[a]Enlarge the place of your tent;
[1]Stretch out the curtains of your
dwellings, spare not;
Lengthen your [b]cords
And strengthen your [b]pegs.
3 "For you will [a]spread abroad to
the right and to the left.
And your [1]descendants will
[b]possess nations
And will [c]resettle the desolate
cities.
4 ¶ "Fear not, for you will [a]not be
put to shame;
And do not feel humiliated, for
you will not be disgraced;
But you will forget the [b]shame
of your youth,
And the [c]reproach of your
widowhood you will
remember no more.
5 "For your [a]husband is your
Maker,
Whose name is the LORD of
hosts;
And your [b]Redeemer is the Holy
One of Israel,
Who is called the [c]God of all
the earth.
6 "For the LORD has called you,
Like a wife [a]forsaken and
grieved in spirit,
Even like a wife of *one's* youth
when she is rejected,"
Says your God.
7 "[1]For a [a]brief moment I forsook
you,
But with great compassion I will
[b]gather you.
8 "In an [1][a]outburst of anger
I hid My face from you for a
moment,
But with everlasting
[b]lovingkindness I will
[c]have compassion on you,"
Says the LORD your [d]Redeemer.
9 ¶ "For [1]this is like the days of
Noah to Me,
When I swore that the waters of
Noah
Would [a]not [2]flood the earth
again;
So I have sworn that I will [b]not
be angry with you
Nor will I rebuke you.
10 "For the [a]mountains may be
removed and the hills may
shake,
But My lovingkindness will not
be removed from you,
And My [b]covenant of peace will
not be shaken,"
Says [c]the LORD who has
compassion on you.
11 ¶ "O [a]afflicted one,
storm-tossed, *and* [b]not
comforted,
Behold, I will set your stones in
antimony,
And your foundations I will [c]lay
in [1][d]sapphires.
12 "Moreover, I will make your
battlements of [1]rubies,
And your gates of [2]crystal,
And your entire [3]wall of
precious stones.
13 "[a]All your sons will be [1]taught of
the LORD;
And the well-being of your sons
will be [b]great.
14 "In [a]righteousness you will be
established;
You will be far from
[b]oppression, for you will
[c]not fear;
And from [d]terror, for it will not
come near you.
15 "If anyone fiercely assails *you* it
will not be from Me.
[a]Whoever assails you will fall
because of you.
16 "Behold, I Myself have created
the smith who blows the
fire of coals
And brings out a weapon for its
work;
And I have created the destroyer
to ruin.

11 [c]Is 53:5,6

12 [1]Lit *His soul* [a]Is 52:13; Phil 2:9-11 [b]Matt 26:38,39,42 [c]Mark 15:28; Luke 22:37 [d]Is 53:6,11; 2 Cor 5:21

54:1 [a]Gal 4:27 [b]Is 62:4 [c]1 Sam 2:5; Is 49:20

2 [1]Lit *Let them stretch out* [a]Is 33:20; 49:19,20 [b]Ex 35:18; 39:40

3 [1]Lit *seed* [a]Gen 28:14; Is 43:5,6; 60:3 [b]Is 14:1,2 [c]Is 49:19

4 [a]Is 45:17 [b]Jer 31:19 [c]Is 4:1; 25:8; 51:7

5 [a]Jer 3:14; Hos 2:19 [b]Is 43:14; 48:17 [c]Is 6:3; 11:9; 65:16

6 [a]Is 49:14-21; 50:1,2; 62:4

7 [1]Lit *In* [a]Is 26:20 [b]Is 11:12; 43:5; 49:18

8 [1]Lit *overflowing* [a]Is 60:10 [b]Is 54:10; 63:7 [c]Is 49:10,13 [d]Is 54:5

9 [1]Some mss read *the waters of Noah this is to Me* [2]Lit *cross over* [a]Gen 9:11 [b]Is 12:1; Ezek 39:29

10 [a]Ps 102:26; Is 51:6 [b]2 Sam 23:5; Ps 89:34; Is 55:3; 59:21; 61:8 [c]Is 54:8

11 [1]Or *lapis lazuli* [a]Is 51:21 [b]Is 51:18,19 [c]Is 14:32; 28:16; 44:28 [d]Job 28:16; Rev 21:19

12 [1]I.e. bright red [2]Or *carbuncles* [3]Lit *border, boundary*

13 [1]Or *disciples* [a]John 6:45 [b]Is 48:18; 66:12

14 [a]Is 1:26,27; 9:7; 62:1 [b]Is 9:4; 14:4 [c]Is 54:4 [d]Is 33:18

15 [a]Is 41:11-16

17 "[a]No weapon that is formed
against you will prosper;
And [b]every tongue that
[1]accuses you in judgment
you will condemn.
This is the heritage of the
servants of the LORD,
And their [c]vindication is from
Me," declares the LORD.

The Free Offer of Mercy

55 "Ho! Every one who [a]thirsts,
come to the waters;
And you who have [b]no [1]money
come, buy and eat.
Come, buy [c]wine and milk
[d]Without money and without
cost.
2 "Why do you [1]spend money for
what is [a]not bread,
And your wages for what does
not satisfy?
Listen carefully to Me, and [b]eat
what is good,
And [c]delight yourself in
abundance.
3 "[a]Incline your ear and come
to Me.
Listen, that [1]you may [b]live;
And I will make [c]an everlasting
covenant with you,
According to the [d]faithful
mercies [2]shown to David.
4 "Behold, I have made [a]him a
witness to the peoples,
A [b]leader and commander for
the peoples.
5 "Behold, you will call a [a]nation
you do not know,
And a nation which knows you
not will [b]run to you,
Because of the LORD your God,
even the Holy One of Israel;
For He has [c]glorified you."
6 ¶ [a]Seek the LORD while He may
be found;
[b]Call upon Him while He is
near.
7 [a]Let the wicked forsake his way
And the unrighteous man his
[b]thoughts;
And let him [c]return to the
LORD,
And He will have [d]compassion
on him,
And to our God,
For He will [e]abundantly pardon.
8 "For My thoughts are not [a]your
thoughts,
Nor are [b]your ways My ways,"
declares the LORD.
9 "For [a]*as* the heavens are higher
than the earth,
So are My ways higher than your
ways
And My thoughts than your
thoughts.
10 "For as the [a]rain and the snow
come down from heaven,
And do not return there without
watering the earth
And making it bear and sprout,
And furnishing [b]seed to the
sower and bread to the
eater;
11 So will My [a]word be which goes
forth from My mouth;
It will [b]not return to Me empty,
Without [c]accomplishing what I
desire,
And without succeeding *in the
matter* for which I sent it.
12 "For you will go out with [a]joy
And be led forth with [b]peace;
The [c]mountains and the hills
will break forth into shouts
of joy before you,
And all the [d]trees of the field
will clap *their* hands.
13 "Instead of the [a]thorn bush the
[b]cypress will come up,
And instead of the [c]nettle the
myrtle will come up,
And [1]it will be a [2d]memorial to
the LORD,
For an everlasting [e]sign which
[f]will not be cut off."

Rewards for Obedience to God

56 Thus says the LORD,
"[a]Preserve justice and do
righteousness,
For My [b]salvation is about to
come
And My righteousness to be
revealed.
2 "How [a]blessed is the man who
does this,
And the son of man who [b]takes
hold of it;
Who [c]keeps from profaning the
sabbath,
And keeps his hand from doing
any evil."
3 Let not the [a]foreigner who has
joined himself to the LORD
say,
"The LORD will surely separate me
from His people."
Nor let the [b]eunuch say,
"Behold, I am a dry tree."
4 For thus says the LORD,
"To the eunuchs who [a]keep My
sabbaths,
And choose what pleases Me,
And [b]hold fast My covenant,

17 [1]Lit *rises against* [a]Is 17:12-14; 29:8 [b]Is 50:8,9 [c]Is 45:24; 46:13

55:1 [1]Lit *silver* [a]Ps 42:1,2; 63:1; 143:6; Is 41:17; 44:3; John 4:14; 7:37; Rev 21:6 [b]Lam 5:4 [c]Song 5:1; Joel 3:18 [d]Hos 14:4; Matt 10:8

2 [1]Lit *weigh out silver* [a]Eccl 6:2; Hos 8:7 [b]Ps 22:26; Is 1:19; 62:8,9 [c]Is 25:6; Jer 31:14

3 [1]Lit *your soul* [2]Lit *of David* [a]Is 51:4 [b]Lev 18:5; Rom 10:5 [c]Is 61:8 [d]Acts 13:34

4 [a]Ps 18:43; Jer 30:9; Hos 3:5 [b]Ezek 34:24; 37:24,25; Dan 9:25; Mic 5:2

5 [a]Is 45:14, 22-24; 49:6,12, 23 [b]Zech 8:22 [c]Is 60:9

6 [a]Ps 32:6; Is 45:19,22; 49:8; Amos 5:6 [b]Is 58:9; 65:24

7 [a]Is 1:16,19; 58:6 [b]Is 32:7; 59:7 [c]Is 31:6; 44:22 [d]Is 14:1; 54:8,10 [e]Is 1:18; 40:2; 43:25; 44:22

8 [a]Is 65:2; 66:18 [b]Is 53:6

9 [a]Ps 103:11

10 [a]Is 30:23 [b]2 Cor 9:10

11 [a]Is 45:23; Matt 24:35 [b]Is 44:26; 59:21 [c]Is 46:10; 53:10

12 [a]Ps 105:43; Is 51:11; 52:9 [b]Is 54:10,13; Jer 29:11 [c]Is 44:23; 49:13 [d]1 Chr 16:33

13 [1]I.e. the transformation of the desert [2]Lit *name* [a]Is 7:19 [b]Is 60:13 [c]Is 5:6; 7:24; 32:13 [d]Is 63:12,14; Jer 33:9 [e]Is 19:20 [f]Is 56:5

56:1 [a]Is 1:17; 33:5; 61:8 [b]Ps 85:9; Is 46:13; 51:5

2 [a]Ps 112:1; 119:1,2 [b]Is 56:4,6 [c]Ex 20:8-11; 31:13-17; Is 56:6; 58:13; Jer 17:21,22; Ezek 20:12,20

3 [a]Is 14:1; 56:6 [b]Deut 23:1; Jer 38:7; Acts 8:27

4 [a]Is 56:2,6 [b]Is 56:6

5 To them I will give in My
[a]house and within My
[b]walls a memorial,
And a name better than that of
sons and daughters;
I will give [1]them an everlasting
[c]name which [d]will not be
cut off.
6 ¶ "Also the [a]foreigners who join
themselves to the LORD,
To minister to Him, and to love
the name of the LORD,
To be His servants, every one
who [b]keeps from profaning
the sabbath
And holds fast My covenant;
7 Even [a]those I will bring to My
[b]holy mountain
And [c]make them joyful in My
house of prayer.
Their burnt offerings and their
sacrifices will be acceptable
on [d]My altar;
For [e]My house will be called a
house of prayer for all the
peoples."
8 The Lord [1]GOD, who [a]gathers
the dispersed of Israel,
declares,
"Yet [b]*others* I will gather to
[2]them, to those *already*
gathered."
9 ¶ All you [a]beasts of the field,
All you beasts in the forest,
Come to eat.
10 His [a]watchmen are [b]blind,
All of them know nothing.
All of them are mute dogs unable
to bark,
[1]Dreamers lying down, who love
to slumber;
11 And the dogs are [1a]greedy, they
[2]are not satisfied.
And they are shepherds who
have [b]no understanding;
They have all [c]turned to their
own way,
Each one to his unjust gain, to
the last one.
12 "Come," *they say,* "let [1]us get
[a]wine, and let us drink
heavily of strong drink;
And [b]tomorrow will be like
today, only more so."

Evil Leaders Rebuked

57 The righteous man perishes,
and no man [a]takes it to
heart;
And devout men are taken away,
while no one understands.
For the righteous man is taken
away from [b]evil,
2 He enters into peace;
They rest in their [1]beds,
Each one who [a]walked in his
upright way.
3 "But come here, you sons of a
[a]sorceress,
[b]Offspring of an adulterer and
[1]a [c]prostitute.
4 "Against whom do you jest?
Against whom do you open wide
your mouth
And stick out your tongue?
Are you not children of
[a]rebellion,
Offspring of deceit,
5 *Who* inflame yourselves among
the [1a]oaks,
[b]Under every luxuriant tree,
Who [c]slaughter the children in
the [2]ravines,
Under the clefts of the crags?
6 "Among the [1a]smooth *stones* of
the [2]ravine
Is your portion, [3]they are your
lot;
Even to them you have [b]poured
out a drink offering,
You have made a grain offering.
Shall I [4c]relent concerning
these things?
7 "Upon a [a]high and lofty mountain
You have [b]made your bed.
You also went up there to offer
sacrifice.
8 "Behind the door and the
doorpost
You have set up your sign;
Indeed, far removed from Me,
you have [a]uncovered
yourself,
And have gone up and made
your bed wide.
And you have made an
agreement for yourself with
them,
You have loved their [1]bed,
You have looked on *their*
[2]manhood.
9 "You have journeyed to the king
with oil
And increased your perfumes;
You have [a]sent your envoys a
great distance
And made *them* go down to
[1]Sheol.
10 "You were tired out by the length
of your road,
Yet you did not say, '[a]It is
hopeless.'
You found [1]renewed strength,
Therefore you did not [2]faint.
11 ¶ "Of [a]whom were you worried
and fearful

5 [1]So DSS; M.T. reads *him* [a]Is 2:2,3; 56:7; 66:20 [b]Is 26:1; 60:18 [c]Is 62:2 [d]Is 48:19; 55:13

6 [a]Is 56:3; 60:10; 61:5 [b]Is 56:2,4

7 [a]Is 2:2,3; 60:11; Mic 4:1,2 [b]Is 11:9; 65:25 [c]Is 61:10 [d]Is 60:7 [e]Matt 21:13; Mark 11:17; Luke 19:46

8 [1]Heb *YHWH,* usually rendered *LORD* [2]Lit *him* [a]Is 11:12 [b]Is 60:3-11; 66:18-21; John 10:16

9 [a]Is 18:6; 46:11

10 [1]So DSS; M.T. *Ravers* [a]Ezek 3:17 [b]Is 29:9-14; Jer 14:13,14

11 [1]Lit *strong of soul/appetite* [2]Lit *do not know satisfaction* [a]Is 28:7; Ezek 13:19; Mic 3:5, 11 [b]Is 1:3 [c]Is 57:17; Jer 22:17

12 [1]So DSS and many versions; M.T. *me* [a]Is 5:11,12,22 [b]Ps 10:6; Luke 12:19,20

57:1 [a]Is 42:25; 47:7 [b]2 Kin 22:20; Is 47:11; Jer 18:11

2 [1]I.e. graves [a]Is 26:7

3 [1]So ancient versions; Heb *she prostitutes herself* [a]Mal 3:5 [b]Is 1:4; Matt 16:4 [c]Is 1:21; 57:7-9

4 [a]Is 48:8

5 [1]Or *terebinths* [2]Or *wadis* [a]Is 1:29 [b]2 Kin 16:4; Jer 2:20; 3:13 [c]2 Kin 23:10; Ps 106:37,38; Jer 7:31

6 [1]I.e. symbols of fertility gods [2]Or *wadi* [3]Lit *they, they* [4]Or *repent* [a]Jer 3:9; Hab 2:19 [b]Jer 7:18 [c]Jer 5:9,29; 9:9

7 [a]Jer 3:6; Ezek 16:16 [b]Ezek 23:41

8 [1]Or *lying down* [2]Lit *hand* [a]Ezek 23:18

9 [1]I.e. the nether world [a]Ezek 23:16,40

10 [1]Lit *the life of your hand* [2]Or *become sick* [a]Jer 2:25; 18:12

11 [a]Prov 29:25; Is 51:12,13

When you lied, and did [b]not
remember Me
[1]Nor [c]give *Me* a thought?
Was I not silent even for a long
time
So you do not fear Me?
12 "I will [a]declare your
righteousness and your
[b]deeds,
But they will not profit you.
13 "When you cry out, [a]let your
collection *of idols* deliver
you.
But the wind will carry all of
them up,
And a breath will take *them*
away.
But he who [b]takes refuge in Me
will [c]inherit the land
And will [d]possess My holy
mountain."

14 ¶ And it will be said,
"[a]Build up, build up, prepare the
way,
Remove *every* obstacle out of the
way of My people."
15 For thus says the [a]high and
exalted One
Who [1b]lives forever, whose
name is Holy,
"I [c]dwell *on* a high and holy
place,
And *also* with the [d]contrite and
lowly of spirit
In order to [e]revive the spirit of
the lowly
And to revive the heart of the
contrite.
16 "For I will [a]not contend forever,
[b]Nor will I always be angry;
For the spirit would grow faint
before Me,
And the [c]breath *of those whom*
I have made.
17 "Because of the iniquity of his
[a]unjust gain I was angry
and struck him;
I hid *My face* and was angry,
And he went on [b]turning away,
in the way of his heart.
18 "I have seen his ways, but I will
[a]heal him;
I will [b]lead him and [c]restore
comfort to him and to his
mourners,
19 Creating the [1a]praise of the
lips.
[b]Peace, peace to him who is
[c]far and to him who is
near,"
Says the LORD, "and I will heal
him."

11 [1]Lit *You did not set it upon your heart* [b]Jer 2:32; 3:21 [c]Ps 50:21; Is 42:14

12 [a]Is 58:1,2 [b]Is 29:15; 59:6; 65:7; 66:18; Mic 3:2-4

13 [a]Jer 22:20; 30:14 [b]Ps 37:3, 9; Is 25:4 [c]Is 49:8; 60:21 [d]Is 65:9

14 [a]Is 62:10; Jer 18:15

15 [1]Or *dwells in eternity* [a]Is 52:13 [b]Deut 33:27; Is 40:28 [c]Is 33:5; 66:1 [d]Ps 34:18; 51:17; Is 66:2 [e]Ps 147:3; Is 61:1-3

16 [a]Gen 6:3 [b]Ps 85:5; 103:9; Mic 7:18 [c]Is 42:5

17 [a]Is 2:7; 56:11; Jer 6:13 [b]Is 1:4; Jer 3:14, 22

18 [a]Is 19:22; 30:26; 53:5 [b]Is 52:12 [c]Is 61:1-3

19 [1]Lit *fruit of the lips* [a]Is 6:7; 51:16; 59:21; Heb 13:15 [b]Is 26:12; 32:17 [c]Acts 2:39; Eph 2:17

20 [a]Job 18:5-14; Is 3:9,11

21 [a]Is 48:22; 59:8 [b]Is 49:4

58:1 [a]Is 40:6 [b]Is 43:27; 50:1; 59:12

2 [a]Is 1:11; Titus 1:16 [b]Is 48:1; Jer 7:9,10 [c]Is 1:4,28; 59:13 [d]Ps 119:151; Is 29:13; 57:3; James 4:8

3 [1]Lit *know* [a]Mal 3:14; Luke 18:12 [b]Is 22:12, 13; Zech 7:5,6

4 [a]Is 3:14,15; 59:6 [b]Is 1:15; 59:2; Joel 2:12-14

5 [1]Lit *his* [a]1 Kin 21:27 [b]Is 49:8; 61:2

6 [a]Neh 5:10-12; Jer 34:8 [b]Is 1:17 [c]Is 58:9

7 [1]Lit *for* [a]Job 31:19,20; Is 58:10; Ezek 18:7,16 [b]Is 16:3,4; Heb 13:2 [c]Matt 25:35,36; Luke 3:11 [d]Deut 22:1-4; Luke 10:31,32

20 But the [a]wicked are like the
tossing sea,
For it cannot be quiet,
And its waters toss up refuse and
mud.
21 "[a]There is no peace," says [b]my
God, "for the wicked."

Observances of Fasts

58 "[a]Cry loudly, do not hold back;
Raise your voice like a trumpet,
And declare to My people their
[b]transgression
And to the house of Jacob their
sins.
2 "Yet they [a]seek Me day by day
and delight to know My
ways,
As a nation that has done
[b]righteousness
And [c]has not forsaken the
ordinance of their God.
They ask Me *for* just decisions,
They delight [d]in the nearness of
God.
3 'Why have we [a]fasted and You
do not see?
Why have we humbled ourselves
and You do not [1]notice?'
Behold, on the [b]day of your fast
you find *your* desire,
And drive hard all your workers.
4 "Behold, you fast for contention
and [a]strife and to strike
with a wicked fist.
You do not fast like *you do* today
to [b]make your voice heard
on high.
5 "Is it a fast like this which I
choose, a day for a man to
humble himself?
Is it for bowing [1]one's head like
a reed
And for spreading out [a]sackcloth
and ashes as a bed?
Will you call this a fast, even an
[b]acceptable day to the
LORD?
6 "Is this not the fast which I
choose,
To [a]loosen the bonds of
wickedness,
To undo the bands of the yoke,
And to [b]let the oppressed go
free
And [c]break every yoke?
7 "Is it not to [a]divide your bread
[1]with the hungry
And [b]bring the homeless poor
into the house;
When you see the [c]naked, to
cover him;
And not to [d]hide yourself from
your own flesh?

8 "Then your [a]light will break out
like the dawn,
And your [b]recovery will speedily
spring forth;
And your [c]righteousness will go
before you;
The glory of the [d]LORD will be
your rear guard.
9 "Then you will [a]call, and the
LORD will answer;
You will cry, and He will say,
'Here I am.'
If you [b]remove the yoke from
your midst,
The [1c]pointing of the finger and
[d]speaking wickedness,
10 And if you [1a]give yourself to
the hungry
And satisfy the [2]desire of the
afflicted,
Then your [b]light will rise in
darkness
And your gloom *will become* like
midday.
11 "And the [a]LORD will continually
guide you,
And [b]satisfy your [1]desire in
scorched places,
And [c]give strength to your
bones;
And you will be like a [d]watered
garden,
And like a [e]spring of water
whose waters do not [2]fail.
12 "Those from among you will
[a]rebuild the ancient ruins;
You will [b]raise up the age-old
foundations;
And you will be called the
repairer of the [c]breach,
The restorer of the [1]streets in
which to dwell.

Keeping the Sabbath

13 ¶ "If because of the sabbath, you
[a]turn your foot
From doing your *own* pleasure
on My holy day,
And call the sabbath a [b]delight,
the holy *day* of the LORD
honorable,
And honor it, desisting from your
[c]*own* ways,
From seeking your *own* pleasure
And [d]speaking *your own* word,
14 Then you will take [a]delight in
the LORD,
And I will make you ride [b]on
the heights of the earth;
And I will feed you *with* the
heritage of Jacob your father,
For the [c]mouth of the LORD has
spoken."

8 [a]Is 58:10 [b]Is 30:26; 33:24; Jer 30:17; 33:6 [c]Ps 85:13; Is 62:1 [d]Ex 14:19; Is 52:12

9 [1]Lit *sending out* [a]Ps 50:15; Is 55:6; 65:24 [b]Is 58:6 [c]Prov 6:13 [d]Ps 12:2; Is 59:13

10 [1]Lit *furnish* [2]Or *soul* [a]Deut 15:7; Is 58:7 [b]Job 11:17; Ps 37:6; Is 42:16; 58:8

11 [1]Or *soul* [2]Or *deceive* [a]Is 49:10; 57:18 [b]Ps 107:9; Is 41:17 [c]Is 66:14 [d]Song 4:15; Is 27:3; Jer 31:12 [e]John 4:14; 7:38

12 [1]Lit *paths* [a]Is 49:8; 61:4; Ezek 36:10 [b]Is 44:28 [c]Is 30:13; Amos 9:11

13 [a]Ex 31:16, 17; 35:2,3; Is 56:2,4,6; Jer 17:21-27 [b]Ps 27:4; 42:4; 84:2, 10 [c]Is 55:8 [d]Is 59:13

14 [a]Job 22:26; Is 61:10 [b]Deut 32:13; 33:29; Is 33:16; Hab 3:19 [c]Is 1:20; 40:5

59:1 [a]Num 11:23; Is 50:2; Jer 32:17 [b]Is 58:9; 65:24; Ezek 8:18

2 [1]So versions; M.T. *faces* [a]Is 1:15; 50:1 [b]Is 58:4

3 [a]Is 1:15,21; Jer 2:30,34; Ezek 7:23; Hos 4:2 [b]Is 28:15; 30:9; 59:13

4 [1]Lit *in truth* [a]Is 5:7; 59:14 [b]Is 59:14,15 [c]Is 30:12; Jer 7:4,8 [d]Job 15:35; Ps 7:14; Is 33:11

5 [a]Job 8:14

6 [1]Lit *palms* [a]Is 28:20 [b]Is 57:12; Jer 6:7 [c]Is 58:4; Ezek 7:11

7 [a]Prov 1:16; 6:17; Rom 3:15-17 [b]Is 65:2; 66:18; Mark 7:21,22

8 [1]Lit *it* [a]Luke 1:79 [b]Is 59:9, 11; Hos 4:1 [c]Is 57:20,21

9 [a]Is 59:14 [b]Is 5:30; 8:21,22

Separation from God

59 Behold, [a]the LORD's hand is not
so short
That it cannot save;
[b]Nor is His ear so dull
That it cannot hear.
2 But your [a]iniquities have made a
separation between you and
your God,
And your sins have hidden *His*
[1]face from you so that He
does [b]not hear.
3 For your [a]hands are defiled with
blood
And your fingers with iniquity;
Your lips have spoken
[b]falsehood,
Your tongue mutters wickedness.
4 [a]No one sues righteously and
[b]no one pleads [1]honestly.
They [c]trust in confusion and
speak lies;
They [d]conceive mischief and
bring forth iniquity.
5 They hatch adders' eggs and
[a]weave the spider's web;
He who eats of their eggs dies,
And *from* that which is crushed
a snake breaks forth.
6 Their webs will not become
clothing,
Nor will they [a]cover themselves
with their works;
Their [b]works are works of
iniquity,
And an [c]act of violence is in
their [1]hands.
7 [a]Their feet run to evil,
And they hasten to shed
innocent blood;
[b]Their thoughts are thoughts of
iniquity,
Devastation and destruction are
in their highways.
8 They do not know the [a]way of
peace,
And there is [b]no justice in their
tracks;
They have made their paths
crooked,
[c]Whoever treads on [1]them does
not know peace.

A Confession of Wickedness

9 ¶ Therefore [a]justice is far
from us,
And righteousness does not
overtake us;
We [b]hope for light, but behold,
darkness,
For brightness, but we walk in
gloom.

10 We [a]grope along the wall like
blind men,
We grope like those who have
no eyes;
We [b]stumble at midday as in the
twilight,
Among those who are vigorous
we are [c]like dead men.
11 All of us growl like bears,
And [a]moan sadly like doves;
We hope for [b]justice, but there
is none,
For salvation, *but* it is far
from us.
12 For our [a]transgressions are
multiplied before You,
And our [b]sins [1]testify
against us;
For our transgressions are
with us,
And [2]we know our iniquities:
13 Transgressing and [a]denying the
LORD,
And turning away from our God,
Speaking [b]oppression and revolt,
Conceiving *in* and [c]uttering
from the heart lying words.
14 [a]Justice is turned back,
And [b]righteousness stands far
away;
For truth has stumbled in the
street,
And uprightness cannot enter.
15 Yes, truth is lacking;
And he who turns aside from
evil [a]makes himself a prey.

¶ Now the LORD saw,
And it was [1]displeasing in His
sight [b]that there was no
justice.
16 And He saw that there was [a]no
man,
And was astonished that there
was no one to intercede;
Then His [b]own arm brought
salvation to Him,
And His righteousness upheld
Him.
17 He put on [a]righteousness like a
breastplate,
And a [b]helmet of salvation on
His head;
And He put on [c]garments of
vengeance for clothing
And wrapped Himself with [d]zeal
as a mantle.
18 [a]According to *their* [1]deeds, [2]so
He will repay,
Wrath to His adversaries,
recompense to His enemies;
To the coastlands He will [3]make
recompense.
19 So they will fear the name of the
LORD from the [a]west
And His glory from the [b]rising
of the sun,
For He will [c]come like a
[1]rushing stream
Which the wind of the LORD
drives.
20 "A [a]Redeemer will come to Zion,
And to those who [b]turn from
transgression in Jacob,"
declares the LORD.
21 ¶ "As for Me, this is My [a]covenant
with them," says the LORD: "My [b]Spirit
which is upon you, and My [c]words
which I have put in your mouth shall not
depart from your mouth, nor from the
mouth of your [1]offspring, nor from the
mouth of your [1]offspring's offspring,"
says the LORD, "from now and forever."

A Glorified Zion

60 "[a]Arise, shine; for your [b]light
has come,
And the [c]glory of the LORD has
risen upon you.
2 "For behold, [a]darkness will cover
the earth
And deep darkness the peoples;
But the LORD will rise upon you
And His [b]glory will appear upon
you.
3 "[a]Nations will come to your light,
And kings to the brightness of
your rising.

4 ¶ "[a]Lift up your eyes round
about and see;
They all gather together, they
[b]come to you.
Your sons will come from afar,
And your [c]daughters will be
[1]carried in the arms.
5 "Then you will see and be
[a]radiant,
And your heart will [1]thrill and
rejoice;
Because the [b]abundance of the
sea will be turned to you,
The [c]wealth of the nations will
come to you.
6 "A multitude of camels will cover
you,
The young camels of Midian and
[a]Ephah;
All those from [b]Sheba will
come;
They will bring [c]gold and
frankincense,
And will [d]bear good news of the
praises of the LORD.
7 "All the flocks of [a]Kedar will be
gathered together to you,

10 [a]Deut 28:29; Job 5:14 [b]Is 8:14,15; 28:13 [c]Lam 3:6

11 [a]Is 38:14; Ezek 7:16 [b]Is 59:9,14

12 [1]Lit *answer* [2]Lit *our iniquities we know them* [a]Ezra 9:6; Is 58:1 [b]Is 3:9; Jer 14:7; Hos 5:5

13 [a]Josh 24:27; Prov 30:9; Matt 10:33; Titus 1:16 [b]Is 5:7; 30:12; Jer 9:3,4 [c]Is 59:3,4; Mark 7:21,22

14 [a]Is 1:21; 5:7 [b]Is 46:12; Hab 1:4

15 [1]Or *evil* [a]Is 5:23; 10:2; 29:21; 32:7 [b]Is 1:21-23

16 [a]Is 41:28; 63:5; Ezek 22:30 [b]Ps 98:1; Is 52:10; 63:5

17 [a]Eph 6:14 [b]Eph 6:17; 1 Thess 5:8 [c]Is 63:2,3 [d]Is 9:7; 37:32; Zech 1:14

18 [1]Lit *recompense* [2]Lit *accordingly* [3]Lit *repay* [a]Job 34:11; Is 65:6,7; 66:6; Jer 17:10

19 [1]Lit *narrow* [a]Is 49:12 [b]Ps 113:3 [c]Is 30:28; 66:12

20 [a]Rom 11:26 [b]Ezek 18:30,31; Acts 2:38,39

21 [1]Lit *seed* [a]Jer 31:31-34; Rom 11:27 [b]Is 11:2; 32:15; 44:3 [c]Is 55:11

60:1 [a]Is 52:2 [b]Is 60:19,20 [c]Is 24:23; 35:2; 58:8

2 [a]Is 58:10; Jer 13:16; Col 1:13 [b]Is 4:5

3 [a]Is 2:3; 45:14, 22-25; 49:23

4 [1]Lit *nursed upon the side* [a]Is 11:12; 49:18 [b]Is 49:20-22 [c]Is 43:6; 49:22

5 [1]Lit *tremble and be enlarged* [a]Ps 34:5 [b]Is 23:18; 24:14 [c]Is 61:6

6 [a]Gen 25:4 [b]Gen 25:3; Ps 72:10 [c]Is 60:9; Matt 2:11 [d]Is 42:10

7 [a]Gen 25:13

The rams of Nebaioth will
minister to you;
They will go up with acceptance
on My [b]altar,
And I shall [1c]glorify My
[2]glorious house.
8 "[a]Who are these who fly like a
cloud
And like the doves to their
[1]lattices?
9 "Surely the [a]coastlands will wait
for Me;
And the [b]ships of Tarshish *will
come* first,
To [c]bring your sons from afar,
Their silver and their gold with
them,
For the name of the LORD your
God,
And for the Holy One of Israel
because He has
[1d]glorified you.

10 ¶ "[a]Foreigners will build up
your walls,
And their [b]kings will minister to
you;
For in My [c]wrath I struck you,
And in My favor I have had
compassion on you.
11 "Your [a]gates will be open
continually;
They will not be closed day or
night,
So that *men* may [b]bring to you
the wealth of the nations,
With [c]their kings led in
procession.
12 "For the [a]nation and the kingdom
which will not serve you
will perish,
And the nations will be utterly
ruined.
13 "The [a]glory of Lebanon will come
to you,
The [b]juniper, the box tree and
the cypress together,
To beautify the place of My
sanctuary;
And I shall make the [c]place of
My feet glorious.
14 "The [a]sons of those who afflicted
you will come bowing to
you,
And all those who despised you
will bow themselves at the
soles of your feet;
And they will call you the [b]city
of the LORD,
The [c]Zion of the Holy One of
Israel.
15 ¶ "Whereas you have been
[a]forsaken and [b]hated
With no one passing through,
I will make you an everlasting
[c]pride,
A joy from generation to
generation.
16 "You will also [a]suck the milk of
nations
And suck the breast of kings;
Then you will know that I, the
LORD, am your [b]Savior
And your [c]Redeemer, the
Mighty One of Jacob.
17 "Instead of bronze I will bring
gold,
And instead of iron I will bring
silver,
And instead of wood, bronze,
And instead of stones, iron.
And I will make peace your
administrators
And righteousness your
overseers.
18 "[a]Violence will not be heard
again in your land,
Nor [b]devastation or destruction
within your borders;
But you will call your [c]walls
salvation, and your [d]gates
praise.
19 "No longer will you have the
[a]sun for light by day,
Nor for brightness will the moon
give you light;
But you will have the [b]LORD for
an everlasting light,
And your [c]God for your [1]glory.
20 "Your [a]sun will no longer set,
Nor will your moon wane;
For you will have the LORD for
an everlasting light,
And the days of your [b]mourning
will be over.
21 "Then all your [a]people *will be*
righteous;
They will [b]possess the land
forever,
The branch of [1]My planting,
The [c]work of My hands,
That I may be [d]glorified.
22 "The [a]smallest one will become a
[1]clan,
And the least one a mighty
nation.
I, the LORD, will hasten it in its
time."

Exaltation of the Afflicted

61 The [a]Spirit of the Lord [1]GOD is
upon me,
Because the LORD has
anointed me
To [b]bring good news to the
[2c]afflicted;
He has sent me to [d]bind up the
brokenhearted,

7 [1]Or *beautify* [2]Or *beautiful* [b]Is 19:19; 56:7 [c]Is 60:13; Hag 2:7,9

8 [1]Or *dovecotes, windows* [a]Is 49:21

9 [1]Lit *beautified* [a]Is 11:11; 24:15; 42:4,10,12; 49:1; 51:5; 66:19 [b]Ps 48:7; Is 2:16 [c]Is 14:2; 43:6; 49:22 [d]Is 55:5

10 [a]Is 14:1,2; 61:5; Zech 6:15 [b]Is 49:23; Rev 21:24 [c]Is 54:8

11 [a]Is 26:2; 60:18; 62:10; Rev 21:25,26 [b]Is 60:5 [c]Ps 149:8; Is 24:21

12 [a]Is 14:2; Zech 14:17

13 [a]Is 35:2 [b]Is 41:19 [c]1 Chr 28:2; Ps 99:5; 132:7

14 [a]Is 14:1,2; 45:14,23; 49:23; Rev 3:9 [b]Is 1:26 [c]Heb 12:22

15 [a]Is 1:7-9; 6:11-13; Jer 30:17 [b]Is 66:5 [c]Is 4:2; 65:18

16 [a]Is 66:11 [b]Is 19:20; 43:3,11; 45:15,21; 63:8 [c]Is 59:20; 63:16

18 [a]Is 54:14 [b]Is 51:19 [c]Is 26:1 [d]Is 60:11

19 [1]Or *beauty* [a]Rev 21:23; 22:5 [b]Is 2:5; 9:2 [c]Is 41:16; 45:25; Zech 2:5

20 [a]Is 30:26 [b]Is 35:10; 65:19; Rev 21:4

21 [1]Lit *His* [a]Is 45:24,25; 52:1 [b]Ps 37:11,22; Is 57:13; 61:7 [c]Is 19:25; 29:23; 45:11; 64:8 [d]Is 61:3

22 [1]Or *thousand* [a]Is 10:22; 51:2

61:1 [1]Heb *YHWH,* usually rendered *LORD* [2]Or *humble* [a]Is 11:2; 48:16; Luke 4:18 [b]Matt 11:5; Luke 7:22 [c]Is 11:4; 29:19; 32:7 [d]Is 57:15

To [e]proclaim liberty to captives
And [3]freedom to prisoners;
2 To [a]proclaim the favorable year
of the LORD
And the [b]day of vengeance of
our God;
To [c]comfort all who mourn,
3 To [a]grant those who mourn *in*
Zion,
Giving them a garland instead of
ashes,
The [b]oil of gladness instead of
mourning,
The mantle of praise instead of a
spirit of fainting.
So they will be called [1c]oaks of
righteousness,
The planting of the LORD, that
He may be glorified.

4 ¶ Then they will [a]rebuild the
ancient ruins,
They will raise up the former
devastations;
And they will repair the ruined
cities,
The desolations of many
generations.
5 [a]Strangers will stand and pasture
your flocks,
And [1]foreigners will be your
farmers and your
vinedressers.
6 But you will be called the
[a]priests of the LORD;
You will be spoken of *as*
[b]ministers of our God.
You will eat the [c]wealth of
nations,
And in their [1]riches you will
boast.
7 Instead of your [a]shame *you will
have a* [b]double *portion,*
And *instead of* humiliation they
will shout for joy over their
portion.
Therefore they will possess a
double *portion* in their land,
[c]Everlasting joy will be theirs.
8 For I, the LORD, [a]love justice,
I hate robbery [1]in the burnt
offering;
And I will faithfully give them
their recompense
And make an [b]everlasting
covenant with them.
9 Then their offspring will be
known among the nations,
And their descendants in the
midst of the peoples.
All who see them will recognize
them
Because they are the [a]offspring
whom the LORD has blessed.

10 ¶ I will [a]rejoice greatly in the
LORD,
My soul will exult in [b]my God;
For He has [c]clothed me with
garments of salvation,
He has wrapped me with a robe
of righteousness,
As a bridegroom decks himself
with a garland,
And [d]as a bride adorns herself
with her jewels.
11 For as the [a]earth brings forth its
sprouts,
And as a garden causes the
things sown in it to
spring up,
So the Lord [1]GOD will [b]cause
[c]righteousness and praise
To spring up before all the
nations.

Zion's Glory and New Name

62 For Zion's sake I will not keep
silent,
And for Jerusalem's sake I will
not keep quiet,
Until her [a]righteousness goes
forth like brightness,
And her [b]salvation like a torch
that is burning.
2 The [a]nations will see your
righteousness,
And all kings your glory;
And you will be called by a new
[b]name
Which the mouth of the LORD
will designate.
3 You will also be a [a]crown of
beauty in the hand of the
LORD,
And a royal [1]diadem in the hand
of your God.
4 It will no longer be said to you,
"[1a]Forsaken,"
Nor to your land will it any
longer be said, "[2]Desolate";
But you will be called, "[3]My
delight is in her,"
And your land, "[4b]Married";
For the [c]LORD delights in you,
And *to Him* your land will be
married.
5 For *as* a young man marries a
virgin,
So your sons will marry you;
And *as* the [1]bridegroom rejoices
over the bride,
So your [a]God will rejoice
over you.

6 ¶ On your walls, O Jerusalem, I
have appointed [a]watchmen;
All day and all night they will
never keep silent.

1 [3]Lit *opening to those who are bound* [e]Is 42:7; 49:9
2 [a]Is 49:8; 60:10 [b]Is 2:12; 13:6; 34:2,8 [c]Is 57:18; Jer 31:13; Matt 5:4
3 [1]Or *terebinths* [a]Is 60:20 [b]Ps 23:5; 45:7; 104:15 [c]Is 60:21; Jer 17:7,8
4 [a]Is 49:8; 58:12; Ezek 36:33; Amos 9:14
5 [1]Lit *sons of the foreigner* [a]Is 14:2; 60:10
6 [1]Or *glory* [a]Is 66:21 [b]Is 56:6 [c]Is 60:5,11
7 [a]Is 54:4 [b]Is 40:2; Zech 9:12 [c]Ps 16:11
8 [1]Or *with iniquity* [a]Is 5:16; 28:17; 30:18 [b]Gen 17:7; Ps 105:10; Is 55:3; Jer 32:40
9 [a]Is 44:3
10 [a]Is 12:1,2; 25:9; 41:16; 51:3 [b]Is 49:4 [c]Is 49:18; 52:1 [d]Rev 21:2
11 [1]Heb *YHWH,* usually rendered *LORD* [a]Is 4:2; 55:10 [b]Is 45:23, 24; 60:18,21 [c]Ps 72:3; 85:11
62:1 [a]Is 1:26; 58:8; 61:11 [b]Is 46:13; 52:10
2 [a]Is 60:3 [b]Is 56:5; 62:4,12; 65:15
3 [1]Lit *turban* [a]Is 28:5; Zech 9:16; 1 Thess 2:19
4 [1]I.e. Azubah [2]I.e. Shemamah [3]I.e. Hephzibah [4]I.e. Beulah [a]Is 54:6,7; 60:15,18 [b]Hos 2:19,20 [c]Jer 32:41; Zeph 3:17
5 [1]Lit *exultation of the bridegroom* [a]Is 65:19
6 [a]Is 52:8; Jer 6:17; Ezek 3:17; 33:7

You who [b]remind the LORD, take no rest for yourselves;
7 And [a]give Him no rest until He establishes
And makes [b]Jerusalem a praise in the earth.
8 [a]The LORD has sworn by His right hand and by His strong arm,
"I will [b]never again give your grain *as* food for your enemies;
Nor will [1]foreigners drink your new wine for which you have labored."
9 But those who [a]garner it will eat it and praise the LORD;
And those who gather it will drink it in the courts of My sanctuary.

10 ¶ Go through, [a]go through the gates,
Clear the way [1]for the people;
[b]Build up, build up the [c]highway,
Remove the stones, lift up a [d]standard over the peoples.
11 Behold, the LORD has proclaimed to the [a]end of the earth,
[b]Say to the daughter of Zion, "Lo, your [c]salvation comes;
[d]Behold His reward is with Him, and His recompense before Him."
12 And they will call them, "[a]The holy people,
The [b]redeemed of the LORD";
And you will be called, "Sought out, a city [c]not forsaken."

God's Vengeance on the Nations

63 Who is this who comes from [a]Edom,
With [b]garments of [1]glowing colors from [c]Bozrah,
This One who is majestic in His apparel,
[2]Marching in the greatness of His strength?
"It is I who speak in righteousness, [d]mighty to save."
2 Why is Your apparel red,
And Your garments like the one who [a]treads in the wine press?
3 "[a]I have trodden the wine trough alone,
And from the peoples there was no man with Me.
I also [b]trod them in My anger
And [c]trampled them in My wrath;
And [d]their [1]lifeblood is sprinkled on My garments,
And I [2]stained all My raiment.
4 "For the [a]day of vengeance was in My heart,
And My year of redemption has come.
5 "I looked, and there was [a]no one to help,
And I was astonished and there was no one to uphold;
So My [b]own arm brought salvation to Me,
And My wrath upheld Me.
6 "I [a]trod down the peoples in My anger
And made them [b]drunk in My wrath,
And I [1]poured out their lifeblood on the earth."

God's Ancient Mercies Recalled

7 ¶ I shall make mention of the [a]lovingkindnesses of the LORD, the praises of the LORD,
According to all that the LORD has granted us,
And the great [b]goodness toward the house of Israel,
Which He has granted them according to His [c]compassion
And according to the abundance of His lovingkindnesses.
8 For He said, "Surely, they are [a]My people,
Sons who will not deal falsely."
So He became their [b]Savior.
9 In all their affliction [1][a]He was afflicted,
And the [b]angel of His presence saved them;
In His [c]love and in His mercy He [d]redeemed them,
And He [e]lifted them and carried them all the days of old.
10 But they [a]rebelled
And grieved His [b]Holy Spirit;
Therefore He turned Himself to become their enemy,
He fought against them.
11 Then [a]His people remembered the days of old, of Moses.
Where is [b]He who brought them up out of the sea with the [1]shepherds of His flock?
Where is He who [c]put His Holy Spirit in the midst of [2]them,
12 Who caused His [a]glorious arm to go at the right hand of Moses,

6 [b]Ps 74:2; Jer 14:21; Lam 5:1, 20
7 [a]Luke 18:1-8 [b]Is 60:18; Jer 33:9; Zeph 3:19, 20
8 [1]Lit *sons of foreigners* [a]Is 45:23; 54:9 [b]Lev 26:16; Deut 28:31,33; Judg 6:3-6; Is 1:7; Jer 5:17
9 [a]Is 65:13, 21-23
10 [1]Lit *of* [a]Is 26:1; 60:11,18 [b]Is 57:14 [c]Is 11:16; 19:23; 35:8; 49:11 [d]Is 11:10,12; 49:22
11 [a]Is 42:10; 49:6 [b]Matt 21:5; Zech 9:9 [c]Is 51:5 [d]Is 40:10; Rev 22:12
12 [a]Deut 7:6; Is 4:3; 1 Pet 2:9 [b]Is 35:9; 51:10 [c]Is 41:17; 42:16; 62:4
63:1 [1]Or *crimson* [2]Lit *Inclining* [a]Ps 137:7; Is 34:5,6; Ezek 25:12-14; 35:1-15; Obad 1-14; Mal 1:2-5 [b]Is 63:2 [c]Is 34:6; Jer 49:13; Amos 1:12 [d]Zeph 3:17
2 [a]Rev 19:13,15
3 [1]Lit *juice* [2]Lit *defiled* [a]Rev 14:20; 19:15 [b]Is 22:5; 28:3 [c]Mic 7:10 [d]Rev 19:13
4 [a]Is 34:8; 35:4; 61:2; Jer 51:6
5 [a]Is 59:16 [b]Ps 44:3; Is 40:10; 52:10
6 [1]Lit *brought down their juice to the earth* [a]Is 22:5; 34:2; 65:12 [b]Is 29:9; 51:17,21
7 [a]Ps 25:6; 92:2; Is 54:8,10 [b]1 Kin 8:66; Neh 9:25,35 [c]Ps 51:1; 86:5,15; Is 54:7,8; Eph 2:4
8 [a]Ex 6:7; Is 3:15; 51:4 [b]Is 60:16
9 [1]Another reading is *He was not an adversary* [a]Judg 10:16 [b]Ex 23:20-23; 33:14, 15 [c]Deut 7:7,8 [d]Is 43:1; 52:9 [e]Deut 1:31; 32:10-12; Is 46:3
10 [a]Ps 78:40; 106:33; Acts 7:51; Eph 4:30 [b]Ps 51:11; Is 63:11
11 [1]Some mss read *shepherd* [2]Lit *him* [a]Ps 106:44,45 [b]Is 51:10 [c]Num 11:17,25,29; Hag 2:5
12 [a]Ex 6:6; 15:16

Who [b]divided the waters before
them to make for Himself an
everlasting name,
13 Who led them through the
depths?
Like the horse in the wilderness,
they did not [a]stumble;
14 As the cattle which go down into
the valley,
The Spirit of the [a]LORD gave
[1]them rest.
So You [b]led Your people,
To make for Yourself a glorious
name.

"You Are Our Father"

15 ¶ [a]Look down from heaven and
see from Your holy and
glorious [b]habitation;
Where are Your [c]zeal and Your
mighty deeds?
The [d]stirrings of Your heart and
Your compassion are
restrained toward me.
16 For You are our [a]Father, though
[b]Abraham does not know us
And Israel does not recognize us.
You, O LORD, are our Father,
Our [c]Redeemer from of old is
Your name.
17 Why, O LORD, do You [a]cause us
to stray from Your ways
And [b]harden our heart from
fearing You?
[c]Return for the sake of Your
servants, the tribes of Your
heritage.
18 Your holy people possessed Your
sanctuary for a little while,
Our adversaries have [a]trodden *it*
down.
19 We have become *like* those over
whom You have never ruled,
Like those who were not called
by Your name.

Prayer for Mercy and Help

64 [1]Oh, that You would rend the
heavens *and* [a]come down,
That the mountains might
[b]quake at Your presence—
2 [1]As fire kindles the brushwood,
as fire causes water to
boil—
To make Your name known to
Your adversaries,
That the [a]nations may tremble
at Your presence!
3 When You did [a]awesome things
which we did not expect,
You came down, the mountains
quaked at Your presence.
4 For from days of old [a]they have
not heard or perceived by
ear,
Nor has the eye seen a God
besides You,
Who acts in behalf of the one
who [b]waits for Him.
5 You [a]meet him who rejoices in
[b]doing righteousness,
Who [c]remembers You in Your
ways.
Behold, [d]You were angry, for we
sinned,
We continued in them a long
time;
And shall we be saved?
6 For all of us have become like
one who is [a]unclean,
And all our [b]righteous deeds are
like a filthy garment;
And all of us [c]wither like a leaf,
And our [d]iniquities, like the
wind, take us away.
7 There is [a]no one who calls on
Your name,
Who arouses himself to take hold
of You;
For You have [b]hidden Your face
from us
And have [1]delivered us into the
power of our iniquities.
8 ¶ But now, O LORD, [a]You are
our Father,
We are the [b]clay, and You our
potter;
And all of us are the [c]work of
Your hand.
9 Do not be [a]angry beyond
measure, O LORD,
[b]Nor remember iniquity forever;
Behold, look now, all of us are
[c]Your people.
10 Your [a]holy cities have become a
[b]wilderness,
Zion has become a wilderness,
Jerusalem a desolation.
11 Our holy and beautiful [a]house,
Where our fathers praised You,
Has been burned *by* fire;
And [b]all our precious things
have become a ruin.
12 Will You [a]restrain Yourself at
these things, O LORD?
Will You keep silent and afflict
us beyond measure?

A Rebellious People

65 "I permitted Myself to be
sought by [a]those who did
not ask *for Me;*
I permitted Myself to be found
by those who did not
seek Me.

12 [b]Ex 14:21, 22; Is 11:15; 51:10
13 [a]Jer 31:9
14 [1]Lit *him* [a]Josh 21:44; 23:1 [b]Deut 32:12
15 [a]Deut 26:15; Ps 80:14 [b]Ps 68:5; 123:1 [c]Is 9:7; 26:11; 37:32; 42:13; 59:17 [d]Jer 31:20; Hos 11:8
16 [a]Is 1:2; 64:8 [b]Is 29:22; 41:8; 51:2 [c]Is 41:14; 44:6; 60:16
17 [a]Is 30:28; Ezek 14:7-9 [b]Is 29:13,14 [c]Num 10:36
18 [a]Ps 74:3-7; Is 64:11
64:1 [1]Ch 63:19b in Heb [a]Ex 19:18; Ps 18:9; 144:5; Mic 1:3,4; Hab 3:13 [b]Judg 5:5; Ps 68:8; Nah 1:5
2 [1]Ch 64:1 in Heb [a]Ps 99:1; Jer 5:22; 33:9
3 [a]Ps 65:5; 66:3,5; 106:22
4 [a]1 Cor 2:9 [b]Is 25:9; 30:18; 40:31
5 [a]Ex 20:24 [b]Is 56:1 [c]Is 26:13; 63:7 [d]Is 12:1
6 [a]Is 6:5 [b]Is 46:12; 48:1 [c]Ps 90:5,6; Is 1:30 [d]Is 50:1
7 [1]Reading with the DSS and versions; M.T. *melted* [a]Is 59:4; Ezek 22:30 [b]Deut 31:18; Is 1:15; 54:8
8 [a]Is 63:16 [b]Is 29:16; 45:9 [c]Ps 100:3; Is 60:21
9 [a]Is 57:17; 60:10 [b]Is 43:25; Mic 7:18 [c]Ps 79:13; Is 63:8
10 [a]Is 48:2; 52:1 [b]Is 1:7; 6:11
11 [a]2 Kin 25:9; Ps 74:5-7; Is 63:18 [b]Lam 1:7, 10,11
12 [a]Ps 74:10, 11,18,19; Is 42:14; 63:15
65:1 [a]Rom 9:24-26; 10:20

I said, 'Here am I, here am I,'
To a nation which [b]did not call on My name.
2 "[a]I have spread out My hands all day long to a [b]rebellious people,
Who walk *in* the way which is not good, [1]following their own [c]thoughts,
3 A people who continually [a]provoke Me to My face,
Offering sacrifices in [b]gardens and [c]burning incense on bricks;
4 Who sit among graves and spend the night in secret places;
Who [a]eat swine's flesh,
And the broth of unclean meat is *in* their pots.
5 "Who say, '[a]Keep to yourself, do not come near me,
For I am holier than you!'
These are smoke in My [1]nostrils,
A fire that burns all the day.
6 "Behold, it is written before Me,
I will [a]not keep silent, but [b]I will repay;
I will even repay into their bosom,
7 Both [1]their own [a]iniquities and the iniquities of their fathers together," says the LORD.
"Because they have [b]burned incense on the mountains
And [c]scorned Me on the hills,
Therefore I will [d]measure their former work into their bosom."
8 ¶ Thus says the LORD,
"As the new wine is found in the cluster,
And one says, 'Do not destroy it, for there is [1]benefit in it,'
So I will act on behalf of My servants
In order [a]not to destroy [2]all of them.
9 "I will bring forth [a]offspring from Jacob,
And an [b]heir of My mountains from Judah;
Even [c]My chosen ones shall inherit it,
And [d]My servants will dwell there.
10 "[a]Sharon will be a pasture land for flocks,
And the [b]valley of Achor a resting place for herds,
For My people who [c]seek Me.
11 "But you who [a]forsake the LORD,
Who forget My [b]holy mountain,
Who set a table for [1]Fortune,
And who fill *cups* with mixed wine for [2]Destiny,
12 I will destine you for the [a]sword,
And all of you will bow down to the [b]slaughter.
Because I called, but you [c]did not answer;
I spoke, but you did not hear.
And you did evil in My sight
And chose that in which I did not delight."
13 ¶ Therefore, thus says the Lord [1]GOD,
"Behold, My servants will [a]eat, but you will be [b]hungry.
Behold, My servants will [c]drink, but you will be [d]thirsty.
Behold, My servants will [e]rejoice, but you will be [f]put to shame.
14 "Behold, My servants will [a]shout joyfully with a glad heart,
But you will [b]cry out with a [1]heavy heart,
And you will wail with a broken spirit.
15 "You will leave your name for a [a]curse to My chosen ones,
And the Lord [1]GOD will slay you.
But [2]My servants will be called by [b]another name.
16 "Because he who [1]is blessed in the earth
Will [1]be blessed by the [a]God of truth;
And he who swears in the earth
Will [b]swear by the God of truth;
Because the former troubles are forgotten,
And because they are hidden from My sight!

New Heavens and a New Earth

17 ¶ "For behold, I create [a]new heavens and a new earth;
And the [b]former things will not be remembered or come to [1]mind.
18 "But be [a]glad and rejoice forever in what I create;
For behold, I create Jerusalem *for* rejoicing
And her people *for* gladness.
19 "I will also [a]rejoice in Jerusalem and be glad in My people;
And there will no longer be heard in her
The voice of [b]weeping and the sound of crying.

1 [b]Is 63:19; Hos 1:10
2 [1]Lit *after* [a]Rom 10:21 [b]Is 1:2,23; 30:1,9 [c]Ps 81:11,12; Is 59:7; 66:18
3 [a]Job 1:11; 2:5; Is 3:8 [b]Is 1:29; 66:17 [c]Is 66:3
4 [a]Lev 11:7; Is 66:3,17
5 [1]Lit *nose* [a]Matt 9:11; Luke 7:39; 18:9-12
6 [a]Ps 50:3,21; Is 42:14; 64:12 [b]Jer 16:18
7 [1]Lit *your* [a]Is 13:11; 22:14; 26:21; 30:13,14 [b]Is 57:7; Hos 2:13 [c]Ezek 20:27,28 [d]Jer 5:29; 13:25
8 [1]Lit *blessing* [2]Lit *the whole* [a]Is 1:9; 10:21, 22; 48:9
9 [a]Is 45:19,25; Jer 31:36,37 [b]Is 49:8; 60:21; Amos 9:11-15 [c]Is 57:13 [d]Is 32:18
10 [a]Is 33:9; 35:2 [b]Josh 7:24, 26; Hos 2:15 [c]Is 51:1; 55:6
11 [1]Heb *Gad* [2]Heb *Meni* [a]Deut 29:24,25; Is 1:4,28 [b]Is 2:2, 3; 66:20
12 [a]Is 27:1; 34:5,6; 66:16 [b]Is 63:6 [c]2 Chr 36:15,16; Prov 1:24; Is 41:28; 50:2; 66:4; Jer 7:13
13 [1]Heb *YHWH,* usually rendered *LORD* [a]Is 1:19 [b]Is 8:21 [c]Is 41:17, 18; 49:10 [d]Is 5:13 [e]Is 61:7; 66:14 [f]Is 42:17; 44:9,11; 66:5
14 [1]Lit *pain of* [a]Ps 66:4; Is 51:11; James 5:13 [b]Is 13:6; Matt 8:12
15 [1]Heb *YHWH,* usually rendered *LORD* [2]So with Gr; Heb *He will call His servants* [a]Jer 24:9; 25:18; Zech 8:13 [b]Is 62:2
16 [1]Or *bless(es) himself* [a]Ex 34:6; Ps 31:5 [b]Is 19:18; 45:23
17 [1]Lit *heart* [a]Is 66:22; 2 Pet 3:13; Rev 21:1 [b]Is 43:18; Jer 3:16
18 [a]Ps 98; Is 12:1,2; 25:9; 35:10; 41:16; 51:3; 61:10
19 [a]Is 62:4,5; Jer 32:41 [b]Is 25:8; 30:19; 35:10; 51:11; Rev 7:17; 21:4

20 "No longer will there be [1]in it an
infant *who lives but a few*
days,
Or an old man who does [a]not
[2]live out his days;
For the youth will die at the age
of one hundred
And the [3][b]one who does not
reach the age of one
hundred
Will be *thought* accursed.
21 "They will [a]build houses and
inhabit *them;*
They will also [b]plant vineyards
and eat their fruit.
22 "They will not build and [a]another
inhabit,
They will not plant and another
eat;
For [b]as the [1]lifetime of a tree,
so will be the days of My
people,
And My chosen ones will [c]wear
out the work of their hands.
23 "They will [a]not labor in vain,
Or bear *children* for calamity;
For they are the [1][b]offspring of
those blessed by the LORD,
And their descendants with
them.
24 "It will also come to pass that before
they call, I will [a]answer; and while they
are still speaking, I will hear.
25 "The [a]wolf and the lamb will graze
together, and the [b]lion will eat straw like
the ox; and [c]dust will be the serpent's
food. They will [d]do no evil or harm in all
My [e]holy mountain," says the LORD.

Heaven Is God's Throne

66 Thus says the LORD,
"[a]Heaven is My throne and
the earth is My footstool.
Where then is a [b]house you
could build for Me?
And where is a place that [1]I
may rest?
2 "For [a]My hand made all these
things,
Thus all these things came into
being," declares the LORD.
"But to this one I will look,
To him who is humble and
[b]contrite of spirit, and who
[c]trembles at My word.

Hypocrisy Rebuked

3 ¶ "*But* he who kills an ox is *like*
one who slays a man;
He who sacrifices a lamb is *like*
the one who breaks a dog's
neck;
He who offers a grain offering *is*
like one who offers [a]swine's
blood;
He who [1][b]burns incense is *like*
the one who blesses an idol.
As they have chosen their [c]*own*
ways,
And their soul delights in their
[d]abominations,
4 So I will [a]choose their
[1]punishments
And will [b]bring on them what
they dread.
Because I called, but [c]no one
answered;
I spoke, but they did not listen.
And they did [d]evil in My sight
And chose that in which I did
not delight."
5 Hear the word of the LORD, you
who [a]tremble at His word:
"Your brothers who [b]hate you,
who [c]exclude you for My
name's sake,
Have said, 'Let the LORD be
glorified, that we may see
your joy.'
But [d]they will be put to shame.
6 "A voice of uproar from the city, a
voice from the temple,
The voice of the LORD who is
[a]rendering recompense to
His enemies.
7 ¶ "Before she travailed, [a]she
brought forth;
Before her pain came, [b]she gave
birth to a boy.
8 "[a]Who has heard such a thing?
Who has seen such things?
Can a land be [1]born in one day?
Can a nation be brought forth all
at once?
As soon as Zion travailed, she
also brought forth her sons.
9 "Shall I bring to the point of birth
and [a]not give delivery?"
says the LORD.
"Or shall I who gives delivery
shut *the womb?*" says your
God.

Joy in Jerusalem's Future

10 "Be [a]joyful with Jerusalem and
rejoice for her, all you who
[b]love her;
Be exceedingly [c]glad with her,
all you who mourn over her,
11 That you may nurse and [a]be
satisfied with her comforting
breasts,
That you may suck and be
delighted with her
[b]bountiful bosom."

20 [1]Lit *from there* [2]Lit *fill out* [3]Lit *one who misses the mark* [a]Deut 4:40; Job 5:26; Ps 34:12 [b]Eccl 8:12,13; Is 3:11; 22:14

21 [a]Is 32:18; Amos 9:14 [b]Is 30:23; 37:30; Jer 31:5

22 [1]Lit *days* [a]Is 62:8,9 [b]Ps 92:12-14 [c]Ps 21:4; 91:16

23 [1]Lit *seed* [a]Deut 28:3-12; Is 55:2 [b]Is 61:9; Jer 32:38,39; Acts 2:39

24 [a]Ps 91:15; Is 55:6; 58:9; Dan 9:20-23; 10:12

25 [a]Is 11:6 [b]Is 11:7 [c]Gen 3:14; Mic 7:17 [d]Is 11:9; Mic 4:3 [e]Is 65:11

66:1 [1]Lit *is My resting place?* [a]1 Kin 8:27; Ps 11:4; Matt 5:34, 35; 23:22 [b]2 Sam 7:5-7; Jer 7:4; John 4:20, 21; Acts 7:48-50

2 [a]Is 40:26 [b]Ps 34:18; Is 57:15; Matt 5:3,4; Luke 18:13,14 [c]Ps 119:120; Is 66:5

3 [1]Lit *offers a memorial of incense* [a]Is 65:4 [b]Lev 2:2; Is 1:13 [c]Is 57:17; 65:2 [d]Is 44:19

4 [1]Lit *ill treatments* [a]Prov 1:31,32; Is 65:7 [b]Prov 10:24 [c]Prov 1:24; Is 65:12; Jer 7:13 [d]2 Kin 21:2,6; Is 59:7; 65:12; Jer 7:30

5 [a]Is 66:2 [b]Ps 38:20; Is 60:15 [c]Matt 5:10-12; 10:22; John 9:34; 15:18-20 [d]Luke 13:17

6 [a]Is 59:18; 65:6; Joel 3:7

7 [a]Is 37:3; 54:1 [b]Rev 12:5

8 [1]Lit *travailed with* [a]Is 64:4

9 [a]Is 37:3

10 [a]Deut 32:43; Is 65:18; Rom 15:10 [b]Ps 26:8; 122:6 [c]Ps 137:6

11 [a]Is 49:23; 60:16; Joel 3:18 [b]Is 60:1,2; 62:2

12 For thus says the LORD, "Behold,
I extend [a]peace to her like
a river,
And the [b]glory of the nations
like an overflowing stream;
And you will [1]be nursed, you
will be [c]carried on the [2]hip
and fondled on the knees.
13 "As one whom his mother
comforts, so I will [a]comfort
you;
And you will be comforted in
Jerusalem."
14 Then you will [a]see *this,* and
your [b]heart will be glad,
And your [c]bones will flourish
like the new grass;
And the [d]hand of the LORD will
be made known to His
servants,
But He will be [e]indignant
toward His enemies.
15 For behold, the LORD will come
in [a]fire
And His [b]chariots like the
whirlwind,
To render His anger with fury,
And His rebuke with flames of
fire.
16 For the LORD will execute
judgment by [a]fire
And by His [b]sword on all flesh,
And those slain by the LORD will
be many.
17 "Those who sanctify and purify
themselves *to go* to the
[a]gardens,
[1]Following one in the center,
Who eat [b]swine's flesh,
detestable things and mice,
Will [c]come to an end
altogether," declares the
LORD.

18 ¶ "For I [1]know their works and
their [a]thoughts; [2]the time is coming to
[b]gather all nations and tongues. And
they shall come and see My glory.
19 "I will set a [a]sign among them and
will send survivors from them to the
nations: [b]Tarshish, [1]Put, [c]Lud, [2]Me-
shech, Rosh, [d]Tubal and [3]Javan, to the
distant [e]coastlands that have neither
heard My fame nor seen My glory. And
they will [f]declare My glory among the
nations.
20 "Then they shall [a]bring all your
brethren from all the nations as a grain
offering to the LORD, on horses, in chariots, in litters, on mules and on camels, to
My [b]holy mountain Jerusalem," says the
LORD, "just as the sons of Israel bring
their grain offering in a [c]clean vessel to
the house of the LORD.
21 "I will also take some of them for
[a]priests *and* for Levites," says the LORD.
22 "For just as the [a]new heavens
and the new earth
Which I make will endure before
Me," declares the LORD,
"So your [b]offspring and your
[c]name will endure.
23 "And it shall be from [a]new moon
to new moon
And from sabbath to sabbath,
All [1]mankind will come to
[b]bow down before Me,"
says the LORD.
24 "Then they will go forth and look
On the [a]corpses of the men
Who have [1b]transgressed
against Me.
For their [c]worm will not die
[d]And their fire will not be
quenched;
And they will be an [e]abhorrence
to all [2]mankind."

12 [1]Lit *nurse* [2]Lit *side* [a]Ps 72:3; Is 48:18 [b]Is 60:5 [c]Is 60:4
13 [a]Is 12:1; 2 Cor 1:3
14 [a]Is 33:20 [b]Zech 10:7 [c]Prov 3:8; Is 58:11 [d]Ezra 7:9 [e]Is 10:5
15 [a]Is 10:17 [b]Ps 68:17; Is 5:28; Hab 3:8
16 [a]Is 30:30; Ezek 38:22 [b]Is 65:12; Ezek 38:21
17 [1]Lit *After* [a]Is 1:29 [b]Lev 11:7; Is 65:4 [c]Is 1:28
18 [1]So with Gr; Heb omits *know* [2]Lit *it is coming* [a]Is 59:7 [b]Is 45:22-25; Jer 3:17
19 [1]So with Gr; Heb *Pul* [2]So with Gr; Heb *those who draw the bow* [3]I.e. Greece [a]Is 11:10 [b]Is 2:16 [c]Ezek 27:10 [d]Gen 10:2 [e]Is 11:11 [f]1 Chr 16:24; Is 42:12
20 [a]Is 43:6 [b]Is 2:2 [c]Is 52:11
21 [a]Ex 19:6; Is 61:6; 1 Pet 2:5
22 [a]Is 65:17; Heb 12:26; 2 Pet 3:13; Rev 21:1 [b]Is 61:8; John 10:27-29; 1 Pet 1:4 [c]Is 56:5
23 [1]Lit *flesh* [a]Is 1:13; Ezek 46:1 [b]Is 19:21
24 [1]Or *rebelled* [2]Lit *flesh* [a]Is 5:25 [b]Is 1:28 [c]Is 14:11; Mark 9:48 [d]Is 1:31; Matt 3:12 [e]Dan 12:2

Jeremiah

Title and Background

The book is named after the prophet whose ministry it records. Jeremiah prophesied in Judah during the reigns of Josiah and succeeding kings up to the Babylonian exile. It was a period of storm and stress, when the doom of entire nations—including Judah itself—was being sealed. After Josiah's reign, Jeremiah was often in danger from political and religious leaders who were angry because of his messages. Through all this, God protected Jeremiah so he could continue to warn the wicked and comfort those who trusted in God.

Author and Date of Writing

The book preserves an account of the prophetic ministry of Jeremiah, whose personal life and struggles are known to us in greater depth and detail than those of any other Old Testament prophet. His prophetic ministry began in 626 B.C. and ended sometime after 586.

Theme and Message

Jeremiah was always conscious of his call from the Lord to be a prophet, and as such he proclaimed words that were spoken first by God Himself and were therefore certain of fulfillment.

Judgment is one of the all-pervasive themes in his writings, though he was careful to point out that repentance, if sincere, would postpone the inevitable.

For Jeremiah, God was ultimate. His theology conceived of the Lord as the Creator of all that exists, as all-powerful and as everywhere present. At the same time God is very much concerned about individual people and their accountability to Him.

Outline

I. The Call of Jeremiah (1:1–19)
II. Warnings and Exhortations to Judah (2:1—29:32)
III. Promises of Restoration (30:1—33:26)
IV. Historical Insertion (34:1—35:19)
V. The Sufferings of Jeremiah (36:1—38:28)
VI. The Fall of Jerusalem and Its Aftermath (39:1—45:5)
VII. Judgment Against the Nations (46:1—51:64)
VIII. Historical Appendix (52:1–34)

Jeremiah's Call and Commission

1 The words of [a]Jeremiah the son of
Hilkiah, of the priests who were in
[b]Anathoth in the land of Benjamin,
2 to whom the word of the LORD
came in the days of [a]Josiah the son of
[b]Amon, king of Judah, in the [c]thirteenth
year of his reign.
3 It came also in the days of [a]Jehoia-
kim the son of Josiah, king of Judah, until
the end of the eleventh year of [b]Zedeki-
ah the son of Josiah, king of Judah, until
the exile of Jerusalem in the fifth month.
4 ¶ Now the word of the LORD came
to me saying,

5 "Before I [a]formed you in the
womb I knew you,
And [b]before you were born I
consecrated you;
I have [c]appointed you a prophet
to the nations."
6 Then [a]I said, "Alas, Lord [1]GOD!
Behold, I do not know how to speak,
Because [b]I am a youth."
7 But the LORD said to me,
"Do not say, 'I am a youth,'
[a]Because everywhere I send
you, you shall go,
And [b]all that I command you,
you shall speak.
8 "[a]Do not be afraid of them,
For [b]I am with you to deliver
you," declares the LORD.
9 Then the LORD stretched out His
hand and [a]touched my mouth, and the
LORD said to me,

1:1 [a]2 Chr 35:25; Ezra 1:1; Dan 9:2; Matt 2:17 [b]Josh 21:18; 1 Kin 2:26; 1 Chr 6:60; Is 10:30; Jer 11:21
2 [a]1 Kin 13:2; 2 Kin 21:24; 2 Chr 34:1; Jer 3:6 [b]2 Kin 21:18 [c]Jer 25:3
3 [a]2 Kin 23:34; 1 Chr 3:15; 2 Chr 36:5-8; Jer 25:1 [b]2 Kin 24:17; 1 Chr 3:15; 2 Chr 36:11-13; Jer 39:2
5 [a]Ps 139:15 [b]Is 49:1; Luke 1:15 [c]Jer 1:10
6 [1]Heb *YHWH*, usually rendered *LORD* [a]Ex 4:10 [b]1 Kin 3:7
7 [a]Ezek 2:3 [b]Num 22:20; Jer 1:17
8 [a]Ex 3:12; Deut 31:6; Josh 1:5; Jer 15:20 [b]Ezek 2:6
9 [a]Is 6:7; Mark 7:33-35

"Behold, I have [b]put My words in
your mouth.
10 "See, [a]I have appointed you this
day over the nations and
over the kingdoms,
[b]To pluck up and to break
down,
To destroy and to overthrow,
[c]To build and to plant."

The Almond Rod and Boiling Pot

11 ¶ The word of the LORD came to me
saying, "What do you see, [a]Jeremiah?"
And I said, "I see a rod of an [1]almond
tree."
12 Then the LORD said to me, "You
have seen well, for [a]I am [1]watching over
My word to perform it."
13 ¶ The word of the LORD came to me
a second time saying, "[a]What do you
see?" And I said, "I see a boiling [b]pot,
facing away from the north."
14 Then the LORD said to me, "[a]Out of
the north the evil [1]will break forth on all
the inhabitants of the land.
15 "For, behold, I am calling [a]all the
families of the kingdoms of the north,"
declares the LORD; "and they will come
and they will [b]set each one his throne at
the entrance of the gates of Jerusalem,
and against all its walls round about and
against all the [c]cities of Judah.
16 "I will [1]pronounce My judgments
on them concerning all their wickedness,
whereby they have [a]forsaken Me and
have [2b]offered sacrifices to other gods,
and worshiped the [c]works of their own
hands.
17 "Now, [a]gird up your loins and arise,
and speak to them all which I command
you. [b]Do not be dismayed before them,
or I will dismay you before them.
18 "Now behold, I have made you today
as a fortified city and as a pillar of iron
and as walls of bronze against the whole
land, to the kings of Judah, to its princes,
to its priests and to the people of the
land.
19 "They will fight against you, but they
will not overcome you, for [a]I am with
you to deliver you," declares the LORD.

Judah's Apostasy

2 Now the word of the LORD came to
me saying,
2 "Go and [a]proclaim in the ears of
Jerusalem, saying, 'Thus says the LORD,
"I remember concerning you the
[1b]devotion of your youth,
The love of your betrothals,
[c]Your following after Me in the
wilderness,
Through a land not sown.
3 "Israel was [a]holy to the LORD,
The [b]first of His harvest.
[c]All who ate of it became guilty;
Evil came upon them," declares
the LORD.' "
4 ¶ Hear the word of the LORD,
O house of Jacob, and all the families of
the house of Israel.
5 Thus says the LORD,
"[a]What injustice did your fathers
find in Me,
That they went far from Me
And walked after [b]emptiness
and became empty?
6 "They did not say, 'Where is the
LORD
Who [a]brought us up out of the
land of Egypt,
Who [b]led us through the
wilderness,
Through a land of deserts and of
pits,
Through a land of drought and of
[1]deep darkness,
Through a land that no one
crossed
And where no man dwelt?'
7 "I brought you into the [a]fruitful
land
To eat its fruit and its good
things.
But you came and [b]defiled My
land,
And My inheritance you made
an abomination.
8 "The [a]priests did not say, 'Where
is the LORD?'
And those who handle the law
[b]did not know Me;
The [1]rulers also transgressed
against Me,
And the [c]prophets prophesied
by Baal
And walked after [d]things that
did not profit.
9 ¶ "Therefore I will yet [a]contend
with you," declares the
LORD,
"And with your sons' sons I will
contend.
10 "For [a]cross to the coastlands of
[1]Kittim and see,
And send to [b]Kedar and observe
closely
And see if there has been such *a*
thing as this!
11 "Has a nation changed gods
When [a]they were not gods?
But My people have [b]changed
their glory
For that which does not profit.
12 "Be appalled, [a]O heavens, at this,

9 [b]Ex 4:11-16; Deut 18:18; Is 51:16

10 [a]Rev 11:3-6 [b]Jer 18:7-10; Ezek 32:18; 2 Cor 10:4 [c]Is 44:26-28; Jer 24:6; 31:28, 40

11 [1]Heb *shaqed* [a]Jer 24:3; Amos 7:8

12 [1]Heb *shoqed* [a]Jer 31:28

13 [a]Zech 4:2 [b]Ezek 11:3,7

14 [1]Lit *will be opened* [a]Is 41:25; Jer 4:6; 10:22

15 [a]Jer 25:9 [b]Is 22:7; Jer 39:3 [c]Jer 4:16; 9:11

16 [1]Lit *speak* [2]Or *burned incense* [a]Deut 28:20 [b]Jer 7:9; 19:4; 44:17 [c]Is 2:8; 37:19; Jer 10:3-5

17 [a]1 Kin 18:46; Job 38:3 [b]Ezek 2:6; 3:16-18

19 [a]Num 14:9; Jer 1:8; 20:11

2:2 [1]Or *lovingkindness* [a]Is 58:1; Jer 7:2; 11:6 [b]Ezek 16:8; Hos 2:15 [c]Deut 2:7; Jer 2:6

3 [a]Ex 19:5,6; Deut 7:6; 14:2 [b]James 1:18; Rev 14:4 [c]Is 41:11; Jer 30:16; 50:7

5 [a]Is 5:4; Mic 6:3 [b]2 Kin 17:15; Jer 8:19; Rom 1:21

6 [1]Or *the shadow of death* [a]Ex 20:2; Is 63:11 [b]Deut 8:15; 32:10

7 [a]Deut 8:7-9; 11:10-12 [b]Ps 106:38; Jer 3:2; 16:18

8 [1]Lit *shepherds* [a]Jer 10:21 [b]Jer 4:22; Mal 2:7,8 [c]Jer 23:13 [d]Jer 16:19; Hab 2:18

9 [a]Jer 2:35; Ezek 20:35,36

10 [1]I.e. Cyprus and other islands [a]Is 23:12 [b]Ps 120:5; Is 21:16; Jer 49:28

11 [a]Is 37:19; Jer 5:7; 16:20 [b]Ps 106:20; Rom 1:23

12 [a]Is 1:2; Jer 4:23

And shudder, be very desolate,"
declares the LORD.
13 "For My people have committed
two evils:
They have forsaken Me,
The [a]fountain of living waters,
To hew for themselves [b]cisterns,
Broken cisterns
That can hold no water.

14 ¶ "Is Israel [a]a slave? Or is he a
homeborn servant?
Why has he become a prey?
15 "The young [a]lions have roared at
him,
They have [1]roared loudly.
And they have [b]made his land a
waste;
His cities have been destroyed,
without inhabitant.
16 "Also the [1]men of [a]Memphis
and Tahpanhes
Have [2]shaved the [b]crown of
your head.
17 "Have you not [a]done this to
yourself
By your forsaking the LORD your
God
When He [a]led you in the way?
18 "But now what are you doing [a]on
the road to Egypt,
To drink the waters of the
[1][b]Nile?
Or what are you doing on the
road to Assyria,
To drink the waters of the
[2]Euphrates?
19 "[a]Your own wickedness will
correct you,
And your [b]apostasies will
reprove you;
Know therefore and see that it is
evil and [c]bitter
For you to forsake the LORD your
God,
And [d]the dread of Me is not in
you," declares the Lord
[1]GOD of hosts.

20 ¶ "For long ago [1][a]I broke your
yoke
And tore off your bonds;
But you said, 'I will not serve!'
For on every [b]high hill
And under every green tree
You have lain down as a harlot.
21 "Yet I [a]planted you a choice vine,
A completely faithful seed.
How then have you turned
yourself before Me
Into the [b]degenerate shoots of a
foreign vine?
22 "Although you [a]wash yourself
with lye
And [1]use much soap,
The [b]stain of your iniquity is
before Me," declares the
Lord [2]GOD.
23 "[a]How can you say, 'I am not
defiled,
I have not gone after the
[b]Baals'?
Look at your way in the [c]valley!
Know what you have done!
You are a swift young camel
[d]entangling her ways,
24 A [a]wild donkey accustomed to
the wilderness,
That sniffs the wind in her
passion.
In *the time of* her [1]heat who
can turn her away?
All who seek her will not
become weary;
In her month they will find her.
25 "Keep your feet from being
unshod
And your throat from thirst;
But you said, '[a]It is [1]hopeless!
No! For I have [b]loved strangers,
And after them I will walk.'

26 ¶ "As the [a]thief is shamed when
he is discovered,
So the house of Israel is shamed;
They, their kings, their princes
And their priests and their
prophets,
27 Who say to a tree, 'You are my
father,'
And to a stone, 'You gave me
birth.'
For they have turned *their* [a]back
to Me,
And not *their* face;
But in the [b]time of their
[1]trouble they will say,
'Arise and save us.'
28 "But where are your [a]gods
Which you made for yourself?
Let them arise, if they can
[b]save you
In the time of your [1]trouble;
For [c]*according to* the number of
your cities
Are your gods, O Judah.

29 ¶ "Why do you contend
with Me?
You have [a]all transgressed
against Me," declares the
LORD.
30 "[a]In vain I have struck your sons;
They accepted no chastening.
Your [b]sword has devoured your
prophets
Like a destroying lion.
31 "O generation, heed the word of
the LORD.

13 [a]Ps 36:9; Jer 17:13; John 4:14 [b]Jer 14:3
14 [a]Jer 5:19; 17:4
15 [1]Lit *given their voice* [a]Jer 50:17 [b]Jer 4:7
16 [1]Or *sons* [2]Lit *grazed* [a]Is 19:13; Jer 44:1; Hos 9:6 [b]Deut 33:20; Jer 48:45
17 [a]Deut 32:10; Jer 4:18
18 [1]Heb *Shihor* [2]Lit *River* [a]Is 30:2 [b]Josh 13:3
19 [1]Heb *YHWH,* usually rendered LORD [a]Is 3:9; Jer 4:18; Hos 5:5 [b]Jer 3:6,8,11,14; Hos 11:7 [c]Job 20:12-16; Amos 8:10 [d]Ps 36:1; Jer 5:24
20 [1]Or *you* [a]Lev 26:13 [b]Deut 12:2; Is 57:5,7; Jer 3:2,6; 17:2
21 [a]Ex 15:17; Ps 44:2; 80:8; Is 5:2 [b]Is 5:4
22 [1]Lit *cause to be great to you* [2]Heb *YHWH,* usually rendered LORD [a]Jer 4:14 [b]Job 14:17; Hos 13:12
23 [a]Prov 30:12 [b]Jer 9:14 [c]Jer 7:31 [d]Jer 2:33, 36; 31:22
24 [1]Lit *occasion* [a]Jer 14:6
25 [1]Or *desperate* [a]Jer 18:12 [b]Deut 32:16; Jer 14:10
26 [a]Jer 48:27
27 [1]Or *evil* [a]Jer 18:17; 32:33 [b]Judg 10:10; Is 26:16
28 [1]Or *evil* [a]Deut 32:37; Judg 10:14; Is 45:20; Jer 1:16 [b]Jer 11:12 [c]2 Kin 17:30,31; Jer 11:13
29 [a]Jer 5:1; 6:13; Dan 9:11
30 [a]Is 1:5; Jer 5:3; 7:28 [b]Neh 9:26; Jer 26:20-24; Acts 7:52; 1 Thess 2:15

Have I been a wilderness to
Israel,
Or a [a]land of thick darkness?
Why do My people say, '[b]We
are free to roam;
We will no longer come to You'?
32 "Can a virgin forget her
ornaments,
Or a bride her attire?
Yet My people have
[a]forgotten Me
Days without number.
33 "How well you prepare your way
To seek love!
Therefore even [1]the wicked
women
You have taught your ways.
34 "Also on your skirts is found
The [a]lifeblood of the innocent
poor;
You did not find them
[b]breaking in.
But in spite of all these things,
35 Yet you said, 'I am innocent;
Surely His anger is turned away
from me.'
Behold, I will [a]enter into
judgment with you
Because you [b]say, 'I have not
sinned.'
36 "Why do you [a]go around so
much
Changing your way?
Also, [b]you will be put to shame
by Egypt
As you were put to shame by
[c]Assyria.
37 "From this *place* also you will
go out
With [a]your hands on your head;
For the LORD has rejected [b]those
in whom you trust,
And you will not prosper with
them."

The Polluted Land

3 *God* [1]says, "[a]If a husband
divorces his wife
And she goes from him
And belongs to another man,
Will he still return to her?
Will not that land be completely
[2]polluted?
But you [b]are a harlot *with* many
[3]lovers;
Yet you [c]turn to Me," declares
the LORD.
2 "Lift up your eyes to the [a]bare
heights and see;
Where have you not been
violated?
By the roads you have [b]sat for
them
Like an Arab in the desert,

31 [a]Is 45:19 [b]Deut 32:15; Jer 2:20,25

32 [a]Ps 106:21; Is 17:10; Jer 3:21; 13:25; Hos 8:14

33 [1]Or *in wickedness*

34 [a]2 Kin 21:16; 24:4; Ps 106:38; Jer 7:6; 19:4 [b]Ex 22:2

35 [a]Jer 25:31 [b]Prov 28:13; 1 John 1:8,10

36 [a]Jer 2:23; 31:22; Hos 12:1 [b]Is 30:3 [c]2 Chr 28:16,20,21

37 [a]2 Sam 13:19; Jer 14:3,4 [b]Jer 37:7-10

3:1 [1]Lit *saying* [2]Or *alienated* [3]Lit *companions* [a]Deut 24:1-4 [b]Jer 2:20; Ezek 16:26,28,29 [c]Jer 4:1; Zech 1:3

2 [a]Deut 12:2; Jer 2:20; 3:21; 7:29 [b]Gen 38:14; Ezek 16:25 [c]Jer 2:7

3 [a]Lev 26:19; Jer 14:3-6 [b]Jer 6:15; 8:12

4 [1]Lit *leader* [a]Jer 3:19; 31:9 [b]Ps 71:17; Prov 2:17 [c]Jer 2:2; Hos 2:15

5 [1]Lit *keep it* [2]Lit *been able* [a]Ps 103:9; Is 57:16; Jer 3:12

6 [a]Jer 17:2; Ezek 23:4-10

7 [1]Lit *said* [a]2 Kin 17:13 [b]Jer 3:11; Ezek 16:47

8 [a]Deut 24:1,3; Is 50:1 [b]Ezek 16:46,47; 23:11

9 [a]Jer 2:7; 3:2 [b]Is 57:6; Jer 2:27; 10:8

10 [a]Jer 12:2; Hos 7:14

11 [a]Ezek 16:51, 52; 23:11

12 [1]Lit *cause My countenance to fall* [a]Jer 3:14, 22; Ezek 33:11 [b]Jer 3:5 [c]Ps 86:15; Jer 12:15; 31:20; 33:26

13 [1]Lit *know* [2]Lit *ways* [a]Deut 30:1-3; Jer 3:25; 14:20; 1 John 1:9 [b]Jer 2:20,25; 3:2,6 [c]Deut 12:2

And you have [c]polluted a land
With your harlotry and with your
wickedness.
3 "Therefore the [a]showers have
been withheld,
And there has been no spring
rain.
Yet you had a [b]harlot's forehead;
You refused to be ashamed.
4 "Have you not just now called
to Me,
'[a]My Father, You are the
[1b]friend of my [c]youth?
5 '[a]Will He be angry forever?
Will He [1]be indignant to
the end?'
Behold, you have spoken
And have done evil things,
And you have [2]had your way."

Faithless Israel

6 ¶ Then the LORD said to me in the
days of Josiah the king, "Have you seen
what faithless Israel did? She [a]went up
on every high hill and under every green
tree, and she was a harlot there.
7 "[a]I [1]thought, 'After she has done all
these things she will return to Me'; but
she did not return, and her [b]treacherous
sister Judah saw it.
8 "And I saw that for all the adulteries
of faithless Israel, I had sent her away and
[a]given her a writ of divorce, yet her
[b]treacherous sister Judah did not fear;
but she went and was a harlot also.
9 "Because of the lightness of her harlotry, she [a]polluted the land and committed adultery with [b]stones and trees.
10 "Yet in spite of all this her treacherous sister Judah did not return to Me with
all her heart, but rather in [a]deception,"
declares the LORD.

God Invites Repentance

11 ¶ And the LORD said to me,
"[a]Faithless Israel has proved herself
more righteous than treacherous Judah.
12 "Go and proclaim these words toward the north and say,
'[a]Return, faithless Israel,'
declares the LORD;
'[b]I will not [1]look upon you in
anger.
For I am [c]gracious,' declares the
LORD;
'I will not be angry forever.
13 'Only [1a]acknowledge your
iniquity,
That you have transgressed
against the LORD your God
And have [b]scattered your
[2]favors to the strangers
[c]under every green tree,

And you have not obeyed My
voice,' declares the LORD.
14 'Return, O faithless sons,'
declares the LORD;
'For I am a [a]master to you,
And I will take you one from a
city and two from a family,
And [b]I will bring you to Zion.'
15 ¶ "Then I will give you [a]shepherds
after My own heart, who will [b]feed you
on knowledge and understanding.
16 "It shall be in those days when you
are multiplied and increased in the land,"
declares the LORD, "they will [a]no longer
say, 'The ark of the covenant of the
LORD.' And it will not come to mind, nor
will they remember it, nor will they miss
it, nor will it be made again.
17 "At that time they will call Jerusalem
'The [a]Throne of the LORD,' and [b]all the
nations will be gathered to it, to Jerusalem, for the [c]name of the LORD; nor will
they [d]walk anymore after the stubbornness of their evil heart.
18 "[a]In those days the house of Judah
will walk with the house of Israel, and
they will come together [b]from the land of
the north to the [c]land that I gave your
fathers as an inheritance.
19 ¶ "Then I said,
'How I would set you among
[1]My sons
And give you a pleasant land,
The most [a]beautiful inheritance
of the nations!'
And I said, 'You shall call Me,
[b]My Father,
And not turn away from
following Me.'
20 "Surely, as a woman treacherously
departs from her [1]lover,
So you have [a]dealt treacherously
with Me,
O house of Israel," declares the
LORD.
21 ¶ A voice is heard on the [a]bare
heights,
The weeping *and* the
supplications of the sons of
Israel;
Because they have perverted
their way,
They have [b]forgotten the LORD
their God.
22 "Return, O faithless sons,
[a]I will heal your faithlessness."
"Behold, we come to You;
For You are the LORD our God.
23 "Surely, [a]the hills are a
deception,
A tumult *on* the mountains.
Surely in the [b]LORD our God
Is the salvation of Israel.
24 ¶ "But [a]the shameful thing has
consumed the labor of our fathers since
our youth, their flocks and their herds,
their sons and their daughters.
25 "Let us lie down in our [a]shame, and
let our humiliation cover us; for we have
sinned against the LORD our God, we and
our fathers, [b]from our youth even to this
day. And we have not obeyed the voice of
the LORD our God."

Judah Threatened with Invasion

4 "If you will [a]return, O Israel,"
declares the LORD,
"*Then* you should return to Me.
And [b]if you will put away your
detested things from My
presence,
And will not waver,
2 And you will [a]swear, 'As the
LORD lives,'
[b]In truth, in justice and in
righteousness;
Then the [c]nations will bless
themselves in Him,
And [d]in Him they will glory."
3 ¶ For thus says the LORD to the men
of Judah and to Jerusalem,
"[1a]Break up your fallow ground,
And [b]do not sow among thorns.
4 "[a]Circumcise yourselves to the
LORD
And remove the foreskins of
your heart,
Men of Judah and inhabitants of
Jerusalem,
Or else My [b]wrath will go forth
like fire
And burn with [c]none to
quench it,
Because of the evil of your
deeds."
5 ¶ Declare in Judah and proclaim
in Jerusalem, and say,
"[a]Blow the trumpet in the land;
Cry aloud and say,
'[b]Assemble yourselves, and let
us go
Into the fortified cities.'
6 "Lift up a [a]standard toward Zion!
Seek refuge, do not stand *still*,
For I am bringing [b]evil from the
north,
And great destruction.
7 "A [a]lion has gone up from his
thicket,
And a [b]destroyer of nations has
set out;
He has gone out from his place
To [c]make your land a waste.
Your cities will be ruins
Without inhabitant.
8 "For this, [a]put on sackcloth,

14 [a]Jer 31:32; Hos 2:19 [b]Jer 31:6,12
15 [a]Jer 23:4; 31:10; Ezek 34:23; Eph 4:11 [b]Acts 20:28
16 [a]Is 65:17
17 [a]Jer 17:12; Ezek 43:7 [b]Jer 3:19; 4:2; 12:15, 16; 16:19 [c]Is 60:9 [d]Jer 11:8
18 [a]Is 11:13; Jer 50:4,5; Hos 1:11 [b]Jer 16:15; 31:8 [c]Amos 9:15
19 [1]Lit *the* [a]Ps 16:6 [b]Is 63:16; Jer 3:4
20 [1]Or *companion* [a]Is 48:8
21 [a]Is 15:2; Jer 3:2; 7:29 [b]Is 17:10; Jer 2:32; 13:25
22 [a]Jer 30:17; 33:6; Hos 6:1; 14:4
23 [a]Jer 17:2 [b]Ps 3:8; Jer 17:14; 31:7
24 [a]Hos 9:10
25 [a]Ezra 9:6,7 [b]Jer 22:21
4:1 [a]Jer 3:22; 15:19; Joel 2:12 [b]Jer 7:3,7; 35:15
2 [a]Deut 10:20; Is 45:23; 65:16; Jer 12:16 [b]Is 48:1 [c]Gen 22:18; Jer 3:17; 12:15,16; Gal 3:8 [d]Is 45:25; Jer 9:24; 1 Cor 1:31
3 [1]Lit *Plow for yourselves plowed ground* [a]Hos 10:12 [b]Matt 13:7
4 [a]Deut 10:16; 30:6; Jer 9:25, 26; Rom 2:28, 29; Col 2:11 [b]Is 30:27,33; Jer 21:12; Zeph 2:2 [c]Amos 5:6; Mark 9:43,48
5 [a]Jer 6:1; Hos 8:1 [b]Josh 10:20; Jer 8:14
6 [a]Is 62:10; Jer 4:21; 50:2 [b]Jer 1:14,15; 6:1,22
7 [a]Jer 5:6; 25:38; 50:17 [b]Jer 25:9; Ezek 26:7-10 [c]Is 1:7; 6:11; Jer 2:15
8 [a]Is 22:12; Jer 6:26

Lament and wail;
For the [b]fierce anger of the LORD
Has not turned back from us."

9 "It shall come about in that day,"
declares the LORD, "that the [a]heart of the
king and the heart of the princes will fail;
and the priests will be appalled and the
[b]prophets will be astounded."
10 ¶ Then I said, "Ah, Lord [1]GOD!
Surely You have utterly [a]deceived this
people and Jerusalem, saying, '[b]You will
have peace'; whereas a sword touches
the [2]throat."
11 ¶ In that time it will be said to this
people and to Jerusalem, "A [a]scorching
wind from the bare heights in the wilderness in the direction of the daughter of
My people—not to winnow and not to
cleanse,
12 a wind too strong for [1]this—will
come [2]at My command; now I will also
pronounce judgments against them.

13 "Behold, he [a]goes up like clouds,
And his [b]chariots like the whirlwind;
His horses are [c]swifter than eagles.
Woe to us, for [d]we are ruined!"

14 ¶ Wash your heart from evil, O Jerusalem,
That you may be saved.
How long will your [a]wicked thoughts
Lodge within you?
15 For a voice declares from [a]Dan,
And proclaims wickedness from Mount Ephraim.
16 "Report *it* to the nations, now!
Proclaim over Jerusalem,
'Besiegers come from a [a]far country,
And [b]lift their voices against the cities of Judah.
17 'Like watchmen of a field they are [a]against her round about,
Because she has [b]rebelled against Me,' declares the LORD.
18 "Your [a]ways and your deeds
Have [1]brought these things to you.
This is your evil. How [b]bitter!
How it has touched your heart!"

Lament over Judah's Devastation

19 ¶ [a]My [1]soul, my [1]soul! I am in anguish! [2]Oh, my heart!
My [b]heart is pounding in me;
I cannot be silent,
Because [3]you have heard, O my soul,
The [c]sound of the trumpet,
The alarm of war.
20 [a]Disaster on disaster is proclaimed,
For the [b]whole land is devastated;
Suddenly my [c]tents are devastated,
My curtains in an instant.
21 How long must I see the standard
And hear the sound of the trumpet?
22 "[a]For My people are foolish,
They know Me not;
They are stupid children
And have no understanding.
They are shrewd to [b]do evil,
But to do good they do not know."

23 ¶ I looked on the earth, and behold, *it was* [1a]formless and void;
And to the heavens, and they had no light.
24 I looked on the mountains, and behold, they were [a]quaking,
And all the hills [1]moved to and fro.
25 I looked, and behold, there was no man,
And all the [a]birds of the heavens had fled.
26 I looked, and behold, [1]the [a]fruitful land was a wilderness,
And all its cities were pulled down
Before the LORD, before His fierce anger.

27 ¶ For thus says the LORD,
"The [a]whole land shall be a desolation,
Yet I will [b]not execute a complete destruction.
28 "For this the [a]earth shall mourn
And the [b]heavens above be dark,
Because I have [c]spoken, I have purposed,
And I will not [1]change My mind, nor will I turn from it."
29 At the sound of the horseman and bowman [a]every city flees;
They [b]go into the thickets and climb among the rocks;
[c]Every city is forsaken,
And no man dwells in them.
30 And you, O desolate one, [a]what will you do?
Although you dress in scarlet,

8 [b]Is 5:25; 10:4; Jer 30:24
9 [a]Is 22:3-5; Jer 48:41 [b]Is 29:9, 10; Ezek 13:9-16
10 [1]Heb *YHWH,* usually rendered LORD [2]Or *life* [a]Ezek 14:9; 2 Thess 2:11 [b]Jer 5:12; 14:13
11 [a]Jer 13:24; 51:1; Ezek 17:10; Hos 13:15
12 [1]Lit *these* [2]Lit *for Me*
13 [a]Is 19:1; Nah 1:3 [b]Is 5:28; 66:15 [c]Lam 4:19; Hab 1:8 [d]Is 3:8
14 [a]Prov 1:22; Jer 6:19; 13:27; James 4:8
15 [a]Jer 8:16
16 [a]Is 39:3; Jer 5:15 [b]Ezek 21:22
17 [a]2 Kin 25:1, 4 [b]Is 1:20,23; Jer 5:23
18 [1]Lit *done* [a]Ps 107:17; Is 50:1; Jer 2:17,19 [b]Jer 2:19
19 [1]Lit *inward parts* [2]Lit *The walls of my heart* [3]Or *I, my soul, heard* [a]Is 15:5; 16:11; 21:3; 22:4; Jer 9:1,10; 20:9 [b]Hab 3:16 [c]Num 10:9
20 [a]Ps 42:7; Ezek 7:26 [b]Jer 4:27 [c]Jer 10:20
22 [a]Jer 5:4,21; 10:8; Rom 1:22 [b]Jer 9:3; 13:23; Rom 16:19; 1 Cor 14:20
23 [1]Or *a waste and emptiness* [a]Gen 1:2; Is 24:19
24 [1]Lit *moved lightly* [a]Is 5:25; Jer 10:10; Ezek 38:20
25 [a]Jer 9:10; 12:4; Zeph 1:3
26 [1]Or *Carmel* [a]Jer 9:10
27 [a]Jer 12:11, 12; 25:11 [b]Jer 5:10,18; 30:11; 46:28
28 [1]Lit *be sorry* [a]Jer 12:4,11; 14:2; Hos 4:3 [b]Is 5:30; 50:3; Joel 2:30,31 [c]Num 23:19; Jer 23:20; 30:24
29 [a]2 Kin 25:4 [b]Is 2:19-21; Jer 16:16 [c]Jer 4:7
30 [a]Is 10:3; 20:6; Jer 13:21

Although you decorate *yourself*
with ornaments of gold,
Although you [b]enlarge your eyes
with paint,
In vain you make yourself
beautiful.
Your [1c]lovers despise you;
They seek your life.
31 For I heard a [1]cry as of a
woman in labor,
The anguish as of one giving
birth to her first child,
The [1]cry of the daughter of Zion
[a]gasping for breath,
[b]Stretching out her [2]hands,
saying,
"Ah, woe is me, for [3]I faint
before murderers."

Jerusalem's Godlessness

5 "[a]Roam to and fro through the
streets of Jerusalem,
And look now and take note.
And seek in her open squares,
If you can [b]find a man,
[c]If there is one who does
justice, who seeks [1]truth,
Then I will pardon her.
2 "And [a]although they say, 'As the
LORD lives,'
Surely they swear falsely."
3 O LORD, do not [a]Your eyes *look*
for [1]truth?
You have [b]smitten them,
But they did not [2]weaken;
You have consumed them,
But they [c]refused to take
correction.
They have [d]made their faces
harder than rock;
They have refused to repent.
4 ¶ Then I said, "They are only the
poor,
They are foolish;
For they [a]do not know the way
of the LORD
Or the ordinance of their God.
5 "I will go to the great
And will speak to them,
For [a]they know the way of the
LORD
And the ordinance of their God."
But they too, with one accord,
have [b]broken the yoke
And burst the bonds.
6 Therefore [a]a lion from the forest
will slay them,
A [b]wolf of the deserts will
destroy them,
A [c]leopard is watching their
cities.
Everyone who goes out of them
will be torn in pieces,
Because their [d]transgressions are
many,
Their apostasies are numerous.
7 ¶ "Why should I pardon you?
Your sons have forsaken Me
And [a]sworn by those who are
[b]not gods.
When I had fed them to the full,
They [c]committed adultery
And trooped to the harlot's
house.
8 "They were well-fed lusty horses,
Each one neighing after his
[a]neighbor's wife.
9 "Shall I not punish [1]these
people," declares the LORD,
"And on a nation such as this
[a]Shall I not avenge Myself?
10 ¶ "Go up through her vine rows
and destroy,
But do not execute a complete
destruction;
Strip away her branches,
For they are not the LORD's.
11 "For the [a]house of Israel and the
house of Judah
Have dealt very treacherously
with Me," declares the
LORD.
12 They have [a]lied about the LORD
And said, "[1b]Not He;
Misfortune will [c]not come
on us,
And we [d]will not see sword or
famine.
13 "The [a]prophets are *as* wind,
And the word is not in them.
Thus it will be done to them!"

Judgment Proclaimed

14 ¶ Therefore, thus says the LORD,
the God of hosts,
"Because you have spoken this
word,
Behold, I am [a]making My words
in your mouth fire
And this people wood, and it
will consume them.
15 "Behold, I am [a]bringing a nation
against you from afar,
O house of Israel," declares
the LORD.
"It is an enduring nation,
It is an ancient nation,
A nation whose [b]language you
do not know,
Nor can you understand what
they say.
16 "Their [a]quiver is like an [b]open
grave,
All of them are mighty men.
17 "They will [a]devour your harvest
and your food;

---

30 [1]Lit *paramours* [b]2 Kin 9:30; Ezek 23:40 [c]Jer 22:20,22; Lam 1:2,19; Ezek 23:9,10,22

31 [1]Lit *sound* [2]Lit *palms* [3]Lit *my soul faints* [a]Is 42:14 [b]Is 1:15; Lam 1:17

5:1 [1]Lit *faithfulness* [a]2 Chr 16:9; Dan 12:4 [b]Ezek 22:30 [c]Gen 18:26,32

2 [a]Is 48:1; Titus 1:16

3 [1]Lit *faithfulness* [2]Or *become sick* [a]2 Chr 16:9 [b]Is 1:5; 9:13; Jer 2:30 [c]Jer 7:28; 8:5; Zeph 3:2 [d]Jer 7:26; 19:15; Ezek 3:8

4 [a]Is 27:11; Jer 8:7; Hos 4:6

5 [a]Mic 3:1 [b]Ex 32:25; Ps 2:3; Jer 2:20

6 [a]Jer 4:7 [b]Ezek 22:27; Hab 1:8; Zeph 3:3 [c]Hos 13:7 [d]Jer 30:14, 15

7 [a]Josh 23:7; Jer 12:16; Zeph 1:5 [b]Deut 32:21; Jer 2:11; Gal 4:8 [c]Jer 7:9

8 [a]Jer 13:27; 29:23; Ezek 22:11

9 [1]Or *for these things* [a]Jer 9:9

11 [a]Jer 3:6,7,20

12 [1]Lit *He is not* [a]2 Chr 36:16 [b]Prov 30:9; Jer 14:22; 43:1-4 [c]Jer 23:17 [d]Jer 14:13

13 [a]Job 8:2; Jer 14:13,15; 22:22

14 [a]Is 24:6; Jer 1:9; 23:29; Hos 6:5; Zech 1:6

15 [a]Deut 28:49; Is 5:26; Jer 4:16 [b]Is 28:11

16 [a]Is 5:28; 13:18 [b]Ps 5:9

17 [a]Lev 26:16; Deut 28:31,33; Jer 8:16; 50:7,17

They will devour your sons and
your daughters;
They will devour your flocks and
your herds;
They will devour your [b]vines
and your fig trees;
They will demolish with the
sword your [c]fortified cities
in which you trust.
18 ¶ "Yet even in those days," declares the LORD, "I will not make you a
complete destruction.
19 "It shall come about [a]when [1]they
say, 'Why has the LORD our God done all
these things to us?' then you shall say
to them, 'As you have forsaken Me and
served foreign gods in your land, so you
will [b]serve strangers in a land that is not
yours.'
20 ¶ "Declare this in the house of
Jacob
And proclaim it in Judah, saying,
21 'Now hear this, O foolish and
[1]senseless people,
Who have [a]eyes but do not see;
Who have ears but do not hear.
22 'Do you not [a]fear Me?' declares
the LORD.
'Do you not tremble in My
presence?
For I have [b]placed the sand as a
boundary for the sea,
An eternal decree, so it cannot
cross over it.
Though the waves toss, yet they
cannot prevail;
Though they roar, yet they
cannot cross over it.
23 'But this people has a [a]stubborn
and rebellious heart;
They have turned aside and
departed.
24 'They do not say in their heart,
"Let us now fear the LORD our
God,
Who [a]gives rain in its season,
Both [b]the autumn rain and the
spring rain,
Who keeps for us
The [c]appointed weeks of the
harvest."
25 'Your [a]iniquities have turned
these away,
And your sins have withheld
good from you.
26 'For wicked men are found
among My people,
They [a]watch like fowlers [1]lying
in wait;
They set a trap,
They catch men.
27 'Like a cage full of birds,
So their houses are full of
[a]deceit;

17 [b]Jer 8:13 [c]Hos 8:14

19 [1]Or *you* [a]Deut 29:24-26; 1 Kin 9:8,9; Jer 13:22; 16:10-13 [b]Deut 28:48; Jer 16:13

21 [1]Lit *without heart* [a]Is 6:9; 43:8; Ezek 12:2; Matt 13:14; Mark 8:18; John 12:40; Acts 28:26; Rom 11:8

22 [a]Deut 28:58; Ps 119:120; Jer 2:19; 10:7; Rev 15:4 [b]Job 38:8-11; Ps 104:9; Prov 8:29

23 [a]Deut 21:18; Ps 78:8; Jer 4:17; 6:28

24 [a]Ps 147:8; Jer 3:3; Matt 5:45; Acts 14:17 [b]Joel 2:23 [c]Gen 8:22

25 [a]Jer 2:17; 4:18

26 [1]Perhaps, *crouching down* [a]Ps 10:9; Prov 1:11; Jer 18:22; Hab 1:15

27 [a]Jer 9:6

28 [1]Lit *pass over,* or, *overlook deeds* [2]Or *fatherless* [3]Lit *judge* [a]Deut 32:15 [b]Is 1:23; Jer 7:6; 22:3; Zech 7:10

29 [1]Or *for these things* [a]Jer 5:9; Mal 3:5

30 [a]Jer 23:14; Hos 6:10

31 [1]Lit *over their own hands* [a]Ezek 13:6 [b]Mic 2:11

6:1 [1]I.e. house of the vineyard [a]Josh 18:28 [b]Neh 3:14 [c]Jer 1:14; 4:6; 6:22

2 [a]Deut 28:56 [b]Is 1:8; Jer 4:31

3 [1]Lit *against her round about* [2]Lit *hand* [a]Jer 12:10 [b]2 Kin 25:1; Jer 4:17; Luke 19:43

4 [1]Lit *Sanctify* [2]Lit *go up* [a]Jer 6:23; Joel 3:9 [b]Jer 15:8; Zeph 2:4

5 [1]Lit *go up* [2]Or *fortified towers* [a]Is 32:14; Jer 52:13

6 [a]Deut 20:19, 20 [b]Jer 32:24; 33:4 [c]Jer 22:17

7 [1]Lit *keeps cold* [a]James 3:11f

Therefore they have become
great and rich.
28 'They are [a]fat, they are sleek,
They also [1]excel in deeds of
wickedness;
They do not plead the cause,
The cause of the [2b]orphan, that
they may prosper;
And they do not [3]defend the
rights of the poor.
29 '[a]Shall I not punish [1]these
people?' declares the LORD,
'On a nation such as this
Shall I not avenge Myself?'
30 ¶ "An appalling and [a]horrible
thing
Has happened in the land:
31 The [a]prophets prophesy falsely,
And the priests rule [1]on their
own authority;
And My people [b]love it so!
But what will you do at the end
of it?

Destruction of Jerusalem Impending

6 "Flee for safety, O sons of
[a]Benjamin,
From the midst of Jerusalem!
Now blow a trumpet in Tekoa
And raise a signal over
[1b]Beth-haccerem;
For evil looks down from the
[c]north,
And a great destruction.
2 "The comely and [a]dainty one,
[b]the daughter of Zion, I will
cut off.
3 "[a]Shepherds and their flocks will
come to her,
They will [b]pitch *their* tents
[1]around her,
They will pasture each in his
[2]place.
4 "[1a]Prepare war against her;
Arise, and let us [2]attack at
[b]noon.
Woe to us, for the day declines,
For the shadows of the evening
lengthen!
5 "Arise, and let us [1]attack by
night
And [a]destroy her [2]palaces!"
6 For thus says the LORD of hosts,
"[a]Cut down her trees
And cast up a [b]siege against
Jerusalem.
This is the city to be punished,
In whose midst there is only
[c]oppression.
7 "[a]As a well [1]keeps its waters
fresh,
So she [1]keeps fresh her
wickedness.

[b]Violence and destruction are
heard in her;
[c]Sickness and wounds are ever
before Me.
8 "[a]Be warned, O Jerusalem,
Or [1b]I shall be alienated from
you,
And make you a desolation,
A land not inhabited."

9 ¶ Thus says the LORD of hosts,
"They will [a]thoroughly glean as
the vine the [b]remnant of
Israel;
Pass your hand again like a grape
gatherer
Over the branches."
10 To whom shall I speak and give
warning
That they may hear?
Behold, their [a]ears are [1]closed
And they cannot listen.
Behold, [b]the word of the LORD
has become a reproach to
them;
They have no delight in it.
11 But I am [a]full of the wrath of
the LORD;
I am [b]weary with holding *it* in.
"[c]Pour *it* out on the children in
the street
And on the [1]gathering of young
men together;
For both husband and wife shall
be taken,
The aged [2]and the very old.
12 "Their [a]houses shall be turned
over to others,
Their fields and their wives
together;
For I will [b]stretch out My hand
Against the inhabitants of the
land," declares the LORD.
13 "For [a]from the least of them even
to the greatest of them,
Everyone is [b]greedy for gain,
And from the prophet even to
the priest
Everyone [1]deals falsely.
14 "They have [a]healed the
brokenness of My people
superficially,
Saying, 'Peace, peace,'
But there is no peace.
15 "Were they [a]ashamed because of
the abomination they have
done?
They were not even ashamed at
all;
They did not even know how to
blush.
Therefore they shall fall among
those who fall;
At the time that I punish them,

7 [b]Jer 20:8; Ezek 7:11,23 [c]Jer 30:12,13

8 [1]Lit *my soul* [a]Jer 7:28; 17:23 [b]Ezek 23:18; Hos 9:12

9 [a]Jer 16:16; 49:9; Obad 5,6 [b]Jer 8:3; 11:23

10 [1]Lit *uncircumcised* [a]Jer 5:21; 7:26; Acts 7:51 [b]Jer 20:8

11 [1]Lit *council* [2]Lit *with fullness of days* [a]Job 32:18,19; Mic 3:8 [b]Jer 15:6; 20:9 [c]Jer 7:20; 9:21

12 [a]Deut 28:30; Jer 8:10; 38:22,23 [b]Jer 15:6

13 [1]Or *makes lies* [a]Jer 8:10 [b]Is 56:11; 57:17; Jer 8:10; 22:17

14 [a]Jer 8:11; Ezek 13:10

15 [a]Jer 3:3; 8:12

16 [a]Is 8:20; Jer 12:16; 18:15; 31:21; Mal 4:4; Luke 16:29 [b]Matt 11:29

17 [a]Is 21:11; 58:1; Jer 25:4; Ezek 3:17; Hab 2:1

19 [1]Or *devices* [a]Is 1:2; Jer 19:3,15; 22:29 [b]Prov 1:31 [c]Jer 8:9

20 [1]Lit *good* [a]Ps 50:7-9; Is 1:11; 66:3; Mic 6:6 [b]Is 60:6 [c]Ex 30:23 [d]Ps 40:6; Amos 5:22

21 [1]Lit *giving* [2]Lit *his friend* [a]Is 8:14; Jer 13:16 [b]Is 9:14-17; Jer 9:21,22

22 [a]Jer 1:15; 10:22; 50:41-43 [b]Neh 1:9

23 [a]Is 13:18; Jer 4:29 [b]Jer 50:42 [c]Is 5:30

24 [a]Is 28:19; Jer 4:19-21

They shall be cast down," says
the LORD.
16 ¶ Thus says the LORD,
"Stand by the ways and see and
ask for the [a]ancient paths,
Where the good way is, and
walk in it;
And [b]you will find rest for your
souls.
But they said, 'We will not walk
in it.'
17 "And I set [a]watchmen over you,
saying,
'Listen to the sound of the
trumpet!'
But they said, 'We will not
listen.'
18 "Therefore hear, O nations,
And know, O congregation, what
is among them.
19 "[a]Hear, O earth: behold, I am
bringing disaster on this
people,
The [b]fruit of their [1]plans,
Because they have not listened
to My words,
And as for My law, they have
[c]rejected it also.
20 "[a]For what purpose does
[b]frankincense come to Me
from Sheba
And the [1c]sweet cane from a
distant land?
[d]Your burnt offerings are not
acceptable
And your sacrifices are not
pleasing to Me."
21 Therefore, thus says the LORD,
"Behold, [a]I am [1]laying stumbling
blocks before this people.
And they will stumble against
them,
[b]Fathers and sons together;
Neighbor and [2]friend will
perish."

The Enemy from the North

22 ¶ Thus says the LORD,
"Behold, [a]a people is coming
from the north land,
And a great nation will be
aroused from the [b]remote
parts of the earth.
23 "They seize [a]bow and spear;
They are [b]cruel and have no
mercy;
Their voice [c]roars like the sea,
And they ride on horses,
Arrayed as a man for the battle
Against you, O daughter of
Zion!"
24 We have [a]heard the report of it;
Our hands are limp.

[b]Anguish has seized us,
Pain as of a woman in childbirth.
25 [a]Do not go out into the field
And [b]do not walk on the road,
For the enemy has a sword,
[c]Terror is on every side.
26 O daughter of my people, [a]put
on sackcloth
And [b]roll in ashes;
[1c]Mourn as for an only son,
A lamentation most bitter.
For suddenly the destroyer
Will come upon us.

27 ¶ "I have [a]made you an assayer
and a tester among My
people,
That you may know and assay
their way."
28 All of them are stubbornly
rebellious,
[a]Going about as a talebearer.
They are [b]bronze and iron;
They, all of them, are corrupt.
29 The bellows blow fiercely,
The lead is consumed by the
fire;
In vain the refining goes on,
But the [a]wicked are not
[1]separated.
30 [a]They call them rejected silver,
Because the [b]LORD has rejected
them.

Message at the Temple Gate

7 The word that came to Jeremiah
from the LORD, saying,
2 "[a]Stand in the gate of the LORD's
house and proclaim there this word and
say, 'Hear the word of the LORD, all you
of Judah, who enter by these gates to worship the LORD!' "
3 Thus says the LORD of hosts, the
God of Israel, "[a]Amend your ways and
your deeds, and I will let you dwell in this
place.
4 "[a]Do not trust in deceptive words,
saying, '[1]This is the temple of the LORD,
the temple of the LORD, the temple of the
LORD.'
5 "For [a]if you truly amend your ways
and your deeds, if you truly [b]practice justice between a man and his neighbor,
6 *if* you do not oppress the alien, the
[1a]orphan, or the widow, and do not
shed [b]innocent blood in this place, nor
[c]walk after other gods to your own ruin,
7 then I will let you [a]dwell in this
place, in the [b]land that I gave to your
fathers forever and ever.
8 ¶ "Behold, you are trusting in [a]de-
ceptive words to no avail.
9 "Will you steal, murder, and commit
adultery and swear falsely, and [1a]offer
sacrifices to Baal and walk after [b]other
gods that you have not known,
10 then [a]come and stand before Me in
[b]this house, which is called by My name,
and say, 'We are delivered!'—that you
may do all these abominations?
11 "Has [a]this house, which is called by
My name, become a [b]den of robbers in
your sight? Behold, [c]I, even I, have seen
it," declares the LORD.
12 ¶ "But go now to My place which
was in [a]Shiloh, where I [b]made My name
dwell at the first, and [c]see what I did to
it because of the wickedness of My people Israel.
13 "And now, because you have done
all these things," declares the LORD, "and
I spoke to you, [a]rising up early and
[b]speaking, but you did not hear, and I
[c]called you but you did not answer,
14 therefore, I will do to the [a]house
which is called by My name, [b]in which
you trust, and to the place which I gave
you and your fathers, as I [c]did to Shiloh.
15 "I will [a]cast you out of My sight, as
I have cast out all your brothers, all the
[1]offspring of [b]Ephraim.
16 ¶ "As for you, [a]do not pray for this
people, and do not lift up cry or prayer for
them, and do not intercede with Me; for
I do not hear you.
17 "Do you not see what they are doing
in the cities of Judah and in the streets of
Jerusalem?
18 "The [1]children gather wood, and
the fathers kindle the fire, and the wom-
en knead dough to make cakes for the
queen of heaven; and *they* [a]pour out
drink offerings to other gods in order to
[b]spite Me.
19 "[a]Do they spite Me?" declares the
LORD. "Is it not themselves *they spite,* to
[1]their own [b]shame?"
20 Therefore thus says the Lord
[1]GOD, "Behold, My [a]anger and My
wrath will be poured out on this place, on
man and on beast and on the [b]trees of
the field and on the fruit of the ground;
and it will burn and not be quenched."
21 ¶ Thus says the LORD of hosts, the
God of Israel, "Add your [a]burnt offerings
to your sacrifices and [b]eat flesh.
22 "For I did not [a]speak to your fathers,
or command them in the day that I
brought them out of the land of Egypt,
concerning burnt offerings and sacrifices.
23 "But this is [1]what I commanded
them, saying, '[a]Obey My voice, and [b]I
will be your God, and you will be My
people; and you will walk in all the way
which I command you, that it may [c]be
well with you.'
24 "Yet they [a]did not obey or incline
their ear, but walked in *their own* coun-

24 [b]Is 21:3; Jer 4:31
25 [a]Jer 14:18 [b]Judg 5:6 [c]Jer 20:10
26 [1]Lit *Make for yourself mourning* [a]Jer 4:8 [b]Jer 25:34; Mic 1:10 [c]Amos 8:10; Zech 12:10
27 [a]Jer 1:18
28 [a]Jer 9:4 [b]Ezek 22:18
29 [1]Or *drawn off* [a]Jer 15:19
30 [a]Ps 119:119; Is 1:22 [b]Jer 7:29; Hos 9:17; Zech 11:8
7:2 [a]Jer 17:19
3 [a]Jer 4:1
4 [1]Lit *They are* [a]Jer 7:8; Mic 3:11
5 [a]Is 1:19; Jer 4:1 [b]1 Kin 6:12; Jer 21:12
6 [1]Or *fatherless* [a]Ex 22:21-24; Jer 5:28 [b]Jer 2:34 [c]Deut 6:14; Jer 13:10
7 [a]Deut 4:40 [b]Jer 3:18
8 [a]Jer 7:4
9 [1]Or *burn incense* [a]Jer 11:13 [b]Ex 20:3; Jer 7:6
10 [a]Ezek 23:39 [b]Jer 7:11
11 [a]Is 56:7 [b]Matt 21:13; Mark 11:17; Luke 19:46 [c]Jer 29:23
12 [a]Judg 18:31; Jer 26:6 [b]Josh 18:1 [c]1 Sam 4:10; Ps 78:60-64
13 [a]Jer 7:25 [b]Jer 35:17 [c]Prov 1:24; Is 65:12
14 [a]Deut 12:5; 1 Kin 9:7 [b]Jer 7:4 [c]Jer 7:12
15 [1]Lit *seed* [a]Jer 15:1 [b]Ps 78:67; Hos 7:13
16 [a]Ex 32:10; Deut 9:14; Jer 11:14
18 [1]Lit *sons* [a]Jer 19:13 [b]Deut 32:16; 1 Kin 14:9; Jer 11:17; Ezek 8:17
19 [1]Lit *their faces'* [a]Job 35:6; 1 Cor 10:22 [b]Jer 9:19
20 [1]Heb *YHWH,* usually rendered LORD [a]Is 42:25; Jer 6:11; Lam 2:3-5 [b]Jer 8:13
21 [a]Is 1:11; Jer 6:20; Amos 5:22 [b]Ezek 33:25; Hos 8:13
22 [a]1 Sam 15:22; Ps 51:16; Hos 6:6
23 [1]Lit *the word which* [a]Ex 15:26; Deut 6:3 [b]Ex 19:5; Lev 26:12; Jer 11:4 [c]Is 3:10; Jer 38:20
24 [a]Deut 29:19; Ps 81:11; Jer 11:8; Ezek 20:8

sels *and* in the stubbornness of their evil
heart, and [1b]went backward and not forward.
25 "Since the day that your fathers
came out of the land of Egypt until this
day, I have [a]sent you all My servants the
prophets, daily rising early and sending
them.
26 "Yet they did not listen to Me or
incline their ear, but [a]stiffened their
neck; they [b]did more evil than their fathers.
27 ¶ "You shall [a]speak all these words
to them, but they will not listen to you;
and you shall call to them, but they will
[b]not answer you.
28 "You shall say to them, 'This is the
nation that [a]did not obey the voice of the
LORD their God or accept correction;
[1b]truth has perished and has been cut
off from their mouth.
29 '[a]Cut off [1]your hair and cast *it*
away,
And [b]take up a lamentation on
the bare heights;
For the LORD has [c]rejected and
forsaken
The generation of His wrath.'
30 "For the sons of Judah have done
that which is evil in My sight," declares
the LORD, "they have [a]set their detestable things in the house which is called
by My name, to defile it.
31 "They have [a]built the high places of
Topheth, which is in the valley of the son
of Hinnom, to [b]burn their sons and their
daughters in the fire, which I [c]did not
command, and it did not come into My
[1]mind.
32 ¶ "[a]Therefore, behold, days are
coming," declares the LORD, "when it
will no longer be called Topheth, or the
valley of the son of Hinnom, but the valley of the Slaughter; for they will [b]bury
in Topheth [1]because there is no *other*
place.
33 "The [a]dead bodies of this people
will be food for the birds of the sky and
for the beasts of the earth; and no one
will frighten *them away.*
34 "Then I will make to [a]cease from
the cities of Judah and from the streets of
Jerusalem the voice of joy and the voice
of gladness, the voice of the bridegroom
and the voice of the bride; for the [b]land
will become a ruin.

The Sin and Treachery of Judah

8 "At that time," declares the LORD,
"they will [a]bring out the bones of
the kings of Judah and the bones of its
princes, and the bones of the priests and
the bones of the prophets, and the bones
of the inhabitants of Jerusalem from their
graves.
2 "They will spread them out to the
sun, the moon and to all the [a]host of
heaven, which they have loved and
which they have served, and which they
have gone after and which they have
sought, and which they have worshiped.
They will not be gathered [b]or buried;
[c]they will be as dung on the face of the
ground.
3 "And [a]death will be chosen rather
than life by all the remnant that remains
of this evil family, that remains in all the
[b]places to which I have driven them,"
declares the LORD of hosts.
4 "You shall say to them, 'Thus says
the LORD,
"Do *men* [a]fall and not get up
again?
Does one turn away and not
[1]repent?
5 "Why then has this people,
Jerusalem,
[a]Turned away in continual
apostasy?
They [b]hold fast to deceit,
They [c]refuse to return.
6 "I [a]have listened and heard,
They have spoken what is not
right;
[b]No man repented of his
wickedness,
Saying, 'What have I done?'
Everyone turned to his course,
Like a [c]horse charging into the
battle.
7 "Even the stork in the sky
[a]Knows her seasons;
And the [b]turtledove and the
swift and the thrush
Observe the time of their
[1]migration;
But [c]My people do not know
The ordinance of the LORD.
8 ¶ "[a]How can you say, 'We are
wise,
And the law of the LORD is
with us'?
But behold, the lying pen of the
scribes
Has made *it* into a lie.
9 "The wise men are [a]put to
shame,
They are dismayed and caught;
Behold, they have [b]rejected the
word of the LORD,
And what kind of wisdom do
they have?
10 "Therefore I will [a]give their
wives to others,
Their fields to [1]new owners;

24 [1]Lit *they were* [b]Jer 15:6
25 [a]2 Chr 36:15; Jer 25:4; 29:19; Luke 11:49
26 [a]Neh 9:16; Jer 17:23; 19:15 [b]Jer 16:12; Matt 23:32
27 [a]Jer 1:7; 26:2; Ezek 2:7 [b]Is 50:2; 65:12; Zech 7:13
28 [1]Lit *faithfulness* [a]Jer 6:17; 11:10 [b]Is 59:14, 15; Jer 9:5
29 [1]Lit *your crown* [a]Job 1:20; Is 15:2; 22:12; Jer 16:6; Mic 1:16 [b]Jer 3:21; 9:17,18 [c]Jer 6:30; 14:19
30 [a]2 Kin 21:3f; 2 Chr 33:3-5,7; Jer 32:34,35; Ezek 7:20; Dan 9:27; 11:31
31 [1]Lit *heart* [a]2 Kin 23:10; Jer 19:5; 32:35 [b]Lev 18:21; 2 Kin 17:17; Ps 106:38 [c]Deut 17:3
32 [1]Or *until there is no place left* [a]Jer 19:6,11 [b]2 Kin 23:10
33 [a]Deut 28:26; Ps 79:2; Jer 12:9; 19:7
34 [a]Is 24:7,8; Jer 16:9; 25:10; Ezek 26:13; Hos 2:11; Rev 18:23 [b]Lev 26:33; Is 1:7; Jer 4:27
8:1 [a]Ezek 6:5
2 [a]2 Kin 23:5; Jer 19:13; Zeph 1:5; Acts 7:42 [b]Jer 22:19; 36:30 [c]2 Kin 9:37; Ps 83:10; Jer 9:22
3 [a]Job 3:21,22; 7:15,16; Jon 4:3; Rev 9:6 [b]Deut 30:1,4; Jer 23:3, 8; 29:14
4 [1]Lit *turn back* [a]Prov 24:16; Amos 5:2; Mic 7:8
5 [a]Jer 5:6; 7:24 [b]Jer 5:27; 9:6 [c]Jer 5:3
6 [a]Ps 14:2; Mal 3:16 [b]Ezek 22:30; Mic 7:2; Rev 9:20 [c]Job 39:21-25
7 [1]Lit *coming* [a]Prov 6:6-8; Is 1:3 [b]Song 2:12 [c]Jer 5:4
8 [a]Job 5:12,13; Jer 4:22; Rom 1:22
9 [a]Is 19:11; Jer 6:15; 1 Cor 1:27 [b]Jer 6:19
10 [1]Lit *possessing ones* [a]Deut 28:30; Jer 6:12, 13; 38:22f

Because from the least even to
the greatest
Everyone is [b]greedy for gain;
From the prophet even to the
priest
Everyone practices deceit.
11 "They [a]heal the brokenness of
the daughter of My people
superficially,
Saying, 'Peace, peace,'
But there is no peace.
12 "Were they [a]ashamed because of
the abomination they had
done?
They certainly were not
ashamed,
And they did not know how to
blush;
Therefore they shall [b]fall among
those who fall;
At the [c]time of their
punishment they shall be
brought down,"
Says the LORD.

13 ¶ "I will [a]surely snatch them
away," declares the LORD;
"There will be [b]no grapes on the
vine
And [c]no figs on the fig tree,
And the leaf will wither;
And what I have given them will
pass away." ' "
14 Why are we sitting still?
[a]Assemble yourselves, and let us
[b]go into the fortified cities
And let us perish there,
Because the LORD our God has
doomed us
And given us [c]poisoned water to
drink,
For [d]we have sinned against the
LORD.
15 *We* [a]waited for peace, but no
good *came;*
For a time of healing, but
behold, terror!
16 From [a]Dan is heard the snorting
of his horses;
At the sound of the neighing of
his [b]stallions
The whole land quakes;
For they come and [c]devour the
land and its fullness,
The city and its inhabitants.
17 "For behold, I am [a]sending
serpents against you,
Adders, for which there is [b]no
charm,
And they will bite you," declares
the LORD.

18 ¶ [1]My [a]sorrow is beyond
healing,
My [b]heart is faint *within me!*
19 Behold, listen! The cry of the
daughter of my people from
a [a]distant land:
"Is the LORD not in Zion? Is her
King not within her?"
"Why have they [b]provoked Me
with their graven images,
with foreign [1c]idols?"
20 "Harvest is past, summer is
ended,
And we are not saved."
21 For the [a]brokenness of the
daughter of my people I am
broken;
I [b]mourn, dismay has taken hold
of me.
22 Is there no [a]balm in Gilead?
Is there no physician there?
[b]Why then has not the [1]health
of the daughter of my people
[2]been restored?

A Lament over Zion

9 [1a]Oh that my head were waters
And my eyes a fountain of tears,
That I might weep day and night
For the slain of the [b]daughter of
my people!
2 [1a]Oh that I had in the desert
A wayfarers' lodging place;
That I might leave my people
And go from them!
For all of them are [b]adulterers,
An assembly of [c]treacherous
men.
3 "They [a]bend their tongue *like*
their bow;
Lies and not truth prevail in the
land;
For they [b]proceed from evil to
evil,
And they [c]do not know Me,"
declares the LORD.
4 "Let everyone [a]be on guard
against his neighbor,
And [b]do not trust any brother;
Because every [c]brother deals
[1]craftily,
And every neighbor [d]goes about
as a slanderer.
5 "Everyone [a]deceives his neighbor
And does not speak the truth,
They have taught their tongue to
speak lies;
They [b]weary themselves
committing iniquity.
6 "Your [a]dwelling is in the midst of
deceit;
Through deceit they [b]refuse to
know Me," declares the
LORD.

7 ¶ Therefore thus says the LORD of
hosts,

10 [b]Is 56:11; 57:17; Jer 6:13
11 [a]Jer 6:14; 14:13,14; Lam 2:14; Ezek 13:10
12 [a]Ps 52:1,7; Is 3:9; Jer 3:3; 6:15; Zeph 3:5 [b]Is 9:14; Jer 6:21; Hos 4:5 [c]Deut 32:35; Jer 10:15
13 [a]Jer 14:12; Ezek 22:20,21 [b]Jer 5:17; 7:20; Joel 1:7 [c]Matt 21:19; Luke 13:6
14 [a]Jer 4:5 [b]2 Sam 20:6; Jer 35:11 [c]Deut 29:18; Ps 69:21; Jer 9:15; 23:15; Lam 3:19; Matt 27:34 [d]Jer 3:25; 14:20
15 [a]Jer 8:11; 14:19
16 [a]Judg 18:29; Jer 4:15 [b]Judg 5:22 [c]Jer 3:24; 10:25
17 [a]Num 21:6; Deut 32:24 [b]Ps 58:4,5
18 [1]So Gr and versions [a]Is 22:4; Lam 1:16, 17 [b]Jer 23:9; Lam 5:17
19 [1]Lit *vanities* [a]Is 13:5; 39:3; Jer 4:16; 9:16 [b]Deut 32:21; Jer 7:19 [c]Ps 31:6
21 [a]Jer 4:19; 9:1; 14:17 [b]Jer 14:2; Joel 2:6; Nah 2:10
22 [1]Or *healing* [2]Lit *gone up* [a]Gen 37:25; Jer 46:11 [b]Jer 14:19; 30:13
9:1 [1]Ch 8:23 in Heb [a]Is 22:4; Jer 8:18; 13:17; Lam 2:18 [b]Jer 6:26; 8:21,22
2 [1]Ch 9:1 in Heb [a]Ps 55:6,7; 120:5,6 [b]Jer 5:7, 8; 23:10; Hos 4:2 [c]Jer 5:11; 12:1,6
3 [a]Ps 64:3; Is 59:4; Jer 9:8 [b]Jer 4:22 [c]Judg 2:10; 1 Sam 2:12; Jer 4:22; 5:4,5; Hos 4:1; 1 Cor 15:34
4 [1]I.e. like Jacob (a play on words) [a]Ps 12:2; Prov 26:24,25; Jer 9:8; Mic 7:5,6 [b]Jer 12:6 [c]Gen 27:35 [d]Ps 15:3; Prov 10:18; Jer 6:28
5 [a]Mic 6:12 [b]Jer 12:13; 51:58,64
6 [a]Ps 120:5,6; Jer 5:27; 8:5 [b]Job 21:14,15; Prov 1:24; Jer 11:10; 13:10; John 3:19,20

"Behold, I will refine them and
[a]assay them;
For [b]what *else* can I do, because
of the daughter of My
people?
8 "Their [a]tongue is a deadly arrow;
It speaks deceit;
With his mouth one [b]speaks
peace to his neighbor,
But inwardly he [c]sets an
ambush for him.
9 "[a]Shall I not punish them for
these things?" declares the
LORD.
"On a nation such as this
Shall I not avenge Myself?

10 ¶ "For the [a]mountains I will
take up a weeping and
wailing,
And for the pastures of the
[b]wilderness a dirge,
Because they are [c]laid waste so
that no one passes through,
And the lowing of the cattle is
not heard;
Both the [d]birds of the sky and
the beasts have fled; they
are gone.
11 "I will make Jerusalem a [a]heap of
ruins,
A haunt of [b]jackals;
And I will make the cities of
Judah a [c]desolation, without
inhabitant."

12 ¶ Who is the [a]wise man that may understand this? And *who is* he to whom [b]the mouth of the LORD has spoken, that he may declare it? [c]Why is the land ruined, laid waste like a desert, so that no one passes through?

13 The LORD said, "Because they have [a]forsaken My law which I set before them, and have not obeyed My voice nor walked according to it,

14 but have [a]walked after the stubbornness of their heart and after the [b]Baals, as their [c]fathers taught them,"

15 therefore thus says the LORD of hosts, the God of Israel, "behold, [a]I will feed them, this people, with wormwood and give them [b]poisoned water to drink.

16 "I will [a]scatter them among the nations, whom neither they nor their fathers have known; and I will send the [b]sword after them until I have annihilated them."

17 ¶ Thus says the LORD of hosts,
"Consider and call for the
[a]mourning women, that
they may come;
And send for the [1][b]wailing
women, that they may
come!
18 "Let them make haste and take up
a wailing for us,
That our [a]eyes may shed tears
And our eyelids flow with water.
19 "For a voice of [a]wailing is heard
from Zion,
'[b]How are we ruined!
We are put to great shame,
For we have [c]left the land,
Because they have cast down our
dwellings.' "
20 Now hear the word of the LORD,
O you [a]women,
And let your ear receive the
word of His mouth;
Teach your daughters wailing,
And everyone her neighbor a
dirge.
21 For [a]death has come up through
our windows;
It has entered our palaces
To cut off the [b]children from
the streets,
The young men from the town
squares.
22 Speak, "Thus says the LORD,
'The corpses of men will fall
[a]like dung on the open
field,
And like the sheaf after the
reaper,
But no one will gather *them.*' "

23 ¶ Thus says the LORD, "[a]Let not a wise man boast of his wisdom, and let not the [b]mighty man boast of his might, let not a [c]rich man boast of his riches;

24 but let him who boasts [a]boast of this, that he understands and knows Me, that I am the LORD who [b]exercises lovingkindness, justice and righteousness on earth; for I [c]delight in these things," declares the LORD.

25 ¶ "Behold, the days are coming," declares the LORD, "that I will punish all who are circumcised and yet [a]uncircumcised—

26 Egypt and Judah, and Edom and the sons of Ammon, and Moab and [a]all those inhabiting the desert who clip the hair on their temples; for all the nations are uncircumcised, and all the house of Israel are [b]uncircumcised of heart."

A Satire on Idolatry

10 Hear the word which the LORD speaks to you, O house of Israel.

2 Thus says the LORD,
"[a]Do not learn the way of the
nations,
And do not be terrified by the
signs of the heavens
Although the nations are terrified
by them;

7 [a]Is 1:25; Jer 6:27; Mal 3:3 [b]Hos 11:8
8 [a]Jer 9:3 [b]Ps 28:3 [c]Jer 5:26
9 [a]Is 1:24; Jer 5:9,29
10 [a]Jer 4:24; 7:29 [b]Jer 4:26; Hos 4:3 [c]Jer 12:4,10; Ezek 14:15; 29:11; 33:28 [d]Jer 4:25; 12:4; Hos 4:3
11 [a]Is 25:2; Jer 51:37 [b]Is 13:22; 34:13 [c]Jer 4:27; 26:9
12 [a]Ps 107:43; Is 42:23; Hos 14:9 [b]Jer 9:20; 23:16 [c]Ps 107:34; Jer 23:10
13 [a]2 Chr 7:19; Ps 89:30; Jer 5:19; 22:9
14 [a]Jer 7:24; 11:8; Rom 1:21-24 [b]Jer 2:8, 23; 23:27 [c]Gal 1:14; 1 Pet 1:18
15 [a]Ps 80:5 [b]Deut 29:18; Jer 8:14; 23:15; Lam 3:15
16 [a]Lev 26:33; Deut 28:64; Jer 13:24 [b]Jer 44:27; Ezek 5:2, 12
17 [1]Lit *skilled* [a]2 Chr 35:25; Eccl 12:5 [b]Amos 5:16
18 [a]Is 22:4; Jer 9:1; 14:17
19 [a]Jer 7:29; Ezek 7:16-18 [b]Deut 28:29; Jer 4:13 [c]Jer 7:15; 15:1
20 [a]Is 32:9
21 [a]2 Chr 36:17; Jer 15:7; 18:21; Ezek 9:5, 6; Amos 6:9,10 [b]Jer 6:11
22 [a]Ps 83:10; Is 5:25; Jer 8:2; 16:4; 25:33
23 [a]Eccl 9:11; Is 47:10; Ezek 28:3-7 [b]1 Kin 20:10,11; Is 10:8-12 [c]Job 31:24,25; Ps 49:6-9
24 [a]Ps 20:7; 44:8; Is 41:16; Jer 4:2; 1 Cor 1:31; 2 Cor 10:17; Gal 6:14 [b]Ex 34:6,7; Ps 36:5,7; 51:1 [c]Is 61:8; Mic 7:18
25 [a]Jer 4:4; Rom 2:28,29
26 [a]Jer 25:23 [b]Lev 26:41; Jer 4:4; 6:10; Ezek 44:7; Rom 2:28
10:2 [a]Lev 18:3; 20:23; Deut 12:30

3 For the customs of the peoples are [1a]delusion;
Because [b]it is wood cut from the forest,
The work of the hands of a craftsman with a cutting tool.
4 "They [a]decorate *it* with silver and with gold;
They [b]fasten it with nails and with hammers
So that it will not totter.
5 "Like a scarecrow in a cucumber field are they,
And they [a]cannot speak;
They must be [b]carried,
Because they cannot walk!
Do not fear them,
For they [c]can do no harm,
Nor can they do any good."

6 ¶ [a]There is none like You, O LORD;
You are [b]great, and great is Your name in might.
7 [a]Who would not fear You, O [b]King of the nations?
Indeed it is Your due!
For among all the [c]wise men of the nations
And in all their kingdoms,
There is none like You.
8 But they are altogether [a]stupid and foolish
In their discipline of [1]delusion—[2]their idol is wood!
9 Beaten [a]silver is brought from [b]Tarshish,
And [c]gold from Uphaz,
The work of a craftsman and of the hands of a goldsmith;
Violet and purple are their clothing;
They are all the [d]work of skilled men.
10 But the LORD is the [a]true God;
He is the [b]living God and the [c]everlasting King.
At His wrath the [d]earth quakes,
And the nations cannot [e]endure His indignation.
11 ¶ [1]Thus you shall say to them,
"The [a]gods that did not make the heav-
ens and the earth will [b]perish from the
earth and from under the [2]heavens."
12 ¶ *It is* [a]He who made the earth by His power,
Who [b]established the world by His wisdom;
And by His understanding He has [c]stretched out the heavens.

13 When He utters His [a]voice, *there is* a tumult of waters in the heavens,
And He causes the [b]clouds to ascend from the end of the earth;
He makes lightning for the rain,
And brings out the [c]wind from His storehouses.
14 Every man is [a]stupid, devoid of knowledge;
Every goldsmith is put to shame by his [1]idols;
For his molten images are deceitful,
And there is no breath in them.
15 They are [a]worthless, a work of mockery;
In the [b]time of their punishment they will perish.
16 The [a]portion of Jacob is not like these;
For the [1b]Maker of all is He,
And [c]Israel is the tribe of His inheritance;
The [d]LORD of hosts is His name.

17 ¶ [a]Pick up your bundle from the ground,
You who dwell under siege!
18 For thus says the LORD,
"Behold, I am [a]slinging out the inhabitants of the land
At this time,
And will cause them distress,
That they may [1]be found."

19 ¶ [a]Woe is me, because of my [1]injury!
My [b]wound is incurable.
But I said, "Truly this is a sickness,
And I [c]must bear it."
20 My [a]tent is destroyed,
And all my ropes are broken;
My [b]sons have gone from me and are no more.
There is [c]no one to stretch out my tent again
Or to set up my curtains.
21 For the shepherds have become stupid
And [a]have not sought the LORD;
Therefore they have not prospered,
And [b]all their flock is scattered.
22 The sound of a [a]report! Behold, it comes—
A great commotion [b]out of the land of the north—
To [c]make the cities of Judah
A desolation, a haunt of jackals.
23 ¶ I know, O LORD, that [a]a man's way is not in himself,

3 [1]Lit *vanity* [a]Jer 14:22 [b]Is 44:9-20
4 [a]Is 40:19 [b]Is 40:20; 41:7
5 [a]Ps 115:5; Is 46:7; Jer 10:14; 1 Cor 12:2 [b]Ps 115:7; Is 46:1,7 [c]Is 41:23,24
6 [a]Ex 15:11; Deut 33:26; Ps 86:8,10; Jer 10:16 [b]Ps 48:1; 96:4; Is 12:6; Jer 32:18
7 [a]Rev 15:4 [b]Ps 22:28 [c]Dan 2:27,28; 1 Cor 1:19,20
8 [1]Lit *vanities, or idols* [2]Lit *it is* [a]Jer 4:22; 5:4; 10:14
9 [a]Is 40:19 [b]Ps 72:10; Is 23:6 [c]Dan 10:5 [d]Ps 115:4
10 [a]Is 65:16 [b]Jer 4:2 [c]Ps 10:16; 29:10 [d]Jer 4:24; 50:46 [e]Ps 76:7
11 [1]This verse is in Aram [2]Or *these heavens* [a]Ps 96:5 [b]Is 2:18; Zeph 2:11
12 [a]Gen 1:1,6; Job 38:4-7; Ps 136:5; 148:4,5; Jer 51:15,19 [b]Ps 78:69; Is 45:18 [c]Job 9:8; Is 40:22
13 [a]Ps 29:3-9 [b]Job 36:27-29 [c]Ps 135:7
14 [1]Or *graven image* [a]Jer 10:8; 51:17,18
15 [a]Is 41:24; Jer 8:19; 14:22 [b]Jer 8:12; 51:18
16 [1]Lit *Fashioner* [a]Ps 16:5; 73:26; 119:57; Jer 51:19; Lam 3:24 [b]Is 45:7; Jer 10:12 [c]Deut 32:9; Ps 74:2 [d]Jer 31:35; 32:18
17 [a]Ezek 12:3-12
18 [1]Lit *find* [a]1 Sam 25:29
19 [1]Lit *breaking* [a]Jer 4:31 [b]Jer 14:17 [c]Mic 7:9
20 [a]Jer 4:20; Lam 2:4 [b]Jer 31:15; Lam 1:5 [c]Is 51:18
21 [a]Jer 2:8 [b]Jer 23:2
22 [a]Jer 4:15 [b]Jer 1:14; 25:9 [c]Jer 9:11; 49:33
23 [a]Prov 16:1; 20:24

[b]Nor is it in a man who walks
to direct his steps.
24 [a]Correct me, O LORD, but with
justice;
Not with Your anger, or You will
[1]bring me to nothing.
25 [a]Pour out Your wrath on the
nations that [b]do not
know You
And on the families that [c]do not
call Your name;
For they have devoured Jacob;
They have [d]devoured him and
consumed him
And have laid waste his
[1]habitation.

The Broken Covenant

11 The word which came to Jeremiah from the LORD, saying,
2 "[a]Hear the words of this [b]cov-
enant, and speak to the men of Judah and
to the inhabitants of Jerusalem;
3 and say to them, 'Thus says the
LORD, the God of Israel, "[a]Cursed is the
man who does not heed the words of this
covenant
4 which I commanded your forefathers in the [a]day that I brought them out
of the land of Egypt, from the [b]iron furnace, saying, '[c]Listen to My voice, and
[1]do according to all which I command
you; so you shall be [d]My people, and I
will be your God,'
5 in order to confirm the [a]oath
which I swore to your forefathers, to
give them a land flowing with milk and
honey, as *it is* this day." ' " Then I said,
"[b]Amen, O LORD."
6 ¶ And the LORD said to me, "[a]Pro-
claim all these words in the cities of Judah and in the streets of Jerusalem, saying, '[b]Hear the words of this covenant
and [c]do them.
7 'For I solemnly [a]warned your fathers in the [b]day that I brought them up
from the land of Egypt, even to this day,
[1c]warning persistently, saying, "[d]Lis-
ten to My voice."
8 'Yet they [a]did not obey or incline
their ear, but walked, each one, in the
stubbornness of his evil heart; therefore I
brought on them all the [b]words of this
covenant, which I commanded *them* to
do, but they did not.' "
9 ¶ Then the LORD said to me, "A
[a]conspiracy has been found among the
men of Judah and among the inhabitants
of Jerusalem.
10 "They have [a]turned back to the iniquities of their [1]ancestors who [b]refused
to hear My words, and they [c]have gone
after other gods to serve them; the house
of Israel and the house of Judah have
[d]broken My covenant which I made with
their fathers."
11 Therefore thus says the LORD, "Behold I am [a]bringing disaster on them
which they will [b]not be able to escape;
though they will [c]cry to Me, yet I will not
listen to them.
12 "Then the cities of Judah and the
inhabitants of Jerusalem will [a]go and cry
to the gods to whom they burn incense,
but they surely will not save them in the
time of their disaster.
13 "For your gods are [1a]as many as
your cities, O Judah; and [1]as many as the
streets of Jerusalem are the altars you
have set up to the [b]shameful thing, altars
to [c]burn incense to Baal.
14 ¶ "Therefore [a]do not pray for this
people, nor lift up a cry or prayer for
them; for I will [b]not listen when they call
to Me because of their disaster.
15 "What right has My [a]beloved in
My house
When [b]she has done many vile
deeds?
Can the sacrificial flesh take
away from you your disaster,
[1]So *that* you can rejoice?"
16 The LORD called your name,
"A [a]green olive tree, beautiful in
fruit and form";
With the [b]noise of a great
tumult
He has [c]kindled fire on it,
And its branches are worthless.
17 The LORD of hosts, who [a]planted
you, has [b]pronounced evil against you
because of the evil of the house of Israel
and of the house of Judah, which they
have [1]done to provoke Me by [2c]offering
up sacrifices to Baal.

Plots against Jeremiah

18 ¶ Moreover, the LORD [a]made it
known to me and I knew it;
Then You showed me their
deeds.
19 But I was like a gentle [a]lamb led
to the slaughter;
And I did not know that they
had [b]devised plots against
me, *saying,*
"Let us destroy the tree with its
[1]fruit,
And [c]let us cut him off from the
[d]land of the living,
That his [e]name be remembered
no more."
20 But, O LORD of hosts, who
[a]judges righteously,
Who [b]tries the [1]feelings and
the heart,
Let me see Your vengeance on
them,

---

23 [b]Is 26:7
24 [1]Lit *diminish me* [a]Ps 6:1
25 [1]Or *pasture* [a]Ps 79:6; Zeph 3:8 [b]Job 18:21; 1 Thess 4:5; 2 Thess 1:8 [c]Zeph 1:6 [d]Jer 8:16
11:2 [a]Jer 11:6 [b]Ex 19:5
3 [a]Deut 27:26; Jer 17:5; Gal 3:10
4 [1]Lit *do them* [a]Ex 24:3-8; Jer 31:32 [b]Deut 4:20; 1 Kin 8:51 [c]Lev 26:3; Deut 11:27; Jer 7:23 [d]Jer 24:7; Zech 8:8
5 [a]Ex 13:5; Deut 7:12; Ps 105:9; Jer 32:22 [b]Jer 28:6
6 [a]Jer 3:12 [b]Jer 11:2 [c]John 13:17; Rom 2:13; James 1:22
7 [1]Lit *rising early and warning* [a]1 Sam 8:9 [b]Jer 11:4 [c]Ex 15:26; 2 Chr 36:15; Jer 7:25 [d]Jer 11:7
8 [a]Jer 7:24; Ezek 20:8 [b]Lev 26:14-43
9 [a]Ezek 22:25; Hos 6:9
10 [1]Lit *former fathers* [a]1 Sam 15:11; Jer 3:10; Ezek 20:18 [b]Deut 9:7; Ps 78:8-10; Jer 13:10 [c]Judg 2:11-13 [d]Jer 3:6-11; Ezek 16:59
11 [a]2 Kin 22:16; Jer 6:19 [b]Is 24:17; Jer 25:35 [c]Ps 18:41; Prov 1:28; Is 1:15; Jer 11:14; Ezek 8:18; Mic 3:4; Zech 7:13
12 [a]Deut 32:37; Jer 44:17
13 [1]Lit *the number of* [a]2 Kin 23:13; Jer 2:28 [b]Jer 3:24 [c]Jer 7:9
14 [a]Ex 32:10; Jer 7:16; 1 John 5:16 [b]Ps 66:18; Jer 11:11; Hos 5:6
15 [1]Lit *Then* [a]Jer 13:27 [b]Ezek 16:25
16 [a]Ps 52:8; Rom 11:17 [b]Ps 83:2 [c]Ps 80:16; Is 27:11; Jer 21:14
17 [1]Or *done for themselves* [2]Or *burning incense* [a]Is 5:2; Jer 2:21 [b]Jer 1:14 [c]Jer 7:9
18 [a]1 Sam 23:11; 2 Kin 6:9; Ezek 8:6
19 [1]Lit *bread* [a]Is 53:7 [b]Jer 18:18 [c]Ps 83:4; Is 53:8 [d]Job 28:13; Ps 52:5 [e]Ps 109:13
20 [1]Lit *kidneys* [a]Gen 18:25; Ps 7:8; Jer 20:12 [b]1 Sam 16:7; Ps 7:9; Jer 17:10

For to You have I [2]committed
my cause.

21 ¶ Therefore thus says the LORD concerning the men of [a]Anathoth, who [b]seek your life, saying, "[c]Do not prophesy in the name of the LORD, so that you will not [d]die at our hand";

22 therefore, thus says the LORD of hosts, "Behold, I am about to [a]punish them! The [b]young men will die by the sword, their sons and daughters will die by famine;

23 and a remnant [a]will not be left to them, for I will [b]bring disaster on the men of Anathoth—[c]the year of their punishment."

Jeremiah's Prayer

12 [a]Righteous are You, O LORD,
that I would plead *my* case
with You;
Indeed I would [b]discuss matters
of justice with You:
Why has the [c]way of the wicked
prospered?
Why are all those who [d]deal in
treachery at ease?
2 You have [a]planted them, they
have also taken root;
They grow, they have even
produced fruit.
You are [b]near [1]to their lips
But far from their [2]mind.
3 But You [a]know me, O LORD;
You see me;
And You [b]examine my heart's
attitude toward You.
Drag them off like sheep for the
slaughter
And [1]set them apart for a [c]day
of carnage!
4 How long is the [a]land to mourn
And the [b]vegetation of the
countryside to wither?
For the [c]wickedness of those
who dwell in it,
[d]Animals and birds have been
snatched away,
Because *men* have said, "He will
not see our latter [e]ending."

5 ¶ "If you have run with footmen
and they have tired you out,
Then how can you compete with
horses?
If you fall down in a land of
peace,
How will you do in the
[1a]thicket of the Jordan?
6 "For even your [a]brothers and the
household of your father,
Even they have dealt
treacherously with you,
Even they have cried aloud after
you.
Do not believe them, although
they may say [b]nice things
to you."

God's Answer

7 ¶ "I have [a]forsaken My house,
I have abandoned My
inheritance;
I have given the [b]beloved of My
soul
Into the hand of her enemies.
8 "My inheritance has become
to Me
Like a lion in the forest;
She has [1a]roared against Me;
Therefore I have come to [b]hate
her.
9 "Is My inheritance like a speckled
bird of prey to Me?
Are the [a]birds of prey against
her on every side?
Go, gather all the [b]beasts of the
field,
Bring them to devour!
10 "Many [a]shepherds have ruined
My [b]vineyard,
They have [c]trampled down My
field;
They have made My [d]pleasant
field
A desolate wilderness.
11 "[1]It has been made a desolation,
Desolate, it [a]mourns
[2]before Me;
The [b]whole land has been made
desolate,
Because no man [c]lays it to
heart.
12 "On all the [1a]bare heights in the
wilderness
Destroyers have come,
For a [b]sword of the LORD is
devouring
From one end of the land even
to the [2]other;
There is [c]no peace for [3]anyone.
13 "They have [a]sown wheat and
have reaped thorns,
They have [b]strained themselves
[1]to no profit.
But be ashamed of your
[2c]harvest
Because of the [d]fierce anger of
the LORD."

14 ¶ Thus says the LORD concerning all My [a]wicked neighbors who [b]strike at the inheritance with which I have endowed My people Israel, "Behold I am about to uproot them from their land and will [c]uproot the house of Judah from among them.

15 "And it will come about that after I

---

20 [2]Lit *revealed*
21 [a]Jer 1:1 [b]Jer 12:5,6; 20:10 [c]Amos 2:12 [d]Jer 26:8; 38:4
22 [a]Jer 21:14 [b]2 Chr 36:17; Jer 18:21
23 [a]Jer 6:9 [b]Jer 23:12; Hos 9:7; Mic 7:4 [c]Luke 19:44
12:1 [a]Ezra 9:15; Ps 51:4; 129:4; Jer 11:20 [b]Job 13:3 [c]Job 12:6; Jer 5:27,28; Hab 1:4; Mal 3:15 [d]Jer 3:7,20; 5:11
2 [1]Lit *in their mouth* [2]Lit *kidneys* [a]Jer 11:17; 45:4; Ezek 17:5-10 [b]Is 29:13; Jer 3:10; Ezek 33:31; Titus 1:16
3 [1]Lit *sanctify them* [a]Ps 139:1-4 [b]Ps 7:9; 11:5; Jer 11:20 [c]Jer 17:18; 50:27; James 5:5
4 [a]Jer 4:28; 9:10; 23:10 [b]Joel 1:10-17 [c]Ps 107:34 [d]Jer 4:25; 7:20; 9:10; Hos 4:3; Hab 3:17 [e]Jer 5:31; Ezek 7:2
5 [1]Lit *pride* [a]Jer 49:19; 50:44
6 [a]Gen 37:4-11; Job 6:15; Ps 69:8; Jer 9:4,5 [b]Ps 12:2; Prov 26:25
7 [a]Is 2:6; Jer 7:29; 23:39 [b]Jer 11:15; Hos 11:1-8
8 [1]Lit *raised her voice* [a]Is 59:13 [b]Hos 9:15; Amos 6:8
9 [a]2 Kin 24:2; Ezek 23:22-25 [b]Is 56:9; Jer 7:33; 15:3; 34:20
10 [a]Jer 6:3; 23:1 [b]Ps 80:8-16; Is 5:1-7 [c]Is 63:18 [d]Jer 3:19
11 [1]Lit *One has made it* [2]Or *upon* [a]Jer 12:4; 14:2; 23:10 [b]Jer 4:20,27; 25:11 [c]Is 42:25
12 [1]Or *caravan trails* [2]Lit *other end of the land* [3]Lit *all flesh* [a]Jer 3:2,21 [b]Is 34:6; Jer 47:6; Amos 9:4 [c]Jer 16:5; 30:5
13 [1]Lit *they do not profit* [2]Lit *products* [a]Lev 26:16; Deut 28:38; Mic 6:15; Hag 1:6 [b]Is 55:2; Jer 9:5 [c]Jer 17:10 [d]Jer 4:26; 25:37,38
14 [a]Jer 49:1,7; Zeph 2:8-10 [b]Jer 2:3; 50:11,12; Zech 2:8 [c]Deut 30:3; Ps 106:47; Is 11:11-16

have uprooted them, I will [a]again have
compassion on them; and I will [b]bring
them back, each one to his inheritance
and each one to his land.
16 "Then if they will really [a]learn the
ways of My people, to [b]swear by My
name, 'As the LORD lives,' even as they
taught My people to [c]swear by Baal, they
will be [d]built up in the midst of My people.
17 "But if they will not listen, then I
will [a]uproot that nation, uproot and destroy it," declares the LORD.

The Ruined Waistband

13 Thus the LORD said to me, "Go
and [a]buy yourself a linen waistband and put it around your waist, but do
not put it in water."
2 So I bought the waistband in accordance with the [a]word of the LORD and
put it around my waist.
3 Then the word of the LORD came to
me a second time, saying,
4 "Take the waistband that you have
bought, which is around your waist, and
arise, go to [1]the [a]Euphrates and hide it
there in a crevice of the rock."
5 So I went and hid it by the Euphrates, [a]as the LORD had commanded me.
6 After many days the LORD said to
me, "Arise, go to the Euphrates and take
from there the waistband which I commanded you to hide there."
7 Then I went to the Euphrates and
dug, and I took the waistband from the
place where I had hidden it; and lo, the
waistband was ruined, it was totally
worthless.
8 ¶ Then the word of the LORD came
to me, saying,
9 "Thus says the LORD, 'Just so will I
destroy the [a]pride of Judah and the great
pride of Jerusalem.
10 'This wicked people, who [a]refuse
to listen to My words, who [b]walk in the
stubbornness of their hearts and have
gone after other gods to serve them and
to bow down to them, let them be just
like this waistband which is totally worthless.
11 'For as the waistband clings to the
waist of a man, so I made the whole
household of Israel and the whole household of Judah [a]cling to Me,' declares the
LORD, 'that they might be for Me a people, for [1b]renown, for [c]praise and for
glory; but they [d]did not listen.'

Captivity Threatened

12 ¶ "Therefore you are to speak this
word to them, 'Thus says the LORD, the
God of Israel, "Every jug is to be filled
with wine." ' And when they say to you,

15 [a]Jer 48:47; 49:6,39 [b]Amos 9:14

16 [a]Is 42:6; 49:6 [b]Jer 4:2; Zeph 1:5 [c]Josh 23:7; Jer 5:7 [d]Jer 3:17; 4:2; 16:19

17 [a]Ps 2:8-12; Is 60:12

13:1 [a]Jer 13:11

2 [a]Is 20:2; Ezek 2:8

4 [1]Or *Parah,* cf Josh 18:23; so through v 7 [a]Jer 51:63

5 [a]Ex 39:42,43; 40:16

9 [a]Lev 26:19; Is 2:10-17; 23:9; Jer 13:15-17; Zeph 3:11

10 [a]Num 14:11; 2 Chr 36:15,16; Jer 11:10 [b]Jer 9:14; 11:8; 16:12

11 [1]Lit *a name* [a]Ex 19:5,6; Deut 32:10,11 [b]Jer 32:20 [c]Is 43:21; Jer 33:9 [d]Ps 81:11; Jer 7:13, 24,26

13 [a]Ps 60:3; 75:8; Is 51:17; 63:6; Jer 25:27; 51:7,57

14 [a]Is 9:20,21; Jer 19:9-11 [b]Jer 6:21; Ezek 5:10 [c]Deut 29:20; Is 27:11; Jer 16:5; 21:7

15 [a]Prov 16:5; Is 28:14-22

16 [a]Josh 7:19; Ps 96:8 [b]Is 5:30; 8:22; 59:9; Amos 5:18; 8:9 [c]Prov 4:19; Jer 23:12 [d]Ps 44:19; 107:10,14; Jer 2:6

17 [a]Mal 2:2 [b]Ps 119:136; Jer 9:1; 14:17; Luke 19:41,42 [c]Ps 80:1; Jer 23:1,2

18 [a]2 Kin 24:12,15; Jer 22:26 [b]2 Chr 33:12,19 [c]Ex 39:28; Is 3:20; Ezek 24:17,23; 44:18

19 [a]Jer 32:44 [b]Jer 20:4; 52:27-30

20 [a]Jer 1:15; 6:22; Hab 1:6 [b]Jer 13:17; 23:2

21 [1]Or *chieftains* [a]Jer 2:25; 38:22 [b]Is 13:8; Jer 4:31

22 [a]Deut 7:17 [b]Jer 5:19; 16:10

'Do we not very well know that every jug
is to be filled with wine?'
13 then say to them, 'Thus says the
LORD, "Behold I am about to fill all the
inhabitants of this land—the kings that
sit for David on his throne, the priests,
the prophets and all the inhabitants of
Jerusalem—with [a]drunkenness!
14 "I will [a]dash them against each other, both the [b]fathers and the sons together," declares the LORD. "I will [c]not show
pity nor be sorry nor have compassion so
as not to destroy them." ' "

15 ¶ Listen and give heed, do not
be [a]haughty,
For the LORD has spoken.
16 [a]Give glory to the LORD your
God,
Before He brings [b]darkness
And before your [c]feet stumble
On the dusky mountains,
And while you are hoping for
light
He makes it into [d]deep
darkness,
And turns *it* into gloom.
17 But [a]if you will not listen to it,
My soul will [b]sob in secret for
such pride;
And my eyes will bitterly weep
And flow down with tears,
Because the [c]flock of the LORD
has been taken captive.
18 Say to the [a]king and the queen
mother,
"[b]Take a lowly seat,
For your beautiful [c]crown
Has come down from your
head."
19 The [a]cities of the Negev have
been locked up,
And there is no one to open
them;
All [b]Judah has been carried into
exile,
Wholly carried into exile.

20 ¶ "Lift up your eyes and see
Those coming [a]from the north.
Where is the [b]flock that was
given you,
Your beautiful sheep?
21 "What will you say when He
appoints over you—
And you yourself had taught
them—
Former [1a]companions to be
head over you?
Will not [b]pangs take hold of you
Like a woman in childbirth?
22 "If you [a]say in your heart,
'[b]Why have these things
happened to me?'

Because of the [c]magnitude of
your iniquity
[d]Your skirts have been removed
And your heels have [1]been
exposed.
23 "[a]Can the Ethiopian change his
skin
Or the leopard his spots?
Then you also can [b]do good
Who are accustomed to doing
evil.
24 "Therefore I will [a]scatter them
like drifting straw
To the desert [b]wind.
25 "This is your [a]lot, the portion
measured to you
From Me," declares the LORD,
"Because you have [b]forgotten Me
And trusted in falsehood.
26 "So I Myself have also [a]stripped
your skirts off over your
face,
That your shame may be seen.
27 "As for your [a]adulteries and your
lustful neighings,
The [b]lewdness of your
prostitution
On the [c]hills in the field,
I have seen your abominations.
Woe to you, O Jerusalem!
[d]How long will you remain
unclean?"

Drought and a Prayer for Mercy

14 That which came as the word of the LORD to Jeremiah in regard to the [a]drought:
2 "Judah mourns
And [a]her gates languish;
They sit on the ground [b]in
mourning,
And the [c]cry of Jerusalem has
ascended.
3 "Their nobles have [a]sent their
[1]servants for water;
They have come to the [b]cisterns
and found no water.
They have returned with their
vessels empty;
They have been [c]put to shame
and humiliated,
And they [d]cover their heads.
4 "Because the [a]ground is
[1]cracked,
For there has been [b]no rain on
the land;
The [c]farmers have been put to
shame,
They have covered their heads.
5 "For even the doe in the field has
given birth only to abandon
her young,
Because there is [a]no grass.
6 "The [a]wild donkeys stand on the
bare heights;
They pant for air like jackals,
Their eyes fail
For there is [b]no vegetation.
7 "Although our [a]iniquities testify
against us,
O LORD, act [b]for Your name's
sake!
Truly our [c]apostasies have been
many,
We have [d]sinned against You.
8 "O [a]Hope of Israel,
Its [b]Savior in [c]time of distress,
Why are You like a stranger in
the land
Or like a traveler who has
pitched his *tent* for the
night?
9 "Why are You like a man
dismayed,
Like a mighty man who [a]cannot
save?
Yet [b]You are in our midst,
O LORD,
And we are [c]called by Your
name;
Do not forsake us!"
10 ¶ Thus says the LORD to this people,
"Even so they have [a]loved to wander;
they have not [b]kept their feet in check.
Therefore the LORD does [c]not accept
them; now He will [d]remember their iniquity and call their sins to account."
11 So the LORD said to me, "[a]Do not
pray for the welfare of this people.
12 "When they fast, I am [a]not going to
listen to their cry; and when they offer
[b]burnt offering and grain offering, I am
not going to accept them. Rather I am
going to [c]make an end of them by the
[d]sword, famine and pestilence."

False Prophets

13 ¶ But, "Ah, Lord [1]GOD!" I said,
"Look, the prophets are telling them,
'You [a]will not see the sword nor will you
have famine, but I will give you [2]lasting
[b]peace in this place.' "
14 Then the LORD said to me, "The
[a]prophets are prophesying falsehood in
My name. [b]I have neither sent them nor
commanded them nor spoken to them;
they are prophesying to you a [c]false vision, divination, futility and the deception of their own [1]minds.
15 "Therefore thus says the LORD concerning the prophets who are prophesying in My name, although it was not I
who sent them—yet they keep saying,
'There will be no sword or famine in this
land'—[a]by sword and famine those
prophets shall [1]meet their end!
16 "The people also to whom they are

22 [1]Or *suffered violence* [c]Jer 2:17-19; 9:2-9 [d]Is 47:2; Ezek 16:37; Nah 3:5

23 [a]Prov 27:22; Is 1:5 [b]Jer 4:22; 9:5

24 [a]Lev 26:33; Jer 9:16; Ezek 5:2,12 [b]Jer 4:11; 18:17

25 [a]Job 20:29; Ps 11:6; Matt 24:51 [b]Ps 9:17; Jer 2:32; 3:21

26 [a]Lam 1:8; Ezek 23:29; Hos 2:10

27 [a]Jer 5:7,8 [b]Jer 11:15 [c]Is 65:7; Jer 2:20; Ezek 6:13 [d]Prov 1:22; Hos 8:5

14:1 [a]Jer 17:8

2 [a]Is 3:26 [b]Jer 8:21 [c]1 Sam 5:12; Jer 11:11; 46:12; Zech 7:13

3 [1]Lit *little ones* [a]1 Kin 18:5 [b]2 Kin 18:31; Jer 2:13 [c]Job 6:20; Ps 40:14 [d]2 Sam 15:30

4 [1]Lit *shattered* [a]Joel 1:19,20 [b]Jer 3:3 [c]Joel 1:11

5 [a]Is 15:6

6 [a]Job 39:5,6; Jer 2:24 [b]Joel 1:18

7 [a]Is 59:12; Hos 5:5 [b]Ps 25:11; Jer 14:21 [c]Jer 5:6; 8:5 [d]Jer 3:25; 8:14; 14:20

8 [a]Jer 17:13 [b]Is 43:3; 63:8 [c]Ps 9:9; 50:15

9 [a]Num 11:23; Is 50:2; 59:1 [b]Ex 29:45; Ps 46:5; Jer 8:19 [c]Is 63:19; Jer 15:16

10 [a]Jer 2:25; 3:13 [b]Ps 119:101 [c]Jer 6:20; Amos 5:22 [d]Jer 44:21-23; Hos 8:13; 9:9

11 [a]Ex 32:10; Jer 7:16; 11:14

12 [a]Prov 1:28; Is 1:15; Jer 11:11; Ezek 8:18; Mic 3:4; Zech 7:13 [b]Jer 6:20; 7:21 [c]Jer 8:13 [d]Jer 21:9

13 [1]Heb *YHWH,* usually rendered LORD [2]Lit *peace of truth* [a]Jer 5:12; 23:17 [b]Jer 6:14; 8:11

14 [1]Lit *hearts* [a]Jer 5:31; 23:25 [b]Jer 23:21 [c]Jer 23:16,26; 27:9, 10; Ezek 12:24

15 [1]Lit *be finished* [a]Jer 23:15; Ezek 14:10

prophesying will be [a]thrown out into the streets of Jerusalem because of the famine and the sword; and there will be no one to [b]bury them—*neither* them, *nor* their wives, nor their sons, nor their daughters—for I will [c]pour out their *own* wickedness on them.

17 "You will say this word to them,
'[a]Let my eyes flow down with
tears night and day,
And let them not cease;
For the virgin [b]daughter of my
people has been crushed
with a mighty blow,
With a sorely [c]infected wound.
18 'If I [a]go out to the country,
Behold, those [1]slain with the
sword!
Or if I enter the city,
Behold, diseases of famine!
For [b]both prophet and priest
Have [2]gone roving about in the
land that they do not
know.' "

19 ¶ Have You completely [a]rejected
Judah?
Or have [1]You loathed Zion?
Why have You stricken us so
that we [b]are beyond
healing?
We [c]waited for peace, but
nothing good *came;*
And for a time of healing, but
behold, terror!
20 We [a]know our wickedness,
O LORD,
The iniquity of our fathers, for
[b]we have sinned
against You.
21 Do not despise *us,* [a]for Your
own name's sake;
Do not disgrace the [b]throne of
Your glory;
Remember *and* do not annul
Your covenant with us.
22 Are there any among the
[1a]idols of the nations who
[b]give rain?
Or can the heavens grant
showers?
Is it not You, O LORD our God?
Therefore we [2c]hope in You,
For You are the one who has
done all these things.

Judgment Must Come

15 Then the LORD said to me, "Even [a]though [b]Moses and [c]Samuel were to [d]stand before Me, My [1]heart would not be [2]with this people; [e]send them away from My presence and let them go!

2 "And it shall be that when they say to you, 'Where should we go?' then you are to tell them, 'Thus says the LORD:
"Those *destined* [a]for death, to
death;
And those *destined* for the
sword, to the sword;
And those *destined* for famine,
to famine;
And those *destined* for captivity,
to captivity." '

3 "I will [a]appoint over them four kinds *of doom,*" declares the LORD: "the sword to slay, the [b]dogs to drag off, and the [c]birds of the sky and the beasts of the earth to devour and destroy.

4 "I will [a]make them an object of horror among all the kingdoms of the earth because of [b]Manasseh, the son of Hezekiah, the king of Judah, for what he did in Jerusalem.

5 ¶ "Indeed, who will have [a]pity
on you, O Jerusalem,
Or who will [b]mourn for you,
Or who will turn aside to ask
about your welfare?
6 "You who have [a]forsaken Me,"
declares the LORD,
"You keep [b]going backward.
So I will [c]stretch out My hand
against you and destroy you;
I am [d]tired of relenting!
7 "I will [a]winnow them with a
winnowing fork
At the gates of the land;
I will [b]bereave *them* of children,
I will destroy My people;
[c]They did not [1]repent of their
ways.
8 "Their [a]widows will be more
numerous before Me
Than the sand of the seas;
I will bring against them, against
the mother of a young man,
A [b]destroyer at noonday;
I will suddenly bring down
on her
Anguish and dismay.
9 "She who [a]bore seven *sons* pines
away;
[1]Her breathing is labored.
Her [b]sun has set while it was
yet day;
She has been [c]shamed and
humiliated.
So I will [d]give over their
survivors to the sword
Before their enemies," declares
the LORD.

10 ¶ [a]Woe to me, my mother, that
you have borne me
As a [b]man of strife and a man of
contention to all the land!

16 [a]Ps 79:2,3; Jer 7:33; 15:2,3 [b]Jer 8:1,2 [c]Prov 1:31; Jer 13:22-25

17 [a]Jer 9:1; 13:17; Lam 1:16 [b]Is 37:22; Jer 8:21; Lam 1:15; 2:13 [c]Jer 10:19; 30:14

18 [1]Lit *pierced* [2]Or *gone around trading* [a]Jer 6:25; Lam 1:20; Ezek 7:15 [b]Jer 6:13; 8:10

19 [1]Lit *Your soul* [a]Jer 6:30; 7:29; 12:7; Lam 5:22 [b]Jer 30:13 [c]Job 30:26; Jer 8:15; 1 Thess 5:3

20 [a]Neh 9:2; Ps 32:5; Jer 3:25 [b]Jer 8:14; 14:7; Dan 9:8

21 [a]Ps 25:11; Jer 14:7 [b]Jer 3:17; 17:12

22 [1]Lit *vanities* [2]Or *wait for* [a]Is 41:29; Jer 10:3 [b]1 Kin 17:1; Jer 5:24 [c]Lam 3:26

15:1 [1]Lit *soul* [2]Lit *toward* [a]Ps 99:6; Ezek 14:14,20 [b]Ex 32:11-14; Num 14:13-20; Ps 99:6; 106:23 [c]1 Sam 7:9; 12:23 [d]Jer 15:19; 18:20; 35:19 [e]2 Kin 17:20; Jer 7:15; 10:18; 52:3

2 [a]Jer 14:12; 24:10; 43:11; Ezek 5:2,12; Zech 11:9; Rev 13:10

3 [a]Lev 26:16,22,25; Ezek 14:21 [b]1 Kin 21:23,24 [c]Deut 28:26; Is 18:6; Jer 7:33

4 [a]Lev 26:33; Jer 24:9; 29:18; Ezek 23:46 [b]2 Kin 21:1-18; 23:26,27; 24:3,4; 2 Chr 33:1-9

5 [a]Ps 69:20; Is 51:19; Jer 13:14; 21:7 [b]Nah 3:7

6 [a]Jer 6:19; 8:9 [b]Is 1:4; Jer 7:24 [c]Jer 6:12; Zeph 1:4 [d]Jer 6:11; 7:16

7 [1]Lit *turn back from* [a]Ps 1:4; Jer 51:2 [b]Jer 18:21; Hos 9:12-16 [c]Is 9:13

8 [a]Is 3:25,26; 4:1 [b]Jer 22:7

9 [1]Or *She has breathed out her soul* [a]1 Sam 2:5; Is 47:9 [b]Jer 6:4; Amos 8:9 [c]Jer 50:12 [d]Jer 21:7

10 [a]Job 3:1,3; Jer 20:14 [b]Jer 1:18,19; 15:20; 20:7,8

I have not [c]lent, nor have men
lent money to me,
Yet everyone curses me.
11 The LORD said, "Surely I will
[a]set you free for *purposes*
of good;
Surely I will cause the [b]enemy
to make supplication to you
In a time of disaster and a time
of distress.
12 ¶ "Can anyone smash iron,
[a]Iron from the north, or bronze?
13 "Your [a]wealth and your treasures
I will give for booty [b]without
cost,
Even for all your sins
And within all your borders.
14 "Then I will cause your enemies
to bring [1]*it*
Into a [a]land you do not know;
For a [b]fire has been kindled in
My anger,
It will burn upon you."

Jeremiah's Prayer and God's Answer

15 ¶ [a]You who know, O LORD,
Remember me, take notice
of me,
And [b]take vengeance for me on
my persecutors.
Do not, in view of Your patience,
take me away;
Know that [c]for Your sake I
endure reproach.
16 Your words were found and I
[a]ate them,
And Your [b]words became for me
a joy and the delight of my
heart;
For I have been [c]called by Your
name,
O LORD God of hosts.
17 I [a]did not sit in the circle of
merrymakers,
Nor did I exult.
Because of Your hand *upon me* I
sat [b]alone,
For You [c]filled me with
indignation.
18 Why has my pain been perpetual
And my [a]wound incurable,
refusing to be healed?
Will You indeed be to me [b]like
a deceptive *stream*
With water that is unreliable?
19 ¶ Therefore, thus says the LORD,
"[a]If you return, then I will
restore you—
[b]Before Me you will stand;
And [c]if you extract the precious
from the worthless,
You will become [1]My
spokesman.
They for their part may turn to
you,
But as for you, you must not
turn to them.
20 "Then I will [a]make you to this
people
A fortified wall of bronze;
And though they fight against
you,
They will not prevail over you;
For [b]I am with you to save you
And deliver you," declares the
LORD.
21 "So I will [a]deliver you from the
hand of the wicked,
And I will [b]redeem you from
the [1]grasp of the violent."

Distresses Foretold

16 The word of the LORD also came
to me saying,
2 "You shall not take a wife for yourself nor have sons or daughters in this
place."
3 For thus says the LORD concerning
the sons and daughters born in this place,
and concerning their [a]mothers who bear
them, and their [b]fathers who beget them
in this land:
4 "They will [a]die of deadly diseases,
they [b]will not be lamented or buried;
they will be as [c]dung on the surface of
the ground and come to an end by sword
and famine, and their carcasses will become food for the [d]birds of the sky and
for the beasts of the earth."
5 ¶ For thus says the LORD, "Do not
enter a house of [1a]mourning, or go to
lament or to console them; for I have
[b]withdrawn My peace from this people,"
declares the LORD, "*My* [c]lovingkindness
and compassion.
6 "Both [a]great men and small will die
in this land; they will not be buried, they
will not be lamented, nor will anyone
[b]gash himself or [c]shave his head for
them.
7 "Men will not [a]break *bread* in
mourning for them, to comfort anyone for
the dead, nor give them a cup of consolation to drink for anyone's father or
mother.
8 "Moreover you shall [a]not go into a
house of feasting to sit with them to eat
and drink."
9 For thus says the LORD of hosts, the
God of Israel: "Behold, I am going to
[1a]eliminate from this place, before your
eyes and in your time, the voice of rejoicing and the voice of gladness, the voice of
the groom and the voice of the bride.
10 ¶ "Now when you tell this people

10 [c]Ex 22:25; Lev 25:36,37; Deut 23:19

11 [a]Ps 138:3; Is 41:10 [b]Jer 21:2; 37:3; 38:14; 42:2

12 [a]Jer 28:14

13 [a]Jer 17:3; 20:5 [b]Ps 44:12; Is 52:3

14 [1]I.e. your possessions [a]Deut 28:36,64; Jer 16:13 [b]Deut 32:22; Ps 21:9; Jer 17:4

15 [a]Jer 12:3 [b]Jer 11:20 [c]Ps 44:22; 69:7-9; Jer 20:8

16 [a]Ezek 3:3 [b]Job 23:12; Ps 119:103 [c]Jer 14:9

17 [a]Ps 1:1; Jer 16:8; 2 Cor 6:17 [b]Ps 102:7; Jer 13:17; Lam 3:28; Ezek 3:24, 25 [c]Jer 6:11

18 [a]Job 34:6; Jer 30:12,15; Mic 1:9 [b]Job 6:15, 20; Jer 14:3

19 [1]Lit *as My mouth* [a]Jer 4:1; Zech 3:7 [b]1 Kin 17:1; Jer 15:1; 35:19 [c]Jer 6:29; Ezek 22:26; 44:23

20 [a]Jer 1:18,19; Ezek 3:9 [b]Ps 46:7; Is 41:10; Jer 1:8,19; 15:15; 20:11

21 [1]Lit *palm* [a]Ps 37:40; Is 49:25; Jer 20:13; 39:11, 12 [b]Gen 48:16; Is 49:26; 60:16; Jer 31:11; 50:34

16:3 [a]Jer 15:8 [b]Jer 6:21

4 [a]Jer 15:2 [b]Jer 25:33 [c]Ps 83:10; Jer 9:22; 25:33 [d]Ps 79:2; Is 18:6; Jer 15:3; 34:20

5 [1]Or *banqueting* [a]Ezek 24:16-23 [b]Jer 12:12; 15:1-4 [c]Ps 25:6; Is 27:11; Jer 13:14

6 [a]2 Chr 36:17; Ezek 9:6 [b]Deut 14:1; Jer 41:5; 47:5 [c]Is 22:12

7 [a]Deut 26:14; Ezek 24:17; Hos 9:4

8 [a]Eccl 7:2-4; Is 22:12-14; Jer 15:17; Amos 6:4-6

9 [1]Lit *cause to cease* [a]Jer 7:34; 25:10; Ezek 26:13; Hos 2:11; Rev 18:23

all these words, they will say to you,
'[a]For what reason has the LORD declared
all this great calamity against us? And
what is our iniquity, or what is our sin
which we have committed against the
LORD our God?'
11 "Then you are to say to them, '*It is*
[a]because your forefathers have forsaken
Me,' declares the LORD, 'and have followed [b]other gods and served them and
bowed down to them; but Me they have
forsaken and have not kept My law.
12 'You too have done evil, *even*
[a]more than your forefathers; for behold,
you are each one walking according to
the [b]stubbornness of his own [c]evil
heart, without listening to Me.
13 'So I will [a]hurl you out of this land
into the [b]land which you have not
known, neither you nor your fathers; and
there you will [c]serve other gods day and
night, for I will grant you no favor.'

God Will Restore Them

14 ¶ "[a]Therefore behold, days are
coming," declares the LORD, "when it
will no longer be said, 'As the LORD lives,
who [b]brought up the sons of Israel out of
the land of Egypt,'
15 but, 'As the LORD lives, who
brought up the sons of Israel from the
[a]land of the north and from all the countries where He had banished them.' For
I will restore them to their own land
which I gave to their fathers.
16 ¶ "Behold, I am going to send for
many [a]fishermen," declares the LORD,
"and they will fish for them; and afterwards I will send for many hunters, and
they will [b]hunt them [c]from every mountain and every hill and from the clefts of
the rocks.
17 "[a]For My eyes are on all their ways;
they are not hidden from My face, [b]nor
is their iniquity concealed from My eyes.
18 "I will first [a]doubly repay their iniquity and their sin, because they have
[b]polluted My land; they have filled My
inheritance with the carcasses of their
[c]detestable idols and with their abominations."

19 ¶ O LORD, my [a]strength and my
stronghold,
And my [b]refuge in the day of
distress,
To You the [c]nations will come
From the ends of the earth and
say,
"Our fathers have inherited
nothing but [d]falsehood,
Futility and [1e]things of no
profit."
20 Can man make gods for himself?
Yet they are [a]not gods!
21 ¶ "Therefore behold, I am going
to make them know—
This time I will [a]make them
know
My [1]power and My might;
And they shall [b]know that My
name is the LORD."

The Deceitful Heart

17 The [a]sin of Judah is written
down with an [b]iron stylus;
With a diamond point it is
[c]engraved upon the tablet
of their heart
And on the horns of [1]their
altars,
2 As they remember their
[a]children,
So they *remember* their altars
and their [1b]Asherim
By [c]green trees on the high
hills.
3 O [a]mountain of Mine in the
countryside,
I will [b]give over your wealth
and all your treasures for
booty,
Your high places for sin
throughout your borders.
4 And you will, even of yourself,
[a]let go of your inheritance
That I gave you;
And I will make you serve your
[b]enemies
In the [c]land which you do not
know;
For you have [d]kindled a fire in
My anger
Which will burn forever.
5 ¶ Thus says the LORD,
"[a]Cursed is the man who trusts
in mankind
And makes [b]flesh his [1]strength,
And whose heart turns away
from the LORD.
6 "For he will be like a [a]bush in
the desert
And will not see when prosperity
comes,
But will live in stony wastes in
the wilderness,
A [b]land of salt [1]without
inhabitant.
7 "[a]Blessed is the man who trusts
in the LORD
And whose [b]trust is the LORD.
8 "For he will be like a [a]tree
planted by the water,
That extends its roots by a
stream
And will not fear when the heat
comes;
But its leaves will be green,

10 [a]Deut 29:24; 1 Kin 9:8; Jer 5:19
11 [a]Deut 29:25; 1 Kin 9:9; 2 Chr 7:22; Neh 9:26-29; Jer 22:9 [b]Deut 29:26; 1 Kin 9:9; Ps 106:35-41; Jer 5:7-9; Ezek 11:21; 1 Pet 4:3
12 [a]Jer 7:26 [b]1 Sam 15:23; Jer 7:24 [c]Eccl 9:3; Mark 7:21
13 [a]Deut 4:26; 2 Chr 7:20; Jer 15:1 [b]Jer 15:14 [c]Deut 4:28; Jer 5:19
14 [a]Is 43:18; Jer 23:7 [b]Ex 20:2; Deut 15:15
15 [a]Ps 106:47; Is 11:11-16; Jer 3:18
16 [a]Amos 4:2; Hab 1:14 [b]1 Sam 26:20; Mic 7:2 [c]Is 2:21; Amos 9:3
17 [a]2 Chr 16:9; Job 34:21; Ps 90:8; Prov 5:21; Jer 23:24; Zech 4:10; Luke 12:2; 1 Cor 4:5; Heb 4:13 [b]Jer 2:22
18 [a]Jer 17:18; Rev 18:6 [b]Num 35:33; Jer 2:7 [c]Jer 7:30; Ezek 11:18
19 [1]Lit *there is nothing profitable in them* [a]Ps 18:1; Is 25:4 [b]Nah 1:7 [c]Ps 22:27; Is 2:2; Jer 3:17 [d]Is 44:20; Hab 2:18 [e]Is 44:10
20 [a]Ps 115:4-8; Is 37:19; Jer 2:11; Hos 8:4-6; Gal 4:8
21 [1]Lit *hand* [a]Ps 9:16 [b]Ps 83:18; Is 43:3; Jer 33:2; Amos 5:8
17:1 [1]So ancient versions; M.T. *your* [a]Jer 2:22 [b]Job 19:24 [c]Prov 3:3; Is 49:16; 2 Cor 3:3
2 [1]I.e. wooden symbols of a female deity [a]Jer 7:18 [b]Ex 34:13; 2 Chr 24:18; Is 17:8 [c]Jer 3:6
3 [a]Jer 26:18; Mic 3:12 [b]2 Kin 24:13; Is 39:4-6; Jer 15:13
4 [a]Jer 12:7; Lam 5:2 [b]Deut 28:48; Is 14:3; Jer 15:14 [c]Jer 16:13 [d]Is 5:25; Jer 7:20
5 [1]Lit *arm* [a]Ps 146:3; Is 2:22; Ezek 29:7 [b]2 Chr 32:8; Is 31:3
6 [1]Lit *and is not inhabited* [a]Jer 48:6 [b]Deut 29:23; Job 39:6
7 [a]Ps 2:12; Prov 16:20 [b]Ps 40:4
8 [a]Ps 1:3; Ezek 31:3-9

And it will not be anxious in a
year of [b]drought
Nor cease to yield fruit.
9 ¶ "The [a]heart is more [b]deceitful
than all else
And is desperately [c]sick;
Who can understand it?
10 "I, the LORD, [a]search the heart,
I test the [1]mind,
Even [b]to give to each man
according to his ways,
According to the [2]results of his
deeds.
11 "As a partridge that hatches eggs
which it has not laid,
So is he who [a]makes a fortune,
but unjustly;
In the midst of his days it will
forsake him,
And in [1]the end he will be a
[b]fool."
12 ¶ [a]A glorious throne on high
from the beginning
Is the place of our sanctuary.
13 O LORD, the [a]hope of Israel,
All who [b]forsake You will be put
to shame.
Those who turn [1]away on earth
will be [c]written down,
Because they have forsaken the
fountain of living water,
even the LORD.
14 [a]Heal me, O LORD, and I will be
healed;
[b]Save me and I will be saved,
For You are my [c]praise.
15 Look, they keep [a]saying to me,
"Where is the word of the LORD?
Let it come now!"
16 But as for me, I have not hurried
away from *being* a shepherd
after You,
Nor have I longed for the woeful
day;
[a]You Yourself know that the
utterance of my lips
Was in Your presence.
17 Do not be a [a]terror to me;
You are my [b]refuge in the day of
disaster.
18 Let those who persecute me be
[a]put to shame, but as for
me, [b]let me not be put to
shame;
Let them be dismayed, but let
me not be dismayed.
[c]Bring on them a day of
disaster,
And crush them with twofold
destruction!

The Sabbath Must Be Kept

19 ¶ Thus the LORD said to me, "Go
and stand in the [1]public gate, through
which the kings of Judah come in and go
out, as well as in all the gates of Jerusalem;
20 and say to them, '[a]Listen to the
word of the LORD, [b]kings of Judah, and all
Judah and all inhabitants of Jerusalem
who come in through these gates:
21 'Thus says the LORD, "[a]Take heed
for yourselves, and [b]do not carry any load
on the sabbath day or bring anything in
through the gates of Jerusalem.
22 "You shall not bring a load out of
your houses on the sabbath day [a]nor do
any work, but keep the sabbath day holy,
as I [b]commanded your [1]forefathers.
23 "Yet they [a]did not listen or incline
their ears, but [b]stiffened their necks in
order not to listen or take correction.
24 ¶ "But it will come about, if you
[a]listen attentively to Me," declares the
LORD, "to [b]bring no load in through the
gates of this city on the sabbath day, [c]but
to keep the sabbath day holy by doing no
work on it,
25 [a]then there will come in through
the gates of this city kings and princes
[b]sitting on the throne of David, riding in
chariots and on horses, they and their
princes, the men of Judah and the inhabitants of Jerusalem, and this [c]city will be
inhabited forever.
26 "They will come in from the [a]cities
of Judah and from the environs of Jerusalem, from the land of Benjamin, from the
[b]lowland, from the hill country and from
the [c]Negev, bringing burnt offerings,
sacrifices, grain offerings and incense,
and bringing sacrifices of thanksgiving to
the house of the LORD.
27 "But [a]if you do not listen to Me to
keep the sabbath day holy by not carrying
a load and coming in through the gates of
Jerusalem on the sabbath day, then [b]I
will kindle a fire in its gates and it will
[c]devour the palaces of Jerusalem and
[d]not be quenched." ' "

The Potter and the Clay

18 The word which came to Jeremiah from the LORD saying,
2 "Arise and [a]go down to the potter's
house, and there I will announce My
words to you."
3 Then I went down to the potter's
house, and there he was, making something on the [1]wheel.
4 But the vessel that he was making
of clay was spoiled in the hand of the
potter; so he remade it into another vessel, as it pleased the potter to make.
5 ¶ Then the word of the LORD came
to me saying,
6 "Can I not, O house of Israel, deal

8 [b]Jer 14:1-6
9 [a]Eccl 9:3; Mark 7:21,22 [b]Rom 7:11; Eph 4:22 [c]Is 1:5,6; 6:10; Matt 13:15; Mark 2:17; Rom 1:21
10 [1]Lit *kidneys* [2]Lit *fruit* [a]1 Sam 16:7; 1 Chr 28:9; Ps 139:23; Prov 17:3; Jer 11:20; 20:12; Rom 8:27; Rev 2:23 [b]Ps 62:12; Jer 32:19; Rom 2:6
11 [1]Lit *his* [a]Jer 6:13; 8:10; 22:13,17 [b]Luke 12:20
12 [a]Jer 3:17; 14:21
13 [1]Lit *away from Me* [a]Jer 14:8; 50:7 [b]Is 1:28 [c]Luke 10:20
14 [a]Jer 30:17; 33:6 [b]Ps 54:1; 60:5 [c]Deut 10:21; Ps 109:1
15 [a]Is 5:19; 2 Pet 3:4
16 [a]Jer 12:3
17 [a]Ps 88:15 [b]Jer 16:19; Nah 1:7
18 [a]Ps 35:4,26; Jer 17:13; 20:11 [b]Jer 1:17 [c]Ps 35:8
19 [1]Lit *gate of the sons of the people*
20 [a]Ezek 2:7 [b]Ps 49:1,2; Jer 19:3,4
21 [a]Deut 4:9, 15,23; Mark 4:24 [b]Num 15:32-36; Neh 13:15-21; John 5:9-12
22 [1]Lit *fathers* [a]Ex 16:23-29; 20:8-10; Deut 5:12-14; Is 56:2-6; 58:13 [b]Ex 31:13-17; Ezek 20:12; Zech 1:4
23 [a]Jer 7:24,28; 11:10 [b]Prov 29:1; Jer 7:26; 19:15
24 [a]Ex 15:26; Deut 11:13; Is 21:7; 55:2 [b]Jer 17:21,22 [c]Ex 20:8-11; Ezek 20:20
25 [a]Jer 22:4 [b]2 Sam 7:16; Is 9:7; Jer 33:15, 17,21; Luke 1:32 [c]Ps 132:13,14; Heb 12:22
26 [a]Jer 32:44; 33:13 [b]Zech 7:7 [c]Ps 107:22; Jer 33:11
27 [a]Is 1:20; Jer 22:5; 26:4; Zech 7:11-14 [b]Lam 4:11 [c]2 Kin 25:9; Jer 39:8; Amos 2:5 [d]Jer 7:20; Ezek 20:47
18:2 [a]Jer 19:1,2
3 [1]Lit *pair of stone discs*

with you as this potter *does?*" declares
the LORD. "Behold, like the [a]clay in the
potter's hand, so are you in My hand,
O house of Israel.
7 "At one moment I might speak concerning a nation or concerning a kingdom
to [a]uproot, to pull down, or to destroy *it;*
8 [a]if that nation against which I have
spoken turns from its evil, I will [1b]relent
concerning the calamity I planned to
bring on it.
9 "Or at another moment I might
speak concerning a nation or concerning
a kingdom to [a]build up or to plant *it;*
10 if it does [a]evil in My sight by not
obeying My voice, then I will [1b]think
better of the good with which I had promised to [2]bless it.
11 "So now then, speak to the men of
Judah and against the inhabitants of Jerusalem saying, 'Thus says the LORD, "Behold, I am [a]fashioning calamity against
you and devising a plan against you. Oh
[b]turn back, each of you from his evil
way, and [1]reform your ways and your
deeds." '
12 "But [a]they will say, 'It's hopeless!
For we are going to follow our own plans,
and each of us will act according to the
[b]stubbornness of his evil heart.'
13 ¶ "Therefore thus says the LORD,
'[a]Ask now among the nations,
Who ever heard the like of
[1]this?
The [b]virgin of Israel
Has done a most [c]appalling
thing.
14 'Does the snow of Lebanon
forsake the rock of the open
country?
Or is the cold flowing water
from a foreign *land* ever
snatched away?
15 'For [a]My people have
forgotten Me,
[b]They burn incense [1]to
worthless gods
And they [2]have stumbled [3]from
their ways,
[3]From the [c]ancient paths,
To walk in bypaths,
Not on a [d]highway,
16 To make their land a
[a]desolation,
An object of perpetual [b]hissing;
Everyone who passes by it will
be astonished
And [c]shake his head.
17 'Like an [a]east wind I will
[b]scatter them
Before the enemy;
I will [1]show them [c]My back
and not *My* face
[d]In the day of their calamity.' "

18 ¶ Then they said, "Come and let us
[a]devise plans against Jeremiah. Surely
the [b]law is not going to be lost to the
priest, nor [c]counsel to the sage, nor the
divine [d]word to the prophet! Come on
and let us [e]strike at him with *our* tongue,
and let us [f]give no heed to any of his
words."
19 ¶ Do give heed to me, O LORD,
And listen to [1]what my
opponents are saying!
20 [a]Should good be repaid with
evil?
For they have [b]dug a pit
for [1]me.
Remember how I [c]stood
before You
To speak good on their behalf,
So as to turn away Your wrath
from them.
21 Therefore, [a]give their children
over to famine
And deliver them up to the
[1]power of the sword;
And let their wives become
[b]childless and [c]widowed.
Let their men also be smitten to
death,
Their [d]young men struck down
by the sword in battle.
22 May an [a]outcry be heard from
their houses,
When You suddenly bring raiders
upon them;
[b]For they have dug a pit to
capture me
And [c]hidden snares for my feet.
23 Yet You, O LORD, know
All their [1]deadly designs
against me;
[a]Do not [2]forgive their iniquity
Or blot out their sin from Your
sight.
But may they be [3b]overthrown
before You;
Deal with them in the [c]time of
Your anger!

The Broken Jar

19 Thus says the LORD, "Go and buy
a [a]potter's earthenware [b]jar, and
take some of the [c]elders of the people
and some of the [1d]senior priests.
2 "Then go out to the [a]valley of Ben-
hinnom, which is by the entrance of the
potsherd gate, and [b]proclaim there the
words that I tell you,
3 and say, 'Hear the word of the
LORD, O [a]kings of Judah and inhabitants
of Jerusalem: thus says the LORD of hosts,
the God of Israel, "Behold I am about
to bring a [b]calamity upon this place, at
which the [c]ears of everyone that hears of
it will tingle.

6 [a]Is 45:9; Matt 20:15; Rom 9:21
7 [a]Jer 1:10
8 [1]Lit *repent of* [a]Jer 7:3-7; Ezek 18:21 [b]Ps 106:45; Jer 26:3; Hos 11:8; Joel 2:13; Jon 3:10
9 [a]Jer 1:10; Amos 9:11-15
10 [1]Lit *repent* [2]Lit *do it good* [a]Ps 125:5; Jer 7:24-28; Ezek 33:18 [b]1 Sam 2:30
11 [1]Lit *make good* [a]Is 5:5; Jer 4:6 [b]2 Kin 17:13; Is 1:16-19; Jer 4:1; Acts 26:20
12 [a]Is 57:10; Jer 2:25 [b]Deut 29:19; Jer 7:24
13 [1]Lit *these* [a]Is 66:8; Jer 2:10 [b]Jer 14:17 [c]Jer 5:30; Hos 6:10
15 [1]Lit *to worthlessness* [2]So ancient versions; Heb *caused them to* [3]Or *in* [a]Jer 2:32 [b]Is 65:7; Jer 7:9 [c]Jer 6:16 [d]Is 57:14
16 [a]Jer 25:9; Ezek 33:28 [b]1 Kin 9:8; Lam 2:15; Mic 6:16 [c]Ps 22:7; Is 37:22; Jer 48:27
17 [1]So ancient versions; M.T. reads *look them in the back and not in the face* [a]Ps 48:7 [b]Job 27:21; Jer 13:24 [c]Jer 2:27 [d]Jer 46:21
18 [a]Jer 11:19 [b]Jer 2:8; Mal 2:7 [c]Job 5:13; Jer 8:8 [d]Jer 5:13 [e]Ps 52:2; Jer 20:10 [f]Jer 43:2
19 [1]Lit *the voice of my opponents*
20 [1]Lit *my soul* [a]Ps 109:4 [b]Ps 35:7; Jer 5:26 [c]Ps 106:23
21 [1]Lit *hands of* [a]Ps 109:9-20; Jer 11:22 [b]1 Sam 15:33; Is 13:18 [c]Jer 15:8; Ezek 22:25 [d]Jer 9:21
22 [a]Jer 6:26 [b]Jer 18:20 [c]Ps 140:5
23 [1]Lit *unto death* [2]Lit *cover over, atone for* [3]Lit *ones made to stumble* [a]Neh 4:5; Ps 109:14; Is 2:9 [b]Jer 6:15 [c]Jer 7:20
19:1 [1]Or *elders of* [a]Jer 18:2 [b]Jer 19:10 [c]Num 11:16 [d]2 Kin 19:2; Ezek 8:11
2 [a]Josh 15:8; 2 Kin 23:10; Jer 7:31 [b]Prov 1:20
3 [a]Jer 17:20 [b]Jer 6:19 [c]1 Sam 3:11

4 "Because they have [a]forsaken Me and have [b]made this an alien place and have burned [1]sacrifices in it to [c]other gods, that neither they nor their forefathers nor the kings of Judah had *ever* known, and *because* they have filled this place with the [d]blood of the innocent

5 and have built the [a]high places of Baal to burn their [b]sons in the fire as burnt offerings to Baal, a thing which I never commanded or spoke of, nor did it *ever* enter My [1]mind;

6 therefore, behold, [a]days are coming," declares the LORD, "when this place will no longer be called [b]Topheth or [c]the valley of Ben-hinnom, but rather the valley of Slaughter.

7 "I will [a]make void the counsel of Judah and Jerusalem in this place, and [b]I will cause them to fall by the sword before their enemies and by the hand of those who seek their life; and I will give over their [c]carcasses as food for the birds of the sky and the beasts of the earth.

8 "I will also make this city a [a]desolation and an *object of* hissing; [b]everyone who passes by it will be astonished and hiss because of all its [1]disasters.

9 "I will make them [a]eat the flesh of their sons and the flesh of their daughters, and they will eat one another's flesh in the siege and in the distress with which their enemies and those who seek their life will distress them." '

10 ¶ "Then you are to break the [a]jar in the sight of the men who accompany you

11 and say to them, 'Thus says the LORD of hosts, "Just so will I [a]break this people and this city, even as one breaks a potter's vessel, which cannot again be repaired; and they will [b]bury in Topheth [1]because there is no *other* place for burial.

12 "This is how I will treat this place and its inhabitants," declares the LORD, "so as to make this city like Topheth.

13 "The [a]houses of Jerusalem and the houses of the kings of Judah will be [b]defiled like the place Topheth, because of all the [c]houses on whose rooftops they burned [1]sacrifices to [d]all the heavenly host and [e]poured out drink offerings to other gods." ' "

14 ¶ Then Jeremiah came from Topheth, where the LORD had sent him to prophesy; and he stood in the [a]court of the LORD's house and said to all the people:

15 "Thus says the LORD of hosts, the God of Israel, 'Behold, I am about to bring on this city and all its towns the entire calamity that I have declared against it, because they have [a]stiffened their necks so [b]as not to heed My words.' "

Pashhur Persecutes Jeremiah

20 When Pashhur the priest, the son of [a]Immer, who was [b]chief officer in the house of the LORD, heard Jeremiah prophesying these things,

2 Pashhur had Jeremiah the prophet [a]beaten and put him in the [b]stocks that were at the upper [c]Benjamin Gate, which was by the house of the LORD.

3 On the next day, when Pashhur released Jeremiah from the stocks, Jeremiah said to him, "Pashhur is not the name the LORD has [a]called you, but rather [1b]Magor-missabib.

4 "For thus says the LORD, 'Behold, I am going to make you a [a]terror to yourself and to all your friends; and while [b]your eyes look on, they will fall by the sword of their enemies. So I will [c]give over all Judah to the hand of the king of Babylon, and he will carry them away as [d]exiles to Babylon and will slay them with the sword.

5 'I will also give over all the [a]wealth of this city, all its produce and all its costly things; even all the treasures of the kings of Judah I will give over to the [b]hand of their enemies, and they will plunder them, take them away and bring them to Babylon.

6 'And you, [a]Pashhur, and all who live in your house will go into captivity; and you will enter Babylon, and there you will die and there you will be buried, you and all your [b]friends to whom you have [c]falsely prophesied.' "

Jeremiah's Complaint

7 ¶ O LORD, You have deceived me
and I was deceived;
You have [a]overcome me and
prevailed.
I have become a [b]laughingstock
all day long;
Everyone [c]mocks me.
8 For each time I speak, I cry
aloud;
I [a]proclaim violence and
destruction,
Because for me the [b]word of the
LORD has [1]resulted
In reproach and derision all day
long.
9 But if I say, "I will not
[a]remember Him
Or speak anymore in His name,"
Then in [b]my heart it becomes
like a burning fire
Shut up in my bones;
And I am weary of holding *it* in,
And [c]I cannot endure *it*.

---

4 [1]Or *incense* [a]Deut 28:20; Is 65:11; Jer 2:13 [b]Ezek 7:22; Dan 11:31 [c]Jer 7:9 [d]2 Kin 21:6; Jer 2:34
5 [1]Lit *heart* [a]Num 22:41; Jer 32:35 [b]Lev 18:21; 2 Kin 17:17; Ps 106:37
6 [a]Jer 7:32 [b]Is 30:33 [c]Josh 15:8
7 [a]Ps 33:10; Is 28:17; Jer 8:8 [b]Lev 26:17; Deut 28:25; Jer 15:2 [c]Ps 79:2; Jer 16:4
8 [1]Lit *blows* [a]Jer 18:16 [b]1 Kin 9:8; 2 Chr 7:21
9 [a]Lev 26:29; Deut 28:53; Is 9:20; Lam 4:10; Ezek 5:10
10 [a]Jer 19:1
11 [1]Or *until there is no place left to bury* [a]Ps 2:9; Is 30:14; Lam 4:2; Rev 2:27 [b]Jer 7:32
13 [1]Or *incense* [a]Jer 52:13 [b]2 Kin 23:10; Ps 74:7; Ezek 7:21 [c]Jer 32:29; Zeph 1:5 [d]Deut 4:19; 2 Kin 17:16; Jer 8:2 [e]Jer 7:18; Ezek 20:28
14 [a]2 Chr 20:5; Jer 26:2
15 [a]Neh 9:17; Jer 7:26 [b]Ps 58:4
20:1 [a]1 Chr 24:14; Ezra 2:37 [b]2 Kin 25:18
2 [a]1 Kin 22:27; 2 Chr 16:10; Jer 1:19; Amos 7:10-13 [b]Job 13:27 [c]Jer 37:13; Zech 14:10
3 [1]I.e. terror on every side [a]Is 8:3; Hos 1:4 [b]Jer 6:25
4 [a]Job 18:11-21; Jer 6:25; Ezek 26:21 [b]Jer 29:21 [c]Jer 21:4-10 [d]Jer 13:10
5 [a]Jer 15:13 [b]2 Kin 20:17; 2 Chr 36:10; Jer 27:21
6 [a]Jer 20:1 [b]Jer 20:4 [c]Jer 14:14; Lam 2:14
7 [a]Ezek 3:14 [b]Job 12:4; Lam 3:14 [c]Ps 22:7; Jer 38:19
8 [1]Lit *become* [a]Jer 6:7 [b]2 Chr 36:16; Jer 6:10
9 [a]1 Kin 19:3; Jon 1:2 [b]Job 32:18-20; Ps 39:3; Jer 4:19; Ezek 3:14; Acts 4:20 [c]Job 32:18-20

10 For [a]I have heard the
whispering of many,
"[b]Terror on every side!
[c]Denounce *him;* yes, let us
denounce him!"
[1]All my [d]trusted friends,
Watching for my fall, say:
"Perhaps he will be [2]deceived, so
that we may [e]prevail
against him
And take our revenge on him."
11 But the [a]LORD is with me like a
dread champion;
Therefore my [b]persecutors will
stumble and not prevail.
They will be utterly ashamed,
because they have [1]failed,
With an [c]everlasting disgrace
that will not be forgotten.
12 Yet, O LORD of hosts, You who
[a]test the righteous,
Who see the [1]mind and the
heart;
Let me [b]see Your vengeance on
them;
For [c]to You I have set forth my
cause.
13 [a]Sing to the LORD, praise the
LORD!
For He has [b]delivered the soul
of the needy one
From the hand of evildoers.

14 ¶ Cursed be the [a]day when I
was born;
Let the day not be blessed when
my mother bore me!
15 Cursed be the man who brought
the news
To my father, saying,
"A [1a]baby boy has been born
to you!"
And made him very happy.
16 But let that man be like the
cities
Which the LORD [a]overthrew
without [1]relenting,
And let him hear an [b]outcry in
the morning
And a [2]shout of alarm at noon;
17 Because he did not [a]kill me
[1]before birth,
So that my mother would have
been my grave,
And her womb ever pregnant.
18 Why did I ever come forth from
the womb
To [a]look on trouble and sorrow,
So that my [b]days have been
spent in [c]shame?

Jeremiah's Message for Zedekiah

21 The word which came to Jeremiah from the LORD when [a]King
Zedekiah sent to him [b]Pashhur the son of
Malchijah, and [c]Zephaniah the priest,
the son of Maaseiah, saying,
2 "Please [a]inquire of the LORD on our
behalf, for [b]Nebuchadnezzar king of
[c]Babylon is warring against us; perhaps
the LORD will deal with us [d]according to
all His [1]wonderful acts, so that *the ene-*
my will withdraw from us."
3 ¶ Then Jeremiah said to them,
"You shall say to Zedekiah as follows:
4 'Thus says the LORD God of Israel,
"Behold, I am about to [a]turn back the
weapons of war which are in your hands,
with which you are warring against the
king of Babylon and the Chaldeans who
are besieging you outside the wall; and I
will [b]gather them into the center of this
city.
5 "I [a]Myself will war against you with
an [b]outstretched hand and a mighty arm,
even in [c]anger and wrath and great indignation.
6 "I will also strike down the inhabitants of this city, both man and beast;
they will die of a great [a]pestilence.
7 "Then afterwards," declares the
LORD, "[a]I will give over Zedekiah king of
Judah and his servants and the people,
even those who survive in this city from
the pestilence, the sword and the famine,
into the hand of Nebuchadnezzar king of
Babylon, and into the hand of their foes
and into the hand of those who seek their
lives; and he will strike them down with
the edge of the sword. He [b]will not spare
them nor have pity nor compassion." '
8 ¶ "You shall also say to this people,
'Thus says the LORD, "Behold, I [a]set before you the way of life and the way of
death.
9 "He who [a]dwells in this city will die
by the [b]sword and by famine and by pestilence; but he who goes out and falls
away to the Chaldeans who are besieging
you will live, and he will have his own life
as booty.
10 "For I have [a]set My face against this
city for [1]harm and not for good," declares the LORD. "It will be [b]given into
the hand of the king of Babylon and he
will [c]burn it with fire." '
11 ¶ "Then *say* to the household of the
[a]king of Judah, 'Hear the word of the
LORD,
12 O [a]house of David, thus says the
LORD:
"[b]Administer justice [1]every
[c]morning;
And deliver the *person* who has
been robbed from the
[2]power of *his* oppressor,
[d]That My wrath may not go
forth like fire

10 [1]Lit *Every man of my peace* [2]Or *persuaded* [a]Ps 31:13 [b]Jer 6:25 [c]Neh 6:6-13; Is 29:21; Jer 18:18 [d]Ps 41:9 [e]1 Kin 19:2

11 [1]Lit *not succeeded*; or *not acted wisely* [a]Jer 1:8; Rom 8:31 [b]Deut 32:35; Jer 15:15 [c]Jer 23:40

12 [1]Lit *kidneys* [a]Ps 7:9; Jer 11:20 [b]Ps 54:7; Jer 11:20 [c]Ps 62:8

13 [a]Jer 31:7 [b]Ps 34:6; Jer 15:21

14 [a]Job 3:3-6; Jer 15:10

15 [1]Lit *male child* [a]Gen 21:6

16 [1]Lit *being sorry* [2]Or *trumpet blast* [a]Gen 19:25 [b]Jer 18:22

17 [1]Lit *from the womb* [a]Job 3:10

18 [a]Job 3:20; Jer 15:10; Lam 3:1 [b]Ps 90:9 [c]Ps 69:19; Jer 3:25; 1 Cor 4:9-13

21:1 [a]2 Kin 24:17; Jer 32:1-3 [b]1 Chr 9:12; Jer 38:1 [c]2 Kin 25:18; Jer 29:25

2 [1]Or *miracles* [a]Ex 9:28; Jer 37:3; Ezek 14:7 [b]2 Kin 25:1 [c]Gen 10:10; 2 Kin 17:24 [d]Ps 44:1-3; Jer 32:17

4 [a]Jer 32:5 [b]Is 5:5; Jer 39:3; Lam 2:5; Zech 14:2

5 [a]Is 63:10 [b]Ex 6:6; Deut 4:34; Jer 6:12 [c]Is 5:25; Jer 32:37

6 [a]Jer 14:12

7 [a]2 Kin 25:5-7; Jer 37:17 [b]2 Chr 36:17; Jer 13:14; Ezek 7:9; Hab 1:6-10

8 [a]Deut 30:15; Is 1:19

9 [a]Jer 38:2 [b]Jer 14:12

10 [1]Lit *evil* [a]Lev 17:10; Jer 44:11; Amos 9:4 [b]Jer 32:28 [c]2 Chr 36:19; Jer 34:2

11 [a]Jer 17:20

12 [1]Or *in the* [2]Lit *hand* [a]Is 7:2 [b]Ps 72:1; Is 1:17; Jer 7:5; Zech 7:9 [c]Ps 101:8; Zeph 3:5 [d]Jer 4:4; Ezek 20:47; Nah 1:6

And [e]burn with none to
extinguish *it*,
Because of the evil of their
deeds.
13 ¶ "Behold, [a]I am against you,
O [b]valley dweller,
O [1]rocky plain," declares the
LORD,
"You men who say, '[c]Who will
come down against us?
Or who will enter into our
habitations?'
14 "But I will punish you [a]according
to the [1]results of your
deeds," declares the LORD,
"And I will [b]kindle a fire in its
forest
That it may devour all its
environs." ' "

Warning of Jerusalem's Fall

22 Thus says the LORD, "Go down to
the house of the king of Judah,
and there speak this word
2 and say, 'Hear the word of the
LORD, O king of Judah, who [a]sits on David's throne, you and your servants and
your people who enter these gates.
3 'Thus says the LORD, "[a]Do justice
and righteousness, and deliver the one
who has been robbed from the power of
his [b]oppressor. Also [c]do not mistreat *or*
do violence to the stranger, the orphan,
or the widow; and do not [d]shed innocent
blood in this place.
4 "For if you men will indeed perform
this thing, then [a]kings will enter the
gates of this house, sitting [1]in David's
place on his throne, riding in chariots and
on horses, *even the king* himself and his
servants and his people.
5 "[a]But if you will not obey these
words, I [b]swear by Myself," declares the
LORD, "that this house will become a desolation." ' "
6 For thus says the LORD concerning
the house of the king of Judah:
"You are *like* [a]Gilead to Me,
Like the summit of Lebanon;
Yet most assuredly I will make
you like a [b]wilderness,
Like cities which are not
inhabited.
7 "For I will set apart [a]destroyers
against you,
Each with his weapons;
And they will [b]cut down your
choicest cedars
And [c]throw *them* on the fire.
8 ¶ "Many nations will pass by this
city; and they will [a]say to one another,
'Why has the LORD done thus to this great
city?'

12 [e]Is 1:31; Jer 7:20
13 [1]Lit *rock of the level place* [a]Jer 23:30-32; Ezek 13:8 [b]Ps 125:2; Is 22:1 [c]2 Sam 5:6,7; Jer 49:4; Lam 4:12; Obad 3,4
14 [1]Lit *fruit* [a]Is 3:10,11; Jer 17:10; 32:19 [b]2 Chr 36:19; Is 10:16,18; Jer 11:16; 17:27; 52:13; Ezek 20:47,48
22:2 [a]Is 9:7; Jer 17:25; 22:4,30; Luke 1:32
3 [a]Is 58:6,7; Jer 7:5,23; 21:12; Mic 6:8; Zech 7:9; 8:16; Matt 23:23 [b]Ps 72:4 [c]Ex 22:21-24 [d]Jer 7:6; 19:4; 22:17
4 [1]Lit *for David* [a]Jer 17:25
5 [a]Jer 17:27; 26:4 [b]Gen 22:16; Amos 6:8; Heb 6:13
6 [a]Gen 37:25; Num 32:1; Song 4:1 [b]Ps 107:34; Is 6:11; Jer 7:34; Mic 3:12
7 [a]Is 10:3-6; Jer 4:6,7 [b]Is 10:33, 34; 37:24 [c]Jer 21:14
8 [a]Deut 29:24-26; 1 Kin 9:8,9; 2 Chr 7:20-22; Jer 16:10
9 [1]Lit *say* [a]2 Kin 22:17; 2 Chr 34:25; Jer 11:3
10 [a]Eccl 4:2; Is 57:1; Jer 16:7; 22:18 [b]Jer 25:27; 44:14
11 [1]I.e. Jehoahaz [a]2 Kin 23:30-34; 1 Chr 3:15; 2 Chr 36:1-4
12 [a]2 Kin 23:34; Jer 22:18
13 [1]Or *roof chambers* [a]Jer 17:11; Mic 3:10; Hab 2:9 [b]Lev 19:13; James 5:4
14 [1]Or *roof chambers* [2]Or *Paneled* [3]Or *vermilion* [a]Is 5:8 [b]2 Sam 7:2; Hag 1:4
15 [a]2 Kin 23:25; Jer 7:5; 21:12 [b]Ps 128:2; Is 3:10; Jer 42:6
16 [a]Ps 72:1-4, 12,13 [b]1 Chr 28:9; Jer 9:24
17 [a]Jer 6:13; 8:10; Luke 12:15-20 [b]2 Kin 24:4; Jer 22:3
18 [a]2 Kin 23:36-24:6; 2 Chr 36:5 [b]Jer 22:10; 34:5 [c]1 Kin 13:30

9 "Then they will [1]answer, 'Because
they [a]forsook the covenant of the LORD
their God and bowed down to other gods
and served them.' "
10 ¶ [a]Do not weep for the dead or
mourn for him,
But weep continually for the one
who goes away;
For [b]he will never return
Or see his native land.
11 ¶ For thus says the LORD in regard
to [1a]Shallum the son of Josiah, king of
Judah, who became king in the place of
Josiah his father, who went forth from
this place, "He will never return there;
12 but in the place where they led him
captive, there he will [a]die and not see
this land again.

Messages about the Kings

13 ¶ "Woe to him who builds his
house [a]without
righteousness
And his [1]upper rooms without
justice,
Who uses his neighbor's services
without pay
And [b]does not give him his
wages,
14 Who says, 'I will [a]build myself a
roomy house
With spacious [1]upper rooms,
And cut out its windows,
[2]Paneling *it* with [b]cedar and
painting *it* [3]bright red.'
15 "Do you become a king because
you are competing in cedar?
Did not your father eat and drink
And [a]do justice and
righteousness?
Then it was [b]well with him.
16 "He pled the cause of the
[a]afflicted and needy;
Then it was well.
[b]Is not that what it means to
know Me?"
Declares the LORD.
17 "But your eyes and your heart
Are *intent* only upon your own
[a]dishonest gain,
And on [b]shedding innocent
blood
And on practicing oppression and
extortion."
18 ¶ Therefore thus says the LORD in
regard to [a]Jehoiakim the son of Josiah,
king of Judah,
"They will not [b]lament for him:
'[c]Alas, my brother!' or, 'Alas,
sister!'
They will not lament for him:
'Alas for the master!' or, 'Alas for
his splendor!'

19 "He will be [a]buried with a
donkey's burial,
Dragged off and thrown out
beyond the gates of
Jerusalem.
20 "Go up to Lebanon and cry out,
And lift up your voice in Bashan;
Cry out also from [a]Abarim,
For all your [b]lovers have been
crushed.
21 "I spoke to you in your prosperity;
But [a]you said, 'I will not listen!'
[b]This has been your practice
[c]from your youth,
That you have not obeyed My
voice.
22 "The wind will sweep away all
your [a]shepherds,
And your [b]lovers will go into
captivity;
Then you will surely be
[c]ashamed and humiliated
Because of all your wickedness.
23 "You who dwell in Lebanon,
Nested in the cedars,
How you will groan when pangs
come upon you,
[a]Pain like a woman in
childbirth!

24 ¶ "As I live," declares the LORD, "even though [1a]Coniah the son of Jehoiakim king of Judah were a [b]signet *ring* on My right hand, yet I would pull [1]you [2]off;
25 and I will [a]give you over into the hand of those who are seeking your life, yes, into the hand of those whom you dread, even into the hand of Nebuchadnezzar king of Babylon and into the hand of the Chaldeans.
26 "I will [a]hurl you and your [b]mother who bore you into another country where you were not born, and there you will die.
27 "But as for the land to which they desire to return, they will not return to it.
28 "Is this man Coniah a despised,
shattered jar?
Or is he an [a]undesirable vessel?
Why have he and his
descendants been
[b]hurled out
And cast into a [c]land that they
had not known?
29 "[a]O land, land, land,
Hear the word of the LORD!
30 "Thus says the LORD,
'Write this man down [a]childless,
A man who will [b]not prosper in
his days;
For no man of his [c]descendants
will prosper
Sitting on the throne of David
Or ruling again in Judah.' "

19 [a]1 Kin 21:23,24; Jer 36:30
20 [a]Num 27:12; Deut 32:49 [b]Jer 2:25; 3:1
21 [a]Jer 13:10; 19:15 [b]Jer 3:25 [c]Jer 3:24; 32:30
22 [a]Jer 23:1 [b]Jer 30:14 [c]Is 65:13; Jer 20:11
23 [a]Jer 4:31; 6:24
24 [1]I.e. Jehoiachin [2]Lit *off from there* [a]2 Kin 24:6; 1 Chr 3:16; 2 Chr 36:9; Jer 37:1 [b]Song 8:6; Is 49:16; Hag 2:23
25 [a]2 Kin 24:15,16; Jer 21:7; 34:20,21
26 [a]2 Kin 24:15; Jer 10:18; 16:13 [b]2 Kin 24:8
28 [a]Ps 31:12; Jer 48:38; Hos 8:8 [b]Jer 15:1 [c]Jer 17:4
29 [a]Deut 4:26; Jer 6:19; Mic 1:2
30 [a]1 Chr 3:17; Matt 1:12 [b]Jer 2:37; 10:21 [c]Ps 94:20; Jer 36:30
23:1 [a]Ezek 13:3; 34:2; Zech 11:17 [b]Is 56:9-12; Jer 10:21; 50:6 [c]Ezek 34:31
2 [1]Lit *shepherding* [a]Ex 32:34 [b]Jer 21:12; 44:22
3 [a]Is 11:11,12, 16; Jer 31:7,8; 32:37
4 [1]Or *shepherd* [a]Jer 3:15; 31:10; Ezek 34:23 [b]Jer 30:10; 46:27,28 [c]John 6:39; 10:28; 1 Pet 1:5
5 [1]Lit *Sprout* [2]Or *succeed* [a]Jer 33:14 [b]Is 4:2; 11:1-5; 53:2; Jer 30:9; 33:15,16; Zech 3:8; 6:12, 13 [c]Is 9:7; 52:13; Luke 1:32,33 [d]Ps 72:2; Is 9:7; 32:1; Dan 9:24
6 [a]Deut 33:28; Jer 30:10; Zech 14:11 [b]Is 7:14; 9:6; Matt 1:21-23 [c]Is 45:24; Jer 33:16; Dan 9:24; Rom 3:22; 1 Cor 1:30
7 [a]Is 43:18,19; Jer 16:14,15
8 [a]Jer 16:15 [b]Is 43:5,6; Ezek 34:13; Amos 9:14,15
9 [a]Jer 8:18; Hab 3:16
10 [a]Jer 9:2; Hos 4:2,3; Mal 3:5 [b]Jer 12:4

The Coming Messiah: the Righteous Branch

23 "[a]Woe to the shepherds who are [b]destroying and scattering the [c]sheep of My pasture!" declares the LORD.
2 Therefore thus says the LORD God of Israel concerning the shepherds who are [1]tending My people: "You have scattered My flock and driven them away, and have not attended to them; behold, I am about to [a]attend to you for the [b]evil of your deeds," declares the LORD.
3 "Then I Myself will [a]gather the remnant of My flock out of all the countries where I have driven them and bring them back to their pasture, and they will be fruitful and multiply.
4 "I will also raise up [a]shepherds over them and they will [1]tend them; and they will [b]not be afraid any longer, nor be terrified, [c]nor will any be missing," declares the LORD.
5 ¶ "Behold, *the* [a]days are
coming," declares the LORD,
"When I will raise up for David a
righteous [1b]Branch;
And He will [c]reign as king and
[2]act wisely
And [d]do justice and
righteousness in the land.
6 "In His days Judah will be saved,
And [a]Israel will dwell securely;
And this is His [b]name by which
He will be called,
'The [c]LORD our righteousness.'
7 ¶ "[a]Therefore behold, *the* days are coming," declares the LORD, "when they will no longer say, 'As the LORD lives, who brought up the sons of Israel from the land of Egypt,'
8 [a]but, 'As the LORD lives, who [b]brought up and led back the descendants of the household of Israel from *the* north land and from all the countries where I had driven them.' Then they will live on their own soil."

False Prophets Denounced

9 ¶ As for the prophets:
My [a]heart is broken within me,
All my bones tremble;
I have become like a drunken
man,
Even like a man overcome with
wine,
Because of the LORD
And because of His holy words.
10 For the land is full of
[a]adulterers;
For the land [b]mourns because of
the curse.

The [c]pastures of the wilderness
have dried up.
Their course also is evil
And their might is not right.
11 "For [a]both prophet and priest are
polluted;
Even in My house I have found
their wickedness," declares
the LORD.
12 "Therefore their way will be like
[a]slippery paths to them,
They will be driven away into
the [b]gloom and fall down
in it;
For I will bring [c]calamity upon
them,
The year of their punishment,"
declares the LORD.

13 ¶ "Moreover, among the
prophets of Samaria I saw an
[a]offensive thing:
They [b]prophesied by Baal and
[c]led My people Israel astray.
14 "Also among the prophets of
Jerusalem I have seen a
[a]horrible thing:
The committing of [b]adultery and
walking in falsehood;
And they strengthen the hands
of [c]evildoers,
So that no one has turned back
from his wickedness.
All of them have become to Me
like [d]Sodom,
And her inhabitants like
Gomorrah.
15 "Therefore thus says the LORD of
hosts concerning the prophets,
'Behold, I am going to [a]feed
them wormwood
And make them drink poisonous
water,
For from the prophets of
Jerusalem
Pollution has gone forth into all
the land.' "

16 ¶ Thus says the LORD of hosts,
"[a]Do not listen to the words of
the prophets who are
prophesying to you.
They are [b]leading you into
futility;
They speak a [c]vision of their
own [1]imagination,
Not [d]from the mouth of the
LORD.
17 "They keep saying to those who
[a]despise Me,
'The LORD has said, "[b]You will
have peace" ';
And as for everyone who walks
in the [c]stubbornness of his
own heart,

10 [c]Ps 107:34; Jer 9:10

11 [a]Jer 6:13; Zeph 3:4

12 [a]Ps 35:6; Prov 4:19; Jer 13:16 [b]Is 8:22; John 12:35 [c]Jer 11:23

13 [a]Hos 9:7,8 [b]1 Kin 18:18-21; Jer 2:8; 23:32 [c]Is 9:16

14 [a]Jer 5:30 [b]Jer 29:23 [c]Jer 23:22; Ezek 13:22,23 [d]Gen 18:20; Deut 32:32; Is 1:9,10; Jer 20:16; 49:18; Matt 11:24

15 [a]Deut 29:18; Jer 8:14; 9:15

16 [1]Lit *heart* [a]Jer 27:9,10, 14-17; 1 John 4:1 [b]Matt 7:15; 2 Cor 11:13-15; Gal 1:8,9 [c]Jer 14:14; Ezek 13:3,6 [d]Jer 9:12, 20

17 [a]Mic 2:11 [b]Jer 8:11; Ezek 13:10 [c]Jer 13:10; 18:12 [d]Jer 5:12; Amos 9:10; Mic 3:11

18 [1]Another reading is *My* [a]Job 15:8,9; Jer 23:22; 1 Cor 2:16 [b]Job 33:31

19 [a]Jer 25:32; 30:23; Amos 1:14

20 [a]2 Kin 23:26,27; Jer 30:24 [b]Is 55:11; Zech 1:6 [c]Gen 49:1

21 [a]Jer 14:14; 23:32; 27:15

22 [a]Jer 9:12; 23:18 [b]Jer 35:15; Zech 1:4

23 [a]Ps 139:1-10

24 [a]Job 22:13, 14; 34:21,22; Ps 139:7-12; Is 29:15; Jer 49:10; Heb 4:13 [b]1 Kin 8:27; 2 Chr 2:6; Is 66:1

25 [a]Jer 8:6; 1 Cor 4:5 [b]Jer 14:14 [c]Num 12:6; Jer 23:28, 32; 29:8; Joel 2:28

26 [a]1 Tim 4:1,2

27 [a]Deut 13:1-3; Jer 29:8 [b]Judg 3:7; 8:33, 34

28 [a]Jer 9:12,20 [b]1 Cor 3:12,13

29 [a]Jer 5:14; 20:9 [b]2 Cor 10:4,5

30 [a]Deut 18:20; Ps 34:16; Jer 14:14,15; Ezek 13:8

They say, '[d]Calamity will not
come upon you.'
18 "But [a]who has stood in the
council of the LORD,
That he should see and hear His
word?
Who has given [b]heed to [1]His
word and listened?
19 "Behold, the [a]storm of the LORD
has gone forth in wrath,
Even a whirling tempest;
It will swirl down on the head of
the wicked.
20 "The [a]anger of the LORD will not
turn back
Until He has [b]performed and
carried out the purposes of
His heart;
[c]In the last days you will clearly
understand it.
21 "[a]I did not send *these* prophets,
But they ran.
I did not speak to them,
But they prophesied.
22 "But if they had [a]stood in My
council,
Then they would have
[b]announced My words to
My people,
And would have turned them
back from their evil way
And from the evil of their deeds.

23 ¶ "Am I a God who is [a]near,"
declares the LORD,
"And not a God far off?
24 "Can a man [a]hide himself in
hiding places
So I do not see him?" declares
the LORD.
"[b]Do I not fill the heavens and
the earth?" declares the
LORD.

25 ¶ "I have [a]heard what the prophets have said who [b]prophesy falsely in
My name, saying, 'I had a [c]dream, I had
a dream!'
26 "How long? Is there *anything* in the
hearts of the prophets who prophesy
falsehood, even *these* prophets of the
[a]deception of their own heart,
27 who intend to [a]make My people
forget My name by their dreams which
they relate to one another, just as their
fathers [b]forgot My name because of Baal?
28 "The prophet who has a dream may
relate *his* dream, but let him who has
[a]My word speak My word in truth.
[b]What does straw have *in common* with
grain?" declares the LORD.
29 "Is not My word like [a]fire?" declares the LORD, "and like a [b]hammer
which shatters a rock?
30 "Therefore behold, [a]I am against

the prophets," declares the LORD, "who steal My words from each other.

31 "Behold, I am against the prophets," declares the LORD, "who use their tongues and declare, '*The Lord* declares.'

32 "Behold, I am against those who have prophesied [a]false dreams," declares the LORD, "and related them and led My people astray by their falsehoods and [b]reckless boasting; yet [c]I did not send them or command them, nor do they [d]furnish this people the slightest benefit," declares the LORD.

33 ¶ "Now when this people or the prophet or a priest asks you saying, 'What is the [1a]oracle of the LORD?' then you shall say to them, 'What [1]oracle?' The LORD declares, 'I will [b]abandon you.'

34 "Then as for the prophet or the priest or the people who say, 'The [a]oracle of the LORD,' I will bring punishment upon that man and his household.

35 "Thus will each of you say to his neighbor and to his brother, '[a]What has the LORD answered?' or, 'What has the LORD spoken?'

36 "For you will no longer remember the oracle of the LORD, because every man's own word will become the oracle, and you have [a]perverted the words of the [b]living God, the LORD of hosts, our God.

37 "Thus you will say to *that* prophet, 'What has the LORD answered you?' and, 'What has the LORD spoken?'

38 "For if you say, 'The oracle of the LORD!' surely thus says the LORD, 'Because you said this word, "The oracle of the LORD!" I have also sent to you, saying, "You shall not say, 'The oracle of the LORD!' " '

39 "Therefore behold, [a]I will surely forget you and cast you away from My presence, along with the city which I gave you and your fathers.

40 "I will put an everlasting [a]reproach on you and an everlasting humiliation which will not be forgotten."

Baskets of Figs and the Returnees

24 After [a]Nebuchadnezzar king of Babylon had carried away captive Jeconiah the son of Jehoiakim, king of Judah, and the officials of Judah with the craftsmen and smiths from Jerusalem and had brought them to Babylon, the LORD showed me: behold, two [b]baskets of figs set before the temple of the LORD!

2 One basket had very good figs, like [a]first-ripe figs, and the other basket had [b]very bad figs which could not be eaten due to rottenness.

3 Then the LORD said to me, "[a]What do you see, Jeremiah?" And I said, "Figs, the good figs, very good; and the bad *figs*, very bad, which cannot be eaten due to rottenness."

4 ¶ Then the word of the LORD came to me, saying,

5 "Thus says the LORD God of Israel, 'Like these good figs, so I will regard [a]as good the captives of Judah, whom I have sent out of this place *into* the land of the Chaldeans.

6 'For I will set My eyes on them for good, and I will [a]bring them again to this land; and I will [b]build them up and not overthrow them, and I will [c]plant them and not pluck them up.

7 'I will give them a [a]heart to know Me, for I am the LORD; and they will be [b]My people, and I will be their God, for they will [c]return to Me with their whole heart.

8 ¶ 'But like the [a]bad figs which cannot be eaten due to rottenness—indeed, thus says the LORD—so I will [1]abandon [b]Zedekiah king of Judah and his officials, and the [c]remnant of Jerusalem who remain in this land and the ones who dwell in the land of [d]Egypt.

9 'I will [a]make them a terror *and an* evil for all the kingdoms of the earth, as a [b]reproach and a proverb, a taunt and a [c]curse in all places where I will scatter them.

10 'I will send the [a]sword, the famine and the pestilence upon them until they are destroyed from the land which I gave to them and their forefathers.' "

Prophecy of the Captivity

25 The word that came to Jeremiah concerning all the people of Judah, in the [a]fourth year of [b]Jehoiakim the son of Josiah, king of Judah (that was the [c]first year of Nebuchadnezzar king of Babylon),

2 which Jeremiah the prophet spoke to all the [a]people of Judah and to all the inhabitants of Jerusalem, saying,

3 "From the [a]thirteenth year of [b]Josiah the son of Amon, king of Judah, even to this day, [1]these [c]twenty-three years the word of the LORD has come to me, and I have spoken to you [2d]again and again, but you have not listened.

4 "And the LORD has sent to you all His [a]servants the prophets [1]again and again, but you have not listened nor inclined your ear to hear,

5 saying, '[a]Turn now everyone from his evil way and from the evil of your deeds, and dwell on the land which the LORD has given to you and your forefathers [b]forever and ever;

6 and [a]do not go after other gods to [1]serve them and to [2]worship them, and

32 [a]Deut 13:1, 2; Jer 23:25 [b]Zeph 3:4 [c]Jer 23:21; Lam 3:37 [d]Jer 7:8; Lam 2:14
33 [1]Or *burden*, and so throughout the ch [a]Is 13:1; Nah 1:1; Hab 1:1; Zech 9:1; Mal 1:1 [b]Jer 12:7; 23:39
34 [a]Lam 2:14; Zech 13:3
35 [a]Jer 33:3; 42:4
36 [a]Gal 1:7,8; 2 Pet 3:16 [b]2 Kin 19:4; Jer 10:10
39 [a]Jer 7:14,15; 23:33; Ezek 8:18
40 [a]Jer 20:11; 42:18; Ezek 5:14,15
24:1 [a]2 Kin 24:10-16; 2 Chr 36:10; Jer 27:20; 29:1,2 [b]Amos 8:1
2 [a]Mic 7:1; Nah 3:12 [b]Is 5:4,7; Jer 29:17
3 [a]Jer 1:11,13; Amos 8:2; Zech 4:2
5 [a]Nah 1:7; Zech 13:9
6 [a]Jer 12:15; 29:10; 32:37; Ezek 11:17 [b]Jer 31:4; 32:41; 33:7; 42:10 [c]Jer 32:41
7 [a]Deut 30:6; Jer 31:33; 32:40; Ezek 11:19; 36:26 [b]Is 51:16; Jer 7:23; 30:22; 31:33; 32:38; Ezek 14:11; Zech 8:8; Heb 8:10 [c]1 Sam 7:3; Ps 119:2; Jer 29:13
8 [1]Lit *give up* [a]Jer 29:17 [b]Jer 39:5; Ezek 12:12,13 [c]Jer 39:9 [d]Jer 44:1, 26-30
9 [a]Jer 15:4; 29:18; 34:17 [b]1 Kin 9:7; Ps 44:13,14 [c]Is 65:15
10 [a]Is 51:19; Jer 21:9; 27:8; Ezek 5:12-17
25:1 [a]Jer 36:1; 46:2 [b]2 Kin 24:1,2; 2 Chr 36:4-6; Dan 1:1, 2 [c]Jer 32:1
2 [a]Jer 18:11
3 [1]Lit *this* [2]Lit *rising early and speaking* [a]Jer 1:2 [b]2 Chr 34:1-3,8 [c]Jer 36:2 [d]Jer 7:25; 11:7; 26:5
4 [1]Lit *rising early and sending* [a]2 Chr 36:15; Jer 26:5
5 [a]2 Kin 17:13; Is 55:6,7; Jer 4:1; 35:15; Ezek 18:30; Jon 3:8-10 [b]Gen 17:8; Jer 7:7; 17:25
6 [1]Or *worship* [2]Or *bow down to* [a]Deut 6:14; 8:19; 2 Kin 17:35; Jer 35:15

do not provoke Me to anger with the
work of your hands, and I will do you no
harm.'
7 "Yet you have not listened to Me,"
declares the LORD, "in order that you
might [a]provoke Me to anger with the
work of your hands to your own harm.
8 ¶ "Therefore thus says the LORD of
hosts, 'Because you have not obeyed My
words,
9 behold, I will [a]send and take all the
families of the north,' declares the LORD,
'and *I will send* to Nebuchadnezzar king
of Babylon, [b]My servant, and will bring
them against this land and against its inhabitants and against all these nations
round about; and I will [1]utterly destroy
them and [c]make them a horror and a
hissing, and an everlasting desolation.
10 'Moreover, I will [1a]take from them
the voice of joy and the voice of gladness,
the voice of the bridegroom and the voice
of the bride, the [b]sound of the millstones
and the light of the lamp.
11 '[a]This whole land will be a desolation and a horror, and these nations will
serve the king of Babylon [b]seventy years.

Babylon Will Be Judged

12 ¶ 'Then it will be [a]when seventy
years are completed I will [b]punish the
king of Babylon and that nation,' declares
the LORD, 'for their iniquity, and the land
of the Chaldeans; and [c]I will make it an
everlasting desolation.
13 'I will bring upon that land all My
words which I have pronounced against
it, all that is written in [a]this book which
Jeremiah has prophesied against [b]all the
nations.
14 '([1]For [a]many nations and great
kings will make slaves of them, even
them; and I will [b]recompense them according to their deeds and according to
the work of their hands.)' "
15 ¶ For thus the LORD, the God of Israel, says to me, "Take this [a]cup of the
wine of wrath from My hand and cause
all the nations to whom I send you to
drink it.
16 "They will [a]drink and stagger and
go mad because of the sword that I will
send among them."
17 ¶ Then I took the cup from the
LORD'S hand and [a]made all the nations to
whom the LORD sent me drink it:
18 [a]Jerusalem and the cities of Judah
and its kings *and* its princes, to make
them a ruin, a horror, a hissing and a
curse, as it is this day;
19 [a]Pharaoh king of Egypt, his servants, his princes and all his people;
20 and all the [1a]foreign people, all
the kings of the [b]land of Uz, all the kings
of the land of the [c]Philistines (even Ashkelon, Gaza, Ekron and the remnant of
[d]Ashdod);
21 [a]Edom, [b]Moab and the sons of
[c]Ammon;
22 and all the kings of [a]Tyre, all the
kings of Sidon and the kings of [b]the
coastlands which are beyond the sea;
23 and [a]Dedan, Tema, [b]Buz and all
who [c]cut the corners *of their hair;*
24 and all the kings of [a]Arabia and all
the kings of the [1b]foreign people who
dwell in the desert;
25 and all the kings of Zimri, all the
kings of [a]Elam and all the kings of [b]Me-
dia;
26 and all the kings of the north, near
and far, one with another; and [a]all the
kingdoms of the earth which are upon
the face of the ground, and the king of
[1b]Sheshach shall drink after them.
27 ¶ "You shall say to them, 'Thus says
the LORD of hosts, the God of Israel,
"[a]Drink, be drunk, vomit, fall and rise no
more because of the [b]sword which I will
send among you." '
28 "And it will be, if they [a]refuse to
take the cup from your hand to drink,
then you will say to them, 'Thus says the
LORD of hosts: "[b]You shall surely drink!
29 "For behold, I am [a]beginning to
work calamity in *this* city which is
[b]called by My name, and shall you be
completely free from punishment? You
will not be free from punishment; for [c]I
am summoning a sword against all the
inhabitants of the earth," declares the
LORD of hosts.'
30 ¶ "Therefore you shall prophesy
against them all these words, and you
shall say to them,

'The [a]LORD will [b]roar from on
high
And utter His voice from His
holy habitation;
He will roar mightily against His
[1]fold.
He will shout like those who
tread *the grapes,*
Against all the inhabitants of the
earth.
31 'A clamor has come to the end of
the earth,
Because the LORD has [a]a
controversy with the
nations.
He is entering into [b]judgment
with all flesh;
As for the wicked, He has given
them to the sword,' declares
the LORD."

32 ¶ Thus says the LORD of hosts,
"Behold, evil is going forth

7 [a]2 Kin 17:17; Jer 7:19
9 [1]Or *put them under the ban* [a]Jer 1:15 [b]Is 13:3; Jer 27:6 [c]1 Kin 9:7; Jer 18:16
10 [1]Lit *cause to perish* [a]Is 24:8-11; Jer 7:34; Ezek 26:13; Rev 18:23 [b]Eccl 12:4; Is 47:2
11 [a]Jer 4:27 [b]2 Chr 36:21; Jer 29:10; Dan 9:2; Zech 7:5
12 [a]Ezra 1:1; Jer 29:10; Dan 9:2 [b]Is 13:14; Jer ch 50 [c]Is 13:19
13 [a]Jer 36:4 [b]Jer 1:5
14 [1]Or *For they have served many nations and great kings* [a]Jer 27:7 [b]Jer 51:6
15 [a]Job 21:20; Ps 75:8; Is 51:17; Jer 51:7
16 [a]Nah 3:11
17 [a]Jer 1:10
18 [a]Ps 60:3; Is 51:17
19 [a]Jer 46:2-28; Nah 3:8-10
20 [1]Or *mixed multitude* [a]Jer 25:24; Ezek 30:5 [b]Job 1:1; Lam 4:21 [c]Jer 47:1-7 [d]Is 20:1
21 [a]Ps 137:7; Jer 49:7-22 [b]Jer 48:1-47; Amos 2:1-3 [c]Jer 49:1-6; Amos 1:13-15
22 [a]Jer 47:4; Zech 9:2-4 [b]Jer 31:10
23 [a]Is 21:13; Jer 49:7 [b]Gen 22:21 [c]Jer 9:26
24 [1]Or *mixed multitude* [a]2 Chr 9:14 [b]Jer 25:20; Ezek 30:5
25 [a]Gen 10:22; Is 11:11; Jer 49:34 [b]Is 13:17; Jer 51:11
26 [1]Cryptic name for Babylon [a]Jer 25:9 [b]Jer 51:41
27 [a]Jer 25:16; Hab 2:16 [b]Ezek 21:4
28 [a]Job 34:33 [b]Jer 49:12
29 [a]Prov 11:31; Is 10:12; Jer 13:13; Ezek 9:6; 1 Pet 4:17 [b]1 Kin 8:43 [c]Ezek 38:21
30 [1]Or *pasture* [a]Is 42:13; Jer 25:38 [b]Joel 2:11; Amos 1:2
31 [a]Hos 4:1; Mic 6:2 [b]Is 66:16; Ezek 20:35; Joel 3:2

From [a]nation to nation,
And a great [b]storm is being
stirred up
From the remotest parts of the
earth.
33 ¶ "Those [a]slain by the LORD on
that day will be from one end of the earth
to the [1]other. They will [b]not be lamented, gathered or buried; they will be like
[c]dung on the face of the ground.
34 "Wail, you shepherds, and cry;
And [a]wallow *in ashes,* you
masters of the flock;
For the days of your [b]slaughter
and your dispersions [1]have
come,
And you will fall like a choice
vessel.
35 "[a]Flight will perish from the
shepherds,
And escape from the masters of
the flock.
36 "*Hear* the sound of the cry of the
shepherds,
And the wailing of the masters of
the flock!
For the LORD is destroying their
pasture,
37 "And the peaceful [1a]folds are
made silent
Because of the [b]fierce anger of
the LORD.
38 "He has left His hiding place
[a]like the lion;
For their land has become a
horror
Because of the fierceness of the
[1]oppressing *sword*
And because of His fierce anger."

Cities of Judah Warned

26 In the beginning of the reign of
[a]Jehoiakim the son of Josiah,
king of Judah, this word came from the
LORD, saying,
2 "Thus says the LORD, '[a]Stand in the
court of the LORD'S house, and speak to all
the cities of Judah who have [b]come to
worship *in* the LORD'S house [c]all the
words that I have commanded you to
speak to them. [d]Do not omit a word!
3 '[a]Perhaps they will listen and everyone will turn from his evil way, that [b]I
may repent of the calamity which I am
planning to do to them because of the evil
of their deeds.'
4 "And you will say to them, 'Thus
says the LORD, "[a]If you will not listen to
Me, to [b]walk in My law which I have set
before you,
5 to listen to the words of [a]My servants the prophets, whom I have been
sending to you [1]again and again, but you
have not listened;
6 then I will make this house like
[a]Shiloh, and this city I will make a
[b]curse to all the nations of the earth." ' "

A Plot to Murder Jeremiah

7 ¶ The [a]priests and the prophets
and all the people heard Jeremiah speaking these words in the house of the LORD.
8 When Jeremiah finished speaking
all that the LORD had commanded *him* to
speak to all the people, the priests and
the prophets and all the people seized
him, saying, "[a]You must die!
9 "Why have you prophesied in the
name of the LORD saying, 'This house will
be like Shiloh and this city will be [a]deso-
late, without inhabitant'?" And [b]all the
people gathered about Jeremiah in the
house of the LORD.
10 ¶ When the [a]officials of Judah
heard these things, they came up from
the king's house to the house of the LORD
and sat in the [b]entrance of the New Gate
of the LORD'S *house.*
11 Then the priests and the prophets
[a]spoke to the officials and to all the people, saying, "A [b]death sentence for this
man! For he has prophesied [c]against this
city as you have heard in your hearing."
12 ¶ Then Jeremiah spoke to all the
officials and to all the people, saying,
"[a]The LORD sent me to prophesy against
this house and against this city all the
words that you have heard.
13 "Now therefore [a]amend your ways
and your deeds and obey the voice of
the LORD your God; and the LORD will
[1]change His mind about the misfortune
which He has pronounced against you.
14 "But as for me, behold, [a]I am in
your hands; do with me as is good and
right in your sight.
15 "Only know for certain that if you
put me to death, you will bring [a]inno-
cent blood on yourselves, and on this city
and on its inhabitants; for truly the LORD
has sent me to you to speak all these
words in your hearing."

Jeremiah Is Spared

16 ¶ Then the officials and all the people [a]said to the priests and to the prophets, "No [b]death sentence for this man!
For he has spoken to us in the name of
the LORD our God."
17 Then [a]some of the elders of the
land rose up and spoke to all the assembly
of the people, saying,
18 "[1a]Micah of Moresheth prophesied
in the days of Hezekiah king of Judah; and
he spoke to all the people of Judah, saying, 'Thus the LORD of hosts has said,
"[b]Zion will be plowed *as* a field,

32 [a]2 Chr 15:6; Is 34:2 [b]Is 30:30; Jer 23:19
33 [1]Lit *other end of the earth* [a]Is 34:2,3; 66:16 [b]Ps 79:3; Jer 16:4; Ezek 39:4, 17 [c]Is 5:25
34 [1]Lit *are full* [a]Jer 6:26; Ezek 27:30 [b]Is 34:6, 7; Jer 50:27
35 [a]Job 11:20; Jer 11:11; Amos 2:14
37 [1]Or *pastures* [a]Is 27:10,11; Jer 5:17; 13:20 [b]Ps 97:1-3; Is 66:15; Heb 12:29
38 [1]Or *oppressor* [a]Jer 4:7; 5:6; Hos 5:14; 13:7,8
26:1 [a]2 Kin 23:36; 2 Chr 36:4,5
2 [a]2 Chr 24:20, 21; Jer 7:2; 19:14 [b]Deut 12:5 [c]Jer 1:17; 42:4; Matt 28:20; Acts 20:20,27 [d]Deut 4:2
3 [a]Is 1:16-19; Jer 36:3-7 [b]Jer 18:8; Jon 3:8
4 [a]Lev 26:14; 1 Kin 9:6; Is 1:20; Jer 17:27; 22:5 [b]Jer 32:23; 44:10,23
5 [1]Lit *rising early and sending* [a]2 Kin 9:7; Ezra 9:11; Jer 7:13; 25:3,4
6 [a]Josh 18:1; 1 Sam 4:12; Ps 78:60,61; Jer 7:12,14 [b]2 Kin 22:19; Is 65:15; Jer 24:9; 25:18
7 [a]Jer 5:31; Mic 3:11
8 [a]Jer 11:19; 18:23; Lam 4:13,14; Matt 21:35,36; 23:34, 35; 27:20
9 [a]Jer 9:11; 33:10 [b]Acts 3:11; 5:12
10 [a]Jer 26:21 [b]Jer 36:10
11 [a]Jer 18:23 [b]Deut 18:20; Matt 26:66 [c]Jer 38:4; Acts 6:11-14
12 [a]Jer 1:17,18; 26:15; Amos 7:15; Acts 4:19; 5:29
13 [1]Lit *be sorry for* [a]Jer 7:3,5; 18:8,11; 26:3; 35:15; Joel 2:14; Jon 3:9; 4:2
14 [a]Jer 38:5
15 [a]Num 35:33; Prov 6:16,17; Jer 7:6
16 [a]Jer 26:11; 36:19,25; 38:7, 13 [b]Acts 5:34-39; 23:9, 29; 25:25; 26:31
17 [a]Acts 5:34
18 [1]Lit *Micaiah the Morasthite* [a]Mic 1:1 [b]Neh 4:2; Ps 79:1; Jer 9:11; Mic 3:12

And Jerusalem will become
ruins,
And the [c]mountain of the house
as the [2]high places of a
forest." '
19 "Did Hezekiah king of Judah and all
Judah put him to death? Did he not [a]fear
the LORD and entreat the favor of the
LORD, and [b]the LORD [1]changed His mind
about the misfortune which He had pronounced against them? But we are [c]com-
mitting a great evil against ourselves."
20 ¶ Indeed, there was also a man
who prophesied in the name of the LORD,
Uriah the son of Shemaiah from [a]Kiriath-
jearim; and he prophesied against this
city and against this land words similar to
all those of Jeremiah.
21 When King Jehoiakim and all his
mighty men and all the officials heard his
words, then the [a]king sought to put him
to death; but Uriah heard *it,* and he was
afraid and [b]fled and went to Egypt.
22 Then King Jehoiakim sent men to
Egypt: [a]Elnathan the son of Achbor and
certain men with him *went* into Egypt.
23 And they brought Uriah from Egypt
and led him to King Jehoiakim, who
[a]slew him with a sword and cast his dead
body into the [1]burial place of the [2]com-
mon people.
24 ¶ But the hand of [a]Ahikam the son
of Shaphan was with Jeremiah, so that he
was [b]not given into the hands of the people to put him to death.

The Nations to Submit to Nebuchadnezzar

27 In the beginning of the reign of
[1a]Zedekiah the son of Josiah,
king of Judah, this word came to Jeremiah
from the LORD, saying—
2 thus says the LORD to me—"Make
for yourself [a]bonds and [b]yokes and put
them on your neck,
3 and send [1]word to the king of
[a]Edom, to the king of [a]Moab, to the king
of the sons of [a]Ammon, to the king of
[a]Tyre and to the king of [a]Sidon [2]by the
messengers who come to Jerusalem to
Zedekiah king of Judah.
4 "Command them *to go* to their masters, saying, 'Thus says the LORD of hosts,
the God of Israel, thus you shall say to
your masters,
5 "[a]I have made the earth, the men
and the beasts which are on the face of
the earth [b]by My great power and by My
outstretched arm, and I will [c]give it to
the one who is [1]pleasing in My sight.
6 "Now I [a]have given all these lands
into the hand of Nebuchadnezzar king of
Babylon, [b]My servant, and I have given
him also the [c]wild animals of the field to
serve him.
7 "[a]All the nations shall serve him
and his son and his grandson [b]until the
time of his own land comes; then [c]many
nations and great kings will [1]make him
their servant.
8 ¶ "It will be, *that* the nation or the
kingdom which [a]will not serve him,
Nebuchadnezzar king of Babylon, and
which will not put its neck under the
yoke of the king of Babylon, I will punish
that nation with the [b]sword, with famine
and with pestilence," declares the LORD,
"until I have destroyed [1]it by his hand.
9 "But as for you, [a]do not listen to
your prophets, your diviners, your
[1]dreamers, your soothsayers or your sorcerers who speak to you, saying, 'You will
not serve the king of Babylon.'
10 "For they prophesy a [a]lie to you in
order to [b]remove you far from your land;
and I will drive you out and you will perish.
11 "But the nation which will [a]bring
its neck under the yoke of the king of
Babylon and serve him, I will [b]let remain
on its land," declares the LORD, "and they
will till it and dwell in it." ' "
12 ¶ I spoke words like all these to
[a]Zedekiah king of Judah, saying, "Bring
your necks under the yoke of the king of
Babylon and serve him and his people,
and live!
13 "Why will you [a]die, you and your
people, by the sword, famine and pestilence, as the LORD has spoken to that nation which will not serve the king of Babylon?
14 "So [a]do not listen to the words of
the prophets who speak to you, saying,
'You will not serve the king of Babylon,'
for they prophesy a [b]lie to you;
15 for [a]I have not sent them," declares the LORD, "but they [b]prophesy
falsely in My name, in order that I may
[c]drive you out and that you may perish,
[d]you and the prophets who prophesy to
you."
16 ¶ *Then* I spoke to the priests and to
all this people, saying, "Thus says the
LORD: Do not listen to the words of your
prophets who prophesy to you, saying,
'Behold, the [a]vessels of the LORD's house
will now shortly be brought again from
Babylon'; for they are prophesying a [b]lie
to you.
17 "Do not listen to them; serve the
king of Babylon, and live! Why should
this city [a]become a ruin?
18 "But [a]if they are prophets, and if the
word of the LORD is with them, let them
now [b]entreat the LORD of hosts that the
vessels which are left in the house of the

18 [2]Or *a wooded height* [c]Is 2:2; Jer 17:3; Mic 4:1; Zech 8:3
19 [1]Lit *was sorry for* [a]2 Chr 29:6-11; Is 37:1 [b]Ex 32:14; 2 Sam 24:16 [c]Jer 44:7; Hab 2:10
20 [a]Josh 9:17; 1 Sam 6:21
21 [a]2 Chr 16:10; Jer 36:26; Matt 14:5 [b]1 Kin 19:2-4; Matt 10:23
22 [a]Jer 36:12
23 [1]Lit *graves* [2]Lit *sons of the people* [a]Jer 2:30
24 [a]2 Kin 22:12-14; Jer 39:14 [b]1 Kin 18:4; Jer 1:18
27:1 [1]Many mss read *Jehoiakim* [a]2 Kin 24:18-20; 2 Chr 36:11-13
2 [a]Jer 30:8 [b]Jer 28:10
3 [1]Lit *them* [2]Lit *by the hand of* [a]Jer 25:21
5 [1]Or *upright* [a]Ps 96:5; Is 42:5; Jer 10:12 [b]Deut 9:29; Jer 32:17; Dan 4:17 [c]Ps 115:15; Acts 17:26
6 [a]Jer 21:7; Ezek 29:18-20 [b]Is 44:28; Jer 25:9 [c]Jer 28:14; Dan 2:38
7 [1]Or *enslave him* [a]2 Chr 36:20; Jer 44:30 [b]Dan 5:26; Zech 2:8 [c]Is 14:4-6; Jer 25:12
8 [1]Lit *them* [a]Jer 38:17-19; Ezek 17:19-21 [b]Jer 24:10; Ezek 14:21
9 [1]Lit *dreams* [a]Ex 22:18; Deut 18:10; Prov 19:27; Is 8:19; Mal 3:5; Eph 5:6
10 [a]Jer 23:25 [b]Jer 8:19
11 [a]Jer 27:2 [b]Jer 21:9
12 [a]Jer 27:3
13 [a]Prov 8:36; Jer 27:8; Ezek 18:31
14 [a]Jer 27:9; 2 Cor 11:13-15 [b]Jer 14:14; Ezek 13:22
15 [a]Jer 23:21 [b]Jer 23:25 [c]2 Chr 25:16; Jer 27:10 [d]Jer 6:13-15
16 [a]2 Kin 24:13; 2 Chr 36:7; Jer 28:3; Dan 1:2 [b]Jer 27:10
17 [a]Jer 7:34
18 [a]1 Kin 18:24 [b]1 Sam 7:8; Jer 18:20

LORD, in the house of the king of Judah
and in Jerusalem may not go to Babylon.
19 "For thus says the LORD of hosts concerning the [a]pillars, concerning the sea,
concerning the stands and concerning
the rest of the vessels that are left in this
city,
20 which Nebuchadnezzar king of
Babylon did not take when he [a]carried
into exile Jeconiah the son of Jehoiakim,
king of Judah, from Jerusalem to Babylon,
and all the nobles of Judah and Jerusalem.
21 "Yes, thus says the LORD of hosts, the
God of Israel, concerning the vessels that
are left in the house of the LORD and in
the house of the king of Judah and in
Jerusalem,
22 'They will be [a]carried to Babylon
and they will be there until the [b]day I
visit them,' declares the LORD. 'Then I
will [c]bring them [1]back and restore them
to this place.' "

Hananiah's False Prophecy

28 Now in the same year, [a]in the
beginning of the reign of [b]Zede-
kiah king of Judah, in the fourth year, in
the fifth month, [c]Hananiah the son of
Azzur, the prophet, who was from [d]Gib-
eon, spoke to me in the house of the LORD
in the presence of the priests and all the
people, saying,
2 "[a]Thus says the LORD of hosts, the
God of Israel, 'I have broken the yoke of
the king of Babylon.
3 'Within two years I am going to
bring back to this place [a]all the vessels of
the LORD'S house, which Nebuchadnezzar king of Babylon took away from this
place and carried to Babylon.
4 'I am [a]also going to bring back to
this place [b]Jeconiah the son of Jehoiakim, king of Judah, and all the [c]exiles of
Judah who went to Babylon,' declares the
LORD, 'for I will break the [d]yoke of the
king of Babylon.' "
5 ¶ Then the prophet Jeremiah spoke
to the prophet Hananiah in the presence
of the priests and in the presence of all
the people who were standing in the
[a]house of the LORD,
6 and the prophet Jeremiah said,
"[a]Amen! May the LORD do so; may the
LORD [1]confirm your words which you
have prophesied to bring back the vessels
of the LORD'S house and all the exiles,
from Babylon to this place.
7 "Yet [a]hear now this word which I
am about to speak in your hearing and in
the hearing of all the people!
8 "The prophets who were before me
and before you from ancient times
[a]prophesied against many lands and
against great kingdoms, of war and of calamity and of pestilence.
9 "The prophet who prophesies of
peace, [a]when the word of the prophet
comes to pass, then that prophet will be
known *as* one whom the LORD has truly
sent."
10 ¶ Then Hananiah the prophet took
the [a]yoke from the neck of Jeremiah the
prophet and broke it.
11 Hananiah spoke in the presence of
all the people, saying, "[a]Thus says the
LORD, 'Even so will I break within two
full years the yoke of Nebuchadnezzar
king of Babylon from the neck of all the
nations.' " Then the prophet Jeremiah
went his way.
12 ¶ The [a]word of the LORD came to
Jeremiah after Hananiah the prophet had
broken the yoke from off the neck of the
prophet Jeremiah, saying,
13 "Go and speak to Hananiah, saying,
'Thus says the LORD, "You have broken
the yokes of wood, but you have made
instead of them [a]yokes of iron."
14 'For thus says the LORD of hosts, the
God of Israel, "I have put a [a]yoke of iron
on the neck of all these nations, that they
may serve Nebuchadnezzar king of Babylon; and they will [b]serve him. And [c]I
have also given him the beasts of the
field." ' "
15 Then Jeremiah the prophet said to
Hananiah the prophet, "Listen now, Hananiah, the LORD has not sent you, and
[a]you have made this people trust in a lie.
16 "Therefore thus says the LORD, '[a]Be-
hold, I am about to [1]remove you from the
face of the earth. This year you are going
to [b]die, because you have [2c]counseled
rebellion against the LORD.' "
17 ¶ So Hananiah the prophet died in
the same year in the seventh month.

Message to the Exiles

29 Now these are the words of the
[a]letter which Jeremiah the
prophet sent from Jerusalem to the rest of
the elders of the exile, the priests, the
prophets and all the people whom Nebuchadnezzar had taken into exile from Jerusalem to Babylon.
2 (This was after King [a]Jeconiah and
the [b]queen mother, the court officials,
the princes of Judah and Jerusalem, the
craftsmen and the smiths had departed
from Jerusalem.)
3 *The letter was sent* by the hand of
Elasah the son of Shaphan, and Gemariah
the son of [a]Hilkiah, whom Zedekiah king
of Judah sent to Babylon to Nebuchadnezzar king of Babylon, saying,
4 "Thus says the LORD of hosts, the
God of Israel, to all the exiles whom I

19 [a]1 Kin 7:15; 2 Kin 25:13,17; Jer 52:17-23
20 [a]2 Kin 24:12,14-16; 2 Chr 36:10,18; Jer 22:28; 24:1
22 [1]Lit *up* [a]Jer 34:2,3 [b]Jer 25:11,12; 27:7; 29:10; 32:5 [c]Ezra 1:7-11; 5:13-15; 7:19
28:1 [a]Jer 27:1; 49:34 [b]2 Kin 24:18-20; 2 Chr 36:11-13; Jer 27:3,12 [c]Jer 28:17 [d]Josh 9:3; 10:12; 1 Kin 3:4
2 [a]Jer 27:12; 28:11
3 [a]2 Kin 24:13; 2 Chr 36:10; Jer 27:16; Dan 1:2
4 [a]Jer 22:26,27 [b]2 Kin 25:27; Jer 22:24; 24:1 [c]Jer 22:10 [d]Jer 27:8
5 [a]Jer 28:1
6 [1]Or *fulfill* [a]1 Kin 1:36; Ps 41:13; Jer 11:5
7 [a]1 Kin 22:28
8 [a]Lev 26:14-39; 1 Kin 14:15; 17:1; 22:17; Is 5:5-7; Joel 1:20; Amos 1:2; Nah 1:2
9 [a]Deut 18:22
10 [a]Jer 27:2
11 [a]Jer 14:14; 27:10; 28:15
12 [a]Jer 1:2
13 [a]Ps 107:16; Is 45:2
14 [a]Deut 28:48; Jer 27:8 [b]Jer 25:11 [c]Jer 27:6
15 [a]Jer 20:6; 29:31; Lam 2:14; Ezek 13:2, 3,22; 22:28; Zech 13:3
16 [1]Lit *send you away* [2]Lit *spoken* [a]Gen 7:4; Ex 32:12; Deut 6:15; 1 Kin 13:34 [b]Jer 20:6 [c]Deut 13:5; Jer 29:32
29:1 [a]2 Chr 30:1,6; Esth 9:20; Jer 29:25, 29
2 [a]2 Kin 24:12-16; 2 Chr 36:9,10; Jer 22:24-28; 24:1; 27:20 [b]2 Kin 24:12,15; Jer 13:18; 22:26
3 [a]1 Chr 6:13

have [a]sent into exile from Jerusalem to
Babylon,
5 '[a]Build houses and live *in them;*
and plant gardens and eat their [1]produce.
6 'Take [a]wives and [1]become the fathers of sons and daughters, and take
wives for your sons and give your daughters to husbands, that they may bear sons
and daughters; and multiply there and do
not decrease.
7 '[a]Seek the [1]welfare of the city
where I have sent you into exile, and
[b]pray to the LORD on its behalf; for in its
[1]welfare you will have [1]welfare.'
8 "For thus says the LORD of hosts, the
God of Israel, 'Do not let your [a]prophets
who are in your midst and your diviners
[b]deceive you, and do not listen to [1c]the
dreams which [2]they dream.
9 'For they [a]prophesy falsely to you in
My name; [b]I have not sent them,' declares the LORD.
10 ¶ "For thus says the LORD, 'When
[a]seventy years have been completed for
Babylon, I will visit you and fulfill My
[b]good word to you, to bring you back to
this place.
11 'For I know the [a]plans that I [1]have
for you,' declares the LORD, 'plans for
[b]welfare and not for calamity to give you
a future and a [c]hope.
12 'Then you will [a]call upon Me and
come and pray to Me, and I will [b]listen
to you.
13 'You will [a]seek Me and find *Me*
when you [b]search for Me with all your
heart.
14 'I will be [a]found by you,' declares
the LORD, 'and I will [b]restore your [1]fortunes and will [c]gather you from all the
nations and from all the places where I
have driven you,' declares the LORD, 'and
I will [d]bring you back to the place from
where I sent you into exile.'
15 ¶ "Because you have said, 'The
LORD has raised up [a]prophets for us in
Babylon'—
16 for thus says the LORD concerning
the king who sits on the throne of David,
and concerning all the people who dwell
in this city, your brothers who did [a]not
go with you into exile—
17 thus says the LORD of hosts, 'Behold, I am sending upon them the
[a]sword, famine and pestilence, and I will
make them like [b]split-open figs that cannot be eaten due to rottenness.
18 'I will pursue them with the sword,
with famine and with pestilence; and I
will [a]make them a terror to all the kingdoms of the earth, to be a [b]curse and a
horror and a [c]hissing, and a reproach

4 [a]Jer 24:5
5 [1]Lit *fruit* [a]Jer 29:28
6 [1]Lit *beget* [a]Jer 16:2-4
7 [1]Or *peace* [a]Dan 4:27 [b]Ezra 6:10; Dan 4:19; 1 Tim 2:1
8 [1]Lit *your* [2]Lit *you* [a]Jer 27:9 [b]Jer 14:14; Eph 5:6 [c]Jer 23:25
9 [a]Jer 27:15 [b]Jer 29:31
10 [a]2 Chr 36:21-23; Jer 25:12; Dan 9:2; Zech 7:5 [b]Jer 24:6; Zeph 2:7
11 [1]Lit *am planning* [a]Ps 40:5; Jer 23:5 [b]Is 40:9-11; Jer 30:18-22 [c]Jer 31:17; Hos 2:15
12 [a]Ps 50:15; Jer 33:3; Dan 9:3 [b]Ps 145:19
13 [a]Deut 4:29; Ps 32:6; Matt 7:7 [b]1 Chr 22:19; 2 Chr 22:9; Jer 24:7
14 [1]Or *captivity* [a]Deut 30:1-10; Ps 32:6; Is 55:6 [b]Jer 30:3 [c]Is 43:5; Jer 23:8 [d]Jer 3:14
15 [a]Jer 29:21
16 [a]Jer 38:2
17 [a]Jer 27:8 [b]Jer 24:3
18 [a]Deut 28:25; 2 Chr 29:8; Jer 15:4; Ezek 12:15 [b]Is 65:15; Jer 42:18 [c]Jer 25:9; Lam 2:15
19 [a]Jer 6:19 [b]Jer 25:4
20 [a]Jer 24:5; Ezek 11:9; Mic 4:10
21 [a]Jer 14:14; Lam 2:14; 2 Pet 2:1
22 [1]Lit *taken* [a]Is 65:15 [b]Dan 3:6
23 [a]Gen 34:7; 2 Sam 13:12 [b]Jer 5:8 [c]Jer 29:8 [d]Prov 5:21; Jer 7:11; Mal 3:5; Heb 4:13
24 [a]Jer 29:31
25 [a]Jer 29:1 [b]2 Kin 25:18; Jer 21:1
26 [1]Lit *overseers* [a]Jer 20:1 [b]2 Kin 9:11; Hos 9:7; Mark 3:21; John 10:20; Acts 26:24; 2 Cor 5:13 [c]Deut 13:1-5; Zech 13:1-5 [d]Jer 20:1; Acts 16:24
27 [a]Jer 1:1
28 [1]Lit *fruit* [a]Jer 29:1 [b]Jer 29:10 [c]Jer 29:5
29 [1]Lit *in the ears of* [a]Jer 29:25
31 [a]Jer 29:20 [b]Jer 29:24 [c]Jer 14:14; Ezek 13:8-16 [d]Jer 28:15
32 [a]Jer 36:31

among all the nations where I have driven them,
19 because they have [a]not listened to
My words,' declares the LORD, 'which I
sent to them again and again by [b]My
servants the prophets; but you did not
listen,' declares the LORD.
20 "You, therefore, hear the word of
the LORD, all you exiles, whom I have
[a]sent away from Jerusalem to Babylon.
21 ¶ "Thus says the LORD of hosts, the
God of Israel, concerning Ahab the son of
Kolaiah and concerning Zedekiah the son
of Maaseiah, who are [a]prophesying to
you falsely in My name, 'Behold, I will
deliver them into the hand of Nebuchadnezzar king of Babylon, and he will slay
them before your eyes.
22 'Because of them a [a]curse will be
[1]used by all the exiles from Judah who
are in Babylon, saying, "May the LORD
make you like Zedekiah and like Ahab,
whom the king of Babylon [b]roasted in
the fire,
23 because they have [a]acted foolishly
in Israel, and [b]have committed adultery
with their neighbors' wives and have
[c]spoken words in My name falsely,
which I did not command them; and I am
He who [d]knows and am a witness," declares the LORD.' "
24 ¶ To [a]Shemaiah the Nehelamite
you shall speak, saying,
25 "Thus says the LORD of hosts, the
God of Israel, 'Because you have sent
[a]letters in your own name to all the people who are in Jerusalem, and to [b]Zephaniah the son of Maaseiah, the priest, and
to all the priests, saying,
26 "The LORD has made you priest instead of Jehoiada the priest, to be the
[1a]overseer in the house of the LORD over
every [b]madman who [c]prophesies, to
[d]put him in the stocks and in the iron
collar,
27 now then, why have you not rebuked Jeremiah of [a]Anathoth who
prophesies to you?
28 "For he has [a]sent to us in Babylon,
saying, '*The exile* will be [b]long; [c]build
houses and live *in them* and plant gardens and eat their [1]produce.' " ' "
29 ¶ [a]Zephaniah the priest read this
letter [1]to Jeremiah the prophet.
30 Then came the word of the LORD to
Jeremiah, saying,
31 "Send to [a]all the exiles, saying,
'Thus says the LORD concerning [b]Shemaiah the Nehelamite, "Because Shemaiah
has [c]prophesied to you, although I did
not send him, and he has [d]made you
trust in a lie,"
32 therefore thus says the LORD, "Behold, I am about to [a]punish Shemaiah

the Nehelamite and his [1]descendants;
he will [b]not have anyone living among
this people, [c]and he will not see the
good that I am about to do to My people," declares the LORD, "because he
has [2d]preached rebellion against the
LORD." ' "

Deliverance from Captivity Promised

30 The word which came to Jeremiah from the LORD, saying,
2 "Thus says the LORD, the God of Israel, '[a]Write all the words which I have
spoken to you in a book.
3 'For behold, [a]days are coming,' declares the LORD, 'when I will [b]restore the
[1]fortunes of My people [c]Israel and Judah.' The LORD says, 'I will also [d]bring
them back to the land that I gave to their
forefathers and they shall possess it.' "
4 ¶ Now these are the words which
the LORD spoke concerning Israel and
concerning Judah:
5 ¶ "For thus says the LORD,
'[1]I have heard a sound of
[a]terror,
Of dread, and there is no peace.
6 'Ask now, and see
If a male can give birth.
Why do I see every man
With his hands on his loins, [a]as
a woman in childbirth?
And *why* have all faces turned
pale?
7 'Alas! for that [a]day is great,
There is [b]none like it;
And it is the time of Jacob's
[c]distress,
But he will be [d]saved from it.
8 ¶ 'It shall come about on that day,'
declares the LORD of hosts, 'that I will
[a]break his yoke from off [1]their neck and
will tear off [1]their [b]bonds; and strangers
will no longer [c]make [2]them their slaves.
9 'But they shall serve the LORD their
God and [a]David their king, whom I will
raise up for them.
10 '[a]Fear not, O Jacob My servant,'
declares the LORD,
'And do not be dismayed,
O Israel;
For behold, I will save you
[b]from afar
And your [1]offspring from the
land of their captivity.
And Jacob will return and will be
[c]quiet and at ease,
And [d]no one will make him
afraid.
11 'For [a]I am with you,' declares
the LORD, 'to save you;
For I will [b]destroy completely all
the nations where I have
scattered you,
Only I will [c]not destroy you
completely.
But I will [d]chasten you justly
And will by no means leave you
unpunished.'
12 ¶ "For thus says the LORD,
'Your wound is incurable
And your [a]injury is serious.
13 'There is no one to plead your
cause;
No healing for *your* sore,
[a]No recovery for you.
14 'All your [a]lovers have forgotten
you,
They do not seek you;
For I have [b]wounded you with
the wound of an enemy,
With the [c]punishment of a
[d]cruel one,
Because your [e]iniquity is great
And your [f]sins are numerous.
15 'Why do you cry out over your
injury?
Your pain is incurable.
Because your iniquity is great
And your sins are numerous,
I have done these things to you.
16 'Therefore all who [a]devour you
will be devoured;
And all your adversaries, every
one of them, [b]will go into
captivity;
And those who plunder you will
be for plunder,
And all who prey upon you I will
give for prey.
17 'For I will [1]restore you to
[2a]health
And I will heal you of your
wounds,' declares the LORD,
'Because they have called you an
[b]outcast, saying:
"It is Zion; no one [3]cares
for her." '

Restoration of Jacob

18 ¶ "Thus says the LORD,
'Behold, I will [a]restore the
[1]fortunes of the tents of
Jacob
And [b]have compassion on his
dwelling places;
And the [c]city will be rebuilt on
its ruin,
And the [d]palace will stand on its
rightful place.
19 'From them will proceed
[a]thanksgiving
And the voice of those who
[1b]celebrate;

32 [1]Lit *seed* [2]Lit *spoken* [b]1 Sam 2:30-34; Jer 22:30 [c]2 Kin 7:2,19,20; Jer 17:6; 29:10 [d]Deut 13:5; Jer 28:16
30:2 [a]Is 30:8; Jer 25:13; 36:4, 28,32; Hab 2:2
3 [1]Or *captivity* [a]Jer 29:10 [b]Ps 53:6; Jer 29:14; 30:18; 32:44; Ezek 39:25; Amos 9:14; Zeph 3:20 [c]Jer 3:18 [d]Jer 16:15; 23:7, 8; Ezek 20:42; 36:24
5 [1]Lit *We* [a]Is 5:30; Jer 6:25; 8:16; Amos 5:16-18
6 [a]Jer 4:31; 6:24; 22:23
7 [a]Is 2:12; Hos 1:11; Joel 2:11; Amos 5:18; Zeph 1:14 [b]Lam 1:12; Dan 9:12; 12:1 [c]Jer 2:27,28; 14:8 [d]Jer 30:10; 50:19
8 [1]So Gr; Heb *your* [2]Lit *him their slave* [a]Is 9:4; Jer 2:20; Ezek 34:27 [b]Jer 27:2 [c]Ezek 34:27
9 [a]Is 55:3-5; Ezek 34:23,24; 37:24,25; Hos 3:5; Luke 1:69; Acts 2:30; 13:23,34
10 [1]Lit *seed* [a]Is 41:13; 43:5; 44:2; Jer 46:27, 28 [b]Is 60:4; Jer 23:3,8; 29:14 [c]Is 35:9; Jer 33:16; Hos 2:18 [d]Mic 4:4
11 [a]Jer 1:8,19 [b]Jer 46:28; Amos 9:8 [c]Jer 4:27; 5:10,18 [d]Ps 6:1; Jer 10:24
12 [a]2 Chr 36:16; Jer 15:18; 30:15
13 [a]Jer 14:19; 46:11
14 [a]Jer 22:20, 22; Lam 1:2 [b]Lam 2:4,5 [c]Job 30:21 [d]Jer 6:23; 50:42 [e]Jer 32:30-35; 44:22 [f]Jer 5:6
16 [a]Jer 2:3; 8:16; 10:25 [b]Is 14:2; Joel 3:8
17 [1]Lit *cause to go up* [2]Or *healing* [3]Lit *is seeking* [a]Ex 15:26; Ps 107:20; Is 30:26; Jer 8:22; 33:6 [b]Is 11:12; 56:8; Jer 33:24
18 [1]Or *captivity* [a]Jer 30:3; 31:23 [b]Ps 102:13 [c]Jer 31:4,38-40 [d]1 Chr 29:1,19; Ps 48:3,13; 122:7
19 [1]Or *dance* [a]Is 12:1; 35:10; 51:3; Jer 17:26; 33:11 [b]Ps 126:1, 2; Is 51:11; Jer 31:4; Zeph 3:14

the LORD, "for I will [c]forgive their iniquity, and their [d]sin I will remember no
more."
35 ¶ Thus says the LORD,
Who [a]gives the sun for light
by day
And the [1]fixed order of the
moon and the stars for light
by night,
Who [b]stirs up the sea so that its
waves roar;
[c]The LORD of hosts is His name:
36 "[a]If [1]this fixed order departs
From before Me," declares the
LORD,
"Then the offspring of Israel also
will [b]cease
From being a nation before Me
[2]forever."
37 Thus says the LORD,
"[a]If the heavens above can be
measured
And the foundations of the earth
searched out below,
Then I will also [b]cast off all the
offspring of Israel
For all that they have done,"
declares the LORD.
38 ¶ "Behold, days are coming," declares the LORD, "when the [a]city will be
rebuilt for the LORD from the [b]Tower of
Hananel to the [c]Corner Gate.
39 "The [a]measuring line will go out
farther straight ahead to the hill Gareb;
then it will turn to Goah.
40 "And [a]the whole valley of the dead
bodies and of the ashes, and all the fields
as far as the brook [b]Kidron, to the corner
of the [c]Horse Gate toward the east, shall
be [d]holy to the LORD; it will not be
plucked up or overthrown anymore forever."

Jeremiah Imprisoned

32 The word that came to Jeremiah
from the LORD in the [a]tenth year
of Zedekiah king of Judah, which was the
eighteenth year of Nebuchadnezzar.
2 Now at that time the army of the
king of Babylon was besieging Jerusalem,
and Jeremiah the prophet was shut up in
the [a]court of the guard, which *was in* the
house of the king of Judah,
3 because Zedekiah king of Judah
had [a]shut him up, saying, "Why do
you [b]prophesy, saying, '[c]Thus says the
LORD, "Behold, I am about to [d]give this
city into the hand of the king of Babylon,
and he will take it;
4 and Zedekiah king of Judah will
[a]not escape out of the hand of the Chaldeans, but he will surely be given into the
hand of the king of Babylon, and he will
[b]speak with him [1]face to face and see
him eye to eye;
5 and he will [a]take Zedekiah to Babylon, and he will be there until I visit
him," declares the LORD. "If you fight
against the Chaldeans, you will [b]not succeed"'?"
6 ¶ And Jeremiah said, "The word of
the LORD came to me, saying,
7 'Behold, Hanamel the son of Shallum your uncle is coming to you, saying,
"Buy for yourself my field which is at
[a]Anathoth, for you have the [b]right of
redemption to buy *it*."'
8 "Then Hanamel my uncle's son
came to me in the [a]court of the guard
according to the word of the LORD and
said to me, 'Buy my field, please, that is
at [b]Anathoth, which is in the land of
Benjamin; for you have the right of possession and the redemption is yours; buy
it for yourself.' Then I knew that this was
the [c]word of the LORD.
9 ¶ "I bought the field which was at
Anathoth from Hanamel my uncle's son,
and I [a]weighed out the silver for him,
seventeen [b]shekels of silver.
10 "I [1a]signed and [b]sealed the deed,
and [c]called in witnesses, and weighed
out the silver on the scales.
11 "Then I took the deeds of purchase,
both the sealed *copy containing* the
[a]terms and conditions and the open
copy;
12 and I gave the deed of purchase to
[a]Baruch the son of [b]Neriah, the son of
Mahseiah, in the sight of Hanamel my
uncle's *son* and in the sight of the witnesses who signed the deed of purchase,
before all the Jews who were sitting in
the court of the guard.
13 "And I commanded Baruch in their
presence, saying,
14 'Thus says the LORD of hosts, the
God of Israel, "Take these deeds, this
sealed deed of purchase and this open
deed, and put them in an earthenware
jar, that they may [1]last a long time."
15 'For thus says the LORD of hosts, the
God of Israel, "[a]Houses and fields and
vineyards will again be bought in this
land."'

Jeremiah Prays and God Explains

16 ¶ "After I had given the deed of
purchase to Baruch the son of Neriah,
then I [a]prayed to the LORD, saying,
17 '[a]Ah Lord [1]GOD! Behold, You have
[b]made the heavens and the earth by
Your great power and by Your outstretched arm! [c]Nothing is too difficult
for You,
18 who [a]shows lovingkindness to
thousands, but [b]repays the iniquity of fa-

34 [c]Jer 33:8; Mic 7:18; Rom 11:27 [d]Is 43:25; Heb 10:17
35 [1]Lit *statutes* [a]Gen 1:14-18; Deut 4:19; Ps 19:1-6 [b]Is 51:15 [c]Jer 10:16
36 [1]Lit *these statutes* [2]Lit *all the days* [a]Ps 89:36; Is 54:9; Jer 33:20-26 [b]Amos 9:8
37 [a]Is 40:12; Jer 33:22 [b]Jer 33:24-26; Rom 11:2-5
38 [a]Jer 30:18 [b]Neh 3:1; Zech 14:10 [c]2 Kin 14:13; 2 Chr 26:9
39 [a]Zech 2:1
40 [a]Jer 7:32 [b]2 Sam 15:23; 2 Kin 23:6; John 18:1 [c]2 Kin 11:16; 2 Chr 23:15; Neh 3:28 [d]Joel 3:17; Zech 14:20
32:1 [a]2 Kin 25:1; Jer 39:1
2 [a]Neh 3:25; Jer 33:1
3 [a]2 Kin 6:32 [b]Jer 26:8 [c]Jer 21:3-7 [d]Jer 21:4-7
4 [1]Lit *mouth to mouth* [a]2 Kin 25:4-7; Jer 37:17 [b]Jer 39:5
5 [a]Jer 27:22; Ezek 12:12 [b]Ezek 17:9
7 [a]Jer 1:1 [b]Lev 25:25; Ruth 4:3
8 [a]Jer 32:2 [b]Jer 1:1 [c]1 Sam 9:16; 1 Kin 22:25; Jer 32:25
9 [a]Gen 23:16; Zech 11:12 [b]Gen 24:22; Ex 21:32; Neh 5:15; Ezek 4:10
10 [1]Or *wrote...on the document* [a]Is 44:5; Jer 32:44 [b]Deut 32:34; Job 14:17 [c]Ruth 4:1; Is 8:2
11 [a]Luke 2:27
12 [a]Jer 32:16 [b]Jer 51:59
14 [1]Lit *stand many days*
15 [a]Jer 30:18; Amos 9:14; Zech 3:10
16 [a]Gen 32:9-12; Jer 12:1; Phil 4:6
17 [1]Heb *YHWH,* usually rendered *LORD* [a]Jer 1:6 [b]2 Kin 19:15; Ps 102:25; Is 40:26-29; Jer 27:5 [c]Gen 18:14; Jer 32:27; Zech 8:6; Matt 19:26; Mark 10:27; Luke 1:37
18 [a]Ex 20:6; Deut 5:9 [b]1 Kin 14:9; Matt 23:32-36

thers into the bosom of their children after them, O [c]great and [d]mighty God. The [e]LORD of hosts is His name;

19 [a]great in counsel and mighty in deed, whose [b]eyes are open to all the ways of the sons of men, [c]giving to everyone according to his ways and according to the fruit of his deeds;

20 who has [a]set signs and wonders in the land of Egypt, *and* even to this day both in Israel and among mankind; and You have [b]made a name for Yourself, as at this day.

21 'You [a]brought Your people Israel out of the land of Egypt with signs and with wonders, and with a strong hand and with an outstretched arm and with great terror;

22 and gave them this land, which You [a]swore to their forefathers to give them, a land flowing with milk and honey.

23 'They [a]came in and took possession of it, but they [b]did not obey Your voice or [c]walk in Your law; they have done nothing of all that You commanded them to do; therefore You have made [d]all this calamity come upon them.

24 'Behold, the [a]siege ramps have reached the city to take it; and the city is [b]given into the hand of the Chaldeans who fight against it, because of the [c]sword, the famine and the pestilence; and what You have spoken has [d]come to pass; and behold, You see *it*.

25 'You have said to me, O Lord [1]GOD, "Buy for yourself the field with money and call in witnesses"—although the city is given into the hand of the Chaldeans.' "

26 ¶ Then the word of the LORD came to Jeremiah, saying,

27 "Behold, I am the LORD, the [a]God of all flesh; is anything [b]too difficult for Me?"

28 Therefore thus says the LORD, "Behold, I am about to [a]give this city into the hand of the Chaldeans and into the hand of Nebuchadnezzar king of Babylon, and he will take it.

29 "The Chaldeans who are fighting against this city will enter and [a]set this city on fire and burn it, with the [b]houses where *people* have offered incense to Baal on their roofs and poured out drink offerings to other gods to provoke Me to anger.

30 "Indeed the sons of Israel and the sons of Judah have been doing only [a]evil in My sight from their youth; for the sons of Israel have been only [b]provoking Me to anger by the work of their hands," declares the LORD.

31 "Indeed this city has been to Me *a* [a]*provocation of* My anger and My wrath from the day that they built it, even to this day, so that it should be [b]removed from before My face,

32 because of all the evil of the sons of Israel and the sons of Judah which they have done to provoke Me to anger—they, their [a]kings, their leaders, their priests, their prophets, the men of Judah and the inhabitants of Jerusalem.

33 "They have turned *their* back to Me and not *their* face; though *I* taught them, [1a]teaching again and again, they would not listen [2]and receive instruction.

34 "But they [a]put their detestable things in the house which is called by My name, to defile it.

35 "They built the [a]high places of Baal that are in the valley of Ben-hinnom to cause their sons and their daughters to pass through *the fire* to [b]Molech, which I had not commanded them nor had it [1]entered My mind that they should do this abomination, to cause Judah to sin.

36 ¶ "Now therefore thus says the LORD God of Israel concerning this city of which you say, 'It is [a]given into the hand of the king of Babylon by sword, by famine and by pestilence.'

37 "Behold, I will [a]gather them out of all the lands to which I have driven them in My anger, in My wrath and in great indignation; and I will bring them back to this place and [b]make them dwell in safety.

38 "They shall be [a]My people, and I will be their God;

39 and I will [a]give them one heart and one way, that they may fear Me always, for their own [b]good and for *the good of* their children after them.

40 "I will make an [a]everlasting covenant with them that I will [b]not turn away from them, to do them good; and I will [c]put the fear of Me in their hearts so that they will not turn away from Me.

41 "I will [a]rejoice over them to do them good and will [1]faithfully [b]plant them in this land with [c]all My heart and with all My soul.

42 "For thus says the LORD, '[a]Just as I brought all this great disaster on this people, so I am going to [b]bring on them all the good that I am promising them.

43 '[a]Fields will be bought in this land of which you say, "[b]It is a desolation, without man or beast; it is given into the hand of the Chaldeans."

44 'Men will buy fields for money, [1a]sign and seal deeds, and call in witnesses in the [b]land of Benjamin, in the environs of Jerusalem, in the cities of Ju-

18 [c]Ps 145:3 [d]Ps 50:1; Is 9:6; Jer 20:11 [e]Jer 10:16
19 [a]Is 9:6 [b]Job 34:21; Jer 23:24 [c]Ps 62:12; Jer 17:10; Matt 16:27; John 5:29
20 [a]Ps 78:43 [b]Ex 9:16; Is 63:12; Dan 9:15
21 [a]Ex 6:6; Deut 4:34; 2 Sam 7:23; 1 Chr 17:21; Ps 136:11
22 [a]Ex 3:8; Deut 1:8; Ps 105:9-11; Jer 11:5
23 [a]Ps 44:2; Jer 2:7 [b]Neh 9:26; Jer 11:8; Dan 9:10-14 [c]Ezra 9:7; Jer 26:4 [d]Lam 1:18; Dan 9:11
24 [a]Jer 33:4; Ezek 21:22 [b]Jer 20:5 [c]Jer 14:12; Ezek 14:21 [d]Deut 4:26; Josh 23:15; Zech 1:6
25 [1]Heb *YHWH*, usually rendered LORD
27 [a]Num 16:22 [b]Jer 32:17; Matt 19:26
28 [a]2 Kin 25:11; 2 Chr 36:17-21; Jer 19:7-12
29 [a]2 Chr 36:19; Jer 21:10 [b]Jer 19:13
30 [a]Deut 9:7-12; Is 63:10; Jer 2:7 [b]Jer 8:19
31 [a]1 Kin 11:7; 2 Kin 21:4-7; Jer 5:9-11; Matt 23:37 [b]2 Kin 23:27; Jer 27:10
32 [a]Ezra 9:7; Is 1:4-6; Jer 2:26; Dan 9:8
33 [1]Lit *rising up early and teaching* [2]Lit *to* [a]2 Chr 36:15; Jer 7:13; John 8:2
34 [a]2 Kin 21:1-7; Jer 7:30; Ezek 8:5
35 [1]Lit *come up into My heart* [a]2 Chr 28:2; Jer 7:31 [b]Lev 18:21; 1 Kin 11:7; 2 Kin 23:10; Acts 7:43
36 [a]Jer 32:24
37 [a]Deut 30:3; Ps 106:47; Is 11:11-16; Jer 16:14; Ezek 11:17; Hos 1:11; Amos 9:14 [b]Jer 23:6; Ezek 34:25; Zech 14:11
38 [a]Jer 24:7
39 [a]2 Chr 30:12; Jer 31:33; Ezek 11:19; John 17:21; Acts 4:32 [b]Deut 11:18-21; Ezek 37:25
40 [a]Is 55:3; Jer 31:33; Ezek 37:26 [b]Deut 31:6; Ezek 39:29 [c]Jer 24:7
41 [1]Or *truly* [a]Deut 30:9; Is 62:5 [b]Jer 24:6; Amos 9:15 [c]Hos 2:19
42 [a]Jer 31:28; Zech 8:14 [b]Jer 33:14
43 [a]Jer 32:15; Ezek 37:11-14 [b]Jer 33:10
44 [1]Or *write...on the document* [a]Jer 32:10 [b]Jer 17:26

dah, in the cities of the hill country, in
the cities of the lowland and in the cities
of the [2]Negev; for I will [c]restore their
[3]fortunes,' declares the LORD."

Restoration Promised

33 Then the word of the LORD came
to Jeremiah the second time,
while he was still [1][a]confined in the
court of the guard, saying,
2 "Thus says [a]the LORD who made
[1]*the earth,* the LORD who formed it to
establish it, the [b]LORD is His name,
3 '[a]Call to Me and I will answer you,
and I will tell you [b]great and mighty
things, [c]which you do not know.'
4 "For thus says the LORD God of Israel
concerning the [a]houses of this city, and
concerning the houses of the kings of Judah which are broken down *to make a*
defense against the [b]siege ramps and
against the sword,
5 'While *they* are coming to [a]fight
with the Chaldeans and to fill them with
the corpses of men whom I have slain in
My anger and in My wrath, and I have
[b]hidden My face from this city because
of all their wickedness:
6 'Behold, I will bring to it [a]health
and healing, and I will heal them; and I
will reveal to them an [b]abundance of
peace and truth.
7 'I will [a]restore the [1]fortunes of Judah and the fortunes of Israel and will
[b]rebuild them as they were at first.
8 'I will [a]cleanse them from all their
iniquity by which they have sinned
against Me, and I will pardon all their
iniquities by which they have sinned
against Me and by which they have transgressed against Me.
9 '[1]It will be to Me a [a]name of joy,
praise and glory before [b]all the nations of
the earth which will hear of all the [c]good
that I do for them, and they will [d]fear and
tremble because of all the good and all the
peace that I make for it.'
10 ¶ "Thus says the LORD, 'Yet again
there will be heard in this place, of which
you say, "It is a [a]waste, without man and
without beast," *that is,* in the cities of
Judah and in the streets of Jerusalem that
are [b]desolate, without man and without
inhabitant and without beast,
11 the voice of [a]joy and the voice of
gladness, the voice of the bridegroom and
the voice of the bride, the voice of those
who say,

"[b]Give thanks to the LORD of
hosts,
For the LORD is good,
For His lovingkindness is
everlasting";

and of those who bring a [c]thank offering
into the house of the LORD. For I will
restore the [1]fortunes of the land as they
were at first,' says the LORD.
12 ¶ "Thus says the LORD of hosts,
'There will again be in this place which is
waste, [a]without man or beast, and in all
its cities, a [1]habitation of shepherds who
rest their [b]flocks.
13 'In the [a]cities of the hill country, in
the cities of the lowland, in the cities of
the Negev, in the land of Benjamin, in the
environs of Jerusalem and in the cities of
Judah, the flocks will again [b]pass under
the hands of the one who numbers
them,' says the LORD.

The Davidic Kingdom

14 ¶ 'Behold, [a]days are coming,' declares the LORD, 'when I will [b]fulfill the
good word which I have spoken concerning the house of Israel and the house of
Judah.
15 'In those days and at that time I will
cause a [a]righteous Branch of David to
spring forth; and He shall execute [b]jus-
tice and righteousness on the earth.
16 'In those days [a]Judah will be saved
and Jerusalem will dwell in safety; and
this is *the name* by which she will be
called: the [b]LORD is our righteousness.'
17 "For thus says the LORD, '[1]David
shall [a]never lack a man to sit on the
throne of the house of Israel;
18 [1]and the [a]Levitical priests shall
never lack a man before Me to offer burnt
offerings, to burn grain offerings and to
[b]prepare sacrifices [2]continually.' "
19 ¶ The word of the LORD came to
Jeremiah, saying,
20 "Thus says the LORD, 'If you can
[a]break My covenant for the day and My
covenant for the night, so that day and
night will not be at their appointed time,
21 then [a]My covenant may also be
broken with David My servant so that he
will not have a son to reign on his throne,
and with the Levitical priests, My ministers.
22 'As the [a]host of heaven cannot be
counted and the [b]sand of the sea cannot
be measured, so I will [c]multiply the
[1]descendants of David My servant and
the [d]Levites who minister to Me.' "
23 ¶ And the word of the LORD came
to Jeremiah, saying,
24 "Have you not observed what this
people have spoken, saying, 'The [a]two
families which the LORD chose, He has
[b]rejected them'? Thus they [c]despise My
people, no longer are they as a nation [1]in
their sight.

44 [2]I.e. South country [3]Or *captivity* [c]Jer 31:23
33:1 [1]Lit *shut up* [a]Jer 32:2
2 [1]Lit *it* [a]Jer 51:19 [b]Ex 3:15; Jer 10:16
3 [a]Ps 50:15; Is 55:6; Jer 29:12 [b]Jer 32:17 [c]Is 48:6
4 [a]Is 32:13 [b]Jer 32:24; Ezek 4:2; Hab 1:10
5 [a]Jer 21:4-7 [b]Is 8:17; Jer 21:10; Mic 3:4
6 [a]Jer 17:14; Hos 6:1 [b]Is 66:12; Gal 5:22
7 [1]Or *captivity* [a]Ps 85:1; Jer 30:18; Amos 9:14 [b]Is 1:26; Jer 30:18; Amos 9:14
8 [a]Ps 51:2; Is 44:22; Jer 50:20; Ezek 36:25; Mic 7:18; Zech 13:1; Heb 9:11-14
9 [1]I.e. This city [a]Is 62:2; Jer 13:11 [b]Jer 3:17 [c]Jer 24:6 [d]Neh 6:16; Ps 40:3; Is 60:5; Hos 3:5
10 [a]Jer 32:43 [b]Jer 26:9
11 [1]Or *captivity* [a]Is 35:10 [b]1 Chr 16:8; 2 Chr 5:13; Ezra 3:11; Ps 100:4 [c]Lev 7:12; Ps 107:22; Jer 17:26; Heb 13:15
12 [1]Or *pasture* [a]Jer 32:43 [b]Is 65:10; Jer 31:12; Ezek 34:12-15; Zeph 2:6
13 [a]Jer 17:26 [b]Lev 27:32; Luke 15:4
14 [a]Jer 23:5 [b]Is 32:1; Jer 29:10; Ezek 34:23-25; Hag 2:6-9
15 [a]Is 4:2; Jer 23:5; Zech 3:8 [b]Ps 72:1-5
16 [a]Is 45:17; Jer 23:6 [b]Is 45:24; Jer 23:6; 1 Cor 1:30; 2 Cor 5:21; Phil 3:9
17 [1]Lit *There shall not be cut off for David* [a]2 Sam 7:16; 1 Kin 2:4; 1 Chr 17:11-14; Ps 89:29-37
18 [1]Lit *there shall not be cut off for the Levitical priests* [2]Lit *all the days* [a]Num 3:5-10; Deut 18:1; Josh 3:3; Ezek 44:15 [b]Ezra 3:5; Heb 13:15
20 [a]Ps 89:37; Is 54:9; Jer 31:35-37
21 [a]2 Sam 23:5; 2 Chr 7:18
22 [1]Lit *seed* [a]Gen 15:5; Jer 31:37 [b]Gen 22:17 [c]Ezek 37:24-27 [d]Is 66:21; Jer 33:18
24 [1]Lit *to their faces* [a]Is 7:17; Jer 3:7; Ezek 37:22 [b]Jer 30:17 [c]Neh 4:2-4; Esth 3:6; Ps 44:13

25 "Thus says the LORD, 'If My [a]covenant *for* day and night *stand* not, *and* the [1]fixed patterns of heaven and earth I have [b]not established,

26 then I would [a]reject the [1]descendants of Jacob and David My servant, [2]not taking from his [1]descendants [b]rulers over the [1]descendants of Abraham, Isaac and Jacob. But I will [c]restore their [3]fortunes and will have [d]mercy on them.' "

A Prophecy against Zedekiah

34 The word which came to Jeremiah from the LORD, when [a]Nebuchadnezzar king of Babylon and all his army, with [b]all the kingdoms of the earth that were under his dominion and all the peoples, were fighting against Jerusalem and against all its cities, saying,

2 "Thus says the LORD God of Israel, '[a]Go and speak to Zedekiah king of Judah and say to him: "Thus says the LORD, 'Behold, [b]I am giving this city into the hand of the king of Babylon, and [c]he will burn it with fire.

3 '[a]You will not escape from his hand, for you will surely be captured and delivered into his hand; and you will [b]see the king of Babylon eye to eye, and he will speak with you [1]face to face, and you will go to Babylon.' " '

4 "Yet hear the word of the LORD, O Zedekiah king of Judah! Thus says the LORD concerning you, 'You will not die by the sword.

5 'You will die in peace; and as *spices* were burned for your fathers, the former kings who were before you, so they will [a]burn *spices* for you; and [b]they will lament for you, "Alas, lord!" ' For I have spoken the word," declares the LORD.

6 ¶ Then Jeremiah the prophet spoke [a]all these words to Zedekiah king of Judah in Jerusalem

7 when the army of the king of Babylon was fighting against Jerusalem and against all the remaining cities of Judah, *that is,* [a]Lachish and [b]Azekah, for they *alone* remained as [c]fortified cities among the cities of Judah.

8 ¶ The word which came to Jeremiah from the LORD after King Zedekiah had [a]made a covenant with all the people who were in Jerusalem to [b]proclaim [1]*release to them:*

9 that each man should set free his male servant and each man his female servant, a [a]Hebrew man or a Hebrew woman; so that [b]no one should keep them, a Jew his brother, in bondage.

10 And all the [a]officials and all the people obeyed who had entered into the covenant that each man should set free his male servant and each man his female servant, so that no one should keep them any longer in bondage; they obeyed, and set *them free.*

11 But afterward they turned around and took back the male servants and the female servants whom they had set free, and brought them into subjection for male servants and for female servants.

12 ¶ Then the word of the LORD came to Jeremiah from the LORD, saying,

13 "Thus says the LORD God of Israel, 'I [a]made a covenant with your forefathers in the day that I [b]brought them out of the land of Egypt, from the house of bondage, saying,

14 "[a]At the end of seven years each of you shall set free his Hebrew brother who [1]has been sold to you and has served you six years, you shall send him out free from you; but your forefathers [b]did not obey Me or incline their ear to Me.

15 "Although recently you *had* turned and [a]done what is right in My sight, each man proclaiming [1]release to his neighbor, and you had [b]made a covenant before Me [c]in the house which is called by My name.

16 "Yet you [a]turned and [b]profaned My name, and each man [1]took back his male servant and each man his female servant whom you had set free according to their desire, and you brought them into subjection to be your male servants and female servants." '

17 ¶ "Therefore thus says the LORD, 'You have not obeyed Me in proclaiming [1]release each man to his brother and each man to his neighbor. Behold, I am [a]proclaiming a [1]release to you,' declares the LORD, 'to the [b]sword, to the pestilence and to the famine; and I will make you a [c]terror to all the kingdoms of the earth.

18 'I will give the men who have [a]transgressed My covenant, who have not fulfilled the words of the covenant which they made before Me, *when* they [b]cut the calf in two and passed between its parts—

19 the [a]officials of Judah and the officials of Jerusalem, the court officers and the priests and all the people of the land who passed between the parts of the calf—

20 I will give them into the hand of their enemies and into the hand of those who [a]seek their life. And their [b]dead bodies will be food for the birds of the sky and the beasts of the earth.

21 '[a]Zedekiah king of Judah and his officials I will give into the hand of their enemies and into the hand of those who

25 [1]Lit *statutes* [a]Gen 8:22; Jer 31:35,36; 33:20 [b]Ps 74:16,17
26 [1]Lit *seed* [2]Lit *from taking* [3]Or *captivity* [a]Jer 31:37 [b]Gen 49:10 [c]Jer 33:7 [d]Is 14:1; 54:8; Jer 31:20; Ezek 39:25; Hos 1:7; 2:23
34:1 [a]2 Kin 25:1; Jer 32:2; 39:1; 52:4 [b]Jer 1:15; 27:7; Dan 2:37,38
2 [a]2 Chr 36:11, 12; Jer 22:1,2; 37:1,2 [b]Jer 21:10; 32:3; 34:22; 37:8-10 [c]Jer 32:29
3 [1]Lit *mouth to mouth* [a]2 Kin 25:4,5; Jer 21:7; 32:4; 34:21 [b]2 Kin 25:6,7; Jer 39:6,7
5 [a]2 Chr 16:14; 21:19 [b]Jer 22:18
6 [a]1 Sam 3:18; 15:16-24
7 [a]Josh 10:3,5; 2 Kin 14:19; 18:14; Is 36:2 [b]Josh 10:10; 2 Chr 11:9 [c]2 Chr 11:5-10
8 [1]Or *liberty* [a]2 Kin 11:17; 23:2,3 [b]Ex 21:2; Lev 25:10,39-46; Neh 5:1-13; Is 58:6; Jer 34:14, 17
9 [a]Gen 14:13; Ex 2:6 [b]Lev 25:39
10 [a]Jer 26:10,16
13 [a]Ex 24:3,7,8; Deut 5:2,3,27; Jer 31:32 [b]Ex 20:2
14 [1]Or *has sold himself* [a]Ex 21:2; Deut 15:12; 1 Kin 9:22 [b]1 Sam 8:7, 8; 2 Kin 17:13, 14
15 [1]Or *liberty* [a]Jer 34:8 [b]2 Kin 23:3; Neh 10:29 [c]Jer 7:10f; 32:34
16 [1]Lit *caused them to return* [a]1 Sam 15:11; Jer 34:11; Ezek 3:20; 18:24 [b]Ex 20:7; Lev 19:12
17 [1]Or *liberty* [a]Lev 26:34,35; Esth 7:10; Dan 6:24; Matt 7:2 [b]Jer 32:24; 38:2 [c]Deut 28:25; Jer 29:18
18 [a]Deut 17:2; Hos 6:7; 8:1; Rom 2:8 [b]Gen 15:10
19 [a]Jer 34:10; Ezek 22:27; Zeph 3:3,4
20 [a]Jer 11:21; 21:7; 22:25 [b]Deut 28:26; 1 Sam 17:44,46; 1 Kin 14:11; 16:4; Ps 79:2; Jer 7:33; 16:4; 19:7
21 [a]2 Kin 25:18-21; Jer 32:3,4; 39:6; 52:10,24-27; Ezek 17:16

seek their life, and into the hand of the army of the king of Babylon which has [b]gone away from you.

22 'Behold, I am going to command,' declares the LORD, 'and I will bring them back to this city; and they will fight against it and [a]take it and burn it with fire; and I will make the cities of Judah a [b]desolation [c]without inhabitant.' "

The Rechabites' Obedience

35 The word which came to Jeremiah from the LORD in the days of [a]Jehoiakim the son of Josiah, king of Judah, saying,

2 "Go to the house of the [a]Rechabites and speak to them, and bring them into the house of the LORD, into one of the [b]chambers, and give them wine to drink."

3 Then I took Jaazaniah the son of Jeremiah, son of Habazziniah, and his brothers and all his sons and the whole house of the Rechabites,

4 and I brought them into the house of the LORD, into the chamber of the sons of Hanan the son of Igdaliah, the [a]man of God, which was near the chamber of the officials, which was above the chamber of Maaseiah the son of Shallum, [b]the doorkeeper.

5 Then I set before the [1]men of the house of the Rechabites pitchers full of wine and cups; and I said to them, "[a]Drink wine!"

6 But they said, "We will not drink wine, for [a]Jonadab the son of [b]Rechab, our father, commanded us, saying, 'You shall [c]not drink wine, you or your sons, forever.

7 'You shall not build a house, and you shall not sow seed and you shall not plant a vineyard or own one; but in [a]tents you shall dwell all your days, that you may live [b]many days in the land where you [c]sojourn.'

8 "We have [a]obeyed the voice of Jonadab the son of Rechab, our father, in all that he commanded us, not to drink wine all our days, we, *our wives, our sons or* our daughters,

9 nor to build ourselves houses to dwell in; and we [a]do not have vineyard or field or seed.

10 "We have only [a]dwelt in tents, and have obeyed and have done according to all that [b]Jonadab our father commanded us.

11 "But when [a]Nebuchadnezzar king of Babylon came up against the land, we said, 'Come and let us [b]go to Jerusalem before the army of the Chaldeans and before the army of the Arameans.' So we have dwelt in Jerusalem."

21 [b]Jer 37:5-11
22 [a]Jer 34:2 [b]Jer 4:7 [c]Jer 33:10
35:1 [a]2 Kin 23:34-36; 2 Chr 36:5-7; Jer 1:3; Dan 1:1
2 [a]2 Kin 10:15; 1 Chr 2:55 [b]1 Kin 6:5; 1 Chr 9:26
4 [a]Deut 33:1; Josh 14:6; 1 Kin 12:22; 2 Kin 1:9-13 [b]1 Chr 9:18f
5 [1]Lit *sons* [a]Amos 2:12
6 [a]2 Kin 10:15 [b]1 Chr 2:55 [c]Lev 10:9; Num 6:2-4; Judg 13:7; Luke 1:15
7 [a]Gen 25:27; Heb 11:9 [b]Ex 20:12; Eph 6:2 [c]Gen 36:7
8 [a]Prov 1:8; Eph 6:1; Col 3:20
9 [a]Ps 37:16; Jer 35:7; 1 Tim 6:6
10 [a]Jer 35:7 [b]Jer 35:6
11 [a]2 Kin 24:1; Dan 1:1 [b]Jer 4:5-7
13 [a]Is 28:9-12; Jer 5:3
14 [1]Lit *rising early and speaking* [a]Jer 35:6-10 [b]2 Chr 36:15; Jer 7:13 [c]Is 30:9
15 [1]Lit *rising early and speaking* [a]Jer 7:25 [b]Is 1:16; Jer 4:1; Ezek 18:30-32; Acts 26:20 [c]Deut 6:14; Jer 7:6 [d]Jer 7:7 [e]Jer 7:24
16 [a]Jer 35:14; Mal 1:6
17 [a]Josh 23:15; Jer 19:3; Mic 3:12 [b]Prov 1:24; Is 65:12; Jer 7:13; Luke 13:34; Rom 10:21
18 [a]Ex 20:12; Eph 6:1-3
19 [1]Lit *all the days* [a]1 Chr 2:55; Jer 33:17 [b]Jer 15:19; Luke 21:36
36:1 [a]2 Kin 24:1; 2 Chr 36:5-7; Jer 25:1; Dan 1:1
2 [1]Lit *scroll of a book* [a]Ex 17:14; Is 8:1; Jer 36:6; Zech 5:1 [b]Jer 1:9; Hab 2:2 [c]Jer 3:3-10 [d]Jer 1:5 [e]Jer 1:2
3 [a]Jer 26:3; Ezek 12:3

Judah Rebuked

12 ¶ Then the word of the LORD came to Jeremiah, saying,

13 "Thus says the LORD of hosts, the God of Israel, 'Go and say to the men of Judah and the inhabitants of Jerusalem, "[a]Will you not receive instruction by listening to My words?" declares the LORD.

14 "The [a]words of Jonadab the son of Rechab, which he commanded his sons not to drink wine, are observed. So they do not drink *wine* to this day, for they have obeyed their father's command. But I have spoken to you [1b]again and again; yet you have [c]not listened to Me.

15 "Also I have sent to you all My [a]servants the prophets, sending *them* [1]again and again, saying: '[b]Turn now every man from his evil way and amend your deeds, and [c]do not go after other gods to worship them. Then you will [d]dwell in the land which I have given to you and to your forefathers; but you have not [e]inclined your ear or listened to Me.

16 'Indeed, the sons of Jonadab the son of Rechab have [a]observed the command of their father which he commanded them, but this people has not listened to Me.' " '

17 "Therefore thus says the LORD, the God of hosts, the God of Israel, 'Behold, [a]I am bringing on Judah and on all the inhabitants of Jerusalem all the disaster that I have pronounced against them; because I [b]spoke to them but they did not listen, and I have called them but they did not answer.' "

18 ¶ Then Jeremiah said to the house of the Rechabites, "Thus says the LORD of hosts, the God of Israel, 'Because you have [a]obeyed the command of Jonadab your father, kept all his commands and done according to all that he commanded you;

19 therefore thus says the LORD of hosts, the God of Israel, "Jonadab the son of Rechab [a]shall not lack a man to [b]stand before Me [1]always." ' "

Jeremiah's Scroll Read in the Temple

36 In the [a]fourth year of Jehoiakim the son of Josiah, king of Judah, this word came to Jeremiah from the LORD, saying,

2 "Take a [1a]scroll and write on it all the [b]words which I have spoken to you concerning [c]Israel and concerning Judah, and concerning all the [d]nations, from the [e]day I *first* spoke to you, from the days of Josiah, even to this day.

3 "[a]Perhaps the house of Judah will hear all the calamity which I plan to bring

on them, in order that every man will [b]turn from his evil way; then I will [c]forgive their iniquity and their sin."

4 ¶ Then Jeremiah called [a]Baruch the son of Neriah, and Baruch wrote on a [1b]scroll [2]*at the dictation* of Jeremiah all the words of the LORD which He had spoken to him.

5 Jeremiah commanded Baruch, saying, "I am [1a]restricted; I cannot go into the house of the LORD.

6 "So you go and [a]read from the scroll which you have [b]written [1]at my dictation the words of the LORD [2]to the people in the LORD's house on a [c]fast day. And also you shall read them [2]to all *the people of* Judah who come from their cities.

7 "[a]Perhaps their supplication will [1]come before the LORD, and everyone will turn from his evil way, for [b]great is the anger and the wrath that the LORD has pronounced against this people."

8 Baruch the son of Neriah did according to all that Jeremiah the prophet commanded him, [a]reading from the book the words of the LORD in the LORD's house.

9 ¶ Now in the [a]fifth year of Jehoiakim the son of Josiah, king of Judah, in the [b]ninth month, all the people in Jerusalem and all the people who [c]came from the cities of Judah to Jerusalem proclaimed a [d]fast before the LORD.

10 Then Baruch read from the book the words of Jeremiah in the house of the LORD in the [a]chamber of [b]Gemariah the son of Shaphan the [c]scribe, in the upper court, at the [d]entry of the New Gate of the LORD's house, to all the people.

11 ¶ Now when [a]Micaiah the son of Gemariah, the son of Shaphan, had heard all the words of the LORD from the book,

12 he went down to the king's house, into the scribe's chamber. And behold, all the officials were sitting there—[a]Elishama the scribe, and [b]Delaiah the son of Shemaiah, and [c]Elnathan the son of Achbor, and Gemariah the son of Shaphan, and Zedekiah the son of Hananiah, and all the *other* officials.

13 Micaiah [a]declared to them all the words that he had heard when Baruch read from the book to the people.

14 Then all the officials sent [a]Jehudi the son of Nethaniah, the son of Shelemiah, the son of Cushi, to Baruch, saying, "Take in your hand the scroll from which you have read to the people and come." So Baruch the son of Neriah [b]took the scroll in his hand and went to them.

15 They said to him, "Sit down, please, and read it to us." So Baruch [a]read it to them.

16 When they had heard all the words, they turned in [a]fear one to another and said to Baruch, "We will surely [b]report all these words to the king."

17 And they asked Baruch, saying, "Tell us, please, [a]how did you write all these words? *Was it* [1]at his dictation?"

18 Then Baruch said to them, "He [a]dictated all these words to me, and I wrote them with ink on the book."

19 Then the officials said to Baruch, "Go, [a]hide yourself, you and Jeremiah, and do not let anyone know where you are."

The Scroll Is Burned

20 ¶ So they went to the [a]king in the court, but they had deposited the scroll in the chamber of [a]Elishama the scribe, and they reported all the words to the king.

21 Then the king sent Jehudi to get the scroll, and he took it out of the chamber of Elishama the scribe. And Jehudi [a]read it to the king as well as to all the officials who stood beside the king.

22 Now the king was sitting in the [a]winter house in the [b]ninth month, with *a fire* burning in the brazier before him.

23 When Jehudi had read three or four columns, *the king* cut it with a scribe's knife and [a]threw *it* into the fire that was in the brazier, until all the scroll was consumed in the fire that was in the brazier.

24 Yet the king and all his servants who heard all these words were [a]not afraid, nor did they [b]rend their garments.

25 Even though Elnathan and Delaiah and Gemariah [a]pleaded with the king not to burn the scroll, he would not listen to them.

26 And the king commanded Jerahmeel the king's son, Seraiah the son of Azriel, and Shelemiah the son of Abdeel to [a]seize Baruch the scribe and Jeremiah the prophet, but the [b]LORD hid them.

The Scroll Is Replaced

27 ¶ Then the word of the LORD came to Jeremiah after the king had [a]burned the scroll and the words which [b]Baruch had written at the dictation of Jeremiah, saying,

28 "[a]Take again another scroll and write on it all the former words that were [b]on the first scroll which Jehoiakim the king of Judah burned.

29 "And concerning Jehoiakim king of Judah you shall say, 'Thus says the LORD, "You have [a]burned this scroll, saying, '[b]Why have you written on it [1]that the [c]king of Babylon will certainly come and destroy this land, and will make man and beast to cease from it?'"

3 [b]Deut 30:2; 1 Sam 7:3; Is 55:7; Jer 18:8; Jon 3:8 [c]Jon 3:10; Mark 4:12; Acts 3:19
4 [1]Lit *scroll of a book* [2]Lit *from the mouth of* [a]Jer 32:12 [b]Jer 36:14; Ezek 2:9
5 [1]Lit *shut up* [a]Jer 32:2; 2 Cor 11:23
6 [1]Lit *from my mouth* [2]Lit *in the ears of,* and so throughout this context [a]Jer 36:8 [b]Jer 36:4 [c]Jer 36:9; Zech 8:19
7 [1]Lit *fall* [a]1 Kin 8:33; 2 Chr 33:12; Jer 26:3 [b]Deut 28:15; 2 Kin 22:13; Jer 4:4; Lam 4:11
8 [a]Jer 1:17
9 [a]Jer 36:1 [b]Jer 36:22 [c]Jer 36:6 [d]Judg 20:26; 1 Sam 7:6; 2 Chr 20:3; Esth 4:16; Joel 1:14; Jon 3:5
10 [a]Jer 35:4 [b]Jer 36:11 [c]2 Sam 8:17; Jer 52:25 [d]Jer 26:10
11 [a]Jer 36:13
12 [a]Jer 36:20 [b]Jer 36:25 [c]Jer 26:22
13 [a]2 Kin 22:10
14 [a]Jer 36:21 [b]Jer 36:2; Ezek 2:7-10
15 [a]Jer 36:21
16 [a]Jer 36:24; Acts 24:25 [b]Jer 13:18; Amos 7:10
17 [1]Lit *from his mouth,* and so throughout this context [a]John 9:10
18 [a]Jer 36:4
19 [a]1 Kin 17:3; Jer 26:20-24
20 [a]Jer 36:12
21 [a]2 Kin 22:10; 2 Chr 34:18; Ezek 2:4
22 [a]Judg 3:20; Amos 3:15 [b]Jer 36:9
23 [a]1 Kin 22:8; Prov 1:30; Is 5:18; Jer 36:29
24 [a]Ps 36:1; Jer 36:16 [b]Gen 37:29; 2 Sam 1:11; 1 Kin 21:27; 2 Kin 19:1; Is 36:22; Jon 3:6
25 [a]Gen 37:22; Acts 5:34-39
26 [a]1 Kin 19:1-3; Matt 23:34 [b]Ps 91:1
27 [a]Jer 36:23 [b]Jer 36:4
28 [a]Zech 1:5 [b]Jer 36:4
29 [1]Lit *saying* [a]Deut 29:19; Job 15:24; Is 45:9 [b]Is 29:21; Jer 26:9 [c]Jer 25:9-11

30 'Therefore thus says the LORD concerning Jehoiakim king of Judah, "He shall have [a]no one to sit on the throne of David, and his [b]dead body shall be cast out to the heat of the day and the frost of the night.
31 "I will also [a]punish him and his [1]descendants and his servants for their iniquity, and I will [b]bring on them and the inhabitants of Jerusalem and the men of Judah all the calamity that I have declared to them—but they did not listen."' "
32 ¶ Then Jeremiah took another scroll and gave it to Baruch the son of Neriah, the scribe, and he [a]wrote on it at the dictation of Jeremiah all the words of the book which Jehoiakim king of Judah had burned in the fire; and many [1]similar words were added to them.

Jeremiah Warns against Trust in Pharaoh

37 Now [a]Zedekiah the son of Josiah whom Nebuchadnezzar king of Babylon had [b]made king in the land of Judah, reigned as king in place of [c]Coniah the son of Jehoiakim.
2 But [a]neither he nor his servants nor the people of the land listened to the words of the LORD which He spoke through Jeremiah the prophet.
3 ¶ Yet [a]King Zedekiah sent Jehucal the son of Shelemiah, and [b]Zephaniah the son of Maaseiah, the priest, to Jeremiah the prophet, saying, "[c]Please pray to the LORD our God on our behalf."
4 Now Jeremiah was *still* coming in and going out among the people, for they had not *yet* [a]put him in the prison.
5 Meanwhile, [a]Pharaoh's army had set out from Egypt; and when the Chaldeans who had been besieging Jerusalem heard the report about them, they [b]lifted the *siege* from Jerusalem.
6 ¶ Then the word of the LORD came to Jeremiah the prophet, saying,
7 "Thus says the LORD God of Israel, '[a]Thus you are to say to the king of Judah, who sent you to Me to inquire of Me: "Behold, [b]Pharaoh's army which has come out for your assistance is going to return to its own land of Egypt.
8 "The Chaldeans will also [a]return and fight against this city, and they will capture it and burn it with fire." '
9 "Thus says the LORD, 'Do not [a]deceive yourselves, saying, "The Chaldeans will surely go away from us," for they will not go.
10 'For [a]even if you had defeated the entire army of Chaldeans who were fighting against you, and there were *only* wounded men left among them, each man in his tent, they would rise up and [b]burn this city with fire.' "

Jeremiah Imprisoned

11 ¶ Now it happened when the army of the Chaldeans had lifted *the siege* from Jerusalem because of Pharaoh's army,
12 that Jeremiah went out from Jerusalem to go to the land of Benjamin in order to [a]take [1]possession of *some* property there among the people.
13 While he was at the [a]Gate of Benjamin, a captain of the guard whose name was Irijah, the son of Shelemiah the son of Hananiah was there; and he [b]arrested Jeremiah the prophet, saying, "You are [1]going over to the Chaldeans!"
14 But Jeremiah said, "[a]A lie! I am not [1]going over to the Chaldeans"; yet he would not listen to him. So Irijah arrested Jeremiah and brought him to the officials.
15 Then the officials were [a]angry at Jeremiah and beat him, and they [b]put him in jail in the house of Jonathan the scribe, which they had made into the prison.
16 For Jeremiah had come into the [1a]dungeon, that is, the vaulted cell; and Jeremiah stayed there many days.
17 ¶ Now King Zedekiah sent and took him *out;* and in his palace the king [a]secretly asked him and said, "Is there a [b]word from the LORD?" And Jeremiah said, "There is!" Then he said, "You will be [c]given into the hand of the king of Babylon!"
18 Moreover Jeremiah said to King Zedekiah, "[a]*In* what *way* have I sinned against you, or against your servants, or against this people, that you have put me in prison?
19 "[a]Where then are your prophets who prophesied to you, saying, 'The [b]king of Babylon will not come against you or against this land'?
20 "But now, please listen, O my lord the king; please let my [a]petition [1]come before you and do not make me return to the house of Jonathan the scribe, that I may not die there."
21 Then King Zedekiah gave commandment, and they committed Jeremiah to the [a]court of the guardhouse and gave him a loaf of [b]bread daily from the bakers' street, until all the bread in the city was [c]gone. So Jeremiah remained in the court of the guardhouse.

Jeremiah Thrown into the Cistern

38 Now Shephatiah the son of Mattan, and Gedaliah the son of Pashhur, and Jucal the [a]son of Shelemiah, and [b]Pashhur the son of Malchijah heard the

---

30 [a]2 Kin 24:12-15; Jer 22:30 [b]Jer 22:19
31 [1]Lit *seed* [a]Jer 23:34 [b]Deut 28:15; Prov 29:1; Jer 19:15
32 [1]Lit *like those* [a]Ex 4:15; Jer 36:4
37:1 [a]2 Kin 24:17; 1 Chr 3:15; 2 Chr 36:10 [b]Ezek 17:12-21 [c]2 Kin 24:12; 1 Chr 3:16; 2 Chr 36:9; Jer 22:24
2 [a]2 Kin 24:19; 2 Chr 36:12-16; Prov 29:12
3 [a]Jer 21:1 [b]Jer 29:25 [c]1 Kin 13:6; Jer 2:27; Acts 8:24
4 [a]Jer 32:2
5 [a]2 Kin 24:7; Jer 37:7; Ezek 17:15 [b]Jer 37:11
7 [a]2 Kin 22:18; Jer 21:1 [b]Is 30:1-3; Jer 2:18; Lam 4:17; Ezek 17:17
8 [a]Jer 34:22
9 [a]Jer 29:8; Obad 3; Matt 24:4; Eph 5:6
10 [a]Lev 26:36-38; Is 30:17; Jer 21:4 [b]Jer 37:8
12 [1]Or *part in a dividing* [a]Jer 32:8
13 [1]Lit *falling* [a]Jer 38:7; Zech 14:10 [b]Jer 18:18; Luke 23:2; Acts 6:11
14 [1]Lit *falling* [a]Ps 27:12; Jer 40:4-6; Matt 5:11
15 [a]Jer 18:23; Matt 21:35 [b]Gen 39:20; 2 Chr 16:10; Jer 38:26; Acts 5:18
16 [1]Lit *house of the cistern-pit* [a]Jer 38:6
17 [a]1 Kin 14:1-4; Jer 38:5 [b]1 Kin 22:15; 2 Kin 3:11; Jer 15:11 [c]Jer 21:7; Ezek 12:12
18 [a]1 Sam 24:9; Dan 6:22; John 10:32; Acts 25:8
19 [a]Deut 32:37; 2 Kin 3:13; Jer 2:28 [b]Jer 27:14
20 [1]Lit *fall* [a]Jer 36:7
21 [a]Jer 32:2 [b]1 Kin 17:6; Job 5:20; Ps 33:18; Is 33:16 [c]2 Kin 25:3; Jer 38:9
38:1 [a]Jer 37:3 [b]Jer 21:1

words that Jeremiah was speaking to all the people, saying,

2 "Thus says the LORD, 'He who [a]stays in this city will die by the [b]sword and by famine and by pestilence, but he who goes out to the Chaldeans will live and have his *own* [c]life as booty and stay alive.'

3 "Thus says the LORD, 'This city will certainly be [a]given into the hand of the army of the king of Babylon and he will capture it.' "

4 Then the [a]officials said to the king, "Now let this man be put to death, inasmuch as he is [1b]discouraging the men of war who are left in this city and [2]all the people, by speaking such words to them; for this man [c]is not seeking the well-being of this people but rather their harm."

5 So King Zedekiah said, "Behold, he is in your [1]hands; for the king [a]can *do* nothing against you."

6 Then they took Jeremiah and cast him into the [a]cistern *of* Malchijah the king's son, which was in the court of the guardhouse; and they let Jeremiah down with ropes. Now in the cistern there was no water but only [b]mud, and Jeremiah sank into the mud.

7 But [a]Ebed-melech the Ethiopian, [1]a [b]eunuch, while he was in the king's palace, heard that they had put Jeremiah into the cistern. Now the king was sitting in the [c]Gate of Benjamin;

8 and Ebed-melech went out from the king's palace and spoke to the king, saying,

9 "My lord the king, these men have acted wickedly in all that they have done to Jeremiah the prophet whom they have cast into the cistern; and he [1]will die right where he is because of the famine, for there is [a]no more bread in the city."

10 Then the king commanded Ebed-melech the Ethiopian, saying, "Take thirty men from here [1]under your authority and bring up Jeremiah the prophet from the cistern before he dies."

11 So Ebed-melech took the men under his [1]authority and went into the king's palace to *a place* beneath the storeroom and took from there worn-out clothes and worn-out rags and let them down by ropes into the cistern to Jeremiah.

12 Then Ebed-melech the Ethiopian said to Jeremiah, "Now put these worn-out clothes and rags under your armpits under the ropes"; and Jeremiah did so.

13 So they pulled Jeremiah up with the ropes and lifted him out of the cistern, and Jeremiah stayed in the [a]court of the guardhouse.

14 ¶ Then King Zedekiah [a]sent and [1]had Jeremiah the prophet brought to him at the third entrance that is in the house of the LORD; and the king said to Jeremiah, "I am going to [b]ask you something; do not hide anything from me."

15 Then Jeremiah said to Zedekiah, "[a]If I tell you, will you not certainly put me to death? Besides, if I give you advice, you will not listen to me."

16 But King Zedekiah swore to Jeremiah in [a]secret saying, "As the LORD lives, who made this [1b]life for us, surely I will not put you to death nor will I give you over to the hand of [c]these men who are seeking your [1]life."

Interview with Zedekiah

17 ¶ Then Jeremiah said to Zedekiah, "Thus says the LORD [a]God of hosts, the [b]God of Israel, 'If you will indeed [c]go out to the officers of the king of Babylon, then [1]you will live, this city will not be burned with fire, and you and your household will [2]survive.

18 'But if you will [a]not go out to the officers of the king of Babylon, then this city [b]will be given over to the hand of the Chaldeans; and they will burn it with fire, and [c]you yourself will not escape from their hand.' "

19 Then King Zedekiah said to Jeremiah, "I [a]dread the Jews who have [1b]gone over to the Chaldeans, for they may give me over into their hand and they will [c]abuse me."

20 But Jeremiah said, "They will not give you over. Please [1a]obey the LORD in what I am saying to you, that it may go [b]well with you and [2c]you may live.

21 "But if you keep refusing to go out, this is the word which the LORD has shown me:

22 'Then behold, all of the [a]women who have been left in the palace of the king of Judah are going to be brought out to the [1]officers of the king of Babylon; and those women will say,

"[2]Your close friends
Have misled and overpowered
you;
While your feet were sunk in the
mire,
They turned back."

23 'They will also bring out all your wives and your [a]sons to the Chaldeans, and [b]you yourself will not escape from their hand, but will be seized by the hand of the king of Babylon, and [b]this city will be burned with fire.' "

24 ¶ Then Zedekiah said to Jeremiah, "Let no man know about these words and you will not die.

25 "But if the [a]officials hear that I have

2 [a]Jer 21:9 [b]Jer 34:17; 42:17 [c]Jer 21:9; 39:18; 45:5
3 [a]Jer 21:10; 32:3-5
4 [1]Lit *weakening the hands of* [2]Lit *the hands of all* [a]Jer 18:23; 26:11,21; 36:12 [b]Ex 5:4; 1 Kin 18:17,18; 21:20; Neh 6:9; Amos 7:10; Acts 16:20 [c]Jer 29:7
5 [1]Lit *hand* [a]2 Sam 3:39
6 [a]Jer 37:16,21; Acts 16:24 [b]Ps 40:2; 69:2,14, 15; Jer 38:22; Zech 9:11
7 [1]Or *an official* [a]Jer 39:16 [b]Jer 29:2; Acts 8:27 [c]Deut 21:19; Job 29:7; Jer 37:13; Amos 5:10
9 [1]M.T. reads *has died* [a]Jer 37:21; 52:6
10 [1]Lit *in your hand*
11 [1]Lit *hand*
13 [a]Neh 3:25; Jer 32:2; 37:21; 38:6; 39:14,15; Acts 23:35; 24:27; 28:16,30
14 [1]Lit *took Jeremiah the prophet to him* [a]Jer 21:1,2; 37:17 [b]1 Sam 3:17,18; 1 Kin 22:16; Jer 15:11; 42:2-5,20
15 [a]Luke 22:67, 68
16 [1]Lit *soul* [a]Jer 37:17; John 3:2 [b]Num 16:22; 27:16; Is 42:5; 57:16; Zech 12:1; Acts 17:25,28 [c]Jer 34:20; 38:4-6
17 [1]Lit *your soul* [2]Lit *live* [a]Ps 80:7,14; Amos 5:27 [b]1 Chr 17:24; Ezek 8:4 [c]2 Kin 24:12; 25:27-30; Jer 21:8-10; 27:12, 17; 38:2; 39:3
18 [a]Jer 27:8 [b]2 Kin 25:4-10; Jer 24:8-10; 32:3-5; 37:8; 38:3 [c]Jer 32:4; 34:3
19 [1]Lit *fallen* [a]Is 51:12,13; 57:11; John 12:42; 19:12,13 [b]Jer 39:9 [c]2 Chr 30:10; Neh 4:1; Jer 38:22
20 [1]Lit *listen to the voice of* [2]Lit *your soul* [a]2 Chr 20:20; Jer 11:4, 8; 26:13; Dan 4:27; Acts 26:29 [b]Jer 7:23 [c]Gen 19:20; Is 55:3
22 [1]Or *princes* [2]Lit *The men of your peace* [a]Jer 6:12; 8:10; 43:6
23 [a]2 Kin 25:7; Jer 39:6; 41:10 [b]Jer 38:18
25 [a]Jer 38:4-6, 27

talked with you and come to you and say
to you, 'Tell us now what you said to the
king and what the king said to you; do not
hide *it* from us and we will not put you to
death,'
26 then you are to say to them, 'I was
[a]presenting my petition before the king,
not to make me return to the house of
Jonathan to die there.' "
27 Then all the officials came to Jeremiah and questioned him. So he reported
to them in accordance with all these
words which the king had commanded;
and they ceased speaking with him, since
the [1]conversation had not been over-
heard.
28 So Jeremiah [a]stayed in the court of
the guardhouse until the day that Jerusalem was captured.

Jerusalem Captured

39 [1]Now when Jerusalem was captured [2a]in the ninth year of Zedekiah king of Judah, in the tenth month,
Nebuchadnezzar king of Babylon and all
his army came to Jerusalem and laid siege
to it;
2 in the eleventh year of Zedekiah, in
the fourth month, in the ninth *day* of the
month, the city *wall* was [a]breached.
3 Then all the [a]officials of the king of
Babylon came in and sat down at the
[b]Middle Gate: Nergal-sar-ezer, Samgar-
nebu, Sar-sekim the [1]Rab-saris, Nergal-
sar-ezer *the* [2]Rab-mag, and all the rest of
the officials of the king of Babylon.
4 When Zedekiah the king of Judah
and all the men of war saw them, they
[a]fled and went out of the city at night by
way of the king's garden through the gate
[b]between the two walls; and he went out
toward the [1]Arabah.
5 But the army of the [a]Chaldeans
pursued them and overtook Zedekiah in
the [b]plains of Jericho; and they seized
him and brought him up to Nebuchadnezzar king of Babylon at [c]Riblah in the
land of Hamath, and he passed sentence
on him.
6 Then the [a]king of Babylon slew the
sons of *Zedekiah* [b]*before his eyes at Rib-*
lah; the king of Babylon also slew all the
nobles of Judah.
7 He then [a]blinded Zedekiah's eyes
and bound him in [b]fetters of bronze to
bring him to [c]Babylon.
8 The Chaldeans also [a]burned with
fire the king's palace and the houses of
the people, and they [b]broke down the
walls of Jerusalem.
9 As for the rest of the people who
were left in the city, the [1a]deserters
who had gone over to him and [b]the rest
of the people who remained, [c]Nebuzara-
dan the [d]captain of the bodyguard carried *them* into exile in Babylon.
10 But some of the [a]poorest people
who had nothing, [a]Nebuzaradan the captain of the bodyguard left behind in the
land of Judah, and gave them vineyards
and fields [1]at that time.

Jeremiah Spared

11 ¶ Now Nebuchadnezzar king of
Babylon gave orders about [a]Jeremiah
through Nebuzaradan the captain of the
bodyguard, saying,
12 "Take him and [1]look after him, and
[a]do nothing harmful to him, but rather
deal with him just as he tells you."
13 So Nebuzaradan the captain of the
bodyguard sent *word,* along with Nebu-
shazban the [1]Rab-saris, and Nergal-sar-
ezer the [2]Rab-mag, and all the leading
officers of the king of Babylon;
14 they even sent and [a]took Jeremiah
out of the court of the guardhouse and
entrusted him to [b]Gedaliah, the son of
[c]Ahikam, the son of Shaphan, to take
him home. So he stayed among the people.
15 ¶ Now the word of the LORD had
come to Jeremiah while he was [a]con-
fined in the court of the guardhouse, saying,
16 "Go and speak to [a]Ebed-melech the
Ethiopian, saying, 'Thus says the LORD of
hosts, the God of Israel, "Behold, I am
about to bring My words on this city [b]for
disaster and not for [1]prosperity; and they
will [c]take place before you on that day.
17 "But I will [a]deliver you on that
day," declares the LORD, "and you will
not be given into the hand of the men
whom you dread.
18 "For I will certainly rescue you, and
you will not fall by the sword; but you will
have your *own* [a]life as booty, because
you have [b]trusted in Me," declares the
LORD.' "

Jeremiah Remains in Judah

40 The word which came to Jeremiah from the LORD after [a]Nebuzar-
adan captain of the bodyguard had released him from [b]Ramah, when he had
taken him bound in [c]chains among all
the exiles of Jerusalem and Judah who
were being exiled to Babylon.
2 Now the captain of the bodyguard
had taken Jeremiah and said to him, "The
[a]LORD your God promised this calamity
against this place;
3 and the LORD has brought *it* on and
done just as He promised. Because you
people [a]sinned against the LORD and did
not listen to His voice, therefore this
thing has happened to you.

26 [a]Jer 37:20
27 [1]Lit *word*
28 [a]Ps 23:4; Jer 15:20,21; 37:20, 21; 38:13; 39:13,14
39:1 [1]Ch 38:28-b in Heb [2]Ch 39:1 in Heb [a]2 Kin 25:1-12; Jer 52:4; Ezek 24:1, 2
2 [a]2 Kin 25:4; Jer 52:7
3 [1]I.e. chief official [2]I.e. title of a high official [a]Jer 38:17 [b]Jer 21:4
4 [1]I.e. Jordan valley [a]2 Kin 25:4; Is 30:16; Jer 52:7; Amos 2:14 [b]2 Chr 32:5
5 [a]Jer 32:4,5; 38:18,23; 52:8 [b]Josh 4:13; 5:10 [c]2 Kin 23:33; Jer 52:9,26,27
6 [a]2 Kin 25:7; Jer 52:10 [b]Deut 28:34 [c]Jer 21:7; 24:8-10; 34:19-21
7 [a]2 Kin 25:7; Jer 52:11; Ezek 12:13 [b]Judg 16:21 [c]Jer 32:5
8 [a]2 Kin 25:9; Jer 21:10; 38:18; 52:13 [b]2 Kin 25:10; Neh 1:3; Jer 52:14
9 [1]Lit *fallers who had fallen* [a]Jer 38:19; 52:15 [b]Jer 24:8 [c]2 Kin 25:11,20; Jer 39:13; 40:1; 52:12-16,26 [d]Gen 37:36
10 [1]Lit *on that day* [a]2 Kin 25:12; Jer 52:16
11 [a]Job 5:15,16; Jer 1:8; 15:20, 21; Acts 24:23
12 [1]Lit *set your eyes on* [a]Ps 105:14,15; Prov 16:7; 21:1; 1 Pet 3:13
13 [1]I.e. chief official [2]I.e. title of a high official
14 [a]Jer 38:28; 40:1-6 [b]Jer 40:5 [c]2 Kin 22:12,14; 2 Chr 34:20; Jer 26:24
15 [a]Jer 38:28
16 [1]Lit *good* [a]Jer 38:7 [b]Jer 21:10; Dan 9:12; Zech 1:6 [c]Ps 91:8
17 [a]Ps 41:1,2; 50:15
18 [a]Jer 21:9; 38:2; 45:5 [b]Ps 34:22; Jer 17:7,8
40:1 [a]Jer 39:9, 11 [b]Jer 31:15 [c]Acts 12:6,7; 21:13; 28:20; Eph 6:20
2 [a]Lev 26:14-38; Deut 28:15-68; 29:24-28; 31:17; 32:19-25; Jer 22:8,9
3 [a]Jer 50:7; Dan 9:11; Rom 2:5

4 "But now, behold, I am [a]freeing you today from the chains which are on your hands. If [1]you would prefer to come with me to Babylon, come *along*, and I will [2]look after you; but if [3]you would prefer not to come with me to Babylon, [4]never mind. Look, the [b]whole land is before you; go wherever it seems good and right for you to go."

5 As [1]Jeremiah was still not going back, [2]*he said*, "Go on back then to [a]Gedaliah the son of Ahikam, the son of Shaphan, whom the king of Babylon has [b]appointed over the cities of Judah, and stay with him among the people; or else go anywhere it seems right for you to go." So the captain of the bodyguard gave him a [c]ration and a [d]gift and let him go.

6 Then Jeremiah went to [a]Mizpah to [b]Gedaliah the son of Ahikam and stayed with him among the people who were left in the land.

7 ¶ [a]Now all the [1]commanders of the forces that were in the field, they and their men, heard that the king of Babylon had appointed Gedaliah the son of Ahikam over the land and that he had put him in charge of the men, women and [2]children, those of the [b]poorest of the land who had not been exiled to Babylon.

8 So they came to Gedaliah at Mizpah, along with [a]Ishmael the son of Nethaniah, and [b]Johanan and Jonathan the sons of Kareah, and Seraiah the son of Tanhumeth, and the sons of Ephai the [c]Netophathite, and [d]Jezaniah the son of the [e]Maacathite, *both* they and their men.

9 Then Gedaliah the son of Ahikam, the son of Shaphan, [a]swore to them and to their men, saying, "[b]Do not be afraid of serving the Chaldeans; stay in the land and serve the king of Babylon, that it may go well with you.

10 "Now as for me, behold, I am going to stay at Mizpah to [a]stand *for you* before the Chaldeans who come to us; but as for you, [b]gather in wine and [c]summer fruit and oil and put *them* in your *storage* vessels, and live in your cities that you have taken over."

11 Likewise, also all the Jews who were in [a]Moab and among the sons of [b]Ammon and in [c]Edom and who were in all the *other* countries, heard that the *king of Babylon had left* a remnant for Judah, and that he had appointed over them Gedaliah the son of Ahikam, the son of Shaphan.

12 Then all the Jews [a]returned from all the places to which they had been driven away and came to the land of Judah, to Gedaliah at Mizpah, and gathered in wine and summer fruit in great abundance.

13 ¶ Now Johanan the son of Kareah and all the commanders of the forces that were in the field came to Gedaliah at Mizpah

14 and said to him, "Are you well aware that Baalis the king of the sons of [a]Ammon has sent Ishmael the son of Nethaniah to take your life?" But Gedaliah the son of Ahikam did not believe them.

15 Then Johanan the son of Kareah spoke secretly to Gedaliah in Mizpah, saying, "[a]Let me go and kill Ishmael the son of Nethaniah, and not a man will know! Why should he [b]take your life, so that all the Jews who are gathered to you would be scattered and the [c]remnant of Judah would perish?"

16 But Gedaliah the son of Ahikam said to Johanan the son of Kareah, "[a]Do not do this thing, for you are telling a lie about Ishmael."

Gedaliah Is Murdered

41 [a]In the seventh month [b]Ishmael the son of Nethaniah, the son of Elishama, of the royal [1]family and *one* of the chief officers of the king, along with ten men, came to Mizpah to [c]Gedaliah the son of Ahikam. While they [d]were eating bread together there in Mizpah,

2 Ishmael the son of Nethaniah and the ten men who were with him arose and [a]struck down Gedaliah the son of Ahikam, the son of Shaphan, with the sword and [b]put to death the one [c]whom the king of Babylon had appointed over the land.

3 Ishmael also struck down all the Jews who were with him, *that is* with Gedaliah at Mizpah, and the Chaldeans who were found there, the men of war.

4 ¶ Now it happened on the [1]next day after the killing of Gedaliah, when no one knew about *it*,

5 that eighty men [a]came from [b]Shechem, from [c]Shiloh, and from [d]Samaria with [e]their beards shaved off and their clothes torn and [1]their bodies [f]gashed, having grain offerings and incense in their hands to bring to the [g]house of the LORD.

6 Then Ishmael the son of Nethaniah went out from Mizpah to meet them, [a]weeping as he went; and as he met them, he said to them, "Come to Gedaliah the son of Ahikam!"

7 Yet it turned out that as soon as they came inside the city, Ishmael the son of Nethaniah and the men that were with him [a]slaughtered them *and cast them* into the cistern.

4 [1]Lit *it is good in your eyes* [2]Lit *set my eyes on* [3]Lit *it is evil in your eyes* [4]Lit *refrain!* [a]Jer 39:11, 12 [b]Gen 13:9; 20:15; 47:6

5 [1]Lit *he* [2]I.e. Nebuzaradan [a]Jer 39:14 [b]2 Kin 25:23 [c]Jer 52:34 [d]2 Kin 8:7-9

6 [a]Judg 20:1; 21:1; 1 Sam 7:5; 2 Chr 16:6 [b]Jer 39:14

7 [1]Or *princes* [2]Lit *infants* [a]2 Kin 25:23 [b]Jer 39:10; 52:16

8 [a]Jer 40:14; 41:2 [b]Jer 40:13, 15; 42:1; 43:2 [c]2 Sam 23:28, 29; Ezra 2:22; Neh 7:26 [d]Jer 42:1 [e]Deut 3:14; Josh 12:5; 2 Sam 10:6,8

9 [a]1 Sam 20:16, 17; 2 Kin 25:24 [b]Jer 27:11; 38:17-20

10 [a]Deut 1:38; 1 Kin 10:8; Jer 35:19 [b]Deut 16:13; Jer 39:10 [c]Is 16:9; Jer 40:12; 48:32

11 [a]Num 22:1; 25:1,2; Is 16:4; Jer 9:26 [b]1 Sam 11:1; 12:12 [c]Gen 36:8; Is 11:14

12 [a]Jer 43:5

14 [a]1 Sam 11:1-3; 2 Sam 10:1-6; Jer 25:21; 41:10

15 [a]1 Sam 26:8 [b]2 Sam 21:17 [c]Jer 42:2

16 [a]Matt 10:16; 1 Cor 13:5

41:1 [1]Lit *seed* [a]2 Kin 25:25 [b]Jer 40:8,14 [c]Jer 39:14; 40:5,6 [d]Ps 41:9; Jer 40:13,14

2 [a]2 Sam 3:27; 20:9,10; 2 Kin 25:25; Ps 41:9; 109:5; John 13:18 [b]2 Kin 25:25 [c]Jer 40:5

4 [1]Or *second*

5 [1]Lit *having cut themselves* [a]2 Kin 10:13,14 [b]Gen 33:18; 37:12; Judg 9:1; 1 Kin 12:1,25 [c]Josh 18:1; Judg 18:31; 1 Sam 3:21; Ps 78:60 [d]1 Kin 16:24,29 [e]Lev 19:27; Deut 14:1 [f]Deut 14:1; Jer 16:6 [g]1 Sam 1:7; 2 Kin 25:9

6 [a]2 Sam 3:16; Jer 50:4

7 [a]Ps 55:23; Is 59:7; Ezek 22:27; 33:24,26

8 But ten men who were found
among them said to Ishmael, "Do not put
us to death; for we have [a]stores of wheat,
barley, oil and honey hidden in the field."
So he refrained and did not put them to
death along with their companions.
9 ¶ Now as for the cistern where Ishmael had cast all the corpses of the men
whom he had struck down [1]because of
Gedaliah, it was the [a]one that King Asa
had made on [b]account of Baasha, king of
Israel; Ishmael the son of Nethaniah filled
it with the slain.
10 Then Ishmael took captive all the
[a]remnant of the people who were in
Mizpah, the [b]king's daughters and all the
people who were left in Mizpah, whom
Nebuzaradan the captain of the bodyguard had put under the charge of Gedaliah the son of Ahikam; thus Ishmael the
son of Nethaniah took them captive and
proceeded to cross over to the sons of
[c]Ammon.

Johanan Rescues the People

11 ¶ But Johanan the son of Kareah
and all the [a]commanders of the forces
that were with him heard of all the evil
that Ishmael the son of Nethaniah had
done.
12 So they took all the men and went
to [a]fight with Ishmael the son of Nethaniah and they found him by the [b]great
[1]pool that is in Gibeon.
13 Now as soon as all the people who
were with Ishmael saw Johanan the son
of Kareah and the commanders of the
forces that were with him, they were
glad.
14 So all the people whom Ishmael
had taken captive from Mizpah turned
around and came back, and went to Johanan the son of Kareah.
15 But Ishmael the son of Nethaniah
[a]escaped from Johanan with eight men
and went to the sons of Ammon.
16 Then Johanan the son of Kareah
and all the commanders of the forces that
were with him took from Mizpah [a]all the
remnant of the people whom he had [1]re-
covered from Ishmael the son of Nethaniah, after he had struck down Gedaliah the
son of Ahikam, *that is,* the men who were
[2]soldiers, *the* women, *the* [3]children,
and *the* eunuchs, whom he had brought
back from Gibeon.
17 And they went and stayed in
[1a]Geruth Chimham, which is beside
Bethlehem, in order to [b]proceed into
Egypt
18 because of the Chaldeans; for they
were [a]afraid of them, since Ishmael the
son of Nethaniah had struck down Gedaliah the son of Ahikam, whom [b]the king
of Babylon had appointed over the land.

Warning against Going to Egypt

42 Then all the [1]commanders of the
forces, [a]Johanan the son of Kareah, Jezaniah the son of Hoshaiah, and all
the people [b]both small and great approached
2 and said to Jeremiah the prophet,
"Please let our [a]petition [1]come before
you, and [b]pray for us to the LORD your
God, *that is* for all this remnant; because
we are left *but* a [c]few out of many, as
your own eyes *now* see us,
3 that the LORD your God may tell us
the [a]way in which we should walk and
the thing that we should do."
4 Then Jeremiah the prophet said to
them, "I have heard *you.* Behold, I am
going to [a]pray to the LORD your God in
accordance with your words; and I will
tell you the whole [1]message which the
[b]LORD will answer you. I will [c]not keep
back a word from you."
5 Then they said to Jeremiah, "May
the [a]LORD be a true and faithful witness
against us if we do not act in accordance
with the whole [1]message with which the
LORD your God will send you to us.
6 "Whether *it* is [1]pleasant or [2]un-
pleasant, we will [a]listen to the voice of
the LORD our God to whom we are sending you, so that it may go [b]well with us
when we listen to the voice of the LORD
our God."
7 ¶ Now at the [a]end of ten days the
word of the LORD came to Jeremiah.
8 Then he called for Johanan the son
of Kareah and all the [1]commanders of
the forces that were with him, and for all
the people both small and great,
9 and said to them, "Thus [a]says the
LORD the God of Israel, to whom you sent
me to present your petition before Him:
10 'If you will indeed stay in this land,
then I will [a]build you up and not tear you
down, and I will plant you and not uproot
you; for I [1]will [b]relent concerning the
calamity that I have inflicted on you.
11 '[a]Do not be afraid of the king of
Babylon, whom you are *now* fearing; do
not be afraid of him,' declares the LORD,
'for [b]I am with you to save you and deliver you from his hand.
12 'I will also show you compassion, so
that [a]he will have compassion on you
and restore you to your own soil.
13 'But if you are going to say, "We will
[a]not stay in this land," so as not to listen
to the voice of the LORD your God,
14 saying, "No, but we will [a]go to the
land of Egypt, where we will not see war

8 [a]Is 45:3
9 [1]Or *by the side of* [a]1 Kin 15:17-22; 2 Chr 16:1-6 [b]Judg 6:2; 1 Sam 13:6; 2 Sam 17:9; Heb 11:38
10 [a]Jer 40:11 [b]Jer 43:6 [c]Neh 2:10; Jer 40:14
11 [a]Jer 40:7
12 [1]Lit *waters* [a]Gen 14:14-16; 1 Sam 30:1-8 [b]2 Sam 2:13
15 [a]1 Sam 30:17; 1 Kin 20:20; Job 21:30; Prov 28:17
16 [1]Lit *brought back* [2]Lit *men of war* [3]Lit *infants* [a]Jer 42:8
17 [1]Or *the lodging place of Chimham* [a]2 Sam 19:37 [b]Jer 42:14
18 [a]Is 51:12; Jer 42:11; Luke 12:4 [b]Jer 40:5
42:1 [1]Or *princes* [a]Jer 40:8 [b]Jer 6:13; Acts 8:10
2 [1]Lit *fall* [a]Jer 36:7 [b]Ex 8:28; 1 Sam 7:8; 1 Kin 13:6; Is 37:4; Jer 37:3; Acts 8:24; James 5:16 [c]Lev 26:22; Deut 28:62; Is 1:9; Lam 1:1
3 [a]Ps 86:11; Prov 3:6; Jer 6:16; Mic 4:2
4 [1]Lit *word* [a]Ex 8:29; 1 Sam 12:23 [b]1 Kin 22:14; Jer 23:28 [c]1 Sam 3:17; Ps 40:10; Acts 20:20
5 [1]Lit *word* [a]Gen 31:50; Judg 11:10; Jer 43:2; Mic 1:2; Mal 2:14
6 [1]Lit *good* [2]Lit *evil* [a]Ex 24:7; Deut 5:27; Josh 24:24 [b]Deut 5:29; Jer 7:23
7 [a]Ps 27:14; Is 30:18
8 [1]Or *princes*
9 [a]2 Kin 19:4
10 [1]Or *shall have changed my mind about* [a]Jer 24:6; Ezek 36:36 [b]Jer 18:7; Hos 11:8; Joel 2:13; Amos 7:3; Jon 3:10
11 [a]Jer 1:8 [b]Num 14:9; 2 Chr 32:7; Ps 46:7; Is 8:9; Jer 1:19; Rom 8:31
12 [a]Neh 1:11; Ps 106:46; Prov 16:7
13 [a]Ex 5:2; Jer 44:16
14 [a]Is 31:1; Jer 41:17

or [b]hear the sound of a trumpet or hunger for bread, and we will stay there";
15 then [1]in that case listen to the
word of the LORD, O remnant of Judah.
Thus says the LORD of hosts, the God of
Israel, "If you really set your [2]mind to
enter [a]Egypt and go in to reside there,
16 then the [a]sword, which you are
afraid of, will overtake you there in the
land of Egypt; and the famine, about
which you are anxious, will follow closely
after you there *in* Egypt, and you will die
there.
17 "So all the men who set their [1]mind
to go to Egypt to reside there will die by
the [a]sword, by famine and by pestilence;
and they will [b]have no survivors or refugees from the calamity that I am going to
bring on them." ' "
18 ¶ For thus says the LORD of hosts,
the God of Israel, "As My [a]anger and
wrath have been poured out on the inhabitants of Jerusalem, so My wrath will
be poured out on you when you enter
Egypt. And you will become a [b]curse, an
object of horror, an imprecation and a
reproach; and [c]you will see this place no
more."
19 The LORD has spoken to you,
O remnant of Judah, "Do not [a]go into
Egypt!" You should clearly [b]understand
that today I have [c]testified against you.
20 For you have *only* [1a]deceived
yourselves; for it is you who sent me to
the LORD your God, saying, "Pray for us
to the LORD our God; and whatever the
LORD our God says, tell us so, and we will
do it."
21 So I have [a]told you today, but you
have [b]not [1]obeyed the LORD your God,
even in whatever He has sent me to *tell*
you.
22 Therefore you should now clearly
understand that you will [a]die by the
sword, by famine and by pestilence, in
the [b]place where you wish to go to reside.

In Egypt Jeremiah Warns of Judgment

43 But as soon as Jeremiah, whom
the LORD their God had sent, had
[a]finished telling all the people all the
words of the LORD their God—that is, all
these words—
2 Azariah the [a]son of Hoshaiah, and
Johanan the son of Kareah, and all the
arrogant men said to Jeremiah, "You are
[b]telling a lie! The LORD our God has not
sent you to say, 'You are not to enter
Egypt to reside there';
3 but [a]Baruch the son of Neriah is
inciting you against us to give us over into
the hand of the Chaldeans, so they will
put us to death or exile us to Babylon."
4 So [a]Johanan the son of Kareah and
all the [1]commanders of the forces, and
all the people, [b]did not obey the voice of
the LORD to [c]stay in the land of Judah.
5 But Johanan the son of Kareah and
all the [1]commanders of the forces took
the [a]entire remnant of Judah who had
returned from all the nations to which
they had been driven away, in order to
reside in the land of Judah—
6 the men, the women, the [1]chil-
dren, the [a]king's daughters and [b]every
person that Nebuzaradan the captain of
the bodyguard had left with Gedaliah the
son of Ahikam [2]and grandson of Shaphan, together with [c]Jeremiah the
prophet and Baruch the son of Neriah—
7 and they entered the land of Egypt
(for they did not obey the voice of the
LORD) and went in as far as [a]Tahpanhes.
8 ¶ Then the word of the LORD came
to Jeremiah in [a]Tahpanhes, saying,
9 "Take *some* large stones in your
[1]hands and hide them in the mortar in
the [2]brick *terrace* which is at the entrance of Pharaoh's [3]palace in Tahpanhes, in the sight of [4]some *of the* Jews;
10 and say to them, 'Thus says the
LORD of hosts, the God of Israel, "Behold,
I am going to send and get [a]Nebuchad-
nezzar the king of Babylon, [b]My servant,
and I am going to set his throne *right* over
these stones that I have hidden; and he
will spread his [c]canopy over them.
11 "He will also come and [a]strike the
land of Egypt; those who are *meant* for
death *will be given over* to death, and
those for captivity to captivity, and
[b]those for the sword to the sword.
12 "And [1]I shall set fire to the temples
of the [a]gods of Egypt, and he will burn
them and take them captive. So he will
[b]wrap himself with the land of Egypt as
a shepherd wraps himself with his garment, and he will depart from there
safely.
13 "He will also shatter the [1]obelisks
of [2]Heliopolis, which is in the land of
Egypt; and the temples of the gods of
Egypt he will burn with fire." ' "

Conquest of Egypt Predicted

44 The word that came to Jeremiah
for all the Jews living in the land
of Egypt, those who were living in [a]Mig-
dol, [b]Tahpanhes, [c]Memphis, and the
land of [d]Pathros, saying,
2 "Thus says the LORD of hosts, the
God of Israel, 'You yourselves have seen
all the calamity that I have brought on
Jerusalem and all the cities of Judah; and

14 [b]Ex 16:3; Num 11:4; Jer 4:19
15 [1]Lit *now therefore* [2]Lit *face* [a]Deut 17:16; Jer 42:17
16 [a]Jer 44:13; Ezek 11:8; Amos 9:1-4
17 [1]Lit *face* [a]Jer 24:10 [b]Jer 44:14
18 [a]2 Chr 36:16-19; Jer 7:20 [b]Deut 29:21; Is 65:15; Jer 18:16 [c]Jer 22:10
19 [a]Deut 17:16; Is 30:1-7 [b]Ezek 2:5 [c]Neh 9:26
20 [1]Or *acted errantly in your souls* [a]Jer 43:2; Ezek 14:3
21 [1]Lit *listened to the voice of* [a]Deut 11:26; Jer 43:1; Ezek 2:7; Zech 7:11; Acts 20:26 [b]Jer 43:4
22 [a]Jer 43:11; Ezek 6:11 [b]Hos 9:6
43:1 [a]Jer 26:8
2 [a]Jer 42:1 [b]2 Chr 36:13; Is 7:9; Jer 5:12
3 [a]Jer 36:4
4 [1]Or *princes* [a]Jer 42:8 [b]2 Chr 25:16; Jer 42:5 [c]Ps 37:3; Jer 42:10-12
5 [1]Or *princes* [a]Jer 40:11
6 [1]Lit *infants* [2]Lit *the son* [a]Jer 41:10 [b]Jer 39:10 [c]Eccl 9:1; Lam 3:1
7 [a]Jer 2:16
8 [a]Jer 2:16; Ezek 30:18
9 [1]Lit *hand* [2]Or *brickwork* [3]Lit *house* [4]Lit *men*
10 [a]Jer 25:9 [b]Is 44:28; Jer 25:9 [c]Ps 18:11
11 [a]Is 19:1-25; Jer 25:15-19; Ezek 29:19 [b]Jer 15:2
12 [1]Some ancient versions read *He will set* [a]Ex 12:12; Is 19:1; Jer 46:25; Ezek 30:13 [b]Ps 104:2; Is 49:18
13 [1]Or *stone pillars* [2]Heb *Beth-shemesh*; i.e. the house of the sun-god
44:1 [a]Ex 14:2; Jer 46:14 [b]Jer 43:7; Ezek 30:18 [c]Is 19:13; Jer 2:16; Ezek 30:13; Hos 9:6 [d]Is 11:11; Ezek 29:14

behold, this day they are in [a]ruins and no
one lives in them,
3 [a]because of their wickedness
which they committed so as to [b]provoke
Me to anger by continuing to [c]burn
[1]sacrifices *and* to [d]serve other gods
whom they had not known, *neither* they,
you, nor your fathers.
4 'Yet I [a]sent you all My servants the
prophets, [1]again and again, saying, "Oh,
do not do this [b]abominable thing which
I hate."
5 'But [a]they did not listen or incline
their ears to turn from their wickedness,
so as not to burn [1]sacrifices to other
gods.
6 'Therefore My [a]wrath and My anger were poured out and burned in the
[b]cities of Judah and in the streets of Jerusalem, so they have become a ruin and a
[c]desolation as it is this day.
7 'Now then thus says the LORD God
of hosts, the God of Israel, "Why are you
[a]doing great harm to yourselves, so as to
[b]cut off from you man and woman, child
and infant, from among Judah, leaving
yourselves without remnant,
8 [a]provoking Me to anger with the
works of your hands, [b]burning [1]sacri-
fices to other gods in the land of Egypt,
where you are entering to reside, so that
you might be cut off and become a [c]curse
and a reproach among all the nations of
the earth?
9 "Have you forgotten the [a]wicked-
ness of your fathers, the wickedness of
the kings of Judah, and the wickedness of
their wives, your own wickedness, and
the wickedness of your wives, which
they committed in the land of Judah and
in the streets of Jerusalem?
10 "But they [a]have not become [1]con-
trite even to this day, nor have they
feared nor [b]walked in My law or My statutes, which I have set before you and
before your fathers." '
11 ¶ "Therefore thus says the LORD of
hosts, the God of Israel, 'Behold, I am
going to [a]set My face against you for
[1]woe, even to cut off all Judah.
12 'And I will [a]take away the remnant
of Judah who have set their [1]mind on
entering the land of Egypt to reside there,
and they will all [2b]meet their end in the
land of Egypt; they will fall by the sword
and meet their end by famine. Both small
and great will die by the sword and famine; and they will become a [c]curse, an
object of horror, an imprecation and a
reproach.
13 'And I will [a]punish those who live
in the land of Egypt, as I have punished
Jerusalem, with the sword, with famine
and with pestilence.
14 'So there will be [a]no refugees or
survivors for the remnant of Judah who
have entered the land of Egypt to reside
there and then to return to the land of
Judah, to which they are [1b]longing to
return and live; for none will [c]return except *a few* refugees.' "
15 ¶ Then [a]all the men who were
aware that their wives were burning
[1]sacrifices to other gods, along with all
the women who were standing by, *as* a
large assembly, [2]including all the people
who were living in Pathros in the land of
Egypt, responded to Jeremiah, saying,
16 "As for the [1a]message that you
have spoken to us in the name of the
LORD, [b]we are not going to listen to you!
17 "But rather we will certainly [a]carry
out every word that has proceeded from
our mouths, [1]by burning [2]sacrifices to
the [b]queen of heaven and pouring out
drink offerings to her, just as [c]we ourselves, our forefathers, our kings and our
princes did in the cities of Judah and in
the streets of Jerusalem; for *then* we had
[d]plenty of [3]food and were well off and
saw no [4]misfortune.
18 "But since we stopped burning [1]sac-
rifices to the queen of heaven and pouring out drink offerings to her, we have
[a]lacked everything and have [2]met our
end by the sword and by famine."
19 "And," *said the women,* "when we
were [a]burning [1]sacrifices to the queen
of heaven and [2]were pouring out drink
offerings to her, was it [b]without our husbands that we made for her *sacrificial*
cakes [3]in her image and poured out
drink offerings to her?"

Calamity for the Jews

20 ¶ Then Jeremiah said to all the people, to the men and women—even to all
the people who were giving him *such* an
answer—saying,
21 "As for the [1a]smoking sacrifices
that you burned in the cities of Judah and
in the [b]streets of Jerusalem, you and your
forefathers, your kings and your princes,
and the people of the land, did not the
LORD [c]remember them and did not *all
this* come into His [2]mind?
22 "So the LORD was [a]no longer able to
endure *it,* [b]because of the evil of your
deeds, because of the abominations
which you have committed; thus your
land has become a [c]ruin, an object of
horror and a curse, without an inhabitant, as *it is* this day.
23 "Because you have burned [1]sacri-
fices and have sinned against the LORD
and [a]not obeyed the voice of the LORD or
[b]walked in His law, His statutes or His

2 [a]Is 6:11; Jer 4:7; Mic 3:12
3 [1]Or *incense* [a]Neh 9:33; Jer 2:17-19; Ezek 8:17; Dan 9:5 [b]Is 3:8; Jer 7:19 [c]Jer 19:4 [d]Deut 13:6
4 [1]Lit *rising early and sending* [a]Jer 7:13; Zech 7:7 [b]Jer 16:18; Ezek 8:10
5 [1]Or *incense* [a]Jer 11:8
6 [a]Is 51:17-20; Jer 42:18; Ezek 8:18 [b]Jer 7:17 [c]Jer 4:27
7 [a]Num 16:38; Jer 26:19; Ezek 33:11; Hab 2:10 [b]Jer 3:24
8 [1]Or *incense* [a]2 Kin 17:15-17; Jer 25:6; 1 Cor 10:21 [b]Jer 7:9; Hos 4:13; Hab 1:16 [c]1 Kin 9:7; 2 Chr 7:20; Jer 42:18
9 [a]Jer 7:9
10 [1]Lit *crushed* [a]Jer 6:15 [b]Jer 26:4
11 [1]Lit *evil* [a]Lev 17:10; Jer 21:10; Amos 9:4
12 [1]Lit *face* [2]Lit *be finished* [a]Jer 42:15-18 [b]Is 1:28; Jer 16:4 [c]Is 65:15; Jer 18:16; Zech 8:13
13 [a]Jer 11:22
14 [1]Lit *lifting up their soul* [a]Jer 22:10 [b]Jer 22:26 [c]Is 4:2; Jer 44:28; Rom 9:27
15 [1]Or *incense* [2]Lit *and* [a]Prov 11:21; Is 1:5; Jer 5:1-5
16 [1]Lit *word* [a]Jer 43:2 [b]Prov 1:24-27; Jer 11:8
17 [1]Or *so as to burn* [2]Or *incense* [3]Lit *bread* [4]Lit *evil* [a]Num 30:12; Deut 23:23 [b]2 Kin 17:16; Jer 7:18 [c]Neh 9:34; Jer 32:32 [d]Ex 16:3; Hos 2:5-9; Phil 3:19
18 [1]Or *incense* [2]Lit *been finished* [a]Num 11:5; Jer 40:12; Mal 3:13-15
19 [1]Or *incense* [2]Lit *to pour* [3]Lit *to make an image of her* [a]Jer 7:18 [b]Num 30:6; Jer 44:15
21 [1]Or *incense* [2]Lit *heart* [a]Ezek 8:10 [b]Jer 11:13 [c]Ps 79:8; Is 64:9; Jer 14:10; Hos 7:2; Amos 8:7
22 [a]Is 7:13; Mal 2:17 [b]Jer 4:4 [c]Gen 19:13; Ps 107:33; Jer 25:11
23 [1]Or *incense* [a]Jer 7:13-15 [b]Jer 44:10; Ps 119:136

testimonies, therefore this [c]calamity has
befallen you, as *it has* this day."
24 ¶ Then Jeremiah said to all the people, including all the women, "[a]Hear the
word of the LORD, all Judah who are [b]in
the land of Egypt,
25 thus says the LORD of hosts, the God
of Israel, as follows: 'As for you and your
wives, you have spoken with your
mouths and fulfilled *it* with your hands,
saying, "We will [a]certainly perform our
vows that we have vowed, to burn [1]sacri-
fices to the queen of heaven and pour out
drink offerings to her." [2b]Go ahead and
confirm your vows, and certainly perform
your vows!'
26 "[1]Nevertheless hear the word of the
LORD, all Judah who are living in the land
of Egypt, 'Behold, I have [a]sworn by My
great name,' says the LORD, '[b]never shall
My name be invoked again by the mouth
of any man of Judah in all the land
of Egypt, saying, "[c]As the Lord [2]GOD
lives."
27 'Behold, I am watching over them
[a]for harm and not for good, and [b]all the
men of Judah who are in the land of Egypt
will [1]meet their end by the sword and by
famine until they [2]are completely gone.
28 '[a]Those who escape the sword will
return out of the land of Egypt to the land
of Judah [1b]few in number. Then all the
remnant of Judah who have gone to the
land of Egypt to reside there will know
[c]whose word will stand, Mine or theirs.
29 'This will be the [a]sign to you,' declares the LORD, 'that I am going to punish you in this place, so that you may
know that [b]My words will surely stand
against you for harm.'
30 "Thus says the LORD, 'Behold, I am
going to give over [a]Pharaoh Hophra king
of Egypt to the hand of his enemies, to
the hand of those who seek his life, just
as I gave over [b]Zedekiah king of Judah to
the hand of Nebuchadnezzar king of Babylon, *who was* his enemy and was seeking his life.'"

Message to Baruch

45 *This is* the message which Jeremiah the prophet spoke to [a]Baruch
the son of Neriah, when he had [b]written
down these words in a book [1]at Jeremiah's dictation, in the [c]fourth year of Jehoiakim the son of Josiah, king of Judah,
saying:
2 "Thus says the LORD the God of Israel to you, O Baruch:
3 'You said, "Ah, woe is me! For the
LORD has added sorrow to my pain; I
am [a]weary with my groaning and have
found no rest."'
4 "Thus you are to say to him, 'Thus
says the LORD, "Behold, [a]what I have
built I am about to tear down, and what
I have planted I am about to uproot, that
is, the whole land."
5 'But you, are you [a]seeking great
things for yourself? Do not seek *them;* for
behold, I am going to [b]bring disaster on
all flesh,' declares the LORD, 'but I will
[c]give your life to you as booty in all the
places where you may go.'"

Defeat of Pharaoh Foretold

46 That which came as the word of
the LORD to Jeremiah the prophet
[a]concerning the nations.
2 ¶ To [a]Egypt, concerning the army
of [b]Pharaoh Neco king of Egypt, which
was by the Euphrates River at [c]Carche-
mish, which Nebuchadnezzar king of
Babylon defeated in the [d]fourth year of
Jehoiakim the son of Josiah, king of Judah:

3 "[a]Line up the shield and
[1]buckler,
And draw near for the battle!
4 "Harness the horses,
And [1]mount the steeds,
And take your stand with
helmets *on!*
[a]Polish the spears,
Put on the [b]scale-armor!
5 "Why have I seen *it?*
They are terrified,
They are [a]drawing back,
And their [b]mighty men are
defeated
And have taken refuge in flight,
Without facing back;
[1c]Terror is on every side!"
Declares the LORD.
6 Let not the [a]swift man flee,
Nor the mighty man escape;
In the north beside the river
Euphrates
They have [b]stumbled and fallen.
7 Who is this that [a]rises like the
Nile,
Like the rivers whose waters
surge about?
8 Egypt rises like the Nile,
Even like the rivers whose
waters surge about;
And He has said, "I will [a]rise
and cover *that* land;
I will surely [b]destroy the city
and its inhabitants."
9 Go up, you horses, and [1a]drive
madly, you chariots,
That the mighty men may
[2]march forward:
Ethiopia and [3b]Put, that handle
the shield,
And the [4c]Lydians, that handle
and bend the bow.

23 [c]1 Kin 9:9; Neh 13:18; Jer 44:2; Dan 9:11
24 [a]Jer 42:15 [b]Jer 43:7
25 [1]Or *incense* [2]Lit *Surely cause to stand* [a]Jer 44:17; Matt 14:9; Acts 23:12 [b]Ezek 20:39
26 [1]Lit *Therefore* [2]Heb *YHWH,* usually rendered *LORD* [a]Gen 22:16; Deut 32:40; Jer 22:5; Amos 6:8; Heb 6:13 [b]Ps 50:16; Ezek 20:39 [c]Is 48:1; Jer 5:2
27 [1]Lit *be finished* [2]Lit *come to an end* [a]Jer 1:10 [b]2 Kin 21:14; Jer 44:14
28 [1]Lit *men of number* [a]Jer 44:14 [b]Is 10:19 [c]Ps 33:11; Is 14:27; Zech 1:6
29 [a]Is 7:11; Jer 44:30; Matt 24:15 [b]Prov 19:21; Is 40:8
30 [a]Jer 43:9-13; Ezek 29:3 [b]2 Kin 25:4-7; Jer 34:21
45:1 [1]Lit *from the mouth of Jeremiah* [a]Jer 32:12 [b]Jer 36:4 [c]2 Kin 24:1; 2 Chr 36:5-7; Jer 25:1; Dan 1:1
3 [a]Ps 6:6; 2 Cor 4:1; Gal 6:9
4 [a]Is 5:5; Jer 1:10
5 [a]1 Kin 3:9; 2 Kin 5:26; Matt 6:25; Rom 12:16 [b]Is 66:16; Jer 25:31 [c]Jer 21:9
46:1 [a]Jer 1:10
2 [a]Jer 46:14; Ezek chs 29-32 [b]2 Kin 18:21; Jer 25:19 [c]2 Chr 35:20; Is 10:9 [d]Jer 45:1
3 [1]I.e. small shield [a]Is 21:5; Jer 51:11; Joel 3:9; Nah 2:1
4 [1]Or *go up, you horsemen* [a]Ezek 21:9-11 [b]1 Sam 17:5; 2 Chr 26:14; Neh 4:16; Jer 51:3
5 [1]Heb *Magor-missabib;* i.e. Terror is on every side [a]Is 42:17; Jer 46:21 [b]Is 5:25; Ezek 39:18 [c]Jer 6:25
6 [a]Is 30:16 [b]Jer 46:12; Dan 11:19
7 [a]Jer 47:2
8 [a]Is 37:24 [b]Is 10:13
9 [1]Lit *act like madmen* [2]Lit *go forth* [3]I.e. Libya (or Somaliland) [4]Heb *Ludim* [a]Jer 47:3; Nah 2:4 [b]Nah 3:9 [c]Is 66:19

10 For [a]that day belongs to the
Lord [1]GOD of hosts,
A day of [b]vengeance, so as to
avenge Himself on His foes;
And the [c]sword will devour and
be satiated
And [2]drink its fill of their blood;
For there will be a [d]slaughter for
the Lord [1]GOD of hosts,
In the land of the north by the
river Euphrates.
11 Go [a]up to Gilead and obtain
balm,
[b]O virgin daughter of Egypt!
In vain have you multiplied
[1]remedies;
There is [c]no healing for you.
12 The nations have heard of your
[a]shame,
And the earth is full of your [b]cry
of distress;
For one [c]warrior has stumbled
over [1]another,
And both of them have fallen
down together.

13 ¶ *This is* the [1]message which the
LORD spoke to Jeremiah the prophet
about the [a]coming of Nebuchadnezzar
king of Babylon to [b]smite the land of
Egypt:

14 "Declare in Egypt and proclaim in
[a]Migdol,
Proclaim also in Memphis and
[b]Tahpanhes;
Say, 'Take your stand and get
yourself ready,
For the [c]sword has devoured
those around you.'
15 "Why have your [a]mighty ones
become prostrate?
They do not stand because the
LORD has [b]thrust them
down.
16 "They have repeatedly [a]stumbled;
Indeed, they have fallen one
against another.
Then they said, 'Get up! And
[b]let us go back
To our own people and our
native land
Away from the [1c]sword of the
oppressor.'
17 "[1]They cried there, 'Pharaoh king
of Egypt *is but* [a]a big noise;
He has let the appointed time
pass by!'
18 "As I live," declares the [a]King
Whose name is the LORD of
hosts,
"Surely one shall come *who looms
up* like [b]Tabor among the
mountains,
Or like [c]Carmel by the sea.
19 "Make your baggage ready for
[a]exile,
O [b]daughter dwelling in Egypt,
For [c]Memphis will become a
desolation;
It will even be burned down *and*
[1]bereft of inhabitants.
20 "Egypt is a pretty [a]heifer,
But a [1]horsefly is coming [b]from
the north—it is coming!
21 "Also her [a]mercenaries in her
midst
Are like [1]fattened [b]calves,
For even they too have turned
back *and* have fled away
together;
They did not stand *their ground.*
For the day of their calamity has
come upon them,
The time of their [c]punishment.
22 "Its sound moves along like a
serpent;
For they move on [1]like an army
And come to her as woodcutters
with axes.
23 "They have cut down her
[a]forest," declares the LORD;
"Surely it will no *more* be found,
Even though [1]they are *now*
more numerous than
[b]locusts
And are without number.
24 "The daughter of Egypt has been
put to shame,
Given over to the [1]power of the
[a]people of the north."

25 ¶ The LORD of hosts, the God of
Israel, says, "Behold, I am going to punish Amon of [a]Thebes, and [b]Pharaoh,
and Egypt along with her [c]gods and her
kings, even Pharaoh and those who
[d]trust in him.
26 "I shall give them over to the [1]pow-
er of those who are [a]seeking their lives,
even into the hand of Nebuchadnezzar
king of Babylon and into the hand of his
[2]officers. [b]Afterwards, however, it will
be inhabited as in the days of old," declares the LORD.

27 ¶ "But as for you, O Jacob My
servant, [a]do not fear,
Nor be dismayed, O Israel!
For, see, I am going to [b]save
you from afar,
And your descendants from the
land of their captivity;
And Jacob will return and be
[c]undisturbed
And secure, with no one making
him tremble.
28 "O Jacob My servant, do not
fear," declares the LORD,
"For [a]I am with you.

10 [1]Heb *YHWH,* usually rendered *LORD* [2]Lit *be saturated with* [a]Joel 1:15 [b]Jer 50:15, 18 [c]Deut 32:42; Is 31:8; Jer 12:12 [d]Is 34:6; Zeph 1:7
11 [1]Lit *healings* [a]Jer 8:22 [b]Is 47:1; Jer 31:4,21 [c]Jer 30:13; Mic 1:9; Nah 3:19
12 [1]Lit *warrior* [a]Jer 2:36; Nah 3:8-10 [b]Jer 14:2 [c]Is 19:2
13 [1]Lit *word* [a]Jer 43:10-13 [b]Is 19:1
14 [a]Jer 44:1 [b]Jer 43:8 [c]Is 1:20; Jer 2:30; 46:10; Nah 2:13
15 [a]Is 66:15,16; Jer 46:5 [b]Ps 18:14,39; 68:1,2
16 [1]Lit *oppressing sword* [a]Lev 26:36,37; Jer 46:6 [b]Jer 51:9 [c]Jer 50:16
17 [1]Some ancient versions read *Call the name of Pharaoh a big noise* [a]Ex 15:9,10; 1 Kin 20:10,11; Is 19:11-16
18 [a]Jer 48:15; Mal 1:14 [b]Josh 19:22; Judg 4:6; Ps 89:12 [c]Josh 12:22; 1 Kin 18:42
19 [1]Lit *without* [a]Is 20:4 [b]Jer 48:18 [c]Jer 46:14; Ezek 30:13
20 [1]Or possibly *mosquito* [a]Hos 10:11 [b]Jer 1:14; 47:2
21 [1]Lit *of the stall* [a]2 Sam 10:6; 2 Kin 7:6; Jer 46:5 [b]Is 34:7 [c]Jer 48:44; Hos 9:7; Obad 13; Mic 7:4
22 [1]Or *in force*
23 [1]I.e. trees of the forest, the Egyptians [a]Jer 21:14 [b]Judg 6:5; 7:12; Joel 2:25
24 [1]Lit *hand* [a]Jer 1:15
25 [a]Ezek 30:14-16; Nah 3:8 [b]Jer 44:30 [c]Ex 12:12; Jer 43:12,13; Ezek 30:13; Zeph 2:11 [d]Is 20:5
26 [1]Lit *hand* [2]Lit *servants* [a]Jer 44:30; Ezek 32:11 [b]Ezek 29:8-14
27 [a]Is 41:13,14; Jer 30:10,11 [b]Is 11:11; Jer 23:3, 4; 29:14; Mic 7:12 [c]Jer 23:6; 50:19
28 [a]Ps 46:7,11; Is 8:10; 43:2; Jer 1:19

For I will make a full end of all
the nations
Where I have driven you,
Yet I will [b]not make a full end
of you;
But I will [c]correct you properly
And by no means leave you
unpunished."

Prophecy against Philistia

47 That which came as the word of
the LORD to Jeremiah the prophet
concerning the [a]Philistines, before Pharaoh [1]conquered [b]Gaza.
2 Thus says the LORD:
"Behold, waters are going to rise
from [a]the north
And become an overflowing
torrent,
And [b]overflow the land and all
its fullness,
The city and those who live
in it;
And the men will [c]cry out,
And every inhabitant of the land
will wail.
3 "Because of the noise of the
[1a]galloping hoofs of his
[2]stallions,
The tumult of his chariots, *and*
the rumbling of his wheels,
The fathers have not turned back
for *their* children,
Because of the limpness of *their*
hands,
4 On account of the day that is
coming
To [a]destroy all the Philistines,
To cut off from [b]Tyre and Sidon
Every ally that is left;
For the LORD is going to destroy
the Philistines,
The remnant of the coastland of
[c]Caphtor.
5 "[a]Baldness has come upon Gaza;
[b]Ashkelon has been ruined.
O remnant of their valley,
How long will you [c]gash
yourself?
6 "Ah, [a]sword of the LORD,
How long will you not be quiet?
Withdraw into your sheath;
Be at rest and stay still.
7 "How can [1]it be quiet,
When the LORD has [a]given it an
order?
Against Ashkelon and against the
seacoast—
There He has [b]assigned it."

Prophecy against Moab

48 Concerning [a]Moab. Thus says
the LORD of hosts, the God of
Israel,
"Woe to [b]Nebo, for it has been
destroyed;
[c]Kiriathaim has been put to
shame, it has been captured;
The lofty stronghold has been
put to shame and
[1]shattered.
2 "There is praise for Moab no
longer;
In [a]Heshbon they have devised
calamity against her:
'Come and let us cut her off from
being a nation!'
You too, [1]Madmen, will be
silenced;
The sword will follow after you.
3 "The sound of an outcry from
[a]Horonaim,
'Devastation and great
destruction!'
4 "Moab is broken,
Her little ones have sounded out
a cry *of distress.*
5 "For by the ascent of [a]Luhith
They will ascend with continual
weeping;
For at the descent of Horonaim
They have heard the [1]anguished
cry of destruction.
6 "[a]Flee, save your lives,
That you may be like a juniper in
the wilderness.
7 "For because of your [a]trust in
your own achievements and
treasures,
Even you yourself will be
captured;
And [b]Chemosh will go off into
exile
Together with his priests and his
princes.
8 "A destroyer will come to every
city,
So that no city will escape;
The valley also will be ruined
And the [a]plateau will be
destroyed,
As the LORD has said.
9 "Give [1a]wings to Moab,
For she will [2]flee away;
And her cities will become a
[b]desolation,
Without inhabitants in them.
10 "[a]Cursed be the one who does
the LORD'S work
[b]negligently,
And cursed be the one who
restrains his [c]sword from
blood.
11 ¶ "Moab has been [a]at ease since
his youth;
He has also been [b]undisturbed,
like wine on [1]its dregs,

28 [b]Jer 4:27; Amos 9:8,9 [c]Jer 10:24; Hab 3:2

47:1 [1]Lit *smote* [a]Jer 25:20; Zech 9:6 [b]Gen 10:19; 1 Kin 4:24; Jer 25:20; Amos 1:6; Zeph 2:4

2 [a]Is 14:31; Jer 1:14; 6:22; 46:20,24 [b]Is 8:7,8 [c]Is 15:2-5; Jer 46:12

3 [1]Lit *stamping of the* [2]Lit *mighty ones* [a]Judg 5:22; Jer 8:16; Nah 3:2

4 [a]Is 14:31 [b]Is 23:5; Jer 25:22; Joel 3:4; Amos 1:9,10; Zech 9:2-4 [c]Gen 10:14; Deut 2:23; Amos 9:7

5 [a]Jer 48:37; Mic 1:16 [b]Judg 1:18; Jer 25:20; Amos 1:7,8; Zeph 2:4,7; Zech 9:5 [c]Jer 16:6; 41:5

6 [a]Judg 7:20; Jer 12:12; Ezek 21:3-5

7 [1]Lit *you* [a]Is 10:6; Ezek 14:17 [b]Mic 6:9

48:1 [1]Or *dismayed* [a]Is 15:1; Ezek 25:9 [b]Num 32:3,38; Jer 48:22 [c]Num 32:37; Jer 48:23; Ezek 25:9

2 [1]I.e. a city of Moab [a]Num 21:25; Jer 48:34, 45; 49:3

3 [a]Is 15:5; Jer 48:5,34

5 [1]Lit *distresses of outcry* [a]Is 15:5

6 [a]Jer 51:6

7 [a]Ps 52:7; Is 59:4; Jer 9:23 [b]Num 21:29; 1 Kin 11:33; Jer 48:13,46

8 [a]Josh 13:9,17, 21

9 [1]Or *salt* [2]Or *fall in ruins* [a]Ps 11:1; Is 16:2; Jer 48:28 [b]Jer 44:22

10 [a]Jer 11:3 [b]1 Kin 20:39,40, 42; 2 Kin 13:19 [c]Jer 47:6,7

11 [1]Lit *his* [a]Jer 22:21; Ezek 16:49; Zech 1:15 [b]Zeph 1:12

And he has not been [c]emptied
from vessel to vessel,
Nor has he gone into exile.
Therefore [2]he retains his flavor,
And his aroma has not changed.
12 "Therefore behold, the days are
coming," declares the LORD, "when I will
send to him those who tip *vessels,* and
they will tip him over, and they will empty his vessels and shatter [1]his jars.
13 "And Moab will be [a]ashamed of
[b]Chemosh, as the house of Israel was
ashamed of [c]Bethel, their confidence.
14 "How can you say, 'We are
[a]mighty warriors,
And men valiant for battle'?
15 "Moab has been destroyed and
[1]men have gone up to [2]his
cities;
His choicest [3a]young men have
also gone down to the
slaughter,"
Declares the [b]King, whose name
is the LORD of hosts.
16 "The disaster of Moab will [a]soon
come,
And his calamity has swiftly
hastened.
17 "Mourn for him, all you who *live*
around him,
Even all of you who know his
name;
Say, 'How has the mighty
[1a]scepter been broken,
A staff of splendor!'
18 "[a]Come down from your glory
And sit [1]on the parched ground,
O [b]daughter dwelling in
[c]Dibon,
For the destroyer of Moab has
come up against you,
He has ruined your strongholds.
19 "Stand by the road and keep
watch,
O inhabitant of [a]Aroer;
[b]Ask him who flees and her
who escapes
And say, 'What has happened?'
20 "Moab has been put to shame, for
it has been [1]shattered.
Wail and cry out;
Declare by the [a]Arnon
That Moab has been destroyed.
21 ¶ "Judgment has also come upon
the plain, upon Holon, [a]Jahzah and
against [b]Mephaath,
22 against Dibon, Nebo and Beth-
diblathaim,
23 against Kiriathaim, Beth-gamul and
[a]Beth-meon,
24 against [a]Kerioth, Bozrah and all
the cities of the land of Moab, far and
near.
25 "The [a]horn of Moab has been cut
off and his [b]arm broken," declares the
LORD.
26 "[a]Make him drunk, for he has [1]be-
come [b]arrogant toward the LORD; so
Moab will [2]wallow in his vomit, and he
also will become a laughingstock.
27 "Now was not Israel a [a]laughing-
stock to you? Or was he [1b]caught among
thieves? For each time you speak about
him you [c]shake *your head in scorn.*
28 "Leave the cities and dwell among
the [a]crags,
O inhabitants of Moab,
And be like a [b]dove that nests
Beyond the mouth of the chasm.
29 "[a]We have heard of the pride of
Moab—he *is* very proud—
Of his haughtiness, his [b]pride,
his arrogance and [1]his
self-exaltation.
30 "I know his [a]fury," declares the
LORD,
"But it is futile;
His idle boasts have
accomplished nothing.
31 "Therefore I will [a]wail for Moab,
Even for all Moab will I cry out;
[1]I will moan for the men of
[b]Kir-heres.
32 "More than the [a]weeping for
[b]Jazer
I will weep for you, O vine of
Sibmah!
Your tendrils stretched across the
sea,
They reached to the sea of Jazer;
Upon your summer fruits and
your grape harvest
The destroyer has fallen.
33 "So [a]gladness and joy are taken
away
From the fruitful field, even from
the land of Moab.
And I have made the wine to
[b]cease from the wine
presses;
No one will tread *them* with
shouting,
The shouting will not be shouts
of joy.
34 "[a]From the outcry at Heshbon even
to [b]Elealeh, even to Jahaz they have
[1]raised their voice, from [c]Zoar even to
Horonaim *and to* Eglath-shelishiyah; for
even the waters of Nimrim will become
desolate.
35 "I will make an end of Moab," declares the LORD, "the one who offers *sac-*
rifice on the [a]high place and the one
who [1b]burns incense to his gods.
36 ¶ "Therefore My [a]heart [1]wails for
Moab like flutes; My heart also [1]wails
like flutes for the men of Kir-heres.

11 [2]Lit *his flavor has stayed in him* [c]Nah 2:2
12 [1]Lit *their*
13 [a]Is 45:16; Jer 48:39 [b]Judg 11:24 [c]1 Kin 12:29; Hos 8:5,6
14 [a]Ps 33:16; Is 10:13-16
15 [1]Lit *one has* [2]Lit *her* [3]I.e. warriors [a]Is 40:30,31; Jer 50:27 [b]Jer 46:18; 51:57; Mal 1:14
16 [a]Is 13:22
17 [1]Or *rod* [a]Is 9:4; 14:5
18 [1]Lit *in thirst* [a]Is 47:1 [b]Jer 46:19 [c]Num 21:30; Josh 13:9, 17; Is 15:2; Jer 48:22
19 [a]Deut 2:36; Josh 12:2 [b]1 Sam 4:13,14, 16
20 [1]Or *dismayed* [a]Num 21:13
21 [a]Num 21:23; Is 15:4; Jer 48:34 [b]Josh 13:18
23 [a]Josh 13:17
24 [a]Jer 48:41; Amos 2:2
25 [a]Ps 75:10; Zech 1:19-21 [b]Job 22:9; Ps 10:15
26 [1]Or *magnified himself against* [2]Or *splash into* [a]Jer 25:15 [b]Ex 5:2; Jer 48:42; Dan 5:23
27 [1]Or *found* [a]Lam 2:15-17; Mic 7:8-10 [b]Jer 2:26 [c]Job 16:4; Jer 18:16
28 [a]Judg 6:2; Is 2:19; Jer 49:16; Obad 3 [b]Ps 55:6; Song 2:14
29 [1]Lit *elevation of his heart* [a]Is 16:6; Zeph 2:8 [b]Job 40:11,12; Ps 138:6
30 [a]Is 37:28
31 [1]Another reading is *He* [a]Is 15:5; 16:7,11 [b]2 Kin 3:25; Is 16:7,11; Jer 48:36
32 [a]Is 16:8,9 [b]Num 21:32
33 [a]Is 16:10; Jer 25:10; Joel 1:12 [b]Is 5:10; Hag 2:16
34 [1]Lit *given forth* [a]Is 15:4-6 [b]Num 32:3,37 [c]Gen 13:10; 14:2; Is 15:5,6
35 [1]Or *offers up in smoke* [a]Is 15:2; 16:12 [b]Jer 7:9; 11:13
36 [1]Lit *sounds* [a]Is 15:5; 16:11

Therefore they have [b]lost the abundance
it produced.
37 "For [a]every head is bald and every
beard cut short; there are gashes on all
the hands and [b]sackcloth on the loins.
38 "On all the [a]housetops of Moab and
in its streets [1]there is lamentation everywhere; for I have broken Moab like an
undesirable [b]vessel," declares the LORD.
39 "How [1]shattered it is! *How* they
have wailed! How Moab has turned his
back—he is ashamed! So Moab will become a laughingstock and an [a]object of
terror to all around him."
40 ¶ For thus says the LORD:
"Behold, one will [a]fly swiftly like
an eagle
And [b]spread out his wings
against Moab.
41 "Kerioth has been captured
And the strongholds have been
seized,
So the [a]hearts of the mighty
men of Moab in that day
Will be like the heart of a
[b]woman in labor.
42 "Moab will be [a]destroyed from
being a people
Because he has [1]become
[b]arrogant toward the LORD.
43 "[a]Terror, pit and snare are
coming upon you,
O inhabitant of Moab," declares
the LORD.
44 "The one who [a]flees from the
terror
Will fall into the pit,
And the one who climbs up out
of the pit
Will be caught in the snare;
For I shall bring upon her, *even*
upon Moab,
The year of their [b]punishment,"
declares the LORD.

45 ¶ "In the shadow of Heshbon
The fugitives stand without
strength;
For a fire has gone forth from
Heshbon
And a [a]flame from the midst of
[b]Sihon,
And it has devoured the
[c]forehead of Moab
And the scalps of the [1]riotous
revelers.
46 "[a]Woe to you, Moab!
The people of [b]Chemosh have
perished;
For your sons have been taken
away captive
And your daughters into
captivity.

47 "Yet I will [a]restore the [1]fortunes
of Moab
In the [2]latter days," declares the
LORD.
¶ Thus far the judgment on Moab.

Prophecy against Ammon

49 Concerning the sons of [a]Ammon.
Thus says the LORD:
"Does Israel have no sons?
Or has he no heirs?
Why then has [1]Malcam taken
possession of Gad
And his people settled in its
cities?
2 "Therefore behold, the days are
coming," declares the LORD,
"That I will cause a [1a]trumpet
blast of war to be heard
Against [b]Rabbah of the sons of
Ammon;
And it will become a desolate
heap,
And her [c]towns will be set on
fire.
Then Israel will take [d]possession
of his possessors,"
Says the LORD.
3 "Wail, O [a]Heshbon, for [b]Ai has
been destroyed!
Cry out, O daughters of Rabbah,
[c]Gird yourselves with sackcloth
and lament,
And rush back and forth inside
the walls;
For [1]Malcam will [d]go into exile
Together with his priests and his
princes.
4 "How [a]boastful you are about the
valleys!
Your valley is flowing *away,*
O [b]backsliding daughter
Who trusts in her [c]treasures,
saying,
'[d]Who will come against me?'
5 "Behold, I am going to bring
[a]terror upon you,"
Declares the Lord [1]GOD of hosts,
"From all *directions* around you;
And each of you will be [b]driven
out [2]headlong,
With no one to gather the
[c]fugitives together.
6 "But afterward I will [a]restore
The [1]fortunes of the sons of
Ammon,"
Declares the LORD.

Prophecy against Edom

7 ¶ Concerning [a]Edom.
Thus says the LORD of hosts,
"Is there no longer any [b]wisdom
in [c]Teman?

36 [b]Is 15:7
37 [a]Is 15:2; Jer 16:6; 41:5; 47:5 [b]Gen 37:34; Is 15:3; 20:2
38 [1]Lit *all of it is lamentation* [a]Is 22:1 [b]Jer 19:10,11; 22:28; 25:34
39 [1]Or *dismayed* [a]Ezek 26:16
40 [a]Deut 28:49; Jer 49:22; Hos 8:1; Hab 1:8 [b]Is 8:8
41 [a]Jer 49:22 [b]Is 13:8; 21:3; Jer 30:6; Mic 4:9,10
42 [1]Or *magnified himself against* [a]Ps 83:4; Jer 48:2 [b]Is 37:23; Jer 48:26
43 [a]Is 24:17,18; Lam 3:47
44 [a]1 Kin 19:17; Is 24:18; Amos 5:19 [b]Jer 46:21
45 [1]Lit *sons of tumult* [a]Num 21:28,29 [b]Num 21:21,26; Ps 135:11 [c]Num 24:17
46 [a]Num 21:29 [b]Judg 11:24; 1 Kin 11:7; Jer 48:7
47 [1]Or *captivity* [2]Lit *end of the days* [a]Jer 12:14-17; 49:6, 39
49:1 [1]In 1 Kin 11:5, 33 and Zeph 1:5, *Milcom* [a]Deut 23:3, 4; 2 Chr 20:1; Ezek 21:28-32; 25:2-10; Amos 1:13-15; Zeph 2:8-11
2 [1]Or *shout of* [a]Num 10:9; Jer 4:19 [b]Deut 3:11; 2 Sam 11:1; Ezek 21:20 [c]Josh 17:11,16 [d]Is 14:2
3 [1]Cf v 1 [a]Jer 48:2 [b]Josh 7:2-5; 8:1-29; Ezra 2:28 [c]Is 32:11; Jer 48:37 [d]Jer 46:25; 48:7
4 [a]Jer 9:23 [b]Jer 31:22 [c]Ps 62:10; Ezek 28:4,5; 1 Tim 6:17 [d]Jer 21:13
5 [1]Heb *YHWH,* usually rendered LORD [2]Lit *before him* [a]Jer 48:43f; 49:29 [b]Jer 16:16; 46:5 [c]Lam 4:15
6 [1]Or *captivity* [a]Jer 48:47; 49:39
7 [a]Gen 25:30; 32:3; Is 34:5,6; Jer 25:21; Ezek 25:12; Amos 1:11; Obad 1-21 [b]Job 2:11; Jer 8:9 [c]Gen 36:11, 15,34; Jer 49:20

Has good counsel been lost to
the prudent?
Has their wisdom decayed?
8 "Flee away, turn back, dwell in
the depths,
O inhabitants of [a]Dedan,
For I [1]will bring the [b]disaster of
Esau upon him
At the time I [2]punish him.
9 "[a]If grape gatherers came to you,
Would they not leave gleanings?
If thieves *came* by night,
They would destroy *only* [1]until
they had enough.
10 "But I have [a]stripped Esau bare,
I have uncovered his hiding
places
So that he will not be able to
conceal himself;
His [1]offspring has been
destroyed along with his
[2]relatives
And his neighbors, and [b]he is
no more.
11 "Leave your [1a]orphans behind, I
will keep *them* alive;
And let your [b]widows trust
in Me."
12 ¶ For thus says the LORD, "Behold,
those [1]who were not sentenced to drink
the [a]cup will certainly drink *it,* and are
you the one who will be [b]completely acquitted? You will not be acquitted, but
you will certainly drink *it.*
13 "For I have [a]sworn by Myself," declares the LORD, "that [b]Bozrah will become an [c]object of horror, a reproach, a
ruin and a curse; and all its cities will
become perpetual ruins."
14 ¶ I have [a]heard a message from
the LORD,
And an [b]envoy is sent among
the nations, *saying,*
"[c]Gather yourselves together and
come against her,
And rise up for battle!"
15 "For behold, I have made you
small among the nations,
Despised among men.
16 "As for the terror of you,
The arrogance of your heart has
deceived you,
O you who live in the clefts of
[1]the [a]rock,
Who occupy the height of the
hill.
Though you make your nest as
[b]high as an eagle's,
I will [c]bring you down from
there," declares the LORD.
17 ¶ "Edom will become an [a]object of
horror; everyone who passes by it will be
horrified and will [b]hiss at all its wounds.
18 "Like the [a]overthrow of Sodom and
Gomorrah with its neighbors," says the
LORD, "[b]no one will live there, nor will
a son of man reside in it.
19 "[a]Behold, one will come up like a
lion from the [1b]thickets of the Jordan
against [2]a perennially watered pasture;
for in an instant I will make him run away
from it, and whoever is [c]chosen I shall
appoint over it. For who is [d]like Me, and
who will summon Me *into court?* And
who then is the shepherd [e]who can
stand against Me?"
20 ¶ Therefore hear the [a]plan of the
LORD which He has planned against
Edom, and His purposes which He has
purposed against the inhabitants of Teman: surely they will drag them off, *even*
the little ones of the flock; surely He will
make their [1]pasture [b]desolate because
of them.
21 The [a]earth has quaked at the noise
of their downfall. There is an outcry!
The noise of it has been heard at the
[1]Red Sea.
22 Behold, [1]He will mount up and
[a]swoop like an eagle and spread out His
wings [2]against Bozrah; and the [b]hearts
of the mighty men of Edom in that day
will be like the heart of a woman in labor.

Prophecy against Damascus

23 ¶ Concerning [a]Damascus.
"[b]Hamath and [c]Arpad are put to
shame,
For they have heard bad news;
They are [d]disheartened.
There is anxiety by the sea,
It [e]cannot be calmed.
24 "Damascus has become helpless;
She has turned away to flee,
And panic has gripped her;
[a]Distress and pangs have taken
hold of her
Like a woman in childbirth.
25 "How [1]the [a]city of praise has not
been deserted,
The town of My joy!
26 "Therefore, her [a]young men will
fall in her streets,
And all the men of war will be
[1]silenced in that day,"
declares the LORD of hosts.
27 "I will [a]set fire to the wall of
Damascus,
And it will devour the [1]fortified
towers of [b]Ben-hadad."

Prophecy against Kedar and Hazor

28 ¶ Concerning [a]Kedar and the kingdoms of Hazor, which Nebuchadnezzar
king of Babylon defeated. Thus says the
LORD,
"Arise, go up to Kedar

8 [1]Or *brought* [2]Or *punished* [a]Is 21:13; Jer 25:23 [b]Jer 46:21; Mal 1:3,4
9 [1]Lit *their sufficiency* [a]Obad 5
10 [1]Lit *seed* [2]Lit *brothers* [a]Jer 13:26 [b]Is 17:14
11 [1]Or *fatherless* [a]Ps 68:5; Hos 14:3 [b]Ps 68:5; Zech 7:10
12 [1]Lit *whose judgment was not to* [a]Jer 25:15 [b]Jer 25:28,29; 1 Pet 4:17
13 [a]Gen 22:16; Is 45:23; Jer 44:26; Amos 6:8 [b]Gen 36:33; 1 Chr 1:44; Is 34:6; 63:1; Amos 1:12 [c]Is 34:9-15; Jer 18:16
14 [a]Obad 1-4 [b]Is 18:2; 30:4 [c]Jer 50:14
16 [1]Or *Sela* [a]2 Kin 14:7; Jer 48:28 [b]Job 39:27; Is 14:13-15 [c]Amos 9:2
17 [a]Jer 18:16; 49:13; 50:13; Ezek 35:7 [b]1 Kin 9:8; Jer 51:37
18 [a]Gen 19:24, 25; Deut 29:23; Jer 50:40; Amos 4:11; Zeph 2:9 [b]Job 18:15-18; Jer 49:33
19 [1]Lit *pride* [2]Or *an enduring habitation* [a]Jer 50:44 [b]Josh 3:15; Jer 12:5 [c]Num 16:5 [d]Ex 15:11; Is 46:9 [e]Job 41:10
20 [1]Or *habitation* [a]Is 14:24, 27; Jer 50:45 [b]Mal 1:3,4
21 [1]Lit *Sea of Reeds* [a]Jer 50:46; Ezek 26:15,18
22 [1]Or *one* [2]Or *over* [a]Jer 4:13; 48:40; Hos 8:1 [b]Is 13:8; Jer 30:6; 48:41
23 [a]Gen 14:15; 15:2; 2 Kin 5:12; 2 Chr 16:2; Is 7:8; 17:1; Amos 1:3; Acts 9:2 [b]Num 13:21; Is 10:9; Jer 39:5; Amos 6:2 [c]2 Kin 18:34; 19:13; Is 10:9 [d]Ex 15:15; Nah 2:10 [e]Is 57:20
24 [a]Is 13:8
25 [1]Or *deserted is the city of praise* [a]Jer 33:9; 51:41
26 [1]Or *destroyed* [a]Jer 11:22; 50:30; Amos 4:10
27 [1]Or *palaces* [a]Jer 43:12; Amos 1:3-5 [b]1 Kin 15:18-20; 2 Kin 13:3
28 [a]Gen 25:13; Ps 120:5; Is 21:16,17; Jer 2:10; Ezek 27:21

And devastate the [1][b]men of the
east.
29 "They will take away their tents
and their flocks;
They will carry off for themselves
Their tent [a]curtains, all their
goods and their [b]camels,
And they will call out to one
another, '[c]Terror on every
side!'
30 "Run away, flee! Dwell in the
depths,
O inhabitants of Hazor," declares
the LORD;
"For [a]Nebuchadnezzar king of
Babylon has formed a plan
against you
And devised a scheme against
you.
31 "Arise, go up against a nation
which is [a]at ease,
Which lives securely," declares
the LORD.
"It has [b]no gates or bars;
They [c]dwell alone.
32 "Their camels will become
plunder,
And their many cattle for booty,
And I will [a]scatter to all the
winds those who [b]cut the
corners *of their hair;*
And I will bring their disaster
from every side," declares
the LORD.
33 "Hazor will become a [a]haunt of
jackals,
A desolation forever;
No one will live there,
Nor will a son of man reside
in it."

Prophecy against Elam

34 ¶ That which came as the word of
the LORD to Jeremiah the prophet concerning [a]Elam, [b]at the beginning of the
reign of Zedekiah king of Judah, saying:
35 ¶ "Thus says the LORD of hosts,
'Behold, I am going to [a]break the
bow of Elam,
The [1]finest of their might.
36 'I will bring upon Elam the [a]four
winds
From the four ends of heaven,
And will [b]scatter them to all
these winds;
And there will be no nation
To which the outcasts of Elam
will not go.
37 'So I will [1]shatter Elam before
their enemies
And before those who seek their
lives;
And I will [a]bring calamity upon
them,
Even My [b]fierce anger,' declares
the LORD,
'And I will [c]send out the sword
after them
Until I have consumed them.
38 'Then I will set My throne in
Elam
And destroy [1]out of it king and
princes,'
Declares the LORD.
39 'But it will come about in the last
days
That I will [a]restore the
[1]fortunes of Elam,' "
Declares the LORD.

Prophecy against Babylon

50 The word which the LORD spoke
concerning [a]Babylon, the land of
the Chaldeans, through Jeremiah the
prophet:
2 "[a]Declare and proclaim among
the nations.
Proclaim it and [b]lift up a
standard.
Do not conceal *it but* say,
'[c]Babylon has been captured,
[d]Bel has been put to shame,
[1]Marduk has been
[2]shattered;
Her [e]images have been put to
shame, her idols have been
shattered.'
3 "For a nation has come up against
her out of the [a]north; it will make her
land [b]an object of horror, and there will
be [c]no inhabitant in it. Both man and
beast have wandered off, they have gone
away!
4 ¶ "In those days and at that time,"
declares the LORD, "the sons of Israel will
come, *both* they and the sons of Judah
[a]as well; they will go along [b]weeping as
they go, and it will be [c]the LORD their
God they will seek.
5 "They will [a]ask for the way to Zion,
turning their faces [1]in its direction;
[2]they [3]will come that they may join
themselves to the LORD *in* an [b]everlast-
ing covenant that will not be forgotten.
6 ¶ "My people have become [a]lost
sheep;
[b]Their shepherds have led them
astray.
They have made them turn aside
on the [c]mountains;
They have gone along from
mountain to hill
And have forgotten their
[d]resting place.
7 "All who came upon them have
devoured them;
And their adversaries have said,
'[a]We are not guilty,

28 [1]Lit *sons* [b]Job 1:3; Is 11:14

29 [a]Hab 3:7 [b]1 Chr 5:21 [c]Jer 46:5

30 [a]Jer 25:9; 27:6

31 [a]Judg 18:7; Is 47:8 [b]Is 42:11 [c]Num 23:9; Deut 33:28; Mic 7:14

32 [a]Ezek 5:10; 12:14,15 [b]Jer 9:26; 25:23

33 [a]Is 13:20-22; Jer 9:11; 10:22; 51:37; Zeph 2:9, 13-15; Mal 1:3

34 [a]Gen 10:22; 14:1,9; Is 11:11; Jer 25:25; Ezek 32:24; Dan 8:2 [b]2 Kin 24:17,18; Jer 28:1

35 [1]Lit *first* [a]Ps 46:9; Is 22:6; Jer 51:56

36 [a]Dan 7:2; 8:8; Rev 7:1 [b]Jer 49:32; Ezek 5:10; Amos 9:9

37 [1]Or *dismay* [a]Jer 6:19 [b]Jer 30:24 [c]Jer 9:16; 48:2

38 [1]Or *from there*

39 [1]Or *captivity* [a]Jer 48:47

50:1 [a]Gen 10:10; 11:9; 2 Kin 17:24; Is 13:1; 47:1; Dan 1:1; Rev 14:8

2 [1]Heb *Merodach* [2]Or *dismayed* [a]Jer 4:16 [b]Jer 51:27 [c]Jer 51:31 [d]Is 46:1 [e]Jer 51:47

3 [a]Is 13:17; Jer 50:9; 51:11,27 [b]Is 14:22,23; Jer 50:13 [c]Jer 9:10, 11; Zeph 1:3

4 [a]Is 11:12,13; Jer 3:18; 31:31; 33:7; Hos 1:11 [b]Ezra 3:12,13; Ps 126:5; Jer 31:9 [c]Hos 3:5

5 [1]Lit *hither* [2]M.T. reads *come ye!* [3]Or *will have come* [a]Is 35:8; Jer 6:16 [b]Is 55:3; Jer 32:40; Heb 8:6-10

6 [a]Is 53:6; Ezek 34:15,16; Matt 9:36; 10:6 [b]Jer 23:11-14 [c]Jer 13:16; Ezek 34:6 [d]Jer 33:12; 50:19

7 [a]Jer 2:3; Zech 11:5

Inasmuch as they have sinned
against the LORD *who is* the
[b]habitation of righteousness,
Even the LORD, the [c]hope of
their fathers.'

8 ¶ "Wander away from the
[a]midst of Babylon
And [1]go forth from the land of
the Chaldeans;
Be also like male goats [2]at the
head of the flock.
9 "For behold, I am going to
[a]arouse and bring up
against Babylon
A horde of great nations from
the land of the north,
And they will draw up *their*
battle lines against her;
From there she will be taken
captive.
Their arrows will be like [1]an
expert warrior
Who does not return
empty-handed.
10 "[1a]Chaldea will become plunder;
All who plunder her will have
enough," declares the LORD.
11 ¶ "Because you are glad, because
you are jubilant,
O you who [a]pillage My heritage,
Because you skip about [1]like a
threshing [b]heifer
And neigh like [2]stallions,
12 Your [a]mother [1]will be greatly
ashamed,
She who gave you birth [1]will be
humiliated.
Behold, *she will be* the least of
the nations,
A [b]wilderness, a parched land
and a desert.
13 "Because of the indignation of the
LORD she will [a]not be
inhabited,
But she will be [b]completely
desolate;
Everyone who passes by Babylon
[c]will be horrified
And will hiss because of all her
wounds.
14 "Draw up your battle lines against
Babylon on every side,
All you who [1]bend the bow;
Shoot at her, do not be sparing
with *your* arrows,
For she has [a]sinned against the
LORD.
15 "Raise your battle cry against her
on every side!
She has [a]given [1]herself up, her
pillars have fallen,
Her [b]walls have been torn
down.
For this is the [c]vengeance of the
LORD:
Take vengeance on her;
[d]As she has done *to others, so*
do to her.
16 "Cut off the [a]sower from Babylon
And the one who wields the
sickle at the time of harvest;
From before [1]the [b]sword of the
oppressor
[c]They will each turn back to his
own people
And they will each flee to his
own land.

17 ¶ "Israel is a [a]scattered [1]flock, the
[b]lions have driven *them* away. The first
one *who* devoured him was the [c]king of
Assyria, and this last one *who* has broken
his bones is [d]Nebuchadnezzar king of
Babylon.
18 "Therefore thus says the LORD of
hosts, the God of Israel: 'Behold, I am
going to punish the king of Babylon and
his land, just as I [a]punished the king of
Assyria.
19 'And I will [a]bring Israel back to his
pasture and he will graze on Carmel and
Bashan, and his [1]desire will be satisfied
in the [b]hill country of Ephraim and Gilead.
20 'In those days and at that time,' declares the LORD, 'search will be made for
the iniquity of Israel, but [a]there will be
none; and for the sins of Judah, but they
will not be found; for I will pardon those
[b]whom I leave as a remnant.'
21 ¶ "Against the land of
[1]Merathaim, go up
against it,
And against the inhabitants of
[2a]Pekod.
Slay and [3]utterly destroy them,"
declares the LORD,
"And do according to all that I
have commanded you.
22 "The [a]noise of battle is in the
land,
And great destruction.
23 "How the [a]hammer of the whole
earth
Has been cut off and broken!
How Babylon has become
An object of horror among the
nations!
24 "I [a]set a snare for you and you
were also [b]caught,
O Babylon,
While you yourself were not
aware;
You have been found and also
seized
Because you have engaged in
[c]conflict with the LORD."
25 The LORD has opened His armory

7 [b]Jer 31:23; 40:2,3 [c]Ps 22:4; Jer 14:8; 17:13

8 [1]Another reading is *let them go forth* [2]Or *in front of* [a]Is 48:20; Jer 51:6; Rev 18:4

9 [1]So some mss and versions; M.T. reads *a warrior who makes childless* [a]Jer 51:1

10 [1]Or *the Chaldeans* [a]Jer 51:24,35; Ezek 11:24

11 [1]Another reading is *in the grass* [2]Lit *mighty ones* [a]Jer 12:14 [b]Jer 46:20

12 [1]Or *has become* [a]Jer 15:9 [b]Jer 22:6; 51:43

13 [a]Jer 34:22 [b]Jer 51:26 [c]Jer 18:16; 49:17

14 [1]Lit *tread* (in order to string) [a]Hab 2:8,17

15 [1]Lit *her hand* [a]1 Chr 29:24; 2 Chr 30:8; Lam 5:6 [b]Jer 50:44; 51:58 [c]Jer 46:10 [d]Ps 137:8; Rev 18:6

16 [1]Or *the oppressing sword* [a]Joel 1:11 [b]Jer 25:38; 46:16 [c]Is 13:14

17 [1]Lit *sheep* [a]Joel 3:2 [b]Jer 2:15; 4:7 [c]2 Kin 15:19; 17:6; 18:9-13 [d]2 Kin 24:1,10-12; 25:1-7

18 [a]Is 10:12; Ezek 31:3,11,12; Nah 3:7,18,19

19 [1]Lit *soul* [a]Is 65:10; Jer 31:10; 33:12; Ezek 34:13 [b]Jer 31:6

20 [a]Is 43:25; Jer 31:34; Mic 7:19 [b]Is 1:9

21 [1]Or *Double Rebellion* [2]Or *Punishment* [3]Lit *put under the ban* [a]Ezek 23:23

22 [a]Jer 4:19-21; 51:54-56

23 [a]Jer 51:20-24

24 [a]Jer 48:43,44 [b]Jer 51:31; Dan 5:30,31 [c]Job 9:4; 40:2,9

And has brought forth the
[a]weapons of His
indignation,
For it is a [b]work of the Lord
[1]GOD of hosts
In the land of the Chaldeans.
26 Come to her from the [1]farthest
border;
[a]Open up her barns,
Pile her up like heaps
And [2b]utterly destroy her,
Let nothing be left to her.
27 [a]Put all her young bulls to the
sword;
Let them [b]go down to the
slaughter!
Woe be upon them, for their
[c]day has come,
The time of their punishment.

28 ¶ There is a [a]sound of fugitives
and refugees from the land
of Babylon,
To declare in Zion the
[b]vengeance of the LORD our
God,
Vengeance for His [c]temple.

29 ¶ "Summon [1]many against
Babylon,
All those who [2]bend the bow:
Encamp against her on every
side,
Let there be no escape[3].
Repay her according to her work;
[a]According to all that she has
done, *so* do to her;
For she has become [b]arrogant
against the LORD,
Against the Holy One of Israel.
30 "Therefore her [a]young men will
fall in her streets,
And all her men of war will be
[1b]silenced in that day,"
declares the LORD.
31 "Behold, [a]I am against you,
O [1]arrogant one,"
Declares the Lord [2]GOD of hosts,
"For your day has come,
The time [3]when I will punish
you.
32 "The [1a]arrogant one will stumble
and fall
With no one to raise him up;
And I will [b]set fire to his cities
And it will devour all his
environs."

33 ¶ Thus says the LORD of hosts,
"The sons of Israel are oppressed,
And the sons of Judah as well;
And [a]all who took them captive
have held them fast,
They have refused to let
them go.
34 "Their [a]Redeemer is strong, [b]the
LORD of hosts is His name;
He will vigorously [c]plead their
case
So that He may [d]bring rest to
[1]the earth,
But turmoil to the inhabitants of
Babylon.
35 "A [a]sword against the
Chaldeans," declares the
LORD,
"And against the inhabitants of
Babylon
And against her [b]officials and
her [c]wise men!
36 "A sword against the [a]oracle
priests, and they will
become fools!
A sword against her [b]mighty
men, and they will be
[1c]shattered!
37 "A sword against [1]their [a]horses
and against [1]their chariots
And against all the [2b]foreigners
who are in the midst of her,
And they will become [c]women!
A sword against her treasures,
and they will be plundered!
38 "A [1a]drought on her waters, and
they will be dried up!
For it is a land of [b]idols,
And they are mad over fearsome
idols.

39 ¶ "Therefore the [a]desert
creatures will live *there*
along with the jackals;
The ostriches also will live in it,
And it will [b]never again be
inhabited
Or dwelt in from generation to
generation.
40 "As when God overthrew [a]Sodom
And Gomorrah with its
neighbors," declares the
LORD,
"No man will live there,
Nor will *any* son of man reside
in it.

41 ¶ "Behold, a people is coming
[a]from the north,
And a great nation and many
kings
Will be aroused from the remote
parts of the earth.
42 "They [a]seize *their* bow and
javelin;
They are [b]cruel and have no
mercy.
Their [c]voice roars like the sea;
And they ride on [d]horses,
[e]Marshalled like a man for the
battle

25 [1]Heb *YHWH,* usually rendered *LORD* [a]Is 13:5 [b]Jer 50:15; 51:12,25,55
26 [1]Lit *end* [2]Lit *put under the ban* [a]Is 45:3; Jer 50:10 [b]Is 14:23
27 [a]Is 34:7 [b]Jer 48:10 [c]Ps 37:13; Jer 46:21; 48:44; Ezek 7:7
28 [a]Is 48:20 [b]Ps 149:6-9; Jer 50:15; 51:10 [c]Lam 1:10; 2:6,7
29 [1]Another reading is *archers* [2]Lit *tread* (in order to string) [3]Some mss add *to her* [a]Ps 137:8; Jer 50:15; 51:56; 2 Thess 1:6 [b]Ex 10:3; Jer 49:16; Dan 4:37
30 [1]Or *made lifeless* or *destroyed* [a]Is 13:17,18; Jer 9:21; 18:21; 49:26; 51:4 [b]Jer 51:57
31 [1]Lit *arrogance* [2]Heb *YHWH,* usually rendered *LORD* [3]Another reading is *of your punishment* [a]Jer 21:13; Nah 2:13
32 [1]Lit *arrogance* [a]Is 10:12-15 [b]Jer 21:14; 49:27
33 [a]Is 14:17; 58:6
34 [1]Or their *land* [a]Prov 23:11; Is 43:14; Jer 15:21; 31:11; Rev 18:8 [b]Is 47:4; Jer 32:18; 51:19 [c]Jer 51:36; Mic 7:9 [d]Is 14:3-7
35 [a]Jer 47:6; Hos 11:6 [b]Dan 5:1,2 [c]Dan 5:7,8
36 [1]Or *dismayed* [a]Is 44:25 [b]Jer 49:22 [c]Nah 3:13
37 [1]Lit *his* [2]Lit *mixed multitude* [a]Ps 20:7,8; Jer 51:21,22 [b]Jer 25:20; Ezek 30:5 [c]Jer 48:41; 51:30; Nah 3:13
38 [1]Another reading is *sword* [a]Is 44:27; Jer 51:32,36; Rev 16:12 [b]Is 46:1, 6,7
39 [a]Is 13:21; 34:14; Rev 18:2 [b]Is 13:20; Jer 25:12
40 [a]Gen 19:24, 25; Is 13:19; Jer 49:18; Luke 17:28-30; 2 Pet 2:6; Jude 7
41 [a]Is 13:2-5; Jer 6:22; 50:3,9; 51:27,28
42 [a]Jer 6:23 [b]Is 13:17,18; 47:6 [c]Is 5:30 [d]Jer 8:16; 47:3; Hab 1:8 [e]Jer 50:9,14; Joel 2:5

Against you, O daughter of
Babylon.
43 "The [a]king of Babylon has heard
the report about them,
And his hands hang limp;
[b]Distress has gripped him,
Agony like a woman in
childbirth.
44 ¶ "[a]Behold, one will come up like
a lion from the [1]thicket of the Jordan to
[2]a perennially watered pasture; for in an
instant I will make them run away from
it, and whoever is [b]chosen I will appoint
over it. For who is [c]like Me, and who
will summon Me *into court?* And who
then is the shepherd who can [d]stand before Me?"
45 Therefore hear the [a]plan of the
LORD which He has planned against Babylon, and His purposes which He has purposed against the land of the Chaldeans:
[b]surely they will drag them off, *even* the
little ones of the flock; surely He will
make their [1]pasture desolate because of
them.
46 At the [1]shout, "Babylon has been
seized!" the [a]earth is shaken, and an
[b]outcry is heard among the nations.

Babylon Judged for Sins against Israel

51 Thus says the LORD:
"Behold, I am going to arouse
against Babylon
And against the inhabitants of
[1]Leb-kamai
[2]The [a]spirit of a destroyer.
2 "I will dispatch [1]foreigners to
Babylon that they may
[a]winnow her
And may devastate her land;
For on every side they will be
opposed to her
In the day of *her* calamity.
3 "[1]Let not [2]him who [3a]bends
his bow [3]bend *it,*
[1]Nor let him rise up in his
[b]scale-armor;
So do not spare her young men;
Devote all her army to
destruction.
4 "They will fall down [1]slain in the
land of the Chaldeans,
And [a]pierced through in their
streets."
5 ¶ For [a]neither Israel nor Judah
has been [1]forsaken
By his God, the LORD of hosts,
Although their land is [b]full of
guilt
[2]Before the Holy One of Israel.
6 [a]Flee from the midst of Babylon,
And each of you save his life!
Do not be [1b]destroyed in her
[2]punishment,
For this is the [c]LORD's time of
vengeance;
He is going to [d]render
recompense to her.
7 Babylon has been a golden [a]cup
in the hand of the LORD,
Intoxicating all the earth.
The [b]nations have drunk of her
wine;
Therefore the nations are [c]going
mad.
8 Suddenly [a]Babylon has fallen
and been broken;
[b]Wail over her!
[c]Bring [1]balm for her pain;
Perhaps she may be healed.
9 We applied healing to Babylon,
but she was not healed;
Forsake her and [a]let us each go
to his own country,
For her judgment has [b]reached
to heaven
And [1]towers up to the very
skies.
10 The LORD has [a]brought [1]about
our vindication;
Come and let us [b]recount in
Zion
The work of the LORD our God!
11 ¶ [a]Sharpen the arrows, fill the
quivers!
The LORD has aroused the spirit
of the kings of the Medes,
Because His purpose is against
Babylon to destroy it;
For it is the [b]vengeance of the
LORD, vengeance for His
temple.
12 [a]Lift up a [1]signal against the
walls of Babylon;
Post a strong guard,
Station [2]sentries,
Place men in ambush!
For the LORD has both
[b]purposed and performed
What He spoke concerning the
inhabitants of Babylon.
13 O you who [a]dwell by many
waters,
Abundant in [b]treasures,
Your end has come,
The [1]measure of your [2c]end.
14 The [a]LORD of hosts has sworn
by Himself:
"Surely I will fill you with a
[1]population like [b]locusts,
And they will cry out with
[2]shouts of victory
over you."
15 ¶ *It is* [a]He who made the earth
by His power,

43 [a]Jer 51:31 [b]Jer 30:6
44 [1]Lit *pride* [2]Or *an enduring habitation* [a]Jer 49:19-21 [b]Num 16:5 [c]Is 46:9 [d]Job 41:10; Jer 30:21
45 [1]Or *habitation* [a]Ps 33:11; Is 14:24; Jer 51:10 [b]Jer 49:20
46 [1]Lit *voice* [a]Jer 10:10; Ezek 26:18 [b]Is 5:7; Jer 46:12; Ezek 27:28
51:1 [1]Cryptic name for Chaldea; or *the heart of those who rise up against Me* [2]Or *a destroying wind* [a]Jer 4:11; Hos 13:15
2 [1]Some versions read *winnowers* [a]Is 41:16; Jer 15:7; Matt 3:12
3 [1]M.T. reads *Against him who* [2]I.e. the Chaldean defender [3]Lit *tread(s)* (in order to string) [a]Jer 50:14 [b]Jer 46:4
4 [1]Or *wounded* [a]Is 13:15; Jer 49:26
5 [1]Lit *widowed* [2]Lit *From* [a]Is 54:7; Jer 33:24-26 [b]Hos 4:1
6 [1]Or *silenced* or *made lifeless* [2]Or *penalty for iniquity* [a]Jer 50:8; Rev 18:4 [b]Num 16:26 [c]Jer 50:15 [d]Jer 25:14
7 [a]Jer 25:15; Hab 2:16; Rev 14:8 [b]Rev 14:8 [c]Jer 25:16
8 [1]Or *balsam resin* [a]Is 21:9; Jer 50:2; Rev 14:8 [b]Is 13:6; Rev 18:9 [c]Jer 46:11
9 [1]Lit *is lifted* [a]Is 13:14; Jer 46:16 [b]Ezra 9:6; Rev 18:5
10 [1]Lit *forth* [a]Ps 37:6; Mic 7:9 [b]Is 40:2; Jer 50:28
11 [a]Jer 46:4; Joel 3:9 [b]Jer 50:28
12 [1]Or *standard* [2]Or *watchmen* [a]Is 13:2; Jer 50:2 [b]Jer 4:28
13 [1]Lit *cubit* [2]Lit *being cut off* [a]Rev 17:1 [b]Is 45:3 [c]Is 57:17; Hab 2:9-11
14 [1]Or *mankind* [2]I.e. like the song of grape treaders [a]Jer 49:13 [b]Jer 51:27; Nah 3:15
15 [a]Gen 1:1; Jer 10:12-16

Who established the world by
His wisdom,
And by His understanding He
[b]stretched out the heavens.
16 When He utters His [a]voice,
there is a tumult of waters
in the heavens,
And He causes the [b]clouds to
ascend from the end of the
earth;
He makes lightning for the rain
And brings forth the [c]wind from
His storehouses.
17 [a]All mankind is stupid, devoid of
knowledge;
Every goldsmith is put to shame
by his [1]idols,
For his molten images are
[b]deceitful,
And there is no breath in them.
18 They are [a]worthless, a work of
mockery;
In the time of their punishment
they will perish.
19 The [a]portion of Jacob is not like
these;
For the [1]Maker of all is He,
And of the [2]tribe of His
inheritance;
The [b]LORD of hosts is His name.
20 *He says,* "You are My
[1a]war-club, *My* weapon of
war;
And with you I [b]shatter nations,
And with you I destroy
kingdoms.
21 "With you I [a]shatter the horse
and his rider,
And with you I shatter the
[b]chariot and its rider,
22 And with you I shatter [a]man
and woman,
And with you I shatter old man
and [b]youth,
And with you I shatter young
man and virgin,
23 And with you I shatter the
shepherd and his flock,
And with you I shatter the
farmer and his team,
And with you I shatter governors
and prefects.
24 ¶ "But I will repay Babylon and all
the inhabitants of [a]Chaldea for [b]all their
evil that they have done in Zion before
your eyes," declares the LORD.
25 "Behold, [a]I am against you,
[b]O destroying mountain,
Who destroys the whole earth,"
declares the LORD,
"And I will stretch out My hand
against you,
And roll you down from the
crags,
And I will make you a [c]burnt
out mountain.
26 "They will not take from you *even*
a stone for a corner
Nor a stone for foundations,
But you will be [a]desolate
forever," declares the LORD.

27 ¶ [a]Lift up a [1]signal in the land,
Blow a trumpet among the
nations!
Consecrate the nations against
her,
Summon against her the
[b]kingdoms of [c]Ararat,
Minni and [d]Ashkenaz;
Appoint a marshal against her,
Bring up the [e]horses like bristly
locusts.
28 Consecrate the nations against
her,
The kings of the Medes,
[1]Their governors and all [1]their
[2]prefects,
And every land of [3]their
dominion.
29 So the [a]land quakes and
writhes,
For the purposes of the LORD
against Babylon stand,
To make the land of Babylon
[1]A [b]desolation without
inhabitants.
30 The [a]mighty men of Babylon
have ceased fighting,
They stay in the strongholds;
[b]Their strength is [1]exhausted,
They are becoming [b]*like*
women;
Their dwelling places are set on
fire,
The [c]bars of her *gates* are
broken.
31 One [1a]courier runs to meet
[1]another,
And one [2b]messenger to meet
[2]another,
To tell the king of Babylon
That his city has been captured
from end *to end;*
32 The fords also have been seized,
And they have burned the
marshes with fire,
And the men of war are terrified.

33 ¶ For thus says the LORD of hosts,
the God of Israel:
"The daughter of Babylon is like a
[a]threshing floor
At the time [1]it is stamped firm;
Yet in a little while the time of
[b]harvest will come for her."

15 [b]Job 9:8; Ps 146:5,6; Jer 32:17; Acts 14:15; Rom 1:20
16 [a]Job 37:2-6; Ps 18:13 [b]Ps 135:7; Jer 10:13 [c]Jon 1:4
17 [1]Or *graven images* [a]Is 44:18-20; Jer 10:14 [b]Hab 2:18,19
18 [a]Jer 18:15
19 [1]Lit *Fashioner* [2]Or *Scepter;* cf Num 24:17 [a]Ps 73:26; Jer 10:16 [b]Jer 50:34
20 [1]Lit *shatterer* [a]Is 10:5; 41:15, 16; Jer 50:23 [b]Is 8:9; 41:15,16; Mic 4:12,13
21 [a]Ex 15:1 [b]Ex 15:4; Is 43:17
22 [a]2 Chr 36:17; Is 13:15, 16 [b]Is 13:18
24 [a]Jer 50:10 [b]Jer 50:15,29
25 [a]Jer 50:31 [b]Is 13:2; Zech 4:7 [c]Rev 8:8
26 [a]Is 13:19-22; Jer 50:13; 51:29
27 [1]Or *standard* [a]Is 13:2-5; 18:3; Jer 50:2; 51:12 [b]Jer 50:3,9 [c]Gen 8:4; 2 Kin 19:37; Is 37:38 [d]Gen 10:3 [e]Jer 50:42
28 [1]Lit *Her* [2]I.e. lieutenant governors [3]Lit *his*
29 [1]Or *An object of horror* [a]Jer 8:16; 10:10; 50:46; Amos 8:8 [b]Is 13:19,20; 47:11; Jer 50:13; 51:26,43
30 [1]Lit *dried up* [a]Ps 76:5; Jer 50:15,36,37 [b]Is 13:7,8; Nah 3:13 [c]Is 45:1,2; Lam 2:9; Amos 1:5; Nah 3:13
31 [1]Lit *runner* [2]Lit *announcer* [a]2 Chr 30:6 [b]2 Sam 18:19-31
33 [1]Lit *of treading it* [a]Is 21:10; 41:15,16; Mic 4:13 [b]Is 17:5; Hos 6:11; Joel 3:13; Rev 14:15

34 ¶ "Nebuchadnezzar king of
Babylon has [a]devoured me
and crushed me,
He has set me down *like* an
[b]empty vessel;
He has [c]swallowed me like a
monster,
He has filled his stomach with
my delicacies;
He has washed me away.
35 "May the [a]violence *done* to me
and to my flesh be upon
Babylon,"
The [1]inhabitant of Zion will say;
And, "May my blood be upon
the inhabitants of Chaldea,"
Jerusalem will say.
36 Therefore thus says the LORD,
"Behold, I am going to [a]plead
your case
And [b]exact full vengeance for
you;
And [c]I will dry up her [1]sea
And make her fountain dry.
37 "[a]Babylon will become a heap *of*
ruins, a haunt of jackals,
An [b]object of horror and hissing,
without inhabitants.
38 "They will roar together like
[a]young lions,
They will growl like lions' cubs.
39 "When they become heated up, I
will serve *them* their
banquet
And [a]make them drunk, that
they may become jubilant
And may [b]sleep a perpetual
sleep
And not wake up," declares the
LORD.
40 "I will bring them down like
[1]lambs [a]to the slaughter,
Like rams together with male
goats.

41 ¶ "How [1a]Sheshak has been
captured,
And [b]the praise of the whole
earth been seized!
How Babylon has become an
object of horror among the
nations!
42 "The [1a]sea has come up over
Babylon;
She has been engulfed with its
tumultuous waves.
43 "Her cities have become an
[a]object of horror,
A parched land and a desert,
A land in which [b]no man lives
And through which no son of
man passes.
44 "[a]I will punish Bel in Babylon,
And I will make what he has
swallowed [b]come out of his
mouth;
And the nations will no longer
[c]stream to him.
Even the [d]wall of Babylon has
fallen down!
45 ¶ "[a]Come forth from her midst,
My people,
And each of you [b]save
yourselves
From the fierce anger of the
LORD.
46 "Now [a]so that your heart does
not grow faint,
And you are not afraid at the
[b]report that *will be* heard in
the land—
For the report will come [1]one
year,
And after that [2]another report in
[2]another year,
And violence *will be* in the land
With [c]ruler against ruler—
47 Therefore behold, days are
coming
When I will punish the [a]idols of
Babylon;
And her whole land will be [b]put
to shame
And all her slain will fall in her
midst.
48 "Then [a]heaven and earth and all
that is in them
Will shout for joy over Babylon,
For [b]the destroyers will come to
her from the north,"
Declares the LORD.

49 ¶ [a]Indeed Babylon is to fall *for*
the slain of Israel,
As also for Babylon [b]the slain of
all the earth have fallen.
50 You [a]who have escaped the
sword,
Depart! Do not stay!
[b]Remember the LORD from afar,
And let Jerusalem [1]come to your
mind.
51 [a]We are ashamed because we
have heard reproach;
Disgrace has covered our faces,
For [b]aliens have entered
The holy places of the LORD'S
house.

52 ¶ "Therefore behold, the days
are coming," declares the
LORD,
"When I will punish her [a]idols,
And the mortally wounded will
groan throughout her land.
53 "Though Babylon should [a]ascend
to the heavens,

---

34 [a]Jer 50:17 [b]Is 24:1-3 [c]Job 20:15; Jer 51:44
35 [1]Lit *inhabitress* [a]Ps 137:8
36 [1]Or *broad river* [a]Ps 140:12 [b]Jer 51:6,11; Rom 12:19 [c]Jer 50:38
37 [a]Rev 18:2 [b]Jer 25:9
38 [a]Jer 2:15
39 [a]Jer 25:27; 48:26; 51:57 [b]Ps 76:5
40 [1]Or *young rams* [a]Jer 48:15; 50:27
41 [1]Cryptic name for Babylon [a]Jer 25:26 [b]Jer 49:25
42 [1]Or *broad river* [a]Is 8:7,8; Jer 51:55; Dan 9:26
43 [a]Jer 50:12 [b]Is 13:20; Jer 2:6
44 [a]Is 46:1; Jer 50:2 [b]Ezra 1:7,8 [c]Is 2:2 [d]Jer 50:15; 51:58
45 [a]Is 48:20; Jer 50:8,28; 51:6; Rev 18:4 [b]Gen 19:12-16; Acts 2:40
46 [1]Lit *in the* [2]Lit *the* [a]Is 43:5; Jer 46:27,28 [b]2 Kin 19:7; Is 13:3-5 [c]Is 19:2
47 [a]Is 21:9; 46:1,2; Jer 50:2; 51:52 [b]Jer 50:12,35-37
48 [a]Is 44:23; 48:20; 49:13; Rev 18:20 [b]Jer 50:3
49 [a]Ps 137:8; Jer 50:29 [b]Rev 18:24
50 [1]Lit *come upon your heart* [a]Jer 44:28 [b]Deut 4:29-31; Ps 137:6
51 [a]Ps 44:15 [b]Ps 74:3-8; Lam 1:10
52 [a]Jer 50:38
53 [a]Gen 11:4; Job 20:6; Ps 139:8-10; Is 14:12-14; Jer 49:16; Amos 9:2; Obad 4

And though she should fortify
[1]her lofty stronghold,
From [b]Me destroyers will come
to her," declares the LORD.

54 ¶ The [a]sound of an outcry from
Babylon,
And of great destruction from
the land of the Chaldeans!
55 For the LORD is going to destroy
Babylon,
And He will make *her* loud
[1]noise vanish from her.
And their [a]waves will roar like
many waters;
The tumult of their voices
[2]sounds forth.
56 For the [a]destroyer is coming
against her, against Babylon,
And her mighty men will be
captured,
Their [b]bows are shattered;
For the LORD is a God of
[c]recompense,
He will fully repay.
57 "I will [a]make her princes and her
wise men drunk,
Her governors, her prefects and
her mighty men,
That they may sleep a
[b]perpetual sleep and not
wake up,"
[c]Declares the King, whose name
is the LORD of hosts.
58 Thus says the LORD of hosts,
"The broad [a]wall of Babylon will
be completely razed
And her high [b]gates will be set
on fire;
So the peoples will [c]toil for
nothing,
And the nations become
[d]exhausted *only* for fire."

59 ¶ The [1]message which Jeremiah the prophet commanded Seraiah the son of [a]Neriah, the grandson of Mahseiah, when he went with [b]Zedekiah the king of Judah to Babylon in the fourth year of his reign. (Now Seraiah was quartermaster.)

60 So Jeremiah [a]wrote in a single [1]scroll all the calamity which would come upon Babylon, *that is,* all these words which have been written concerning Babylon.

61 Then Jeremiah said to Seraiah, "As soon as you come to Babylon, then see that you read all these words aloud,

62 and say, 'You, O LORD, have [1]promised concerning this place to [a]cut it off, so that there will be [b]nothing dwelling in it, [2]whether man or beast, but it will be a perpetual desolation.'

63 "And as soon as you finish reading this [1]scroll, you will tie a stone to it and [a]throw it into the middle of the Euphrates,

64 and say, 'Just so shall Babylon sink down and [a]not rise again because of the calamity that I am going to bring upon her; and they will become [b]exhausted.' " [c]Thus far are the words of Jeremiah.

The Fall of Jerusalem

52

[a]Zedekiah was twenty-one years old when he became king, and he reigned eleven years in Jerusalem; and his mother's name was [1b]Hamutal the daughter of Jeremiah of [c]Libnah.

2 He did [a]evil in the sight of the LORD like all that [b]Jehoiakim had done.

3 For through the [a]anger of the LORD *this* came about in Jerusalem and Judah until He cast them out from His presence. And Zedekiah [b]rebelled against the king of Babylon.

4 [a]Now it came about in the ninth year of his reign, on the tenth *day* of the tenth month, that Nebuchadnezzar king of Babylon came, he and all his army, against Jerusalem, camped against it and built a [b]siege wall all around [1]it.

5 [a]So the city was under siege until the eleventh year of King Zedekiah.

6 On the ninth *day* of the [a]fourth month the [b]famine was so severe in the city that there was no food for the people of the land.

7 Then the city was [a]broken into, and all the [b]men of war fled and went forth from the city at night by way of the gate between the two walls which *was* by the king's garden, though the Chaldeans were [1c]all around the city. And they went by way of the Arabah.

8 But the army of the Chaldeans pursued the king and [a]overtook Zedekiah in the [1]plains of Jericho, and all his army was scattered from him.

9 Then they captured the king and [a]brought him up to the king of Babylon at [b]Riblah in the land of [c]Hamath, and he [1]passed sentence on him.

10 The king of Babylon [a]slaughtered the sons of Zedekiah before his eyes, and he also slaughtered all the [1]princes of Judah in Riblah.

11 Then he [a]blinded the eyes of Zedekiah; and the king of Babylon bound him with bronze fetters and brought him to Babylon and put him in prison until the day of his death.

12 ¶ [a]Now on the tenth *day* of the fifth month, which was the [b]nineteenth year of King Nebuchadnezzar, king of Babylon, [c]Nebuzaradan the captain of the bodyguard, [1]who was in the service of the king of Babylon, came to Jerusalem.

---

53 [1]Lit *the height of her strength* [b]Is 13:3
54 [a]Jer 48:3-5; 50:22,46
55 [1]Or *voice* [2]Lit *is given* [a]Ps 18:4; 69:2; 124:2,4,5; Jer 51:42
56 [a]Jer 51:48, 53; Hab 2:8 [b]Ps 46:9; 76:3 [c]Deut 32:35; Ps 94:1,2; Jer 51:6,24
57 [a]Jer 25:27 [b]Ps 76:5,6 [c]Jer 46:18; 48:15
58 [a]Jer 50:15 [b]Is 45:1,2 [c]Hab 2:13 [d]Jer 9:5; 51:64; Lam 5:5
59 [1]Lit *word* [a]Jer 32:12; 36:4; 45:1 [b]Jer 28:1; 52:1
60 [1]Or *book* [a]Is 30:8; Jer 30:2,3; 36:2,4,32
62 [1]Lit *spoken* [2]Lit *from man even to beast* [a]Is 13:19-22; 14:22, 23; Jer 50:3,13, 39,40 [b]Jer 51:43; Ezek 35:9
63 [1]Or *book* [a]Jer 19:10,11; Rev 18:21
64 [a]Nah 1:8,9 [b]Jer 51:58 [c]Job 31:40; Ps 72:20
52:1 [1]Another reading is *Hamital* [a]2 Kin 24:18; 2 Chr 36:11 [b]2 Kin 23:31; 24:18 [c]Josh 10:29; 2 Kin 8:22; Is 37:8
2 [a]1 Kin 14:22; 2 Kin 24:19; 2 Chr 36:12 [b]Jer 36:30,31
3 [a]2 Kin 24:20; Is 3:1,4,5 [b]2 Chr 36:13; Ezek 17:12-16
4 [1]Lit *against it* [a]2 Kin 25:1; Jer 39:1; Ezek 24:1, 2; Zech 8:19 [b]Jer 32:24
5 [a]2 Kin 25:2
6 [a]Jer 39:2 [b]2 Kin 25:3; Is 3:1; Jer 38:9; Ezek 4:16; 5:16; 14:13
7 [1]Lit *against the city on every side* [a]2 Kin 25:4; Jer 39:2 [b]Jer 39:4-7; 51:32 [c]Ezek 33:21
8 [1]Lit *Arabah* [a]Jer 21:7; 32:4; 34:21; 37:17; 38:23
9 [1]Lit *spoke judgments with* [a]2 Kin 25:6; Jer 32:4; 39:5 [b]Num 34:11; Jer 39:5 [c]Num 13:21; Josh 13:5
10 [1]Or *commanders* [a]2 Kin 25:7; Jer 22:30; 39:6
11 [a]Jer 39:7; Ezek 12:13
12 [1]Lit *stood before the king* [a]2 Kin 25:8-21; Zech 7:5; 8:19 [b]2 Kin 24:12; 25:8; Jer 52:29 [c]Jer 39:9

13 He [a]burned the house of the LORD, the [b]king's house and all the houses of Jerusalem; even every large house he burned with fire.

14 So all the army of the Chaldeans who *were* with the captain of the guard [a]broke down all the walls around Jerusalem.

15 Then Nebuzaradan the captain of the guard [a]carried away into exile some of the poorest of the people, the rest of the people who were left in the city, the [1b]deserters who had deserted to the king of Babylon and the rest of the artisans.

16 But [a]Nebuzaradan the captain of the guard left some of the poorest of the land to be vinedressers and [1]plowmen.

17 ¶ Now the bronze [a]pillars which belonged to the house of the LORD and the [b]stands and the bronze [c]sea, which were in the house of the LORD, the Chaldeans broke in pieces and carried all their bronze to Babylon.

18 They also took away the [a]pots, the shovels, the snuffers, the basins, the [1]pans and all the bronze vessels which were used in *temple* service.

19 The captain of the guard also took away the [a]bowls, the firepans, the basins, the pots, the lampstands, the [1]pans and the drink offering bowls, what was fine gold and what was fine silver.

20 The two pillars, the one sea, and the twelve bronze bulls that were under [1]the sea, *and* the stands, which King Solomon had made for the house of the LORD—the bronze of all these vessels was [a]beyond weight.

21 As for the pillars, the [a]height of each pillar *was* eighteen [1]cubits, and [2]it *was* twelve cubits in [a]circumference and four fingers in thickness, *and* hollow.

22 Now a [a]capital of bronze was on it; and the height of each capital was five cubits, with network and [b]pomegranates upon the capital all around, all of bronze. And the second pillar was like these, including pomegranates.

23 There were ninety-six [1]exposed pomegranates; all [a]the pomegranates *numbered* a hundred on the network all around.

24 ¶ Then the captain of the guard took [a]Seraiah the chief priest and [b]Zephaniah the second priest, with the three [1c]officers of the temple.

25 He also took from the city one official who was overseer of the men of war, and seven [1]of the [a]king's advisers who were found in the city, and the scribe of the commander of the army who mustered the people of the land, and sixty men of the people of the land who were found in the midst of the city.

26 Nebuzaradan the captain of the guard took them and [a]brought them to the king of Babylon at Riblah.

27 Then the king of Babylon [a]struck them down and put them to death at Riblah in the land of Hamath. So Judah was [b]led away into exile from its land.

28 ¶ These are the people whom [a]Nebuchadnezzar carried away into exile: in the [1]seventh year 3,023 Jews;

29 in the eighteenth year of Nebuchadnezzar 832 persons from Jerusalem;

30 in the twenty-third year of Nebuchadnezzar, [a]Nebuzaradan the captain of the guard carried into exile 745 Jewish people; there were 4,600 persons in all.

31 ¶ [a]Now it came about in the thirty-seventh year of the exile of Jehoiachin king of Judah, in the twelfth month, on the twenty-fifth of the month, that [1]Evil-merodach king of Babylon, in the *first* year of his reign, [2b]showed favor to Jehoiachin king of Judah and brought him out of prison.

32 [a]Then he spoke kindly to him and set his throne above the thrones of the kings who *were* with him in Babylon.

33 So [1]Jehoiachin [a]changed his prison clothes, and [2b]had his meals in [3]the king's presence regularly all the days of his life.

34 For his allowance, a [a]regular allowance was given him by the king of Babylon, a daily portion all the days of his life until the day of his death.

13 [a]1 Kin 9:8; 2 Kin 25:9; 2 Chr 36:19; Ps 74:6-8; Is 64:10; Lam 2:7; Mic 3:12 [b]Jer 39:8 **14** [a]2 Kin 25:10; Neh 1:3 **15** [1]Lit *fallers who had fallen* [a]2 Kin 25:11 [b]Jer 39:9 **16** [1]Or *unpaid laborers* [a]2 Kin 25:12; Jer 39:10 **17** [a]1 Kin 7:15-22; 2 Kin 25:13; Jer 27:19-22 [b]1 Kin 7:27-37 [c]1 Kin 7:23-26 **18** [1]Or *spoons* for incense [a]Ex 27:3; 1 Kin 7:40; 2 Kin 25:14 **19** [1]Or *spoons* for incense [a]1 Kin 7:49; 2 Kin 25:15 **20** [1]So Gr and Syriac; Heb omits *the sea* [a]1 Kin 7:47; 2 Kin 25:16 **21** [1]I.e. One cubit equals approx 18 in. [2]Lit *a line of 12 cubits would encircle it* [a]1 Kin 7:15; 2 Kin 25:17; 2 Chr 3:15 **22** [a]1 Kin 7:16; 2 Kin 25:17 [b]1 Kin 7:20 **23** [1]Lit *windward* [a]1 Kin 7:20 **24** [1]Lit *keepers of the door* [a]2 Kin 25:18; 1 Chr 6:14; Ezra 7:1 [b]2 Kin 25:18; Jer 21:1 [c]1 Chr 9:19; Jer 35:4 **25** [1]Lit *men of those seeing the king's face* [a]2 Kin 25:19; Esth 1:14 **26** [a]2 Kin 25:20 **27** [a]2 Kin 25:21; Ezek 8:11-18 [b]Is 6:11; Jer 13:19; Ezek 33:28; Mic 4:10 **28** [1]Or possibly *seventeenth* [a]2 Kin 24:2; 2 Chr 36:20; Ezra 2:1; Neh 7:6; Dan 1:1-3 **30** [a]2 Kin 25:11; Jer 39:9 **31** [1]Or *Awil-Marduk* ("Man of Marduk") [2]Lit *lifted up the head of* [a]2 Kin 25:27 [b]Gen 40:13; Ps 3:3 **32** [a]2 Kin 25:28 **33** [1]Lit *he* [2]Lit *ate* [3]Lit *his presence* [a]Gen 41:14; 2 Kin 25:29 [b]2 Sam 9:7; 1 Kin 2:7 **34** [a]2 Sam 9:10; 2 Kin 25:30

Lamentations

Title and Background

Because of its subject matter, the book is referred to in Jewish tradition as "Lamentations." It was written as a reminder of the fall of Jerusalem and of the burning of the temple.

Author and Date of Writing

Although the writer of Lamentations is anonymous, ancient Jewish and Christian tradition ascribes it to Jeremiah. Since he was an eyewitness to the divine judgment on Jerusalem in 586 B.C., it is reasonable to assume he was the author. The book was probably written shortly after 586.

Theme and Message

Lamentations is the only Old Testament book that consists solely of laments. Jeremiah recognizes that the judgment on Jerusalem and the temple is the judgment of a righteous God. The book that begins with a lament (1:1–2) rightly ends in repentance (5:21–22). Knowing that God is merciful, the author appeals for mercy in prayer to God. In the middle of the book, the theology of Lamentations reaches its apex as it focuses on God's goodness. In spite of all evidence to the contrary, "His compassions never fail."

Outline

I. Jerusalem's Misery and Desolation (1:1–22)
II. The Lord's Anger Against His People (2:1–22)
III. Judah's Complaint and the Basis for Consolation (3:1–66)
IV. The Contrast Between Zion's Past and Present (4:1–22)
V. Judah's Appeal for God's Forgiveness (5:1–22)

The Sorrows of Zion

1 How [a]lonely sits the city
That was [b]full of people!
She has become like a [c]widow
Who was *once* [d]great among the nations!
She who was a princess among the [1]provinces
Has become a [e]forced laborer!
2 She [a]weeps bitterly in the night
And her tears are on her cheeks;
She has none to comfort her
Among all her [b]lovers.
All her friends have [c]dealt treacherously with her;
They have become her enemies.
3 [a]Judah has gone into exile [1]under affliction
And [1]under [2]harsh servitude;
She dwells [b]among the nations,
But she has found no rest;
All [c]her pursuers have overtaken her
In the midst of [3]distress.
4 The roads [1]of Zion are in mourning
Because [a]no one comes to the appointed feasts.
All her gates are [b]desolate;
Her priests are groaning,
Her [c]virgins are afflicted,
And she herself [2]is [d]bitter.
5 Her adversaries have become [1]her masters,
Her enemies [2]prosper;
For the LORD has [a]caused her grief
Because of the multitude of her transgressions;
Her little ones have gone away
As captives before the adversary.
6 All her [a]majesty
Has departed from the daughter of Zion;
Her princes have become like deer
That have found no pasture;
And they have [1][b]fled without strength
Before the pursuer.
7 In the days of her affliction and homelessness
[a]Jerusalem remembers all her precious things

1:1 [1]Or *districts* [a]Is 3:26 [b]Is 22:2 [c]Is 54:4 [d]1 Kin 4:21; Ezra 4:20; Jer 31:7 [e]2 Kin 23:35; Jer 40:9

2 [a]Ps 6:6; 77:2-6; Lam 1:16 [b]Jer 2:25; 3:1; 22:20-22 [c]Job 19:13,14; Ps 31:11; Mic 7:5

3 [1]Or *by reason of* [2]Lit *great* [3]Or *narrow places* [a]Jer 13:19 [b]Lev 26:39; Deut 28:64-67 [c]2 Kin 25:4,5

4 [1]Or *to* [2]Or *suffers bitterly* [a]Is 24:4-6; Lam 2:6,7 [b]Jer 9:11; 10:22 [c]Lam 2:10,21 [d]Joel 1:8-13

5 [1]Lit *head* [2]Or *are at ease* [a]Ps 90:7,8; Ezek 8:17,18; 9:9,10

6 [1]Lit *gone* [a]Jer 13:18 [b]2 Kin 25:4,5

7 [a]Ps 42:4; 77:5-9

That were from the days of old,
When her people fell into the
hand of the adversary
And [b]no one helped her.
The adversaries saw her,
They [c]mocked at her [1]ruin.
8 Jerusalem sinned [a]greatly,
Therefore [b]she has become an
unclean thing.
All who honored her despise her
Because they have seen her
nakedness;
Even [c]she herself groans and
turns away.
9 Her [a]uncleanness was in her
skirts;
She [1]did not consider her
[b]future.
Therefore she has [2c]fallen
astonishingly;
[d]She has no comforter.
"[e]See, O LORD, my affliction,
For the enemy has [f]magnified
himself!"
10 The adversary has stretched out
his hand
Over all her precious things,
For she has seen the [a]nations
enter her sanctuary,
The ones whom You commanded
That they should [b]not enter into
Your congregation.
11 All her people groan [a]seeking
bread;
They have given their precious
things for food
To [b]restore their [1]lives
themselves.
"See, O LORD, and look,
For I am [c]despised."
12 "Is [a]it nothing to all you who
pass this way?
Look and see if there is any
[1]pain like my [1]pain
Which was severely dealt out
to me,
Which the [b]LORD inflicted on
the day of His [c]fierce anger.
13 "From on high He sent fire into
my [a]bones,
And it [1]prevailed *over them.*
He has spread a [b]net for my
feet;
He has turned me back;
He has made me [c]desolate,
[2]Faint all day long.
14 "The [a]yoke of my transgressions
is bound;
By His hand they are knit
together.
They have [b]come upon my
neck;
He has made my strength [1]fail.
The Lord [c]has given me into the
hands
Of *those against whom* I am not
able to stand.
15 "The [a]Lord has rejected all my
strong men
In my midst;
He has called an appointed
[1]time against me
To crush my [b]young men;
The Lord has [c]trodden *as in* a
wine press
The virgin daughter of Judah.
16 "For these things I [a]weep;
[1]My eyes run down with water;
Because far from me is a
[b]comforter,
One who restores my soul.
My children are desolate
Because the enemy has
prevailed."
17 Zion [a]stretches out her hands;
There is no one to comfort her;
The LORD has [b]commanded
concerning Jacob
That the ones round about him
should be his adversaries;
[c]Jerusalem has become an
unclean thing among them.
18 "The LORD is [a]righteous;
For I have [b]rebelled against His
[1]command;
Hear now, all peoples,
And [c]behold my [2]pain;
[d]My virgins and my young men
Have gone into captivity.
19 "I [a]called to my lovers, *but* they
deceived me;
My [b]priests and my elders
perished in the city
While they sought food to
[c]restore [1]their strength
themselves.
20 "See, O LORD, for I am in distress;
My [1a]spirit is greatly troubled;
My heart is overturned
within me,
For I have been very [b]rebellious.
In the street the sword [2]slays;
In the house it is like death.
21 "They have heard that I [a]groan;
There is no one to comfort me;
All my enemies have heard of
my [1]calamity;
They are [b]glad that You have
done *it.*
Oh, that You would bring the
day which You have
proclaimed,
That they may become [c]like me.
22 "Let all their wickedness come
before You;
And [a]deal with them as You
have dealt with me

7 [1]Lit *cessation* [b]Jer 37:7; Lam 4:17 [c]Ps 79:4; Jer 48:27

8 [a]Is 59:2-13; Lam 1:5,20 [b]Lam 1:17 [c]Lam 1:11,21,22

9 [1]Lit *did not remember her latter end* [2]Lit *come down* [a]Jer 2:34; Ezek 24:13 [b]Deut 32:29; Is 47:7 [c]Is 3:8; Jer 13:17,18 [d]Eccl 4:1; Jer 16:7 [e]Ps 25:18; 119:153 [f]Ps 74:23; Zeph 2:10

10 [a]Ps 74:4-8; Is 64:10,11; Jer 51:51 [b]Deut 23:3

11 [1]Lit *soul* [a]Jer 38:9; 52:6 [b]1 Sam 30:12 [c]Jer 15:19

12 [1]Or *sorrow* [a]Jer 18:16; 48:27 [b]Jer 30:23,24 [c]Is 13:13; Jer 4:8

13 [1]Or *descended, overthrew* [2]Or *Sick* [a]Job 30:30; Ps 22:14; Hab 3:16 [b]Job 19:6; Ps 66:11 [c]Jer 44:6

14 [1]Lit *stumble* [a]Prov 5:22; Is 47:6 [b]Jer 28:13, 14 [c]Jer 32:3,5; Ezek 25:4,7

15 [1]Or *feast* [a]Is 41:2; Jer 13:24; 37:10 [b]Jer 6:11; 18:21 [c]Mal 4:3

16 [1]Lit *My eye, my eye* [a]Jer 14:17; Lam 2:11,18; 3:48,49 [b]Ps 69:20; Eccl 4:1; Lam 1:2

17 [a]Is 1:15; Jer 4:31 [b]2 Kin 24:2-4; Jer 12:9 [c]Lam 1:8

18 [1]Lit *mouth* [2]Or *sorrow* [a]Ps 119:75; Jer 12:1 [b]1 Sam 12:14, 15; Jer 4:17 [c]Lam 1:12 [d]Deut 28:32,41

19 [1]Lit *their soul* [a]Job 19:13-19; Lam 1:2 [b]Jer 14:15; Lam 2:20 [c]Lam 1:11

20 [1]Lit *inward parts are in ferment* [2]Lit *bereaves* [a]Is 16:11; Lam 2:11 [b]Jer 14:20

21 [1]Lit *evil* [a]Lam 1:4,8,22 [b]Ps 35:15; Jer 50:11; Lam 2:15 [c]Is 14:5,6; 47:6, 11; Jer 30:16

22 [a]Neh 4:4,5; Ps 137:7,8

For all my transgressions;
For my groans are many and my
heart is faint."

God's Anger over Israel

2 How the Lord has [a]covered the
daughter of Zion
With a cloud in His anger!
He has [b]cast from heaven to
earth
The [c]glory of Israel,
And has not remembered His
[d]footstool
In the day of His anger.
2 The Lord has [a]swallowed up; He
has not spared
All the habitations of Jacob.
In His wrath He has [b]thrown
down
The strongholds of the daughter
of Judah;
He has [c]brought *them* down to
the ground;
He has [d]profaned the kingdom
and its princes.
3 In fierce anger He has cut off
[1]All the [a]strength of Israel;
He has [b]drawn back His right
hand
From before the enemy.
And He has [c]burned in Jacob
like a flaming fire
Consuming round about.
4 He has bent His [a]bow like an
enemy;
He has set His right hand like an
adversary
And slain all that were [b]pleasant
to the eye;
In the tent of the daughter of
Zion
He has [c]poured out His wrath
like fire.
5 The Lord has become like an
[a]enemy.
He has [b]swallowed up Israel;
He has swallowed up all its
[c]palaces,
He has destroyed its strongholds
And [d]multiplied in the daughter
of Judah
Mourning and moaning.
6 And He has violently treated His
[1]tabernacle like a garden
booth;
He has [a]destroyed His appointed
[2]meeting place.
The LORD has [b]caused to be
forgotten
The appointed feast and sabbath
in Zion,
And He has [c]despised king and
priest
In the indignation of His anger.
7 The Lord has [a]rejected His altar,
He has abandoned His sanctuary;
He [b]has delivered into the hand
of the enemy
The walls of her palaces.
They have made a [c]noise in the
house of the LORD
As in the day of an appointed
feast.
8 The LORD [1]determined to
destroy
The wall of the daughter of Zion.
He has [a]stretched out a line,
He has not restrained His hand
from [2]destroying,
And He has [b]caused rampart
and wall to lament;
They have languished together.
9 Her [a]gates have sunk into the
ground,
He has destroyed and broken her
bars.
Her king and her princes are
among the nations;
The [b]law is no more.
Also, her prophets find
[c]No vision from the LORD.
10 The elders of the daughter of
Zion
[a]Sit on the ground, they [b]are
silent.
They have thrown [c]dust on
their heads;
They have girded themselves
with [d]sackcloth.
The [e]virgins of Jerusalem
Have bowed their heads to the
ground.
11 My [a]eyes fail because of tears,
My [1b]spirit is greatly troubled;
My [2c]heart is poured out on
the earth
[d]Because of the [3]destruction of
the daughter of my people,
When [e]little ones and infants
faint
In the streets of the city.
12 They say to their mothers,
"[a]Where is grain and wine?"
As they faint like a
wounded man
In the streets of the city,
As their [b]life is poured out
On their mothers' bosom.
13 How shall I admonish you?
To what [a]shall I compare you,
O daughter of Jerusalem?
To what shall I liken you as I
comfort you,
O [b]virgin daughter of Zion?
For your [1]ruin is as vast as the
sea;
Who can [c]heal you?

2:1 [a]Ezek 30:18 [b]Is 14:12-15; Ezek 28:14-16 [c]Is 64:11 [d]Ps 99:5; 132:7

2 [a]Ps 21:9; Lam 3:43 [b]Lam 2:5; Mic 5:11,14 [c]Is 25:12; 26:5 [d]Ps 89:39,40; Is 43:28

3 [1]Lit *Every horn* [a]Ps 75:5, 10; Jer 48:25 [b]Ps 74:11; Jer 21:4,5 [c]Is 42:25; Jer 21:14

4 [a]Job 6:4; 16:13; Lam 3:12,13 [b]Ezek 24:25 [c]Is 42:25; Jer 7:20

5 [a]Jer 30:14 [b]Lam 2:2 [c]Jer 52:13; Lam 2:2 [d]Jer 9:17-20

6 [1]Lit *booth* [2]Or *feast* [a]Jer 52:13 [b]Jer 17:27; Lam 1:4; Zeph 3:18 [c]Lam 4:16

7 [a]Ps 78:59-61; Is 64:11; Ezek 7:20-22 [b]Jer 33:4,5; 52:13 [c]Ps 74:3-8

8 [1]Lit *thought* [2]Lit *swallowing up* [a]2 Kin 21:13; Is 34:11; Amos 7:7-9 [b]Is 3:26; Jer 14:2

9 [a]Neh 1:3 [b]Hos 3:4 [c]Jer 14:14; 23:16; Ezek 7:26

10 [a]Job 2:13; Is 3:26; 47:1 [b]Amos 8:3 [c]Job 2:12; Ezek 27:30 [d]Is 15:3; Jon 3:6-8 [e]Lam 1:4

11 [1]Lit *inward parts are in ferment* [2]Lit *liver* [3]Lit *breaking* [a]Lam 1:16; 3:48, 51 [b]Jer 4:19 [c]Job 16:13 [d]Is 22:4; Lam 4:10 [e]Jer 44:7; Lam 2:19

12 [a]Jer 5:17 [b]Job 30:16; Ps 42:4; 62:8

13 [1]Lit *breaking* [a]Lam 1:12 [b]Is 37:22 [c]Jer 8:22; 30:12-15

14 Your [a]prophets have seen
for you
False and foolish *visions;*
And they have not [b]exposed
your iniquity
So as to restore you from
captivity,
But they have [c]seen for you
false and misleading
[1]oracles.
15 All who pass along the way
[a]Clap their hands *in derision* at
you;
They [b]hiss and shake their
heads
At the daughter of Jerusalem,
"Is this the city of which they
said,
'[c]The perfection of beauty,
[d]A joy to all the earth'?"
16 All [a]your enemies
Have opened their mouths wide
against you;
They hiss and [b]gnash *their*
teeth.
They say, "We have [c]swallowed
her up!
Surely this is the [d]day for which
we waited;
We have reached *it,* we have
seen *it.*"
17 The LORD has [a]done what He
purposed;
He has accomplished His word
Which He commanded from days
of old.
He has thrown down [b]without
sparing,
And He has caused the enemy to
[c]rejoice over you;
He has [d]exalted the [1]might of
your adversaries.
18 Their [a]heart cried out to the
Lord,
"O [b]wall of the daughter of Zion,
Let *your* [c]tears run down like a
river day and night;
Give yourself no relief,
Let [1]your eyes have no rest.
19 "Arise, cry aloud in the [a]night
At the beginning of the night
watches;
[b]Pour out your heart like water
Before the presence of the Lord;
Lift up your hands to Him
For the [c]life of your little ones
Who are [d]faint because of
hunger
At the head of every street."
20 See, O LORD, and look!
With [a]whom have You dealt
thus?
Should women [b]eat their
[1]offspring,
The little ones who were [2]born
healthy?
Should [c]priest and prophet be
slain
In the sanctuary of the Lord?
21 On the ground in the streets
Lie [a]young and old;
My [b]virgins and my young men
Have fallen by the sword.
You have slain *them* in the day
of Your anger,
You have slaughtered, [c]not
sparing.
22 You called as in the day of an
appointed feast
My [a]terrors on every side;
And there was [b]no one who
escaped or survived
In the day of the LORD'S anger.
Those [c]whom I [1]bore and
reared,
My enemy annihilated them.

Jeremiah Shares Israel's Affliction

3 I am the man who has [a]seen
affliction
Because of the rod of His wrath.
2 He has driven me and made me
walk
In [a]darkness and not in light.
3 Surely against me He has
[a]turned His hand
Repeatedly all the day.
4 He has caused my [a]flesh and my
skin to waste away,
He has [b]broken my bones.
5 He has [a]besieged and
encompassed me with
[b]bitterness and hardship.
6 In [a]dark places He has made me
dwell,
Like those who have long been
dead.
7 He has [a]walled me in so that I
cannot go out;
He has made my [1b]chain heavy.
8 Even when I cry out and call for
help,
He [a]shuts out my prayer.
9 He has [a]blocked my ways with
hewn stone;
He has made my paths crooked.
10 He is to me like a bear lying in
wait,
Like a lion in secret places.
11 He has turned aside my ways
and [a]torn me to pieces;
He has made me desolate.
12 He [a]bent His bow
And [b]set me as a target for the
arrow.
13 He made the [1]arrows of His
[a]quiver
To enter into my [2]inward parts.

14 [1]Lit *burdens* [a]Jer 23:25-29; 29:8,9 [b]Is 58:1; Ezek 23:36; Mic 3:8 [c]Jer 23:36; Ezek 22:25,28
15 [a]Job 27:23; Ezek 25:6 [b]Ps 22:7; Is 37:22; Jer 18:16; 19:8; Zeph 2:15 [c]Ps 50:2 [d]Ps 48:2
16 [a]Job 16:10; Ps 22:13; Lam 3:46 [b]Job 16:9; Ps 35:16; 37:12 [c]Ps 56:2; 124:3; Jer 51:34 [d]Obad 12-15
17 [1]Lit *horn* [a]Jer 4:28 [b]Lam 2:1,2; Ezek 5:11; 7:8,9; 8:18 [c]Ps 35:24,26; 89:42; Is 14:29 [d]Deut 28:43,44; Lam 1:5
18 [1]Lit *the daughter of your eye* [a]Ps 119:145; Hos 7:14 [b]Lam 2:8; Hab 2:11 [c]Ps 119:136; Jer 9:1; Lam 1:2,16; 3:48,49
19 [a]Ps 42:3; Is 26:9 [b]1 Sam 1:15; Ps 42:4; 62:8 [c]Lam 2:11 [d]Is 51:20
20 [1]Lit *fruit* [2]Or *tenderly cared for* [a]Ex 32:11; Deut 9:26 [b]Jer 19:9; Lam 4:10 [c]Ps 78:64; Jer 14:15; 23:11,12
21 [a]2 Chr 36:17; Jer 6:11 [b]Ps 78:62,63 [c]Jer 13:14; Zech 11:6
22 [1]Lit *bore healthy* or, *tenderly cared for* [a]Ps 31:13; Is 24:17; Jer 6:25 [b]Jer 11:11 [c]Jer 16:2-4; 44:7
3:1 [a]Ps 88:7,15,16
2 [a]Job 30:26; Is 59:9; Jer 4:23
3 [a]Ps 38:2; Is 5:25
4 [a]Ps 31:9,10; 38:2-8; 102:3-5 [b]Ps 51:8; Is 38:13
5 [a]Job 19:8 [b]Jer 23:15; Lam 3:19
6 [a]Ps 88:5,6; 143:3
7 [1]Lit *bronze piece* [a]Job 3:23; 19:8 [b]Jer 40:4
8 [a]Job 30:20; Ps 22:2
9 [a]Is 63:17; Hos 2:6
11 [a]Job 16:12,13; Jer 15:3; Hos 6:1
12 [a]Ps 7:12; Lam 2:4 [b]Job 6:4; 7:20; Ps 38:2
13 [1]Lit *sons* [2]Lit *kidneys* [a]Jer 5:16

14 I have become a [a]laughingstock
to all my people,
Their *mocking* [b]song all the
day.
15 He has [a]filled me with
bitterness,
He has made me drunk with
wormwood.
16 He has [a]broken my teeth with
[b]gravel;
He has made me cower in the
[c]dust.
17 My soul has been rejected [a]from
peace;
I have forgotten [1]happiness.
18 So I say, "My strength has
perished,
And *so has* my [a]hope from the
LORD."

Hope of Relief in God's Mercy

19 ¶ Remember my affliction and
my [1]wandering, the
[a]wormwood and bitterness.
20 Surely [a]my soul remembers
And is [b]bowed down within me.
21 This I recall to my mind,
Therefore I have [a]hope.
22 The LORD's [a]lovingkindnesses
[1]indeed never cease,
[b]For His compassions never
fail.
23 *They* are new [a]every morning;
Great is [b]Your faithfulness.
24 "The LORD is my [a]portion," says
my soul,
"Therefore I [b]have hope in Him."
25 The LORD is good to those who
[a]wait for Him,
To the [1]person who [b]seeks
Him.
26 *It is* good that he [a]waits silently
For the salvation of the LORD.
27 *It is* good for a man that he
should bear
The yoke in his youth.
28 Let him [a]sit alone and be silent
Since He has laid *it* on him.
29 Let him [1]put his mouth in the
[a]dust,
Perhaps there is [b]hope.
30 Let him give his [a]cheek to [1]the
smiter,
Let him be filled with reproach.
31 For the Lord will [a]not reject
forever,
32 For if He causes grief,
Then He will have [a]compassion
According to His abundant
lovingkindness.
33 For He [a]does not afflict
[1]willingly
Or grieve the sons of men.
34 To crush under His feet
All the prisoners of the [1]land,
35 To [1]deprive a man of [a]justice
In the presence of the Most
High,
36 To [1a]defraud a man in his
lawsuit—
Of these things the Lord does
not [2]approve.
37 Who is [1]there who speaks and it
[a]comes to pass,
Unless the Lord has
commanded *it?*
38 *Is it* not from the mouth of the
Most High
That [1a]both good and ill go
forth?

39 ¶ Why should *any* living
[1]mortal, or *any* man,
Offer [a]complaint [2]in view of his
sins?
40 Let us [a]examine and probe our
ways,
And let us return to the LORD.
41 We [a]lift up our heart [1]and
hands
Toward God in heaven;
42 We have [a]transgressed and
rebelled,
You have [b]not pardoned.
43 You have covered *Yourself* with
[a]anger
And [b]pursued us;
You have slain *and* [c]have not
spared.
44 You have [a]covered Yourself with
a cloud
So that [b]no prayer can pass
through.
45 *You have made us mere*
[a]offscouring and refuse
In the midst of the peoples.
46 All our enemies have [a]opened
their mouths against us.
47 [a]Panic and pitfall have
befallen us,
Devastation and destruction;
48 My [1a]eyes run down with
streams of water
Because of the destruction of the
daughter of my people.
49 My eyes pour down
[a]unceasingly,
Without stopping,
50 Until the LORD [a]looks down
And sees from heaven.
51 My eyes bring pain to my soul
Because of all the daughters of
my city.
52 My enemies [a]without cause
Hunted me down [b]like a bird;
53 They have silenced [1]me [a]in
the pit

14 [a]Ps 22:6; Jer 20:7 [b]Job 30:9; Lam 3:63
15 [a]Jer 9:15
16 [a]Ps 3:7 [b]Prov 20:17 [c]Jer 6:26
17 [1]Lit *good* [a]Is 59:11; Jer 12:12
18 [a]Job 17:15; Ezek 37:11
19 [1]Or *bitterness* [a]Jer 9:15; Lam 3:5
20 [a]Job 21:6 [b]Ps 42:5
21 [a]Ps 130:7
22 [1]Or *that we are not consumed* [a]Ps 78:38; Jer 3:12 [b]Mal 3:6
23 [a]Is 33:2; Zeph 3:5 [b]Heb 10:23
24 [a]Ps 16:5 [b]Ps 33:18
25 [1]Lit *soul* [a]Ps 27:14; Is 25:9 [b]Is 26:9
26 [a]Ps 37:7
28 [a]Jer 15:17
29 [1]Lit *give* [a]Job 16:15 [b]Jer 31:17
30 [1]Lit *his* [a]Job 16:10; Is 50:6
31 [a]Ps 77:7; Is 54:7-10
32 [a]Ps 78:38; Hos 11:8
33 [1]Lit *from His heart* [a]Ps 119:67; Ezek 33:11; Heb 12:10
34 [1]Or *earth*
35 [1]Or *turn aside a man's case* [a]Ps 140:12; Prov 17:15
36 [1]Lit *make crooked* [2]Lit *see* [a]Jer 22:3; Hab 1:13
37 [1]Lit *this* [a]Ps 33:9-11
38 [1]Lit *the evil things and the good* [a]Job 2:10; Is 45:7; Jer 32:42
39 [1]Or *human being* [2]Or *on the basis of* [a]Jer 30:15; Mic 7:9; Heb 12:5
40 [a]Ps 119:59; 2 Cor 13:5
41 [1]Lit *toward our* [a]Ps 25:1
42 [a]Neh 9:26; Jer 14:20; Dan 9:5 [b]2 Kin 24:4; Jer 5:7
43 [a]Lam 2:21 [b]Ps 83:15; Lam 3:66 [c]Lam 2:2
44 [a]Ps 97:2 [b]Lam 3:8; Zech 7:13
45 [a]1 Cor 4:13
46 [a]Job 30:9; Ps 22:6-8; Lam 2:16
47 [a]Is 24:17; Jer 48:43
48 [1]Lit *eye brings* [a]Ps 119:136; Jer 9:1; Lam 1:16
49 [a]Ps 77:2; Jer 14:17
50 [a]Ps 80:14; Is 63:15; Lam 5:1
52 [a]Ps 35:7 [b]1 Sam 26:20; Ps 11:1
53 [1]Lit *my life* [a]Jer 37:16

And have [2b]placed a stone
on me.
54 Waters flowed [a]over my head;
I said, "I am cut off!"
55 I [a]called on Your name, O LORD,
Out of the lowest pit.
56 You have [a]heard my voice,
"[b]Do not hide Your ear from my
prayer for relief,
From my cry for help."
57 You [a]drew near when I called
on You;
You said, "[b]Do not fear!"
58 O Lord, You [a]have pleaded my
soul's cause;
You have [b]redeemed my life.
59 O LORD, You have [a]seen my
oppression;
[b]Judge my case.
60 You have seen all their
vengeance,
All their [a]schemes against me.
61 You have heard their [a]reproach,
O LORD,
All their schemes against me.
62 The [a]lips of my assailants and
their whispering
Are against me all day long.
63 Look on their [a]sitting and their
rising;
[b]I am their mocking song.
64 You will [a]recompense them,
O LORD,
According to the work of their
hands.
65 You will give them [1a]hardness
of heart,
Your curse will be on them.
66 You will [a]pursue them in anger
and destroy them
From under the [b]heavens of the
LORD!

Distress of the Siege Described

4 How [a]dark the gold has become,
How the pure gold has changed!
The sacred stones are poured out
At the [1]corner of every street.
2 The precious sons of Zion,
Weighed against fine gold,
How they are regarded as
[a]earthen jars,
The work of a potter's hands!
3 Even [a]jackals offer the breast,
They nurse their young;
But the daughter of my people
has become [b]cruel
Like [c]ostriches in the
wilderness.
4 The [a]tongue of the infant
cleaves
To the roof of its mouth because
of [b]thirst;
The little ones [c]ask for bread,
But no one breaks *it* for them.
5 Those who ate [a]delicacies
Are desolate in the streets;
Those [1]reared in purple
Embrace ash pits.
6 For the [1]iniquity of the daughter
of my people
Is greater than the [2a]sin of
Sodom,
Which was [b]overthrown as in a
moment,
And no hands were [3]turned
toward her.
7 Her [1]consecrated ones were
[a]purer than snow,
They were whiter than milk;
They were more ruddy *in* [2]body
than corals,
Their polishing *was like* [3b]lapis
lazuli.
8 Their appearance is [a]blacker
than soot,
They are not recognized in the
streets;
Their [b]skin is shriveled on their
bones,
It is withered, it has become like
wood.
9 Better are those [1a]slain with
the sword
Than those [1]slain with hunger;
For they [2b]pine away, being
stricken
For lack of the fruits of [3]the
field.
10 The hands of compassionate
women
[a]Boiled their own children;
They became [b]food for them
Because of the destruction of the
daughter of my people.
11 The LORD has [a]accomplished His
wrath,
He has poured out His fierce
anger;
And He has [b]kindled a fire in
Zion
Which has consumed its
foundations.
12 The kings of the earth did not
believe,
Nor *did* any of [a]the inhabitants
of the world,
That the adversary and the
enemy
Could [b]enter the gates of
Jerusalem.
13 Because of the sins of her
[a]prophets
And the iniquities of her priests,
Who have shed in her midst
The [b]blood of the righteous;
14 They wandered, [a]blind, in the
streets;

53 [2]Or *cast stones* [b]Dan 6:17
54 [a]Ps 69:2; Jon 2:3-5
55 [a]Ps 130:1; Jon 2:2
56 [a]Job 34:28 [b]Ps 55:1
57 [a]Ps 145:18 [b]Is 41:10,14
58 [a]Jer 50:34 [b]Ps 34:22
59 [a]Jer 18:19,20 [b]Ps 26:1; 43:1
60 [a]Jer 11:19
61 [a]Ps 74:18; 89:50; Lam 5:1; Zeph 2:8
62 [a]Ps 59:7,12; 140:3; Ezek 36:3
63 [a]Ps 139:2 [b]Job 30:9; Lam 3:14
64 [a]Ps 28:4; Jer 51:6,24,56
65 [1]Or *insolence* [a]Ex 14:8; Deut 2:30; Is 6:10
66 [a]Lam 3:43 [b]Ps 8:3
4:1 [1]Lit *head* [a]Ezek 7:19-22
2 [a]Is 30:14; Jer 19:1,11
3 [a]Is 13:22; 34:13 [b]Is 49:15; Ezek 5:10 [c]Job 39:14-17
4 [a]Ps 22:15 [b]Jer 14:3 [c]Lam 2:12
5 [1]Lit *established in crimson* [a]Jer 6:2; Amos 6:3-7
6 [1]Or *punishment for iniquity* [2]Or *punishment for sin* [3]Or *wrung over her* [a]Gen 19:24 [b]Gen 19:25; Jer 20:16
7 [1]Or *Nazirites* [2]Lit *bones* [3]Heb *sappir* [a]Ps 51:7 [b]Ex 24:10; Job 28:16
8 [a]Job 30:30; Lam 5:10 [b]Job 19:20; Ps 102:3-5
9 [1]Lit *pierced* [2]Lit *flow away* [3]Lit *my fields* [a]Jer 16:4 [b]Lev 26:39; Ezek 24:23
10 [a]Lev 26:29; Deut 28:57; 2 Kin 6:29; Jer 19:9; Lam 2:20; Ezek 5:10 [b]Deut 28:53-55
11 [a]Jer 7:20; Lam 2:17; Ezek 22:31 [b]Deut 32:22; Jer 17:27
12 [a]Deut 29:24 [b]Jer 21:13
13 [a]Jer 5:31; 6:13; Lam 2:14; Ezek 22:26-28 [b]Jer 2:30; 26:8, 9; Matt 23:31
14 [a]Deut 28:28, 29; Is 29:10; 56:10; 59:9,10

They were defiled with [b]blood
So that no one could touch their
[c]garments.
15 "Depart! [a]Unclean!" [1]they cried
of themselves.
"Depart, depart, do not touch!"
So they [b]fled and wandered;
Men among the nations said,
"They shall not continue to dwell
with us."
16 The presence of the LORD has
scattered them,
He will not continue to regard
them;
They did not [1a]honor the
priests,
They did not favor the elders.
17 Yet our eyes failed,
Looking for [1]help was [a]useless;
In our watching we have
watched
For a [b]nation that could not
save.
18 They [a]hunted our steps
So that we could not walk in our
streets;
Our [b]end drew near,
Our days were [1]finished
For our end had come.
19 Our pursuers were [a]swifter
Than the eagles of the sky;
They chased us on the
mountains,
They waited in ambush for us in
the wilderness.
20 The [a]breath of our nostrils, the
[b]LORD's anointed,
Was [c]captured in their pits,
Of whom we had said, "Under
his [d]shadow
We shall live among the
nations."
21 Rejoice and be glad, O daughter
of [a]Edom,
Who dwells in the land of Uz;
But the [b]cup will come around
to you as well,
You will become drunk and
make yourself naked.
22 *The punishment* of your iniquity
has been [a]completed,
O daughter of Zion;
He will exile you no longer.
But He [b]will punish your
iniquity, O daughter of
Edom;
He will expose your sins!

A Prayer for Mercy

5 Remember, O LORD, what has
befallen us;
Look, and see our [a]reproach!
2 Our inheritance has been turned
over to [a]strangers,
Our [b]houses to aliens.
3 We have become orphans
[a]without a father,
Our mothers are like widows.
4 [1]We have to pay for our
drinking [a]water,
Our wood comes *to us* at a
price.
5 [1]Our pursuers are at our necks;
We are worn out, there is [a]no
rest for us.
6 We have [1]submitted to [a]Egypt
and Assyria [2]to get enough
bread.
7 Our [a]fathers sinned, *and* are no
more;
It is we who have borne their
iniquities.
8 [a]Slaves rule over us;
There is [b]no one to deliver us
from their hand.
9 We get our bread [1]at the [a]risk
of our lives
[2]Because of the sword in the
wilderness.
10 Our skin has become as [a]hot as
an oven,
Because of [1]the burning heat of
famine.
11 They ravished the [a]women in
Zion,
The virgins in the cities of
Judah.
12 Princes were hung by their
hands;
[1a]Elders were not respected.
13 Young men [1a]worked at the
grinding mill,
And youths [b]stumbled under
loads of wood.
14 Elders [1]are gone from the
gate,
Young men from their [a]music.
15 The joy of our hearts has
[a]ceased;
Our dancing has been turned
into mourning.
16 The [a]crown has fallen from our
head;
[b]Woe to us, for we have sinned!
17 Because of this our [a]heart is
faint,
Because of these things our
[b]eyes are dim;
18 Because of [a]Mount Zion which
lies desolate,
[b]Foxes prowl in it.
19 ¶ [a]You, O LORD, [1]rule forever;
Your [b]throne is from generation
to generation.

14 [b]Is 1:15 [c]Jer 2:34
15 [1]Or *they* (men) *cried to them* [a]Lev 13:45,46 [b]Jer 49:5
16 [1]Lit *lift up the faces of* [a]Is 9:14-16; Jer 52:24-27
17 [1]Lit *our help* [a]Jer 37:7; Lam 1:7 [b]Ezek 29:6, 7,16
18 [1]Lit *full* [a]Jer 16:16 [b]Jer 5:31; Ezek 7:2-12; Amos 8:2
19 [a]Is 5:26-28; 30:16,17; Jer 4:13; Hab 1:8
20 [a]Gen 2:7 [b]2 Sam 1:14; 19:21 [c]Jer 39:5; 52:9 [d]Dan 4:12
21 [a]Ps 137:7; Jer 25:21 [b]Obad 16
22 [a]Is 40:2; Jer 33:7,8 [b]Jer 49:10; Mal 1:3,4
5:1 [a]Ps 44:13-16
2 [a]Is 1:7; Hos 8:7,8 [b]Zeph 1:13
3 [a]Ex 22:24; Jer 15:8; 18:21
4 [1]Lit *We drink our water for silver* [a]Is 3:1
5 [1]Lit *We have been pursued upon* [a]Neh 9:36, 37
6 [1]Lit *given the hand to* [2]Lit *to be satisfied with* [a]Hos 9:3; 12:1
7 [a]Jer 14:20; 16:12
8 [a]Neh 5:15 [b]Ps 7:2; Zech 11:6
9 [1]Lit *with our soul* [2]Or *In the face of* [a]Jer 40:9-12
10 [1]Or *the ravages of hunger* [a]Job 30:30; Lam 4:8
11 [a]Is 13:16; Zech 14:2
12 [1]Lit *The faces of elders* [a]Is 47:6; Lam 4:16
13 [1]Lit *carry* [a]Judg 16:21 [b]Jer 7:18
14 [1]Lit *have ceased* [a]Is 24:8; Jer 7:34
15 [a]Jer 25:10; Amos 8:10
16 [a]Job 19:9; Ps 89:39; Jer 13:18 [b]Is 3:9-11
17 [a]Is 1:5 [b]Job 17:7; Lam 2:11
18 [a]Mic 3:12 [b]Neh 4:3
19 [1]Lit *sit* [a]Ps 102:12,25-27 [b]Ps 45:6

20 Why do You [a]forget us forever?
Why do You forsake us [1]so long?
21 [a]Restore us to You, O LORD, that we may be restored;
Renew [b]our days as of old,
22 Unless [a]You have utterly rejected us
And are exceedingly [b]angry with us.

20 [1]Lit *to length of days* [a]Ps 13:1; 44:24
21 [a]Ps 80:3; Jer 31:18 [b]Is 60:20-22
22 [a]Ps 60:1,2; Jer 7:29 [b]Is 64:9

Ezekiel

Title and Background

This book is named after the prophet Ezekiel, whose name means "God is strong." The Babylonians laid siege to Jerusalem in 588 B.C., and in 586 the city and temple were burned. Israel's monarchy was ended; the City of David and the Lord's temple were no more.

Author and Date of Writing

Ezekiel was among the more than 3,000 Jews exiled to Babylon by Nebuchadnezzar in 597 B.C., and there among the exiles he received his call to become a prophet. As a priest-prophet called to minister to the exiles, his message had much to do with the temple and its ritual.

Since the book of Ezekiel contains more dates than any other Biblical book, its prophecies can be dated with considerable precision. Ezekiel's period of activity coincides with Jerusalem's darkest hour. His messages are dated between 593 and 571 B.C.

Theme and Message

Nowhere in the Bible are God's initiative and control over all creation expressed more clearly and pervasively than in Ezekiel. This sovereign God resolved that He would be known and acknowledged, for at least 65 times we read the clause (or variations): "Thus they will know that I am the LORD." God's total sovereignty is also evident in His mobility. He was not limited to the temple; He can respond to His people under any circumstance.

Outline

I. Ezekiel's Call and Commission (1:1—3:27)
II. Judgment Against Judah and Jerusalem (4:1—24:27)
III. Judgment Against the Nations (25:1—32:32)
IV. Preparation for Restoration (33:1—39:29)
V. Renewed Worship (40:1—48:35)

The Vision of Four Figures

1 Now it came about in the thirtieth
year, on the fifth *day* of the fourth
month, while I was by the [a]river Chebar
among the exiles, the [b]heavens were
opened and I saw [1c]visions of God.
2 (On the fifth of the month [1]in the
[a]fifth year of King Jehoiachin's exile,
3 the [a]word of the LORD came ex-
pressly to Ezekiel the priest, son of Buzi,
in the [b]land of the Chaldeans by the river
Chebar; and there [c]the hand of the LORD
came upon him.)
4 ¶ As I looked, behold, a [a]storm
wind was coming from the north, a great
cloud with fire flashing forth continually
and a bright light around it, and in its
midst something like [b]glowing metal in
the midst of the fire.
5 Within it there were figures resembling [a]four living beings. And this was
their appearance: they had human
[b]form.
6 Each of them had [a]four faces and
[b]four wings.
7 Their legs were straight and [1]their
feet were like a calf's hoof, and they
gleamed like [a]burnished bronze.
8 Under their wings on their [a]four
sides *were* human [b]hands. As for the
faces and wings of the four of them,
9 their wings touched one another;
their faces did [a]not turn when they
moved, each [b]went straight forward.
10 As for the [a]form of their faces,
each had the [b]face of a man; [1]all four
had the face of a lion on the right and the
face of a bull on the left, and [1]all four had
the face of an eagle.
11 Such were their faces. Their wings
were spread out above; each had two
touching another *being,* and [a]two covering their bodies.
12 And [a]each went straight forward;

1:1 [1]Some ancient mss and versions read *a vision* [a]Ezek 3:23 [b]Matt 3:16; Mark 1:10; Luke 3:21; Acts 7:56; Rev 4:1 [c]Ex 24:10; Num 12:6; Is 1:1; Ezek 8:3; Dan 8:1
2 [1]Lit *it was* [a]2 Kin 24:12-15; Ezek 8:1
3 [a]2 Pet 1:21 [b]Ezek 12:13 [c]1 Kin 18:46; 2 Kin 3:15; Ezek 3:14
4 [a]Is 21:1; Jer 23:19; Ezek 13:11 [b]Ezek 1:27
5 [a]Ezek 10:15; Rev 4:6-8 [b]Ezek 1:26
6 [a]Ezek 1:10 [b]Ezek 1:23
7 [1]Lit *the soles of their feet* [a]Dan 10:6; Rev 1:15
8 [a]Ezek 1:17 [b]Ezek 10:8
9 [a]Ezek 1:17 [b]Ezek 1:12
10 [1]Lit *the four of them* [a]Rev 4:7 [b]Ezek 10:14 **11** [a]Is 6:2; Ezek 1:23 **12** [a]Ezek 1:9

[b]wherever the spirit was about to go,
they would go, without turning as they
went.
13 [1]In the midst of the living beings
there was something that looked like
burning coals of [a]fire, [2]like torches dart-
ing back and forth among the living beings. The fire was bright, and lightning
was [3]flashing from the fire.
14 And the living beings [a]ran to and
fro like bolts of [b]lightning.
15 ¶ Now as I looked at the living beings, behold, there was one [a]wheel on
the earth beside the living beings, [1]for
each of the four of them.
16 The [a]appearance of the wheels and
their workmanship *was* like [1]sparkling
[b]beryl, and all four of them had the same
form, their appearance and workmanship
being as if [2]one wheel were within another.
17 Whenever they [1]moved, they
[1]moved in any of their four [2]directions
without [a]turning as they [1]moved.
18 As for their rims they were lofty
and awesome, and the rims of all four of
them were [a]full of eyes round about.
19 [a]Whenever the living beings
[1]moved, the wheels [1]moved with them.
And whenever the living beings [b]rose
from the earth, the wheels rose *also.*
20 [a]Wherever the spirit was about to
go, they would go in that direction[1]. And
the wheels rose close beside them; for
the spirit of the living [2]beings *was* in the
wheels.
21 [a]Whenever those went, these
went; and whenever those stood still,
these stood still. And whenever those
rose from the earth, the wheels rose close
beside them; for the spirit of the living
[1]beings *was* in the wheels.

Vision of Divine Glory

22 ¶ Now [a]over the heads of the living [1]beings *there was* something like an
expanse, like the awesome gleam of
[2]crystal, spread out over their heads.
23 Under the expanse their wings
were stretched out straight, one toward
the other; each one also had [a]two wings
covering its body on the one side and on
the other.
24 I also heard the sound of their
wings like the [a]sound of abundant waters as they went, like the [b]voice of [1]the
Almighty, a sound of tumult like the
[c]sound of an army camp; whenever they
stood still, they dropped their wings.
25 And there came a voice from above
the [a]expanse that was over their heads;
whenever they stood still, they dropped
their wings.
26 ¶ Now [a]above the expanse that
was over their heads there was something [b]resembling a throne, like [1c]lapis
lazuli in appearance; and on that which
resembled a throne, high up, *was* a figure
with the appearance of a [d]man.
27 Then I [1]noticed from the appearance of His loins and upward something
[a]like [2]glowing metal that looked like fire
all around within it, and from the appearance of His loins and downward I saw
something like fire; and *there was* a radiance around Him.
28 As the appearance of the [a]rainbow
[1]in the clouds on a rainy day, so *was* the
appearance of the surrounding radiance.
Such *was* the appearance of the likeness
of the [b]glory of the LORD. And when I
saw *it,* I [c]fell on my face and heard a
voice speaking.

The Prophet's Call

2 Then He said to me, "Son of man,
[a]stand on your feet that I may speak
with you!"
2 As He spoke to me the [a]Spirit entered me and set me on my feet; and I
heard *Him* speaking to me.
3 Then He said to me, "Son of man,
I am sending you to the sons of Israel, to
a rebellious people who have [a]rebelled
against Me; [b]they and their fathers have
transgressed against Me to this very day.
4 "I am sending you to them who are
[1a]stubborn and obstinate children, and
you shall say to them, 'Thus says the
Lord [2]GOD.'
5 "As for them, [a]whether they listen or [1]not—for they are a rebellious
house—they will [b]know that a prophet
has been among them.
6 "And you, son of man, [a]neither fear
them nor fear their words, though [b]this-
tles and thorns are with you and you sit
on scorpions; neither fear their words nor
be dismayed at their presence, for they
are a rebellious house.
7 "But you shall [a]speak My words to
them [b]whether they listen or [1]not, for
they are rebellious.
8 ¶ "Now you, son of man, listen to
what I am speaking to you; do not be
rebellious like that rebellious house.
Open your mouth and [a]eat what I am
giving you."
9 Then I looked, and behold, a [a]hand
was extended to me; and lo, a [1b]scroll
was in it.
10 When He spread it out before me,
it was written on the front and back, and
written on it were lamentations, mourning and [a]woe.

12 [b]Ezek 1:20
13 [1]So with some ancient versions; Heb *as the likeness of the living beings* [2]Lit *like the appearance of* [3]Lit *coming out* [a]Ps 104:4; Rev 4:5
14 [a]Zech 4:10 [b]Matt 24:27; Luke 17:24
15 [1]Lit *for his four faces* [a]Ezek 1:19-21
16 [1]Lit *the look of beryl* [2]Lit *the wheel in the midst of the wheel* [a]Ezek 10:9-11 [b]Ezek 10:9; Dan 10:6
17 [1]Lit *went* [2]Lit *sides* [a]Ezek 1:9
18 [a]Ezek 10:12; Rev 4:6
19 [1]Lit *went* [a]Ezek 10:16 [b]Ezek 10:19
20 [1]M.T. adds *the spirit to go* [2]M.T. reads *being* [a]Ezek 1:12
21 [1]M.T. reads *being* [a]Ezek 10:17
22 [1]So some ancient mss and versions; M.T. reads *being* [2]Or *ice* [a]Ezek 10:1
23 [a]Ezek 1:6
24 [1]Heb *Shaddai* [a]Ezek 43:2; Rev 1:15 [b]Ezek 10:5 [c]2 Kin 7:6; Dan 10:6
25 [a]Ezek 1:22
26 [1]Heb *eben-sappir* [a]Ezek 1:22 [b]Is 6:1; Ezek 10:1; Dan 7:9 [c]Ex 24:10; Is 54:11 [d]Ezek 43:6; Rev 1:13
27 [1]Lit *saw* [2]Or *electrum* [a]Ezek 1:4
28 [1]Lit *which occurs in* [a]Gen 9:13; Rev 4:3 [b]Ex 24:16; Ezek 8:4 [c]Gen 17:3; Ezek 3:23; Dan 8:17; Rev 1:17
2:1 [a]Dan 10:11; Acts 9:6
2 [a]Ezek 3:24; Dan 8:18
3 [a]1 Sam 8:7; Jer 3:25 [b]Ezek 20:18
4 [1]Lit *the sons, stiff-faced and hard-hearted* [2]Heb *YHWH,* usually rendered *LORD* [a]Ps 95:8; Is 48:4; Jer 5:3; Ezek 3:7
5 [1]Lit *forbear* [a]Ezek 2:7; Matt 10:12-15; Acts 13:46 [b]Ezek 33:33; Luke 10:10; John 15:22
6 [a]Is 51:12; Jer 1:8; Ezek 3:9 [b]2 Sam 23:6; Ezek 28:24; Mic 7:4
7 [1]Lit *forbear* [a]Jer 1:7; Ezek 3:10 [b]Ezek 2:5
8 [a]Jer 15:16; Ezek 3:3; Rev 10:9
9 [1]Lit *scroll of a book* [a]Ezek 8:3 [b]Jer 36:2; Ezek 3:1; Rev 5:1-5
10 [a]Is 3:11; Rev 8:13

Ezekiel's Commission

3 Then He said to me, "Son of man, eat what you find; [a]eat this scroll, and go, speak to the house of Israel."

2 So I [a]opened my mouth, and He fed me this scroll.

3 He said to me, "Son of man, feed your stomach and [a]fill your [1]body with this scroll which I am giving you." Then I [b]ate it, and it was sweet as [c]honey in my mouth.

4 ¶ Then He said to me, "Son of man, [1]go to the house of Israel and speak with My words to them.

5 "For [a]you are not being sent to a people of [1b]unintelligible speech or difficult language, *but* to the house of Israel,

6 nor to many peoples of [1]unintelligible speech or difficult language, whose words you cannot understand. [2]But I have sent you to them [3]who should listen to you;

7 yet the house of Israel will not be willing to listen to you, since they are [a]not willing to listen to Me. Surely the whole house of Israel is [1]stubborn and obstinate.

8 "Behold, I have made your face as hard as their faces and your forehead as hard as their foreheads.

9 "Like [1]emery harder than flint I have made your forehead. Do not be afraid of them or be dismayed before them, though they are a rebellious house."

10 Moreover, He said to me, "Son of man, take into your heart all My [a]words which I will speak to you and listen [1]closely.

11 "[1]Go to the exiles, to the sons of your people, and speak to them and tell them, whether they listen or [2]not, 'Thus says the Lord [3]GOD.' "

12 ¶ Then the [a]Spirit lifted me up, and I heard a great [b]rumbling sound behind me, "Blessed be the glory of the LORD [1]in His place."

13 And I *heard* the sound of the wings of the living beings touching one another and the sound of the [a]wheels beside them, even a great rumbling sound.

14 So the Spirit lifted me up and took me away; and I went embittered in the rage of my spirit, and [a]the hand of the LORD was strong on me.

15 Then I came to the exiles who lived beside the river Chebar at Tel-abib, and I sat there [a]seven days where they were living, causing consternation among them.

16 ¶ [a]At the end of seven days the word of the LORD came to me, saying,

17 "Son of man, I have appointed you a [a]watchman to the house of Israel; whenever you hear a word from My mouth, [b]warn them from Me.

18 "When I say to the wicked, 'You will surely die,' and you do not warn him or speak out to warn the wicked from his wicked way that he may live, that wicked man shall die in his iniquity, but his [a]blood I will require at your hand.

19 "Yet if you have [a]warned the wicked and he does not turn from his wickedness or from his wicked way, he shall die in his iniquity; but you have [b]delivered yourself.

20 "Again, [a]when a righteous man turns away from his righteousness and commits iniquity, and I place an [b]obstacle before him, he will die; since you have not warned him, he shall die in his sin, and his righteous deeds which he has done shall not be remembered; but his blood I will require at your hand.

21 "However, if you have [a]warned [1]the righteous man that the righteous should not sin and he does not sin, he shall surely live because he took warning; and you have delivered yourself."

22 ¶ The hand of the LORD was on me there, and He said to me, "Get up, go out to the plain, and there I will [a]speak to you."

23 So I got up and went out to the plain; and behold, the [a]glory of the LORD was standing there, like the glory which [b]I saw by the river Chebar, and I fell on my face.

24 The [a]Spirit then entered me and made me stand on my feet, and He spoke with me and said to me, "Go, shut yourself up in your house.

25 "As for you, son of man, they will [a]put ropes on you and bind you with them so that you cannot go out among them.

26 "Moreover, [a]I will make your tongue stick to [1]the roof of your mouth so that you will be mute and cannot be a man who rebukes them, for they are a rebellious house.

27 "But [a]when I speak to you, I will open your mouth and you will say to them, 'Thus says the Lord [1]GOD.' He who hears, let him hear; and he who refuses, let him refuse; [b]for they are a rebellious house.

Siege of Jerusalem Predicted

4 "Now you son of man, [a]get yourself a brick, place it before you and inscribe a city on it, Jerusalem.

2 "Then [a]lay siege against it, build a siege wall, [1]raise up a ramp, pitch camps and place battering rams against it all around.

3:1 [a]Ezek 2:9
2 [a]Jer 25:17
3 [1]Lit *inward parts* [a]Jer 6:11; 20:9 [b]Jer 15:16 [c]Ps 19:10; 119:103; Rev 10:9,10
4 [1]Lit *go, come*
5 [1]Lit *deepness of lip and heaviness of tongue* [a]Jon 1:2; Acts 14:11; 26:17 [b]Is 28:11; 33:19
6 [1]Lit *deepness of lip and heaviness of tongue* [2]Or *If I had sent you to them, they would listen to you* [3]Lit *they*
7 [1]Lit *of a hard forehead and a stiff heart* [a]1 Sam 8:7
9 [1]Lit *corundum*
10 [1]Lit *with your ears* [a]Job 22:22; Ezek 2:8; 3:1-3
11 [1]Lit *Go, come* [2]Lit *forbear* [3]Heb *YHWH*, usually rendered *LORD*
12 [1]Or *from* [a]Ezek 3:14; 8:3; Acts 8:39 [b]Acts 2:2
13 [a]Ezek 1:15; 10:16,17
14 [a]2 Kin 3:15
15 [a]Job 2:13
16 [a]Jer 42:7
17 [a]Is 52:8; 56:10; 62:6; Jer 6:17; Ezek 33:7-9 [b]2 Chr 19:10; Is 58:1; Hab 2:1
18 [a]Ezek 3:20; 33:6,8
19 [a]2 Kin 17:13,14; Ezek 33:3,9 [b]Ezek 14:14,20; Acts 18:6; 1 Tim 4:16
20 [a]Ps 125:5; Ezek 18:24; 33:18; Zeph 1:6 [b]Is 8:14; Jer 6:21; Ezek 14:3, 7-9
21 [1]Lit *him, the righteous* [a]Acts 20:31
22 [a]Acts 9:6
23 [a]Ezek 1:28; Acts 7:55 [b]Ezek 1:1
24 [a]Ezek 2:2
25 [a]Ezek 4:8
26 [1]Lit *your palate* [a]Luke 1:20, 22
27 [1]Heb *YHWH*, usually rendered *LORD* [a]Ezek 24:27; 33:22 [b]Ezek 12:2,3
4:1 [a]Is 20:2; Jer 13:1; 18:2; 19:1
2 [1]Lit *cast* [a]Jer 6:6; Ezek 21:22

3 "Then get yourself an iron plate and set it up as an iron wall between you and the city, and set your face toward it so that [a]it is under siege, and besiege it. This is a [b]sign to the house of Israel.

4 ¶ "As for you, lie down on your left side and lay the iniquity of the house of Israel on it; you shall [a]bear their iniquity for the number of days that you lie on it.

5 "For I have assigned you a number of days corresponding to the years of their iniquity, three hundred and ninety days; thus [a]you shall bear the iniquity of the house of Israel.

6 "When you have completed these, you shall lie down a second time, *but* on your right side and bear the iniquity of the house of Judah; I have assigned it to you for forty days, a day for [a]each year.

7 "Then you shall set your face toward the siege of Jerusalem with your arm bared and [a]prophesy against it.

8 "Now behold, I will [a]put ropes on you so that you cannot turn from one side to the other until you have completed the days of your siege.

Defiled Bread

9 ¶ "But as for you, take wheat, barley, beans, lentils, millet and [a]spelt, put them in one vessel and make them into bread for yourself; you shall eat it according to the number of the days that you lie on your side, three hundred and ninety days.

10 "Your food which you eat *shall be* [a]twenty shekels a day by weight; you shall eat it from time to time.

11 "The water you drink shall be the sixth part of a hin by measure; you shall drink it from time to time.

12 "You shall eat it as a barley cake, having baked *it* in their sight over human [a]dung."

13 Then the LORD said, "Thus will the sons of Israel eat their bread [a]unclean among the nations where I will banish them."

14 But I said, "[a]Ah, Lord [1]GOD! Behold, I have [b]never been defiled; for from my youth until now I have never eaten what [c]died of itself or was torn by beasts, nor has any [d]unclean meat ever entered my mouth."

15 Then He said to me, "See, I will give you cow's dung in place of human dung over which you will prepare your bread."

16 Moreover, He said to me, "Son of man, behold, I am going to [a]break the staff of bread in Jerusalem, and they will eat bread by [b]weight and with anxiety, and drink water by [c]measure and in horror,

17 because bread and water will be scarce; and they will be appalled with one another and [a]waste away in their iniquity.

Jerusalem's Desolation Foretold

5 "As for you, son of man, take a [a]sharp sword; take and [1]use it *as* a barber's razor on your head and beard. Then take [b]scales for weighing and divide [2]the hair.

2 "One third you shall burn in the fire at the center of the city, when the [a]days of the siege are completed. Then you shall take one third and strike *it* with the sword all around [1]the city, and one third you shall scatter to the wind; and I will [b]unsheathe a sword behind them.

3 "Take also a few in number from [1]them and bind them in the edges of your *robes.*

4 "Take again some of them and throw them into the fire and burn them in the fire; from it a fire will [1]spread to all the house of Israel.

5 ¶ "Thus says the Lord [1]GOD, 'This is [a]Jerusalem; I have set her at the [b]center of the nations, with lands around her.

6 'But she has rebelled against My ordinances more wickedly than the nations and against My statutes [a]more than the lands which surround her; for they have [b]rejected My ordinances and have not walked [1]in My statutes.'

7 "Therefore, thus says the Lord GOD, 'Because you have [a]more turmoil than the nations which surround you *and* have not walked in My statutes, nor observed My ordinances, nor observed the ordinances of the nations which surround you,'

8 therefore, thus says the Lord GOD, 'Behold, I, even I, am [a]against you, and I will [b]execute judgments among you in the sight of the nations.

9 'And because of all your abominations, I will do among you what I have [a]not done, and the like of which I will never do again.

10 'Therefore, [a]fathers will eat *their* sons among you, and sons will eat their fathers; for I will execute judgments on you and [b]scatter all your remnant to every wind.

11 'So as I live,' declares the Lord GOD, 'surely, because you have [a]defiled My sanctuary with all your [b]detestable idols and with all your abominations, therefore I will also withdraw, and My eye will have no pity and I will not spare.

12 'One third of you will die by [a]plague or be consumed by famine among you, one third will fall by the sword around you, and one third I will

3 [a]Jer 39:1,2; Ezek 5:2 [b]Is 8:18; 20:3; Ezek 12:6,11; 24:24-27
4 [a]Lev 10:17; 16:22; Num 18:1
5 [a]Num 14:34
6 [a]Num 14:34; Dan 9:24-26; 12:11,12; Rev 11:2,3
7 [a]Ezek 21:2
8 [a]Ezek 3:25
9 [a]Ex 9:32; Is 28:25
10 [a]Ezek 45:12
12 [a]Is 36:12
13 [a]Dan 1:8; Hos 9:3
14 [1]Heb *YHWH,* usually rendered LORD [a]Jer 1:6; Ezek 9:8; 20:49 [b]Acts 10:14 [c]Lev 17:15; 22:8; Ezek 44:31 [d]Deut 14:3; Is 65:4; 66:17
16 [a]Lev 26:26; Is 3:1; Ezek 5:16; 14:13 [b]Ezek 4:10,11; 12:19 [c]Lam 5:4; Ezek 12:18,19
17 [a]Lev 26:39; Ezek 24:23; 33:10
5:1 [1]Lit *make it pass over your head* [2]Lit *them* [a]Lev 21:5; Is 7:20; Ezek 44:20 [b]Dan 5:27
2 [1]Lit *it* [a]Jer 39:1,2; Ezek 4:2-8 [b]Lev 26:33
3 [1]Lit *there*
4 [1]Lit *go out*
5 [1]Heb *YHWH,* usually rendered LORD, and so throughout the ch [a]Jer 6:6; Ezek 4:1 [b]Deut 4:6; Lam 1:1; Ezek 16:14
6 [1]Lit *in them, My statutes* [a]2 Kin 17:8-20; Ezek 16:47,48, 51 [b]Neh 9:16, 17; Ps 78:10; Jer 11:10; Zech 7:11
7 [a]2 Kin 21:9-11; 2 Chr 33:9; Jer 2:10,11
8 [a]Jer 21:5,13; Ezek 15:7; 21:3; Zech 14:2 [b]Jer 24:9; Ezek 5:15; 11:9
9 [a]Dan 9:12; Amos 3:2; Matt 24:21
10 [a]Lev 26:29; Jer 19:9; Lam 4:10 [b]Ps 44:11; Ezek 5:2,12; 6:8; 12:14; Amos 9:9; Zech 2:6; 7:14
11 [a]Jer 7:9-11; Ezek 8:5,6,16 [b]Jer 16:18; Ezek 7:20
12 [a]Jer 15:2; 21:9; Ezek 5:17; 6:11,12

[b]scatter to every wind, and I will [c]unsheathe a sword behind them.

13 ¶ 'Thus My anger will be spent and I will [1]satisfy My wrath on them, and I will be [2a]appeased; then they will know that I, the LORD, have [b]spoken in My zeal when I have spent My wrath upon them.

14 'Moreover, I will make you a desolation and a [a]reproach among the nations which surround you, in the sight of all who pass by.

15 'So [1]it will be a reproach, a reviling, a [a]warning and an object of horror to the nations who surround you when I [b]execute judgments against you in anger, wrath and raging rebukes. I, the LORD, have spoken.

16 'When I send against them the [1]deadly arrows of famine which [2]were for the destruction of those whom I will send to destroy you, then I will also intensify the famine upon you and break the staff of bread.

17 'Moreover, [a]I will send on you famine and wild beasts, and they will bereave you of children; [b]plague and bloodshed also will pass through you, and I will bring the sword on you. I, the LORD, have spoken.' "

Idolatrous Worship Denounced

6 And the word of the LORD came to me saying,

2 "Son of man, set your face toward the [a]mountains of Israel, and prophesy against them

3 and say, 'Mountains of Israel, listen to the word of the Lord [1]GOD! Thus says the Lord [1]GOD to the mountains, the hills, the ravines and the valleys: "Behold, I Myself am going to bring a sword on you, and [a]I will destroy your high places.

4 "So your [a]altars will become desolate and your incense altars will be smashed; and I will make your slain fall in front of your idols.

5 "I will also lay the dead bodies of the sons of Israel in front of their idols; and I will scatter your [a]bones around your altars.

6 "In all your dwellings, [a]cities will become waste and the high places will be desolate, that your altars may become waste and [1]desolate, your [b]idols may be broken and brought to an end, your incense altars may be cut down, and your works may be blotted out.

7 "The slain will fall among you, and you will know that I am the LORD.

8 ¶ "However, I will leave a [a]remnant, for you will have those who [b]escaped the sword among the nations when you are scattered among the countries.

9 "Then those of you who escape will [a]remember Me among the nations to which they will be carried captive, how I have [1b]been hurt by their adulterous hearts which turned away from Me, and by their eyes which played the harlot after their idols; and they will [c]loathe themselves in their own sight for the evils which they have committed, for all their abominations.

10 "Then they will know that I am the LORD; I have not said in vain [1]that I would inflict this disaster on them." '

11 ¶ "Thus says the Lord [1]GOD, 'Clap your hand, [a]stamp your foot and say, "[b]Alas, because of all the evil abominations of the house of Israel, which will fall by [c]sword, famine and plague!

12 "He who is [a]far off will die by the plague, and he who is near will fall by the sword, and he who remains and is besieged will die by the famine. Thus will I [b]spend My wrath on them.

13 "Then you will know that I am the LORD, when their [a]slain are among their idols around their altars, on [b]every high hill, on all the tops of the mountains, under every green tree and under every leafy oak—the places where they offered soothing aroma to all their idols.

14 "So throughout all their habitations I will [a]stretch out My hand against them and make the land more desolate and waste than the wilderness toward Diblah; thus they will know that I am the LORD." ' "

Punishment for Wickedness Foretold

7 Moreover, the word of the LORD came to me saying,

2 "And you, son of man, thus says the Lord [1]GOD to the land of Israel, 'An [a]end! The end is coming on the four corners of the land.

3 'Now the end is upon you, and I will send My anger against you; I will judge you according to your ways and bring all your abominations upon you.

4 'For My eye will have no pity on you, nor will I spare *you,* but I will [a]bring your ways upon you, and your abominations will be among you; then you will [b]know that I am the LORD!'

5 ¶ "Thus says the Lord [1]GOD, 'A [a]disaster, unique disaster, behold it is coming!

6 'An end is coming; the end has come! It has [a]awakened against you; behold, it has come!

7 'Your doom has come to you, O inhabitant of the land. The [a]time has

12 [b]Ezek 5:2, 10; Amos 9:9; Zech 2:6 [c]Jer 43:10,11; 44:27; Ezek 5:2; 12:14
13 [1]Lit *cause to rest* [2]Lit *comforted* [a]Is 1:24 [b]Is 59:17; Ezek 36:5,6; 38:19
14 [a]Ps 74:3-10; 79:1-4; Ezek 22:4
15 [1]Ancient versions read *you* [a]Is 26:9; Jer 22:8,9; 1 Cor 10:11 [b]Is 66:15, 16; Ezek 5:8; 25:17
16 [1]Lit *evil* [2]Or *are for destruction, which I will send*
17 [a]Lev 26:22; Rev 6:8 [b]Ezek 38:22
6:2 [a]Ezek 36:1
3 [1]Heb *YHWH,* usually rendered *LORD* [a]Lev 26:30
4 [a]Lev 26:30; 2 Chr 14:5; Is 27:9; Ezek 6:6
5 [a]2 Kin 23:14, 16,20; Jer 8:1,2
6 [1]So some ancient versions; Heb *bear their guilt* [a]Lev 26:31; Is 6:11; Ezek 5:14 [b]Ezek 6:4; Mic 1:7; Zech 13:2
8 [a]Is 6:13; Jer 30:11 [b]Jer 44:14,28; Ezek 7:16; 14:22
9 [1]Lit *been broken,* or, *broken for Myself their* [a]Deut 4:29; 30:2; Jer 51:50 [b]Ps 78:40; Is 7:13; 43:24; Hos 11:8 [c]Job 42:6; Ezek 20:43; 36:31
10 [1]Lit *to do this evil to*
11 [1]Heb *YHWH,* usually rendered *LORD* [a]Ezek 25:6 [b]Ezek 9:4 [c]Ezek 5:12; 7:15
12 [a]Dan 9:7 [b]Lam 4:11,22; Ezek 5:13
13 [a]Ezek 6:4-7 [b]1 Kin 14:23; 2 Kin 16:4; Is 57:5-7; Ezek 20:28; Hos 4:13
14 [a]Is 5:25; 9:12; Ezek 14:13; 20:33,34
7:2 [1]Heb *YHWH,* usually rendered *LORD* [a]Ezek 7:3,5,6; 11:13; Amos 8:2,10
4 [a]Ezek 11:21; 22:31; Hos 9:7 [b]Ezek 6:7,14; 7:27
5 [1]Heb *YHWH,* usually rendered *LORD* [a]2 Kin 21:12,13; Nah 1:9
6 [a]Zech 13:7
7 [a]Ezek 7:12; 12:23-25,28

come, the [b]day is near—tumult rather
than joyful shouting on the mountains.
8 'Now I will shortly [a]pour out My
wrath on you and spend My anger against
you; [b]judge you according to your ways
and bring on you all your abominations.
9 'My eye will show no pity nor will I
spare. I will [1]repay you according to your
ways, while your abominations are in
your midst; then you will know that I, the
LORD, do the smiting.
10 ¶ 'Behold, the day! Behold, it is
coming! *Your* doom has gone forth; the
[a]rod has budded, arrogance has blos-
somed.
11 'Violence [1]has grown into a rod of
[a]wickedness. None of them *shall re-*
main, none of their people, none of their
[b]wealth, nor anything eminent among
them.
12 'The [a]time has come, the day has
arrived. Let not the [b]buyer rejoice nor
the seller mourn; for [c]wrath is against all
their multitude.
13 'Indeed, the seller will not [1a]re-
gain [2]what he sold as long as [3]they *both*
live; for the vision regarding all their multitude will not [4]be averted, nor will any
of them maintain his life by his iniquity.
14 ¶ 'They have [a]blown the trumpet
and made everything ready, but no one
is going to the battle, for My wrath is
against all [1]their multitude.
15 'The [a]sword is outside and the
plague and the famine are within. He
who is in the field will die by the sword;
famine and the plague will also consume
those in the city.
16 'Even when their survivors [a]es-
cape, they will be on the mountains like
[b]doves of the valleys, all of them
[1c]mourning, each over his own iniquity.
17 'All [a]hands will hang limp and all
knees will [1]become *like* water.
18 'They will [a]gird themselves with
sackcloth and [b]shuddering will over-
whelm them; and shame *will be* on all
faces and [c]baldness on all their heads.
19 'They will [a]fling their silver into the
streets and their gold will become an abhorrent thing; their [b]silver and their gold
will not be able to deliver them in the day
of the wrath of the LORD. They cannot
satisfy their [1]appetite nor can they fill
their stomachs, for their iniquity has become an occasion of stumbling.

The Temple Profaned

20 'They transformed the beauty of His
ornaments into pride, and [a]they made
the images of their abominations *and*
their detestable things with it; therefore
I will make it an abhorrent thing to them.
21 'I will give it into the hands of the
[a]foreigners as plunder and to the wicked
of the earth as spoil, and they will profane it.
22 'I will also turn My [a]face from
them, and they will profane My secret
place; then robbers will enter and profane it.
23 ¶ '[a]Make the chain, for the land is
full of [1b]bloody crimes and the city is
[c]full of violence.
24 'Therefore, I will bring the worst of
the [a]nations, and they will possess their
houses. I will also make the [b]pride of the
strong ones cease, and their [c]holy places
will be profaned.
25 'When anguish comes, they will
seek [a]peace, but there will be none.
26 '[a]Disaster will come upon disaster
and [b]rumor will be *added* to rumor; then
they will seek a [c]vision from a prophet,
but the [d]law will be lost from the priest
and [e]counsel from the elders.
27 'The king will mourn, the prince
will be [a]clothed with horror, and the
hands of the people of the land will
[1]tremble. According to their conduct I
will deal with them, and by their judgments I will judge them. And they will
know that I am the LORD.' "

Vision of Abominations in Jerusalem

8 It came about in the sixth year, on
the fifth *day* of the sixth month, as I
was sitting in my house with the elders of
Judah sitting before me, that the hand of
the Lord [1]GOD fell on me there.
2 Then I looked, and behold, a likeness as the appearance of [1]a man; from
His loins and downward *there was* the
[a]appearance of fire, and from His loins
and upward the appearance of brightness, like the appearance [b]of [2]glowing
metal.
3 He stretched out the form of a hand
and caught me by a lock of my head; and
the [a]Spirit lifted me up between earth
and heaven and brought me in the visions
of God to Jerusalem, to the entrance of
the [1]north gate of the inner *court,* where
the seat of the idol of jealousy, which
[b]provokes to jealousy, was *located.*
4 And behold, the [a]glory of the God
of Israel *was* there, like the appearance
which I saw in the plain.
5 ¶ Then He said to me, "Son of man,
[a]raise your eyes now toward the north."
So I raised my eyes toward the north, and
behold, to the north of the altar gate *was*
this [b]idol of jealousy at the entrance.
6 And He said to me, "Son of man, do
you see what they are doing, the great
[a]abominations which the house of Israel

7 [b]Is 22:5
8 [a]Is 42:25; Ezek 9:8; Nah 1:6 [b]Ezek 7:3
9 [1]Lit *give*
10 [a]Ps 89:32; Is 10:5
11 [1]Lit *has risen* [a]Ps 73:8; Is 59:6-8 [b]Zeph 1:18
12 [a]Ezek 7:5-7; 1 Cor 7:29-31; James 5:8 [b]Prov 20:14; 1 Cor 7:30 [c]Is 5:13; Ezek 6:11
13 [1]Lit *return to* [2]Lit *thing sold,* i.e. his inherited land [3]Lit *their life among the living ones* [4]Lit *return* [a]Lev 25:24-28
14 [1]Lit *her* [a]Num 10:9; Jer 4:5
15 [a]Jer 14:18; Ezek 5:12
16 [1]Lit *moaning* [a]Ezra 9:15; Is 37:31; Ezek 6:8 [b]Is 38:14 [c]Is 59:11; Nah 2:7
17 [1]Lit *run with water* [a]Is 13:7; Ezek 21:7; Heb 12:12
18 [a]Is 15:3; Ezek 27:31; Amos 8:10 [b]Job 21:6; Ps 55:5 [c]Ezek 27:31
19 [1]Lit *soul* [a]Is 2:20 [b]Prov 11:4; Zeph 1:18
20 [a]Jer 7:30
21 [a]2 Kin 24:13; Ps 74:2-8; Jer 52:13
22 [a]Jer 18:17; Ezek 39:23
23 [1]Lit *judgment of blood* [a]Jer 27:2 [b]Ezek 9:9; Hos 4:2 [c]Ezek 8:17
24 [a]Ezek 21:31 [b]Ezek 33:28 [c]2 Chr 7:20; Ezek 24:21
25 [a]Ezek 13:10
26 [a]Is 47:11; Jer 4:20 [b]Ezek 21:7 [c]Jer 21:2 [d]Ps 74:9; Ezek 22:26; Mic 3:6 [e]Jer 18:18; Ezek 11:2
27 [1]Lit *be terrified* [a]Job 8:22; Ps 35:26; Ezek 26:16
8:1 [1]Heb *YHWH,* usually rendered *LORD*
2 [1]Lit *fire* [2]Or *electrum* [a]Ezek 1:27 [b]Ezek 1:4
3 [1]Lit *facing north* [a]Ezek 3:12 [b]Ex 20:4; Deut 32:16
4 [a]Ezek 1:28
5 [a]Jer 3:2; Zech 5:5 [b]Ps 78:58; Jer 7:30; Ezek 8:3
6 [a]2 Kin 23:4; Ezek 5:11

are committing here, so that I would be far from My sanctuary? But yet you will see still greater abominations."

7 ¶ Then He brought me to the entrance of the court, and when I looked, behold, a hole in the wall.

8 He said to me, "Son of man, now [a]dig through the wall." So I dug through the wall, and behold, an entrance.

9 And He said to me, "Go in and see the wicked abominations that they are committing here."

10 So I entered and looked, and behold, every form of creeping things and beasts *and* detestable things, with all the idols of the house of Israel, were carved on the wall all around.

11 Standing in front of them were [a]seventy [b]elders of the house of Israel, with Jaazaniah the son of Shaphan standing among them, each man with his [c]censer in his hand and the fragrance of the cloud of incense rising.

12 Then He said to me, "Son of man, do you see what the elders of the house of Israel are committing in the dark, each man in the room of his carved images? For they say, '[a]The LORD does not see us; the LORD has [b]forsaken the land.' "

13 And He said to me, "Yet you will see still greater abominations which they are committing."

14 ¶ Then He brought me to the entrance of the [a]gate of the LORD'S house which *was* toward the north; and behold, women were sitting there weeping for Tammuz.

15 He said to me, "Do you see *this,* son of man? Yet you will see still greater abominations than these."

16 ¶ Then He brought me into the inner court of the LORD'S house. And behold, at the entrance to the temple of the LORD, between the porch and the altar, *were* about twenty-five men with their [a]backs to the temple of the LORD and their faces toward the east; and [b]they were [1]prostrating themselves eastward toward the sun.

17 He said to me, "Do you see *this,* son of man? Is it too light a thing for the house of Judah to commit the abominations which they have committed here, that they have [a]filled the land with violence and [b]provoked Me repeatedly? For behold, they are putting the twig to their nose.

18 "Therefore, I indeed will deal in wrath. My eye will have no pity nor will I spare; and [a]though they cry in My ears with a loud voice, yet I will not listen to them."

The Vision of Slaughter

9 Then He cried out in my hearing with a loud [a]voice saying, "Draw near, [1]O executioners of the city, each with his destroying weapon in his hand."

2 Behold, six men came from the direction of the upper gate which faces north, each with his shattering weapon in his hand; and among them was [a]a certain man clothed in linen with a [1]writing case at his loins. And they went in and stood beside the bronze altar.

3 ¶ Then the [a]glory of the God of Israel went up from the cherub on which it had been, to the threshold of the [1]temple. And He called to the man clothed in linen at whose loins was the writing case.

4 The LORD said to him, "Go through the midst of the city, *even* through the midst of Jerusalem, and put a [a]mark on the foreheads of the men who [b]sigh and groan over all the abominations which are being committed in its midst."

5 But to the others He said in my hearing, "Go through the city after him and strike; do not let your eye have pity and do not spare.

6 "[1]Utterly [a]slay old men, young men, maidens, little children, and women, but do not [b]touch any man on whom is the mark; and you shall [c]start from My sanctuary." So they started with the [2]elders who *were* before the [3]temple.

7 And He said to them, "[a]Defile the [1]temple and fill the courts with the slain. Go out!" Thus they went out and struck down *the people* in the city.

8 As they were striking *the people* and I *alone* was left, I [a]fell on my face and cried out [1]saying, "[b]Alas, Lord [2]GOD! Are You destroying the whole remnant of Israel [3]by pouring out Your wrath on Jerusalem?"

9 ¶ Then He said to me, "The iniquity of the house of Israel and Judah is very, very great, and the land is [a]filled with blood and the city is [b]full of perversion; for [c]they say, 'The LORD has forsaken the land, and the LORD does not see!'

10 "But as for Me, [a]My eye will have no pity nor will I spare, but [b]I will bring their conduct upon their heads."

11 ¶ Then behold, the man clothed in linen at whose loins was the [1]writing case [2]reported, saying, "I have done just as You have commanded me."

Vision of God's Glory Departing from the Temple

10 Then I looked, and behold, in the [1a]expanse that was over the heads of the cherubim something like a

8 [a]Is 29:15

11 [a]Num 11:16, 25; Luke 10:1 [b]Jer 19:1 [c]Num 16:17,35

12 [a]Ps 14:1; Is 29:15; Ezek 9:9 [b]Ps 10:11

14 [a]Ezek 44:4; 46:9

16 [1]I.e. worshiping [a]2 Chr 29:6; Jer 2:27; Ezek 23:39 [b]Deut 4:19; 17:3; Job 31:26-28; Jer 44:17

17 [a]Ezek 7:11, 23; 9:9; Amos 3:10; Mic 2:2 [b]Jer 7:18,19; Ezek 16:26

18 [a]Is 1:15; Jer 11:11; Mic 3:4; Zech 7:13

9:1 [1]Lit *you who punish* [a]Is 6:8

2 [1]Or *scribal inkhorn* [a]Lev 16:4

3 [1]Lit *house* [a]Ezek 10:4; 11:22,23

4 [a]Ex 12:7,13; Ezek 9:6; 2 Cor 1:22; 2 Tim 2:19; Rev 7:2,3; 9:4; 14:1 [b]Ps 119:53,136; Jer 13:17; Ezek 6:11; 21:6

6 [1]Lit To *destruction* [2]Or *old men* [3]Lit *house* [a]2 Chr 36:17 [b]Ex 12:23; Rev 9:4 [c]Jer 25:29; Amos 3:2; Luke 12:47

7 [1]Lit *house* [a]2 Chr 36:17; Ezek 7:20-22

8 [1]Lit *and said* [2]Heb *YHWH,* usually rendered *LORD* [3]Lit *by Your pouring* [a]1 Chr 21:16 [b]Ezek 11:13; Amos 7:2-6

9 [a]2 Kin 21:16; Jer 2:34; Ezek 7:23; 22:2,3 [b]Ezek 22:29; Mic 3:1-3; 7:3 [c]Job 22:13; Ps 10:11; 94:7; Is 29:15; Ezek 8:12

10 [a]Is 65:6; Ezek 8:18; 24:14 [b]Ezek 7:4; 11:21; Hos 9:7

11 [1]Or *inkhorn* [2]Lit *brought back word*

10:1 [1]Or *firmament* [a]Ezek 1:22,26

[b]sapphire stone, in appearance resembling a [c]throne, appeared above them.
2 And He spoke to the man clothed
in linen and said, "Enter between the
[a]whirling wheels under the [1]cherubim
and fill your hands with [b]coals of fire
from between the cherubim and scatter
them over the city." And he entered in
my sight.
3 ¶ Now the cherubim were standing
on the right side of the [1]temple when the
man entered, and the cloud filled the [a]in-
ner court.
4 Then the [a]glory of the LORD went
up from the cherub to the threshold of
the temple, and the [b]temple was filled
with the cloud and the court was filled
with the [c]brightness of the glory of the
LORD.
5 Moreover, the sound of the wings
of the cherubim was heard as far as the
outer court, like the [a]voice of [1]God Almighty when He speaks.
6 ¶ It came about when He commanded the man clothed in linen, saying,
"Take fire from between the whirling
wheels, from between the cherubim," he
entered and stood beside a wheel.
7 Then the cherub stretched out his
hand from between the cherubim to the
fire which was between the cherubim,
took *some* and put *it* into the hands of the
one clothed in linen, who took *it* and
went out.
8 The cherubim appeared to have the
form of a man's hand under their wings.
9 ¶ Then I looked, and behold, [a]four
wheels beside the cherubim, one wheel
beside each cherub; and the appearance
of the wheels *was* like the gleam of a
[1b]Tarshish stone.
10 As for their appearance, all four of
them had the same likeness, as if one
wheel were within another wheel.
11 When they moved, they went [a]in
any of their four [1]directions without
turning as they went; but they followed
in the direction which [2]they faced, without turning as they went.
12 Their [a]whole body, their backs,
their hands, their wings and the [b]wheels
were full of eyes all around, the wheels
belonging to all four of them.
13 The wheels were called in my hearing, the whirling wheels.
14 And [a]each one had four faces. The
first face *was* the face of a cherub, the
second face *was* the face of a man, the
third the face of a lion, and the fourth
the face of an eagle.
15 ¶ Then the cherubim rose up. They
are the [a]living beings that I saw by the
river Chebar.
16 Now when the cherubim moved,
the wheels would go beside them; also
when the cherubim lifted up their wings
to rise from the ground, the wheels
would not turn from beside them.
17 When [1]the cherubim [a]stood still,
[1]the wheels would stand still; and when
they rose up, [1]the wheels would rise
with them, for the spirit of the living beings *was* in them.
18 ¶ Then the glory of the LORD departed from the threshold of the temple
and stood [a]over the cherubim.
19 When [a]the cherubim departed,
they lifted their wings and rose up from
the earth in my sight with the wheels
beside them; and they stood still at the
entrance of the east gate of the LORD'S
house, and the glory of the God of Israel
[1]hovered over them.
20 ¶ These are the [a]living beings that
I saw beneath the God of Israel by [b]the
river Chebar; so I knew that they *were*
cherubim.
21 [a]Each one had four faces and each
one four wings, and beneath their wings
was the form of human hands.
22 As for the likeness of their faces,
they were the same faces whose appearance I had seen by the river Chebar. Each
one went straight ahead.

Evil Rulers to Be Judged

11 Moreover, the [a]Spirit lifted me
up and brought me to the east
gate of the LORD'S house which faced
eastward. And behold, *there were*
twenty-five men at the entrance of the
gate, and among them I saw Jaazaniah
son of Azzur and [b]Pelatiah son of Benaiah, leaders of the people.
2 He said to me, "Son of man, these
are the men who devise iniquity and
[a]give evil advice in this city,
3 who say, '[1]Is not *the time* near to
build houses? [2]This [a]*city* is the pot and
we are the flesh.'
4 "Therefore, [a]prophesy against them,
son of man, prophesy!"
5 ¶ Then the Spirit of the LORD fell
upon me, and He said to me, "Say, 'Thus
says the LORD, "So you think, house of
Israel, for [a]I know [1]your [b]thoughts.
6 "You have [a]multiplied your slain in
this city, filling its streets with [1]them."
7 'Therefore, thus says the Lord
[1]GOD, "Your [a]slain whom you have laid
in the midst of [2]the city are the flesh and
this *city* is the pot; but [3]I will [b]bring you
out of it.
8 "You have [a]feared a sword; so I will
[b]bring a sword upon you," the Lord GOD
declares.
9 "And I will bring you out of the
midst of [1]the city and deliver you into

---

1 [b]Ex 24:10 [c]Rev 4:2,3
2 [1]So with Gr; Heb *cherub* [a]Ezek 1:15-21; 10:13 [b]Ps 18:10-13; Is 6:6; Ezek 1:13; Rev 8:5
3 [1]Lit *house,* and so throughout the ch [a]Ezek 8:3,16
4 [a]Ezek 9:3; 11:22,23 [b]Ex 40:34,35; Is 6:1-4 [c]Ezek 1:28
5 [1]Heb *El Shaddai* [a]Job 40:9; Ezek 1:24; Rev 10:3
9 [1]Perhaps, *beryl* [a]Ezek 1:15-17 [b]Dan 10:6; Rev 21:20
11 [1]Lit *sides* [2]Lit *the head turned* [a]Ezek 1:17
12 [a]Rev 4:6,8 [b]Ezek 1:18
14 [a]1 Kin 7:29, 36; Ezek 1:6,10; 10:21; Rev 4:7
15 [a]Ezek 1:3,5
17 [1]Lit *they* [a]Ezek 1:21
18 [a]Ps 18:10
19 [1]Lit *over them from above* [a]Ezek 11:22
20 [a]Ezek 1:5,22, 26; 10:15 [b]Ezek 1:1
21 [a]Ezek 1:6,8; 10:14; 41:18,19
11:1 [a]Ezek 3:12,14; 8:3; 11:24; 43:5 [b]Ezek 11:13
2 [a]Ps 2:1,2; 52:2; Is 30:1; Jer 5:5; Mic 2:1
3 [1]Or *The time is not near* [2]Or *This is* [a]Jer 1:13; Ezek 11:7,11; 24:3,6
4 [a]Ezek 3:4,17
5 [1]Lit *what comes up in your spirit* [a]Jer 11:20; 17:10 [b]Ezek 38:10
6 [1]Lit *the slain* [a]Is 1:15; Ezek 7:23; 22:2-6,9, 12,27
7 [1]Heb *YHWH,* usually rendered LORD, and so throughout the ch [2]Lit *it* [3]So with Gr; Heb *he will bring you out* [a]Ezek 24:3-13; Mic 3:2,3 [b]2 Kin 25:18-22; Jer 52:24-27; Ezek 11:9
8 [a]Prov 10:24; Is 66:4 [b]Job 3:25; Is 24:17, 18
9 [1]Lit *it*

the hands of [a]strangers and [b]execute judgments against you.

10 "You will [a]fall by the sword. I will judge you to the [b]border of Israel; so you shall know that I am the LORD.

11 "This *city* will [a]not be a pot for you, nor will you be flesh in the midst of it, *but* I will judge you to the border of Israel.

12 "Thus you will know that I am the LORD; for you have not walked in My statutes nor have you [a]executed My ordinances, but have acted according to the ordinances of the [b]nations around you." ' "

13 ¶ Now it came about as I prophesied, that [a]Pelatiah son of Benaiah died. Then I fell on my face and cried out with a loud voice and said, "[b]Alas, Lord GOD! Will You bring the remnant of Israel to a complete end?"

Promise of Restoration

14 ¶ Then the word of the LORD came to me, saying,

15 "Son of man, your brothers, your [1]relatives, [2]your fellow exiles and the whole house of Israel, all of them, *are those* to whom the inhabitants of Jerusalem have said, 'Go far from the LORD; this land has been given [a]us as a possession.'

16 "Therefore say, 'Thus says the Lord GOD, "Though I had removed them far away among the nations and though I had scattered them among the countries, yet I was a [a]sanctuary for them a little while in the countries where they had gone." '

17 "Therefore say, 'Thus says the Lord GOD, "I will [a]gather you from the peoples and assemble you out of the countries among which you have been scattered, and I will give you the land of Israel." '

18 "When they come there, they will [a]remove all its [b]detestable things and all its abominations from it.

19 "And I will [a]give them one heart, and put a new spirit within [1]them. And I will take the [b]heart of stone out of their flesh and give them a [c]heart of flesh,

20 that they may [a]walk in My statutes and keep My ordinances and do them. Then they will be [b]My people, and I shall be their God.

21 "[1]But as for those whose hearts go after their [a]detestable things and abominations, I will [b]bring their conduct down on their heads," declares the Lord GOD.

22 ¶ Then the cherubim [a]lifted up their wings with the wheels beside them, and [b]the glory of the God of Israel [1]hovered over them.

23 The [a]glory of the LORD went up from the midst of the city and [b]stood over the mountain which is east of the city.

24 And the [a]Spirit lifted me up and brought me in a vision by the Spirit of God to the exiles [1]in Chaldea. So the vision that I had seen [2b]left me.

25 Then I [a]told the exiles all the things that the LORD had shown me.

Ezekiel Prepares for Exile

12 Then the word of the LORD came to me, saying,

2 "Son of man, you live in the [a]midst of the [b]rebellious house, who [c]have eyes to see but do not see, ears to hear but do not hear; for they are a rebellious house.

3 "Therefore, son of man, prepare for yourself baggage for exile and go into exile by day in their sight; even go into exile from your place to another place in their sight. [a]Perhaps they will [1]understand though they are a rebellious house.

4 "Bring your baggage out by day in their sight, as baggage for exile. Then you will go out [a]at evening in their sight, as those going into exile.

5 "Dig a hole through the wall in their sight and [1]go out through it.

6 "Load *the baggage* on *your* shoulder in their sight *and* carry *it* out in the dark. You shall [a]cover your face so that you cannot see the land, for I have set you as a [b]sign to the house of Israel."

7 ¶ I [a]did so, as I had been commanded. By day I [b]brought out my baggage like the baggage of an exile. Then in the evening I dug through the wall with my hands; I went out in the dark *and* carried *the baggage* on *my* shoulder in their sight.

8 ¶ In the morning the word of the LORD came to me, saying,

9 "Son of man, has not the house of Israel, the [a]rebellious house, said to you, '[b]What are you doing?'

10 "Say to them, 'Thus says the Lord [1]GOD, "This [2a]burden *concerns* the prince in Jerusalem as well as all the house of Israel who are [3]in it." '

11 "Say, 'I am [1]a [a]sign to you. As I have done, so it will be done to them; they will [b]go into exile, into captivity.'

12 "The [a]prince who is among them will load *his baggage* on *his* shoulder in the dark and go out. [1]They will dig a hole through the wall to bring *it* out. He will cover his face so that he can not see the land with *his* eyes.

13 "I will also spread My [a]net over him, and he will be caught in My snare. And I will bring him to Babylon in the

9 [a]Deut 28:36; Ps 106:41 [b]Ezek 5:8
10 [a]Jer 52:9 [b]2 Kin 14:25
11 [a]Ezek 11:3
12 [a]Ezek 18:8 [b]Ezek 8:10
13 [a]Ezek 11:1 [b]Ezek 9:8
15 [1]Lit *brothers* [2]So with Gr and some ancient versions; Heb *the men of your redemption* [a]Ezek 33:24
16 [a]Ps 31:20; Is 8:14; Jer 29:7
17 [a]Is 11:11-16; Jer 3:12; Ezek 20:41
18 [a]Ezek 37:23 [b]Ezek 5:11
19 [1]So with Gr and many mss; Heb *you* [a]Jer 24:7; Ezek 18:31 [b]Zech 7:12; Rom 2:4 [c]2 Cor 3:3
20 [a]Ps 105:45; Ezek 36:27 [b]Ezek 14:11
21 [1]Lit *And to the heart of their detestable things and their abomination their heart goes* [a]Jer 16:18; Ezek 11:18 [b]Ezek 9:10
22 [1]Lit *over them from above* [a]Ezek 10:19 [b]Ezek 43:2
23 [a]Ezek 8:4 [b]Zech 14:4
24 [1]I.e. Babylonia [2]Lit *went up from* [a]Ezek 8:3; 2 Cor 12:2-4 [b]Acts 10:16
25 [a]Ezek 2:7
12:2 [a]Is 6:5 [b]Ps 78:40; Is 1:23; Ezek 2:7 [c]Is 6:9f; Jer 5:21; Matt 13:13; Mark 4:12; Luke 8:10; John 9:39-41; Acts 28:26f; Rom 11:8
3 [1]Or *see that they are* [a]Jer 26:3; Luke 20:13; 2 Tim 2:25
4 [a]2 Kin 25:4; Jer 39:4; Ezek 12:12
5 [1]Lit *bring it out*
6 [a]1 Sam 28:8; Ezek 12:12 [b]Is 8:18; Ezek 4:3
7 [a]Ezek 24:18 [b]Ezek 12:3-6
9 [a]Ezek 2:5-8 [b]Ezek 17:12
10 [1]Heb *YHWH*, usually rendered LORD, and so throughout the ch [2]Or *oracle* [3]Lit *in their midst* [a]2 Kin 9:25; Is 13:1; Ezek 12:3-8
11 [1]Lit *your sign* [a]Ezek 12:6 [b]Jer 15:2; Ezek 12:3
12 [1]I.e. the king's attendants [a]2 Kin 25:4; Jer 39:4; Ezek 12:6
13 [a]Is 24:17; Ezek 17:20; Hos 7:12

land of the Chaldeans; yet he will [b]not
see it, though he will die there.
14 "I will [a]scatter to every wind all
who are around him, his helpers and all
his troops; and I will draw out a sword
after them.
15 "So they will [a]know that I am the
LORD when I scatter them among the nations and spread them among the countries.
16 "But I will [1]spare a few of them
from the [a]sword, the famine and the pestilence that they may tell all their abominations among the nations where they
go, and [2]may [b]know that I am the
LORD."
17 ¶ Moreover, the word of the LORD
came to me saying,
18 "Son of man, [a]eat your bread with
trembling and drink your water with
quivering and anxiety.
19 "Then say to the people of the land,
'Thus says the Lord GOD concerning
the inhabitants of Jerusalem in the land
of Israel, "They will eat their bread
with anxiety and drink their water with
horror, because [1]their land will be
[2a]stripped of its fullness on account of
the violence of all who live in it.
20 "The inhabited [a]cities will be laid
waste and the [b]land will be a desolation.
So you will know that I am the LORD." ' "
21 ¶ Then the word of the LORD came
to me, saying,
22 "Son of man, what is this [a]proverb
you *people* have concerning the land of
Israel, saying, 'The [b]days are long and
every [c]vision fails'?
23 "Therefore say to them, 'Thus says
the Lord GOD, "I will make this proverb
cease so that they will no longer use it as
a proverb in Israel." But tell them, "[a]The
days draw near as well as the [1]fulfillment
of every vision.
24 "For there will no longer be any
[1a]false vision or flattering divination
within the house of Israel.
25 "For I the LORD will speak, and whatever [a]word I speak will be performed. It
will no longer be delayed, for in [b]your
days, O [c]rebellious house, I will speak
the word and perform it," declares the
Lord GOD.' "
26 ¶ Furthermore, the word of the
LORD came to me, saying,
27 "Son of man, behold, the house of
Israel is saying, 'The vision that he sees
is for [a]many [1]years *from now,* and he
prophesies of times far off.'
28 "Therefore say to them, 'Thus says
the Lord GOD, "None of My words will be
delayed any longer. Whatever word I
speak will be performed," ' " declares the
Lord GOD.

False Prophets Condemned

13 Then the word of the LORD came
to me saying,
2 "Son of man, prophesy against the
[a]prophets of Israel who prophesy, and
say to those who prophesy from their
own [1]inspiration, '[b]Listen to the word
of the LORD!
3 'Thus says the Lord [1]GOD, "Woe to
the [a]foolish prophets who are following
their own spirit and have [b]seen nothing.
4 "O Israel, your prophets have been
like foxes among ruins.
5 "You have not [a]gone up into the
[b]breaches, nor did you build the wall
around the house of Israel to stand in the
battle on the [c]day of the LORD.
6 "They see [1a]falsehood and lying
divination who are saying, 'The LORD declares,' when the LORD has not sent
them; [b]yet they hope for the fulfillment
of *their* word.
7 "[a]Did you not see a false vision and
speak a lying divination when you said,
'The LORD declares,' but it is not I who
have spoken?" ' "
8 ¶ Therefore, thus says the Lord
GOD, "Because you have spoken [1]false-
hood and seen a lie, therefore behold, [a]I
am against you," declares the Lord GOD.
9 "So My hand will be against the
[a]prophets who see false visions and utter
lying divinations. They will [1]have no
place in the council of My people, [b]nor
will they be written down in the register
of the house of Israel, nor will they enter
the land of Israel, [2]that you may know
that I am the Lord GOD.
10 "It is definitely because they have
[a]misled My people by saying, '[b]Peace!'
when there is [c]no peace. And when anyone builds a wall, behold, they plaster it
over with whitewash;
11 *so* tell those who plaster *it* over
with whitewash, that it will fall. A
[a]flooding rain will come, and you,
O hailstones, will fall; and a violent wind
will break out.
12 "Behold, when the wall has fallen,
will you not be asked, 'Where is the plaster with which you plastered *it?*' "
13 Therefore, thus says the Lord GOD,
"I will make a violent wind break out in
My wrath. There will also be in My anger
a flooding rain and [a]hailstones to consume *it* in wrath.
14 "So I will tear down the wall which
you plastered over with whitewash and
bring it down to the ground, so that its
[a]foundation is laid bare; and when it
falls, you will be [b]consumed in its midst.
And you will [c]know that I am the LORD.
15 "Thus I will spend My wrath on the

13 [b]Jer 39:7; 52:11
14 [a]2 Kin 25:4, 5; Ezek 5:2; 17:21
15 [a]Ezek 6:7,14; 12:16,20
16 [1]Lit *leave over* [2]Or *they will know* [a]Ezek 7:15; 14:21 [b]Jer 22:8,9
18 [a]Lam 5:9; Ezek 4:16
19 [1]Lit *her* [2]Lit *desolate* [a]Jer 10:22; Ezek 6:6, 7,14; Mic 7:13; Zech 7:14
20 [a]Is 3:26; Jer 4:7; Ezek 5:14 [b]Is 7:23,24; Jer 25:9; Ezek 36:3
22 [a]Ezek 16:44; 18:2,3 [b]Jer 5:12; Ezek 11:3; 12:27; Amos 6:3; 2 Pet 3:4 [c]Ezek 7:26
23 [1]Lit *word* [a]Ps 37:13; Joel 2:1; Zeph 1:14
24 [1]Lit *vain* [a]Jer 14:13-16; Ezek 13:6,23; Zech 13:2-4
25 [a]Num 14:28-34; Is 14:24; Ezek 6:10; 12:28 [b]Jer 16:9; Hab 1:5 [c]Ezek 12:2
27 [1]Lit *days* [a]Ezek 12:22; Dan 10:14
13:2 [1]Lit *heart* [a]Is 9:15; Jer 37:19; Ezek 22:25,28 [b]Is 1:10; Amos 7:16
3 [1]Heb *YHWH,* usually rendered LORD, and so throughout the ch [a]Lam 2:14; Hos 9:7; Zech 11:15 [b]Jer 23:28-32
5 [a]Ps 106:23; Jer 23:22; Ezek 22:30 [b]Is 58:12 [c]Is 13:6,9; Ezek 7:19
6 [1]Lit *vanity* [a]Jer 29:8; Ezek 22:28 [b]Jer 28:15; 37:19
7 [a]Ezek 22:28
8 [1]Lit *vanity* [a]Ezek 5:8; 21:3; Nah 2:13
9 [1]Lit *not be in* [2]Or *and you will know* [a]Jer 20:3-6; 28:15-17 [b]Ps 69:28; 87:6; Jer 17:13; Dan 12:1
10 [a]Jer 23:32; 50:6 [b]Jer 6:14; 8:11; 14:13 [c]Ezek 7:25; 13:16
11 [a]Ezek 38:22
13 [a]Ex 9:24,25; Ps 18:12,13; Is 30:30; Rev 11:19; 16:21
14 [a]Mic 1:6; Hab 3:13 [b]Jer 6:15; 14:15 [c]Ezek 13:9

wall and on those who have plastered it
over with whitewash; and I will say to
you, 'The wall [1]is gone and its plasterers
are gone,
16 *along with* the prophets of Israel
who prophesy to Jerusalem, and who
[a]see visions of peace for her when there
is [b]no peace,' declares the Lord GOD.
17 ¶ "Now you, son of man, set your
face against the daughters of your people
who are [a]prophesying [b]from their own
[1]inspiration. Prophesy against them
18 and say, 'Thus says the Lord GOD,
"Woe to the women who sew *magic*
bands on [1]all wrists and make veils for
the heads of *persons* of every stature to
[a]hunt down [2]lives! Will you hunt down
the [2]lives of My people, but preserve the
[2]lives *of others* for yourselves?
19 "[a]For handfuls of barley and fragments of bread, you have profaned Me to
My people to put to death [1]some who
should not die and to [b]keep [1]others alive
who should not live, by your lying to My
people who listen to lies." ' "
20 ¶ Therefore, thus says the Lord
GOD, "Behold, I am against your *magic*
bands by which you hunt [1]lives there as
[2]birds and I will tear them from your
arms; and I will let [1]them go, even those
[1]lives whom you hunt as [2]birds.
21 "I will also tear off your veils and
[a]deliver My people from your hands, and
they will no longer be in your hands to be
hunted; and you will know that I am the
LORD.
22 "Because you [a]disheartened the
righteous with falsehood when I did not
cause him grief, but have [1b]encouraged
the wicked not to [c]turn from his wicked
way *and* preserve his life,
23 therefore, you women will no longer see [1a]false visions or practice divination, and I will [b]deliver My people out of
your hand. Thus you will [c]know that I
am the LORD."

Idolatrous Elders Condemned

14 Then some [a]elders of Israel came
to me and [b]sat down before me.
2 And the word of the LORD came to
me, saying,
3 "Son of man, these men have [a]set
up their idols in their hearts and have
[b]put right before their faces the stumbling block of their iniquity. Should I be
[c]consulted by them at all?
4 "Therefore speak to them and tell
them, 'Thus says the Lord [1]GOD, "Any
man of the house of Israel who sets up his
idols in his heart, puts right before his
face the stumbling block of his iniquity,
and *then* comes to the prophet, I the
LORD will be brought to give him an answer in [2]the matter in view of the [a]mul-
titude of his idols,
5 in order to lay hold of [1a]the hearts
of the house of Israel who are [2b]es-
tranged from Me through all their
idols." '
6 ¶ "Therefore say to the house of Israel, 'Thus says the Lord GOD, "[a]Repent
and turn away from your idols and turn
your faces away from all your [b]abomina-
tions.
7 "For anyone of the house of Israel or
of the [a]immigrants who stay in Israel
who separates himself from Me, sets up
his idols in his heart, puts right before his
face the stumbling block of his iniquity,
and *then* comes to the prophet to inquire
of Me for himself, [b]I the LORD will be
brought to answer him in My own person.
8 "I will [a]set My face against that man
and make him a [b]sign and [1]a proverb,
and I will cut him off from among My
people. So you will know that I am the
LORD.
9 ¶ "But if the prophet is [1]prevailed
upon to speak a word, it is I, the LORD,
who have [1]prevailed upon that prophet,
and I will stretch out My hand against
him and [a]destroy him from among My
people Israel.
10 "They will bear *the punishment of*
their iniquity; as the iniquity of the in-
quirer is, so the iniquity of the prophet
will be,
11 in order that the house of Israel
may no longer [a]stray from Me and no
longer [b]defile themselves with all their
transgressions. Thus they will be [c]My
people, and I shall be their God," ' declares the Lord GOD."

The City Will Not Be Spared

12 ¶ Then the word of the LORD came
to me saying,
13 "Son of man, if a country sins against
Me by [a]committing unfaithfulness, and I
stretch out My hand against it, [1]destroy
its [b]supply of bread, send famine against
it and cut off from it both man and beast,
14 even [a]*though* these three men,
[b]Noah, [c]Daniel and [d]Job were in its
midst, by their *own* righteousness they
could *only* deliver [e]themselves," declares the Lord GOD.
15 "If I were to cause [a]wild beasts to
pass through the land and they [1]depopu-
lated it, and it became desolate so that no
one would pass through it because of the
beasts,
16 *though* these three men were in its
midst, as I live," declares the Lord GOD,
"they could not deliver either *their* sons
or *their* daughters. [a]They alone would be

15 [1]Lit *is not...are not*
16 [a]Jer 6:14; Ezek 13:10 [b]Is 57:21
17 [1]Lit *heart* [a]Judg 4:4; 2 Kin 22:14; Luke 2:36; Acts 21:9 [b]Ezek 13:2; Rev 2:20
18 [1]Lit *all joints of the hand;* M.T. reads *of my hands* [2]Or *souls* [a]2 Pet 2:14
19 [1]Or *souls* [a]Prov 28:21; Mic 3:5 [b]Jer 23:14
20 [1]Lit *souls* [2]Or *flying ones*
21 [a]Ps 91:3
22 [1]Lit *strengthen the hands of* [a]Amos 5:12 [b]Jer 23:14 [c]Ezek 18:21
23 [1]Lit *vanity* [a]Ezek 12:24; Mic 3:6; Zech 13:3 [b]Ezek 13:21 [c]Ezek 13:9
14:1 [a]2 Kin 6:32; Ezek 8:1 [b]Is 29:13; Ezek 33:31
3 [a]Ezek 20:16 [b]Ezek 7:19; Zeph 1:3 [c]Is 1:15; Jer 11:11; Ezek 20:3
4 [1]Heb *YHWH,* usually rendered *LORD,* and so throughout the ch [2]Lit *it* [a]1 Kin 21:20-24; 2 Kin 1:16; Is 66:4
5 [1]Lit *their* [2]Or *all estranged from Me through their idols* [a]Jer 17:10; Zech 7:12 [b]Is 1:4; Jer 2:11; Zech 11:8
6 [a]1 Sam 7:3; Neh 1:9; Is 2:20; Ezek 18:30 [b]Ezek 8:6
7 [a]Ex 12:48 [b]Ezek 14:4
8 [1]Lit *proverbs* [a]Jer 44:11; Ezek 15:7 [b]Is 65:15; Ezek 5:15
9 [1]Or *enticed* [a]Jer 6:14
11 [a]Ezek 44:10 [b]Ezek 11:18 [c]Ezek 11:20
13 [1]Lit *break the staff* [a]Ezek 15:8 [b]Lev 26:26; Is 3:1; Ezek 4:16
14 [a]Jer 15:1 [b]Gen 6:8; Heb 11:7 [c]Ezek 28:3; Dan 1:6 [d]Job 1:1 [e]Ezek 16:18
15 [1]Lit *bereave of children* [a]Lev 26:22; Num 21:6; Ezek 5:17
16 [a]Gen 19:29; Ezek 18:20

delivered, but the country would be desolate.
17 "Or *if* I should [a]bring a sword on
that country and say, 'Let the sword pass
through the country and [b]cut off man
and beast from it,'
18 even *though* these three men were
in its midst, as I live," declares the Lord
GOD, "they could not deliver either *their*
sons or *their* daughters, but they alone
would be delivered.
19 "Or *if* I should send a [a]plague
against that country and pour out My
wrath in blood on it to cut off man and
beast from it,
20 even *though* Noah, Daniel and Job
were in its midst, as I live," declares the
Lord GOD, "they could not deliver either
their son or *their* daughter. They would
deliver only themselves by their righteousness."
21 ¶ For thus says the Lord GOD,
"How much more when [a]I send My four
[1]severe judgments against Jerusalem:
sword, famine, wild beasts and plague to
cut off man and beast from it!
22 "Yet, behold, [1]survivors will be left
in it who will be brought out, *both* sons
and daughters. Behold, they are going to
come forth to you and you will [a]see their
conduct and actions; then you will be
[b]comforted for the calamity which I have
brought against Jerusalem for everything
which I have brought upon it.
23 "Then they will comfort you when
you see their conduct and actions, for you
will know that I have not done [a]in vain
whatever I did [1]to it," declares the
Lord GOD.

Jerusalem like a Useless Vine

15 Then the word of the LORD came
to me, saying,
2 "Son of man, how is the wood of the
[a]vine *better* than any wood of a branch
which is among the trees of the forest?
3 "Can wood be taken from it to make
[1]anything, or can *men* take a peg from it
on which to hang any vessel?
4 "[1]If it has been put into the [a]fire for
fuel, *and* the fire has consumed both of
its ends and its middle part has been
charred, is it *then* useful for [2]anything?
5 "Behold, while it is intact, it is not
made into [1]anything. How much less,
when the fire has consumed it and it is
charred, can it still be made into [1]any-
thing!
6 "Therefore, thus says the Lord
[1]GOD, 'As the wood of the vine among
the trees of the forest, which I have given
to the fire for fuel, so have I given up the
inhabitants of Jerusalem;
7 and I [a]set My face against them.
Though they have [b]come out of the fire,
yet the fire will consume them. Then you
will know that I am the LORD, when I set
My face against them.
8 'Thus I will make the land desolate,
because they have [a]acted unfaithfully,'"
declares the Lord GOD.

God's Grace to Unfaithful Jerusalem

16 Then the word of the LORD came
to me, saying,
2 "Son of man, [a]make known to Jerusalem her abominations
3 and say, 'Thus says the Lord [1]GOD
to Jerusalem, "Your origin and your birth
are from the land of the Canaanite, your
father was an Amorite and your mother a
Hittite.
4 "As for your birth, [a]on the day you
were born your navel cord was not cut,
nor were you washed with water for
cleansing; you were not rubbed with salt
or even wrapped in cloths.
5 "No eye looked with pity on you to
do any of these things for you, to have
compassion on you. Rather you were
thrown out into the [1a]open field, [2]for
you were abhorred on the day you were
born.
6 ¶ "When I passed by you and saw
you squirming in your blood, I said to you
while you were in your blood, 'Live!' Yes,
I said to you *while you were* in your
blood, 'Live!'
7 "I [a]made you [1]numerous like
plants of the field. Then you grew up,
became tall and reached the age for fine
ornaments; *your* breasts were formed and
your hair had grown. Yet you were naked
and bare.
8 ¶ "Then I passed by you and saw
you, and behold, [1]you were at the time
for love; so I [a]spread My skirt over you
and covered your nakedness. I also
[b]swore to you and [c]entered into a covenant with you so that you [d]became
Mine," declares the Lord GOD.
9 "Then I bathed you with water,
washed off your blood from you and
[a]anointed you with oil.
10 "I also clothed you with [a]embroi-
dered cloth and put sandals of porpoise
skin on your feet; and I wrapped you with
fine linen and covered you with silk.
11 "I adorned you with ornaments, put
[a]bracelets on your hands and a [b]neck-
lace around your neck.
12 "I also put a [a]ring in your nostril,
earrings in your ears and a [b]beautiful
crown on your head.
13 "Thus you were adorned with [a]gold
and silver, and your dress was of fine lin-

17 [a]Lev 26:25; Ezek 5:12; 21:3, 4 [b]Ezek 25:13; Zeph 1:3
19 [a]Jer 14:12; Ezek 5:12; 14:21
21 [1]Lit *evil* [a]Ezek 5:17; 33:27; Amos 4:6-10; Rev 6:8
22 [1]Lit *escaped ones* [a]Ezek 12:16; 36:20 [b]Ezek 16:54; 31:16; 32:31
23 [1]Or *in* [a]Jer 22:8,9
15:2 [a]Ps 80:8-16; Is 5:1-7; Hos 10:1
3 [1]Lit *a work*
4 [1]Or *Behold* [2]Lit *a work* [a]Is 27:11; Ezek 15:6; 19:14
5 [1]Lit *a work*
6 [1]Heb *YHWH,* usually rendered *LORD,* and so throughout the ch
7 [a]Lev 26:17; Ps 34:16; Jer 21:10; Ezek 14:8 [b]1 Kin 19:17; Is 24:18; Amos 9:1-4
8 [a]Ezek 14:13; 17:20
16:2 [a]Is 58:1; Ezek 20:4; 22:2
3 [1]Heb *YHWH,* usually rendered *LORD,* and so throughout the ch
4 [a]Hos 2:3
5 [1]Lit *surface* [2]Lit *in the loathing of your soul* [a]Deut 32:10
7 [1]Lit *a myriad* [a]Ex 1:7; Deut 1:10
8 [1]Lit *your time was* [a]Ruth 3:9; Jer 2:2 [b]Gen 22:16-18 [c]Ex 24:7,8 [d]Ex 19:5; Ezek 20:5; Hos 2:19,20
9 [a]Ruth 3:3
10 [a]Ex 26:36; Ezek 16:13,18; 26:16; 27:7,16
11 [a]Gen 24:22, 47; Is 3:19; Ezek 23:42 [b]Gen 41:42; Prov 1:9
12 [a]Gen 24:47; Is 3:21 [b]Is 28:5; Jer 13:18; Ezek 16:14
13 [a]Ps 45:13, 14; Ezek 16:17

en, silk and embroidered cloth. You ate fine flour, honey and oil; so you were exceedingly beautiful and advanced to [b]royalty.

14 "Then your [a]fame went forth among the nations on account of your beauty, for it was [b]perfect because of My splendor which I bestowed on you," declares the Lord GOD.

15 ¶ "But you [a]trusted in your beauty and [b]played the harlot because of your fame, and you poured out your harlotries on every passer-by [1]who might be *willing.*

16 "You took some of your clothes, made for yourself high places of various colors and played the harlot on them, [1]which should never come about nor happen.

17 "You also took your beautiful [1a]jewels *made* of My gold and of My silver, which I had given you, and made for yourself male images that you might play the harlot with them.

18 "Then you took your embroidered cloth and covered them, and offered My oil and My incense before them.

19 "Also [a]My bread which I gave you, fine flour, oil and honey with which I fed you, [1]you would offer before them for a soothing aroma; so it happened," declares the Lord GOD.

20 "Moreover, you took your sons and daughters whom you had borne to [a]Me and [b]sacrificed them to [1]idols to be devoured. Were your harlotries so small a matter?

21 "You slaughtered [a]My children and offered them up to [1]idols by [b]causing them to pass through *the fire.*

22 "Besides all your abominations and harlotries you did not remember the days of [a]your youth, when you were naked and bare and squirming in your blood.

23 ¶ "Then it came about after all your wickedness ('Woe, woe to you!' declares the Lord GOD),

24 that you built yourself a [a]shrine and made yourself a [b]high place in every square.

25 "You built yourself a high place at the top of [a]every street and made your beauty abominable, and you spread your legs to every passer-by to multiply your harlotry.

26 "You also played the harlot with the Egyptians, your [1]lustful neighbors, and multiplied your harlotry to [a]make Me angry.

27 "Behold now, I have stretched out My hand against you and diminished your rations. And I delivered you up to the desire of those who hate you, the [a]daughters of the Philistines, who are ashamed of your lewd conduct.

28 "Moreover, you played the harlot with the [a]Assyrians because you were not satisfied; you played the harlot with them and still were not satisfied.

29 "You also multiplied your harlotry with the land of merchants, Chaldea, yet even with this you were not satisfied." ' "

30 ¶ "How [a]languishing is your heart," declares the Lord GOD, "while you do all these things, the actions of a [1b]bold-faced harlot.

31 "When you built your shrine at the beginning of every street and made your high place in every square, in [a]disdaining money, you were not like a harlot.

32 "You adulteress wife, who takes strangers instead of her husband!

33 "[1]Men give gifts to all harlots, but you [a]give your gifts to all your lovers to bribe them to come to you from every direction for your harlotries.

34 "Thus you are different from those women in your harlotries, in that no one plays the harlot [1]as you do, because you give money and no money is given you; thus you are different."

35 ¶ Therefore, O harlot, hear the word of the LORD.

36 Thus says the Lord GOD, "Because your lewdness was poured out and your nakedness uncovered through your harlotries with your lovers and with all your detestable [a]idols, and because of the blood of your sons which you gave to [1]idols,

37 therefore, behold, I will [a]gather all your lovers with whom you took pleasure, even all those whom you loved *and* all those whom you [b]hated. So I will gather them against you from every direction and [c]expose your nakedness to them that they may see all your nakedness.

38 "Thus I will [a]judge you like women who commit adultery or shed blood are judged; and I will bring on you the blood of [b]wrath and jealousy.

39 "I will also give you into [1]the hands of your lovers, and they will tear down your shrines, demolish your high places, [a]strip you of your clothing, take away your [2]jewels, and will leave you naked and bare.

40 "They will [1]incite a [a]crowd against you and they will stone you and cut you to pieces with their swords.

41 "They will [a]burn your houses with fire and execute judgments on you in the sight of many women. Then I will [b]stop you from playing the harlot, and you will also no longer pay [1]your lovers.

42 "So I [a]will calm My fury against you

13 [b]1 Sam 10:1; 1 Kin 4:21
14 [a]1 Kin 10:1, 24 [b]Ps 50:2; Lam 2:15
15 [1]Lit *to whom it might be* [a]Ezek 16:25; 27:3 [b]Is 57:8; Jer 2:20
16 [1]Lit *things which had not happened nor will it be*
17 [1]Lit *articles of beauty* [a]Ezek 16:11,12
19 [1]Lit *and you...offer it* [a]Hos 2:8
20 [1]Lit *them* [a]Ex 13:2,12; Deut 29:11,12 [b]Ps 106:37,38; Jer 7:31; Ezek 20:31; 23:37
21 [1]Lit *them* [a]Ex 13:2 [b]2 Kin 17:17; Jer 19:5
22 [a]Jer 2:2
24 [a]Jer 11:13; Ezek 16:31,39; 20:28,29 [b]Ps 78:58; Is 57:7
25 [a]Prov 9:14
26 [1]Lit *great of flesh* [a]Jer 7:18, 19; Ezek 8:17
27 [a]Is 9:12; Ezek 16:57
28 [a]2 Kin 16:7, 10-18; 2 Chr 28:16,20-23; Jer 2:18,36; Ezek 23:12; Hos 10:6
30 [1]Lit *domineering* [a]Prov 9:13; Is 1:3; Jer 4:22 [b]Is 3:9; Jer 3:3
31 [a]Is 52:3
33 [1]Lit *They* [a]Is 57:9; Ezek 16:41; Hos 8:9, 10
34 [1]Lit *after you*
36 [1]Lit *them* [a]Jer 19:5; Ezek 20:31; 23:37
37 [a]Jer 13:22, 26; Ezek 23:9, 22; Hos 2:3,10; Nah 3:5,6 [b]Ezek 23:17,28 [c]Is 47:3
38 [a]Ezek 23:45 [b]Ps 79:3,5; Jer 18:21; Ezek 23:25; Zeph 1:17
39 [1]Lit *their hands, and they* [2]Lit *articles of beauty* [a]Ezek 23:26; Hos 2:3
40 [1]Lit *bring up an assembly* [a]Ezek 23:47; Hab 1:6-10
41 [1]Lit *a harlot's hire* [a]2 Kin 25:9; Jer 39:8; 52:13 [b]Ezek 23:48
42 [a]2 Sam 24:25; Ezek 5:13; 21:17; Zech 6:8

and My jealousy will depart from you, and
I will be pacified and angry [b]no more.
43 "Because you have [a]not remembered the days of your youth but [1]have
[b]enraged Me by all these things, behold,
I in turn will [c]bring your conduct down
on your own head," declares the Lord
GOD, "so that you will not commit this
lewdness on top of all your *other* abominations.
44 ¶ "Behold, everyone who quotes
[a]proverbs will quote *this* proverb concerning you, saying, '[1]Like mother, [1]like
daughter.'
45 "You are the daughter of your mother, who loathed her husband and children. You are also the [a]sister of your
sisters, who [b]loathed their husbands and
children. Your mother was a Hittite and
your father an Amorite.
46 "Now your [a]older sister is Samaria,
who lives [1]north of you with her
[2]daughters; and your younger sister,
who lives [3]south of you, is [b]Sodom with
her [2]daughters.
47 "Yet you have not merely walked in
their ways or done according to their
abominations; but, as if that were [a]too
little, you acted [b]more corruptly in all
your conduct than they.
48 "As I live," declares the Lord GOD,
"Sodom, your sister and her daughters
have [a]not done as you and your daughters have done.
49 "Behold, this was the guilt of your
sister Sodom: she and her daughters had
[a]arrogance, [b]abundant food and [c]care-
less ease, but she did not [1]help the
[d]poor and needy.
50 "Thus they were haughty and committed [a]abominations before Me. Therefore I [b]removed them [1]when I saw *it.*
51 "Furthermore, Samaria did not commit half of your sins, for you have multiplied your abominations more than they.
Thus you have made your sisters appear
[a]righteous by all your abominations
which you have committed.
52 "Also bear your disgrace in that you
have [1]made judgment favorable for your
sisters. Because of your sins in which you
acted [a]more abominably than they, they
are more in the right than you. Yes, be
also ashamed and bear your disgrace, in
that you made your sisters appear righteous.
53 ¶ "Nevertheless, I will restore their
captivity, the captivity of Sodom and her
daughters, the captivity of Samaria and
her daughters, and [1]along with them
[2]your own captivity,
54 in order that you may bear your humiliation and feel [a]ashamed for all that
you have done when you become [b]a consolation to them.
55 "Your sisters, Sodom with her
daughters and Samaria with her daughters, [1]will return to their former state,
and you with your daughters will *also* return to your former state.
56 "As *the name of* your sister Sodom
was not heard from your lips in your day
of pride,
57 before your [a]wickedness was uncovered, [1]so now you have become the
[b]reproach of the daughters of [2]Edom
and of all who are around her, of the
daughters of the Philistines—those surrounding *you* who despise you.
58 "You have [a]borne *the penalty of*
your lewdness and abominations," the
LORD declares.
59 For thus says the Lord GOD, "I will
also do with you as you have done, you
who have [a]despised the oath by breaking
the covenant.

The Covenant Remembered

60 ¶ "Nevertheless, I will remember
My covenant with you in the days of your
youth, and I will establish an [a]everlast-
ing covenant with you.
61 "Then you will [a]remember your
ways and be ashamed when you receive
your sisters, *both* your older and your
younger; and I will give them to you as
daughters, but not because of your covenant.
62 "Thus I will [a]establish My covenant
with you, and you shall [b]know that I am
the LORD,
63 so that you may [a]remember and be
ashamed and [b]never open your mouth
anymore because of your humiliation,
when I have [c]forgiven you for all that
you have done," the Lord GOD declares.

Parable of Two Eagles and a Vine

17 Now the word of the LORD came
to me saying,
2 "Son of man, propound a riddle and
speak a [a]parable to the house of Israel,
3 [1]saying, 'Thus says the Lord [2]GOD,
"A great [a]eagle with [b]great wings, long
pinions and a full plumage of many
colors came to [c]Lebanon and took away
the top of the cedar.
4 "He plucked off the topmost of its
young twigs and brought it to a land of
merchants; he set it in a city of traders.
5 "He also took some of the seed of the
land and planted it in [1][a]fertile soil. He
[2]placed *it* beside abundant waters; he set
it *like* a [b]willow.
6 "Then it sprouted and became a low,
spreading vine with its branches turned
toward him, but its roots remained under

42 [b]Is 40:1; Ezek 39:29
43 [1]So with ancient versions; Heb *are angry against* [a]Ps 78:42; Ezek 16:22 [b]Is 63:10; Ezek 6:9 [c]Ezek 11:21
44 [1]Lit *Her* [a]1 Sam 24:13; Ezek 12:22
45 [a]Ezek 23:2 [b]Is 1:4; Ezek 23:37-39; Zech 11:8
46 [1]Lit *on your left* [2]I.e. environs; so through v 55 [3]Lit *from your right* [a]Jer 3:8-11; Ezek 23:4 [b]Gen 13:10-13; Ezek 16:48
47 [a]1 Kin 16:31 [b]2 Kin 21:9; Ezek 5:6
48 [a]Matt 10:15
49 [1]Lit *grasp the hand of* [a]Gen 19:9; Ps 138:6; Is 3:9; Ezek 28:2 [b]Gen 13:10; Is 22:13; Amos 6:4-6 [c]Luke 12:16-20 [d]Ezek 18:7
50 [1]Many ancient mss and versions read *as you have seen* [a]Gen 13:13 [b]Gen 19:24
51 [a]Jer 3:8-11
52 [1]Lit *mediated for* [a]Ezek 16:47
53 [1]Lit *in their midst* [2]Lit *the captivity of your captivity*
54 [a]Jer 2:26 [b]Ezek 14:22
55 [1]Heb includes *will return...state* after Sodom also
57 [1]Lit *as at the time of* [2]So with many mss and one version; M.T. *Aram* [a]Ezek 16:36 [b]2 Kin 16:5-7; 2 Chr 28:5; Ezek 5:14
58 [a]Ezek 23:49
59 [a]Is 24:5; Ezek 17:19
60 [a]Is 55:3; Jer 32:38-41; Ezek 37:26
61 [a]Jer 50:4; Ezek 6:9
62 [a]Ezek 20:37 [b]Jer 24:7; Ezek 20:43
63 [a]Ezek 36:31; Dan 9:7 [b]Ps 39:9; Rom 3:19 [c]Ps 65:3
17:2 [a]Ezek 20:49
3 [1]Lit *and you shall say* [2]Heb *YHWH,* usually rendered *LORD,* and so throughout the ch [a]Jer 48:40; Ezek 17:12; Hos 8:1 [b]Dan 4:22 [c]Jer 22:23
5 [1]Lit *a field of seed* [2]Lit *took* [a]Deut 8:7-9 [b]Is 44:4

it. So it became a vine and yielded shoots
and sent out branches.
7 ¶ "But there was [1]another great
eagle with great wings and much plumage; and behold, this vine bent its roots
toward him and sent out its branches toward him from the beds where it was
[a]planted, that he might water it.
8 "It was planted in good [1]soil beside
abundant waters, that it might yield
branches and bear fruit *and* become a
splendid vine." '
9 "Say, 'Thus says the Lord GOD, "Will
it thrive? Will he not pull up its roots and
cut off its fruit, so that it withers—so that
all its sprouting leaves wither? And neither by great [1]strength nor by many people can it be raised from its roots *again.*
10 "Behold, though it is planted, will it
thrive? Will it not [a]completely wither as
soon as the east wind strikes it—wither
on the beds where it grew?" ' "

Zedekiah's Rebellion

11 ¶ Moreover, the word of the LORD
came to me, saying,
12 "Say now to the [a]rebellious house,
'Do you not [b]know what these things
mean?' Say, 'Behold, the [c]king of Babylon came to Jerusalem, took its king and
princes and brought them to him in Babylon.
13 'He took one of the royal [1a]family
and made a covenant with him, [2]putting
him under [b]oath. He also took away the
[c]mighty of the land,
14 that the kingdom might [a]be [1]in
subjection, not exalting itself, *but* keeping his covenant that it might continue.
15 'But he [a]rebelled against him by
sending his envoys to Egypt that they
might give him horses and many [1]troops.
Will he succeed? Will he who does such
things [b]escape? Can he indeed break the
covenant and escape?
16 'As I live,' declares the Lord GOD,
'Surely in the [1]country of the king who
[2]put him on the throne, whose oath he
[a]despised and whose covenant he broke,
[3b]in Babylon he shall die.
17 '[a]Pharaoh with *his* mighty army
and great company will not [1]help him in
the war, when they cast up ramps and
build siege walls to cut off many lives.
18 'Now he despised the oath by breaking the covenant, and behold, he
[1a]pledged his allegiance, yet did all
these things; he shall not escape.' "
19 Therefore, thus says the Lord GOD,
"As I live, surely My oath which he despised and My covenant which he broke,
I will [1]inflict on his head.
20 "I will spread My [a]net over him,
and he will be [b]caught in My snare. Then
I will bring him to Babylon and [c]enter
into judgment with him there *regarding*
the unfaithful act which he has committed against Me.
21 "All the [1a]choice men in all his
troops will fall by the sword, and the survivors will be scattered to every wind;
and you will know that I, the LORD, have
spoken."
22 ¶ Thus says the Lord GOD, "I will
also take *a sprig* from the lofty top of the
cedar and set *it* out; I will pluck from the
topmost of its young twigs a tender one
and I will plant *it* on a [a]high and lofty
mountain.
23 "On the high mountain of Israel I
will plant it, that it may bring forth
boughs and bear fruit and become a stately [a]cedar. And birds of every [1]kind will
[2]nest under it; they will [2]nest in the
shade of its branches.
24 "All the [a]trees of the field will know
that I am the LORD; I bring down the high
tree, exalt the low tree, dry up the green
tree and make the dry tree [b]flourish. I
am the LORD; I have spoken, and I will
perform *it.*"

God Deals Justly with Individuals

18 Then the word of the LORD came
to me, saying,
2 "[a]What do you mean by using this
proverb concerning the land of Israel,
saying,
'[b]The fathers eat the sour grapes,
But the children's teeth [1]are set
on edge'?
3 "As I live," declares the Lord [1]GOD,
"you are surely not going to use this proverb in Israel anymore.
4 "Behold, [a]all [1]souls are Mine; the
[2]soul of the father as well as the [2]soul of
the son is Mine. The [3]soul who [b]sins
will die.
5 ¶ "But if a man is righteous and
practices justice and righteousness,
6 and does not [a]eat at the mountain
shrines or [b]lift up his eyes to the idols of
the house of Israel, or [c]defile his neighbor's wife or approach a woman during
her menstrual period—
7 if a man does not oppress anyone,
but [a]restores to the debtor his pledge,
[b]does not commit robbery, *but* [c]gives
his bread to the hungry and covers the
naked with clothing,
8 if he does not lend *money* on [a]in-
terest or take [b]increase, *if* he keeps his
hand from iniquity *and* [c]executes true
justice between man and man,
9 *if* he walks in [a]My statutes and My
ordinances so as to deal faithfully—[b]he
is righteous *and* will surely [c]live," declares the Lord GOD.

7 [1]So with several ancient versions; M.T. *one* [a]Ezek 31:4
8 [1]Lit *field*
9 [1]Lit *arm*
10 [a]Ezek 19:14; Hos 13:15
12 [a]Ezek 2:3-5 [b]Ezek 12:9-11 [c]2 Kin 24:11; Ezek 1:2
13 [1]Lit *seed* [2]Lit *and caused him to enter into an oath* [a]2 Kin 24:17; Ezek 17:5 [b]2 Chr 36:13 [c]2 Kin 24:15
14 [1]Lit *low* [a]Ezek 29:14
15 [1]Lit *people* [a]2 Kin 24:20; 2 Chr 36:13; Jer 52:3; Ezek 17:7 [b]Jer 34:3; Ezek 17:18
16 [1]Lit *place* [2]Lit *made him king* [3]Lit *with him in Babylon* [a]2 Kin 24:17; Ezek 16:59 [b]Jer 52:11; Ezek 12:13
17 [1]Lit *act with* [a]Is 36:6; Jer 37:5; Ezek 29:6
18 [1]Lit *gave his hand* [a]1 Chr 29:24
19 [1]Lit *give it*
20 [a]Ezek 12:13 [b]Jer 39:5-7 [c]Jer 2:35; Ezek 20:35
21 [1]So many ancient mss and versions; M.T. *fugitives* [a]2 Kin 25:5; Ezek 5:2
22 [a]Ps 72:16; Ezek 20:40
23 [1]Lit *wing* [2]Lit *dwell* [a]Ps 92:12
24 [a]Ps 96:12; Is 55:12 [b]Amos 9:11
18:2 [1]Lit *become dull* [a]Is 3:15 [b]Jer 31:29; Lam 5:7
3 [1]Heb *YHWH,* usually rendered LORD, and so throughout the ch
4 [1]Or *lives* [2]Or *life* [3]Or *person* [a]Num 16:22; Is 42:5 [b]Ezek 18:20; Rom 6:23
6 [a]Ezek 6:13 [b]Deut 4:19; Ezek 18:12 [c]Ezek 18:15
7 [a]Deut 24:13; Ezek 33:15; Amos 2:8 [b]Lev 19:13; Amos 3:10 [c]Deut 15:11; Ezek 18:16; Matt 25:35-40; Luke 3:11
8 [a]Ex 22:25; Deut 23:19 [b]Lev 25:36 [c]Zech 7:9
9 [a]Lev 18:5 [b]Rom 8:1 [c]Amos 5:4; Hab 2:4; Rom 1:17

10 ¶ "Then he may [1]have a violent son who sheds blood and who does any of these things to a brother

11 (though he himself did not do any of these things), that is, he even eats at the mountain *shrines,* and [a]defiles his neighbor's wife,

12 oppresses the [a]poor and needy, [b]commits robbery, does not restore a pledge, but lifts up his eyes to the idols *and* [c]commits abomination,

13 he [a]lends *money* on interest and takes increase; will he live? He will not live! He has committed all these abominations, he will surely be put to death; his [b]blood will be [1]on his own head.

14 ¶ "Now behold, he [1]has a son who has observed all his father's sins which he committed, and [a]observing does not do likewise.

15 "He does not eat at the mountain *shrines* or lift up his eyes to the idols of the house of Israel, or defile his neighbor's wife,

16 or oppress anyone, or retain a pledge, or commit robbery, *but* he [a]gives his bread to the hungry and covers the naked with clothing,

17 he keeps his hand from [1]the poor, does not take interest or increase, *but* executes My ordinances, and walks in My statutes; [a]he will not die for his father's iniquity, he will surely live.

18 "As for his father, because he practiced extortion, robbed *his* brother and did what was not good among his people, behold, he will die for his iniquity.

19 ¶ "Yet you say, '[a]Why should the son not bear the punishment for the father's iniquity?' When the son has practiced [b]justice and righteousness and has observed all My statutes and done them, he shall surely live.

20 "The person who [a]sins will die. The [b]son will not bear the punishment for the father's iniquity, nor will the father bear the punishment for the son's iniquity; the [c]righteousness of the righteous will be upon himself, and the wickedness of the wicked will be upon himself.

21 ¶ "But if the [a]wicked man turns from all his sins which he has committed and observes all My statutes and practices justice and righteousness, he shall surely live; he shall not die.

22 "[a]All his transgressions which he has committed will not be remembered against him; because of his [b]righteousness which he has practiced, he will live.

23 "[a]Do I have any pleasure in the death of the wicked," declares the Lord GOD, "[1]rather than that he should [b]turn from his ways and live?

24 ¶ "But when a righteous man [a]turns away from his righteousness, commits iniquity and does according to all the abominations that a wicked man does, will he live? [b]All his righteous deeds which he has done will not be remembered for his [c]treachery which he has committed and his sin which he has committed; for them he will die.

25 "Yet you say, '[a]The way of the Lord is not right.' Hear now, O house of Israel! Is [b]My way not right? Is it not your ways that are not right?

26 "When a righteous man turns away from his righteousness, commits iniquity and dies because of it, for his iniquity which he has committed he will die.

27 "Again, when a wicked man turns away [a]from his wickedness which he has committed and practices justice and righteousness, he will save his life.

28 "Because he considered and turned away from all his transgressions which he had committed, he shall surely live; he shall not die.

29 "But the house of Israel says, 'The way of the Lord is not right.' Are My ways not right, O house of Israel? Is it not your ways that are not right?

30 ¶ "Therefore I will judge you, O house of Israel, each according to his conduct," declares the Lord GOD. "[a]Repent and turn away from all your transgressions, so that iniquity may not become a stumbling block to you.

31 "[a]Cast away from you all your transgressions which you have committed and make yourselves a [b]new heart and a new spirit! For why will you die, O house of Israel?

32 "For I have [a]no pleasure in the death of anyone who dies," declares the Lord GOD. "Therefore, repent and live."

Lament for the Princes of Israel

19 "As for you, take up a [a]lamentation for the [b]princes of Israel
2 and say,
'[1]What was your mother?
A lioness among lions!
She lay down among young lions,
She reared her cubs.
3 'When she brought up one of her cubs,
He became a lion,
And he learned to tear *his* prey;
He devoured men.
4 'Then nations heard about him;
He was captured in their pit,
And they [a]brought him with hooks
To the land of Egypt.
5 'When she saw, as she waited,

---

10 [1]Lit *beget*
11 [a]1 Cor 6:9
12 [a]Amos 4:1; Zech 7:10 [b]Is 59:6,7; Jer 22:3, 17; Ezek 7:23; 18:7,16,18 [c]2 Kin 21:11; Ezek 8:6,17
13 [1]Lit *on him* [a]Ex 22:25 [b]Ezek 33:4,5
14 [1]Lit *begets* [a]2 Chr 29:6-10; 34:21
16 [a]Job 31:16, 20; Ps 41:1; Is 58:7,10; Ezek 18:7
17 [1]So M.T.; Gr reads *iniquity* as in v 8 [a]Rom 2:7
19 [a]Ex 20:5; Jer 15:4; Ezek 18:2 [b]Ezek 18:9; 20:18-20; Zech 1:3-6
20 [a]2 Kin 14:6; 22:18-20; Ezek 18:4 [b]Deut 24:16; Jer 31:30 [c]1 Kin 8:32; Is 3:10,11; Matt 16:27; Rom 2:6-9
21 [a]Ezek 18:27, 28; 33:12,19
22 [a]Is 43:25; Jer 50:20; Ezek 18:24; 33:16; Mic 7:19 [b]Ps 18:20-24
23 [1]Lit *is it not* [a]Ezek 18:32; 33:11 [b]Ps 147:11; Mic 7:18
24 [a]1 Sam 15:11; 2 Chr 24:2,17-22; Ezek 3:20; 18:26; 33:18 [b]Ezek 18:22; Gal 3:3,4 [c]Prov 21:16; Ezek 17:20; 20:27
25 [a]Ezek 18:29; 33:17,20; Mal 2:17; 3:13-15 [b]Gen 18:25; Jer 12:1; Zeph 3:5
27 [a]Is 1:18; 55:7
30 [a]Ezek 14:6; 33:11; Hos 12:6
31 [a]Is 1:16,17; 55:7 [b]Ps 51:10; Ezek 11:19; 36:26
32 [a]Ezek 18:23; 33:11
19:1 [a]Ezek 2:10; 19:14 [b]2 Kin 23:29,30, 34; 24:6,12; 25:5-7
2 [1]Or *Why did your mother, a lioness, lie down among lions; among young lions rear her cubs?*
4 [a]2 Kin 23:34; 2 Chr 36:4,6

That her hope was lost,
She took [1]another of her cubs
And made him a young lion.
6 ‘And he [a]walked about among
the lions;
He became a young lion,
He learned to tear *his* prey;
He devoured men.
7 ‘He [1]destroyed their [2]fortified
towers
And laid waste their cities;
And the land and its fullness
were appalled
Because of the sound of his
roaring.
8 ‘Then [a]nations set against him
On every side from *their*
provinces,
And they spread their net over
him;
He was captured in their pit.
9 ‘[a]They put him in a cage with
hooks
And [b]brought him to the king of
Babylon;
They brought him in hunting
nets
So that his voice would be heard
no more
On the mountains of Israel.
10 ‘Your mother was [a]like a vine in
your [1]vineyard,
Planted by the waters;
It was fruitful and full of
branches
Because of abundant waters.
11 ‘And it had [1a]strong branches *fit*
for scepters of rulers,
And its [b]height was raised above
the clouds
So that it was seen in its height
with the mass of its
branches.
12 ‘But it was [a]plucked up in fury;
It was [b]cast down to the ground;
And the [c]east wind dried up its
fruit.
Its [1d]strong branch [2]was
torn off
So that [3]it withered;
The fire consumed it.
13 ‘And now it is planted in the
[a]wilderness,
In a dry and thirsty land.
14 ‘And [a]fire has gone out from *its*
branch;
It has consumed its shoots *and*
fruit,
So that there is not in it a
[1]strong branch,
A scepter to rule.’ ”

This is a lamentation, and has become a lamentation.

5 [1]Lit *one*

6 [a]2 Kin 24:9; 2 Chr 36:9

7 [1]So Targum; M.T. *knew* [2]Or *widows*

8 [a]2 Kin 24:11

9 [a]2 Chr 36:6 [b]2 Kin 24:15

10 [1]So with some ancient mss; M.T. *blood* [a]Ps 80:8-11

11 [1]Lit *rods of strength* [a]Ps 80:15 [b]Ezek 31:3

12 [1]Lit *rods of her strength* [2]So Gr; M.T. *they were* [3]So Gr; M.T. *they* [a]Jer 31:28 [b]Lam 2:1; Ezek 28:17 [c]Ezek 17:10; Hos 13:15 [d]Is 27:11; Ezek 19:11

13 [a]2 Kin 24:12-16; Ezek 19:10; 20:35; Hos 2:3

14 [1]Lit *rod of strength* [a]Ezek 15:4; 20:47,48

20:1 [1]Lit *men* [a]Ezek 8:1,11,12

3 [1]Heb *YHWH,* usually rendered *LORD,* and so throughout the ch [a]Ezek 14:3

4 [a]Ezek 16:2; 22:2; Matt 23:32

5 [1]Lit *lifted up My hand,* and so throughout the ch [2]Lit *seed* [a]Ex 6:6-8 [b]Ex 6:2,3

6 [1]Lit *spied out* [a]Jer 32:22 [b]Ex 13:5; 33:3 [c]Ps 48:2

7 [a]Ex 20:4,5; 22:20 [b]Lev 18:3; Deut 29:16-18 [c]Ex 20:2

8 [1]Lit *each one* [2]Lit *said* [a]Deut 9:7; Is 63:10 [b]Ex 32:1-9 [c]Ezek 5:13; 7:8; 20:13,21

9 [a]Ex 32:11-14; Ezek 20:14,22; 36:21,22 [b]Ezek 39:7

10 [a]Ex 19:1

11 [1]Lit *does* [a]Ex 20:1-23:33 [b]Lev 18:5; Ezek 20:13

12 [a]Ex 31:13, 17; Ezek 20:20

13 [1]Lit *does* [a]Num 14:11,12, 22; Ezek 20:8 [b]Lev 18:5

God’s Dealings with Israel Rehearsed

20 Now in the seventh year, in the
fifth *month,* on the tenth of the
month, [1]certain of the [a]elders of Israel
came to inquire of the LORD, and sat before me.
2 And the word of the LORD came to
me saying,
3 “Son of man, speak to the elders of
Israel and say to them, ‘Thus says the
Lord [1]GOD, “Do you come to inquire of
Me? As I live,” declares the Lord GOD,
“[a]I will not be inquired of by you.” ’
4 “Will you judge them, will you judge
them, son of man? [a]Make them know
the abominations of their fathers;
5 and say to them, ‘Thus says the
Lord GOD, “On the day when I [a]chose
Israel and [1]swore to the [2]descendants
of the house of Jacob and made Myself
known to them in the land of Egypt,
when I [1]swore to them, saying, [b]I am
the LORD your God,
6 on that day I swore to them, [a]to
bring them out from the land of Egypt
into a land that I had [1]selected for them,
[b]flowing with milk and honey, which is
[c]the glory of all lands.
7 “I said to them, ‘[a]Cast away, each of
you, the detestable things of his eyes, and
[b]do not defile yourselves with the idols
of Egypt; [c]I am the LORD your God.’
8 “But they [a]rebelled against Me and
were not willing to listen to Me; [1]they
did not cast away the detestable things of
their eyes, nor did they forsake the [b]idols
of Egypt.
¶ Then I [2]resolved to [c]pour out My
wrath on them, to accomplish My anger
against them in the midst of the land of
Egypt.
9 “But I acted [a]for the sake of My
name, that it should [b]not be profaned in
the sight of the nations among whom
they *lived,* in whose sight I made Myself
known to them by bringing them out of
the land of Egypt.
10 “So I took them out of the land of
Egypt and brought them into the [a]wil-
derness.
11 “I gave them My [a]statutes and informed them of My ordinances, by
[b]which, if a man [1]observes them, he
will live.
12 “Also I gave them My sabbaths to be
a [a]sign between Me and them, that they
might know that I am the LORD who sanctifies them.
13 “But the house of Israel [a]rebelled
against Me in the wilderness. They did
not walk in My statutes and they rejected
My ordinances, [b]by which, if a man [1]ob-

serves them, he will live; and My [c]sabbaths they greatly profaned. Then I [2]resolved to [d]pour out My wrath on them in the wilderness, to annihilate them.

14 "But I acted for the sake of My name, that it should not be profaned in the sight of the nations, before whose sight I had brought them out.

15 "Also [a]I swore to them in the wilderness that I would not bring them into the land which I had given them, flowing with milk and honey, which is the glory of all lands,

16 because they rejected My ordinances, and as for My statutes, they did not walk in them; they even profaned My sabbaths, for their [a]heart continually went after their idols.

17 "Yet My eye spared them rather than destroying them, and I did not cause their [a]annihilation in the wilderness.

18 ¶ "I said to their [1a]children in the wilderness, '[b]Do not walk in the statutes of your fathers or keep their ordinances or defile yourselves with their idols.

19 '[a]I am the LORD your God; [b]walk in My statutes and keep My ordinances and [1]observe them.

20 '[a]Sanctify My sabbaths; and they shall be a sign between Me and you, that you may know that I am the LORD your God.'

21 "But the [a]children rebelled against Me; they did not walk in My statutes, nor were they careful to observe My ordinances, by which, *if* a man observes them, he will live; they profaned My sabbaths. So I [1]resolved to pour out My wrath on them, to accomplish My anger against them in the wilderness.

22 "But I [a]withdrew My hand and acted [b]for the sake of My name, that it should not be profaned in the sight of the nations in whose sight I had brought them out.

23 "Also I swore to them in the wilderness that I would [a]scatter them among the nations and disperse them among the lands,

24 because they had not observed My ordinances, but had rejected My statutes and had profaned My sabbaths, and [a]their eyes were [1]on the idols of their fathers.

25 "I also gave them statutes that were [a]not good and ordinances by which they could not live;

26 and I pronounced them [a]unclean because of their gifts, in that they [b]caused all [1]their firstborn to pass through *the fire* so that I might make them desolate, in order that they might [c]know that I am the LORD." '

27 ¶ "Therefore, son of man, [a]speak to the house of Israel and say to them, 'Thus says the Lord GOD, "Yet in this your fathers have [b]blasphemed Me by [c]acting treacherously against Me.

28 "When I had [a]brought them into the land which I swore to give to them, then they saw every [b]high hill and every leafy tree, and they offered there their sacrifices and there they presented the provocation of their offering. There also they made their soothing aroma and there they poured out their drink offerings.

29 "Then I said to them, 'What is the high place to which you go?' So its name is called [1]Bamah to this day." '

30 "Therefore, say to the house of Israel, 'Thus says the Lord GOD, "Will you defile yourselves [1]after the manner of your [a]fathers and play the harlot after their detestable things?

31 "[1]When you offer your gifts, when you [a]cause your sons to pass through the fire, you are defiling yourselves with all your idols to this day. And shall I be inquired of by you, O house of Israel? As I live," declares the Lord GOD, "I will not be inquired of by you.

32 "What [a]comes [1]into your mind will not come about, when you say: 'We will be like the nations, like the tribes of the lands, [b]serving wood and stone.'

God Will Restore Israel to Her Land

33 ¶ "As I live," declares the Lord GOD, "surely with a mighty hand and with an [a]outstretched arm and with wrath poured out, I shall be [b]king over you.

34 "I will [a]bring you out from the peoples and gather you from the lands where you are scattered, with a mighty hand and with an outstretched arm and with [b]wrath poured out;

35 and I will bring you into the [a]wilderness of the peoples, and there I will enter into judgment with you face to face.

36 "As I [a]entered into judgment with your fathers in the [b]wilderness of the land of Egypt, so I will enter into judgment with you," declares the Lord GOD.

37 "I will make you [a]pass under the rod, and I will bring you into the bond of the covenant;

38 and I will [a]purge from you the rebels and those who transgress against Me; I will bring them out of the land where they sojourn, but they will [b]not enter the [1]land of Israel. Thus you will know that I am the LORD.

39 ¶ "As for you, O house of Israel," thus says the Lord GOD, "[a]Go, serve everyone his idols; [1]but later you will surely listen to Me, and My holy name you

13 [2]Lit *said* [c]Is 56:6; Ezek 20:21 [d]Ex 32:10; Deut 9:8; Ezek 20:8
15 [a]Num 14:30; Ps 95:11
16 [a]Ezek 11:21
17 [a]Jer 4:27; Ezek 11:13
18 [1]Lit *sons* [a]Num 14:31; Deut 4:3-6 [b]Zech 1:4
19 [1]Lit *do* [a]Ex 6:7 [b]Deut 5:32
20 [a]Jer 17:22
21 [1]Lit *said* [a]Num 21:5
22 [a]Job 13:21; Ps 78:38; Ezek 20:17 [b]Is 48:9-11; Jer 14:7; Ezek 20:9
23 [a]Lev 26:33; Deut 4:27
24 [1]Lit *after* [a]Ezek 6:9
25 [a]Ps 81:12; Is 66:4; Rom 1:21-25
26 [1]Lit *that which opens the womb* [a]Lev 18:21; Is 63:17; Ezek 20:30; Rom 11:8 [b]Jer 7:31 [c]Ezek 6:7
27 [a]Ezek 2:7 [b]Num 15:30; Rom 2:24 [c]Ezek 18:24
28 [a]Josh 23:3; Neh 9:22-26; Ps 78:55; Jer 2:7 [b]1 Kin 14:23; Ps 78:58; Is 57:5-7; Jer 3:6; Ezek 6:13
29 [1]Or *High Place*
30 [1]Lit *in the way of* [a]Judg 2:19; Jer 7:26
31 [1]Lit *In your lifting up* [a]Ps 106:37-39; Jer 7:31; Ezek 16:20
32 [1]Lit *upon your spirit* [a]Ezek 11:5 [b]Jer 2:25
33 [a]Jer 21:5 [b]Jer 51:57
34 [a]Is 27:12; Ezek 20:38 [b]Jer 42:18; Lam 2:4
35 [a]Ezek 19:13; Hos 2:14
36 [a]Num 11:1-35; Ps 106:15; Ezek 20:13; 1 Cor 10:5-10 [b]Deut 32:10
37 [a]Lev 27:32; Jer 33:13
38 [1]Lit *ground or soil* [a]Ezek 34:17-22; Amos 9:9; Zech 13:8; Mal 3:3 [b]Num 14:29; Ps 95:11; Ezek 13:9; Heb 4:3
39 [1]Or *and afterwards, if you will not listen to Me, but* [a]Jer 44:25

will [b]profane no longer with your gifts and with your idols.

40 "For on My holy mountain, on the high mountain of Israel," declares the Lord GOD, "there the whole house of Israel, [a]all of them, will serve Me in the land; there I will [b]accept them and there I will [1]seek your contributions and the choicest of your gifts, with all your holy things.

41 "[1]As a soothing aroma I will accept you when I [a]bring you out from the peoples and gather you from the lands where you are scattered; and I will prove Myself [b]holy among you in the sight of the nations.

42 "And [a]you will know that I am the LORD, [b]when I bring you into the land of Israel, into the [c]land which I swore to give to your forefathers.

43 "There you will [a]remember your ways and all your deeds with which you have defiled yourselves; and you will [b]loathe yourselves in your own [1]sight for all the evil things that you have done.

44 "Then [a]you will know that I am the LORD when I have dealt with you [b]for My name's sake, not according to your evil ways or according to your corrupt deeds, O house of Israel," declares the Lord GOD.' "

45 ¶ [1]Now the word of the LORD came to me, saying,

46 "Son of man, set your face toward [1]Teman, and speak out against the [a]south and [b]prophesy against the [c]forest [2]land of the Negev,

47 and say to the forest of the Negev, 'Hear the word of the LORD: thus says the Lord GOD, "Behold, I am about to [a]kindle a fire in you, and it will consume every [1]green tree in you, as well as every dry tree; the blazing flame will not be quenched and [2b]the whole surface from south to north will be burned by it.

48 "All flesh will see that I, the LORD, have kindled it; it shall [a]not be quenched." ' "

49 Then I said, "Ah Lord GOD! They are saying of me, 'Is he not *just* speaking [a]parables?' "

Parable of the Sword of the LORD

21 [1]And the word of the LORD came to me saying,

2 "Son of man, [a]set your face toward Jerusalem, and [1b]speak against the sanctuaries and prophesy against the land of Israel;

3 and say to the land of Israel, 'Thus says the LORD, "Behold, [a]I am against you; and I will draw My sword out of its sheath and cut off from you the [b]righteous and the wicked.

4 "Because I will cut off from you the righteous and the wicked, therefore My sword will go forth from its sheath against [a]all flesh from south *to* north.

5 "Thus all flesh will know that I, the LORD, have drawn My sword out of its sheath. It will [a]not return *to its sheath* again." '

6 "As for you, son of man, groan with breaking [1]heart and bitter grief, groan in their sight.

7 "And when they say to you, 'Why do you groan?' you shall say, 'Because of the [a]news that is coming; and [b]every heart will melt, all hands will be feeble, every spirit will [1]faint and all knees will [2]be weak as water. Behold, it comes and it will happen,' declares the Lord [3]GOD."

8 ¶ Again the word of the LORD came to me, saying,

9 "Son of man, prophesy and say, 'Thus says the LORD.' Say,

'[a]A sword, a sword sharpened
And also polished!
10 'Sharpened to make a [a]slaughter,
Polished [1]to flash like lightning!'

Or shall we rejoice, the [2]rod of My son [b]despising every tree?

11 "It is given to be polished, that it may be handled; the sword is sharpened and polished, to give it into the hand of the slayer.

12 "[a]Cry out and wail, son of man; for it is against My people, it is against all the [b]officials of Israel. They are delivered over to the sword with My people, therefore strike *your* thigh.

13 "For *there is* a testing; and what if even the [1]rod which despises will be no more?" declares the Lord GOD.

14 ¶ "You therefore, son of man, prophesy and clap *your* hands together; and let the sword be [a]doubled the third time, the sword for the slain. It is the sword for the great one slain, which surrounds them,

15 that *their* [a]hearts may melt, and many [b]fall at all their [c]gates. I have given the glittering sword. Ah! It is made *for striking* like lightning, it is wrapped up *in readiness* for slaughter.

16 "[1]Show yourself sharp, go to the right; set yourself; go to the left, wherever your [2]edge is appointed.

17 "I will also clap My hands together, and I will [1a]appease My wrath; I, the LORD, have spoken."

The Instrument of God's Judgment

18 ¶ The word of the LORD came to me saying,

19 "As for you, son of man, [1a]make two ways for the sword of the king of Babylon to come; both of them will go

39 [b]Is 1:13-15; Ezek 23:38,39; 43:7
40 [1]Or *require* [a]Is 66:23; Ezek 37:22,24 [b]Is 56:7; 60:7; Ezek 43:12,27
41 [1]Lit *With* [a]Is 27:12,13; Ezek 11:17; 28:25 [b]Is 5:16; Ezek 28:25; 36:23
42 [a]Ezek 36:23; 38:23 [b]Ezek 11:17; 34:13; 36:24 [c]Ezek 20:6,15
43 [1]Lit *faces* [a]Ezek 6:9; 16:61,63; Hos 5:15 [b]Jer 31:18; Ezek 36:31; Zech 12:10
44 [a]Ezek 24:24 [b]Ezek 36:22
45 [1]Ch 21:1 in Heb
46 [1]Or *the South* [2]Lit *of the field* [a]Jer 13:19; Ezek 21:4 [b]Ezek 21:2; Amos 7:16 [c]Is 30:6-11
47 [1]Lit *moist* [2]Or *all the faces* [a]Is 9:18,19; Jer 21:14 [b]Is 13:8
48 [a]Jer 7:20; 17:27
49 [a]Ezek 17:2; Matt 13:13; John 16:25
21:1 [1]Ch 21:6 in Heb
2 [1]Lit *flow* [a]Ezek 20:46; 25:2; 28:21 [b]Job 29:22; Ezek 20:46
3 [a]Jer 21:13; Ezek 5:8; Nah 2:13; 3:5 [b]Is 57:1
4 [a]Jer 12:12; Ezek 7:2; 20:47
5 [a]1 Sam 3:12; Jer 23:20; Ezek 21:30; Nah 1:9
6 [1]Lit *loins*
7 [1]Lit *be dim* [2]Lit *flow* [3]Heb *YHWH,* usually rendered *LORD,* and so throughout the ch [a]Ezek 7:26 [b]Is 13:7; Nah 2:10
9 [a]Deut 32:41
10 [1]Lit *lightning to be to her* [2]Or *scepter* [a]Is 34:5, 6 [b]Ps 110:5,6; Ezek 20:47
12 [a]Ezek 21:6; Joel 1:13 [b]Ezek 21:25; 22:6
13 [1]Or *scepter*
14 [a]Lev 26:21, 24; 2 Kin 24:1, 10-16; 25:1
15 [a]Josh 2:11; 2 Sam 17:10; Ps 22:14; Ezek 21:7 [b]Is 59:10; Jer 13:16; 18:15 [c]Jer 17:27; Ezek 21:19
16 [1]Or *Unite yourself* [2]Lit *face*
17 [1]Lit *cause to rest* [a]Ezek 5:13
19 [1]Or *set for yourself* [a]Jer 1:10; Ezek 4:1-3

out of one land. And [2]make a signpost;
[3]make it at the head of the way to the
city.
20 "You shall [1]mark a way for the
sword to come to [a]Rabbah of the sons of
Ammon, and to Judah into [b]fortified Jerusalem.
21 "For the king of Babylon stands at
the [1]parting of the way, at the head of
the two ways, to use [a]divination; he
[b]shakes the arrows, he consults the
[2c]household idols, he looks at the liver.
22 "Into his right hand came the divination, 'Jerusalem,' to [a]set battering rams,
to open the mouth [1]for slaughter, to lift
up the voice with a battle cry, to set battering rams against the gates, to cast up
ramps, to build a siege wall.
23 "And it will be to them like a false
divination in their eyes; [a]they have
sworn solemn oaths. But he [b]brings iniquity to remembrance, that they may be
seized.
24 ¶ "Therefore, thus says the Lord
GOD, 'Because you have made your iniquity to be remembered, in that your
transgressions are uncovered, so that in
all your deeds your sins appear—because
you have come to remembrance, you will
be seized with the hand.
25 'And you, O slain, wicked one, the
prince of Israel, whose [a]day has come, in
the time of the [1]punishment of the end,'
26 thus says the Lord GOD, 'Remove
the turban and take off the [a]crown; this
will [1]no longer *be* the same. [b]Exalt that
which is low and abase that which is
high.
27 '[a]A ruin, a ruin, a ruin, I will make
it. This also will be no more until [b]He
comes whose right it is, and I will give it
to Him.'
28 ¶ "And you, son of man, prophesy
and say, 'Thus says the Lord GOD concerning the sons of Ammon and concerning their [a]reproach,' and say: 'A sword,
a sword is drawn, polished for the slaughter, to cause it [1]to [b]consume, that it may
be like lightning—
29 while they see for you [a]false visions, while they divine lies for you—to
place you on the necks of the wicked who
are slain, whose day has come, in the
[b]time of the [1]punishment of the end.
30 '[a]Return *it* to its sheath. In the
[b]place where you were created, in the
land of your origin, I will judge you.
31 'I will [a]pour out My indignation on
you; I will [b]blow on you with the fire of
My wrath, and I will give you into the
hand of brutal men, [1c]skilled in destruction.
32 'You will be [1a]fuel for the fire; your
blood will be in the midst of the land. You

19 [2]Lit *cut out a hand* [3]Lit *cut it*
20 [1]Lit *set* [a]Deut 3:11; Jer 49:2; Ezek 25:5; Amos 1:14 [b]Ps 48:12
21 [1]Lit *mother* [2]Heb *teraphim* [a]Num 22:7 [b]Prov 16:33 [c]Gen 31:19; Judg 17:5
22 [1]Lit *in* [a]Ezek 4:2
23 [a]Ezek 17:16 [b]Num 5:15; Ezek 21:24
25 [1]Or *iniquity* [a]Ps 37:13; Ezek 7:2
26 [1]Lit *not this* [a]Jer 13:18; Ezek 16:12 [b]Ps 75:7; Ezek 17:24
27 [a]Hag 2:21 [b]Ps 2:6; Jer 23:5; Ezek 34:24
28 [1]Lit *to finish* [a]Ezek 36:15; Zeph 2:8-10 [b]Is 31:8; Jer 12:12
29 [1]Or *iniquity* [a]Jer 27:9; Ezek 13:6-9 [b]Ezek 21:25
30 [a]Jer 47:6 [b]Ezek 25:5
31 [1]Or *artisans of* [a]Ezek 14:19; Nah 1:6 [b]Ps 18:15; Is 30:33; Ezek 22:20; Hag 1:9 [c]Jer 4:7; Hab 1:6
32 [1]Lit *food* [a]Ezek 20:47; Mal 4:1 [b]Ezek 25:10
22:3 [1]Heb *YHWH,* usually rendered *LORD,* and so throughout the ch [a]Ezek 22:6
4 [1]Lit *your* [2]Lit *days* [a]2 Kin 21:16; Ezek 24:7 [b]Ps 44:13; Ezek 5:14
5 [a]Is 22:2
6 [1]Lit *arm* [a]Is 1:23; Ezek 22:27
7 [a]Ex 20:12; Lev 20:9; Deut 5:16 [b]Ex 22:21f; Deut 24:17; Jer 7:6; Zech 7:10 [c]Ex 22:22; Ezek 22:25; Mal 3:5
8 [a]Ezek 22:26 [b]Ezek 20:13
9 [a]Ezek 23:29; Hos 4:2
10 [1]Lit *he has* [a]Lev 18:8 [b]Lev 18:19; Ezek 18:6
11 [a]Ezek 18:11 [b]Lev 18:15 [c]2 Sam 13:11-14
12 [a]Ex 23:8; Deut 16:19; Mic 7:2 [b]Lev 25:36; Deut 23:19 [c]Lev 19:13 [d]Ps 106:21; Ezek 23:35
13 [1]Lit *your* [a]Is 33:15; Amos 2:6-8; Mic 2:2
14 [a]Ezek 21:7 [b]Ezek 17:24
15 [a]Deut 4:27; Neh 1:8; Ezek 20:23; Zech 7:14

will [b]not be remembered, for I, the
LORD, have spoken.' "

The Sins of Israel

22 Then the word of the LORD came
to me, saying,
2 "And you, son of man, will you
judge, will you judge the bloody city?
Then cause her to know all her abominations.
3 "You shall say, 'Thus says the Lord
[1]GOD, "A city [a]shedding blood in her
midst, so that her time will come, and
that makes idols, contrary to her *interest,*
for defilement!
4 "You have become [a]guilty by [1]the
blood which you have shed, and defiled
by your idols which you have made. Thus
you have brought your [2]day near and
have come to your years; therefore I have
made you a [b]reproach to the nations and
a mocking to all the lands.
5 "Those who are near and those who
are far from you will mock you, you of ill
repute, full of [a]turmoil.
6 ¶ "Behold, the [a]rulers of Israel,
each according to his [1]power, have been
in you for the purpose of shedding blood.
7 "They have [a]treated father and
mother lightly within you. The [b]alien
they have oppressed in your midst; the
[c]fatherless and the widow they have
wronged in you.
8 "You have [a]despised My holy things
and [b]profaned My sabbaths.
9 "Slanderous men have been in you
for the purpose of shedding blood, and
in you they have eaten at the mountain
shrines. In your midst they have [a]com-
mitted acts of lewdness.
10 "In you [1]they have [a]uncovered
their fathers' nakedness; in you they have
humbled her who was [b]unclean in her
menstrual impurity.
11 "One has committed abomination
with his [a]neighbor's wife and another
has lewdly defiled his [b]daughter-in-law.
And another in you has [c]humbled his
sister, his father's daughter.
12 "In you they have [a]taken bribes to
shed blood; you have taken [b]interest and
profits, and you have injured your neighbors for gain by [c]oppression, and you
have [d]forgotten Me," declares the Lord
GOD.
13 ¶ "Behold, then, I smite My hand
at your [a]dishonest gain which you have
acquired and at [1]the bloodshed which is
among you.
14 "Can [a]your heart endure, or can
your hands be strong in the days that I
will deal with you? [b]I, the LORD, have
spoken and will act.
15 "I will [a]scatter you among the na-

tions and I will disperse you through the
lands, and I will [b]consume your uncleanness from you.
16 "You will profane yourself in the
sight of the nations, and you will [a]know
that I am the LORD." ' "
17 ¶ And the word of the LORD came
to me, saying,
18 "Son of man, the house of Israel has
become [a]dross to Me; all of them are
[b]bronze and tin and iron and lead in the
[c]furnace; they are the dross of silver.
19 "Therefore, thus says the Lord GOD,
'Because all of you have become dross,
therefore, behold, I am going to gather
you into the midst of Jerusalem.
20 'As they gather silver and bronze
and iron and lead and tin into the [a]fur-
nace to blow fire on it in order to melt *it,*
so I will gather *you* in My anger and in
My wrath and I will lay you *there* and
melt you.
21 'I will gather you and blow on you
with the fire of My wrath, and you will be
melted in the midst of it.
22 'As silver is melted in the furnace,
so you will be melted in the midst of it;
and you will know that I, the LORD, have
[a]poured out My wrath on you.' "
23 ¶ And the word of the LORD came
to me, saying,
24 "Son of man, say to her, 'You are a
land that is [a]not cleansed or rained on in
the day of indignation.'
25 "There is a [a]conspiracy of her
prophets in her midst like a roaring lion
tearing the prey. They have [b]devoured
lives; they have taken treasure and precious things; they have made many [c]wid-
ows in the midst of her.
26 "Her [a]priests have done violence to
My law and have [b]profaned My holy
things; they have made no [c]distinction
between the holy and the profane, and
they have not taught the difference between the [d]unclean and the clean; and
they hide their eyes from My sabbaths,
and I am profaned among them.
27 "Her princes within her are like
wolves tearing the prey, by shedding
blood *and* [a]destroying lives in order to
get [b]dishonest gain.
28 "Her prophets have smeared whitewash for them, seeing [a]false visions and
divining lies for them, saying, 'Thus says
the Lord GOD,' when the LORD has not
spoken.
29 "The people of the land have practiced [a]oppression and committed robbery, and they have wronged the poor
and needy and have [b]oppressed the sojourner without justice.
30 "I [a]searched for a man among them
who would [b]build up the wall and
[c]stand in the gap before Me for the land,
so that I would not destroy it; but I found
[1]no one.
31 "Thus I have poured out My [a]indig-
nation on them; I have consumed them
with the fire of My wrath; [b]their way I
have brought upon their heads," declares
the Lord GOD.

Oholah and Oholibah's Sin and Its Consequences

23 The word of the LORD came to me
again, saying,
2 "Son of man, there were [a]two wom-
en, the daughters of one mother;
3 and they played the harlot in Egypt.
They [a]played the harlot in their youth;
there their breasts were pressed and
there their virgin bosom was handled.
4 "Their names were Oholah the elder
and Oholibah her sister. And they became Mine, and they bore sons and
daughters. And *as for* their names, Samaria is Oholah and Jerusalem is Oholibah.
5 ¶ "Oholah played the harlot
[1]while she was Mine; and she lusted after her lovers, after the [a]Assyrians, *her*
neighbors,
6 who were clothed in purple, [a]gov-
ernors and officials, all of them desirable
young men, horsemen riding on horses.
7 "She bestowed her harlotries on
them, all of whom *were* the choicest
[1]men of Assyria; and with all whom she
lusted after, with all their idols she [a]de-
filed herself.
8 "She did not forsake her harlotries
[a]from *the time in* Egypt; for in her youth
[1]men had lain with her, and they handled her virgin bosom and poured out
their [2]lust on her.
9 "Therefore, I gave her into the hand
of her [a]lovers, into the hand of the [1]As-
syrians, after whom she lusted.
10 "They [a]uncovered her nakedness;
they took her sons and her daughters, but
they slew her with the sword. Thus she
became a [1]byword among women, and
they executed judgments on her.
11 ¶ "Now her sister Oholibah saw
this, yet she was [a]more corrupt in her
lust than she, and her harlotries were
more than the harlotries of her sister.
12 "She lusted after the [1a]Assyrians,
governors and officials, the ones near,
magnificently dressed, horsemen riding
on horses, all of them desirable young
men.
13 "I saw that she had defiled herself;
they both took [1]the same way.
14 "So she increased her harlotries.
And she saw men [a]portrayed on the

15 [b]Ezek 23:27, 48
16 [a]Ps 83:18; Ezek 6:7
18 [a]Ps 119:119; Is 1:22; Lam 4:1 [b]Jer 6:28-30 [c]Prov 17:3; Is 48:10
20 [a]Is 1:25
22 [a]Ezek 20:8, 33; Hos 5:10
24 [a]Is 9:13; Jer 2:30; Ezek 24:13; Zeph 3:2
25 [a]Jer 11:9; Hos 6:9 [b]Jer 2:34; Ezek 13:19; 22:27 [c]Jer 15:8; Ezek 22:7
26 [a]Jer 2:8,26; Ezek 7:26 [b]1 Sam 2:12-17, 22; Ezek 22:8 [c]Lev 10:10; Ezek 44:23 [d]Hag 2:11-14
27 [a]Ezek 22:25 [b]Ezek 22:13
28 [a]Jer 23:25-32; Ezek 13:6
29 [a]Is 5:7; Ezek 9:9; 22:7; Amos 3:10 [b]Ex 23:9
30 [1]Lit *not* [a]Is 59:16; 63:5; Jer 5:1 [b]Ezek 13:5 [c]Ps 106:23; Jer 15:1
31 [a]Is 10:5; 13:5; 30:27; Ezek 22:20 [b]Ezek 7:3,8,9; 9:10; 16:43; Rom 2:8,9
23:2 [a]Ezek 16:46
3 [a]Lev 17:7; Jer 3:9
5 [1]Lit *under Me* [a]2 Kin 15:19; 16:7; 17:3; Ezek 16:28; Hos 5:13; 8:9,10
6 [a]Ezek 23:12, 13
7 [1]Lit *sons of Asshur* [a]Ezek 20:7; 22:3,4; Hos 5:3; 6:10
8 [1]Lit *they* [2]Lit *harlotry* [a]Ex 32:4; 1 Kin 12:28; 2 Kin 10:29; 17:16; Ezek 23:3,19
9 [1]Lit *sons of Asshur* [a]Ezek 16:37; 23:22
10 [1]Lit *name* [a]Ezek 16:37,41
11 [a]Jer 3:8-11; Ezek 16:51
12 [1]Lit *sons of Asshur* [a]2 Kin 16:7
13 [1]Lit *one*
14 [a]Ezek 8:10

wall, images of the [b]Chaldeans portrayed with vermilion,

15 girded with belts on their loins, with flowing turbans on their heads, all of them looking like officers, [1]like the [2]Babylonians *in* Chaldea, the land of their birth.

16 "[1]When she saw them she [a]lusted after them and sent messengers to them in Chaldea.

17 "The [1a]Babylonians came to her to the bed of love and defiled her with their harlotry. And when she had been defiled by them, [2]she became disgusted with them.

18 "She [a]uncovered her harlotries and uncovered her nakedness; then [1]I became [b]disgusted with her, as [1]I had become disgusted with her [c]sister.

19 "Yet she multiplied her harlotries, remembering the days of her youth, when she played the harlot in the land of Egypt.

20 "She [a]lusted after their paramours, whose flesh is *like* the flesh of donkeys and whose issue is *like* the issue of horses.

21 "Thus you longed for the [a]lewdness of your youth, when [1]the Egyptians handled your bosom because of the breasts of your youth.

22 ¶ "Therefore, O Oholibah, thus says the Lord [1]GOD, 'Behold I will arouse your lovers against you, from whom [2]you were alienated, and I will bring them against you from every side:

23 the [1a]Babylonians and all the [b]Chaldeans, [c]Pekod and Shoa and Koa, *and* all the [2d]Assyrians with them; desirable young men, governors and officials all of them, officers and [3]men of renown, all of them riding on horses.

24 'They will come against you with weapons, [a]chariots and [1]wagons, and with a company of peoples. They will set themselves against you on every side with buckler and shield and helmet; and I will commit the [b]judgment to them, and they will judge you according to their customs.

25 'I will set My [a]jealousy against you, that they may deal with you in wrath. They will remove your nose and your ears; and your [1]survivors will fall by the sword. They will take your [b]sons and your daughters; and your [1]survivors will be consumed by the fire.

26 'They will also [a]strip you of your clothes and take away your [b]beautiful jewels.

27 'Thus [a]I will make your lewdness and your harlotry *brought* from the land of Egypt to cease from you, so that you will not lift up your eyes to them or remember Egypt anymore.'

28 "For thus says the Lord GOD, 'Behold, I will give you into the hand of those whom you [a]hate, into the hand of those from whom [1]you were alienated.

29 'They will [a]deal with you in hatred, take all your property, and leave you naked and bare. And the nakedness of your harlotries will be uncovered, both your lewdness and your harlotries.

30 'These things will be done to you because you have [a]played the harlot with the nations, because you have defiled yourself with their idols.

31 'You have walked in the way of your sister; therefore I will give [a]her cup into your hand.'

32 "Thus says the Lord GOD,

'You will [a]drink your sister's
cup,
Which is deep and wide.
[1]You will be [b]laughed at and
held in derision;
It contains much.

33 'You will be filled with
[a]drunkenness and sorrow,
The cup of horror and
desolation,
The cup of your sister Samaria.

34 'You will [a]drink it and drain it.
Then you will gnaw its fragments
And tear your breasts;

for I have spoken,' declares the Lord GOD.

35 "Therefore, thus says the Lord GOD, 'Because you have [a]forgotten Me and [b]cast Me behind your back, bear now the *punishment* of your lewdness and your harlotries.' "

36 ¶ Moreover, the LORD said to me, "Son of man, will you [a]judge Oholah and Oholibah? Then [b]declare to them their abominations.

37 "For they have committed adultery, and blood is on their hands. Thus they have committed adultery with their idols and even caused their sons, [a]whom they bore to Me, to pass through *the fire* to [1]them as food.

38 "Again, they have done this to Me: they have [a]defiled My sanctuary on the same day and have [b]profaned My sabbaths.

39 "For when they had slaughtered their children for their idols, they entered My [a]sanctuary on the same day to profane it; and lo, thus they did within My house.

40 ¶ "Furthermore, [1]they have even sent for men who come from afar, to whom a messenger was sent; and lo, they came—for whom you bathed, [a]painted

14 [b]Ezek 16:29
15 [1]Lit *the likeness of* [2]Lit *sons of Babel*
16 [1]Lit *at the sight of her eyes* [a]Ezek 23:20; Matt 5:28
17 [1]Lit *sons of Babel* [2]Lit *her soul* [a]2 Kin 24:17
18 [1]Lit *My soul* [a]Jer 8:12; Ezek 21:24 [b]Ps 78:59; Jer 12:8 [c]Ezek 23:9; Amos 5:21
20 [a]Ezek 16:26
21 [1]So two mss; M.T. *from Egypt* [a]Jer 3:9; Ezek 23:3
22 [1]Heb *YHWH,* usually rendered LORD, and so throughout the ch [2]Lit *your soul was alienated*
23 [1]Lit *sons of Babylon* [2]Lit *sons of Assyria* [3]Lit *the called ones* [a]2 Kin 20:14-17; Ezek 21:19 [b]2 Kin 24:2; Job 1:17; Is 23:13 [c]Jer 50:21 [d]Gen 2:14; Ezra 6:22
24 [1]Lit *wheels* [a]Jer 47:3; Ezek 26:10; Nah 2:3 [b]Jer 39:5; Ezek 16:38
25 [1]Lit *remainder* [a]Ex 34:14; Ezek 5:13; Zeph 1:18 [b]Ezek 23:47; Hos 2:4
26 [a]Jer 13:22; Ezek 16:39 [b]Is 3:18-23
27 [a]Ezek 16:41
28 [1]Lit *your soul was alienated* [a]Jer 21:7-10; Ezek 16:37
29 [a]Deut 28:48; Ezek 23:25
30 [a]Ezek 6:9
31 [a]2 Kin 21:13; Jer 7:14; Ezek 23:33
32 [1]Or *It will be for jesting and deriding because of its great size* [a]Ps 60:3; Is 51:17; Jer 25:15 [b]Ezek 5:14
33 [a]Jer 25:15; Hab 2:16
34 [a]Ps 75:8; Is 51:17
35 [a]Is 17:10; Jer 3:21; Ezek 22:12; Hos 8:14 [b]1 Kin 14:9; Jer 2:27
36 [a]Jer 1:10; Ezek 20:4 [b]Is 58:1; Ezek 16:2; Mic 3:8
37 [1]I.e. idols [a]Ezek 16:20
38 [a]2 Kin 21:4; Ezek 5:11 [b]Jer 17:27; Ezek 20:13
39 [a]Jer 7:9-11
40 [1]Or *you* (women) [a]2 Kin 9:30; Jer 4:30

your eyes and [b]decorated yourselves
with ornaments;
41 and you sat on a splendid [a]couch
with a [b]table arranged before it on which
you had set My [c]incense and My [c]oil.
42 "The sound of a [1a]carefree multitude was with her; and [b]drunkards were
brought from the wilderness with men of
the [2]common sort. And they put [c]brace-
lets on [3]the hands of the women and
beautiful crowns on their heads.
43 ¶ "Then I said concerning her who
was [a]worn out by adulteries, '[1]Will they
now commit adultery with her when she
is *thus?'*
44 "[1]But they went in to her as they
would go in to a harlot. Thus they went
in to Oholah and to Oholibah, the lewd
women.
45 "But they, righteous men, will
[a]judge them with the judgment of adulteresses and with the judgment of wom-
en who shed blood, because they are
adulteresses and blood is on their hands.
46 ¶ "For thus says the Lord GOD,
'Bring up a company against them and
give them over to [a]terror and plunder.
47 'The company will [a]stone them
with stones and cut them down with
their swords; they will slay their sons and
their daughters and [b]burn their houses
with fire.
48 'Thus I will make lewdness cease
from the land, that all women may be
admonished and not commit [1]lewdness
as you have done.
49 'Your lewdness [1]will be [a]requited
upon you, and you will bear the penalty
of *worshiping* your idols; thus you will
know that I am the Lord GOD.' "

Parable of the Boiling Pot

24 And the word of the LORD came to
me in the ninth year, in the tenth
month, on the tenth of the month, saying,
2 "Son of man, write the name of the
day, this very day. The king of Babylon
[1]has [a]laid siege to Jerusalem this very
day.
3 "Speak a [a]parable to the [b]rebellious
house and say to them, 'Thus says the
Lord [1]GOD,
"Put on the [c]pot, put *it* on and
also pour water in it;
4 [1a]Put in it the pieces,
Every good piece, the thigh and
the shoulder;
Fill *it* with choice bones.
5 "Take the [a]choicest of the flock,
And also pile [1]wood under [2]the
pot.
Make it boil vigorously.
Also seethe its bones in it."

6 ¶ 'Therefore, thus says the
Lord GOD,
"Woe to the [a]bloody city,
To the pot in which there is rust
And whose rust has not gone out
of it!
Take out of it piece after piece,
[1]Without making a choice.
7 "For her blood is in her midst;
She placed it on the bare rock;
She did not [a]pour it on the
ground
To cover it with dust.
8 "That it may [a]cause wrath to
come up to take vengeance,
I have put her blood on the bare
rock,
That it may not be covered."
9 'Therefore, thus says the Lord GOD,
"[a]Woe to the bloody city!
I also will make the pile great.
10 "Heap on the wood, kindle the
fire,
[1]Boil the flesh well
And mix in the spices,
And let the bones be burned.
11 "Then [a]set it empty on its coals
So that it may be hot
And its bronze may [1]glow
And its [b]filthiness may be
melted in it,
Its rust consumed.
12 "She has [a]wearied *Me* with toil,
Yet her great rust has not gone
from her;
Let her rust *be* in the fire!
13 "In your filthiness is lewdness.
Because I *would* have cleansed
you,
Yet you are [a]not clean,
You will not be cleansed from
your filthiness again
Until I have [1b]spent My wrath
on you.
14 "I, the LORD, have spoken; it is
[a]coming and I will act. I will not relent,
and I will not [b]pity and I will not be
sorry; [c]according to your ways and according to your deeds [1]I will judge you,"
declares the Lord GOD.' "

Death of Ezekiel's Wife Is a Sign

15 ¶ And the word of the LORD came
to me saying,
16 "Son of man, behold, I am about to
take from you the [a]desire of your eyes
with a [b]blow; but you shall not [c]mourn
and you shall not weep, and your [d]tears
shall not come.
17 "Groan silently; make [a]no mourning for the dead. Bind on your turban and
put your shoes on your feet, and do not
cover *your* mustache and [b]do not eat the
bread of men."

40 [b]Is 3:18-23; Ezek 16:13-16
41 [a]Esth 1:6; Is 57:7; Amos 6:4 [b]Is 65:11; Ezek 44:16 [c]Jer 44:17; Hos 2:8
42 [1]Lit *at ease* [2]Lit *multitude of mankind* [3]Lit *their hands* [a]Ezek 16:49; Amos 6:3-6 [b]Jer 51:7 [c]Gen 24:30; Ezek 16:11,12
43 [1]Or *Now they will commit adultery with her, and she with them* [a]Ezek 23:3
44 [1]Or *And*
45 [a]Ezek 16:38
46 [a]Jer 15:4; 24:9; 29:18
47 [a]Lev 20:10; Ezek 16:40 [b]Jer 39:8
48 [1]Lit *according to your lewdness*
49 [1]Lit *they will give* [a]Is 59:18; Ezek 7:4,9; 9:10; 23:35
24:2 [1]Lit *leaned on* [a]2 Kin 25:1; Jer 39:1; 52:4
3 [1]Heb *YHWH,* usually rendered *LORD,* and so throughout the ch [a]Ps 78:2; Ezek 17:2; 20:49 [b]Is 1:2; 30:1,9; Ezek 2:3,6,8 [c]Jer 1:13,14; Ezek 11:3,7,11; 24:6
4 [1]Lit *Gather her pieces* [a]Mic 3:2,3
5 [1]Lit *bones* [2]Lit *it* [a]Jer 39:6; 52:10,24-27
6 [1]Lit *No lot has fallen on it* [a]2 Kin 24:3,4; Ezek 22:2,3,27; Mic 7:2; Nah 3:1
7 [a]Lev 17:13; Deut 12:16
8 [a]Is 26:21
9 [a]Ezek 24:6; Hab 2:12
10 [1]Lit *Complete*
11 [1]Lit *become hot* [a]Jer 21:10; Mal 4:1 [b]Ezek 22:15; 23:27
12 [a]Jer 9:5
13 [1]Lit *caused to rest* [a]Jer 6:28-30; Ezek 22:24 [b]Ezek 5:13; 8:18
14 [1]So with several ancient mss and versions; M.T. *they* [a]Ps 33:9; Is 55:11 [b]Jer 13:14; Ezek 9:10 [c]Is 3:11; Ezek 18:30; 36:19
16 [a]Song 7:10; Ezek 24:18 [b]Job 23:2 [c]Jer 16:5; 22:10 [d]Jer 13:17
17 [a]Lev 21:10-12 [b]Jer 16:7; Hos 9:4

18 So I spoke to the people in the
morning, and in the evening my wife
died. And in the morning I did as I was
commanded.
19 The people said to me, "Will you
not tell us what these things that you are
doing mean for us?"
20 Then I said to them, "The word of
the LORD came to me saying,
21 'Speak to the house of Israel, "Thus
says the Lord GOD, 'Behold, I am about to
profane My sanctuary, the pride of your
power, the [a]desire of your eyes and the
delight of your soul; and your [b]sons and
your daughters whom you have left behind will fall by the sword.
22 'You will do as I have done; you will
not cover *your* mustache and you will not
eat the bread of men.
23 'Your turbans will be on your heads
and your shoes on your feet. You [a]will
not mourn and you will not weep, but
[b]you will rot away in your iniquities and
you will groan [1]to one another.
24 'Thus Ezekiel will be a [a]sign to you;
according to all that he has done you will
do; when it comes, then you will know
that I am the Lord GOD.' "
25 ¶ 'As for you, son of man, will *it* not
be on the day when I take from them
their [a]stronghold, the joy of their [1]pride,
the desire of their eyes and [2]their heart's
delight, their sons and their daughters,
26 that on that day he who [a]escapes
will come to you with information for
your ears?
27 'On that day your [a]mouth will be
opened to him who escaped, and you will
speak and be mute no longer. Thus you
will be a sign to them, and they will know
that I am the LORD.' "

Judgment on Gentile Nations—Ammon

25 And the word of the LORD came to
me saying,
2 "Son of man, set your face toward
the [a]sons of Ammon and prophesy
against them,
3 and say to the sons of Ammon,
'Hear the word of the Lord [1]GOD! Thus
says the Lord GOD, "Because you said,
'[a]Aha!' against My sanctuary when it
was profaned, and against the land of Israel when it was made desolate, and against
the house of Judah when they went into
exile,
4 therefore, behold, I am going to
give you to the [a]sons of the east for a
possession, and they will set their encampments among you and make their
dwellings among you; they will [b]eat your
fruit and drink your milk.

21 [a]Ps 27:4; 84:1; Ezek 24:16 [b]Jer 6:11; 16:3, 4; Ezek 23:25,47
23 [1]Lit *a man to his brother* [a]Job 27:15; Ps 78:64 [b]Lev 26:39; Ezek 33:10
24 [a]Ezek 4:3; Luke 11:29,30
25 [1]Or *beauty* [2]Lit *the lifting up of their soul* [a]Ps 48:2; 50:2; Ezek 24:21
26 [a]1 Sam 4:12; Job 1:15-19
27 [a]Ezek 3:26; 33:22
25:2 [a]Jer 49:1-6; Amos 1:13-15; Zeph 2:9
3 [1]Heb *YHWH,* usually rendered *LORD,* and so throughout the ch [a]Ps 70:2,3; Ezek 21:28; 25:6; 26:2; 36:2
4 [a]Judg 6:3,33; 1 Kin 4:30 [b]Deut 28:33,51; Is 1:7
5 [a]Deut 3:11; 2 Sam 12:26; Jer 49:2; Ezek 21:20
6 [a]Job 27:23; Nah 3:19 [b]Obad 12; Zeph 2:8,10
7 [a]Ezek 25:13, 16; Zeph 1:4 [b]Is 33:4; Ezek 26:5 [c]Ezek 21:32 [d]Amos 1:14,15 [e]Ezek 6:14
8 [a]Is 15:1; Jer 48:1; Amos 2:1, 2
9 [1]Lit *open* [2]Lit *end* [a]Num 33:49; Josh 12:3; 13:20 [b]Num 32:3,38; Josh 13:17; 1 Chr 5:8; Jer 48:23 [c]Num 32:37; Josh 13:19; Jer 48:1,23
10 [a]Ezek 25:4
12 [a]2 Chr 28:17; Ps 137:7; Jer 49:7-22
13 [a]Jer 49:8,13 [b]Ezek 29:8; Mal 1:3,4 [c]Gen 36:34; Jer 49:7; Amos 1:12 [d]Jer 25:23; 49:8
14 [a]Is 11:14 [b]Ezek 35:11
15 [a]Is 14:29-31; Ezek 25:6,12; Joel 3:4
16 [a]Jer 25:20; 47:1-7

5 "I will make [a]Rabbah a pasture for
camels and the sons of Ammon a resting
place for flocks. Thus you will know that
I am the LORD."
6 'For thus says the Lord GOD, "Because you have [a]clapped your hands and
stamped your feet and [b]rejoiced with all
the scorn of your soul against the land of
Israel,
7 therefore, behold, I have
[a]stretched out My hand against you and
I will give you for [b]spoil to the nations.
And I will [c]cut you off from the peoples
and [d]make you perish from the lands; I
will destroy you. Thus you will [e]know
that I am the LORD."

Moab

8 ¶ 'Thus says the Lord GOD, "Because [a]Moab and Seir say, 'Behold, the
house of Judah is like all the nations,'
9 therefore, behold, I am going to
[1]deprive the flank of Moab of *its* cities,
of its cities which are on its [2]frontiers,
the glory of the land, [a]Beth-jeshimoth,
[b]Baal-meon and [c]Kiriathaim,
10 and I will give it for a possession
along with the sons of Ammon to the
[a]sons of the east, so that the sons of Ammon will not be remembered among the
nations.
11 "Thus I will execute judgments on
Moab, and they will know that I am the
LORD."

Edom

12 ¶ 'Thus says the Lord GOD, "Because [a]Edom has acted against the house
of Judah by taking vengeance, and has
incurred grievous guilt, and avenged
themselves upon them,"
13 therefore thus says the Lord GOD,
"I will also [a]stretch out My hand against
Edom and [b]cut off man and beast from it.
And I will lay it waste; from [c]Teman
even to [d]Dedan they will fall by the
sword.
14 "[a]I will lay My vengeance on Edom
by the hand of My people Israel. Therefore, they will act in Edom [b]according to
My anger and according to My wrath;
thus they will know My vengeance," declares the Lord GOD.

Philistia

15 ¶ 'Thus says the Lord GOD, "Because the Philistines have acted in [a]re-
venge and have taken vengeance with
scorn of soul to destroy with everlasting
enmity,"
16 therefore thus says the Lord GOD,
"Behold, I will [a]stretch out My hand
against the Philistines, even cut off the

[b]Cherethites and destroy the remnant of
the seacoast.
17 "I will execute great vengeance on
them with wrathful rebukes; and they
will [a]know that I am the LORD when I lay
My vengeance on them." ' "

Judgment on Tyre

26 Now in the eleventh year, on the
first of the month, the word of the
LORD came to me saying,
2 "Son of man, because [a]Tyre has said
concerning Jerusalem, 'Aha, the [b]gate-
way of the peoples is broken; it has
[1c]opened to me. I shall be filled, *now
that* she is laid waste,'
3 therefore thus says the Lord [1]GOD,
'Behold, I am against you, O Tyre, and I
will bring up [a]many nations against you,
as the [b]sea brings up its waves.
4 'They will [a]destroy the walls of
Tyre and break down her towers; and I
will scrape her debris from her and make
her a bare rock.
5 'She will be a place for the spreading
of nets in the midst of the sea, for I have
spoken,' declares the Lord GOD, 'and she
will become [a]spoil for the nations.
6 'Also her [a]daughters who are [1]on
the mainland will be slain by the sword,
and they will know that I am the LORD.' "
7 ¶ For thus says the Lord GOD, "Behold, I will bring upon Tyre from the
north Nebuchadnezzar king of Babylon,
[a]king of kings, with horses, [b]chariots,
cavalry and [1]a great army.
8 "He will slay your daughters [1]on the
mainland with the sword; and he will
make [a]siege walls against you, cast up a
[b]ramp against you and raise up a large
shield against you.
9 "The blow of his battering rams he
will direct against your walls, and with
his [1]axes he will break down your towers.
10 "Because of the multitude of his
[a]horses, the dust *raised by* them will cover you; your walls will [b]shake at the
noise of cavalry and [1]wagons and chariots when he [c]enters your gates as men
enter a city that is breached.
11 "With the hoofs of his [a]horses he
will trample all your streets. He will slay
your people with the sword; and your
strong pillars will [b]come down to the
ground.
12 "Also they will make a spoil of your
riches and a prey of your [a]merchandise,
[b]break down your walls and destroy your
[c]pleasant houses, and [1]throw your
stones and your timbers and your debris
[d]into the water.
13 "So I will [1]silence the sound of your
[a]songs, and the sound of your [b]harps
will be heard no more.
14 "I will make you a bare rock; you
will be a place for the spreading of nets.
You will be [a]built no more, for I the
[b]LORD have spoken," declares the Lord
GOD.
15 ¶ Thus says the Lord GOD to Tyre,
"Shall not the [a]coastlands [b]shake at the
sound of your fall when the wounded
groan, when the slaughter occurs in your
midst?
16 "Then all the princes of the sea will
[a]go down from their thrones, remove
their robes and strip off their embroidered garments. They will [b]clothe themselves with [1]trembling; they will sit on
the ground, [c]tremble every moment and
be appalled at you.
17 "They will take up a [a]lamentation
over you and say to you,
'[b]How you have perished,
O inhabited one,
From the seas, O renowned city,
Which was [c]mighty on the sea,
She and her inhabitants,
Who [1]imposed [2]her terror
On all her inhabitants!
18 'Now the [a]coastlands will
tremble
On the day of your fall;
Yes, the coastlands which are by
the sea
Will be terrified at your
[b]passing.' "
19 ¶ For thus says the Lord GOD,
"When I make you a desolate city, like
the cities which are not inhabited, when
I [a]bring up the deep over you and the
great waters cover you,
20 then I will bring you down with
those who [a]go down to the pit, to the
people of old, and I will make you dwell
in the [b]lower parts of the earth, like the
ancient waste places, with those who go
down to the pit, so that you will not [1]be
inhabited; but I will set [c]glory in the land
of the living.
21 "I will [1]bring [a]terrors on you and
you will be no more; though you will be
sought, [b]you will never be found again,"
declares the Lord GOD.

Lament over Tyre

27 Moreover, the word of the LORD
came to me saying,
2 "And you, son of man, [a]take up a
lamentation over Tyre;
3 and say to Tyre, [a]who dwells at the
[1]entrance to the sea, [b]merchant of the
peoples to many coastlands, 'Thus says
the Lord [2]GOD,
"O Tyre, you have said, 'I am
perfect in beauty.'

---

16 [b]1 Sam 30:14; Zeph 2:5
17 [a]Ps 9:16
26:2 [1]Lit *turned* [a]2 Sam 5:11; Is 23:1; Jer 25:22 [b]Is 62:10 [c]Ezek 25:8
3 [1]Heb *YHWH,* usually rendered *LORD,* and so throughout the ch [a]Mic 4:11 [b]Is 5:30; Jer 50:42
4 [a]Is 23:11; Ezek 26:9; Amos 1:10
5 [a]Ezek 25:7
6 [1]Lit *in the field* [a]Ezek 16:46
7 [1]Lit *an assembly, even many people* [a]Ezra 7:12; Is 10:8; Jer 52:32; Dan 2:37 [b]Ezek 23:24; Nah 2:3
8 [1]Lit *in the field* [a]Jer 52:4; Ezek 21:22 [b]Jer 32:24
9 [1]Lit *swords*
10 [1]Lit *wheels* [a]Jer 4:13 [b]Ezek 26:15 [c]Jer 39:3
11 [a]Is 5:28; Hab 1:8 [b]Is 26:5; Jer 43:13
12 [1]Lit *put* [a]Is 23:8; Ezek 27:3-27; Zech 9:3 [b]Jer 52:14 [c]2 Chr 32:27; Amos 5:11 [d]Ezek 27:27
13 [1]Lit *cause to cease* [a]Is 23:16; Amos 6:5 [b]Is 5:12; Rev 18:22
14 [a]Deut 13:16; Job 12:14; Mal 1:4 [b]Is 14:27
15 [a]Ezek 26:18 [b]Jer 49:21; Ezek 31:16
16 [1]Lit *tremblings* [a]Jon 3:6 [b]Job 8:22; Ps 35:26; Ezek 7:27; 1 Pet 5:5 [c]Ezek 32:10; Hos 11:10
17 [1]Lit *put* [2]Lit *their* [a]Ezek 19:1 [b]Is 14:12; Jer 48:39 [c]Ezek 27:3
18 [a]Is 41:5; Ezek 26:15 [b]Is 23:5-7
19 [a]Is 8:7; Ezek 26:3
20 [1]Or *return* [a]Is 14:9; Ezek 32:30 [b]Ps 88:6; Amos 9:2; Jon 2:2 [c]Jer 33:9; Zech 2:8
21 [1]Lit *give you terrors* [a]Ezek 26:15 [b]Rev 18:21
27:2 [a]Jer 9:10; Ezek 28:12
3 [1]Lit *entrances* [2]Heb *YHWH,* usually rendered *LORD,* and so throughout the ch [a]Ezek 28:2 [b]Is 23:3

4 "Your borders are in the heart of
the seas;
Your builders have perfected
your beauty.
5 "They have [1]made all *your* planks
of fir trees from [a]Senir;
They have taken a cedar from
Lebanon to make a mast for
you.
6 "Of [a]oaks from [b]Bashan they
have made your oars;
With ivory they have [1]inlaid
your deck of boxwood from
the coastlands of [c]Cyprus.
7 "Your sail was of fine
embroidered linen from
Egypt
So that it became your
[1]distinguishing mark;
Your [2]awning was [3a]blue and
purple from the coastlands
of [b]Elishah.
8 "The inhabitants of Sidon and
[a]Arvad were your rowers;
Your [b]wise men, O Tyre, were
[1]aboard; they were your
pilots.
9 "The elders of [a]Gebal and her
wise men were with you
repairing your seams;
All the ships of the sea and their
sailors were with you in
order to deal in your
merchandise.

10 ¶ "[a]Persia and [a]Lud and [a]Put
were in your army, your men of war.
They hung shield and helmet in you; they
set forth your splendor.
11 "The sons of Arvad and your army
were on your walls, *all* around, and the
[1]Gammadim were in your towers. They
hung their shields on your walls *all*
around; they perfected your beauty.
12 ¶ "Tarshish was your customer because of the abundance of all *kinds* of
wealth; with silver, iron, tin and lead
they paid for your wares.
13 "[a]Javan, [a]Tubal and [b]Meshech,
they were your traders; with the [c]lives of
men and vessels of bronze they paid for
your merchandise.
14 "Those from [a]Beth-togarmah gave
horses and war horses and mules for your
wares.
15 "The sons of [a]Dedan were your
traders. Many coastlands were [1]your
market; [b]ivory tusks and ebony they
brought as your payment.
16 "[a]Aram was your customer because
of the abundance of your [1]goods; they
paid for your wares with [b]emeralds, purple, [c]embroidered work, fine linen, coral
and rubies.
17 "Judah and the land of Israel, they
were your traders; with the wheat of
[a]Minnith, [1]cakes, honey, oil and balm
they paid for your merchandise.
18 "[a]Damascus was your customer because of the abundance of your [1]goods,
because of the abundance of all *kinds* of
wealth, because of the wine of Helbon
and white wool.
19 "Vedan and Javan paid for your
wares [1]from Uzal; wrought iron, cassia
and [2]sweet cane were among your merchandise.
20 "[a]Dedan traded with you in saddle-
cloths for riding.
21 "[a]Arabia and all the princes of Kedar, they were [1]your customers for
[b]lambs, rams and goats; for these they
were your customers.
22 "The traders of [a]Sheba and Raamah,
they traded with you; they paid for your
wares with the best of all *kinds* of
[b]spices, and with all *kinds* of precious
stones and gold.
23 "Haran, Canneh, [a]Eden, the traders
of Sheba, Asshur *and* Chilmad traded
with you.
24 "They traded with you in choice garments, in clothes of [1]blue and embroidered work, and in carpets of many colors
and tightly wound cords, *which were*
among your merchandise.
25 "The [a]ships of Tarshish were [1]the
carriers for your merchandise.
And you were filled and were
very [2]glorious
In the heart of the seas.

26 ¶ "Your rowers have brought you
Into [a]great waters;
The [b]east wind has broken you
In the heart of the seas.
27 "Your wealth, your wares, your
merchandise,
Your sailors and your pilots,
Your repairers of seams, your
dealers in merchandise
And all your men of war who are
in you,
With all your company that is in
your midst,
Will fall into the heart of the
seas
On the day of your overthrow.
28 "At the sound of the cry of your
pilots
The pasture lands will [a]shake.
29 "All who handle the oar,
The [a]sailors *and* all the pilots of
the sea
Will come down from their
ships;
They will stand on the land,
30 And they will [a]make their voice
heard over you

5 [1]Lit *built* [a]Deut 3:9; 1 Chr 5:23; Song 4:8
6 [1]Lit *made* [a]Is 2:13; Zech 11:2 [b]Num 21:33; Is 2:13; Jer 22:20 [c]Gen 10:4; Is 23:1,12; Jer 2:10
7 [1]Or *standard* [2]Lit *covering* [3]Or *violet* [a]Ex 25:4; Jer 10:9 [b]Gen 10:4
8 [1]Lit *in you* [a]Gen 10:18; 1 Chr 1:16; Ezek 27:11 [b]1 Kin 9:27
9 [a]Josh 13:5; 1 Kin 5:18
10 [a]Ezek 30:5; 38:5
11 [1]Or *valorous ones*
13 [a]Gen 10:2; Is 66:19; Ezek 27:19 [b]Gen 10:2; Ezek 38:2; 39:1 [c]Joel 3:3; Rev 18:13
14 [a]Gen 10:3; Ezek 38:6
15 [1]Lit *the market of your hand* [a]Jer 25:23; Ezek 25:13; 27:20 [b]1 Kin 10:22; Rev 18:12
16 [1]Lit *works* [a]Judg 10:6; Is 7:1-8; Ezek 16:57 [b]Ezek 28:13 [c]Ezek 16:13,18
17 [1]Heb *pannag* [a]Judg 11:33
18 [1]Lit *works* [a]Gen 14:15; Is 7:8; Jer 49:23; Ezek 47:16-18
19 [1]Or *with yarn* [2]Or *calamus*
20 [a]Gen 25:3
21 [1]Lit *customers of your hand* [a]Is 21:13 [b]Is 60:7
22 [a]Gen 10:7; Is 60:6; Ezek 38:13 [b]Gen 43:11; 1 Kin 10:2
23 [a]2 Kin 19:12; Is 37:12; Amos 1:5
24 [1]Or *violet*
25 [1]Lit *your travelers* [2]Lit *honored* [a]Is 2:16
26 [a]Ezek 26:19 [b]Ps 48:7; Jer 18:17; Acts 27:14
28 [a]Ezek 26:10, 15,18
29 [a]Rev 18:17-19
30 [a]Is 23:1-6; Ezek 26:17

And will cry bitterly.
They will [b]cast dust on their
heads,
They will [c]wallow in ashes.
31 "Also they will make themselves
[a]bald for you
And [b]gird themselves with
sackcloth;
And they will [c]weep for you in
bitterness of soul
With bitter mourning.
32 "Moreover, in their wailing they
will take up a [a]lamentation
for you
And lament over you:
'Who is like Tyre,
Like her who is silent in the
midst of the sea?
33 'When your wares went out from
the seas,
You satisfied many peoples;
With the [a]abundance of your
wealth and your
merchandise
You enriched the kings of earth.
34 '[1]Now that you are [a]broken by
the seas
In the depths of the waters,
Your [b]merchandise and all your
company
Have fallen in the midst of you.
35 'All the [a]inhabitants of the
coastlands
Are appalled at you,
And their kings are horribly
afraid;
They are troubled in
countenance.
36 'The merchants among the
peoples [a]hiss at you;
You have become [1]terrified
And you [b]will cease to be
forever.' " ' "

Tyre's King Overthrown

28 The word of the LORD came again
to me, saying,
2 "Son of man, say to the [1]leader of
Tyre, 'Thus says the Lord [2]GOD,
"Because your heart is lifted up
And you have said, '[a]I am a god,
I sit in the seat of [3]gods
In the heart of the seas';
Yet you are a [b]man and not
God,
Although you make your heart
like the heart of God—
3 Behold, you are wiser than
[a]Daniel;
There is no secret that is a
match for you.
4 "By your wisdom and
understanding
You have acquired [a]riches for
yourself
And have acquired gold and
silver for your treasuries.
5 "By your great wisdom, by your
[a]trade
You have increased your riches
And your [b]heart is lifted up
because of your riches—
6 Therefore thus says the Lord GOD,
'Because you have [a]made your
heart
Like the heart of God,
7 Therefore, behold, I will bring
[a]strangers upon you,
The [b]most ruthless of the
nations.
And they will draw their swords
Against the beauty of your
wisdom
And defile your splendor.
8 'They will bring you down to the
pit,
And you will die the [a]death of
those who are slain
In the heart of the seas.
9 'Will you still say, "I am a god,"
In the presence of your slayer,
Though you are a man and not
God,
In the hands of those who
wound you?
10 'You will die the death of the
[a]uncircumcised
By the hand of strangers,
For I have spoken!' declares the
Lord GOD!" ' "
11 ¶ Again the word of the LORD came
to me saying,
12 "Son of man, [a]take up a lamentation
over the king of Tyre and say to him,
'Thus says the Lord GOD,
"You [1]had the seal of perfection,
Full of wisdom and perfect in
beauty.
13 "You were in [a]Eden, the garden
of God;
[b]Every precious stone was your
covering:
The [c]ruby, the topaz and the
diamond;
The beryl, the onyx and the
jasper;
The lapis lazuli, the turquoise
and the emerald;
And the gold, the workmanship
of your [1d]settings and
[2]sockets,
Was in you.
On the day that you were
created
They were prepared.
14 "You were the [a]anointed cherub
who [1]covers,

30 [b]1 Sam 4:12; 2 Sam 1:2; Lam 2:10; Rev 18:19 [c]Jer 6:26; Jon 3:6

31 [a]Is 15:2; Ezek 29:18 [b]Is 22:12; Ezek 7:18 [c]Is 16:9; 22:4

32 [a]Ezek 26:17; 27:2; 28:12

33 [a]Ezek 27:12, 18; 28:4,5

34 [1]Lit *The time* [a]Ezek 26:12; 27:26,27 [b]Zech 9:3,4

35 [a]Is 23:6; Ezek 26:16

36 [1]Lit *terrors* [a]Jer 18:16; 19:8; 49:17; 50:13; Zeph 2:15 [b]Ps 37:10,36

28:2 [1]Or *ruler, prince* [2]Heb *YHWH,* usually rendered *LORD,* and so throughout the ch [3]Or *God* [a]Is 14:14; 47:8; Ezek 28:9; 2 Thess 2:4 [b]Ps 9:20; 82:6,7; Is 31:3; Ezek 28:9

3 [a]Dan 1:20; 2:20-23,28; 5:11,12

4 [a]Ezek 27:33; Zech 9:2,3

5 [a]Ezek 27:12; Hos 12:7,8 [b]Job 31:24,25; Ps 52:7; Ezek 28:2; Hos 13:6

6 [a]Ex 9:17; Ezek 28:2

7 [a]Ezek 26:7 [b]Ezek 30:11; 31:12; 32:12; Hab 1:6-8

8 [a]Ezek 27:26, 27,34

10 [a]1 Sam 17:26,36; Ezek 31:18; 32:30

12 [1]Lit *were the one sealing a pattern* [a]Ezek 19:1; 26:17; 27:2

13 [1]Or *tambourines* [2]Or *flutes* [a]Gen 2:8; Is 51:3; Ezek 31:8, 9,16; 36:35 [b]Ezek 27:16,22 [c]Ex 28:17-20 [d]Is 24:8; 30:32

14 [1]Or *guards* [a]Ex 25:17-20; 30:26; 40:9; Ezek 28:16

And I placed you *there.*
You were on the holy [b]mountain
of God;
You walked in the midst of the
[c]stones of fire.
15 "You were [a]blameless in your
ways
From the day you were created
Until [b]unrighteousness was
found in you.
16 "By the [a]abundance of your trade
[1]You were internally [b]filled
with violence,
And you sinned;
Therefore I have cast you as
profane
From the mountain of God.
And I have destroyed you,
O [2]covering cherub,
From the midst of the stones of
fire.
17 "Your heart was lifted up because
of your [a]beauty;
You [b]corrupted your wisdom by
reason of your splendor.
I cast you to the ground;
I put you before [c]kings,
That they may see you.
18 "By the multitude of your
iniquities,
In the unrighteousness of your
trade
You profaned your sanctuaries.
Therefore I have brought [a]fire
from the midst of you;
It has consumed you,
And I have turned you to [b]ashes
on the earth
In the eyes of all who see you.
19 "All who know you among the
peoples
Are appalled at you;
You have become [1a]terrified
And you will cease to be
[b]forever." ' "

Judgment of Sidon

20 ¶ And the word of the LORD came
to me saying,
21 "Son of man, [a]set your face toward
[b]Sidon, prophesy against her
22 and say, 'Thus says the Lord GOD,
"Behold, I am against you,
O Sidon,
And I will [1]be glorified in your
midst.
Then they will know that I am
the LORD when I [a]execute
judgments in her,
And I will manifest My holiness
in her.
23 "For [a]I will send pestilence
to her
And blood to her streets,

14 [b]Ezek 20:40; 28:16 [c]Ezek 28:13,16; Rev 18:16

15 [a]Ezek 27:3,4; 28:3-6,12 [b]Ezek 28:17,18

16 [1]Lit *They filled your midst* [2]Or *guardian* [a]Ezek 27:12 [b]Ezek 8:17; Hab 2:8,17

17 [a]Ezek 27:3,4; 28:7 [b]Is 19:11 [c]Ezek 26:16

18 [a]Amos 1:9, 10 [b]Mal 4:3

19 [1]Lit *terrors* [a]Ezek 26:21; 27:36 [b]Jer 51:64

21 [a]Ezek 6:2; 25:2 [b]Gen 10:15,19; Is 23:2,4; Ezek 27:8

22 [1]Or *glorify Myself* [a]Ezek 28:26; 30:19

23 [1]Or *be judged* [a]Ezek 38:22 [b]Jer 51:52

24 [a]Num 33:55; Josh 23:13; Is 55:13; Ezek 2:6

25 [1]Lit *ground* [a]Ps 106:47; Is 11:12,13; Jer 32:37; Ezek 20:41; 34:13,27 [b]Jer 23:8; 27:11

26 [a]Jer 23:6; Ezek 34:25-28; 38:8 [b]Jer 32:15, 43,44; Amos 9:13,14 [c]Ezek 25:11; 28:22

29:1 [a]Ezek 26:1; 29:17; 30:20

2 [a]Jer 44:30 [b]Is 19:1-17; Jer 46:2-26; Ezek 30:1-32:32

3 [1]Heb *YHWH,* usually rendered *LORD,* and so throughout the ch [2]Lit *tannim* [3]Or *Nile* [a]Is 27:1; Ezek 32:2 [b]Ezek 29:9; 30:12

4 [1]Or *Nile* [a]2 Kin 19:28; Ezek 38:4

5 [1]Or *Nile* [2]Lit *faces of the field* [3]Or with several mss and Targum, *buried* [a]Ezek 32:4-6 [b]Jer 8:2; 25:33 [c]Jer 7:33; 34:20; Ezek 39:4

And the [b]wounded will [1]fall in
her midst
By the sword upon her on every
side;
Then they will know that I am
the LORD.
24 "And there will be no more for the
house of Israel a [a]prickling brier or a
painful thorn from any round about them
who scorned them; then they will know
that I am the Lord GOD."

Israel Regathered

25 ¶ 'Thus says the Lord GOD, "When
I [a]gather the house of Israel from the
peoples among whom they are scattered,
and will manifest My holiness in them in
the sight of the nations, then they will
[b]live in their [1]land which I gave to My
servant Jacob.
26 "They will [a]live in it securely; and
they will [b]build houses, plant vineyards
and live securely when I [c]execute judgments upon all who scorn them round
about them. Then they will know that I
am the LORD their God." ' "

Judgment of Egypt

29 In the [a]tenth year, in the tenth
month, on the twelfth of the
month, the word of the LORD came to me
saying,
2 "Son of man, set your face against
[a]Pharaoh king of Egypt and prophesy
against him and against all [b]Egypt.
3 "Speak and say, 'Thus says the
Lord [1]GOD,
"Behold, I am against you,
Pharaoh king of Egypt,
The great [2a]monster that lies in
the midst of his [3]rivers,
That [b]has said, 'My Nile is
mine, and I myself have
made *it.*'
4 "I will put [a]hooks in your jaws
And make the fish of your
[1]rivers cling to your scales.
And I will bring you up out of
the midst of your [1]rivers,
And all the fish of your [1]rivers
will cling to your scales.
5 "I will [a]abandon you to the
wilderness, you and all the
fish of your [1]rivers;
You will fall on the [2]open field;
you will not be brought
together or [3b]gathered.
I have given you for [c]food to the
beasts of the earth and to
the birds of the sky.
6 "Then all the inhabitants of Egypt
will know that I am the
LORD,

Because they have been *only* a
[a]staff *made* of reed to the
house of Israel.
7 "When they took hold of you with
the hand,
You [a]broke and tore all their
[1]hands;
And when they leaned on you,
You broke and made all their
loins [2]quake."
8 ¶ 'Therefore thus says the Lord
GOD, "Behold, I will [a]bring upon you a
sword and I will cut off from you man and
beast.
9 "The [a]land of Egypt will become a
desolation and waste. Then they will
know that I am the LORD.
¶ Because [1]you [b]said, 'The Nile is
mine, and I have made *it,*'
10 therefore, behold, I am [a]against
you and against your [1]rivers, and I will
make the land of Egypt an utter waste and
desolation, from Migdol *to* Syene and
even to the border of [2]Ethiopia.
11 "A man's foot will [a]not pass through
it, and the foot of a beast will not pass
through it, and it will not be inhabited for
forty years.
12 "So I will make the land of Egypt a
desolation in the [a]midst of desolated
lands. And her cities, in the midst of cities that are laid waste, will be desolate
forty years; and I will [b]scatter the Egyptians among the nations and disperse
them among the lands."
13 ¶ 'For thus says the Lord GOD, "At
the end of forty years I will [a]gather the
Egyptians from the peoples [1]among
whom they were scattered.
14 "I will turn the fortunes of Egypt and
make them return to the land of [a]Pa-
thros, to the land of their origin, and
there they will be a lowly kingdom.
15 "It will be the [a]lowest of the kingdoms, and it will never again lift itself up
above the nations. And I will make them
so small that they will not [b]rule over the
nations.
16 "And it will never again be the
[a]confidence of the house of Israel,
[1b]bringing to mind the iniquity of their
having turned [2]to Egypt. Then they will
know that I am the Lord GOD." ' "
17 ¶ Now in the [a]twenty-seventh
year, in the first *month,* on the first of the
month, the word of the LORD came to me
saying,
18 "Son of man, [a]Nebuchadnezzar
king of Babylon made his army labor
[1]hard against Tyre; every head was made
[b]bald and every shoulder was rubbed
bare. But he and his army had no wages
from Tyre for the labor that he had [2]per-
formed against it."
19 Therefore thus says the Lord GOD,
"Behold, I [a]will give the land of Egypt to
Nebuchadnezzar king of Babylon. And he
will carry off her [1b]wealth and capture
her spoil and seize her plunder; and it
will be wages for his army.
20 "I have given him the land of Egypt
for his labor which he [1a]performed, because they acted for Me," declares the
Lord GOD.
21 ¶ "On that day I will make a [a]horn
sprout for the house of Israel, and I will
[1b]open your mouth in their midst. Then
they will know that I am the LORD."

Lament over Egypt

30 The word of the LORD came again
to me saying,
2 "Son of man, prophesy and say,
'Thus says the Lord [1]GOD,
"[a]Wail, 'Alas for the day!'
3 "For the day is near,
Even [a]the day of the LORD is
near;
It will be a day of [b]clouds,
A time *of doom* for the nations.
4 "A sword will come upon Egypt,
And anguish will be in
[1]Ethiopia;
When the slain fall in Egypt,
They [a]take away her [2]wealth,
And her foundations are torn
down.
5 "[1]Ethiopia, Put, Lud, all [2a]Arabia,
[3]Libya and the [4]people of the land [5]that
is in league will fall with them by the
sword."
6 ¶ 'Thus says the LORD,
"Indeed, those who support
[a]Egypt will fall
And the pride of her power will
come down;
From Migdol *to* Syene
They will fall within her by the
sword,"
Declares the Lord GOD.
7 "They will be desolate
In the [a]midst of the desolated
lands;
And her cities will be
In the midst of the devastated
cities.
8 "And they will [a]know that I am
the LORD,
When I set a [b]fire in Egypt
And all her helpers are broken.
9 "On that day [a]messengers will go
forth from Me in ships to frighten [b]se-
cure [1]Ethiopia; and [c]anguish will be on
them as on the day of Egypt; for behold,
it comes!"
10 ¶ 'Thus says the Lord GOD,
"[a]I will also make the [1]hordes of
Egypt cease

6 [a]2 Kin 18:21; Is 36:6
7 [1]So with some ancient versions; M.T. *shoulders* [2]Lit *stand* [a]2 Kin 18:21; Is 36:6; Ezek 17:15-17
8 [a]Jer 46:13; Ezek 14:17
9 [1]Lit *he* [a]Ezek 29:10-12 [b]Prov 16:18; Ezek 29:3
10 [1]Or *Nile* [2]Lit *Cush* [a]Ezek 13:8
11 [a]Jer 43:11; Ezek 32:13
12 [a]Jer 25:15-19; Ezek 30:7 [b]Jer 46:19; Ezek 30:23
13 [1]Lit *where* [a]Is 19:22; Jer 46:26
14 [a]Is 11:11; Jer 44:1; Ezek 30:14
15 [a]Ezek 17:6; Zech 10:11 [b]Ezek 31:2; Nah 3:8-10
16 [1]Lit *causing to remember* [2]Lit *after them* [a]Is 20:5; Ezek 17:15 [b]Is 64:9; Jer 14:10; Ezek 21:23; Hos 8:13
17 [a]Ezek 24:1
18 [1]Lit *a great labor* [2]Lit *labored* [a]Jer 25:9; Ezek 26:7-12 [b]Jer 48:37; Ezek 27:31
19 [1]Or *multitude* [a]Ezek 30:10 [b]Jer 43:10-13; Ezek 30:14
20 [1]Lit *labored* [a]Is 10:6; Jer 25:9
21 [1]Lit *give you an opening of the mouth* [a]1 Sam 2:10; Ps 92:10 [b]Ezek 3:27; Amos 3:7; Luke 21:15
30:2 [1]Heb *YHWH,* usually rendered *LORD,* and so throughout the ch [a]Is 13:6; Ezek 21:12; Joel 1:5
3 [a]Ezek 7:19; Joel 1:15; Obad 15 [b]Ezek 30:18
4 [1]Lit *Cush* [2]Or *multitude* [a]Ezek 29:19
5 [1]Lit *Cush* [2]Or *the mixed people* [3]Or *Cub* [4]Lit *sons* [5]Lit *of the covenant* [a]Jer 25:20
6 [a]Is 20:3-6
7 [a]Jer 25:18-26; Ezek 29:12
8 [a]Ps 58:11; Ezek 29:6 [b]Ezek 22:31; Amos 1:4
9 [1]Lit *Cush* [a]Is 18:1 [b]Is 47:8; Ezek 38:11 [c]Is 19:17; Ezek 32:9
10 [1]Or *people;* lit *crowd,* and so throughout the ch [a]Ezek 29:19

By the hand of Nebuchadnezzar
king of Babylon.
11 "He and his people with him,
[a]The most ruthless of the
nations,
Will be brought in to destroy the
land;
And they will draw their swords
against Egypt
And fill the land with the slain.
12 "Moreover, I will make the [a]Nile
canals dry
And [b]sell the land into the
hands of evil men.
And I will make the land
desolate
And [1]all that is in it,
By the hand of strangers; I the
LORD have spoken."

13 ¶ 'Thus says the Lord GOD,
"I will also [a]destroy the idols
And make the [1]images cease
from [2b]Memphis.
And there will no longer be a
prince in the land of Egypt;
And I will put fear in the land of
Egypt.
14 "I will make [a]Pathros desolate,
Set a fire in [b]Zoan
And execute judgments on
[1c]Thebes.
15 "I will pour out My wrath
on [1]Sin,
The stronghold of Egypt;
I will also cut off the hordes of
[2]Thebes.
16 "I will set a fire in Egypt;
[1]Sin will writhe in anguish,
[2]Thebes will be breached
And [3]Memphis *will have*
[4]distresses daily.
17 "The young men of [1a]On and of
Pi-beseth
Will fall by the sword,
And [2]the women will go into
captivity.
18 "In [a]Tehaphnehes the day will
[1]be [b]dark
When I [c]break there the yoke
bars of Egypt.
Then the pride of her power will
cease in her;
A cloud will cover her,
And her daughters will go into
captivity.
19 "Thus I will [a]execute judgments
on Egypt,
And they will know that I am
the LORD." ' "

Victory for Babylon

20 ¶ In the [a]eleventh year, in the first
month, on the seventh of the month, the
word of the LORD came to me saying,
21 "Son of man, I have [a]broken the
arm of Pharaoh king of Egypt; and, behold, it has not been [b]bound up [1]for
healing [2]or wrapped with a bandage,
that it may be strong to hold the sword.
22 "Therefore thus says the Lord GOD,
'Behold, I am [a]against Pharaoh king of
Egypt and will break his arms, both the
strong and the [b]broken; and I will make
the sword [c]fall from his hand.
23 'I will [a]scatter the Egyptians among
the nations and disperse them among the
lands.
24 'For I will [a]strengthen the arms of
the king of Babylon and put [b]My sword
in his hand; and I will break the arms of
Pharaoh, so that he will groan before him
with the groanings of a wounded man.
25 'Thus I will strengthen the arms of
the king of Babylon, but the arms of Pharaoh will fall. Then they will know that I
am the LORD, when I put My sword into
the hand of the king of Babylon and he
[a]stretches it out against the land of
Egypt.
26 'When I scatter the Egyptians
among the nations and disperse them
among the lands, then they will know
that I am the LORD.' "

Pharaoh Warned of Assyria's Fate

31 In the [a]eleventh year, in the
third *month,* on the first of the
month, the word of the LORD came to me
saying,
2 "Son of man, say to Pharaoh king of
Egypt and to his [a]hordes,
'Whom are you like in your
greatness?
3 'Behold, Assyria *was* a [a]cedar in
Lebanon
With beautiful branches and
forest shade,
And [1b]very high,
And its top was among the
[2]clouds.
4 'The [a]waters made it grow, the
[1]deep made it high.
With its rivers it continually
[2]extended all around its
planting place,
And sent out its channels to all
the trees of the field.
5 'Therefore [a]its height was loftier
than all the trees of the field
And its boughs became many
and its branches long
Because of [b]many waters [1]as it
spread them out.
6 'All the [a]birds of the heavens
nested in its boughs,

11 [a]Ezek 28:7
12 [1]Lit *her fullness* [a]Ezek 29:3, 9 [b]Is 19:4
13 [1]Or *futile ones* [2]Or *Noph* [a]Is 2:18 [b]Is 19:13; Jer 2:16; 44:1; 46:14; Ezek 30:16
14 [1]Or *No* [a]Is 11:11; Jer 44:1, 15; Ezek 29:14 [b]Ps 78:12,43; Is 19:11,13 [c]Jer 46:25; Ezek 30:15,16; Nah 3:8
15 [1]Or *Pelusium* [2]Or *No*
16 [1]Or *Pelusium* [2]Or *No* [3]Or *Noph* [4]Or *adversaries*
17 [1]Or *Aven* [2]Lit *they* [a]Gen 41:45; 46:20
18 [1]So with many mss and ancient versions; M.T. *restrain* [a]Jer 43:8-13 [b]Ezek 30:3 [c]Lev 26:13; Is 10:27; Jer 27:2; 28:10, 13; 30:8; Ezek 34:27
19 [a]Ps 9:16; Ezek 5:8,15; 25:11; 30:14
20 [a]Ezek 26:1; 29:1,17; 31:1
21 [1]Lit *to give healing* [2]Lit *to put a bandage, to wrap it* [a]Ps 10:15; 37:17; Ezek 30:24 [b]Jer 30:13; 46:11
22 [a]Jer 46:25; Ezek 29:3 [b]2 Kin 24:7; Jer 37:7 [c]Jer 46:21
23 [a]Ezek 29:12; 30:17,18,26
24 [a]Neh 6:9; Is 45:1,5; Ezek 30:10,25; Zech 10:12 [b]Ezek 30:11,25; Zeph 2:12
25 [a]Josh 8:18; 1 Chr 21:16; Is 5:25
31:1 [a]Jer 52:5, 6; Ezek 30:20; 32:1
2 [a]Ezek 29:19; 30:10; Nah 3:9
3 [1]Lit *high of stature* [2]So Gr; M.T. *thick boughs* [a]Is 10:33,34; Ezek 17:3,4,22; 31:16; Dan 4:10, 20-23 [b]Is 10:33; Ezek 31:5,10
4 [1]I.e. subterranean waters [2]Lit *was going* [a]Ezek 17:5,8; Rev 17:1,15
5 [1]Lit *in its sending forth* [a]Dan 4:11 [b]Ps 1:3; Ezek 17:5
6 [a]Ezek 17:23; 31:13; Dan 4:12, 21; Matt 13:32

And under its branches all the
beasts of the field gave birth,
And all great nations lived under
its shade.
7 'So it was beautiful in its
greatness, in the length of
its branches;
For its [1]roots extended to many
waters.
8 'The [a]cedars in [b]God's garden
[1]could not match it;
The [2]cypresses [1]could not
compare with its boughs,
And the plane trees [3]could not
match its branches.
No tree in [b]God's garden [1]could
compare with it in its
beauty.
9 'I made it beautiful with the
multitude of its branches,
And all the trees of [a]Eden,
which were in the [a]garden
of God, were jealous of it.
10 ¶ 'Therefore thus says the Lord
[1]GOD, "Because [2]it is high in stature and
has set its top among the [3]clouds, and its
[a]heart is haughty in its loftiness,
11 therefore I will give it into the hand
of a [1a]despot of the nations; he will thoroughly deal with it. According to its wickedness I have [b]driven it away.
12 "[a]Alien [b]tyrants of the nations have
cut it down and left it; on the [c]mountains
and in all the valleys its branches have
fallen and its boughs have been broken in
all the ravines of the land. And all the
peoples of the earth have [d]gone down
from its shade and left it.
13 "On its ruin all the [a]birds of the
heavens will dwell, and all the beasts of
the field will be on its *fallen* branches
14 so that all the trees by the waters
may not be exalted in their stature, nor
set their top among the [1]clouds, nor
their [2]well-watered mighty ones stand
erect in their height. For they have all
been given over to death, to the [a]earth
beneath, among the sons of men, with
those who go down to the pit."
15 ¶ 'Thus says the Lord GOD, "On
the day when it went down to Sheol
I [a]caused lamentations; I closed the
[1]deep over it and held back its rivers.
And *its* many waters were stopped up,
and I made Lebanon [2]mourn for it, and
all the trees of the field wilted away on
account of it.
16 "I made the nations [a]quake at the
sound of its fall when I made it [b]go down
to Sheol with those who go down to the
pit; and all the [1]well-watered trees of
Eden, the choicest and best of [c]Lebanon,
were [d]comforted in the earth beneath.
17 "They also [a]went down with it to
Sheol to those who were [b]slain by the
sword; and those who were its [1]strength
lived [c]under its shade among the nations.
18 ¶ "To which among the trees of
Eden are you thus [1]equal in glory and
greatness? Yet you will be brought down
with the trees of Eden to the earth beneath; you will lie in the midst of the
[a]uncircumcised, with those who were
slain by the sword. [b]So is Pharaoh and all
his hordes!" ' declares the Lord GOD."

Lament over Pharaoh and Egypt

32 In the [a]twelfth year, in the
twelfth *month*, on the first of the
month, the word of the LORD came to me
saying,
2 "Son of man, take up a [a]lamentation
over Pharaoh king of Egypt and say to
him,
'You [1]compared yourself to a
young [b]lion of the nations,
Yet you are like the [c]monster in
the seas;
And you [d]burst forth in your
rivers
And muddied the waters with
your feet
And [2]fouled their rivers.' "
3 ¶ Thus says the Lord [1]GOD,
"Now I will [a]spread My net
over you
With a company of many
peoples,
And they shall lift you up in My
net.
4 "I will leave you on the land;
I will cast you on the [1]open
field.
And I will cause all the [a]birds of
the heavens to dwell on you,
And I will satisfy the beasts of
the whole earth [2]with you.
5 "I will lay your flesh [a]on the
mountains
And fill the valleys with your
refuse.
6 "I will also make the land drink
the discharge of your [a]blood
As far as the mountains,
And the ravines will be full of
you.
7 "And when *I* [a]extinguish you,
I will [b]cover the heavens and
darken their [c]stars;
I will cover the [d]sun with a
cloud
And the moon will not give its
light.
8 "All the shining [a]lights in the
heavens
I will darken over you

7 [1]Lit *root was*
8 [1]Lit *did* [2]Or *Phoenician junipers* [3]Lit *were not like* [a]Ps 80:10; Ezek 31:3 [b]Gen 2:8; Is 51:3; Ezek 28:13
9 [a]Gen 2:8; Is 51:3; Ezek 28:13
10 [1]Heb *YHWH,* usually rendered LORD, and so throughout the ch [2]Lit *you are* [3]Or *thick boughs* [a]2 Chr 32:25; Is 10:12; Ezek 28:17; Dan 5:20
11 [1]Or *mighty one* [a]Ezek 30:10; Dan 5:18 [b]Deut 18:12; Nah 3:18
12 [a]Ezek 7:21; Hab 1:6 [b]Ezek 28:7 [c]Ezek 32:5 [d]Ezek 31:17; Dan 4:14; Nah 3:17
13 [a]Is 18:6; Ezek 29:5
14 [1]Or *thick boughs* [2]Lit *drinkers of water* [a]Num 16:30; Ps 63:9; Ezek 26:20; Amos 9:2; Jon 2:2; Eph 4:9
15 [1]I.e. subterranean waters [2]Lit *be darkened* [a]Ezek 32:7; Nah 2:10
16 [1]Lit *drinkers of water* [a]Ezek 26:15; Hag 2:7 [b]Is 14:15; Ezek 32:18 [c]Is 14:8; Hab 2:17 [d]Ezek 14:22
17 [1]Lit *arm* [a]Ps 9:17 [b]Ezek 32:20f [c]Ezek 31:3; Dan 4:12
18 [1]Lit *like* [a]Jer 9:25; Ezek 28:10 [b]Ps 52:7; Matt 13:19
32:1 [a]Ezek 30:20
2 [1]Or *were like* [2]Lit *fouled by stamping* [a]Ezek 19:1 [b]Jer 4:7; Ezek 19:2-6; Nah 2:11-13 [c]Is 27:1; Ezek 29:3 [d]Jer 46:7
3 [1]Heb *YHWH,* usually rendered LORD, and so throughout the ch [a]Ezek 12:13
4 [1]Lit *surface of the field* [2]Lit *from* [a]Is 18:6
5 [a]Ezek 31:12
6 [a]Ex 7:17; Is 34:3; Ezek 35:6; Rev 14:20
7 [a]Job 18:5; Prov 13:9 [b]Ex 10:21-23; Is 34:4; Ezek 30:3 [c]Is 13:10 [d]Joel 2:2; Amos 8:9; Matt 24:29; Mark 13:24f; Luke 21:25; Rev 6:12
8 [a]Gen 1:14

And will set darkness on your
land,"
Declares the Lord GOD.
9 "I will also [a]trouble the hearts of
many peoples when I [b]bring your destruction among the nations, into lands
which you have not known.
10 "I will make many peoples [a]ap-
palled at you, and their kings will be horribly afraid of you when I brandish My
sword before them; and [b]they will tremble every moment, every man for his own
life, on the day of your fall."
11 ¶ For [a]thus says the Lord GOD,
"The sword of the king of Babylon will
come upon you.
12 "By the swords of the mighty ones I
will cause your hordes to fall; all of them
are [a]tyrants of the nations,
And they will [b]devastate the
pride of Egypt,
And all its hordes will be
destroyed.
13 "I will also destroy all its cattle
from beside many waters;
And [a]the foot of man will not
muddy them anymore
And the hoofs of beasts will not
muddy them.
14 "Then I will make their waters
settle
And will cause their rivers to run
like oil,"
Declares the Lord GOD.
15 "When I make the land of Egypt a
[a]desolation,
And the land is destitute of that
which filled it,
When I smite all those who live
in it,
Then they shall [b]know that I am
the LORD.
16 "This is a [a]lamentation and they
shall [1]chant it. The daughters of the nations shall [1]chant it. Over Egypt and over
all her hordes they shall [1]chant it," declares the Lord GOD.
17 ¶ In the [a]twelfth year, on the [a]fif-
teenth of the month, the word of the
LORD came to me saying,
18 "Son of man, [a]wail for the hordes of
Egypt and [b]bring it down, her and the
daughters of the powerful nations, to the
[c]nether world, with those who go down
to the pit;
19 'Whom do you surpass in beauty?
Go down and make your bed
with the [a]uncircumcised.'
20 "They shall fall in the midst of those
who are slain by the sword. [1]She is given
over to the sword; they have [a]drawn her
and all her hordes away.
21 "The [a]strong among the mighty
ones shall speak of him *and* his helpers
from the midst of Sheol, 'They have gone
down, they lie still, the uncircumcised,
slain by the sword.'
22 ¶ "[a]Assyria is there and all her
company; [1]her graves are round about
[2]her. All of them are slain, fallen by the
sword,
23 whose [a]graves are set in the remotest parts of the pit and her company is
round about her grave. All of them are
slain, fallen by the sword, who [1]spread
terror in the land of the living.
24 ¶ "[a]Elam is there and all her
hordes around her grave; all of them
slain, fallen by the sword, who went
down uncircumcised to the [b]lower parts
of the earth, who instilled their terror in
the [c]land of the living and [d]bore their
disgrace with those who went down to
the pit.
25 "They have made a [a]bed for her
among the slain with all her hordes. Her
graves are around it, they are all uncircumcised, slain by the sword (although
their terror was [1]instilled in the land of
the living), and they bore their disgrace
with those who go down to the pit; [2]they
were put in the midst of the slain.
26 ¶ "[a]Meshech, [b]Tubal and all their
hordes are there; their graves [1]surround
them. All of them were slain by the sword
[c]uncircumcised, though they instilled
their terror in the land of the living.
27 "[a]Nor do they lie beside the fallen
[1b]heroes of the uncircumcised, who
went down to Sheol with their weapons
of war and whose swords were laid under
their heads; but the punishment for their
[c]iniquity rested on their bones, though
the terror of *these* [1]heroes *was once* in
the land of the living.
28 "But in the midst of the uncircumcised you will be broken and lie with
those slain by the sword.
29 ¶ "There also is [a]Edom, its kings
and all its [1]princes, who [2]for *all* their
might are laid with those slain by the
sword; they will lie with the uncircumcised and with those who go down to the
pit.
30 ¶ "There also are the [1]chiefs of the
[a]north, all of them, and all the [b]Sidoni-
ans, who in spite of the terror resulting
from their might, in shame went down
with the slain. So they lay down uncircumcised with those slain by the sword
and bore their disgrace with those who
go down to the pit.
31 ¶ "These Pharaoh will see, and he
will be [a]comforted for all his hordes slain
by the sword, *even* Pharaoh and all his
army," declares the Lord GOD.
32 "Though I instilled a terror of him in
the land of the living, yet he will be made

9 [a]Ezek 27:29-32; 28:19; Rev 18:10-15 [b]Ex 15:14-16
10 [a]Ezek 27:35 [b]Ezek 26:16
11 [a]Jer 46:26
12 [a]Ezek 28:7 [b]Ezek 28:19
13 [a]Ezek 29:11
15 [a]Ps 107:33, 34; Ezek 29:12, 19,20 [b]Ex 7:5; 14:4,18; Ps 9:16; 83:17,18; Ezek 6:7; 30:19,26
16 [1]Or *lament* [a]2 Sam 1:17; 3:33,34; 2 Chr 35:25; Jer 9:17; Ezek 26:17; 32:2
17 [a]Ezek 31:1; 32:1; 33:21
18 [a]Is 16:9; Ezek 21:6; 32:2, 16; Mic 1:8 [b]Jer 1:10; Ezek 43:3; Hos 6:5 [c]Ezek 31:14,16,18; 32:24
19 [a]Jer 9:25,26; Ezek 31:18; 32:21,24,29,30
20 [1]Or *The sword is given* [a]Ps 28:3
21 [a]Is 14:9-12; Ezek 32:27
22 [1]Lit *his* [2]Lit *him* [a]Ezek 27:23; 31:3,16
23 [1]Lit *gave,* and so throughout the ch [a]Is 14:15
24 [a]Gen 10:22; 14:1; Is 11:11; Jer 25:25; 49:34-39 [b]Ezek 26:20; 31:14,18; 32:18 [c]Job 28:13; Ps 27:13; 52:5; 142:5; Is 38:11; Jer 11:19 [d]Ezek 16:52,54; 32:25,30
25 [1]Lit *given* [2]So with ancient versions; M.T. reads *he was* [a]Ps 139:8
26 [1]Lit *are around him* [a]Gen 10:2; Ezek 27:13; 38:2,3; 39:1 [b]Gen 10:2; Is 66:19; Ezek 27:13; 38:2,3; 39:1 [c]Ezek 32:19
27 [1]Or *mighty ones* [a]Is 14:18, 19 [b]Job 3:13-15; Ezek 32:21 [c]Job 20:11; Ps 109:18
29 [1]Or *leaders* [2]Or *in* [a]Is 34:5-15; Jer 49:7-22; Ezek 25:13; 35:9,15
30 [1]Or *princes* [a]Jer 1:15; 25:26; Ezek 38:6,15; 39:2 [b]Jer 25:22; Ezek 28:21-23
31 [a]Ezek 14:22; 31:16

to lie down among *the* uncircumcised *along* with those slain by the sword, *even* Pharaoh and all his hordes," declares the Lord GOD.

The Watchman's Duty

33 And the word of the LORD came to me, saying,

2 "Son of man, speak to the [a]sons of your people and say to them, 'If I bring a sword upon a land, and the people of the land take one man from among them and make him their watchman,

3 and he sees the sword coming upon the land and [a]blows on the trumpet and warns the people,

4 then he who hears the sound of the trumpet and [a]does not take warning, and a sword comes and takes him away, his [b]blood will be on his *own* head.

5 'He heard the sound of the trumpet but did not take warning; his blood will be on himself. But had he taken warning, he would have [a]delivered his life.

6 'But if the watchman sees the sword coming and does not blow the trumpet and the people are not warned, and a sword comes and takes a person from them, he is [a]taken away [1]in his iniquity; but his [b]blood I will require from the watchman's hand.'

7 ¶ "Now as for you, son of man, I have [1a]appointed you a watchman for the house of Israel; so you will hear a [2]message from My mouth and give them [b]warning from Me.

8 "When I say to the wicked, 'O wicked man, you will [a]surely die,' and you do not speak to warn the wicked from his way, that wicked man shall die in his iniquity, but his blood I will require from your hand.

9 "But if you on your part warn a wicked man to turn from his way and he [a]does not turn from his way, he will die in his iniquity, but you have [b]delivered your life.

10 ¶ "Now as for you, son of man, say to the house of Israel, 'Thus you have spoken, saying, "Surely our transgressions and our sins are upon us, and we are [a]rotting away in them; [b]how then can we [1]survive?"'

11 "Say to them, '[a]As I live!' declares the Lord [1]GOD, 'I take [b]no pleasure in the death of the wicked, but rather that the wicked [c]turn from his way and live. [d]Turn back, turn back from your evil ways! Why then will you die, O house of Israel?'

12 "And you, son of man, say to [1]your fellow citizens, 'The [a]righteousness of a righteous man will not deliver him in the day of his transgression, and as for the wickedness of the wicked, he will [b]not stumble because of it in the day when he turns from his wickedness; whereas a righteous man will not be able to live [2]by his righteousness on the day when he commits sin.'

13 "When I say to the righteous he will surely live, and he *so* trusts in his righteousness that he [a]commits iniquity, none of his righteous deeds will be remembered; but in that same iniquity of his which he has committed he will die.

14 "But when I say to the wicked, 'You will surely die,' and he [a]turns from his sin and practices [b]justice and righteousness,

15 *if a* wicked man restores a pledge, [a]pays back what he has taken by robbery, walks by the [b]statutes [1]which ensure life without committing iniquity, he shall surely live; he shall not die.

16 "[a]None of his sins that he has committed will be remembered against him. He has practiced justice and righteousness; he shall surely live.

17 ¶ "Yet [1]your fellow citizens say, 'The way of the Lord is not right,' when it is their own way that is not right.

18 "When the righteous turns from his righteousness and [a]commits iniquity, then he shall die in [1]it.

19 "But when the wicked turns from his wickedness and practices justice and righteousness, he will live by them.

20 "Yet you say, '[a]The way of the Lord is not right.' O house of Israel, I will judge each of you according to his ways."

Word of Jerusalem's Capture

21 ¶ Now [a]in the [b]twelfth year of our exile, on the fifth of the tenth month, the [1]refugees from Jerusalem came to me, saying, "[c]The city has been [2]taken."

22 Now the [a]hand of the LORD had been upon me in the evening, before the [1]refugees came. And He [b]opened my mouth [2]at the time *they* came to me in the morning; so my mouth was [c]opened and I was no longer [3]speechless.

23 ¶ Then the word of the LORD came to me saying,

24 "Son of man, they who [a]live in these waste places in the land of Israel are saying, '[b]Abraham was *only* one, yet he possessed the land; so to [c]us who are many the land has been given as a possession.'

25 "Therefore say to them, 'Thus says the Lord GOD, "You eat *meat* with the [a]blood *in it,* lift up your eyes to your idols as you shed blood. [b]Should you then possess the land?

26 "You [1a]rely on your sword, you commit abominations and each of you de-

33:2 [a]Ezek 3:11
3 [a]Neh 4:18-20; Is 58:1; Ezek 33:9; Hos 8:1; Joel 2:1
4 [a]2 Chr 25:16; Jer 6:17; Zech 1:4 [b]Ezek 18:13; Acts 18:6
5 [a]Ex 9:19-21; Heb 11:7
6 [1]Or *for,* and so throughout the ch [a]Ezek 18:20 [b]Ezek 3:18
7 [1]Or *given* [2]Lit *word* [a]Is 62:6; Ezek 3:17-21 [b]Jer 1:17; Ezek 2:7; Acts 5:20
8 [a]Is 3:11; Ezek 18:4
9 [a]Acts 13:40 [b]Ezek 3:19; Acts 20:26
10 [1]Lit *live* [a]Lev 26:39; Ezek 4:17 [b]Is 49:14; Ezek 37:11
11 [1]Heb *YHWH,* usually rendered *LORD,* and so throughout the ch [a]Is 49:18; Ezek 5:11 [b]Ezek 18:23; Hos 11:8 [c]Jer 31:20; 1 Tim 2:4; 2 Pet 3:9 [d]Is 55:6; Jer 3:22; Ezek 18:30; Hos 14:1; Acts 3:19
12 [1]Lit *the sons of your people* [2]Lit *by it* [a]Ezek 3:18 [b]2 Chr 7:14; Ezek 18:21
13 [a]Ezek 18:26; Heb 10:38; 2 Pet 2:20
14 [a]Is 55:7; Jer 18:7; Ezek 18:27; Hos 14:1 [b]Mic 6:8
15 [1]Lit *of life* [a]Ex 22:1-4; Lev 6:4; Luke 19:8 [b]Ps 119:59; Ezek 20:11
16 [a]Is 1:18; Ezek 18:22
17 [1]Lit *the sons of your people*
18 [1]Lit *them* [a]Ezek 3:20
20 [a]Ezek 18:25
21 [1]Or *refugee* [2]Lit *smitten* [a]Ezek 31:1 [b]Jer 39:1; Ezek 24:1 [c]2 Kin 25:10; Jer 39:8
22 [1]Lit *refugee* [2]Lit *until he came* [3]Or *mute* [a]Ezek 1:3 [b]Ezek 3:26 [c]Luke 1:64
24 [a]Jer 39:10; Ezek 33:27 [b]Is 51:2; Luke 3:8; Acts 7:5; Rom 4:12 [c]Ezek 11:15
25 [a]Lev 17:10; Deut 12:16 [b]Jer 7:9
26 [1]Lit *stand* [a]Mic 2:1; Zeph 3:3

files his neighbor's wife. Should you then
possess the land?" '
27 "Thus you shall say to them, 'Thus
says the Lord GOD, "As I live, surely those
who are in the waste places will [a]fall by
the sword, and whoever is in the [1]open
field I will give to the beasts to be devoured, and those who are in the strongholds and in the [b]caves will die of pestilence.
28 "I will [a]make the land a desolation
and a waste, and the [b]pride of her power
will cease; and the mountains of Israel
will be desolate so that no one will pass
through.
29 "Then they will know that I am the
LORD, when I make the land a desolation
and a waste because of all their abominations which they have committed." '
30 ¶ "But as for you, son of man,
[1]your fellow citizens who talk about you
by the walls and in the doorways of the
houses, speak to one another, each to his
brother, saying, '[a]Come now and hear
what the [2]message is which comes forth
from the LORD.'
31 "They come to you as people come,
and sit before you *as* My people and hear
your words, but they do not do them, for
they do the lustful desires *expressed* by
their [a]mouth, *and* their heart goes after
their [b]gain.
32 "Behold, you are to them like a sensual song by one who has a [a]beautiful
voice and plays well on an instrument; for
they hear your words but they do not
practice them.
33 "So when it [a]comes to pass—[1]as
surely it will—then they will know that a
prophet has been in their midst."

Prophecy against the Shepherds of Israel

34 Then the word of the LORD came
to me saying,
2 "Son of man, prophesy against the
[a]shepherds of Israel. Prophesy and say to
[1]those shepherds, 'Thus says the Lord
[2]GOD, "Woe, shepherds of Israel who
have been [3b]feeding themselves! Should
not the shepherds [3c]feed the flock?
3 "You [a]eat the fat and clothe yourselves with the wool, you [b]slaughter the
fat *sheep* without [1]feeding the flock.
4 "Those who are sickly you have not
strengthened, the [1]diseased you have
not healed, [a]the broken you have not
bound up, the scattered you have not
brought back, nor have you [b]sought for
the lost; but with force and with severity
you have dominated them.
5 "They were [a]scattered for lack of a
shepherd, and they became [b]food for every beast of the field and were scattered.
6 "My flock [a]wandered through all
the mountains and on every high hill;
[b]My flock was scattered over all the surface of the earth, and there was [c]no one
to search or seek *for them*." ' "
7 ¶ Therefore, you shepherds, hear
the word of the LORD:
8 "As I live," declares the Lord GOD,
"surely because My flock has become a
[a]prey, My flock has even become food
for all the beasts of the field for lack of
a shepherd, and My shepherds did not
search for My flock, but *rather* the shepherds fed themselves and did not feed My
flock;
9 therefore, you shepherds, hear the
word of the LORD:
10 'Thus says the Lord GOD, "Behold, I
am [a]against the shepherds, and I will
demand My [1]sheep [2]from them and
make them [b]cease from feeding [1]sheep.
So the shepherds will not [3]feed themselves anymore, but I will [c]deliver My
flock from their mouth, so that they will
not be food for them." ' "

The Restoration of Israel

11 ¶ For thus says the Lord GOD, "Behold, I Myself will [a]search for My sheep
and seek them out.
12 "[a]As a shepherd [1]cares for his herd
in the day when he is among his scattered
[2]sheep, so I will [1b]care for My [2]sheep
and will deliver them from all the places
to which they were scattered on a
[c]cloudy and gloomy day.
13 "I will bring them out from the peoples and gather them from the countries
and bring them to their own land; and I
will [a]feed them on the mountains of Israel, by the [b]streams, and in all the inhabited places of the land.
14 "I will feed them in a [a]good pasture,
and their grazing ground will be on the
mountain heights of Israel. There they
will lie down on good grazing ground and
feed in [1b]rich pasture on the mountains
of Israel.
15 "I will [a]feed My flock and I will
[1]lead them to rest," declares the Lord
GOD.
16 "I will seek the lost, bring back the
scattered, bind up the broken and
strengthen the sick; but the [a]fat and the
strong I will destroy. I will [b]feed them
with judgment.
17 ¶ "As for you, My flock, thus says
the Lord GOD, 'Behold, I will [a]judge between one [1]sheep and another, between
the rams and the male goats.
18 'Is it too [a]slight a thing for you that
you should feed in the good pasture, that
you must tread down with your feet the

---

27 [1]Lit *surface of the field* [a]Jer 15:2; Ezek 5:12 [b]1 Sam 13:6; Is 2:19
28 [a]Ezek 5:14; Mic 7:13 [b]Ezek 7:24
30 [1]Lit *the sons of your people* [2]Lit *word* [a]Is 29:13; Ezek 14:3
31 [a]Ps 78:36; Is 29:13; 1 John 3:18 [b]Ezek 22:13; Luke 12:15
32 [a]Mark 6:20
33 [1]Lit *behold, it is coming* [a]Jer 28:9; Ezek 33:29
34:2 [1]Lit *them, the shepherds* [2]Heb *YHWH*, usually rendered *LORD*, and so throughout the ch [3]Lit *pasturing, pasture* [a]Jer 2:8 [b]Jer 23:1; Ezek 22:25; Mic 3:1-3 [c]Ps 78:71; Is 40:11; Ezek 34:14; John 10:11
3 [1]Lit *pasturing* [a]Zech 11:16 [b]Ezek 22:25
4 [1]Lit *sick* [a]Zech 11:16 [b]Matt 9:36; Luke 15:4
5 [a]Num 27:17; 2 Chr 18:16; Jer 10:21; Matt 9:36; Mark 6:34 [b]Ezek 34:8
6 [a]Jer 40:11; Ezek 7:16; 1 Pet 2:25 [b]John 10:16 [c]Ps 142:4
8 [a]Acts 20:29
10 [1]Or (a) *flock* [2]Lit *from their hand* [3]Lit *pasture*, and so throughout the ch [a]Jer 21:13; Ezek 5:8; Zech 10:3 [b]1 Sam 2:29; Jer 52:24-27 [c]Ps 72:12-14; Ezek 13:23
11 [a]Ezek 11:17
12 [1]Or *seek(s) out* [2]Or *flock* [a]Jer 31:10 [b]Is 40:11; Jer 23:3; Luke 19:10; John 10:16 [c]Jer 13:16; Ezek 30:3; Joel 2:2
13 [a]Ezek 34:23; Mic 7:14 [b]Is 30:25
14 [1]Lit *fat* [a]Ps 23:2; Jer 31:12-14; John 10:9 [b]Ezek 28:25
15 [1]Lit *cause them to lie down* [a]Ps 23:1; Ezek 34:23
16 [a]Is 10:16 [b]Is 49:26
17 [1]Or *lamb* [a]Ezek 20:38; Mal 4:1; Matt 25:32
18 [a]Num 16:9; 2 Sam 7:19; Is 7:13

rest of your pastures? Or that you should
drink of the clear waters, that you must
[1]foul the rest with your feet?
19 'As for My flock, they must eat what
you tread down with your feet and drink
what you [1]foul with your feet!' "
20 ¶ Therefore, thus says the Lord
GOD to them, "Behold, I, even I, will
judge between the fat sheep and the lean
sheep.
21 "Because you push with side and
with shoulder, and [a]thrust at all the
[1]weak with your horns until you have
scattered them [2]abroad,
22 therefore, I will [a]deliver My flock,
and they will no longer be a prey; and I
will judge between one sheep and another.
23 ¶ "Then I will [a]set over them one
[b]shepherd, My servant [c]David, and he
will feed them; he will feed them himself
and be their shepherd.
24 "And I, the LORD, will be their God,
and My servant [a]David will be prince
among them; I the LORD have spoken.
25 ¶ "I will make a [a]covenant of
peace with them and [b]eliminate harmful
beasts from the land so that they may
[c]live securely in the wilderness and
sleep in the woods.
26 "I will make them and the places
around My hill a [a]blessing. And I will
cause [b]showers to come down in their
season; they will be showers of [c]bless-
ing.
27 "Also the tree of the field will yield
its fruit and the earth will yield its increase, and they will be [a]secure on their
land. Then they will know that I am the
LORD, when I have [b]broken the bars of
their yoke and have delivered them from
the hand of those who enslaved them.
28 "They will no longer be a prey to the
nations, and the beasts of the earth will
not devour them; but they will [a]live securely, and no one will make *them* afraid.
29 "I will establish for them a [a]re-
nowned planting place, and they will
[b]not again be [1]victims of famine in the
land, and they will not [c]endure the insults of the nations anymore.
30 "Then they will know that [a]I, the
LORD their God, am with them, and that
they, the house of Israel, are My people,"
declares the Lord GOD.
31 "As for you, My [a]sheep, the [b]sheep
of My pasture, you are men, and I am
your God," declares the Lord GOD.

Prophecy against Mount Seir

35 Moreover, the word of the LORD
came to me saying,
2 "Son of man, set your face against
[a]Mount Seir, and prophesy against it
3 and say to it, 'Thus says the
Lord [1]GOD,
"Behold, I am against you, Mount
Seir,
And I will [a]stretch out My hand
against you
And make you a [b]desolation and
a waste.
4 "I will [a]lay waste your cities
And you will become a
desolation.
Then you will know that I am
the LORD.
5 "Because you have had everlasting
[a]enmity and have [1]delivered the sons of
Israel to the power of the sword at the
time of their calamity, at the time of the
[2b]punishment of the end,
6 therefore as I live," declares the
Lord GOD, "I will [1]give you over to
[a]bloodshed, and bloodshed will pursue
you; since you have not hated bloodshed,
therefore bloodshed will pursue you.
7 "I will make Mount Seir a waste and
a desolation and I will cut off from it the
one who passes through and returns.
8 "I will [a]fill its mountains with its
slain; on your hills and in your valleys and
in all your ravines those slain by the
sword will [1]fall.
9 "I will make you an everlasting
[a]desolation and your cities will not be
inhabited. Then you will know that I am
the LORD.
10 ¶ "Because you have [a]said, 'These
two nations and these two lands will be
mine, and we will possess [1]them,' although the [b]LORD was there,
11 therefore as I live," declares the
Lord GOD, "I will deal *with you* [a]accord-
ing to your anger and according to your
envy which you showed because of your
hatred against them; so I will [b]make Myself known among them when I judge
you.
12 "Then you will know [1]that I, the
LORD, have heard all your revilings which
you have spoken against the mountains of
Israel saying, 'They are laid desolate; they
are [a]given to us for food.'
13 "And you have [1a]spoken arrogantly
against Me and have multiplied your
words against Me; [b]I have heard *it*."
14 'Thus says the Lord GOD, "As all the
[a]earth rejoices, I will make you a desolation.
15 "As you [a]rejoiced over the inheritance of the house of Israel because it was
desolate, [b]so I will do to you. You will
be a [c]desolation, O Mount Seir, and all
Edom, all of it. Then they will know that
I am the LORD." '

18 [1]Lit *foul by trampling*
19 [1]Lit *foul by trampling*
21 [1]Or *sick* [2]Lit *to the outside* [a]Deut 33:17; Dan 8:4; Luke 13:14-16
22 [a]Ps 72:12-14; Jer 23:3; Ezek 34:10
23 [a]Rev 7:17 [b]Is 40:11; John 10:11 [c]Jer 30:9; Ezek 37:24
24 [a]Is 55:3; Jer 30:9; Ezek 37:24; Hos 3:5
25 [a]Ezek 16:60 [b]Job 5:22; Is 11:6-9 [c]Jer 33:16; Ezek 28:26
26 [a]Gen 12:2; Ezek 34:14 [b]Deut 11:13-15 [c]Lev 25:21; Is 44:3
27 [a]Ezek 38:8 [b]Lev 26:13; Is 52:2; Jer 30:8
28 [a]Jer 30:10; Ezek 39:26
29 [1]Lit *those gathered* [a]Is 4:2 [b]Ezek 34:26 [c]Ezek 36:6
30 [a]Ps 46:7; Ezek 14:11
31 [a]Ps 78:52; Ezek 36:38 [b]Ps 100:3; Jer 23:1
35:2 [a]Gen 36:8; Ezek 25:12
3 [1]Heb *YHWH,* usually rendered *LORD,* and so throughout the ch [a]Jer 6:12; Ezek 25:13 [b]Jer 49:13; Ezek 35:7
4 [a]Ezek 6:6; Mal 1:3
5 [1]Lit *poured* [2]Or *iniquity* [a]Ps 137:7; Ezek 25:12; Amos 1:11; Obad 10 [b]Ezek 7:2
6 [1]Lit *prepare you for* [a]Is 63:2-6; Ezek 16:38
8 [1]Lit *fall in them* [a]Is 34:5; Ezek 31:12
9 [a]Jer 49:13; Ezek 25:13
10 [1]Lit *it* [a]Ps 83:4-12; Ezek 36:2 [b]Ps 48:1-3; Is 12:6; Ezek 48:35; Zeph 3:15
11 [a]Ps 137:7; Ezek 25:14; Amos 1:11 [b]Ps 9:16
12 [1]Or *that I am the LORD: I have heard* [a]Jer 50:7; Ezek 36:2
13 [1]Lit *made great with your mouth* [a]Is 10:13; Jer 48:26; Dan 11:36 [b]Jer 7:11
14 [a]Is 44:23; Jer 51:48
15 [a]Jer 50:11; Lam 4:21 [b]Obad 15 [c]Is 34:5; Ezek 35:3

The Mountains of Israel to Be Blessed

36 "And you, son of man, prophesy to the mountains of Israel and say, 'O mountains of Israel, hear the word of the LORD.

2 'Thus says the Lord [1]GOD, "Because the enemy has spoken against you, 'Aha!' and, 'The everlasting [2a]heights have become our possession,'

3 therefore prophesy and say, 'Thus says the Lord GOD, "[1]For good reason they have made you [a]desolate and crushed you from every side, that you would become a possession of the rest of the nations and you have been taken up in the [2b]talk and the whispering of the people." ' "

4 'Therefore, O [a]mountains of Israel, hear the word of the Lord GOD. Thus says the Lord GOD to the mountains and to the hills, to the ravines and to the valleys, to the desolate wastes and to the forsaken cities which have become a [b]prey and a derision to the rest of the nations which are round about,

5 therefore thus says the Lord GOD, "Surely in the fire of My [a]jealousy I have spoken against the [b]rest of the nations, and against all Edom, who [1]appropriated My land for themselves as a possession with wholehearted [c]joy *and* with scorn of soul, to drive it out for a prey."

6 'Therefore prophesy concerning the land of Israel and say to the mountains and to the hills, to the ravines and to the valleys, "Thus says the Lord GOD, 'Behold, I have spoken in My jealousy and in My wrath because you have [a]endured the insults of the nations.'

7 "Therefore thus says the Lord GOD, 'I have [1]sworn that surely the nations which are around you will themselves endure their insults.

8 'But you, O mountains of Israel, you will [a]put forth your branches and bear your fruit for My people Israel; for they will soon come.

9 'For, behold, I am for you, and I will turn to you, and you will be [b]cultivated and sown.

10 'I will multiply men on you, [a]all the house of Israel, all of it; and the [b]cities will be inhabited and the waste places will be rebuilt.

11 'I will multiply on you man and beast; and they will increase and be fruitful; and I will cause you to be inhabited as you were [a]formerly and will [1]treat you [b]better than at the first. Thus you will know that I am the LORD.

12 'Yes, I will cause [a]men—My people Israel—to walk on you and possess you, so that you will become their [b]inheritance and never again [c]bereave them of children.'

13 ¶ "Thus says the Lord GOD, 'Because they say to you, "You are a [a]devourer of men and have bereaved your [1]nation of children,"

14 therefore you will no longer devour men and no longer bereave your nation of children,' declares the Lord GOD.

15 "I will not let you hear [a]insults from the nations anymore, nor will you bear [b]disgrace from the peoples any longer, nor will you cause your nation to [c]stumble any longer," declares the Lord GOD.' "

16 ¶ Then the word of the LORD came to me saying,

17 "Son of man, when the house of Israel was living in their own land, they [a]defiled it by their ways and their deeds; their way before Me was like [b]the uncleanness of a woman in her impurity.

18 "Therefore I [a]poured out My wrath on them for the blood which they had shed on the land, because they had defiled it with their idols.

19 "Also I [a]scattered them among the nations and they were dispersed throughout the lands. [b]According to their ways and their deeds I judged them.

20 "When they came to the nations where they went, they [a]profaned My holy name, because it was said of them, 'These are the [b]people of the LORD; yet they have come out of His land.'

21 "But I had [1]concern for My [a]holy name, which the house of Israel had profaned among the nations where they went.

Israel to Be Renewed for His Name's Sake

22 ¶ "Therefore say to the house of Israel, 'Thus says the Lord GOD, "It is [a]not for your sake, O house of Israel, that I am about to act, but for My holy name, which you have profaned among the nations where you went.

23 "I will [a]vindicate the holiness of My great name which has been profaned among the nations, which you have profaned in their midst. Then the [b]nations will know that I am the LORD," declares the Lord GOD, "when I prove Myself holy among you in their sight.

24 "For I will [a]take you from the nations, gather you from all the lands and bring you into your own land.

25 "Then I will [a]sprinkle clean water on you, and you will be clean; I will cleanse you from all your [b]filthiness and from all your [c]idols.

36:2 [1]Heb *YHWH,* usually rendered *LORD,* and so throughout the ch [2]Heb *Bamoth* [a]Deut 32:13; Ps 78:69; Is 58:14; Hab 3:19
3 [1]Lit *Because;* or *By the cause* [2]Lit *lip of the tongue* [a]Jer 2:15 [b]Ps 44:13,14; Jer 18:16; Ezek 35:13
4 [a]Deut 11:11; Ezek 36:1,6,8 [b]Ezek 34:8,28
5 [1]Lit *gave* [a]Ezek 5:13; 36:6; 38:19 [b]Jer 25:9,15-29; Ezek 36:3 [c]Jer 50:11; Ezek 35:15; Mic 7:8
6 [a]Ps 74:10; 123:3,4; Ezek 34:29
7 [1]Lit *lifted up My hand*
8 [a]Is 4:2; 27:6; Ezek 17:23; 34:26-29
9 [a]Lev 26:9 [b]Ezek 28:26; 34:14; 36:34
10 [a]Is 27:6; 49:17-23; Ezek 37:21,22 [b]Jer 31:27,28; 33:12; Ezek 36:33
11 [1]Lit *cause good* [a]Jer 30:18; Ezek 16:55; Mic 7:14 [b]Job 42:12; Is 51:3
12 [a]Ezek 34:13, 14 [b]Ezek 47:14 [c]Jer 15:7; Ezek 22:12,27
13 [1]Or *nations,* and so throughout the ch [a]Num 13:32
15 [a]Is 60:14; Ezek 34:29; 36:7 [b]Ps 89:50; Is 54:4; Ezek 22:4 [c]Is 63:13; Jer 13:16; 18:15
17 [a]Jer 2:7 [b]Lev 15:19
18 [a]2 Chr 34:21,25; Lam 2:4; 4:11; Ezek 22:20,22
19 [a]Deut 28:64; Ezek 5:12; 22:15; Amos 9:9 [b]Ezek 24:14; 39:24; Rom 2:6
20 [a]Is 52:5; Ezek 12:16; Rom 2:24 [b]Jer 33:24
21 [1]Lit *compassion* [a]Ps 74:18; Is 48:9; Ezek 20:44
22 [a]Deut 7:7,8; 9:5,6; Ezek 36:32
23 [a]Is 5:16; Ezek 20:41; 38:23; 39:7,25 [b]Ps 102:15; 126:2
24 [a]Is 43:5,6; Ezek 34:13; 37:21
25 [a]Num 19:17-19; Ps 51:7; Titus 3:5, 6; Heb 9:13,19; 10:22 [b]Is 4:4; Zech 13:1 [c]Is 2:18,20; Hos 14:3,8

26 "Moreover, I will give you a [a]new
heart and put a new spirit within you;
and I will remove the [b]heart of stone
from your flesh and give you a heart of
flesh.
27 "I will [a]put My Spirit within you
and cause you to walk in My statutes, and
you will be careful to observe My ordinances.
28 "You will live in the land that I gave
to your forefathers; so you will be [a]My
people, and I will be your God.
29 "Moreover, I will save you from all
your uncleanness; and I will call for the
grain and multiply it, and I [a]will not
[1]bring a famine on you.
30 "I will [a]multiply the fruit of the tree
and the produce of the field, so that you
will not receive again the disgrace of famine among the nations.
31 "Then you will [a]remember your evil
ways and your deeds that were not good,
and you will loathe yourselves in your
own sight for your iniquities and your
abominations.
32 "I am not doing *this* [a]for your sake,"
declares the Lord GOD, "let it be known
to you. Be ashamed and confounded for
your ways, O house of Israel!"
33 ¶ 'Thus says the Lord GOD, "On the
day that I cleanse you from all your iniquities, I will cause the [a]cities to be inhabited, and the [b]waste places will be rebuilt.
34 "The desolate land will be cultivated
instead of being a desolation in the sight
of everyone who passes by.
35 "They will say, 'This desolate land
has become like the [a]garden of Eden;
and the waste, desolate and ruined cities
are fortified *and* inhabited.'
36 "Then the nations that are left round
about you will know that I, the LORD,
have rebuilt the ruined places *and* planted that which was desolate; I, the LORD,
have spoken and [a]will do it."
37 ¶ 'Thus says the Lord GOD, "This
also I will let the house of Israel ask Me
to do for them: I will increase their men
like a flock.
38 "Like the [a]flock [1]for sacrifices, like
the flock at Jerusalem during her appointed feasts, so will the waste cities be filled
with [b]flocks of men. Then they will
know that I am the LORD." ' "

Vision of the Valley of Dry Bones

37 The [a]hand of the LORD was upon
me, and He [b]brought me out [1]by
the Spirit of the LORD and set me down in
the middle of the [c]valley; and it was full
of bones.
2 He caused me to pass among them
round about, and behold, *there were* very
many on the surface of the valley; and lo,
they were very dry.
3 He said to me, "Son of man, [a]can
these bones live?" And I answered,
"O Lord [1]GOD, [b]You know."
4 Again He said to me, "[a]Prophesy
over these bones and say to them, 'O dry
bones, [b]hear the word of the LORD.'
5 "Thus says the Lord GOD to these
bones, 'Behold, I will cause [1a]breath to
enter you that you may come to life.
6 'I will put sinews on you, make flesh
grow back on you, cover you with skin
and put breath in you that you may come
alive; and you will [a]know that I am the
LORD.' "
7 ¶ So I prophesied [a]as I was commanded; and as I prophesied, there was a
[1]noise, and behold, a rattling; and the
bones came together, bone to its bone.
8 And I looked, and behold, sinews
were on them, and flesh grew and skin
covered them; but there was no breath in
them.
9 Then He said to me, "Prophesy to
the breath, prophesy, son of man, and say
to the breath, 'Thus says the Lord GOD,
"Come from the four winds, O breath,
and [a]breathe on these slain, that they
[b]come to life." ' "
10 So I prophesied as He commanded
me, and the [a]breath came into them, and
they came to life and stood on their feet,
an [b]exceedingly great army.

The Vision Explained

11 ¶ Then He said to me, "Son of man,
these bones are the [a]whole house of Israel; behold, they say, 'Our [b]bones are
dried up and our hope has perished. We
are [1]completely [c]cut off.'
12 "Therefore prophesy and say to
them, 'Thus says the Lord GOD, "Behold,
I will open your graves and [a]cause you to
come up out of your graves, My people;
and I will bring you into the land of Israel.
13 "Then you will know that I am the
LORD, when I have opened your graves
and caused you to come up out of your
graves, My people.
14 "I will [a]put My [1]Spirit within you
and you will come to life, and I will place
you on your own land. Then you will
know that I, the LORD, have spoken and
done it," declares the LORD.' "

Reunion of Judah and Israel

15 ¶ The word of the LORD came again
to me saying,
16 "And you, son of man, take for yourself [a]one stick and write on it, 'For [b]Ju-
dah and for the sons of Israel, his companions'; then take another stick and write
on it, 'For [c]Joseph, the stick of Ephraim

26 [a]Ps 51:10; Ezek 11:19; 18:31; John 3:3, 5; 2 Cor 5:17 [b]Ezek 11:19; Zech 7:12
27 [a]Is 44:3; 59:21; Ezek 37:14; 39:29; Joel 2:28,29
28 [a]Ezek 14:11; 37:23,27
29 [1]Lit *put* [a]Ezek 34:27,29; Hos 2:21-23
30 [a]Lev 26:4; Ezek 34:27
31 [a]Ezek 16:61-63; 20:43
32 [a]Deut 9:5
33 [a]Ezek 36:10; Zech 8:7,8 [b]Is 58:12
35 [a]Is 51:3; Ezek 31:9; Joel 2:3
36 [a]Ezek 17:24; 22:14; 37:14; Hos 14:4-9
38 [1]Lit *of holy things* [a]1 Kin 8:63; 2 Chr 35:7-9; John 2:14 [b]Ps 74:1; 100:3; Jer 23:1; John 10:7,9,16
37:1 [1]Or *in* [a]Ezek 1:3; 33:22; 40:1 [b]Ezek 8:3; 11:24; 43:5; Acts 8:39 [c]Jer 7:32-8:2
3 [1]Heb *YHWH,* usually rendered LORD, and so throughout the ch [a]Ezek 26:19 [b]Deut 32:39; 1 Sam 2:6
4 [a]Ezek 37:9,12 [b]Jer 22:29; Ezek 36:1
5 [1]Or *spirit,* and so throughout the ch [a]Gen 2:7; Ps 104:29,30; Ezek 37:9,10,14
6 [a]Is 49:23; Ezek 35:9; 38:23; 39:6; Joel 2:27; 3:17
7 [1]Lit *voice;* or *thunder* [a]Jer 13:5-7
9 [a]Ps 104:30 [b]Hos 13:14
10 [a]Rev 11:11 [b]Jer 30:19; 33:22
11 [1]Lit *cut off to ourselves* [a]Jer 33:24; Ezek 36:10; 39:25 [b]Ps 141:7 [c]Ps 88:5; Lam 3:54
12 [a]Deut 32:39; 1 Sam 2:6; Is 26:19; 66:14; Hos 13:14
14 [1]Or *breath* [a]Is 32:15; Ezek 11:19; 36:27; 37:6,9; 39:29; Joel 2:28,29; Zech 12:10
16 [a]Num 17:2,3 [b]2 Chr 10:17; 11:11-17; 15:9 [c]1 Kin 12:16-20; 2 Chr 10:19

and all the house of Israel, his companions.'
17 "Then [a]join them for yourself one to
another into one stick, that they may become one in your hand.
18 "When the sons of your people
speak to you saying, 'Will you not declare
to us [a]what you mean by these?'
19 say to them, 'Thus says the Lord
GOD, "Behold, I will take the stick of Joseph, which is in the hand of Ephraim,
and the tribes of Israel, his companions;
and I will put them with it, with the stick
of Judah, and make them one stick, and
they will be one in My hand." '
20 "The sticks on which you write will
be in your hand before their eyes.
21 "Say to them, 'Thus says the Lord
GOD, "Behold, I will [a]take the sons of
Israel from among the nations where they
have gone, and I will gather them from
every side and bring them into their own
land;
22 and I will make them [a]one nation
in the land, on the mountains of Israel;
and [b]one king will be king for all of them;
and they will no longer be two nations
and no longer be divided into two kingdoms.
23 "They will [a]no longer defile themselves with their idols, or with their detestable things, or with any of their transgressions; but [b]I will deliver them from
all their [1]dwelling places in which they
have sinned, and will cleanse them. And
they will be My people, and I will be their
God.

The Davidic Kingdom

24 ¶ "My servant [a]David will be king
over them, and they will all have [b]one
shepherd; and they will walk in My ordinances and keep My statutes and observe
them.
25 "They will live on the land that I
gave to Jacob My servant, in which your
fathers lived; and they will live on it,
they, and their sons and their sons' sons,
forever; and [a]David My servant will be
their prince forever.
26 "I will make a [a]covenant of peace
with them; it will be an [b]everlasting covenant with them. And I will [1]place them
and [c]multiply them, and will set My
[d]sanctuary in their midst forever.
27 "My [a]dwelling place also will be
with them; and [b]I will be their God, and
they will be My people.
28 "And the nations will know that I am
the LORD [a]who sanctifies Israel, when
My sanctuary is in their midst forever." ' "

17 [a]Is 11:13; Jer 50:4; Ezek 37:22-24; Hos 1:11; Zeph 3:9
18 [a]Ezek 12:9
21 [a]Is 43:5; Jer 29:14; Ezek 36:24; Amos 9:14
22 [a]Jer 3:18; Ezek 36:10 [b]Ezek 34:23
23 [1]Another reading is *backslidings* [a]Ezek 36:25 [b]Ezek 36:28
24 [a]Jer 30:9; Ezek 34:24; Hos 3:5 [b]Ps 78:71; Is 40:11; Ezek 34:23
25 [a]Is 11:1; Ezek 37:24; Zech 6:12
26 [1]Lit *give* [a]Ezek 16:62 [b]Ps 89:3; Is 55:3; Ezek 16:60 [c]Jer 30:19; Ezek 36:10 [d]Ezek 20:40
27 [a]John 1:14; Rev 21:3 [b]Ezek 37:23; 2 Cor 6:16
28 [a]Ex 31:13; Ezek 20:12
38:2 [1]Or *chief prince of Meshech* [a]Ezek 38:3; Rev 20:8 [b]Gen 10:2; Ezek 39:6; Rev 20:8 [c]Ezek 38:3 [d]Ezek 27:13
3 [1]Heb *YHWH,* usually rendered LORD, and so throughout the ch [2]Or *chief prince of Meshech*
4 [1]Or *clothed in full armor* [a]Is 43:17 [b]Ezek 38:15; Dan 11:40
5 [1]Lit *Cush* [a]2 Chr 36:20; Ezra 1:1; Ezek 27:10; Dan 8:20 [b]Gen 10:6-8; Ezek 30:4 [c]Ezek 27:10
6 [a]Gen 10:2 [b]Gen 10:3; Ezek 27:14
7 [a]Is 8:9
8 [1]Lit *peoples* [2]Lit *it was* [a]Is 24:22 [b]Is 11:11; Ezek 36:24 [c]Ezek 34:13 [d]Ezek 38:11
9 [a]Is 5:28; Jer 4:13 [b]Ezek 30:18; Joel 2:2
10 [1]Lit *words* [a]Ps 36:4; Mic 2:1
11 [1]Or *open country* [a]Zech 2:4 [b]Jer 49:31
12 [1]Lit *navel* [a]Is 10:6; Ezek 29:19
13 [1]Or *young lions* [a]Ezek 27:22 [b]Ezek 25:13 [c]Ezek 27:12 [d]Is 10:6; Jer 15:13

Prophecy about Gog and Future Invasion of Israel

38 And the word of the LORD came to
me saying,
2 "Son of man, set your face toward
[a]Gog of the land of [b]Magog, the [1]prince
of [c]Rosh, [d]Meshech and [d]Tubal, and
prophesy against him
3 and say, 'Thus says the Lord [1]GOD,
"Behold, I am against you, O Gog,
[2]prince of Rosh, Meshech and Tubal.
4 "I will turn you about and put hooks
into your jaws, and I will [a]bring you out,
and all your army, [b]horses and horsemen, all of them [1]splendidly attired, a
great company *with* buckler and shield,
all of them wielding swords;
5 [a]Persia, [1b]Ethiopia and [c]Put with
them, all of them *with* shield and helmet;
6 [a]Gomer with all its troops; [b]Beth-
togarmah *from* the remote parts of the
north with all its troops—many peoples
with you.
7 ¶ "[a]Be prepared, and prepare
yourself, you and all your companies that
are assembled about you, and be a guard
for them.
8 "[a]After many days you will be summoned; in the latter years you will come
into the land that is restored from the
sword, *whose inhabitants* have been
[b]gathered from many [1]nations to the
[c]mountains of Israel which had been a
continual waste; but [2]its people were
brought out from the [1]nations, and they
are [d]living securely, all of them.
9 "You will go up, you will come [a]like
a storm; you will be like a [b]cloud covering the land, you and all your troops, and
many peoples with you."
10 ¶ 'Thus says the Lord GOD, "It will
come about on that day, that [1]thoughts
will come into your mind and you will
[a]devise an evil plan,
11 and you will say, 'I will go up
against the land of [1a]unwalled villages.
I will go against those who are [b]at rest,
that live securely, all of them living without walls and having no bars or gates,
12 to [a]capture spoil and to seize plunder, to turn your hand against the waste
places which are *now* inhabited, and
against the people who are gathered from
the nations, who have acquired cattle and
goods, who live at the [1]center of the
world.'
13 "[a]Sheba and [b]Dedan and the merchants of [c]Tarshish with all its [1]villages
will say to you, 'Have you come to capture spoil? Have you assembled your company to seize plunder, to carry away silver and gold, to take away cattle and
goods, to capture great [d]spoil?' " '

14 ¶ "Therefore prophesy, son of man,
and say to Gog, 'Thus says the Lord GOD,
"On that day when My people Israel are
[a]living securely, will you not know *it?*
15 "[a]You will come from your place out
of the remote parts of the north, you and
many peoples with you, all of them riding
on horses, a great assembly and a mighty
army;
16 and you will come up against My
people Israel like a cloud to cover the
land. It shall come about in the last days
that I will bring you against My land, so
that the nations may [a]know Me when I
am [b]sanctified through you before their
eyes, O Gog."
17 ¶ 'Thus says the Lord GOD, "Are
you the one of whom I spoke in former
days through My servants the prophets of
Israel, who [a]prophesied in those days for
many years that I would bring you against
them?
18 "It will come about on that day,
when Gog comes against the land of Israel," declares the Lord GOD, "that My fury
will mount up in My [a]anger.
19 "In My [a]zeal and in My blazing
wrath I declare *that* on that day there will
surely be a great [1b]earthquake in the
land of Israel.
20 "[a]The fish of the sea, the birds of
the heavens, the beasts of the field, all the
creeping things that creep on the earth,
and all the men who are on the face of the
earth will shake at My presence; the
[b]mountains also will be thrown down,
the steep pathways will [1]collapse and every wall will fall to the ground.
21 "I will call for a [a]sword against
[1]him on all My mountains," declares the
Lord GOD. "[b]Every man's sword will be
against his brother.
22 "With pestilence and with blood I
will enter into [a]judgment with him; and
I will rain on him and on his troops, and
on the many peoples who are with him,
[1]a torrential rain, with [b]hailstones, fire
and brimstone.
23 "I will magnify Myself, sanctify Myself, and [a]make Myself known in the
sight of many nations; and they will know
that I am the LORD."'

Prophecy against Gog—Invaders Destroyed

39 "And [a]you, son of man, prophesy
against Gog and say, 'Thus says
the Lord [1]GOD, "Behold, I am against
you, O Gog, [2]prince of Rosh, Meshech
and Tubal;
2 and I will turn you around, drive
you on, take you up from the remotest
parts of the north and bring you against
the mountains of Israel.
3 "I will [a]strike your bow from your
left hand and dash down your arrows
from your right hand.
4 "You will [a]fall on the mountains of
Israel, you and all your troops and the
peoples who are with you; I will give you
as [b]food to every [1]kind of predatory bird
and beast of the field.
5 "You will fall on the [1]open field; for
it is I who have spoken," declares the
Lord GOD.
6 "And I will send [a]fire upon Magog
and those who inhabit the [b]coastlands in
safety; and they will know that I am the
LORD.
7 ¶ "My [a]holy name I will make
known in the midst of My people Israel;
and I will not let My holy name be [b]pro-
faned anymore. And the [c]nations will
know that I am the LORD, the [d]Holy One
in Israel.
8 "Behold, it is coming and it shall be
done," declares the Lord GOD. "That is
the day of which I have spoken.
9 ¶ "Then those who inhabit the cities of Israel will [a]go out and make [b]fires
with the weapons and burn *them,* both
shields and bucklers, bows and arrows,
war clubs and spears, and for seven years
they will make fires of them.
10 "They will not take wood from the
field or gather firewood from the forests,
for they will make fires with the weapons; and they will take the spoil of those
who despoiled them and seize the [a]plun-
der of those who plundered them," declares the Lord GOD.
11 ¶ "On that day I will give Gog a
burial ground there in Israel, the valley of
those who pass by east of the sea, and it
will block off those who would pass by.
So they will bury Gog there with all his
[1]horde, and they will call *it* the valley of
[2]Hamon-gog.
12 "For seven months the house of Israel will be burying them in order to
[a]cleanse the land.
13 "Even all the people of the land will
bury *them;* and it will be [1]to their [a]re-
nown *on* the day that I [b]glorify Myself,"
declares the Lord GOD.
14 "They will set apart men who will
constantly pass through the land, [a]bury-
ing those who were passing through,
even those left on the surface of the
ground, in order to cleanse it. At the end
of seven months they will make a search.
15 "As those who pass through the land
pass through and anyone sees a man's
bone, then he will [1]set up a marker by it
until the buriers have buried it in the
valley of [2]Hamon-gog.

14 [a]Jer 23:6; Ezek 38:8,11; Zech 2:5,8
15 [a]Ezek 39:2
16 [a]Ps 83:18; Ezek 36:23; 38:23 [b]Is 5:16; 8:13; 29:23; Ezek 28:22
17 [a]Is 5:26-29; 34:1-6; 63:1-6; 66:15,16; Joel 3:9-14
18 [a]Ps 18:8,15
19 [1]Or *shaking* [a]Deut 32:22; Ps 18:7,8; Ezek 5:13; 36:5,6; Nah 1:2; Heb 12:29 [b]Joel 3:16; Hag 2:6,7, 21
20 [1]Lit *fall* [a]Jer 4:24,25; Hos 4:3; Nah 1:4-6 [b]Zech 14:4
21 [1]I.e. Gog [a]Ezek 14:17 [b]Judg 7:22; 1 Sam 14:20; 2 Chr 20:23; Hag 2:22
22 [1]Lit *an overflowing* [a]Is 66:16; Jer 25:31 [b]Ps 11:6; 18:12-14; Is 28:17
23 [a]Ps 9:16; Ezek 37:28; 38:16
39:1 [1]Heb *YHWH,* usually rendered *LORD,* and so throughout the ch [2]Or *chief prince of Meshech* [a]Ezek 38:2
3 [a]Ps 76:3; Jer 21:4,5; Ezek 30:21-24; Hos 1:5
4 [1]Lit *wing* [a]Is 14:24,25; Ezek 39:17-20 [b]Ezek 29:5; 32:4,5; 33:27
5 [1]Lit *face of the*
6 [a]Ezek 30:8,16; 38:19,22; Amos 1:4,7,10; Nah 1:6 [b]Ps 72:10; Is 66:19; Jer 25:22
7 [a]Ezek 36:20-22; 39:25 [b]Ex 20:7; Ezek 20:9,14,39 [c]Ezek 38:16,23 [d]Is 12:6; 43:3, 14; 55:5; 60:9, 14
9 [a]Is 66:24; Mal 1:5 [b]Josh 11:6; Ps 46:9
10 [a]Is 14:2; 33:1; Mic 5:8; Hab 2:8
11 [1]Lit *crowd* [2]Or *the multitude of Gog*
12 [a]Deut 21:23; Ezek 39:14,16
13 [1]Or *a memorial for them* [a]Jer 33:9; Zeph 3:19, 20 [b]Ezek 28:22
14 [a]Jer 14:16
15 [1]Lit *build* [2]Or *the multitude of Gog*

16 "And even *the* name of *the* city will
be Hamonah. So they will cleanse the
land." '
17 ¶ "As for you, son of man, thus says
the Lord GOD, 'Speak to every [1]kind of
[a]bird and to every [a]beast of the field,
"Assemble and come, gather from every
side to My sacrifice which I am going to
[b]sacrifice for you, as a great sacrifice on
the mountains of Israel, that you may eat
flesh and drink blood.
18 "You will [a]eat the flesh of mighty
men and drink the blood of the princes of
the earth, as *though they were* [b]rams,
lambs, goats and [c]bulls, all of them fatlings of [d]Bashan.
19 "So you will eat fat until you are glutted, and drink blood until you are drunk,
from My sacrifice which I have sacrificed
for you.
20 "You will be glutted at My table with
[a]horses and charioteers, with mighty
men and all the men of war," declares the
Lord GOD.
21 ¶ "And I will set My [a]glory among
the nations; and all the nations will see
My judgment which I have executed and
My hand which I have laid on them.
22 "And the house of Israel will [a]know
that I am the LORD their God from that
day onward.
23 "The nations will know that the
house of Israel went into exile for their
[a]iniquity because they acted treacherously against Me, and I [b]hid My face
from them; so I gave them into the hand
of their adversaries, and all of them fell by
the sword.
24 "[a]According to their uncleanness
and according to their transgressions I
dealt with them, and I hid My face from
them." ' "

Israel Restored

25 ¶ Therefore thus says the Lord
GOD, "Now I will [1a]restore the fortunes
of Jacob and have mercy on the whole
[b]house of Israel; and I will be [c]jealous
for My holy name.
26 "They will [1a]forget their disgrace
and all their treachery which they [2]per-
petrated against Me, when they [b]live securely on their *own* land with [c]no one to
make *them* afraid.
27 "When I [a]bring them back from the
peoples and gather them from the lands
of their enemies, then I shall be [b]sancti-
fied [1]through them in the sight of the
many nations.
28 "Then they will know that I am the
LORD their God because I made them go
into exile among the nations, and then
gathered them *again* to their own land;
and I will leave none of them there any
longer.
29 "I will not hide My face from them
any longer, for I will have [a]poured out
My Spirit on the house of Israel," declares
the Lord GOD.

Vision of the Man with a Measuring Rod

40 In the [a]twenty-fifth year of our
exile, at the beginning of the
year, on the tenth of the month, in the
fourteenth year after the [b]city was
[1]taken, on that same day the [c]hand of
the LORD was upon me and He brought
me there.
2 In the [a]visions of God He brought
me into the land of Israel and set me on
a very [b]high mountain, and on it [c]to the
south *there was* a [d]structure like a city.
3 So He brought me there; and behold, there was a man whose appearance
was like the appearance of [a]bronze, with
a [b]line of flax and a [c]measuring [1]rod in
his hand; and he was standing in the gateway.
4 The man said to me, "[a]Son of man,
[b]see with your eyes, hear with your ears,
and give attention to all that I am going to
show you; for you have been brought
here in order to show *it* to you. [c]Declare
to the house of Israel all that you see."

Measurements Relating to the Temple

5 ¶ And behold, there was a [a]wall on
the outside of the [1]temple all around,
and in the man's hand was a measuring
rod of six cubits, *each of which was* a
cubit and a [2]handbreadth. So he measured the thickness of the [3]wall, one rod;
and the height, one rod.
6 Then he went to the gate which
faced [a]east, went up its steps and measured the threshold of the gate, one rod
[1]in width; and the other threshold *was*
one rod [1]in width.
7 The [a]guardroom *was* one rod long
and one rod wide; and *there were* five
cubits between the guardrooms. And the
threshold of the gate by the porch of the
gate [1]facing inward *was* one rod.
8 Then he measured the porch of the
gate [1]facing inward, one rod.
9 He measured the porch of the gate,
eight cubits; and its side pillars, two cubits. And the porch of the gate was
[1]faced inward.
10 The guardrooms of the gate toward
the east *numbered* three on each side;
the three of them had the same measurement. The side pillars also had the same
measurement on each side.

17 [1]Lit *wing* [a]Is 56:9; Jer 12:9; Ezek 39:4; Rev 19:17,18 [b]Is 34:6,7; Jer 46:10; Zeph 1:7
18 [a]Ezek 29:5; Rev 19:18 [b]Jer 51:40 [c]Jer 50:27 [d]Ps 22:12; Amos 4:1
20 [a]Ps 76:5,6; Ezek 38:4; Hag 2:22; Rev 19:18
21 [a]Ex 9:16; Is 37:20; Ezek 36:23; 38:16,23; 39:13
22 [a]Jer 24:7
23 [a]Jer 22:8,9; 44:22; Ezek 36:18,19 [b]Is 1:15; 59:2; Ezek 39:29
24 [a]2 Kin 17:7; Jer 2:17,19; 4:18; Ezek 36:19
25 [1]Or *return the captivity* [a]Is 27:12,13; Jer 33:7; Ezek 34:13 [b]Jer 31:1; Ezek 36:10; 37:21,22; Hos 1:11 [c]Ex 20:5; Nah 1:2
26 [1]Another reading is *bear* [2]Lit *did treacherously* [a]Ezek 16:63; 20:43; 36:31 [b]1 Kin 4:25; Ezek 34:25-28 [c]Is 17:2; Mic 4:4
27 [1]Lit *in* [a]Ezek 36:24; 37:21 [b]Ezek 36:23; 38:16,23
29 [a]Is 32:15; Ezek 36:27; 37:14; Joel 2:28
40:1 [1]Lit *struck* [a]Ezek 32:1,17; 33:21 [b]2 Kin 25:1-7; Jer 39:1-9; 52:4-11; Ezek 33:21 [c]Ezek 1:3; 3:14, 22; 37:1
2 [a]Ezek 1:1; 8:3; Dan 7:1,7 [b]Is 2:2,3; Ezek 17:23; 20:40; 37:22; Mic 4:1; Rev 21:10 [c]Ps 48:2; Is 14:13 [d]1 Chr 28:12,19
3 [1]Lit *reed,* and so throughout the ch [a]Ezek 1:7; Dan 10:6; Rev 1:15 [b]Ezek 47:3; Zech 2:1,2 [c]Rev 11:1; 21:15
4 [a]Ezek 2:1,3,6, 8; 44:5 [b]Ezek 2:7,8; 44:5 [c]Is 21:10; Jer 26:2; Acts 20:27
5 [1]Lit *house* [2]I.e. 204 in. [3]Lit *building* [a]Is 26:1; Ezek 42:20
6 [1]Or *in depth* [a]Ezek 8:16; 11:1; 40:20; 43:1
7 [1]Lit *from the house* [a]Ezek 40:10-16,21,29, 33,36
8 [1]Lit *from the house*
9 [1]Lit *from the house*

11 And he measured the width of the [1]gateway, ten cubits, and the length of the gate, thirteen cubits.

12 *There was* a [1]barrier *wall* one cubit *wide* in front of the guardrooms on each side; and the guardrooms *were* six cubits *square* on each side.

13 He measured the gate from the roof of the one guardroom to the roof of the other, a width of twenty-five cubits from *one* door to *the* door opposite.

14 He made the side pillars sixty cubits *high;* the gate *extended* round about to the side pillar of the [a]courtyard.

15 *From* the front of the entrance gate to the front of the inner porch of the gate *was* fifty cubits.

16 *There were* [1a]shuttered windows *looking* toward the guardrooms, and toward their side pillars within the gate all around, and likewise for the porches. And *there were* windows all around inside; and on *each* side pillar *were* [b]palm tree ornaments.

17 ¶ Then he brought me into the [a]outer court, and behold, *there were* [b]chambers and a pavement made for the court all around; thirty chambers [1]faced the pavement.

18 The pavement (*that is,* the lower pavement) *was* by the [1]side of the gates, corresponding to the length of the gates.

19 Then he measured the width from the front of the [a]lower gate to the front of the exterior of the inner court, a [b]hundred cubits on the east and on the north.

20 ¶ *As for* the [a]gate of the outer court which faced the north, he measured its length and its width.

21 [1]It had three [a]guardrooms on each side; and its [b]side pillars and its porches [2]had the same measurement as the first gate. Its length *was* [c]fifty cubits and the width [d]twenty-five cubits.

22 Its [a]windows and its porches and its palm tree ornaments *had* the same measurements as the [b]gate which faced toward the east; and [1]it was reached by seven [c]steps, and its [2]porch *was* in front of them.

23 The inner court had a gate opposite the gate on the north as well as *the gate* on the east; and he measured a [a]hundred cubits from gate to gate.

24 ¶ Then he led me toward the south, and behold, there was a [a]gate toward the south; and he measured its [b]side pillars and its porches according to [1]those same measurements.

25 [1]The gate and its porches had [a]windows all around like [2]those other windows; the length *was* [b]fifty cubits and the width twenty-five cubits.

26 *There were* seven [a]steps going up to it, and its porches *were* in front of them; and it had [b]palm tree ornaments on its side pillars, one on each side.

27 The inner court had a gate toward the [a]south; and he measured from gate to gate toward the south, a [b]hundred cubits.

28 ¶ Then he brought me to the inner court by the south gate; and he measured the south gate [a]according to those same measurements.

29 Its [a]guardrooms also, its side pillars and its [b]porches *were* according to those same measurements. And [1]the gate and its porches had [b]windows all around; it *was* [c]fifty cubits long and twenty-five cubits wide.

30 *There were* [a]porches all around, twenty-five cubits long and five cubits wide.

31 Its porches *were* toward the outer court; and [a]palm tree ornaments *were* on its side pillars, and its stairway *had* eight [b]steps.

32 ¶ He brought me into the [a]inner court toward the east. And he measured the gate [b]according to those same measurements.

33 Its [a]guardrooms also, its side pillars and its porches *were* according to those same measurements. And [1]the gate and its porches had [b]windows all around; it *was* [c]fifty cubits long and twenty-five cubits wide.

34 Its [a]porches *were* toward the outer court; and [a]palm tree ornaments *were* on its side pillars, on each side, and its stairway *had* eight [b]steps.

35 ¶ Then he brought me to the [a]north gate; and he measured *it* according to those same measurements,

36 *with* its [a]guardrooms, its side pillars and its [b]porches. And [1]the gate had [b]windows all around; the length *was* [c]fifty cubits and the width twenty-five cubits.

37 Its side pillars *were* toward the outer court; and [a]palm tree ornaments *were* on its side pillars on each side, and its stairway had eight [b]steps.

38 ¶ A [a]chamber with its doorway was by the side pillars at the gates; there they [b]rinse the burnt offering.

39 In the porch of the gate *were* two [a]tables on each side, on which to slaughter the [b]burnt offering, the sin offering and the guilt offering.

40 On the outer [1]side, [2]as one went up to the [3]gateway toward the north, *were* two tables; and on the other [1]side of the porch of the gate *were* two tables.

41 Four [a]tables *were* on each side [1]next to the gate; *or,* eight tables on which they slaughter *sacrifices.*

---

11 [1]Lit *entrance of the gate*
12 [1]Lit *border*
14 [a]Ex 27:9; 1 Chr 28:6; Ps 100:4; Is 62:9; Ezek 8:7
16 [1]Or *beveled inwards* [a]1 Kin 6:4; Ezek 41:16 [b]1 Kin 6:29; 2 Chr 3:5; Ezek 40:22
17 [1]Lit *to* [a]Ezek 10:5; Rev 11:2 [b]2 Kin 23:11; 1 Chr 9:26; 2 Chr 31:11; Ezek 40:38
18 [1]Lit *shoulder*
19 [a]Ezek 40:23 [b]Ezek 40:23
20 [a]Ezek 40:6
21 [1]Lit *its guardrooms were three* [2]Lit *were* [a]Ezek 40:7 [b]Ezek 40:16 [c]Ezek 40:15 [d]Ezek 40:13
22 [1]Lit *they were going up into it* [2]Or *porches* [a]Ezek 40:16 [b]Ezek 40:6 [c]Ezek 40:26
23 [a]Ezek 40:19
24 [1]Lit *these measurements,* and so throughout the ch [a]Ezek 40:6 [b]Ezek 40:21
25 [1]Lit *It* [2]Lit *these windows* [a]Ezek 40:16 [b]Ezek 40:21
26 [a]Ezek 40:6 [b]Ezek 40:16
27 [a]Ezek 40:23 [b]Ezek 40:19
28 [a]Ezek 40:32
29 [1]Lit *it* [a]Ezek 40:7 [b]Ezek 40:16 [c]Ezek 40:21
30 [a]Ezek 40:16
31 [a]Ezek 40:16 [b]Ezek 40:22
32 [a]Ezek 40:28-31 [b]Ezek 40:28
33 [1]Lit *it* [a]Ezek 40:29 [b]Ezek 40:16 [c]Ezek 40:21
34 [a]Ezek 40:16 [b]Ezek 40:22
35 [a]Ezek 40:27
36 [1]Lit *it* [a]Ezek 40:7 [b]Ezek 40:16 [c]Ezek 40:21
37 [a]Ezek 40:16 [b]Ezek 40:34
38 [a]1 Chr 28:12; Neh 13:5; Jer 35:4; Ezek 40:17 [b]2 Chr 4:6
39 [a]Ezek 40:42 [b]Lev 1:3-17; Ezek 46:2
40 [1]Lit *shoulder* [2]Lit *to the one going up* [3]Lit *entrance of the gate*
41 [1]Lit *by the shoulder of* [a]Ezek 40:39

42 For the burnt offering *there were*
four [a]tables of [b]hewn stone, a cubit and
a half long, a cubit and a half wide and
one cubit high, on which they lay the
instruments with which they slaughter
the [a]burnt offering and the sacrifice.
43 The double [1]hooks, one handbreadth in length, were installed [2]in the
house all around; and on the tables *was*
the flesh of the offering.
44 ¶ From the outside to the [a]inner
gate were [1b]chambers for the [c]singers
in the inner court, *one of* which was at
the [2]side of the north gate, with [3]its
front toward the south, and one at the
[2]side of the [4]south gate facing toward
the north.
45 He said to me, "This is the [a]cham-
ber which faces toward the south, *intended* for the priests who [b]keep charge of
the [1]temple;
46 but the [a]chamber which faces toward the north is for the priests who
[b]keep charge of the altar. These are the
[c]sons of Zadok, who from the sons of
Levi [d]come near to the LORD to minister
to Him."
47 He measured the court, a *perfect*
square, a [a]hundred cubits long and a
hundred cubits wide; and the altar was in
front of the [1]temple.
48 ¶ Then he brought me to the
[a]porch of the [1]temple and measured
each side pillar of the porch, five cubits
on each side; and the width of the gate
was three cubits on each side.
49 The length of the porch *was* twenty
cubits and the width eleven cubits; and at
the [a]stairway by which it was ascended
were [b]columns belonging to the side pillars, one on each side.

The Inner Temple

41 Then he [a]brought me to the
[1b]nave and measured the [c]side
pillars; six cubits wide on each side *was*
the width of the [2]side pillar.
2 The width of the entrance *was* ten
cubits and the [1]sides of the entrance
were five cubits on each side. And he
measured [2]the length of the nave, [a]forty
cubits, and the width, [a]twenty cubits.
3 Then he went [1a]inside and measured each [b]side pillar of the doorway,
two cubits, and the doorway, six cubits
high; and the width of the doorway, sev-
en cubits.
4 He measured its length, [a]twenty
cubits, and the width, twenty cubits, before the [b]nave; and he said to me, "This
is the [c]most holy *place.*"
5 ¶ Then he measured the wall of the
[1]temple, six cubits; and the width of the
[a]side chambers, four cubits, all around
about the house on every side.
6 [a]The side chambers were in three
stories, [1]one above another, and [2]thirty
in each story; and [3]the side chambers
[b]extended to the wall which *stood* on
[4]their inward side all around, that they
might be fastened, and not be fastened
into the wall of the temple *itself.*
7 The side chambers surrounding the
temple were wider at each successive story. Because the [a]structure surrounding
the temple went upward by stages on all
sides of the temple, therefore the width
of the temple *increased* as it went higher;
and thus one went up from the lowest
story to the highest by way of the [1]sec-
ond *story.*
8 I saw also that the house had a
raised [1]platform all around; the foundations of the side chambers were a full rod
of [a]six [2]long cubits *in height.*
9 The [1]thickness of the outer wall of
the side chambers *was* five cubits. But
the [a]free space between the side chambers belonging to the temple
10 and the *outer* [a]chambers *was*
twenty cubits in width all around the
temple on every side.
11 The [1]doorways of the [2]side chambers toward the [a]free space *consisted of*
one doorway toward the north and another doorway toward the south; and the
width of the [a]free space *was* five cubits
all around.
12 ¶ The [a]building that *was* in front of
the [b]separate area at the side toward the
west *was* seventy cubits wide; and the
wall of the building *was* five cubits [1]thick
all around, and its length *was* ninety cubits.
13 ¶ Then he measured the temple, a
[a]hundred cubits long; the [b]separate area
with the [c]building and its walls *were* also
a [a]hundred cubits long.
14 Also the width of the front of the
temple and *that of* the separate [1]areas
along the east *side totaled* a hundred cubits.
15 ¶ He measured the length of the
[a]building [1]along the front of the [b]sepa-
rate area behind it, with a [2c]gallery on
each side, a hundred cubits; *he* also *measured* the inner nave and the porches of
the court.
16 The [a]thresholds, the [1b]latticed
windows and the [2c]galleries round
about their [d]three stories, opposite the
threshold, were [e]paneled with wood all
around, and *from* the ground to the windows (but the windows were covered),
17 over the entrance, and to the inner
house, and on the outside, and on all the

42 [a]Ezek 40:39 [b]Ex 20:25
43 [1]Or *ledges* [2]Or *inside*
44 [1]Gr reads *in two chambers* [2]Lit *shoulder* [3]Lit *their* [4]Gr reads *east* [a]Ezek 40:23 [b]Ezek 40:17 [c]1 Chr 6:31
45 [1]Or *house* [a]Ezek 40:17 [b]1 Chr 9:23; Ps 134:1
46 [a]Ezek 40:17 [b]Lev 6:12; Ezek 44:15 [c]1 Kin 2:35; Ezek 43:19 [d]Lev 10:3; Num 16:5; Ezek 42:13
47 [1]Lit *house* [a]Ezek 40:19
48 [1]Lit *house* [a]1 Kin 6:3; 2 Chr 3:4
49 [a]Ezek 40:31 [b]1 Kin 7:15-22; 2 Chr 3:17; Jer 52:17-23; Rev 3:12
41:1 [1]I.e. the main inner hall [2]Lit *tent* [a]Ezek 40:2 [b]Ezek 41:21 [c]Ezek 40:9
2 [1]Lit *shoulders* [2]Lit *its length,* [a]1 Kin 6:2; 2 Chr 3:3
3 [1]I.e. of the inner sanctuary [a]Ezek 40:16 [b]Ezek 41:1
4 [a]1 Kin 6:20 [b]1 Kin 6:5 [c]Ex 26:33; 1 Kin 6:16; 2 Chr 5:7; Heb 9:3-8
5 [1]Lit *house,* and so throughout the ch [a]1 Kin 6:5; Ezek 41:6-11
6 [1]Lit *chamber upon chamber* [2]Lit *thirty times* [3]Lit *they were coming* [4]Lit *the inside of the side chambers* [a]1 Kin 6:5-10 [b]1 Kin 6:6
7 [1]Lit *middle* [a]1 Kin 6:8
8 [1]Lit *height* [2]Or *to the joint* [a]Ezek 40:5
9 [1]Lit *width* [a]Ezek 41:11
10 [a]Ezek 40:17
11 [1]Lit *doorway* [2]Lit *side chamber* [a]Ezek 41:9
12 [1]Lit *wide* [a]Ezek 41:13 [b]Ezek 41:14
13 [a]Ezek 40:47 [b]Ezek 41:13-15 [c]Ezek 41:12
14 [1]Lit *area*
15 [1]Lit *to* [2]Or *passageway* [a]Ezek 41:12 [b]Ezek 41:14 [c]Ezek 41:16
16 [1]Or *framed* [2]Or *passageways* [a]Is 6:4; Ezek 10:18 [b]1 Kin 6:4; Ezek 40:16 [c]Ezek 41:15 [d]Ezek 42:3 [e]1 Kin 6:15

wall all around inside and outside, by
measurement.
18 It was [1]carved with [a]cherubim
and [b]palm trees; and a palm tree was
between cherub and cherub, and every
cherub had two faces,
19 a [a]man's face toward the palm tree
on one side and a young [a]lion's face toward the palm tree on the other side;
they were [1]carved on all the house all
around.
20 From the ground to above the entrance [a]cherubim and [a]palm trees were
[1]carved, as well as *on* the wall of the
nave.
21 ¶ The [a]doorposts of the [b]nave
were square; as for the front of the sanctuary, the appearance of one doorpost
was like that of the other.
22 The [a]altar *was* of wood, three cubits high and its length two cubits; its
corners, its [1]base and its [2]sides *were* of
wood. And he said to me, "This is the
[b]table that is before the LORD."
23 The [a]nave and the [b]sanctuary
each had a double [c]door.
24 Each of the doors had two leaves,
two [1a]swinging leaves; two *leaves* for
one door and two leaves for the other.
25 Also there were [1]carved on them,
on the doors of the nave, [a]cherubim and
[a]palm trees like those [1]carved on the
walls; and *there was* a [2b]threshold of
wood on the front of the porch outside.
26 *There were* [1a]latticed windows
and [b]palm trees on one side and on the
other, on the sides of the [c]porch; thus
were the [d]side chambers of the house
and the [2]thresholds.

Chambers of the Temple

42 Then he [a]brought me out into
the [b]outer court, the way [c]to-
ward the north; and he brought me to the
[d]chamber which *was* opposite the [e]sep-
arate area and opposite the [f]building toward the north.
2 Along the length, *which was* a
[a]hundred cubits, *was* the north door; the
width *was* fifty cubits.
3 Opposite the [a]twenty *cubits* which
belonged to the inner court, and opposite
the [b]pavement which belonged to the
outer court, *was* [1c]gallery corresponding to [1]gallery in three stories.
4 Before the [a]chambers *was* an inner
walk ten cubits wide, a way of one *hundred* cubits; and their openings *were* on
the north.
5 Now the upper chambers *were*
[1]smaller because the [2a]galleries took
more *space* away from them than from
the lower and middle ones in the building.

18 [1]Lit *made* [a]1 Kin 6:29,32, 35; 7:36; Ezek 41:20,25 [b]2 Chr 3:5; Ezek 40:16
19 [1]Lit *made* [a]Ezek 1:10; 10:14
20 [1]Lit *made* [a]Ezek 41:18
21 [a]1 Kin 6:33; Ezek 40:9,14,16; 41:1 [b]Ezek 41:1
22 [1]Lit *length* [2]Lit *walls* [a]Ex 30:1-3; 1 Kin 6:20; Rev 8:3 [b]Ex 25:23,30; Lev 24:6; Ezek 23:41; 44:16; Mal 1:7,12
23 [a]Ezek 41:1 [b]Ezek 41:4 [c]1 Kin 6:31-35
24 [1]Or *turning* [a]1 Kin 6:34
25 [1]Lit *made* [2]Or *canopy of wood over* [a]Ezek 41:18 [b]Ezek 41:16
26 [1]Or *framed* [2]Or *canopies* [a]Ezek 41:16 [b]Ezek 40:16 [c]Ezek 40:9,48 [d]Ezek 41:5
42:1 [a]Ezek 40:17,28,48; 41:1 [b]Ezek 40:17,20 [c]Ezek 40:20 [d]Ezek 40:17; 42:4 [e]Ezek 41:12; 42:10,13 [f]Ezek 41:12
2 [a]Ezek 41:13
3 [1]Or *passage-way* [a]Ezek 41:10 [b]Ezek 40:17 [c]Ezek 41:15,16; 42:5
4 [a]Ezek 46:19
5 [1]Lit *shorter* [2]Or *passageways* [a]Ezek 42:3
6 [1]Or *reduced* [a]Ezek 41:6
7 [a]Ezek 42:10, 12
8 [a]Ezek 41:13, 14
9 [a]Ezek 44:5; 46:19
10 [1]Lit *width* [a]Ezek 42:7 [b]Ezek 42:1,13 [c]Ezek 40:17
11 [a]Ezek 42:4
12 [a]Ezek 42:7
13 [a]Ezek 42:1, 10 [b]Ex 29:31; Lev 7:6; 10:13, 14,17 [c]Lev 10:3; Deut 21:5; Ezek 40:46 [d]Lev 6:25, 29; 14:13; Num 18:9,10
14 [1]Lit *but there they shall lay* [a]Ezek 44:19 [b]Ex 29:4-9; Lev 8:7, 13; Is 61:10; Zech 3:4,5
15 [a]Ezek 40:6; 43:1
16 [a]Ezek 40:3
20 [1]Lit *toward the four winds* [a]Is 60:18; Ezek 40:5; Zech 2:5 [b]Ezek 45:2; Rev 21:16

6 For they *were* in [a]three stories and
had no pillars like the pillars of the courts;
therefore *the upper chambers* were [1]set
back from the ground upward, more than
the lower and middle ones.
7 As for the [a]outer wall by the side of
the chambers, toward the outer court facing the chambers, its length *was* fifty cubits.
8 For the length of the chambers
which *were* in the outer court *was* fifty
cubits; and behold, *the length of those*
facing the temple *was* a [a]hundred cubits.
9 Below these chambers *was* the
[a]entrance on the east side, as one enters
them from the outer court.
10 ¶ In the [1]thickness of the [a]wall
of the court toward the east, facing the
[b]separate area and facing the building,
there were [c]chambers.
11 The [a]way in front of them *was* like
the appearance of the chambers which
were on the north, according to their
length so was their width, and all their
exits *were* both according to their ar-
rangements and openings.
12 Corresponding to the openings of
the chambers which were toward the
south was an opening at the head of the
way, the way in front of the [a]wall toward
the east, as one enters them.
13 ¶ Then he said to me, "The north
chambers *and* the south chambers,
which are opposite the [a]separate area,
they are the [b]holy chambers where the
priests who are [c]near to the LORD shall
eat the [d]most holy things. There they
shall lay the most holy things, the grain
offering, the sin offering and the guilt offering; for the place is holy.
14 "When the priests enter, then they
shall not go out into the outer court from
the sanctuary [1]without [a]laying there
their [b]garments in which they minister,
for they are holy. They shall put on other
garments; then they shall approach that
which is for the people."
15 ¶ Now when he had finished measuring the inner house, he brought me
out by the way of the [a]gate which faced
toward the east and measured it all
around.
16 He measured on the east side with
the measuring reed five hundred reeds by
the [a]measuring reed.
17 He measured on the north side five
hundred reeds by the measuring reed.
18 On the south side he measured five
hundred reeds with the measuring reed.
19 He turned to the west side *and*
measured five hundred reeds with the
measuring reed.
20 He measured it [1]on the four sides;
it had a [a]wall all around, the [b]length five

hundred and the [c]width five hundred, to [d]divide between the holy and the profane.

Vision of the Glory of God Filling the Temple

43 Then he led me to the [a]gate, the gate facing toward the east;

2 and behold, the [a]glory of the God of Israel was coming from the way of the [b]east. And His [c]voice was like the sound of many waters; and the earth [d]shone with His glory.

3 And *it was* like the appearance of the vision which I saw, like the [a]vision which I saw when [1]He came to [b]destroy the city. And the visions *were* like the vision which I saw by the [c]river Chebar; and I [d]fell on my face.

4 And the glory of the LORD came into the house by the way of the gate facing toward the [a]east.

5 And the [a]Spirit lifted me up and brought me into the inner court; and behold, the [b]glory of the LORD filled the house.

6 ¶ Then I heard one speaking to me from the house, while a [a]man was standing beside me.

7 He said to me, "Son of man, *this is* the place of My [a]throne and the place of the soles of My feet, where I will [b]dwell among the sons of Israel forever. And the house of Israel will not again defile My holy name, neither they nor their kings, by their harlotry and by the [1c]corpses of their kings [2]when they die,

8 by setting their threshold by My threshold and their door post beside My door post, with *only* the wall between Me and them. And they have [a]defiled My holy name by their abominations which they have committed. So I have consumed them in My anger.

9 "Now let them [a]put away their harlotry and the [1]corpses of their kings far from Me; and I will [b]dwell among them forever.

10 ¶ "As for you, son of man, [1a]describe the [2]temple to the house of Israel, that they may be [b]ashamed of their iniquities; and let them measure the [3c]plan.

11 "If they are ashamed of all that they have done, make known to them the [1]design of the house, its structure, its [a]exits, its entrances, all its designs, all its statutes[2], and all its laws. And write *it* [b]in their sight, so that they may observe its whole [1]design and all its statutes and [c]do them.

12 "This is the [1]law of the house: its entire [2]area on the top of the [a]mountain all around *shall be* most holy. Behold, this is the [1]law of the house.

The Altar of Sacrifice

13 ¶ "And these are the measurements of the [a]altar by cubits (the [b]cubit being a cubit and a handbreadth): the [1]base *shall be* a cubit and the width a cubit, and its border on its edge round about one span; and this *shall be* the *height* of the [2]base of the altar.

14 "From the base on the ground to the lower [a]ledge *shall be* two cubits and the width one cubit; and from the smaller ledge to the larger ledge *shall be* four cubits and the width [1]one cubit.

15 "The [1]altar hearth *shall be* four cubits; and from the [1]altar hearth shall extend upwards four [a]horns.

16 "Now the [1]altar hearth *shall be* twelve *cubits* long by twelve wide, [a]square in its four sides.

17 "The ledge *shall be* fourteen *cubits* long by fourteen wide in its four sides, the border around it *shall be* half a cubit and its base *shall be* a cubit round about; and its [a]steps shall [1b]face the east."

The Offerings

18 ¶ And He said to me, "[a]Son of man, thus says the Lord [1]GOD, 'These are the statutes for the altar on the day it is built, to offer [b]burnt offerings on it and to [c]sprinkle blood on it.

19 'You shall give to the Levitical priests who are from the offspring of [a]Zadok, who draw [b]near to Me to minister to Me,' declares the Lord GOD, 'a [c]young bull for a [d]sin offering.

20 'You shall take some of its blood and put it on its four [a]horns and on the four corners of the [b]ledge and on the border round about; thus you shall [c]cleanse it and make atonement for it.

21 'You shall also take the bull for the sin offering, and it *shall be* [a]burned in the appointed place of the house, outside the sanctuary.

22 ¶ 'On the second day you shall offer a [a]male goat without blemish for a sin offering, and they shall [b]cleanse the altar as they cleansed *it* with the bull.

23 'When you have finished cleansing *it*, you shall present a [a]young bull without blemish and a [b]ram without blemish from the flock.

24 'You shall present them before the LORD, and the priests shall throw [a]salt on them, and they shall offer them up as a burnt offering to the LORD.

25 '[a]For seven days you shall prepare daily a goat for a sin offering; also a young

20 [c]Ezek 45:2; Rev 21:16 [d]Ezek 22:26
43:1 [a]Ezek 10:19
2 [a]Is 6:3; Ezek 1:28 [b]Ezek 11:23 [c]Ezek 1:24; Rev 1:15 [d]Ezek 1:28; Rev 18:1
3 [1]So with some mss and some ancient versions; M.T. *I* [a]Ezek 1:4-28 [b]Jer 1:10; Ezek 9:1 [c]Ezek 1:3 [d]Ezek 1:28
4 [a]Ezek 10:19
5 [a]Ezek 3:14; 2 Cor 12:2-4 [b]Ezek 10:4
6 [a]Ezek 1:26
7 [1]Or *monuments* as in Ugaritic [2]Or *in their high places* [a]Ps 47:8; Ezek 1:26 [b]Ezek 37:26 [c]Lev 26:30; Ezek 6:5
8 [a]Ezek 8:3
9 [1]Or *monuments* as in Ugaritic [a]Ezek 18:30 [b]Ezek 37:26-28
10 [1]Lit *declare* [2]Lit *house* [3]Lit *perfection* or *pattern* [a]Ezek 40:4 [b]Ezek 16:61 [c]Ezek 28:12
11 [1]Or *form(s)* [2]M.T. repeats *and all its designs* after *statutes* [a]Ezek 44:5 [b]Ezek 12:3 [c]Ezek 11:20
12 [1]Or *instruction for* [2]Lit *border* [a]Ezek 40:2
13 [1]Lit *lap* [2]Or *back* [a]Ex 27:1-8; 2 Chr 4:1 [b]Ezek 40:5
14 [1]Lit *the* [a]Ezek 43:17
15 [1]Or *ariel* shall [a]Ex 27:2; Lev 9:9; 1 Kin 1:50; Ps 118:27
16 [1]Or *ariel* shall [a]Ex 27:1
17 [1]Or *be on the east side* [a]Ex 20:26 [b]Ezek 40:6
18 [1]Heb *YHWH*, usually rendered *LORD*, and so throughout the ch [a]Ezek 2:1 [b]Ex 40:29 [c]Lev 1:5; Heb 9:21
19 [a]1 Kin 2:35; Ezek 40:46 [b]Num 16:5 [c]Lev 4:3; Ezek 43:23 [d]Ezek 45:19; Heb 7:27
20 [a]Lev 8:15; Ezek 43:15 [b]Ezek 43:14 [c]Lev 16:19; Ezek 43:22
21 [a]Ex 29:14; Lev 4:12; Heb 13:11
22 [a]Ezek 43:25 [b]Ezek 43:20
23 [a]Ex 29:1; Ezek 45:18 [b]Ex 29:1
24 [a]Lev 2:13; Num 18:19; Mark 9:49; Col 4:6

25 [a]Ex 29:35-37; Lev 8:33

bull and a ram from the flock, without blemish, shall be prepared.

26 'For seven days they shall make atonement for the altar and purify it; so shall they [1]consecrate it.

27 'When they have completed the days, it shall be that on the [a]eighth day and onward, the priests shall [1]offer your burnt offerings on the altar, and your [b]peace offerings; and I will [c]accept you,' declares the Lord GOD."

Gate for the Prince

44 Then He brought me back by the way of the [a]outer gate of the sanctuary, which faces the east; and it was shut.

2 The LORD said to me, "This gate shall be shut; it shall not be opened, and no one shall enter by it, for the [a]LORD God of Israel has entered by it; therefore it shall be shut.

3 "As for the [a]prince, he shall sit in it as prince to [b]eat bread before the LORD; he shall [c]enter by way of the [d]porch of the gate and shall go out [1]by the same way."

4 ¶ Then He brought me by way of the [a]north gate to the front of the house; and I looked, and behold, the [b]glory of the LORD filled the house of the LORD, and I [c]fell on my face.

5 The LORD said to me, "Son of man, [1a]mark well, see with your eyes and hear with your ears all that I say to you concerning all the [b]statutes of the house of the LORD and concerning all its laws; and [1]mark well the entrance of the house, with all exits of the sanctuary.

6 "You shall say to the [1a]rebellious ones, to the house of Israel, 'Thus says the Lord [2]GOD, "[b]Enough of all your abominations, O house of Israel,

7 when you brought in [a]foreigners, [b]uncircumcised in heart and uncircumcised in flesh, to be in My sanctuary to profane it, *even* My house, when you [c]offered My food, the fat and the blood; for they [d]made My covenant void—*this* in addition to all your abominations.

8 "And you have not [a]kept charge of My holy things yourselves, but you have set *foreigners* [1]to keep charge of My sanctuary."

9 ¶ 'Thus says the Lord GOD, "[a]No foreigner uncircumcised in heart and uncircumcised in flesh, of all the foreigners who are among the sons of Israel, shall enter My sanctuary.

10 "But the Levites who went far from Me when Israel went astray, who [a]went astray from Me after their idols, shall [b]bear the punishment for their iniquity.

11 "Yet they shall be [a]ministers in My sanctuary, having [b]oversight at the gates of the house and [c]ministering in the house; they shall [d]slaughter the burnt offering and the sacrifice for the people, and they shall [e]stand before them to minister to them.

12 "Because they ministered to them [a]before their idols and became a [b]stumbling block of iniquity to the house of Israel, therefore I have [1c]sworn against them," declares the Lord GOD, "that they shall [d]bear *the punishment for* their iniquity.

13 "And they shall [a]not come near to Me to serve as a priest to Me, nor come near to any of My holy things, to the things that are most holy; but they will [b]bear their shame and their abominations which they have committed.

14 "Yet I will [1]appoint them [2]to [a]keep charge of the house, of all its service and of all that shall be done in it.

Ordinances for the Levites

15 ¶ "But the [a]Levitical priests, the sons of [b]Zadok, who [c]kept charge of My sanctuary when the sons of Israel [d]went astray from Me, shall come near to Me to minister to Me; and they shall [e]stand before Me to offer Me the [f]fat and the blood," declares the Lord GOD.

16 "They shall [a]enter My sanctuary; they shall come near to My [b]table to minister to Me and keep My charge.

17 "It shall be that when they enter at the gates of the inner court, they shall be clothed with [a]linen garments; and wool shall not [1]be on them while they are ministering in the gates of the inner court and in the house.

18 "Linen [a]turbans shall be on their heads and [b]linen undergarments shall be on their loins; they shall not gird themselves with *anything which makes them* sweat.

19 "When they go out into the outer court, into the outer court to the people, they shall [a]put off their garments in which they have been ministering and lay them in the holy chambers; then they shall put on other garments so that they will [b]not transmit holiness to the people with their garments.

20 "Also they shall [a]not shave their heads, yet they shall not [b]let their locks [1]grow long; they shall only trim *the hair of* their heads.

21 "[a]Nor shall any of the priests drink wine when they enter the inner court.

22 "And they shall not [1]marry a widow or a [a]divorced woman but shall [b]take virgins from the offspring of the house of Israel, or a widow who is the widow of a priest.

26 [1]Lit *fill its hands*
27 [1]Lit *make* [a]Lev 9:1 [b]Lev 3:1 [c]Ezek 20:40
44:1 [a]Ezek 40:6
2 [a]Ezek 43:2-4
3 [1]Lit *by his way* [a]Ezek 34:24 [b]Gen 31:54; Ex 24:9-11 [c]Ezek 46:2 [d]Ezek 40:9
4 [a]Ezek 40:20 [b]Is 6:3; Ezek 1:28; Hag 2:7 [c]Ezek 1:28
5 [1]Lit *set your heart on* [a]Deut 32:46; Ezek 40:4 [b]Deut 12:32; Ezek 43:10
6 [1]Lit *rebellion* [2]Heb *YHWH,* usually rendered *LORD,* and so throughout the ch [a]Ezek 2:5-7 [b]Ezek 45:9; 1 Pet 4:3
7 [a]Ex 12:43-49 [b]Lev 26:41; Deut 10:16; Jer 4:4 [c]Lev 22:25 [d]Gen 17:14
8 [1]Lit *as keepers of My charge in My* [a]Lev 22:2; Num 18:7
9 [a]Ezek 44:7; Joel 3:17; Zech 14:21
10 [a]2 Kin 23:8; Ezek 22:26 [b]Num 18:23
11 [a]Num 3:5-37 [b]1 Chr 26:1-19 [c]Ezek 40:45 [d]2 Chr 29:34 [e]Num 16:9
12 [1]Lit *lifted up My hand* [a]2 Kin 16:10-16 [b]Ezek 14:3 [c]Ezek 20:15 [d]Ezek 44:10
13 [a]Num 18:3 [b]Ezek 16:61
14 [1]Lit *give* [2]Lit *keepers of the charge* [a]Num 18:4; 1 Chr 23:28-32; Ezek 44:11
15 [a]Jer 33:18-22 [b]Ezek 40:46 [c]Num 18:7; Ezek 40:45 [d]Ezek 44:10 [e]Zech 3:1 [f]Lev 3:16; Ezek 44:7
16 [a]Num 18:5 [b]Ezek 41:22; Mal 1:7
17 [1]Lit *come upon* [a]Ex 28:42; Rev 19:8
18 [a]Ex 28:40; Is 3:20; Ezek 24:17 [b]Ex 28:42; Lev 16:4
19 [a]Lev 6:10; Ezek 42:14 [b]Lev 6:27; Ezek 46:20
20 [1]Or *hang loose* [a]Lev 21:5 [b]Num 6:5
21 [a]Lev 10:9
22 [1]Lit *take as wives for themselves* [a]Lev 21:7 [b]Lev 21:13

23 "Moreover, they shall teach My people *the* [a]*difference* between the holy and
the profane, and cause them to discern
between the unclean and the clean.
24 "In a dispute [a]they shall take their
stand to judge; they shall judge it according to My ordinances. They shall also
keep My laws and My statutes in all My
[b]appointed feasts and [c]sanctify My sabbaths.
25 "[1a]They shall not go to a dead person to defile *themselves;* however, for father, for mother, for son, for daughter, for
brother, or for a sister who has not had a
husband, they may defile themselves.
26 "After he is [a]cleansed, seven days
shall [1]elapse for him.
27 "On the day that he goes into the
sanctuary, into the [a]inner court to minister in the sanctuary, he shall offer his
[b]sin offering," declares the Lord GOD.
28 ¶ "And it shall be with regard to an
inheritance for them, *that* [a]I am their
inheritance; and you shall give them no
possession in Israel—I am their possession.
29 "They shall [a]eat the grain offering,
the sin offering and the guilt offering; and
every [1b]devoted thing in Israel shall be
theirs.
30 "The first of all the [a]first fruits of
every kind and every [1]contribution of every kind, from all your [1]contributions,
shall be for the priests; you shall also give
to the priest the [b]first of your [2]dough to
cause a [c]blessing to rest on your house.
31 "The priests shall not eat any bird or
beast that has [a]died a natural death or
has been torn to pieces.

The LORD's Portion of the Land

45 "And when you [a]divide by lot the
land for inheritance, you shall offer [1]an [b]allotment to the LORD, a [c]holy
portion of the land; the length shall be
the length of 25,000 [d]*cubits,* and the
width shall be [2]20,000. It shall be holy
within all its boundary round about.
2 "Out of this there shall be for the
holy place a square round about [a]five
hundred by five hundred *cubits,* and fifty
cubits for its [1b]open space round about.
3 "From this [1]area you shall measure
a length of 25,000 *cubits* and a width of
10,000 *cubits;* and in it shall be the sanctuary, the most holy place.
4 "It shall be the holy portion of the
land; it shall be for the [a]priests, the ministers of the sanctuary, who [b]come near
to minister to the LORD, and it shall be a
place for their houses and a holy place for
the sanctuary.
5 "*An area* [a]25,000 *cubits* in length
and 10,000 in width shall be for the Levites, the ministers of the house, *and* for
their possession [1]cities to dwell in.
6 ¶ "You shall give the [a]city possession of *an area* 5,000 *cubits* wide and
25,000 *cubits* long, alongside the [1]allot-
ment of the holy portion; it shall be for
the whole house of Israel.

Portion for the Prince

7 ¶ "The [a]prince shall have *land* on
either side of the holy [1]allotment and the
[2]property of the city, adjacent to the holy
[1]allotment and the [2]property of the city,
on the west side toward the west and
on the east side toward the east, and in
length comparable to one of the portions,
from the west border to the east border.
8 "This shall be his land for a possession in Israel; so My princes shall no longer [a]oppress My people, but they shall
give *the rest of* the land to the house of
Israel [b]according to their tribes."
9 ¶ 'Thus says the Lord [1]GOD,
"[a]Enough, you princes of Israel; put
away [b]violence and destruction, and
[c]practice justice and righteousness. Stop
your [d]expropriations from My people,"
declares the Lord GOD.
10 ¶ "You shall have [a]just balances, a
just [b]ephah and a just [b]bath.
11 "The ephah and the bath shall be
[1]the same quantity, so that the bath will
contain a tenth of a [a]homer and the
ephah a tenth of a homer; [2]their standard shall be according to the homer.
12 "The [a]shekel shall be twenty [a]ge-
rahs; twenty shekels, twenty-five shekels, *and* fifteen shekels shall be your
[1]maneh.
13 ¶ "This is the offering that you shall
offer: a sixth of an ephah from a homer of
wheat; a sixth of an ephah from a homer
of barley;
14 and the prescribed portion of oil
(*namely,* the bath of oil), a tenth of a bath
from *each* kor (*which is* ten baths *or* a
homer, for ten baths are a homer);
15 and one sheep from *each* flock of
two hundred from the watering places of
Israel—for a [a]grain offering, for a burnt
offering and for peace offerings, to [b]make
atonement for them," declares the
Lord GOD.
16 "[a]All the people of the land shall
[1]give to this offering for the [b]prince in
Israel.
17 "It shall be the [a]prince's part *to provide* the [b]burnt offerings, the grain offerings and the drink offerings, at the
[c]feasts, on the [d]new moons and on the
sabbaths, at all the appointed feasts of
the house of Israel; he shall provide the

23 [a]Lev 10:10; Ezek 22:26; Hos 4:6; Mic 3:9-11; Zeph 3:4; Hag 2:11-13; Mal 2:6-8
24 [a]Deut 17:8; 1 Chr 23:4; 2 Chr 19:8-10 [b]Lev 23:2 [c]Ezek 20:12
25 [1]Lit *He* [a]Lev 21:1-4
26 [1]Lit *be counted* [a]Num 19:13-19
27 [a]Ezek 44:17 [b]Lev 5:3; Num 6:9-11
28 [a]Num 18:20; Deut 10:9; Josh 13:33
29 [1]Or *dedicated* [a]Num 18:9; Josh 13:14 [b]Lev 27:21; Num 18:14
30 [1]Or *heave offering(s)* [2]Or *coarse meal* [a]Num 18:12; 2 Chr 31:4-6; Neh 10:35-37 [b]Num 15:20 [c]Mal 3:10
31 [a]Lev 22:8; Deut 14:21; Ezek 4:14
45:1 [1]Or *a contribution* [2]Or with Gr *10,000* [a]Num 34:13; Josh 13:7; Ezek 47:21 [b]Ezek 48:8 [c]Zech 14:20 [d]Ezek 42:16
2 [1]Or *pasture land* [a]Ezek 42:20 [b]Ezek 27:28
3 [1]Lit *measure*
4 [a]Ezek 48:10 [b]Num 16:5; Ezek 40:45
5 [1]So with Gr; M.T. *twenty chambers* [a]Ezek 48:13
6 [1]Or *contribution* [a]Ezek 48:15-18
7 [1]Or *contribution* [2]Lit *possession* [a]Ezek 34:24
8 [a]Is 11:3-5; Jer 23:5; Ezek 19:7 [b]Josh 11:23
9 [1]Heb *YHWH,* usually rendered LORD, and so throughout the ch [a]Ezek 44:6 [b]Jer 6:7; Ezek 7:11 [c]Jer 22:3; Zech 8:16 [d]Neh 5:1-5
10 [a]Lev 19:36; Deut 25:15; Prov 16:11; Amos 8:4-6; Mic 6:10 [b]Is 5:10
11 [1]Lit *one* [2]Lit *its measure* [a]Is 5:10
12 [1]Or *mina* [a]Ex 30:13; Lev 27:25; Num 3:47
15 [a]Ezek 45:17 [b]Lev 1:4
16 [1]Lit *be* [a]Ex 30:14 [b]Is 16:1
17 [a]Ezek 46:4-12 [b]1 Kin 8:64; 1 Chr 16:2; 2 Chr 31:3 [c]Lev 23:1-44; Num 28:1-29:39 [d]Is 66:23

sin offering, the grain offering, the burnt offering and the [e]peace offerings, to make atonement for the house of Israel."

18 ¶ 'Thus says the Lord GOD, "In the [a]first *month,* on the first of the month, you shall take a young bull [b]without blemish and [c]cleanse the sanctuary.

19 "The priest shall take some of the blood from the sin offering and put *it* on the door posts of the house, on the [a]four corners of the [b]ledge of the altar and on the posts of the gate of the inner court.

20 "Thus you shall do on the seventh *day* of the month for everyone who goes [a]astray or is [1]naive; so you shall make [b]atonement for the house.

21 ¶ "In the [a]first *month,* on the fourteenth day of the month, you shall have the [b]Passover, a feast of seven days; unleavened bread shall be eaten.

22 "On that day the prince shall provide for himself and all the people of the land a [a]bull for a sin offering.

23 "*During* the [a]seven days of the feast he shall provide as a [b]burnt offering to the LORD [c]seven bulls and seven rams without blemish on every day of the seven days, and a male goat daily for a sin offering.

24 "He shall provide as a [a]grain offering an ephah [1]with a bull, an ephah [1]with a ram and a hin of oil [1]with an ephah.

25 "In the [a]seventh *month,* on the fifteenth day of the month, at the feast, he shall provide like this, seven days [1]for the sin offering, the burnt offering, the grain offering and the oil."

The Prince's Offerings

46 'Thus says the Lord [1]GOD, "The [a]gate of the [b]inner court facing east shall be [c]shut the six [d]working days; but it shall be opened on the [e]sabbath day and opened on the day of the [f]new moon.

2 "The [a]prince shall enter by way of the porch of the gate from outside and stand by the [b]post of the gate. Then the priests shall provide his burnt offering and his peace offerings, and he shall worship at the threshold of the gate and then go out; but the gate shall not be [c]shut until the evening.

3 "The [a]people of the land shall also worship at the doorway of that gate before the LORD on the sabbaths and on the [b]new moons.

4 "The [a]burnt offering which the prince shall offer to the LORD on the sabbath day shall be [b]six lambs without blemish and a ram without blemish;

5 and the [a]grain offering shall be an ephah [1]with the ram, and the grain offering [1]with the lambs [2]as much as he is [b]able to give, and a hin of oil [1]with an ephah.

6 "On the day of the [a]new moon *he shall offer* a young bull without blemish, also six lambs and a ram, *which* shall be without blemish.

7 "And he shall provide a [a]grain offering, an ephah [1]with the bull and an ephah [1]with the ram, and [1]with the lambs as [2]much as he is [b]able, and a hin of oil [1]with an ephah.

8 "When the [a]prince enters, he shall go in by way of the porch of the gate and go out [1]by the same way.

9 "But when the people of the land come [a]before the LORD at the appointed feasts, he who enters by way of the north gate to worship shall go out by way of the south gate. And he who enters by way of the south gate shall go out by way of the north gate. [1]No one shall return by way of the gate by which he entered but shall go straight out.

10 "When they go in, the prince shall go in [a]among them; and when they go out, [1]he shall go out.

11 ¶ "At the [a]festivals and the appointed feasts the [b]grain offering shall be an ephah [1]with a bull and an ephah [1]with a ram, and [1]with the lambs as [2]much as one is able to give, and a hin of oil [1]with an ephah.

12 "When the prince provides a [a]freewill offering, a burnt offering, or peace offerings *as* a freewill offering to the LORD, the gate facing east shall be [b]opened for him. And he shall provide his burnt offering and his peace offerings as he does on the [c]sabbath day. Then he shall go out, and the gate shall be shut after he goes out.

13 ¶ "And you shall provide a [a]lamb a year old without blemish for a burnt offering to the LORD daily; [b]morning by morning you shall provide it.

14 "Also you shall provide a grain offering with it morning by morning, a [a]sixth of an ephah and a third of a hin of oil to moisten the fine flour, a grain offering to the LORD continually by a perpetual [1]ordinance.

15 "Thus they shall provide the lamb, the grain offering and the oil, morning by morning, for a [a]continual burnt offering."

16 ¶ 'Thus says the Lord GOD, "If the prince gives a [a]gift *out of* his inheritance to any of his sons, it shall belong to his sons; it is their possession by inheritance.

17 "But if he gives a gift from his inheritance to one of his servants, it shall be his until the [a]year of liberty; then it shall return to the prince. His inheritance *shall*

---

17 [e]1 Kin 8:63; Ezek 43:27
18 [a]Ex 12:2 [b]Lev 22:20; Heb 9:14 [c]Lev 16:16, 33; Ezek 43:22, 26
19 [a]Lev 16:18-20; Ezek 43:20 [b]Ezek 43:14,17,20
20 [1]Lit *simple* [a]Lev 4:27; Ps 19:12 [b]Lev 16:20; Ezek 45:15,18
21 [a]Num 28:16f [b]Ex 12:1-24; Lev 23:5-8
22 [a]Lev 4:14
23 [a]Lev 23:8 [b]Num 28:16-25 [c]Num 23:1,2; Job 42:8
24 [1]Lit *for* [a]Num 28:12-15; Ezek 46:5-7
25 [1]Lit *according to* [a]Lev 23:33-43; Num 29:12-38; 2 Chr 5:3; 7:8,10
46:1 [1]Heb *YHWH,* usually rendered LORD, and so throughout the ch [a]Ezek 45:19 [b]Ezek 8:16; 10:3 [c]Ezek 44:1,2 [d]Ex 20:9 [e]Is 66:23; Ezek 45:17 [f]Ezek 45:18; 46:3,6
2 [a]Ezek 44:3; 46:8 [b]Ezek 45:19 [c]Ezek 46:12
3 [a]Luke 1:10 [b]Ezek 46:1
4 [a]Ezek 45:17 [b]Num 28:9
5 [1]Lit *for* [2]Lit *a gift of his hand* [a]Num 28:12; Ezek 45:24; 46:7,11 [b]Ezek 46:7
6 [a]Ezek 46:1
7 [1]Lit *for* [2]Lit *his hand can reach* [a]Ezek 46:5 [b]Lev 14:21; Deut 16:17; Ezek 46:5
8 [1]Lit *by its way* [a]Ezek 44:3; 46:2
9 [1]Lit *He shall not* [a]Ex 34:23; Ps 84:7; Mic 6:6
10 [1]So with many mss and the ancient versions; M.T. *they* [a]2 Sam 6:14,15; 1 Chr 29:20,22; 2 Chr 6:3; 7:4; Ps 42:4
11 [1]Lit *for* [2]Lit *a gift of his hand* [a]Ezek 45:17 [b]Ezek 46:5,7
12 [a]Lev 23:38; 2 Chr 29:31 [b]Ezek 44:3; 46:1,2,8 [c]Ezek 45:17
13 [a]Num 28:3-5 [b]Is 50:4
14 [1]Lit *statute* [a]Num 28:5
15 [a]Ex 29:42; Num 28:6
16 [a]2 Chr 21:3
17 [a]Lev 25:10

be only his sons'; it shall belong to them.
18 "The prince shall [a]not take from the
people's inheritance, [1b]thrusting them
out of their possession; he shall give his
sons inheritance from his own possession
so that My people will not be scattered,
anyone from his possession." ' "

The Boiling Places

19 ¶ Then he brought me through the
[a]entrance, which *was* at the side of the
gate, into the holy chambers for the
priests, which faced north; and behold,
there *was* a place at the extreme rear
toward the west.
20 He said to me, "This is the place
where the priests shall boil the [a]guilt
offering and the sin offering *and* where
they shall [b]bake the grain offering, in
order that they may not bring *them* out
into the outer court to transmit holiness
to the people."
21 ¶ Then he brought me out into the
outer court and led me across to the four
corners of the court; and behold, in every
corner of the court *there was* a *small*
court.
22 In the four corners of the court
there were enclosed courts, forty *cubits*
long and thirty wide; these four in the
corners *were* [1]the same size.
23 *There was* a row *of masonry* round
about in them, around the four of them,
and boiling places were made under the
rows round about.
24 Then he said to me, "These are the
boiling [1]places where the ministers of
the house shall boil the sacrifices of the
people."

Water from the Temple

47 Then he brought me back to the
[a]door of the house; and behold,
[b]water was flowing from under the
threshold of the house toward the east,
for the house faced east. And the water
was flowing down from under, from the
right side of the house, from south of the
altar.
2 He brought me out by way of the
north gate and led me around [1]on the
outside to the outer gate by way of *the
gate* that faces east. And behold, water
was trickling from the south side.
3 ¶ When the man went out toward
the east with a line in his hand, he measured a thousand cubits, and he led me
through the water, water *reaching* the
ankles.
4 Again he measured a thousand and
led me through the water, water *reaching*
the knees. Again he measured a thousand
and led me through *the water,* water
reaching the loins.
5 Again he measured a thousand; *and
it was* a river that I could not ford, for the
water had risen, *enough* water to swim
in, a [a]river that could not be forded.
6 He said to me, "Son of man, have
you [a]seen *this?"* Then he brought me
[1]back to the bank of the river.
7 Now when I had returned, behold,
on the bank of the river there *were* very
many [a]trees on the one side and on the
other.
8 Then he said to me, "These waters
go out toward the eastern region and go
down into the [a]Arabah; then they go toward the sea, being made to flow into the
[b]sea, and the waters *of the sea* become
[1]fresh.
9 "It will come about that every living
creature which swarms in every place
where the [1]river goes, will live. And
there will be very many fish, for these
waters go there and *the others* [2]become
fresh; so [a]everything will live where the
river goes.
10 "And it will come about that [a]fisher-
men will stand beside it; from [b]Engedi to
Eneglaim there will be a place for the
[c]spreading of nets. Their fish will be according to their kinds, like the fish of the
[d]Great Sea, [e]very many.
11 "But its swamps and marshes will
not become [1]fresh; they will be [2]left for
[a]salt.
12 "[a]By the river on its bank, on one
side and on the other, will grow all *kinds
of* [b]trees for food. Their [c]leaves will not
wither and their fruit will not fail. They
will bear every month because their water flows from the sanctuary, and their
fruit will be for food and their [d]leaves for
healing."

Boundaries and Division of the Land

13 ¶ Thus says the Lord [1]GOD, "This
shall be the [a]boundary by which you
shall divide the land for an inheritance
among the twelve tribes of Israel; Joseph
shall have two [b]portions.
14 "You shall divide it for an inheritance, each one [1]equally with the other;
for I [2a]swore to give it to your forefathers, and this land shall fall to you [3]as an
inheritance.
15 ¶ "This *shall be* the boundary of the
land: on the [a]north side, from the Great
Sea *by* the way of Hethlon, to the entrance of [1b]Zedad;
16 [1a]Hamath, Berothah, Sibraim,
which is between the border of [b]Damas-
cus and the border of Hamath; Hazer-
hatticon, which is by the border of Hauran.

18 [1]Lit *oppressing* [a]Ezek 45:8 [b]1 Kin 21:19; Ezek 22:27; Mic 2:1,2
19 [a]Ezek 42:9; 44:5
20 [a]2 Chr 35:13; Ezek 44:29 [b]Lev 2:4-7
22 [1]Lit *one measure*
24 [1]Lit *houses*
47:1 [a]Ezek 41:2,23-25 [b]Ps 46:4; Is 30:25; 55:1; Jer 2:13; Joel 3:18; Zech 13:1; 14:8; Rev 22:1,17
2 [1]Lit *by way of*
5 [a]Is 11:9; Hab 2:14
6 [1]Lit *and caused me to return* [a]Ezek 8:6; 40:4; 44:5
7 [a]Is 60:13,21; 61:3; Ezek 47:12
8 [1]Lit *healed* [a]Deut 3:17; Is 35:6,7; 41:17-19; 44:3 [b]Josh 3:16
9 [1]Lit *two rivers* [2]Lit *are healed* [a]Is 12:3; 55:1; John 4:14; 7:37, 38
10 [a]Matt 4:19; 13:47; Luke 5:10 [b]Gen 14:7; Josh 15:62; 1 Sam 23:29; 24:1; 2 Chr 20:2 [c]Ezek 26:5,14 [d]Num 34:6; Ps 104:25; Ezek 47:15; 48:28 [e]Luke 5:5-9; John 21:6
11 [1]Lit *healed* [2]Lit *given* [a]Deut 29:23
12 [a]Ezek 47:7; Rev 22:2 [b]Gen 2:9 [c]Ps 1:3; Jer 17:8 [d]Rev 22:2
13 [1]Heb *YHWH,* usually rendered LORD, and so throughout the ch [a]Num 34:2-12 [b]Gen 48:5; Ezek 48:4, 5
14 [1]Lit *like his brother* [2]Lit *lifted up My hand* [3]Lit *in* [a]Deut 1:8; Ezek 20:6
15 [1]Or *Hamath* [a]Num 34:7-9 [b]Num 34:8
16 [1]Or *Zedad* [a]Num 13:21; Is 10:9; Ezek 47:17,20; 48:1; Zech 9:2 [b]Gen 14:15; Ezek 47:17,18; 48:1

17 "The boundary shall [1]extend from the sea *to* [a]Hazar-enan *at* the border of Damascus, and on the north toward the north is the border of Hamath. This is the north side.

18 ¶ "The [a]east side, from between Hauran, Damascus, [b]Gilead and the land of Israel, *shall be* the [c]Jordan; from the *north* border to the eastern sea you shall measure. This is the east side.

19 ¶ "The [a]south side toward the south *shall extend* from [b]Tamar as far as the waters of [c]Meribath-kadesh, to the [d]brook *of Egypt and* to the [e]Great Sea. This is the south side toward the south.

20 ¶ "The [a]west side *shall be* the Great Sea, from the *south* border to a point opposite [1][b]Lebo-hamath. This is the west side.

21 ¶ "So you shall divide this land among yourselves according to the tribes of Israel.

22 "You shall divide it by [a]lot for an inheritance among yourselves and among the [b]aliens who stay in your midst, who bring forth sons in your midst. And they shall be to you as the native-born among the sons of Israel; they shall be allotted an [c]inheritance with you among the tribes of Israel.

23 "And in the tribe with which the alien stays, there you shall give *him* his inheritance," declares the Lord GOD.

Division of the Land

48 "Now [a]these are the names of the tribes: from the northern extremity, [1]beside the way of Hethlon to [2]Lebo-hamath, *as far as* Hazar-enan *at* the border of Damascus, toward the north [1]beside Hamath, [3]running from east to west, [b]Dan, one *portion.*

2 "Beside the border of Dan, from the east side to the west side, [a]Asher, one *portion.*

3 "Beside the border of Asher, from the east side to the west side, [a]Naphtali, one *portion.*

4 "Beside the border of Naphtali, from the east side to the west side, [a]Manasseh, one *portion.*

5 "Beside the border of Manasseh, from the east side to the west side, [a]Ephraim, one *portion.*

6 "Beside the border of Ephraim, from the east side to the west side, [a]Reuben, one *portion.*

7 "Beside the border of Reuben, from the east side to the west side, [a]Judah, one *portion.*

8 ¶ "And beside the border of Judah, from the east side to the west side, shall be the [1]allotment which you shall [2]set apart, 25,000 [3]*cubits* in width, and in length like one of the portions, from the east side to the west side; and the [a]sanctuary shall be in the middle of it.

9 "The allotment that you shall set apart to the LORD *shall be* 25,000 *cubits* in length and 10,000 in width.

Portion for the Priests

10 "The holy allotment shall be for these, *namely* for the [a]priests, toward the north 25,000 *cubits in length,* toward the west 10,000 in width, toward the east 10,000 in width, and toward the south 25,000 in length; and the sanctuary of the LORD shall be in its midst.

11 "*It shall be* for the priests who are sanctified of the [a]sons of Zadok, who have kept My charge, who did not go astray when the sons of Israel went astray as the [b]Levites went astray.

12 "It shall be an allotment to them from the allotment of the land, a most holy place, by the border of the Levites.

13 "Alongside the border of the priests the Levites *shall have* 25,000 *cubits* in length and 10,000 in width. The whole length *shall be* 25,000 *cubits* and the width 10,000.

14 "Moreover, they [a]shall not sell or exchange any of it, or alienate this [1]choice *portion* of land; for it is holy to the LORD.

15 ¶ "The remainder, 5,000 *cubits* in width and 25,000 [1]in length, shall be for [a]common use for the city, for dwellings and for [2]open spaces; and the city shall be in its midst.

16 "These *shall be* its measurements: the north side 4,500 *cubits,* the south side [a]4,500 *cubits,* the east side 4,500 *cubits,* and the west side 4,500 *cubits.*

17 "The city shall have [1]open spaces: on the north 250 *cubits,* on the south 250 *cubits,* on the east 250 *cubits,* and on the west 250 *cubits.*

18 "The remainder of the length alongside the holy allotment shall be 10,000 *cubits* toward the east and 10,000 toward the west; and it shall be [1]alongside the holy allotment. And its produce shall be food for the workers of the city.

19 "The workers of the city, out of all the tribes of Israel, shall cultivate it.

20 "The whole allotment *shall be* 25,000 by 25,000 *cubits;* you shall [1]set apart the holy allotment, a [2]square, with the [3]property of the city.

Portion for the Prince

21 ¶ "The [a]remainder *shall be* for the prince, on the one side and on the other of the holy allotment and of the [1]property of the city; in front of the 25,000 *cubits* of the allotment toward the east border

---

17 [1]Lit *be* [a]Num 34:9

18 [a]Num 34:10-12 [b]Gen 37:25; Jer 50:19 [c]Gen 13:10,11

19 [a]Num 34:3-5 [b]Ezek 48:28 [c]Deut 32:51 [d]Num 34:5; 1 Kin 8:65; Is 27:12 [e]Ezek 47:10,15

20 [1]Or *entrance of Hamath* [a]Num 34:6 [b]Judg 3:3; 2 Chr 7:8; Ezek 48:1; Amos 6:14

22 [a]Num 26:55, 56 [b]Is 14:1; 56:6,7 [c]Acts 11:18; 15:9; Eph 2:12-14; 3:6; Col 3:11

48:1 [1]Lit *at the hand of* [2]Or *the entrance of Hamath* [3]Lit *and there shall be to it an east and west side* [a]Ex 1:1 [b]Josh 19:40-48

2 [a]Josh 19:24-31

3 [a]Josh 19:32-39

4 [a]Josh 13:29-31; 17:1-11

5 [a]Josh 16:5-9; 17:8-10,14-18

6 [a]Josh 13:15-21

7 [a]Josh 15:1-63; 19:9

8 [1]Or *contribution,* and so throughout the ch [2]Lit *offer* [3]Or possibly *reeds,* and so throughout the ch [a]Is 12:6; 33:20-22; Ezek 45:3,4

10 [a]Ezek 44:28; 45:4

11 [a]Ezek 40:46; 44:15 [b]Ezek 44:10,12

14 [1]Lit *first* or *first fruits* [a]Lev 25:32-34; 27:10, 28,33

15 [1]Lit *in front* [2]Or *pasture land* [a]Ezek 42:20; 45:6

16 [a]Rev 21:16

17 [1]Or *pasture land*

18 [1]Or *exactly as*

20 [1]Lit *offer* [2]Lit *fourth* [3]Or *possession*

21 [1]Or *possession* [a]Ezek 34:24; 45:7; 48:22

and westward in front of the 25,000 toward the west border, alongside the portions, *it shall be* for the prince. And the
holy allotment and the sanctuary of the
house shall be in the middle of it.
22 "Exclusive of the [1]property of the
Levites and the [1]property of the city,
which are in the middle of that which
belongs to the prince, *everything* between the border of Judah and the border
of Benjamin shall be for the prince.

Portion for Other Tribes

23 ¶ "As for the rest of the tribes: from
the east side to the west side, [a]Benjamin,
one *portion.*
24 "Beside the border of Benjamin,
from the east side to the west side, [a]Sim-
eon, one *portion.*
25 "Beside the border of Simeon, from
the east side to the west side, [a]Issachar,
one *portion.*
26 "Beside the border of Issachar, from
the east side to the west side, [a]Zebulun,
one *portion.*
27 "Beside the border of Zebulun, from
the east side to the west side, [a]Gad, one
portion.
28 "And beside the border of Gad, at
the south side toward the south, the border shall be from [a]Tamar to the waters of
Meribath-kadesh, to the brook *of Egypt,*
to the [b]Great Sea.
29 "This is the [a]land which you shall
divide by lot to the tribes of Israel for an
inheritance, and these are their *several*
portions," declares the Lord [1]GOD.

The City Gates

30 ¶ "These are the exits of the city:
on the [a]north side, 4,500 *cubits* by measurement,
31 [1]shall be the gates of the city,
[2a]named for the tribes of Israel, three
gates toward the north: the gate of Reuben, one; the gate of Judah, one; the gate
of Levi, one.
32 "On the east side, 4,500 *cubits,*
[1]shall be three gates: the gate of Joseph,
one; the gate of Benjamin, one; the gate
of Dan, one.
33 "On the south side, 4,500 *cubits* by
measurement, [1]shall be three gates: the
gate of Simeon, one; the gate of Issachar,
one; the gate of Zebulun, one.
34 "On the west side, 4,500 *cubits,*
shall be three gates: the gate of Gad, one;
the gate of Asher, one; the gate of Naphtali, one.
35 "*The city shall be* 18,000 *cubits*
round about; and the [a]name of the city
from *that* day *shall be,* '[1]The [b]LORD is
there.' "

22 [1]Or *possession*
23 [a]Josh 18:21-28
24 [a]Josh 19:1-9
25 [a]Josh 19:17-23
26 [a]Josh 19:10-16
27 [a]Josh 13:24-28
28 [a]Gen 14:7; 2 Chr 20:2; Ezek 47:19 [b]Ezek 47:10,15,19,20
29 [1]Heb *YHWH,* usually rendered *LORD* [a]Ezek 47:13-20
30 [a]Ezek 48:32-34
31 [1]Lit *and* [2]Lit *according to the names of* [a]Rev 21:12,13
32 [1]Lit *and*
33 [1]Lit *and*
35 [1]Heb *YHWH-shammah* [a]Jer 23:6; 33:16 [b]Is 12:6; 14:32; 24:23; Jer 3:17; 8:19; 14:9; Ezek 35:10; Joel 3:21; Zech 2:10; Rev 21:3; 22:3

Daniel

Title and Background

Daniel records events that took place during Israel's captivity and encourages the people to trust in the God who controls all history.

Author and Date of Writing

In several passages, such as 9:2 and 10:2, the book itself mentions Daniel as the author. Jesus Himself referred to Daniel as the author (Matthew 24:15). Objective evidence indicates that the book was written about 530 B.C., shortly after the capture of Babylon by Cyrus in 539.

Theme and Message

The theological theme of the book is God's sovereignty: "The Most High God is ruler over the realm of mankind" (5:21). Daniel's visions always show God as triumphant. The climax of His sovereignty is described in Revelation 11:15 (compare Daniel 2:44; 7:27).

Outline

I. Introduction: The Setting (1:1–21)
II. The Destinies of the Nations (2:1—7:28)
  A. Nebuchadnezzar's Dreams (2:1—4:37)
  B. Belshazzar's and Babylon's Downfall (5:1–31)
  C. Daniel's Deliverance and Dream (6:1—7:28)
III. The Destiny of Israel (8:1—12:13)
  A. Daniel's Vision of a Ram and a Goat (8:1–27)
  B. Daniel's Prayer and the Seventy "Weeks" (9:1–27)
  C. Daniel's Vision of Israel's Future (10:1—12:13)

The Choice Young Men

1 In the third year of the reign of [a]Je-
hoiakim king of Judah, [b]Nebuchad-
nezzar king of Babylon came to Jerusalem
and besieged it.
2 The [a]Lord gave Jehoiakim king of
Judah into his hand, along with some of
the [b]vessels of the house of God; and he
brought them to the land of [c]Shinar, to
the house of his [1]god, and he brought the
vessels into the treasury of his [1d]god.
3 ¶ Then the king [1]ordered Ashpe-
naz, the chief of his [2]officials, to bring in
some of the sons of Israel, including some
of the [3]royal [a]family and of the nobles,
4 youths in whom was [a]no defect,
who were good-looking, showing [b]intel-
ligence in every *branch of* wisdom, endowed with understanding and discerning knowledge, and who had ability for
[1]serving in the king's [2]court; and *he ordered him* to teach them the [3]literature
and [c]language of the [d]Chaldeans.
5 The king appointed for them a daily
ration from the [a]king's choice food and
from the wine which he drank, and *appointed* that they should be [1]educated
three years, at the end of which they
were to [2b]enter the king's personal service.
6 Now among them from the sons of
Judah were [a]Daniel, Hananiah, Mishael
and Azariah.
7 Then the commander of the officials assigned *new* names to them; and to
Daniel he assigned *the name* [a]Belteshaz-
zar, to Hananiah [b]Shadrach, to Mishael
[b]Meshach and to Azariah [b]Abed-nego.

Daniel's Resolve

8 ¶ But Daniel [1]made up his mind
that he would not [a]defile himself with
the [b]king's choice food or with the
[c]wine which he drank; so he sought *permission* from the commander of the officials that he might not defile himself.
9 Now God granted Daniel [1a]favor
and compassion in the sight of the commander of the officials,
10 and the commander of the officials
said to Daniel, "I am afraid of my lord the

1:1 [a]2 Kin 24:1; 2 Chr 36:5 [b]Jer 25:1
2 [1]Or *gods* [a]Is 42:24; Dan 2:37 [b]2 Chr 36:7; Jer 27:19; Dan 5:2 [c]Gen 10:10; Is 11:11; Zech 5:11 [d]Jer 50:2
3 [1]Or *said to* [2]Or *eunuchs,* and so throughout the ch [3]Lit *seed of the* [a]2 Kin 24:15; Is 39:7
4 [1]Lit *standing* [2]Lit *palace* [3]Or *writing* [a]2 Sam 14:25 [b]Dan 1:17 [c]Is 36:11; Jer 5:15; Dan 2:4 [d]Dan 2:2
5 [1]Or *reared* [2]Lit *stand before the king* [a]Dan 1:8 [b]1 Sam 16:22; Dan 1:19
6 [a]Ezek 14:14; Matt 24:15
7 [a]Dan 2:26 [b]Dan 2:49
8 [1]Lit *set upon his heart* [a]Lev 11:47; Ezek 4:13; Hos 9:3 [b]Ps 141:4; Dan 1:5 [c]Deut 32:38; Dan 5:4
9 [1]Lit *lovingkindness* [a]Gen 39:21; 1 Kin 8:50; Job 5:15; Ps 106:46; Prov 16:7

king, who has appointed your food and
your drink; for why should he see your
faces looking more haggard than the
youths who are your own age? Then you
would [1]make me forfeit my head to the
king."
11 But Daniel said to the overseer
whom the commander of the officials had
appointed over Daniel, Hananiah, Mishael and Azariah,
12 "Please test your servants for ten
days, and let us be [a]given some vegetables to eat and water to drink.
13 "Then let our appearance be [1]ob-
served in your presence and the appearance of the youths who are eating the
king's choice food; and deal with your
servants according to what you see."
14 ¶ So he listened to them in this
matter and tested them for ten days.
15 At the end of ten days their appearance seemed [a]better and [1]they were fat-
ter than all the youths who had been eating the king's choice food.
16 So the overseer continued to
[1]withhold their choice food and the
wine they were to drink, and kept [a]giv-
ing them vegetables.
17 ¶ As for these four youths, [a]God
gave them knowledge and intelligence in
every *branch of* [1]literature and wisdom;
Daniel even understood all *kinds of* [b]vi-
sions and dreams.
18 ¶ Then at the end of the days which
the king had [1]specified [2]for presenting
them, the commander of the officials
[3]presented them before Nebuchadnezzar.
19 The king talked with them, and out
of them all not one was found like [a]Dan-
iel, Hananiah, Mishael and Azariah; so
they [1b]entered the king's personal service.
20 As for every matter of [a]wisdom
[1]and understanding about which the
king consulted them, he found them
[b]ten times [c]better than all the [2d]magi-
cians *and* conjurers who *were* in all his
realm.
21 And Daniel [1]continued until the
[a]first year of Cyrus the king.

The King's Forgotten Dream

2 Now in the second year of the reign
of Nebuchadnezzar, Nebuchadnezzar [1a]had dreams; and his spirit was
troubled and his [b]sleep [2]left him.
2 Then the king [1]gave orders to call
in the [2a]magicians, the conjurers, the
sorcerers and the [3]Chaldeans to tell the
king his dreams. So they came in and
stood before the king.
3 The king said to them, "I [1a]had a
dream and my spirit [2]is anxious to [3]un-
derstand the dream."
4 ¶ Then the Chaldeans spoke to the
king in [1a]Aramaic: "[b]O king, live forever! [c]Tell the dream to your servants, and
we will declare the interpretation."
5 The king replied to the Chaldeans,
"[1]The command from me is firm: if you
do not make known to me the dream and
its interpretation, you will be [2a]torn
limb from limb and your houses will be
made a rubbish heap.
6 "But if you declare the dream and its
interpretation, you will receive from me
[a]gifts and a reward and great honor;
therefore declare to me the dream and its
interpretation."
7 They answered a second time and
said, "Let the king [a]tell the dream to his
servants, and we will declare the interpretation."
8 The king replied, "I know for certain that you are [1]bargaining for time,
inasmuch as you have seen that [2]the
command from me is firm,
9 that if you do not make the dream
known to me, there is only [a]one [1]decree
for you. For you have agreed together to
speak lying and corrupt [2]words before
me until the [3]situation is changed; therefore tell me the dream, that I may [b]know
that you can declare to me its interpretation."
10 The Chaldeans answered [1]the king
and said, "There is not a man on earth
who could declare the matter [2]for the
king, inasmuch as no great king or ruler
has *ever* asked anything like this of any
[3a]magician, conjurer or Chaldean.
11 "Moreover, the thing which the king
demands is [1]difficult, and there is no one
else who could declare it [2]to the king
except [a]gods, whose [b]dwelling place is
not with *mortal* flesh."
12 ¶ Because of this the king became
[a]indignant and very furious and gave orders to destroy all the wise men of Babylon.
13 So the [1]decree went forth that the
wise men should be slain; and they
looked for [a]Daniel and his friends to
[2]kill *them.*
14 ¶ Then Daniel replied with discretion and discernment to [a]Arioch, the
captain of the king's [1]bodyguard, who
had gone forth to slay the wise men of
Babylon;
15 he said to Arioch, the king's commander, "For what reason is the [1]decree
from the king *so* [2]urgent?" Then Arioch
informed Daniel about the matter.
16 So Daniel went in and requested of
the king that he would [1]give him time, in

10 [1]Lit *make my head guilty*
12 [a]Dan 1:16
13 [1]Lit *seen*
15 [1]Lit *fat of flesh* [a]Ex 23:25; Prov 10:22
16 [1]Lit *take away* [a]Dan 1:12
17 [1]Or *writing* [a]1 Kin 3:12; Job 32:8; Dan 1:20; Acts 7:22 [b]Dan 2:19
18 [1]Lit *said* [2]Lit *to bring them in* [3]Lit *brought in*
19 [1]Lit *stood before the king* [a]Dan 1:6 [b]Gen 41:46; Dan 1:5
20 [1]Lit *of* [2]Or *soothsayer priests* [a]1 Kin 4:30; Dan 1:17 [b]Gen 31:7; Num 14:22; Neh 4:12; Job 19:3 [c]Dan 2:27 [d]Is 19:3; Dan 2:2
21 [1]Lit *was until* [a]Dan 6:28
2:1 [1]Lit *dreamed dreams* [2]Lit *was gone upon him* [a]Gen 40:5-8; Job 33:15-17; Dan 2:3 [b]Esth 6:1; Dan 6:18
2 [1]Lit *said to call* [2]Or *soothsayer priests* [3]Or *master astrologers,* and so throughout the ch [a]Gen 41:8; Ex 7:11; Is 47:12; Dan 1:20
3 [1]Lit *dreamed* [2]Lit *was troubled* [3]Lit *know* [a]Gen 40:8; Dan 4:5
4 [1]The text is in Aramaic from here through 7:28 [a]Ezra 4:7; Is 36:11 [b]Dan 3:9 [c]Dan 2:7
5 [1]Another reading is *The word has gone from me* [2]Lit *made into limbs* [a]Ezra 6:11; Dan 2:12
6 [a]Dan 2:48
7 [a]Dan 2:4
8 [1]Lit *buying* [2]V 5, note 1
9 [1]Or *law* [2]Lit *word* [3]Lit *time* [a]Esth 4:11; Dan 3:15 [b]Is 41:23
10 [1]Lit *before the* [2]Lit *of* [3]Or *soothsayer priest* [a]Dan 2:2
11 [1]Or *rare* [2]Lit *before* [a]Gen 41:39; Dan 5:11 [b]Ex 29:45; Is 57:15
12 [a]Ps 76:10; Dan 2:5
13 [1]Or *law* [2]Lit *be killed* [a]Dan 1:19
14 [1]Or *executioners* [a]Dan 2:24
15 [1]Or *law* [2]Or *harsh*
16 [1]Or *appoint a time for him*

order that he might declare the interpretation to the king.

17 ¶ Then Daniel went to his house and informed his friends, [a]Hananiah, Mishael and Azariah, about the matter,

18 so that they might [a]request compassion from the God of heaven concerning this mystery, so that Daniel and his friends would not be [b]destroyed with the rest of the wise men of Babylon.

The Secret Is Revealed to Daniel

19 Then the mystery was revealed to Daniel in a night [a]vision. Then Daniel blessed the God of heaven;

20 Daniel said,
"Let the name of God be [a]blessed
forever and ever,
For [b]wisdom and power belong
to Him.
21 "It is He who [a]changes the times
and the epochs;
He [b]removes kings and
[1]establishes kings;
He gives [c]wisdom to wise men
And knowledge to [2]men of
understanding.
22 "It is He who [a]reveals the
profound and hidden things;
[b]He knows what is in the
darkness,
And the [c]light dwells with Him.
23 "To You, O [a]God of my fathers, I
give thanks and praise,
For You have given me [b]wisdom
and power;
Even now You have made known
to me what we [c]requested
of You,
For You have made known to us
the king's matter."

24 ¶ Therefore, Daniel went in to Arioch, whom the king had appointed to destroy the wise men of Babylon; he went and spoke to him as follows: "[a]Do not destroy the wise men of Babylon! Take me [1]into the king's presence, and I will declare the interpretation to the king."

25 ¶ Then Arioch hurriedly [a]brought Daniel [1]into the king's presence and spoke to him as follows: "I have found a man among the [2b]exiles from Judah who can make the interpretation known to the king!"

26 The king said to Daniel, whose name was [a]Belteshazzar, "Are you able to make known to me the dream which I have seen and its interpretation?"

27 Daniel answered before the king and said, "As for the mystery about which the king has inquired, neither [a]wise men, conjurers, [1]magicians *nor* diviners are able to declare *it* to the king.

28 "However, there is a [a]God in heaven who reveals mysteries, and He has made known to King Nebuchadnezzar what will take place in the [1b]latter days. This was your dream and the [c]visions [2]in your mind *while* on your bed.

29 "As for you, O king, *while* on your bed your thoughts [1]turned to what would take place [2]in the future; and [a]He who reveals mysteries has made known to you what will take place.

30 "But as for me, this mystery has not been revealed to me for any [a]wisdom [1]residing in me more than *in* any *other* living man, but for the purpose of making the interpretation known to the king, and that you may [2]understand the [b]thoughts of your [3]mind.

The King's Dream

31 ¶ "You, O king, were looking and behold, there was a single great statue; that statue, which was large and [1]of extraordinary splendor, was standing in front of you, and its appearance was [a]awesome.

32 "The [a]head of that statue *was made* of fine gold, its breast and its arms of silver, its belly and its thighs of bronze,

33 its legs of iron, its feet partly of iron and partly of clay.

34 "You [1]continued looking until a [a]stone was cut out [b]without hands, and it struck the statue on its feet of iron and clay and [c]crushed them.

35 "Then the iron, the clay, the bronze, the silver and the gold were crushed [1]all at the same time and became [a]like chaff from the summer threshing floors; and the wind carried them away so that [b]not a trace of them was found. But the stone that struck the statue became a great [c]mountain and filled the whole earth.

The Interpretation—Babylon the First Kingdom

36 ¶ "This *was* the dream; now we will tell [a]its interpretation before the king.

37 "You, O king, are the [a]king of kings, to whom the God of heaven has given the [1]kingdom, the [b]power, the strength and the glory;

38 and wherever the sons of men dwell, *or* the [a]beasts of the field, or the birds of the sky, He has given *them* into your hand and has caused you to rule over them all. You are the head of gold.

Medo-Persia and Greece

39 "After you there will arise another kingdom inferior to you, then another third kingdom of bronze, which will rule over all the earth.

17 [a]Dan 1:6
18 [a]Esth 4:15, 16; Is 37:4; Jer 33:3; Ezek 36:37; Dan 2:23 [b]Gen 18:28; Mal 3:18
19 [a]Num 12:6; Job 33:15,16; Dan 1:17; 7:2,7, 13
20 [a]Ps 103:1,2; 113:1,2; 115:18; 145:1,2,21 [b]1 Chr 29:11,12; Job 12:13,16-22; Dan 2:21-23
21 [1]Or *sets up* [2]Lit *knowers* [a]Ps 31:15; Dan 2:9; 7:25 [b]Job 12:18; Ps 75:6,7; Dan 4:17,32 [c]1 Kin 3:9,10; 4:29; James 1:5
22 [a]Job 12:22; Ps 25:14; Dan 2:19,28 [b]Job 26:6; Ps 139:12; Is 45:7; Jer 23:24; Heb 4:13 [c]Ps 36:9; Dan 5:11,14; James 1:17; 1 John 1:5
23 [a]Gen 31:42; Ex 3:15 [b]Dan 1:17; 2:21 [c]Ps 21:2,4; Dan 2:18,29,30
24 [1]Lit *in before the king* [a]Dan 2:12,13; Acts 27:24
25 [1]Lit *in before the king* [2]Lit *sons of the exile of* [a]Gen 41:14 [b]Dan 1:6; 5:13; 6:13
26 [a]Dan 1:7; 4:8; 5:12
27 [1]Or *soothsayer priests* [a]Dan 2:2,10,11; 5:7,8
28 [1]Lit *end of the days* [2]Lit *of your head* [a]Gen 40:8; 41:16; Dan 2:22,45 [b]Gen 49:1; Is 2:2; Dan 10:14; Mic 4:1 [c]Dan 4:5
29 [1]Lit *came up* [2]Lit *after this* [a]Dan 2:23,47
30 [1]Lit *which is* [2]Lit *know* [3]Lit *heart* [a]Gen 41:16; Dan 1:17 [b]Ps 139:2; Amos 4:13
31 [1]Lit *its splendor was surpassing* [a]Hab 1:7
32 [a]Dan 2:38
34 [1]Lit *were* [a]Dan 2:45 [b]Dan 8:25; Zech 4:6 [c]Ps 2:9; Is 60:12
35 [1]Lit *like one* [a]Ps 1:4; Is 17:13; 41:15,16; Hos 13:3 [b]Ps 37:10,36 [c]Is 2:2; Mic 4:1
36 [a]Dan 2:24
37 [1]Or *sovereignty* [a]Is 47:5; Jer 27:6,7; Ezek 26:7 [b]Ps 62:11
38 [a]Ps 50:10, 11; Dan 4:21,22

Rome

40 "Then there will be a [a]fourth kingdom as strong as iron; inasmuch as iron crushes and shatters all things, so, like iron that breaks in pieces, it will crush and break all these in pieces.

41 "In that you saw the feet and toes, partly of potter's clay and partly of iron, it will be a divided kingdom; but it will have in it the toughness of iron, inasmuch as you saw the iron mixed with [1]common clay.

42 "*As* the toes of the feet *were* partly of iron and partly of pottery, *so* some of the kingdom will be strong and part of it will be brittle.

43 "And in that you saw the iron mixed with [1]common clay, they will combine with one another [2]in the seed of men; but they will not adhere to one another, even as iron does not combine with pottery.

The Divine Kingdom

44 "In the days of those kings the [a]God of heaven will [b]set up a [c]kingdom which will never be destroyed, and *that* kingdom will not be [1]left for another people; it will [d]crush and put an end to all these kingdoms, but it will itself endure forever.

45 "Inasmuch as you saw that a [a]stone was cut out of the mountain without hands and that it crushed the iron, the bronze, the clay, the silver and the gold, the [b]great God has made known to the king what [c]will take place [1]in the future; so the dream is true and its interpretation is trustworthy."

Daniel Promoted

46 ¶ Then King Nebuchadnezzar fell on his face and did [a]homage to Daniel, and gave orders to present to him an offering and [1b]fragrant incense.

47 The king answered Daniel and said, "Surely [a]your God is a [b]God of gods and a Lord of kings and a [c]revealer of mysteries, since you have been able to reveal this mystery."

48 Then the king [1a]promoted Daniel and gave him many great gifts, and he made him ruler over the whole [b]province of Babylon and chief [2]prefect over all the wise men of Babylon.

49 And Daniel made request of the king, and he [a]appointed [b]Shadrach, Meshach and Abed-nego over the administration of the province of Babylon, while Daniel *was* at the king's [1c]court.

The King's Golden Image

3 Nebuchadnezzar the king made an [a]image of gold, the height of which *was* sixty [1]cubits *and* its width six [1]cubits; he set it up on the plain of Dura in the [b]province of Babylon.

2 Then Nebuchadnezzar the king sent *word* to assemble the [a]satraps, the prefects and the governors, the counselors, the treasurers, the judges, the magistrates and all the rulers of the provinces to come to the dedication of the image that Nebuchadnezzar the king had set up.

3 Then the satraps, the prefects and the governors, the counselors, the treasurers, the judges, the magistrates and all the rulers of the provinces were assembled for the dedication of the image that Nebuchadnezzar the king had set up; and they stood before the image that Nebuchadnezzar had set up.

4 Then the herald loudly proclaimed: "To you [1]the command is given, [a]O peoples, nations and *men of every* [2]language,

5 that at the moment you [a]hear the sound of the horn, flute, [1]lyre, [2]trigon, [3]psaltery, bagpipe and all kinds of music, you are to fall down and worship the golden image that Nebuchadnezzar the king has set up.

6 "But whoever does not fall down and worship shall [1]immediately be [a]cast into the midst of a [b]furnace of blazing fire."

7 Therefore at that time, when all the peoples heard the sound of the horn, flute, [1]lyre, trigon, psaltery, bagpipe and all kinds of music, all the peoples, nations and *men of every* [2]language fell down *and* worshiped the golden image that Nebuchadnezzar the king had set up.

Worship of the Image Refused

8 ¶ For this reason at that time certain [a]Chaldeans came forward and [1b]brought charges against the Jews.

9 They responded and said to Nebuchadnezzar the king: "[a]O king, live forever!

10 "You, O king, have [a]made a decree that every man who hears the sound of the horn, flute, [1]lyre, trigon, psaltery, and bagpipe and all kinds of music, is to [b]fall down and worship the golden image.

11 "But whoever does not fall down and worship shall be cast into the midst of a furnace of blazing fire.

12 "There are certain Jews whom you have [a]appointed over the administration of the province of Babylon, *namely* Shadrach, Meshach and Abed-nego. These

40 [a]Dan 7:23
41 [1]Lit *clay of mud*
43 [1]Lit *clay of mud* [2]Or *with*
44 [1]Or *passed on to* [a]Dan 2:28, 37 [b]Is 9:6,7 [c]Ps 145:13; Ezek 37:25; Dan 4:3, 34; 6:26; 7:14, 27; Mic 4:7; Luke 1:32,33 [d]Ps 2:9; Is 60:12; Dan 2:34, 35
45 [1]Lit *after this* [a]Dan 2:34 [b]Deut 10:17; 2 Sam 7:22; Ps 48:1; Jer 32:18,19; Dan 2:29; Mal 1:11 [c]Gen 41:28,32
46 [1]Lit *sweet odors* [a]Dan 3:5, 7; Acts 10:25; 14:13; Rev 19:10; 22:8 [b]Lev 26:31; Ezra 6:10
47 [a]Dan 3:15; 4:25 [b]Deut 10:17; Ps 136:2, 3; Dan 11:36 [c]Dan 2:22,30; Amos 3:7
48 [1]Lit *made great* [2]Lit *of the prefects* [a]Gen 41:39-43; Dan 2:6; 5:16,29 [b]Dan 3:1,12,30
49 [1]Lit *gate* [a]Dan 3:12 [b]Dan 1:7 [c]Esth 2:19, 21; Amos 5:15
3:1 [1]I.e. One cubit equals approx 18 in. [a]1 Kin 12:28; Is 46:6; Jer 16:20; Dan 2:31; Hos 2:8; 8:4; Hab 2:19 [b]Dan 2:48; 3:30
2 [a]Dan 3:3,27; 6:1-7
4 [1]Lit *they command* [2]Lit *tongue* [a]Dan 3:7; 4:1; 6:25
5 [1]Or *zither* [2]I.e. triangular lyre [3]Or *a type of harp* [a]Dan 3:7,10,15
6 [1]Or *in the same hour* [a]Dan 3:11,15,21; 6:7 [b]Jer 29:22; Ezek 22:18-22; Matt 13:42,50; Rev 9:2; 14:11
7 [1]V 5, notes 1, 2, 3 [2]Lit *tongue*
8 [1]Lit *ate the pieces of* [a]Dan 2:2,10; 4:7 [b]Ezra 4:12-16; Esth 3:8,9; Dan 6:12,13
9 [a]Dan 2:4; 5:10; 6:6,21
10 [1]V 5, notes 1, 2, 3 [a]Esth 3:12-14; Dan 3:4-6; 6:12 [b]Dan 3:5,7,15
12 [a]Dan 2:49

men, O king, have disregarded you; they
do not serve your gods or worship the
golden image which you have set up."
13 ¶ Then Nebuchadnezzar in [a]rage
and anger gave orders to bring Shadrach,
Meshach and Abed-nego; then these men
were brought before the king.
14 Nebuchadnezzar responded and
said to them, "Is it true, Shadrach, Meshach and Abed-nego, that you do not
serve [a]my gods or worship the golden
image that I have set up?
15 "Now if you are ready, [a]at the moment you hear the sound of the horn,
flute, [1]lyre, trigon, psaltery and bagpipe
and all kinds of music, to fall down and
worship the image that I have made, *very*
well. But if you do not worship, you will
[2]immediately be [b]cast into the midst of
a furnace of blazing fire; and [c]what god
is there who can deliver you out of my
hands?"
16 ¶ [a]Shadrach, Meshach and Abed-
nego replied to the king, "O Nebuchadnezzar, we do not need to give you an
answer concerning this matter.
17 "[1]If it be *so,* our [a]God whom we
serve is able to deliver us from the furnace of blazing fire; [2]and [b]He will deliver us out of your hand, O king.
18 "[a]But *even* if *He does* not, [b]let it be
known to you, O king, that we are not
going to serve your gods or worship the
golden image that you have set up."

Daniel's Friends Protected

19 ¶ Then Nebuchadnezzar was filled
with [a]wrath, and his facial expression
was altered toward Shadrach, Meshach
and Abed-nego. He answered [1]by giving
orders to heat the furnace seven times
more than it was usually heated.
20 He commanded certain valiant warriors who *were* in his army to tie up Shadrach, Meshach and Abed-nego in order
to cast *them* into the furnace of blazing
fire.
21 Then these men were tied up in
their [1a]trousers, their [2]coats, their caps
and their *other* clothes, and were cast
into the midst of the furnace of blazing
fire.
22 For this reason, because the king's
[1]command *was* [2a]urgent and the furnace had been made extremely hot, the
flame of the fire slew those men who
carried up Shadrach, Meshach and Abed-
nego.
23 But these three men, Shadrach,
Meshach and Abed-nego, [a]fell into the
midst of the furnace of blazing fire *still*
tied up.
24 ¶ Then Nebuchadnezzar the king
was astounded and stood up in haste; he
said to his high officials, "Was it not three
men we cast bound into the midst of the
fire?" They replied to the king, "Certainly, O king."
25 He said, "Look! I see four men
loosed *and* [a]walking *about* in the midst
of the fire [1]without harm, and the appearance of the fourth is like a son of *the*
[b]gods!"
26 Then Nebuchadnezzar came near
to the door of the furnace of blazing fire;
he responded and said, "Shadrach, Meshach and Abed-nego, come out, you servants of the [a]Most High God, and come
here!" Then Shadrach, Meshach and
Abed-nego [b]came out of the midst of the
fire.
27 The [a]satraps, the prefects, the governors and the king's high officials gathered around *and* saw in regard to these
men that the [b]fire had no [1]effect on
[2]the bodies of these men nor was the
hair of their head singed, nor were their
[3c]trousers [4]damaged, nor had the smell
of fire *even* come upon them.
28 ¶ Nebuchadnezzar responded and
said, "Blessed be the [a]God of Shadrach,
Meshach and Abed-nego, who has [b]sent
His angel and delivered His servants who
put their [c]trust in Him, [1]violating the
king's command, and yielded up their
bodies so as [d]not to serve or worship any
god except their own God.
29 "Therefore I [a]make a decree that
any people, nation or tongue that speaks
anything offensive against the God of
[b]Shadrach, Meshach and Abed-nego
shall be torn limb from limb and their
[c]houses reduced to a rubbish heap, inasmuch as there is [d]no other god who is
able to deliver in this way."
30 Then the king [a]caused Shadrach,
Meshach and Abed-nego to prosper in
the province of Babylon.

The King Acknowledges God

4 [1]Nebuchadnezzar the king to all the
peoples, nations, and *men of every*
[2]language that live in all the earth: "May
your [3a]peace abound!
2 "It has seemed good to me to declare
the signs and wonders which the [a]Most
High God has done for me.
3 "How great are His [a]signs
And how mighty are His
wonders!
His [b]kingdom is an everlasting
kingdom
And His dominion is from
generation to generation.

The Vision of a Great Tree

4 ¶ "[1]I, Nebuchadnezzar, was at

---

13 [a]Dan 2:12; 3:19

14 [a]Is 46:1; Jer 50:2; Dan 3:1; 4:8

15 [1]V 5, notes 1, 2, 3 [2]Or *in the same hour* [a]Dan 3:5 [b]Dan 3:6 [c]Ex 5:2; Is 36:18-20; Dan 2:47

16 [a]Dan 1:7; 3:12

17 [1]Or *If our God...is able* [2]Or *then* [a]Job 5:19; Ps 27:1,2; Is 26:3,4; Jer 1:8; 15:20,21 [b]1 Sam 17:37; Mic 7:7; 2 Cor 1:10

18 [a]Josh 24:15; 1 Kin 19:14,18; Is 51:12,13; Dan 3:28 [b]Heb 11:25

19 [1]Lit *and ordered to* [a]Esth 7:7; Dan 3:13

21 [1]Or *leggings* [2]Or *cloaks* [a]Dan 3:27

22 [1]Lit *word* [2]Or *harsh* [a]Ex 12:33; Dan 2:15

23 [a]Is 43:2

25 [1]Lit *there is no injury in them* [a]Ps 91:3-9; Is 43:2 [b]Jer 1:8, 19; 15:21

26 [a]Dan 3:17; 4:2 [b]Deut 4:20; 1 Kin 8:51; Jer 11:4

27 [1]Lit *power over* [2]Lit *their* [3]Or *cloaks* [4]Lit *changed* [a]Dan 3:2,3 [b]Is 43:2; Heb 11:34 [c]Dan 3:21

28 [1]Lit *and changed the king's word* [a]Dan 2:47; 3:15-17 [b]Ps 34:7,8; Is 37:36; Dan 3:25; 6:22; Acts 5:19; 12:7 [c]Ps 22:4,5; 40:4; 84:12; Is 12:2; 26:3,4; 50:10; Jer 17:7 [d]Dan 3:16-18

29 [a]Dan 6:26 [b]Dan 1:7,19; 2:17,49; 3:12 [c]Ezra 6:11; Dan 2:5 [d]Dan 2:47; 3:15

30 [a]Dan 2:49; 3:12

4:1 [1]Ch 3:31 in Aram [2]Lit *tongue* [3]Or *welfare* or *prosperity* [a]Ezra 4:17; Dan 6:25

2 [a]Dan 3:26; 4:17,24,25,32, 34

3 [a]Ps 77:19; 105:27; Is 25:1; Dan 6:27 [b]Dan 2:44; 4:34; 6:26

4 [1]Ch 4:1 in Aram

ease in my house and [a]flourishing in my palace.

5 "I saw a [a]dream and it made me fearful; and *these* fantasies *as I lay* on my bed and the [b]visions [1]in my mind kept alarming me.

6 "So I gave orders to [a]bring into my presence all the wise men of Babylon, that they might make known to me the interpretation of the dream.

7 "Then the [1a]magicians, the conjurers, the [2]Chaldeans and the diviners came in and I related the dream [3]to them, but they could not make its [b]interpretation known to me.

8 "But finally Daniel came in before me, whose name is [a]Belteshazzar according to the name of my god, and in whom is [1b]a spirit of the holy gods; and I related the dream [2]to him, *saying,*

9 'O Belteshazzar, [a]chief of the magicians, since I know that [b]a spirit of the holy gods is in you and [c]no mystery baffles you, [d]tell *me* the visions of my dream which I have seen, along with its interpretation.

10 ¶ 'Now *these were* the [a]visions [1]in my mind *as I lay* on my bed: I was looking, and behold, *there was* a [b]tree in the midst of the [2]earth and its height *was* great.

11 'The tree grew large and became
  strong
And its height [a]reached to the
  sky,
And it *was* visible to the end of
  the whole earth.
12 'Its foliage *was* [a]beautiful and its
  fruit abundant,
And in it *was* food for all.
The [b]beasts of the field found
  [c]shade under it,
And the [d]birds of the sky dwelt
  in its branches,
And all [1]living creatures fed
  themselves from it.

13 ¶ 'I was looking in the [a]visions [1]in my mind *as I lay* on my bed, and behold, [b]an *angelic* watcher, a [c]holy one, descended from heaven.

14 'He shouted out and spoke as
  follows:
"[a]Chop down the tree and cut off
  its branches,
Strip off its foliage and scatter its
  fruit;
Let the [b]beasts flee from
  under it
And the birds from its branches.
15 "Yet [a]leave the stump [1]with its
  roots in the ground,
But with a band of iron and
  bronze *around it*
In the new grass of the field;
And let him be drenched with
  the dew of heaven,
And let [2]him share with the
  beasts in the grass of the
  earth.
16 "Let his [1]mind be changed from
  that of a man
And let a beast's [1]mind be given
  to him,
And let [a]seven [2]periods of time
  pass over him.
17 "This sentence is by the decree of
  the *angelic* watchers
And the decision is a command
  of the holy ones,
In order that the living may
  [a]know
That the Most High is ruler over
  the realm of mankind,
And [b]bestows it on whom He
  wishes
And sets over it the [c]lowliest of
  men."

18 'This is the dream *which* I, King Nebuchadnezzar, have seen. Now you, Belteshazzar, tell *me* its interpretation, inasmuch as none of the [a]wise men of my kingdom is able to make known to me the interpretation; but you are able, for a [b]spirit of the holy gods is in you.'

Daniel Interprets the Vision

19 ¶ "Then Daniel, whose name is Belteshazzar, was appalled for a while as his [a]thoughts alarmed him. The king responded and said, 'Belteshazzar, do not [b]let the dream or its interpretation alarm you.' Belteshazzar replied, '[c]My lord, *if only* the dream applied to those who hate you and its interpretation to [d]your adversaries!

20 'The [a]tree that you saw, which became large and grew strong, whose height reached to the sky and was visible to all the earth

21 and whose foliage *was* beautiful and its fruit abundant, and in which *was* food for all, under which the beasts of the field dwelt and in whose branches the birds of the sky lodged—

22 it is [a]you, O king; for you have become great and grown strong, and your [1]majesty has become great and reached to the sky and your [b]dominion to the end of the earth.

23 'In that the king saw an *angelic* watcher, a holy one, descending from heaven and saying, "[a]Chop down the tree and destroy it; yet leave the stump [1]with its roots in the ground, but with a band of iron and bronze *around it* in the new grass of the field, and let him be drenched with the dew of heaven, and let [2]him share with the beasts of the field

4 [a]Ps 30:6; Is 47:7

5 [1]Lit *of my head* [a]Dan 2:3 [b]Dan 2:1

6 [a]Gen 41:8; Dan 2:2

7 [1]Or *soothsayer priests,* and so throughout the ch [2]Or *master astrologers* [3]Lit *before* [a]Gen 41:8; Dan 2:10 [b]Is 44:25; Jer 27:9; Dan 2:7

8 [1]Or possibly *the Spirit of the holy God,* and so throughout the ch [2]Lit *before* [a]Dan 1:7 [b]Dan 4:9

9 [a]Dan 1:20 [b]Gen 41:38; Dan 4:8 [c]Ezek 28:3; Dan 2:47 [d]Gen 41:15; Dan 2:4

10 [1]Lit *of my head* [2]Or *land,* and so throughout the ch [a]Dan 4:5 [b]Ezek 31:3

11 [a]Deut 9:1; Dan 4:21

12 [1]Lit *flesh* [a]Ezek 31:7 [b]Jer 27:6; Ezek 31:6 [c]Lam 4:20 [d]Ezek 17:23; Matt 13:32; Luke 13:19

13 [1]Lit *of my head* [a]Dan 7:1 [b]Dan 4:17 [c]Deut 33:2; Ps 89:7; Dan 8:13

14 [a]Ezek 31:10-14; Dan 4:23; Matt 3:10; Luke 13:7-9 [b]Ezek 31:12; Dan 4:12

15 [1]Lit *of* [2]Lit *his portion be with* [a]Job 14:7-9

16 [1]Lit *heart* [2]I.e. years [a]Dan 4:23

17 [a]Ps 9:16; Dan 2:21 [b]Jer 27:5-7; Dan 4:25 [c]1 Sam 2:8; Dan 11:21

18 [a]Gen 41:8; Dan 4:7 [b]Dan 4:8

19 [a]Jer 4:19; Dan 7:15 [b]1 Sam 3:17; Dan 4:4 [c]2 Sam 18:31; Dan 4:24 [d]2 Sam 18:32

20 [a]Dan 4:10-12

22 [1]Lit *greatness* [a]2 Sam 12:7; Dan 2:37 [b]Jer 27:6

23 [1]Lit *of* [2]Lit *his portion be with* [a]Dan 4:14

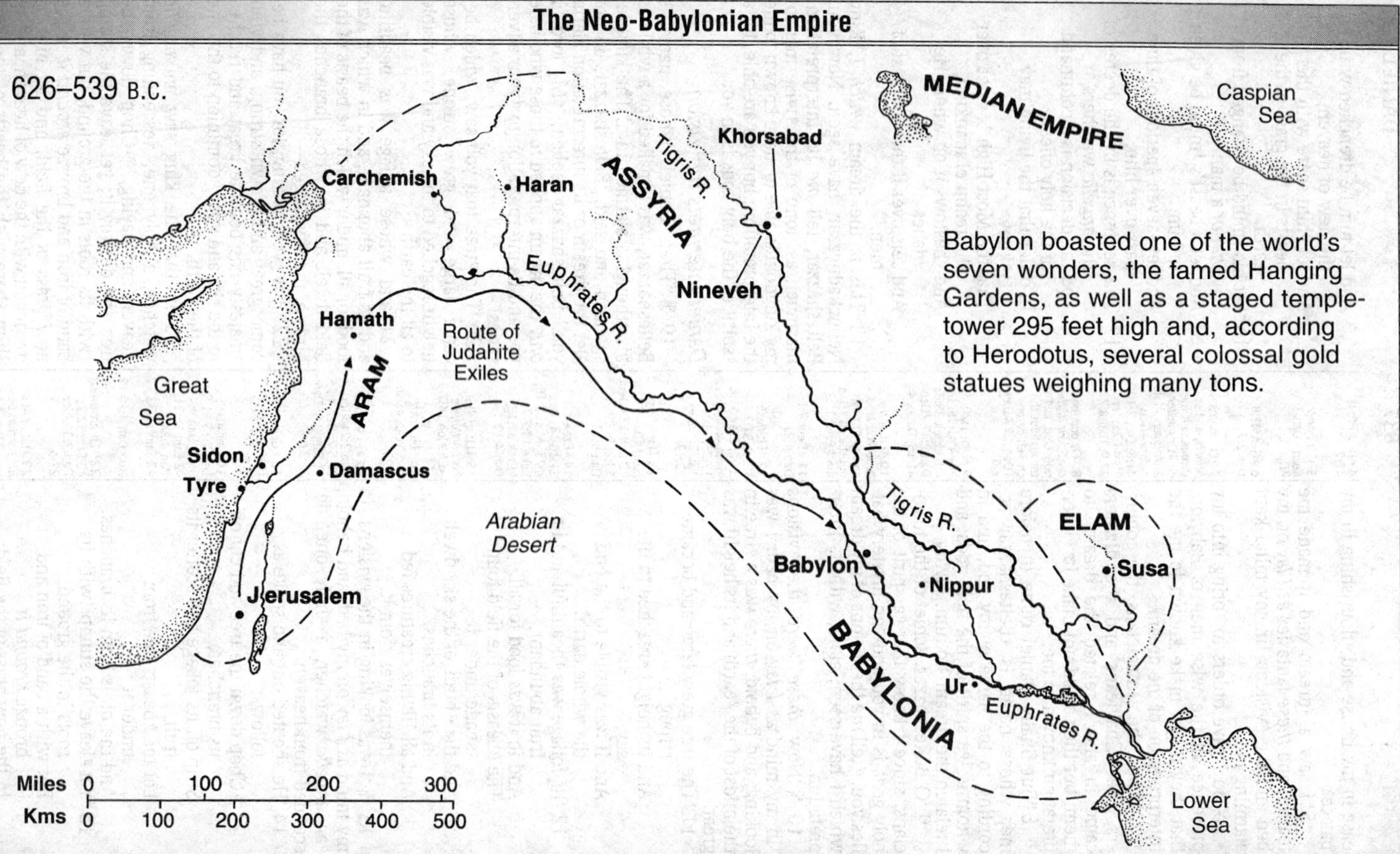
The Neo-Babylonian Empire
626–539 B.C.
MEDIAN EMPIRE
Caspian Sea
Khorsabad
Tigris R.
ASSYRIA
Carchemish
Haran
Euphrates R.
Nineveh
Babylon boasted one of the world's seven wonders, the famed Hanging Gardens, as well as a staged temple-tower 295 feet high and, according to Herodotus, several colossal gold statues weighing many tons.
Hamath
Route of Judahite Exiles
ARAM
Great Sea
Sidon
Tyre
Damascus
Arabian Desert
Tigris R.
ELAM
Susa
Babylon
Nippur
Jerusalem
BABYLONIA
Ur
Euphrates R.
Lower Sea
Miles 0 100 200 300
Kms 0 100 200 300 400 500

until [b]seven [3]periods of time pass over
him,"
24 this is the interpretation, O king,
and this is the decree of the Most High,
which has [a]come upon my lord the king:
25 that you be [a]driven away from
mankind and your dwelling place be with
the beasts of the field, and you be given
grass to eat like cattle and be drenched
with the dew of heaven; and seven [1]peri-
ods of time will pass over you, until you
recognize that the [b]Most High is ruler
over the realm of mankind and [c]bestows
it on whomever He wishes.
26 'And in that it was commanded to
[a]leave the stump [1]with the roots of the
tree, your kingdom will be [2]assured to
you after you recognize that *it is* [b]Heaven
that rules.
27 'Therefore, O king, may my [a]ad-
vice be pleasing to you: [1b]break away
now from your sins by *doing* righteousness and from your iniquities by [c]show-
ing mercy to *the* poor, in case there may
be a [d]prolonging of your prosperity.'

The Vision Fulfilled

28 ¶ "All *this* [a]happened to Nebuchadnezzar the king.
29 "[a]Twelve months later he was walking on the *roof of* the royal palace of Babylon.
30 "The king [1]reflected and said, 'Is
this not Babylon the [a]great, which I myself have built as a royal [2]residence by
the might of my power and for the glory
of my majesty?'
31 "While the word *was* in the king's
mouth, a voice [1]came from heaven, *saying,* 'King Nebuchadnezzar, to you it is
declared: [2]sovereignty has been removed from you,
32 and [a]you will be driven away from
mankind, and your dwelling place *will be*
with the beasts of the field. You will be
given grass to eat like cattle, and [b]seven
[1]periods of time will pass over you until
you recognize that the [c]Most High is ruler over the realm of mankind and be-
stows it on whomever He wishes.'
33 "Immediately the word concerning
Nebuchadnezzar was fulfilled; and he
was [a]driven away from mankind and began eating grass like cattle, and his body
was drenched with the dew of heaven
until his hair had grown like eagles' *feathers* and his nails like birds' *claws.*
34 ¶ "But at the end of [1]that period, I,
Nebuchadnezzar, raised my eyes toward
heaven and my [2]reason returned to me,
and I blessed the [a]Most High and praised
and honored [b]Him who lives forever;

For His dominion is an
[c]everlasting dominion,
And His kingdom *endures* from
generation to generation.
35 "[a]All the inhabitants of the earth
are accounted as nothing,
But [b]He does according to His
will in the host of heaven
And *among* the inhabitants of
earth;
And [c]no one can [1]ward off His
hand
Or say to Him, '[d]What have You
done?'

36 "At that time my [1a]reason returned
to me. And my majesty and [b]splendor
were [2]restored to me for the glory of my
kingdom, and my counselors and my nobles began seeking me out; so I was rees-
tablished in my [3]sovereignty, and surpassing [c]greatness was added to me.
37 "Now I, Nebuchadnezzar, praise,
exalt and honor the King of [a]heaven, for
[b]all His works are [1]true and His ways
[2]just, and He is able to humble those
who [c]walk in pride."

Belshazzar's Feast

5 Belshazzar the king [1]held a great
[a]feast for a thousand of his nobles,
and he was drinking wine in the presence
of the thousand.
2 When Belshazzar tasted the wine,
he gave orders to bring the gold and silver
[a]vessels which Nebuchadnezzar his [1]fa-
ther had taken out of the temple which
was in Jerusalem, so that the king and his
nobles, his wives and his concubines
might drink from them.
3 Then they brought the gold vessels
that had been taken out of the temple,
the house of God which *was* in Jerusalem; and the king and his nobles, his
wives and his concubines drank from
them.
4 They [a]drank the wine and praised
the gods of [b]gold and silver, of bronze,
iron, wood and stone.
5 ¶ Suddenly the fingers of a man's
hand emerged and began writing opposite the lampstand on the plaster of the
wall of the king's palace, and the king saw
the [1]back of the hand that did the writing.
6 Then the king's [1a]face grew pale
and his thoughts alarmed him, and his
[b]hip joints went slack and his [c]knees
began knocking together.
7 The king called aloud to bring in
the [a]conjurers, the [1]Chaldeans and the
diviners. The king spoke and said to the
wise men of Babylon, "Any man who can
read this inscription and explain its interpretation to me shall be [b]clothed with
purple and *have* a [c]necklace of gold

23 [3]I.e. years [b]Dan 4:16
24 [a]Job 40:11; Ps 107:40
25 [1]I.e. years [a]Dan 4:33 [b]Ps 83:18; Jer 27:5; Dan 4:2 [c]Dan 2:37
26 [1]Lit *of* [2]Lit *enduring* [a]Dan 4:15 [b]Dan 2:18
27 [1]Or *redeem now your sins* [a]Gen 41:33-37 [b]Prov 28:13; Is 55:6; Ezek 18:7; Acts 8:22 [c]Ps 41:1-3; Is 58:6 [d]1 Kin 21:29; Jon 3:9
28 [a]Num 23:19; Zech 1:6
29 [a]2 Pet 3:9
30 [1]Lit *answered* [2]Lit *house* [a]Hab 2:4
31 [1]Lit *fell* [2]Or *kingdom*
32 [1]I.e. years [a]Dan 4:25 [b]Dan 4:16 [c]Dan 4:17
33 [a]Dan 4:25
34 [1]Lit *the days* [2]Lit *knowledge* [a]Dan 4:2 [b]Ps 102:24-27; Dan 6:26; Rev 4:10 [c]Ps 145:13; Jer 10:10; Dan 4:3; Mic 4:7; Luke 1:33
35 [1]Lit *strike against* [a]Ps 39:5; Is 40:15 [b]Ps 33:11; Dan 6:27 [c]Job 42:2; Is 43:13 [d]Job 9:12; Is 45:9; Rom 9:20
36 [1]Lit *knowledge* [2]Lit *returning* [3]Or *kingdom* [a]2 Chr 33:12; Dan 4:34 [b]Dan 2:31 [c]Prov 22:4; Dan 4:22
37 [1]Lit *truth* [2]Lit *justice* [a]Dan 4:26 [b]Deut 32:4; Ps 33:4; Is 5:16 [c]Ex 18:11; Job 40:11; Dan 5:20
5:1 [1]Lit *made* [a]Esth 1:3; Is 22:12-14
2 [1]Or *forefather,* and so throughout the ch [a]2 Kin 24:13; Ezra 1:7-11; Dan 1:2
4 [a]Is 42:8; Dan 5:23; Rev 9:20 [b]Ps 115:4; Is 40:19; Dan 3:1; Hab 2:19
5 [1]Or *palm*
6 [1]Lit *brightness changed for him* [a]Dan 5:9 [b]Ps 69:23 [c]Ezek 7:17; Nah 2:10
7 [1]Or *master astrologers* [a]Is 44:25; Dan 4:6 [b]Gen 41:42-44; Dan 5:16 [c]Ezek 16:11

around his neck, and have authority as [2d]third *ruler* in the kingdom."

8 Then all the king's wise men came in, but [a]they could not read the inscription or make known its interpretation to the king.

9 Then King Belshazzar was greatly [a]alarmed, his [1b]face grew *even* paler, and his nobles were perplexed.

10 ¶ The queen entered the banquet [1]hall because of the words of the king and his nobles; the queen spoke and said, "[a]O king, live forever! Do not let your thoughts alarm you or your [2]face be pale.

11 "There is a [a]man in your kingdom in whom is [1]a [b]spirit of the holy gods; and in the days of your father, illumination, insight and wisdom like the wisdom of the gods were found in him. And King Nebuchadnezzar, your father, your father [2c]the king, appointed him chief of the [3]magicians, conjurers, [4]Chaldeans *and* diviners.

12 "*This was* because an [a]extraordinary spirit, knowledge and insight, interpretation of dreams, explanation of enigmas and solving of difficult problems were found in this Daniel, whom the king named [b]Belteshazzar. Let Daniel now be summoned and he will declare the interpretation."

Daniel Interprets Handwriting on the Wall

13 ¶ Then Daniel was brought in before the king. The king spoke and said to Daniel, "Are you that Daniel who is one of the [1a]exiles from Judah, whom my father the king [b]brought from Judah?

14 "Now I have heard about you that [1]a spirit of the gods is in you, and that illumination, insight and extraordinary wisdom have been found in you.

15 "Just now the [a]wise men *and* the conjurers were brought in before me that they might read this inscription and make its interpretation known to me, but they [b]could not declare the interpretation of the [1]message.

16 "But I personally have heard about you, that you are able to give interpretations and solve difficult problems. Now if you are able to read the inscription and make its [a]interpretation known to me, you will be [b]clothed with purple and *wear* a necklace of gold around your neck, and you will have authority as the [1]third *ruler* in the kingdom."

17 ¶ Then Daniel answered and said before the king, "[1]Keep your [a]gifts for yourself or give your rewards to someone else; however, I will read the inscription to the king and make the interpretation known to him.

18 "[1]O king, the [a]Most High God [b]granted [2]sovereignty, [c]grandeur, glory and majesty to Nebuchadnezzar your father.

19 "Because of the grandeur which He bestowed on him, all the peoples, nations and *men of every* [1]language feared and trembled before him; [a]whomever he wished he killed and whomever he wished he spared alive; and whomever he wished he elevated and whomever he wished he humbled.

20 "But when his heart was [a]lifted up and his spirit became so [1b]proud that he behaved arrogantly, he was [c]deposed from his royal throne and *his* glory was taken away from him.

21 "He was also [a]driven away from [1]mankind, and his heart was made like *that of* beasts, and his dwelling place *was* with the [b]wild donkeys. He was given grass to eat like cattle, and his body was drenched with the dew of heaven until he recognized that the [c]Most High God is ruler over the realm of mankind and *that* He sets over it whomever He wishes.

22 "Yet you, his [1]son, Belshazzar, have [a]not humbled your heart, [2]even though you knew all this,

23 but you have [a]exalted yourself against the [b]Lord of heaven; and they have brought the vessels of His house before you, and you and your nobles, your wives and your concubines have been drinking wine from them; and you have praised the [c]gods of silver and gold, of bronze, iron, wood and stone, which do not see, hear or understand. But the God [d]in whose hand are your life-breath and your [e]ways, you have not glorified.

24 "Then the [1a]hand was sent from Him and this inscription was written out.

25 ¶ "Now this is the inscription that was written out: '[1]MENĒ, [1]MENĒ, [2]TEKĒL, [3]UPHARSIN.'

26 "This is the interpretation of the [1]message: 'MENĒ'—God has numbered your kingdom and [a]put an end to it.

27 " 'TEKĒL'—you have been [a]weighed on the scales and found deficient.

28 " 'PERĒS'—your kingdom has been divided and given over to the [a]Medes and [1]Persians."

29 ¶ Then Belshazzar gave orders, and they [a]clothed Daniel with purple and *put* a necklace of gold around his neck, and issued a proclamation concerning him that he *now* had authority as the [1]third *ruler* in the kingdom.

7 [2]Or *a triumvir* [d]Dan 2:48
8 [a]Gen 41:8; Dan 2:27
9 [1]Lit *brightness was changing upon him* [a]Job 18:11; Is 21:2-4; Jer 6:24; Dan 2:1 [b]Is 13:6-8
10 [1]Lit *house* [2]Lit *brightness be changed* [a]Dan 3:9
11 [1]Or possibly *the Spirit of the holy God* [2]Or *O king* [3]Or *soothsayer priests* [4]Or *master astrologers* [a]Gen 41:11-15; Dan 2:47 [b]Dan 4:8 [c]Dan 2:48
12 [a]Dan 5:14 [b]Dan 1:7
13 [1]Lit *sons of the exile* [a]Ezra 4:1; Dan 2:25 [b]Dan 1:1
14 [1]Or possibly *the Spirit of God*
15 [1]Lit *word* [a]Dan 5:7 [b]Is 47:12f; Dan 5:8
16 [1]Or *triumvir* [a]Gen 40:8 [b]Dan 5:7
17 [1]Lit *Let...be for* [a]2 Kin 5:16
18 [1]Lit *You, O king* [2]Or *the kingdom* [a]Dan 4:2 [b]Dan 2:37 [c]Jer 25:9
19 [1]Lit *tongue* [a]Dan 2:12
20 [1]Lit *strong* [a]Ex 9:17; Job 15:25; Is 14:13-15; Dan 4:30 [b]2 Kin 17:14; 2 Chr 36:13 [c]Job 40:11; Jer 13:18
21 [1]Lit *the sons of man* [a]Job 30:3-7; Dan 4:32 [b]Job 39:5-8 [c]Ex 9:14-16; Ps 83:17; Ezek 17:24; Dan 4:17
22 [1]Or *descendant* [2]Lit *inasmuch as you* [a]Ex 10:3; 2 Chr 33:23
23 [a]2 Kin 14:10; Is 2:12; Jer 50:29; Dan 5:3 [b]Dan 4:37 [c]Ps 115:4-8; Is 37:19; Hab 2:18 [d]Job 12:10 [e]Job 31:4; Ps 139:3; Prov 20:24; Jer 10:23
24 [1]Lit *palm of the hand* [a]Dan 5:5
25 [1]Or *a mina* (50 shekels) from verb "to number" [2]Or *a shekel* from verb "to weigh" [3]Or *and half-shekels* (sing: *perēs*) from verb "to divide"
26 [1]Lit *word* [a]Is 13:6; Jer 50:41-43
27 [a]Job 31:6; Ps 62:9
28 [1]Aram: *Pāras* [a]Is 13:17; Dan 5:31; Acts 2:9
29 [1]Or *triumvir* [a]Dan 5:7

30 ¶ That same night [a]Belshazzar the Chaldean king was [b]slain.

31 [1]So [a]Darius the Mede received the kingdom at about the age of sixty-two.

Daniel Serves Darius

6 [1]It seemed good to Darius to appoint 120 satraps over the kingdom, that they would be in charge of the whole kingdom,

2 and over them three commissioners (of whom [a]Daniel was one), that these satraps might be accountable to them, and that the king might not suffer [b]loss.

3 Then this Daniel began distinguishing himself [1]among the commissioners and satraps because [2]he possessed an [a]extraordinary spirit, and the king planned to appoint him over the [b]entire kingdom.

4 Then the commissioners and satraps began [a]trying to find a ground of accusation against Daniel in regard to [1]government affairs; but they could find [b]no ground of accusation or *evidence of* corruption, inasmuch as he was faithful, and no negligence or corruption was *to be* found in him.

5 Then these men said, "We will not find any ground of accusation against this Daniel unless we find *it* against him with regard to the [a]law of his God."

6 ¶ Then these commissioners and satraps came [1]by agreement to the king and spoke to him as follows: "King Darius, [a]live forever!

7 "All the [a]commissioners of the kingdom, the prefects and the satraps, the high officials and the governors have [b]consulted together that the king should establish a statute and enforce an injunction that anyone who makes a petition to any god or man besides you, O king, for thirty days, shall [c]be cast into the lions' [1]den.

8 "Now, O king, [a]establish the injunction and sign the document so that it may not be changed, according to the [b]law of the Medes and Persians, which [1]may not be revoked."

9 Therefore King Darius [a]signed the document, that is, the injunction.

10 ¶ Now when Daniel knew that the document was signed, he entered his house (now in his roof chamber he had windows open [a]toward Jerusalem); and he continued [b]kneeling on his knees three times a day, [c]praying and [d]giving thanks before his God, [1]as he had been doing previously.

11 Then these men came [1a]by agreement and found Daniel making petition and supplication before his God.

12 Then they approached and [a]spoke before the king about the king's injunction, "Did you not sign an injunction that any man who makes a petition to any god or man besides you, O king, for thirty days, is to be cast into the lions' den?" The king replied, "The statement is true, according to the [b]law of the Medes and Persians, which [1]may not be revoked."

13 Then they answered and spoke before the king, "[a]Daniel, who is one of the [1]exiles from Judah, pays [b]no attention to you, O king, or to the injunction which you signed, but keeps making his petition three times a day."

14 ¶ Then, as soon as the king heard this statement, he was deeply [a]distressed and set *his* mind on delivering Daniel; and even until sunset he kept exerting himself to rescue him.

15 Then these men came [1]by agreement to the king and said to the king, "Recognize, O king, that it is a [a]law of the Medes and Persians that no injunction or statute which the king establishes may be changed."

Daniel in the Lions' Den

16 ¶ Then the king gave orders, and Daniel was brought in and [a]cast into the lions' den. The king spoke and said to Daniel, "[1b]Your God whom you constantly serve will Himself deliver you."

17 A [a]stone was brought and laid over the mouth of the den; and the king sealed it with his own signet ring and with the signet rings of his nobles, so that nothing would be changed in regard to Daniel.

18 Then the king went off to his palace and spent the night [a]fasting, and no entertainment was brought before him; and his [b]sleep fled from him.

19 ¶ Then the king arose at dawn, at the break of day, and went in haste to the lions' den.

20 When he had come near the den to Daniel, he cried out with a troubled voice. The king spoke and said to Daniel, "Daniel, servant of the living God, has [a]your God, whom you constantly serve, been [b]able to deliver you from the lions?"

21 Then Daniel spoke [1]to the king, "[a]O king, live forever!

22 "My God [a]sent His angel and [b]shut the lions' mouths and they have not harmed me, inasmuch as [1]I was found innocent before Him; and also [2]toward you, O king, I have committed no crime."

23 Then the king was very pleased and gave orders for Daniel to be taken up out

30 [a]Dan 5:1 [b]Is 21:4-9; Jer 51:11
31 [1]Ch 6:1 in Aram [a]Dan 6:1
6:1 [1]Ch 6:2 in Aram
2 [a]Dan 2:48 [b]Ezra 4:22; Esth 7:4
3 [1]Lit *above* [2]Lit *there was in him* [a]Dan 5:12 [b]Gen 41:40; Esth 10:3
4 [1]Lit *the kingdom* [a]Gen 43:18; Judg 14:4; Jer 20:10; Dan 3:8; Luke 20:20 [b]Dan 6:22; Luke 20:26; Phil 2:15; 1 Pet 2:12
5 [a]Acts 24:13-16
6 [1]Or *thronging* [a]Neh 2:3; Dan 2:4
7 [1]Or *pit,* and so throughout the ch [a]Dan 3:2 [b]Ps 59:3 [c]Ps 10:9; Dan 3:6
8 [1]Lit *does not pass away* [a]Esth 3:12; Is 10:1 [b]Esth 1:19; Dan 6:12
9 [a]Ps 118:9
10 [1]Or *because* [a]1 Kin 8:44; Ps 5:7; Jon 2:4 [b]Ps 55:17 [c]Dan 9:4-19 [d]Ps 34:1; Phil 4:6; 1 Thess 5:17
11 [1]Or *thronging* [a]Ps 37:32; Dan 6:6
12 [1]Lit *does not pass away* [a]Dan 3:8-12; Acts 16:19-21 [b]Esth 1:19; Dan 6:8
13 [1]Lit *sons of the exile* [a]Dan 2:25 [b]Esth 3:8; Dan 3:12; Acts 5:29
14 [a]Mark 6:26
15 [1]Or *thronging* [a]Esth 8:8; Ps 94:20; Dan 6:8
16 [1]Or *May your God...Himself deliver you* [a]2 Sam 3:39; Jer 38:5; Dan 6:7 [b]Job 5:19; Ps 37:39; Is 41:10; Dan 3:17; 2 Cor 1:10
17 [a]Lam 3:53; Matt 27:66
18 [a]2 Sam 12:16 [b]Esth 6:1; Ps 77:4; Dan 2:1
20 [a]Dan 6:16 [b]Gen 18:14; Num 11:23; Jer 32:17; Dan 3:17
21 [1]Lit *with* [a]Dan 2:4
22 [1]Lit *innocence was found for me* [2]Lit *before* [a]Num 20:16; Is 63:9; Dan 3:28; Acts 12:11; Heb 1:14 [b]Ps 91:11-13; 2 Tim 4:17; Heb 11:33

of the den. So Daniel was taken up out of
the den and [a]no injury whatever was
found on him, because he had [b]trusted
in his God.
24 The king then gave orders, and
they brought those men who had [1]mali-
ciously accused Daniel, and they [a]cast
them, their [b]children and their wives
into the lions' den; and they had not
reached the bottom of the den before the
lions overpowered them and crushed all
their bones.
25 ¶ Then Darius the king wrote to all
the [a]peoples, nations and *men of every*
[1]language who were living in all the
land: "[b]May your [2]peace abound!
26 "[1]I [a]make a decree that in all the
dominion of my kingdom men are to fear
and tremble before the God of Daniel;
For He is the [b]living God and
[c]enduring forever,
And [d]His kingdom is one which
will not be destroyed,
And His dominion *will be*
[2]forever.
27 "He delivers and rescues and
performs [a]signs and
wonders
In heaven and on earth,
Who has *also* delivered Daniel
from the [1]power of the
lions."
28 ¶ So this [a]Daniel enjoyed success
in the reign of Darius and in the reign of
[b]Cyrus the Persian.

Vision of the Four Beasts

7 In the first year of Belshazzar king of
Babylon Daniel saw a [a]dream and
visions [1]in his mind *as he lay* on his bed;
then he [b]wrote the dream down *and* related the [2]*following* summary of [3]it.
2 Daniel [1]said, "I was [a]looking in
my vision by night, and behold, the [b]four
winds of heaven were stirring up the
great sea.
3 "And four great [a]beasts were coming up from the sea, different from one
another.
4 "The first *was* [a]like a lion and had
the wings of an eagle. I kept looking until
its wings were plucked, and it was lifted
up from the ground and made to stand on
two feet like a man; a human [1]mind also
was given to it.
5 "And behold, another beast, a second one, resembling a bear. And it was
raised up on one side, and three ribs *were*
in its mouth between its teeth; and thus
they said to it, 'Arise, devour much
meat!'
6 "After this I kept looking, and behold, another one, [a]like a leopard, which
had on its [1]back four wings of a bird; the
beast also had [b]four heads, and dominion
was given to it.
7 "After this I kept looking in the night
visions, and behold, a [a]fourth beast,
dreadful and terrifying and extremely
strong; and it had large iron teeth. It devoured and crushed and trampled down
the remainder with its feet; and it was
different from all the beasts that were
before it, and it had [b]ten horns.
8 "While I was contemplating the
horns, behold, [a]another horn, a little
one, came up among them, and three of
the first horns were pulled out by the
roots before it; and behold, [1]this horn
possessed eyes like the eyes of a man and
[b]a mouth uttering great *boasts*.

The Ancient of Days Reigns

9 ¶ "I kept looking
Until [a]thrones were set up,
And the Ancient of Days took
His seat;
His [b]vesture *was* like white
snow
And the [c]hair of His head like
pure wool.
His [d]throne *was* [1]ablaze with
flames,
Its [e]wheels *were* a burning fire.
10 "A river of [a]fire was flowing
And coming out from before
Him;
[b]Thousands upon thousands
were attending Him,
And myriads upon myriads were
standing before Him;
The [c]court sat,
And [d]the books were opened.
11 "Then I kept looking because of the
sound of the [1]boastful words which the
horn was speaking; I kept looking until
the beast was slain, and its body was destroyed and given to the [a]burning [2]fire.
12 "As for the rest of the beasts, their
dominion was taken away, but an exten-
sion of life was granted to them for an
appointed period of time.

The Son of Man Presented

13 ¶ "I kept looking in the night
visions,
And behold, with the clouds of
heaven
One like a [a]Son of Man was
coming,
And He came up to the Ancient
of Days
And was presented before Him.
14 "And to Him was given
[a]dominion,
Glory and [1b]a kingdom,
[c]That all the peoples, nations
and *men of every* [2]language

23 [a]Dan 3:25,27 [b]1 Chr 5:20; 2 Chr 20:20; Ps 118:8,9; Is 26:3; Dan 3:17,28
24 [1]Lit *eaten the pieces of Daniel* [a]Deut 19:18,19; Esth 7:10 [b]Deut 24:16; 2 Kin 14:6; Esth 9:10
25 [1]Lit *tongue* [2]Or *welfare* or *prosperity* [a]Ezra 1:1,2; Esth 3:12; 8:9; Dan 4:1 [b]Ezra 4:17; 1 Pet 1:2
26 [1]Lit *From me a decree is made* [2]Lit *to the end* [a]Ezra 6:8-12; 7:13,21; Dan 3:29 [b]Dan 4:34; 6:20; Hos 1:10; Rom 9:26 [c]Ps 93:1,2; Mal 3:6 [d]Dan 2:44; 4:3; 7:14,27; Luke 1:33
27 [1]Lit *hand* [a]Dan 4:2,3
28 [a]Dan 1:21 [b]2 Chr 36:22,23; Dan 10:1
7:1 [1]Lit *of his head* [2]Or *beginning* [3]Lit *words* [a]Job 33:14-16; Dan 1:17; 2:1, 26-28; 4:5-9; Joel 2:28 [b]Jer 36:4,32
2 [1]Lit *spoke and said* [a]Dan 7:7,13 [b]Rev 7:1
3 [a]Dan 7:17; Rev 13:1; 17:8
4 [1]Lit *heart* [a]Jer 4:7
6 [1]Or *sides* [a]Rev 13:2 [b]Dan 8:22
7 [a]Dan 7:19,20, 23 [b]Rev 12:3; 13:1
8 [1]Lit *in this horn were eyes* [a]Dan 8:9 [b]Rev 13:5,6
9 [1]Lit *flames of fire* [a]Rev 20:4 [b]Mark 9:3 [c]Rev 1:14 [d]Ezek 1:13, 26 [e]Ezek 10:2,6
10 [a]Ps 18:8; 50:3; 97:3; Is 30:27,33 [b]Deut 33:2; 1 Kin 22:19; Rev 5:11 [c]Ps 96:11-13; Dan 7:22,26 [d]Dan 12:1; Rev 20:11-15
11 [1]Lit *great* [2]Lit *of the fire* [a]Rev 19:20; 20:10
13 [a]Matt 24:30; 26:64; Mark 13:26; 14:62; Luke 21:27; Rev 1:7,13; 14:14
14 [1]Or *sovereignty* [2]Lit *tongue* [a]Dan 7:27; John 3:35; 1 Cor 15:27; Eph 1:20-22; Phil 2:9-11; Rev 1:6; 11:15 [b]Dan 2:37 [c]Ps 72:11; 102:22

Might serve Him.
[d]His dominion is an everlasting
dominion
Which will not pass away;
[e]And His kingdom is one
Which will not be destroyed.

The Vision Interpreted

15 ¶ "As for me, Daniel, my spirit was
distressed [1]within me, and the [a]visions
[2]in my mind kept [b]alarming me.
16 "I approached one of those who
were [a]standing by and began asking him
the [1]exact meaning of all this. So he
[b]told me and made known to me the
interpretation of these things:
17 'These great beasts, which are four
in number, are four kings *who* will arise
from the earth.
18 'But the [1a]saints of the Highest
One will [b]receive the kingdom and possess the kingdom forever, [2]for all ages to
come.'
19 ¶ "Then I desired to know the [1]ex-
act meaning of the [a]fourth beast, which
was different from all [2]the others, exceedingly dreadful, with its teeth of iron
and its claws of bronze, *and which* devoured, crushed and trampled down the
remainder with its feet,
20 and *the meaning* of the ten horns
that *were* on its head and the other *horn*
which came up, and before which three
of them fell, namely, that horn which had
eyes and a mouth uttering great *boasts*
and [1]which was larger in appearance
than its associates.
21 "I kept looking, and that horn was
[a]waging war with the [1]saints and over-
powering them
22 until the Ancient of Days came and
[a]judgment was [1]passed in favor of the
[2]saints of the Highest One, and the time
arrived when the [2]saints took possession
of the kingdom.
23 ¶ "Thus he said: 'The fourth beast
will be a fourth kingdom on the earth,
which will be different from all the *other*
kingdoms and will devour the whole
earth and tread it down and crush it.
24 'As for the [a]ten horns, out of this
kingdom ten kings will arise; and another
will arise after them, and he will be different from the previous ones and will subdue three kings.
25 'He will [a]speak [1]out against the
[b]Most High and [c]wear down the [2]saints
of the Highest One, and he will intend to
make [d]alterations in times and in law;
and [3]they will be given into his hand for
a [4e]time, [4]times, and half a [4]time.
26 'But the court will sit *for judgment,*
and his dominion will be [a]taken away,
[1]annihilated and destroyed [2]forever.
27 'Then the [1a]sovereignty, the dominion and the greatness of *all* the kingdoms under the whole heaven will be
given to the people of the [2]saints of the
Highest One; His kingdom *will be* an
[b]everlasting kingdom, and all the dominions will [c]serve and obey Him.'
28 ¶ "[1]At this point the revelation
ended. As for me, Daniel, my thoughts
were [a]greatly alarming me and my [2]face
grew pale, but I [b]kept the matter [3]to
myself."

Vision of the Ram and Goat

8 In the third year of the reign of Belshazzar the king a vision appeared
to me, [1]Daniel, subsequent to the one
which appeared to me [2]previously.
2 I [a]looked in the vision, and while
I was looking I was in the citadel of
[b]Susa, which is in the province of
[c]Elam; and I looked in the vision and I
myself was beside the Ulai [1]Canal.
3 Then I lifted my eyes and looked,
and behold, a [a]ram which had two horns
was standing in front of the [1]canal. Now
the two horns *were* [2]long, but one *was*
[2]longer than the other, with the [2]longer
one coming up last.
4 I saw the ram [a]butting westward,
northward, and southward, and no *other*
beasts could stand before him nor was
there anyone to rescue from his [1]power,
but [b]he did as he pleased and magnified
himself.
5 ¶ While I was observing, behold, a
male goat was coming from the west over
the surface of the whole earth without
touching the ground; and the [1]goat *had*
a [a]conspicuous horn between his eyes.
6 He came up to the ram that had the
two horns, which I had seen standing in
front of the [1]canal, and rushed at him in
his mighty wrath.
7 I saw him come beside the ram,
and he was enraged at him; and he struck
the ram and shattered his two horns, and
the ram had no strength to withstand
him. So he hurled him to the ground and
trampled on him, and there was none to
rescue the ram from his [1]power.
8 Then the male goat magnified *him-*
self exceedingly. But as soon as [a]he was
mighty, the [b]large horn was broken; and
in its place there came up four conspicu-
ous *horns* toward the [c]four winds of
heaven.

The Little Horn

9 ¶ Out of one of them came forth a
rather [a]small horn which grew exceedingly great toward the south, toward the
east, and toward the [1b]Beautiful *Land.*
10 It grew up to the host of heaven and

14 [d]Mic 4:7; Luke 1:33 [e]Heb 12:28
15 [1]Lit *in the midst of* its *sheath* [2]Lit *of my head* [a]Dan 7:1 [b]Dan 4:19
16 [1]Lit *truth concerning* [a]Zech 1:9; Rev 5:5 [b]Dan 8:16
18 [1]Lit *holy ones* [2]Lit *and unto the age of the ages* [a]Dan 7:22 [b]Ps 149:5-9; Is 60:12-14; Dan 7:14; Rev 2:26
19 [1]Lit *truth concerning* [2]Lit *of them* [a]Dan 7:7
20 [1]Lit *its appearance was larger*
21 [1]Lit *holy ones* [a]Rev 11:7
22 [1]Lit *given for* [2]Lit *holy ones* [a]Dan 7:10; 1 Cor 6:2
24 [a]Dan 7:7; Rev 17:12
25 [1]Lit *words* [2]Lit *holy ones* [3]I.e. the saints [4]I.e. year(s) [a]Dan 11:36; Rev 13:6 [b]Dan 3:26 [c]Rev 13:7 [d]Dan 2:21 [e]Dan 12:7; Rev 12:14
26 [1]Lit *to annihilate and to destroy* [2]Lit *to the end* [a]Rev 17:14
27 [1]Or *kingdom* [2]Lit *holy ones* [a]Is 54:3; Dan 7:14; Rev 20:4 [b]Ps 145:13; Is 9:7; Dan 2:44; Luke 1:33; Rev 11:15 [c]Ps 2:6-12; Is 60:12; Rev 11:1
28 [1]Lit *To here the end of the word* [2]Lit *brightness was changing upon me* [3]Lit *in my heart* [a]Dan 4:19 [b]Luke 2:19
8:1 [1]Lit *I, Daniel* [2]Lit *at the beginning*
2 [1]Or *river* [a]Num 12:6; Dan 7:2 [b]Neh 1:1; Esth 1:2 [c]Gen 10:22; Is 11:11; Jer 25:25; Ezek 32:24
3 [1]Or *river* [2]Lit *high(er)* [a]Dan 8:20
4 [1]Lit *hand* [a]Deut 33:17; 1 Kin 22:11; Ezek 34:21 [b]Dan 11:3
5 [1]Lit *buck* [a]Dan 8:8
6 [1]Or *river*
7 [1]Lit *hand*
8 [a]2 Chr 26:16; Dan 5:20 [b]Dan 8:22 [c]Dan 7:2; Rev 7:1
9 [1]I.e. Palestine [a]Dan 8:23 [b]Ps 48:2; Dan 11:16

caused some of the host and some of the [a]stars to fall to the earth, and it [b]trampled them down.

11 It even [a]magnified *itself* [1]to be equal with the [2]Commander of the host; and it removed the [b]regular sacrifice from Him, and the place of His sanctuary was thrown down.

12 And on account of transgression the host will be given over *to the horn* along with the regular sacrifice; and it will [a]fling truth to the ground and perform *its will* and prosper.

13 Then I heard a [a]holy one speaking, and another holy one said to that particular one who was speaking, "[b]How long will the vision *about* the regular sacrifice apply, [1]while the transgression causes horror, so as to allow both the holy place and the host [2]to be [c]trampled?"

14 He said to me, "For [a]2,300 evenings *and* mornings; then the holy place will be [1]properly restored."

Interpretation of the Vision

15 ¶ When [a]I, Daniel, had seen the vision, I sought [1]to understand it; and behold, standing before me was one [2]who looked like a [b]man.

16 And I heard the voice of a man between *the banks of* Ulai, and he called out and said, "[a]Gabriel, give this *man* an understanding of the vision."

17 So he came near to where I was standing, and when he came I was frightened and [a]fell on my face; but he said to me, "Son of man, understand that the vision pertains to the [b]time of the end."

18 ¶ Now while he was talking with me, I [a]sank into a deep sleep with my face to the ground; but he [b]touched me and made me stand [1]upright.

19 He said, "Behold, I am going to [a]let you know what will occur at the final period of the indignation, for *it* pertains to the appointed time of the end.

The Ram's Identity

20 "The [a]ram which you saw with the two horns represents the kings of Media and Persia.

The Goat

21 "The shaggy [1]goat *represents* the [2]kingdom of Greece, and the large horn that is between his eyes is the first king.

22 "The [a]broken *horn* and the four *horns that* arose in its place *represent* four kingdoms *which* will arise from *his* nation, although not with his power.

23 "In the latter period of their
[1]rule,
When the transgressors have
[2]run *their course,*
A king will arise,
[3]Insolent and skilled in
[4]intrigue.
24 "His power will be mighty, but not by his *own* power,
And he will [1a]destroy to an extraordinary degree
And prosper and perform *his will;*
He will [1]destroy mighty men and [2]the holy people.
25 "And through his shrewdness
He will cause deceit to succeed by his [1]influence;
And he will magnify *himself* in his heart,
And he will [2]destroy many while *they are* [3]at ease.
He will even [4a]oppose the Prince of princes,
But he will be broken [b]without [1]human agency.
26 "The vision of the evenings and mornings
Which has been told is [a]true;
But [b]keep the vision secret,
For *it* pertains to many [c]days *in the future.*"

27 ¶ Then I, Daniel, was [1a]exhausted and sick for days. Then I got up *again* and [b]carried on the king's business; but I was astounded at the vision, and there was none to [2]explain *it.*

Daniel's Prayer for His People

9 In the first year of [a]Darius the son of Ahasuerus, of Median descent, who was made king over the kingdom of the Chaldeans—

2 in the first year of his reign, I, Daniel, observed in the books the number of the years which was *revealed as* the word of the LORD to [a]Jeremiah the prophet for the completion of the desolations of Jerusalem, *namely,* [a]seventy years.

3 So I [1]gave my attention to the Lord God to seek *Him by* prayer and supplications, with fasting, sackcloth and ashes.

4 I prayed to the LORD my God and confessed and said, "Alas, O Lord, the [a]great and awesome God, who [b]keeps His covenant and lovingkindness for those who love Him and keep His commandments,

5 [a]we have sinned, committed iniquity, acted wickedly and [b]rebelled, even [c]turning aside from Your commandments and ordinances.

6 "Moreover, we have not [a]listened to Your servants the prophets, who spoke in Your name to our kings, our princes, our fathers and all the people of the land.

7 ¶ "[a]Righteousness belongs to You, O Lord, but to us [1b]open shame, as it is

10 [a]Is 14:13; Jer 48:26; Rev 12:4 [b]Dan 7:7
11 [1]Lit *up to the* [2]Or *Prince* [a]2 Kin 19:22; 2 Chr 32:15-17; Is 37:23; Dan 8:25 [b]Ezek 46:14; Dan 11:31
12 [a]Is 59:14
13 [1]Or possibly *and the transgression that horrifies* [2]Lit *as a trampling* [a]Dan 4:13; 1 Pet 1:12 [b]Ps 74:10; Is 6:11; Dan 12:6; Rev 6:10 [c]Is 63:18; Jer 12:10; Luke 21:24; Heb 10:29; Rev 11:2
14 [1]Lit *vindicated* [a]Dan 7:25; Rev 11:2
15 [1]Lit *understanding* [2]Lit *like the appearance of a man* [a]Dan 8:1 [b]Dan 7:13
16 [a]Dan 9:21; Luke 1:19
17 [a]Ezek 1:28; Dan 2:46; Rev 1:17 [b]Dan 8:19
18 [1]Lit *on my standing* [a]Dan 10:9; Luke 9:32 [b]Ezek 2:2; Dan 10:10
19 [a]Dan 8:15-17
20 [a]Dan 8:3
21 [1]Lit *buck* [2]Lit *king*
22 [a]Dan 8:8
23 [1]Or *kingdom* [2]Lit *finished* [3]Lit *Strong of face* [4]Or *ambiguous speech*
24 [1]Or *corrupt* [2]Lit *people of the saints* [a]Dan 8:11-13
25 [1]Lit *hand* [2]Or *corrupt* [3]Or *secure* [4]Lit *stand against* [a]Dan 8:11 [b]Job 34:20; Dan 2:34
26 [a]Dan 10:1 [b]Ezek 12:27; Dan 12:4; Rev 22:10 [c]Dan 10:14
27 [1]Or *done in* [2]Lit *make me understand* [a]Dan 7:28; Hab 3:16 [b]Dan 2:48
9:1 [a]Dan 5:31
2 [a]2 Chr 36:21; Ezra 1:1; Jer 25:11; Zech 7:5
3 [1]Lit *set my face*
4 [a]Deut 7:21; Neh 9:32 [b]Deut 7:9
5 [a]1 Kin 8:48; Neh 9:33; Ps 106:6; Is 64:5-7; Jer 14:7 [b]Lam 1:18 [c]Ps 119:176; Is 53:6; Dan 9:11
6 [a]2 Chr 36:16; Jer 44:4
7 [1]Lit *the shame of face* [a]Jer 23:6; Dan 9:18 [b]Ps 44:15; Jer 2:26

this day—to the men of Judah, the inhabitants of Jerusalem and all Israel, those who are nearby and those who are far away in [c]all the countries to which You have driven them, because of their unfaithful deeds which they have committed against You.

8 "[1]Open shame belongs to us, O Lord, to our kings, our princes and our fathers, because we have sinned against You.

9 "To the Lord our God *belong* [a]compassion and forgiveness, [1]for we have [b]rebelled against Him;

10 nor have we obeyed the voice of the LORD our God, to walk in His [1]teachings which He [a]set before us through His servants the prophets.

11 "Indeed [a]all Israel has transgressed Your law and turned aside, not obeying Your voice; so the [b]curse has been poured out on us, along with the oath which is written in the law of Moses the servant of God, for we have sinned against Him.

12 "Thus He has [a]confirmed His words which He had spoken against us and against our [1b]rulers who ruled us, to bring on us great calamity; for under the whole heaven there has [c]not been done *anything* like what was done to Jerusalem.

13 "As it is written in the [a]law of Moses, all this calamity has come on us; yet we have [b]not [1]sought the favor of the LORD our God by [c]turning from our iniquity and [2]giving attention to Your truth.

14 "Therefore the LORD has [1a]kept the calamity in store and brought it on us; for the LORD our God is [b]righteous with respect to all His deeds which He has done, but we have not obeyed His voice.

15 ¶ "And now, O Lord our God, who have [a]brought Your people out of the land of Egypt with a mighty hand and have [b]made a name for Yourself, as it is this day—we have sinned, we have been wicked.

16 "O Lord, in accordance with all Your [1]righteous acts, let now Your [a]anger and Your wrath turn away from Your city Jerusalem, Your [b]holy mountain; for because of our sins and the iniquities of our fathers, Jerusalem and Your people *have become* a [c]reproach to all those around us.

17 "So now, our God, listen to the prayer of Your servant and to his supplications, and for [1]Your sake, O Lord, [a]let Your face shine on Your [b]desolate sanctuary.

18 "O my God, [a]incline Your ear and hear! Open Your eyes and [b]see our desolations and the city which is [c]called by Your name; for we are not [1d]presenting our supplications before You on account of [2]any merits of our own, but on account of Your great compassion.

19 "O Lord, hear! O Lord, forgive! O Lord, listen and take action! For Your own sake, O my God, [a]do not delay, because Your city and Your people are called by Your name."

Gabriel Brings an Answer

20 ¶ Now while I was [a]speaking and praying, and [b]confessing my sin and the sin of my people Israel, and [1]presenting my supplication before the LORD my God in behalf of the holy mountain of my God,

21 while I was still speaking in prayer, then the man [a]Gabriel, whom I had seen in the vision [1]previously, [2]came to me [3]in *my* extreme weariness about the time of the [b]evening offering.

22 He gave *me* instruction and talked with me and said, "O Daniel, I have now come forth to give you insight with [a]understanding.

23 "At the [a]beginning of your supplications the [1]command was issued, and I have come to tell *you,* for you are [2b]highly esteemed; so give heed to the message and gain [c]understanding of the vision.

Seventy Weeks and the Messiah

24 ¶ "Seventy [1a]weeks have been decreed for your people and your holy city, to [2]finish the transgression, to [3]make an end of sin, to [b]make atonement for iniquity, to bring in [c]everlasting righteousness, to seal up vision and [4]prophecy and to anoint the most holy *place.*

25 "So you are to know and discern *that* from the issuing of a [1a]decree to restore and rebuild Jerusalem until [2b]Messiah the [c]Prince *there will be* seven weeks and sixty-two weeks; it will be built again, with [3]plaza and moat, even in times of distress.

26 "Then after the sixty-two weeks the [1]Messiah will be [a]cut off and have [2]nothing, and the people of the prince who is to come will [b]destroy the city and the sanctuary. And [3]its end *will come* with a [c]flood; even to the end [4]there will be war; desolations are determined.

27 "And he will make a firm covenant with the many for one week, but in the middle of the week he will put a stop to sacrifice and grain offering; and on the wing of [1a]abominations *will come* one

7 [c]Deut 4:27 **8** [1]Lit *The shame of face* **9** [1]Or *though* [a]Neh 9:17; Ps 130:4 [b]Ps 106:43; Jer 14:7; Dan 9:5 **10** [1]Or *laws* [a]2 Kin 17:13-15 **11** [a]Is 1:3; Jer 8:5-10 [b]Deut 27:15-26 **12** [1]Lit *judges who judged us* [a]Is 44:26; Jer 44:2-6; Lam 2:17; Zech 1:6 [b]Job 12:17; Ps 82:2-7 [c]Lam 1:12; Ezek 5:9 **13** [1]Lit *softened the face of* [2]Or *having insight into* [a]Lev 26:14-45; Deut 28:15-68; Dan 9:11 [b]Job 36:13; Is 9:13; Jer 2:30 [c]Jer 31:18 **14** [1]Lit *watched over the evil* [a]Jer 31:28 [b]Ps 51:14; Dan 9:7 **15** [a]Deut 5:15 [b]Neh 9:10; Jer 32:20 **16** [1]Lit *righteousnesses* [a]Jer 32:31 [b]Ps 87:1-3; Dan 9:20; Joel 3:17; Zech 8:3 [c]Ezek 5:14 **17** [1]Lit *the sake of the Lord* [a]Num 6:24-26; Ps 80:3 [b]Lam 5:18 **18** [1]Lit *causing to fall* [2]Lit *our righteousnesses* [a]Is 37:17 [b]Ps 80:14 [c]Jer 7:10-12 [d]Jer 36:7 **19** [a]Ps 44:23 **20** [1]Lit *causing to fall* [a]Ps 145:18; Is 58:9; Dan 9:3 [b]Is 6:5 **21** [1]Lit *at the beginning* [2]Lit *was reaching*; or *touching* [3]Lit *wearied with weariness* [a]Dan 8:16; Luke 1:19 [b]Ex 29:39; 1 Kin 18:36; Ezra 9:4 **22** [a]Dan 8:16; Zech 1:9 **23** [1]Lit *word went out* [2]Lit *desirable*; or *precious* [a]Dan 10:12 [b]Dan 10:11 [c]Matt 24:15 **24** [1]Or *units of seven,* and so throughout the ch [2]Or *restrain* [3]Another reading is *seal up sins* [4]Lit *prophet* [a]Lev 25:8; Num 14:34; Ezek 4:5 [b]2 Chr 29:24; Is 53:10; Rom 5:10 [c]Is 51:6; Jer 23:5; Rom 3:21 **25** [1]Lit *word* [2]Or *an anointed one* [3]Or *streets* [a]Ezra 4:24; Neh 2:1-8 [b]John 1:41 [c]Is 9:6; Dan 8:11

26 [1]Or *anointed one* [2]Or *no one* [3]Or *his* [4]Or *war will be decreed for desolations* [a]Is 53:8; Mark 9:12; Luke 24:26 [b]Matt 24:2; Mark 13:2; Luke 19:43 [c]Nah 1:8 **27** [1]Or *detestable things* [a]Dan 11:31; Matt 24:15; Mark 13:14; Luke 21:20

who [2]makes desolate, even until a [b]complete destruction, one that is decreed, is poured out on the one who [2]makes desolate."

Daniel Is Terrified by a Vision

10 In the third year of [a]Cyrus king of Persia a [1]message was revealed to [b]Daniel, who was named Belteshazzar; and the [1c]message was true and *one of* great [2]conflict, but he understood the [1]message and had an [d]understanding of the vision.

2 ¶ In those days, I, Daniel, had been [a]mourning for three entire weeks.

3 I [a]did not eat any [1]tasty food, nor did meat or wine enter my mouth, nor did I use any ointment at all until the entire three weeks were completed.

4 On the twenty-fourth day of the first month, while I was by the bank of the great [a]river, that is, the [1]Tigris,

5 I lifted my eyes and looked, and behold, there was a certain man [a]dressed in linen, whose waist was [b]girded with *a belt of* pure [c]gold of Uphaz.

6 His body also *was* like [1]beryl, his face [2]had the appearance of lightning, [a]his eyes were like flaming torches, his arms and feet like the gleam of polished bronze, and the sound of his words like the sound of a [3]tumult.

7 Now I, Daniel, [a]alone saw the vision, while the [b]men who were with me did not see the vision; nevertheless, a great [c]dread fell on them, and they ran away to hide themselves.

8 So I was [a]left alone and saw this great vision; yet [b]no strength was left in me, for my [1]natural color turned to [2]a deathly pallor, and I retained no strength.

9 But I heard the sound of his words; and as soon as I heard the sound of his words, I [a]fell into a deep sleep on my face, with my face to the ground.

Daniel Comforted

10 ¶ Then behold, a hand [a]touched me and set me trembling on my [1]hands and knees.

11 He said to me, "O [a]Daniel, man of [1]high esteem, [b]understand the words that I am about to tell you and [c]stand [2]upright, for I have now been sent to you." And when he had spoken this word to me, I stood up [d]trembling.

12 Then he said to me, "[a]Do not be afraid, Daniel, for from the first day that you set your heart on understanding *this* and on [b]humbling yourself before your God, your words were heard, and I have come in response [c]to your words.

13 "But the prince of the kingdom of Persia was [1]withstanding me for twenty-one days; then behold, [a]Michael, one of the chief princes, came to help me, for I had been left there with the kings of Persia.

14 "Now I have come to [a]give you an understanding of what will happen to your people in the [1b]latter days, for the vision pertains to [c]the days yet *future.*"

15 ¶ When he had spoken to me according to these words, I [1]turned my face toward the ground and became [a]speechless.

16 And behold, [1a]one who resembled a human being was [b]touching my lips; then I opened my mouth and spoke and said to him who was standing before me, "O my lord, as a result of the vision [2c]anguish has come upon me, and I have retained no strength.

17 "For [a]how can such a servant of my lord talk with such as my lord? As for me, there remains just now [b]no strength in me, nor has any breath been left in me."

18 ¶ Then *this* one with human appearance touched me again and [a]strengthened me.

19 He said, "O man of [1]high esteem, [a]do not be afraid. Peace [2]be with you; take [b]courage and be courageous!" Now as soon as he spoke to me, I received strength and said, "May my lord speak, for you have [c]strengthened me."

20 Then he said, "Do you [1]understand why I came to you? But I shall now return to fight against the [2]prince of Persia; so I am going forth, and behold, the [2a]prince of [3]Greece is about to come.

21 "However, I will tell you what is inscribed in the writing of [a]truth. Yet there is no one who [1]stands firmly with me against these *forces* except [b]Michael your prince.

Conflicts to Come

11 "In the [a]first year of Darius the Mede, [1]I arose to be [2]an encouragement and a protection for him.

2 "And now I will tell you the [a]truth. Behold, three more kings are going to arise [1]in Persia. Then a fourth will gain far more riches than all *of them;* as soon as he becomes strong through his riches, [2]he will arouse the whole *empire* against the realm of [3b]Greece.

3 "And a [a]mighty king will arise, and he will rule with great authority and [b]do as he pleases.

4 "But as soon as he has arisen, his kingdom will be broken up and parceled out [a]toward the [b]four [1]points of the compass, though not to his *own* descen-

27 [2]Or *causes horror* [b]Is 10:23
10:1 [1]Lit *word* [2]Or *warfare* [a]Dan 1:21 [b]Dan 1:7 [c]Dan 8:26 [d]Dan 1:17
2 [a]Ezra 9:4; Neh 1:4
3 [1]Lit *bread of desirability* [a]Dan 6:18
4 [1]Heb *Hiddekel* [a]Ezek 1:3; Dan 8:2
5 [a]Ezek 9:2; Dan 12:6 [b]Rev 1:13 [c]Jer 10:9
6 [1]Or *yellow serpentine* [2]Lit *like* [3]Or *roaring* [a]Rev 1:14
7 [a]2 Kin 6:17-20 [b]Acts 9:7 [c]Ezek 12:18
8 [1]Lit *splendor* [2]Lit *corruption* [a]Gen 32:24 [b]Dan 7:28; Hab 3:16
9 [a]Gen 15:12; Job 4:13; Dan 8:18
10 [1]Lit *knees and the palms of my hands* [a]Jer 1:9; Dan 8:18
11 [1]Lit *desirability;* or *preciousness* [2]Lit *upon your standing* [a]Dan 10:19 [b]Dan 8:16 [c]Ezek 2:1 [d]Job 4:14
12 [a]Is 41:10; Dan 10:19 [b]Dan 9:20-23 [c]Acts 10:30
13 [1]Lit *standing opposite* [a]Dan 10:21; Jude 9; Rev 12:7
14 [1]Lit *end of the days* [a]Dan 8:16 [b]Deut 31:29; Dan 2:28 [c]Dan 8:26
15 [1]Lit *set* [a]Ezek 3:26; Luke 1:20
16 [1]Lit *as a likeness of sons of man* [2]Lit *my pains have* [a]Dan 8:15 [b]Is 6:7; Jer 1:9 [c]Dan 7:15
17 [a]Ex 24:10; Is 6:1-5 [b]Dan 10:8
18 [a]Is 35:3
19 [1]Lit *desirability;* or *preciousness* [2]Lit *to you* [a]Judg 6:23; Is 43:1; Dan 10:12 [b]Josh 1:6; Is 35:4 [c]Ps 138:3; 2 Cor 12:9
20 [1]Lit *know* [2]I.e. Satanic angel [3]Heb *Javan* [a]Dan 8:21
21 [1]Lit *shows himself strong* [a]Dan 12:4 [b]Dan 10:13; Rev 12:7
11:1 [1]Lit *my standing up* was [2]Lit *for a strengthener* [a]Dan 5:31
2 [1]Lit *for* [2]Or they *all will stir up the realm of Greece* [3]Heb *Javan* [a]Dan 8:26 [b]Dan 8:21
3 [a]Dan 8:5 [b]Dan 5:19
4 [1]Lit *winds of the heaven* [a]Dan 8:8 [b]Jer 49:36; Ezek 37:9; Dan 7:2; Zech 2:6; Rev 7:1

dants, nor according to his authority
which he wielded, for his sovereignty
will be [c]uprooted and *given* to others
besides [2]them.
5 ¶ "Then the [a]king of the South will
grow strong, [1]along with *one* of his
princes [2]who will gain ascendancy over
him and obtain dominion; his domain
will be a great dominion *indeed.*
6 "After some years they will form an
alliance, and the daughter of the king of
the South will come to the [a]king of the
North to carry out [1]a peaceful arrangement. But she will not retain her [2]posi-
tion of power, nor will he remain with his
[3]power, but she will be given up, along
with those who brought her in and the
one who sired her as well as he who supported her in *those* times.
7 "But one of the [1]descendants of her
line will arise in his place, and he will
come against *their* army and enter the
[a]fortress of the king of the North, and he
will deal with them and display *great*
strength.
8 "Also their [a]gods with their [1]metal
images *and* their precious vessels of silver
and gold he will take into captivity to
Egypt, and he on his part will [2]refrain
from *attacking* the king of the North for
some years.
9 "Then [1]the latter will enter the
realm of the king of the South, but will
return to his *own* land.
10 ¶ "His sons will [1]mobilize and assemble a multitude of great forces; and
one of them will keep on coming and
[a]overflow and pass through, that he may
[2]again wage war up to his *very* fortress.
11 "The [a]king of the South will be enraged and go forth and fight [1]with the
king of the North. Then the latter will
raise a great multitude, but *that* multitude will be given into [2]the hand of the
former.
12 "When the multitude is carried
away, his heart will be lifted up, and he
will cause tens of thousands to fall; yet he
will not prevail.
13 "For the king of the North will again
raise a greater multitude than the former,
and [1]after an [a]interval of some years he
will [2]press on with a great army and
much equipment.
14 ¶ "Now in those times many will
rise up against the king of the South; the
violent ones among your people will also
lift themselves up in order to fulfill the
vision, but they will [1]fall down.
15 "Then the king of the North will
come, cast up a [a]siege ramp and capture
a well-fortified city; and the forces of the
South will not stand *their ground,* not
even [1]their choicest troops, for there
will be no strength to make a stand.
16 "But he who comes against him will
[a]do as he pleases, and [b]no one will *be
able to* withstand him; he will also stay
for a time in the [1c]Beautiful Land, with
destruction in his hand.
17 "He will [a]set his face to come with
the power of his whole kingdom, [1]bring-
ing with him [2]a proposal of peace which
he will put into effect; he will also give
him the daughter of women to ruin it. But
she will not take a stand *for him* or be
[3]on his side.
18 "Then he will turn his face to the
[a]coastlands and capture many. But a
commander will put a stop to his scorn
against him; moreover, he will [b]repay
him for his scorn.
19 "So he will turn his face toward the
fortresses of his own land, but he will
[a]stumble and fall and be [b]found no
more.
20 ¶ "Then in his place one will arise
who will [a]send an [1]oppressor through
the [2]Jewel of *his* kingdom; yet within a
few days he will be shattered, though not
in anger nor in battle.
21 "In his place a despicable person will
arise, on whom the honor of kingship has
not been conferred, but he will come in
a time of tranquility and [a]seize the kingdom by intrigue.
22 "The overflowing [a]forces will be
flooded away before him and shattered,
and also the prince of the covenant.
23 "After an alliance is made with him
he will practice deception, and he will go
up and gain power with a small *force of*
people.
24 "[1]In a time of tranquility he will enter the [a]richest *parts* of the [2]realm, and
he will accomplish what his fathers never
did, nor his [3]ancestors; he will distribute
plunder, booty and possessions among
them, and he will devise his schemes
against strongholds, but *only* for a time.
25 "He will stir up his strength and
[1]courage against the [a]king of the South
with a large army; so the king of the
South will mobilize an extremely large
and mighty army for war; but he will not
stand, for schemes will be devised against
him.
26 "Those who eat his choice food will
[1]destroy him, and his army will [2a]over-
flow, but many will fall down slain.
27 "As for both kings, their hearts will
be *intent* on [a]evil, and they will [b]speak
lies *to each other* at the same table; but
it will not succeed, for the [c]end is still *to
come* at the appointed time.
28 "Then he will return to his land with
much [1]plunder; but his heart will be *set*

4 [2]I.e. his descendants [c]Jer 12:15,17; 18:7
5 [1]Lit *and* [2]Lit *and he* [a]Dan 11:9,11,14,25,40
6 [1]Or *an equitable agreement* [2]Lit *strength of arm* [3]Lit *arm* [a]Dan 11:7,13,15,40
7 [1]Lit *branch of her roots* [a]Dan 11:19,38,39
8 [1]Lit *cast images* [2]Or *stand against the king* [a]Is 37:19; 46:1,2; Jer 43:12,13
9 [1]Lit *he will,* and so throughout the ch
10 [1]Or *wage war* [2]Or *return and wage* [a]Is 8:8; Jer 46:7,8; 51:42; Dan 11:26,40
11 [1]Lit *with him, with* [2]Lit *his hand* [a]Dan 11:5
13 [1]Lit *at the end of the times, years* [2]Or *keep on coming* [a]Dan 4:16; 12:7
14 [1]Lit *stumble,* and so throughout the ch
15 [1]Lit *the people of its choice ones* [a]Jer 6:6; Ezek 4:2; 17:17
16 [1]I.e. Palestine [a]Dan 5:19; 11:3,36 [b]Josh 1:5 [c]Dan 8:9; 11:41
17 [1]Lit *and* [2]Lit *equitable things* [3]Lit *for him;* i.e. for her father [a]2 Kin 12:17; Ezek 4:3,7
18 [a]Gen 10:5; Is 66:19; Jer 2:10; 31:10; Zeph 2:11 [b]Hos 12:14
19 [a]Ps 27:2; Jer 46:6 [b]Job 20:8; Ps 37:36; Ezek 26:21
20 [1]Or *exactor of tribute* [2]Lit *adornment;* i.e. probably Jerusalem and its temple [a]Is 60:17
21 [a]2 Sam 15:6
22 [a]Dan 9:26; 11:10
24 [1]Lit *Into tranquility and the richest...he will enter* [2]Or *province* [3]Lit *fathers' fathers* [a]Num 13:20; Neh 9:25; Ezek 34:14
25 [1]Lit *heart* [a]Dan 11:5
26 [1]Lit *break* [2]Or *be swept away, and many* [a]Dan 11:10,40
27 [a]Ps 52:1; 64:6 [b]Ps 12:2; Jer 9:3-5; 41:1-3 [c]Dan 8:19; 11:35,40; Hab 2:3
28 [1]Lit *possessions*

against the holy covenant, and he will
take action and *then* return to his *own*
land.
29 ¶ "At the appointed time he will
return and come into the South, but [1]this
last time it will not turn out the way it did
before.
30 "For ships of [1a]Kittim will come
against him; therefore he will be disheart-
ened and will return and become enraged
at the holy covenant and take action; so
he will come back and show regard for
those who forsake the holy covenant.
31 "Forces from him will arise, [a]dese-
crate the sanctuary fortress, and do away
with the regular sacrifice. And they will
set up the [b]abomination [1]of desolation.
32 "By [a]smooth *words* he will [1]turn to
godlessness those who act wickedly toward the covenant, but the people who
know their God will display [b]strength
and take action.
33 "[1a]Those who have insight among
the people will give understanding to the
many; yet they will [b]fall by sword and by
flame, by captivity and by plunder for
many days.
34 "Now when they fall they will be
granted a little help, and many will [a]join
with them in [b]hypocrisy.
35 "Some of [1]those who have insight
will fall, in order to [a]refine, [b]purge and
make them [2c]pure until the [d]end time;
because *it is* still *to come* at the appointed
time.
36 ¶ "Then the king will [a]do as he
pleases, and he will exalt and [b]magnify
himself above every god and will [c]speak
[1]monstrous things against the [d]God of
gods; and he will prosper until the [e]in-
dignation is finished, for that which is
[f]decreed will be done.
37 "He will show no regard for the
[1]gods of his fathers or for the desire of
women, nor will he show regard for any
other god; for he will magnify himself
above *them* all.
38 "But [1]instead he will honor a god of
fortresses, a god whom his fathers did not
know; he will honor *him* with gold, silver, costly stones and treasures.
39 "He will take action against the
strongest of fortresses with *the help of* a
foreign god; he will give great honor to
[1]those who acknowledge *him* and will
cause them to rule over the many, and
will parcel out land for a price.
40 ¶ "At the [a]end time the [b]king of
the South will collide with him, and the
[c]king of the North will [d]storm against
him with chariots, with horsemen and
with many ships; and he will enter countries, [e]overflow *them* and pass through.
41 "He will also enter the [1a]Beautiful
Land, and many *countries* will fall; but
these will be rescued out of his hand:
Edom, [b]Moab and the foremost of the
sons of [c]Ammon.
42 "Then he will stretch out his hand
against *other* countries, and the land of
Egypt will not escape.
43 "But he will [1]gain control over the
hidden treasures of gold and silver and
over all the precious things of Egypt; and
[a]Libyans and [b]Ethiopians *will follow* at
his [2]heels.
44 "But rumors from the East and from
the North will disturb him, and he will go
forth with great wrath to destroy and
[1]annihilate many.
45 "He will pitch the tents of his royal
pavilion between the seas and the beautiful [a]Holy Mountain; yet he will come to
his end, and no one will help him.

The Time of the End

12 "Now at that time [a]Michael, the
great prince who stands *guard*
over the sons of your people, will arise.
And there will be a [b]time of distress
[c]such as never occurred since there was
a nation until that time; and at that time
your people, everyone who is found written in the [d]book, will be rescued.
2 "[a]Many of those who sleep in the
dust of the ground will awake, [b]these to
everlasting life, but the others to disgrace
and everlasting [1]contempt.
3 "[1]Those who have [a]insight will
[b]shine brightly like the brightness of the
[2]expanse of heaven, and those who
[c]lead the many to righteousness, like the
stars forever and ever.
4 "But as for you, Daniel, [a]conceal
these words and [b]seal up the book until
the [c]end of time; [d]many will go back and
forth, and knowledge will increase."
5 ¶ Then I, Daniel, looked and behold, two others were standing, one on
this bank of the river and the other on
that bank of the river.
6 And [a]one said to the man [b]dressed
in linen, who was above the waters of the
river, "[c]How long *will it be* until the end
of *these* wonders?"
7 I heard the man dressed in linen,
who was above the waters of the river,
[1]as he [a]raised his right hand and his left
toward heaven, and swore by [b]Him who
lives forever that it would be for a
[2c]time, [2]times, and half *a* [2]*time;* and
as soon as [3]they finish [d]shattering the
[4]power of the holy people, all these
events will be completed.

29 [1]Lit *it will not happen as the first and as the last*
30 [1]I.e. Cyprus [a]Gen 10:4; Num 24:24; Is 23:1; Jer 2:10
31 [1]Lit *that makes desolate;* or *that causes horror* [a]Dan 8:11-13 [b]Dan 9:27; Matt 24:15; Mark 13:14
32 [1]Or *pollute those* [a]Dan 11:21 [b]Mic 5:7-9; Zech 9:13-16
33 [1]Or *Instructors of* the *people* [a]Mal 2:7 [b]Matt 24:9; John 16:2; Heb 11:36-38
34 [a]Matt 7:15; Acts 20:29 [b]Dan 11:21; Rom 16:18
35 [1]Or *the instructors* [2]Lit *white* [a]Deut 8:16; Prov 17:3; Dan 12:10; Zech 13:9; Mal 3:2 [b]John 15:2 [c]Rev 7:14 [d]Dan 11:27
36 [1]Lit *extraordinary* [a]Dan 5:19 [b]Is 14:13; Dan 5:20; 2 Thess 2:4 [c]Rev 13:5 [d]Deut 10:17; Ps 136:2; Dan 2:47 [e]Is 10:25; Dan 8:19 [f]Dan 9:27
37 [1]Or *God*
38 [1]Lit *in his place*
39 [1]Lit *the one who acknowledges*
40 [a]Dan 11:27 [b]Dan 11:11 [c]Dan 11:7 [d]Is 5:28; Jer 4:13 [e]Dan 11:10
41 [1]I.e. Palestine [a]Dan 8:9 [b]Jer 48:47 [c]Jer 49:6
43 [1]Or *rule over* [2]Lit *footsteps* [a]2 Chr 12:3; Nah 3:9 [b]2 Chr 12:3; Ezek 30:4; Nah 3:9
44 [1]Lit *devote to destruction*
45 [a]Is 11:9; Dan 9:16
12:1 [a]Dan 10:13; Rev 12:7 [b]Rev 7:14 [c]Jer 30:7; Ezek 5:9; Dan 9:12; Matt 24:21; Mark 13:19 [d]Dan 7:10
2 [1]Lit *abhorrence* [a]Is 26:19; Ezek 37:12-14 [b]Matt 25:46; John 5:28
3 [1]Or *The instructors will* [2]Or *firmament* [a]Dan 11:33 [b]John 5:35 [c]Is 53:11; Dan 11:33
4 [a]Dan 8:26 [b]Is 8:16; Dan 12:9; Rev 22:10 [c]Dan 8:17 [d]Is 11:9; Dan 11:33
6 [a]Dan 8:16; Zech 1:12 [b]Ezek 9:2; Dan 10:5 [c]Dan 8:13; Matt 24:3; Mark 13:4 **7** [1]Lit *and* [2]I.e. year(s) [3]Lit *to finish* [4]Lit *hand* [a]Ezek 20:5; Rev 10:5 [b]Dan 4:34 [c]Dan 7:25; Rev 12:14 [d]Dan 8:24; Luke 21:24

8 As for me, I heard but could not
understand; so I said, "My lord, what *will
be* the [1]outcome of these *events?*"
9 He said, "Go *your way,* Daniel, for
these words are concealed and [a]sealed
up until the end time.
10 "[a]Many will be purged, [1]purified
and refined, but the [b]wicked will act
wickedly; and none of the wicked will
understand, but [2]those who [c]have insight will understand.
11 "From the time that the regular sacrifice is abolished and the [1a]abomination of desolation is set up, *there will be*
1,290 days.
12 "How [a]blessed is he who keeps
waiting and attains to the [b]1,335 days!
13 "But as for you, go *your way* to the
[1]end; then you will enter into [a]rest and
rise *again* for your [b]allotted portion at
the end of the [2]age."

8 [1]Or *final end* **9** [a]Dan 12:4 **10** [1]Lit *made white* [2]Or *the instructors will* [a]Zech 13:9 [b]Is 32:6; Rev 22:11 [c]Dan 12:3; Hos 14:9; John 7:17 **11** [1]Or *horrible abomination* [a]Dan 9:27; Matt 24:15; Mark 13:14 **12** [a]Is 30:18 [b]Dan 8:14; Rev 11:2 **13** [1]I.e. end of your life [2]Lit *days* [a]Is 57:2; Rev 14:13 [b]Ps 16:5

Hosea

Title and Background

The book is named after the prophet whose message it preserves. Hosea's time encompasses the tragic last days of the northern kingdom (Israel), during which six kings reigned within twenty-five years. Assyria was expanding westward, and in about 733 B.C. they dismembered Israel. Then in 722–721 B.C. Samaria was captured and its people exiled. The northern kingdom was at an end.

Author and Date of Writing

Hosea prophesied about the middle of the eighth century B.C., shortly after the ministry of Amos. Amos threatened God's judgment on Israel at the hands of an unnamed enemy; Hosea identifies that enemy as Assyria. Hosea stands first in the division of the Bible called the Minor Prophets (Hosea–Malachi).

Theme and Message

In the first half of the book Hosea's family life is made a symbolic action to convey the message Hosea had from the Lord for His people. The Lord loved His covenant people and would take them back, however often they would wander.

The second half of the book gives the details of Israel's involvement in Canaanite religion. Like other prophetic books, Hosea carried a call to repentance. The alternative to destruction is to forsake idols and return to the Lord.

Outline

I. The Unfaithful Wife and the Faithful Husband (1:1—3:5)
II. The Unfaithful Nation and the Faithful God (4:1—14:9)
  A. Israel's Unfaithfulness (4:1—6:3)
  B. Israel's Punishment (6:4—10:15)
  C. The Lord's Faithful Love (11:1—14:9)

Hosea's Wife and Children

1 The word of the LORD which came to
[a]Hosea the son of Beeri, during the
days of [b]Uzziah, [c]Jotham, [d]Ahaz *and*
[e]Hezekiah, kings of Judah, and during
the days of [f]Jeroboam the son of Joash,
king of Israel.
2 ¶ When the LORD first spoke
through Hosea, the LORD said to Hosea,
"[a]Go, take to yourself a wife of harlotry
and *have* children of harlotry; for [b]the
land commits flagrant harlotry, [1]forsak-
ing the LORD."
3 So he went and took Gomer the
daughter of Diblaim, and she conceived
and [a]bore him a son.
4 And the LORD said to him, "Name
him [a]Jezreel; for yet a little while, and [b]I
will [1]punish the house of Jehu for the
bloodshed of Jezreel, and [c]I will put an
end to the kingdom of the house of Israel.
5 "On that day I will [a]break the bow
of Israel in the [b]valley of Jezreel."
6 ¶ Then she conceived again and
gave birth to a daughter. And [1]the LORD
said to him, "Name her [2]Lo-ruhamah,
for I will no longer [a]have compassion on
the house of Israel, that I would ever forgive them.
7 "But I will have [a]compassion on the
house of Judah and [b]deliver them by the
LORD their God, and will not deliver them
by [c]bow, sword, battle, horses or horsemen."
8 ¶ When she had weaned Lo-
ruhamah, she conceived and gave birth to
a son.
9 And [1]the LORD said, "Name him
[2]Lo-ammi, for you are not My people and
I am not [3]your God."
10 ¶ [1]Yet the number of the sons of
Israel
Will be like the [a]sand of the
sea,
Which cannot be measured or
numbered;
And [b]in the place
Where it is said to them,

1:1 [a]Rom 9:25 [b]2 Chr 26:1-23; Is 1:1; Amos 1:1 [c]2 Kin 15:5; 2 Chr 27:1-9 [d]2 Kin 16:1-20; 2 Chr 28:1-27; Is 1:1; Mic 1:1 [e]2 Kin 18:1-20:21; 2 Chr 29:1-32:33; Mic 1:1 [f]2 Kin 13:13; Amos 1:1
2 [1]Lit *from not following after* [a]Hos 3:1 [b]Deut 31:16; Jer 3:1; Ezek 23:3-21; Hos 2:5
3 [a]Ezek 23:4
4 [1]Lit *visit the bloodshed of Jezreel on the house of Jehu* [a]Hos 2:22 [b]2 Kin 10:11 [c]2 Kin 15:8-10
5 [a]Jer 49:35; Ezek 39:3 [b]Josh 17:16; Judg 6:33
6 [1]Lit *He* [2]I.e. she has not obtained compassion [a]Hos 2:4
7 [a]2 Kin 19:29-35; Is 30:18 [b]Jer 25:5; Zech 9:9 [c]Ps 44:3-7; Zech 4:6

9 [1]Lit *He* [2]I.e. not my people [3]Lit *yours* **10** [1]Ch 2:1 in Heb [a]Gen 22:17; Jer 33:22 [b]Rom 9:26

"You are [c]not My people,"
It will be said to them,
"*You are* the [d]sons of the living
God."
11 And the [a]sons of Judah and the
sons of Israel will be
[b]gathered together,
And they will appoint for
themselves [c]one leader,
And they will go up from the
land,
For great will be the day of
Jezreel.

Israel's Unfaithfulness Condemned

2 [1]Say to your brothers, "[2]Ammi,"
and to your sisters, "[3]Ruhamah."
2 "Contend with your mother,
[a]contend,
For she is [b]not my wife, and I
am not her husband;
And let her put away her
[c]harlotry from her face
And her adultery from between
her breasts,
3 Or I will strip her [a]naked
And expose her as on the [b]day
when she was born.
I will also [c]make her like a
wilderness,
Make her like desert land
And slay her with [d]thirst.
4 "Also, I will have no compassion
on her children,
Because they are [a]children of
harlotry.
5 "For their mother has [a]played the
harlot;
She who conceived them has
acted shamefully.
For she said, '[a]I will go after my
lovers,
Who [b]give *me* my bread and my
water,
My wool and my flax, my [c]oil
and my drink.'
6 "Therefore, behold, I will [a]hedge
up [1]her way with [b]thorns,
And I will build [2]a wall against
her so that she cannot find
her [c]paths.
7 "She will [a]pursue her lovers, but
she will not overtake them;
And she will seek them, but will
not find *them.*
Then she will say, '[b]I will go
back to my [c]first husband,
For it was [d]better for me then
than now!'
8 ¶ "For she does [a]not know that
it was [b]I who gave her the
grain, the new wine and the
oil,
And lavished on her silver and
gold,
Which they [1]used for Baal.
9 "Therefore, I will [a]take back My
grain at [1]harvest time
And My new wine in its season.
I will also take away My wool
and My flax
Given to cover her nakedness.
10 "And then I will [a]uncover her
lewdness
In the sight of her lovers,
And no one will rescue her out
of My hand.
11 "I will also [a]put an end to all her
gaiety,
Her [b]feasts, her [c]new moons,
her sabbaths
And all her festal assemblies.
12 "I will [a]destroy her vines and fig
trees,
Of which she said, 'These are
my wages
Which my lovers have given me.'
And I will [b]make them a forest,
And the [c]beasts of the field will
devour them.
13 "I will punish her for the [a]days
of the Baals
When she used to [1b]offer
sacrifices to them
And [c]adorn herself with her
[2]earrings and jewelry,
And follow her lovers, so that
she [d]forgot Me," declares
the LORD.

Restoration of Israel

14 ¶ "Therefore, behold, I will
allure her,
[a]Bring her into the wilderness
And speak [1]kindly to her.
15 "Then I will give her her
[a]vineyards from there,
And [b]the valley of Achor as a
door of hope.
And she will [1c]sing there as in
the days of her youth,
As in the [d]day when she came
up from the land of Egypt.
16 "It will come about in that day,"
declares the LORD,
"That you will call Me [1a]Ishi
And will no longer call Me
[2]Baali.
17 "For [a]I will remove the names of
the Baals from her mouth,
So that they will be [1]mentioned
by their names no more.
18 "In that day I will also make a
covenant for them
With the [a]beasts of the field,
The birds of the sky

10 [c]Is 65:1; Hos 1:9 [d]Is 63:16; 64:8; John 1:12; 1 Pet 2:10

11 [a]Is 11:12 [b]Jer 23:5,6; 50:4,5; Ezek 37:21-24 [c]Jer 30:21; Hos 3:5

2:1 [1]Ch 2:3 in Heb [2]I.e. my people [3]I.e. she has obtained compassion

2 [a]Ezek 23:45; Hos 2:5; 4:5 [b]Is 50:1 [c]Jer 3:1,9, 13

3 [a]Jer 13:22; Ezek 16:7,22,39 [b]Ezek 16:4 [c]Is 32:13,14; Hos 13:15 [d]Jer 14:3; Amos 8:11-13

4 [a]Jer 13:14

5 [a]Is 1:21; Jer 2:25; 3:1,2; Hos 3:1 [b]Jer 44:17, 18; Hos 2:12 [c]Hos 2:8

6 [1]So with some ancient versions; Heb *your* [2]Lit *her wall so that* [a]Job 19:8; Lam 3:7,9 [b]Hos 9:6; 10:8 [c]Jer 18:15

7 [a]Hos 5:13 [b]Luke 15:17,18 [c]Jer 2:2; 3:1; Ezek 16:8; 23:4 [d]Jer 14:22; Hos 13:6

8 [1]Or *made into the* [a]Is 1:3 [b]Ezek 16:19

9 [1]Lit *its time* [a]Hos 8:7; 9:2

10 [a]Ezek 16:37

11 [a]Jer 7:34; 16:9 [b]Hos 3:4; Amos 5:21; 8:10 [c]Is 1:13,14

12 [a]Jer 5:17; 8:13 [b]Is 5:5; 7:23 [c]Hos 13:8

13 [1]Or *burn incense* [2]Or *nose rings* [a]Hos 4:13; 11:2 [b]Jer 7:9 [c]Ezek 16:12,17; 23:40 [d]Hos 4:6; 8:14; 13:6

14 [1]Lit *upon her heart* [a]Ezek 20:33-38

15 [1]Or *give answer* [a]Ezek 28:25,26 [b]Josh 7:26 [c]Jer 2:1-3; Ezek 16:8-14 [d]Hos 11:1; 12:9, 13; 13:4

16 [1]I.e. my husband [2]I.e. my master, or my Baal [a]Is 54:5; Hos 2:7

17 [1]Or *remembered* [a]Ex 23:13; Josh 23:7; Ps 16:4

18 [a]Job 5:23; Is 11:6-9; Ezek 34:25

And the creeping things of the
ground.
And I will [1b]abolish the bow,
the sword and war from the
land,
And will make them [c]lie down
in safety.
19 "I will [a]betroth you to Me
forever;
Yes, I will betroth you to Me in
[b]righteousness and in
justice,
In lovingkindness and in
compassion,
20 And I will betroth you to Me in
faithfulness.
Then you will [a]know the LORD.

21 ¶ "It will come about in that day
that [a]I will respond,"
declares the LORD.
"I will respond to the heavens,
and they will respond to the
earth,
22 And the [a]earth will respond to
the grain, to the new wine
and to the oil,
And they will respond to
[1]Jezreel.
23 "I will [a]sow her for Myself in the
land.
[b]I will also have compassion on
[1]her who had not obtained
compassion,
And [c]I will say to [2]those who
were [d]not My people,
'You are My people!'
And [3]they will say, '*You are* my
God!' "

Hosea's Second Symbolic Marriage

3 Then the LORD said to me, "Go again,
love a [1]woman *who* is loved by *her*
[2]husband, yet an adulteress, even [a]as
the LORD loves the sons of Israel, though
they turn to other gods and love raisin
[b]cakes."
2 So I [a]bought her for myself for fifteen *shekels* of silver and a homer and a
[1]half of barley.
3 Then I said to her, "You shall [a]stay
with me for many days. You shall not play
the harlot, nor shall you have a [1]man; so
I will also be toward you."
4 For the sons of Israel will remain
for many days [a]without king or prince,
[b]without sacrifice or *sacred* [c]pillar and
without [d]ephod or [1e]household idols.
5 Afterward the sons of Israel will
[a]return and seek the LORD their God and
[b]David their king; and [c]they will come
trembling to the LORD and to His goodness in the last days.

God's Controversy with Israel

4 [a]Listen to the word of the LORD,
O sons of Israel,
For the LORD has a [b]case against
the inhabitants of the land,
Because there is [c]no
[1]faithfulness or [2]kindness
Or [d]knowledge of God in the
land.
2 *There is* [a]swearing, [b]deception,
[c]murder, [d]stealing and
[e]adultery.
They employ violence, so that
[f]bloodshed [1]follows
bloodshed.
3 Therefore the land [a]mourns,
And everyone who lives in it
languishes
Along with the beasts of the field
and the birds of the sky,
And also the fish of the sea
[1]disappear.

4 ¶ Yet let no one [1a]find fault,
and let none offer reproof;
For your people are like those
who [b]contend with the
priest.
5 So you will [a]stumble by day,
And the prophet also will
stumble with you by night;
And I will destroy your [b]mother.
6 [a]My people are destroyed for
lack of knowledge.
Because you have [b]rejected
knowledge,
I also will [c]reject you from
being My priest.
Since you have [d]forgotten the
[e]law of your God,
I also will forget your children.

7 ¶ The more they [a]multiplied,
the more they sinned
against Me;
I will [b]change their glory into
shame.
8 They [a]feed on the [1]sin of My
people
And [b]direct their desire toward
their iniquity.
9 And it will be, like people, [a]like
priest;
So I will [b]punish them for their
ways
And repay them for their deeds.
10 [a]They will eat, but not have
enough;
They will [b]play the harlot, but
not increase,
Because they have [1c]stopped
giving heed to the LORD.

18 [1]Lit *break* [b]Is 2:4; Ezek 39:1-10 [c]Lev 26:5; Jer 23:6; Ezek 34:25
19 [a]Is 62:4,5 [b]Is 1:27; 54:6-8
20 [a]Jer 31:33, 34; Hos 6:6; 13:4
21 [a]Is 55:10; Zech 8:12; Mal 3:10,11
22 [1]I.e. God sows [a]Jer 31:12; Joel 2:19
23 [1]Heb *Lo-ruhamah* [2]Heb *Lo-ammi* [3]Lit *he* [a]Jer 31:27 [b]Hos 1:6 [c]Rom 9:25; 1 Pet 2:10 [d]Hos 1:9
3:1 [1]I.e. Gomer [2]Lit *companion* [a]Jer 3:20 [b]2 Sam 6:19; 1 Chr 16:3; Song 2:5
2 [1]Heb *lethech* [a]Ruth 4:10
3 [1]Or *husband* [a]Deut 21:13
4 [1]Heb *teraphim* [a]Hos 10:3; 13:10,11 [b]Dan 9:27; 11:31; 12:11; Hos 2:11 [c]Hos 10:1,2 [d]Ex 28:4-12; 1 Sam 23:9-12 [e]Gen 31:19,34; Judg 17:5; 18:14,17; 1 Sam 15:23
5 [a]Jer 50:4,5 [b]Jer 30:9; Ezek 34:24 [c]Is 2:2,3; Jer 31:9
4:1 [1]Or *truth* [2]Or *loyalty* [a]Hos 5:1 [b]Hos 12:2; Mic 6:2 [c]Is 59:4; Jer 7:28 [d]Jer 4:22
2 [1]Lit *touches* [a]Deut 5:11; Hos 10:4 [b]Hos 7:3; 10:13; 11:12 [c]Gen 4:8; Hos 6:9 [d]Deut 5:19; Hos 7:1 [e]Deut 5:18; Hos 7:4 [f]Hos 6:8; 12:14
3 [1]Lit *are taken away* [a]Is 24:4; 33:9; Amos 5:16; Zeph 1:3
4 [1]Lit *contend* [a]Ezek 3:26; Amos 5:10,13 [b]Deut 17:12
5 [a]Ezek 14:3,7; Hos 5:5 [b]Jer 15:8; Hos 2:2,5
6 [a]Is 5:13 [b]Hos 4:14; Mal 2:7,8 [c]Zech 11:8,9, 15-17 [d]Hos 2:13; 8:14; 13:6 [e]Hos 8:1,12
7 [a]Hos 10:1; 13:6 [b]Hab 2:16
8 [1]Or *sin offering* [a]Hos 10:13 [b]Is 56:11; Mic 3:11
9 [a]Is 24:2; Jer 5:31 [b]Hos 8:13; 9:9
10 [1]Lit *forsaken giving heed*; or *forsaken the LORD to practice* (v 11) *harlotry* [a]Lev 26:26; Is 65:13; Mic 6:14 [b]Hos 7:4 [c]Hos 9:17

11 ¶ Harlotry, [a]wine and new wine
take away the
[1]understanding.
12 My people [a]consult their
wooden idol, and their
diviner's wand informs
them;
For a spirit of harlotry has led
them astray,
And they have played the harlot,
departing [1]from their God.
13 They offer sacrifices on the
[a]tops of the mountains
And [1b]burn incense on the
hills,
[c]Under oak, poplar and
terebinth,
Because their shade is pleasant.
Therefore your daughters play
the harlot
And your [2]brides commit
adultery.
14 I will not punish your daughters
when they play the harlot
Or your [1]brides when they
commit adultery,
For *the men* themselves go apart
with harlots
And offer sacrifices with [a]temple
prostitutes;
So the people without
understanding are [2]ruined.
15 ¶ Though you, Israel, play the
harlot,
Do not let Judah become guilty;
Also do not go to [a]Gilgal,
Or go up to Beth-aven
[b]And take the oath:
"As the LORD lives!"
16 Since Israel is [a]stubborn
Like a stubborn heifer,
[1]Can the LORD now [b]pasture
them
Like a lamb in a large field?
17 Ephraim is joined to [a]idols;
[b]Let him alone.
18 Their liquor gone,
They play the harlot continually;
[a]Their [1]rulers dearly love
shame.
19 [a]The wind wraps them in its
wings,
And they will be ashamed
because of their sacrifices.

The People's Apostasy Rebuked

5 Hear this, O priests!
Give heed, O house of Israel!
Listen, O house of the king!
For the judgment applies to you,
For you have been a [a]snare at
Mizpah
And a net spread out on Tabor.
2 The [a]revolters have [1b]gone
deep in depravity,
But I will chastise all of them.
3 I [a]know Ephraim, and Israel is
not hidden from Me;
For now, O Ephraim, you have
played the harlot,
Israel has defiled itself.
4 Their deeds will not allow them
To return to their God.
For a [a]spirit of harlotry is within
them,
And they [b]do not know the
LORD.
5 Moreover, the [a]pride of Israel
testifies against him,
And Israel and Ephraim stumble
in their iniquity;
[b]Judah also has stumbled with
them.
6 They will [a]go with their flocks
and herds
To seek the LORD, but they will
[b]not find *Him;*
He has [c]withdrawn from them.
7 They have [a]dealt treacherously
against the LORD,
For they have borne
[1b]illegitimate children.
Now the [c]new moon will
devour them with their
[2]land.

8 ¶ [a]Blow the horn in [b]Gibeah,
The trumpet in Ramah.
Sound an alarm at Beth-aven:
"[c]Behind you, Benjamin!"
9 Ephraim will become a
[a]desolation in the [b]day of
rebuke;
Among the tribes of Israel I
[c]declare what is sure.
10 The princes of Judah have
become like those who
[a]move a boundary;
On them I will [b]pour out My
wrath [c]like water.
11 Ephraim is [a]oppressed, crushed
in judgment,
[b]Because he was determined to
[1]follow *man's* command.
12 Therefore I am like a [a]moth to
Ephraim
And like rottenness to the house
of Judah.
13 When Ephraim saw his sickness,
And Judah his [1]wound,
Then Ephraim went to [a]Assyria
And sent to [2b]King Jareb.
But he is [c]unable to heal you,
Or to cure you of your [1]wound.
14 For I *will be* [a]like a lion to
Ephraim

11 [1]Lit *heart* [a]Prov 20:1; Is 5:12; 28:7
12 [1]Lit *from under* [a]Is 44:19; Jer 2:27
13 [1]Or *offer sacrifices* [2]Or *daughters-in-law* [a]Jer 3:6 [b]Hos 2:13; 11:2 [c]Is 1:29; Jer 2:20
14 [1]Or *daughters-in-law* [2]Lit *thrust down* [a]Deut 23:17
15 [a]Hos 9:15; 12:11 [b]Jer 5:2; 44:26; Amos 8:14
16 [1]Or *Now the LORD will pasture...field* [a]Ps 78:8 [b]Is 5:17; 7:25
17 [a]Hos 13:2 [b]Ps 81:12; Hos 4:4
18 [1]Lit *shields* [a]Mic 3:11
19 [a]Hos 12:1; 13:15
5:1 [a]Hos 9:8
2 [1]Or *waded deep in slaughter* [a]Hos 9:15 [b]Is 29:15; Hos 4:2; 6:9
3 [a]Amos 3:2; 5:12
4 [a]Hos 4:12 [b]Hos 4:6,14
5 [a]Hos 7:10 [b]Ezek 23:31-35
6 [a]Hos 8:13; Mic 6:6,7 [b]Prov 1:28; Is 1:15; Jer 14:12 [c]Ezek 8:6
7 [1]Lit *strange* [2]Lit *portions* [a]Is 48:8; Jer 3:20; Hos 6:7 [b]Hos 2:4 [c]Is 1:14; Hos 2:11
8 [a]Joel 2:1 [b]Hos 9:9; 10:9 [c]Judg 5:14
9 [a]Is 28:1-4; Hos 9:11-17 [b]Is 37:3 [c]Is 46:10; Zech 1:6
10 [a]Deut 19:14; 27:17 [b]Ezek 7:8 [c]Ps 32:6; 93:3,4
11 [1]Or with some ancient versions, *follow nothingness* [a]Deut 28:33 [b]Mic 6:16
12 [a]Ps 39:11; Is 51:8
13 [1]Or *ulcer* [2]Or *the avenging king* or *the great king* [a]Hos 7:11; 8:9; 12:1 [b]Hos 10:6 [c]Jer 30:12-15
14 [a]Ps 7:2; Hos 13:7,8; Amos 3:4

And like a young lion to the
house of Judah.
[b]I, even I, will tear to pieces
and go away,
I will carry away, and there will
be [c]none to deliver.
15 I will go away *and* return to My
place
Until they [1a]acknowledge their
guilt and seek My face;
In their affliction they will
earnestly [b]seek Me.

The Response to God's Rebuke

6 "[a]Come, let us return to the
LORD.
For [b]He has torn *us,* but [c]He
will heal us;
He has [1]wounded *us,* but He
will [d]bandage us.
2 "He will [a]revive us after two
days;
He will [b]raise us up on the third
day,
That we may live before Him.
3 "So let us [a]know, let us press on
to know the LORD.
His [b]going forth is as certain as
the dawn;
And He will come to us like the
[c]rain,
Like the spring rain watering the
earth."
4 ¶ What shall I do with you,
O [a]Ephraim?
What shall I do with you,
O Judah?
For your [1]loyalty is like a
[b]morning cloud
And like the dew which goes
away early.
5 Therefore I have [a]hewn *them* in
pieces by the prophets;
I have slain them by the [b]words
of My mouth;
And the judgments on you are
like the light that goes forth.
6 For [a]I delight in loyalty [b]rather
than sacrifice,
And in the knowledge of God
rather than burnt offerings.
7 But [a]like [1]Adam they have
[b]transgressed the covenant;
There they have [c]dealt
treacherously against Me.
8 [a]Gilead is a city of wrongdoers,
Tracked with [b]bloody *footprints.*
9 And as [a]raiders wait for a man,
So a band of priests [b]murder on
the way to Shechem;
Surely they have committed
[1c]crime.
10 In the house of Israel I have
seen a [a]horrible thing;
Ephraim's [b]harlotry is there,
Israel has defiled itself.
11 Also, O Judah, there is a
[a]harvest appointed for you,
When I [b]restore the fortunes of
My people.

Ephraim's Iniquity

7 When I [a]would heal Israel,
The iniquity of Ephraim is
uncovered,
And the evil deeds of Samaria,
For they deal [b]falsely;
The thief enters in,
[c]Bandits raid outside,
2 And they do not [1]consider in
their hearts
That I [a]remember all their
wickedness.
Now their [b]deeds are all around
them;
They are before My face.
3 [a]With their wickedness they
make the [b]king glad,
And the princes with their [c]lies.
4 They are [a]all adulterers,
Like an oven heated by the
baker
Who ceases to stir up *the fire*
From the kneading of the dough
until it is leavened.
5 On the [1]day of our king, the
princes [a]became sick with
the heat of wine;
He stretched out his hand with
[b]scoffers,
6 For their hearts are like an
[a]oven
As they approach their [1]plotting;
Their [2]anger [3]smolders all
night,
In the morning it burns like a
flaming fire.
7 All of them are hot like an oven,
And they consume their [a]rulers;
All their kings have fallen.
[b]None of them calls on Me.
8 ¶ Ephraim [a]mixes himself with
the [1]nations;
Ephraim has become a cake not
turned.
9 [a]Strangers devour his strength,
Yet he [b]does not know *it;*
Gray hairs also are sprinkled on
him,
Yet he does not know *it.*
10 Though the [a]pride of Israel
testifies against him,
Yet [b]they have not returned to
the LORD their God,

14 [b]Ps 50:22 [c]Mic 5:8
15 [1]Or *bear their punishment* [a]Is 64:7-9; Jer 3:13,14 [b]Ps 50:15; 78:34; Jer 2:27; Hos 3:5
6:1 [1]Lit *struck* [a]Jer 50:4,5 [b]Deut 32:39; Hos 5:14 [c]Jer 30:17; Hos 14:4 [d]Is 30:26
2 [a]Ps 30:5 [b]1 Cor 15:4
3 [a]Is 2:3; Mic 4:2 [b]Ps 19:6; Mic 5:2 [c]Job 29:23; Ps 72:6; Joel 2:23
4 [1]Or *loving kindness* [a]Hos 7:1; 11:8 [b]Ps 78:34-37; Hos 13:3
5 [a]1 Sam 15:32, 33; Jer 1:10; 5:14 [b]Jer 23:29
6 [a]Matt 9:13; 12:7 [b]Is 1:11
7 [1]Or *men* [a]Job 31:33 [b]Hos 8:1 [c]Hos 5:7
8 [a]Hos 12:11 [b]Hos 4:2
9 [1]Or *lewdness* [a]Hos 7:1 [b]Jer 7:9,10; Hos 4:2 [c]Ezek 22:9; 23:27; Hos 2:10
10 [a]Jer 5:30,31; 23:14 [b]Hos 5:3
11 [a]Jer 51:33; Joel 3:13 [b]Zeph 2:7
7:1 [a]Ezek 24:13; Hos 6:4; 7:13; 11:8 [b]Hos 4:2 [c]Hos 6:9
2 [1]Lit *say to their heart* [a]Ps 25:7; Jer 14:10; 17:1; Hos 8:13; 9:9; Amos 8:7 [b]Jer 2:19; 4:18; Hos 4:9
3 [a]Rom 1:32 [b]Jer 28:1-4; Hos 7:5; Mic 7:3 [c]Hos 4:2; 11:12
4 [a]Jer 9:2; 23:10
5 [1]I.e. a festive occasion [a]Is 28:1,7 [b]Is 28:14
6 [1]Lit *ambush* [2]So with some ancient versions; M.T. *baker* [3]Lit *sleeps* [a]Ps 21:9
7 [a]Hos 13:10 [b]Is 64:7
8 [1]Lit *peoples* [a]Ps 106:35
9 [a]Is 1:7; Hos 8:7 [b]Hos 4:6
10 [a]Hos 5:5 [b]Is 9:13

Nor have they sought Him, for
all this.
11 So [a]Ephraim has become like a
silly dove, [b]without [1]sense;
They call to [c]Egypt, they go to
[d]Assyria.
12 When they go, I will [a]spread My
net over them;
I will bring them down like the
birds of the sky.
I will [b]chastise them in
accordance with the
[1]proclamation to their
assembly.
13 [a]Woe to them, for they have
[b]strayed from Me!
Destruction is theirs, for they
have rebelled against Me!
I [c]would redeem them, but they
speak lies against Me.
14 And [a]they do not cry to Me
from their heart
When they wail on their beds;
For the sake of grain and new
wine they [1b]assemble
themselves,
They [c]turn away from Me.
15 Although I trained *and*
strengthened their arms,
Yet they [a]devise evil against Me.
16 They turn, *but* not [1]upward,
They are like a [a]deceitful bow;
Their princes will fall by the
sword
Because of the [2b]insolence of
their tongue.
This *will be* their [c]derision in
the land of Egypt.

Israel Reaps the Whirlwind

8 [a]*Put* the trumpet to your [1]lips!
[b]Like an eagle *the enemy comes*
[c]against the house of the
LORD,
Because they have [d]transgressed
My covenant
And rebelled against My [e]law.
2 [a]They cry out to Me,
"My God, [b]we of Israel
know You!"
3 Israel has rejected the good;
The enemy will pursue him.
4 [a]They have set up kings, but not
by Me;
They have appointed princes, but
I did not know *it*.
With their [b]silver and gold they
have made idols for
themselves,
That [1]they might be cut off.
5 [1]He has rejected your [a]calf,
O Samaria, *saying,*
"My anger burns against them!"
How long will they be incapable
of [b]innocence?
6 For from Israel is even this!
A [a]craftsman made it, so it is
not God;
Surely the calf of Samaria will be
broken to [1]pieces.
7 For [a]they sow the wind
And they reap the [b]whirlwind.
The standing grain has no
[1]heads;
It yields [c]no [2]grain.
Should it yield, strangers would
swallow it up.

8 ¶ Israel is [a]swallowed up;
They are now among the nations
Like a [b]vessel in which no one
delights.
9 For they have gone up to
[a]Assyria,
Like [b]a wild donkey all alone;
Ephraim has [c]hired [1]lovers.
10 Even though they hire *allies*
among the nations,
Now I will [a]gather them up;
And they will begin [b]to
[1]diminish
Because of the burden of the
[c]king of princes.

11 ¶ Since Ephraim has [a]multiplied
altars for sin,
They have become altars of
sinning for him.
12 Though [a]I wrote for him ten
thousand *precepts* of
My [b]law,
They are regarded as a strange
thing.
13 As for My [a]sacrificial gifts,
They [b]sacrifice the flesh and
eat *it,*
But the LORD has taken no
delight in them.
Now He will [c]remember their
iniquity,
And [d]punish *them* for their sins;
They will return to [e]Egypt.
14 For Israel has [a]forgotten his
Maker and [b]built palaces;
And Judah has multiplied
fortified cities,
But I will send a [c]fire on its
cities that it may consume
its palatial dwellings.

Ephraim Punished

9 [a]Do not rejoice, O Israel, [1]with
exultation like the [2]nations!
For you have [b]played the harlot,
[3]forsaking your God.
You have loved *harlots'* earnings
on [4]every threshing floor.

---

11 [1]Lit *heart* [a]Hos 11:11 [b]Hos 4:6,11,14; 5:4 [c]Hos 8:13; 9:3,6 [d]Hos 5:13; 8:9; 12:1

12 [1]Lit *report* [a]Ezek 12:13 [b]Lev 26:14-39; Deut 28:15

13 [a]Hos 9:12 [b]Jer 14:10; Ezek 34:6; Hos 9:17 [c]Jer 51:9; Hos 7:1; Matt 23:37

14 [1]Or with Gr and many ancient mss *gash themselves* [a]Job 35:9-11; Hos 8:2; Zech 7:5 [b]Judg 9:27; Amos 2:8; Mic 2:11 [c]Hos 13:16

15 [a]Nah 1:9

16 [1]Or possibly *to the Most High* [2]Lit *indignation;* or *cursing* [a]Ps 78:57 [b]Ps 12:3, 4; 17:10; 73:9; Dan 7:25; Mal 3:13,14 [c]Ezek 23:32; Hos 9:3,6

8:1 [1]Lit *palate* [a]Jer 4:13; Hos 5:8 [b]Hab 1:8 [c]Deut 28:49 [d]Hos 6:7 [e]Hos 4:6

2 [a]Ps 78:34; Hos 7:14 [b]Titus 1:16

4 [1]Lit *he* [a]2 Kin 15:13,17,25; Hos 13:10,11 [b]Hos 2:8; 13:1,2

5 [1]Or *Your calf has rejected you* [a]Hos 10:5; 13:2 [b]Ps 19:13; Jer 13:27

6 [1]Or *splinters* [a]Hos 13:2

7 [1]Lit *growth* [2]Or *meal* [a]Prov 22:8 [b]Is 66:15; Nah 1:3 [c]Hos 2:9

8 [a]2 Kin 17:6; Jer 51:34 [b]Jer 22:28; 25:34

9 [1]Lit *loves* [a]Hos 7:11 [b]Jer 2:24 [c]Ezek 16:33,34

10 [1]Or *suffer for awhile* [a]Ezek 16:37; 22:20 [b]Jer 42:2 [c]Is 10:8

11 [a]Hos 10:1

12 [a]Deut 4:6,8 [b]Hos 4:6

13 [a]Hos 5:6 [b]Jer 6:20; 7:21 [c]Jer 14:10; Hos 7:2; Luke 12:2; 1 Cor 4:5 [d]Hos 4:9; 9:7 [e]Hos 9:3,6

14 [a]Deut 32:18; Hos 2:13; 4:6; 13:6 [b]Is 9:9,10 [c]Jer 17:27

9:1 [1]Lit *to* [2]Lit *peoples* [3]Lit *away from your God* [4]Lit *all threshing floors of grain* [a]Is 22:12,13; Hos 10:5 [b]Hos 4:12

2 Threshing floor and wine press
will [a]not feed them,
And the new wine will fail
[1]them.
3 They will not remain in [a]the
LORD's land,
But Ephraim will return to
[b]Egypt,
And in [c]Assyria they will eat
[d]unclean *food.*
4 They will not pour out drink
offerings of [a]wine to the
LORD,
[b]Their sacrifices will not please
Him.
Their bread will [1]*be* like
[2]mourners' bread;
All who eat of it will be
[c]defiled,
For their bread will be for
[3]themselves *alone;*
It will not enter the house of the
LORD.
5 [a]What will you do on the day of
the appointed festival
And on the day of the [b]feast of
the LORD?
6 For behold, they will go because
of destruction;
Egypt will gather them up,
[a]Memphis will bury them.
Weeds will take over their
treasures of silver;
[b]Thorns *will be* in their tents.

7 ¶ The days of [a]punishment have
come,
The days of [b]retribution have
come;
[1]Let Israel know *this!*
The prophet is a [c]fool,
The [2]inspired man is
[d]demented,
Because of the grossness of your
[e]iniquity,
And *because* your hostility is *so*
great.
8 Ephraim *was* a watchman with
my God, a prophet;
Yet the snare of a bird catcher is
in all his ways,
And there is *only* hostility in the
house of his God.
9 They have gone [a]deep [1]in
depravity
As in the days of [b]Gibeah;
He will [c]remember their
iniquity,
He will punish their sins.

10 ¶ I found Israel like [a]grapes in
the wilderness;
I saw your forefathers as the
[b]earliest fruit on the fig tree
in its first *season.*
But they came to [c]Baal-peor and
devoted themselves to
[1d]shame,
And they became as [e]detestable
as that which they loved.
11 As for Ephraim, their [a]glory will
fly away like a bird—
No birth, no pregnancy and no
conception!
12 Though they bring up their
children,
Yet I will bereave them [1]until
not a man is left.
Yes, [a]woe to them indeed when
I depart from them!
13 Ephraim, as I have seen,
Is planted in a pleasant meadow
like [a]Tyre;
But Ephraim will bring out his
children for slaughter.
14 Give them, O LORD—what will
You give?
Give them a [a]miscarrying womb
and dry breasts.

15 ¶ All their evil is at [a]Gilgal;
Indeed, I came to hate them
there!
Because of the [b]wickedness of
their deeds
I will drive them out of My
house!
I will love them no more;
All their princes are [c]rebels.
16 [a]Ephraim is stricken, their root
is dried up,
They will bear [b]no fruit.
Even though they bear children,
I will slay the [c]precious ones of
their womb.
17 My God will cast them away
Because they have [a]not listened
to Him;
And they will be [b]wanderers
among the nations.

Retribution for Israel's Sin

10 Israel is a [1]luxuriant [a]vine;
He produces fruit for himself.
The more his fruit,
The more altars he [b]made;
The [2]richer his land,
The better [3]he made the *sacred*
[c]pillars.
2 Their heart is [1a]faithless;
Now they must bear their [b]guilt.
[2]The LORD will [c]break down
their altars
And destroy their *sacred* pillars.

3 ¶ Surely now they will say, "We
have [a]no king,
For we do not revere the LORD.
As for the king, what can he do
for us?"

2 [1]Lit *her* [a]Hos 2:9

3 [a]Lev 25:23; Jer 2:7 [b]Hos 7:16; 8:13 [c]Hos 7:11 [d]Ezek 4:13

4 [1]Lit be *to them* [2]Or *bread of misfortune* [3]Lit *their appetite* [a]Ex 29:40 [b]Jer 6:20; Hos 8:13 [c]Hag 2:13, 14

5 [a]Is 10:3; Jer 5:31 [b]Hos 2:11; Joel 1:13

6 [a]Is 19:13; Jer 2:16; 44:1; 46:14,19; Ezek 30:13,16 [b]Is 5:6; 7:23; Hos 10:8

7 [1]Or *Israel will know it* [2]Lit *man of the spirit* [a]Is 10:3; Jer 10:15; Mic 7:4; Luke 21:22 [b]Is 34:8; Jer 16:18; 25:14 [c]Lam 2:14; Ezek 13:3,10 [d]Is 44:25 [e]Ezek 14:9,10

9 [1]Lit *they have corrupted* [a]Is 31:6 [b]Judg 19:12,16-30; Hos 10:9 [c]Hos 7:2; 8:13

10 [1]I.e. Baal [a]Mic 7:1 [b]Jer 24:2 [c]Num 25:1-5; Ps 106:28,29 [d]Jer 11:13; Hos 4:18 [e]Ps 115:8; Ezek 20:8

11 [a]Hos 4:7; 10:5

12 [1]Lit *without a man* [a]Deut 31:17; Hos 7:13

13 [a]Ezek 26:1-21

14 [a]Hos 9:11

15 [a]Hos 4:15; 12:11 [b]Hos 4:9; 7:2; 12:2 [c]Is 1:23; Hos 5:2

16 [a]Hos 5:11 [b]Hos 8:7 [c]Ezek 24:21

17 [a]Hos 4:10 [b]Hos 7:13

10:1 [1]Or *degenerate* [2]Or *better* [3]Lit *they* [a]Is 5:1-7; Ezek 15:1-6 [b]Jer 2:28; Hos 8:11; 12:11 [c]1 Kin 14:23; Hos 3:4

2 [1]Lit *smooth* [2]Lit *He* [a]1 Kin 18:21; Zeph 1:5 [b]Hos 13:16 [c]Hos 10:8; Mic 5:13

3 [a]Ps 12:4; Is 5:19

4 They speak *mere* words,
[1]With [a]worthless oaths they
make covenants;
And [b]judgment sprouts like
poisonous weeds in the
furrows of the field.
5 The inhabitants of Samaria will
fear
For the [1a]calf of [b]Beth-aven.
Indeed, its people will mourn
for it,
And its [c]idolatrous priests [2]will
cry out over it,
Over its [d]glory, since it has
departed from it.
6 The thing itself will be carried to
[a]Assyria
As tribute to [1b]King Jareb;
Ephraim will [2]be [c]seized with
shame
And Israel will be ashamed of its
[d]own counsel.
7 Samaria will be [a]cut off *with* her
king
Like a stick on the surface of the
water.
8 Also the [a]high places of Aven,
the [b]sin of Israel, will be
destroyed;
[c]Thorn and thistle will grow on
their altars;
Then they will [d]say to the
mountains,
"Cover us!" And to the hills, "Fall
on us!"
9 From the days of Gibeah you
have sinned, O Israel;
There they stand!
Will not the battle against the
sons of iniquity overtake
them in Gibeah?
10 When it is My [a]desire, I will
[1b]chastise them;
And [c]the peoples will be
gathered against them
When they are bound for their
double guilt.

11 ¶ Ephraim is a trained [a]heifer
that loves to thresh,
But I will [b]come over her fair
neck *with a yoke;*
I will harness Ephraim,
Judah will plow, Jacob will
harrow for himself.
12 [a]Sow with a view to
righteousness,
Reap in accordance with
[1]kindness;
[b]Break up your fallow ground,
For it is time to [c]seek the LORD
Until He [d]comes to [2e]rain
righteousness on you.
13 You have [a]plowed wickedness,
you have reaped injustice,
You have eaten the fruit of [b]lies.
Because you have trusted in your
way, in your [c]numerous
warriors,
14 Therefore a tumult will arise
among your people,
And all your [a]fortresses will be
destroyed,
As Shalman destroyed Beth-arbel
on the day of battle,
When [b]mothers were dashed in
pieces with *their* children.
15 Thus it will be done to you at
Bethel because of your great
wickedness.
At dawn the king of Israel will
be completely cut off.

God Yearns over His People

11 When Israel *was* a youth I loved
him,
And [a]out of Egypt I [b]called My
son.
2 The more [1a]they called them,
The more they went from
[1]them;
They kept [b]sacrificing to the
Baals
And [c]burning incense to idols.
3 Yet it is I who taught Ephraim to
walk,
[1]I [a]took them in My arms;
But they did not know that I
[b]healed them.
4 I [a]led them with cords of a man,
with bonds of love,
And [b]I became to them as one
who lifts the yoke from their
jaws;
And I bent down *and* [c]fed them.

5 ¶ [1]They will not return to the
land of Egypt;
But Assyria—he will be [2]their
king
Because they [a]refused to return
to Me.
6 The [a]sword will whirl against
[1]their cities,
And will demolish [1]their gate
bars
And [b]consume *them* because of
their [c]counsels.
7 So My people are bent on
[a]turning from Me.
Though [1]they call [2]them to *the
One* on high,
None at all exalts *Him.*

8 ¶ [a]How can I give you up,
O Ephraim?
How can I surrender you,
O Israel?

4 [1]Or *Swearing falsely in making a covenant* [a]Ezek 17:13-19; Hos 4:2 [b]Deut 31:16, 17; 2 Kin 17:3,4; Amos 5:7

5 [1]So with some ancient versions; Heb *calves* [2]Or who *used to rejoice over* [a]Hos 8:5,6 [b]Hos 4:15; 5:8 [c]2 Kin 23:5 [d]Hos 9:11

6 [1]Or *the avenging king* or *the great king* [2]Lit *receive shame* [a]Hos 11:5 [b]Hos 5:13 [c]Hos 4:7 [d]Is 30:3; Jer 7:24

7 [a]Hos 13:11

8 [a]Hos 4:13 [b]1 Kin 12:28-30; 13:34 [c]Is 32:13; Hos 9:6; 10:2 [d]Is 2:19; Luke 23:30; Rev 6:16

10 [1]Or *bind* [a]Ezek 5:13 [b]Hos 4:9 [c]Jer 16:16

11 [a]Jer 50:11; Hos 4:16; Mic 4:13 [b]Jer 28:14

12 [1]Or *loyalty* [2]Or *teach* [a]Prov 11:18 [b]Jer 4:3 [c]Hos 12:6 [d]Hos 6:3 [e]Is 44:3; 45:8

13 [a]Job 4:8; Prov 22:8; Gal 6:7,8 [b]Hos 4:2; 7:3; 11:12 [c]Ps 33:16

14 [a]Is 17:3 [b]Hos 13:16

11:1 [a]Hos 2:15; 12:9,13; 13:4 [b]Ex 4:22,23; Matt 2:15

2 [1]I.e. God's prophets [a]2 Kin 17:13-15 [b]Hos 2:13; 4:13 [c]Is 65:7; Jer 18:15

3 [1]So ancient versions; Heb *He...His* [a]Deut 1:31; 32:10,11 [b]Ps 107:20; Jer 30:17

4 [a]Jer 31:2,3 [b]Lev 26:13 [c]Ex 16:32; Ps 78:25

5 [1]Lit *He* [2]Lit *his* [a]Hos 7:16

6 [1]Lit *his* [a]Hos 13:16 [b]Lam 2:9 [c]Hos 4:16,17

7 [1]I.e. God's prophets [2]Lit *him;* i.e. Israel [a]Jer 3:6,7; 8:5

8 [a]Hos 6:4; 7:1

How can I [1]make you like
[b]Admah?
How can I treat you like
[b]Zeboiim?
My heart is turned over
within Me,
[2]All My compassions are
kindled.
9 I will [a]not execute My fierce
anger;
I will not destroy Ephraim
[b]again.
For [c]I am God and not man, the
[d]Holy One in your midst,
And I will not come in [1]wrath.
10 They will [a]walk after the LORD,
He will [b]roar like a lion;
Indeed He will roar
And *His* sons will come
[c]trembling from the west.
11 They will come trembling like
birds from [a]Egypt
And like [b]doves from the land of
[a]Assyria;
And I will [c]settle them in their
houses, declares the LORD.

12 ¶ [1]Ephraim surrounds Me with
[a]lies
And the house of Israel with
deceit;
Judah is also unruly against God,
Even against the Holy One who
is faithful.

Ephraim Reminded

12 [1]Ephraim feeds on [a]wind,
And pursues the [b]east wind
continually;
He multiplies lies and violence.
Moreover, [2]he makes a covenant
with Assyria,
And oil is carried to Egypt.
2 The LORD also has a [a]dispute
with Judah,
And will punish Jacob
[b]according to his ways;
He will repay him according to
his deeds.
3 In the womb he [a]took his
brother by the heel,
And in his maturity he
[b]contended with God.
4 Yes, he wrestled with the angel
and prevailed;
He wept and [a]sought His favor.
He found Him at [b]Bethel
And there He spoke with us,
5 Even the LORD, the God of
hosts,
The LORD is His [1a]name.
6 Therefore, [a]return to your God,
[b]Observe [1]kindness and justice,
And [c]wait for your God
continually.
7 A [1]merchant, in whose hands
are false [a]balances,
He loves to oppress.
8 And Ephraim said, "Surely I have
become [a]rich,
I have found wealth for myself;
In all my labors they will find
in me
[b]No iniquity, which *would be*
sin."
9 But I *have been* the LORD your
God since the land of Egypt;
I will make you [a]live in tents
again,
As in the days of the appointed
festival.
10 I have also spoken to the
[a]prophets,
And I [1]gave numerous visions,
And through the prophets I gave
[b]parables.
11 Is there iniquity *in* Gilead?
Surely they are worthless.
In Gilgal they sacrifice bulls,
Yes, [a]their altars are like the
stone heaps
Beside the furrows of the field.
12 ¶ Now [a]Jacob fled to the [1]land
of Aram,
And [b]Israel worked for a wife,
And for a wife he kept *sheep.*
13 But by a [a]prophet the LORD
brought Israel from Egypt,
And by a prophet he was kept.
14 [a]Ephraim has provoked to bitter
anger;
So his Lord will leave his
[b]bloodguilt on him
And bring back his [c]reproach to
him.

Ephraim's Idolatry

13 [a]When Ephraim [1]spoke, *there
was* trembling.
He [b]exalted himself in Israel,
But through [c]Baal he [2]did
wrong and died.
2 And now they sin more and
more,
And make for themselves
[a]molten images,
Idols [1b]skillfully made from
their silver,
All of them the [c]work of
craftsmen.
They say of them, "Let the
[2]men who sacrifice kiss the
[d]calves!"
3 Therefore they will be like the
[a]morning cloud

8 [1]Lit *give* [2]Lit *Together* [b]Gen 14:8; Deut 29:23

9 [1]Lit *excitement* [a]Deut 13:17 [b]Jer 26:3; 30:11 [c]Num 23:19 [d]Is 5:24; 12:6; 41:14,16

10 [a]Hos 3:5; 6:1-3 [b]Is 31:4; Joel 3:16; Amos 1:2 [c]Is 66:2,5

11 [a]Is 11:11 [b]Is 60:8; Hos 7:11 [c]Ezek 28:25,26; 34:27,28

12 [1]Ch 12:1 in Heb [a]Hos 4:2; 7:3

12:1 [1]Ch 12:2 in Heb [2]Lit *they make* [a]Jer 22:22 [b]Gen 41:6; Ezek 17:10

2 [a]Hos 4:1; Mic 6:2 [b]Hos 4:9; 7:2

3 [a]Gen 25:26 [b]Gen 32:28

4 [a]Gen 32:26 [b]Gen 28:13-19; 35:10-15

5 [1]Lit *memorial* [a]Ex 3:15

6 [1]Or *loyalty* [a]Hos 6:1-3; 10:12 [b]Mic 6:8 [c]Mic 7:7

7 [1]Or *Canaanite* [a]Prov 11:1; Amos 8:5; Mic 6:11

8 [a]Ps 62:10; Hos 13:6; Rev 3:17 [b]Hos 4:8; 14:1

9 [a]Lev 23:42

10 [1]Lit *multiplied the vision* [a]2 Kin 17:13; Jer 7:25 [b]Ezek 17:2; 20:49

11 [a]Hos 8:11; 10:1,2

12 [1]Lit *field* [a]Gen 28:5 [b]Gen 29:20

13 [a]Ex 14:19-22; Is 63:11-14

14 [a]2 Kin 17:7-18 [b]Ezek 18:10-13 [c]Dan 11:18; Mic 6:16

13:1 [1]Or *spoke with trembling* [2]Or *became guilty* [a]Job 29:21,22 [b]Judg 8:1; 12:1 [c]Hos 2:8-17; 11:2

2 [1]Or *according to their own understanding* [2]Lit *sacrificers of* or, *(among) mankind* [a]Is 46:6; Jer 10:4; Hos 2:8 [b]Is 44:17-20 [c]Hos 8:6 [d]Hos 8:5,6; 10:5

3 [a]Hos 6:4

And like dew which [1]soon disappears,
Like [b]chaff which is blown away from the threshing floor
And like [c]smoke from a [2]chimney.

4 ¶ Yet I *have been* the [a]LORD your God
Since the land of Egypt;
And you were not to know [b]any god except Me,
For there is no savior [c]besides Me.
5 I [1a]cared for you in the wilderness,
[b]In the land of drought.
6 As *they had* their pasture, they became [a]satisfied,
And being satisfied, their [b]heart became proud;
Therefore they [c]forgot Me.
7 So I will be [a]like a lion to them;
Like a [b]leopard I will [1]lie in wait by the wayside.
8 I will encounter them [a]like a bear robbed of her cubs,
And I will tear open [1]their chests;
There I will also [b]devour them like a lioness,
As a wild beast would tear them.

9 ¶ *It is* your destruction, O Israel,
[1]That *you are* [a]against Me, against your [b]help.
10 Where now is your [a]king
That he may save you in all your cities,
And your [b]judges of whom you [1]requested,
"Give me a king and princes"?
11 I [a]gave you a king in My anger
And [b]took him away in My wrath.

12 ¶ The iniquity of Ephraim is bound up;
His sin is [a]stored up.
13 The pains of [a]childbirth come upon him;
He is [b]not a wise son,
For [1]it is not the time that he should [c]delay at the opening of the womb.
14 Shall I [a]ransom them from the [1]power of Sheol?
Shall I redeem them from death?
[b]O Death, where are your thorns?
O Sheol, where is your sting?
[c]Compassion will be hidden from My sight.

3 [1]Lit *goes away early* [2]Lit *window* [b]Ps 1:4; Is 17:13; Dan 2:35 [c]Ps 68:2
4 [a]Hos 12:9 [b]Ex 20:3; 2 Kin 18:35 [c]Is 43:11
5 [1]Or *knew* [a]Deut 2:7 [b]Deut 8:15
6 [a]Deut 8:12; Jer 5:7 [b]Hos 7:14 [c]Hos 2:13
7 [1]Or *watch* [a]Lam 3:10; Hos 5:14 [b]Jer 5:6
8 [1]Lit *the enclosure of their heart* [a]2 Sam 17:8 [b]Ps 50:22
9 [1]Or *But in Me is your help* [a]Jer 2:17; Mal 1:12 [b]Deut 33:26
10 [1]Lit *said* [a]2 Kin 17:4; Hos 8:4 [b]1 Sam 8:5
11 [a]1 Sam 8:7 [b]1 Sam 15:26; 1 Kin 14:7-10; Hos 10:7
12 [a]Deut 32:34; Job 14:17; Rom 2:5
13 [1]Lit *it is the time that he should not tarry at the breaking forth of children* [a]Is 13:8; Mic 4:9 [b]Deut 32:6; Hos 5:4 [c]Is 37:3
14 [1]Lit *hand* [a]Ps 49:15; Ezek 37:12 [b]1 Cor 15:55 [c]Jer 20:16
15 [1]Or *brothers* [a]Gen 49:22; Hos 10:1 [b]Gen 41:6; Jer 4:11; Ezek 17:10 [c]Jer 51:36 [d]Jer 20:5
16 [1]Ch 14:1 in Heb [a]Hos 10:2 [b]Hos 7:14 [c]2 Kin 8:12 [d]Hos 11:6 [e]Hos 10:14 [f]2 Kin 15:16
14:1 [1]Ch 14:2 in Heb [2]Or *in* [a]Hos 6:1; Joel 2:13 [b]Hos 4:8
2 [1]Or *accept that which is good* [2]So with ancient versions; M.T. *our lips as bulls* [a]Mic 7:18 [b]Ps 51:16; Hos 6:6; Heb 13:15
3 [1]Or *fatherless* [a]Ps 33:17; Is 31:1 [b]Hos 8:6 [c]Hos 4:12 [d]Ps 10:14
4 [a]Is 57:18; Hos 6:1 [b]Zeph 3:17 [c]Is 12:1
5 [1]Lit *strike his roots* [a]Prov 19:12; Is 26:19 [b]Song 2:1; Matt 6:28 [c]Is 35:2
6 [1]Lit *go* [2]Or *splendor* [a]Jer 11:16 [b]Song 4:11
7 [1]Or *return, they will raise grain* [a]Ezek 17:23 [b]Hos 2:21
8 [a]Job 34:32; Hos 14:3

15 ¶ Though he [a]flourishes among the [1]reeds,
An [b]east wind will come,
The wind of the LORD coming up from the wilderness;
And his fountain will [c]become dry
And his spring will be dried up;
It will [d]plunder *his* treasury of every precious article.
16 [1]Samaria will be held [a]guilty,
For she has [b]rebelled against her God.
[c]They will fall by the [d]sword,
Their little ones will be [e]dashed in pieces,
And their pregnant [f]women will be ripped open.

Israel's Future Blessing

14 [1a]Return, O Israel, to the LORD your God,
For you have stumbled [2]because of your [b]iniquity.
2 Take words with you and return to the LORD.
Say to Him, "[a]Take away all iniquity
And [1]receive *us* graciously,
That we may [b]present [2]the fruit of our lips.
3 "Assyria will not save us,
We will [a]not ride on horses;
Nor will we say again,
'[b]Our god,'
To the [c]work of our hands;
For in [d]You the [1]orphan finds mercy."

4 ¶ I will [a]heal their apostasy,
I will [b]love them freely,
For My anger has [c]turned away from them.
5 I will be like the [a]dew to Israel;
He will blossom like the [b]lily,
And he will [1]take root like *the cedars of* [c]Lebanon.
6 His shoots will [1]sprout,
And his [2]beauty will be like the [a]olive tree
And his fragrance like *the cedars of* [b]Lebanon.
7 Those who [a]live in his shadow
Will [1]again raise [b]grain,
And they will blossom like the vine.
His renown *will be* like the wine of Lebanon.

8 ¶ O Ephraim, what more have I to do with [a]idols?

It is I who answer and look
after [1]you.
I am like a luxuriant [b]cypress;
From [c]Me comes your fruit.

9 ¶ [a]Whoever is wise, let him
understand these things;
Whoever is discerning, let him
know them.
For the [b]ways of the LORD are right,
And the [c]righteous will walk in
them,
But [d]transgressors will stumble
in them.

8 [1]Lit *him* [b]Is 41:19 [c]Ezek 17:23

9 [a]Ps 107:43; Jer 9:12 [b]Ps 111:7,8; Prov 10:29; Zeph 3:5 [c]Is 26:7 [d]Is 1:28

Joel

Title and Background

Joel was a common Old Testament name meaning "The LORD is God." Locust plagues were frequent occurrences in the Near East for millennia, and Joel envisions one coming on Israel as a judgment from God.

Author and Date of Writing

The book contains no references to datable historical events, but a good case can be made for its being written about 830 B.C., during the reign of King Joash and at a time when Jehoiada the high priest was regent in Judah.

Theme and Message

Joel sees in the massive locust plague and severe drought devastating Judah a harbinger of the "great and awesome day of the LORD" (2:31). Confronted with this crisis, he calls on everyone to repent. He sees this day as a day of punishment for unfaithful Israel as well as for her neighbors. Restoration and blessing will come only after judgment and repentance.

Outline

I. A Foretaste of the Day of the Lord (1:1—2:17)
- A. A Call to Mourning and Prayer (1:1–14)
- B. The Announcement of the Day of the Lord (1:15—2:11)
- C. A Call to Repentance (2:12–17)

II. Salvation in the Day of the Lord (2:18—3:21)
- A. The Lord's Restoration of Judah (2:18–27)
- B. The Lord's Renewal of His People (2:28–32)
- C. The Coming of the Day of the Lord (3:1–21)

The Devastation of Locusts

1 The [a]word of the LORD that came to [b]Joel, the son of Pethuel:

2 [a]Hear this, O [b]elders,
And listen, all inhabitants of the land.
[c]Has *anything like* this happened in your days
Or in your fathers' days?
3 [a]Tell your sons about it,
And *let* your sons *tell* their sons,
And their sons the next generation.

4 ¶ What the [a]gnawing locust has left, the swarming locust has eaten;
And what the [b]swarming locust has left, the creeping locust has eaten;
And what the creeping locust has left, the [c]stripping locust has eaten.
5 Awake, [a]drunkards, and weep;
And wail, all you wine drinkers,
On account of the sweet wine
That is [b]cut off from your mouth.
6 For a [a]nation has [1]invaded my land,
Mighty and without number;
[b]Its teeth are the teeth of a lion,
And it has the fangs of a lioness.
7 It has [a]made my vine a waste
And my fig tree [1]splinters.
It has stripped them bare and cast *them* away;
Their branches have become white.

8 ¶ [a]Wail like a virgin [b]girded with sackcloth
For the bridegroom of her youth.
9 The [a]grain offering and the drink offering are cut off
From the house of the LORD.
The [b]priests mourn,
The ministers of the LORD.
10 The field is [a]ruined,
[b]The land mourns;
For the grain is ruined,
The new wine dries up,
Fresh oil [1]fails.

1:1 [a]Jer 1:2; Ezek 1:3; Hos 1:1 [b]Acts 2:16
2 [a]Hos 4:1; 5:1 [b]Job 8:8; Joel 1:14 [c]Jer 30:7; Joel 2:2
3 [a]Ex 10:2; Ps 78:4
4 [a]Deut 28:38; Joel 2:25; Amos 4:9 [b]Nah 3:15, 16 [c]Is 33:4
5 [a]Joel 3:3 [b]Is 32:10
6 [1]Lit *come up against* [a]Joel 2:2, 11,25 [b]Rev 9:8
7 [1]Or *a stump* [a]Is 5:6; Amos 4:9
8 [a]Is 22:12 [b]Joel 1:13; Amos 8:10
9 [a]Hos 9:4; Joel 1:13; 2:14 [b]Joel 2:17
10 [1]Lit *wastes away* [a]Is 24:4,7 [b]Jer 12:11

11 [1][a]Be ashamed, O farmers,
Wail, O vinedressers,
For the wheat and the barley;
Because the [b]harvest of the field
is destroyed.
12 The [a]vine dries up
And the fig tree [1]fails;
The [b]pomegranate, the [c]palm
also, and the [2][d]apple tree,
All the trees of the field dry up.
Indeed, [e]rejoicing dries up
From the sons of men.

13 ¶ [a]Gird yourselves *with*
sackcloth
And lament, O priests;
[b]Wail, O ministers of the altar!
Come, [c]spend the night in
sackcloth
O ministers of my God,
For the grain offering and the
drink offering
Are withheld from the house of
your God.

Starvation and Drought

14 [a]Consecrate a fast,
Proclaim a [b]solemn assembly;
Gather the elders
And all the inhabitants of the
land
To the house of the LORD your
God,
And [c]cry out to the LORD.
15 [a]Alas for the day!
For the [b]day of the LORD is near,
And it will come as [c]destruction
from the [1]Almighty.
16 Has not [a]food been cut off
before our eyes,
Gladness and [b]joy from the
house of our God?
17 The [1][a]seeds shrivel under their
[2]clods;
The storehouses are desolate,
The barns are torn down,
For the grain is dried up.
18 How [a]the beasts groan!
The herds of cattle wander
aimlessly
Because there is no pasture for
them;
Even the flocks of sheep [1]suffer.
19 [a]To You, O LORD, I cry;
For [b]fire has devoured the
pastures of the wilderness
And the flame has burned up all
the trees of the field.
20 Even the beasts of the field
[1][a]pant for You;
For the [b]water brooks are
dried up
And fire has devoured the
pastures of the wilderness.

The Terrible Visitation

2 [a]Blow a trumpet in Zion,
And sound an alarm on My holy
mountain!
Let all the inhabitants of the land
tremble,
For the [b]day of the LORD is
coming;
Surely it is near,
2 A day of [a]darkness and gloom,
A day of clouds and thick
darkness.
As the dawn is spread over the
mountains,
So there is a [b]great and mighty
people;
There has [c]never been *anything*
like it,
Nor will there be again after it
To the years of many
generations.
3 A [a]fire consumes before them
And behind them a flame burns.
The land is [b]like the garden of
Eden before them
But a [c]desolate wilderness
behind them,
And nothing at all escapes them.
4 Their [a]appearance is like the
appearance of horses;
And like war horses, so they run.
5 [1]With a [a]noise as of chariots
They leap on the tops of the
mountains,
Like the [2]crackling of a [b]flame
of fire consuming the
stubble,
Like a mighty people arranged
for battle.
6 Before them the people are in
[a]anguish;
All [b]faces [1]turn pale.
7 They run like mighty men,
They climb the wall like soldiers;
And they each [a]march [1]in line,
Nor do they deviate from their
paths.
8 They do not crowd each other,
They march everyone in his
path;
When they [1]burst through the
[2]defenses,
They do not break ranks.
9 They rush on the city,
They run on the wall;
They climb into the [a]houses,
They [b]enter through the
windows like a thief.
10 Before them the earth [a]quakes,
The heavens tremble,
The [b]sun and the moon grow
dark

11 [1]Or *The farmers are ashamed, The vinedressers wail* [a]Jer 14:4; Amos 5:16 [b]Is 17:11; Jer 9:12

12 [1]Lit *wastes away* [2]Or *apricot* [a]Joel 1:10; Hab 3:17 [b]Hag 2:19 [c]Song 7:8 [d]Song 2:3 [e]Is 16:10; 24:11; Jer 48:33

13 [a]Jer 4:8; Ezek 7:18 [b]Jer 9:10 [c]1 Kin 21:27

14 [a]Joel 2:15,16 [b]Lev 23:36 [c]Jon 3:8

15 [1]Heb *Shaddai* [a]Is 13:9; Jer 30:7; Amos 5:16 [b]Joel 2:1,11,31 [c]Is 13:6; Ezek 7:2-12

16 [a]Is 3:7; Amos 4:6 [b]Deut 12:7; Ps 43:4

17 [1]Or *dried figs* [2]Or *shovels* [a]Is 17:10,11

18 [1]Lit *bear punishment* [a]1 Kin 8:5; Jer 12:4; 14:5,6; Hos 4:3

19 [a]Ps 50:15; Mic 7:7 [b]Jer 9:10; Amos 7:4

20 [1]Lit *long for* [a]Ps 104:21; 147:9; Joel 1:18 [b]1 Kin 17:7; 18:5

2:1 [a]Jer 4:5; Joel 2:15; Zeph 1:16 [b]Joel 1:15; 2:11, 31; 3:14; Obad 15; Zeph 1:14

2 [a]Joel 2:10,31; Amos 5:18; Zeph 1:15 [b]Joel 1:6; 2:11,25 [c]Lam 1:12; Dan 9:12; 12:1; Joel 1:2

3 [a]Ps 97:3; Is 9:18,19 [b]Is 51:3; Ezek 36:35 [c]Ex 10:5,15; Ps 105:34,35; Zech 7:14

4 [a]Rev 9:7

5 [1]Lit *Like the noise of chariots* [2]Lit *noise* [a]Rev 9:9 [b]Is 5:24; 30:30

6 [1]Or *become flushed* [a]Is 13:8; Nah 2:10 [b]Jer 30:6

7 [1]Lit *in his ways* [a]Prov 30:27

8 [1]Lit *fall* [2]Lit *weapon,* probably *javelin*

9 [a]Ex 10:6 [b]Jer 9:21; John 10:1

10 [a]Ps 18:7; Joel 3:16; Nah 1:5 [b]Is 13:10; 34:4; Jer 4:23; Ezek 32:7,8; Joel 2:31; 3:15; Matt 24:29; Rev 8:12

And the stars lose their
brightness.
11 The LORD [a]utters His voice
before [b]His army;
Surely His camp is very great,
For [c]strong is he who carries
out His word.
The [d]day of the LORD is indeed
great and very awesome,
And [e]who can endure it?
12 "Yet even now," declares the
LORD,
"[a]Return to Me with all your
heart,
And with [b]fasting, weeping and
mourning;
13 And [a]rend your heart and not
[b]your garments."
Now return to the LORD your
God,
For He is [c]gracious and
compassionate,
Slow to anger, abounding in
lovingkindness
And [d]relenting of evil.
14 Who knows [a]whether He will
not turn and relent
And leave a [b]blessing behind
Him,
Even [c]a grain offering and a
drink offering
For the LORD your God?
15 [a]Blow a trumpet in Zion,
[b]Consecrate a fast, proclaim a
solemn assembly,
16 Gather the people, [a]sanctify the
congregation,
Assemble the elders,
Gather the children and the
nursing infants.
Let the [b]bridegroom come out of
his room
And the bride out of her *bridal*
chamber.
17 Let the priests, the LORD's
ministers,
Weep [a]between the porch and
the altar,
And let them say, "[b]Spare Your
people, O LORD,
And do not make Your
inheritance a [c]reproach,
A byword among the nations.
Why should they among the
peoples say,
'[d]Where is their God?' "

Deliverance Promised

18 ¶ Then the LORD [1]will be
[a]zealous for His land
And [2]will have [b]pity on His
people.
19 The LORD [1]will answer and say
to His people,

11 [a]Ps 46:6; Is 13:4; Jer 25:30; Joel 3:16 [b]Joel 2:25 [c]Jer 50:34; Rev 18:8 [d]Jer 30:7; Joel 1:15; 2:1,31; 3:14; Zeph 1:14,15; Rev 6:17 [e]Ezek 22:14; Mal 3:2

12 [a]Deut 4:29; Jer 4:1,2; Ezek 33:11; Hos 12:6 [b]Dan 9:3

13 [a]Ps 34:18; 51:17; Is 57:15 [b]Gen 37:34; 2 Sam 1:11; Job 1:20; Jer 41:5 [c]Ex 34:6 [d]Jer 18:8; 42:10; Amos 7:3,6

14 [a]Jer 26:3; Jon 3:9 [b]Hag 2:19 [c]Joel 1:9,13

15 [a]Num 10:3; 2 Kin 10:20 [b]Joel 1:14

16 [a]1 Sam 16:5; 2 Chr 29:5 [b]Ps 19:5

17 [a]2 Chr 8:12; Ezek 8:16 [b]Ex 32:11,12; Is 37:20; Amos 7:2,5 [c]Ps 44:13; 74:10 [d]Ps 42:10; 79:10; 115:2

18 [1]Or *was zealous* [2]Or *had pity* [a]Zech 1:14; 8:2 [b]Is 60:10; 63:9, 15

19 [1]Or *answered and said* [2]Lit *it* [a]Jer 31:12; Hos 2:21, 22; Joel 1:10; Mal 3:10 [b]Ezek 34:29; 36:15

20 [a]Jer 1:14,15 [b]Zech 14:8 [c]Deut 11:24 [d]Is 34:3; Amos 4:10

21 [a]Is 54:4; Jer 30:10; Zeph 3:16,17 [b]Ps 126:3; Joel 2:26

22 [1]Lit *their wealth* [a]Ps 65:12,13

23 [1]I.e. autumn; or possibly *the teacher for righteousness* [2]I.e. autumn [3]I.e. spring [4]So with ancient versions; Heb *in the first* [a]Ps 149:2 [b]Is 12:2-6 [c]Deut 11:14; Is 41:16; Jer 5:24; Hab 3:18; Zech 10:7 [d]Lev 26:4; Hos 6:3; Zech 10:1

24 [a]Lev 26:10; Amos 9:13; Mal 3:10

25 [a]Joel 1:4-7; 2:2-11

26 [a]Lev 26:5; Deut 11:15; Is 62:9 [b]Deut 12:7; Ps 67:5-7 [c]Ps 126:2,3; Is 25:1 [d]Is 45:17

27 [a]Lev 26:11, 12; Joel 3:17,21

"Behold, I am going to [a]send you
grain, new wine and oil,
And you will be satisfied *in full*
with [2]them;
And I will [b]never again make
you a reproach among the
nations.
20 "But I will remove the [a]northern
army far from you,
And I will drive it into a parched
and desolate land,
And its vanguard into the
[b]eastern sea,
And its rear guard into the
[c]western sea.
And its [d]stench will arise and its
foul smell will come up,
For it has done great things."

21 ¶ [a]Do not fear, O land, rejoice
and be glad,
For the LORD has done [b]great
things.
22 Do not fear, beasts of the field,
For the [a]pastures of the
wilderness have turned
green,
For the tree has borne its fruit,
The fig tree and the vine have
yielded [1]in full.
23 So rejoice, O [a]sons of Zion,
And [b]be glad in the LORD your
God;
For He has [c]given you [1]the
early rain for *your*
vindication.
And He has poured down for you
the rain,
The [2]early and [3][d]latter rain [4]as
before.
24 The threshing floors will be full
of grain,
And the vats will [a]overflow with
the new wine and oil.
25 "Then I will make up to you for
the years
That the swarming [a]locust has
eaten,
The creeping locust, the
stripping locust and the
gnawing locust,
My great army which I sent
among you.
26 "You will have plenty to [a]eat and
be satisfied
And [b]praise the name of the
LORD your God,
Who has [c]dealt wondrously with
you;
Then My people will [d]never be
put to shame.
27 "Thus you will [a]know that I am
in the midst of Israel,

And that I am the LORD your
God,
And there is [b]no other;
And My people will never be
[c]put to shame.

The Promise of the Spirit

28 ¶ "[1a]It will come about after
this
That I will [b]pour out My Spirit
on all [2c]mankind;
And your sons and daughters will
prophesy,
Your old men will dream dreams,
Your young men will see visions.
29 "Even on the [a]male and female
servants
I will pour out My Spirit in those
days.

The Day of the LORD

30 "I will [a]display wonders in the
sky and on the earth,
Blood, fire and columns of
smoke.
31 "The [a]sun will be turned into
darkness
And the moon into blood
Before the [b]great and awesome
day of the LORD comes.
32 "And it will come about that
[a]whoever calls on the name
of the LORD
Will be delivered;
For [b]on Mount Zion and in
Jerusalem
There will be those who
[c]escape,
As the LORD has said,
Even among the [d]survivors
whom the LORD calls.

The Nations Will Be Judged

3 "[1]For behold, [a]in those days and
at that time,
When I [b]restore the fortunes of
Judah and Jerusalem,
2 I will [a]gather all the nations
And bring them down to the
[b]valley of [1]Jehoshaphat.
Then I will [c]enter into judgment
with them there
On behalf of My people and My
inheritance, Israel,
Whom they have [d]scattered
among the nations;
And they have [e]divided up My
land.
3 "They have also [a]cast lots for My
people,
[1b]Traded a boy for a harlot
And sold a girl for wine that they
may drink.
4 "Moreover, what are you to Me,
O [a]Tyre, Sidon and all the regions of
[b]Philistia? Are you rendering Me a recompense? But if you do recompense Me,
swiftly and speedily I will [c]return your
recompense on your head.
5 "Since you have [a]taken My silver
and My gold, brought My precious [1]trea-
sures to your temples,
6 and sold the [a]sons of Judah and
Jerusalem to the [1]Greeks in order to remove them far from their territory,
7 behold, I am going to [a]arouse them
from the place where you have sold
them, and return your recompense on
your head.
8 "Also I will [a]sell your sons and your
daughters into the hand of the sons of
Judah, and they will sell them to the [b]Sa-
beans, to a distant nation," for the LORD
has spoken.
9 ¶ [a]Proclaim this among the
nations:
[b]Prepare a war; [c]rouse the
mighty men!
Let all the soldiers draw near, let
them come up!
10 [a]Beat your plowshares into
swords
And your pruning hooks into
spears;
[b]Let the weak say, "I am a
mighty man."
11 [1a]Hasten and come, all you
surrounding nations,
And gather yourselves there.
Bring down, O LORD, Your
[b]mighty ones.
12 Let the nations be aroused
And come up to the [a]valley of
[1]Jehoshaphat,
For there I will sit to [b]judge
All the surrounding nations.
13 [a]Put in the sickle, for the
[b]harvest is ripe.
Come, [c]tread, for the [d]wine
press is full;
The vats overflow, for their
[e]wickedness is great.
14 [a]Multitudes, multitudes in the
[b]valley of [1]decision!
For the [c]day of the LORD is near
in the valley of [1]decision.
15 The [a]sun and moon grow dark
And the stars lose their
brightness.
16 The LORD [a]roars from Zion
And [b]utters His voice from
Jerusalem,
And the [c]heavens and the earth
tremble.
But the LORD is a [d]refuge for His
people
And a [e]stronghold to the sons of
Israel.

27 [b]Is 45:5 [c]Is 49:23
28 [1]Ch 3:1 in Heb [2]Lit *flesh* [a]Acts 2:17-21 [b]Is 32:15; Ezek 39:29; Zech 12:10 [c]Is 40:5
29 [a]1 Cor 12:13; Gal 3:28
30 [a]Matt 24:29; Mark 13:24; Luke 21:11; Acts 2:19
31 [a]Is 13:10; Joel 2:10; Matt 24:29; Mark 13:24; Luke 21:25; Acts 2:20; Rev 6:12 [b]Is 13:9; Zeph 1:14-16; Mal 4:1
32 [a]Jer 33:3; Acts 2:21; Rom 10:13 [b]Is 46:13; Rom 11:26 [c]Is 4:2; Obad 17 [d]Is 11:11; Jer 31:7; Mic 4:7; Rom 9:27
3:1 [1]Ch 4:1 in Heb [a]Jer 30:3; Ezek 38:14 [b]Jer 16:15
2 [1]I.e. YHWH judges [a]Is 66:18; Mic 4:12; Zech 14:2 [b]Joel 3:12 [c]Is 66:16; Jer 25:31; Ezek 38:22 [d]Jer 50:17; Ezek 34:6 [e]Ezek 35:10
3 [1]Lit *Given* [a]Obad 11; Nah 3:10 [b]Amos 2:6
4 [a]Is 23:1-18; Amos 1:9; Zech 9:2-4; Matt 11:21; Luke 10:13 [b]Is 14:29-31; Jer 47:1-7; Ezek 25:15-17; Amos 1:6-8; Zech 9:5-7 [c]Is 34:8
5 [1]Lit *goodly things* [a]2 Kin 12:18; 2 Chr 21:16
6 [1]Lit *sons of Javan* [a]Ezek 27:13
7 [a]Is 43:5; Jer 23:8; Zech 9:13
8 [a]Is 14:2 [b]Job 1:15; Ps 72:10; Ezek 38:13
9 [a]Jer 51:27 [b]Jer 6:4; Ezek 38:7; Mic 3:5 [c]Is 8:9; Jer 46:3; Zech 14:2
10 [a]Is 2:4; Mic 4:3 [b]Zech 12:8
11 [1]Or *Lend aid* [a]Ezek 38:15 [b]Is 13:3
12 [1]I.e. YHWH judges [a]Joel 3:2 [b]Ps 7:6; Is 2:4
13 [a]Rev 14:14-19 [b]Jer 51:33; Hos 6:11 [c]Rev 14:19 [d]Is 63:3; Lam 1:15 [e]Gen 18:20
14 [1]I.e. God's verdict [a]Is 34:2-8 [b]Joel 3:2 [c]Joel 1:15
15 [a]Joel 2:10
16 [a]Hos 11:10; Amos 1:2 [b]Joel 2:11 [c]Ezek 38:19; Joel 2:10; Hag 2:6 [d]Ps 61:3; Is 33:16; Jer 17:17 [e]Jer 16:19; Nah 1:7

17 Then you will [a]know that I am
the LORD your God,
Dwelling in Zion, My [b]holy
mountain.
So Jerusalem will be [c]holy,
And [d]strangers will pass through
it no more.

Judah Will Be Blessed

18 ¶ And in that day
The [a]mountains will drip with
[1]sweet wine,
And the hills will [b]flow with
milk,
And all the [c]brooks of Judah will
flow with water;
And a [d]spring will go out from
the house of the LORD
To water the valley of [2]Shittim.
19 Egypt will become a waste,
And Edom will become a
desolate wilderness,
Because of the [a]violence [1]done
to the sons of Judah,
In whose land they have shed
innocent blood.
20 But Judah will be [a]inhabited
forever
And Jerusalem for all
generations.
21 And I will [a]avenge their blood
which I have not avenged,
For the LORD dwells in Zion.

17 [a]Joel 2:27 [b]Is 11:9; 56:7; Ezek 20:40 [c]Is 4:3; Obad 17 [d]Is 52:1; Nah 1:15

18 [1]Lit *freshly pressed out grape juice* [2]Or *acacias* [a]Amos 9:13 [b]Ex 3:8 [c]Is 30:25; 35:6 [d]Ezek 47:1-12

19 [1]Lit *of the sons* [a]Obad 10

20 [a]Ezek 37:25; Amos 9:15

21 [a]Is 4:4

Amos

Title and Background

The concurrent reigns of Uzziah of Judah and Jeroboam II of Israel were marked by a period of peace and prosperity. Prosperity was accompanied by an almost unprecedented degree of social corruption, and it is to this that the book of Amos is addressed.

Author and Date of Writing

Amos was a herdsman from the small town of Tekoa; he was not a man of the court like Isaiah, or a priest like Jeremiah. Though he lived in Judah, he was sent to announce God's judgment on the northern kingdom (Israel).

Amos prophesied during the reigns of Uzziah and Jeroboam II. The main part of his ministry was probably carried out about 760–750 B.C. and this book can be dated during that time.

Theme and Message

The dominant theme is clearly stated in 5:24, which calls for social justice as the indispensable expression of true piety. Amos was a vigorous spokesman for God's justice and righteousness. He condemns all who make themselves powerful or rich at the expense of others.

Outline

I. Judgments on Israel's Neighbors (1:1—2:5)
II. Judgment on Israel (2:6–16)
III. Oracles Against Israel (3:1—5:17)
IV. Announcements of Exile (5:18—6:14)
V. Visions of Divine Retribution (7:1—9:10)
VI. Restoration of Israel (9:11–15)

Judgment on Neighbor Nations

1 The words of Amos, who was among the [a]sheepherders from [b]Tekoa, which he [1]envisioned in visions concerning Israel in the days of [c]Uzziah king of Judah, and in the days of [d]Jeroboam son of Joash, king of Israel, two years before the [e]earthquake.

2 He said,
"The [a]LORD roars from Zion
And from Jerusalem He utters
His voice;
And the shepherds' [b]pasture
grounds mourn,
And the [1c]summit of Carmel
dries up."

3 ¶ Thus says the LORD,
"For [a]three transgressions of
[b]Damascus and for four
I will not [1]revoke its
punishment,
Because they threshed Gilead
with *implements* of sharp
iron.
4 "So I will send fire upon the
house of Hazael
And it will consume the citadels
of [a]Ben-hadad.
5 "I will also [a]break the *gate* bar of
Damascus,
And cut off the inhabitant from
the [1]valley of Aven,
And him who holds the scepter,
from Beth-eden;
So the people of Aram will go
exiled to [b]Kir,"
Says the LORD.

6 ¶ Thus says the LORD,
"For three transgressions of
[a]Gaza and for four
I will not revoke its *punishment,*
Because they deported an entire
population
To [b]deliver *it* up to Edom.
7 "So I will send fire upon the wall
of Gaza
And it will consume her citadels.
8 "I will also cut off the inhabitant
from [a]Ashdod,
And him who holds the scepter,
from [b]Ashkelon;
I will even [1]unleash My [2]power
upon Ekron,

1:1 [1]Lit *saw concerning* [a]Amos 7:14 [b]2 Sam 14:2; Jer 6:1 [c]2 Chr 26:1-23; Is 1:1 [d]2 Kin 14:23-29; Hos 1:1; Amos 7:10,11 [e]Zech 14:5

2 [1]Lit *head* [a]Is 42:13; Jer 25:30; Joel 3:16 [b]Jer 12:4; Joel 1:18, 19 [c]Amos 9:3

3 [1]Lit *cause it to turn back,* and so throughout the ch [a]Amos 2:1,4, 6 [b]Is 8:4; 17:1-3; Jer 49:23-27; Zech 9:1

4 [a]1 Kin 20:1; 2 Kin 6:24

5 [1]Possibly *Baal-bek* [a]Jer 51:30; Lam 2:9 [b]2 Kin 16:9; Amos 9:7

6 [a]1 Sam 6:17; Jer 47:1,5; Zeph 2:4 [b]Ezek 35:5; Obad 11

8 [1]Lit *cause to return* [2]Lit *hand* [a]2 Chr 26:6; Amos 3:9; Zech 9:6 [b]Jer 47:5; Zeph 2:4

And the remnant of the
[c]Philistines will perish,"
Says the Lord [3]GOD.

9 ¶ Thus says the LORD,
"For three transgressions of [a]Tyre
and for four
I will not revoke its *punishment,*
Because they delivered up an
entire population to Edom
And did not remember *the*
covenant of [1b]brotherhood.
10 "So I will [a]send fire upon the
wall of Tyre
And it will consume her
citadels."

11 ¶ Thus says the LORD,
"For three transgressions of
[a]Edom and for four
I will not revoke its *punishment,*
Because he [b]pursued his brother
with the sword,
While he [1]stifled his
compassion;
His anger also [c]tore continually,
And he maintained his fury
forever.
12 "So I will send fire upon [a]Teman
And it will consume the citadels
of Bozrah."

13 ¶ Thus says the LORD,
"For three transgressions of the
sons of [a]Ammon and for
four
I will not revoke its *punishment,*
Because they [b]ripped open the
pregnant women of Gilead
In order to [c]enlarge their
borders.
14 "So I will kindle a fire on the wall
of [a]Rabbah
And it will consume her citadels
Amid [1b]war cries on the day of
battle,
And a [c]storm on the day of
tempest.
15 "Their [a]king will go into exile,
He and his princes together,"
says the LORD.

Judgment on Judah and Israel

2 Thus says the LORD,
"For three transgressions of
[a]Moab and for four
I will not [1]revoke its
punishment,
Because he [b]burned the bones
of the king of Edom to lime.
2 "So I will send fire upon Moab
And it will consume the citadels
of [a]Kerioth;
And Moab will die amid
[b]tumult,
With [1]war cries and the sound
of a trumpet.
3 "I will also cut off the [1a]judge
from her midst
And slay all her [b]princes with
him," says the LORD.

4 ¶ Thus says the LORD,
"For three transgressions of
[a]Judah and for four
I will not revoke its *punishment,*
Because they [b]rejected the law
of the LORD
And have not kept His statutes;
Their [1c]lies also have led them
astray,
Those after which their [d]fathers
walked.
5 "So I will [a]send fire upon Judah
And it will consume the citadels
of Jerusalem."

6 ¶ Thus says the LORD,
"For three transgressions of
[a]Israel and for four
I will not revoke its *punishment,*
Because they [b]sell the righteous
for money
And the needy for a pair of
sandals.
7 "These who [1]pant after the *very*
dust of the earth on the
head of the [a]helpless
Also [b]turn aside the way of the
humble;
And a [c]man and his father
[2]resort to the same [3]girl
In order to profane My holy
name.
8 "On garments [a]taken as pledges
they stretch out beside
[b]every altar,
And in the house of their God
they [c]drink the wine of
those who have been fined.

9 ¶ "Yet it was I who destroyed
the [a]Amorite before them,
[1]Though his [b]height *was* like
the height of cedars
And he *was* strong as the oaks;
I even destroyed his [c]fruit above
and his root below.
10 "It was I who [a]brought you up
from the land of Egypt,
And I led you in the wilderness
[b]forty years
[1]That you might take possession
of the land of the [c]Amorite.
11 "Then I [a]raised up some of your
sons to be prophets
And some of your young men to
be [b]Nazirites.
Is this not so, O sons of Israel?"
declares the LORD.

8 [3]Heb *YHWH,* usually rendered *LORD* [c]Is 14:29-31; Jer 47:1-7; Ezek 25:16; Joel 3:4-8; Zeph 2:4-7; Zech 9:5-7
9 [1]Lit *brothers* [a]Is 23:1-18; Jer 25:22; Ezek 26:2-4; Joel 3:4-8; Zech 9:1-4; Matt 11:21; Luke 10:13 [b]1 Kin 9:11-14
10 [a]Zech 9:4
11 [1]Lit *corrupted* [a]Is 34:5; Jer 49:7-22; Ezek 25:12-14; Obad 1-14; Mal 1:2-5 [b]Num 20:14-21; 2 Chr 28:17; Obad 10-12 [c]Is 57:16; Mic 7:18
12 [a]Jer 49:7; Obad 9
13 [a]Jer 49:1-6; Ezek 21:28-32; Zeph 2:8 [b]2 Kin 15:16; Hos 13:16 [c]Is 5:8; Ezek 35:10
14 [1]Or *shouts* [a]Deut 3:11; 1 Chr 20:1; Jer 49:2 [b]Ezek 21:22; Amos 2:2 [c]Is 29:6
15 [a]Jer 49:3
2:1 [1]Lit *cause it to turn back,* and so throughout the ch [a]Is 15:1-16:14; Jer 48:1-47; Ezek 25:8-11; Zeph 2:8 [b]2 Kin 3:26
2 [1]Or *shouts* [a]Jer 48:24 [b]Jer 48:45
3 [1]Or *executive officer* [a]Ps 2:10; Amos 5:7 [b]Job 12:21; Is 40:23
4 [1]Or *false gods* [a]2 Kin 17:19; Hos 12:2; Amos 3:2 [b]Judg 2:17-20; 2 Kin 22:11-17; Jer 6:19 [c]Is 9:15; Jer 16:19; Hab 2:18 [d]Jer 9:14; Ezek 20:18
5 [a]Jer 17:27; Hos 8:14
6 [a]2 Kin 18:11 [b]Joel 3:3; Amos 5:11
7 [1]Or *trample* or, *snap at the head of the helpless on the dust* [2]Lit *go* [3]Possibly a harlot, or a temple prostitute [a]Amos 8:4; Mic 2:2 [b]Amos 5:12 [c]Hos 4:14
8 [a]Ex 22:26 [b]Amos 3:14 [c]Amos 4:1
9 [1]Lit *Whose height* [a]Num 21:23-25; Josh 10:12 [b]Num 13:32 [c]Ezek 17:9; Mal 4:1
10 [1]Lit *To possess* [a]Ex 12:51; Amos 3:1 [b]Deut 2:7 [c]Ex 3:8
11 [a]Deut 18:18; Jer 7:25 [b]Num 6:2; Judg 13:5

12 "But you made the Nazirites drink
wine,
And you commanded the
prophets saying, 'You [a]shall
not prophesy!'
13 "Behold, I am [1a]weighted down
beneath you
As a wagon [2]is weighted down
when filled with sheaves.
14 "[1a]Flight will perish from the
swift,
And the stalwart will not
strengthen his power,
Nor the [b]mighty man save his
[2]life.
15 "He who [a]grasps the bow will
not stand *his ground,*
The swift of foot will not escape,
Nor will he who rides the
[b]horse save his [1]life.
16 "Even the [1]bravest among the
warriors will [a]flee naked in
that day," declares the LORD.

All the Tribes Are Guilty

3 Hear this word which the LORD has
spoken against you, sons of Israel,
against the entire [1a]family which [2]He
brought up from the land of Egypt:
2 "[a]You only have I [1]chosen
among all the families of the
earth;
Therefore I will [2b]punish you
for all your iniquities."
3 Do two men walk together
unless they have made an
[1]appointment?
4 Does a [a]lion roar in the forest
when he has no prey?
Does a young lion [1]growl from
his den unless he has
captured *something?*
5 Does a bird fall into a trap on
the ground when there is no
[1]bait in it?
Does a trap spring up from the
earth when it captures
nothing at all?
6 If a [a]trumpet is blown in a city
will not the people tremble?
If a [b]calamity occurs in a city
has not the LORD done it?
7 [1]Surely the Lord [2]GOD does
nothing
Unless He [a]reveals His secret
counsel
To His servants the prophets.
8 A [a]lion has roared! Who will not
fear?
The [b]Lord [1]GOD has spoken!
[c]Who can but prophesy?
9 ¶ Proclaim on the citadels in [a]Ash-
dod and on the citadels in the land of
Egypt and say, "Assemble yourselves on
the [b]mountains of Samaria and see *the*
great tumults within her and *the* [c]op-
pressions in her midst.
10 "But they [a]do not know how to do
what is right," declares the LORD, "these
who [b]hoard up [1]violence and devastation in their citadels."
11 ¶ Therefore, thus says the Lord
GOD,
"An [a]enemy, even one
surrounding the land,
Will pull down your [1]strength
from you
And your [b]citadels will be
looted."
12 Thus says the LORD,
"Just as the shepherd [1a]snatches
from the lion's mouth a
couple of legs or a piece of
an ear,
So will the sons of Israel
dwelling in Samaria be
[2]snatched away—
With *the* [b]corner of a bed and
the [3c]cover of a couch!
13 "Hear and [a]testify against the
house of Jacob,"
Declares the Lord GOD, the God
of hosts.
14 "For on the day that I punish
Israel's transgressions,
I will also punish the altars of
[a]Bethel;
The horns of the altar will be
cut off
And they will fall to the ground.
15 "I will also smite the [1a]winter
house together with the
[b]summer house;
The houses of [2c]ivory will also
perish
And the [d]great houses will come
to an end,"
Declares the LORD.

"Yet You Have Not Returned to Me"

4 Hear this word, you cows of
[a]Bashan who are on the
[b]mountain of Samaria,
Who [c]oppress the poor, who
crush the needy,
Who say to [1]your husbands,
"Bring now, that we may
[d]drink!"
2 The Lord [1]GOD has [a]sworn by
His [b]holiness,
"Behold, the days are coming
upon you
When [2]they will take you away
with [c]meat hooks,
And the last of you with [d]fish
hooks.

12 [a]Is 30:10; Jer 11:21; Amos 7:13,16; Mic 2:6
13 [1]Or *tottering* [2]Or *totters* [a]Is 1:14
14 [1]Or *A place of refuge* [2]Lit *soul* [a]Is 30:16, 17 [b]Ps 33:16; Jer 9:23
15 [1]Lit *soul* [a]Jer 51:56; Ezek 39:3 [b]Is 31:3
16 [1]Lit *stout of heart* [a]Judg 4:17
3:1 [1]I.e. nation [2]Lit *I* [a]Jer 8:3; 13:11
2 [1]Lit *known* [2]Lit *visit* [a]Gen 18:19; Ex 19:5, 6; Deut 4:32-37; 7:6 [b]Jer 14:10; Ezek 20:36; Dan 9:12; Rom 2:9
3 [1]Or *agreement*
4 [1]Lit *give his voice* [a]Ps 104:21; Hos 5:14; 11:10
5 [1]Or *striker-bar set*
6 [a]Jer 4:5,19,21; 6:1; Hos 5:8; Zeph 1:16 [b]Is 14:24-27; 45:7
7 [1]Or *For* [2]Heb *YHWH* [a]Gen 6:13; 18:17; Jer 23:22; Dan 9:22; John 15:15
8 [1]Heb *YHWH,* usually rendered *LORD,* and so throughout the ch [a]Amos 1:2 [b]Jon 1:1-3; 3:1-3 [c]Jer 20:9; Acts 4:20
9 [a]1 Sam 5:1 [b]Amos 4:1; 6:1 [c]Amos 5:11; 8:6
10 [1]I.e. the booty from violence [a]Ps 14:4; Jer 4:22; Amos 5:7; 6:12 [b]Hab 2:8-10; Zeph 1:9; Zech 5:3,4
11 [1]Or *stronghold* [a]Amos 6:14 [b]Amos 2:5
12 [1]Or *delivers* [2]Or *delivered* [3]Lit *damask* [a]1 Sam 17:34-37 [b]Ps 132:3 [c]Esth 1:6; 7:8; Amos 6:4
13 [a]Ezek 2:7
14 [a]2 Kin 23:15; Hos 10:5-8,14,15; Amos 4:4; 5:5,6; 7:10,13
15 [1]Or *autumn* [2]I.e. ivory inlay [a]Jer 36:22 [b]Judg 3:20 [c]1 Kin 22:39; Ps 45:8 [d]Amos 2:5; 6:11
4:1 [1]Lit *their lords* [a]Ps 22:12; Ezek 39:18 [b]Amos 3:9; 6:1 [c]Amos 5:11; 8:6 [d]Amos 2:8; 6:6
2 [1]Heb *YHWH,* usually rendered *LORD,* and so throughout the ch [2]Lit *he* [a]Amos 6:8; 8:7 [b]Ps 89:35 [c]Is 37:29; Ezek 38:4 [d]Jer 16:16; Ezek 29:4; Hab 1:15

3 "You will [a]go out *through*
breaches *in the walls,*
Each one straight before her,
And you [1]will be cast to
Harmon," declares the LORD.

4 ¶ "Enter Bethel and transgress;
In Gilgal multiply transgression!
[a]Bring your sacrifices every
morning,
Your tithes every three days.
5 "[1]Offer a [a]thank offering also
from that which is leavened,
And proclaim [b]freewill offerings,
make them known.
For so you [c]love *to do,* you sons
of Israel,"
Declares the Lord GOD.

6 ¶ "But I gave you also
[a]cleanness of teeth in all
your cities
And lack of bread in all your
places,
Yet you have [b]not returned to
Me," declares the LORD.
7 "Furthermore, I [a]withheld the
rain from you
While *there were* still three
months until harvest.
Then I would send rain on one
city
And on [b]another city I would
not send rain;
One part would be rained on,
While the part not rained on
would dry up.
8 "So two or three cities would
stagger to another city to
drink [a]water,
But would [b]not be satisfied;
Yet you have [c]not returned to
Me," declares the LORD.
9 "I [a]smote you with scorching
wind and mildew;
And the [b]caterpillar was
devouring
Your many gardens and
vineyards, fig trees and olive
trees;
Yet you have [c]not returned to
Me," declares the LORD.
10 "I sent a [a]plague among you after
the manner of Egypt;
I [b]slew your young men by the
sword along with your
[c]captured horses,
And I made the [d]stench of your
camp rise up in your
nostrils;
Yet you have [e]not returned to
Me," declares the LORD.
11 "I overthrew you, as [a]God
overthrew Sodom and
Gomorrah,
And you were like a [b]firebrand
snatched from a blaze;
Yet you have [c]not returned to
Me," declares the LORD.
12 "Therefore thus I will do to you,
O Israel;
Because I will do this to you,
Prepare to [a]meet your God,
O Israel."
13 For behold, He who [a]forms
mountains and [b]creates the
wind
And [c]declares to man what are
His thoughts,
He who [d]makes dawn into
darkness
And [e]treads on the high places
of the earth,
[f]The LORD God of hosts is His
name.

"Seek Me that You May Live"

5 Hear this word which I take up
for you as a [a]dirge, O house
of Israel:
2 She has fallen, she will [a]not rise
again—
The [b]virgin Israel.
She *lies* neglected on her land;
There is [c]none to raise her up.
3 For thus says the Lord [1]GOD,
"The city which goes forth a
thousand *strong*
Will have a [a]hundred left,
And the one which goes forth a
hundred *strong*
Will have [b]ten left to the house
of Israel."

4 ¶ For thus says the LORD to the
house of Israel,
"[a]Seek Me [b]that you may live.
5 "But do not [1]resort to [a]Bethel
And do not come to [b]Gilgal,
Nor cross over to [c]Beersheba;
For Gilgal will certainly go into
captivity
And Bethel will [2]come to
trouble.
6 "[a]Seek the LORD that you may
live,
Or He will break forth like a
[b]fire, [1]O house of Joseph,
And it will consume with none
to quench *it* for Bethel,
7 *For* those who turn [a]justice into
wormwood
And [1]cast righteousness down to
the earth."
8 ¶ He who made the [a]Pleiades
and Orion
And [b]changes deep darkness
into morning,

3 [1]So Gr; M.T. reads *will cast* [a]Jer 52:7
4 [a]Num 28:3; Amos 5:21,22
5 [1]Lit *Offer up in smoke* [a]Lev 7:13 [b]Lev 22:18-21 [c]Jer 7:9,10; Hos 9:1, 10
6 [a]Is 3:1; Jer 14:18 [b]Is 9:13; Jer 5:3; Hag 2:17
7 [a]Deut 11:17; 2 Chr 7:13; Is 5:6 [b]Ex 9:4,26; 10:22,23
8 [a]1 Kin 18:5; Jer 14:4 [b]Ezek 4:16,17; Hag 1:6 [c]Jer 3:7
9 [a]Deut 28:22; Hag 2:17 [b]Joel 1:4,7; Amos 7:1, 2 [c]Jer 3:10
10 [a]Ex 9:3; Lev 26:25; Deut 28:27,60; Ps 78:50 [b]Jer 11:22; 18:21; 48:15 [c]2 Kin 13:3,7 [d]Joel 2:20 [e]Is 9:13
11 [a]Gen 19:24, 25; Deut 29:23; Is 13:19 [b]Zech 3:2 [c]Jer 23:14
12 [a]Is 32:11; 64:2; Jer 5:22
13 [a]Job 38:4-7; Ps 65:6; Is 40:12 [b]Ps 135:7; Jer 10:13 [c]Dan 2:28,30 [d]Jer 13:16; Joel 2:2; Amos 5:8 [e]Mic 1:3 [f]Is 47:4; Jer 10:16; Amos 5:8,27; 9:6
5:1 [a]Jer 7:29; 9:10,17; Ezek 19:1
2 [a]Amos 8:14 [b]Jer 14:17 [c]Is 51:18; Jer 50:32
3 [1]Heb *YHWH,* usually rendered *LORD,* and so throughout the ch [a]Is 6:13 [b]Amos 6:9
4 [a]Deut 4:29; 32:46,47; Jer 29:13 [b]Is 55:3
5 [1]Lit *seek* [2]Or *become iniquity* [a]1 Kin 12:28,29; Amos 3:14; 4:4; 7:10,13 [b]1 Sam 7:16; 11:14 [c]Gen 21:31-33; Amos 8:14
6 [1]Or in *the house* [a]Is 55:3,6, 7; Amos 5:14 [b]Deut 4:24
7 [1]Lit *they have put down* [a]Amos 2:3; 5:12; 6:12
8 [a]Job 9:9; 38:31 [b]Job 12:22; 38:12; Is 42:16

[1]Who also [c]darkens day *into*
night,
Who [d]calls for the waters of
the sea
And pours them out on the
surface of the earth,
The [e]LORD is His name.
9 It is He who [a]flashes forth *with*
destruction upon the strong,
So that [b]destruction comes upon
the fortress.

10 ¶ They hate him who [a]reproves
in the [1]gate,
And they [b]abhor him who
speaks *with* integrity.
11 Therefore because you [1]impose
heavy rent on the poor
And exact a tribute of grain from
them,
Though you have built [a]houses
of well-hewn stone,
Yet you will not live in them;
You have planted pleasant
vineyards, yet you will [b]not
drink their wine.
12 For I know your transgressions
are many and your sins are
great,
You who [a]distress the righteous
and accept bribes
And [1]turn aside the poor in the
[2]gate.
13 Therefore at [1]such a time the
prudent person [a]keeps
silent, for it is an evil time.

14 ¶ Seek good and not evil, that
you may live;
And thus may the LORD God of
hosts be with you,
[a]Just as you have said!
15 [a]Hate evil, love good,
And establish justice in the
[1]gate!
Perhaps the LORD God of hosts
[b]May be gracious to the
[c]remnant of Joseph.

16 ¶ Therefore thus says the LORD God
of hosts, the Lord,
"There is [a]wailing in all the
plazas,
And in all the streets they say,
'Alas! Alas!'
They also call the [b]farmer to
mourning
And [1c]professional mourners to
lamentation.
17 "And in all the [a]vineyards *there*
is wailing,
Because I will pass through the
midst of you," says the
LORD.

18 ¶ Alas, you who are longing for
the [a]day of the LORD,
For what purpose *will* the day of
the LORD *be* to you?
It *will be* [b]darkness and not
light;
19 As when a man [a]flees from a
lion
And a bear meets him,
[1]Or goes home, leans his hand
against the wall
And a snake bites him.
20 *Will* not the day of the LORD *be*
[a]darkness instead of light,
Even gloom with no brightness
in it?

21 ¶ "I hate, I [a]reject your festivals,
Nor do I [1b]delight in your
solemn assemblies.
22 "Even though you [a]offer up to
Me burnt offerings and your
grain offerings,
I will not accept *them;*
And I will not *even* look at the
[b]peace offerings of your
fatlings.
23 "Take away from Me the noise of
your songs;
I will not even listen to the
sound of your harps.
24 "But let [a]justice roll down like
waters
And righteousness like an
ever-flowing stream.
25 ¶ "[1a]Did you present Me with sacrifices and grain offerings in the wilderness for forty years, O house of Israel?
26 "[a]You also carried along [1]Sikkuth
your king and [2]Kiyyun, your images,
[3]the star of your gods which you made
for yourselves.
27 "Therefore, I will make you go into
exile beyond Damascus," says the LORD,
whose name is the God of hosts.

"Those at Ease in Zion"

6 [a]Woe to those who are at ease
in Zion
And to those who *feel* secure in
the mountain of Samaria,
The [b]distinguished men of the
foremost of nations,
To whom the house of Israel
comes.
2 Go over to [a]Calneh and look,
And go from there to [b]Hamath
the great,
Then go down to [c]Gath of the
Philistines.
Are [1]they better than these
kingdoms,
Or is their territory greater than
yours?

8 [1]Lit *And He darkened* [c]Ps 104:20 [d]Ps 104:6-9; Amos 9:6 [e]Amos 4:13
9 [a]Is 29:5; Amos 2:14 [b]Mic 5:11
10 [1]I.e. the place where court was held [a]Is 29:21; Amos 5:15 [b]1 Kin 22:8; Is 59:15; Jer 17:16-18
11 [1]Another reading is *trample upon* [a]Amos 3:15; 6:11 [b]Mic 6:15
12 [1]Lit *they turn* [2]I.e. the place where court was held [a]Is 1:23; 5:23; Amos 2:6
13 [1]Lit *that time* [a]Eccl 3:7; Hos 4:4
14 [a]Mic 3:11
15 [1]I.e. the place where court was held [a]Ps 97:10; Rom 12:9 [b]Joel 2:14 [c]Mic 5:3,7,8
16 [1]Lit *those who know lamentation* [a]Jer 9:10,18-20; Amos 8:3 [b]Joel 1:11 [c]2 Chr 35:25; Jer 9:17
17 [a]Is 16:10; Jer 48:33
18 [a]Is 5:19; Jer 30:7; Joel 1:15; 2:1,11,31 [b]Is 5:30; Joel 2:2
19 [1]Or *Then* [a]Job 20:24; Is 24:17,18; Jer 15:2,3; 48:44
20 [a]Is 13:10; Zeph 1:15
21 [1]Lit *like to smell* [a]Is 1:11-16; 66:3; Amos 4:4,5; 8:10 [b]Lev 26:31; Jer 14:12; Hos 5:6
22 [a]Is 66:3; Mic 6:6,7 [b]Lev 7:11-15; Amos 4:5
24 [a]Jer 22:3; Ezek 45:9; Mic 6:8
25 [1]Or *You presented Me with the sacrifices and a grain offering* [a]Deut 32:17; Josh 24:14; Neh 9:18-21; Acts 7:42,43
26 [1]Or *Sakkuth (Saturn)* or *shrine of your Moloch* [2]Or *Kaiwan (Saturn)* or *stands of* [3]Or *your star gods* [a]Acts 7:43
6:1 [a]Is 32:9-11; Zeph 1:12; Luke 6:24 [b]Ex 19:5; Amos 3:2
2 [1]Or *you* [a]Gen 10:10; Is 10:9 [b]1 Kin 8:65; 2 Kin 18:34; Is 10:9 [c]1 Sam 5:8; 2 Chr 26:6

3 Do you [a]put off the day of
calamity,
And would you [b]bring near the
seat of violence?
4 ¶ Those who recline on beds of
ivory
And sprawl on their [a]couches,
And [b]eat lambs from the flock
And calves from the midst of the
stall,
5 Who improvise to the sound of
the harp,
And like David have [1]composed
[a]songs for themselves,
6 Who [a]drink wine from
[1]sacrificial bowls
While they anoint themselves
with the finest of oils,
Yet they have not [b]grieved over
the ruin of Joseph.
7 Therefore, they will now [a]go
into exile at the head of the
exiles,
And the [b]sprawlers'
[1]banqueting will [2]pass
away.

8 ¶ The Lord [1]GOD has [a]sworn by
Himself, the LORD God of
hosts has declared:
"I [b]loathe the arrogance of Jacob,
And [2]detest his [c]citadels;
Therefore I will [d]deliver up *the*
city and [3]all it contains."
9 And it will be, if [a]ten men are left
in one house, they will die.
10 Then one's [1]uncle, or his [2a]un-
dertaker, will lift him up to carry out *his*
bones from the house, and he will say to
the one who is in the innermost part of
the house, "Is anyone else with you?"
And that one will say, "No one." Then he
will [3]answer, "[b]Keep quiet. For [4]the
name of the LORD is [c]not to be mentioned."
11 For behold, the LORD is going to
[a]command that the [b]great house be
smashed to pieces and the small house to
fragments.
12 ¶ Do horses run on rocks?
Or does one plow [1]them with
oxen?
Yet you have turned [a]justice
into poison
And the fruit of righteousness
into [2]wormwood,
13 You who rejoice in [1a]Lodebar,
[2]And say, "Have we not [b]by
our *own* strength taken
[3]Karnaim for ourselves?"
14 "For behold, [a]I am going to raise
up a nation against you,
O house of Israel," declares the
LORD God of hosts,
"And they will afflict you from the
[b]entrance of Hamath
To the [b]brook of the Arabah."

Warning Through Visions

7 Thus the Lord [1]GOD showed me,
and behold, He was forming a
[a]locust-swarm [2]when the spring crop
began to sprout. And behold, the spring
crop *was* after the king's [3]mowing.
2 And it came about, [1]when it had
[a]finished eating the vegetation of the
land, that I said,
"[b]Lord GOD, please pardon!
[2]How can Jacob stand,
For he is [c]small?"
3 The LORD [1a]changed His mind
about this.
"It shall not be," said the LORD.
4 ¶ Thus the Lord GOD showed me,
and behold, the Lord GOD was calling to
contend *with them* by [a]fire, and it consumed the great deep and began to consume the [1]farm land.
5 Then I said,
"[a]Lord GOD, please stop!
[b]How can Jacob stand, for he is
small?"
6 The LORD [1a]changed His mind
about this.
"This too shall not be," said the
Lord GOD.
7 ¶ Thus He showed me, and behold,
the Lord was standing [1]by a [2]vertical
wall with a plumb line in His hand.
8 The LORD said to me, "[a]What do
you see, Amos?" And I said, "A plumb
line." Then the Lord said,
"Behold I am about to put a
[b]plumb line
In the midst of My people Israel.
I will [1c]spare them no longer.
9 "The [a]high places of Isaac will be
desolated
And the [b]sanctuaries of Israel
laid waste.
Then I will [c]rise up against the
house of Jeroboam with the
sword."

Amos Accused, Answers

10 ¶ Then Amaziah, the [a]priest of
Bethel, sent *word* to [b]Jeroboam king of
Israel, saying, "Amos has [c]conspired
against you in the midst of the house of
Israel; the land is unable to endure all his
words.
11 "For thus Amos says, 'Jeroboam will
die by the sword and Israel will certainly
go from its land into exile.' "
12 Then Amaziah said to Amos, "[a]Go,

3 [a]Is 56:12; Amos 9:10 [b]Amos 3:10
4 [a]Amos 3:12 [b]Ezek 34:2
5 [1]Or *invented musical instruments* [a]1 Chr 15:16; Is 5:12
6 [1]Lit *sprinkling basins* [a]Amos 2:8 [b]Ezek 9:4
7 [1]Or *cultic feasts* [2]Lit *turn aside* [a]Amos 7:11 [b]1 Kin 20:16-21; Dan 5:4-6
8 [1]Heb *YHWH,* usually rendered LORD [2]Lit *hate* [3]Lit *its fullness* [a]Gen 22:16; Jer 22:5; Amos 4:2 [b]Lev 26:30; Deut 32:19; Ps 106:40; Amos 5:21 [c]Amos 3:10 [d]Hos 11:6
9 [a]Amos 5:3
10 [1]Or *beloved one* [2]Lit *one who burns him* [3]Lit *say* [4]Lit *not to make mention of the name of* [a]1 Sam 31:12 [b]Amos 5:13 [c]Jer 44:26; Ezek 20:39
11 [a]Is 55:11 [b]2 Kin 25:9; Amos 3:15
12 [1]Another reading is *the sea with oxen* [2]I.e. bitterness [a]1 Kin 21:7-13; Is 59:13; Hos 10:4; Amos 5:7
13 [1]Lit *a thing of nothing* [2]Lit *Who* [3]Lit *a pair of horns* [a]Job 8:14; Ps 2:2-4; Luke 12:19 [b]Ps 75:4; Is 28:14
14 [a]Jer 5:15 [b]Num 34:7; 1 Kin 8:65; 2 Kin 14:25
7:1 [1]Heb *YHWH,* usually rendered *LORD,* and so throughout the ch [2]Lit *at the beginning of the coming up of* [3]Or *shearings* [a]Joel 1:4; Amos 4:9; Nah 3:15
2 [1]Lit *if* [2]Lit *As who* [a]Ex 10:15 [b]Jer 14:7; Ezek 9:8 [c]Is 37:4; Jer 42:2
3 [1]Or *relented* [a]Deut 32:36; Jer 26:19; Hos 11:8; Amos 5:15; Jon 3:10
4 [1]Lit *portion* [a]Deut 32:22; Is 66:15; Amos 2:5
5 [a]Ps 85:4; Joel 2:17 [b]Amos 7:2
6 [1]Or *relented* [a]Ps 106:45; Amos 7:3; Jon 3:10
7 [1]Or *upon* [2]Lit *wall of a plumb line*
8 [1]Lit *pass him by* [a]Jer 1:11; Amos 8:2 [b]2 Kin 21:13; Is 28:17; Lam 2:8 [c]Jer 15:6; Ezek 7:4-9; Amos 8:2 **9** [a]Gen 46:1; Hos 10:8; Mic 1:5 [b]Lev 26:31; Is 63:18; Jer 51:51; Amos 7:13 [c]2 Kin 15:8-10; Amos 7:11
10 [a]1 Kin 12:31 [b]2 Kin 14:23 [c]Jer 26:8-11 **12** [a]Matt 8:34

you seer, flee away to the land of Judah
and there eat bread and there do your
prophesying!
13 "But [a]no longer prophesy at Bethel,
for it is a [b]sanctuary of the king and a
royal [1]residence."
14 ¶ Then Amos replied to Amaziah,
"I am not a prophet, nor am I the [a]son of
a prophet; for I am a herdsman and a
[1]grower of sycamore figs.
15 "But the LORD took me from [1]fol-
lowing the flock and the LORD said to me,
'Go [a]prophesy to My people Israel.'
16 "Now hear the word of the LORD:
you are saying, 'You [a]shall not prophesy
against Israel [b]nor shall you [1]speak
against the house of Isaac.'
17 "Therefore, thus says the LORD,
'Your [a]wife will become a harlot in the
city, your [b]sons and your daughters will
fall by the sword, your land will be parceled up by a *measuring* line and you
yourself will die [1]upon [c]unclean soil.
Moreover, Israel will certainly go from its
land into exile.' "

Basket of Fruit and Israel's Captivity

8 Thus the Lord [1]GOD showed me,
and behold, *there was* a basket of
summer fruit.
2 He said, "What do you see, Amos?"
And [a]I said, "A basket of summer fruit."
Then the LORD said to me, "The [b]end has
come for My people Israel. I will [1c]spare
them no longer.
3 "[1]The [a]songs of the palace will turn
to [b]wailing in that day," declares the
Lord GOD. "Many *will be* the [c]corpses; in
every place [2]they will cast them forth
[3]in silence."
4 ¶ Hear this, you who [1a]trample
the needy, to do away with the humble of
the land,
5 saying,
"When will the [a]new moon [1]be
over,
So that we may sell grain,
And the [b]sabbath, that we may
open the wheat *market*,
To make the [2]bushel smaller
and the shekel bigger,
And to [c]cheat with [3]dishonest
scales,
6 So as to [a]buy the helpless for
[1]money
And the needy for a pair of
sandals,
And *that* we may sell the refuse
of the wheat?"

7 ¶ The LORD has [a]sworn by the
[b]pride of Jacob,
"Indeed, I will [c]never forget any
of their deeds.
8 "Because of this will not the land
[a]quake
And everyone who dwells in it
[b]mourn?
Indeed, all of it will [c]rise up like
the Nile,
And it will be tossed about
And subside like the Nile of
Egypt.
9 "It will come about in that day,"
declares the Lord GOD,
"That I will make the [a]sun go
down at noon
And [b]make the earth dark in
[1]broad daylight.
10 "Then I will [a]turn your festivals
into mourning
And all your songs into
[1]lamentation;
And I will bring [b]sackcloth on
everyone's loins
And baldness on every head.
And I will make it [c]like *a time
of* mourning for an only son,
And the end of it will be like a
bitter day.

11 ¶ "Behold, days are coming,"
declares the Lord GOD,
"When I will send a famine on
the land,
Not a famine for bread or a thirst
for water,
But rather [a]for hearing the
words of the LORD.
12 "People will stagger from sea
to sea
And from the north even to the
east;
They will go to and fro to [a]seek
the word of the LORD,
But they will not find *it*.
13 "In that day the beautiful [a]virgins
And the young men will [b]faint
from thirst.
14 "*As for* those who swear by the
[1a]guilt of Samaria,
Who say, 'As your god lives,
O [b]Dan,'
And, 'As the way of [c]Beersheba
lives,'
They will fall and [d]not rise
again."

God's Judgment Unavoidable

9 I saw the Lord standing beside the
[a]altar, and He said,
"Smite the capitals so that the
[b]thresholds will shake,
And [c]break them on the heads
of them all!

13 [1]Lit *house* [a]Amos 2:12; Acts 4:18 [b]1 Kin 12:29,32; Amos 7:9
14 [1]Or *nipper* [a]1 Kin 20:35; 2 Kin 2:3,5; 4:38; 2 Chr 19:2
15 [1]Lit *behind* [a]Jer 1:7; Ezek 2:3,4
16 [1]Lit *flow* [a]Amos 2:12; 7:13 [b]Deut 32:2; Ezek 20:46; 21:2
17 [1]Or *in an unclean land* [a]Hos 4:13,14 [b]Jer 14:16 [c]2 Kin 17:6; Ezek 4:13; Hos 9:3
8:1 [1]Heb *YHWH*, usually rendered LORD, and so throughout the ch
2 [1]Lit *pass him by* [a]Jer 24:3 [b]Ezek 7:2,3,6 [c]Amos 7:8
3 [1]Or *They will howl the palace songs* [2]Lit *he has thrown* [3]Or *hush!* [a]Amos 5:23; 6:4,5; 8:10 [b]Amos 5:16 [c]Amos 6:8-10
4 [1]Or *snap at* [a]Ps 14:4; Prov 30:14; Amos 2:7; 5:11,12
5 [1]Lit *pass by* [2]Lit *ephah* [3]Lit *balances of deception* [a]Num 28:11; 2 Kin 4:23 [b]Ex 31:13-17; Neh 13:15 [c]Hos 12:7; Mic 6:11
6 [1]Lit *silver* [a]Amos 2:6
7 [a]Amos 4:2 [b]Deut 33:26,29; Ps 68:34; Amos 6:8 [c]Ps 10:11; Hos 7:2; 8:13
8 [a]Ps 18:7; 60:2; Is 5:25 [b]Hos 4:3 [c]Jer 46:7,8; Amos 9:5
9 [1]Lit *a day of light* [a]Job 5:14; Is 13:10; Jer 15:9; Mic 3:6 [b]Is 59:9,10; Amos 4:13; 5:8
10 [1]Or *a dirge* [a]Job 20:23; Amos 5:21 [b]Is 15:2,3; Jer 48:37; Ezek 7:18; 27:31 [c]Jer 6:26; Zech 12:10
11 [a]1 Sam 3:1; 2 Chr 15:3; Ps 74:9; Ezek 7:26; Mic 3:6
12 [a]Ezek 20:3, 31
13 [a]Lam 1:18; 2:21 [b]Is 41:17; Hos 2:3
14 [1]Or *Ashimah* [a]Hos 8:5 [b]1 Kin 12:28,29 [c]Amos 5:5 [d]Amos 5:2
9:1 [a]Amos 3:14 [b]Zeph 2:14 [c]Ps 68:21; Hab 3:13

Then I will [d]slay the rest of
them with the sword;
They will [e]not have a fugitive
who will flee,
Or a refugee who will escape.
2 "Though they dig into [a]Sheol,
From there will My hand take
them;
And though they [b]ascend to
heaven,
From there will I bring them
down.
3 "Though they hide on the summit
of Carmel,
I will [a]search them out and take
them from there;
And though they [b]conceal
themselves from My sight on
the floor of the sea,
From there I will command the
[c]serpent and it will bite
them.
4 "And though they go into
[a]captivity before their
enemies,
From there I will command the
sword that it slay them,
And I will [b]set My eyes against
them for evil and not for
good."

5 ¶ The Lord [1]GOD of hosts,
The One who [a]touches the land
so that it melts,
And [b]all those who dwell in it
mourn,
And all of it rises up like the
Nile
And subsides like the Nile of
Egypt;
6 The One who builds His
[1a]upper chambers in the
heavens
And has founded His vaulted
dome over the earth,
He who [b]calls for the waters of
the sea
And [c]pours them out on the
face of the earth,
[d]The LORD is His name.

7 ¶ "Are you not as the sons of
[a]Ethiopia to Me,
O sons of Israel?" declares the
LORD.
"Have I not brought up Israel
from the land of Egypt,
And the [b]Philistines from
Caphtor and the [c]Arameans
from [d]Kir?
8 "Behold, the [a]eyes of the Lord
GOD are on the sinful
kingdom,
And I will [b]destroy it from the
face of the earth;
Nevertheless, I will [c]not totally
destroy the house of Jacob,"
Declares the LORD.
9 "For behold, I am commanding,
And I will [a]shake the house of
Israel among all nations
As *grain* is shaken in a sieve,
But not a [1]kernel will fall to the
ground.
10 "All the [a]sinners of My people
will die by the sword,
Those who say, '[b]The calamity
will not overtake or
confront us.'

The Restoration of Israel

11 ¶ "In that day I will [a]raise up
the fallen [1b]booth of David,
And wall up its [c]breaches;
I will also raise up its ruins
And rebuild it as in the [d]days of
old;
12 [a]That they may possess the
remnant of [b]Edom
And all the [1]nations who are
[c]called by My name,"
Declares the LORD who does this.

13 ¶ "Behold, days are coming,"
declares the LORD,
"When the [a]plowman will
overtake the reaper
And the treader of grapes him
who sows seed;
When the [b]mountains will drip
sweet [c]wine
And all the hills will be
dissolved.
14 "Also I will [a]restore the
[1]captivity of My people
Israel,
And they will [b]rebuild the
ruined cities and live *in
them;*
They will also [c]plant vineyards
and drink their wine,
And make gardens and eat their
fruit.
15 "I will also plant them on their
land,
And [a]they will not again be
rooted out from their land
Which I have given them,"
Says the LORD your God.

---

1 [d]Amos 7:17 [e]Jer 11:11

2 [a]Ps 139:8 [b]Jer 51:53; Obad 4

3 [a]Jer 16:16 [b]Job 34:22; Ps 139:9,10 [c]Is 27:1

4 [a]Lev 26:33 [b]Lev 17:10; Jer 21:10; 39:16; 44:11

5 [1]Heb *YHWH,* usually rendered *LORD,* and so throughout the ch [a]Ps 104:32; 144:5; Is 64:1; Mic 1:4 [b]Amos 8:8

6 [1]Or *stairs* [a]Ps 104:3,13 [b]Amos 5:8 [c]Ps 104:6 [d]Amos 4:13

7 [a]2 Chr 14:9, 12; Is 20:4; 43:3 [b]Deut 2:23; Jer 47:4 [c]Amos 1:5 [d]2 Kin 16:9; Is 22:6

8 [a]Jer 44:27; Amos 9:4 [b]Amos 7:17; 9:10 [c]Jer 5:10; 30:11; 31:35,36; Joel 2:32; Amos 3:12; Obad 17

9 [1]Or *pebble* [a]Is 30:28; Luke 22:31

10 [a]Is 33:14; Zech 13:8 [b]Amos 6:3

11 [1]Or *shelter* or *tabernacle* [a]Acts 15:16-18 [b]Is 16:5 [c]Ps 80:12 [d]Is 63:11; Jer 46:26

12 [1]Or *Gentiles* [a]Obad 19 [b]Num 24:18; Is 11:14 [c]Is 43:7

13 [a]Lev 26:5 [b]Joel 3:18 [c]Gen 49:11

14 [1]Or *fortunes* [a]Ps 53:6; Is 60:4; Jer 30:3,18 [b]Is 61:4; 65:21 [c]Jer 24:6; 31:28

15 [a]Is 60:21; Ezek 34:28; 37:25

Obadiah

Title and Background

Obadiah's name means "servant of the LORD." The prophecy centers around an ancient feud between Edom and Israel. The Edomites were descendants of Esau, and carried a grudge against Israel because Jacob had cheated their ancestor out of his birthright.

Author and Date of Writing

The author is Obadiah. The date and place of composition are uncertain. A date between 853 and 841 B.C. is suggested by relating verses 11–14 to the invasion of Jerusalem by Philistines and Arabians during Jehoram's reign (2 Kings 8:20–22). An exilic date is arrived at by relating those verses to the Babylonian attacks on Jerusalem (605–586 B.C.).

Theme and Message

The book's theme is that Edom is proud of her own security and has gloated over God's people when Israel was devastated by foreign powers, but her participation in that disaster will bring on God's wrath. Edom herself will be destroyed, but Mount Zion and Israel will be delivered, and God's kingdom will triumph.

Outline

I. The Doom of Edom (1–14)
II. Edom in the Day of the Lord (15–21)

Edom Will Be Humbled

1 The vision of Obadiah.
¶ Thus says the Lord [1]GOD concerning [a]Edom—
[b]We have heard a report from the LORD,
And an [c]envoy has been sent among the nations *saying,*
"[d]Arise and let us go against her for battle"—
2 "Behold, I will make you [a]small among the nations;
You are greatly despised.
3 "The [a]arrogance of your heart has deceived you,
You who live in the clefts of [1]the [b]rock,
In the loftiness of your dwelling place,
Who say in your heart,
'[c]Who will bring me down to earth?'
4 "Though you [a]build high like the eagle,
Though you set your nest among the [b]stars,
From there I will bring you down," declares the LORD.
5 "If [a]thieves came to you,
If [1]robbers by night—
O how you will be ruined!—
Would they not steal *only* [2]until they had enough?
If grape gatherers came to you,
[b]Would they not leave *some* gleanings?
6 "O how Esau will be [a]ransacked,
And his hidden treasures searched out!
7 "All the [a]men [1]allied with you
Will send you forth to the border,
And the men at peace with you
Will deceive you and overpower you.
They who eat your [b]bread
Will set an ambush for you.
(There is [c]no understanding [2]in him.)
8 "Will I not on that day," declares the LORD,
"[a]Destroy wise men from Edom
And understanding from the mountain of Esau?
9 "Then your [a]mighty men will be dismayed, O [b]Teman,
So that everyone may be [c]cut off from the mountain of Esau by slaughter.

10 ¶ "Because of [a]violence to your brother Jacob,

1:1 [1]Heb *YHWH,* usually rendered *LORD* [a]Ps 137:7; Is 21:11,12; 34:1-17; 63:1-6; Jer 49:7-22; Ezek 25:12-14; 35:15; Joel 3:19; Amos 1:11,12; Mal 1:4 [b]Jer 49:14-16; Obad 1-4 [c]Is 18:2; 30:4 [d]Jer 6:4,5
2 [a]Num 24:18; Is 23:9
3 [1]Or *Sela* [a]Is 16:6; Jer 49:16 [b]2 Kin 14:7; 2 Chr 25:11f [c]Is 14:13-15; Rev 18:7
4 [a]Job 20:6,7; Hab 2:9 [b]Is 14:12-15
5 [1]Lit *devastators of* the *night* [2]Lit *their sufficiency* [a]Jer 49:9 [b]Deut 24:21
6 [a]Jer 49:10
7 [1]Lit *of your covenant* [2]I.e. in Esau; or *of it* [a]Jer 30:14 [b]Ps 41:9 [c]Is 19:11; Jer 49:7
8 [a]Job 5:12-14; Is 29:14
9 [a]Jer 49:22 [b]Gen 36:11; 1 Chr 1:45; Job 2:11; Jer 49:7; Ezek 25:13; Amos 1:12; Hab 3:3 [c]Is 34:5-8; 63:1-3; Obad 5
10 [a]Gen 27:41; Ezek 25:12; Joel 3:19; Amos 1:11

[1]You will be covered *with*
shame,
[b]And you will be cut off forever.
11 "On the day that you [a]stood
aloof,
On the day that strangers carried
off his wealth,
And foreigners entered his gate
And [b]cast lots for Jerusalem—
[c]You too were as one of them.
12 "[a]Do not [1]gloat over your
brother's day,
The day of his misfortune.
And [b]do not rejoice over the
sons of Judah
In the day of their destruction;
Yes, [c]do not [2]boast
In the day of *their* distress.
13 "Do not enter the gate of My
people
In the [a]day of their disaster.
Yes, you, do not [1]gloat over
their calamity
In the day of their disaster.
And do not [b]loot their wealth
In the day of their disaster.
14 "Do not [a]stand at the fork of the
road
To cut down their fugitives;
And do not imprison their
survivors
In the day of their distress.

The Day of the LORD and the Future

15 ¶ "For the [a]day of the LORD
draws near on all the
nations.
[b]As you have done, it will be
done to you.
Your [c]dealings will return on
your own head.
16 "Because just as you [a]drank on
[b]My holy mountain,
All the nations [c]will drink
continually.
They will drink and [1]swallow
And become as if they had never
existed.
17 "But on Mount [a]Zion there will
be those who escape,
And it will be holy.
And the house of Jacob will
[b]possess their possessions.
18 "Then the house of Jacob will be
a [a]fire
And the house of Joseph a flame;
But the house of Esau *will be* as
stubble.
And they will set [1]them on fire
and consume [1]them,
So that there will be [b]no
survivor of the house of
Esau,"
For the LORD has spoken.
19 Then *those of* the [1]Negev will
[a]possess the mountain of
Esau,
And *those of* the [2]Shephelah the
[b]Philistine *plain;*
Also, [c]possess the territory of
Ephraim and the territory of
Samaria,
And Benjamin *will possess*
Gilead.
20 And the exiles of this host of the
sons of Israel,
Who are *among* the Canaanites
as far as [a]Zarephath,
And the exiles of Jerusalem who
are in Sepharad
Will possess the [b]cities of the
Negev.
21 The [a]deliverers will ascend
Mount Zion
To judge the mountain of Esau,
And the [b]kingdom will be the
LORD'S.

10 [1]Lit *Shame will cover you* [b]Ezek 35:9

11 [a]Ps 83:5,6; 137:7; Amos 1:6,9 [b]Joel 3:3; Nah 3:10 [c]Ezek 35:10

12 [1]Lit *look on* [2]Lit *make your mouth large* [a]Mic 4:11; 7:10 [b]Prov 17:5; Ezek 35:15; 36:5 [c]Ps 31:18; Ezek 35:12

13 [1]Lit *look on* [a]Ezek 35:5 [b]Ezek 35:10; 36:2,3

14 [a]Is 16:3,4

15 [a]Ezek 30:3; Joel 1:15; 2:1, 11,31; Amos 5:18,20 [b]Jer 50:29; 51:56; Hab 2:8 [c]Ezek 35:11

16 [1]Or *stagger* [a]Jer 49:12 [b]Joel 3:17 [c]Is 51:22, 23; Jer 25:15,16

17 [a]Is 4:2,3 [b]Is 14:1,2; Amos 9:11-15

18 [1]I.e. the people of Esau [a]Is 5:24; 9:18,19; Zech 12:6 [b]Jer 11:23; Amos 1:8

19 [1]I.e. South country [2]I.e. the foothills [a]Is 11:14; Amos 9:12 [b]Is 11:14 [c]Jer 31:5; 32:44

20 [a]1 Kin 17:9; Luke 4:26 [b]Jer 32:44; 33:13

21 [a]Neh 9:27 [b]Ps 22:28; 47:7-9; 67:4; Zech 14:9; Rev 11:15

Jonah

Title and Background

The book is named after its principal character, whose name means "dove." The events in the book took place probably during the eighth century, when the Assyrians were a feared and despised enemy.

Author and Date of Writing

Traditionally, the book has been ascribed to Jonah son of Amittai, though nowhere in the book is it plainly stated. To accept that the book is authored by Jonah would necessitate a date no later than the third quarter of the eighth century B.C.

Theme and Message

The theme that runs throughout the four chapters of the book is God's great mercy to Gentile nations through repentance. The book also depicts the larger scope of God's purpose for Israel: that she might rediscover the truth of His concern for the whole creation and that she might better understand her own role in carrying out that concern.

Outline

I. Jonah Flees His Mission (1:1—2:10)
  - A. Jonah's Commission and Flight (1:1–3)
  - B. The Endangered Sailors' Cry to Their Gods (1:4–6)
  - C. Jonah's Disobedience Exposed (1:7–10)
  - D. Jonah's Punishment, Deliverance and Prayer of Thanksgiving (1:11—2:10)

II. Jonah Reluctantly Fulfills His Mission (3:1—4:11)
  - A. Jonah's Renewed Commission and Obedience (3:1–4)
  - B. The Endangered Ninevites' Repentant Appeal to the Lord (3:5–9)
  - C. The Ninevites' Repentance Acknowledged (3:10—4:4)
  - D. Jonah's Deliverance and Rebuke (4:5–11)

Jonah's Disobedience

1 The word of the LORD came to [a]Jo-
nah the son of Amittai saying,
2 "Arise, go to [a]Nineveh the great city
and [b]cry against it, for their [c]wicked-
ness has come up before Me."
3 But Jonah rose up to flee to [a]Tar-
shish [b]from the presence of the LORD. So
he went down to [c]Joppa, found a ship
which was going to Tarshish, paid the
fare and went down into it to go with
them to Tarshish from the presence of
the LORD.
4 ¶ The [a]LORD hurled a great wind
on the sea and there was a great storm on
the sea so that the ship was about to
[1]break up.
5 Then the sailors became afraid and
every man cried to [a]his god, and they
[b]threw the [1]cargo which was in the ship
into the sea to lighten *it* [2]for them.
But Jonah had gone below into the hold
of the ship, lain down and fallen sound
asleep.
6 So the captain approached him and
said, "How is it that you are sleeping? Get
up, [a]call on your god. Perhaps *your* [b]god
will be concerned about us so that we
will not perish."
7 ¶ Each man said to his mate,
"Come, let us [a]cast lots so we may
[1]learn on whose account this calamity
has struck us." So they cast lots and the
[b]lot fell on Jonah.
8 Then they said to him, "[a]Tell us,
now! On whose account *has* this calamity
struck us? What is your [b]occupation?
And where do you come from? What is
your country? From what people are
you?"
9 He said to them, "I am a [a]Hebrew,
and I [b]fear the LORD [c]God of heaven
who [d]made the sea and the dry land."
10 ¶ Then the men became extremely
frightened and they said to him, "[1]How
could you do this?" For the men knew

1 [a]2 Kin 14:25; Matt 12:39-41; Luke 11:29
2 [a]Gen 10:11; 2 Kin 19:36; Is 37:37; Nah 1:1; Zeph 2:13 [b]Is 58:1 [c]Gen 18:20; Hos 7:2
3 [a]Is 23:1; Jer 10:9 [b]Gen 4:16; Ps 139:7 [c]Josh 19:46; 2 Chr 2:16; Ezra 3:7; Acts 9:36
4 [1]Lit *be broken* [a]Ps 107:23-28
5 [1]Lit *vessels* [2]Lit *from upon them* [a]1 Kin 18:26 [b]Acts 27:18
6 [a]Ps 107:28 [b]2 Sam 12:22; Amos 5:15; Jon 3:9
7 [1]Lit *know* [a]Josh 7:14-18; 1 Sam 10:20; Acts 1:23-26 [b]Num 32:23; Prov 16:33
8 [a]Josh 7:19; 1 Sam 14:43 [b]Gen 47:3; 1 Sam 30:13
9 [a]Gen 14:13; Ex 1:15 [b]2 Kin 17:25 [c]Ezra 1:2; Neh 1:4; Ps 136:26; Dan 2:18 [d]Neh 9:6; Ps 95:5
10 [1]Lit *What is this you have done*

that he was [a]fleeing from the presence of
the LORD, because he had told them.
11 So they said to him, "What should
we do to you that the sea may become
calm [1]for us?"—for the sea was becoming increasingly stormy.
12 He said to them, "Pick me up and
throw me into the sea. Then the sea will
become calm [1]for you, for I know that
[a]on account of me this great storm *has*
come upon you."
13 However, the men [1]rowed *desper-*
ately to return to land but they could not,
for the sea was becoming *even* stormier
against them.
14 Then they called on the [a]LORD and
said, "We earnestly pray, O LORD, do not
let us perish on account of this man's life
and do not put innocent blood on us; for
[b]You, O LORD, have done as You have
pleased."
15 ¶ So they picked up Jonah, threw
him into the sea, and the sea [a]stopped its
raging.
16 Then the men feared the LORD
greatly, and they offered a sacrifice to the
LORD and made [a]vows.
17 ¶ [1]And the LORD appointed a great
fish to swallow Jonah, and Jonah was in
the [a]stomach of the fish three days and
three nights.

Jonah's Prayer

2 [1]Then Jonah prayed to the LORD his
God [a]from the stomach of the fish,
2 and he said,
"I [a]called out of my distress to
the LORD,
And He answered me.
I cried for help from the [1]depth
of [b]Sheol;
You heard my voice.
3 "For You had [a]cast me into the
deep,
Into the heart of the seas,
And the current [1]engulfed me.
All Your [b]breakers and billows
passed over me.
4 "So I said, 'I have been [a]expelled
from [1]Your sight.
Nevertheless I will look again
[b]toward Your holy temple.'
5 "[a]Water encompassed me to the
[1]point of death.
The great [b]deep [2]engulfed me,
Weeds were wrapped around my
head.
6 "I [a]descended to the roots of the
mountains.
The earth with its [b]bars *was*
around me forever,
But You have [c]brought up my
life from [1]the pit, O LORD
my God.

10 [a]Job 27:22; Jon 1:3
11 [1]Lit *from upon us*
12 [1]Lit *from upon you* [a]2 Sam 24:17; 1 Chr 21:17
13 [1]Lit *dug their oars into the water*
14 [a]Ps 107:28; Jon 1:16 [b]Ps 115:3; Dan 4:34
15 [a]Ps 65:7
16 [a]Ps 50:14
17 [1]Ch 2:1 in Heb [a]Matt 12:40
2:1 [1]Ch 2:2 in Heb [a]Job 13:15; Ps 130:1; Lam 3:53-56
2 [1]Lit *belly* [a]1 Sam 30:6; Ps 18:4-6 [b]Ps 18:5
3 [1]Lit *surrounded* [a]Ps 69:1; Lam 3:54 [b]Ps 42:7
4 [1]Lit *before Your eyes* [a]Ps 31:22; Jer 7:15 [b]1 Kin 8:38; 2 Chr 6:38; Ps 5:7
5 [1]Lit *soul* [2]Lit *surrounded* [a]Lam 3:54 [b]Ps 69:1
6 [1]Or *corruption* [a]Ps 18:5 [b]Is 38:10; Matt 16:18 [c]Job 33:28; Ps 16:10; Is 38:17
7 [1]Lit *my soul...within me* [a]Ps 142:3 [b]Ps 77:10 [c]2 Chr 30:27; Ps 18:6 [d]Ps 11:4; Jon 2:4; Mic 1:2; Hab 2:20
8 [1]Lit *empty vanities* [a]2 Kin 17:15; Ps 31:6; Jer 10:8
9 [a]Ps 50:14; Jer 33:11; Hos 14:2 [b]Job 22:27; Eccl 5:4 [c]Ps 3:8; Is 45:17
10 [a]Jon 1:17
3:2 [a]Zeph 2:13 [b]Jer 1:17; Ezek 2:7
3 [1]Lit *a great city to God* [a]Jon 1:2
4 [a]Matt 12:41; Luke 11:32
5 [a]Dan 9:3; Joel 1:14
6 [1]Or *dust* [a]Esth 4:1-4; Jer 6:26; Ezek 27:30
7 [a]2 Chr 20:3; Ezra 8:21; Jon 3:5
8 [1]Lit *them* [2]Lit *their* [a]Ps 130:1; Jon 1:6 [b]Is 1:16-19; Jer 18:11
9 [a]2 Sam 12:22; Joel 2:14
10 [1]Lit *do* [a]1 Kin 21:27-29; Jer 31:18 [b]Ex 32:14; Jer 18:8; Amos 7:3
4:1 [a]Jon 4:4; Matt 20:15; Luke 15:28
2 [1]Lit *my word* [a]Jer 20:7

7 "While [1]I was [a]fainting away,
I [b]remembered the LORD,
And my [c]prayer came to You,
Into [d]Your holy temple.
8 "Those who [a]regard [1]vain idols
Forsake their faithfulness,
9 But I will [a]sacrifice to You
With the voice of thanksgiving.
That which I have vowed I
will [b]pay.
[c]Salvation is from the LORD."
10 ¶ Then the LORD commanded the
[a]fish, and it vomited Jonah up onto the
dry land.

Nineveh Repents

3 Now the word of the LORD came to
Jonah the second time, saying,
2 "Arise, go to [a]Nineveh the great city
and [b]proclaim to it the proclamation
which I am going to tell you."
3 So Jonah arose and went to Nineveh according to the word of the LORD.
Now Nineveh was [1]an [a]exceedingly
great city, a three days' walk.
4 Then Jonah began to go through the
city one day's walk; and he [a]cried out
and said, "Yet forty days and Nineveh will
be overthrown."
5 ¶ Then the people of Nineveh believed in God; and they called a [a]fast and
put on sackcloth from the greatest to the
least of them.
6 When the word reached the king
of Nineveh, he arose from his throne,
laid aside his robe from him, [a]covered
himself with sackcloth and sat on the
[1]ashes.
7 He issued a [a]proclamation and it
said, "In Nineveh by the decree of the
king and his nobles: Do not let man,
beast, herd, or flock taste a thing. Do not
let them eat or drink water.
8 "But both man and beast must be
covered with sackcloth; and let [1]men
[a]call on God earnestly that each may
[b]turn from his wicked way and from the
violence which is in [2]his hands.
9 "[a]Who knows, God may turn and
relent and withdraw His burning anger so
that we will not perish."
10 ¶ When God saw their deeds, that
they [a]turned from their wicked way,
then [b]God relented concerning the calamity which He had declared He would
[1]bring upon them. And He did not
do *it*.

Jonah's Displeasure Rebuked

4 But it greatly displeased Jonah and he
became [a]angry.
2 He [a]prayed to the LORD and said,
"Please LORD, was not this [1]what I said

while I was still in my *own* country?
Therefore [2]in order to forestall this I
[b]fled to Tarshish, for I knew that You are
a [c]gracious and compassionate God, slow
to anger and abundant in lovingkindness,
and one who relents concerning calamity.
3 "Therefore now, O LORD, please
[a]take my [1]life from me, for death is
[b]better to me than life."
4 The LORD said, "Do you have good
reason to be angry?"
5 ¶ Then Jonah went out from the
city and sat east of [1]it. There he made a
shelter for himself and [a]sat under it in
the shade until he could see what would
happen in the city.
6 So the LORD God appointed a
[1]plant and it grew up over Jonah to be a
shade over his head to deliver him from
his discomfort. And Jonah was [2]extreme-
ly happy about the [1]plant.
7 But God appointed a worm when
dawn came the next day and it attacked
the plant and it [a]withered.
8 When the sun came up God appointed a scorching [a]east wind, and the
[b]sun beat down on Jonah's head so that
he became faint and begged with *all* his
soul to die, saying, "[c]Death is better to
me than life."
9 ¶ Then God said to Jonah, "Do you
have good reason to be angry about the
plant?" And he said, "I have good reason
to be angry, even to death."
10 Then the LORD said, "You had compassion on the plant for which you did
not work and *which* you did not cause to
grow, which [1]came up overnight and
perished [2]overnight.
11 "Should I not [a]have compassion on
Nineveh, the great city in which there
are more than 120,000 persons who do
not [b]know *the difference* between their
right and left hand, as well as many [c]ani-
mals?"

2 [2]Lit *I was beforehand in fleeing* [b]Jon 1:3 [c]Ex 34:6; Num 14:18; Ps 86:5, 15; Joel 2:13

3 [1]Lit *soul* [a]1 Kin 19:4; Job 6:8,9 [b]Job 7:15, 16; Eccl 7:1

5 [1]Lit *the city* [a]1 Kin 19:9,13

6 [1]Probably a castor oil plant, and so in vv 7, 9 and 10 [2]Lit *greatly*

7 [a]Joel 1:12

8 [a]Ezek 19:12; Hos 13:15 [b]Ps 121:6; Is 49:10 [c]Jon 4:3

10 [1]Lit *was a son of a night* [2]Lit *a son of a night*

11 [a]Jon 3:10 [b]Deut 1:39; Is 7:16 [c]Ps 36:6

Micah

Title and Background

The book is named after Micah, a shortened form of Micaiah, meaning "Who is like the LORD?" Judah had enjoyed comparative economic prosperity when Micah came on the scene. This prosperity placed wealth and power in the hands of a few and brought with it social injustice.

Author and Date of Writing

Little is known about Micah beyond what can be learned from the book itself. He was deeply sensitive to the social ills of his day, especially as they affected the small towns and villages of his homeland. Micah prophesied sometime between 750 and 686 B.C., and his book was written prior to 686.

Theme and Message

Micah's message alternated between oracles of doom and oracles of hope. The theme is judgment and deliverance by God. Micah also stresses that God hates idolatry, injustice, rebellion and empty ritualism, but He delights in pardoning the penitent.

Outline

I. Judgment Against Israel and Judah (1:1—3:12)
II. Hope for Israel and Judah (4:1—5:15)
III. The Lord's Case Against Israel (6:1–16)
IV. Gloom Turns to Triumph (7:1–20)

Destruction in Israel and Judah

1 The [a]word of the LORD which came
to [b]Micah of Moresheth in the days
of [c]Jotham, [d]Ahaz *and* [e]Hezekiah, kings
of Judah, which he saw concerning Samaria and Jerusalem.

2 Hear, O peoples, all of [1]you;
[a]Listen, O earth and [2]all it contains,
And let the Lord [3]GOD be a [b]witness against you,
The Lord from His holy temple.
3 For behold, the LORD is [a]coming forth from His place.
He will come down and [b]tread on the high places of the [1]earth.
4 [a]The mountains will melt under Him
And the valleys will be split,
Like wax before the fire,
Like water poured down a steep place.
5 All this is for the rebellion of Jacob
And for the sins of the house of Israel.
What is the [a]rebellion of Jacob?
Is it not [b]Samaria?
What is the [c]high [1]place of Judah?
Is it not Jerusalem?
6 For I will make Samaria a [a]heap of ruins [1]in the open country,
[b]Planting places for a vineyard.
I will [c]pour her stones down into the valley
And will [d]lay bare her foundations.
7 All of her [a]idols will be smashed,
All of her earnings will be burned with fire
And all of her images I will make desolate,
For she collected *them* from a [b]harlot's earnings,
And to the earnings of a harlot they will return.

8 ¶ Because of this I must lament and wail,
I must go [a]barefoot and naked;
I must make a lament like the [b]jackals
And a mourning like the ostriches.
9 For her [1a]wound is incurable,
For [b]it has come to Judah;
It has reached the [c]gate of my people,
Even to Jerusalem.

1:1 [a]2 Pet 1:21 [b]Jer 26:18 [c]2 Kin 15:5, 32-38; 2 Chr 27:1-9; Is 1:1; Hos 1:1 [d]2 Kin 16:1-20; 2 Chr 28:1-27; Is 7:1-12 [e]2 Kin 18:1-20; 2 Chr 29:1-31

2 [1]Lit *them* [2]Lit *its fullness* [3]Heb *YHWH,* usually rendered *LORD* [a]Jer 6:19; 22:29 [b]Is 50:7

3 [1]Or *land* [a]Is 26:21 [b]Amos 4:13

4 [a]Ps 97:5; Is 64:1,2; Nah 1:5

5 [1]Lit *places* [a]Jer 2:19 [b]Is 7:9; Amos 8:14 [c]2 Chr 34:3,4

6 [1]Lit *of the field* [a]2 Kin 19:25; Mic 3:12 [b]Jer 31:5; Amos 5:11 [c]Lam 4:1 [d]Ezek 13:14

7 [a]Deut 9:21; 2 Chr 34:7 [b]Deut 23:18; Is 23:17

8 [a]Is 32:11 [b]Is 13:21,22

9 [1]Lit *wounds* [a]Is 3:26; Jer 30:12,15 [b]2 Kin 18:13; Is 8:7,8 [c]Mic 1:12

10 [a]Tell it not in Gath,
Weep not at all.
At [1]Beth-le-aphrah roll yourself
in the dust.
11 [1]Go on your way, inhabitant of
[2]Shaphir, in [a]shameful
nakedness.
The inhabitant of [3][b]Zaanan does
not [4]escape.
The lamentation of [5]Bethezel:
"He will take from you its
[6]support."
12 For the inhabitant of [1]Maroth
Becomes weak [a]waiting for
good,
Because a calamity has come
down from the LORD
To the [b]gate of Jerusalem.
13 Harness the chariot to the team
of horses,
O inhabitant of [a]Lachish—
She was the beginning of sin
To the daughter of Zion—
Because in you were found
The [b]rebellious acts of Israel.
14 Therefore you will give parting
[a]gifts
On behalf of Moresheth-gath;
The houses of [b]Achzib *will*
become a [c]deception
To the kings of Israel.
15 Moreover, I will bring on you
The one who takes possession,
O inhabitant of [1][a]Mareshah.
The glory of Israel will enter
[b]Adullam.
16 Make yourself [a]bald and cut off
your hair,
Because of the children of your
delight;
Extend your baldness like the
eagle,
For they will [b]go from you into
exile.

Woe to Oppressors

2 Woe to those who [a]scheme
iniquity,
Who work out evil on their beds!
[1][b]When morning comes, they
do it,
For it is in the [c]power of their
hands.
2 They [a]covet fields and then
[b]seize *them,*
And houses, and take *them*
away.
They [1][c]rob a man and his
house,
A man and his inheritance.
3 Therefore thus says the LORD,
"Behold, I am [a]planning against
this [b]family a calamity
From which you [c]cannot remove
your necks;
And you will not walk
[d]haughtily,
For it will be an [e]evil time.
4 "On that day they will [a]take up
against you a [1]taunt
And [2][b]utter a bitter lamentation
and say,
'We are completely [c]destroyed!
He exchanges the portion of my
people;
How He removes it from me!
To the apostate He [d]apportions
our fields.'
5 "Therefore you will have no one
[1][a]stretching a measuring
line
For you by lot in the assembly of
the LORD.
6 ¶ '[a]Do not [1]speak out,' *so* they
[1]speak out.
But if [2]they do [b]not [1]speak out
concerning these things,
[c]Reproaches will not be turned
back.
7 "Is it being said, O house of
Jacob:
'Is the Spirit of the LORD
[a]impatient?
Are these His doings?'
Do not My words [b]do good
To the one [c]walking uprightly?
8 "[1]Recently My people have arisen
as an [a]enemy—
You [b]strip the [2]robe off the
garment
From [c]unsuspecting passers-by,
From those returned from war.
9 "The women of My people you
[a]evict,
Each *one* from her pleasant
house.
From her children you take My
[b]splendor forever.
10 "Arise and go,
For this is no place [a]of rest
Because of the [b]uncleanness that
brings on destruction,
A painful destruction.
11 "If a man walking after wind and
[a]falsehood
Had told lies *and said,*
'I will [1]speak out to you
concerning [b]wine and
liquor,'
He would be [2]spokesman to
[c]this people.
12 ¶ "I will surely [a]assemble all of
you, Jacob,
I will surely gather the [b]remnant
of Israel.

10 [1]I.e. house of dust [a]2 Sam 1:20

11 [1]I.e. Go into captivity [2]I.e. pleasantness [3]I.e. going out [4]Lit *go out* [5]I.e. house of removal [6]Lit *standing place* [a]Ezek 23:29 [b]Josh 15:37

12 [1]I.e. bitterness [a]Is 59:9-11; Jer 14:19 [b]Mic 1:9

13 [a]Josh 10:3; 2 Kin 14:19; Is 36:2 [b]Mic 1:5

14 [a]2 Kin 16:8 [b]Josh 15:44 [c]Jer 15:18

15 [1]I.e. possession [a]Josh 15:44 [b]Josh 12:15; 15:35; 2 Sam 23:13

16 [a]Is 22:12 [b]2 Kin 17:6; Amos 7:11,17

2:1 [1]Lit *In the light of the morning* [a]Ps 36:4; Is 32:7; Nah 1:11 [b]Hos 7:6,7 [c]Gen 31:29; Deut 28:32; Prov 3:27

2 [1]Lit *oppress* [a]Jer 22:17; Amos 8:4 [b]Is 5:8 [c]1 Kin 21:1-15

3 [a]Deut 28:48; Jer 18:11 [b]Jer 8:3; Amos 3:1,2 [c]Lam 1:14; 5:5 [d]Is 2:11,12 [e]Amos 5:13

4 [1]Or *proverb* [2]Lit *lament* [a]Hab 2:6 [b]Jer 9:10, 17-21; Mic 1:8 [c]Is 6:11; 24:3; Jer 4:13 [d]Jer 6:12; 8:10

5 [1]Lit *casting* [a]Num 34:13, 16-29; Deut 32:8; Josh 18:4, 10

6 [1]Lit *flow* [2]I.e. God's prophets [a]Is 30:10; Amos 2:12; 7:16 [b]Is 29:10; Mic 3:6 [c]Mic 6:16

7 [a]Is 50:2; 59:1 [b]Ps 119:65,68, 116; Jer 15:16 [c]Ps 15:2; 84:11

8 [1]Lit *And yesterday* [2]Or *ornaments* [a]Jer 12:8 [b]Mic 3:2,3; 7:2, 3 [c]Ps 120:6,7

9 [a]Jer 10:20 [b]Ezek 39:21; Hab 2:14

10 [a]Deut 12:9 [b]Ps 106:38

11 [1]Lit *flow* [2]Lit *one who flows oracles* [a]Jer 5:31 [b]Is 28:7 [c]Is 30:10,11

12 [a]Mic 4:6,7 [b]Mic 5:7,8; 7:18

I will put them together like
sheep in the fold;
Like a flock in the midst of its
pasture
They will be noisy with men.
13 "The breaker goes up before
them;
They break out, pass through the
gate and go out by it.
So their king goes on before
them,
And the LORD at their head."

Rulers Denounced

3 And I said,
"[a]Hear now, heads of Jacob
And rulers of the house of Israel.
Is it not for you to [b]know
justice?
2 "You who hate good and love evil,
Who [a]tear off their skin from
them
And their flesh from their bones,
3 Who [a]eat the flesh of my
people,
Strip off their skin from them,
Break their bones
And [b]chop *them* up as for
the pot
And as meat in a kettle."
4 Then they will [a]cry out to the
LORD,
But He will not answer them.
Instead, He will [b]hide His face
from them at that time
Because they have [c]practiced
evil deeds.

5 ¶ Thus says the LORD concerning
the prophets who [a]lead my people astray;
When they have *something* to
bite with their teeth,
They [b]cry, "Peace,"
But against him who puts
nothing in their mouths
They declare holy war.
6 Therefore *it will be* [a]night for
you—without vision,
And darkness for you—without
divination.
The [b]sun will go down on the
prophets,
And the day will become dark
over them.
7 The seers will be [a]ashamed
And the [b]diviners will be
embarrassed.
Indeed, they will all [c]cover *their*
[1]mouths
Because there is [d]no answer
from God.
8 On the other hand [a]I am filled
with power—
With the Spirit of the LORD—
And with justice and courage
To [b]make known to Jacob his
rebellious act,
Even to Israel his sin.
9 Now hear this, [a]heads of the
house of Jacob
And rulers of the house of Israel,
Who [b]abhor justice
And twist everything that is
straight,
10 Who [a]build Zion with bloodshed
And Jerusalem with violent
injustice.
11 Her leaders pronounce
[a]judgment for a bribe,
Her [b]priests instruct for a price
And her prophets divine for
money.
Yet they lean on the LORD
saying,
"[c]Is not the LORD in our midst?
Calamity will not come
upon us."
12 Therefore, on account of you
[a]Zion will be plowed as a field,
[b]Jerusalem will become a heap
of ruins,
And the [c]mountain of the
[1]temple *will become* high
places of a forest.

Peaceful Latter Days

4 And it will come about in the
[a]last days
That the [b]mountain of the house
of the LORD
Will be established [1]as the chief
of the mountains.
It will be raised above the hills,
And the [c]peoples will stream
to it.
2 [a]Many nations will come and
say,
"[b]Come and let us go up to the
mountain of the LORD
And to the house of the God of
Jacob,
That [c]He may teach us about
His ways
And that we may walk in His
paths."
For [d]from Zion will go forth the
law,
Even the word of the LORD from
Jerusalem.
3 And He will [a]judge between
many peoples
And render decisions for mighty,
[1]distant nations.
Then they will hammer their
swords [b]into plowshares
And their spears into pruning
hooks;

3:1 [a]Is 1:10; Mic 3:9 [b]Ps 82:1-5; Jer 5:5
2 [a]Ps 53:4; Ezek 22:27; Mic 2:8; 7:2,3
3 [a]Ps 14:4; 27:2; Zeph 3:3 [b]Ezek 11:3,6,7
4 [a]Ps 18:41; Prov 1:28; Is 1:15; Jer 11:11 [b]Deut 31:17; Is 59:2 [c]Is 3:11; Mic 7:13
5 [a]Is 3:12; 9:15, 16; Jer 14:14,15 [b]Jer 6:14
6 [a]Is 8:20-22; 29:10-12 [b]Is 59:10
7 [1]Lit *mustache* [a]Zech 13:4 [b]Is 44:25; 47:12-14 [c]Mic 7:16 [d]1 Sam 28:6; Mic 3:4
8 [a]Is 61:1,2; Jer 1:18 [b]Is 58:1
9 [a]Mic 1:1 [b]Ps 58:1,2; Is 1:23
10 [a]Jer 22:13, 17; Hab 2:12
11 [a]Is 1:23; Mic 7:3 [b]Jer 6:13 [c]Is 48:2
12 [1]Lit *house* [a]Jer 26:18 [b]Ps 79:1; Jer 9:11 [c]Mic 4:1
4:1 [1]Lit *on* [a]Is 2:2-4; Dan 2:28; 10:14; Hos 3:5 [b]Ezek 43:12; Mic 3:12; Zech 8:3 [c]Ps 22:27; 86:9; Jer 3:17
2 [a]Zech 2:11; 14:16 [b]Is 2:3; Jer 31:6 [c]Ps 25:8,9,12; Is 54:13 [d]Is 42:1-4; Zech 14:8,9
3 [1]Lit *at a distance* [a]Is 2:4; 11:3-5 [b]Joel 3:10

Nation will not lift up sword
against nation,
And never again will they [2]train
for war.
4 Each of them will [a]sit under his
vine
And under his fig tree,
With [b]no one to make *them*
afraid,
For the [c]mouth of the LORD of
hosts has spoken.
5 Though all the peoples walk
Each in the [a]name of his god,
As for us, [b]we will walk
In the name of the [c]LORD our
God forever and ever.

6 ¶ "In that day," declares the
LORD,
"I will assemble the [a]lame
And [b]gather the outcasts,
Even those whom I have
afflicted.
7 "I will make the lame a [a]remnant
And the outcasts a strong nation,
And the [b]LORD will reign over
them in Mount Zion
From now on and forever.
8 "As for you, [1a]tower of the flock,
[2]Hill of the daughter of Zion,
To you it will come—
Even the [b]former dominion will
come,
The kingdom of the daughter of
Jerusalem.

9 ¶ "Now, why do you [a]cry out
loudly?
Is there no king among you,
Or has your [b]counselor
perished,
That agony has gripped you like
a woman in childbirth?
10 "[a]Writhe and labor to give birth,
Daughter of Zion,
Like a woman in childbirth;
For now you will [b]go out of the
city,
Dwell in the field,
And go to Babylon.
[c]There you will be rescued;
[d]There the LORD will
redeem you
From the hand of your enemies.
11 "And now [a]many nations have
been assembled against you
Who say, 'Let her be polluted,
And let our eyes [1]gloat over
Zion.'
12 "But they do not [a]know the
thoughts of the LORD,
And they do not understand His
purpose;
For He has gathered them like
sheaves to the threshing
floor.
13 "Arise and [a]thresh, daughter of
Zion,
For your horn I will make iron
And your hoofs I will make
bronze,
That you may [b]pulverize many
peoples,
That you may [c]devote to the
LORD their unjust gain
And their wealth to the Lord of
all the earth.

Birth of the King in Bethlehem

5 "[1]Now muster yourselves in
troops, daughter of troops;
[2]They have laid siege against us;
With a rod they will [a]smite the
judge of Israel on the cheek.
2 "[1]But as for [a]you, Bethlehem
Ephrathah,
Too little to be among the clans
of Judah,
From [b]you One will go forth for
Me to be [c]ruler in Israel.
[2]His goings forth are [d]from long
ago,
From the days of eternity."
3 Therefore He will [a]give them *up*
until the time
When she [b]who is in labor has
borne a child.
Then the [c]remainder of His
brethren
Will return to the sons of Israel.
4 And He will arise and [a]shepherd
His flock
In the strength of the LORD,
In the majesty of the name of
the LORD His God.
And they will [1]remain,
Because [2]at that time He will be
great
To the [b]ends of the earth.
5 This One [a]will be *our* peace.

¶ When the [b]Assyrian invades
our land,
When he tramples on our
[1]citadels,
Then we will raise against him
Seven shepherds and eight
leaders of men.
6 They will [a]shepherd the land of
Assyria with the sword,
The land of [b]Nimrod at its
entrances;
And He will [c]deliver *us* from
the Assyrian
When he attacks our land
And when he tramples our
territory.

3 [2]Lit *learn*

4 [a]1 Kin 4:25; Zech 3:10 [b]Lev 26:6; Jer 30:10 [c]Is 1:20; 40:5

5 [a]2 Kin 17:29 [b]Zech 10:12 [c]Josh 24:15; Is 26:8,13

6 [a]Zeph 3:19 [b]Ps 147:2; Ezek 34:13,16; 37:21

7 [a]Mic 5:7,8; 7:18 [b]Is 24:23

8 [1]Heb *Migdal-eder* [2]Heb *Ophel of* [a]Ps 48:3,12; 61:3; Mic 2:12 [b]Is 1:26; Zech 9:10

9 [a]Jer 8:19 [b]Is 3:1-3

10 [a]Mic 5:3 [b]2 Kin 20:18; Hos 2:14 [c]Is 43:14; 45:13; Mic 7:8-12 [d]Is 48:20; 52:9-12

11 [1]Lit *look on* [a]Is 5:25-30; 17:12-14

12 [a]Ps 147:19, 20

13 [a]Is 41:15 [b]Jer 51:20-23 [c]Is 60:9

5:1 [1]Ch 4:14 in Heb [2]Lit *He has* [a]1 Kin 22:24; Job 16:10; Lam 3:30

2 [1]Ch 5:1 in Heb [2]Or *His appearances are from long ago, from days of old* [a]Gen 35:19; 48:7; Ruth 4:11; Matt 2:6 [b]Is 11:1; Luke 2:4; John 7:42 [c]Jer 30:21; Zech 9:9 [d]Ps 102:25; Prov 8:22,23

3 [a]Hos 11:8; Mic 4:10; 7:13 [b]Mic 4:9,10 [c]Is 10:20-22; Mic 5:7,8

4 [1]Or *live* in safety [2]Lit *now* [a]Is 40:11; 49:9; Ezek 34:13-15, 23,24; Mic 7:14 [b]Is 45:22; 52:10

5 [1]Or *palaces* [a]Is 9:6; Luke 2:14; Eph 2:14; Col 1:20 [b]Is 8:7, 8; 10:24-27

6 [a]Nah 2:11-13; Zeph 2:13 [b]Gen 10:8-11 [c]Is 14:25; 37:36,37

7 ¶ Then the [a]remnant of Jacob
Will be among many peoples
Like [b]dew from the LORD,
Like [c]showers on vegetation
Which do not wait for man
Or delay for the sons of men.
8 The remnant of Jacob
Will be among the nations,
Among many peoples
[a]Like a lion among the beasts of
the forest,
Like a young lion among flocks
of sheep,
Which, if he passes through,
[b]Tramples down and [c]tears,
And there is [d]none to rescue.
9 Your hand will be [a]lifted up
against your adversaries,
And all your enemies will be
cut off.
10 ¶ "It will be in that day,"
declares the LORD,
"[a]That I will cut off your [b]horses
from among you
And destroy your chariots.
11 "I will also cut off the [a]cities of
your land
And tear down all your
[b]fortifications.
12 "I will cut off [a]sorceries from
your hand,
And you will have fortune-tellers
no more.
13 "[a]I will cut off your carved
images
And your *sacred* pillars from
among you,
So that you will no longer bow
down
To the work of your hands.
14 "I will root out your [1a]Asherim
from among you
And destroy your cities.
15 "And I will [a]execute vengeance
in anger and wrath
On the nations which have not
obeyed."

God's Indictment of His People

6 Hear now what the LORD is
saying,
"Arise, plead your case [1]before
the mountains,
And let the hills hear your voice.
2 "Listen, you mountains, to the
indictment of the LORD,
And you enduring [a]foundations
of the earth,
Because the [b]LORD has a case
against His people;
Even with Israel He will dispute.
3 "[a]My people, [b]what have I done
to you,
And [c]how have I wearied you?
Answer Me.
4 "Indeed, I [a]brought you up from
the land of Egypt
And [b]ransomed you from the
house of slavery,
And I sent before you [c]Moses,
Aaron and [d]Miriam.
5 "My people, remember now
What [a]Balak king of Moab
counseled
And what Balaam son of Beor
answered him,
And from [b]Shittim to [c]Gilgal,
So [1]that you might know the
[d]righteous acts of the
LORD."

What God Requires of Man

6 ¶ [a]With what shall I come to
the LORD
And bow myself before the God
on high?
Shall I come to Him with [b]burnt
offerings,
With yearling calves?
7 Does the LORD take delight in
[a]thousands of rams,
In ten thousand rivers of oil?
Shall I present my [b]firstborn *for*
my rebellious acts,
The fruit of my body for the sin
of my soul?
8 He has [a]told you, O man, what
is good;
And [b]what does the LORD
require of you
But to [c]do justice, to [d]love
[1]kindness,
And to walk [2e]humbly with
your God?
9 ¶ The voice of the LORD will call
to the city—
And it is sound wisdom to fear
Your name:
"Hear, O tribe. Who has
appointed [1]its time?
10 "Is there yet a man in the wicked
house,
Along with treasures of
[a]wickedness
And a [1b]short measure *that is*
cursed?
11 "Can I justify wicked [a]scales
And a bag of deceptive weights?
12 "For the rich men of *the* [1]city are
full of [a]violence,
Her residents speak [b]lies,
And their [c]tongue is deceitful in
their mouth.
13 "So also I will make *you* [a]sick,
striking you down,

7 [a]Mic 2:12; 4:7; 5:3; 7:18 [b]Deut 32:2; Ps 110:3; Hos 14:5 [c]Ps 72:6; Is 44:3

8 [a]Gen 49:9; Num 24:9 [b]Ps 44:5; Is 41:15, 16; Mic 4:13; Zech 10:5 [c]Hos 5:14 [d]Ps 50:22

9 [a]Ps 10:12; 21:8; Is 26:11

10 [a]Zech 9:10 [b]Deut 17:16; Is 2:7; Hos 14:3

11 [a]Is 1:7; 6:11 [b]Is 2:12-17; Hos 10:14; Amos 5:9

12 [a]Deut 18:10-12; Is 2:6; 8:19

13 [a]Is 2:18; 17:8; Ezek 6:9

14 [1]I.e. wooden symbols of a female deity [a]Ex 34:13; Is 17:8; 27:9

15 [a]Is 1:24; 65:12

6:1 [1]Lit *with*

2 [a]2 Sam 22:16; Ps 104:5 [b]Is 1:18; Hos 4:1; 12:2

3 [a]Ps 50:7 [b]Jer 2:5 [c]Is 43:22,23

4 [a]Ex 12:51; 20:2 [b]Deut 7:8 [c]Ex 4:10-16; Ps 77:20 [d]Ex 15:20

5 [1]Lit *to know* [a]Num 22:5,6 [b]Num 25:1; Josh 2:1; 3:1 [c]Josh 4:19; 5:9,10 [d]1 Sam 12:7; Is 1:27

6 [a]Ps 40:6-8 [b]Ps 51:16,17

7 [a]Ps 50:9; Is 1:1; 40:16 [b]Lev 18:21; 20:1-5; 2 Kin 16:3; Jer 7:31

8 [1]Or *loyalty* [2]Or *circumspectly* [a]Deut 30:15 [b]Deut 10:12 [c]Is 56:1; Jer 22:3 [d]Hos 6:6 [e]Is 57:15; 66:2

9 [1]Lit *it*

10 [1]Lit *shrunken ephah* [a]Jer 5:26, 27; Amos 3:10 [b]Ezek 45:9,10; Amos 8:5

11 [a]Lev 19:36; Hos 12:7

12 [1]Lit *her* [a]Is 1:23; 5:7; Amos 6:3,4; Mic 2:1,2 [b]Jer 9:2-6,8; Hos 7:13; Amos 2:4 [c]Is 3:8

13 [a]Mic 1:9

[b]Desolating *you* because of your sins.
14 "You will eat, but you will [a]not be satisfied,
And your [1]vileness will be in your midst.
You will *try to* remove *for safekeeping,*
But you will [b]not preserve *anything,*
And what you do preserve I will give to the sword.
15 "You will sow but you will [a]not reap.
You will tread the olive but will not anoint yourself with oil;
And the grapes, but you will [b]not drink wine.
16 "The statutes of [a]Omri
And all the works of the house of [b]Ahab are observed;
And in their devices you [c]walk.
Therefore I will give you up for [d]destruction
And [1]your inhabitants for [e]derision,
And you will bear the [f]reproach of My people."

The Prophet Acknowledges

7 Woe is me! For I am
Like the fruit pickers, like the [a]grape gatherers.
There is not a cluster of grapes to eat,
Or a [b]first-ripe fig *which* [1]I crave.
2 The [1]godly person has [a]perished from the land,
And there is no upright *person* among men.
All of them lie in wait for [b]bloodshed;
Each of them hunts the other with a [c]net.
3 Concerning evil, both hands do it [a]well.
The prince asks, also the judge, for a [b]bribe,
And a great man speaks the desire of his soul;
So they weave it together.
4 The best of them is like a [a]briar,
The most upright like a [b]thorn hedge.
The day when you post your watchmen,
Your [c]punishment will come.
Then their [d]confusion will occur.
5 Do not [a]trust in a neighbor;
Do not have confidence in a friend.
From her who lies in your bosom
Guard [1]your lips.
6 For [a]son treats father contemptuously,
Daughter rises up against her mother,
Daughter-in-law against her mother-in-law;
[b]A man's enemies are the men of his own household.

God Is the Source of Salvation and Light

7 ¶ But as for me, I will [a]watch expectantly for the LORD;
I will [b]wait for the God of my salvation.
My [c]God will hear me.
8 [a]Do not rejoice over me, O [b]my enemy.
Though I fall I will [c]rise;
Though I dwell in darkness, the LORD is a [d]light for me.
9 ¶ I will bear the indignation of the LORD
Because I have sinned against Him,
Until He [a]pleads my case and executes justice for me.
He will bring me out to the [b]light,
And I will see His [1c]righteousness.
10 Then my enemy will see,
And shame will cover her who [a]said to me,
"Where is the LORD your God?"
My eyes will look on her;
[1]At that time she will [2]be [b]trampled down
Like mire of the streets.
11 *It will be* a day for [a]building your walls.
On that day will your boundary be extended.
12 It *will be* a day when [1]they will [a]come to you
From Assyria and the cities of Egypt,
From Egypt even to the [2]Euphrates,
Even from sea to sea and mountain to mountain.
13 And the earth will become [a]desolate because of her inhabitants,
On account of the [b]fruit of their deeds.
14 ¶ [a]Shepherd Your people with Your [b]scepter,

---

13 [b]Is 1:7; 6:11
14 [1]Or possibly *garbage* or *excreta* [a]Is 9:20 [b]Is 30:6
15 [a]Deut 28:38-40; Jer 12:13 [b]Amos 5:11; Zeph 1:13
16 [1]Lit *her* [a]1 Kin 16:25,26 [b]1 Kin 16:29-33 [c]Jer 7:24 [d]Jer 18:16; Mic 6:13 [e]Jer 19:8; 25:9, 18; 29:18 [f]Ps 44:13; Jer 51:51; Hos 12:14
7:1 [1]Lit *my soul* [a]Is 24:13 [b]Is 28:4; Hos 9:10
2 [1]Or *loyal* [a]Is 57:1 [b]Is 59:7; Mic 3:10 [c]Jer 5:26; Hos 5:1
3 [a]Prov 4:16,17 [b]Amos 5:12; Mic 3:11
4 [a]Ezek 2:6; 28:24 [b]Nah 1:10 [c]Is 10:3; Hos 9:7 [d]Is 22:5
5 [1]Lit *openings of your mouth* [a]Jer 9:4
6 [a]Matt 10:21, 35; Luke 12:53 [b]Matt 10:36
7 [a]Hab 2:1 [b]Ps 130:5; Is 25:9 [c]Ps 4:3
8 [a]Prov 24:17; Obad 12 [b]Mic 7:10 [c]Amos 9:11 [d]Is 9:2
9 [1]I.e. right dealing [a]Jer 50:34 [b]Ps 37:6; Is 42:7,16 [c]Is 46:13; 56:1
10 [1]Lit *Now* [2]Lit *become a trampled* place [a]Joel 2:17 [b]Is 51:23; Zech 10:5
11 [a]Is 54:11; Amos 9:11
12 [1]Lit *he* [2]Lit *River* [a]Is 19:23-25; 60:4,9
13 [a]Jer 25:11; Mic 6:13 [b]Is 3:10,11; Mic 3:4
14 [a]Ps 95:7; Is 40:11; 49:10; Mic 5:4 [b]Lev 27:32; Ps 23:4

The flock of Your [1]possession
Which dwells by itself in the
woodland,
In the midst of [2]a fruitful
field.
Let them feed in [c]Bashan
and Gilead
[d]As in the days of old.
15 "As in the days when you came
out from the land of Egypt,
I will show [1a]you miracles."
16 Nations [a]will see and be
ashamed
Of all their might.
They will [b]put *their* hand on
their mouth,
Their ears will be deaf.
17 They will [a]lick the dust like a
serpent,
Like [b]reptiles of the earth.
They will come [c]trembling out
of their [1]fortresses;
To the LORD our God they will
come in [d]dread
And they will be afraid
before You.
18 Who is a God like You, who
[a]pardons iniquity
And passes over the rebellious
act of the [b]remnant of His
[1]possession?
He does not [c]retain His anger
forever,
Because He [d]delights in
[2]unchanging love.
19 He will again have compassion
on us;
[a]He will tread our iniquities
under foot.
Yes, You will [b]cast all [1]their
sins
Into the depths of the sea.
20 You will give [1a]truth to Jacob
And [2]unchanging love to
Abraham,
Which You [b]swore to our
forefathers
From the days of old.

14 [1]Or *inheritance* [2]Or *Carmel* [c]Jer 50:19 [d]Amos 9:11

15 [1]Lit *him* [a]Ex 3:20; 34:10; Ps 78:12

16 [a]Is 26:11 [b]Mic 3:7

17 [1]Lit *fastnesses* [a]Ps 72:9; Is 49:23 [b]Deut 32:24 [c]Ps 18:45 [d]Is 25:3; 59:19

18 [1]Or *inheritance* [2]Or *lovingkindness* [a]Ex 34:7,9; Is 43:25 [b]Mic 2:12; 4:7; 5:7,8 [c]Ps 103:8, 9,13 [d]Jer 32:41

19 [1]Several ancient versions read *our* [a]Jer 50:20 [b]Is 38:17; 43:25; Jer 31:34

20 [1]Or *faithfulness* [2]Or *lovingkindness* [a]Gen 24:27; 32:10 [b]Deut 7:8,12

Nahum

Title and Background

The name Nahum means "comfort," or "consolation." During Jonah's time Nineveh repented and their destruction was temporarily averted. Not long after that, however, Nineveh reverted to its extreme wickedness, brutality and pride.

Author and Date of Writing

Nothing is known about Nahum except his hometown (Elkosh), but even its precise location is uncertain. In all three chapters Nahum prophesied Nineveh's fall, which was fulfilled in 612 B.C. Nahum therefore probably uttered this oracle between 663 and 612, perhaps near the end of this period.

Theme and Message

The focal point of the book is the Lord's judgment on Nineveh for her oppression, cruelty, idolatry and wickedness. God's righteous and just kingdom will ultimately triumph, for kingdoms built on wickedness and tyranny must eventually fall, as Assyria did.

Finally, Nahum declares the universal sovereignty of God. God is Lord of history and of all nations; as such He controls their destinies.

Outline

I. The Lord's Anger Against Nineveh (1:1–15)
II. Nineveh's Fall (2:1–13)
III. Woe to Nineveh (3:1–19)

God Is Awesome

1 The [1a]oracle of [b]Nineveh. The book of the vision of Nahum the Elkoshite.

2 ¶ A [a]jealous and avenging God
is the LORD;
The LORD is [b]avenging and
[1]wrathful.
The LORD takes [c]vengeance on
His adversaries,
And He reserves wrath for His
enemies.
3 The LORD is [a]slow to anger and
great in power,
And the LORD will by no means
leave *the guilty* unpunished.
In [b]whirlwind and storm is His
way,
And [c]clouds are the dust
beneath His feet.
4 He [a]rebukes the sea and makes
it dry;
He dries up all the rivers.
[b]Bashan and Carmel wither;
The blossoms of Lebanon
wither.
5 Mountains [a]quake because
of Him
And the hills [b]dissolve;
Indeed the earth is [c]upheaved
by His presence,
The [d]world and all the
inhabitants in it.
6 [a]Who can stand before His
indignation?
Who can endure the [b]burning of
His anger?
His [c]wrath is poured out like
fire
And the [d]rocks are broken up by
Him.
7 The LORD is [a]good,
A stronghold in the day of
trouble,
And [b]He knows those who take
refuge in Him.
8 But with an [a]overflowing flood
He will make a complete end of
[1]its site,
And will pursue His enemies
into [b]darkness.

9 ¶ Whatever you [a]devise against
the LORD,
He will make a [b]complete end
of it.
Distress will not rise up twice.
10 Like tangled [a]thorns,

1:1 [1]Or *burden* [a]Is 13:1; 19:1; Jer 23:33,34; Hab 1:1; Zech 9:1; Mal 1:1 [b]2 Kin 19:36; Jon 1:2; Nah 2:8; Zeph 2:13
2 [1]Lit *a possessor of wrath* [a]Ex 20:5; Josh 24:19 [b]Deut 32:35,41 [c]Ps 94:1
3 [a]Ex 34:6,7; Neh 9:17; Ps 103:8 [b]Ex 19:16; Is 29:6 [c]Ps 104:3; Is 19:1
4 [a]Josh 3:15,16; Ps 106:9; Is 50:2; Matt 8:26 [b]Is 33:9
5 [a]Ex 19:18; 2 Sam 22:8; Ps 18:7 [b]Mic 1:4 [c]Is 24:1,20 [d]Ps 98:7
6 [a]Jer 10:10; Mal 3:2 [b]Is 13:13 [c]Is 66:15 [d]1 Kin 19:11
7 [a]Ps 25:8; 37:39,40; Jer 33:11 [b]Ps 1:6; John 10:14; 2 Tim 2:19
8 [1]I.e. Nineveh's [a]Is 28:2,17f; Amos 8:8 [b]Is 13:9,10
9 [a]Ps 2:1; Nah 1:11 [b]Is 28:22
10 [a]2 Sam 23:6; Mic 7:4

And like those who are
[b]drunken with their drink,
They are [c]consumed
As stubble completely withered.
11 From you has gone forth
One who [a]plotted evil against
the LORD,
A [1b]wicked counselor.
12 Thus says the LORD,
"Though they are at full *strength*
and likewise many,
Even so, they will be [a]cut off
and pass away.
Though I have afflicted you,
I will afflict you [b]no longer.
13 "So now, I will [a]break his yoke
bar from upon you,
And I will tear off your
shackles."
14 ¶ The LORD has issued a
command concerning [1]you:
"[2]Your name will [a]no longer be
perpetuated.
I will cut off [3b]idol and [4]image
From the house of your gods.
I will prepare your [c]grave,
For you are contemptible."

15 ¶ [1]Behold, [a]on the mountains
the feet of him who brings
good news,
Who announces peace!
[b]Celebrate your feasts, O Judah;
Pay your vows.
For [c]never again will the
[2]wicked one pass through
you;
He is [d]cut off completely.

The Overthrow of Nineveh

2 [1]The one who [a]scatters has
come up against [2]you.
Man the fortress, watch the
road;
[3]Strengthen your back,
[4]summon all *your* strength.
2 For the LORD will restore the
[a]splendor of Jacob
[b]Like the splendor of Israel,
Even though devastators have
devastated them
And [c]destroyed their vine
branches.

3 ¶ The shields of [1]his mighty
men are *colored* red,
The warriors are dressed in
[a]scarlet,
The chariots are *enveloped* in
[2]flashing steel
[3]When he is prepared *to march,*
And the cypress [b]*spears* are
brandished.
4 The [a]chariots race madly in the
streets,
They rush wildly in the
[1]squares,
Their appearance is like torches,
They dash to and fro like
lightning flashes.
5 He remembers his [a]nobles;
They [b]stumble in their march,
They hurry to her wall,
And the [1]mantelet is set up.
6 The gates of the rivers are
opened
And the palace is dissolved.
7 It is fixed:
She is stripped, she is carried
away,
And her handmaids are
[a]moaning like the sound of
doves,
[b]Beating on their [1]breasts.

8 ¶ Though Nineveh *was* like a
pool of water throughout her
days,
Now they are fleeing;
"Stop, stop,"
But [a]no one turns back.
9 Plunder the silver!
Plunder the [a]gold!
For there is no limit to the
treasure—
Wealth from every kind of
desirable object.
10 She is [a]emptied! Yes, she is
desolate and waste!
[b]Hearts are melting and knees
knocking!
Also anguish is in [1]the whole
body
And all their [c]faces are grown
pale!
11 Where is the den of the lions
And the feeding place of the
[a]young lions,
Where the lion, lioness and
lion's cub prowled,
With nothing to disturb *them?*
12 The lion tore enough for his
cubs,
[1]Killed *enough* for his lionesses,
And filled his lairs with prey
And his dens with torn flesh.
13 ¶ "Behold, [a]I am against you," declares the LORD of hosts. "I will [b]burn up
her chariots in smoke, a sword will devour your young lions; I will [c]cut off your
prey from the land, and no longer will the
voice of your messengers be heard."

Nineveh's Complete Ruin

3 [a]Woe to the bloody city,
completely full of lies *and*
pillage;

10 [b]Is 56:12; Nah 3:11 [c]Is 5:24; 10:17; Mal 4:1

11 [1]Or *worthless*; Heb *Belial* [a]Is 10:7-11; Nah 1:9 [b]Ezek 11:2

12 [a]Is 10:16-19, 33,34 [b]Lam 3:31,32

13 [a]Is 9:4; 10:27; Jer 2:20

14 [1]I.e. the king of Nineveh [2]Lit *No more of your name will be sown* [3]Or *a graven image* [4]Lit *cast* metal *image* [a]Job 18:17; Ps 109:13; Is 14:22 [b]Is 46:1,2; Mic 5:13,14 [c]Ezek 32:22,23

15 [1]Ch 2:1 in Heb [2]Or *worthless one*; Heb *Belial* [a]Is 40:9; 52:7; Rom 10:15 [b]Lev 23:2,4 [c]Is 52:1; Joel 3:17 [d]Is 29:7,8

2:1 [1]Ch 2:2 in Heb [2]Lit *your face* [3]Lit *Make strong your loins* [4]Lit *strengthen power greatly* [a]Jer 51:20-23

2 [a]Is 60:15 [b]Ezek 37:21-23 [c]Ps 80:12,13

3 [1]I.e. those attacking Nineveh [2]Lit *fire of steel* [3]Lit *On the day of his preparation* [a]Ezek 23:14,15 [b]Job 39:23

4 [1]Lit *broad places* [a]Is 66:15; Jer 4:13; Ezek 26:10; Nah 3:2,3

5 [1]Lit *covering* used in a siege [a]Nah 3:18 [b]Jer 46:12

7 [1]Lit *hearts* [a]Is 38:14; 59:11 [b]Is 32:12

8 [a]Jer 46:5; 47:3

9 [a]Rev 18:12,16

10 [1]Lit *all the loin* [a]Is 24:1; 34:10-13; Nah 2:2 [b]Ps 22:14; Is 13:7,8; Ezek 21:7 [c]Joel 2:6

11 [a]Is 5:29

12 [1]Lit *Strangled*

13 [a]Jer 21:13; Ezek 5:8; Nah 3:5 [b]Josh 11:6,9; Ps 46:9 [c]Is 49:24,25; Nah 3:1

3:1 [a]Ezek 24:6,9

Her prey never departs.
2 The [a]noise of the whip,
The noise of the rattling of the
wheel,
Galloping horses
And [1]bounding chariots!
3 Horsemen charging,
Swords flashing, [a]spears
gleaming,
[b]Many slain, a mass of corpses,
And [1c]countless dead bodies—
They stumble over [2]the dead
bodies!
4 *All* because of the [a]many
harlotries of the harlot,
The charming one, the [b]mistress
of sorceries,
Who [c]sells nations by her
harlotries
And families by her sorceries.
5 "Behold, [a]I am against you,"
declares the LORD of hosts;
"And I will [1b]lift up your skirts
over your face,
And [c]show to the nations your
nakedness
And to the kingdoms your
disgrace.
6 "I will [a]throw [1]filth on you
And [b]make you vile,
And set you up as a [c]spectacle.
7 "And it will come about that all
who see you
Will [1]shrink from you and say,
'Nineveh is devastated!
[a]Who will grieve for her?'
Where will I seek comforters
for you?"

8 ¶ Are you better than
[1a]No-amon,
Which was situated by the
[b]waters of the Nile,
With water surrounding her,
Whose rampart *was* [2]the sea,
Whose wall *consisted* of
[2]the sea?
9 [a]Ethiopia was *her* might,
And Egypt too, without limits.
[b]Put and [c]Lubim were among
[1]her helpers.
10 Yet she [a]became an exile,
She went into captivity;
Also her [b]small children were
dashed to pieces
[c]At the head of every street;
They [d]cast lots for her honorable
men,
And all her great men were
bound with fetters.
11 You too will become [a]drunk,
You will be [b]hidden.
You too will search for a refuge
from the enemy.
12 All your fortifications are [a]fig
trees with [1b]ripe fruit—
When shaken, they fall into the
eater's mouth.
13 Behold, your people are [a]women
in your midst!
The gates of your land are
[b]opened wide to your
enemies;
Fire consumes your gate bars.
14 [a]Draw for yourself water for the
siege!
[b]Strengthen your fortifications!
Go into the clay and tread the
mortar!
Take hold of the brick mold!
15 There [a]fire will consume you,
The sword will cut you down;
It will [b]consume you as the
locust *does.*

¶ Multiply yourself like the
creeping locust,
Multiply yourself like the
swarming locust.
16 You have increased your
[a]traders more than the stars
of heaven—
The creeping locust [1]strips and
flies away.
17 Your [1a]guardsmen are like the
swarming locust.
Your [b]marshals are like hordes
of grasshoppers
Settling in the stone walls on a
cold day.
The sun rises and they flee,
And the place where they are is
not known.
18 Your shepherds are [a]sleeping,
O [b]king of Assyria;
Your [c]nobles are lying down.
Your people are [d]scattered on
the mountains
And there is no one to regather
them.
19 There is [a]no relief for your
breakdown,
Your [b]wound is incurable.
All who hear [1]about you
Will [c]clap *their* hands over you,
For on whom has not your evil
passed continually?

2 [1]Lit *skipping* [a]Job 39:22-25; Jer 47:3; Nah 2:3,4
3 [1]Lit *there is no end to* [2]Lit *their* [a]Hab 3:11 [b]Is 34:3; 66:16 [c]Is 37:36; Ezek 39:4
4 [a]Is 23:17; Ezek 16:25-29; Rev 17:1,2 [b]Is 47:9,12,13 [c]Rev 18:3
5 [1]Lit *uncover your* [a]Jer 50:31; Ezek 26:3; Nah 2:13 [b]Is 47:2,3; Jer 13:26 [c]Ezek 16:37
6 [1]Lit *detestable things* [a]Job 9:31 [b]Job 30:8; Mal 2:9 [c]Is 14:16; Jer 51:37
7 [1]Lit *flee* [a]Is 51:19; Jer 15:5
8 [1]I.e. the city of Amon: Thebes [2]I.e. the Nile [a]Jer 46:25; Ezek 30:14-16 [b]Is 19:6-8
9 [1]Lit *your* [a]Is 20:5 [b]Jer 46:9; Ezek 27:10; 30:5; 38:5 [c]2 Chr 12:3; 16:8
10 [a]Is 19:4; 20:4 [b]Ps 137:9; Is 13:16; Hos 13:16 [c]Lam 2:19 [d]Joel 3:3; Obad 11
11 [a]Is 49:26; Jer 25:27; Nah 1:10 [b]Is 2:10,19; Hos 10:8
12 [1]Lit *first fruits* [a]Rev 6:13 [b]Is 28:4
13 [a]Is 19:16; Jer 50:37; 51:30 [b]Is 45:1,2; Nah 2:6
14 [a]2 Chr 32:3, 4 [b]Nah 2:1
15 [a]Is 66:15,16; Nah 2:13; 3:13 [b]Joel 1:4
16 [1]I.e. strips vegetation; or *molts* [a]Is 23:8
17 [1]Or *officials* [a]Rev 9:7 [b]Jer 51:27
18 [a]Ps 76:5,6; Is 56:10; Jer 51:57 [b]Jer 50:18 [c]Nah 2:5 [d]1 Kin 22:17; Is 13:14
19 [1]Lit *your report* [a]Jer 46:11; Mic 1:9 [b]Jer 30:12 [c]Job 27:23; Lam 2:15

Habakkuk

Title and Background

The title of the book is the author's name, and apparently comes from a Hebrew root meaning "to clasp" or "to embrace." Habakkuk prayed and prophesied in times of crisis. The international scene was shocked by events of far-reaching import. Internally the people of God were caught up in a crisis of religious and moral bewilderment.

Author and Date of Writing

Little is known about the author except his name and that he was a contemporary of Jeremiah. He was a man of vigorous faith, a faith rooted deeply in the religious traditions of Israel. The prophecy is generally dated a little before or after the battle of Carchemish (605 B.C.).

Theme and Message

Habakkuk was written as a dialogue or conversation between God and the prophet. He saw that the leaders were oppressing the poor, so he asked why God allowed the wicked to prosper. Having received replies, he responds with a beautiful confession of faith. His confession became a public expression and appears to have been used as a psalm.

Outline

I. Habakkuk's First Question and God's Answer (1:1–11)
II. Habakkuk's Second Question and God's Answer (1:12—2:20)
III. Habakkuk's Prayer (3:1–19)

Chaldeans Used to Punish Judah

1 The [1a]oracle which Habakkuk the prophet saw.

2 ¶ [a]How long, O LORD, will I call
for help,
And You will not hear?
I cry out to You, "Violence!"
Yet You do [b]not save.
3 Why do You make me [a]see
iniquity,
And cause *me* to look on
wickedness?
Yes, [b]destruction and violence
are before me;
[c]Strife exists and contention
arises.
4 Therefore the [a]law is [1]ignored
And justice [2]is never upheld.
For the wicked [b]surround the
righteous;
Therefore justice comes out
[c]perverted.

5 ¶ "[a]Look among the nations!
Observe!
Be astonished! [b]Wonder!
Because *I am* doing [c]something
in your days—
You would not believe if [1]you
were told.

6 "For behold, I am [a]raising up the
Chaldeans,
That [1]fierce and impetuous
people
Who march [2]throughout the
earth
To [3b]seize dwelling places
which are not theirs.
7 "They are dreaded and [a]feared;
Their [b]justice and [1]authority
[2]originate with themselves.
8 "Their [a]horses are swifter than
leopards
And [1]keener than [b]wolves in
the evening.
Their [2]horsemen come
galloping,
Their horsemen come from
afar;
They fly like an [c]eagle swooping
down to devour.
9 "All of them come for violence.
[1]Their horde of [a]faces *moves*
forward.
They collect captives like sand.
10 "They [a]mock at kings
And rulers are a laughing matter
to them.
They [b]laugh at every fortress
And [c]heap up rubble to
capture it.

1:1 [1]Or *burden* [a]Is 13:1; Nah 1:1
2 [a]Ps 13:1,2; 22:1,2 [b]Jer 14:9
3 [a]Ps 55:9-11; Jer 20:18 [b]Jer 20:8 [c]Jer 15:10
4 [1]Or *ineffective*; lit *numbed* [2]Lit *never goes forth* [a]Ps 58:1,2; 119:126; Is 59:12-14 [b]Ps 22:12; Is 1:21-23 [c]Is 5:20; Ezek 9:9
5 [1]Lit *it* [a]Acts 13:41 [b]Is 29:9 [c]Is 29:14; Ezek 12:22-28
6 [1]Lit *bitter* [2]Lit *the breadth of* [3]Lit *take possession of* [a]2 Kin 24:2; Jer 4:11-13 [b]Jer 8:10
7 [1]Lit *eminence* [2]Lit *proceeds from* [a]Is 18:2,7 [b]Jer 39:5-9
8 [1]Or *more eager* to attack [2]Or *steeds paw* the ground [a]Jer 4:13 [b]Zeph 3:3 [c]Ezek 17:3; Hos 8:1
9 [1]Or *The eagerness of their faces* [a]2 Kin 12:17; Dan 11:17
10 [a]2 Chr 36:6, 10; Is 37:13 [b]Is 10:9; 14:16 [c]Jer 32:24; Ezek 26:8

11 "Then they will sweep through
like the [a]wind and pass on.
But they will be held [b]guilty,
They whose [c]strength is
their god."

12 ¶ Are You not from [a]everlasting,
O LORD, my God, my Holy One?
We will not die.
You, O LORD, have [b]appointed
them to judge;
And You, O [c]Rock, have
established them to correct.
13 *Your* eyes are too [a]pure to
[1]approve evil,
And You can not look on
wickedness *with favor.*
Why do You [b]look with favor
On those who deal
[c]treacherously?
Why are You [d]silent when the
wicked [e]swallow up
Those more righteous than they?
14 *Why* have You made men like
the fish of the sea,
Like creeping things without a
ruler over them?
15 *The Chaldeans* [a]bring all of
them up with a hook,
[b]Drag them away with their net,
And gather them together in
their fishing net.
Therefore they rejoice and are
glad.
16 Therefore they offer a sacrifice to
their net
And [1]burn incense to their
fishing net;
Because through [a]these things
their [2]catch is [3]large,
And their food is [4]plentiful.
17 Will they therefore empty
their [a]net
And continually [b]slay nations
without sparing?

God Answers the Prophet

2 I will [a]stand on my guard post
And station myself on the
rampart;
And I will [b]keep watch to see
[c]what He will speak to me,
And how I may reply [1]when I
am reproved.
2 Then the LORD answered me and
said,
"[a]Record the vision
And inscribe *it* on tablets,
That [1]the one who [2]reads it
may run.
3 "For the vision is yet for the
[a]appointed time;
It [1]hastens toward the goal and
it will not [2]fail.
Though it tarries, [b]wait for it;
For it will certainly come, it
[c]will not delay.

4 ¶ "Behold, as for the [a]proud
one,
His soul is not right within him;
But the [b]righteous will live by
his [1]faith.
5 "Furthermore, [a]wine betrays the
[b]haughty man,
So that he does not [c]stay at
home.
He [d]enlarges his appetite like
Sheol,
And he is like death, never
satisfied.
He also gathers to himself all
nations
And collects to himself all
peoples.

6 ¶ "Will not all of these [a]take up
a taunt-song against him,
Even mockery *and* insinuations
against him
And say, '[b]Woe to him who
increases what is not his—
For how long—
And makes himself [1]rich with
loans?'
7 "Will not [1]your creditors [a]rise up
suddenly,
And those who [2]collect from
you awaken?
Indeed, you will become plunder
for them.
8 "Because you have [a]looted many
nations,
All the remainder of the peoples
will loot you—
Because of human bloodshed and
violence [1]done to the land,
To the town and all its
inhabitants.

9 ¶ "Woe to him who gets [a]evil
gain for his house
To [b]put his nest on high,
To be delivered from the hand of
calamity!
10 "You have devised a [a]shameful
thing for your house
By cutting off many peoples;
So you are [b]sinning against
yourself.
11 "Surely the [a]stone will cry out
from the wall,
And the rafter will answer it
from the [1]framework.

12 ¶ "Woe to him who [a]builds a
city with bloodshed
And founds a town with
[1]violence!

11 [a]Jer 4:11,12 [b]Jer 2:3 [c]Dan 4:30; Hab 1:16

12 [a]Deut 33:27; Ps 90:2; Mal 3:6 [b]Is 10:5,6; Mal 3:5 [c]Deut 32:4

13 [1]Lit *look at* [a]Ps 11:4-6; 34:15,16 [b]Jer 12:1,2 [c]Is 24:16 [d]Ps 50:21 [e]Ps 35:25

15 [a]Jer 16:16; Amos 4:2 [b]Ps 10:9

16 [1]Or *sacrifice* [2]Lit *portion* [3]Lit *fat;* or *plentiful* [4]Lit *the fat portion* [a]Jer 44:17

17 [a]Is 19:8 [b]Is 14:5,6

2:1 [1]Lit *upon my reproof* [a]Is 21:8 [b]Ps 5:3 [c]Ps 85:8

2 [1]Or *one may read it fluently* [2]Or *is to proclaim it* [a]Deut 27:8; Rom 15:4; Rev 1:19

3 [1]Lit *pants* [2]Or *lie* [a]Dan 8:17, 19; 10:14 [b]Ps 27:14 [c]Ezek 12:25; Heb 10:37

4 [1]Or *faithfulness* [a]Ps 49:18; Is 13:11 [b]Rom 1:17; Gal 3:11; Heb 10:38

5 [a]Prov 20:1 [b]Prov 21:24 [c]2 Kin 14:10 [d]Prov 27:20; 30:16; Is 5:11-15

6 [1]Lit *heavy* [a]Is 14:4-10; Jer 50:13 [b]Job 20:15-29; Hab 2:12

7 [1]Lit *those who bite you* [2]Lit *violently shake you* [a]Prov 29:1

8 [1]Lit *of the land* [a]Is 33:1; Jer 27:7; Zech 2:8

9 [a]Jer 22:13; Ezek 22:27 [b]Jer 49:16

10 [a]2 Kin 9:26; Nah 1:14; Hab 2:16 [b]Jer 26:19

11 [1]Lit *wood* [a]Josh 24:27; Luke 19:40

12 [1]Or *injustice* [a]Mic 3:10; Nah 3:1

13 "Is it not indeed from the LORD of hosts
That peoples [a]toil for fire,
And nations grow weary for nothing?
14 "For the earth will be [a]filled
With the knowledge of the glory of the LORD,
As the waters cover the sea.

15 ¶ "Woe to you who make [1]your neighbors drink,
Who mix in your venom even to make *them* drunk
So as to look on their nakedness!
16 "You will be filled with disgrace rather than honor.
Now you yourself [a]drink and [1]expose your *own* nakedness.
The [b]cup in the LORD'S right hand will come around to you,
And [c]utter disgrace *will come* upon your glory.
17 "For the [a]violence [1]done to Lebanon will [2]overwhelm you,
And the devastation of *its* beasts [3]by which you terrified them,
[b]Because of human bloodshed and [c]violence [4]done to the land,
To the town and all its inhabitants.

18 ¶ "What [a]profit is the [1]idol when its maker has carved it,
Or [2]an image, a [b]teacher of falsehood?
For *its* maker [c]trusts in his *own* handiwork
When he fashions speechless idols.
19 "Woe to him who [a]says to a *piece of* wood, '[b]Awake!'
To a mute stone, 'Arise!'
And that is *your* teacher?
Behold, it is overlaid with [c]gold and silver,
And there is [d]no breath at all inside it.
20 "But the [a]LORD is in His holy temple.
[1]Let all the earth [b]be silent before Him."

God's Deliverance of His People

3 A prayer of Habakkuk the prophet, according to [1]Shigionoth.
2 ¶ LORD, I have [a]heard [1]the report about You *and* [2]I [b]fear.
O LORD, [c]revive [d]Your work in the midst of the years,
In the midst of the years make it known;
In wrath remember [3e]mercy.

3 ¶ God comes from [a]Teman,
And the Holy One from Mount [b]Paran. Selah.
His [c]splendor covers the heavens,
And the [d]earth is full of His praise.
4 *His* [a]radiance is like the sunlight;
He has rays *flashing* from His hand,
And there is the hiding of His [b]power.
5 Before Him goes [a]pestilence,
And [b]plague comes [1]after Him.
6 He stood and surveyed the earth;
He looked and [a]startled the nations.
Yes, the perpetual mountains were shattered,
The ancient hills [1]collapsed.
His ways are [b]everlasting.
7 I saw the tents of Cushan under [a]distress,
The tent curtains of the land of [b]Midian were trembling.

8 ¶ Did the LORD rage against the [a]rivers,
Or *was* Your anger against the rivers,
Or *was* Your wrath against the [b]sea,
That You [c]rode on Your horses,
On Your [d]chariots of salvation?
9 Your [a]bow was made bare,
The rods of [1]chastisement were sworn. Selah.
You [b]cleaved the earth with rivers.
10 The mountains saw You *and* quaked;
The downpour of waters swept by.
The deep [a]uttered forth its voice,
It lifted high its hands.
11 [a]Sun *and* moon stood in their places;
They went away at the [b]light of Your arrows,
At the radiance of Your gleaming spear.
12 In indignation You [a]marched through the earth;
In anger You [1b]trampled the nations.

13 [a]Is 50:11; Jer 51:58
14 [a]Ps 22:27; Is 11:9; Zech 14:9
15 [1]Lit *his neighbor*
16 [1]Lit *show yourself uncircumcised*; or *stagger*; so DSS and ancient versions [a]Lam 4:21 [b]Jer 25:15 [c]Nah 3:6
17 [1]Lit *of Lebanon* [2]Lit *cover* [3]Lit which *terrified them* [4]Lit *of the land* [a]Joel 3:19; Zech 11:1 [b]Ps 55:23; Hab 2:8 [c]Jer 51:35; Hab 2:8
18 [1]Or *a graven image* [2]Lit a *cast* metal *image* [a]Is 42:17; Jer 2:27 [b]Jer 10:8; Zech 10:2 [c]Ps 115:4
19 [a]Jer 2:27 [b]1 Kin 18:26-29 [c]Ps 135:15-18; Jer 10:4 [d]Ps 135:17
20 [1]Lit *Hush before Him, all the earth* [a]Mic 1:2 [b]Zeph 1:7; Zech 2:13
3:1 [1]I.e. a highly emotional poetic form
2 [1]Or *Your report* [2]Or *I stand in awe of Your work, O LORD; In the midst of the years revive it,* [3]Or *compassion* [a]Job 42:5 [b]Ps 119:120; Jer 10:7 [c]Ps 71:20 [d]Ps 44:1-8; Hab 1:5 [e]Num 14:19; 2 Sam 24:15-17; Is 54:8
3 [a]Jer 49:7; Amos 1:12; Obad 9 [b]Gen 21:21; Deut 33:2 [c]Ps 113:4 [d]Ps 48:10
4 [a]Ps 18:12 [b]Job 26:14
5 [1]Lit *at His feet* [a]Ex 12:29; Num 16:46-49 [b]Num 11:1-3; Ps 18:12
6 [1]Lit *bowed*; or *sank down* [a]Job 21:18; Ps 35:5 [b]Hab 1:12
7 [a]Ex 15:14-16 [b]Num 31:7; Judg 7:24
8 [a]Ex 7:19; Josh 3:16; Is 50:2 [b]Ex 14:16; Ps 114:3 [c]Deut 33:26; Ps 18:10; Hab 3:15 [d]Ps 68:17
9 [1]Lit *word* [a]Ps 7:12; Hab 3:11 [b]Ps 78:16
10 [a]Ps 93:3
11 [a]Josh 10:12-14 [b]Ps 18:14
12 [1]Or *thresh* [a]Ps 68:7 [b]Is 41:15; Jer 51:33; Mic 4:13

13 You went forth for the [a]salvation
of Your people,
For the salvation of Your
[b]anointed.
You struck the [c]head of the
house of the evil
To lay him open from [1]thigh to
neck. Selah.
14 You pierced with his [a]own
[1]spears
The head of his [2]throngs.
They [b]stormed in to scatter
[3]us;
Their exultation *was* like those
Who [c]devour the oppressed in
secret.
15 You [a]trampled on the sea with
Your horses,
On the [b]surge of many waters.

16 ¶ I heard and my [1]inward parts
[a]trembled,
At the sound my lips quivered.
Decay enters my [b]bones,
And in my place I tremble.
Because I must [c]wait quietly for
the day of distress,
[2]For the [d]people to arise *who*
will invade us.
17 Though the [a]fig tree should not
blossom
And there be no [1]fruit on the
vines,
Though the yield of the [b]olive
should fail
And the fields produce no food,
Though the [c]flock should be cut
off from the fold
And there be [d]no cattle in the
stalls,
18 Yet I will [a]exult in the LORD,
I will [b]rejoice in the [c]God of
my salvation.
19 The Lord [1]GOD is my [a]strength,
And [b]He has made my feet like
hinds' *feet,*
And makes me walk on my
[c]high places.

For the choir director, on my stringed instruments.

13 [1]Lit *foundation* [a]Ex 15:2; 2 Sam 5:20; Ps 68:19 [b]Ps 20:6 [c]Ps 68:21
14 [1]Lit *shafts* [2]Or *warriors* or *villagers* [3]Lit *me* [a]Judg 7:22 [b]Dan 11:40; Zech 9:14 [c]Ps 10:8
15 [a]Ps 77:19; Hab 3:8 [b]Ex 15:8
16 [1]Lit *belly* [2]Or *To come upon the people* who *will* [a]Dan 10:8; Hab 3:2 [b]Job 30:17; Jer 23:9 [c]Luke 21:19 [d]Jer 5:15
17 [1]Lit *produce* [a]Joel 1:10-12; Amos 4:9; 2 Cor 4:8 [b]Mic 6:15 [c]Joel 1:18 [d]Jer 5:17
18 [a]Ex 15:1; Job 13:15; Is 61:10; Rom 5:2 [b]Ps 46:1-5; Phil 4:4 [c]Ps 25:5; Is 12:2
19 [1]Heb *YHWH,* usually rendered *LORD* [a]Ps 18:32; Is 45:24 [b]2 Sam 22:34 [c]Deut 33:29

Zephaniah

Title and Background

The name Zephaniah means "The LORD hides (or protects)."

The religious condition of Judah declined markedly following the death of Hezekiah, but Josiah launched a sweeping reform. He was backed by Jeremiah and Nahum, but their calls for repentance fell on deaf ears. Judah became ripe for judgment.

Author and Date of Writing

The prophet was evidently a person of considerable social standing in Judah. He was a fourth-generation descendant of King Hezekiah. Zephaniah shows great familiarity with court circles and current political issues.

According to 1:1, Zephaniah prophesied during the reign of King Josiah (640–609 B.C.), so this prophecy could have been written about 630 B.C.

Theme and Message

The intent of the author was to announce to Judah God's approaching judgment. His main theme was the coming of the day of the Lord, when God would severely punish the nations. He portrays the stark horror of that ordeal, but also makes it clear that God will yet be merciful toward His people.

Outline

I. Introduction (1:1–3)
II. The Day of the Lord Coming on Judah and the Nations (1:4–18)
III. God's Judgment on the Nations (2:1—3:8)
IV. Redemption of the Remnant (3:9–20)

Day of Judgment on Judah

1 The word of the LORD which came to Zephaniah son of Cushi, son of Gedaliah, son of Amariah, son of Hezekiah, in the days of [a]Josiah son of [b]Amon, king of Judah:

2 ¶ "I will completely [a]remove all *things*
From the face of the [1]earth,"
declares the LORD.
3 "I will remove [a]man and beast;
I will remove the [b]birds of the sky
And the fish of the sea,
And the [1c]ruins along with the wicked;
And I will cut off man from the face of the [2]earth," declares the LORD.
4 "So I will [a]stretch out My hand against Judah
And against all the inhabitants of Jerusalem.
And I will [b]cut off the remnant of Baal from this place,
And the names of the [c]idolatrous priests along with the priests.
5 "And those who bow down on the [a]housetops to the host of heaven,
And those who bow down *and* [b]swear to the LORD and *yet* swear by [1c]Milcom,
6 And those who have [a]turned back from following the LORD,
And those who have [b]not sought the LORD or inquired of Him."

7 ¶ [1a]Be silent before the Lord [2]GOD!
For the [b]day of the LORD is near,
For the LORD has prepared a [c]sacrifice,
He has [d]consecrated His guests.
8 "Then it will come about on the day of the LORD's sacrifice
That I will [a]punish the princes, the king's sons
And all who clothe themselves with [b]foreign garments.
9 "And I will punish on that day all who leap on the *temple* threshold,

1:1 [a]2 Kin 22:1, 2; 2 Chr 34:1-33; Jer 1:2; 22:11 [b]2 Kin 21:18-26; 2 Chr 33:20-25
2 [1]Lit *ground* [a]Gen 6:7; Jer 7:20; Ezek 33:27,28
3 [1]Or *stumbling blocks* [2]Lit *ground* [a]Is 6:11, 12 [b]Jer 4:25; 9:10 [c]Ezek 7:19; 14:3,4,8
4 [a]Jer 6:12; Ezek 6:14 [b]Mic 5:13 [c]2 Kin 23:5; Hos 10:5
5 [1]Or *their king;* M.T. *Malcam,* probably a variant spelling of Milcom [a]2 Kin 23:12; Jer 19:13 [b]Jer 5:2,7; 7:9, 10 [c]1 Kin 11:5, 33; Jer 49:1
6 [a]Is 1:4; Hos 7:10 [b]Is 9:13
7 [1]Lit *Hush* [2]Heb *YHWH,* usually rendered *LORD* [a]Hab 2:20; Zech 2:13 [b]Zeph 1:14 [c]Is 34:6; Jer 46:10 [d]1 Sam 16:5; Is 13:3
8 [a]Is 24:21; Hab 1:10 [b]Is 2:6

Who fill the house of their [1]lord
with [a]violence and deceit.
10 "On that day," declares the LORD,
"There will be the sound of a cry
from the [a]Fish Gate,
A wail from the [1b]Second
Quarter,
And a loud crash from the [c]hills.
11 "Wail, O inhabitants of the
[1]Mortar,
For all the [2]people of [a]Canaan
will be silenced;
All who weigh out [b]silver will
be cut off.
12 "It will come about at that time
That I will [a]search Jerusalem
with lamps,
And I will punish the men
Who are [1b]stagnant in spirit,
Who say in their hearts,
'The LORD will [c]not do good or
evil!'
13 "Moreover, their wealth will
become [a]plunder
And their houses desolate;
Yes, [b]they will build houses but
not inhabit *them*,
And plant vineyards but not
drink their wine."
14 ¶ Near is the [a]great [b]day of the
LORD,
Near and coming very quickly;
Listen, the day of the LORD!
[1]In it the warrior [c]cries out
bitterly.
15 A day of wrath is that day,
A day of [a]trouble and distress,
A day of destruction and
desolation,
A day of [b]darkness and gloom,
A day of clouds and thick
darkness,
16 A day of [a]trumpet and battle cry
Against the [b]fortified cities
And the high corner towers.
17 I will bring [a]distress on men
So that they will walk [b]like the
blind,
Because they have sinned against
the LORD;
And their [c]blood will be poured
out like dust
And their [d]flesh like dung.
18 Neither their [a]silver nor their
gold
Will be able to deliver them
On the day of the LORD's wrath;
And [b]all the earth will be
devoured
In the fire of His jealousy,
For He will [c]make a complete
end,
Indeed a terrifying one,
Of all the inhabitants of the
earth.

Judgments on Judah's Enemies

2 Gather yourselves together, yes,
[a]gather,
O nation [b]without [1]shame,
2 Before the decree [1]takes
effect—
The day passes [a]like the chaff—
Before the [b]burning anger of the
LORD comes upon you,
Before the [c]day of the LORD's
anger comes upon you.
3 [a]Seek the LORD,
All you [b]humble of the [1]earth
Who have carried out His
[2]ordinances;
[c]Seek righteousness, seek
humility.
Perhaps you will be [d]hidden
In the day of the LORD's anger.
4 ¶ For [a]Gaza will be abandoned
And Ashkelon a desolation;
[a]Ashdod will be driven out at
noon
And [a]Ekron will be uprooted.
5 Woe to the inhabitants of the
seacoast,
The nation of the
[1a]Cherethites!
The word of the LORD is
[b]against you,
O [c]Canaan, land of the
Philistines;
And I will [d]destroy you
So that there will be [e]no
inhabitant.
6 So the seacoast will be
[a]pastures,
With [1]caves for shepherds and
folds for flocks.
7 And the coast will be
For the [a]remnant of the house
of Judah,
They will [b]pasture on it.
In the houses of Ashkelon they
will lie down at evening;
For the LORD their God will
[c]care for them
And [d]restore their fortune.
8 ¶ "I have heard the [1a]taunting
of Moab
And the [b]revilings of the sons of
Ammon,
With which they have [2]taunted
My people
And [3c]become arrogant against
their territory.
9 "Therefore, as I live," declares the
LORD of hosts,
The God of Israel,

9 [1]Or *Lord* [a]Jer 5:27; Amos 3:10

10 [1]I.e. a district of Jerusalem [a]2 Chr 33:14; Neh 3:3; 12:39 [b]2 Chr 34:22 [c]Ezek 6:13

11 [1]I.e. a district of Jerusalem [2]Or *merchant people will* [a]Zeph 2:5; Zech 14:21 [b]Job 27:16,17; Hos 9:6

12 [1]Lit *thickening on their lees* [a]Jer 16:16,17; Ezek 9:4-11; Amos 9:1-3 [b]Jer 48:11; Amos 6:1 [c]Ezek 8:12; 9:9

13 [a]Jer 15:13; 17:3 [b]Amos 5:11; Mic 6:15

14 [1]Lit *There* [a]Jer 30:7; Joel 2:11; Mal 4:5 [b]Ezek 7:7,12; 30:3; Joel 1:15; 3:14; Zeph 1:7 [c]Ezek 7:16-18

15 [a]Is 22:5 [b]Joel 2:2,31; Amos 5:18-20

16 [a]Is 27:13; Jer 4:19 [b]Is 2:12-15

17 [a]Jer 10:18 [b]Deut 28:29 [c]Ezek 24:7,8 [d]Jer 8:2; 9:22

18 [a]Ezek 7:19 [b]Zeph 3:8 [c]Gen 6:7; Ezek 7:5-7

2:1 [1]Or *longing* [a]2 Chr 20:4; Joel 1:14 [b]Jer 3:3; 6:15

2 [1]Lit *is born* [a]Is 17:13; Hos 13:3 [b]Lam 4:11; Nah 1:6 [c]Zeph 1:18

3 [1]Or *land* [2]Or *justice* [a]Ps 105:4; Amos 5:6 [b]Ps 22:26; Is 11:4 [c]Amos 5:14,15 [d]Ps 57:1; Is 26:20

4 [a]Amos 1:7,8; Zech 9:5-7

5 [1]I.e. a segment of the Philistines with roots in Crete [a]Ezek 25:16 [b]Amos 3:1 [c]Zeph 1:11 [d]Is 14:29,30 [e]Zeph 3:6

6 [1]Or *meadows* or *wells* [a]Is 5:17; 7:25

7 [a]Is 11:16 [b]Is 32:14 [c]Ex 4:31; Ps 80:14 [d]Jer 32:44; Zeph 3:20

8 [1]Lit *reproach* [2]Lit *reproached* [3]Lit *made* themselves *great* [a]Ezek 25:8 [b]Ezek 25:3 [c]Amos 1:13

"Surely [a]Moab will be like
[b]Sodom
And the sons of [c]Ammon like
[d]Gomorrah—
A place possessed by nettles and
salt pits,
And a perpetual desolation.
The remnant of My people will
[e]plunder them
And the remainder of My nation
will inherit them."
10 This they will have in return for
their [a]pride, because they have [1b]taunt-
ed and [2]become arrogant against the
people of the LORD of hosts.
11 The LORD will be [a]terrifying to
them, for He will [1]starve [b]all the gods of
the earth; and all the [c]coastlands of the
nations will [d]bow down to Him, everyone from his *own* place.
12 ¶ "You also, O [a]Ethiopians, will
be slain by My sword."
13 And He will [a]stretch out His
hand against the north
And destroy [b]Assyria,
And He will make [c]Nineveh a
desolation,
Parched like the wilderness.
14 Flocks will lie down in her
midst,
[1]All beasts which range in
herds;
Both the [2a]pelican and the
hedgehog
Will lodge in [3]the tops of her
pillars;
[4]Birds will sing in the window,
Desolation *will be* on the
threshold;
For He has laid bare the cedar
work.
15 This is the [a]exultant city
Which [b]dwells securely,
Who says in her heart,
"[c]I am, and there is no one
besides me."
How she has become a
[d]desolation,
A resting place for beasts!
[e]Everyone who passes by her
will hiss
And wave his hand *in contempt.*

Woe to Jerusalem and the Nations

3 Woe to her who is [a]rebellious
and [b]defiled,
The [c]tyrannical city!
2 She [a]heeded no voice,
She [b]accepted no instruction.
She did not [c]trust in the LORD,
She did not [d]draw near to her
God.
3 Her [a]princes within her are
roaring lions,
Her judges are [b]wolves at
evening;
They leave nothing for the
morning.
4 Her prophets are [a]reckless,
treacherous men;
Her [b]priests have profaned the
sanctuary.
They have done violence to the
law.
5 The LORD is [a]righteous [b]within
her;
He will [c]do no injustice.
[d]Every morning He brings His
justice to light;
He does not fail.
But the unjust [e]knows no
shame.
6 "I have cut off nations;
Their corner towers are in ruins.
I have made their streets
[a]desolate,
With no one passing by;
Their [b]cities are laid waste,
Without a man, [c]without an
inhabitant.
7 "I said, 'Surely you will
revere Me,
[a]Accept instruction.'
So her dwelling will [b]not be
cut off
According to all that I have
appointed concerning her.
But they were eager to [c]corrupt
all their deeds.
8 ¶ "Therefore [a]wait for Me,"
declares the LORD,
"For the day when I rise up as a
witness.
Indeed, My decision is to
[b]gather nations,
To assemble kingdoms,
To pour out on them My
indignation,
All My burning anger;
For [c]all the earth will be
devoured
By the fire of My zeal.
9 "For then I will [1]give to the
peoples [a]purified lips,
That all of them may [b]call on
the name of the LORD,
To serve Him [2]shoulder to
shoulder.
10 "From beyond the rivers of
[a]Ethiopia
My [1]worshipers, [2]My dispersed
ones,
Will [b]bring My offerings.
11 "In that day you will [a]feel no
shame
Because of all your deeds

---

9 [a]Is 15:1-9; Jer 48:1-47; Amos 2:1-3 [b]Gen 19:24 [c]Jer 49:1-6; Ezek 25:1-10 [d]Deut 29:23 [e]Is 11:14

10 [1]Lit *re-proached* [2]Lit *made* themselves *great* [a]Is 16:6 [b]Zeph 2:8

11 [1]Lit *make lean* [a]Joel 2:11 [b]Zeph 1:4 [c]Is 24:15 [d]Ps 72:8-11; Zeph 3:9

12 [a]Is 18:1-7; 20:4,5; Ezek 30:4-9

13 [a]Is 14:26; Zeph 1:4 [b]Is 10:16; Mic 5:6 [c]Nah 3:7

14 [1]Or *All* kinds of *beasts in crowds;* lit *Every* kind of *beast of a nation* [2]Or *owl* or *jackdaw* [3]Lit *her capitals* [4]Lit *A voice* [a]Is 14:23; 34:11

15 [a]Is 22:2 [b]Is 32:9,11; 47:8 [c]Is 47:8; Ezek 28:2, 9 [d]Is 32:14 [e]Jer 18:16; 19:8

3:1 [a]Jer 5:23 [b]Ezek 23:30 [c]Jer 6:6

2 [a]Jer 7:23-28 [b]Jer 2:30; 5:3; 2 Tim 3:16 [c]Ps 78:22; Jer 13:25 [d]Ps 73:28

3 [a]Ezek 22:27 [b]Jer 5:6; Hab 1:8

4 [a]Judg 9:4 [b]Ezek 22:26; Mal 2:7,8

5 [a]Deut 32:4 [b]Zeph 3:15,17 [c]Ps 92:15 [d]Job 7:18 [e]Zeph 2:1

6 [a]Jer 9:12; Zech 7:14; Matt 23:38 [b]Lev 26:31; Is 6:11 [c]Zeph 2:5

7 [a]Job 36:10; Ps 32:8; 1 Tim 1:5 [b]Jer 7:7 [c]Hos 9:9

8 [a]Ps 27:14; Is 30:18; Hab 2:3 [b]Ezek 38:14-23; Joel 3:2 [c]Zeph 1:18

9 [1]Lit *change* [2]Lit *with one shoulder* [a]Is 19:18; 57:19 [b]Ps 22:27; 86:9; Hab 2:14; Zeph 2:11

10 [1]Or *suppli-ants* [2]Lit *the daughter of My dispersed ones* [a]Ps 68:31; Is 18:1 [b]Is 60:6,7

11 [a]Is 45:17; 54:4; Joel 2:26, 27

By which you have rebelled
against Me;
For then I will remove from your
midst
Your [b]proud, exulting ones,
And you will never again be
haughty
On My [c]holy mountain.

A Remnant of Israel

12 "But I will leave among you
A [a]humble and lowly people,
And they will [b]take refuge in
the name of the LORD.
13 "The [a]remnant of Israel will [b]do
no wrong
And [c]tell no lies,
Nor will a deceitful tongue
Be found in their mouths;
For they will [d]feed and lie down
With no one to make them
tremble."

14 ¶ Shout for joy, O daughter of
Zion!
[a]Shout *in triumph,* O Israel!
Rejoice and exult with all *your*
heart,
O daughter of Jerusalem!
15 The LORD has taken away [a]*His*
judgments against you,
He has cleared away your
enemies.
The King of Israel, the LORD, is
[b]in your midst;
You will [c]fear disaster no more.

16 [a]In that day it will be said to
Jerusalem:
"[b]Do not be afraid, O Zion;
[c]Do not let your hands fall limp.
17 "The LORD your God is [a]in your
midst,
A [1b]victorious warrior.
He will [c]exult over you with
joy,
He will [2]be quiet in His love,
He will rejoice over you with
shouts of joy.
18 "I will gather those who [a]grieve
about the appointed feasts—
They [1]came from you, *O Zion;*
The reproach *of exile* is a burden
on [2]them.
19 "Behold, I am going to deal at
that time
With all your [a]oppressors,
I will save the [b]lame
And gather the outcast,
And I will turn their [c]shame
into [d]praise and renown
In all the earth.
20 "At that time I will [a]bring you in,
Even at the time when I gather
you together;
Indeed, I will give you [b]renown
and praise
Among all the peoples of the
earth,
When I [c]restore your fortunes
before your eyes,"
Says the LORD.

11 [b]Is 2:12; 5:15 [c]Is 11:9; 56:7; Ezek 20:40

12 [a]Is 14:30 [b]Is 14:32; 50:10; Nah 1:7; Zech 13:8,9

13 [a]Is 10:20-22; Mic 4:7; Zeph 2:7 [b]Ps 119:3; Jer 31:33; Zeph 3:5 [c]Zech 8:3, 16; Rev 14:5 [d]Ezek 34:13-15

14 [a]Zech 9:9

15 [a]Ps 19:9; John 5:30; Rev 18:20 [b]Ezek 37:26-28; Zeph 3:5 [c]Is 54:14

16 [a]Is 25:9 [b]Is 35:3,4 [c]Job 4:3; Heb 12:12

17 [1]Lit *A warrior who saves* [2]Or with some ancient versions, *renew* you *in* [a]Zeph 3:5,15 [b]Is 63:1 [c]Is 62:5

18 [1]Lit *were* [2]Lit *her* [a]Ps 42:2-4; Ezek 9:4

19 [a]Is 60:14 [b]Ezek 34:16; Mic 4:6 [c]Ezek 16:27,57 [d]Is 60:18; 62:7; Zech 8:23

20 [a]Ezek 37:12, 21 [b]Deut 26:18, 19; Is 56:5; 66:22 [c]Jer 29:14; Joel 3:1; Zeph 2:7

Haggai

Title and Background

The book is named for its author, and the name means "festal" or "festival."

In 538 B.C. Cyrus issued a decree allowing the Jews to return to Jerusalem and rebuild the temple. The Samaritans and other neighbors opposed the project vigorously and managed to halt work until Darius the Great became king. Haggai began to preach in Darius's second year.

Author and Date of Writing

Haggai was a prophet who, along with Zechariah, encouraged the returned exiles to rebuild the temple. Based on 2:3, Haggai may have witnessed the destruction of Solomon's temple. If so, he was about 80 years old during his ministry recorded in this book. The messages of Haggai were given during a four-month period in 520 B.C.

Theme and Message

Haggai clearly shows the consequences of disobedience and the blessings of obedience. When the people give priority to God and His house, they are blessed. Obedience brings the encouragement and strength of the Spirit of God.

Outline

I. First Message: The Call to Rebuild the Temple (1:1–11)
II. The Response of Zerubbabel and the People (1:12–15)
III. Second Message: The Temple to Be Filled With Glory (2:1–9)
IV. Third Message: A Defiled People Purified and Blessed (2:10–19)
V. Fourth Message: The Promise to Zerubbabel (2:20–23)

Haggai Begins Temple Building

1 In the [a]second year of Darius the
king, on the first day of the sixth
month, the word of the LORD came by the
prophet [b]Haggai to [c]Zerubbabel the son
of Shealtiel, [d]governor of Judah, and to
[e]Joshua the son of Jehozadak, the high
priest, saying,
2 "Thus says the LORD of [1]hosts, 'This
people says, "The time has not come,
even the time for the house of the LORD
to be rebuilt." ' "
3 Then the word of the LORD came by
Haggai the prophet, saying,
4 "Is it time for you yourselves to
dwell in your paneled houses while this
house [a]*lies* desolate?"
5 Now therefore, thus says the LORD
of hosts, "[1]Consider your ways!
6 "You have [a]sown much, but [1]har-
vest little; *you* eat, but *there is* not
enough to be satisfied; *you* drink, but
there is [2]not *enough* to become drunk;
you put on clothing, but no one is warm
enough; and he who earns, earns wages
to put into a purse with holes."

1:1 [a]Ezra 4:24 [b]Ezra 5:1; Hag 1:3 [c]Ezra 2:2; Neh 7:7; Hag 1:12; Zech 4:6; Matt 1:12 [d]1 Kin 10:15; Ezra 5:3 [e]Zech 6:11
2 [1]Lit *hosts, saying*
4 [a]Jer 33:10; Hag 1:9
5 [1]Lit *Set your heart on*
6 [1]Lit *bring in* [2]Lit *not becoming drunk* [a]Deut 28:38-40; Hos 8:7; Hag 1:9
7 [1]Lit *Set your heart on*
8 [1]Lit *mountain* [2]Lit *house* [a]1 Kin 6:1 [b]Ps 132:13 [c]Hag 2:7
9 [a]Prov 27:20; Eccl 1:8 [b]Is 40:7 [c]Hag 1:4
10 [1]Lit *from dew* [a]Deut 28:23; 1 Kin 17:1; Joel 1:18-20
11 [1]Lit *the palms* [a]Jer 14:2-6; Mal 3:9 [b]Deut 28:22 [c]Hag 2:17
12 [a]Hag 1:1

7 ¶ Thus says the LORD of hosts,
"[1]Consider your ways!
8 "Go up to the [1]mountains, bring
wood and [a]rebuild the [2]temple, that I
may be [b]pleased with it and be [c]glori-
fied," says the LORD.
9 "[a]*You* look for much, but behold, *it*
comes to little; when you bring *it* home,
I [b]blow it *away.* Why?" declares the
LORD of hosts, "Because of My house
which [c]*lies* desolate, while each of you
runs to his own house.
10 "Therefore, because of you the [a]sky
has withheld [1]its dew and the earth has
withheld its produce.
11 "I called for a [a]drought on the land,
on the mountains, on the grain, on the
new wine, on the oil, on what the ground
produces, on [b]men, on cattle, and on
[c]all the labor of [1]your hands."
12 ¶ Then [a]Zerubbabel the son of
Shealtiel, and [b]Joshua the son of Jehozadak, the high priest, with all the remnant
of the people, [c]obeyed the voice of the
LORD their God and the words of Haggai

[b]Hag 1:14 [c]Is 1:19; 1 Thess 2:13

the prophet, as the LORD their God had
sent him. And the people [1d]showed reverence for the LORD.
13 Then Haggai, the [a]messenger of
the LORD, spoke [1]by the commission of
the LORD to the people saying, " '[b]I am
with you,' declares the LORD."
14 So the LORD stirred up the spirit of
[a]Zerubbabel the son of Shealtiel, [a]gover-
nor of Judah, and the spirit of Joshua the
son of Jehozadak, the high priest, and the
spirit of all the [b]remnant of the people;
and they came and [c]worked on the
house of the LORD of hosts, their God,
15 on the twenty-fourth day of the
sixth month in the second year of Darius
the king.

The Builders Encouraged

2 On the twenty-first of the seventh
month, the word of the LORD came
by [a]Haggai the prophet saying,
2 "Speak now to [a]Zerubbabel the son
of Shealtiel, [a]governor of Judah, and to
[a]Joshua the son of Jehozadak, the high
priest, and to the [b]remnant of the people
saying,
3 'Who is [a]left among you who saw
this [1]temple in its [b]former glory? And
how do you see it now? Does it not
[2]seem to you like nothing [3]in comparison?
4 'But now [1a]take courage, Zerubbabel,' declares the LORD, 'take courage
also, Joshua son of Jehozadak, the high
priest, and all you people of the land take
courage,' declares the LORD, 'and work;
for [b]I am with you,' declares the LORD of
hosts.
5 'As for the [1a]promise which I
[2]made you when you came out of Egypt,
[3]My [b]Spirit is abiding in your midst;
[c]do not fear!'
6 "For thus says the LORD of hosts,
'[a]Once more [1]in a [b]little while, I am
going to [c]shake the heavens and the
earth, the sea also and the dry land.
7 'I will shake [a]all the nations; and
[1]they will come with the [b]wealth of all
nations, and I will [c]fill this house with
glory,' says the LORD of hosts.
8 'The [a]silver is Mine and the gold is
Mine,' declares the LORD of hosts.
9 'The latter [a]glory of this house will
be greater than the [b]former,' says the
LORD of hosts, 'and in this place I will give
[c]peace,' declares the LORD of hosts."
10 ¶ On the [a]twenty-fourth of the
ninth *month,* in the second year of Darius, the word of the LORD came to Haggai
the prophet, saying,
11 "Thus says the LORD of hosts, '[a]Ask
now the priests *for* a [1]ruling:
12 'If a man carries [a]holy meat in the
[1]fold of his garment, and touches bread
with [2]this fold, or cooked food, wine, oil,
or any *other* food, will it become holy?' "
And the priests answered, "No."
13 Then Haggai said, "[a]If one who is
unclean from a [1]corpse touches any of
these, will *the latter* become unclean?"
And the priests answered, "It will become unclean."
14 Then Haggai said, " '[a]So is this
people. And so is this nation before Me,'
declares the LORD, 'and so is every work
of their hands; and what they offer there
is unclean.
15 'But now, do [1a]consider from this
day [2]onward: before one [b]stone was
placed on another in the temple of the
LORD,
16 [1]from that time *when* one came to
a *grain* heap of twenty *measures,* there
would be only ten; and *when* one came to
the wine vat to draw fifty [2]measures,
there would be *only* twenty.
17 'I smote you *and* every work of your
hands with [a]blasting wind, mildew and
hail; [1]yet you *did* not *come back* to Me,'
declares the LORD.
18 'Do [1a]consider from this day [2]on-
ward, from the [b]twenty-fourth day of the
ninth *month;* from the day when the temple of the LORD was [c]founded, [1]con-
sider:
19 'Is the seed still in the barn? Even
including the vine, the fig tree, the pomegranate and the olive tree, it has not
borne *fruit.* Yet from this day on I will
[a]bless *you.*' "
20 ¶ Then the word of the LORD came
a second time to Haggai on the [a]twenty-
fourth *day* of the month, saying,
21 "Speak to [a]Zerubbabel governor of
Judah, saying, 'I am going to [b]shake the
heavens and the earth.
22 'I will [a]overthrow the thrones of
kingdoms and destroy the [b]power of the
kingdoms of the [1]nations; and I will
[c]overthrow the chariots and their riders,
and the [d]horses and their riders will go
down, [e]everyone by the sword of another.'
23 'On that day,' declares the LORD of
hosts, 'I will take you, Zerubbabel, son of
Shealtiel, My servant,' declares the LORD,
'and I will make you like a [1a]signet *ring,*
for [b]I have chosen you,' " declares the
LORD of hosts.

12 [1]Lit *feared before* [d]Deut 31:12; Ps 112:1; Is 50:10
13 [1]Or *the message* [a]Is 44:26; Ezek 3:17; Mal 2:7 [b]Ps 46:11; Is 41:10
14 [a]Hag 1:1 [b]Hag 1:12 [c]Ezra 5:2; Neh 4:6
2:1 [a]Hag 1:1
2 [a]Hag 1:1 [b]Hag 1:12
3 [1]Lit *house* [2]Lit *in your eyes* [3]Lit *like it* [a]Ezra 3:12 [b]Hag 2:9
4 [1]Lit *be strong* [a]Deut 31:23; 1 Chr 22:13; Zech 8:9; Eph 6:10 [b]2 Sam 5:10; Acts 7:9
5 [1]Lit *word* [2]Lit *cut with* [3]Or *while...was standing* [a]Ex 19:4-6 [b]Neh 9:20; Is 63:11 [c]Is 41:10; Zech 8:13
6 [1]Lit *it is a little* [a]Heb 12:26 [b]Is 10:25 [c]Hag 2:21
7 [1]Or *the desire of all nations will come* [a]Dan 2:44; Joel 3:9 [b]Is 60:4-9 [c]1 Kin 8:11; Is 60:7
8 [a]1 Chr 29:14; Is 60:17
9 [a]Zech 2:5 [b]Hag 2:3 [c]Is 9:6
10 [a]Hag 2:20
11 [1]Lit *law* [a]Deut 17:8-11; Mal 2:7
12 [1]Lit *wing* [2]Lit *his wing* [a]Ex 29:37; Lev 6:27; Ezek 44:19; Matt 23:19
13 [1]Lit *soul* [a]Lev 22:4-6; Num 19:22
14 [a]Prov 15:8; Is 1:11-15
15 [1]Lit *set your heart* [2]Or *backward* [a]Hag 1:5 [b]Ezra 3:10
16 [1]Lit *since they were* [2]Or *troughs full*
17 [1]Or *but what did we have in common?* [a]Deut 28:22; 1 Kin 8:37; Amos 4:9
18 [1]Lit *set your heart* [2]Or *backward* [a]Deut 32:29; Hag 2:15 [b]Hag 2:10 [c]Ezra 5:1; Zech 8:9
19 [a]Ps 128:1-6; Jer 31:12; Mal 3:10
20 [a]Hag 2:10
21 [a]Ezra 5:2; Hag 1:1; Zech 4:6-10 [b]Hag 2:6; Heb 12:26
22 [1]Or *Gentiles* [a]Ezek 26:16; Zeph 3:8 [b]Mic 7:16 [c]Ps 46:9; Ezek 39:20; Mic 5:10 [d]Amos 2:15 [e]Judg 7:22; 2 Chr 20:23
23 [1]Or *seal* [a]Song 8:6; Jer 22:24 [b]Is 42:1

Zechariah

Title and Background

The book is named after its author, and the title means "The LORD remembers." Zechariah's prophetic ministry took place in the postexilic period, the time of the Jewish restoration from Babylonian captivity. His prophecies began two months after Haggai's first message.

Author and Date of Writing

Zechariah was not only a prophet but also a priest. He was among those who returned to Judah in 538 B.C. He was a contemporary of Haggai but continued his ministry long after him. The book of Zechariah was probably written sometime before 480 B.C.

Theme and Message

Zechariah was concerned about the rebuilding of the temple, and in his first message he warned the people they were to listen to God's message through the prophets. He was also interested in their spiritual renewal.

Zechariah also contains many Messianic passages: he predicted Christ's coming in lowliness (6:12), His humanity (6:12; 13:7), His rejection and betrayal for thirty pieces of silver (11:12–13), His being struck by the sword of the Lord (13:7), His priesthood (6:13), His kingship (6:13; 9:9; 14:9,16), His coming in glory (14:4), His building of the Lord's temple (6:12–13), His reign (9:10,14) and His establishment of enduring peace and prosperity (3:10; 9:9–10).

Outline

I. A Call to Repentance (1:1–6)
II. Eight Visions (1:7—6:8)
III. The Crowning of Joshua the High Priest (6:9–15)
IV. Fasting and the Future (7:1—8:23)
V. The Advent and Rejection of the Messiah (9:1—11:17)
VI. The Advent and Redemption of the Messiah (12:1—14:21)

A Call to Repentance

1 In the eighth month of the second
year of [a]Darius, the word of the
LORD came to [b]Zechariah the prophet,
the son of Berechiah, the son of [c]Iddo
saying,
2 "The LORD was very [a]angry with
your fathers.
3 "Therefore say to them, 'Thus says
the LORD of hosts, "[a]Return to Me," declares the LORD of hosts, "that I may return to you," says the LORD of hosts.
4 "Do not be [a]like your fathers, to
whom the [b]former prophets proclaimed,
saying, 'Thus says the LORD of hosts,
"[c]Return now from your evil ways and
from your evil deeds." ' But they did [d]not
listen or give heed to Me," declares the
LORD.
5 "Your [a]fathers, where are they?
And the [b]prophets, do they live forever?
6 "But did not My words and My statutes, which I commanded My servants
the prophets, [a]overtake your fathers?
Then they repented and said, '[b]As the
LORD of hosts purposed to do to us in
accordance with our ways and our deeds,
so He has dealt with us.' " ' "

Patrol of the Earth

7 ¶ On the twenty-fourth day of the
eleventh month, which is the month She-
bat, in the second year of Darius, the
word of the LORD came to Zechariah the
prophet, the son of Berechiah, the son of
Iddo, as follows:
8 I saw at night, and behold, a man
was riding on a [a]red horse, and he was
standing among the [b]myrtle trees which
were in the ravine, with red, sorrel and
[c]white horses behind him.
9 Then I said, "My [a]lord, what are
these?" And the [b]angel who was speaking with me said to me, "I will show you
what these are."
10 And the man who was standing
among the myrtle trees answered and
said, "These are those whom the LORD
has sent to [1][a]patrol the earth."

1:1 [a]Ezra 4:24; 6:15; Hag 1:15; 2:10; Zech 1:7; 7:1 [b]Ezra 5:1; 6:14; Zech 7:1; Matt 23:35; Luke 11:51 [c]Neh 12:4,16
2 [a]2 Chr 36:16; Jer 44:6; Ezek 8:18; Zech 1:15
3 [a]Is 31:6; 44:22; Mal 3:7
4 [a]Ps 78:8; 106:6,7 [b]2 Chr 24:19; 36:15 [c]Is 1:16-19; Jer 4:1; Ezek 33:11 [d]Jer 6:17; 11:7,8
5 [a]Lam 5:7 [b]John 8:52
6 [a]Jer 12:16,17; 44:28,29; Amos 9:10 [b]Lam 2:17
8 [a]Zech 6:2; Rev 6:4 [b]Neh 8:15; Is 41:19; 55:13; Zech 1:10,11 [c]Zech 6:3; Rev 6:2
9 [a]Zech 1:19; 4:4,5,13; 6:4 [b]Zech 2:3; 5:5
10 [1]Lit *walk about through* [a]Job 1:7; Zech 1:11; 4:10; 6:5-8

11 So they answered the angel of the
LORD who was [a]standing among the myrtle trees and said, "We have [1]patrolled
the earth, and behold, [b]all the earth is
[2]peaceful and quiet."
12 ¶ Then the angel of the LORD said,
"O LORD of hosts, [a]how long will You
[b]have no compassion for Jerusalem and
the cities of Judah, with which You have
been [c]indignant these [d]seventy years?"
13 The LORD answered the [a]angel
who was speaking with me with [1]gra-
cious words, [b]comforting words.
14 So the angel who was speaking
with me said to me, "[a]Proclaim, saying,
'Thus says the LORD of hosts, "I am [b]ex-
ceedingly jealous for Jerusalem and Zion.
15 "But I am very [a]angry with the nations who are [b]at ease; for while I was
only a little angry, they [1c]furthered the
disaster."
16 'Therefore thus says the LORD, "I
will [a]return to Jerusalem with compassion; My [b]house will be built in it,"
declares the LORD of hosts, "and a measuring [c]line will be stretched over Jerusalem." '
17 "Again, proclaim, saying, 'Thus says
the LORD of hosts, "My [a]cities will again
overflow with prosperity, and the LORD
will again [b]comfort Zion and again
[c]choose Jerusalem." ' "
18 ¶ [1]Then I lifted up my eyes and
looked, and behold, *there were* four
horns.
19 So I said to the angel who was
speaking with me, "What are these?"
And he answered me, "These are the
[a]horns which have scattered Judah, Israel and Jerusalem."
20 Then the LORD showed me four
[a]craftsmen.
21 I said, "What are these coming to
do?" And he said, "These are the [a]horns
which have scattered Judah so that no
man lifts up his head; but these *craftsmen*
have come to terrify them, to [b]throw
down the horns of the nations who have
lifted up *their* horns against the land of
Judah in order to scatter it."

God's Favor to Zion

2 [1]Then I lifted up my eyes and
looked, and behold, *there was* a man
with a [a]measuring line in his hand.
2 So I said, "Where are you going?"
And he said to me, "To [a]measure Jerusalem, to see how wide it is and how long
it is."
3 And behold, the [a]angel who was
speaking with me was going out, and another angel was coming out to meet him,
4 and said to him, "Run, speak to that
[a]young man, saying, '[b]Jerusalem will be
inhabited [1c]without walls because of
the [d]multitude of men and cattle within it.
5 'For I,' declares the LORD, 'will be a
[a]wall of fire [1]around her, and I will be
the [b]glory in her midst.' "
6 ¶ "[1]Ho there! [a]Flee from the land
of the north," declares the LORD, "for I
have [b]dispersed you as the four winds of
the heavens," declares the LORD.
7 "Ho, Zion! [a]Escape, you who are living with the daughter of Babylon."
8 For thus says the LORD of hosts, "After [1a]glory He has sent me against the
nations which plunder you, for he who
touches you, touches the [2b]apple of His
eye.
9 "For behold, I will [a]wave My hand
over them so that they will be [b]plunder
for their slaves. Then you will know that
the LORD of hosts has sent Me.
10 "[a]Sing for joy and be glad,
O daughter of Zion; for behold I am coming and I will [b]dwell in your midst," declares the LORD.
11 "[a]Many nations will join themselves to the LORD in that day and will
become My people. Then I will [b]dwell in
your midst, and you will [c]know that the
LORD of hosts has sent Me to you.
12 "The LORD will [1a]possess Judah as
His portion in the holy land, and will
again [b]choose Jerusalem.
13 ¶ "[1a]Be silent, all flesh, before the
LORD; for He is [b]aroused from His holy
habitation."

Joshua, the High Priest

3 Then he showed me [a]Joshua the
high priest standing before the angel
of the LORD, and [1b]Satan standing at his
right hand to accuse him.
2 The LORD said to Satan, "[a]The
LORD rebuke you, Satan! Indeed, the
LORD who has [b]chosen Jerusalem rebuke
you! Is this not a [c]brand plucked from
the fire?"
3 Now Joshua was clothed with
[a]filthy garments and standing before the
angel.
4 He spoke and said to those who
were standing before him, saying, "[a]Re-
move the filthy garments from him."
Again he said to him, "See, I have [b]taken
your iniquity away from you and [1]will
[c]clothe you with festal robes."
5 Then I said, "Let them put a clean
[a]turban on his head." So they put a clean
turban on his head and clothed him with
garments, while the angel of the LORD
was standing by.

11 [1]Lit *walked about through* [2]Lit *sitting* [a]Zech 1:8 [b]Is 14:7
12 [a]Ps 74:10; Jer 12:4; Hab 1:2 [b]Ps 102:13; Jer 30:18 [c]Ps 102:10; Jer 15:17 [d]Jer 25:11; Dan 9:2; Zech 7:5
13 [1]Lit *good* [a]Zech 1:9 [b]Is 40:1
14 [a]Is 40:2; Zech 1:17 [b]Zech 8:2
15 [1]Lit *helped for evil* [a]Zech 1:2 [b]Ps 123:4; Jer 48:11 [c]Amos 1:11
16 [a]Is 54:8-10; Zech 2:10 [b]Ezra 6:14; Zech 4:9 [c]Jer 31:39; Zech 2:2
17 [a]Is 44:26 [b]Is 51:3 [c]Zech 2:12
18 [1]Ch 2:1 in Heb
19 [a]1 Kin 22:11; Ps 75:4; Amos 6:13 mg
20 [a]Is 44:12
21 [a]Zech 1:19 [b]Ps 75:10
2:1 [1]Ch 2:5 in Heb [a]Jer 31:39; Ezek 40:3; Zech 1:16
2 [a]Jer 31:39; Ezek 40:3; Rev 21:15-17
3 [a]Zech 1:9
4 [1]Lit like *unwalled villages*; or like *open country* [a]Jer 1:6; Dan 1:4; 1 Tim 4:12 [b]Zech 1:17 [c]Ezek 38:11 [d]Is 49:20; Jer 30:19
5 [1]Lit *to her* [a]Is 4:5 [b]Hag 2:9; Zech 2:10
6 [1]Lit *Ho! Ho!* [a]Jer 3:18 [b]Jer 31:10; Ezek 11:16
7 [a]Is 48:20; Jer 51:6
8 [1]Or *the glory* [2]Lit *pupil* [a]Is 60:7-9 [b]Deut 32:10; Ps 17:8
9 [a]Is 19:16 [b]Is 14:2
10 [a]Is 65:18; Zech 9:9 [b]Zech 2:5
11 [a]Mic 4:2 [b]Zech 2:5 [c]Zech 2:9
12 [1]Or *inherit* [a]Deut 32:9; Ps 33:12; Jer 10:16 [b]2 Chr 6:6; Ps 132:13; Zech 1:17
13 [1]Lit *Hush* [a]Hab 2:20; Zeph 1:7 [b]Ps 78:65; Is 51:9
3:1 [1]Or the *Adversary* or *Accuser* [a]Ezra 5:2; Hag 1:1; Zech 6:11 [b]1 Chr 21:1; Job 1:6; Ps 109:6; Rev 12:10
2 [a]Mark 9:25; Jude 9 [b]Zech 2:12 [c]Amos 4:11; Jude 23
3 [a]Ezra 9:15; Is 4:4
4 [1]Lit *to clothe* [a]Is 43:25; Ezek 36:25 [b]Mic 7:18; Zech 3:9 [c]Is 52:1
5 [a]Job 29:14; Is 3:23

6 ¶ And the angel of the LORD admonished Joshua, saying,

7 "Thus says the LORD of hosts, 'If you will [a]walk in My ways and if you will perform My service, then you will also [b]govern My house and also have charge of My [c]courts, and I will grant you [1]free access among these who are standing *here.*

The Branch

8 'Now listen, Joshua the high priest, you and your friends who are sitting in front of you—indeed they are men who are a [a]symbol, for behold, I am going to bring in My servant the [1b]Branch.

9 'For behold, the stone that I have set before Joshua; on one stone are [a]seven eyes. Behold, I will engrave an inscription on it,' declares the LORD of hosts, 'and I will [b]remove the iniquity of that land in one day.

10 'In that day,' declares the LORD of hosts, 'every one of you will invite his neighbor to *sit* under *his* [a]vine and under *his* fig tree.' "

The Golden Lampstand and Olive Trees

4 Then [a]the angel who was speaking with me returned and [b]roused me, as a man who is awakened from his sleep.

2 He said to me, "[a]What do you see?" And I said, "I see, and behold, a [b]lampstand all of gold with its bowl on the top of it, and its [c]seven lamps on it with seven spouts belonging to each of the lamps which are on the top of it;

3 also [a]two olive trees by it, one on the right side of the bowl and the other on its left side."

4 Then I said to the angel who was speaking with me saying, "What are these, [a]my lord?"

5 So [a]the angel who was speaking with me answered and said to me, "[b]Do you not know what these are?" And I said, "No, my lord."

6 Then he [1]said to me, "This is the word of the LORD to [a]Zerubbabel saying, '[b]Not by might nor by power, but by My [c]Spirit,' says the LORD of hosts.

7 'What are you, O great [a]mountain? Before Zerubbabel *you will become* a plain; and he will bring forth the top stone with [b]shouts of "Grace, grace to it!" ' "

8 ¶ Also the word of the LORD came to me, saying,

9 "The hands of Zerubbabel have [a]laid the foundation of this house, and his hands will [b]finish *it.* Then you will know that the LORD of hosts has sent me to [1]you.

10 "For who has despised the day of [a]small things? [1]But these [b]seven will be glad when they see the [2c]plumb line in the hand of Zerubbabel—*these are* the [d]eyes of the LORD which [e]range to and fro throughout the earth."

11 ¶ Then I said to him, "What are these [a]two olive trees on the right of the lampstand and on its left?"

12 And I answered the second time and said to him, "What are the two olive [1]branches which are beside the two golden pipes, which empty the golden *oil* from themselves?"

13 So he answered me, saying, "[a]Do you not know what these are?" And I said, "No, [b]my lord."

14 Then he said, "These are the two [1a]anointed ones who are [b]standing by the [c]Lord of the whole earth."

The Flying Scroll

5 Then I lifted up my eyes again and looked, and behold, *there was* a flying [a]scroll.

2 And he said to me, "[a]What do you see?" And I answered, "I see a flying scroll; its length is twenty [1]cubits and its width ten cubits."

3 Then he said to me, "This is the [a]curse that is going forth over the face of the whole [1]land; surely everyone who [b]steals will be purged away according to [2]the writing on one side, and everyone who [c]swears will be purged away according to [2]the writing on the other side.

4 "I will [a]make it go forth," declares the LORD of hosts, "and it will [b]enter the house of the [c]thief and the house of the one who swears falsely by My name; and it will spend the night within that house and [d]consume it with its timber and stones."

5 ¶ Then [a]the angel who was speaking with me went out and said to me, "Lift up now your eyes and see what this is going forth."

6 I said, "What is it?" And he said, "This is the [1a]ephah going forth." Again he said, "This is their [2]appearance in all the [3]land

7 (and behold, a lead cover was lifted up); and this is a woman sitting inside the ephah."

8 Then he said, "This is [a]Wickedness!" And he threw her down into the middle of the ephah and cast the lead weight on its [1]opening.

9 Then I lifted up my eyes and looked, and there two women were coming out with the wind in their wings; and

---

7 [1]Lit *goings* [a]1 Kin 3:14 [b]Deut 17:9 [c]Is 62:9
8 [1]Lit *Sprout* [a]Is 8:18; Ezek 12:11 [b]Is 11:1; Jer 23:5; Zech 6:12
9 [a]Zech 4:10 [b]Jer 31:34; Zech 3:4
10 [a]1 Kin 4:25; Is 36:16; Mic 4:4
4:1 [a]Zech 1:9 [b]1 Kin 19:5-7; Jer 31:26
2 [a]Jer 1:13; Zech 5:2 [b]Ex 25:31; Jer 52:19 [c]Rev 4:5
3 [a]Zech 4:11; Rev 11:4
4 [a]Zech 1:9
5 [a]Zech 1:9 [b]Zech 4:13
6 [1]Lit *said to me, saying* [a]Ezra 5:2; Hag 2:4 [b]Is 11:2-4; Hos 1:7 [c]2 Chr 32:7; Eph 6:17
7 [a]Ps 114:4; Is 40:4; Jer 51:25; Nah 1:5; Zech 14:4 [b]Ezra 3:10; Ps 84:11
9 [1]Lit *you* (plural) [a]Neh 3:8-10; Hag 2:18 [b]Ezra 6:14; Zech 6:12
10 [1]Or *But they will rejoice when they see...Zerubbabel. These seven are the eyes of the LORD* [2]Lit *plummet stone* [a]Neh 4:2-4; Amos 7:2; Hag 2:3 [b]Zech 3:9; Rev 8:2 [c]Amos 7:7 [d]2 Chr 16:9; Prov 15:3; Jer 16:17 [e]Zech 1:10; Rev 5:6
11 [a]Zech 4:3; Rev 11:4
12 [1]Or *clusters*
13 [a]Zech 4:5 [b]Zech 4:4
14 [1]Lit *sons of fresh oil* [a]Ex 29:7; 1 Sam 16:1; Is 61:1-3; Dan 9:24-26 [b]Zech 3:1-7 [c]Mic 4:13
5:1 [a]Jer 36:2; Ezek 2:9; Rev 5:1
2 [1]I.e. One cubit equals approx 18 in. [a]Zech 4:2
3 [1]Or *earth* [2]Lit *it* [a]Is 24:6; Jer 26:6 [b]Ex 20:15; Lev 19:11; Mal 3:8 [c]Lev 19:12; Is 48:1; Jer 5:2; Zech 5:4
4 [a]Mal 3:5 [b]Hos 4:2 [c]Jer 2:26 [d]Lev 14:34; Job 18:15
5 [a]Zech 1:9
6 [1]I.e. Approx one bu [2]Lit *eye;* some ancient versions read *iniquity* [3]Or *earth* [a]Lev 19:36; Amos 8:5
8 [1]Lit *mouth* [a]Hos 12:7; Amos 8:5; Mic 6:11

they had wings like the wings of a [a]stork, and they lifted up the ephah between the earth and the heavens.

10 I said to the angel who was speaking with me, "Where are they taking the ephah?"

11 Then he said to me, "To build a [1]temple for her in the land of [a]Shinar; and when it is prepared, she will be set there on her own pedestal."

The Four Chariots

6 Now I lifted up my eyes again and looked, and behold, [a]four chariots were coming forth from between the two mountains; and the mountains *were* bronze mountains.

2 With the first chariot *were* [a]red horses, with the second chariot [b]black horses,

3 with the third chariot [a]white horses, and with the fourth chariot strong [b]dappled horses.

4 Then I spoke and said to the angel who was speaking with me, "[a]What are these, my lord?"

5 The angel replied to me, "These are the [a]four spirits of heaven, going forth after standing before the Lord of all the earth,

6 with one of which the black horses are going forth to the [a]north country; and the white ones go forth after them, while the dappled ones go forth to the [b]south country.

7 "When the strong ones went out, they [1]were eager to go to [2a]patrol the earth." And He said, "Go, [2]patrol the earth." So they [3]patrolled the earth.

8 Then He cried out to me and spoke to me saying, "See, those who are going to the land of the north have [1a]appeased My wrath in the land of the north."

9 ¶ The [a]word of the LORD also came to me, saying,

10 "[a]Take *an offering* from the exiles, from Heldai, Tobijah and Jedaiah; and you go the same day and enter the house of Josiah the son of Zephaniah, where they have arrived from Babylon.

The Symbolic Crowns

11 "Take silver and gold, make an *ornate* [a]crown and set *it* on the head of [b]Joshua the son of Jehozadak, the high priest.

12 "Then say to him, 'Thus says the LORD of hosts, "Behold, a man whose name is [1a]Branch, for He will [2b]branch out from where He is; and He will [c]build the temple of the LORD.

13 "Yes, it is He who will build the temple of the LORD, and He who will [a]bear the honor and sit and [b]rule on His throne. Thus, He will be a [c]priest on His throne, and the counsel of peace will be between the two [1]offices." '

14 "Now the [a]crown will become a reminder in the temple of the LORD to Helem, Tobijah, Jedaiah and [1]Hen the son of Zephaniah.

15 "[a]Those who are far off will come and [1]build the temple of the LORD." Then you will [b]know that the LORD of hosts has sent me to you. And it will take place if you completely [c]obey the LORD your God.

Hearts like Flint

7 In the fourth year of King Darius, the word of the LORD came to Zechariah on the fourth *day* of the ninth month, *which is* [a]Chislev.

2 Now *the town of* Bethel had sent Sharezer and Regemmelech and [1]their men to [2a]seek the favor of the LORD,

3 speaking to the [a]priests who belong to the house of the LORD of hosts, and to the prophets, saying, "Shall I weep in the [b]fifth month [1]and abstain, as I have done these many years?"

4 Then the word of the LORD of hosts came to me, saying,

5 "Say to all the people of the land and to the priests, 'When you fasted and mourned in the fifth and seventh months [1]these [a]seventy years, was it actually for [b]Me that you fasted?

6 'When you eat and drink, [1]do you not eat for yourselves and do you not drink for yourselves?

7 'Are not *these* the words which the LORD [a]proclaimed by the former prophets, when Jerusalem was inhabited and [1b]prosperous along with its cities around it, and the [2c]Negev and the [3]foothills were inhabited?' "

8 ¶ Then the word of the LORD came to Zechariah saying,

9 "Thus has the LORD of hosts said, '[a]Dispense true justice and practice [b]kindness and compassion each to his brother;

10 and [a]do not oppress the widow or the [1]orphan, the [2]stranger or the poor; and do [b]not devise evil in your hearts against one another.'

11 "But they [a]refused to pay attention and [1b]turned a stubborn shoulder and [2c]stopped their ears from hearing.

12 "They made their [a]hearts *like* [1b]flint [2]so that they could not hear the law and the [c]words which the LORD of hosts had sent by His Spirit through the [d]former prophets; therefore great [e]wrath came from the LORD of hosts.

9 [a]Lev 11:13; Ps 104:17; Jer 8:7
11 [1]Lit *house* [a]Gen 10:10; Is 11:11; Dan 1:2
6:1 [a]Dan 7:3; Zech 1:18
2 [a]Zech 1:8; Rev 6:4 [b]Rev 6:5
3 [a]Rev 6:2 [b]Rev 6:8
4 [a]Zech 1:9
5 [a]Jer 49:36; Ezek 37:9; Dan 7:2; Matt 24:31; Rev 7:1
6 [a]Jer 1:14; Ezek 1:4 [b]Is 43:6; Dan 11:5
7 [1]Lit *sought to go* [2]Lit *walk about through* [3]Lit *walked about through* [a]Zech 1:10
8 [1]Lit *caused My spirit to rest in* [a]Ezek 5:13; Zech 1:15
9 [a]Zech 1:1
10 [a]Ezra 7:14-16; Jer 28:6
11 [a]2 Sam 12:30; Ps 21:3; Song 3:11 [b]Ezra 3:2; Hag 1:1; Zech 3:1
12 [1]Lit *Sprout* [2]Lit *sprout up* [a]Is 4:2; Jer 23:5; Zech 3:8 [b]Is 53:2 [c]Ezra 3:8; Amos 9:11; Zech 4:6-9
13 [1]Lit *of them* [a]Is 9:6 [b]Is 9:7 [c]Ps 110:1
14 [1]I.e. Josiah [a]Zech 6:11
15 [1]Lit *build in* [a]Is 56:6-8 [b]Zech 2:9-11 [c]Is 58:10-14; Jer 7:23; Zech 3:7
7:1 [a]Neh 1:1
2 [1]Lit *his* [2]Lit *soften the face of* [a]1 Kin 13:6; Jer 26:19; Zech 8:21
3 [1]Lit *abstaining*; or *dedicating myself* [a]Ezra 3:10-12 [b]Zech 8:19
5 [1]Lit *and these* [a]Zech 1:12 [b]Is 1:11
6 [1]Lit *is it not you who eat and you who drink*
7 [1]Or *at ease* [2]I.e. South country [3]Heb *Shephelah* [a]Is 1:16-20; Jer 7:5; Zech 1:4 [b]Jer 22:21 [c]Jer 13:19
9 [a]Ezek 18:8; Zech 8:16 [b]2 Sam 9:7; Job 6:14; Mic 6:8
10 [1]Or *fatherless* [2]Or *resident alien* [a]Ex 22:22; Ps 72:4; Jer 7:6 [b]Ps 21:11; Mic 2:1; Zech 8:17
11 [1]Lit *gave* [2]Lit *made heavy* [a]Jer 5:3 [b]Jer 7:26 [c]Ps 58:4; Jer 5:21
12 [1]Lit *corundum* [2]Lit *from hearing* [a]2 Chr 36:13; Ezek 2:4 [b]Jer 17:1; Ezek 3:9 [c]Zech 7:7 [d]Neh 9:30 [e]2 Chr 36:16; Dan 9:11

And tell [c]false dreams;
They comfort in vain.
Therefore *the people* [3]wander
like [d]sheep,
They are afflicted, because there
is no shepherd.
3 "My [a]anger is kindled against the
shepherds,
And I will punish the [1]male
goats;
For the LORD of hosts has
[b]visited His flock, the house
of Judah,
And will make them like His
majestic horse in battle.
4 "From [1]them will come the
[a]cornerstone,
From [1]them the tent peg,
From [1]them the bow of [b]battle,
From [1]them every [2]ruler, *all* of
them together.
5 "They will be as mighty men,
[a]Treading down *the enemy* in
the mire of the streets in
battle;
And they will fight, for the LORD
will be with them;
And the [b]riders on horses will
be put to shame.
6 "I will [a]strengthen the house of
Judah,
And I will [b]save the house of
Joseph,
And I will [1c]bring them back,
Because I have had [d]compassion
on them;
And they will be as though I had
[e]not rejected them,
For I am the LORD their God and
I will [f]answer them.
7 "Ephraim will be like a mighty
man,
And their heart will be glad as if
from wine;
Indeed, their [a]children will see
it and be glad,
[1]Their heart will rejoice in the
LORD.
8 "I will [a]whistle for them to
gather them together,
For I have redeemed them;
And they will be as [b]numerous
as they [1c]were before.
9 "When I [1]scatter them among the
peoples,
They will [a]remember Me in far
countries,
And they with their children will
live and come back.
10 "I will [a]bring them back from the
land of Egypt
And gather them from Assyria;
And I will bring them into the
land of [b]Gilead and Lebanon
[1]Until [c]no *room* can be found
for them.
11 "And they will pass through the
[a]sea *of* distress
And He will strike the waves in
the sea,
So that all the depths of the
[b]Nile will dry up;
And the pride of [c]Assyria will
be brought down
And the scepter of [d]Egypt will
depart.
12 "And I will [a]strengthen them in
the LORD,
And in His name [b]they will
walk," declares the LORD.

The Doomed Flock

11 Open your doors, O Lebanon,
That a [a]fire may feed on your
[b]cedars.
2 Wail, O [1]cypress, for the cedar
has fallen,
Because the glorious *trees* have
been destroyed;
Wail, O oaks of Bashan,
For the [2]impenetrable forest has
come down.
3 There is a sound of the
shepherds' [a]wail,
For their glory is ruined;
There is a [b]sound of the young
lions' roar,
For the [1]pride of the Jordan is
ruined.
4 ¶ Thus says the LORD my God, "Pasture the flock *doomed* to [a]slaughter.
5 "Those who buy them slay them and
[1]go [a]unpunished, and *each of* those
who sell them says, 'Blessed be the LORD,
for [b]I have become rich!' And their
[c]own shepherds have no pity on them.
6 "For I will [a]no longer have pity on
the inhabitants of the land," declares the
LORD; "but behold, I will [b]cause the men
to [1]fall, each into another's [2]power and
into the [2]power of his king; and they will
strike the land, and I will [c]not deliver
them from their [2]power."
7 ¶ So I [a]pastured the flock *doomed*
to slaughter, [1]hence the [b]afflicted of the
flock. And I took for myself two [c]staffs:
the one I called [2d]Favor and the other I
called [3e]Union; so I pastured the flock.
8 Then I annihilated the three shepherds in [a]one month, for my soul was
impatient with them, and their soul also
[1]was weary of me.
9 Then I said, "I will not pasture you.
What is to [a]die, [1]let it die, and what is
to be annihilated, [2]let it be annihilated;
and [3]let those who are left eat one another's flesh."
10 I took my staff [1a]Favor and cut it

2 [3]Lit *journey* [c]Jer 23:32 [d]Ezek 34:5,8; Matt 9:36; Mark 6:34
3 [1]I.e. leaders [a]Jer 25:34-36 [b]Ezek 34:12
4 [1]Lit *him* [2]Or *oppressor* [a]Luke 20:17; Eph 2:20; 1 Pet 2:6 [b]Jer 51:20; Zech 9:10
5 [a]2 Sam 22:43 [b]Amos 2:15; Hag 2:22
6 [1]Or *make them dwell* [a]Zech 10:12 [b]Zech 8:7; 9:16 [c]Zech 8:8 [d]Is 54:8; Zech 1:16 [e]Is 54:4 [f]Zech 13:9
7 [1]Or *Let their heart rejoice* [a]Is 54:13; Ezek 37:25
8 [1]Lit *were numerous* [a]Is 5:26; 7:18,19 [b]Jer 33:22; Rev 7:9 [c]Jer 30:20; Ezek 36:11
9 [1]Lit *sow* [a]1 Kin 8:47,48; Ezek 6:9
10 [1]Lit *And* [a]Is 11:11 [b]Jer 50:19 [c]Is 49:19,20
11 [a]Is 51:9,10 [b]Is 19:5-7 [c]Zeph 2:13 [d]Ezek 30:13
12 [a]Zech 10:6 [b]Mic 4:5
11:1 [a]Jer 22:6,7 [b]Ezek 31:3
2 [1]Or *juniper* [2]Another reading is *forest of the vintage*
3 [1]Or *jungle* [a]Jer 25:34-36 [b]Jer 2:15; 50:44
4 [a]Ps 44:22; Zech 11:7
5 [1]Lit *are not held guilty* [a]Jer 50:7 [b]Hos 12:8; 1 Tim 6:9 [c]Ezek 34:2,3
6 [1]Lit *find* [2]Lit *hand* [a]Jer 13:14 [b]Is 9:19-21; Mic 7:2-6; Zech 14:13 [c]Ps 50:22; Mic 5:8
7 [1]Another reading is *for the sheep dealers* [2]Or *Pleasantness* [3]Or *Cords* [a]Zech 11:4 [b]Jer 39:10; Zeph 3:12 [c]Ezek 37:16 [d]Ps 27:4; 90:17; Zech 11:10 [e]Ps 133:1; Ezek 37:16-23; Zech 11:14
8 [1]Or *detested* [a]Hos 5:7
9 [1]Or *will die* [2]Or *will be annihilated* [3]Or *those...will eat* [a]Jer 15:2
10 [1]Or *Pleasantness* [a]Zech 11:7

in pieces, to [2b]break my covenant which
I had made with all the peoples.
11 So it was [1]broken on that day, and
[2]thus the [a]afflicted of the flock who
were watching me realized that it was the
word of the LORD.
12 I said to them, "If it is good in your
sight, give *me* my [a]wages; but if not,
[1]never mind!" So they weighed out
[b]thirty *shekels* of silver as my wages.
13 Then the LORD said to me, "Throw
it to the [a]potter, *that* magnificent price at
which I was valued by them." So I took
the thirty *shekels* of silver and threw
them to the potter in the house of the
LORD.
14 Then I cut in pieces my second staff
[1a]Union, to [b]break the brotherhood between Judah and Israel.
15 ¶ The LORD said to me, "Take again
for yourself the equipment of a [1a]foolish
shepherd.
16 "For behold, I am going to raise up a
shepherd in the land who will [a]not care
for the perishing, seek the scattered, heal
the broken, or sustain the one standing,
but will [b]devour the flesh of the fat *sheep*
and tear off their hoofs.
17 "[a]Woe to the worthless shepherd
Who leaves the flock!
A [b]sword will be on his arm
And on his right eye!
His [c]arm will be totally withered
And his right eye will be
[1]blind."

Jerusalem to Be Attacked

12 The [1]burden of the word of the
LORD concerning Israel.
¶ *Thus* declares the LORD who
[a]stretches out the heavens, [b]lays the
foundation of the earth, and [c]forms the
spirit of man within him,
2 "Behold, I am going to make Jerusalem a [a]cup [1]that causes reeling to all the
peoples around; and when the siege is
against Jerusalem, it will also be against
[b]Judah.
3 "It will come about in that day that
I will make Jerusalem a heavy [a]stone for
all the peoples; all who lift it will be [b]se-
verely [1]injured. And all the [c]nations of
the earth will be gathered against it.
4 "In that day," declares the LORD, "I
will strike every horse with bewilderment and his rider with madness. But I
will [1]watch over the house of Judah,
while I strike every horse of the peoples
with blindness.
5 "Then the clans of Judah will say in
their hearts, '[1]A strong support for us are
the inhabitants of Jerusalem through the
LORD of hosts, their God.'
6 ¶ "In that day I will make the clans
of Judah like a [a]firepot among pieces of
wood and a flaming torch among sheaves,
so they will consume on the right hand
and on the left all the surrounding peoples, while the [b]inhabitants of Jerusalem
again dwell on their own sites in Jerusalem.
7 "The LORD also will [a]save the tents
of Judah first, so that the glory of the
house of [b]David and the glory of the inhabitants of Jerusalem will not be magnified above Judah.
8 "In that day the LORD will [a]defend
the inhabitants of Jerusalem, and the one
who [1b]is feeble among them in that day
will be like David, and the house of David
will be like [c]God, like the [d]angel of the
LORD before them.
9 "And in that day I will [1a]set about
to destroy all the nations that come
against Jerusalem.
10 ¶ "I will [a]pour out on the house of
David and on the inhabitants of Jerusalem, [1]the Spirit of grace and of supplication, so that they will look on Me whom
they have [b]pierced; and they will mourn
for Him, as one [c]mourns for an only son,
and they will weep bitterly over Him like
the bitter weeping over a firstborn.
11 "In that day there will be great
[a]mourning in Jerusalem, like the mourning of Hadadrimmon in the [1]plain of
[2]Megiddo.
12 "The land will mourn, every family
by itself; the family of the house of David
by itself and their wives by themselves;
the family of the house of Nathan by itself
and their wives by themselves;
13 the family of the house of Levi by
itself and their wives by themselves; the
family of the Shimeites by itself and their
wives by themselves;
14 all the families that remain, every
family by itself and their wives by themselves.

False Prophets Ashamed

13 "In that day a [a]fountain will be
opened for the house of David
and for the inhabitants of Jerusalem, for
[b]sin and for [c]impurity.
2 ¶ "It will come about in that day,"
declares the LORD of hosts, "that I will
[a]cut off the names of the idols from the
land, and they will no longer be remembered; and I will also remove the [b]proph-
ets and the [c]unclean spirit from the land.
3 "And if anyone still [a]prophesies,
then his father and mother who gave
birth to him will say to him, 'You shall
[b]not live, for you have spoken [c]falsely in
the name of the LORD'; and his [d]father
and mother who gave birth to him will
pierce him through when he prophesies.

10 [2]Or *annul* [b]Ps 89:39; Jer 14:21
11 [1]Or *annulled* [2]Another reading is *the sheep dealers who* [a]Zeph 3:12
12 [1]Lit *cease* [a]1 Kin 5:6; Mal 3:5 [b]Gen 37:28; Ex 21:32; Matt 26:15; 27:9,10
13 [a]Matt 27:3-10; Acts 1:18,19
14 [1]Or *Cords* [a]Zech 11:7 [b]Is 9:21; Zech 11:6
15 [1]Or *useless* [a]Is 6:10-12; Zech 11:17
16 [a]Jer 23:2 [b]Ezek 34:2-6
17 [1]Lit *completely dimmed* [a]Jer 23:1; Zech 10:2; 11:15 [b]Jer 50:35-37 [c]Ezek 30:21,22
12:1 [1]Or *oracle* [a]Is 42:5; 44:24; Jer 51:15 [b]Job 26:7; Ps 102:25, 26; Heb 1:10-12 [c]Is 57:16; Heb 12:9
2 [1]Lit *of reeling* [a]Ps 75:8; Is 51:22,23 [b]Zech 14:14
3 [1]Lit *scratched* [a]Dan 2:34,35, 44,45 [b]Matt 21:44 [c]Zech 14:2
4 [1]Lit *open My eyes*
5 [1]Lit *My strength is*
6 [a]Is 10:17,18; Obad 18; Zech 11:1 [b]Zech 2:4; 8:3-5
7 [a]Jer 30:18 [b]Amos 9:11
8 [1]Or *stumbles* [a]Joel 3:16; Zech 9:14,15 [b]Lev 26:8; Josh 23:10; Mic 7:8 [c]Ps 8:5; 82:6 [d]Ex 14:19; 33:2
9 [1]Lit *seek to* [a]Zech 14:2,3
10 [1]Or *a spirit* [a]Is 44:3; Ezek 39:29; Joel 2:28, 29 [b]John 19:37; Rev 1:7 [c]Jer 6:26; Amos 8:10
11 [1]I.e. broad valley [2]Heb *Megiddon* [a]Matt 24:30; Rev 1:7
13:1 [a]Jer 2:13; 17:13 [b]Ps 51:2, 7; Is 1:16-18; John 1:29 [c]Num 19:17; Is 4:4; Ezek 36:25
2 [a]Ex 23:13; Hos 2:17 [b]Jer 23:14,15 [c]1 Kin 22:22; Ezek 36:25,29
3 [a]Jer 23:34 [b]Deut 18:20; Ezek 14:9 [c]Jer 23:25 [d]Deut 13:6-11; Matt 10:37

4 "Also it will come about in that day
that the prophets will each be [a]ashamed
of his vision when he prophesies, and
they will not put on a [b]hairy robe in
order to deceive;
5 but he will say, 'I am [a]not a prophet;
I am a tiller of the ground, for a man
[1]sold me as a slave in my youth.'
6 "And one will say to him, 'What are
these wounds [a]between your [1]arms?'
Then he will say, '*Those* with which I
was wounded in the house of [2]my
friends.'
7 ¶ "Awake, O [a]sword, against My
[b]Shepherd,
And against the man, My
[c]Associate,"
Declares the LORD of hosts.
"[d]Strike the Shepherd that the
sheep may be scattered;
And I will [e]turn My hand
[1]against the little ones.
8 "It will come about in all the
land,"
Declares the LORD,
"That [a]two parts in it will be cut
off *and* perish;
But the third will be left in it.
9 "And I will bring the third part
through the [a]fire,
Refine them as silver is refined,
And test them as gold is tested.
They will [b]call on My name,
And I will [c]answer them;
I will say, 'They are [d]My
people,'
And they will say, 'The LORD is
my God.' "

God Will Battle Jerusalem's Foes

14 Behold, a [a]day is coming for the
LORD when [b]the spoil taken from
you will be divided among you.
2 For I will [a]gather all the nations
against Jerusalem to battle, and the city
will be captured, the [b]houses plundered,
the women ravished and half of the city
exiled, but the rest of the people will not
be cut off from the city.
3 Then the LORD will go forth and
[a]fight against those nations, as [1]when
He fights on a day of battle.
4 In that day His feet will [a]stand on
the Mount of Olives, which is in front of
Jerusalem on the east; and the Mount of
Olives will be [b]split in its middle from
east to west by a very large valley, so that
half of the mountain will move toward
the north and the other half toward the
south.
5 You will flee by the valley of My
mountains, for the valley of the mountains
will reach to Azel; yes, you will flee
just as you fled before the [a]earthquake in
the days of Uzziah king of Judah. [b]Then
the LORD, my God, will come, *and* all the
holy ones with [1]Him!
6 ¶ In that day there will be [a]no
light; the [1]luminaries will dwindle.
7 For it will be [a]a unique day which
is [b]known to the LORD, neither day nor
night, but it will come about that at [c]evening
time there will be light.
8 ¶ And in that day [a]living waters
will flow out of Jerusalem, half of them
toward the eastern sea and the other half
toward the western sea; it will be in summer
as well as in winter.

God Will Be King over All

9 ¶ And the LORD will be [a]king over
all the earth; in that day the LORD will be
the only [b]one, and His name *the only*
one.
10 ¶ All the land will be changed into
a plain from [a]Geba to [b]Rimmon south of
Jerusalem; but [1]Jerusalem will [c]rise and
[d]remain on its site from [e]Benjamin's
Gate as far as the place of the First Gate
to the [f]Corner Gate, and from the [g]Tower
of Hananel to the king's wine presses.
11 [1]People will live in it, and there
will [a]no longer be a curse, for Jerusalem
will [b]dwell in security.
12 ¶ Now this will be the plague with
which the LORD will strike all the peoples
who have gone to war against Jerusalem;
their flesh will [a]rot while they stand on
their feet, and their eyes will rot in their
sockets, and their tongue will rot in their
mouth.
13 It will come about in that day that
a great panic from the LORD will [1]fall on
them; and they will [a]seize one another's
hand, and the hand of one will [2]be lifted
against the hand of another.
14 [a]Judah also will fight at Jerusalem;
and the [b]wealth of all the surrounding
nations will be gathered, gold and silver
and garments in great abundance.
15 So also like this [a]plague will be the
plague on the horse, the mule, the camel,
the donkey and all the cattle that will be
in those camps.
16 ¶ Then it will come about that any
who are left of all the nations that went
against Jerusalem will [a]go up from year
to year to worship the King, the LORD
of hosts, and to celebrate the [b]Feast of
Booths.
17 And it will be that whichever of the
families of the earth does not go up to
Jerusalem to worship the [a]King, the
LORD of hosts, there will be [b]no rain on
them.
18 If the family of Egypt does not go up
or enter, then no *rain will fall* on them; it
will be the [a]plague with which the LORD

---

4 [a]Jer 6:15; 8:9; Mic 3:7 [b]2 Kin 1:8; Is 20:2; Matt 3:4
5 [1]Lit *caused another to buy me* [a]Amos 7:14
6 [1]Lit *hands* [2]Lit *those who love me* [a]2 Kin 9:24
7 [1]Or *upon* [a]Jer 47:6; Ezek 21:3-5 [b]Is 40:11; Ezek 34:23,24; 37:24; Mic 5:2,4 [c]Ps 2:2; Jer 23:5,6 [d]Is 53:4, 5,10; Matt 26:31; Mark 14:27 [e]Is 1:25
8 [a]Is 6:13; Ezek 5:2-4,12
9 [a]Is 48:10; Mal 3:3 [b]Ps 34:15-17; 50:15; Zech 12:10 [c]Is 58:9; 65:24; Jer 29:11-13; Zech 10:6 [d]Hos 2:23
14:1 [a]Is 13:6,9; Joel 2:1; Mal 4:1 [b]Zech 14:14
2 [a]Zech 12:2,3 [b]Is 13:16
3 [1]Lit *His day of fighting* [a]Zech 9:14,15
4 [a]Ezek 11:23 [b]Is 64:1,2; Ezek 47:1-10; Mic 1:3,4; Hab 3:6; Zech 4:7; 14:8
5 [1]So the versions; Heb *You* [a]Is 29:6; Amos 1:1 [b]Ps 96:13; Is 66:15,16; Matt 16:27; 25:31
6 [1]Lit *glorious ones will congeal* [a]Is 13:10; Jer 4:23; Ezek 32:7, 8; Joel 2:30,31; Acts 2:16,19
7 [a]Jer 30:7; Amos 8:9 [b]Is 45:21; Acts 15:18 [c]Is 58:10; Rev 22:5
8 [a]Ezek 47:1-12; Joel 3:18; John 7:38; Rev 22:1,2
9 [a]Is 2:2-4; 45:23; Zech 9:9; 14:16,17 [b]Deut 6:4; Is 45:21-24
10 [1]Lit *it* [a]1 Kin 15:22 [b]Josh 15:32; Judg 20:45,47 [c]Is 2:2; Amos 9:11 [d]Jer 30:18; Zech 12:6 [e]Jer 37:13; 38:7 [f]2 Kin 14:13 [g]Jer 31:38
11 [1]Lit *They* [a]Zech 8:13; Rev 22:3 [b]Jer 23:5,6; Ezek 34:25-28
12 [a]Lev 26:16; Deut 28:21,22
13 [1]Lit *be among* [2]Lit *rise up against* [a]Zech 11:6
14 [a]Zech 12:2,5 [b]Is 23:18; Zech 14:1
15 [a]Zech 14:12
16 [a]Is 60:6-9; 66:18-21,23 [b]Lev 23:34-44
17 [a]Zech 14:9, 16 [b]Jer 14:3-6; Amos 4:7
18 [a]Zech 14:12, 15

smites the nations who do not go up to
celebrate the Feast of Booths.
19 This will be the [1]punishment of
Egypt, and the [1]punishment of all the
nations who do not go up to celebrate the
Feast of Booths.
20 ¶ In that day there will *be inscribed*
on the bells of the horses, "[a]HOLY
TO THE LORD." And the [b]cooking pots
in the LORD's house will be like the bowls
before the altar.
21 Every cooking pot in Jerusalem and
in Judah will be [a]holy to the LORD of
hosts; and all who sacrifice will come
and take of them and boil in them. And
there will no longer be a [1b]Canaanite
in the house of the LORD of hosts in that
day.

19 [1]Lit *sin*

20 [a]Ex 28:36-38 [b]Ezek 46:20

21 [1]Or *merchant* [a]Neh 8:10; Rom 14:6, 7; 1 Cor 10:31 [b]Zeph 1:11

Malachi

Title and Background

The temple had been rebuilt, but times of prosperity had not come. The people were suffering drought, famine and blighted crops, and they met these conditions with indifference and spiritual lethargy. They had forgotten God and treated Him with dishonor. They had also married foreign women. Against such a background Malachi, meaning "My messenger," was written.

Author and Date of Writing

Since the term "My messenger" occurs in 3:1, and since both prophets and priests were called messengers of the Lord, some have thought "Malachi" only a title that tradition has given the author. There is no certainty about this, however, and it seems likely that Malachi was in fact the author's name. The book was probably written around 433–430 B.C.

Theme and Message

Malachi's message is filled with indictments and warnings. He rebukes the Jews for doubting God's love (1:2–5) and for the faithlessness of both priests (1:6—2:9) and people (2:10–16). How quickly the nation had forgotten! Only through repentance and reformation will the people again experience God's blessing (3:6–12). That "great and terrible day of the LORD" (4:5) was coming, and Malachi both reassures and warns his people.

Outline

I. God's Covenant Love for Israel (1:1–5)
II. Israel's Unfaithfulness (1:6—2:16)
  A. The Unfaithfulness of the Priests (1:6—2:9)
  B. The Unfaithfulness of the People (2:10–16)
III. The Lord's Coming (2:17—4:6)

God's Love for Jacob

1 The [1a]oracle of the word of the
LORD to [b]Israel through [2]Malachi.
2 ¶ "I have [a]loved you," says the
LORD. But you say, "How have You loved
us?" "*Was* not Esau Jacob's brother?" declares the LORD. "Yet I [b]have loved Jacob;
3 but I have hated Esau, and I have
[a]made his mountains a desolation and
appointed his inheritance for the jackals
of the wilderness."
4 Though Edom says, "We have been
[a]beaten down, but we will [1b]return and
build up the ruins"; thus says the LORD of
hosts, "They may [c]build, but I will tear
down; and *men* will call them the [2]wick-
ed territory, and the people [3]toward
whom the LORD is indignant [d]forever."
5 Your eyes will see this and you will
say, "[a]The LORD [1]be magnified beyond
the [2]border of Israel!"

Sin of the Priests

6 ¶ " 'A son [a]honors *his* father, and
a servant his master. Then if I am a [b]fa-
ther, where is My honor? And if I am a
master, where is My [1]respect?' says the
LORD of hosts to you, O [c]priests who despise My name. But you say, 'How have
we despised Your name?'
7 "*You* are presenting [a]defiled [1b]food
upon My altar. But you say, 'How have
we defiled You?' In that you say, 'The
[c]table of the LORD is to be despised.'
8 "But when you present the [a]blind
for sacrifice, is it not evil? And when you
present the lame and sick, is it not evil?
[1]Why not offer it to your [b]governor?
Would he be pleased with you? Or would
he receive you kindly?" says the LORD of
hosts.
9 "But now [1]will you not [a]entreat
God's favor, that He may be gracious to
us? [2]With such an offering on your part,
will He [b]receive any of you kindly?" says
the LORD of hosts.
10 "Oh that there were one among you
who would [a]shut the [1]gates, that you
might not uselessly kindle *fire on* My altar! I am not pleased with you," says the

1:1 [1]Lit *burden* [2]Or *My messenger* [a]Is 13:1; Nah 1:1; Hab 1:1; Zech 9:1 [b]Mal 2:11
2 [a]Deut 4:37; Is 41:8; Jer 31:3; John 15:12 [b]Rom 9:13
3 [a]Jer 49:10; Ezek 35:3
4 [1]Or *rebuild the ruins* [2]Lit *border of wickedness* [3]Or *whom the LORD has cursed* [a]Jer 5:17 [b]Is 9:9 [c]Amos 3:15 [d]Ezek 35:9; Obad 10
5 [1]Or *will be great* [2]Or *territory* [a]Ps 35:27; Mic 5:4
6 [1]Lit *fear* [a]Ex 20:12; Prov 30:11 [b]Deut 1:31; Is 1:2; Jer 3:4; Mal 2:10 [c]Zeph 3:4; Mal 2:1-9
7 [1]Lit *bread* [a]Mal 1:8 [b]Lev 3:11 [c]Mal 1:12
8 [1]Lit *Offer it, please* [a]Lev 22:22; Deut 15:21 [b]Hag 1:1
9 [1]Lit *entreat, please* [2]Lit *This has been from your hand* [a]Jer 27:18; Joel 2:12-14 [b]Amos 5:22
10 [1]Or *doors* [a]Is 1:13

LORD of hosts, "[b]nor will I accept an offering from [2]you.

11 "For from the [a]rising of the sun even to its setting, [b]My name *will be* [c]great among the nations, and in every place [d]incense is going to be offered to My name, and a grain offering *that is* pure; for My name *will be* [e]great among the nations," says the LORD of hosts.

12 "But you are [a]profaning it, in that you say, 'The table of the Lord is defiled, and as for its fruit, its food is to be despised.'

13 "You also say, '[1]My, how [a]tiresome it is!' And you disdainfully sniff at it," says the LORD of hosts, "and you bring what was taken by [b]robbery and *what is* [c]lame or sick; so you bring the offering! Should I [d]receive that from your hand?" says the LORD.

14 "But cursed be the [a]swindler who has a male in his flock and vows it, but sacrifices a [b]blemished animal to the Lord, for I am a great [c]King," says the LORD of hosts, "and My name is [1d]feared among the [2]nations."

Priests to Be Disciplined

2 "And now this commandment is for you, O priests.

2 "If you do [a]not listen, and if you do not take it to heart to give honor to My name," says the LORD of hosts, "then I will send the [b]curse upon you and I will curse your blessings; and indeed, I have [c]cursed them *already,* because you are not taking *it* to heart.

3 "Behold, I am going to [a]rebuke your [1]offspring, and I will [b]spread [2]refuse on your faces, the [2]refuse of your [c]feasts; and you will be taken away [3]with it.

4 "Then you will know that I have sent this commandment to you, [1]that My [a]covenant may [2]continue with Levi," says the LORD of hosts.

5 "My covenant with him was *one of* life and [a]peace, and I gave them to him *as an object of* [1]reverence; so he [2b]revered Me and stood in awe of My name.

6 "[1a]True instruction was in his mouth and unrighteousness was not found on his lips; he walked [b]with Me in peace and uprightness, and he [c]turned many back from iniquity.

7 "For the lips of a priest should preserve [a]knowledge, and [1]men should [b]seek [2]instruction from his mouth; for he is the [c]messenger of the LORD of hosts.

8 "But as for you, you have turned aside from the way; you have caused many to [a]stumble [1]by the instruction; you have [2b]corrupted the covenant of Levi," says the LORD of hosts.

9 "So [a]I also have made you despised and [b]abased [1]before all the people, just as you are not keeping My ways but are showing [c]partiality in the [2]instruction.

Sin in the Family

10 ¶ "Do we not all have [a]one father? [b]Has not one God created us? Why do we deal [c]treacherously each against his brother so as to profane the [d]covenant of our fathers?

11 "Judah has dealt [a]treacherously, and an abomination has been committed in Israel and in Jerusalem; for Judah has [b]profaned the sanctuary of the LORD [1]which He loves and has married the daughter of a foreign god.

12 "*As* for the man who does this, may the [a]LORD cut off from the tents of Jacob *everyone* who awakes and answers, or who [b]presents [1]an offering to the LORD of hosts.

13 ¶ "This is [1]another thing you do: you cover the altar of the LORD with tears, with weeping and with groaning, because He [a]no longer regards the [2]offering or accepts *it with* favor from your hand.

14 "Yet you say, 'For what reason?' Because the LORD has been a witness between you and the [a]wife of your youth, against whom you have dealt [b]treacherously, though she is your companion and your wife by covenant.

15 "[1]But not one has [a]done *so* who has a remnant of the Spirit. And [2]what did *that* one *do* while he was seeking a [b]godly [3]offspring? Take heed then to your spirit, and let no one deal [c]treacherously against the wife of your youth.

16 "For [1]I hate [2a]divorce," says the LORD, the God of Israel, "and [3]him who covers his garment with [4b]wrong," says the LORD of hosts. "So take heed to your spirit, that you do not deal treacherously."

17 ¶ You have [a]wearied the LORD with your words. Yet you say, "How have we wearied *Him?*" In that you say, "[b]Everyone who does evil is good in the sight of the LORD, and He [c]delights in them," or, "[d]Where is the God of [e]justice?"

The Purifier

3 "[a]Behold, I am going to send [b]My [1]messenger, and he will [2c]clear the way before Me. And the Lord, whom you seek, will suddenly come to His temple; [3]and the [1d]messenger of the covenant, in whom you delight, behold, He is coming," says the LORD of hosts.

---

10 [2]Lit *your hand* [b]Jer 14:10; Hos 5:6
11 [a]Is 45:6 [b]Ps 111:9 [c]Is 66:18 [d]Is 60:6 [e]Is 12:4; Jer 10:6
12 [a]Mal 1:7
13 [1]Lit *Behold* it is *weariness* [a]Is 43:22 [b]Lev 6:4; Is 61:8 [c]Mal 1:8 [d]Mal 1:10
14 [1]Or *revered* [2]Or *Gentiles* [a]Acts 5:1-4 [b]Lev 22:18-20 [c]Zech 14:9 [d]Zeph 2:11
2:2 [a]Lev 26:14; Deut 28:15 [b]Deut 28:16-20 [c]Mal 3:9
3 [1]Lit *seed* [2]Or *vomit* [3]Lit *to* [a]Lev 26:16; Deut 28:38 [b]Nah 3:6 [c]Ex 29:14
4 [1]Or *to be My covenant with* [2]Lit *be* [a]Num 3:11-13; Neh 13:29; Mal 3:1
5 [1]Or *fear* [2]Or *feared* [a]Num 25:12 [b]Num 25:7
6 [1]Or *Law of truth* [a]Ps 119:142 [b]Deut 33:8; Ps 37:37 [c]Jer 23:22
7 [1]Lit *they* [2]Or *law* [a]Lev 10:11; Neh 8:7 [b]Num 27:21; Deut 17:8-11; Jer 18:18; Ezek 7:26 [c]Hag 1:13
8 [1]Or *in the law* [2]Or *violated* [a]Jer 18:15 [b]Num 25:12; Neh 13:29; Ezek 44:10
9 [1]Lit *to* [2]Or *law* [a]Nah 3:6 [b]Ezek 7:26 [c]Deut 1:17; Mic 3:11
10 [a]Is 63:16; Jer 31:9; 1 Cor 8:6; Eph 4:6 [b]Acts 17:24f [c]Jer 9:4 [d]Ex 19:4-6
11 [1]Or *in that He has loved and married* [a]Jer 3:7-9 [b]Ezra 9:1
12 [1]Or *a grain offering* [a]Ezek 24:21; Hos 9:12 [b]Mal 1:10
13 [1]Lit *second* [2]Or *grain offering* [a]Jer 11:14
14 [a]Is 54:6 [b]Jer 9:2; Mal 3:5
15 [1]Or *Did He not make one, although He had the remnant* [2]Or *why one? He sought a godly offspring* [3]Lit *seed* [a]Gen 2:24; Matt 19:4 [b]Ruth 4:12; 1 Sam 2:20 [c]Ex 20:14; Lev 20:10
16 [1]Lit *He hates* [2]Lit *sending away* [3]Lit *he covers* [4]Or *violence* [a]Deut 24:1; Matt 5:31 [b]Ps 73:6; Is 59:6
17 [a]Is 43:22 [b]Is 5:20; Zeph 1:12 [c]Job 9:24 [d]2 Pet 3:4 [e]Is 5:19; Jer 17:15
3:1 [1]Or *angel* [2]Or *prepare* [3]Or *even* [a]Matt 11:10; Mark 1:2; Luke 1:76 [b]Hag 1:13; John 1:6 [c]Is 40:3 [d]Is 63:9

2 "But who can [a]endure the day of His coming? And who can stand when He appears? For He is like a [b]refiner's fire and like [1]fullers' soap.

3 "He will sit as a smelter and purifier of silver, and He will [a]purify the sons of Levi and refine them like gold and silver, so that they may [b]present to the LORD [1]offerings in righteousness.

4 "Then the [1]offering of Judah and Jerusalem will be [a]pleasing to the LORD as in the [b]days of old and as in former years.

5 ¶ "Then I will draw near to you for judgment; and I will be a swift witness against the [a]sorcerers and against the [b]adulterers and against those who [c]swear falsely, and against those who oppress the [d]wage earner in his wages, the [e]widow and the [1]orphan, and those who turn aside the [2f]alien and do not [3]fear Me," says the LORD of hosts.

6 "For [1]I, the LORD, [a]do not change; therefore you, O sons of Jacob, [2]are not consumed.

7 ¶ "From the [a]days of your fathers you have turned aside from My statutes and have not kept *them.* [b]Return to Me, and I will return to you," says the LORD of hosts. "But you say, 'How shall we return?'

You Have Robbed God

8 ¶ "Will a man [1]rob God? Yet you are robbing Me! But you say, 'How have we robbed You?' In [a]tithes and [2]offerings.

9 "You are [a]cursed with a curse, for you are [1]robbing Me, the whole nation *of you!*

10 "[a]Bring the whole tithe into the storehouse, so that there may be [1]food in My house, and test Me now in this," says the LORD of hosts, "if I will not [b]open for you the windows of heaven and [c]pour out for you a blessing until [2d]it overflows.

11 "Then I will rebuke the [a]devourer for you, so that it will not [1]destroy the fruits of the ground; nor will your vine in the field cast *its grapes,*" says the LORD of hosts.

12 "[a]All the nations will call you blessed, for you shall be a [b]delightful land," says the LORD of hosts.

13 ¶ "Your words have been [1]arrogant against Me," says the LORD. "Yet you say, 'What have we spoken against You?'

14 "You have said, 'It is [a]vain to serve God; and what [b]profit is it that we have kept His charge, and that we have walked in mourning before the LORD of hosts?

15 'So now we [a]call the arrogant blessed; not only are the doers of wickedness built up but they also test God and [b]escape.' "

The Book of Remembrance

16 ¶ Then those who [1]feared the LORD spoke to one another, and the LORD [a]gave attention and heard *it,* and a [b]book of remembrance was written before Him for those who [1]fear the LORD and who esteem His name.

17 "They will be [a]Mine," says the LORD of hosts, "on the [b]day that I [1]prepare *My* [2c]own possession, and I will [3]spare them as a man [3d]spares his own son who serves him."

18 So you will again [a]distinguish between the righteous and the wicked, between one who serves God and one who does not serve Him.

Final Admonition

4 "[1]For behold, the day is coming, [a]burning like a furnace; and all the arrogant and every evildoer will be [b]chaff; and the day that is coming will [c]set them ablaze," says the LORD of hosts, "so that it will leave them neither root nor branch."

2 "But for you who [1]fear My name, the [a]sun of righteousness will rise with [b]healing in its wings; and you will go forth and [c]skip about like calves from the stall.

3 "You will [a]tread down the wicked, for they will be [b]ashes under the soles of your feet [c]on the day [1]which I am preparing," says the LORD of hosts.

4 ¶ "[1a]Remember the law of Moses My servant, *even the* statutes and ordinances which I commanded him in Horeb for all Israel.

5 ¶ "Behold, I am going to send you [a]Elijah the prophet before the coming of the great and terrible day of the LORD.

6 "He will [1a]restore the hearts of the fathers to *their* children and the hearts of the children to their fathers, so that I will not come and [b]smite the land with a [2]curse."

2 [1]Lit *laundrymen's* [a]Is 33:14; Ezek 22:14; Rev 6:17 [b]Zech 13:9; Matt 3:10-12; 1 Cor 3:13-15
3 [1]Or *grain offerings* [a]Is 1:25; Dan 12:10 [b]Ps 4:5
4 [1]Or *grain offering* [a]Ps 51:17-19 [b]2 Chr 7:1-3
5 [1]Or *fatherless* [2]Or *sojourner* [3]Or *revere* [a]Deut 18:10; Jer 27:9 [b]Ezek 22:9-11 [c]Jer 5:2; Zech 5:4 [d]Lev 19:13 [e]Ex 22:22-24 [f]Deut 27:19
6 [1]Or *I am the LORD; I do not* [2]Or *have not come to an end* [a]Num 23:19; James 1:17
7 [a]Jer 7:25 [b]Zech 1:3
8 [1]Or *defraud* [2]Or *heave offerings* [a]Neh 13:11
9 [1]Or *defrauding* [a]Mal 2:2
10 [1]Lit *prey* [2]Or *there is not* room *enough* [a]Lev 27:30; Num 18:21-24; Deut 12:6; Neh 13:12 [b]Ps 78:23-29 [c]Ezek 34:26 [d]Lev 26:3-5
11 [1]Lit *ruin* [a]Joel 1:4
12 [a]Is 61:9 [b]Is 62:4
13 [1]Lit *strong*
14 [a]Jer 2:25 [b]Is 58:3
15 [a]Is 2:22; Mal 4:1 [b]Jer 7:10
16 [1]Or *revere(d)* [a]Ps 34:15; Jer 31:18-20 [b]Is 4:3; Dan 12:1
17 [1]Lit *make* [2]Or *special treasure* [3]Or *have (has) compassion on* [a]Is 43:1 [b]Is 4:2 [c]Ex 19:5; Deut 7:6; Is 43:21; 1 Pet 2:9 [d]Ps 103:13
18 [a]Gen 18:25; Amos 5:15
4:1 [1]Ch 3:19 in Heb [a]Ps 21:9; Nah 1:5; Mal 3:2; 2 Pet 3:7 [b]Is 5:24; Obad 18 [c]Is 9:18
2 [1]Or *revere* [a]2 Sam 23:4; Is 30:26 [b]Jer 30:17 [c]Is 35:6
3 [1]Or *when I act* [a]Job 40:12; Is 26:6; Mic 5:8 [b]Ezek 28:18 [c]Mal 3:17
4 [1]Ch 3:22 in Heb [a]Deut 4:23
5 [a]Matt 11:14; Mark 9:11-13; Luke 1:17; John 1:21
6 [1]Or *turn* [2]Or *ban of destruction* [a]Luke 1:17 [b]Is 11:4; Rev 19:15

From Malachi to Christ

THE PERSIAN PERIOD 450-330 B.C.

For about 200 years after Nehemiah's time the Persians controlled Judah, but the Jews were allowed to carry on their religious observances and were not interfered with. During this time Judah was ruled by high priests who were responsible to the Jewish government.

Rule of Alexander the Great

THE HELLENISTIC PERIOD 330-166 B.C.

In 333 B.C. the Persian armies stationed in Macedonia were defeated by Alexander the Great. He was convinced that Greek culture was the one force that could unify the world. Alexander permitted the Jews to observe their laws and even granted them exemption from tribute or tax during their sabbath years. When he built Alexandria in Egypt, he encouraged Jews to live there and gave them some of the same privileges he gave his Greek subjects.The Greek conquest prepared the way for the translation of the OT into Greek (Septuagint version) c.250 B.C.

Rule of the Ptolemies of Egypt

Rule of the Seleucids of Syria

THE HASMONEAN PERIOD 166-63 B.C.

When this historical period began, the Jews were being greatly oppressed. The Ptolemies had been tolerant of the Jews and their religious practices, but the Seleucid rulers were determined to force Hellenism on them. Copies of the Scriptures were ordered destroyed and laws were enforced with extreme cruelty. The oppressed Jews revolted, led by Judas the Maccabee.

Hasmonean Dynasty

THE ROMAN PERIOD 63 B.C. . . .

In the year 63 B.C. Pompey, the Roman general, captured Jerusalem, and the provinces of Palestine became subject to Rome. The local government was entrusted part of the time to princes and the rest of the time to procurators who were appointed by the emperors. Herod the Great was ruler of all Palestine at the time of Christ's birth.

Herod the Great rules as king; subject to Rome

410	Malachi c. 430 B.C.
400B.C.	
390	
380	
370	
360	
350	
340	
330	334-323 Alexander the Great conquers the East
	330-328 Alexander's years of power
320	320 Ptolemy (I) Soter conquers Jerusalem
310	311 Seleucus conquers Babylon; Seleucid dynasty begins
300	
290	
280	
270	
260	
250	
240	
230	226 Antiochus III (the Great) of Syria overpowers Palestine
220	223-187 Antiochus becomes Seleucid ruler of Syria
210	
200	198 Antiochus defeats Egypt and gains control of Palestine
190	
180	175-164 Antiochus (IV) Epiphanes rules Syria; Judaism is prohibited
170	
160	167 Mattathias and his sons rebel against Antiochus; Maccabean revolt begins
	166-160 Judas Maccabeus's leadership
150	160-143 Jonathan is high priest
140	142 Tower of Jerusalem cleansed
130	142-134 Simon becomes high priest; establishes Hasmonean dynasty
120	134-104 John Hyrcanus enlarges the independent Jewish state
110	
100	103 Aristobulus's rule
90	102-76 Alexander Janneus's rule
80	75-67 Rule of Salome Alexandra with Hyrcanus II as high priest
70	
60	66-63 Battle between Aristobulus II and Hyrcanus II
	63 Pompey invades Palestine; Roman rule begins
50	63-40 Hyrcanus II rules but is subject to Rome
40	40-37 Parthians conquer Jerusalem
30	37 Jerusalem besieged for six months
20	32 Herod defeated
10	19 Herod's temple begun
	16 Herod visits Agrippa
	4 Herod dies; Archelaus succeeds
10	
20	
A.D. 30	

NEW TESTAMENT

Matthew

Title and Background

The Gospel of Matthew was so named to distinguish it from the other Gospel accounts. There is only one gospel, but four accounts of it. So we have here Matthew's version of the "good news" from God. Matthew's name means "gift of the LORD."

Author and Date of Writing

All four of the canonical Gospels are anonymous, but the early church fathers were unanimous in holding that Matthew was the author of this Gospel. He was a tax collector and was also known as Levi. The Gospel was most likely written before the destruction of Jerusalem in A.D. 70.

Theme and Message

Matthew's main purpose is to prove to his Jewish readers that Jesus is their Messiah. He quotes the Old Testament often and uses the phrase "kingdom of heaven" frequently. The whole Gospel is woven around five great discourses: (1) chapters 5—7; (2) chapter 10; (3) chapter 13; (4) chapter 18; (5) chapters 24—25.

Outline

I. The Birth and Early Years of Jesus (1:1—2:23)
II. The Beginnings of Jesus' Ministry (3:1—4:11)
III. Jesus' Ministry in Galilee (4:12—14:12)
IV. Jesus' Withdrawals From Galilee (14:13—17:20)
V. Jesus' Last Ministry in Galilee (17:22—18:35)
VI. Jesus' Ministry in Judea and Perea (19:1—20:34)
VII. Passion Week (21:1—27:66)
VIII. The Resurrection (28:1–20)

The Genealogy of Jesus the Messiah

1 The [1]record of the genealogy of
[2]Jesus [3]the Messiah, [a]the son of
David, [b]the son of Abraham:
2 ¶ Abraham [1]was the father of
Isaac, [2]Isaac the father of Jacob, and Ja-
cob the father of [3]Judah and his brothers.
3 Judah was the father of Perez and
Zerah by Tamar, [a]Perez was the father of
Hezron, and Hezron the father of [1]Ram.
4 Ram was the father of Amminadab,
Amminadab the father of Nahshon, and
Nahshon the father of Salmon.
5 Salmon was the father of Boaz by
Rahab, Boaz was the father of Obed by
Ruth, and Obed the father of Jesse.
6 Jesse was the father of David the
king.
¶ David [a]was the father of Solomon by
[1]Bathsheba who had been the wife of
Uriah.
7 Solomon [a]was the father of Rehoboam, Rehoboam the father of Abijah,
and Abijah the father of [1]Asa.
8 Asa was the father of Jehoshaphat,
Jehoshaphat the father of [1]Joram, and Joram the father of Uzziah.
9 Uzziah was the father of [1]Jotham,
Jotham the father of Ahaz, and Ahaz the
father of Hezekiah.
10 Hezekiah was the father of Manasseh, Manasseh the father of [1]Amon, and
Amon the [a]father of Josiah.
11 Josiah became the father of [1]Jeco-
niah and his brothers, at the time of the
[a]deportation to Babylon.
12 ¶ After the [a]deportation to Babylon: Jeconiah became the father of [1]She-
altiel, and Shealtiel the father of Zerubbabel.
13 Zerubbabel was the father of [1]Abi-
hud, Abihud the father of Eliakim, and
Eliakim the father of Azor.
14 Azor was the father of Zadok, Zadok
the father of Achim, and Achim the father
of Eliud.
15 Eliud was the father of Eleazar, Ele-

1:1 [1]Lit *book* [2]Heb *Yeshua* (*Joshua*), meaning *The LORD saves* [3]Gr *Christos* (*Christ*), Gr for *Messiah*, which means *Anointed One* [a]2 Sam 7:12-16; Ps 89:3f; Is 9:6f; Matt 9:27; Luke 1:32; John 7:42; Acts 13:23; Rom 1:3; Rev 22:16 [b]Matt 1:1-6: *Luke 3:32-34*; Gen 22:18; Gal 3:16 **2** [1]Lit *fathered*, and throughout the genealogy [2]Lit *and...*, and throughout the genealogy [3]Gr *Judas*; names of people in the Old Testament are given in their Old Testament form **3** [1]Gr *Aram* [a]Ruth 4:18-22; 1 Chr 2:1-15; Matt 1:3-6 **6** [1]Lit *her of Uriah* [a]2 Sam 11:27 **7** [1]Gr *Asaph* [a]1 Chr 3:10ff **8** [1]Also Gr for *Jehoram* in 2 King 8:16; cf 1 Chron 3:11 **9** [1]Gr *Joatham* **10** [1]Gr *Amos* [a]1 Chr 3:14 **11** [1]*Jehoiachin* in 2 Kin 24:15 [a]2 Kin 24:14f; Jer 27:20; Matt 1:17 **12** [1]Gr *Salathiel* [a]2 Kin 24:14f; Jer 27:20; Matt 1:17 **13** [1]Gr *Abioud*, usually spelled *Abiud*

azar the father of Matthan, and Matthan the father of Jacob.

16 Jacob was the father of Joseph the husband of Mary, by whom Jesus was born, [a]who is called [1]the Messiah.

17 ¶ So all the generations from Abraham to David are fourteen generations; from David to the [a]deportation to Babylon, fourteen generations; and from the [a]deportation to Babylon to [1]the Messiah, fourteen generations.

Conception and Birth of Jesus

18 ¶ Now the birth of Jesus [1]Christ was as follows: when His [a]mother Mary had been [2]betrothed to Joseph, before they came together she was [b]found to be with child by the Holy Spirit.

19 And Joseph her husband, being a righteous man and not wanting to disgrace her, planned [1a]to send her away secretly.

20 But when he had considered this, behold, an angel of the Lord appeared to him in a dream, saying, "[a]Joseph, son of David, do not be afraid to take Mary as your wife; for [1]the Child who has been [2]conceived in her is of the Holy Spirit.

21 "She will bear a Son; and [a]you shall call His name Jesus, for [1]He [b]will save His people from their sins."

22 Now all this [1]took place to fulfill what was [a]spoken by the Lord through the prophet:

23 "[a]BEHOLD, THE VIRGIN SHALL BE WITH [b]CHILD AND SHALL BEAR A SON, AND THEY SHALL CALL HIS NAME [1]IMMANUEL," which translated means, "[c]GOD WITH US."

24 And Joseph [1]awoke from his sleep and did as the angel of the Lord commanded him, and took *Mary* as his wife,

25 [1]but kept her a virgin until she [a]gave birth to a Son; and [b]he called His name Jesus.

The Visit of the Magi

2 Now after Jesus was [a]born in Bethlehem of Judea in the days of [b]Herod the king, [1]magi from the east arrived in Jerusalem, saying,

2 "Where is He who has been born [a]King of the Jews? For we saw [b]His star in the east and have come to worship Him."

3 When Herod the king heard *this,* he was troubled, and all Jerusalem with him.

4 Gathering together all the chief priests and scribes of the people, he inquired of them where the [1]Messiah was to be born.

5 They said to him, "[a]In Bethlehem of Judea; for this is what has been written [1]by the prophet:

6 '[a]AND YOU, BETHLEHEM, LAND OF JUDAH,
ARE BY NO MEANS LEAST AMONG THE LEADERS OF JUDAH;
FOR OUT OF YOU SHALL COME FORTH A RULER
WHO WILL [b]SHEPHERD MY PEOPLE ISRAEL.' "

7 ¶ Then Herod secretly called the magi and determined from them [1]the exact time [a]the star appeared.

8 And he sent them to Bethlehem and said, "Go and search carefully for the Child; and when you have found *Him,* report to me, so that I too may come and worship Him."

9 After hearing the king, they went their way; and the star, which they had seen in the east, went on before them until it came and stood over *the place* where the Child was.

10 When they saw the star, they rejoiced exceedingly with great joy.

11 After coming into the house they saw the Child with [a]Mary His mother; and they [1]fell to the ground and [b]worshiped Him. Then, opening their treasures, they presented to Him gifts of gold, frankincense, and myrrh.

12 And having been [a]warned *by God* [b]in a dream not to return to Herod, the magi left for their own country by another way.

The Flight to Egypt

13 ¶ Now when they had gone, behold, an [a]angel of the Lord *[b]appeared to Joseph in a dream and said, "Get up! Take the Child and His mother and flee to Egypt, and remain there until I tell you; for Herod is going to search for the Child to destroy Him."

14 ¶ So [1]Joseph got up and took the Child and His mother while it was still night, and left for Egypt.

15 He [1]remained there until the death of Herod. *This was* to fulfill what had been spoken by the Lord through the prophet: "[a]OUT OF EGYPT I CALLED [b]MY SON."

Herod Slaughters Babies

16 ¶ Then when Herod saw that he had been tricked by [a]the magi, he became very enraged, and sent and [b]slew all the male children who were in Bethlehem and all its vicinity, from two years old and under, according to the time which he had determined from the magi.

17 Then what had been spoken through Jeremiah the prophet was fulfilled:

18 "[a]A VOICE WAS HEARD IN RAMAH,
WEEPING AND GREAT MOURNING,

---

16 [1]Gr *Christos (Christ)* [a]Matt 27:17,22; Luke 2:11; John 4:25
17 [1]Gr *Christos (Christ)* [a]2 Kin 24:14f; Jer 27:20; Matt 1:11,12
18 [1]I.e. The Messiah [2]The first stage of marriage in Jewish culture, usually lasting for a year before the wedding night, more legal than an engagement [a]Matt 12:46; Luke 1:27 [b]Luke 1:35
19 [1]Or *to divorce her* [a]Deut 22:20-24; 24:1-4; John 8:4, 5
20 [1]Lit *that which* [2]Lit *begotten* [a]Luke 2:4
21 [1]Lit *He Himself* [a]Luke 1:31; 2:21 [b]Luke 2:11; John 1:29; Acts 4:12; 5:31; 13:23,38,39; Col 1:20-23
22 [1]Lit *has happened* [a]Luke 24:44; Rom 1:2-4
23 [1]Or *Emmanuel* [a]Is 7:14 [b]Is 9:6,7 [c]Is 8:10
24 [1]Lit *got up*
25 [1]Lit *and was not knowing her* [a]Luke 2:7 [b]Matt 1:21; Luke 2:21
2:1 [1]A caste of wise men specializing in astronomy, astrology, and natural science [a]Mic 5:2; Luke 2:4-7 [b]Luke 1:5
2 [a]Jer 23:5; 30:9; Zech 9:9; Matt 27:11; Luke 19:38; 23:38; John 1:49 [b]Num 24:17
4 [1]Gr *Christos (Christ)*
5 [1]Or *through* [a]John 7:42
6 [a]Mic 5:2; John 7:42 [b]John 21:16
7 [1]Lit *the time of the appearing star* [a]Num 24:17
11 [1]Lit *prostrated;* i.e. face down in a prone position to indicate worship [a]Matt 1:18; 12:46 [b]Matt 14:33
12 [a]Matt 2:13, 19,22; Luke 2:26; Acts 10:22; Heb 8:5; 11:7 [b]Job 33:15, 16; Matt 1:20
13 [a]Acts 5:19; 10:7; 12:7-11 [b]Matt 2:12,19
14 [1]Lit *he*
15 [1]Lit *was* [a]Hos 11:1; Num 24:8 [b]Ex 4:22f
16 [a]Matt 2:1 [b]Is 59:7
18 [a]Jer 31:15

RACHEL WEEPING FOR HER
CHILDREN;
AND SHE REFUSED TO BE
COMFORTED,
BECAUSE THEY WERE NO MORE."
19 ¶ But when Herod died, behold, an
angel of the Lord *[a]appeared in a dream
to Joseph in Egypt, and said,
20 "Get up, take the Child and His
mother, and go into the land of Israel; for
those who sought the Child's life are
dead."
21 So [1]Joseph got up, took the Child
and His mother, and came into the land
of Israel.
22 But when he heard that Archelaus
was reigning over Judea in place of his
father Herod, he was afraid to go there.
Then after being [a]warned *by God* in a
dream, he left for the regions of Galilee,
23 and came and lived in a city called
[a]Nazareth. *This was* to fulfill what was
spoken through the prophets: "He shall
be called a [b]Nazarene."

The Preaching of John the Baptist

3 Now [a]in those days [b]John the Baptist *[1]came, [2]preaching in the [c]wil-
derness of Judea, saying,
2 "[a]Repent, for [b]the kingdom of
heaven [1]is at hand."
3 For this is the [a]one referred to [1]by
Isaiah the prophet when he said,
"[b]THE VOICE OF ONE [2]CRYING IN
THE WILDERNESS,
'[c]MAKE READY THE WAY OF THE
LORD,
MAKE HIS PATHS STRAIGHT!' "
4 Now John himself had [1a]a garment of camel's hair and a leather belt
around his waist; and his food was [b]lo-
custs and wild honey.
5 Then Jerusalem [a]was going out to
him, and all Judea and all [b]the district
around the Jordan;
6 and they were being [a]baptized by
him in the Jordan River, as they confessed their sins.
7 ¶ But when he saw many of the
[a]Pharisees and [b]Sadducees coming for
baptism, he said to them, "You [c]brood of
vipers, who warned you to flee from [d]the
wrath to come?
8 "[a]Therefore bear fruit [b]in keeping
with repentance;
9 and do not suppose that you can say
to yourselves, '[a]We have Abraham for
our father'; for I say to you that from
these stones God is able to raise up children to Abraham.
10 "The [a]axe is already laid at the root
of the trees; therefore [b]every tree that
does not bear good fruit is cut down and
thrown into the fire.
11 ¶ "As for me, [a]I baptize you [1]with
water for repentance, but He who is coming after me is mightier than I, and I am
not fit to remove His sandals; [b]He will
baptize you [1]with the Holy Spirit and
fire.
12 "His [a]winnowing fork is in His
hand, and He will thoroughly clear His
threshing floor; and He will [b]gather
His wheat into the barn, but He will
burn up the [c]chaff with [d]unquenchable
fire."

The Baptism of Jesus

13 ¶ [a]Then Jesus *arrived [b]from Galilee at the Jordan *coming* to John, to be
baptized by him.
14 But John tried to prevent Him, saying, "I have need to be baptized by You,
and do You come to me?"
15 But Jesus answering said to him,
"Permit *it* at this time; for in this way it
is fitting for us [a]to fulfill all righteousness." Then he *permitted Him.
16 After being baptized, Jesus came up
immediately from the water; and behold,
the heavens were opened, and [1a]he saw
the Spirit of God descending as a dove
and [2]lighting on Him,
17 and behold, a voice out of the heavens said, "[a]This is [1]My beloved Son, in
whom I am well-pleased."

The Temptation of Jesus

4 [a]Then Jesus was led up by the Spirit
into the wilderness [b]to be tempted
by the devil.
2 And after He had [a]fasted forty days
and forty nights, He [1]then became hungry.
3 And [a]the tempter came and said to
Him, "If You are the [b]Son of God, command that these stones become bread."
4 But He answered and said, "It is
written, '[a]MAN SHALL NOT LIVE ON BREAD
ALONE, BUT ON EVERY WORD THAT PROCEEDS
OUT OF THE MOUTH OF GOD.' "
5 ¶ Then the devil *took Him into
[a]the holy city and had Him stand on the
pinnacle of the temple,
6 and *said to Him, "If You are the
Son of God, throw Yourself down; for it is
written,
'[a]HE WILL COMMAND HIS ANGELS
CONCERNING YOU';
and
'ON *their* HANDS THEY WILL BEAR
YOU UP,
SO THAT YOU WILL NOT STRIKE
YOUR FOOT AGAINST A STONE.' "
7 Jesus said to him, "[1]On the other

19 [a]Matt 1:20 **21** [1]Lit *he* **22** [a]Matt 2:12 **23** [a]Luke 1:26; John 1:45 [b]Mark 1:24; John 18:5 **3:1** [1]Or *arrived*, or *appeared* [2]Or *proclaiming as a herald* [a]Matt 3:1-12: *Mark 1:3-8; Luke 3:2-17*; John 1:6-8 [b]Matt 11:11-14 [c]Josh 15:61; Judg 1:16 **2** [1]Lit *has come near* [a]Matt 4:17 [b]Dan 2:44; Matt 4:17; Mark 1:15; Luke 10:9f **3** [1]Or *through* [2]Or *shouting* [a]Luke 1:17 [b]Is 40:3 [c]John 1:23 **4** [1]Lit *his garment* [a]2 Kin 1:8; Zech 13:4; Matt 11:8; Mark 1:6 [b]Lev 11:22 **5** [a]Mark 1:5 [b]Luke 3:3 **6** [a]Matt 3:11; Mark 1:5; John 1:25; Acts 1:5 **7** [a]Matt 16:1ff [b]Matt 22:23; Acts 4:1 [c]Matt 12:34 [d]1 Thess 1:10 **8** [a]Luke 3:8; Eph 5:8 [b]Acts 26:20 **9** [a]Luke 3:8; John 8:33; Acts 13:26; Rom 4:1; Gal 3:29 **10** [a]Luke 3:9 [b]Ps 92:12-14; Matt 7:19; John 15:2 **11** [1]The Gr here can be translated *in*, *with* or *by* [a]Mark 1:4; Luke 3:16; John 1:26f; Acts 1:5 [b]John 1:33; Acts 2:3; Titus 3:5 **12** [a]Is 30:24; Jer 15:7; Luke 3:17 [b]Matt 13:30 [c]Ps 1:4 [d]Is 66:24; Jer 7:20; Matt 13:41; Mark 9:43 **13** [a]Matt 3:13-17: *Mark 1:9-11; Luke 3:21,22*; John 1:31-34 [b]Matt 2:22 **15** [a]Ps 40:7; John 4:34 **16** [1]Or *He* [2]Lit *coming upon Him* [a]Mark 1:10; Luke 3:22; John 1:32; Acts 7:56 **17** [1]Or *My Son, the Beloved* [a]Ps 2:7; Is 42:1; Matt 12:18; Mark 9:7; Luke 9:35; John 12:28 **4:1** [a]Matt 4:1-11: *Mark 1:12,13; Luke 4:1-13* [b]Heb 4:15; James 1:14 **2** [1]Lit *later became*; or *afterward became* [a]Ex 34:28; 1 Kin 19:8 **3** [a]1 Thess 3:5 [b]Matt 14:33; Mark 3:11; Luke 1:35; John 1:34; Acts 9:20 **4** [a]Deut 8:3 **5** [a]Neh 11:1; Dan 9:24; Matt 27:53 **6** [a]Ps 91:11 **7** [1]Lit *Again*

hand, it is written, '[a]YOU SHALL NOT PUT
THE LORD YOUR GOD TO THE TEST.' "
8 ¶ [a]Again, the devil *took Him to a
very high mountain and *showed Him
all the kingdoms of the world and their
glory;
9 and he said to Him, "[a]All these
things I will give You, if You fall down and
[1]worship me."
10 Then Jesus *said to him, "Go, Satan! For it is written, '[a]YOU SHALL WOR-
SHIP THE LORD YOUR GOD, AND [1]SERVE HIM
ONLY.' "
11 Then the devil *left Him; and behold, [a]angels came and *began* to minister
to Him.

Jesus Begins His Ministry

12 ¶ Now when Jesus heard that
[a]John had been taken into custody, [b]He
withdrew into Galilee;
13 and leaving Nazareth, He came and
[a]settled in Capernaum, which is by the
sea, in the region of Zebulun and Naphtali.
14 *This was* to fulfill what was spoken
through Isaiah the prophet:
15 "[a]THE LAND OF ZEBULUN AND THE
LAND OF NAPHTALI,
[1]BY THE WAY OF THE SEA, BEYOND
THE JORDAN, GALILEE OF THE
[2]GENTILES—
16 "[a]THE PEOPLE WHO WERE SITTING IN
DARKNESS SAW A GREAT LIGHT,
AND THOSE WHO WERE SITTING IN
THE LAND AND SHADOW OF
DEATH,
UPON THEM A LIGHT DAWNED."
17 ¶ [a]From that time Jesus began to
[1]preach and say, "[b]Repent, for the kingdom of heaven is at hand."

The First Disciples

18 ¶ [a]Now as Jesus was walking by
[b]the Sea of Galilee, He saw two brothers,
[c]Simon who was called Peter, and Andrew his brother, casting a net into the
sea; for they were fishermen.
19 And He *said to them, "[1]Follow
Me, and I will make you fishers of men."
20 Immediately they left their nets and
followed Him.
21 Going on from there He saw two
other brothers, [1a]James the *son* of Zebedee, and [2]John his brother, in the boat
with Zebedee their father, mending their
nets; and He called them.
22 Immediately they left the boat and
their father, and followed Him.

Ministry in Galilee

23 ¶ Jesus was going [a]throughout all
Galilee, [b]teaching in their synagogues
and [c]proclaiming the [1]gospel of the
kingdom, and [d]healing every kind of disease and every kind of sickness among
the people.
24 ¶ The news about Him spread
[a]throughout all Syria; and they brought
to Him all who were ill, those suffering
with various diseases and pains, [b]demo-
niacs, [1c]epileptics, [d]paralytics; and He
healed them.
25 Large crowds [a]followed Him from
Galilee and [b]*the* Decapolis and Jerusalem
and Judea and *from* [c]beyond the Jordan.

The Sermon on the Mount
The Beatitudes

5 [a]When Jesus saw the crowds, He
went up on [b]the [1]mountain; and after He sat down, His disciples came to
Him.
2 [a]He opened His mouth and *began*
to teach them, saying,
3 ¶ "[1a]Blessed are the [2]poor in
spirit, for [b]theirs is the kingdom of
heaven.
4 ¶ "Blessed are [a]those who mourn,
for they shall be comforted.
5 ¶ "Blessed are [a]the [1]gentle, for
they shall inherit the earth.
6 ¶ "Blessed are [a]those who hunger
and thirst for righteousness, for they shall
be satisfied.
7 ¶ "Blessed are [a]the merciful, for
they shall receive mercy.
8 ¶ "Blessed are [a]the pure in heart,
for [b]they shall see God.
9 ¶ "Blessed are the peacemakers, for
[a]they shall be called sons of God.
10 ¶ "Blessed are those who have
been [a]persecuted for the sake of righteousness, for [b]theirs is the kingdom of
heaven.
11 ¶ "Blessed are you when *people*
[a]insult you and persecute you, and falsely say all kinds of evil against you because
of Me.
12 "Rejoice and be glad, for your reward in heaven is great; for [a]in the same
way they persecuted the prophets who
were before you.

Disciples and the World

13 ¶ "You are the salt of the earth; but
[a]if the salt has become tasteless, how
[1]can it be made salty *again*? It is no longer good for anything, except to be thrown
out and trampled under foot by men.
14 ¶ "You are [a]the light of the world.
A city set on a [1]hill cannot be hidden;

7 [a]Deut 6:16 **8** [a]Matt 16:26; 1 John 2:15-17 **9** [1]Lit *prostrate Yourself* [a]1 Cor 10:20f **10** [1]Or *fulfill religious duty to Him* [a]Deut 6:13 **11** [a]Matt 26:53; Luke 22:43; Heb 1:14 **12** [a]Matt 14:3; Mark 1:14; Luke 3:20; John 3:24 [b]Mark 1:14; Luke 4:14; John 1:43 **13** [a]Matt 11:23; Mark 1:21; Luke 4:23; John 2:12 **15** [1]Or *Toward the sea* [2]Lit *nations*, usually non-Jewish [a]Is 9:1 **16** [a]Is 9:2; Luke 2:32 **17** [1]Or *proclaim* [a]Mark 1:14 [b]Matt 3:2 **18** [a]Matt 4:18-22: *Mark 1:16-20*; Luke 5:2-11; John 1:40-42 [b]Matt 15:29; Mark 7:31; Luke 5:1; John 6:1 [c]Matt 10:2; John 1:40-42 **19** [1]Lit *Come here after Me* **21** [1]Or *Jacob*; James is the Eng form of Jacob [2]Gr *Joannes*, Heb *Johanan* [a]Matt 10:2 **23** [1]Or *good news* [a]Mark 1:39; Luke 4:14 [b]Matt 9:35; Mark 1:21; Luke 4:15; John 6:59 [c]Matt 3:2; Mark 1:14; Luke 4:43; Acts 20:25 [d]Matt 8:16; Mark 1:34; Luke 4:40; Acts 10:38 **24** [1]Lit *moonstruck* [a]Mark 7:26; Luke 2:2; Acts 15:23; Gal 1:21 [b]Matt 8:16; Mark 1:32; Luke 8:36; John 10:21 [c]Matt 17:15 [d]Matt 8:6; Mark 2:3-5; Luke 5:24 **25** [a]Mark 3:7; Luke 6:17 [b]Mark 5:20 [c]Matt 4:15
5:1 [1]Or *hill* [a]Matt ch 5-7; Luke 6:20-49 [b]Mark 3:13; Luke 6:17; John 6:3 **2** [a]Matt 13:35; Acts 8:35 **3** [1]I.e. fortunate or prosperous, and so throughout v 11 [2]I.e. those who are not spiritually arrogant [a]Matt 5:3-12; Luke 6:20-23 [b]Matt 5:10; Mark 10:14; Luke 6:20 **4** [a]Is 61:2; John 16:20; Rev 7:17 **5** [1]Or *humble, meek* [a]Ps 37:11 **6** [a]Is 55:1; John 4:14 **7** [a]Prov 11:17; Matt 6:14 **8** [a]Ps 24:4 [b]Heb 12:14; 1 John 3:2; Rev 22:4 **9** [a]Matt 5:45; Luke 6:35; Rom 8:14 **10** [a]1 Pet 3:14 [b]Matt 5:3; Mark 10:14; Luke 6:20 **11** [a]1 Pet 4:14 **12** [a]2 Chr 36:16; Matt 23:37; Acts 7:52; 1 Thess 2:15; Heb 11:33ff; James 5:10 **13** [1]Lit *will* [a]Mark 9:50; Luke 14:34f **14** [1]Or *mountain* [a]Prov 4:18; John 8:12

15 [a]nor does *anyone* light a lamp and put it under a [1]basket, but on the lampstand, and it gives light to all who are in the house.

16 "Let your light shine before men in such a way that they may [a]see your good works, and [b]glorify your Father who is in heaven.

17 ¶"Do not think that I came to abolish the [a]Law or the Prophets; I did not come to abolish but to fulfill.

18 "For truly I say to you, [a]until heaven and earth pass away, not [1]the smallest letter or stroke shall pass from the Law until all is accomplished.

19 "Whoever then annuls one of the least of these commandments, and teaches [1]others *to do* the same, shall be called least [a]in the kingdom of heaven; but whoever [2]keeps and teaches *them*, he shall be called great in the kingdom of heaven.

20 ¶"For I say to you that unless your [a]righteousness surpasses *that* of the scribes and Pharisees, you will not enter the kingdom of heaven.

Personal Relationships

21 ¶"[a]You have heard that [1]the ancients were told, '[b]YOU SHALL NOT COMMIT MURDER' and 'Whoever commits murder shall be [2]liable to [c]the court.'

22 "But I say to you that everyone who is angry with his brother shall be [1]guilty before [a]the court; and whoever says to his brother, '[2]You good-for-nothing,' shall be [1]guilty before [3b]the supreme court; and whoever says, 'You fool,' shall be [1]guilty *enough to go* into the [4c]fiery hell.

23 "Therefore if you are [a]presenting your [1]offering at the altar, and there remember that your brother has something against you,

24 leave your [1]offering there before the altar and go; first be [a]reconciled to your brother, and then come and present your [1]offering.

25 "[a]Make friends quickly with your opponent at law while you are with him on the way, so that your opponent may not hand you over to the judge, and the judge to the officer, and you be thrown into prison.

26 "Truly I say to you, [a]you will not come out of there until you have paid up the last [1]cent.

27 ¶"[a]You have heard that it was said, '[b]YOU SHALL NOT COMMIT ADULTERY';

28 but I say to you that everyone who looks at a woman [a]with lust for her has already committed adultery with her in his heart.

29 "[a]If your right eye makes you [1]stumble, tear it out and throw it from you; for it is better for you [2]to lose one of the parts of your body, [3]than for your whole body to be thrown into [4b]hell.

30 "[a]If your right hand makes you [1]stumble, cut it off and throw it from you; for it is better for you [2]to lose one of the parts of your body, [3]than for your whole body to go into [4b]hell.

31 ¶"It was said, '[a]WHOEVER SENDS HIS WIFE AWAY, LET HIM GIVE HER A CERTIFICATE OF DIVORCE';

32 [a]but I say to you that everyone who [1]divorces his wife, except for *the* reason of unchastity, makes her commit adultery; and whoever marries a [2]divorced woman commits adultery.

33 ¶"Again, [a]you have heard that [1]the ancients were told, '[2b]YOU SHALL NOT [3]MAKE FALSE VOWS, BUT SHALL FULFILL YOUR [4]VOWS TO THE LORD.'

34 "But I say to you, [a]make no oath at all, either by heaven, for it is [b]the throne of God,

35 or by the earth, for it is the [a]footstool of His feet, or [1]by Jerusalem, for it is [b]THE CITY OF THE GREAT KING.

36 "Nor shall you make an oath by your head, for you cannot make one hair white or black.

37 "But let your statement be, 'Yes, yes' *or* 'No, no'; anything beyond these is [1]of [a]evil.

38 ¶"[a]You have heard that it was said, '[b]AN EYE FOR AN EYE, AND A TOOTH FOR A TOOTH.'

39 "But I say to you, do not resist an evil person; but [a]whoever slaps you on your right cheek, turn the other to him also.

40 "If anyone wants to sue you and take your [1]shirt, let him have your [2]coat also.

41 "Whoever [1]forces you to go one mile, go with him two.

42 "[a]Give to him who asks of you, and do not turn away from him who wants to borrow from you.

43 ¶"[a]You have heard that it was said, '[b]YOU SHALL LOVE YOUR NEIGHBOR [c]and hate your enemy.'

44 "But I say to you, [a]love your enemies and pray for those who persecute you,

45 so that you may [1]be [a]sons of your Father who is in heaven; for He causes His sun to rise on *the* evil and *the* good, and sends rain on *the* righteous and *the* unrighteous.

15 [1]Or *peck-measure* [a]Mark 4:21; Luke 8:16; Phil 2:15
16 [a]1 Pet 2:12 [b]Matt 9:8
17 [a]Matt 7:12
18 [1]Lit *one iota* (Heb yodh) or *one projection of a letter* (serif) [a]Matt 24:35; Luke 16:17
19 [1]Gr *anthropoi* [2]Lit *does* [a]Matt 11:11
20 [a]Luke 18:11
21 [1]Lit *it was said to the ancients* [2]Or *guilty before* [a]Matt 5:27 [b]Ex 20:13; Deut 5:17 [c]Deut 16:18; 2 Chr 19:5f
22 [1]Or *liable to* [2]Or *empty-head*; Gr *Raka (Raca)* fr Aram *reqa* [3]Lit *the Sanhedrin* [4]Lit *Gehenna of fire* [a]Deut 16:18; 2 Chr 19:5f [b]Matt 10:17; Mark 13:9; Luke 22:66; John 11:47; Acts 4:15 [c]Matt 5:29f; Mark 9:43ff; Luke 12:5; James 3:6
23 [1]Or *gift* [a]Matt 5:24
24 [1]Or *gift* [a]Rom 12:17
25 [a]Prov 25:8f; Luke 12:58
26 [1]Lit *quadrans* (equaling two mites); i.e. 1/64 of a daily wage [a]Luke 12:59
27 [a]Matt 5:21 [b]Ex 20:14; Deut 5:18
28 [a]2 Sam 11:2-5; Job 31:1; Matt 15:19; James 1:14
29 [1]I.e. sin [2]Lit *that one...be lost* [3]Lit *not your whole body* [4]Gr *Gehenna* [a]Matt 18:9; Mark 9:47 [b]Matt 5:22
30 [1]I.e. sin [2]Lit *that one...be lost* [3]Lit *not your whole body* [4]Gr *Gehenna* [a]Matt 18:8; Mark 9:43 [b]Matt 5:22
31 [a]Deut 24:1; Jer 3:1; Matt 19:7; Mark 10:4
32 [1]Or *sends away* [2]Or *sent away* [a]Matt 19:9; Mark 10:11f; Luke 16:18; 1 Cor 7:11f
33 [1]Lit *it was said to the ancients* [2]*you* and *your* are singular here [3]Or *break your vows* [4]Lit *oaths* [a]Matt 5:21 [b]Lev 19:12; Num 30:2; Deut 23:21
34 [a]James 5:12 [b]Is 66:1; Matt 23:22
35 [1]Or *toward* [a]Is 66:1; Acts 7:49 [b]Ps 48:2
37 [1]Or *from the evil one* [a]Matt 6:13; John 17:15; 2 Thess 3:3; 1 John 2:13f
38 [a]Matt 5:21 [b]Ex 21:24; Lev 24:20; Deut 19:21 **39** [a]Matt 5:39-42: Luke 6:29; 1 Cor 6:7 **40** [1]Lit *tunic*; i.e. a garment worn next to the body [2]Lit *cloak*; i.e. an outer garment
41 [1]Lit *will force* **42** [a]Deut 15:7-11; Luke 6:34f; 1 Tim 6:18
43 [a]Matt 5:21 [b]Lev 19:18 [c]Deut 23:3-6 **44** [a]Luke 6:27f; Acts 7:60; Rom 12:20 **45** [1]Or *show yourselves to be* [a]Matt 5:9; Luke 6:35; Acts 14:17

46 "For [a]if you love those who love you, what reward do you have? Do not even the tax collectors do the same?

47 "If you greet only your brothers, what more are you doing *than others*? Do not even the Gentiles do the same?

48 "Therefore [1a]you are to be perfect, as your heavenly Father is perfect.

Giving to the Poor and Prayer

6 "Beware of practicing your righteousness before men [a]to be noticed by them; otherwise you have no reward with your Father who is in heaven.

2 ¶ "So when you [1]give to the poor, do not sound a trumpet before you, as the hypocrites do in the synagogues and in the streets, so that they [a]may be honored by men. [b]Truly I say to you, they have their reward in full.

3 "But when you [1]give to the poor, do not let your left hand know what your right hand is doing,

4 so that your [1]giving will be in secret; and [a]your Father who sees *what is done* in secret will reward you.

5 ¶ "When you pray, you are not to be like the hypocrites; for they love to [a]stand and pray in the synagogues and on the street corners [1b]so that they may be seen by men. [c]Truly I say to you, they have their reward in full.

6 "But you, when you pray, [a]go into your inner room, close your door and pray to your Father who is in secret, and [b]your Father who sees *what is done* in secret will reward you.

7 ¶ "And when you are praying, do not use meaningless repetition as the Gentiles do, for they suppose that they will be heard for their [a]many words.

8 "So do not be like them; for [a]your Father knows what you need before you ask Him.

9 ¶ "[a]Pray, then, in this way:
'Our Father who is in heaven,
Hallowed be Your name.
10 '[a]Your kingdom come.
[b]Your will be done,
On earth as it is in heaven.
11 '[a]Give us this day [1]our daily bread.
12 'And [a]forgive us our debts, as we also have forgiven our debtors.
13 'And do not lead us into temptation, but [a]deliver us from [1b]evil. [2][For Yours is the kingdom and the power and the glory forever. Amen.]'

14 "[a]For if you forgive [1]others for their transgressions, your heavenly Father will also forgive you.

46 [a]Luke 6:32 **48** [1]Lit *you shall be* [a]Lev 19:2; Deut 18:13; 2 Cor 7:1; Phil 3:12-15
6:1 [a]Matt 6:5
2 [1]Or *give alms* [a]Matt 6:5 [b]Matt 6:5; Luke 6:24
3 [1]Or *give alms*
4 [1]Or *alms* [a]Jer 17:10; Matt 6:6; Heb 4:13
5 [1]Lit *to be apparent to men* [a]Mark 11:25; Luke 18:11 [b]Matt 6:1 [c]Matt 6:2; Luke 6:24
6 [a]Is 26:20; Matt 26:36-39; Acts 9:40 [b]Matt 6:4
7 [a]1 Kin 18:26f
8 [a]Ps 38:9; Matt 6:32; Luke 12:30
9 [a]Matt 6:9-13: *Luke 11:2-4*
10 [a]Matt 3:2 [b]Matt 26:42; Luke 22:42; Acts 21:14
11 [1]Or *our bread for tomorrow* [a]Prov 30:8; Is 33:16; Luke 11:3
12 [a]Ex 34:7; Ps 32:1; Matt 9:2; Eph 1:7; 1 John 1:7-9
13 [1]Or *the evil one* [2]This clause not found in early mss [a]John 17:15; 1 Cor 10:13; 2 Thess 3:3; 2 Tim 4:18; 2 Pet 2:9; 1 John 5:18 [b]Matt 5:37
14 [1]Gr *anthropoi* [a]Matt 7:2; Mark 11:25f; Eph 4:32; Col 3:13
15 [1]Gr *anthropoi* [a]Matt 18:35
16 [1]Lit *distort their faces*, i.e. discolor their faces with make-up [a]Is 58:5 [b]Matt 6:2
17 [a]Ruth 3:3; 2 Sam 12:20
18 [a]Matt 6:4
19 [a]Prov 23:4; Matt 19:21; Luke 12:21; 1 Tim 6:9; Heb 13:5; James 5:2
20 [a]Matt 19:21; Luke 12:33; 1 Tim 6:19
21 [a]Luke 12:34
22 [1]Or *healthy*; or *sincere* [a]Matt 6:22: *Luke 11:34*
23 [1]Or *evil* [a]Matt 20:15; Mark 7:22
24 [1]*mamona*, Gr for Ara *mammon;* i.e. wealth, etc, personified as an object of worship [a]1 Kin 18:21; Luke 16:13; Gal 1:10; James 4:4 [b]Luke 16:9
25 [1]Or *stop being worried* [2]Lit *soul* [a]Matt 6:25-33: *Luke 12:22-31* [b]Matt 6:27; Luke 10:41; Phil 4:6; 1 Pet 5:7 **26** [1]Lit *heaven* [a]Job 35:11; Ps 104:27; Matt 10:29ff; Luke 12:24 **27** [1]Lit *cubit* (approx 18 in.) [2]Or *height* [a]Matt 6:25; Luke 10:41; Phil 4:6; 1 Pet 5:7 [b]Ps 39:5 **28** [a]Matt 6:25; Luke 10:41; Phil 4:6; 1 Pet 5:7

15 "But [a]if you do not forgive [1]others, then your Father will not forgive your transgressions.

Fasting
The True Treasure
Wealth (Mammon)

16 ¶ "[a]Whenever you fast, do not put on a gloomy face as the hypocrites *do*, for they [1]neglect their appearance so that they will be noticed by men when they are fasting. [b]Truly I say to you, they have their reward in full.

17 "But you, when you fast, [a]anoint your head and wash your face

18 so that your fasting will not be noticed by men, but by your Father who is in secret; and your [a]Father who sees *what is done* in secret will reward you.

19 ¶ "[a]Do not store up for yourselves treasures on earth, where moth and rust destroy, and where thieves break in and steal.

20 "But store up for yourselves [a]treasures in heaven, where neither moth nor rust destroys, and where thieves do not break in or steal;

21 for [a]where your treasure is, there your heart will be also.

22 ¶ "[a]The eye is the lamp of the body; so then if your eye is [1]clear, your whole body will be full of light.

23 "But if [a]your eye is [1]bad, your whole body will be full of darkness. If then the light that is in you is darkness, how great is the darkness!

24 ¶ "[a]No one can serve two masters; for either he will hate the one and love the other, or he will be devoted to one and despise the other. You cannot serve God and [1b]wealth.

The Cure for Anxiety

25 ¶ "[a]For this reason I say to you, [1]do not be [b]worried about your [2]life, *as to* what you will eat or what you will drink; nor for your body, *as to* what you will put on. Is not life more than food, and the body more than clothing?

26 "[a]Look at the birds of the [1]air, that they do not sow, nor reap nor gather into barns, and *yet* your heavenly Father feeds them. Are you not worth much more than they?

27 "And who of you by being [a]worried can [b]add a *single* [1]hour to his [2]life?

28 "And why are you [a]worried about clothing? Observe how the lilies of the field grow; they do not toil nor do they spin,

29 yet I say to you that not even [a]Solomon in all his glory clothed himself like one of these.

30 "But if God so clothes the [a]grass of the field, which is *alive* today and tomorrow is thrown into the furnace, *will He* not much more *clothe* you? [b]You of little faith!

31 "Do not [a]worry then, saying, 'What will we eat?' or 'What will we drink?' or 'What will we wear for clothing?'

32 "For the Gentiles eagerly seek all these things; for [a]your heavenly Father knows that you need all these things.

33 "But [1]seek first [2]His kingdom and His righteousness, and [a]all these things will be [3]added to you.

34 ¶ "So do not [a]worry about tomorrow; for tomorrow will [1]care for itself. [2]Each day has enough trouble of its own.

Judging Others

7 "[a]Do not judge so that you will not be judged.

2 "For in the way you judge, you will be judged; and [1a]by your standard of measure, it will be measured to you.

3 "Why do you [a]look at the speck that is in your brother's eye, but do not notice the log that is in your own eye?

4 "[a]Or how [1]can you say to your brother, 'Let me take the speck out of your eye,' and behold, the log is in your own eye?

5 "You hypocrite, first take the log out of your own eye, and then you will see clearly to take the speck out of your brother's eye.

6 ¶ "[a]Do not give what is holy to dogs, and do not throw your pearls before swine, or they will trample them under their feet, and turn and tear you to pieces.

Prayer and the Golden Rule

7 ¶ "[1a]Ask, and [b]it will be given to you; [2]seek, and you will find; [3]knock, and it will be opened to you.

8 "For everyone who asks receives, and he who seeks finds, and to him who knocks it will be opened.

9 "Or what man is there among you [1]who, when his son asks for a loaf, [2]will give him a stone?

10 "Or [1]if he asks for a fish, he will not give him a snake, will he?

11 "If you then, being evil, know how to give good gifts to your children, [a]how much more will your Father who is in heaven give what is good to those who ask Him!

12 ¶ "In everything, [a]therefore, [1]treat people the same way you want [2]them to treat you, for [b]this is the Law and the Prophets.

29 [a]1 Kin 10:4-7; 2 Chr 9:4-6
30 [a]James 1:10; 1 Pet 1:24 [b]Matt 8:26
31 [a]Matt 6:25; Luke 10:41; Phil 4:6; 1 Pet 5:7
32 [a]Matt 6:8; Phil 4:19
33 [1]Or *continually seek* [2]Or *the kingdom* [3]Or *provided* [a]Matt 19:28; Mark 10:29f; Luke 18:29f; 1 Tim 4:8
34 [1]Lit *worry about itself* [2]Lit *Sufficient for the day is its evils* [a]Matt 6:25; Luke 10:41; Phil 4:6; 1 Pet 5:7
7:1 [a]Matt 7:1-5: *Luke 6:37f,41f*; Rom 14:10
2 [1]Lit *by what measure you measure* [a]Mark 4:24; Luke 6:38
3 [a]Rom 2:1
4 [1]Lit *will* [a]Luke 6:42
6 [a]Matt 15:26
7 [1]Or *Keep asking* [2]Or *keep seeking* [3]Or *keep knocking* [a]Matt 7:7-11: *Luke 11:9-13* [b]Matt 18:19; Mark 11:24; John 14:13; James 1:5f; 1 John 3:22
9 [1]Lit *whom his son will ask* [2]Lit *he will not give him a stone, will he?*
10 [1]Lit *also will ask*
11 [a]Ps 84:11; Is 63:7; Rom 8:32; James 1:17
12 [1]Lit *you, too, do so for them* [2]Lit *people*; Gr *anthropoi* [a]Luke 6:31 [b]Matt 22:40; Rom 13:8ff; Gal 5:14
13 [a]Luke 13:24
15 [a]Matt 24:11; Mark 13:22; Luke 6:26; Acts 13:6; 2 Pet 2:1; 1 John 4:1; Rev 16:13 [b]Ezek 22:27; John 10:12; Acts 20:29
16 [1]Or *recognize* [2]Lit *They do not gather* [a]Matt 7:20; Luke 6:44; James 3:12
17 [a]Matt 12:33
19 [a]Matt 3:10; Luke 3:9; John 15:2
20 [1]Or *recognize* [a]Matt 7:16; Luke 6:44; James 3:12
21 [a]Luke 6:46
22 [1]Or *works of power* [a]Matt 25:11f; Luke 13:25ff [b]Matt 10:15
23 [a]Ps 6:8; Matt 25:41; Luke 13:27
24 [1]Lit *does* [2]Lit *will* [a]Matt 7:24-27: *Luke*

The Narrow and Wide Gates

13 ¶ "[a]Enter through the narrow gate; for the gate is wide and the way is broad that leads to destruction, and there are many who enter through it.

14 "For the gate is small and the way is narrow that leads to life, and there are few who find it.

A Tree and Its Fruit

15 ¶ "Beware of the [a]false prophets, who come to you in sheep's clothing, but inwardly are [b]ravenous wolves.

16 "You will [1a]know them by their fruits. [2]Grapes are not gathered from thorn *bushes* nor figs from thistles, are they?

17 "So [a]every good tree bears good fruit, but the bad tree bears bad fruit.

18 "A good tree cannot produce bad fruit, nor can a bad tree produce good fruit.

19 "[a]Every tree that does not bear good fruit is cut down and thrown into the fire.

20 "So then, you will [1]know them [a]by their fruits.

21 ¶ "[a]Not everyone who says to Me, 'Lord, Lord,' will enter the kingdom of heaven, but he who does the will of My Father who is in heaven *will enter*.

22 "[a]Many will say to Me on [b]that day, 'Lord, Lord, did we not prophesy in Your name, and in Your name cast out demons, and in Your name perform many [1]miracles?'

23 "And then I will declare to them, 'I never knew you; [a]DEPART FROM ME, YOU WHO PRACTICE LAWLESSNESS.'

The Two Foundations

24 ¶ "Therefore [a]everyone who hears these words of Mine and [1]acts on them, [2]may be compared to a wise man who built his house on the rock.

25 "And the rain fell, and the [1]floods came, and the winds blew and slammed against that house; and *yet* it did not fall, for it had been founded on the rock.

26 "Everyone who hears these words of Mine and does not [1]act on them, will be like a foolish man who built his house on the sand.

27 "The rain fell, and the [1]floods came, and the winds blew and slammed against that house; and it fell—and great was its fall."

28 ¶ [1a]When Jesus had finished these words, [b]the crowds were amazed at His teaching;

6:47-49; Matt 16:18; James 1:22-25 **25** [1]Lit *rivers* **26** [1]Lit *do* **27** [1]Lit *rivers* **28** [1]Lit *And it happened when* [a]Matt 11:1 [b]Matt 13:54; Mark 1:22; Luke 4:32; John 7:46

29 for He was teaching them as *one*
having authority, and not as their scribes.

Jesus Cleanses a Leper
The Centurion's Faith

8 When [1]Jesus came down from the
mountain, [2]large crowds followed
Him.
2 And [a]a leper came to Him and
[1b]bowed down before Him, and said,
"Lord, if You are willing, You can make
me clean."
3 Jesus stretched out His hand and
touched him, saying, "I am willing; be
cleansed." And immediately his [a]leprosy
was cleansed.
4 And Jesus *said to him, "[a]See that
you tell no one; but [b]go, [c]show yourself
to the priest and present the [1]offering
that Moses commanded, as a testimony to
them."
5 ¶ And [a]when [1]Jesus entered Capernaum, a centurion came to Him, imploring Him,
6 and saying, "[1]Lord, my [2]servant is
[3]lying [a]paralyzed at home, fearfully tormented."
7 Jesus *said to him, "I will come and
heal him."
8 But the centurion said, "[1]Lord, I
am not worthy for You to come under my
roof, but just [2]say the word, and my
[3]servant will be healed.
9 "For I also am a man under [a]authori-
ty, with soldiers under me; and I say to
this one, 'Go!' and he goes, and to another, 'Come!' and he comes, and to my
slave, 'Do this!' and he does *it*."
10 Now when Jesus heard *this*, He
marveled and said to those who were following, "Truly I say to you, I have not
found such great faith [1]with anyone in
Israel.
11 "I say to you that many [a]will come
from east and west, and [1]recline *at the
table* with Abraham, Isaac and Jacob in
the kingdom of heaven;
12 but [a]the sons of the kingdom will
be cast out into [b]the outer darkness; in
that place [c]there will be weeping and
gnashing of teeth."
13 And Jesus said to the centurion,
"Go; [1]it shall be done for you [a]as you
have believed." And the [2]servant was
healed that *very* [3]moment.

Peter's Mother-in-law and Many
Others Healed

14 ¶ [a]When Jesus came into Peter's
[1]home, He saw his mother-in-law lying
sick in bed with a fever.
15 He touched her hand, and the fever
left her; and she got up and [1]waited on
Him.
16 When evening came, they brought
to Him many [a]who were demon-
possessed; and He cast out the spirits
with a word, and [b]healed all who were
ill.
17 *This was* to fulfill what was spoken
through Isaiah the prophet: "[a]HE
HIMSELF TOOK OUR INFIRMITIES AND [1]CAR-
RIED AWAY OUR DISEASES."

Discipleship Tested

18 ¶ Now when Jesus saw a crowd
around Him, [a]He gave orders to depart to
the other side *of the sea*.
19 [a]Then a scribe came and said to
Him, "Teacher, I will follow You wherever You go."
20 Jesus *said to him, "The foxes have
holes and the birds of the [1]air *have*
[2]nests, but [a]the Son of Man has nowhere to lay His head."
21 Another of the disciples said to
Him, "Lord, permit me first to go and
bury my father."
22 But Jesus *said to him, "[a]Follow
Me, and allow the dead to bury their own
dead."
23 ¶ [a]When He got into the boat, His
disciples followed Him.
24 And behold, there arose [1]a great
storm on the sea, so that the boat was
being covered with the waves; but Jesus
Himself was asleep.
25 And they came to *Him* and woke
Him, saying, "[a]Save *us*, Lord; we are perishing!"
26 He *said to them, "Why are you
[1]afraid, [a]you men of little faith?" Then
He got up and rebuked the winds and the
sea, and [2]it became perfectly calm.
27 The men were amazed, and said,
"What kind of a man is this, that even the
winds and the sea obey Him?"

Jesus Casts Out Demons

28 ¶ [a]When He came to the other
side into the country of the Gadarenes,
two men who were [b]demon-possessed
met Him as they were coming out of the
tombs. *They were* so extremely violent
that no one could pass by that way.
29 And they cried out, saying,
"[1a]What business do we have with each
other, Son of God? Have You come here
to torment us before [2]the time?"
30 Now there was a herd of many
swine feeding at a distance from them.
31 The demons *began* to entreat Him,
saying, "If You *are going to* cast us out,
send us into the herd of swine."
32 And He said to them, "Go!" And
they came out and went into the swine,

8:1 [1]Lit *He* [2]Lit *many*
2 [1]Or *worshiped* [a]Matt 8:2-4: *Mark 1:40-44; Luke 5:12-14* [b]Matt 9:18; John 9:38; Acts 10:25
3 [a]Matt 11:5; Luke 4:27
4 [1]Lit *gift* [a]Matt 9:30; Mark 1:44; Luke 4:41 [b]Mark 1:44; Luke 5:14 [c]Lev 13:49
5 [1]Lit *He* [a]Matt 8:5-13: *Luke 7:1-10*
6 [1]Or *Sir* [2]Lit *boy* [3]Lit *thrown down* [a]Matt 4:24
8 [1]Or *Sir* [2]Lit *say with a word* [3]Lit *boy*
9 [a]Mark 1:27; Luke 9:1
10 [1]One early ms reads *not even in Israel*
11 [1]Or *dine* [a]Is 49:12; Mal 1:11; Luke 13:29
12 [a]Matt 13:38 [b]Matt 22:13 [c]Matt 13:42; Luke 13:28
13 [1]Or *let it be done*; i.e. a command [2]Lit *boy* [3]Lit *hour* [a]Matt 9:22
14 [1]Or *house* [a]Matt 8:14-16: *Mark 1:29-34; Luke 4:38-41*
15 [1]Or *served*
16 [a]Matt 4:24 [b]Matt 4:23
17 [1]Or *removed* [a]Is 53:4
18 [a]Mark 4:35; Luke 8:22
19 [a]Matt 8:19-22: *Luke 9:57-60*
20 [1]Or *sky* [2]Or *roosting places* [a]Dan 7:13; Matt 9:6; Mark 8:38; Luke 12:8; John 1:51; Acts 7:56
22 [a]Matt 9:9; Mark 2:14; Luke 9:59; John 1:43
23 [a]Matt 8:23-27: *Mark 4:36-41; Luke 8:22-25*
24 [1]Lit *a shaking*
25 [a]Matt 8:2
26 [1]Or *cowardly* [2]Lit *a great calm occurred* [a]Matt 6:30
28 [a]Matt 8:28-34: *Mark 5:1-17; Luke 8:26-37* [b]Matt 4:24
29 [1]Lit *What is to us and to you* (a Heb idiom) [2]I.e. the appointed time of judgment [a]Judg 11:12; 2 Sam 16:10; 1 Kin 17:18; 2 Kin 3:13; 2 Chr 35:21; Mark 1:24; Luke 4:34; John 2:4

and the whole herd rushed down the
steep bank into the sea and perished in
the waters.
33 The herdsmen ran away, and went
to the city and reported everything, [1]in-
cluding what had happened to the
[a]demoniacs.
34 And behold, the whole city came
out to meet Jesus; and when they saw
Him, [a]they implored Him to leave their
region.

A Paralytic Healed

9 Getting into a boat, Jesus crossed
over *the sea* and came to [a]His own
city.
2 ¶ [a]And they brought to Him a
[b]paralytic lying on a bed. Seeing their
faith, Jesus said to the paralytic, "[c]Take
courage, [1]son; [d]your sins are forgiven."
3 And some of the scribes said [1]to
themselves, "This *fellow* [a]blasphemes."
4 And Jesus [a]knowing their thoughts
said, "Why are you thinking evil in your
hearts?
5 "Which is easier, to say, '[a]Your sins
are forgiven,' or to say, 'Get up, and
walk'?
6 "But so that you may know that [a]the
Son of Man has authority on earth to forgive sins"—then He *said to the [b]para-
lytic, "Get up, pick up your bed and go
home."
7 And he got up and [1]went home.
8 But when the crowds saw *this,* they
were [1]awestruck, and [a]glorified God,
who had given such authority to men.

Matthew Called

9 ¶ [a]As Jesus went on from there,
He saw a man called [b]Matthew, sitting in
the tax collector's booth; and He *said to
him, "[c]Follow Me!" And he got up and
followed Him.
10 ¶ Then it happened that as [1]Jesus
was reclining *at the table* in the house,
behold, many tax collectors and [2]sinners
came and were dining with Jesus and His
disciples.
11 When the Pharisees saw *this,* they
said to His disciples, "[a]Why is your
Teacher eating with the tax collectors
and sinners?"
12 But when Jesus heard *this,* He said,
"*It is* not [a]those who are healthy who
need a physician, but those who are sick.
13 "But go and learn [1a]what this
means: '[b]I DESIRE [2]COMPASSION, [3]AND
NOT SACRIFICE,' for [c]I did not come to call
the righteous, but sinners."

The Question about Fasting

14 ¶ Then the disciples of John *came
to Him, asking, "Why do we and [a]the
Pharisees fast, but Your disciples do not
fast?"
15 And Jesus said to them, "The [1]at-
tendants of the bridegroom cannot
mourn as long as the bridegroom is with
them, can they? But the days will come
when the bridegroom is taken away from
them, and then they will fast.
16 "But no one puts [1]a patch of unshrunk cloth on an old garment; for [2]the
patch pulls away from the garment, and a
worse tear results.
17 "Nor do *people* put new wine into
old wineskins; otherwise the wineskins
burst, and the wine pours out and the
wineskins are ruined; but they put new
wine into fresh wineskins, and both are
preserved."

Miracles of Healing

18 ¶ [a]While He was saying these
things to them, [1]a *synagogue* [2]official
came and [3b]bowed down before Him,
and said, "My daughter has just died; but
come and lay Your hand on her, and she
will live."
19 Jesus got up and *began* to follow
him, and *so did* His disciples.
20 ¶ And a woman who had been suffering from a hemorrhage for twelve
years, came up behind Him and touched
[a]the [1]fringe of His [2]cloak;
21 for she was saying [1]to herself, "If
I only [a]touch His garment, I will [2]get
well."
22 But Jesus turning and seeing her
said, "Daughter, [a]take courage; [b]your
faith has [1]made you well." [2]At once the
woman was [3]made well.
23 ¶ When Jesus came into the [1]offi-
cial's house, and saw [a]the flute-players
and the crowd in noisy disorder,
24 He said, "Leave; for the girl [a]has
not died, but is asleep." And they *began*
laughing at Him.
25 But [a]when the crowd had been
sent out, He entered and [b]took her by
the hand, and the girl [1]got up.
26 [a]This news spread throughout all
that land.
27 ¶ As Jesus went on from there, two
blind men followed Him, crying out,
"Have mercy on us, [a]Son of David!"
28 When He entered the house, the
blind men came up to Him, and Jesus
*said to them, "Do you believe that I am
able to do this?" They *said to Him, "Yes,
Lord."
29 Then He touched their eyes, saying, "[1]It shall be done to you [a]according
to your faith."

33 [1]Lit *and the things of* [a]Matt 4:24
34 [a]Amos 7:12; Acts 16:39
9:1 [a]Matt 4:13; Mark 5:21
2 [1]Lit *child* [a]Matt 9:2-8: *Mark 2:3-12; Luke 5:18-26* [b]Matt 4:24 [c]Matt 9:22; Mark 6:50; John 16:33; Acts 23:11 [d]Mark 2:5; Luke 5:20
3 [1]Lit *among* [a]Mark 3:28
4 [a]Matt 12:25; Luke 6:8
5 [a]Matt 9:2; Mark 2:5; Luke 5:20
6 [a]Matt 8:20; John 5:27 [b]Matt 4:24
7 [1]Or *departed*
8 [1]Lit *afraid* [a]Matt 5:16; Mark 2:12; Luke 2:20; John 15:8; Acts 4:21; 2 Cor 9:13; Gal 1:24
9 [a]Matt 9:9-17: *Mark 2:14-22* [b]Matt 10:3; Mark 2:14; Luke 6:15; Acts 1:13 [c]Matt 8:22
10 [1]Lit *He* [2]I.e. irreligious Jews
11 [a]Matt 11:19; Mark 2:16; Luke 5:30
12 [a]Mark 2:17; Luke 5:31
13 [1]Lit *what is* [2]Or *mercy* [3]I.e. more than [a]Matt 12:7 [b]Hos 6:6 [c]Mark 2:17; Luke 5:32; 1 Tim 1:15
14 [a]Luke 18:12
15 [1]Lit *sons of the wedding place*
16 [1]Lit *that which is put on* [2]Lit *that which fills up*
18 [1]Or *one* [2]Lit *ruler* [3]Or *worshiped* [a]Matt 9:18-26: *Mark 5:22-43; Luke 8:41-56* [b]Matt 8:2
20 [1]I.e. tassel fringe with a blue cord [2]Or *outer garment* [a]Num 15:38; Deut 22:12; Matt 14:36
21 [1]Lit *in herself* [2]Lit *be saved* [a]Matt 14:36; Mark 3:10; Luke 6:19
22 [1]Lit *saved you* [2]Lit *from that hour* [3]Lit *saved* [a]Matt 9:2 [b]Matt 9:29; Mark 5:34; Luke 7:50
23 [1]Lit *ruler's* [a]2 Chr 35:25; Jer 9:17; Ezek 24:17
24 [a]John 11:13; Acts 20:10
25 [1]Or *was raised up* [a]Acts 9:40 [b]Mark 9:27
26 [a]Matt 4:24; Mark 1:28; Luke 4:14 **27** [a]Matt 1:1; Mark 10:47; Luke 18:38 **29** [1]Or *Let it be done*; Gr command [a]Matt 8:13

30 And their eyes were opened. And Jesus [a]sternly warned them: "See that no one knows *about this!*"

31 But they went out and [a]spread the news about Him throughout all that land.

32 ¶ As they were going out, [a]a mute, [b]demon-possessed man [1]was brought to Him.

33 After the demon was cast out, the mute man spoke; and the crowds were amazed, *and were* saying, "[a]Nothing like this has [1]ever been seen in Israel."

34 But the Pharisees were saying, "He [a]casts out the demons by the ruler of the demons."

35 ¶ Jesus was going through all the cities and villages, [a]teaching in their synagogues and proclaiming the gospel of the kingdom, and healing every kind of disease and every kind of sickness.

36 ¶ [a]Seeing the [1]people, He felt compassion for them, [b]because they were [2]distressed and [3]dispirited like sheep [4]without a shepherd.

37 Then He *said to His disciples, "[a]The harvest is plentiful, but the workers are few.

38 "Therefore beseech the Lord of the harvest to send out workers into His harvest."

The Twelve Disciples
Instructions for Service

10 Jesus [a]summoned His twelve disciples and gave them authority over unclean spirits, to cast them out, and to [b]heal every kind of disease and every kind of sickness.

2 ¶ [a]Now the names of the twelve apostles are these: The first, [b]Simon, who is called Peter, and [b]Andrew his brother; and [1c]James the son of Zebedee, and [2]John his brother;

3 [a]Philip and [1]Bartholomew; [b]Thomas and [c]Matthew the tax collector; [2d]James the son of Alphaeus, and [e]Thaddaeus;

4 Simon the [1]Zealot, and [a]Judas Iscariot, the one who betrayed Him.

5 ¶ [a]These twelve Jesus sent out after instructing them: "Do not [1]go [2]in *the* way of *the* Gentiles, and do not enter *any* city of the [b]Samaritans;

6 but rather go to [a]the lost sheep of the house of Israel.

7 "And as you go, [1]preach, saying, '[a]The kingdom of heaven [2]is at hand.'

8 "Heal *the* sick, raise *the* dead, cleanse *the* lepers, cast out demons. Freely you received, freely give.

9 "[a]Do not acquire gold, or silver, or copper for your money belts,

10 or a [1]bag for *your* journey, or even two [2]coats, or sandals, or a staff; for [a]the worker is worthy of his [3]support.

11 "And whatever city or village you enter, inquire who is worthy in it, and stay [1]at his house until you leave *that city*.

12 "As you enter the [1]house, [a]give it your [2]greeting.

13 "If the house is worthy, [1]give it your *blessing of* peace. But if it is not worthy, [2]take back your *blessing of* peace.

14 "Whoever does not receive you, nor heed your words, as you go out of that house or that city, [a]shake the dust off your feet.

15 "Truly I say to you, [a]it will be more tolerable for *the* land of [b]Sodom and Gomorrah in [c]the day of judgment than for that city.

A Hard Road before Them

16 ¶ "[a]Behold, I send you out as sheep in the midst of wolves; so [1]be [b]shrewd as serpents and [c]innocent as doves.

17 "But beware of men, for they will hand you over to *the* [a]courts and scourge you [b]in their synagogues;

18 and you will even be brought before governors and kings for My sake, as a testimony to them and to the Gentiles.

19 "[a]But when they hand you over, [b]do not worry about how or what you are to say; for it will be given you in that hour what you are to say.

20 "For [a]it is not you who speak, but *it is* the Spirit of your Father who speaks in you.

21 ¶ "[a]Brother will betray brother to death, and a father *his* child; and [b]children will rise up against parents and [1]cause them to be put to death.

22 "[a]You will be hated by all because of My name, but [b]it is the one who has endured to the end who will be saved.

23 ¶ "But whenever they [a]persecute you in [1]one city, flee to [2]the next; for truly I say to you, you will not finish *going through* the cities of Israel [b]until the Son of Man comes.

The Meaning of Discipleship

24 ¶ "[a]A [1]disciple is not above his teacher, nor a slave above his master.

25 "It is enough for the disciple that he become like his teacher, and the slave like his master. [a]If they have called the

30 [a]Matt 8:4 **31** [a]Matt 4:24; Mark 1:28; Luke 4:14 **32** [1]Lit *they brought* [a]Matt 12:22 [b]Matt 4:24 **33** [1]Lit *ever appeared* [a]Mark 2:12 **34** [a]Matt 12:24; Mark 3:22; Luke 11:15; John 7:20f **35** [a]Matt 4:23; Mark 1:14 **36** [1]Lit *crowds* [2]Or *harassed* [3]Lit *thrown down* [4]Lit *not having* [a]Matt 14:14; Mark 6:34 [b]Num 27:17; Ezek 34:5; Zech 10:2; Mark 6:34 **37** [a]Luke 10:2 **10:1** [a]Mark 3:13-15 [b]Matt 9:35; Luke 9:1 **2** [1]Or *Jacob*; James is the Eng form of Jacob [2]Gr *Joannes,* Heb *Johanan* [a]Matt 10:2-4: *Mark 3:16-19; Luke 6:14-16; Acts 1:13* [b]Matt 4:18 [c]Matt 4:21 **3** [1]I.e. son of Talmai (Aram) [2]Or *Jacob* [a]John 1:43ff [b]John 11:16 [c]Matt 9:9 [d]Mark 15:40 [e]Mark 3:18; Luke 6:16; Acts 1:13 **4** [1]Or *Cananaean* [a]Matt 26:14; Luke 22:3; John 6:71 **5** [1]Or *go off* [2]Or *on the road of* (Gr *hodos: way* or *road*) [a]Mark 6:7; Luke 9:2 [b]2 Kin 17:24ff; Luke 9:52; John 4:9; Acts 8:25 **6** [a]Matt 15:24 **7** [1]Or *proclaim* [2]Lit *has come near* [a]Matt 3:2 **9** [a]Matt 10:9-15: *Mark 6:8-11; Luke 9:3-5;* Luke 22:35 **10** [1]Or *knapsack*, or *beggar's bag* [2]Or *inner garments* [3]Lit *nourishment* [a]1 Cor 9:14; 1 Tim 5:18 **11** [1]Lit *there until* **12** [1]Or *household* [2]I.e. the familiar Heb blessing, "Peace be to this house!" [a]1 Sam 25:6; Ps 122:7 **13** [1]Lit *your peace is to come upon it* [2]Lit *your peace is to return to you* **14** [a]Acts 13:51 **15** [a]Matt 11:22 [b]Matt 11:24; 2 Pet 2:6; Jude 7 [c]Matt 7:22; Acts 17:31; 1 Thess 5:4; Heb 10:25; 2 Pet 2:9; 1 John 4:17; Jude 6 **16** [1]Or *show yourselves to be* [a]Luke 10:3 [b]Gen 3:1; Matt 24:25; Rom 16:19 [c]Hos 7:11 **17** [a]Matt 5:22 [b]Matt 23:34; Mark 13:9; Luke 12:11; Acts 5:40 **19** [a]Matt 10:19-22: *Mark 13:11-13; Luke 21:12-17* [b]Matt 6:25; Luke 12:11 **20** [a]Luke 12:12; Acts 4:8; 2 Cor 13:3 **21** [1]Lit *put them to death* [a]Matt 10:35; Mark 13:12 [b]Mic 7:6 **22** [a]Matt 24:9; Luke 21:17; John 15:18ff [b]Matt 24:13; Mark 13:13 **23** [1]Lit *this* [2]Lit *the other* [a]Matt 23:34 [b]Matt 16:27f **24** [1]Or *student* [a]Luke 6:40; John 13:16 **25** [a]Matt 9:34

head of the house [1b]Beelzebul, how much more *will they malign* the members of his household!

26 ¶ "Therefore do not [a]fear them, [b]for there is nothing concealed that will not be revealed, or hidden that will not be known.

27 "[a]What I tell you in the darkness, speak in the light; and what you hear *whispered* in *your* ear, proclaim [b]upon the housetops.

28 "Do not fear those who kill the body but are unable to kill the soul; but rather [a]fear Him who is able to destroy both soul and body in [1b]hell.

29 "[a]Are not two sparrows sold for a [1]cent? And *yet* not one of them will fall to the ground apart from your Father.

30 "But [a]the very hairs of your head are all numbered.

31 "So do not fear; [a]you are more valuable than many sparrows.

32 ¶ "Therefore [a]everyone who [1]confesses Me before men, I will also confess [2]him before My Father who is in heaven.

33 "But [a]whoever [1]denies Me before men, I will also deny him before My Father who is in heaven.

34 ¶ "[a]Do not think that I came to [1]bring peace on the earth; I did not come to bring peace, but a sword.

35 "For I came to [a]SET A MAN AGAINST HIS FATHER, AND A DAUGHTER AGAINST HER MOTHER, AND A DAUGHTER-IN-LAW AGAINST HER MOTHER-IN-LAW;

36 and [a]A MAN'S ENEMIES WILL BE THE MEMBERS OF HIS HOUSEHOLD.

37 ¶ "[a]He who loves father or mother more than Me is not worthy of Me; and he who loves son or daughter more than Me is not worthy of Me.

38 "And [a]he who does not take his cross and follow after Me is not worthy of Me.

39 "[a]He who has found his [1]life will lose it, and he who has lost his [1]life for My sake will find it.

The Reward of Service

40 ¶ "[a]He who receives you receives Me, and [b]he who receives Me receives Him who sent Me.

41 "[a]He who receives a prophet in *the* name of a prophet shall receive a prophet's reward; and he who receives a righteous man in the name of a righteous man shall receive a righteous man's reward.

42 "And [a]whoever in the name of a disciple gives to one of these [1]little ones even a cup of cold water to drink, truly I say to you, he shall not lose his reward."

25 [1]Or *Beezebul*: ruler of demons [b]2 Kin 1:2; Matt 12:24; Mark 3:22; Luke 11:15 **26** [a]Matt 10:26-33: *Luke 12:2-9* [b]Mark 4:22; Luke 8:17; 1 Cor 4:5 **27** [a]Luke 12:3 [b]Matt 24:17; Acts 5:20 **28** [1]Gr *Gehenna* [a]Heb 10:31 [b]Matt 5:22; Luke 12:5 **29** [1]Gr *assarion*, the smallest copper coin [a]Luke 12:6 **30** [a]1 Sam 14:45; 2 Sam 14:11; 1 Kin 1:52; Luke 21:18; Acts 27:34 **31** [a]Matt 12:12 **32** [1]Lit *will confess in Me* [2]Lit *in him* [a]Luke 12:8; Rev 3:5 **33** [1]Lit *will deny* [a]Mark 8:38; Luke 9:26; 2 Tim 2:12 **34** [1]Lit *cast* [a]Matt 10:34: *Luke 12:51-53* **35** [a]Mic 7:6; Matt 10:21; Luke 12:53 **36** [a]Mic 7:6; Matt 10:21 **37** [a]Deut 33:9; Luke 14:26 **38** [a]Matt 16:24; Mark 8:34; Luke 9:23 **39** [1]Or *soul* [a]Matt 16:25; Mark 8:35; Luke 9:24; John 12:25 **40** [a]Matt 18:5; Luke 10:16; John 13:20; Gal 4:14 [b]Mark 9:37; Luke 9:48; John 12:44 **41** [a]Matt 25:44 **42** [1]I.e. humble [a]Matt 25:40; Mark 9:41 **11:1** [1]Or *commanding* [2]Or *proclaim* [a]Matt 7:28 [b]Matt 9:35; Luke 23:5 **2** [1]Lit *in prison* [a]Matt 11:2-19: *Luke 7:18-35*; Matt 4:12 [b]Matt 14:3; Mark 6:17; Luke 9:7ff **3** [1]Lit *Coming One* [a]Ps 118:26; Matt 11:10; John 6:14; Heb 10:37 **5** [1]Or *good news* [a]Is 35:5f; Matt 8:3 [b]Is 61:1; Luke 4:18 **6** [1]Lit *whoever* [2]Or *stumble over Me* [a]Matt 5:29; Mark 6:3; John 6:61 **7** [a]Matt 3:1 **8** [1]Or *Well then,* [2]Lit *houses* **9** [1]Or *Well then,* [a]Matt 14:5; Luke 1:76 **10** [1]Lit *has been written* [2]Lit *before your face* [a]Mal 3:1; Mark 1:2

John's Questions

11 [a]When Jesus had finished [1]giving instructions to His twelve disciples, He departed from there [b]to teach and [2]preach in their cities.

2 ¶ [a]Now when [b]John, [1]while imprisoned, heard of the works of Christ, he sent *word* by his disciples

3 and said to Him, "Are You [a]the [1]Expected One, or shall we look for someone else?"

4 Jesus answered and said to them, "Go and report to John what you hear and see:

5 [a]*the* BLIND RECEIVE SIGHT and *the* lame walk, *the* lepers are cleansed and *the* deaf hear, *the* dead are raised up, and *the* [b]POOR HAVE THE [1]GOSPEL PREACHED TO THEM.

6 "And blessed is he [1]who [a]does not [2]take offense at Me."

Jesus' Tribute to John

7 ¶ As these men were going *away,* Jesus began to speak to the crowds about John, "What did you go out into [a]the wilderness to see? A reed shaken by the wind?

8 "[1]But what did you go out to see? A man dressed in soft *clothing*? Those who wear soft *clothing* are in kings' [2]palaces!

9 "[1]But what did you go out to see? [a]A prophet? Yes, I tell you, and one who is more than a prophet.

10 "This is the one about whom it [1]is written,

'[a]BEHOLD, I SEND MY MESSENGER
[2]AHEAD OF YOU,
WHO WILL PREPARE YOUR WAY
BEFORE YOU.'

11 "Truly I say to you, among those born of women there has not arisen *anyone* greater than John the Baptist! Yet the one who is [1]least in the kingdom of heaven is greater than he.

12 "[a]From the days of John the Baptist until now the kingdom of heaven [1]suffers violence, and violent men [2]take it by force.

13 "For all the prophets and the Law prophesied until John.

14 "And if you are willing to accept *it,* John himself is [a]Elijah who [1]was to come.

15 "[a]He who has ears to hear, [1]let him hear.

16 ¶ "But to what shall I compare this generation? It is like children sitting in the market places, who call out to the other *children,*

11 [1]Or *less* **12** [1]Or *is forcibly entered* [2]Or *seize it for themselves* [a]Luke 16:16 **14** [1]Or *is going to come* [a]Mal 4:5; Matt 17:10-13; Mark 9:11-13; Luke 1:17; John 1:21 **15** [1]Or *hear!* Or *listen!* [a]Matt 13:9; Mark 4:9; Luke 8:8; Rev 2:7

17 and say, 'We played the flute for you, and you did not dance; we sang a dirge, and you did not [1]mourn.'

18"For John came neither [a]eating nor [b]drinking, and they say, '[c]He has a demon!'

19"The Son of Man came eating and drinking, and they say, 'Behold, a gluttonous man and a [1]drunkard, [a]a friend of tax collectors and [2]sinners!' Yet wisdom is vindicated by her deeds."

The Unrepenting Cities

20 ¶ Then He began to denounce the cities in which most of His [1a]miracles were done, because they did not repent.

21"[a]Woe to you, Chorazin! Woe to you, [b]Bethsaida! For if the [1]miracles had occurred in [c]Tyre and [c]Sidon which occurred in you, they would have repented long ago in [2d]sackcloth and ashes.

22"Nevertheless I say to you, [a]it will be more tolerable for Tyre and Sidon in [b]*the* day of judgment than for you.

23"And you, [a]Capernaum, will not be exalted to heaven, will you? You will [b]descend to [c]Hades; for if the [1]miracles had occurred in [d]Sodom which occurred in you, it would have remained to this day.

24"Nevertheless I say to you that [a]it will be more tolerable for the land of [b]Sodom in *the* day of judgment, than for you."

Come to Me

25 ¶ [a]At that [1]time Jesus said, "I praise You, [b]Father, Lord of heaven and earth, that [c]You have hidden these things from *the* wise and intelligent and have revealed them to infants.

26"Yes, [a]Father, for this way was well-pleasing in Your sight.

27"[a]All things have been handed over to Me by My Father; and no one knows the Son except the Father; nor does anyone know the Father [b]except the Son, and anyone to whom the Son wills to reveal *Him.*

28 ¶"[a]Come to Me, all [1]who are weary and heavy-laden, and I will give you rest.

29"Take My yoke upon you and [a]learn from Me, for I am gentle and humble in heart, and [b]YOU WILL FIND REST FOR YOUR SOULS.

30"For [a]My yoke is [1]easy and My burden is light."

Sabbath Questions

12 [a]At that [1]time Jesus went through the grainfields on the Sabbath, and His disciples became hungry and began to [b]pick the heads *of grain* and eat.

2 But when the Pharisees saw *this,* they said to Him, "Look, Your disciples do what [a]is not lawful to do on a Sabbath."

3 But He said to them, "Have you not read what David did when he became hungry, he and his companions,

4 how he entered the house of God, and [a]they ate the [1]consecrated bread, which was not lawful for him to eat nor for those with him, but for the priests alone?

5"Or have you not read in the Law, that on the Sabbath the priests in the temple [1]break the Sabbath and are innocent?

6"But I say to you that something [a]greater than the temple is here.

7"But if you had known what this [1]means, '[a]I DESIRE [2]COMPASSION, AND NOT A SACRIFICE,' you would not have condemned the innocent.

Lord of the Sabbath

8"For [a]the Son of Man is Lord of the Sabbath."

9 ¶ [a]Departing from there, He went into their synagogue.

10 And a man *was there* whose hand was withered. And they questioned [1]Jesus, asking, "[a]Is it lawful to heal on the Sabbath?"—so that they might accuse Him.

11 And He said to them, "[a]What man [1]is there among you who [2]has a sheep, and if it falls into a pit on the Sabbath, will he not take hold of it and lift it out?

12"[a]How much more valuable then is a man than a sheep! So then, it is lawful to do [1]good on the Sabbath."

13 Then He *said to the man, "Stretch out your hand!" [a]He stretched it out, and it was restored to [1]normal, like the other.

14 But the Pharisees went out and [1a]conspired against Him, *as to* how they might destroy Him.

15 ¶ But Jesus, [1]aware of *this,* withdrew from there. Many followed Him, and [a]He healed them all,

16 and [a]warned them not to [1]tell who He was.

17 *This was* to fulfill what was spoken through Isaiah the prophet:

18"[a]BEHOLD, MY [1]SERVANT WHOM I
[2]HAVE CHOSEN;
[b]MY BELOVED IN WHOM MY SOUL
[3]IS WELL-PLEASED;
[c]I WILL PUT MY SPIRIT UPON HIM,

17 [1]Lit *beat the breast*
18 [a]Matt 3:4 [b]Luke 1:15 [c]Matt 9:34; John 7:20
19 [1]Or *wine-drinker* [2]I.e. irreligious Jews [a]Matt 9:11; Luke 5:29-32
20 [1]Or *works of power* [a]Luke 10:13-15
21 [1]Or *works of power* [2]I.e. symbols of mourning [a]Matt 11:21-23: *Luke 10:13-15* [b]Mark 6:45; Luke 9:10; John 1:44 [c]Matt 11:22; Mark 3:8; Luke 4:26; Acts 12:20 [d]Rev 11:3
22 [a]Matt 10:15 [b]Matt 10:15; Rev 20:11
23 [1]Or *works of power* [a]Matt 4:13 [b]Is 14:13; Ezek 26:20 [c]Matt 16:18; Luke 10:15; Acts 2:27; Rev 1:18 [d]Matt 10:15
24 [a]Matt 10:15 [b]Matt 10:15
25 [1]Or *occasion* [a]Matt 11:25-27: *Luke 10:21,22* [b]Luke 22:42; John 11:41 [c]Ps 8:2; 1 Cor 1:26ff
26 [a]Luke 22:42; John 11:41
27 [a]Matt 28:18; John 3:35 [b]John 7:29
28 [1]Or *who work to exhaustion* [a]Jer 31:25; John 7:37
29 [a]John 13:15; Eph 4:20; Phil 2:5; 1 Pet 2:21; 1 John 2:6 [b]Jer 6:16
30 [1]Or *comfortable,* or *pleasant* [a]1 John 5:3
12:1 [1]Or *occasion* [a]Matt 12:1-8: *Mark 2:23-28; Luke 6:1-5* [b]Deut 23:25
2 [a]Matt 12:10; Luke 13:14; John 5:10
4 [1]Or *showbread;* lit *loaves of presentation* [a]1 Sam 21:6
5 [1]Or *profane*
6 [a]2 Chr 6:18; Is 66:1; Matt 12:41
7 [1]Lit *is* [2]Or *mercy* [a]Hos 6:6; Matt 9:13
8 [a]Matt 8:20
9 [a]Matt 12:9-14: *Mark 3:1-6; Luke 6:6-11*
10 [1]Lit *Him* [a]Matt 12:2; Luke 13:14; John 5:10
11 [1]Lit *will be from you* [2]Lit *will have* [a]Luke 14:5
12 [1]Lit *well* [a]Matt 10:31; Luke 14:1-6
13 [1]Lit *health* [a]Matt 8:3; Acts 28:8
14 [1]Lit *took counsel* [a]Matt 26:4; Mark 14:1; Luke 22:2; John 7:30
15 [1]Lit *knowing* [a]Matt 4:23 **16** [1]Lit *make Him known* [a]Matt 8:4 **18** [1]Lit *Child* [2]Lit *chose* [3]Or *took pleasure* [a]Is 42:1 [b]Matt 3:17 [c]Luke 4:18; John 3:34

and said to him, 'Sir, did you not sow good seed in your field? [1]How then does it have tares?'

28 "And he said to them, 'An [1]enemy has done this!' The slaves *said to him, 'Do you want us, then, to go and gather them up?'

29 "But he *said, 'No; for while you are gathering up the tares, you may uproot the wheat with them.

30 'Allow both to grow together until the harvest; and in the time of the harvest I will say to the reapers, "First gather up the tares and bind them in bundles to burn them up; but [a]gather the wheat into my barn." ' "

The Mustard Seed

31 ¶ He presented another parable to them, saying, "[a]The kingdom of heaven is like [b]a mustard seed, which a man took and sowed in his field;

32 and this is smaller than all *other* seeds, but when it is full grown, it is larger than the garden plants and becomes a tree, so that [a]THE BIRDS OF THE [1]AIR come and NEST IN ITS BRANCHES."

The Leaven

33 ¶ He spoke another parable to them, "[a]The kingdom of heaven is like leaven, which a woman took and hid in [b]three [1]pecks of flour until it was all leavened."

34 ¶ All these things Jesus spoke to the crowds in parables, and He did not speak to them [a]without a parable.

35 *This was* to fulfill what was spoken through the prophet:

"[a]I WILL OPEN MY MOUTH IN PARABLES;
I WILL UTTER THINGS HIDDEN SINCE THE FOUNDATION OF THE WORLD."

The Tares Explained

36 ¶ Then He left the crowds and went into [a]the house. And His disciples came to Him and said, "[b]Explain to us the parable of the [1]tares of the field."

37 And He said, "The one who sows the good seed is [a]the Son of Man,

38 and the field is the world; and *as for* the good seed, these are [a]the sons of the kingdom; and the tares are [b]the sons of [c]the evil *one;*

39 and the enemy who sowed them is the devil, and the harvest is [a]the [1]end of the age; and the reapers are angels.

40 "So just as the tares are gathered up and burned with fire, so shall it be at [a]the [1]end of the age.

41 "[a]The Son of Man [b]will send forth His angels, and they will gather out of His kingdom [1]all [c]stumbling blocks, and those who commit lawlessness,

42 and [a]will throw them into the furnace of fire; in that place [b]there will be weeping and gnashing of teeth.

43 "[a]Then THE RIGHTEOUS WILL SHINE FORTH AS THE SUN in the kingdom of their Father. [b]He who has ears, [1]let him hear.

Hidden Treasure

44 ¶ "[a]The kingdom of heaven is like a treasure hidden in the field, which a man found and hid *again;* and from joy over it he goes and [b]sells all that he has and buys that field.

A Costly Pearl

45 ¶ "Again, [a]the kingdom of heaven is like a merchant seeking fine pearls,

46 and upon finding one pearl of great value, he went and sold all that he had and bought it.

A Dragnet

47 ¶ "Again, [a]the kingdom of heaven is like a dragnet cast into the sea, and gathering *fish* of every kind;

48 and when it was filled, they drew it up on the beach; and they sat down and gathered the good *fish* into containers, but the bad they threw away.

49 "So it will be at [a]the [1]end of the age; the angels will come forth and [2]take out the wicked from among the righteous,

50 and [a]will throw them into the furnace of fire; in that place [b]there will be weeping and gnashing of teeth.

51 ¶ "Have you understood all these things?" They *said to Him, "Yes."

52 And [1]Jesus said to them, "Therefore every scribe who has become a disciple of the kingdom of heaven is like a head of a household, who brings out of his treasure things new and old."

Jesus Revisits Nazareth

53 ¶ [a]When Jesus had finished these parables, He departed from there.

54 [a]He came to [1]His hometown and [b]*began* teaching them in their synagogue, so that [c]they were astonished, and said, "Where *did* this man *get* this wisdom and *these* [2]miraculous powers?

55 "Is not this the carpenter's son? Is not [a]His mother called Mary, and His [a]brothers, James and Joseph and Simon and Judas?

56 "And [a]His sisters, are they not all with us? Where then *did* this man *get* all these things?"

57 And they took [a]offense at Him. But Jesus said to them, "[b]A prophet is not

27 [1]Lit *From where*
28 [1]Lit *enemy man*
30 [a]Matt 3:12
31 [a]Matt 13:31, 32: *Mark 4:30-32; Luke 13:18,19;* Matt 13:24 [b]Matt 17:20; Luke 17:6
32 [1]Or *sky* [a]Ezek 17:23; Ps 104:12; Ezek 31:6; Dan 4:12
33 [1]Gr *sata* [a]Matt 13:33: *Luke 13:21;* Matt 13:24 [b]Gen 18:6; Judg 6:19; 1 Sam 1:24
34 [a]Mark 4:34; John 10:6; 16:25
35 [a]Ps 78:2
36 [1]Or *darnel,* a weed resembling wheat [a]Matt 13:1 [b]Matt 15:15
37 [a]Matt 8:20
38 [a]Matt 8:12 [b]John 8:44; Acts 13:10; 1 John 3:10 [c]Matt 5:37
39 [1]Or *consummation* [a]Matt 12:32; 13:22,40, 49; 24:3; 28:20; 1 Cor 10:11; Heb 9:26
40 [1]Or *consummation* [a]Matt 12:32; 13:22,39, 49; 24:3; 28:20; 1 Cor 10:11; Heb 9:26
41 [1]Or *everything that is offensive* [a]Matt 8:20 [b]Matt 24:31 [c]Zeph 1:3
42 [a]Matt 13:50 [b]Matt 8:12
43 [1]Or *hear!* Or *listen!* [a]Dan 12:3 [b]Matt 11:15
44 [a]Matt 13:24 [b]Matt 13:46
45 [a]Matt 13:24
47 [a]Matt 13:44
49 [1]Or *consummation* [2]Or *separate* [a]Matt 13:39,40
50 [a]Matt 13:42 [b]Matt 8:12
52 [1]Lit *He*
53 [a]Matt 7:28
54 [1]Or *His own part of the country* [2]Or *miracles* [a]Matt 13:54-58: *Mark 6:1-6* [b]Matt 4:23 [c]Matt 7:28
55 [a]Matt 12:46
56 [a]Mark 6:3
57 [a]Matt 11:6 [b]Mark 6:4; Luke 4:24; John 4:44

without honor except in his [1]hometown
and in his *own* household."
58 And He did not do many [1]miracles
there because of their unbelief.

John the Baptist Beheaded

14 [a]At that [1]time [b]Herod the tetrarch heard the news about
Jesus,
2 and said to his servants, "[a]This is
John the Baptist; [1]he has risen from the
dead, and that is why miraculous powers
are at work in him."
3 ¶ For when [a]Herod had John arrested, he bound him and put him [b]in
prison because of [c]Herodias, the wife of
his brother Philip.
4 For John had been saying to him,
"[a]It is not lawful for you to have her."
5 Although Herod wanted to put him
to death, he feared the crowd, because
they regarded [1]John as [a]a prophet.
6 ¶ But when Herod's birthday came,
the daughter of [a]Herodias danced [1]be-
fore *them* and pleased [b]Herod,
7 so *much* that he promised with an
oath to give her whatever she asked.
8 Having been prompted by her
mother, she *said, "Give me here on a
platter the head of John the Baptist."
9 Although he was grieved, the king
commanded *it* to be given because of his
oaths, and because of [1]his dinner guests.
10 He sent and had John beheaded in
the prison.
11 And his head was brought on a platter and given to the girl, and she brought
it to her mother.
12 His disciples came and took away
the body and buried [1]it; and they went
and reported to Jesus.

Five Thousand Fed

13 ¶ [a]Now when Jesus heard *about
John,* He withdrew from there in a boat
to a secluded place by Himself; and when
the [1]people heard *of this,* they followed
Him on foot from the cities.
14 When He went [1]ashore, He [a]saw
a large crowd, and felt compassion for
them and [b]healed their sick.
15 ¶ When it was evening, the disciples came to Him and said, "This place is
desolate and the hour is already [1]late; so
send the crowds away, that they may go
into the villages and buy food for themselves."
16 But Jesus said to them, "They do
not need to go away; you give them *something* to eat!"
17 They *said to Him, "We have here
only [a]five loaves and two fish."
18 And He said, "Bring them here
to Me."
19 Ordering the [1]people to [2]sit down
on the grass, He took the five loaves and
the two fish, and looking up toward heav-
en, He [a]blessed *the food,* and breaking
the loaves He gave them to the disciples,
and the disciples *gave them* to the
crowds,
20 and they all ate and were satisfied.
They picked up what was left over of the
broken pieces, twelve full [a]baskets.
21 There were about five thousand
men who ate, besides women and children.

Jesus Walks on the Water

22 ¶ [a]Immediately He [1]made the disciples get into the boat and go ahead of
Him to the other side, while He sent the
crowds away.
23 After He had sent the crowds away,
[a]He went up on the mountain by Himself
to pray; and when it was evening, He was
there alone.
24 But the boat was already [1]a long
distance from the land, [2]battered by the
waves; for the wind was [3a]contrary.
25 And in [a]the [1]fourth watch of the
night He came to them, walking on the
sea.
26 When the disciples saw Him walking on the sea, they were terrified, and
said, "It is [a]a ghost!" And they cried out
[1]in fear.
27 But immediately Jesus spoke to
them, saying, "[a]Take courage, it is I; [b]do
not be afraid."
28 ¶ Peter said to Him, "Lord, if it is
You, command me to come to You on the
water."
29 And He said, "Come!" And Peter
got out of the boat, and walked on the
water and came toward Jesus.
30 But seeing the wind, he became
frightened, and beginning to sink, he
cried out, "Lord, save me!"
31 Immediately Jesus stretched out
His hand and took hold of him, and *said
to him, "[a]You of little faith, why did you
doubt?"
32 When they got into the boat, the
wind stopped.
33 And those who were in the boat
worshiped Him, saying, "You are certainly [a]God's Son!"
34 ¶ [a]When they had crossed over,
they came to land at [b]Gennesaret.
35 And when the men of that place
[1]recognized Him, they sent *word* into all
that surrounding district and brought to
Him all who were sick;
36 and they implored Him that they
might just touch [a]the fringe of His cloak;
and as many as [b]touched *it* were cured.

57 [1]Or *own part of the country*
58 [1]Or *works of power*
14:1 [1]Or *occasion* [a]Matt 14:1-12: *Mark 6:14-29*; Matt 14:1: *Luke 9:7-9* [b]Mark 8:15; Luke 3:1; Acts 4:27
2 [1]Or *he, himself* [a]Matt 16:14; Mark 6:14; Luke 9:7
3 [a]Matt 14:1-12: *Mark 6:14-29*; Mark 8:15; Luke 3:1; Acts 4:27 [b]Matt 4:12 [c]Matt 14:6; Mark 6:17; Luke 3:19f
4 [a]Lev 18:16
5 [1]Lit *him* [a]Matt 11:9
6 [1]Lit *in the midst* [a]Matt 14:3; Mark 6:17; Luke 3:19 [b]Matt 14:1-12: *Mark 6:14-29*; Mark 8:15; Luke 3:1; Acts 4:27
9 [1]Lit *those who reclined* at the table *with him*
12 [1]Lit *him*
13 [1]Lit *the crowds* [a]Matt 14:13-21: *Mark 6:32-44; Luke 9:10-17; John 6:1-13*; Matt 15:32-38
14 [1]*Lit out* [a]Matt 9:36 [b]Matt 4:23
15 [1]Lit *past*
17 [a]Matt 16:9
19 [1]Lit *crowds* [2]Lit *recline* [a]1 Sam 9:13; Matt 15:36; Mark 6:41; Luke 24:30; Acts 27:35; Rom 14:6
20 [a]Matt 16:9; Mark 6:43; Luke 9:17; John 6:13
22 [1]Lit *compelled* [a]Matt 14:22-33: *Mark 6:45-51; John 6:15-21*
23 [a]Mark 6:46; Luke 6:12; John 6:15
24 [1]Lit *many stadia from*; a stadion was about 600 feet or about 182 meters [2]Lit *tormented* [3]Or *adverse* [a]Acts 27:4
25 [1]I.e. 3-6 a.m. [a]Matt 24:43; Mark 13:35
26 [1]Lit *from* [a]Luke 24:37
27 [a]Matt 9:2 [b]Matt 17:7; Mark 6:50; Luke 1:13; John 6:20; Rev 1:17
31 [a]Matt 6:30
33 [a]Matt 4:3
34 [a]Matt 14:34-36: *Mark 6:53-56*; John 6:24 [b]Mark 6:53; Luke 5:1
35 [1]Or *knew*
36 [a]Matt 9:20 [b]Matt 9:21; Mark 3:10; Luke 6:19

Tradition and Commandment

15 [a]Then some Pharisees and scribes *came to Jesus [b]from Jerusalem and said,

2 "Why do Your disciples break the tradition of the elders? For they [a]do not wash their hands when they eat bread."

3 And He answered and said to them, "Why do you yourselves transgress the commandment of God for the sake of your tradition?

4 "For God said, '[a]HONOR YOUR FATHER AND MOTHER,' and, '[b]HE WHO SPEAKS EVIL OF FATHER OR MOTHER IS TO [1]BE PUT TO DEATH.'

5 "But you say, 'Whoever says to *his* father or mother, "Whatever I have that would help you has been [1]given *to God*,"

6 he is not to honor his father or his mother[1].' And *by this* you invalidated the word of God for the sake of your tradition.

7 "You hypocrites, rightly did Isaiah prophesy of you:

8 '[a]THIS PEOPLE HONORS ME WITH
THEIR LIPS,
BUT THEIR HEART IS FAR AWAY
FROM ME.
9 'BUT IN VAIN DO THEY WORSHIP ME,
TEACHING AS [a]DOCTRINES THE
PRECEPTS OF MEN.' "

10 ¶ After Jesus called the crowd to Him, He said to them, "Hear and understand.

11 "[a]*It is* not what enters into the mouth *that* defiles the man, but what proceeds out of the mouth, this defiles the man."

12 ¶ Then the disciples *came and *said to Him, "Do You know that the Pharisees were [1]offended when they heard this statement?"

13 But He answered and said, "[a]Every plant which My heavenly Father did not plant shall be uprooted.

14 "Let them alone; [a]they are blind guides [1]of the blind. And [b]if a blind man guides a blind man, both will fall into a pit."

The Heart of Man

15 ¶ Peter [1]said to Him, "[a]Explain the parable to us."

16 [1]Jesus said, "Are you still lacking in understanding also?

17 "Do you not understand that everything that goes into the mouth passes into the stomach, and is [1]eliminated?

18 "But [a]the things that proceed out of the mouth come from the heart, and those defile the man.

19 "[a]For out of the heart come evil thoughts, murders, adulteries, [1]fornications, thefts, false witness, slanders.

20 "These are the things which defile the man; but to eat with unwashed hands does not defile the man."

The Syrophoenician Woman

21 ¶ [a]Jesus went away from there, and withdrew into the district of [b]Tyre and [b]Sidon.

22 And a Canaanite woman from that region came out and *began* to cry out, saying, "Have mercy on me, Lord, [a]Son of David; my daughter is cruelly [b]demon-possessed."

23 But He did not answer her a word. And His disciples came and implored Him, saying, "Send her away, because she keeps shouting [1]at us."

24 But He answered and said, "I was sent only to [a]the lost sheep of the house of Israel."

25 But she came and [a]*began* [1]to bow down before Him, saying, "Lord, help me!"

26 And He answered and said, "It is not [1]good to take the children's bread and throw it to the dogs."

27 But she said, "Yes, Lord; [1]but even the dogs feed on the crumbs which fall from their masters' table."

28 Then Jesus said to her, "O woman, [a]your faith is great; it shall be done for you as you wish." And her daughter was healed [1]at once.

Healing Crowds

29 ¶ [a]Departing from there, Jesus went along by [b]the Sea of Galilee, and having gone up on the mountain, He was sitting there.

30 And [1]large crowds came to Him, bringing with them *those who were* lame, crippled, blind, mute, and many others, and they laid them down at His feet; and [a]He healed them.

31 So the crowd marveled as they saw the mute speaking, the crippled [1]restored, and the lame walking, and the blind seeing; and they [a]glorified the God of Israel.

Four Thousand Fed

32 ¶ [a]And Jesus called His disciples to Him, and said, "[b]I feel compassion for the [1]people, because they [2]have remained with Me now three days and have nothing to eat; and I do not want to send them away hungry, for they might faint on the way."

33 The disciples *said to Him, "Where would we get so many loaves in *this* desolate place to satisfy such a large crowd?"

34 And Jesus *said to them, "How

15:1 [a]Matt 15:1-20: *Mark 7:1-23* [b]Mark 3:22; 7:1; John 1:19; Acts 25:7
2 [a]Luke 11:38
4 [1]Lit *die the death* [a]Ex 20:12; Deut 5:16 [b]Ex 21:17; Lev 20:9
5 [1]Lit *a gift*; i.e. an offering
6 [1]I.e. by supporting them with it
8 [a]Is 29:13
9 [a]Col 2:22
11 [a]Matt 15:18; Acts 10:14,15; 1 Tim 4:3
12 [1]Lit *caused to stumble*
13 [a]Is 60:21; 61:3; John 15:2; 1 Cor 3:9
14 [1]Later mss add *of the blind* [a]Matt 23:16,24 [b]Luke 6:39
15 [1]Lit *answered and said* [a]Matt 13:36
16 [1]Lit *and He*
17 [1]Lit *thrown out into the latrine*
18 [a]Matt 12:34; Mark 7:20
19 [1]I.e. sexual immorality [a]Gal 5:19ff
21 [a]Matt 15:21-28: *Mark 7:24-30* [b]Matt 11:21
22 [a]Matt 9:27 [b]Matt 4:24
23 [1]Lit *behind us*
24 [a]Matt 10:6
25 [1]Or *worshiped* [a]Matt 8:2
26 [1]Or *proper*
27 [1]Lit *for*
28 [1]Lit *from that hour* [a]Matt 9:22
29 [a]Matt 15:29-31; Mark 7:31-37 [b]Matt 4:18
30 [1]Lit *many* [a]Matt 4:23
31 [1]Or *healthy* [a]Matt 9:8
32 [1]Lit *crowd* [2]Lit *are remaining* [a]Matt 15:32-39: *Mark 8:1-10*; Matt 14:13-21 [b]Matt 9:36

many loaves do you have?" And they said,
"Seven, and a few small fish."
35 And He directed the [1]people to
[2]sit down on the ground;
36 and He took the seven loaves and
the fish; and [a]giving thanks, He broke
them and started giving them to the disciples, and the disciples *gave them* to the
people.
37 And they all ate and were satisfied,
and they picked up what was left over of
the broken pieces, seven large [a]baskets
full.
38 And those who ate were four thousand men, besides women and children.
39 ¶ And sending away the crowds,
Jesus got into [a]the boat and came to the
region of [b]Magadan.

Pharisees Test Jesus

16 [a]The [b]Pharisees and Sadducees
came up, and testing Jesus, they
[c]asked Him to show them a [1]sign from
heaven.
2 But He replied to them, "[1a]When
it is evening, you say, *'It will be* fair
weather, for the sky is red.'
3 "And in the morning, *'There will be*
a storm today, for the sky is red and
threatening.' [a]Do you know how to discern the [1]appearance of the sky, but cannot *discern* the signs of the times?
4 "[a]An evil and adulterous generation
seeks after a [1]sign; and a [1]sign will not
be given it, except the sign of Jonah."
And He left them and went away.
5 ¶ And the disciples came to the
other side *of the sea*, but they had forgotten to bring *any* bread.
6 And Jesus said to them, "Watch out
and [a]beware of the [1]leaven of the
[b]Pharisees and Sadducees."
7 They began to discuss *this* among
themselves, saying, *"He said that* because we did not bring *any* bread."
8 But Jesus, aware of this, said,
"[a]You men of little faith, why do you
discuss among yourselves that you have
no bread?
9 "Do you not yet understand or remember [a]the five loaves of the five thousand, and how many baskets *full* you
picked up?
10 "Or [a]the seven loaves of the four
thousand, and how many large baskets
full you picked up?
11 "How is it that you do not understand that I did not speak to you concerning bread? But [a]beware of the [1]leaven of
the [b]Pharisees and Sadducees."
12 Then they understood that He did
not say to beware of the leaven of bread,
but of the teaching of the [a]Pharisees and
Sadducees.

Peter's Confession of Christ

13 ¶ [a]Now when Jesus came into the
district of [b]Caesarea Philippi, He was
asking His disciples, "Who do people say
that [c]the Son of Man is?"
14 And they said, "Some *say* [a]John
the Baptist; and others, [1b]Elijah; but still
others, [2]Jeremiah, or one of the prophets."
15 He *said to them, "But who do you
say that I am?"
16 Simon Peter answered, "You are
[1a]the Christ, [b]the Son of [c]the living
God."
17 And Jesus said to him, "Blessed are
you, [a]Simon [1]Barjona, because [b]flesh
and blood did not reveal *this* to you, but
My Father who is in heaven.
18 "I also say to you that you are [1a]Pe-
ter, and upon this [2]rock I will build My
church; and the gates of [b]Hades will not
overpower it.
19 "I will give you [a]the keys of the
kingdom of heaven; and [b]whatever you
bind on earth [1]shall have been bound in
heaven, and whatever you loose on earth
[2]shall have been loosed in heaven."
20 [a]Then He [1]warned the disciples
that they should tell no one that He was
[2b]the Christ.

Jesus Foretells His Death

21 ¶ [a]From that time [1]Jesus began to
show His disciples that He must go to
Jerusalem, and [b]suffer many things from
the elders and chief priests and scribes,
and be killed, and be raised up on the
third day.
22 Peter took Him aside and began to
rebuke Him, saying, "[1]God forbid *it*,
Lord! This shall never [2]happen to You."
23 But He turned and said to Peter,
"Get behind Me, [a]Satan! You are a stumbling block to Me; for you are not setting
your mind on [1]God's interests, but
man's."

Discipleship Is Costly

24 ¶ Then Jesus said to His disciples,
"If anyone wishes to come after Me,
he must deny himself, and [a]take up his
cross and follow Me.
25 "For [a]whoever wishes to save his
[1]life will lose it; but whoever loses his
[1]life for My sake will find it.
26 "For what will it profit a man if
he gains the whole world and forfeits
his soul? Or what will a man give in
exchange for his soul?

35 [1]Lit *crowd* [2]Lit *recline* **36** [a]Matt 14:19; Luke 22:17; John 6:11; Acts 27:35; Rom 14:6 **37** [a]Matt 16:10; Mark 8:8; Acts 9:25 **39** [a]Mark 3:9 [b]Mark 8:10 **16:1** [1]Or *attesting miracle* [a]Matt 16:1-12: *Mark 8:11-21* [b]Matt 3:7 [c]Matt 12:38; Luke 11:16 **2** [1]Early mss do not contain the rest of v 2 and v 3 [a]Luke 12:54f **3** [1]Lit *face* [a]Luke 12:56 **4** [1]Or *attesting miracle* [a]Matt 12:39; Luke 11:29 **6** [1]Or *yeast* [a]Mark 8:15; Luke 12:1 [b]Matt 3:7 **8** [a]Matt 6:30 **9** [a]Matt 14:17-21 **10** [a]Matt 15:34-38 **11** [1]Or *yeast* [a]Matt 16:6; Mark 8:15; Luke 12:1 [b]Matt 3:7 **12** [a]Matt 3:7 **13** [a]Matt 16:13-16: *Mark 8:27-29; Luke 9:18-20* [b]Mark 8:27 [c]Matt 8:20 **14** [1]Gr *Elias* [2]Gr *Jeremias* [a]Matt 14:2 [b]Matt 17:10; Mark 6:15; Luke 9:8; John 1:21 **16** [1]I.e. the Messiah [a]Matt 1:16; John 11:27 [b]Matt 4:3 [c]Ps 42:2; Matt 26:63; Acts 14:15; Rom 9:26; 2 Cor 3:3; 1 Thess 1:9; 1 Tim 3:15; Heb 3:12; Rev 7:2 **17** [1]I.e. son of Jonah [a]John 1:42 [b]1 Cor 15:50; Gal 1:16; Eph 6:12; Heb 2:14 **18** [1]Gr *Petros*, a stone [2]Gr *petra*, large rock; bedrock [a]Matt 4:18 [b]Matt 11:23 **19** [1]Gr *estai dedemenon*, fut. pft. pass. [2]Gr *estai lelumenon*, fut. pft. pass. [a]Is 22:22; Rev 1:18 [b]Matt 18:18; John 20:23 **20** [1]Or *strictly admonished* [2]I.e. the Messiah [a]Matt 8:4; Mark 8:30; Luke 9:21 [b]Matt 1:16; John 11:27 **21** [1]Two early mss read *Jesus Christ* [a]Matt 16:21-28: *Mark 8:31-9:1; Luke 9:22-27* [b]Matt 12:40; Mark 9:12; Luke 17:25; John 2:19 **22** [1]Lit (God be) *merciful to You* [2]Lit *be* **23** [1]Lit *the things of God* [a]Matt 4:10 **24** [a]Matt 10:38; Luke 14:27 **25** [1]Or *soul* [a]Matt 10:39

27 “For the [a]Son of Man [b]is going to
come in the glory of His Father with His
angels, and [c]WILL THEN [1]REPAY EVERY MAN
ACCORDING TO HIS [2]DEEDS.
28 ¶ “Truly I say to you, there are
some of those who are standing here who
will not taste death until they see the
[a]Son of Man [b]coming in His kingdom.”

The Transfiguration

17 [a]Six days later Jesus *took with
Him [b]Peter and [1]James and John
his brother, and *led them up on a high
mountain by themselves.
2 And He was transfigured before
them; and His face shone like the sun,
and His garments became as white as
light.
3 And behold, Moses and Elijah appeared to them, talking with Him.
4 Peter said to Jesus, “Lord, it is good
for us to be here; if You wish, [a]I will
make three [1]tabernacles here, one for
You, and one for Moses, and one for Elijah.”
5 While he was still speaking, a
bright cloud overshadowed them, and
behold, [a]a voice out of the cloud said,
“[b]This is My beloved Son, with whom I
am well-pleased; listen to Him!”
6 When the disciples heard *this,* they
fell [1]face down to the ground and were
terrified.
7 And Jesus came to *them* and
touched them and said, “Get up, and [a]do
not be afraid.”
8 And lifting up their eyes, they saw
no one except Jesus Himself alone.
9 ¶ [a]As they were coming down
from the mountain, Jesus commanded
them, saying, “[b]Tell the vision to no one
until [c]the Son of Man has [d]risen from
the dead.”
10 And His disciples asked Him, “Why
then do the scribes say that [a]Elijah must
come first?”
11 And He answered and said, “Elijah
is coming and will restore all things;
12 but I say to you that Elijah already
came, and they did not recognize him,
but did [1]to him whatever they wished.
So also [a]the Son of Man is going to suffer
[2]at their hands.”
13 Then the disciples understood that
He had spoken to them about John the
Baptist.

The Demoniac

14 ¶ [a]When they came to the crowd,
a man came up to Jesus, falling on his
knees before Him and saying,
15 “[1]Lord, have mercy on my son, for
he is a [2a]lunatic and is very ill; for he
often falls into the fire and often into the
water.
16 “I brought him to Your disciples, and
they could not cure him.”
17 And Jesus answered and said, “You
unbelieving and perverted generation,
how long shall I be with you? How long
shall I put up with you? Bring him here
to Me.”
18 And Jesus rebuked him, and the demon came out of him, and the boy was
cured [1]at once.
19 ¶ Then the disciples came to Jesus
privately and said, “Why could we not
drive it out?”
20 And He *said to them, “Because of
the littleness of your faith; for truly I say
to you, [a]if you have faith [1]the size of [b]a
mustard seed, you will say to [c]this mountain, ‘Move from here to there,’ and it
will move; and [d]nothing will be impossible to you.
21 [“[1a]But this kind does not go out
except by prayer and fasting.”]
22 ¶ [a]And while they were gathering
together in Galilee, Jesus said to them,
“The Son of Man is going to be [1]deliv-
ered into the hands of men;
23 and [a]they will kill Him, and He will
be raised on the third day.” And they
were deeply grieved.

The Tribute Money

24 ¶ When they came to Capernaum,
those who collected [a]the [1]two-drachma
tax came to Peter and said, “Does your
teacher not pay [a]the [1]two-drachma
tax?”
25 He *said, “Yes.” And when he
came into the house, Jesus spoke to him
first, saying, “What do you think, Simon?
From whom do the kings of the earth
collect [a]customs or [b]poll-tax, from their
sons or from strangers?”
26 When Peter said, “From strangers,”
Jesus said to him, “Then the sons are
[1]exempt.
27 “However, so that we do not [1a]of-
fend them, go to the sea and throw in a
hook, and take the first fish that comes
up; and when you open its mouth, you
will find [2]a shekel. Take that and give it
to them for you and Me.”

Rank in the Kingdom

18 [a]At that [1]time the disciples
came to Jesus and said, “[b]Who
then is greatest in the kingdom of
heaven?”
2 And He called a child to Himself
and set him [1]before them,

27 [1]Or *recompense* [2]Lit *doing* [a]Matt 8:20 [b]Matt 10:23; Mark 8:38; Luke 21:27; John 21:22; Acts 1:11; 1 Cor 15:23; 1 Thess 1:10; 2 Thess 1:7; James 5:7f; 2 Pet 1:16; 1 John 2:28; Rev 1:7 [c]Ps 62:12; Prov 24:12; Rom 2:6; 1 Cor 3:13; 2 Cor 5:10; Eph 6:8; Col 3:25; Rev 2:23
28 [a]Matt 8:20 [b]Matt 10:23; Mark 8:38; Luke 21:27; John 21:22; Acts 1:11; 1 Cor 15:23; 1 Thess 1:10; 2 Thess 1:7; James 5:7f; 2 Pet 1:16; 1 John 2:28; Rev 1:7
17:1 [1]Or *Jacob* [a]Matt 17:1-8: *Mark 9:2-8; Luke 9:28-36* [b]Matt 26:37; Mark 5:37
4 [1]Or *sacred tents* [a]Mark 9:5; Luke 9:33
5 [a]Mark 1:11; Luke 3:22; 2 Pet 1:17f [b]Is 42:1; Matt 3:17
6 [1]Lit *on their faces*
7 [a]Matt 14:27
9 [a]Matt 17:9-13: *Mark 9:9-13* [b]Matt 8:4 [c]Matt 8:20 [d]Matt 16:21
10 [a]Mal 4:5; Matt 11:14
12 [1]Lit *in him;* or *in his case* [2]Lit *by them* [a]Matt 8:20
14 [a]Matt 17:14-19: *Mark 9:14-28;* Matt 17:14-18: *Luke 9:37-42*
15 [1]Or *Sir* [2]Or moonstruck; Gr *seleniazo* [a]Matt 4:24
18 [1]Lit *from that hour*
20 [1]Lit *as* [a]Matt 21:21f; Mark 11:23f; Luke 17:6 [b]Matt 13:31; Luke 17:6 [c]Matt 17:9; 1 Cor 13:2 [d]Mark 9:23; John 11:40
21 [1]Early mss do not contain this v [a]Mark 9:29
22 [1]Or *betrayed* [a]Matt 17:22: *Mark 9:30-32; Luke 9:44*
23 [a]Matt 16:21
24 [1]Equivalent to two denarii or two days' wages, paid as a temple tax [a]Ex 30:13
25 [a]Rom 13:7 [b]Matt 22:17
26 [1]Or *free*
27 [1]Lit *cause them to stumble* [2]Lit *standard coin,* which was a shekel [a]Matt 5:29; Mark 9:42; Luke 17:2; John 6:61; 1 Cor 8:13 **18:1** [1]Lit *hour* [a]Matt 18:1-5: *Mark 9:33-37; Luke 9:46-48* [b]Luke 22:24 **2** [1]Lit *in their midst*

3 and said, "Truly I say to you, unless
you [1]are converted and [a]become like
children, you will not enter the kingdom
of heaven.
4 "Whoever then humbles himself as
this child, he is the greatest in the kingdom of heaven.
5 "And whoever receives one such
child in My name receives Me;
6 but [a]whoever [b]causes one of these
little ones who believe in Me to stumble,
it [1]would be better for him to have a
[2]heavy millstone hung around his neck,
and to be drowned in the depth of the
sea.

Stumbling Blocks

7 ¶ "Woe to the world because of *its*
stumbling blocks! For [a]it is inevitable
that stumbling blocks come; but woe to
that man through whom the stumbling
block comes!
8 ¶ "[a]If your hand or your foot
causes you to stumble, cut it off and
throw it from you; it is better for you to
enter life crippled or lame, than [1]to have
two hands or two feet and be cast into the
eternal fire.
9 "[a]If your eye causes you to stumble,
pluck it out and throw it from you. It is
better for you to enter life with one eye,
than [1]to have two eyes and be cast into
the [2b]fiery hell.
10 ¶ "See that you do not despise one
of these little ones, for I say to you that
[a]their angels in heaven continually see
the face of My Father who is in heaven.
11 ["[1a]For the Son of Man has come
to save that which was lost.]

Ninety-nine Plus One

12 ¶ "What do you think? [a]If any man
has a hundred sheep, and one of them
has gone astray, does he not leave the
ninety-nine on the mountains and go and
search for the one that is straying?
13 "If it turns out that he finds it, truly
I say to you, he rejoices over it more than
over the ninety-nine which have not
gone astray.
14 "So it is not *the* will [1]of your Father
who is in heaven that one of these little
ones perish.

Discipline and Prayer

15 ¶ "[a]If your brother sins[1], go and
[2]show him his fault [3]in private; if he
listens to you, you have won your
brother.
16 "But if he does not listen *to you,* take
one or two more with you, so that [a]BY
THE MOUTH OF TWO OR THREE WITNESSES EV-
ERY [1]FACT MAY BE CONFIRMED.
17 "If he refuses to listen to them, [a]tell
it to the church; and if he refuses to listen
even to the church, [b]let him be to you as
[1]a Gentile and [1]a tax collector.
18 "Truly I say to you, [a]whatever you
[1]bind on earth [2]shall have been bound
in heaven; and whatever you [3]loose on
earth [2]shall have been loosed in heaven.
19 ¶ "Again I say to you, that if two of
you agree on earth about anything that
they may ask, [a]it shall be done for them
[1]by My Father who is in heaven.
20 "For where two or three have gathered together in My name, [a]I am there in
their midst."

Forgiveness

21 ¶ Then Peter came and said to Him,
"Lord, [a]how often shall my brother sin
against me and I forgive him? Up to [b]sev-
en times?"
22 Jesus *said to him, "I do not say to
you, up to seven times, but up to [a]seven-
ty times seven.
23 ¶ "For this reason [a]the kingdom of
heaven [1]may be compared to a king who
wished to [b]settle accounts with his
slaves.
24 "When he had begun to settle *them,*
one who owed him [1]ten thousand talents was brought to him.
25 "But since he [1a]did not have *the
means* to repay, his lord commanded him
[b]to be sold, along with his wife and children and all that he had, and repayment
to be made.
26 "So the slave fell *to the ground* and
[a]prostrated himself before him, saying,
'Have patience with me and I will repay
you everything.'
27 "And the lord of that slave felt compassion and released him and [a]forgave
him the [1]debt.
28 "But that slave went out and found
one of his fellow slaves who owed him a
hundred [1]denarii; and he seized him and
began to choke *him,* saying, 'Pay back
what you owe.'
29 "So his fellow slave fell *to the ground*
and *began* to plead with him, saying,
'Have patience with me and I will repay
you.'
30 "But he was unwilling [1]and went
and threw him in prison until he should
pay back what was owed.
31 "So when his fellow slaves saw what
had happened, they were deeply grieved
and came and reported to their lord all
that had happened.
32 "Then summoning him, his lord
*said to him, 'You wicked slave, I forgave
you all that debt because you pleaded
with me.
33 '[a]Should you not also have had mer-

3 [1]Lit *are turned* [a]Matt 19:14; Mark 10:15; Luke 18:17; 1 Cor 14:20; 1 Pet 2:2
6 [1]Lit *is better* [2]Lit *millstone turned by a donkey* [a]Mark 9:42; Luke 17:2; 1 Cor 8:12 [b]Matt 17:27
7 [a]Luke 17:1; 1 Cor 11:19; 1 Tim 4:1
8 [1]Lit *having*; Gr part. [a]Matt 5:30; Mark 9:43
9 [1]Lit *having*; Gr part. [2]Lit *Gehenna of fire* [a]Matt 5:29; Mark 9:47 [b]Matt 5:22
10 [a]Luke 1:19; Acts 12:15; Rev 8:2
11 [1]Early mss do not contain this v [a]Luke 19:10
12 [a]Matt 18:12-14: *Luke 15:4-7*
14 [1]Lit *before*
15 [1]Late mss add *against you* [2]Or *reprove* [3]Lit *between you and him alone* [a]Lev 19:17; Luke 17:3; Gal 6:1; 2 Thess 3:15; James 5:19
16 [1]Lit *word* [a]Deut 19:15; John 8:17; 2 Cor 13:1; 1 Tim 5:19; Heb 10:28
17 [1]Lit *the* [a]1 Cor 6:1ff [b]2 Thess 3:6,14f
18 [1]Or *forbid* [2]Gr fut. pft. pass. [3]Or *permit* [a]Matt 16:19; John 20:23
19 [1]Lit *from* [a]Matt 7:7
20 [a]Matt 28:20
21 [a]Matt 18:15 [b]Luke 17:4
22 [a]Gen 4:24
23 [1]Lit *was compared to* [a]Matt 13:24 [b]Matt 25:19
24 [1]A talent was worth more than fifteen years' wages of a laborer
25 [1]Or *was unable to* [a]Luke 7:42 [b]Ex 21:2; Lev 25:39; 2 Kin 4:1; Neh 5:5
26 [a]Matt 8:2
27 [1]Or *loan* [a]Luke 7:42
28 [1]The denarius was a day's wages
30 [1]Lit *but*
33 [a]Matt 6:12; Eph 4:32

cy on your fellow slave, in the same way
that I had mercy on you?'
34 "And his lord, moved with anger,
handed him over to the torturers until he
should repay all that was owed him.
35 "[a]My heavenly Father will also do
the same to you, if each of you does not
forgive his brother from [1]your heart."

Concerning Divorce

19 [a]When Jesus had finished these
words, He departed from Galilee
and [b]came into the region of Judea beyond the Jordan;
2 and [1]large crowds followed Him,
and [a]He healed them there.
3 ¶ *Some* Pharisees came to [1]Jesus,
testing Him and asking, "[a]Is it lawful *for*
a man to [2]divorce his wife for any reason
at all?"
4 And He answered and said, "Have
you not read [a]that He who created *them*
from the beginning MADE THEM MALE AND
FEMALE,
5 and said, '[a]FOR THIS REASON A MAN
SHALL LEAVE HIS FATHER AND MOTHER AND BE
JOINED TO HIS WIFE, AND [b]THE TWO SHALL
BECOME ONE FLESH'?
6 "So they are no longer two, but one
flesh. What therefore God has joined together, let no man separate."
7 They *said to Him, "[a]Why then
did Moses command to GIVE HER A CERTIFI-
CATE OF DIVORCE AND SEND *her* AWAY?"
8 He *said to them, "Because of your
hardness of heart Moses permitted you to
[1]divorce your wives; but from the beginning it has not been this way.
9 "And I say to you, [a]whoever [1]di-
vorces his wife, except for [2]immorality,
and marries another woman [3]commits
adultery [4]."
10 ¶ The disciples *said to Him, "If
the relationship of the man with his wife
is like this, it is better not to marry."
11 But He said to them, "[a]Not all men
can accept this statement, but [b]*only*
those to whom it has been given.
12 "For there are eunuchs who were
born that way from their mother's womb;
and there are eunuchs who were made
eunuchs by men; and there are *also* eunuchs who made themselves eunuchs for
the sake of the kingdom of heaven. He
who is able to accept *this,* let him accept *it.*"

Jesus Blesses Little Children

13 ¶ [a]Then *some* children were
brought to Him so that He might lay His
hands on them and pray; and the disciples rebuked them.
14 But Jesus said, "[1a]Let the children
alone, and do not hinder them from coming to Me; for [b]the kingdom of heaven
belongs to such as these."
15 After laying His hands on them, He
departed from there.

The Rich Young Ruler

16 ¶ [a]And someone came to Him and
said, "Teacher, what good thing shall I do
that I may obtain [b]eternal life?"
17 And He said to him, "Why are you
asking Me about what is good? There is
only One who is good; but [a]if you wish
to enter into life, keep the commandments."
18 *Then* he *said to Him, "Which
ones?" And Jesus said, "[a]YOU SHALL NOT
COMMIT MURDER; YOU SHALL NOT COMMIT
ADULTERY; YOU SHALL NOT STEAL; YOU SHALL
NOT BEAR FALSE WITNESS;
19 [a]HONOR YOUR FATHER AND MOTHER;
and [b]YOU SHALL LOVE YOUR NEIGHBOR AS
YOURSELF."
20 The young man *said to Him, "All
these things I have kept; what am I still
lacking?"
21 Jesus said to him, "If you wish to be
[1]complete, go *and* [a]sell your possessions
and give to *the* poor, and you will have
[b]treasure in heaven; and come, follow Me."
22 But when the young man heard this
statement, he went away grieving; for he
was one who owned much property.
23 ¶ And Jesus said to His disciples,
"Truly I say to you, [a]it is hard for a rich
man to enter the kingdom of heaven.
24 "Again I say to you, [a]it is easier for
a camel to go through the eye of a needle,
than for a rich man to enter the kingdom
of God."
25 When the disciples heard *this,* they
were very astonished and said, "Then
who can be saved?"
26 And looking at *them* Jesus said to
them, "[a]With people this is impossible,
but with God all things are possible."

The Disciples' Reward

27 ¶ Then Peter said to Him, "Behold,
we have left everything and followed
You; what then will there be for us?"
28 And Jesus said to them, "Truly I say
to you, that you who have followed Me,
in the regeneration when [a]the Son of
Man will sit on [1]His glorious throne,
[b]you also shall sit upon twelve thrones,
judging the twelve tribes of Israel.
29 "And [a]everyone who has left houses
or brothers or sisters or father or mother
[1]or children or farms for My name's
sake, will receive [2]many times as much,
and will inherit eternal life.
30 "[a]But many *who are* first will be
last; and *the* last, first.

35 [1]Lit *your hearts* [a]Matt 6:14
19:1 [a]Matt 7:28 [b]Matt 19:1-9: *Mark 10:1-12*
2 [1]Lit *many* [a]Matt 4:23
3 [1]Lit *Him* [2]Or *send away* [a]Matt 5:31
4 [a]Gen 1:27; 5:2
5 [a]Gen 2:24; Eph 5:31 [b]1 Cor 6:16
7 [a]Deut 24:1-4; Matt 5:31
8 [1]Or *send away*
9 [1]Or *sends away* [2]Lit *fornication* [3]Some early mss read *makes her commit adultery* [4]Some early mss add *and he who marries a divorced woman commits adultery* [a]Matt 5:32
11 [a]1 Cor 7:7ff [b]Matt 13:11
13 [a]Matt 19:13-15: *Mark 10:13-16; Luke 18:15-17*
14 [1]Or *Permit the children* [a]Matt 18:3; Mark 10:15; Luke 18:17; 1 Cor 14:20; 1 Pet 2:2 [b]Matt 5:3
16 [a]Matt 19:16-29: *Mark 10:17-30; Luke 18:18-30*; Luke 10:25-28 [b]Matt 25:46
17 [a]Lev 18:5; Neh 9:29; Ezek 20:21
18 [a]Ex 20:13-16; Deut 5:17-20
19 [a]Ex 20:12; Deut 5:16 [b]Lev 19:18
21 [1]Or *perfect* [a]Luke 12:33; 16:9; Acts 2:45; 4:34f [b]Matt 6:20
23 [a]Matt 13:22; Mark 10:23f; Luke 18:24
24 [a]Mark 10:25; Luke 18:25
26 [a]Gen 18:14; Job 42:2; Jer 32:17; Zech 8:6; Mark 10:27; Luke 1:37; 18:27
28 [1]Lit *the throne of His glory* [a]Matt 25:31 [b]Luke 22:30; Rev 3:21; 4:4; 11:16; 20:4
29 [1]One early ms adds *or wife* [2]One early mss reads *a hundred times* [a]Matt 6:33; Mark 10:29f; Luke 18:29f
30 [a]Matt 20:16; Mark 10:31; Luke 13:30

Laborers in the Vineyard

20 “For [a]the kingdom of heaven is like [1]a landowner who went out early in the morning to hire laborers for his [b]vineyard.

2 “When he had agreed with the laborers for a [1]denarius for the day, he sent them into his vineyard.

3 “And he went out about the [1]third hour and saw others standing idle in the market place;

4 and to those he said, ‘You also go into the vineyard, and whatever is right I will give you.’ And *so* they went.

5 “Again he went out about the [1]sixth and the ninth hour, and did [2]the same thing.

6 “And about the [1]eleventh *hour* he went out and found others standing *around*; and he *said to them, ‘Why have you been standing here idle all day long?’

7 “They *said to him, ‘Because no one hired us.’ He *said to them, ‘You go into the vineyard too.’

8 ¶ “When [a]evening came, the [1]owner of the vineyard *said to his [b]foreman, ‘Call the laborers and pay them their wages, beginning with the last *group* to the first.’

9 “When those *hired* about the eleventh hour came, each one received a [1]denarius.

10 “When those *hired* first came, they thought that they would receive more; [1]but each of them also received a denarius.

11 “When they received it, they grumbled at the landowner,

12 saying, ‘These last men have worked *only* one hour, and you have made them equal to us who have borne the burden and the [a]scorching heat of the day.’

13 “But he answered and said to one of them, ‘[a]Friend, I am doing you no wrong; did you not agree with me for a denarius?

14 ‘Take what is yours and go, but I wish to give to this last man the same as to you.

15 ‘Is it not lawful for me to do what I wish with what is my own? Or is your [a]eye [1]envious because I am [2]generous?’

16 “So [a]the last shall be first, and the first last.”

Death, Resurrection Foretold

17 ¶ [a]As Jesus was about to go up to Jerusalem, He took the twelve *disciples* aside by themselves, and on the way He said to them,

18 “Behold, we are going up to Jerusalem; and the Son of Man [a]will be [1]delivered to the chief priests and scribes, and they will condemn Him to death,

19 and [a]will hand Him over to the Gentiles to mock and scourge and crucify *Him*, and on [b]the third day He will be raised up.”

Preferment Asked

20 ¶ [a]Then the mother of [b]the sons of Zebedee came to [1]Jesus with her sons, [c]bowing down and making a request of Him.

21 And He said to her, “What do you wish?” She *said to Him, “Command that in Your kingdom these two sons of mine [a]may sit one on Your right and one on Your left.”

22 But Jesus answered, “You do not know what you are asking. Are you able [a]to drink the cup that I am about to drink?” They *said to Him, “We are able.”

23 He *said to them, “[a]My cup you shall drink; but to sit on My right and on *My* left, this is not Mine to give, [b]but it is for those for whom it has been [c]prepared by My Father.”

24 ¶ And hearing *this*, the ten became indignant with the two brothers.

25 [a]But Jesus called them to Himself and said, “You know that the rulers of the Gentiles lord it over them, and *their* great men exercise authority over them.

26 “It is not this way among you, [a]but whoever wishes to become great among you shall be your servant,

27 and whoever wishes to be first among you shall be your slave;

28 just as [a]the Son of Man [b]did not come to be served, but to serve, and to give His [1]life a ransom for many.”

Sight for the Blind

29 ¶ [a]As they were leaving Jericho, a large crowd followed Him.

30 And two blind men sitting by the road, hearing that Jesus was passing by, cried out, “Lord, [a]have mercy on us, [b]Son of David!”

31 The crowd sternly told them to be quiet, but they cried out all the more, “Lord, [a]Son of David, have mercy on us!”

32 And Jesus stopped and called them, and said, “What do you want Me to do for you?”

33 They *said to Him, “Lord, *we want* our eyes to be opened.”

34 Moved with compassion, Jesus touched their eyes; and immediately they regained their sight and followed Him.

20:1 [1]Lit *a man, a landowner* [a]Matt 13:24 [b]Matt 21:28,33

2 [1]The denarius was a day's wages

3 [1]I.e. 9 a.m.

5 [1]I.e. noon and 3 p.m. [2]Lit *similarly*

6 [1]I.e. 5 p.m.

8 [1]Or *lord* [a]Lev 19:13; Deut 24:15 [b]Luke 8:3

9 [1]The denarius was a day's wages

10 [1]Lit *each one a denarius*

12 [a]Jon 4:8; Luke 12:55; James 1:11

13 [a]Matt 22:12; 26:50

15 [1]Lit *evil* [2]Lit *good* [a]Deut 15:9; Matt 6:23; Mark 7:22

16 [a]Matt 19:30; Mark 10:31; Luke 13:30

17 [a]Matt 20:17-19: *Mark 10:32-34; Luke 18:31-33*

18 [1]Or *betrayed* [a]Matt 16:21

19 [a]Matt 27:2; Acts 2:23; 3:13; 4:27; 21:11 [b]Matt 16:21; 17:23; Luke 18:32f

20 [1]Lit *Him* [a]Matt 20:20-28: *Mark 10:35-45* [b]Matt 4:21; 10:2 [c]Matt 8:2

21 [a]Matt 19:28

22 [a]Is 51:17,22; Jer 49:12; Matt 26:39,42; Luke 22:42; John 18:11

23 [a]Acts 12:2; Rev 1:9 [b]Matt 13:11 [c]Matt 25:34

25 [a]Matt 20:25-28; Luke 22:25-27

26 [a]Matt 23:11; Mark 9:35; 10:43; Luke 22:26

28 [1]Or *soul* [a]Matt 8:20 [b]Matt 26:28; John 13:13ff; 2 Cor 8:9; Phil 2:7; 1 Tim 2:6; Titus 2:14; Heb 9:28; Rev 1:5

29 [a]Matt 20:29-34: *Mark 10:46-52; Luke 18:35-43;* Matt 9:27-31

30 [a]Matt 9:27 [b]Matt 20:31

31 [a]Matt 9:27

The Triumphal Entry

21 [a]When they had approached Jerusalem and had come to Bethphage, at [b]the Mount of Olives, then
Jesus sent two disciples,
2 saying to them, "Go into the village
opposite you, and immediately you will
find a donkey tied *there* and a colt with
her; untie them and bring them to Me.
3 "If anyone says anything to you, you
shall say, 'The Lord has need of them,'
and immediately he will send them."
4 [a]This [1]took place to fulfill what
was spoken through the prophet:
5 "[a]SAY TO THE DAUGHTER OF ZION,
'BEHOLD YOUR KING IS COMING
TO YOU,
GENTLE, AND MOUNTED ON A
DONKEY,
EVEN ON A COLT, THE FOAL OF A
BEAST OF BURDEN.' "
6 The disciples went and did just as
Jesus had instructed them,
7 and brought the donkey and the
colt, and laid their coats on them; and He
sat on [1]the coats.
8 Most of the crowd [a]spread their
coats in the road, and others were cutting
branches from the trees and spreading
them in the road.
9 The crowds going ahead of Him,
and those who followed, were shouting,
"Hosanna to the [a]Son of David;
[b]BLESSED IS HE WHO COMES IN THE
NAME OF THE LORD;
Hosanna [c]in the highest!"
10 When He had entered Jerusalem,
all the city was stirred, saying, "Who is
this?"
11 And the crowds were saying, "This
is [a]the prophet Jesus, from [b]Nazareth in
Galilee."

Cleansing the Temple

12 ¶ [a]And Jesus entered the temple
and drove out all those who were buying
and selling in the temple, and overturned
the tables of the [b]money changers and
the seats of those who were selling
[c]doves.
13 And He *said to them, "It is written, '[a]MY HOUSE SHALL BE CALLED A HOUSE
OF PRAYER'; but you are making it a [b]ROB-
BERS' [1]DEN."
14 ¶ And *the* blind and *the* lame came
to Him in the temple, and [a]He healed
them.
15 But when the chief priests and the
scribes saw the wonderful things that He
had done, and the children who were
shouting in the temple, "Hosanna to the
[a]Son of David," they became indignant
16 and said to Him, "Do You hear

21:1 [a]Matt 21:1-9: *Mark 11:1-10; Luke 19:29-38* [b]Matt 24:3; 26:30; Mark 11:1; 13:3; 14:26; Luke 19:29,37; 21:37; 22:39; John 8:1; Acts 1:12
4 [1]Lit *has happened* [a]Matt 21:4-9: *Mark 11:7-10; Luke 19:35-38; John 12:12-15*
5 [a]Is 62:11; Zech 9:9
7 [1]Lit *them*
8 [a]2 Kin 9:13
9 [a]Matt 9:27 [b]Ps 118:26 [c]Luke 2:14
11 [a]Matt 21:26; Mark 6:15; Luke 7:16,39; 13:33; 24:19; John 1:21,25; 4:19; 6:14; 7:40; 9:17; Acts 3:22f; 7:37 [b]Matt 2:23
12 [a]Matt 21:12-16: *Mark 11:15-18; Luke 19:45-47*; Matt 21:12,13: *John 2:13-16* [b]Ex 30:13 [c]Lev 1:14; 5:7; 12:8
13 [1]Lit *cave* [a]Is 56:7 [b]Jer 7:11
14 [a]Matt 4:23
15 [a]Matt 9:27
16 [a]Ps 8:2; Matt 11:25
17 [a]Matt 26:6; Mark 11:1,11, 12; 14:3; Luke 19:29; 24:50; John 11:1,18; 12:1
18 [a]Matt 21:18-22: *Mark 11:12-14,20-24*
19 [a]Luke 13:6-9
21 [a]Matt 17:20; Mark 11:23; Luke 17:6; James 1:6
22 [a]Matt 7:7
23 [a]Matt 21:23-27: *Mark 11:27-33; Luke 20:1-8* [b]Matt 26:55
24 [1]Lit *word*
26 [1]Lit *crowd* [a]Matt 11:9; Mark 6:20
28 [1]Lit *children* [2]Lit *Child* [a]Matt 20:1; 21:33

what these *children* are saying?" And
Jesus *said to them, "Yes; have you never
read, '[a]OUT OF THE MOUTH OF INFANTS AND
NURSING BABIES YOU HAVE PREPARED PRAISE
FOR YOURSELF'?"
17 And He left them and went out of
the city to [a]Bethany, and spent the night
there.

The Barren Fig Tree

18 ¶ [a]Now in the morning, when He
was returning to the city, He became
hungry.
19 Seeing a lone [a]fig tree by the road,
He came to it and found nothing on it
except leaves only; and He *said to it,
"No longer shall there ever be *any* fruit
from you." And at once the fig tree withered.
20 ¶ Seeing *this,* the disciples were
amazed and asked, "How did the fig tree
wither *all* at once?"
21 And Jesus answered and said to
them, "Truly I say to you, [a]if you have
faith and do not doubt, you will not only
do what was done to the fig tree, but even
if you say to this mountain, 'Be taken up
and cast into the sea,' it will happen.
22 "And [a]all things you ask in prayer,
believing, you will receive."

Authority Challenged

23 ¶ [a]When He entered the temple,
the chief priests and the elders of the
people came to Him [b]while He was
teaching, and said, "By what authority
are You doing these things, and who gave
You this authority?"
24 Jesus said to them, "I will also ask
you one [1]thing, which if you tell Me, I
will also tell you by what authority I do
these things.
25 "The baptism of John was from what
source, from heaven or from men?" And
they *began* reasoning among themselves,
saying, "If we say, 'From heaven,' He will
say to us, 'Then why did you not believe him?'
26 "But if we say, 'From men,' we fear
the [1]people; for they all regard John as
[a]a prophet."
27 And answering Jesus, they said,
"We do not know." He also said to them,
"Neither will I tell you by what authority
I do these things.

Parable of Two Sons

28 ¶ "But what do you think? A man
had two [1]sons, and he came to the first
and said, '[2]Son, go work today in the
[a]vineyard.'
29 "And he answered, 'I will not'; but
afterward he regretted it and went.
30 "The man came to the second and

said the same thing; and he answered, 'I
will, sir'; but he did not go.
31 "Which of the two did the will of his
father?" They *said, "The first." Jesus
*said to them, "Truly I say to you that
[a]the tax collectors and prostitutes [1]will
get into the kingdom of God before you.
32 "For John came to you in the way of
righteousness and you did not believe
him; but [a]the tax collectors and prostitutes did believe him; and you, seeing
this, did not even feel remorse afterward
so as to believe him.

Parable of the Landowner

33 ¶ "Listen to another parable.
[a]There was a [1]landowner who [b]PLANT-
ED A [c]VINEYARD AND PUT A WALL AROUND IT
AND DUG A WINE PRESS IN IT, AND BUILT A
TOWER, and rented it out to [2]vine-
growers and [d]went on a journey.
34 "When the [1]harvest time approached, he [a]sent his slaves to the vine-
growers to receive his produce.
35 "The vine-growers took his slaves
and beat one, and killed another, and
stoned a third.
36 "Again he [a]sent another group of
slaves larger than the first; and they did
the same thing to them.
37 "But afterward he sent his son to
them, saying, 'They will respect my son.'
38 "But when the vine-growers saw the
son, they said among themselves, 'This is
the heir; come, let us kill him and seize
his inheritance.'
39 "They took him, and threw him out
of the vineyard and killed him.
40 "Therefore when the [1]owner of the
vineyard comes, what will he do to those
vine-growers?"
41 They *said to Him, "He will bring
those wretches to a wretched end, and
[a]will rent out the vineyard to other vine-
growers who will pay him the proceeds at
the *proper* seasons."
42 ¶ Jesus *said to them, "Did you
never read in the Scriptures,

'[a]THE STONE WHICH THE BUILDERS
REJECTED,
THIS BECAME THE CHIEF CORNER
stone;
THIS CAME ABOUT FROM THE LORD,
AND IT IS MARVELOUS IN OUR EYES'?

43 "Therefore I say to you, the kingdom
of God will be taken away from you and
given to a [1]people, producing the fruit
of it.
44 "And [a]he who falls on this stone
will be broken to pieces; but on whomever it falls, it will scatter him like dust."
45 ¶ When the chief priests and the
Pharisees heard His parables, they understood that He was speaking about them.
46 When they sought to seize Him,
they [a]feared the [1]people, because they
considered Him to be a [b]prophet.

Parable of the Marriage Feast

22

Jesus spoke to them again in parables, saying,
2 "[a]The kingdom of heaven [1]may be
compared to [2]a king who [3]gave a [b]wed-
ding feast for his son.
3 "And he [a]sent out his slaves to call
those who had been invited to the wedding feast, and they were unwilling to
come.
4 "Again he [a]sent out other slaves
saying, 'Tell those who have been invited, "Behold, I have prepared my dinner;
my oxen and my fattened livestock are *all*
butchered and everything is ready; come
to the wedding feast." '
5 "But they paid no attention and
went their way, one to his own [1]farm,
another to his business,
6 and the rest seized his slaves and
mistreated them and killed them.
7 "But the king was enraged, and he
sent his armies and destroyed those murderers and set their city on fire.
8 "Then he *said to his slaves, 'The
wedding is ready, but those who were
invited were not worthy.
9 'Go therefore to [a]the main highways, and as many as you find *there,* invite to the wedding feast.'
10 "Those slaves went out into the
streets and gathered together all they
found, both evil and good; and the wedding hall was filled with [1]dinner guests.
11 ¶ "But when the king came in to
look over the dinner guests, he saw [a]a
man there who was not dressed in wedding clothes,
12 and he *said to him, '[a]Friend, how
did you come in here without wedding
clothes?' And the man was speechless.
13 "Then the king said to the servants,
'Bind him hand and foot, and throw him
into [a]the outer darkness; in that place
there will be weeping and gnashing of
teeth.'
14 "For many are [1a]called, but few *are*
[a]chosen."

Tribute to Caesar

15 ¶ [a]Then the Pharisees went and
[1]plotted together how they might trap
Him [2]in what He said.
16 And they *sent their disciples to
Him, along with the [a]Herodians, saying,
"Teacher, we know that You are truthful
and teach the way of God in truth, and
[1]defer to no one; for You are not partial
to any.
17 "Tell us then, what do You think? Is

31 [1]Lit *are getting into* [a]Luke 7:29,37-50
32 [a]Luke 3:12; 7:29f
33 [1]Lit *a man, head of a household* [2]Or *tenant farmers,* also vv 34, 35, 38, 40 [a]Matt 21:33-46: *Mark 12:1-12; Luke 20:9-19* [b]Is 5:1,2 [c]Matt 20:1; 21:28 [d]Matt 25:14
34 [1]Lit *the fruit season* [a]Matt 22:3
36 [a]Matt 22:4
40 [1]Lit *lord*
41 [a]Matt 8:11f; Acts 13:46; 18:6; 28:28
42 [a]Ps 118:22f; Acts 4:11; Rom 9:33; 1 Pet 2:7
43 [1]Lit *nation*
44 [a]Is 8:14,15
46 [1]Lit *crowds* [a]Matt 21:26 [b]Matt 21:11
22:2 [1]Lit *was compared to* [2]Lit *a man, a king* [3]Lit *made* [a]Matt 13:24; 22:2-14; Luke 14:16-24 [b]Luke 12:36; John 2:2
3 [a]Matt 21:34
4 [a]Matt 21:36
5 [1]Or *field*
9 [a]Ezek 21:21; Obad 14
10 [1]Lit *those reclining* at the table
11 [a]2 Kin 10:22; Zech 3:3,4
12 [a]Matt 20:13; 26:50
13 [a]Matt 8:12; 25:30; Luke 13:28
14 [1]Or *invited* [a]Matt 24:22; 2 Pet 1:10; Rev 17:14
15 [1]Lit *took counsel* [2]Lit *in word* [a]Matt 22:15-22: *Mark 12:13-17; Luke 20:20-26*
16 [1]Lit *it is not a concern to You about anyone;* i.e. You do not seek anyone's favor [a]Mark 3:6; 8:15; 12:13

it [1]lawful to give a [a]poll-tax to [b]Caesar,
or not?"
18 But Jesus perceived their [1]malice,
and said, "Why are you testing Me, you
hypocrites?
19 "Show Me the [a]coin *used* for the
poll-tax." And they brought Him a [1]de-
narius.
20 And He *said to them, "Whose
likeness and inscription is this?"
21 They *said to Him, "Caesar's."
Then He *said to them, "[a]Then render
to Caesar the things that are Caesar's;
and to God the things that are God's."
22 And hearing *this,* they were
amazed, and [a]leaving Him, they went
away.

Jesus Answers the Sadducees

23 ¶ [a]On that day *some* [b]Sadducees
(who say [c]there is no resurrection) came
to Jesus and questioned Him,
24 asking, "Teacher, Moses said, '[a]IF
A MAN DIES HAVING NO CHILDREN, HIS BROTH-
ER AS NEXT OF KIN SHALL MARRY HIS WIFE,
AND RAISE UP CHILDREN FOR HIS BROTHER.'
25 "Now there were seven brothers
with us; and the first married and died,
and having no children left his wife to his
brother;
26 so also the second, and the third,
down to the seventh.
27 "Last of all, the woman died.
28 "In the resurrection, therefore,
whose wife of the seven will she be? For
they all had *married* her."
29 ¶ But Jesus answered and said to
them, "You are mistaken, [a]not [1]under-
standing the Scriptures nor the power of
God.
30 "For in the resurrection they neither
[a]marry nor are given in marriage, but are
like angels in heaven.
31 "But regarding the resurrection of
the dead, have you not read what was
spoken to you by God:
32 '[a]I AM THE GOD OF ABRAHAM, AND
THE GOD OF ISAAC, AND THE GOD OF
JACOB'? He is not the God of the dead but
of the living."
33 When the crowds heard *this,* [a]they
were astonished at His teaching.
34 ¶ [a]But when the Pharisees heard
that Jesus had silenced [b]the Sadducees,
they gathered themselves together.
35 One of them, [1a]a lawyer, asked
Him *a question,* testing Him,
36 "Teacher, which is the great commandment in the Law?"
37 And He said to him, " '[a]YOU SHALL
LOVE THE LORD YOUR GOD WITH ALL YOUR
HEART, AND WITH ALL YOUR SOUL, AND WITH
ALL YOUR MIND.'
38 "This is the great and [1]foremost
commandment.
39 "The second is like it, '[a]YOU SHALL
LOVE YOUR NEIGHBOR AS YOURSELF.'
40 "[a]On these two commandments depend the whole Law and the Prophets."
41 ¶ [a]Now while the Pharisees were
gathered together, Jesus asked them a
question:
42 "What do you think about [1]the
Christ, whose son is He?" They *said to
Him, "[a]*The son* of David."
43 He *said to them, "Then how does
David [1a]in the Spirit call Him 'Lord,'
saying,
44 '[a]THE LORD SAID TO MY LORD,
"SIT AT MY RIGHT HAND,
UNTIL I PUT YOUR ENEMIES
BENEATH YOUR FEET" '?
45 "If David then calls Him 'Lord,' how
is He his son?"
46 [a]No one was able to answer Him a
word, nor did anyone dare from that day
on to ask Him [1]another question.

Pharisaism Exposed

23 [a]Then Jesus spoke to the crowds
and to His disciples,
2 saying: "[a]The scribes and the Pharisees have seated themselves in the chair
of Moses;
3 therefore all that they tell you, do
and observe, but do not do according to
their deeds; for they say *things* and do not
do *them.*
4 "[a]They tie up heavy burdens and lay
them on men's shoulders, but they themselves are unwilling to move them with
so much as a finger.
5 "But they do all their deeds [a]to be
noticed by men; for they [b]broaden their
[1]phylacteries and lengthen [c]the tassels
of their garments.
6 "They [a]love the place of honor at
banquets and the chief seats in the synagogues,
7 and respectful greetings in the market places, and being called [a]Rabbi by
men.
8 "But [a]do not be called [b]Rabbi; for
One is your Teacher, and you are all
brothers.
9 "Do not call *anyone* on earth your
father; for [a]One is your Father, He who
is in heaven.
10 "Do not be called [1]leaders; for One
is your Leader, *that is,* Christ.
11 "[a]But the greatest among you shall
be your servant.
12 "[a]Whoever exalts himself shall be
humbled; and whoever humbles himself
shall be exalted.

17 [1]Or *permissible* [a]Matt 17:25 [b]Luke 2:1
18 [1]Or *wickedness*
19 [1]The denarius was a day's wages [a]Matt 17:25
21 [a]Mark 12:17; Luke 20:25; Rom 13:7
22 [a]Mark 12:12
23 [a]Matt 22:23-33: *Mark 12:18-27; Luke 20:27-40* [b]Matt 3:7 [c]Acts 23:8
24 [a]Deut 25:5
29 [1]Or *knowing* [a]John 20:9
30 [a]Matt 24:38; Luke 17:27
32 [a]Ex 3:6
33 [a]Matt 7:28
34 [a]Matt 22:34-40: *Mark 12:28-31*; Luke 10:25-37 [b]Matt 3:7
35 [1]I.e. an expert in the Mosaic Law [a]Luke 7:30; Titus 3:13
37 [a]Deut 6:5
38 [1]Or *first*
39 [a]Lev 19:18; Matt 19:19; Gal 5:14
40 [a]Matt 7:12
41 [a]Matt 22:41-46: *Mark 12:35-37; Luke 20:41-44*
42 [1]I.e. the Messiah [a]Matt 9:27
43 [1]Or *by inspiration* [a]2 Sam 23:2; Rev 1:10
44 [a]Ps 110:1; Matt 26:64; Mark 16:19; Acts 2:34f; 1 Cor 15:25; Heb 1:13
46 [1]Lit *any longer* [a]Mark 12:34; Luke 14:6
23:1 [a]Matt 23:1-7: *Mark 12:38,39; Luke 20:45,46*
2 [a]Deut 33:3f; Ezra 7:6; Neh 8:4
4 [a]Luke 11:46; Acts 15:10
5 [1]I.e. small cases containing Scripture texts worn on the left arm and forehead for religious purposes [a]Matt 6:1 [b]Ex 13:9; Deut 6:8 [c]Matt 9:20
6 [a]Luke 11:43
7 [a]Matt 23:8; Mark 9:5; John 1:38
8 [a]James 3:1 [b]Matt 23:7; Mark 9:5; John 1:38
9 [a]Matt 6:9
10 [1]Or *teachers*
11 [a]Matt 20:26
12 [a]Luke 14:11

Jewish Sects

PHARISEES Their roots can be traced to the second century B.C.—to the Hasidim.

1. Along with the Torah, they accepted as equally inspired and authoritative all material contained within the oral tradition.
2. On free will and determination, they held to a mediating view that made it impossible for either free will or the sovereignty of God to cancel out the other.
3. They accepted a rather developed hierarchy of angels and demons.
4. They taught that there was a future for the dead.
5. They believed in the immortality of the soul and in reward and retribution after death.
6. They were champions of human equality.
7. The emphasis of their teaching was ethical rather than theological.

SADDUCEES They probably had their beginning during the Hasmonean period (166-63 B.C.). Their demise occurred c. A.D. 70 with the fall of Jerusalem.

1. They denied that the oral law was authoritative and binding.
2. They interpreted Mosaic law more literally than did the Pharisees.
3. They were very exacting in Levitical purity.
4. They attributed all to free will.
5. They argued there is neither resurrection of the dead nor a future life.
6. They rejected a belief in angels and demons.
7. They rejected the idea of a spiritual world.
8. Only the books of Moses were canonical Scripture.

ESSENES They probably originated among the Hasidim, along with the Pharisees, from whom they later separated (I Maccabees 2:42; 7:13). They were a group of very strict and zealous Jews who took part with the Maccabeans in a revolt against the Syrians, c. 165-155 B.C.

1. They followed a strict observance of the purity laws of the Torah.
2. They were notable for their communal ownership of property.
3. They had a strong sense of mutual responsibility.
4. Daily worship was an important feature along with a daily study of their sacred scriptures.
5. Solemn oaths of piety and obedience had to be taken.
6. Sacrifices were offered on holy days and during sacred seasons.
7. Marriage was not condemned in principle but was avoided.
8. They attributed all that happened to fate.

ZEALOTS They originated during the reign of Herod the Great c. 6 B.C. and ceased to exist in A.D. 73 at Masada.

1. They opposed payment of tribute for taxes to a pagan emperor, saying that allegiance was due only to God.
2. They held a fierce loyalty to the Jewish traditions.
3. They were opposed to the use of the Greek language in Palestine.
4. They prophesied the coming of the time of salvation.

Eight Woes

13 ¶ "[a]But woe to you, scribes and
Pharisees, hypocrites, [b]because you shut
off the kingdom of heaven [1]from [2]peo-
ple; for you do not enter in yourselves,
nor do you allow those who are entering
to go in.
14 ["[1]Woe to you, scribes and Pharisees, hypocrites, because [a]you devour
widows' houses, and for a pretense you
make long prayers; therefore you will receive greater condemnation.]
15 ¶ "Woe to you, scribes and Pharisees, hypocrites, because you travel
around on sea and land to make one
[1a]proselyte; and when he becomes one,
you make him twice as much a son of
[2b]hell as yourselves.
16 ¶ "Woe to you, [a]blind guides, who
say, '[b]Whoever swears by the [1]temple,
that is nothing; but whoever swears by
the gold of the [1]temple is obligated.'
17 "You fools and blind men! [a]Which
is [1]more important, the gold or the
[2]temple that sanctified the gold?
18 "And, 'Whoever swears by the altar,
that is nothing, but whoever swears by
the [1]offering on it, he is obligated.'
19 "You blind men, [a]which is [1]more
important, the [2]offering, or the altar that
sanctifies the [2]offering?
20 "Therefore, [1]whoever swears by
the altar, swears *both* by [2]the altar and
by everything on it.
21 "And [1]whoever swears by the
[2]temple, swears *both* by [3]the temple
and by Him who [a]dwells within it.
22 "And [1]whoever swears by heaven,
[a]swears *both* by the throne of God and
by Him who sits upon it.
23 ¶ "[a]Woe to you, scribes and Pharisees, hypocrites! For you tithe mint and
dill and [1]cummin, and have neglected
the weightier provisions of the law: justice and mercy and faithfulness; but these
are the things you should have done without neglecting the others.
24 "You [a]blind guides, who strain out a
gnat and swallow a camel!
25 ¶ "Woe to you, scribes and Pharisees, hypocrites! For [a]you clean the outside of the cup and of the dish, but inside
they are full [1]of robbery and self-
indulgence.
26 "You blind Pharisee, first [a]clean the
inside of the cup and of the dish, so that
the outside of it may become clean also.
27 ¶ "[a]Woe to you, scribes and Pharisees, hypocrites! For you are like whitewashed tombs which on the outside appear beautiful, but inside they are full of
dead men's bones and all uncleanness.
28 "So you, too, outwardly appear righteous to men, but inwardly you are full of
hypocrisy and lawlessness.
29 ¶ "[a]Woe to you, scribes and Pharisees, hypocrites! For you build the tombs
of the prophets and adorn the monuments of the righteous,
30 and say, 'If we had been *living* in
the days of our fathers, we would not
have been partners with them in *shedding* the blood of the prophets.'
31 "So you testify against yourselves,
that you [a]are [1]sons of those who murdered the prophets.
32 "Fill up, then, the measure *of the
guilt* of your fathers.
33 "You serpents, [a]you brood of vipers,
how [1]will you escape the [2]sentence of
[3b]hell?
34 ¶ "[a]Therefore, behold, [b]I am
sending you prophets and wise men
and scribes; some of them you will kill
and crucify, and some of them you will
[c]scourge in your synagogues, and [d]per-
secute from city to city,
35 so that upon you may fall *the guilt
of* all the righteous blood shed on earth,
from the blood of righteous [a]Abel to the
blood of Zechariah, the [b]son of Berechiah, whom [c]you murdered between
the [1]temple and the altar.
36 "Truly I say to you, all these things
will come upon [a]this generation.

Lament over Jerusalem

37 ¶ "[a]Jerusalem, Jerusalem, who
[b]kills the prophets and stones those who
are sent to her! How often I wanted to
gather your children together, [c]the way
a hen gathers her chicks under her
wings, and you were unwilling.
38 "Behold, [a]your house is being left to
you desolate!
39 "For I say to you, from now on you
will not see Me until you say, '[a]BLESSED
IS HE WHO COMES IN THE NAME OF THE
LORD!' "

Signs of Christ's Return

24 [a]Jesus [b]came out from the temple and was going away [1]when
His disciples came up to point out the
temple buildings to Him.
2 And He said to them, "Do you not
see all these things? Truly I say to you,
[a]not one stone here will be left upon
another, which will not be torn down."
3 ¶ As He was sitting on [a]the Mount
of Olives, the disciples came to Him privately, saying, "Tell us, when will these
things happen, and what *will be* the sign
of [b]Your coming, and of the [1]end of the
age?"
4 ¶ And Jesus answered and said to

13 [1]Lit *in front of* [2]Gr *anthropoi* [a]Matt 23:15 [b]Luke 11:52
14 [1]This v not found in early mss [a]Mark 12:40; Luke 20:47
15 [1]Or *convert* [2]Gr *Gehenna* [a]Acts 2:10 [b]Matt 5:22
16 [1]Or *sanctuary* [a]Matt 15:14 [b]Matt 5:33-35
17 [1]Lit *greater* [2]Or *sanctuary* [a]Ex 30:29
18 [1]Or *gift*
19 [1]Lit *greater* [2]Or *gift* [a]Ex 29:37
20 [1]Lit *he who* [2]Lit *it*
21 [1]Lit *he who* [2]Or *sanctuary* [3]Lit *it* [a]1 Kin 8:13; Ps 26:8
22 [1]Lit *he who* [a]Is 66:1; Matt 5:34
23 [1]Similar to caraway seeds [a]Matt 23:13; Luke 11:42
24 [a]Matt 23:16
25 [1]Or *as a result of* [a]Mark 7:4; Luke 11:39f
26 [a]Mark 7:4; Luke 11:39f
27 [a]Luke 11:44; Acts 23:3
29 [a]Luke 11:47f
31 [1]Or *descendants* [a]Matt 23:34; Acts 7:51f
33 [1]Lit *would* [2]Or *judgment* [3]Gr *Gehenna* [a]Matt 3:7; Luke 3:7 [b]Matt 5:22
34 [a]Matt 23:34-36; Luke 11:49-51 [b]2 Chr 36:15 [c]Matt 10:17 [d]Matt 10:23
35 [1]Or *sanctuary* [a]Gen 4:8ff; Heb 11:4 [b]Zech 1:1 [c]2 Chr 24:21
36 [a]Matt 10:23
37 [a]Matt 23:37-39: *Luke 13:34,35* [b]Matt 5:12 [c]Ruth 2:12
38 [a]1 Kin 9:7f; Jer 22:5
39 [a]Ps 118:26; Matt 21:9
24:1 [1]Lit *and* [a]Matt 24:1-51: *Mark 13; Luke 21:5-36* [b]Matt 21:23
2 [a]Luke 19:44
3 [1]Or *consummation* [a]Matt 21:1 [b]Matt 16:27f

them, "[a]See to it that no one misleads you.

5 "For [a]many will come in My name, saying, 'I am the [1]Christ,' and will mislead many.

6 "You will be hearing of [a]wars and rumors of wars. See that you are not frightened, for *those things* must take place, but *that* is not yet the end.

7 "For [a]nation will rise against nation, and kingdom against kingdom, and in various places there will be [b]famines and earthquakes.

8 "[a]But all these things are *merely* the beginning of birth pangs.

9 ¶ "[a]Then they will deliver you to tribulation, and will kill you, and [b]you will be hated by all nations because of My name.

10 "At that time many will [1a]fall away and will [2]betray one another and hate one another.

11 "Many [a]false prophets will arise and will mislead many.

12 "Because lawlessness is increased, [1]most people's love will grow cold.

13 "[a]But the one who endures to the end, he will be saved.

14 "This [a]gospel of the kingdom [b]shall be preached in the whole [1c]world as a testimony to all the nations, and then the end will come.

Perilous Times

15 ¶ "Therefore when you see the [a]ABOMINATION OF DESOLATION which was spoken of through Daniel the prophet, standing in [b]the holy place ([c]let the reader understand),

16 then those who are in Judea must flee to the mountains.

17 "[1]Whoever is on [a]the housetop must not go down to get the things out that are in his house.

18 "[1]Whoever is in the field must not turn back to get his cloak.

19 "But [a]woe to those who are pregnant and to those who are nursing babies in those days!

20 "But pray that your flight will not be in the winter, or on a Sabbath.

21 "For then there will be a [a]great tribulation, such as has not occurred since the beginning of the world until now, nor ever will.

22 "Unless those days had been cut short, no [1]life would have been saved; but for [a]the sake of the [2]elect those days will be cut short.

23 "[a]Then if anyone says to you, 'Behold, here is the [1]Christ,' or '[2]There *He is,*' do not believe *him.*

24 "For false Christs and [a]false prophets will arise and will [1]show great [2b]signs and wonders, so as to mislead, if possible, even [c]the [3]elect.

25 "Behold, I have told you in advance.

26 "So if they say to you, 'Behold, He is in the wilderness,' do not go out, *or,* 'Behold, He is in the inner rooms,' do not believe *them.*

27 "[a]For just as the lightning comes from the east and flashes even to the west, so will the [b]coming of the [c]Son of Man be.

28 "[a]Wherever the corpse is, there the [1]vultures will gather.

The Glorious Return

29 ¶ "But immediately after the [a]tribulation of those days [b]THE SUN WILL BE DARKENED, AND THE MOON WILL NOT GIVE ITS LIGHT, AND [c]THE STARS WILL FALL from [1]the sky, and the powers of [1]the heavens will be shaken.

30 "And then [a]the sign of the Son of Man will appear in the sky, and then all the tribes of the earth will mourn, and they will see [b]the SON OF MAN COMING ON THE CLOUDS OF THE SKY with power and great glory.

31 "And [a]He will send forth His angels with [b]A GREAT TRUMPET and THEY WILL GATHER TOGETHER His [1c]elect from [d]the four winds, from one end of the sky to the other.

Parable of the Fig Tree

32 ¶ "Now learn the parable from the fig tree: when its branch has already become tender and puts forth its leaves, you know that summer is near;

33 so, you too, when you see all these things, [1]recognize that [2]He is near, *right* [a]at the [3]door.

34 "Truly I say to you, [a]this [1]generation will not pass away until all these things take place.

35 "[a]Heaven and earth will pass away, but My words will not pass away.

36 ¶ "But [a]of that day and hour no one knows, not even the angels of heaven, nor the Son, but the Father alone.

37 "For [1]the [a]coming of the Son of Man will be [b]just like the days of Noah.

38 "For as in those days before the flood they were eating and drinking, [a]marrying and giving in marriage, until the day that [b]Noah entered the ark,

39 and they did not [1]understand until the flood came and took them all away; so will the [a]coming of the Son of Man be.

40 "Then there will be two men in the

4 [a]Jer 29:8 **5** [1]I.e. the Messiah [a]Matt 24:11; Acts 5:36f; 1 John 2:18 **6** [a]Rev 6:4 **7** [a]2 Chr 15:6; Is 19:2; Rev 6:8 [b]Acts 11:28; Rev 6:5 **8** [a]Matt 24:8-20; Luke 21:12-24 **9** [a]Matt 10:17; John 16:2 [b]Matt 10:22; John 15:18ff **10** [1]Lit *be caused to stumble* [2]Or *hand over* [a]Matt 11:6 **11** [a]Matt 7:15 **12** [1]Lit *the love of many* **13** [a]Matt 10:22 **14** [1]Lit *inhabited earth* [a]Matt 4:23 [b]Rom 10:18; Col 1:6 [c]Luke 2:1; Acts 11:28; Rom 10:18; Heb 1:6; Rev 3:10 **15** [a]Dan 9:27 [b]Mark 13:14; Luke 21:20; John 11:48; Acts 6:13f [c]Mark 13:14; Rev 1:3 **17** [1]Lit *He who* [a]1 Sam 9:25; 2 Sam 11:2; Matt 10:27; Luke 5:19; Acts 10:9 **18** [1]Lit *He who* **19** [a]Luke 23:29 **21** [a]Dan 12:1; Joel 2:2; Matt 24:29 **22** [1]Lit *flesh* [2]Or *chosen ones* [a]Matt 22:14; Luke 18:7 **23** [1]I.e. Messiah [2]Lit *here* [a]Luke 17:23f **24** [1]Lit *give* [2]Or *attesting miracles* [3]Or *chosen ones* [a]Matt 7:15 [b]John 4:48; 2 Thess 2:9 [c]Matt 22:14; Luke 18:7 **27** [a]Luke 17:24 [b]Matt 24:3 [c]Matt 8:20 **28** [1]Or *eagles* [a]Job 39:30; Ezek 39:17; Hab 1:8; Luke 17:37 **29** [1]Or *heaven* [a]Matt 24:21 [b]Is 13:10; Ezek 32:7; Joel 2:10; Amos 5:20; Zeph 1:15; Matt 24:29-35; Acts 2:20; Rev 6:12-17 [c]Is 34:4; Rev 6:13 **30** [a]Matt 24:3; Rev 1:7 [b]Dan 7:13; Matt 16:27 **31** [1]Or *chosen ones* [a]Matt 13:41 [b]Ex 19:16; Deut 30:4; Is 27:13; Zech 9:14; 1 Cor 15:52; 1 Thess 4:16; Heb 12:19; Rev 8:2 [c]Matt 24:22 [d]Dan 7:2; Zech 2:6; Rev 7:1 **33** [1]Or *know* [2]Or *it* [3]Lit *doors* [a]James 5:9; Rev 3:20 **34** [1]Or *race* [a]Matt 10:23 **35** [a]Matt 5:18; Mark 13:31; Luke 21:33 **36** [a]Mark 13:32; Acts 1:7 **37** [1]Lit *just as...were the days* [a]Matt 16:27 [b]Gen 6:5; Luke 17:26f **38** [a]Matt 22:30 [b]Gen 7:7 **39** [1]Lit *know* [a]Matt 16:27

field; one [1]will be taken and one [1]will be left.

41 "[a]Two women *will be* grinding at the [1b]mill; one [2]will be taken and one [2]will be left.

Be Ready for His Coming

42 ¶ "Therefore [a]be on the alert, for you do not know which day your Lord is coming.

43 "But [1]be sure of this, that [a]if the head of the house had known [b]at what time of the night the thief was coming, he would have been on the alert and would not have allowed his house to be [2]broken into.

44 "For this reason [a]you also must be ready; for [b]the Son of Man is coming at an hour when you do not think *He will.*

45 ¶ "[a]Who then is the [b]faithful and [c]sensible slave whom his [1]master [d]put in charge of his household to give them their food at the proper time?

46 "Blessed is that slave whom his [1]master finds so doing when he comes.

47 "Truly I say to you that [a]he will put him in charge of all his possessions.

48 "But if that evil slave says in his heart, 'My [1]master [2]is not coming for a long time,'

49 and begins to beat his fellow slaves and eat and drink with drunkards;

50 the [1]master of that slave will come on a day when he does not expect *him* and at an hour which he does not know,

51 and will [1]cut him in pieces and [2]assign him a place with the hypocrites; in that place there will be [a]weeping and gnashing of teeth.

Parable of Ten Virgins

25 "Then [a]the kingdom of heaven will be comparable to ten virgins, who took their [b]lamps and went out to meet the bridegroom.

2 "Five of them were foolish, and five were [a]prudent.

3 "For when the foolish took their lamps, they took no oil with them,

4 but the [a]prudent took oil in flasks along with their lamps.

5 "Now while the bridegroom was delaying, they all got drowsy and *began* to sleep.

6 "But at midnight there was a shout, 'Behold, the bridegroom! Come out to meet *him.*'

7 "Then all those virgins rose and trimmed their lamps.

8 "The foolish said to the prudent, 'Give us some of your oil, for our lamps are going out.'

9 "But the [a]prudent answered, 'No, there will not be enough for us and you *too*; go instead to the dealers and buy *some* for yourselves.'

10 "And while they were going away to make the purchase, the bridegroom came, and those who were [a]ready went in with him to [b]the wedding feast; and [c]the door was shut.

11 "Later the other virgins also came, saying, '[a]Lord, lord, open up for us.'

12 "But he answered, 'Truly I say to you, I do not know you.'

13 "[a]Be on the alert then, for you do not know the day nor the hour.

Parable of the Talents

14 ¶ "[a]For *it is* just like a man [b]*about* to go on a journey, who called his own slaves and entrusted his possessions to them.

15 "To one he gave five [1a]talents, to another, two, and to another, one, each according to his own ability; and he [b]went on his journey.

16 "Immediately the one who had received the five [a]talents went and traded with them, and gained five more talents.

17 "In the same manner the one who *had received* the two *talents* gained two more.

18 "But he who received the one *talent* went away, and dug *a hole* in the ground and hid his [1]master's money.

19 ¶ "Now after a long time the master of those slaves *came and *[a]settled accounts with them.

20 "The one who had received the five [a]talents came up and brought five more talents, saying, 'Master, you entrusted five talents to me. See, I have gained five more talents.'

21 "His master said to him, 'Well done, good and [a]faithful slave. You were faithful with a few things, I will [b]put you in charge of many things; enter into the joy of your [1]master.'

22 ¶ "Also the one who *had received* the two [a]talents came up and said, 'Master, you entrusted two talents to me. See, I have gained two more talents.'

23 "His master said to him, 'Well done, good and [a]faithful slave. You were faithful with a few things, I will put you in charge of many things; enter into the joy of your master.'

24 ¶ "And the one also who had received the one [a]talent came up and said, 'Master, I knew you to be a hard man, reaping where you did not sow and gathering where you scattered no *seed.*

25 'And I was afraid, and went away and hid your talent in the ground. See, you have what is yours.'

26 ¶ "But his master answered and said to him, 'You wicked, lazy slave, you

40 [1]Lit *is*
41 [1]I.e. handmill [2]Lit *is* [a]Luke 17:35 [b]Ex 11:5; Deut 24:6; Is 47:2
42 [a]Matt 24:43, 44; 25:10,13; Luke 12:39f; 21:36
43 [1]Lit *know this* [2]Lit *dug through* [a]Matt 24:42,44; 25:10, 13; Luke 12:39f; 21:36 [b]Matt 14:25; Mark 6:48; 13:35; Luke 12:38
44 [a]Matt 24:42, 43; 25:10,13; Luke 12:39f; 21:36 [b]Matt 24:27
45 [1]Or *lord* [a]Matt 24:45-51: *Luke 12:42-46* [b]Matt 25:21,23; Luke 16:10 [c]Matt 7:24; 10:16; 25:2ff [d]Matt 25:21,23
46 [1]Or *lord*
47 [a]Matt 25:21, 23
48 [1]Or *lord* [2]Lit *lingers*
50 [1]Or *lord*
51 [1]Or *severely scourge him* [2]Lit *appoint his portion* [a]Matt 8:12
25:1 [a]Matt 13:24 [b]John 18:3; Acts 20:8; Rev 4:5; 8:10
2 [a]Matt 7:24; 10:16; 25:2ff
4 [a]Matt 7:24; 10:16; 25:2ff
9 [a]Matt 7:24; 10:16; 25:2ff
10 [a]Matt 24:42ff [b]Luke 12:35f [c]Matt 7:21ff; Luke 13:25
11 [a]Matt 7:21ff; Luke 13:25
13 [a]Matt 24:42ff
14 [a]Matt 25:14-30; Luke 19:12-27 [b]Matt 21:33
15 [1]A talent was worth about fifteen years' wages of a laborer [a]Matt 18:24; Luke 19:13 [b]Matt 21:33
16 [a]Matt 18:24; Luke 19:13
18 [1]Or *lord's*
19 [a]Matt 18:23
20 [a]Matt 18:24; Luke 19:13
21 [1]Or *lord* [a]Matt 24:45,47; 25:23 [b]Luke 12:44; 22:29; Rev 3:21; 21:7
22 [a]Matt 18:24; Luke 19:13
23 [a]Matt 24:45, 47; 25:21
24 [a]Matt 18:24; Luke 19:13

knew that I reap where I did not sow and
gather where I scattered no *seed.*
27 'Then you ought to have put my
money [1]in the bank, and on my arrival
I would have received my *money* back
with interest.
28 'Therefore take away the talent from
him, and give it to the one who has the
ten talents.'
29 ¶ "[a]For to everyone who has, *more*
shall be given, and he will have an abundance; but from the one who does not
have, even what he does have shall be
taken away.
30 "Throw out the worthless slave into
[a]the outer darkness; in that place there
will be weeping and gnashing of teeth.

The Judgment

31 ¶ "But when [a]the Son of Man
comes in His glory, and all the angels
with Him, then [b]He will sit on His glorious throne.
32 "All the nations will be [a]gathered
before Him; and He will separate them
from one another, [b]as the shepherd separates the sheep from the goats;
33 and He will put the sheep [a]on His
right, and the goats [b]on the left.
34 ¶ "Then the King will say to those
on His right, 'Come, you who are blessed
of My Father, [a]inherit the kingdom prepared for you [b]from the foundation of the
world.
35 'For [a]I was hungry, and you gave
Me *something* to eat; I was thirsty, and
you gave Me *something* to drink; [b]I was
a stranger, and you invited Me in;
36 [a]naked, and you clothed Me; I was
sick, and you [b]visited Me; [c]I was in prison, and you came to Me.'
37 "Then the righteous will answer
Him, 'Lord, when did we see You hungry,
and feed You, or thirsty, and give You
something to drink?
38 'And when did we see You a stranger, and invite You in, or naked, and
clothe You?
39 'When did we see You sick, or in
prison, and come to You?'
40 "[a]The King will answer and say to
them, 'Truly I say to you, [b]to the extent
that you did it to one of these brothers of
Mine, *even* the least *of them,* you did it
to Me.'
41 ¶ "Then He will also say to those on
His left, '[a]Depart from Me, accursed
ones, into the [b]eternal fire which has
been prepared for [c]the devil and his angels;
42 for I was hungry, and you gave Me
nothing to eat; I was thirsty, and you gave
Me nothing to drink;
43 I was a stranger, and you did not
invite Me in; naked, and you did not
clothe Me; sick, and in prison, and you
did not visit Me.'
44 "Then they themselves also will answer, 'Lord, when did we see You hungry, or thirsty, or a stranger, or naked, or
sick, or in prison, and did not [1]take care
of You?'
45 "Then He will answer them, 'Truly I
say to you, to the extent that you did not
do it to one of the least of these, you did
not do it to Me.'
46 "These will go away into [a]eternal
punishment, but the righteous into
[b]eternal life."

The Plot to Kill Jesus

26 [a]When Jesus had finished all
these words, He said to His disciples,
2 "[a]You know that after two days
[b]the Passover is coming, and the Son of
Man is *to be* [c]handed over for crucifixion."
3 ¶ [a]Then the chief priests and the
elders of the people were gathered together in [b]the court of the high priest,
named [c]Caiaphas;
4 and they [a]plotted together to seize
Jesus by stealth and kill Him.
5 But they were saying, "Not during
the festival, [a]otherwise a riot might occur among the people."

The Precious Ointment

6 ¶ [a]Now when Jesus was in [b]Beth-
any, at the home of Simon the leper,
7 [a]a woman came to Him with an
alabaster vial of very costly perfume, and
she poured it on His head as He reclined
at the table.
8 But the disciples were indignant
when they saw *this,* and said, "Why this
waste?
9 "For this *perfume* might have been
sold for a high price and *the money* given
to the poor."
10 But Jesus, aware of this, said to
them, "Why do you bother the woman?
For she has done a good deed to Me.
11 "For you always have [a]the poor
with you; but you do not always
have Me.
12 "For when she poured this perfume
on My body, she did it [a]to prepare Me for
burial.
13 "Truly I say to you, [a]wherever this
gospel is preached in the whole world,
what this woman has done will also be
spoken of in memory of her."

Judas's Bargain

14 ¶ [a]Then one of the twelve, named
[b]Judas Iscariot, went to the chief priests

---

27 [1]Lit *to the bankers*
29 [a]Matt 13:12; Mark 4:25; Luke 8:18; John 15:2
30 [a]Matt 8:12; Luke 13:28
31 [a]Matt 16:27f; 1 Thess 4:16; 2 Thess 1:7; Heb 9:28; Jude 14; Rev 1:7 [b]Matt 19:28
32 [a]Matt 13:49; 2 Cor 5:10 [b]Ezek 34:17
33 [a]1 Kin 2:19; Ps 45:9 [b]Eccl 10:2
34 [a]Matt 5:3; Luke 12:32; 1 Cor 6:9; Gal 5:21; James 2:5 [b]Matt 13:35; Luke 11:50; John 17:24; Eph 1:4; Heb 4:3; 1 Pet 1:20; Rev 13:8
35 [a]Is 58:7; Ezek 18:7; James 2:15 [b]Job 31:32; Heb 13:2
36 [a]Is 58:7; Ezek 18:7; James 2:15 [b]James 1:27 [c]2 Tim 1:16f
40 [a]Matt 25:34; Luke 19:38; Rev 17:14 [b]Prov 19:17; Matt 10:42; Heb 6:10
41 [a]Matt 7:23 [b]Mark 9:48; Luke 16:24; Jude 7 [c]Matt 4:10; Rev 12:9
44 [1]Or *serve*
46 [a]Dan 12:2; John 5:29; Acts 24:15 [b]Matt 19:29; John 3:15f; Acts 13:46; Rom 2:7; Gal 6:8; 1 John 5:11
26:1 [a]Matt 7:28
2 [a]Matt 26:2-5: *Mark 14:1,2; Luke 22:1,2* [b]John 11:55 [c]Matt 10:4
3 [a]John 11:47 [b]Matt 26:58; Mark 14:54; Luke 22:55; John 18:15 [c]Matt 26:57; Luke 3:2; John 11:49; Acts 4:6
4 [a]Matt 12:14
5 [a]Matt 27:24
6 [a]Matt 26:6-13: *Mark 14:3-9;* Luke 7:37-39; John 12:1-8 [b]Matt 21:17
7 [a]Luke 7:37f
11 [a]Deut 15:11; Mark 14:7; John 12:8
12 [a]John 19:40
13 [a]Mark 14:9
14 [a]Matt 26:14-16: *Mark 14:10,11; Luke 22:3-6* [b]Matt 10:4; John 6:71; Acts 1:16

15 and said, "What are you willing to give me [1]to [2][a]betray Him to you?" And [b]they weighed out thirty [3]pieces of silver to him.
16 From then on he *began* looking for a good opportunity to [1]betray [2]Jesus.
17 ¶ [a]Now on the first *day* of [b]Unleavened Bread the disciples came to Jesus and asked, "Where do You want us to prepare for You to eat the Passover?"
18 And He said, "Go into the city to [a]a certain man, and say to him, 'The Teacher says, "[b]My time is near; I *am to* keep the Passover at your house with My disciples." ' "
19 The disciples did as Jesus had directed them; and they prepared the Passover.

The Last Passover

20 ¶ [a]Now when evening came, Jesus was reclining *at the table* with the twelve disciples.
21 As they were eating, He said, "[a]Truly I say to you that one of you will betray Me."
22 Being deeply grieved, they [1]each one began to say to Him, "Surely not I, Lord?"
23 And He answered, "[a]He who dipped his hand with Me in the bowl is the one who will betray Me.
24 "The Son of Man *is to* go, [a]just as it is written of Him; but woe to that man by whom the Son of Man is betrayed! [b]It would have been good [1]for that man if he had not been born."
25 And [a]Judas, who was betraying Him, said, "Surely it is not I, [b]Rabbi?" Jesus *said to him, "[c]You have said *it* yourself."

The Lord's Supper Instituted

26 ¶ [a]While they were eating, Jesus took *some* bread, and [1][b]after a blessing, He broke *it* and gave *it* to the disciples, and said, "Take, eat; this is My body."
27 And when He had taken a cup and given thanks, He gave *it* to them, saying, "Drink from it, all of you;
28 for [a]this is My blood of the covenant, which is poured out for [b]many for forgiveness of sins.
29 "But I say to you, I will not drink of this fruit of the vine from now on until that day when I drink it new with you in My Father's kingdom."
30 ¶ [a]After singing a hymn, they went out to [b]the Mount of Olives.
31 ¶ Then Jesus *said to them, "You will all [1][a]fall away because of Me this night, for it is written, '[b]I WILL STRIKE DOWN THE SHEPHERD, AND THE SHEEP OF THE FLOCK SHALL BE [c]SCATTERED.'
32 "But after I have been raised, [a]I will go ahead of you to Galilee."
33 But Peter said to Him, "*Even* though all may [1]fall away because of You, I will never fall away."
34 Jesus said to him, "[a]Truly I say to you that [b]this *very* night, before a rooster crows, you will deny Me three times."
35 Peter *said to Him, "[a]Even if I have to die with You, I will not deny You." All the disciples said the same thing too.

The Garden of Gethsemane

36 ¶ [a]Then Jesus *came with them to a place called [b]Gethsemane, and *said to His disciples, "Sit here while I go over there and pray."
37 And He took with Him [a]Peter and the two sons of Zebedee, and began to be grieved and distressed.
38 Then He *said to them, "[a]My soul is deeply grieved, to the point of death; remain here and [b]keep watch with Me."
39 ¶ And He went a little beyond *them,* and fell on His face and prayed, saying, "My Father, if it is possible, let [a]this cup pass from Me; [b]yet not as I will, but as You will."
40 And He *came to the disciples and *found them sleeping, and *said to Peter, "So, you *men* could not [a]keep watch with Me for one hour?
41 "[a]Keep watching and praying that you may not enter into temptation; [b]the spirit is willing, but the flesh is weak."
42 ¶ He went away again a second time and prayed, saying, "My Father, if this [a]cannot pass away unless I drink it, [b]Your will be done."
43 Again He came and found them sleeping, for their eyes were heavy.
44 And He left them again, and went away and prayed a third time, saying the same thing once more.
45 Then He *came to the disciples and *said to them, "[1]Are you still sleeping and resting? Behold, [a]the hour is at hand and the Son of Man is being betrayed into the hands of sinners.
46 "Get up, let us be going; behold, the one who betrays Me is at hand!"

Jesus' Betrayal and Arrest

47 ¶ [a]While He was still speaking, behold, [b]Judas, one of the twelve, came up [1]accompanied by a large crowd with swords and clubs, *who came* from the chief priests and elders of the people.
48 Now he who was betraying Him gave them a sign, saying, "Whomever I kiss, He is the one; seize Him."

15 [1]Lit *and I will* [2]Or *deliver* [3]I.e. *silver shekels* [a]Matt 10:4 [b]Ex 21:32; Zech 11:12
16 [1]Or *deliver* [2]Lit *Him*
17 [a]Matt 26:17-19: *Mark 14:12-16; Luke 22:7-13* [b]Ex 12:18-20
18 [a]Mark 14:13; Luke 22:10 [b]John 7:6
20 [a]Matt 26:20-24: *Mark 14:17-21*
21 [a]Luke 22:21-23; John 13:21f
22 [1]Or *one after another*
23 [a]Ps 41:9; John 13:18
24 [1]Lit *for him if that man had not been born* [a]Matt 26:31; Mark 9:12; Luke 24:25-27; Acts 17:2f; 1 Cor 15:3; 1 Pet 1:10f [b]Matt 18:7; Mark 14:21
25 [a]Matt 26:14 [b]Matt 23:7 [c]Matt 26:64; Luke 22:70
26 [1]Lit *having blessed* [a]Matt 26:26-29: *Mark 14:22-25; Luke 22:17-20; 1 Cor 11:23-25*; 1 Cor 10:16 [b]Matt 14:19
28 [a]Ex 24:8; Heb 9:20 [b]Matt 20:28
30 [a]Matt 26:30-35: *Mark 14:26-31; Luke 22:31-34* [b]Matt 21:1
31 [1]Or *stumble* [a]Matt 11:6 [b]Zech 13:7 [c]John 16:32
32 [a]Matt 28:7; Mark 16:7
33 [1]Or *stumble*
34 [a]Matt 26:75; John 13:38 [b]Mark 14:30
35 [a]John 13:37
36 [a]Matt 26:36-46: *Mark 14:32-42; Luke 22:40-46* [b]Mark 14:32; Luke 22:39; John 18:1
37 [a]Matt 4:21; Mark 5:37
38 [a]John 12:27 [b]Matt 26:40
39 [a]Matt 20:22 [b]Matt 26:42; Mark 14:36; Luke 22:42; John 6:38
40 [a]Matt 26:38
41 [a]Matt 26:38 [b]Mark 14:38
42 [a]Matt 20:22 [b]Matt 26:39; Mark 14:36; Luke 22:42; John 6:38
45 [1]Or *Keep on sleeping therefore* [a]Mark 14:41; John 12:27
47 [1]Lit *and with him* [a]Matt 26:47-56: *Mark 14:43-50; Luke 22:47-53; John 18:3-11* [b]Matt 26:14

49 Immediately Judas went to Jesus and said, "Hail, [a]Rabbi!" and kissed Him.
50 And Jesus said to him, "[a]Friend, *do* what you have come for." Then they came and laid hands on Jesus and seized Him.
51 ¶ And behold, [a]one of those who were with Jesus [1]reached and drew out his [b]sword, and struck the [a]slave of the high priest and [2]cut off his ear.
52 Then Jesus *said to him, "Put your sword back into its place; for [a]all those who take up the sword shall perish by the sword.
53 "Or do you think that I cannot appeal to My Father, and He will at once put at My disposal more than twelve [1a]legions of [b]angels?
54 "How then will [a]the Scriptures be fulfilled, *which say* that it must happen this way?"
55 ¶ At that time Jesus said to the crowds, "Have you come out with swords and clubs to arrest Me as *you would* against a robber? [a]Every day I used to sit in the temple teaching and you did not seize Me.
56 "But all this has taken place to fulfill [a]the Scriptures of the prophets." Then all the disciples left Him and fled.

Jesus before Caiaphas

57 ¶ [a]Those who had seized Jesus led Him away to [b]Caiaphas, the high priest, where the scribes and the elders were gathered together.
58 But [a]Peter was following Him at a distance as far as the [b]courtyard of the high priest, and entered in, and sat down with the [1c]officers to see the outcome.
59 ¶ Now the chief priests and the whole [1a]Council kept trying to obtain false testimony against Jesus, so that they might put Him to death.
60 They did not find *any*, even though many false witnesses came forward. But later on [a]two came forward,
61 and said, "This man stated, '[a]I am able to destroy the [1]temple of God and to rebuild it [2]in three days.'"
62 The high priest stood up and said to Him, "Do You not answer? What is it that these men are testifying against You?"
63 But [a]Jesus kept silent. [b]And the high priest said to Him, "I [1c]adjure You by [d]the living God, that You tell us whether You are [2]the Christ, [e]the Son of God."
64 Jesus *said to him, "[a]You have said it *yourself*; nevertheless I tell you, [1]hereafter you will see [b]THE SON OF MAN SITTING AT THE RIGHT HAND OF POWER, and [c]COMING ON THE CLOUDS OF HEAVEN."
65 ¶ Then the high priest [a]tore his [1]robes and said, "He has blasphemed! What further need do we have of witnesses? Behold, you have now heard the blasphemy;
66 what do you think?" They answered, "[a]He deserves death!"
67 ¶ [a]Then they [b]spat in His face and beat Him with their fists; and others [1]slapped Him,
68 and said, "[a]Prophesy to us, You [1]Christ; who is the one who hit You?"

Peter's Denials

69 ¶ [a]Now Peter was sitting outside in the [b]courtyard, and a servant-girl came to him and said, "You too were with Jesus the Galilean."
70 But he denied *it* before them all, saying, "I do not know what you are talking about."
71 When he had gone out to the gateway, another *servant-girl* saw him and *said to those who were there, "This man was with Jesus of Nazareth."
72 And again he denied *it* with an oath, "I do not know the man."
73 A little later the bystanders came up and said to Peter, "Surely you too are *one* of them; [a]for even the way you talk [1]gives you away."
74 Then he began to curse and swear, "I do not know the man!" And immediately a rooster crowed.
75 And Peter remembered the word which Jesus had said, "[a]Before a rooster crows, you will deny Me three times." And he went out and wept bitterly.

Judas's Remorse

27 [a]Now when morning came, all the chief priests and the elders of the people conferred together against Jesus to put Him to death;
2 and they bound Him, and led Him away and [a]delivered Him to [b]Pilate the governor.
3 ¶ Then when [a]Judas, who had betrayed Him, saw that He had been condemned, he felt remorse and returned [b]the thirty [1]pieces of silver to the chief priests and elders,
4 saying, "I have sinned by betraying innocent blood." But they said, "What is that to us? [a]See *to that* yourself!"
5 And he threw the pieces of silver into [a]the temple sanctuary and departed; and [b]he went away and hanged himself.
6 The chief priests took the pieces of silver and said, "It is not lawful to put them into the temple treasury, since it is the price of blood."
7 And they conferred together and

49 [a]Matt 23:7
50 [a]Matt 20:13
51 [1]Lit *extended the hand* [2]Lit *took off* [a]Mark 14:47; Luke 22:50; John 18:10 [b]Luke 22:38
52 [a]Gen 9:6; Rev 13:10
53 [1]A legion equaled 6,000 troops [a]Mark 5:9; Luke 8:30 [b]Matt 4:11
54 [a]Matt 26:24
55 [a]Mark 12:35; Luke 4:20; John 7:14
56 [a]Matt 26:24
57 [a]Matt 26:57-68: *Mark 14:53-65; John 18:12f,19-24* [b]Matt 26:3
58 [1]Or *servants* [a]John 18:15 [b]Matt 26:3 [c]Matt 5:25; John 7:32; Acts 5:22
59 [1]Or *Sanhedrin* [a]Matt 5:22
60 [a]Deut 19:15
61 [1]Or *sanctuary* [2]Or *after* [a]Matt 27:40; Mark 14:58; John 2:19; Acts 6:14
63 [1]Or *charge You under oath* [2]I.e. the Messiah [a]Matt 27:12; John 19:9 [b]Matt 26:63-66; Luke 22:67-71 [c]Lev 5:1 [d]Matt 16:16 [e]Matt 4:3
64 [1]Or *from now on* [a]Matt 26:25 [b]Ps 110:1; Mark 14:62 [c]Dan 7:13; Matt 16:27f
65 [1]Or *outer garments* [a]Num 14:6; Mark 14:63; Acts 14:14
66 [a]Lev 24:16; John 19:7
67 [1]Or *beat Him with rods* [a]Is 50:6; Matt 26:67; Luke 22:63-65; John 18:22 [b]Matt 27:30; Mark 10:34
68 [1]I.e. the Messiah [a]Mark 14:65; Luke 22:64
69 [a]Matt 26:69-75: *Mark 14:66-72; Luke 22:55-62; John 18:16-18,25-27* [b]Matt 26:3
73 [1]Lit *makes you evident* [a]Mark 14:70; Luke 22:59; John 18:26
75 [a]Matt 26:34
27:1 [a]Mark 15:1; Luke 22:66; John 18:28
2 [a]Matt 20:19 [b]Luke 3:1; Acts 3:13; 1 Tim 6:13
3 [1]Or *silver shekels* [a]Matt 26:14 [b]Matt 26:15
4 [a]Matt 27:24
5 [a]Matt 26:61; Luke 1:9 [b]Acts 1:18

[1]with the money bought the Potter's
Field as a burial place for strangers.
8 [a]For this reason that field has been
called the Field of Blood to this day.
9 Then that which was spoken
through Jeremiah the prophet was fulfilled: "[a]AND [1]THEY TOOK THE THIRTY
PIECES OF SILVER, THE PRICE OF THE ONE
WHOSE PRICE HAD BEEN SET by the sons of
Israel;
10 [a]AND [1]THEY GAVE THEM FOR THE
POTTER'S FIELD, AS THE LORD DIRECT-
ED ME."

Jesus before Pilate

11 ¶ [a]Now Jesus stood before the governor, and the governor questioned Him,
saying, "Are You the [b]King of the Jews?"
And Jesus said to him, "[c]*It is as* you say."
12 And while He was being accused by
the chief priests and elders, [a]He did not
answer.
13 Then Pilate *said to Him, "Do You
not hear how many things they testify
against You?"
14 And [a]He did not answer him with
regard to even a *single* [1]charge, so the
governor was quite amazed.
15 ¶ [a]Now at *the* feast the governor
was accustomed to release for the [1]peo-
ple *any* one prisoner whom they wanted.
16 At that time they were holding a
notorious prisoner, called Barabbas.
17 So when the people gathered together, Pilate said to them, "Whom do
you want me to release for you? Barabbas,
or Jesus [a]who is called Christ?"
18 For he knew that because of envy
they had handed Him over.
19 ¶ [a]While he was sitting on the
judgment seat, his wife sent him *a message*, saying, "Have nothing to do with
that [b]righteous Man; for [1]last night I
suffered greatly [c]in a dream because of
Him."
20 But the chief priests and the elders
persuaded the crowds to [a]ask for Barabbas and to put Jesus to death.
21 But the governor [1]said to them,
"Which of the two do you want me to
release for you?" And they said, "Barabbas."
22 Pilate *said to them, "Then what
shall I do with Jesus [a]who is called
Christ?" They all *said, "[1]Crucify Him!"
23 And he said, "Why, what evil has
He done?" But they kept shouting all the
more, saying, "[1]Crucify Him!"
24 ¶ When Pilate saw that he was accomplishing nothing, but rather that [a]a
riot was starting, he took water and
[b]washed his hands in front of the crowd,
saying, "I am innocent of [c]this Man's
blood; [d]see *to that* yourselves."
25 And all the people said, "[a]His
blood shall be on us and on our children!"
26 Then he released Barabbas [1]for
them; but after having Jesus [a]scourged,
he handed Him over to be crucified.

Jesus Is Mocked

27 ¶ [a]Then the soldiers of the governor took Jesus into [b]the [1]Praetorium
and gathered the whole *Roman* [2c]cohort
around Him.
28 They stripped Him and [a]put a scarlet robe on Him.
29 [a]And after twisting together a
crown of thorns, they put it on His head,
and a [1]reed in His right hand; and they
knelt down before Him and mocked Him,
saying, "[b]Hail, King of the Jews!"
30 [a]They spat on Him, and took the
reed and *began* to beat Him on the head.
31 [a]After they had mocked Him, they
took the *scarlet* robe off Him and put His
own garments back on Him, and led Him
away to crucify Him.
32 ¶ [a]As they were coming out, they
found a man of [b]Cyrene named Simon,
[1]whom they pressed into service to bear
His cross.

The Crucifixion

33 ¶ [a]And when they came to a place
called [b]Golgotha, which means Place of
a Skull,
34 [a]they gave Him [b]wine to drink
mixed with gall; and after tasting *it,* He
was unwilling to drink.
35 ¶ And when they had crucified
Him, [a]they divided up His garments
among themselves by casting [1]lots.
36 And sitting down, they *began* to
[a]keep watch over Him there.
37 And above His head they put up the
charge against Him [1]which read, "[a]THIS
IS JESUS THE KING OF THE JEWS."
38 ¶ At that time two robbers *were
crucified with Him, one on the right and
one on the left.
39 And those passing by were [1]hurl-
ing abuse at Him, [a]wagging their heads
40 and saying, "[a]You who *are going to*
destroy the temple and rebuild it in three
days, save Yourself! [b]If You are the Son of
God, come down from the cross."
41 In the same way the chief priests
also, along with the scribes and elders,
were mocking *Him* and saying,
42 "[a]He saved others; [1]He cannot save
Himself. [b]He is the King of Israel; let
Him now come down from the cross, and
we will believe in Him.
43 "[a]HE TRUSTS IN GOD; LET GOD RESCUE

7 [1]Lit *from them*
8 [a]Acts 1:19
9 [1]Or *I took*; cf Zech 11:13 [a]Zech 11:12
10 [1]Some early mss read *I gave* [a]Zech 11:13
11 [a]Matt 27:11-14: *Mark 15:2-5; Luke 23:2,3; John 18:29-38* [b]Matt 2:2 [c]Matt 26:25
12 [a]Matt 26:63; John 19:9
14 [1]Lit *word* [a]Matt 27:12; Mark 15:5; Luke 23:9; John 19:9
15 [1]Lit *crowd* [a]Matt 27:15-26: *Mark 15:6-15; Luke 23:17-25*; John 18:39-19:16
17 [a]Matt 1:16
19 [1]Lit *today* [a]John 19:13; Acts 12:21 [b]Matt 27:24 [c]Gen 20:6; Num 12:6; Job 33:15; Matt 1:20
20 [a]Acts 3:14
21 [1]Lit *answered and said to them*
22 [1]Lit *Let Him be crucified* [a]Matt 1:16
23 [1]Lit *Let Him be crucified*
24 [a]Matt 26:5 [b]Deut 21:6-8 [c]Matt 27:19 [d]Matt 27:4
25 [a]Josh 2:19; Acts 5:28
26 [1]Or *to them* [a]Mark 15:15; Luke 23:16; John 19:1
27 [1]I.e. the governor's official residence [2]Or *battalion* [a]Matt 27:27-31: *Mark 15:16-20* [b]Matt 26:3; John 18:28 [c]Acts 10:1
28 [a]Mark 15:17; John 19:2
29 [1]Or *staff*; i.e. to mimic a king's scepter [a]Mark 15:17; John 19:2 [b]Mark 15:18; John 19:3
30 [a]Matt 26:67; Mark 10:34
31 [a]Mark 15:20
32 [1]Lit *this one* [a]Matt 27:32: *Mark 15:21; Luke 23:26*; John 19:17 [b]Acts 2:10
33 [a]Matt 27:34-44: *Mark 15:22-32; Luke 23:33-43; John 19:17-24* [b]Luke 23:33; John 19:17
34 [a]Ps 69:21 [b]Mark 15:23
35 [1]Lit *a lot* [a]Ps 22:18
36 [a]Matt 27:54
37 [1]Lit *written* [a]Mark 15:26; Luke 23:38; John 19:19
39 [1]Or *blaspheming* [a]Job 16:4; Ps 22:7; Lam 2:15; Mark 15:29
40 [a]Matt 26:61; John 2:19 [b]Matt 27:42
42 [1]Or *can He not save Himself?* [a]Mark 15:31; Luke 23:35 [b]Matt 27:37; Luke 23:37; John 1:49
43 [a]Ps 22:8

Him now, IF HE [1]DELIGHTS IN HIM; for He said, 'I am the Son of God.' "

44 [a]The robbers who were crucified with Him were also insulting Him with the same words.

45 ¶ [a]Now from the [1]sixth hour darkness [2]fell upon all the land until the [3]ninth hour.

46 About the ninth hour Jesus cried out with a loud voice, saying, "[a]ELI, ELI, LAMA SABACHTHANI?" that is, "MY GOD, MY GOD, WHY HAVE YOU FORSAKEN ME?"

47 And some of those who were standing there, when they heard it, *began* saying, "This man is calling for Elijah."

48 [a]Immediately one of them ran, and taking a sponge, he filled it with sour wine and put it on a reed, and gave Him a drink.

49 But the rest *of them* said, "[1]Let us see whether Elijah will come to save Him."[2]

50 And Jesus [a]cried out again with a loud voice, and yielded up His spirit.

51 [a]And behold, [b]the [1]veil of the temple was torn in two from top to bottom; and [c]the earth shook and the rocks were split.

52 The tombs were opened, and many bodies of the [1]saints who had [a]fallen asleep were raised;

53 and coming out of the tombs after His resurrection they entered [a]the holy city and appeared to many.

54 [a]Now the centurion, and those who were with him [b]keeping guard over Jesus, when they saw [c]the earthquake and the things that were happening, became very frightened and said, "Truly this was [1d]the Son of God!"

55 ¶ [a]Many women were there looking on from a distance, who had followed Jesus from Galilee while [1b]ministering to Him.

56 Among them was [a]Mary Magdalene, and Mary the mother of James and Joseph, and [b]the mother of the sons of Zebedee.

Jesus Is Buried

57 ¶ [a]When it was evening, there came a rich man from Arimathea, named Joseph, who himself had also become a disciple of Jesus.

58 This man went to Pilate and asked for the body of Jesus. Then Pilate ordered it to be given *to him.*

59 And Joseph took the body and wrapped it in a clean linen cloth,

60 and laid it in his own new tomb, which he had hewn out in the rock; and he rolled [a]a large stone against the entrance of the tomb and went away.

61 And [a]Mary Magdalene was there, and the other Mary, sitting opposite the grave.

62 ¶ Now on the next day, [1]the day after [a]the preparation, the chief priests and the Pharisees gathered together with Pilate,

63 and said, "Sir, we remember that when He was still alive that deceiver said, '[a]After three days I *am to* rise again.'

64 "Therefore, give orders for the grave to be made secure until the third day, otherwise His disciples may come and steal Him away and say to the people, 'He has risen from the dead,' and the last deception will be worse than the first."

65 Pilate said to them, "You have a [a]guard; go, make it *as* secure as you know how."

66 And they went and made the grave secure, and along with [a]the guard they set a [b]seal on [c]the stone.

Jesus Is Risen!

28 [a]Now after the Sabbath, as it began to dawn toward the first *day* of the week, [b]Mary Magdalene and the other Mary came to look at the grave.

2 And behold, a severe earthquake had occurred, for [a]an angel of the Lord descended from heaven and came and rolled away [b]the stone and sat upon it.

3 And [a]his appearance was like lightning, and his clothing as white as snow.

4 The guards shook for fear of him and became like dead men.

5 The angel said to the women, "[1a]Do not be afraid; for I know that you are looking for Jesus who has been crucified.

6 "He is not here, for He has risen, [a]just as He said. Come, see the place where He was lying.

7 "Go quickly and tell His disciples that He has risen from the dead; and behold, He is going ahead of you [a]into Galilee, there you will see Him; behold, I have told you."

8 ¶ And they left the tomb quickly with fear and great joy and ran to report it to His disciples.

9 And behold, Jesus met them [1]and greeted them. And they came up and took hold of His feet and worshiped Him.

10 Then Jesus *said to them, "[1a]Do not be afraid; go and take word to [b]My brethren to leave [c]for Galilee, and there they will see Me."

11 ¶ Now while they were on their way, some of [a]the guard came into the city and reported to the chief priests all that had happened.

43 [1]Or *takes pleasure in;* or *cares for him*
44 [a]Luke 23:39-43
45 [1]I.e. noon [2]Or *occurred* [3]I.e. 3 p.m. [a]Matt 27:45-56: *Mark 15:33-41; Luke 23:44-49*
46 [a]Ps 22:1
48 [a]Ps 69:21; Mark 15:36; Luke 23:36; John 19:29
49 [1]Lit *Permit that we see* [2]Some early mss read *And another took a spear and pierced His side, and there came out water and blood* (cf John 19:34)
50 [a]Mark 15:37; Luke 23:46; John 19:30
51 [1]Or *curtain* [a]Matt 27:51-56: *Mark 15:38-41;* Luke 23:47-49 [b]Ex 26:31ff; Mark 15:38; Luke 23:45; Heb 9:3 [c]Matt 27:54
52 [1]Or *holy ones* [a]Acts 7:60
53 [a]Matt 4:5
54 [1]Or *a son of God* or *a son of a god* [a]Mark 15:39; Luke 23:47 [b]Matt 27:36 [c]Matt 27:51 [d]Matt 4:3
55 [1]Or *caring for Him* [a]Mark 15:40f; Luke 23:49; John 19:25 [b]Mark 15:41; Luke 8:2
56 [a]Matt 28:1; Mark 15:40; Luke 8:2; John 19:25 [b]Matt 20:20
57 [a]Matt 27:57-61: *Mark 15:42-47; Luke 23:50-56; John 19:38-42*
60 [a]Matt 27:66; Mark 16:4
61 [a]Matt 27:56
62 [1]Lit *which is after* [a]Mark 15:42; Luke 23:54; John 19:14
63 [a]Matt 16:21; Mark 8:31; Luke 9:22
65 [a]Matt 27:66
66 [a]Matt 27:65 [b]Dan 6:17 [c]Matt 27:60; Mark 16:4
28:1 [a]Matt 28:1-8: *Mark 16:1-8; Luke 24:1-10;* John 20:1-8 [b]Matt 27:56
2 [a]Luke 24:4; John 20:12 [b]Matt 27:66; Mark 16:4
3 [a]Dan 7:9; Mark 9:3; John 20:12; Acts 1:10
5 [1]Or *Stop being afraid* [a]Matt 14:27; Rev 1:17
6 [a]Matt 12:40
7 [a]Matt 26:32; Mark 16:7
9 [1]Lit *saying hello*
10 [1]Or *Stop being afraid* [a]Matt 14:27 [b]John 20:17; Rom 8:29; Heb 2:11f [c]Matt 26:32
11 [a]Matt 27:65

12 And when they had assembled with
the elders and consulted together, they
gave a large sum of money to the soldiers,
13 and said, "You are to say, 'His disciples came by night and stole Him away
while we were asleep.'
14 "And if this should come to [a]the
governor's ears, we will win him over
and [1]keep you out of trouble."
15 And they took the money and did as
they had been instructed; and this story
was widely [a]spread among the Jews, *and
is* [b]to this day.

The Great Commission

16 ¶ But the eleven disciples proceeded [a]to Galilee, to the mountain which
Jesus had designated.
17 When they saw Him, they worshiped *Him*; but [a]some were doubtful.
18 And Jesus came up and spoke to
them, saying, "[a]All authority has been
given to Me in heaven and on earth.
19 "[1a]Go therefore and [b]make disciples of [c]all the nations, [d]baptizing them
in the name of the Father and the Son and
the Holy Spirit,
20 teaching them to observe all that
I commanded you; and lo, [a]I am with
you [1]always, even to [b]the end of the
age."

14 [1]Lit *make you free from care* [a]Matt 27:2
15 [a]Matt 9:31; Mark 1:45 [b]Matt 27:8
16 [a]Matt 26:32; Mark 15:41
17 [a]Mark 16:11
18 [a]Dan 7:13f; Matt 11:27; Rom 14:9; Eph 1:20-22; Phil 2:9f; Col 2:10; 1 Pet 3:22
19 [1]Or *Having gone*; Gr aorist part. [a]Mark 16:15f [b]Matt 13:52; Acts 1:8 [c]Matt 25:32; Luke 24:47 [d]Acts 2:38; Rom 6:3; 1 Cor 1:13; Gal 3:27
20 [1]Lit *all the days* [a]Matt 18:20; Acts 18:10 [b]Matt 13:39

Mark

Title and Background

The early church fathers agreed that Mark's Gospel reproduces the preaching of Peter. Peter's personality can be found on almost every page, and the main characteristic of this Gospel is action.

Author and Date of Writing

Mark was the son of Mary (Acts 12:12) and the cousin of Barnabas (Colossians 4:10). He accompanied Paul and Barnabas on their first missionary journey. Paul speaks of him as his companion in Rome and pays high tribute to his service. It is believed that Mark is the first of the Gospels, and therefore it can be dated about A.D. 55.

Theme and Message

The book of Mark stresses facts and actions rather than themes or topics. Although it is the shortest of the four Gospels, it is often the most detailed. Jewish customs are carefully explained for Roman readers, and one of Mark's purposes was to demonstrate the deity of Jesus. He tells the stories of Jesus' ministry, especially His miracles. Mark spends one-third of the book telling the events of Jesus' last week on earth, ending with His death and resurrection.

Outline

I. The Beginnings of Jesus' Ministry (1:1–13)
II. Jesus' Ministry in Galilee (1:14—6:29)
III. Jesus' Withdrawals From Galilee (6:30—9:32)
IV. Jesus' Final Ministry in Galilee (9:33–50)
V. Jesus' Ministry in Judea and Perea (10:1–52)
VI. The Passion of Jesus (11:1—15:47)
VII. The Resurrection of Jesus (16:1–20)

Preaching of John the Baptist

1 The beginning of the gospel of Jesus
Christ, [a]the Son of God.
2 ¶ [a]As it is written in Isaiah the
prophet:
"[b]BEHOLD, I SEND MY MESSENGER
[1]AHEAD OF YOU,
WHO WILL PREPARE YOUR WAY;
3 [a]THE VOICE OF ONE CRYING IN THE
WILDERNESS,
'MAKE READY THE WAY OF THE
LORD,
MAKE HIS PATHS STRAIGHT.' "
4 John the Baptist appeared in the
wilderness [1a]preaching a baptism of repentance for the [b]forgiveness of sins.
5 And all the country of Judea was
going out to him, and all the people of
Jerusalem; and they were being baptized
by him in the Jordan River, confessing
their sins.
6 John was clothed with camel's hair
and *wore* [a]a leather belt around his
waist, and [1]his diet was locusts and wild
honey.

1:1 [a]Matt 4:3
2 [1]Lit *before your face* [a]Mark 1:2-8: *Matt 3:1-11; Luke 3:2-16* [b]Mal 3:1; Matt 11:10; Luke 7:27
3 [a]Is 40:3; Matt 3:3; Luke 3:4; John 1:23
4 [1]Or *proclaiming* [a]Acts 13:24 [b]Luke 1:77
6 [1]Lit *he was eating* [a]2 Kin 1:8
7 [1]Or *proclaiming*
8 [1]The Gr here can be translated *in, with* or *by*
9 [a]Mark 1:9-11: *Matt 3:13-17; Luke 3:21,22* [b]Matt 2:23; Luke 2:51
10 [1]Or *being parted*
11 [a]Ps 2:7; Is 42:1; Matt 3:17; 12:18; Mark 9:7; Luke 3:22
12 [a]Mark 1:12, 13: *Matt 4:1-11; Luke 4:1-13*
13 [a]Matt 4:10

7 And he was [1]preaching, and saying, "After me One is coming who is
mightier than I, and I am not fit to stoop
down and untie the thong of His sandals.
8 "I baptized you [1]with water; but He
will baptize you [1]with the Holy Spirit."

The Baptism of Jesus

9 ¶ [a]In those days Jesus [b]came from
Nazareth in Galilee and was baptized by
John in the Jordan.
10 Immediately coming up out of the
water, He saw the heavens [1]opening,
and the Spirit like a dove descending
upon Him;
11 and a voice came out of the heavens: "[a]You are My beloved Son, in You I
am well-pleased."
12 ¶ [a]Immediately the Spirit *impelled Him *to go* out into the wilderness.
13 And He was in the wilderness forty
days being tempted by [a]Satan; and He
was with the wild beasts, and the angels
were ministering to Him.

Jesus Preaches in Galilee

14 ¶ [a]Now after John had been [1]tak-
en into custody, Jesus came into Galilee,
[2b]preaching the gospel of God,
15 and saying, "[a]The time is fulfilled,
and the kingdom of God [1]is at hand; [b]re-
pent and [2]believe in the gospel."
16 ¶ [a]As He was going along by the
Sea of Galilee, He saw Simon and Andrew, the brother of Simon, casting a net
in the sea; for they were fishermen.
17 And Jesus said to them, "Follow
Me, and I will make you become fishers
of men."
18 Immediately they left their nets and
followed Him.
19 Going on a little farther, He saw
[1]James the son of Zebedee, and John his
brother, who were also in the boat mending the nets.
20 Immediately He called them; and
they left their father Zebedee in the boat
with the hired servants, and went away
[1]to follow Him.
21 ¶ [a]They *went into Capernaum;
and immediately on the Sabbath [b]He entered the synagogue and *began* to teach.
22 [a]They were amazed at His teaching; for He was teaching them as *one*
having authority, and not as the scribes.
23 Just then there was a man in their
synagogue with an unclean spirit; and he
cried out,
24 saying, "[a]What [1]business do we
have with each other, Jesus [2]of [b]Naza-
reth? Have You come to destroy us? I
know who You are—[c]the Holy One of
God!"
25 And Jesus rebuked him, saying, "Be
quiet, and come out of him!"
26 Throwing him into convulsions,
the unclean spirit cried out with a loud
voice and came out of him.
27 They were all [a]amazed, so that
they debated among themselves, saying,
"What is this? A new teaching with authority! He commands even the unclean
spirits, and they obey Him."
28 Immediately the news about Him
spread everywhere into all the surrounding district of Galilee.

Crowds Healed

29 ¶ [a]And immediately after they
came [b]out of the synagogue, they came
into the house of Simon and Andrew,
with [1]James and John.
30 Now Simon's mother-in-law was
lying sick with a fever; and immediately
they *spoke to [1]Jesus about her.
31 And He came to her and raised her
up, taking her by the hand, and the fever
left her, and she [1]waited on them.
32 ¶ [ab]When evening came, [b]after
the sun had set, they *began* bringing to
Him all who were ill and those who were
[c]demon-possessed.
33 And the whole [a]city had gathered
at the door.
34 And He [a]healed many who were ill
with various diseases, and cast out many
demons; and He was not permitting the
demons to speak, because they knew
who He was.
35 ¶ [a]In the early morning, while it
was still dark, Jesus got up, left *the house*,
and went away to a secluded place, and
[b]was praying there.
36 Simon and his companions
searched for Him;
37 they found Him, and *said to Him,
"Everyone is looking for You."
38 He *said to them, "Let us go somewhere else to the towns nearby, so that I
may [1]preach there also; for that is what
I came for."
39 [a]And He went into their synagogues throughout all Galilee, [1]preach-
ing and casting out the demons.
40 ¶ [a]And a leper *came to Jesus, be-
seeching Him and [b]falling on his knees
before Him, and saying, "If You are willing, You can make me clean."
41 Moved with compassion, Jesus
stretched out His hand and touched him,
and *said to him, "I am willing; be
cleansed."
42 Immediately the leprosy left him
and he was cleansed.
43 And He sternly warned him and immediately sent him away,
44 and He *said to him, "[a]See that
you say nothing to anyone; but [a]go, show
yourself to the priest and [b]offer for your
cleansing what Moses commanded, as a
testimony to them."
45 But he went out and began to [a]pro-
claim it freely and to [a]spread the news
around, to such an extent that [1]Jesus
could no longer publicly enter a city, but
[2]stayed out in unpopulated areas; and
[b]they were coming to Him from everywhere.

The Paralytic Healed

2 When He had come back to Capernaum several days afterward, it was
heard that He was at home.
2 And [a]many were gathered together, so that there was no longer room, not
even near the door; and He was speaking
the word to them.
3 [a]And they *came, bringing to Him
a [b]paralytic, carried by four men.
4 Being unable to [1]get to Him because of the crowd, they [a]removed the
roof [2]above Him; and when they had dug

14 [1]Lit *delivered up* [2]Or *proclaiming* [a]Matt 4:12 [b]Matt 4:23
15 [1]Lit *has come near* [2]Or *put your trust in* [a]Gal 4:4; Eph 1:10; 1 Tim 2:6; Titus 1:3 [b]Matt 3:2; Acts 20:21
16 [a]Mark 1:16-20: *Matt 4:18-22*; Luke 5:2-11; John 1:40-42
19 [1]Or *Jacob*
20 [1]Lit *after Him*
21 [a]Mark 1:21-28: *Luke 4:31-37* [b]Matt 4:23; Mark 1:39; 10:1
22 [a]Matt 7:28
24 [1]Lit *What to us and to You* (a Heb idiom) [2]Lit *the Nazarene* [a]Matt 8:29 [b]Matt 2:23; Mark 10:47; 14:67; 16:6; Luke 4:34; 24:19; Acts 24:5 [c]Luke 1:35; 4:34; John 6:69; Acts 3:14
27 [a]Mark 10:24, 32; 16:5,6
29 [1]*Or Jacob* [a]Mark 1:29-31: *Matt 8:14,15; Luke 4:38,39* [b]Mark 1:21,23
30 [1]Lit *Him*
31 [1]Or *served*
32 [a]Mark 1:32-34: *Matt 8:16,17; Luke 4:40,41* [b]Matt 8:16; Luke 4:40 [c]Matt 4:24
33 [a]Mark 1:21
34 [a]Matt 4:23
35 [a]Mark 1:35-38: *Luke 4:42,43* [b]Matt 14:23; Luke 5:16
38 [1]Or *proclaim*
39 [1]Or *proclaiming* [a]Matt 4:23; 9:35; Mark 1:23; 3:1
40 [a]Mark 1:40-44: *Matt 8:2-4; Luke 5:12-14* [b]Matt 8:2; Mark 10:17; Luke 5:12
44 [a]Matt 8:4 [b]Lev 14:1-32
45 [1]Lit *He* [2]Lit *was* [a]Matt 28:15; Luke 5:15 [b]Mark 2:2,13; 3:7; Luke 5:17; John 6:2
2:2 [a]Mark 1:45; 2:13
3 [a]Mark 2:3-12: *Matt 9:2-8; Luke 5:18-26* [b]Matt 4:24
4 [1]Lit *bring to* [2]Lit *where He was* [a]Luke 5:19

an opening, they let down the pallet on which the [b]paralytic was lying.

5 And Jesus seeing their faith *said to the paralytic, "[1]Son, [a]your sins are forgiven."

6 But some of the scribes were sitting there and reasoning in their hearts,

7 "Why does this man speak that way? He is blaspheming; [a]who can forgive sins [1]but God alone?"

8 Immediately Jesus, aware [1]in His spirit that they were reasoning that way within themselves, *said to them, "Why are you reasoning about these things in your hearts?

9 "Which is easier, to say to the [a]paralytic, 'Your sins are forgiven'; or to say, 'Get up, and pick up your pallet and walk'?

10 "But so that you may know that the Son of Man has authority on earth to forgive sins"—He *said to the paralytic,

11 "I say to you, get up, pick up your pallet and go home."

12 And he got up and immediately picked up the pallet and went out in the sight of everyone, so that they were all amazed and [a]were glorifying God, saying, "[b]We have never seen anything like this."

13 ¶ And He went out again by the seashore; and [a]all the [1]people were coming to Him, and He was teaching them.

Levi (Matthew) Called

14 [a]As He passed by, He saw [1][b]Levi the *son* of Alphaeus sitting in the tax booth, and He *said to him, "[c]Follow Me!" And he got up and followed Him.

15 ¶ And it [1]*happened that He was reclining *at the table* in his house, and many tax collectors and [2]sinners [3]were dining with Jesus and His disciples; for there were many of them, and they were following Him.

16 When [a]the scribes of the Pharisees saw that He was eating with the sinners and tax collectors, they said to His disciples, "[b]Why is He eating and drinking with tax collectors and [1]sinners?"

17 And hearing *this*, Jesus *said to them, "[a]*It is* not those who are healthy who need a physician, but those who are sick; I did not come to call the righteous, but sinners."

18 ¶ [a]John's disciples and the Pharisees were fasting; and they *came and *said to Him, "Why do John's disciples and the disciples of the Pharisees fast, but Your disciples do not fast?"

19 And Jesus said to them, "While the bridegroom is with them, [1]the attendants of the bridegroom cannot fast, can they? So long as they have the bridegroom with them, they cannot fast.

20 "But the [a]days will come when the bridegroom is taken away from them, and then they will fast in that day.

21 ¶ "No one sews [1]a patch of unshrunk cloth on an old garment; otherwise [2]the patch pulls away from it, the new from the old, and a worse tear results.

22 "No one puts new wine into old wineskins; otherwise the wine will burst the skins, and the wine is lost and the skins *as well*; but *one puts* new wine into fresh wineskins."

Question of the Sabbath

23 ¶ [a]And it happened that He was passing through the grainfields on the Sabbath, and His disciples began to make their way along while [b]picking the heads *of grain.*

24 The Pharisees were saying to Him, "Look, [a]why are they doing what is not lawful on the Sabbath?"

25 And He *said to them, "Have you never read what David did when he was in need and he and his companions became hungry;

26 how he entered the house of God in the time of [a]Abiathar *the* high priest, and ate the [1]consecrated bread, which [b]is not lawful for *anyone* to eat except the priests, and he also gave it to those who were with him?"

27 Jesus said to them, "[a]The Sabbath [1]was made [2]for man, and [b]not man [2]for the Sabbath.

28 "So the Son of Man is Lord even of the Sabbath."

Jesus Heals on the Sabbath

3 [a]He [b]entered again into a synagogue; and a man was there whose hand was withered.

2 [a]They were watching Him *to see* if He would heal him on the Sabbath, [b]so that they might accuse Him.

3 He *said to the man with the withered hand, "[1]Get up and come forward!"

4 And He *said to them, "Is it lawful to do good or to do harm on the Sabbath, to save a life or to kill?" But they kept silent.

5 After [a]looking around at them with anger, grieved at their hardness of heart, He *said to the man, "Stretch out your hand." And he stretched it out, and his hand was restored.

6 The Pharisees went out and immediately *began* [1]conspiring with the [a]Herodians against Him, *as to* how they might destroy Him.

7 ¶ [a]Jesus withdrew to the sea with

4 [b]Matt 4:24
5 [1]Lit *child* [a]Matt 9:2
7 [1]Lit *if not one, God* [a]Is 43:25
8 [1]Lit *by*
9 [a]Matt 4:24
12 [a]Matt 9:8 [b]Matt 9:33
13 [1]Lit *crowd* [a]Mark 1:45
14 [1]also called *Matthew* [a]Mark 2:14-17: *Matt 9:9-13; Luke 5:27-32* [b]Matt 9:9 [c]Matt 8:22
15 [1]Lit *happens* [2]I.e. irreligious Jews [3]Lit *were reclining with*
16 [1]I.e. irreligious Jews [a]Luke 5:30; Acts 23:9 [b]Matt 9:11
17 [a]Matt 9:12, 13; Luke 5:31,32
18 [a]Mark 2:18-22: *Matt 9:14-17; Luke 5:33-38*
19 [1]Lit *sons of the bridal-chamber*
20 [a]Matt 9:15; Luke 17:22
21 [1]Lit *that which is put on* [2]Lit *that which fills up*
23 [a]Mark 2:23-28: *Matt 12:1-8; Luke 6:1-5* [b]Deut 23:25
24 [a]Matt 12:2
26 [1]Or *showbread*; lit *loaves of presentation* [a]1 Sam 21:1; 2 Sam 8:17; 1 Chr 24:6 [b]Lev 24:9
27 [1]Or *came into being* [2]Lit *because for the sake of* [a]Ex 23:12; Deut 5:14 [b]Col 2:16
3:1 [a]Mark 3:1-6: *Matt 12:9-14; Luke 6:6-11* [b]Mark 1:21,39
2 [a]Luke 6:7; 14:1; 20:20 [b]Matt 12:10; Luke 6:7; 11:54
3 [1]Lit *Arise into the midst*
5 [a]Luke 6:10
6 [1]Lit *giving counsel* [a]Matt 22:16; Mark 12:13
7 [a]Mark 3:7-12: *Matt 12:15,16; Luke 6:17-19*

His disciples; and [b]a great multitude
from Galilee followed; and *also* from Judea,
8 and from Jerusalem, and from [a]Id-
umea, and beyond the Jordan, and the
vicinity of [b]Tyre and Sidon, a great number of people heard of all that He was
doing and came to Him.
9 [a]And He told His disciples that a
boat should stand ready for Him because
of the crowd, so that they would not
crowd Him;
10 for He had [a]healed many, with the
result that all those who had [b]afflictions
pressed around Him in order to [c]touch
Him.
11 Whenever the unclean spirits saw
Him, they would fall down before Him
and shout, "You are [a]the Son of God!"
12 And He [a]earnestly warned them
not to [1]tell who He was.

The Twelve Are Chosen

13 ¶ And He *went up on [a]the mountain and * [b]summoned those whom He
Himself wanted, and they came to Him.
14 And He appointed twelve, so that
they would be with Him and that He
could send them out to preach,
15 and to have authority to cast out the
demons.
16 And He appointed the twelve: [a]Si-
mon (to whom He gave the name Peter),
17 and [1]James, the *son* of Zebedee,
and John the brother of [1]James (to them
He gave the name Boanerges, which
means, "Sons of Thunder");
18 and Andrew, and Philip, and Bartholomew, and Matthew, and Thomas,
and [1]James the son of Alphaeus, and
Thaddaeus, and Simon the [2]Zealot;
19 and Judas Iscariot, who betrayed
Him.
20 ¶ And He *came [1a]home, and the
[b]crowd *gathered again, [c]to such an extent that they could not even eat [2]a meal.
21 When [a]His own [1]people heard *of*
this, they went out to take custody of
Him; for they were saying, "[b]He has lost
His senses."
22 The scribes who came down [a]from
Jerusalem were saying, "He is possessed
by [1b]Beelzebul," and "[c]He casts out the
demons by the ruler of the demons."
23 [a]And He called them to Himself
and began speaking to them in [b]parables,
"How can [c]Satan cast out Satan?
24 "If a kingdom is divided against itself, that kingdom cannot stand.
25 "If a house is divided against itself,
that house will not be able to stand.
26 "If [a]Satan has risen up against himself and is divided, he cannot stand, but
[1]he is finished!
27 "[a]But no one can enter the strong
man's house and plunder his property unless he first binds the strong man, and
then he will plunder his house.
28 ¶ "[a]Truly I say to you, all sins shall
be forgiven the sons of men, and whatever blasphemies they utter;
29 but [a]whoever blasphemes against
the Holy Spirit never has forgiveness, but
is guilty of an eternal sin"—
30 because they were saying, "He has
an unclean spirit."
31 ¶ [a]Then His mother and His brothers *arrived, and standing outside they
sent *word* to Him and called Him.
32 A crowd was sitting around Him,
and they *said to Him, "Behold, Your
mother and Your brothers are outside
looking for You."
33 Answering them, He *said, "Who
are My mother and My brothers?"
34 Looking about at those who were
sitting around Him, He *said, "[a]Behold
My mother and My brothers!
35 "For whoever [a]does the will of God,
he is My brother and sister and mother."

Parable of the Sower and Soils

4 [a]He began to teach again [b]by the
sea. And such a very large crowd
gathered to Him that [c]He got into a boat
in the sea and sat down; and the whole
crowd was by the sea on the land.
2 And He was teaching them many
things in [a]parables, and was saying to
them in His teaching,
3 "Listen *to this*! Behold, the sower
went out to sow;
4 as he was sowing, some *seed* fell
beside the road, and the birds came and
ate it up.
5 "Other *seed* fell on the rocky *ground*
where it did not have much soil; and immediately it sprang up because it had no
depth of soil.
6 "And after the sun had risen, it was
scorched; and because it had no root, it
withered away.
7 "Other *seed* fell among the thorns,
and the thorns came up and choked it,
and it yielded no crop.
8 "Other *seeds* fell into the good soil,
and as they grew up and increased, they
yielded a crop and produced thirty, sixty,
and a hundredfold."
9 And He was saying, "[a]He who has
ears to hear, [1]let him hear."
10 ¶ As soon as He was alone, [1]His
followers, along with the twelve, *began*
asking Him *about* the parables.
11 And He was saying to them, "To
you has been given the mystery of the
kingdom of God, but [a]those who are outside get everything [b]in parables,

7 [b]Matt 4:25; Luke 6:17
8 [a]Josh 15:1,21; Ezek 35:15; 36:5 [b]Matt 11:21
9 [a]Mark 4:1; Luke 5:1-3
10 [a]Matt 4:23 [b]Mark 5:29,34; Luke 7:21 [c]Matt 9:21; 14:36; Mark 6:56; 8:22
11 [a]Matt 4:3
12 [1]Lit *make Him known* [a]Matt 8:4
13 [a]Matt 5:1; Luke 6:12 [b]Matt 10:1; Mark 6:7; Luke 9:1
16 [a]Mark 3:16-19: *Matt 10:2-4; Luke 6:14-16*; Acts 1:13
17 [1]Or *Jacob*
18 [1]Or *Jacob* [2]Or *Cananaean*
20 [1]Lit *into a house* [2]Lit *bread* [a]Mark 2:1; 7:17; 9:28 [b]Mark 1:45; 3:7 [c]Mark 6:31
21 [1]Or *kinsmen* [a]Mark 3:31f [b]John 10:20; Acts 26:24
22 [1]Or *Beezebul*; others read *Beelzebub* [a]Matt 15:1 [b]Matt 10:25; 11:18 [c]Matt 9:34
23 [a]Mark 3:23-27: *Matt 12:25-29; Luke 11:17-22* [b]Matt 13:3ff; Mark 4:2ff [c]Matt 4:10
26 [1]Lit *he has an end* [a]Matt 4:10
27 [a]Is 49:24,25
28 [a]Matt 12:31, 32; Mark 3:28-30; Luke 12:10
29 [a]Luke 12:10
31 [a]Mark 3:31-35: *Matt 12:46-50; Luke 8:19-21*
34 [a]Matt 12:49
35 [a]Eph 6:6; Heb 10:36; 1 Pet 4:2; 1 John 2:17
4:1 [a]Mark 4:1-12: *Matt 13:1-15; Luke 8:4-10* [b]Mark 2:13; 3:7 [c]Luke 5:1-3
2 [a]Matt 13:3ff; Mark 3:23; 4:2ff
9 [1]Or *hear!*; or *listen!* [a]Matt 11:15; Mark 4:23; Rev 2:7, 11,17,29
10 [1]Lit *those about Him*
11 [a]1 Cor 5:12f; Col 4:5; 1 Thess 4:12; 1 Tim 3:7 [b]Mark 3:23; 4:2

12 so that [a]WHILE SEEING, THEY MAY SEE AND NOT PERCEIVE, AND WHILE HEARING, THEY MAY HEAR AND NOT UNDERSTAND, OTHERWISE THEY MIGHT RETURN AND BE FORGIVEN."

Explanation

13 ¶ [a]And He *said to them, "Do you not understand this parable? How will you understand all the parables?

14"The sower sows the word.

15"These are the ones who are beside the road where the word is sown; and when they hear, immediately [a]Satan comes and takes away the word which has been sown in them.

16"In a similar way these are the ones on whom seed was sown on the rocky *places,* who, when they hear the word, immediately receive it with joy;

17 and they have no *firm* root in themselves, but are *only* temporary; then, when affliction or persecution arises because of the word, immediately they [1]fall away.

18"And others are the ones on whom seed was sown among the thorns; these are the ones who have heard the word,

19 but the worries of [a]the [1]world, and the [b]deceitfulness of riches, and the desires for other things enter in and choke the word, and it becomes unfruitful.

20"And those are the ones on whom seed was sown on the good soil; and they hear the word and accept it and [a]bear fruit, thirty, sixty, and a hundredfold."

21 ¶ And He was saying to them, "[a]A lamp is not brought to be put under a [1]basket, is it, or under a bed? Is it not *brought* to be put on the lampstand?

22"[a]For nothing is hidden, except to be revealed; nor has *anything* been secret, but that it would come to light.

23"[a]If anyone has ears to hear, let him hear."

24 And He was saying to them, "Take care what you listen to. [1a]By your standard of measure it will be measured to you; and more will be given you besides.

25"[a]For whoever has, to him *more* shall be given; and whoever does not have, even what he has shall be taken away from him."

Parable of the Seed

26 ¶ And He was saying, "The kingdom of God is like a man who casts seed upon the soil;

27 and he goes to bed at night and gets up by day, and the seed sprouts and grows—how, he himself does not know.

28"The soil produces crops by itself;

12 [a]Is 6:9f; 43:8; Jer 5:21; Ezek 12:2; Matt 13:14; Luke 8:10; John 12:40; Rom 11:8

13 [a]Mark 4:13-20: *Matt 13:18-23; Luke 8:11-15*

15 [a]Matt 4:10f; 1 Pet 5:8; Rev 20:2,3,7-10

17 [1]Lit *are caused to stumble*

19 [1]Or *age* [a]Matt 13:22; Rom 12:2; Eph 2:2; 6:12 [b]Prov 23:4; 1 Tim 6:9, 10,17

20 [a]John 15:2ff; Rom 7:4

21 [1]Or *peck-measure* [a]Matt 5:15; Luke 8:16; 11:33

22 [a]Matt 10:26; Luke 8:17; 12:2

23 [a]Matt 11:15; 13:9,43; Mark 4:9; Luke 8:8; 14:35; Rev 3:6, 13,22; 13:9

24 [1]Lit *By what measure you measure* [a]Matt 7:2; Luke 6:38

25 [a]Matt 13:12; 25:29; Luke 8:18; 19:26

29 [1]Lit *sends forth* [a]Joel 3:13

30 [1]Lit *compare* [a]Mark 4:30-32: *Matt 13:31,32; Luke 13:18,19* [b]Matt 13:24

32 [1]Or *sky* [a]Ezek 17:23; Ps 104:12; Ezek 31:6; Dan 4:12

34 [a]Matt 13:34; John 10:6; 16:25 [b]Luke 24:27

35 [a]Mark 4:35-41: *Matt 8:18,23-27; Luke 8:22,25*

36 [1]Or *Sending away* [a]Mark 3:9; 4:1; 5:2,21

39 [1]Lit *a great calm occurred* [a]Ps 65:7; 89:9; 107:29; Matt 8:26; Luke 8:24

40 [1]Or *cowardly* [a]Matt 14:31; Luke 8:25

5:1 [a]Mark 5:1-17: *Matt 8:28-34; Luke 8:26-37*

2 [a]Mark 3:9; 4:1,36; 5:21 [b]Mark 1:23

first the blade, then the head, then the mature grain in the head.

29"But when the crop permits, he immediately [1a]puts in the sickle, because the harvest has come."

Parable of the Mustard Seed

30 ¶ [a]And He said, "How shall we [1b]picture the kingdom of God, or by what parable shall we present it?

31"*It is* like a mustard seed, which, when sown upon the soil, though it is smaller than all the seeds that are upon the soil,

32 yet when it is sown, it grows up and becomes larger than all the garden plants and forms large branches; so that [a]THE BIRDS OF THE [1]AIR can NEST UNDER ITS SHADE."

33 ¶ With many such parables He was speaking the word to them, so far as they were able to hear it;

34 and He did not speak to them [a]without a parable; but He was [b]explaining everything privately to His own disciples.

Jesus Stills the Sea

35 ¶ [a]On that day, when evening came, He *said to them, "Let us go over to the other side."

36 [1]Leaving the crowd, they *took Him along with them [a]in the boat, just as He was; and other boats were with Him.

37 And there *arose a fierce gale of wind, and the waves were breaking over the boat so much that the boat was already filling up.

38 Jesus Himself was in the stern, asleep on the cushion; and they *woke Him and *said to Him, "Teacher, do You not care that we are perishing?"

39 And He got up and [a]rebuked the wind and said to the sea, "Hush, be still." And the wind died down and [1]it became perfectly calm.

40 And He said to them, "Why are you [1]afraid? [a]Do you still have no faith?"

41 They became very much afraid and said to one another, "Who then is this, that even the wind and the sea obey Him?"

The Gerasene Demoniac

5 [a]They came to the other side of the sea, into the country of the Gerasenes.

2 When He got out of [a]the boat, immediately a man from the tombs [b]with an unclean spirit met Him,

3 and he had his dwelling among the tombs. And no one was able to bind him anymore, even with a chain;

4 because he had often been bound
with shackles and chains, and the chains
had been torn apart by him and the
shackles broken in pieces, and no one
was strong enough to subdue him.
5 Constantly, night and day, he was
screaming among the tombs and in the
mountains, and gashing himself with
stones.
6 Seeing Jesus from a distance, he ran
up and bowed down before Him;
7 and shouting with a loud voice, he
*said, "[1][a]What business do we have
with each other, Jesus, [b]Son of [c]the
Most High God? I implore You by God, do
not torment me!"
8 For He had been saying to him,
"Come out of the man, you unclean
spirit!"
9 And He was asking him, "What is
your name?" And he *said to Him, "My
name is [a]Legion; for we are many."
10 And he *began* to implore Him earnestly not to send them out of the country.
11 Now there was a large herd of
swine feeding [1]nearby on the mountain.
12 *The demons* implored Him, saying,
"Send us into the swine so that we may
enter them."
13 Jesus gave them permission. And
coming out, the unclean spirits entered
the swine; and the herd rushed down the
steep bank into the sea, about two thousand *of them*; and they were drowned in
the sea.
14 ¶ Their herdsmen ran away and reported it in the city and in the country.
And *the people* came to see what it was
that had happened.
15 They *came to Jesus and *observed
the man who had been [a]demon-
possessed sitting down, [b]clothed and
[c]in his right mind, the very man who
had had the "[d]legion"; and they became
frightened.
16 Those who had seen it described
to them how it had happened to the
[a]demon-possessed man, and *all* about
the swine.
17 And they began to [a]implore Him to
leave their region.
18 [a]As He was getting into the boat,
the man who had been [b]demon-
possessed was imploring Him that he
might [1]accompany Him.
19 And He did not let him, but He
*said to him, "[a]Go home to your people
and report to them [1]what great things
the Lord has done for you, and *how* He
had mercy on you."
20 And he went away and began to
[a]proclaim in [b]Decapolis [1]what great
things Jesus had done for him; and everyone was amazed.

Miracles and Healing

21 ¶ [a]When Jesus had crossed over
again in [b]the boat to the other side, a
large crowd gathered around Him; and so
He [1]stayed [c]by the seashore.
22 [a]One of [b]the synagogue [1]officials
named Jairus *came up, and on seeing
Him, *fell at His feet
23 and *implored Him earnestly, saying, "My little daughter is at the point of
death; *please* come and [a]lay Your hands
on her, so that she will [1]get well and
live."
24 And He went off with him; and a
large crowd was following Him and pressing in on Him.
25 ¶ A woman who had had a hemorrhage for twelve years,
26 and had endured much at the
hands of many physicians, and had spent
all that she had and was not helped at all,
but rather had grown worse—
27 after hearing about Jesus, she came
up in the crowd behind *Him* and touched
His [1]cloak.
28 For she [1]thought, "If I just touch
His garments, I will [2]get well."
29 Immediately the flow of her blood
was dried up; and she felt in her body that
she was healed of her [a]affliction.
30 Immediately Jesus, perceiving in
Himself that [a]the power *proceeding*
from Him had gone forth, turned around
in the crowd and said, "Who touched My
garments?"
31 And His disciples said to Him, "You
see the crowd pressing in on You, and
You say, 'Who touched Me?' "
32 And He looked around to see the
woman who had done this.
33 But the woman fearing and trembling, aware of what had happened to
her, came and fell down before Him and
told Him the whole truth.
34 And He said to her, "Daughter,
[a]your faith has [1]made you well; [b]go in
peace and be healed of your [c]affliction."
35 ¶ While He was still speaking, they
*came from the *house of* the [a]synagogue
official, saying, "Your daughter has died;
why trouble the Teacher anymore?"
36 But Jesus, overhearing what was
being spoken, *said to the [a]synagogue
official, "[b]Do not be afraid *any longer*,
only [1]believe."
37 And He allowed no one to accompany Him, except [a]Peter and [1]James and
John the brother of [1]James.
38 They *came to the house of the
[a]synagogue official; and He *saw a com-

7 [1]Lit *What to me and to you* (a Heb idiom) [a]Matt 8:29 [b]Matt 4:3 [c]Luke 8:28; Acts 16:17; Heb 7:1
9 [a]Matt 26:53; Mark 5:15; Luke 8:30
11 [1]Lit *there*
15 [a]Matt 4:24; Mark 5:16,18 [b]Luke 8:27 [c]Luke 8:35 [d]Mark 5:9
16 [a]Matt 4:24; Mark 5:15
17 [a]Matt 8:34; Acts 16:39
18 [1]Lit *be with Him* [a]Mark 5:18-20: *Luke 8:38,39* [b]Matt 4:24; Mark 5:15, 16
19 [1]Or *everything that* [a]Luke 8:39
20 [1]Or *everything that* [a]Ps 66:16 [b]Matt 4:25; Mark 7:31
21 [1]Lit *was* [a]Matt 9:1; Luke 8:40 [b]Mark 4:36 [c]Mark 4:1
22 [1]Or *rulers* [a]Mark 5:22-43: *Matt 9:18-26; Luke 8:41-56* [b]Matt 9:18; Mark 5:35,36, 38; Luke 8:49; 13:14; Acts 13:15; 18:8,17
23 [1]Lit *be saved* [a]Mark 6:5; 7:32; 8:23; 16:18; Luke 4:40; 13:13; Acts 6:6; 9:17; 28:8
27 [1]Or *outer garment*
28 [1]Lit *was saying* [2]Lit *be saved*
29 [a]Mark 3:10; 5:34
30 [a]Luke 5:17
34 [1]Lit *saved you* [a]Matt 9:22 [b]Luke 7:50; 8:48; Acts 16:36; James 2:16 [c]Mark 3:10; 5:29
35 [a]Mark 5:22
36 [1]Or *keep on believing* [a]Mark 5:22 [b]Luke 8:50
37 [1]Or *Jacob*; James is the Eng form of Jacob [a]Matt 17:1; 26:37
38 [a]Mark 5:22

motion, and *people* loudly weeping and
wailing.
39 And entering in, He *said to them,
"Why make a commotion and weep? The
child has not died, but is asleep."
40 They *began* laughing at Him. But
putting them all out, He *took along the
child's father and mother and His own
companions, and *entered *the room*
where the child was.
41 Taking the child by the hand, He
*said to her, "Talitha kum!" (which
translated means, "Little girl, [a]I say to
you, get up!").
42 Immediately the girl got up and *began* to walk, for she was twelve years old.
And immediately they were completely
astounded.
43 And He [a]gave them strict orders
that no one should know about this, and
He said that *something* should be given
her to eat.

Teaching at Nazareth

6 [a]Jesus went out from there and
*came into [1b]His hometown; and
His disciples *followed Him.
2 When the Sabbath came, He began
[a]to teach in the synagogue; and the
[b]many listeners were astonished, saying,
"Where did this man *get* these things,
and what is *this* wisdom given to Him,
and such [1]miracles as these performed
by His hands?
3 "Is not this [a]the carpenter, [b]the son
of Mary, and brother of [1]James and Joses
and Judas and Simon? Are not [c]His sisters here with us?" And they took [d]of-
fense at Him.
4 Jesus said to them, "[a]A prophet
is not without honor except in [1b]his
hometown and among his *own* relatives
and in his *own* household."
5 And He could do no [1]miracle there
except that He [a]laid His hands on a few
sick people and healed them.
6 And He wondered at their unbelief.
¶ [a]And He was going around the villages teaching.

The Twelve Sent Out

7 ¶ [a]And [b]He *summoned the
twelve and began to send them out [c]in
pairs, and gave them authority over the
unclean spirits;
8 [a]and He instructed them that they
should take nothing for *their* journey, except a mere staff—no bread, no [1]bag, no
money in their belt—
9 but [1]*to* wear sandals; and *He added*, "Do not put on two [2]tunics."
10 And He said to them, "Wherever
you enter a house, stay there until you
[1]leave town.
11 "Any place that does not receive you
or listen to you, as you go out from there,
[a]shake the dust [1]off the soles of your
feet for a testimony against them."
12 [a]They went out and [1]preached
that *men* should repent.
13 And they were casting out many
demons and [a]were anointing with oil
many sick people and healing them.

John's Fate Recalled

14 ¶ [a]And King Herod heard *of it*, for
His name had become well known; and
people were saying, "[b]John the Baptist
has risen from the dead, and that is why
these miraculous powers are at work in
Him."
15 But others were saying, "He is [a]Eli-
jah." And others were saying, "*He is* [b]a
prophet, like one of the prophets *of old*."
16 But when Herod heard *of it*, he
kept saying, "John, whom I beheaded,
has risen!"
17 ¶ For Herod himself had sent and
had John arrested and bound in prison on
account of [a]Herodias, the wife of his
brother Philip, because he had married
her.
18 For John had been saying to Herod,
"[a]It is not lawful for you to have your
brother's wife."
19 [a]Herodias had a grudge against
him and wanted to put him to death and
could not *do so;*
20 for [a]Herod was afraid of John,
knowing that he was a righteous and holy
man, and he kept him safe. And when he
heard him, he was very perplexed; [1]but
he [2]used to enjoy listening to him.
21 A strategic day came when Herod
on his birthday [a]gave a banquet for his
lords and [1]military commanders and the
leading men [b]of Galilee;
22 and when the daughter of [a]Herodi-
as herself came in and danced, she
pleased Herod and [1]his dinner guests;
and the king said to the girl, "Ask me for
whatever you want and I will give it to
you."
23 And he swore to her, "Whatever
you ask of me, I will give it to you; up to
[a]half of my kingdom."
24 And she went out and said to her
mother, "What shall I ask for?" And she
said, "The head of John the Baptist."
25 Immediately she came in a hurry to
the king and asked, saying, "I want you to
give me at once the head of John the
Baptist on a platter."
26 And although the king was very sorry, *yet* because of his oaths and because
of [1]his dinner guests, he was unwilling
to refuse her.
27 Immediately the king sent an exe-

41 [a]Luke 7:14; Acts 9:40
43 [a]Matt 8:4
6:1 [1]Or *His own part of the country* [a]Mark 6:1-6: *Matt 13:54-58* [b]Matt 13:54,57; Luke 4:16,23
2 [1]Or *works of power* [a]Matt 4:23; Mark 10:1 [b]Matt 7:28
3 [1]Or *Jacob* [a]Matt 13:55 [b]Matt 12:46 [c]Matt 13:56 [d]Matt 11:6
4 [1]Or *his own part of the country* [a]Matt 13:57; John 4:44 [b]Mark 6:1
5 [1]Or *work of power* [a]Mark 5:23
6 [a]Matt 9:35; Mark 1:39; 10:1; Luke 13:22
7 [a]Mark 6:7-11: *Matt 10:1,9-14; Luke 9:1,3-5;* Luke 10:4-11 [b]Matt 10:1,5; Mark 3:13; Luke 9:1 [c]Luke 10:1
8 [1]Or *knapsack or beggar's bag* [a]Matt 10:10
9 [1]Lit *being shod with* [2]Or *inner garments*
10 [1]Lit *go out from there*
11 [1]Lit *under your feet* [a]Matt 10:14; Acts 13:51
12 [1]Or *proclaimed as a herald* [a]Matt 11:1; Luke 9:6
13 [a]James 5:14
14 [a]Mark 6:14-29: *Matt 14:1-12;* Mark 6:14-16: *Luke 9:7-9* [b]Matt 14:2; Luke 9:19
15 [a]Matt 16:14; Mark 8:28 [b]Matt 21:11
17 [a]Matt 14:3; Luke 3:19
18 [a]Matt 14:4
19 [a]Matt 14:3
20 [1]Lit *and* [2]Lit *was hearing him gladly* [a]Matt 21:26
21 [1]I.e. chiliarchs, in command of a thousand troops [a]Esth 1:3; 2:18 [b]Luke 3:1
22 [1]Lit *those who reclined at the table with him* [a]Matt 14:3
23 [a]Esth 5:3,6; 7:2
26 [1]Lit *those reclining at the table*

cutioner and commanded *him* to bring
back his head. And he went and had him
beheaded in the prison,
28 and brought his head on a platter,
and gave it to the girl; and the girl gave it
to her mother.
29 When his disciples heard *about*
this, they came and took away his body
and laid it in a tomb.
30 ¶ [a]The [b]apostles *gathered together with Jesus; and they reported to
Him all that they had done and taught.
31 And He *said to them, "Come away
by yourselves to a secluded place and rest
a while." (For there were many *people*
coming and going, and [a]they did not
even have time to eat.)
32 [a]They went away in [b]the boat to a
secluded place by themselves.

Five Thousand Fed

33 *The people* saw them going, and
many recognized *them* and ran there together on foot from all the cities, and got
there ahead of them.
34 When Jesus went [1]ashore, He
[a]saw a large crowd, and He felt compassion for them because [b]they were like
sheep without a shepherd; and He began
to teach them many things.
35 When it was already quite late, His
disciples came to Him and said, "[1]This
place is desolate and it is already quite
late;
36 send them away so that they may
go into the surrounding countryside and
villages and buy themselves [1]something
to eat."
37 But He answered them, "You give
them *something* to eat!" [a]And they *said
to Him, "Shall we go and spend two hundred [1b]denarii on bread and give them
something to eat?"
38 And He *said to them, "How many
loaves do you have? Go look!" And when
they found out, they *said, "Five, and
two fish."
39 And He commanded them all to
[1]sit down by groups on the green grass.
40 They [1]sat down in groups of hundreds and of fifties.
41 And He took the five loaves and the
two fish, and looking up toward heaven,
He [a]blessed *the food* and broke the
loaves and He kept giving *them* to the
disciples to set before them; and He divided up the two fish among them all.
42 They all ate and were satisfied,
43 and they picked up twelve full
[a]baskets of the broken pieces, and also of
the fish.
44 There were [a]five thousand men
who ate the loaves.

30 [a]Luke 9:10 [b]Matt 10:2; Mark 3:14; Luke 6:13; 9:10; 17:5; 22:14; 24:10; Acts 1:2,26
31 [a]Mark 3:20
32 [a]Mark 6:32-44: *Matt 14:13-21; Luke 9:10-17; John 6:5-13;* Mark 8:2-9 [b]Mark 3:9; 4:36; 6:45
34 [1]Lit *out* [a]Matt 9:36 [b]Num 27:17; 1 Kin 22:17; 2 Chr 18:16; Zech 10:2
35 [1]Lit *The*
36 [1]Lit *what they may eat*
37 [1]The denarius was equivalent to one day's wage [a]John 6:7 [b]Matt 18:28; Luke 7:41
39 [1]Lit *recline*
40 [1]Lit *reclined*
41 [a]Matt 14:19
43 [a]Matt 14:20
44 [a]Matt 14:21
45 [a]Mark 6:45-51: *Matt 14:22-32; John 6:15-21* [b]Mark 6:32 [c]Matt 11:21; Mark 8:22
46 [a]Acts 18:18, 21; 2 Cor 2:13 [b]Matt 14:23
48 [1]Lit *harassed in rowing* [2]I.e. 3-6 a.m. [a]Matt 24:43; Mark 13:35
50 [1]Or *troubled* [a]Matt 9:2 [b]Matt 14:27
51 [a]Mark 6:32
52 [1]Lit *had not understood on the basis of* [2]Or *their mind was closed, made dull,* or *insensible* [a]Mark 8:17ff [b]Rom 11:7
53 [a]Mark 6:53-56: *Matt 14:34-36;* John 6:24,25
55 [1]Lit *where they were hearing that He was*
56 [a]Mark 3:10 [b]Matt 9:20; Num 15:37-40
7:1 [a]Mark 7:1-23: *Matt 15:1-20* [b]Matt 15:1
2 [a]Matt 15:2; Mark 7:5; Luke 11:38; Acts 10:14,28; 11:8; Rom 14:14; Heb 10:29; Rev 21:27
3 [1]Lit *with the fist* [a]Mark 7:5,8, 9,13; Gal 1:14
4 [1]Or *sprinkle*

Jesus Walks on the Water

45 ¶ [a]Immediately Jesus made His
disciples get into [b]the boat and go ahead
of *Him* to the other side to [c]Bethsaida,
while He Himself was sending the crowd
away.
46 After [a]bidding them farewell, He
left [b]for the mountain to pray.
47 ¶ When it was evening, the boat
was in the middle of the sea, and He was
alone on the land.
48 Seeing them [1]straining at the oars,
for the wind was against them, at about
the [2a]fourth watch of the night He
*came to them, walking on the sea; and
He intended to pass by them.
49 But when they saw Him walking on
the sea, they supposed that it was a ghost,
and cried out;
50 for they all saw Him and were [1]ter-
rified. But immediately He spoke with
them and *said to them, "[a]Take courage;
it is I, [b]do not be afraid."
51 Then He got into [a]the boat with
them, and the wind stopped; and they
were utterly astonished,
52 for [a]they [1]had not gained any insight from the *incident of* the loaves, but
[2]their heart [b]was hardened.

Healing at Gennesaret

53 ¶ [a]When they had crossed over
they came to land at Gennesaret, and
moored to the shore.
54 When they got out of the boat, immediately *the people* recognized Him,
55 and ran about that whole country
and began to carry here and there on
their pallets those who were sick, to [1]the
place they heard He was.
56 Wherever He entered villages, or
cities, or countryside, they were laying
the sick in the market places, and imploring Him that they might just [a]touch [b]the
fringe of His cloak; and as many as
touched it were being cured.

Followers of Tradition

7 [a]The Pharisees and some of the
scribes gathered around Him when
they had come [b]from Jerusalem,
2 and had seen that some of His disciples were eating their bread with [a]im-
pure hands, that is, unwashed.
3 (For the Pharisees and all the Jews
do not eat unless they [1]carefully wash
their hands, *thus* observing the [a]tradi-
tions of the elders;
4 and *when they come* from the market place, they do not eat unless they
[1]cleanse themselves; and there are many
other things which they have received in

order to observe, such as the [2]washing of
[a]cups and pitchers and copper pots.)
5 The Pharisees and the scribes
*asked Him, "Why do Your disciples not
walk according to the [a]tradition of the
elders, but eat their bread with [b]impure
hands?"
6 And He said to them, "Rightly did
Isaiah prophesy of you hypocrites, as it is
written:
'[a]THIS PEOPLE HONORS ME WITH
THEIR LIPS,
BUT THEIR HEART IS FAR AWAY
FROM ME.
7 '[a]BUT IN VAIN DO THEY
WORSHIP ME,
TEACHING AS DOCTRINES THE
PRECEPTS OF MEN.'
8 "Neglecting the commandment of
God, you hold to the [a]tradition of men."
9 ¶ He was also saying to them, "You
are experts at setting aside the commandment of God in order to keep your [a]tradi-
tion.
10 "For Moses said, '[a]HONOR YOUR FA-
THER AND YOUR MOTHER'; and, '[b]HE WHO
SPEAKS EVIL OF FATHER OR MOTHER, IS TO
[1]BE PUT TO DEATH';
11 but you say, 'If a man says to *his*
father or *his* mother, whatever I have that
would help you is [a]Corban (that is to say,
[1]given *to God*),'
12 you no longer permit him to do anything for *his* father or *his* mother;
13 *thus* invalidating the word of God
by your [a]tradition which you have handed down; and you do many things such as
that."

The Heart of Man

14 ¶ After He called the crowd to Him
again, He *began* saying to them, "Listen
to Me, all of you, and understand:
15 there is nothing outside the man
which can defile him if it goes into him;
but the things which proceed out of the
man are what defile the man.
16 ["[1]If anyone has ears to hear, let
him hear."]
17 ¶ When he had left the crowd *and*
entered [a]the house, [b]His disciples questioned Him about the parable.
18 And He *said to them, "Are you so
lacking in understanding also? Do you not
understand that whatever goes into the
man from outside cannot defile him,
19 because it does not go into his
heart, but into his stomach, and [1]is elim-
inated?" (*Thus He* declared [a]all foods
[b]clean.)
20 And He was saying, "[a]That which
proceeds out of the man, that is what
defiles the man.
21 "For from within, out of the heart of
men, proceed the evil thoughts, [1]fornica-
tions, thefts, murders, adulteries,
22 deeds of coveting *and* wickedness,
as well as deceit, sensuality, [1a]envy,
slander, [2]pride *and* foolishness.
23 "All these evil things proceed from
within and defile the man."

The Syrophoenician Woman

24 ¶ [a]Jesus got up and went away
from there to the region of [b]Tyre[1]. And
when He had entered a house, He wanted no one to know *of it*; [2]yet He could
not escape notice.
25 But after hearing of Him, a woman
whose little daughter had an unclean
spirit immediately came and fell at His
feet.
26 Now the woman was a [1]Gentile, of
the Syrophoenician race. And she kept
asking Him to cast the demon out of her
daughter.
27 And He was saying to her, "Let the
children be satisfied first, for it is not
[1]good to take the children's bread and
throw it to the dogs."
28 But she answered and *said to Him,
"Yes, Lord, *but* even the dogs under the
table feed on the children's crumbs."
29 And He said to her, "Because of this
[1]answer go; the demon has gone out of
your daughter."
30 And going back to her home, she
found the child [1]lying on the bed, the
demon having left.
31 ¶ [a]Again He went out from the region of [b]Tyre, and came through Sidon to
[c]the Sea of Galilee, within the region of
[d]Decapolis.
32 They *brought to Him one who was
deaf and spoke with difficulty, and they
*implored Him to [a]lay His hand on him.
33 [a]Jesus took him aside from the
crowd, by himself, and put His fingers
into his ears, and after [a]spitting, He
touched his tongue *with the saliva;*
34 and looking up to heaven with a
deep [a]sigh, He *said to him, "Ephpha-
tha!" that is, "Be opened!"
35 And his ears were opened, and the
[1]impediment of his tongue [2]was removed, and he *began* speaking plainly.
36 And [a]He gave them orders not to
tell anyone; but the more He ordered
them, the more widely they [b]continued
to proclaim it.
37 They were utterly astonished, saying, "He has done all things well; He
makes even the deaf to hear and the mute
to speak."

Four Thousand Fed

8 In those days, when there was again
a large crowd and they had nothing

4 [2]Lit *baptizing* [a]Matt 23:25
5 [a]Mark 7:3,8,9, 13; Gal 1:14 [b]Mark 7:2
6 [a]Is 29:13
7 [a]Is 29:13
8 [a]Mark 7:3,5,9, 13; Gal 1:14
9 [a]Mark 7:3,5,8, 13; Gal 1:14
10 [1]Lit *die the death* [a]Ex 20:12; Deut 5:16 [b]Ex 21:17; Lev 20:9
11 [1]Or *a gift,* i.e. an offering [a]Lev 1:2; Matt 27:6
13 [a]Mark 7:3,5, 8,9; Gal 1:14
16 [1]Early mss do not contain this verse
17 [a]Mark 2:1; 3:20; 9:28 [b]Matt 15:15
19 [1]Lit *goes out into the latrine* [a]Rom 14:1-12; Col 2:16 [b]Luke 11:41; Acts 10:15; 11:9
20 [a]Matt 15:18; Mark 7:23
21 [1]I.e. acts of sexual immorality
22 [1]Lit *an evil eye* [2]Or *arrogance* [a]Matt 6:23; 20:15
24 [1]Two early mss add *and Sidon* [2]Lit *and* [a]Mark 7:24-30: *Matt 15:21-28* [b]Matt 11:21; Mark 7:31
26 [1]Lit *Greek*
27 [1]Or *proper*
29 [1]Lit *word*
30 [1]Lit *thrown*
31 [a]Mark 7:31-37: *Matt 15:29-31* [b]Matt 11:21; Mark 7:24 [c]Matt 4:18 [d]Matt 4:25; Mark 5:20
32 [a]Mark 5:23
33 [a]Mark 8:23
34 [a]Mark 8:12
35 [1]Or *bond* [2]Lit *was loosed*
36 [a]Matt 8:4 [b]Mark 1:45

to eat, [a]Jesus called His disciples and
*said to them,
2 "[a]I feel compassion for the [1]people
because they have remained with Me
now three days and have nothing to eat.
3 "If I send them away hungry to their
homes, they will faint on the way; and
some of them have come from a great
distance."
4 And His disciples answered Him,
"Where will anyone be able *to find
enough* [1]bread here in *this* desolate
place to satisfy these people?"
5 And He was asking them, "How
many loaves do you have?" And they said,
"Seven."
6 And He *directed the [1]people to
[2]sit down on the ground; and taking the
seven loaves, He gave thanks and broke
them, and started giving them to His disciples to [3]serve to them, and they served
them to the [1]people.
7 They also had a few small fish; and
[a]after He had blessed them, He ordered
these to be [1]served as well.
8 And they ate and were satisfied;
and they picked up seven large [a]baskets
full of what was left over of the broken
pieces.
9 About four thousand were *there*;
and He sent them away.
10 And immediately He entered the
boat with His disciples and came to the
district of [a]Dalmanutha.
11 ¶ [a]The Pharisees came out and began to argue with Him, [b]seeking from
Him a [1]sign from heaven, [2]to test Him.
12 [a]Sighing deeply [1]in His spirit, He
*said, "Why does this generation seek for
a [2]sign? Truly I say to you, [3b]no [2]sign
will be given to this generation."
13 Leaving them, He again embarked
and went away to the other side.
14 ¶ And they had forgotten to take
bread, and did not have more than one
loaf in the boat with them.
15 And He was giving orders to them,
saying, "[a]Watch out! Beware of the leav-
en of the Pharisees and the leaven of
[b]Herod."
16 They *began* to discuss with one another *the fact* that they had no bread.
17 And Jesus, aware of this, *said to
them, "Why do you discuss *the fact* that
you have no bread? [a]Do you not yet see
or understand? Do you have a [1]hardened
heart?
18 "[a]HAVING EYES, DO YOU NOT SEE? AND
HAVING EARS, DO YOU NOT HEAR? And do
you not remember,
19 when I broke [a]the five loaves for
the five thousand, how many [b]baskets
full of broken pieces you picked up?"
They *said to Him, "Twelve."

8:1 [a]Mark 8:1-9: *Matt 15:32-39;* Mark 6:34-44
2 [1]Lit *crowd* [a]Matt 9:36; Mark 6:34
4 [1]Lit *loaves*
6 [1]Lit *crowd* [2]Lit *recline* [3]Lit *set before*
7 [1]Lit *set before them* [a]Matt 14:19
8 [a]Matt 15:37; Mark 8:20
10 [a]Matt 15:39
11 [1]Or *attesting miracle* [2]Lit *testing Him* [a]Mark 8:11-21: *Matt 16:1-12* [b]Matt 12:38
12 [1]Or *to Himself* [2]Or *attesting miracle* [3]Lit *if a sign shall be given* [a]Mark 7:34 [b]Matt 12:39
15 [a]Matt 16:6; Luke 12:1 [b]Matt 14:1; 22:16
17 [1]Or *dull, insensible* [a]Mark 6:52
18 [a]Jer 5:21; Ezek 12:2; Mark 4:12
19 [a]Mark 6:41-44 [b]Matt 14:20
20 [a]Mark 8:6-9 [b]Mark 8:8
21 [a]Mark 6:52
22 [a]Matt 11:21; Mark 6:45 [b]Mark 3:10
23 [a]Mark 7:33 [b]Mark 5:23
24 [1]Or *gained sight* [2]Or *they look to me*
26 [a]Mark 8:23
27 [a]Mark 8:27-29: *Matt 16:13-16; Luke 9:18-20* [b]Matt 16:13
28 [a]Mark 6:14; Luke 9:7,8
29 [1]I.e. the Messiah [a]John 6:68,69
30 [1]Or *strictly admonished* [a]Matt 8:4; 16:20; Luke 9:21
31 [a]Mark 8:31-9:1: *Matt 16:21-28; Luke 9:22-27* [b]Matt 16:21
32 [a]John 10:24; 11:14; 16:25,29; 18:20
33 [1]Lit *the things of God* [a]Matt 4:10
34 [a]Matt 10:38; Luke 14:27
35 [1]Or *soul* [a]Matt 10:39; Luke 17:33; John 12:25

20 "When *I broke* [a]the seven for the
four thousand, how many large [b]baskets
full of broken pieces did you pick up?"
And they *said to Him, "Seven."
21 And He was saying to them, "[a]Do
you not yet understand?"
22 ¶ And they *came to [a]Bethsaida.
And they *brought a blind man to Jesus
and *implored Him to [b]touch him.
23 Taking the blind man by the hand,
He [a]brought him out of the village; and
after [a]spitting on his eyes and [b]laying
His hands on him, He asked him, "Do you
see anything?"
24 And he [1]looked up and said, "I see
men, for [2]I see *them* like trees, walking
around."
25 Then again He laid His hands on his
eyes; and he looked intently and was restored, and *began* to see everything
clearly.
26 And He sent him to his home, saying, "Do not even enter [a]the village."

Peter's Confession of Christ

27 ¶ [a]Jesus went out, along with His
disciples, to the villages of [b]Caesarea
Philippi; and on the way He questioned
His disciples, saying to them, "Who do
people say that I am?"
28 [a]They told Him, saying, "John the
Baptist; and others *say* Elijah; but others,
one of the prophets."
29 And He *continued* by questioning
them, "But who do you say that I am?"
[a]Peter *answered and *said to Him,
"You are [1]the Christ."
30 And [a]He [1]warned them to tell no
one about Him.
31 ¶ [a]And He began to teach them
that [b]the Son of Man must suffer many
things and be rejected by the elders and
the chief priests and the scribes, and be
killed, and after three days rise again.
32 And He was stating the matter
[a]plainly. And Peter took Him aside and
began to rebuke Him.
33 But turning around and seeing His
disciples, He rebuked Peter and *said,
"Get behind Me, [a]Satan; for you are not
setting your mind on [1]God's interests,
but man's."
34 ¶ And He summoned the crowd
with His disciples, and said to them, "If
anyone wishes to come after Me, he must
deny himself, and [a]take up his cross and
follow Me.
35 "For [a]whoever wishes to save his
[1]life will lose it, but whoever loses his
[1]life for My sake and the gospel's will
save it.
36 "For what does it profit a man to gain
the whole world, and forfeit his soul?

37 "For what will a man give in exchange for his soul?
38 "For [a]whoever is ashamed of Me
and My words in this adulterous and sinful generation, [b]the Son of Man will also
be ashamed of him when He [c]comes in
the glory of His Father with the holy angels."

The Transfiguration

9 And Jesus was saying to them,
"[a]Truly I say to you, there are some
of those who are standing here who will
not taste death until they see the kingdom of God after it has come with
power."
2 ¶ [a]Six days later, Jesus *took with
Him [b]Peter and [1]James and John, and
*brought them up on a high mountain by
themselves. And He was transfigured before them;
3 and [a]His garments became radiant
and exceedingly white, as no launderer
on earth can whiten them.
4 Elijah appeared to them along with
Moses; and they were talking with Jesus.
5 Peter *said to Jesus, "[a]Rabbi, it is
good for us to be here; [b]let us make three
[1]tabernacles, one for You, and one for
Moses, and one for Elijah."
6 For he did not know what to answer; for they became terrified.
7 Then a cloud [1]formed, overshadowing them, and [a]a voice [1]came out of
the cloud, "[b]This is My beloved Son,
[2]listen to Him!"
8 All at once they looked around and
saw no one with them anymore, except
Jesus alone.
9 ¶ [a]As they were coming down
from the mountain, He [b]gave them orders not to relate to anyone what they
had seen, [1]until the Son of Man rose
from the dead.
10 They [1]seized upon [2]that statement, discussing with one another
[3]what rising from the dead meant.
11 They asked Him, saying, *"Why is it*
that the scribes say that [a]Elijah must
come first?"
12 And He said to them, "Elijah does
first come and restore all things. And *yet*
how is it written of [a]the Son of Man that
[b]He will suffer many things and be treated with contempt?
13 "But I say to you that Elijah has [1]in-
deed come, and they did to him whatever
they wished, just as it is written of him."

All Things Possible

14 ¶ [a]When they came *back* to the
disciples, they saw a large crowd around
them, and *some* scribes arguing with
them.
15 Immediately, when the entire
crowd saw Him, they were [a]amazed and
began running up to greet Him.
16 And He asked them, "What are you
discussing with them?"
17 And one of the crowd answered
Him, "Teacher, I brought You my son,
possessed with a spirit which makes him
mute;
18 and [1]whenever it seizes him, it
[2]slams him *to the ground* and he foams
at the mouth, and grinds his teeth and
[3]stiffens out. I told Your disciples to cast
it out, and they could not *do it."*
19 And He *answered them and *said,
"O unbelieving generation, how long
shall I be with you? How long shall I put
up with you? Bring him to Me!"
20 They brought [1]the boy to Him.
When he saw Him, immediately the spirit threw him into a convulsion, and falling
to the ground, he *began* rolling around
and foaming *at the mouth.*
21 And He asked his father, "How long
has this been happening to him?" And he
said, "From childhood.
22 "It has often thrown him both into
the fire and into the water to destroy him.
But if You can do anything, take pity on
us and help us!"
23 And Jesus said to him, " 'If You
can?' [a]All things are possible to him who
believes."
24 Immediately the boy's father cried
out and said, "I do believe; help my unbelief."
25 When Jesus saw that [a]a crowd was
[1]rapidly gathering, He rebuked the unclean spirit, saying to it, "You deaf and
mute spirit, I [2]command you, come out
of him and do not enter him [3]again."
26 After crying out and throwing him
into terrible convulsions, it came out; and
the boy became so much like a corpse
that most *of them* said, "He is dead!"
27 But Jesus took him by the hand and
raised him; and he got up.
28 When He came [a]into *the* house,
His disciples *began* questioning Him privately, "Why could we not drive it out?"
29 And He said to them, "This kind
cannot come out by anything but prayer."

Death and Resurrection Foretold

30 ¶ [a]From there they went out and
began to go through Galilee, and He did
not want anyone to know *about it.*
31 For He was teaching His disciples
and telling them, "[a]The Son of Man is to
be [1]delivered into the hands of men, and
they will kill Him; and when He has been
killed, He will rise three days later."
32 But [a]they [1]did not understand *this*

38 [a]Matt 10:33; Luke 9:26; Heb 11:16 [b]Matt 8:20 [c]Matt 16:27; Mark 13:26; Luke 9:26

9:1 [a]Matt 16:28; Mark 13:26; Luke 9:27

2 [1]Or *Jacob* [a]Mark 9:2-8: *Matt 17:1-8; Luke 9:28-36* [b]Mark 5:37

3 [a]Matt 28:3

5 [1]Or *sacred tents* [a]Matt 23:7 [b]Matt 17:4; Luke 9:33

7 [1]Or *occurred* [2]Or *give constant heed* [a]2 Pet 1:17f [b]Matt 3:17; Mark 1:11; Luke 3:22

9 [1]Lit *except when* [a]Mark 9:9-13: *Matt 17:9-13* [b]Matt 8:4; Mark 5:43; 7:36; 8:30

10 [1]Or *kept to themselves* [2]Lit *the statement* [3]Lit *what was the rising from the dead*

11 [a]Mal 4:5; Matt 11:14

12 [a]Mark 9:31 [b]Matt 16:21; 26:24

13 [1]Lit *also*

14 [a]Mark 9:14-28: *Matt 17:14-19; Luke 9:37-42*

15 [a]Mark 14:33; 16:5,6

18 [1]Or *wherever* [2]Or *tears him* [3]Or *withers away*

20 [1]Lit *him*

23 [a]Matt 17:20; John 11:40

25 [1]Or *running together* [2]Or *I Myself command* [3]Or *from now on* [a]Mark 9:15

28 [a]Mark 2:1; 7:17

30 [a]Mark 9:30-32: *Matt 17:22,23; Luke 9:43-45*

31 [1]Or *betrayed* [a]Matt 16:21; Mark 8:31; 9:12

32 [1]Lit *were not knowing* [a]Luke 2:50; 9:45; 18:34; John 12:16

statement, and they were afraid to ask
Him.
33 ¶ [a]They came to Capernaum; and
when He [1]was in [b]the house, He *began*
to question them, "What were you discussing on the way?"
34 But they kept silent, for on the way
[a]they had discussed with one another
which *of them was* the greatest.
35 Sitting down, He called the twelve
and *said to them, "[a]If anyone wants to
be first, [1]he shall be last of all and servant
of all."
36 Taking a child, He set him [1]before
them, and taking him in His arms, He
said to them,
37 "[a]Whoever receives [1]one child like
this in My name receives Me; and whoever receives Me does not receive Me,
but Him who sent Me."

Dire Warnings

38 ¶ [a]John said to Him, "Teacher, we
saw someone casting out demons in Your
name, and [b]we tried to prevent him because he was not following us."
39 But Jesus said, "Do not hinder him,
for there is no one who will perform a
miracle in My name, and be able soon
afterward to speak evil of Me.
40 "[a]For he who is not against us is
[1]for us.
41 "For [a]whoever gives you a cup of
water to drink [1]because of your name as
followers of Christ, truly I say to you, he
will not lose his reward.
42 ¶ "[a]Whoever causes one of these
[1]little ones who believe to stumble, it
[2]would be better for him if, with a heavy
millstone hung around his neck, he [3]had
been cast into the sea.
43 "[a]If your hand causes you to stumble, cut it off; it is better for you to enter
life crippled, than, having your two
hands, to go into [1b]hell, into the [c]un-
quenchable fire,
44 [[1]where THEIR WORM DOES NOT DIE,
AND THE FIRE IS NOT QUENCHED.]
45 "If your foot causes you to stumble,
cut it off; it is better for you to enter life
lame, than, having your two feet, to be
cast into [1a]hell,
46 [[1]where THEIR WORM DOES NOT DIE,
AND THE FIRE IS NOT QUENCHED.]
47 "[a]If your eye causes you to stumble,
throw it out; it is better for you to enter
the kingdom of God with one eye, than,
having two eyes, to be cast into [1b]hell,
48 [a]where THEIR WORM DOES NOT DIE,
AND [b]THE FIRE IS NOT QUENCHED.
49 ¶ "For everyone will be salted with
fire.
50 "Salt is good; but [a]if the salt becomes unsalty, with what will you [1]make
it salty *again*? [b]Have salt in yourselves,
and [c]be at peace with one another."

Jesus' Teaching about Divorce

10 [a]Getting up, He *went from
there to the region of Judea and
beyond the Jordan; crowds *gathered
around Him again, and, [b]according to
His custom, He once more *began* to teach
them.
2 ¶ *Some* Pharisees came up to Jesus,
testing Him, and *began* to question Him
whether it was lawful for a man to [1]di-
vorce a wife.
3 And He answered and said to them,
"What did Moses command you?"
4 They said, "[a]Moses permitted *a
man* TO WRITE A CERTIFICATE OF DIVORCE
AND [1]SEND *her* AWAY."
5 But Jesus said to them, "[1a]Because
of your hardness of heart he wrote you
this commandment.
6 "But [a]from the beginning of creation, *God* [b]MADE THEM MALE AND FEMALE.
7 "[a]FOR THIS REASON A MAN SHALL LEAVE
HIS FATHER AND MOTHER,[1]
8 [a]AND THE TWO SHALL BECOME ONE
FLESH; so they are no longer two, but one
flesh.
9 "What therefore God has joined together, let no man separate."
10 ¶ In the house the disciples *began*
questioning Him about this again.
11 And He *said to them, "[a]Whoever
[1]divorces his wife and marries another
woman commits adultery against her;
12 and [a]if she herself [1]divorces her
husband and marries another man, she is
committing adultery."

Jesus Blesses Little Children

13 ¶ [a]And they were bringing children to Him so that He might touch
them; but the disciples rebuked them.
14 But when Jesus saw this, He was
indignant and said to them, "Permit the
children to come to Me; do not hinder
them; [a]for the kingdom of God belongs
to such as these.
15 "Truly I say to you, [a]whoever does
not receive the kingdom of God like a
child will not enter it *at all*."
16 And He [a]took them in His arms
and *began* blessing them, laying His
hands on them.

The Rich Young Ruler

17 ¶ [a]As He was setting out on a journey, a man ran up to Him and [b]knelt
before Him, and asked Him, "Good

33 [1]Lit *had come* [a]Mark 9:33-37: *Matt 18:1-5; Luke 9:46-48* [b]Mark 3:19
34 [a]Matt 18:4; Mark 9:50; Luke 22:24
35 [1]Or *let him be* [a]Matt 20:26; Mark 10:43; Luke 22:26
36 [1]Lit *in their midst*
37 [1]Lit *one of such children* [a]Matt 10:40; Luke 10:16; John 13:20
38 [a]Mark 9:38-40: *Luke 9:49,50* [b]Num 11:27-29
40 [1]Or *on our side* [a]Matt 12:30; Luke 11:23
41 [1]Lit *in a name that you are Christ's* [a]Matt 10:42
42 [1]I.e. humble [2]Lit *is better for him if a millstone turned by a donkey is hung* [3]Lit *has been thrown* [a]Matt 18:6; Luke 17:2; 1 Cor 8:12
43 [1]Gr *Gehenna* [a]Matt 5:30 [b]Matt 5:22 [c]Matt 3:12
44 [1]Vv 44 and 46, which are identical to v 48, are not found in the early mss
45 [1]Gr *Gehenna* [a]Matt 5:22
46 [1]V 44, note 1
47 [1]Gr *Gehenna* [a]Matt 5:29 [b]Matt 5:22
48 [a]Is 66:24 [b]Matt 3:12
50 [1]Lit *season it* [a]Matt 5:13; Luke 14:34f [b]Col 4:6 [c]Mark 9:34; Rom 12:18; 2 Cor 13:11; 1 Thess 5:13
10:1 [a]Mark 10:1-12: *Matt 19:1-9* [b]Matt 4:23; Mark 1:21
2 [1]Or *send away*
4 [1]Or *divorce* her [a]Deut 24:1; Matt 5:31
5 [1]Or *With reference to* [a]Matt 19:8
6 [a]Mark 13:19; 2 Pet 3:4 [b]Gen 1:27
7 [1]Many late mss add *and shall cling to his wife* [a]Gen 2:24
8 [a]Gen 2:24
11 [1]Or *sends away* [a]Matt 5:32
12 [1]Or *sends away* [a]1 Cor 7:11
13 [a]Mark 10:13-16: *Matt 19:13-15; Luke 18:15-17*
14 [a]Matt 5:3
15 [a]Matt 18:3; Luke 18:17; 1 Cor 14:20; 1 Pet 2:2
16 [a]Mark 9:36

17 [a]Mark 10:17-31: *Matt 19:16-30; Luke 18:18-30* [b]Mark 1:40

Teacher, what shall I do to [c]inherit eternal life?"
18 And Jesus said to him, "Why do you
call Me good? No one is good except God
alone.
19 "You know the commandments,
'[a]DO NOT MURDER, DO NOT COMMIT ADUL-
TERY, DO NOT STEAL, DO NOT BEAR FALSE
WITNESS, Do not defraud, HONOR YOUR FA-
THER AND MOTHER.' "
20 And he said to Him, "Teacher, I
have kept [a]all these things from my
youth up."
21 Looking at him, Jesus felt a love for
him and said to him, "One thing you lack:
go and sell all you possess and give to the
poor, and you will have [a]treasure in
heaven; and come, follow Me."
22 But at these words [1]he was sad-
dened, and he went away grieving, for he
was one who owned much property.
23 ¶ And Jesus, looking around, *said
to His disciples, "[a]How hard it will be for
those who are wealthy to enter the kingdom of God!"
24 The disciples [a]were amazed at His
words. But Jesus *answered again and
*said to them, "Children, how hard it is
to enter the kingdom of God!
25 "[a]It is easier for a camel to go
through the eye of a needle than for a rich
man to enter the kingdom of God."
26 They were even more astonished
and said to Him, "[1]Then who can be
saved?"
27 Looking at them, Jesus *said,
"[a]With people it is impossible, but not
with God; for all things are possible with
God."
28 ¶ [a]Peter began to say to Him, "Behold, we have left everything and followed You."
29 Jesus said, "Truly I say to you,
[a]there is no one who has left house or
brothers or sisters or mother or father or
children or farms, for My sake and for the
gospel's sake,
30 [1]but that he will receive a hundred
times as much now in [2]the present age,
houses and brothers and sisters and
mothers and children and farms, along
with persecutions; and in [a]the age to
come, eternal life.
31 "But [a]many *who are* first will be
last, and the last, first."

Jesus' Sufferings Foretold

32 ¶ [a]They were on the road going up
to Jerusalem, and Jesus was walking on
ahead of them; and they [b]were amazed,
and those who followed were fearful.
And again He took the twelve aside and
began to tell them what was going to happen to Him,
33 *saying,* "Behold, we are going up to
Jerusalem, and [a]the Son of Man will be
[1]delivered to the chief priests and the
scribes; and they will condemn Him to
death and will [2]hand Him over to the
Gentiles.
34 "They will mock Him and [a]spit on
Him, and scourge Him and kill *Him,* and
three days later He will rise again."
35 ¶ [1a]James and John, the two sons
of Zebedee, *came up to Jesus, saying,
"Teacher, we want You to do for us whatever we ask of You."
36 And He said to them, "What do you
want Me to do for you?"
37 They said to Him, "[1]Grant that we
[a]may sit, one on Your right and one on
Your left, in Your glory."
38 But Jesus said to them, "You do not
know what you are asking. Are you able
[a]to drink the cup that I drink, or [b]to be
baptized with the baptism with which I
am baptized?"
39 They said to Him, "We are able."
And Jesus said to them, "The cup that I
drink [a]you shall drink; and you shall be
baptized with the baptism with which I
am baptized.
40 "But to sit on My right or on *My* left,
this is not Mine to give; [a]but it is for
those for whom it has been prepared."
41 ¶ [a]Hearing *this,* the ten began to
feel indignant with [1]James and John.
42 Calling them to Himself, Jesus
*said to them, "You know that those who
are recognized as rulers of the Gentiles
lord it over them; and their great men
exercise authority over them.
43 "But it is not this way among you,
[a]but whoever wishes to become great
among you shall be your servant;
44 and whoever wishes to be first
among you shall be slave of all.
45 "For even the Son of Man [a]did not
come to be served, but to serve, and to
give His [1]life a ransom for many."

Bartimaeus Receives His Sight

46 ¶ [a]Then they *came to Jericho.
And [b]as He was leaving Jericho with His
disciples and a large crowd, a blind beggar *named* Bartimaeus, the son of Timae-
us, was sitting by the road.
47 When he heard that it was Jesus the
[a]Nazarene, he began to cry out and say,
"Jesus, [b]Son of David, have mercy
on me!"
48 Many were sternly telling him to be
quiet, but he kept crying out all the more,
"[a]Son of David, have mercy on me!"
49 And Jesus stopped and said, "Call
him *here.*" So they *called the blind man,
saying to him, "[a]Take courage, stand up!
He is calling for you."

17 [c]Matt 25:34; Luke 10:25; 18:18; Acts 20:32; Eph 1:18; 1 Pet 1:4
19 [a]Ex 20:12-16; Deut 5:16-20
20 [a]Matt 19:20
21 [a]Matt 6:20
22 [1]Or *he became gloomy*
23 [a]Matt 19:23
24 [a]Mark 1:27
25 [a]Matt 19:24
26 [1]Lit *And*
27 [a]Matt 19:26
28 [a]Matt 4:20-22
29 [a]Matt 6:33; 19:29; Luke 18:29f
30 [1]Lit *if not* [2]Lit *this time* [a]Matt 12:32
31 [a]Matt 19:30; 20:16; Luke 13:30
32 [a]Mark 10:32-34: *Matt 20:17-19; Luke 18:31-33* [b]Mark 1:27
33 [1]Or *betrayed* [2]Or *betray* [a]Mark 8:31; 9:12
34 [a]Matt 16:21; 26:67; 27:30; Mark 9:31; 14:65
35 [1]Or *Jacob* [a]Mark 10:35-45: *Matt 20:20-28*
37 [1]Lit *Give to us* [a]Matt 19:28
38 [a]Matt 20:22 [b]Luke 12:50
39 [a]Acts 12:2; Rev 1:9
40 [a]Matt 13:11
41 [1]Or *Jacob* [a]Mark 10:42-45; Luke 22:25-27
43 [a]Matt 20:26; 23:11; Mark 9:35; Luke 22:26
45 [1]Or *soul* [a]Matt 20:28
46 [a]Mark 10:46-52: *Matt 20:29-34; Luke 18:35-43* [b]Luke 18:35; 19:1
47 [a]Mark 1:24 [b]Matt 9:27
48 [a]Matt 9:27
49 [a]Matt 9:2

50 Throwing aside his cloak, he jumped up and came to Jesus.

51 And answering him, Jesus said, "What do you want Me to do for you?" And the blind man said to Him, "[1][a]Rabboni, *I want* to regain my sight!"

52 And Jesus said to him, "Go; [a]your faith has [1]made you well." Immediately he regained his sight and *began* following Him on the road.

The Triumphal Entry

11 [a]As they *approached Jerusalem, at Bethphage and [b]Bethany, near [c]the Mount of Olives, He *sent two of His disciples,

2 and *said to them, "Go into the village opposite you, and immediately as you enter it, you will find a colt tied *there,* on which no one yet has ever sat; untie it and bring it *here.*

3 "If anyone says to you, 'Why are you doing this?' you say, 'The Lord has need of it'; and immediately he [1]will send it back here."

4 They went away and found a colt tied at the door, outside in the street; and they *untied it.

5 Some of the bystanders were saying to them, "What are you doing, untying the colt?"

6 They spoke to them just as Jesus had told *them,* and they gave them permission.

7 [a]They *brought the colt to Jesus and put their coats on it; and He sat on it.

8 And many spread their coats in the road, and others *spread* leafy branches which they had cut from the fields.

9 Those who went in front and those who followed were shouting:

"Hosanna!
[a]BLESSED IS HE WHO COMES IN THE NAME OF THE LORD;
10 Blessed *is* the coming kingdom of our father David;
Hosanna [a]in the highest!"

11 ¶ [a]Jesus entered Jerusalem *and came* into the temple; and after looking around at everything, [b]He left for Bethany with the twelve, since it was already late.

12 ¶ [a]On the next day, when they had left Bethany, He became hungry.

13 Seeing at a distance a fig tree in leaf, He went *to see* if perhaps He would find anything on it; and when He came to it, He found nothing but leaves, for it was not the season for figs.

14 He said to it, "May no one ever eat fruit from you again!" And His disciples were listening.

Jesus Drives Money Changers from the Temple

15 ¶ [a]Then they *came to Jerusalem. And He entered the temple and began to drive out those who were buying and selling in the temple, and overturned the tables of the money changers and the seats of those who were selling [1]doves;

16 and He would not permit anyone to carry [1]merchandise through the temple.

17 And He *began* to teach and say to them, "Is it not written, '[a]MY HOUSE SHALL BE CALLED A HOUSE OF PRAYER FOR ALL THE NATIONS'? [b]But you have made it a ROBBERS' [1]DEN."

18 The chief priests and the scribes heard *this,* and [a]*began* seeking how to destroy Him; for they were afraid of Him, for [b]the whole crowd was astonished at His teaching.

19 ¶ [a]When evening came, [1]they would go out of the city.

20 ¶ [a]As they were passing by in the morning, they saw the fig tree withered from the roots *up.*

21 Being reminded, Peter *said to Him, "[a]Rabbi, look, the fig tree which You cursed has withered."

22 And Jesus *answered saying to them, "[a]Have faith in God.

23 "[a]Truly I say to you, whoever says to this mountain, 'Be taken up and cast into the sea,' and does not doubt in his heart, but believes that what he says is going to happen, it will be *granted* him.

24 "Therefore I say to you, [a]all things for which you pray and ask, believe that you have received them, and they will be *granted* you.

25 "Whenever you [a]stand praying, [b]forgive, if you have anything against anyone, so that your Father who is in heaven will also forgive you your transgressions.

26 ["[1][a]But if you do not forgive, neither will your Father who is in heaven forgive your transgressions."]

Jesus' Authority Questioned

27 ¶ They *came again to Jerusalem. [a]And as He was walking in the temple, the chief priests and the scribes and the elders *came to Him,

28 and *began* saying to Him, "By what authority are You doing these things, or who gave You this authority to do these things?"

29 And Jesus said to them, "I will ask you one question, and you answer Me, and *then* I will tell you by what authority I do these things.

30 "Was the baptism of John from heaven, or from men? Answer Me."

51 [1]I.e. My Master [a]Matt 23:7; John 20:16
52 [1]Lit *saved you* [a]Matt 9:22
11:1 [a]Mark 11:1-10: *Matt 21:1-9; Luke 19:29-38* [b]Matt 21:17 [c]Matt 21:1
3 [1]Lit *sends*
7 [a]Mark 11:7-10: *Matt 21:4-9; Luke 19:35-38; John 12:12-15*
9 [a]Ps 118:26; Matt 21:9
10 [a]Matt 21:9
11 [a]Matt 21:12 [b]Matt 21:17
12 [a]Mark 11:12-14,20-24: *Matt 21:18-22*
15 [1]Lit *the doves* [a]Mark 11:15-18: *Matt 21:12-16; Luke 19:45-47;* John 2:13-16
16 [1]Lit *a vessel;* i.e. a receptacle or implement of any kind
17 [1]Lit *cave* [a]Is 56:7 [b]Jer 7:11
18 [a]Matt 21:46; Mark 12:12; Luke 20:19; John 7:1 [b]Matt 7:28
19 [1]I.e. Jesus and His disciples [a]Matt 21:17; Mark 11:11; Luke 21:37
20 [a]Mark 11:12-14,20-24: *Matt 21:19-22*
21 [a]Matt 23:7
22 [a]Matt 17:20; 21:21f
23 [a]Matt 17:20; 1 Cor 13:2
24 [a]Matt 7:7f
25 [a]Matt 6:5 [b]Matt 6:14
26 [1]Early mss do not contain this v [a]Matt 6:15; 18:35
27 [a]Mark 11:27-33: *Matt 21:23-27; Luke 20:1-8*

31 They *began* reasoning among themselves, saying, "If we say, 'From heaven,'
He will say, 'Then why did you not believe him?'
32 "But [1]shall we say, 'From men'?"—
they were afraid of the people, for everyone considered John to have been a real
prophet.
33 Answering Jesus, they *said, "We
do not know." And Jesus *said to them,
"Nor [1]will I tell you by what authority I
do these things."

Parable of the Vine-growers

12 [a]And He began to speak to them
in parables: "[b]A man [c]PLANTED A
VINEYARD AND PUT A [1]WALL AROUND IT, AND
DUG A VAT UNDER THE WINE PRESS AND BUILT
A TOWER, and rented it out to [2]vine-
growers and went on a journey.
2 "At the *harvest* time he sent a slave
to the vine-growers, in order to receive
some of the produce of the vineyard from
the vine-growers.
3 "They took him, and beat him and
sent him away empty-handed.
4 "Again he sent them another slave,
and they wounded him in the head, and
treated him shamefully.
5 "And he sent another, and that one
they killed; and *so with* many others,
beating some and killing others.
6 "He had one more *to send,* a beloved
son; he sent him last *of all* to them, saying, 'They will respect my son.'
7 "But those vine-growers said to one
another, 'This is the heir; come, let us kill
him, and the inheritance will be ours!'
8 "They took him, and killed him and
threw him out of the vineyard.
9 "What will the [1]owner of the vineyard do? He will come and destroy the
vine-growers, and will give the vineyard
to others.
10 "Have you not even read this Scripture:
'[a]THE STONE WHICH THE BUILDERS
REJECTED,
THIS BECAME THE CHIEF CORNER
stone;
11 [a]THIS CAME ABOUT FROM THE
LORD,
AND IT IS MARVELOUS IN OUR
EYES'?"
12 ¶ [a]And they were seeking to seize
Him, and *yet* they feared the [1]people, for
they understood that He spoke the parable against them. And *so* [b]they left Him
and went away.

Jesus Answers the Pharisees, Sadducees and Scribes

13 ¶ [a]Then they *sent some of the
Pharisees and [b]Herodians to Him in order to [c]trap Him in a statement.
14 They *came and *said to Him,
"Teacher, we know that You are truthful
and [1]defer to no one; for You are not
partial to any, but teach the way of God
in truth. Is it [2]lawful to pay a poll-tax to
Caesar, or not?
15 "Shall we pay or shall we not pay?"
But He, knowing their hypocrisy, said to
them, "Why are you testing Me? Bring
Me a [1]denarius to look at."
16 They brought *one.* And He *said to
them, "Whose likeness and inscription is
this?" And they said to Him, "Caesar's."
17 And Jesus said to them, "[a]Render
to Caesar the things that are Caesar's,
and to God the things that are God's."
And they [1]were amazed at Him.
18 ¶ [a]*Some* Sadducees (who say that
there is no resurrection) *came to Jesus,
and *began* questioning Him, saying,
19 "Teacher, Moses wrote for us that
[a]IF A MAN'S BROTHER DIES and leaves behind a wife AND LEAVES NO CHILD, HIS
BROTHER SHOULD [1]MARRY THE WIFE AND
RAISE UP CHILDREN TO HIS BROTHER.
20 "There were seven brothers; and the
first took a wife, and died leaving no children.
21 "The second one [1]married her, and
died leaving behind no children; and the
third likewise;
22 and *so* [1]all seven left no children.
Last of all the woman died also.
23 "In the resurrection, [1]when they
rise again, which one's wife will she be?
For [2]all seven had married her."
24 Jesus said to them, "Is this not the
reason you are mistaken, that you do not
[1]understand the Scriptures or the power
of God?
25 "For when they rise from the dead,
they neither marry nor are given in marriage, but are like angels in heaven.
26 "But [1]regarding the fact that the
dead rise again, have you not read in the
book of Moses, [a]in the *passage* about *the
burning* bush, how God spoke to him,
saying, '[b]I AM THE GOD OF ABRAHAM, AND
THE GOD OF ISAAC, and the God of Jacob'?
27 "[a]He is not the God [1]of the dead,
but of the living; you are greatly mistaken."
28 ¶ [a]One of the scribes came and
heard them arguing, and [b]recognizing
that He had answered them well, asked
Him, "What commandment is the [1]fore-
most of all?"
29 Jesus answered, "The foremost is,
'[a]HEAR, O ISRAEL! THE LORD OUR GOD IS
ONE LORD;
30 [a]AND YOU SHALL LOVE THE LORD YOUR
GOD WITH ALL YOUR HEART, AND WITH ALL

32 [1]Or *if we say*
33 [1]Lit *do I tell*
12:1 [1]Or *fence* [2]Or *tenant farmers,* also vv 2, 7, 9 [a]Mark 3:23; 4:2ff [b]Mark 12:1-12: *Matt 21:33-46; Luke 20:9-19* [c]Is 5:1,2
9 [1]Lit *lord*
10 [a]Ps 118:22
11 [a]Ps 118:23
12 [1]Lit *crowd* [a]Mark 11:18 [b]Matt 22:22
13 [a]Mark 12:13-17: *Matt 22:15-22; Luke 20:20-26* [b]Matt 22:16 [c]Luke 11:54
14 [1]Lit *it is not a concern to You about anyone*; i.e. You do not seek anyone's favor [2]Or *permissible*
15 [1]The denarius was a day's wages
17 [1]Or *were greatly marveling* [a]Matt 22:21
18 [a]Mark 12:18-27: *Matt 22:23-33; Luke 20:27-38*; Acts 23:8
19 [1]Lit *take* [a]Deut 25:5
21 [1]Lit *took*
22 [1]Lit *the seven*
23 [1]Early mss do not contain *when they rise again* [2]Lit *the seven*
24 [1]Or *know*
26 [1]Lit *concerning the dead, that they rise* [a]Luke 20:37; Rom 11:2 [b]Ex 3:6
27 [1]Or *of corpses* [a]Matt 22:32; Luke 20:38
28 [1]Or *first* [a]Mark 12:28-34: *Matt 22:34-40*; Luke 10:25-28; 20:39f [b]Matt 22:34; Luke 20:39
29 [a]Deut 6:4
30 [a]Deut 6:5

YOUR SOUL, AND WITH ALL YOUR MIND, AND WITH ALL YOUR STRENGTH.'

31 "The second is this, '[a]YOU SHALL LOVE YOUR NEIGHBOR AS YOURSELF.' There is no other commandment greater than these."

32 The scribe said to Him, "Right, Teacher; You have truly stated that [a]HE IS ONE, AND THERE IS NO ONE ELSE BESIDES HIM;

33 [a]AND TO LOVE HIM WITH ALL THE HEART AND WITH ALL THE UNDERSTANDING AND WITH ALL THE STRENGTH, AND TO LOVE ONE'S NEIGHBOR AS HIMSELF, [b]is much more than all burnt offerings and sacrifices."

34 When Jesus saw that he had answered intelligently, He said to him, "You are not far from the kingdom of God." [a]After that, no one would venture to ask Him any more questions.

35 ¶ [a]And Jesus *began* to say, as He [b]taught in the temple, "How *is it that* the scribes say that [1]the Christ is the [c]son of David?

36 "David himself said [1]in the Holy Spirit,

'[a]THE LORD SAID TO MY LORD,
"SIT AT MY RIGHT HAND,
UNTIL I PUT YOUR ENEMIES
BENEATH YOUR FEET." '

37 "David himself calls Him 'Lord'; so in what sense is He his son?" And [a]the large crowd [1]enjoyed listening to Him.

38 ¶ [a]In His teaching He was saying: "Beware of the scribes who like to walk around in long robes, and *like* [b]respectful greetings in the market places,

39 and chief seats in the synagogues and places of honor at banquets,

40 [a]who devour widows' houses, and for appearance's sake offer long prayers; these will receive greater condemnation."

The Widow's Mite

41 ¶ [a]And He sat down opposite [b]the treasury, and *began* observing how the people were [c]putting [1]money into the treasury; and many rich people were putting in large sums.

42 A poor widow came and put in two [1]small copper coins, which amount to a [2]cent.

43 Calling His disciples to Him, He said to them, "Truly I say to you, this poor widow put in more than all [1]the contributors to the treasury;

44 for they all put in out of their [1]surplus, but she, out of her poverty, put in all she owned, [2]all she had [a]to live on."

Things to Come

13 [a]As He was going out of the temple, one of His disciples *said to Him, "Teacher, behold [1]what wonderful stones and [1]what wonderful buildings!"

2 And Jesus said to him, "Do you see these great buildings? [a]Not one stone will be left upon another which will not be torn down."

3 ¶ As He was sitting on [a]the Mount of Olives opposite the temple, [b]Peter and [1]James and John and Andrew were questioning Him privately,

4 "Tell us, when will these things be, and what *will be* the [1]sign when all these things are going to be fulfilled?"

5 And Jesus began to say to them, "See to it that no one misleads you.

6 "Many will come in My name, saying, '[a]I am *He!*' and will mislead many.

7 "When you hear of wars and rumors of wars, do not be frightened; *those things* must take place; but *that is* not yet the end.

8 "For nation will rise up against nation, and kingdom against kingdom; there will be earthquakes in various places; there will *also* be famines. These things are *merely* the beginning of birth pangs.

9 ¶ "But [1]be on your guard; for they will [a]deliver you to *the* [2]courts, and you will be flogged [a]in *the* synagogues, and you will stand before governors and kings for My sake, as a testimony to them.

10 "[a]The gospel must first be preached to all the nations.

11 "[a]When they [1]arrest you and hand you over, do not worry beforehand about what you are to say, but say whatever is given you in that hour; for it is not you who speak, but *it is* the Holy Spirit.

12 "Brother will betray brother to death, and a father *his* child; and children will rise up against parents and [1]have them put to death.

13 "[a]You will be hated by all because of My name, but the one who endures to the end, he will be saved.

14 ¶ "But [a]when you see the [b]ABOMINATION OF DESOLATION standing where it should not be (let the reader understand), then those who are in Judea must flee to the mountains.

15 "[a]The one who is on the housetop must not go down, or go in to get anything out of his house;

16 and the one who is in the field must not turn back to get his coat.

17 "But woe to those who are pregnant and to those who are nursing babies in those days!

31 [a]Lev 19:18
32 [a]Deut 4:35
33 [a]Deut 6:5 [b]1 Sam 15:22; Hos 6:6; Mic 6:6-8; Matt 9:13; 12:7
34 [a]Matt 22:46
35 [1]I.e. the Messiah [a]Mark 12:35-37: *Matt 22:41-46; Luke 20:41-44* [b]Matt 26:55; Mark 10:1 [c]Matt 9:27
36 [1]Or *by* [a]Ps 110:1
37 [1]Lit *was gladly hearing Him* [a]John 12:9
38 [a]Mark 12:38-40: *Matt 23:1-7; Luke 20:45-47* [b]Matt 23:7; Luke 11:43
40 [a]Luke 20:47
41 [1]I.e. copper coins [a]Mark 12:41-44: *Luke 21:1-4* [b]John 8:20 [c]2 Kin 12:9
42 [1]Gr *lepta* [2]Gr *quadrans*; i.e. 1/64 of a denarius
43 [1]Lit *those who were putting in*
44 [1]Or *abundance* [2]Lit *her whole livelihood* [a]Luke 8:43; 15:12,30; 21:4
13:1 [1]Lit *how great* [a]Mark 13:1-37: *Matt 24; Luke 21:5-36*
2 [a]Luke 19:44
3 [1]Or *Jacob* [a]Matt 21:1 [b]Matt 17:1
4 [1]Or *attesting miracle*
6 [a]John 8:24
9 [1]Lit *look to yourselves* [2]Or *Sanhedrin* or *council* [a]Matt 10:17
10 [a]Matt 24:14
11 [1]Lit *lead* [a]Mark 13:11-13: *Matt 10:19-22; Luke 21:12-17*
12 [1]Lit *put them to death*
13 [a]Matt 10:22; John 15:21
14 [a]Matt 24:15f [b]Dan 9:27; 11:31; 12:11
15 [a]Luke 17:31

18 "But pray that it may not happen in the winter.

19 "For those days will be a *time of* tribulation such as has not occurred [a]since the beginning of the creation which God created until now, and never will.

20 "Unless the Lord had shortened *those* days, no [1]life would have been saved; but for the sake of the [2]elect, whom He chose, He shortened the days.

21 "And then if anyone says to you, 'Behold, here is [1]the Christ'; or, 'Behold, *He is* there'; do not believe *him;*

22 for false Christs and [a]false prophets will arise, and will show [1b]signs and [b]wonders, in order to lead astray, if possible, the elect.

23 "But take heed; behold, I have told you everything in advance.

The Return of Christ

24 ¶ "But in those days, after that tribulation, [a]THE SUN WILL BE DARKENED AND THE MOON WILL NOT GIVE ITS LIGHT,

25 [a]AND THE STARS WILL BE FALLING from heaven, and the powers that are in [1]the heavens will be shaken.

26 "Then they will see [a]THE SON OF MAN [b]COMING IN CLOUDS with great power and glory.

27 "And then He will send forth the angels, and [a]will gather together His [1]elect from the four winds, [b]from the farthest end of the earth to the farthest end of heaven.

28 ¶ "Now learn the parable from the fig tree: when its branch has already become tender and puts forth its leaves, you know that summer is near.

29 "Even so, you too, when you see these things happening, [1]recognize that [2]He is near, *right* at the [3]door.

30 "Truly I say to you, this [1]generation will not pass away until all these things take place.

31 "Heaven and earth will pass away, but My words will not pass away.

32 "[a]But of that day or hour no one knows, not even the angels in heaven, nor the Son, but the Father *alone.*

33 ¶ "Take heed, [a]keep on the alert; for you do not know when the *appointed* time [1]will come.

34 "[a]*It is* like a man away on a journey, *who* upon leaving his house and [1]putting his slaves in charge, *assigning* to each one his task, also commanded the doorkeeper to stay on the alert.

35 "Therefore, [a]be on the alert—for you do not know when the [1]master of the house is coming, whether in the evening, at midnight, or [b]when the rooster crows, or [c]in the morning—

36 in case he should come suddenly and find you [a]asleep.

37 "What I say to you I say to all, '[a]Be on the alert!' "

Death Plot and Anointing

14 [a]Now [b]the Passover and Unleavened Bread were two days away; and the chief priests and the scribes [c]were seeking how to seize Him by stealth and kill *Him;*

2 for they were saying, "Not during the festival, otherwise there might be a riot of the people."

3 ¶ [a]While He was in [b]Bethany at the home of Simon the leper, and reclining *at the table,* there came a woman with an alabaster vial of very [c]costly perfume of pure [1]nard; *and* she broke the vial and poured it over His head.

4 But some were indignantly *remarking* to one another, "Why has this perfume been wasted?

5 "For this perfume might have been sold for over three hundred [1]denarii, and *the money* given to the poor." And they were scolding her.

6 But Jesus said, "Let her alone; why do you bother her? She has done a good deed to Me.

7 "For you always have [a]the poor with you, and whenever you wish you can do good to them; but you do not always have Me.

8 "She has done what she could; [a]she has anointed My body beforehand for the burial.

9 "Truly I say to you, [a]wherever the gospel is preached in the whole world, what this woman has done will also be spoken of in memory of her."

10 ¶ [a]Then Judas Iscariot, [b]who was one of the twelve, went off to the chief priests in order to [1]betray Him to them.

11 They were glad when they heard *this,* and promised to give him money. And he *began* seeking how to betray Him at an opportune time.

The Last Passover

12 ¶ [a]On the first day of [b]Unleavened Bread, when [1]the Passover *lamb* was being [c]sacrificed, His disciples *said to Him, "Where do You want us to go and prepare for You to eat the Passover?"

13 And He *sent two of His disciples and *said to them, "Go into the city, and a man will meet you carrying a pitcher of water; follow him;

14 and wherever he enters, say to the owner of the house, 'The Teacher says, "Where is My [a]guest room in which I may eat the Passover with My disciples?" '

---

19 [a]Dan 12:1; Mark 10:6

20 [1]Lit *flesh* [2]Or *chosen ones*

21 [1]I.e. the Messiah

22 [1]Or *attesting miracles* [a]Matt 7:15 [b]Matt 24:24; John 4:48

24 [a]Is 13:10; Ezek 32:7; Joel 2:10,31; 3:15; Rev 6:12

25 [1]Or *heaven* [a]Is 34:4; Rev 6:13

26 [a]Dan 7:13; Rev 1:7 [b]Matt 16:27; Mark 8:38

27 [1]Or *chosen ones* [a]Deut 30:4 [b]Zech 2:6

29 [1]Or *know* [2]Or *it* [3]Lit *doors*

30 [1]Or *race*

32 [a]Matt 24:36; Acts 1:7

33 [1]Lit *is* [a]Eph 6:18; Col 4:2

34 [1]Lit *giving the authority to* [a]Luke 12:36-38

35 [1]Lit *lord* [a]Matt 24:42; Mark 13:37 [b]Mark 14:30 [c]Matt 14:25; Mark 6:48

36 [a]Rom 13:11

37 [a]Matt 24:42; Mark 13:35

14:1 [a]Mark 14:1,2: *Matt 26:2-5; Luke 22:1,2* [b]Ex 22:1-27; Mark 14:12; John 11:55; 13:1 [c]Matt 12:14

3 [1]An aromatic oil extracted from an East Indian plant [a]Mark 14:3-9: *Matt 26:6-13;* Luke 7:37-39; John 12:1-8 [b]Matt 21:17 [c]Matt 26:6f; John 12:3

5 [1]The denarius was equivalent to a day's wages

7 [a]Deut 15:11; Matt 26:11; John 12:8

8 [a]John 19:40

9 [a]Matt 26:13

10 [1]Or *hand Him over* [a]Mark 14:10,11: *Matt 26:14-16; Luke 22:3-6* [b]John 6:71

12 [1]Lit *they were sacrificing* [a]Mark 14:12-16: *Matt 26:17-19; Luke 22:7-13* [b]Matt 26:17 [c]Deut 16:5; Mark 14:1; Luke 22:7; 1 Cor 5:7

14 [a]Luke 22:11

15 "And he himself will show you a
large upper room furnished *and* ready;
prepare for us there."
16 The disciples went out and came to
the city, and found *it* just as He had told
them; and they prepared the Passover.
17 ¶ [a]When it was evening He *came
with the twelve.
18 As they were reclining *at the table*
and eating, Jesus said, "Truly I say to you
that one of you will [1]betray Me—[2]one
who is eating with Me."
19 They began to be grieved and to say
to Him one by one, "Surely not I?"
20 And He said to them, "*It is* one of
the twelve, [1]one who dips with Me in
the bowl.
21 "For the Son of Man *is to* go just as
it is written of Him; but woe to that man
[1]by whom the Son of Man is betrayed! *It*
would have been good [2]for that man if he
had not been born."

The Lord's Supper

22 ¶ [a]While they were eating, He
took *some* bread, and [1]after a [b]blessing
He broke *it*, and gave *it* to them, and said,
"Take *it*; this is My body."
23 And when He had taken a cup *and*
given thanks, He gave *it* to them, and
they all drank from it.
24 And He said to them, "This is My
[a]blood of the [b]covenant, which is
poured out for many.
25 "Truly I say to you, I will never again
drink of the fruit of the vine until that day
when I drink it new in the kingdom of
God."
26 ¶ [a]After singing a hymn, they went
out to [b]the Mount of Olives.
27 ¶ [a]And Jesus *said to them, "You
will all [1]fall away, because it is written,
'[b]I WILL STRIKE DOWN THE SHEPHERD, AND
THE SHEEP SHALL BE SCATTERED.'
28 "But after I have been raised, [a]I will
go ahead of you to Galilee."
29 But Peter said to Him, "*Even*
though all may [1]fall away, yet I will not."
30 And Jesus *said to him, "Truly I say
to you, that [1a]this very night, before [b]a
rooster crows twice, you yourself will
deny Me three times."
31 But *Peter* kept saying insistently,
"*Even* if I have to die with You, I will not
deny You!" And they all were saying the
same thing also.

Jesus in Gethsemane

32 ¶ [a]They *came to a place named
Gethsemane; and He *said to His disciples, "Sit here until I have prayed."
33 And He *took with Him Peter and
[1]James and John, and began to be very
[a]distressed and troubled.
34 And He *said to them, "[a]My soul is
deeply grieved to the point of death; remain here and keep watch."
35 And He went a little beyond *them,*
and fell to the ground and *began* to pray
that if it were possible, [a]the hour might
[1]pass Him by.
36 And He was saying, "[a]Abba! Father! All things are possible for You; remove this cup from Me; [b]yet not what I
will, but what You will."
37 And He *came and *found them
sleeping, and *said to Peter, "Simon, are
you asleep? Could you not keep watch for
one hour?
38 "[a]Keep watching and praying that
you may not come into temptation; the
spirit is willing, but the flesh is weak."
39 Again He went away and prayed,
saying the same [1]words.
40 And again He came and found them
sleeping, for their eyes were very heavy;
and they did not know what to answer
Him.
41 And He *came the third time, and
*said to them, "[1]Are you still sleeping
and resting? It is enough; [a]the hour has
come; behold, the Son of Man is being
[2]betrayed into the hands of sinners.
42 "Get up, let us be going; behold, the
one who betrays Me is at hand!"

Betrayal and Arrest

43 ¶ [a]Immediately while He was still
speaking, Judas, one of the twelve, *came
up [1]accompanied by a crowd with
swords and clubs, *who were* from the
chief priests and the scribes and the elders.
44 Now he who was betraying Him
had given them a signal, saying, "Whomever I kiss, He is the one; seize Him and
lead Him away [1]under guard."
45 After coming, Judas immediately
went to Him, saying, "[a]Rabbi!" and
kissed Him.
46 They laid hands on Him and seized
Him.
47 But one of those who stood by drew
his sword, and struck the slave of the
high priest and [1]cut off his ear.
48 And Jesus said to them, "Have you
come out with swords and clubs to arrest
Me, as *you would* against a robber?
49 "Every day I was with you [a]in the
temple teaching, and you did not seize
Me; but *this has taken place* to fulfill the
Scriptures."
50 And they all left Him and fled.
51 ¶ A young man was following Him,
wearing *nothing but* a linen sheet over
his naked *body*; and they *seized him.
52 But he [1]pulled free of the linen
sheet and escaped naked.

17 [a]Mark 14:17-21: *Matt 26:20-24; Luke 22:14,21-23;* John 13:18ff

18 [1]Or *deliver Me over* [2]Or *the one*

20 [1]Or *the one*

21 [1]Or *through* [2]Lit *for him if that man had not been born*

22 [1]Lit *having blessed* [a]Mark 14:22-25: *Matt 26:26-29; Luke 22:17-20; 1 Cor 11:23-25;* Mark 10:16 [b]Matt 14:19

24 [a]Ex 24:8 [b]Jer 31:31-34

26 [a]Matt 26:30 [b]Matt 21:1

27 [1]Or *stumble* [a]Mark 14:27-31: *Matt 26:31-35* [b]Zech 13:7

28 [a]Matt 28:16

29 [1]Or *stumble*

30 [1]Lit *today, on this night* [a]Matt 26:34 [b]Mark 14:68,72; John 13:38

32 [a]Mark 14:32-42: *Matt 26:36-46; Luke 22:40-46*

33 [1]Or *Jacob* [a]Mark 9:15; 16:5,6

34 [a]Matt 26:38; John 12:27

35 [1]Lit *pass from Him* [a]Matt 26:45; Mark 14:41

36 [a]Rom 8:15; Gal 4:6 [b]Matt 26:39

38 [a]Matt 26:41

39 [1]Lit *word*

41 [1]Or *Keep on sleeping therefore* [2]Or *delivered* [a]Mark 14:35

43 [1]Lit *and with him* [a]Mark 14:43-50: *Matt 26:47-56; Luke 22:47-53; John 18:3-11*

44 [1]Lit *safely*

45 [a]Matt 23:7

47 [1]Lit *took off*

49 [a]Mark 12:35; Luke 19:47; 21:37

52 [1]Lit *left behind*

Jesus before His Accusers

53 ¶ [a]They led Jesus away to the high
priest; and all the chief priests and the
elders and the scribes *gathered together.
54 Peter had followed Him at a distance, [a]right into [b]the courtyard of the
high priest; and he was sitting with the
[1]officers and [c]warming himself at
the [2]fire.
55 Now the chief priests and the
whole [1a]Council kept trying to obtain
testimony against Jesus to put Him to
death, and they were not finding any.
56 For many were giving false testimony against Him, but their testimony was
not consistent.
57 Some stood up and *began* to give
false testimony against Him, saying,
58 "We heard Him say, '[a]I will destroy
this [1]temple made with hands, and in
three days I will build another made without hands.' "
59 Not even in this respect was their
testimony consistent.
60 The high priest stood up *and came*
forward and questioned Jesus, saying,
"Do You not answer? [1]What is it that
these men are testifying against You?"
61 [a]But He kept silent and did not answer. [b]Again the high priest was questioning Him, and [1]saying to Him, "Are
You [2]the Christ, the Son of the
Blessed *One?*"
62 And Jesus said, "I am; and you shall
see [a]THE SON OF MAN SITTING AT THE RIGHT
HAND OF POWER, and [b]COMING WITH THE
CLOUDS OF HEAVEN."
63 [a]Tearing his clothes, the high
priest *said, "What further need do we
have of witnesses?
64 "You have heard the [a]blasphemy;
how does it seem to you?" And they all
condemned Him to be deserving of
death.
65 Some began to [a]spit at Him, and
[1b]to blindfold Him, and to beat Him
with their fists, and to say to Him,
"[c]Prophesy!" And the officers [2]received
Him with [3]slaps *in the face.*

Peter's Denials

66 ¶ [a]As Peter was below in [b]the
courtyard, one of the servant-girls of the
high priest *came,
67 and seeing Peter [a]warming himself, she looked at him and *said, "You
also were with Jesus the [b]Nazarene."
68 But he denied *it,* saying, "I neither
know nor understand what you are talking about." And he [a]went out onto the
[1]porch, and a rooster crowed.[2]
69 The servant-girl saw him, and began once more to say to the bystanders,
"This is *one* of them!"
70 But again [a]he denied it. And after
a little while the bystanders were again
saying to Peter, "Surely you are *one* of
them, [b]for you are a Galilean too."
71 But he began to [1]curse and swear,
"I do not know this man you are talking
about!"
72 Immediately a rooster crowed a
second time. And Peter remembered
how Jesus had made the remark to him,
"Before [a]a rooster crows twice, you will
deny Me three times." [1]And he began to
weep.

Jesus before Pilate

15 [a]Early in the morning the chief
priests with the elders and scribes
and the whole [1b]Council, immediately
held a consultation; and binding Jesus,
they led Him away and delivered Him to
Pilate.
2 [a]Pilate questioned Him, "Are You
the King of the Jews?" And He *answered
him, "*It is as* you say."
3 The chief priests *began* to accuse
Him [1]harshly.
4 Then Pilate questioned Him again,
saying, "Do You not answer? See how
many charges they bring against You!"
5 But Jesus [a]made no further answer; so Pilate was amazed.
6 ¶ [a]Now at *the* feast he used to release for them *any* one prisoner whom
they requested.
7 The man named Barabbas had been
imprisoned with the insurrectionists who
had committed murder in the insurrection.
8 The crowd went up and began asking him *to do* as he had been accustomed
to do for them.
9 Pilate answered them, saying, "Do
you want me to release for you the King
of the Jews?"
10 For he was aware that the chief
priests had handed Him over because of
envy.
11 But the chief priests stirred up the
crowd [a]*to ask* him to release Barabbas
for them instead.
12 Answering again, Pilate said to
them, "Then what shall I do with Him
whom you call the King of the Jews?"
13 They shouted [1]back, "Crucify
Him!"
14 But Pilate said to them, "Why, what
evil has He done?" But they shouted all
the more, "Crucify Him!"
15 Wishing to satisfy the crowd, Pilate
released Barabbas for them, and after
having Jesus [a]scourged, he handed Him
over to be crucified.

53 [a]Mark 14:53-65: *Matt 26:57-68; John 18:12f,19-24*

54 [1]Or *servants* [2]Lit *light* [a]Mark 14:68 [b]Matt 26:3 [c]Mark 14:67; John 18:18

55 [1]Or *Sanhedrin* [a]Matt 5:22

58 [1]Or *sanctuary* [a]Matt 26:61; Mark 15:29; John 2:19

60 [1]Or *what do these testify?*

61 [1]Lit *says* [2]I.e. the Messiah [a]Matt 26:63 [b]Mark 14:61-63: *Matt 26:63ff; Luke 22:67-71*

62 [a]Ps 110:1; Mark 13:26 [b]Dan 7:13

63 [a]Num 14:6; Matt 26:65; Acts 14:14

64 [a]Lev 24:16

65 [1]Or *cover over His face* [2]Or *treated* [3]Or *blows with rods* [a]Matt 26:67; Mark 10:34 [b]Esth 7:8 [c]Matt 26:68; Luke 22:64

66 [a]Mark 14:66-72: *Matt 26:69-75; Luke 22:56-62; John 18:16-18,25-27* [b]Mark 14:54

67 [a]Mark 14:54 [b]Mark 1:24

68 [1]Or *forecourt, gateway* [2]Later mss add *and a rooster crowed* [a]Mark 14:54

70 [a]Mark 14:68 [b]Matt 26:73; Luke 22:59

71 [1]Or *put himself under a curse*

72 [1]Or *Thinking of this, he began weeping* or *Rushing out, he began weeping* [a]Mark 14:30,68

15:1 [1]Or *Sanhedrin* [a]Matt 27:1 [b]Matt 5:22

2 [a]Mark 15:2-5: *Matt 27:11-14; Luke 23:2,3; John 18:29-38*

3 [1]Or *of many things*

5 [a]Matt 27:12

6 [a]Mark 15:6-15: *Matt 27:15-26; Luke 23:18-25; John 18:39-19:16*

11 [a]Acts 3:14

13 [1]Or *again*

15 [a]Matt 27:26

Jesus Is Mocked

16 ¶ [a]The soldiers took Him away into [b]the [1]palace (that is, the Praetorium), and they *called together the whole *Roman* [2c]cohort.

17 They *dressed Him up in purple, and after twisting a crown of thorns, they put it on Him;

18 and they began to acclaim Him, "Hail, King of the Jews!"

19 They kept beating His head with a [1]reed, and spitting on Him, and kneeling and bowing before Him.

20 After they had mocked Him, they took the purple robe off Him and put His *own* garments on Him. And they *led Him out to crucify Him.

21 ¶ [a]They *pressed into service a passer-by coming from the country, Simon of Cyrene (the father of Alexander and [b]Rufus), to bear His cross.

The Crucifixion

22 ¶ [a]Then they *brought Him to the place [b]Golgotha, which is translated, Place of a Skull.

23 They tried to give Him [a]wine mixed with myrrh; but He did not take it.

24 And they *crucified Him, and *[a]divided up His garments among themselves, casting [1]lots for them *to decide* [2]what each man should take.

25 It was the [1a]third hour [2]when they crucified Him.

26 The inscription of the charge against Him [1]read, "[a]THE KING OF THE JEWS."

27 ¶ They *crucified two robbers with Him, one on His right and one on His left.

28 [[1]And the Scripture was fulfilled which says, "And He was numbered with transgressors."]

29 Those passing by were [1]hurling abuse at Him, [a]wagging their heads, and saying, "Ha! You who *are going to* [b]destroy the temple and rebuild it in three days,

30 save Yourself, and come down from the cross!"

31 In the same way the chief priests also, along with the scribes, were mocking *Him* among themselves and saying, "[a]He saved others; [1]He cannot save Himself.

32 "Let *this* Christ, [a]the King of Israel, now come down from the cross, so that we may see and believe!" [b]Those who were crucified with Him were also insulting Him.

33 ¶ [a]When the [1b]sixth hour came, darkness [2]fell over the whole land until the [3b]ninth hour.

34 At the [a]ninth hour Jesus cried out with a loud voice, "[b]ELOI, ELOI, LAMA SABACHTHANI?" which is translated, "MY GOD, MY GOD, WHY HAVE YOU FORSAKEN ME?"

35 When some of the bystanders heard it, they *began* saying, "Behold, He is calling for Elijah."

36 Someone ran and filled a sponge with sour wine, put it on a reed, and gave Him a drink, saying, "[1]Let us see whether Elijah will come to take Him down."

37 [a]And Jesus uttered a loud cry, and breathed His last.

38 [a]And the veil of the temple was torn in two from top to bottom.

39 [a]When the centurion, who was standing [1]right in front of Him, saw [2]the way He breathed His last, he said, "Truly this man was [3]the Son of God!"

40 ¶ [a]There were also *some* women looking on from a distance, among whom *were* Mary Magdalene, and Mary the mother of [1]James [b]the [2]Less and Joses, and [c]Salome.

41 When He was in Galilee, they used to follow Him and [1a]minister to Him; and *there were* many other women who came up with Him to Jerusalem.

Jesus Is Buried

42 ¶ [a]When evening had already come, because it was [b]the preparation day, that is, the day before the Sabbath,

43 Joseph of Arimathea came, a [a]prominent member of the Council, who himself was [b]waiting for the kingdom of God; and he [c]gathered up courage and went in before Pilate, and asked for the body of Jesus.

44 Pilate wondered if He was dead by this time, and summoning the centurion, he questioned him as to whether He was already dead.

45 And ascertaining this from [a]the centurion, he granted the body to Joseph.

46 Joseph bought a linen cloth, took Him down, wrapped Him in the linen cloth and laid Him in a tomb which had been hewn out in the rock; and he rolled a stone against the entrance of the tomb.

47 [a]Mary Magdalene and Mary the *mother* of Joses were looking on *to see* where He was laid.

The Resurrection

16 [a]When the Sabbath was over, [b]Mary Magdalene, and Mary the *mother* of [1]James, and Salome, [c]bought spices, so that they might come and anoint Him.

---

16 [1]Or *court* [2]Or *battalion* [a]Mark 15:16-20: *Matt 27:27-31* [b]Matt 26:3 [c]Acts 10:1
19 [1]Or *staff* (made of a reed)
21 [a]Mark 15:21: *Matt 27:32; Luke 23:26* [b]Rom 16:13
22 [a]Mark 15:22-32: *Matt 27:33-44; Luke 23:33-43; John 19:17-24* [b]Luke 23:33; John 19:17
23 [a]Matt 27:34
24 [1]Lit *a lot upon* [2]Lit *who should take what* [a]Ps 22:18; John 19:24
25 [1]I.e. 9 a.m. [2]Lit *and* [a]Mark 15:33
26 [1]Lit *had been inscribed* [a]Matt 27:37
28 [1]Early mss do not contain this v
29 [1]Or *blaspheming* [a]Ps 22:7; Matt 27:39 [b]Mark 14:58; John 2:19
31 [1]Or *can He not save Himself?* [a]Matt 27:42; Luke 23:35
32 [a]Matt 27:42; Mark 15:26 [b]Matt 27:44; Mark 15:27; Luke 23:39-43
33 [1]I.e. noon [2]Or *occurred* [3]I.e. 3 p.m. [a]Mark 15:33-41: *Matt 27:45-56; Luke 23:44-49* [b]Matt 27:45f; Mark 15:25; Luke 23:44
34 [a]Matt 27:45f; Mark 15:25; Luke 23:44 [b]Ps 22:1; Matt 27:46
36 [1]Lit *Permit that we see*; or *Hold off, let us see*
37 [a]Matt 27:50; Luke 23:46; John 19:30
38 [a]Ex 26:31-33; Matt 27:51; Luke 23:45
39 [1]Or *opposite Him* [2]Lit *that He thus* [3]Or *a son of God* or *son of a god* [a]Matt 27:54; Mark 15:45; Luke 23:47
40 [1]Or *Jacob* [2]Lit *little* (either in stature or age) [a]Mark 15:40: *Matt 27:55f;* Luke 23:49; John 19:25 [b]Luke 19:3 [c]Mark 16:1
41 [1]Or *wait on* [a]Matt 27:55f
42 [a]Mark 15:42-47: *Matt 27:57-61; Luke 23:50-56; John 19:38-42* [b]Matt 27:62
43 [a]Matt 27:57; Luke 23:50; Acts 13:50 [b]Matt 27:57; Luke 2:25; John 19:38 [c]John 19:38
45 [a]Mark 15:39
47 [a]Matt 27:56; Mark 15:40
16:1 [1]Or *Jacob* [a]Mark 16:1-8: *Matt 28:1-8; Luke 24:1-10*; John 20:1-8 [b]Mark 15:47 [c]Luke 23:56; John 19:39f

2 Very early on the first day of the
week, they *came to the tomb when the
sun had risen.
3 They were saying to one another,
"Who will roll away [a]the stone for us
from the entrance of the tomb?"
4 Looking up, they *saw that the
stone had been rolled away, [1]although it
was extremely large.
5 [a]Entering the tomb, they saw a
young man sitting at the right, wearing a
white robe; and they [b]were amazed.
6 And he *said to them, "[a]Do not be
amazed; you are looking for Jesus the
[b]Nazarene, who has been crucified. [c]He
has risen; He is not here; behold, *here is*
the place where they laid Him.
7 "But go, tell His disciples and Peter,
'[a]He is going ahead of you to Galilee;
there you will see Him, just as He
told you.' "
8 They went out and fled from the
tomb, for trembling and astonishment
had gripped them; and they said nothing
to anyone, for they were afraid.
9 ¶ [[1]Now after He had risen early
on the first day of the week, He first appeared to [a]Mary Magdalene, from whom
He had cast out seven demons.
10 [a]She went and reported to those
who had been with Him, while they were
mourning and weeping.
11 When they heard that He was alive
and had been seen by her, [a]they refused
to believe it.
12 ¶ After that, [a]He appeared in a different form [b]to two of them while they
were walking along on their way to the
country.
13 They went away and reported it to
the others, but they [a]did not believe
them either.

The Disciples Commissioned

14 ¶ Afterward [a]He appeared [b]to the
eleven themselves as they were reclining
at the table; and He reproached them for
their [c]unbelief and hardness of heart, because they had not believed those who
had seen Him after He had risen.
15 And He said to them, "[a]Go into all
the world and preach the gospel to all
creation.
16 "[a]He who has believed and has
been baptized shall be saved; but he who
has disbelieved shall be condemned.
17 "These [1]signs will accompany those
who have believed: [a]in My name they
will cast out demons, they will [b]speak
with new tongues;
18 they will [a]pick up serpents, and if
they drink any deadly *poison*, it will not
hurt them; they will [b]lay hands on the
sick, and they will recover."
19 ¶ So then, when the Lord Jesus had
[a]spoken to them, He [b]was received up
into heaven and [c]sat down at the right
hand of God.
20 And they went out and preached
everywhere, while the Lord worked with
them, and confirmed the word by the
[1]signs that followed.]
¶ [[2]*And they promptly reported all
these instructions to Peter and his companions. And after that, Jesus Himself
sent out through them from east to west
the sacred and imperishable proclamation of eternal salvation.*]

3 [a]Matt 27:60; Mark 15:46
4 [1]Lit *for*
5 [a]John 20:11 [b]Mark 9:15
6 [a]Mark 9:15 [b]Mark 1:24 [c]Matt 28:6; Luke 24:6
7 [a]Matt 26:32; Mark 14:28
9 [1]Later mss add vv 9-20 [a]Matt 27:56; John 20:14
10 [a]John 20:18
11 [a]Matt 28:17; Mark 16:13; Luke 24:11; John 20:25
12 [a]Mark 16:14; John 21:1 [b]Luke 24:13-35
13 [a]Matt 28:17; Mark 16:11; Luke 24:11; John 20:25
14 [a]Mark 16:12; John 21:1 [b]Luke 24:36; John 20:19; 1 Cor 15:5 [c]Matt 28:17; Mark 16:11; Luke 24:11; John 20:25
15 [a]Matt 28:19; Acts 1:8
16 [a]John 3:18; Acts 16:31
17 [1]Or *attesting miracles* [a]Mark 9:38; Luke 10:17; Acts 5:16 [b]Acts 2:4; 1 Cor 12:10
18 [a]Luke 10:19; Acts 28:3-5 [b]Mark 5:23
19 [a]Acts 1:3 [b]Luke 9:51; John 6:62; Acts 1:2; 1 Tim 3:16 [c]Ps 110:1; Luke 22:69; Acts 7:55f; Rom 8:34; Eph 1:20; Col 3:1; Heb 1:3; 1 Pet 3:22
20 [1]Or *attesting miracles* [2]A few late mss and versions contain this paragraph, usually after v 8; a few have it at the end of ch

Luke

Title and Background

The Gospel of Luke has been called the most beautiful book ever written. Luke's writing shows him to be a highly educated man, one who wrote from a Greek background and viewpoint. He wrote especially with Gentiles in mind, for he explained Jewish customs and traced the genealogy of Jesus back to Adam.

Author and Date of Writing

The author's name does not appear in the book, but much unmistakable evidence points to Luke. This Gospel is a companion volume to the book of Acts, and the language and structure of these books indicate that both were written by the same person. Luke was probably a Gentile by birth, well educated in Greek culture, a physician by profession and a companion of Paul at various times. The book was probably written between A.D. 59 and 63.

Theme and Message

Luke tells us in the first four verses of his book that he wrote this Gospel to give the true and complete story of Jesus' life. He wrote the fullest and most orderly story of His life. One of Luke's interests in writing this book was to show that Jesus loved all kinds of people. In the parables especially, he wrote about the poor and oppressed. The theme of joy is felt throughout the book, as Jesus' coming brought joy as well as hope and salvation to a sinful world.

Outline

I. The Preface (1:1–4)
II. The Coming of Jesus (1:5—2:52)
III. Jesus' Preparation for His Ministry (3:1—4:13)
IV. Jesus' Ministry in Galilee (4:14—9:9)
V. Jesus' Withdrawals From Galilee (9:10–50)
VI. Jesus' Ministry in Judea (9:51—13:21)
VII. Jesus' Ministry in and Near Perea (13:22—19:27)
VIII. Jesus' Sacrifice and Triumph (19:28—24:53)

Introduction

1 Inasmuch as many have undertaken
to compile an account of the things
[1a]accomplished among us,
2 just as they were handed down to
us by those who [a]from the beginning
[1]were [b]eyewitnesses and [2c]servants of
[d]the [3]word,
3 it seemed fitting for me as well,
[a]having [1]investigated everything carefully from the beginning, to write *it* out
for you [b]in consecutive order, [c]most excellent [d]Theophilus;
4 so that you may know the exact
truth about the things you have been
[1a]taught.

Birth of John the Baptist Foretold

5 ¶ [a]In the days of Herod, king of
Judea, there was a priest named [1]Zacha-
rias, of the [b]division of [2]Abijah; and he
had a wife [3]from the daughters of Aaron,
and her name was Elizabeth.
6 They were both [a]righteous in the
sight of God, walking [b]blamelessly in all
the commandments and requirements of
the Lord.
7 But they had no child, because Elizabeth was barren, and they were both
advanced in [1]years.
8 ¶ Now it happened *that* while [a]he
was performing his priestly service before God in the *appointed* order of his
division,
9 according to the custom of the
priestly office, he was chosen by lot [a]to
enter the temple of the Lord and burn
incense.

1:1 [1]Or *on which there is full conviction* [a]Rom 4:21; Col 2:2; 1 Thess 1:5; 2 Tim 4:17; Heb 6:11
2 [1]Lit *became* [2]Or *ministers* [3]I.e. gospel [a]John 15:27; Acts 1:21f [b]2 Pet 1:16; 1 John 1:1 [c]Acts 26:16; 1 Cor 4:1; Heb 2:3 [d]Mark 4:14; Acts 8:4
3 [1]Or *followed* [a]1 Tim 4:6 [b]Acts 11:4 [c]Acts 23:26 [d]Acts 1:1
4 [1]Or *orally instructed in* [a]Acts 18:25; Rom 2:18; 1 Cor 14:19; Gal 6:6
5 [1]I.e. Zechariah [2]Gr *Abia* [3]I.e. of priestly descent [a]Matt 2:1 [b]1 Chr 24:10
6 [a]Gen 7:1; Acts 2:25 [b]Phil 2:15; 1 Thess 3:13 **7** [1]Lit *days* **8** [a]1 Chr 24:19; 2 Chr 8:14 **9** [a]Ex 30:7f

10 And the whole multitude of the
people were in prayer [a]outside at the
hour of the incense offering.
11 And [a]an angel of the Lord appeared to him, standing to the right of the
altar of incense.
12 Zacharias was troubled when he
saw *the angel,* and [a]fear [1]gripped him.
13 But the angel said to him, "[a]Do not
be afraid, Zacharias, for your petition has
been heard, and your wife Elizabeth will
bear you a son, and [b]you will [1]give him
the name John.
14 "You will have joy and gladness, and
many will rejoice at his birth.
15 "For he will be great in the sight of
the Lord; and he will [a]drink no wine or
liquor, and he will be filled with the Holy
Spirit [1]while yet in his mother's womb.
16 "And he will [a]turn many of the sons
of Israel back to the Lord their God.
17 "It is he who will [a]go *as a forerun-
ner* before Him in the spirit and power of
[b]Elijah, [c]TO TURN THE HEARTS OF THE FA-
THERS BACK TO THE CHILDREN, and the disobedient to the attitude of the righteous,
so as to [a]make ready a people prepared
for the Lord."
18 ¶ Zacharias said to the angel, "How
will I know this *for certain*? For [a]I am
an old man and my wife is advanced in
[1]years."
19 The angel answered and said to
him, "I am [a]Gabriel, who [1b]stands in
the presence of God, and I have been sent
to speak to you and to bring you this good
news.
20 "And behold, you shall be silent and
unable to speak until the day when these
things take place, because you did not
believe my words, which will be fulfilled
in their proper time."
21 ¶ The people were waiting for
Zacharias, and were wondering at his delay in the temple.
22 But when he came out, he was unable to speak to them; and they realized
that he had seen a vision in the temple;
and he [a]kept [1]making signs to them, and
remained mute.
23 When the days of his priestly service were ended, he went back home.
24 ¶ After these days Elizabeth his
wife became pregnant, and she [1]kept
herself in seclusion for five months, saying,
25 "This is the way the Lord has dealt
with me in the days when He looked *with
favor* upon *me,* to [a]take away my disgrace among men."

Jesus' Birth Foretold

26 ¶ Now in the sixth month the angel
[a]Gabriel was sent from God to a city in
Galilee called [b]Nazareth,
27 to [a]a virgin [1]engaged to a man
whose name was Joseph, [b]of the
[2]descendants of David; and the virgin's
name was [3]Mary.
28 And coming in, he said to her,
"Greetings, [1]favored one! The Lord [2]*is*
with you."
29 But she [a]was very perplexed at *this*
statement, and kept pondering what kind
of salutation this was.
30 The angel said to her, "[a]Do not be
afraid, Mary; for you have found favor
with God.
31 "And behold, you will conceive in
your womb and bear a son, and you
[a]shall name Him Jesus.
32 "He will be great and will be called
the Son of [a]the Most High; and the Lord
God will give Him [b]the throne of His
father David;
33 [a]and He will reign over the house
of Jacob forever, [b]and His kingdom will
have no end."
34 Mary said to the angel, "How [1]can
this be, since I [2]am a virgin?"
35 The angel answered and said to
her, "[a]The Holy Spirit will come upon
you, and the power of [b]the Most High
will overshadow you; and for that reason
[c]the [1]holy Child shall be called [d]the
Son of God.
36 "And behold, even your relative Elizabeth has also conceived a son in her old
age; and [1]she who was called barren is
now in her sixth month.
37 "For [1a]nothing will be impossible
with God."
38 And Mary said, "Behold, the
[1]bondslave of the Lord; may it be done to
me according to your word." And the angel departed from her.

Mary Visits Elizabeth

39 ¶ Now [1]at this time Mary arose
and went in a hurry to [a]the hill country,
to a city of Judah,
40 and entered the house of Zacharias
and greeted Elizabeth.
41 When Elizabeth heard Mary's
greeting, the baby leaped in her womb;
and Elizabeth was [a]filled with the Holy
Spirit.
42 And she cried out with a loud voice
and said, "Blessed *are* you among wom-
en, and blessed *is* the fruit of your womb!
43 "And [1]how has it *happened* to me,
that the mother of [a]my Lord would come
to me?
44 "For behold, when the sound of your
greeting reached my ears, the baby
leaped in my womb for joy.
45 "And [a]blessed *is* she who [1]believed

10 [a]Lev 16:17
11 [a]Luke 2:9; Acts 5:19
12 [1]Or *fell upon* [a]Luke 2:9
13 [1]Lit *call his name* [a]Matt 14:27; Luke 1:30 [b]Luke 1:60
15 [1]Lit *from* [a]Num 6:3; Judg 13:4; Matt 11:18; Luke 7:33
16 [a]Matt 3:2; Luke 3:3
17 [a]Luke 1:76 [b]Matt 11:14 [c]Mal 4:6
18 [1]Lit *days* [a]Gen 17:17
19 [1]Lit *stand beside* [a]Dan 8:16; Luke 1:26 [b]Matt 18:10
22 [1]Or *beckoning to* or *nodding to* [a]Luke 1:62
24 [1]Lit *was hidden*
25 [a]Gen 30:23; Is 4:1
26 [a]Luke 1:19 [b]Matt 2:23
27 [1]Or *betrothed*; i.e. the first stage of marriage in Jewish culture, usually lasting for a year before the wedding night. More legal than engagement [2]Lit *house* [3]Gr *Mariam*; i.e. Heb Miriam; so throughout Luke [a]Matt 1:18 [b]Matt 1:16; Luke 2:4
28 [1]Or *Woman richly blessed* [2]Or *be*
29 [a]Luke 1:12
30 [a]Matt 14:27; Luke 1:13
31 [a]Is 7:14; Matt 1:21; Luke 2:21
32 [a]Mark 5:7; Luke 1:35; Acts 7:48 [b]2 Sam 7:12; Is 9:7
33 [a]Matt 1:1 [b]2 Sam 7:13; Ps 89:36; Dan 2:44; Matt 28:18
34 [1]Lit *will* [2]Lit *know no man*
35 [1]Lit *the holy thing begotten* [a]Matt 1:18 [b]Luke 1:32 [c]Mark 1:24 [d]Matt 4:3; John 1:34
36 [1]Lit *this is the sixth month to her who*
37 [1]Lit *not any word* [a]Gen 18:14; Jer 32:17; Matt 19:26
38 [1]I.e. female slave
39 [1]Lit *in these days* [a]Josh 20:7; Luke 1:65
41 [a]Luke 1:67; Acts 2:4
43 [1]Lit *from where this to me* [a]Luke 2:11
45 [1]Or *believed, because there will be* [a]Luke 1:20

that there would be a fulfillment of what
had been spoken to her [2]by the Lord."

The Magnificat

46 ¶ And Mary said:
"[a]My soul [1b]exalts the Lord,
47 And [a]my spirit has rejoiced in
[b]God my Savior.
48 "For [a]He has had regard for the
humble state of His
[1]bondslave;
For behold, from this time on all
generations will count me
[b]blessed.
49 "For the Mighty One has done
great things for me;
And holy is His name.
50 "[a]AND HIS MERCY IS [1]UPON
GENERATION AFTER
GENERATION
TOWARD THOSE WHO FEAR HIM.
51 "[a]He has done [1]mighty deeds
with His arm;
He has scattered *those who were*
proud in the [2]thoughts of
their heart.
52 "He has brought down rulers from
their thrones,
And has [a]exalted those who
were humble.
53 "[a]HE HAS FILLED THE HUNGRY WITH
GOOD THINGS;
And sent away the rich
empty-handed.
54 "He has given help to Israel His
servant,
[1]In remembrance of His mercy,
55 [a]As He spoke to our fathers,
[b]To Abraham and his
[1]descendants forever."
56 ¶ And Mary stayed with her about
three months, and *then* returned to her
home.

John Is Born

57 ¶ Now the time [1]had come for
Elizabeth to give birth, and she gave birth
to a son.
58 Her neighbors and her relatives
heard that the Lord had [1a]displayed His
great mercy toward her; and they were
rejoicing with her.
59 ¶ And it happened that on [a]the
eighth day they came to circumcise the
child, and they were going to call him
Zacharias, [1]after his father.
60 But his mother answered and said,
"No indeed; but [a]he shall be called
John."
61 And they said to her, "There is no
one among your relatives who is called by
that name."
62 And they [a]made signs to his father,
as to what he wanted him called.

45 [2]Lit *from*
46 [1]Lit *makes great* [a]Luke 1:46-53: *1 Sam 2:1-10* [b]Ps 34:2f
47 [a]Ps 35:9; Hab 3:18 [b]1 Tim 1:1; 2:3; Titus 1:3; 2:10; 3:4; Jude 25
48 [1]I.e. female slave [a]Ps 138:6 [b]Luke 1:45
50 [1]Lit *unto generations and generations* [a]Ps 103:17
51 [1]Lit *might* [2]Lit *thought, attitude* [a]Ps 98:1; 118:15
52 [a]Job 5:11
53 [a]Ps 107:9
54 [1]Lit *So as to remember*
55 [1]Lit *seed* [a]Gen 17:19; Ps 132:11; Gal 3:16 [b]Gen 17:7
57 [1]Lit *was fulfilled*
58 [1]Lit *magnified* [a]Gen 19:19
59 [1]Lit *after the name of* [a]Gen 17:12; Lev 12:3; Luke 2:21; Phil 3:5
60 [a]Luke 1:13, 63
62 [a]Luke 1:22
63 [a]Luke 1:13, 60
64 [a]Luke 1:20
65 [a]Luke 1:39
66 [a]Acts 11:21
67 [a]Luke 1:41; Acts 2:4,8; 9:17 [b]Joel 2:28
68 [a]1 Kin 1:48; Ps 41:13; 72:18; 106:48 [b]Luke 1:71; 2:38; Heb 9:12
69 [a]1 Sam 2:1, 10; Ps 18:2; 89:17; 132:17; Ezek 29:21 [b]Matt 1:1
70 [a]Rom 1:2 [b]Acts 3:21
71 [1]Or *Deliverance* [a]Luke 1:68 [b]Ps 106:10
72 [a]Mic 7:20 [b]Ps 105:8f,42; 106:45
73 [a]Gen 22:16ff; Heb 6:13
75 [a]Eph 4:24
76 [a]Matt 11:9 [b]Luke 1:32 [c]Mal 3:1; Matt 11:10; Mark 1:2; Luke 7:27 [d]Luke 1:17
77 [1]Or *Consisting in* [a]Jer 31:34; Mark 1:4
78 [a]Mal 4:2; Eph 5:14; 2 Pet 1:19
79 [a]Is 9:2 [b]Is 59:8; Matt 4:16

63 And he asked for a tablet and wrote
as follows, "[a]His name is John." And
they were all astonished.
64 [a]And at once his mouth was
opened and his tongue *loosed,* and he
began to speak in praise of God.
65 Fear came on all those living
around them; and all these matters were
being talked about in all [a]the hill country
of Judea.
66 All who heard them kept them in
mind, saying, "What then will this child
turn out to be?" For [a]the hand of the
Lord was certainly with him.

Zacharias's Prophecy

67 ¶ And his father Zacharias [a]was
filled with the Holy Spirit, and [b]prophe-
sied, saying:
68 "[a]Blessed *be* the Lord God of
Israel,
For He has visited us and
accomplished [b]redemption
for His people,
69 And has raised up a [a]horn of
salvation for us
In the house of David [b]His
servant—
70 [a]As He spoke by the mouth of
His holy prophets [b]from
of old—
71 [1a]Salvation [b]FROM OUR ENEMIES,
And FROM THE HAND OF ALL WHO
HATE US;
72 [a]To show mercy toward our
fathers,
[b]And to remember His holy
covenant,
73 [a]The oath which He swore to
Abraham our father,
74 To grant us that we, being
rescued from the hand of
our enemies,
Might serve Him without fear,
75 [a]In holiness and righteousness
before Him all our days.
76 "And you, child, will be called the
[a]prophet of [b]the Most
High;
For you will go on [c]BEFORE THE
LORD TO [d]PREPARE HIS WAYS;
77 To give to His people *the*
knowledge of salvation
[1]By [a]the forgiveness of their
sins,
78 Because of the tender mercy of
our God,
With which [a]the Sunrise from
on high will visit us,
79 [a]TO SHINE UPON THOSE WHO SIT IN
DARKNESS AND THE SHADOW OF
DEATH,
To guide our feet into the [b]way
of peace."

80 ¶ [a]And the child continued to grow and to become strong in spirit, and he lived in the deserts until the day of his public appearance to Israel.

Jesus' Birth in Bethlehem

2 Now in those days a decree went out from [a]Caesar Augustus, that a census be taken of [b]all [1]the inhabited earth.

2 [1]This was the first census taken while [2]Quirinius was governor of [a]Syria.

3 And everyone was on his way to register for the census, each to his own city.

4 Joseph also went up from Galilee, from the city of Nazareth, to Judea, to the city of David which is called Bethlehem, because [a]he was of the house and family of David,

5 in order to register along with Mary, who was engaged to him, and was with child.

6 While they were there, the days were completed for her to give birth.

7 And she [a]gave birth to her firstborn son; and she wrapped Him in cloths, and laid Him in a [1]manger, because there was no room for them in the inn.

8 ¶ In the same region there were *some* shepherds staying out in the fields and keeping watch over their flock by night.

9 And [a]an angel of the Lord suddenly [b]stood before them, and the glory of the Lord shone around them; and they were terribly frightened.

10 But the angel said to them, "[a]Do not be afraid; for behold, I bring you good news of great joy which will be for all the people;

11 for today in the city of David there has been born for you a [a]Savior, who is [1b]Christ [c]the Lord.

12 "[a]This *will be* a sign for you: you will find a baby wrapped in cloths and lying in a [1]manger."

13 And suddenly there appeared with the angel a multitude of the heavenly host praising God and saying,

14 "[a]Glory to God in the highest,
And on earth peace among men
[1b]with whom He is
pleased."

15 ¶ When the angels had gone away from them into heaven, the shepherds *began* saying to one another, "Let us go straight to Bethlehem then, and see this thing that has happened which the Lord has made known to us."

16 So they came in a hurry and found their way to Mary and Joseph, and the baby as He lay in the [1]manger.

17 When they had seen this, they made known the statement which had been told them about this Child.

18 And all who heard it wondered at the things which were told them by the shepherds.

19 But Mary [a]treasured all these things, pondering them in her heart.

20 The shepherds went back, [a]glorifying and praising God for all that they had heard and seen, just as had been told them.

Jesus Presented at the Temple

21 ¶ And when [a]eight days had passed, [1]before His circumcision, [b]His name was *then* called Jesus, the name given by the angel before He was conceived in the womb.

22 ¶ [a]And when the days for their purification according to the law of Moses were completed, they brought Him up to Jerusalem to present Him to the Lord

23 (as it is written in the Law of the Lord, "[a]EVERY *firstborn* MALE THAT OPENS THE WOMB SHALL BE CALLED HOLY TO THE LORD"),

24 and to offer a sacrifice according to what was said in the Law of the Lord, "[a]A PAIR OF TURTLEDOVES OR TWO YOUNG PIGEONS."

25 ¶ And there was a man in Jerusalem whose name was Simeon; and this man was [a]righteous and devout, [b]looking for the consolation of Israel; and the Holy Spirit was upon him.

26 And [a]it had been revealed to him by the Holy Spirit that he would not [b]see death before he had seen the Lord's [1]Christ.

27 And he came in the Spirit into the temple; and when the parents brought in the child Jesus, [1a]to carry out for Him the custom of the Law,

28 then he took Him into his arms, and blessed God, and said,

29 "Now Lord, You are releasing
Your bond-servant to depart
in peace,
[a]According to Your word;

30 For my eyes have [a]seen Your
salvation,

31 Which You have prepared in the
presence of all peoples,

32 [a]A LIGHT [1]OF REVELATION TO THE
GENTILES,
And the glory of Your people
Israel."

33 ¶ And His father and [a]mother were amazed at the things which were being said about Him.

34 And Simeon blessed them and said to Mary [a]His mother, "Behold, this *Child* is appointed for [b]the fall and [1]rise of

80 [a]Luke 2:40
2:1 [1]I.e. the Roman empire [a]Matt 22:17; Luke 3:1 [b]Matt 24:14
2 [1]Or *This took place as a first census* [2]Gr *Kyrenios* [a]Matt 4:24
4 [a]Luke 1:27
7 [1]Or *feeding trough* [a]Matt 1:25
9 [a]Luke 1:11; Acts 5:19 [b]Luke 24:4; Acts 12:7
10 [a]Matt 14:27
11 [1]I.e. Messiah [a]Matt 1:21; John 4:42; Acts 5:31 [b]Matt 1:16; 16:16,20; John 11:27 [c]Luke 1:43; Acts 2:36; 10:36
12 [1]Or *feeding trough* [a]1 Sam 2:34; 2 Kin 19:29; 20:8f; Is 7:11,14
14 [1]Lit *of good pleasure*; or *of good will* [a]Matt 21:9; Luke 19:38 [b]Luke 3:22; Eph 1:9; Phil 2:13
16 [1]Or *feeding trough*
19 [a]Luke 2:51
20 [a]Matt 9:8
21 [1]Lit *so as to circumcise Him* [a]Gen 17:12; Lev 12:3; Luke 1:59 [b]Matt 1:21,25; Luke 1:31
22 [a]Lev 12:6-8
23 [a]Ex 13:2,12; Num 3:13; 8:17
24 [a]Lev 5:11; 12:8
25 [a]Luke 1:6 [b]Mark 15:43; Luke 2:38; 23:51
26 [1]I.e. Messiah [a]Matt 2:12 [b]Ps 89:48; John 8:51; Heb 11:5
27 [1]Lit *to do for Him according to* [a]Luke 2:22
29 [a]Luke 2:26
30 [a]Ps 119:166, 174; Is 52:10; Luke 3:6
32 [1]Or *for* [a]Is 9:2; 42:6; 49:6, 9; 51:4; 60:1-3; Matt 4:16; Acts 13:47; 26:23
33 [a]Matt 12:46
34 [1]Or *resurrection* [a]Matt 12:46 [b]Matt 21:44; 1 Cor 1:23; 2 Cor 2:16; 1 Pet 2:8

many in Israel, and for a sign to be opposed—

35 and a sword will pierce even your own soul—to the end that thoughts from many hearts may be revealed."

36 ¶ And there was a [a]prophetess, [1]Anna the daughter of Phanuel, of [b]the tribe of Asher. She was advanced in [2]years [c]and had lived with *her* husband seven years after her [3]marriage,

37 and then as a widow to the age of eighty-four. She never left the temple, serving night and day with [a]fastings and prayers.

38 At that very [1]moment she came up and *began* giving thanks to God, and continued to speak of Him to all those who were [a]looking for the redemption of Jerusalem.

Return to Nazareth

39 ¶ When they had performed everything according to the Law of the Lord, they returned to Galilee, to [a]their own city of Nazareth.

40 [a]The Child continued to grow and become strong, [1]increasing in wisdom; and the grace of God was upon Him.

Visit to Jerusalem

41 ¶ Now His parents went to Jerusalem every year at [a]the Feast of the Passover.

42 And when He became twelve, they went up *there* according to the custom of the Feast;

43 and as they were returning, after spending the [a]full number of days, the boy Jesus stayed behind in Jerusalem. But His parents were unaware of it,

44 but supposed Him to be in the caravan, and went a day's journey; and they *began* looking for Him among their relatives and acquaintances.

45 When they did not find Him, they returned to Jerusalem looking for Him.

46 Then, after three days they found Him in the temple, sitting in the midst of the teachers, both listening to them and asking them questions.

47 And all who heard Him [a]were amazed at His understanding and His answers.

48 When they saw Him, they were astonished; and [a]His mother said to Him, "[1]Son, why have You treated us this way? Behold, [b]Your father and I [2]have been anxiously looking for You."

49 And He said to them, "Why is it that you were looking for Me? Did you not know that [a]I had to be in My Father's [1]*house?"*

50 But [a]they did not understand the statement which He [1]had made to them.

51 And He went down with them and came to [a]Nazareth, and He continued in subjection to them; and [b]His mother [c]treasured all *these* [1]things in her heart.

52 ¶ And Jesus kept increasing in wisdom and [1]stature, and in [a]favor with God and men.

John the Baptist Preaches

3 Now in the fifteenth year of the reign of Tiberius Caesar, when [a]Pontius Pilate was governor of Judea, and [b]Herod was tetrarch of Galilee, and his brother Philip was tetrarch of the region of Iturea and Trachonitis, and Lysanias was tetrarch of Abilene,

2 in the high priesthood of [a]Annas and [b]Caiaphas, [c]the word of God came to John, the son of Zacharias, in the wilderness.

3 And he came into all [a]the district around the Jordan, preaching a baptism of repentance for the forgiveness of sins;

4 as it is written in the book of the words of Isaiah the prophet,

"[a]THE VOICE OF ONE CRYING IN THE
WILDERNESS,
'MAKE READY THE WAY OF THE
LORD,
MAKE HIS PATHS STRAIGHT.
5 '[a]EVERY RAVINE WILL BE FILLED,
AND EVERY MOUNTAIN AND HILL
WILL BE [1]BROUGHT LOW;
THE CROOKED WILL BECOME
STRAIGHT,
AND THE ROUGH ROADS SMOOTH;
6 [a]AND ALL [1]FLESH WILL [b]SEE THE
SALVATION OF GOD.' "

7 ¶ So he *began* saying to the crowds who were going out to be baptized by him, "[a]You brood of vipers, who warned you to flee from the wrath to come?

8 "Therefore bear fruits in keeping with repentance, and [a]do not begin to say [1]to yourselves, '[b]We have Abraham for our father,' for I say to you that from these stones God is able to raise up children to Abraham.

9 "Indeed the axe is already laid at the root of the trees; so [a]every tree that does not bear good fruit is cut down and thrown into the fire."

10 ¶ And the crowds were questioning him, saying, "[a]Then what shall we do?"

11 And he would answer and say to them, "The man who has two tunics is to [a]share with him who has none; and he who has food is to do likewise."

12 And *some* [a]tax collectors also came to be baptized, and they said to him, "Teacher, what shall we do?"

13 And he said to them, "[1]Collect no

---

36 [1]Or *Hannah* [2]Lit *days* [3]Lit *virginity* [a]Luke 2:38; Acts 21:9 [b]Josh 19:24 [c]1 Tim 5:9

37 [a]Luke 5:33; Acts 13:3; 14:23; 1 Tim 5:5

38 [1]Lit *hour* [a]Luke 1:68; 2:25

39 [a]Matt 2:23; Luke 1:26; 2:51; 4:16

40 [1]Lit *becoming full of* [a]Luke 1:80; 2:52

41 [a]Ex 12:11; 23:15; Deut 16:1-6

43 [a]Ex 12:15

47 [a]Matt 7:28; 13:54; 22:33; Mark 1:22; 6:2; 11:18; Luke 4:32; John 7:15

48 [1]Or *Child* [2]Lit *are looking* [a]Matt 12:46 [b]Luke 2:49; 3:23; 4:22

49 [1]Or *affairs*; lit *in the things of My Father* [a]John 4:34; 5:36

50 [1]Lit *had spoken* [a]Mark 9:32; Luke 9:45; 18:34

51 [1]Lit *words* [a]Luke 2:39 [b]Matt 12:46 [c]Luke 2:19

52 [1]Or *age* [a]Luke 2:40

3:1 [a]Matt 27:2 [b]Matt 14:1

2 [a]John 18:13, 24; Acts 4:6 [b]Matt 26:3 [c]Luke 3:3-10: *Matt 3:1-10; Mark 1:3-5*

3 [a]Matt 3:5

4 [a]Is 40:3

5 [1]Or *leveled* [a]Is 40:4

6 [1]Or *mankind* [a]Is 40:5 [b]Luke 2:30

7 [a]Matt 12:34; 23:33

8 [1]Or *in* [a]Luke 5:21; 13:25,26; 14:9 [b]John 8:33

9 [a]Matt 7:19; Luke 13:6-9

10 [a]Luke 3:12, 14; Acts 2:37,38

11 [a]Is 58:7; 1 Tim 6:17,18; James 2:14-20

12 [a]Luke 7:29

13 [1]Or *Exact*

more than what you have been ordered to."
14 *Some* soldiers were questioning
him, saying, "And *what about* us, what
shall we do?" And he said to them, "Do
not take money from anyone by force, or
[a]accuse *anyone* falsely, and [b]be content
with your wages."
15 ¶ Now while the people were in a
state of expectation and all were [1]won-
dering in their hearts about John, [a]as to
whether he was [2]the Christ,
16 [a]John answered and said to them
all, "As for me, I baptize you with water;
but One is coming who is mightier than
I, and I am not fit to untie the thong of
His sandals; He will baptize you [1]with the
Holy Spirit and fire.
17 "His [a]winnowing fork is in His hand
to thoroughly clear His threshing floor,
and to gather the wheat into His barn; but
He will burn up the chaff with [b]un-
quenchable fire."
18 ¶ So with many other exhortations
he preached the gospel to the people.
19 But when [a]Herod the tetrarch was
reprimanded by him because of [a]Herodi-
as, his brother's wife, and because of all
the wicked things which [b]Herod had
done,
20 Herod also added this to them all:
[a]he locked John up in prison.

Jesus Is Baptized

21 ¶ [a]Now when all the people were
baptized, Jesus was also baptized, and
while He was [b]praying, heaven was
opened,
22 and the Holy Spirit descended upon
Him in bodily form like a dove, and a
voice came out of heaven, "[a]You are My
beloved Son, in You I am well-pleased."

Genealogy of Jesus

23 ¶ [a]When He began His ministry,
Jesus Himself was about thirty years of
age, being, [1]as was supposed, the son of
[b]Joseph, [2]the son of [3]Eli,
24 the son of Matthat, the son of Levi,
the son of Melchi, the son of Jannai, the
son of Joseph,
25 the son of Mattathias, the son of
Amos, the son of Nahum, the son of
[1]Hesli, the son of Naggai,
26 the son of Maath, the son of Mattathias, the son of Semein, the son of
Josech, the son of Joda,
27 the son of Joanan, the son of Rhesa,
[a]the son of Zerubbabel, the son of [1]She-
altiel, the son of Neri,
28 the son of Melchi, the son of Addi,
the son of Cosam, the son of Elmadam,
the son of Er,
29 the son of [1]Joshua, the son of Eliezer, the son of Jorim, the son of Matthat,
the son of Levi,
30 the son of Simeon, the son of [1]Ju-
dah, the son of Joseph, the son of Jonam,
the son of Eliakim,
31 the son of Melea, the son of Menna,
the son of Mattatha, the son of Nathan,
the son of David,
32 [a]the son of Jesse, the son of Obed,
the son of Boaz, the son of [1]Salmon, the
son of [2]Nahshon,
33 the son of Amminadab, the son of
Admin, the son of [1]Ram, the son of Hezron, the son of Perez, the son of Judah,
34 the son of Jacob, the son of Isaac,
[a]the son of Abraham, the son of Terah,
the son of Nahor,
35 the son of Serug, the son of [1]Reu,
the son of Peleg, the son of [2]Heber, the
son of Shelah,
36 the son of Cainan, the son of Ar-
phaxad, the son of Shem, [a]the son of
Noah, the son of Lamech,
37 the son of Methuselah, the son of
Enoch, the son of Jared, the son of
Mahalaleel, the son of Cainan,
38 the son of Enosh, the son of Seth,
the son of Adam, the son of God.

The Temptation of Jesus

4 [a]Jesus, full of the Holy Spirit, [b]re-
turned from the Jordan and was led
around [1]by the Spirit in the wilderness
2 for [a]forty days, being tempted by
the devil. And He ate nothing during
those days, and when they had ended, He
became hungry.
3 And the devil said to Him, "If You
are the Son of God, tell this stone to become bread."
4 And Jesus answered him, "It is
written, '[a]MAN SHALL NOT LIVE ON BREAD
ALONE.'"
5 ¶ [a]And he led Him up and showed
Him all the kingdoms of [1b]the world in
a moment of time.
6 And the devil said to Him, "I will
give You all this domain and [1]its glory;
[a]for it has been handed over to me, and
I give it to whomever I wish.
7 "Therefore if You [1]worship before
me, it shall all be Yours."
8 Jesus answered him, "It is written,
'[a]YOU SHALL WORSHIP THE LORD YOUR GOD
AND SERVE HIM ONLY.'"
9 ¶ [a]And he led Him to Jerusalem
and had Him stand on the pinnacle of the
temple, and said to Him, "If You are the
Son of God, throw Yourself down from
here;
10 for it is written,

> '[a]HE WILL COMMAND HIS ANGELS
> CONCERNING YOU TO
> GUARD YOU,'

---

14 [a]Ex 20:16; 23:1 [b]Phil 4:11
15 [1]Or *reasoning* or *debating* [2]I.e. the Messiah [a]John 1:19f
16 [1]The Gr here can be translated *in, with* or *by* [a]Luke 3:16,17: *Matt 3:11,12; Mark 1:7,8*
17 [a]Is 30:24 [b]Mark 9:43,48
19 [a]Matt 14:3; Mark 6:17 [b]Matt 14:1; Luke 3:1
20 [a]John 3:24
21 [a]Luke 3:21, 22: *Matt 3:13-17; Mark 1:9-11* [b]Matt 14:23; Luke 5:16; 9:18,28f
22 [a]Ps 2:7; Is 42:1; Matt 3:17; 17:5; Mark 1:11; Luke 9:35; 2 Pet 1:17
23 [1]Lit *as it was being thought* [2]Lit *of Eli* and so throughout the genealogy [3]Also spelled *Heli* [a]Matt 4:17; Acts 1:1 [b]Matt 1:16; Luke 3:23-27
25 [1]Also spelled *Esli*
27 [1]Gr *Salathiel*; names of people in the Old Testament are given in their Old Testament form throughout v 38 [a]Matt 1:12
29 [1]Gr *Jesus*
30 [1]Gr *Judas*
32 [1]Gr *Sala* [2]Gr *Naasson* [a]Luke 3:32-34: *Matt 1:1-6*
33 [1]Gr *Arni*
34 [a]Luke 3:34-36: *Gen 11:26-30; 1 Chr 1:24-27*
35 [1]Gr *Ragau* [2]Gr *Eber*
36 [a]Luke 3:36-38: *Gen 5:3-32; 1 Chr 1:1-4*
4:1 [1]Or *under the influence of*; lit *in* [a]Luke 4:1-13: *Matt 4:1-11; Mark 1:12,13* [b]Luke 3:3
2 [a]Ex 34:28; 1 Kin 19:8
4 [a]Deut 8:3
5 [1]Lit *the inhabited earth* [a]Matt 4:8-10 [b]Matt 24:14
6 [1]Lit *their* (referring to the kingdoms in v 5) [a]1 John 5:19
7 [1]Or *bow down before*
8 [a]Deut 6:13; 10:20; Matt 4:10
9 [a]Matt 4:5-7
10 [a]Ps 91:11

11 and,
‘[a]ON *their* HANDS THEY WILL BEAR
YOU UP,
SO THAT YOU WILL NOT STRIKE
YOUR FOOT AGAINST A
STONE.’ ”
12 And Jesus answered and said to
him, “It is said, ‘[a]YOU SHALL NOT PUT THE
LORD YOUR GOD TO THE TEST.’ ”
13 ¶ When the devil had finished every temptation, he left Him until an opportune time.

Jesus' Public Ministry

14 ¶ And [a]Jesus returned to Galilee in
the power of the Spirit, and [b]news about
Him spread through all the surrounding
district.
15 And He *began* [a]teaching in their
synagogues and was praised by all.
16 ¶ And He came to [a]Nazareth,
where He had been brought up; and as
was His custom, [b]He entered the synagogue on the Sabbath, and [c]stood up to
read.
17 And the [1]book of the prophet Isaiah was handed to Him. And He opened
the [1]book and found the place where it
was written,
18“[a]THE SPIRIT OF THE LORD IS
UPON ME,
BECAUSE HE ANOINTED ME TO
PREACH THE GOSPEL TO THE
POOR.
HE HAS SENT ME TO PROCLAIM
RELEASE TO THE CAPTIVES,
AND RECOVERY OF SIGHT TO THE
BLIND,
TO SET FREE THOSE WHO ARE
OPPRESSED,
19 [a]TO PROCLAIM THE FAVORABLE YEAR
OF THE LORD.”
20 And He [a]closed the [1]book, gave it
back to the attendant and [b]sat down; and
the eyes of all in the synagogue were
fixed on Him.
21 And He began to say to them, “Today this Scripture has been fulfilled in
your [1]hearing.”
22 And all were [1]speaking well of
Him, and wondering at the [2]gracious
words which [3]were falling from His lips;
and they were saying, “[a]Is this not Joseph's son?”
23 And He said to them, “No doubt
you will quote this proverb to Me, ‘Physician, heal yourself! Whatever we heard
was done [a]at Capernaum, do here in
[b]your hometown as well.’ ”
24 And He said, “Truly I say to you,
[a]no prophet is welcome in his hometown.
25“But I say to you in truth, there were
many widows in Israel [a]in the days of
Elijah, when the sky was shut up for
three years and six months, when a great
famine came over all the land;
26 and yet Elijah was sent to none of
them, but [a]only to [1]Zarephath, *in the
land* of [b]Sidon, to a woman who was a
widow.
27“And there were many lepers in Israel in the time of Elisha the prophet; and
none of them was cleansed, but [a]only
Naaman the Syrian.”
28 And all *the people* in the synagogue
were filled with rage as they heard these
things;
29 and they got up and [a]drove Him
out of the city, and led Him to the brow
of the hill on which their city had been
built, in order to throw Him down the
cliff.
30 But [a]passing through their midst,
He went His way.
31 ¶ And [a]He came down to [b]Caper-
naum, a city of Galilee, and He was teaching them on the Sabbath;
32 and [a]they were amazed at His
teaching, for [b]His [1]message was with
authority.
33 In the synagogue there was a man
[1]possessed by the spirit of an unclean
demon, and he cried out with a loud
voice,
34“Let us alone! [1a]What business do
we have with each other, Jesus [2]of [b]Naz-
areth? Have You come to destroy us? I
know who You are—[b]the Holy One of
God!”
35 But Jesus [a]rebuked him, saying,
“Be quiet and come out of him!” And
when the demon had thrown him down
in the midst *of the people*, he came out
of him without doing him any harm.
36 And amazement came upon them
all, and they *began* talking with one another saying, “What is [1]this message?
For [a]with authority and power He commands the unclean spirits and they come
out.”
37 And [a]the report about Him was
spreading into every locality in the surrounding district.

Many Are Healed

38 ¶ [a]Then He got up and *left* the synagogue, and entered Simon's home. Now
Simon's mother-in-law was [b]suffering
from a high fever, and they asked Him
[1]to help her.
39 And standing over her, He [a]re-
buked the fever, and it left her; and she
immediately got up and [1]waited on
them.
40 ¶ [a]While [b]the sun was setting, all
those who had any *who were* sick with
various diseases brought them to Him;

11 [a]Ps 91:12
12 [a]Deut 6:16
14 [a]Matt 4:12 [b]Matt 9:26; Luke 4:37
15 [a]Matt 4:23
16 [a]Luke 2:39, 51 [b]Matt 13:54; Mark 6:1f [c]Acts 13:14-16
17 [1]Or *scroll*
18 [a]Is 61:1; Matt 11:5; 12:18; John 3:34
19 [a]Is 61:2; Lev 25:10
20 [1]Or *scroll* [a]Luke 4:17 [b]Matt 26:55
21 [1]Lit *ears*
22 [1]Or *testifying* [2]Or *words of grace* [3]Lit *were proceeding out of His mouth* [a]Matt 13:55; Mark 6:3; John 6:42
23 [a]Matt 4:13; Mark 1:21ff; 2:1ff; Luke 4:35ff; John 4:46ff [b]Mark 6:1; Luke 2:39, 51; 4:16
24 [a]Matt 13:57; Mark 6:4; John 4:44
25 [a]1 Kin 17:1; 18:1; James 5:17
26 [1]Gr *Sarepta* [a]1 Kin 17:9 [b]Matt 11:21
27 [a]2 Kin 5:1-14
29 [a]Num 15:35; Acts 7:58; Heb 13:12
30 [a]John 10:39
31 [a]Luke 4:31-37: *Mark 1:21-28* [b]Matt 4:13; Luke 4:23
32 [1]Lit *word* [a]Matt 7:28 [b]Luke 4:36; John 7:46
33 [1]Lit *having a spirit*
34 [1]Lit *What to us and to you* (a Heb idiom) [2]Lit *the Nazarene* [a]Matt 8:29 [b]Mark 1:24
35 [a]Matt 8:26; Mark 4:39; Luke 4:39,41; 8:24
36 [1]Or *this word, that with authority...come out?* [a]Luke 4:32
37 [a]Luke 4:14
38 [1]Lit *about her* [a]Luke 4:38, 39: *Matt 8:14, 15; Mark 1:29-31* [b]Matt 4:24
39 [1]Or *served* [a]Luke 4:35,41
40 [a]Luke 4:40, 41: *Matt 8:16, 17; Mark 1:32-34* [b]Mark 1:32

and [c]laying His hands on each one of
them, He was [d]healing them.
41 Demons also were coming out of
many, shouting, "You are [a]the Son of
God!" But [b]rebuking them, He would
[c]not allow them to speak, because they
knew Him to be [1]the Christ.
42 ¶ [a]When day came, Jesus left and
went to a secluded place; and the crowds
were searching for Him, and came to Him
and tried to keep Him from going away
from them.
43 But He said to them, "I must preach
the kingdom of God to the other cities
also, [a]for I was sent for this purpose."
44 ¶ So He kept on preaching in the
synagogues [a]of [1]Judea.

The First Disciples

5 [a]Now it happened that while the
crowd was pressing around Him and
listening to the word of God, He was
standing by [b]the lake of Gennesaret;
2 and He saw two boats lying at the
edge of the lake; but the fishermen had
gotten out of them and were washing
their nets.
3 And [a]He got into one of the boats,
which was Simon's, and asked him to put
out a little way from the land. And He sat
down and *began* teaching the [1]people
from the boat.
4 When He had finished speaking,
He said to Simon, "Put out into the deep
water and [a]let down your nets for a
catch."
5 Simon answered and said, "[a]Mas-
ter, [b]we worked hard all night and
caught nothing, but [1]I will do as You say
and let down the nets.
6 When they had done this, [a]they
enclosed a great quantity of fish, and their
nets *began* to break;
7 so they signaled to their partners in
the other boat for them to come and help
them. And they came and filled both of
the boats, so that they began to sink.
8 But when Simon Peter saw *that*, he
fell down at Jesus' [1]feet, saying, "Go
away from me Lord, for I am a sinful man,
O Lord!"
9 For amazement had seized him and
all his companions because of the catch of
fish which they had taken;
10 and so also *were* [1]James and John,
sons of Zebedee, who were partners with
Simon. And Jesus said to Simon, "[a]Do
not fear, from now on you will be [b]catch-
ing men."
11 When they had brought their boats
to land, [a]they left everything and followed Him.

The Leper and the Paralytic

12 ¶ [a]While He was in one of the cities, behold, *there was* a man [1]covered
with leprosy; and when he saw Jesus, he
fell on his face and implored Him, saying,
"Lord, if You are willing, You can make
me clean."
13 And He stretched out His hand and
touched him, saying, "I am willing; be
cleansed." And immediately the leprosy
left him.
14 And He ordered him to tell no one,
"But go and [a]show yourself to the priest
and make an offering for your cleansing,
just as Moses commanded, as a testimony
to them."
15 But [a]the news about Him was
spreading even farther, and large crowds
were gathering to hear *Him* and to be
healed of their sicknesses.
16 But Jesus Himself would *often* slip
away [1]to the [2]wilderness and [a]pray.
17 ¶ [1]One day He was teaching; and
[a]there were *some* Pharisees and [b]teach-
ers of the law sitting *there*, who had
[c]come from every village of Galilee and
Judea and *from* Jerusalem; and [d]the power of the Lord was *present* for Him to
perform healing.
18 [a]And *some* men *were* carrying on
a [1]bed a man who was paralyzed; and
they were trying to bring him in and to
set him down in front of Him.
19 But not finding any *way* to bring
him in because of the crowd, they went
up on [a]the roof and let him down
[b]through the tiles with his stretcher, into
the middle *of the crowd*, in front of Jesus.
20 Seeing their faith, He said,
"[1]Friend, [a]your sins are forgiven you."
21 The scribes and the Pharisees [a]be-
gan to reason, saying, "[b]Who is this *man*
who speaks blasphemies? [c]Who can forgive sins, but God alone?"
22 But Jesus, [1]aware of their reasonings, answered and said to them, "Why
are you reasoning in your hearts?
23 "Which is easier, to say, 'Your sins
have been forgiven you,' or to say, 'Get
up and walk'?
24 "But, so that you may know that the
Son of Man has authority on earth to forgive sins,"—He said to the [a]paralytic—
"I say to you, get up, and pick up your
stretcher and go home."
25 Immediately he got up before
them, and picked up what he had been
lying on, and went home [a]glorifying
God.
26 [1]They were all struck with astonishment and *began* [a]glorifying God; and
they were filled [b]with fear, saying, "We
have seen remarkable things today."

40 [c]Mark 5:23 [d]Matt 4:23
41 [1]I.e. the Messiah [a]Matt 4:3 [b]Luke 4:35 [c]Matt 8:16; Mark 1:34
42 [a]Luke 4:42, 43: *Mark 1:35-38*
43 [a]Mark 1:38
44 [1]I.e. the country of the Jews (including Galilee) [a]Matt 4:23
5:1 [a]Matt 4:18-22; Mark 1:16-20; Luke 5:1-11; John 1:40-42 [b]Num 34:11; Deut 3:17; Josh 12:3; 13:27; Matt 4:18
3 [1]Lit *crowds* [a]Matt 13:2; Mark 3:9,10; 4:1
4 [a]John 21:6
5 [1]Lit *upon Your word* [a]Luke 8:24; 9:33,49; 17:13 [b]John 21:3
6 [a]John 21:6
8 [1]Lit *knees*
10 [1]Or *Jacob* [a]Matt 14:27 [b]2 Tim 2:26
11 [a]Matt 4:20, 22; 19:29; Mark 1:18,20; Luke 5:28
12 [1]Lit *full of* [a]Luke 5:12-14: *Matt 8:2-4; Mark 1:40-44*
14 [a]Lev 13:49; 14:2ff
15 [a]Matt 9:26
16 [1]Lit *in* [2]Or *deserted places* [a]Matt 14:23; Mark 1:35; Luke 6:12
17 [1]Lit *On one of the days* [a]Matt 15:1 [b]Luke 2:46 [c]Mark 1:45 [d]Mark 5:30; Luke 6:19; 8:46
18 [1]Or *stretcher* [a]Luke 5:18-26: *Matt 9:2-8; Mark 2:3-12*
19 [a]Matt 24:17 [b]Mark 2:4
20 [1]Lit *Man* [a]Matt 9:2
21 [a]Luke 3:8 [b]Luke 7:49 [c]Is 43:25
22 [1]Or *perceiving*
24 [a]Matt 4:24
25 [a]Matt 9:8
26 [1]Lit *Astonishment took them all* [a]Matt 9:8 [b]Luke 1:65; 7:16

Call of Levi (Matthew)

27 ¶ [a]After that He went out and noticed a tax collector named [1b]Levi sitting in the tax booth, and He said to him, "Follow Me."

28 And he [a]left everything behind, and got up and *began* to follow Him.

29 ¶ And [a]Levi gave a big reception for Him in his house; and there was a great crowd of [b]tax collectors and other *people* who were reclining *at the table* with them.

30 [a]The Pharisees and their scribes *began* grumbling at His disciples, saying, "Why do you eat and drink with the tax collectors and [1]sinners?"

31 And Jesus answered and said to them, "[a]*It is* not those who are well who need a physician, but those who are sick.

32 "I have not come to call the righteous but sinners to repentance."

33 ¶ And they said to Him, "[a]The disciples of John often fast and offer prayers, the *disciples* of the Pharisees also do [1]the same, but Yours eat and drink."

34 And Jesus said to them, "You cannot make the [1]attendants of the bridegroom fast while the bridegroom is with them, can you?

35 "[a]But *the* days will come; and when the bridegroom is taken away from them, then they will fast in those days."

36 And He was also telling them a parable: "No one tears a piece of cloth from a new garment and puts it on an old garment; otherwise he will both tear the new, and the piece from the new will not match the old.

37 "And no one puts new wine into old wineskins; otherwise the new wine will burst the skins and it will be spilled out, and the skins will be ruined.

38 "But new wine must be put into fresh wineskins.

39 "And no one, after drinking old *wine* wishes for new; for he says, 'The old is good *enough*.'"

Jesus Is Lord of the Sabbath

6 [a]Now it happened that He was passing through *some* grainfields on a Sabbath; and His disciples [b]were picking the heads of grain, rubbing them in their hands, and eating *the grain*.

2 But some of the Pharisees said, "Why do you do what [a]is not lawful on the Sabbath?"

3 And Jesus answering them said, "Have you not even read [a]what David did when he was hungry, he and those who were with him,

4 how he entered the house of God, and took and ate the [1]consecrated bread which [a]is not lawful for any to eat except the priests alone, and gave it to his companions?"

5 And He was saying to them, "The Son of Man is Lord of the Sabbath."

6 ¶ [a]On another Sabbath He entered [b]the synagogue and was teaching; and there was a man there [1]whose right hand was withered.

7 The scribes and the Pharisees [a]were watching Him closely *to see* if He healed on the Sabbath, so that they might find *reason* to accuse Him.

8 But He [a]knew [1]what they were thinking, and He said to the man with the withered hand, "Get up and [2]come forward!" And he got up and [3]came forward.

9 And Jesus said to them, "I ask you, is it lawful to do good or to do harm on the Sabbath, to save a life or to destroy it?"

10 After [a]looking around at them all, He said to him, "Stretch out your hand!" And he did *so*; and his hand was restored.

11 But they themselves were filled with [1]rage, and discussed together what they might do to Jesus.

Choosing the Twelve

12 ¶ It was [1]at this time that He went off to [a]the mountain to [b]pray, and He spent the whole night in prayer to God.

13 And when day came, [a]He called His disciples to Him and chose twelve of them, whom He also named as [b]apostles:

14 Simon, whom He also named Peter, and Andrew his brother; and [1]James and John; and Philip and Bartholomew;

15 and [a]Matthew and Thomas; James *the son* of Alphaeus, and Simon who was called the Zealot;

16 Judas *the son* of James, and Judas Iscariot, who became a traitor.

17 ¶ Jesus [a]came down with them and stood on a level place; and *there was* [b]a large crowd of His disciples, and a great throng of people from all Judea and Jerusalem and the coastal region of [c]Tyre and Sidon,

18 who had come to hear Him and to be healed of their diseases; and those who were troubled with unclean spirits were being cured.

19 And all the [1]people were trying to [a]touch Him, for [b]power was coming from Him and healing *them* all.

The Beatitudes

20 ¶ And turning His gaze toward His disciples, He *began* to say, "[a]Blessed *are* [1]you *who are* poor, for [b]yours is the kingdom of God.

21 "Blessed *are* [1]you who hunger now,

27 [1]Also called *Matthew* [a]Luke 5:27-39: *Matt 9:9-17; Mark 2:14-22* [b]Matt 9:9
28 [a]Luke 5:11
29 [a]Matt 9:9 [b]Luke 15:1
30 [1]I.e. irreligious Jews [a]Mark 2:16; Luke 15:2; Acts 23:9
31 [a]Matt 9:12, 13; Mark 2:17
33 [1]Or *likewise* [a]Matt 9:14; Mark 2:18
34 [1]Lit *sons of the bridal-chamber*
35 [a]Matt 9:15; Mark 2:20; Luke 17:22
6:1 [a]Luke 6:1-5: *Matt 12:1-8; Mark 2:23-28* [b]Deut 23:25
2 [a]Matt 12:2
3 [a]1 Sam 21:6
4 [1]Or *showbread*; lit *loaves of presentation* [a]Lev 24:9
6 [1]Lit *and his* [a]Luke 6:6-11: *Matt 12:9-14; Mark 3:1-6;* Luke 6:1 [b]Matt 4:23
7 [a]Mark 3:2
8 [1]Lit *their thoughts* [2]Lit *stand into the middle* [3]Lit *stood* [a]Matt 9:4
10 [a]Mark 3:5
11 [1]Lit *folly*
12 [1]Lit *in these days* [a]Matt 5:1 [b]Matt 14:23; Luke 5:16; 9:18, 28
13 [a]Luke 6:13-16: *Matt 10:2-4; Mark 3:16-19; Acts 1:13* [b]Mark 6:30
14 [1]Or *Jacob*, also vv 15 and 16
15 [a]Matt 9:9
17 [a]Luke 6:12 [b]Matt 4:25; Mark 3:7,8 [c]Matt 11:21
19 [1]Lit *crowd* [a]Matt 9:21; 14:36; Mark 3:10 [b]Luke 5:17
20 [1]Lit *the* [a]Matt 5:3-12; Luke 6:20-23 [b]Matt 5:3
21 [1]Lit *the*

for you shall be satisfied. Blessed *are* you who weep now, for you shall laugh.

22“[a]Blessed are you when men hate you, and [b]ostracize you, and insult you, and scorn your name as evil, for the sake of the Son of Man.

23“Be glad in that day and [a]leap *for joy,* for behold, your reward is great in heaven. For [b]in the same way their fathers used to [1]treat the prophets.

24“But woe to [a]you who are rich, for [b]you are receiving your comfort in full.

25“Woe to you who [1]are well-fed now, for you shall be hungry. Woe *to you* who laugh now, for you shall mourn and weep.

26“Woe *to you* when all men speak well of you, for their fathers used to [1]treat the [a]false prophets in the same way.

27 ¶ “But I say to you who hear, [a]love your enemies, do good to those who hate you,

28 bless those who curse you, [a]pray for those who [1]mistreat you.

29“[a]Whoever hits you on the cheek, offer him the other also; and whoever takes away your [1]coat, do not withhold your [2]shirt from him either.

30“Give to everyone who asks of you, and whoever takes away what is yours, do not demand it back.

31“[1a]Treat others the same way you want [2]them to treat you.

32“[a]If you love those who love you, what credit is *that* to you? For even sinners love those who love them.

33“If you do good to those who do good to you, what credit is *that* to you? For even sinners do the same.

34“[a]If you lend to those from whom you expect to receive, what credit is *that* to you? Even sinners lend to sinners in order to receive back the same *amount.*

35“But [a]love your enemies, and do good, and lend, [1]expecting nothing in return; and your reward will be great, and you will be [b]sons of [c]the Most High; for He Himself is kind to ungrateful and evil *men.*

36“[1]Be merciful, just as your Father is merciful.

37 ¶ “[a]Do not judge, and you will not be judged; and do not condemn, and you will not be condemned; [1b]pardon, and you will be pardoned.

38“Give, and it will be given to you. They will [1]pour [a]into your lap a [b]good measure—pressed down, shaken together, *and* running over. For by your standard of measure it will be measured to you in return.”

39 ¶ And He also spoke a parable to them: “[a]A blind man cannot guide a blind man, can he? Will they not both fall into a pit?

40“[a]A [1]pupil is not above his teacher; but everyone, after he has been fully trained, will [2]be like his teacher.

41“Why do you look at the speck that is in your brother’s eye, but do not notice the log that is in your own eye?

42“Or how can you say to your brother, ‘Brother, let me take out the speck that is in your eye,’ when you yourself do not see the log that is in your own eye? You hypocrite, first take the log out of your own eye, and then you will see clearly to take out the speck that is in your brother’s eye.

43“[a]For there is no good tree which produces bad fruit, nor, [1]on the other hand, a bad tree which produces good fruit.

44“[a]For each tree is known by its own fruit. For men do not gather figs from thorns, nor do they pick grapes from a briar bush.

45“[a]The good man out of the good [1]treasure of his heart brings forth what is good; and the evil *man* out of the evil *treasure* brings forth what is evil; [b]for his mouth speaks from [2]that which fills his heart.

Builders and Foundations

46 ¶ “[a]Why do you call Me, ‘Lord, Lord,’ and do not do what I say?

47“[a]Everyone who comes to Me and hears My words and [1]acts on them, I will show you whom he is like:

48 he is like a man building a house, who [1]dug deep and laid a foundation on the rock; and when a flood occurred, the [2]torrent burst against that house and could not shake it, because it had been well built.

49“But the one who has heard and has not acted *accordingly,* is like a man who built a house on the ground without any foundation; and the [1]torrent burst against it and immediately it collapsed, and the ruin of that house was great.”

Jesus Heals a Centurion’s Servant

7 [a]When He had completed all His discourse in the hearing of the people, [b]He went to Capernaum.

2 ¶ And a centurion’s slave, [1]who was highly regarded by him, was sick and about to die.

3 When he heard about Jesus, [a]he sent some [1]Jewish elders asking Him to come and [2]save the life of his slave.

4 When they came to Jesus, they earnestly implored Him, saying, “He is worthy for You to grant this to him;

22 [a]1 Pet 4:14 [b]John 9:22; 16:2
23 [1]Lit *do to* [a]Mal 4 [b]2 Chr 36:16; Acts 7:52
24 [a]Luke 16:25; James 5:1 [b]Matt 6:2
25 [1]Lit *having been filled*
26 [1]Lit *do to* [a]Matt 7:15
27 [a]Matt 5:44; Luke 6:35
28 [1]Or *revile* [a]Matt 5:44; Luke 6:35
29 [1]I.e. outer garment [2]Or *tunic;* i.e. garment worn next to body [a]Luke 6:29, 30: *Matt 5:39-42*
31 [1]Lit *Do to* [2]Lit *people* [a]Matt 7:12
32 [a]Matt 5:46
34 [a]Matt 5:42
35 [1]Or *not despairing at all* [a]Luke 6:27 [b]Matt 5:9 [c]Luke 1:32
36 [1]Or *Become*
37 [1]Lit *release* [a]Luke 6:37-42: *Matt 7:1-5* [b]Matt 6:14; Luke 23:16; Acts 3:13
38 [1]Lit *give* [a]Mark 4:24 [b]Ps 79:12; Is 65:6,7; Jer 32:18
39 [a]Matt 15:14
40 [1]Or *disciple* [2]Or *reach his teacher’s level* [a]Matt 10:24; John 13:16; 15:20
43 [1]Lit *again* [a]Luke 6:43,44: *Matt 7:16,18,20*
44 [a]Matt 7:16; 12:33
45 [1]Or *treasury, storehouse* [2]Lit *the abundance of* [a]Matt 12:35 [b]Matt 12:34
46 [a]Mal 1:6; Matt 7:21
47 [1]Lit *does* [a]Luke 6:47-49: *Matt 7:24-27;* James 1:22ff
48 [1]Lit *dug and went deep* [2]Lit *river*
49 [1]Lit *river*
7:1 [a]Matt 7:28 [b]Luke 7:1-10: *Matt 8:5-13*
2 [1]Lit *to whom he was honorable*
3 [1]Lit *elders of the Jews* [2]Lit *bring safely through, rescue* [a]Matt 8:5

5 for he loves our nation and it was
he who built us our synagogue."
6 Now Jesus *started* on His way with
them; and when He was not far from the
house, the centurion sent friends, saying
to Him, "[1]Lord, do not trouble Yourself
further, for I am not worthy for You to
come under my roof;
7 for this reason I did not even consider myself worthy to come to You, but
just [1]say the word, and my [2]servant will
be healed.
8 "For I also am a man placed under
authority, with soldiers under me; and I
say to this one, 'Go!' and he goes, and to
another, 'Come!' and he comes, and to
my slave, 'Do this!' and he does it."
9 Now when Jesus heard this, He
marveled at him, and turned and said to
the crowd that was following Him, "I say
to you, [a]not even in Israel have I found
such great faith."
10 When those who had been sent returned to the house, they found the slave
in good health.
11 ¶ Soon afterwards He went to a city
called Nain; and His disciples were going
along with Him, [1]accompanied by a large
crowd.
12 Now as He approached the gate of
the city, [1]a dead man was being carried
out, the [2]only son of his mother, and she
was a widow; and a sizeable crowd from
the city was with her.
13 When [a]the Lord saw her, He felt
compassion for her, and said to her,
"[1]Do not weep."
14 And He came up and touched the
coffin; and the bearers came to a halt.
And He said, "Young man, I say to you,
arise!"
15 The [1]dead man sat up and began to
speak. And *Jesus* gave him back to his
mother.
16 [a]Fear gripped them all, and they
began [b]glorifying God, saying, "A great
[c]prophet has arisen among us!" and,
"God has [1]visited His people!"
17 [a]This report concerning Him went
out all over Judea and in all the surrounding district.

A Deputation from John

18 ¶ [a]The disciples of John reported
to him about all these things.
19 Summoning [1]two of his disciples,
John sent them to [a]the Lord, saying,
"Are You the [2]Expected One, or do we
look for someone else?"
20 When the men came to Him, they
said, "John the Baptist has sent us to You,
to ask, 'Are You the [1]Expected One, or
do we look for someone else?' "
21 At that [1]very time He [a]cured
many *people* of diseases and [b]afflictions
and evil spirits; and He gave sight to
many *who were* blind.
22 And He answered and said to them,
"Go and report to John what you have
seen and heard: *the* [a]BLIND RECEIVE SIGHT,
the lame walk, *the* lepers are cleansed,
and *the* deaf hear, *the* dead are raised up,
the [b]POOR HAVE THE GOSPEL PREACHED TO
THEM.
23 "Blessed is he [1]who does not take
offense at Me."
24 ¶ When the messengers of John
had left, He began to speak to the crowds
about John, "What did you go out into the
wilderness to see? A reed shaken by the
wind?
25 "[1]But what did you go out to see?
A man dressed in soft [2]clothing? Those
who are splendidly clothed and live in
luxury are *found* in royal palaces!
26 "But what did you go out to see? A
prophet? Yes, I say to you, and one who
is more than a prophet.
27 "This is the one about whom it is
written,

'[a]BEHOLD, I SEND MY MESSENGER
[1]AHEAD OF YOU,
WHO WILL PREPARE YOUR WAY
BEFORE YOU.'

28 "I say to you, among those born of
women there is no one greater than John;
yet he who is [1]least in the kingdom of
God is greater than he."
29 When all the people and the tax
collectors heard *this,* they [1]acknowl-
edged [a]God's justice, [b]having been baptized with [c]the baptism of John.
30 But the Pharisees and the [1a]law-
yers rejected God's purpose for themselves, not having been baptized by
[2]John.
31 ¶ "To what then shall I compare
the men of this generation, and what are
they like?
32 "They are like children who sit in
the market place and call to one another,
and they say, 'We played the flute for
you, and you did not dance; we sang a
dirge, and you did not weep.'
33 "For John the Baptist has come [a]eat-
ing no bread and drinking no wine, and
you say, 'He has a demon!'
34 "The Son of Man has come eating
and drinking, and you say, 'Behold, a gluttonous man and a [1]drunkard, a friend of
tax collectors and [2]sinners!'
35 "Yet wisdom [a]is vindicated by all
her children."
36 ¶ Now one of the Pharisees was requesting Him to [1]dine with him, and He
entered the Pharisee's house and reclined *at the table.*
37 [a]And there was a woman in the

6 [1]Or *Sir*
7 [1]Lit *say with a word* [2]Or *boy*
9 [a]Matt 8:10; Luke 7:50
11 [1]Lit *and*
12 [1]Lit *one who had died* [2]Or *only begotten*
13 [1]Or *Stop weeping* [a]Luke 7:19; 10:1; 11:1, 39; 12:42; 13:15; 17:5,6; 18:6; 19:8; 22:61; 24:34; John 4:1; 6:23; 11:2
15 [1]Or *corpse*
16 [1]Or *cared for* [a]Luke 5:26 [b]Matt 9:8 [c]Matt 21:11; Luke 7:39
17 [a]Matt 9:26
18 [a]Luke 7:18-35: *Matt 11:2-19*
19 [1]Lit *a certain two* [2]Lit *Coming One* [a]Luke 7:13; 10:1; 11:1,39; 12:42; 13:15; 17:5,6; 18:6; 19:8; 22:61; 24:34; John 4:1; 6:23; 11:2
20 [1]Lit *Coming One*
21 [1]Lit *hour* [a]Matt 4:23 [b]Mark 3:10
22 [a]Is 35:5 [b]Is 61:1
23 [1]Lit *whoever*
25 [1]Or *Well then, what* [2]Or *garments*
27 [1]Lit *before Your face* [a]Mal 3:1; Matt 11:10; Mark 1:2
28 [1]Or *less*
29 [1]Or *justified God* [a]Luke 7:35 [b]Matt 21:32; Luke 3:12 [c]Acts 18:25; 19:3
30 [1]I.e. experts in the Mosaic Law [2]Lit *him* [a]Matt 22:35
33 [a]Luke 1:15
34 [1]Or *wine-drinker* [2]I.e. irreligious Jews
35 [a]Luke 7:29
36 [1]Lit *eat*
37 [a]Matt 26:6-13; Mark 14:3-9; Luke 7:37-39; John 12:1-8

city who was a [1]sinner; and when she
learned that He was reclining *at the table*
in the Pharisee's house, she brought an
alabaster vial of perfume,
38 and standing behind *Him* at His
feet, weeping, she began to wet His feet
with her tears, and kept wiping them
with the hair of her head, and kissing His
feet and anointing them with the perfume.
39 Now when the Pharisee who had
invited Him saw this, he said to himself,
"If this man were [a]a prophet He would
know who and what sort of person this
woman is who is touching Him, that she
is a [1]sinner."

Parable of Two Debtors

40 And Jesus answered him, "Simon, I
have something to say to you." And he
[1]replied, "Say it, Teacher."
41 "A moneylender had two debtors:
one owed five hundred [1a]denarii, and
the other fifty.
42 "When they [a]were unable to repay,
he graciously forgave them both. So
which of them will love him more?"
43 Simon answered and said, "I suppose the one whom he forgave more."
And He said to him, "You have judged
correctly."
44 Turning toward the woman, He
said to Simon, "Do you see this woman?
I entered your house; you [a]gave Me no
water for My feet, but she has wet My
feet with her tears and wiped them with
her hair.
45 "You [a]gave Me no kiss; but she,
since the time I came in, has not ceased
to kiss My feet.
46 "[a]You did not anoint My head with
oil, but she anointed My feet with perfume.
47 "For this reason I say to you, her
sins, which are many, have been forgiv-
en, for she loved much; but he who is
forgiven little, loves little."
48 Then He said to her, "[a]Your sins
have been forgiven."
49 Those who were reclining *at the*
table with Him began to say [1]to themselves, "[a]Who is this *man* who even forgives sins?"
50 And He said to the woman, "[a]Your
faith has saved you; [b]go in peace."

Ministering Women

8 Soon afterwards, He *began* going
around from one city and village to
another, [a]proclaiming and preaching the
kingdom of God. The twelve were with
Him,
2 and *also* [a]some women who had
been healed of evil spirits and sicknesses:
[b]Mary who was called Magdalene, from
whom seven demons had gone out,
3 and Joanna the wife of Chuza,
[a]Herod's [b]steward, and Susanna, and
many others who were contributing to
their support out of their private means.

Parable of the Sower

4 ¶ [a]When a large crowd was coming together, and those from the various
cities were journeying to Him, He spoke
by way of a parable:
5 "The sower went out to sow his
seed; and as he sowed, some fell beside
the road, and it was trampled under foot
and the birds of the [1]air ate it up.
6 "Other *seed* fell on rocky *soil,* and as
soon as it grew up, it withered away, because it had no moisture.
7 "Other *seed* fell among the thorns;
and the thorns grew up with it and
choked it out.
8 "Other *seed* fell into the good soil,
and grew up, and produced a crop a hundred times as great." As He said these
things, He would call out, "[a]He who has
ears to hear, [1]let him hear."
9 ¶ [a]His disciples *began* questioning
Him as to what this parable meant.
10 And He said, "[a]To you it has been
granted to know the mysteries of the
kingdom of God, but to the rest *it is* in
parables, so that [b]SEEING THEY MAY NOT
SEE, AND HEARING THEY MAY NOT UNDER-
STAND.
11 ¶ "Now the parable is this: [a]the
seed is the word of God.
12 "Those beside the road are those
who have heard; then the devil comes
and takes away the word from their
heart, so that they will not believe and be
saved.
13 "Those on the rocky *soil are* those
who, when they hear, receive the word
with joy; and these have no *firm* root;
[1]they believe for a while, and in time of
temptation fall away.
14 "The *seed* which fell among the
thorns, these are the ones who have
heard, and as they go on their way they
are choked with worries and riches and
pleasures of *this* life, and bring no fruit to
maturity.
15 "But the *seed* in the good soil, these
are the ones who have heard the word in
an honest and good heart, and hold it fast,
and bear fruit with [1]perseverance.

Parable of the Lamp

16 ¶ "Now [a]no one after lighting a
lamp covers it over with a container, or
puts it under a bed; but he puts it on a
lampstand, so that those who come in
may see the light.

37 [1]I.e. an immoral woman
39 [1]I.e. an immoral woman [a]Luke 7:16; John 4:19
40 [1]Lit *says*
41 [1]The denarius was equivalent to a day's wages [a]Matt 18:28; Mark 6:37
42 [a]Matt 18:25
44 [a]Gen 18:4; 19:2; 43:24; Judg 19:21; 1 Tim 5:10
45 [a]2 Sam 15:5
46 [a]2 Sam 12:20; Ps 23:5; Eccl 9:8; Dan 10:3
48 [a]Matt 9:2; Mark 2:5,9; Luke 5:20,23
49 [1]Or *among* [a]Luke 5:21
50 [a]Matt 9:22; Luke 17:19; 18:42 [b]Mark 5:34; Luke 8:48
8:1 [a]Matt 4:23
2 [a]Matt 27:55; Mark 15:40,41; Luke 23:49,55 [b]Matt 27:56; Mark 16:9
3 [a]Matt 14:1 [b]Matt 20:8
4 [a]Luke 8:4-8: *Matt 13:2-9; Mark 4:1-9*
5 [1]Lit *heaven*
8 [1]Or *hear!* Or *listen!* [a]Matt 11:15; Mark 7:16; Luke 14:35; Rev 2:7, 11,17,29; 3:6, 13,22; 13:9
9 [a]Luke 8:9-15: *Matt 13:10-23; Mark 4:10-20*
10 [a]Matt 13:11 [b]Is 6:9; Matt 13:14; Acts 28:26
11 [a]1 Pet 1:23
13 [1]Lit *who believe*
15 [1]Or *steadfastness*
16 [a]Matt 5:15; Mark 4:21; Luke 11:33

17 “[a]For nothing is hidden that will not
become evident, nor *anything* secret that
will not be known and come to light.
18 “So take care how you listen; [a]for
whoever has, to him *more* shall be given;
and whoever does not have, even what
he [1]thinks he has shall be taken away
from him.”
19 ¶ [a]And His mother and brothers
came to Him, and they were unable to get
to Him because of the crowd.
20 And it was reported to Him, “Your
mother and Your brothers are standing
outside, wishing to see You.”
21 But He answered and said to them,
“My mother and My brothers are these
[a]who hear the word of God and do it.”

Jesus Stills the Sea

22 ¶ [a]Now on one of *those* days Jesus
and His disciples got into a boat, and He
said to them, “Let us go over to the other
side of [b]the lake.” So they launched out.
23 But as they were sailing along He
fell asleep; and a fierce gale of wind descended on [a]the lake, and they *began* to
be swamped and to be in danger.
24 They came to Jesus and woke Him
up, saying, “[a]Master, Master, we are
perishing!” And He got up and [b]rebuked
the wind and the surging waves, and they
stopped, and [1]it became calm.
25 And He said to them, “Where is
your faith?” They were fearful and
amazed, saying to one another, “Who
then is this, that He commands even the
winds and the water, and they obey
Him?”

The Demoniac Cured

26 ¶ [a]Then they sailed to the country
of the Gerasenes, which is opposite Galilee.
27 And when He came out onto the
land, He was met by a man from the city
who was possessed with demons; and
who had not put on any clothing for a
long time, and was not living in a house,
but in the tombs.
28 Seeing Jesus, he cried out and fell
before Him, and said in a loud voice,
“[1a]What business do we have with each
other, Jesus, Son of [b]the Most High God?
I beg You, do not torment me.”
29 For He had commanded the unclean spirit to come out of the man. For
it had seized him many times; and he was
bound with chains and shackles and kept
under guard, and *yet* he would break his
bonds and be driven by the demon into
the desert.
30 And Jesus asked him, “What is your
name?” And he said, “[a]Legion”; for
many demons had entered him.
31 They were imploring Him not to
command them to go away into [a]the
abyss.
32 ¶ Now there was a herd of many
swine feeding there on the mountain;
and *the demons* implored Him to permit
them to enter [1]the swine. And He gave
them permission.
33 And the demons came out of the
man and entered the swine; and the herd
rushed down the steep bank into [a]the
lake and was drowned.
34 ¶ When the herdsmen saw what
had happened, they ran away and reported it in the city and *out* in the country.
35 *The people* went out to see what
had happened; and they came to Jesus,
and found the man from whom the demons had gone out, sitting down [a]at the
feet of Jesus, clothed and in his right
mind; and they became frightened.
36 Those who had seen it reported to
them how the man who was [a]demon-
possessed had been [1]made well.
37 And all the people of the country of
the Gerasenes and the surrounding district asked Him to leave them, for they
were gripped with great fear; and He got
into a boat and returned.
38 [a]But the man from whom the demons had gone out was begging Him that
he might [1]accompany Him; but He sent
him away, saying,
39 “Return to your house and describe
what great things God has done for you.”
So he went away, proclaiming throughout the whole city what great things Jesus
had done for him.

Miracles of Healing

40 ¶ [a]And as Jesus returned, the
[1]people welcomed Him, for they had all
been waiting for Him.
41 [a]And there came a man named Jairus, and he was an [1b]official of the synagogue; and he fell at Jesus' feet, and *began* to implore Him to come to his house;
42 for he had an [1]only daughter,
about twelve years old, and she was dying. But as He went, the crowds were
pressing against Him.
43 ¶ And a woman who had a hemorrhage for twelve years, and could not be
healed by anyone,
44 came up behind Him and touched
the fringe of His [1]cloak, and immediately
her hemorrhage stopped.
45 And Jesus said, “Who is the one
who touched Me?” And while they were
all denying it, Peter said, “[a]Master, the
[1]people are crowding and pressing in
on You.”
46 But Jesus said, “Someone did touch

17 [a]Matt 10:26; Mark 4:22; Luke 12:2
18 [1]Or *seems to have* [a]Matt 13:12; 25:29; Luke 19:26
19 [a]Luke 8:19-21: *Matt 12:46-50; Mark 3:31-35*
21 [a]Luke 11:28
22 [a]Luke 8:22-25: *Matt 8:23-27; Mark 4:36-41* [b]Luke 5:1f; 8:23
23 [a]Luke 5:1f; 8:22
24 [1]Lit *a calm occurred* [a]Luke 5:5 [b]Luke 4:39
26 [a]Luke 8:26-37: *Matt 8:28-34; Mark 5:1-17*
28 [1]Lit *What to me and to you* (a Heb idiom) [a]Matt 8:29 [b]Mark 5:7
30 [a]Matt 26:53
31 [a]Rom 10:7; Rev 9:1f,11; 11:7; 17:8; 20:1, 3
32 [1]Lit *them*
33 [a]Luke 5:1f; 8:22
35 [a]Luke 10:39
36 [1]Or *saved* [a]Matt 4:24
38 [1]Lit *be with* [a]Luke 8:38,39: *Mark 5:18-20*
40 [1]Lit *crowd* [a]Matt 9:1; Mark 5:21
41 [1]Lit *ruler* [a]Luke 8:41-56: *Matt 9:18-26; Mark 5:22-43* [b]Mark 5:22; Luke 8:49
42 [1]Or *only begotten*
44 [1]Or *outer garment*
45 [1]Lit *crowds* [a]Luke 5:5

Me, for I was aware that [a]power had
gone out of Me."
47 When the woman saw that she had
not escaped notice, she came trembling
and fell down before Him, and declared
in the presence of all the people the reason why she had touched Him, and how
she had been immediately healed.
48 And He said to her, "Daughter,
[a]your faith has [1]made you well; [b]go in
peace."
49 ¶ While He was still speaking,
someone *came from *the house of* [a]the
synagogue official, saying, "Your daughter has died; do not trouble the Teacher
anymore."
50 But when Jesus heard *this,* He answered him, "[a]Do not be afraid *any longer*; only believe, and she will be [1]made
well."
51 When He came to the house, He
did not allow anyone to enter with Him,
except Peter and John and James, and the
girl's father and mother.
52 Now they were all weeping and
[a]lamenting for her; but He said, "Stop
weeping, for she has not died, but [b]is
asleep."
53 And they *began* laughing at Him,
knowing that she had died.
54 He, however, took her by the hand
and called, saying, "Child, arise!"
55 And her spirit returned, and she got
up immediately; and He gave orders for
something to be given her to eat.
56 Her parents were amazed; but He
[a]instructed them to tell no one what had
happened.

Ministry of the Twelve

9 [a]And He called the twelve together,
and gave them power and authority
over all the demons and to heal diseases.
2 And He sent them out to [a]proclaim
the kingdom of God and to perform healing.
3 And He said to them, "[a]Take nothing for *your* journey, [b]neither a staff, nor
a [1]bag, nor bread, nor money; and do not
even have [2]two tunics apiece.
4 "Whatever house you enter, stay
there [1]until you leave that city.
5 "And as for those who do not receive
you, as you go out from that city, [a]shake
the dust off your feet as a testimony
against them."
6 Departing, they *began* going
[1]throughout the villages, [a]preaching the
gospel and healing everywhere.
7 ¶ [a]Now [b]Herod the tetrarch heard
of all that was happening; and he was
greatly perplexed, because it was said by
some that [c]John had risen from the dead,
8 and by some that [a]Elijah had appeared, and by others that one of the
prophets of old had risen again.
9 Herod said, "I myself had John beheaded; but who is this man about whom
I hear such things?" And [a]he kept trying
to see Him.
10 ¶ [a]When the apostles returned,
they gave an account to Him of all that
they had done. [b]Taking them with Him,
He withdrew by Himself to a city called
[c]Bethsaida.
11 But the crowds were aware of this
and followed Him; and welcoming them,
He *began* speaking to them about the
kingdom of God and curing those who
had need of healing.

Five Thousand Fed

12 ¶ Now the day [1]was ending, and
the twelve came and said to Him, "Send
the crowd away, that they may go into
the surrounding villages and countryside
and find lodging and get [2]something to
eat; for here we are in a desolate place."
13 But He said to them, "You give
them *something* to eat!" And they said,
"We have no more than five loaves and
two fish, unless perhaps we go and buy
food for all these people."
14 (For there were about five thousand men.) And He said to His disciples,
"Have them [1]sit down *to eat* [a]in groups
of about fifty each."
15 They did so, and had them all [1]sit
down.
16 Then He took the five loaves and
the two fish, and looking up to heaven,
He blessed them, and broke *them,* and
kept giving *them* to the disciples to set
before the [1]people.
17 And they all ate and were satisfied;
and [1]the broken pieces which they had
left over were picked up, twelve [a]baskets
full.
18 ¶ [a]And it happened that while He
was [b]praying alone, the disciples were
with Him, and He questioned them, saying, "Who do the [1]people say that I am?"
19 They answered and said, "John the
Baptist, and others *say* Elijah; but others,
that one of the prophets of old has risen
again."
20 And He said to them, "But who do
you say that I am?" And Peter answered
and said, "[a]The [1]Christ of God."
21 But He [1a]warned them and instructed *them* not to tell this to anyone,
22 [a]saying, "[b]The Son of Man must
suffer many things and be rejected by the
elders and chief priests and scribes, and
be killed and be raised up on the third
day."
23 ¶ And He was saying to *them* all,
"[a]If anyone wishes to come after Me, he

8:46 [a]Luke 5:17
48 [1]Or *saved you* [a]Matt 9:22 [b]Mark 5:34; Luke 7:50
49 [a]Luke 8:41
50 [1]Or *saved* [a]Mark 5:36
52 [a]Matt 11:17; Luke 23:27 [b]John 11:13
56 [a]Matt 8:4
9:1 [a]Matt 10:5; Mark 6:7
2 [a]Matt 10:7
3 [1]Or *knapsack* or *beggar's bag* [2]Or *inner garments* [a]Luke 9:3-5: *Matt 10:9-15; Mark 6:8-11*; Luke 10:4-12; 22:35 [b]Matt 10:10; Mark 6:8; Luke 22:35f
4 [1]Lit *and leave from there*
5 [a]Luke 10:11; Acts 13:51
6 [1]Or *from village to village* [a]Mark 6:12; Luke 8:1
7 [a]Luke 9:7-9: *Matt 14:1,2;* Mark 6:14f [b]Matt 14:1; Luke 3:1; 13:31; 23:7 [c]Matt 14:2
8 [a]Matt 16:14
9 [a]Luke 23:8
10 [a]Mark 6:30 [b]Luke 9:10-17: *Matt 14:13-21; Mark 6:32-44; John 6:5-13* [c]Matt 11:21
12 [1]Lit *began to decline* [2]Lit *provisions*
14 [1]Lit *recline* [a]Mark 6:39
15 [1]Lit *recline*
16 [1]Lit *crowd*
17 [1]Lit *that which was left over to them of the broken pieces was* [a]Matt 14:20
18 [1]Lit *crowds* [a]Luke 9:18-20: *Matt 16:13-16; Mark 8:27-29* [b]Matt 14:23; Luke 6:12; 9:28
20 [1]I.e. Messiah [a]John 6:68f
21 [1]Or *strictly admonished* [a]Matt 8:4; 16:20; Mark 8:30
22 [a]Luke 9:22-27: *Matt 16:21-28; Mark 8:31-9:1* [b]Matt 16:21; Luke 9:44
23 [a]Matt 10:38; Luke 14:27

must deny himself, and take up his cross
daily and follow Me.
24 "For [a]whoever wishes to save his
[1]life will lose it, but whoever loses his
[1]life for My sake, he is the one who will
save it.
25 "For what is a man profited if he
gains the whole world, and [a]loses or forfeits himself?
26 "[a]For whoever is ashamed of Me
and My words, the Son of Man will be
ashamed of him when He comes in His
glory, and *the glory* of the Father and of
the holy angels.
27 "But I say to you truthfully, [a]there
are some of those standing here who will
not taste death until they see the kingdom of God."

The Transfiguration

28 ¶ [a]Some eight days after these sayings, He took along [b]Peter and John and
James, and [c]went up on the mountain
[d]to pray.
29 And while He was [a]praying, the
appearance of His face [b]became different, and His clothing *became* white *and*
[1]gleaming.
30 And behold, two men were talking
with Him; and they were Moses and Elijah,
31 who, appearing in [1]glory, were
speaking of His [a]departure which He
was about to accomplish at Jerusalem.
32 Now Peter and his companions
[a]had been overcome with sleep; but
when they were fully awake, they saw
His glory and the two men standing with
Him.
33 And as [1]these were leaving Him,
Peter said to Jesus, "[a]Master, it is good
for us to be here; [b]let us make three
[2]tabernacles: one for You, and one for
Moses, and one for Elijah"—[c]not realizing what he was saying.
34 While he was saying this, a cloud
[1]formed and *began* to overshadow them;
and they were afraid as they entered the
cloud.
35 Then [a]a voice came out of the
cloud, saying, "[b]This is My Son, *My* Chosen One; listen to Him!"
36 And when the voice [1]had spoken,
Jesus was found alone. And [a]they kept
silent, and reported to no one in those
days any of the things which they had
seen.
37 ¶ [a]On the next day, when they
came down from the mountain, a large
crowd met Him.
38 And a man from the crowd shouted, saying, "Teacher, I beg You to look at
my son, for he is my [1]only *boy,*
39 and a spirit seizes him, and he suddenly screams, and it throws him into a
convulsion with foaming *at the mouth*;
and only with difficulty does it leave him,
mauling him *as it leaves*.
40 "I begged Your disciples to cast it
out, and they could not."
41 And Jesus answered and said, "You
unbelieving and perverted generation,
how long shall I be with you and put up
with you? Bring your son here."
42 While he was still approaching, the
demon [1]slammed him *to the ground* and
threw him into a convulsion. But Jesus
rebuked the unclean spirit, and healed
the boy and gave him back to his father.
43 And they were all amazed at the
[1][a]greatness of God.
¶ [b]But while everyone was marveling
at all that He was doing, He said to His
disciples,
44 "Let these words sink into your ears;
[a]for the Son of Man is going to be [1]deliv-
ered into the hands of men."
45 But [a]they [1]did not understand this
statement, and it was concealed from
them so that they would not perceive it;
and they were afraid to ask Him about
this statement.

The Test of Greatness

46 ¶ [a]An argument [1]started among
them as to which of them might be the
greatest.
47 But Jesus, [a]knowing [1]what they
were thinking in their heart, took a child
and stood him by His side,
48 and said to them, "[a]Whoever receives this child in My name receives
Me, and whoever receives Me receives
Him who sent Me; [b]for the one who is
least among all of you, this is the one who
is great."
49 ¶ [a]John answered and said,
"[b]Master, we saw someone casting out
demons in Your name; and we tried to
prevent him because he does not follow
along with us."
50 But Jesus said to him, "Do not hinder *him;* [a]for he who is not against you
is [1]for you."
51 ¶ When the days were approaching
for [a]His [1]ascension, He [2]was determined [b]to go to Jerusalem;
52 and He sent messengers on ahead
of Him, and they went and entered a village of the [a]Samaritans to [1]make ar-
rangements for Him.
53 But they did not receive Him, [a]be-
cause [1]He was traveling toward Jerusalem.
54 When His disciples [a]James and
John saw *this,* they said, "Lord, do You
want us to [b]command fire to come down
from heaven and consume them?"

24 [1]Or *soul* [a]Matt 10:39; Luke 17:33; John 12:25
25 [a]Heb 10:34
26 [a]Matt 10:33; Luke 12:9
27 [a]Matt 16:28
28 [a]Luke 9:28-36: *Matt 17:1-8; Mark 9:2-8* [b]Matt 17:1 [c]Matt 5:1 [d]Luke 3:21; 5:16; 6:12; 9:18
29 [1]Lit *flashing like lightning* [a]Luke 3:21; 5:16; 6:12; 9:18 [b]Mark 16:12
31 [1]Or *splendor* [a]2 Pet 1:15
32 [a]Matt 26:43; Mark 14:40
33 [1]Lit *they* [2]Or *sacred tents* [a]Luke 5:5; 9:49 [b]Matt 17:4; Mark 9:5 [c]Mark 9:6
34 [1]Lit *occurred*
35 [a]2 Pet 1:17f [b]Is 42:1; Matt 3:17; 12:18; Mark 1:11; Luke 3:22
36 [1]Lit *occurred* [a]Matt 17:9; Mark 9:9f
37 [a]Luke 9:37-42: *Matt 17:14-18; Mark 9:14-27*
38 [1]Or *only begotten*
42 [1]Or *tore him*
43 [1]Or *majesty* [a]2 Pet 1:16 [b]Luke 9:43-45: *Matt 17:22f; Mark 9:30-32*
44 [1]Or *betrayed* [a]Luke 9:22
45 [1]Lit *were not knowing* [a]Mark 9:32
46 [1]Lit *entered in* [a]Luke 9:46-48: *Matt 18:1-5; Mark 9:33-37*; Luke 22:24
47 [1]Lit *the reasoning*; or *argument* [a]Matt 9:4
48 [a]Matt 10:40; Luke 10:16; John 13:20 [b]Luke 22:26
49 [a]Luke 9:49, 50: *Mark 9:38-40* [b]Luke 5:5; 9:33
50 [1]Or *on your side* [a]Matt 12:30; Luke 11:23
51 [1]Lit *taking up* [2]Lit *set His face* [a]Mark 16:19 [b]Luke 13:22; 17:11; 18:31; 19:11,28
52 [1]Or *prepare* [a]Matt 10:5; Luke 10:33; 17:16; John 4:4
53 [1]Lit *His face was proceeding toward* [a]John 4:9
54 [a]Mark 3:17 [b]2 Kin 1:9-16

55 But He turned and rebuked them, [[1]and said, "You do not know what kind of spirit you are of;

56 for the Son of Man did not come to destroy men's lives, but to save them."] And they went on to another village.

Exacting Discipleship

57 ¶ [a]As they were going along the road, [b]someone said to Him, "I will follow You wherever You go."

58 And Jesus said to him, "The foxes have holes and the birds of the [1]air *have* [2]nests, but [a]the Son of Man has nowhere to lay His head."

59 And He said to another, "[a]Follow Me." But he said, "Lord, permit me first to go and bury my father."

60 But He said to him, "Allow the dead to bury their own dead; but as for you, go and [a]proclaim everywhere the kingdom of God."

61 Another also said, "I will follow You, Lord; but [a]first permit me to say good-bye to those at home."

62 But Jesus said to him, "[a]No one, after putting his hand to the plow and looking back, is fit for the kingdom of God."

The Seventy Sent Out

10 Now after this [a]the Lord appointed [1]seventy [b]others, and sent them [c]in pairs ahead of Him to every city and place where He Himself was going to come.

2 And He was saying to them, "[a]The harvest is plentiful, but the laborers are few; therefore beseech the Lord of the harvest to send out laborers into His harvest.

3 "Go; [a]behold, I send you out as lambs in the midst of wolves.

4 "[a]Carry no money belt, no [1]bag, no shoes; and greet no one on the way.

5 "Whatever house you enter, first say, 'Peace *be* to this house.'

6 "If a [1]man of peace is there, your peace will rest on him; but if not, it will return to you.

7 "Stay in [1]that house, eating and drinking [2]what they give you; for [a]the laborer is worthy of his wages. Do not keep moving from house to house.

8 "Whatever city you enter and they receive you, [a]eat what is set before you;

9 and heal those in it who are sick, and say to them, '[a]The kingdom of God has come near to you.'

10 "But whatever city you enter and they do not receive you, go out into its streets and say,

11 '[a]Even the dust of your city which clings to our feet we wipe off *in protest* against you; yet [1]be sure of this, that [b]the kingdom of God has come near.'

12 "I say to you, [a]it will be more tolerable in that day for [b]Sodom than for that city.

13 ¶ "[a]Woe to you, [b]Chorazin! Woe to you, [b]Bethsaida! For if the [1]miracles had been performed in [b]Tyre and Sidon which occurred in you, they would have repented long ago, sitting in [2c]sackcloth and ashes.

14 "But it will be more tolerable for [a]Tyre and Sidon in the judgment than for you.

15 "And you, [a]Capernaum, will not be exalted to heaven, will you? You will be brought down to Hades!

16 ¶ "[a]The one who listens to you listens to Me, and [b]the one who rejects you rejects Me; and he who rejects Me rejects the One who sent Me."

The Happy Results

17 ¶ The [1]seventy returned with joy, saying, "Lord, even [a]the demons are subject to us in Your name."

18 And He said to them, "I was watching [a]Satan fall from heaven like lightning.

19 "Behold, I have given you authority to [a]tread on serpents and scorpions, and over all the power of the enemy, and nothing will injure you.

20 "Nevertheless do not rejoice in this, that the spirits are subject to you, but rejoice that [a]your names are recorded in heaven."

21 ¶ [a]At that very [1]time He rejoiced greatly in the Holy Spirit, and said, "I [2]praise You, O Father, Lord of heaven and earth, that You have hidden these things from *the* wise and intelligent and have revealed them to infants. Yes, Father, for this way was well-pleasing in Your sight.

22 "[a]All things have been handed over to Me by My Father, and [b]no one knows who the Son is except the Father, and who the Father is except the Son, and anyone to whom the Son wills to reveal *Him.*"

23 ¶ [a]Turning to the disciples, He said privately, "Blessed *are* the eyes which see the things you see,

24 for I say to you, that many prophets and kings wished to see the things which you see, and did not see *them,* and to hear the things which you hear, and did not hear *them.*"

25 ¶ [a]And a [1b]lawyer stood up and put Him to the test, saying, "Teacher, what shall I do to inherit eternal life?"

26 And He said to him, "What is writ-

55 [1]Early mss do not contain bracketed portion
57 [a]Luke 9:51 [b]Luke 9:57-60: *Matt 8:19-22*
58 [1]Or *sky* [2]Or *roosting-places* [a]Matt 8:20
59 [a]Matt 8:22
60 [a]Matt 4:23
61 [a]1 Kin 19:20
62 [a]Phil 3:13
10:1 [1]Some mss read *seventy-two* [a]Luke 7:13 [b]Luke 9:1f,52 [c]Mark 6:7
2 [a]Matt 9:37,38; John 4:35
3 [a]Matt 10:16
4 [1]Or *knapsack* or *beggar's bag* [a]Matt 10:9-14; Mark 6:8-11; Luke 9:3-5; 10:4-12
6 [1]Lit *son of peace*; i.e. a person inclined toward peace
7 [1]Lit *the house itself* [2]Lit *the things from them* [a]Matt 10:10; 1 Cor 9:14; 1 Tim 5:18
8 [a]1 Cor 10:27
9 [a]Matt 3:2; 10:7; Luke 10:11
11 [1]Lit *know* [a]Matt 10:14; Mark 6:11; Luke 9:5; Acts 13:51 [b]Matt 3:2; 10:7; Luke 10:9
12 [a]Gen 19:24-28; Matt 10:15; 11:24 [b]Matt 10:15
13 [1]Or *works of power* [2]Symbols of mourning [a]Luke 10:13-15: *Matt 11:21-23* [b]Is 23:1-18; Ezek 26:1-28:26; Joel 3:4-8; Matt 11:21 [c]Rev 11:3
14 [a]Matt 11:21
15 [a]Is 14:13-15; Matt 4:13; 11:23
16 [a]Matt 10:40; Mark 9:37; Luke 9:48; John 13:20; Gal 4:14 [b]John 12:48; 1 Thess 4:8
17 [1]Some mss read *seventy-two* [a]Mark 16:17
18 [a]Matt 4:10
19 [a]Ps 91:13; Mark 16:18
20 [a]Ex 32:32; Ps 69:28; Is 4:3; Ezek 13:9; Dan 12:1; Phil 4:3; Heb 12:23; Rev 3:5; 13:8; 17:8; 20:12,15; 21:27
21 [1]Lit *hour* [2]Or *acknowledge to You* [a]Luke 10:21,22: *Matt 11:25-27*
22 [a]John 3:35 [b]John 10:15
23 [a]Luke 10:23, 24: *Matt 13:16, 17*
25 [1]I.e. an expert in the Mosaic Law [a]Luke 10:25-28: *Matt 22:34-40; Mark 12:28-31*; Matt 19:16-19 [b]Matt 22:35

ten in the Law? [1]How does it read to
you?"
27 And he answered, "[a]YOU SHALL
LOVE THE LORD YOUR GOD WITH ALL YOUR
HEART, AND WITH ALL YOUR SOUL, AND WITH
ALL YOUR STRENGTH, AND WITH ALL YOUR
MIND; AND YOUR NEIGHBOR AS YOURSELF."
28 And He said to him, "You have answered correctly; [a]DO THIS AND YOU WILL
LIVE."
29 But wishing [a]to justify himself, he
said to Jesus, "And who is my neighbor?"

The Good Samaritan

30 Jesus replied and said, "A man was
[a]going down from Jerusalem to Jericho,
and fell among robbers, and they stripped
him and [1]beat him, and went away leaving him half dead.
31 "And by chance a priest was going
down on that road, and when he saw
him, he passed by on the other side.
32 "Likewise a Levite also, when he
came to the place and saw him, passed by
on the other side.
33 "But a [a]Samaritan, who was on a
journey, came upon him; and when he
saw him, he felt compassion,
34 and came to him and bandaged up
his wounds, pouring oil and wine on
them; and he put him on his own beast,
and brought him to an inn and took care
of him.
35 "On the next day he took out two
[1]denarii and gave them to the innkeeper
and said, 'Take care of him; and whatever
more you spend, when I return I will repay you.'
36 "Which of these three do you think
proved to be a neighbor to the man who
fell into the robbers' *hands?*"
37 And he said, "The one who showed
mercy toward him." Then Jesus said to
him, "Go and do [1]the same."

Martha and Mary

38 ¶ Now as they were traveling
along, He entered a village; and a woman
named [a]Martha welcomed Him into her
home.
39 She had a sister called [a]Mary, who
was [b]seated at the Lord's feet, listening
to His word.
40 But [a]Martha was distracted with
[1]all her preparations; and she came up *to*
Him and said, "Lord, do You not care that
my sister has left me to do all the serving
alone? Then tell her to help me."
41 But the Lord answered and said to
her, "[a]Martha, Martha, you are [b]wor-
ried and bothered about so many things;
42 [a]but *only* one thing is necessary,
for [b]Mary has chosen the good part,
which shall not be taken away from her."

Instruction about Prayer

11 It happened that while [1]Jesus
was praying in a certain place, after He had finished, one of His disciples
said to Him, "Lord, teach us to pray just
as John also taught his disciples."
2 And He said to them, "[a]When you
pray, say:
'[1]Father, hallowed be Your
name.
Your kingdom come.
3 'Give us [a]each day our [1]daily
bread.
4 'And forgive us our sins,
For we ourselves also forgive
everyone who [a]is indebted
to us.
And lead us not into
temptation.' "
5 ¶ Then He said to them, "[1]Sup-
pose one of you has a friend, and goes to
him at midnight and says to him, 'Friend,
lend me three loaves;
6 for a friend of mine has come to me
from a journey, and I have nothing to set
before him';
7 and from inside he answers and
says, 'Do not bother me; the door has
already been shut and my children [1]and
I are in bed; I cannot get up and give you
anything.'
8 "I tell you, even though he will not
get up and give him *anything* because he
is his friend, yet [a]because of his [1]persis-
tence he will get up and give him as much
as he needs.
9 ¶ "So I say to you, [1a]ask, and it
will be given to you; [2]seek, and you will
find; [3]knock, and it will be opened to
you.
10 "For everyone who asks, receives;
and he who seeks, finds; and to him who
knocks, it will be opened.
11 "Now [1]suppose one of you fathers is
asked by his son for a [2]fish; he will not
give him a snake instead of a fish,
will he?
12 "Or *if* he is asked for an egg, he will
not give him a scorpion, will he?
13 "[a]If you then, being evil, know how
to give good gifts to your children, how
much more will *your* [1]heavenly Father
give the Holy Spirit to those who ask
Him?"

Pharisees' Blasphemy

14 ¶ [a]And He was casting out a demon, and it was mute; when the demon
had gone out, the mute man spoke; and
the crowds were amazed.
15 But some of them said, "He casts
out demons [a]by [b]Beelzebul, the ruler of
the demons."

26 [1]Lit *How do you read?*
27 [a]Deut 6:5; Lev 19:18
28 [a]Lev 18:5; Ezek 20:11; Matt 19:17
29 [a]Luke 16:15
30 [1]Lit *laid blows upon* [a]Luke 18:31; 19:28
33 [a]Matt 10:5; Luke 9:52
35 [1]The denarius was equivalent to a day's wages
37 [1]Or *likewise*
38 [a]Luke 10:40f; John 11:1,5,19ff,30, 39; 12:2
39 [a]Luke 10:42; John 11:1f,19f, 28,31f,45; 12:3 [b]Luke 8:35; Acts 22:3
40 [1]Lit *much service* [a]Luke 10:38,41; John 11:1,5,19ff,30, 39; 12:2
41 [a]Luke 10:38, 40; John 11:1,5, 19ff,30,39; 12:2 [b]Matt 6:25
42 [a]Ps 27:4; John 6:27 [b]Luke 10:39; John 11:1f,19f,28,31f, 45; 12:3
11:1 [1]Lit *He*
2 [1]Later mss add phrases from Matt 6:9-13 to make the two passages closely similar [a]Luke 11:2-4: *Matt 6:9-13*
3 [1]Or *bread for the coming day* or *needful bread* [a]Acts 17:11
4 [a]Luke 13:4 mg
5 [1]Lit *Which one of you will have*
7 [1]Lit *with me*
8 [1]Lit *shamelessness* [a]Luke 18:1-5
9 [1]Or *keep asking* [2]Or *keep seeking* [3]Or *keep knocking* [a]Luke 11:9-13: *Matt 7:7-11*
11 [1]Lit *which of you, a son, will ask the father* [2]Two early mss insert *loaf, he will not give him a stone, will he, or for a*
13 [1]Lit *Father from heaven* [a]Matt 7:11; Luke 18:7f
14 [a]Luke 11:14, 15: *Matt 12:22, 24*; Matt 9:32-34
15 [a]Matt 9:34 [b]Matt 10:25

16 Others, [1]to test *Him,* [a]were demanding of Him a [2]sign from heaven.

17 [a]But He knew their thoughts and said to them, "[1]Any kingdom divided against itself is laid waste; and a house *divided* against [2]itself falls.

18 "If [a]Satan also is divided against himself, how will his kingdom stand? For you say that I cast out demons by [b]Beelzebul.

19 "And if I by [a]Beelzebul cast out demons, by whom do your sons cast them out? So they will be your judges.

20 "But if I cast out demons by the [a]finger of God, then [b]the kingdom of God has come upon you.

21 "When [1]a strong *man,* fully armed, guards his own house, his possessions are [2]undisturbed.

22 "But when someone stronger than he attacks him and overpowers him, he takes away from him all his armor on which he had relied and distributes his plunder.

23 "[a]He who is not with Me is against Me; and he who does not gather with Me, scatters.

24 ¶ "[a]When the unclean spirit goes out of [1]a man, it passes through waterless places seeking rest, and not finding any, it says, 'I will return to my house from which I came.'

25 "And when it comes, it finds it swept and put in order.

26 "Then it goes and takes *along* seven other spirits more evil than itself, and they go in and live there; and the last state of that man becomes worse than the first."

27 ¶ While [1]Jesus was saying these things, one of the women in the crowd raised her voice and said to Him, "[a]Blessed is the womb that bore You and the breasts at which You nursed."

28 But He said, "On the contrary, blessed are [a]those who hear the word of God and observe it."

The Sign of Jonah

29 ¶ As the crowds were increasing, He began to say, "[a]This generation is a wicked generation; it [b]seeks for a [1]sign, and *yet* no [1]sign will be given to it but the [1]sign of Jonah.

30 "For just as [a]Jonah became a [1]sign to the Ninevites, so will the Son of Man be to this generation.

31 "The [a]Queen of the South will rise up with the men of this generation at the judgment and condemn them, because she came from the ends of the earth to hear the wisdom of Solomon; and behold, something greater than Solomon is here.

32 "The men of Nineveh will stand up with this generation at the judgment and condemn it, because [a]they repented at the preaching of Jonah; and behold, something greater than Jonah is here.

33 ¶ "[a]No one, after lighting a lamp, puts it away in a cellar nor under a basket, but on the lampstand, so that those who enter may see the light.

34 "[a]The eye is the lamp of your body; when your eye is [1]clear, your whole body also is full of light; but when it is [2]bad, your body also is full of darkness.

35 "Then watch out that the light in you is not darkness.

36 "If therefore your whole body is full of light, with no dark part in it, it will be wholly illumined, as when the lamp illumines you with its rays."

Woes upon the Pharisees

37 ¶ Now when He had spoken, a Pharisee *asked Him to have lunch with him; and He went in, and reclined *at the table.*

38 When the Pharisee saw it, he was surprised that He had not first [1a]ceremonially washed before the [2]meal.

39 But [a]the Lord said to him, "Now [b]you Pharisees clean the outside of the cup and of the platter; but [1]inside of you, you are full of robbery and wickedness.

40 "[a]You foolish ones, did not He who made the outside make the inside also?

41 "But [a]give that which is within as charity, and [1]then all things are [b]clean for you.

42 ¶ "[a]But woe to you Pharisees! For you [b]pay tithe of mint and rue and every *kind of* garden herb, and *yet* disregard justice and the love of God; but these are the things you should have done without neglecting the others.

43 "Woe to you Pharisees! For you [a]love the chief seats in the synagogues and the respectful greetings in the market places.

44 "[a]Woe to you! For you are like [1]concealed tombs, and the people who walk over *them* are unaware *of it.*"

45 ¶ One of the [1a]lawyers *said to Him in reply, "Teacher, when You say this, You insult us too."

46 But He said, "Woe to you [a]lawyers as well! For [b]you weigh men down with burdens hard to bear, [1]while you yourselves will not even touch the burdens with one of your fingers.

47 "[a]Woe to you! For you build the [1]tombs of the prophets, and *it was* your fathers *who* killed them.

48 "So you are witnesses and approve the deeds of your fathers; because it was they who killed them, and you build *their tombs.*

16 [1]Lit *testing* [2]Or *attesting miracle* [a]Matt 12:38; 16:1; Mark 8:11

17 [1]Lit *every* [2]Lit *a house* [a]Luke 11:17-22: *Matt 12:25-29; Mark 3:23-27*

18 [a]Matt 4:10 [b]Matt 10:25

19 [a]Matt 10:25

20 [a]Ex 8:19 [b]Matt 3:2

21 [1]Lit *the* [2]Lit *in peace*

23 [a]Matt 12:30; Mark 9:40

24 [1]Lit *the* [a]Luke 11:24-26: *Matt 12:43-45*

27 [1]Lit *He* [a]Luke 23:29

28 [a]Luke 8:21

29 [1]Or *attesting miracle* [a]Luke 11:29-32: *Matt 12:39-42;* Matt 16:4; Mark 8:12 [b]Matt 12:38; Luke 11:16

30 [1]Or *attesting miracle* [a]Jon 3:4

31 [a]1 Kin 10:1-10; 2 Chr 9:1-12

32 [a]Jon 3:5

33 [a]Matt 5:15; Mark 4:21; Luke 8:16

34 [1]Or *healthy* [2]Or *evil* [a]Luke 11:34,35: *Matt 6:22,23*

38 [1]Lit *baptized* [2]Or *lunch* [a]Matt 15:2; Mark 7:3f

39 [1]Lit *your inside is full* [a]Luke 7:13 [b]Matt 23:25f

40 [a]Luke 12:20; 1 Cor 15:36

41 [1]Lit *behold* [a]Luke 12:33; 16:9 [b]Mark 7:19; Titus 1:15

42 [a]Matt 23:23 [b]Lev 27:30; Luke 18:12

43 [a]Matt 23:6f; Mark 12:38f; Luke 14:7; 20:46

44 [1]Or *indistinct, unseen* [a]Matt 23:27

45 [1]I.e. experts in the Mosaic Law [a]Matt 22:35; Luke 11:46,52

46 [1]Lit *and* [a]Matt 22:35; Luke 11:45,52 [b]Matt 23:4

47 [1]Or *monuments to* [a]Matt 23:29ff

49 "For this reason also [a]the wisdom of
God said, '[b]I will send to them prophets
and apostles, and *some* of them they will
kill and *some* they will [1]persecute,
50 so that the blood of all the prophets,
shed [a]since the foundation of the world,
may be [1]charged against this generation,
51 from [a]the blood of Abel to [b]the
blood of Zechariah, who was killed between the altar and the house *of God*;
yes, I tell you, it shall be [1]charged against
this generation.'
52 "Woe to you [1a]lawyers! For you
have taken away the key of knowledge;
[b]you yourselves did not enter, and you
hindered those who were entering."
53 ¶ When He left there, the scribes
and the Pharisees began to be very hostile
and to question Him closely on many subjects,
54 [a]plotting against Him [b]to catch
[1]*Him* in something He might say.

God Knows and Cares

12 Under these circumstances, after
[1]so many thousands of [2]people
had gathered together that they were
stepping on one another, He began saying
to His disciples first *of all*, "[a]Beware of
the leaven of the Pharisees, which is hypocrisy.
2 "[a]But there is nothing covered up
that will not be revealed, and hidden that
will not be known.
3 "Accordingly, whatever you have
said in the dark will be heard in the light,
and what you have [1]whispered in the
inner rooms will be proclaimed upon
[a]the housetops.
4 ¶ "I say to you, [a]My friends, do not
be afraid of those who kill the body and
after that have no more that they can do.
5 "But I will [1]warn you whom to fear:
[a]fear the One who, after He has killed,
has authority to cast into [2b]hell; yes, I
tell you, fear Him!
6 "Are not [a]five sparrows sold for two
[1]cents? *Yet* not one of them is forgotten
before God.
7 "[a]Indeed, the very hairs of your
head are all numbered. Do not fear; you
are more valuable than many sparrows.
8 ¶ "And I say to you, everyone who
[a]confesses Me before men, the Son of
Man will confess him also before the angels of God;
9 but [a]he who denies Me before
men will be denied [b]before the angels of
God.
10 "[a]And everyone who [1]speaks a
word against the Son of Man, it will be
forgiven him; but he who blasphemes
against the Holy Spirit, it will not be forgiven him.
11 "When they bring you before [a]the
synagogues and the rulers and the authorities, do not [b]worry about how or what
you are to speak in your defense, or what
you are to say;
12 for [a]the Holy Spirit will teach you
in that very hour what you ought to say."

Covetousness Denounced

13 ¶ Someone [1]in the crowd said to
Him, "Teacher, tell my brother to divide
the *family* inheritance with me."
14 But He said to him, "[a]Man, who
appointed Me a judge or arbitrator over
you?"
15 Then He said to them, "[a]Beware,
and be on your guard against every form
of greed; for not *even* when one has an
abundance does his life consist of his possessions."
16 And He told them a parable, saying,
"The land of a rich man was very productive.
17 "And he began reasoning to himself,
saying, 'What shall I do, since I have no
place to store my crops?'
18 "Then he said, 'This is what I will
do: I will tear down my barns and build
larger ones, and there I will store all my
grain and my goods.
19 'And I will say to my soul, "Soul,
[a]you have many goods laid up for many
years *to come*; take your ease, eat, drink
and be merry." '
20 "But God said to him, '[a]You fool!
This *very* night [1b]your soul is required of
you; and [c]*now* who will own what you
have prepared?'
21 "So is the man who [a]stores up treasure for himself, and is not rich toward
God."
22 ¶ And He said to His disciples,
"[a]For this reason I say to you, [1]do not
worry about *your* [2]life, *as to* what you
will eat; nor for your body, *as to* what you
will put on.
23 "For life is more than food, and the
body more than clothing.
24 "Consider the [a]ravens, for they neither sow nor reap; they have no storeroom nor [b]barn, and *yet* God feeds them;
how much more valuable you are than
the birds!
25 "And which of you by worrying can
add a *single* [1a]hour to his [2]life's span?
26 "If then you cannot do even a very
little thing, why do you worry about other
matters?
27 "Consider the lilies, how they grow:
they neither toil nor spin; but I tell you,
not even [a]Solomon in all his glory
clothed himself like one of these.
28 "But if God so clothes the grass in
the field, which is *alive* today and tomor-

49 [1]Or *drive out* [a]1 Cor 1:24,30; Col 2:3 [b]Matt 23:34-36
50 [1]Or *required of* [a]Matt 25:34
51 [1]Or *required of* [a]Gen 4:8 [b]2 Chr 24:20,21
52 [1]I.e. experts in the Mosaic Law [a]Matt 22:35; Luke 11:45,46 [b]Matt 23:13
54 [1]Lit *something out of His mouth* [a]Mark 3:2; Luke 20:20; Acts 23:21 [b]Mark 12:13
12:1 [1]Lit *myriads* [2]Lit *the crowd* [a]Matt 16:6,11f; Mark 8:15
2 [a]Luke 12:2-9: *Matt 10:26-33*; Matt 10:26; Mark 4:22; Luke 8:17
3 [1]Lit *spoken in the ear* [a]Matt 10:27; 24:17
4 [a]John 15:13-15
5 [1]Or *show* [2]Gr *Gehenna* [a]Heb 10:31 [b]Matt 5:22
6 [1]Gr *assaria*, the smallest of copper coins [a]Matt 10:29
7 [a]Matt 10:30
8 [a]Matt 10:32; Luke 15:10; Rom 10:9
9 [a]Matt 10:33; Luke 9:26 [b]Luke 15:10
10 [1]Lit *will speak* [a]Matt 12:31,32; Mark 3:28-30
11 [a]Matt 10:17 [b]Matt 6:25; 10:19; Mark 13:11; Luke 12:22; 21:14
12 [a]Matt 10:20; Luke 21:15
13 [1]Lit *out of*
14 [a]Mic 6:8; Rom 2:1,3; 9:20
15 [a]1 Tim 6:6-10
19 [a]Eccl 11:9
20 [1]Lit *they are demanding your soul from you* [a]Jer 17:11; Luke 11:40 [b]Job 27:8 [c]Ps 39:6
21 [a]Luke 12:33
22 [1]Or *stop being worried* [2]Lit *soul* [a]Luke 12:22-31: *Matt 6:25-33*
24 [a]Job 38:41 [b]Luke 12:18
25 [1]Lit *cubit* (approx 18 in.) [2]Or *height* [a]Ps 39:5
27 [a]1 Kin 10:4-7; 2 Chr 9:3-6

row is thrown into the furnace, how
much more *will He clothe* you? [a]You
men of little faith!
29 "And do not seek what you will eat
and what you will drink, and do not
[a]keep worrying.
30 "For [1]all these things the nations of
the world eagerly seek; but your Father
knows that you need these things.
31 "But seek His kingdom, and [a]these
things will be added to you.
32 "[a]Do not be afraid, [b]little flock, for
[c]your Father has chosen gladly to give
you the kingdom.
33 ¶ "[a]Sell your possessions and give
to charity; make yourselves money belts
which do not wear out, [b]an unfailing
treasure in heaven, where no thief comes
near nor moth destroys.
34 "For [a]where your treasure is, there
your heart will be also.

Be in Readiness

35 ¶ "[1a]Be dressed in [b]readiness, and
keep your lamps lit.
36 "Be like men who are waiting for
their master when he returns from the
wedding feast, so that they may immediately open *the door* to him when he
comes and knocks.
37 "Blessed are those slaves whom the
master will find [a]on the alert when he
comes; truly I say to you, that [b]he will
gird himself *to serve,* and have them recline *at the table,* and will come up and
wait on them.
38 "[a]Whether he comes in the [1]sec-
ond watch, or even in the [2]third, and
finds *them* so, blessed are those *slaves.*
39 ¶ "[a]But [1]be sure of this, that if the
head of the house had known at what
hour the thief was coming, he would not
have allowed his house to be [2b]broken
into.
40 "[a]You too, be ready; for the Son of
Man is coming at an hour that you do not
[1]expect."
41 ¶ Peter said, "Lord, are You addressing this parable to us, or [a]to everyone *else* as well?"
42 And [a]the Lord said, "[b]Who then is
the faithful and sensible [c]steward, whom
his master will put in charge of his [1]ser-
vants, to give them their rations at the
proper time?
43 "Blessed is that [a]slave whom his
[1]master finds so doing when he comes.
44 "Truly I say to you that he will put
him in charge of all his possessions.
45 "But if that slave says in his heart,
'My master [1]will be a long time in coming,' and begins to beat the slaves, *both*
men and women, and to eat and drink
and get drunk;
46 the master of that slave will come
on a day when he does not expect *him*
and at an hour he does not know, and will
cut him in pieces, and assign him a place
with the unbelievers.
47 "And that slave who knew his master's will and did not get ready or act in
accord with his will, will [a]receive many
lashes,
48 but the one who did not [a]know *it,*
and committed deeds worthy of [1]a flog-
ging, will receive but few. [b]From everyone who has been given much, much will
be required; and to whom they entrusted
much, of him they will ask all the more.

Christ Divides Men

49 ¶ "I [1]have come to cast fire upon
the earth; and [2]how I wish it were already kindled!
50 "But I have a [a]baptism to [1]undergo,
and how distressed I am until it is accomplished!
51 "[a]Do you suppose that I came to
grant peace on earth? I tell you, no, but
rather division;
52 for from now on five *members* in
one household will be divided, three
against two and two against three.
53 "They will be divided, [a]father
against son and son against father, mother against daughter and daughter against
mother, mother-in-law against daughter-
in-law and daughter-in-law against
mother-in-law."
54 ¶ And He was also saying to the
crowds, "[a]When you see a cloud rising
in the west, immediately you say, 'A
shower is coming,' and so it turns out.
55 "And when *you see* a south wind
blowing, you say, 'It will be a [a]hot day,'
and it turns out *that way.*
56 "You hypocrites! [a]You know how to
analyze the appearance of the earth and
the sky, but [1]why do you not analyze this
present time?
57 ¶ "And [a]why do you not even on
your own initiative judge what is right?
58 "For [a]while you are going with your
opponent to appear before the magistrate, on *your* way *there* make an effort to
[1]settle with him, so that he may not drag
you before the judge, and the judge turn
you over to the officer, and the officer
throw you into prison.
59 "I say to you, you will not get out of
there until you have paid the very last
[1a]cent."

Call to Repent

13 Now on the same occasion there
were some present who reported
to Him about the Galileans whose blood
[a]Pilate had [1]mixed with their sacrifices.

28 [a]Matt 6:30
29 [a]Matt 6:31
30 [1]Or *these things all the nations of the world*
31 [a]Matt 6:33
32 [a]Matt 14:27 [b]John 21:15-17 [c]Eph 1:5,9
33 [a]Matt 19:21; Luke 11:41; 18:22 [b]Matt 6:20; Luke 12:21
34 [a]Matt 6:21
35 [1]Lit *Let your loins be girded* [a]Matt 25:1ff [b]Eph 6:14; 1 Pet 1:13
37 [a]Matt 24:42 [b]Luke 17:8; John 13:4
38 [1]I.e. 9 p.m. to midnight [2]I.e. midnight to 3 a.m. [a]Matt 24:43
39 [1]Lit *know* [2]Lit *dug through* [a]Luke 12:39,40: *Matt 24:43,44* [b]Matt 6:19
40 [1]Lit *think, suppose* [a]Mark 13:33; Luke 21:36
41 [a]Luke 12:47, 48
42 [1]Lit *service* [a]Luke 7:13 [b]Luke 12:42-46: *Matt 24:45-51* [c]Matt 24:45; Luke 16:1ff
43 [1]Or *lord* [a]Luke 12:42
45 [1]Lit *is delaying to come*
47 [a]Deut 25:2; James 4:17
48 [1]Lit *blows* [a]Lev 5:17; Num 15:29f [b]Matt 13:12
49 [1]Or *came* [2]Lit *what do I wish if...?*
50 [1]Lit *be baptized with* [a]Mark 10:38
51 [a]Luke 12:51-53: *Matt 10:34-36*
53 [a]Mic 7:6; Matt 10:21
54 [a]Matt 16:2f
55 [a]Matt 20:12
56 [1]Lit *how* [a]Matt 16:3
57 [a]Luke 21:30
58 [1]Lit *be released from him* [a]Luke 12:58,59: *Matt 5:25,26*
59 [1]Gr *lepton*; i.e. 1/128 of a denarius [a]Mark 12:42
13:1 [1]I.e. *shed along with* [a]Matt 27

2 And Jesus said to them, “[a]Do you
suppose that these Galileans were *greater*
sinners than all *other* Galileans because
they suffered this *fate?*
3 “I tell you, no, but unless you [1]re-
pent, you will all likewise perish.
4 “Or do you suppose that those eighteen on whom the tower in [a]Siloam fell
and killed them were *worse* [1b]culprits
than all the men who live in Jerusalem?
5 “I tell you, no, but unless you repent, you will all likewise perish.”
6 ¶ And He *began* telling this parable: “A man had [a]a fig tree which had
been planted in his vineyard; and he
came looking for fruit on it and did not
find any.
7 “And he said to the vineyard-keeper,
‘Behold, for three years I have come looking for fruit on this fig tree [1]without finding any. [a]Cut it down! Why does it even
use up the ground?’
8 “And he answered and said to him,
‘Let it alone, sir, for this year too, until I
dig around it and put in fertilizer;
9 and if it bears fruit next year, *fine*;
but if not, cut it down.’ ”

Healing on the Sabbath

10 ¶ And He was [a]teaching in one of
the synagogues on the Sabbath.
11 And there was a woman who for
eighteen years had had [a]a sickness
caused by a spirit; and she was bent double, and could not straighten up at all.
12 When Jesus saw her, He called her
over and said to her, “Woman, you are
freed from your sickness.”
13 And He [a]laid His hands on her; and
immediately she was made erect again
and *began* [b]glorifying God.
14 But [a]the synagogue official, indignant because Jesus [b]had healed on the
Sabbath, *began* saying to the crowd in
response, “[c]There are six days in which
work should be done; so come during
them and get healed, and not on the Sabbath day.”
15 But [a]the Lord answered him and
said, “You hypocrites, [b]does not each of
you on the Sabbath untie his ox or his
donkey from the stall and lead him away
to water *him?*
16 “And this woman, [a]a daughter of
Abraham as she is, whom [b]Satan has
bound for eighteen long years, should she
not have been released from this bond on
the Sabbath day?”
17 As He said this, all His opponents
were being humiliated; and [a]the entire
crowd was rejoicing over all the glorious
things being done by Him.

Parables of Mustard Seed and Leaven

18 ¶ So [a]He was saying, “[b]What is
the kingdom of God like, and to what
shall I compare it?
19 “It is like a mustard seed, which a
man took and threw into his own garden;
and it grew and became a tree, and [a]THE
BIRDS OF THE [1]AIR NESTED IN ITS BRANCHES.”
20 ¶ And again He said, “[a]To what
shall I compare the kingdom of God?
21 “[a]It is like leaven, which a woman
took and hid in [b]three [1]pecks of flour
until it was all leavened.”

Teaching in the Villages

22 ¶ And He was passing through from
one city and village to another, teaching,
and [a]proceeding on His way to Jerusalem.
23 And someone said to Him, “Lord,
are there *just* a few who are being
saved?” And He said to them,
24 “[a]Strive to enter through the narrow door; for many, I tell you, will seek
to enter and will not be able.
25 “Once the head of the house gets up
and [a]shuts the door, and you begin to
stand outside and knock on the door, saying, ‘[b]Lord, open up to us!’ then He will
answer and say to you, ‘[c]I do not know
where you are from.’
26 “Then you will [a]begin to say, ‘We
ate and drank in Your presence, and You
taught in our streets’;
27 and He will say, ‘I tell you, [a]I do
not know where you are from; [b]DEPART
FROM ME, ALL YOU EVILDOERS.’
28 “[a]In that place there will be weeping and gnashing of teeth when you see
Abraham and Isaac and Jacob and all the
prophets in the kingdom of God, but
yourselves being thrown out.
29 “And they [a]will come from east and
west and from north and south, and will
recline *at the table* in the kingdom of
God.
30 “And behold, [a]*some* are last who
will be first and *some* are first who will
be last.”
31 ¶ Just at that time some Pharisees
approached, saying to Him, “Go away,
leave here, for [a]Herod wants to kill
You.”
32 And He said to them, “Go and tell
that fox, ‘Behold, I cast out demons and
perform cures today and tomorrow, and
the third *day* I [1a]reach My goal.’
33 “Nevertheless [a]I must journey on
today and tomorrow and the next *day*; for
it cannot be that a [b]prophet would perish
outside of Jerusalem.
34 “[a]O Jerusalem, Jerusalem, *the city*

---

2 [a]John 9:2f
3 [1]Or *are repentant*
4 [1]Lit *debtors* [a]Neh 3:15; Is 8:6; John 9:7,11 [b]Matt 6:12; Luke 11:4
6 [a]Matt 21:19
7 [1]Lit *and I do not find* [a]Matt 3:10; 7:19; Luke 3:9
10 [a]Matt 4:23
11 [a]Luke 13:16
13 [a]Mark 5:23 [b]Matt 9:8
14 [a]Mark 5:22 [b]Matt 12:2; Luke 14:3 [c]Ex 20:9; Deut 5:13
15 [a]Luke 7:13 [b]Luke 14:5
16 [a]Luke 19:9 [b]Matt 4:10; Luke 13:11
17 [a]Luke 18:43
18 [a]Luke 13:18, 19: *Matt 13:31, 32; Mark 4:30-32* [b]Matt 13:24; Luke 13:20
19 [1]Or *sky* [a]Ezek 17:23
20 [a]Matt 13:24; Luke 13:18
21 [1]Gr *sata* [a]Luke 13:20,21: *Matt 13:33* [b]Matt 13:33
22 [a]Luke 9:51
24 [a]Matt 7:13
25 [a]Matt 25:10 [b]Matt 7:22; 25:11 [c]Matt 7:23; 25:12; Luke 13:27
26 [a]Luke 3:8
27 [a]Luke 13:25 [b]Ps 6:8; Matt 25:41
28 [a]Matt 8:12; 22:13; 25:30
29 [a]Matt 8:11
30 [a]Matt 19:30; 20:16; Mark 10:31
31 [a]Matt 14:1; Luke 3:1; 9:7; 23:7
32 [1]Or *am perfected* [a]Heb 2:10; 5:9; 7:28
33 [a]John 11:9 [b]Matt 21:11
34 [a]Luke 13:34, 35: *Matt 23:37-39*; Luke 19:41

that kills the prophets and stones those
sent to her! How often I wanted to gather
your children together, [b]just as a hen
gathers her brood under her wings, and
you would not *have it!*
35 "Behold, your house is left to you
desolate; and I say to you, you will not see
Me until *the time* comes when you say,
'[a]BLESSED IS HE WHO COMES IN THE NAME
OF THE LORD!' "

Jesus Heals on the Sabbath

14 It happened that when He went
into the house of one of the
[1]leaders of the Pharisees on *the* Sabbath
to eat bread, [a]they were watching Him
closely.
2 And [1]there in front of Him was a
man suffering from dropsy.
3 And Jesus answered and spoke to
the [1a]lawyers and Pharisees, saying,
"[b]Is it lawful to heal on the Sabbath, or
not?"
4 But they kept silent. And He took
hold of him and healed him, and sent him
away.
5 And He said to them, "[1a]Which
one of you will have a son or an ox fall
into a well, and will not immediately pull
him out on a Sabbath day?"
6 [a]And they could make no reply to
this.

Parable of the Guests

7 ¶ And He *began* speaking a parable
to the invited guests when He noticed
how [a]they had been picking out the
places of honor *at the table,* saying to
them,
8 "When you are invited by someone
to a wedding feast, [a]do not [1]take the
place of honor, for someone more distinguished than you may have been invited
by him,
9 and he who invited you both will
come and say to you, 'Give *your* place
to this man,' and then [a]in disgrace you
[1]proceed to occupy the last place.
10 "But when you are invited, go and
recline at the last place, so that when the
one who has invited you comes, he may
say to you, 'Friend, [a]move up higher';
then you will have honor in the sight of
all who [1]are at the table with you.
11 "[a]For everyone who exalts himself
will be humbled, and he who humbles
himself will be exalted."
12 ¶ And He also went on to say to the
one who had invited Him, "When you
give a luncheon or a dinner, do not invite
your friends or your brothers or your relatives or rich neighbors, otherwise they
may also invite you in return and *that* will
be your repayment.
13 "But when you give a [1]reception,
invite *the* poor, *the* crippled, *the* lame,
the blind,
14 and you will be blessed, since they
[1]do not have *the means* to repay you; for
you will be repaid at [a]the resurrection of
the righteous."
15 ¶ When one of those who were reclining *at the table* with Him heard this,
he said to Him, "[a]Blessed is everyone
who will eat bread in the kingdom of
God!"

Parable of the Dinner

16 But He said to him, "[a]A man was
giving a big dinner, and he invited many;
17 and at the dinner hour he sent his
slave to say to those who had been invited, 'Come; for everything is ready now.'
18 "But they all alike began to make
excuses. The first one said to him, 'I have
bought a [1]piece of land and I need to go
out and look at it; [2]please consider me
excused.'
19 "Another one said, 'I have bought
five yoke of oxen, and I am going to try
them out; [1]please consider me excused.'
20 "Another one said, '[a]I have married
a wife, and for that reason I cannot
come.'
21 "And the slave came *back* and reported this to his master. Then the head
of the household became angry and said
to his slave, 'Go out at once into the
streets and lanes of the city and bring in
here the poor and crippled and blind and
lame.'
22 "And the slave said, 'Master, what
you commanded has been done, and still
there is room.'
23 "And the master said to the slave,
'Go out into the highways and along the
hedges, and compel *them* to come in, so
that my house may be filled.
24 'For I tell you, none of those men
who were invited shall taste of my dinner.' "

Discipleship Tested

25 ¶ Now [1]large crowds were going
along with Him; and He turned and said
to them,
26 "[a]If anyone comes to Me, and does
not [1]hate his own father and mother and
wife and children and brothers and sisters, yes, and even his own life, he cannot
be My disciple.
27 "Whoever does not [a]carry his own
cross and come after Me cannot be My
disciple.
28 "For which one of you, when he
wants to build a tower, does not first sit
down and calculate the cost to see if he
has enough to complete it?

34 [b]Matt 23:37
35 [a]Ps 118:26; Matt 21:9; Luke 19:38
14:1 [1]I.e. members of the Sanhedrin [a]Mark 3:2
2 [1]Lit *behold*
3 [1]I.e. experts in Mosaic Law [a]Matt 22:35 [b]Matt 12:2; Luke 13:14
5 [1]Lit *Whose son of you...will fall* [a]Matt 12:11; Luke 13:15
6 [a]Matt 22:46; Luke 20:40
7 [a]Matt 23:6
8 [1]Lit *recline at* [a]Prov 25:6,7
9 [1]Lit *begin* [a]Luke 3:8
10 [1]Lit *recline* at the table [a]Prov 25:6,7
11 [a]2 Sam 22:28; Prov 29:23; Matt 23:12; Luke 1:52; 18:14; James 4:10
13 [1]Or *banquet*
14 [1]Or *are unable to* [a]John 5:29; Acts 24:15; Rev 20:4,5
15 [a]Rev 19:9
16 [a]Matt 22:2-14; Luke 14:16-24
18 [1]Or *field* [2]Lit *I request you*
19 [1]Lit *I request you*
20 [a]Deut 24:5; 1 Cor 7:33
25 [1]Lit *many*
26 [1]I.e. by comparison of his love for Me [a]Matt 10:37
27 [a]Matt 10:38; 16:24; Mark 8:34; Luke 9:23

29"Otherwise, when he has laid a foundation and is not able to finish, all who observe it begin to ridicule him,
30 saying, 'This man began to build and was not able to finish.'
31"Or what king, when he sets out to meet another king in battle, will not first sit down and [a]consider whether he is strong enough with ten thousand *men* to encounter the one coming against him with twenty thousand?
32"Or else, while the other is still far away, he sends [1]a delegation and asks for terms of peace.
33"So then, none of you can be My disciple who [a]does not give up all his own possessions.
34 ¶ "Therefore, salt is good; but [a]if even salt has become tasteless, with what will it be seasoned?
35"It is useless either for the soil or for the manure pile; it is thrown out. [a]He who has ears to hear, [1]let him hear."

The Lost Sheep

15 Now all the [a]tax collectors and the [1]sinners were coming near Him to listen to Him.
2 Both the Pharisees and the scribes *began* to grumble, saying, "This man receives sinners and [a]eats with them."
3 ¶ So He told them this parable, saying,
4"[a]What man among you, if he has a hundred sheep and has lost one of them, does not leave the ninety-nine in the [1]open pasture and go after the one which is lost until he finds it?
5"When he has found it, he lays it on his shoulders, rejoicing.
6"And when he comes home, he calls together his friends and his neighbors, saying to them, 'Rejoice with me, for I have found my sheep which was lost!'
7"I tell you that in the same way, there will be *more* joy in heaven over one sinner who repents than over ninety-nine righteous persons who need no repentance.

The Lost Coin

8 ¶ "Or what woman, if she has ten [1]silver coins and loses one coin, does not light a lamp and sweep the house and search carefully until she finds it?
9"When she has found it, she calls together her friends and neighbors, saying, 'Rejoice with me, for I have found the coin which I had lost!'
10"In the same way, I tell you, there is joy [a]in the presence of the angels of God over one sinner who repents."

The Prodigal Son

11 ¶ And He said, "A man had two sons.
12"The younger of them said to his father, 'Father, give me [a]the share of the estate that falls to me.' So he divided his [1b]wealth between them.
13"And not many days later, the younger son gathered everything together and went on a journey into a distant country, and there he squandered his estate with loose living.
14"Now when he had spent everything, a severe famine occurred in that country, and he began to be impoverished.
15"So he went and [1]hired himself out to one of the citizens of that country, and he sent him into his fields to feed swine.
16"And he would have gladly filled his stomach with the [1]pods that the swine were eating, and no one was giving *anything* to him.
17"But when he came to [1]his senses, he said, 'How many of my father's hired men have more than enough bread, but I am dying here with hunger!
18 'I will get up and go to my father, and will say to him, "Father, I have sinned against heaven, and [1]in your sight;
19 I am no longer worthy to be called your son; make me as one of your hired men." '
20"So he got up and came to [1]his father. But while he was still a long way off, his father saw him and felt compassion *for him*, and ran and [2a]embraced him and kissed him.
21"And the son said to him, 'Father, I have sinned against heaven and in your sight; I am no longer worthy to be called your son.'
22"But the father said to his slaves, 'Quickly bring out [a]the best robe and put it on him, and [b]put a ring on his hand and sandals on his feet;
23 and bring the fattened calf, kill it, and let us eat and celebrate;
24 for this son of mine was [a]dead and has come to life again; he was lost and has been found.' And they began to celebrate.
25 ¶ "Now his older son was in the field, and when he came and approached the house, he heard music and dancing.
26"And he summoned one of the servants and *began* inquiring what these things could be.
27"And he said to him, 'Your brother has come, and your father has killed the fattened calf because he has received him back safe and sound.'

31 [a]Prov 20:18
32 [1]Or *an embassy*
33 [a]Phil 3:7; Heb 11:26
34 [a]Matt 5:13; Mark 9:50
35 [1]Or *hear!* Or *listen!* [a]Matt 11:15
15:1 [1]I.e. irreligious Jews [a]Luke 5:29
2 [a]Matt 9:11
4 [1]Lit *wilderness* [a]Matt 18:12-14; Luke 15:4-7
8 [1]Gr *drachmas,* one drachma was a day's wages
10 [a]Matt 10:32; Luke 15:7
12 [1]Lit *living* [a]Deut 21:17 [b]Mark 12:44; Luke 15:30
15 [1]Lit *was joined to*
16 [1]I.e. of the carob tree
17 [1]Lit *himself*
18 [1]Lit *before you*
20 [1]Lit *his own* [2]Lit *fell on his neck* [a]Gen 45:14; 46:29; Acts 20:37
22 [a]Zech 3:4; Rev 6:11 [b]Gen 41:42
24 [a]Matt 8:22; Luke 9:60; 15:32; Rom 11:15; Eph 2:1, 5; 5:14; Col 2:13; 1 Tim 5:6

28 "But he became angry and was not willing to go in; and his father came out and *began* pleading with him.

29 "But he answered and said to his father, 'Look! For so many years I have been serving you and I have never [1]neglected a command of yours; and *yet* you have never given me a young goat, so that I might celebrate with my friends;

30 but when this son of yours came, who has devoured your [1a]wealth with prostitutes, you killed the fattened calf for him.'

31 "And he said to him, 'Son, you [1]have always been with me, and all that is mine is yours.

32 'But we had to celebrate and rejoice, for this brother of yours was [a]dead and *has begun* to live, and *was* lost and has been found.' "

The Unrighteous Steward

16 Now He was also saying to the disciples, "There was a rich man who had a manager, and this *manager* was [1]reported to him as [a]squandering his possessions.

2 "And he called him and said to him, 'What is this I hear about you? Give an accounting of your management, for you can no longer be manager.'

3 "The manager said to himself, 'What shall I do, since my [1]master is taking the management away from me? I am not strong enough to dig; I am ashamed to beg.

4 'I know what I shall do, so that when I am removed from the management people will welcome me into their homes.'

5 "And he summoned each one of his [1]master's debtors, and he *began* saying to the first, 'How much do you owe my master?'

6 "And he said, 'A hundred [1]measures of oil.' And he said to him, 'Take your bill, and sit down quickly and write fifty.'

7 "Then he said to another, 'And how much do you owe?' And he said, 'A hundred [1]measures of wheat.' He *said to him, 'Take your bill, and write eighty.'

8 "And his [1]master praised the unrighteous manager because he had acted shrewdly; for the sons of [a]this age are more shrewd in relation to their own [2]kind than the [b]sons of light.

9 "And I say to you, [a]make friends for yourselves by means of the [1b]wealth of unrighteousness, so that when it fails, [c]they will receive you into the eternal dwellings.

10 ¶ "[a]He who is faithful in a very little thing is faithful also in much; and he who is unrighteous in a very little thing is unrighteous also in much.

11 "Therefore if you have not been faithful in the *use of* unrighteous [1a]wealth, who will entrust the true *riches* to you?

12 "And if you have not been faithful in *the use of* that which is another's, who will give you that which is your own?

13 "[a]No [1]servant can serve two masters; for either he will hate the one and love the other, or else he will be devoted to one and despise the other. You cannot serve God and [2b]wealth."

14 ¶ Now the Pharisees, who were [a]lovers of money, were listening to all these things and [b]were scoffing at Him.

15 And He said to them, "You are those who [a]justify yourselves [1]in the sight of men, but [b]God knows your hearts; for that which is highly esteemed among men is detestable [1]in the sight of God.

16 ¶ "[a]The Law and the Prophets *were proclaimed* until John; since that time [b]the gospel of the kingdom of God [1]has been preached, and everyone is forcing his way into it.

17 "[a]But it is easier for heaven and earth to pass away than for one [1]stroke of a letter of the Law to fail.

18 ¶ "[a]Everyone who [1]divorces his wife and marries another commits adultery, and he who marries one who is [2]divorced from a husband commits adultery.

The Rich Man and Lazarus

19 ¶ "Now there was a rich man, and he habitually dressed in purple and fine linen, joyously living in splendor every day.

20 "And a poor man named Lazarus [a]was laid at his gate, covered with sores,

21 and longing to be fed with the *crumbs* which were falling from the rich man's table; besides, even the dogs were coming and licking his sores.

22 "Now the poor man died and was carried away by the angels to [a]Abraham's bosom; and the rich man also died and was buried.

23 "In [a]Hades he lifted up his eyes, being in torment, and *saw Abraham far away and Lazarus in his bosom.

24 "And he cried out and said, '[a]Father Abraham, have mercy on me, and send Lazarus so that he may dip the tip of his finger in water and cool off my tongue, for I am in agony in [b]this flame.'

25 "But Abraham said, 'Child, remember that [a]during your life you received your good things, and likewise Lazarus bad things; but now he is being comforted here, and you are in agony.

---

29 [1]Or *disobeyed*
30 [1]Lit *living* [a]Prov 29:3; Luke 15:12
31 [1]Lit *are always with me*
32 [a]Luke 15:24
16:1 [1]Or *accused* [a]Luke 15:13
3 [1]Or *lord*
5 [1]Or *lord's*
6 [1]Gr *baths,* a Heb unit of measure equaling about 7 1/2 gal.
7 [1]Gr *kors,* one kor equals between 10 and 12 bu
8 [1]Or *lord* [2]Lit *generation* [a]Matt 12:32; Luke 20:34 [b]John 12:36; Eph 5:8; 1 Thess 5:5
9 [1]Gr *mammon,* fr Aram *mamona,* signifying riches, wealth, etc, personified as an object of worship [a]Matt 19:21; Luke 11:41; 12:33 [b]Matt 6:24; Luke 16:11,13 [c]Luke 16:4
10 [a]Matt 25:21, 23
11 [1]Gr *mammon,* fr Aram *mamona,* signifying riches, wealth, etc, personified as an object of worship [a]Luke 16:9
13 [1]Or *house-servant* [2]Gr *mammon,* fr Aram *mamona,* signifying riches, wealth, etc, personified as an object of worship [a]Matt 6:24 [b]Luke 16:9
14 [a]2 Tim 3:2 [b]Luke 23:35
15 [1]Lit *before* [a]Luke 10:29; 18:9,14 [b]1 Sam 16:7; Prov 21:2; Acts 1:24; Rom 8:27
16 [1]Lit *is preached* [a]Matt 11:12f [b]Matt 4:23
17 [1]I.e. projection of a letter (serif) [a]Matt 5:18
18 [1]Or *sends away* [2]Or *sent away* [a]Matt 5:32; 1 Cor 7:10,11
20 [a]Acts 3:2
22 [a]John 1:18; 13:23
23 [a]Matt 11:23
24 [a]Luke 3:8; 16:30; 19:9 [b]Matt 25:41
25 [a]Luke 6:24

26 'And [1]besides all this, between us
and you there is a great chasm fixed, so
that those who wish to come over from
here to you will not be able, and *that*
none may cross over from there to us.'
27 "And he said, 'Then I beg you, father, that you send him to my father's
house—
28 for I have five brothers—in order
that he may [a]warn them, so that they
will not also come to this place of torment.'
29 "But Abraham *said, 'They have
[a]Moses and the Prophets; let them hear
them.'
30 "But he said, 'No, [a]father Abraham,
but if someone goes to them from the
dead, they will repent!'
31 "But he said to him, 'If they do not
listen to Moses and the Prophets, they
will not be persuaded even if someone
rises from the dead.' "

Instructions

17 He said to His disciples, "[a]It is
inevitable that [1]stumbling blocks
come, but woe to him through whom
they come!
2 "[a]It [1]would be better for him if a
millstone were hung around his neck and
he were thrown into the sea, than that he
would cause one of these little ones to
stumble.
3 "[1]Be on your guard! [a]If your brother sins, rebuke him; and if he repents,
forgive him.
4 "And if he sins against you [a]seven
times a day, and returns to you seven
times, saying, 'I repent,' [1]forgive him."
5 ¶ [a]The apostles said to [b]the Lord,
"Increase our faith!"
6 And [a]the Lord said, "If you [1]had
faith like [b]a mustard seed, you would say
to this [c]mulberry tree, 'Be uprooted and
be planted in the sea'; and it would
[2]obey you.
7 ¶ "Which of you, having a slave
plowing or tending sheep, will say to him
when he has come in from the field,
'Come immediately and [1]sit down to
eat'?
8 "But will he not say to him, '[a]Pre-
pare something for me to eat, and *proper-*
ly [1]clothe yourself and serve me while I
eat and drink; and [2]afterward you [3]may
eat and drink'?
9 "He does not thank the slave because he did the things which were commanded, does he?
10 "So you too, when you do all the
things which are commanded you, say,
'We are unworthy slaves; we have done
only that which we ought to have
done.' "

26 [1]Lit *in all these things*
28 [a]Acts 2:40; 8:25; 10:42; 18:5; 20:21ff; 23:11; 28:23; Gal 5:3; Eph 4:17; 1 Thess 2:11; 4:6
29 [a]Luke 4:17; John 5:45-47; Acts 15:21
30 [a]Luke 3:8; 16:24; 19:9
17:1 [1]Or *temptations to sin* [a]Matt 18:7; 1 Cor 11:19; 1 Tim 4:1
2 [1]Lit *is* [a]Matt 18:6; Mark 9:42; 1 Cor 8:12
3 [1]Lit *Take heed to yourselves* [a]Matt 18:15
4 [1]Lit *you shall forgive* [a]Matt 18:21f
5 [a]Mark 6:30 [b]Luke 7:13
6 [1]Lit *have* [2]Lit *have obeyed* [a]Luke 7:13 [b]Matt 13:31; 17:20; Mark 4:31; Luke 13:19 [c]Luke 19:4
7 [1]Lit *recline*
8 [1]Lit *gird* [2]Lit *after these things* [3]Lit *will* [a]Luke 12:37
11 [1]Lit *through the middle of*; or *along the borders of* [a]Luke 9:51 [b]Luke 9:52ff; John 4:3f
12 [a]Lev 13:45f
13 [a]Luke 5:5
14 [a]Lev 14:1-32; Matt 8:4; Luke 5:14
15 [a]Matt 9:8
16 [a]Matt 10:5
18 [1]Lit *Were there not found those who* [a]Matt 9:8
19 [1]Lit *has saved you* [a]Matt 9:22; Luke 18:42
20 [1]Lit *observation* [a]Luke 19:11; Acts 1:6 [b]Luke 14:1
21 [1]Or *within you* [a]Luke 17:23
22 [a]Matt 9:15; Mark 2:20; Luke 5:35
23 [a]Matt 24:23; Mark 13:21; Luke 21:8
24 [1]Lit *under heaven* [a]Matt 24:27
25 [a]Matt 16:21; Luke 9:22
26 [a]Luke 17:26, 27: *Matt 24:37-39* [b]Gen 6:5-8; 7
28 [1]Lit *In the same way as* [a]Gen 19

Ten Lepers Cleansed

11 ¶ While He was [a]on the way to
Jerusalem, [b]He was passing [1]between
Samaria and Galilee.
12 As He entered a village, ten leprous
men who [a]stood at a distance met Him;
13 and they raised their voices, saying,
"Jesus, [a]Master, have mercy on us!"
14 When He saw them, He said to
them, "[a]Go and show yourselves to the
priests." And as they were going, they
were cleansed.
15 Now one of them, when he saw
that he had been healed, turned back,
[a]glorifying God with a loud voice,
16 and he fell on his face at His feet,
giving thanks to Him. And he was a [a]Sa-
maritan.
17 Then Jesus answered and said,
"Were there not ten cleansed? But the
nine—where are they?
18 "[1]Was no one found who returned
to [a]give glory to God, except this foreigner?"
19 And He said to him, "Stand up and
go; [a]your faith [1]has made you well."
20 ¶ Now having been questioned by
the Pharisees [a]as to when the kingdom
of God was coming, He answered them
and said, "The kingdom of God is not
coming with [1b]signs to be observed;
21 nor will [a]they say, 'Look, here *it*
is!' or, 'There *it is!*' For behold, the kingdom of God is [1]in your midst."

Second Coming Foretold

22 ¶ And He said to the disciples,
"[a]The days will come when you will long
to see one of the days of the Son of Man,
and you will not see it.
23 "[a]They will say to you, 'Look there!
Look here!' Do not go away, and do not
run after *them.*
24 "[a]For just like the lightning, when it
flashes out of one part [1]of the sky, shines
to the other part [1]of the sky, so will the
Son of Man be in His day.
25 "[a]But first He must suffer many
things and be rejected by this generation.
26 "[a]And just as it happened [b]in the
days of Noah, so it will be also in the days
of the Son of Man:
27 they were eating, they were drinking, they were marrying, they were being
given in marriage, until the day that Noah
entered the ark, and the flood came and
destroyed them all.
28 "[1]It was the same as happened in
[a]the days of Lot: they were eating, they
were drinking, they were buying, they
were selling, they were planting,
they were building;
29 but on the day that Lot went out

from Sodom it rained fire and [1]brimstone from heaven and destroyed them all.

30 "It will be [1]just the same on the day that the Son of Man [a]is revealed.

31 "On that day, the one who is [a]on the housetop and whose goods are in the house must not go down to take them out; and likewise the one who is in the field must not turn back.

32 "[a]Remember Lot's wife.

33 "[a]Whoever seeks to keep his [1]life will lose it, and whoever loses *his life* will preserve it.

34 "I tell you, on that night there will be two in one bed; one will be taken and the other will be left.

35 "[a]There will be two women grinding at the same place; one will be taken and the other will be left.

36 ["[1a]Two men will be in the field; one will be taken and the other will be left."]

37 And answering they *said to Him, "Where, Lord?" And He said to them, "[a]Where the body *is,* there also the [1]vultures will be gathered."

Parables on Prayer

18 Now He was telling them a parable to show that at all times they [a]ought to pray and not to [b]lose heart,

2 saying, "In a certain city there was a judge who did not fear God and did not [a]respect man.

3 "There was a widow in that city, and she kept coming to him, saying, '[1]Give me legal protection from my opponent.'

4 "For a while he was unwilling; but afterward he said to himself, 'Even though I do not fear God nor [a]respect man,

5 yet [a]because this widow bothers me, I will [1]give her legal protection, otherwise by continually coming she will [2b]wear me out.' "

6 And [a]the Lord said, "Hear what the unrighteous judge *said;

7 now, will not God [a]bring about justice for His [b]elect who cry to Him day and night, [1]and will He [c]delay long over them?

8 "I tell you that He will bring about justice for them quickly. However, when the Son of Man comes, [a]will He find [1]faith on the earth?"

The Pharisee and the Publican

9 ¶ And He also told this parable to some people who [a]trusted in themselves that they were righteous, and [b]viewed others with contempt:

10 "Two men [a]went up into the temple to pray, one a Pharisee and the other a tax collector.

11 "The Pharisee [a]stood and was praying this to himself: 'God, I thank You that I am not like other people: swindlers, unjust, adulterers, or even like this tax collector.

12 'I [a]fast twice a week; I [b]pay tithes of all that I get.'

13 "But the tax collector, [a]standing some distance away, [b]was even unwilling to lift up his eyes to heaven, but [c]was beating his breast, saying, 'God, be [1]merciful to me, the sinner!'

14 "I tell you, this man went to his house justified rather than the other; [a]for everyone who exalts himself will be humbled, but he who humbles himself will be exalted."

15 ¶ [a]And they were bringing even their babies to Him so that He would touch them, but when the disciples saw it, they *began* rebuking them.

16 But Jesus called for them, saying, "Permit the children to come to Me, and do not hinder them, for the kingdom of God belongs to such as these.

17 "Truly I say to you, [a]whoever does not receive the kingdom of God like a child will not enter it *at all.*"

The Rich Young Ruler

18 ¶ [a]A ruler questioned Him, saying, "Good Teacher, what shall I do to inherit eternal life?"

19 And Jesus said to him, "Why do you call Me good? No one is good except God alone.

20 "You know the commandments, '[a]DO NOT COMMIT ADULTERY, DO NOT MURDER, DO NOT STEAL, DO NOT BEAR FALSE WITNESS, HONOR YOUR FATHER AND MOTHER.' "

21 And he said, "All these things I have kept from *my* youth."

22 When Jesus heard *this,* He said to him, "One thing you still lack; [a]sell all that you possess and distribute it to the poor, and you shall have [b]treasure in heaven; and come, follow Me."

23 But when he had heard these things, he became very sad, for he was extremely rich.

24 And Jesus looked at him and said, "[a]How hard it is for those who are wealthy to enter the kingdom of God!

25 "For [a]it is easier for a camel to [1]go through the eye of a needle than for a rich man to enter the kingdom of God."

26 They who heard it said, "Then who can be saved?"

27 But He said, "[a]The things that are impossible with people are possible with God."

28 ¶ Peter said, "Behold, [a]we have left [1]our own *homes* and followed You."

29 And He said to them, "Truly I say to

---

29 [1]I.e. burning sulfur
30 [1]Lit *according to the same things* [a]Matt 16:27; 1 Cor 1:7; Col 3:4; 2 Thess 1:7; 1 Pet 1:7; 4:13; 1 John 2:28
31 [a]Matt 24:17, 18; Mark 13:15f; Luke 21:21
32 [a]Gen 19:26
33 [1]Or *soul* [a]Matt 10:39
35 [a]Matt 24:41
36 [1]Early mss do not contain this v [a]Matt 24:40
37 [1]Or *eagles* [a]Matt 24:28
18:1 [a]Luke 11:5-10 [b]2 Cor 4:1
2 [a]Luke 18:4; 20:13; Heb 12:9
3 [1]Lit *Do me justice*
4 [a]Luke 18:2; 20:13; Heb 12:9
5 [1]Lit *do her justice* [2]Lit *hit me under the eye* [a]Luke 11:8 [b]1 Cor 9:27
6 [a]Luke 7:13
7 [1]Or *and yet He is very patient toward them* [a]Rev 6:10 [b]Matt 24:22; Rom 8:33; Col 3:12; 2 Tim 2:10; Titus 1:1 [c]2 Pet 3:9
8 [1]Lit *the faith* [a]Luke 17:26ff
9 [a]Luke 16:15 [b]Rom 14:3,10
10 [a]1 Kin 10:5; 2 Kin 20:5,8; Acts 3:1
11 [a]Matt 6:5; Mark 11:25; Luke 22:41
12 [a]Matt 9:14 [b]Luke 11:42
13 [1]Or *propitious* [a]Matt 6:5; Mark 11:25; Luke 22:41 [b]Ezra 9:6 [c]Luke 23:48
14 [a]Matt 23:12; Luke 14:11
15 [a]Luke 18:15-17: *Matt 19:13-15; Mark 10:13-16*
17 [a]Matt 18:3; 19:14; Mark 10:15; 1 Cor 14:20; 1 Pet 2:2
18 [a]Luke 18:18-30: *Matt 19:16-29; Mark 10:17-30*; Luke 10:25-28
20 [a]Ex 20:12-16; Deut 5:16-20
22 [a]Matt 19:21; Luke 12:33 [b]Matt 6:20
24 [a]Matt 19:23; Mark 10:23f
25 [1]Lit *enter* [a]Matt 19:24; Mark 10:25
27 [a]Matt 19:26
28 [1]Lit *our own things* [a]Luke 5:11

you, [a]there is no one who has left house
or wife or brothers or parents or children,
for the sake of the kingdom of God,
30 who will not receive many times as
much at this time and in [a]the age to
come, eternal life."
31 ¶ [a]Then He took the twelve aside
and said to them, "Behold, [b]we are going
up to Jerusalem, and [c]all things which
are written through the prophets about
the Son of Man will be accomplished.
32 "[a]For He will be [1]handed over to
the Gentiles, and will be mocked and
mistreated and spit upon,
33 and after they have scourged Him,
they will kill Him; and the third day He
will rise again."
34 But [a]the disciples understood none
of these things, and *the meaning of* this
statement was hidden from them, and
they did not comprehend the things that
were said.

Bartimaeus Receives Sight

35 ¶ [a]As [1b]Jesus was approaching
Jericho, a blind man was sitting by the
road begging.
36 Now hearing a crowd going by, he
began to inquire what this was.
37 They told him that Jesus of Nazareth was passing by.
38 And he called out, saying, "Jesus,
[a]Son of David, have mercy on me!"
39 Those who led the way were sternly telling him to be quiet; but he kept
crying out all the more, "[a]Son of David,
have mercy on me!"
40 And Jesus stopped and commanded
that he be brought to Him; and when he
came near, He questioned him,
41 "What do you want Me to do for
you?" And he said, "Lord, *I want* to regain my sight!"
42 And Jesus said to him, "[1]Receive
your sight; [a]your faith has [2]made you
well."
43 Immediately he regained his sight
and *began* following Him, [a]glorifying
God; and when [b]all the people saw it,
they gave praise to God.

Zaccheus Converted

19 He [a]entered Jericho and was
passing through.
2 And there was a man called by the
name of Zaccheus; he was a chief tax collector and he was rich.
3 Zaccheus was trying to see who
Jesus was, and was unable because of the
crowd, for he was small in stature.
4 So he ran on ahead and climbed up
into a [1a]sycamore tree in order to see
Him, for He was about to pass through
that way.
5 When Jesus came to the place, He
looked up and said to him, "Zaccheus,
hurry and come down, for today I must
stay at your house."
6 And he hurried and came down
and received Him [1]gladly.
7 When they saw it, they all *began* to
grumble, saying, "He has gone [1]to be the
guest of a man who is a sinner."
8 Zaccheus stopped and said to [a]the
Lord, "Behold, Lord, half of my possessions I [1]will give to the poor, and if I
have [b]defrauded anyone of anything, I
[1]will give back [c]four times as much."
9 And Jesus said to him, "Today salvation has come to this house, because
he, too, is [a]a son of Abraham.
10 "For [a]the Son of Man has come to
seek and to save that which was lost."

Parable of Money Usage

11 ¶ While they were listening to
these things, Jesus went on to tell a parable, because [a]He was near Jerusalem,
and they supposed that [b]the kingdom of
God was going to appear immediately.
12 So He said, "[a]A nobleman went to
a distant country to receive a kingdom for
himself, and *then* return.
13 "And he called ten of his slaves, and
gave them ten [1]minas and said to them,
'Do business *with this* [2]until I come
back.'
14 "But his citizens hated him and sent
[1]a delegation after him, saying, 'We do
not want this man to reign over us.'
15 "When he returned, after receiving
the kingdom, he ordered that these
slaves, to whom he had given the money,
be called to him so that he might know
what business they had done.
16 "The first appeared, saying, '[1]Mas-
ter, your [2]mina has made ten minas
more.'
17 "And he said to him, 'Well done,
good slave, because you have been
[a]faithful in a very little thing, you are to
be in authority over ten cities.'
18 "The second came, saying, 'Your
[1]mina, [2]master, has made five minas.'
19 "And he said to him also, 'And you
are to be over five cities.'
20 "Another came, saying, 'Master,
here is your mina, which I kept put away
in a handkerchief;
21 for I was afraid of you, because you
are an exacting man; you take up what
you did not lay down and reap what you
did not sow.'
22 "He *said to him, '[1]By your own
words I will judge you, you worthless
slave. Did you know that I am an exacting
man, taking up what I did not lay down
and reaping what I did not sow?

29 [a]Matt 6:33; 19:29; Mark 10:29f
30 [a]Matt 12:32
31 [a]Luke 18:31-33: *Matt 20:17-19; Mark 10:32-34* [b]Luke 9:51 [c]Ps 22; Is 53
32 [1]Or *betrayed* [a]Matt 16:21
34 [a]Mark 9:32; Luke 9:45
35 [1]Lit *He* [a]Luke 18:35-43: *Matt 20:29-34; Mark 10:46-52* [b]Matt 20:29; Mark 10:46; Luke 19:1
38 [a]Matt 9:27; Luke 18:39
39 [a]Luke 18:38
42 [1]Lit *Regain your sight* [2]Lit *saved you* [a]Matt 9:22
43 [a]Matt 9:8 [b]Luke 9:43; 13:17; 19:37
19:1 [a]Luke 18:35
4 [1]I.e. fig-mulberry [a]1 Kin 10:27; 1 Chr 27:28; 2 Chr 1:15; 9:27; Ps 78:47; Is 9:10; Luke 17:6
6 [1]Lit *rejoicing*
7 [1]Or *to find lodging*
8 [1]Lit *am giving* [a]Luke 7:13 [b]Luke 3:14 [c]Ex 22:1; Lev 6:5; Num 5:7; 2 Sam 12:6
9 [a]Luke 3:8; 13:16; Rom 4:16; Gal 3:7
10 [a]Matt 18:11
11 [a]Luke 9:51 [b]Luke 17:20
12 [a]Matt 25:14-30; Luke 19:12-27
13 [1]A mina is equal to about 100 days' wages [2]Lit *while I am coming*
14 [1]Or *an embassy*
16 [1]Lit *Lord* [2]V 13, note 1
17 [a]Luke 16:10
18 [1]V 13, note 1 [2]Lit *lord*
22 [1]Lit *Out of your own mouth*

23 'Then why did you not put my money in the bank, and having come, I would
have collected it with interest?'
24"Then he said to the bystanders,
'Take the mina away from him and give
it to the one who has the ten minas.'
25"And they said to him, 'Master, he
has ten minas *already.*'
26"[a]I tell you that to everyone who
has, more shall be given, but from the
one who does not have, even what he
does have shall be taken away.
27"But [a]these enemies of mine, who
did not want me to reign over them,
bring them here and [b]slay them in my
presence."

Triumphal Entry

28 ¶ After He had said these things,
He [a]was going on ahead, [b]going up to
Jerusalem.
29 ¶ [a]When He approached Bethphage and [b]Bethany, near the [1]mount that
is called [c]Olivet, He sent two of the disciples,
30 saying, "Go into the village ahead
of *you;* there, as you enter, you will find
a colt tied on which no one yet has ever
sat; untie it and bring it *here.*
31"If anyone asks you, 'Why are you
untying it?' you shall say, 'The Lord has
need of it.' "
32 So those who were sent went away
and found it just as He had told them.
33 As they were untying the colt, its
[1]owners said to them, "Why are you untying the colt?"
34 They said, "The Lord has need
of it."
35 They brought it to Jesus, [a]and they
threw their coats on the colt and put
Jesus *on it.*
36 As He was going, they were spreading their coats on the road.
37 As soon as He was approaching,
near the descent of [a]the Mount of Olives, the whole crowd of the disciples
began to [b]praise God [1]joyfully with a
loud voice for all the [2]miracles which
they had seen,
38 shouting:
"[a]BLESSED IS THE [b]KING WHO
COMES IN THE NAME OF THE
LORD;
Peace in heaven and [c]glory in
the highest!"
39 [a]Some of the Pharisees [1]in the
crowd said to Him, "Teacher, rebuke
Your disciples."
40 But Jesus answered, "I tell you, if
these become silent, [a]the stones will cry
out!"
41 ¶ When He approached *Jerusalem,*
He saw the city and [a]wept over it,
42 saying, "If you had known in this
day, even you, the things which make for
peace! But now they have been hidden
from your eyes.
43"For the days will come upon you
[1]when your enemies will [a]throw up a
[2]barricade against you, and [b]surround
you and hem you in on every side,
44 and they will level you to the
ground and your children within you, and
[a]they will not leave in you one stone
upon another, because you did not recognize [b]the time of your visitation."

Traders Driven from the Temple

45 ¶ [a]Jesus entered the temple and
began to drive out those who were selling,
46 saying to them, "It is written,
'[a]AND MY HOUSE SHALL BE A HOUSE OF
PRAYER,' [b]but you have made it a ROBBERS'
[1]DEN."
47 ¶ And [a]He was teaching daily in
the temple; but the chief priests and the
scribes and the leading men among the
people [b]were trying to destroy Him,
48 and they could not find [1]anything
that they might do, for all the people
were hanging on to [2]every word He said.

Jesus' Authority Questioned

20 [a]On one of the days while [b]He
was teaching the people in the
temple and [c]preaching the gospel, the
chief priests and the scribes with the elders [d]confronted *Him,*
2 and they spoke, saying to Him,
"Tell us by what authority You are doing
these things, or who is the one who gave
You this authority?"
3 Jesus answered and said to them, "I
will also ask you a [1]question, and you
tell Me:
4"Was the baptism of John from heav-
en or from men?"
5 They reasoned among themselves,
saying, "If we say, 'From heaven,' He will
say, 'Why did you not believe him?'
6"But if we say, 'From men,' all the
people will stone us to death, for they are
convinced that John was a [a]prophet."
7 So they answered that they did not
know where *it came* from.
8 And Jesus said to them, "Nor [1]will
I tell you by what authority I do these
things."

Parable of the Vine-growers

9 ¶ [a]And He began to tell the people
this parable: "A man planted a vineyard
and rented it out to [1]vine-growers, and
went on a journey for a long time.
10"At the *harvest* time he sent a slave
to the vine-growers, so that they would

26 [a]Matt 13:12; Mark 4:25; Luke 8:18
27 [a]Luke 19:14 [b]Matt 22:7; Luke 20:16
28 [a]Mark 10:32 [b]Luke 9:51
29 [1]Or *hill...Olive Grove*; Mount of Olives [a]Luke 19:29-38: *Matt 21:1-9; Mark 11:1-10* [b]Matt 21:17 [c]Luke 21:37; Acts 1:12
33 [1]Lit *lords*
35 [a]Luke 19:35-38: *Matt 21:4-9; Mark 11:7-10; John 12:12-15*
37 [1]Lit *rejoicing* [2]Or *works of power* [a]Matt 21:1; Luke 19:29 [b]Luke 18:43
38 [a]Ps 118:26 [b]Matt 2:2; 25:34 [c]Matt 21:9; Luke 2:14
39 [1]Lit *from* [a]Matt 21:15f
40 [a]Hab 2:11
41 [a]Luke 13:34, 35
43 [1]Lit *and* [2]I.e. a dirt wall or mound for siege purposes [a]Eccl 9:14; Is 29:3; 37:33; Jer 6:6; Ezek 4:2; 26:8 [b]Luke 21:20
44 [a]Matt 24:2; Mark 13:2; Luke 21:6 [b]1 Pet 2:12
45 [a]Luke 19:45, 46: *Matt 21:12, 13; Mark 11:15-17*; John 2:13-16
46 [1]Lit *cave* [a]Is 56:7; Jer 7:11; Matt 21:13; Mark 11:17 [b]Jer 7:11
47 [a]Matt 26:55; Luke 21:37 [b]Luke 20:19
48 [1]Lit *what they would do* [2]Lit *Him, listening*
20:1 [a]Luke 20:1-8: *Matt 21:23-27; Mark 11:27-33* [b]Matt 26:55 [c]Luke 8:1 [d]Acts 4:1; 6:12
3 [1]Lit *word*
6 [a]Matt 11:9; Luke 7:29,30
8 [1]Lit *do I tell*
9 [1]Or *tenant farmers*, also vv 10, 14, 16 [a]Luke 20:9-19: *Matt 21:33-46; Mark 12:1-12*

give him *some* of the produce of the vineyard; but the vine-growers beat him and
sent him away empty-handed.
11 "And he proceeded to send another
slave; and they beat him also and treated
him shamefully and sent him away
empty-handed.
12 "And he proceeded to send a third;
and this one also they wounded and cast
out.
13 "The [1]owner of the vineyard said,
'What shall I do? I will send my beloved
son; perhaps they will [a]respect him.'
14 "But when the vine-growers saw
him, they reasoned with one another,
saying, 'This is the heir; let us kill him so
that the inheritance will be ours.'
15 "So they threw him out of the vineyard and killed him. What, then, will the
[1]owner of the vineyard do to them?
16 "He will come and [a]destroy these
vine-growers and will give the vineyard
to others." When they heard it, they said,
"[b]May it never be!"
17 But [1]Jesus looked at them and said,
"What then is this that is written:

'[a]THE STONE WHICH THE BUILDERS
REJECTED,
THIS BECAME [b]THE CHIEF CORNER
stone'?

18 "[a]Everyone who falls on that stone
will be broken to pieces; but on whomever it falls, it will scatter him like dust."

Tribute to Caesar

19 ¶ The scribes and the chief priests
[a]tried to lay hands on Him that very
hour, and they feared the people; for they
understood that He spoke this parable
against them.
20 [a]So they watched Him, and sent
spies who [1]pretended to be righteous, in
order [b]that they might [2]catch Him in
some statement, so that they *could* deliver Him to the rule and the authority of
[c]the governor.
21 They questioned Him, saying,
"Teacher, we know that You speak and
teach correctly, and You [1]are not partial
to any, but teach the way of God in truth.
22 "Is it [1]lawful for us [a]to pay taxes to
Caesar, or not?"
23 But He detected their trickery and
said to them,
24 "Show Me a [1]denarius. Whose
[2]likeness and inscription does it have?"
They said, "Caesar's."
25 And He said to them, "Then [a]ren-
der to Caesar the things that are Caesar's,
and to God the things that are God's."
26 And they were unable to [1a]catch
Him in a saying in the presence of the
people; and being amazed at His answer,
they became silent.

Is There a Resurrection?

27 ¶ [a]Now there came to Him some
of the [b]Sadducees (who say that there is
no resurrection),
28 and they questioned Him, saying,
"Teacher, Moses wrote for us that [a]IF A
MAN'S BROTHER DIES, having a wife, AND HE
IS CHILDLESS, HIS BROTHER SHOULD [1]MARRY
THE WIFE AND RAISE UP CHILDREN TO HIS
BROTHER.
29 "Now there were seven brothers;
and the first took a wife and died childless;
30 and the second
31 and the third [1]married her; and in
the same way [2]all seven [3]died, leaving
no children.
32 "Finally the woman died also.
33 "In the resurrection therefore,
which one's wife will she be? For [1]all
seven [2]had married her."
34 ¶ Jesus said to them, "The sons of
[a]this age marry and are given in marriage,
35 but those who are considered worthy to attain to [a]that age and the resurrection from the dead, neither marry nor
are given in marriage;
36 for they cannot even die anymore,
because they are like angels, and are
[a]sons of God, being sons of the resurrection.
37 "But that the dead are raised, even
Moses showed, in [a]the *passage about
the burning* bush, where he calls the Lord
[b]THE GOD OF ABRAHAM, AND THE GOD OF
ISAAC, AND THE GOD OF JACOB.
38 "[a]Now He is not the God of the
dead but of the living; for [b]all live to
Him."
39 Some of the scribes answered and
said, "Teacher, You have spoken well."
40 For [a]they did not have courage to
question Him any longer about anything.
41 ¶ [a]Then He said to them, "How *is
it that* they say [1]the Christ is [b]David's
son?
42 "For David himself says in the book
of Psalms,

'[a]THE LORD SAID TO MY LORD,
"SIT AT MY RIGHT HAND,
43 [a]UNTIL I MAKE YOUR ENEMIES A
FOOTSTOOL FOR YOUR FEET." '

44 "Therefore David calls Him 'Lord,'
and how is He his son?"
45 ¶ [a]And while all the people were
listening, He said to the disciples,
46 "Beware of the scribes, [a]who like to
walk around in long robes, and love respectful greetings in the market places,
and chief seats in the synagogues and
places of honor at banquets,
47 who devour widows' houses, and

13 [1]Lit *lord* [a]Luke 18:2
15 [1]Lit *lord*
16 [a]Matt 21:41; Mark 12:9; Luke 19:27 [b]Rom 3:4, 6,31; 6:2,15; 7:7,13; 9:14; 11:1,11; 1 Cor 6:15; Gal 2:17; 3:21; 6:14
17 [1]Lit *He* [a]Ps 118:22 [b]Eph 2:20; 1 Pet 2:6
18 [a]Matt 21:44
19 [a]Luke 19:47
20 [1]Lit *falsely represented themselves* [2]Lit *take hold of His word* [a]Luke 20:20-26: *Matt 22:15-22; Mark 12:13-17*; Mark 3:2 [b]Luke 11:54; 20:26 [c]Matt 27:2
21 [1]Lit *do not receive a face*
22 [1]Or *permissible* [a]Matt 17:25; Luke 23:2
24 [1]The denarius was a day's wages [2]Lit *image*
25 [a]Matt 22:21; Mark 12:17
26 [1]Lit *catch His statement* [a]Luke 11:54
27 [a]Luke 20:27-40: *Matt 22:23-33; Mark 12:18-27* [b]Acts 23:8
28 [1]Lit *take* [a]Deut 25:5
31 [1]Lit *took* [2]Lit *the seven also* [3]Lit *left no children, and died*
33 [1]Lit *the* [2]Lit *had her as wife*
34 [a]Matt 12:32; Luke 16:8
35 [a]Matt 12:32; Luke 16:8
36 [a]Rom 8:16f; 1 John 3:1,2
37 [a]Mark 12:26 [b]Ex 3:6
38 [a]Matt 22:32; Mark 12:27 [b]Rom 14:8
40 [a]Matt 22:46; Luke 14:6
41 [1]I.e. the Messiah [a]Luke 20:41-44: *Matt 22:41-46; Mark 12:35-37* [b]Matt 9:27
42 [a]Ps 110:1
43 [a]Ps 110:1
45 [a]Luke 20:45-47: *Matt 23:1-7; Mark 12:38-40*
46 [a]Luke 11:43; 14:7

for appearance's sake offer long prayers. These will receive greater condemnation."

The Widow's Gift

21 [a]And He looked up and saw the rich putting their gifts into the treasury.

2 And He saw a poor widow putting [1]in [a]two [2]small copper coins.

3 And He said, "Truly I say to you, this poor widow put in more than all *of them;*

4 for they all out of their [1]surplus put into the [2]offering; but she out of her poverty put in all [3]that she had [a]to live on."

5 ¶ [a]And while some were talking about the temple, that it was adorned with beautiful stones and votive gifts, He said,

6 "*As for* these things which you are looking at, the days will come in which [a]there will not be left one stone upon another which will not be torn down."

7 ¶ They questioned Him, saying, "Teacher, when therefore will these things happen? And what *will be* the [1]sign when these things are about to take place?"

8 And He said, "See to it that you are not misled; for many will come in My name, saying, '[a]I am *He,'* and, 'The time is near.' [b]Do not go after them.

9 "When you hear of wars and disturbances, do not be terrified; for these things must take place first, but the end *does* not *follow* immediately."

Things to Come

10 ¶ Then He continued by saying to them, "Nation will rise against nation and kingdom against kingdom,

11 and there will be great earthquakes, and in various places plagues and famines; and there will be terrors and great [1]signs from heaven.

12 ¶ "But before all these things, [a]they will lay their hands on you and will persecute you, delivering you to the synagogues and prisons, [1]bringing you before kings and governors for My name's sake.

13 "[a]It will lead to [1]an opportunity for your testimony.

14 "[a]So make up your minds not to prepare beforehand to defend yourselves;

15 for [a]I will give you [1]utterance and wisdom which none of your opponents will be able to resist or refute.

16 "But you will be betrayed even by parents and brothers and relatives and friends, and they will put *some* of you to death,

17 and you will be hated by all because of My name.

18 "Yet [a]not a hair of your head will perish.

19 "[a]By your endurance you will gain your [1]lives.

20 ¶ "But when you see Jerusalem [a]surrounded by armies, then [1]recognize that her desolation is near.

21 "Then those who are in Judea must flee to the mountains, and those who are in the midst of [1]the city must leave, and [a]those who are in the country must not enter [1]the city;

22 because these are [a]days of vengeance, so that all things which are written will be fulfilled.

23 "Woe to those who are pregnant and to those who are nursing babies in those days; for [a]there will be great distress upon the [1]land and wrath to this people;

24 and they will fall by [a]the edge of the sword, and will be led captive into all the nations; and [b]Jerusalem will be [c]trampled under foot by the Gentiles until [d]the times of the Gentiles are fulfilled.

The Return of Christ

25 ¶ "There will be [1]signs in sun and moon and stars, and on the earth dismay among nations, in perplexity at the roaring of the sea and the waves,

26 men fainting from fear and the expectation of the things which are coming upon the [1]world; for the powers of [2]the heavens will be shaken.

27 "[a]Then they will see [b]THE SON OF MAN COMING IN A CLOUD with power and great glory.

28 "But when these things begin to take place, straighten up and lift up your heads, because [a]your redemption is drawing near."

29 ¶ Then He told them a parable: "Behold the fig tree and all the trees;

30 as soon as they put forth *leaves,* you see it and [a]know for yourselves that summer is now near.

31 "So you also, when you see these things happening, [1]recognize that [a]the kingdom of God is near.

32 "Truly I say to you, this [1]generation will not pass away until all things take place.

33 "[a]Heaven and earth will pass away, but My words will not pass away.

34 ¶ "[a]Be on guard, so that your hearts will not be weighted down with dissipation and drunkenness and the worries of life, and that day will not come on you suddenly like a trap;

35 for it will come upon all those who dwell on the face of all the earth.

36 "But [a]keep on the alert at all times, praying that you may have strength to escape all these things that are about to

21:1 [a]Luke 21:1-4: *Mark 12:41-44*
2 [1]Lit *there* [2]Gr *lepta* [a]Mark 12:42
4 [1]Or *abundance* [2]Lit *gifts* [3]Lit *the living that she had* [a]Mark 12:44
5 [a]Luke 21:5-36: *Matt 24; Mark 13*
6 [a]Luke 19:44
7 [1]Or *attesting miracle*
8 [a]John 8:24 [b]Luke 17:23
11 [1]Or *attesting miracles*
12 [1]Lit *being brought* [a]Luke 21:12-17: *Matt 10:19-22; Mark 13:11-13*
13 [1]Lit *a testimony for you* [a]Phil 1:12
14 [a]Luke 12:11
15 [1]Lit *a mouth* [a]Luke 12:12
18 [a]Matt 10:30; Luke 12:7
19 [1]Lit *souls* [a]Matt 10:22; 24:13; Rom 2:7; 5:3f; Heb 10:36; James 1:3; 2 Pet 1:6
20 [1]Lit *know* [a]Luke 19:43
21 [1]Lit *her* [a]Luke 17:31
22 [a]Is 63:4; Dan 9:24-27; Hos 9:7
23 [1]Or *earth* [a]Dan 8:19; 1 Cor 7:26
24 [a]Gen 34:26; Ex 17:13; Heb 11:34 [b]Is 63:18; Dan 8:13 [c]Rev 11:2 [d]Rom 11:25
25 [1]Or *attesting miracles*
26 [1]Lit *inhabited earth* [2]Or *heaven*
27 [a]Matt 16:27; 24:30; 26:64; Mark 13:26 [b]Dan 7:13; Rev 1:7
28 [a]Luke 18:7
30 [a]Luke 12:57
31 [1]Lit *know* [a]Matt 3:2
32 [1]Or *race*
33 [a]Matt 5:18; Luke 16:17
34 [a]Matt 24:42-44; Mark 4:19; Luke 12:40,45; 1 Thess 5:2ff
36 [a]Mark 13:33; Luke 12:40

take place, and to [b]stand before the Son of Man."

37 ¶ Now [1]during the day He was [a]teaching in the temple, but [2b]at evening He would go out and spend the night on [3c]the mount that is called [4]Olivet.

38 And all the people would get up [a]early in the morning *to come* to Him in the temple to listen to Him.

Preparing the Passover

22 [a]Now the Feast of Unleavened Bread, which is called the [b]Passover, was approaching.

2 The chief priests and the scribes [a]were seeking how they might put Him to death; for they were afraid of the people.

3 ¶ [a]And [b]Satan entered into Judas who was called Iscariot, [1]belonging to the number of the twelve.

4 And he went away and discussed with the chief priests and [a]officers how he might betray Him to them.

5 They were glad and agreed to give him money.

6 So he consented, and *began* seeking a good opportunity to betray Him to them [1]apart from the crowd.

7 ¶ [a]Then came the *first* day of Unleavened Bread on which [b]the Passover *lamb* had to be sacrificed.

8 And Jesus sent [a]Peter and John, saying, "Go and prepare the Passover for us, so that we may eat it."

9 They said to Him, "Where do You want us to prepare it?"

10 And He said to them, "When you have entered the city, a man will meet you carrying a pitcher of water; follow him into the house that he enters.

11 "And you shall say to the owner of the house, 'The Teacher says to you, "Where is the guest room in which I may eat the Passover with My disciples?" '

12 "And he will show you a large, furnished upper room; prepare it there."

13 And they left and found *everything* just as He had told them; and they prepared the Passover.

The Lord's Supper

14 ¶ [a]When the hour had come, He reclined *at the table,* and [b]the apostles with Him.

15 And He said to them, "I have earnestly desired to eat this Passover with you before I suffer;

16 for I say to you, I shall never again eat it [a]until it is fulfilled in the kingdom of God."

17 [a]And when He had taken a cup *and* [b]given thanks, He said, "Take this and share it among yourselves;

18 for [a]I say to you, I will not drink of the fruit of the vine from now on until the kingdom of God comes."

19 And when He had taken *some* bread *and* [a]given thanks, He broke it and gave it to them, saying, "This is My body which is given for you; do this in remembrance of Me."

20 And in the same way *He took* the cup after they had eaten, saying, "This cup which is [a]poured out for you is the [b]new covenant in My blood.

21 "[a]But behold, the hand of the one betraying Me is with [1]Mine on the table.

22 "For indeed, the Son of Man is going [a]as it has been determined; but woe to that man by whom He is betrayed!"

23 And they began to discuss among themselves which one of them it might be who was going to do this thing.

Who Is Greatest

24 ¶ And there arose also [a]a dispute among them *as to* which one of them was regarded to be greatest.

25 [a]And He said to them, "The kings of the Gentiles lord it over them; and those who have authority over them are called 'Benefactors.'

26 "But *it is* not this way with you, [a]but the one who is the greatest among you must become like [b]the youngest, and the leader like the servant.

27 "For [a]who is greater, the one who reclines *at the table* or the one who serves? Is it not the one who reclines *at the table*? But [b]I am among you as the one who serves.

28 ¶ "You are those who have stood by Me in My [a]trials;

29 and just as My Father has granted Me a [a]kingdom, I grant you

30 that you may [a]eat and drink at My table in My [b]kingdom, and [c]you will sit on thrones judging the twelve tribes of Israel.

31 ¶ "Simon, Simon, behold, [a]Satan has [1]demanded *permission* to [b]sift you like wheat;

32 but I [a]have prayed for you, that your faith may not fail; and you, when once you have turned again, [b]strengthen your brothers."

33 [a]But he said to Him, "Lord, with You I am ready to go both to prison and to death!"

34 And He said, "I say to you, Peter, the rooster will not crow today until you have denied three times that you know Me."

35 ¶ And He said to them, "[a]When I sent you out without money belt and bag and sandals, you did not lack anything, did you?" They said, "*No,* nothing."

---

36 [b]Luke 1:19; Rev 7:9
37 [1]Lit *days* [2]Lit *nights* [3]Or *the hill* [4]Or *Olive Grove* [a]Matt 26:55; Luke 19:47 [b]Mark 11:19 [c]Matt 21:1
38 [a]John 8:2
22:1 [a]Luke 22:1: *Matt 26:2-5; Mark 14:1,2;* Ex 12:1-27 [b]John 11:55
2 [a]Matt 12:14
3 [1]Lit *being of* [a]Luke 22:3-6: *Matt 26:14-16; Mark 14:10,11* [b]Matt 4:10; John 13:2
4 [a]1 Chr 9:11; Neh 11:11; Luke 22:52; Acts 4:1
6 [1]Or *without a disturbance*
7 [a]Luke 22:7-13: *Matt 26:17-19; Mark 14:12-16* [b]Mark 14:12
8 [a]Acts 3:1; Gal 2:9
14 [a]Matt 26:20; Mark 14:17 [b]Mark 6:30
16 [a]Luke 14:15; Rev 19:9
17 [a]Luke 22:17-20: *Matt 26:26-29; Mark 14:22-25; 1 Cor 11:23-25;* 1 Cor 10:16 [b]Matt 14:19
18 [a]Matt 26:29; Mark 14:25
19 [a]Matt 14:19
20 [a]Matt 26:28; Mark 14:24 [b]Ex 24:8; Jer 31:31; 1 Cor 11:25; 2 Cor 3:6; Heb 8:8
21 [1]Lit *Me* [a]Luke 22:21-23: *Matt 26:21-24; Mark 14:18-21;* Ps 41:9; John 13:18
22 [a]Acts 2:23
24 [a]Mark 9:34; Luke 9:46
25 [a]Luke 22:25-27: *Matt 20:25-28; Mark 10:42-45*
26 [a]Matt 23:11; Mark 9:35; Luke 9:48 [b]1 Pet 5:5
27 [a]Luke 12:37 [b]Matt 20:28; John 13:12-15
28 [a]Heb 2:18
29 [a]Matt 5:3; 2 Tim 2:12
30 [a]Luke 22:16 [b]Matt 5:3; 2 Tim 2:12 [c]Matt 19:28
31 [1]Or *obtained by asking* [a]Job 1:6-12; Matt 4:10 [b]Amos 9:9
32 [a]John 17:9 [b]John 21:15-17
33 [a]Luke 22:33: *Matt 26:33-35; Mark 14:29-31; John 13:37,38*
35 [a]Matt 10:9f; Mark 6:8; Luke 9:3ff

36 And He said to them, "But now, [1]whoever has a money belt is to take it along, likewise also a bag, and [1]whoever has no sword is to sell his [2]coat and buy one.

37 "For I tell you that this which is written must be fulfilled in Me, '[a]AND HE WAS NUMBERED WITH TRANSGRESSORS'; for [b]that which refers to Me has *its* [1]fulfillment."

38 They said, "Lord, look, here are two [a]swords." And He said to them, "It is enough."

The Garden of Gethsemane

39 ¶ [a]And He came out and proceeded [b]as was His custom to [c]the Mount of Olives; and the disciples also followed Him.

40 [a]When He arrived at the place, He said to them, "[b]Pray that you may not enter into temptation."

41 And He withdrew from them about a stone's throw, and He [a]knelt down and *began* to pray,

42 saying, "Father, if You are willing, remove this [a]cup from Me; [b]yet not My will, but Yours be done."

43 [1]Now an [a]angel from heaven appeared to Him, strengthening Him.

44 And [a]being in agony He was praying very fervently; and His sweat became like drops of blood, falling down upon the ground.

45 When He rose from prayer, He came to the disciples and found them sleeping from sorrow,

46 and said to them, "Why are you sleeping? Get up and [a]pray that you may not enter into temptation."

Jesus Betrayed by Judas

47 ¶ [a]While He was still speaking, behold, a crowd *came,* and the one called Judas, one of the twelve, was preceding them; and he approached Jesus to kiss Him.

48 But Jesus said to him, "Judas, are you betraying the Son of Man with a kiss?"

49 When those who were around Him saw what was going to happen, they said, "Lord, shall we strike with the [a]sword?"

50 And one of them struck the slave of the high priest and cut off his right ear.

51 But Jesus answered and said, "[1]Stop! No more of this." And He touched his ear and healed him.

52 Then Jesus said to the chief priests and [a]officers of the temple and elders who had come against Him, "Have you come out with swords and clubs [b]as you would against a robber?

53 "While I was with you daily in the temple, you did not lay hands on Me; but [1]this hour and the power of darkness are yours."

Jesus' Arrest

54 ¶ [a]Having arrested Him, they led Him *away* and brought Him to the house of the high priest; but [b]Peter was following at a distance.

55 [a]After they had kindled a fire in the middle of [b]the courtyard and had sat down together, Peter was sitting among them.

56 And a servant-girl, seeing him as he sat in the firelight and looking intently at him, said, "This man was with Him too."

57 But he denied *it,* saying, "Woman, I do not know Him."

58 A little later, [a]another saw him and said, "You are *one* of them too!" But Peter said, "Man, I am not!"

59 After about an hour had passed, another man *began* to insist, saying, "Certainly this man also was with Him, [a]for he is a Galilean too."

60 But Peter said, "Man, I do not know what you are talking about." Immediately, while he was still speaking, a rooster crowed.

61 [a]The Lord turned and looked at Peter. And Peter remembered the word of the Lord, how He had told him, "[b]Before a rooster crows today, you will deny Me three times."

62 And he went out and wept bitterly.

63 ¶ [a]Now the men who were holding [1]Jesus in custody were mocking Him and beating Him,

64 and they blindfolded Him and were asking Him, saying, "[a]Prophesy, who is the one who hit You?"

65 And they were saying many other things against Him, [a]blaspheming.

Jesus before the Sanhedrin

66 ¶ [a]When it was day, [b]the [1]Council of elders of the people assembled, both chief priests and scribes, and they led Him away to their [c]council *chamber,* saying,

67 "[a]If You are the [1]Christ, tell us." But He said to them, "If I tell you, you will not believe;

68 and if I ask a question, you will not answer.

69 "[a]But from now on [b]THE SON OF MAN WILL BE SEATED AT THE RIGHT HAND of the power OF GOD."

70 And they all said, "Are You [a]the Son of God, then?" And He said to them, "[1][b]Yes, I am."

71 Then they said, "What further need do we have of testimony? For we have heard it ourselves from His own mouth."

36 [1]Lit *he who* [2]Or *outer garment*
37 [1]Lit *end* [a]Is 53:12 [b]John 17:4; 19:30
38 [a]Luke 22:36, 49
39 [a]Matt 26:30; Mark 14:26; John 18:1 [b]Luke 21:37 [c]Matt 21:1
40 [a]Luke 22:40-46: *Matt 26:36-46; Mark 14:32-42* [b]Matt 6:13; Luke 22:46
41 [a]Matt 26:39; Mark 14:35; Luke 18:11
42 [a]Matt 20:22 [b]Matt 26:39
43 [1]Most early mss do not contain vv 43 and 44 [a]Matt 4:11
44 [a]Heb 5:7
46 [a]Luke 22:40
47 [a]Luke 22:47-53: *Matt 26:47-56; Mark 14:43-50; John 18:3-11*
49 [a]Luke 22:38
51 [1]Or *"Let Me at least do this," and He touched*
52 [a]Luke 22:4 [b]Luke 22:37
53 [1]Lit *this is your hour and power of darkness*
54 [a]Matt 26:57; Mark 14:53 [b]Matt 26:58; Mark 14:54; John 18:15
55 [a]Luke 22:55-62: *Matt 26:69-75; Mark 14:66-72; John 18:16-18,25-27* [b]Matt 26:3
58 [a]John 18:26
59 [a]Matt 26:73; Mark 14:70
61 [a]Luke 7:13 [b]Luke 22:34
63 [1]Lit *Him* [a]Matt 26:67f; Mark 14:65; John 18:22f
64 [a]Matt 26:68; Mark 14:65
65 [a]Matt 27:39
66 [1]Or *Sanhedrin* [a]Matt 27:1f; Mark 15:1; John 18:28 [b]Acts 22:5 [c]Matt 5:22
67 [1]I.e. Messiah [a]Matt 26:63-66; Mark 14:61-63; Luke 22:67-71; John 18:19-21
69 [a]Matt 26:64; Mark 14:62; 16:19 [b]Ps 110:1
70 [1]Lit *You say that I am* [a]Matt 4:3 [b]Matt 26:64; 27:11; Luke 23:3

Jesus before Pilate

23 Then the whole body of them got up and [a]brought Him before Pilate.

2 [a]And they began to accuse Him, saying, "We found this man [b]misleading our nation and [c]forbidding to pay taxes to Caesar, and saying that He Himself is [1]Christ, a King."

3 So Pilate asked Him, saying, "Are You the King of the Jews?" And He answered him and said, "[a]*It is as* you say."

4 Then Pilate said to the chief priests and the crowds, "[a]I find no guilt in this man."

5 But they kept on insisting, saying, "He stirs up the people, teaching all over Judea, [a]starting from Galilee even as far as this place."

6 ¶ When Pilate heard it, he asked whether the man was a Galilean.

7 And when he learned that He belonged to Herod's jurisdiction, he sent Him to [a]Herod, who himself also was in Jerusalem [1]at that time.

Jesus before Herod

8 ¶ Now Herod was very glad when he saw Jesus; for [a]he had wanted to see Him for a long time, because he had been hearing about Him and was hoping to see some [1]sign performed by Him.

9 And he questioned Him [1]at some length; but [a]He answered him nothing.

10 And the chief priests and the scribes were standing there, accusing Him vehemently.

11 And Herod with his soldiers, after treating Him with contempt and mocking Him, [a]dressed Him in a gorgeous robe and sent Him back to Pilate.

12 Now [a]Herod and Pilate became friends with one another that very day; for before they had been enemies with each other.

Pilate Seeks Jesus' Release

13 ¶ Pilate summoned the chief priests and the [a]rulers and the people,

14 and said to them, "You brought this man to me as one who [a]incites the people to rebellion, and behold, having examined Him before you, I [b]have found no guilt in this man regarding the charges which you make against Him.

15 "No, nor has [a]Herod, for he sent Him back to us; and behold, nothing deserving death has been done by Him.

16 "Therefore I will [a]punish Him and release Him."

17 [[1]Now he was obliged to release to them at the feast one prisoner.]

18 ¶ But they cried out all together, saying, "[a]Away with this man, and release for us Barabbas!"

19 (He was one who had been thrown into prison for an insurrection made in the city, and for murder.)

20 Pilate, wanting to release Jesus, addressed them again,

21 but they kept on calling out, saying, "Crucify, crucify Him!"

22 And he said to them the third time, "Why, what evil has this man done? I have found in Him no guilt *demanding* death; therefore I will [a]punish Him and release Him."

23 But they were insistent, with loud voices asking that He be crucified. And their voices *began* to prevail.

24 And Pilate pronounced sentence that their demand be granted.

25 And he released the man they were asking for who had been thrown into prison for insurrection and murder, but he delivered Jesus to their will.

Simon Bears the Cross

26 ¶ [a]When they led Him away, they seized a man, Simon of [b]Cyrene, coming in from the country, and placed on him the cross to carry behind Jesus.

27 ¶ And following Him was a large crowd of the people, and of women who were [1a]mourning and lamenting Him.

28 But Jesus turning to them said, "Daughters of Jerusalem, stop weeping for Me, but weep for yourselves and for your children.

29 "For behold, the days are coming when they will say, '[a]Blessed are the barren, and the wombs that never bore, and the breasts that never nursed.'

30 "Then they will begin TO [a]SAY TO THE MOUNTAINS, 'FALL ON US,' AND TO THE HILLS, 'COVER US.'

31 "For if they do these things [1]when the tree is green, what will happen [2]when it is dry?"

32 ¶ [a]Two others also, who were criminals, were being led away to be put to death with Him.

The Crucifixion

33 ¶ [a]When they came to the place called [1]The Skull, there they crucified Him and the criminals, one on the right and the other on the left.

34 [1]But Jesus was saying, "[a]Father, forgive them; for they do not know what they are doing." [b]And they cast lots, dividing up His garments among themselves.

35 And the people stood by, looking on. And even the [a]rulers were sneering at Him, saying, "He saved others; [b]let

23:1 [a]Matt 27:2; Mark 15:1; John 18:28
2 [1]I.e. Messiah [a]Luke 23:2,3: *Matt 27:11-14; Mark 15:2-5; John 18:29-37* [b]Luke 23:14 [c]Luke 20:22; John 18:33ff; 19:12; Acts 17:7
3 [a]Luke 22:70
4 [a]Matt 27:23; Mark 15:14; Luke 23:14,22; John 18:38; 19:4,6
5 [a]Matt 4:12
7 [1]Lit *in these days* [a]Matt 14:1; Mark 6:14; Luke 3:1; 9:7; 13:31
8 [1]Or *attesting miracle* [a]Luke 9:9
9 [1]Lit *in many words* [a]Matt 27:12,14; Mark 15:5; John 19:9
11 [a]Matt 27:28
12 [a]Acts 4:27
13 [a]Luke 23:35; John 7:26,48; 12:42; Acts 3:17; 4:5,8; 13:27
14 [a]Luke 23:2 [b]Luke 23:4
15 [a]Luke 9:9
16 [a]Matt 27:26; Mark 15:15; Luke 23:22; John 19:1; Acts 16:37
17 [1]Early mss do not contain this v
18 [a]Luke 23:18-25: *Matt 27:15-26; Mark 15:6-15*; John 18:39-19:16
22 [a]Luke 23:16
26 [a]Luke 23:26: *Matt 27:32; Mark 15:21*; John 19:17 [b]Matt 27:32
27 [1]Lit *beating the breast* [a]Luke 8:52
29 [a]Matt 24:19; Luke 11:27; 21:23
30 [a]Hos 10:8; Is 2:19,20; Rev 6:16
31 [1]Lit *in the green tree* [2]Lit *in the dry*
32 [a]Matt 27:38; Mark 15:27; John 19:18
33 [1]In Lat *Calvarius*; or *Calvary* [a]Luke 23:33-43: *Matt 27:33-44; Mark 15:22-32; John 19:17-24*
34 [1]Some early mss do not contain *But Jesus was saying... doing* [a]Matt 11:25; Luke 22:42 [b]Ps 22:18; John 19:24
35 [a]Luke 23:13 [b]Matt 27:43

Resurrection Appearances

EVENT	PLACE	DAY OF THE WEEK	MATTHEW	MARK	LUKE	JOHN	ACTS	1 COR
The empty tomb	Jerusalem	Resurrection Sunday	28:1-10	16:1-8	24:1-12	20:1-9		
To Mary Magdalene in the garden	Jerusalem	Resurrection Sunday		16:9-11		20:11-18		
To other women	Jerusalem	Resurrection Sunday	28:9-10					
To two people going to Emmaus	Road to Emmaus	Resurrection Sunday		16:12-13	24:13-32			
To Peter	Jerusalem	Resurrection Sunday			24:34			15:5
To the ten disciples in the upper room	Jerusalem	Resurrection Sunday			24:36-43	20:19-25		
To the eleven disciples in the upper room	Jerusalem	Following Sunday		16:14		20:26-31		15:5
To seven disciples fishing	Sea of Galilee	Some time later				21:1-23		
To the eleven disciples on a mountain	Galilee	Some time later	28:16-20	16:15-18				
To more than five hundred	Unknown	Some time later						15:6
To James	Unknown	Some time later						15:7
To his disciples at his ascension	Mount of Olives	Forty days after Jesus' resurrection			24:44-49		1:3-8	
To Paul	Damascus	Several years later					9:1-19 22:3-16 26:9-18	9:1

Him save Himself if this is the [1]Christ of
God, His Chosen One."
36 The soldiers also mocked Him,
coming up to Him, [a]offering Him sour
wine,
37 and saying, "[a]If You are the King of
the Jews, save Yourself!"
38 Now there was also an inscription
above Him, "[a]THIS IS THE KING OF
THE JEWS."
39 ¶ [a]One of the criminals who were
hanged *there* was [1]hurling abuse at Him,
saying, "Are You not the [2]Christ? [b]Save
Yourself and us!"
40 But the other answered, and rebuking him said, "Do you not even fear God,
since you are under the same sentence of
condemnation?
41 "And we indeed *are suffering* justly,
for we are receiving [1]what we deserve
for our deeds; but this man has done
nothing wrong."
42 And he was saying, "Jesus, remember me when You come [1]in Your kingdom!"
43 And He said to him, "Truly I say to
you, today you shall be with Me in [a]Para-
dise."
44 ¶ [a]It was now about [1b]the sixth
hour, and darkness [2]fell over the whole
land until [3]the ninth hour,
45 [1]because the sun was obscured;
and [a]the veil of the temple was torn [2]in
two.
46 And Jesus, [a]crying out with a loud
voice, said, "Father, [b]INTO YOUR HANDS I
COMMIT MY SPIRIT." Having said this, He
breathed His last.
47 [a]Now when the centurion saw
what had happened, he *began* [b]praising
God, saying, "Certainly this man was
[1]innocent."
48 And all the crowds who came together for this spectacle, when they observed what had happened, *began* to return, [1a]beating their breasts.
49 [a]And all His acquaintances and
[a]the women who accompanied Him
from Galilee were standing at a distance,
seeing these things.

Jesus Is Buried

50 ¶ [a]And a man named Joseph, who
was a [b]member of the Council, a good
and righteous man
51 (he had not consented to their plan
and action), *a man* from Arimathea, a city
of the Jews, who was [a]waiting for the
kingdom of God;
52 this man went to Pilate and asked
for the body of Jesus.
53 And he took it down and wrapped
it in a linen cloth, and laid Him in a tomb
cut into the rock, where no one had ever
lain.
54 It was [a]the [1]preparation day, and
the Sabbath was about to [2]begin.
55 Now [a]the women who had come
with Him out of Galilee followed, and
saw the tomb and how His body was
laid.
56 Then they returned and [a]prepared
spices and perfumes.
¶ And [b]on the Sabbath they rested according to the commandment.

The Resurrection

24 [a]But on the first day of the week,
at early dawn, they came to the
tomb bringing the spices which they had
prepared.
2 And they found the stone rolled
away from the tomb,
3 but when they entered, they did
not find the body of [a]the Lord Jesus.
4 While they were perplexed about
this, behold, [a]two men suddenly [b]stood
near them in dazzling clothing;
5 and as *the women* were terrified
and bowed their faces to the ground, *the
men* said to them, "Why do you seek the
living One among the dead?
6 "He is not here, but He [a]has [1]risen.
Remember how He spoke to you [b]while
He was still in Galilee,
7 saying that [a]the Son of Man must
be delivered into the hands of sinful men,
and be crucified, and the third day rise
again."
8 And [a]they remembered His words,
9 and returned from the tomb and reported all these things to the eleven and
to all the rest.
10 Now they were [a]Mary Magdalene
and Joanna and Mary the *mother* of
James; also the other women with them
were telling these things to [b]the apostles.
11 But these words appeared [1]to
them as nonsense, and they [a]would not
believe them.
12 But Peter got up and [a]ran to the
tomb; stooping and looking in, he *saw
the linen wrappings [1]only; and he went
away [b]to his home, marveling at what
had happened.

The Road to Emmaus

13 ¶ And behold, [a]two of them were
going that very day to a village named
Emmaus, which was [1]about seven miles
from Jerusalem.
14 And they were talking with each
other about all these things which had
taken place.

35 [1]I.e. Messiah
36 [a]Matt 27:48
37 [a]Matt 27:43
38 [a]Matt 27:37; Mark 15:26; John 19:19
39 [1]Or *blaspheming* [2]I.e. Messiah [a]Matt 27:44; Mark 15:32; Luke 23:39-43 [b]Luke 23:35,37
41 [1]Lit *things worthy of what we have done*
42 [1]Or *into*
43 [a]2 Cor 12:4; Rev 2:7
44 [1]I.e. noon [2]Or *occurred* [3]I.e. 3 p.m. [a]Luke 23:44-49: *Matt 27:45-56; Mark 15:33-41* [b]John 19:14
45 [1]Lit *the sun failing* [2]Lit *in the middle* [a]Ex 26:31-33; Matt 27:51
46 [a]Matt 27:50; Mark 15:37; John 19:30 [b]Ps 31:5
47 [1]Lit *righteous* [a]Matt 27:54; Mark 15:39 [b]Matt 9:8
48 [1]I.e. as a traditional sign of mourning or contrition [a]Luke 8:52; 18:13
49 [a]Matt 27:55f; Mark 15:40f; Luke 8:2; John 19:25
50 [a]Luke 23:50-56: *Matt 27:57-61; Mark 15:42-47; John 19:38-42* [b]Mark 15:43
51 [a]Mark 15:43; Luke 2:25
54 [1]I.e. preparation for the Sabbath [2]Lit *dawn* [a]Matt 27:62; Mark 15:42
55 [a]Luke 23:49
56 [a]Mark 16:1; Luke 24:1 [b]Ex 20:10f; Deut 5:14
24:1 [a]Luke 24:1-10: *Matt 28:1-8; Mark 16:1-8*; John 20:1-8
3 [a]Luke 7:13; Acts 1:21
4 [a]John 20:12 [b]Luke 2:9; Acts 12:7
6 [1]Or *been raised* [a]Mark 16:6 [b]Matt 17:22f; Mark 9:30f; Luke 9:44; 24:44
7 [a]Matt 16:21; Luke 24:46
8 [a]John 2:22
10 [a]Matt 27:56 [b]Mark 6:30
11 [1]Lit *in their sight* [a]Mark 16:11
12 [1]Or *by themselves* [a]John 20:3-6 [b]John 20:10
13 [1]Lit *60 stadia*; one stadion was about 600 ft [a]Mark 16:12

15 While they were talking and discussing, Jesus Himself approached and
began traveling with them.
16 But [a]their eyes were prevented
from recognizing Him.
17 And He said to them, "What are
these words that you are exchanging with
one another as you are walking?" And
they stood still, looking sad.
18 One *of them*, named Cleopas, answered and said to Him, "Are You [1]the
only one visiting Jerusalem and unaware
of the things which have happened here
in these days?"
19 And He said to them, "What
things?" And they said to Him, "The
things about [a]Jesus the Nazarene, who
was a [b]prophet mighty in deed and
word in the sight of God and all the people,
20 and how the chief priests and our
[a]rulers delivered Him to the sentence of
death, and crucified Him.
21 "But we were hoping that it was He
who was going to [a] redeem Israel. Indeed, besides all this, it is the third day
since these things happened.
22 "But also some women among us
amazed us. [a]When they were at the
tomb early in the morning,
23 and did not find His body, they
came, saying that they had also seen a
vision of angels who said that He was
alive.
24 "Some of those who were with us
went to the tomb and found it just exactly
as the women also had said; but Him they
did not see."
25 And He said to them, "O foolish
men and slow of heart to believe in all
that [a]the prophets have spoken!
26 "[a]Was it not necessary for the
[1]Christ to suffer these things and to enter into His glory?"
27 Then beginning [1]with [a]Moses and
[1]with all the [b]prophets, He explained to
them the things concerning Himself in all
the Scriptures.
28 ¶ And they approached the village
where they were going, and [a]He acted as
though He were going farther.
29 But they urged Him, saying, "Stay
with us, for it is *getting* toward evening,
and the day [1]is now nearly over." So He
went in to stay with them.
30 When He had reclined *at the table*
with them, He took the bread and
[a]blessed *it*, and breaking *it*, He *began*
giving *it* to them.
31 Then their [a]eyes were opened and
they recognized Him; and He vanished
from [1]their sight.
32 They said to one another, "[1]Were
not our hearts burning within us while
He was speaking to us on the road, while
He [a]was [2]explaining the Scriptures
to us?"
33 And they got up that very hour and
returned to Jerusalem, and [a]found gathered together the eleven and [b]those who
were with them,
34 saying, "[a]The Lord has really risen
and [b]has appeared to Simon."
35 They *began* to relate [1]their experi-
ences on the road and how [a]He was recognized by them in the breaking of the
bread.

Other Appearances

36 ¶ While they were telling these
things, [a]He Himself stood in their
midst and *said to them, "Peace be to
you."
37 But they were startled and frightened and thought that they were seeing
[a]a spirit.
38 And He said to them, "Why are you
troubled, and why do doubts arise in your
[1]hearts?
39 "[a]See My hands and My feet, that it
is I Myself; [b]touch Me and see, for a
spirit does not have flesh and bones as
you see that I have."
40 And when He had said this, He
showed them His hands and His feet.
41 While they still [1a]could not believe *it* because of their joy and amazement, He said to them, "[b]Have you anything here to eat?"
42 They gave Him a piece of a broiled
fish;
43 and He took it and [a]ate *it* before
them.
44 ¶ Now He said to them, "[a]These
are My words which I spoke to you while
I was still with you, that all things which
are written about Me in the [b]Law of Moses and the Prophets and [c]the Psalms
must be fulfilled."
45 Then He [a]opened their [1]minds to
understand the Scriptures,
46 and He said to them, "[a]Thus it is
written, that the [1]Christ would suffer
and [b]rise again from the dead the third
day,
47 and that [a]repentance [1]for forgiveness of sins would be proclaimed [2]in His
name to [b]all the nations, beginning from
Jerusalem.
48 "You are [a]witnesses of these things.
49 "And behold, [a]I am sending forth
the promise of My Father upon you;
but [b]you are to stay in the city until

16 [a]Luke 24:31; John 20:14
18 [1]Or *visiting Jerusalem alone*
19 [a]Mark 1:24 [b]Matt 21:11
20 [a]Luke 23:13
21 [a]Luke 1:68
22 [a]Luke 24:1ff
25 [a]Matt 26:24
26 [1]I.e. Messiah [a]Luke 24:7; Heb 2:10; 1 Pet 1:11
27 [1]Lit *from* [a]Gen 3:15; Num 21:9 [John 3:14] Deut 18:15 [John 1:45] John 5:46 [b]2 Sam 7:12-16; Is 7:14 [Matt 1:23] Is 9:1f [Matt 4:15f] Is 42:1 [Matt 12:18ff] Is 53:4 [Matt 8:17; Luke 22:37] Dan 7:13 [Matt 24:30] Mic 5:2 [Matt 2:6] Zech 9:9 [Matt 21:5] Acts 13:27
28 [a]Mark 6:48
29 [1]Lit *has now declined*
30 [a]Matt 14:19
31 [1]Lit *them* [a]Luke 24:16
32 [1]Lit *Was not our heart* [2]Lit *opening* [a]Luke 24:45
33 [a]Mark 16:13 [b]Acts 1:14
34 [a]Luke 24:6 [b]1 Cor 15:5
35 [1]Lit *the things* [a]Luke 24:30f
36 [a]Mark 16:14
37 [a]Matt 14:26; Mark 6:49
38 [1]Lit *heart*
39 [a]John 20:20 [b]John 20:27; 1 John 1:1
41 [1]Lit *were disbelieving* [a]Luke 24:11 [b]John 21:5
43 [a]Acts 10:41
44 [a]Luke 9:22 [b]Luke 24:27 [c]Ps 2:7ff [Acts 13:33] Ps 16:10 [Acts 2:27] Ps 22:1-18 [Matt 27:34-46] Ps 69:1-21 [John 19:28ff] Ps 72; Matt 22:43f] Ps 118:22f [Matt 21:42]
45 [1]Lit *mind* [a]Luke 24:32; Acts 16:14; 1 John 5:20
46 [1]I.e. Messiah [a]Luke 24:26 [b]Luke 24:7
47 [1]Later mss read *and forgiveness* [2]Or *on the basis of* [a]Acts 5:31 [b]Matt 28:19
48 [a]Acts 1:8; 1 Pet 5:1
49 [a]John 14:26 [b]Acts 1:4

you are clothed with power from on high."

The Ascension

50 ¶ And He led them out as far as
[a]Bethany, and He lifted up His hands and
blessed them.

51 While He was blessing them, He
parted from them and was carried up into
heaven.
52 And they, after worshiping Him, returned to Jerusalem with great joy,
53 and were continually in the temple
[1]praising God.

50 [a]Matt 21:17; Acts 1:12

53 [1]Lit *blessing*

John

Title and Background

The Gospel of John was greatly influenced by the Old Testament. The prologue, with its account of the origin of light and life, is evocative of the Genesis account of creation. Reminders of the Passover also occur frequently in John. His name means "The LORD is gracious."

Author and Date of Writing

The author is the apostle John, "the disciple whom Jesus loved." He knew Jewish life well and referred often to Jewish customs. John's account has many touches that were obviously based on the recollections of an eyewitness. The date of writing was probably about A.D. 85 or a little later.

Theme and Message

The writer states his main purpose clearly in 20:31. He may have had Greek readers mainly in mind, and his primary intention was evangelism. John's purpose is not so much to present new evidence as it is to clarify issues on which the evidence will be either accepted or rejected. He writes not so much to inform the reader as to confront him with the necessity to "believe."

Outline

I. Prologue (1:1–18)
II. Beginnings of Jesus' Ministry (1:19–51)
III. Jesus' Ministry: Signs and Discourses (2:1—11:57)
IV. Passion Week (12:1—19:42)
V. The Resurrection (20:1–29)
VI. Statement of Purpose (20:30–31)
VII. Epilogue (21:1–25)

The Deity of Jesus Christ

1 [a]In the beginning was [b]the Word,
and the Word was [c]with God, and
[d]the Word was God.
2 [1]He was in the beginning with
God.
3 [a]All things came into being
through Him, and apart from Him nothing came into being that has come into
being.
4 [a]In Him was life, and the life was
[b]the Light of men.
5 [a]The Light shines in the darkness,
and the darkness did not [1]compre-
hend it.

The Witness John

6 ¶ There [1]came a man sent from
God, whose name was [a]John.
7 [1]He came [2a]as a witness, to testify about the Light, [b]so that all might believe through him.
8 [1a]He was not the Light, but *he*
came to testify about the Light.
9 ¶ There was [a]the true Light
[1]which, coming into the world, enlightens every man.
10 He was in the world, and [a]the
world was made through Him, and the
world did not know Him.
11 He came to His [1]own, and those
who were His own did not receive Him.
12 But as many as received Him, to
them He gave the right to become [a]chil-
dren of God, *even* [b]to those who believe
in His name,
13 [a]who were [1]born, not of [2]blood
nor of the will of the flesh nor of the will
of man, but of God.

The Word Made Flesh

14 ¶ And [a]the Word [b]became flesh,
and [1c]dwelt among us, and [d]we saw His
glory, glory as of [2]the only begotten from
the Father, full of [e]grace and [f]truth.
15 John *[a]testified about Him and
cried out, saying, "This was He of whom

1:1 [a]Gen 1:1; Col 1:17; 1 John 1:1 [b]John 1:14; Rev 19:13 [c]John 17:5; 1 John 1:2 [d]Phil 2:6
2 [1]Lit *This one*
3 [a]John 1:10; 1 Cor 8:6; Col 1:16; Heb 1:2
4 [a]John 5:26 [b]John 8:12
5 [1]Or *overpower* [a]John 3:19
6 [1]Or *came into being* [a]Matt 3:1
7 [1]Lit *This one* [2]Lit *for testimony* [a]John 1:15 [b]John 1:12; Acts 19:4; Gal 3:26
8 [1]Lit *That one* [a]John 1:20
9 [1]Or *which enlightens every person coming into the world* [a]1 John 2:8
10 [a]1 Cor 8:6; Col 1:16; Heb 1:2
11 [1]Or *own things, possessions, domain*
12 [a]John 11:52; Gal 3:26 [b]John 1:7; 1 John 3:23
13 [1]Or *begotten* [2]Lit *bloods* [a]John 3:5f; James 1:18; 1 Pet 1:23; 1 John 2:29

14 [1]Or *tabernacled*; i.e. lived temporarily [2]Or *unique, only one of His kind* [a]Rev 19:13 [b]Rom 1:3; Gal 4:4; Phil 2:7f; 1 Tim 3:16; Heb 2:14; 1 John 1:1f; 2 John 7 [c]Rev 21:3 [d]Luke 9:32; John 2:11; 2 Pet 1:16f; 1 John 1:1 [e]John 1:17; Rom 5:21 [f]John 8:32 **15** [a]John 1:7

I said, ‘[b]He who comes after me [1]has a higher rank than I, [c]for He existed before me.’ ”

16 For of His [a]fullness [1]we have all received, and [2]grace upon grace.

17 For [a]the Law was given through Moses; [b]grace and [c]truth [1]were realized through Jesus Christ.

18 [a]No one has seen God at any time; [b]the only begotten God who is [c]in the bosom of the Father, [d]He has explained *Him.*

The Testimony of John

19 ¶ This is [a]the testimony of John, when [b]the Jews sent to him priests and Levites [c]from Jerusalem to ask him, “Who are you?”

20 And he confessed and did not deny, but confessed, “[a]I am not [1]the Christ.”

21 They asked him, “What then? Are you [a]Elijah?” And he *said, “I am not.” “Are you [b]the Prophet?” And he answered, “No.”

22 Then they said to him, “Who are you, so that we may give an answer to those who sent us? What do you say about yourself?”

23 He said, “I am [a]A VOICE OF ONE CRYING IN THE WILDERNESS, ‘MAKE STRAIGHT THE WAY OF THE LORD,’ as Isaiah the prophet said.”

24 ¶ Now they had been sent from the Pharisees.

25 They asked him, and said to him, “Why then are you baptizing, if you are not the [1]Christ, nor Elijah, nor [a]the Prophet?”

26 John answered them saying, “[a]I baptize [1]in water, *but* among you stands One whom you do not know.

27 “*It is* [a]He who comes after me, the [b]thong of whose sandal I am not worthy to untie.”

28 These things took place in Bethany [a]beyond the Jordan, where John was baptizing.

29 ¶ The next day he *saw Jesus coming to him and *said, “Behold, [a]the Lamb of God who [b]takes away the sin of the world!

30 “This is He on behalf of whom I said, ‘[a]After me comes a Man who [1]has a higher rank than I, [b]for He existed before me.’

31 “I did not recognize [1]Him, but so that He might be manifested to Israel, I came baptizing [2]in water.”

32 John [a]testified saying, “[b]I have seen the Spirit descending as a dove out of heaven, and He remained upon Him.

33 “I did not recognize [1]Him, but He who sent me to baptize [2]in water said to me, ‘He upon whom you see the Spirit descending and remaining upon Him, [a]this is the One who baptizes [2]in the Holy Spirit.’

34 “I myself have seen, and have testified that this is [a]the Son of God.”

Jesus’ Public Ministry, First Converts

35 ¶ Again [a]the next day John was standing [1]with two of his disciples,

36 and he looked at Jesus as He walked, and *said, “Behold, [a]the Lamb of God!”

37 The two disciples heard him speak, and they followed Jesus.

38 And Jesus turned and saw them following, and *said to them, “What do you seek?” They said to Him, “[a]Rabbi (which translated means Teacher), where are You staying?”

39 He *said to them, “Come, and you will see.” So they came and saw where He was staying; and they stayed with Him that day, for it was about the [1]tenth hour.

40 [a]One of the two who heard John *speak* and followed Him, was Andrew, Simon Peter’s brother.

41 He *found first his own brother Simon and *said to him, “We have found the [a]Messiah” (which translated means [1]Christ).

42 He brought him to Jesus. Jesus looked at him and said, “You are Simon the son of [1a]John; you shall be called [b]Cephas” (which is translated [2c]Peter).

43 ¶ [a]The next day He purposed to go into [b]Galilee, and He *found [c]Philip. And Jesus *said to him, “[d]Follow Me.”

44 Now [a]Philip was from [b]Bethsaida, of the city of Andrew and Peter.

45 [a]Philip *found [b]Nathanael and *said to him, “We have found Him of whom [c]Moses in the Law and *also* [c]the Prophets wrote—Jesus of [d]Nazareth, [e]the son of Joseph.”

46 Nathanael said to him, “[a]Can any good thing come out of Nazareth?” [b]Philip *said to him, “Come and see.”

47 Jesus saw Nathanael coming to Him, and *said of him, “Behold, an [a]Israelite indeed, in whom there is no deceit!”

48 Nathanael *said to Him, “How do You know me?” Jesus answered and said to him, “Before [a]Philip called you, when you were under the fig tree, I saw you.”

49 Nathanael answered Him, “[a]Rab-

15 [1]Lit *has become before me* [b]Matt 3:11; John 1:27 [c]John 1:30 **16** [1]Lit *we all received* [2]Lit *grace for grace* [a]Eph 1:23; Col 1:19 **17** [1]Lit *came to be* [a]John 7:19 [b]John 1:14; Rom 5:21 [c]John 8:32 **18** [a]Ex 33:20; John 6:46; Col 1:15; 1 Tim 6:16; 1 John 4:12 [b]John 3:16; 1 John 4:9 [c]Luke 16:22; John 13:23 [d]John 3:11 **19** [a]John 1:7 [b]John 2:18 [c]Matt 15:1 **20** [1]I.e. the Messiah [a]Luke 3:15f; John 3:28 **21** [a]Matt 11:14 [b]Deut 18:15; Matt 21:11; John 1:25 **23** [a]Is 40:3; Matt 3:3; Mark 1:3; Luke 3:4 **25** [1]I.e. Messiah [a]Deut 18:15; Matt 21:11; John 1:21 **26** [1]The Gr here can be translated *in, with* or *by* [a]Matt 3:11; Mark 1:8; Luke 3:16; Acts 1:5 **27** [a]Matt 3:11; John 1:30 [b]Matt 3:11; Mark 1:7; Luke 3:16 **28** [a]John 3:26 **29** [a]Is 53:7; John 1:36; Acts 8:32; 1 Pet 1:19; Rev 5:6 [b]Matt 1:21; 1 John 3:5 **30** [1]Lit *has become before me* [a]Matt 3:11; John 1:27 [b]John 1:15 **31** [1]I.e. as the Messiah [2]The Gr here can be translated *in, with* or *by* **32** [a]John 1:7 [b]Matt 3:16; Mark 1:10; Luke 3:22 **33** [1]I.e. as the Messiah [2]The Gr here can be translated *in, with,* or *by* [a]Matt 3:11; Mark 1:8; Luke 3:16; Acts 1:5 **34** [a]Matt 4:3; John 1:49 **35** [1]Lit *and* [a]John 1:29 **36** [a]John 1:29 **38** [a]Matt 23:7f; John 1:49 **39** [1]Perhaps 10 a.m. (Roman time) **40** [a]Matt 4:18-22; Mark 1:16-20; Luke 5:2-11; John 1:40-42 **41** [1]Gr *Anointed One* [a]Dan 9:25; John 4:25 **42** [1]Gr *Joannes* [2]I.e. Rock or Stone [a]Matt 16:17; John 21:15-17 [b]1 Cor 1:12; Gal 1:18 [c]Matt 16:18 **43** [a]John 1:29 [b]Matt 4:12; John 1:28 [c]Matt 10:3; John 1:44-48 [d]Matt 8:22 **44** [a]Matt 10:3; John 1:44-48 [b]Matt 11:21 **45** [a]Matt 10:3; John 1:44-48 [b]John 1:46-49 [c]Luke 24:27 [d]Matt 2:23 [e]Luke 2:48; John 6:42 **46** [a]John 7:41 [b]Matt 10:3; John 1:44-48 **47** [a]Rom 9:4 **48** [a]Matt 10:3; John 1:44-48 **49** [a]John 1:38

bi, You are [b]the Son of God; You are the
[c]King of Israel."
50 Jesus answered and said to him,
"Because I said to you that I saw you
under the fig tree, do you believe? You
will see greater things than these."
51 And He *said to him, "Truly, truly,
I say to you, you will see [a]the heavens
opened and [b]the angels of God ascending
and descending on [c]the Son of Man."

Miracle at Cana

2 On [a]the third day there was a wedding in [b]Cana of Galilee, and the
[c]mother of Jesus was there;
2 and both Jesus and His [a]disciples
were invited to the wedding.
3 When the wine ran out, the mother
of Jesus *said to Him, "They have no
wine."
4 And Jesus *said to her, "[a]Woman,
[1b]what does that have to do with us?
[c]My hour has not yet come."
5 His [a]mother *said to the servants,
"Whatever He says to you, do it."
6 Now there were six stone water-
pots set there [a]for the Jewish custom of
purification, containing [1]twenty or thirty
gallons each.
7 Jesus *said to them, "Fill the water-
pots with water." So they filled them up
to the brim.
8 And He *said to them, "Draw *some*
out now and take it to the [1]headwaiter."
So they took it *to him.*
9 When the headwaiter tasted the
water [a]which had become wine, and did
not know where it came from (but the
servants who had drawn the water
knew), the headwaiter *called the bridegroom,
10 and *said to him, "Every man
serves the good wine first, and when *the*
people [a]have [1]drunk freely, *then he*
serves the poorer *wine*; *but* you have kept
the good wine until now."
11 This beginning of *His* [1a]signs
Jesus did in Cana of [b]Galilee, and manifested His [c]glory, and His disciples believed in Him.
12 ¶ After this He went down to [a]Ca-
pernaum, He and His [b]mother and *His*
[b]brothers and His [c]disciples; and they
stayed there a few days.

First Passover—Cleansing the Temple

13 ¶ [a]The Passover of the Jews was
near, and Jesus [b]went up to Jerusalem.
14 [a]And He found in the temple those
who were selling oxen and sheep and
doves, and the money changers seated *at*
their tables.

49 [b]John 1:34 [c]Matt 2:2; Mark 15:32; John 12:13
51 [a]Ezek 1:1; Matt 3:16; Luke 3:21; Acts 7:56; Rev 19:11 [b]Gen 28:12 [c]Matt 8:20
2:1 [a]John 1:29 [b]John 2:11 [c]Matt 12:46
2 [a]John 1:40-49
4 [1]Lit *what to Me and to you* (a Hebrew idiom) [a]John 19:26 [b]Matt 8:29 [c]John 7:6
5 [a]Matt 12:46
6 [1]Lit *two or three measures* [a]Mark 7:3f; John 3:25
8 [1]Or *steward*
9 [a]John 4:46
10 [1]Or *have become drunk* [a]Matt 24:49; Luke 12:45; Acts 2:15; 1 Cor 11:21; Eph 5:18; 1 Thess 5:7; Rev 17:2
11 [1]Or *attesting miracles*; i.e. one which points to the supernatural power of God in redeeming grace [a]John 2:23 [b]John 1:43 [c]John 1:14
12 [a]Matt 4:13 [b]Matt 12:46 [c]John 2:2
13 [a]Deut 16:1-6; John 5:1 [b]Luke 2:41; John 2:23
14 [a]John 2:14-16: *Matt 21:12ff; Mark 11:15,17; Luke 19:45f*; Mal 3:1ff
16 [1]Lit *house* [a]Matt 21:12 [b]Luke 2:49
17 [a]John 2:2 [b]Ps 69:9
18 [1]Lit *that You do these* [a]John 1:19 [b]Matt 12:38
19 [1]Or *sanctuary* [a]Matt 26:61; Mark 14:58; Acts 6:14
20 [1]Or *sanctuary* [a]John 1:19 [b]Ezra 5:16
21 [1]Or *sanctuary* [a]1 Cor 6:19
22 [a]John 2:2 [b]Luke 24:8; John 2:17 [c]Ps 16:10; Luke 24:26f; John 20:9; Acts 13:33
23 [a]John 2:13 [b]John 2:11
24 [a]Acts 1:24
25 [a]Matt 9:4; John 1:42
3:1 [a]John 7:50 [b]Luke 23:13; John 7:26
2 [1]Or *attesting miracles* [a]Matt 23:7; John 3:26 [b]John 2:11 [c]John 9:33; Acts 2:22
3 [1]Or *from above* [a]2 Cor 5:17; 1 Pet 1:23 [b]Matt 19:24; Mark 9:47; John 3:5
5 [a]Ezek 36:25-27; Eph 5:26; Titus 3:5 [b]Matt 19:24; Mark 9:47; John 3:3
6 [a]John 1:13; 1 Cor 15:50

15 And He made a scourge of cords,
and drove *them* all out of the temple,
with the sheep and the oxen; and He
poured out the coins of the money changers and overturned their tables;
16 and to those who were selling [a]the
doves He said, "Take these things away;
stop making [b]My Father's house a
[1]place of business."
17 His [a]disciples remembered that it
was written, "[b]ZEAL FOR YOUR HOUSE WILL
CONSUME ME."
18 [a]The Jews then said to Him,
"[b]What sign do You show us [1]as your
authority for doing these things?"
19 Jesus answered them, "[a]Destroy
this [1]temple, and in three days I will
raise it up."
20 [a]The Jews then said, "It took
[b]forty-six years to build this [1]temple,
and will You raise it up in three days?"
21 But He was speaking of [a]the [1]tem-
ple of His body.
22 So when He was raised from the
dead, His [a]disciples [b]remembered that
He said this; and they believed [c]the
Scripture and the word which Jesus had
spoken.
23 ¶ Now when He was in Jerusalem
at [a]the Passover, during the feast, many
believed in His name, [b]observing His
signs which He was doing.
24 But Jesus, on His part, was not entrusting Himself to them, for [a]He knew
all men,
25 and because He did not need anyone to testify concerning man, [a]for He
Himself knew what was in man.

The New Birth

3 Now there was a man of the Pharisees, named [a]Nicodemus, a [b]ruler
of the Jews;
2 this man came to Jesus by night and
said to Him, "[a]Rabbi, we know that You
have come from God *as* a teacher; for no
one can do these [1b]signs that You do
unless [c]God is with him."
3 Jesus answered and said to him,
"Truly, truly, I say to you, unless one [a]is
born [1]again he cannot see [b]the kingdom
of God."
4 ¶ Nicodemus *said to Him, "How
can a man be born when he is old? He
cannot enter a second time into his mother's womb and be born, can he?"
5 Jesus answered, "Truly, truly, I say
to you, unless one is born of [a]water and
the Spirit he cannot enter into [b]the kingdom of God.
6 "[a]That which is born of the flesh is

flesh, and that which is born of the Spirit is spirit.

7 "Do not be amazed that I said to you, 'You must be born [1]again.'

8 "[a]The wind blows where it wishes and you hear the sound of it, but do not know where it comes from and where it is going; so is everyone who is born of the Spirit."

9 ¶ Nicodemus said to Him, "How can these things be?"

10 Jesus answered and said to him, "Are you [a]the teacher of Israel and do not understand these things?

11 "Truly, truly, I say to you, [a]we speak of what we know and [b]testify of what we have seen, and [b]you do not accept our testimony.

12 "If I told you earthly things and you do not believe, how will you believe if I tell you heavenly things?

13 "[a]No one has ascended into heaven, but [b]He who descended from heaven: [c]the Son of Man.

14 "As [a]Moses lifted up the serpent in the wilderness, even so must [b]the Son of Man [c]be lifted up;

15 so that whoever [1]believes will [a]in Him have eternal life.

16 ¶ "For God so [a]loved the world, that He [b]gave His [1c]only begotten Son, that whoever [d]believes in Him shall not perish, but have eternal life.

17 "For God [a]did not send the Son into the world [b]to judge the world, but that the world might be saved through Him.

18 "[a]He who believes in Him is not judged; he who does not believe has been judged already, because he has not believed in the name of [b]the [1]only begotten Son of God.

19 "This is the judgment, that [a]the Light has come into the world, and men loved the darkness rather than the Light, for [b]their deeds were evil.

20 "[a]For everyone who does evil hates the Light, and does not come to the Light for fear that his deeds will be exposed.

21 "But he who [a]practices the truth comes to the Light, so that his deeds may be manifested as having been wrought in God."

John's Last Testimony

22 ¶ After these things Jesus and His [a]disciples came into the land of Judea, and there He was spending time with them and [b]baptizing.

23 John also was baptizing in Aenon near Salim, because there was much water there; and *people* were coming and were being baptized—

24 for [a]John had not yet been thrown into prison.

25 ¶ Therefore there arose a discussion on the part of John's disciples with a Jew about [a]purification.

26 And they came to John and said to him, "[a]Rabbi, He who was with you [b]beyond the Jordan, to whom you [c]have testified, behold, He is baptizing and all are coming to Him."

27 John answered and said, "[a]A man can receive nothing unless it [b]has been given him from heaven.

28 "You yourselves [1]are my witnesses that I said, '[a]I am not the [2]Christ,' but, 'I have been sent ahead of Him.'

29 "He who has the bride is [a]the bridegroom; but the friend of the bridegroom, who stands and hears him, rejoices greatly because of the bridegroom's voice. So this [b]joy of mine has been made full.

30 "He must increase, but I must decrease.

31 ¶ "[a]He who comes from above is above all, [b]he who is of the earth is from the earth and speaks of the earth. [a]He who comes from heaven is above all.

32 "What He has seen and heard, of that He [a]testifies; and [a]no one receives His testimony.

33 "He who has received His testimony [a]has set his seal to *this,* that God is true.

34 "For He whom God has [a]sent speaks the words of God; [1b]for He gives the Spirit without measure.

35 "[a]The Father loves the Son and [b]has given all things into His hand.

36 "He who [a]believes in the Son has eternal life; but he who [b]does not [1]obey the Son will not see life, but the wrath of God abides on him."

Jesus Goes to Galilee

4 Therefore when [a]the Lord knew that the Pharisees had heard that Jesus was making and [b]baptizing more disciples than John

2 (although [a]Jesus Himself was not baptizing, but His [b]disciples were),

3 He left [a]Judea and went away [b]again into Galilee.

4 And He had to pass through [a]Samaria.

5 So He *came to a city of [a]Samaria called Sychar, near [b]the parcel of ground that [c]Jacob gave to his son Joseph;

6 and Jacob's well was there. So Jesus, being wearied from His journey, was sitting thus by the well. It was about [1]the sixth hour.

The Woman of Samaria

7 ¶ There *came a woman of Samaria

7 [1]Or *from above*
8 [a]Ps 135:7; Eccl 11:5; Ezek 37:9
10 [a]Luke 2:46; Acts 5:34
11 [a]John 1:18 [b]John 3:32
13 [a]Deut 30:12; Prov 30:4; Acts 2:34; Rom 10:6; Eph 4:9 [b]John 3:31 [c]Matt 8:20
14 [a]Num 21:9 [b]Matt 8:20 [c]John 8:28
15 [1]Or *believes in Him will have eternal life* [a]John 20:31; 1 John 5:11-13
16 [1]Or *unique, only one of His kind* [a]Rom 5:8; Eph 2:4; 2 Thess 2:16; 1 John 4:10; Rev 1:5 [b]Rom 8:32; 1 John 4:9 [c]John 1:18; 1 John 4:9 [d]John 3:36
17 [a]John 3:34 [b]Luke 19:10; John 8:15; 1 John 4:14
18 [1]Or *unique, only one of His kind* [a]Mark 16:16; John 5:24 [b]John 1:18; 1 John 4:9
19 [a]John 1:4 [b]John 7:7
20 [a]John 3:20; Eph 5:11
21 [a]1 John 1:6
22 [a]John 2:2 [b]John 4:1
24 [a]Matt 4:12; Mark 6:17; Luke 3:20
25 [a]John 2:6
26 [a]Matt 23:7; John 3:2 [b]John 1:28 [c]John 1:7
27 [a]1 Cor 4:7; Heb 5:4 [b]James 1:17
28 [1]Lit *testify for me* [2]I.e. Messiah [a]John 1:20
29 [a]Matt 9:15 [b]John 15:11; Phil 2:2; 1 John 1:4; 2 John 12
31 [a]Matt 28:18; John 3:13 [b]1 Cor 15:47; 1 John 4:5
32 [a]John 3:11
33 [a]John 6:27; Rom 4:11; 1 Cor 9:2; 2 Cor 1:22; Eph 1:13; 2 Tim 2:19; Rev 7:3-8
34 [1]Lit *because He does not give the Spirit by measure* [a]John 3:17 [b]Matt 12:18; Luke 4:18; Acts 1:2
35 [a]Matt 28:18; John 5:20 [b]Matt 11:27; Luke 10:22
36 [1]Or *believe* [a]John 3:16 [b]Acts 14:2; Heb 3:18
4:1 [a]Luke 7:13 [b]John 3:22; 1 Cor 1:17
2 [a]John 3:22; 1 Cor 1:17 [b]John 2:2
3 [a]John 3:22 [b]John 2:11f
4 [a]Luke 9:52

5 [a]Luke 9:52 [b]Gen 33:19; Josh 24:32 [c]Gen 48:22; John 4:12 **6** [1]Perhaps 6 p.m. Roman time or noon Jewish time to draw water. Jesus *said to her, "Give Me a drink."

8 For His [a]disciples had gone away into [b]the city to buy food.

9 Therefore the [a]Samaritan woman *said to Him, "How is it that You, being a Jew, ask me for a drink since I am a Samaritan woman?" (For [b]Jews have no dealings with Samaritans.)

10 Jesus answered and said to her, "If you knew the gift of God, and who it is who says to you, 'Give Me a drink,' you would have asked Him, and He would have given you [a]living water."

11 She *said to Him, "[1]Sir, You have nothing to draw with and the well is deep; where then do You get that [a]living water?

12 "You are not greater than our father Jacob, are You, who [a]gave us the well, and drank of it himself and his sons and his cattle?"

13 Jesus answered and said to her, "Everyone who drinks of this water will thirst again;

14 but whoever drinks of the water that I will give him [a]shall never thirst; but the water that I will give him will become in him a well of water springing up to [b]eternal life."

15 ¶ The woman *said to Him, "[1]Sir, [a]give me this water, so I will not be thirsty nor come all the way here to draw."

16 He *said to her, "Go, call your husband and come here."

17 The woman answered and said, "I have no husband." Jesus *said to her, "You have correctly said, 'I have no husband';

18 for you have had five husbands, and the one whom you now have is not your husband; this you have said truly."

19 The woman *said to Him, "[1]Sir, I perceive that You are [a]a prophet.

20 "[a]Our fathers worshiped in [b]this mountain, and you *people* say that [c]in Jerusalem is the place where men ought to worship."

21 Jesus *said to her, "Woman, believe Me, [a]an hour is coming when [b]neither in this mountain nor in Jerusalem will you worship the Father.

22 "[a]You worship what you do not know; we worship what we know, for [b]salvation is from the Jews.

23 "But [a]an hour is coming, and now is, when the true worshipers will worship the Father [b]in spirit and truth; for such people the Father seeks to be His worshipers.

24 "God is [1]spirit, and those who worship Him must worship [a]in spirit and truth."

25 The woman *said to Him, "I know that [a]Messiah is coming ([b]He who is called Christ); when that One comes, He will declare all things to us."

26 Jesus *said to her, "[a]I who speak to you am *He.*"

27 ¶ At this point His [a]disciples came, and they were amazed that He had been speaking with a woman, yet no one said, "What do You seek?" or, "Why do You speak with her?"

28 So the woman left her waterpot, and went into the city and *said to the men,

29 "Come, see a man [a]who told me all the things that I *have* done; [b]this is not [1]the Christ, is it?"

30 They went out of the city, and were coming to Him.

31 ¶ Meanwhile the disciples were urging Him, saying, "[a]Rabbi, eat."

32 But He said to them, "I have food to eat that you do not know about."

33 So the [a]disciples were saying to one another, "No one brought Him *anything* to eat, did he?"

34 Jesus *said to them, "My food is to [a]do the will of Him who sent Me and to [b]accomplish His work.

35 "Do you not say, 'There are yet four months, and *then* comes the harvest'? Behold, I say to you, lift up your eyes and look on the fields, that they are white [a]for harvest.

36 "Already he who reaps is receiving [a]wages and is gathering [b]fruit for [c]life eternal; so that he who sows and he who reaps may rejoice together.

37 "For in this *case* the saying is true, '[a]One sows and another reaps.'

38 "I sent you to reap that for which you have not labored; others have labored and you have entered into their labor."

The Samaritans

39 ¶ From [a]that city many of the Samaritans believed in Him because of the word of the woman who testified, "[b]He told me all the things that I *have* done."

40 So when the Samaritans came to Jesus, they were asking Him to stay with them; and He stayed there two days.

41 Many more believed because of His word;

42 and they were saying to the woman, "It is no longer because of what you said that we believe, for we have heard for ourselves and know that this One is indeed [a]the Savior of the world."

43 ¶ After [a]the two days He went forth from there into Galilee.

44 For Jesus Himself testified that [a]a prophet has no honor in his own country.

8 [a]John 2:2 [b]John 4:5,39
9 [a]Luke 9:52 [b]Ezra 4:3-6,11ff; Matt 10:5; John 8:48; Acts 10:28
10 [a]Jer 2:13; John 4:14; 7:37f; Rev 7:17; 21:6; 22:1,17
11 [1]Or *Lord* [a]Jer 2:13; John 4:14; 7:37f; Rev 7:17; 21:6; 22:1,17
12 [a]John 4:6
14 [a]John 6:35; 7:38 [b]Matt 25:46; John 6:27
15 [1]Or *Lord* [a]John 6:35
19 [1]Or *Lord* [a]Matt 21:11; Luke 7:16,39; 24:19; John 6:14; 7:40; 9:17
20 [a]Gen 33:20; John 4:12 [b]Deut 11:29; Josh 8:33 [c]Luke 9:53
21 [a]John 4:23; 5:25,28; 16:2,32 [b]Mal 1:11; 1 Tim 2:8
22 [a]2 Kin 17:28-41 [b]Is 2:3; Rom 3:1f; 9:4f
23 [a]John 4:21; 5:25,28; 16:2,32 [b]Phil 3:3
24 [1]Or *Spirit* [a]Phil 3:3
25 [a]Dan 9:25; John 1:41 [b]Matt 1:16; 27:17,22; Luke 2:11
26 [a]John 8:24, 28,58; 9:37; 13:19
27 [a]John 4:8
29 [1]I.e. the Messiah [a]John 4:17f [b]Matt 12:23; John 7:26,31
31 [a]Matt 23:7; 26:25,49; Mark 9:5; 11:21; 14:45; John 1:38,49; 3:2,26; 6:25; 9:2; 11:8
33 [a]Luke 6:13-16; John 1:40-49; 2:2
34 [a]John 5:30; 6:38 [b]John 5:36; 17:4; 19:28,30
35 [a]Matt 9:37, 38; Luke 10:2
36 [a]Prov 11:18; 1 Cor 9:17f [b]Rom 1:13 [c]Matt 19:29; John 3:36; 4:14; 5:24; Rom 2:7; 6:23
37 [a]Job 31:8; Mic 6:15
39 [a]John 4:5,30 [b]John 4:29
42 [a]Matt 1:21; Luke 2:11; John 1:29; Acts 5:31; 13:23; 1 Tim 4:10; 1 John 4:14
43 [a]John 4:40
44 [a]Matt 13:57; Mark 6:4; Luke 4:24

45 So when He came to Galilee, the Galileans received Him, [a]having seen all the things that He did in Jerusalem at the feast; for they themselves also went to the feast.

Healing a Nobleman's Son

46 ¶ Therefore He came again to [a]Cana of Galilee [b]where He had made the water wine. And there was a royal official whose son was sick at [c]Capernaum.

47 When he heard that Jesus had come [a]out of Judea into Galilee, he went to Him and was imploring *Him* to come down and heal his son; for he was at the point of death.

48 So Jesus said to him, "Unless you *people* see [1a]signs and [a]wonders, you *simply* will not believe."

49 The royal official *said to Him, "[1]Sir, come down before my child dies."

50 Jesus *said to him, "[a]Go; your son lives." The man believed the word that Jesus spoke to him and started off.

51 As he was now going down, *his* slaves met him, saying that his [1]son was living.

52 So he inquired of them the hour when he began to get better. Then they said to him, "Yesterday at the [1]seventh hour the fever left him."

53 So the father knew that *it was* at that hour in which Jesus said to him, "Your son lives"; and he himself believed and [a]his whole household.

54 This is again a [a]second [1]sign that Jesus performed when He had [b]come out of Judea into Galilee.

The Healing at Bethesda

5 After these things there was [a]a feast of the Jews, and Jesus went up to Jerusalem.

2 ¶ Now there is in Jerusalem by [a]the sheep *gate* a pool, which is called [b]in [1]Hebrew [2]Bethesda, having five porticoes.

3 In these lay a multitude of those who were sick, blind, lame, and withered, [[1]waiting for the moving of the waters;

4 for an angel of the Lord went down at certain seasons into the pool and stirred up the water; whoever then first, after the stirring up of the water, stepped in was made well from whatever disease with which he was afflicted.]

5 A man was there who had been [1]ill for thirty-eight years.

6 When Jesus saw him lying *there*, and knew that he had already been a long time *in that condition,* He *said to him, "Do you wish to get well?"

7 The sick man answered Him, "Sir, I have no man to put me into the pool when [a]the water is stirred up, but while I am coming, another steps down before me."

8 Jesus *said to him, "[a]Get up, pick up your pallet and walk."

9 Immediately the man became well, and picked up his pallet and *began* to walk.

¶ [a]Now it was the Sabbath on that day.

10 So [a]the Jews were saying to the man who was cured, "It is the Sabbath, and [b]it is not permissible for you to carry your pallet."

11 But he answered them, "He who made me well was the one who said to me, 'Pick up your pallet and walk.' "

12 They asked him, "Who is the man who said to you, 'Pick up *your pallet* and walk'?"

13 But the man who was healed did not know who it was, for Jesus had slipped away while there was a crowd in *that* place.

14 Afterward Jesus *found him in the temple and said to him, "Behold, you have become well; do not [a]sin anymore, [b]so that nothing worse happens to you."

15 The man went away, and told [a]the Jews that it was Jesus who had made him well.

16 For this reason [a]the Jews were persecuting Jesus, because He was doing these things on the Sabbath.

17 But He answered them, "My Father is working until now, and I Myself am working."

Jesus' Equality with God

18 For this reason therefore [a]the Jews [b]were seeking all the more to kill Him, because He not only was breaking the Sabbath, but also was calling God His own Father, [c]making Himself equal with God.

19 ¶ Therefore Jesus answered and was saying to them, "Truly, truly, I say to you, [a]the Son can do nothing of Himself, unless *it is* something He sees the Father doing; for whatever [1]the Father does, these things the Son also does in like manner.

20 "[a]For the Father loves the Son, and shows Him all things that He Himself is doing; and *the Father* will show Him [b]greater works than these, so that you will marvel.

21 "For just as the Father raises the dead and [a]gives them life, even so [b]the Son also gives life to whom He wishes.

22 "For not even the Father judges anyone, but [a]He has given all judgment to the Son,

45 [a]John 2:23
46 [a]John 2:1 [b]John 2:9 [c]Luke 4:23; John 2:12
47 [a]John 4:3,54
48 [1]Or *attesting miracles* [a]Dan 4:2f; 6:27; Matt 24:24; Mark 13:22; Acts 2:19,22,43; 4:30; 5:12; 6:8; 7:36; 14:3; 15:12; Rom 15:19; 1 Cor 1:22; 2 Cor 12:12; 2 Thess 2:9; Heb 2:4
49 [1]Or *Lord*
50 [a]Matt 8:13
51 [1]Or *boy*
52 [1]Perhaps 7 p.m. Roman time or 1 p.m. Jewish time
53 [a]Acts 11:14
54 [1]Or *attesting miracle* [a]John 2:11 [b]John 4:45f
5:1 [a]Deut 16:1; John 2:13
2 [1]I.e. Jewish Aramaic [2]Some early mss read *Bethsaida* or *Bethzatha* [a]Neh 3:1,32; 12:39 [b]John 19:13,17, 20; 20:16; Acts 21:40; Rev 9:11; 16:16
3 [1]Early mss do not contain the remainder of v 3, nor v 4
5 [1]Lit *in his sickness*
7 [a]John 5:4
8 [a]Matt 9:6; Mark 2:11; Luke 5:24
9 [a]John 9:14
10 [a]John 1:19; 5:15,16,18 [b]Neh 13:19; Jer 17:21f; Matt 12:2; Luke 6:2; John 7:23; 9:16
14 [a]Mark 2:5; John 8:11 [b]Ezra 9:14
15 [a]John 1:19; 5:16,18
16 [a]John 1:19; 5:10,15,18
18 [a]John 1:19; 5:15,16 [b]John 5:16; 7:1 [c]John 10:33; 19:7
19 [1]Lit *that One* [a]Matt 26:39; John 5:30; 6:38; 8:28; 12:49; 14:10
20 [a]Matt 3:17; John 3:35; 2 Pet 1:17 [b]John 14:12
21 [a]Rom 4:17; 8:11 [b]John 11:25
22 [a]John 5:27; 9:39; Acts 10:42; 17:31

23 so that all will honor the Son even
as they honor the Father. [a]He who does
not honor the Son does not honor the
Father who sent Him.
24 ¶ "Truly, truly, I say to you, he who
hears My word, and [a]believes Him who
sent Me, has eternal life, and [b]does not
come into judgment, but has [c]passed out
of death into life.

Two Resurrections

25 "Truly, truly, I say to you, [a]an hour
is coming and now is, when [b]the dead
will hear the voice of the Son of God, and
those who [c]hear will live.
26 "For just as the Father has life in
Himself, even so He [a]gave to the Son also
to have life in Himself;
27 and He gave Him authority to [a]exe-
cute judgment, because He is [1]*the* Son of
Man.
28 "Do not marvel at this; for [a]an hour
is coming, in which [b]all who are in the
tombs will hear His voice,
29 and will come forth; [a]those who
did the good *deeds* to a resurrection of
life, those who committed the evil *deeds*
to a resurrection of judgment.
30 ¶ "[a]I can do nothing on My own
initiative. As I hear, I judge; and [b]My
judgment is just, because I do not seek
My own will, but [c]the will of Him who
sent Me.
31 ¶ "[a]If I *alone* testify about Myself,
My testimony is not [1]true.
32 "There is [a]another who testifies of
Me, and I know that the testimony which
He gives about Me is true.

Witness of John

33 "You have sent to John, and he [a]has
testified to the truth.
34 "But [a]the testimony which I receive
is not from man, but I say these things so
that you may be saved.
35 "He was [a]the lamp that was burning
and was shining and you [b]were willing to
rejoice for [1]a while in his light.

Witness of Works

36 "But the testimony which I have is
greater than *the testimony of* John; for
[a]the works which the Father has given
Me [b]to accomplish—the very works that
I do—testify about Me, that the Father
[c]has sent Me.

Witness of the Father

37 "And the Father who sent Me, [a]He
has testified of Me. You have neither
heard His voice at any time nor seen His
form.
38 "You do not have [a]His word abiding
in you, for you do not believe Him whom
He [b]sent.

Witness of the Scripture

39 "[1a]You search the Scriptures because you think that in them you have
eternal life; it is [b]these that testify
about Me;
40 and you are unwilling to come to
Me so that you may have life.
41 "[a]I do not receive glory from men;
42 but I know you, that you do not
have the love of God in yourselves.
43 "I have come in My Father's name,
and you do not receive Me; [a]if another
comes in his own name, you will receive
him.
44 "How can you believe, when you
[a]receive [1]glory from one another and
you do not seek [b]the [1]glory that is from
[c]the *one and* only God?
45 "Do not think that I will accuse you
before the Father; the one who accuses
you is [a]Moses, in whom you have set
your hope.
46 "For if you believed Moses, you
would believe Me, for [a]he wrote
about Me.
47 "But [a]if you do not believe his writings, how will you believe My words?"

Five Thousand Fed

6 After these things [a]Jesus went away
to the other side of [b]the Sea of Galilee (or [c]Tiberias).
2 A large crowd followed Him, because they saw the [1a]signs which He
was performing on those who were sick.
3 Then [a]Jesus went up on the mountain, and there He sat down with His disciples.
4 Now [a]the Passover, the feast of the
Jews, was near.
5 Therefore Jesus, lifting up His eyes
and seeing that a large crowd was coming
to Him, *said to [a]Philip, "Where are we
to buy bread, so that these may eat?"
6 This He was saying to [a]test him,
for He Himself knew what He was intending to do.
7 [a]Philip answered Him, "[b]Two
hundred [1]denarii worth of bread is not
sufficient for them, for everyone to receive a little."
8 One of His [a]disciples, [b]Andrew,
Simon Peter's brother, *said to Him,
9 "There is a lad here who has five
barley loaves and two [a]fish, but what are
these for so many people?"
10 Jesus said, "Have the people [1]sit
down." Now there was [a]much grass in
the place. So the men [1]sat down, in number about [b]five thousand.
11 Jesus then took the loaves, and

---

23 [a]Luke 10:16; 1 John 2:23
24 [a]John 3:18; 1 John 5:13 [b]John 3:18 [c]1 John 3:14
25 [a]John 4:21 [b]Luke 15:24 [c]John 6:60
26 [a]John 1:4
27 [1]Or *a son of man* [a]John 9:39; Acts 10:42
28 [a]John 4:21 [b]John 11:24; 1 Cor 15:52
29 [a]Dan 12:2; Matt 25:46; Acts 24:15
30 [a]John 5:19 [b]John 8:16 [c]John 4:34
31 [1]I.e. admissible as legal evidence [a]John 8:14
32 [a]John 5:37
33 [a]John 1:7
34 [a]John 5:32; 1 John 5:9
35 [1]Lit *an hour* [a]2 Sam 21:17; 2 Pet 1:19 [b]Mark 1:5
36 [a]Matt 11:4; John 2:23 [b]John 4:34 [c]John 3:17
37 [a]Matt 3:17; Mark 1:11; Luke 3:22; John 8:18; 1 John 5:9
38 [a]1 John 2:14 [b]John 3:17
39 [1]Or (a command) *Search the Scriptures!* [a]John 7:52; Rom 2:17ff [b]Luke 24:25; Acts 13:27
41 [a]John 5:44; 1 Thess 2:6
43 [a]Matt 24:5
44 [1]Or *honor* or *fame* [a]John 5:41 [b]Rom 2:29 [c]John 17:3; 1 Tim 1:17
45 [a]John 9:28; Rom 2:17ff
46 [a]Luke 24:27
47 [a]Luke 16:29
6:1 [a]John 6:1-13: *Matt 14:13-21; Mark 6:32-44* [b]*Matt 4:18; Luke 5:1* [c]*John 6:23*
2 [1]*Or attesting miracles* [a]John 2:11
3 [a]Matt 5:1; Mark 3:13; Luke 6:12; John 6:15
4 [a]Deut 16:1; John 2:13
5 [a]John 1:43
6 [a]2 Cor 13:5; Rev 2:2
7 [1]The denarius was equivalent to a day's wages [a]John 1:43 [b]Mark 6:37
8 [a]John 2:2 [b]John 1:40
9 [a]John 6:11
10 [1]Lit *recline(d)* [a]Mark 6:39 [b]Matt 14:21

[a]having given thanks, He distributed to
those who were seated; likewise also of
the [b]fish as much as they wanted.
12 When they were filled, He *said to
His [a]disciples, "Gather up the leftover
fragments so that nothing will be lost."
13 So they gathered them up, and
filled twelve [a]baskets with fragments
from the five barley loaves which were
left over by those who had eaten.
14 Therefore when the people saw the
[1]sign which He had performed, they
said, "This is truly the [a]Prophet who is to
come into the world."

Jesus Walks on the Water

15 ¶ So Jesus, perceiving that they
were [1]intending to come and take Him
by force [a]to make Him king, [b]withdrew
again to [c]the mountain by Himself alone.
16 ¶ Now when evening came, His
[a]disciples went down to the sea,
17 and after getting into a boat, they
started to cross the sea [a]to Capernaum.
It had already become dark, and Jesus had
not yet come to them.
18 The sea *began* to be stirred up because a strong wind was blowing.
19 Then, when they had rowed about
[1]three or four miles, they *saw Jesus
walking on the sea and drawing near to
the boat; and they were frightened.
20 But He *said to them, "It is I; [1][a]do
not be afraid."
21 So they were willing to receive Him
into the boat, and immediately the boat
was at the land to which they were going.
22 ¶ The next day [a]the crowd that
stood on the other side of the sea saw that
there was no other small boat there, except one, and that Jesus [b]had not entered
with His disciples into the boat, but *that*
His disciples had gone away alone.
23 There came other small boats from
[a]Tiberias near to the place where they
ate the bread after the [b]Lord [c]had given
thanks.
24 So when the crowd saw that Jesus
was not there, nor His disciples, they
themselves got into the small boats, and
[a]came to Capernaum seeking Jesus.
25 When they found Him on the other
side of the sea, they said to Him, "[a]Rabbi, when did You get here?"

Words to the People

26 ¶ Jesus answered them and said,
"Truly, truly, I say to you, you [a]seek Me,
not because you saw [b]signs, but because
you ate of the loaves and were filled.
27 "Do not [a]work for the food which
perishes, but for the food which endures
to [b]eternal life, which [c]the Son of Man
will give to you, for on Him the Father,
God, [d]has set His seal."
28 Therefore they said to Him, "What
shall we do, so that we may work the
works of God?"
29 Jesus answered and said to them,
"This is [a]the work of God, that you believe in Him whom He [b]has sent."
30 So they said to Him, "[a]What then
do You do for a [b]sign, so that we may see,
and believe You? What work do You perform?
31 "[a]Our fathers ate the manna in the
wilderness; as it is written, '[b]HE GAVE
THEM BREAD OUT OF HEAVEN TO EAT.' "
32 Jesus then said to them, "Truly, truly, I say to you, it is not Moses who has
given you the bread out of heaven, but
it is My Father who gives you the true
bread out of heaven.
33 "For the bread of God is [1]that which
[a]comes down out of heaven, and gives
life to the world."
34 Then they said to Him, "Lord, always [a]give us this bread."
35 ¶ Jesus said to them, "[a]I am the
bread of life; he who comes to Me will
not hunger, and he who believes in Me
[b]will never thirst.
36 "But [a]I said to you that you have
seen Me, and yet do not believe.
37 "[a]All that the Father gives Me will
come to Me, and the one who comes to
Me I will certainly not cast out.
38 "For [a]I have come down from heaven, [b]not to do My own will, but [c]the will
of Him who [d]sent Me.
39 "This is the will of Him who sent
Me, that of [a]all that He has given Me I
[b]lose nothing, but [c]raise it up on the last
day.
40 "For this is the will of My Father,
that everyone who [a]beholds the Son and
[b]believes in Him will have eternal life,
and I Myself will [c]raise him up on the
last day."

Words to the Jews

41 ¶ [a]Therefore the Jews were grumbling about Him, because He said, "I am
the bread that [b]came down out of
heaven."
42 They were saying, "[a]Is not this
Jesus, the son of Joseph, whose father and
mother [b]we know? How does He now
say, '[c]I have come down out of
heaven'?"
43 Jesus answered and said to them,
"Do not grumble among yourselves.
44 "No one can come to Me unless the
Father who sent Me [a]draws him; and I
will [b]raise him up on the last day.
45 "It is written [a]in the prophets,
'[b]AND THEY SHALL ALL BE [c]TAUGHT OF

11 [a]Matt 15:36; John 6:23 [b]John 6:9; 21:9,10,13
12 [a]John 2:2
13 [a]Matt 14:20
14 [1]Or *attesting miracle* [a]Matt 11:3; 21:11; John 1:21
15 [1]Or *about* [a]John 18:36f [b]John 6:15-21: *Matt 14:22-33; Mark 6:45-51* [c]John 6:3
16 [a]John 2:2
17 [a]Mark 6:45; John 6:24,59
19 [1]Lit *25 or 30 stadia*
20 [1]Or *stop being afraid* [a]Matt 14:27
22 [a]John 6:2 [b]John 6:15ff
23 [a]John 6:1 [b]Luke 7:13 [c]John 6:11
24 [a]Matt 14:34; Mark 6:53; John 6:17,59
25 [a]Matt 23:7
26 [a]John 6:24 [b]John 6:2,14,30
27 [a]Is 55:2 [b]John 3:15f; 4:14; 6:40,47, 54; 10:28; 17:2f [c]Matt 8:20; John 6:53,62 [d]John 3:33
29 [a]1 Thess 1:3; James 2:22; 1 John 3:23; Rev 2:26 [b]John 3:17
30 [a]Matt 12:38 [b]John 6:2,14,26
31 [a]Ex 16:4,15, 21; Num 11:8; John 6:49,58 [b]Ps 78:24; Ex 16:4, 15; Neh 9:15; Ps 105:40
33 [1]Or *He who comes* [a]John 6:41,50
34 [a]John 4:15
35 [a]John 6:48, 51 [b]John 4:14
36 [a]John 6:26
37 [a]John 6:39; 17:2,24
38 [a]John 3:13 [b]Matt 26:39 [c]John 4:34; 5:30 [d]John 6:29
39 [a]John 6:37; 17:2,24 [b]John 17:12; 18:9 [c]Matt 10:15; John 6:40,44,54; 11:24
40 [a]John 12:45; 14:17,19 [b]John 3:16 [c]Matt 10:15; John 6:39,44,54; 11:24
41 [a]John 1:19; 6:52 [b]John 6:33, 51,58
42 [a]Luke 4:22 [b]John 7:27f [c]John 6:38,62
44 [a]Jer 31:3; Hos 11:4; John 6:65; 12:32 [b]John 6:39
45 [a]Acts 7:42; 13:40; Heb 8:11 [b]Is 54:13; Jer 31:34 [c]Phil 3:15; 1 Thess 4:9; 1 John 2:27

GOD.' Everyone who has heard and
learned from the Father, comes to Me.
46"[a]Not that anyone has seen the Father, except the One who is from God;
He has seen the Father.
47"Truly, truly, I say to you, he who
believes [a]has eternal life.
48"[a]I am the bread of life.
49"[a]Your fathers ate the manna in the
wilderness, and they died.
50"This is the bread which [a]comes
down out of heaven, so that one may eat
of it and [b]not die.
51"[a]I am the living bread that [b]came
down out of heaven; if anyone eats of this
bread, [c]he will live forever; and the
bread also which I will give [d]for the life
of the world is [e]My flesh."
52 ¶ [a]Then the Jews [b]*began* to argue
with one another, saying, "How can this
man give us *His* flesh to eat?"
53 So Jesus said to them, "Truly, truly,
I say to you, unless you eat the flesh of
[a]the Son of Man and drink His blood, you
have no life in yourselves.
54"He who eats My flesh and drinks
My blood has eternal life, and I will
[a]raise him up on the last day.
55"For My flesh is true food, and My
blood is true drink.
56"He who eats My flesh and drinks
My blood [a]abides in Me, and I in him.
57"As the [a]living Father [b]sent Me,
and I live because of the Father, so he
who eats Me, he also will live because
of Me.
58"This is the bread which [a]came
down out of heaven; not as [b]the fathers
ate and died; he who eats this bread [c]will
live forever."

Words to the Disciples

59 These things He said [a]in the synagogue as He taught [b]in Capernaum.
60 ¶ Therefore many of His [a]disci-
ples, when they heard *this* said, "[b]This
is a difficult statement; who can listen
to it?"
61 But Jesus, [a]conscious that His disciples grumbled at this, said to them,
"Does this [b]cause you to stumble?
62 *"What* then if you see [a]the Son of
Man [b]ascending to where He was before?
63"[a]It is the Spirit who gives life; the
flesh profits nothing; [b]the words that I
have spoken to you are spirit and are life.
64"But there are [a]some of you who do
not believe." For Jesus [b]knew from the
beginning who they were who did not
believe, and [c]who it was that would [1]be-
tray Him.
65 And He was saying, "For this reason I have [a]said to you, that no one can
come to Me unless [b]it has been granted
him from the Father."

Peter's Confession of Faith

66 ¶ As a result of this many of His
[a]disciples [b]withdrew and were not
walking with Him anymore.
67 So Jesus said to [a]the twelve, "You
do not want to go away also, do you?"
68 [a]Simon Peter answered Him,
"Lord, to whom shall we go? You have
[b]words of eternal life.
69"We have believed and have come to
know that You are [a]the Holy One of
God."
70 Jesus answered them, "[a]Did I Myself not choose you, [b]the twelve, and *yet*
one of you is [c]a devil?"
71 Now He meant Judas [a]*the son* of
Simon Iscariot, for he, [b]one of [c]the
twelve, [1]was going to betray Him.

Jesus Teaches at the Feast

7 After these things Jesus [a]was walking in Galilee, for He was unwilling
to walk in Judea because [b]the Jews
[c]were seeking to kill Him.
2 Now the feast of the Jews, [a]the
Feast of Booths, was near.
3 Therefore His [a]brothers said to
Him, "Leave here and go into Judea, so
that Your [b]disciples also may see Your
works which You are doing.
4"For no one does anything in secret
[1]when he himself seeks to be *known*
publicly. If You do these things, show
Yourself to the world."
5 For not even His [a]brothers were
believing in Him.
6 So Jesus *said to them, "[a]My time
is not yet here, but your time is always
opportune.
7"[a]The world cannot hate you, but it
hates Me because I testify of it, that [b]its
deeds are evil.
8"Go up to the feast yourselves; I do
not go up to this feast because [a]My time
has not yet fully come."
9 Having said these things to them,
He stayed in Galilee.
10 ¶ But when His [a]brothers had
gone up to the feast, then He Himself also
went up, not publicly, but as if, in secret.
11 [a]So the Jews [b]were seeking Him
at the feast and were saying, "Where
is He?"
12 There was much grumbling among
the crowds concerning Him; [a]some were
saying, "He is a good man"; others were
saying, "No, on the contrary, He leads the
people astray."
13 Yet no one was speaking openly of
Him for [a]fear of the Jews.
14 ¶ But when it was now the midst of

46 [a]John 1:18
47 [a]John 3:36
48 [a]John 6:35
49 [a]John 6:31
50 [a]John 6:33 [b]John 3:36
51 [a]John 6:35 [b]John 6:41 [c]John 3:36 [d]John 1:29; Heb 10:10; 1 John 4:10 [e]John 6:53-56
52 [a]John 1:19 [b]John 9:16
53 [a]Matt 8:20; John 6:27
54 [a]John 6:39
56 [a]John 15:4f; 1 John 2:24
57 [a]Matt 16:16; John 5:26 [b]John 3:17
58 [a]John 6:33 [b]John 6:31 [c]John 3:36
59 [a]Matt 4:23 [b]John 6:24
60 [a]John 2:2 [b]John 6:52
61 [a]John 6:64 [b]Matt 11:6
62 [a]Matt 8:20; John 6:27 [b]Mark 16:19; John 3:13
63 [a]2 Cor 3:6 [b]John 6:68
64 [1]Or *hand Him over* [a]John 6:60 [b]John 2:25 [c]Matt 10:4; John 6:71
65 [a]John 6:37 [b]Matt 13:11; John 3:27
66 [a]John 2:2 [b]John 6:60
67 [a]Matt 10:2; John 2:2
68 [a]Matt 16:16 [b]John 6:63
69 [a]Mark 1:24; Luke 9:20
70 [a]John 15:16 [b]Matt 10:2; John 2:2 [c]John 8:44
71 [1]Or *was intending to* [a]John 12:4 [b]Mark 14:10 [c]Matt 10:2; John 2:2
7:1 [a]John 4:3 [b]John 1:19 [c]John 5:18
2 [a]Lev 23:34; Deut 16:13; Zech 14:16-19
3 [a]Matt 12:46; Mark 3:21; John 7:5 [b]John 6:60
4 [1]Lit *and*
5 [a]Matt 12:46; Mark 3:21; John 7:3
6 [a]Matt 26:18; John 2:4
7 [a]John 15:18f [b]John 3:19f
8 [a]John 7:6
10 [a]Matt 12:46; Mark 3:21; John 7:3
11 [a]John 7:13 [b]John 11:56
12 [a]John 7:40-43
13 [a]John 9:22

the feast Jesus went up into the temple,
and *began to* [a]teach.
15 [a]The Jews then were astonished,
saying, "How has this man [b]become
learned, having never been educated?"
16 So Jesus answered them and said,
"[a]My teaching is not Mine, but His who
sent Me.
17 "[a]If anyone is willing to do His will,
he will know of the teaching, whether it
is of God or *whether* I speak from Myself.
18 "He who speaks from himself
[a]seeks his own glory; but He who is seeking the glory of the One who sent Him,
He is true, and there is no unrighteousness in Him.
19 ¶ "[a]Did not Moses give you the
Law, and *yet* none of you carries out the
Law? Why do you [b]seek to kill Me?"
20 The crowd answered, "[a]You have
a demon! Who seeks to kill You?"
21 Jesus answered them, "I did [a]one
[1]deed, and you all marvel.
22 "For this reason [a]Moses has given
you circumcision (not because it is from
Moses, but from [b]the fathers), and on *the*
Sabbath you circumcise a man.
23 "[a]If a man receives circumcision on
the Sabbath so that the Law of Moses will
not be broken, are you angry with Me
because I made an entire man well on *the*
Sabbath?
24 "Do not [a]judge according to appearance, but [1]judge with righteous judgment."
25 ¶ So some of the people of Jerusalem were saying, "Is this not the man
whom they are seeking to kill?
26 "Look, He is speaking publicly, and
they are saying nothing to Him. [a]The
rulers do not really know that this is [1]the
Christ, do they?
27 "However, [a]we know where this
man is from; but whenever the Christ
may come, no one knows where He is
from."
28 Then Jesus cried out in the temple,
[a]teaching and saying, "[b]You both know
Me and know where I am from; and [c]I
have not come of Myself, but He who
sent Me is true, whom you do not know.
29 "[a]I know Him, because [b]I am from
Him, and [c]He sent Me."
30 So they [a]were seeking to seize
Him; and no man laid his hand on Him,
because His [b]hour had not yet come.
31 But [a]many of the crowd believed
in Him; and they were saying, "[b]When
[1]the Christ comes, He will not perform
more [2c]signs than those which this man
has, will He?"
32 ¶ The Pharisees heard the crowd
muttering these things about Him, and
the chief priests and the Pharisees sent
[a]officers to [b]seize Him.
33 Therefore Jesus said, "[a]For a little
while longer I am with you, then [b]I go to
Him who sent Me.
34 "[a]You will seek Me, and will not
find Me; and where I am, you cannot
come."
35 [a]The Jews then said to one another, "[b]Where does this man intend to go
that we will not find Him? He is not intending to go to [c]the Dispersion among
[d]the Greeks, and teach the Greeks,
is He?
36 "What is this statement that He said,
'[a]You will seek Me, and will not find Me;
and where I am, you cannot come'?"
37 ¶ Now on [a]the last day, the great
day of the feast, Jesus stood and cried out,
saying, "[1b]If anyone is thirsty, [2]let him
come to Me and drink.
38 "He who believes in Me, [a]as the
Scripture said, 'From [1]his innermost being will flow rivers of [b]living water.' "
39 But this He spoke [a]of the Spirit,
whom those who believed in Him were
to receive; for [b]the Spirit was not yet
given, because Jesus was not yet [c]glori-
fied.

Division of People over Jesus

40 ¶ *Some* of the people therefore,
when they heard these words, were saying, "This certainly is [a]the Prophet."
41 Others were saying, "This is [1]the
Christ." Still others were saying, "[a]Sure-
ly [1]the Christ is not going to come from
Galilee, is He?
42 "Has not the Scripture said that the
Christ comes from [a]the descendants of
David, and from Bethlehem, the village
where David was?"
43 So [a]a division occurred in the
crowd because of Him.
44 [a]Some of them wanted to seize
Him, but no one laid hands on Him.
45 ¶ The [a]officers then came to the
chief priests and Pharisees, and they said
to them, "Why did you not bring Him?"
46 The [a]officers answered, "[b]Never
has a man spoken the way this man
speaks."
47 The Pharisees then answered
them, "[a]You have not also been led
astray, have you?
48 "[a]No one of [b]the rulers or Pharisees has believed in Him, has he?
49 "But this crowd which does not
know the Law is accursed."
50 [a]Nicodemus (he who came to Him
before, being one of them) *said to them,
51 "[a]Our Law does not judge a man

14 [a]Matt 26:55; John 7:28
15 [a]John 1:19 [b]Acts 26:24
16 [a]John 3:11
17 [a]Ps 25:9; Prov 3:32; Dan 12:10; John 3:21
18 [a]John 5:41
19 [a]John 1:17 [b]Mark 11:18; John 7:1
20 [a]Matt 11:18; John 8:48f
21 [1]Or *work* [a]John 5:2-9
22 [a]Lev 12:3 [b]Gen 17:10ff; Acts 7:8
23 [a]Matt 12:2; John 5:9
24 [1]Lit *judge the righteous judgment* [a]Lev 19:15; Is 11:3; Zech 7:9; John 8:15
26 [1]I.e. the Messiah [a]Luke 23:13; John 3:1
27 [a]John 6:42
28 [a]John 7:14 [b]John 6:42 [c]John 8:42
29 [a]Matt 11:27; John 8:55 [b]John 6:46 [c]John 3:17
30 [a]Matt 21:46; John 7:32 [b]John 7:6
31 [1]I.e. the Messiah [2]Or *attesting miracles* [a]John 2:23 [b]John 7:26 [c]John 2:11
32 [a]Matt 26:58; John 7:45f [b]Matt 12:14
33 [a]John 12:35 [b]John 14:12
34 [a]John 7:36
35 [a]John 7:1 [b]John 8:22 [c]Ps 147:2; Is 11:12; Zeph 3:10; James 1:1; 1 Pet 1:1 [d]John 12:20; Acts 14:1; Rom 1:16
36 [a]John 7:34
37 [1]Vv 37-38 may also be read: *If anyone is thirsty,...let him come,... he who believes in me as...* [2]Or *let him keep coming to Me and let him keep drinking* [a]Lev 23:36; Num 29:35; Neh 8:18 [b]John 4:10
38 [1]Lit *out of his belly* [a]Is 44:3 [b]John 4:10
39 [a]Joel 2:28; John 1:33 [b]John 20:22; Acts 1:4f [c]John 12:16
40 [a]Matt 21:11; John 1:21
41 [1]I.e. the Messiah [a]John 1:46
42 [a]Ps 89:4; Mic 5:2; Matt 1:1; Luke 2:4ff
43 [a]John 9:16
44 [a]John 7:30
45 [a]John 7:32
46 [a]John 7:32 [b]Matt 7:28
47 [a]John 7:12
48 [a]John 12:42 [b]Luke 23:13; John 7:26
50 [a]John 3:1
51 [a]Ex 23:1; Deut 17:6; Prov 18:13; Acts 23:3

unless it first hears from him and knows
what he is doing, does it?"
52 They answered him, "[a]You are not
also from Galilee, are you? Search, and
see that no prophet arises out of Galilee."
53 [[1]Everyone went to his home.

The Adulterous Woman

8 But Jesus went to [a]the Mount of Olives.
2 Early in the morning He came again
into the temple, and all the people were
coming to Him; and [a]He sat down and
began to teach them.
3 The scribes and the Pharisees
*brought a woman caught in adultery,
and having set her in the center *of the
court*,
4 they *said to Him, "Teacher, this
woman has been caught in adultery, in
the very act.
5 "Now in the Law [a]Moses commanded us to stone such women; what then do
You say?"
6 They were saying this, [a]testing
Him, [b]so that they might have grounds
for accusing Him. But Jesus stooped down
and with His finger wrote on the ground.
7 But when they persisted in asking
Him, [a]He straightened up, and said to
them, "[b]He who is without sin among
you, let him *be the* [c]first to throw a stone
at her."
8 Again He stooped down and wrote
on the ground.
9 When they heard it, they *began* to
go out one by one, beginning with the
older ones, and He was left alone, and the
woman, where she was, in the center *of
the court*.
10 [a]Straightening up, Jesus said to
her, "Woman, where are they? Did no
one condemn you?"
11 She said, "No one, [1]Lord." And
Jesus said, "[a]I do not condemn you, either. Go. From now on [b]sin no more."]

Jesus Is the Light of the World

12 ¶ Then Jesus again spoke to them,
saying, "[a]I am the Light of the world;
[b]he who follows Me will not walk in the
darkness, but will have the Light of life."
13 So the Pharisees said to Him,
"[a]You are testifying about Yourself; Your
testimony is not [1]true."
14 Jesus answered and said to them,
"[a]Even if I testify about Myself, My testimony is [1]true, for I know [b]where I came
from and where I am going; but [c]you do
not know where I come from or where I
am going.
15 "[a]You judge [1]according to the
flesh; [b]I am not judging anyone.
16 "But even [a]if I do judge, My judgment is true; for I am not alone *in it*, but
I and the Father who sent Me.
17 "Even in [a]your law it has been written that the testimony of [b]two men is
[1]true.
18 "I am He who testifies about Myself,
and [a]the Father who sent Me testifies
about Me."
19 So they were saying to Him,
"Where is Your Father?" Jesus answered,
"You know neither Me nor My Father;
[a]if you knew Me, you would know My
Father also."
20 These words He spoke in [a]the treasury, as [b]He taught in the temple; and no
one seized Him, because [c]His hour had
not yet come.
21 ¶ Then He said again to them, "I go
away, and [a]you will seek Me, and [b]will
die in your sin; where I am going, you
cannot come."
22 So [a]the Jews were saying, "Surely
He will not kill Himself, will He, since He
says, '[b]Where I am going, you cannot
come'?"
23 And He was saying to them, "[a]You
are from below, I am from above; [b]you
are of this world, [c]I am not of this world.
24 "Therefore I said to you that you
[a]will die in your sins; for unless you believe that [1b]I am *He*, [a]you will die in
your sins."
25 So they were saying to Him, "Who
are You?" Jesus said to them, "[1]What
have I been saying to you *from* the beginning?
26 "I have many things to speak and to
judge concerning you, but [a]He who sent
Me is true; and [b]the things which I heard
from Him, these I speak to the world."
27 They did not realize that He had
been speaking to them about the Father.
28 So Jesus said, "When you [a]lift up
the Son of Man, then you will know that
[1b]I am *He*, and [c]I do nothing on My
own initiative, but I speak these things as
the Father taught Me.
29 "And He who sent Me is with Me;
[a]He [1]has not left Me alone, for [b]I always do the things that are pleasing to
Him."
30 As He spoke these things, [a]many
came to believe in Him.

The Truth Will Make You Free

31 ¶ So Jesus was saying to those Jews
who had believed Him, "[a]If you continue
in My word, *then* you are truly [b]disciples
of Mine;
32 and [a]you will know the truth, and
[b]the truth will make you free."
33 They answered Him, "[a]We are
Abraham's descendants and have never

---

52 [a]John 1:46
53 [1]Later mss add the story of the adulterous woman, numbering it as John 7:53-8:11
8:1 [a]Matt 21:1
2 [a]Matt 26:55; John 8:20
5 [a]Lev 20:10; Deut 22:22f
6 [a]Matt 16:1; Mark 8:11; Luke 10:25 [b]Mark 3:2
7 [a]John 8:10 [b]Matt 7:1; Rom 2:1 [c]Deut 17:7
10 [a]John 8:7
11 [1]Or *Sir* [a]John 3:17 [b]John 5:14
12 [a]John 1:4 [b]Matt 5:14
13 [1]Or *valid* [a]John 5:31
14 [1]Or *valid* [a]John 18:37; Rev 1:5 [b]John 8:42 [c]John 7:28
15 [1]I.e. by a carnal standard [a]1 Sam 16:7; John 7:24 [b]John 3:17
16 [a]John 5:30
17 [1]I.e. valid or admissible [a]Deut 17:6 [b]Matt 18:16
18 [a]John 5:37; 1 John 5:9
19 [a]John 7:28
20 [a]Mark 12:41; Luke 21:1 [b]John 7:14 [c]John 7:30
21 [a]John 7:34 [b]John 8:24
22 [a]John 1:19 [b]John 7:35
23 [a]John 3:31 [b]1 John 4:5 [c]John 17:14
24 [1]Most authorities associate this with Ex 3:14, *I AM WHO I AM* [a]John 8:21 [b]Matt 24:5; Mark 13:6; Luke 21:8; John 4:26
25 [1]Or *That which I have been saying to you from the beginning*
26 [a]John 3:33 [b]John 8:40
28 [1]Lit *I AM* (v 24 note) [a]John 3:14 [b]Matt 24:5; Mark 13:6; Luke 21:8; John 4:26 [c]John 3:11
29 [1]Or *did not leave* [a]John 8:16 [b]John 4:34
30 [a]John 7:31
31 [a]John 15:7; 2 John 9 [b]John 2:2
32 [a]John 1:14 [b]John 8:36; Rom 8:2; 2 Cor 3:17; Gal 5:1; James 2:12; 1 Pet 2:16
33 [a]Matt 3:9; Luke 3:8; John 8:37

yet been enslaved to anyone; how is it that You say, 'You will become free'?"

34 ¶ Jesus answered them, "Truly, truly, I say to you, [a]everyone who commits sin is the slave of sin.

35 "[a]The slave does not remain in the house forever; [b]the son does remain forever.

36 "So if the Son [a]makes you free, you will be free indeed.

37 "I know that you are [a]Abraham's descendants; yet [b]you seek to kill Me, because My word [1]has no place in you.

38 "I speak the things which I have seen [1]with *My* Father; therefore you also do the things which you heard from [a]*your* father."

39 ¶ They answered and said to Him, "Abraham is [a]our father." Jesus *said to them, "[b]If you are Abraham's children, do the deeds of Abraham.

40 "But as it is, [a]you are seeking to kill Me, a man who has [b]told you the truth, which I heard from God; this Abraham did not do.

41 "You are doing the deeds of [a]your father." They said to Him, "We were not born of fornication; [b]we have one Father: God."

42 Jesus said to them, "If God were your Father, [a]you would love Me, [b]for I proceeded forth and have come from God, for I have [c]not even come on My own initiative, but [1d]He sent Me.

43 "Why do you not understand [1a]what I am saying? *It is* because you cannot [b]hear My word.

44 "[a]You are of [b]*your* father the devil, and [c]you want to do the desires of your father. [d]He was a murderer from the beginning, and does not stand in the truth because [e]there is no truth in him. Whenever he speaks [1]a lie, he [f]speaks from his own *nature,* for he is a liar and the father of [2]lies.

45 "But because [a]I speak the truth, you do not believe Me.

46 "Which one of you convicts Me of sin? If [a]I speak truth, why do you not believe Me?

47 "[a]He who is of God hears the words of God; for this reason you do not hear *them,* because you are not of God."

48 ¶ [a]The Jews answered and said to Him, "Do we not say rightly that You are a [b]Samaritan and [c]have a demon?"

49 Jesus answered, "I do not [a]have a demon; but I honor My Father, and you dishonor Me.

50 "But [a]I do not seek My glory; there is One who seeks and judges.

51 "Truly, truly, I say to you, if anyone [a]keeps My word he will never [b]see death."

52 [a]The Jews said to Him, "Now we know that You [b]have a demon. Abraham died, and the prophets *also;* and You say, 'If anyone [c]keeps My word, he will never [d]taste of death.'

53 "Surely You [a]are not greater than our father Abraham, who died? The prophets died too; whom do You make Yourself out *to be*?"

54 Jesus answered, "[a]If I glorify Myself, My glory is nothing; [b]it is My Father who glorifies Me, of whom you say, 'He is our God';

55 and [a]you have not come to know Him, [b]but I know Him; and if I say that I do not know Him, I will be [c]a liar like you, [b]but I do know Him and [d]keep His word.

56 "[a]Your father Abraham [b]rejoiced [1]to see My day, and he saw *it* and was glad."

57 [a]So the Jews said to Him, "You are not yet fifty years old, and have You seen Abraham?"

58 Jesus said to them, "Truly, truly, I say to you, before Abraham [1]was born, [a]I am."

59 Therefore they [a]picked up stones to throw at Him, but Jesus [1b]hid Himself and went out of the temple.

Healing the Man Born Blind

9 As He passed by, He saw a man blind from birth.

2 And His disciples asked Him, "[a]Rabbi, who sinned, [b]this man or his [c]parents, that he would be born blind?"

3 Jesus answered, "*It was* neither *that* this man sinned, nor his parents; but *it was* so [a]that the works of God might be displayed in him.

4 "We must work the works of Him who sent Me [a]as long as it is day; night is coming when no one can work.

5 "While I am in the world, I am [a]the Light of the world."

6 When He had said this, He [a]spat on the ground, and made clay of the spittle, and applied the clay to his eyes,

7 and said to him, "Go, wash in [a]the pool of Siloam" (which is translated, Sent). So he went away and [b]washed, and [c]came *back* seeing.

8 Therefore the neighbors, and those who previously saw him as a beggar, were saying, "Is not this the one who used to [a]sit and beg?"

9 Others were saying, "This is he," *still* others were saying, "No, but he is like him." [1]He kept saying, "I am the one."

10 So they were saying to him, "How then were your eyes opened?"

11 He answered, "The man who is

34 [a]Rom 6:16; 2 Pet 2:19
35 [a]Gen 21:10; Gal 4:30 [b]Luke 15:31
36 [a]John 8:32
37 [1]Or *makes no progress* [a]Matt 3:9; John 8:39 [b]John 7:1
38 [1]Or *in the presence of* [a]John 8:41
39 [a]Matt 3:9; John 8:37 [b]Rom 9:7; Gal 3:7
40 [a]John 7:1 [b]John 8:26
41 [a]John 8:38 [b]Deut 32:6; Is 63:16
42 [1]Lit *that One* [a]1 John 5:1 [b]John 13:3 [c]John 7:28 [d]John 3:17
43 [1]Or *My way of speaking* [a]John 8:33 [b]John 5:25
44 [1]Lit *the lie* [2]Lit *it* [a]1 John 3:8 [b]John 8:38 [c]John 7:17 [d]Gen 3:4; 1 John 3:8 [e]1 John 2:4 [f]Matt 12:34
45 [a]John 18:37
46 [a]John 18:37
47 [a]1 John 4:6
48 [a]John 1:19 [b]Matt 10:5; John 4:9 [c]John 7:20
49 [a]John 7:20
50 [a]John 5:41
51 [a]John 8:55 [b]Matt 16:28; Luke 2:26; John 8:52; Heb 2:9
52 [a]John 1:19 [b]John 7:20 [c]John 8:55 [d]John 8:51
53 [a]John 4:12
54 [a]John 8:50 [b]John 7:39
55 [a]John 8:19 [b]John 7:29 [c]John 8:44 [d]John 8:51
56 [1]Lit *in order that he might see* [a]John 8:37 [b]Matt 13:17; Heb 11:13
57 [a]John 1:19
58 [1]Lit *came into being* [a]Ex 3:14; John 1:1
59 [1]Lit *was hidden* [a]Matt 12:14; John 10:31 [b]John 12:36
9:2 [a]Matt 23:7 [b]Luke 13:2; John 9:34; Acts 28:4 [c]Ex 20:5
3 [a]John 11:4
4 [a]John 7:33; Gal 6:10
5 [a]Matt 5:14; John 1:4
6 [a]Mark 7:33
7 [a]Neh 3:15; Is 8:6; Luke 13:4; John 9:11 [b]2 Kin 5:13f [c]Is 29:18; Matt 11:5; John 11:37
8 [a]Acts 3:2
9 [1]Lit *That one*

called Jesus made clay, and anointed my eyes, and said to me, 'Go to [a]Siloam and wash'; so I went away and washed, and I received sight."

12 They said to him, "Where is He?" He *said, "I do not know."

Controversy over the Man

13 ¶ They *brought to the Pharisees the man who was formerly blind.

14 [a]Now it was a Sabbath on the day when Jesus made the clay and opened his eyes.

15 [a]Then the Pharisees also were asking him again how he received his sight. And he said to them, "He applied clay to my eyes, and I washed, and I see."

16 Therefore some of the Pharisees were saying, "This man is not from God, because He [a]does not keep the Sabbath." But others were saying, "How can a man who is a sinner perform such [1b]signs?" And [c]there was a division among them.

17 So they *said to the blind man [a]again, "What do you say about Him, since He opened your eyes?" And he said, "He is a [b]prophet."

18 ¶ [a]The Jews then did not believe *it* of him, that he had been blind and had received sight, until they called the parents of the very one who had received his sight,

19 and questioned them, saying, "Is this your son, who you say was born blind? Then how does he now see?"

20 His parents answered them and said, "We know that this is our son, and that he was born blind;

21 but how he now sees, we do not know; or who opened his eyes, we do not know. Ask him; he is of age, he will speak for himself."

22 His parents said this because they [a]were afraid of the Jews; for the Jews [b]had already agreed that if anyone confessed Him to be [1]Christ, [c]he was to be put out of the synagogue.

23 For this reason his parents said, "[a]He is of age; ask him."

24 ¶ So a second time they called the man who had been blind, and said to him, "[a]Give glory to God; we know that [b]this man is a sinner."

25 He then answered, "Whether He is a sinner, I do not know; one thing I do know, that though I was blind, now I see."

26 So they said to him, "What did He do to you? How did He open your eyes?"

27 He answered them, "[a]I told you already and you did not [b]listen; why do you want to hear *it* again? You do not want to become His disciples too, do you?"

28 They reviled him and said, "You are His disciple, but [a]we are disciples of Moses.

29 "We know that God has spoken to Moses, but as for this man, [a]we do not know where He is from."

30 The man answered and said to them, "Well, here is an amazing thing, that you do not know where He is from, and *yet* He opened my eyes.

31 "We know that [a]God does not hear sinners; but if anyone is God-fearing and does His will, He hears him.

32 "[1]Since the beginning of time it has never been heard that anyone opened the eyes of a person born blind.

33 "[a]If this man were not from God, He could do nothing."

34 They answered him, "[a]You were born entirely in sins, and are you teaching us?" So they [b]put him out.

Jesus Affirms His Deity

35 ¶ Jesus heard that they had [a]put him out, and finding him, He said, "Do you believe in the [b]Son of Man?"

36 He answered, "[a]Who is He, [1]Lord, that I may believe in Him?"

37 Jesus said to him, "You have both seen Him, and [a]He is the one who is talking with you."

38 And he said, "Lord, I believe." And he [a]worshiped Him.

39 And Jesus said, "[a]For judgment I came into this world, so that [b]those who do not see may see, and that [c]those who see may become blind."

40 Those of the Pharisees who were with Him heard these things and said to Him, "[a]We are not blind too, are we?"

41 Jesus said to them, "[a]If you were blind, you would have no sin; but [1]since you say, '[b]We see,' your sin remains.

Parable of the Good Shepherd

10 "Truly, truly, I say to you, he who does not enter by the door into the fold of the sheep, but climbs up some other way, he is [a]a thief and a robber.

2 "But he who enters by the door is [a]a shepherd of the sheep.

3 "To him the doorkeeper opens, and the sheep hear [a]his voice, and he calls his own sheep by name and [b]leads them out.

4 "When he puts forth all his own, he goes ahead of them, and the sheep follow him because they know [a]his voice.

5 "A stranger they simply will not follow, but will flee from him, because they do not know [a]the voice of strangers."

6 This [a]figure of speech Jesus spoke to them, but they did not understand

---

11 [a]John 9:7
14 [a]John 5:9
15 [a]John 9:10
16 [1]Or *attesting miracles* [a]Matt 12:2; Luke 13:14; John 5:10; 7:23 [b]John 2:11 [c]John 6:52; 7:12,43; 10:19
17 [a]John 9:15 [b]Deut 18:15; Matt 21:11
18 [a]John 1:19; 9:22
22 [1]I.e. the Messiah [a]John 7:13 [b]John 7:45-52 [c]Luke 6:22; John 12:42; 16:2
23 [a]John 9:21
24 [a]Josh 7:19; Ezra 10:11; Rev 11:13 [b]John 9:16
27 [a]John 9:15 [b]John 5:25
28 [a]John 5:45; Rom 2:17
29 [a]John 8:14
31 [a]Job 27:8f; 35:13; Ps 34:15f; 66:18; 145:19; Prov 15:29; 28:9; Is 1:15; James 5:16ff
32 [1]Lit *From the age it was not heard*
33 [a]John 3:2; 9:16
34 [a]John 9:2 [b]John 9:22,35; 3 John 10
35 [a]John 9:22, 34; 3 John 10 [b]Matt 4:3
36 [1]Or *Sir* [a]Rom 10:14
37 [a]John 4:26
38 [a]Matt 8:2
39 [a]John 3:19; 5:22,27 [b]Luke 4:18 [c]Matt 13:13; 15:14
40 [a]Rom 2:19
41 [1]Lit *now* [a]John 15:22,24 [b]Prov 26:12
10:1 [a]John 10:8
2 [a]John 10:11f
3 [a]John 10:4f, 16,27 [b]John 10:9
4 [a]John 10:5,16, 27
5 [a]John 10:4,16, 27
6 [a]John 16:25, 29; 2 Pet 2:22

what those things were which He had
been saying to them.
7 ¶ So Jesus said to them again, "Truly, truly, I say to you, I am [a]the door of
the sheep.
8 "All who came before Me are
[a]thieves and robbers, but the sheep did
not hear them.
9 "[a]I am the door; if anyone enters
through Me, he will be saved, and will go
in and out and find pasture.
10 "The thief comes only to steal and
kill and destroy; I came that they [a]may
have life, and [1]have *it* abundantly.
11 ¶ "[a]I am the good shepherd; the
good shepherd [b]lays down His life for the
sheep.
12 "He who is a hired hand, and not a
[a]shepherd, who is not the owner of the
sheep, sees the wolf coming, and leaves
the sheep and flees, and the wolf
snatches them and scatters *them.*
13 *"He flees* because he is a hired hand
and is not concerned about the sheep.
14 "[a]I am the good shepherd, and [b]I
know My own and My own know Me,
15 even as [a]the Father knows Me and
I know the Father; and [b]I lay down My
life for the sheep.
16 "I have [a]other sheep, which are not
of this fold; I must bring them also, and
they will hear My voice; and they will
become [b]one flock *with* [c]one shepherd.
17 "For this reason the Father loves
Me, because I [a]lay down My life so that
I may take it again.
18 "[a]No one has taken it away from
Me, but I [b]lay it down on My own initiative. I have authority to lay it down, and
I have authority to take it up again. [c]This
commandment I received from My Father."
19 ¶ [a]A division occurred again
among the Jews because of these words.
20 Many of them were saying, "He
[a]has a demon and [b]is insane. Why do
you listen to Him?"
21 Others were saying, "These are not
the sayings of one [a]demon-possessed.
[b]A demon cannot open the eyes of the
blind, can he?"

Jesus Asserts His Deity

22 ¶ At that time the Feast of the Dedication took place at Jerusalem;
23 it was winter, and Jesus was walking in the temple in the portico of [a]Solo-
mon.
24 [a]The Jews then gathered around
Him, and were saying to Him, "How long
[1]will You keep us in suspense? If You are
[2]the Christ, tell us [b]plainly."
25 Jesus answered them, "[a]I told you,
and you do not believe; [b]the works that
I do in My Father's name, these testify
of Me.
26 "But you do not believe because
[a]you are not of My sheep.
27 "My sheep [a]hear My voice, and [b]I
know them, and they follow Me;
28 and I give [a]eternal life to them, and
they will never perish; and [b]no one will
snatch them out of My hand.
29 "[1]My Father, who has given *them* to
Me, is greater than all; and no one is able
to snatch *them* out of the Father's hand.
30 "[a]I and the Father are [1]one."
31 ¶ The Jews [a]picked up stones
again to stone Him.
32 Jesus answered them, "I showed
you many good works from the Father;
for which of them are you stoning Me?"
33 The Jews answered Him, "For a
good work we do not stone You, but for
[a]blasphemy; and because You, being a
man, [b]make Yourself out *to be* God."
34 Jesus answered them, "Has it not
been written in [a]your [b]Law, '[c]I SAID,
YOU ARE GODS'?
35 "If he called them gods, to whom the
word of God came (and the Scripture cannot be broken),
36 do you say of Him, whom the Father [a]sanctified and [b]sent into the
world, 'You are blaspheming,' because I
said, '[c]I am the Son of God'?
37 "[a]If I do not do the works of My
Father, do not believe Me;
38 but if I do them, though you do not
believe Me, believe [a]the works, so that
you may [1]know and understand that
[b]the Father is in Me, and I in the Father."
39 Therefore [a]they were seeking
again to seize Him, and [b]He eluded their
grasp.
40 ¶ And He went away [a]again beyond the Jordan to the place where John
was first baptizing, and He was staying
there.
41 Many came to Him and were saying, "While John performed no [a]sign, yet
[b]everything John said about this man
was true."
42 [a]Many believed in Him there.

The Death and Resurrection of Lazarus

11 Now a certain man was sick, Lazarus of [a]Bethany, the village of
Mary and her sister [b]Martha.
2 It was the Mary who [a]anointed
[b]the Lord with ointment, and wiped His
feet with her hair, whose brother Lazarus
was sick.
3 So the sisters sent *word* to Him,

7 [a]John 10:1f
8 [a]Jer 23:1f; Ezek 34:2ff; John 10:1
9 [a]John 10:1f
10 [1]Or *have abundance* [a]John 5:40
11 [a]Is 40:11; Ezek 34:11-16; John 10:14; Heb 13:20; 1 Pet 5:4; Rev 7:17 [b]John 10:15; 1 John 3:16
12 [a]John 10:2
14 [a]John 10:11 [b]John 10:27
15 [a]Matt 11:27; Luke 10:22 [b]John 10:11
16 [a]Is 56:8 [b]John 11:52; Eph 2:13-18; 1 Pet 2:25 [c]Ezek 34:23
17 [a]John 10:11
18 [a]Matt 26:53; John 2:19 [b]John 10:11 [c]John 14:31; Phil 2:8; Heb 5:8
19 [a]John 7:43
20 [a]John 7:20 [b]Mark 3:21
21 [a]Matt 4:24 [b]Ex 4:11; John 9:32f
23 [a]Acts 3:11
24 [1]Lit *do You lift up our soul* [2]I.e. the Messiah [a]John 1:19 [b]Luke 22:67; John 16:25
25 [a]John 8:56 [b]John 5:36
26 [a]John 8:47
27 [a]John 10:4 [b]John 10:14
28 [a]John 17:2f; 1 John 2:25 [b]John 6:37
29 [1]One early ms reads *What My Father has given Me is greater than all*
30 [1]Or *a unity*; or *one essence* [a]John 17:21ff
31 [a]John 8:59
33 [a]Lev 24:16 [b]John 5:18
34 [a]John 8:17 [b]John 12:34; Rom 3:19; 1 Cor 14:21 [c]Ps 82:6
36 [a]Jer 1:5; John 6:69 [b]John 3:17 [c]John 5:17f
37 [a]John 10:25
38 [1]Lit *know and continue knowing* [a]John 10:25 [b]John 14:10f
39 [a]John 7:30 [b]Luke 4:30; John 8:59
40 [a]John 1:28
41 [a]John 2:11 [b]John 1:27
42 [a]John 7:31
11:1 [a]Matt 21:17; John 11:18 [b]Luke 10:38; John 11:5
2 [a]Luke 7:38; John 12:3 [b]Luke 7:13; John 11:3

saying, "[a]Lord, behold, [b]he whom You
love is sick."
4 But when Jesus heard *this*, He said,
"This sickness is not to end in death, but
for [a]the glory of God, so that the Son of
God may be glorified by it."
5 Now Jesus loved [a]Martha and her
sister and Lazarus.
6 So when He heard that he was sick,
He then stayed two days *longer* in the
place where He was.
7 Then after this He *said to the disciples, "[a]Let us go to Judea again."
8 The disciples *said to Him, "[a]Rab-
bi, the Jews were just now seeking [b]to
stone You, and are You going there
again?"
9 Jesus answered, "[a]Are there not
twelve hours in the day? If anyone walks
in the day, he does not stumble, because
he sees the light of this world.
10 "But if anyone walks in the night,
he stumbles, because the light is not in
him."
11 This He said, and after that He
*said to them, "Our [a]friend Lazarus
[b]has fallen asleep; but I go, so that I may
awaken him out of sleep."
12 The disciples then said to Him,
"Lord, if he has fallen asleep, he will [1]re-
cover."
13 Now [a]Jesus had spoken of his
death, but they thought that He was
speaking of [1]literal sleep.
14 So Jesus then said to them plainly,
"Lazarus is dead,
15 and I am glad for your sakes that I
was not there, so that you may believe;
but let us go to him."
16 [a]Therefore Thomas, who is called
[1b]Didymus, said to *his* fellow disciples,
"Let us also go, so that we may die with
Him."
17 ¶ So when Jesus came, He found
that he had already been in the tomb
[a]four days.
18 Now [a]Bethany was near Jerusalem, about [1]two miles off;
19 and many of [a]the Jews had come to
[b]Martha and Mary, [c]to console them
concerning *their* brother.
20 [a]Martha therefore, when she
heard that Jesus was coming, went to
meet Him, but [a]Mary [1]stayed at the
house.
21 Martha then said to Jesus, "[a]Lord,
[b]if You had been here, my brother would
not have died.
22 "Even now I know that [a]whatever
You ask of God, God will give You."
23 Jesus *said to her, "Your brother
will rise again."
24 Martha *said to Him, "[a]I know
that he will rise again in the resurrection
on the last day."
25 Jesus said to her, "[a]I am the resurrection and the life; he who believes in
Me will live even if he dies,
26 and everyone who lives and believes in Me [a]will never die. Do you believe this?"
27 She *said to Him, "Yes, Lord; I have
believed that You are [1a]the Christ, the
Son of God, *even* [2b]He who comes into
the world."
28 ¶ When she had said this, she
[a]went away and called Mary her sister,
saying secretly, "[b]The Teacher is here
and is calling for you."
29 And when she heard it, she *got up
quickly and was coming to Him.
30 ¶ Now Jesus had not yet come into
the village, but [a]was still in the place
where Martha met Him.
31 [a]Then the Jews who were with her
in the house, and [b]consoling her, when
they saw that Mary got up quickly and
went out, they followed her, supposing
that she was going to the tomb to weep
there.
32 Therefore, when Mary came where
Jesus was, she saw Him, and fell at His
feet, saying to Him, "[a]Lord, [b]if You had
been here, my brother would not have
died."
33 When Jesus therefore saw her
weeping, and [a]the Jews who came with
her *also* weeping, He [b]was deeply moved
in spirit and [1c]was troubled,
34 and said, "Where have you laid
him?" They *said to Him, "Lord, come
and see."
35 Jesus [a]wept.
36 So [a]the Jews were saying, "See
how He [b]loved him!"
37 But some of them said, "Could not
this man, who [a]opened the eyes of the
blind man, [1]have kept this man also from
dying?"
38 ¶ So Jesus, again being deeply
moved within, *came to the tomb. Now
it was a [a]cave, and a stone was lying
against it.
39 Jesus *said, "Remove the stone."
Martha, the sister of the deceased, *said
to Him, "Lord, by this time [1]there will be
a stench, for he has been *dead* [a]four
days."
40 Jesus *said to her, "[a]Did I not say
to you that if you believe, you will see the
glory of God?"
41 So they removed the [a]stone. Then
Jesus [b]raised His eyes, and said, "[c]Fa-
ther, I thank You that You have
heard Me.
42 "I knew that You always hear Me;
but [a]because of the [1]people standing

3 [a]Luke 7:13; John 11:2 [b]John 11:5
4 [a]John 9:3
5 [a]John 11:1
7 [a]John 10:40
8 [a]Matt 23:7 [b]John 8:59
9 [a]Luke 13:33; John 9:4
11 [a]John 11:3 [b]Matt 27:52; Mark 5:39; John 11:13; Acts 7:60
12 [1]Lit *be saved*
13 [1]Lit *the slumber of sleep* [a]Matt 9:24; Luke 8:52
16 [1]I.e. the Twin [a]Matt 10:3; Mark 3:18; Luke 6:15; John 14:5; Acts 1:13 [b]John 20:24
17 [a]John 11:39
18 [1]Lit *15 stadia* (9,090 ft) [a]John 11:1
19 [a]John 1:19 [b]John 11:1 [c]1 Sam 31:13; 1 Chr 10:12; Job 2:11; John 11:31
20 [1]Lit *was sitting* [a]Luke 10:38-42
21 [a]John 11:2 [b]John 11:32
22 [a]John 9:31
24 [a]Dan 12:2; John 5:28f; Acts 24:15
25 [a]John 1:4; Rev 1:18
26 [a]John 6:47
27 [1]I.e. the Messiah [2]The Coming One was the Messianic title [a]Matt 16:16; Luke 2:11 [b]John 6:14
28 [a]John 11:30 [b]Matt 26:18; Mark 14:14; Luke 22:11; John 13:13
30 [a]John 11:20
31 [a]John 11:19 [b]John 11:19
32 [a]John 11:2 [b]John 11:21
33 [1]Lit *troubled Himself* [a]John 11:19 [b]John 11:38 [c]John 12:27
35 [a]Luke 19:41; John 11:33
36 [a]John 11:19 [b]John 11:3
37 [1]Lit *have caused that this man also not die* [a]John 9:7
38 [a]Matt 27:60; Mark 15:46; Luke 24:2; John 20:1
39 [1]Lit *he stinks* [a]John 11:17
40 [a]John 11:4
41 [a]Matt 27:60; Mark 15:46; Luke 24:2; John 20:1 [b]John 17:1; Acts 7:55 [c]Matt 11:25
42 [1]Lit *crowd* [a]John 12:30

around I said it, so that they may believe
that [b]You sent Me."
43 When He had said these things, He
cried out with a loud voice, "Lazarus,
come forth."
44 The man who had died came forth,
[a]bound hand and foot with wrappings,
and [b]his face was wrapped around with
a cloth. Jesus *said to them, "Unbind
him, and let him go."
45 ¶ [a]Therefore many of the Jews
[b]who came to Mary, and [c]saw what He
had done, believed in Him.
46 But some of them went to the
[a]Pharisees and told them the things
which Jesus had done.

Conspiracy to Kill Jesus

47 ¶ Therefore [a]the chief priests and
the Pharisees [b]convened a [c]council, and
were saying, "What are we doing? For
this man is performing many [1d]signs.
48 "If we let Him *go on* like this, all
men will believe in Him, and the Romans
will come and take away both our [a]place
and our nation."
49 But one of them, [a]Caiaphas, [b]who
was high priest that year, said to them,
"You know nothing at all,
50 nor do you take into account that
[a]it is expedient for you that one man die
for the people, and that the whole nation
not perish."
51 Now he did not say this [1]on his
own initiative, but [a]being high priest
that year, he prophesied that Jesus was
going to die for the nation,
52 and not for the nation only, but in
order that He might also [a]gather together into one the children of God who are
scattered abroad.
53 So from that day on they [a]planned
together to kill Him.
54 ¶ Therefore Jesus [a]no longer continued to walk publicly among the Jews,
but went away from there to the country
near the wilderness, into a city called
[b]Ephraim; and there He stayed with the
disciples.
55 ¶ Now [a]the Passover of the Jews
was near, and many went up to Jerusalem
out of the country before the Passover
[b]to purify themselves.
56 So they [a]were seeking for Jesus,
and were saying to one another as they
stood in the temple, "What do you think;
that He will not come to the feast at all?"
57 Now [a]the chief priests and the
Pharisees had given orders that if anyone
knew where He was, he was to report it,
so that they might seize Him.

Mary Anoints Jesus

12 [a]Jesus, therefore, six days before
[b]the Passover, came to [c]Bethany
where Lazarus was, whom Jesus had
raised from the dead.
2 So they made Him a supper there,
and [a]Martha was serving; but Lazarus
was one of those reclining *at the table*
with Him.
3 [a]Mary then took a [1]pound of very
costly [b]perfume of pure nard, and anointed the feet of Jesus and wiped His feet
with her hair; and the house was filled
with the fragrance of the perfume.
4 But [a]Judas Iscariot, one of His disciples, who was intending to [1]betray
Him, *said,
5 "Why was this perfume not sold for
[1]three hundred denarii and given to poor
people?"
6 Now he said this, not because he
was concerned about the poor, but because he was a thief, and as he [a]had the
money box, he used to pilfer [b]what was
put into it.
7 Therefore Jesus said, "Let her
alone, so that she may keep [1]it for [a]the
day of My burial.
8 "[a]For you always have the poor
with you, but you do not always
have Me."
9 ¶ The [a]large crowd of the Jews
then learned that He was there; and they
came, not for Jesus' sake only, but that
they might also see Lazarus, [b]whom He
raised from the dead.
10 But the chief priests planned to put
Lazarus to death also;
11 because [a]on account of him
[b]many of the Jews were going away and
were believing in Jesus.

Jesus Enters Jerusalem

12 ¶ On the next day [a]the large crowd
who had come to [b]the feast, when they
heard that Jesus was coming to Jerusalem,
13 took the branches of the palm trees
and went out to meet Him, and *began* to
shout, "[a]Hosanna! BLESSED IS HE WHO
COMES IN THE NAME OF THE LORD, even the
[b]King of Israel."
14 Jesus, finding a young donkey, sat
on it; as it is written,
15 "[a]FEAR NOT, DAUGHTER OF ZION; BE-
HOLD, YOUR KING IS COMING, SEATED ON A
DONKEY'S COLT."
16 [a]These things His disciples did not
understand at the first; but when Jesus
[b]was glorified, then they remembered
that these things were written of Him,
and that they had done these things to
Him.

42 [b]John 3:17
44 [a]John 19:40 [b]John 20:7
45 [a]John 7:31 [b]John 11:19; 12:17f [c]John 2:23
46 [a]John 7:32, 45; 11:57
47 [1]Or *attesting miracles* [a]John 7:32,45; 11:57 [b]Matt 26:3 [c]Matt 5:22 [d]John 2:11
48 [a]Matt 24:15
49 [a]Matt 26:3 [b]John 11:51; 18:13
50 [a]John 18:14
51 [1]Lit *from himself* [a]John 18:13
52 [a]John 10:16
53 [a]Matt 26:4
54 [a]John 7:1 [b]2 Chr 13:19 mg
55 [a]Matt 26:1f; Mark 14:1; Luke 22:1; John 2:13; 12:1; 13:1 [b]Num 9:10; 2 Chr 30:17f; John 18:28
56 [a]John 7:11
57 [a]John 11:47
12:1 [a]John 12:1-8: *Matt 26:6-13; Mark 14:3-9; Luke 7:37-39* [b]John 11:55; 12:20 [c]Matt 21:17; John 11:43f
2 [a]Luke 10:38
3 [1]I.e. a Roman pound, equaling 12 oz [a]Luke 7:37f; John 11:2 [b]Mark 14:3
4 [1]Or *hand Him over* [a]John 6:71
5 [1]Equivalent to 11 months' wages
6 [a]John 13:29 [b]Luke 8:3
7 [1]I.e. the custom of preparing the body for burial [a]John 19:40
8 [a]Deut 15:11; Matt 26:11; Mark 14:7
9 [a]Mark 12:37; John 12:12 mg [b]John 11:43f; 12:1,17f
11 [a]John 11:45f; 12:18 [b]John 7:31; 11:42
12 [a]John 12:12-15: *Matt 21:4-9; Mark 11:7-10; Luke 19:35-38* [b]John 12:1
13 [a]Ps 118:26 [b]John 1:49
15 [a]Zech 9:9
16 [a]Mark 9:32; John 2:22; 14:26 [b]John 7:39; 12:23

17 So [a]the [1]people, who were with Him when He called Lazarus out of the tomb and raised him from the dead, continued to testify *about Him.*

18 [a]For this reason also the [1]people went and met Him, [b]because they heard that He had performed this [2]sign.

19 So the Pharisees said to one another, "You see that you are not doing any good; look, the world has gone after Him."

Greeks Seek Jesus

20 ¶ Now there were some [a]Greeks among those who were going up to worship at [b]the feast;

21 these then came to [a]Philip, who was from [b]Bethsaida of Galilee, and *began to* ask him, saying, "Sir, we wish to see Jesus."

22 Philip *came and *told [a]Andrew; Andrew and Philip *came and *told Jesus.

23 And Jesus *answered them, saying, "[a]The hour has come for the Son of Man to [b]be glorified.

24 "Truly, truly, I say to you, [a]unless a grain of wheat falls into the earth and dies, it remains alone; but if it dies, it bears much fruit.

25 "[a]He who loves his [1]life loses it, and he who [b]hates his [1]life in this world will keep it to life eternal.

26 "If anyone [1]serves Me, he must follow Me; and [a]where I am, there My servant will be also; if anyone [1]serves Me, the Father will [b]honor him.

Jesus Foretells His Death

27 ¶ "[a]Now My soul has become troubled; and what shall I say, '[b]Father, save Me from [c]this hour'? But for this purpose I came to this hour.

28 "[a]Father, glorify Your name." Then a [b]voice came out of heaven: "I have both glorified it, and will glorify it again."

29 So the crowd *of people* who stood by and heard it were saying that it had thundered; others were saying, "[a]An angel has spoken to Him."

30 Jesus answered and said, "[a]This voice has not come for My sake, but for your sakes.

31 "[a]Now judgment is upon this world; now [b]the ruler of this world will be cast out.

32 "And I, if I [a]am lifted up from the earth, will [b]draw all men to Myself."

33 But He was saying this [a]to indicate the kind of death by which He was to die.

34 The crowd then answered Him, "We have heard out of [a]the Law that [1b]the Christ is to remain forever; and how can You say, 'The [c]Son of Man must be [d]lifted up'? Who is this [c]Son of Man?"

35 So Jesus said to them, "[a]For a little while longer [b]the Light is among you. [c]Walk while you have the Light, so that darkness will not overtake you; he who [d]walks in the darkness does not know where he goes.

36 "While you have the Light, [a]believe in the Light, so that you may become [b]sons of Light."

¶ These things Jesus spoke, and He went away and [1c]hid Himself from them.

37 But though He had performed so many [1]signs before them, *yet* they were not believing in Him.

38 *This was* to fulfill the word of Isaiah the prophet which he spoke: "[a]LORD, WHO HAS BELIEVED OUR REPORT? AND TO WHOM HAS THE ARM OF THE LORD BEEN REVEALED?"

39 For this reason they could not believe, for Isaiah said again,

40 "[a]HE HAS BLINDED THEIR EYES AND HE [b]HARDENED THEIR HEART, SO THAT THEY WOULD NOT SEE WITH THEIR EYES AND PERCEIVE WITH THEIR HEART, AND [1]BE CONVERTED AND I HEAL THEM."

41 These things Isaiah said because [a]he saw His glory, and [b]he spoke of Him.

42 Nevertheless [a]many even of [b]the rulers believed in Him, but [c]because of the Pharisees they were not confessing *Him,* for fear that they would be [1d]put out of the synagogue;

43 [a]for they loved the [1]approval of men rather than the [1]approval of God.

44 ¶ And Jesus cried out and said, "[a]He who believes in Me, does not believe in Me but in Him who sent Me.

45 "[a]He who sees Me sees the One who sent Me.

46 "[a]I have come *as* Light into the world, so that everyone who believes in Me will not remain in darkness.

47 "If anyone hears My sayings and does not keep them, I do not judge him; for [a]I did not come to judge the world, but to save the world.

48 "[a]He who rejects Me and does not receive My sayings, has one who judges him; [b]the word I spoke is what will judge him at [c]the last day.

49 "[a]For I did not speak [1]on My own initiative, but the Father Himself who sent Me [b]has given Me a commandment *as to* what to say and what to speak.

50 "I know that [a]His commandment is eternal life; therefore the things I speak, I speak [b]just as the Father has told Me."

17 [1]Lit *crowd* [a]John 11:42
18 [1]Lit *crowd* [2]Or *attesting miracle* [a]Luke 19:37; John 12:12 [b]John 12:11
20 [a]John 7:35 [b]John 12:1
21 [a]John 1:44 [b]Matt 11:21
22 [a]John 1:44
23 [a]Matt 26:45; Mark 14:35; John 13:1 [b]John 7:39
24 [a]Rom 14:9; 1 Cor 15:36
25 [1]Lit *soul* [a]Matt 10:39; Mark 8:35; Luke 9:24 [b]Luke 14:26
26 [1]Or *is serving* [a]John 14:3; 2 Cor 5:8; Phil 1:23; 1 Thess 4:17 [b]1 Sam 2:30; Ps 91:15; Luke 12:37
27 [a]Matt 26:38; Mark 14:34; John 11:33 [b]Matt 11:25 [c]John 12:23
28 [a]Matt 11:25 [b]Matt 3:17; Mark 1:11; Luke 3:22
29 [a]Acts 23:9
30 [a]John 11:42
31 [a]John 3:19 [b]John 14:30; 2 Cor 4:4; Eph 2:2; 1 John 4:4
32 [a]John 3:14 [b]John 6:44
33 [a]John 18:32
34 [1]I.e. the Messiah [a]John 10:34 [b]Ps 110:4; Is 9:7; Ezek 37:25; Dan 7:14 [c]Matt 8:20 [d]John 3:14
35 [a]John 7:33 [b]John 12:46; 1 John 2:10 [c]Gal 6:10; Eph 5:8 [d]1 John 1:6
36 [1]Lit *was hidden* [a]John 12:46 [b]Luke 16:8; John 8:12 [c]John 8:59
37 [1]Or *attesting signs*
38 [a]Is 53:1; Rom 10:16
40 [1]Lit *be turned*; i.e. turn about [a]Is 6:10; Matt 13:14f [b]Mark 6:52
41 [a]Is 6:1ff [b]Luke 24:27
42 [1]I.e. excommunicated [a]John 7:48 [b]Luke 23:13 [c]John 7:13 [d]John 9:22
43 [1]Or *glory* [a]John 5:41
44 [a]Matt 10:40; John 5:24
45 [a]John 14:9
46 [a]John 1:4
47 [a]John 3:17
48 [a]Luke 10:16 [b]Deut 18:18f; John 5:45ff [c]Matt 10:15; John 6:39; Acts 17:31; 1 Pet 1:5; 2 Pet 3:3; Heb 10:25
49 [1]Lit *of Myself* [a]John 3:11 [b]John 14:31
50 [a]John 6:68 [b]John 5:19

The Lord's Supper

13 Now before the Feast of [a]the
Passover, Jesus knowing that
[b]His hour had come that He would depart out of this world [c]to the Father,
having loved His own who were in the
world, He loved them [1]to the end.
2 During supper, [a]the devil having
already put into the heart of [b]Judas Iscariot, *the son* of Simon, to betray Him,
3 *Jesus,* [a]knowing that the Father
had given all things into His hands, and
that [b]He had come forth from God and
was going back to God,
4 *got up from supper, and *laid
aside His garments; and taking a towel,
He [a]girded Himself.

Jesus Washes the Disciples' Feet

5 Then He *poured water into the
basin, and began to [a]wash the disciples'
feet and to wipe them with the towel
with which He was girded.
6 So He *came to Simon Peter. He
*said to Him, "Lord, do You wash my
feet?"
7 Jesus answered and said to him,
"What I do you do not realize now, but
you will understand [a]hereafter."
8 Peter *said to Him, "Never shall
You wash my feet!" Jesus answered him,
"[a]If I do not wash you, [b]you have no part
with Me."
9 Simon Peter *said to Him, "Lord,
then wash not only my feet, but also my
hands and my head."
10 Jesus *said to him, "He who has
bathed needs only to wash his feet, but is
completely clean; and [a]you are clean, but
not all *of you.*"
11 For [a]He knew the one who was
betraying Him; for this reason He said,
"Not all of you are clean."
12 ¶ So when He had washed their
feet, and [a]taken His garments and reclined *at the table* again, He said to them,
"Do you know what I have done to you?
13 "You call Me [a]Teacher and [b]Lord;
and [1]you are right, for *so* I am.
14 "If I then, [a]the Lord and the Teacher, washed your feet, you also ought to
wash one another's feet.
15 "For I gave you [a]an example that
you also should do as I did to you.
16 "Truly, truly, I say to you, [a]a slave is
not greater than his master, nor *is* [b]one
who is sent greater than the one who
sent him.
17 "If you know these things, you are
[a]blessed if you do them.
18 "[a]I do not speak of all of you. I know
the ones I have [b]chosen; but *it is* [c]that
the Scripture may be fulfilled, '[d]HE WHO
EATS MY BREAD HAS LIFTED UP HIS HEEL
AGAINST ME.'
19 "From now on [a]I am telling you before *it* comes to pass, so that when it does
occur, you may believe that [b]I am *He.*
20 "Truly, truly, I say to you, [a]he who
receives whomever I send receives Me;
and he who receives Me receives Him
who sent Me."

Jesus Predicts His Betrayal

21 ¶ When Jesus had said this, He
[a]became troubled in spirit, and testified
and said, "Truly, truly, I say to you, that
[b]one of you will [1]betray Me."
22 The disciples *began* looking at one
another, [a]at a loss *to know* of which one
He was speaking.
23 There was reclining on [a]Jesus' bosom one of His disciples, [b]whom Jesus
loved.
24 So Simon Peter *gestured to him,
and *said to him, "Tell *us* who it is of
whom He is speaking."
25 He, [a]leaning back thus on Jesus'
bosom, *said to Him, "Lord, who is it?"
26 Jesus then *answered, "That is the
one for whom I shall dip the morsel and
give it to him." So when He had dipped
the morsel, He *took and *gave it to Judas, [a]*the son* of Simon Iscariot.
27 After the morsel, [a]Satan then [b]en-
tered into him. Therefore Jesus *said to
him, "What you do, do quickly."
28 Now no one of those reclining *at
the table* knew for what purpose He had
said this to him.
29 For some were supposing, because
Judas [a]had the money box, that Jesus
was saying to him, "Buy the things we
have need of [b]for the feast"; or else, that
he should [c]give something to the poor.
30 So after receiving the morsel he
went out immediately; and [a]it was night.
31 ¶ Therefore when he had gone
out, Jesus *said, "Now [1]is [a]the Son of
Man [b]glorified, and [c]God [1]is glorified in
Him;
32 [1]if God is glorified in Him, [a]God
will also glorify Him in Himself, and will
glorify Him immediately.
33 "[a]Little children, I am with you [b]a
little while longer. [c]You will seek Me;
and as I said to the Jews, now I also say
to you, 'Where I am going, you cannot
come.'
34 "A [a]new commandment I give to
you, [b]that you love one another, [c]even
as I have loved you, that you also love one
another.
35 "[a]By this all men will know that you
are My disciples, if you have love for one
another."
36 ¶ Simon Peter *said to Him, "Lord,

13:1 [1]Or *to the uttermost*; or *eternally* [a]John 2:13 [b]John 12:23 [c]John 13:3
2 [a]John 6:70 [b]John 6:71
3 [a]John 3:35 [b]John 8:42
4 [a]Luke 12:37
5 [a]Gen 18:4; Judg 19:21; Luke 7:44; 1 Tim 5:10
7 [a]John 13:12ff
8 [a]Ps 51:2; Ezek 36:25; Acts 22:16; 1 Cor 6:11; Heb 10:22 [b]Deut 12:12; 2 Sam 20:1; 1 Kin 12:16
10 [a]John 15:3; Eph 5:26
11 [a]John 6:64
12 [a]John 13:4
13 [1]Lit *you say well* [a]John 11:28 [b]John 11:2; 1 Cor 12:3; Phil 2:11
14 [a]John 11:2; 1 Cor 12:3; Phil 2:11
15 [a]1 Pet 5:3
16 [a]Matt 10:24; Luke 6:40; John 15:20 [b]2 Cor 8:23; Phil 2:25
17 [a]Matt 7:24ff; Luke 11:28; James 1:25
18 [a]John 13:10f [b]John 6:70 [c]John 15:25 [d]Ps 41:9; Matt 26:21ff; Mark 14:18f; Luke 22:21ff; John 13:21
19 [a]John 14:29 [b]John 8:24
20 [a]Matt 10:40; Mark 9:37; Luke 9:48; Gal 4:14
21 [1]Or *hand Me over* [a]John 11:33 [b]Matt 26:21f; Mark 14:18ff; Luke 22:21ff; John 13:18
22 [a]Matt 26:21ff; Mark 14:18ff; Luke 22:21ff; John 13:18
23 [a]John 1:18 [b]John 19:26
25 [a]John 21:20
26 [a]John 6:71
27 [a]Matt 4:10 [b]Luke 22:3; John 13:2
29 [a]John 12:6 [b]John 13:1 [c]John 12:5
30 [a]Luke 22:53
31 [1]Or *was* [a]Matt 8:20 [b]John 7:39 [c]John 14:13; 1 Pet 4:11
32 [1]Most early mss do not contain this phrase [a]John 17:1
33 [a]1 John 2:1 [b]John 7:33 [c]John 7:34
34 [a]John 15:12; 1 John 2:7f; 2 John 5 [b]Lev 19:18; Matt 5:44; Gal 5:14; 1 Thess 4:9; Heb 13:1; 1 Pet 1:22; 1 John 4:7 [c]Eph 5:2; 1 John 4:10f
35 [a]1 John 3:14

where are You going?" Jesus answered, "[a]Where I go, you cannot follow Me now; but [b]you will follow later."

37 Peter *said to Him, "Lord, why can I not follow You right now? [a]I will lay down my life for You."

38 Jesus *answered, "Will you lay down your life for Me? Truly, truly, I say to you, [a]a rooster will not crow until you deny Me three times.

Jesus Comforts His Disciples

14 "[a]Do not let your heart be troubled; [1]believe in God, believe also in Me.

2 "In My Father's house are many dwelling places; if it were not so, I would have told you; for [a]I go to prepare a place for you.

3 "If I go and prepare a place for you, [a]I will come again and receive you to Myself, that [b]where I am, *there* you may be also.

4 "And you know the way where I am going."

5 [a]Thomas *said to Him, "Lord, we do not know where You are going, how do we know the way?"

6 Jesus *said to him, "I am [a]the way, and [b]the truth, and [c]the life; no one comes to the Father but through Me.

Oneness with the Father

7 "[a]If you had known Me, you would have known My Father also; from now on you [b]know Him, and have [c]seen Him."

8 ¶ [a]Philip *said to Him, "Lord, show us the Father, and it is enough for us."

9 Jesus *said to him, "Have I been so long with you, and *yet* you have not come to know Me, Philip? [a]He who has seen Me has seen the Father; how *can* you say, 'Show us the Father'?

10 "Do you not believe that [a]I am in the Father, and the Father is in Me? [b]The words that I say to you I do not speak on My own initiative, but the Father abiding in Me does His works.

11 "Believe Me that [a]I am in the Father and the Father is in Me; otherwise [b]believe because of the works themselves.

12 "Truly, truly, I say to you, he who believes in Me, the works that I do, he will do also; and [a]greater *works* than these he will do; because [b]I go to the Father.

13 "[a]Whatever you ask in My name, that will I do, so that [b]the Father may be glorified in the Son.

14 "If you ask Me anything [a]in My name, I will do *it.*

15 ¶ "[a]If you love Me, you will keep My commandments.

Role of the Spirit

16 "I will ask the Father, and He will give you another [1a]Helper, that He may be with you forever;

17 *that is* [a]the Spirit of truth, [b]whom the world cannot receive, because it does not see Him or know Him, *but* you know Him because He abides with you and will be in you.

18 ¶ "I will not leave you as orphans; [a]I will come to you.

19 "[1a]After a little while [b]the world will no longer see Me, but you *will* see Me; [c]because I live, you will live also.

20 "[a]In that day you will know that [b]I am in My Father, and you in Me, and I in you.

21 "[a]He who has My commandments and keeps them is the one who loves Me; and [b]he who loves Me will be loved by My Father, and I will love him and will [c]disclose Myself to him."

22 [a]Judas (not Iscariot) *said to Him, "Lord, what then has happened [b]that You are going to disclose Yourself to us and not to the world?"

23 Jesus answered and said to him, "[a]If anyone loves Me, he will [b]keep My word; and [c]My Father will love him, and We [d]will come to him and make Our abode with him.

24 "He who does not love Me [a]does not keep My words; and [b]the word which you hear is not Mine, but the Father's who sent Me.

25 ¶ "These things I have spoken to you while abiding with you.

26 "But the [a]Helper, the Holy Spirit, [b]whom the Father will send in My name, [c]He will teach you all things, and [d]bring to your remembrance all that I said to you.

27 "[a]Peace I leave with you; My peace I give to you; not as the world gives do I give to you. [b]Do not let your heart be troubled, nor let it be fearful.

28 "[a]You heard that I said to you, 'I go away, and [b]I will come to you.' If you loved Me, you would have rejoiced because [c]I go to the Father, for [d]the Father is greater than I.

29 "Now [a]I have told you before it happens, so that when it happens, you may believe.

30 "I will not speak much more with you, for [a]the ruler of the world is coming, and he has nothing in Me;

31 but so that the world may know that I love the Father, [1]I do exactly as [a]the Father commanded Me. Get up, [b]let us go from here.

---

36 [a]John 13:33 [b]John 21:18f; 2 Pet 1:14
37 [a]John 13:37: *Matt 26:33-35; Mark 14:29-31; Luke 22:33-34*
38 [a]Mark 14:30; John 18:27
14:1 [1]Or *you believe in God* [a]John 14:27
2 [a]John 13:33
3 [a]John 14:18 [b]John 12:26
5 [a]John 11:16
6 [a]John 10:9; Rom 5:2; Eph 2:18; Heb 10:20 [b]John 1:14 [c]John 1:4; 1 John 5:20
7 [a]John 8:19 [b]1 John 2:13 [c]John 6:46
8 [a]John 1:43
9 [a]John 1:14; Col 1:15; Heb 1:3
10 [a]John 10:38 [b]John 5:19
11 [a]John 10:38 [b]John 5:36
12 [a]John 4:37f [b]John 7:33
13 [a]Matt 7:7 [b]John 13:31
14 [a]John 15:16
15 [a]John 14:21; 1 John 5:3; 2 John 6
16 [1]Gr *Paracletos*, one called alongside to help; or *Comforter, Advocate, Intercessor* [a]John 7:39; Rom 8:26; 1 John 2:1
17 [a]John 15:26; 1 John 4:6 [b]1 Cor 2:14
18 [a]John 14:3
19 [1]Lit *Yet a little and the world* [a]John 7:33 [b]John 16:16 [c]John 6:57
20 [a]John 16:23 [b]John 10:38
21 [a]John 14:15; 1 John 5:3; 2 John 6 [b]John 14:23 [c]Ex 33:18f; Prov 8:17
22 [a]Luke 6:16; Acts 1:13 [b]Acts 10:40
23 [a]John 14:15; 1 John 5:3; 2 John 6 [b]John 8:51; 1 John 2:5 [c]John 14:21 [d]2 Cor 6:16; Eph 3:17; 1 John 2:24; Rev 3:20
24 [a]John 14:23 [b]John 7:16
26 [a]John 14:16 [b]Luke 24:49; John 1:33; Acts 2:33 [c]John 16:13f; 1 John 2:20 [d]John 2:22
27 [a]John 16:33; Phil 4:7; Col 3:15 [b]John 14:1
28 [a]John 14:2-4 [b]John 14:3 [c]John 14:12 [d]John 10:29; Phil 2:6
29 [a]John 13:19
30 [a]John 12:31
31 [1]Lit *and as the Father...so I do* [a]John 10:18 [b]John 13:1

Jesus Is the Vine—Followers Are Branches

15 "[a]I am the true vine, and My Father is the [b]vinedresser.

2 "Every branch in Me that does not bear fruit, He takes away; and every *branch* that bears fruit, He [1]prunes it so that it may bear more fruit.

3 "[a]You are already [1]clean because of the word which I have spoken to you.

4 "[a]Abide in Me, and I in you. As the branch cannot bear fruit [1]of itself unless it abides in the vine, so neither *can* you unless you abide in Me.

5 "I am the vine, you are the branches; he who abides in Me and I in him, he [a]bears much fruit, for apart from Me you can do nothing.

6 "If anyone does not abide in Me, he is [a]thrown away as a branch and dries up; and they gather them, and cast them into the fire and they are burned.

7 "If you abide in Me, and My words abide in you, [a]ask whatever you wish, and it will be done for you.

8 "My [a]Father is glorified by this, that you bear much fruit, and *so* [1b]prove to be My disciples.

9 "Just as [a]the Father has loved Me, I have also loved you; abide in My love.

10 "[a]If you keep My commandments, you will abide in My love; just as [b]I have kept My Father's commandments and abide in His love.

11 "[a]These things I have spoken to you so that My joy may be in you, and *that* your [b]joy may be made full.

Disciples' Relation to Each Other

12 ¶ "This is [a]My commandment, that you love one another, just as I have loved you.

13 "[a]Greater love has no one than this, that one [b]lay down his life for his friends.

14 "You are My [a]friends if [b]you do what I command you.

15 "No longer do I call you slaves, for the slave does not know what his master is doing; but I have called you friends, for [a]all things that I have heard from My Father I have made known to you.

16 "[a]You did not choose Me but I chose you, and appointed you that you would go and [b]bear fruit, and *that* your fruit would remain, so that [c]whatever you ask of the Father in My name He may give to you.

17 "This [a]I command you, that you love one another.

Disciples' Relation to the World

18 ¶ "[a]If the world hates you, [1]you know that it has hated Me before *it hated* you.

19 "If you were of the world, the world would love its own; but because you are not of the world, but [a]I chose you out of the world, [b]because of this the world hates you.

20 "Remember the word that I said to you, '[a]A slave is not greater than his master.' If they persecuted Me, [b]they will also persecute you; if they [c]kept My word, they will keep yours also.

21 "But all these things they will do to you [a]for My name's sake, [b]because they do not know the One who sent Me.

22 "[a]If I had not come and spoken to them, they would not have [1]sin, but now they have no excuse for their sin.

23 "He who hates Me hates My Father also.

24 "[a]If I had not done among them [b]the works which no one else did, they would not have [1]sin; but now they have both seen and hated Me and My Father as well.

25 "But *they have done this* to fulfill the word that is written in their [a]Law, '[b]THEY HATED ME WITHOUT A CAUSE.'

26 ¶ "When the [1a]Helper comes, [b]whom I will send to you from the Father, *that is* [c]the Spirit of truth who proceeds from the Father, [d]He will testify about Me,

27 [1]and [a]you *will* testify also, because you have been with Me [b]from the beginning.

Jesus' Warning

16 "[a]These things I have spoken to you so that you may be kept from [b]stumbling.

2 "[1]They will [a]make you outcasts from the synagogue, but [b]an hour is coming for everyone [c]who kills you to think that he is offering service to God.

3 "These things they will do [a]because they have not known the Father or Me.

4 "But these things I have spoken to you, [a]so that when their hour comes, you [1]may remember that I told you of them. These things I did not say to you [b]at the beginning, because I was with you.

The Holy Spirit Promised

5 ¶ "But now [a]I am going to Him who sent Me; and none of you asks Me, '[b]Where are You going?'

6 "But because I have said these things to you, [a]sorrow has filled your heart.

7 "But I tell you the truth, it is to your

15:1 [a]Ps 80:8ff; Is 5:1ff; Ezek 19:10ff; Matt 21:33ff [b]Matt 15:13; Rom 11:17; 1 Cor 3:9
2 [1]Lit *cleans*; used to describe pruning
3 [1]I.e. pruned like a branch [a]John 13:10; Eph 5:26
4 [1]Lit *from* [a]John 6:56; 1 John 2:6
5 [a]John 15:16
6 [a]John 15:2
7 [a]Matt 7:7; John 15:16
8 [1]Or *become My disciples* [a]Matt 5:16 [b]John 8:31
9 [a]John 3:35
10 [a]John 14:15 [b]John 8:29
11 [a]John 17:13 [b]John 3:29
12 [a]John 13:34; 1 John 3:23; 2 John 5
13 [a]Rom 5:7f [b]John 10:11
14 [a]Luke 12:4 [b]Matt 12:50
15 [a]John 8:26
16 [a]John 6:70 [b]John 15:5 [c]John 14:13
17 [a]John 15:12
18 [1]Or (imperative) *know that* [a]John 7:7; 1 John 3:13
19 [a]John 15:16 [b]Matt 10:22; John 17:14
20 [a]Matt 10:24; John 13:16 [b]1 Cor 4:12; 2 Cor 4:9; 2 Tim 3:12 [c]John 8:51
21 [a]Matt 10:22; Mark 13:13; Luke 21:12; Acts 4:17; 1 Pet 4:14; Rev 2:3 [b]John 8:19; Acts 3:17; 1 John 3:1
22 [1]I.e. guilt [a]John 9:41
24 [1]I.e. guilt [a]John 9:41 [b]John 5:36
25 [a]John 10:34 [b]Ps 35:19
26 [1]Gr *Paracletos*, one called alongside to help; or *Comforter, Advocate, Intercessor* [a]John 14:16 [b]John 14:26 [c]John 14:17 [d]1 John 5:7
27 [1]Or (imperative) *and bear witness* [a]Luke 24:48; John 19:35; 1 John 1:2 [b]Luke 1:2
16:1 [a]John 15:18-27 [b]Matt 11:6
2 [1]Or *They will have you excommunicated* [a]John 9:22 [b]John 4:21 [c]Is 66:5; Acts 26:9-11; Rev 6:9
3 [a]John 8:19; Acts 3:17; 1 John 3:1
4 [1]Or *will remember them, that I told you* [a]John 13:19 [b]Luke 1:2
5 [a]John 7:33 [b]John 13:36
6 [a]John 14:1

advantage that I go away; for if I do not go
away, the [1a]Helper will not come to
you; but if I go, [b]I will send Him to you.
8 "And He, when He comes, will convict the world concerning sin and righteousness and judgment;
9 concerning sin, [a]because they do
not believe in Me;
10 and concerning [a]righteousness,
because [b]I go to the Father and you no
longer see Me;
11 [a]and concerning judgment, because the ruler of this world has been
judged.
12 ¶ "I have many more things to say
to you, but you cannot bear *them* now.
13 "But when He, [a]the Spirit of truth,
comes, He will [b]guide you into all the
truth; for He will not speak on His own
initiative, but whatever He hears, He will
speak; and He will disclose to you what is
to come.
14 "He will [a]glorify Me, for He will
take of Mine and will disclose *it* to you.
15 "[a]All things that the Father has are
Mine; therefore I said that He takes of
Mine and will disclose *it* to you.

Jesus' Death and Resurrection Foretold

16 ¶ "[a]A little while, and [b]you will
no longer see Me; and again a little while,
and [c]you will see Me."
17 *Some* of His disciples then said to
one another, "What is this thing He is
telling us, '[a]A little while, and you will
not see Me; and again a little while, and
you will see Me'; and, 'because [b]I go to
the Father'?"
18 So they were saying, "What is this
that He says, 'A little while'? We do not
know what He is talking about."
19 [a]Jesus knew that they wished to
question Him, and He said to them, "Are
you deliberating together about this, that
I said, 'A little while, and you will not see
Me, and again a little while, and you will
see Me'?
20 "Truly, truly, I say to you, that [a]you
will weep and lament, but the world will
rejoice; you will grieve, but [b]your grief
will be turned into joy.
21 "[a]Whenever a woman is in labor
she has [1]pain, because her hour has
come; but when she gives birth to the
child, she no longer remembers the anguish because of the joy that a [2]child has
been born into the world.
22 "Therefore [a]you too have grief now;
but [b]I will see you again, and your heart
will rejoice, and no one *will* take your joy
away from you.

Prayer Promises

23 "[a]In that day [b]you will not question
Me about anything. Truly, truly, I say to
you, [c]if you ask the Father for anything
in My name, He will give it to you.
24 "[a]Until now you have asked for
nothing in My name; ask and you will
receive, so that your [b]joy may be made
full.
25 ¶ "These things I have spoken to
you in [1a]figurative language; [b]an hour
is coming when I will no longer speak to
you in [1]figurative language, but will tell
you plainly of the Father.
26 "[a]In that day [b]you will ask in My
name, and I do not say to you that I will
request of the Father on your behalf;
27 for [a]the Father Himself loves you,
because you have loved Me and [b]have
believed that [c]I came forth from the Father.
28 "[a]I came forth from the Father and
have come into the world; I am leaving
the world again and [b]going to the Father."
29 ¶ His disciples *said, "Lo, now You
are speaking plainly and are not [1]using
[a]a figure of speech.
30 "Now we know that You know all
things, and have no need for anyone to
question You; by this we [a]believe that
You [b]came from God."
31 Jesus answered them, "Do you now
believe?
32 "Behold, [a]an hour is coming, and
has *already* come, for [b]you to be scattered, each to [c]his own *home,* and to
leave Me alone; and *yet* [d]I am not alone,
because the Father is with Me.
33 "These things I have spoken to you,
so that [a]in Me you may have peace. [b]In
the world you have tribulation, but [c]take
courage; [d]I have overcome the world."

The High Priestly Prayer

17 Jesus spoke these things; and
[a]lifting up His eyes to heaven, He
said, "Father, the hour has come; [b]glorify
Your Son, that the Son may glorify You,
2 even as [a]You gave Him authority
over all flesh, that [b]to [1]all whom You
have given Him, [c]He may give eternal
life.
3 "This is eternal life, that they may
know You, [a]the only true God, and Jesus
Christ whom [b]You have sent.
4 "[a]I glorified You on the earth,
[1b]having accomplished the work which
You have given Me to do.
5 "Now, Father, [a]glorify Me together
with Yourself, with the glory which I had
[b]with You before the world was.
6 ¶ "[a]I have manifested Your name

7 [1]Gr *Paracletos, one called along-side to help; or Comforter, Advocate, Intercessor* [a]John 14:16 [b]John 14:26
9 [a]John 15:22
10 [a]Acts 3:14; 1 Pet 3:18 [b]John 16:5
11 [a]John 12:31
13 [a]John 14:17 [b]John 14:26
14 [a]John 7:39
15 [a]John 17:10
16 [a]John 7:33 [b]John 14:18-24 [c]John 16:22
17 [a]John 16:16 [b]John 16:5
19 [a]Mark 9:32; John 6:61
20 [a]Mark 16:10; Luke 23:27 [b]John 20:20
21 [1]Lit *grief* [2]Lit *human being* [a]Is 13:8; Hos 13:13; Mic 4:9; 1 Thess 5:3
22 [a]John 16:6 [b]John 16:16
23 [a]John 14:20 [b]John 16:19 [c]John 15:16
24 [a]John 14:14 [b]John 3:29
25 [1]Lit *proverbs;* or *figures of speech* [a]Matt 13:34; John 10:6 [b]John 16:2
26 [a]John 14:20 [b]John 16:19
27 [a]John 14:21 [b]John 2:11 [c]John 8:42
28 [a]John 8:42 [b]John 13:1
29 [1]Lit *saying a proverb* [a]Matt 13:34; John 10:6
30 [a]John 2:11 [b]John 8:42
32 [a]John 4:23 [b]Zech 13:7; Matt 26:31 [c]John 19:27 [d]John 8:29
33 [a]John 14:27 [b]John 15:18ff [c]Matt 9:2 [d]Rom 8:37; 2 Cor 2:14; Rev 3:21
17:1 [a]John 11:41 [b]John 7:39
2 [1]Lit *everything that You have given Him, to them He may* [a]John 3:35 [b]John 10:28 [c]John 6:37
3 [a]John 5:44 [b]John 3:17
4 [1]Or *by accomplishing* [a]John 13:31 [b]Luke 22:37; John 4:34
5 [a]John 17:1 [b]John 1:1; Phil 2:6
6 [a]John 17:26

to the men whom [b]You gave Me out of
the world; they were [c]Yours and You
gave them to Me, and they have [d]kept
Your word.
7 "Now they have come to know that
everything You have given Me is from
You;
8 for [a]the words which You gave Me
[b]I have given to them; and they received
them and truly understood that [c]I came
forth from You, and they believed that
[d]You sent Me.
9 "[a]I ask on their behalf; [b]I do not ask
on behalf of the world, but of those whom
[c]You have given Me; for [d]they are
Yours;
10 and [a]all things that are Mine are
Yours, and Yours are Mine; and I have
been glorified in them.
11 "I am no longer in the world; and *yet*
[a]they themselves are in the world, and
[b]I come to You. [c]Holy Father, keep them
in Your name, *the name* [d]which You
have given Me, that [e]they may be one
even as We *are*.
12 "While I was with them, I was keeping them in Your name [a]which You have
given Me; and I guarded them and [b]not
one of them perished but [c]the [1]son of
perdition, so that the [d]Scripture would
be fulfilled.

The Disciples in the World

13 "But now [a]I come to You; and
[b]these things I speak in the world so that
they may have My [c]joy made full in
themselves.
14 "I have given them Your word; and
[a]the world has hated them, because
[b]they are not of the world, even as I am
not of the world.
15 "I do not ask You to take them out
of the world, but to keep them [1]from
[2a]the evil *one*.
16 "[a]They are not of the world, even as
I am not of the world.
17 "[a]Sanctify them in the truth; Your
word is truth.
18 "As [a]You sent Me into the world, [b]I
also have sent them into the world.
19 "For their sakes I [a]sanctify Myself,
that they themselves also may be [b]sancti-
fied [c]in truth.
20 ¶ "I do not ask on behalf of these
alone, but for those also who believe in
Me through their word;
21 that they may all be one; [a]even as
You, Father, *are* in Me and I in You, that
they also may be in Us, [b]so that the
world may [1]believe that [c]You sent Me.

Their Future Glory

22 "The [a]glory which You have given
Me I have given to them, that they may
be one, just as We are one;
23 [a]I in them and You in Me, that
they may be perfected [1]in unity, so that
the world may [2]know that [b]You sent
Me, and [c]loved them, even as You have
loved Me.
24 "Father, I desire that [a]they also,
whom You have given Me, [b]be with Me
where I am, so that they may see My
[c]glory which You have given Me, for You
loved Me before [d]the foundation of the
world.
25 ¶ "O [a]righteous Father, [1]although
[b]the world has not known You, yet I
have known You; and these have known
that [c]You sent Me;
26 and [a]I have made Your name
known to them, and will make it known,
so that [b]the love with which You loved
Me may be in them, and I in them."

Judas Betrays Jesus

18 When Jesus had spoken these
words, [a]He went forth with His
disciples over [b]the [1]ravine of the Kidron, where there was [c]a garden, in
which He entered [2]with His disciples.
2 Now Judas also, who was [1]betray-
ing Him, knew the place, for Jesus had
[a]often met there with His disciples.
3 [a]Judas then, having received [b]the
Roman [1]cohort and [c]officers from the
chief priests and the Pharisees, *came
there with lanterns and [d]torches and
weapons.
4 So Jesus, [a]knowing all the things
that were coming upon Him, went forth
and *said to them, "[b]Whom do you
seek?"
5 They answered Him, "Jesus the
Nazarene." He *said to them, "I am *He*."
And Judas also, who was betraying Him,
was standing with them.
6 So when He said to them, "I am
He," they drew back and fell to the
ground.
7 Therefore He again asked them,
"[a]Whom do you seek?" And they said,
"Jesus the Nazarene."
8 Jesus answered, "I told you that I
am *He*; so if you seek Me, let these go
their way,"
9 to fulfill the word which He spoke,
"[a]Of those whom You have given Me I
lost not one."
10 Simon Peter then, [a]having a
sword, drew it and struck the high
priest's slave, and cut off his right ear;
and the slave's name was Malchus.
11 So Jesus said to Peter, "Put the

6 [b]John 6:37 [c]John 17:9 [d]John 8:51
8 [a]John 6:68 [b]John 15:15 [c]John 8:42 [d]John 3:17
9 [a]Luke 22:32; John 14:16 [b]Luke 23:34; John 17:20f [c]John 6:37 [d]John 17:6
10 [a]John 16:15
11 [a]John 13:1 [b]John 7:33 [c]John 17:25 [d]John 17:6; Phil 2:9; Rev 19:12 [e]John 17:21f; Rom 12:5; Gal 3:28
12 [1]Heb idiom for one destined to perish [a]John 17:6; Phil 2:9; Rev 19:12 [b]John 6:39 [c]John 6:70 [d]Ps 41:9; John 13:18
13 [a]John 7:33 [b]John 15:11 [c]John 3:29
14 [a]John 15:19 [b]John 8:23
15 [1]Or *out of the power of* [2]Or *evil* [a]Matt 5:37
16 [a]John 17:14
17 [a]John 15:3
18 [a]John 3:17 [b]Matt 10:5; John 4:38
19 [a]John 15:13 [b]John 15:3 [c]2 Cor 7:14; Col 1:6; 1 John 3:18
21 [1]Gr tense indicates *continually believe* [a]John 10:38 [b]John 17:8 [c]John 3:17
22 [a]John 1:14
23 [1]Lit *into one* [2]Gr tense indicates *continually know* [a]John 10:38 [b]John 3:17 [c]John 16:27
24 [a]John 17:2 [b]John 12:26 [c]John 1:14 [d]Matt 25:34; John 17:5
25 [1]Lit *even the world* [a]John 17:11; 1 John 1:9 [b]John 7:29 [c]John 3:17
26 [a]John 17:6 [b]John 15:9
18:1 [1]Lit *winter-torrent* [2]Lit *and* [a]Matt 26:30; Mark 14:26; Luke 22:39 [b]2 Sam 15:23; 1 Kin 2:37; 2 Kin 23:4; 2 Chr 15:16; Jer 31:40 [c]Matt 26:36; Mark 14:32; John 18:26
2 [1]Or *handing Him over* [a]Luke 21:37
3 [1]Normally 600 men; *a battalion* [a]John 18:3-11: *Matt 26:47-56; Mark 14:43-50; Luke 22:47-53* [b]John 18:12; Acts 10:1 [c]John 7:32 [d]Matt 25:1
4 [a]John 6:64 [b]John 18:7
7 [a]John 18:4
9 [a]John 17:12 **10** [a]Matt 26:51; Mark 14:47

sword into the sheath; [a]the cup which
the Father has given Me, shall I not
drink it?"

Jesus before the Priests

12 ¶ [a]So [b]the *Roman* [1]cohort and
the [2]commander and the [b]officers of the
Jews, arrested Jesus and bound Him,
13 and led Him to [a]Annas first; for he
was father-in-law of [b]Caiaphas, who was
high priest that year.
14 Now Caiaphas was the one who
had advised the Jews that [a]it was expedient for one man to die on behalf of the
people.
15 ¶ [a]Simon Peter was following
Jesus, and *so was* another disciple. Now
that disciple was known to the high
priest, and entered with Jesus into [b]the
court of the high priest,
16 [a]but Peter was standing at the door
outside. So the other disciple, who was
known to the high priest, went out and
spoke to the doorkeeper, and brought Peter in.
17 [a]Then the slave-girl who kept the
door *said to Peter, "[b]You are not also
one of this man's disciples, are you?" He
*said, "I am not."
18 Now the slaves and the [a]officers
were standing *there,* having made [b]a
charcoal fire, for it was cold and they
were [c]warming themselves; and Peter
was also with them, standing and warming himself.
19 ¶ [a]The high priest then questioned
Jesus about His disciples, and about His
teaching.
20 Jesus answered him, "I [a]have spoken openly to the world; I always [b]taught
in [1]synagogues and [c]in the temple,
where all the Jews come together; and I
spoke nothing in secret.
21 "Why do you question Me? Question
those who have heard what I spoke to
them; they know what I said."
22 When He had said this, one of the
[a]officers standing nearby [b]struck Jesus,
saying, "Is that the way You answer the
high priest?"
23 [a]Jesus answered him, "If I have
spoken wrongly, testify of the wrong; but
if rightly, why do you strike Me?"
24 [a]So Annas sent Him bound to [a]Ca-
iaphas the high priest.

Peter's Denial of Jesus

25 ¶ [a]Now [b]Simon Peter was standing and warming himself. So they said to
him, "[c]You are not also *one* of His disciples, are you?" He denied *it,* and said, "I
am not."
26 One of the slaves of the high priest,
being a relative of the one [a]whose ear
Peter cut off, *said, "Did I not see you in
[b]the garden with Him?"
27 Peter then denied *it* again, and immediately [a]a rooster crowed.

Jesus before Pilate

28 ¶ [a]Then they *led Jesus from [b]Ca-
iaphas into [c]the [1]Praetorium, and it was
early; and they themselves did not enter
into [c]the [1]Praetorium so that [d]they
would not be defiled, but might eat the
Passover.
29 [a]Therefore Pilate went out to them
and *said, "What accusation do you bring
against this Man?"
30 They answered and said to him, "If
this Man were not an evildoer, we would
not have delivered Him to you."
31 So Pilate said to them, "Take Him
yourselves, and judge Him according to
your law." The Jews said to him, "We are
not permitted to put anyone to death,"
32 to fulfill [a]the word of Jesus which
He spoke, signifying by what kind of
death He was about to die.
33 ¶ Therefore Pilate [a]entered again
into the Praetorium, and summoned
Jesus and said to Him, "[b]Are You the
King of the Jews?"
34 Jesus answered, "Are you saying
this [1]on your own initiative, or did others tell you about Me?"
35 Pilate answered, "I am not a Jew,
am I? Your own nation and the chief
priests delivered You to me; what have
You done?"
36 Jesus answered, "[a]My kingdom
[1]is not of this world. If My kingdom were
of this world, then My servants would be
fighting so that I would not be handed
over to the Jews; but as it is, My kingdom
is not [2]of this realm."
37 Therefore Pilate said to Him, "So
You are a king?" Jesus answered, "[a]You
say *correctly* that I am a king. For this I
have been born, and for this I have come
into the world, [b]to testify to the truth.
[c]Everyone who is of the truth hears My
voice."
38 Pilate *said to Him, "What is
truth?"
¶ And when he had said this, he [a]went
out again to the Jews and *said to them,
"[b]I find no guilt in Him.
39 "[a]But you have a custom that I release someone [1]for you at the Passover;
do you wish then that I release [1]for you
the King of the Jews?"
40 So they cried out again, saying,
"[a]Not this Man, but Barabbas." Now
Barabbas was a robber.

11 [a]Matt 20:22; Mark 14:36; Luke 22:42
12 [1]Or *battalion* [2]I.e. chiliarch, in command of a thousand troops [a]John 18:12f: *Matt 26:57ff* [b]John 18:3
13 [a]Luke 3:2; John 18:24 [b]Matt 26:3; John 11:49
14 [a]John 11:50
15 [a]Matt 26:58; Mark 14:54; Luke 22:54 [b]Matt 26:3; John 18:24
16 [a]John 18:16-18: *Matt 26:69f; Mark 14:66-68; Luke 22:55-57*
17 [a]Acts 12:13 [b]John 18:25
18 [a]John 18:3 [b]John 21:9 [c]Mark 14:54
19 [a]John 18:19-24: *Matt 26:59-68; Mark 14:55-65; Luke 22:63-71*
20 [1]Lit *a synagogue* [a]John 7:26 [b]Matt 4:23; John 6:59 [c]Matt 26:55
22 [a]John 18:3 [b]John 19:3
23 [a]Matt 5:39; Acts 23:2-5
24 [a]John 18:13
25 [a]John 18:25-27: *Matt 26:71-75; Mark 14:69-72; Luke 22:58-62* [b]John 18:18 [c]John 18:17
26 [a]John 18:10 [b]John 18:1
27 [a]John 13:38
28 [1]I.e. governor's official residence [a]Matt 27:2; Mark 15:1; Luke 23:1 [b]John 18:13 [c]Matt 27:27; John 18:33 [d]John 11:55; Acts 11:3
29 [a]John 18:29-38: *Matt 27:11-14; Mark 15:2-5; Luke 23:2,3*
32 [a]Matt 20:19; Mark 10:33f; Luke 18:32f; John 3:14
33 [a]John 18:28 [b]Luke 23:3; John 19:12
34 [1]Lit *from yourself*
36 [1]Or *is not derived from* [2]Lit *from here* [a]Matt 26:53; Luke 17:21; John 6:15
37 [a]Matt 27:11; Mark 15:2; Luke 22:70 [b]John 1:14 [c]John 8:47; 1 John 4:6
38 [a]John 18:33 [b]Luke 23:4; John 19:4
39 [1]Or *to you* [a]John 18:39-19:16: *Matt 27:15-26; Mark 15:6-15; Luke 23:18-25*
40 [a]Acts 3:14

The Crown of Thorns

19 Pilate then took Jesus and [1a]scourged Him.

2 [a]And the soldiers twisted together a crown of thorns and put it on His head, and put a purple robe on Him;

3 and they *began* to come up to Him and say, "[a]Hail, King of the Jews!" and to [b]give Him slaps *in the face.*

4 Pilate [a]came out again and *said to them, "Behold, I am bringing Him out to you so that you may know that [b]I find no guilt in Him."

5 Jesus then came out, [a]wearing the crown of thorns and the purple robe. *Pilate* *said to them, "Behold, the Man!"

6 So when the chief priests and the [a]officers saw Him, they cried out saying, "Crucify, crucify!" Pilate *said to them, "Take Him yourselves and crucify Him, for [b]I find no guilt in Him."

7 The Jews answered him, "[a]We have a law, and by that law He ought to die because He [b]made Himself out *to be* the Son of God."

8 ¶ Therefore when Pilate heard this statement, he was *even* more afraid;

9 and he [a]entered into the [1]Praetorium again and *said to Jesus, "Where are You from?" But [b]Jesus gave him no answer.

10 So Pilate *said to Him, "You do not speak to me? Do You not know that I have authority to release You, and I have authority to crucify You?"

11 Jesus answered, "[a]You would have no authority [1]over Me, unless it had been given you from above; for this reason [b]he who delivered Me to you has *the* greater sin."

12 As a result of this Pilate [1]made efforts to release Him, but the Jews cried out saying, "[a]If you release this Man, you are no friend of Caesar; everyone who makes himself out *to be* a king [2]opposes Caesar."

13 ¶ Therefore when Pilate heard these words, he brought Jesus out, and [a]sat down on the judgment seat at a place called [1]The Pavement, but [b]in [2]Hebrew, Gabbatha.

14 Now it was [a]the day of preparation for the Passover; it was about the [1b]sixth hour. And he *said to the Jews, "Behold, [c]your King!"

15 So they cried out, "[a]Away with *Him,* away with *Him,* crucify Him!" Pilate *said to them, "Shall I crucify your King?" The chief priests answered, "We have no king but Caesar."

19:1 [1]Or *had Him scourged* [a]Matt 27:26
2 [a]Matt 27:27-30; *Mark 15:16-19*
3 [a]Matt 27:29; Mark 15:18 [b]John 18:22
4 [a]John 18:33 [b]Luke 23:4; John 18:38
5 [a]John 19:2
6 [a]Matt 26:58; John 18:3 [b]Luke 23:4; John 18:38
7 [a]Lev 24:16; Matt 26:63-66 [b]John 5:18
9 [1]I.e. governor's official residence [a]John 18:33 [b]Matt 26:63; John 18:34-37
11 [1]Lit *against* [a]Rom 13:1 [b]John 18:13f; Acts 3:13
12 [1]Lit *was seeking to* [2]Or *speaks against* [a]Luke 23:2; John 18:33ff
13 [1]Gr *The Lithostrotos* [2]I.e. Jewish Aramaic [a]Matt 27:19 [b]John 5:2
14 [1]Perhaps 6 a.m. [a]Matt 27:62; John 19:31 [b]Matt 27:45; Mark 15:25 [c]John 19:19
15 [a]Luke 23:18
16 [a]Matt 27:26; Mark 15:15; Luke 23:25
17 [1]Lit *bearing the cross for Himself* [2]I.e. Jewish Aramaic [a]John 19:17-24: *Matt 27:33-44; Mark 15:22-32; Luke 23:33-43* [b]Matt 27:32; Mark 15:21; Luke 14:27 [c]Luke 23:33 [d]John 19:13
18 [a]Luke 23:32
19 [a]Matt 27:37; Mark 15:26; Luke 23:38 [b]John 19:14
20 [1]I.e. Jewish Aramaic [a]John 19:13
21 [a]John 19:14
22 [a]Gen 43:14; Esth 4:16
23 [1]Gr *khiton,* the garment worn next to the skin [2]Lit *from the upper part through the whole* [a]Matt 27:35; Mark 15:24; Luke 23:34 [b]Acts 12:4
24 [1]Lit *a lot* [a]Ex 28:32; Matt 27:35; Mark 15:24; Luke 23:34 [b]John 19:28 [c]Ps 22:18
25 [a]Matt 27:55f; Mark 15:40f; Luke 23:49 [b]Matt 12:46 [c]Luke 8:2; John 20:1
26 [a]John 13:23 [b]John 2:4
27 [a]Luke 18:28; John 1:11; Acts 21:6
28 [a]John 13:1 [b]John 19:24 [c]Ps 69:21
29 [a]John 19:29: *Matt 27:48,50; Mark 15:36f; Luke 23:36*

The Crucifixion

16 So he then [a]handed Him over to them to be crucified.

17 ¶ [a]They took Jesus, therefore, and He went out, [1b]bearing His own cross, to the place called [c]the Place of a Skull, which is called [d]in [2]Hebrew, Golgotha.

18 There they crucified Him, and with Him [a]two other men, one on either side, and Jesus in between.

19 Pilate also wrote an inscription and put it on the cross. It was written, "[a]JESUS THE NAZARENE, [b]THE KING OF THE JEWS."

20 Therefore many of the Jews read this inscription, for the place where Jesus was crucified was near the city; and it was written [a]in [1]Hebrew, Latin *and* in Greek.

21 So the chief priests of the Jews were saying to Pilate, "Do not write, '[a]The King of the Jews'; but that He said, 'I am [a]King of the Jews.'"

22 Pilate answered, "[a]What I have written I have written."

23 ¶ Then [a]the soldiers, when they had crucified Jesus, took His outer garments and made [b]four parts, a part to every soldier and *also* the [1]tunic; now the tunic was seamless, woven [2]in one piece.

24 So they said to one another, "[a]Let us not tear it, but cast lots for it, *to decide* whose it shall be"; [b]*this was* to fulfill the Scripture: "THEY [c]DIVIDED MY OUTER GARMENTS AMONG THEM, AND FOR MY CLOTHING THEY CAST [1]LOTS."

25 Therefore the soldiers did these things.

¶ [a]But standing by the cross of Jesus were [b]His mother, and His mother's sister, Mary the *wife* of Clopas, and [c]Mary Magdalene.

26 When Jesus then saw His mother, and [a]the disciple whom He loved standing nearby, He *said to His mother, "[b]Woman, behold, your son!"

27 Then He *said to the disciple, "Behold, your mother!" From that hour the disciple took her into [a]his own *household.*

28 ¶ After this, Jesus, [a]knowing that all things had already been accomplished, [b]to fulfill the Scripture, *said, "[c]I am thirsty."

29 A jar full of sour wine was standing there; so [a]they put a sponge full of the sour wine upon *a branch of* hyssop and brought it up to His mouth.

30 Therefore when Jesus had received

the sour wine, He said, "[a]It is finished!" And He bowed His head and [b]gave up His spirit.

Care of the Body of Jesus

31 ¶ Then the Jews, because it was [a]the day of preparation, so that [b]the bodies would not remain on the cross on the Sabbath ([1]for that Sabbath was a [c]high day), asked Pilate that their legs might be broken, and *that* they might be taken away.

32 So the soldiers came, and broke the legs of the first man and of the other who was [a]crucified with Him;

33 but coming to Jesus, when they saw that He was already dead, they did not break His legs.

34 But one of the soldiers pierced His side with a spear, and immediately [a]blood and water came out.

35 And he who has seen has [a]testified, and his testimony is true; and he knows that he is telling the truth, so that you also may believe.

36 For these things came to pass [a]to fulfill the Scripture, "[b]NOT A BONE OF HIM SHALL BE [1]BROKEN."

37 And again another Scripture says, "[a]THEY SHALL LOOK ON HIM WHOM THEY PIERCED."

38 ¶ [a]After these things Joseph of Arimathea, being a disciple of Jesus, but a [b]secret *one* for [c]fear of the Jews, asked Pilate that he might take away the body of Jesus; and Pilate granted permission. So he came and took away His body.

39 [a]Nicodemus, who had first come to Him by night, also came, [b]bringing a [1]mixture of [c]myrrh and aloes, about a [d]hundred [2]pounds *weight*.

40 So they took the body of Jesus and [a]bound it in [b]linen wrappings with the spices, as is the burial custom of the Jews.

41 Now in the place where He was crucified there was a garden, and in the garden a [a]new tomb [b]in which no one had yet been laid.

42 Therefore because of the Jewish day of [a]preparation, since the tomb was [b]nearby, they laid Jesus there.

The Empty Tomb

20 [a]Now on the first *day* of the week [b]Mary Magdalene *came early to the tomb, while it *was still dark, and *saw [c]the stone *already* taken away from the tomb.

2 So she *ran and *came to Simon Peter and to the other [a]disciple whom Jesus loved, and *said to them, "[b]They have taken away the Lord out of the tomb, and we do not know where they have laid Him."

3 [a]So Peter and the other disciple went forth, and they were going to the tomb.

4 The two were running together; and the other disciple ran ahead faster than Peter and came to the tomb first;

5 and [a]stooping and looking in, he *saw the [b]linen wrappings lying *there*; but he did not go in.

6 And so Simon Peter also *came, following him, and entered the tomb; and he *saw the linen wrappings lying *there*,

7 and [a]the face-cloth which had been on His head, not lying with the [b]linen wrappings, but rolled up in a place by itself.

8 So the other disciple who [a]had first come to the tomb then also entered, and he saw and believed.

9 For as yet [a]they did not understand the Scripture, [b]that He must rise again from the dead.

10 So the disciples went away again [a]to their own homes.

11 ¶ [a]But Mary was standing outside the tomb weeping; and so, as she wept, she [b]stooped and looked into the tomb;

12 and she *saw [a]two angels in white sitting, one at the head and one at the feet, where the body of Jesus had been lying.

13 And they *said to her, "[a]Woman, why are you weeping?" She *said to them, "Because [b]they have taken away my Lord, and I do not know where they have laid Him."

14 When she had said this, she turned around and *[a]saw Jesus standing *there*, and [b]did not know that it was Jesus.

15 Jesus *said to her, "[a]Woman, why are you weeping? Whom are you seeking?" Supposing Him to be the gardener, she *said to Him, "Sir, if you have carried Him away, tell me where you have laid Him, and I will take Him away."

16 Jesus *said to her, "Mary!" She turned and *said to Him [a]in [1]Hebrew, "[b]Rabboni!" (which means, Teacher).

17 Jesus *said to her, "Stop clinging to Me, for I have not yet ascended to the Father; but go to [a]My brethren and say to them, 'I [b]ascend to My Father and your Father, and My God and your God.' "

18 [a]Mary Magdalene *came, [b]announcing to the disciples, "I have seen the Lord," and *that* He had said these things to her.

Jesus among His Disciples

19 ¶ So when it was evening on that day, the first *day* of the week, and when the doors were shut where the disciples were, for [a]fear of the Jews, Jesus came

---

30 [a]John 17:4 [b]Matt 27:50; Mark 15:37; Luke 23:46
31 [1]Lit *for the day of that Sabbath was great* [a]John 19:14,42 [b]Deut 21:23; Josh 8:29; 10:26f [c]Ex 12:16
32 [a]John 19:18
34 [a]1 John 5:6,8
35 [a]John 15:27; 21:24
36 [1]Or *crushed* or *shattered* [a]John 19:24,28 [b]Ex 12:46; Num 9:12; Ps 34:20
37 [a]Zech 12:10; Rev 1:7
38 [a]John 19:38-42: *Matt 27:57-61; Mark 15:42-47; Luke 23:50-56* [b]Mark 15:43 [c]John 7:13
39 [1]Two early mss read *package of* [2]Lit *100 litras* (12 oz each) [a]John 3:1 [b]Mark 16:1 [c]Ps 45:8; Prov 7:17; Song 4:14; Matt 2:11 [d]John 12:3
40 [a]Matt 26:12; Mark 14:8; John 11:44 [b]Luke 24:12; John 20:5,7
41 [a]Matt 27:60 [b]Luke 23:53
42 [a]John 19:14, 31 [b]John 19:20, 41
20:1 [a]John 20:1-8: *Matt 28:1-8; Mark 16:1-8; Luke 24:1-10* [b]John 19:25; 20:18 [c]Matt 27:60,66; 28:2; Mark 15:46; 16:3f; Luke 24:2; John 11:38
2 [a]John 13:23 [b]John 20:13
3 [a]Luke 24:12; John 20:3-10
5 [a]John 20:11 [b]John 19:40
7 [a]John 11:44 [b]John 19:40
8 [a]John 20:4
9 [a]Matt 22:29; John 2:22 [b]Luke 24:26ff,46
10 [a]Luke 24:12
11 [a]Mark 16:5 [b]John 20:5
12 [a]Matt 28:2f; Mark 16:5; Luke 24:4
13 [a]John 20:15 [b]John 20:2
14 [a]Matt 28:9; Mark 16:9 [b]John 21:4
15 [a]John 20:13
16 [1]I.e. Jewish Aramaic [a]John 5:2 [b]Matt 23:7; Mark 10:51
17 [a]Matt 28:10 [b]Mark 12:26; 16:19; John 7:33
18 [a]John 20:1 [b]Mark 16:10; Luke 24:10,23
19 [a]John 7:13

and stood in their midst and *said to
them, "[1b]Peace *be* with you."
20 And when He had said this, [a]He
showed them both His hands and His
side. The disciples then [b]rejoiced when
they saw the Lord.
21 So Jesus said to them again,
"[a]Peace *be* with you; [b]as the Father has
sent Me, I also send you."
22 And when He had said this, He
breathed on them and *said to them, "Receive the Holy Spirit.
23 "[a]If you forgive the sins of any, *their*
sins [1]have been forgiven them; if you
retain the *sins* of any, they have been
retained."
24 ¶ But [a]Thomas, one of [b]the
twelve, called [1a]Didymus, was not with
them when Jesus came.
25 So the other disciples were saying
to him, "We have seen the Lord!" But he
said to them, "Unless I see in [a]His hands
the imprint of the nails, and put my finger
into the place of the nails, and put my
hand into His side, [b]I will not believe."
26 ¶ [1]After eight days His disciples
were again inside, and Thomas with
them. Jesus *came, the doors having
been [2]shut, and stood in their midst and
said, "[a]Peace *be* with you."
27 Then He *said to Thomas, "[a]Reach
here with your finger, and see My hands;
and reach here your hand and put it into
My side; and do not be unbelieving, but
believing."
28 Thomas answered and said to Him,
"My Lord and my God!"
29 Jesus *said to him, "Because you
have seen Me, have you believed?
[a]Blessed *are* they who did not see, and
yet believed."

Why This Gospel Was Written

30 ¶ [a]Therefore many other [1b]signs
Jesus also performed in the presence of
the disciples, which are not written in
this book;
31 but these have been written [a]so
that you may believe that Jesus is [1]the
Christ, [b]the Son of God; and that [c]be-
lieving you may have life in His name.

Jesus Appears at the Sea of Galilee

21 After these things Jesus [1a]mani-
fested Himself [b]again to the disciples at the [c]Sea of Tiberias, and He manifested *Himself* in this way.
2 Simon Peter, and [a]Thomas called
[1]Didymus, and [b]Nathanael of [c]Cana in
Galilee, and [d]the *sons* of Zebedee, and
two others of His disciples were together.
3 Simon Peter *said to them, "I am
going fishing." They *said to him, "We
will also come with you." They went out
and got into the boat; and [a]that night
they caught nothing.
4 ¶ But when the day was now breaking, Jesus stood on the beach; yet the
disciples did not [a]know that it was Jesus.
5 So Jesus *said to them, "Children,
[a]you do not have [1]any fish, do you?"
They answered Him, "No."
6 And He said to them, "[a]Cast the
net on the right-hand side of the boat and
you will find *a catch*." So they cast, and
then they were not able to haul it in because of the great number of fish.
7 [a]Therefore that disciple whom
Jesus loved *said to Peter, "It is the
Lord." So when Simon Peter heard that it
was the Lord, he put his outer garment
on (for he was stripped *for work*), and
threw himself into the sea.
8 But the other disciples came in the
little boat, for they were not far from the
land, but about [1]one hundred yards
away, dragging the net *full* of fish.
9 ¶ So when they got out on the land,
they *saw a charcoal [a]fire *already* laid
and [b]fish placed on it, and bread.
10 Jesus *said to them, "Bring some of
the [a]fish which you have now caught."
11 Simon Peter went up and drew the
net to land, full of large fish, a hundred
and fifty-three; and although there were
so many, the net was not torn.

Jesus Provides

12 Jesus *said to them, "Come *and*
have [a]breakfast." None of the disciples
ventured to question Him, "Who are
You?" knowing that it was the Lord.
13 Jesus *came and *took [a]the bread
and *gave *it* to them, and the [b]fish likewise.
14 This is now the [a]third time that
Jesus [1]was manifested to the disciples,
after He was raised from the dead.

The Love Motivation

15 ¶ So when they had [a]finished
breakfast, Jesus *said to Simon Peter, "Simon, *son* of John, do you [1b]love Me
more than these?" He *said to Him, "Yes,
Lord; You know that I [2]love You." He
*said to him, "Tend [c]My lambs."
16 He *said to him again a second
time, "Simon, *son* of John, do you [1]love
Me?" He *said to Him, "Yes, Lord; You
know that I [2]love You." He *said to him,
"[a]Shepherd My sheep."
17 He *said to him the third time, "Simon, *son* of John, do you [1]love Me?"
Peter was grieved because He said to him
[a]the third time, "Do you [1]love Me?"
And he said to Him, "Lord, [b]You know

19 [1]Lit *Peace to you* [b]Luke 24:36; John 14:27; 20:21,26
20 [a]Luke 24:39, 40; John 19:34 [b]John 16:20,22
21 [a]Luke 24:36; John 14:27; 20:19,26 [b]John 17:18
23 [1]I.e. have previously been forgiven [a]Matt 16:19; 18:18
24 [1]I.e. the Twin [a]John 11:16 [b]John 6:67
25 [a]John 20:20 [b]Mark 16:11
26 [1]Or *A week later* [2]Or *locked* [a]Luke 24:36; John 14:27; 20:19,21
27 [a]Luke 24:40; John 20:25
29 [a]1 Pet 1:8
30 [1]Or *attesting miracles* [a]John 21:25 [b]John 2:11
31 [1]I.e. the Messiah [a]John 19:35 [b]Matt 4:3 [c]John 3:15
21:1 [1]Or *made Himself visible* [a]Mark 16:12; John 21:14 [b]John 20:19,26 [c]John 6:1
2 [1]I.e. the Twin [a]John 11:16 [b]John 1:45ff [c]John 2:1 [d]Matt 4:21; Mark 1:19; Luke 5:10
3 [a]Luke 5:5
4 [a]Luke 24:16; John 20:14
5 [1]Lit *something eaten with bread* [a]Luke 24:41
6 [a]Luke 5:4ff
7 [a]John 13:23; 21:20
8 [1]Lit *200 cubits*
9 [a]John 18:18 [b]John 6:9,11; 21:10,13
10 [a]John 6:9,11; 21:9,13
12 [a]John 21:15
13 [a]John 21:9 [b]John 6:9,11; 21:9,10
14 [1]Or *made Himself visible* [a]John 20:19,26
15 [1]Gr *agapao* [2]Gr *phileo* [a]John 21:12 [b]Matt 26:33; Mark 14:29; John 13:37 [c]Luke 12:32
16 [1]Gr *agapao* [2]Gr *phileo* [a]Matt 2:6; Acts 20:28; 1 Pet 5:2; Rev 7:17
17 [1]Gr *phileo* [a]John 13:38 [b]John 16:30

all things; You know that I [1]love You."
Jesus *said to him, "[c]Tend My sheep.

Our Times Are in His Hand

18 "Truly, truly, I say to you, when you
were younger, you used to gird yourself
and walk wherever you wished; but
when you grow old, you will stretch out
your hands and someone else will gird
you, and bring you where you do not
wish to *go.*"
19 Now this He said, [a]signifying by
[b]what kind of death he would glorify
God. And when He had spoken this, He
*said to him, "[c]Follow Me!"
20 ¶ Peter, turning around, *saw the
[a]disciple whom Jesus loved following
them; the one who also had [b]leaned back
on His bosom at the supper and said,
"Lord, who is the one who betrays You?"
21 So Peter seeing him *said to Jesus,
"Lord, and what about this man?"
22 Jesus *said to him, "If I want him to
remain [a]until I come, what *is that* to
you? You [b]follow Me!"
23 Therefore this saying went out
among [a]the brethren that that disciple
would not die; yet Jesus did not say to
him that he would not die, but *only*, "If
I want him to remain [b]until I come, what
is that to you?"
24 ¶ This is the disciple who [a]is testifying to these things and wrote these
things, and we know that his testimony is
true.
25 ¶ And there are also [a]many other
things which Jesus did, which if they
*were written in detail, I suppose that
even the world itself *would not contain
the books that *would be written.

17 [1]Gr *phileo* [c]John 21:15,16

19 [a]John 12:33; 18:32 [b]2 Pet 1:14 [c]Matt 8:22; 16:24; John 21:22

20 [a]John 21:7 [b]John 13:25

22 [a]Matt 16:27f; 1 Cor 4:5; 11:26; James 5:7; Rev 2:25 [b]Matt 8:22; 16:24; John 21:19

23 [a]Acts 1:15 [b]Matt 16:27f; 1 Cor 4:5; 11:26; James 5:7; Rev 2:25

24 [a]John 15:27

25 [a]John 20:30

Acts

Title and Background

The book of Acts provides the basic history of the spread of Christianity during the thirty years immediately following the death and resurrection of Jesus Christ. It serves as a link between the Gospels and the Letters. It can be called "The Acts of the Holy Spirit," because it teaches about the coming and work of the Spirit.

Author and Date of Writing

Although the author does not name himself, evidence outside the Scriptures and inferences from the book itself lead to the conclusion that the author was Luke. A likely date for the book of Acts is A.D. 63.

Theme and Message

The theme of the work is best summarized in 1:8. Luke weaves together different interests and emphases as he relates the beginnings and expansion of the church. The design of the book revolves around (1) key persons: Peter and Paul; (2) important topics and events: the role of the Holy Spirit, pioneer missionary outreach to new fields, conversions, the growth of the church, and life in the Christian community; (3) significant problems: conflict between Jew and Gentile, persecution of the church by some Jewish elements, trials before Jews and Romans, confrontations with Gentiles, and other hardships in the ministry; (4) geographical advances: from Jerusalem to Rome.

Outline

I. Peter and the Beginnings of the Church in Palestine (1:1—12:25)
   A. "Throughout all Judea and Galilee and Samaria" (1:1—9:31; see 9:31)
   B. "To Phoenicia and Cyprus and Antioch" (9:32—12:25; see 11:19)

II. Paul and the Expansion of the Church From Antioch to Rome (13:1—28:31)
   A. "Through the Phrygian and Galatian Region" (13:1—15:35; see 16:6)
   B. "Over to Macedonia" (15:36—21:16; see 16:9)
   C. "To Rome" (21:17—28:31; see 28:14)

Introduction

1 The first account I [1]composed,
[a]Theophilus, about all that Jesus
[b]began to do and teach,
2 until the day when He [a]was taken
up *to heaven*, after He [b]had [1]by the Holy
Spirit given orders to [c]the apostles
whom He had [d]chosen.
3 To [1]these [a]He also presented Himself alive after His suffering, by many con-
vincing proofs, appearing to them over *a
period of* forty days and speaking of [b]the
things concerning the kingdom of God.
4 [1]Gathering them together, He
commanded them [a]not to leave Jerusalem, but to wait for [2b]what the Father
had promised, "Which," *He said,* "you
heard of from Me;
5 for [a]John baptized with water, but
you will be baptized [1]with the Holy Spirit [2b]not many days from now."
6 ¶ So when they had come together,
they were asking Him, saying, "Lord, [a]is
it at this time You are restoring the kingdom to Israel?"
7 He said to them, "It is not for you
to know times or epochs which [a]the Father has fixed by His own authority;
8 but you will receive power [a]when
the Holy Spirit has come upon you; and
you shall be [b]My witnesses both in Jerusalem, and in all Judea and [c]Samaria, and
even to [d]the remotest part of the earth."

The Ascension

9 And after He had said these things,
[a]He was lifted up while they were looking on, and a cloud received Him out of
their sight.
10 And as they were gazing intently
into [1]the sky while He was going, be-

1:1 [1]Lit *made* [a]Luke 1:3 [b]Luke 3:23 **2** [1]Or *through* [a]Mark 16:19; Acts 1:9 [b]Matt 28:19f; Mark 16:15; John 20:21f; Acts 10:42 [c]Mark 6:30 [d]John 13:18; Acts 10:41 **3** [1]Lit *whom* [a]Matt 28:17; Mark 16:12; Luke 24:34; John 20:19; 1 Cor 15:5-7 [b]Acts 8:12 **4** [1]Or *eating with*; or *lodging with* [2]Lit *the promise of the Father* [a]Luke 24:49 [b]John 14:16; Acts 2:33 **5** [1]Or *in* [2]Lit *not* long *after these many days* [a]Matt 3:11; Mark 1:8; Luke 3:16; John 1:33; Acts 11:16 [b]Acts 2:1-4 **6** [a]Matt 17:11; Mark 9:12; Luke 17:20 **7** [a]Matt 24:36; Mark 13:32 **8** [a]Acts 2:1-4 [b]Luke 24:48; John 15:27 [c]Acts 8:1 [d]Matt 28:19; Mark 16:15; Rom 10:18; Col 1:23 **9** [a]Luke 24:50; Acts 1:2 **10** [1]Or *heaven*

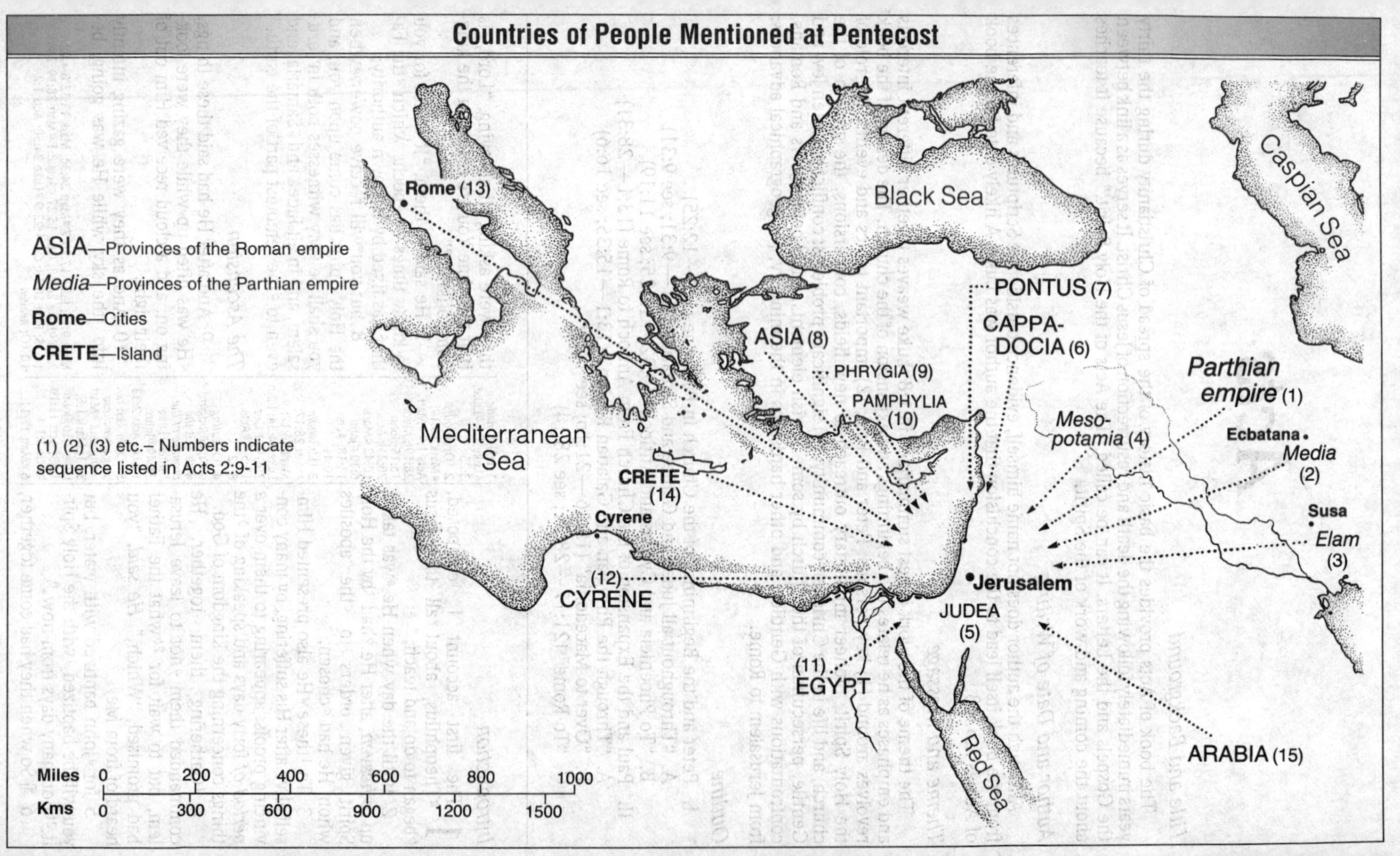
Countries of People Mentioned at Pentecost
ASIA—Provinces of the Roman empire
Media—Provinces of the Parthian empire
Rome—Cities
CRETE—Island
(1) (2) (3) etc.– Numbers indicate sequence listed in Acts 2:9-11
Rome (13)
Black Sea
Caspian Sea
PONTUS (7)
CAPPA-DOCIA (6)
ASIA (8)
PHRYGIA (9)
PAMPHYLIA (10)
Parthian empire (1)
Meso-potamia (4)
Ecbatana
Media (2)
Susa
Elam (3)
Mediterranean Sea
CRETE (14)
Cyrene
(12) CYRENE
Jerusalem
JUDEA (5)
(11) EGYPT
Red Sea
ARABIA (15)
Miles 0 200 400 600 800 1000
Kms 0 300 600 900 1200 1500

hold, [a]two men in white clothing stood beside them.

11 They also said, "[a]Men of Galilee, why do you stand looking into [1]the sky? This Jesus, who [b]has been taken up from you into heaven, will [c]come in just the same way as you have watched Him go into heaven."

The Upper Room

12 ¶ Then they [a]returned to Jerusalem from the [1b]mount called [2]Olivet, which is near Jerusalem, a [3]Sabbath day's journey away.

13 When they had entered *the city,* they went up to [a]the upper room where they were staying; [b]that is, Peter and John and [1]James and Andrew, Philip and Thomas, Bartholomew and Matthew, [1]James *the son* of Alphaeus, and Simon the Zealot, and [c]Judas *the* [2]*son* of [1]James.

14 These all with one mind [a]were continually devoting themselves to prayer, along with [b]*the* women, and Mary the [c]mother of Jesus, and with His [c]brothers.

15 ¶ [1]At this time Peter stood up in the midst of [a]the brethren (a gathering of about one hundred and twenty [2]persons was there together), and said,

16 "Brethren, [a]the Scripture had to be fulfilled, which the Holy Spirit foretold by the mouth of David concerning Judas, [b]who became a guide to those who arrested Jesus.

17 "For he was [a]counted among us and received his share in [b]this ministry."

18 (Now this man [a]acquired a field with [b]the price of his wickedness, and falling headlong, he burst open in the middle and all his intestines gushed out.

19 And it became known to all who were living in Jerusalem; so that in [a]their own language that field was called Hakeldama, that is, Field of Blood.)

20 "For it is written in the book of Psalms,

'[a]LET HIS HOMESTEAD BE MADE
DESOLATE,
AND LET NO ONE DWELL IN IT';

and,

'[b]LET ANOTHER MAN TAKE HIS
[1]OFFICE.'

21 "Therefore it is necessary that of the men who have accompanied us all the time that [a]the Lord Jesus went in and out [1]among us—

22 [a]beginning [1]with the baptism of John until the day that He [b]was taken up from us—one of these *must* become a [c]witness with us of His resurrection."

23 So they put forward two men, Joseph called Barsabbas (who was also called Justus), and [a]Matthias.

24 And they [a]prayed and said, "You, Lord, [b]who know the hearts of all men, show which one of these two You have chosen

25 to [1]occupy [a]this ministry and [b]apostleship from which Judas turned aside to go to his own place."

26 And they [1a]drew lots for them, and the lot fell [2]to [b]Matthias; and he was [3]added to [c]the eleven apostles.

The Day of Pentecost

2 When [a]the day of Pentecost [1]had come, they were all together in one place.

2 And suddenly there came from heaven a noise like a violent rushing wind, and it filled [a]the whole house where they were sitting.

3 And there appeared to them tongues as of fire [1]distributing themselves, and [2]they [3]rested on each one of them.

4 And they were all [a]filled with the Holy Spirit and began to [b]speak with other [1]tongues, as the Spirit was giving them [2]utterance.

5 ¶ Now there were Jews living in Jerusalem, [a]devout men from every nation under heaven.

6 And when [a]this sound occurred, the crowd came together, and were bewildered because each one of them was hearing them speak in his own [1]language.

7 [a]They were amazed and astonished, saying, "[1]Why, are not all these who are speaking [b]Galileans?

8 "And how is it that we each hear *them* in our own [1]language [2]to which we were born?

9 "Parthians and Medes and Elamites, and residents of Mesopotamia, Judea and [a]Cappadocia, [b]Pontus and [1c]Asia,

10 [a]Phrygia and [b]Pamphylia, Egypt and the districts of Libya around [c]Cyrene, and [1d]visitors from Rome, both Jews and [2e]proselytes,

11 Cretans and Arabs—we hear them in our *own* tongues speaking of the mighty deeds of God."

12 And [a]they all continued in amazement and great perplexity, saying to one another, "What does this mean?"

13 But others were mocking and saying, "[a]They are full of [1]sweet wine."

10 [a]Luke 24:4; John 20:12 **11** [1]Or *heaven* [a]Acts 2:7 [b]Mark 16:19; Acts 1:9 [c]Matt 16:27f; Acts 3:21 **12** [1]Or *hill* [2]Or *Olive Grove* [3]I.e. 2K cubits, or approx 3/5 mile [a]Luke 24:52 [b]Matt 21:1 **13** [1]Or *Jacob* [2]Or *brother* [a]Mark 14:15; Luke 22:12; Acts 9:37 [b]Acts 1:13: *Matt 10:2-4; Mark 3:16-19; Luke 6:14-16* [c]John 14:22 **14** [a]Acts 2:42; Rom 12:12; Eph 6:18; Col 4:2 [b]Luke 8:2f [c]Matt 12:46 **15** [1]Lit *in these days* [2]Lit *names* [a]John 21:23; Acts 6:3; Rom 1:13 **16** [a]John 13:18; Acts 1:20 [b]Matt 26:47; Mark 14:43; Luke 22:47; John 18:3 **17** [a]John 6:70f [b]Acts 1:25 **18** [a]Matt 27:3-10 [b]Matt 26:14f **19** [a]Matt 27:8; Acts 21:40 **20** [1]Lit *position as overseer* [a]Ps 69:25 [b]Ps 109:8 **21** [1]Lit *to us* [a]Luke 24:3 **22** [1]Lit *from* [a]Matt 3:16; Mark 1:1-4; Luke 3:21 [b]Mark 16:19; Acts 1:2 [c]Acts 1:8 **23** [a]Acts 1:26 **24** [a]Acts 6:6 [b]1 Sam 16:7; Jer 17:10; Acts 15:8; Rom 8:27 **25** [1]Lit *take the place of* [a]Acts 1:17 [b]Rom 1:5; 1 Cor 9:2; Gal 2:8 **26** [1]Lit *gave* [2]Or *upon* [3]Lit *voted together with* [a]Lev 16:8; Josh 14:2; 1 Sam 14:41f; Neh 10:34; Prov 16:33 [b]Acts 1:23 [c]Acts 2:14 **2:1** [1]Lit *was being fulfilled* [a]Lev 23:15f; Acts 20:16; 1 Cor 16:8 **2** [a]Acts 4:31 **3** [1]Or *being distributed* [2]Lit *it* [3]Or *sat* **4** [1]Or *languages* [2]Or *ability to speak out* [a]Matt 10:20; Acts 1:5 [b]Mark 16:17; 1 Cor 12:10f **5** [a]Luke 2:25; Acts 8:2 **6** [1]Or *dialect* [a]Acts 2:2 **7** [1]Lit *Behold* [a]Acts 2:12 [b]Matt 26:73; Acts 1:11 **8** [1]Or *dialect* [2]Lit *in* **9** [1]I.e. west coast province of Asia Minor [a]1 Pet 1:1 [b]Acts 18:2; 1 Pet 1:1 [c]Acts 6:9; Rom 16:5; 1 Cor 16:19; 2 Cor 1:8; 2 Tim 1:15; Rev 1:4 **10** [1]Lit *the sojourning Romans* [2]I.e. Gentile converts to Judaism [a]Acts 16:6 [b]Acts 13:13 [c]Matt 27:32 [d]Acts 17:21 [e]Matt 23:15 **12** [a]Acts 2:7 **13** [1]I.e. new wine [a]1 Cor 14:23

Peter's Sermon

14 ¶ But Peter, [1]taking his stand with
[a]the eleven, raised his voice and declared to them: "Men of Judea and all you
who live in Jerusalem, let this be known
to you and give heed to my words.
15 "For these men are not drunk, as you
suppose, [a]for it is *only* the [1]third hour of
the day;
16 but this is what was spoken of
through the prophet Joel:
17 '[a]AND IT SHALL BE IN THE LAST
DAYS,' God says,
'THAT I WILL POUR FORTH OF MY
SPIRIT ON ALL [1]MANKIND;
AND YOUR SONS AND YOUR
DAUGHTERS SHALL PROPHESY,
AND YOUR YOUNG MEN SHALL SEE
VISIONS,
AND YOUR OLD MEN SHALL DREAM
DREAMS;
18 EVEN ON MY BONDSLAVES, BOTH
MEN AND WOMEN,
I WILL IN THOSE DAYS POUR FORTH
OF MY SPIRIT
And they shall prophesy.
19 'AND I WILL GRANT WONDERS IN THE
SKY ABOVE
AND SIGNS ON THE EARTH BELOW,
BLOOD, AND FIRE, AND VAPOR OF
SMOKE.
20 'THE SUN WILL BE TURNED INTO
DARKNESS
AND THE MOON INTO BLOOD,
BEFORE THE GREAT AND GLORIOUS
DAY OF THE LORD SHALL COME.
21 'AND IT SHALL BE THAT [a]EVERYONE
WHO CALLS ON THE NAME OF
THE LORD WILL BE SAVED.'
22 ¶ "Men of Israel, listen to these
words: [a]Jesus the Nazarene, [b]a man [1]at-
tested to you by God with [2]miracles and
[c]wonders and [3]signs which God performed through Him in your midst, just
as you yourselves know—
23 this *Man*, delivered over by the
[a]predetermined plan and foreknowledge
of God, [b]you nailed to a cross by the
hands of [1]godless men and put *Him* to
death.
24 "[1]But [a]God raised Him up again,
putting an end to the [2]agony of death,
since it [b]was impossible for Him to be
held [3]in its power.
25 "For David says of Him,
'[a]I SAW THE LORD ALWAYS IN MY
PRESENCE;
FOR HE IS AT MY RIGHT HAND, SO
THAT I WILL NOT BE SHAKEN.
26 'THEREFORE MY HEART WAS GLAD
AND MY TONGUE EXULTED;
MOREOVER MY FLESH ALSO WILL LIVE
IN HOPE;
27 BECAUSE YOU WILL NOT ABANDON
MY SOUL TO [a]HADES,
[b]NOR [1]ALLOW YOUR [2]HOLY ONE
TO [3]UNDERGO DECAY.
28 'YOU HAVE MADE KNOWN TO ME THE
WAYS OF LIFE;
YOU WILL MAKE ME FULL OF
GLADNESS WITH YOUR
PRESENCE.'
29 ¶ "[1]Brethren, I may confidently
say to you regarding the [a]patriarch David
that he both [b]died and [c]was buried, and
[d]his tomb is [2]with us to this day.
30 "And so, because he was [a]a prophet
and knew that [b]GOD HAD SWORN TO HIM
WITH AN OATH TO SEAT *one* [1]OF HIS DESCEN-
DANTS ON HIS THRONE,
31 he looked ahead and spoke of the
resurrection of [1]the Christ, that [a]HE
WAS NEITHER ABANDONED TO HADES, NOR
DID His flesh [2]SUFFER DECAY.
32 "This Jesus [a]God raised up again, to
which we are all [b]witnesses.
33 "Therefore having been exalted
[1a]to the right hand of God, and [b]having
received from the Father [c]the promise of
the Holy Spirit, He has [d]poured forth this
which you both see and hear.
34 "For it was not David who ascended
into [1]heaven, but he himself says:
'[a]THE LORD SAID TO MY LORD,
"SIT AT MY RIGHT HAND,
35 UNTIL I MAKE YOUR ENEMIES A
FOOTSTOOL FOR YOUR FEET." '
36 "Therefore let all the [a]house of Israel know for certain that God has made
Him both [b]Lord and [1]Christ—this Jesus
[c]whom you crucified."

The Ingathering

37 ¶ Now when they heard *this*, they
were [1]pierced to the heart, and said to
Peter and the rest of the apostles,
"[2]Brethren, [3a]what shall we do?"
38 Peter *said* to them, "[a]Repent, and
each of you be [b]baptized in the name of
Jesus Christ for the forgiveness of your
sins; and you will receive the gift of the
Holy Spirit.
39 "For [a]the promise is for you and
your children and for all who are [b]far off,
as many as the Lord our God will call to
Himself."
40 And with many other words he solemnly [a]testified and kept on exhorting
them, saying, "[1]Be saved from this [b]per-
verse generation!"
41 So then, those who had received
his word were baptized; and that day
there were added about three thousand
[1a]souls.

14 [1]Or *being put forward* as spokesman [a]Acts 1:26
15 [1]I.e. 9 a.m. [a]1 Thess 5:7
17 [1]Lit *flesh* [a]Joel 2:28-32
21 [a]Rom 10:13
22 [1]Or *exhibited* or *accredited* [2]Or *works of power* [3]Or *attesting miracles* [a]Acts 3:6 [b]John 3:2 [c]John 4:48; Acts 2:19
23 [1]Lit *men without the Law*; i.e. pagan [a]Luke 22:22; Acts 3:18; 1 Pet 1:20 [b]Matt 27:35; Mark 15:24; Luke 23:33; John 19:18; Acts 3:13
24 [1]Lit *Whom God raised up* [2]Lit *birth pains* [3]Lit *by it* [a]Matt 28:5; Mark 16:6; Luke 24:5; Acts 2:32; Rom 4:24; 1 Cor 6:14; 2 Cor 4:14; Gal 1:1; Eph 1:20; Col 2:12; 1 Thess 1:10; Heb 13:20; 1 Pet 1:21 [b]John 20:9
25 [a]Ps 16:8-11
27 [1]Lit *give* [2]Or *devout* or *pious* [3]Lit *see corruption* [a]Matt 11:23; Acts 2:31 [b]Acts 13:35
29 [1]Lit *Men brothers* [2]Lit *among* [a]Acts 7:8f; Heb 7:4 [b]Acts 13:36 [c]1 Kin 2:10 [d]Neh 3:16
30 [1]Lit *of the fruit of his loins* [a]Matt 22:43 [b]Ps 132:11; 2 Sam 7:12f; Ps 89:3f
31 [1]I.e. the Messiah [2]Lit *see corruption* [a]Matt 11:23; Acts 2:27
32 [a]Acts 2:24; Rom 4:24; 1 Cor 6:14; 2 Cor 4:14; Gal 1:1; Eph 1:20; Col 2:12; 1 Thess 1:10; Heb 13:20; 1 Pet 1:21 [b]Acts 1:8
33 [1]Or *by* [a]Mark 16:19; Acts 5:31 [b]Acts 1:4 [c]John 7:39; Gal 3:14 [d]Acts 2:17
34 [1]Lit *the heavens* [a]Ps 110:1; Matt 22:44f
36 [1]I.e. Messiah [a]Ezek 36:22 [b]Acts 2:23 [c]Luke 2:11
37 [1]Or *wounded in conscience* [2]Lit *Men brothers* [3]Or *what are we to do* [a]Luke 3:10
38 [a]Mark 1:15; Luke 24:47; Acts 3:19 [b]Mark 16:16; Acts 8:12
39 [a]Is 44:3; Joel 2:32; Rom 9:4; Eph 2:12 [b]Eph 2:13
40 [1]Or *Escape* [a]Luke 16:28 [b]Deut 32:5; Matt 17:17; Phil 2:15 **41** [1]I.e. persons [a]Acts 3:23; Rom 13:1; 1 Pet 3:20; Rev 16:3

42 They were [a]continually devoting themselves to the apostles' teaching and to fellowship, to [b]the breaking of bread and [1a]to prayer.

43 ¶ [1]Everyone kept feeling a sense of awe; and many [a]wonders and [2]signs were taking place through the apostles.

44 And all those who had believed [1]were together and [a]had all things in common;

45 and they [a]*began* selling their property and possessions and were sharing them with all, as anyone might have need.

46 [a]Day by day continuing with one mind in the temple, and [b]breaking bread [1]from house to house, they were taking their [2]meals together with gladness and [3]sincerity of heart,

47 praising God and [a]having favor with all the people. And the Lord [b]was adding [1]to their number day by day [c]those who were being saved.

Healing the Lame Beggar

3 Now [a]Peter and John were going up to the temple at the [1]ninth *hour,* [b]the hour of prayer.

2 And [a]a man who had been lame from his mother's womb was being carried along, whom they [b]used to set down every day at the gate of the temple which is called Beautiful, [c]in order to beg [1]alms of those who were entering the temple.

3 When he saw [a]Peter and John about to go into the temple, he *began* asking to receive alms.

4 But Peter, along with John, [a]fixed his gaze on him and said, "Look at us!"

5 And he *began* to give them his attention, expecting to receive something from them.

6 But Peter said, "I do not possess silver and gold, but what I do have I give to you: [a]In the name of Jesus Christ the Nazarene—walk!"

7 And seizing him by the right hand, he raised him up; and immediately his feet and his ankles were strengthened.

8 [1a]With a leap he stood upright and *began* to walk; and he entered the temple with them, walking and leaping and praising God.

9 And [a]all the people saw him walking and praising God;

10 and they were taking note of him as being the one who used to [a]sit at the Beautiful Gate of the temple to *beg* alms, and they were filled with wonder and amazement at what had happened to him.

Peter's Second Sermon

11 ¶ While he was clinging to [a]Peter and John, all the people ran together to them at the so-called [1b]portico of Solomon, full of amazement.

12 But when Peter saw *this*, he replied to the people, "Men of Israel, why are you amazed at this, or why do you gaze at us, as if by our own power or piety we had made him walk?

13 "[a]The God of Abraham, Isaac and Jacob, [b]the God of our fathers, has glorified His [1c]servant Jesus, *the one* whom [d]you delivered and disowned in the presence of [e]Pilate, when he had [f]decided to release Him.

14 "But you disowned [a]the Holy and Righteous One and [b]asked for a murderer to be granted to you,

15 but put to death the [1a]Prince of life, *the one* whom [b]God raised from the dead, *a fact* to which we are [c]witnesses.

16 "And on the basis of faith [a]in His name, *it is* [1]the name of Jesus which has strengthened this man whom you see and know; and the faith which *comes* through Him has given him this perfect health in the presence of you all.

17 ¶ "And now, brethren, I know that you acted [a]in ignorance, just as your [b]rulers did also.

18 "But the things which [a]God announced beforehand by the mouth of all the prophets, [b]that His [1]Christ would suffer, He has thus fulfilled.

19 "Therefore [a]repent and return, so that your sins may be wiped away, in order that [b]times of refreshing may come from the presence of the Lord;

20 and that He may send Jesus, the [1]Christ appointed for you,

21 [a]whom heaven must receive until *the* [1]period of [b]restoration of all things about which [c]God spoke by the mouth of His holy prophets from ancient time.

22 "Moses said, '[a]THE LORD GOD WILL RAISE UP FOR YOU A PROPHET [1]LIKE ME FROM YOUR BRETHREN; TO HIM YOU SHALL GIVE HEED to everything He says to you.

23 '[a]And it will be that every [b]soul that does not heed that prophet [c]shall be utterly destroyed from among the people.'

24 "And likewise, [a]all the prophets who have spoken, from Samuel and *his* successors onward, also announced these days.

25 "It is you who are [a]the sons of the prophets and of the [b]covenant which God [1]made with your fathers, saying to

42 [1]Lit *the prayers* [a]Acts 1:14 [b]Luke 24:30; Acts 2:46; 1 Cor 10:16
43 [1]Lit *fear was occurring to every soul* [2]Or *attesting miracles* [a]Acts 2:22
44 [1]One early ms does not contain *were* and *and* [a]Acts 4:32
45 [a]Matt 19:21; Acts 4:34
46 [1]Or *in the various private homes* [2]Lit *food* [3]Or *simplicity* [a]Acts 5:42 [b]Luke 24:30; Acts 2:42; 1 Cor 10:16
47 [1]Lit *together* [a]Acts 5:13 [b]Acts 2:41 [c]1 Cor 1:18
3:1 [1]I.e. 3 p.m. [a]Luke 22:8; Acts 3:3 [b]Ps 55:17; Matt 27:45; Acts 10:30
2 [1]Or *a gift of charity* [a]Acts 14:8 [b]Luke 16:20 [c]John 9:8; Acts 3:10
3 [a]Luke 22:8; Acts 3:1
4 [a]Acts 10:4
6 [a]Acts 2:22
8 [1]Lit *leaping up* [a]Acts 14:10
9 [a]Acts 4:16
10 [a]John 9:8; Acts 3:2
11 [1]Or *colonnade* [a]Luke 22:8; Acts 3:3 [b]John 10:23; Acts 5:12
13 [1]Or *Son* [a]Matt 22:32 [b]Ex 3:13; Acts 5:30 [c]Acts 3:26 [d]Matt 20:19; John 19:11; Acts 2:23 [e]Matt 27:2 [f]Luke 23:4
14 [a]Mark 1:24; Acts 4:27; 2 Cor 5:21 [b]Matt 27:20; Mark 15:11; Luke 23:18
15 [1]Or *Author* [a]Acts 5:31; Heb 2:10 [b]Acts 2:24 [c]Luke 24:48
16 [1]Lit *His name* [a]Acts 3:6
17 [a]Luke 23:34; John 15:21; Acts 13:27; Eph 4:18 [b]Luke 23:13
18 [1]Or *Anointed One*; i.e. Messiah [a]Acts 2:23 [b]Luke 24:27; Acts 17:3
19 [a]Acts 2:38 [b]2 Thess 1:7; Heb 4:1ff
20 [1]Or *Anointed One*; i.e. Messiah
21 [1]Lit *periods, times* [a]Acts 1:11 [b]Matt 17:11; Rom 8:21 [c]Luke 1:70
22 [1]Or *as* He raised up *me* [a]Deut 18:15; Acts 7:37
23 [a]Deut 18:19 [b]Acts 2:41 [c]Lev 23:29
24 [a]Luke 24:27; Acts 17:3 **25** [1]Lit *covenanted* [a]Acts 2:39 [b]Rom 9:4f

Abraham, '[c]AND IN YOUR SEED ALL THE FAMILIES OF THE EARTH SHALL BE BLESSED.'

26 "For you [a]first, God [b]raised up His [1]Servant and sent Him to bless you by turning every one *of you* from your wicked ways."

Peter and John Arrested

4 As they were speaking to the people, the priests and [a]the captain of the temple *guard* and [b]the Sadducees [c]came up to them,

2 being greatly disturbed because they were teaching the people and proclaiming [1a]in Jesus the resurrection from the dead.

3 And they laid hands on them and [a]put them in jail until the next day, for it was already evening.

4 But many of those who had heard the [1]message believed; and [a]the number of the men came to be about five thousand.

5 ¶ On the next day, their [a]rulers and elders and scribes were gathered together in Jerusalem;

6 and [a]Annas the high priest *was there,* and [b]Caiaphas and John and Alexander, and all who were of high-priestly descent.

7 When they had placed them in the center, they *began to* inquire, "By what power, or in what name, have you done this?"

8 Then Peter, [1a]filled with the Holy Spirit, said to them, "[2b]Rulers and elders of the people,

9 if we are [1]on trial today for [a]a benefit done to a sick man, [2]as to how this man has been made well,

10 let it be known to all of you and to all the people of Israel, that [1a]by the name of Jesus Christ the Nazarene, whom you crucified, whom [b]God raised from the dead—[1]by [2]this *name* this man stands here before you in good health.

11 "[1a]He is the [b]STONE WHICH WAS [c]REJECTED by you, THE BUILDERS, *but* WHICH BECAME THE CHIEF CORNER *stone.*

12 "And there is salvation in [a]no one else; for there is no other name under heaven that has been given among men by which we must be saved."

Threat and Release

13 ¶ Now as they observed the [a]confidence of [b]Peter and John and understood that they were uneducated and untrained men, they were amazed, and [c]*began* to recognize them [1]as having been with Jesus.

14 And seeing the man who had been healed standing with them, they had nothing to say in reply.

15 But when they had ordered them to leave the [1a]Council, they *began* to confer with one another,

16 saying, "[a]What shall we do with these men? For the fact that a [b]noteworthy [1]miracle has taken place through them is apparent to all who live in Jerusalem, and we cannot deny it.

17 "But so that it will not spread any further among the people, let us warn them to speak no longer to any man [a]in this name."

18 And when they had summoned them, they [a]commanded them not to speak or teach at all [1]in the name of Jesus.

19 But [a]Peter and John answered and said to them, "[b]Whether it is right in the sight of God to give heed to you rather than to God, you be the judge;

20 for [a]we cannot stop speaking about what we have seen and heard."

21 When they had threatened them further, they let them go (finding no basis on which to punish them) [a]on account of the people, because they were all [b]glorifying God for what had happened;

22 for the man was more than forty years old on whom this [1]miracle of healing had been performed.

23 ¶ When they had been released, they went to their own *companions* and reported all that the chief priests and the elders had said to them.

24 And when they heard *this,* they lifted their voices to God with one accord and said, "O [1]Lord, it is You who [a]MADE THE HEAVEN AND THE EARTH AND THE SEA, AND ALL THAT IS IN THEM,

25 who [a]by the Holy Spirit, *through* the mouth of our father David Your servant, said,

'[b]WHY DID THE [1]GENTILES RAGE,
AND THE PEOPLES DEVISE FUTILE THINGS?

26 '[a]THE KINGS OF THE EARTH [1]TOOK THEIR STAND,
AND THE RULERS WERE GATHERED TOGETHER
AGAINST THE LORD AND AGAINST HIS [2b]CHRIST.'

27 "For truly in this city there were gathered together against Your holy [1a]servant Jesus, whom You anointed, both [b]Herod and [c]Pontius Pilate, along with [d]the [2]Gentiles and the peoples of Israel,

28 to do whatever Your hand and [a]Your purpose predestined to occur.

29 "And [1]now, Lord, take note of their threats, and grant that Your bond-

25 [c]Gen 22:18
26 [1]Or *Son* [a]Matt 15:24; John 4:22; Acts 13:46; Rom 1:16; 2:9f [b]Acts 2:24
4:1 [a]Luke 22:4 [b]Matt 3:7 [c]Luke 20:1; Acts 6:12
2 [1]Or *in the case of* [a]Acts 3:15; 17:18
3 [a]Acts 5:18
4 [1]Lit *word* [a]Acts 2:41
5 [a]Luke 23:13; Acts 4:8
6 [a]Luke 3:2 [b]Matt 26:3
8 [1]Or *having just been filled* [2]Lit *Rulers of the people and elders* [a]Acts 2:4; 13:9 [b]Luke 23:13; Acts 4:5
9 [1]Lit *answering* [2]Or *by whom* [a]Acts 3:7f
10 [1]Or *in* [2]Or *Him* [a]Acts 2:22; 3:6 [b]Acts 2:24
11 [1]Lit *This One* [a]Matt 21:42 [b]Ps 118:22 [c]Mark 9:12
12 [a]Matt 1:21; Acts 10:43; 1 Tim 2:5
13 [1]Lit *that they had been* [a]Acts 4:31 [b]Luke 22:8; Acts 4:19 [c]John 7:15
15 [1]Or *Sanhedrin* [a]Matt 5:22
16 [1]Or *sign* [a]John 11:47 [b]Acts 3:7-10
17 [a]John 15:21
18 [1]Or *on the basis of* [a]Acts 5:28f
19 [a]Acts 4:13 [b]Acts 5:28f
20 [a]1 Cor 9:16
21 [a]Acts 5:26 [b]Matt 9:8
22 [1]Or *sign*
24 [1]Or *Master* [a]Ex 20:11; Neh 9:6; Ps 146:6
25 [1]Or *nations* [a]Acts 1:16 [b]Ps 2:1
26 [1]Or *approached* [2]Or *Anointed One*; i.e. Messiah [a]Ps 2:2 [b]Dan 9:24f; Luke 4:18; Acts 10:38; Heb 1:9
27 [1]Or *Son* [2]Or *nations* [a]Acts 3:13; 4:30 [b]Matt 14:1; Luke 23:7-11 [c]Matt 27:2; Mark 15:1; Luke 23:1,12; John 18:28,29 [d]Matt 20:19
28 [a]Acts 2:23
29 [1]Or *as for the present situation*

servants may [a]speak Your word with all
[b]confidence,
30 while You extend Your hand to
heal, and [1a]signs and wonders take
place through the name of Your holy
[2b]servant Jesus."
31 And when they had prayed, the
[a]place where they had gathered together
was shaken, and they were all [b]filled
with the Holy Spirit and *began* to [c]speak
the word of God with [d]boldness.

Sharing among Believers

32 ¶ And the [1]congregation of those
who believed were of one heart and soul;
and not one *of them* [2]claimed that anything belonging to him was his own, but
[a]all things were common property to
them.
33 And [a]with great power the apostles were giving [b]testimony to the resurrection of the Lord Jesus, and abundant
grace was upon them all.
34 For there was not a needy person
among them, for all who were owners of
land or houses [a]would sell them and
bring the [1]proceeds of the sales
35 and [a]lay them at the apostles' feet,
and they would be [b]distributed to each
as any had need.
36 ¶ Now Joseph, a Levite of [a]Cyprian
birth, who was also called [b]Barnabas by
the apostles (which translated means Son
of [1c]Encouragement),
37 and who owned a tract of land, sold
it and brought the money and [a]laid it at
the apostles' feet.

Fate of Ananias and Sapphira

5 But a man named Ananias, with his
wife Sapphira, sold a piece of property,
2 and [a]kept back *some* of the price
for himself, with his wife's [1]full knowledge, and bringing a portion of it, he
[b]laid it at the apostles' feet.
3 But Peter said, "Ananias, why has
[a]Satan filled your heart to lie [b]to the
Holy Spirit and to [c]keep back *some* of the
price of the land?
4 "While it remained *unsold,* did it not
remain your own? And after it was sold,
was it not [1]under your control? Why is it
that you have [2]conceived this deed in
your heart? You have not lied to men but
[a]to God."
5 And as he heard these words, Ananias [a]fell down and breathed his last; and
[b]great fear came over all who heard of it.
6 The young men got up and [a]cov-
ered him up, and after carrying him out,
they buried him.
7 ¶ Now there elapsed an interval of
about three hours, and his wife came in,
not knowing what had happened.
8 And Peter responded to her, "Tell
me whether you sold the land [1a]for such
and such a price?" And she said, "Yes,
[1]that was the price."
9 Then Peter *said* to her, "Why is it
that you have agreed together to [a]put
[b]the Spirit of the Lord to the test? Behold, the feet of those who have buried
your husband are at the door, and they
will carry you out *as well.*"
10 And immediately she [a]fell at his
feet and breathed her last, and the young
men came in and found her dead, and
they carried her out and buried her beside her husband.
11 And [a]great fear came over the
whole church, and over all who heard of
these things.
12 ¶ [1]At the hands of the apostles
many [a]signs and wonders were taking
place among the people; and they were
all with one accord in [b]Solomon's portico.
13 But none of the rest dared to associate with them; however, [a]the people
held them in high esteem.
14 And all the more [a]believers in the
Lord, multitudes of men and women,
were constantly [b]added to *their number,*
15 to such an extent that they even
carried the sick out into the streets and
laid them on cots and pallets, so that
when Peter came by [a]at least his shadow
might fall on any one of them.
16 Also the [1]people from the cities in
the vicinity of Jerusalem were coming together, bringing people who were sick
[2]or afflicted with unclean spirits, and
they were all being healed.

Imprisonment and Release

17 ¶ But the high priest rose up, along
with all his associates (that is [a]the sect of
[b]the Sadducees), and they were filled
with jealousy.
18 They laid hands on the apostles and
[a]put them in a public jail.
19 But during the night [a]an angel of
the Lord opened the gates of the prison,
and taking them out he said,
20 "Go, stand and [1]speak to the people
in the temple [2a]the whole message of
this Life."
21 Upon hearing *this,* they entered
into the temple [a]about daybreak and *began* to teach.
¶ Now when [b]the high priest and his
associates came, they called [c]the [1]Coun-
cil together, even all the Senate of the
sons of Israel, and sent *orders* to the prison house for them to be brought.
22 But [a]the officers who came did not

29 [a]Phil 1:14 [b]Acts 4:13,31; 14:3
30 [1]Or *attesting miracles* [2]Or *Son* [a]John 4:48 [b]Acts 3:13; 4:27
31 [a]Acts 2:1 [b]Acts 2:4 [c]Phil 1:14 [d]Acts 4:13; 14:3
32 [1]Or *multitude* [2]Lit *was saying* [a]Acts 2:44
33 [a]Acts 1:8 [b]Luke 24:48
34 [1]Lit *the prices of the things being sold* [a]Matt 19:21; Acts 2:45
35 [a]Acts 4:37; 5:2 [b]Acts 2:45; 6:1
36 [1]Or *Exhortation* or *Consolation* [a]Acts 11:19f; 13:4; 15:39; 21:3,16; 27:4 [b]Acts 9:27; 11:22,30; 12:25; 13:1,2,7; 1 Cor 9:6; Gal 2:1,9, 13; Col 4:10 [c]Acts 2:40; 11:23; 13:15; 1 Cor 14:3; 1 Thess 2:3
37 [a]Acts 4:35; 5:2
5:2 [1]Or *collusion* [a]Acts 5:3 [b]Acts 4:35,37
3 [a]Matt 4:10; Luke 22:3; John 13:2,27 [b]Acts 5:4,9 [c]Acts 5:2
4 [1]Or *in your authority* [2]Lit *placed* [a]Acts 5:3, 9
5 [a]Ezek 11:13; Acts 5:10 [b]Acts 2:43; 5:11
6 [a]John 19:40
8 [1]Lit *for so much* [a]Acts 5:2
9 [a]Acts 15:10 [b]Acts 5:3,4
10 [a]Ezek 11:13; Acts 5:5
11 [a]Acts 2:43; 5:5
12 [1]Lit *Through* [a]John 4:48 [b]John 10:23; Acts 3:11
13 [a]Acts 2:47; 4:21
14 [a]2 Cor 6:15 [b]Acts 2:47; 11:24
15 [a]Acts 19:12
16 [1]Lit *multitude* [2]Lit *and*
17 [a]Acts 15:5 [b]Matt 3:7; Acts 4:1
18 [a]Acts 4:3
19 [a]Matt 1:20, 24; 2:13,19; 28:2; Luke 1:11; 2:9; Acts 8:26; 10:3; 12:7,23; 27:23
20 [1]Or *continue to speak* [2]Lit *all the words* [a]John 6:63,68
21 [1]Or *Sanhedrin* [a]John 8:2 [b]Acts 4:6 [c]Matt 5:22; Acts 5:27, 34,41
22 [a]Matt 26:58; Acts 5:26

find them in the prison; and they returned and reported back,
23 saying, "We found the prison house
locked quite securely and the guards
standing at the doors; but when we had
opened up, we found no one inside."
24 Now when [a]the captain of the temple *guard* and the chief priests heard
these words, they were greatly perplexed
about them as to what [1]would come of
this.
25 But someone came and reported to
them, "The men whom you put in prison
are standing in the temple and teaching
the people!"
26 Then [a]the captain went along with
[b]the officers and *proceeded* to bring
them *back* without violence (for [c]they
were afraid of the people, that they might
be stoned).
27 ¶ When they had brought them,
they stood them [1]before [a]the Council.
The high priest questioned them,
28 saying, "We gave you [a]strict orders
not to continue teaching in this name,
and [1]yet, you have filled Jerusalem with
your teaching and [b]intend to bring this
man's blood upon us."
29 But Peter and the apostles answered, "[a]We must obey God rather
than men.
30 "[a]The God of our fathers [b]raised up
Jesus, [1]whom you had [c]put to death by
hanging Him on a [2]cross.
31 "[a]He is the one whom God exalted
[1]to His right hand as a [2b]Prince and a
[c]Savior, to grant [d]repentance to Israel,
and forgiveness of sins.
32 "And we are [a]witnesses [1]of these
things; and [b]*so is* the Holy Spirit, whom
God has given to those who obey Him."

Gamaliel's Counsel

33 ¶ But when they heard this, they
were [a]cut [1]to the quick and intended to
kill them.
34 But a Pharisee named [a]Gamaliel, a
[b]teacher of the Law, respected by all the
people, stood up in [c]the Council and
gave orders to put the men outside for a
short time.
35 And he said to them, "Men of Israel, take care what you propose to do with
these men.
36 "For some time ago Theudas rose up,
[a]claiming to be somebody, and a group of
about four hundred men joined up with
him. [1]But he was killed, and all who
[2]followed him were dispersed and came
to nothing.
37 "After this man, Judas of Galilee rose
up in the days of [a]the census and drew
away *some* people after him; he too perished, and all those who [1]followed him
were scattered.
38 "So in the present case, I say to you,
stay away from these men and let them
alone, for if this plan or [1]action [a]is of
men, it will be overthrown;
39 but if it is of God, you will not be
able to overthrow them; or else you may
even be found [a]fighting against God."
40 ¶ They [1]took his advice; and after
calling the apostles in, they [a]flogged
them and ordered them not to [2]speak
in the name of Jesus, and *then* released
them.
41 So they went on their way from the
presence of the [1a]Council, [b]rejoicing
that they had been considered worthy to
suffer shame [c]for *His* name.
42 [a]And every day, in the temple and
[1]from house to house, they [2]kept right
on teaching and [3b]preaching Jesus *as*
the [4]Christ.

Choosing of the Seven

6 Now [1]at this time while the [a]disci-
ples were [b]increasing *in number,* a
complaint arose on the part of the [2c]Hel-
lenistic *Jews* against the *native* [d]He-
brews, because their [e]widows were being overlooked in [f]the daily serving *of
food.*
2 So the twelve summoned the [1]con-
gregation of the disciples and said, "It is
not desirable for us to neglect the word of
God in order to serve tables.
3 "Therefore, [a]brethren, select from
among you seven men of good reputation, [b]full of the Spirit and of wisdom,
whom we may put in charge of this task.
4 "But we will [a]devote ourselves to
prayer and to the [1]ministry of the word."
5 The statement found approval with
the whole [1]congregation; and they chose
[a]Stephen, a man [b]full of faith and of the
Holy Spirit, and [c]Philip, Prochorus, Nica-
nor, Timon, Parmenas and [2]Nicolas, a
[3d]proselyte from [e]Antioch.
6 And these they brought before the
apostles; and after [a]praying, they [b]laid
their hands on them.
7 ¶ [a]The word of God kept on
spreading; and [b]the number of the disciples continued to increase greatly in Jerusalem, and a great many of the priests
were becoming obedient to [c]the faith.
8 ¶ And Stephen, full of grace and
power, was performing great [a]wonders
and [1]signs among the people.
9 But some men from what was
called the Synagogue of the Freedmen,
including both [a]Cyrenians and [b]Alexan-

24 [1]Lit *this would become* [a]Acts 4:1
26 [a]Acts 5:24 [b]Acts 5:22 [c]Acts 4:21
27 [1]Lit *in* [a]Matt 5:22; Acts 5:21
28 [1]Lit *behold* [a]Acts 4:18 [b]Matt 23:35; Acts 2:23
29 [a]Acts 4:19
30 [1]Or *on whom you had laid violent hands* [2]Lit *wood* [a]Acts 3:13 [b]Acts 2:24 [c]Acts 10:39; Gal 3:13; 1 Pet 2:24
31 [1]Or *by* [2]Or *Leader* [a]Acts 2:33 [b]Acts 3:15 [c]Luke 2:11 [d]Luke 24:47; Acts 2:38
32 [1]One early ms adds *in Him* [a]Luke 24:48 [b]John 15:26; Acts 15:28; Rom 8:16; Heb 2:4
33 [1]Or *in their hearts* [a]Acts 2:37
34 [a]Acts 22:3 [b]Luke 2:46 [c]Acts 5:21
36 [1]Lit *Who was killed* [2]Lit *were obeying* [a]Acts 8:9; Gal 2:6
37 [1]Lit *were obeying* [a]Luke 2:2
38 [1]Or *work* [a]Mark 11:30
39 [a]Prov 21:30; Acts 11:17
40 [1]Lit *were persuaded by him* [2]Lit *be speaking* [a]Matt 10:17
41 [1]Or *Sanhedrin* [a]Acts 5:21 [b]1 Pet 4:14 [c]John 15:21
42 [1]Or *in the various private homes* [2]Lit *were not ceasing to* [3]Lit *telling the good news of* [4]I.e. Messiah [a]Acts 2:46 [b]Acts 8:35; Gal 1:16
6:1 [1]Lit *in these days* [2]Jews who adopted the Gr language and much of Gr culture through acculturation [a]Acts 11:26 [b]Acts 2:47 [c]Acts 9:29 [d]2 Cor 11:22; Phil 3:5 [e]Acts 9:39; 1 Tim 5:3 [f]Acts 4:35
2 [1]Lit *multitude*
3 [a]John 21:23; Acts 1:15 [b]Acts 2:4
4 [1]Or *service* [a]Acts 1:14
5 [1]Lit *multitude* [2]Gr *Nikolaos* [3]I.e. a Gentile convert to Judaism [a]Acts 6:8ff [b]Acts 6:3 [c]Acts 8:5ff [d]Matt 23:15 [e]Acts 11:19
6 [a]Acts 1:24 [b]Num 8:10; Deut 34:9; Mark 5:23; Acts 8:17ff; 1 Tim 4:14; 2 Tim 1:6; Heb 6:2
7 [a]Acts 12:24 [b]Acts 6:1 [c]Acts 13:8; Gal 1:23; Jude 3
8 [1]Or *attesting miracles* [a]John 4:48
9 [a]Matt 27:32; Acts 2:10 [b]Acts 18:24

drians, and some from [c]Cilicia and
[1d]Asia, rose up and argued with Stephen.
10 But they were unable to cope with
the wisdom and the Spirit with which he
was speaking.
11 Then they secretly induced men to
say, "We have heard him speak blasphe-
mous words against Moses and *against*
God."
12 And they stirred up the people, the
elders and the scribes, and they [a]came
up to him and dragged him away and
brought him [1]before [b]the [2]Council.
13 They put forward [a]false witnesses
who said, "This man incessantly speaks
against this [b]holy place and the Law;
14 for we have heard him say that
[a]this Nazarene, Jesus, will destroy this
place and alter [b]the customs which Moses handed down to us."
15 And fixing their gaze on him, all
who were sitting in the [1a]Council saw
his face like the face of an angel.

Stephen's Defense

7 The high priest said, "Are these
things so?"
2 ¶ And he said, "Hear me, [a]breth-
ren and fathers! [b]The God of glory [c]ap-
peared to our father Abraham when he
was in Mesopotamia, before he lived in
[1]Haran,
3 and said to him, '[a]LEAVE YOUR
COUNTRY AND YOUR RELATIVES, AND COME
INTO THE LAND THAT I WILL SHOW YOU.'
4 "[a]Then he left the land of the Chaldeans and settled in [1]Haran. [b]From
there, after his father died, *God* had him
move to this country in which you are
now living.
5 "But He gave him no inheritance in
it, not even a foot of ground, and *yet,*
even when he had no child, [a]He promised that HE WOULD GIVE IT TO HIM AS A
POSSESSION, AND TO HIS DESCENDANTS AF-
TER HIM.
6 "But [a]God spoke to this effect, that
his DESCENDANTS WOULD BE ALIENS IN A FOR-
EIGN LAND, AND THAT THEY WOULD [1]BE EN-
SLAVED AND MISTREATED FOR FOUR HUNDRED
YEARS.
7 " 'AND WHATEVER NATION TO WHICH
THEY WILL BE IN BONDAGE I MYSELF WILL
JUDGE,' said God, 'AND [a]AFTER THAT THEY
WILL COME OUT AND [1]SERVE ME IN THIS
PLACE.'
8 "And He [a]gave him [1]the covenant
of circumcision; and so [b]*Abraham* became the father of Isaac, and circumcised
him on the eighth day; and [c]Isaac *became the father of* Jacob, and [d]Jacob *of*
the twelve [e]patriarchs.
9 ¶ "The patriarchs [a]became jealous
of Joseph and sold him into Egypt. *Yet*
God was with him,
10 and rescued him from all his afflictions, and [a]granted him favor and wisdom in the sight of Pharaoh, king of
Egypt, and he made him governor over
Egypt and all his household.
11 ¶ "Now [a]a famine came over all
Egypt and Canaan, and great affliction
with it, and our fathers [1]could find no
food.
12 "But [a]when Jacob heard that there
was grain in Egypt, he sent our fathers
there the first time.
13 "On the second *visit* [a]Joseph [1]made
himself known to his brothers, and [b]Jo-
seph's family was disclosed to Pharaoh.
14 "Then [a]Joseph sent *word* and invited Jacob his father and all his relatives to
come to him, [b]seventy-five [1c]persons
in all.
15 "And [a]Jacob went down to Egypt
and *there* he and our fathers died.
16 "*From there* they were removed to
[1a]Shechem and laid in the tomb which
Abraham had purchased for a sum of
money from the sons of [2]Hamor in [1]She-
chem.
17 ¶ "But as the [a]time of the promise
was approaching which God had assured
to Abraham, [b]the people increased and
multiplied in Egypt,
18 until [a]THERE AROSE ANOTHER KING
OVER EGYPT WHO KNEW NOTHING ABOUT
JOSEPH.
19 "It was he who took [a]shrewd advantage of our race and mistreated our fathers so that they would [1b]expose their
infants and they would not survive.
20 "It was at this time that [a]Moses was
born; and he was lovely [1]in the sight of
God, and he was nurtured three months
in his father's home.
21 "And after he had been set outside,
[a]Pharaoh's daughter [1]took him away
and nurtured him as her own son.
22 "Moses was educated in all [a]the
learning of the Egyptians, and he was a
man of power in words and deeds.
23 "But when he was approaching the
age of forty, [a]it entered his [1]mind to
visit his brethren, the sons of Israel.
24 "And when he saw one *of them* being treated unjustly, he defended him and
took vengeance for the oppressed by
striking down the Egyptian.
25 "And he supposed that his brethren
understood that God was granting them
[1]deliverance [2]through him, but they did
not understand.
26 "[a]On the following day he appeared
to them as they were fighting together,
and he tried to reconcile them in peace,

9 [1]I.e. west coast province of Asia Minor [c]Acts 15:23,41; 21:39; 22:3; 23:34; 27:5; Gal 1:21 [d]Acts 16:6; 19:10; 21:27; 24:18
12 [1]Lit *into* [2]Or *Sanhedrin* [a]Luke 20:1; Acts 4:1 [b]Matt 5:22
13 [a]Matt 26:59-61; Acts 7:58 [b]Matt 24:15; Acts 21:28; 25:8
14 [a]Matt 26:61 [b]Acts 15:1; 21:21; 26:3; 28:17
15 [1]Or *Sanhedrin* [a]Matt 5:22
7:2 [1]Gr *Charran* [a]Acts 22:1 [b]Ps 29:3; 1 Cor 2:8 [c]Gen 11:31; 15:7
3 [a]Gen 12:1
4 [1]Gr *Charran* [a]Gen 11:31; 15:7 [b]Gen 12:4, 5
5 [a]Gen 12:7; 13:15; 15:18; 17:8
6 [1]Lit *enslave them and mistreat them* [a]Gen 15:13f
7 [1]Or *worship* [a]Ex 3:12
8 [1]Or *a* [a]Gen 17:10ff [b]Gen 21:2-4 [c]Gen 25:26 [d]Gen 29:31ff; 30:5ff; 35:23ff [e]Acts 2:29
9 [a]Gen 37:11, 28; 39:2,21f; 45:4
10 [a]Gen 39:21; 41:40-46; Ps 105:21
11 [1]Lit *were not finding* [a]Gen 41:54f; 42:5
12 [a]Gen 42:2
13 [1]Or *was made known* [a]Gen 45:1-4 [b]Gen 45:16
14 [1]Lit *souls* [a]Gen 45:9,10, 17,18 [b]Gen 46:26f; Ex 1:5; Deut 10:22 [c]Acts 2:41
15 [a]Gen 46:1-7; 49:33; Ex 1:6
16 [1]Gr *Sychem* [2]Gr *Emmor* [a]Gen 23:16; 33:19; 50:13; Josh 24:32
17 [a]Gen 15:13 [b]Ex 1:7f
18 [a]Ex 1:8
19 [1]Or *put out to die* [a]Ex 1:10f, 16ff [b]Ex 1:22
20 [1]Lit *to God* [a]Ex 2:2; Heb 11:23
21 [1]Or *adopted him* [a]Ex 2:5f,10
22 [a]1 Kin 4:30; Is 19:11
23 [1]Lit *heart* [a]Ex 2:11f; Heb 11:24-26
25 [1]Or *salvation* [2]Lit *through his hand*
26 [a]Ex 2:13f

saying, 'Men, you are brethren, why do
you injure one another?'
27 "But the one who was injuring his
neighbor pushed him away, saying,
'[a]WHO MADE YOU A RULER AND JUDGE
OVER US?
28 '[a]YOU DO NOT MEAN TO KILL ME AS
YOU KILLED THE EGYPTIAN YESTERDAY,
DO YOU?'
29 "At this remark, [a]MOSES FLED AND
BECAME AN ALIEN IN THE LAND OF [1]MIDIAN,
where he [b]became the father of two
sons.
30 ¶ "After forty years had passed,
[a]AN ANGEL APPEARED TO HIM IN THE WILDER-
NESS OF MOUNT Sinai, IN THE FLAME OF A
BURNING THORN BUSH.
31 "When Moses saw it, he marveled at
the sight; and as he approached to look
more closely, there came the voice of the
Lord:
32 '[a]I AM THE GOD OF YOUR FATHERS, THE
GOD OF ABRAHAM AND ISAAC AND JACOB.'
Moses shook with fear and would not
venture to look.
33 "[a]BUT THE LORD SAID TO HIM, '[b]TAKE
OFF THE SANDALS FROM YOUR FEET, FOR THE
PLACE ON WHICH YOU ARE STANDING IS HOLY
GROUND.
34 '[a]I HAVE CERTAINLY SEEN THE OPPRES-
SION OF MY PEOPLE IN EGYPT AND HAVE
HEARD THEIR GROANS, AND I HAVE COME
DOWN TO RESCUE THEM; [1b]COME NOW, AND
I WILL SEND YOU TO EGYPT.'
35 ¶ "This Moses whom they [a]dis-
owned, saying, 'WHO MADE YOU A RULER
AND A JUDGE?' is the one whom God [1]sent
to be both a ruler and a deliverer with the
[2]help of the angel who appeared to him
in the thorn bush.
36 "[a]This man led them out, performing [b]wonders and [1]signs in the land of
Egypt and in the Red Sea and in the [c]wil-
derness for forty years.
37 "This is the Moses who said to the
sons of Israel, '[a]GOD WILL RAISE UP FOR
YOU A PROPHET [1]LIKE ME FROM YOUR BRETH-
REN.'
38 "This is the one who was in [a]the
[1]congregation in the wilderness together
with [b]the angel who was speaking to him
on Mount Sinai, and *who was* with our
fathers; and he received [c]living [d]oracles
to pass on to you.
39 "Our fathers were unwilling to be
obedient to him, but [a]repudiated him
and in their hearts turned back to Egypt,
40 [a]SAYING TO AARON, 'MAKE FOR US
GODS WHO WILL GO BEFORE US; FOR THIS
MOSES WHO LED US OUT OF THE LAND OF
EGYPT—WE DO NOT KNOW WHAT HAPPENED
TO HIM.'
41 "[1]At that time [a]they made a [2]calf
and brought a sacrifice to the idol, and
were rejoicing in [b]the works of their
hands.
42 "But God [a]turned away and delivered them up to [1]serve the [2]host of
heaven; as it is written in the book of the
prophets, '[b]IT WAS NOT TO ME THAT YOU
OFFERED VICTIMS AND SACRIFICES [c]FORTY
YEARS IN THE WILDERNESS, WAS IT, O HOUSE
OF ISRAEL?
43 '[a]YOU ALSO TOOK ALONG THE TABER-
NACLE OF MOLOCH AND THE STAR OF THE
GOD [1]ROMPHA, THE IMAGES WHICH YOU
MADE TO WORSHIP. I ALSO WILL REMOVE YOU
BEYOND BABYLON.'
44 ¶ "Our fathers had [a]the tabernacle
of testimony in the wilderness, just as He
who spoke to Moses directed *him* to
make it [b]according to the pattern which
he had seen.
45 "And having received it in their
turn, our fathers [a]brought it in with
[1]Joshua upon dispossessing the [2]nations
whom God drove out before our fathers,
until the time of David.
46 "[a]*David* found favor in God's sight,
and [b]asked that he might find a dwelling
place for the [1]God of Jacob.
47 "But it was [a]Solomon who built a
house for Him.
48 "However, [a]the Most High does not
dwell in *houses* made by *human* hands;
as the prophet says:
49 '[a]HEAVEN IS MY THRONE,
AND EARTH IS THE FOOTSTOOL OF
MY FEET;
WHAT KIND OF HOUSE WILL YOU
BUILD FOR ME?' says the
Lord,
'OR WHAT PLACE IS THERE FOR MY
REPOSE?
50 '[a]WAS IT NOT MY HAND WHICH
MADE ALL THESE THINGS?'
51 ¶ "You men who are [a]stiff-necked
and uncircumcised in heart and ears are
always resisting the Holy Spirit; you are
doing just as your fathers did.
52 "[a]Which one of the prophets did
your fathers not persecute? They killed
those who had previously announced the
coming of [b]the Righteous One, whose
betrayers and murderers [c]you have now
become;
53 you who received the law as [a]or-
dained by angels, and *yet* did not
keep it."

Stephen Put to Death

54 ¶ Now when they heard this, they
were [a]cut to the quick, and they *began*
gnashing their teeth at him.
55 But being [a]full of the Holy Spirit,
he [b]gazed intently into heaven and saw
the glory of God, and Jesus standing [c]at
the right hand of God;

27 [a]Ex 2:14; Acts 7:35
28 [a]Ex 2:14
29 [1]Gr *Madiam* [a]Ex 2:15 [b]Ex 18:3
30 [a]Ex 3:1f; Is 63:9
32 [a]Ex 3:6; Matt 22:32
33 [a]Ex 3:5 [b]Josh 5:15
34 [1]Lit *and now come!* [a]Ex 3:7f [b]Ex 3:10
35 [1]Lit *has sent* [2]Lit *hand* [a]Ex 2:14; Acts 7:27
36 [1]Or *attesting miracles* [a]Ex 12:41; Heb 8:9 [b]Ex 7:3; John 4:48 [c]Ex 16:35; Num 14:33; Ps 95:8-10; Acts 7:42; Heb 3:8f
37 [1]Or *as* He raised up *me* [a]Deut 18:15; Acts 3:22
38 [1]Gr *ekklesia* [a]Ex 19:17 [b]Acts 7:53 [c]Deut 32:47; Heb 4:12 [d]Rom 3:2; Heb 5:12; 1 Pet 4:11
39 [a]Num 14:3f
40 [a]Ex 32:1
41 [1]Lit *in those days* [2]Or *young bull* [a]Ex 32:4 [b]Rev 9:20
42 [1]Or *worship* [2]I.e. heavenly bodies [a]Josh 24:20; Is 63:10; Jer 19:13; Ezek 20:39 [b]Amos 5:25 [c]Acts 7:36
43 [1]Other mss spell it: *Romphan,* or *Remphan,* or *Raiphan,* or *Rephan* [a]Amos 5:26
44 [a]Ex 25:8 [b]Ex 25:40
45 [1]Gr *Jesus* [2]Or *Gentiles* [a]Deut 32:49; Josh 3:14ff; Ps 44:2f
46 [1]The earliest mss read *house* instead of *God*; the Septuagint reads *God* [a]2 Sam 7:8ff; Ps 132:1-5; Acts 13:22 [b]2 Sam 7:1-16; 1 Chr 17:1-14
47 [a]1 Kin 6:1-38; 2 Chr 3:1-17
48 [a]Luke 1:32
49 [a]Is 66:1; Matt 5:34f
50 [a]Is 66:2
51 [a]Ex 32:9; Lev 26:41; Num 27:14; Is 63:10; Jer 6:10
52 [a]2 Chr 36:15f; Matt 5:12 [b]Acts 3:14; 1 John 2:1 [c]Acts 3:14
53 [a]Deut 33:2; Acts 7:38; Gal 3:19; Heb 2:2
54 [a]Acts 5:33
55 [a]Acts 2:4 [b]John 11:41 [c]Mark 16:19

56 and he said, "Behold, I see the [a]heavens opened up and [b]the Son of Man standing at the right hand of God."

57 But they cried out with a loud voice, and covered their ears and rushed at him with one impulse.

58 When they had [a]driven him out of the city, they *began* stoning *him*; and [b]the witnesses [c]laid aside their robes at the feet of [d]a young man named Saul.

59 They went on stoning Stephen as he [a]called on *the Lord* and said, "Lord Jesus, receive my spirit!"

60 Then [a]falling on his knees, he cried out with a loud voice, "Lord, [b]do not hold this sin against them!" Having said this, he [1c]fell asleep.

Saul Persecutes the Church

8 [a]Saul was in hearty agreement with putting him to death.

¶ And on that day a great persecution [1]began against [b]the church in Jerusalem, and they were all [c]scattered throughout the regions of Judea and [d]Samaria, except the apostles.

2 *Some* devout men buried Stephen, and made loud lamentation over him.

3 But [a]Saul *began* ravaging the church, entering house after house, and [b]dragging off men and women, he would put them in prison.

Philip in Samaria

4 ¶ Therefore, those [a]who had been scattered went about [1b]preaching the word.

5 [a]Philip went down to the city of Samaria and *began* proclaiming [1]Christ to them.

6 The crowds with one accord were giving attention to what was said by Philip, as they heard and saw the [1]signs which he was performing.

7 For *in the case of* many who had [a]unclean spirits, they were coming out *of them* shouting with a loud voice; and many who had been [b]paralyzed and lame were healed.

8 So there was [a]much rejoicing in that city.

9 ¶ Now there was a man named Simon, who formerly was practicing [a]magic in the city and astonishing the people of Samaria, [b]claiming to be someone great;

10 and they all, from smallest to greatest, were giving attention to him, saying, "[a]This man is what is called the Great Power of God."

11 And they were giving him attention because he had for a long time astonished them with his [a]magic arts.

12 But when they believed Philip [a]preaching the good news about the kingdom of God and the name of Jesus Christ, they were being [b]baptized, men and women alike.

13 Even Simon himself believed; and after being baptized, he continued on with Philip, and as he observed [a]signs and [b]great miracles taking place, he was constantly amazed.

14 ¶ Now when [a]the apostles in Jerusalem heard that Samaria had received the word of God, they sent them [b]Peter and John,

15 who came down and prayed for them [a]that they might receive the Holy Spirit.

16 For He had [a]not yet fallen upon any of them; they had simply been [b]baptized [1]in the name of the Lord Jesus.

17 Then they [a]*began* laying their hands on them, and they were [b]receiving the Holy Spirit.

18 Now when Simon saw that the Spirit was bestowed through the laying on of the apostles' hands, he offered them money,

19 saying, "Give this authority to me as well, so that everyone on whom I lay my hands may receive the Holy Spirit."

20 But Peter said to him, "May your silver perish with you, because you thought you could [a]obtain the gift of God with money!

21 "You have [a]no part or portion in this [1]matter, for your heart is not [b]right before God.

22 "Therefore repent of this wickedness of yours, and pray the Lord that, [a]if possible, the intention of your heart may be forgiven you.

23 "For I see that you are in the gall of bitterness and in [a]the [1]bondage of iniquity."

24 But Simon answered and said, "[a]Pray to the Lord for me yourselves, so that nothing of what you have said may come upon me."

An Ethiopian Receives Christ

25 ¶ So, when they had solemnly [a]testified and spoken [b]the word of the Lord, they started back to Jerusalem, and were [c]preaching the gospel to many villages of the [d]Samaritans.

26 ¶ But [a]an angel of the Lord spoke to [b]Philip saying, "Get up and go south to the road that descends from Jerusalem to [c]Gaza." ([1]This is a desert *road*.)

27 So he got up and went; and [a]there was an Ethiopian eunuch, a court official of Candace, queen of the Ethiopians, who was in charge of all her treasure; and he [b]had come to Jerusalem to worship,

28 and he was returning and sitting in

---

56 [a]John 1:51 [b]Matt 8:20
58 [a]Lev 24:14, 16; Luke 4:29 [b]Deut 13:9f; 17:7; Acts 6:13 [c]Acts 22:20 [d]Acts 8:1; 22:20; 26:10
59 [a]Acts 9:14, 21; 22:16; Rom 10:12-14; 1 Cor 1:2; 2 Tim 2:22
60 [1]I.e. died [a]Luke 22:41 [b]Matt 5:44; Luke 23:34 [c]Dan 12:2; Matt 27:52; John 11:11f; Acts 13:36; 1 Cor 15:6,18,20; 1 Thess 4:13ff; 2 Pet 3:4
8:1 [1]Lit *occurred* [a]Acts 7:58; 22:20; 26:10 [b]Acts 9:31 [c]Acts 8:4; 11:19 [d]Acts 1:8; 8:5, 14; 9:31
3 [a]Acts 9:1,13, 21; 22:4,19; 26:10f; 1 Cor 15:9; Gal 1:13; Phil 3:6; 1 Tim 1:13 [b]James 2:6
4 [1]Or *bringing the good news of* [a]Acts 8:1 [b]Acts 8:12; 15:35
5 [1]I.e. the Messiah [a]Acts 6:5; 8:26,30
6 [1]Or *attesting miracles*
7 [a]Mark 16:17 [b]Matt 4:24
8 [a]John 4:40-42; Acts 8:39
9 [a]Acts 8:11; 13:6 [b]Acts 5:36
10 [a]Acts 14:11; 28:6
11 [a]Acts 8:9; 13:6
12 [a]Acts 1:3; 8:4 [b]Acts 2:38
13 [a]Acts 8:6 [b]Acts 19:11
14 [a]Acts 8:1 [b]Luke 22:8
15 [a]Acts 2:38; 19:2
16 [1]Lit *into* [a]Matt 28:19; Acts 19:2 [b]Acts 2:38; 10:48
17 [a]Mark 5:23; Acts 6:6 [b]Acts 2:4
20 [a]2 Kin 5:16; Is 55:1; Dan 5:17; Matt 10:8; Acts 2:38
21 [1]Or *teaching*; lit *word* [a]Deut 10:9; 12:12; Eph 5:5 [b]Ps 78:37
22 [a]Is 55:7
23 [1]Lit *bond* [a]Is 58:6
24 [a]Gen 20:7; Ex 8:8; Num 21:7; James 5:16
25 [a]Luke 16:28 [b]Acts 13:12 [c]Acts 8:40 [d]Matt 10:5
26 [1]Or *This city is deserted* [a]Acts 5:19; 8:29 [b]Acts 8:5 [c]Gen 10:19
27 [a]Ps 68:31; 87:4; Is 56:3ff [b]1 Kin 8:41f; John 12:20

his [1]chariot, and was reading the prophet Isaiah.
29 Then [a]the Spirit said to Philip, "Go
up and join this [1]chariot."
30 Philip ran up and heard him reading Isaiah the prophet, and said, "Do you
understand what you are reading?"
31 And he said, "Well, how could I,
unless someone guides me?" And he invited Philip to come up and sit with him.
32 Now the passage of Scripture
which he was reading was this:
"[a]HE WAS LED AS A SHEEP TO
SLAUGHTER;
AND AS A LAMB BEFORE ITS SHEARER
IS SILENT,
SO HE DOES NOT OPEN HIS MOUTH.
33 "[a]IN HUMILIATION HIS JUDGMENT
WAS TAKEN AWAY;
WHO WILL [1]RELATE HIS
[2]GENERATION?
FOR HIS LIFE IS REMOVED FROM THE
EARTH."
34 The eunuch answered Philip and
said, "Please *tell me*, of whom does the
prophet say this? Of himself or of someone else?"
35 Then Philip [a]opened his mouth,
and [b]beginning from this Scripture he
[c]preached Jesus to him.
36 As they went along the road they
came to some water; and the eunuch
*said, "Look! Water! [a]What prevents me
from being baptized?"
37 [[1]And Philip said, "If you believe
with all your heart, you may." And he
answered and said, "I believe that Jesus
Christ is the Son of God."]
38 And he ordered the [1]chariot to
stop; and they both went down into the
water, Philip as well as the eunuch, and
he baptized him.
39 When they came up out of the water, [a]the Spirit of the Lord snatched Philip away; and the eunuch no longer saw
him, [1]but went on his way rejoicing.
40 But Philip [1]found himself at
[2a]Azotus, and as he passed through he
[b]kept preaching the gospel to all the cities until he came to [c]Caesarea.

The Conversion of Saul

9 [a]Now [1]Saul, still [b]breathing [2]threats
and murder against the disciples of
the Lord, went to the high priest,
2 and asked for [a]letters from him to
[b]the synagogues at [c]Damascus, so that if
he found any belonging to [d]the Way,
both men and women, he might bring
them bound to Jerusalem.
3 As he was traveling, it happened
that he was approaching Damascus, and
[a]suddenly a light from heaven flashed
around him;
4 and [a]he fell to the ground and
heard a voice saying to him, "Saul, Saul,
why are you persecuting Me?"
5 And he said, "Who are You, Lord?"
And He *said*, "I am Jesus whom you are
persecuting,
6 but get up and enter the city, and
[a]it will be told you what you must do."
7 The men who traveled with him
[a]stood speechless, [b]hearing the [1]voice
but seeing no one.
8 Saul got up from the ground, and
[a]though his eyes were open, he [1]could
see nothing; and leading him by the
hand, they brought him into [b]Damascus.
9 And he was three days without
sight, and neither ate nor drank.
10 ¶ Now there was a disciple at [a]Da-
mascus named [b]Ananias; and the Lord
said to him in [c]a vision, "Ananias." And
he said, "Here I am, Lord."
11 And the Lord *said* to him, "Get up
and go to the street called Straight, and
inquire at the house of Judas for a man
from [a]Tarsus named Saul, for he is praying,
12 and he has seen [1]in a vision a man
named Ananias come in and [a]lay his
hands on him, so that he might regain his
sight."
13 But Ananias answered, "Lord, I
have heard from many about this man,
[a]how much harm he did to [b]Your
[1]saints at Jerusalem;
14 and here he [a]has authority from
the chief priests to bind all who [b]call on
Your name."
15 But the Lord said to him, "Go, for
[a]he is a chosen [1]instrument of Mine, to
bear My name before [b]the Gentiles and
[c]kings and the sons of Israel;
16 for [a]I will show him how much he
must suffer for My name's sake."
17 So Ananias departed and entered
the house, and after [a]laying his hands on
him said, "[b]Brother Saul, the Lord Jesus,
who appeared to you on the road by
which you were coming, has sent me so
that you may regain your sight and be
[c]filled with the Holy Spirit."
18 And immediately there fell from his
eyes something like scales, and he regained his sight, and he got up and was
baptized;
19 and he took food and was strengthened.

Saul Begins to Preach Christ

¶ Now [a]for several days he was with
[b]the disciples who were at Damascus,
20 and immediately he *began* to proclaim Jesus [a]in the synagogues, [1]saying,
"He is [b]the Son of God."
21 All those hearing him continued to

28 [1]Or *carriage*
29 [1]Or *carriage* [a]Acts 8:39; Heb 3:7
32 [a]Is 53:7
33 [1]Or *describe* [2]Or *family* or *origin* [a]Is 53:8
35 [a]Matt 5:2 [b]Luke 24:27; Acts 17:2 [c]Acts 5:42
36 [a]Acts 10:47
37 [1]Early mss do not contain this v
38 [1]Or *carriage*
39 [1]Lit *for he was going* [a]1 Kin 18:12; 2 Kin 2:16; Ezek 3:12; 2 Cor 12:2
40 [1]Or *was found* [2]OT: Ashdod [a]Josh 11:22; 1 Sam 5:1 [b]Acts 8:25 [c]Acts 9:30
9:1 [1]Later called Paul [2]Lit *threat* [a]Acts 9:1-22 [b]Acts 8:3
2 [a]Acts 9:14 [b]Matt 10:17 [c]Gen 14:15; 2 Cor 11:32; Gal 1:17 [d]John 14:6; Acts 18:25f
3 [a]1 Cor 15:8
4 [a]Acts 22:7
6 [a]Acts 9:16
7 [1]Or *sound* [a]Acts 26:14 [b]John 12:29f; Acts 22:9
8 [1]Lit *was seeing* [a]Acts 9:18 [b]Gen 14:15; 2 Cor 11:32; Gal 1:17
10 [a]Gen 14:15; 2 Cor 11:32; Gal 1:17 [b]Acts 22:12 [c]Acts 10:3
11 [a]Acts 9:30
12 [1]A few early mss do not contain *in a vision* [a]Mark 5:23; Acts 6:6
13 [1]Or *holy ones* [a]Acts 8:3 [b]Acts 9:32; Rom 1:7; 1 Cor 1:2
14 [a]Acts 9:2 [b]Acts 7:59
15 [1]Or *vessel* [a]Acts 13:2; Rom 1:1; Gal 1:15; Eph 3:7 [b]Acts 22:21; Rom 1:5; Gal 1:16; Eph 3:1; 1 Tim 2:7; 2 Tim 4:17 [c]Acts 25:22f; 2 Tim 4:17
16 [a]Acts 20:23; 2 Cor 6:4f; 1 Thess 3:3
17 [a]Mark 5:23; Acts 6:6 [b]Acts 22:13 [c]Acts 2:4
19 [a]Acts 26:20 [b]Acts 9:26
20 [1]Lit *that* [a]Acts 13:5 [b]Matt 4:3; Acts 9:22

be amazed, and were saying, "Is this not
he who in Jerusalem [a]destroyed those
who [b]called on this name, and *who* had
come here for the purpose of bringing
them bound before the chief priests?"
22 But Saul kept increasing in strength
and confounding the Jews who lived at
Damascus by proving that this *Jesus* is the
[1]Christ.
23 ¶ When [a]many days had elapsed,
[b]the Jews plotted together to do away
with him,
24 but [a]their plot became known to
Saul. [b]They were also watching the gates
day and night so that they might put him
to death;
25 but his disciples took him by night
and let him down through *an opening in*
the wall, lowering him in a large basket.
26 ¶ [a]When he came to Jerusalem, he
was trying to associate with the disciples;
[1]but they were all afraid of him, not believing that he was a disciple.
27 But [a]Barnabas took hold of him
and brought him to the apostles and described to them how he had [b]seen the
Lord on the road, and that He had talked
to him, and how [c]at Damascus he had
[d]spoken out boldly in the name of Jesus.
28 And he was with them, [1]moving
about freely in Jerusalem, [a]speaking out
boldly in the name of the Lord.
29 And he was talking and arguing
with the [1a]Hellenistic *Jews*; but they
were attempting to put him to death.
30 But when [a]the brethren learned *of
it*, they brought him down to [b]Caesarea
and [c]sent him away to [d]Tarsus.
31 ¶ So [a]the church throughout all Judea and Galilee and Samaria [1]enjoyed
peace, being built up; and going on in the
fear of the Lord and in the comfort of the
Holy Spirit, it continued to increase.

Peter's Ministry

32 ¶ Now as Peter was traveling
through all *those regions,* he came down
also to [a]the [1]saints who lived at
[2b]Lydda.
33 There he found a man named Aeneas, who had been bedridden eight years,
for he was paralyzed.
34 Peter said to him, "Aeneas, Jesus
Christ heals you; get up and make your
bed." Immediately he got up.
35 And all who lived at [1a]Lydda and
[b]Sharon saw him, and they [c]turned to
the Lord.
36 ¶ Now in [a]Joppa there was a disciple named Tabitha (which translated *in
Greek* is called [1]Dorcas); this woman
was abounding with deeds of kindness
and charity which she continually did.
37 And it happened [1]at that time that
she fell sick and died; and when they had
washed her body, they laid it in an [a]up-
per room.
38 Since Lydda was near [a]Joppa, [b]the
disciples, having heard that Peter was
there, sent two men to him, imploring
him, "Do not delay in coming to us."
39 So Peter arose and went with them.
When he arrived, they brought him into
the [a]upper room; and all the [b]widows
stood beside him, weeping and showing
all the [1]tunics and garments that Dorcas
used to make while she was with them.
40 But Peter [a]sent them all out and
[b]knelt down and prayed, and turning to
the body, he said, "[c]Tabitha, arise." And
she opened her eyes, and when she saw
Peter, she sat up.
41 And he gave her his hand and
raised her up; and calling [a]the [1]saints
and [b]widows, he presented her alive.
42 It became known all over [a]Joppa,
and [b]many believed in the Lord.
43 And Peter stayed many days in
[a]Joppa with [b]a tanner *named* Simon.

Cornelius's Vision

10 Now *there was* a man at [a]Caesa-
rea named Cornelius, a centurion
of what was [b]called the Italian [1]cohort,
2 a devout man and [a]one who feared
God with all his household, and [b]gave
many [1]alms to the *Jewish* people and
prayed to God continually.
3 About [a]the [1]ninth hour of the day
he clearly saw [b]in a vision [c]an angel of
God who had *just* come in and said to
him, "Cornelius!"
4 And [a]fixing his gaze on him and
being much alarmed, he said, "What is it,
Lord?" And he said to him, "Your prayers
and [1]alms [b]have ascended [c]as a memorial before God.
5 "Now dispatch *some* men to [a]Joppa
and send for a man *named* Simon, who is
also called Peter;
6 he is staying with a tanner *named*
[a]Simon, whose house is by the sea."
7 When the angel who was speaking
to him had left, he summoned two of his
[1]servants and a devout soldier of those
who were his personal attendants,
8 and after he had explained everything to them, he sent them to [a]Joppa.
9 ¶ On the next day, as they were on
their way and approaching the city, [a]Pe-
ter went up on [b]the housetop about [c]the
[1]sixth hour to pray.
10 But he became hungry and was
desiring to eat; but while they were making preparations, he [a]fell into a trance;
11 and he *saw [a]the [1]sky opened up,

21 [a]Acts 8:3; Gal 1:13 [b]Acts 9:14
22 [1]I.e. Messiah
23 [a]Gal 1:17 [b]1 Thess 2:16
24 [a]Acts 20:3 [b]2 Cor 11:32f
26 [1]Lit *and* [a]Acts 22:17-20
27 [a]Acts 4:36 [b]Acts 9:3-6 [c]Acts 9:20 [d]Acts 4:13
28 [1]Lit *going in and going out* [a]Acts 4:13
29 [1]Jews who adopted the Gr language and much of Gr culture through acculturation [a]Acts 6:1
30 [a]Acts 1:15 [b]Acts 8:40 [c]Gal 1:21 [d]Acts 9:11
31 [1]Lit *was having* [a]Acts 5:11
32 [1]Or *holy ones* [2]OT: Lod [a]Acts 9:13 [b]1 Chr 8:12; Ezra 2:33; Neh 7:37
35 [1]OT: Lod [a]1 Chr 8:12; Ezra 2:33; Neh 7:37 [b]1 Chr 5:16; Is 33:9 [c]Acts 2:47
36 [1]I.e. *Gazelle* [a]Josh 19:46; 2 Chr 2:16; Ezra 3:7; Jon 1:3; Acts 9:38
37 [1]Lit *in those days* [a]Acts 1:13
38 [a]Josh 19:46; 2 Chr 2:16; Ezra 3:7; Jon 1:3; Acts 9:36 [b]Acts 11:26
39 [1]Or *inner garments* [a]Acts 1:13 [b]Acts 6:1
40 [a]Matt 9:25 [b]Luke 22:41; Acts 7:60 [c]Mark 5:41
41 [1]Or *holy ones* [a]Acts 9:13 [b]Acts 6:1
42 [a]Josh 19:46; 2 Chr 2:16; Jon 1:3; Acts 9:38 [b]Acts 9:35
43 [a]Josh 19:46; 2 Chr 2:16; Ezra 3:7; Jon 1:3; Acts 9:38 [b]Acts 10:6
10:1 [1]Or *battalion* [a]Acts 8:40 [b]Matt 27:27; Mark 15:16; John 18:3; Acts 21:31
2 [1]Or *gifts of charity* [a]Acts 10:22 [b]Luke 7:4f
3 [1]I.e. 3 p.m. [a]Acts 3:1 [b]Acts 9:10 [c]Acts 5:19
4 [1]Or *deeds of charity* [a]Acts 3:4 [b]Rev 8:4 [c]Matt 26:13; Phil 4:18; Heb 6:10
5 [a]Acts 9:36
6 [a]Acts 9:43
7 [1]Or *household slaves*
8 [a]Acts 9:36
9 [1]I.e. noon [a]Acts 10:9-32 [b]Jer 19:13; Zeph 1:5; Matt 24:17 [c]Ps 55:17; Acts10:3
10 [a]Acts 11:5
11 [1]Or *heaven* [a]John 1:51

and an [2]object like a great sheet coming down, lowered by four corners to the ground,

12 and there were in it all *kinds of* four-footed animals and [1]crawling creatures of the earth and birds of the [2]air.

13 A voice came to him, "Get up, Peter, [1]kill and eat!"

14 But Peter said, "By no means, [a]Lord, for [b]I have never eaten anything [1]unholy and unclean."

15 Again a voice *came* to him a second time, "[a]What God has cleansed, no *longer* consider [1]unholy."

16 This happened three times, and immediately the [1]object was taken up into the [2]sky.

17 ¶ Now while Peter was greatly perplexed in [1]mind as to what [a]the vision which he had seen might be, behold, [b]the men who had been sent by Cornelius, having asked directions for Simon's house, appeared at the gate;

18 and calling out, they were asking whether Simon, who was also called Peter, was staying there.

19 While Peter was reflecting on [a]the vision, [b]the Spirit said to him, "Behold, [1]three men are looking for you.

20 "But get up, go downstairs and [a]accompany them [1]without misgivings, for I have sent them Myself."

21 Peter went down to the men and said, "Behold, I am the one you are looking for; what is the reason for which you have come?"

22 They said, "Cornelius, a centurion, a righteous and [a]God-fearing man well spoken of by the entire nation of the Jews, [b]was *divinely* directed by a [c]holy angel to send for you *to come* to his house and hear [1d]a message from you."

23 So he invited them in and gave them lodging.

Peter at Caesarea

¶ And on the next day he got up and went away with them, and [a]some of [b]the brethren from [c]Joppa accompanied him.

24 On the following day he entered [a]Caesarea. Now Cornelius was waiting for them and had called together his relatives and close friends.

25 When Peter entered, Cornelius met him, and fell at his feet and [1a]worshiped *him.*

26 But Peter raised him up, saying, "[a]Stand up; I too am *just* a man."

27 As he talked with him, he entered and *found [a]many people assembled.

28 And he said to them, "You yourselves know how [a]unlawful it is for a man who is a Jew to associate with a foreigner or to visit him; and *yet* [b]God has shown me that I should not call any man [1]unholy or unclean.

29 "That is why I came without even raising any objection when I was sent for. So I ask for what reason you have sent for me."

30 ¶ Cornelius said, "[a]Four days ago to this hour, I was praying in my house during [b]the [1]ninth hour; and behold, [c]a man stood before me in shining garments,

31 and he *said, 'Cornelius, your prayer has been heard and your [1]alms have been remembered before God.

32 'Therefore send to [a]Joppa and invite Simon, who is also called Peter, to come to you; he is staying at the house of Simon *the* tanner by the sea.'

33 "So I sent for you immediately, and you have [1]been kind enough to come. Now then, we are all here present before God to hear all that you have been commanded by the Lord."

Gentiles Hear Good News

34 ¶ [a]Opening his mouth, Peter said:
¶ "I most certainly understand *now* that [b]God is not one to show partiality,

35 but [a]in every nation the man who [1b]fears Him and [2]does what is right is welcome to Him.

36 "The word which He sent to the sons of Israel, [a]preaching [1b]peace through Jesus Christ (He is [c]Lord of all)—

37 you yourselves know the thing which took place throughout all Judea, starting from Galilee, after the baptism which John proclaimed.

38 "[1]*You know of* [a]Jesus of Nazareth, how God [b]anointed Him with the Holy Spirit and with power, [2c]and *how* He went about doing good and healing all who were oppressed by the devil, for [d]God was with Him.

39 "We are [a]witnesses of all the things He did both in the [1]land of the Jews and in Jerusalem. They also [b]put Him to death by hanging Him on a [2]cross.

40 "[a]God raised Him up on the third day and granted that He become visible,

41 [a]not to all the people, but to [b]witnesses who were chosen beforehand by God, *that is,* to us [c]who ate and drank with Him after He arose from the dead.

42 "And He [a]ordered us to [1]preach to the people, and solemnly to [b]testify that this is the One who has been [c]appointed by God as [d]Judge of the living and the dead.

11 [2]Or *vessel*
12 [1]Or *reptiles* [2]Or *heaven*
13 [1]Or *sacrifice*
14 [1]Or *profane;* lit *common* [a]Matt 8:2ff; John 4:11ff; Acts 9:5 [b]Lev 11:20-25; Deut 14:4-20; Ezek 4:14; Dan 1:8; Acts 10:28
15 [1]Lit *make common* [a]Matt 15:11; Mark 7:19; Rom 14:14; 1 Cor 10:25ff; 1 Tim 4:4f; Titus 1:15
16 [1]Or *vessel* [2]Or *heaven*
17 [1]Lit *himself* [a]Acts 10:3 [b]Acts 10:8
19 [1]One early ms reads *two* [a]Acts 10:3 [b]Acts 8:29
20 [1]Lit *doubting nothing* [a]Acts 15:7-9
22 [1]Lit *words* [a]Acts 10:2 [b]Matt 2:12 [c]Mark 8:38; Luke 9:26; Rev 14:10 [d]Acts 11:14
23 [a]Acts 10:45 [b]Acts 1:15 [c]Acts 9:36
24 [a]Acts 8:40
25 [1]Or *prostrated himself in reverence* [a]Matt 8:2
26 [a]Acts 14:15; Rev 19:10
27 [a]Acts 10:24
28 [1]Or *profane;* lit *common* [a]John 4:9; Acts 11:3 [b]Acts 10:14f
30 [1]I.e. 3 to 4 p.m. [a]Acts 10:9 [b]Acts 3:1 [c]Acts 10:3-6
31 [1]Or *deeds of charity*
32 [a]John 4:9; Acts 11:3
33 [1]Lit *done well in coming*
34 [a]Matt 5:2 [b]Deut 10:17; 2 Chr 19:7; Rom 2:11; Gal 2:6; Eph 6:9; Col 3:25; 1 Pet 1:17
35 [1]Or *reverences* [2]Lit *works righteousness* [a]Acts 10:28 [b]Acts 10:2
36 [1]Or *the gospel of peace* [a]Acts 13:32 [b]Luke 1:79; Rom 5:1; Eph 2:17 [c]Matt 28:18; Acts 2:36; Rom 10:12
38 [1]Or *How God anointed Jesus of Nazareth* [2]Lit *who went* [a]Acts 2:22 [b]Acts 4:26 [c]Matt 4:23 [d]John 3:2
39 [1]Or *countryside* [2]Lit *wood* [a]Luke 24:48; Acts 10:41 [b]Acts 5:30
40 [a]Acts 2:24
41 [a]John 14:19 [b]Luke 24:48; Acts 10:39 [c]Luke 24:43; Acts 1:4 mg
42 [1]Or *proclaim* [a]Acts 1:2 [b]Luke 16:28 [c]Luke 22:22 [d]John 5:22; Acts 17:31; 2 Tim 4:1; 1 Pet 4:5

43 "Of Him [a]all the prophets bear witness that through [b]His name everyone
who believes in Him receives forgiveness
of sins."
44 ¶ While Peter was still speaking
these words, [a]the Holy Spirit fell upon all
those who were listening to the [1]mes-
sage.
45 [a]All the [1]circumcised believers
who came with Peter were amazed, because the gift of the Holy Spirit had been
[b]poured out on the Gentiles also.
46 For they were hearing them
[a]speaking with tongues and exalting
God. Then Peter answered,
47 "[a]Surely no one can refuse the water for these to be baptized who [b]have
received the Holy Spirit just as we *did*,
can he?"
48 And he [a]ordered them to be baptized [b]in the name of Jesus Christ. Then
they asked him to stay on for a few days.

Peter Reports at Jerusalem

11 Now the apostles and [a]the brethren who were throughout Judea
heard that the Gentiles also had received
the word of God.
2 And when Peter came up to Jerusalem, [1a]those who were circumcised
took issue with him,
3 saying, "[a]You [1]went to uncircumcised men and ate with them."
4 But Peter began *speaking* [1]and
proceeded to explain to them [a]in orderly
sequence, saying,
5 "[a]I was in the city of Joppa praying;
and in a trance I saw [b]a vision, an [1]ob-
ject coming down like a great sheet lowered by four corners from [2]the sky; and
it came right down to me,
6 and when I had fixed my gaze on it
and was observing it [1]I saw the four-
footed animals of the earth and the wild
beasts and the [2]crawling creatures and
the birds of the [3]air.
7 "I also heard a voice saying to me,
'Get up, Peter; [1]kill and eat.'
8 "But I said, 'By no means, Lord, for
nothing [1]unholy or unclean has ever entered my mouth.'
9 "But a voice from heaven answered
a second time, '[a]What God has cleansed,
no longer [1]consider unholy.'
10 "This happened three times, and everything was drawn back up into [1]the
sky.
11 "And behold, at that moment three
men appeared at the house in which we
were *staying*, having been sent to me
from [a]Caesarea.
12 "[a]The Spirit told me to go with
them [1b]without misgivings. [c]These six
brethren also went with me and we entered the man's house.
13 "And he reported to us how he had
seen the angel [1]standing in his house,
and saying, 'Send to Joppa and have Simon, who is also called Peter, brought
here;
14 and he will speak [a]words to you by
which you will be saved, you and [b]all
your household.'
15 "And as I began to speak, [a]the Holy
Spirit fell upon them just [b]as *He did* upon
us at the beginning.
16 "And I remembered the word of the
Lord, how He used to say, '[a]John baptized with water, but you will be baptized
[1]with the Holy Spirit.'
17 "Therefore if [a]God gave to them the
same gift as *He gave* to us also after believing in the Lord Jesus Christ, [b]who
was I that I could [1]stand in God's way?"
18 When they heard this, they [1]quiet-
ed down and [a]glorified God, saying,
"Well then, God has granted to the Gentiles also the [b]repentance *that leads* to
life."

The Church at Antioch

19 ¶ [a]So then those who were scattered because of the [1]persecution that
occurred in connection with Stephen
made their way [2]to [b]Phoenicia and [c]Cy-
prus and [d]Antioch, speaking the word to
no one except to Jews alone.
20 But there were some of them, men
of [a]Cyprus and [b]Cyrene, who came to
[c]Antioch and *began* speaking to the
[1d]Greeks also, [2e]preaching the Lord
Jesus.
21 And [a]the hand of the Lord was
with them, and [b]a large number who
believed turned to the Lord.
22 The [1]news about them [2]reached
the ears of the church at Jerusalem, and
they sent [a]Barnabas off [3]to [b]Antioch.
23 Then when he arrived and [1]wit-
nessed [a]the grace of God, he rejoiced
and *began* to encourage them all with
[2]resolute heart to remain *true* to the
Lord;
24 for he was a good man, and [a]full of
the Holy Spirit and of faith. And [b]consid-
erable [1]numbers were [2]brought to the
Lord.
25 And he left for [a]Tarsus to look for
Saul;
26 and when he had found him, he
brought him to [a]Antioch. And for an entire year they [1]met with the church and
taught considerable [2]numbers; and [b]the

43 [a]Acts 3:18 [b]Luke 24:47; Acts 2:38
44 [1]Lit *word* [a]Acts 11:15
45 [1]Lit *believers from among the circumcision*; i.e. Jewish Christians [a]Acts 10:23 [b]Acts 2:33
46 [a]Mark 16:17; Acts 2:4
47 [a]Acts 8:36 [b]Acts 2:4
48 [a]1 Cor 1:14-17 [b]Acts 2:38
11:1 [a]Acts 1:15
2 [1]Lit *those of the circumcision*; i.e. Jewish Christians [a]Acts 10:45
3 [1]Or *entered the house of* [a]Matt 9:11; Acts 10:28; Gal 2:12
4 [1]Lit *and was explaining* [a]Luke 1:3
5 [1]Or *vessel* [2]Or *heaven* [a]Acts 10:9-32 [b]Acts 9:10
6 [1]Lit *and I saw* [2]Or *reptiles* [3]Or *heaven*
7 [1]Or *sacrifice*
8 [1]Or *profane*; lit *common*
9 [1]Lit *make common* [a]Acts 10:15
10 [1]Or *heaven*
11 [a]Acts 8:40
12 [1]Or *without making any distinction* [a]Acts 8:29 [b]Acts 15:9; Rom 3:22 [c]Acts 10:23
13 [1]Or *after he had stood in his house and said*
14 [a]Acts 10:22 [b]John 4:53; Acts 10:2; 1 Cor 1:16
15 [a]Acts 10:44 [b]Acts 2:4
16 [1]Or *in* [a]Acts 1:5
17 [1]Lit *prevent God* [a]Acts 10:45 [b]Acts 5:39
18 [1]Lit *became silent* [a]Matt 9:8 [b]2 Cor 7:10
19 [1]Lit *tribulation* [2]Lit *as far as* [a]Acts 8:1 [b]Acts 15:3 [c]Acts 4:36 [d]Acts 6:5; Gal 2:11
20 [1]Lit *Hellenists*; people who lived by Greek customs and culture [2]Or *bringing the good news of* [a]Acts 4:36 [b]Matt 27:32; Acts 2:10 [c]Acts 6:5; Gal 2:11 [d]John 7:35; Acts 6:1 [e]Acts 5:42
21 [a]Luke 1:66 [b]Acts 2:47
22 [1]Lit *word* [2]Lit *was heard in* [3]Lit *as far as* [a]Acts 4:36 [b]Acts 6:5; Gal 2:11
23 [1]Lit *saw* [2]Lit *purpose of heart* [a]Acts 13:43
24 [1]Lit *crowd was* [2]Lit *added* [a]Acts 2:4 [b]Acts 2:47

25 [a]Acts 9:11 **26** [1]Or *were gathered together* [2]Lit *crowd* [a]Acts 6:5 [b]John 2:2; Acts 1:15

disciples were first called [c]Christians in
[d]Antioch.
27 ¶ Now [1]at this time [a]some prophets came down from Jerusalem to [b]Anti-
och.
28 One of them named [a]Agabus stood
up and *began* to indicate [1]by the Spirit
that there would certainly be a great famine [b]all over the [2]world. [3]And this took
place in the *reign* of [c]Claudius.
29 And in the proportion that any of
[a]the disciples had means, each of them
determined to send *a contribution* for the
[1]relief of [b]the brethren living in Judea.
30 [a]And this they did, sending it [1]in
charge of [b]Barnabas and Saul to the [c]el-
ders.

Peter's Arrest and Deliverance

12 Now about that time [1]Herod the
king laid hands on some who belonged to the church in order to mistreat
them.
2 And he [a]had James the brother of
John [b]put to death with a sword.
3 When he saw that it [a]pleased the
Jews, he proceeded to arrest Peter also.
Now [1]it was during [b]the days of Unleavened Bread.
4 When he had seized him, he put
him in prison, delivering him to four
[1a]squads of soldiers to guard him, intending after [b]the Passover to bring him
out before the people.
5 So Peter was kept in the prison, but
prayer for him was being made fervently
by the church to God.
6 ¶ On [1]the very night when Herod
was about to bring him forward, Peter
was sleeping between two soldiers,
[a]bound with two chains, and guards in
front of the door were watching over the
prison.
7 And behold, [a]an angel of the Lord
suddenly [b]appeared and a light shone in
the cell; and he struck Peter's side and
woke him up, saying, "Get up quickly."
And [c]his chains fell off his hands.
8 And the angel said to him, "Gird
yourself and [1]put on your sandals." And
he did so. And he *said to him, "Wrap
your cloak around you and follow me."
9 And he went out and continued to
follow, and he did not know that what
was being done by the angel was real, but
thought he was seeing [a]a vision.
10 When they had passed the first and
second guard, they came to the iron gate
that leads into the city, which [a]opened
for them by itself; and they went out and
went along one street, and immediately
the angel departed from him.
11 When Peter [a]came [1]to himself, he
said, "Now I know for sure that [b]the
Lord has sent forth His angel and rescued
me from the hand of Herod and from all
[2]that the Jewish people were expecting."
12 And when he realized *this*, he went
to the house of Mary, the mother of
[a]John who was also called Mark, where
many were gathered together and [b]were
praying.
13 When he knocked at the door of the
gate, [a]a servant-girl named Rhoda came
to answer.
14 When she recognized Peter's voice,
[a]because of her joy she did not open the
gate, but ran in and announced that Peter
was standing in front of the gate.
15 They said to her, "You are out of
your mind!" But she kept insisting that it
was so. They kept saying, "It is [a]his angel."
16 But Peter continued knocking; and
when they had opened *the door*, they
saw him and were amazed.
17 But [a]motioning to them with his
hand to be silent, he described to them
how the Lord had led him out of the prison. And he said, "Report these things to
[1b]James and [c]the brethren." Then he
left and went to another place.
18 ¶ Now when day came, there was
no small disturbance among the soldiers
as to [1]what could have become of Peter.
19 When Herod had searched for him
and had not found him, he examined the
guards and ordered that they [a]be led
away *to execution*. Then he went down
from Judea to [b]Caesarea and was spending time there.

Death of Herod

20 ¶ Now he was very angry with the
people of [a]Tyre and Sidon; and with one
accord they came to him, and having won
over Blastus the king's chamberlain, they
were asking for peace, because [b]their
country was fed by the king's country.
21 On an appointed day Herod, having
put on his royal apparel, took his seat on
the [1]rostrum and *began* delivering an address to them.
22 The people kept crying out, "The
voice of a god and not of a man!"
23 And immediately [a]an angel of the
Lord struck him because he did not give
God the glory, and he was eaten by
worms and [1]died.
24 ¶ But [a]the word of the Lord continued to grow and to be multiplied.
25 ¶ And [a]Barnabas and [a]Saul returned [1]from Jerusalem [b]when they had
fulfilled their [2]mission, taking along with
them [c]John, who was also called Mark.

26 [c]Acts 26:28; 1 Pet 4:16 [d]Acts 6:5
27 [1]Lit *in these days* [a]Luke 11:49; Acts 2:17; 1 Cor 12:10 [b]Acts 6:5; Gal 2:11
28 [1]Or *through* [2]Lit *inhabited earth* [3]Lit *which* [a]Acts 21:10 [b]Matt 24:14 [c]Acts 18:2
29 [1]Lit *service* [a]John 2:2; Acts 1:15 [b]Acts 11:1
30 [1]Lit *by the hand of* [a]Acts 12:25 [b]Acts 4:36 [c]Acts 14:23; 1 Tim 5:17; Titus 1:5; James 5:14; 1 Pet 5:1; 2 John 1; 3 John 1
12:1 [1]I.e. Herod Agrippa I
2 [a]Matt 4:21 [b]Mark 10:39
3 [1]Lit *they were the days* [a]Acts 24:27 [b]Ex 12:15; Acts 20:6
4 [1]Lit *quaternions;* a quaternion was composed of four soldiers [a]John 19:23 [b]Ex 12:1-27; Mark 14:1; Acts 12:3
6 [1]Lit *that night* [a]Acts 21:33
7 [a]Acts 5:19 [b]Luke 2:9 [c]Acts 16:26
8 [1]Lit *bind*
9 [a]Acts 9:10
10 [a]Acts 5:19
11 [1]Lit *in himself* [2]Lit *the expectation of the people of the Jews* [a]Luke 15:17 [b]Dan 3:28
12 [a]Acts 12:25; Col 4:10; 2 Tim 4:11; Philem 24; 1 Pet 5:13 [b]Acts 12:5
13 [a]John 18:16f
14 [a]Luke 24:41
15 [a]Matt 18:10
17 [1]Or *Jacob* [a]Acts 13:16 [b]Mark 6:3; Acts 15:13; 1 Cor 15:7; Gal 1:19 [c]Acts 1:15
18 [1]Lit *what therefore had become*
19 [a]Acts 16:27 [b]Acts 8:40
20 [a]Matt 11:21 [b]1 Kin 5:11; Ezra 3:7; Ezek 27:17
21 [1]Or *judgment seat*
23 [1]Lit *breathed his last breath* [a]2 Sam 24:16; 2 Kin 19:35; Acts 5:19
24 [a]Acts 6:7
25 [1]Two early mss read *to Jerusalem* [2]Lit *ministry* [a]Acts 4:36 [b]Acts 11:30 [c]Acts 12:12

First Missionary Journey

13 Now there were at [a]Antioch, in the [b]church that was *there,* [c]prophets and [d]teachers: [e]Barnabas, and Simeon who was called Niger, and Lucius of [f]Cyrene, and Manaen who had been brought up with [g]Herod the tetrarch, and Saul.

2 While they were ministering to the Lord and fasting, [a]the Holy Spirit said, "Set apart for Me [b]Barnabas and Saul for [c]the work to which I have called them."

3 Then, when they had fasted and [a]prayed and [b]laid their hands on them, [c]they sent them away.

4 ¶ So, being [a]sent out by the Holy Spirit, they went down to Seleucia and from there they sailed to [b]Cyprus.

5 When they reached Salamis, they *began* to proclaim the word of God in [a]the synagogues of the Jews; and they also had [b]John as their helper.

6 When they had gone through the whole island as far as Paphos, they found a [a]magician, a Jewish [b]false prophet whose name was Bar-Jesus,

7 who was with the [a]proconsul, Sergius Paulus, a man of intelligence. This man summoned Barnabas and Saul and sought to hear the word of God.

8 But Elymas the [a]magician (for so his name is translated) was opposing them, seeking to turn the [b]proconsul away from [c]the faith.

9 But Saul, who was also *known as* Paul, [1a]filled with the Holy Spirit, fixed his gaze on him,

10 and said, "You who are full of all deceit and fraud, you [a]son of the devil, you enemy of all righteousness, will you not cease to make crooked [b]the straight ways of the Lord?

11 "Now, behold, [a]the hand of the Lord is upon you, and you will be blind and not see the sun for a time." And immediately a mist and a darkness fell upon him, and he went about seeking those who would lead him by the hand.

12 Then the [a]proconsul believed when he saw what had happened, being amazed at [b]the teaching of the Lord.

13 ¶ Now Paul and his companions put out to sea from [a]Paphos and came to [b]Perga in [c]Pamphylia; but [d]John left them and returned to Jerusalem.

14 But going on from Perga, they arrived at [a]Pisidian [b]Antioch, and on [c]the Sabbath day they went into [d]the synagogue and sat down.

15 After [a]the reading of the Law and [b]the Prophets [c]the synagogue officials sent to them, saying, "Brethren, if you have any word of exhortation for the people, say it."

16 Paul stood up, and [a]motioning with his hand said,

¶ "Men of Israel, and [b]you who fear God, listen:

17 "The God of this people Israel [a]chose our fathers and [1b]made the people great during their stay in the land of Egypt, and with an uplifted arm [c]He led them out from it.

18 "For [a]a period of about forty years [b]He put up with them in the wilderness.

19 "[a]When He had destroyed [b]seven nations in the land of Canaan, He [c]distributed their land as an inheritance—*all of which took* [d]about four hundred and fifty years.

20 "After these things He [a]gave *them* judges until [b]Samuel the prophet.

21 "Then they [a]asked for a king, and God gave them [b]Saul the son of Kish, a man of the tribe of Benjamin, for forty years.

22 "After He had [a]removed him, He raised up David to be their king, concerning whom He also testified and said, '[b]I HAVE FOUND DAVID the son of Jesse, A MAN AFTER MY HEART, who will do all My [1]will.'

23 "[a]From the descendants of this man, [b]according to promise, God has brought to Israel [c]a Savior, Jesus,

24 after [a]John had proclaimed before [1]His coming a [b]baptism of repentance to all the people of Israel.

25 "And while John [a]was completing his course, [b]he kept saying, 'What do you suppose that I am? I am not *He.* But behold, one is coming after me the sandals of whose feet I am not worthy to untie.'

26 ¶ "Brethren, sons of Abraham's family, and those among you who fear God, to us the message of [a]this salvation has been sent.

27 "For those who live in Jerusalem, and their [a]rulers, [b]recognizing neither Him nor the [1]utterances of [c]the prophets which are [d]read every Sabbath, fulfilled *these* by condemning *Him.*

28 "And though they found no ground for *putting Him to* death, they [a]asked Pilate that He be [1]executed.

29 "When they had [a]carried out all that was written concerning Him, [b]they took Him down from [c]the [1]cross and [d]laid Him in a tomb.

30 "But God [a]raised Him from the dead;

13:1 [a]Acts 11:19 [b]Acts 11:26 [c]Acts 11:27; 1 Cor 11:4f [d]Rom 12:6f; 1 Cor 12:28f; Eph 4:11; James 3:1 [e]Acts 4:36 [f]Matt 27:32; Acts 11:20 [g]Matt 14:1
2 [a]Acts 8:29 [b]Acts 4:36 [c]Acts 9:15
3 [a]Acts 1:24 [b]Acts 6:6 [c]Acts 13:4
4 [a]Acts 13:2f [b]Acts 4:36
5 [a]Acts 9:20 [b]Acts 12:12
6 [a]Acts 8:9 [b]Matt 7:15
7 [a]Acts 13:8
8 [a]Acts 8:9 [b]Acts 13:7 [c]Acts 6:7
9 [1]Or *having just been filled* [a]Acts 2:4
10 [a]Matt 13:38; John 8:44 [b]Hos 14:9; 2 Pet 2:15
11 [a]Ex 9:3; 1 Sam 5:6f; Job 19:21; Ps 32:4; Heb 10:31
12 [a]Acts 13:7 [b]Acts 8:25
13 [a]Acts 13:6 [b]Acts 14:25 [c]Acts 2:10 [d]Acts 12:12
14 [a]Acts 14:24 [b]Acts 14:19; 2 Tim 3:11 [c]Acts 13:42 [d]Acts 9:20
15 [a]Acts 15:21; 2 Cor 3:14f [b]Acts 13:27 [c]Mark 5:22
16 [a]Acts 12:17 [b]Acts 10:2
17 [1]Or *exalted* [a]Ex 6:1; Deut 7:6-8; Acts 7:17ff [b]Ex 1:7 [c]Ex 12:51
18 [a]Num 14:34; Acts 7:36 [b]Deut 1:31
19 [a]Acts 7:45 [b]Deut 7:1 [c]Josh 14:1; Ps 78:55 [d]Judg 11:26; 1 Kin 6:1
20 [a]Judg 2:16 [b]1 Sam 3:20; Acts 3:24
21 [a]1 Sam 8:5 [b]1 Sam 9:1f
22 [1]Lit *wishes* [a]1 Sam 15:23 [b]1 Sam 13:14; Ps 89:20; Acts 7:46
23 [a]Matt 1:1 [b]Acts 13:32f [c]Luke 2:11; John 4:42
24 [1]Lit *the face of His entering* [a]Mark 1:1-4; Acts 1:22 [b]Luke 3:3
25 [a]Acts 20:24 [b]Matt 3:11; Mark 1:7; Luke 3:16; John 1:20
26 [a]John 6:68; Acts 4:12
27 [1]Lit *voices* [a]Luke 23:13 [b]Acts 3:17 [c]Luke 24:27 [d]Acts 13:15
28 [1]Lit *destroyed* [a]Matt 27:22; Mark 15:13; Luke 23:21-23; John 19:15; Acts 3:14
29 [1]Lit *wood* [a]Acts 26:22 [b]Luke 23:53 [c]Acts 5:30 [d]Matt 27:57-61; Mark 15:42-47; Luke 23:50-56; John 19:38-42
30 [a]Acts 2:24

31 and for many days [a]He appeared to those who came up with Him from Galilee to Jerusalem, the very ones who are now [b]His witnesses to the people.

32 "And we [a]preach to you the good news of [b]the promise made to the fathers,

33 that God has fulfilled this *promise* [1]to our children in that He [a]raised up Jesus, as it is also written in the second Psalm, '[b]YOU ARE MY SON; TODAY I HAVE BEGOTTEN YOU.'

34 "*As for the fact* that He [a]raised Him up from the dead, no longer to return to decay, He has spoken in this way: '[b]I WILL GIVE YOU THE HOLY *and* [1]SURE *blessings* OF DAVID.'

35 "Therefore He also says in another *Psalm,* '[a]YOU WILL NOT [1]ALLOW YOUR [2]HOLY ONE TO [3]UNDERGO DECAY.'

36 "For [a]David, after he had [1]served [b]the purpose of God in his own generation, [c]fell asleep, and was laid among his fathers and [2]underwent decay;

37 but He whom God [a]raised did not [1]undergo decay.

38 "Therefore let it be known to you, brethren, that [a]through [1]Him forgiveness of sins is proclaimed to you,

39 and [1]through Him [a]everyone who believes is [2]freed [3]from all things, from which you could not be [2]freed [3]through the Law of Moses.

40 "Therefore take heed, so that the thing spoken of [a]in the Prophets may not come upon *you*:

41 '[a]BEHOLD, YOU SCOFFERS, AND
MARVEL, AND [1]PERISH;
FOR I AM ACCOMPLISHING A WORK
IN YOUR DAYS,
A WORK WHICH YOU WILL NEVER
BELIEVE, THOUGH SOMEONE
SHOULD DESCRIBE IT TO YOU.' "

42 ¶ As [1]Paul and Barnabas were going out, the people kept begging that these [2]things might be spoken to them the next [a]Sabbath.

43 Now when *the meeting of* the synagogue had broken up, many of the Jews and of the [a]God-fearing [1b]proselytes followed Paul and Barnabas, who, speaking to them, were urging them to continue in [c]the grace of God.

Paul Turns to the Gentiles

44 ¶ The next [a]Sabbath nearly the whole city assembled to hear the word of [1]the Lord.

45 But when [a]the Jews saw the crowds, they were filled with jealousy and *began* contradicting the things spoken by Paul, and were [1]blaspheming.

46 Paul and Barnabas spoke out boldly and said, "It was necessary that the word of God be spoken to you [a]first; since you repudiate it and judge yourselves unworthy of eternal life, behold, [b]we are turning to the Gentiles.

47 "For so the Lord has commanded us,
'[a]I HAVE PLACED YOU AS A [b]LIGHT
FOR THE GENTILES,
THAT YOU MAY [1]BRING SALVATION
TO THE END OF THE EARTH.' "

48 ¶ When the Gentiles heard this, they *began* rejoicing and glorifying [a]the word of [1]the Lord; and as many as [b]had been appointed to eternal life believed.

49 And [a]the word of the Lord was being spread through the whole region.

50 But [a]the Jews incited the [1b]devout women [c]of prominence and the leading men of the city, and instigated a persecution against Paul and Barnabas, and drove them out of their [2]district.

51 But [a]they shook off the dust of their feet *in protest* against them and went to [b]Iconium.

52 And the disciples were continually [a]filled with joy and with the Holy Spirit.

Acceptance and Opposition

14 In [a]Iconium [b]they entered the synagogue of the Jews together, and spoke in such a manner [c]that a large number of people believed, both of Jews and of [d]Greeks.

2 But [a]the Jews who [1b]disbelieved stirred up the [2]minds of the Gentiles and embittered them against [c]the brethren.

3 Therefore they spent a long time *there* [a]speaking boldly *with reliance* upon the Lord, who was testifying to the word of His grace, granting that [1b]signs and wonders be done by their hands.

4 [a]But the [1]people of the city were divided; and some [2]sided with [b]the Jews, and some with [c]the apostles.

5 And when an attempt was made by both the Gentiles and [a]the Jews with their rulers, to mistreat and to [b]stone them,

6 they became aware of it and fled to the cities of [a]Lycaonia, [b]Lystra and [c]Derbe, and the surrounding region;

7 and there they continued to [a]preach the gospel.

8 ¶ At [a]Lystra [b]a man was sitting who had no strength in his feet, lame from his mother's womb, who had never walked.

9 This man was listening to Paul as he spoke, who, [a]when he had fixed his gaze on him and had seen that he had [b]faith to be [1]made well,

31 [a]Acts 1:3 [b]Luke 24:48
32 [a]Acts 5:42 [b]Acts 13:23; Rom 1:2
33 [1]Late mss read *to us their children* [a]Acts 2:24 [b]Ps 2:7
34 [1]Lit *trustworthy* [a]Acts 2:24 [b]Is 55:3
35 [1]Lit *give* [2]Or *Devout* or *Pious* [3]Lit *see corruption* [a]Ps 16:10; Acts 2:27
36 [1]Or *served his own generation by the purpose of God* [2]Lit *saw corruption* [a]Acts 2:29 [b]Acts 13:22 [c]1 Kin 2:10; Acts 8:1
37 [1]Lit *see corruption* [a]Acts 2:24
38 [1]Lit *this One* [a]Luke 24:47; Acts 2:38
39 [1]Lit *in* or *by* [2]Lit *justified* [3]Lit *by* [a]Acts 10:43; Rom 3:28
40 [a]Luke 24:44; John 6:45; Acts 7:42
41 [1]Lit *disappear* [a]Hab 1:5
42 [1]Lit *they* [2]Lit *words* [a]Acts 13:14
43 [1]I.e. Gentile converts to Judaism [a]Acts 13:50 [b]Matt 23:15 [c]Acts 11:23
44 [1]One early ms reads *God* [a]Acts 13:14
45 [1]Or *slandering* him [a]Acts 13:50; 1 Thess 2:16
46 [a]Acts 3:26 [b]Acts 18:6
47 [1]Lit *be for salvation* [a]Is 42:6 [b]Luke 2:32
48 [1]Two early mss read *God* [a]Acts 13:12 [b]Rom 8:28ff; Eph 1:4f
49 [a]Acts 13:12
50 [1]Or *worshiping* [2]Lit *boundaries* [a]Acts 13:45; 1 Thess 2:14ff [b]Acts 13:43 [c]Mark 15:43
51 [a]Matt 10:14; Mark 6:11; Luke 9:5; Acts 18:6 [b]Acts 14:1; 2 Tim 3:11
52 [a]Acts 2:4
14:1 [a]Acts 13:51; 2 Tim 3:11 [b]Acts 13:5 [c]Acts 2:47 [d]John 7:35; Acts 18:4
2 [1]Or *disobeyed* [2]Lit *souls* [a]Acts 13:45; 1 Thess 2:14ff [b]John 3:36 [c]Acts 1:15
3 [1]Or *attesting miracles* [a]Acts 4:29f; Heb 2:4 [b]John 4:48
4 [1]Lit *multitude* [2]Lit *were* [a]Acts 17:4f [b]Acts 13:45; 1 Thess 2:14ff [c]Acts 14:14

5 [a]Acts 13:45; 1 Thess 2:14ff [b]Acts 14:19 **6** [a]Acts 14:11 [b]Acts 14:8; 2 Tim 3:11 [c]Acts 14:20 **7** [a]Acts 14:15 **8** [a]Acts 14:6; 2 Tim 3:11 [b]Acts 3:2 **9** [1]Lit *saved* [a]Acts 3:4 [b]Matt 9:28

10 said with a loud voice, "Stand upright on your feet." [a]And he leaped up
and *began* to walk.
11 When the crowds saw what Paul
had done, they raised their voice, saying
in the [a]Lycaonian language, "[b]The gods
have become like men and have come
down to us."
12 And they *began* calling Barnabas,
[1]Zeus, and Paul, [2]Hermes, because he
was [3]the chief speaker.
13 The priest of Zeus, whose *temple*
was [1]just outside the city, brought oxen
and garlands to the gates, and [a]wanted to
offer sacrifice with the crowds.
14 But when [a]the apostles Barnabas
and Paul heard of it, they [b]tore their
[1]robes and rushed out into the crowd,
crying out
15 and saying, "Men, why are you doing these things? We are also [a]men of the
same nature as you, and [b]preach the gospel to you that you should turn from these
[1][c]vain things to a [d]living God, [e]WHO
MADE THE HEAVEN AND THE EARTH AND THE
SEA AND ALL THAT IS IN THEM.
16 "[1]In the generations gone by He
[a]permitted all the [2]nations to [b]go their
own ways;
17 and yet [a]He did not leave Himself
without witness, in that He did good and
[b]gave you rains from heaven and fruitful
seasons, [1]satisfying your hearts with
food and gladness."
18 *Even* saying these things, with difficulty they restrained the crowds from offering sacrifice to them.
19 ¶ But [a]Jews came from [b]Antioch
and [c]Iconium, and having won over the
crowds, they [d]stoned Paul and dragged
him out of the city, supposing him to be
dead.
20 But while [a]the disciples stood
around him, he got up and entered the
city. The next day he went away with
Barnabas to [b]Derbe.
21 After they had [a]preached the gospel to that city and had [b]made many disciples, they returned to [c]Lystra and to
[d]Iconium and to [e]Antioch,
22 strengthening the souls of [a]the disciples, encouraging them to continue in
[b]the faith, and *saying*, "[c]Through many
tribulations we must enter the kingdom
of God."
23 When [a]they had appointed [b]el-
ders for them in every church, having
[c]prayed with fasting, they [d]commended
them to the Lord in whom they had believed.
24 ¶ They passed through [a]Pisidia
and came into [b]Pamphylia.
25 When they had spoken the word in
[a]Perga, they went down to Attalia.

10 [a]Acts 3:8
11 [a]Acts 14:6 [b]Acts 8:10
12 [1]Lat *Jupiter*, the chief pagan god [2]Lat *Mercury*, considered the messenger or spokesman for the pagan gods of Greece and Rome [3]Lit *the leader of the speaking*
13 [1]Lit *in front of* [a]Dan 2:46
14 [1]Or *outer garments* [a]Acts 14:4 [b]Num 14:6; Matt 26:65; Mark 14:63
15 [1]I.e. idols [a]Acts 10:26; James 5:17 [b]Acts 13:32 [c]Deut 32:21; 1 Sam 12:21; Jer 8:19; 1 Cor 8:4 [d]Matt 16:16 [e]Ex 20:11; Ps 146:6; Acts 4:24; Rev 14:7
16 [1]Lit *Who in the generations gone by permitted* [2]Or *Gentiles* [a]Acts 17:30 [b]Ps 81:12; Mic 4:5
17 [1]Lit *filling* [a]Acts 17:26f; Rom 1:19f [b]Deut 11:14; Job 5:10; Ps 65:10f; Ezek 34:26f; Joel 2:23
19 [a]Acts 13:45; 1 Thess 2:14ff [b]Acts 13:14 [c]Acts 13:51 [d]Acts 14:5; 2 Cor 11:25; 2 Tim 3:11
20 [a]Acts 11:26 [b]Acts 14:6
21 [a]Acts 14:7 [b]Acts 2:47 [c]Acts 14:6 [d]Acts 13:51 [e]Acts 13:14
22 [a]Acts 11:26 [b]Acts 6:7 [c]Mark 10:30; John 15:18; Acts 9:16; 1 Thess 3:3; 2 Tim 3:12; 1 Pet 2:21; Rev 1:9
23 [a]2 Cor 8:19; Titus 1:5 [b]Acts 11:30 [c]Acts 1:24 [d]Acts 20:32
24 [a]Acts 13:14 [b]Acts 13:13
25 [a]Acts 13:13
26 [1]Lit *fulfilled* [a]Acts 11:19 [b]Acts 13:3 [c]Acts 11:23
27 [1]Lit *that* [a]Acts 15:3 [b]1 Cor 16:9; 2 Cor 2:12; Col 4:3; Rev 3:8
28 [1]Lit *not a little* [a]Acts 11:26
15:1 [a]Acts 15:24 [b]Acts 1:15 [c]Lev 12:3; Acts 15:5; 1 Cor 7:18; Gal 2:11 [d]Acts 6:14
2 [1]Lit *not a little* [a]Acts 15:7 [b]Gal 2:2 [c]Acts 11:30
3 [a]Acts 20:38; Rom 15:24; 1 Cor 16:6; 2 Cor 1:16; Titus 3:13; 3 John 6 [b]Acts 11:19

26 From there they sailed to [a]Anti-
och, from [b]which they had been [c]com-
mended to the grace of God for the work
that they had [1]accomplished.
27 When they had arrived and gathered the church together, they *began* to
[a]report all things that God had done with
them and [1]how He had opened a [b]door
of faith to the Gentiles.
28 And they spent [1]a long time with
[a]the disciples.

The Council at Jerusalem

15 [a]Some men came down from Judea and *began* teaching [b]the
brethren, "Unless you are [c]circumcised
according to [d]the custom of Moses, you
cannot be saved."
2 And when Paul and Barnabas had
[1]great dissension and [a]debate with
them, [b]*the brethren* determined that
Paul and Barnabas and some others of
them should go up to Jerusalem to the
[c]apostles and elders concerning this issue.
3 Therefore, being [a]sent on their
way by the church, they were passing
through both [b]Phoenicia and Samaria,
[c]describing in detail the conversion of
the Gentiles, and were bringing great joy
to all [d]the brethren.
4 When they arrived at Jerusalem,
they were received by the church and
[a]the apostles and the elders, and they
[b]reported all that God had done with
them.
5 But some of [a]the sect of the [b]Phar-
isees who had believed stood up, saying,
"It is necessary to [c]circumcise them and
to direct them to observe the Law of Moses."
6 ¶ [a]The apostles and the elders
came together to [1]look into this [2]matter.
7 After there had been much [a]de-
bate, Peter stood up and said to them,
"Brethren, you know that [1]in the early
days [b]God made a choice among you,
that by my mouth the Gentiles would
hear the word of [c]the gospel and believe.
8 "And God, [a]who knows the heart,
testified to them [b]giving them the Holy
Spirit, just as He also did to us;
9 and [a]He made no distinction between us and them, [b]cleansing their
hearts by faith.
10 "Now therefore why do you [a]put
God to the test by placing upon the neck
of the disciples a yoke which [b]neither

[c]Acts 14:27 [d]Acts 1:15 **4** [a]Acts 11:30 [b]Acts 14:27 **5** [a]Acts 5:17 [b]Matt 3:7; Acts 26:5 [c]1 Cor 7:18; Gal 2:11 **6** [1]Lit *see about* [2]Lit *word* [a]Acts 11:30 **7** [1]Lit *from days of old* [a]Acts 15:2 [b]Acts 10:19f [c]Acts 20:24 **8** [a]Acts 1:24 [b]Acts 2:4 **9** [a]Acts 10:28 [b]Acts 10:43 **10** [a]Acts 5:9 [b]Matt 23:4; Gal 5:1

our fathers nor we have been able to
bear?
11 "But we believe that we are saved
through [a]the grace of the Lord Jesus, in
the same way as they also are."
12 ¶ All the people kept silent, and
they were listening to Barnabas and Paul
as they were [a]relating what [b]signs and
wonders God had done through them
among the Gentiles.

James's Judgment

13 After they had stopped speaking,
[1a]James answered, saying, "Brethren,
listen to me.
14 "[a]Simeon has related how God first
concerned Himself about taking from
among the Gentiles a people for His
name.
15 "With this the words of [a]the Prophets agree, just as it is written,
16 '[a]AFTER THESE THINGS [b]I will
return,
AND I WILL REBUILD THE
[1]TABERNACLE OF DAVID WHICH
HAS FALLEN,
AND I WILL REBUILD ITS RUINS,
AND I WILL RESTORE IT,
17 [a]SO THAT THE REST OF [1]MANKIND
MAY SEEK THE LORD,
AND ALL THE GENTILES [2b]WHO ARE
CALLED BY MY NAME,'
18 [a]SAYS THE LORD, WHO [1b]MAKES
THESE THINGS KNOWN FROM
LONG AGO.
19 "Therefore it is [a]my judgment that
we do not trouble those who are turning
to God from among the Gentiles,
20 but that we write to them that they
abstain from [1a]things contaminated by
idols and from [b]fornication and from
[c]what is strangled and from blood.
21 "For [a]Moses from ancient generations has in every city those who preach
him, since [1]he is read in the synagogues
every Sabbath."
22 ¶ Then it seemed good to [a]the
apostles and the elders, with the whole
church, to choose men from among them
to send to [b]Antioch with Paul and Barnabas—Judas called Barsabbas, and [c]Silas,
leading men among [d]the brethren,
23 and they [1]sent this letter by them,
"[a]The apostles and the brethren
who are elders, to [b]the brethren
in [c]Antioch and [d]Syria and [e]Ci-
licia who are from the Gentiles,
[f]greetings.
24 "Since we have heard that [a]some
[1]of our number to whom we
gave no instruction have [b]dis-
turbed you with *their* words, un-
settling your souls,
25 [a]it seemed good to us, having
[1]become of one mind, to select
men to send to you with our beloved Barnabas and Paul,
26 men who have [1a]risked their
lives for the name of our Lord
Jesus Christ.
27 "Therefore we have sent [a]Judas
and [b]Silas, who themselves will
also report the same things by
word *of mouth*.
28 "For [a]it seemed good to [b]the
Holy Spirit and to [c]us to lay upon
you no greater burden than these
essentials:
29 that you abstain from [a]things
sacrificed to idols and from
[a]blood and from [a]things strangled and from [a]fornication; [1]if
you keep yourselves free from
such things, you will do well.
Farewell."
30 ¶ So when they were sent away,
[a]they went down to Antioch; and having
gathered the [1]congregation together,
they delivered the letter.
31 When they had read it, they rejoiced because of its [1]encouragement.
32 [a]Judas and [b]Silas, also being
[c]prophets themselves, [1]encouraged and
strengthened [d]the brethren with a
lengthy message.
33 After they had spent time *there*,
they were sent away from the brethren
[a]in peace to those who had [b]sent them
out.
34 [[1]But it seemed good to Silas to remain there.]
35 But [a]Paul and Barnabas stayed in
Antioch, teaching and [b]preaching with
many others also, [c]the word of the Lord.

Second Missionary Journey

36 ¶ After some days Paul said to Barnabas, "Let us return and visit the brethren in [a]every city in which we proclaimed [b]the word of the Lord, *and see*
how they are."
37 Barnabas wanted to take [a]John,
called Mark, along with them also.
38 But Paul kept insisting that they
should not take him along who had [a]de-
serted them [1]in Pamphylia and had not
gone with them to the work.
39 And there occurred such a sharp
disagreement that they separated from
one another, and Barnabas took [a]Mark
with him and sailed away to [b]Cyprus.
40 But Paul chose [a]Silas and left, being [b]committed by the brethren to the
grace of the Lord.
41 And he was traveling through

11 [a]Rom 3:24; 2 Cor 13:14; Eph 2:5-8
12 [a]Acts 14:27 [b]John 4:48
13 [1]Or *Jacob* [a]Acts 12:17
14 [a]Acts 15:7; 2 Pet 1:1
15 [a]Acts 13:40
16 [1]Or *tent* [a]Amos 9:11 [b]Jer 12:15
17 [1]Gr *anthropoi* [2]Lit *upon whom My name is called* [a]Amos 9:12 [b]Deut 28:10; Is 63:19; Jer 14:9; Dan 9:19; James 2:7
18 [1]Or *does these things which were known* [a]Amos 9:12 [b]Is 45:21
19 [a]Acts 15:28
20 [1]Lit *the pollutions of* [a]Ex 34:15-17; Dan 1:8; Acts 15:29; 1 Cor 8:7; Rev 2:14 [b]Lev 18:6-23 [c]Gen 9:4; Lev 3:17; Deut 12:16; 1 Sam 14:33
21 [1]I.e. the books of Moses, Gen through Deut [a]Acts 13:15; 2 Cor 3:14f
22 [a]Acts 15:2 [b]Acts 11:20 [c]Acts 15:27; 2 Cor 1:19; 1 Thess 1:1; 2 Thess 1:1; 1 Pet 5:12 [d]Acts 15:1
23 [1]Lit *wrote by their hand* [a]Acts 15:2 [b]Acts 15:1 [c]Acts 11:20 [d]Matt 4:24; Acts 15:41; Gal 1:21 [e]Acts 6:9 [f]Acts 23:26; James 1:1; 2 John 10f
24 [1]Lit *from us* [a]Acts 15:1 [b]Gal 1:7
25 [1]Or *met together* [a]Acts 15:28
26 [1]Lit *given over* [a]Acts 9:23ff
27 [a]Acts 15:22 [b]Acts 15:22
28 [a]Acts 15:25 [b]Acts 5:32 [c]Acts 15:19
29 [1]Lit *from which keeping yourselves free* [a]Acts 15:20
30 [1]Or *multitude* [a]Acts 15:22f
31 [1]Or *exhortation*
32 [1]Or *exhorted* [a]Acts 15:22 [b]Acts 15:22 [c]Acts 13:1 [d]Acts 15:1
33 [a]Mark 5:34; Acts 16:36; 1 Cor 16:11; Heb 11:31 [b]Acts 15:22
34 [1]Early mss do not contain this v
35 [a]Acts 12:25 [b]Acts 8:4 [c]Acts 13:12

36 [a]Acts 13:4 [b]Acts 13:12 **37** [a]Acts 12:12 **38** [1]Lit *from* [a]Acts 13:13 **39** [a]Acts 12:12; Col 4:10 [b]Acts 4:36 **40** [a]Acts 15:22 [b]Acts 11:23

[a]Syria and [b]Cilicia, strengthening the
churches.

The Macedonian Vision

16 Paul came also to [a]Derbe and to
[a]Lystra. And a disciple was there,
named [b]Timothy, the son of a [c]Jewish
woman who was a believer, but his father
was a Greek,
2 and he was well spoken of by [a]the
brethren who were in [b]Lystra and [c]Ico-
nium.
3 Paul wanted this man to [1]go with
him; and he [a]took him and circumcised
him because of the Jews who were in
those parts, for they all knew that his
father was a Greek.
4 Now while they were passing
through the cities, they were delivering
[a]the decrees which had been decided
upon by [b]the apostles and [c]elders who
were in Jerusalem, for them to observe.
5 So [a]the churches were being
strengthened [1]in the faith, and were
[b]increasing in number daily.
6 ¶ They passed through the
[1a]Phrygian and [b]Galatian region, having been forbidden by the Holy Spirit to
speak the word in [2c]Asia;
7 and after they came to [a]Mysia,
they were trying to go into [b]Bithynia,
and the [c]Spirit of Jesus did not permit
them;
8 and passing by [a]Mysia, they came
down to [b]Troas.
9 [a]A vision appeared to Paul in the
night: a man of [b]Macedonia was standing
and appealing to him, and saying, "Come
over to Macedonia and help us."
10 When he had seen [a]the vision, immediately [b]we sought to [1]go into Macedonia, concluding that God had called us
to [c]preach the gospel to them.
11 ¶ So putting out to sea from [a]Tro-
as, we ran [b]a straight course to Samothrace, and on the day following to Neapolis;
12 and from there to [a]Philippi, which
is a leading city of the district of [b]Mace-
donia, [c]a *Roman* colony; and we were
staying in this city for some days.
13 And on [a]the Sabbath day we went
outside the gate to a riverside, where we
were supposing that there would be a
place of prayer; and we sat down and
began speaking to the women who had
assembled.

First Convert in Europe

14 A woman named Lydia, from the
city of [a]Thyatira, a seller of purple fabrics, [b]a worshiper of God, was listening;
[1]and the Lord [c]opened her heart to respond to the things spoken by Paul.
15 And when she and [a]her household
had been baptized, she urged us, saying,
"If you have judged me to be faithful to
the Lord, come into my house and stay."
And she prevailed upon us.
16 ¶ It happened that as we were going to [a]the place of prayer, a slave-girl
having [b]a spirit of divination met us,
who was bringing her masters much profit by fortune-telling.
17 Following after Paul and us, she
kept crying out, saying, "These men are
bond-servants of [a]the Most High God,
who are proclaiming to you [1]the way of
salvation."
18 She continued doing this for many
days. But Paul was greatly annoyed, and
turned and said to the spirit, "I command
you [a]in the name of Jesus Christ to come
out of her!" And it came out at that very
[1]moment.
19 ¶ But when her masters saw that
their hope of [a]profit was [1]gone, they
seized [b]Paul and Silas and [c]dragged
them into the market place before the
authorities,
20 and when they had brought them
to the chief magistrates, they said,
"These men are throwing our city into
confusion, being Jews,
21 and [a]are proclaiming customs
which it is not lawful for us to accept or
to observe, being [b]Romans."

Paul and Silas Imprisoned

22 The crowd rose up together against
them, and the chief magistrates tore their
[1]robes off them and proceeded to order
[2]*them* to be [a]beaten with rods.
23 When they had struck them with
many blows, they threw them into prison, commanding [a]the jailer to guard
them securely;
24 [1]and he, having received such a
command, threw them into the inner
prison and fastened their feet in [a]the
[2]stocks.
25 ¶ But about midnight [a]Paul and Silas were praying and [b]singing hymns of
praise to God, and the prisoners were
listening to them;
26 and suddenly [a]there came a great
earthquake, so that the foundations of the
prison house were shaken; and immediately [b]all the doors were opened and everyone's [c]chains were unfastened.
27 When [a]the jailer awoke and saw
the prison doors opened, he drew his
sword and was about [b]to kill himself,
supposing that the prisoners had escaped.
28 But Paul cried out with a loud

41 [a]Matt 4:24; Acts 15:23 [b]Acts 6:9
16:1 [a]Acts 14:6 [b]Acts 17:14f; Rom 16:21; 1 Cor 4:17; 2 Cor 1:1; Phil 1:1; Col 1:1; 1 Thess 1:1; 2 Thess 1:1; 1 Tim 1:2; 2 Tim 1:2; Philem 1; Heb 13:23 [c]2 Tim 1:5
2 [a]Acts 16:40 [b]Acts 14:6 [c]Acts 13:51
3 [1]Lit *go out* [a]Gal 2:3
4 [a]Acts 15:28f [b]Acts 15:2 [c]Acts 11:30
5 [1]Or *in faith* [a]Acts 9:31 [b]Acts 2:47
6 [1]Or *Phrygia and the Galatian region* [2]I.e. west coast province of Asia Minor [a]Acts 2:10 [b]Acts 18:23; 1 Cor 16:1; Gal 1:2; 2 Tim 4:10; 1 Pet 1:1 [c]Acts 2:9
7 [a]Acts 16:8 [b]1 Pet 1:1 [c]Luke 24:49; Acts 8:29; Rom 8:9; Gal 4:6; Phil 1:19; 1 Pet 1:11
8 [a]Acts 16:7 [b]Acts 16:11; 2 Cor 2:12; 2 Tim 4:13
9 [a]Acts 9:10 [b]Acts 16:10; Rom 15:26
10 [1]Lit *go out* [a]Acts 9:10 [b][we] Acts 16:10-17 [c]Acts 14:7
11 [a]Acts 16:8; 2 Cor 2:12; 2 Tim 4:13 [b]Acts 21:1
12 [a]Acts 20:6; Phil 1:1; 1 Thess 2:2 [b]Acts 16:9; Rom 15:26 [c]Acts 16:21
13 [a]Acts 13:14
14 [1]Lit *whose heart the Lord opened* [a]Rev 1:11 [b]Acts 13:43 [c]Luke 24:45
15 [a]Acts 11:14
16 [a]Acts 16:13 [b]Lev 19:31; Deut 18:11; 1 Sam 28:3; 2 Kin 21:6; 1 Chr 10:13; Is 8:19
17 [1]Lit *a way* [a]Mark 5:7
18 [1]Lit *hour* [a]Mark 16:17
19 [1]Lit *gone out* [a]Acts 16:16 [b]Acts 15:22 [c]Acts 8:3; James 2:6
21 [a]Esth 3:8 [b]Acts 16:12
22 [1]Or *outer garments* [2]Lit *to beat with rods* [a]2 Cor 11:25; 1 Thess 2:2
23 [a]Acts 16:27
24 [1]Lit *who* [2]Lit *wood* [a]Job 13:27; Jer 20:2f
25 [a]Acts 16:19 [b]Eph 5:19
26 [a]Acts 4:31 [b]Acts 12:10 [c]Acts 12:7 **27** [a]Acts 16:23 [b]Acts 12:19

voice, saying, "Do not harm yourself, for we are all here!"

29 And he called for lights and rushed in, and trembling with fear he fell down before [a]Paul and Silas,

30 and after he brought them out, he said, "Sirs, [a]what must I do to be saved?"

The Jailer Converted

31 They said, "[a]Believe in the Lord Jesus, and you will be saved, you and [b]your household."

32 And they spoke the word of [1]the Lord to him together with all who were in his house.

33 And he took them [a]that *very* hour of the night and washed their wounds, and immediately he was baptized, he and all his *household.*

34 And he brought them into his house and set [1]food before them, and rejoiced [2]greatly, having believed in God with [a]his whole household.

35 ¶ Now when day came, the chief magistrates sent their policemen, saying, "Release those men."

36 And [a]the jailer reported these words to Paul, *saying,* "The chief magistrates have sent to release you. Therefore come out now and go [b]in peace."

37 But Paul said to them, "They have beaten us in public without trial, [a]men who are Romans, and have thrown us into prison; and now are they sending us away secretly? No indeed! But let them come themselves and bring us out."

38 The policemen reported these words to the chief magistrates. [a]They were afraid when they heard that they were Romans,

39 and they came and appealed to them, and when they had brought them out, they kept begging them [a]to leave the city.

40 They went out of the prison and entered *the house of* [a]Lydia, and when they saw [b]the brethren, they [1]encouraged them and departed.

Paul at Thessalonica

17 Now when they had traveled through Amphipolis and Apollonia, they came to [a]Thessalonica, where there was a synagogue of the Jews.

2 And [a]according to Paul's custom, he went to them, and for three [b]Sabbaths reasoned with them from [c]the Scriptures,

3 [1]explaining and [2]giving evidence that the [3]Christ [a]had to suffer and [b]rise again from the dead, and *saying,* "[c]This Jesus whom I am proclaiming to you is the [3]Christ."

4 [a]And some of them were persuaded and joined [b]Paul and Silas, [1]along with a large number of the [c]God-fearing [d]Greeks and [2]a number of the [e]leading women.

5 But [a]the Jews, becoming jealous and taking along some wicked men from the market place, formed a mob and set the city in an uproar; and attacking the house of [b]Jason, they were seeking to bring them out to the people.

6 When they did not find them, they *began* [a]dragging Jason and some brethren before the city authorities, shouting, "These men who have upset [1b]the world have come here also;

7 [1]and Jason [a]has welcomed them, and they all act [b]contrary to the decrees of Caesar, saying that there is another king, Jesus."

8 They stirred up the crowd and the city authorities who heard these things.

9 And when they had received a [1]pledge from [a]Jason and the others, they released them.

Paul at Berea

10 ¶ [a]The brethren immediately sent [b]Paul and Silas away by night to [c]Berea, [1]and when they arrived, they went into [d]the synagogue of the Jews.

11 Now these were more noble-minded than those in [a]Thessalonica, [1]for they received the word with [2]great eagerness, examining the Scriptures daily *to see* whether these things were so.

12 Therefore [a]many of them believed, [1]along with a number of [b]prominent Greek [c]women and men.

13 But when the Jews of [a]Thessalonica found out that the word of God had been proclaimed by Paul in [b]Berea also, they came there as well, agitating and stirring up the crowds.

14 Then immediately [a]the brethren sent Paul out to go as far as the sea; and [b]Silas and [c]Timothy remained there.

15 Now [a]those who escorted Paul brought him as far as [b]Athens; and receiving a command for [c]Silas and Timothy to [d]come to him as soon as possible, they left.

Paul at Athens

16 ¶ Now while Paul was waiting for them at [a]Athens, his spirit was being provoked within him as he was observing the city full of idols.

17 So he was reasoning [a]in the synagogue with the Jews and [b]the God-fearing *Gentiles,* and in the market place every day with those who happened to be present.

18 And also some of the Epicurean and Stoic philosophers were [1]conversing

---

29 [a]Acts 16:19
30 [a]Acts 2:37; 22:10
31 [a]Mark 16:16 [b]Acts 11:14; 16:15
32 [1]Two early mss read *God*
33 [a]Acts 16:25
34 [1]Lit *a table* [2]Or *greatly with his whole household, having believed in God* [a]Acts 11:14; 16:15
36 [a]Acts 16:27 [b]Acts 15:33
37 [a]Acts 22:25-29
38 [a]Acts 22:29
39 [a]Matt 8:34
40 [1]Or *exhorted* [a]Acts 16:14 [b]Acts 1:15; 16:2
17:1 [a]Acts 17:11,13; 20:4; 27:2; Phil 4:16; 1 Thess 1:1; 2 Thess 1:1; 2 Tim 4:10
2 [a]Acts 9:20; 17:10,17 [b]Acts 13:14 [c]Acts 8:35
3 [1]Lit *opening* [2]Lit *placing before* [3]I.e. Messiah [a]Acts 3:18 [b]John 20:9 [c]Acts 9:22; 18:5,28
4 [1]Lit *and a large* [2]Lit *not a few* [a]Acts 14:4 [b]Acts 15:22,40; 17:10,14f [c]Acts 13:43; 17:17 [d]John 7:35 [e]Acts 13:50
5 [a]Acts 17:13; 1 Thess 2:14ff [b]Acts 17:6,7,9; Rom 16:21
6 [1]Lit *the inhabited earth* [a]Acts 16:19f [b]Matt 24:14; Acts 17:31
7 [1]Lit *whom Jason has welcomed* [a]Luke 10:38; James 2:25 [b]Luke 23:2
9 [1]Or *bond* [a]Acts 17:5
10 [1]Lit *who when...arrived went* [a]Acts 1:15; 17:6,14f [b]Acts 17:4 [c]Acts 17:13; 20:4 [d]Acts 17:1f
11 [1]Lit *who received* [2]Lit *all* [a]Acts 17:1
12 [1]Lit *and not a few* [a]Acts 2:47 [b]Mark 15:43 [c]Acts 13:50
13 [a]Acts 17:1 [b]Acts 17:10; 20:4
14 [a]Acts 1:15; 17:6,10 [b]Acts 15:22; 17:4,10 [c]Acts 16:1
15 [a]Acts 15:3 [b]Acts 17:16,21f; 18:1; 1 Thess 3:1 [c]Acts 17:14 [d]Acts 18:5
16 [a]Acts 17:15, 21f; 18:1; 1 Thess 3:1
17 [a]Acts 9:20; 17:2 [b]Acts 17:4
18 [1]Or *disputing*

with him. Some were saying, "What
would [a]this [2]idle babbler wish to say?"
Others, "He seems to be a proclaimer
of strange deities,"—because he was
preaching [b]Jesus and the resurrection.
19 And they [a]took him and brought
him [1]to the [2b]Areopagus, saying, "May
we know what [c]this new teaching is
[3]which you are proclaiming?
20 "For you are bringing some strange
things to our ears; so we want to know
what these things mean."
21 (Now all the Athenians and the
strangers [a]visiting there used to spend
their time in nothing other than telling or
hearing something new.)

Sermon on Mars Hill

22 ¶ So Paul stood in the midst of the
[1]Areopagus and said, "Men of [a]Athens,
I observe that you are very [b]religious in
all respects.
23 "For while I was passing through
and examining the [a]objects of your worship, I also found an altar with this inscription, 'TO AN UNKNOWN GOD.'
Therefore what [b]you worship in ignorance, this I proclaim to you.
24 "[a]The God who made the world and
all things in it, since He is [b]Lord of heav-
en and earth, does not [c]dwell in temples
made with hands;
25 nor is He served by human hands,
[a]as though He needed anything, since
He Himself gives to all *people* life and
breath and all things;
26 and [a]He made from one *man* every
nation of mankind to live on all the face
of the earth, having [b]determined *their*
appointed times and the boundaries of
their habitation,
27 that they would seek God, if perhaps they might grope for Him and find
Him, [a]though He is not far from each one
of us;
28 for [a]in Him we live and move and
[1]exist, as even some of your own poets
have said, 'For we also are His children.'
29 "Being then the children of God, we
[a]ought not to think that the Divine Nature is like gold or silver or stone, an
image formed by the art and thought of
man.
30 "Therefore having [a]overlooked
[b]the times of ignorance, God is [c]now
declaring to men that all *people* everywhere should repent,
31 because He has fixed [a]a day in
which [b]He will judge [1c]the world in
righteousness [2]through a Man whom He
has [d]appointed, having furnished proof
to all men [3]by [e]raising Him from the
dead."
32 ¶ Now when they heard of [a]the
resurrection of the dead, some *began* to
sneer, but others said, "We shall hear you
[1]again concerning this."
33 So Paul went out of their midst.
34 But some men joined him and believed, among whom also were Dionysius
the [a]Areopagite and a woman named
Damaris and others with them.

Paul at Corinth

18 After these things he left [a]Athens
and went to [b]Corinth.
2 And he found a Jew named [a]Aqui-
la, a native of [b]Pontus, having recently
come from [c]Italy with his wife [a]Priscilla,
because [d]Claudius had commanded all
the Jews to leave Rome. He came to
them,
3 and because he was of the same
trade, he stayed with them and [a]they
were working, for by trade they were
tent-makers.
4 And he was reasoning [a]in the synagogue every [b]Sabbath and trying to persuade [c]Jews and Greeks.
5 ¶ But when [a]Silas and Timothy
[b]came down from [c]Macedonia, Paul *began* devoting himself completely to the
word, solemnly [d]testifying to the Jews
that [e]Jesus was the [1]Christ.
6 But when they resisted and blasphemed, he [a]shook out his garments and
said to them, "Your [b]blood *be* on your
own heads! I am clean. From now on I
will go [c]to the Gentiles."
7 Then he left there and went to the
house of a man named [1]Titius Justus, [a]a
worshiper of God, whose house was next
to the synagogue.
8 [a]Crispus, [b]the leader of the synagogue, believed in the Lord [c]with all his
household, and many of the [d]Corinthi-
ans when they heard were believing and
being baptized.
9 And the Lord said to Paul in the
night by [a]a vision, "Do not be afraid *any
longer*, but go on speaking and do not be
silent;
10 for I am with you, and no man will
attack you in order to harm you, for I have
many people in this city."
11 And he settled *there* a year and six
months, teaching the word of God among
them.
12 ¶ But while Gallio was [a]proconsul
of [b]Achaia, [c]the Jews with one accord
rose up against Paul and brought him before [d]the judgment seat,
13 saying, "This man persuades men
to worship God contrary to [a]the law."

18 [2]I.e. one who makes his living by picking up scraps [a]1 Cor 1:20 [b]Acts 4:2
19 [1]Or *before* [2]Or *Hill of Ares*, god of war [3]Lit *which is being spoken by you* [a]Acts 23:19 [b]Acts 17:22 [c]Mark 1:27
21 [a]Acts 2:10
22 [1]Or *the Council of the Areopagus* [a]Acts 17:15 [b]Acts 25:19
23 [a]2 Thess 2:4 [b]John 4:22
24 [a]Is 42:5; Acts 14:15 [b]Deut 10:14; Ps 115:16; Matt 11:25 [c]1 Kin 8:27; Acts 7:48
25 [a]Job 22:2; Ps 50:10-12
26 [a]Mal 2:10 [b]Deut 32:8; Job 12:23
27 [a]Deut 4:7; Jer 23:23f; Acts 14:17
28 [1]Lit *are* [a]Job 12:10; Dan 5:23
29 [a]Is 40:18ff; Rom 1:23
30 [a]Acts 14:16; Rom 3:25 [b]Acts 17:23 [c]Luke 24:47; Acts 26:20; Titus 2:11f
31 [1]Lit *the inhabited earth* [2]Lit *by* or *in* [3]Or *when He raised* [a]Matt 10:15 [b]Ps 9:8; John 5:22; Acts 10:42 [c]Matt 24:14; Acts 17:6 [d]Luke 22:22 [e]Acts 2:24
32 [1]Lit *also again* [a]Acts 17:18
34 [a]Acts 17:19
18:1 [a]Acts 17:15 [b]Acts 18:8; 1 Cor 1:2; 2 Cor 1:1; 2 Tim 4:20
2 [a]Acts 18:18; Rom 16:3; 1 Cor 16:19; 2 Tim 4:19 [b]Acts 2:9 [c]Acts 27:1; Heb 13:24 [d]Acts 11:28
3 [a]Acts 20:34; 1 Cor 4:12; 2 Cor 11:7; 1 Thess 2:9; 2 Thess 3:8
4 [a]Acts 9:20 [b]Acts 13:14 [c]Acts 14:1
5 [1]I.e. Messiah [a]Acts 15:22 [b]Acts 17:15 [c]Acts 16:9 [d]Luke 16:28; Acts 20:21 [e]Acts 17:3
6 [a]Neh 5:13; Acts 13:51 [b]2 Sam 1:16; 1 Kin 2:33; Ezek 18:13; Matt 27:25; Acts 20:26 [c]Acts 13:46
7 [1]One early ms reads *Titus*; two other early mss omit the name [a]Acts 13:43

8 [a]1 Cor 1:14 [b]Mark 5:22 [c]Acts 11:14 [d]Acts 18:1; 1 Cor 1:2; 2 Cor 1:1; 2 Tim 4:20 **9** [a]Acts 9:10 **12** [a]Acts 13:7 [b]Acts 18:27; Rom 15:26; 1 Cor 16:15; 2 Cor 1:1; 1 Thess 1:7f [c]1 Thess 2:14ff [d]Matt 27:19 **13** [a]John 19:7; Acts 18:15

14 But when Paul was about to [a]open his mouth, Gallio said to the Jews, "If it were a matter of wrong or of vicious crime, O Jews, it would be reasonable for me to put up with you;

15 but if there are [a]questions about words and names and your own law, look after it yourselves; I am unwilling to be a judge of these matters."

16 And he drove them away from [a]the judgment seat.

17 And they all took hold of [a]Sosthenes, [b]the leader of the synagogue, and *began* beating him in front of [c]the judgment seat. But Gallio was not concerned about any of these things.

18 ¶ Paul, having remained many days longer, [a]took leave of [b]the brethren and put out to sea for [c]Syria, and with him were [d]Priscilla and [d]Aquila. In [e]Cenchrea [1]he [f]had his hair cut, for he was keeping a vow.

19 They came to [a]Ephesus, and he left them there. Now he himself entered [b]the synagogue and reasoned with the Jews.

20 When they asked him to stay for a longer time, he did not consent,

21 but [a]taking leave of them and saying, "I will return to you again [b]if God wills," he set sail from [c]Ephesus.

22 ¶ When he had landed at [a]Caesarea, he went up and greeted the church, and went down to [b]Antioch.

Third Missionary Journey

23 And having spent some time *there,* he left and passed successively through the [a]Galatian region and Phrygia, strengthening all the disciples.

24 ¶ Now a Jew named [a]Apollos, an [b]Alexandrian by birth, [1]an eloquent man, came to [c]Ephesus; and he was mighty in the Scriptures.

25 This man had been instructed in [a]the way of the Lord; and being fervent in spirit, he was speaking and teaching accurately the things concerning Jesus, being acquainted only with [b]the baptism of John;

26 and [1]he began to speak out boldly in the synagogue. But when [a]Priscilla and Aquila heard him, they took him aside and explained to him [b]the way of God more accurately.

27 And when he wanted to go across to [a]Achaia, [b]the brethren encouraged him and wrote to [c]the disciples to welcome him; and when he had arrived, he greatly [1]helped those who had believed through grace,

28 for he powerfully refuted the Jews in public, demonstrating [a]by the Scriptures that [b]Jesus was the [1]Christ.

Paul at Ephesus

19 It happened that while [a]Apollos was at [b]Corinth, Paul passed through the [c]upper country and came to [d]Ephesus, and found some disciples.

2 He said to them, "[a]Did you receive the Holy Spirit when you believed?" And they *said* to him, "No, [b]we have not even heard whether [1]there is a Holy Spirit."

3 And he said, "Into what then were you baptized?" And they said, "[a]Into John's baptism."

4 Paul said, "[a]John baptized with the baptism of repentance, telling the people [b]to believe in Him who was coming after him, that is, in Jesus."

5 When they heard this, they were [a]baptized [1]in the name of the Lord Jesus.

6 And when Paul had [a]laid his hands upon them, the Holy Spirit came on them, and they *began* [b]speaking with tongues and [c]prophesying.

7 There were in all about twelve men.

8 ¶ And he entered [a]the synagogue and continued speaking out boldly for three months, reasoning and persuading *them* [b]about the kingdom of God.

9 But when [a]some were becoming hardened and disobedient, speaking evil of [b]the Way before the [1]people, he withdrew from them and took away [c]the disciples, reasoning daily in the school of Tyrannus.

10 This took place for [a]two years, so that all who lived in [1b]Asia heard [c]the word of the Lord, both Jews and Greeks.

Miracles at Ephesus

11 ¶ God was performing [a]extraordinary [1]miracles by the hands of Paul,

12 [a]so that handkerchiefs or aprons were even carried from his body to the sick, and the diseases left them and [b]the evil spirits went out.

13 But also some of the Jewish [a]exorcists, who went from place to place, attempted to name over those who had the evil spirits the name of the Lord Jesus, saying, "I adjure you by Jesus whom Paul preaches."

14 Seven sons of one Sceva, a Jewish chief priest, were doing this.

15 And the evil spirit answered and said to them, "I recognize Jesus, and I know about Paul, but who are you?"

16 And the man, in whom was the evil spirit, leaped on them and subdued all of them and overpowered them, so that they fled out of that house naked and wounded.

14 [a]Matt 5:2
15 [a]Acts 23:29
16 [a]Matt 27:19
17 [a]1 Cor 1:1 [b]Acts 18:8 [c]Matt 27:19
18 [1]Lit *having his hair cut* [a]Mark 6:46 [b]Acts 1:15 [c]Matt 4:24 [d]Acts 18:2 [e]Rom 16:1 [f]Num 6:2; Acts 21:24
19 [a]Acts 18:21; 1 Cor 15:32; Eph 1:1; 1 Tim 1:3; 2 Tim 1:18; Rev 1:11 [b]Acts 18:4
21 [a]Mark 6:46 [b]Rom 1:10; 1 Cor 4:19; Heb 6:3; James 4:15; 1 Pet 3:17 [c]Acts 18:19; 1 Cor 15:32; Eph 1:1; 1 Tim 1:3; 2 Tim 1:18; Rev 1:11
22 [a]Acts 8:40 [b]Acts 11:19
23 [a]Acts 16:6
24 [1]Or a *learned man* [a]Acts 19:1; 1 Cor 1:12; Titus 3:13 [b]Acts 6:9 [c]Acts 18:19
25 [a]Acts 9:2 [b]Luke 7:29; Acts 19:3
26 [1]Lit *this man* [a]Acts 18:2 [b]Acts 18:25
27 [1]Or *helped greatly through grace those who had believed* [a]Acts 18:12 [b]Acts 18:18 [c]Acts 11:26
28 [1]I.e. Messiah [a]Acts 8:35 [b]Acts 18:5
19:1 [a]Acts 18:24; 1 Cor 1:12; Titus 3:13 [b]Acts 18:1 [c]Acts 18:23 [d]Acts 18:21; 1 Cor 15:32; Eph 1:1; 1 Tim 1:3; 2 Tim 1:18; Rev 1:11
2 [1]Or *the Holy Spirit has been given* [a]Acts 8:15f [b]John 7:39
3 [a]Luke 7:29; Acts 18:25
4 [a]Matt 3:11; Mark 1:4; Luke 3:16; John 1:26; Acts 13:24 [b]John 1:7
5 [1]Lit *into* [a]Acts 8:12
6 [a]Acts 6:6 [b]Mark 16:17; Acts 2:4 [c]Acts 13:1
8 [a]Acts 9:20 [b]Acts 1:3
9 [1]Lit *multitude* [a]Acts 14:4 [b]Acts 9:2 [c]Acts 11:26
10 [1]I.e. west coast province of Asia Minor [a]Acts 19:8 [b]Acts 16:6 [c]Acts 13:12
11 [1]Or *works of power* [a]Acts 8:13
12 [a]Acts 5:15 [b]Mark 16:17
13 [a]Matt 12:27; Luke 11:19

17 This became known to all, both
Jews and Greeks, who lived in [a]Ephesus;
and fear fell upon them all and the name
of the Lord Jesus was being magnified.
18 Many also of those who had believed kept coming, confessing and disclosing their practices.
19 And many of those who practiced
magic brought their books together and
began burning them in the sight of everyone; and they counted up the price of
them and found it [1]fifty thousand
[a]pieces of silver.
20 So [1a]the word of the Lord [b]was
growing mightily and prevailing.
21 ¶ Now after these things were finished, Paul purposed in the [1]spirit to [a]go
to Jerusalem [b]after he had passed
through [c]Macedonia and [d]Achaia, saying, "After I have been there, [e]I must
also see Rome."
22 And having sent into [a]Macedonia
two of [b]those who ministered to him,
[c]Timothy and [d]Erastus, he himself
stayed in [1e]Asia for a while.
23 ¶ About that time there occurred
no small disturbance concerning [a]the
Way.
24 For a man named Demetrius, a silversmith, who made silver shrines of
[1]Artemis, [a]was bringing no little [2]busi-
ness to the craftsmen;
25 these he gathered together with
the workmen of similar *trades,* and said,
"Men, you know that our prosperity [1]de-
pends upon this business.
26 "You see and hear that not only in
[a]Ephesus, but in almost all of [1b]Asia,
this Paul has persuaded and turned away
a considerable number of people, saying
that [2c]gods made with hands are no
gods *at all.*
27 "Not only is there danger that this
trade of ours fall into disrepute, but also
that the temple of the great goddess [1]Ar-
temis be regarded as worthless and that
she whom all of [2a]Asia and [b]the [3]world
worship will even be dethroned from her
magnificence."
28 ¶ When they heard *this* and were
filled with rage, they *began* crying out,
saying, "Great is [1]Artemis of the [a]Ephe-
sians!"
29 The city was filled with the confusion, and they rushed [1]with one accord
into the theater, dragging along [a]Gaius
and [b]Aristarchus, Paul's traveling [c]com-
panions from [d]Macedonia.
30 And when Paul wanted to go into
the [1]assembly, [a]the disciples would not
let him.
31 Also some of the [1]Asiarchs who
were friends of his sent to him and repeatedly urged him not to [2]venture into
the theater.
32 [a]So then, some were shouting one
thing and some another, for the [1]assem-
bly was in confusion and the majority did
not know [2]for what reason they had
come together.
33 Some of the crowd [1]concluded *it*
was Alexander, since the Jews had put
him forward; and having [a]motioned with
his hand, Alexander was intending to
make a defense to the [2]assembly.
34 But when they recognized that he
was a Jew, a *single* outcry arose from
them all as they shouted for about two
hours, "Great is [1]Artemis of the Ephesians!"
35 After quieting the crowd, the town
clerk *said, "Men of [a]Ephesus, what
man is there after all who does not know
that the city of the Ephesians is guardian
of the temple of the great [1]Artemis and
of the *image* which fell down from
[2]heaven?
36 "So, since these are undeniable
facts, you ought to keep calm and to do
nothing rash.
37 "For you have brought these men
here who are neither [a]robbers of temples nor blasphemers of our goddess.
38 "So then, if Demetrius and the
craftsmen who are with him have a complaint against any man, the courts are in
session and [1a]proconsuls are *available;*
let them bring charges against one another.
39 "But if you want anything beyond
this, it shall be settled in the [1]lawful [2]as-
sembly.
40 "For indeed we are in danger of being accused of a riot in connection with
today's events, since there is no *real*
cause *for it,* and in this connection we
will be unable to account for this disorderly gathering."
41 After saying this he dismissed the
[1]assembly.

Paul in Macedonia and Greece

20 After the uproar had ceased, Paul
sent for [a]the disciples, and when
he had exhorted them and taken his leave
of them, he left [b]to go to [c]Macedonia.
2 When he had gone through those
districts and had given them much exhortation, he came to Greece.
3 And *there* he spent three months,
and when [a]a plot was formed against
him by the Jews as he was about to set
sail for [b]Syria, he decided to return
through [c]Macedonia.
4 And [1]he was accompanied by So-
pater of [a]Berea, *the son* of Pyrrhus, and
by [b]Aristarchus and Secundus of the

17 [a]Acts 18:19
19 [1]Probably fifty thousand Greek drachmas; a drachma approximated a day's wage [a]Luke 15:8
20 [1]Or *according to the power of the Lord the word was growing* [a]Acts 19:10 [b]Acts 6:7
21 [1]Or *Spirit* [a]Acts 20:16; Rom 15:25; 2 Cor 1:16 [b]Acts 20:1; 1 Cor 16:5 [c]Acts 16:9; Rom 15:26; 1 Thess 1:7f [d]Acts 18:12 [e]Acts 23:11; Rom 15:24
22 [1]I.e. west coast province of Asia Minor [a]Acts 16:9 [b]Acts 13:5; 2 Cor 8:19 [c]Acts 16:1 [d]Rom 16:23; 2 Tim 4:20 [e]Acts 19:10
23 [a]Acts 19:9
24 [1]Lat *Diana* [2]Or *profit* [a]Acts 16:16
25 [1]Lit *is from*
26 [1]V 22, note 1 [2]Lit *those* [a]Acts 18:19 [b]Acts 19:10 [c]Deut 4:28; Ps 115:4; Is 44:10-20; Jer 10:3ff; Acts 17:29; 1 Cor 8:4; Rev 9:20
27 [1]Lat *Diana* [2]V 22, note 1 [3]Lit *the inhabited earth* [a]Acts 19:10 [b]Matt 24:14
28 [1]Lat *Diana* [a]Acts 18:19
29 [1]Or *together* [a]Acts 20:4 [b]Acts 20:4; Col 4:10; Philem 24 [c]Acts 13:5; 2 Cor 8:19 [d]Acts 16:9
30 [1]Lit *people* [a]Acts 19:9
31 [1]I.e. political or religious officials of the province of Asia [2]Lit *give himself*
32 [1]Gr *ekklesia* [2]Or *on whose account* [a]Acts 21:34
33 [1]Or *advised Alexander* [2]Lit *people* [a]Acts 12:17
34 [1]Lat *Diana*
35 [1]Lat *Diana* [2]Lit *Zeus;* Lat *Jupiter* [a]Acts 18:19
37 [a]Rom 2:22
38 [1]Or *provincial governors* [a]Acts 13:7
39 [1]Or *regular* [2]Gr *ekklesia*
41 [1]Gr *ekklesia*
20:1 [a]Acts 11:26 [b]Acts 19:21 [c]Acts 16:9
3 [a]Acts 9:23f [b]Matt 4:24 [c]Acts 16:9
4 [1]Lit *there accompanied him* [a]Acts 17:10 [b]Acts 19:29

[c]Thessalonians, and [d]Gaius of [e]Derbe,
and [f]Timothy, and [g]Tychicus and
[h]Trophimus of [2][i]Asia.
5 But these had gone on ahead and
were waiting for [a]us at [b]Troas.
6 [a]We sailed from [b]Philippi after
[c]the days of Unleavened Bread, and
came to them at [d]Troas within five days;
and there we stayed seven days.
7 ¶ On [a]the first day of the week,
when [b]we were gathered together to
[c]break bread, Paul *began* talking to
them, intending to leave the next day,
and he prolonged his [1]message until
midnight.
8 There were many [a]lamps in the
[b]upper room where we were gathered
together.
9 And there was a young man named
[1]Eutychus sitting [2]on the window sill,
sinking into a deep sleep; and as Paul
kept on talking, he was overcome by
sleep and fell down from the third floor
and was picked up dead.
10 But Paul went down and [a]fell upon
him, and after embracing him, he [b]said,
"[1]Do not be troubled, for his life is in
him."
11 When he had gone *back* up and had
[a]broken the bread and [1]eaten, he talked
with them a long while until daybreak,
and then left.
12 They took away the boy alive, and
were [1]greatly comforted.

Troas to Miletus

13 ¶ But [a]we, going ahead to the ship,
set sail for Assos, intending from there to
take Paul on board; for so he had arranged
it, intending himself to go [1]by land.
14 And when he met us at Assos, we
took him on board and came to Mitylene.
15 Sailing from there, we arrived the
following day opposite Chios; and the
next day we crossed over to Samos; and
the day following we came to [a]Miletus.
16 For Paul had decided to sail past
[a]Ephesus so that he would not have to
spend time in [1][b]Asia; for he was hurry-
ing [c]to be in Jerusalem, if possible, [d]on
the day of Pentecost.

Farewell to Ephesus

17 ¶ From Miletus he sent to [a]Ephe-
sus and called to him [b]the elders of the
church.
18 And when they had come to him,
he said to them,
¶ "You yourselves know, [a]from the
first day that I set foot in [1]Asia, how I
was with you the whole time,
19 serving the Lord with all humility
and with tears and with trials which
came upon me [1]through [a]the plots of
the Jews;
20 how I [a]did not shrink from declaring to you anything that was profitable,
and teaching you publicly and [1]from
house to house,
21 solemnly [a]testifying to both Jews
and Greeks of [b]repentance toward God
and [c]faith in our Lord Jesus Christ.
22 "And now, behold, bound in [1]spirit,
[a]I am on my way to Jerusalem, not knowing what will happen to me there,
23 except that [a]the Holy Spirit solemnly [b]testifies to me in every city, saying that [c]bonds and afflictions await me.
24 "But [a]I do not consider my life of
any account as dear to myself, so that I
may [b]finish my course and [c]the ministry
which I received from the Lord Jesus, to
[d]testify solemnly of the gospel of [e]the
grace of God.
25 ¶ "And now, behold, I know that
all of you, among whom I went about
[a]preaching the kingdom, will no longer
see my face.
26 "Therefore, I [1]testify to you this day
that [a]I am [2]innocent of the blood of all
men.
27 "For I [a]did not shrink from declaring to you the whole [b]purpose of God.
28 "Be on guard for yourselves and for
all [a]the flock, among which the Holy
Spirit has made you [1]overseers, to shepherd [b]the church of God which [c]He
[2]purchased [3]with His own blood.
29 "I know that after my departure
[a]savage wolves will come in among you,
not sparing [b]the flock;
30 and from among your own selves
men will arise, speaking perverse things,
to draw away [a]the disciples after them.
31 "Therefore be on the alert, remembering that night and day for a period of
[a]three years I did not cease to admonish
each one [b]with tears.
32 "And now I [a]commend you to God
and to [b]the word of His grace, which is
able to [c]build *you* up and to give *you*
[d]the inheritance among all those who
are sanctified.
33 "[a]I have coveted no one's silver or
gold or clothes.
34 "You yourselves know that [a]these
hands ministered to my *own* needs and to
the [b]men who were with me.
35 "In everything I showed you that by
working hard in this manner you must
help the weak and remember the words
of the Lord Jesus, that He Himself said, 'It

4 [2]I.e. west coast province of Asia Minor [c]Acts 17:1 [d]Acts 19:29 [e]Acts 14:6 [f]Acts 16:1 [g]Eph 6:21; Col 4:7; 2 Tim 4:12; Titus 3:12 [h]Acts 21:29; 2 Tim 4:20 [i]Acts 16:6
5 [a]Acts 16:10 [b]Acts 16:8
6 [a]Acts 16:10 [b]Acts 16:12 [c]Acts 12:3 [d]Acts 16:8
7 [1]Lit *word, speech* [a]1 Cor 16:2; Rev 1:10 [b]Acts 16:10 [c]Acts 2:42
8 [a]Matt 25:1 [b]Acts 1:13
9 [1]*Eutychus* means *Good fortune*, i.e. *'Lucky'* [2]Or *at the window*
10 [1]Or *Stop being troubled* [a]1 Kin 17:21; 2 Kin 4:34 [b]Matt 9:23f; Mark 5:39
11 [1]Lit *tasted* [a]Acts 2:42
12 [1]Lit *not moderately*
13 [1]Or *on foot* [a]Acts 16:10
15 [a]Acts 20:17; 2 Tim 4:20
16 [1]I.e. west coast province of Asia Minor [a]Acts 18:19 [b]Acts 16:6 [c]Acts 19:21; 1 Cor 16:8 [d]Acts 2:1
17 [a]Acts 18:19 [b]Acts 11:30
18 [1]V 16, note 1 [a]Acts 18:19
19 [1]Lit *by* [a]Acts 20:3
20 [1]Or *in the various private homes* [a]Acts 20:27
21 [a]Luke 16:28; Acts 18:5 [b]Acts 2:38 [c]Acts 24:24; Eph 1:15; Col 2:5; Philem 5
22 [1]Or *the Spirit* [a]Acts 17:16
23 [a]Acts 8:29 [b]Luke 16:28; Acts 18:5 [c]Acts 9:16
24 [a]Acts 21:13 [b]Acts 13:25; 2 Tim 4:7 [c]Acts 1:17 [d]Luke 16:28; Acts 18:5 [e]Acts 11:23
25 [a]Matt 4:23; Acts 28:31
26 [1]Or *call you to witness* [2]Lit *pure from* [a]Acts 18:6
27 [a]Acts 20:20 [b]Acts 13:36
28 [1]Or *bishops* [2]Lit *acquired* [3]Lit *through* [a]Luke 12:32; John 21:15-17; Acts 20:29; 1 Pet 5:2f [b]Matt 16:18; Rom 16:16; 1 Cor 10:32 [c]Eph 1:7; Titus 2:14; 1 Pet 1:19; Rev 5:9
29 [a]Ezek 22:27; Matt 7:15 [b]Luke 12:32; John 21:15-17; Acts 20:28; 1 Pet 5:2f **30** [a]Acts 11:26 **31** [a]Acts 19:8 [b]Acts 20:19 **32** [a]Acts 14:23 [b]Acts 14:3 [c]Acts 9:31 [d]Acts 26:18; Eph 1:14; Col 1:12; Heb 9:15; 1 Pet 1:4 **33** [a]1 Cor 9:4-18; 2 Cor 11:7-12; 1 Thess 2:5f **34** [a]Acts 18:3 [b]Acts 19:22

is more blessed to give than to receive.' "

36 ¶ When he had said these things, he [a]knelt down and prayed with them all.

37 And [1]they *began* to weep aloud and [2a]embraced Paul, and repeatedly kissed him,

38 [1]grieving especially over [a]the word which he had spoken, that they would not see his face again. And they were [b]accompanying him to the ship.

Paul Sails from Miletus

21 When [a]we had parted from them and had set sail, we ran [b]a straight course to Cos and the next day to Rhodes and from there to Patara;

2 and having found a ship crossing over to [a]Phoenicia, we went aboard and set sail.

3 When we came in sight of [a]Cyprus, leaving it on the left, we kept sailing to [b]Syria and landed at [c]Tyre; for there the ship was to unload its cargo.

4 After looking up [a]the disciples, we stayed there seven days; and they kept telling Paul [1b]through the Spirit not to set foot in Jerusalem.

5 When [1]our days there were ended, we left and started on our journey, while they all, with wives and children, [a]escorted us until *we were* out of the city. After [b]kneeling down on the beach and praying, we said farewell to one another.

6 Then we went on board the ship, and they returned [a]home again.

7 ¶ When we had finished the voyage from [a]Tyre, we arrived at Ptolemais, and after greeting [b]the brethren, we stayed with them for a day.

8 On the next day we left and came to [a]Caesarea, and entering the house of [b]Philip the [c]evangelist, who was [b]one of the seven, we stayed with him.

9 Now this man had four virgin daughters who were [a]prophetesses.

10 As we were staying there for some days, a prophet named [a]Agabus came down from Judea.

11 And coming to us, he [a]took Paul's belt and bound his own feet and hands, and said, "This [b]is what the Holy Spirit says: 'In this way the Jews at Jerusalem will [c]bind the man who owns this belt and [d]deliver him into the hands of the Gentiles.' "

12 When we had heard this, we as well as the local residents *began* begging him [a]not to go up to Jerusalem.

13 Then Paul answered, "What are you doing, weeping and breaking my heart? For [a]I am ready not only to be bound, but even to die at Jerusalem for [b]the name of the Lord Jesus."

14 And since he would not be persuaded, we fell silent, remarking, "[a]The will of the Lord be done!"

Paul at Jerusalem

15 ¶ After these days we got ready and [a]started on our way up to Jerusalem.

16 *Some* of [a]the disciples from [b]Caesarea also came with us, taking us to Mnason of [c]Cyprus, a [d]disciple of long standing with whom we were to lodge.

17 ¶ After we arrived in Jerusalem, [a]the brethren received us gladly.

18 And the following day Paul went in with us to [1a]James, and all [b]the elders were present.

19 After he had greeted them, he [a]*began* to relate one by one the things which God had done among the Gentiles through his [b]ministry.

20 And when they heard it they *began* [a]glorifying God; and they said to him, "You see, brother, how many [1]thousands there are among the Jews of those who have believed, and they are all [b]zealous for the Law;

21 and they have been told about you, that you are [a]teaching all the Jews who are among the Gentiles to forsake Moses, telling them [b]not to circumcise their children nor to [1]walk according to [c]the customs.

22 "What, then, is *to be done*? They will certainly hear that you have come.

23 "Therefore do this that we tell you. We have four men who [1a]are under a vow;

24 take them and [a]purify yourself along with them, and [1]pay their expenses so that they may [b]shave their [2]heads; and all will know that there is nothing to the things which they have been told about you, but that you yourself also walk orderly, keeping the Law.

25 "But concerning the Gentiles who have believed, we wrote, [a]having decided that they should abstain from [1]meat sacrificed to idols and from blood and from what is strangled and from fornication."

26 Then Paul [1]took the men, and the next day, [a]purifying himself along with them, [b]went into the temple giving notice of the completion of the days of purification, until the sacrifice was offered for each one of them.

Paul Seized in the Temple

27 ¶ When [a]the seven days were almost over, [b]the Jews from [1c]Asia, upon seeing him in the temple, *began* to stir up all the crowd and laid hands on him,

28 crying out, "Men of Israel, come to our aid! [a]This is the man who preaches

36 [a]Acts 9:40; Luke 22:41
37 [1]Lit *a considerable weeping of all occurred* [2]Lit *threw themselves on Paul's neck* [a]Luke 15:20
38 [1]Lit *suffering pain* [a]Acts 20:25 [b]Acts 15:3
21:1 [a][we] Acts 16:10 [b]Acts 16:11
2 [a]Acts 11:19
3 [a]Acts 4:36 [b]Matt 4:24 [c]Acts 12:20
4 [1]I.e. because of impressions made by the Spirit [a]Acts 11:26 [b]Acts 20:23
5 [1]Lit *we had completed the days* [a]Acts 15:3 [b]Luke 22:41; Acts 9:40
6 [a]John 19:27
7 [a]Acts 12:20 [b]Acts 1:15
8 [a]Acts 8:40 [b]Acts 6:5 [c]Eph 4:11; 2 Tim 4:5
9 [a]Luke 2:36; Acts 13:1; 1 Cor 11:5
10 [a]Acts 11:28
11 [a]1 Kin 22:11; Is 20:2; Jer 13:1-11; John 18 [b]Acts 8:29 [c]Acts 9:16 [d]Matt 20:19
12 [a]Acts 21:15
13 [a]Acts 20:24 [b]Acts 5:41
14 [a]Luke 22:42
15 [a]Acts 21:12
16 [a]Acts 21:4 [b]Acts 8:40 [c]Acts 4:36 [d]Acts 15:7
17 [a]Acts 1:15
18 [1]Or *Jacob* [a]Acts 12:17 [b]Acts 11:30
19 [a]Acts 14:27 [b]Acts 1:17
20 [1]Lit *ten thousands* [a]Matt 9:8 [b]Acts 15:1; Rom 10:2; Gal 1:14
21 [1]I.e. observe or live by [a]Acts 21:28 [b]Acts 15:19ff; 1 Cor 7:18f [c]Acts 6:14
23 [1]Lit *have a vow on them* [a]Num 6:13-21; Acts 18:18
24 [1]Lit *spend on them* [2]Lit *head* [a]John 11:55; Acts 21:26 [b]Acts 18:18
25 [1]Lit *the thing* [a]Acts 15:19f
26 [1]Or *took the men the next day, and purifying himself* [a]John 11:55; Acts 21:24 [b]Num 6:13; Acts 24:18
27 [1]I.e. west coast province of Asia Minor [a]Num 6:9 [b]Acts 20:19 [c]Acts 16:6
28 [a]Acts 6:13

to all men everywhere against our people and the Law and this place; and besides he has even brought Greeks into the temple and has [b]defiled this holy place."

29 For they had previously seen [a]Trophimus the [b]Ephesian in the city with him, and they supposed that Paul had brought him into the temple.

30 Then all the city was provoked, and [1]the people rushed together, and taking hold of Paul they [a]dragged him out of the temple, and immediately the doors were shut.

31 While they were seeking to kill him, a report came up to the [1]commander of the [a]*Roman* [2]cohort that all Jerusalem was in confusion.

32 At once he [a]took along *some* soldiers and centurions and ran down to them; and when they saw the [1]commander and the soldiers, they stopped beating Paul.

33 Then the [1]commander came up and took hold of him, and ordered him to be [a]bound with [b]two chains; and he *began* asking who he was and what he had done.

34 But among the crowd [a]some were shouting one thing *and* some another, and when he could not find out the [1]facts because of the uproar, he ordered him to be brought into [b]the barracks.

35 When he got to [a]the stairs, he was carried by the soldiers because of the violence of the [1]mob;

36 for the multitude of the people kept following them, shouting, "[a]Away with him!"

37 ¶ As Paul was about to be brought into [a]the barracks, he said to the [1]commander, "May I say something to you?" And he *said, "Do you know Greek?

38 "Then you are not [a]the Egyptian who some [1]time ago stirred up a revolt and led the four thousand men of the Assassins out [b]into the wilderness?"

39 But Paul said, "[a]I am a Jew of Tarsus in [b]Cilicia, a citizen of no insignificant city; and I beg you, allow me to speak to the people."

40 When he had given him permission, Paul, standing on [a]the stairs, [b]motioned to the people with his hand; and when there [1]was a great hush, he spoke to them in the [2c]Hebrew dialect, saying,

Paul's Defense before the Jews

22 "[a]Brethren and fathers, hear my defense which I now *offer* to you."

2 ¶ And when they heard that he was addressing them in the [1a]Hebrew dialect, they became even more quiet; and he *said,

3 ¶ "[a]I am [b]a Jew, born in [c]Tarsus of [d]Cilicia, but brought up in this city, educated [1]under [e]Gamaliel, [2f]strictly according to the law of our fathers, being zealous for God just as [g]you all are today.

4 "[a]I persecuted this [b]Way to the death, binding and putting both men and women into prisons,

5 as also [a]the high priest and all [b]the Council of the elders [1]can testify. From them I also [c]received letters to [d]the brethren, and started off for [c]Damascus in order to bring even those who were there to Jerusalem [2]as prisoners to be punished.

6 ¶ "[a]But it happened that as I was on my way, approaching Damascus about noontime, a very bright light suddenly flashed from heaven all around me,

7 and I fell to the ground and heard a voice saying to me, 'Saul, Saul, why are you persecuting Me?'

8 "And I answered, 'Who are You, Lord?' And He said to me, 'I am [a]Jesus the Nazarene, whom you are persecuting.'

9 "And those who were with me [a]saw the light, to be sure, but [b]did not [1]understand the voice of the One who was speaking to me.

10 "And I said, '[a]What shall I do, Lord?' And the Lord said to me, 'Get up and go on into Damascus, and there you will be told of all that has been appointed for you to do.'

11 "But since I [a]could not see because of the [1]brightness of that light, I was led by the hand by those who were with me and came into Damascus.

12 ¶ "A certain [a]Ananias, a man who was devout by the standard of the Law, *and* [b]well spoken of by all the Jews who lived there,

13 came to me, and standing near said to me, '[a]Brother Saul, receive your sight!' And [1b]at that very time I looked up at him.

14 "And he said, '[a]The God of our fathers has [b]appointed you to know His will and to [c]see the [d]Righteous One and to hear an [1]utterance from His mouth.

15 'For you will be [a]a witness for Him to all men of [b]what you have seen and heard.

16 'Now why do you delay? [a]Get up and be baptized, and [b]wash away your sins, [c]calling on His name.'

17 ¶ "It happened when I [a]returned to Jerusalem and was praying in the temple, that I [b]fell into a trance,

18 and I saw Him saying to me, '[a]Make haste, and get out of Jerusalem quickly, because they will not accept your testimony about Me.'

28 [b]Matt 24:15; Acts 6:13f
29 [a]Acts 20:4 [b]Acts 18:19
30 [1]Lit *a running together of the people occurred* [a]2 Kin 11:15; Acts 16:19
31 [1]I.e. chiliarch, in command of one thousand troops [2]Or *battalion* [a]Acts 10:1
32 [1]V 31, note 1 [a]Acts 23:27
33 [1]V 31, note 1 [a]Acts 20:23; Eph 6:20; 2 Tim 1:16 [b]Acts 12:6
34 [1]Lit *certainty* [a]Acts 19:32 [b]Acts 21:37
35 [1]Lit *crowd* [a]Acts 21:40
36 [a]Luke 23:18; John 19:15; Acts 22:22
37 [1]V 31, note 1 [a]Acts 21:34
38 [1]Lit *days* [a]Acts 5:36 [b]Matt 24:26
39 [a]Acts 9:11 [b]Acts 6:9
40 [1]Lit *occurred* [2]I.e. Jewish Aramaic [a]Acts 21:35 [b]Acts 12:17 [c]John 5:2; Acts 1:19
22:1 [a]Acts 7:2
2 [1]I.e. Jewish Aramaic [a]Acts 21:40
3 [1]Lit *at the feet of* [2]Lit *according to the strictness of the ancestral law* [a]Acts 9:1-22 [b]Acts 21:39 [c]Acts 9:11 [d]Acts 6:9 [e]Acts 5:34 [f]Acts 23:6; Phil 3:6 [g]Acts 21:20
4 [a]Acts 8:3 [b]Acts 9:2
5 [1]Lit *testifies for me* [2]Lit *having been bound* [a]Acts 9:1 [b]Luke 22:66; Acts 5:21; 1 Tim 4:14 [c]Acts 9:2 [d]Acts 2:29; Rom 9:3
6 [a]Acts 22:6-11: *Acts 9:3-8*
8 [a]Acts 26:9
9 [1]Or *hear* (with comprehension) [a]Acts 26:13 [b]Acts 9:7
10 [a]Acts 16:30
11 [1]Lit *glory* [a]Acts 9:8
12 [a]Acts 9:10 [b]Acts 6:3
13 [1]Or *instantly*; lit *at the very hour* [a]Acts 9:17 [b]Acts 9:18
14 [1]Or *message*; lit *voice* [a]Acts 3:13 [b]Acts 9:15 [c]Acts 9:17; 1 Cor 9:1 [d]Acts 7:52
15 [a]Acts 23:11 [b]Acts 22:14
16 [a]Acts 9:18 [b]Acts 2:38; 1 Cor 6:11; Eph 5:26; Heb 10:22 [c]Acts 7:59
17 [a]Acts 9:26 [b]Acts 10:10
18 [a]Acts 9:29

19 "And I said, 'Lord, they themselves understand that in one synagogue after another [a]I used to imprison and [b]beat those who believed in You.

20 'And [a]when the blood of Your witness Stephen was being shed, I also was standing by approving, and watching out for the coats of those who were slaying him.'

21 "And He said to me, 'Go! For I will send you far away [a]to the Gentiles.' "

22 ¶ They listened to him up to this statement, and *then* they raised their voices and said, "[a]Away with such a fellow from the earth, for [b]he should not be allowed to live!"

23 And as they were crying out and [a]throwing off their cloaks and [b]tossing dust into the air,

24 the [1]commander ordered him to be brought into [a]the barracks, stating that he should be [b]examined by scourging so that he might find out the reason why they were shouting against him that way.

25 But when they stretched him out [1]with thongs, Paul said to the centurion who was standing by, "Is it [2]lawful for you to scourge [a]a man who is a Roman and uncondemned?"

26 When the centurion heard *this,* he went to the [1]commander and told him, saying, "What are you about to do? For this man is a Roman."

27 The [1]commander came and said to him, "Tell me, are you a Roman?" And he said, "Yes."

28 The [1]commander answered, "I acquired this citizenship with a large sum of money." And Paul said, "But I was actually born *a citizen.*"

29 Therefore those who were about to [a]examine him immediately [1]let go of him; and the [2]commander also [b]was afraid when he found out that he was a Roman, and because he had [3c]put him in chains.

30 ¶ But on the next day, [a]wishing to know for certain why he had been accused by the Jews, he [b]released him and ordered the chief priests and all [c]the [1]Council to assemble, and brought Paul down and set him before them.

Paul before the Council

23 Paul, looking intently at [a]the [1]Council, said, "[b]Brethren, [c]I have [2]lived my life with a perfectly good conscience before God up to this day."

2 The high priest [a]Ananias commanded those standing beside him [b]to strike him on the mouth.

3 Then Paul said to him, "God is going to strike you, [a]you whitewashed wall! Do you [b]sit to try me according to the Law, and in violation of the Law order me to be struck?"

4 But the bystanders said, "Do you revile God's high priest?"

5 And Paul said, "I was not aware, brethren, that he was high priest; for it is written, '[a]YOU SHALL NOT SPEAK EVIL OF A RULER OF YOUR PEOPLE.' "

6 ¶ But perceiving that one group were [a]Sadducees and the other Pharisees, Paul *began* crying out in [b]the [1]Council, "[c]Brethren, [d]I am a Pharisee, a son of Pharisees; I am on trial for [e]the hope and resurrection of the dead!"

7 As he said this, there occurred a dissension between the Pharisees and Sadducees, and the assembly was divided.

8 For [a]the Sadducees say that there is no resurrection, nor an angel, nor a spirit, but the Pharisees acknowledge them all.

9 And there occurred a great uproar; and some of [a]the scribes of the Pharisaic party stood up and *began* to argue heatedly, saying, "[b]We find nothing wrong with this man; [c]suppose a spirit or an angel has spoken to him?"

10 And as a great dissension was developing, the [1]commander was afraid Paul would be torn to pieces by them and ordered the troops to go down and take him away from them by force, and bring him into [a]the barracks.

11 ¶ But on [a]the night *immediately* following, the Lord stood at his side and said, "[b]Take courage; for [c]as you have [d]solemnly witnessed to My cause at Jerusalem, so you must witness at Rome also."

A Conspiracy to Kill Paul

12 ¶ When it was day, [a]the Jews formed a [1]conspiracy and [b]bound themselves under an oath, saying that they would neither eat nor drink until they had killed Paul.

13 There were more than forty who formed this plot.

14 They came to the chief priests and the elders and said, "We have [a]bound ourselves under a solemn oath to taste nothing until we have killed Paul.

15 "Now therefore, you [1]and [a]the [2]Council notify the [3]commander to bring him down to you, as though you were going to determine his case by a more thorough investigation; and we for our part are ready to slay him before he comes near *the place.*"

16 ¶ But the son of Paul's sister heard of their ambush, [1]and he came and entered [a]the barracks and told Paul.

19 [a]Acts 8:3; 22:4 [b]Matt 10:17; Acts 26:11
20 [a]Acts 7:58f; 8:1; 26:10
21 [a]Acts 9:15
22 [a]Acts 21:36; 1 Thess 2:16 [b]Acts 25:24
23 [a]Acts 7:58 [b]2 Sam 16:13
24 [1]I.e. chiliarch, in command of one thousand troops [a]Acts 21:34 [b]Acts 22:29
25 [1]Or *for the whip* [2]Interrogation by torture was a procedure used with slaves [a]Acts 16:37
26 [1]V 24, note 1
27 [1]V 24, note 1
28 [1]V 24, note 1
29 [1]Lit *withdrew from* [2]V 24, note 1 [3]Lit *bound him* [a]Acts 22:24 [b]Acts 16:38 [c]Acts 21:33
30 [1]Or *Sanhedrin* [a]Acts 23:28 [b]Acts 21:33 [c]Matt 5:22
23:1 [1]Or *Sanhedrin* [2]Or *conducted myself as a citizen* [a]Acts 22:30; 23:6,15, 20,28 [b]Acts 22:5 [c]Acts 24:16; 2 Cor 1:12; 2 Tim 1:3
2 [a]Acts 24:1 [b]John 18:22
3 [a]Matt 23:27 [b]Lev 19:15; Deut 25:2; John 7:51
5 [a]Ex 22:28
6 [1]Or *Sanhedrin* [a]Matt 3:7; 22:23 [b]Acts 22:30; 23:1,15,20,28 [c]Acts 22:5 [d]Acts 26:5; Phil 3:5 [e]Acts 24:15,21; 26:8
8 [a]Matt 22:23; Mark 12:18; Luke 20:27
9 [a]Mark 2:16; Luke 5:30 [b]Acts 23:29 [c]John 12:29; Acts 22:6ff
10 [1]I.e. chiliarch, in command of one thousand troops [a]Acts 21:34; 23:16,32
11 [a]Acts 18:9 [b]Matt 9:2 [c]Acts 19:21 [d]Luke 16:28; Acts 28:23
12 [1]Or *mob* [a]Acts 9:23; 23:30; 1 Thess 2:16 [b]Acts 23:14,21
14 [a]Acts 23:12, 21
15 [1]Lit *with* [2]Or *Sanhedrin* [3]V 10, note 1 [a]Acts 22:30; 23:1,6, 20,28
16 [1]Or *having been present with them, and he entered* [a]Acts 21:34; 23:10,32

17 Paul called one of the centurions to
him and said, "Lead this young man to
the [1]commander, for he has something
to report to him."
18 So he took him and led him to the
[1]commander and *said, "Paul [a]the prisoner called me to him and asked me to
lead this young man to you since he has
something to tell you."
19 The [1]commander took him by the
hand and stepping aside, *began* to inquire
of him privately, "What is it that you have
to report to me?"
20 And he said, "[a]The Jews have
agreed to ask you to bring Paul down
tomorrow to [b]the [1]Council, as though
they were going to inquire somewhat
more thoroughly about him.
21 "So do not [1]listen to them, for more
than forty of them are [a]lying in wait for
him who have [b]bound themselves under
a curse not to eat or drink until they slay
him; and now they are ready and waiting
for the promise from you."
22 So the [1]commander let the young
man go, instructing him, "Tell no one
that you have notified me of these
things."

Paul Moved to Caesarea

23 And he called to him two of the
centurions and said, "Get two hundred
soldiers ready by [1]the third hour of the
night to proceed to [a]Caesarea, [2]with
seventy horsemen and two hundred
[3]spearmen."
24 *They were* also to provide mounts
to put Paul on and bring him safely to
[a]Felix the governor.
25 And he wrote a letter having this
form:
26 ¶ "Claudius Lysias, to the [a]most
excellent governor Felix, [b]greet-
ings.
27 ¶ "When this man was arrested
by the Jews and was about to be
slain by them, [a]I came up to
them with the troops and rescued him, [b]having learned that
he was a Roman.
28 "And [a]wanting to ascertain the
charge for which they were accusing him, I [b]brought him
down to their [1c]Council;
29 and I found him to be accused
over [a]questions about their Law,
but [1]under [b]no accusation deserving death or [2]imprisonment.
30 ¶ "When I was [a]informed that
there would be [b]a plot against
the man, I sent him to you at
once, also instructing [c]his accusers to [1]bring charges against him
before you."

31 ¶ So the soldiers, in accordance
with their orders, took Paul and brought
him by night to Antipatris.
32 But the next day, leaving [a]the
horsemen to go on with him, they returned to [b]the barracks.
33 When these had come to [a]Caesa-
rea and delivered the letter to [b]the governor, they also presented Paul to him.
34 When he had read it, he asked from
what [a]province he was, and when he
learned that [b]he was from Cilicia,
35 he said, "I will give you a hearing
after your [a]accusers arrive also," giving
orders for him to be [b]kept in Herod's
[1]Praetorium.

Paul before Felix

24 After [a]five days the high priest
[b]Ananias came down with some
elders, [1]with an [2]attorney *named* Tertullus, and they [3]brought charges to [c]the
governor against Paul.
2 After *Paul* had been summoned,
Tertullus began to accuse him, saying *to
the governor,*
¶ "Since we have through you attained
much peace, and since by your provi-
dence reforms are being carried out for
this nation,
3 we acknowledge *this* in every way
and everywhere, [a]most excellent Felix,
with all thankfulness.
4 "But, that I may not weary you any
further, I beg you [1]to grant us, by your
kindness, a brief hearing.
5 "For we have found this man a real
pest and a fellow who stirs up dissension
among all the Jews throughout [1]the
world, and a ringleader of the [a]sect of the
Nazarenes.
6 "And he even tried to [a]desecrate
the temple; and [1]then we arrested him.
[[2]We wanted to judge him according to
our own Law.
7 "But Lysias the commander came
along, and with much violence took him
out of our hands,
8 ordering his accusers to come before you.] By examining him yourself concerning all these matters you will be able
to ascertain the things of which we accuse him."
9 [a]The Jews also joined in the attack,
asserting that these things were so.
10 ¶ When [a]the governor had nodded
for him to speak, Paul responded:
¶ "Knowing that for many years you
have been a judge to this nation, I cheer-
fully make my defense,
11 since you can take note of the fact
that no more than [a]twelve days ago I
went up to Jerusalem to worship.
12 "[a]Neither in the temple, nor in the

17 [1]V 10, note 1
18 [1]V 10, note 1 [a]Eph 3:1
19 [1]V 10, note 1
20 [1]Or *Sanhedrin* [a]Acts 23:14f [b]Acts 22:30; 23:1,6, 15,28
21 [1]Lit *be persuaded by them* [a]Acts 23:12,14 [b]Luke 11:54
22 [1]V 10, note 1
23 [1]I.e. 9 p.m. [2]Lit *and* [3]Or *slingers* or *bowmen* [a]Acts 8:40; 23:33
24 [a]Acts 23:26, 33; 24:1,3,10; 25:14
26 [a]Luke 1:3; Acts 24:3; 26:25 [b]Acts 15:23
27 [a]Acts 21:32f [b]Acts 22:25-29
28 [1]Or *Sanhedrin* [a]Acts 22:30 [b]Acts 23:10 [c]Acts 23:1
29 [1]Lit *having* [2]Lit *bonds* [a]Acts 18:15; 25:19 [b]Acts 23:9; 25:25; 26:31; 28:18
30 [1]Lit *speak against him* [a]Acts 23:20f [b]Acts 9:24; 23:12 [c]Acts 23:35; 24:19; 25:16
32 [a]Acts 23:23 [b]Acts 23:10
33 [a]Acts 8:40; 23:23 [b]Acts 23:24,26; 24:1, 3,10; 25:14
34 [a]Acts 25:1 [b]Acts 6:9; 21:39
35 [1]I.e. governor's official residence [a]Acts 23:30; 24:19; 25:16 [b]Acts 24:27
24:1 [1]Lit *and* [2]Lit *orator* [3]Or *presented their evidence* or *case* [a]Acts 24:11 [b]Acts 23:2 [c]Acts 23:24
3 [a]Acts 23:26; 26:25
4 [1]Lit *to hear...briefly*
5 [1]Lit *the inhabited earth* [a]Acts 15:5; 24:14
6 [1]Lit *also* [2]The early mss do not contain the remainder of v 6, v 7, nor the first part of v 8 [a]Acts 21:28
9 [a]1 Thess 2:16
10 [a]Acts 23:24
11 [a]Acts 21:18, 27; 24:1
12 [a]Acts 25:8

synagogues, nor in the city *itself* did they find me carrying on a discussion with anyone or [b]causing [1]a riot.

13 “[a]Nor can they prove to you *the charges* of which they now accuse me.

14 “But this I admit to you, that according to [a]the Way which they call a [b]sect I do serve [1][c]the God of our fathers, [d]believing everything that is in accordance with the Law and that is written in the Prophets;

15 having a hope in God, which [a]these men cherish themselves, that there shall certainly be a resurrection of both the righteous and the wicked.

16 “In view of this, [a]I also [1]do my best to maintain always a blameless conscience *both* before God and before men.

17 “Now [a]after several years I [b]came to bring [1]alms to my nation and to present offerings;

18 in which they found me *occupied* in the temple, having been [a]purified, without *any* [b]crowd or uproar. But *there were* some [c]Jews from [1]Asia—

19 who ought to have been present before you and to [a]make accusation, if they should have anything against me.

20 “Or else let these men themselves tell what misdeed they found when I stood before [a]the [1]Council,

21 other than for this one statement which [a]I shouted out while standing among them, ‘For the resurrection of the dead I am on trial before you today.’ ”

22 ¶ But Felix, [1]having a more exact knowledge about [a]the Way, put them off, saying, “When Lysias the [2]commander comes down, I will decide your case.”

23 Then he gave orders to the centurion for him to be [a]kept in custody and *yet* [b]have *some* freedom, and not to prevent any of [c]his friends from ministering to him.

24 ¶ But some days later Felix arrived with Drusilla, his [1]wife who was a Jewess, and sent for Paul and heard him *speak* about [a]faith in Christ Jesus.

25 But as he was discussing [a]righteousness, [b]self-control and [c]the judgment to come, Felix became frightened and said, “Go away for the present, and when I find time I will summon you.”

26 At the same time too, he was hoping that [a]money would be given him by Paul; therefore he also used to send for him quite often and converse with him.

27 But after two years had passed, Felix [1]was succeeded by Porcius [a]Festus, and [b]wishing to do the Jews a favor, Felix left Paul [c]imprisoned.

Paul before Festus

25 Festus then, having arrived in [a]the province, three days later went up to Jerusalem from [b]Caesarea.

2 And the chief priests and the leading men of the Jews [a]brought charges against Paul, and they were urging him,

3 requesting a [1]concession against [2]Paul, that he might [3]have him brought to Jerusalem (*at the same time,* [a]setting an ambush to kill him on the way).

4 Festus then [a]answered that Paul [b]was being kept in custody at [c]Caesarea and that he himself was about to leave shortly.

5 “Therefore,” he *said, “let the influential men among you [1]go there with me, and if there is anything wrong [2]about the man, let them [3]prosecute him.”

6 ¶ After he had spent not more than eight or ten days among them, he went down to [a]Caesarea, and on the next day he took his seat on [b]the tribunal and ordered Paul to be brought.

7 After Paul arrived, the Jews who had come down from Jerusalem stood around him, bringing [a]many and serious charges against him [b]which they could not prove,

8 while Paul said in his own defense, “[a]I have committed no offense either against the Law of the Jews or against the temple or against Caesar.”

9 But Festus, [a]wishing to do the Jews a favor, answered Paul and said, “[b]Are you willing to go up to Jerusalem and [1]stand trial before me on these *charges*?”

10 But Paul said, “I am standing before Caesar’s [a]tribunal, where I ought to be tried. I have done no wrong to *the* Jews, as you also very well know.

11 “If, then, I am a wrongdoer and have committed anything worthy of death, I do not refuse to die; but if none of those things is *true* of which these men accuse me, no one can hand me over to them. I [a]appeal to Caesar.”

12 Then when Festus had conferred with [1]his council, he answered, “You have appealed to Caesar, to Caesar you shall go.”

13 ¶ Now when several days had elapsed, King Agrippa and Bernice arrived at [a]Caesarea [1]and paid their respects to Festus.

14 While they were spending many days there, Festus laid Paul’s case before the king, saying, “There is a man who was [a]left as a prisoner by Felix;

15 and when I was at Jerusalem, the chief priests and the elders of the Jews [a]brought charges against him, asking for

12 [1]Lit *an attack of a mob* [b]Acts 24:18
13 [a]Acts 25:7
14 [1]Lit *the ancestral God* [a]Acts 9:2 [b]Acts 15:5 [c]Acts 3:13 [d]Acts 25:8
15 [a]Dan 12:2; John 5:28f; Acts 23:6
16 [1]Lit *practice myself* [a]Acts 23:1
17 [1]Or *gifts to charity* [a]Acts 20:31 [b]Acts 11:29f; Rom 15:25-28; 1 Cor 16:1-4; 2 Cor 8:1-4; Gal 2:10
18 [1]I.e. west coast province of Asia Minor [a]Acts 21:26 [b]Acts 24:12 [c]Acts 21:27
19 [a]Acts 23:30
20 [1]Or *Sanhedrin* [a]Matt 5:22
21 [a]Acts 23:6
22 [1]Lit *knowing more accurately* [2]I.e. chiliarch, in command of one thousand troops [a]Acts 24:14
23 [a]Acts 23:35 [b]Acts 28:16 [c]Acts 23:16
24 [1]Lit *own wife* [a]Acts 20:21
25 [a]Titus 2:12 [b]Gal 5:23; Titus 1:8; 2 Pet 1:6 [c]Acts 10:42
26 [a]Acts 24:17
27 [1]Lit *received a successor, Porcius Festus* [a]Acts 25:1 [b]Acts 12:3 [c]Acts 23:35
25:1 [a]Acts 23:34 [b]Acts 8:40
2 [a]Acts 24:1
3 [1]Or *favor* [2]Lit *him* [3]Lit *send for him to Jerusalem* [a]Acts 9:24
4 [a]Acts 25:16 [b]Acts 24:23 [c]Acts 8:40
5 [1]Lit *go down* [2]Lit *in* [3]Or *accuse*
6 [a]Acts 8:40 [b]Matt 27:19; Acts 25:10
7 [a]Acts 24:5f [b]Acts 24:13
8 [a]Acts 6:13
9 [1]Lit *be judged* [a]Acts 12:3 [b]Acts 25:20
10 [a]Matt 27:19; Acts 25:6
11 [a]Acts 25:21
12 [1]A different group from that mentioned in Acts 4:15 and 24:20
13 [1]Lit *greeting Festus* [a]Acts 8:40
14 [a]Acts 24:27
15 [a]Acts 24:1

a sentence of condemnation against him.
16 "I [a]answered them that it is not the
custom of the Romans to hand over any
man before [b]the accused meets his accusers face to face and has an opportunity
to make his defense against the charges.
17 "So after they had assembled here, I
did not delay, but on the next day took
my seat on [a]the tribunal and ordered the
man to be brought before me.
18 "When the accusers stood up, they
began bringing charges against him not of
such crimes as I was expecting,
19 but they *simply* had some [a]points
of disagreement with him about their
own [1b]religion and about a dead man,
Jesus, whom Paul asserted to be alive.
20 "[a]Being at a loss how to investigate
[1]such matters, I asked whether he was
willing to go to Jerusalem and there stand
trial on these matters.
21 "But when Paul [a]appealed to be
held in custody for [1]the Emperor's decision, I ordered him to be kept in custody
until I send him to Caesar."
22 Then [a]Agrippa *said* to Festus, "I
also would like to hear the man myself."
"Tomorrow," he *said, "you shall hear
him."

Paul before Agrippa

23 ¶ So, on the next day when [a]Agrip-
pa came [1]together with [a]Bernice amid
great pomp, and entered the auditorium
[2]accompanied by the [3]commanders and
the prominent men of the city, at the
command of Festus, Paul was brought in.
24 Festus *said, "King Agrippa, and all
you gentlemen here present with us, you
see this man about whom [a]all the people
of the Jews appealed to me, both at Jerusalem and here, loudly declaring that [b]he
ought not to live any longer.
25 "But I found that he had committed
[a]nothing worthy of death; and since he
himself [b]appealed to [1]the Emperor, I decided to send him.
26 "[1]Yet I have nothing definite about
him to write to my lord. Therefore I have
brought him before you *all* and especially
before you, King Agrippa, so that after the
investigation has taken place, I may have
something to write.
27 "For it seems absurd to me in sending a prisoner, not to indicate also the
charges against him."

Paul's Defense before Agrippa

26 [a]Agrippa said to Paul, "You are
permitted to speak for yourself."
Then Paul stretched out his hand and *pro-*
ceeded to make his defense:
2 ¶ "In regard to all the things of
which I am accused by the Jews, I consider myself fortunate, King Agrippa, that I
am about to make my defense before you
today;
3 [1]especially because you are an expert in all [a]customs and [2]questions
among *the* Jews; therefore I beg you to
listen to me patiently.
4 ¶ "So then, all Jews know [a]my
manner of life from my youth up, which
from the beginning was spent among my
own nation and at Jerusalem;
5 since they have known about me
for a long time, if they are willing to testify, that I lived *as* a [a]Pharisee [b]according
to the strictest [c]sect of our religion.
6 "And now I am [1]standing trial [a]for
the hope of [b]the promise made by God to
our fathers;
7 *the promise* [a]to which our twelve
tribes hope to attain, as they earnestly
serve *God* night and day. And for this
[b]hope, O King, I am being [c]accused by
Jews.
8 "Why is it considered incredible
among you *people* [a]if God does raise the
dead?
9 ¶ "So then, [a]I thought to myself
that I had to do many things hostile to
[b]the name of Jesus of Nazareth.
10 "And this is [1]just what I [a]did in
Jerusalem; not only did I lock up many of
the [2]saints in prisons, having [b]received
authority from the chief priests, but also
when they were being put to death I
[c]cast my vote against them.
11 "And [a]as I punished them often in
all the synagogues, I tried to force them
to blaspheme; and being [b]furiously enraged at them, I kept pursuing them
[c]even to [1]foreign cities.
12 ¶ "[1]While so engaged [a]as I was
journeying to Damascus with the authority and commission of the chief priests,
13 at midday, O King, I saw on the
way a light from heaven, [1]brighter than
the sun, shining all around me and those
who were journeying with me.
14 "And when we had [a]all fallen to the
ground, I heard a voice saying to me in
the [1b]Hebrew dialect, 'Saul, Saul, why
are you persecuting Me? [2]It is hard for
you to kick against the goads.'
15 "And I said, 'Who are You, Lord?'
And the Lord said, 'I am Jesus whom you
are persecuting.
16 'But get up and [a]stand on your feet;
for this purpose I have appeared to you,
to [b]appoint you a [c]minister and [d]a witness not only to the things which you
have [1]seen, but also to the things in
which I will appear to you;
17 [a]rescuing you [b]from the *Jewish*
people and from the Gentiles, to whom I
am sending you,

16 [a]Acts 25:4f [b]Acts 23:30
17 [a]Matt 27:19; Acts 25:6,10
19 [1]Or *superstition* [a]Acts 18:15; 23:29 [b]Acts 17:22
20 [1]Lit *these* [a]Acts 25:9
21 [1]Lit *the Augustus's* (in this case Nero) [a]Acts 25:11f
22 [a]Acts 9:15
23 [1]Lit *and Bernice* [2]Lit *and with* [3]I.e. chiliarchs, in command of one thousand troops [a]Acts 25:13; 26:30
24 [a]Acts 25:2,7 [b]Acts 22:22
25 [1]V 21, note 1 [a]Luke 23:4; Acts 23:29 [b]Acts 25:11f
26 [1]Lit *About whom I have nothing definite*
26:1 [a]Acts 9:15
3 [1]Or *because you are especially expert* [2]Or *controversial issues* [a]Acts 6:14; 25:19; 26:7
4 [a]Gal 1:13f; Phil 3:5
5 [a]Acts 23:6; Phil 3:5 [b]Acts 22:3 [c]Acts 15:5
6 [1]Lit *being tried* [a]Acts 24:15; 28:20 [b]Acts 13:32
7 [a]James 1:1 [b]Acts 24:15; 28:20 [c]Acts 26:2
8 [a]Acts 23:6
9 [a]John 16:2; 1 Tim 1:13 [b]John 15:21
10 [1]Lit *also* [2]Or *holy ones* [a]Acts 8:3; 9:13 [b]Acts 9:1f [c]Acts 22:20
11 [1]Or *outlying* [a]Matt 10:17; Acts 22:19 [b]Acts 9:1 [c]Acts 22:5
12 [1]Lit *In which things* [a]Acts 26:12-18: *9:3-8; 22:6-11*
13 [1]Lit *above the brightness of*
14 [1]I.e. Jewish Aramaic [2]An idiom referring to an animal's futile resistance to being prodded with goads [a]Acts 9:7 [b]Acts 21:40
16 [1]Two early mss read *seen Me* [a]Ezek 2:1; Dan 10:11 [b]Acts 22:14 [c]Luke 1:2 [d]Acts 22:15
17 [a]Jer 1:8,19 [b]1 Chr 16:35; Acts 9:15

18 to [a]open their eyes so that they
may turn from [b]darkness to light and
from the dominion of [c]Satan to God, that
they may receive [d]forgiveness of sins and
an [e]inheritance among those who have
been sanctified by [f]faith in Me.'
19 ¶ "So, King Agrippa, I did not prove
disobedient to the heavenly vision,
20 but *kept* declaring both [a]to those
of Damascus first, and *also* [b]at Jerusalem
and *then* throughout all the region of Judea, and *even* [c]to the Gentiles, that they
should [d]repent and turn to God, performing deeds [e]appropriate to repentance.
21 "For this reason *some* Jews [a]seized
me in the temple and tried [b]to put me to
death.
22 "So, having obtained help from God,
I stand to this day [a]testifying both to
small and great, stating nothing but what
[b]the Prophets and Moses said was going
to take place;
23 [1a]that [2]the Christ was [3]to suffer,
and [1]that [b]by reason of *His* resurrection
from the dead He would be the first to
proclaim [c]light both to the *Jewish* people
and to the Gentiles."
24 ¶ While *Paul* was saying this in his
defense, Festus *said in a loud voice,
"Paul, you are out of your mind! [1]*Your*
great [a]learning is [2]driving you mad."
25 But Paul *said, "I am not out of my
mind, [a]most excellent Festus, but I utter
words [1]of sober truth.
26 "For the king [1a]knows about these
matters, and I speak to him also with confidence, since I am persuaded that none
of these things escape his notice; for this
has not been done in a [2]corner.
27 "King Agrippa, do you believe the
Prophets? I know that you [1]do."
28 Agrippa *replied* to Paul, "[1]In a
short time you [2]will persuade me to [3]be-
come a [a]Christian."
29 And Paul *said,* "[1]I would wish to
God, that whether [2]in a short or long
time, not only you, but also all who hear
me this day, might become such as I am,
except for these [a]chains."
30 ¶ [a]The king stood up and the governor and Bernice, and those who were
sitting with them,
31 and when they had gone aside, they
began talking to one another, saying,
"[a]This man is not doing anything worthy
of death or [1]imprisonment."
32 And Agrippa said to Festus, "This
man might have been [a]set free if he had
not [b]appealed to Caesar."

Paul Is Sent to Rome

27 When it was decided that [a]we
[b]would sail for [c]Italy, they proceeded to deliver Paul and some other
prisoners to a centurion of the Augustan
[1d]cohort named Julius.
2 And embarking in an Adramyttian
ship, which was about to sail to the regions along the coast of [1a]Asia, we put
out to sea accompanied by [b]Aristarchus,
a [c]Macedonian of [d]Thessalonica.
3 The next day we put in at [a]Sidon;
and Julius [b]treated Paul with consideration and [c]allowed him to go to his
friends and receive care.
4 From there we put out to sea and
sailed under the shelter of [a]Cyprus because [b]the winds were contrary.
5 When we had sailed through the
sea along the coast of [a]Cilicia and [b]Pam-
phylia, we landed at Myra in Lycia.
6 There the centurion found an [a]Al-
exandrian ship sailing for [b]Italy, and he
put us aboard it.
7 When we had sailed slowly for a
good many days, and with difficulty had
arrived off Cnidus, [a]since the wind did
not permit us *to go* farther, we sailed
under the shelter of [b]Crete, off Salmone;
8 and with difficulty [a]sailing past it
we came to a place called Fair Havens,
near which was the city of Lasea.
9 ¶ When considerable time had
passed and the voyage was now dangerous, since even [a]the [1]fast was already
over, Paul *began* to admonish them,
10 and said to them, "Men, I perceive
that the voyage will certainly be with
[a]damage and great loss, not only of the
cargo and the ship, but also of our lives."
11 But the centurion was more persuaded by the [a]pilot and the [1]captain of
the ship than by what was being said by
Paul.
12 Because the harbor was not suitable for wintering, the majority reached a
decision to put out to sea from there, if
somehow they could reach Phoenix, a
harbor of [a]Crete, facing southwest and
northwest, and spend the winter *there.*
13 ¶ [1]When a moderate south wind
came up, supposing that they had attained their purpose, they weighed anchor and *began* [a]sailing along [b]Crete,
close *inshore.*

Shipwreck

14 But before very long there [a]rushed
down from [1]the land a violent wind,
called [2]Euraquilo;
15 and when the ship was caught *in it*
and could not face the wind, we gave way
to it and let ourselves be driven along.
16 Running under the shelter of a

18 [a]Is 35:5; Eph 5:8; Col 1:13; 1 Pet 2:9 [b]John 1:5; Eph 5:8; Col 1:12f; 1 Thess 5:5; 1 Pet 2:9 [c]Matt 4:10 [d]Luke 24:47; Acts 2:38 [e]Acts 20:32 [f]Acts 20:21
20 [a]Acts 9:19ff [b]Acts 9:26-29 [c]Acts 9:15 [d]Acts 3:19 [e]Matt 3:8; Luke 3:8
21 [a]Acts 21:27 [b]Acts 21:31
22 [a]Luke 16:28 [b]Acts 10:43
23 [1]Lit *whether* [2]I.e. the Messiah [3]Lit *subject to suffering* [a]Matt 26:24; Acts 3:18 [b]1 Cor 15:20; Col 1:18; Rev 1:5 [c]Is 42:6; Luke 2:32; 2 Cor 4:4
24 [1]Lit *The many letters* [2]Lit *turning you to madness* [a]John 7:15; 2 Tim 3:15
25 [1]Lit *of truth and rationality* [a]Acts 23:26
26 [1]Or *understands* [2]I.e. a hidden or secret place [a]Acts 26:3
27 [1]Lit *believe*
28 [1]Or *With a little* [2]Or *are trying to convince* [3]Lit *make* [a]Acts 11:26
29 [1]Or *I would pray to* [2]Or *with a little or with much* [a]Acts 21:33
30 [a]Acts 25:23
31 [1]Lit *bonds* [a]Acts 23:29
32 [a]Acts 28:18 [b]Acts 25:11
27:1 [1]Or *battalion* [a][we] Acts 16:10 [b]Acts 25:12 [c]Acts 18:2 [d]Acts 10:1
2 [1]I.e. west coast province of Asia Minor [a]Acts 2:9 [b]Acts 19:29 [c]Acts 16:9 [d]Acts 17:1
3 [a]Matt 11:21 [b]Acts 27:43 [c]Acts 24:23
4 [a]Acts 4:36 [b]Acts 27:7
5 [a]Acts 6:9 [b]Acts 13:13
6 [a]Acts 28:11 [b]Acts 18:2
7 [a]Acts 27:4 [b]Acts 2:11; Titus 1:5
8 [a]Acts 27:13
9 [1]I.e. Day of Atonement in September or October, which was a dangerous time of year for navigation [a]Lev 16:29-31; Num 29:7
10 [a]Acts 27:21
11 [1]Or *owner* [a]Rev 18:17
12 [a]Acts 2:11; Titus 1:5
13 [1]Lit *a south wind having gently blown*

[a]Acts 27:8 [b]Acts 2:11; Titus 1:5 **14** [1]Lit *it* [2]I.e. a northeaster [a]Mark 4:37

small island called Clauda, we were
scarcely able to get the *ship's* [1]boat under control.
17 After they had hoisted it up, they
used [1]supporting cables in undergirding
the ship; and fearing that they might
[a]run aground on *the shallows* of Syrtis,
they let down the [2]sea anchor and in this
way let themselves be driven along.
18 The next day as we were being violently storm-tossed, [1]they began to [a]jet-
tison the cargo;
19 and on the third day they threw the
ship's tackle overboard with their own
hands.
20 Since neither sun nor stars appeared for many days, and no small storm
was assailing *us*, from then on all hope
of our being saved was gradually abandoned.
21 ¶ [1]When they had gone a long
time without food, then Paul stood up in
their midst and said, "[a]Men, you ought
to have [2]followed my advice and not to
have set sail from [b]Crete and [3]incurred
this [a]damage and loss.
22 "*Yet* now I urge you to [a]keep up
your courage, for there will be no loss of
life among you, but *only* of the ship.
23 "For this very night [a]an angel of the
God to whom I belong and [b]whom I
serve [c]stood before me,
24 saying, 'Do not be afraid, Paul;
[a]you must stand before Caesar; and behold, God has granted you [b]all those who
are sailing with you.'
25 "Therefore, [a]keep up your courage,
men, for I believe God that [1]it will turn
out exactly as I have been told.
26 "But we must [a]run aground on a
certain [b]island."
27 ¶ But when the fourteenth night
came, as we were being driven about in
the Adriatic Sea, about midnight the sailors *began* to surmise that [1]they were approaching some land.
28 They took soundings and found *it to
be* twenty fathoms; and a little farther on
they took another sounding and found *it
to be* fifteen fathoms.
29 Fearing that we might [a]run
aground somewhere on the [1]rocks, they
cast four anchors from the stern and
[2]wished for daybreak.
30 But as the sailors were trying to escape from the ship and had let down [a]the
ship's boat into the sea, on the pretense
of intending to lay out anchors from the
bow,
31 Paul said to the centurion and to
the soldiers, "Unless these men remain
in the ship, you yourselves cannot be
saved."
32 Then the soldiers cut away the
[a]ropes of the *ship's* boat and let it fall
away.
33 ¶ Until the day was about to dawn,
Paul was encouraging them all to take
some food, saying, "Today is the fourteenth day that you have been constantly
watching and going without eating, having taken nothing.
34 "Therefore I encourage you to take
some food, for this is for your preserva-
tion, for [a]not a hair from the head of any
of you will perish."
35 Having said this, he took bread and
[a]gave thanks to God in the presence of
all, and he broke it and began to eat.
36 All [a]of them [1]were encouraged
and they themselves also took food.
37 All of us in the ship were two hundred and seventy-six [1a]persons.
38 When they had eaten enough, they
began to lighten the ship by [a]throwing
out the wheat into the sea.
39 ¶ When day came, [a]they [1]could
not recognize the land; but they did observe a bay with a beach, and they resolved to drive the ship onto it if they
could.
40 And casting off [a]the anchors, they
left them in the sea while at the same
time they were loosening the ropes of the
rudders; and hoisting the foresail to the
wind, they were heading for the beach.
41 But striking a [1]reef where two seas
met, they ran the vessel aground; and the
prow stuck fast and remained immovable, but the stern *began* to be broken up
by the force *of the waves.*
42 The soldiers' plan was to [a]kill the
prisoners, so that none *of them* would
swim away and escape;
43 but the centurion, [a]wanting to
bring Paul safely through, kept them from
their intention, and commanded that
those who could swim should [1]jump
overboard first and get to land,
44 and the rest *should follow*, some on
planks, and others on various things from
the ship. And so it happened that [a]they
all were brought safely to land.

Safe at Malta

28 When [a]they had been brought
safely through, [b]then we found
out that [c]the island was called [1]Malta.
2 [a]The [1]natives showed us extraordinary kindness; for because of the rain
that had set in and because of the cold,
they kindled a fire and [b]received us all.
3 But when Paul had gathered a bundle of sticks and laid them on the fire, a
viper came out [1]because of the heat and
fastened itself on his hand.
4 When [a]the [1]natives saw the creature hanging from his hand, they *began*

16 [1]Or *skiff*: a small boat in tow or carried on board for emergency use, transportation to and from shore, etc

17 [1]Lit *helps* [2]Or *gear* [a]Acts 27:26,29

18 [1]Lit *they were doing a throwing out* [a]Jon 1:5; Acts 27:38

21 [1]Lit *there being much abstinence from food* [2]Lit *obeyed me* [3]Lit *gained* [a]Acts 27:10 [b]Acts 27:7

22 [a]Acts 27:25, 36

23 [a]Acts 5:19 [b]Rom 1:9 [c]Acts 18:9; 23:11; 2 Tim 4:17

24 [a]Acts 23:11 [b]Acts 27:31,42, 44

25 [1]Lit *it will be* [a]Acts 27:22,36

26 [a]Acts 27:17, 29 [b]Acts 28:1

27 [1]Lit *some land was approaching them*

29 [1]Lit *rough places* [2]Lit *they were praying for it to become day* [a]Acts 27:17,26

30 [a]Acts 27:16

32 [a]John 2:15

34 [a]Matt 10:30

35 [a]Matt 14:19

36 [1]Lit *became cheerful* [a]Acts 27:22,25

37 [1]Lit *souls* [a]Acts 2:41

38 [a]Jon 1:5; Acts 27:18

39 [1]Lit *were not recognizing* [a]Acts 28:1

40 [a]Acts 27:29

41 [1]Lit *place*

42 [a]Acts 12:19

43 [1]Lit *throw themselves* [a]Acts 27:3

44 [a]Acts 27:22, 31

28:1 [1]Or *Melita* [a][they] Acts 16:10; 27:1 [b]Acts 27:39 [c]Acts 27:26

2 [1]Lit *barbarians* [a]Acts 28:4; Rom 1:14; 1 Cor 14:11; Col 3:11 [b]Rom 14:1

3 [1]Or *from the heat*

4 [1]Lit *barbarians* [a]Acts 28:2

saying to one another, "[b]Undoubtedly
this man is a murderer, and though he
has been saved from the sea, [2]justice has
not allowed him to live."
5 However [a]he shook the creature
off into the fire and suffered no harm.
6 But they were expecting that he
was about to swell up or suddenly fall
down dead. But after they had waited a
long time and had seen nothing unusual
happen to him, they changed their minds
and [a]*began* to say that he was a god.
7 ¶ Now in the neighborhood of that
place were lands belonging to the leading
man of the island, named Publius, who
welcomed us and entertained us courte-
ously three days.
8 And it happened that the father of
Publius was lying *in bed* afflicted with
recurrent fever and dysentery; and Paul
went in *to see* him and after he had
[a]prayed, he [b]laid his hands on him and
healed him.
9 After this had happened, the rest of
the people on the island who had diseases were coming to him and getting
cured.
10 They also honored us with many
[1]marks of respect; and when we were
setting sail, they [2]supplied *us* with [3]all
we needed.

Paul Arrives at Rome

11 ¶ At the end of three months we
set sail on [a]an Alexandrian ship which
had wintered at the island, and which
had [1]the Twin Brothers for its figure-
head.
12 After we put in at Syracuse, we
stayed there for three days.
13 From there we sailed around and
arrived at Rhegium, and a day later a
south wind sprang up, and on the second
day we came to Puteoli.
14 [1]There we found *some* [a]brethren,
and were invited to stay with them for
seven days; and thus we came to Rome.
15 And the [a]brethren, when they
heard about us, came from there as far as
the [1]Market of Appius and [2]Three Inns
to meet us; and when Paul saw them, he
thanked God and took courage.
16 ¶ When we entered Rome, Paul
was [a]allowed to stay by himself, with the
soldier who was guarding him.
17 ¶ After three days [1]Paul called together those who were [a]the leading men
of the Jews, and when they came together, he *began* saying to them, "[b]Brethren,
[c]though I had done nothing against our
people or [d]the customs of our [2]fathers,
yet I was delivered as a prisoner from
Jerusalem into the hands of the Romans.
18 "And when they had [a]examined
me, they [b]were willing to release me because there was [c]no ground [1]for putting
me to death.
19 "But when the Jews [1]objected, I
was forced to [a]appeal to Caesar, not that
I had any accusation against my nation.
20 "For this reason, therefore, I [1]re-
quested to see you and to speak with you,
for I am wearing [a]this chain for [b]the
sake of the hope of Israel."
21 They said to him, "We have neither
received letters from Judea concerning
you, nor have any of [a]the brethren come
here and reported or spoken anything
bad about you.
22 "But we desire to hear from you
what [1]your views are; for concerning
this [a]sect, it is known to us that [b]it is
spoken against everywhere."
23 ¶ When they had set a day for Paul,
they came to him at [a]his lodging in large
numbers; and he was explaining to them
by solemnly [b]testifying about the kingdom of God and trying to persuade them
concerning Jesus, [c]from both the Law
of Moses and from the Prophets, from
morning until evening.
24 [a]Some were being persuaded by
the things spoken, but others would not
believe.
25 And when they did not agree with
one another, they *began* leaving after
Paul had spoken one *parting* word, "The
Holy Spirit rightly spoke through Isaiah
the prophet to your fathers,
26 saying,
'[a]GO TO THIS PEOPLE AND SAY,
"[1][b]YOU WILL KEEP ON HEARING,
[2]BUT WILL NOT UNDERSTAND;
AND [3]YOU WILL KEEP ON SEEING,
BUT WILL NOT PERCEIVE;
27 [a]FOR THE HEART OF THIS PEOPLE
HAS BECOME DULL,
AND WITH THEIR EARS THEY
SCARCELY HEAR,
AND THEY HAVE CLOSED THEIR EYES;
OTHERWISE THEY MIGHT SEE WITH
THEIR EYES,
AND HEAR WITH THEIR EARS,
AND UNDERSTAND WITH THEIR
HEART AND RETURN,
AND I WOULD HEAL THEM."'
28 "Therefore let it be known to you
that [a]this salvation of God has been sent
[b]to the Gentiles; they will also listen."
29 [[1]When he had spoken these
words, the Jews departed, having a great
dispute among themselves.]
30 ¶ And he stayed two full years [1]in
his own rented quarters and was welcoming all who came to him,
31 [1][a]preaching the kingdom of God
and teaching concerning the Lord Jesus
Christ [b]with all openness, unhindered.

4 [2]Or *Justice,* i.e. the personification of a goddess [b]Luke 13:2, 4
5 [a]Mark 16:18
6 [a]Acts 14:11
8 [a]Acts 9:40; James 5:14f [b]Matt 9:18; Mark 5:23; 6:5
10 [1]Lit *honors* [2]Or *put on board* [3]Lit *the things pertaining to the needs*
11 [1]Gr *Dioscuri;* i.e. Castor and Pollux, twin sons of Zeus [a]Acts 27:6
14 [1]Lit *Where* [a]John 21:23; Acts 1:15; 6:3; 9:30; 28:15; Rom 1:13
15 [1]Lat *Appii Forum,* a station about 43 miles from Rome [2]Lat *Tres Tabernae,* a station about 33 miles from Rome [a]Acts 1:15; 10:23; 11:1,12, 29; 12:17
16 [a]Acts 24:23
17 [1]Lit *he* [2]Or *forefathers* [a]Acts 13:50; 25:2 [b]Acts 22:5 [c]Acts 25:8 [d]Acts 6:14
18 [1]Lit *of death in me* [a]Acts 22:24 [b]Acts 26:32 [c]Acts 23:29; 25:25; 26:31
19 [1]Lit *spoke against* [a]Acts 25:11,21,25; 26:32
20 [1]Or *invited you to see me and speak with me* [a]Acts 21:33 [b]Acts 26:6f
21 [a]Acts 3:17; 22:5; 28:14; Rom 9:3
22 [1]Lit *you think* [a]Acts 24:14 [b]1 Pet 2:12; 3:16; 4:14, 16
23 [a]Philem 22 [b]Luke 16:28; Acts 1:3; 23:11 [c]Acts 8:35
24 [a]Acts 14:4
26 [1]Lit *with a hearing* [2]Lit *and* [3]Lit *seeing you will see* [a]Is 6:9 [b]Matt 13:14f
27 [a]Is 6:10
28 [a]Ps 98:3; Luke 2:30; Acts 13:26 [b]Acts 9:15; 13:46
29 [1]Early mss do not contain this v
30 [1]Or *at his own expense*
31 [1]Or *proclaiming* [a]Matt 4:23; Acts 20:25; 28:23 [b]2 Tim 2:9

Romans

Title and Background

When Paul wrote this letter, he was probably in Corinth on his third missionary journey. His work in the eastern Mediterranean was almost finished, and he greatly desired to visit the Roman church. At this time, however, he could not go to Rome, so he sent a letter there, intending to visit Rome while en route on a mission to Spain. This letter served as a theological introduction to that hoped-for personal ministry.

Author and Date of Writing

The writer of this letter was the apostle Paul, and it was probably written in the early spring of A.D. 57.

Theme and Message

Paul's primary theme in Romans is the basic gospel, God's plan of salvation and righteousness for all mankind, Jew and Gentile alike. "The gospel of God" (1:1) includes justification by faith, but it also embraces such related ideas as guilt, sanctification and security. Romans is the most comprehensive and systematic statement of the Christian faith in the Bible.

Outline

I. Introduction (1:1–15)
II. Theme: Righteousness From God (1:16–17)
III. The Unrighteousness of All Mankind (1:18—3:20)
IV. Righteousness Imputed: Justification (3:21—5:21)
V. Righteousness Imparted: Sanctification (6:1—8:39)
VI. God's Righteousness Vindicated: The Problem of Israel's Rejection (9:1—11:36)
VII. Righteousness Practiced (12:1—15:13)
VIII. Conclusion (15:14–33)
IX. Commendation and Greetings (16:1–27)

The Gospel Exalted

1 Paul, a bond-servant of Christ Jesus, [1a]called *as* an apostle, [b]set apart for [c]the gospel of God,

2 which He [a]promised beforehand through His [b]prophets in the holy Scriptures,

3 concerning His Son, who was born [a]of a [1]descendant of David [b]according to the flesh,

4 who was declared [a]the Son of God with power [1]by the resurrection from the dead, according to the [2]Spirit of holiness, Jesus Christ our Lord,

5 through whom we have received grace and [a]apostleship [1]to bring about *the* [b]obedience of faith among [c]all the Gentiles for His name's sake,

6 among whom you also are the [a]called of Jesus Christ;

7 ¶ to all who are [a]beloved of God in Rome, called *as* [1b]saints: [c]Grace to you and peace from God our Father and the Lord Jesus Christ.

8 ¶ First, [a]I thank my God through Jesus Christ [1]for you all, because [b]your faith is being proclaimed throughout the whole world.

9 For [a]God, whom I [b]serve in my spirit in the *preaching of the* gospel of His Son, is my witness *as to* how unceasingly [c]I make mention of you,

10 always in my prayers making request, if perhaps now at last by [a]the will of God I may succeed in coming to you.

11 For [a]I long to see you so that I may impart some spiritual gift to you, that you may be [1]established;

12 that is, that I may be encouraged together with you *while* among you, each of us by the other's faith, both yours and mine.

13 [a]I do not want you to be unaware, [b]brethren, that often I [c]have planned to

1:1 [1]Lit *a called apostle* [a]1 Cor 1:1; 2 Cor 1:1 [b]Acts 9:15; Gal 1:15 [c]Mark 1:14; Rom 15:16 **2** [a]Titus 1:2 [b]Luke 1:70; Rom 3:21 **3** [1]Lit *seed* [a]Matt 1:1 [b]John 1:14; Rom 4:1; 1 Cor 10:18 **4** [1]Or *as a result of* [2]Or *spirit* [a]Matt 4:3 **5** [1]Lit *for obedience* [a]Acts 1:25; Gal 1:16 [b]Acts 6:7; Rom 16:26 [c]Acts 9:15 **6** [a]Jude 1; Rev 17:14 **7** [1]Or *holy ones* [a]Rom 5:5ff [b]Acts 9:13; Rom 8:28ff; 1 Cor 1:2 [c]Num 6:25f; 1 Cor 1:3; 2 Cor 1:2; Gal 1:3; Eph 1:2; Phil 1:2; Col 1:2; 1 Thess 1:1; 2 Thess 1:2 **8** [1]Or *concerning you all, that...* [a]1 Cor 1:4; Eph 1:15f; Phil 1:3f; Col 1:3f; 1 Thess 1:2

[b]Acts 28:22; Rom 16:19 **9** [a]Rom 9:1 [b]Acts 24:14; 2 Tim 1:3 [c]Eph 1:16; Phil 1:3f **10** [a]Acts 18:21; Rom 15:32 **11** [1]Or *strengthened* [a]Acts 19:21; Rom 15:23 **13** [a]Rom 11:25; 1 Cor 10:1; 2 Cor 1:8; 1 Thess 4:13 [b]Acts 1:15; Rom 7:1; 1 Cor 1:10; Gal 3:15 [c]Acts 19:21; Rom 15:22f

come to you (and have been prevented
so far) so that I may obtain some [d]fruit
among you also, even as among the rest
of the Gentiles.
14 [a]I am [1]under obligation both to
Greeks and to [b]barbarians, both to the
wise and to the foolish.
15 So, for my part, I am eager to
[a]preach the gospel to you also who are in
Rome.
16 ¶ For I am not [a]ashamed of the gospel, for [b]it is the power of God for salvation to everyone who believes, to the
[c]Jew first and also to [d]the Greek.
17 For in it [a]*the* righteousness of God
is revealed [1]from faith to faith; as it is
written, "[2b]BUT THE RIGHTEOUS *man*
SHALL LIVE BY FAITH."

Unbelief and Its Consequences

18 ¶ For [a]the wrath of God is revealed
from heaven against all ungodliness and
unrighteousness of men who [b]suppress
the truth [1]in unrighteousness,
19 because [a]that which is known
about God is evident [1]within them; for
God made it evident to them.
20 For [a]since the creation of the
world His invisible attributes, His eternal
power and divine nature, have been
clearly seen, [b]being understood through
what has been made, so that they are
without excuse.
21 For even though they knew God,
they did not [1]honor Him as God or give
thanks, but they became [a]futile in their
speculations, and their foolish heart was
darkened.
22 [a]Professing to be wise, they became fools,
23 and [a]exchanged the glory of the
incorruptible God for an image in the
form of corruptible man and of birds and
four-footed animals and [1]crawling creatures.
24 ¶ Therefore [a]God gave them over
in the lusts of their hearts to impurity, so
that their bodies would be [b]dishonored
among them.
25 For they exchanged the truth of
God for [1]a [a]lie, and worshiped and
served the creature rather than the Creator, [b]who is blessed [2]forever. Amen.
26 ¶ For this reason [a]God gave them
over to [b]degrading passions; for their
women exchanged the natural function
for that which is [1]unnatural,
27 and in the same way also the men
abandoned the natural function of the
woman and burned in their desire toward
one another, [a]men with men committing [1]indecent acts and receiving in
[2]their own persons the due penalty of
their error.

13 [d]John 4:36; Phil 1:22; Col 1:6
14 [1]Lit *debtor* [a]1 Cor 9:16 [b]Acts 28:2
15 [a]Rom 15:20
16 [a]Mark 8:38; 2 Tim 1:8 [b]1 Cor 1:18 [c]Acts 3:26; Rom 2:9 [d]John 7:35
17 [1]Or *by* [2]Or *But he who is righteous by faith shall live* [a]Rom 3:21; Phil 3:9 [b]Hab 2:4; Gal 3:11; Heb 10:38
18 [1]Or *by* [a]Rom 5:9; Eph 5:6; Col 3:6 [b]2 Thess 2:6f
19 [1]Or *among* [a]Acts 14:17
20 [a]Mark 10:6 [b]Job 12:7-9; Ps 19:1-6; Jer 5:21f
21 [1]Lit *glorify* [a]2 Kin 17:15; Jer 2:5; Eph 4:17f
22 [a]Jer 10:14; 1 Cor 1:20
23 [1]Or *reptiles* [a]Deut 4:16-18; Ps 106:20; Jer 2:11; Acts 17:29
24 [a]Rom 1:26; Eph 4:19 [b]Eph 2:3
25 [1]Lit *the lie* [2]Lit *unto the ages* [a]Is 44:20; Jer 10:14 [b]Rom 9:5; 2 Cor 11:31
26 [1]Lit *against nature* [a]Rom 1:24 [b]1 Thess 4:5
27 [1]Lit *the shameless deed* [2]Lit *themselves* [a]Lev 18:22; 1 Cor 6:9
28 [1]Lit *to have God in knowledge* [a]Rom 1:24
29 [a]2 Cor 12:20
30 [1]Or *hateful to God* [a]Ps 5:5 [b]2 Tim 3:2
31 [a]2 Tim 3:3
32 [a]Rom 6:21 [b]Luke 11:48; Acts 8:1
2:1 [1]Lit *O man, everyone who* [a]Rom 1:20 [b]Luke 12:14; Rom 2:3 [c]2 Sam 12:5-7; Matt 7:1; Luke 6:37; Rom 14:22
2 [1]Lit *is according to truth against*
3 [1]Lit *who passes judgment* [a]Luke 12:14; Rom 2:1
4 [a]Rom 9:23; 2 Cor 8:2; Eph 1:7; Phil 4:19; Col 1:27; Titus 3:6 [b]Rom 11:22 [c]Rom 3:25 [d]Ex 34:6; Rom 9:22; 1 Tim 1:16; 1 Pet 3:20; 2 Pet 3:9
5 [1]Or *in accordance with* [a]Deut 32:34f; Prov 1:18 [b]Ps 110:5; 2 Cor 5:10; 2 Thess 1:5; Jude 6
6 [a]Ps 62:12; Prov 24:12; Matt

28 ¶ And just as they did not see fit
[1]to acknowledge God any longer, [a]God
gave them over to a depraved mind, to do
those things which are not proper,
29 being filled with all unrighteousness, wickedness, greed, evil; full of
envy, murder, strife, deceit, malice; *they
are* [a]gossips,
30 slanderers, [1a]haters of God, insolent, arrogant, boastful, inventors of evil,
[b]disobedient to parents,
31 without understanding, untrustworthy, [a]unloving, unmerciful;
32 and although they know the ordinance of God, that those who practice
such things are worthy of [a]death, they
not only do the same, but also [b]give
hearty approval to those who practice
them.

The Impartiality of God

2 Therefore you have [a]no excuse,
[1b]everyone of you who passes judgment, for in that which [c]you judge another, you condemn yourself; for you
who judge practice the same things.
2 And we know that the judgment of
God [1]rightly falls upon those who practice such things.
3 But do you suppose this, [a]O man,
[1]when you pass judgment on those who
practice such things and do the same
yourself, that you will escape the judgment of God?
4 Or do you think lightly of [a]the
riches of His [b]kindness and [c]tolerance
and [d]patience, not knowing that the
kindness of God leads you to repentance?
5 But [1]because of your stubbornness
and unrepentant heart [a]you are storing
up wrath for yourself [b]in the day of wrath
and revelation of the righteous judgment
of God,
6 [a]who WILL RENDER TO EACH PERSON
ACCORDING TO HIS DEEDS:
7 to those who by [a]perseverance in
doing good seek for [b]glory and honor and
[c]immortality, [d]eternal life;
8 but to those who are [a]selfishly am-
bitious and [b]do not obey the truth, but
obey unrighteousness, wrath and indignation.
9 *There will be* [a]tribulation and distress [1]for every soul of man who does
evil, of the Jew [b]first and also of the
Greek,
10 but [a]glory and honor and peace
to everyone who does good, to the Jew
[b]first and also to the Greek.

16:27 **7** [a]Luke 8:15; Heb 10:36 [b]Rom 2:10; Heb 2:7; 1 Pet 1:7 [c]1 Cor 15:42; Eph 6:24; 2 Tim 1:10 [d]Matt 25:46
8 [a]2 Cor 12:20; Gal 5:20; Phil 1:17; James 3:14 [b]2 Thess 2:12 **9** [1]Lit *upon* [a]Rom 8:35 [b]Acts 3:26; Rom 1:16; 1 Pet 4:17 **10** [a]Rom 2:7; Heb 2:7; 1 Pet 1:7 [b]Rom 2:9

11 For [a]there is no partiality with God.

12 ¶ For all who have sinned [1a]without the Law will also perish [1]without the Law, and all who have sinned [2]under the Law will be judged [3]by the Law;

13 for *it is* [a]not the hearers [1]of the Law *who* are [2]just before God, but the doers [1]of the Law will be justified.

14 For when Gentiles who do not have [1]the Law do [2a]instinctively the things of the Law, these, not having [1]the Law, are a law to themselves,

15 in that they show [a]the work of the Law written in their hearts, their conscience bearing witness and their thoughts alternately accusing or else defending them,

16 on the day when, [a]according to my gospel, [b]God will judge the secrets of men through Christ Jesus.

The Jew Is Condemned by the Law

17 ¶ But if you bear the name "Jew" and [a]rely [1]upon the Law and boast in God,

18 and know *His* will and [1a]approve the things that are essential, being instructed out of the Law,

19 and are confident that you yourself are a guide to the blind, a light to those who are in darkness,

20 a [1]corrector of the foolish, a teacher of [2]the immature, having in the Law [a]the embodiment of knowledge and of the truth,

21 you, therefore, [a]who teach another, do you not teach yourself? You who [1]preach that one shall not steal, do you steal?

22 You who say that one should not commit adultery, do you commit adultery? You who abhor idols, do you [a]rob temples?

23 You who [a]boast [1]in the Law, through your breaking the Law, do you dishonor God?

24 For "[a]THE NAME OF GOD IS BLASPHEMED AMONG THE GENTILES [b]BECAUSE OF YOU," just as it is written.

25 ¶ For indeed circumcision is of value if you [a]practice [1]the Law; but if you are a transgressor [2]of the Law, [b]your circumcision has become uncircumcision.

26 [a]So if [b]the [1]uncircumcised man [c]keeps the requirements of the Law, will not his uncircumcision be regarded as circumcision?

27 And [a]he who is physically uncircumcised, if he keeps the Law, will he not [b]judge you who [1]though having the letter *of the Law* and circumcision are a transgressor [2]of the Law?

28 For [a]he is not a Jew who is one outwardly, nor is circumcision that which is outward in the flesh.

29 But [a]he is a Jew who is one inwardly; and [b]circumcision is that which is of the heart, by the [c]Spirit, not by the letter; [d]and his praise is not from men, but from God.

All the World Guilty

3 Then what [1]advantage has the Jew? Or what is the benefit of circumcision?

2 Great in every respect. First of all, that [a]they were entrusted with the [b]oracles of God.

3 What then? If [a]some [1]did not believe, their [2]unbelief will not nullify the faithfulness of God, will it?

4 [a]May it never be! Rather, let God be found true, though every man *be found* [b]a liar, as it is written,

"[c]THAT YOU MAY BE JUSTIFIED IN
YOUR WORDS,
AND PREVAIL WHEN YOU [1]ARE
JUDGED."

5 But if our unrighteousness [1a]demonstrates the righteousness of God, [b]what shall we say? The God who inflicts wrath is not unrighteous, is He? ([c]I am speaking in human terms.)

6 [a]May it never be! For otherwise, how will [b]God judge the world?

7 But if through my lie [a]the truth of God abounded to His glory, [b]why am I also still being judged as a sinner?

8 And why not *say* (as we are slanderously reported and as some claim that we say), "[a]Let us do evil that good may come"? [1]Their condemnation is just.

9 ¶ What then? [1a]Are we better than they? Not at all; for we have already charged that both [b]Jews and [c]Greeks are [d]all under sin;

10 as it is written,
"[a]THERE IS NONE RIGHTEOUS, NOT
EVEN ONE;
11 THERE IS NONE WHO UNDERSTANDS,
THERE IS NONE WHO SEEKS
FOR GOD;
12 ALL HAVE TURNED ASIDE, TOGETHER
THEY HAVE BECOME USELESS;
THERE IS NONE WHO DOES GOOD,
THERE IS NOT EVEN ONE."
13 "[a]THEIR THROAT IS AN OPEN GRAVE,
WITH THEIR TONGUES THEY KEEP
DECEIVING,"
"[b]THE POISON OF ASPS IS UNDER
THEIR LIPS";
14 "[a]WHOSE MOUTH IS FULL OF
CURSING AND BITTERNESS";

---

11 [a]Deut 10:17; Acts 10:34
12 [1]Or *without law* [2]Or *under law* [3]Or *by law* [a]Acts 2:23; 1 Cor 9:21
13 [1]Or *of law* [2]Or *righteous* [a]Matt 7:21; John 13:17; James 1:22f
14 [1]Or *law* [2]Lit *by nature* [a]Acts 10:35; Rom 1:19
15 [a]Rom 2:14
16 [a]Rom 16:25; 1 Cor 15:1; Gal 1:11; 1 Tim 1:11; 2 Tim 2:8 [b]Acts 10:42; Rom 3:6
17 [1]Or *upon law* [a]Mic 3:11; John 5:45; Rom 2:23
18 [1]Or *distinguish between the things which differ* [a]Phil 1:10
20 [1]Or *instructor* [2]Lit *infants* [a]Rom 3:31; 2 Tim 1:13
21 [1]Or *proclaim* [a]Matt 23:3ff
22 [a]Acts 19:37
23 [1]Or *in law* [a]Mic 3:11; John 5:45; Rom 2:17
24 [a]Is 52:5; Ezek 36:20ff [b]2 Pet 2:2
25 [1]Or *law* [2]Or *of law* [a]Rom 2:13f [b]Jer 4:4
26 [1]Lit *uncircumcision* [a]1 Cor 7:19 [b]Rom 3:30; Eph 2:11 [c]Rom 2:25
27 [1]Lit *through the letter* [2]Or *of law* [a]Rom 3:30; Eph 2:11 [b]Matt 12:41
28 [a]John 8:39; Rom 2:17; Gal 6:15
29 [a]Phil 3:3; Col 2:11 [b]Deut 30:6 [c]Rom 2:27; 2 Cor 3:6 [d]John 5:44; 1 Cor 4:5; 2 Cor 10:18
3:1 [1]Lit *is the advantage of the Jew*
2 [a]Deut 4:8; Ps 147:19; Rom 9:4 [b]Acts 7:38
3 [1]Or *were unfaithful* [2]Or *unfaithfulness* [a]Rom 10:16; Heb 4:2
4 [1]Lit *in Your judging* [a]Luke 20:16; Rom 3:6 [b]Ps 116:11; Rom 3:7 [c]Ps 51:4
5 [1]Or *commends* [a]Rom 5:8; 2 Cor 6:4 [b]Rom 4:1 [c]Rom 6:19; 1 Cor 9:8; Gal 3:15
6 [a]Luke 20:16; Rom 3:4 [b]Rom 2:16
7 [a]Rom 3:4 [b]Rom 9:19
8 [1]Lit *Whose* [a]Rom 6:1
9 [1]Or *Are we worse* [a]Rom 3:1 [b]Rom 2:1-29 [c]Rom 1:18-32 [d]Rom 3:19; Gal 3:22
10 [a]Ps 14:1-3
13 [a]Ps 5:9 [b]Ps 140:3
14 [a]Ps 10:7

15 “[a]THEIR FEET ARE SWIFT TO SHED
BLOOD,
16 DESTRUCTION AND MISERY ARE IN
THEIR PATHS,
17 AND THE PATH OF PEACE THEY HAVE
NOT KNOWN.”
18 “[a]THERE IS NO FEAR OF GOD BEFORE
THEIR EYES.”
19 ¶ Now we know that whatever the
[a]Law says, it speaks to [b]those who are
[1]under the Law, so that every mouth
may be closed and [c]all the world may
become accountable to God;
20 because [a]by the works [1]of the Law
no flesh will be justified in His sight; for
[2b]through the Law *comes* the knowledge of sin.

Justification by Faith

21 ¶ But now apart [1]from the Law
[a]*the* righteousness of God has been
manifested, being [b]witnessed by the Law
and the Prophets,
22 even *the* [a]righteousness of God
through [b]faith [c]in Jesus Christ for [d]all
those [1]who believe; for [e]there is no distinction;
23 for all [1a]have sinned and fall short
of the glory of God,
24 being justified as a gift [a]by His
grace through [b]the redemption which is
in Christ Jesus;
25 whom God displayed publicly as [a]a
[1]propitiation [2b]in His blood through
faith. *This was* to demonstrate His righteousness, [3]because in the [c]forbearance
of God He [d]passed over the sins previously committed;
26 for the demonstration, *I say,* of His
righteousness at the present time, so that
He would be just and the justifier of the
one who [1]has faith in Jesus.
27 ¶ Where then is [a]boasting? It is excluded. By [b]what kind of law? Of works?
No, but by a law of faith.
28 [1]For [a]we maintain that a man is
justified by faith apart from works [2]of the
Law.
29 Or [a]is God *the God* of Jews only? Is
He not *the God* of Gentiles also? Yes, of
Gentiles also,
30 since indeed [a]God [b]who will justify the [1]circumcised [2]by faith and the
[3]uncircumcised through faith [c]is one.
31 ¶ Do we then nullify [1]the Law
through faith? [a]May it never be! On the
contrary, we [b]establish the Law.

Justification by Faith Evidenced in Old Testament

4 What then shall we say that Abraham, [1]our forefather [a]according to
the flesh, has found?
2 For if Abraham was justified [1]by
works, he has something to boast about,
but [a]not [2]before God.
3 For what does the Scripture say?
“[a]ABRAHAM BELIEVED GOD, AND IT WAS
CREDITED TO HIM AS RIGHTEOUSNESS.”
4 Now to the one who [a]works, his
wage is not credited as a favor, but as
what is due.
5 But to the one who does not work,
but [a]believes in Him who justifies the
ungodly, his faith is credited as righteousness,
6 just as David also speaks of the
blessing on the man to whom God credits
righteousness apart from works:
7 “[a]BLESSED ARE THOSE WHOSE
LAWLESS DEEDS HAVE BEEN
FORGIVEN,
AND WHOSE SINS HAVE BEEN
COVERED.
8 “[a]BLESSED IS THE MAN WHOSE SIN
THE LORD WILL NOT [b]TAKE
INTO ACCOUNT.”
9 ¶ Is this blessing then on [1a]the
circumcised, or on [2]the uncircumcised
also? For [b]we say, “[c]FAITH WAS CREDITED
TO ABRAHAM AS RIGHTEOUSNESS.”
10 How then was it credited? While he
was [1]circumcised, or [2]uncircumcised?
Not while [1]circumcised, but while [2]un-
circumcised;
11 and he [a]received the sign of circumcision, [b]a seal of the righteousness of
the faith which [1]he had while uncircumcised, so that he might be [c]the father of
[d]all who believe without being circumcised, that righteousness might be credited to them,
12 and the father of circumcision to
those who not only are of the circumcision, but who also follow in the steps of
the faith of our father Abraham which
[1]he had while uncircumcised.
13 ¶ For [a]the promise to Abraham or
to his [1]descendants [b]that he would be
heir of the world was not [2]through the
Law, but through the righteousness of
faith.
14 For [a]if those who are [1]of the Law
are heirs, faith is made void and the
promise is nullified;
15 for [a]the Law brings about wrath,
but [b]where there is no law, there also is
no violation.
16 ¶ For this reason *it is* [1]by faith, in
order that *it may be* in accordance with
[a]grace, so that the promise will be guaranteed to [b]all the [2]descendants, not only

15 [a]Is 59:7f
18 [a]Ps 36:1
19 [1]Lit *in* [a]John 10:34 [b]Rom 2:12 [c]Rom 3:9
20 [1]Or *of law* [2]Or *through law* [a]Ps 143:2; Acts 13:39; Gal 2:16 [b]Rom 4:15
21 [1]Or *from law* [a]Rom 1:17 [b]Acts 10:43; Rom 1:2
22 [1]Or *who believe For there is no distinction, since they all have sinned...and are being justified* [a]Rom 1:17 [b]Rom 4:5 [c]Acts 3:16; Gal 2:16; Eph 3:12 [d]Rom 4:11 [e]Rom 10:12; Gal 3:28; Col 3:11
23 [1]Or *sinned* [a]Rom 3:9
24 [a]Rom 4:4f; Eph 2:8 [b]1 Cor 1:30; Eph 1:7; Col 1:14; Heb 9:15
25 [1]Or *a propitiatory sacrifice* [2]Or *by* [3]Lit *because of the passing over of the sins previously committed in the forbearance of God* [a]1 John 2:2 [b]1 Cor 5:7; Heb 9:14; 1 Pet 1:19; Rev 1:5 [c]Rom 2:4 [d]Acts 14:16
26 [1]Lit *is of the faith of Jesus*
27 [a]Rom 2:17; 1 Cor 1:29ff [b]Rom 9:31
28 [1]One early ms reads *Therefore* [2]Or *of law* [a]Acts 13:39; Rom 3:20; Eph 2:9; James 2:20
29 [a]Acts 10:34f; Rom 9:24; Gal 3:28
30 [1]Lit *circumcision* [2]Lit *out of* [3]Lit *uncircumcision* [a]Rom 10:12; Gal 3:20 [b]Rom 3:22; Gal 3:8 [c]Deut 6:4
31 [1]Or *law* [a]Luke 20:16; Rom 3:4 [b]Matt 5:17; Rom 3:4
4:1 [1]Or *our forefather, has found according to the flesh* [a]Rom 1:3
2 [1]Lit *out of* [2]Lit *toward* [a]1 Cor 1:31
3 [a]Gen 15:6; Rom 4:9; Gal 3:6; James 2:23
4 [a]Rom 11:6
5 [a]John 6:29; Rom 3:22
7 [a]Ps 32:1
8 [a]Ps 32:2 [b]2 Cor 5:19
9 [1]Lit *circumcision* [2]Lit *uncircumcision* [a]Rom 3:30 [b]Rom 4:3 [c]Gen 15:6
10 [1]Lit *in circumcision* [2]Lit *in uncircumcision*
11 [1]Lit *was in uncircumcision* [a]Gen 17:10f [b]John 3:33 [c]Luke 19:9; Rom 4:16f [d]Rom 3:22
12 [1]Lit *was in uncircumcision* **13** [1]Lit *seed* [2]Or *through law* [a]Rom 9:8; Gal 3:16 [b]Gen 17:4-6 **14** [1]Or *of law* [a]Gal 3:18
15 [a]Rom 7:7; 1 Cor 15:56; Gal 3:10 [b]Rom 3:20 **16** [1]Or *out of* [2]Lit *seed* [a]Rom 3:24 [b]Rom 4:11

to [3]those who are of the Law, but also to
[3c]those who are of the faith of Abraham,
who is [d]the father of us all,
17 (as it is written, "[a]A FATHER OF
MANY NATIONS HAVE I MADE YOU") in the
presence of Him whom he believed, *even*
God, [b]who gives life to the dead and
[1c]calls into being [d]that which does not
exist.
18 In hope against hope he believed,
so that he might become [a]a father of
many nations according to that which
had been spoken, "[b]SO SHALL YOUR
[1]DESCENDANTS BE."
19 Without becoming weak in faith he
contemplated his own body, now [a]as
good as dead since [b]he was about a hundred years old, and [c]the deadness of Sarah's womb;
20 yet, with respect to the promise of
God, he did not waver in unbelief but
grew strong in faith, [a]giving glory to
God,
21 and [a]being fully assured that
[b]what God had promised, He was able
also to perform.
22 Therefore [a]IT WAS ALSO CREDITED TO
HIM AS RIGHTEOUSNESS.
23 Now [a]not for his sake only was it
written that it was credited to him,
24 but for our sake also, to whom it
will be credited, as those [a]who believe in
Him who [b]raised Jesus our Lord from the
dead,
25 *He* who was [a]delivered over because of our transgressions, and was
[b]raised because of our justification.

Results of Justification

5 [a]Therefore, having been justified by
faith, [1b]we have peace with God
through our Lord Jesus Christ,
2 through whom also we have [a]ob-
tained our introduction by faith into this
grace [b]in which we stand; and [1]we exult
in hope of the glory of God.
3 [a]And not only this, but [1]we also
[b]exult in our tribulations, knowing that
tribulation brings about [c]perseverance;
4 and [a]perseverance, [b]proven character; and proven character, hope;
5 and hope [a]does not disappoint, because the love of God has been [b]poured
out within our hearts through the Holy
Spirit who was given to us.
6 ¶ For while we were still [a]help-
less, [b]at the right time [c]Christ died for
the ungodly.
7 For one will hardly die for a righteous man; [1]though perhaps for the good
man someone would dare even to die.
8 But God [a]demonstrates [b]His own
love toward us, in that while we were yet
sinners, [c]Christ died for us.
9 Much more then, having now been
justified [1a]by His blood, we shall be
saved [b]from the wrath *of God* through
Him.
10 For if while we were [a]enemies we
were reconciled to God through the
death of His Son, much more, having
been reconciled, we shall be saved [1b]by
His life.
11 [a]And not only this, [1]but we also
exult in God through our Lord Jesus
Christ, through whom we have now received [b]the reconciliation.
12 ¶ Therefore, just as through [a]one
man sin entered into the world, and
[b]death through sin, and [c]so death
spread to all men, because all sinned—
13 for [1]until the Law sin was in the
world, but [a]sin is not imputed when
there is no law.
14 Nevertheless death reigned from
Adam until Moses, even over those who
had not sinned [a]in the likeness of the
offense of Adam, who is a [1b]type of Him
who was to come.
15 ¶ But [1]the free gift is not like the
transgression. For if by the transgression
of [a]the one [b]the many died, much more
did the grace of God and the gift by [c]the
grace of the one Man, Jesus Christ,
abound to the many.
16 The gift is not like *that which came*
through the one who sinned; for on the
one hand [a]the judgment *arose* from one
transgression [1]resulting in condemnation, but on the other hand the free gift
arose from many transgressions [2]result-
ing in justification.
17 For if by the transgression of the
one, death reigned [a]through the one,
much more those who receive the abundance of grace and of the gift of righteousness will [b]reign in life through the One,
Jesus Christ.
18 ¶ So then as through [a]one transgression [1]there resulted condemnation
to all men, even so through one [b]act of
righteousness [2]there resulted [c]justifica-
tion of life to all men.
19 For as through the one man's disobedience [a]the many [b]were made sinners, even so through [c]the obedience of
the One [a]the many will be made righteous.
20 [1a]The Law came in so that the
transgression would increase; but where
sin increased, [b]grace abounded all the
more,
21 so that, as [a]sin reigned in death,

16 [3]Lit *that which is* [c]Gal 3:7 [d]Luke 19:9; Rom 4:11
17 [1]Lit *calls the things which do not exist as existing* [a]Gen 17:5 [b]John 5:21 [c]Is 48:13 [d]1 Cor 1:28
18 [1]Lit *seed* [a]Rom 4:17 [b]Gen 15:5
19 [a]Heb 11:12 [b]Gen 17:17 [c]Gen 18:11
20 [a]Matt 9:8
21 [a]Rom 14:5 [b]Gen 18:14; Heb 11:19
22 [a]Gen 15:6; Rom 4:3
23 [a]Rom 15:4; 1 Cor 9:9f; 2 Tim 3:16f
24 [a]Rom 10:9; 1 Pet 1:21 [b]Acts 2:24
25 [a]Is 53:4; Rom 5:6; Gal 2:20; Eph 5:2 [b]Rom 5:18; 1 Cor 15:17; 2 Cor 5:15
5:1 [1]Two early mss read *let us have* [a]Rom 3:28 [b]Rom 5:11
2 [1]Or *let us exult* [a]Eph 2:18; Heb 10:19f; 1 Pet 3:18 [b]1 Cor 15:1
3 [1]Or *let us also exult* [a]Rom 5:11; 2 Cor 8:19 [b]Matt 5:12; James 1:2f [c]Luke 21:19
4 [a]Luke 21:19 [b]Phil 2:22; James 1:12
5 [a]Ps 119:116; Rom 9:33; Heb 6:18f [b]Acts 2:33; Gal 4:6; Titus 3:6
6 [a]Rom 5:8 [b]Gal 4:4 [c]Rom 4:25; Gal 2:20; Eph 5:2
7 [1]Lit *for*
8 [a]Rom 3:5 [b]John 3:16; Rom 8:39 [c]Rom 4:25; Gal 2:20; Eph 5:2
9 [1]Or *in* [a]Rom 3:25 [b]Rom 1:18; 1 Thess 1:10
10 [1]Or *in* [a]Rom 11:28; 2 Cor 5:18f; Eph 2:3; Col 1:21f [b]Rom 8:34; Heb 7:25; 1 John 2:1
11 [1]Lit *but also exulting* [a]Rom 5:3; 2 Cor 8:19 [b]Rom 5:10; 2 Cor 5:18f
12 [a]Gen 2:17; Rom 5:15-17; 1 Cor 15:21f [b]Rom 6:23; 1 Cor 15:56; James 1:15 [c]Rom 5:14; 1 Cor 15:22
13 [1]Or *until law* [a]Rom 4:15
14 [1]Or *foreshadowing* [a]Hos 6:7 [b]1 Cor 15:45
15 [1]Lit *not as the transgression, so also is the free gift* [a]Rom 5:12 [b]Rom 5:19 [c]Acts 15:11
16 [1]Lit *to condemnation* [2]Lit *to an act of righteousness* [a]1 Cor 11:32
17 [a]Gen 2:17; Rom 5:12; 1 Cor 15:21f [b]2 Tim 2:12; Rev 22:5
18 [1]Lit *to condemnation* [2]Lit *to justification* [a]Rom 5:12 [b]Rom 3:25 [c]Rom 4:25
19 [a]Rom 5:15 [b]Rom 5:12 [c]Phil 2:8
20 [1]Or *law* [a]Rom 3:20; Gal 3:19 [b]Rom 6:1; 1 Tim 1:14
21 [a]Rom 5:12

even so [b]grace would reign through righteousness to eternal life through Jesus Christ our Lord.

Believers Are Dead to Sin, Alive to God

6 [a]What shall we say then? Are we to [b]continue in sin so that grace may increase?

2 [a]May it never be! How shall we who [b]died to sin still live in it?

3 Or do you not know that all of us who have been [a]baptized into [b]Christ Jesus have been baptized into His death?

4 Therefore we have been [a]buried with Him through baptism into death, so that as Christ was [b]raised from the dead through the [c]glory of the Father, so we too might walk in [d]newness of life.

5 For [a]if we have become [1]united with *Him* in the likeness of His death, certainly we shall also be [2]*in the likeness* of His resurrection,

6 knowing this, that our [a]old [1]self was [b]crucified with *Him,* in order that our [c]body of sin might be [2]done away with, so that we would no longer be slaves to sin;

7 for [a]he who has died is [1]freed from sin.

8 ¶ Now [a]if we have died with Christ, we believe that we shall also live with Him,

9 knowing that Christ, having been [a]raised from the dead, [1]is never to die again; [b]death no longer is master over Him.

10 For the death that He died, He died to sin once for all; but the life that He lives, He lives to God.

11 Even so consider yourselves to be [a]dead to sin, but alive to God in Christ Jesus.

12 ¶ Therefore do not let sin [a]reign in your mortal body so that you obey its lusts,

13 and do not go on [a]presenting [1]the members of your body to sin *as* [2]instruments of unrighteousness; but [b]present yourselves to God as those alive from the dead, and your members *as* [2]instruments of righteousness to God.

14 For [a]sin shall not [b]be master over you, for [c]you are not under law but [d]under grace.

15 ¶ What then? [a]Shall we sin because we are not under law but under grace? [b]May it never be!

16 Do you not [a]know that when you present yourselves to someone *as* [b]slaves for obedience, you are slaves of the one whom you obey, either of [c]sin [1]resulting in death, or of obedience [2]resulting in righteousness?

17 But [a]thanks be to God that [1]though you were slaves of sin, you became obedient from the heart to that [b]form of teaching to which you were committed,

18 and having been [a]freed from sin, you became slaves of righteousness.

19 [a]I am speaking in human terms because of the weakness of your flesh. For just [b]as you presented your members as slaves to impurity and to lawlessness, [1]resulting in *further* lawlessness, so now present your members as slaves to righteousness, [2]resulting in sanctification.

20 ¶ For [a]when you were slaves of sin, you were free in regard to righteousness.

21 Therefore what [1a]benefit were you then [2]deriving [3]from the things of which you are now ashamed? For the outcome of those things is [b]death.

22 But now having been [a]freed from sin and [b]enslaved to God, you [1]derive your [2c]benefit, [3]resulting in sanctification, and [d]the outcome, eternal life.

23 For the wages of [a]sin is death, but the free gift of God is [b]eternal life in Christ Jesus our Lord.

Believers United to Christ

7 Or do you not know, [a]brethren (for I am speaking to those who know the law), that the law has jurisdiction over a person as long as he lives?

2 For [a]the married woman is bound by law to her [1]husband while he is living; but if her husband dies, she is released from the law [2]concerning the husband.

3 So then, if while her husband is living she is joined to another man, she shall be called an adulteress; but if her husband dies, she is free from the law, so that she is not an adulteress though she is joined to another man.

4 ¶ Therefore, my brethren, you also were [a]made to die [b]to the Law [c]through the body of Christ, so that you might be joined to another, to Him who was raised from the dead, in order that we might bear fruit for God.

5 For while we were [a]in the flesh, the sinful passions, which were [b]*aroused* by the Law, were at work [c]in [1]the members of our body to bear fruit for death.

6 But now we have been [a]released from the Law, having [b]died to that by which we were bound, so that we serve

21 [b]John 1:17; Rom 6:23 **6:1** [a]Rom 3:5 [b]Rom 3:8 **2** [a]Luke 20:16; Rom 6:15 [b]Rom 6:11; Gal 2:19; Col 2:20; 1 Pet 2:24 **3** [a]Matt 28:19 [b]Acts 2:38; Gal 3:27 **4** [a]Col 2:12 [b]Acts 2:24; Rom 6:9 [c]John 11:40; 2 Cor 13:4 [d]Rom 7:6; 2 Cor 5:17; Gal 6:15; Eph 4:23f; Col 3:10 **5** [1]Or *united with the likeness* [2]Or *with* [a]2 Cor 4:10; Phil 3:10f; Col 2:12 **6** [1]Gr *anthropos* [2]Or *made powerless* [a]Eph 4:22; Col 3:9 [b]Gal 2:20 [c]Rom 7:24 **7** [1]Or *acquitted* [a]1 Pet 4:1 **8** [a]Rom 6:4; 2 Cor 4:10; 2 Tim 2:11 **9** [1]Lit *no longer dies* [a]Acts 2:24; Rom 6:4 [b]Rev 1:18 **11** [a]Rom 6:2; Gal 2:19; Col 2:20; 1 Pet 2:24 **12** [a]Rom 6:14 **13** [1]Lit *your members to sin* [2]Or *weapons* [a]Rom 6:16; Col 3:5 [b]Rom 12:1; 2 Cor 5:14f; 1 Pet 2:24 **14** [a]Rom 8:2 [b]Rom 6:12 [c]Rom 5:18; Gal 4:21 [d]Rom 5:17 **15** [a]Rom 6:1 [b]Luke 20:16; Rom 6:2 **16** [1]Lit *to death* [2]Lit *to righteousness* [a]Rom 11:2; 1 Cor 3:16 [b]John 8:34; 2 Pet 2:19 [c]Rom 6:21 **17** [1]Lit *you were slaves...but you became* [a]Rom 1:8; 2 Cor 2:14 [b]2 Tim 1:13 **18** [a]John 8:32; Rom 6:22 **19** [1]Lit *to lawlessness* [2]Lit *to sanctification* [a]Rom 3:5 [b]Rom 6:13 **20** [a]Matt 6:24; Rom 6:16 **21** [1]Lit *fruit* [2]Lit *having* [3]Lit *in* [a]Jer 12:13; Ezek 16:63; Rom 7:5 [b]Rom 1:32; Gal 6:8 **22** [1]Lit *have* [2]Lit *fruit* [3]Lit *to sanctification* [a]John 8:32; Rom 6:18 [b]1 Cor 7:22; 1 Pet 2:16 [c]Rom 7:4 [d]1 Pet 1:9 **23** [a]Rom 1:32; Gal 6:8 [b]Matt 25:46; Rom 5:21 **7:1** [a]Rom 1:13 **2** [1]Lit *living husband* [2]Lit *of* [a]1 Cor 7:39 **4** [a]Rom 6:2 [b]Rom 8:2; Gal 2:19 [c]Col 1:22

5 [1]Lit *our members to bear* [a]Rom 8:8f; 2 Cor 10:3 [b]Rom 7:7f [c]Rom 6:13 **6** [a]Rom 7:2 [b]Rom 6:2

in [c]newness of [d]the [1]Spirit and not in
oldness of the letter.
7 ¶ [a]What shall we say then? Is the
Law sin? [b]May it never be! On the contrary, [c]I would not have come to know
sin except [1]through the Law; for I would
not have known about [2]coveting if the
Law had not said, "[d]YOU SHALL NOT
[2]COVET."
8 But sin, [a]taking opportunity
[b]through the commandment, produced
in me [1]coveting of every kind; for [c]apart
[2]from the Law sin *is* dead.
9 I was once alive apart [1]from the
Law; but when the commandment came,
sin became alive and I died;
10 and this commandment, which was
[1a]to result in life, proved [2]to result in
death for me;
11 for sin, [a]taking an opportunity
[b]through the commandment, [c]deceived
me and through it killed me.
12 [a]So then, the Law is holy, and the
commandment is holy and righteous and
good.
13 ¶ Therefore did that which is good
become *a cause of* death for me? [a]May it
never be! Rather it was sin, in order that
it might be shown to be sin by effecting
my death through that which is good,
so that through the commandment sin
would become utterly sinful.

The Conflict of Two Natures

14 ¶ For we know that the Law is
[a]spiritual, but I am [a]of flesh, [b]sold
[1c]into bondage to sin.
15 For what I am doing, [a]I do not understand; for I am not practicing [b]what I
would like to *do,* but I am doing the very
thing I hate.
16 But if I do the very thing I do not
want *to do,* I agree with [a]the Law, *confessing* that the Law is good.
17 So now, [a]no longer am I the one
doing it, but sin which dwells in me.
18 For I know that nothing good
dwells in me, that is, in my [a]flesh; for the
willing is present in me, but the doing of
the good *is* not.
19 For [a]the good that I want, I do not
do, but I practice the very evil that I do
not want.
20 But if I am doing the very thing I do
not want, [a]I am no longer the one doing
it, but sin which dwells in me.
21 ¶ I find then [a]the [1]principle that
evil is present in me, the one who wants
to do good.
22 For I joyfully concur with the law of
God [1]in [a]the inner man,
23 but I see [a]a different law in [1]the
members of my body, waging war against
the [b]law of my mind and making me a
prisoner [2]of [c]the law of sin which is in
my members.
24 Wretched man that I am! Who will
set me free from [1a]the body of this
[b]death?
25 [a]Thanks be to God through Jesus
Christ our Lord! So then, on the one hand
I myself with my mind am serving the law
of God, but on the other, with my flesh
[b]the law of sin.

Deliverance from Bondage

8 Therefore there is now no [a]condem-
nation for those who are [b]in [c]Christ
Jesus.
2 For [a]the law of the Spirit of life [1]in
[b]Christ Jesus [c]has set you free from the
law of sin and of death.
3 For [a]what the Law could not do,
[1b]weak as it was through the flesh, God
did: sending His own Son in [c]the likeness of [2]sinful flesh and *as an offering* for
sin, He condemned sin in the flesh,
4 so that the [a]requirement of the
Law might be fulfilled in us, who [b]do not
walk according to the flesh but according
to the Spirit.
5 For those who are according to the
flesh set their minds on [a]the things of
the flesh, but those who are according to
the Spirit, [b]the things of the Spirit.
6 [a]For the mind set on the flesh is
[b]death, but the mind set on the Spirit
is life and peace,
7 because the mind set on the flesh is
[a]hostile toward God; for it does not subject itself to the law of God, for it is not
even able *to do so,*
8 and those who are [a]in the flesh
cannot please God.
9 ¶ However, you are not [a]in the
flesh but in the Spirit, if indeed the Spirit
of God [b]dwells in you. But [c]if anyone
does not have the Spirit of Christ, he does
not belong to Him.
10 [a]If Christ is in you, though the
body is dead because of sin, yet the spirit
is [1]alive because of righteousness.
11 But if the Spirit of Him who [a]raised
Jesus from the dead dwells in you, [b]He
who raised [c]Christ Jesus from the dead
will also give life to your mortal bodies
[1]through His Spirit who dwells in you.
12 ¶ So then, brethren, we are under
obligation, not to the flesh, to live according to the flesh—
13 for [a]if you are living according to
the flesh, you [1]must die; but if by the
Spirit you are [b]putting to death the deeds
of the body, you will live.

6 [1]Or *spirit* [c]Rom 6:4 [d]Rom 2:29
7 [1]Or *through law* [2]Or *lust* [a]Rom 3:5 [b]Luke 20:16 [c]Rom 3:20 [d]Ex 20:17; Deut 5:21
8 [1]Or *lust* [2]Or *from law* [a]Rom 7:11 [b]Rom 3:20 [c]1 Cor 15:56
9 [1]Or *from law*
10 [1]Lit *to life* [2]Lit *to death* [a]Lev 18:5; Luke 10:28; Rom 10:5; Gal 3:12
11 [a]Rom 7:8 [b]Rom 3:20 [c]Gen 3:13
12 [a]Rom 7:16; 1 Tim 1:8
13 [a]Luke 20:16
14 [1]Lit *under sin* [a]1 Cor 3:1 [b]1 Kin 21:20; 2 Kin 17:17; Rom 6:6; Gal 4:3 [c]Rom 3:9
15 [a]John 15:15 [b]Rom 7:19; Gal 5:17
16 [a]Rom 7:12; 1 Tim 1:8
17 [a]Rom 7:20
18 [a]John 3:6; Rom 7:25
19 [a]Rom 7:15
20 [a]Rom 7:17
21 [1]Lit *law* [a]Rom 7:23
22 [1]Or *concerning* [a]2 Cor 4:16; Eph 3:16; 1 Pet 3:4
23 [1]Lit *my members* [2]Lit *in* [a]Rom 6:19; Gal 5:17; James 4:1; 1 Pet 2:11 [b]Rom 7:25 [c]Rom 7:21
24 [1]Or *this body of death* [a]Rom 6:6; Col 2:11 [b]Rom 8:2
25 [a]1 Cor 15:57 [b]Rom 7:21
8:1 [a]Rom 5:16 [b]Rom 8:9f [c]Rom 8:2
2 [1]Or *has set you free in Christ Jesus* [a]1 Cor 15:45 [b]Rom 8:1 [c]John 8:32; Rom 6:14
3 [1]Lit *in which it was weak* [2]Lit *flesh of sin* [a]Acts 13:39; Heb 10:1ff [b]Rom 7:18f; Heb 7:18 [c]Phil 2:7; Heb 2:14
4 [a]Luke 1:6; Rom 2:26 [b]Gal 5:16
5 [a]Gal 5:19-21 [b]Gal 5:22-25
6 [a]Gal 6:8 [b]Rom 6:21
7 [a]James 4:4
8 [a]Rom 7:5
9 [a]Rom 7:5 [b]John 14:23; Rom 8:11; 1 Cor 3:16; 2 Cor 6:16; Gal 4:6; Phil 1:19; 2 Tim 1:14; 1 John 4:13 [c]John 14:17
10 [1]Lit *life* [a]John 17:23; Gal 2:20; Eph 3:17; Col 1:27
11 [1]One early ms reads *because of* [a]Acts 2:24; Rom 6:4 [b]John 5:21 [c]Rom 8:1
13 [1]Or *are going to* [a]Rom 8:6 [b]Col 3:5

14 For all who are [a]being led by the Spirit of God, these are [b]sons of God.

15 For you [a]have not received a spirit of slavery [1]leading to fear again, but you [b]have received [2]a spirit of adoption as sons by which we cry out, "[c]Abba! Father!"

16 The Spirit Himself [a]testifies with our spirit that we are [b]children of God,

17 and if children, [a]heirs also, heirs of God and fellow heirs with Christ, [b]if indeed we suffer with *Him* so that we may also be glorified with *Him.*

18 ¶ For I consider that the sufferings of this present time [a]are not worthy to be compared with the [b]glory that is to be revealed to us.

19 For the [a]anxious longing of the creation waits eagerly for [b]the revealing of the [c]sons of God.

20 For the creation [a]was subjected to [b]futility, not willingly, but [c]because of Him who subjected it, [1]in hope

21 that [a]the creation itself also will be set free from its slavery to corruption into the freedom of the glory of the children of God.

22 For we know that the whole creation [a]groans and suffers the pains of childbirth together until now.

23 [a]And not only this, but also we ourselves, having [b]the first fruits of the Spirit, even we ourselves [c]groan within ourselves, [d]waiting eagerly for *our* adoption as sons, [e]the redemption of our body.

24 For [a]in hope we have been saved, but [b]hope that is seen is not hope; for who hopes for what he *already* sees?

25 But [a]if we hope for what we do not see, with perseverance we wait eagerly for it.

Our Victory in Christ

26 ¶ In the same way the Spirit also helps our weakness; for [a]we do not know how to pray as we should, but [b]the Spirit Himself intercedes for *us* with groanings too deep for words;

27 and [a]He who searches the hearts knows what [b]the mind of the Spirit is, because He [c]intercedes for the [1]saints according to *the will of* God.

28 ¶ And we know that [1]God causes [a]all things to work together for good to those who love God, to those who are [b]called according to *His* purpose.

29 For those whom He [a]foreknew, He also [b]predestined *to become* [c]conformed to the image of His Son, so that He would be the [d]firstborn among many brethren;

30 and these whom He [a]predestined, He also [b]called; and these whom He called, He also [c]justified; and these whom He justified, He also [d]glorified.

31 ¶ [a]What then shall we say to these things? [b]If God *is* for us, who *is* against us?

32 He who [a]did not spare His own Son, but [b]delivered Him over for us all, how will He not also with Him freely give us all things?

33 Who will bring a charge against [a]God's elect? [b]God is the one who justifies;

34 who is the one who [a]condemns? Christ Jesus is He who [b]died, yes, rather who was [1][c]raised, who is [d]at the right hand of God, who also [e]intercedes for us.

35 Who will separate us from [a]the love of [1]Christ? Will [b]tribulation, or distress, or [c]persecution, or [c]famine, or [c]nakedness, or [c]peril, or sword?

36 Just as it is written,

"[a]For Your sake we are being put
to death all day long;
We were considered as sheep to
be slaughtered."

37 But in all these things we overwhelmingly [a]conquer through [b]Him who loved us.

38 For I am convinced that neither [a]death, nor life, nor [b]angels, nor principalities, nor [a]things present, nor things to come, nor powers,

39 nor height, nor depth, nor any other created thing, will be able to separate us from [a]the love of God, which is [b]in Christ Jesus our Lord.

Solicitude for Israel

9 [a]I am telling the truth in Christ, I am not lying, my conscience testifies with me in the Holy Spirit,

2 that I have great sorrow and unceasing grief in my heart.

3 For [a]I could [1]wish that I myself were [b]accursed, *separated* from Christ for the sake of my brethren, my kinsmen [c]according to the flesh,

4 who are [a]Israelites, to whom belongs [b]the adoption as sons, and [c]the glory and [d]the covenants and [e]the giving of the Law and [f]the *temple* service and [g]the promises,

14 [a]Gal 5:18 [b]Hos 1:10; Matt 5:9; John 1:12; Rom 8:16; 2 Cor 6:18; Gal 3:26; 1 John 3:1; Rev 21:7 **15** [1]Lit *for fear again* [2]Or *the Spirit* [a]2 Tim 1:7; Heb 2:15 [b]Rom 8:23; Gal 4:5f [c]Mark 14:36; Gal 4:6 **16** [a]Acts 5:32 [b]Hos 1:10; Matt 5:9; John 1:12; Rom 8:14; 2 Cor 6:18; Gal 3:26; 1 John 3:1; Rev 21:7 **17** [a]Acts 20:32; Gal 3:29; Eph 3:6; Titus 3:7; Heb 1:14; Rev 21:7 [b]2 Cor 1:5; Phil 3:10; Col 1:24; 2 Tim 2:12; 1 Pet 4:13 **18** [a]2 Cor 4:17; 1 Pet 4:13 [b]Col 3:4; Titus 2:13; 1 Pet 1:5 **19** [a]Phil 1:20 [b]Rom 8:18; 1 Cor 1:7f; Col 3:4; 1 Pet 1:7; 1 John 3:2 [c]Hos 1:10; Matt 5:9; John 1:12; Rom 8:14; 2 Cor 6:18; Gal 3:26; 1 John 3:1; Rev 21:7 **20** [1]Or *in hope; because the creation* [a]Gen 3:17-19 [b]Ps 39:5f; Eccl 1:2 [c]Gen 3:17 **21** [a]Acts 3:21; 2 Pet 3:13; Rev 21:1 **22** [a]Jer 12:4 **23** [a]Rom 5:3 [b]Rom 8:16; 2 Cor 1:22 [c]2 Cor 5:2 [d]Rom 8:15; Gal 5:5 [e]Rom 7:24 **24** [a]Rom 8:20; 1 Thess 5:8; Titus 3:7 [b]Rom 4:18; 2 Cor 5:7; Heb 11:1 **25** [a]1 Thess 1:3 **26** [a]Matt 20:22; 2 Cor 12:8 [b]John 14:16; Rom 8:15f; Eph 6:18 **27** [1]Or *holy ones* [a]Ps 139:1f; Luke 16:15; Acts 1:24; Rev 2:23 [b]Rom 8:6 [c]Rom 8:34 **28** [1]One early ms reads *all things work together for good* [a]Rom 8:32 [b]Rom 8:30; 1 Cor 1:9; Gal 1:6; Eph 1:11; 2 Thess 2:14; Heb 9:15; 1 Pet 2:9 **29** [a]Rom 11:2; 1 Cor 8:3; 2 Tim 1:9; 1 Pet 1:2 [b]Rom 9:23; 1 Cor 2:7; Eph 1:5 [c]1 Cor 15:49; Phil 3:21 [d]Col 1:18; Heb 1:6 **30** [a]Rom 9:23; 1 Cor 2:7; Eph 1:5 [b]Rom 8:28; 1 Cor 1:9; Gal 1:6; Eph 1:11; 2 Thess 2:14; Heb 9:15; 1 Pet 2:9 [c]1 Cor 6:11 [d]John 17:22; Rom 8:21 **31** [a]Rom 3:5 [b]Ps 118:6; Matt 1:23 **32** [a]John 3:16; Rom 5:8 [b]Rom 4:25 **33** [a]Luke 18:7 [b]Is 50:8f **34** [1]One early ms reads *raised from the dead* [a]Rom 8:1 [b]Rom 5:6f [c]Acts 2:24 [d]Mark 16:19 [e]Rom 8:27; Heb 7:25 **35** [1]Two early mss read *God* [a]Rom 8:37f [b]Rom 2:9; 2 Cor 4:8 [c]1 Cor 4:11; 2 Cor 11:26f **36** [a]Ps 44:22; Acts 20:24; 1 Cor 4:9; 2 Cor 1:9 **37** [a]John 16:33; 1 Cor 15:57 [b]Gal 2:20; Eph 5:2; Rev 1:5 **38** [a]1 Cor 3:22 [b]1 Cor 15:24; Eph 1:21; 1 Pet 3:22 **39** [a]Rom 5:8 [b]Rom 8:1 **9:1** [a]2 Cor 11:10; Gal 1:20; 1 Tim 2:7 **3** [1]Lit *pray* [a]Ex 32:32 [b]1 Cor 12:3; Gal 1:8f [c]Rom 1:3; Eph 6:5 **4** [a]Deut 7:6; Rom 9:6 [b]Ex 4:22; Rom 8:15 [c]Ex 40:34; 1 Kin 8:11; Ezek 1:28; Heb 9:5 [d]Gen 17:2; Deut 29:14; Luke 1:72; Acts 3:25; Eph 2:12 [e]Deut 4:13f; Ps 147:19 [f]Heb 9:1 [g]Acts 2:39; Eph 2:12

5 whose are [a]the fathers, and [b]from
whom is [1]the Christ according to the
flesh, [c]who is over all, [d]God [e]blessed
[2]forever. Amen.
6 ¶ But *it is* not as though [a]the word
of God has failed. [b]For they are not all
Israel who are *descended* from Israel;
7 nor are they all children [a]because
they are Abraham's [1]descendants, but:
"[2][b]THROUGH ISAAC YOUR [1]DESCENDANTS
WILL BE NAMED."
8 That is, it is not the children of the
flesh who are [a]children of God, but the
[b]children of the promise are regarded as
[1]descendants.
9 For this is the word of promise:
"[a]AT THIS TIME I WILL COME, AND SARAH
SHALL HAVE A SON."
10 [a]And not only this, but there was
[b]Rebekah also, when she had conceived
twins by one man, our father Isaac;
11 for though *the twins* were not yet
born and had not done anything good or
bad, so that [a]God's purpose according to
His choice would [1]stand, not [2]because
of works but [2]because of Him who calls,
12 it was said to her, "[a]THE OLDER
WILL SERVE THE YOUNGER."
13 Just as it is written, "[a]JACOB I
LOVED, BUT ESAU I HATED."
14 ¶ [a]What shall we say then?
[b]There is no injustice with God, is there?
[c]May it never be!
15 For He says to Moses, "[a]I WILL
HAVE MERCY ON WHOM I HAVE MERCY, AND
I WILL HAVE COMPASSION ON WHOM I HAVE
COMPASSION."
16 So then it *does* not *depend* on the
man who wills or the man who [a]runs,
but on [b]God who has mercy.
17 For the Scripture says to Pharaoh,
"[a]FOR THIS VERY PURPOSE I RAISED YOU UP,
TO DEMONSTRATE MY POWER IN YOU, AND
THAT MY NAME MIGHT BE PROCLAIMED
[1]THROUGHOUT THE WHOLE EARTH."
18 So then He has mercy on whom He
desires, and He [a]hardens whom He desires.
19 ¶ [a]You will say to me then, "[b]Why
does He still find fault? For [c]who resists
His will?"
20 On the contrary, who are you,
[a]O man, who [b]answers back to God?
[c]The thing molded will not say to the
molder, "Why did you make me like
this," will it?
21 Or does not the potter have a right
over the clay, to make from the same
lump one vessel [1]for honorable use and
another [2]for common use?
22 [1]What if God, although willing to
demonstrate His wrath and to make His
power known, endured with much [a]pa-
tience vessels of wrath [b]prepared for destruction?
23 And *He did so* to make known [a]the
riches of His glory upon [b]vessels of mercy, which He [c]prepared beforehand for
glory,
24 *even* us, whom He also [a]called,
[b]not from among Jews only, but also
from among Gentiles.
25 As He says also in Hosea,
"[a]I WILL CALL THOSE WHO WERE NOT
MY PEOPLE, 'MY PEOPLE,'
AND HER WHO WAS NOT BELOVED,
'BELOVED.'"
26 "[a]AND IT SHALL BE THAT IN THE
PLACE WHERE IT WAS SAID TO
THEM, 'YOU ARE NOT MY
PEOPLE,'
THERE THEY SHALL BE CALLED SONS
OF [b]THE LIVING GOD."
27 ¶ Isaiah cries out concerning Israel,
"[a]THOUGH THE NUMBER OF THE SONS OF
ISRAEL BE [b]LIKE THE SAND OF THE SEA, IT IS
[c]THE REMNANT THAT WILL BE SAVED;
28 [a]FOR THE LORD WILL EXECUTE HIS
WORD ON THE EARTH, [1]THOROUGHLY AND
[2]QUICKLY."
29 And just as Isaiah foretold,
"[a]UNLESS [b]THE LORD OF [1]SABAOTH
HAD LEFT TO US A [2]POSTERITY,
[c]WE WOULD HAVE BECOME LIKE
SODOM, AND WOULD HAVE
[3]RESEMBLED GOMORRAH."
30 ¶ [a]What shall we say then? That
Gentiles, who did not pursue righteousness, attained righteousness, even [b]the
righteousness which is [1]by faith;
31 but Israel, [a]pursuing a law of righteousness, did not [b]arrive at *that* law.
32 Why? Because *they did* not *pursue*
it [1]by faith, but as though *it were* [1]by
works. They stumbled over [a]the stumbling stone,
33 just as it is written,
"[a]BEHOLD, I LAY IN ZION [b]A STONE
OF STUMBLING AND A ROCK OF
OFFENSE,
[c]AND HE WHO BELIEVES IN HIM
[d]WILL NOT BE
[1]DISAPPOINTED."

The Word of Faith Brings Salvation

10 Brethren, my heart's desire and
my prayer to God for them is for
their salvation.
2 For I testify about them that they
have [a]a zeal for God, but not in accordance with knowledge.
3 For not knowing about [a]God's
righteousness and [b]seeking to establish
their own, they did not subject themselves to the righteousness of God.

5 [1]I.e. the Messiah [2]Lit *unto the ages* [a]Acts 3:13; Rom 11:28 [b]Matt 1:1-16; Rom 1:3 [c]Col 1:16-19 [d]John 1:1 [e]Rom 1:25
6 [a]Num 23:19 [b]John 1:47; Rom 2:28f; Gal 6:16
7 [1]Lit *seed* [2]Lit *in* [a]John 8:33; Gal 4:23 [b]Gen 21:12; Heb 11:18
8 [1]Lit *seed* [a]Rom 8:14 [b]Rom 4:13; Gal 3:29; Heb 11:11
9 [a]Gen 18:10
10 [a]Rom 5:3 [b]Gen 25:21
11 [1]Lit *remain* [2]Lit *from* [a]Rom 4:17
12 [a]Gen 25:23
13 [a]Mal 1:2f
14 [a]Rom 3:5 [b]2 Chr 19:7; Rom 2:11 [c]Luke 20:16
15 [a]Ex 33:19
16 [a]Gal 2:2 [b]Eph 2:8
17 [1]Lit *in* [a]Ex 9:16
18 [a]Ex 4:21; Deut 2:30; Josh 11:20; John 12:40; Rom 11:7
19 [a]Rom 11:19; 1 Cor 15:35; James 2:18 [b]Rom 3:7 [c]2 Chr 20:6; Job 9:12; Dan 4:35
20 [a]Rom 2:1 [b]Job 33:13 [c]Is 29:16; Jer 18:6; Rom 9:22f; 2 Tim 2:20
21 [1]Lit *for honor* [2]Lit *for dishonor*
22 [1]Lit *But* [a]Rom 2:4 [b]Prov 16:4; 1 Pet 2:8
23 [a]Rom 2:4; Eph 3:16 [b]Acts 9:15 [c]Rom 8:29f
24 [a]Rom 8:28 [b]Rom 3:29
25 [a]Hos 2:23; 1 Pet 2:10
26 [a]Hos 1:10 [b]Matt 16:16
27 [a]Is 10:22 [b]Gen 22:17; Hos 1:10 [c]Rom 11:5
28 [1]Lit *finishing it* [2]Lit *cutting it short* [a]Is 10:23
29 [1]I.e. Hosts [2]Lit *seed* [3]Lit *been made like* [a]Is 1:9 [b]James 5:4 [c]Deut 29:23; Is 13:19; Jer 49:18; Amos 4:11
30 [1]Lit *out of* [a]Rom 9:14 [b]Rom 1:17; Gal 2:16; Phil 3:9; Heb 11:7
31 [a]Is 51:1; Rom 9:30 [b]Gal 5:4
32 [1]Lit *out of* [a]Is 8:14; 1 Pet 2:6
33 [1]Lit *put to shame* [a]Is 28:16 [b]Is 8:14 [c]Rom 10:11 [d]Rom 5:5
10:2 [a]Acts 21:20
3 [a]Rom 1:17 [b]Is 51:1; Rom 10:2f

4 For [a]Christ is the [1]end of the law for righteousness to [b]everyone who believes.

5 ¶ For Moses writes that the man who practices the righteousness which is [1]based on law [a]shall live [2]by that righteousness.

6 But [a]the righteousness [1]based on faith speaks as follows: "[b]DO NOT SAY IN YOUR HEART, 'WHO WILL ASCEND INTO HEAVEN?' (that is, to bring Christ down),

7 or 'WHO WILL DESCEND INTO THE [a]ABYSS?' (that is, to [b]bring Christ up from the dead)."

8 But what does it say? "[a]THE WORD IS NEAR YOU, in your mouth and in your heart"—that is, the word of faith which we are preaching,

9 [1]that [a]if you confess with your mouth Jesus *as* Lord, and [b]believe in your heart that [c]God raised Him from the dead, you will be saved;

10 for with the heart a person believes, [1]resulting in righteousness, and with the mouth he confesses, [2]resulting in salvation.

11 For the Scripture says, "[a]WHOEVER BELIEVES IN HIM WILL NOT BE [1]DISAPPOINTED."

12 For [a]there is no distinction between Jew and Greek; for the same *Lord* is [b]Lord of [c]all, abounding in riches for all who call on Him;

13 for "[a]WHOEVER WILL CALL ON THE NAME OF THE LORD WILL BE SAVED."

14 ¶ How then will they call on Him in whom they have not believed? How will they believe in Him [a]whom they have not heard? And how will they hear without [b]a preacher?

15 How will they preach unless they are sent? Just as it is written, "[a]HOW BEAUTIFUL ARE THE FEET OF THOSE WHO [1][b]BRING GOOD NEWS OF GOOD THINGS!"

16 ¶ However, they [a]did not all heed the [1]good news; for Isaiah says, "[b]LORD, WHO HAS BELIEVED OUR REPORT?"

17 So faith *comes* from [a]hearing, and hearing by [b]the word [1]of Christ.

18 ¶ But I say, surely they have never heard, have they? Indeed they have;

"[a]THEIR VOICE HAS GONE OUT INTO
ALL THE EARTH,
AND THEIR WORDS TO THE ENDS OF
THE [1]WORLD."

19 But I say, surely Israel did not know, did they? First Moses says,

"[a]I WILL [b]MAKE YOU JEALOUS BY
THAT WHICH IS NOT A NATION,
BY A NATION WITHOUT
UNDERSTANDING WILL I
ANGER YOU."

20 And Isaiah is very bold and says,

"[a]I WAS FOUND BY THOSE WHO DID
NOT SEEK ME,
I BECAME MANIFEST TO THOSE WHO
DID NOT ASK FOR ME."

21 But as for Israel He says, "[a]ALL THE DAY LONG I HAVE STRETCHED OUT MY HANDS TO A DISOBEDIENT AND OBSTINATE PEOPLE."

Israel Is Not Cast Away

11 I say then, God has not [a]rejected His people, has He? [b]May it never be! For [c]I too am an Israelite, [1]a descendant of Abraham, of the tribe of Benjamin.

2 God [a]has not rejected His people whom He [b]foreknew. [c]Or do you not know what the Scripture says in *the passage about* Elijah, how he pleads with God against Israel?

3 "Lord, [a]THEY HAVE KILLED YOUR PROPHETS, THEY HAVE TORN DOWN YOUR ALTARS, AND I ALONE AM LEFT, AND THEY ARE SEEKING MY LIFE."

4 But what [1]is the divine response to him? "[a]I HAVE KEPT for Myself SEVEN THOUSAND MEN WHO HAVE NOT BOWED THE KNEE TO BAAL."

5 In the same way then, there has also come to be at the present time [a]a remnant according to *God's* [1]gracious choice.

6 But [a]if it is by grace, it is no longer [1]on the basis of works, otherwise grace is no longer grace.

7 ¶ What then? What [a]Israel is seeking, it has not obtained, but [1]those who were chosen obtained it, and the rest were [b]hardened;

8 just as it is written,

"[a]GOD GAVE THEM A SPIRIT OF
STUPOR,
EYES TO SEE NOT AND EARS TO
HEAR NOT,
DOWN TO THIS VERY DAY."

9 And David says,

"[a]LET THEIR TABLE BECOME A SNARE
AND A TRAP,
AND A STUMBLING BLOCK AND A
RETRIBUTION TO THEM.
10 "[a]LET THEIR EYES BE DARKENED TO
SEE NOT,
AND BEND THEIR BACKS FOREVER."

11 ¶ [a]I say then, they did not stumble so as to fall, did they? [b]May it never be! But by their transgression [c]salvation *has come* to the Gentiles, to [d]make them jealous.

12 Now if their transgression is riches for the world and their failure is riches for the Gentiles, how much more will their [1][a]fulfillment be!

13 But I am speaking to you who are Gentiles. Inasmuch then as [a]I am an

---

4 [1]Or *goal* [a]Rom 7:1-4; Gal 3:24; 4:5 [b]Rom 3:22
5 [1]Lit *out of, from* [2]Lit *by it* [a]Lev 18:5; Neh 9:29; Ezek 20:11,13,21; Rom 7:10
6 [1]Lit *out of, from* [a]Rom 9:30 [b]Deut 30:12
7 [a]Luke 8:31 [b]Heb 13:20
8 [a]Deut 30:14
9 [1]Or *because* [a]Matt 10:32; Luke 12:8; Rom 14:9; 1 Cor 12:3; Phil 2:11 [b]Acts 16:31; Rom 4:24 [c]Acts 2:24
10 [1]Lit *to righteousness* [2]Lit *to salvation*
11 [1]Lit *put to shame* [a]Is 28:16; Rom 9:33
12 [a]Rom 3:22, 29 [b]Acts 10:36 [c]Rom 3:29
13 [a]Joel 2:32; Acts 2:21
14 [a]Eph 2:17; 4:21 [b]Acts 8:31; Titus 1:3
15 [1]Or *preach the gospel* [a]Is 52:7 [b]Rom 1:15; 15:20
16 [1]Or *gospel* [a]Rom 3:3 [b]Is 53:1; John 12:38
17 [1]Or *concerning Christ* [a]Gal 3:2,5 [b]Col 3:16
18 [1]Or *inhabited earth* [a]Ps 19:4; Rom 1:8; Col 1:6,23; 1 Thess 1:8
19 [a]Deut 32:21 [b]Rom 11:11,14
20 [a]Is 65:1; Rom 9:30
21 [a]Is 65:2
11:1 [1]Lit *of the seed of Abraham* [a]1 Sam 12:22; Jer 31:37; 33:24-26 [b]Luke 20:16 [c]2 Cor 11:22; Phil 3:5
2 [a]Ps 94:14 [b]Rom 8:29 [c]Rom 6:16
3 [a]1 Kin 19:10, 14
4 [1]Lit *says* [a]1 Kin 19:18
5 [1]Lit *choice of grace* [a]2 Kin 19:4; Rom 9:27
6 [1]Lit *out of* [a]Rom 4:4
7 [1]Lit *the election* [a]Rom 9:31 [b]Mark 6:52; Rom 9:18; 11:25; 2 Cor 3:14
8 [a]Deut 29:4; Is 29:10; Matt 13:13f
9 [a]Ps 69:22
10 [a]Ps 69:23
11 [a]Rom 11:1 [b]Luke 20:16 [c]Acts 28:28 [d]Rom 11:14
12 [1]Or *fullness* [a]Rom 11:25
13 [a]Acts 9:15

apostle of Gentiles, I magnify my ministry,
14 if somehow I might [a]move to jealousy [b]my [1]fellow countrymen and
[c]save some of them.
15 For if their rejection is the [a]recon-
ciliation of the world, what will *their* acceptance be but [b]life from the dead?
16 If the [a]first piece *of dough* is holy,
the lump is also; and if the root is holy,
the branches are too.
17 ¶ But if some of the [a]branches
were broken off, and [b]you, being a wild
olive, were grafted in among them and
became partaker with them of the [1]rich
root of the olive tree,
18 do not be arrogant toward the
branches; but if you are arrogant, *remember that* [a]it is not you who supports the
root, but the root *supports* you.
19 [a]You will say then, "Branches
were broken off so that I might be grafted in."
20 Quite right, they were broken off
for their unbelief, but you [a]stand by your
faith. [b]Do not be conceited, but fear;
21 for if God did not spare the natural
branches, He will not spare you, either.
22 Behold then the kindness and severity of God; to those who fell, severity,
but to you, God's [a]kindness, [b]if you continue in His kindness; otherwise you also
[c]will be cut off.
23 And they also, [a]if they do not continue in their unbelief, will be grafted in,
for God is able to graft them in again.
24 For if you were cut off from what is
by nature a wild olive tree, and were
grafted contrary to nature into a cultivated olive tree, how much more will these
who are the natural *branches* be grafted
into their own olive tree?
25 ¶ For [a]I do not want you, brethren,
to be uninformed of this [b]mystery—so
that you will not be [c]wise in your own
estimation—that a partial [d]hardening
has happened to Israel until the [e]fullness
of the Gentiles has come in;
26 and so all Israel will be saved; just
as it is written,
"[a]THE DELIVERER WILL COME FROM
ZION,
HE WILL REMOVE UNGODLINESS
FROM JACOB."
27 "[a]THIS IS [1]MY COVENANT WITH
THEM,
[b]WHEN I TAKE AWAY THEIR SINS."
28 [1]From the standpoint of the gospel
they are [a]enemies for your sake, but
[2]from the standpoint of *God's* choice
they are beloved for [b]the sake of the fathers;
29 for the gifts and the [a]calling of God
[b]are irrevocable.
30 For just as you once were disobedient to God, but now have been shown
mercy because of their disobedience,
31 so these also now have been disobedient, that because of the mercy
shown to you they also may now be
shown mercy.
32 For [a]God has shut up all in disobedience so that He may show mercy to all.
33 ¶ Oh, the depth of [a]the riches
[1]both of the [b]wisdom and knowledge of
God! [c]How unsearchable are His judgments and unfathomable His ways!
34 For [a]WHO HAS KNOWN THE MIND OF
THE LORD, OR WHO BECAME HIS COUNSELOR?
35 Or [a]WHO HAS FIRST GIVEN TO HIM
[1]THAT IT MIGHT BE PAID BACK TO HIM AGAIN?
36 For [a]from Him and through Him
and to Him are all things. [b]To Him *be* the
glory [1]forever. Amen.

Dedicated Service

12 Therefore [a]I urge you, brethren,
by the mercies of God, to
[b]present your bodies a living and holy
sacrifice, [1]acceptable to God, *which is*
your [2]spiritual service of worship.
2 And do not [a]be conformed to [b]this
[1]world, but be transformed by the [c]re-
newing of your mind, so that you may
[2d]prove what the will of God is, that
which is good and [3]acceptable and perfect.
3 ¶ For through [a]the grace given to
me I say to everyone among you [b]not
to think more highly of himself than he
ought to think; but to think so as to have
sound judgment, as God has allotted to
[c]each a measure of faith.
4 For [a]just as we have many members in one body and all the members do
not have the same function,
5 so we, [a]who are many, are [b]one
body in Christ, and individually members
one of another.
6 Since we have gifts that [a]differ according to the grace given to us, *each
of us is to exercise them accordingly*: if
[b]prophecy, [1]according to the proportion
of his faith;
7 if [1a]service, in his serving; or he
who [b]teaches, in his teaching;
8 or he who [a]exhorts, in his exhortation; he who gives, with [1b]liberality;
[c]he who [2]leads, with diligence; he who
shows mercy, with [d]cheerfulness.
9 ¶ *Let* [a]love *be* without hypocrisy.

14 [1]Lit *flesh* [a]Rom 11:11 [b]Gen 29:14; 2 Sam 19:12f; Rom 9:3 [c]1 Cor 1:21; 1 Tim 1:15; 2 Tim 1:9; Titus 3:5
15 [a]Rom 5:11 [b]Luke 15:24
16 [a]Num 15:18ff; Neh 10:37; Ezek 44:30
17 [1]Lit *root of the fatness* [a]Jer 11:16; John 15:2 [b]Eph 2:11ff
18 [a]John 4:22
19 [a]Rom 9:19
20 [a]Rom 5:2; 1 Cor 10:12; 2 Cor 1:24 [b]Rom 12:16; 1 Tim 6:17; 1 Pet 1:17
22 [a]Rom 2:4 [b]1 Cor 15:2; Heb 3:6 [c]John 15:2
23 [a]2 Cor 3:16
25 [a]Rom 1:13 [b]Matt 13:11; Rom 16:25; 1 Cor 2:7-10; Eph 3:3-5 [c]Rom 12:16 [d]Rom 11:7 [e]Luke 21:24; John 10:16; Rom 11:12
26 [a]Is 59:20
27 [1]Lit *the covenant from Me* [a]Is 59:21; Jer 31:33; Heb 8:10 [b]Is 27:9; Heb 8:12
28 [1]Lit *According to the gospel* [2]Lit *according to the election* [a]Rom 5:10 [b]Deut 7:8; Rom 9:5
29 [a]Rom 8:28; 1 Cor 1:26; Eph 1:18; Phil 3:14; 2 Thess 1:11; 2 Tim 1:9; Heb 3:1; 2 Pet 1:10 [b]Heb 7:21
32 [a]Rom 3:9; Gal 3:22f
33 [1]Or *and the wisdom* [a]Rom 2:4; Eph 3:8 [b]Eph 3:10; Col 2:3 [c]Job 5:9
34 [a]Is 40:13f; 1 Cor 2:16
35 [1]Lit *and it will be paid back* [a]Job 35:7
36 [1]Lit *to the ages* [a]1 Cor 8:6; Col 1:16; Heb 2:10 [b]Rom 16:27; Eph 3:21; Phil 4:20; 1 Tim 1:17; 2 Tim 4:18; 1 Pet 4:11; 2 Pet 3:18; Jude 25; Rev 1:6
12:1 [1]Or *well-pleasing* [2]Or *rational* [a]1 Cor 1:10; 2 Cor 10:1-4; Eph 4:1; 1 Pet 2:11 [b]Rom 6:13; 1 Cor 6:20; Heb 13:15; 1 Pet 2:5
2 [1]Or *age* [2]Or *approve* [3]Or *well-pleasing* [a]1 Pet 1:14 [b]Matt 13:22; Gal 1:4; 1 John 2:15 [c]Eph 4:23; Titus 3:5 [d]Eph 5:10; Col 1:9
3 [a]Rom 1:5; 1 Cor 3:10; Gal 2:9; Eph 3:7f [b]Rom 11:20 [c]1 Cor 7:17; 2 Cor 10:13; Eph 4:7; 1 Pet 4:11
4 [a]1 Cor 12:12-14; Eph 4:4
5 [a]1 Cor 10:17 [b]1 Cor 12:20; Eph 4:12
6 [1]Or *in agreement with the faith* [a]Rom 12:3; 1 Cor 7:7; 1 Pet 4:10 [b]Acts 13:1; 1 Cor 12:10
7 [1]Or *office of service* [a]Acts 6:1; 1 Cor 12:5 [b]Acts 13:1; 1 Cor 12:28
8 [1]Or *simplicity* [2]Or *gives aid* [a]Acts 4:36 [b]2 Cor 8:2 [c]1 Cor 12:28; 1 Tim 5:17 [d]2 Cor 9:7
9 [a]2 Cor 6:6; 1 Tim 1:5

[b]Abhor what is evil; cling to what is
good.
10 *Be* [a]devoted to one another in
brotherly love; [1]give preference to one
another [b]in honor;
11 not lagging behind in diligence,
[a]fervent in spirit, [b]serving the Lord;
12 [a]rejoicing in hope, [b]persevering
in tribulation, [c]devoted to prayer,
13 [a]contributing to the needs of the
[1]saints, [2b]practicing hospitality.
14 ¶ [a]Bless those who persecute
[1]you; bless and do not curse.
15 [a]Rejoice with those who rejoice,
and weep with those who weep.
16 [a]Be of the same mind toward one
another; [b]do not be haughty in mind, but
[1]associate with the lowly. [c]Do not be
wise in your own estimation.
17 [a]Never pay back evil for evil to
anyone. [1b]Respect what is right in the
sight of all men.
18 If possible, [a]so far as it depends on
you, [b]be at peace with all men.
19 [a]Never take your own revenge, beloved, but [1]leave room for the wrath *of*
God, for it is written, "[b]VENGEANCE IS
MINE, I WILL REPAY," says the Lord.
20 "[a]BUT IF YOUR ENEMY IS HUNGRY, FEED
HIM, AND IF HE IS THIRSTY, GIVE HIM A DRINK;
FOR IN SO DOING YOU WILL HEAP BURNING
COALS ON HIS HEAD."
21 Do not be overcome by evil, but
overcome evil with good.

Be Subject to Government

13 Every [1a]person is to be in [b]sub-
jection to the governing authorities. For [c]there is no authority except
[2]from God, and those which exist are
established by God.
2 Therefore [1]whoever resists authority has opposed the ordinance of God;
and they who have opposed will receive
condemnation upon themselves.
3 For [a]rulers are not a cause of fear
for [1]good behavior, but for evil. Do you
want to have no fear of authority? Do
what is good and you will have praise
from the same;
4 for it is a minister of God to you for
good. But if you do what is evil, be afraid;
for it does not bear the sword for nothing;
for it is a minister of God, an [a]avenger
who brings wrath on the one who practices evil.
5 Therefore it is necessary to be in
subjection, not only because of wrath, but
also [a]for conscience' sake.
6 For because of this you also pay
taxes, for *rulers* are servants of God, devoting themselves to this very thing.
7 [a]Render to all what is due them:
[b]tax to whom tax *is due;* [c]custom to
whom custom; fear to whom fear; honor
to whom honor.
8 ¶ Owe nothing to anyone except to
love one another; for [a]he who loves [1]his
neighbor has fulfilled *the* law.
9 For this, "[a]YOU SHALL NOT COMMIT
ADULTERY, YOU SHALL NOT MURDER, YOU
SHALL NOT STEAL, YOU SHALL NOT COVET,"
and if there is any other commandment,
it is summed up in this saying, "[b]YOU
SHALL LOVE YOUR NEIGHBOR AS YOURSELF."
10 Love [1]does no wrong to a neighbor; therefore [a]love is the fulfillment of
the law.
11 ¶ *Do* this, knowing the time, that it
is [a]already the hour for you to [b]awaken
from sleep; for now [1]salvation is nearer
to us than when we believed.
12 [a]The night is almost gone, and
[b]the day is near. Therefore let us lay
aside [c]the deeds of darkness and put on
[d]the armor of light.
13 Let us [1a]behave properly as in the
day, [b]not in carousing and drunkenness,
not in sexual promiscuity and sensuality,
not in strife and jealousy.
14 But [a]put on the Lord Jesus Christ,
and make no provision for the flesh [b]in
regard to *its* lusts.

Principles of Conscience

14 Now [a]accept the one who is
[b]weak in faith, *but* not for *the*
purpose of passing judgment on his opinions.
2 [a]One person has faith that he may
eat all things, but he who is [b]weak eats
vegetables *only.*
3 The one who eats is not to [a]regard
with contempt the one who does not eat,
and the one who does not eat is not to
[b]judge the one who eats, for God has
[c]accepted him.
4 [a]Who are you to judge the [1]ser-
vant of another? To his own [2]master he
stands or falls; and he will stand, for the
Lord is able to make him stand.
5 ¶ [a]One person [1]regards one day
above another, another regards every day
alike. Each person must be [b]fully convinced in his own mind.
6 He who observes the day, observes
it for the Lord, and he who eats, [1]does so
for the Lord, for he [a]gives thanks to God;
and he who eats not, for the Lord he does
not eat, and gives thanks to God.

9 [b]1 Thess 5:21f
10 [1]Or *outdo one another in showing honor* [a]John 13:34; 1 Thess 4:9; Heb 13:1; 2 Pet 1:7 [b]Rom 13:7; Phil 2:3; 1 Pet 2:17
11 [a]Acts 18:25 [b]Acts 20:19
12 [a]Rom 5:2 [b]Heb 10:32 [c]Acts 1:14
13 [1]Or *holy ones* [2]Lit *pursuing* [a]Rom 15:25; 1 Cor 16:15; 2 Cor 9:1; Heb 6:10 [b]Matt 25:35; 1 Tim 3:2
14 [1]Two early mss do not contain *you* [a]Matt 5:44; Luke 6:28; 1 Cor 4:12
15 [a]Job 30:25; Heb 13:3
16 [1]Or *accommodate yourself to lowly things* [a]Rom 15:5; 2 Cor 13:11; Phil 2:2; 1 Pet 3:8 [b]Rom 11:20 [c]Prov 3:7; Rom 11:25
17 [1]Lit *Take thought for* [a]Prov 20:22; Rom 12:19 [b]2 Cor 8:21
18 [a]Rom 1:15 [b]Mark 9:50; Rom 14:19
19 [1]Lit *give a place* [a]Prov 20:22; Rom 12:17 [b]Deut 32:35; Ps 94:1; 1 Thess 4:6; Heb 10:30
20 [a]2 Kin 6:22; Prov 25:21f; Matt 5:44; Luke 6:27
13:1 [1]Or *soul* [2]Lit *by* [a]Acts 2:41 [b]Titus 3:1; 1 Pet 2:13f [c]Dan 2:21; John 19:11
2 [1]Lit *he who*
3 [1]Lit *good work* [a]1 Pet 2:14
4 [a]1 Thess 4:6
5 [a]Eccl 8; 1 Pet 2:13
7 [a]Matt 22:21; Mark 12:17; Luke 20:25 [b]Luke 20:22 [c]Matt 17:25
8 [1]Lit *the other* [a]Matt 7:12; John 13:34; Rom 13:10; Gal 5:14; James 2:8
9 [a]Ex 20:13ff; Deut 5:17ff [b]Lev 19:18; Matt 19:19
10 [1]Lit *works no evil* [a]Matt 7:12; John 13:34; Rom 13:8; Gal 5:14; James 2:8
11 [1]Or *our salvation is nearer than when* [a]1 Cor 7:29f; James 5:8; 1 Pet 4:7; 2 Pet 3:9; 1 John 2:18; Rev 1:3 [b]Mark 13:37; 1 Cor 15:34; Eph 5:14; 1 Thess 5:6
12 [a]1 Cor 7:29f; James 5:8; 1 Pet 4:7; 2 Pet 3:9; 1 John 2:18; Rev 1:3 [b]Heb 10:25; 1 John 2:8; Rev 1:3 [c]Eph 5:11 [d]2 Cor 6:7; Eph 6:11; 1 Thess 5:8
13 [1]Lit *walk* [a]1 Thess 4:12 [b]Luke 21:34; Gal 5:21; Eph 5:18; 1 Pet 4:3 **14** [a]Job 29:14; Gal 3:27; Eph 4:24; Col 3:10 [b]Gal 5:16; 1 Pet 2:11 **14:1** [a]Acts 28:2; Rom 11:15 [b]Rom 14:2; 1 Cor 8:9ff **2** [a]Rom 14:14 [b]Rom 14:1; 1 Cor 8:9ff
3 [a]Luke 18:9; Rom 14:10 [b]Rom 14:10; Col 2:16 [c]Acts 28:2; Rom 11:15 **4** [1]Or *house-servant* [2]Lit *lord* [a]Rom 9:20; James 4:12 **5** [1]Lit *judges* [a]Gal 4:10 [b]Luke 1:1; Rom 4:21 **6** [1]Lit *eats* [a]Matt 14:19; 1 Cor 10:30; 1 Tim 4:3f

7 For not one of us [a]lives for himself,
and not one dies for himself;
8 for if we live, we live for the Lord,
or if we die, we die for the Lord; therefore [a]whether we live or die, we are the
Lord's.
9 For to this end [a]Christ died and
lived again, that He might be [b]Lord both
of the dead and of the living.
10 ¶ But you, why do you judge your
brother? Or you again, why do you [a]re-
gard your brother with contempt? For
[b]we will all stand before the judgment
seat of God.
11 For it is written,
"[a]AS I LIVE, SAYS THE LORD, [b]EVERY
KNEE SHALL BOW TO ME,
AND EVERY TONGUE SHALL [1]GIVE
PRAISE TO GOD."
12 So then [a]each one of us will give an
account of himself to God.
13 ¶ Therefore let us not [a]judge one
another anymore, but rather determine
this—[b]not to put an obstacle or a stumbling block in a brother's way.
14 I know and am convinced [1]in the
Lord Jesus that [a]nothing is unclean in
itself; but to him who [b]thinks anything to
be unclean, to him it is unclean.
15 For if because of food your brother
is hurt, you are no longer [a]walking according to love. [b]Do not destroy with
your food him for whom Christ died.
16 Therefore [a]do not let what is for
you a good thing be [1]spoken of as evil;
17 for the kingdom of God [a]is not eating and drinking, but righteousness and
[b]peace and [b]joy in the Holy Spirit.
18 For he who in this *way* [a]serves
Christ is [b]acceptable to God and approved by men.
19 So then [1]we [a]pursue the things
which make for peace and the [b]building
up of one another.
20 [a]Do not tear down the work of God
for the sake of food. [b]All things indeed
are clean, but [c]they are evil for the man
who eats [1]and gives offense.
21 [a]It is good not to eat meat or to
drink wine, or *to do anything* by which
your brother stumbles.
22 The faith which you have, have [1]as
your own conviction before God. Happy
is he who [a]does not condemn himself in
what he approves.
23 But [a]he who doubts is condemned
if he eats, because *his eating is* not from
faith; and whatever is not from faith is
sin.

Self-denial on Behalf of Others

15 Now we who are strong ought to
bear the weaknesses of [a]those
without strength and not *just* please ourselves.
2 Each of us is to [a]please his neighbor [1]for his good, to his [b]edification.
3 For even [a]Christ did not please
Himself; but as it is written, "[b]THE RE-
PROACHES OF THOSE WHO REPROACHED YOU
FELL ON ME."
4 For [a]whatever was written in earlier times was written for our instruction,
so that through perseverance and the encouragement of the Scriptures we might
have hope.
5 Now may the [a]God [1]who gives
perseverance and encouragement grant
you [b]to be of the same mind with one
another according to Christ Jesus,
6 so that with one accord you may
with one [1]voice glorify [a]the God and
Father of our Lord Jesus Christ.
7 ¶ Therefore, [a]accept one another,
just as Christ also accepted [1]us to the
glory of God.
8 For I say that Christ has become a
servant to [a]the circumcision on behalf of
the truth of God to confirm [b]the promises *given* to the fathers,
9 and for [a]the Gentiles to [b]glorify
God for His mercy; as it is written,
"[c]THEREFORE I WILL [1]GIVE PRAISE
TO YOU AMONG THE GENTILES,
AND I WILL SING TO YOUR NAME."
10 Again he says,
"[a]REJOICE, O GENTILES, WITH HIS
PEOPLE."
11 And again,
"[a]PRAISE THE LORD ALL YOU
GENTILES,
AND LET ALL THE PEOPLES
PRAISE HIM."
12 Again Isaiah says,
"[a]THERE SHALL COME [b]THE ROOT OF
JESSE,
AND HE WHO ARISES TO RULE OVER
THE GENTILES,
[c]IN HIM SHALL THE GENTILES
HOPE."
13 Now may the God of hope fill you
with all [a]joy and peace in believing, so
that you will abound in hope [b]by the
power of the Holy Spirit.
14 ¶ And concerning you, my brethren, I myself also am convinced that you
yourselves are full of [a]goodness, filled
with [b]all knowledge and able also to admonish one another.
15 But I have written very boldly to
you on some points so as to remind you
again, because of [a]the grace that was giv-
en me [1]from God,
16 to be [a]a minister of Christ Jesus to

7 [a]Rom 8:38f; 2 Cor 5:15; Gal 2:20; Phil 1:20f
8 [a]Luke 20:38; Phil 1:20; 1 Thess 5:10; Rev 14:13
9 [a]Rev 1:18 [b]Matt 28:18; John 12:24; Phil 2:11; 1 Thess 5:10
10 [a]Luke 18:9; Rom 14:3 [b]Rom 2:16; 2 Cor 5:10
11 [1]Or *confess* [a]Is 45:23 [b]Phil 2:10f
12 [a]Matt 12:36; 1 Pet 4:5
13 [a]Matt 7:1; Rom 14:3 [b]1 Cor 8:13
14 [1]Lit *through* [a]Acts 10:15; Rom 14:2 [b]1 Cor 8:7
15 [a]Eph 5:2 [b]Rom 14:20; 1 Cor 8:11
16 [1]Lit *blasphemed* [a]1 Cor 10:30; Titus 2:5
17 [a]1 Cor 8:8 [b]Rom 15:13; Gal 5:22
18 [a]Rom 16:18 [b]2 Cor 8:21; Phil 4:8; 1 Pet 2:12
19 [1]Later mss read *let us pursue* [a]Ps 34:14; Rom 12:18; 1 Cor 7:15; 2 Tim 2:22; Heb 12:14 [b]Rom 15:2; 1 Cor 10:23; 2 Cor 12:19; Eph 4:12
20 [1]Lit *with offense* [a]Rom 14:15 [b]Acts 10:15; Rom 14:2 [c]1 Cor 8:9-12
21 [a]1 Cor 8:13
22 [1]Lit *according to yourself* [a]1 John 3:21
23 [a]Rom 14:5
15:1 [a]Rom 14:1; Gal 6:2; 1 Thess 5:14
2 [1]Lit *for what is good to edification* [a]1 Cor 9:22; 2 Cor 13:9 [b]Rom 14:19; 1 Cor 10:23; 2 Cor 12:19; Eph 4:12
3 [a]2 Cor 8:9 [b]Ps 69:9
4 [a]Rom 4:23f; 2 Tim 3:16
5 [1]Lit *of perseverance* [a]2 Cor 1:3 [b]Rom 12:16
6 [1]Lit *mouth* [a]Rev 1:6
7 [1]One early ms reads *you* [a]Rom 14:1
8 [a]Matt 15:24; Acts 3:26 [b]Rom 4:16; 2 Cor 1:20
9 [1]Or *confess* [a]Rom 3:29 [b]Matt 9:8 [c]2 Sam 22:50; Ps 18:49
10 [a]Deut 32:43
11 [a]Ps 117:1
12 [a]Is 11:10 [b]Rev 5:5 [c]Matt 12:21
13 [a]Rom 14:17 [b]Rom 15:19; 1 Cor 2:4; 1 Thess 1:5

14 [a]Eph 5:9; 2 Thess 1:11 [b]1 Cor 1:5 **15** [1]One early ms reads *by God* [a]Rom 12:3 **16** [a]Acts 9:15; Rom 11:13

the Gentiles, ministering as a priest the
[b]gospel of God, so that *my* [c]offering of
the Gentiles may become acceptable,
sanctified by the Holy Spirit.
17 Therefore in Christ Jesus I have
found [a]reason for boasting in [b]things
pertaining to God.
18 For I will not presume to speak of
anything [1]except what [a]Christ has accomplished through me, [2]resulting in
the obedience of the Gentiles by word
and deed,
19 in the power of [1a]signs and wonders, [b]in the power of the Spirit; so that
[c]from Jerusalem and round about as [d]far
as Illyricum I have [2]fully preached the
gospel of Christ.
20 And thus I aspired to [a]preach the
gospel, not where Christ was *already*
named, [b]so that I would not build on
another man's foundation;
21 but as it is written,
"[a]THEY WHO HAD NO NEWS OF HIM
SHALL SEE,
AND THEY WHO HAVE NOT HEARD
SHALL UNDERSTAND."
22 ¶ For this reason [a]I have often
been prevented from coming to you;
23 but now, with no further place for
me in these regions, and since I [a]have
had for many years a longing to come
to you
24 whenever I [a]go to Spain—for I
hope to see you in passing, and to be
[b]helped on my way there by you, when
I have first [c]enjoyed your company [1]for
a while—
25 but now, [a]I am going to Jerusalem
[b]serving the [1]saints.
26 For [a]Macedonia and [b]Achaia have
been pleased to make a contribution for
the poor among the [1]saints in Jerusalem.
27 Yes, they were pleased *to do so,*
and they are indebted to them. For [a]if
the Gentiles have shared in their spiritual
things, they are indebted to minister to
them also in material things.
28 Therefore, when I have finished
this, and [a]have [1]put my seal on this fruit
of theirs, I will [b]go on by way of you to
Spain.
29 I know that when [a]I come to you,
I will come in the fullness of the blessing
of Christ.
30 ¶ Now I urge you, brethren, by our
Lord Jesus Christ and by [a]the love of the
Spirit, to [b]strive together with me in
your prayers to God for me,
31 that I may be [a]rescued from those
who are disobedient in Judea, and *that*
my [b]service for Jerusalem may prove acceptable to the [1c]saints;
32 so that [a]I may come to you in joy
by [b]the will of God and find *refreshing*
rest in your company.
33 Now [a]the God of peace be with
you all. Amen.

Greetings and Love Expressed

16 I [a]commend to you our sister
Phoebe, who is a [1]servant of the
church which is at [b]Cenchrea;
2 that you [a]receive her in the Lord in
a manner worthy of the [1b]saints, and
that you help her in whatever matter she
may have need of you; for she herself has
also been a helper of many, [2]and of myself as well.
3 ¶ Greet [a]Prisca and Aquila, my fellow workers [b]in [c]Christ Jesus,
4 who for my life risked their own
necks, to whom not only do I give thanks,
but also all the churches of the Gentiles;
5 also *greet* [a]the church that is in
their house. Greet Epaenetus, my beloved, who is the [b]first convert to Christ
from [1c]Asia.
6 Greet Mary, who has worked hard
for you.
7 Greet Andronicus and [1]Junias, my
[a]kinsmen and my [b]fellow prisoners,
who are outstanding among the apostles,
who also [2]were [c]in Christ before me.
8 Greet Ampliatus, my beloved in the
Lord.
9 Greet Urbanus, our fellow worker
[a]in Christ, and Stachys my beloved.
10 Greet Apelles, the approved [a]in
Christ. Greet those who are of the *household* of Aristobulus.
11 Greet Herodion, my [a]kinsman.
Greet those of the *household* of Narcis-
sus, who are in the Lord.
12 Greet Tryphaena and Tryphosa,
workers in the Lord. Greet Persis the beloved, who has worked hard in the Lord.
13 Greet [a]Rufus, a choice man in the
Lord, also his mother and mine.
14 Greet Asyncritus, Phlegon, Hermes, Patrobas, Hermas and the brethren
with them.
15 Greet Philologus and Julia, Nereus
and his sister, and Olympas, and all [a]the
[1]saints who are with them.
16 [a]Greet one another with a holy
kiss. All the churches of Christ greet you.
17 ¶ Now I urge you, brethren, keep
your eye on those who cause dissensions
and [1]hindrances [a]contrary to the teaching which you learned, and [b]turn away
from them.
18 For such men are [a]slaves, not of

16 [b]Rom 1:1 [c]Rom 12:1; Eph 5:2; Phil 2:17
17 [a]Phil 3:3 [b]Heb 2:17
18 [1]Lit *which Christ has not accomplished* [2]Lit *to the obedience* [a]Acts 15:12; Rom 1:5; 2 Cor 3:5
19 [1]Or *attesting miracles* [2]Lit *fulfilled* [a]John 4:48 [b]Rom 15:13; 1 Cor 2:4; 1 Thess 1:5 [c]Acts 22:17-21 [d]Acts 20:1f
20 [a]Rom 1:15 [b]1 Cor 3:10; 2 Cor 10:15f
21 [a]Is 52:15
22 [a]Rom 1:13; 1 Thess 2:18
23 [a]Acts 19:21; Rom 1:10f
24 [1]Lit *in part* [a]Rom 15:28 [b]Acts 15:3 [c]Rom 1:12
25 [1]Or *holy ones* [a]Acts 19:21 [b]Acts 24:17
26 [1]V 25, note 1 [a]Acts 16:9; 1 Cor 16:5; 2 Cor 1:16; Phil 4:15; 1 Thess 1:7f; 1 Tim 1:3 [b]Acts 18:12
27 [a]1 Cor 9:11
28 [1]Lit *sealed to them this fruit* [a]John 3:33 [b]Rom 15:24
29 [a]Acts 19:21; Rom 1:10f
30 [a]Gal 5:22; Col 1:8 [b]2 Cor 1:11; Col 4:12
31 [1]V 25, note 1 [a]2 Cor 1:10; 2 Thess 3:2; 2 Tim 3:11 [b]Rom 15:25f; 2 Cor 8:4 [c]Acts 9:13
32 [a]Rom 15:23 [b]Acts 18:21; Rom 1:10
33 [a]Rom 16:20; 2 Cor 13:11; Phil 4:9; 1 Thess 5:23; 2 Thess 3:16; Heb 13:20
16:1 [1]Or *deaconess* [a]2 Cor 3:1 [b]Acts 18:18
2 [1]Or *holy ones* [2]Lit *and of me, myself* [a]Phil 2:29 [b]Acts 9:13
3 [a]Acts 18:2 [b]Rom 8:1ff; 2 Cor 5:17; Gal 1:22 [c]Rom 8:1
5 [1]I.e. west coast province of Asia Minor [a]1 Cor 16:19; Col 4:15; Philem 2 [b]1 Cor 16:15 [c]Acts 16:6
7 [1]Or *Junia* (fem) [2]Lit *have become* [a]Rom 9:3 [b]Col 4:10; Philem 23 [c]Rom 8:1ff; 2 Cor 5:17; Gal 1:22
9 [a]Rom 8:1ff; 2 Cor 5:17; Gal 1:22
10 [a]Rom 8:1ff; 2 Cor 5:17; Gal 1:22
11 [a]Rom 9:3

13 [a]Mark 15:21 **15** [1]V 2, note 1 [a]Rom 16:2 **16** [a]1 Cor 16:20; 2 Cor 13:12; 1 Thess 5:26; 1 Pet 5:14 **17** [1]Lit *occasions of stumbling* [a]1 Tim 1:3 [b]Matt 7:15; Gal 1:8f; 2 Thess 3:6; Titus 3:10; 2 John 10 **18** [a]Rom 14:18

our Lord Christ but of [b]their own [1]appe-
tites; and by their [c]smooth and flattering
speech they deceive the hearts of the un-
suspecting.
19 For the report of your obedience
[a]has reached to all; therefore I am rejoicing over you, but [b]I want you to be wise
in what is good and innocent in what is
evil.
20 [a]The God of peace will soon crush
[b]Satan under your feet.
¶ [c]The grace of our Lord Jesus be with
you.
21 ¶ [a]Timothy my fellow worker
greets you, and *so do* [b]Lucius and [c]Jason
and [d]Sosipater, my [e]kinsmen.
22 ¶ I, Tertius, who [a]write this letter,
greet you in the Lord.
23 ¶ [a]Gaius, host to me and to the
whole church, greets you. [b]Erastus, the
city treasurer greets you, and Quartus,
the brother.
24 [[1]The grace of our Lord Jesus
Christ be with you all. Amen.]
25 ¶ [a]Now to Him who is able to establish you [b]according to my gospel and
the preaching of Jesus Christ, according
to the revelation of [c]the mystery which
has been kept secret for [d]long ages past,
26 but now is manifested, and by [a]the
Scriptures of the prophets, according to
the commandment of the eternal God,
has been made known to all the nations,
leading to [b]obedience of faith;
27 to the only wise God, through Jesus
Christ, [a]be the glory forever. Amen.

18 [1]Lit *belly* [b]Phil 3:19 [c]Col 2:4; 2 Pet 2:3 **19** [a]Rom 1:8 [b]Jer 4:22; Matt 10:16; 1 Cor 14:20 **20** [a]Rom 15:33 [b]Matt 4:10 [c]1 Cor 16:23; 2 Cor 13:14; Gal 6:18; Phil 4:23; 1 Thess 5:28; 2 Thess 3:18; Rev 22:21 **21** [a]Acts 16:1 [b][Acts 13:1] [c][Acts 17:5] [d][Acts 20:4] [e]Rom 9:3 **22** [a]1 Cor 16:21; Gal 6:11; Col 4:18; 2 Thess 3:17; Philem 19 **23** [a]Acts 19:29; 1 Cor 1:14 [b]Acts 19:22; 2 Tim 4:20 **24** [1]Early mss do not contain this v **25** [a]Eph 3:20; Jude 24 [b]Rom 2:16 [c]Matt 13:35; Rom 11:25; 1 Cor 2:1; Eph 1:9; Col 1:26f; 1 Tim 3:16 [d]2 Tim 1:9; Titus 1:2 **26** [a]Rom 1:2 [b]Rom 1:5 **27** [a]Rom 11:36

1 Corinthians

Title and Background

Located between the Corinthian Gulf and the Saronic Gulf, the city of Corinth was a wealthy trading center. It was also a wicked city and was known for that throughout the Roman world. Because the church in Corinth was new, it was hard for the Christians there not to act like their neighbors; consequently the church was having some problems.

Author and Date of Writing

Paul is acknowledged as the author both in the letter itself and by the early church fathers. This book was written about A.D. 55, toward the close of Paul's three-year residency in Ephesus.

Theme and Message

The letter revolves around the theme of problems in Christian conduct. It thus has to do with progressive sanctification, the continuing development of holiness of character. Obviously Paul was personally concerned with the Corinthians' problems, revealing a true pastor's (shepherd's) heart. In spite of the concentration on problems, the book contains some of the most familiar and beloved chapters in the entire Bible—for example, chapter 13 (on love) and chapter 15 (on resurrection).

Outline

I. Introduction: Greetings and Thanksgiving (1:1–9)
II. Divisions in the Church (1:10—4:21)
III. Moral and Ethical Disorders (5:1—6:20)
IV. Instruction on Marriage (7:1–40)
V. Instruction on Questionable Practices (8:1—11:1)
VI. Instruction on Public Worship (11:2—14:40)
    A. Propriety in Worship (11:2–16)
    B. The Lord's Supper (11:17–34)
    C. Spiritual Gifts (12:1—14:40)
VII. Instruction on the Resurrection (15:1–58)
VIII. Conclusion: Practical and Personal Matters (16:1–24)

Appeal to Unity

1 Paul, [a]called *as* an apostle of Jesus
Christ [1]by [b]the will of God, and
[c]Sosthenes our [d]brother,
2 ¶To [a]the church of God which is
at [b]Corinth, to those who have been
sanctified in Christ Jesus, [1]saints [c]by
calling, with all who in every place [d]call
on the name of our Lord Jesus Christ,
their *Lord* and ours:
3 ¶ [a]Grace to you and peace from
God our Father and the Lord Jesus Christ.
4 ¶ [a]I thank [1]my God always concerning you for the grace of God which
was given you in Christ Jesus,
5 that in everything you were [a]en-
riched in Him, in all [b]speech and [b]all
knowledge,
6 even as [a]the testimony concerning
Christ was confirmed [1]in you,
7 so that you are not lacking in any
gift, [a]awaiting eagerly the revelation of
our Lord Jesus Christ,
8 [a]who will also confirm you to the
end, blameless in [b]the day of our Lord
Jesus Christ.
9 [a]God is faithful, through whom
you were [b]called into [c]fellowship with
His Son, Jesus Christ our Lord.
10 ¶ Now [a]I exhort you, [b]brethren,
by the name of our Lord Jesus Christ, that
you all [1]agree and that there be no [2c]di-
visions among you, but that you be
[3]made complete in [d]the same mind and
in the same judgment.
11 For I have been informed concerning you, my brethren, by Chloe's *people*,
that there are quarrels among you.
12 Now I mean this, that [a]each one of

1:1 [1]Lit *through* [a]Rom 1:1 [b]Rom 1:10; 2 Tim 1:1 [c]Acts 18:17 [d]Acts 1:15
2 [1]Or *holy ones* [a]1 Cor 10:32 [b]Acts 18:1 [c]Rom 1:7 [d]Acts 7:59
3 [a]Rom 1:7
4 [1]Two early mss do not contain *my* [a]Rom 1:8
5 [a]2 Cor 9:11 [b]Rom 15:14; 2 Cor 8:7
6 [1]Or *among* [a]2 Thess 1:10; 1 Tim 2:6; 2 Tim 1:8; Rev 1:2
7 [a]Luke 17:30; Rom 8:19; Phil 3:20; 2 Pet 3:12
8 [a]Rom 8:19; Phil 1:6; Col 2:7; 1 Thess 3:13 [b]Luke 17:24; 1 Cor 5:5; 2 Cor 1:14; Phil 1:6; 1 Thess 5:2; 2 Thess 2:2
9 [a]Deut 7:9; Is 49:7; 1 Cor 10:13; 2 Cor 1:18; 1 Thess 5:24; 2 Thess 3:3 [b]Rom 8:28 [c]1 John 1:3
10 [1]Lit *speak the same thing* [2]Lit *schisms* [3]Or *united* [a]Rom 12:1 [b]Rom 1:13 [c]1 Cor 11:18 [d]Rom 12:16; Phil 1:27
12 [a]Matt 23:8-10; 1 Cor 3:4

you is saying, "I am of Paul," and "I of [b]Apollos," and "I of [c]Cephas," and "I of Christ."

13 [1]Has Christ been divided? Paul was not crucified for you, was he? Or were you [a]baptized [2]in the name of Paul?

14 [1]I thank God that I [a]baptized none of you except [a]Crispus and [b]Gaius,

15 so that no one would say you were baptized [1]in my name.

16 Now I did baptize also the [a]household of Stephanas; beyond that, I do not know whether I baptized any other.

17 [a]For Christ did not send me to baptize, but to preach the gospel, [b]not in [1]cleverness of speech, so that the cross of Christ would not be made void.

The Wisdom of God

18 ¶ For the word of the cross is [a]foolishness to [b]those who [1]are perishing, but to us who [2]are being saved it is [c]the power of God.

19 For it is written,

"[a]I WILL DESTROY THE WISDOM OF
THE WISE,
AND THE CLEVERNESS OF THE CLEVER
I WILL SET ASIDE."

20 [a]Where is the wise man? Where is the scribe? Where is the debater of [b]this age? Has not God [c]made foolish the wisdom of [d]the world?

21 For since in the wisdom of God [a]the world through its wisdom did not *come to* know God, [b]God was well-pleased through the [c]foolishness of the [1]message preached to [d]save those who believe.

22 For indeed [a]Jews ask for [1]signs and Greeks search for wisdom;

23 but we preach [1a]Christ crucified, [b]to Jews a stumbling block and to Gentiles [c]foolishness,

24 but to those who are [a]the called, both Jews and Greeks, Christ [b]the power of God and [c]the wisdom of God.

25 Because the [a]foolishness of God is wiser than men, and [b]the weakness of God is stronger than men.

26 ¶ For [1]consider your [a]calling, brethren, that there were [b]not many wise according to [2]the flesh, not many mighty, not many noble;

27 but [a]God has chosen the foolish things of [b]the world to shame the wise, and God has chosen the weak things of [b]the world to shame the things which are strong,

28 and the base things of [a]the world and the despised God has chosen, [b]the things that are not, so that He may [c]nullify the things that are,

29 so that [a]no [1]man may boast before God.

30 But [1]by His doing you are in [a]Christ Jesus, who became to us [b]wisdom from God, [2]and [c]righteousness and [d]sanctification, and [e]redemption,

31 so that, just as it is written, "[a]LET HIM WHO BOASTS, BOAST IN THE LORD."

Paul's Reliance upon the Spirit

2 And when I came to you, brethren, I [a]did not come with superiority of speech or of wisdom, proclaiming to you [b]the [1]testimony of God.

2 For I determined to know nothing among you except [a]Jesus Christ, and Him crucified.

3 I was with you in [a]weakness and in [b]fear and in much trembling,

4 and my [1]message and my preaching were [a]not in persuasive words of wisdom, but in demonstration of [b]the Spirit and of power,

5 so that your faith would not [1]rest on the wisdom of men, but on [a]the power of God.

6 ¶ Yet we do speak wisdom among those who are [a]mature; a wisdom, however, not of [b]this age nor of the rulers of [b]this age, who are [c]passing away;

7 but we speak God's wisdom in a [a]mystery, the hidden *wisdom* which God [b]predestined before the [c]ages to our glory;

8 *the wisdom* [a]which none of the rulers of [b]this age has understood; for if they had understood it they would not have crucified [c]the Lord of glory;

9 but just as it is written,

"[a]THINGS WHICH EYE HAS NOT SEEN
AND EAR HAS NOT HEARD,
AND *which* HAVE NOT ENTERED THE
HEART OF MAN,
ALL THAT GOD HAS PREPARED FOR
THOSE WHO LOVE HIM."

10 [1a]For to us God revealed *them* [b]through the Spirit; for the Spirit searches all things, even the [c]depths of God.

11 For who among men knows the *thoughts* of a man except the [a]spirit of the man which is in him? Even so the *thoughts* of God no one knows except the Spirit of God.

12 Now we [a]have received, not the spirit of [b]the world, but the Spirit who is from God, so that we may know the things freely given to us by God,

12 [b]Acts 18:24; 1 Cor 3:22 [c]John 1:42; 1 Cor 3:22 **13** [1]Or *Christ has been divided!* or *Christ is divided!* [2]Lit *into* [a]Matt 28:19; Acts 2:38 **14** [1]Two early mss read *I give thanks that* [a]Acts 18:8 [b]Rom 16:23 **15** [1]Lit *into* **16** [a]1 Cor 16:15 **17** [1]Lit *wisdom* [a]John 4:2; Acts 10:48 [b]1 Cor 2:1; 2 Cor 10:10 **18** [1]Or *perish* [2]Or *are saved* [a]1 Cor 1:21 [b]Acts 2:47; 2 Cor 2:15; 2 Thess 2:10 [c]Rom 1:16; 1 Cor 1:24 **19** [a]Is 29:14 **20** [a]Job 12:17; Is 19:11f [b]Matt 13:22; 1 Cor 2:6 [c]Rom 1:20ff [d]John 12:31; 1 Cor 1:27f; James 4:4 **21** [1]Lit *preaching* [a]John 12:31; 1 Cor 1:27f; James 4:4 [b]Luke 12:32; Gal 1:15; Col 1:19 [c]1 Cor 1:18 [d]Rom 11:14; James 5:20 **22** [1]Or *attesting miracles* [a]Matt 12:38 **23** [1]I.e. Messiah [a]1 Cor 2:2; Gal 3:1 [b]Luke 2:34; 1 Pet 2:8 [c]1 Cor 1:18 **24** [a]Rom 8:28 [b]Rom 1:16; 1 Cor 1:18 [c]Luke 11:49; 1 Cor 1:30 **25** [a]1 Cor 1:18 [b]2 Cor 13:4 **26** [1]Lit *see* [2]I.e. *human standards* [a]Rom 11:29 [b]Matt 11:25; 1 Cor 1:20 **27** [a]James 2:5 [b]1 Cor 1:20 **28** [a]1 Cor 1:20 [b]Rom 4:17 [c]Job 34:19; 1 Cor 2:6; 2 Thess 2:8; Heb 2:14 **29** [1]Lit *flesh* [a]Eph 2:9 **30** [1]Lit *of Him* [2]Or *both* [a]Rom 8:1; 1 Cor 4:15 [b]1 Cor 1:24 [c]Jer 23:5f; 2 Cor 5:21; Phil 3:9 [d]1 Cor 1:2; 1 Thess 5:23 [e]Rom 3:24; Eph 1:7; Col 1:14 **31** [a]Jer 9:23f; 2 Cor 10:17 **2:1** [1]One early ms reads *mystery* [a]1 Cor 1:17 [b]1 Cor 2:7 **2** [a]1 Cor 1:23; Gal 6:14 **3** [a]1 Cor 4:10; 2 Cor 11:30 [b]Is 19:16; 2 Cor 7:15; Eph 6:5 **4** [1]Lit *word* [a]1 Cor 1:17 [b]Rom 15:19; 1 Cor 4:20 **5** [1]Lit *be* [a]2 Cor 4:7 **6** [a]Eph 4:13; Phil 3:15; Heb 5:14 [b]Matt 13:22; 1 Cor 1:20 [c]1 Cor 1:28 **7** [a]Rom 11:25; 1 Cor 2:1 [b]Rom 8:29f [c]Heb 1:2 **8** [a]1 Cor 1:26 [b]Matt 13:22; 1 Cor 1:20 [c]Acts 7:2; James 2:1 **9** [a]Is 64:4 **10** [1]One early ms reads *But* [a]Matt 11:25; Gal 1:12; Eph 3:3 [b]John 14:26 [c]Rom 11:33ff **11** [a]Prov 20:27 **12** [a]Rom 8:15 [b]1 Cor 1:27

13 which things we also speak, [a]not
in words taught by human wisdom, but in
those taught by the Spirit, [1]combining
spiritual *thoughts* with spiritual *words.*
14 ¶ But [1]a [a]natural man [b]does not
accept the things of the Spirit of God, for
they are [c]foolishness to him; and he cannot understand them, because they are
spiritually [2]appraised.
15 But he who is [a]spiritual appraises
all things, yet he himself is appraised by
no one.
16 For [a]WHO HAS KNOWN THE MIND OF
THE LORD, THAT HE WILL INSTRUCT HIM? But
[b]we have the mind of Christ.

Foundations for Living

3 And I, brethren, could not speak to
you as to [a]spiritual men, but as to
[b]men of flesh, as to [c]infants in Christ.
2 I gave you [a]milk to drink, not solid
food; for you [b]were not yet able *to receive it.* Indeed, even now you are not yet
able,
3 for you are still fleshly. For since
there is [a]jealousy and strife among you,
are you not fleshly, and are you not walking [1b]like mere men?
4 For when [a]one says, "I am of
Paul," and another, "I am of Apollos," are
you not *mere* [b]men?
5 ¶ What then is Apollos? And what
is Paul? [a]Servants through whom you believed, even [b]as the Lord gave *opportunity* to each one.
6 [a]I planted, [b]Apollos watered, but
[c]God was causing the growth.
7 So then neither the one who plants
nor the one who waters is anything, but
God who causes the growth.
8 Now he who plants and he who
waters are one; but each will [a]receive his
own [1]reward according to his own labor.
9 For we are God's [a]fellow workers;
you are God's [1b]field, God's [c]building.
10 ¶ According to [a]the grace of God
which was given to me, like a wise master builder [b]I laid a foundation, and [c]an-
other is building on it. But each man must
be careful how he builds on it.
11 For no man can lay a [a]foundation
other than the one which is laid, which is
Jesus Christ.
12 Now if any man builds on the foundation with gold, silver, [1]precious
stones, wood, hay, straw,
13 [a]each man's work will become evident; for [b]the day will show it because it
is *to be* revealed with fire, and the fire
itself will test [1]the quality of each man's
work.
14 If any man's work which he has
built on it remains, he will [a]receive a
reward.
15 If any man's work is burned up, he
will suffer loss; but he himself will be
saved, yet [a]so as through fire.
16 ¶ [a]Do you not know that [b]you are
a [1]temple of God and *that* the Spirit of
God dwells in you?
17 If any man destroys the [1]temple of
God, God will destroy him, for the [1]tem-
ple of God is holy, and [2]that is what you
are.
18 ¶ [a]Let no man deceive himself. [b]If
any man among you thinks that he is wise
in [c]this age, he must become foolish, so
that he may become wise.
19 For [a]the wisdom of this world is
foolishness before God. For it is written,
"*He is* [b]THE ONE WHO CATCHES THE WISE IN
THEIR CRAFTINESS";
20 and again, "[a]THE LORD KNOWS THE
REASONINGS of the wise, THAT THEY ARE USE-
LESS."
21 So then [a]let no one boast in men.
For [b]all things belong to you,
22 [a]whether Paul or Apollos or Cephas or the world or [b]life or death or
things present or things to come; all
things belong to you,
23 and [a]you belong to Christ; and
[b]Christ belongs to God.

Servants of Christ

4 Let a man regard us in this manner,
as [a]servants of Christ and [b]stewards
of [c]the mysteries of God.
2 In this case, moreover, it is required [1]of stewards that one be found
trustworthy.
3 But to me it is a very small thing
that I may be examined by you, or by *any*
human [1]court; in fact, I do not even examine myself.
4 For I [a]am conscious of nothing
against myself, yet I am not by this [b]ac-
quitted; but the one who examines me is
the Lord.
5 Therefore [a]do not go on [1]passing
judgment before [2]the time, *but wait*
[b]until the Lord comes who will both
[c]bring to light the things hidden in the
darkness and disclose the motives of
men's hearts; and then each man's
[d]praise will come to him from God.
6 ¶ Now these things, brethren, I
have figuratively applied to myself and
Apollos for your sakes, so that in us you
may learn not to exceed [a]what is written, so that no one of you will [b]become
[1]arrogant [c]in behalf of one against the
other.

13 [1]Or *interpreting spiritual things for spiritual men* [a]1 Cor 1:17
14 [1]Or *an unspiritual* [2]Or *examined* [a]1 Cor 15:44; James 3:15; Jude 19 mg [b]John 14:17 [c]1 Cor 1:18
15 [a]1 Cor 3:1; Gal 6:1
16 [a]Is 40:13; Rom 11:34 [b]John 15:15
3:1 [a]1 Cor 2:15; Gal 6:1 [b]Rom 7:14; 1 Cor 2:14 [c]1 Cor 2:6; Eph 4:14; Heb 5:13
2 [a]Heb 5:12f; 1 Pet 2:2 [b]John 16:12
3 [1]Lit *according to man* [a]Rom 13:13; 1 Cor 1:10f [b]1 Cor 3:4
4 [a]1 Cor 1:12 [b]1 Cor 3:3
5 [a]Rom 15:16; 2 Cor 3:3; Eph 3:7; Col 1:25; 1 Tim 1:12 [b]Rom 12:6; 1 Cor 3:10
6 [a]1 Cor 4:15; 2 Cor 10:14f [b]Acts 18:24-27; 1 Cor 1:12 [c]1 Cor 15:10
8 [1]Or *wages* [a]1 Cor 3:14; Gal 6:4
9 [1]Or *cultivated land* [a]Mark 16:20; 2 Cor 6:1 [b]Is 61:3; Matt 15:13 [c]1 Cor 3:16; Eph 2:20-22; Col 2:7; 1 Pet 2:5
10 [a]Rom 12:3; 1 Cor 15:10 [b]Rom 15:20; 1 Cor 3:11f [c]1 Thess 3:2
11 [a]Is 28:16; Eph 2:20; 1 Pet 2:4ff
12 [1]Or *costly*
13 [1]Lit *of what sort each man's work is* [a]1 Cor 4:5 [b]Matt 10:15; 1 Cor 1:8; 2 Thess 1:7-10; 2 Tim 1:12
14 [a]1 Cor 3:8; Gal 6:4
15 [a]Job 23:10; Ps 66:10; Jude 23
16 [1]Or *sanctuary* [a]Rom 6:16 [b]Rom 8:9; 1 Cor 6:19; 2 Cor 6:16; Eph 2:21f
17 [1]Or *sanctuary* [2]Lit *who you are*
18 [a]Is 5:21 [b]1 Cor 8:2; Gal 6:3 [c]1 Cor 1:20
19 [a]1 Cor 1:20 [b]Job 5:13
20 [a]Ps 94:11
21 [a]1 Cor 4:6 [b]Rom 8:32
22 [a]1 Cor 1:12 [b]Rom 8:38
23 [a]1 Cor 15:23; 2 Cor 10:7; Gal 3:29 [b]1 Cor 11:3
4:1 [a]Luke 1:2 [b]1 Cor 9:17; Titus 1:7; 1 Pet 4:10 [c]Rom 11:25 **2** [1]Lit *in* **3** [1]Lit *day* **4** [a]Acts 23:1; 2 Cor 1:12 [b]Ps 143:2; Rom 2:13 **5** [1]Lit *judging anything* [2]I.e. the appointed time of judgment [a]Matt 7:1; Rom 2:1 [b]John 21:22; Rom 2:16 [c]1 Cor 3:13 [d]Rom 2:29; 1 Cor 3:8; 2 Cor 10:18 **6** [1]Lit *puffed up* [a]1 Cor 1:19 [b]1 Cor 4:18f [c]1 Cor 1:12

7 For who regards you as superior? [a]What do you have that you did not receive? And if you did receive it, why do you boast as if you had not received it?

8 ¶ You are [a]already filled, you have already become rich, you have become kings without us; and indeed, *I* wish that you had become kings so that we also might reign with you.

9 For, I think, God has exhibited us apostles last of all, as men [a]condemned to death; because we [b]have become a spectacle to the world, [1]both to angels and to men.

10 We are [a]fools for Christ's sake, but [b]you are prudent in Christ; [c]we are weak, but you are strong; you are distinguished, but we are without honor.

11 To this present hour we are both [a]hungry and thirsty, and are poorly clothed, and are roughly treated, and are homeless;

12 and we toil, [a]working with our own hands; when we are [b]reviled, we bless; when we are [c]persecuted, we endure;

13 when we are slandered, we try to [1]conciliate; we have [a]become as the scum of the world, the dregs of all things, *even* until now.

14 ¶ I do not write these things to [a]shame you, but to admonish you as my beloved [b]children.

15 For if you were to have countless [a]tutors in Christ, yet *you would* not *have* many fathers, for in [b]Christ Jesus I [c]became your father through the [d]gospel.

16 Therefore I exhort you, be [a]imitators of me.

17 For this reason I [a]have sent to you [b]Timothy, who is my [c]beloved and faithful child in the Lord, and he will remind you of my ways which are in Christ, [d]just as I teach everywhere in every church.

18 Now some have become [1a]arrogant, as though I were not [b]coming to you.

19 But I [a]will come to you soon, [b]if the Lord wills, and I shall find out, not the [1]words of those who are [c]arrogant but their power.

20 For the kingdom of God does [a]not consist in [1]words but in power.

21 What do you desire? [a]Shall I come to you with a rod, or with love and a spirit of gentleness?

Immorality Rebuked

5 It is actually reported that there is immorality among you, and immorality of such a kind as does not exist even among the Gentiles, that someone has [a]his father's wife.

2 [1]You [a]have become [2]arrogant and [1]have not [b]mourned instead, so that the one who had done this deed would be [c]removed from your midst.

3 ¶ For I, on my part, though [a]absent in body but present in spirit, have already judged him who has so committed this, as though I were present.

4 [a]In the name of our Lord Jesus, when you are assembled, and [1]I with you in spirit, [b]with the power of our Lord Jesus,

5 *I have decided* to [a]deliver such a one to [b]Satan for the destruction of his flesh, so that his spirit may be saved in [c]the day of the Lord [1]Jesus.

6 ¶ [a]Your boasting is not good. [b]Do you not know that [c]a little leaven leavens the whole lump *of dough*?

7 Clean out the old leaven so that you may be a new lump, just as you are *in fact* unleavened. For Christ our [a]Passover also has been sacrificed.

8 Therefore let us celebrate the feast, [a]not with old leaven, nor with the leaven of malice and wickedness, but with the unleavened bread of sincerity and truth.

9 ¶ I wrote you in my letter [a]not to associate with immoral people;

10 I *did* not at all *mean* with the immoral people of this world, or with the covetous and swindlers, or with [a]idolaters, for then you would have to go out of the world.

11 But [1]actually, I wrote to you not to associate [2]with any so-called [a]brother if he is an immoral person, or covetous, or [b]an idolater, or a reviler, or a drunkard, or a swindler—not even to eat with such a one.

12 For what have I to do with judging [a]outsiders? [b]Do you not judge those who are within *the church*?

13 But those who are outside, God [1]judges. [a]REMOVE THE WICKED MAN FROM AMONG YOURSELVES.

Lawsuits Discouraged

6 Does any one of you, when he has a [1]case against his neighbor, dare to go to law before the unrighteous and [a]not before the [2]saints?

2 Or [a]do you not know that [b]the [1]saints will judge [c]the world? If the world is judged by you, are you not competent *to* [2]*constitute* the smallest law courts?

3 [a]Do you not know that we will judge angels? How much more matters of this life?

4 So if you have law courts dealing

4:7 [a]John 3:27; Rom 12:3; 1 Pet 4:10
8 [a]Rev 3:17f
9 [1]Or *and to angels and to men* [a]Rom 8:36; 1 Cor 15:31; 2 Cor 11:23 [b]Heb 10:33
10 [a]Acts 17:18; 1 Cor 1:18 [b]1 Cor 1:19f; 2 Cor 11:19 [c]1 Cor 2:3; 2 Cor 13:9
11 [a]Rom 8:35; 2 Cor 11:23-27
12 [a]Acts 18:3 [b]1 Pet 3:9 [c]John 15:20; Rom 8:35
13 [1]Or *console* [a]Lam 3:45
14 [a]1 Cor 6:5 [b]2 Cor 6:13; 1 Thess 2:11; 1 John 2:1; 3 John 4
15 [a]Gal 3:24f [b]1 Cor 1:30 [c]Num 11:12; 1 Cor 3:8; Gal 4:19; Philem 10 [d]1 Cor 9:12
16 [a]1 Cor 11:1; Phil 3:17; 1 Thess 1:6; 2 Thess 3:9
17 [a]1 Cor 16:10 [b]Acts 16:1 [c]1 Cor 4:14; 1 Tim 1:2; 2 Tim 1:2 [d]1 Cor 7:17; Titus 1:5
18 [1]Lit *puffed up* [a]1 Cor 4:6 [b]1 Cor 4:21
19 [1]Lit *word* [a]Acts 19:21; 1 Cor 11:34; 2 Cor 1:15f [b]Acts 18:21 [c]1 Cor 4:6
20 [1]Lit *word* [a]1 Cor 2:4
21 [a]2 Cor 1:23
5:1 [a]Lev 18:8; Deut 22:30
2 [1]Or *have you...?* [2]Lit *puffed up* [a]1 Cor 4:6 [b]2 Cor 7:7-10 [c]1 Cor 5:13
3 [a]Col 2:5; 1 Thess 2:17
4 [1]Lit *my spirit, with the power* [a]2 Thess 3:6 [b]John 20:23; 2 Cor 2:10
5 [1]Two early mss do not contain *Jesus* [a]Prov 23:14; Luke 22:31; 1 Tim 1:20 [b]Matt 4:10 [c]1 Cor 1:8
6 [a]1 Cor 5:2; James 4:16 [b]Rom 6:16 [c]Hos 7:4; Matt 16:6; Gal 5:9
7 [a]Mark 14:12; 1 Pet 1:19
8 [a]Ex 12:19; Deut 16:3
9 [a]2 Cor 6:14; Eph 5:11; 2 Thess 3:6
10 [a]1 Cor 10:27
11 [1]Lit *now* [2]Lit *together if any man called a brother is* [a]Acts 1:15; 2 Thess 3:6 [b]1 Cor 10:7
12 [a]Mark 4:11 [b]1 Cor 5:3-5

13 [1]Or *will judge* [a]Deut 13:5; 1 Cor 5:2 **6:1** [1]Lit *matter* [2]Or *holy ones* [a]Matt 18:17 **2** [1]V 1, note 2 [2]Or try *the trivial cases?* [a]Rom 6:16 [b]Dan 7:18; Matt 19:28 [c]1 Cor 1:20 **3** [a]Rom 6:16

with matters of this life, [1]do you appoint them as judges who are of no account in the church?

5 [a]I say *this* to your shame. *Is it* so, *that* there is not among you one wise man who will be able to decide between his [b]brethren,

6 but brother goes to law with brother, and that before [a]unbelievers?

7 ¶ Actually, then, it is already a defeat for you, that you have lawsuits with one another. [a]Why not rather be wronged? Why not rather be defrauded?

8 On the contrary, you yourselves wrong and defraud. *You do* this even to *your* [a]brethren.

9 ¶ Or [a]do you not know that the unrighteous will not [b]inherit the kingdom of God? [c]Do not be deceived; [d]neither fornicators, nor idolaters, nor adulterers, nor [1]effeminate, nor homosexuals,

10 nor thieves, nor *the* covetous, nor drunkards, nor revilers, nor swindlers, will [a]inherit the kingdom of God.

11 [a]Such were some of you; but you were [b]washed, but you were [c]sanctified, but you were [d]justified in the name of the Lord Jesus Christ and in the Spirit of our God.

The Body Is the Lord's

12 ¶ [a]All things are lawful for me, but not all things are profitable. All things are lawful for me, but I will not be mastered by anything.

13 [a]Food is for the [1]stomach and the [1]stomach is for food, but God will [b]do away with both [2]of them. Yet the body is not for immorality, but [c]for the Lord, and [d]the Lord is for the body.

14 Now God has not only [a]raised the Lord, but [b]will also raise us up through His power.

15 [a]Do you not know that [b]your bodies are members of Christ? Shall I then take away the members of Christ and make them members of a prostitute? [c]May it never be!

16 Or [a]do you not know that the one who joins himself to a prostitute is one body *with her*? For He says, "[b]THE TWO SHALL BECOME ONE FLESH."

17 But the one who joins himself to the Lord is [a]one spirit *with Him.*

18 [a]Flee immorality. Every *other* sin that a man commits is outside the body, but the [1]immoral man sins against his own body.

19 Or [a]do you not know that [b]your body is a [1]temple of the Holy Spirit who is in you, whom you have from [2]God, and that [c]you are not your own?

20 For [a]you have been bought with a price: therefore glorify God in [b]your body.

Teaching on Marriage

7 Now concerning the things about which you wrote, it is [a]good for a man not to touch a woman.

2 But because of immoralities, each man is to have his own wife, and each woman is to have her own husband.

3 The husband must [1]fulfill his duty to his wife, and likewise also the wife to her husband.

4 The wife does not have authority over her own body, but the husband *does*; and likewise also the husband does not have authority over his own body, but the wife *does.*

5 [a]Stop depriving one another, except by agreement for a time, so that you may devote yourselves to prayer, and [1]come together again so that [b]Satan will not tempt you because of your lack of self-control.

6 But this I say by way of concession, [a]not of command.

7 [1]Yet I wish that all men were [a]even as I myself am. However, [b]each man has his own gift from God, one in this manner, and another in that.

8 ¶ But I say to the unmarried and to widows that it is [a]good for them if they remain [b]even as I.

9 But if they do not have self-control, [a]let them marry; for it is better to marry than to burn *with passion.*

10 ¶ But to the married I give instructions, [a]not I, but the Lord, that the wife should not [1]leave her husband

11 (but if she does leave, she must remain unmarried, or else be reconciled to her husband), and that the husband should not [1]divorce his wife.

12 ¶ But to the rest [a]I say, not the Lord, that if any brother has a wife who is an unbeliever, and she consents to live with him, he must not [1]divorce her.

13 And a woman who has an unbelieving husband, and he consents to live with her, she must not [1]send her husband away.

14 For the unbelieving husband is sanctified through his wife, and the unbelieving wife is sanctified through [1]her believing husband; for otherwise your children are unclean, but now they are [a]holy.

15 Yet if the unbelieving one leaves, let him leave; the brother or the sister is not under bondage in such *cases,* but God has called [1]us [2a]to peace.

4 [1]Or *appoint them...church*
5 [a]1 Cor 4:14 [b]Acts 1:15; 1 Cor 6:1
6 [a]2 Cor 6:14f; 1 Tim 5:8
7 [a]Matt 5:39f
8 [a]1 Thess 4:6
9 [1]I.e. effeminate by perversion [a]Rom 6:16 [b]Acts 20:32; 1 Cor 15:50; Gal 5:21; Eph 5:5 [c]Luke 21:8; 1 Cor 15:33; Gal 6:7; James 1:16; 1 John 3:7 [d]Rom 13:13; 1 Cor 5:11; Gal 5:19-21; Eph 5:5; 1 Tim 1:10; Rev 21:8
10 [a]Acts 20:32; 1 Cor 15:50; Gal 5:21; Eph 5:5
11 [a]1 Cor 12:2; Eph 2:2f; Col 3:5-7; Titus 3:3-7 [b]Acts 22:16; Eph 5:26 [c]1 Cor 1:2 [d]Rom 8:30
12 [a]1 Cor 10:23
13 [1]Lit *belly* [2]Lit *it and them* [a]Matt 15:17 [b]Col 2:22 [c]1 Cor 6:15 [d]Gal 5:24; Eph 5:23
14 [a]Acts 2:24 [b]John 6:39f; 1 Cor 15:23
15 [a]1 Cor 6:3 [b]Rom 12:5; 1 Cor 6:13; Eph 5:30 [c]Luke 20:16
16 [a]1 Cor 6:3 [b]Gen 2:24; Matt 19:5; Mark 10:8; Eph 5:31
17 [a]John 17:21-23; Rom 8:9-11; 1 Cor 6:15; Gal 2:20
18 [1]Or *one who practices immorality* [a]1 Cor 6:9; 2 Cor 12:21; Eph 5:3; Col 3:5; Heb 13:4
19 [1]Or *sanctuary* [2]Or *God? And you...own* [a]1 Cor 6:3 [b]John 2:21; 1 Cor 3:16; 2 Cor 6:16 [c]Rom 14:7f
20 [a]Acts 20:28; 1 Cor 7:23; 1 Pet 1:18f; 2 Pet 2:1; Rev 5:9 [b]Rom 12:1; Phil 1:20
7:1 [a]1 Cor 7:8
3 [1]Lit *render*
5 [1]Lit *be* [a]Ex 19:15; 1 Sam 21:5 [b]Matt 4:10
6 [a]2 Cor 8:8
7 [1]One early ms reads *For* [a]1 Cor 7:8 [b]Matt 19:11f; Rom 12:6; 1 Cor 12:4
8 [a]1 Cor 7:1 [b]1 Cor 7:7
9 [a]1 Tim 5:14
10 [1]Lit *depart from* [a]Mal 2:16; Matt 5:32; Mark 10:2-12; Luke 16:18; 1 Cor 7:6
11 [1]Or *leave his wife*
12 [1]Or *leave her* [a]1 Cor 7:6; 2 Cor 11:17

13 [1]Or *leave her husband* 14 [1]Lit *the brother* [a]Ezra 9:2; Mal 2:15 15 [1]One early ms reads *you* [2]Lit *in* [a]Rom 14:19

16 For how do you know, O wife,
whether you will [a]save your husband?
Or how do you know, O husband, whether you will save your wife?
17 ¶ Only, [a]as the Lord has assigned
to each one, as God has called each, in
this manner let him walk. And [b]so I direct in [c]all the churches.
18 Was any man called *when he was*
already circumcised? He is not to become
uncircumcised. Has anyone been called
in uncircumcision? [a]He is not to be circumcised.
19 [a]Circumcision is nothing, and uncircumcision is nothing, but *what matters*
is [b]the keeping of the commandments of
God.
20 [a]Each man must remain in that
[1]condition in which he was called.
21 ¶ Were you called while a slave?
[1]Do not worry about it; but if you are
able also to become free, rather [2]do that.
22 For he who was called in the Lord
while a slave, is [a]the Lord's freedman;
likewise he who was called while free, is
[b]Christ's slave.
23 [a]You were bought with a price; do
not become slaves of men.
24 Brethren, [a]each one is to remain
with God in that *condition* in which he
was called.
25 ¶ Now concerning virgins I have
[a]no command of the Lord, but I give an
opinion as one who [1b]by the mercy of
the Lord is trustworthy.
26 I think then that this is good in
view of the [1]present [a]distress, that [b]it is
good for a man [2]to remain as he is.
27 Are you bound to a wife? Do not
seek to be released. Are you released
from a wife? Do not seek a wife.
28 But if you marry, you have not
sinned; and if a virgin marries, she has
not sinned. Yet such will have [1]trouble
in this life, and I am trying to spare you.
29 But this I say, brethren, [a]the time
has been shortened, so that from now
on those who have wives should be as
though they had none;
30 and those who weep, as though
they did not weep; and those who rejoice, as though they did not rejoice; and
those who buy, as though they did not
possess;
31 and those who use the world, as
though they did not [a]make full use of it;
for [b]the form of this world is passing
away.
32 ¶ But I want you to be free from
concern. One who is [a]unmarried is concerned about the things of the Lord, how
he may please the Lord;
33 but one who is married is concerned about the things of the world,
how he may please his wife,
34 and *his interests* are divided. The
woman who is unmarried, and the virgin,
is concerned about the things of the Lord,
that she may be holy both in body and
spirit; but one who is married is concerned about the things of the world,
how she may please her husband.
35 This I say for your own benefit; not
to put a restraint upon you, but [1]to promote what is appropriate and *to secure*
undistracted devotion to the Lord.
36 ¶ But if any man thinks that he is
acting unbecomingly toward his virgin
daughter, if she is past her youth, and if
it must be so, let him do what he wishes,
he does not sin; let [1]her marry.
37 But he who stands firm in his heart,
[1]being under no constraint, but has authority [2]over his own will, and has decided this in his own heart, to keep his own
virgin *daughter,* he will do well.
38 So then both he who gives his own
virgin *daughter* in marriage does well,
and he who does not give her in marriage
will do better.
39 ¶ [a]A wife is bound as long as her
husband lives; but if her husband [1]is
dead, she is free to be married to whom
she wishes, only [b]in the Lord.
40 But [a]in my opinion she is happier
if she remains as she is; and I think that
I also have the Spirit of God.

Take Care with Your Liberty

8 Now concerning [a]things sacrificed
to idols, we know that we all have
[b]knowledge. Knowledge [1c]makes arrogant, but love [d]edifies.
2 [a]If anyone supposes that he knows
anything, he has not yet [b]known as he
ought to know;
3 but if anyone loves God, he [a]is
known by Him.
4 ¶ Therefore concerning the eating
of [a]things sacrificed to idols, we know
that [1]there is [b]no such thing as an idol
in the world, and that [c]there is no God
but one.
5 For even if [a]there are so-called
gods whether in heaven or on earth, as
indeed there are many gods and many
lords,
6 yet for us [a]there is *but* one God,
[b]the Father, [c]from whom are all things
and we *exist* for Him; and [d]one Lord,
Jesus Christ, [e]by whom are all things,
and we *exist* through Him.
7 ¶ However not all men [a]have this
knowledge; but [b]some, being accustomed to the idol until now, eat *food* as
if it were sacrificed to an idol; and their
conscience being weak is defiled.

16 [a]Rom 11:14; 1 Pet 3:1
17 [a]Rom 12:3 [b]1 Cor 4:17 [c]1 Cor 11:16; 14:33; 2 Cor 8:18; 11:28; Gal 1:22; 1 Thess 2:14; 2 Thess 1:4
18 [a]Acts 15:1ff
19 [a]Rom 2:27, 29; Gal 3:28; 5:6; 6:15; Col 3:11 [b]Rom 2:25
20 [1]Lit *calling* [a]1 Cor 7:24
21 [1]Lit *Let it not be a care to you* [2]Lit *use*
22 [a]John 8:32, 36; Philem 16 [b]Eph 6:6; Col 3:24; 1 Pet 2:16
23 [a]1 Cor 6:20
24 [a]1 Cor 7:20
25 [1]Lit *has had mercy shown on him by the Lord to be trustworthy* [a]1 Cor 7:6 [b]2 Cor 4:1; 1 Tim 1:13,16
26 [1]Or *impending* [2]Lit *so to be* [a]Luke 21:23; 2 Thess 2:2 [b]1 Cor 7:1,8
28 [1]Lit *tribulation in the flesh*
29 [a]Rom 13:11f; 1 Cor 7:31
31 [a]1 Cor 9:18 [b]1 Cor 7:29; 1 John 2:17
32 [a]1 Tim 5:5
35 [1]Lit *for what is seemly*
36 [1]Lit *them*
37 [1]Lit *having no necessity* [2]Lit *pertaining to*
39 [1]Lit *falls asleep* [a]Rom 7:2 [b]2 Cor 6:14
40 [a]1 Cor 7:6, 25
8:1 [1]Lit *puffs up* [a]Acts 15:20; 1 Cor 8:4,7,10 [b]Rom 15:14; 1 Cor 8:7,10; 10:15 [c]1 Cor 4:6 [d]Rom 14:19
2 [a]1 Cor 3:18 [b]1 Cor 13:8-12; 1 Tim 6:4
3 [a]Ps 1:6; Jer 1:5; Amos 3:2; Rom 8:29; 11:2; Gal 4:9
4 [1]Lit *nothing is an idol in the world*; i.e. an idol has no real existence [a]Acts 15:20; 1 Cor 8:1,7,10 [b]Acts 14:15; 1 Cor 10:19; Gal 4:8 [c]Deut 4:35,39; 6:4; 1 Cor 8:6
5 [a]2 Thess 2:4
6 [a]Deut 4:35,39; 6:4; Is 46:9; Jer 10:6,7; 1 Cor 8:4 [b]Mal 2:10; Eph 4:6 [c]Rom 11:36 [d]John 13:13; 1 Cor 1:2; Eph 4:5; 1 Tim 2:5 [e]John 1:3; Col 1:16
7 [a]1 Cor 8:4ff [b]Rom 14:14,22f

8 But [a]food will not [1]commend us to God; we are neither [2]the worse if we do not eat, nor [3]the better if we do eat.

9 But [a]take care that this [1]liberty of yours does not somehow become a stumbling block to the [b]weak.

10 For if someone sees you, who have [a]knowledge, dining in an idol's temple, will not his conscience, if he is weak, be strengthened to eat [b]things sacrificed to idols?

11 For through [a]your knowledge he who is weak [b]is ruined, the brother for whose sake Christ died.

12 [a]And so, by sinning against the brethren and wounding their conscience when it is weak, you sin [b]against Christ.

13 Therefore, [a]if food causes my brother to stumble, I will never eat meat again, so that I will not cause my brother to stumble.

Paul's Use of Liberty

9 Am I not [a]free? Am I not an [b]apostle? Have I not [c]seen Jesus our Lord? Are you not [d]my work in the Lord?

2 If to others I am not an apostle, at least I am to you; for you are the [a]seal of my [b]apostleship in the Lord.

3 ¶ My defense to those who examine me is this:

4 [1a]Do we not have a right to eat and drink?

5 [1a]Do we not have a right to take along a [2]believing wife, even as the rest of the apostles and the [b]brothers of the Lord and [c]Cephas?

6 Or do only [1a]Barnabas and I not have a right to refrain from working?

7 Who at any time serves [a]as a soldier at his own expense? Who [b]plants a vineyard and does not eat the fruit of it? Or who tends a flock and does not [1]use the milk of the flock?

8 ¶ I am not speaking these things [a]according to [1]human judgment, am I? Or does not the Law also say these things?

9 For it is written in the Law of Moses, "[a]YOU SHALL NOT MUZZLE THE OX WHILE HE IS THRESHING." God is not concerned about [b]oxen, is He?

10 Or is He speaking altogether for our sake? Yes, [a]for our sake it was written, because [b]the plowman ought to plow in hope, and the thresher *to thresh* in hope of sharing *the crops.*

11 [a]If we sowed spiritual things in you, is it too much if we reap material things from you?

12 If others share the right over you, do we not more? Nevertheless, we [a]did not use this right, but we endure all things [b]so that we will cause no hindrance to the [c]gospel of Christ.

13 [a]Do you not know that those who [b]perform sacred services eat the *food* of the temple, *and* those who attend regularly to the altar have their share [1]from the altar?

14 So also [a]the Lord directed those who proclaim the [b]gospel to [c]get their living from the gospel.

15 ¶ But I have [a]used none of these things. And I am not writing these things so that it will be done so in my case; for it would be better for me to die than have any man make [b]my boast an empty one.

16 For if I preach the gospel, I have nothing to boast of, for [a]I am under compulsion; for woe is me if I do not preach [b]the gospel.

17 For if I do this voluntarily, I have a [a]reward; but if against my will, I have a [b]stewardship entrusted to me.

18 What then is my [a]reward? That, when I preach the gospel, I may offer the gospel [b]without charge, so as [c]not to make full use of my right in the gospel.

19 ¶ For though I am [a]free from all *men,* I have made myself [b]a slave to all, so that I may [c]win more.

20 [a]To the Jews I became as a Jew, so that I might win Jews; to those who are under [1]the Law, as under [1]the Law though [b]not being myself under [1]the Law, so that I might win those who are under [1]the Law;

21 to those who are [a]without law, [b]as without law, though not being without the law of God but [c]under the law of Christ, so that I might win those who are without law.

22 To the [a]weak I became weak, that I might win the weak; I have become [b]all things to all men, [c]so that I may by all means save some.

23 I do all things for the sake of the gospel, so that I may become a fellow partaker of it.

24 ¶ [a]Do you not know that those who run in a race all run, but *only* one receives [b]the prize? [c]Run in such a way that you may win.

25 Everyone who [a]competes in the games exercises self-control in all things. They then *do it* to receive a perishable [b]wreath, but we an imperishable.

26 Therefore I [a]run in such a way, as not without aim; I box in such a way, as not [b]beating the air;

8 [1]Or *present* [2]Lit *lacking* [3]Lit *abounding* [a]Rom 14:17
9 [1]Lit *right* [a]Rom 14:13; 1 Cor 10:28; Gal 5:13 [b]Rom 14:1; 1 Cor 8:10f
10 [a]1 Cor 8:4ff [b]Acts 15:20; 1 Cor 8:1
11 [a]1 Cor 8:4ff [b]Rom 14:15
12 [a]Matt 18:6; Rom 14:20 [b]Matt 25:45
13 [a]Rom 14:21; 1 Cor 10:32; 2 Cor 6:3
9:1 [a]1 Cor 9:19 [b]Acts 14:14; Rom 1:1; 2 Cor 12:12; 1 Thess 2:6; 1 Tim 2:7; 2 Tim 1:11 [c]Acts 9:3; 1 Cor 15:8 [d]1 Cor 3:6
2 [a]John 3:33; 2 Cor 3:2f [b]Acts 1:25
4 [1]Lit *It is not that we have no right to eat and drink, is it?* [a]1 Cor 9:14; 1 Thess 2:6; 2 Thess 3:8f
5 [1]Lit *It is not that we have no right to take along...Cephas, is it?* [2]Lit *sister, as wife* [a]1 Cor 7:7f [b]Matt 12:46 [c]Matt 8:14; John 1:42
6 [1]Lit *I and Barnabas* [a]Acts 4:36
7 [1]Lit *eat of* [a]2 Cor 10:4; 1 Tim 1:18; 2 Tim 2:3f [b]Deut 20:6; Prov 27:18; 1 Cor 3:6
8 [1]Lit *man* [a]Rom 3:5
9 [a]Deut 25:4; 1 Tim 5:18 [b]Deut 22:1-4; Prov 12:10
10 [a]Rom 4:23f [b]2 Tim 2:6
11 [a]Rom 15:27; 1 Cor 9:14
12 [a]Acts 18:3; 1 Cor 9:15 [b]2 Cor 6:3 [c]1 Cor 4:15; 2 Cor 2:12
13 [1]Lit *with* [a]Rom 6:16 [b]Lev 6:16; Num 5:9f; Deut 18:1
14 [a]Matt 10:10; Luke 10:7; 1 Tim 5:18 [b]1 Cor 4:15; 2 Cor 2:12 [c]Luke 10:8; 1 Cor 9:4
15 [a]Acts 18:3; 1 Cor 9:12 [b]2 Cor 11:10
16 [a]Acts 9:15; Rom 1:14 [b]1 Cor 4:15; 2 Cor 2:12
17 [a]John 4:36; 1 Cor 3:8 [b]1 Cor 4:1; Gal 2:7; Eph 3:2; Phil 1:16; Col 1:25
18 [a]John 4:36; 1 Cor 3:8 [b]Acts 18:3; 2 Cor 11:7 [c]1 Cor 7:31
19 [a]1 Cor 9:1 [b]2 Cor 4:5; Gal 5:13 [c]Matt 18:15; 1 Pet 3:1
20 [1]Or *law* [a]Acts 16:3; Rom 11:14 [b]Gal 2:19 **21** [a]Rom 2:12 [b]Gal 2:3 [c]1 Cor 7:22; Gal 6:2 **22** [a]Rom 14:1; 2 Cor 11:29 [b]1 Cor 10:33 [c]Rom 11:14 **24** [a]1 Cor 9:13 [b]Phil 3:14; Col 2:18 [c]Gal 2:2; 2 Tim 4:7; Heb 12:1 **25** [a]Eph 6:12; 1 Tim 6:12; 2 Tim 2:5 [b]2 Tim 4:8; James 1:12; 1 Pet 5:4; Rev 2:10 **26** [a]Gal 2:2; 2 Tim 4:7; Heb 12:1 [b]1 Cor 14:9

27 but I [1]discipline [a]my body and
make it my slave, so that, after I have
preached to others, I myself will not be
disqualified.

Avoid Israel's Mistakes

10 For [a]I do not want you to be unaware, brethren, that our fathers
were all [b]under the cloud and all
[c]passed through the sea;
2 and all were [a]baptized into Moses
in the cloud and in the sea;
3 and all [a]ate the same spiritual food;
4 and all [a]drank the same spiritual
drink, for they were drinking from a spiritual rock which followed them; and the
rock was [1]Christ.
5 Nevertheless, with most of them
God was not well-pleased; for [a]they
were laid low in the wilderness.
6 ¶ Now these things happened as
[a]examples for us, so that we would not
crave evil things as [b]they also craved.
7 Do not be [a]idolaters, as some of
them were; as it is written, "[b]THE PEOPLE
SAT DOWN TO EAT AND DRINK, AND STOOD UP
TO [c]PLAY."
8 Nor let us act immorally, as [a]some
of them [1]did, and [b]twenty-three thousand fell in one day.
9 Nor let us try the Lord, as [a]some of
them [1]did, and were destroyed by the
serpents.
10 Nor [a]grumble, as some of them
[1]did, and [b]were destroyed by the [c]de-
stroyer.
11 Now these things happened to
them as an [a]example, and [b]they were
written for our instruction, upon whom
[c]the ends of the ages have come.
12 Therefore let him who [a]thinks he
stands take heed that he does not fall.
13 No temptation has overtaken you
but such as is common to man; and [a]God
is faithful, who will not allow you to be
[b]tempted beyond what you are able, but
with the temptation will provide the way
of escape also, so that you will be able to
endure it.
14 ¶ Therefore, my [a]beloved, flee
from [b]idolatry.
15 I speak as to wise men; you judge
what I say.
16 Is not the [a]cup of blessing which
we bless a sharing in the blood of Christ?
Is not the [1b]bread which we break a
sharing in the body of Christ?
17 Since there is one [1]bread, we
[a]who are many are one body; for we all
partake of the one [1]bread.
18 Look at [1]the nation [a]Israel; are not
those who [b]eat the sacrifices sharers in
the altar?
19 What do I mean then? That a thing

27 [1]Lit *bruise* [a]Rom 8:13
10:1 [a]Rom 1:13 [b]Ex 13:21; Ps 105:39 [c]Ex 14:22; Neh 9:11; Ps 66:6
2 [a]Rom 6:3; 1 Cor 1:13; Gal 3:27
3 [a]Ex 16:4; Deut 8:3; Neh 9:15; Ps 78:24f; John 6:31
4 [1]I.e. the Messiah [a]Ex 17:6; Num 20:11; Ps 78:15
5 [a]Num 14:29ff; Heb 3:17; Jude 5
6 [a]1 Cor 10:11 [b]Num 11:4; Ps 106:14
7 [a]Ex 32:4; 1 Cor 5:11 [b]Ex 32:6 [c]Ex 32:19
8 [1]Lit *acted immorally* [a]Num 25:1ff [b]Num 25:9
9 [1]Lit *made trial* [a]Num 21:5f
10 [1]Lit *grumbled* [a]Num 16:41 [b]Num 16:49 [c]Ex 12:23; 2 Sam 24:16; 1 Chr 21:15; Heb 11:28
11 [a]1 Cor 10:6 [b]Rom 4:23 [c]Rom 13:11
12 [a]Rom 11:20; 2 Pet 3:17
13 [a]1 Cor 1:9 [b]2 Pet 2:9
14 [a]Heb 6:9 [b]1 Cor 10:7; 1 John 5:21
16 [1]Lit *loaf* [a]Matt 26:27f; Mark 14:23f; Luke 22:20; 1 Cor 11:25 [b]Matt 26:26; Luke 22:19; Acts 2:42; 1 Cor 11:23f
17 [1]Lit *loaf* [a]Rom 12:5; 1 Cor 12:12f; Eph 4:4; Col 3:15
18 [1]Lit *Israel according to the flesh* [a]Rom 1:3 [b]Lev 7:6; Deut 12:17f
19 [a]1 Cor 8:4
20 [a]Deut 32:17; Ps 106:37; Gal 4:8; Rev 9:20
21 [a]2 Cor 6:16 [b]Is 65:11
22 [a]Deut 32:21 [b]Eccl 6:10; Is 45:9
23 [a]1 Cor 6:12 [b]Rom 14:19
24 [1]Lit *the other* [a]Rom 15:2; 1 Cor 10:33; 2 Cor 12:14; Phil 2:21
25 [a]Acts 10:15; 1 Cor 8:7
26 [1]Lit *its fullness* [a]Ps 24:1; 1 Tim 4:4
27 [a]1 Cor 5:10 [b]Luke 10:8
28 [a]1 Cor 8:7
29 [a]Rom 14:16; 1 Cor 9:19
30 [a]1 Cor 9:1 [b]Rom 14:6
31 [a]Col 3:17; 1 Pet 4:11
32 [a]Acts 24:16;

sacrificed to idols is anything, or [a]that an
idol is anything?
20 *No,* but *I say* that the things which
the Gentiles sacrifice, they [a]sacrifice to
demons and not to God; and I do not
want you to become sharers in demons.
21 [a]You cannot drink the cup of the
Lord and the cup of demons; you cannot
partake of the table of the Lord and [b]the
table of demons.
22 Or do we [a]provoke the Lord to jealousy? We are not [b]stronger than He,
are we?
23 ¶ [a]All things are lawful, but not all
things are profitable. All things are lawful, but not all things [b]edify.
24 Let no one [a]seek his own *good,* but
that of his [1]neighbor.
25 [a]Eat anything that is sold in the
meat market without asking questions for
conscience' sake;
26 [a]FOR THE EARTH IS THE LORD'S, AND
[1]ALL IT CONTAINS.
27 If [a]one of the unbelievers invites
you and you want to go, [b]eat anything
that is set before you without asking
questions for conscience' sake.
28 But [a]if anyone says to you, "This is
meat sacrificed to idols," do not eat *it,* for
the sake of the one who informed *you,*
and for conscience' sake;
29 I mean not your own conscience,
but the other *man's;* for [a]why is my freedom judged by another's conscience?
30 If I partake with thankfulness,
[a]why am I slandered concerning that for
which I [b]give thanks?
31 ¶ Whether, then, you eat or drink
or [a]whatever you do, do all to the glory
of God.
32 [a]Give no offense either to Jews or
to Greeks or to [b]the church of God;
33 just as I also [a]please all men in all
things, [b]not seeking my own profit but
the *profit* of the many, [c]so that they may
be saved.

Christian Order

11 [a]Be imitators of me, just as I also
am of Christ.
2 ¶ Now [a]I praise you because you
[b]remember me in everything and [c]hold
firmly to the traditions, just as I delivered
them to you.
3 But I want you to understand that
[1]Christ is the [a]head of every man, and
[b]the man is the head of a woman, and
God is the [c]head of [1]Christ.
4 Every man who has *something* on

1 Cor 8:13 [b]Acts 20:28; 1 Cor 1:2; 2 Cor 1:1; Gal 1:13; Phil 3:6; 1 Tim 3:5 **33** [a]Rom 15:2; 1 Cor 9:22; Gal 1:10 [b]Rom 15:2; 1 Cor 13:5; 2 Cor 12:14; Phil 2:21 [c]Rom 11:14; 1 Thess 2:16 **11:1** [a]1 Cor 4:16; Phil 3:17 **2** [a]1 Cor 11:17 [b]1 Cor 4:17; 1 Thess 1:6 [c]2 Thess 2:15 **3** [1]I.e. the Messiah [a]Eph 1:22; Col 1:18 [b]Gen 3:16; Eph 5:23 [c]1 Cor 3:23

his head while praying or [a]prophesying
disgraces his head.
5 But every [a]woman who has her
head uncovered while praying or prophesying disgraces her head, for she is one
and the same as the woman [1]whose head
is [b]shaved.
6 For if a woman does not cover [1]her
head, let her also [2]have her hair cut off;
but if it is disgraceful for a woman to
[2]have her hair cut off or [1]her head
shaved, let her cover [1]her head.
7 For a man ought not to have his
head covered, since he is the [a]image and
glory of God; but the woman is the glory
of man.
8 For [a]man [1]does not originate from
woman, but woman from man;
9 for indeed man was not created for
the woman's sake, but [a]woman for the
man's sake.
10 Therefore the woman ought to
have *a symbol of* authority on her head,
because of the angels.
11 However, in the Lord, neither is
woman [1]independent of man, nor is man
[1]independent of woman.
12 For as the woman [1]originates from
the man, so also the man *has his birth*
through the woman; and [a]all things
[2]originate [b]from God.
13 [a]Judge [1]for yourselves: is it proper
for a woman to pray to God *with her head*
uncovered?
14 Does not even nature itself teach
you that if a man has long hair, it is a
dishonor to him,
15 but if a woman has long hair, it is a
glory to her? For her hair is given to her
for a covering.
16 But if one is inclined to be contentious, [a]we have no [1]other practice, nor
have [b]the churches of God.
17 ¶ But in giving this instruction, [a]I
do not praise you, because you come together not for the better but for the
worse.
18 For, in the first place, when you
come together [1]as a church, I hear that
[2a]divisions exist among you; and in part
I believe it.
19 For there [a]must also be factions
among you, [b]so that those who are approved may become [1]evident among
you.
20 Therefore when you meet together,
it is not to eat the Lord's Supper,
21 for in your eating each one takes his
own supper first; and one is hungry and
[a]another is drunk.
22 What! Do you not have houses in
which to eat and drink? Or do you despise the [a]church of God and [b]shame
those who have nothing? What shall I say
to you? Shall [c]I praise you? In this I will
not praise you.

The Lord's Supper

23 ¶ For [a]I received from the Lord
that which I also delivered to you, that
[b]the Lord Jesus in the night in which He
was betrayed took bread;
24 and when He had given thanks, He
broke it and said, "This is My body,
which is for you; do this in remembrance
of Me."
25 In the same way *He took* [a]the cup
also after supper, saying, "This cup is the
[b]new covenant in My blood; do this, as
often as you drink *it,* in remembrance
of Me."
26 For as often as you eat this bread
and drink the cup, you proclaim the
Lord's death [a]until He comes.
27 ¶ Therefore whoever eats the
bread or drinks the cup of the Lord in an
unworthy manner, shall be [a]guilty of the
body and the blood of the Lord.
28 But a man must [a]examine himself,
and in so doing he is to eat of the bread
and drink of the cup.
29 For he who eats and drinks, eats
and drinks judgment to himself if he does
not judge the body rightly.
30 For this reason many among you
are weak and sick, and a number
[1a]sleep.
31 But if we judged ourselves rightly,
we would not be judged.
32 But when we are judged, we are
[a]disciplined by the Lord so that we will
not be condemned along with [b]the
world.
33 ¶ So then, my brethren, when you
come together to eat, wait for one another.
34 If anyone is [a]hungry, let him eat
[b]at home, so that you will not come together for judgment. The remaining matters I will [c]arrange [d]when I come.

The Use of Spiritual Gifts

12 Now concerning [a]spiritual *gifts,*
brethren, [b]I do not want you to
be unaware.
2 [a]You know that when you were
pagans, *you were* [b]led astray to the
[c]mute idols, however you were led.
3 Therefore I make known to you
that no one speaking [1a]by the Spirit of
God says, "Jesus is [2b]accursed"; and no
one can say, "Jesus is [c]Lord," except
[1a]by the Holy Spirit.
4 ¶ Now there are [a]varieties of gifts,
but the same Spirit.
5 And there are varieties of minis-
tries, and the same Lord.
6 There are varieties of effects, but

4 [a]Acts 13:1; 1 Thess 5:20
5 [1]Lit *who is shaved* [a]Luke 2:36; Acts 21:9; 1 Cor 14:34 [b]Deut 21:12
6 [1]Lit *herself* [2]Lit *shear herself*
7 [a]Gen 1:26; 5:1; 9:6; James 3:9
8 [1]Lit *is not from* [a]Gen 2:21-23; 1 Tim 2:13
9 [a]Gen 2:18
11 [1]Lit *without*
12 [1]Lit *is* [2]Lit *are* [a]2 Cor 5:18 [b]Rom 11:36
13 [1]Lit *in* [a]Luke 12:57
16 [1]Lit *such* [a]1 Cor 4:5; 9:1-3,6 [b]1 Cor 7:17
17 [a]1 Cor 11:2, 22
18 [1]Lit *in church* [2]Lit *schisms* [a]1 Cor 1:10; 3:3
19 [1]Or *manifest* [a]Matt 18:7; Luke 17:1; 1 Tim 4:1; 2 Pet 2:1 [b]Deut 13:3; 1 John 2:19
21 [a]Jude 12
22 [a]1 Cor 10:32 [b]James 2:6 [c]1 Cor 11:2,17
23 [a]1 Cor 15:3; Gal 1:12; Col 3:24 [b]1 Cor 11:23-25: *Matt 26:26-28; Mark 14:22-24; Luke 22:17-20;* 1 Cor 10:16
25 [a]1 Cor 10:16 [b]Ex 24:6-8; Luke 22:20; 2 Cor 3:6
26 [a]John 21:22; 1 Cor 4:5
27 [a]Heb 10:29
28 [a]Matt 26:22; 2 Cor 13:5; Gal 6:4
30 [1]I.e. are dead [a]Acts 7:60
32 [a]2 Sam 7:14; Ps 94:12; Heb 12:7-10; Rev 3:19 [b]1 Cor 1:20
34 [a]1 Cor 11:21 [b]1 Cor 11:22 [c]1 Cor 4:17; 7:17; 16:1 [d]1 Cor 4:19
12:1 [a]1 Cor 12:4; 14:1 [b]Rom 1:13
2 [a]1 Cor 6:11; Eph 2:11f; 1 Pet 4:3 [b]1 Thess 1:9 [c]Ps 115:5; Is 46:7; Jer 10:5; Hab 2:18f
3 [1]Or *in* [2]Gr *anathema* [a]Matt 22:43; 1 John 4:2f; Rev 1:10 [b]Rom 9:3 [c]John 13:13; Rom 10:9
4 [a]Rom 12:6f; 1 Cor 12:11; Eph 4:4ff,11; Heb 2:4

the same [a]God who works all things in
all *persons.*
7 But to each one is given the manifestation of the Spirit [a]for the common
good.
8 For to one is given the word of
[a]wisdom through the Spirit, and to another the word of [b]knowledge according
to the same Spirit;
9 to another [a]faith [1]by the same
Spirit, and to another [b]gifts of [2]healing
[1]by the one Spirit,
10 and to another the [1]effecting of
[2a]miracles, and to another [b]prophecy,
and to another the [3c]distinguishing of
spirits, to another *various* [d]kinds of
tongues, and to another the [e]interpreta-
tion of tongues.
11 But one and the same Spirit works
all these things, [a]distributing to each one
individually just as He wills.
12 ¶ For even [a]as the body is one and
yet has many members, and all the members of the body, though they are many,
are one body, [b]so also is Christ.
13 For [1a]by one Spirit we were all
baptized into one body, whether [b]Jews
or Greeks, whether slaves or free, and we
were all made to [c]drink of one Spirit.
14 ¶ For [a]the body is not one member, but many.
15 If the foot says, "Because I am not
a hand, I am not *a part* of the body," it is
not for this reason [1]any the less *a part* of
the body.
16 And if the ear says, "Because I am
not an eye, I am not *a part* of the body,"
it is not for this reason [1]any the less *a*
part of the body.
17 If the whole body were an eye,
where would the hearing be? If the whole
were hearing, where would the sense of
smell be?
18 But now God has [a]placed the
members, each one of them, in the body,
[b]just as He desired.
19 If they were all one member, where
would the body be?
20 But now [a]there are many members, but one body.
21 And the eye cannot say to the hand,
"I have no need of you"; or again the
head to the feet, "I have no need of you."
22 On the contrary, [1] it is much truer
that the members of the body which
seem to be weaker are necessary;
23 and those *members* of the body
which we [1]deem less honorable, [2]on
these we bestow more abundant honor,
and our less presentable members become much more presentable,
24 whereas our more presentable
members have no need *of it.* But God has
so composed the body, giving more abundant honor to that *member* which lacked,
25 so that there may be no [1]division
in the body, but *that* the members may
have the same care for one another.
26 And if one member suffers, all the
members suffer with it; if *one* member
is [1]honored, all the members rejoice
with it.
27 ¶ Now you are [a]Christ's body, and
[b]individually members of it.
28 And God has [1a]appointed in [b]the
church, first [c]apostles, second [d]proph-
ets, third [e]teachers, then [2f]miracles,
then [g]gifts of healings, helps, [h]adminis-
trations, *various* [i]kinds of tongues.
29 All are not apostles, are they? All
are not prophets, are they? All are not
teachers, are they? All are not *workers of*
[1]miracles, are they?
30 All do not have gifts of healings, do
they? All do not speak with tongues, do
they? All do not [a]interpret, do they?
31 But [a]earnestly desire the greater
gifts.
¶ And I show you a still more excellent
way.

The Excellence of Love

13 If I speak with the [a]tongues of
men and of [b]angels, but do not
have love, I have become a noisy gong or
a [c]clanging cymbal.
2 If I have *the gift of* [a]prophecy, and
know all [b]mysteries and all [c]knowledge;
and if I have [d]all faith, so as to [e]remove
mountains, but do not have love, I am
nothing.
3 And if I [a]give all my possessions to
feed *the poor,* and if I [b]surrender my
body [1]to be burned, but do not have
love, it profits me nothing.
4 ¶ Love [a]is patient, love is kind *and*
[b]is not jealous; love does not brag *and* is
not [c]arrogant,
5 does not act unbecomingly; it
[a]does not seek its own, is not provoked,
[b]does not take into account a wrong *suf-*
fered,
6 [a]does not rejoice in unrighteousness, but [b]rejoices with the truth;
7 [1a]bears all things, believes all things,
hopes all things, endures all things.
8 ¶ Love never fails; but if *there are*
gifts of [1a]prophecy, they will be done
away; if *there are* [b]tongues, they will
cease; if *there is* knowledge, it will be
done away.
9 For we [a]know in part and we
prophesy in part;

6 [a]1 Cor 15:28; Eph 1:23
7 [a]1 Cor 12:12-30; Eph 4:12
8 [a]1 Cor 2:6; 2 Cor 1:12 [b]Rom 15:14; 1 Cor 2:11; 2 Cor 2:14
9 [1]Or *in* [2]Lit *healings* [a]1 Cor 13:2; 2 Cor 4:13 [b]1 Cor 12:28
10 [1]Lit *effects* [2]Or *works of power* [3]Lit *distinguishings* [a]1 Cor 12:28f; Gal 3:5 [b]1 Cor 11:4 [c]1 Cor 14:29; 1 John 4:1 [d]Mark 16:17; 1 Cor 12:28 [e]1 Cor 12:30
11 [a]1 Cor 12:4
12 [a]Rom 12:4f; 1 Cor 10:17 [b]1 Cor 12:27
13 [1]Or *in* [a]Eph 2:18 [b]Rom 3:22; Gal 3:28; Eph 2:13-18; Col 3:11 [c]John 7:37-39
14 [a]1 Cor 12:20
15 [1]Lit *not a part*
16 [1]Lit *not a part*
18 [a]1 Cor 12:28 [b]Rom 12:6; 1 Cor 12:11
20 [a]1 Cor 12:12
22 [1]Lit *to a much greater degree the members*
23 [1]Or *think to be* [2]Or *these we clothe with*
25 [1]Lit *schism*
26 [1]Lit *glorified*
27 [a]1 Cor 1:2; Eph 1:23; Col 1:18 [b]Rom 12:5; Eph 5:30
28 [1]Lit *set some in* [2]Or *works of power* [a]1 Cor 12:18 [b]1 Cor 10:32 [c]Eph 4:11 [d]Acts 13:1; Eph 2:20 [e]Acts 13:1 [f]1 Cor 12:10 [g]1 Cor 12:9 [h]Rom 12:8 [i]1 Cor 12:10
29 [1]Or *works of power*
30 [a]1 Cor 12:10
31 [a]1 Cor 14:1
13:1 [a]1 Cor 12:10 [b]2 Cor 12:4; Rev 14:2 [c]Ps 150:5
2 [a]Matt 7:22; Acts 13:1; 1 Cor 11:4 [b]1 Cor 14:2 [c]Rom 15:14 [d]1 Cor 12:9 [e]Matt 17:20; Mark 11:23
3 [1]Early mss read *that I may boast* [a]Matt 6:2 [b]Dan 3:28
4 [a]Prov 10:12; 1 Thess 5:14; 1 Pet 4:8 [b]Acts 7:9 [c]1 Cor 4:6
5 [a]1 Cor 10:24; Phil 2:21 [b]2 Cor 5:19
6 [a]2 Thess 2:12 [b]2 John 4; 3 John 3f
7 [1]Or *covers* [a]1 Cor 9:12
8 [1]Lit *prophecies* [a]1 Cor 13:2 [b]1 Cor 13:1
9 [a]1 Cor 8:2

10 but when the perfect comes, the partial will be done away.

11 When I was a child, I used to speak like a child, think like a child, reason like a child; when I [1]became a man, I did away with childish things.

12 For now we [a]see in a mirror [1]dimly, but then [b]face to face; now I know in part, but then I will know fully just as I also [c]have been fully known.

13 But now faith, hope, love, abide these three; but the [1]greatest of these is [a]love.

Prophecy a Superior Gift

14 [a]Pursue love, yet [b]desire earnestly [c]spiritual *gifts,* but especially that you may [d]prophesy.

2 For one who [a]speaks in a tongue does not speak to men but to God; for no one [1]understands, but [2]in *his* spirit he speaks [b]mysteries.

3 But one who prophesies speaks to men for [a]edification and [b]exhortation and consolation.

4 One who [a]speaks in a tongue [b]edifies himself; but one who [c]prophesies [b]edifies the church.

5 Now I wish that you all [a]spoke in tongues, but [b]*even* more that you would prophesy; and greater is one who prophesies than one who [a]speaks in tongues, unless he interprets, so that the church may receive [c]edifying.

6 ¶ But now, brethren, if I come to you speaking in tongues, what will I profit you unless I speak to you either by way of [a]revelation or of [b]knowledge or of [c]prophecy or of [d]teaching?

7 Yet *even* lifeless things, either flute or harp, in producing a sound, if they do not produce a distinction in the tones, how will it be known what is played on the flute or on the harp?

8 For if [a]the [1]bugle produces an indistinct sound, who will prepare himself for battle?

9 So also you, unless you utter by the tongue speech that is clear, how will it be known what is spoken? For you will be [a]speaking into the air.

10 There are, perhaps, a great many kinds of [1]languages in the world, and no *kind* is without meaning.

11 If then I do not know the meaning of the language, I will be to the one who speaks a [1a]barbarian, and the one who speaks will be a [1]barbarian [2]to me.

12 So also you, since you are zealous of [1]spiritual *gifts,* seek to abound for the [a]edification of the church.

13 ¶ Therefore let one who speaks in a tongue pray that he may interpret.

14 For if I pray in a tongue, my spirit prays, but my mind is unfruitful.

15 [a]What is *the outcome* then? I will pray with the spirit and I will pray with the mind also; I will [b]sing with the spirit and I will sing with the mind also.

16 Otherwise if you bless [1]in the spirit *only,* how will the one who fills the place of the [2]ungifted say [a]the "Amen" at your [b]giving of thanks, since he does not know what you are saying?

17 For you are giving thanks well enough, but the other person is not [a]edified.

18 I thank God, I speak in tongues more than you all;

19 however, in the church I desire to speak five words with my mind so that I may instruct others also, rather than ten thousand words in a tongue.

Instruction for the Church

20 ¶ [a]Brethren, [b]do not be children in your thinking; yet in evil [c]be infants, but in your thinking be mature.

21 In [a]the Law it is written, "[b]BY MEN OF STRANGE TONGUES AND BY THE LIPS OF STRANGERS I WILL SPEAK TO THIS PEOPLE, AND EVEN SO THEY WILL NOT LISTEN TO ME," says the Lord.

22 So then tongues are for a sign, not to those who believe but to unbelievers; but [a]prophecy *is for a sign,* not to unbelievers but to those who believe.

23 Therefore if the whole church assembles together and all speak in tongues, and [1]ungifted men or unbelievers enter, will they not say that [a]you are mad?

24 But if all [a]prophesy, and an unbeliever or an [1]ungifted man enters, he is [b]convicted by all, he is called to account by all;

25 [a]the secrets of his heart are disclosed; and so he will [b]fall on his face and worship God, [c]declaring that God is certainly among you.

26 ¶ [a]What is *the outcome* then, [b]brethren? When you assemble, [c]each one has a [d]psalm, has a [e]teaching, has a [e]revelation, has a [f]tongue, has an [g]interpretation. Let [h]all things be done for edification.

27 If anyone speaks in a [a]tongue, *it should be* by two or at the most three, and *each* in turn, and one must [b]interpret;

28 but if there is no interpreter, he must keep silent in the church; and let him speak to himself and to God.

29 Let two or three [a]prophets speak, and let the others [b]pass judgment.

11 [1]Lit *have become...have done away with*
12 [1]Lit *in a riddle* [a]2 Cor 5:7; Phil 3:12; James 1:23 [b]Gen 32:30; Num 12:8; 1 John 3:2 [c]1 Cor 8:3
13 [1]Lit *greater* [a]Gal 5:6
14:1 [a]1 Cor 16:14 [b]1 Cor 12:31 [c]1 Cor 12:1 [d]1 Cor 13:2
2 [1]Lit *hears* [2]Or *by the Spirit* [a]Mark 16:17; 1 Cor 12:10 [b]1 Cor 13:2
3 [a]Rom 14:19; 1 Cor 14:5 [b]Acts 4:36
4 [a]Mark 16:17; 1 Cor 12:10 [b]Rom 14:19; 1 Cor 14:5 [c]1 Cor 13:2
5 [a]Mark 16:17; 1 Cor 12:10 [b]Num 11:29 [c]Rom 14:19; 1 Cor 14:4
6 [a]1 Cor 14:26; Eph 1:17 [b]1 Cor 12:8 [c]1 Cor 13:2 [d]Acts 2:42; Rom 6:17; 1 Cor 14:26
8 [1]Lit *trumpet* [a]Num 10:9; Jer 4:19; Ezek 33:3-6; Joel 2:1
9 [a]1 Cor 9:26
10 [1]Lit *voices*
11 [1]Or *foreigner* [2]Or *in my estimation* [a]Acts 28:2
12 [1]Lit *spirits* [a]Rom 14:19; 1 Cor 14:4
15 [a]Acts 21:22; 1 Cor 14:26 [b]Eph 5:19; Col 3:16
16 [1]Or *with the* [2]I.e. unversed in spiritual gifts [a]Deut 27:15-26; 1 Chr 16:36; Neh 5:13; Ps 106:48; Jer 11:5; Rev 5:14 [b]Matt 15:36
17 [a]Rom 14:19; 1 Cor 14:4
20 [a]Rom 1:13 [b]Eph 4:14; Heb 5:12f [c]Ps 131:2; Matt 18:3; Rom 16:19; 1 Pet 2:2
21 [a]John 10:34; 1 Cor 14:34 [b]Is 28:11f
22 [a]1 Cor 14:1
23 [1]V 16, note 2 [a]Acts 2:13
24 [1]V 16, note 2 [a]1 Cor 14:1 [b]John 16:8
25 [a]John 4:19 [b]Luke 17:16 [c]Is 45:14; Dan 2:47; Zech 8:23; Acts 4:13
26 [a]1 Cor 14:15 [b]Rom 1:13 [c]1 Cor 12:8-10 [d]Eph 5:19 [e]1 Cor 14:6 [f]1 Cor 14:2 [g]1 Cor 12:10 [h]Rom 14:19
27 [a]1 Cor 14:2 [b]1 Cor 12:10

29 [a]1 Cor 13:2 [b]1 Cor 12:10

30 But if a revelation is made to another who is seated, the first one must keep silent.

31 For you can all prophesy one by one, so that all may learn and all may be exhorted;

32 and the spirits of prophets are subject to prophets;

33 for God is not *a God* of [a]confusion but of [1]peace, as in [b]all the churches of the [c]saints.

34 ¶ The women are to [a]keep silent in the churches; for they are not permitted to speak, but [b]are to subject themselves, just as [c]the Law also says.

35 If they desire to learn anything, let them ask their own husbands at home; for it is [1]improper for a woman to speak in church.

36 [1]Was it from you that the word of God *first* went forth? Or has it come to you only?

37 ¶ [a]If anyone thinks he is a prophet or [b]spiritual, let him recognize that the things which I write to you [c]are the Lord's commandment.

38 But if anyone does not recognize *this*, he [1]is not recognized.

39 ¶ Therefore, my brethren, [a]desire earnestly to [b]prophesy, and do not forbid to speak in tongues.

40 But [a]all things must be done properly and in an orderly manner.

The Fact of Christ's Resurrection

15 Now [a]I make known to you, brethren, the [b]gospel which I preached to you, which also you received, [c]in which also you stand,

2 by which also you are saved, [a]if you hold fast [1]the word which I preached to you, [b]unless you believed in vain.

3 ¶ For [a]I delivered to you [1]as of first importance what I also received, that Christ died [b]for our sins [c]according to the Scriptures,

4 and that He was buried, and that He was [a]raised on the third day [b]according to the Scriptures,

5 and that [a]He appeared to [b]Cephas, then [c]to the twelve.

6 After that He appeared to more than five hundred brethren at one time, most of whom remain until now, but some [a]have fallen asleep;

7 then He appeared to [1a]James, then to [b]all the apostles;

8 and last of all, as [1]to one untimely born, [a]He appeared to me also.

9 For I am [a]the least of the apostles, [1]and not fit to be called an apostle, because I [b]persecuted the church of God.

10 But by [a]the grace of God I am what I am, and His grace toward me did not prove vain; but I [b]labored even more than all of them, yet [c]not I, but the grace of God with me.

11 Whether then *it was* I or they, so we preach and so you believed.

12 ¶ Now if Christ is preached, that He has been raised from the dead, how do some among you say that there [a]is no resurrection of the dead?

13 But if there is no resurrection of the dead, not even Christ has been raised;

14 and [a]if Christ has not been raised, then our preaching is vain, your faith also is vain.

15 Moreover we are even found *to be* false witnesses of God, because we testified [1]against God that He [a]raised [2]Christ, whom He did not raise, if in fact the dead are not raised.

16 For if the dead are not raised, not even Christ has been raised;

17 and if Christ has not been raised, your faith is worthless; [a]you are still in your sins.

18 Then those also who [a]have fallen asleep in Christ have perished.

19 If we have hoped in Christ in this life only, we are [a]of all men most to be pitied.

The Order of Resurrection

20 ¶ But now Christ [a]has been raised from the dead, the [b]first fruits of those who [c]are asleep.

21 For since [a]by a man *came* death, by a man also *came* the resurrection of the dead.

22 For [a]as in Adam all die, so also in [1]Christ all will be made alive.

23 But each in his own order: Christ [a]the first fruits, after that [b]those who are Christ's at [c]His coming,

24 then *comes* the end, when He hands over [a]the kingdom to the [b]God and Father, when He has abolished [c]all rule and all authority and power.

25 For He must reign [a]until He has put all His enemies under His feet.

26 The last enemy that will be [a]abolished is death.

27 For [a]HE HAS PUT ALL THINGS IN SUBJECTION UNDER HIS FEET. But when He says, "[b]All things are put in subjection," it is evident that He is excepted who put all things in subjection to Him.

28 When [a]all things are subjected to Him, then the Son Himself also will be subjected to the One who subjected

33 [1]Or *peace. As in all...saints, let* [a]1 Cor 14:40 [b]1 Cor 4:17 [c]Acts 9:13 **34** [a]1 Cor 11:5 [b]1 Tim 2:11f; 1 Pet 3:1 [c]1 Cor 14:21 **35** [1]Or *disgraceful* **36** [1]Lit *Or was* **37** [a]2 Cor 10:7 [b]1 Cor 2:15 [c]1 John 4:6 **38** [1]Two early mss read *is not to be recognized* **39** [a]1 Cor 12:31 [b]1 Cor 13:2 **40** [a]1 Cor 14:33 **15:1** [a]Rom 2:16; Gal 1:11 [b]Rom 2:16; 1 Cor 3:6 [c]Rom 5:2; 2 Cor 1:24 **2** [1]Lit *to what word I* [a]Rom 11:22 [b]Gal 3:4 **3** [1]Lit *among the first* [a]1 Cor 11:23 [b]John 1:29; Gal 1:4; Heb 5:1; 1 Pet 2:24 [c]Is 53:5-12; Matt 26:24; Luke 24:25-27; Acts 8:32f **4** [a]Matt 16:21; John 2:20ff; Acts 2:24 [b]Ps 16:8ff; Acts 2:31 **5** [a]Luke 24:34 [b]1 Cor 1:12 [c]Mark 16:14; Luke 24:36; John 20:19 **6** [a]Acts 7:60; 1 Cor 15:18 **7** [1]Or *Jacob* [a]Acts 12:17 [b]Luke 24:33; Acts 1:3f **8** [1]Lit *to an untimely birth* [a]Acts 9:3-8; 1 Cor 9:1 **9** [1]Lit *who am* [a]2 Cor 12:11; Eph 3:8; 1 Tim 1:15 [b]Acts 8:3 **10** [a]Rom 12:3 [b]2 Cor 11:23; Col 1:29; 1 Tim 4:10 [c]1 Cor 3:6; 2 Cor 3:5; Phil 2:13 **12** [a]Acts 17:32; 2 Tim 2:18 **14** [a]1 Thess 4:14 **15** [1]Or *concerning* [2]I.e. the Messiah [a]Acts 2:24 **17** [a]Rom 4:25 **18** [a]1 Cor 15:6; 1 Thess 4:16; Rev 14:13 **19** [a]1 Cor 4:9; 2 Tim 3:12 **20** [a]Acts 2:24; 1 Pet 1:3 [b]Acts 26:23; 1 Cor 15:23; Rev 1:5 [c]1 Cor 15:6; 1 Thess 4:16; Rev 14:13 **21** [a]Rom 5:12 **22** [1]I.e. the Messiah [a]Rom 5:14-18 **23** [a]Acts 26:23; 1 Cor 15:20; Rev 1:5 [b]1 Cor 6:14; 1 Thess 4:16 [c]1 Thess 2:19 **24** [a]Dan 2:44; 2 Pet 1:11 [b]Eph 5:20 [c]Rom 8:38 **25** [a]Ps 110:1; Matt 22:44 **26** [a]2 Tim 1:10; Rev 20:14 **27** [a]Ps 8:6 [b]Matt 11:27; Eph 1:22; Heb 2:8 **28** [a]Phil 3:21

all things to Him, so that [b]God may be all in all.

29 ¶ Otherwise, what will those do who are baptized for the dead? If the dead are not raised at all, why then are they baptized for them?

30 Why are we also [a]in danger every hour?

31 I affirm, brethren, by the boasting in you which I have in Christ Jesus our Lord, [a]I die daily.

32 If [1]from human motives I [a]fought with wild beasts at [b]Ephesus, what does it profit me? If the dead are not raised, [c]LET US EAT AND DRINK, FOR TOMORROW WE DIE.

33 [a]Do not be deceived: "Bad company corrupts good morals."

34 [a]Become sober-minded [1]as you ought, and stop sinning; for some have [b]no knowledge of God. [c]I speak *this* to your shame.

35 ¶ But [a]someone will say, "How are [b]the dead raised? And with what kind of body do they come?"

36 [a]You fool! That which you [b]sow does not come to life unless it dies;

37 and that which you sow, you do not sow the body which is to be, but a bare grain, perhaps of wheat or of [1]something else.

38 But God gives it a body just as He wished, and [a]to each of the seeds a body of its own.

39 All flesh is not the same flesh, but there is one *flesh* of men, and another flesh of beasts, and another flesh of birds, and another of fish.

40 There are also heavenly bodies and earthly bodies, but the glory of the heavenly is one, and the *glory* of the earthly is another.

41 There is one glory of the sun, and another glory of the moon, and another glory of the stars; for star differs from star in glory.

42 ¶ [a]So also is the resurrection of the dead. It is sown [1b]a perishable *body*, it is raised [2c]an imperishable *body*;

43 it is sown in dishonor, it is raised in [a]glory; it is sown in weakness, it is raised in power;

44 it is sown a [a]natural body, it is raised a [b]spiritual body. If there is a natural body, there is also a spiritual *body*.

45 So also it is written, "The first [a]MAN, Adam, BECAME A LIVING SOUL." The [b]last Adam *became* a [c]life-giving spirit.

46 However, the spiritual is not first, but the natural; then the spiritual.

47 The first man is [a]from the earth, [1b]earthy; the second man is from heaven.

48 As is the earthy, so also are those who are earthy; and as is the heavenly, [a]so also are those who are heavenly.

49 Just as we have [a]borne the image of the earthy, [1]we [b]will also bear the image of the heavenly.

The Mystery of Resurrection

50 ¶ Now I say this, brethren, that [a]flesh and blood cannot [b]inherit the kingdom of God; nor does [1]the perishable inherit [2c]the imperishable.

51 Behold, I tell you a [a]mystery; we will not all sleep, but we will all be [b]changed,

52 in a moment, in the twinkling of an eye, at the last trumpet; for [a]the trumpet will sound, and [b]the dead will be raised [1]imperishable, and [c]we will be changed.

53 For this [1]perishable must put on [2a]the imperishable, and this [b]mortal must put on immortality.

54 But when this [1]perishable will have put on [2]the imperishable, and this mortal will have put on immortality, then will come about the saying that is written, "[a]DEATH IS SWALLOWED UP in victory.

55 "[a]O DEATH, WHERE IS YOUR VICTORY? O DEATH, WHERE IS YOUR STING?"

56 The sting of [a]death is sin, and [b]the power of sin is the law;

57 but [a]thanks be to God, who gives us the [b]victory through our Lord Jesus Christ.

58 ¶ [a]Therefore, my beloved brethren, be steadfast, immovable, always abounding in [b]the work of the Lord, knowing that your toil is not *in* vain in the Lord.

Instructions and Greetings

16 Now concerning [a]the collection for [b]the saints, as [c]I directed the churches of [d]Galatia, so do you also.

2 On [a]the first day of every week each one of you is to [1]put aside and save, as he may prosper, so that [b]no collections be made when I come.

3 When I arrive, [a]whomever you may approve, I will send them with letters to carry your gift to Jerusalem;

4 and if it is fitting for me to go also, they will go with me.

5 ¶ But I [a]will come to you after I go through [b]Macedonia, for I [c]am going through Macedonia;

6 and perhaps I will stay with you, or even spend the winter, so that you may [a]send me on my way wherever I may go.

7 For I do not wish to see you now [a]*just* in passing; for I hope to remain with you for some time, [b]if the Lord permits.

---

28 [b]1 Cor 3:23
30 [a]2 Cor 11:26
31 [a]Rom 8:36
32 [1]Lit *according to man* [a]2 Cor 1:8 [b]Acts 18:19; 1 Cor 16:8 [c]Is 22:13; 56:12; Luke 12:19
33 [a]1 Cor 6:9
34 [1]Lit *righteously* [a]Rom 13:11 [b]Matt 22:29; Acts 26:8 [c]1 Cor 6:5
35 [a]Rom 9:19 [b]Ezek 37:3
36 [a]Luke 11:40 [b]John 12:24
37 [1]Lit *some of the rest*
38 [a]Gen 1:11
42 [1]Lit *in corruption* [2]Lit *in incorruption* [a]Dan 12:3; Matt 13:43 [b]Rom 8:21; 1 Cor 15:50; Gal 6:8 [c]Rom 2:7
43 [a]Phil 3:21; Col 3:4
44 [a]1 Cor 2:14 [b]1 Cor 15:50
45 [a]Gen 2:7 [b]Rom 5:14 [c]John 5:21; 6:57f; Rom 8:2
47 [1]Lit *made of dust* [a]John 3:31 [b]Gen 2:7; 3:19
48 [a]Phil 3:20f
49 [1]Two early mss read *let us also* [a]Gen 5:3 [b]Rom 8:29
50 [1]Lit *corruption* [2]Lit *incorruption* [a]Matt 16:17; John 3:5f [b]1 Cor 6:9 [c]Rom 2:7
51 [a]1 Cor 13:2 [b]2 Cor 5:2,4
52 [1]Lit *incorruptible* [a]Matt 24:31 [b]John 5:28 [c]1 Thess 4:15,17
53 [1]Lit *corruptible* [2]Lit *incorruption* [a]Rom 2:7 [b]2 Cor 5:4
54 [1]V 53, note 1 [2]V 53, note 2 [a]Is 25:8
55 [a]Hos 13:14
56 [a]Rom 5:12 [b]Rom 3:20; 4:15; 7:8
57 [a]Rom 7:25; 2 Cor 2:14 [b]Rom 8:37; Heb 2:14f; 1 John 5:4; Rev 21:4
58 [a]2 Pet 3:14 [b]1 Cor 16:10
16:1 [a]Acts 24:17; Rom 15:25f [b]Acts 9:13 [c]1 Cor 4:17 [d]Acts 16:6
2 [1]Lit *put by himself* [a]Acts 20:7 [b]2 Cor 9:4f
3 [a]2 Cor 3:1; 8:18f
5 [a]1 Cor 4:19 [b]Rom 15:26 [c]Acts 19:21
6 [a]Acts 15:3; 1 Cor 16:11
7 [a]2 Cor 1:15f [b]Acts 18:21

8 But I will remain in [a]Ephesus until
[b]Pentecost;
9 for a [a]wide door [1]for effective *service* has opened to me, and [b]there are
many adversaries.
10 ¶ Now if [a]Timothy comes, see that
he is with you without [1]cause to be
afraid, for he is doing [b]the Lord's work,
as I also am.
11 [a]So let no one despise him. But
[b]send him on his way [c]in peace, so that
he may come to me; for I expect him with
the brethren.
12 ¶ But concerning [a]Apollos our
brother, I encouraged him greatly to
come to you with the brethren; and it was
not at all *his* desire to come now, but he
will come when he has opportunity.
13 ¶ [a]Be on the alert, [b]stand firm in
the faith, [c]act like men, [d]be strong.
14 Let all that you do be done [a]in love.
15 ¶ Now I urge you, brethren (you
know the [a]household of Stephanas, that
[1]they were the [b]first fruits of [c]Achaia,
and that they have devoted themselves
for [d]ministry to [e]the saints),
16 that [a]you also be in subjection to
such men and to everyone who helps in
the work and labors.
17 I rejoice over the [1a]coming of
Stephanas and Fortunatus and Achaicus,
because they have [2]supplied [b]what was
lacking on your part.
18 For they [a]have refreshed my spirit
and yours. Therefore [b]acknowledge such
men.
19 ¶ The churches of [a]Asia greet you.
[b]Aquila and Prisca greet you heartily in
the Lord, with [c]the church that is in
their house.
20 All the brethren greet you. [a]Greet
one another with a holy kiss.
21 ¶ The greeting is in [a]my own
hand—[1]Paul.
22 If anyone does not love the Lord, he
is to be [1a]accursed. [2b]Maranatha.
23 [a]The grace of the Lord Jesus be
with you.
24 My love be with you all in Christ
Jesus. Amen.

8 [a]Acts 18:19 [b]Acts 2:1 **9** [1]Lit *and* [a]Acts 14:27 [b]Acts 19:9 **10** [1]Lit *fear; for* [a]Acts 16:1; 1 Cor 4:17; 2 Cor 1:1 [b]1 Cor 15:58 **11** [a]1 Tim 4:12; Titus 2:15 [b]Acts 15:3; 1 Cor 16:6 [c]Acts 15:33 **12** [a]Acts 18:24; 1 Cor 1:12 **13** [a]Matt 24:42 [b]1 Cor 15:1; Gal 5:1; Phil 1:27; 1 Thess 3:8; 2 Thess 2:15 [c]1 Sam 4:9; 2 Sam 10:12 [d]Ps 31:24; Eph 3:16; Col 1:11 **14** [a]1 Cor 14:1 **15** [1]Lit *it was* [a]1 Cor 1:16 [b]Rom 16:5 [c]Acts 18:12 [d]Rom 15:31 [e]1 Cor 16:1 **16** [a]1 Thess 5:12; Heb 13:17 **17** [1]Or *presence* [2]Or *made up for your absence* [a]2 Cor 7:6f [b]2 Cor 11:9; Phil 2:30 **18** [a]2 Cor 7:13; Philem 7 [b]Phil 2:29; 1 Thess 5:12 **19** [a]Acts 16:6 [b]Acts 18:2 [c]Rom 16:5 **20** [a]Rom 16:16 **21** [1]Lit *Paul's* [a]Rom 16:22; Gal 6:11; Col 4:18; 2 Thess 3:17; Philem 19 **22** [1]Gr *anathema* [2]I.e. O[our] Lord come! [a]Rom 9:3 [b]Phil 4:5; Rev 22:20 **23** [a]Rom 16:20

2 Corinthians

Title and Background

This letter seems to have been written a few months after the first letter. The divisions and problems spoken of in 1 Corinthians were still present in the church at Corinth. False teachers were challenging both Paul's personal integrity and his authority as an apostle. They were saying that he was not a genuine apostle and that he was putting into his own pocket the money they had collected for the poverty-stricken believers in Jerusalem.

Author and Date of Writing

Paul was the author of this letter. It is stamped with his style and contains more autobiographical material than any of his other writings. The available evidence indicates that 1 Corinthians was written in the spring of A.D. 55 and that 2 Corinthians was written in the fall of that same year.

Theme and Message

Paul shows his feelings in this letter more than in any other. He goes from despair to ecstatic joy. The letter falls naturally into three sections: (1) Paul explains the reasons for the change of his itinerary (chapters 1—7); (2) he encourages the Corinthians to complete the collection in preparation for his arrival (chapters 8—9); (3) he stresses the certainty of his coming, his authenticity as an apostle and his readiness as an apostle to exercise discipline if necessary (chapters 10—13).

Outline

I. Introduction: Greetings and Thanksgiving (1:1–11)
II. Paul's Explanation of His Conduct and Apostolic Ministry (1:12—7:16)
III. The Collection for the Christians at Jerusalem (8:1—9:15)
IV. Paul's Vindication of His Apostolic Authority (10:1—13:10)
V. Conclusion (13:11–14)

Introduction

1 Paul, [a]an apostle of [b]Christ Jesus
[c]by the will of God, and [d]Timothy
our brother,
¶ To [e]the church of God which is at
[f]Corinth with all the [1]saints who are
throughout [g]Achaia:
2 ¶ [a]Grace to you and peace from
God our Father and the Lord Jesus Christ.
3 ¶ [a]Blessed *be* the God and Father
of our Lord Jesus Christ, the Father of
mercies and [b]God of all comfort,
4 who [a]comforts us in all our affliction so that we will be able to comfort
those who are in [1]any affliction with the
comfort with which we ourselves are
comforted by God.
5 For just [a]as the sufferings of Christ
are [1]ours in abundance, so also our comfort is abundant through Christ.
6 But if we are afflicted, it is [a]for
your comfort and salvation; or if we are
comforted, it is for your comfort, which is
effective in the patient enduring of the
same sufferings which we also suffer;
7 and our hope for you is firmly
grounded, knowing that [a]as you are sharers of our sufferings, so also you are *sharers* of our comfort.
8 ¶ For [a]we do not want you to be
unaware, brethren, of our [b]affliction
which came *to us* in [1c]Asia, that we
were burdened excessively, beyond our
strength, so that we despaired even of
life;
9 [1]indeed, we had the sentence of
death within ourselves so that we would
not trust in ourselves, but in God who
raises the dead;
10 who [a]delivered us from so great a
peril of death, and will deliver *us,* [1]He
[b]on whom we have set our hope. And He
will yet deliver us,
11 you also joining in [a]helping us

1:1 [1]Or *holy ones* [a]Rom 1:1; Gal 1:1; Eph 1:1; Col 1:1; 2 Tim 1:1; Titus 1:1 [b]Gal 3:26 [c]1 Cor 1:1 [d]Acts 16:1; 1 Cor 16:10; 2 Cor 1:19 [e]1 Cor 10:32 [f]Acts 18:1 [g]Acts 18:12
2 [a]Rom 1:7
3 [a]Eph 1:3; 1 Pet 1:3 [b]Rom 15:5
4 [1]Lit *every* [a]Is 51:12; 2 Cor 7:6
5 [1]Lit *to us* [a]2 Cor 4:10; Phil 3:10; Col 1:24
6 [a]2 Cor 4:15; Eph 3:1; 2 Tim 2:10
7 [a]Rom 8:17
8 [1]I.e. west coast province of Asia Minor [a]Rom 1:13 [b]Acts 19:23; 1 Cor 15:32 [c]Acts 16:6
9 [1]Lit *but we ourselves*
10 [1]One early ms reads *on whom we have set our hope that He will also* [a]Rom 15:31 [b]1 Tim 4:10
11 [a]Rom 15:30; Phil 1:19; Philem 22

through your prayers, so that thanks may
be given by [b]many persons on our behalf
for the favor bestowed on us through *the
prayers of* many.

Paul's Integrity

12 ¶ For our [1]proud confidence is
this: the testimony of [a]our conscience,
that in holiness and [b]godly sincerity,
[c]not in fleshly wisdom but in the grace of
God, we have conducted ourselves in the
world, and especially toward you.
13 For we write nothing else to you
than what you read and understand, and
I hope you will understand [a]until the
end;
14 just as you also partially did understand us, that we are your reason to be
proud as you also are ours, in [a]the day of
our Lord Jesus.
15 ¶ In this confidence I intended at
first to [a]come to you, so that you might
[1]twice receive a [2b]blessing;
16 [1]that is, to [a]pass [2]your way into
[b]Macedonia, and again from Macedonia
to come to you, and by you to be [c]helped
on my journey to Judea.
17 Therefore, I was not vacillating
when I intended to do this, was I? Or
what I purpose, do I purpose [a]according
to the flesh, so that with me there will be
yes, yes and no, no *at the same time*?
18 But as [a]God is faithful, [b]our word
to you is not yes and no.
19 For [a]the Son of God, Christ Jesus,
who was preached among you by us—by
me and [b]Silvanus and [c]Timothy—was
not yes and no, but is yes [d]in Him.
20 For [a]as many as are the promises of
God, [b]in Him they are yes; therefore also
through Him is [c]our Amen to the glory of
God through us.
21 Now He who [a]establishes us with
you in Christ and [b]anointed us is God,
22 who also [a]sealed us and [b]gave *us*
the Spirit in our hearts as a [1]pledge.
23 ¶ But [a]I call God as witness [1]to my
soul, that [b]to spare you I did not come
again to [c]Corinth.
24 Not that we [a]lord it over your faith,
but are workers with you for your joy; for
in your faith you are [b]standing firm.

Reaffirm Your Love

2 But I determined this [1]for my own
sake, that I [a]would not come to you
in sorrow again.
2 For if I [a]cause you sorrow, who
then makes me glad but the one whom I
made sorrowful?
3 This is the very thing I [a]wrote you,
so that [b]when I came, I would not have
sorrow from those who ought to make me
rejoice; having [c]confidence in you all
that my joy would be *the joy* of you all.
4 For out of much affliction and anguish of heart I [a]wrote to you with many
tears; not so that you would be made sorrowful, but that you might know the love
which I have especially for you.
5 ¶ But [a]if any has caused sorrow, he
has caused sorrow not to me, but in some
degree—[1]in order not to say too much—
to all of you.
6 Sufficient for such a one is [a]this
punishment which *was inflicted* by the
majority,
7 so that on the contrary you should
rather [a]forgive and comfort *him*, otherwise such a one might be overwhelmed
by excessive sorrow.
8 Wherefore I urge you to reaffirm
your love for him.
9 For to this end also [a]I wrote, so
that I might [1b]put you to the test,
whether you are [c]obedient in all things.
10 But one whom you forgive anything, I *forgive* also; for indeed what I
have forgiven, if I have forgiven anything,
I did it for your sakes [a]in the presence of
Christ,
11 so that no advantage would be tak-
en of us by [a]Satan, for [b]we are not ignorant of his schemes.
12 ¶ Now when I came to [a]Troas for
the [b]gospel of Christ and when a [c]door
was opened for me in the Lord,
13 I [a]had no rest for my spirit, not
finding [b]Titus my brother; but [c]taking
my leave of them, I went on to [d]Macedo-
nia.
14 ¶ [a]But thanks be to God, who always [b]leads us in triumph in Christ, and
manifests through us the [c]sweet aroma
of the [d]knowledge of Him in every place.
15 For we are a [a]fragrance of Christ to
God among [b]those who are being saved
and among those who are perishing;
16 [a]to the one an aroma from death to
death, to the other an aroma from life
to life. And who is [b]adequate for these
things?
17 For we are not like many, [1a]ped-
dling the word of God, but [b]as from sincerity, but as from God, we speak in
Christ [c]in the sight of God.

Ministers of a New Covenant

3 Are we beginning to [a]commend ourselves again? Or do we need, as
some, [b]letters of commendation to you
or from you?

11 [b]2 Cor 4:15 **12** [1]Lit *boasting* [a]Acts 23:1; 1 Thess 2:10; Heb 13:18 [b]2 Cor 2:17 [c]1 Cor 1:17; James 3:15 **13** [a]1 Cor 1:8 **14** [a]1 Cor 1:8 **15** [1]Lit *have a second grace* [2]One early ms reads *joy* [a]1 Cor 4:19 [b]Rom 1:11 **16** [1]Lit *and* [2]Lit *through you into* [a]Acts 19:21; 1 Cor 16:5-7 [b]Acts 19:21; Rom 15:26 [c]Acts 15:3; 1 Cor 16:6 **17** [a]2 Cor 10:2f **18** [a]1 Cor 1:9 [b]2 Cor 2:17 **19** [a]Matt 4:3 [b]Acts 15:22; 1 Thess 1:1; 2 Thess 1:1; 1 Pet 5:12 [c]Acts 18:5; 2 Cor 1:1 [d]Heb 13:8 **20** [a]Rom 15:8 [b]Heb 13:8 [c]1 Cor 14:16; Rev 3:14 **21** [a]1 Cor 1:8 [b]1 John 2:20 **22** [1]Or *down payment* [a]John 3:33 [b]Rom 8:16; 2 Cor 5:5; Eph 1:14 **23** [1]Lit *upon* [a]Rom 1:9; Gal 1:20 [b]1 Cor 4:21; 2 Cor 2:1 [c]2 Cor 1:1 **24** [a]2 Cor 4:5; 1 Pet 5:3 [b]Rom 11:20; 1 Cor 15:1 **2:1** [1]Or *as far as I am concerned* [a]1 Cor 4:21; 2 Cor 12:21 **2** [a]2 Cor 7:8 **3** [a]2 Cor 2:9 [b]1 Cor 4:21; 2 Cor 12:21 [c]Gal 5:10; 2 Thess 3:4; Philem 21 **4** [a]2 Cor 2:9 **5** [1]Lit *so that I not be burdensome* [a]1 Cor 5:1f **6** [a]1 Cor 5:4f; 2 Cor 7:11 **7** [a]Gal 6:1; Eph 4:32 **9** [1]Lit *know the proof of you* [a]2 Cor 2:3f [b]2 Cor 8:2; Phil 2:22 [c]2 Cor 7:15 **10** [a]1 Cor 5:4; 2 Cor 4:6 **11** [a]Matt 4:10 [b]Luke 22:31; 2 Cor 4:4; 1 Pet 5:8 **12** [a]Acts 16:8 [b]Rom 1:1; 2 Cor 4:3; 1 Thess 3:2 [c]Acts 14:27 **13** [a]2 Cor 7:5 [b]2 Cor 7:6; Gal 2:1; 2 Tim 4:10; Titus 1:4 [c]Mark 6:46 [d]Rom 15:26 **14** [a]Rom 1:8; 1 Cor 15:57; 2 Cor 8:16 [b]Col 2:15 [c]Song 1:3; Ezek 20:41; Eph 5:2; Phil 4:18 [d]1 Cor 12:8 **15** [a]Song 1:3; Ezek 20:41; Eph 5:2; Phil 4:18 [b]1 Cor 1:18 **16** [a]Luke 2:34; John 9:39; 1 Pet 2:7f [b]2 Cor 3:5f **17** [1]Or *corrupting* [a]2 Cor 4:2; Gal 1:6-9 [b]1 Cor 5:8; 2 Cor 1:12; 1 Thess 2:4; 1 Pet 4:11 [c]2 Cor 12:19 **3:1** [a]2 Cor 5:12 [b]Acts 18:27; 1 Cor 16:3

2 [a]You are our letter, written in our
hearts, known and read by all men;
3 being manifested that you are a letter of Christ, [1a]cared for by us, written
not with ink but with the Spirit of [b]the
living God, not on [c]tablets of stone but
on [d]tablets of [2e]human hearts.
4 ¶ Such [a]confidence we have through
Christ toward God.
5 Not that we are adequate in ourselves to consider anything as *coming*
from ourselves, but [a]our adequacy is
from God,
6 who also made us adequate *as* [a]ser-
vants of a [b]new covenant, not of [c]the
letter but of the Spirit; for the letter kills,
but [d]the Spirit gives life.
7 ¶ But if the [a]ministry of death, [b]in
letters engraved on stones, came [1]with
glory, [c]so that the sons of Israel could not
look intently at the face of Moses because
of the glory of his face, fading *as* it was,
8 how will the ministry of the Spirit
fail to be even more with glory?
9 For if [a]the ministry of condemnation has glory, much more does the
[b]ministry of righteousness abound in
glory.
10 For indeed what had glory, in this
case has no glory because of the glory that
surpasses *it.*
11 For if that which fades away *was*
[1]with glory, much more that which remains *is* in glory.
12 ¶ [a]Therefore having such a hope,
[b]we use great boldness in *our* speech,
13 and *are* not like Moses, [a]*who* used
to put a veil over his face so that the sons
of Israel would not look intently at the
end of what was fading away.
14 But their minds were [a]hardened;
for until this very day at the [b]reading of
[c]the old covenant the same veil [1]re-
mains unlifted, because it is removed in
Christ.
15 But to this day whenever Moses is
read, a veil lies over their heart;
16 [a]but whenever a person turns to
the Lord, the veil is taken away.
17 Now the Lord is the Spirit, and
where [a]the Spirit of the Lord is, [b]*there*
is liberty.
18 But we all, with unveiled face, [a]be-
holding as in a mirror the [b]glory of the
Lord, are being [c]transformed into the
same image from glory to glory, just as
from [d]the Lord, the Spirit.

Paul's Apostolic Ministry

4 Therefore, since we have this [a]min-
istry, as we [b]received mercy, we
[c]do not lose heart,
2 but we have renounced the [a]things
hidden because of shame, not walking in
craftiness or [b]adulterating the word of
God, but by the manifestation of truth
[c]commending ourselves to every man's
conscience in the sight of God.
3 And even if our [a]gospel is [b]veiled,
it is veiled [1]to [c]those who are perishing,
4 in whose case [a]the god of [b]this
[1]world has [c]blinded the minds of the
unbelieving [2]so that they might not see
the [d]light of the gospel of the [e]glory of
Christ, who is the [f]image of God.
5 For we [a]do not preach ourselves
but Christ Jesus as Lord, and ourselves as
your bond-servants [1]for Jesus' sake.
6 For God, who said, "[a]Light shall
shine out of darkness," is the One who
has [b]shone in our hearts to give the
[c]Light of the knowledge of the glory of
God in the face of Christ.
7 ¶ But we have this treasure in
[a]earthen vessels, so that the surpassing
greatness of [b]the power will be of God
and not from ourselves;
8 *we are* [a]afflicted in every way, but
not [b]crushed; [c]perplexed, but not despairing;
9 [a]persecuted, but not [b]forsaken;
[c]struck down, but not destroyed;
10 [a]always carrying about in the body
the dying of Jesus, so that [b]the life of
Jesus also may be manifested in our body.
11 For we who live are constantly being delivered over to death for Jesus'
sake, so that the life of Jesus also may be
manifested in our mortal flesh.
12 So death works in us, but life in
you.
13 ¶ But having the same [a]spirit of
faith, according to what is written, "[b]I
BELIEVED, THEREFORE I SPOKE," we also believe, therefore we also speak,
14 knowing that He who [a]raised the
Lord Jesus [b]will raise us also with Jesus
and will [c]present us with you.
15 For all things *are* [a]for your sakes,
so that the grace which is [1b]spreading to
more and more people may cause the giving of thanks to abound to the glory of
God.
16 ¶ Therefore we [a]do not lose heart,
but though our outer man is decaying, yet
our [b]inner man is [c]being renewed day
by day.
17 For momentary, [a]light affliction is
producing for us an eternal weight of glory far beyond all comparison,
18 while we [a]look not at the things
which are seen, but at the things which

2 [a]1 Cor 9:2 **3** [1]Lit *served* [2]Lit *hearts of flesh* [a]2 Cor 3:6 [b]Matt 16:16 [c]Ex 24:12; 2 Cor 3:7 [d]Prov 3:3; Jer 17:1 [e]Jer 31:33; Ezek 11:19 **4** [a]Eph 3:12 **5** [a]1 Cor 15:10 **6** [a]1 Cor 3:5 [b]Jer 31:31; Luke 22:20 [c]Rom 2:29 [d]John 6:63; Rom 7:6 **7** [1]Or *in glory* [a]Rom 4:15; 2 Cor 3:9; Gal 3:10 [b]Ex 24:12; 2 Cor 3:3 [c]Ex 34:29-35; 2 Cor 3:13 **9** [a]Deut 27:26; 2 Cor 3:7; Heb 12:18-21 [b]Rom 1:17 **11** [1]Lit *through* **12** [a]2 Cor 7:4 [b]Acts 4:13; 2 Cor 7:4; Eph 6:19; 1 Thess 2:2 **13** [a]Ex 34:33-35; 2 Cor 3:7 **14** [1]Or *remains, it not being revealed that it is done away in Christ* [a]Rom 11:7; 2 Cor 4:4 [b]Acts 13:15 [c]2 Cor 3:6 **16** [a]Ex 34:34; Rom 11:23 **17** [a]Is 61:1f; Gal 4:6 [b]John 8:32; Gal 5:1 **18** [a]1 Cor 13:12 [b]John 17:22; 2 Cor 4:4 [c]Rom 8:29 [d]2 Cor 3:17 **4:1** [a]1 Cor 3:5 [b]1 Cor 7:25 [c]Luke 18:1; 2 Cor 4:16; Gal 6:9; Eph 3:13; 2 Thess 3:13 **2** [a]Rom 6:21; 1 Cor 4:5 [b]2 Cor 2:17 [c]2 Cor 5:11f **3** [1]Lit *in* [a]2 Cor 2:12 [b]1 Cor 2:6ff; 2 Cor 3:14 [c]1 Cor 1:18; 2 Cor 2:15 **4** [1]Lit *age* [2]Or *that the light...image of God, would not dawn* upon them [a]John 12:31 [b]Matt 13:22 [c]2 Cor 3:14 [d]Acts 26:18; 2 Cor 4:6 [e]2 Cor 3:18 [f]John 1:18; Phil 2:6; Col 1:15; Heb 1:3 **5** [1]Two early mss read *through Jesus* [a]1 Cor 4:15f; 1 Thess 2:6f **6** [a]Gen 1:3 [b]2 Pet 1:19 [c]Acts 26:18; 2 Cor 4:4 **7** [a]Job 4:19; Lam 4:2; 2 Cor 5:1; 2 Tim 2:20 [b]Judg 7:2; 1 Cor 2:5 **8** [a]2 Cor 1:8 [b]2 Cor 6:12 [c]Gal 4:20

9 [a]John 15:20; Rom 8:35f [b]Ps 129:2; Heb 13:5 [c]Ps 37:24; Prov 24:16; Mic 7:8 **10** [a]Rom 6:5; Gal 6:17 [b]Rom 6:8 **13** [a]1 Cor 12:9 [b]Ps 116:10 **14** [a]Acts 2:24 [b]1 Thess 4:14 [c]Luke 21:36; Eph 5:27; Col 1:22; Jude 24 **15** [1]Lit *being multiplied through the many* [a]Rom 8:28; 2 Cor 1:6 [b]1 Cor 9:19; 2 Cor 1:11 **16** [a]2 Cor 4:1 [b]Rom 7:22 [c]Is 40:29; Col 3:10 **17** [a]Rom 8:18 **18** [a]Rom 8:24; 2 Cor 5:7; Heb 11:1

are not seen; for the things which are seen are temporal, but the things which are not seen are eternal.

The Temporal and Eternal

5 For we know that if [1]the [a]earthly [b]tent which is our house is torn down, we have a building from God, a house [c]not made with hands, eternal in the heavens.

2 For indeed in this *house* we [a]groan, longing to be [b]clothed with our dwelling from heaven,

3 inasmuch as we, having put it on, will not be found naked.

4 For indeed while we are in this tent, we [a]groan, being burdened, because we do not want to be unclothed but to be [b]clothed, so that what is [c]mortal will be swallowed up by life.

5 Now He who prepared us for this very purpose is God, who [a]gave to us the Spirit as a [1]pledge.

6 ¶ Therefore, being always of good courage, and knowing that [a]while we are at home in the body we are absent from the Lord—

7 for [a]we walk by faith, not by [1]sight—

8 we are of good courage, I say, and [a]prefer rather to be absent from the body and [b]to be at home with the Lord.

9 Therefore we also have as our ambition, whether at home or absent, to be [a]pleasing to Him.

10 For we must all appear before [a]the judgment seat of Christ, so that each one may be recompensed for [1]his deeds in the body, according to what he has done, whether good or bad.

11 ¶ Therefore, knowing the [a]fear of the Lord, we persuade men, but we are made manifest to God; and I hope that we are [b]made manifest also in your consciences.

12 We are not [a]again commending ourselves to you but *are* giving you an [b]occasion to be proud of us, so that you will have *an answer* for those who take pride in appearance and not in heart.

13 For if we [1]are [a]beside ourselves, it is for God; if we are of sound mind, it is for you.

14 For the love of Christ [a]controls us, having concluded this, that [b]one died for all, therefore all died;

15 and He died for all, so that they who live might no longer [a]live for themselves, but for Him who died and rose again on their behalf.

16 ¶ Therefore from now on we recognize no one [1a]according to the flesh; even though we have known Christ [1]according to the flesh, yet now we know *Him in this way* no longer.

17 Therefore if anyone is [a]in Christ, [1]*he is* [b]a new creature; [c]the old things passed away; behold, new things have come.

18 Now [a]all *these* things are from God, [b]who reconciled us to Himself through Christ and gave us the [c]ministry of reconciliation,

19 namely, that [a]God was in Christ reconciling the world to Himself, [b]not counting their trespasses against them, and [1]He has [2]committed to us the word of reconciliation.

20 ¶ Therefore, we are [a]ambassadors for Christ, [b]as though God were making an appeal through us; we beg you on behalf of Christ, be [c]reconciled to God.

21 He made Him who [a]knew no sin *to be* [b]sin on our behalf, so that we might become the [c]righteousness of God in Him.

Their Ministry Commended

6 And [a]working together *with Him,* [b]we also urge you not to receive [c]the grace of God in vain—

2 for He says,

"[a]AT THE ACCEPTABLE TIME I
LISTENED TO YOU,
AND ON THE DAY OF SALVATION I
HELPED YOU."

Behold, now is "THE ACCEPTABLE TIME," behold, now is "THE DAY OF SALVATION"—

3 [a]giving no cause for offense in anything, so that the ministry will not be discredited,

4 but in everything [a]commending ourselves as [1b]servants of God, [c]in much endurance, in afflictions, in hardships, in distresses,

5 in [a]beatings, in imprisonments, in [b]tumults, in labors, in sleeplessness, in [c]hunger,

6 in purity, in [a]knowledge, in [b]patience, in kindness, in the [c]Holy Spirit, in [d]genuine love,

7 in [a]the word of truth, in [b]the power of God; by [c]the weapons of righteousness for the right hand and the left,

8 by glory and [a]dishonor, by [b]evil report and good report; *regarded* as [c]deceivers and yet [d]true;

9 as unknown [1]yet well-known, as [a]dying [1]yet behold, [b]we live; as [2]punished [1]yet not put to death,

10 as [a]sorrowful yet always [a]rejoicing, as [b]poor yet making many rich, as

5:1 [1]Lit *our earthly house of the tent* [a]Job 4:19; 1 Cor 15:47; 2 Cor 4:7 [b]2 Pet 1:13f [c]Mark 14:58; Acts 7:48; Heb 9:11
2 [a]Rom 8:23; 2 Cor 5:4 [b]1 Cor 15:53f; 2 Cor 5:4
4 [a]2 Cor 5:2 [b]1 Cor 15:53f; 2 Cor 5:2 [c]1 Cor 15:54
5 [1]Or *down payment* [a]Rom 8:23; 2 Cor 1:22
6 [a]Heb 11:13f
7 [1]Or *appearance* [a]1 Cor 13:12; 2 Cor 4:18
8 [a]Phil 1:23 [b]John 12:26; Phil 1:23
9 [a]Rom 14:18; Col 1:10; 1 Thess 4:1
10 [1]Lit *the things through the body* [a]Matt 16:27; Acts 10:42; Rom 2:16; Eph 6:8
11 [a]Heb 10:31; Jude 23 [b]2 Cor 4:2
12 [a]2 Cor 3:1 [b]2 Cor 1:14; Phil 1:26
13 [1]Lit *were* [a]Mark 3:21; 2 Cor 11:1
14 [a]Acts 18:5 [b]Rom 5:15; Gal 2:20; Col 3:3
15 [a]Rom 14:7-9
16 [1]I.e. by what he is in the flesh [a]John 8:15; 2 Cor 11:18; Phil 3:4
17 [1]Or there is *a new creation* [a]Rom 16:7 [b]John 3:3; Rom 6:4; Gal 6:15 [c]Is 43:18f; Eph 4:24; Rev 21:4f
18 [a]1 Cor 11:12 [b]Rom 5:10; Col 1:20 [c]1 Cor 3:5
19 [1]Lit *having* [2]Lit *placed in us* [a]Col 2:9 [b]Rom 4:8; 1 Cor 13:5
20 [a]Mal 2:7; Eph 6:20 [b]2 Cor 6:1 [c]Rom 5:10; Col 1:20
21 [a]Acts 3:14; Heb 4:15; 1 Pet 2:22; 1 John 3:5 [b]Rom 3:25; Gal 3:13 [c]Rom 1:17; 1 Cor 1:30
6:1 [a]1 Cor 3:9 [b]2 Cor 5:20 [c]Acts 11:23
2 [a]Is 49:8
3 [a]1 Cor 8:9
4 [1]Or *ministers* [a]Rom 3:5 [b]1 Cor 3:5; 2 Tim 2:24f [c]Acts 9:16; 2 Cor 4:8-11
5 [a]Acts 16:23 [b]Acts 19:23ff [c]1 Cor 4:11
6 [a]1 Cor 12:8; 2 Cor 11:6 [b]2 Cor 1:23 [c]1 Cor 2:4; 1 Thess 1:5 [d]Rom 12:9
7 [a]2 Cor 2:17 [b]1 Cor 2:5 [c]Rom 13:12; 2 Cor 10:4; Eph 6:11ff
8 [a]1 Cor 4:10 [b]Rom 3:8; 1 Cor 4:13; 2 Cor 12:16 [c]Matt 27:63 [d]2 Cor 1:18; 1 Thess 2:3f
9 [1]Lit *and* [2]Or *disciplined* [a]Rom 8:36 [b]2 Cor 1:8
10 [a]John 16:22; 2 Cor 7:4; Phil 2:17; Col 1:24; 1 Thess 1:6 [b]1 Cor 1:5; 2 Cor 8:9

[c]having nothing [1]yet possessing [d]all things.

11 ¶ [a]Our mouth [1]has spoken freely to you, O Corinthians, our [b]heart is opened wide.

12 You are not restrained [1]by us, but [a]you are restrained in your own [2]affections.

13 Now in a like [a]exchange—I speak as to [b]children—open wide *to us* also.

14 ¶ [a]Do not be [1]bound together with [b]unbelievers; for what [c]partnership have righteousness and lawlessness, or what fellowship has light with darkness?

15 Or what [a]harmony has Christ with [1]Belial, or [2]what has a [b]believer in common with an [c]unbeliever?

16 Or [a]what agreement has the temple of God with idols? For we are [b]the temple of [c]the living God; just as God said,

“[d]I WILL [e]DWELL IN THEM AND
[f]WALK AMONG THEM;
AND I WILL BE THEIR GOD, AND
THEY SHALL BE MY PEOPLE.
17 “[a]Therefore, [b]COME OUT FROM
THEIR MIDST AND BE
SEPARATE,” says the Lord.
“AND DO NOT TOUCH WHAT IS
UNCLEAN;
And I will welcome you.
18 “[a]And I will be a father to you,
And you shall be [b]sons and
daughters to Me,”
Says the Lord Almighty.

Paul Reveals His Heart

7 Therefore, having these promises, [a]beloved, [b]let us cleanse ourselves from all defilement of flesh and spirit, perfecting holiness in the fear of God.

2 ¶ [a]Make room for us *in your hearts*; we wronged no one, we corrupted no one, we took advantage of no one.

3 I do not speak to condemn you, for I have said [a]before that you are [b]in our hearts to die together and to live together.

4 Great is my [a]confidence [1]in you; great is my [b]boasting on your behalf. I am filled with [c]comfort; I am overflowing with [d]joy in all our affliction.

5 ¶ For even when we came into [a]Macedonia our flesh had no rest, but we were [b]afflicted on every side: [c]conflicts without, fears within.

6 But [a]God, who comforts the [1]depressed, [b]comforted us by the coming of [c]Titus;

7 and not only by his coming, but also by the comfort with which he was comforted in you, as he reported to us your longing, your mourning, your zeal for me; so that I rejoiced even more.

8 For though I [a]caused you sorrow by my letter, I do not regret it; though I did regret it—*for* I see that that letter caused you sorrow, though only for a while—

9 I now rejoice, not that you were made sorrowful, but that you were made sorrowful to *the point of* repentance; for you were made sorrowful according to *the will of* God, so that you might not suffer loss in anything [1]through us.

10 For the sorrow that is according to *the will of* God produces a [a]repentance [1]without regret, *leading* to salvation, but the sorrow of the world produces death.

11 For behold what earnestness this very thing, this [1]godly sorrow, has produced in you: what vindication of yourselves, what indignation, what fear, what [a]longing, what zeal, what [b]avenging of wrong! In everything you [c]demonstrated yourselves to be innocent in the matter.

12 So although [a]I wrote to you, *it was* not for the sake of [b]the offender nor for the sake of the one offended, but that your earnestness on our behalf might be made known to you in the sight of God.

13 For this reason we have been [a]comforted.

¶ And besides our comfort, we rejoiced even much more for the joy of [b]Titus, because his [c]spirit has been refreshed by you all.

14 For if in anything I have [a]boasted to him about you, I was not put to shame; but as we spoke all things to you in truth, so also our boasting before [b]Titus proved to be *the* truth.

15 His [1]affection abounds all the more toward you, as he remembers the [a]obedience of you all, how you received him with [b]fear and trembling.

16 I rejoice that in everything [a]I have confidence in you.

Great Generosity

8 Now, brethren, we *wish to* make known to you the grace of God which has been [a]given in the churches of [b]Macedonia,

2 that in a great ordeal of affliction their abundance of joy and their deep poverty overflowed in the [a]wealth of their liberality.

3 For I testify that [a]according to their ability, and beyond their ability, *they gave* of their own accord,

4 begging us with much urging for the [a]favor [1]of participation in the [2b]support of the [3]saints,

5 and *this,* not as we had [1]expected,

10 [1]Lit *and* [c]Acts 3:6 [d]Rom 8:32; 1 Cor 3:21
11 [1]Lit *is open to you* [a]Ezek 33:22; Eph 6:19 [b]Is 60:5; 2 Cor 7:3
12 [1]Or *in us* [2]Lit *inward parts* [a]2 Cor 7:2
13 [a]Gal 4:12 [b]1 Cor 4:14
14 [1]Lit *unequally yoked* [a]Deut 22:10; 1 Cor 5:9f [b]1 Cor 6:6 [c]Eph 5:7; 1 John 1:6
15 [1]Gr *Beliar* [2]Lit *what part has a believer with an unbeliever* [a]1 Cor 10:21 [b]Acts 5:14; 1 Pet 1:21 [c]1 Cor 6:6
16 [a]1 Cor 10:21 [b]1 Cor 3:16 [c]Matt 16:16 [d]Ex 29:45; Lev 26:12; Jer 31:1; Ezek 37:27 [e]Ex 25:8; John 14:23 [f]Rev 2:1
17 [a]Is 52:11 [b]Rev 18:4
18 [a]2 Sam 7:14; 1 Chr 17:13; Is 43:6; Hos 1:10 [b]Rom 8:14
7:1 [a]Heb 6:9 [b]1 Pet 1:15f
2 [a]2 Cor 6:12f
3 [a]2 Cor 6:11f [b]Phil 1:7
4 [1]Lit *toward* [a]2 Cor 3:12 [b]2 Cor 7:14; Phil 1:26; 2 Thess 1:4 [c]2 Cor 1:4 [d]2 Cor 6:10
5 [a]Rom 15:26; 2 Cor 2:13 [b]2 Cor 4:8 [c]Deut 32:25
6 [1]Or *humble* [a]2 Cor 1:3f [b]2 Cor 7:13 [c]2 Cor 2:13
8 [a]2 Cor 2:2
9 [1]Lit *from*
10 [1]Or leading *to a salvation without regret* [a]Acts 11:18
11 [1]Lit *sorrow according to God* [a]2 Cor 7:7 [b]2 Cor 2:6 [c]Rom 3:5
12 [a]2 Cor 2:3 [b]1 Cor 5:1f
13 [a]2 Cor 7:6 [b]2 Cor 2:13 [c]1 Cor 16:18
14 [a]2 Cor 7:4; Phil 1:26; 2 Thess 1:4 [b]2 Cor 2:13
15 [1]Lit *inward parts* [a]2 Cor 2:9 [b]1 Cor 2:3; Phil 2:12
16 [a]2 Cor 2:3
8:1 [a]2 Cor 8:5 [b]Acts 16:9
2 [a]Rom 2:4
3 [a]1 Cor 16:2; 2 Cor 8:11
4 [1]Lit *and* [2]Lit *service to the saints* [3]Or *holy ones* [a]Acts 24:17; Rom 15:25f [b]Rom 15:31; 2 Cor 8:19f
5 [1]Lit *hoped*

but they first [a]gave themselves to the Lord and to us by [b]the will of God.

6 So we [a]urged [b]Titus that as he had previously [c]made a beginning, so he would also complete in you [d]this gracious work as well.

7 ¶ But just as you [a]abound [b]in everything, in faith and utterance and knowledge and in all earnestness and in the [1]love we inspired in you, *see* that you [a]abound in this gracious work also.

8 I [a]am not speaking *this* as a command, but as proving through the earnestness of others the sincerity of your love also.

9 For you know [a]the grace of our Lord Jesus Christ, that [b]though He was rich, yet for your sake He became poor, so that you through His poverty might become rich.

10 I [a]give *my* opinion in this matter, for this is to your advantage, who were the first to begin [b]a year ago not only to do *this,* but also to desire *to do it.*

11 But now finish [1]doing it also, so that just as *there was* the [a]readiness to desire it, so *there may be* also the completion of it by your ability.

12 For if the readiness is present, it is acceptable [a]according to what *a person* has, not according to what he does not have.

13 For *this* is not for the ease of others *and* for your affliction, but by way of equality—

14 at this present time your abundance *being a supply* for [a]their need, so that their abundance also may become *a supply* for [a]your need, that there may be equality;

15 as it is written, "[a]HE WHO *gathered* MUCH DID NOT HAVE TOO MUCH, AND HE WHO *gathered* LITTLE HAD NO LACK."

16 ¶ But [a]thanks be to God who [b]puts the same earnestness on your behalf in the heart of [c]Titus.

17 For he not only accepted our [a]appeal, but being himself very earnest, he has gone to you of his own accord.

18 We have sent along with him [a]the brother whose fame in *the things of* the [b]gospel *has spread* through [c]all the churches;

19 [a]and not only *this,* but he has also been [b]appointed by the churches to travel with us in [c]this gracious work, which is being administered by us for the glory of the Lord Himself, and *to show* our [d]readiness,

20 [1]taking precaution so that no one will discredit us in our administration of this generous gift;

21 for we [a]have regard for what is honorable, not only in [b]the sight of the Lord, but also in the sight of men.

22 We have sent with them our brother, whom we have often tested and found diligent in many things, but now even more diligent because of *his* great confidence in you.

23 As for [a]Titus, *he is* my [b]partner and fellow worker [1]among you; as for our [c]brethren, *they are* [2][d]messengers of the churches, [e]a glory to Christ.

24 Therefore [1]openly before the churches, [2]show them the proof of your love and of our [a]reason for boasting about you.

God Gives Most

9 For [a]it is superfluous for me to write to you about this [b]ministry to the [1]saints;

2 for I know your readiness, of which I [a]boast about you to the [b]Macedonians, *namely,* that [c]Achaia has been prepared since [d]last year, and your zeal has stirred up most of them.

3 But I have sent the brethren, in order that our [a]boasting about you may not be made empty in this case, so that, [b]as I was saying, you may be prepared;

4 otherwise if any [a]Macedonians come with me and find you unprepared, we—not to speak of you—will be put to shame by this confidence.

5 So I thought it necessary to urge the [a]brethren that they would go on ahead to you and arrange beforehand your previously promised [1][b]bountiful gift, so that the same would be ready as a [1][c]bountiful gift and not [2][d]affected by covetousness.

6 ¶ Now this *I say,* [a]he who sows sparingly will also reap sparingly, and he who sows [1]bountifully will also reap [1]bountifully.

7 Each one *must do* just as he has purposed in his heart, not [a]grudgingly or under compulsion, for [b]God loves a cheerful giver.

8 And [a]God is able to make all grace abound to you, so that always having all sufficiency in everything, you may have an abundance for every good deed;

9 as it is written,

"[a]HE SCATTERED ABROAD, HE GAVE
TO THE POOR,
HIS RIGHTEOUSNESS [1]ENDURES
FOREVER."

10 Now He who supplies [a]seed to the sower and bread for food will supply and multiply your seed for sowing and [b]increase the harvest of your righteousness;

11 you will be [a]enriched in everything for all liberality, which through us is producing [b]thanksgiving to God.

---

5 [a]2 Cor 8:1 [b]1 Cor 1:1
6 [a]2 Cor 8:17 [b]2 Cor 2:13 [c]2 Cor 8:10 [d]Acts 24:17; Rom 15:25f
7 [1]Lit *love from us in you*; one early ms reads *your love for us* [a]2 Cor 9:8 [b]Rom 15:14; 1 Cor 1:5
8 [a]1 Cor 7:6
9 [a]2 Cor 13:14 [b]Matt 20:28; 2 Cor 6:10; Phil 2:6f
10 [a]1 Cor 7:25 [b]1 Cor 16:2f; 2 Cor 9:2
11 [1]Lit *the doing* [a]2 Cor 8:12
12 [a]Mark 12:43f; Luke 21:3; 2 Cor 9:7
14 [a]Acts 4:34; 2 Cor 9:12
15 [a]Ex 16:18
16 [a]2 Cor 2:14 [b]Rev 17:17 [c]2 Cor 2:13
17 [a]2 Cor 8:6
18 [a]1 Cor 16:3; 2 Cor 12:18 [b]2 Cor 2:12 [c]1 Cor 4:17
19 [a]Rom 5:3 [b]Acts 14:23; 1 Cor 16:3f [c]2 Cor 8:4 [d]2 Cor 8:11
20 [1]Lit *avoiding this*
21 [a]Rom 12:17 [b]Prov 3:4; Rom 14:18
23 [1]Lit *for you* [2]Lit *apostles* [a]2 Cor 8:6 [b]Philem 17 [c]2 Cor 8:18 [d]John 13:16; Phil 2:25 [e]1 Cor 11:7
24 [1]Lit *in the face of the churches* [2]Or *show the proof...for boasting to them about you* [a]2 Cor 7:4
9:1 [1]Or *holy ones* [a]1 Thess 4:9 [b]2 Cor 8:4
2 [a]2 Cor 7:4 [b]Rom 15:26 [c]Acts 18:12 [d]2 Cor 8:10
3 [a]2 Cor 7:4 [b]1 Cor 16:2
4 [a]Rom 15:26
5 [1]Lit *blessing* [2]Lit *as covetousness* [a]2 Cor 9:3 [b]Gen 33:11; Judg 1:15; 2 Cor 9:6 [c]Phil 4:17 [d]2 Cor 12:17f
6 [1]Lit *with blessings* [a]Prov 11:24f; Gal 6:7
7 [a]Deut 15:10; 1 Chr 29:17; Rom 12:8; 2 Cor 8:12 [b]Ex 25:2
8 [a]Eph 3:20
9 [1]Lit *abides* [a]Ps 112:9
10 [a]Is 55:10 [b]Hos 10:12
11 [a]1 Cor 1:5 [b]2 Cor 1:11

12 For the ministry of this service is not only fully supplying [a]the needs of the [1]saints, but is also overflowing [b]through many thanksgivings to God.

13 Because of the proof given by this [a]ministry, they will [b]glorify God for *your* obedience to your [c]confession of the [d]gospel of Christ and for the liberality of your [1]contribution to them and to all,

14 while they also, by prayer on your behalf, yearn for you because of the surpassing grace of God in you.

15 [a]Thanks be to God for His indescribable [b]gift!

Paul Describes Himself

10 Now [a]I, Paul, myself [b]urge you by the [c]meekness and gentleness of Christ—I who [d]am [1]meek when face to face with you, but bold toward you when absent!

2 I ask that [a]when I am present I *need* not be bold with the confidence with which I propose to be courageous against [b]some, who regard us as if we walked [c]according to the flesh.

3 For though we walk in the flesh, we do not war [a]according to the flesh,

4 for the [a]weapons of our warfare are not of the flesh, but [1]divinely powerful [b]for the destruction of fortresses.

5 *We are* destroying speculations and every [a]lofty thing raised up against the knowledge of God, and *we are* taking every thought captive to the [b]obedience of Christ,

6 and we are ready to punish all disobedience, whenever [a]your obedience is complete.

7 ¶ [1a]You are looking at [2]things as they are outwardly. [b]If anyone is confident in himself that he is Christ's, let him consider this again within himself, that just as he is Christ's, [c]so also are we.

8 For even if [a]I boast somewhat [1]further about our [b]authority, which the Lord gave for building you up and not for destroying you, I will not be put to shame,

9 [1]for I do not wish to seem as if I would terrify you by my letters.

10 For they say, "His letters are weighty and strong, but his [1]personal presence is [a]unimpressive and [b]his speech contemptible."

11 Let such a person consider this, that what we are in word by letters when absent, such persons *we are* also in deed when present.

12 ¶ For we are not bold to class or compare ourselves with [1]some of those who [a]commend themselves; but when they measure themselves by themselves and compare themselves with themselves, they are without understanding.

13 But we will not boast [a]beyond *our* measure, but [1b]within the measure of the sphere which God apportioned to us as a measure, to reach even as far as you.

14 For we are not overextending ourselves, as if we did not reach to you, for [a]we were the first to come even as far as you in the [b]gospel of Christ;

15 not boasting [a]beyond *our* measure, *that is,* in [b]other men's labors, but with the hope that as [c]your faith grows, we will be, [1]within our sphere, [d]enlarged even more by you,

16 so as to [a]preach the gospel even to [b]the regions beyond you, *and* not to boast [1c]in what has been accomplished in the sphere of another.

17 But [a]HE WHO BOASTS IS TO BOAST IN THE LORD.

18 For it is not he who [a]commends himself that is approved, but he [b]whom the Lord commends.

Paul Defends His Apostleship

11 I wish that you would [a]bear with me in a little [b]foolishness; but [1]indeed you are bearing with me.

2 For I am jealous for you with a godly jealousy; for I [a]betrothed you to one husband, so that to Christ I might [b]present you *as* a pure virgin.

3 But I am afraid that, as the [a]serpent deceived Eve by his craftiness, your minds will be led astray from the simplicity and purity *of devotion* to Christ.

4 For if [1]one comes and preaches [a]another Jesus whom we have not preached, or you receive a [b]different spirit which you have not received, or a [c]different gospel which you have not accepted, you [d]bear *this* [e]beautifully.

5 For I consider myself [a]not in the least inferior to the [1]most eminent apostles.

6 But even if I am [a]unskilled in speech, yet I am not *so* in [b]knowledge; in fact, in every way we have [c]made *this* evident to you in all things.

7 ¶ Or [a]did I commit a sin in humbling myself so that you might be exalted, because I preached the [b]gospel of God to you [c]without charge?

8 I robbed other churches by [a]taking wages *from them* to serve you;

9 and when I was present with you and was in need, I was [a]not a burden to anyone; for when [b]the brethren came

12 [1]Or *holy ones* [a]2 Cor 8:14 [b]2 Cor 1:11
13 [1]Or *sharing with them* [a]Rom 15:31; 2 Cor 8:4 [b]Matt 9:8 [c]1 Tim 6:12f; Heb 3:1 [d]2 Cor 2:12
15 [a]2 Cor 2:14 [b]Rom 5:15f
10:1 [1]Lit *lowly* [a]Gal 5:2; Eph 3:1; Col 1:23 [b]Rom 12:1 [c]Matt 11:29; 1 Cor 4:21; Phil 4:5 [d]1 Cor 2:3f; 2 Cor 10:10
2 [a]1 Cor 4:21; 2 Cor 13:2 [b]1 Cor 4:18f [c]Rom 8:4; 2 Cor 1:17
3 [a]Rom 8:4; 2 Cor 1:17
4 [1]Or *mighty before God* [a]1 Cor 9:7; 2 Cor 6:7; 1 Tim 1:18 [b]Jer 1:10; 2 Cor 10:8
5 [a]Is 2:11f [b]2 Cor 9:13
6 [a]2 Cor 2:9
7 [1]Or *Look at...* or *Do you look at...?* [2]Lit *what is before your face* [a]John 7:24; 2 Cor 5:12 [b]1 Cor 1:12 [c]1 Cor 9:1; 2 Cor 11:23; Gal 1:12
8 [1]Or *more abundantly* [a]2 Cor 7:4 [b]2 Cor 13:10
9 [1]Lit *so that I may not seem*
10 [1]Lit *bodily presence is weak* [a]1 Cor 2:3; 2 Cor 12:7; Gal 4:13f [b]1 Cor 1:17; 2 Cor 11:6
12 [1]Or *any* [a]2 Cor 3:1
13 [1]Lit *according to the measure* [a]2 Cor 10:15 [b]Rom 12:3; 2 Cor 10:15f
14 [a]1 Cor 3:6 [b]2 Cor 2:12
15 [1]Lit *according to our sphere* [a]2 Cor 10:13 [b]Rom 15:20 [c]2 Thess 1:3 [d]Acts 5:13
16 [1]Lit *to the things prepared in the* [a]2 Cor 11:7 [b]Acts 19:21 [c]Rom 15:20
17 [a]Jer 9:24; 1 Cor 1:31
18 [a]2 Cor 10:12 [b]Rom 2:29; 1 Cor 4:5
11:1 [1]Or *do indeed bear with me* [a]Matt 17:17; 2 Cor 11:4 [b]2 Cor 5:13
2 [a]Hos 2:19f; Eph 5:26f [b]2 Cor 4:14
3 [a]Gen 3:4; John 8:44; 1 Thess 3:5; 1 Tim 2:14; Rev 12:9
4 [1]Lit *the one who comes preaches* [a]1 Cor 3:11 [b]Rom 8:15 [c]Gal 1:6 [d]2 Cor 11:1 [e]Mark 7:9
5 [1]Or *super-apostles* [a]2 Cor 12:11; Gal 2:6
6 [a]1 Cor 1:17 [b]1 Cor 12:8; Eph 3:4 [c]2 Cor 4:2
7 [a]2 Cor 12:13 [b]Rom 1:1; 2 Cor 2:12 [c]Acts 18:3; 1 Cor 9:18
8 [a]1 Cor 4:12; Phil 4:15
9 [a]2 Cor 12:13f [b]Acts 18:5

from [c]Macedonia they fully supplied my
need, and in everything I kept myself
from [d]being a burden to you, [1]and will
continue to do so.
10 [a]As the truth of Christ is in me,
[b]this boasting of mine will not be
stopped in the regions of [c]Achaia.
11 Why? [a]Because I do not love you?
[b]God knows *I do!*
12 ¶ But what I am doing I will continue to do, [a]so that I may cut off opportunity from those who desire an opportunity
to be [1]regarded just as we are in the
matter about which they are boasting.
13 For such men are [a]false apostles,
[b]deceitful workers, disguising themselves as apostles of Christ.
14 No wonder, for even [a]Satan disguises himself as an [b]angel of light.
15 Therefore it is not surprising if his
servants also disguise themselves as servants of righteousness, [a]whose end will
be according to their deeds.
16 ¶ [a]Again I say, let no one think me
foolish; but if *you do,* receive me even as
foolish, so that I also may boast a little.
17 What I am saying, I am not saying
[1a]as the Lord would, but as [b]in foolishness, in this confidence of boasting.
18 Since [a]many boast [b]according to
the flesh, I will boast also.
19 For you, [a]being *so* wise, tolerate
the foolish gladly.
20 For you tolerate it if anyone [a]en-
slaves you, anyone [b]devours you, anyone
[c]takes advantage of you, anyone [d]exalts
himself, anyone [e]hits you in the face.
21 To *my* [a]shame I *must* say that we
have been [b]weak *by comparison.*
¶ But in whatever respect anyone *else*
[c]is bold—I [d]speak in foolishness—I am
just as bold myself.
22 Are they [a]Hebrews? [b]So am I. Are
they [c]Israelites? [c]So am I. Are they
[1d]descendants of Abraham? [e]So am I.
23 Are they [a]servants of Christ?—I
speak as if insane—I more so; in [1b]far
more labors, in [1c]far more imprisonments, [2d]beaten times without number,
often in [e]danger of death.
24 Five times I received from the Jews
[a]thirty-nine *lashes.*
25 Three times I was [a]beaten with
rods, once I was [b]stoned, three times I
was shipwrecked, a night and a day I have
spent in the deep.
26 *I have been* on frequent journeys,
in dangers from rivers, dangers from robbers, dangers from *my* [a]countrymen,
dangers from the [b]Gentiles, dangers in
the [c]city, dangers in the wilderness, dangers on the sea, dangers among [d]false
brethren;
27 *I have been* in [a]labor and hardship,
[1]through many sleepless nights, in
[b]hunger and thirst, often [c]without food,
in cold and [2d]exposure.
28 Apart from *such* [1]external things,
there is the daily pressure on me *of* concern for [a]all the churches.
29 Who is [a]weak without my being
weak? Who is [1]led into sin [2]without my
intense concern?
30 ¶ If I have to boast, I will boast of
what pertains to my [a]weakness.
31 The God and Father of the Lord
Jesus, [a]He who is blessed forever,
[b]knows that I am not lying.
32 In [a]Damascus the ethnarch under
Aretas the king was [b]guarding the city of
the Damascenes in order to seize me,
33 and I was let down in a basket
[a]through a window [1]in the wall, and *so*
escaped his hands.

Paul's Vision

12 [a]Boasting is necessary, though it
is not profitable; but I will go on
to visions and [b]revelations [1]of the Lord.
2 I know a man [a]in Christ who fourteen years ago—whether in the body I do
not know, or out of the body I do not
know, [b]God knows—such a man was
[c]caught up to the [d]third heaven.
3 And I know how such a man—
whether in the body or apart from the
body I do not know, [a]God knows—
4 was [a]caught up into [b]Paradise and
heard inexpressible words, which a man
is not permitted to speak.
5 [a]On behalf of such a man I will
boast; but on my own behalf I will not
boast, except in regard to *my* [b]weak-
nesses.
6 For if I do wish to boast I will not
be [a]foolish, [b]for I will be speaking the
truth; but I refrain *from this,* so that no
one will credit me with more than he
sees *in* me or hears from me.

A Thorn in the Flesh

7 Because of the surpassing greatness
of the [a]revelations, for this reason, to
keep me from exalting myself, there was
given me a [b]thorn in the flesh, a [c]mes-
senger of Satan to [1]torment me—to keep
me from exalting myself!
8 Concerning this I implored the
Lord [a]three times that it might leave me.
9 And He has said to me, "My grace
is sufficient for you, for [a]power is perfected in weakness." Most gladly, therefore, I will rather [b]boast [1]about my

9 [1]Lit *and I will keep* [c]Rom 15:26; Phil 4:15-18 [d]2 Cor 12:13f
10 [a]Rom 1:9; 2 Cor 1:23; Gal 2:20 [b]1 Cor 9:15 [c]Acts 18:12
11 [a]2 Cor 12:15 [b]Rom 1:9; 2 Cor 2:17
12 [1]Lit *found* [a]1 Cor 9:12
13 [a]Acts 20:30; Gal 1:7; Phil 1:15; Titus 1:10f; 2 Pet 2:1; Rev 2:2 [b]Phil 3:2
14 [a]Matt 4:10; Eph 6:12; Col 1:13 [b]Col 1:12
15 [a]Rom 2:6
16 [a]2 Cor 11:1
17 [1]Lit *in accordance with the Lord* [a]1 Cor 7:12 [b]2 Cor 11:21
18 [a]Phil 3:3f [b]2 Cor 5:16
19 [a]1 Cor 4:10
20 [a]2 Cor 1:24; Gal 2:4 [b]Mark 12:40 [c]2 Cor 11:3 [d]2 Cor 10:5 [e]1 Cor 4:11
21 [a]2 Cor 6:8 [b]2 Cor 10:10 [c]2 Cor 10:2 [d]2 Cor 11:17
22 [1]Lit *seed* [a]Acts 6:1 [b]Phil 3:5 [c]Rom 9:4 [d]Gal 3:16 [e]Rom 11:1
23 [1]Lit *more abundant* [2]Lit *exceedingly in stripes* [a]1 Cor 3:5; 2 Cor 3:6 [b]1 Cor 15:10 [c]2 Cor 6:5 [d]Acts 16:23; 2 Cor 6:5 [e]Rom 8:36
24 [a]Deut 25:3
25 [a]Acts 16:22 [b]Acts 14:19
26 [a]Acts 9:23; 1 Thess 2:15 [b]Acts 14:5 [c]Acts 21:31 [d]Gal 2:4
27 [1]Lit *often in wakefulness* [2]Lit *nakedness*; i.e. lack of clothing [a]1 Thess 2:9; 2 Thess 3:8 [b]1 Cor 4:11; Phil 4:12 [c]2 Cor 6:5 [d]1 Cor 4:11
28 [1]Or *the things unmentioned* [a]1 Cor 7:17
29 [1]Lit *made to stumble* [2]Lit *and I do not burn* [a]1 Cor 8:9
30 [a]1 Cor 2:3
31 [a]Rom 1:25 [b]2 Cor 11:11
32 [a]Acts 9:2 [b]Acts 9:24
33 [1]Lit *through* [a]Acts 9:25
12:1 [1]Or *from* [a]2 Cor 11:16 [b]1 Cor 14:6; 2 Cor 12:7; Gal 1:12; Eph 3:3
2 [a]Rom 16:7 [b]2 Cor 11:11 [c]Ezek 8:3; Acts 8:39; 2 Cor 12:4; 1 Thess 4:17; Rev 12:5 [d]Deut 10:14; Ps 148:4; Eph 4:10; Heb 4:14
3 [a]2 Cor 11:11
4 [a]Ezek 8:3; Acts 8:39; 2 Cor 12:2; 1 Thess 4:17; Rev 12:5 [b]Luke 23:43
5 [a]2 Cor 12:1 [b]1 Cor 2:3; 2 Cor 12:9f
6 [a]2 Cor 5:13 [b]2 Cor 7:14
7 [1]Lit *beat* [a]2 Cor 12:1 [b]Num 33:55; Ezek 28:24; Hos 2:6 [c]Job 2:6; Matt 4:10; 1 Cor 5:5
8 [a]Matt 26:44
9 [1]Lit *in* [a]1 Cor 2:5; Eph 3:16; Phil 4:13 [b]1 Cor 2:3; 2 Cor 12:5

weaknesses, so that the power of Christ
may dwell in me.
10 Therefore [a]I am well content with
weaknesses, with [1]insults, with [b]dis-
tresses, with [c]persecutions, with [b]diffi-
culties, [d]for Christ's sake; for [e]when I
am weak, then I am strong.
11 ¶ I have become [a]foolish; you
yourselves compelled me. Actually I
should have been commended by you,
for [b]in no respect was I inferior to the
[1]most eminent apostles, even though [c]I
am a nobody.
12 The [1a]signs [2]of a true apostle
were performed among you with all perseverance, by [1]signs and wonders and
[3]miracles.
13 For in what respect were you treated as inferior to the rest of the churches,
except that [a]I myself did not become a
burden to you? Forgive me [b]this wrong!
14 ¶ Here [a]for this third time I am
ready to come to you, and I [b]will not be
a burden to you; for I [c]do not seek what
is yours, but [d]you; for [e]children are not
responsible to save up for *their* parents,
but [f]parents for *their* children.
15 I will [a]most gladly spend and be
expended for your souls. If [b]I love you
more, am I to be loved less?
16 But be that as it may, I [a]did not
burden you myself; nevertheless, crafty
fellow that I am, I [b]took you in by deceit.
17 [a]*Certainly* I have not taken advantage of you through any of those whom I
have sent to you, have I?
18 I [a]urged [b]Titus *to go,* and I sent
[c]the brother with him. Titus did not take
any advantage of you, did he? Did we not
[1]conduct ourselves [2]in the same [d]spirit
and walk [e]in the same steps?
19 ¶ All this time [1]you have been
thinking that we are defending ourselves to you. *Actually,* [a]it is in the sight
of God that we have been speaking in
Christ; and [b]all for your upbuilding, [c]be-
loved.
20 For I am afraid that perhaps [a]when
I come I may find you to be not what I
wish and may be found by you to be not
what you wish; that perhaps *there will be*
[b]strife, jealousy, [c]angry tempers, [d]dis-
putes, [e]slanders, [f]gossip, [g]arrogance,
[h]disturbances;
21 I am afraid that when I come again
my God may humiliate me before you,
and I may mourn over many of those
who have [a]sinned in the past and not
repented of the [b]impurity, [1]immoral-
ity and sensuality which they have practiced.

Examine Yourselves

13 [a]This is the third time I am coming to you. [b]EVERY [1]FACT [2]IS TO
BE CONFIRMED BY THE [3]TESTIMONY OF TWO
OR THREE WITNESSES.
2 I have previously said when
present the second time, and though now
absent I say in advance to those who have
[a]sinned in the past and to all the rest *as
well,* that [b]if I come again I will not
[c]spare *anyone,*
3 since you are [a]seeking for proof of
the [b]Christ who speaks in me, and who
is not weak toward you, but [c]mighty in
you.
4 For indeed He was [a]crucified because of weakness, yet He lives [b]because
of the power of God. For we also are
[c]weak [1]in Him, yet [d]we will live with
Him because of the power of God *directed* toward you.
5 ¶ [a]Test yourselves *to see* if you are
in the faith; [b]examine yourselves! Or do
you not recognize this about yourselves,
that Jesus Christ is in you—unless indeed
you [1c]fail the test?
6 But I trust that you will realize that
we ourselves [1]do not fail the test.
7 Now we pray to God that you do
no wrong; not that we ourselves may appear approved, but that you may do what
is right, even though we may [1]appear
unapproved.
8 For we can do nothing against the
truth, but *only* for the truth.
9 For we rejoice when we ourselves
are [a]weak but you are strong; this we
also pray for, [1]that you be [b]made complete.
10 For this reason I am writing these
things while absent, so that when present
[a]I *need* not use [b]severity, in accordance
with the [c]authority which the Lord gave
me for building up and not for tearing
down.
11 ¶ [a]Finally, brethren, [1]rejoice, [2b]be
made complete, be comforted, [c]be like-
minded, [d]live in peace; and [e]the God of
love and peace will be with you.
12 [a]Greet one another with a holy
kiss.
13 [a]All the [1]saints greet you.
14 ¶ [a]The grace of the Lord Jesus
Christ, and the [b]love of God, and the
[c]fellowship of the Holy Spirit, be with
you all.

10 [1]Or *mistreatment* [a]Rom 5:3 [b]2 Cor 6:4 [c]2 Thess 1:4; 2 Tim 3:11 [d]2 Cor 5:15 [e]2 Cor 13:4
11 [1]Or *super-apostles* [a]2 Cor 5:13 [b]1 Cor 15:10; 2 Cor 11:5 [c]1 Cor 3:7
12 [1]Or *attesting miracles* [2]Lit *of the apostle* [3]Or *works of power* [a]John 4:48; Rom 15:19; 1 Cor 9:1
13 [a]1 Cor 9:12; 2 Cor 11:9 [b]2 Cor 11:7
14 [a]2 Cor 1:15 [b]1 Cor 9:12; 2 Cor 11:9 [c]1 Cor 10:24 [d]1 Cor 9:19 [e]1 Cor 4:14f; Gal 4:19 [f]Prov 19:14; Ezek 34:2
15 [a]Rom 9:3; 2 Cor 1:6; Phil 2:17; Col 1:24; 1 Thess 2:8; 2 Tim 2:10 [b]2 Cor 11:11
16 [a]2 Cor 11:9 [b]2 Cor 11:20
17 [a]2 Cor 9:5
18 [1]Lit *walk* [2]Or *by the same Spirit* [a]2 Cor 8:6 [b]2 Cor 2:13 [c]2 Cor 8:18 [d]1 Cor 4:21 [e]Rom 4:12
19 [1]Or *have you been thinking...?* [a]Rom 9:1; 2 Cor 2:17 [b]Rom 14:19; 2 Cor 10:8; 1 Thess 5:11 [c]Heb 6:9
20 [a]1 Cor 4:21; 2 Cor 2:1-4 [b]1 Cor 1:11 [c]Gal 5:20 [d]Rom 2:8; 1 Cor 11:19 [e]Rom 1:30; James 4:11; 1 Pet 2:1 [f]Rom 1:29 [g]1 Cor 4:6 [h]1 Cor 14:33
21 [1]I.e. sexual immorality [a]2 Cor 13:2 [b]1 Cor 6:9; Gal 5:19; Col 3:5
13:1 [1]Lit *word* [2]Lit *shall be* [3]Lit *mouth* [a]2 Cor 12:14 [b]Deut 17:6; Matt 18:16
2 [a]2 Cor 12:21 [b]1 Cor 4:21; 2 Cor 13:10 [c]2 Cor 1:23
3 [a]2 Cor 10:1 [b]Matt 10:20; 1 Cor 5:4 [c]2 Cor 9:8
4 [1]One early ms reads *with Him* [a]Phil 2:7f; 1 Pet 3:18 [b]Rom 1:4; 1 Cor 6:14 [c]1 Cor 2:3; 2 Cor 13:9 [d]Rom 6:8
5 [1]Lit *are unapproved* [a]John 6:6 [b]1 Cor 11:28 [c]1 Cor 9:27
6 [1]Lit *are not unapproved*
7 [1]Lit *be as*
9 [1]Lit *your completion* [a]2 Cor 12:10 [b]1 Cor 1:10; 2 Cor 13:11; Eph 4:12; 1 Thess 3:10
10 [a]2 Cor 2:3 [b]Titus 1:13 [c]1 Cor 5:4; 2 Cor 10:8
11 [1]Or *farewell* [2]Or *put yourselves in order* [a]1 Thess 4:1; 2 Thess 3:1 [b]1 Cor 1:10; 2 Cor 13:9; Eph 4:12; 1 Thess 3:10 [c]Rom 12:16 [d]Mark 9:50 [e]Rom 15:33; Eph 6:23
12 [a]Rom 16:16
13 [1]Or *holy ones* [a]Phil 4:22
14 [a]Rom 16:20; 2 Cor 8:9 [b]Rom 5:5; Jude 21 [c]Phil 2:1

Galatians

Title and Background

Judaizers were Jewish Christians who believed, among other things, that a number of the ceremonial practices of the Old Testament were still binding on the New Testament church. Following Paul's successful campaign in Galatia, they insisted that Gentile converts to Christianity abide by certain Old Testament rites, especially circumcision. The Judaizers argued that Paul was not an authentic apostle and that out of a desire to make the message more appealing to Gentiles he had removed from the gospel certain legal requirements. Paul responds by writing this letter.

Author and Date of Writing

The opening verse identifies the author as the apostle Paul. Various dates have been given for the writing of this letter, but it was probably written around A.D. 50.

Theme and Message

Galatians stands as an eloquent and vigorous defense for the essential New Testament truth that we are justified by faith in Jesus Christ—by nothing less and nothing more—and that we are sanctified by the obedience that comes from faith in God's work for us, in us and through us by the grace and power of Jesus Christ and the Holy Spirit. Some have called the letter the *Magna Charta* of Christian liberty.

Outline

I. Introduction: Greetings and Denunciation (1:1–9)
II. Authentication of the Apostle of Liberty and Faith (1:10—2:21)
III. Justification of the Doctrine of Liberty and Faith (3:1—4:31)
IV. Practice of the Life of Liberty and Faith (5:1—6:10)
V. Conclusion (6:11–18)

Introduction

1 Paul, [a]an apostle ([b]not *sent* from
men nor through the agency of man,
but [c]through Jesus Christ and God the
Father, who [d]raised Him from the dead),
2 and all [a]the brethren who are
with me,
¶ To [b]the churches of Galatia:
3 ¶ [a]Grace to you and peace from
[1]God our Father and the Lord Jesus
Christ,
4 who [a]gave Himself for our sins so
that He might rescue us from [b]this
present evil [1]age, according to the will of
[c]our God and Father,
5 [a]to whom *be* the glory forevermore. Amen.

Perversion of the Gospel

6 ¶ I am amazed that you are so
quickly deserting [a]Him who called you
[1]by the grace of Christ, for a [b]different
gospel;
7 which is *really* not another; only
there are some who are [a]disturbing you
and want to distort the gospel of Christ.
8 But even if we, or [a]an angel from
heaven, should preach to you a gospel
[1]contrary to what we have preached to
you, he is to be [2b]accursed!
9 As we [a]have said before, so I say
again now, [b]if any man is preaching to
you a gospel [1]contrary to what you received, he is to be [2c]accursed!
10 ¶ For am I now [a]seeking the favor
of men, or of God? Or am I striving to
please men? If I were still trying to please
men, I would not be a [b]bond-servant of
Christ.

Paul Defends His Ministry

11 ¶ For [a]I would have you know,
brethren, that the gospel which was
preached by me is [b]not according to
man.
12 For [a]I neither received it from
man, nor was I taught it, but *I received it*
through a [b]revelation of Jesus Christ.
13 ¶ For you have heard of [a]my for-

1:1 [a]2 Cor 1:1 [b]Gal 1:11f [c]Acts 9:15; Gal 1:15f [d]Acts 2:24
2 [a]Phil 4:21 [b]Acts 16:6; 1 Cor 16:1
3 [1]Two early mss read *God the Father, and our Lord Jesus Christ* [a]Rom 1:7
4 [1]Or *world* [a]Gal 2:20 [b]Matt 13:22; Rom 12:2; 2 Cor 4:4 [c]Phil 4:20
5 [a]Rom 11:36
6 [1]Lit *in* [a]Rom 8:28; Gal 1:15 [b]2 Cor 11:4; Gal 1:7; 1 Tim 1:3
7 [a]Acts 15:24; Gal 5:10
8 [1]Or *other than, more than* [2]Gr *anathema* [a]2 Cor 11:14 [b]Rom 9:3
9 [1]Or *other than, more than* [2]Gr *anathema* [a]Acts 18:23 [b]Rom 16:17 [c]Rom 9:3
10 [a]1 Cor 10:33; 1 Thess 2:4 [b]Rom 1:1; Phil 1:1
11 [a]Rom 2:16; 1 Cor 15:1 [b]1 Cor 3:4 **12** [a]1 Cor 11:23; Gal 1:1 [b]1 Cor 2:10; 2 Cor 12:1; Gal 1:16 **13** [a]Acts 26:4f

mer manner of life in Judaism, how I
[b]used to persecute [c]the church of God
beyond measure and [d]tried to destroy it;
14 and I [a]was advancing in Judaism
beyond many of my contemporaries
among my [1]countrymen, being more extremely zealous for my [b]ancestral traditions.
15 But when God, who had set me
apart *even* from my mother's womb and
[a]called me through His grace, was
pleased
16 to reveal His Son in me so that I
might [a]preach Him among the Gentiles,
[b]I did not immediately consult with
[1c]flesh and blood,
17 [a]nor did I go up to Jerusalem to
those who were apostles before me; but
I went away to Arabia, and returned once
more to [b]Damascus.
18 ¶ Then [a]three years later I went up
[b]to Jerusalem to [1]become acquainted
with [c]Cephas, and stayed with him fifteen days.
19 But I did not see any other of the
apostles except [1a]James, the Lord's
brother.
20 (Now in what I am writing to you,
[1]I assure you [a]before God that I am not
lying.)
21 Then [a]I went into the regions of
[b]Syria and [c]Cilicia.
22 I was *still* unknown by [1]sight to
[a]the churches of Judea which were [b]in
Christ;
23 but only, they kept hearing, "He
who once persecuted us is now preaching
[a]the faith which he once [b]tried to destroy."
24 And they [a]were glorifying God
[1]because of me.

The Council at Jerusalem

2 Then after an interval of fourteen
years I [a]went up again to Jerusalem
with [b]Barnabas, taking [c]Titus along also.
2 [1]It was because of a [a]revelation
that I went up; and I submitted to them
the [b]gospel which I preach among the
Gentiles, but *I did so* in private to those
who were of reputation, for fear that I
might be [c]running, or had run, in vain.
3 But not even [a]Titus, who was with
me, though he was a Greek, was [b]com-
pelled to be circumcised.
4 But *it was* because of the [a]false
brethren secretly brought in, who [b]had
sneaked in to spy out our [c]liberty which
we have in Christ Jesus, in order to
[d]bring us into bondage.
5 But we did not yield in subjection
to them for even an hour, so that [a]the
truth of the gospel would remain with
you.
6 But from those who [1]were of high
[a]reputation (what they were makes no
difference to me; [b]God [2]shows no partiality)—well, those who were of reputation contributed nothing to me.
7 But on the contrary, seeing that I
had been [a]entrusted with the [b]gospel
[1]to the uncircumcised, just as [c]Peter
had been [2]to the circumcised
8 (for He who effectually worked for
Peter in *his* [a]apostleship [1]to the circumcised effectually worked for me also to
the Gentiles),
9 and recognizing [a]the grace that
had been given to me, [1b]James and [c]Ce-
phas and John, who were [d]reputed to
be [e]pillars, gave to me and [f]Barnabas
the [g]right [2]hand of fellowship, so that
we *might* [h]*go* to the Gentiles and they to
the circumcised.
10 *They* only *asked* us to remember
the poor—[a]the very thing I also was eager to do.

Peter (Cephas) Opposed by Paul

11 ¶ But when [a]Cephas came to [b]An-
tioch, I opposed him to his face, because
he [1]stood condemned.
12 For prior to the coming of certain
men from [1a]James, he used to [b]eat with
the Gentiles; but when they came, he
began to withdraw and hold himself
aloof, [c]fearing [2]the party of the circumcision.
13 The rest of the Jews joined him in
hypocrisy, with the result that even [a]Bar-
nabas was carried away by their hypocrisy.
14 But when I saw that they [a]were
not [1]straightforward about [b]the truth of
the gospel, I said to [c]Cephas in the presence of all, "If you, being a Jew, [d]live like
the Gentiles and not like the Jews, how *is
it that* you compel the Gentiles to live like
Jews?[2]
15 ¶ "We *are* [a]Jews by nature and not
[b]sinners from among the Gentiles;
16 nevertheless knowing that [a]a man
is not justified by the works of [1]the Law
but through faith in Christ Jesus, even we
have believed in Christ Jesus, so that we
may be justified by [b]faith in Christ and
not by the works of [1]the Law; since [c]by
the works of [1]the Law no [2]flesh will be
justified.
17 "But if, while seeking to be justified
in Christ, we ourselves have also been

13 [b]Acts 8:3 [c]1 Cor 10:32 [d]Acts 9:21
14 [1]Lit *race* [a]Acts 22:3 [b]Jer 9:14; Matt 15:2; Mark 7:3; Col 2:8
15 [a]Is 49:1; Jer 1:5; Acts 9:15; Rom 1:1; Gal 1:6
16 [1]I.e. human beings [a]Acts 9:15; Gal 2:9 [b]Acts 9:20 [c]Matt 16:17
17 [a]Acts 9:19-22 [b]Acts 9:2
18 [1]Or *visit Cephas* [a]Acts 9:22f [b]Acts 9:26 [c]John 1:42; Gal 2:9
19 [1]Or *Jacob* [a]Matt 12:46; Acts 12:17
20 [1]Lit *behold before God* [a]Rom 9:1; 2 Cor 1:23
21 [a]Acts 9:30 [b]Acts 15:23 [c]Acts 6:9
22 [1]Lit *face* [a]1 Cor 7:17; 1 Thess 2:14 [b]Rom 16:7
23 [a]Acts 6:7; Gal 6:10 [b]Acts 9:21
24 [1]Lit *in me* [a]Matt 9:8
2:1 [a]Acts 15:2 [b]Acts 4:36; Gal 2:9 [c]2 Cor 2:13; Gal 2:3
2 [1]Lit *according to revelation I went up* [a]Acts 15:2; Gal 1:12 [b]Gal 1:6 [c]Rom 9:16; 1 Cor 9:24ff; Gal 5:7; Phil 2:16; 2 Tim 4:7; Heb 12:1
3 [a]2 Cor 2:13; Gal 2:1 [b]Acts 16:3; 1 Cor 9:21
4 [a]Acts 15:1; 2 Cor 11:13; Gal 1:7 [b]2 Pet 2:1; Jude 4 [c]Gal 5:1; James 1:25 [d]Rom 8:15; 2 Cor 11:20
5 [a]Gal 1:6; Col 1:5
6 [1]Lit *seemed to be something* [2]Lit *does not receive a face* [a]2 Cor 11:5; Gal 2:9 [b]Acts 10:34
7 [1]Lit *of the uncircumcision* [2]Lit *of the circumcision* [a]1 Cor 9:17; 1 Thess 2:4; 1 Tim 1:11 [b]Acts 9:15; Gal 1:16 [c]Gal 1:18
8 [1]Lit *of the circumcision* [a]Acts 1:25
9 [1]Or *Jacob* [2]Lit *hands* [a]Rom 12:3 [b]Acts 12:17; Gal 2:12 [c]Luke 22:8; Gal 1:18 [d]2 Cor 11:5; Gal 2:2 [e]1 Tim 3:15; Rev 3:12 [f]Acts 4:36; Gal 2:1 [g]2 Kin 10:15 [h]Gal 1:16
10 [a]Acts 24:17
11 [1]Or *was to be condemned*; lit *was one who was condemned*, or, *was self-condemned* [a]Gal 1:18 [b]Acts 11:19 **12** [1]Or *Jacob* [2]Or converts *from the circumcised*; lit *those from the circumcision* [a]Acts 12:17; Gal 2:9 [b]Acts 11:3 [c]Acts 11:2
13 [a]Acts 4:36; Gal 2:1 **14** [1]Or *progressing toward*; lit *walking straightly* [2]Some close the direct quotation here, others extend it through v 21 [a]Heb 12:13 [b]Gal 1:6; Col 1:5 [c]Gal 1:18 [d]Acts 10:28; Gal 2:12 **15** [a]Phil 3:4f [b]1 Sam 15:18; Luke 24:7 **16** [1]Or *law* [2]Or *mortal man* [a]Acts 13:39; Gal 3:11 [b]Rom 3:22 [c]Ps 143:2; Rom 3:20

found [a]sinners, is Christ then a minister
of sin? [b]May it never be!
18 "For if I rebuild what I have *once*
destroyed, I [a]prove myself to be a transgressor.
19 "For through [1]the Law I [a]died to
[1]the Law, so that I might live to God.
20 "I have been [a]crucified with Christ;
and it is no longer I who live, but [b]Christ
lives in me; and [1]the *life* which I now
live in the flesh I live by faith in [c]the Son
of God, who [d]loved me and [e]gave Himself up for me.
21 "I do not nullify the grace of God, for
[a]if righteousness *comes* through [1]the
Law, then Christ died needlessly."

Faith Brings Righteousness

3 [1]You foolish [a]Galatians, who has
bewitched you, before whose eyes
Jesus Christ [b]was publicly portrayed *as*
crucified?
2 This is the only thing I want to find
out from you: did you receive the Spirit
by the works of [1]the Law, or by [2a]hearing with faith?
3 Are you so foolish? Having begun
[1]by the Spirit, are you now [2]being perfected by the flesh?
4 Did you [1]suffer so many things in
vain—[a]if indeed it was in vain?
5 So then, does He who [a]provides
you with the Spirit and [b]works [1]miracles among you, do it by the works of
[2]the Law, or by [3c]hearing with faith?
6 ¶ [1]Even so [a]Abraham [b]BELIEVED
GOD, AND IT WAS RECKONED TO HIM AS RIGHTEOUSNESS.
7 Therefore, [1]be sure that [a]it is
those who are of faith who are [b]sons of
Abraham.
8 The Scripture, foreseeing that God
[1]would justify the [2]Gentiles by faith,
preached the gospel beforehand to Abraham, *saying*, "[a]ALL THE NATIONS WILL BE
BLESSED IN YOU."
9 So then [a]those who are of faith are
blessed with [1]Abraham, the believer.
10 ¶ For as many as are of the works of
[1]the Law are under a curse; for it is written, "[a]CURSED IS EVERYONE WHO DOES NOT
ABIDE BY ALL THINGS WRITTEN IN THE BOOK
OF THE LAW, TO PERFORM THEM."
11 Now that [a]no one is justified [1]by
[2]the Law before God is evident; for,
"[3b]THE RIGHTEOUS MAN SHALL LIVE BY
FAITH."
12 [1]However, the Law is not [2]of
faith; on the contrary, "[a]HE WHO PRACTICES THEM SHALL LIVE [3]BY THEM."
13 Christ [a]redeemed us from the
curse of the Law, having become a curse
for us—for it is written, "[b]CURSED IS EVERYONE WHO HANGS ON [c]A [1]TREE"—
14 in order that [a]in Christ Jesus the
blessing of Abraham might [1]come to the
Gentiles, so that we [b]would receive [c]the
promise of the Spirit through faith.

Intent of the Law

15 ¶ [a]Brethren, [b]I speak [1]in terms of
human relations: [c]even though it is *only*
a man's [2]covenant, yet when it has been
ratified, no one sets it aside or adds [3]conditions to it.
16 Now the promises were spoken [a]to
Abraham and to his seed. He does not
say, "And to seeds," as *referring* to many,
but *rather* to one, "[b]And to your seed,"
that is, Christ.
17 What I am saying is this: the Law,
which came [a]four hundred and thirty
years later, does not invalidate a covenant
previously ratified by God, so as to nullify
the promise.
18 For [a]if the inheritance is [1]based
on law, it is no longer [1]based on a promise; but [b]God has granted it to Abraham
by means of a promise.
19 ¶ [a]Why the Law then? It was added [1]because of transgressions, having
been [b]ordained through angels [c]by the
[2]agency of a mediator, until [d]the seed
would come to whom the promise had
been made.
20 Now [a]a mediator is not [1]for one
party only; whereas God is *only* one.
21 Is the Law then contrary to the
promises of God? [a]May it never be! For
[b]if a law had been given which was able
to impart life, then righteousness [1]would
indeed have been [2]based on law.
22 But the Scripture has [a]shut up [1]everyone under sin, so that the promise by
faith in Jesus Christ might be given to
those who believe.
23 ¶ But before faith came, we were
kept in custody under the law, [a]being
shut up to the faith which was later to be
revealed.
24 Therefore the Law has become our
[a]tutor *to lead us* to Christ, so that [b]we
may be justified by faith.
25 But now that faith has come, we are
no longer under a [1a]tutor.
26 For you are all [a]sons of God
through faith in [b]Christ Jesus.
27 For all of you who were [a]baptized
into Christ have [b]clothed yourselves
with Christ.
28 [a]There is neither Jew nor Greek,
there is neither slave nor free man, there

17 [a]Gal 2:15 [b]Luke 20:16; Gal 3:21
18 [a]Rom 3:5
19 [1]Or *law* [a]Rom 6:2; 1 Cor 9:20
20 [1]Or *insofar as I* [a]Rom 6:6; Gal 5:24 [b]Rom 8:10 [c]Matt 4:3 [d]Rom 8:37 [e]Gal 1:4
21 [1]Or *law* [a]Gal 3:21
3:1 [1]Lit *O* [a]Gal 1:2 [b]1 Cor 1:23; Gal 5:11
2 [1]Or *law* [2]Lit *the hearing of faith* [a]Rom 10:17
3 [1]Or *with* [2]Or *ending with*
4 [1]Or *experience* [a]1 Cor 15:2
5 [1]Or *works of power* [2]Or *law* [3]Lit *the hearing of faith* [a]2 Cor 9:10; Phil 1:19 [b]1 Cor 12:10 [c]Rom 10:17
6 [1]Lit *Just as* [a]Rom 4:3 [b]Gen 15:6
7 [1]Lit *know* [a]Rom 4:16; Gal 3:9 [b]Luke 19:9; Gal 6:16
8 [1]Lit *justifies* [2]Lit *nations* [a]Gen 12:3
9 [1]Lit *the believing Abraham* [a]Gal 3:7
10 [1]Or *law* [a]Deut 27:26
11 [1]Or *in* [2]Or *law* [3]Or *But he who is righteous by faith shall live* [a]Gal 2:16 [b]Hab 2:4; Rom 1:17; Heb 10:38
12 [1]Or *And* [2]Or *based on* [3]Or *in* [a]Lev 18:5; Rom 10:5
13 [1]Or *cross*; lit *wood* [a]Gal 4:5 [b]Deut 21:23 [c]Acts 5:30
14 [1]Or *occur* [a]Rom 4:9; Gal 3:28 [b]Gal 3:2 [c]Acts 2:33; Eph 1:13
15 [1]Lit *according to man* [2]Or *will* or *testament* [3]Or *a codicil* [a]Acts 1:15; Rom 1:13; Gal 6:18 [b]Rom 3:5 [c]Heb 6:16
16 [a]Luke 1:55; Rom 4:13 [b]Acts 3:25
17 [a]Gen 15:13f; Ex 12:40; Acts 7:6
18 [1]Lit *out of, from* [a]Rom 4:14 [b]Heb 6:14
19 [1]Or *for the sake of defining* [2]Lit *hand* [a]Rom 5:20 [b]Acts 7:53 [c]Ex 20:19; Deut 5:5 [d]Gal 3:16
20 [1]Lit *of one* [a]1 Tim 2:5; Heb 8:6
21 [1]Or *would indeed be* [2]Lit *out of, from* [a]Luke 20:16; Gal 2:17 [b]Gal 2:21

22 [1]Lit *things* [a]Rom 11:32 **23** [a]Rom 11:32 **24** [a]1 Cor 4:15 [b]Gal 2:16 **25** [1]Lit *child-conductor* [a]1 Cor 4:15 **26** [a]Rom 8:14; Gal 4:5 [b]Rom 8:1; Gal 3:28; Eph 1:1; Phil 1:1; Col 1:4; 1 Tim 1:12; 2 Tim 1:1; Titus 1:4 **27** [a]Matt 28:19; Rom 6:3; 1 Cor 10:2 [b]Rom 13:14 **28** [a]Rom 3:22; 1 Cor 12:13; Col 3:11

is [1]neither male nor female; for [b]you are all one in [c]Christ Jesus.

29 And if [a]you [1]belong to Christ, then you are Abraham's [2]descendants, heirs according to [b]promise.

Sonship in Christ

4 Now I say, as long as the heir is a [1]child, he does not differ at all from a slave although he is [2]owner of everything,

2 but he is under guardians and [1]managers until the date set by the father.

3 So also we, while we were children, were held [a]in bondage under the [1b]elemental things of the world.

4 But when [a]the fullness of the time came, God sent forth His Son, [b]born of a woman, born [c]under [1]the Law,

5 so that He might redeem those who were under [1]the Law, that we might receive the adoption as [a]sons.

6 Because you are sons, [a]God has sent forth the Spirit of His Son into our hearts, crying, "[b]Abba! Father!"

7 Therefore you are no longer a slave, but a son; and [a]if a son, then an heir [1]through God.

8 ¶ However at that time, [a]when you did not know God, you were [b]slaves to [c]those which by nature are no gods.

9 But now that you have come to know God, or rather to be [a]known by God, [b]how is it that you turn back again to the weak and worthless [1c]elemental things, to which you desire to be enslaved all over again?

10 You [a]observe days and months and seasons and years.

11 I fear for you, that perhaps I have labored [1]over you in vain.

12 ¶ I beg of you, [a]brethren, [b]become as I *am*, for I also *have become* as you *are*. You have done me no wrong;

13 but you know that it was because of a [1]bodily illness that I preached the gospel to you the [2]first time;

14 and that which was a [1]trial to you in my [2]bodily condition you did not despise or [3]loathe, but [a]you received me as an angel of God, as [b]Christ Jesus *Himself*.

15 Where then is [1]that sense of blessing you had? For I bear you witness that, if possible, you would have plucked out your eyes and given them to me.

16 So have I become your enemy [a]by [1]telling you the truth?

17 They eagerly seek you, not commendably, but they wish to shut you out so that you will seek them.

18 But it is good always to be eagerly sought in a commendable [1]manner, and [a]not only when I am present with you.

19 [a]My children, with whom [b]I am again in labor until [c]Christ is formed in you—

20 but I could wish to be present with you now and to change my tone, for [a]I am perplexed about you.

Bond and Free

21 ¶ Tell me, you who want to be under law, do you not [a]listen to the law?

22 For it is written that Abraham had two sons, [a]one by the bondwoman and [b]one by the free woman.

23 But [a]the son by the bondwoman [1]was born according to the flesh, and [b]the son by the free woman through the promise.

24 [1a]This is allegorically speaking, for these *women* are two covenants: one *proceeding* from [b]Mount Sinai bearing children [2]who are to be [c]slaves; [3]she is Hagar.

25 Now this Hagar is Mount Sinai in Arabia and corresponds to the present Jerusalem, for she is in slavery with her children.

26 But [a]the Jerusalem above is free; [1]she is our mother.

27 For it is written,

"[a]REJOICE, BARREN WOMAN WHO
DOES NOT BEAR;
BREAK FORTH AND SHOUT, YOU WHO
ARE NOT IN LABOR;
FOR MORE NUMEROUS ARE THE
CHILDREN OF THE DESOLATE
THAN OF THE ONE WHO HAS A
HUSBAND."

28 And you brethren, [a]like Isaac, are [b]children of promise.

29 But as at that time [a]he who was born according to the flesh [b]persecuted him *who was born* according to the Spirit, [c]so it is now also.

30 But what does the Scripture say?

"[a]CAST OUT THE BONDWOMAN AND
HER SON,
FOR [b]THE SON OF THE BONDWOMAN
SHALL NOT BE AN HEIR WITH
THE SON OF THE FREE WOMAN."

31 So then, brethren, we are not children of a bondwoman, [1]but of the free woman.

Walk by the Spirit

5 [1a]It was for freedom that Christ set us free; therefore [b]keep standing firm and do not be subject again to a [c]yoke of slavery.

28 [1]Lit *not male and female* [b]John 17:11; Eph 2:15 [c]Rom 8:1; Gal 3:26; Eph 1:1; Phil 1:1; Col 1:4; 1 Tim 1:12; 2 Tim 1:1; Titus 1:4 **29** [1]Lit *are Christ's* [2]Lit *seed* [a]Rom 4:13; 1 Cor 3:23 [b]Rom 9:8; Gal 3:18 **4:1** [1]Or *minor* [2]Lit *lord* **2** [1]Or *stewards* **3** [1]Or *rudimentary teachings* or *principles* [a]Gal 2:4 [b]Gal 4:9; Col 2:8; Heb 5:12 **4** [1]Or *law* [a]Mark 1:15 [b]John 1:14; Rom 1:3; Phil 2:7 [c]Luke 2:21f **5** [1]Or *law* [a]Rom 8:14; Gal 3:26 **6** [a]Acts 16:7; Rom 5:5; 2 Cor 3:17 [b]Mark 14:36; Rom 8:15 **7** [1]I.e. through the gracious act of [a]Rom 8:17 **8** [a]1 Cor 1:21; Eph 2:12; 1 Thess 4:5; 2 Thess 1:8 [b]Gal 4:3 [c]2 Chr 13:9; Is 37:19; Jer 2:11; 1 Cor 8:4f **9** [1]Or *rudimentary teachings* or *principles* [a]1 Cor 8:3 [b]Col 2:20 [c]Gal 4:3 **10** [a]Rom 14:5; Col 2:16 **11** [1]Or *for* **12** [a]Gal 6:18 [b]2 Cor 6:11 **13** [1]Lit *weakness of the flesh* [2]Or *former* **14** [1]Or *temptation* [2]Lit *flesh* [3]Lit *spit out at* [a]Matt 10:40; 1 Thess 2:13 [b]Gal 3:26 **15** [1]Lit *the congratulation of yourselves* **16** [1]Or *dealing truthfully with you* [a]Amos 5:10 **18** [1]Or *thing* [a]Gal 4:13f **19** [a]1 John 2:1 [b]1 Cor 4:15 [c]Eph 4:13 **20** [a]2 Cor 4:8 **21** [a]Luke 16:29 **22** [a]Gen 16:15 [b]Gen 21:2 **23** [1]Lit *has been born* [a]Rom 9:7; Gal 4:29 [b]Gen 17:16ff; Gal 4:28; Heb 11:11 **24** [1]Lit *Which* [2]Lit *into slavery* [3]Lit *which* [a]1 Cor 10:11 [b]Deut 33:2 [c]Gal 4:3 **26** [1]Lit *which* [a]Heb 12:22; Rev 3:12 **27** [a]Is 54:1 **28** [a]Gal 4:23 [b]Rom 9:7ff; Gal 3:29 **29** [a]Gal 4:23 [b]Gen 21:9 [c]Gal 5:11 **30** [a]Gen 21:10 [b]John 8:35

31 [1]V 5:1, note 1 **5:1** [1]Some authorities prefer to join with 4:31 and render *but with the freedom of the free woman Christ set us free* [a]John 8:32; Rom 8:15; 2 Cor 3:17; Gal 2:4 [b]1 Cor 16:13 [c]Acts 15:10; Gal 2:4

2 ¶ Behold I, [a]Paul, say to you that if
you receive [b]circumcision, Christ will be
of no benefit to you.
3 And I [a]testify again to every man
who receives [b]circumcision, that he is
under obligation to [c]keep the whole Law.
4 You have been severed from Christ,
you who [1]are seeking to be justified by
law; you have [a]fallen from grace.
5 For we [1]through the Spirit, [2]by
faith, are [a]waiting for the hope of righteousness.
6 For in [a]Christ Jesus [b]neither circumcision nor uncircumcision means
anything, but [c]faith working through
love.
7 ¶ You were [a]running well; who
hindered you from obeying the truth?
8 This persuasion *did* not *come* from
[a]Him who calls you.
9 [a]A little leaven leavens the whole
lump *of dough.*
10 [a]I have confidence [1]in you in the
Lord that you [b]will adopt no other view;
but the one who is [c]disturbing you will
bear his judgment, whoever he is.
11 But I, brethren, if I still preach circumcision, why am I still [a]persecuted?
Then [b]the stumbling block of the cross
has been abolished.
12 I wish that [a]those who are troubling you would even [1b]mutilate themselves.
13 ¶ For you were called to [a]freedom,
brethren; [b]only *do* not *turn* your freedom into an opportunity for the flesh, but
through love [c]serve one another.
14 For [a]the whole Law is fulfilled in
one word, in the *statement*, "[b]YOU SHALL
LOVE YOUR NEIGHBOR AS YOURSELF."
15 But if you [a]bite and devour one
another, take care that you are not consumed by one another.
16 ¶ But I say, [a]walk by the Spirit, and
you will not carry out [b]the desire of the
flesh.
17 For [a]the flesh [1]sets its desire
against the Spirit, and the Spirit against
the flesh; for these are in opposition to
one another, [b]so that you may not do the
things that you [2]please.
18 But if you are [a]led by the Spirit,
[b]you are not under the Law.
19 Now the deeds of the flesh are evident, which are: [1a]immorality, impurity, sensuality,
20 idolatry, [a]sorcery, enmities, [b]strife,
jealousy, outbursts of anger, [c]disputes,
dissensions, [1d]factions,
21 envying, [a]drunkenness, carousing,
and things like these, of which I forewarn
you, just as I have forewarned you, that
those who practice such things will not
[b]inherit the kingdom of God.

2 [a]2 Cor 10:1 [b]Acts 15:1; Gal 5:3
3 [a]Luke 16:28 [b]Acts 15:1; Gal 5:2 [c]Rom 2:25
4 [1]Or *would be* [a]Heb 12:15; 2 Pet 3:17
5 [1]Lit *by* [2]Lit *out of* [a]Rom 8:23; 1 Cor 1:7
6 [a]Gal 3:26 [b]1 Cor 7:19; Gal 6:15 [c]Col 1:4f; 1 Thess 1:3; James 2:18
7 [a]Gal 2:2
8 [a]Rom 8:28; Gal 1:6
9 [a]1 Cor 5:6
10 [1]Lit *toward* [a]2 Cor 2:3 [b]Gal 5:7; Phil 3:15 [c]Gal 1:7
11 [a]Gal 4:29 [b]Rom 9:33; 1 Cor 1:23
12 [1]Or *cut themselves off* [a]Gal 2:4 [b]Deut 23:1
13 [a]Gal 5:1 [b]1 Cor 8:9; 1 Pet 2:16 [c]1 Cor 9:19; Eph 5:21
14 [a]Matt 7:12; Rom 13:8; Gal 6:2 [b]Lev 19:18; Matt 19:19; John 13:34
15 [a]Gal 5:20; Phil 3:2
16 [a]Rom 8:4; Gal 5:24f [b]Rom 13:14; Eph 2:3
17 [1]Lit *lusts against* [2]Lit *wish* [a]Rom 7:18 [b]Rom 7:15ff
18 [a]Rom 8:14 [b]Rom 6:14; 1 Tim 1:9
19 [1]I.e. sexual immorality [a]1 Cor 6:9; 2 Cor 12:21
20 [1]Or *heresies* [a]Rev 21:8 [b]2 Cor 12:20 [c]Rom 2:8; James 3:14ff [d]1 Cor 11:19
21 [a]Rom 13:13 [b]1 Cor 6:9
22 [a]Matt 7:16ff; Eph 5:9 [b]Rom 5:1-5; 1 Cor 13:4; Col 3:12-15
23 [a]Acts 24:25 [b]Gal 5:18
24 [1]Lit *are of Christ Jesus* [a]Gal 3:26 [b]Rom 6:6; Gal 2:20 [c]Gal 5:16f
25 [1]Or *follow the Spirit* [a]Gal 5:16
26 [a]Phil 2:3
6:1 [1]Gr *anthropos* [a]Gal 6:18; 1 Thess 4:1 [b]1 Cor 2:15 [c]2 Cor 2:7; 2 Thess 3:15; Heb 12:13; James 5:19f [d]1 Cor 4:21
2 [a]Rom 15:1 [b]Rom 8:2; 1 Cor 9:21; James 1:25; 2 Pet 3:2
3 [a]Acts 5:36; 1 Cor 3:18; 2 Cor 12:11
4 [a]1 Cor 11:28 [b]Phil 1:26
5 [a]Prov 9:12;

22 But [a]the fruit of the Spirit is [b]love,
joy, peace, patience, kindness, goodness,
faithfulness,
23 gentleness, [a]self-control; against
such things [b]there is no law.
24 Now those who [1]belong to [a]Christ
Jesus have [b]crucified the flesh with its
passions and [c]desires.
25 ¶ If we live by the Spirit, let us also
[1]walk [a]by the Spirit.
26 Let us not become [a]boastful, challenging one another, envying one another.

Bear One Another's Burdens

6 [a]Brethren, even if [1]anyone is
caught in any trespass, you who are
[b]spiritual, [c]restore such a one [d]in a
spirit of gentleness; *each one* looking
to yourself, so that you too will not be
tempted.
2 [a]Bear one another's burdens, and
thereby fulfill [b]the law of Christ.
3 For [a]if anyone thinks he is something when he is nothing, he deceives
himself.
4 But each one must [a]examine his
own work, and then he will have *reason
for* [b]boasting in regard to himself alone,
and not in regard to another.
5 For [a]each one will bear his own
load.
6 ¶ [a]The one who is taught [b]the
word is to share all good things with the
one who teaches *him.*
7 [a]Do not be deceived, [b]God is not
mocked; for [c]whatever a man sows, this
he will also reap.
8 [a]For the one who sows to his own
flesh will from the flesh reap [b]corruption, but [c]the one who sows to the Spirit
will from the Spirit reap eternal life.
9 [a]Let us not lose heart in doing
good, for in due time we will reap if we
[b]do not grow weary.
10 So then, [1a]while we have opportunity, let us do good to all people, and
especially to those who are of the
[b]household of [c]the faith.
11 ¶ See with what large letters I [1]am
writing to you [a]with my own hand.
12 Those who desire [a]to make a good
showing in the flesh try to [b]compel you
to be circumcised, simply so that they
[c]will not be persecuted [1]for the cross of
Christ.
13 For those who [1]are circumcised do

Rom 14:12; 1 Cor 3:8 **6** [a]1 Cor 9:11 [b]2 Tim 4:2 **7** [a]1 Cor 6:9 [b]Job 13:9 [c]2 Cor 9:6 **8** [a]Job 4:8; Hos 8:7; Rom 6:21 [b]1 Cor 15:42 [c]Rom 8:11; James 3:18 **9** [a]1 Cor 15:58; 2 Cor 4:1 [b]Matt 10:22; Heb 12:3; James 5:7f **10** [1]Or *as* [a]Prov 3:27; John 12:35 [b]Eph 2:19; Heb 3:6; 1 Pet 2:5 [c]Acts 6:7; Gal 1:23 **11** [1]Or *have written* [a]1 Cor 16:21 **12** [1]Or *because of* [a]Matt 23:27f [b]Acts 15:1 [c]Gal 5:11 **13** [1]Two early mss read *have been*

not even [a]keep [2]the Law themselves,
but they desire to have you circumcised
so that they may [b]boast in your flesh.
14 But [a]may it never be that I would
boast, [b]except in the cross of our Lord
Jesus Christ, [c]through [1]which the world
has been crucified to me, and [d]I to the
world.
15 For [a]neither is circumcision anything, nor uncircumcision, but a [b]new
[1]creation.
16 And those who will [1]walk by this
rule, peace and mercy *be* upon them, and
upon the [a]Israel of God.
17 ¶ From now on let no one cause
trouble for me, for I bear on my body the
[a]brand-marks of Jesus.
18 ¶ [a]The grace of our Lord Jesus
Christ be [b]with your spirit, [c]brethren.
Amen.

13 [2] Or *law* [a]Rom 2:25 [b]Phil 3:3
14 [1]Or *whom* [a]Luke 20:16; Gal 2:17 [b]1 Cor 2:2 [c]Gal 2:20; Col 2:20 [d]Rom 6:2; Gal 2:19f
15 [1]Or *creature* [a]Rom 2:26; 1 Cor 7:19; Gal 5:6 [b]2 Cor 5:17; Eph 2:10; Col 3:10
16 [1]Or *follow this rule* [a]Rom 9:6; Gal 3:7; Phil 3:3
17 [a]Is 44:5; Ezek 9:4; 2 Cor 4:10; Rev 13:16
18 [a]Rom 16:20 [b]2 Tim 4:22 [c]Acts 1:15; Rom 1:13; Gal 3:15

Ephesians

Title and Background

Ephesus was the most important city in western Asia Minor (now Turkey). Because it was at an intersection of major trade routes, it became a commercial center. It also boasted a pagan temple dedicated to the Roman goddess Diana (Greek *Artemis*). Paul made Ephesus a center for evangelism for about three years. This letter was probably not sent merely to the church at Ephesus but also to the various churches in the province of Asia, where Paul conducted his third missionary journey.

Author and Date of Writing

The more widely held position is that Paul wrote this letter about A.D. 60, during his two-year imprisonment in Rome.

Theme and Message

Unlike several of Paul's other letters, Ephesians does not address any particular error or heresy. Paul wrote to help his readers better understand the dimensions of God's eternal purpose and grace and come to appreciate the high goals God has for the church. One of Paul's themes is that of unity—all Christians are one family in Jesus, and they should act with love toward each other. He also writes about the church—not a church building, but the church that is made up of all Christians through all the ages.

Outline

I. Greetings (1:1–2)
II. The Glory and Headship of Jesus Christ (1:3–14)
III. Prayer That Christians May Realize God's Purpose and Power (1:15–23)
IV. Steps Toward the Fulfillment of God's Purpose (2:1—3:21)
V. Ways to Fulfill God's Purpose in the Church (4:1—6:20)
VI. Conclusion (6:21–24)

The Blessings of Redemption

1 Paul, [a]an apostle of [b]Christ Jesus
[1c]by the will of God,
¶ To the [2d]saints who are [3]at [e]Ephe-
sus and [f]*who are* faithful in [b]Christ
Jesus:
2 [a]Grace to you and peace from God
our Father and the Lord Jesus Christ.
3 ¶ [a]Blessed *be* the God and Father
of our Lord Jesus Christ, who has blessed
us with every spiritual blessing in [b]the
heavenly *places* in Christ,
4 just as [a]He chose us in Him before
[b]the foundation of the world, that we
would be [c]holy and blameless before
[1]Him. [d]In love
5 [1]He [a]predestined us to [b]adoption
as sons through Jesus Christ to Himself,
[c]according to the [2]kind intention of His
will,
6 [a]to the praise of the glory of His
grace, which He freely bestowed on us in
[b]the Beloved.
7 [a]In [1]Him we have [b]redemption
[c]through His blood, the [d]forgiveness of
our trespasses, according to [e]the riches
of His grace
8 which He [1]lavished on [2]us. In all
wisdom and insight
9 He [1a]made known to us the mystery of His will, [b]according to His [2]kind
intention which He [c]purposed in Him
10 with a view to an administration
[1]suitable to [a]the fullness of the times,
that is, [b]the summing up of all things in
Christ, things [2]in the heavens and things
on the earth. In Him
11 [1]also we [2a]have obtained an inheritance, having been [b]predestined
[c]according to His purpose who works all
things [d]after the counsel of His will,
12 to the end that we who were the
first to hope in [1]Christ would be [a]to the
praise of His glory.

1:1 [1]Lit *through* [2]Or *holy ones* [3]Three early mss do not contain *at Ephesus* [a]2 Cor 1:1 [b]Rom 8:1 [c]1 Cor 1:1 [d]Acts 9:13 [e]Acts 18:19 [f]Col 1:2
2 [a]Rom 1:7
3 [a]2 Cor 1:3 [b]Eph 1:20
4 [1]Or *Him, in love* [a]Eph 2:10; 2 Thess 2:13f [b]Matt 25:34 [c]Eph 5:27; Col 1:22 [d]Eph 4:2
5 [1]Lit *having predestined* [2]Lit *good pleasure* [a]Acts 13:48; Rom 8:29f [b]Rom 8:14ff [c]Phil 2:13; Col 1:19
6 [a]Eph 1:12 [b]Matt 3:17
7 [1]Lit *whom* [a]Col 1:14 [b]Rom 3:24; 1 Cor 1:30; Eph 1:14 [c]Acts 20:28; Rom 3:25 [d]Acts 2:38 [e]Rom 2:4; Eph 1:18
8 [1]Lit *made abundant toward* [2]Or *us, in all wisdom and insight*
9 [1]Lit *making known* [2]Lit *good pleasure* [a]Rom 11:25; Eph 3:3 [b]1 Cor 1:21; Gal 1:15 [c]Rom 8:28; Eph 1:11
10 [1]Lit *of* [2]Lit *upon* [a]Mark 1:15 [b]Eph 3:15; Phil 2:9f; Col 1:16
11 [1]Lit *in whom also* [2]Or *were made a heritage* [a]Deut 4:20; Eph 1:14; Titus 2:14 [b]Eph 1:5 [c]Rom 8:28f; Eph 3:11 [d]Rom 9:11; Heb 6:17
12 [1]I.e. the Messiah [a]Eph 1:6

13 In [1]Him, you also, after listening to
[a]the message of truth, the gospel of your
salvation—having also [2]believed, you
were [b]sealed in [1]Him with [c]the Holy
Spirit of promise,
14 who is [1a]given as a pledge of [b]our
inheritance, with a view to the [c]redemp-
tion of [d]*God's own* possession, [e]to the
praise of His glory.
15 ¶ For this reason I too, [a]having
heard of the faith in the Lord Jesus which
exists among you and [1]your love for [b]all
the [2]saints,
16 [a]do not cease giving thanks for
you, [b]while making mention *of you* in
my prayers;
17 that the [a]God of our Lord Jesus
Christ, [b]the Father of glory, may give to
you a spirit of [c]wisdom and of [d]revela-
tion in the [1]knowledge of Him.
18 *I pray that* [a]the eyes of your heart
[1]may be enlightened, so that you will
know what is the [b]hope of His [c]calling,
what are [d]the riches of the glory of [e]His
inheritance in [f]the [2]saints,
19 and what is the surpassing greatness of His power toward us who believe.
[a]*These are* in accordance with the working of the [b]strength of His might
20 which He brought about in Christ,
when He [a]raised Him from the dead and
[b]seated Him at His right hand in [c]the
heavenly *places*,
21 far above [a]all rule and authority
and power and dominion, and every
[b]name that is named, not only in [c]this
age but also in the one to come.
22 And He [a]put all things in subjection under His feet, and gave Him as
[b]head over all things to the church,
23 which is His [a]body, the [b]fullness
of Him who [c]fills [d]all in all.

Made Alive in Christ

2 And you [1]were [a]dead [2]in your trespasses and sins,
2 in which you [a]formerly walked according to the [1]course of [b]this world,
according to [c]the prince of the power of
the air, of the spirit that is now working
in [d]the sons of disobedience.
3 Among them we too all [a]formerly
lived in [b]the lusts of our flesh, [1]indulg-
ing the desires of the flesh and of the
[2]mind, and were [c]by nature [d]children
of wrath, [e]even as the rest.
4 But God, being [a]rich in mercy, because of [b]His great love with which He
loved us,
5 even when we were [a]dead [1]in our
transgressions, made us alive together
[2]with Christ ([b]by grace you have been
saved),
6 and [a]raised us up with Him, and

13 [1]Lit *whom* [2]Or *believed in Him, you were sealed* [a]Eph 4:21; Col 1:5 [b]Eph 4:30 [c]Acts 2:33
14 [1]Or *a down payment* [a]2 Cor 1:22 [b]Acts 20:32 [c]Eph 1:7 [d]Eph 1:11 [e]Eph 1:6
15 [1]Three early mss do not contain *your love* [2]V 1, note 2 [a]Col 1:4; Philem 5 [b]Eph 1:1
16 [a]Rom 1:8f; Col 1:9 [b]Rom 1:9
17 [1]Or *true knowledge* [a]John 20:17; Rom 15:6 [b]Acts 7:2; 1 Cor 2:8 [c]Col 1:9 [d]1 Cor 14:6
18 [1]Lit *being* [2]Or *holy ones* [a]Acts 26:18; 2 Cor 4:6; Heb 6:4 [b]Eph 4:4 [c]Rom 11:29 [d]Eph 1:7 [e]Eph 1:11 [f]Col 1:12
19 [a]Eph 3:7; Col 1:29 [b]Eph 6:10
20 [a]Acts 2:24 [b]Mark 16:19 [c]Eph 1:3
21 [a]Matt 28:18; Col 1:16 [b]Phil 2:9; Rev 19:12 [c]Matt 12:32
22 [a]Ps 8:6; 1 Cor 15:27 [b]1 Cor 11:3; Eph 4:15; Col 1:18
23 [a]1 Cor 12:27; Eph 4:12; Col 1:18 [b]John 1:16; Eph 3:19 [c]Eph 4:10 [d]Col 3:11
2:1 [1]Lit *being* [2]Or *by reason of* [a]Eph 2:5; Col 2:13
2 [1]Lit *age* [a]1 Cor 6:11; Eph 2:3 [b]Eph 1:21 [c]John 12:31; Eph 6:12 [d]Eph 5:6
3 [1]Lit *doing* [2]Lit *thoughts* [a]Eph 2:2 [b]Gal 5:16f [c]Rom 2:14; Gal 2:15 [d]Rom 5:9; Col 1:21; 2 Pet 2:14 [e]Rom 5:12
4 [a]Eph 1:7 [b]John 3:16
5 [1]Or *by reason of* [2]Two early mss read *in Christ* [a]Eph 2:1 [b]Acts 15:11
6 [a]Col 2:12 [b]Eph 1:20 [c]Eph 1:3 [d]Eph 1:1
7 [a]Rom 2:4; Eph 1:7 [b]Titus 3:4
8 [1]I.e. that salvation [a]Acts 15:11; Eph 2:5 [b]1 Pet 1:5 [c]John 4:10
9 [a]Rom 3:28; 2 Tim 1:9 [b]1 Cor 1:29
10 [a]Eph 2:15; Col 3:10 [b]Eph 1:1 [c]Titus 2:14 [d]Eph 1:4 [e]Eph 4:1
11 [a]Eph 2:2 [b]1 Cor 12:2; Eph 5:8 [c]Rom 2:28f;

[b]seated us with Him in [c]the heavenly
places in [d]Christ Jesus,
7 so that in the ages to come He
might show the surpassing [a]riches of His
grace in [b]kindness toward us in Christ
Jesus.
8 For [a]by grace you have been saved
[b]through faith; and [1]that not of yourselves, *it is* [c]the gift of God;
9 [a]not as a result of works, so that
[b]no one may boast.
10 For we are His workmanship, [a]cre-
ated in [b]Christ Jesus for [c]good works,
which God [d]prepared beforehand so that
we would [e]walk in them.
11 ¶ Therefore remember that [a]for-
merly [b]you, the Gentiles in the flesh,
who are called "[c]Uncircumcision" by
the so-called "[c]Circumcision," *which is*
performed in the flesh by human
hands—
12 *remember* that you were at that
time separate from Christ, [1a]excluded
from the commonwealth of Israel, and
strangers to [b]the covenants of promise,
having [c]no hope and [d]without God in
the world.
13 But now in [a]Christ Jesus you who
[b]formerly were [c]far off [1]have [c]been
brought near [2d]by the blood of Christ.
14 For He Himself is [a]our peace,
[b]who made both *groups into* one and
broke down the [1]barrier of the dividing
wall,
15 [1]by [a]abolishing in His flesh the enmity, *which is* [b]the Law of commandments *contained* in ordinances, so that
in Himself He might [2c]make the two
into [d]one new man, *thus* establishing
[e]peace,
16 and might [a]reconcile them both in
[b]one body to God through the cross, [1]by
it having [c]put to death the enmity.
17 AND [a]HE CAME AND PREACHED
[b]PEACE TO YOU WHO WERE [c]FAR AWAY, AND
PEACE TO THOSE WHO WERE [c]NEAR;
18 for through Him we both have
[a]our access in [b]one Spirit to [c]the Father.
19 So then you are no longer [a]strang-
ers and aliens, but you are [b]fellow citizens with the [1]saints, and are of [c]God's
household,

Col 2:11 **12** [1]Or *alienated* [a]Rom 9:4; Col 1:21 [b]Gal 3:17; Heb 8:6 [c]1 Thess 4:13 [d]Gal 4:8; 1 Thess 4:5 **13** [1]Lit *became*; or *were made* [2]Or *in* [a]Eph 1:1 [b]Eph 2:2 [c]Is 57:19; Acts 2:39; Eph 2:17 [d]Rom 3:25; Col 1:20 **14** [1]Lit *the dividing wall of the barrier* [a]Is 9:6; Eph 2:15; Col 3:15 [b]1 Cor 12:13; Gal 3:28; Col 3:11 **15** [1]Or *the enmity, by abolishing in His flesh the Law* [2]Lit *create* [a]Eph 2:16; Col 1:21f [b]Col 2:14 [c]Gal 3:28; Eph 2:10; Col 3:10 [d]Gal 3:28; Col 3:10f [e]Is 9:6; Eph 2:14; Col 3:15 **16** [1]Or *in Himself* [a]2 Cor 5:18; Col 1:20 [b]1 Cor 10:17; Eph 4:4 [c]Eph 2:15 **17** [a]Is 57:19; Rom 10:14 [b]Acts 10:36; Eph 2:14 [c]Eph 2:13 **18** [a]Rom 5:2; Eph 3:12 [b]1 Cor 12:13; Eph 4:4 [c]Col 1:12 **19** [1]Or *holy ones* [a]Eph 2:12; Heb 11:13; 1 Pet 2:11 [b]Phil 3:20; Heb 12:22f [c]Gal 6:10

20 having been [a]built on [b]the foundation of [c]the apostles and prophets,
[d]Christ Jesus Himself being the [e]corner
stone,
21 [a]in whom the whole building, being fitted together, is growing into [b]a
holy [1]temple in the Lord,
22 in whom you also are being [a]built
together into a [b]dwelling of God in the
Spirit.

Paul's Stewardship

3 For this reason I, Paul, [a]the prisoner
of [b]Christ Jesus [c]for the sake of you
[d]Gentiles—
2 if indeed you have heard of the
[a]stewardship of God's grace which was
given to me for you;
3 [a]that [b]by revelation there was
[c]made known to me [d]the mystery, [e]as
I wrote before in brief.
4 [1]By referring to this, when you
read you can understand [a]my insight
[2]into the [b]mystery of Christ,
5 which in other generations was not
made known to the sons of men, as it has
now been revealed to His holy [a]apostles
and prophets [1]in the Spirit;
6 *to be specific,* that the Gentiles are
[a]fellow heirs and [b]fellow members of
the body, and [c]fellow partakers of the
promise in [d]Christ Jesus through the gospel,
7 [a]of which I was made a [b]minister,
according to the gift of [c]God's grace
which was given to me [d]according to the
working of His power.
8 To me, [a]the very least of all
[1]saints, this grace was given, to [b]preach
to the Gentiles the unfathomable [c]riches
of Christ,
9 and to [1]bring to light what is the
administration of the [a]mystery which for
ages has been [b]hidden in God [c]who created all things;
10 so that the manifold [a]wisdom of
God might now be [b]made known
through the church to the [c]rulers and
the authorities in [d]the heavenly *places.*
11 *This was* in [a]accordance with the
[1]eternal purpose which He [2]carried out
in [b]Christ Jesus our Lord,
12 in whom we have boldness and
[1a]confident [b]access through faith [2]in
Him.
13 Therefore I ask [1]you not [a]to lose
heart at my tribulations [b]on your behalf,
[2]for they are your glory.
14 ¶ For this reason I [a]bow my knees
before the Father,
15 from whom [1]every family in heav-
en and on earth derives its name,
16 that He would grant you, according
to [a]the riches of His glory, to be

20 [a]1 Cor 3:9 [b]Matt 16:18; 1 Cor 3:10; Rev 21:14 [c]1 Cor 12:28; Eph 3:5 [d]1 Cor 3:11 [e]Ps 118:22; Luke 20:17
21 [1]Or *sanctuary* [a]Eph 4:15f; Col 2:19 [b]1 Cor 3:16f
22 [a]1 Cor 3:9; 2 Cor 6:16 [b]Eph 3:17
3:1 [a]Acts 23:18; Eph 4:1; 2 Tim 1:8; Philem 1 [b]Gal 5:24 [c]2 Cor 1:6; Eph 3:13 [d]Eph 3:8
2 [a]Eph 1:10; Col 1:25; 1 Tim 1:4
3 [a]Acts 22:17 [b]Gal 1:12 [c]Eph 1:9 [d]Rom 11:25; Eph 3:4; Col 1:26f [e]Eph 1:9f; Heb 13:22; 1 Pet 5:12
4 [1]Lit *To which, when you read* [2]Lit *in* [a]2 Cor 11:6 [b]Rom 11:25; Eph 3:3; Col 1:26f
5 [1]Or *by* [a]1 Cor 12:28; Eph 2:20
6 [a]Gal 3:29 [b]Eph 2:16 [c]Eph 5:7 [d]Gal 5:24
7 [a]Col 1:23 [b]1 Cor 3:5 [c]Acts 9:15; Rom 12:3; Eph 3:2 [d]Eph 1:19
8 [1]Or *holy ones* [a]1 Cor 15:9 [b]Acts 9:15; Eph 3:1f [c]Rom 2:4; Eph 1:7
9 [1]Two early mss read *make all know* [a]Rom 11:25; Eph 3:3; Col 1:26f [b]Col 3:3 [c]Rev 4:11
10 [a]Rom 11:33; 1 Cor 2:7 [b]Eph 1:23; 1 Pet 1:12 [c]Eph 1:21; Col 2:10 [d]Eph 1:3
11 [1]Lit *purpose of the ages* [2]Or *formed* [a]Eph 1:11 [b]Gal 5:24; Eph 3:1
12 [1]Lit *access in confidence* [2]Lit *of Him* [a]2 Cor 3:4; Heb 4:16; 1 John 2:28 [b]Eph 2:18
13 [1]Or *that I may not lose* [2]Lit *which are* [a]2 Cor 4:1 [b]Eph 3:1
14 [a]Phil 2:10
15 [1]Or *the whole*
16 [a]Eph 1:18 [b]1 Cor 16:13; Phil 4:13; Col 1:11 [c]Rom 7:22
17 [a]John 14:23; Rom 8:9f; 2 Cor 13:5; Eph 2:22 [b]1 Cor 3:6; Col 2:7 [c]Col 1:23
18 [1]V 8, note 1 [a]Eph 1:15 [b]Job 11:8f
19 [a]Rom 8:35 [b]Phil 4:7 [c]Col 2:10 [d]Eph 1:23
20 [a]Rom 16:25 [b]2 Cor 9:8 [c]Eph 3:7
21 [1]Lit *of the*

[b]strengthened with power through His
Spirit in [c]the inner man,
17 so that [a]Christ may dwell in your
hearts through faith; *and* that you, being
[b]rooted and [c]grounded in love,
18 may be able to comprehend with
[a]all the [1]saints what is [b]the breadth and
length and height and depth,
19 and to know [a]the love of Christ
which [b]surpasses knowledge, that you
may be [c]filled up to all the [d]fullness of
God.
20 ¶ [a]Now to Him who is [b]able to do
far more abundantly beyond all that we
ask or think, [c]according to the power
that works within us,
21 [a]to Him *be* the glory in the church
and in Christ Jesus to all generations
[1]forever and ever. Amen.

Unity of the Spirit

4 Therefore I, [a]the prisoner of the
Lord, [b]implore you to [c]walk in a
manner worthy of the [d]calling with
which you have been [e]called,
2 with all [a]humility and gentleness,
with patience, showing tolerance for one
another [b]in love,
3 being diligent to preserve the unity
of the Spirit in the [a]bond of peace.
4 *There is* [a]one body and one Spirit,
just as also you were called in one [b]hope
of your calling;
5 [a]one Lord, one faith, one baptism,
6 one God and Father of all [a]who is
over all and through all and in all.
7 ¶ But [a]to each one of us [b]grace
was given [c]according to the measure of
Christ's gift.
8 Therefore [1]it says,
"[a]WHEN HE ASCENDED ON HIGH,
HE [b]LED CAPTIVE A HOST OF
CAPTIVES,
AND HE GAVE GIFTS TO MEN."
9 (Now this *expression,* "He [a]as-
cended," what [1]does it mean except that
He also [2]had descended into [b]the lower
parts of the earth?
10 He who descended is Himself also
He who ascended [a]far above all the heavens, so that He might [b]fill all things.)
11 And He [a]gave [b]some *as* apostles,
and some *as* prophets, and some *as*
[c]evangelists, and some *as* pastors and
[d]teachers,
12 [a]for the equipping of the [1]saints

age of the ages [a]Rom 11:36 **4:1** [a]Eph 3:1 [b]Rom 12:1 [c]Eph 2:10; Col 1:10; 1 Thess 2:12 [d]Rom 11:29 [e]Rom 8:28f
2 [a]Col 3:12f [b]Eph 1:4 **3** [a]Col 3:14f **4** [a]1 Cor 12:4ff; Eph 2:16 [b]Eph 1:18 **5** [a]1 Cor 8:6 **6** [a]Rom 11:36 **7** [a]1 Cor 12:7 [b]Eph 3:2 [c]Rom 12:3 **8** [1]Or *He* [a]Ps 68:18 [b]Col 2:15 **9** [1]Lit *is it except* [2]One early ms reads *had first descended* [a]John 3:13 [b]Is 44:23 **10** [a]Eph 1:20f; Heb 4:14 [b]Eph 1:23
11 [a]Eph 4:8 [b]Acts 13:1; 1 Cor 12:28 [c]Acts 21:8 [d]Acts 13:1
12 [1]Or *holy ones* [a]2 Cor 13:9

for the work of service, to the building up of [b]the body of Christ;

13 until we all attain to [a]the unity of the faith, and of the [1b]knowledge of the Son of God, to a [c]mature man, to the measure of the stature [2]which belongs to the [d]fullness of Christ.

14 [1]As a result, we are [a]no longer to be children, [b]tossed here and there by waves and carried about by every wind of doctrine, by the trickery of men, by [c]craftiness [2]in [d]deceitful scheming;

15 but [1]speaking the truth [a]in love, [2]we are to [b]grow up in all *aspects* into Him who is the [c]head, *even* Christ,

16 from whom [a]the whole body, being fitted and held together [1]by what every joint supplies, according to the [2]proper working of each individual part, causes the growth of the body for the building up of itself [b]in love.

The Christian's Walk

17 ¶ [a]So this I say, and affirm together with the Lord, [b]that you walk no longer just as the Gentiles also walk, in the [c]futility of their mind,

18 being [a]darkened in their understanding, [1b]excluded from the life of God because of the [c]ignorance that is in them, because of the [d]hardness of their heart;

19 and they, having [a]become callous, [b]have given themselves over to [c]sensuality [1]for the practice of every kind of impurity with greediness.

20 But you did not [a]learn [1]Christ in this way,

21 if indeed you [a]have heard Him and have [b]been taught in Him, just as truth is in Jesus,

22 that, in reference to your former manner of life, you [a]lay aside the [b]old [1]self, which is being corrupted in accordance with the [c]lusts of deceit,

23 and that you be [a]renewed in the spirit of your mind,

24 and [a]put on the [b]new [1]self, which [2c]in *the likeness of* God has been created in righteousness and holiness of the truth.

25 ¶ Therefore, [a]laying aside falsehood, [b]SPEAK TRUTH EACH ONE *of you* WITH HIS NEIGHBOR, for we are [c]members of one another.

26 [a]BE ANGRY, AND *yet* DO NOT SIN; do not let the sun go down on your anger,

27 and do not [a]give the devil [1]an opportunity.

28 He who steals must steal no longer; but rather [a]he must labor, [b]performing with his own hands what is good, [c]so that he will have *something* to share with [1]one who has need.

29 Let no [1a]unwholesome word proceed from your mouth, but only such *a word* as is good for [b]edification [2]according to the need *of the moment,* so that it will give grace to those who hear.

30 [a]Do not grieve the Holy Spirit of God, [1]by whom you were [b]sealed for the day of redemption.

31 [a]Let all bitterness and wrath and anger and clamor and slander be [b]put away from you, along with all [c]malice.

32 [a]Be kind to one another, tenderhearted, forgiving each other, [b]just as God in Christ also has forgiven [1]you.

Be Imitators of God

5 [a]Therefore be imitators of God, as beloved children;

2 and [a]walk in love, just as Christ also [b]loved [1]you and [c]gave Himself up for us, an [d]offering and a sacrifice to God [2]as a [e]fragrant aroma.

3 ¶ But [a]immorality [1]or any impurity or greed must not even be named among you, as is proper among [2]saints;

4 and *there must be no* [a]filthiness and silly talk, or coarse jesting, which [b]are not fitting, but rather [c]giving of thanks.

5 For this you know with certainty, that [a]no [1]immoral or impure person or covetous man, who is an idolater, has an inheritance in the kingdom [b]of Christ and God.

6 ¶ [a]Let no one deceive you with empty words, for because of these things [b]the wrath of God comes upon [c]the sons of disobedience.

7 Therefore do not be [a]partakers with them;

8 for [a]you were formerly [b]darkness, but now you are Light in the Lord; walk as [c]children of Light

9 (for [a]the fruit of the Light *consists* in all [b]goodness and righteousness and truth),

10 [1a]trying to learn what is pleasing to the Lord.

11 [a]Do not participate in the unfruitful [b]deeds of [c]darkness, but instead even [1d]expose them;

12 for it is disgraceful even to speak of the things which are done by them in secret.

12 [b]1 Cor 12:27; Eph 1:23 **13** [1]Or *true knowledge* [2]Lit *of the fullness* [a]Eph 4:3 [b]John 6:69; Eph 1:17; Phil 3:10 [c]1 Cor 14:20; Col 1:28; Heb 5:14 [d]John 1:16; Eph 1:23 **14** [1]Lit *So that we will no longer be* [2]Lit *with regard to the scheming of deceit* [a]1 Cor 14:20 [b]James 1:6; Jude 12 [c]1 Cor 3:19; 2 Cor 4:2 [d]Eph 6:11 **15** [1]Or *holding to* or *being truthful in* [2]Or *let us grow up* [a]Eph 1:4 [b]Eph 2:21 [c]Eph 1:22 **16** [1]Lit *through every joint of the supply* [2]Lit *working in measure* [a]Rom 12:4f; Col 2:19 [b]Eph 1:4 **17** [a]Col 2:4 [b]Eph 2:2 [c]Rom 1:21; Col 2:18; 1 Pet 1:18; 2 Pet 2:18 **18** [1]Or *alienated* [a]Rom 1:21 [b]Eph 2:1 [c]Acts 3:17; 1 Cor 2:8; Heb 5:2; 1 Pet 1:14 [d]Mark 3:5; Rom 11:7; 2 Cor 3:14 **19** [1]Or *greedy for the practice of every kind of impurity* [a]1 Tim 4:2 [b]Rom 1:24 [c]Col 3:5 **20** [1]I.e. the Messiah [a]Matt 11:29 **21** [a]Rom 10:14; Eph 1:13; Col 1:5 [b]Col 2:7 **22** [1]Lit *man* [a]Eph 4:25; Col 3:8; Heb 12:1; James 1:21; 1 Pet 2:1 [b]Rom 6:6 [c]2 Cor 11:3; Heb 3:13 **23** [a]Rom 12:2 **24** [1]Lit *man* [2]Lit *according to God* [a]Rom 13:14 [b]Rom 6:4; 2 Cor 5:17; Col 3:10 [c]Eph 2:10 **25** [a]Eph 4:22; Col 3:8; Heb 12:1; James 1:21; 1 Pet 2:1 [b]Zech 8:16; Eph 4:15; Col 3:9 [c]Rom 12:5 **26** [a]Ps 4:4 **27** [1]Lit *a place* [a]Rom 12:19; James 4:7 **28** [1]Lit *the one* [a]Acts 20:35; 1 Cor 4:12; Gal 6:10 [b]1 Thess 4:11; 2 Thess 3:8; Titus 3:8 [c]Luke 3:11; 1 Thess 4:12 **29** [1]Lit *rotten* [2]Lit *of the need* [a]Matt 12:34; Eph 5:4; Col 3:8 [b]Eccl 10:12; Rom 14:19; Col 4:6 **30** [1]Lit *in* [a]Is 63:10; 1 Thess 5:19 [b]John 3:33; Eph 1:13 **31** [a]Rom 3:14; Col 3:8 [b]Eph 4:22 [c]1 Pet 2:1 **32** [1]Two early mss read *us* [a]1 Cor 13:4; Col 3:12f; 1 Pet 3:8 [b]Matt 6:14f; 2 Cor 2:10
5:1 [a]Matt 5:48; Luke 6:36; Eph 4:32 **2** [1]One early ms reads *us* [2]Lit *for an odor of fragrance* [a]Rom 14:15; Col 3:14 [b]John 13:34; Rom 8:37 [c]John 6:51; Rom 4:25; Gal 2:20; Eph 5:25 [d]Heb 7:27 [e]Ex 29:18; 2 Cor 2:14 **3** [1]Lit *and all* [2]Or *holy ones* [a]Col 3:5 **4** [a]Matt 12:34; Eph 4:29; Col 3:8 [b]Rom 1:28 [c]Eph 5:20 **5** [1]I.e. one who commits sexual immorality [a]1 Cor 6:9; Col 3:5 [b]Col 1:13 **6** [a]Col 2:8 [b]Rom 1:18; Col 3:6 [c]Eph 2:2 **7** [a]Eph 3:6 **8** [a]Eph 2:2 [b]Acts 26:18; Col 1:12f [c]John 12:36; Rom 13:12 **9** [a]Gal 5:22 [b]Rom 15:14 **10** [1]Lit *proving what* [a]Rom 12:2 **11** [1]Or *reprove* [a]1 Cor 5:9; 2 Cor 6:14 [b]Rom 13:12 [c]Acts 26:18; Col 1:12f [d]1 Tim 5:20

13 But all things become visible
[a]when they are [1]exposed by the light,
for everything that becomes visible is
light.
14 For this reason [1]it says,
"[a]Awake, sleeper,
And arise from [b]the dead,
And Christ [c]will shine on you."
15 ¶ Therefore [1]be careful how you
[a]walk, not [b]as unwise men but as wise,
16 [1a]making the most of your time,
because [b]the days are evil.
17 So then do not be foolish, but [a]un-
derstand what the will of the Lord is.
18 And [a]do not get drunk with wine,
[1]for that is [b]dissipation, but be [c]filled
with the Spirit,
19 [a]speaking to [1]one another in
[b]psalms and [c]hymns and spiritual
[d]songs, [e]singing and making melody
with your heart to the Lord;
20 [a]always giving thanks for all things
in the name of our Lord Jesus Christ to
[1b]God, even the Father;
21 [1a]and be subject to one another in
the [2b]fear of Christ.

Marriage Like Christ and the Church

22 ¶ [a]Wives, [b]*be subject* to your own
husbands, [c]as to the Lord.
23 For [a]the husband is the head of the
wife, as Christ also is the [b]head of the
church, He Himself [c]*being* the Savior of
the body.
24 But as the church is subject to
Christ, so also the wives *ought to be* to
their husbands in everything.
25 ¶ [a]Husbands, love your wives, just
as Christ also loved the church and [b]gave
Himself up for her,
26 [a]so that He might sanctify her, having [b]cleansed her by the [c]washing of
water with [d]the word,
27 that He might [a]present to Himself
the church [1]in all her glory, having no
spot or wrinkle or any such thing; but
that she would be [b]holy and blameless.
28 So husbands ought also to [a]love
their own wives as their own bodies. He
who loves his own wife loves himself;
29 for no one ever hated his own flesh,
but nourishes and cherishes it, just as
Christ also *does* the church,
30 because we are [a]members of His
[b]body.
31 [a]FOR THIS REASON A MAN SHALL LEAVE
HIS FATHER AND MOTHER AND SHALL BE
JOINED TO HIS WIFE, AND THE TWO SHALL BE-
COME ONE FLESH.
32 This mystery is great; but I am
speaking with reference to Christ and the
church.
33 Nevertheless, each individual
among you also is to [a]love his own wife
even as himself, and the wife must *see to
it* that she [1b]respects her husband.

Family Relationships

6 [a]Children, obey your parents in the
Lord, for this is right.
2 [a]HONOR YOUR FATHER AND MOTHER
(which is the first commandment with a
promise),
3 SO THAT IT MAY BE WELL WITH YOU,
AND THAT YOU MAY LIVE LONG ON THE EARTH.
4 ¶ [a]Fathers, do not provoke your
children to anger, but [b]bring them up in
the discipline and instruction of the Lord.
5 ¶ [a]Slaves, be obedient to those
who are your [1]masters according to the
flesh, with [b]fear and trembling, in the
sincerity of your heart, [c]as to Christ;
6 [a]not [1]by way of eyeservice, as
[b]men-pleasers, but as [c]slaves of Christ,
[d]doing the will of God from the [2]heart.
7 With good will [1]render service,
[a]as to the Lord, and not to men,
8 [a]knowing that [b]whatever good
thing each one does, this he will receive
back from the Lord, [c]whether slave or
free.
9 ¶ And masters, do the same things
to them, and [a]give up threatening,
knowing that [b]both their Master and
yours is in heaven, and there is [c]no partiality with Him.

The Armor of God

10 ¶ Finally, [a]be strong in the Lord
and in [b]the strength of His might.
11 [a]Put on the full armor of God, so
that you will be able to stand firm against
the [b]schemes of the devil.
12 For our [a]struggle is not against
[1b]flesh and blood, but [c]against the rulers, against the powers, against the
[d]world forces of this [e]darkness, against
the [f]spiritual *forces* of wickedness in
[g]the heavenly *places.*
13 Therefore, take up [a]the full armor
of God, so that you will be able to [b]resist
in [c]the evil day, and having done everything, to stand firm.
14 Stand firm therefore, [a]HAVING GIRD-
ED YOUR LOINS WITH TRUTH, and HAVING
[b]PUT ON THE BREASTPLATE OF RIGHTEOUS-
NESS,
15 and having [a]shod YOUR FEET WITH
THE PREPARATION OF THE GOSPEL OF PEACE;
16 [1]in addition to all, taking up the

13 [1]Or *reproved* [a]John 3:20f **14** [1]Or *He* [a]Is 26:19; Rom 13:11 [b]Eph 2:1 [c]Luke 1:78f **15** [1]Lit *look carefully* [a]Eph 5:2 [b]Col 4:5 **16** [1]Lit *redeeming the time* [a]Col 4:5 [b]Gal 1:4; Eph 6:13 **17** [a]Rom 12:2; Col 1:9; 1 Thess 4:3 **18** [1]Lit *in which is* [a]Prov 20:1; Rom 13:13; 1 Cor 5:11; 1 Thess 5:7 [b]Titus 1:6; 1 Pet 4:4 [c]Luke 1:15 **19** [1]Or *yourselves* [a]Col 3:16 [b]1 Cor 14:26 [c]Acts 16:25 [d]Rev 5:9 [e]1 Cor 14:15 **20** [1]Lit *the God and Father* [a]Rom 1:8; Eph 5:4; Col 3:17 [b]1 Cor 15:24 **21** [1]Lit *being subject* [2]Or *reverence* [a]Gal 5:13; Phil 2:3; 1 Pet 5:5 [b]2 Cor 5:11 **22** [a]Eph 5:22-6:9: *Col 3:18-4:1* [b]1 Cor 14:34f; Titus 2:5; 1 Pet 3:1 [c]Eph 6:5 **23** [a]1 Cor 11:3 [b]Eph 1:22 [c]1 Cor 6:13 **25** [a]Eph 5:28; Col 3:19; 1 Pet 3:7 [b]Eph 5:2 **26** [a]Titus 2:14; Heb 10:10 [b]2 Pet 1:9 [c]Acts 22:16; 1 Cor 6:11; Titus 3:5 [d]John 15:3; Rom 10:8f; Eph 6:17 **27** [1]Lit *glorious* [a]2 Cor 4:14; Col 1:22 [b]Eph 1:4 **28** [a]Eph 5:25; 1 Pet 3:7 **30** [a]1 Cor 6:15 [b]Eph 1:23 **31** [a]Gen 2:24; Matt 19:5; Mark 10:7f **33** [1]Lit *fear* [a]Eph 5:25; 1 Pet 3:7 [b]1 Pet 3:2 **6:1** [a]Prov 6:20; Col 3:20 **2** [a]Ex 20:12; Deut 5:16 **4** [a]Col 3:21 [b]Gen 18:19; Deut 6:7; Ps 78:4; Prov 22:6; 2 Tim 3:15 **5** [1]I.e. earthly masters, with fear [a]Col 3:22; 1 Tim 6:1; Titus 2:9 [b]1 Cor 2:3 [c]Eph 5:22 **6** [1]Lit *according to* [2]Lit *soul* [a]Col 3:22 [b]Gal 1:10 [c]1 Cor 7:22 [d]Mark 3:35 **7** [1]Lit *rendering* [a]Col 3:23 **8** [a]Col 3:24 [b]Matt 16:27; 2 Cor 5:10; Col 3:24f [c]1 Cor 12:13; Col 3:11

9 [a]Lev 25:43 [b]Job 31:13ff; John 13:13; Col 4:1 [c]Deut 10:17; Acts 10:34; Col 3:25 **10** [a]1 Cor 16:13; 2 Tim 2:1 [b]Eph 1:19 **11** [a]Rom 13:12; Eph 6:13 [b]Eph 4:14 **12** [1]Lit *blood and flesh* [a]1 Cor 9:25 [b]Matt 16:17 [c]Eph 1:21 [d]John 12:31 [e]Acts 26:18; Col 1:13 [f]Eph 3:10 [g]Eph 1:3 **13** [a]Eph 6:11 [b]James 4:7 [c]Eph 5:16 **14** [a]Is 11:5; Luke 12:35; 1 Pet 1:13 [b]Is 59:17; Rom 13:12; Eph 6:13; 1 Thess 5:8 **15** [a]Is 52:7; Rom 10:15 **16** [1]Lit *in all*

[a]shield of faith with which you will be
able to extinguish all the [b]flaming arrows
of [c]the evil *one.*
17 And take [a]THE HELMET OF SALVA-
TION, and the [b]sword of the Spirit, which
is [c]the word of God.
18 ¶ [1]With all [a]prayer and petition
[2b]pray at all times [c]in the Spirit, and
with this in view, [3d]be on the alert with
all [e]perseverance and [f]petition for all
the saints,
19 and [a]*pray* on my behalf, that utterance may be given to me [b]in the opening
of my mouth, to make known with [c]bold-
ness [d]the mystery of the gospel,
20 for which I am an [a]ambassador [b]in
[1]chains; that [2]in *proclaiming* it I may
speak [c]boldly, [d]as I ought to speak.
21 ¶ [a]But that you also may know
about my circumstances, [1]how I am doing, [b]Tychicus, [c]the beloved brother
and faithful minister in the Lord, will
make everything known to you.
22 [1a]I have sent him to you for this
very purpose, so that you may know
[2]about us, and that he may [b]comfort
your hearts.
23 ¶ [a]Peace be to the brethren, and
[b]love with faith, from God the Father
and the Lord Jesus Christ.
24 Grace be with all those who love
our Lord Jesus Christ [1]with incorruptible
love.

16 [a]1 Thess 5:8 [b]Ps 7:13 [c]Matt 5:37 **17** [a]Is 59:17 [b]Is 49:2; Hos 6:5; Heb 4:12 [c]Eph 5:26; Heb 6:5 **18** [1]Lit *Through* [2]Lit *praying* [3]Lit *being* [a]Phil 4:6 [b]Luke 18:1; Col 1:3; 1 Thess 5:17 [c]Rom 8:26f [d]Mark 13:33 [e]Acts 1:14 [f]1 Tim 2:1 **19** [a]Col 4:3; 1 Thess 5:25 [b]2 Cor 6:11 [c]2 Cor 3:12 [d]Eph 3:3 **20** [1]Lit *a chain* [2]Two early mss read *I may speak it boldly* [a]2 Cor 5:20; Philem 9 mg [b]Acts 21:33; Eph 3:1; Phil 1:7; Col 4:3 [c]2 Cor 3:12 [d]Col 4:4 **21** [1]Lit *what* [a]Eph 6:21,22: *Col 4:7-9* [b]Acts 20:4; 2 Tim 4:12 [c]Col 4:7 **22** [1]Lit *Whom I have sent to you* [2]Lit *the things about us* [a]Col 4:8 [b]Col 2:2 **23** [a]Rom 15:33; Gal 6:16; 2 Thess 3:16; 1 Pet 5:14 [b]Gal 5:6; 1 Thess 5:8 **24** [1]Lit *in incorruption*

Philippians

Title and Background

Philippians was written during Paul's first Roman imprisonment and is known as a "Prison Letter" (along with Ephesians, Colossians and Philemon). The church at Philippi had sent Paul a gift by way of Epaphroditus, their messenger. Epaphroditus had become sick in Rome, and the Philippian Christians were concerned about him. This made Epaphroditus all the more eager to return home. Paul therefore wrote this letter to his Christian friends in Philippi, expressing his gratitude for their love and help.

Author and Date of Writing

The first verse of Philippians tells us Paul wrote the letter, and the writing itself reveals the stamp of genuineness. The many personal references of the author fit what we know of Paul from other New Testament books. The most widely accepted date for the writing of the letter is about A.D. 61.

Theme and Message

The theme of the book is "joy," or "rejoicing in the Lord." The word "joy" in its various forms occurs sixteen times. There were also perils to watch for, because there were enemies of the church, both inside and outside. Paul warns the Philippians of the present dangers of a self-seeking attitude and an attitude of pride, both of which could lead to harmful divisions. The book of Philippians also contains the most profound statement of the meaning of the incarnation (2:5–11).

Outline

I. Greetings, Thanksgiving and Prayer (1:1–11)
II. Paul's Personal Circumstances (1:12–26)
III. Exhortations (1:27—2:18)
  A. Live a Life Worthy of the Gospel (1:27–30)
  B. Follow the Servant Attitude of Christ Jesus (2:1–18)
IV. Paul's Associates in the Gospel (2:19–30)
V. Warnings Against Judaizers and Libertines (3:1—4:1)
VI. Final Exhortations, Thanks and Conclusion (4:2–23)

Thanksgiving

1 [a]Paul and [b]Timothy, [c]bond-
servants of [d]Christ Jesus,
¶ To [e]all the [1f]saints in Christ Jesus
who are in [g]Philippi, [2]including the
[h]overseers and [i]deacons:
2 [a]Grace to you and peace from God
our Father and the Lord Jesus Christ.
3 ¶ [a]I thank my God in all my remembrance of you,
4 always offering prayer with joy in
[a]my every prayer for you all,
5 in view of your [1a]participation in
the [b]gospel [c]from the first day until
now.
6 *For I am* confident of this very
thing, that He who began a good work in
you will perfect it until [a]the day of Christ
Jesus.
7 [1]For [a]it is only right for me to feel
this way about you all, because I [b]have
you in my heart, since both in my [2c]im-
prisonment and in the [d]defense and confirmation of the [e]gospel, you all are partakers of grace with me.
8 For [a]God is my witness, how I long
for you all with the [1]affection of [b]Christ
Jesus.
9 And this I pray, that [a]your love
may abound still more and more in [b]real
knowledge and all discernment,
10 so that you may [1a]approve the
things that are excellent, in order to be
sincere and blameless [2]until [b]the day of
Christ;
11 having been filled with the [a]fruit
of righteousness which *comes* through
Jesus Christ, to the glory and praise of
God.

1:1 [1]Or *holy ones* [2]Lit *with* [a]2 Cor 1:1 [b]Acts 16:1 [c]Rom 1:1; Gal 1:10 [d]Gal 3:26 [e]2 Cor 1:1; Col 1:2 [f]Acts 9:13 [g]Acts 16:12 [h]Acts 20:28; 1 Tim 3:1f; Titus 1:7 [i]1 Tim 3:8ff **2** [a]Rom 1:7 **3** [a]Rom 1:8 **4** [a]Rom 1:9 **5** [1]Or *sharing in the preaching of the gospel* [a]Acts 2:42; Phil 4:15 [b]Phil 1:7 [c]Acts 16:12-40; Phil 2:12 **6** [a]1 Cor 1:8; Phil 1:10 **7** [1]Lit *Just as it is right* [2]Lit *bonds* [a]2 Pet 1:13 [b]2 Cor 7:3 [c]Acts 21:33; Eph 6:20; Phil 1:13f [d]Phil 1:16 [e]Phil 1:5 **8** [1]Lit *inward parts* [a]Rom 1:9 [b]Gal 3:26

9 [a]1 Thess 3:12 [b]Col 1:9 **10** [1]Or *discover*; or *distinguish between the things which differ* [2]Or *for* [a]Rom 2:18 [b]1 Cor 1:8; Phil 1:6 **11** [a]James 3:18

The Gospel Is Preached

12 ¶ Now I want you to know, brethren, that my circumstances [a]have turned out for the greater progress of the [b]gospel,
13 so that my [1a]imprisonment in *the cause of* Christ has become well known throughout the whole [2]praetorian guard and to [b]everyone else,
14 and that most of the [1]brethren, trusting in the Lord because of my [2a]imprisonment, have [b]far more courage to speak the word of God without fear.
15 [a]Some, to be sure, are preaching Christ even [1]from envy and strife, but some also [1]from good will;
16 the latter *do it* out of love, knowing that I am appointed for the defense of the [a]gospel;
17 the former proclaim Christ [a]out of selfish ambition [1]rather than from pure motives, thinking to cause me distress in my [2b]imprisonment.
18 What then? Only that in every way, whether in pretense or in truth, Christ is proclaimed; and in this I rejoice.
¶ Yes, and I will rejoice,
19 for I know that this will turn out for my [1]deliverance [a]through your [2]prayers and the provision of [b]the Spirit of Jesus Christ,
20 according to my [a]earnest expectation and [b]hope, that I will not be put to shame in anything, but *that* with [c]all boldness, Christ will even now, as always, be [d]exalted in my body, [e]whether by life or by death.

To Live Is Christ

21 For to me, [a]to live is Christ and to die is gain.
22 [1]But if *I am* to live *on* in the flesh, this *will mean* [a]fruitful labor for me; and I do not know [2]which to choose.
23 But I am hard-pressed from both *directions,* having the [a]desire to depart and [b]be with Christ, for *that* is very much better;
24 yet to remain on in the flesh is more necessary for your sake.
25 [a]Convinced of this, I know that I will remain and continue with you all for your progress and joy [1]in the faith,
26 so that your [a]proud confidence in me may abound in Christ Jesus through my coming to you again.
27 ¶ Only conduct yourselves in a manner [a]worthy of the [b]gospel of Christ, so that whether I come and see you or remain absent, I will hear of you that you are [c]standing firm in [d]one spirit, with one [1]mind [e]striving together for the faith of the gospel;
28 in no way alarmed by *your* opponents—which is a [a]sign of destruction for them, but of salvation for you, and that *too,* from God.
29 For to you [a]it has been granted for Christ's sake, not only to believe in Him, but also to [b]suffer for His sake,
30 experiencing the same [a]conflict which [b]you saw in me, and now hear *to be* in me.

Be Like Christ

2 Therefore if there is any encouragement in Christ, if there is any consolation of love, if there is any [a]fellowship of the Spirit, if any [1b]affection and compassion,
2 [a]make my joy complete [1]by [b]being of the same mind, maintaining the same love, united in spirit, intent on one purpose.
3 Do nothing [1]from [2a]selfishness or [b]empty conceit, but with humility of mind [c]regard one another as more important than yourselves;
4 [a]do not *merely* look out for your own personal interests, but also for the interests of others.
5 [a]Have this attitude [1]in yourselves which was also in [b]Christ Jesus,
6 who, although He [a]existed in the [b]form of God, [c]did not regard equality with God a thing to be [1]grasped,
7 but [1a]emptied Himself, taking the form of a [b]bond-servant, *and* [c]being made in the likeness of men.
8 Being found in appearance as a man, [a]He humbled Himself by becoming [b]obedient to the point of death, even [c]death [1]on a cross.
9 [a]For this reason also, God [b]highly exalted Him, and bestowed on Him [c]the name which is above every name,
10 so that at the name of Jesus [a]EVERY KNEE WILL BOW, of [b]those who are in heaven and on earth and under the earth,
11 and that every tongue will confess that Jesus Christ is [a]Lord, to the glory of God the Father.
12 ¶ So then, my beloved, [a]just as you have always obeyed, not as in my presence only, but now much more in my absence, work out your [b]salvation with [c]fear and trembling;
13 for it is [a]God who is at work in you, both to will and to work [b]for *His* good pleasure.
14 ¶ Do all things without [a]grumbling or disputing;
15 so that you will [1]prove yourselves

---

12 [a]Luke 21:13 [b]Phil 1:5 **13** [1]Lit *bonds* [2]Or *governor's palace* [a]Phil 1:7; 2 Tim 2:9 [b]Acts 28:30 **14** [1]Or *brethren in the Lord, trusting because of my bonds* [2]Lit *bonds* [a]Phil 1:7; 2 Tim 2:9 [b]Acts 4:31; 2 Cor 3:12; Phil 1:20 **15** [1]Lit *because of* [a]2 Cor 11:13 **16** [a]Phil 1:5 **17** [1]Lit *not sincerely* [2]Lit *bonds* [a]Rom 2:8; Phil 2:3 [b]Phil 1:7; 2 Tim 2:9 **19** [1]Or *salvation* [2]Lit *supplication* [a]2 Cor 1:11 [b]Acts 16:7 **20** [a]Rom 8:19 [b]Rom 5:5; 1 Pet 4:16 [c]Acts 4:31; 2 Cor 3:12; Phil 1:14 [d]1 Cor 6:20 [e]Rom 14:8 **21** [a]Gal 2:20 **22** [1]Or *But if to live in the flesh, this will be fruitful labor for me, then I* [2]Lit *what I shall choose* [a]Rom 1:13 **23** [a]2 Cor 5:8; 2 Tim 4:6 [b]John 12:26 **25** [1]Lit *of* [a]Phil 2:24 **26** [a]2 Cor 5:12; Phil 2:16 **27** [1]Lit *soul* [a]Eph 4:1 [b]Phil 1:5 [c]1 Cor 16:13; Phil 4:1 [d]Acts 4:32 [e]Jude 3 **28** [a]2 Thess 1:5 **29** [a]Matt 5:11 [b]Acts 14:22 **30** [a]Col 1:29; 1 Thess 2:2; 1 Tim 6:12; 2 Tim 4:7; Heb 10:32 [b]Acts 16:19-40; Phil 1:13
2:1 [1]Lit *inward parts* [a]2 Cor 13:14 [b]Col 3:12 **2** [1]Lit *that you be* [a]John 3:29 [b]Rom 12:16; Phil 4:2 **3** [1]Lit *according to* [2]Or *contentiousness* [a]Rom 2:8; Phil 1:17 [b]Gal 5:26 [c]Rom 12:10; Eph 5:21 **4** [a]Rom 15:1f **5** [1]Or *among* [a]Matt 11:29; Rom 15:3 [b]Phil 1:1 **6** [1]I.e. utilized or asserted [a]John 1:1 [b]2 Cor 4:4 [c]John 5:18 **7** [1]I.e. laid aside His privileges [a]2 Cor 8:9 [b]Matt 20:28 [c]John 1:14; Rom 8:3; Gal 4:4; Heb 2:17 **8** [1]Lit *of* [a]2 Cor 8:9 [b]Matt 26:39; John 10:18; Rom 5:19; Heb 5:8 [c]Heb 12:2 **9** [a]Heb 1:9 [b]Matt 28:18; Acts 2:33; Heb 2:9 [c]Eph 1:21 **10** [a]Is 45:23; Rom 14:11 [b]Eph 1:10 **11** [a]John 13:13; Rom 10:9 **12** [a]Phil 1:5 [b]Heb 5:9 [c]2 Cor 7:15 **13** [a]Rom 12:3; 1 Cor 12:6; Heb 13:21 [b]Eph 1:5 **14** [a]1 Cor 10:10; 1 Pet 4:9 **15** [1]Or *become*

to be [a]blameless and innocent, [b]chil-
dren of God above reproach in the midst
of a [c]crooked and perverse generation,
among whom you [2d]appear as [3]lights in
the world,
16 holding [1]fast the word of life, so
that in [a]the day of Christ I will have
reason to glory because I did not [b]run in
vain nor [c]toil in vain.
17 But even if I am being [a]poured out
as a drink offering upon [b]the sacrifice
and service of your faith, I rejoice and
share my joy with you all.
18 You too, *I urge you,* rejoice in the
same way and share your joy with me.

Timothy and Epaphroditus

19 ¶ But I hope [1]in the Lord Jesus to
[a]send [b]Timothy to you shortly, so that I
also may be encouraged when I learn of
your condition.
20 For I have no one *else* [a]of kindred
spirit who will genuinely be concerned
for your welfare.
21 For they all [a]seek after their own
interests, not those of Christ Jesus.
22 But you know [a]of his proven
worth, that [b]he served with me in the
furtherance of the gospel [c]like a child
serving his father.
23 [a]Therefore I hope to send him immediately, as soon as I see how things *go*
with me;
24 and [a]I trust in the Lord that I myself also will be coming shortly.
25 But I thought it necessary to send to
you [a]Epaphroditus, my brother and [b]fel-
low worker and [c]fellow soldier, who is
also your [1d]messenger and [a]minister to
my need;
26 because he was longing [1]for you
all and was distressed because you had
heard that he was sick.
27 For indeed he was sick to the point
of death, but God had mercy on him, and
not on him only but also on me, so that
I would not have sorrow upon sorrow.
28 Therefore I have sent him all the
more eagerly so that when you see him
again you may rejoice and I may be less
concerned *about you.*
29 [a]Receive him then in the Lord
with all joy, and [b]hold men like him in
high regard;
30 because he came close to death
[1a]for the work of Christ, risking his life
to [b]complete [2]what was deficient in
your service to me.

The Goal of Life

3 Finally, my brethren, [a]rejoice in the
Lord. To write the same things *again*
is no trouble to me, and it is a safeguard
for you.

15 [2]Or *shine* [3]Or *luminaries, stars* [a]Luke 1:6; Phil 3:6 [b]Matt 5:45; Eph 5:1 [c]Deut 32:5; Acts 2:40 [d]Matt 5:14-16
16 [1]Or *forth* [a]Phil 1:6 [b]Gal 2:2 [c]Is 49:4; Gal 4:11; 1 Thess 3:5
17 [a]2 Cor 12:15; 2 Tim 4:6 [b]Num 28:6; Rom 15:16
19 [1]Or *trusting in* [a]Phil 2:23 [b]Phil 1:1
20 [a]1 Cor 16:10; 2 Tim 3:10
21 [a]1 Cor 10:24; Phil 2:4
22 [a]Rom 5:4; Acts 16:2 [b]Acts 16:3; 1 Cor 16:10; 2 Tim 3:10 [c]1 Cor 4:17
23 [a]Phil 2:19
24 [a]Phil 1:25
25 [1]Lit *apostle* [a]Phil 4:18 [b]Rom 16:3; Phil 4:3; Philem 1 [c]Philem 2 [d]John 13:16; 2 Cor 8:23
26 [1]One early ms reads *to see you all*
29 [a]Rom 16:2 [b]1 Cor 16:18
30 [1]Lit *because of* [2]Lit *your deficiency of service* [a]Acts 20:24 [b]1 Cor 16:17; Phil 4:10
3:1 [a]Phil 2:18
2 [1]Lit *mutilation*; Gr *katatome* [a]Ps 22:16; Gal 5:15; Rev 22:15 [b]2 Cor 11:13
3 [1]Gr *peritome* [a]Rom 2:29; Gal 6:15 [b]Gal 5:25 [c]Rom 15:17; Gal 6:14 [d]Rom 8:39; Phil 1:1
4 [a]2 Cor 5:16
5 [a]Luke 1:59 [b]Rom 11:1; 2 Cor 11:22 [c]Rom 11:1 [d]Acts 22:3
6 [a]Acts 8:3 [b]Phil 3:9 [c]Phil 2:15
7 [a]Luke 14:33
8 [1]Lit *because of* [2]Lit *the knowledge of* [a]Jer 9:23f; John 17:3; Eph 4:13; Phil 3:10; 2 Pet 1:3 [b]Rom 8:39; Phil 1:1
9 [a]Rom 10:5; Phil 3:6 [b]Rom 9:30; 1 Cor 1:30
10 [1]Or *participation in* [a]Jer 9:23f; John 17:3; Eph 4:13; Phil 3:8; 2 Pet 1:13 [b]Rom 6:5 [c]Rom 8:17 [d]Rom 6:5; Gal 6:17
11 [1]Lit *if somehow* [a]Acts 26:7; 1 Cor 15:23; Rev 20:5f
12 [1]Lit *if I may even* [2]Or *because also* [a]1 Cor 9:24f;

2 ¶ Beware of the [a]dogs, beware of
the [b]evil workers, beware of the [1]false
circumcision;
3 for [a]we are the *true* [1]circumci-
sion, who [b]worship in the Spirit of God
and [c]glory in [d]Christ Jesus and put no
confidence in the flesh,
4 although [a]I myself might have confidence even in the flesh. If anyone else
has a mind to put confidence in the flesh,
I far more:
5 [a]circumcised the eighth day, of the
[b]nation of Israel, of the [c]tribe of Benjamin, a [b]Hebrew of Hebrews; as to the
Law, [d]a Pharisee;
6 as to zeal, [a]a persecutor of the
church; as to the [b]righteousness which is
in the Law, found [c]blameless.
7 ¶ But [a]whatever things were gain
to me, those things I have counted as loss
for the sake of Christ.
8 More than that, I count all things to
be loss [1]in view of the surpassing value
of [2a]knowing [b]Christ Jesus my Lord,
[1]for whom I have suffered the loss of all
things, and count them but rubbish so
that I may gain Christ,
9 and may be found in Him, not having [a]a righteousness of my own derived
from *the* Law, but that which is through
faith in Christ, [b]the righteousness which
comes from God on the basis of faith,
10 that I may [a]know Him and [b]the
power of His resurrection and [1c]the fellowship of His sufferings, being [d]con-
formed to His death;
11 [1]in order that I may [a]attain to the
resurrection from the dead.
12 ¶ Not that I have already [a]obtained
it or have already [b]become perfect, but I
press on [1]so that I may [c]lay hold of that
[2]for which also I [d]was laid hold of by
[e]Christ Jesus.
13 Brethren, I do not regard myself as
having laid hold of *it* yet; but one thing
I do: [a]forgetting what *lies* behind and
reaching forward to what *lies* ahead,
14 I [a]press on toward the goal for the
prize of the [b]upward call of God in
[c]Christ Jesus.
15 Let us therefore, as many as are
[1a]perfect, have this attitude; and if in
anything you have a [b]different attitude,
[c]God will reveal that also to you;
16 however, let us keep [1a]living by
that same *standard* to which we have attained.
17 ¶ Brethren, [a]join in following my
example, and observe those who walk ac-

1 Tim 6:12 [b]1 Cor 13:10 [c]1 Tim 6:12 [d]Acts 9:5f [e]Rom 8:39; Phil 1:1 **13** [a]Luke 9:62 **14** [a]1 Cor 9:24; Heb 6:1 [b]Rom 8:28; 2 Tim 1:9 [c]Phil 3:3 **15** [1]Or *mature* [a]Matt 5:48; 1 Cor 2:6 [b]Gal 5:10 [c]John 6:45; Eph 1:17; 1 Thess 4:9 **16** [1]Lit *following in line* [a]Gal 6:16 **17** [a]1 Cor 4:16; Phil 4:9

cording to the [b]pattern you have in us.
18 For [a]many walk, of whom I often
told you, and now tell you even [b]weep-
ing, *that they are* enemies of [c]the cross
of Christ,
19 whose end is destruction, whose
god is *their* [1a]appetite, and *whose* [b]glo-
ry is in their shame, who [c]set their
minds on earthly things.
20 For [a]our [1]citizenship is in heaven,
from which also we eagerly [b]wait for a
Savior, the Lord Jesus Christ;
21 who will [a]transform [1]the body of
our humble state into [b]conformity with
[2]the [c]body of His glory, [d]by the exer-
tion of the power that He has even to
[e]subject all things to Himself.

Think of Excellence

4 Therefore, my beloved brethren
[1]whom I [a]long *to see,* my joy and
crown, in this way [b]stand firm in the
Lord, my beloved.
2 ¶ I urge Euodia and I urge Syntyche
to [1a]live in harmony in the Lord.
3 Indeed, true companion, I ask you
also to help these women who have
shared my struggle in *the cause of* the
gospel, together with Clement also and
the rest of my [a]fellow workers, whose
[b]names are in the book of life.
4 ¶ [a]Rejoice in the Lord always;
again I will say, rejoice!
5 Let your gentle *spirit* be known to
all men. [a]The Lord is [1]near.
6 [a]Be anxious for nothing, but in everything by [b]prayer and supplication
with thanksgiving let your requests be
made known to God.
7 And [a]the peace of God, which surpasses all [1]comprehension, will [b]guard
your hearts and your [c]minds in [d]Christ
Jesus.
8 ¶ Finally, brethren, [a]whatever is
true, whatever is honorable, whatever
is right, whatever is pure, whatever is
[1]lovely, whatever is of good repute, if
there is any excellence and if anything
worthy of praise, [2]dwell on these things.
9 The things you have learned and
received and heard and seen [a]in me,
practice these things, and [b]the God of
peace will be with you.

God's Provisions

10 ¶ But I rejoiced in the Lord greatly,
that now at last [a]you have revived your
concern for me; indeed, you were concerned *before,* but you lacked opportunity.
11 Not that I speak [1]from want, for I
have learned to be [2a]content in whatever circumstances I am.
12 I know how to get along with humble means, and I also know how to live
in prosperity; in any and every circumstance I have learned the secret of being
filled and going [a]hungry, both of having
abundance and [b]suffering need.
13 I can do all things [1]through Him
who [a]strengthens me.
14 Nevertheless, you have done well
to [a]share *with me* in my affliction.
15 ¶ You yourselves also know, Philippians, that at the [1a]first preaching of
the gospel, after I left [b]Macedonia, no
church [c]shared with me in the matter of
giving and receiving but you alone;
16 for even in [a]Thessalonica you sent
a gift more than once for my needs.
17 [a]Not that I seek the gift itself, but
I seek for the [1]profit which increases to
your account.
18 But I have received everything in
full and have an abundance; I am [1]amply
supplied, having received from [a]Epaph-
roditus [2]what you have sent, [3b]a fragrant aroma, an acceptable sacrifice,
well-pleasing to God.
19 And [a]my God will supply [1]all your
needs according to His [b]riches in glory in
Christ Jesus.
20 Now to [a]our God and Father [b]*be*
the glory [1]forever and ever. Amen.
21 ¶ Greet every [1]saint in Christ
Jesus. [a]The brethren who are with me
greet you.
22 [a]All the [1b]saints greet you, especially those of Caesar's household.
23 ¶ [a]The grace of the Lord Jesus
Christ [b]be with your spirit.

17 [b]1 Pet 5:3 **18** [a]2 Cor 11:13 [b]Acts 20:31 [c]Gal 6:14 **19** [1]Lit *belly* [a]Rom 16:18; Titus 1:12 [b]Rom 6:21; Jude 13 [c]Rom 8:5f; Col 3:2 **20** [1]Lit *commonwealth* [a]Eph 2:19; Phil 1:27; Col 3:1; Heb 12:22 [b]1 Cor 1:7 **21** [1]Or *our lowly body* [2]Or *His glorious body* [a]1 Cor 15:43-53 [b]Rom 8:29; Col 3:4 [c]1 Cor 15:43 [d]Eph 1:19 [e]1 Cor 15:28 **4:1** [1]Lit *and longed for* [a]Phil 1:8 [b]1 Cor 16:13; Phil 1:27 **2** [1]Or *be of the same mind* [a]Phil 2:2 **3** [a]Phil 2:25 [b]Luke 10:20 **4** [a]Phil 3:1 **5** [1]Or *at hand* [a]1 Cor 16:22 mg; Heb 10:37; James 5:8f **6** [a]Matt 6:25 [b]Eph 6:18; 1 Tim 2:1 **7** [1]Lit *mind* [a]Is 26:3; John 14:27; Phil 4:9; Col 3:15 [b]1 Pet 1:5 [c]2 Cor 10:5 [d]Phil 1:1 **8** [1]Or *lovable and gracious* [2]Lit *ponder these things* [a]Rom 14:18; 1 Pet 2:12 **9** [a]Phil 3:17 [b]Rom 15:33 **10** [a]2 Cor 11:9; Phil 2:30 **11** [1]Lit *according to* [2]Or *self-sufficient* [a]2 Cor 9:8; 1 Tim 6:6; Heb 13:5 **12** [a]1 Cor 4:11 [b]2 Cor 11:9 **13** [1]Lit *in* [a]2 Cor 12:9; Eph 3:16; Col 1:11 **14** [a]Heb 10:33; Rev 1:9 **15** [1]Lit *beginning of* [a]Phil 1:5 [b]Rom 15:26 [c]2 Cor 11:9 **16** [a]Acts 17:1; 1 Thess 2:9 **17** [1]Lit *fruit* [a]1 Cor 9:11f; 2 Cor 9:5 **18** [1]Lit *made full* [2]Lit *the things from you* [3]Lit *an odor of fragrance* [a]Phil 2:25 [b]Ex 29:18; 2 Cor 2:14; Eph 5:2 **19** [1]Or *every need of yours* [a]2 Cor 9:8 [b]Rom 2:4 **20** [1]Lit *to the ages of the ages* [a]Gal 1:4 [b]Rom 11:36 **21** [1]Or *holy one* [a]Gal 1:2 **22** [1]V 21, note 1 [a]2 Cor 13:13 [b]Acts 9:13 **23** [a]Rom 16:20 [b]2 Tim 4:22

Colossians

Title and Background

During Paul's three-year ministry in Ephesus, Epaphras had been converted and had carried the gospel to Colosse. The young church that resulted then became the target of heretical attack (the Colossian heresy), which led to Epaphras's visit to Paul in Rome and ultimately to the penning of this letter.

Author and Date of Writing

Some have argued that Paul wrote Colossians from Ephesus or Caesarea, but most of the evidence favors Rome as the place. It should be dated about A.D. 60, during Paul's first Roman imprisonment.

Theme and Message

Paul's purpose is to refute the Colossian heresy. To accomplish this goal, he exalts Jesus Christ and states that He is completely adequate. The theme is the complete adequacy of Christ as contrasted with the emptiness of mere human philosophy. In Christ we "have been made complete" (2:10).

Outline

I. Greetings, Thanksgiving and Prayer (1:1–14)
II. The Supremacy of Christ (1:15–23)
III. Paul's Labor for the Church (1:24—2:7)
IV. Freedom From Human Regulations Through Life With Christ (2:8–23)
V. Rules for Holy Living (3:1—4:6)
VI. Final Greetings and Conclusion (4:7–18)

Thankfulness for Spiritual Attainments

1 [a]Paul, [b]an apostle of Jesus Christ
[1c]by the will of God, and [d]Timothy
[2]our brother,
2 ¶ To the [1a]saints and faithful
brethren in Christ *who are* at Colossae:
[b]Grace to you and peace from God our
Father.
3 ¶ [a]We give thanks to God, [b]the
Father of our Lord Jesus Christ, praying
always for you,
4 [a]since we heard of your faith in
Christ Jesus and the [b]love which you
have [1]for [c]all the [2]saints;
5 because of the [a]hope [b]laid up for
you in [1]heaven, of which you previously
[c]heard in the word of truth, [2]the gospel
6 which has come to you, just as
[1a]in all the world also it is constantly
bearing [b]fruit and [2]increasing, even as *it
has been doing* in you also since the day
you [c]heard *of it* and [3]understood the
grace of God in truth;
7 just as you learned *it* from [a]Epa-
phras, our [b]beloved fellow bond-servant,
who is a faithful servant of Christ on our
behalf,
8 and he also informed us of your
[a]love in the Spirit.
9 ¶ For this reason also, [a]since the
day we heard *of it*, [b]we have not ceased
to pray for you and to ask that you may be
filled with the [1c]knowledge of His will
in all spiritual [d]wisdom and understanding,
10 so that you will [a]walk in a manner
worthy of the Lord, [1b]to please *Him* in
all respects, [c]bearing fruit in every good
work and [2]increasing in the [3]knowledge
of God;
11 [a]strengthened with all power, according to [1]His glorious might, [2]for the
attaining of all steadfastness and [3]pa-
tience; [b]joyously
12 giving thanks to [a]the Father, who
has qualified us [1]to share in [b]the inheritance of the [2]saints in [c]Light.

1:1 [1]Lit *through* [2]Lit *the* [a]Phil 1:1 [b]2 Cor 1:1 [c]1 Cor 1:1 [d]2 Cor 1:1; 1 Thess 3:2 **2** [1]Or *holy ones* [a]Acts 9:13 [b]Rom 1:7 **3** [a]Rom 1:8 [b]Rom 15:6; 2 Cor 1:3 **4** [1]Or *toward* [2]Or *holy ones* [a]Eph 1:15 [b]Gal 5:6 [c]Eph 6:18 **5** [1]Lit *the heavens* [2]Or *of the gospel* [a]Acts 23:6 [b]2 Tim 4:8 [c]Eph 1:13 **6** [1]Or *it is in the world* [2]Or *spreading abroad* [3]Or *came really to know* [a]Rom 10:18 [b]Rom 1:13 [c]Eph 4:21 **7** [a]Col 4:12 [b]Col 4:7 **8** [a]Rom 15:30 **9** [1]Or *real knowledge* [a]Col 1:4 [b]Eph 1:16 [c]Phil 1:9 [d]Eph 1:17 **10** [1]Lit *unto all pleasing* [2]Or *growing by the knowledge* [3]Or *real knowledge* [a]Eph 4:1 [b]Eph 5:10 [c]Rom 1:13 **11** [1]Lit *the might of His glory* [2]Lit *unto all* [3]Or *patience with joy* [a]1 Cor 16:13 [b]Eph 4:2 **12** [1]Lit *unto the portion of* [2]Or *holy ones* [a]Eph 2:18 [b]Acts 20:32 [c]Acts 26:18

The Incomparable Christ

13 [1]For He rescued us from the [2a]domain of darkness, and transferred us to the kingdom of [3b]His beloved Son,

14 [a]in whom we have redemption, the forgiveness of sins.

15 ¶ [1]He is the [a]image of the [b]invisible God, the [c]firstborn of all creation.

16 For [1a]by Him all things were created, [a]*both* in the heavens and on earth, visible and invisible, whether [b]thrones or dominions or rulers or authorities—[c]all things have been created through Him and for Him.

17 He [1a]is before all things, and in Him all things [2]hold together.

18 He is also [a]head of [b]the body, the church; and He is [c]the beginning, [d]the firstborn from the dead, so that He Himself will come to have first place in everything.

19 For [1]it was [a]the *Father's* good pleasure for all [b]the [2]fullness to dwell in Him,

20 and through Him to [a]reconcile all things to Himself, having made [b]peace through [c]the blood of His cross; through Him, *I say*, [d]whether things on earth or things in [1]heaven.

21 ¶ And although you were [a]formerly alienated and hostile in mind, *engaged* in evil deeds,

22 yet He has now [a]reconciled you in His fleshly [b]body through death, in order to [c]present you before Him [d]holy and blameless and beyond reproach—

23 if indeed you continue in [1]the faith firmly [a]established and steadfast, and not moved away from the [b]hope of the gospel that you have heard, which was proclaimed [c]in all creation under heaven, [d]and of which I, Paul, [2]was made a [3e]minister.

24 ¶ [a]Now I rejoice in my sufferings for your sake, and in my flesh [b]I [1]do my share on behalf of [c]His body, which is the church, in filling up what is lacking [2]in Christ's afflictions.

25 [a]Of *this church* I [1]was made a minister according to the [b]stewardship from God bestowed on me for your benefit, so that I might [2]fully carry out the *preaching of* the word of God,

26 *that is,* [a]the mystery which has been hidden from the *past* ages and generations, but has now been manifested to His [1]saints,

27 to whom [a]God willed to make known what is [b]the riches of the glory of this mystery among the Gentiles, which is [c]Christ in you, the [d]hope of glory.

28 We proclaim Him, [a]admonishing every man and teaching every man [1]with all [b]wisdom, so that we may [c]present every man [2d]complete in Christ.

29 For this purpose also I [a]labor, [b]striving [c]according to His [1]power, which [2]mightily works within me.

You Are Built Up in Christ

2 For I want you to know how great a [a]struggle I have on your behalf and for those who are at [b]Laodicea, and for all those who have not [1]personally seen my face,

2 that their [a]hearts may be encouraged, having been [b]knit together in love, and *attaining* to all [c]the wealth [1]that comes from the full assurance of understanding, *resulting* in a [d]true knowledge of [e]God's mystery, *that is,* Christ *Himself,*

3 in whom are hidden all [a]the treasures of wisdom and knowledge.

4 [a]I say this so that no one will delude you with [b]persuasive argument.

5 For even though I am [a]absent in body, nevertheless I am with you in spirit, rejoicing [1]to see [2]your [b]good discipline and the [c]stability of your faith in Christ.

6 ¶ Therefore as you have received [a]Christ Jesus the Lord, *so* [1b]walk in Him,

7 having been firmly [a]rooted *and now* being [b]built up in Him and [c]established [1]in your faith, just as you [d]were instructed, *and* overflowing [2]with gratitude.

8 ¶ [a]See to it that no one takes you captive through [b]philosophy and empty deception, according to the tradition of men, according to the [c]elementary principles of the world, [1]rather than according to Christ.

9 For in Him all the [a]fullness of Deity dwells in bodily form,

10 and in Him you have been [a]made [1]complete, and [b]He is the head [2]over all [c]rule and authority;

11 and in Him [a]you were also circumcised with a circumcision made without hands, in the removal of [b]the body of the flesh by the circumcision of Christ;

12 having been [a]buried with Him in baptism, in which you were also [b]raised up with Him through faith in the working of God, who [c]raised Him from the dead.

13 When you were [a]dead [1]in your transgressions and the uncircumcision of

1:13 [1]Lit *Who rescued* [2]Lit *authority* [3]Lit *the Son of His love* [a]Eph 6:12 [b]Eph 1:6 **14** [a]Rom 3:24 **15** [1]Lit *Who is* [a]2 Cor 4:4 [b]John 1:1 [c]Rom 8:29 **16** [1]Or *in* [a]Eph 1:10 [b]Eph 1:20f; Col 2:15 [c]John 1:3; Rom 11:36; 1 Cor 8:6 **17** [1]Or *has existed prior to* [2]Or *endure* [a]John 1:1 **18** [a]Eph 1:22 [b]Eph 1:23; Col 1:24 [c]Rev 3:14 [d]Acts 26:23 **19** [1]Or *all the fullness was pleased to dwell* [2]I.e. fullness of deity [a]Eph 1:5 [b]John 1:16 **20** [1]Lit *the heavens* [a]2 Cor 5:18; Eph 2:16 [b]Rom 5:1; Eph 2:14 [c]Eph 2:13 [d]Col 1:16 **21** [a]Rom 5:10; Eph 2:3 **22** [a]2 Cor 5:18; Eph 2:16 [b]Rom 7:4 [c]Eph 5:27; Col 1:28 [d]Eph 1:4 **23** [1]Or *in faith* [2]Lit *became* [3]Or *servant* [a]Eph 3:17; Col 2:7 [b]Col 1:5 [c]Mark 16:15; Acts 2:5; Col 1:6 [d]Eph 3:7; Col 1:25 [e]1 Cor 3:5 **24** [1]Or *representatively...fill up* [2]Lit *of* [a]Rom 8:17; 2 Cor 1:5; Phil 2:17 [b]2 Tim 1:8 [c]Col 1:18 **25** [1]Lit *became* [2]Lit *make full the word of God* [a]Col 1:23 [b]Eph 3:2 **26** [1]Or *holy ones* [a]Rom 16:25f; Eph 3:3f; Col 2:2 **27** [a]Matt 13:11 [b]Eph 1:7 [c]Rom 8:10 [d]1 Tim 1:1 **28** [1]Lit *in* [2]Or *perfect* [a]Acts 20:31; Col 3:16 [b]1 Cor 2:6f; Col 2:3 [c]Col 1:22 [d]Matt 5:48; Eph 4:13 **29** [1]Lit *working* [2]Lit *in power* [a]1 Cor 15:10 [b]Col 2:1 [c]Eph 1:19; Col 2:12 **2:1** [1]Lit *in the flesh* [a]Col 1:29 [b]Col 4:13; Rev 1:11 **2** [1]Lit *of the full assurance* [a]1 Cor 14:31; Eph 6:22; Col 4:8 [b]Col 2:19 [c]Eph 1:7 [d]Matt 13:11 [e]Rom 16:25f; Eph 3:3f; Col 1:26 **3** [a]Is 11:2; Rom 11:33 **4** [a]Eph 4:17 [b]Rom 16:18 **5** [1]Lit *and seeing* [2]Or *your good order* [a]1 Cor 5:3 [b]1 Cor 14:40 [c]1 Pet 5:9 **6** [1]Or *lead your life* [a]Gal 3:26 [b]Col 1:10 **7** [1]Or *by* [2]One early ms reads *in it with* [a]Eph 3:17 [b]1 Cor 3:9; Eph 2:20 [c]1 Cor 1:8 [d]Eph 4:21 **8** [1]Lit *and not* [a]1 Cor 8:9; Gal 5:15; Heb 3:12 [b]Eph 5:6; Col 2:23; 1 Tim 6:20 [c]Gal 4:3; Col 2:20 **9** [a]2 Cor 5:19; Col 1:19 **10** [1]Lit *full* [2]Lit *of* [a]Eph 3:19 [b]Eph 1:21f [c]1 Cor 15:24; Eph 3:10; Col 2:15 **11** [a]Rom 2:29; Eph 2:11 [b]Rom 6:6; Gal 5:24; Col 3:5 **12** [a]Rom 6:4f [b]Rom 6:5; Eph 2:6; Col 2:13 [c]Acts 2:24 **13** [1]Or *by reason of* [a]Eph 2:1

your flesh, He [b]made you alive together
with Him, having forgiven us all our
transgressions,
14 having canceled out [a]the certificate of debt consisting of decrees against
us, which was hostile to us; and [b]He has
taken it out of the way, having nailed it to
the cross.
15 When He had [1a]disarmed the
[b]rulers and authorities, He [a]made a public display of them, having [c]triumphed
over them through [2]Him.
16 ¶ Therefore no one is to [1a]act as
your judge in regard to [b]food or [b]drink
or in respect to a [c]festival or a [d]new
moon or a [e]Sabbath [2]day—
17 things which are [a]a *mere* shadow
of what is to come; but the [1]substance
[2]belongs to Christ.
18 Let no one keep [1a]defrauding you
of your prize by [b]delighting in [2]self-
abasement and the worship of the angels,
[3]taking his stand on *visions* he has seen,
[4c]inflated without cause by his [d]fleshly
mind,
19 and not holding fast to [a]the head,
from whom [b]the entire body, being supplied and held together by the joints and
[1]ligaments, grows with a growth [2]which
is from God.
20 ¶ [a]If you have died with Christ [1]to
the [b]elementary principles of the world,
[c]why, as if you were living in the world,
do you submit yourself to [d]decrees,
such as,
21 "Do not handle, do not taste, do not
touch!"
22 (which all *refer* [a]*to* things destined
to perish [1]with use)—in accordance
with the [b]commandments and teachings
of men?
23 These are matters which have, to
be sure, the [1]appearance of wisdom in
[2a]self-made religion and self-abasement
and [b]severe treatment of the body, *but
are* of no value against [c]fleshly indulgence.

Put On the New Self

3 Therefore if you have been [a]raised
up with Christ, keep seeking the
things above, where Christ is, [b]seated at
the right hand of God.
2 [1a]Set your mind on the things
above, not on the things that are on
earth.
3 For you have [a]died and your life is
hidden with Christ in God.
4 When Christ, [a]who is our life, is
revealed, [b]then you also will be revealed
with Him in glory.
5 ¶ [a]Therefore [1]consider [b]the members of your earthly body as dead to [2c]im-
morality, impurity, passion, evil desire
and greed, which [3]amounts to idolatry.
6 For it is because of these things that
[a]the wrath of God will come [1]upon the
sons of disobedience,
7 and [a]in them you also once
walked, when you were living [1]in them.
8 But now you also, [a]put them all
aside: [b]anger, wrath, malice, slander,
and [c]abusive speech from your mouth.
9 [1a]Do not lie to one another, since
you [b]laid aside the old [2]self with its *evil*
practices,
10 and have [a]put on the new self who
is being [1b]renewed to a true knowledge
[c]according to the image of the One who
[d]created him—
11 *a renewal* in which [a]there is no
distinction between Greek and Jew, [b]cir-
cumcised and uncircumcised, [1c]barbari-
an, Scythian, [d]slave and freeman, but
[e]Christ is all, and in all.
12 ¶ So, as those who have been [a]cho-
sen of God, holy and beloved, [b]put on a
[c]heart of compassion, kindness, [d]humil-
ity, gentleness and [1e]patience;
13 [a]bearing with one another, and
[b]forgiving each other, whoever has a
complaint against anyone; [b]just as the
Lord forgave you, so also should you.
14 Beyond all these things *put on* love,
which is [1a]the perfect bond of [b]unity.
15 Let [a]the peace of Christ [1]rule in
your hearts, to which [2]indeed you were
called in [b]one body; and [3]be thankful.
16 Let [a]the word of [1]Christ richly
dwell within you, [2]with all wisdom
[b]teaching and admonishing [3]one another [c]with psalms *and* hymns *and* spiritual
songs, [d]singing [4]with thankfulness in
your hearts to God.
17 [a]Whatever you do in word or deed,
do all in the name of the Lord Jesus, [b]giv-
ing thanks through Him to God the Father.

Family Relations

18 ¶ [a]Wives, [b]be subject to your husbands, as is fitting in the Lord.
19 [a]Husbands, love your wives and do
not be embittered against them.
20 [a]Children, be obedient to your par-

13 [b]Eph 2:5; Col 2:12 **14** [a]Eph 2:15; Col 2:20 [b]1 Pet 2:24 **15** [1]Or *divested Himself of* [2]Or *it;* i.e. the cross [a]Eph 4:8 [b]John 12:31; 1 Cor 15:24; Eph 3:10; Col 2:10 [c]2 Cor 2:14 **16** [1]Lit *judge you* [2]Or *days* [a]Rom 14:3 [b]Mark 7:19; Rom 14:17; Heb 9:10 [c]Lev 23:2; Rom 14:5 [d]1 Chr 23:31; 2 Chr 31:3; Neh 10:33 [e]Mark 2:27f; Gal 4:10 **17** [1]Lit *body* [2]Lit *of Christ* [a]Heb 8:5 **18** [1]Or *deciding against you* [2]Or *humility* [3]Or *going into detail about* [4]Or *conceited* [a]1 Cor 9:24; Phil 3:14 [b]Col 2:23 [c]1 Cor 4:6 [d]Rom 8:7 **19** [1]Lit *bonds* [2]Lit *of God* [a]Eph 1:22 [b]Eph 1:23 **20** [1]Lit *from* [a]Rom 6:2 [b]Col 2:8 [c]Gal 4:9 [d]Col 2:14 **22** [1]Or *by being consumed* [a]1 Cor 6:13 [b]Is 29:13; Matt 15:9; Titus 1:14 **23** [1]Lit *report;* Gr *logos* [2]Or *would-be religion* [a]Col 2:18 [b]1 Tim 4:3 [c]Rom 13:14; 1 Tim 4:8 **3:1** [a]Col 2:12 [b]Ps 110:1; Mark 16:19 **2** [1]Or *Be intent on* [a]Matt 16:23; Phil 3:19 **3** [a]Rom 6:2; 2 Cor 5:14; Col 2:20 **4** [a]John 11:25; Gal 2:20 [b]1 Cor 1:7; Phil 3:21; 1 Pet 1:13; 1 John 2:28 **5** [1]Lit *put to death the members which are upon the earth* [2]Lit *fornication* [3]Lit *is* [a]Rom 8:13 [b]Col 2:11 [c]Mark 7:21f; 1 Cor 6:9f; 2 Cor 12:21; Gal 5:19f; Eph 4:19 **6** [1]Two early mss do not contain *upon the sons of disobedience* [a]Rom 1:18; Eph 5:6 **7** [1]Or *among these* [a]Eph 2:2 **8** [a]Eph 4:22 [b]Eph 4:31 [c]Eph 4:29 **9** [1]Or *Stop lying* [2]Gr *anthropos* [a]Eph 4:25 [b]Eph 4:22 **10** [1]Lit *renovated* [a]Eph 4:24 [b]Rom 12:2; 2 Cor 4:16; Eph 4:23 [c]Gen 1:26; Rom 8:29 [d]Eph 2:10 **11** [1]I.e. those who were not Greeks, either by birth or by culture [a]Rom 10:12; 1 Cor 12:13; Gal 3:28 [b]1 Cor 7:19; Gal 5:6 [c]Acts 28:2 [d]Eph 6:8 [e]Eph 1:23 **12** [1]I.e. forbearance toward others [a]Luke 18:7 [b]Eph 4:24 [c]Luke 1:78; Gal 5:22f; Phil 2:1 [d]Eph 4:2; Phil 2:3 [e]1 Cor 13:4; 2 Cor 6:6 **13** [a]Eph 4:2 [b]Rom 15:7; Eph 4:32 **14** [1]Lit *the uniting bond of perfection* [a]Eph 4:3 [b]John 17:23; Heb 6:1 **15** [1]Or *act as arbiter* [2]Lit *also* [3]Or *show yourselves thankful* [a]John 14:27 [b]Eph 2:16 **16** [1]One early ms reads *the Lord* [2]Or *in* [3]Or *one another, singing with psalms...* [4]Or *by;* lit *in His grace* [a]Rom 10:17; Eph 5:26; 1 Thess 1:8 [b]Col 1:28 [c]Eph 5:19 [d]1 Cor 14:15 **17** [a]1 Cor 10:31 [b]Eph 5:20; Col 3:15 **18** [a]Col 3:18-4:1: *Eph 5:22-6:9* [b]Eph 5:22 **19** [a]Eph 5:25; 1 Pet 3:7 **20** [a]Eph 6:1

11 Therefore [1]encourage one another
and [a]build up one another, just as you
also are doing.

Christian Conduct

12 ¶ But we request of you, brethren,
that you [1a]appreciate those [b]who diligently labor among you, and [c]have
charge over you in the Lord and give you
[2]instruction,
13 and that you esteem them very
highly in love because of their work.
[a]Live in peace with one another.
14 We urge you, brethren, admonish
[a]the [1]unruly, encourage [b]the fainthearted, help [c]the weak, be [d]patient
with everyone.
15 See that [a]no one repays another
with evil for evil, but always [b]seek after
that which is good for one another and for
all people.
16 [a]Rejoice always;
17 [a]pray without ceasing;
18 in everything [a]give thanks; for this
is God's will for you in Christ Jesus.
19 [a]Do not quench the Spirit;
20 do not despise [a]prophetic [1]utter-
ances.
21 But [a]examine everything *carefully*;
[b]hold fast to that which is good;
22 abstain from every [1]form of evil.
23 ¶ Now [a]may the God of peace
[b]Himself sanctify you entirely; and may
your [c]spirit and soul and body be preserved complete, [d]without blame at
[e]the coming of our Lord Jesus Christ.
24 [a]Faithful is He who [b]calls you, and
He also will bring it to pass.
25 ¶ Brethren, [a]pray for us[1].
26 ¶ [a]Greet all the brethren with a
holy kiss.
27 I adjure you by the Lord to [a]have
this letter read to all the [b]brethren.
28 ¶ [a]The grace of our Lord Jesus
Christ be with you.

11 [1]Or *comfort* [a]Eph 4:29 **12** [1]Lit *know* [2]Or *admonition* [a]1 Cor 16:18; 1 Tim 5:17 [b]Rom 16:6; 1 Cor 15:10 [c]Heb 13:17 **13** [a]Mark 9:50 **14** [1]Or *undisciplined* [a]2 Thess 3:6 [b]Is 35:4 [c]Rom 14:1f; 1 Cor 8:7ff; Rom 15:1 [d]1 Cor 13:4 **15** [a]Matt 5:44; Rom 12:17; 1 Pet 3:9 [b]Rom 12:9; Gal 6:10; 1 Thess 5:21 **16** [a]Phil 4:4 **17** [a]Eph 6:18 **18** [a]Eph 5:20 **19** [a]Eph 4:30 **20** [1]Or *gifts* [a]Acts 13:1; 1 Cor 14:31 **21** [a]1 Cor 14:29; 1 John 4:1 [b]Rom 12:9; Gal 6:10; 1 Thess 5:15 **22** [1]Or *appearance* **23** [a]Rom 15:33 [b]1 Thess 3:11 [c]Luke 1:46f; Heb 4:12 [d]James 1:4; 2 Pet 3:14 [e]1 Thess 2:19 **24** [a]1 Cor 1:9; 2 Thess 3:3 [b]1 Thess 2:12 **25** [1]Two early mss add *also* [a]Eph 6:19; 2 Thess 3:1; Heb 13:18 **26** [a]Rom 16:16 **27** [a]Col 4:16 [b]Acts 1:15 **28** [a]Rom 16:20; 2 Thess 3:18

2 Thessalonians

Title and Background

See Introduction to 1 Thessalonians.

Author and Date of Writing

Because of its similarity to 1 Thessalonians, it must have been written not long after the first letter, about A.D. 51 or 52.

Theme and Message

Like 1 Thessalonians, this letter deals extensively with eschatology. In fact, in 2 Thessalonians eighteen of the forty-seven verses deal with this subject. Some people had misunderstood Paul and were sure Jesus was coming very soon. In fact, they had stopped working and were just waiting for Jesus to return. Paul writes to correct this misunderstanding.

Outline

I. Greetings, Thanksgiving and Prayer (1:1–12)
II. Instruction on Jesus' Coming and Christian Conduct (2:1–17)
III. Request for Prayer and Warning Against Idleness (3:1–15)
IV. Final Greetings and Benediction (3:16–18)

Thanksgiving for Faith and Perseverance

1 [a]Paul and [b]Silvanus and [c]Timothy,
¶ To the [d]church of the Thessalonians in God our Father and the Lord Jesus
Christ:
2 [a]Grace to you and peace from God
the Father and the Lord Jesus Christ.
3 ¶ We ought always [a]to give thanks
to God for you, [b]brethren, as is *only*
fitting, because your faith is greatly
enlarged, and the [c]love of each one of
you toward one another grows *ever*
greater;
4 therefore, we ourselves [a]speak
proudly of you among [b]the churches of
God for your [1]perseverance and faith [b]in
the midst of all your persecutions and afflictions which you endure.
5 *This is* a [a]plain indication of God's
righteous judgment so that you will be
[b]considered worthy of the kingdom of
God, for which indeed you are suffering.
6 [1]For after all [a]it is *only* just [2]for
God to repay with affliction those who
afflict you,
7 and *to give* relief to you who are
afflicted [1]and to us as well [2a]when the
Lord Jesus will be revealed [b]from heaven
[c]with [3]His mighty angels [d]in flaming
fire,
8 dealing out retribution to those
who [a]do not know God and to those who
[b]do not obey the gospel of our Lord
Jesus.
9 These will pay the penalty of [a]eter-
nal destruction, [b]away from the presence of the Lord and from the glory of His
power,
10 when He comes to be [a]glorified
[1]in His [2]saints on that [b]day, and to
be marveled at among all who have believed—for our [c]testimony to you was
believed.
11 To this end also we [a]pray for you
always, that our God will [1b]count you
worthy of your [c]calling, and fulfill every
desire for [d]goodness and the [e]work of
faith with power,
12 so that the [a]name of our Lord Jesus
will be glorified in you, and you in Him,
according to the grace of our God and *the*
Lord Jesus Christ.

Man of Lawlessness

2 Now we request you, [a]brethren,
with regard to the [1b]coming of our
Lord Jesus Christ and our [c]gathering together to Him,
2 that you not be quickly shaken from
your [1]composure or be disturbed either

1:1 [a]1 Thess 1:1 [b]2 Cor 1:19 [c]Acts 16:1 [d]Acts 17:1; 1 Thess 1:1 **2** [a]Rom 1:7 **3** [a]Rom 1:8; Eph 5:20; 1 Thess 1:2; 2 Thess 2:13 [b]1 Thess 4:1; 2 Thess 2:1 [c]1 Thess 3:12 **4** [1]Or *steadfastness* [a]2 Cor 7:4; 1 Thess 2:19 [b]1 Cor 7:17; 1 Thess 2:14 **5** [a]Phil 1:28 [b]Luke 20:35; 2 Thess 1:11 **6** [1]Lit *If indeed* [2]Or *in the sight of* [a]Ex 23:22; Col 3:25; Heb 6:10 **7** [1]Lit *along with us* [2]Lit *at the revelation of the Lord Jesus* [3]Lit *the angels of His power* [a]Luke 17:30 [b]1 Thess 4:16 [c]Jude 14 [d]Ex 3:2; Is 66:15; Ezek 1:13; Dan 7:9; Matt 25:41; 1 Cor 3:13; Heb 10:27; 2 Pet 3:7; Jude 7; Rev 14:10 **8** [a]Gal 4:8 [b]Rom 2:8 **9** [a]Phil 3:19; 1 Thess 5:3 [b]Is 2:10; 2 Thess 2:8 **10** [1]Or *in the persons of* [2]Or *holy ones* [a]Is 49:3; John 17:10; 1 Thess 2:12 [b]Is 2:11ff; 1 Cor 3:13 [c]1 Cor 1:6; 1 Thess 2:1 **11** [1]Or *make* [a]Col 1:9 [b]2 Thess 1:5 [c]Rom 11:29 [d]Rom 15:14 [e]1 Thess 1:3 **12** [a]Is 24:15; Mal 1:11; Phil 2:9ff **2:1** [1]Or *presence* [a]2 Thess 1:3 [b]1 Thess 2:19 [c]Mark 13:27; 1 Thess 4:15-17 **2** [1]Lit *mind*

by a [a]spirit or a [2b]message or a [c]letter
as if from us, to the effect that [d]the day
of the Lord [e]has come.
3 [a]Let no one in any way deceive
you, for *it will not come* unless the
[1b]apostasy comes first, and the [c]man of
lawlessness is revealed, the [d]son of destruction,
4 who opposes and exalts himself
above [1a]every so-called god or object of
worship, so that he takes his seat in the
temple of God, [b]displaying himself as being God.
5 Do you not remember that [a]while
I was still with you, I was telling you
these things?
6 And you know [a]what restrains him
now, so that in his time he will be revealed.
7 For [a]the mystery of lawlessness is
already at work; only [b]he who now restrains *will do so* until he is taken out of
the way.
8 Then that lawless one [a]will be revealed whom the Lord will slay [b]with the
breath of His mouth and bring to an end
by the [c]appearance of His [1]coming;
9 *that is,* the one whose [1]coming is
in accord with the activity of [a]Satan,
with all power and [2b]signs and false
wonders,
10 and with [1]all the deception of
wickedness for [a]those who perish, because they did not receive the love of
[b]the truth so as to be saved.
11 For this reason [a]God [1]will send
upon them [2]a [b]deluding influence so
that they will believe [3]what is false,
12 in order that they all may be
[1]judged who [a]did not believe the truth,
but [2b]took pleasure in wickedness.
13 ¶ [a]But we should always give
thanks to God for you, [b]brethren beloved
by the Lord, because [c]God has chosen
you [1]from the beginning [d]for salvation
[2e]through sanctification [3]by the Spirit
and faith in the truth.
14 It was for this He [a]called you
through [b]our gospel, [1]that you may gain
the glory of our Lord Jesus Christ.
15 So then, brethren, [a]stand firm and
[b]hold to the traditions which you were
taught, whether [c]by word *of mouth* or
[c]by letter [1]from us.
16 ¶ [a]Now may our Lord Jesus Christ
[a]Himself and God our Father, who has
[b]loved us and given us eternal comfort
and [c]good hope by grace,
17 [a]comfort and [b]strengthen your
hearts in every good work and word.

Exhortation

3 [a]Finally, brethren, [b]pray for us that
[c]the word of the Lord will [1]spread
rapidly and be glorified, just as *it did* also
with you;
2 and that we will be [a]rescued from
[1]perverse and evil men; for not all have
[2]faith.
3 But [a]the Lord is faithful, [1]and He
will strengthen and protect you [2]from
[b]the evil *one.*
4 We have [a]confidence in the Lord
concerning you, that you [b]are doing
and will *continue to* do what we command.
5 May the Lord [a]direct your hearts
into the love of God and into the steadfastness of Christ.
6 ¶ Now we command you, brethren, [a]in the name of our Lord Jesus
Christ, that you [1b]keep away from every
brother who [2]leads an [3c]unruly life and
not according to [d]the tradition which
[4]you received from us.
7 For you yourselves know how you
ought to [1a]follow our example, because
we did not act in an undisciplined manner among you,
8 nor did we [a]eat [1]anyone's bread
[2]without paying for it, but with [b]labor
and hardship we *kept* [c]working night
and day so that we would not be a burden
to any of you;
9 not because we do not have [a]the
right *to this,* but in order to offer ourselves [b]as a model for you, so that you
would [1]follow our example.
10 For even [a]when we were with
you, we used to give you this order: [b]if
anyone is not willing to work, then he is
not to eat, either.
11 For we hear that some among you
are [a]leading an undisciplined life, doing
no work at all, but acting like [b]busybod-
ies.
12 Now such persons we command
and [a]exhort in the Lord Jesus Christ to
[b]work in quiet fashion and eat their own
bread.
13 But as for you, [a]brethren, [b]do not
grow weary of doing good.
14 ¶ If anyone does not obey our [1]in-
struction [2a]in this letter, take special
note of that person [3b]and do not associate with him, so that he will be [c]put to
shame.
15 *Yet* [a]do not regard him as an enemy, but [1b]admonish him as a [c]brother.

2 [2]Lit *word* [a]1 Cor 14:32; 1 John 4:1 [b]1 Thess 5:2; 2 Thess 2:15 [c]2 Thess 3:17 [d]1 Cor 1:8 [e]1 Cor 7:26
3 [1]Or *falling away* from the faith [a]Eph 5:6 [b]1 Tim 4:1 [c]Dan 7:25; 2 Thess 2:8; Rev 13:5ff [d]John 17:12
4 [1]Or *everyone who is called God* [a]1 Cor 8:5 [b]Is 14:14; Ezek 28:2
5 [a]1 Thess 3:4
6 [a]2 Thess 2:7
7 [a]Rev 17:5 [b]2 Thess 2:6
8 [1]Or *presence* [a]Dan 7:25; 2 Thess 2:3; Rev 13:5ff [b]Is 11:4; Rev 2:16 [c]1 Tim 6:14; 2 Tim 1:10; Titus 2:13
9 [1]Or *presence* [2]Or *attesting miracles* [a]Matt 4:10 [b]Matt 24:24; John 4:48
10 [1]Or *every deception* [a]1 Cor 1:18 [b]2 Thess 2:12
11 [1]Lit *is sending* [2]Lit *an activity of error* [3]Or *the lie* [a]1 Kin 22:22; Rom 1:28 [b]1 Thess 2:3; 2 Tim 4:4
12 [1]Or *condemned* [2]Or *approved* [a]Rom 2:8 [b]Rom 1:32; 1 Cor 13:6
13 [1]One early ms reads *first fruits* [2]Lit *in* [3]Lit *of* [a]2 Thess 1:3 [b]1 Thess 1:4 [c]Eph 1:4ff [d]1 Cor 1:21; 1 Thess 2:12; 1 Pet 1:5 [e]1 Thess 4:7; 1 Pet 1:2
14 [1]Lit *to the gaining of* [a]1 Thess 2:12 [b]1 Thess 1:5
15 [1]Lit *of* [a]1 Cor 16:13 [b]1 Cor 11:2; 2 Thess 3:6 [c]2 Thess 2:2
16 [a]1 Thess 3:11 [b]John 3:16 [c]Titus 3:7; 1 Pet 1:3
17 [a]1 Thess 3:2 [b]2 Thess 3:3
3:1 [1]Lit *run* [a]1 Thess 4:1 [b]1 Thess 5:25 [c]1 Thess 1:8
2 [1]Lit *improper* [2]Or *the faith* [a]Rom 15:31
3 [1]Lit *who will* [2]Or *from evil* [a]1 Cor 1:9; 1 Thess 5:24 [b]Matt 5:37
4 [a]2 Cor 2:3 [b]1 Thess 4:10
5 [a]1 Thess 3:11
6 [1]Or *avoid* [2]Lit *walks disorderly* [3]Or *undisciplined* [4]One early ms reads *they* [a]1 Cor 5:4 [b]Rom 16:17; 1 Cor 5:11; 2 Thess 3:14 [c]1 Thess 5:14; 2 Thess 3:7 [d]1 Cor 11:2; 2 Thess 2:15
7 [1]Lit *imitate us* [a]1 Thess 1:6; 2 Thess 3:9
8 [1]Lit *from anyone* [2]Lit *freely* [a]1 Cor 9:4 [b]1 Thess 2:9 [c]Acts 18:3; Eph 4:28
9 [1]Lit *imitate us* [a]1 Cor 9:4ff [b]2 Thess 3:7
10 [a]1 Thess 3:4 [b]1 Thess 4:11
11 [a]2 Thess 3:6 [b]1 Tim 5:13; 1 Pet 4:15
12 [a]1 Thess 4:1 [b]1 Thess 4:11
13 [a]1 Thess 4:1 [b]2 Cor 4:1; Gal 6:9
14 [1]Lit *word* [2]Lit *through* [3]Lit *not to associate* [a]Col 4:16 [b]2 Thess 3:6 [c]1 Cor 4:14
15 [1]Or *keep admonishing* [a]Gal 6:1 [b]1 Thess 5:14 [c]2 Thess 3:6

16 ¶ Now [a]may the Lord of peace
[b]Himself continually grant you peace in
every [1]circumstance. [c]The Lord be with
you all!
17 ¶ [1]I, Paul, write this greeting
[a]with my own hand, and this is a distinguishing mark in every letter; this is the
way I write.
18 [a]The grace of our Lord Jesus Christ
be with you all.

16 [1]Lit *way* [a]Rom 15:33 [b]1 Thess 3:11 [c]Ruth 2:4

17 [1]Lit *The greeting by my hand of Paul* [a]1 Cor 16:21

18 [a]Rom 16:20; 1 Thess 5:28

1 Timothy

Title and Background

During his fourth missionary journey, Paul had instructed Timothy to care for the church at Ephesus while he went on to Macedonia. When Paul realized he might not return to Ephesus in the near future, he wrote this first letter to Timothy. He repeatedly states his desire and determination to visit Timothy, which shows he was not in prison when he wrote the letter.

Author and Date of Writing

Both early church tradition and the salutations of the Pastoral Letters (1,2 Timothy, Titus) themselves confirm Paul as the author of this letter. 1 Timothy was written about A.D. 64, at least eight years after Paul's three-year stay in Ephesus.

Theme and Message

The letter was written to Timothy to give him instructions regarding the church. Paul wrote to develop the charge he had given his young assistant: to refute false teachings and to supervise the affairs of the growing Ephesian church. A major problem in this church was a heresy that combined Gnosticism (whose central teaching was that spirit is entirely good and matter is entirely evil), decadent Judaism and false asceticism (with its belief that the body should be treated harshly).

Outline

I. Warning Against False Teachers (1:1–11)
II. The Lord's Grace to Paul (1:12–17)
III. The Purpose of Paul's Instructions (1:18–20)
IV. Instructions for the Church (2:1—3:16)
V. Dealing With False Teachers (4:1–16)
VI. Dealing With Different Groups (5:1—6:2)
VII. Miscellaneous Matters (6:3–21)

Misleadings in Doctrine and Living

1 Paul, [a]an apostle of [b]Christ Jesus [c]according to the commandment of [c]God our Savior, and of [b]Christ Jesus, *who is* our [d]hope,

2 ¶ To [a]Timothy, [a]*my* true child in *the* faith: [b]Grace, mercy *and* peace from God the Father and [c]Christ Jesus our Lord.

3 ¶ As I urged you [1]upon my departure for [a]Macedonia, [2]remain on at [b]Ephesus so that you may instruct certain men not to [c]teach strange doctrines,

4 nor to [1]pay attention to [a]myths and endless [b]genealogies, which give rise to mere [c]speculation rather than [d]*furthering* [2]the administration of God which is by faith.

5 But the goal of our [1a]instruction is love [b]from a pure heart and a [c]good conscience and a sincere [d]faith.

6 For some men, straying from these things, have turned aside to [a]fruitless discussion,

7 [a]wanting to be [b]teachers of the Law, even though they do not understand either what they are saying or the matters about which they make confident assertions.

8 ¶ But we know that [a]the Law is good, if one uses it lawfully,

9 realizing the fact that [a]law is not made for a righteous person, but for those who are lawless and [b]rebellious, for the [c]ungodly and sinners, for the unholy and [d]profane, for those who kill their fathers or mothers, for murderers

10 [1]and [2a]immoral men [1]and [b]homosexuals [1]and [c]kidnappers [1]and [d]liars [1]and [e]perjurers, and whatever else is contrary to [f]sound teaching,

11 according to [a]the glorious gospel of [b]the blessed God, with which I have been [c]entrusted.

12 ¶ I thank [a]Christ Jesus our Lord, who has [b]strengthened me, because He

1:1 [a]2 Cor 1:1 [b]1 Tim 1:12 [c]Titus 1:3 [d]Col 1:27
2 [a]2 Tim 1:2 [b]Rom 1:7; 2 Tim 1:2; Titus 1:4 [c]1 Tim 1:12
3 [1]Lit *while going to* [2]Lit *to remain* [a]Rom 15:26 [b]Acts 18:19 [c]Rom 16:17; 2 Cor 11:4; Gal 1:6f; 1 Tim 6:3
4 [1]Or *occupy themselves with* [2]Lit *God's provision* [a]1 Tim 4:7; 2 Tim 4:4; Titus 1:14; 2 Pet 1:16 [b]Titus 3:9 [c]2 Tim 2:23 [d]Eph 3:2
5 [1]Lit *commandment* [a]1 Tim 1:18 [b]2 Tim 2:22 [c]1 Tim 1:19; 2 Tim 1:3; 1 Pet 3:16 [d]2 Tim 1:5
6 [a]Titus 1:10
7 [a]James 3:1 [b]Luke 2:46
8 [a]Rom 7:12
9 [a]Gal 5:23 [b]Titus 1:6 [c]1 Pet 4:18; Jude 15 [d]1 Tim 4:7; Heb 12:16
10 [1]Lit *for* [2]Or *fornicators* [a]1 Cor 6:9 [b]Lev 18:22 [c]Ex 21:16; Rev 18:13 [d]Rev 21:8 [e]Matt 5:33 [f]1 Tim 4:6; 2 Tim 4:3; Titus 1:9
11 [a]2 Cor 4:4 [b]1 Tim 6:15 [c]Gal 2:7
12 [a]Gal 3:26 [b]Acts 9:22; Phil 4:13; 2 Tim 4:17

considered me faithful, [c]putting me into
service,
13 even though I was formerly a blas-
phemer and a [a]persecutor and a violent
aggressor. Yet I was [b]shown mercy because [c]I acted ignorantly in unbelief;
14 and the [a]grace of our Lord was
more than abundant, with the [b]faith and
love which are *found* in Christ Jesus.
15 [a]It is a trustworthy statement, deserving full acceptance, that [b]Christ
Jesus came into the world to [c]save sinners, among whom [d]I am foremost *of all.*
16 Yet for this reason I [a]found mercy,
so that in me as the foremost, Jesus Christ
might [b]demonstrate His perfect patience
as an example for those [1]who would believe in Him for eternal life.
17 Now to the [a]King [1]eternal, [b]im-
mortal, [c]invisible, the [d]only God, [e]*be*
honor and glory [2]forever and ever.
Amen.
18 ¶ This [a]command I entrust to you,
Timothy, [b]*my* [1]son, in accordance with
the [c]prophecies previously made concerning you, that by them you [d]fight the
good fight,
19 keeping [a]faith and a good conscience, which some have rejected and
suffered shipwreck in regard to [1b]their
faith.
20 [1]Among these are [a]Hymenaeus
and [b]Alexander, whom I have [c]handed
over to Satan, so that they will be [d]taught
not to blaspheme.

A Call to Prayer

2 First of all, then, I urge that [a]entrea-
ties *and* prayers, petitions *and*
thanksgivings, be made on behalf of all
men,
2 [a]for kings and all who are in [1]au-
thority, so that we may lead a tranquil
and quiet life in all godliness and [2]dig-
nity.
3 This is good and acceptable in the
sight of [a]God our Savior,
4 [a]who desires all men to be [b]saved
and to [c]come to the [1]knowledge of the
truth.
5 For there is [a]one God, *and* [b]one
mediator also between God and men, *the*
[c]man Christ Jesus,
6 who [a]gave Himself as a ransom
for all, the [b]testimony [1]*given* at [2c]the
proper time.
7 [a]For this I was appointed a
[1]preacher and [b]an apostle ([c]I am telling
the truth, I am not lying) as a teacher of
[d]the Gentiles in faith and truth.
8 ¶ Therefore [a]I want the men [b]in
every place to pray, [c]lifting up [d]holy
hands, without wrath and dissension.

Women Instructed

9 Likewise, *I want* [a]women to adorn
themselves with proper clothing, [1]mod-
estly and discreetly, not with braided hair
and gold or pearls or costly garments,
10 but rather by means of good works,
as is proper for women making a claim to
godliness.
11 [a]A woman must quietly receive instruction with entire submissiveness.
12 [a]But I do not allow a woman to
teach or exercise authority over a man,
but to remain quiet.
13 [a]For it was Adam who was first
[1]created, *and* then Eve.
14 And *it was* not Adam *who* was deceived, but [a]the woman being deceived,
[1]fell into transgression.
15 But *women* will be [1]preserved
through the bearing of children if they
continue in [a]faith and love and sanctity
with [2]self-restraint.

Overseers and Deacons

3 [a]It is a trustworthy statement: if any
man aspires to the [b]office of [1]over-
seer, it is a fine work he desires *to do.*
2 [1a]An overseer, then, must be
above reproach, [b]the husband of one
wife, [c]temperate, prudent, respectable,
[d]hospitable, [e]able to teach,
3 [a]not addicted to wine [1]or pugnacious, but gentle, peaceable, [b]free from
the love of money.
4 *He must be* one who [a]manages his
own household well, keeping his children under control with all dignity
5 (but if a man does not know how to
manage his own household, how will he
take care of [a]the church of God?),
6 *and* not a new convert, so that he
will not become [a]conceited and fall into
the [b]condemnation [1]incurred by the
devil.
7 And he must [a]have a good reputation with [b]those outside *the church,* so
that he will not fall into reproach and
[c]the snare of the devil.
8 ¶ [a]Deacons likewise *must be* men
of dignity, not [1]double-tongued, [2b]or
addicted to much wine [2c]or fond of sordid gain,
9 [a]*but* holding to the mystery of the
faith with a clear conscience.

12 [c]Acts 9:15 **13** [a]Acts 8:3 [b]1 Cor 7:25 [c]Acts 26:9 **14** [a]Rom 5:20; 1 Cor 3:10; 2 Cor 4:15; Gal 1:13-16 [b]1 Thess 1:3; 1 Tim 2:15; 2 Tim 1:13; Titus 2:2 **15** [a]1 Tim 3:1; 2 Tim 2:11; Titus 3:8 [b]Mark 2:17; Luke 15:2ff [c]Rom 11:14 [d]1 Cor 15:9; Eph 3:8 **16** [1]Or *destined to* [a]1 Cor 7:25; 1 Tim 1:13 [b]Eph 2:7 **17** [1]Lit *of the ages* [2]Lit *to the ages of the ages* [a]Rev 15:3 [b]1 Tim 6:16 [c]Col 1:15 [d]John 5:44; 1 Tim 6:15; Jude 25 [e]Rom 2:7; Heb 2:7 **18** [1]Or *child* [a]1 Tim 1:5 [b]1 Tim 1:2 [c]1 Tim 4:14 [d]2 Cor 10:4; 1 Tim 6:12; 2 Tim 2:3f **19** [1]Lit *the* [a]1 Tim 1:5 [b]1 Tim 6:12; 2 Tim 2:18 **20** [1]Lit *Of* [a]2 Tim 2:17 [b]2 Tim 4:14 [c]1 Cor 5:5 [d]1 Cor 11:32; Heb 12:5ff **2:1** [a]Eph 6:18 **2** [1]Or *a high position* [2]Or *seriousness* [a]Ezra 6:10; Rom 13:1 **3** [a]Luke 1:47; 1 Tim 1:1 **4** [1]Or *recognition* [a]Ezek 18:23; John 3:17; 1 Tim 4:10; Titus 2:11; 2 Pet 3:9 [b]Rom 11:14 [c]2 Tim 2:25; Titus 1:1; Heb 10:26 **5** [a]Rom 3:30; 1 Cor 8:4 [b]1 Cor 8:6; Gal 3:20 [c]Matt 1:1; Rom 1:3 **6** [1]Or *to be given* [2]Lit *its own times* [a]Matt 20:28; Gal 1:4 [b]1 Cor 1:6 [c]Mark 1:15; Gal 4:4; 1 Tim 6:15; Titus 1:3 **7** [1]Or *herald* [a]Eph 3:8; 1 Tim 1:11; 2 Tim 1:11 [b]1 Cor 9:1 [c]Rom 9:1 [d]Acts 9:15 **8** [a]Phil 1:12; 1 Tim 5:14; Titus 3:8 [b]John 4:21; 1 Cor 1:2; 2 Cor 2:14; 1 Thess 1:8 [c]Ps 63:4; Luke 24:50 [d]Ps 24:4; James 4:8 **9** [1]Lit *with modesty* [a]1 Pet 3:3 **11** [a]1 Cor 14:34; Titus 2:5 **12** [a]1 Cor 14:34; Titus 2:5 **13** [1]Or *formed* [a]Gen 2:7; 1 Cor 11:8ff **14** [1]Lit *has come* [a]Gen 3:6; 2 Cor 11:3 **15** [1]Lit *saved* [2]Or *discretion* [a]1 Tim 1:14 **3:1** [1]Or *bishop* [a]1 Tim 1:15 [b]Acts 20:28; Phil 1:1 **2** [1]Lit *The* [a]1 Tim 3:2-4; Titus 1:6-8 [b]Luke 2:36f; 1 Tim 5:9; Titus 1:6 [c]1 Tim 3:8; Titus 2:2 [d]Rom 12:13; Titus 1:8; Heb 13:2; 1 Pet 4:9 [e]2 Tim 2:24 **3** [1]Lit *not* [a]Titus 1:7 [b]1 Tim 3:8; Titus 1:7; Heb 13:5 **4** [a]1 Tim 3:12 **5** [a]1 Cor 10:32; 1 Tim 3:15 **6** [1]Lit *of the devil* [a]1 Tim 6:4; 2 Tim 3:4 [b]1 Tim 3:7 **7** [a]2 Cor 8:21 [b]Mark 4:11 [c]1 Tim 6:9; 2 Tim 2:26 **8** [1]Or *given to double-talk* [2]Lit *not* [a]Phil 1:1; 1 Tim 3:12 [b]1 Tim 5:23; Titus 2:3 [c]1 Tim 3:3; Titus 1:7; 1 Pet 5:2 **9** [a]1 Tim 1:5

10 [a]These men must also first be tested; then let them serve as deacons if they are beyond reproach.

11 [1]Women *must* likewise *be* dignified, [a]not malicious gossips, but [b]temperate, faithful in all things.

12 [a]Deacons must be [b]husbands of *only* one wife, *and* [1c]good managers of *their* children and their own households.

13 For those who have served well as deacons [a]obtain for themselves a [1]high standing and great confidence in the faith that is in Christ Jesus.

14 ¶ I am writing these things to you, hoping to come to you before long;

15 but [1]in case I am delayed, *I write* so that you will know how [2]one ought to conduct himself in [a]the household of God, which is the [b]church of [c]the living God, the [d]pillar and support of the truth.

16 By common confession, great is [a]the mystery of godliness:

He who was [b]revealed in the flesh,
Was [1c]vindicated [2]in the Spirit,
[d]Seen by angels,
[e]Proclaimed among the nations,
[f]Believed on in the world,
[g]Taken up in glory.

Apostasy

4 But [a]the Spirit explicitly says that [b]in later times some will [1]fall away from the faith, paying attention to [c]deceitful spirits and [d]doctrines of demons,

2 by means of the hypocrisy of liars [a]seared in their own conscience as with a branding iron,

3 *men* who [a]forbid marriage *and advocate* [b]abstaining from foods which [c]God has created to be [d]gratefully shared in by those who believe and know the truth.

4 For [a]everything created by God is good, and nothing is to be rejected if it is [b]received with gratitude;

5 for it is sanctified by means of [a]the word of God and prayer.

A Good Minister's Discipline

6 ¶ In pointing out these things to [a]the brethren, you will be a good [b]servant of Christ Jesus, *constantly* nourished on the words of the faith and of the [1c]sound doctrine which you [d]have been following.

7 But [1]have nothing to do with [a]worldly [b]fables fit only for old women. On the other hand, discipline yourself for the purpose of [c]godliness;

8 for [a]bodily discipline is only of little profit, but [b]godliness is profitable for all things, since it [c]holds promise for the [d]present life and *also* for the *life* to come.

9 [a]It is a trustworthy statement deserving full acceptance.

10 For it is for this we labor and strive, because we have fixed [a]our hope on [b]the living God, who is [c]the Savior of all men, especially of believers.

11 ¶ [1a]Prescribe and teach these things.

12 [a]Let no one look down on your youthfulness, but *rather* in speech, conduct, [b]love, faith *and* purity, show yourself [c]an example [1]of those who believe.

13 [a]Until I come, give attention to the *public* [b]reading *of Scripture,* to exhortation and teaching.

14 Do not neglect the spiritual gift within you, which was bestowed on you through [a]prophetic utterance with [b]the laying on of hands by the [1c]presbytery.

15 Take pains with these things; be *absorbed* in them, so that your progress will be evident to all.

16 [a]Pay close attention to yourself and to your teaching; persevere in these things, for as you do this you will [1b]ensure salvation both for yourself and for those who hear you.

Honor Widows

5 [a]Do not sharply rebuke an [b]older man, but *rather* appeal to *him* as a father, *to* [c]the younger men as brothers,

2 the older women as mothers, *and* the younger women as sisters, in all purity.

3 ¶ Honor widows who are [a]widows indeed;

4 but if any widow has children or grandchildren, [a]they must first learn to practice piety in regard to their own family and to [1]make some return to their parents; for this is [b]acceptable in the sight of God.

5 Now she who is a [a]widow indeed and who has been left alone, [b]has fixed her hope on God and continues in [c]entreaties and prayers night and day.

6 But she who [a]gives herself to wanton pleasure is [b]dead even while she lives.

7 [1a]Prescribe these things as well, so that they may be above reproach.

8 But if anyone does not provide for his own, and especially for those of his household, he has [a]denied the faith and is worse than an unbeliever.

9 ¶ A widow is to be [a]put on the list

---

10 [a]1 Tim 5:22 **11** [1]I.e. either deacons' wives or deaconesses [a]2 Tim 3:3; Titus 2:3 [b]1 Tim 3:2 **12** [1]Lit *managing well* [a]Phil 1:1; 1 Tim 3:8 [b]1 Tim 3:2 [c]1 Tim 3:4 **13** [1]Lit *good* [a]Matt 25:21 **15** [1]Lit *if I delay* [2]Or *you ought to conduct yourself* [a]1 Cor 3:16; 2 Cor 6:16; Eph 2:21f; 1 Pet 2:5 [b]1 Tim 3:5 [c]Matt 16:16; 1 Tim 4:10 [d]Gal 2:9; 2 Tim 2:19 **16** [1]Or *justified* [2]Or *by* [a]Rom 16:25 [b]John 1:14; 1 Pet 1:20; 1 John 3:5 [c]Rom 3:4 [d]Luke 2:13; 1 Pet 1:12 [e]Rom 16:26; 2 Cor 1:19; Col 1:23 [f]2 Thess 1:10 [g]Mark 16:19; Acts 1:9

4:1 [1]I.e. apostacize [a]John 16:13; Acts 20:23; 1 Cor 2:10f [b]2 Thess 2:3ff; 2 Tim 3:1; 2 Pet 3:3; Jude 18 [c]1 John 4:6 [d]James 3:15 **2** [a]Eph 4:19 **3** [a]Heb 13:4 [b]Col 2:16 [c]Gen 1:29 [d]Rom 14:6; 1 Cor 10:30f; 1 Tim 4:4 **4** [a]1 Cor 10:26 [b]Rom 14:6; 1 Cor 10:30f; 1 Tim 4:3 **5** [a]Gen 1:25; Heb 11:3 **6** [1]Lit *good* [a]Acts 1:15 [b]2 Cor 11:23 [c]1 Tim 1:10 [d]Luke 1:3; Phil 2:20; 2 Tim 3:10 **7** [1]Or *reject* [a]1 Tim 1:9 [b]1 Tim 1:4 [c]1 Tim 4:8; 2 Tim 3:5 **8** [a]Col 2:23 [b]1 Tim 4:7; 2 Tim 3:5 [c]Ps 37:9; Prov 19:23; Matt 6:33 [d]Matt 6:33; Mark 10:30 **9** [a]1 Tim 1:15 **10** [a]2 Cor 1:10; 1 Tim 6:17 [b]1 Tim 3:15 [c]John 4:42; 1 Tim 2:4 **11** [1]Or *Keep commanding and teaching* [a]1 Tim 5:7 **12** [1]Or *to* [a]1 Cor 16:11; Titus 2:15 [b]Titus 2:7; 1 Pet 5:3 [c]1 Tim 1:14 **13** [a]1 Tim 3:14 [b]2 Tim 3:15ff **14** [1]Or *board of elders* [a]1 Tim 1:18 [b]Acts 6:6; 1 Tim 5:22; 2 Tim 1:6 [c]Acts 11:30 **16** [1]Lit *save both yourself and those* [a]Acts 20:28 [b]1 Cor 1:21

5:1 [a]Lev 19:32 [b]Titus 2:2 [c]Titus 2:6 **3** [a]Acts 6:1; 1 Tim 5:5 **4** [1]Lit *give back recompenses* [a]Eph 6:2 [b]1 Tim 2:3 **5** [a]Acts 6:1; 1 Tim 5:3 [b]1 Cor 7:34; 1 Pet 3:5 [c]Luke 2:37; 1 Tim 2:1; 2 Tim 1:3 **6** [a]James 5:5 [b]Luke 15:24; 2 Tim 3:6; Rev 3:1 **7** [1]Or *Keep commanding* [a]1 Tim 4:11 **8** [a]2 Tim 2:12; Titus 1:16; 2 Pet 2:1 **9** [a]1 Tim 5:16

only if she is not less than sixty years old, *having been* [b]the wife of one man,

10 having a reputation for [a]good works; *and* if she has brought up children, if she has [b]shown hospitality to strangers, if she [c]has washed the [1]saints' feet, if she has [d]assisted those in distress, *and* if she has devoted herself to every good work.

11 But refuse *to put* younger widows *on the list,* for when they feel [a]sensual desires in disregard of Christ, they want to get married,

12 *thus* incurring condemnation, because they have set aside their previous [1]pledge.

13 At the same time they also learn *to be* idle, as they go around from house to house; and not merely idle, but also [a]gossips and [b]busybodies, talking about [c]things not proper *to mention.*

14 Therefore, I want younger *widows* to get [a]married, bear children, [b]keep house, *and* [c]give the enemy no occasion for reproach;

15 for some [a]have already turned aside to follow [b]Satan.

16 If any woman who is a believer [a]has *dependent* widows, she must [b]assist them and the church must not be burdened, so that it may assist those who are [c]widows indeed.

Concerning Elders

17 ¶ [a]The elders who [b]rule well are to be considered worthy of double honor, especially those who [c]work hard [1]at preaching and teaching.

18 For the Scripture says, "[a]YOU SHALL NOT MUZZLE THE OX WHILE HE IS THRESHING," and "[b]The laborer is worthy of his wages."

19 Do not receive an accusation against an [a]elder except on the basis of [b]two or three witnesses.

20 Those who continue in sin, [a]rebuke in the presence of all, [b]so that the rest also will be fearful *of sinning.*

21 [a]I solemnly charge you in the presence of God and of Christ Jesus and of *His* chosen angels, to maintain these *principles* without bias, doing nothing in a *spirit of* partiality.

22 [a]Do not lay hands upon anyone *too* hastily and [1]thereby share [b]*responsibility for* the sins of others; keep yourself [2]free from sin.

23 ¶ No longer drink water *exclusively,* but [a]use a little wine for the sake of your stomach and your frequent ailments.

24 ¶ The sins of some men are quite evident, going before them to judgment; for others, their *sins* [a]follow after.

25 Likewise also, deeds that are good are quite evident, and [a]those which are otherwise cannot be concealed.

Instructions to Those Who Minister

6 [a]All who are under the yoke as slaves are to regard their own masters as worthy of all honor so [b]that the name of God and *our* doctrine will not be [1]spoken against.

2 Those who have believers as their masters must not be disrespectful to them because they are [a]brethren, but must serve them all the more, because those who [1]partake of the benefit are believers and beloved. [b]Teach and [2]preach these *principles.*

3 ¶ If anyone [a]advocates a different doctrine and does not [1]agree with [b]sound words, those of our Lord Jesus Christ, and with the doctrine [c]conforming to godliness,

4 he is [a]conceited *and* understands nothing; but he [1]has a morbid interest in [b]controversial questions and [c]disputes about words, out of which arise envy, strife, abusive language, evil suspicions,

5 and constant friction between [a]men of depraved mind and deprived of the truth, who [b]suppose that [1]godliness is a means of gain.

6 [a]But godliness *actually* is a means of [b]great gain when accompanied by [c]contentment.

7 For [a]we have brought nothing into the world, so we cannot take anything out of it either.

8 If we [a]have food and covering, with these we shall be content.

9 [a]But those who want to get rich fall into temptation and [b]a snare and many foolish and harmful desires which plunge men into ruin and destruction.

10 For [a]the love of money is a root of all [1]sorts of evil, and some by longing for it have [b]wandered away from the faith and pierced themselves with many griefs.

11 ¶ But [a]flee from these things, you [b]man of God, and pursue righteousness, godliness, [c]faith, [d]love, [1]perseverance *and* gentleness.

12 [a]Fight the good fight of [b]faith; [c]take hold of the eternal life [d]to which you were called, and you made the good [e]confession in the presence of [f]many witnesses.

13 [a]I charge you in the presence of God, who [1]gives life to all things, and of [b]Christ Jesus, who testified the [c]good confession [d]before Pontius Pilate,

---

9 [b]1 Tim 3:2
10 [1]Or *holy ones* [a]Acts 9:36; 1 Tim 6:18; Titus 2:7; 1 Pet 2:12 [b]1 Tim 3:2 [c]Luke 7:44; John 13:14 [d]1 Tim 5:16
11 [a]Rev 18:7
12 [1]Lit *faith*
13 [a]3 John 10 [b]2 Thess 3:11 [c]Titus 1:11
14 [a]1 Cor 7:9; 1 Tim 4:3 [b]Titus 2:5 [c]1 Tim 6:1
15 [a]1 Tim 1:20 [b]Matt 4:10
16 [a]1 Tim 5:4 [b]1 Tim 5:10 [c]1 Tim 5:3
17 [1]Lit *in word* [a]Acts 11:30; 1 Tim 4:14 [b]Rom 12:8 [c]1 Thess 5:12
18 [a]Deut 25:4; 1 Cor 9:9 [b]Lev 19:13; Deut 24:15; Matt 10:10; Luke 10:7; 1 Cor 9:14
19 [a]Acts 11:30; 1 Tim 4:14 [b]Deut 17:6; Matt 18:16
20 [a]Gal 2:14; Eph 5:11; 2 Tim 4:2 [b]2 Cor 7:11
21 [a]Luke 9:26; 1 Tim 6:13; 2 Tim 2:14
22 [1]Lit *do not share* [2]Lit *pure* [a]1 Tim 3:10 [b]Eph 5:11; 1 Tim 3:2-7
23 [a]1 Tim 3:8
24 [a]Rev 14:13
25 [a]Prov 10:9
6:1 [1]Or *blasphemed* [a]Eph 6:5; Titus 2:9; 1 Pet 2:18 [b]Titus 2:5
2 [1]Or *devote themselves to kindness* [2]Lit *exhort, urge* [a]Acts 1:15; Gal 3:28; Philem 16 [b]1 Tim 4:11
3 [1]Lit *come to;* or *come with* [a]1 Tim 1:3 [b]1 Tim 1:10 [c]Titus 1:1
4 [1]Lit *is sick about* [a]1 Tim 3:6 [b]1 Tim 1:4 [c]Acts 18:15; 2 Tim 2:14
5 [1]Or *religion* [a]2 Tim 3:8; Titus 1:15 [b]Titus 1:11; 2 Pet 2:3
6 [a]Luke 12:15-21; 1 Tim 6:6-10 [b]1 Tim 4:8 [c]Phil 4:11; Heb 13:5
7 [a]Job 1:21; Eccl 5:15
8 [a]Prov 30:8
9 [a]Prov 15:27; Luke 12:21; 1 Tim 6:17 [b]1 Tim 3:7
10 [1]Lit *the evils* [a]Col 3:5; 1 Tim 3:3 [b]James 5:19
11 [1]Or *steadfastness* [a]2 Tim 2:22 [b]2 Tim 3:17 [c]1 Tim 1:14 [d]2 Tim 3:10
12 [a]1 Cor 9:25f; Phil 1:30; 1 Tim 1:18 [b]1 Tim 1:19 [c]Phil 3:12; 1 Tim 6:19 [d]Col 3:15 [e]2 Cor 9:13; 1 Tim 6:13 [f]1 Tim 4:14; 2 Tim 2:2
13 [1]Or *preserves alive* [a]1 Tim 5:21 [b]Gal 3:26; 1 Tim 1:12 [c]2 Cor 9:13; 1 Tim 6:12 [d]Matt 27:2; John 18:37

14 that you keep the commandment
without stain or reproach until the [a]ap-
pearing of our Lord Jesus Christ,
15 which He will [1]bring about at [a]the
proper time—He who is [b]the blessed
and [c]only Sovereign, [d]the King of
[2]kings and [e]Lord of [3]lords,
16 [a]who alone possesses immortality
and [b]dwells in unapproachable light,
[c]whom no man has seen or can see. [a]To
Him *be* honor and eternal dominion!
Amen.
17 ¶ Instruct those who are rich in
[a]this present world [b]not to be conceited
or to [c]fix their hope on the uncertainty
of riches, but on God, [d]who richly supplies us with all things to enjoy.
18 *Instruct them* to do good, to be rich
in [a]good [1]works, [b]to be generous and
ready to share,
19 [a]storing up for themselves the
treasure of a good foundation for the future, so that they may [b]take hold of that
which is life indeed.
20 ¶ O [a]Timothy, guard [b]what has
been entrusted to you, avoiding [c]worldly
and empty chatter *and* the opposing arguments of what is falsely called "knowledge"—
21 which some have professed and
thus [a]gone astray [1]from [b]the faith.
¶ [c]Grace be with you.

14 [a]2 Thess 2:8 **15** [1]Lit *show* [2]Lit *those who reign as kings* [3]Lit *those who rule as lords* [a]1 Tim 2:6 [b]1 Tim 1:11 [c]1 Tim 1:17 [d]Deut 10:17; Rev 17:14 [e]Ps 136:3 **16** [a]1 Tim 1:17 [b]Ps 104:2; James 1:17; 1 John 1:5 [c]John 1:18 **17** [a]Matt 12:32; 2 Tim 4:10; Titus 2:12 [b]Ps 62:10; Luke 12:20; Rom 11:20; 1 Tim 6:9 [c]1 Tim 4:10 [d]Acts 14:17 **18** [1]Or *deeds* [a]1 Tim 5:10 [b]Rom 12:8; Eph 4:28

19 [a]Matt 6:20 [b]1 Tim 6:12 **20** [a]1 Tim 1:2 [b]2 Tim 1:12 [c]1 Tim 1:9; 2 Tim 2:16 **21** [1]Lit *concerning* [a]2 Tim 2:18 [b]1 Tim 1:19 [c]Col 4:18

2 Timothy

Title and Background

After Paul's release from prison in Rome in A.D. 62–63 and after his fourth missionary journey, during which he wrote 1 Timothy and Titus, he was again imprisoned in Rome under Emperor Nero about A.D. 66–67. He was languishing in a cold dungeon, chained like a common criminal. Paul knew that his work was done and that his life was nearly at an end.

Author and Date of Writing

The first verse states that the author is Paul, and numerous references in the letter confirm this. 2 Timothy was written about A.D. 66.

Theme and Message

Paul had three reasons for writing to Timothy at this time: (1) Paul was lonely because many of his friends had deserted him. Paul wanted very much for Timothy to join him; (2) he was concerned about the welfare of the churches during this time of persecution under Nero, and he admonishes Timothy to guard the gospel and, if necessary, to suffer for it; (3) he wanted to write to the Ephesian church through Timothy.

Outline

I. Paul's Concern for Timothy (1:1–14)
II. Paul's Situation (1:15–18)
III. Instructions to Timothy (2:1–26)
IV. Warning About the Last Days (3:1–17)
V. Paul's Charge, Requests and Greetings (4:1–22)

Timothy Charged to Guard His Trust

1 Paul, [a]an apostle of [b]Christ Jesus
[1c]by the will of God, according to
the promise of [d]life in Christ Jesus,
2 ¶ To [a]Timothy, my beloved [1b]son:
[c]Grace, mercy *and* peace from God
the Father and Christ Jesus our Lord.
3 ¶ [a]I thank God, whom I [b]serve
with a [c]clear conscience [1]the way my
forefathers did, [d]as I constantly remember you in my [2]prayers night and day,
4 [a]longing to see you, [b]even as I recall your tears, so that I may be filled with
joy.
5 [1]For I am mindful of the [a]sincere
faith within you, which first dwelt in your
grandmother Lois and [b]your mother Eu-
nice, and I am sure that *it is* in you as
well.
6 For this reason I remind you to kindle afresh [a]the gift of God which is in you
through [a]the laying on of my hands.
7 For God has not given us a [a]spirit
of [1]timidity, but of power and love and
[2]discipline.
8 ¶ Therefore [a]do not be ashamed of
the [b]testimony of our Lord or of me [c]His
prisoner, but join with *me* in [d]suffering
for the [e]gospel according to the power of
God,
9 who has [a]saved us and [b]called us
with a holy [c]calling, [d]not according to
our works, but according to His own
[b]purpose and grace which was granted
us in [e]Christ Jesus from [f]all eternity,
10 but [a]now has been revealed by the
[b]appearing of our Savior [c]Christ Jesus,
who [d]abolished death and brought life
and immortality to light through the gospel,
11 [a]for which I was appointed a
preacher and an apostle and a teacher.
12 For this reason I also suffer these
things, but [a]I am not ashamed; for I
know [b]whom I have believed and I am
convinced that He is able to [c]guard what
I have entrusted to Him [1]until [d]that day.
13 [1a]Retain the [b]standard of [c]sound
words [d]which you have heard from me,
in the [e]faith and love which are in
[f]Christ Jesus.
14 Guard, through the Holy Spirit who

1:1 [1]Lit *through* [a]2 Cor 1:1 [b]Gal 3:26 [c]1 Cor 1:1 [d]1 Tim 6:19
2 [1]Or *child* [a]Acts 16:1; 1 Tim 1:2 [b]1 Tim 1:2; 2 Tim 2:1; Titus 1:4 [c]Rom 1:7
3 [1]Lit *from my forefathers* [2]Or *petitions* [a]Rom 1:8 [b]Acts 24:14 [c]Acts 23:1; 1 Tim 1:5 [d]Rom 1:9
4 [a]2 Tim 4:9 [b]Acts 20:37
5 [1]Lit *Receiving remembrance of* [a]1 Tim 1:5 [b]Acts 16:1; 2 Tim 3:15
6 [a]1 Tim 4:14
7 [1]Or *cowardice* [2]Or *sound judgment* [a]John 14:27; Rom 8:15
8 [a]Mark 8:38; Rom 1:16; 2 Tim 1:12 [b]1 Cor 1:6 [c]Eph 3:1; 2 Tim 1:16 [d]2 Tim 2:3 [e]2 Tim 1:10
9 [a]Rom 11:14 [b]Rom 8:28ff [c]Rom 11:29 [d]Eph 2:9 [e]2 Tim 1:1 [f]Rom 16:25; Eph 1:4; Titus 1:2
10 [a]Rom 16:26 [b]2 Thess 2:8; 2 Tim 4:1; Titus 2:11 [c]2 Tim 1:1 [d]1 Cor 15:26; Heb 2:14f
11 [a]1 Tim 2:7
12 [1]Or *for* [a]2 Tim 1:8 [b]Titus 3:8 [c]1 Tim 6:20; 2 Tim 1:14 [d]1 Cor 1:8; 2 Tim 1:18
13 [1]Or *Hold the example* [a]2 Tim 3:14; Titus 1:9 [b]Rom 2:20 [c]1 Tim 1:10 [d]2 Tim 2:2 [e]1 Tim 1:14 [f]2 Tim 1:1

[a]dwells in us, the [1b]treasure which has been entrusted to *you.*

15 ¶ You are aware of the fact that all who are in [1a]Asia [b]turned away from me, among whom are Phygelus and Hermogenes.

16 The Lord grant mercy to [a]the house of Onesiphorus, for he often refreshed me and [b]was not ashamed of my [1c]chains;

17 but when he was in Rome, he eagerly searched for me and found me—

18 the Lord grant to him to find mercy from the Lord on [a]that day—and you know very well what services he rendered at [b]Ephesus.

Be Strong

2 You therefore, my [1a]son, [b]be strong in the grace that is in [c]Christ Jesus.

2 The things [a]which you have heard from me in the presence of [b]many witnesses, [c]entrust these to [d]faithful men who will be [e]able to teach others also.

3 [a]Suffer hardship with *me,* as a good [b]soldier of [c]Christ Jesus.

4 No soldier in active service [a]entangles himself in the affairs of everyday life, so that he may please the one who enlisted him as a soldier.

5 Also if anyone [a]competes as an athlete, he [1]does not win the prize unless he competes according to the rules.

6 [a]The hard-working farmer ought to be the first to receive his share of the crops.

7 Consider what I say, for the Lord will give you understanding in everything.

8 ¶ Remember Jesus Christ, [a]risen from the dead, [b]descendant of David, [c]according to my gospel,

9 [1]for which I [a]suffer hardship even to [b]imprisonment as a [c]criminal; but [d]the word of God [e]is not imprisoned.

10 For this reason [a]I endure all things for [b]the sake of those who are chosen, [c]so that they also may obtain the [d]salvation which is in [e]Christ Jesus *and* with *it* [f]eternal glory.

11 [a]It is a trustworthy statement:
For [b]if we died with Him, we
will also live with Him;
12 If we endure, [a]we will also
reign with Him;
If we [1b]deny Him, He also will
deny us;
13 If we are faithless, [a]He remains
faithful, for [b]He cannot
deny Himself.

An Unashamed Workman

14 ¶ Remind *them* of these things, and solemnly [a]charge *them* in the presence of God not to [b]wrangle about words, which is useless *and leads* to the ruin of the hearers.

15 Be diligent to [a]present yourself approved to God as a workman who does not need to be ashamed, accurately handling [b]the word of truth.

16 But [a]avoid [b]worldly *and* empty chatter, for [1]it will lead to further ungodliness,

17 and their [1]talk will spread like [2]gangrene. Among them are [a]Hymenaeus and Philetus,

18 *men* who have gone astray from the truth saying that [a]the resurrection has already taken place, and they upset [b]the faith of some.

19 Nevertheless, the [a]firm foundation of God stands, having this [b]seal, "[c]The Lord knows those who are His," and, "[d]Everyone who names the name of the Lord is to abstain from wickedness."

20 ¶ Now in a large house there are not only gold and silver vessels, but also vessels of wood and of earthenware, and [a]some to honor and some to dishonor.

21 Therefore, if anyone cleanses himself from [a]these *things,* he will be a vessel for honor, sanctified, useful to the Master, [b]prepared for every good work.

22 Now [a]flee from youthful lusts and pursue righteousness, [b]faith, love *and* peace, with those who [c]call on the Lord [d]from a pure heart.

23 But refuse foolish and ignorant [a]speculations, knowing that they [b]produce [1]quarrels.

24 [a]The Lord's bond-servant must not be quarrelsome, but be kind to all, [b]able to teach, patient when wronged,

25 [a]with gentleness correcting those who are in opposition, [b]if perhaps God may grant them repentance leading to [c]the knowledge of the truth,

26 and they may come to their senses *and escape* from [a]the snare of the devil, having been [b]held captive [1]by him to do his will.

"Difficult Times Will Come"

3 But realize this, that [a]in the last days difficult times will come.

2 For men will be [a]lovers of self, [b]lovers of money, [c]boastful, [c]arrogant, [d]revilers, [c]disobedient to parents, [e]ungrateful, [f]unholy,

3 [a]unloving, irreconcilable, [b]mali-

14 [1]Lit *good deposit* [a]Rom 8:9 [b]1 Tim 6:20; 2 Tim 1:12 **15** [1]I.e. the province of Asia [a]Acts 2:9 [b]2 Tim 4:10 **16** [1]Lit *chain* [a]2 Tim 4:19 [b]2 Tim 1:8 [c]Eph 6:20 **18** [a]1 Cor 1:8; 2 Tim 1:12 [b]Acts 18:19; 1 Tim 1:3 **2:1** [1]Or *child* [a]2 Tim 1:2 [b]Eph 6:10 [c]2 Tim 1:1 **2** [a]2 Tim 1:13 [b]1 Tim 6:12 [c]1 Tim 1:18 [d]1 Tim 1:12 [e]2 Cor 2:14ff **3** [a]2 Tim 1:8 [b]1 Cor 9:7; 1 Tim 1:18 [c]2 Tim 1:1 **4** [a]2 Pet 2:20 **5** [1]Lit *is not crowned* [a]1 Cor 9:25 **6** [a]1 Cor 9:10 **8** [a]Acts 2:24 [b]Matt 1:1 [c]Rom 2:16 **9** [1]Lit *in which* [a]2 Tim 1:8 [b]Phil 1:7 [c]Luke 23:32 [d]1 Thess 1:8 [e]Acts 28:31; 2 Tim 4:17 **10** [a]Col 1:24 [b]Luke 18:7; Titus 1:1 [c]2 Cor 1:6; 1 Thess 5:9 [d]1 Cor 1:21 [e]2 Tim 1:1 [f]2 Cor 4:17; 1 Pet 5:10 **11** [a]1 Tim 1:15 [b]Rom 6:8; 1 Thess 5:10 **12** [1]Lit *will deny* [a]Matt 19:28; Luke 22:29; Rom 5:17 [b]Matt 10:33; Luke 12:9; 1 Tim 5:8 **13** [a]Rom 3:3; 1 Cor 1:9 [b]Num 23:19; Titus 1:2 **14** [a]1 Tim 5:21; 2 Tim 4:1 [b]1 Tim 6:4; 2 Tim 2:23; Titus 3:9 **15** [a]Rom 6:13; James 1:12 [b]Eph 1:13; James 1:18 **16** [1]Lit *they will make further progress in ungodliness* [a]Titus 3:9 [b]1 Tim 1:9 **17** [1]Lit *word* [2]Or *cancer* [a]1 Tim 1:20 **18** [a]1 Cor 15:12 [b]1 Tim 1:19; Titus 1:11 **19** [a]Is 28:16f; 1 Tim 3:15 [b]John 3:33 [c]John 10:14; 1 Cor 8:3 [d]Luke 13:27; 1 Cor 1:2 **20** [a]Rom 9:21 **21** [a]1 Tim 6:11; 2 Tim 2:16-18 [b]2 Cor 9:8; Eph 2:10; 2 Tim 3:17 **22** [a]1 Tim 6:11 [b]1 Tim 1:14 [c]Acts 7:59 [d]1 Tim 1:5 **23** [1]Lit *fightings* [a]1 Tim 6:4; 2 Tim 2:14; Titus 3:9 [b]Titus 3:9; James 4:1 **24** [a]1 Tim 3:3; Titus 1:7 [b]1 Tim 3:2 **25** [a]Gal 6:1; Titus 3:2; 1 Pet 3:15 [b]Acts 8:22 [c]1 Tim 2:4 **26** [1]Or *by him, to do His will* [a]1 Tim 3:7 [b]Luke 5:10 **3:1** [a]1 Tim 4:1 **2** [a]Phil 2:21 [b]Luke 16:14; 1 Tim 3:3 [c]Rom 1:30 [d]2 Pet 2:10-12 [e]Luke 6:35 [f]1 Tim 1:9 **3** [a]Rom 1:31 [b]1 Tim 3:11

cious gossips, without self-control, brutal, [1c]haters of good,
4 [a]treacherous, [b]reckless, [c]conceit-
ed, [d]lovers of pleasure rather than lovers
of God,
5 holding to a form of [1a]godliness,
although they have [b]denied its power;
[c]Avoid such men as these.
6 For among them are those who
[1a]enter into households and captivate
[2b]weak women weighed down with
sins, led on by [c]various impulses,
7 always learning and never able to
[a]come to the [1]knowledge of the truth.
8 Just as [a]Jannes and Jambres [b]op-
posed Moses, so these *men* also oppose
the truth, [c]men of depraved mind, rejected in regard to the faith.
9 But they will not make further
progress; for their [a]folly will be obvious
to all, just [b]as [1]Jannes's and Jambres's folly
was also.
10 ¶ Now you [a]followed my teaching,
conduct, purpose, faith, patience, [b]love,
[1]perseverance,
11 [a]persecutions, *and* [b]sufferings,
such as happened to me at [c]Antioch, at
[d]Iconium *and* at [e]Lystra; what [f]perse-
cutions I endured, and out of them all
[g]the Lord rescued me!
12 Indeed, all who desire to live godly
in Christ Jesus [a]will be persecuted.
13 But evil men and impostors [a]will
proceed *from bad* to worse, [b]deceiving
and being deceived.
14 You, however, [a]continue in the
things you have learned and become convinced of, knowing from whom you have
learned *them*,
15 and that [a]from childhood you have
known [b]the sacred writings which are
able to [c]give you the wisdom that leads
to [d]salvation through faith which is in
[e]Christ Jesus.
16 [a]All Scripture is [1]inspired by God
and profitable for teaching, for reproof,
for correction, for [2]training in righteousness;
17 so that [a]the man of God may be
adequate, [b]equipped for every good
work.

"Preach the Word"

4 [a]I solemnly charge *you* in the presence of God and of Christ Jesus, who
is to [b]judge the living and the dead, and
by His [c]appearing and His kingdom:
2 preach [a]the word; be ready in season *and* out of season; [b]reprove, rebuke,
exhort, with [1]great [c]patience and instruction.
3 For [a]the time will come when they
will not endure [b]sound doctrine; but
wanting to have their ears tickled, they
will accumulate for themselves teachers
in accordance to their own desires,
4 and [a]will turn away their ears from
the truth and [b]will turn aside to myths.
5 But you, [a]be sober in all things,
[b]endure hardship, do the work of an
[c]evangelist, fulfill your [d]ministry.
6 ¶ For I am already being [a]poured
out as a drink offering, and the time of
[b]my departure has come.
7 [a]I have fought the good fight, I
have finished [b]the course, I have kept
[c]the faith;
8 in the future there [a]is laid up for
me [b]the crown of righteousness, which
the Lord, the righteous Judge, will award
to me on [c]that day; and not only to me,
but also to [d]all who have loved His [e]ap-
pearing.

Personal Concerns

9 ¶ [a]Make every effort to come to
me soon;
10 for [a]Demas, having loved [b]this
present [1]world, has deserted me and
gone to [c]Thessalonica; Crescens *has
gone* to [2d]Galatia, [e]Titus to Dalmatia.
11 [a]Only [b]Luke is with me. Pick up
[c]Mark and bring him with you, [d]for he
is useful to me for service.
12 But [a]Tychicus I have sent to [b]Eph-
esus.
13 When you come bring the cloak
which I left at [a]Troas with Carpus,
and the books, especially the parch-
ments.
14 [a]Alexander the coppersmith did
me much harm; [b]the Lord will repay him
according to his deeds.
15 Be on guard against him yourself,
for he vigorously opposed our [1]teach-
ing.
16 ¶ At my first defense no one supported me, but all deserted me; [a]may it
not be counted against them.
17 But the Lord stood with me and
[a]strengthened me, so that through me
[b]the proclamation might [1]be [c]fully accomplished, and that all [d]the Gentiles
might hear; and I was [e]rescued out of
[f]the lion's mouth.
18 The Lord will rescue me from every
evil deed, and will [1a]bring me safely to
His [b]heavenly kingdom; [c]to [2]Him *be*
the glory forever and ever. Amen.

3 [1]Lit *not loving good* [c]Titus 1:8
4 [a]Acts 7:52 [b]Acts 19:36 [c]1 Tim 3:6 [d]Phil 3:19
5 [1]Or *religion* [a]1 Tim 4:7 [b]1 Tim 5:8 [c]Matt 7:15; 2 Thess 3:6
6 [1]Or *creep into* [2]Or *idle* [a]Jude 4 [b]1 Tim 5:6; Titus 3:3 [c]Titus 3:3
7 [1]Or *recognition* [a]2 Tim 2:25
8 [a]Ex 7:11 [b]Acts 13:8 [c]1 Tim 6:5
9 [1]Lit *that of those* [a]Luke 6:11 [b]Ex 7:11
10 [1]Or *steadfastness* [a]Phil 2:20; 1 Tim 4:6 [b]1 Tim 6:11
11 [a]2 Cor 12:10 [b]2 Cor 1:5 [c]Acts 13:14 [d]Acts 14:1-7 [e]Acts 14:8-20 [f]2 Cor 11:23-27 [g]Rom 15:31
12 [a]John 15:20; Acts 14:22; 2 Cor 4:9f
13 [a]2 Tim 2:16 [b]Titus 3:3
14 [a]2 Tim 1:13; Titus 1:9
15 [a]2 Tim 1:5 [b]John 5:47; Rom 2:27 [c]Ps 119:98f [d]1 Cor 1:21 [e]2 Tim 1:1
16 [1]Lit *God-breathed* [2]Lit *training which is in* [a]Rom 4:23f; 2 Pet 1:20f
17 [a]1 Tim 6:11 [b]2 Tim 2:21; Heb 13:21
4:1 [a]1 Tim 5:21; 2 Tim 2:14 [b]Acts 10:42 [c]2 Thess 2:8; 2 Tim 1:10
2 [1]Lit *all* [a]Gal 6:6; Col 4:3; 1 Thess 1:6 [b]1 Tim 5:20; Titus 1:13 [c]2 Tim 3:10
3 [a]2 Tim 3:1 [b]1 Tim 1:10; 2 Tim 1:13
4 [a]2 Thess 2:11; Titus 1:14 [b]1 Tim 1:4
5 [a]1 Pet 1:13 [b]2 Tim 1:8 [c]Acts 21:8 [d]Eph 4:12; Col 4:17
6 [a]Phil 2:17 [b]Phil 1:23; 2 Pet 1:14
7 [a]1 Cor 9:25f; Phil 1:30; 1 Tim 1:18 [b]Acts 20:24; 1 Cor 9:24 [c]2 Tim 3:10
8 [a]Col 1:5; 1 Pet 1:4 [b]1 Cor 9:25; 2 Tim 2:5; James 1:12 [c]2 Tim 1:12 [d]Phil 3:11 [e]2 Tim 4:1
9 [a]2 Tim 1:4; Titus 3:12
10 [1]Or *age* [2]One early ms reads *Gaul* [a]Col 4:14 [b]1 Tim 6:17 [c]Acts 17:1 [d]Acts 16:6 [e]2 Cor 2:13; Gal 2:3; Titus 1:4
11 [a]2 Tim 1:15 [b]Col 4:14; Philem 24 [c]Acts 12:12; Col 4:10 [d]2 Tim 2:21
12 [a]Acts 20:4; Eph 6:21; Col 4:7f [b]Acts 18:19
13 [a]Acts 16:8
14 [a]Acts 19:33; 1 Tim 1:20 [b]Ps 62:12; Rom 2:6
15 [1]Lit *words*
16 [a]Acts 7:60; 1 Cor 13:5
17 [1]Or *be fulfilled* [a]1 Tim 1:12; 2 Tim 2:1 [b]Titus 1:3 [c]2 Tim 4:5 [d]Acts 9:15; Phil 1:12ff [e]Rom 15:31; 2 Tim 3:11 [f]1 Sam 17:37; Ps 22:21
18 [1]Or *save me for* [2]Lit *Whom* [a]1 Cor 1:21 [b]1 Cor 15:50; 2 Tim 4:1; Heb 11:16 [c]Rom 11:36; 2 Pet 3:18

19 ¶ Greet Prisca and [a]Aquila, and
[b]the household of Onesiphorus.
20 [a]Erastus remained at [b]Corinth,
but [c]Trophimus I left sick at [d]Miletus.
21 [a]Make every effort to come before
[b]winter. Eubulus greets you, also Pudens
and Linus and Claudia and all the brethren.
22 ¶ [a]The Lord be with your spirit.
[b]Grace be with you.

19 [a]Acts 18:2 [b]2 Tim 1:16 **20** [a]Acts 19:22; Rom 16:23 [b]Acts 18:1 [c]Acts 20:4 [d]Acts 20:15 **21** [a]2 Tim 4:9 [b]Titus 3:12 **22** [a]Gal 6:18; Phil 4:23; Philem 25 [b]Col 4:18

Titus

Title and Background

When Paul left Antioch to discuss "his" gospel with the Jerusalem leaders, he took Titus with him. Presumably Titus, who is not referred to in the book of Acts, worked with Paul at Ephesus during the third missionary journey. From there the apostle sent him to Corinth to help that church with its work. Following Paul's release from his first Roman imprisonment, he and Titus worked briefly in Crete, after which he commissioned Titus to remain there as his representative and complete some needed work.

Author and Date of Writing

Paul probably wrote this letter to Titus from Corinth about A.D. 64.

Theme and Message

Paul wrote Titus to give him personal authorization and guidance in meeting opposition, instructions about faith and conduct, and warnings about false teachers. He also informed Titus of his future plans for him.

Outline

I. Concerning Elders (1:1–9)
II. Concerning False Teachers (1:10–16)
III. Concerning Various Groups (2:1–15)
IV. Concerning Believers in General (3:1–8)
V. Concerning Response to Spiritual Error (3:9–15)

Salutation

1 Paul, [a]a bond-servant of God and an
[b]apostle of Jesus Christ, [1]for the
faith of those [c]chosen of God and [d]the
knowledge of the truth which is [e]accord-
ing to godliness,
2 in [a]the hope of eternal life, which
God, [b]who cannot lie, [c]promised
[1d]long ages ago,
3 but [a]at the proper time manifested, *even* His word, in [b]the proclamation [c]with which I was entrusted [d]ac-
cording to the commandment of [e]God
our Savior,
4 ¶ To [a]Titus, [b]my true child [1]in a
[c]common faith: [d]Grace and peace from
God the Father and [e]Christ Jesus our
Savior.

Qualifications of Elders

5 ¶ For this reason I left you in
[a]Crete, that you would set in order what
remains and [b]appoint [c]elders in every
city as I directed you,
6 *namely,* [a]if any man is above reproach, the [b]husband of one wife, having
children who believe, not accused of
[c]dissipation or [d]rebellion.
7 For the [1a]overseer must be above
reproach as [b]God's steward, not [c]self-
willed, not quick-tempered, not [d]addict-
ed to wine, not pugnacious, [e]not fond of
sordid gain,
8 but [a]hospitable, [b]loving what is
good, sensible, just, devout, self-
controlled,
9 [a]holding fast the faithful word
which is in accordance with the teaching,
so that he will be able both to exhort in
[b]sound doctrine and to refute those who
contradict.
10 ¶ [a]For there are many [b]rebellious
men, [c]empty talkers and deceivers, especially [d]those of the circumcision,
11 who must be silenced because they
are upsetting [a]whole families, teaching
[b]things they should not *teach* [c]for the
sake of sordid gain.
12 One of themselves, a prophet of
their own, said, "[a]Cretans are always liars, evil beasts, lazy gluttons."
13 This testimony is true. For this reason [a]reprove them [b]severely so that
they may be [c]sound in the faith,
14 not paying attention to Jewish

1:1 [1]Or *according to* [a]Rom 1:1; James 1:1; Rev 1:1 [b]2 Cor 1:1 [c]Luke 18:7 [d]1 Tim 2:4 [e]1 Tim 6:3 **2** [1]Lit *before times eternal* [a]2 Tim 1:1; Titus 3:7 [b]2 Tim 2:13; Heb 6:18 [c]Rom 1:2 [d]2 Tim 1:9 **3** [a]1 Tim 2:6 [b]Rom 16:25; 2 Tim 4:17 [c]1 Tim 1:11 [d]1 Tim 1:1 [e]Luke 1:47; 1 Tim 1:1; Titus 2:10 **4** [1]Lit *according to* [a]2 Cor 2:13; Gal 2:3; 2 Tim 4:10 [b]2 Tim 1:2 [c]2 Pet 1:1 [d]Rom 1:7 [e]1 Tim 1:12; 2 Tim 1:1 **5** [a]Acts 27:7; Titus 1:12 [b]Acts 14:23 [c]Acts 11:30 **6** [a]1 Tim 3:2-4; Titus 1:6-8 [b]1 Tim 3:2 [c]Eph 5:18 [d]Titus 1:10 **7** [1]Or *bishop* [a]1 Tim 3:2 [b]1 Cor 4:1 [c]2 Pet 2:10 [d]1 Tim 3:3 [e]1 Tim 3:3 **8** [a]1 Tim 3:2 [b]2 Tim 3:3 **9** [a]2 Thess 2:15; 1 Tim 1:19; 2 Tim 1:13 [b]1 Tim 1:10; Titus 2:1 **10** [a]2 Cor 11:13 [b]Titus 1:6 [c]1 Tim 1:6 [d]Acts 11:2 **11** [a]1 Tim 5:4; 2 Tim 3:6 [b]1 Tim 5:13 [c]1 Tim 6:5 **12** [a]Acts 2:11 **13** [a]1 Tim 5:20; 2 Tim 4:2; Titus 2:15 [b]2 Cor 13:10 [c]Titus 2:2

[a]myths and [b]commandments of men who [c]turn away from the truth.

15 [a]To the pure, all things are pure; but [b]to those who are defiled and unbelieving, nothing is pure, but both their [c]mind and their conscience are defiled.

16 [a]They profess to know God, but by *their* deeds they [b]deny *Him*, being [c]detestable and [d]disobedient and [e]worthless [f]for any good deed.

Duties of the Older and Younger

2 But as for you, speak the things which are fitting for [a]sound doctrine.

2 [a]Older men are to be [b]temperate, dignified, sensible, [c]sound [d]in faith, in love, in [1]perseverance.

3 ¶ Older women likewise are to be reverent in their behavior, [a]not malicious gossips nor [b]enslaved to much wine, teaching what is good,

4 so that they may [1]encourage the young women to love their husbands, to love their children,

5 *to be* sensible, pure, [a]workers at home, kind, being [b]subject to their own husbands, [c]so that the word of God will not be dishonored.

6 ¶ Likewise urge [a]the young men to be [1]sensible;

7 in all things show yourself to be [a]an example of good deeds, *with* [1]purity in doctrine, dignified,

8 sound *in* speech which is beyond reproach, so [a]that the opponent will be put to shame, having nothing bad to say about us.

9 ¶ *Urge* [a]bondslaves to be subject to their own masters in everything, to be well-pleasing, not [1]argumentative,

10 not pilfering, but showing all good faith so that they will adorn the doctrine of [a]God our Savior in every respect.

11 ¶ For the grace of God has [a]appeared, [1b]bringing salvation to all men,

12 [1]instructing us to deny ungodliness and [a]worldly desires and [b]to live sensibly, righteously and godly [c]in the present age,

13 looking for the blessed hope and the [a]appearing of the glory of [1b]our great God and Savior, Christ Jesus,

14 who [a]gave Himself for us [b]to redeem us from every lawless deed, and to [c]purify for Himself a [d]people for His own possession, [e]zealous for good deeds.

15 ¶ These things speak and [a]exhort and [a]reprove with all [1]authority. [b]Let no one disregard you.

Godly Living

3 [a]Remind them [b]to be subject to rulers, to authorities, to be obedient, to be [c]ready for every good deed,

2 to malign no one, [a]to be peaceable, [a]gentle, [b]showing every consideration for all men.

3 [a]For we also once were foolish ourselves, [b]disobedient, [c]deceived, [d]enslaved to [e]various lusts and pleasures, spending our life in [f]malice and [f]envy, hateful, hating one another.

4 But when the [a]kindness of [b]God our Savior and *His* love for mankind [c]appeared,

5 [a]He saved us, [b]not on the basis of deeds which we have done in righteousness, but [c]according to His mercy, by the [d]washing of regeneration and [e]renewing by the Holy Spirit,

6 [a]whom He poured out upon us [b]richly through Jesus Christ our Savior,

7 so that being justified by His grace we would be made [a]heirs [1]according to *the* hope of eternal life.

8 [a]This is a trustworthy statement; and concerning these things I [b]want you to speak confidently, so that those who have [c]believed God will be careful to [d]engage in good deeds. These things are good and profitable for men.

9 But [a]avoid [b]foolish controversies and [c]genealogies and strife and [d]disputes about the Law, for they are [e]unprofitable and worthless.

10 [a]Reject a [b]factious man [c]after a first and second warning,

11 knowing that such a man is [a]perverted and is sinning, being self-condemned.

Personal Concerns

12 ¶ When I send Artemas or [a]Tychicus to you, [b]make every effort to come to me at Nicopolis, for I have decided to [c]spend the winter there.

13 Diligently help Zenas the [a]lawyer and [b]Apollos on their way so that nothing is lacking for them.

14 [a]Our people must also learn to [b]engage in good [1]deeds to meet [c]pressing needs, so that they will not be [d]unfruitful.

15 ¶ [a]All who are with me greet you. Greet those who love us [b]in *the* faith.

¶ [c]Grace be with you all.

14 [a]1 Tim 1:4 [b]Col 2:22 [c]2 Tim 4:4 **15** [a]Luke 11:41; Rom 14:20 [b]Rom 14:14 [c]1 Tim 6:5 **16** [a]1 John 2:4 [b]1 Tim 5:8 [c]Rev 21:8 [d]Titus 3:3 [e]2 Tim 3:8 [f]2 Tim 3:17; Titus 3:1
2:1 [a]Titus 1:9 **2** [1]Or *steadfastness* [a]Philem 9 [b]1 Tim 3:2 [c]Titus 1:13 [d]1 Tim 1:2 **3** [a]1 Tim 3:11 [b]1 Tim 3:8 **4** [1]Or *train* **5** [a]1 Tim 5:14 [b]Eph 5:22 [c]1 Tim 6:1 **6** [1]Or *sensible in all things; show* [a]1 Tim 5:1 **7** [1]Or *soundness*; lit *uncorruptness* [a]1 Tim 4:12 **8** [a]2 Thess 3:14; 1 Pet 2:12 **9** [1]Lit *contradicting* [a]Eph 6:5; 1 Tim 6:1 **10** [a]Titus 1:3 **11** [1]Or *to all men, bringing* [a]2 Tim 1:10; Titus 3:4 [b]1 Tim 2:4 **12** [1]Or *disciplining* [a]1 Tim 6:9; Titus 3:3 [b]2 Tim 3:12 [c]1 Tim 6:17 **13** [1]Or *the great God and our Savior* [a]2 Thess 2:8 [b]1 Tim 1:1; 2 Tim 1:2; Titus 1:4; 2 Pet 1:1 **14** [a]1 Tim 2:6 [b]Ps 130:8; 1 Pet 1:18f [c]Ezek 37:23; Heb 1:3; 1 John 1:7 [d]Ex 19:5; Deut 4:20; Eph 1:11; 1 Pet 2:9 [e]Eph 2:10; Titus 3:8; 1 Pet 3:13 **15** [1]Lit *command* [a]1 Tim 4:13; 2 Tim 4:2 [b]1 Tim 4:12
3:1 [a]2 Tim 2:14 [b]Rom 13:1 [c]2 Tim 2:21 **2** [a]1 Tim 3:3; 1 Pet 2:18 [b]2 Tim 2:25 **3** [a]Rom 11:30; Col 3:7 [b]Titus 1:16 [c]2 Tim 3:13 [d]Rom 6:6 [e]2 Tim 3:6; Titus 2:12 [f]Rom 1:29 **4** [a]Rom 2:4; Eph 2:7; 1 Pet 2:3 [b]Titus 2:10 [c]Titus 2:11 **5** [a]Rom 11:14; 2 Tim 1:9 [b]Eph 2:9 [c]Eph 2:4; 1 Pet 1:3 [d]John 3:5; Eph 5:26; 1 Pet 3:21 [e]Rom 12:2 **6** [a]Rom 5:5 [b]Rom 2:4; 1 Tim 6:17 **7** [1]Or *of eternal life according to hope* [a]Matt 25:34; Mark 10:17; Rom 8:17; Titus 1:2 **8** [a]1 Tim 1:15 [b]1 Tim 2:8 [c]2 Tim 1:12 [d]Titus 2:7 **9** [a]2 Tim 2:16 [b]1 Tim 1:4; 2 Tim 2:23 [c]1 Tim 1:4 [d]James 4:1 [e]2 Tim 2:14 **10** [a]2 John 10 [b]Rom 16:17 [c]Matt 18:15f **11** [a]Titus 1:14 **12** [a]Acts 20:4; Eph 6:21f; Col 4:7f; 2 Tim 4:12 [b]2 Tim 4:9 [c]2 Tim 4:21 **13** [a]Matt 22:35 [b]Acts 18:24; 1 Cor 16:12 **14** [1]Or *occupations* [a]Titus 2:8 [b]Titus 3:8 [c]Rom 12:13; Phil 4:16 [d]Matt 7:19; Phil 1:11; Col 1:10 **15** [a]Acts 20:34 [b]1 Tim 1:2 [c]Col 4:18

Philemon

Title and Background

Philemon was a believer in Colosse who, along with other Christians, was a slave owner. One of his slaves, Onesimus, had apparently stolen from him and then run away, which under Roman law was punishable by death. But Onesimus met Paul and through his ministry became a Christian. Now he was willing to return to his master.

Author and Date of Writing

Paul wrote this short letter about A.D. 60 from prison and sent it to Colosse with Onesimus and Tychicus.

Theme and Message

Paul writes this personal appeal to ask Philemon to accept Onesimus as a Christian brother, not as a slave. Now that Onesimus (whose name means useful) was a believer, he was really useful (see verses 10 and 11 and the footnote on verse 10).

Outline

I. Greetings (1–3)
II. Thanksgiving and Prayer (4–7)
III. Paul's Plea for Onesimus (8–21)
IV. Conclusion (22–25)

Salutation

1 [a]Paul, [b]a prisoner of [c]Christ Jesus,
and [d]Timothy [1]our brother,
¶ To Philemon our beloved *brother* and
[e]fellow worker,
2 and to Apphia [1a]our sister, and to
[b]Archippus our [c]fellow soldier, and to
[d]the church in your house:
3 [a]Grace to you and peace from God
our Father and the Lord Jesus Christ.

Philemon's Love and Faith

4 ¶ [a]I thank my God always, making
mention of you in my prayers,
5 because I [a]hear of your love and of
the faith which you have toward the Lord
Jesus and toward all the [1]saints;
6 *and I pray* that the fellowship of
your faith may become effective
[1]through the [a]knowledge of every good
thing which is in you [2]for Christ's sake.
7 For I have come to have much [a]joy
and comfort in your love, because the
[1]hearts of the [2]saints have been [b]re-
freshed through you, brother.
8 ¶ Therefore, [a]though I have
[1]enough confidence in Christ to order
you *to do* what is [b]proper,
9 yet for love's sake I rather [a]appeal
to you—since I am such a person as Paul,
[1]the [b]aged, and now also [c]a prisoner of
[d]Christ Jesus—

Plea for Onesimus, a Free Man

10 I [a]appeal to you for my [b]child
[1c]Onesimus, whom I have begotten in
my [2]imprisonment,
11 who formerly was useless to you,
but now is useful both to you and to me.
12 I have sent him back to you in person, that is, *sending* my very heart,
13 whom I wished to keep with me, so
that on your behalf he might minister to
me in my [1a]imprisonment for the gospel;
14 but without your consent I did not
want to do anything, so that your goodness would [a]not be, in effect, by compulsion but of your own free will.
15 For perhaps [a]he was for this reason
separated *from you* for a while, that you
would have him back forever,
16 [a]no longer as a slave, but more
than a slave, [b]a beloved brother, especially to me, but how much more to you,
both [c]in the flesh and in the Lord.
17 ¶ If then you regard me a [a]partner,
accept him as *you would* me.
18 But if he has wronged you in any
way or owes you anything, charge that to
my account;

1:1 [1]Lit *the* [a]Phil 1:1 [b]Eph 3:1 [c]Gal 3:26 [d]2 Cor 1:1; Col 1:1 [e]Phil 2:25; Philem 24
2 [1]Lit *the* [a]Rom 16:1 [b]Col 4:17 [c]Phil 2:25; 2 Tim 2:3 [d]Rom 16:5
3 [a]Rom 1:7
4 [a]Rom 1:8f
5 [1]Or *holy ones* [a]Eph 1:15; Col 1:4; 1 Thess 3:6
6 [1]Or *in* [2]Lit *toward Christ* [a]Phil 1:9; Col 1:9
7 [1]Lit *inward parts* [2]Or *holy ones* [a]2 Cor 7:4 [b]1 Cor 16:18; Philem 20
8 [1]Lit *much* [a]2 Cor 3:12; 1 Thess 2:6 [b]Eph 5:4
9 [1]Or *an ambassador* [a]Rom 12:1 [b]Titus 2:2 [c]Philem 1 [d]Gal 3:26; 1 Tim 1:12; Philem 23
10 [1]I.e. useful [2]Lit *bonds* [a]Rom 12:1 [b]1 Cor 4:14f [c]Col 4:9
13 [1]Lit *bonds* [a]Phil 1:7; Philem 10
14 [a]2 Cor 9:7; 1 Pet 5:2
15 [a]Gen 45:5
16 [a]1 Cor 7:22 [b]Matt 23:8; 1 Tim 6:2 [c]Eph 6:5; Col 3:22
17 [a]2 Cor 8:23

19 [a]I, Paul, am writing this with my
own hand, I will repay it ([b]not to [1]men-
tion to you that you owe to me even your
own self as well).
20 Yes, brother, let me benefit from
you in the Lord; [a]refresh my heart in
Christ.
21 ¶ [a]Having confidence in your obedience, I write to you, since I know that
you will do even more than what I say.
22 ¶ At the same time also prepare me
a [a]lodging, for [b]I hope that through
[c]your prayers [d]I will be given to you.
23 ¶ [a]Epaphras, my [b]fellow prisoner
in Christ Jesus, greets you,
24 *as do* [a]Mark, [b]Aristarchus, [c]De-
mas, [c]Luke, my [d]fellow workers.
25 ¶ [a]The grace of the Lord Jesus
Christ be [b]with your spirit.[1]

19 [1]Lit *say* [a]1 Cor 16:21; 2 Cor 10:1; Gal 5:2 [b]2 Cor 9:4
20 [a]Philem 7
21 [a]2 Cor 2:3
22 [a]Acts 28:23 [b]Phil 1:25 [c]2 Cor 1:11 [d]Acts 27:24; Heb 13:19
23 [a]Col 1:7 [b]Rom 16:7; Philem 1
24 [a]Acts 12:12; Col 4:10 [b]Acts 19:29; Col 4:10 [c]Col 4:14; 2 Tim 4:10f [d]Philem 1
25 [1]One early ms adds *Amen* [a]Gal 6:18 [b]2 Tim 4:22

Hebrews

Title and Background

The first-century church underwent much persecution, and this letter was written in that setting. The persecution had not yet resulted in martyrdom, but it was severe. The intended readers seem to have been Jewish Christians who were thinking of abandoning their faith and of lapsing back into Judaism. So the author exhorts them to hold fast to their confession of Jesus Christ as Savior and Lord.

Author and Date of Writing

The author of this letter does not identify himself, but he was obviously well known to the original recipients. For many years Paul was considered to be the author, but since the Reformation it has been widely recognized that Paul could not have been the author. Apollos and Barnabas are those most often suggested. The book was written prior to the fall of Jerusalem in A.D. 70.

Theme and Message

The theme of Hebrews is the absolute supremacy and sufficiency of Jesus Christ as revealer and as mediator of God's grace. The prologue presents Jesus as God's full and final revelation. Hebrews could be called "the book of better things," since the two Greek words for "better" and "superior" occur 15 times in the letter. Practical applications of this theme are given throughout the book.

Outline

I. Christ's Superior Revelation (1:1–4)
II. Christ's Superiority Over Angels (1:5—2:18)
III. Christ's Superiority Over Moses (3:1—4:13)
IV. Christ's Superiority Over Aaronic Priests (4:14—7:28)
V. Christ's Superior Sacrifice (8:1—10:39)
VI. Plea for Persevering Faith (11:1—12:29)
VII. Conclusion (13:1–25)

God's Final Word in His Son

1 God, after He [a]spoke long ago to the
fathers in [b]the prophets in many
portions and [c]in many ways,
2 [1a]in these last days [b]has spoken
to us [2]in [c]His Son, whom He appointed
[d]heir of all things, [e]through whom also
He made the [3f]world.
3 [1]And He is the radiance of His
glory and the exact [a]representation of
His nature, and [2b]upholds all things by
the word of His power. When He had
made [c]purification of sins, He [d]sat down
at the right hand of the [e]Majesty on
high,
4 having become as much better than
the angels, as He has inherited a more
excellent [a]name than they.
5 ¶ For to which of the angels did He
ever say,
"[a]YOU ARE MY SON,
TODAY I HAVE BEGOTTEN YOU"?
And again,
"[b]I WILL BE A FATHER TO HIM
AND HE SHALL BE A SON TO ME"?
6 And [1]when He again [a]brings the
firstborn into [2b]the world, He says,
"[c]AND LET ALL THE ANGELS OF GOD
WORSHIP HIM."
7 And of the angels He says,
"[a]WHO MAKES HIS ANGELS WINDS,
AND HIS MINISTERS A FLAME OF
FIRE."
8 But of the Son *He says,*
"[a]YOUR THRONE, O GOD, IS
FOREVER AND EVER,
AND THE RIGHTEOUS SCEPTER IS THE
SCEPTER OF [1]HIS KINGDOM.
9 "[a]YOU HAVE LOVED RIGHTEOUSNESS
AND HATED LAWLESSNESS;
[b]THEREFORE GOD, YOUR GOD, HAS
[c]ANOINTED YOU

1:1 [a]John 9:29; Heb 2:2f [b]Acts 2:30 [c]Num 12:6; Joel 2:28
2 [1]Or *at the end of these days* [2]Lit *in Son*; or in the person of a Son [3]Lit *ages* [a]Matt 13:39; 1 Pet 1:20 [b]John 9:29 [c]John 5:26; Heb 3:6 [d]Ps 2:8; Matt 28:18; Mark 12:7; Rom 8:17; Heb 2:8 [e]John 1:3; 1 Cor 8:6; Col 1:16 [f]1 Cor 2:7; Heb 11:3
3 [1]Lit *Who being* [2]Lit *upholding* [a]2 Cor 4:4 [b]Col 1:17 [c]Titus 2:14; Heb 9:14 [d]Mark 16:19; Heb 8:1 [e]2 Pet 1:17
4 [a]Eph 1:21
5 [a]Ps 2:7; Acts 13:33; Heb 5:5 [b]2 Sam 7:14
6 [1]Or *again when He brings* [2]Lit *the inhabited earth* [a]Heb 10:5 [b]Matt 24:14 [c]Ps 97:7 **7** [a]Ps 104:4
8 [1]Late mss read *Your* [a]Ps 45:6 **9** [a]Ps 45:7 [b]John 10:17; Phil 2:9; Heb 2:9 [c]Is 61:1

WITH THE OIL OF GLADNESS ABOVE
YOUR COMPANIONS."
10 And,
"[a]YOU, LORD, IN THE BEGINNING
LAID THE FOUNDATION OF THE
EARTH,
AND THE HEAVENS ARE THE WORKS
OF YOUR HANDS;
11 [a]THEY WILL PERISH, BUT YOU
REMAIN;
[b]AND THEY ALL WILL BECOME OLD
LIKE A GARMENT,
12 [a]AND LIKE A MANTLE YOU WILL
ROLL THEM UP;
LIKE A GARMENT THEY WILL ALSO BE
CHANGED.
BUT YOU ARE [b]THE SAME,
AND YOUR YEARS WILL NOT COME
TO AN END."
13 But to which of the angels has He
ever said,
"[a]SIT AT MY RIGHT HAND,
[b]UNTIL I MAKE YOUR ENEMIES
A FOOTSTOOL FOR YOUR FEET"?
14 Are they not all [a]ministering spir-
its, sent out to render service for the sake
of those who will [b]inherit [c]salvation?

Give Heed

2 For this reason we must pay much
closer attention to [1]what we have
heard, so that [a]we do not drift away
from it.
2 For if the word [a]spoken through
[b]angels proved [1]unalterable, and [c]ev-
ery transgression and disobedience received a just [2d]penalty,
3 [a]how will we escape if we neglect
so great a [b]salvation? [1]After it was at the
first [c]spoken through the Lord, it was
[d]confirmed to us by those who heard,
4 God also testifying with them, both
by [a]signs and wonders and by [b]various
[1]miracles and by [2c]gifts of the Holy
Spirit [d]according to His own will.

Earth Subject to Man

5 ¶ For He did not subject to angels
[1a]the world to come, concerning which
we are speaking.
6 But one has testified [a]somewhere,
saying,
"[b]WHAT IS MAN, THAT YOU
REMEMBER HIM?
OR THE SON OF MAN, THAT YOU ARE
CONCERNED ABOUT HIM?
7 "[a]YOU HAVE MADE HIM [1]FOR A
LITTLE WHILE LOWER THAN THE
ANGELS;
YOU HAVE CROWNED HIM WITH
GLORY AND HONOR,
[2]AND HAVE APPOINTED HIM OVER
THE WORKS OF YOUR HANDS;
8 [a]YOU HAVE PUT ALL THINGS IN
SUBJECTION UNDER HIS FEET."
For in subjecting all things to him, He left
nothing that is not subject to him. But
now [b]we do not yet see all things subject-
ed to him.

Jesus Briefly Humbled

9 But we do see Him who was [a]made
[1]for a little while lower than the angels,
namely, Jesus, [b]because of the suffering
of death [c]crowned with glory and honor,
so that [d]by the grace of God He might
[e]taste death [f]for everyone.
10 ¶ For [a]it was fitting for Him, [b]for
whom are all things, and through whom
are all things, in bringing many sons to
glory, to [c]perfect the [1d]author of their
salvation through sufferings.
11 For both He who [a]sanctifies and
those who [b]are [1]sanctified are all [c]from
one *Father*; for which reason He is not
ashamed to call them [d]brethren,
12 saying,
"[a]I WILL PROCLAIM YOUR NAME TO
MY BRETHREN,
IN THE MIDST OF THE
CONGREGATION I WILL SING
YOUR PRAISE."
13 And again,
"[a]I WILL PUT MY TRUST IN HIM."
And again,
"[b]BEHOLD, I AND THE CHILDREN
WHOM GOD HAS GIVEN ME."
14 ¶ Therefore, since the children
share in [1a]flesh and blood, [b]He Himself
likewise also partook of the same, that
[c]through death He might render powerless [d]him who had the power of death,
that is, the devil,
15 and might free those who through
[a]fear of death were subject to slavery all
their lives.
16 For assuredly He does not [1]give
help to angels, but He gives help to the
[2]descendant of Abraham.
17 Therefore, He [1]had [a]to be made
like His brethren in all things, so that He
might [b]become a merciful and faithful
[c]high priest in [d]things pertaining to
God, to [e]make propitiation for the sins of
the people.
18 For since He Himself was [a]tempt-
ed in that which He has suffered, He is
able to come to the aid of those who are
tempted.

Jesus Our High Priest

3 Therefore, [a]holy brethren, partakers
of a [b]heavenly calling, consider

10 [a]Ps 102:25 **11** [a]Ps 102:26 [b]Is 51:6; Heb 8:13 **12** [a]Ps 102:26 [b]Heb 13:8 **13** [a]Ps 110:1; Matt 22:44; Heb 1:3 [b]Josh 10:24; Heb 10:13 **14** [a]Ps 103:20f; Dan 7:10 [b]Matt 25:34; Mark 10:17; Titus 3:7; Heb 6:12 [c]Rom 11:14; 1 Cor 1:21; Heb 2:3 **2:1** [1]Lit *the things that have been heard* [a]Prov 3:21 **2** [1]Or *steadfast* [2]Or *recompense* [a]Heb 1:1 [b]Acts 7:53 [c]Heb 10:28 [d]Heb 10:35 **3** [1]Lit *Which was* [a]Heb 10:29 [b]Rom 11:14; 1 Cor 1:21; Heb 1:14 [c]Heb 1:1 [d]Mark 16:20; Luke 1:2; 1 John 1:1 **4** [1]Or *works of power* [2]Lit *distributions* [a]John 4:48 [b]Mark 6:14 [c]1 Cor 12:4; Eph 4:7 [d]Eph 1:5 **5** [1]Lit *the inhabited earth* [a]Matt 24:14; Heb 6:5 **6** [a]Heb 4:4 [b]Ps 8:4 **7** [1]Or *...him a little lower than...* [2]Two early mss do not contain *And...hands* [a]Ps 8:5 **8** [a]Ps 8:6; 1 Cor 15:27 [b]1 Cor 15:25 **9** [1]Or *a little lower* [a]Heb 2:7 [b]Acts 2:33; 1 Pet 1:21 [c]Phil 2:9; Heb 1:9 [d]John 3:16 [e]Matt 16:28; John 8:52 [f]Heb 7:25 **10** [1]Or *leader* [a]Luke 24:26 [b]Rom 11:36 [c]Heb 5:9 [d]Acts 3:15 **11** [1]Or *being sanctified* [a]Heb 13:12 [b]Heb 10:10 [c]Acts 17:28 [d]Matt 25:40; Mark 3:34f; John 20:17 **12** [a]Ps 22:22 **13** [a]Is 8:17 [b]Is 8:18 **14** [1]Lit *blood and flesh* [a]Matt 16:17 [b]John 1:14 [c]1 Cor 15:54-57; 2 Tim 1:10 [d]John 12:31; 1 John 3:8 **15** [a]Rom 8:15 **16** [1]Lit *take hold of angels, but He takes hold of* [2]Lit *seed* **17** [1]Lit *was obligated to be* [a]Phil 2:7; Heb 2:14 [b]Heb 4:15f [c]Heb 3:1 [d]Rom 15:17; Heb 5:1 [e]Dan 9:24; 1 John 2:2

18 [a]Heb 4:15 **3:1** [a]Acts 1:15; Heb 2:11 [b]Phil 3:14

Jesus, [c]the Apostle and [d]High Priest of our [e]confession;

2 [1]He was faithful to Him who appointed Him, as [a]Moses also was in all His house.

3 [a]For He has been counted worthy of more glory than Moses, by just so much as the builder of the house has more honor than the house.

4 For every house is built by someone, but the builder of all things is God.

5 Now [a]Moses was faithful in all His house as [b]a servant, [c]for a testimony of those things [d]which were to be spoken later;

6 but Christ *was faithful* as [a]a Son over His house—[b]whose house we are, [c]if we hold fast our [d]confidence and the boast of our [e]hope firm until the end.

7 ¶ Therefore, just as [a]the Holy Spirit says,

"[b]TODAY IF YOU HEAR HIS VOICE,
8 [a]DO NOT HARDEN YOUR HEARTS AS
[1]WHEN THEY PROVOKED ME,
AS IN THE DAY OF TRIAL IN THE
WILDERNESS,
9 [a]WHERE YOUR FATHERS TRIED *ME*
BY TESTING *ME*,
AND SAW MY WORKS FOR [b]FORTY
YEARS.
10 "[a]THEREFORE I WAS ANGRY WITH
THIS GENERATION,
AND SAID, 'THEY ALWAYS GO ASTRAY
IN THEIR HEART,
AND THEY DID NOT KNOW MY
WAYS';
11 [a]AS I SWORE IN MY WRATH,
'THEY SHALL NOT ENTER MY REST.' "

The Peril of Unbelief

12 [a]Take care, brethren, that there not be in any one of you an evil, unbelieving heart [1]that falls away from [b]the living God.

13 But [a]encourage one another day after day, as long as it is *still* called "Today," so that none of you will be hardened by the [b]deceitfulness of sin.

14 For we have become partakers of Christ, [a]if we hold fast the beginning of our [b]assurance firm until the end,

15 while it is said,

"[a]TODAY IF YOU HEAR HIS VOICE,
DO NOT HARDEN YOUR HEARTS, AS
[1]WHEN THEY PROVOKED ME."

16 For who [a]provoked *Him* when they had heard? Indeed, [b]did not all those who came out of Egypt *led* by Moses?

17 And with whom was He angry for forty years? Was it not with those who sinned, [a]whose bodies fell in the wilderness?

18 And to whom did He swear [a]that they would not enter His rest, but to those who were [b]disobedient?

19 *So* we see that they were not able to enter because of [a]unbelief.

The Believer's Rest

4 Therefore, let us fear if, while a promise remains of entering His rest, any one of you may seem to have [a]come short of it.

2 For indeed we have had good news preached to us, just as they also; but [a]the word [1]they heard did not profit them, because [2]it was not united by faith in those who heard.

3 For we who have believed enter that rest, just as He has said,

"[a]AS I SWORE IN MY WRATH,
THEY SHALL NOT ENTER MY REST,"

although His works were finished [b]from the foundation of the world.

4 For He has said [a]somewhere concerning the seventh *day*: "[b]AND GOD [c]RESTED ON THE SEVENTH DAY FROM ALL HIS WORKS";

5 and again in this *passage*, "[a]THEY SHALL NOT ENTER MY REST."

6 Therefore, since it remains for some to enter it, and those who formerly had good news preached to them failed to enter because of [a]disobedience,

7 He again fixes a certain day, "Today," saying [1]through David after so long a time just [a]as has been said before,

"[b]TODAY IF YOU HEAR HIS VOICE,
DO NOT HARDEN YOUR HEARTS."

8 For [a]if [1]Joshua had given them rest, He would not have spoken of another day after that.

9 So there remains a Sabbath rest for the people of God.

10 For the one who has entered His rest has himself also [a]rested from his works, as [b]God did from His.

11 Therefore let us be diligent to enter that rest, so that no one will fall, through *following* the same [a]example of [b]disobedience.

12 For [a]the word of God is [b]living and [c]active and sharper than any two-edged [d]sword, and piercing as far as the division of [e]soul and [e]spirit, of both joints and marrow, and [f]able to judge the thoughts and intentions of the heart.

13 And [a]there is no creature hidden from His sight, but all things are [b]open and laid bare to the eyes of Him with whom we have to do.

14 ¶ Therefore, since we have a great [a]high priest who has [b]passed through the heavens, Jesus [c]the Son of God, let us hold fast our [d]confession.

1 [c]John 17:3 [d]Heb 2:17 [e]2 Cor 9:13; Heb 4:14
2 [1]Lit *Being faithful* [a]Ex 40:16; Num 12:7; Heb 3:5
3 [a]2 Cor 3:7-11
5 [a]Ex 40:16; Num 12:7; Heb 3:2 [b]Ex 14:31; Num 12:7 [c]Deut 18:18f [d]Heb 1:1
6 [a]Heb 1:2 [b]1 Cor 3:16; 1 Tim 3:15 [c]Rom 11:22; Heb 3:14 [d]Eph 3:12; Heb 4:16 [e]Heb 6:11; 1 Pet 1:3
7 [a]Acts 28:25; Heb 9:8 [b]Ps 95:7; Heb 3:15
8 [1]Lit *in the provocation* [a]Ps 95:8
9 [a]Ps 95:9-11 [b]Acts 7:36
10 [a]Ps 95:10
11 [a]Ps 95:11; Heb 4:3
12 [1]Lit *in falling* [a]Col 2:8; Heb 12:25 [b]Matt 16:16; Heb 9:14
13 [a]Heb 10:24f [b]Eph 4:22
14 [a]Heb 3:6 [b]Heb 11:1
15 [1]Lit *in the rebellion* [a]Ps 95:7f; Heb 3:7
16 [a]Jer 32:29 [b]Num 14:2; Deut 1:35
17 [a]Num 14:29; 1 Cor 10:5
18 [a]Num 14:23; Deut 1:34f; Heb 4:2 [b]Rom 11:30-32; Heb 4:6
19 [a]John 3:18; Rom 11:23; Heb 3:12
4:1 [a]2 Cor 6:1; Gal 5:4; Heb 12:15
2 [1]Lit *of hearing* [2]Two early mss read *they were...faith with those who heard* [a]Rom 10:17; Gal 3:2; 1 Thess 2:13
3 [a]Ps 95:11; Heb 3:11 [b]Matt 25:34
4 [a]Heb 2:6 [b]Gen 2:2 [c]Ex 20:11
5 [a]Ps 95:11; Heb 3:11
6 [a]Heb 3:18
7 [1]Or *in* [a]Heb 3:7f [b]Ps 95:7f
8 [1]Gr *Jesus* [a]Josh 22:4
10 [a]Rev 14:13 [b]Gen 2:2; Heb 4:4
11 [a]2 Pet 2:6 [b]Heb 3:18
12 [a]Jer 23:29; Eph 5:26; Heb 6:5; 1 Pet 1:23 [b]Acts 7:38 [c]1 Thess 2:13 [d]Eph 6:17 [e]1 Thess 5:23 [f]John 12:48; 1 Cor 14:24f
13 [a]2 Chr 16:9; Ps 33:13-15 [b]Job 26:6
14 [a]Heb 2:17 [b]Eph 4:10; Heb 6:20 [c]Matt 4:3; Heb 1:2 [d]Heb 3:1

15 For we do not have [a]a high priest who cannot sympathize with our weaknesses, but One who has been [b]tempted in all things as *we are, yet* [c]without sin.
16 Therefore let us [a]draw near with [b]confidence to the throne of grace, so that we may receive mercy and find grace to help in time of need.

The Perfect High Priest

5 For every high priest [a]taken from among men is appointed on behalf of men in [b]things pertaining to God, in order to [c]offer both gifts and sacrifices [d]for sins;
2 [1a]he can deal gently with the [b]ignorant and [c]misguided, since he himself also is [2d]beset with weakness;
3 and because of it he is obligated to offer *sacrifices* [a]for sins, [b]as for the people, so also for himself.
4 And [a]no one takes the honor to himself, but *receives it* when he is called by God, even [b]as Aaron was.
5 ¶ So also Christ [a]did not glorify Himself so as to become a [b]high priest, but He who [c]said to Him,

"[d]YOU ARE MY SON,
TODAY I HAVE BEGOTTEN YOU";

6 just as He says also in another *passage*,

"[a]YOU ARE A PRIEST FOREVER
ACCORDING TO [b]THE ORDER OF
MELCHIZEDEK."

7 [1]In the days of His flesh, [2a]He offered up both prayers and supplications with [b]loud crying and tears to the One [c]able to save Him [3]from death, and He [4]was heard because of His [d]piety.
8 Although He was [a]a Son, He learned [b]obedience from the things which He suffered.
9 And having been made [a]perfect, He became to all those who obey Him the source of eternal salvation,
10 being designated by God as [a]a high priest according to [b]the order of Melchizedek.
11 ¶ Concerning [1]him we have much to say, and *it is* hard to explain, since you have become dull of hearing.
12 For though [1]by this time you ought to be teachers, you have need again for someone to teach you [a]the [2b]elementary principles of the [c]oracles of God, and you have come to need [d]milk and not solid food.
13 For everyone who partakes *only* of milk is not accustomed to the word of righteousness, for he is an [a]infant.
14 But solid food is for [a]the mature, who because of practice have their senses [b]trained to [c]discern good and evil.

15 [a]Heb 2:17 [b]Heb 2:18 [c]2 Cor 5:21; Heb 7:26 **16** [a]Heb 7:19 [b]Heb 3:6 **5:1** [a]Ex 28:1 [b]Heb 2:17 [c]Heb 7:27 [d]1 Cor 15:3; Heb 7:27 **2** [1]Lit *being able to* [2]Or *subject to weakness* [a]Heb 2:18 [b]Eph 4:18; Heb 9:7 mg [c]James 5:19; 1 Pet 2:25 [d]Heb 7:28 **3** [a]1 Cor 15:3; Heb 7:27 [b]Lev 9:7; Heb 7:27 **4** [a]Num 16:40; 2 Chr 26:18 [b]Ex 28:1; 1 Chr 23:13 **5** [a]John 8:54 [b]Heb 2:17 [c]Heb 1:1 [d]Ps 2:7 **6** [a]Ps 110:4; Heb 7:17 [b]Heb 5:10 **7** [1]I.e. during Christ's earthly life [2]Lit *who having offered up* [3]Or *out of* [4]Lit *having been heard* [a]Matt 26:39; Mark 14:36; Luke 22:41 [b]Matt 27:46; Mark 15:34; Luke 23:46 [c]Mark 14:36 [d]Heb 11:7 **8** [a]Heb 1:2 [b]Phil 2:8 **9** [a]Heb 2:10 **10** [a]Heb 2:17 [b]Heb 5:6 **11** [1]Lit *whom* or *which* **12** [1]Lit *because of the time* [2]Lit *elements of the beginning* [a]Gal 4:3 [b]Heb 6:1 [c]Acts 7:38 [d]1 Cor 3:2; 1 Pet 2:2 **13** [a]1 Cor 3:1; 1 Pet 2:2 **14** [a]1 Cor 2:6; Eph 4:13; Heb 6:1 [b]1 Tim 4:7 [c]Rom 14:1ff **6:1** [1]Lit *word of the beginning* [2]I.e. Messiah [3]Or *perfection* [a]Phil 3:13f [b]Heb 5:12 [c]Heb 5:14 [d]Heb 9:14 **2** [a]John 3:25; Acts 19:3f [b]Acts 6:6 [c]Acts 17:31f **3** [a]Acts 18:21 **4** [a]2 Cor 4:4; Heb 10:32 [b]John 4:10; Eph 2:8 [c]Gal 3:2; Heb 2:4 **5** [a]1 Pet 2:3 [b]Eph 6:17 [c]Heb 2:5 **6** [1]Or *while* [a]Matt 19:26; Heb 10:26f; 2 Pet 2:21; 1 John 5:16 [b]Heb 10:29 **7** [1]Lit *comes* [a]2 Tim 2:6 **8** [1]Lit *near to a curse* [2]Lit *whose end is for burning* [a]Gen 3:17f; Deut 29:22ff **9** [1]Or *belong to*

The Peril of Falling Away

6 Therefore [a]leaving [b]the [1]elementary teaching about the [2]Christ, let us press on to [3c]maturity, not laying again a foundation of repentance from [d]dead works and of faith toward God,
2 of [a]instruction about washings and [b]laying on of hands, and the [c]resurrection of the dead and [c]eternal judgment.
3 And this we will do, [a]if God permits.
4 For in the case of those who have once been [a]enlightened and have tasted of [b]the heavenly gift and have been made [c]partakers of the Holy Spirit,
5 and [a]have tasted the good [b]word of God and the powers of [c]the age to come,
6 and *then* have fallen away, it is [a]impossible to renew them again to repentance, [1b]since they again crucify to themselves the Son of God and put Him to open shame.
7 For ground that drinks the rain which often [1]falls on it and brings forth vegetation useful to those [a]for whose sake it is also tilled, receives a blessing from God;
8 but if it yields thorns and thistles, it is worthless and [a]close [1]to being cursed, and [2]it ends up being burned.

Better Things for You

9 ¶ But, [a]beloved, we are convinced of better things concerning you, and things that [1]accompany salvation, though we are speaking in this way.
10 For [a]God is not unjust so as to forget [b]your work and the love which you have shown toward His name, in having [c]ministered and in still ministering to the [1]saints.
11 And we desire that each one of you show the same diligence [1]so as to realize the [a]full assurance of [b]hope until the end,
12 so that you will not be sluggish, but [a]imitators of those who through [b]faith and patience [c]inherit the promises.
13 ¶ For [a]when God made the promise to Abraham, since He could swear by no one greater, He [b]swore by Himself,
14 saying, "[a]I WILL SURELY BLESS YOU AND I WILL SURELY MULTIPLY YOU."
15 And so, [a]having patiently waited, he obtained the promise.
16 [a]For men swear by [1]one greater *than themselves*, and with them [b]an oath

[a]1 Cor 10:14; 2 Cor 7:1; 1 Pet 2:11; 2 Pet 3:1; 1 John 2:7; Jude 3 **10** [1]Or *holy ones* [a]Prov 19:17; Matt 10:42; Acts 10:4 [b]1 Thess 1:3 [c]Rom 15:25; Heb 10:32-34 **11** [1]Lit *to the full* [a]Heb 10:22 [b]Heb 3:6 **12** [a]Heb 13:7 [b]2 Thess 1:4; James 1:3; Rev 13:10 [c]Heb 1:14 **13** [a]Gal 3:15 [b]Gen 22:16; Luke 1:73 **14** [a]Gen 22:17 **15** [a]Gen 12:4 **16** [1]Or *Him who is greater* [a]Gal 3:15 [b]Ex 22:11

given as confirmation is an end of every
dispute.
17 [1]In the same way God, desiring
even more to show to [a]the heirs of the
promise [b]the unchangeableness of His
purpose, [2]interposed with an oath,
18 so that by two unchangeable things
in which [a]it is impossible for God to lie,
we who have [1]taken refuge would have
strong encouragement to take hold of
[b]the hope set before us.
19 [1]This [a]hope we have as an anchor
of the soul, a *hope* both sure and steadfast
and one which [b]enters [2]within the veil,
20 [a]where Jesus has entered as a fore-
runner for us, having become a [b]high
priest forever according to the order of
Melchizedek.

Melchizedek's Priesthood Like Christ's

7 For this [a]Melchizedek, king of Salem, priest of the [b]Most High God,
who met Abraham as he was returning
from the slaughter of the kings and
blessed him,
2 to whom also Abraham appor-
tioned a tenth part of all *the spoils*, was
first of all, by the translation *of his name*,
king of righteousness, and then also king
of Salem, which is king of peace.
3 Without father, without mother,
[a]without genealogy, having neither beginning of days nor end of life, but made
like [b]the Son of God, he remains a priest
perpetually.
4 ¶ Now observe how great this man
was to whom Abraham, the [a]patriarch,
[b]gave a tenth of the choicest spoils.
5 And those indeed of [a]the sons of
Levi who receive the priest's office have
commandment [1]in the Law to collect [2]a
tenth from the people, that is, from their
brethren, although these [3]are descended
from Abraham.
6 But the one [a]whose genealogy is
not traced from them [b]collected [1]a tenth
from Abraham and [2b]blessed the one
who [c]had the promises.
7 But without any dispute the lesser
is blessed by the greater.
8 In this case mortal men receive
tithes, but in that case one *receives them*,
[a]of whom it is witnessed that he
lives on.
9 And, so to speak, through Abraham
even Levi, who received tithes, paid
tithes,
10 for he was still in the loins of his
father when Melchizedek met him.
11 ¶ [a]Now if perfection was through
the Levitical priesthood (for on the basis
of it [b]the people received the Law), what
further need *was there* for another priest
to arise [c]according to the order of Melchizedek, and not be designated according to the order of Aaron?
12 For when the priesthood is
changed, of necessity there takes place a
change of law also.
13 For [a]the one concerning whom
[b]these things are spoken belongs to another tribe, from which no one has of-
ficiated at the altar.
14 For it is evident that our Lord [1]was
[a]descended from Judah, a tribe with reference to which Moses spoke nothing
concerning priests.
15 And this is clearer still, if another
priest arises according to the likeness of
Melchizedek,
16 who has become *such* not on the
basis of a law of [1a]physical requirement,
but according to the power of [b]an inde-
structible life.
17 For it is attested *of Him*,
"[a]YOU ARE A PRIEST FOREVER
ACCORDING TO THE ORDER OF
MELCHIZEDEK."
18 For, on the one hand, there is a
setting aside of a former commandment
[a]because of its weakness and uselessness
19 (for [a]the Law made nothing perfect), and on the other hand there is a
bringing in of a better [b]hope, through
which we [c]draw near to God.
20 And inasmuch as *it was* not without
an oath
21 (for they indeed became priests
without an oath, but He with an oath
through the One who said to Him,
"[a]THE LORD HAS SWORN
AND [b]WILL NOT CHANGE HIS MIND,
'YOU ARE A PRIEST [c]FOREVER' ");
22 so much the more also Jesus has
become the [a]guarantee of [b]a better covenant.
23 ¶ [1]The *former* priests, on the one
hand, existed in greater numbers because
they were prevented by death from continuing,
24 but Jesus, on the other hand, because He continues [a]forever, holds His
priesthood permanently.
25 Therefore He is able also to [a]save
[1]forever those who [b]draw near to God
through Him, since He always lives to
[c]make intercession for them.
26 ¶ For it was fitting for us to have
such a [a]high priest, [b]holy, [c]innocent,
undefiled, separated from sinners and
[d]exalted above the heavens;
27 who does not need daily, like those
high priests, to [a]offer up sacrifices, [b]first
for His own sins and then for the *sins* of
the people, because this He did [c]once for
all when He [d]offered up Himself.

17 [1]Lit *In which* [2]Or *guaranteed* [a]Heb 11:9 [b]Ps 110:4; Prov 19:21; Heb 6:18
18 [1]Lit *in which* [a]Num 23:19; Titus 1:2 [b]Heb 3:6
19 [1]Lit *Which hope we have* [2]Or *inside* [a]Ps 39:7; Acts 23:6; Rom 4:18; 1 Cor 13:13; Col 1:27; 1 Pet 1:3 [b]Lev 16:2; Heb 9:3
20 [a]John 14:2; Heb 4:14 [b]Ps 110:4; Heb 2:17
7:1 [a]Gen 14:18-20; Heb 7:6 [b]Mark 5:7
3 [a]Heb 7:6 [b]Matt 4:3; Heb 7:1
4 [a]Acts 2:29 [b]Gen 14:20
5 [1]Lit *according to* [2]Or *tithes* [3]Lit *have come out of the loins of* [a]Num 18:21; 2 Chr 31:4f
6 [1]Or *tithes* [2]Lit *has blessed* [a]Heb 7:3 [b]Heb 7:1f [c]Rom 4:13
8 [a]Heb 5:6
11 [a]Heb 7:18f [b]Heb 9:6 [c]Heb 5:6
13 [a]Heb 7:14 [b]Heb 7:11
14 [1]Lit *has arisen from* [a]Num 24:17; Is 11:1; Mic 5:2; Matt 2:6; Rev 5:5
16 [1]Lit *fleshly commandment*; i.e. to be a descendant of Levi [a]Heb 9:10 [b]Heb 9:14
17 [a]Ps 110:4; Heb 5:6
18 [a]Rom 8:3; Gal 3:21; Heb 7:11
19 [a]Acts 13:39; Rom 3:20; Gal 2:16; Heb 9:9 [b]Heb 3:6 [c]Lam 3:57; Heb 4:16; James 4:8
21 [a]Ps 110:4; Heb 5:6 [b]Num 23:19; 1 Sam 15:29; Rom 11:29 [c]Heb 7:23f
22 [a]Ps 119:122; Is 38:14 [b]Heb 8:6
23 [1]Lit *The greater number have become priests...*
24 [a]Is 9:7; John 12:34; Rom 9:5; Heb 7:23f
25 [1]Or *completely* [a]1 Cor 1:21 [b]Heb 7:19 [c]Rom 8:34; Heb 9:24
26 [a]Heb 2:17 [b]2 Cor 5:21; Heb 4:15 [c]1 Pet 2:22 [d]Heb 4:14
27 [a]Heb 5:1 [b]Lev 9:7; Heb 5:3 [c]Heb 9:12 [d]Eph 5:2; Heb 9:14

28 For the Law appoints men as high
priests [a]who are weak, but the word of
the oath, which came after the Law, *ap-*
points [b]a Son, [c]made perfect forever.

A Better Ministry

8 Now the main point in what has
been said *is this*: we have such a
[a]high priest, who has taken His seat at
[b]the right hand of the throne of the
[b]Majesty in the heavens,
2 a [a]minister [1]in the sanctuary and
[1]in the [b]true [2]tabernacle, which the
Lord [c]pitched, not man.
3 For every [a]high priest is appointed
[b]to offer both gifts and sacrifices; so it is
necessary that this *high priest* also have
something to offer.
4 Now if He were on earth, He would
not be a priest at all, since there are those
who [a]offer the gifts according to the
Law;
5 who serve [a]a copy and [b]shadow of
the heavenly things, just as Moses [1]was
[c]warned *by God* when he was about to
erect the [2]tabernacle; for, "[d]SEE," He
says, "THAT YOU MAKE all things ACCORD-
ING TO THE PATTERN WHICH WAS SHOWN YOU
ON THE MOUNTAIN."
6 But now He has obtained a more
excellent ministry, by as much as He is
also the [a]mediator of [b]a better covenant,
which has been enacted on better promises.

A New Covenant

7 For [a]if that first *covenant* had been
faultless, there would have been no occasion sought for a second.
8 For finding fault with them, He
says,

"[a]BEHOLD, DAYS ARE COMING, SAYS
THE LORD,
[1]WHEN I WILL EFFECT [b]A NEW
COVENANT
WITH THE HOUSE OF ISRAEL AND
WITH THE HOUSE OF JUDAH;
9 [a]NOT LIKE THE COVENANT WHICH I
MADE WITH THEIR FATHERS
ON THE DAY WHEN I TOOK THEM BY
THE HAND
TO LEAD THEM OUT OF THE LAND OF
EGYPT;
FOR THEY DID NOT CONTINUE IN MY
COVENANT,
AND I DID NOT CARE FOR THEM,
SAYS THE LORD.
10 "[a]FOR THIS IS THE COVENANT THAT I
WILL MAKE WITH THE HOUSE OF
ISRAEL
AFTER THOSE DAYS, SAYS THE LORD:
[1]I WILL PUT MY LAWS INTO THEIR
MINDS,

28 [a]Heb 5:2 [b]Heb 1:2 [c]Heb 2:10
8:1 [a]Col 3:1; Heb 2:17 [b]Ps 110:1; Heb 1:3
2 [1]Or *of* [2]Or *sacred tent* [a]Heb 10:11 [b]Heb 9:11 [c]Ex 33:7
3 [a]Heb 2:17 [b]Rom 4:25; Gal 2:20; Eph 5:2; Heb 5:1
4 [a]Heb 5:1
5 [1]Lit *has been* [2]Or *sacred tent* [a]Heb 9:23 [b]Col 2:17; Heb 10:1 [c]Matt 2:12; Heb 11:7 [d]Ex 25:40
6 [a]1 Tim 2:5 [b]Luke 22:20; Heb 7:22
7 [a]Heb 7:11
8 [1]Lit *And* [a]Jer 31:31 [b]Luke 22:20; 2 Cor 3:6; Heb 7:22
9 [a]Ex 19:5; Deut 5:2; Jer 31:32
10 [1]Lit *Putting my laws into...* [a]Jer 31:33; Rom 11:27; Heb 10:16 [b]2 Cor 3:3
11 [1]Lit *small to great of them* [a]Jer 31:34 [b]Is 54:13; John 6:45; 1 John 2:27
12 [a]Is 43:25; Jer 31:34; Mic 7:18 [b]Heb 10:17
13 [1]Or *In His saying* [2]Or *near* [a]Luke 22:20; 2 Cor 3:6; Heb 7:22 [b]2 Cor 5:17; Heb 1:11
9:1 [a]Heb 9:10 [b]Ex 25:8; Heb 8:2
2 [1]Or *sacred tent* [2]Lit *first* [3]Lit *loaves of presentation* [a]Ex 25:8 [b]Ex 25:31-39 [c]Ex 25:23-29 [d]Ex 25:30; Lev 24:5ff; Matt 12:4
3 [1]Or *sacred tent* [a]Ex 26:31-33 [b]Ex 26:33
4 [1]Or *censer* [a]Ex 30:1-5 [b]Ex 25:10ff [c]Ex 16:32f [d]Num 17:10 [e]Ex 25:16; Deut 9:9
5 [a]Ex 25:18ff [b]Ex 25:17; Lev 16:2; 1 Kin 8:7
6 [1]Lit *first* [2]Or *sacred tent* [a]Num 18:2-6
7 [1]Lit *ignorance of the people* [a]Heb 9:3 [b]Lev 16:12ff [c]Ex 30:10; Lev 16:34; Heb 10:3 [d]Lev 16:11 [e]Heb 5:3 [f]Num 15:25; Heb 5:2
8 [1]Lit *first* [a]Heb 3:7 [b]John 14:6; Heb 10:20
9 [a]Heb 5:1 [b]Heb 7:19
10 [a]Lev 11:2ff; Col 2:16 [b]Num 6:3 [c]Lev 11:25; Num 19:13; Mark 7:4 [d]Heb 7:16

AND I WILL WRITE THEM [b]ON THEIR
HEARTS.
AND I WILL BE THEIR GOD,
AND THEY SHALL BE MY PEOPLE.
11 "[a]AND THEY SHALL NOT TEACH
EVERYONE HIS FELLOW CITIZEN,
AND EVERYONE HIS BROTHER,
SAYING, 'KNOW THE LORD,'
FOR [b]ALL WILL KNOW ME,
FROM [1]THE LEAST TO THE GREATEST
OF THEM.
12 "[a]FOR I WILL BE MERCIFUL TO THEIR
INIQUITIES,
[b]AND I WILL REMEMBER THEIR SINS
NO MORE."

13 [1]When He said, "[a]A new *cov-*
enant," He has made the first obsolete.
[b]But whatever is becoming obsolete and
growing old is [2]ready to disappear.

The Old and the New

9 Now even the first *covenant* had
[a]regulations of divine worship and
[b]the earthly sanctuary.
2 For there was [a]a [1]tabernacle prepared, the [2]outer one, in which *were*
[b]the lampstand and [c]the table and [d]the
[3]sacred bread; this is called the holy place.
3 Behind [a]the second veil there was
a [1]tabernacle which is called the [b]Holy
of Holies,
4 having a golden [1a]altar of incense
and [b]the ark of the covenant covered on
all sides with gold, in which was [c]a gold-
en jar holding the manna, and [d]Aaron's
rod which budded, and [e]the tables of the
covenant;
5 and above it *were* the [a]cherubim of
glory [b]overshadowing the mercy seat;
but of these things we cannot now speak
in detail.
6 ¶ Now when these things have
been so prepared, the priests [a]are continually entering the [1]outer [2]tabernacle
performing the divine worship,
7 but into [a]the second, only [b]the
high priest *enters* [c]once a year, [d]not
without *taking* blood, which he [e]offers
for himself and for the [1f]sins of the people committed in ignorance.
8 [a]The Holy Spirit *is* signifying this,
[b]that the way into the holy place has not
yet been disclosed while the [1]outer tabernacle is still standing,
9 which *is* a symbol for the present
time. Accordingly [a]both gifts and sacrifices are offered which [b]cannot make the
worshiper perfect in conscience,
10 since they *relate* only to [a]food and
[b]drink and various [c]washings, [d]regula-

tions for the [1]body imposed until [e]a time of reformation.

11 ¶ But when Christ appeared *as* a [a]high priest of the [b]good things [1]to come, *He entered* through [c]the greater and more perfect [2]tabernacle, [d]not made with hands, that is to say, [e]not of this creation;

12 and not through [a]the blood of goats and calves, but [b]through His own blood, He [c]entered the holy place [d]once for all, [1]having obtained [e]eternal redemption.

13 For if [a]the blood of goats and bulls and [b]the ashes of a heifer sprinkling those who have been defiled sanctify for the [1]cleansing of the flesh,

14 how much more will [a]the blood of Christ, who through [1b]the eternal Spirit [c]offered Himself without blemish to God, [d]cleanse [2]your conscience from [e]dead works to serve [f]the living God?

15 ¶ For this reason [a]He is the [b]mediator of a [c]new covenant, so that, since a death has taken place for the redemption of the transgressions that were *committed* under the first covenant, those who have been [d]called may [e]receive the promise of [f]the eternal inheritance.

16 For where a [1]covenant is, there must of necessity [2]be the death of the one who made it.

17 For a [1]covenant is valid *only* when [2]men are dead, [3]for it is never in force while the one who made it lives.

18 Therefore even the first *covenant* was not inaugurated without blood.

19 For when every commandment had been [a]spoken by Moses to all the people according to the Law, [b]he took the [c]blood of the calves and the goats, with [d]water and scarlet wool and hyssop, and sprinkled both [e]the book itself and all the people,

20 saying, "[a]THIS IS THE BLOOD OF THE COVENANT WHICH GOD COMMANDED YOU."

21 And in the same way he [a]sprinkled both the [1]tabernacle and all the vessels of the ministry with the blood.

22 And according to the [1]Law, *one may* [a]almost *say*, all things are cleansed with blood, and [b]without shedding of blood there is no forgiveness.

23 ¶ Therefore it was necessary for the [a]copies of the things in the heavens to be cleansed with these, but [a]the heavenly things themselves with better sacrifices than these.

24 For Christ [a]did not enter a holy place made with hands, a *mere* copy of [b]the true one, but into [c]heaven itself, now [d]to appear in the presence of God for us;

25 nor was it that He would offer Himself often, as [a]the high priest enters [b]the holy place [a]year by year with blood that is not his own.

26 Otherwise, He would have needed to suffer often since [a]the foundation of the world; but now [b]once at [c]the consummation of the ages He has been [d]manifested to put away sin [1e]by the sacrifice of Himself.

27 And inasmuch as [a]it is [1]appointed for men to die once and after this [b]*comes* judgment,

28 so Christ also, having been [a]offered once to [b]bear the sins of many, will appear [c]a second time for [d]salvation [e]without *reference to* sin, to those who [f]eagerly await Him.

One Sacrifice of Christ Is Sufficient

10 For the Law, since it has *only* [a]a shadow of [b]the good things to come *and* not the very [1]form of things, [2]can [c]never, by the same sacrifices which they offer continually year by year, [d]make perfect those who draw near.

2 Otherwise, would they not have ceased to be offered, because the worshipers, having once been cleansed, would no longer have had [a]consciousness of sins?

3 But [a]in [1]those *sacrifices* there is a reminder of sins year by year.

4 For it is [a]impossible for the [b]blood of bulls and goats to take away sins.

5 Therefore, [a]when He comes into the world, He says,

"[b]SACRIFICE AND OFFERING YOU
HAVE NOT DESIRED,
BUT [c]A BODY YOU HAVE PREPARED
FOR ME;

6 [a]IN WHOLE BURNT OFFERINGS AND
sacrifices FOR SIN YOU HAVE
TAKEN NO PLEASURE.

7 "[a]THEN I SAID, 'BEHOLD, I HAVE
COME
(IN [b]THE SCROLL OF THE BOOK IT IS
WRITTEN OF ME)
TO DO YOUR WILL, O GOD.' "

8 After saying above, "[a]SACRIFICES AND OFFERINGS AND [b]WHOLE BURNT OFFERINGS AND *sacrifices* [c]FOR SIN YOU HAVE NOT DESIRED, NOR HAVE YOU TAKEN PLEASURE *in them*" (which are offered according to the Law),

9 then He [1]said, "[a]BEHOLD, I HAVE COME TO DO YOUR WILL." He takes away the first in order to establish the second.

10 By [1]this will we have been [a]sanctified through [b]the offering of [c]the body of Jesus Christ [d]once for all.

10 [1]Lit *flesh* [e]Heb 7:12
11 [1]Two early mss read *that have come* [2]Or *sacred tent* [a]Heb 2:17 [b]Heb 10:1 [c]Heb 8:2 [d]Mark 14:58; 2 Cor 5:1 [e]2 Cor 4:18; Heb 12:27
12 [1]Or *obtaining* [a]Lev 4:3; Heb 9:19 [b]Heb 9:14 [c]Heb 9:24 [d]Heb 7:27 [e]Heb 5:9
13 [1]Lit *purity* [a]Lev 16:15; Heb 9:19 [b]Num 19:9
14 [1]Or His *eternal spirit* [2]One early ms reads *our* [a]Heb 9:12 [b]1 Cor 15:45; 1 Pet 3:18 [c]Eph 5:2; Heb 7:27 [d]Acts 15:9; Titus 2:14; Heb 1:3 [e]Heb 6:1 [f]Matt 16:16; Heb 3:12
15 [a]Rom 3:24 [b]1 Tim 2:5; Heb 8:6 [c]Heb 8:8 [d]Matt 22:3ff; Rom 8:28f; Heb 3:1 [e]Heb 6:15 [f]Acts 20:32
16 [1]Or *testament* [2]Lit *be brought*
17 [1]Or *testament* [2]Lit *over the dead* [3]Two early mss read *for is it then...lives?*
19 [a]Heb 1:1 [b]Ex 24:6ff [c]Heb 9:12 [d]Lev 14:4; Num 19:6 [e]Ex 24:7
20 [a]Ex 24:8; Matt 26:28
21 [1]Or *sacred tent* [a]Ex 24:6; Lev 8:15
22 [1]Or *Law, almost all things* [a]Lev 5:11f [b]Lev 17:11
23 [a]Heb 8:5
24 [a]Heb 4:14 [b]Heb 8:2 [c]Heb 9:12 [d]Matt 18:10; Heb 7:25
25 [a]Heb 9:7 [b]Heb 9:2
26 [1]Or *by His sacrifice* [a]Matt 25:34; Heb 4:3 [b]Heb 7:27 [c]Matt 13:39; Heb 1:2 [d]1 John 3:5 [e]Heb 9:12
27 [1]Lit *laid up* [a]Gen 3:19 [b]2 Cor 5:10; 1 John 4:17
28 [a]Heb 7:27 [b]Is 53:12; 1 Pet 2:24 [c]Acts 1:11 [d]Heb 5:9 [e]Heb 4:15 [f]1 Cor 1:7; Titus 2:13
10:1 [1]Lit *image* [2]Two early mss read *they can* [a]Heb 8:5 [b]Heb 9:11 [c]Rom 8:3; Heb 9:9 [d]Heb 7:19
2 [a]1 Pet 2:19
3 [1]Lit *them there is* [a]Heb 9:7
4 [a]Heb 10:1 [b]Heb 9:12f
5 [a]Heb 1:6 [b]Ps 40:6 [c]Heb 2:14; 1 Pet 2:24

6 [a]Ps 40:6 **7** [a]Ps 40:7 [b]Ezra 6:2; Jer 36:2; Ezek 2:9 **8** [a]Ps 40:6; Heb 10:5f [b]Mark 12:33 [c]Rom 8:3 **9** [1]Lit *has said* [a]Ps 40:7; Heb 10:7 **10** [1]Lit *which* [a]John 17:19; Eph 5:26; Heb 2:11 [b]John 6:51; Eph 5:2; Heb 7:27 [c]Heb 2:14; 1 Pet 2:24 [d]Heb 7:27

11 ¶ Every priest stands daily ministering and [a]offering time after time the
same sacrifices, which [b]can never take
away sins;
12 but He, having offered one sacrifice
[a]for [1]sins [b]for all time, [c]SAT DOWN AT
THE RIGHT HAND OF GOD,
13 waiting from that time onward
[a]UNTIL HIS ENEMIES BE MADE A FOOTSTOOL
FOR HIS FEET.
14 For by one offering He has [a]per-
fected [b]for all time those who are [1]sanc-
tified.
15 And [a]the Holy Spirit also testifies
to us; for after saying,
16 "[a]THIS IS THE COVENANT THAT I
WILL MAKE WITH THEM
AFTER THOSE DAYS, SAYS THE LORD:
I WILL PUT MY LAWS UPON THEIR
HEART,
AND ON THEIR MIND I WILL WRITE
THEM,"
He then says,
17 "[a]AND THEIR SINS AND THEIR
LAWLESS DEEDS
I WILL REMEMBER NO MORE."
18 Now where there is forgiveness of
these things, there is no longer *any* offering for sin.

A New and Living Way

19 ¶ Therefore, brethren, since we
[a]have confidence to [b]enter the holy
place by the blood of Jesus,
20 by [a]a new and living way which He
inaugurated for us through [b]the veil, that
is, His flesh,
21 and since *we have* [a]a great priest
[b]over the house of God,
22 let us [a]draw near with a [1]sincere
heart in [b]full assurance of faith, having
our hearts [c]sprinkled *clean* from an evil
conscience and our bodies [d]washed with
pure water.
23 Let us hold fast the [a]confession of
our [b]hope without wavering, for [c]He
who promised is faithful;
24 and let us consider how [a]to stimu-
late one another to love and [b]good deeds,
25 not forsaking our own [a]assembling
together, as is the habit of some, but [b]en-
couraging *one another;* and all the more
as you see [c]the day drawing near.

Christ or Judgment

26 ¶ For if we go on [a]sinning willfully
after receiving [b]the knowledge of the
truth, there no longer remains a sacrifice
for sins,
27 but a terrifying expectation of
[a]judgment and [b]THE FURY OF A FIRE WHICH
WILL CONSUME THE ADVERSARIES.
28 [a]Anyone who has set aside the
Law of Moses dies without mercy on *the
testimony of* two or three witnesses.
29 [a]How much severer punishment
do you think he will deserve [b]who has
trampled under foot the Son of God, and
has regarded as unclean [c]the blood of the
covenant [d]by which he was sanctified,
and has [e]insulted the Spirit of grace?
30 For we know Him who said,
"[a]VENGEANCE IS MINE, I WILL REPAY." And
again, "[b]THE LORD WILL JUDGE HIS PEO-
PLE."
31 It is a [a]terrifying thing to fall into
the hands of the [b]living God.
32 ¶ But remember [a]the former days,
[1]when, after being [b]enlightened, you
endured a great [c]conflict of sufferings,
33 partly by being [a]made a public
spectacle through reproaches and tribulations, and partly by becoming [b]sharers
with those who were so treated.
34 For you [a]showed sympathy to the
prisoners and accepted [b]joyfully the sei-
zure of your property, knowing that you
have for yourselves [c]a better possession
and a lasting one.
35 Therefore, do not throw away your
[a]confidence, which has a great [b]reward.
36 For you have need of [a]endurance,
so that when you have [b]done the will of
God, you may [c]receive [1]what was promised.
37 [a]FOR YET IN A VERY LITTLE WHILE,
[b]HE WHO IS COMING WILL COME,
AND WILL NOT DELAY.
38 [a]BUT MY RIGHTEOUS ONE SHALL
LIVE BY FAITH;
AND IF HE SHRINKS BACK, MY SOUL
HAS NO PLEASURE IN HIM.
39 But [1]we are not of those who
shrink back to destruction, but of those
who have faith to the [2]preserving of the
soul.

The Triumphs of Faith

11 Now faith is the [1a]assurance of
things [2b]hoped for, the [3]convic-
tion of [c]things not seen.
2 For by it the [a]men of old [1b]gained
approval.
3 ¶ By faith we understand that the
[1a]worlds were prepared [b]by the word
of God, so that what is seen [c]was not
made out of things which are visible.
4 By faith [a]Abel offered to God a better sacrifice than Cain, through which he
[b]obtained the testimony that he was
righteous, God testifying [1]about his

11 [a]Heb 5:1 [b]Mic 6:6-8; Heb 10:1 **12** [1]Or *sins, forever sat down* [a]Heb 5:1 [b]Heb 10:14 [c]Ps 110:1; Heb 1:3 **13** [a]Ps 110:1; Heb 1:13 **14** [1]Or *being sanctified* [a]Heb 10:1 [b]Heb 10:12 **15** [a]Heb 3:7 **16** [a]Jer 31:33; Heb 8:10 **17** [a]Jer 31:34; Heb 8:12 **19** [a]Heb 3:6 [b]Heb 9:25 **20** [a]Heb 9:8 [b]Heb 6:19 **21** [a]Heb 2:17 [b]1 Tim 3:15; Heb 3:6 **22** [1]Lit *true* [a]Heb 7:19 [b]Heb 6:11 [c]Ezek 36:25; Heb 9:19; 1 Pet 1:2 [d]Acts 22:16; 1 Cor 6:11; Eph 5:26; Titus 3:5; 1 Pet 3:21 **23** [a]Heb 3:1 [b]Heb 3:6 [c]1 Cor 1:9; Heb 11:11 **24** [a]Heb 13:1 [b]Titus 3:8 **25** [a]Acts 2:42 [b]Heb 3:13 [c]1 Cor 3:13 **26** [a]Num 15:30; Heb 6:4-8; 2 Pet 2:20f [b]1 Tim 2:4 **27** [a]John 5:29; Heb 9:27 [b]Is 26:11; 2 Thess 1:7 **28** [a]Deut 17:2-6; Matt 18:16; Heb 2:2 **29** [a]Heb 2:3 [b]Heb 6:6 [c]Ex 24:8; Matt 26:28; Heb 13:20 [d]Eph 5:26; Heb 9:13f; Rev 1:5 [e]1 Cor 6:11; Eph 4:30; Heb 6:4 **30** [a]Deut 32:35; Rom 12:19 [b]Deut 32:36 **31** [a]2 Cor 5:11 [b]Matt 16:16; Heb 3:12 **32** [1]Lit *in which* [a]Heb 5:12 [b]Heb 6:4 [c]Phil 1:30 **33** [a]1 Cor 4:9; Heb 12:4 [b]Phil 4:14; 1 Thess 2:14 **34** [a]Heb 13:3 [b]Matt 5:12 [c]Heb 9:15; 1 Pet 1:4f **35** [a]Heb 10:19 [b]Heb 2:2 **36** [1]Lit *the promise* [a]Luke 21:19; Heb 12:1 [b]Mark 3:35 [c]Heb 9:15 **37** [a]Hab 2:3; Heb 10:25; Rev 22:20 [b]Matt 11:3 **38** [a]Hab 2:4; Rom 1:17; Gal 3:11 **39** [1]Lit *we are not of shrinking back...but of faith* [2]Or *possessing* **11:1** [1]Or *substance* [2]Or *expected* [3]Or *evidence* [a]Heb 3:14 [b]Heb 3:6 [c]Rom 8:24; 2 Cor 4:18; Heb 11:7 **2** [1]Lit *obtained a* good *testimony* [a]Heb 1:1 [b]Heb 11:4 **3** [1]Lit *ages* [a]John 1:3; Heb 1:2 [b]Gen ch 1; Ps 33:6; Heb 6:5; 2 Pet 3:5 [c]Rom 4:17 **4** [1]I.e. by receiving his gifts [a]Gen 4:4; Matt 23:35; 1 John 3:12 [b]Heb 11:2

[c]gifts, and through [2]faith, though [d]he is dead, he still speaks.

5 By faith [a]Enoch was taken up so that he would not [b]see death; AND HE WAS NOT FOUND BECAUSE GOD TOOK HIM UP; for he obtained the witness that before his being taken up he was pleasing to God.

6 And without faith it is impossible to please *Him*, for he who [a]comes to God must believe that He is and *that* He is a rewarder of those who seek Him.

7 By faith [a]Noah, being [b]warned *by God* about [c]things not yet seen, [1d]in reverence [e]prepared an ark for the salvation of his household, by which he condemned the world, and became an heir of [f]the righteousness which is according to faith.

8 ¶ By faith [a]Abraham, when he was called, obeyed [1]by going out to a place which he was to [b]receive for an inheritance; and he went out, not knowing where he was going.

9 By faith he lived as an alien in [a]the land of promise, as in a foreign *land*, [b]dwelling in tents with Isaac and Jacob, [c]fellow heirs of the same promise;

10 for he was looking for [a]the city which has [b]foundations, [c]whose architect and builder is God.

11 By faith even [a]Sarah herself received [1]ability to conceive, even beyond the proper time of life, since she considered Him [b]faithful who had promised.

12 Therefore there was born even of one man, and [a]him as good as dead [1]at that, *as many descendants* [b]AS THE STARS OF HEAVEN IN NUMBER, AND INNUMERABLE AS THE SAND WHICH IS BY THE SEASHORE.

13 ¶ [a]All these died in faith, [b]without receiving the promises, but [c]having seen them and having welcomed them from a distance, and [d]having confessed that they were strangers and exiles on the earth.

14 For those who say such things make it clear that they are seeking a country of their own.

15 And indeed if they had been [1]thinking of that *country* from which they went out, [a]they would have had opportunity to return.

16 But as it is, they desire a better *country*, that is, a [a]heavenly one. Therefore [b]God is not [1]ashamed to be [c]called their God; for [d]He has prepared a city for them.

17 ¶ By faith [a]Abraham, when he was tested, offered up Isaac, and he who had [b]received the promises was offering up his only begotten *son*;

18 *it was he* to whom it was said, "[a]IN ISAAC YOUR [1]DESCENDANTS SHALL BE CALLED."

19 [1]He considered that [a]God is able to raise *people* even from the dead, from which he also received him back [2]as a [b]type.

20 By faith [a]Isaac blessed Jacob and Esau, even regarding things to come.

21 By faith [a]Jacob, as he was dying, blessed each of the sons of Joseph, and [b]worshiped, *leaning* on the top of his staff.

22 By faith [a]Joseph, when he was dying, made mention of the exodus of the sons of Israel, and gave orders concerning his bones.

23 ¶ By faith [a]Moses, when he was born, was hidden for three months by his parents, because they saw he was a beautiful child; and they were not afraid of the [b]king's edict.

24 By faith Moses, [a]when he had grown up, refused to be called the son of Pharaoh's daughter,

25 choosing rather to [a]endure ill-treatment with the people of God than to enjoy the passing pleasures of sin,

26 [a]considering the reproach of [1]Christ greater riches than the treasures of Egypt; for he was looking to the [b]reward.

27 By faith he [a]left Egypt, not [b]fearing the wrath of the king; for he endured, as [c]seeing Him who is unseen.

28 By faith he [1a]kept the Passover and the sprinkling of the blood, so that [b]he who destroyed the firstborn would not touch them.

29 By faith they [a]passed through the Red Sea as though *they were passing* through dry land; and the Egyptians, when they attempted it, were [1]drowned.

30 ¶ By faith [a]the walls of Jericho fell down [b]after they had been encircled for seven days.

31 By faith [a]Rahab the harlot did not perish along with those who were disobedient, after she had welcomed the spies [1]in peace.

32 ¶ And what more shall I say? For time will fail me if I tell of [a]Gideon, [b]Barak, [c]Samson, [d]Jephthah, of [e]David and [f]Samuel and the prophets,

33 who by faith [a]conquered kingdoms, [b]performed *acts of* righteousness, [c]obtained promises, [d]shut the mouths of lions,

34 [a]quenched the power of fire, [b]escaped the edge of the sword, from weak-

4 [2]Lit *it* [c]Heb 5:1 [d]Gen 4:8-10; Heb 12:24
5 [a]Gen 5:21-24 [b]Luke 2:26; John 8:51; Heb 2:9
6 [a]Heb 7:19
7 [1]Lit *having become reverent* [a]Gen 6:13-22 [b]Heb 8:5 [c]Heb 11:1 [d]Heb 5:7 [e]1 Pet 3:20 [f]Gen 6:9; Ezek 14:14; Rom 4:13
8 [1]Lit *to go out* [a]Gen 12:1-4; Acts 7:2-4 [b]Gen 12:7
9 [a]Acts 7:5 [b]Gen 12:8 [c]Heb 6:17
10 [a]Heb 12:22 [b]Rev 21:14ff [c]Heb 11:16
11 [1]Lit *power for the laying down of seed* [a]Gen 17:19 [b]Heb 10:23
12 [1]Lit *in these things* [a]Rom 4:19 [b]Gen 15:5
13 [a]Matt 13:17 [b]Heb 11:39 [c]John 8:56; Heb 11:27 [d]Gen 23:4; 1 Chr 29:15; Ps 39:12; Eph 2:19; 1 Pet 1:1
15 [1]Or *remembering* [a]Gen 24:6-8
16 [1]Lit *ashamed of them, to be* [a]2 Tim 4:18 [b]Mark 8:38; Heb 2:11 [c]Gen 26:24; Ex 3:6 [d]Heb 11:10; Rev 21:2
17 [a]Gen 22:1-10; James 2:21 [b]Heb 11:13
18 [1]Lit *seed* [a]Gen 21:12; Rom 9:7
19 [1]Lit *Considering* [2]Or *figuratively speaking*; lit *in a parable* [a]Rom 4:21 [b]Heb 9:9
20 [a]Gen 27:27-29
21 [a]Gen 48:1 [b]Gen 47:31; 1 Kin 1:47
22 [a]Gen 50:24f; Ex 13:19
23 [a]Ex 2:2 [b]Ex 1:16
24 [a]Ex 2:10
25 [a]Heb 11:37
26 [1]I.e. the Messiah [a]Luke 14:33; Phil 3:7f [b]Heb 2:2
27 [a]Ex 2:15 [b]Ex 2:14 [c]Col 1:15; Heb 11:1
28 [1]Lit *has kept* [a]Ex 12:21ff [b]Ex 12:23; 1 Cor 10:10
29 [1]Lit *swallowed up* [a]Ex 14:22-29
30 [a]Josh 6:20 [b]Josh 6:15f
31 [1]Lit *with* [a]Josh 2:9ff; James 2:25
32 [a]Judg ch 6-8 [b]Judg ch 4 [c]Judg ch 13-16 [d]Judg ch 11 [e]1 Sam 16:1 [f]1 Sam 1:20
33 [a]Judg ch 4; 2 Sam 5:17-20 [b]1 Sam 12:4; 2 Sam 8:15 [c]2 Sam 7:11f [d]Judg 14:6; 1 Sam 17:34ff; Dan 6:22
34 [a]Dan 3:23ff [b]Ex 18:4; 1 Sam 18:11; 1 Kin ch 19; 2 Kin ch 6; Ps 144:10

ness were made strong, [c]became mighty
in war, [c]put foreign armies to flight.
35 [a]Women received *back* their dead
by resurrection; and others were tor-
tured, not accepting their [1]release, so
that they might obtain a better resurrection;
36 and others [1]experienced mockings
and scourgings, yes, also [a]chains and imprisonment.
37 They were [a]stoned, they were
[b]sawn in two, [1]they were tempted, they
were [c]put to death with the sword; they
went about [d]in sheepskins, in goatskins,
being destitute, afflicted, [e]ill-treated
38 (*men* of whom the world was not
worthy), [a]wandering in deserts and
mountains and caves and holes [1]in the
ground.
39 ¶ And all these, having [1a]gained
approval through their faith, [b]did not receive [2]what was promised,
40 because God had [1]provided [a]some-
thing better for us, so that [b]apart from
us they would not be made perfect.

Jesus, the Example

12 Therefore, since we have so great
a cloud of witnesses surrounding
us, let us also [a]lay aside every encum-
brance and the sin which so easily entan-
gles us, and let us [b]run with [c]endurance
the race that is set before us,
2 [1]fixing our eyes on Jesus, the
[2a]author and perfecter of faith, who
for the joy set before Him [b]endured
the cross, [c]despising the shame, and has
[d]sat down at the right hand of the throne
of God.
3 ¶ For [a]consider Him who has endured such hostility by sinners against
Himself, so that you will not grow weary
[1b]and lose heart.

A Father's Discipline

4 [a]You have not yet resisted [1b]to
the point of shedding blood in your striving against sin;
5 and you have forgotten the exhortation which is addressed to you as sons,
"[a]MY SON, DO NOT REGARD LIGHTLY
THE DISCIPLINE OF THE LORD,
NOR [b]FAINT WHEN YOU ARE
REPROVED BY HIM;
6 [a]FOR THOSE [b]WHOM THE LORD
LOVES HE DISCIPLINES,
AND HE SCOURGES EVERY SON
WHOM HE RECEIVES."
7 It is for discipline that you endure;
[a]God deals with you as with sons; for
what son is there whom *his* father does
not discipline?
8 But if you are without discipline,
[a]of which all have become partakers,
then you are illegitimate children and not
sons.
9 Furthermore, we had [1]earthly fathers to discipline us, and we [a]respected
them; shall we not much rather be subject to [b]the Father of [2]spirits, and [c]live?
10 For they disciplined us for a short
time as seemed best to them, but He *disciplines us* for *our* good, [a]so that we may
share His holiness.
11 All discipline [a]for the moment
seems not to be joyful, but sorrowful; yet
to those who have been trained by it,
afterwards it yields the [b]peaceful fruit of
righteousness.
12 ¶ Therefore, [1a]strengthen the hands
that are weak and the knees that are
feeble,
13 and [a]make straight paths for your
feet, so that *the limb* which is lame may
not be put out of joint, but rather [b]be
healed.
14 ¶ [a]Pursue peace with all men, and
the [b]sanctification without which no one
will [c]see the Lord.
15 See to it that no one [a]comes short
of the grace of God; that no [b]root of bitterness springing up causes trouble, and
by it many be [c]defiled;
16 that *there be* no [a]immoral or [b]god-
less person like Esau, [c]who sold his own
birthright for a *single* meal.
17 For you know that even afterwards,
[a]when he desired to inherit the blessing,
he was rejected, for he found no place for
repentance, though he sought for it with
tears.

Contrast of Sinai and Zion

18 ¶ [a]For you have not come to [b]*a
mountain* that can be touched and to a
blazing fire, and to darkness and gloom
and whirlwind,
19 and to the [a]blast of a trumpet and
the [b]sound of words which *sound was
such that* those who heard [c]begged that
no further word be spoken to them.
20 For they could not bear the command, "[a]IF EVEN A BEAST TOUCHES THE
MOUNTAIN, IT WILL BE STONED."
21 And so terrible was the sight, *that*
Moses said, "[a]I AM FULL OF FEAR and trembling."
22 But [a]you have come to Mount Zion
and to [b]the city of [c]the living God, [d]the
heavenly Jerusalem, and to [e]myriads of
[1]angels,
23 to the general assembly and
[a]church of the firstborn who [b]are enrolled in heaven, and to God, [c]the Judge

34 [c]Judg 7:21; 1 Sam 17:51f; 2 Sam 8:1-6 **35** [1]Lit *redemption* [a]1 Kin 17:23; 2 Kin 4:36f **36** [1]Lit *received the trial of* [a]Gen 39:20; 1 Kin 22:27; 2 Chr 18:26; Jer 20:2 **37** [1]One early ms does not contain *they were tempted* [a]1 Kin 21:13; 2 Chr 24:21 [b]2 Sam 12:31; 1 Chr 20:3 [c]1 Kin 19:10; Jer 26:23 [d]1 Kin 19:13; 2 Kin 2:8; Zech 13:4 [e]Heb 11:25 **38** [1]Lit *of* [a]1 Kin 18:4 **39** [1]Lit *obtained a testimony* [2]Lit *the promise* [a]Heb 11:2 [b]Heb 10:36 **40** [1]Or *foreseen* [a]Heb 11:16 [b]Rev 6:11
12:1 [a]Rom 13:12; Eph 4:22 [b]1 Cor 9:24; Gal 2:2 [c]Heb 10:36 **2** [1]Lit *looking to* [2]Or *leader* [a]Heb 2:10 [b]Phil 2:8f; Heb 2:9 [c]1 Cor 1:18; Heb 13:13 [d]Heb 1:3 **3** [1]Lit *fainting in your souls* [a]Rev 2:3 [b]Gal 6:9; Heb 12:5 **4** [1]Lit *as far as blood* [a]Heb 10:32ff [b]Phil 2:8 **5** [a]Job 5:17; Prov 3:11 [b]Heb 12:3 **6** [a]Prov 3:12 [b]Ps 119:75; Rev 3:19 **7** [a]Deut 8:5; 2 Sam 7:14; Prov 13:24 **8** [a]1 Pet 5:9 **9** [1]Lit *fathers of our flesh* [2]Or *our spirits* [a]Luke 18:2 [b]Num 16:22; Rev 22:6 [c]Is 38:16 **10** [a]2 Pet 1:4 **11** [a]1 Pet 1:6 [b]Is 32:17; 2 Tim 4:8; James 3:17f **12** [1]Lit *make straight* [a]Is 35:3 **13** [a]Prov 4:26; Gal 2:14 [b]Gal 6:1; James 5:16 **14** [a]Rom 14:19 [b]Rom 6:22; Heb 12:10 [c]Matt 5:8; Heb 9:28 **15** [a]2 Cor 6:1; Gal 5:4; Heb 4:1 [b]Deut 29:18 [c]Titus 1:15 **16** [a]Heb 13:4 [b]1 Tim 1:9 [c]Gen 25:33f **17** [a]Gen 27:30-40 **18** [a]2 Cor 3:7-13; Heb 12:18ff [b]Ex 19:12; Deut 4:11 **19** [a]Ex 19:16; Matt 24:31 [b]Ex 19:19; Deut 4:12 [c]Ex 20:19; Deut 5:25 **20** [a]Ex 19:12f

21 [a]Deut 9:19 **22** [1]Or *angels in festive gathering, and to the church* [a]Rev 14:1 [b]Eph 2:19; Phil 3:20; Heb 11:10; Rev 21:2 [c]Heb 3:12 [d]Gal 4:26; Heb 11:16 [e]Rev 5:11 **23** [a]Ex 4:22; Heb 2:12 [b]Luke 10:20 [c]Gen 18:25; Ps 50:6

of all, and to the [d]spirits of *the* righteous made perfect,
24 and to Jesus, the [a]mediator of a new covenant, and to the [b]sprinkled blood, which speaks better than [c]*the blood* of Abel.

The Unshaken Kingdom

25 ¶ [a]See to it that you do not refuse Him who is [b]speaking. For [c]if those did not escape when they [d]refused him who [e]warned *them* on earth, [1]much less *will* we *escape* who turn away from Him who [e]*warns* from heaven.
26 And [a]His voice shook the earth then, but now He has promised, saying, "[b]YET ONCE MORE I WILL SHAKE NOT ONLY THE EARTH, BUT ALSO THE HEAVEN."
27 This *expression*, "Yet once more," denotes [a]the removing of those things which can be shaken, as of created things, so that those things which cannot be shaken may remain.
28 Therefore, since we receive a [a]kingdom which cannot be shaken, let us [1]show gratitude, by which we may [b]offer to God an acceptable service with reverence and awe;
29 for [a]our God is a consuming fire.

The Changeless Christ

13 Let [a]love of the brethren continue.
2 Do not neglect to [a]show hospitality to strangers, for by this some have [b]entertained angels without knowing it.
3 [a]Remember [b]the prisoners, as though in prison with them, *and* those who are ill-treated, since you yourselves also are in the body.
4 [a]Marriage *is to be held* in honor among all, and the *marriage* bed *is to be* undefiled; [b]for fornicators and adulterers God will judge.
5 *Make sure that* your character is [a]free from the love of money, [b]being content with what you have; for He Himself has said, "[c]I WILL NEVER DESERT YOU, NOR WILL I EVER FORSAKE YOU,"
6 so that we confidently say,
"[a]THE LORD IS MY HELPER, I WILL NOT BE AFRAID.
WHAT WILL MAN DO TO ME?"
7 ¶ Remember [a]those who led you, who spoke [b]the word of God to you; and considering the [1]result of their conduct, [c]imitate their faith.
8 [a]Jesus Christ *is* the same yesterday and today and forever.
9 [a]Do not be carried away by varied and strange teachings; for it is good for the heart to [b]be strengthened by grace, not by [c]foods, [d]through which those who [1]were so occupied were not benefited.
10 We have an altar [a]from which those [b]who serve the [1]tabernacle have no right to eat.
11 For [a]the bodies of those animals whose blood is brought into the holy place by the high priest *as an offering* for sin, are burned outside the camp.
12 Therefore Jesus also, [a]that He might sanctify the people [b]through His own blood, suffered [c]outside the gate.
13 So, let us go out to Him outside the camp, [a]bearing His reproach.
14 For here [a]we do not have a lasting city, but we are seeking [b]*the city* which is to come.

God-pleasing Sacrifices

15 [a]Through Him then, let us continually offer up a [b]sacrifice of praise to God, that is, [c]the fruit of lips that [1]give thanks to His name.
16 And do not neglect doing good and [a]sharing, for [b]with such sacrifices God is pleased.
17 ¶ [a]Obey your leaders and submit *to them*, for [b]they keep watch over your souls as those who will give an account. [1]Let them do this with joy and not [2]with grief, for this would be unprofitable for you.
18 ¶ [a]Pray for us, for we are sure that we have a [b]good conscience, desiring to conduct ourselves honorably in all things.
19 And I urge *you* all the more to do this, [a]so that I may be restored to you the sooner.

Benediction

20 ¶ Now [a]the God of peace, who [b]brought up from the dead the [c]great Shepherd of the sheep [1]through [d]the blood of the [e]eternal covenant, *even* Jesus our Lord,
21 [a]equip you in every good thing to do His will, [b]working in us that [c]which is pleasing in His sight, through Jesus Christ, [d]to whom *be* the glory forever and ever. Amen.
22 ¶ But [a]I urge you, [b]brethren, [1]bear with [2]this [b]word of exhortation, for [c]I have written to you briefly.
23 [1]Take notice that [a]our brother Timothy has been released, with whom, if he comes soon, I will see you.
24 Greet [a]all of your leaders and all the [1][b]saints. Those from [c]Italy greet you.
25 ¶ [a]Grace be with you all.

12:23 [d]Heb 11:40; Rev 6:9 **24** [a]1 Tim 2:5; Heb 8:6 [b]Heb 9:19; 1 Pet 1:2 [c]Gen 4:10; Heb 11:4 **25** [1]Lit *much rather we* will not escape... [a]Heb 3:12 [b]Heb 1:1 [c]Heb 2:2f [d]Heb 12:19 [e]Ex 20:22; Heb 8:5 **26** [a]Ex 19:18; Judg 5:4f [b]Hag 2:6 **27** [a]Is 34:4; Rom 8:19; 1 Cor 7:31; Heb 1:10ff **28** [1]Lit *have* [a]Dan 2:44 [b]Heb 13:15 **29** [a]Deut 4:24; Is 33:14; 2 Thess 1:7; Heb 10:27 **13:1** [a]Rom 12:10; 1 Thess 4:9; 1 Pet 1:22 **2** [a]Matt 25:35; Rom 12:13; 1 Pet 4:9 [b]Gen 18:1ff **3** [a]Col 4:18 [b]Matt 25:36; Heb 10:34 **4** [a]1 Cor 7:38; 1 Tim 4:3 [b]1 Cor 6:9; Gal 5:19; 1 Thess 4:6 **5** [a]Eph 5:3; Col 3:5; 1 Tim 3:3 [b]Phil 4:11 [c]Deut 31:6; Josh 1:5 **6** [a]Ps 118:6 **7** [1]Or *end of their life* [a]Heb 13:17 [b]Luke 5:1 [c]Heb 6:12 **8** [a]2 Cor 1:19; Heb 1:12 **9** [1]Lit *walked* [a]Eph 4:14; Jude 12 [b]2 Cor 1:21; Col 2:7 [c]Col 2:16 [d]Heb 9:10 **10** [1]Or *sacred tent* [a]1 Cor 10:18 [b]Heb 8:5 **11** [a]Ex 29:14; Lev 4:12; Num 19:3 **12** [a]Eph 5:26; Heb 2:11 [b]Heb 9:12 [c]John 19:17 **13** [a]Luke 9:23; Heb 11:26 **14** [a]Heb 10:34 [b]Eph 2:19; Heb 2:5 **15** [1]Lit *confess* [a]1 Pet 2:5 [b]Lev 7:12 [c]Is 57:19; Hos 14:2 **16** [a]Rom 12:13 [b]Phil 4:18 **17** [1]Lit *in order that they may do this* [2]Lit *groaning* [a]1 Cor 16:16; Heb 13:7 [b]Is 62:6; Ezek 3:17; Acts 20:28 **18** [a]1 Thess 5:25 [b]Acts 24:16; 1 Tim 1:5 **19** [a]Philem 22 **20** [1]Lit *in* [a]Rom 15:33 [b]Acts 2:24; Rom 10:7 [c]Is 63:11; John 10:11; 1 Pet 2:25 [d]Zech 9:11; Heb 10:29 [e]Is 55:3; Jer 32:40; Ezek 37:26 **21** [a]1 Pet 5:10 [b]Phil 2:13 [c]Heb 12:28; 1 John 3:22 [d]Rom 11:36 **22** [1]Or *listen to* [2]Lit *the* [a]Acts 13:15; Heb 3:13 [b]Heb 3:1 [c]1 Pet 5:12 **23** [1]Lit *Know* [a]Acts 16:1; Col 1:1 **24** [1]Or *holy ones* [a]1 Cor 16:16; Heb 13:7 [b]Acts 9:13 [c]Acts 18:2 **25** [a]Col 4:18

James

Title and Background

The book of James has a distinctively Jewish nature that suggests it was composed when the church was still predominantly Jewish. It reflects a simple church order, and no reference is made to the controversy over Gentile circumcision. The seven New Testament letters from the book of James through the book of Jude are called the General Letters because they are addressed to Christians in general and not to a particular church.

Author and Date of Writing

The author identifies himself as James, and he was probably the brother of Jesus and the leader of the Jerusalem council. At first James did not believe in Jesus and even challenged him and misunderstood his mission. Later he became very prominent in the church. The book of James was written about A.D. 48, at least before A.D. 50.

Theme and Message

As leader of the Jerusalem church, James wrote as a pastor to instruct and encourage his dispersed people in the face of their difficulties. The letter is concerned mainly with the practical aspects of the Christian faith, consisting of maxims and counsel for everyday conduct. There is very little reference to any of the central doctrines of the Christian faith. The letter discusses true religion, true faith and true wisdom.

Outline

I. Trials and Temptations (1:1–18)
II. Listening and Doing (1:19–27)
III. Favoritism Forbidden (2:1–13)
IV. Faith and Works (2:14–26)
V. Taming the Tongue (3:1–12)
VI. Two Kinds of Wisdom (3:13–18)
VII. Warning Against Worldliness (4:1–17)
VIII. Warning to Rich Oppressors (5:1–6)
IX. Miscellaneous Exhortations (5:7–20)

Testing Your Faith

1 [1a]James, a [b]bond-servant of God and
[c]of the Lord Jesus Christist,
¶ To [d]the twelve tribes who are
[2e]dispersed abroad: [f]Greetings.
2 ¶ [a]Consider it all joy, my brethren,
when you encounter [b]various [1]trials,
3 knowing that [a]the testing of your
[b]faith produces [1c]endurance.
4 And let [1a]endurance have *its* perfect [2]result, so that you may be [3b]per-
fect and complete, lacking in nothing.
5 ¶ But if any of you [a]lacks wisdom,
let him ask of God, who gives to all generously and [1]without reproach, and [b]it
will be given to him.
6 But he must [a]ask in faith [b]without
any doubting, for the one who doubts
is like the surf of the sea, [c]driven and
tossed by the wind.
7 For that man ought not to expect
that he will receive anything from the
Lord,
8 *being* a [1a]double-minded man,
[b]unstable in all his ways.
9 ¶ [a]But the [1]brother of humble circumstances is to glory in his high position;
10 and the rich man *is to glory* in his
humiliation, because [a]like [1]flowering
grass he will pass away.
11 For the sun rises with [1a]a scorching wind and [b]withers the grass; and its
flower falls off and the beauty of its appearance is destroyed; so too the rich
man in the midst of his pursuits will fade
away.
12 ¶ [a]Blessed is a man who perseveres under trial; for once he has [1]been
approved, he will receive [b]the crown of

1:1 [1]Or *Jacob* [2]Lit *in the Dispersion* [a]Acts 12:17 [b]Titus 1:1 [c]Rom 1:1 [d]Luke 22:30 [e]John 7:35 [f]Acts 15:23
2 [1]Or *temptations* [a]Matt 5:12; James 1:12 [b]1 Pet 1:6
3 [1]Or *steadfastness* [a]1 Pet 1:7 [b]Heb 6:12 [c]Luke 21:19
4 [1]V 3, note 1 [2]Lit *work* [3]Or *mature* [a]Luke 21:19 [b]Matt 5:48; Col 4:12
5 [1]Lit *does not reproach* [a]1 Kin 3:9ff; James 3:17 [b]Matt 7:7
6 [a]Matt 21:21 [b]Mark 11:23; Acts 10:20 [c]Matt 14:28-31; Eph 4:14
8 [1]Or *doubting, hesitating* [a]James 4:8 [b]2 Pet 2:14
9 [1]I.e. church member [a]Luke 14:11

10 [1]Lit *the flower of the grass* [a]1 Cor 7:31; 1 Pet 1:24
11 [1]Lit *the* [a]Matt 20:12 [b]Ps 102:4; Is 40:7f **12** [1]Or *passed the test* [a]Luke 6:22; James 5:11; 1 Pet 3:14 [b]1 Cor 9:25

life which *the Lord* [c]has promised to those who [d]love Him.

13 Let no one say when he is tempted, "[a]I am being tempted [1]by God"; for God cannot be tempted [2]by evil, and He Himself does not tempt anyone.

14 But each one is tempted when he is carried away and enticed by his own lust.

15 Then [a]when lust has conceived, it gives birth to sin; and when [b]sin [1]is accomplished, it brings forth death.

16 [a]Do not be [1]deceived, [b]my beloved brethren.

17 Every good thing given and every perfect gift is [a]from above, coming down from [b]the Father of lights, [c]with whom there is no variation or [1]shifting shadow.

18 In the exercise of [a]His will He [b]brought us forth by [c]the word of truth, so that we would be [1]a kind of [d]first fruits [2]among His creatures.

19 ¶ [1]*This* [a]you know, [b]my beloved brethren. But everyone must be quick to hear, [c]slow to speak *and* [d]slow to anger;

20 for [a]the anger of man does not achieve the righteousness of God.

21 Therefore, [a]putting aside all filthiness and *all* [1]that remains of wickedness, in [2]humility receive [b]the word implanted, which is able to save your souls.

22 [a]But prove yourselves doers of the word, and not merely hearers who delude themselves.

23 For if anyone is a hearer of the word and not a doer, he is like a man who looks at his [1]natural face [a]in a mirror;

24 for *once* he has looked at himself and gone away, [1]he has immediately forgotten what kind of person he was.

25 But one who looks intently at the perfect law, [a]the *law* of liberty, and abides by it, not having become a forgetful hearer but [1]an effectual doer, this man will be [b]blessed in [2]what he does.

26 ¶ If anyone thinks himself to be religious, and yet does not [1a]bridle his tongue but deceives his *own* heart, this man's religion is worthless.

27 Pure and undefiled religion [a]in the sight of *our* God and Father is this: to [b]visit [c]orphans and widows in their distress, *and* to keep oneself unstained [1]by [d]the world.

The Sin of Partiality

2 [a]My brethren, [b]do not hold your faith in our [c]glorious Lord Jesus Christ with *an attitude of* [d]personal favoritism.

2 For if a man comes into your [1]assembly with a gold ring and dressed in [2a]fine clothes, and there also comes in a poor man in [b]dirty clothes,

3 and you [1]pay special attention to the one who is wearing the [a]fine clothes, and say, "You sit here in a good place," and you say to the poor man, "You stand over there, or sit down by my footstool,"

4 have you not made distinctions among yourselves, and become judges [a]with evil [1]motives?

5 Listen, [a]my beloved brethren: did not [b]God choose the poor [1]of this world *to be* [c]rich in faith and [d]heirs of the kingdom which He [e]promised to those who love Him?

6 But you have dishonored the poor man. Is it not the rich who oppress you and [1]personally [a]drag you into [2]court?

7 [a]Do they not blaspheme the fair name [1]by which you have been called?

8 ¶ If, however, you [a]are fulfilling the [1]royal law according to the Scripture, "[b]YOU SHALL LOVE YOUR NEIGHBOR AS YOURSELF," you are doing well.

9 But if you [a]show partiality, you are committing sin *and* are convicted by the [1]law as transgressors.

10 For whoever keeps the whole [1]law and yet [a]stumbles in one *point,* he has become [b]guilty of all.

11 For He who said, "[a]DO NOT COMMIT ADULTERY," also said, "[b]DO NOT COMMIT MURDER." Now if you do not commit adultery, but do commit murder, you have become a transgressor of the [1]law.

12 So speak and so act as those who are to be judged by [a]*the* law of liberty.

13 For [a]judgment *will be* merciless to one who has shown no mercy; mercy [1]triumphs over judgment.

Faith and Works

14 ¶ [a]What use is it, [b]my brethren, if someone says he has faith but he has no works? Can [1]that faith save him?

15 [a]If a brother or sister is without clothing and in need of daily food,

16 and one of you says to them, "[a]Go in peace, [1]be warmed and be filled," and yet you do not give them what is necessary for *their* body, what use is that?

17 Even so [a]faith, if it has no works, is [1]dead, *being* by itself.

18 ¶ [a]But someone [1]may *well* say, "You have faith and I have works; show me your [b]faith without the works, and I will [c]show you my faith [d]by my works."

19 You believe that [1a]God is one.

12 [c]Ex 20:6; James 2:5 [d]1 Cor 2:9 **13** [1]Lit *from* [2]Lit *of evil things* [a]Gen 22:1 **15** [1]Lit *is brought to completion* [a]Job 15:35; Ps 7:14; Is 59:4 [b]Rom 5:12 **16** [1]Or *misled* [a]1 Cor 6:9 [b]Acts 1:15; James 1:2 **17** [1]Lit *shadow of turning* [a]John 3:3; James 3:15 [b]Ps 136:7; 1 John 1:5 [c]Mal 3:6 **18** [1]Or *a certain first fruits* [2]Lit *of* [a]John 1:13 [b]James 1:15; 1 Pet 1:3 [c]2 Cor 6:7; Eph 1:13; 2 Tim 2:15 [d]Jer 2:3; Rev 14:4 **19** [1]Or *Know this* [a]1 John 2:21 [b]Acts 1:15; James 1:2 [c]Prov 10:19 [d]Prov 16:32; Eccl 7:9 **20** [a]Matt 5:22; Eph 4:26 **21** [1]Lit *abundance of malice* [2]Or *gentleness* [a]Eph 4:22; 1 Pet 2:1 [b]Eph 1:13; 1 Pet 1:22f **22** [a]Matt 7:24-27; Luke 6:46-49; Rom 2:13; James 1:22-25 **23** [1]Lit *the face of his birth*; or *nature* [a]1 Cor 13:12 **24** [1]Lit *and he* **25** [1]Lit *a doer of a work* [2]Lit *his doing* [a]John 8:32; Rom 8:2; Gal 2:4; James 2:12; 1 Pet 2:16 [b]John 13:17 **26** [1]Or *control* [a]Ps 39:1; James 3:2-12 **27** [1]Lit *from* [a]Rom 2:13; Gal 3:11 [b]Matt 25:36 [c]Deut 14:29; Job 31:16; Ps 146:9; Is 1:17 [d]Matt 12:32; Eph 2:2; Titus 2:12; James 4:4; 2 Pet 1:4; 1 John 2:15-17 **2:1** [a]James 1:16 [b]Heb 12:2 [c]Acts 7:2; 1 Cor 2:8 [d]Acts 10:34; James 2:9 **2** [1]Or *synagogue* [2]Or *bright* [a]Luke 23:11; James 2:3 [b]Zech 3:3f **3** [1]Lit *look at* [a]Luke 23:11 **4** [1]Lit *reasonings* [a]Luke 18:6; John 7:24 **5** [1]Lit *to the* [a]James 1:16 [b]Job 34:19; 1 Cor 1:27f [c]Luke 12:21; Rev 2:9 [d]Matt 5:3 [e]James 1:12 **6** [1]Lit *they themselves* [2]Lit *courts* [a]Acts 8:3 **7** [1]Lit *which has been called upon you* [a]Acts 11:26; 1 Pet 4:16 **8** [1]Or *law of our King* [a]Matt 7:12 [b]Lev 19:18 **9** [1]Or *Law* [a]Acts 10:34; James 2:1 **10** [1]Or *Law* [a]James 3:2; 2 Pet 1:10; Jude 24 [b]Matt 5:19; Gal 5:3 **11** [1]Or *Law* [a]Ex 20:14; Deut 5:18 [b]Ex 20:13; Deut 5:17 **12** [a]James 1:25 **13** [1]Lit *boasts against* [a]Prov 21:13; Matt 5:7; Luke 6:37f **14** [1]Lit *the* [a]James 1:22ff [b]James 1:16 **15** [a]Matt 25:35f; Luke 3:11 **16** [1]Or *warm yourselves and fill yourselves* [a]1 John 3:17f **17** [1]Or *dead by its own standards* [a]Gal 5:6; James 2:20 **18** [1]Lit *will* [a]Rom 9:19 [b]Rom 3:28; Heb 11:33 [c]James 3:13 [d]Matt 7:16f; Gal 5:6 **19** [1]One early ms reads *there is one God* [a]Deut 6:4; Mark 12:29

[b]You do well; [c]the demons also believe,
and shudder.
20 But are you willing to recognize,
[a]you foolish fellow, that [b]faith without
works is useless?
21 [a]Was not Abraham our father justified by works when he offered up Isaac
his son on the altar?
22 You see that [a]faith was working
with his works, and [1]as a result of the
[b]works, faith was [2]perfected;
23 and the Scripture was fulfilled
which says, "[a]AND ABRAHAM BELIEVED
GOD, AND IT WAS RECKONED TO HIM AS RIGH-
TEOUSNESS," and he was called [b]the
friend of God.
24 You see that a man is justified by
works and not by faith alone.
25 In the same way, was not [a]Rahab
the harlot also justified by works [b]when
she received the messengers and sent
them out by another way?
26 For just as the body without *the*
spirit is dead, so also [a]faith without
works is dead.

The Tongue Is a Fire

3 [a]Let not many *of you* become teachers, [b]my brethren, knowing that as
such we will incur a [1]stricter judgment.
2 For we all [a]stumble in many *ways.*
[b]If anyone does not stumble in [1]what he
says, he is a [c]perfect man, able to [d]bridle
the whole body as well.
3 Now [a]if we put the bits into the
horses' mouths so that they will obey us,
we direct their entire body as well.
4 Look at the ships also, though they
are so great and are driven by strong
winds, are still directed by a very small
rudder wherever the inclination of the
pilot desires.
5 So also the tongue is a small part
of the body, and *yet* it [a]boasts of great
things.
¶ [b]See how great a forest is set aflame
by such a small fire!
6 And [a]the tongue is a fire, the *very*
world of iniquity; the tongue is set among
our members as that which [b]defiles the
entire body, and sets on fire the course of
our [1]life, and is set on fire by [2c]hell.
7 For every [1]species of beasts and
birds, of reptiles and creatures of the sea,
is tamed and has been tamed by the human [1]race.
8 But no one can tame the tongue; *it*
is a restless evil *and* full of [a]deadly poison.
9 With it we bless [a]*our* Lord and Father, and with it we curse men, [b]who
have been made in the likeness of God;
10 from the same mouth come *both*
blessing and cursing. My brethren, these
things ought not to be this way.
11 Does a fountain send out from the
same opening *both* [1]fresh and bitter *wa-*
ter?
12 [a]Can a fig tree, my brethren, produce olives, or a vine produce figs? Nor
can salt water produce [1]fresh.

Wisdom from Above

13 ¶ Who among you is wise and understanding? [a]Let him show by his
[b]good behavior his deeds in the gentleness of wisdom.
14 But if you have bitter [a]jealousy and
[1]selfish ambition in your heart, do not be
arrogant and *so* lie against [b]the truth.
15 This wisdom is not that which
comes down [a]from above, but is [b]earth-
ly, [1c]natural, [d]demonic.
16 For where [a]jealousy and [1]selfish
ambition exist, [2]there is disorder and every evil thing.
17 But the wisdom [a]from above is first
[b]pure, then [c]peaceable, [d]gentle, [1]rea-
sonable, [e]full of mercy and good fruits,
[f]unwavering, without [g]hypocrisy.
18 And the [1a]seed whose fruit is righteousness is sown in peace [2]by those
who make peace.

Things to Avoid

4 [1]What is the source of quarrels and
[a]conflicts among you? [2]Is not the
source your pleasures that wage [b]war in
your members?
2 You lust and do not have; *so* you
[a]commit murder. You are envious and
cannot obtain; *so* you fight and quarrel.
You do not have because you do not ask.
3 You ask and [a]do not receive, because you ask [1]with wrong motives, so
that you may spend *it* [2]on your pleasures.
4 You [a]adulteresses, do you not
know that friendship with [b]the world is
[c]hostility toward God? [d]Therefore whoever wishes to be a friend of the world
makes himself an enemy of God.
5 Or do you think that the Scripture
[a]speaks to no purpose: "[1]He [2]jealously
desires [b]the Spirit which He has made to
dwell in us"?
6 But [a]He gives a greater grace.
Therefore *it* says, "[b]GOD IS OPPOSED TO
THE PROUD, BUT GIVES GRACE TO THE HUM-
BLE."
7 [a]Submit therefore to God. [b]Resist
the devil and he will flee from you.

19 [b]James 2:8 [c]Matt 8:29; Mark 1:24; Luke 4:34; Acts 19:15 **20** [a]Rom 9:20; 1 Cor 15:36 [b]Gal 5:6; James 2:17 **21** [a]Gen 22:9 **22** [1]Or *by the deeds* [2]Or *completed* [a]John 6:29; Heb 11:17 [b]1 Thess 1:3 **23** [a]Gen 15:6; Rom 4:3 [b]2 Chr 20:7; Is 41:8 **25** [a]Heb 11:31 [b]Josh 2:4 **26** [a]Gal 5:6; James 2:17 **3:1** [1]Or *greater condemnation* [a]Matt 23:8; Rom 2:20f; 1 Tim 1:7 [b]James 1:16 **2** [1]Lit *word* [a]James 2:10 [b]Matt 12:34-37; James 3:2-12 [c]James 1:4 [d]James 1:26 **3** [a]Ps 32:9 **5** [a]Ps 12:3f [b]Prov 26:20f **6** [1]Or *existence, origin* [2]Gr *Gehenna* [a]Ps 120:2; Prov 16:27 [b]Matt 12:36f [c]Matt 5:22 **7** [1]Lit *nature* **8** [a]Ps 140:3; Eccl 10:11; Rom 3:13 **9** [a]James 1:27 [b]Gen 1:26; 1 Cor 11:7 **11** [1]Lit *sweet* **12** [1]V 11, note 1 [a]Matt 7:16 **13** [a]James 2:18 [b]1 Pet 2:12 **14** [1]Or *strife* [a]Rom 2:8; 2 Cor 12:20; James 3:16 [b]1 Tim 2:4; James 1:18 **15** [1]Or *unspiritual* [a]James 1:17 [b]1 Cor 2:6 [c]2 Cor 1:12; Jude 19 [d]2 Thess 2:9f; 1 Tim 4:1; Rev 2:24 **16** [1]V 14, note 1 [2]I.e. in that place [a]Rom 2:8; 2 Cor 12:20; James 3:14 **17** [1]Or *willing to yield* [a]James 1:17 [b]2 Cor 7:11; James 4:8 [c]Matt 5:9; Heb 12:11 [d]Titus 3:2 [e]Luke 6:36; James 2:13 [f]James 2:4 [g]Rom 12:9; 2 Cor 6:6 **18** [1]Lit *fruit of righteousness* [2]Or *for* [a]Prov 11:18; Is 32:17; Hos 10:12; Amos 6:12; Gal 6:8; Phil 1:11 **4:1** [1]Lit *From where wars and from where fightings* [2]Lit Are they *not from here,* from your [a]Titus 3:9 [b]Rom 7:23 **2** [a]James 5:6; 1 John 3:15 **3** [1]Lit *wickedly* [2]Lit *in* [a]1 John 3:22 **4** [a]Jer 2:2; Ezek 16:32 [b]James 1:27 [c]Rom 8:7; 1 John 2:15 [d]Matt 6:24; John 15:19 **5** [1]Or *The spirit which He has made to dwell in us lusts with envy* [2]Lit *desires to jealousy* [a]Num 23:19 [b]1 Cor 6:19; 2 Cor 6:16 **6** [a]Is 54:7f; Matt 13:12 [b]Ps 138:6; Prov 3:34; Matt 23:12; 1 Pet 5:5 **7** [a]1 Pet 5:6 [b]Eph 4:27; 1 Pet 5:8f

8 [a]Draw near to God and He will draw near to you. [b]Cleanse your hands, you sinners; and [c]purify your hearts, you [d]double-minded.

9 [a]Be miserable and mourn and weep; let your laughter be turned into mourning and your joy to gloom.

10 [a]Humble yourselves in the presence of the Lord, and He will exalt you.

11 ¶ [a]Do not speak against one another, [b]brethren. He who speaks against a brother or [c]judges his brother, speaks against [d]the law and judges the law; but if you judge the law, you are not [e]a doer of the law but a judge *of it.*

12 There is *only* one [a]Lawgiver and Judge, the One who is [b]able to save and to destroy; but [c]who are you who judge your neighbor?

13 ¶ [a]Come now, you who say, "[b]Today or tomorrow we will go to such and such a city, and spend a year there and engage in business and make a profit."

14 [1]Yet you do not know [2]what your life will be like tomorrow. [a]You are *just* a vapor that appears for a little while and then vanishes away.

15 [1]Instead, *you ought* to say, "[a]If the Lord wills, we will live and also do this or that."

16 But as it is, you boast in your [1]arrogance; [a]all such boasting is evil.

17 Therefore, [a]to one who knows *the* [1]right thing to do and does not do it, to him it is sin.

Misuse of Riches

5 [a]Come now, [b]you rich, [c]weep and howl for your miseries which are coming upon you.

2 [a]Your riches have rotted and your garments have become moth-eaten.

3 Your gold and your silver have rusted; and their rust will be a witness against you and will consume your flesh like fire. It is [a]in the last days that you have stored up your treasure!

4 Behold, [a]the pay of the laborers who mowed your fields, *and* which has been withheld by you, cries out *against you;* and [b]the outcry of those who did the harvesting has reached the ears of [c]the Lord of [1]Sabaoth.

5 You have [a]lived luxuriously on the earth and led a life of wanton pleasure; you have [1]fattened your hearts in [b]a day of slaughter.

6 You have condemned and [1a]put to death [b]the righteous *man;* he does not resist you.

Exhortation

7 ¶ Therefore be patient, [a]brethren, [b]until the coming of the Lord. [c]The farmer waits for the precious produce of the soil, being patient about it, until [1]it gets [d]the early and late rains.

8 [a]You too be patient; [b]strengthen your hearts, for [c]the coming of the Lord is [d]near.

9 [a]Do not [1]complain, [b]brethren, against one another, so that you yourselves may not be judged; behold, [c]the Judge is standing [2d]right at the [3]door.

10 As an example, [a]brethren, of suffering and patience, take [b]the prophets who spoke in the name of the Lord.

11 We count those [a]blessed who endured. You have heard of [b]the [1]endurance of Job and have seen [c]the [2]outcome of the Lord's dealings, that [d]the Lord is full of compassion and *is* merciful.

12 ¶ But above all, [a]my brethren, [b]do not swear, either by heaven or by earth or with any other oath; but [1]your yes is to be yes, and your no, no, so that you may not fall under judgment.

13 ¶ Is anyone among you [a]suffering? [b]*Then* he must pray. Is anyone cheerful? He is to [c]sing praises.

14 Is anyone among you sick? *Then* he must call for [a]the elders of the church and they are to pray over him, [1b]anointing him with oil in the name of the Lord;

15 and the [a]prayer [1]offered in faith will [2b]restore the one who is sick, and the Lord will [c]raise him up, and if he has committed sins, [3]they will be forgiven him.

16 Therefore, [a]confess your sins to one another, and pray for one another so that you may be [b]healed. [c]The effective [1]prayer of a righteous man can accomplish much.

17 Elijah was [a]a man with a nature like ours, and [b]he prayed [1]earnestly that it would not rain, and it did not rain on the earth for [c]three years and six months.

18 Then he [a]prayed again, and [b]the [1]sky [2]poured rain and the earth produced its fruit.

19 ¶ My brethren, [a]if any among you strays from [b]the truth and one turns him back,

20 let him know that [1]he who turns a sinner from the error of his way will [a]save his soul from death and will [b]cover a multitude of sins.

8 [a]2 Chr 15:2; Zech 1:3; Mal 3:7; Heb 7:19 [b]Job 17:9; Is 1:16; 1 Tim 2:8 [c]Jer 4:14; James 3:17; 1 Pet 1:22; 1 John 3:3 [d]James 1:8 **9** [a]Neh 8:9; Prov 14:13; Luke 6:25 **10** [a]Job 5:11; Ezek 21:26; Luke 1:52; James 4:6 **11** [a]2 Cor 12:20; James 5:9; 1 Pet 2:1 [b]James 1:16 [c]Matt 7:1; Rom 14:4 [d]James 2:8 [e]James 1:22 **12** [a]Is 33:22; James 5:9 [b]Matt 10:28 [c]Rom 14:4 **13** [a]James 5:1 [b]Prov 27:1; Luke 12:18-20 **14** [1]Lit *Who do not* [2]Or *what will happen tomorrow What kind of life is yours?* [a]Job 7:7; Ps 39:5 **15** [1]Lit *Instead of your saying* [a]Acts 18:21 **16** [1]Or *pretensions* [a]1 Cor 5:6 **17** [1]Or *good* [a]Luke 12:47; John 9:41; 2 Pet 2:21 **5:1** [a]James 4:13 [b]Luke 6:24; 1 Tim 6:9 [c]Is 13:6; Ezek 30:2 **2** [a]Job 13:28; Is 50:9; Matt 6:19f **3** [a]James 5:7 **4** [1]I.e. Hosts [a]Lev 19:13; Job 24:10f; Jer 22:13; Mal 3:5 [b]Ex 2:23; Deut 24:15; Job 31:38f [c]Rom 9:29; Is 5:9 **5** [1]Lit *nourished* [a]Ezek 16:49; Luke 16:19; 1 Tim 5:6; 2 Pet 2:13 [b]Jer 12:3 **6** [1]Or *murdered* [a]James 4:2 [b]Heb 10:38; 1 Pet 4:18 **7** [1]Or *he* [a]James 4:11 [b]John 21:22; 1 Thess 2:19 [c]Gal 6:9 [d]Deut 11:14; Jer 5:24; Joel 2:23 **8** [a]Luke 21:19 [b]1 Thess 3:13 [c]John 21:22; 1 Thess 2:19 [d]Rom 13:11; 1 Pet 4:7 **9** [1]Lit *groan* [2]Lit *before* [3]Lit *doors* [a]James 4:11 [b]James 5:7 [c]1 Cor 4:5; James 4:12; 1 Pet 4:5 [d]Matt 24:33; Mark 13:29 **10** [a]James 4:11 [b]Matt 5:12 **11** [1]Or *steadfastness* [2]Lit *end of the Lord* [a]Matt 5:10; 1 Pet 3:14 [b]Job 1:21f [c]Job 42:10 [d]Ex 34:6; Ps 103:8

12 [1]Lit *yours is to be yes, yes, and no, no* [a]James 1:16 [b]Matt 5:34-37 **13** [a]James 5:10 [b]Ps 50:15 [c]1 Cor 14:15; Col 3:16 **14** [1]Lit *having anointed* [a]Acts 11:30 [b]Mark 6:13 **15** [1]Lit *of* [2]Or *save* [3]Lit *it* [a]James 1:6 [b]1 Cor 1:21; James 5:20 [c]John 6:39; 2 Cor 4:14 **16** [1]Lit *supplication* [a]Matt 3:6; Mark 1:5; Acts 19:18 [b]Heb 12:13; 1 Pet 2:24 [c]Gen 18:23-32; John 9:31 **17** [1]Lit *with prayer* [a]Acts 14:15 [b]1 Kin 17:1 [c]Luke 4:25 **18** [1]Lit *heaven* [2]Lit *gave* [a]1 Kin 18:42 [b]1 Kin 18:45 **19** [a]Matt 18:15; Gal 6:1 [b]James 3:14 **20** [1]Lit *he who has turned* [a]Rom 11:14; 1 Cor 1:21; James 1:21 [b]Prov 10:12; 1 Pet 4:8

1 Peter

Title and Background

The recipients of this letter had been suffering various trials and afflictions, and the possibility of greater and more severe difficulties was very real. This letter is addressed to Christians who were scattered throughout the Roman world. In fact, the readers were called "aliens."

Author and Date of Writing

The author identifies himself as the apostle Peter, and the contents and character of the letter support his authorship. Moreover, the letter reflects the history and terminology of the Gospels and Acts, notably Peter's speeches. The book was written about A.D. 64.

Theme and Message

1 Peter touches on various doctrines and has much to say about Christian life and duties. It has been characterized as a letter of separation, of suffering and persecution, of suffering and glory, of hope, of pilgrimage, of courage, and as a letter dealing with the true grace of God. The letter is composed also of a series of exhortations focusing on the call to holy living, especially in anticipation of the end times.

Outline

I. Greetings (1:1–2)
II. Praise for God's Grace and Salvation (1:3–12)
III. Holy Living (1:13—5:11)
IV. The Purpose of the Letter (5:12)
V. Closing Greetings (5:13–14)

A Living Hope, and a Sure Salvation

1 [a]Peter, an apostle of Jesus Christ,
¶ To those who reside as [b]aliens,
[c]scattered throughout [d]Pontus, [e]Gala-
tia, [d]Cappadocia, [d]Asia, and [f]Bithynia,
[g]who are chosen
2 according to the [a]foreknowledge of
God the Father, [b]by the sanctifying work
of the Spirit, [1]to [c]obey Jesus Christ and
be [d]sprinkled with His blood: [e]May
grace and peace [2]be yours in the fullest
measure.
3 ¶ [a]Blessed be the God and Father
of our Lord Jesus Christ, who [b]according
to His great mercy [c]has caused us to be
born again to [d]a living hope through the
[e]resurrection of Jesus Christ from the
dead,
4 to *obtain* an [a]inheritance *which is*
imperishable and undefiled and [b]will not
fade away, [c]reserved in heaven for you,
5 who are [a]protected by the power
of God [b]through faith for [c]a salvation
ready [d]to be revealed in the last time.
6 [a]In this you greatly rejoice, even
though now [b]for a little while, [c]if necessary, you have been distressed by [d]vari-
ous [1]trials,
7 so that the [1a]proof of your faith,
being more precious than gold which [2]is
perishable, [b]even though tested by fire,
[c]may be found to result in praise and
glory and honor at [d]the revelation of
Jesus Christ;
8 and [a]though you have not seen
Him, you [b]love Him, and though you do
not see Him now, but believe in Him, you
greatly rejoice with joy inexpressible and
[1]full of glory,
9 obtaining as [a]the outcome of your
faith the salvation of [1]your souls.
10 ¶ [a]As to this salvation, the prophets who [b]prophesied of the [c]grace that
would come to you made careful searches
and inquiries,
11 [1]seeking to know what person or
time [a]the Spirit of Christ within them
was indicating as He [b]predicted the sufferings of Christ and the glories [2]to follow.
12 It was revealed to them that they

1:1 [a]2 Pet 1:1 [b]1 Pet 2:11 [c]James 1:1 [d]Acts 2:9 [e]Acts 16:6 [f]Acts 16:7 [g]Matt 24:22; Luke 18:7
2 [1]Lit *unto obedience and sprinkling* [2]Lit *be multiplied for you* [a]Rom 8:29; 1 Pet 1:20 [b]2 Thess 2:13 [c]1 Pet 1:14 [d]Heb 10:22 [e]2 Pet 1:2
3 [a]2 Cor 1:3 [b]Gal 6:16; Titus 3:5 [c]James 1:18; 1 Pet 1:23 [d]1 Pet 1:13; 1 John 3:3 [e]1 Cor 15:20; 1 Pet 3:21
4 [a]Acts 20:32; Rom 8:17; Col 3:24 [b]1 Pet 5:4 [c]2 Tim 4:8
5 [a]John 10:28; Phil 4:7 [b]Eph 2:8 [c]1 Cor 1:21; 2 Thess 2:13 [d]1 Pet 4:13
6 [1]Or *temptations* [a]Rom 5:2 [b]1 Pet 5:10 [c]1 Pet 3:17 [d]James 1:2; 1 Pet 4:12
7 [1]Or *genuineness* [2]Lit *perishes* [a]James 1:3 [b]1 Cor 3:13 [c]Rom 2:7 [d]Luke 17:30; 1 Pet

1:13 **8** [1]Lit *glorified* [a]John 20:29 [b]Eph 3:19 **9** [1]One early ms does not contain *your* [a]Rom 6:22 **10** [a]Matt 13:17; Luke 10:24 [b]Matt 26:24 [c]1 Pet 1:13 **11** [1]Or *inquiring* [2]Lit *after these* [a]2 Pet 1:21 [b]Matt 26:24

were not serving themselves, but you,
in these things which now have been
announced to you through those who
[a]preached the gospel to you by [b]the
Holy Spirit sent from heaven—things
into which [c]angels long to [1]look.
13 ¶ Therefore, [1a]prepare your minds
for action, [2b]keep sober *in spirit,* fix
your [c]hope completely on the [d]grace
[3]to be brought to you at [e]the revelation
of Jesus Christ.
14 As [1a]obedient children, do not
[2b]be conformed to the former lusts
which were yours in your [c]ignorance,
15 but [1a]like the Holy One who
called you, [2b]be holy yourselves also [c]in
all *your* behavior;
16 because it is written, "[a]YOU SHALL
BE HOLY, FOR I AM HOLY."
17 ¶ If you [a]address as Father the One
who [b]impartially [c]judges according to
each one's work, conduct yourselves [d]in
fear during the time of your [e]stay *on
earth;*
18 knowing that you were not [1a]re-
deemed with perishable things like silver
or gold from your [b]futile way of life inherited from your forefathers,
19 but with precious [a]blood, as of a
[b]lamb unblemished and spotless, *the
blood* of Christ.
20 For He was [a]foreknown before
[b]the foundation of the world, but has
[c]appeared [1]in these last times [d]for the
sake of you
21 who through Him are [a]believers in
God, who raised Him from the dead and
[b]gave Him glory, so that your faith and
[c]hope are in God.
22 ¶ Since you have [a]in obedience
to the truth [b]purified your souls for a
[1c]sincere love of the brethren, fervently
love one another from [2]the heart,
23 for you have been [a]born again
[b]not of seed which is perishable but imperishable, *that is,* through the living and
enduring [c]word of God.
24 For,

"[a]ALL FLESH IS LIKE GRASS,
AND ALL ITS GLORY LIKE THE FLOWER
OF GRASS.
THE GRASS WITHERS,
AND THE FLOWER FALLS OFF,
25 [a]BUT THE WORD OF THE LORD
ENDURES FOREVER."

And this is [b]the word which was
[1]preached to you.

As Newborn Babes

2 Therefore, [a]putting aside all [1]mal-
ice and all deceit and [2]hypocrisy and
[2]envy and all [2b]slander,
2 [a]like newborn babies, long for the
[1b]pure [2]milk of the word, so that by it
you may [c]grow [3]in respect to salvation,
3 if you have [a]tasted [1b]the kindness
of the Lord.

As Living Stones

4 ¶ And coming to Him as to a living
stone which has been [a]rejected by men,
but is [1]choice and precious in the sight
of God,
5 [a]you also, as living stones, [1]are being built up as a [b]spiritual house for a
holy [c]priesthood, to [d]offer up spiritual
sacrifices acceptable to God through
Jesus Christ.
6 For *this* is contained in [1]Scripture:

"[a]BEHOLD, I LAY IN ZION A CHOICE
STONE, A [b]PRECIOUS CORNER
stone,
AND HE WHO BELIEVES IN [2]HIM
WILL NOT BE [3]DISAPPOINTED."

7 [a]This precious value, then, is for
you who believe; but for those who dis-
believe,

"[b]THE STONE WHICH THE BUILDERS
[c]REJECTED,
THIS BECAME THE VERY CORNER
stone,"

8 and,

"[a]A STONE OF STUMBLING AND A
ROCK OF OFFENSE";

[b]for they stumble because they are disobedient to the word, [c]and to this *doom*
they were also appointed.
9 ¶ But you are [a]A CHOSEN RACE, A
royal [b]PRIESTHOOD, A [c]HOLY NATION, [d]A
PEOPLE FOR *God's* OWN POSSESSION, so that
you may proclaim the excellencies of Him
who has called you [e]out of darkness into
His marvelous light;
10 [a]for you once were NOT A PEOPLE,
but now you are THE PEOPLE OF GOD; you
had NOT RECEIVED MERCY, but now you
have RECEIVED MERCY.
11 ¶ [a]Beloved, [b]I urge you as [c]aliens
and strangers to abstain from [d]fleshly
lusts which wage [e]war against the soul.
12 [a]Keep your behavior excellent
among the Gentiles, so that in the thing
in which they [b]slander you as evildoers,
they may [1]because of your good deeds, as
they observe *them,* [c]glorify God [d]in the
day of [2]visitation.

12 [1]Or *gain a clear glimpse* [a]1 Pet 1:25 [b]Acts 2:2-4 [c]1 Tim 3:16 **13** [1]Lit *gird the loins of your mind* [2]Lit *be sober* [3]Or *which is announced* [a]Eph 6:14 [b]1 Thess 5:6; 2 Tim 4:5; 1 Pet 4:7 [c]1 Pet 1:3 [d]1 Pet 1:10 [e]1 Pet 1:7 **14** [1]Lit *children of obedience* [2]Or *conform yourselves* [a]1 Pet 1:2 [b]Rom 12:2; 1 Pet 4:2f [c]Eph 4:18 **15** [1]Lit *according to* [2]Or *become* [a]1 Thess 4:7; 1 John 3:3 [b]2 Cor 7:1 [c]James 3:13 **16** [a]Lev 11:44f **17** [a]Ps 89:26; Jer 3:19; Matt 6:9 [b]Acts 10:34 [c]Matt 16:27 [d]2 Cor 7:1; Heb 12:28; 1 Pet 3:15 [e]1 Pet 2:11 **18** [1]Or *ransomed* [a]Is 52:3; 1 Cor 6:20; Titus 2:14; Heb 9:12 [b]Eph 4:17 **19** [a]Acts 20:28; 1 Pet 1:2 [b]John 1:29 **20** [1]Lit *at the end of the times* [a]Acts 2:23; Eph 1:4; 1 Pet 1:2; Rev 13:8 [b]Matt 25:34 [c]Heb 9:26 [d]Heb 2:14 **21** [a]Rom 4:24 [b]John 17:5; 1 Tim 3:16; Heb 2:9 [c]1 Pet 1:3 **22** [1]Lit *unhypocritical* [2]Two early mss read *a clean heart* [a]1 Pet 1:2 [b]James 4:8 [c]John 13:34; Rom 12:10; Heb 13:1; 1 Pet 2:17 **23** [a]John 3:3; 1 Pet 1:3 [b]John 1:13 [c]Heb 4:12 **24** [a]Is 40:6ff; James 1:10f **25** [1]Lit *preached as good news to you* [a]Is 40:8 [b]Heb 6:5 **2:1** [1]Or *wickedness* [2]plural nouns [a]Eph 4:22; James 1:21 [b]James 4:11 **2** [1]Or *unadulterated* [2]Or *spiritual* (Gr *logikos*) *milk* [3]Or *up to salvation* [a]Matt 18:3; Mark 10:15; Luke 18:17; 1 Cor 14:20 [b]1 Cor 3:2 [c]Eph 4:15f **3** [1]Lit *that the Lord is kind* [a]Heb 6:5 [b]Ps 34:8; Titus 3:4 **4** [1]Lit *chosen;* or *elect* [a]1 Pet 2:7 **5** [1]Or *allow yourselves to be built up;* or *build yourselves up* [a]1 Cor 3:9 [b]Gal 6:10; 1 Tim 3:15 [c]Is 61:6; 1 Pet 2:9; Rev 1:6 [d]Rom 15:16; Heb 13:15 **6** [1]Or *a scripture* [2]Or *it* [3]Or *put to shame* [a]Is 28:16; Rom 9:32; 1 Pet 2:8 [b]Eph 2:20 **7** [a]2 Cor 2:16; 1 Pet 2:7 [b]Ps 118:22; Matt 21:42; Luke 2:34 [c]1 Pet 2:4 **8** [a]Is 8:14 [b]1 Cor 1:23; Gal 5:11 [c]Rom 9:22 **9** [a]Is 43:20f; Deut 10:15 [b]Is 61:6; 1 Pet 2:5; Rev 1:6 [c]Ex 19:6; Deut 7:6 [d]Ex 19:5; Deut 4:20; Titus 2:14 [e]Is 9:2; Acts 26:18; 2 Cor 4:6 **10** [a]Hos 1:10; Rom 9:25 **11** [a]Heb 6:9; 1 Pet 4:12 [b]Rom 12:1 [c]Lev 25:23; Ps 39:12; Eph 2:19; Heb 11:13; 1 Pet 1:17 [d]Rom 13:14; Gal 5:16 [e]James 4:1 **12** [1]Or *as a result of* [2]I.e. Christ's coming again in judgment [a]2 Cor 8:21; Phil 2:15; Titus 2:8; 1 Pet 2:15 [b]Acts 28:22 [c]Matt 5:16; John 13:31; 1 Pet 4:11 [d]Is 10:3; Luke 19:44

Honor Authority

13 ¶ [a]Submit yourselves for the
Lord's sake to every human institution,
whether to a king as the one in authority,
14 or to governors as sent [1]by him
[a]for the punishment of evildoers and the
[b]praise of those who do right.
15 For [1a]such is the will of God that
by doing right you may [b]silence the ignorance of foolish men.
16 *Act* as [a]free men, and [1]do not use
your freedom as a covering for evil, but
use it as [b]bondslaves of God.
17 [a]Honor all people, [b]love the brotherhood, [c]fear God, [d]honor the [1]king.
18 ¶ [a]Servants, be submissive to your
masters with all respect, not only to those
who are good and [b]gentle, but also to
those who are [1]unreasonable.
19 For this *finds* [1]favor, if for the sake
of [a]conscience toward God a person
bears up under sorrows when suffering
unjustly.
20 For what credit is there if, when
you sin and are harshly treated, you endure it with patience? But if [a]when you
do what is right and suffer *for it* you patiently endure it, this *finds* [1]favor with
God.

Christ Is Our Example

21 For [a]you have been called for this
purpose, [b]since Christ also suffered for
you, leaving you [c]an example for you to
follow in His steps,
22 WHO [a]COMMITTED NO SIN, NOR WAS
ANY DECEIT FOUND IN HIS MOUTH;
23 [1]and while being [a]reviled, He did
not revile in return; while suffering, He
uttered no threats, but kept entrusting
Himself to Him who judges righteously;
24 and He Himself [1a]bore our sins in
His body on the [2b]cross, so that we
[c]might die to [3]sin and live to righteousness; for [d]by His [4]wounds you were
[e]healed.
25 For you were [a]continually straying
like sheep, but now you have returned to
the [b]Shepherd and [1]Guardian of your
souls.

Godly Living

3 [a]In the same way, you wives, [b]be
submissive to your own husbands so
that even if any *of them* are disobedient
to the word, they may be [c]won without
a word by the behavior of their wives,
2 as they observe your chaste and
[1]respectful behavior.
3 [a]Your adornment must not be
merely external—braiding the hair, and
wearing gold jewelry, or putting on
dresses;
4 but *let it be* [a]the hidden person of
the heart, with the imperishable quality
of a gentle and quiet spirit, which is precious in the sight of God.
5 For in this way in former times the
holy women also, [a]who hoped in God,
used to adorn themselves, being submissive to their own husbands;
6 just as Sarah obeyed Abraham,
[a]calling him lord, and you have become
her children if you do what is right
[1b]without being frightened by any fear.
7 ¶ [a]You husbands in the same way,
live with *your wives* in an understanding
way, as with [1b]someone weaker, since
she is a woman; and show her honor as
a fellow heir of the grace of life, so that
your prayers will not be hindered.
8 ¶ [1]To sum up, [a]all of you be har-
monious, sympathetic, [b]brotherly, [c]kind-
hearted, and [d]humble in spirit;
9 [a]not returning evil for evil or [b]in-
sult for insult, but [1]giving a [c]blessing
instead; for [d]you were called for the very
purpose that you might [e]inherit a blessing.
10 For,
"[a]THE ONE WHO DESIRES LIFE, TO
LOVE AND SEE GOOD DAYS,
MUST KEEP HIS TONGUE FROM EVIL
AND HIS LIPS FROM SPEAKING
DECEIT.
11 "[a]HE MUST TURN AWAY FROM EVIL
AND DO GOOD;
HE MUST SEEK PEACE AND
PURSUE IT.
12 "[a]FOR THE EYES OF THE LORD ARE
TOWARD THE RIGHTEOUS,
AND HIS EARS ATTEND TO THEIR
PRAYER,
BUT THE FACE OF THE LORD IS
AGAINST THOSE WHO DO EVIL."
13 ¶ [a]Who is [1]there to harm you if
you prove zealous for what is good?
14 But even if you should [a]suffer for
the sake of righteousness, [b]you [1]are
blessed. [c]AND DO NOT FEAR THEIR [2]INTIMI-
DATION, AND DO NOT BE TROUBLED,
15 but [1]sanctify [a]Christ as Lord in
your hearts, always *being* ready [b]to make
a [2]defense to everyone who asks you to
give an account for the [a]hope that is in
you, yet [c]with gentleness and [3d]rever-
ence;
16 [1]and keep a [a]good conscience so
that in the thing in which [b]you are slandered, those who revile your good behavior in Christ will be put to shame.
17 For [a]it is better, [b]if [1]God should
will it so, that you suffer for doing what

13 [a]Rom 13:1
14 [1]Lit *through* [a]Rom 13:4 [b]Rom 13:3
15 [1]Lit *so* [a]1 Pet 3:17 [b]1 Pet 2:12
16 [1]Lit *not having* [a]John 8:32; James 1:25 [b]Rom 6:22; 1 Cor 7:22
17 [1]Or *emperor* [a]Rom 12:10 [b]1 Pet 1:22 [c]Prov 24:21 [d]Matt 22:21; 1 Pet 2:13
18 [1]Or *perverse* [a]Eph 6:5 [b]James 3:17
19 [1]Or *grace* [a]Rom 13:5; 1 Pet 3:14
20 [1]V 19, note 1 [a]1 Pet 3:17
21 [a]Acts 14:22; 1 Pet 3:9 [b]1 Pet 3:18 [c]Matt 11:29
22 [a]Is 53:9; 2 Cor 5:21
23 [1]Lit *who* [a]Is 53:7; Heb 12:3; 1 Pet 3:9
24 [1]Or *carried...up to the cross* [2]Lit *wood* [3]Lit *sins* [4]Lit *wound; or welt* [a]Is 53:4; 1 Cor 15:3; Heb 9:28 [b]Acts 5:30 [c]Rom 6:2 [d]Is 53:5 [e]Heb 12:13; James 5:16
25 [1]Or *Bishop, Overseer* [a]Is 53:6 [b]John 10:11; 1 Pet 5:4
3:1 [a]1 Pet 3:7 [b]Eph 5:22; Col 3:18 [c]1 Cor 9:19
2 [1]Lit *with respect*
3 [a]Is 3:18ff; 1 Tim 2:9
4 [a]Rom 7:22
5 [a]1 Tim 5:5; 1 Pet 1:3
6 [1]Lit *and are not* [a]Gen 18:12 [b]1 Pet 3:14
7 [1]Lit *a weaker vessel* [a]Eph 5:25; Col 3:19 [b]1 Thess 4:4
8 [1]Or *Finally* [a]Rom 12:16 [b]1 Pet 1:22 [c]Eph 4:32 [d]Eph 4:2; Phil 2:3; 1 Pet 5:5
9 [1]Lit *blessing instead* [a]Rom 12:17; 1 Thess 5:15 [b]1 Cor 4:12; 1 Pet 2:23 [c]Luke 6:28; Rom 12:14; 1 Cor 4:12 [d]1 Pet 2:21 [e]Gal 3:14; Heb 6:14
10 [a]Ps 34:12
11 [a]Ps 34:14
12 [a]Ps 34:15
13 [1]Lit *the one who will harm you* [a]Prov 16:7
14 [1]Or *would be* [2]Lit *fear* [a]Matt 5:10; 1 Pet 2:19ff [b]James 5:11 [c]Is 8:12f; 1 Pet 3:6
15 [1]I.e. set apart [2]Or *argument; or explanation* [3]Or *fear* [a]1 Pet 1:3

[b]Col 4:6 [c]2 Tim 2:25 [d]1 Pet 1:17 **16** [1]Lit *having a good* [a]1 Tim 1:5; Heb 13:18; 1 Pet 3:21 [b]1 Pet 2:12 **17** [1]Lit *the will of God* [a]1 Pet 2:20 [b]Acts 18:21; 1 Pet 1:6

is right rather than for doing what is
wrong.
18 For [a]Christ also died for sins
[b]once for all, *the* just for *the* unjust, so
that He might [c]bring us to God, having
been put to death [d]in the flesh, but made
alive [e]in the [1]spirit;
19 in [1]which also He went and made
proclamation to the spirits *now* in prison,
20 who once were disobedient, when
the [a]patience of God [b]kept waiting in
the days of Noah, during the construction
of [c]the ark, in which a few, that is,
[d]eight [e]persons, were brought safely
through *the* [1]water.
21 [a]Corresponding to that, baptism
now saves you—[b]not the removal of dirt
from the flesh, but an appeal to God [1]for
a [c]good conscience—through [d]the resurrection of Jesus Christ,
22 [a]who is at the right hand of God,
[b]having gone into heaven, [c]after angels
and authorities and powers had been subjected to Him.

Keep Fervent in Your Love

4 Therefore, since [a]Christ has [1]suf-
fered in the flesh, [b]arm yourselves
also with the same purpose, because [c]he
who has [1]suffered in the flesh has ceased
from sin,
2 [a]so as to live [b]the rest of the time
in the flesh no longer for the lusts of men,
but for the [c]will of God.
3 For [a]the time already past is sufficient *for you* to have carried out the desire of the Gentiles, [1b]having pursued a
course of sensuality, lusts, drunkenness,
carousing, drinking parties and [2]abomi-
nable idolatries.
4 In *all* this, they are surprised that
you do not run with *them* into the same
excesses of [a]dissipation, and they [b]ma-
lign *you*;
5 but they will give account to Him
who is ready to judge [a]the living and the
dead.
6 For [a]the gospel has for this purpose
been [1]preached even to those who are
dead, that though they are judged in the
flesh as men, they may live in the spirit
according to *the will of* God.
7 ¶ [a]The end of all things [1]is near;
therefore, [b]be of sound judgment and sober *spirit* for the purpose of [2]prayer.
8 Above all, [a]keep fervent in your
love for one another, because [b]love covers a multitude of sins.
9 [a]Be hospitable to one another
without [b]complaint.
10 [a]As each one has received a *special* gift, employ it in serving one another
as good [b]stewards of the manifold grace
of God.
11 [a]Whoever speaks, *is to do so* [1]as
one who is speaking the [b]utterances of
God; whoever serves *is to do so* as one
who is serving [2c]by the strength which
God supplies; so that [d]in all things God
may be glorified through Jesus Christ,
[e]to whom belongs the glory and dominion forever and ever. Amen.

Share the Sufferings of Christ

12 ¶ [a]Beloved, do not be surprised
at the [b]fiery ordeal among you, which
comes upon you for your testing, as
though some strange thing were happening to you;
13 but to the degree that you [a]share
the sufferings of Christ, keep on rejoicing, so that also at the [b]revelation of His
glory [c]you may rejoice with exultation.
14 If you are reviled [1a]for the name of
Christ, [b]you are blessed, [c]because the
Spirit of glory and of God rests on you.
15 Make sure that [a]none of you suffers as a murderer, or thief, or evildoer,
or a [1b]troublesome meddler;
16 but if *anyone suffers* as a [a]Chris-
tian, he is not to be ashamed, but is to
[b]glorify God in this name.
17 For *it is* time for judgment [a]to begin [1]with [b]the household of God; and if
it [c]*begins* with us first, what *will be* the
outcome for those [d]who do not obey the
[e]gospel of God?
18 [a]AND IF IT IS WITH DIFFICULTY THAT
THE RIGHTEOUS IS SAVED, [1]WHAT WILL BE-
COME OF THE [b]GODLESS MAN AND THE SIN-
NER?
19 Therefore, those also who suffer according to [a]the will of God shall entrust
their souls to a faithful Creator in doing
what is right.

Serve God Willingly

5 [a]Therefore, I exhort the elders
among you, as *your* [b]fellow elder
and [c]witness of the sufferings of Christ,
and a [d]partaker also of the glory that is to
be revealed,
2 shepherd [a]the flock of God among
you, exercising oversight [b]not under
compulsion, but voluntarily, according to
the will of God; and [c]not for sordid gain,
but with eagerness;
3 nor yet as [a]lording it over [1]those
allotted to your charge, but [2]proving to
be [b]examples to the flock.
4 And when the Chief [a]Shepherd

18 [1]Or *Spirit* [a]1 Pet 2:21 [b]Heb 9:26 [c]Rom 5:2; Eph 3:12 [d]Col 1:22; 1 Pet 4:1 [e]1 Pet 4:6 **19** [1]Or *whom* **20** [1]I.e. the great flood [a]Rom 2:4 [b]Gen 6:3 [c]Heb 11:7 [d]Gen 8:18; 2 Pet 2:5 [e]Acts 2:41; 1 Pet 1:9 **21** [1]Or *from* [a]Acts 16:33; Titus 3:5 [b]Heb 9:14 [c]1 Tim 1:5; Heb 13:18; 1 Pet 3:16 [d]1 Pet 1:3 **22** [a]Mark 16:19 [b]Heb 4:14 [c]Rom 8:38f; Heb 1:6 **4:1** [1]I.e. suffered death [a]1 Pet 2:21 [b]Eph 6:13 [c]Rom 6:7 **2** [a]Rom 6:2; Col 3:3 [b]1 Pet 1:14 [c]Mark 3:35 **3** [1]Lit *having gone in* [2]Lit *lawless* [a]1 Cor 12:2 [b]Rom 13:13; Eph 2:2 **4** [a]Eph 5:18 [b]1 Pet 3:16 **5** [a]Acts 10:42; Rom 14:9; 2 Tim 4:1 **6** [1]I.e. preached in their lifetimes [a]1 Pet 3:18 **7** [1]Lit *has come near* [2]Lit *prayers* [a]Rom 13:11; Heb 9:26; James 5:8; 1 John 2:18 [b]1 Pet 1:13 **8** [a]1 Pet 1:22 [b]Prov 10:12; 1 Cor 13:4ff; James 5:20 **9** [a]1 Tim 3:2; Heb 13:2 [b]Phil 2:14 **10** [a]Rom 12:6f [b]1 Cor 4:1 **11** [1]Lit *as utterances* [2]Lit *from* [a]1 Thess 2:4; Titus 2:1; Heb 13:7 [b]Acts 7:38 [c]Eph 1:19 [d]1 Cor 10:31; 1 Pet 2:12 [e]Rom 11:36; 1 Pet 5:11; Rev 1:6 **12** [a]1 Pet 2:11 [b]1 Pet 1:6f **13** [a]Rom 8:17; 2 Cor 1:5; Phil 3:10 [b]2 Tim 2:12 [c]1 Pet 1:7 **14** [1]Lit *in* [a]John 15:21; Heb 11:26; 1 Pet 4:16 [b]Matt 5:11; Luke 6:22; Acts 5:41 [c]2 Cor 4:10f **15** [1]Lit *one who oversees others' affairs* [a]1 Pet 2:19f [b]1 Thess 4:11; 2 Thess 3:11; 1 Tim 5:13 **16** [a]Acts 5:41; James 2:7 [b]1 Pet 4:11 **17** [1]Lit *from* [a]Jer 25:29; Ezek 9:6; Amos 3:2 [b]1 Tim 3:15; Heb 3:6; 1 Pet 2:5 [c]Rom 2:9 [d]2 Thess 1:8 [e]Rom 1:1 **18** [1]Lit *where will appear* [a]Prov 11:31; Luke 23:31 [b]1 Tim 1:9 **19** [a]1 Pet 3:17 **5:1** [a]Acts 11:30 [b]2 John 1; 3 John 1 [c]Luke 24:48; Heb 12:1 [d]1 Pet 1:5; Rev 1:9 **2** [a]John 21:16; Acts 20:28 [b]Philem 14 [c]1 Tim 3:8 **3** [1]Lit *the allotments* [2]Or *becoming* [a]Ezek 34:4; Matt 20:25f [b]John 13:15; Phil 3:17; 1 Thess 1:7; 2 Thess 3:9; 1 Tim 4:12; Titus 2:7 **4** [a]1 Pet 2:25

appears, you will receive the [b]unfading
[1c]crown of glory.
5 [a]You younger men, likewise, [b]be
subject to *your* elders; and all of you,
clothe yourselves with [c]humility toward
one another, for [d]GOD IS OPPOSED TO THE
PROUD, BUT GIVES GRACE TO THE HUMBLE.
6 ¶ Therefore [a]humble yourselves
under the mighty hand of God, that He
may exalt you at the proper time,
7 casting all your [a]anxiety on Him,
because He cares for you.
8 [a]Be of sober *spirit*, [b]be on the
alert. Your adversary, [c]the devil, prowls
around like a roaring [d]lion, seeking
someone to devour.
9 [1a]But resist him, [b]firm in *your*
faith, knowing that [c]the same experi-
ences of suffering are being accomplished
by your [2]brethren who are in the world.
10 After you have suffered [a]for a little
while, the [b]God of all grace, who [c]called
you to His [d]eternal glory in Christ, will
Himself [e]perfect, [f]confirm, strengthen
and establish you.
11 [a]To Him *be* dominion forever and
ever. Amen.
12 ¶ Through [a]Silvanus, our faithful
brother [1](for so I regard *him*), [b]I have
written to you briefly, exhorting and testifying that this is [c]the true grace of God.
[d]Stand firm in it!
13 She who is in Babylon, chosen together with you, sends you greetings, and
so does my son, [a]Mark.
14 [a]Greet one another with a kiss of
love.
¶ [b]Peace be to you all who are in
Christ.

4 [1]Lit *wreath* [b]1 Pet 1:4 [c]1 Cor 9:25 **5** [a]Luke 22:26; 1 Tim 5:1 [b]Eph 5:21 [c]1 Pet 3:8 [d]Prov 3:34; James 4:6 **6** [a]Matt 23:12; Luke 14:11; James 4:10 **7** [a]Ps 55:22; Matt 6:25 **8** [a]1 Pet 1:13 [b]Matt 24:42 [c]James 4:7 [d]2 Tim 4:17 **9** [1]Lit *whom resist* [2]Lit *brotherhood* [a]James 4:7 [b]Col 2:5 [c]Acts 14:22 **10** [a]1 Pet 1:6 [b]1 Pet 4:10 [c]1 Cor 1:9; 1 Thess 2:12 [d]2 Cor 4:17; 2 Tim 2:10 [e]1 Cor 1:10; Heb 13:21 [f]Rom 16:25; 2 Thess 2:17 **11** [a]Rom 11:36; 1 Pet 4:11 **12** [1]Lit *(as I consider)* [a]2 Cor 1:19 [b]Heb 13:22 [c]Acts 11:23; 1 Pet 1:13 [d]1 Cor 15:1 **13** [a]Acts 12:12; Col 4:10; Philem 24 **14** [a]Rom 16:16 [b]Eph 6:23

2 Peter

Title and Background

The recipients of this letter were the same group of Christians addressed in Peter's first letter. They were in danger of being confused by false teachers.

Author and Date of Writing

The author identifies himself as Simon Peter. He asserts that this is his second letter to the readers (3:1) and refers to Paul as "our beloved brother" (3:15). The character of the letter is compatible with the claim that it was written by Peter. It was written about A.D. 66.

Theme and Message

Peter, as a "shepherd" of Christ's sheep is particularly concerned about the false teachers and evildoers who have come into the church. He teaches the church how to deal with these false teachers but also seeks to commend to his readers a wholesome combination of Christian faith and practice. The Lord is certain to return, so the believers are to be watchful.

Outline

I. Introduction (1:1–2)
II. Growth in Christian Virtues (1:3–11)
III. Peter's Message (1:12–21)
IV. Warning Against False Teachers (2:1–22)
V. Jesus' Return (3:1–16)
VI. Conclusion (3:17–18)

Growth in Christian Virtue

1 [1]Simon Peter, a [a]bond-servant and [b]apostle of Jesus Christ,

¶ To those who have received [c]a faith of the same [2]kind as ours, [3]by [d]the righteousness of [e]our God and Savior, Jesus Christ:

2 [a]Grace and peace be multiplied to you in [b]the knowledge of God and of Jesus our Lord;

3 seeing that His [a]divine power has granted to us everything pertaining to life and godliness, through the true [b]knowledge of Him who [c]called us [1]by His own glory and [2]excellence.

4 [1]For by these He has granted to us His precious and magnificent [a]promises, so that by them you may become [b]partakers of *the* divine nature, having [c]escaped the [d]corruption that is in [e]the world by lust.

5 Now for this very reason also, applying all diligence, in your faith [a]supply [b]moral [1]excellence, and in *your* moral excellence, [c]knowledge,

6 and in *your* knowledge, [a]self-control, and in *your* self-control, [b]perseverance, and in *your* perseverance, [c]godliness,

7 and in *your* godliness, [a]brotherly kindness, and in *your* brotherly kindness, love.

8 For if these *qualities* are yours and are increasing, they render you neither useless nor [a]unfruitful in the true [b]knowledge of our Lord Jesus Christ.

9 For he who lacks these *qualities* is [a]blind *or* short-sighted, having forgotten *his* [b]purification from his former sins.

10 Therefore, brethren, be all the more diligent to make certain about His [a]calling and [b]choosing you; for as long as you practice these things, you will never [c]stumble;

11 for in this way the entrance into [a]the eternal kingdom of our [b]Lord and Savior Jesus Christ will be [c]abundantly [d]supplied to you.

12 ¶ Therefore, [a]I will always be ready to remind you of these things, even though you *already* know *them*, and have been established in [b]the truth which is present with *you.*

13 I consider it [a]right, as long as I am

1:1 [1]Two early mss read *Simeon* [2]Or *value* [3]Or *in* [a]Rom 1:1; Phil 1:1; James 1:1; Jude 1 [b]1 Pet 1:1 [c]Rom 1:12; 2 Cor 4:13; Titus 1:4 [d]Rom 3:21-26 [e]Titus 2:13
2 [a]Rom 1:7; 1 Pet 1:2 [b]John 17:3; Phil 3:8; 2 Pet 1:3
3 [1]Or *to* [2]Or *virtue* [a]1 Pet 1:5 [b]John 17:3; Phil 3:8; 2 Pet 1:2 [c]1 Thess 2:12; 2 Thess 2:14; 1 Pet 5:10
4 [1]Lit *Through which* (things) [a]2 Pet 3:9 [b]Eph 4:13; Heb 12:10; 1 John 3:2 [c]2 Pet 2:18 [d]2 Pet 2:19 [e]James 1:27
5 [1]Or *virtue* [a]2 Pet 1:11 [b]2 Pet 1:3 [c]Col 2:3; 2 Pet 1:2
6 [a]Acts 24:25 [b]Luke 21:19 [c]2 Pet 1:3
7 [a]Rom 12:10; 1 Pet 1:22
8 [a]Col 1:10 [b]John 17:3; Phil 3:8; 2 Pet 1:2
9 [a]1 John 2:11 [b]Eph 5:26; Titus 2:14
10 [a]Matt 22:14; Rom 11:29; 2 Pet 1:3 [b]1 Thess 1:4 [c]James 2:10; 2 Pet 3:17; Jude 24
11 [a]2 Tim 4:18 [b]2 Pet 2:20 [c]Rom 2:4; 1 Tim 6:17 [d]2 Pet 1:5
12 [a]Phil 3:1; 1 John 2:21; Jude 5 [b]Col 1:5f; 2 John 2
13 [a]Phil 1:7

in [b]this *earthly* dwelling, to [c]stir you up
by way of reminder,
14 knowing that [a]the laying aside of
my *earthly* dwelling is imminent, [b]as also
our Lord Jesus Christ has made clear
to me.
15 And I will also be diligent that at
any time after my [a]departure you will be
able to call these things to mind.

Eyewitnesses

16 ¶ For we did not follow cleverly devised [a]tales when we made known to
you the [b]power and coming of our Lord
Jesus Christ, but we were [c]eyewitnesses
of His majesty.
17 For when He received honor and
glory from God the Father, such an [1a]ut-
terance as this was [2]made to Him by the
[b]Majestic Glory, "This is My beloved Son
with whom I am well-pleased"—
18 and we ourselves heard this [1]utter-
ance made from heaven when we were
with Him on the [a]holy mountain.
19 ¶ [1]*So* we have [a]the prophetic
word *made* more [b]sure, to which you do
well to pay attention as to [c]a lamp shining in a dark place, until the [d]day dawns
and the [e]morning star arises [f]in your
hearts.
20 But [a]know this first of all, that [b]no
prophecy of Scripture is *a matter* of one's
own interpretation,
21 for [a]no prophecy was ever made by
an act of human will, but men [b]moved by
the Holy Spirit spoke from God.

The Rise of False Prophets

2 But [a]false prophets also arose among
the people, just as there will also be
[b]false teachers [c]among you, who will
[d]secretly introduce [e]destructive heresies, even [f]denying the [g]Master who
[h]bought them, bringing swift destruction
upon themselves.
2 Many will follow their [a]sensuality,
and because of them [b]the way of the
truth will be [c]maligned;
3 and in *their* [a]greed they will [b]ex-
ploit you with [c]false words; [d]their judgment from long ago is not idle, and their
destruction is not asleep.
4 ¶ For [a]if God did not spare angels
when they sinned, but cast them into hell
and [b]committed them to pits of darkness, reserved for judgment;
5 and did not spare [a]the ancient
world, but preserved [b]Noah, a [1]preach-
er of righteousness, with seven others,
when He brought a [c]flood upon the
world of the ungodly;
6 and *if* He [a]condemned the cities of
Sodom and Gomorrah to destruction by
reducing *them* to ashes, having made
them an [b]example to those who would
[c]live ungodly *lives* thereafter;
7 and *if* He [a]rescued righteous Lot,
oppressed by the [b]sensual conduct of
[c]unprincipled men
8 (for by what he saw and heard *that*
[a]righteous man, while living among
them, felt *his* righteous soul tormented
day after day by *their* lawless deeds),
9 [a]*then* the Lord knows how to rescue the godly from [1]temptation, and to
keep the unrighteous under punishment
for the [b]day of judgment,
10 and especially those who [1a]in-
dulge the flesh in *its* corrupt desires and
[b]despise authority.
¶ Daring, [c]self-willed, they do not
tremble when they [b]revile angelic
[2]majesties,
11 [a]whereas angels who are greater
in might and power do not bring a reviling judgment against them before the
Lord.
12 But [a]these, like unreasoning animals, [b]born as creatures of instinct to be
captured and killed, reviling where they
have no knowledge, will in [1]the destruction of those creatures also be destroyed,
13 suffering wrong as [a]the wages of
doing wrong. They count it a pleasure to
[b]revel in the [c]daytime. They are stains
and blemishes, [b]reveling in their
[1]deceptions, as they [d]carouse with you,
14 having eyes full of adultery that
never cease from sin, [a]enticing [b]unsta-
ble souls, having a heart trained in
[c]greed, [d]accursed children;
15 forsaking [a]the right way, they have
gone astray, having followed [b]the way of
Balaam, the *son* of Beor, who loved [c]the
wages of unrighteousness;
16 but he received a rebuke for his
own transgression, [a]*for* a mute donkey,
speaking with a voice of a man, restrained the madness of the prophet.
17 ¶ These are [a]springs without water and mists driven by a storm, [b]for
whom the [1]black darkness has been reserved.
18 For speaking out [a]arrogant *words*
of [b]vanity they [c]entice by fleshly desires, by [d]sensuality, those who barely
[e]escape from the ones who live in error,
19 promising them freedom while
they themselves are slaves of corruption;
for [a]by what a man is overcome, by this
he is enslaved.
20 For if, after they have [a]escaped the
defilements of the world by [b]the knowl-

13 [b]2 Cor 5:1; 2 Pet 1:14 [c]2 Pet 3:1
14 [a]2 Cor 5:1; 2 Tim 4:6 [b]John 13:36
15 [a]Luke 9:31
16 [a]1 Tim 1:4; 2 Pet 2:3 [b]Mark 13:26; 1 Thess 2:19 [c]Matt 17:1ff; Mark 9:2ff; Luke 9:28ff
17 [1]Lit *voice* [2]Lit *brought* [a]Matt 17:5; Mark 9:7; Luke 9:35 [b]Heb 1:3
18 [1]Lit *voice brought* [a]Ex 3:5; Josh 5:15
19 [1]Or *We have the* even *more sure prophetic word* [a]1 Pet 1:10f [b]Heb 2:2 [c]Ps 119:105 [d]Luke 1:78 [e]Rev 22:16 [f]2 Cor 4:6
20 [a]2 Pet 3:3 [b]Rom 12:6
21 [a]Jer 23:26; 2 Tim 3:16 [b]2 Sam 23:2; Luke 1:70; Acts 1:16; 1 Pet 1:11
2:1 [a]Deut 13:1ff; Jer 6:13 [b]2 Cor 11:13 [c]Matt 7:15; 1 Tim 4:1 [d]Gal 2:4; Jude 4 [e]1 Cor 11:19; Gal 5:20 [f]Jude 4 [g]Rev 6:10 [h]1 Cor 6:20
2 [a]Gen 19:5ff; 2 Pet 2:7; Jude 4 [b]Acts 16:17 [c]Rom 2:24
3 [a]1 Tim 6:5; 2 Pet 2:14; Jude 16 [b]2 Cor 2:17; 1 Thess 2:5 [c]Rom 16:18; 2 Pet 1:16 [d]Deut 32:35
4 [a]Jude 6 [b]Rev 20:1f
5 [1]Or *herald* [a]Ezek 26:20; 2 Pet 3:6 [b]Gen 6:8; 1 Pet 3:20 [c]2 Pet 3:6
6 [a]Gen 19:24; Jude 7 [b]Is 1:9; Matt 10:15; Rom 9:29; Jude 7 [c]Jude 15
7 [a]Gen 19:16 [b]Gen 19:5ff; 2 Pet 2:2; Jude 4 [c]2 Pet 3:17
8 [a]Heb 11:4
9 [1]Lit *trial*; or *temptation* [a]1 Cor 10:13; Rev 3:10 [b]Matt 10:15; Jude 6
10 [1]Lit *go after* [2]Lit *glories* [a]2 Pet 3:3; Jude 16 [b]Ex 22:28; Jude 8 [c]Titus 1:7
11 [a]Jude 9
12 [1]Lit *their destruction also* [a]Jude 10 [b]Jer 12:3; Col 2:22
13 [1]One early ms reads *love feasts* [a]2 Pet 2:15 [b]Rom 13:13 [c]1 Thess 5:7 [d]1 Cor 11:21; Jude 12
14 [a]2 Pet 2:18 [b]James 1:8; 2 Pet 3:16 [c]2 Pet 2:3 [d]Eph 2:3
15 [a]Acts 13:10 [b]Num 22:5; Deut 23:4; Neh 13:2; Jude 11; Rev 2:14 [c]2 Pet 2:13
16 [a]Num 22:21
17 [1]Lit *blackness of darkness* [a]Jude 12 [b]Jude 13
18 [a]Jude 16 [b]Eph 4:17 [c]2 Pet 2:14 [d]2 Pet 2:2 [e]2 Pet 1:4
19 [a]John 8:34; Rom 6:16
20 [a]2 Pet 2:18 [b]2 Pet 1:2

edge of the [c]Lord and Savior Jesus Christ, they are again [d]entangled in them and are overcome, [e]the last state has become worse for them than the first.

21 [a]For it would be better for them not to have known the way of righteousness, than having known it, to turn away from [b]the holy commandment [c]handed on to them.

22 [1]It has happened to them according to the true proverb, "[a]A DOG RETURNS TO ITS OWN VOMIT," and, "A sow, after washing, *returns* to wallowing in the mire."

Purpose of This Letter

3 This is now, [a]beloved, the second letter I am writing to you in which I am [b]stirring up your sincere mind by way of reminder,

2 that you should [a]remember the words spoken beforehand by [b]the holy prophets and [c]the commandment of the Lord and Savior *spoken* by your apostles.

The Coming Day of the Lord

3 [a]Know this first of all, that [b]in the last days [c]mockers will come with *their* mocking, [d]following after their own lusts,

4 and saying, "[a]Where is the promise of His [b]coming? For *ever* since the fathers [c]fell asleep, all continues just as it was [d]from the beginning of creation."

5 For [1]when they maintain this, it escapes their notice that [a]by the word of God *the* heavens existed long ago and *the* earth was [b]formed out of water and by water,

6 through which [a]the world at that time was [b]destroyed, being flooded with water.

7 But by His word [a]the present heavens and earth are being reserved for [b]fire, kept for [c]the day of judgment and destruction of ungodly men.

8 ¶ But do not let this one *fact* escape your notice, [a]beloved, that with the Lord one day is like a thousand years, and [b]a thousand years like one day.

9 [a]The Lord is not slow about His promise, as some count slowness, but [b]is patient toward you, [c]not wishing for any to perish but for all to come to repentance.

A New Heaven and Earth

10 But [a]the day of the Lord [b]will come like a thief, in which [c]the heavens [d]will pass away with a roar and the [e]elements will be destroyed with intense heat, and [f]the earth and [1]its works will be [2]burned up.

11 ¶ Since all these things are to be destroyed in this way, what sort of people ought you to be in holy conduct and godliness,

12 [a]looking for and hastening the coming of the day of God, because of which [b]the heavens will be destroyed by burning, and the [c]elements will melt with intense heat!

13 But according to His [a]promise we are looking for [b]new heavens and a new earth, [c]in which righteousness dwells.

14 ¶ [a]Therefore, [b]beloved, since you look for these things, be diligent to be [c]found by Him in peace, [d]spotless and blameless,

15 and regard the [a]patience of our Lord *as* salvation; just as also [b]our beloved brother Paul, [c]according to the wisdom given him, wrote to you,

16 as also in all *his* letters, speaking in them of [a]these things, [b]in which are some things hard to understand, which the untaught and [c]unstable distort, as *they do* also [d]the rest of the Scriptures, to their own destruction.

17 You therefore, [a]beloved, knowing this beforehand, [b]be on your guard so that you are not carried away by [c]the error of [d]unprincipled men and [e]fall from your own steadfastness,

18 but grow in the grace and [a]knowledge of our [b]Lord and Savior Jesus Christ. [c]To Him *be* the glory, both now and to the day of eternity. Amen.

---

20 [c]2 Pet 1:11 [d]2 Tim 2:4 [e]Matt 12:45; Luke 11:26
21 [a]Ezek 18:24; Heb 6:4ff; James 4:17 [b]Gal 6:2; 1 Tim 6:14; 2 Pet 3:2 [c]Jude 3
22 [1]Lit *The thing of the true proverb has happened to them* [a]Prov 26:11
3:1 [a]1 Pet 2:11; 2 Pet 3:8 [b]2 Pet 1:13
2 [a]Jude 17 [b]Luke 1:70; Acts 3:21; Eph 3:5 [c]Gal 6:2; 1 Tim 6:14; 2 Pet 2:21
3 [a]2 Pet 1:20 [b]1 Tim 4:1; Heb 1:2 [c]Jude 18 [d]2 Pet 2:10
4 [a]Is 5:19; Jer 17:15; Ezek 11:3; Mal 2:17; Matt 24:48 [b]1 Thess 2:19; 2 Pet 3:12 [c]Acts 7:60 [d]Mark 10:6
5 [1]Or *they are willfully ignorant of this fact, that* [a]Gen 1:6; Heb 11:3 [b]Ps 24:2
6 [a]2 Pet 2:5 [b]Gen 7:11
7 [a]2 Pet 3:10 [b]Is 66:15; Dan 7:9f; 2 Thess 1:7; Heb 12:29 [c]Matt 10:15; 1 Cor 3:13; Jude 7
8 [a]2 Pet 3:1 [b]Ps 90:4
9 [a]Hab 2:3; Rom 13:11; Heb 10:37 [b]Rom 2:4; Rev 2:21 [c]1 Tim 2:4; Rev 2:21
10 [1]Lit *the works in it* [2]Two early mss read *discovered* [a]1 Cor 1:8 [b]Matt 24:43; Luke 12:39; 1 Thess 5:2; Rev 3:3 [c]Is 34:4; 2 Pet 3:7 [d]Matt 24:35; Rev 21:1 [e]Is 24:19; Mic 1:4 [f]2 Pet 3:7
12 [a]1 Cor 1:7 [b]2 Pet 3:7 [c]Is 24:19; Mic 1:4
13 [a]Is 65:17 [b]Rom 8:21; Rev 21:1 [c]Is 60:21; Rev 21:27
14 [a]1 Cor 15:58; 2 Pet 1:10 [b]2 Pet 3:1 [c]1 Pet 1:7 [d]Phil 2:15; 1 Thess 5:23; 1 Tim 6:14; James 1:27 **15** [a]2 Pet 3:9 [b]Acts 9:17; 2 Pet 3:2 [c]1 Cor 3:10; Eph 3:3 **16** [a]2 Pet 3:14 [b]Heb 5:11 [c]2 Pet 2:14 [d]2 Pet 3:2 **17** [a]2 Pet 3:1 [b]1 Cor 10:12 [c]2 Pet 2:18 [d]2 Pet 2:7 [e]Rev 2:5 **18** [a]2 Pet 1:2 [b]2 Pet 1:11 [c]Rom 11:36; 2 Tim 4:18; Rev 1:6

1 John

Title and Background

False teachers were trying to mislead first-century Christians by denying, among other things, the true humanity of Jesus Christ. This view was incorporated within the system called Gnosticism and is the background of much of 1 John.

Author and Date of Writing

The author is John son of Zebedee—the apostle and the author of the Gospel of John and the book of Revelation. He was a first cousin of Jesus. The letter is difficult to date with precision, but many factors indicate that it was written near the end of the first century, probably around A.D. 90.

Theme and Message

John had two basic purposes in mind in this letter: (1) to expose false teachers, and (2) to give believers assurance of salvation. In keeping with his intention to combat Gnostic teachers, who taught that the spirit is entirely good and matter is entirely evil, John specifically struck at their total lack of morality; and by giving eyewitness testimony to the incarnation, he sought to confirm his readers' belief in the incarnate Christ. He tells his readers that if he is successful in doing this, it would give him great joy.

Outline

I. The Reality of the Incarnation (1:1–4)
II. Fellowship With the Father and the Son (1:5—2:28)
III. Divine Sonship (2:29—4:6)
IV. Ethics and Jesus Christ (4:7—5:12)
V. Great Christian Certainties (5:13–21)

Introduction
The Incarnate Word

1 What was [a]from the beginning, what we have [b]heard, what we have [c]seen with our eyes, what we [d]have looked at and [e]touched with our hands, concerning the [f]Word of Life—

2 and [a]the life was manifested, and we have [b]seen and [c]testify and proclaim to you [d]the eternal life, which was [e]with the Father and was [a]manifested to us—

3 what we have [a]seen and [b]heard we proclaim to you also, so that you too may have fellowship with us; and indeed our [c]fellowship is with the Father, and with His Son Jesus Christ.

4 [a]These things we write, so that our [b]joy may be made complete.

God Is Light

5 ¶ [a]This is the message we have heard from Him and announce to you, that [b]God is Light, and in Him there is no darkness at all.

6 [a]If we say that we have fellowship with Him and *yet* walk in the darkness, we [b]lie and [c]do not practice the truth;

7 but if we [a]walk in the Light as [b]He Himself is in the Light, we have fellowship with one another, and [c]the blood of Jesus His Son cleanses us from all sin.

8 [a]If we say that we have no sin, we are deceiving ourselves and the [b]truth is not in us.

9 [a]If we confess our sins, He is faithful and righteous to forgive us our sins and [b]to cleanse us from all unrighteousness.

10 [a]If we say that we have not sinned, we [b]make Him a liar and [c]His word is not in us.

Christ Is Our Advocate

2 [a]My little children, I am [b]writing these things to you so that you may not sin. And if anyone sins, [c]we have an [1d]Advocate with the Father, Jesus Christ the righteous;

2 and He Himself is [a]the [1]propitiation for our sins; and not for ours only,

1:1 [a]John 1:1f; 1 John 2:13 [b]Acts 4:20; 1 John 1:3 [c]John 19:35; 2 Pet 1:16; 1 John 1:2 [d]John 1:14; 1 John 4:14 [e]Luke 24:39; John 20:27 [f]John 1:1
2 [a]John 1:4; 1 John 3:5 [b]John 19:35; 1 John 1:1 [c]John 15:27; 1 John 4:14 [d]John 10:28; 1 John 2:25 [e]John 1:1
3 [a]John 19:35; 2 Pet 1:16; 1 John 1:1 [b]Acts 4:20; 1 John 1:1 [c]John 17:3; 1 Cor 1:9
4 [a]1 John 2:1 [b]John 3:29
5 [a]John 1:19; 1 John 3:11 [b]1 Tim 6:16; James 1:17
6 [a]John 8:12; 1 John 2:11 [b]John 8:55; 1 John 2:4 [c]John 3:21
7 [a]Is 2:5 [b]1 Tim 6:16 [c]Titus 2:14
8 [a]Job 15:14; Prov 20:9; Rom 3:10ff; James 3:2 [b]John 8:44; 1 John 2:4

9 [a]Ps 32:5; Prov 28:13 [b]Titus 2:14 **10** [a]Job 15:14 [b]John 3:33; 1 John 5:10 [c]1 John 2:14 **2:1** [1]Gr *Paracletos,* one called alongside to help; or *Intercessor* [a]John 13:33; Gal 4:19; 1 John 2:12 [b]1 John 1:4 [c]Rom 8:34; 1 Tim 2:5; Heb 7:25 [d]John 14:16 **2** [1]Or *satisfaction* [a]Rom 3:25; Heb 2:17; 1 John 4:10

but also [b]for *those of* the whole world.

3 ¶ [a]By this we know that we have come to [b]know Him, if we [c]keep His commandments.

4 The one who says, "[a]I have come to [b]know Him," and does not keep His commandments, is a [c]liar, and [d]the truth is not in him;

5 but whoever [a]keeps His word, in him the [b]love of God has truly been perfected. [c]By this we know that we are in Him:

6 the one who says he [a]abides in Him [b]ought himself to walk in the same manner as He walked.

7 ¶ [a]Beloved, I am [b]not writing a new commandment to you, but an old commandment which you have had [c]from the beginning; the old commandment is the word which you have heard.

8 [1]On the other hand, I am writing [a]a new commandment to you, which is true in Him and in you, because [b]the darkness is passing away and [c]the true Light is already shining.

9 The one who says he is in the Light and *yet* [a]hates his [b]brother is in the darkness until now.

10 [a]The one who loves his brother abides in the Light and there is no cause for stumbling in him.

11 But the one who [a]hates his brother is in the darkness and [b]walks in the darkness, and does not know where he is going because the darkness has [c]blinded his eyes.

12 ¶ I am writing to you, [a]little children, because [b]your sins have been forgiven you for His name's sake.

13 I am writing to you, fathers, because you know Him [a]who has been from the beginning. I am writing to you, young men, because [b]you have overcome [c]the evil one. I have written to you, children, because [d]you know the Father.

14 I have written to you, fathers, because you know Him [a]who has been from the beginning. I have written to you, young men, because you are [b]strong, and the [c]word of God abides in you, and [d]you have overcome the evil one.

Do Not Love the World

15 ¶ Do not love [a]the world nor the things in the world. [b]If anyone loves the world, the love of the Father is not in him.

16 For all that is in the world, [a]the lust of the flesh and [b]the lust of the eyes and [c]the boastful pride of life, is not from the Father, but is from the world.

17 [a]The world is passing away, and *also* its lusts; but the one who [b]does the will of God lives forever.

18 ¶ Children, [a]it is the last hour; and just as you heard that [b]antichrist is coming, [c]even now many antichrists have appeared; from this we know that it is the last hour.

19 [a]They went out from us, but they were not *really* of us; for if they had been of us, they would have remained with us; but *they went out,* [b]so that [1]it would be shown that they all are not of us.

20 [1]But you have an [a]anointing from [b]the Holy One, and [c]you all know.

21 I have not written to you because you do not know the truth, but [a]because you do know it, and [1]because no lie is [b]of the truth.

22 Who is the liar but [a]the one who denies that Jesus is the [1]Christ? This is [b]the antichrist, the one who denies the Father and the Son.

23 [a]Whoever denies the Son does not have the Father; the one who confesses the Son has the Father also.

24 As for you, let that abide in you which you heard [a]from the beginning. If what you heard from the beginning abides in you, you also [b]will abide in the Son and in the Father.

The Promise Is Eternal Life

25 [a]This is the promise which He Himself [1]made to us: eternal life.

26 ¶ These things I have written to you concerning those who are trying to [a]deceive you.

27 As for you, the [a]anointing which you received from Him abides in you, and you have no need for anyone to teach you; but as His anointing [b]teaches you about all things, and is [c]true and is not a lie, and just as it has taught you, [1]you abide in Him.

28 ¶ Now, [a]little children, abide in Him, so that when He [b]appears, we may have [c]confidence and [d]not [1]shrink away from Him in shame [2]at His [e]coming.

29 If you know that [a]He is righteous, you know that everyone also who practices righteousness [b]is [1]born of Him.

Children of God Love One Another

3 See [1a]how great a love the Father has bestowed on us, that we would be called [b]children of God; and *such* we

2 [b]John 4:42; 1 John 4:14
3 [a]1 John 2:5 [b]1 John 2:4 [c]John 14:15; 1 John 3:22; Rev 12:17
4 [a]Titus 1:10 [b]1 John 3:6 [c]1 John 1:6 [d]1 John 1:8
5 [a]John 14:23 [b]1 John 4:12 [c]1 John 2:3
6 [a]John 15:4 [b]John 13:15; 1 Pet 2:21
7 [a]Heb 6:9; 1 John 3:2 [b]John 13:34; 1 John 3:11; 2 John 5 [c]1 John 2:24; 2 John 5
8 [1]Lit *Again* [a]John 13:34 [b]Rom 13:12; Eph 5:8; 1 Thess 5:4f [c]John 1:9
9 [a]1 John 2:11 [b]Acts 1:15; 1 John 3:10
10 [a]John 11:9; 1 John 2:10
11 [a]1 John 2:9 [b]John 12:35; 1 John 1:6 [c]2 Cor 4:4; 2 Pet 1:9
12 [a]1 John 2:1 [b]Acts 13:38; 1 Cor 6:11
13 [a]1 John 1:1 [b]John 16:33; 1 John 2:14; Rev 2:7 [c]Matt 5:37; 1 John 2:14 [d]John 14:7; 1 John 2:3
14 [a]1 John 1:1 [b]Eph 6:10 [c]John 5:38; 1 John 1:10 [d]1 John 2:13
15 [a]Rom 12:2; James 1:27 [b]James 4:4
16 [a]Rom 13:14; Eph 2:3; 1 Pet 2:11 [b]Prov 27:20 [c]James 4:16
17 [a]1 Cor 7:31 [b]Mark 3:35
18 [a]Rom 13:11; 1 Tim 4:1; 1 Pet 4:7 [b]Matt 24:5; 1 John 2:22; 2 John 7 [c]Mark 13:22; 1 John 4:1
19 [1]Lit *they would be revealed* [a]Acts 20:30 [b]1 Cor 11:19
20 [1]Lit *And* [a]2 Cor 1:21; 1 John 2:27 [b]Mark 1:24; Acts 10:38 [c]Prov 28:5; Matt 13:11; John 14:26; 1 Cor 2:15f; 1 John 2:27
21 [1]Or know *that* [a]James 1:19; 2 Pet 1:12; Jude 5 [b]John 8:44; 1 John 3:19
22 [1]I.e. Messiah [a]1 John 4:3; 2 John 7 [b]Matt 24:5; 1 John 2:18; 2 John 7
23 [a]John 8:19; 1 John 4:15; 2 John 9
24 [a]1 John 2:7 [b]John 14:23; 1 John 1:3; 2 John 9 **25** [1]Lit *promised us* [a]John 3:15; 1 John 1:2 **26** [a]1 John 3:7; 2 John 7 **27** [1]Or *abide in Him*; Gr command [a]John 14:16; 1 John 2:20 [b]John 14:26; 1 Cor 2:12; 1 Thess 4:9 [c]John 14:17 **28** [1]Lit *be put to shame from Him* [2]Or *in His presence* [a]1 John 2:1 [b]Luke 17:30; Col 3:4; 1 John 3:2 [c]Eph 3:12; 1 John 3:21 [d]Mark 8:38 [e]1 Thess 2:19 **29** [1]Or *begotten* [a]John 7:18; 1 John 3:7 [b]John 1:13; 1 John 3:9; 3 John 11 **3:1** [1]Lit *what kind of love* [a]John 3:16; 1 John 4:10 [b]John 1:12; Rom 8:16; 1 John 3:2

are. For this reason the world does not know us, because [c]it did not know Him.

2 [a]Beloved, now we are [b]children of God, and [c]it has not appeared as yet what we will be. We know that when He [d]appears, we will be [e]like Him, because we will [f]see Him just as He is.

3 And everyone who has this [a]hope *fixed* on Him [b]purifies himself, just as He is pure.

4 ¶ Everyone who practices sin also practices lawlessness; and [a]sin is lawlessness.

5 You know that He [a]appeared in order to [b]take away sins; and [c]in Him there is no sin.

6 No one who abides in Him [a]sins; no one who sins has seen Him or [1b]knows Him.

7 [a]Little children, make sure no one [b]deceives you; [c]the one who practices righteousness is righteous, just as He is righteous;

8 the one who practices sin is [a]of the devil; for the devil [1]has sinned from the beginning. [b]The Son of God [c]appeared for this purpose, [d]to destroy the works of the devil.

9 No one who is [1a]born of God [b]practices sin, because His seed abides in him; and he cannot sin, because he is [1]born of God.

10 By this the [a]children of God and the [b]children of the devil are obvious: [1]anyone who does not practice righteousness is not of God, nor the one who [c]does not love his [d]brother.

11 ¶ [a]For this is the message [b]which you have heard from the beginning, [c]that we should love one another;

12 not as [a]Cain, *who* was of [b]the evil one and slew his brother. And for what reason did he slay him? Because [c]his deeds were evil, and his brother's were righteous.

13 ¶ Do not be surprised, brethren, if [a]the world hates you.

14 We know that we have [a]passed out of death into life, [b]because we love the brethren. He who does not love abides in death.

15 Everyone who [a]hates his brother is a murderer; and you know that [b]no murderer has eternal life abiding in him.

16 We know love by this, that [a]He laid down His life for us; and [b]we ought to lay down our lives for the [c]brethren.

17 But [a]whoever has the world's goods, and sees his brother in need and [b]closes his [1]heart [2]against him, [c]how does the love of God abide in him?

18 [a]Little children, let us not love with word or with tongue, but in deed and [b]truth.

1 [c]John 15:18 **2** [a]1 John 2:7 [b]John 1:12; Rom 8:16; 1 John 3:1 [c]Rom 8:19 [d]Luke 17:30; Col 3:4; 1 John 2:28 [e]Rom 8:29; 2 Pet 1:4 [f]John 17:24; 2 Cor 3:18 **3** [a]Rom 15:12; 1 Pet 1:3 [b]John 17:19; 2 Cor 7:1 **4** [a]Rom 4:15; 1 John 5:17 **5** [a]1 John 1:2 [b]John 1:29; 1 Pet 1:18-20; 1 John 2:2 [c]2 Cor 5:21; 1 John 2:29 **6** [1]Or *has known* [a]1 John 3:9 [b]1 John 2:3; 3 John 11 **7** [a]1 John 2:1 [b]1 John 2:26 [c]1 John 2:29 **8** [1]Lit *sins* [a]Matt 13:38; John 8:44; 1 John 3:10 [b]Matt 4:3 [c]1 John 3:5 [d]John 12:31 **9** [1]Or *begotten* [a]John 1:13; 1 John 2:29; 3 John 11 [b]1 Pet 1:23; 1 John 3:6 **10** [1]Lit *everyone* [a]John 1:12; Rom 8:16; 1 John 3:1 [b]Matt 13:38; John 8:44; 1 John 3:8 [c]Rom 13:8ff; Col 3:14; 1 Tim 1:5; 1 John 4:8 [d]1 John 2:9 **11** [a]1 John 1:5 [b]1 John 2:7 [c]John 13:4f; 1 John 4:7; 2 John 5 **12** [a]Gen 4:8 [b]Matt 5:37; 1 John 2:13f [c]Ps 38:20; Prov 29:10; John 8:40 **13** [a]John 15:18 **14** [a]John 5:24 [b]John 13:35; 1 John 2:10 **15** [a]Matt 5:21f; John 8:44 [b]Gal 5:20f; Rev 21:8 **16** [a]John 10:11 [b]Phil 2:17; 1 Thess 2:8 [c]1 John 2:9 **17** [1]Lit *inward parts* [2]Lit *from* [a]James 2:15f [b]Deut 15:7 [c]1 John 4:20 **18** [a]1 John 2:1 [b]2 John 1; 3 John 1 **19** [1]Lit *persuade* [a]1 John 2:21 **20** [1]Or *that if our heart condemns us, that God...* **21** [1]Lit *toward* [a]1 John 3:2 [b]1 John 2:28 **22** [a]Job 22:26f; Matt 7:7; John 9:31 [b]1 John 2:3 [c]John 8:29; Heb 13:21 **23** [1]Or *believe the name* [2]Lit *gave us a commandment* [a]John 6:29 [b]John 1:12 [c]John 13:34;

19 We will know by this that we are [a]of the truth, and will [1]assure our heart before Him

20 [1]in whatever our heart condemns us; for God is greater than our heart and knows all things.

21 [a]Beloved, if our heart does not condemn us, we have [b]confidence [1]before God;

22 and [a]whatever we ask we receive from Him, because we [b]keep His commandments and do [c]the things that are pleasing in His sight.

23 ¶ This is His commandment, that we [1a]believe in [b]the name of His Son Jesus Christ, and love one another, just as [c]He [2]commanded us.

24 The one who [a]keeps His commandments [b]abides in Him, and He in him. [c]We know by this that [d]He abides in us, by the Spirit whom He has given us.

Testing the Spirits

4 [a]Beloved, do not believe every [b]spirit, but test the spirits to see whether they are from God, because [c]many false prophets have gone out into the world.

2 By this you know the Spirit of God: [a]every spirit that [b]confesses that [c]Jesus Christ has come in the flesh is from God;

3 and every spirit that [a]does not confess Jesus is not from God; this is the *spirit* of the [b]antichrist, of which you have heard that it is coming, and [c]now it is already in the world.

4 You are from God, [a]little children, and [b]have overcome them; because [c]greater is He who is in you than [d]he who is in the world.

5 [a]They are from the world; therefore they speak *as* from the world, and the world listens to them.

6 [a]We are from God; [b]he who knows God listens to us; [c]he who is not from God does not listen to us. By this we know [d]the spirit of truth and [e]the spirit of error.

God Is Love

7 ¶ [a]Beloved, let us [b]love one another, for love is from God; and [c]everyone who loves is [1d]born of God and [e]knows God.

1 John 2:8 **24** [a]1 John 2:3 [b]John 6:56; 1 John 2:6 [c]John 14:17; Rom 8:9; 1 Thess 4:8; 1 John 4:13 [d]1 John 2:5 **4:1** [a]3 John 11 [b]Jer 29:8; 1 Cor 12:10; 1 Thess 5:20f; 2 Thess 2:2 [c]Jer 14:14; 2 Pet 2:1; 1 John 2:18 **2** [a]1 Cor 12:3 [b]1 John 2:23 [c]John 1:14; 1 John 1:2 **3** [a]1 John 2:22; 2 John 7 [b]1 John 2:18 [c]2 Thess 2:3-7; 1 John 2:18 **4** [a]1 John 2:1 [b]1 John 2:13 [c]Rom 8:31; 1 John 3:20 [d]John 12:31 **5** [a]John 15:19 **6** [a]John 8:23; 1 John 4:4 [b]John 8:47 [c]1 Cor 14:37 [d]John 14:17 [e]1 Tim 4:1 **7** [1]Or *begotten* [a]1 John 2:7 [b]1 John 3:11 [c]1 John 5:1 [d]1 John 2:29 [e]1 Cor 8:3; 1 John 2:3

8 The one who does not love does not
know God, for [a]God is love.
9 By this the love of God was manifested [1a]in us, that [b]God has sent His
[2]only begotten Son into the world so that
we might live through Him.
10 In this is love, [a]not that we loved
God, but that [b]He loved us and sent His
Son *to be* [c]the propitiation for our sins.
11 [a]Beloved, if God so loved us, [b]we
also ought to love one another.
12 [a]No one has seen God at any time;
if we love one another, God abides in us,
and His [b]love is perfected in us.
13 [a]By this we know that we abide in
Him and He in us, because He has given
us of His Spirit.
14 We have seen and [a]testify that the
Father has [b]sent the Son *to be* the Savior
of the world.
15 ¶ [a]Whoever confesses that [b]Jesus
is the Son of God, God [c]abides in him,
and he in God.
16 [a]We have come to know and have
believed the love which God has [1b]for
us. [c]God is love, and the one who
[d]abides in love abides in God, and God
abides in him.
17 By this, [a]love is perfected with us,
so that we may have [b]confidence in [c]the
day of judgment; because [d]as He is, so
also are we in this world.
18 There is no fear in love; but [a]per-
fect love casts out fear, because fear [1]in-
volves punishment, and the one who
fears is not [b]perfected in love.
19 [a]We love, because He first
loved us.
20 [a]If someone says, "I love God,"
and [b]hates his brother, he is a [c]liar; for
[d]the one who does not love his brother
whom he has seen, [e]cannot love God
whom he has not seen.
21 And [a]this commandment we have
from Him, that the one who loves God
[b]should love his brother also.

Overcoming the World

5 [a]Whoever believes that Jesus is the
[1]Christ is [2b]born of God, and whoever loves the [3]Father [c]loves the *child*
[2]born of Him.
2 [a]By this we know that [b]we love
the children of God, when we love God
and [1]observe His commandments.
3 For [a]this is the love of God, that we
[b]keep His commandments; and [c]His
commandments are not burdensome.
4 For whatever is [1a]born of God
[b]overcomes the world; and this is the
victory that has overcome the world—
our faith.
5 ¶ Who is the one who overcomes
the world, but he who [a]believes that
Jesus is the Son of God?
6 This is the One who came [a]by
water and blood, Jesus Christ; not
[1]with the water only, but [1]with the water and [1]with the blood. It is [b]the
Spirit who testifies, because the Spirit is
the truth.
7 For there are [a]three that testify:
8 [1]the Spirit and the water and the
blood; and the three are [2]in agreement.
9 [a]If we receive the testimony of
men, the testimony of God is greater; for
the testimony of God is this, that [b]He has
testified concerning His Son.
10 The one who believes in the Son of
God [a]has the testimony in himself; the
one who does not believe God has [b]made
Him a liar, because he has not believed in
the testimony that God has given concerning His Son.
11 And the testimony is this, that God
has given us [a]eternal life, and [b]this life
is in His Son.
12 [a]He who has the Son has the life;
he who does not have the Son of God
does not have the life.

This Is Written That You May Know

13 ¶ [a]These things I have written to
you who [b]believe in the name of the Son
of God, so that you may know that you
have [c]eternal life.
14 This is [a]the confidence which
we have [1]before Him, that, [b]if we ask
anything according to His will, He
hears us.
15 And if we know that He hears us *in*
whatever we ask, [a]we know that we
have the requests which we have asked
from Him.
16 ¶ If anyone sees his brother [1]com-
mitting a sin not *leading* to death, [a]he
shall ask and [2]*God* will for him give life
to those who commit sin not *leading* to
death. [b]There is a sin *leading* to death;
[c]I do not say that he should make request
for this.
17 [a]All unrighteousness is sin, and
[b]there is a sin not *leading* to death.
18 ¶ [a]We know that [b]no one who
is [1]born of God sins; but He who was
[1]born of God [c]keeps him, and [d]the evil
one does not [e]touch him.
19 [a]We know that [b]we are of God,

8 [a]1 John 4:7
9 [1]Or *in our case* [2]Or *unique, only one of His kind* [a]John 9:3; 1 John 4:16 [b]John 3:16f; 1 John 4:10
10 [a]Rom 5:8; 1 John 4:19 [b]John 3:16f; 1 John 4:9 [c]1 John 2:2
11 [a]1 John 2:7 [b]1 John 4:7
12 [a]John 1:18; 1 Tim 6:16; 1 John 4:20 [b]1 John 2:5
13 [a]Rom 8:9; 1 John 3:24
14 [a]John 15:27; 1 John 1:2 [b]John 3:17; 1 John 2:2
15 [a]1 John 2:23 [b]Rom 10:9; 1 John 3:23 [c]1 John 2:24
16 [1]Lit *in* [a]John 6:69 [b]John 9:3; 1 John 4:9 [c]1 John 4:7 [d]1 John 4:12f
17 [a]1 John 2:5 [b]1 John 2:28 [c]Matt 10:15 [d]John 17:22; 1 John 2:6
18 [1]Lit *has* [a]Rom 8:15 [b]1 John 4:12
19 [a]1 John 4:10
20 [a]1 John 1:6 [b]1 John 2:9 [c]1 John 1:6 [d]1 John 3:17 [e]1 Pet 1:8; 1 John 4:12
21 [a]Lev 19:18; Matt 5:43f; John 13:34 [b]1 John 3:11
5:1 [1]I.e. Messiah [2]Or *begotten* [3]Lit *one who begets* [a]1 John 2:22f [b]John 1:3; 1 John 2:29 [c]John 8:42
2 [1]Lit *do* [a]1 John 2:5 [b]1 John 3:14
3 [a]John 14:15; 2 John 6 [b]1 John 2:3 [c]Matt 11:30
4 [1]Or *begotten* [a]John 1:13; 1 John 2:29 [b]1 John 2:13
5 [a]1 John 4:15
6 [1]Lit *in* [a]John 19:34 [b]Matt 3:16f; John 15:26
7 [a]Matt 18:16
8 [1]A few late mss add *...in heaven, the Father, the Word, and the Holy Spirit, and these three are one. And there are three that testify on earth, the Spirit* [2]Lit *for the one thing*
9 [a]John 5:34 [b]Matt 3:17; John 5:32
10 [a]Rom 8:16; Gal 4-6; Rev 12:17 [b]John 3:18; 1 John 1:10
11 [a]John 3:36; 1 John 1:2 [b]John 1:4
12 [a]John 3:15f

13 [a]John 20:31 [b]1 John 3:23 [c]1 John 1:2 **14** [1]Lit *toward* [a]1 John 2:28 [b]Matt 7:7; John 14:13; 1 John 3:22 **15** [a]1 John 5:18-20 **16** [1]Lit *sinning* [2]Or *God will give him life,* that is, *to those who...* [a]James 5:15 [b]Num 15:30; Heb 6:4-6 [c]Jer 7:16 **17** [a]1 John 3:4 [b]1 John 2:1f **18** [1]Or *begotten* [a]1 John 5:15 [b]1 John 3:9 [c]James 1:27; Jude 21 [d]1 John 2:13 [e]John 14:30 **19** [a]1 John 5:15 [b]1 John 4:6

and that [c]the whole world lies in *the*
power of the evil one.
20 And [a]we know that [b]the Son of
God has come, and has [c]given us understanding so that we may know [d]Him who
is true; and we [e]are in Him who is true,
in His Son Jesus Christ. [f]This is the true
God and [g]eternal life.
21 ¶ [a]Little children, guard yourselves from [b]idols.

19 [c]John 12:31; Gal 1:4 **20** [a]1 John 5:15 [b]John 8:42; 1 John 5:5 [c]Luke 24:45 [d]John 17:3; Rev 3:7 [e]John 1:18; 1 John 2:23; Rev 3:7 [f]1 John 1:2 [g]1 John 5:11 **21** [a]1 John 2:1 [b]1 Cor 10:7; 1 Thess 1:9

2 John

Title and Background

During the first two centuries A.D. the gospel was taken from place to place by traveling evangelists and teachers. Believers customarily took these missionaries into their homes and gave them provisions for their journey when they left. Since Gnostic teachers also relied on this practice, 2 John was written to urge discernment in supporting traveling teachers.

Author and Date of Writing

John wrote this letter shortly after his first letter, about A.D. 90.

Theme and Message

John writes of how important it is for Christians to love one another. To love means to obey God's commandments, and God's commandments in turn tell us to live lives of love. John again emphasizes the importance of the doctrine that Jesus is God's Son—both God and man. Christians should separate themselves from those who teach that Jesus is not God's Son.

Outline

I. Greeting (1–3)
II. Commendation (4)
III. Exhortation and Warning (5–11)
IV. Conclusion (12–13)

Walk According to His Commandments

1 [a]The elder to the [b]chosen [c]lady and her children, whom I [d]love in truth; and not only I, but also all who [e]know the truth,

2 for [a]the sake of the truth which abides [b]in us and will be [c]with us forever:

3 [a]Grace, mercy *and* peace will be with us, from God the Father and from Jesus Christ, the Son of the Father, in truth and love.

4 ¶ [a]I was very glad to find *some* of your children walking in truth, just as we have received commandment *to do* from the Father.

5 Now I ask you, lady, [a]not as though *I were* writing to you a new commandment, but the one which we have had [a]from the beginning, that we [b]love one another.

6 And [a]this is love, that we walk according to His commandments. This is the commandment, [b]just as you have heard [c]from the beginning, that you should walk in it.

7 ¶ For [a]many deceivers have [b]gone out into the world, those who [c]do not acknowledge Jesus Christ *as* coming in the flesh. This is [a]the deceiver and the [d]antichrist.

8 [a]Watch yourselves, [b]that you do not lose what we have accomplished, but that you may receive a full reward.

9 [1]Anyone who [2]goes too far and [a]does not abide in the teaching of Christ, does not have God; the one who abides in the teaching, he has both the Father and the Son.

10 If anyone comes to you and does not bring this teaching, [a]do not receive him into *your* house, and do not give him a greeting;

11 for the one who gives him a greeting [a]participates in his evil deeds.

12 ¶ [a]Though I have many things to write to you, I do not want to *do so* with paper and ink; but I hope to come to you and speak face to face, so that [1]your [b]joy may be made full.

13 ¶ The children of your [a]chosen sister greet you.

1:1 [a]Acts 11:30; 1 Pet 5:1; 3 John 1 [b]Rom 16:13; 1 Pet 5:13; 2 John 13 [c]2 John 5 [d]1 John 3:18; 2 John 3; 3 John 1 [e]John 8:32; 1 Tim 2:4
2 [a]2 Pet 1:12 [b]1 John 1:8 [c]John 14:16
3 [a]Rom 1:7; 1 Tim 1:2
4 [a]3 John 3f
5 [a]1 John 2:7 [b]John 13:34; 1 John 3:11
6 [a]1 John 2:5 [b]1 John 2:24 [c]1 John 2:7
7 [a]1 John 2:26 [b]1 John 2:19 [c]1 John 4:2f [d]1 John 2:18
8 [a]Mark 13:9 [b]1 Cor 3:8; Heb 10:35
9 [1]Lit *Everyone* [2]Lit *goes on ahead* [a]John 7:16; 1 John 2:23
10 [a]1 Kin 13:16f; Rom 16:17; 2 Thess 3:6; Titus 3:10
11 [a]Eph 5:11; 1 Tim 5:22; Jude 23
12 [1]One early ms reads *our*
[a]3 John 13 [b]John 3:29; 1 John 1:4 **13** [a]2 John 1

3 John

Title and Background

Itinerant teachers sent out by John were rejected in one of the churches in the province of Asia by a dictatorial leader, Diotrephes. This man had gone so far as to excommunicate members who showed hospitality to John's messengers.

Author and Date of Writing

The letter was probably written about the same time as 1 and 2 John, around A.D. 90. The apostle John is the author.

Theme and Message

John wrote to Gaius, his friend and a leader in the church. He writes to praise and thank Gaius for his help and to give him encouragement. He also reproves Diotrephes for not cooperating and for rebelling against John's leadership. In a later visit John will deal with him personally.

Outline

I. Greeting (1–2)
II. Commendation of Gaius (3–8)
III. Condemnation of Diotrephes (9–10)
IV. Exhortation to Gaius (11)
V. Example of Demetrius (12)
VI. Conclusion (13–14)

You Walk in the Truth

1 [a]The elder to the beloved [b]Gaius,
whom I [c]love in truth.
2 ¶ Beloved, I pray that in all respects
you may prosper and be in good health,
just as your soul prospers.
3 For I [a]was very glad when [b]breth-
ren came and testified to your truth, *that*
is, how you [a]are walking in truth.
4 I have no greater joy than [1]this, to
hear of [a]my children [b]walking in the
truth.
5 ¶ Beloved, you are acting faithfully
in whatever you accomplish for the
[a]brethren, and [1]especially *when they*
are [b]strangers;
6 and they have testified to your love
before the church. You will do well to
[a]send them on their way in a manner
[b]worthy of God.
7 For they went out for the sake of
[a]the Name, [b]accepting nothing from the
Gentiles.
8 Therefore we ought to [1]support
such men, so that we may [2]be fellow
workers [3]with the truth.
9 ¶ I wrote something to the church;
but Diotrephes, who loves to [a]be first
among them, does not accept [1]what we
say.
10 For this reason, [a]if I come, I will
call attention to his deeds which he does,
unjustly accusing us with wicked words;
and not satisfied with this, he himself
does not [b]receive the [c]brethren, either,
and he forbids those who desire *to do so*
and [d]puts *them* out of the church.
11 ¶ Beloved, [a]do not imitate what is
evil, but what is good. [b]The one who
does good is of God; [c]the one who does
evil has not seen God.
12 Demetrius [a]has received a *good*
testimony from everyone, and from the
truth itself; and we add our testimony,
and [b]you know that our testimony is
true.
13 ¶ [a]I had many things to write to
you, but I am not willing to write *them* to
you with pen and ink;
14 but I hope to see you shortly, and
we will speak face to face.
15 ¶ [a]Peace *be* to you. The friends
greet you. Greet the friends [b]by name.

1 [a]2 John 1 [b]Acts 19:29; Rom 16:23; 1 Cor 1:14 [c]1 John 3:18; 2 John 1
3 [a]2 John 4 [b]Acts 1:15; Gal 6:10; 3 John 5
4 [1]Lit *these things, that I hear* [a]1 Cor 4:14f; 2 Cor 6:13; Gal 4:19; 1 Thess 2:11; 1 Tim 1:2; 2 Tim 1:2; Philem 10; 1 John 2:1 [b]2 John 4
5 [1]Lit *this* [a]Acts 1:15; Gal 6:10; 3 John 3 [b]Rom 12:13; Heb 13:2
6 [a]Acts 15:3; Titus 3:13 [b]Col 1:10; 1 Thess 2:12
7 [a]John 15:21; Acts 5:41; Phil 2:9 [b]Acts 20:33
8 [1]Or *receive such men as guests* [2]Or *prove ourselves to be* [3]Or *for*
9 [1]Lit *us* [a]2 John 9
10 [a]2 John 12 [b]2 John 10; 3 John 5 [c]Acts 1:15; Gal 6:10; 3 John 3 [d]John 9:34
11 [a]Ps 34:14 [b]1 John 2:29 [c]1 John 3:6
12 [a]Acts 6:3; 1 Tim 3:7 [b]John 19:35
13 [a]2 John 12
15 [a]John 20:19; Eph 6:23; 1 Pet 5:14 [b]John 10:3

Jude

Title and Background

Jude originated as a personal letter from a leader in the apostolic church to one or more of the congregations dispersed throughout the Roman empire. The dangers facing the church at this time were not those of outright persecution and extinction but of heretics and distorters of the faith.

Author and Date of Writing

The author identifies himself as Jude, another form of the Hebrew name Judah. He was most likely Judas the brother of our Lord. The letter was probably written about A.D. 65.

Theme and Message

Although Jude was eager to write to his readers about salvation, he thought he must instead warn them about certain immoral men circulating among them who were perverting the grace of God. Apparently these false teachers were trying to convince believers that being saved by grace gave them license to sin since their sins would no longer be held against them. It has been thought that these false teachers were Gnostics, who believed that the spirit is entirely good and matter is entirely evil, probably forerunners of second-century, fully developed Gnosticism.

Outline

I. Introduction (1–2)
II. Occasion for the Letter (3–4)
III. Warning Against False Teachers (5–16)
IV. Exhortation to Believers (17–23)
V. Concluding Doxology (24–25)

The Warnings of History to the Ungodly

1 [1][a]Jude, a [b]bond-servant of Jesus
Christ, and brother of [2]James,
¶ To [c]those who are the called, beloved in God the Father, and [d]kept for
Jesus Christ:
2 [a]May mercy and peace and love
[b]be multiplied to you.
3 ¶ [a]Beloved, while I was making every effort to write you about our [b]com-
mon salvation, I felt the necessity to write
to you appealing that you [c]contend earnestly for [d]the faith which was once for
all [e]handed down to [f]the [1]saints.
4 For certain persons have [a]crept in
unnoticed, those who were long beforehand [1][b]marked out for this condemnation, ungodly persons who turn [c]the
grace of our God into [d]licentiousness and
[e]deny our only Master and Lord, Jesus
Christ.
5 ¶ Now I desire to [a]remind you,
though [b]you know all things once for all,
that [1]the Lord, [c]after saving a people out
of the land of Egypt, [2]subsequently destroyed those who did not believe.
6 And [a]angels who did not keep
their own domain, but abandoned their
proper abode, He has [b]kept in eternal
bonds under darkness for the judgment of
the great day,
7 just as [a]Sodom and Gomorrah and
the [b]cities around them, since they in
the same way as these indulged in gross
immorality and [c]went after [1]strange
flesh, are exhibited as an [2][d]example in
undergoing the [e]punishment of eternal
fire.
8 ¶ Yet in the same way these men,
also by dreaming, [a]defile the flesh, and
reject authority, and revile [1]angelic
majesties.
9 But [a]Michael [b]the archangel,
when he disputed with the devil and argued about [c]the body of Moses, did not
dare pronounce against him a railing
judgment, but said, "[d]The Lord rebuke you!"
10 But [a]these men revile the things
which they do not understand; and [b]the

1 [1]Gk *Judas* [2]Or *Jacob* [a]Matt 13:55; Mark 6:3; [Luke 6:16; John 14:22; Acts 1:13] [b]Rom 1:1 [c]Rom 1:6f [d]John 17:11f; 1 Pet 1:5 **2** [a]Gal 6:16; 1 Tim 1:2 [b]1 Pet 1:2; 2 Pet 1:2 **3** [1]Or *holy ones* [a]Heb 6:9; Jude 1 [b]Titus 1:4 [c]1 Tim 6:12 [d]Acts 6:7; Jude 20 [e]2 Pet 2:21 [f]Acts 9:13 **4** [1]Or *written about...long ago* [a]Gal 2:4; 2 Tim 3:6 [b]1 Pet 2:8 [c]Acts 11:23 [d]2 Pet 2:7 [e]2 Tim 2:12; Titus 1:16; 2 Pet 2:1; 1 John 2:22 **5** [1]Two early mss read *Jesus* [2]Lit *the second time* [a]2 Pet 1:12f [b]1 John 2:20 [c]Ex 12:51; 1 Cor 10:5-10; Heb 3:16f **6** [a]2 Pet 2:4 [b]2 Pet 2:9 **7** [1]Lit *different* or *other flesh* [2]Or *example of eternal fire, in undergoing punishment* [a]Gen 19:24f; 2 Pet 2:6 [b]Deut 29:23; Hos 11:8 [c]2 Pet 2:2 [d]2 Pet 2:6 [e]Matt 25:41; 2 Thess 1:8f; 2 Pet 3:7 **8** [1]Lit *glories* [a]2 Pet 2:10 **9** [a]Dan 10:13; Rev 12:7 [b]1 Thess 4:16; 2 Pet 2:11 [c]Deut 34:6 [d]Zech 3:2 **10** [a]2 Pet 2:12 [b]Phil 3:19

things which they know by instinct,
[c]like unreasoning animals, by these
things they are [1]destroyed.
11 Woe to them! For they have gone
[a]the way of Cain, and for pay [1]they have
rushed headlong into [b]the error of Balaam,
and [c]perished in the rebellion of
Korah.
12 These are the men who are [1]hidden
reefs [a]in your love feasts when they
feast with you [b]without fear, caring for
themselves; [c]clouds without water,
[d]carried along by winds; autumn trees
without fruit, [2]doubly dead, [e]uprooted;
13 [a]wild waves of the sea, casting up
[b]their own [1]shame like foam; wandering
stars, [c]for whom the [2]black darkness
has been reserved forever.
14 ¶ *It was* also about these men *that*
[a]Enoch, *in* the seventh *generation* from
Adam, prophesied, saying, "[b]Behold, the
Lord came with [1]many thousands of His
holy ones,
15 [a]to execute judgment upon all, and
to convict all the ungodly of all their ungodly
deeds which they have done in an
ungodly way, and of all the harsh things
which [b]ungodly sinners have spoken
against Him."
16 These are [a]grumblers, finding
fault, [b]following after their *own* lusts;
[1]they speak [c]arrogantly, flattering people
[d]for the sake of *gaining an* advantage.

Keep Yourselves in the Love of God

17 ¶ But you, [a]beloved, [b]ought to remember
the words that were spoken beforehand
by [c]the apostles of our Lord
Jesus Christ,
18 that they were saying to you, "[a]In
the last time there will be mockers, [b]following
after their own ungodly lusts."
19 These are the ones who cause divisions,
[1a]worldly-minded, [2]devoid of the
Spirit.
20 But you, [a]beloved, [b]building yourselves
up on your most holy [a]faith,
[c]praying in the Holy Spirit,
21 keep yourselves in the love of God,
[a]waiting anxiously for the mercy of our
Lord Jesus Christ to eternal life.
22 And have mercy on some, who are
doubting;
23 save others, [a]snatching them out
of the fire; and on some have mercy with
fear, [b]hating even the garment polluted
by the flesh.
24 ¶ [a]Now to Him who is able to keep
you from stumbling, and to [b]make you
stand in the presence of His glory blameless
with [c]great joy,
25 to the [a]only [b]God our Savior,
through Jesus Christ our Lord, [c]*be* glory,
majesty, dominion and authority, [d]before
all time and now and [1]forever.
Amen.

10 [1]Lit *corrupted* [c]2 Pet 2:12
11 [1]Lit *they have poured themselves out* [a]Gen 4:3-8; Heb 11:4; 1 John 3:12 [b]Num 31:16; 2 Pet 2:15; Rev 2:14 [c]Num 16:1-3
12 [1]Or *stains* [2]Lit *twice* [a]1 Cor 11:20ff; 2 Pet 2:13 and mg [b]Ezek 34:2 [c]Prov 25:14; 2 Pet 2:17 [d]Eph 4:14 [e]Matt 15:13
13 [1]Or *shameless deeds* [2]Lit *blackness of darkness*; or *netherworld gloom* [a]Is 57:20 [b]Phil 3:19 [c]2 Pet 2:17; Jude 6
14 [1]Lit *His holy ten thousands* [a]Gen 5:18 [b]Deut 33:2; Dan 7:10; Matt 16:27; Heb 12:22
15 [a]2 Pet 2:6ff [b]1 Tim 1:9
16 [1]Lit *their mouth speaks* [a]Num 16:11; 1 Cor 10:10 [b]2 Pet 2:10; Jude 18 [c]2 Pet 2:18 [d]2 Pet 2:3
17 [a]Jude 3 [b]2 Pet 3:2 [c]Heb 2:3
18 [a]Acts 20:29; 1 Tim 4:1; 2 Tim 3:1f; 2 Pet 3:3 [b]Jude 4
19 [1]Or *merely natural* [2]Lit *not having* [a]1 Cor 2:14f; James 3:15

20 [a]Jude 3 [b]Col 2:7; 1 Thess 5:11 [c]Eph 6:18 **21** [a]Titus 2:13; Heb 9:28; 2 Pet 3:12 **23** [a]Amos 4:11; Zech 3:2; 1 Cor 3:15 [b]Zech 3:3f; Rev 3:4 **24** [a]Rom 16:25 [b]2 Cor 4:14 [c]1 Pet 4:13 **25** [1]Lit *to all the ages* [a]John 5:44; 1 Tim 1:17 [b]Luke 1:47 [c]Rom 11:36 [d]Heb 13:8

Revelation

Title and Background

Because Roman authorities at this time were beginning to enforce the cult of emperor worship, Christians—who held that Jesus, not Caesar, was Lord—were facing increasing hostility. Some in the church were advocating a policy of compromise; this had to be corrected before its subtle influence could undermine believers' determination to stand fast in the perilous days that lay ahead.

Author and Date of Writing

Four times the author identifies himself as John, and John was held to be the author from as early as the second century. Most scholars hold that the book was written about A.D. 95.

Theme and Message

John writes to encourage the faithful to resist staunchly the demands that they worship the emperor. He informs his readers that the final showdown between God and Satan is imminent. Satan will increase his persecution of believers, but they must stand fast, even to death. They are sealed against any spiritual harm and will soon be vindicated when Jesus returns, when the wicked are forever destroyed, and when God's people enter an eternity of glory and blessedness.

Outline

I. Jesus Among the Seven Churches (1:1–20)
II. Letters to the Seven Churches (2:1—3:22)
III. The Throne, the Scroll and the Lamb (4:1—5:14)
IV. The Seven Seals (6:1—8:1)
V. The Seven Trumpets (8:2—11:19)
VI. Various Personages and Events (12:1—14:20)
VII. The Seven Bowls (15:1—16:21)
VIII. Babylon: The Great Harlot (17:1—19:5)
IX. The Marriage of the Lamb (19:6–10)
X. The Return of Jesus (19:11–21)
XI. The Thousand Years (20:1–6)
XII. Satan's Doom (20:7–10)
XIII. Great White Throne Judgment (20:11–15)
XIV. New Heaven, New Earth, New Jerusalem (21:1—22:5)
XV. Conclusion (22:6–21)

The Revelation of Jesus Christ

1 The Revelation of Jesus Christ,
which [a]God gave Him to [b]show to
His bond-servants, [c]the things which
must soon take place; and He sent and
[1]communicated *it* [d]by His angel to His
bond-servant [e]John,
2 who testified to [a]the word of God
and to [b]the testimony of Jesus Christ,
even to all that he saw.
3 [a]Blessed is he who reads and those
who hear the words of the prophecy, and
[1]heed the things which are written in it;
[b]for the time is near.

Message to the Seven Churches

4 ¶ [a]John to [b]the seven churches
that are in [c]Asia: [d]Grace to you and
peace, from [e]Him who is and who was
and who [1]is to come, and from [f]the sev-
en Spirits who are before His throne,
5 and from Jesus Christ, [a]the faithful
witness, the [b]firstborn of the dead, and
the [c]ruler of the kings of the earth. To
Him who [d]loves us and released us from
our sins [1]by His blood—
6 and He has made us *to be* a [a]king-
dom, [a]priests to [1b]His God and Father—[c]to Him *be* the glory and the dominion forever and ever. Amen.
7 [a]BEHOLD, HE IS COMING WITH THE
CLOUDS, and [b]every eye will see Him,

1 [1]Or *signified* [a]John 17:8; Rev 5:7 [b]Rev 22:6 [c]Dan 2:28f; Rev 1:19 [d]Rev 17:1 [e]Rev 1:4
2 [a]Rev 1:9 [b]1 Cor 1:6; Rev 12:17
3 [1]Or *keep* [a]Luke 11:28; Rev 22:7 [b]Rom 13:11; Rev 3:11
4 [1]Or *is coming* [a]Rev 1:1 [b]Rev 1:11 [c]Acts 2:9 [d]Rom 1:7 [e]Rev 1:8 [f]Is 11:2; Rev 3:1
5 [1]Or *in* [a]Rev 3:14 [b]1 Cor 15:20; Col 1:18 [c]Rev 17:14 [d]Rom 8:37
6 [1]Or *God and His Father* [a]Rev 5:10 [b]Rom 15:6 [c]Rom 11:36
7 [a]Dan 7:13; 1 Thess 4:17 [b]Zech 12:10-14; John 19:37

even those who pierced Him; and all the
tribes of the earth will [c]mourn over Him.
So it is to be. Amen.
8 ¶ "I am [a]the Alpha and the Omega," says the [b]Lord God, "[c]who is and
who was and who [1]is to come, the Almighty."

The Patmos Vision

9 ¶ [a]I, John, your [b]brother and [c]fellow partaker in the tribulation and [d]kingdom and [1e]perseverance *which are* in
Jesus, was on the island called Patmos
[f]because of the word of God and the
testimony of Jesus.
10 I was [1a]in the Spirit on [b]the
Lord's day, and I heard behind me a loud
voice [c]like *the sound* of a trumpet,
11 saying, "[a]Write in a [1]book what
you see, and send *it* to the [b]seven
churches: to [c]Ephesus and to [d]Smyrna
and to [e]Pergamum and to [f]Thyatira and
to [g]Sardis and to [h]Philadelphia and to
[i]Laodicea."
12 ¶ Then I turned to see the voice
that was speaking with me. And having
turned I saw [a]seven golden lampstands;
13 and [a]in the middle of the lampstands *I saw* one [b]like [1]a son of man,
[c]clothed in a robe reaching to the feet,
and [d]girded across His chest with a golden sash.
14 His head and His [a]hair were white
like white wool, like snow; and [b]His eyes
were like a flame of fire.
15 His [a]feet *were* like burnished
bronze, when it has been made to glow in
a furnace, and His [b]voice *was* like the
sound of many waters.
16 In His right hand He held [a]seven
stars, and out of His mouth came a
[b]sharp two-edged sword; and His [c]face
was like [d]the sun [1]shining in its
strength.
17 ¶ When I saw Him, I [a]fell at His
feet like a dead man. And He [b]placed His
right hand on me, saying, "[c]Do not be
afraid; [d]I am the first and the last,
18 and the [a]living One; and I [1b]was
dead, and behold, I am alive forevermore,
and I have [c]the keys of death and of Hades.
19 "Therefore [a]write [b]the things
which you have seen, and the things
which are, and the things which will take
place [c]after these things.
20 "As for the [a]mystery of the [b]seven
stars which you saw in My right hand,
and the [c]seven golden lampstands: the
[b]seven stars are the angels of [d]the seven
churches, and the seven [e]lampstands are
the seven churches.

7 [c]Luke 23:28 **8** [1]Or *is coming* [a]Is 41:4; Rev 21:6 [b]Rev 4:8 [c]Rev 1:4 **9** [1]Or *steadfastness* [a]Rev 1:1 [b]Acts 1:15 [c]Matt 20:23; Acts 14:22; 2 Cor 1:7; Phil 4:14 [d]2 Tim 2:12; Rev 1:6 [e]2 Thess 3:5; Rev 3:10 [f]Rev 1:2 **10** [1]Or *in spirit* [a]Matt 22:43; Rev 4:2 [b]Acts 20:7 [c]Rev 4:1 **11** [1]Or *scroll* [a]Rev 1:2 [b]Rev 1:4 [c]Rev 2:1 [d]Rev 2:8 [e]Rev 2:12 [f]Acts 16:14; Rev 2:18 [g]Rev 3:1 [h]Rev 3:7 [i]Col 2:1; Rev 3:14 **12** [a]Ex 25:37; Zech 4:2; Rev 1:20 **13** [1]Or *the Son of Man* [a]Rev 2:1 [b]Ezek 1:26; Dan 7:13; Rev 14:14 [c]Dan 10:5 [d]Rev 15:6 **14** [a]Dan 7:9 [b]Dan 7:9; Rev 2:18 **15** [a]Ezek 1:7; Dan 10:6; Rev 2:18 [b]Ezek 1:24; Rev 14:2 **16** [1]Lit *shines* [a]Rev 1:20 [b]Is 49:2; Heb 4:12; Rev 2:12 [c]Matt 17:2; Rev 10:1 [d]Judg 5:31 **17** [a]Dan 8:17 [b]Dan 8:18 [c]Matt 14:27 [d]Is 41:4; Rev 2:8 **18** [1]Lit *became* [a]Luke 24:5; Rev 4:9f [b]Rom 6:9; Rev 2:8 [c]Job 38:17; Matt 11:23; Rev 9:1 **19** [a]Rev 1:11 [b]Rev 1:12-16 [c]Rev 4:1 **20** [a]Rom 11:25 [b]Rev 1:16 [c]Ex 25:37; Zech 4:2; Rev 1:12 [d]Rev 1:4 [e]Matt 5:14f **2:1** [1]Lit *in the middle of* [a]Rev 1:11 [b]Rev 1:16 [c]Rev 1:12f **2** [1]Or *steadfastness* [a]Rev 2:19 [b]John 6:6; 1 John 4:1 [c]2 Cor 11:13 **3** [1]V 2, note 1 [a]John 15:21 **4** [a]Jer 2:2; Matt 24:12 **5** [1]Lit *first deeds* [a]Rev 2:16 [b]Heb 10:32; Rev 2:2 [c]Matt 5:14ff; Phil 2:15; Rev 1:20 **6** [a]Rev 2:15 **7** [a]Matt 11:15; Rev 2:11 [b]Rev 2:11 [c]Gen 2:9; Prov 3:18; Rev 22:2 [d]Ezek 28:13; Luke 23:43 **8** [1]Lit *became* [a]Rev 1:11 [b]Is 44:6; Rev 1:17 [c]Rev 1:18

Message to Ephesus

2 "To the angel of the church in [a]Ephesus write:
¶ The One who holds [b]the seven stars
in His right hand, the One who walks
[1c]among the seven golden lampstands,
says this:
2 ¶ '[a]I know your deeds and your toil
and [1]perseverance, and that you cannot
tolerate evil men, and you [b]put to the
test those who call themselves [c]apostles,
and they are not, and you found them *to
be* false;
3 and you have [1]perseverance and
have endured [a]for My name's sake, and
have not grown weary.
4 'But I have *this* against you, that you
have [a]left your first love.
5 'Therefore remember from where
you have fallen, and [a]repent and [b]do the
[1]deeds you did at first; or else I am coming to you and will remove your [c]lampstand out of its place—unless you repent.
6 'Yet this you do have, that you hate
the deeds of the [a]Nicolaitans, which I
also hate.
7 '[a]He who has an ear, let him hear
what the Spirit says to the churches. [b]To
him who overcomes, I will grant to eat of
[c]the tree of life which is in the [d]Paradise
of God.'

Message to Smyrna

8 ¶ "And to the angel of the church
in [a]Smyrna write:
¶ [b]The first and the last, who [1c]was
dead, and has come to life, says this:
9 ¶ 'I know your [a]tribulation and
your [b]poverty (but you are [b]rich), and
the blasphemy by those who [c]say they
are Jews and are not, but are a synagogue
of [d]Satan.
10 'Do not fear what you are about to
suffer. Behold, the devil is about to cast
some of you into prison, so that you will
be [a]tested, and you will have tribulation
[b]for ten days. [1]Be [c]faithful until death,
and I will give you [d]the crown of life.
11 '[a]He who has an ear, let him hear
what the Spirit says to the churches. [b]He
who overcomes will not be hurt by the
[c]second death.'

Message to Pergamum

12 ¶ "And to the angel of the church
in [a]Pergamum write:
¶ The One who has [b]the sharp two-edged sword says this:
13 ¶ 'I know where you dwell, where

9 [a]Rev 1:9 [b]2 Cor 6:10; James 2:5 [c]Rev 3:9 [d]Matt 4:10; Rev 2:13 **10** [1]Or *Prove yourself faithful* [a]Rev 3:10 [b]Dan 1:12 [c]Rev 2:13 [d]1 Cor 9:25; Rev 3:11 **11** [a]Matt 11:15; Rev 2:7 [b]Rev 2:7 [c]Rev 20:6 **12** [a]Rev 1:11 [b]Rev 1:16

[a]Satan's throne is; and you hold fast My name, and did not deny [b]My faith even in the days of Antipas, My [c]witness, My [d]faithful one, who was killed among you, [e]where Satan dwells.

14 'But [a]I have a few things against you, because you have there some who hold the [b]teaching of Balaam, who kept teaching Balak to put a stumbling block before the sons of Israel, [c]to eat things sacrificed to idols and to commit *acts of* immorality.

15 'So you also have some who in the same way hold the teaching of the [a]Nicolaitans.

16 'Therefore [a]repent; or else [b]I am coming to you quickly, and I will make war against them with [c]the sword of My mouth.

17 '[a]He who has an ear, let him hear what the Spirit says to the churches. [a]To him who overcomes, to him I will give *some* of the hidden [b]manna, and I will give him a white stone, and a [c]new name written on the stone [d]which no one knows but he who receives it.'

Message to Thyatira

18 ¶ "And to the angel of the church in [a]Thyatira write:

¶ [b]The Son of God, [c]who has [1]eyes like a flame of fire, and His feet are like burnished bronze, says this:

19 ¶ '[a]I know your deeds, and your love and faith and service and [1]perseverance, and that your [2]deeds of late are greater than [3]at first.

20 'But [a]I have *this* against you, that you tolerate the woman [b]Jezebel, who calls herself a prophetess, and she teaches and leads My bond-servants astray so that they [c]commit *acts of* immorality and eat things sacrificed to idols.

21 '[a]I gave her time to repent, and she [b]does not want to repent of her immorality.

22 'Behold, I will throw her [1]on a bed *of sickness*, and those who [a]commit adultery with her into great tribulation, unless they repent of [2]her deeds.

23 'And I will kill her children with [1]pestilence, and all the churches will know that I am He who [a]searches the [2]minds and hearts; and [b]I will give to each one of you according to your deeds.

24 'But I say to you, the rest who are in [a]Thyatira, who do not hold this teaching, who have not known the [b]deep things of Satan, as they call them—I [c]place no other burden on you.

25 'Nevertheless [a]what you have, hold fast [b]until I come.

26 '[a]He who overcomes, and he who keeps My deeds [b]until the end, [c]TO HIM I WILL GIVE AUTHORITY OVER THE [1]NATIONS;

27 AND HE SHALL [1a]RULE THEM WITH A ROD OF IRON, [b]AS THE VESSELS OF THE POTTER ARE BROKEN TO PIECES, as I also have received *authority* from My Father;

28 and I will give him [a]the morning star.

29 '[a]He who has an ear, let him hear what the Spirit says to the churches.'

Message to Sardis

3 "To the angel of the church in [a]Sardis write:

¶ He who has [b]the seven Spirits of God and [c]the seven stars, says this: '[d]I know your deeds, that you have a name that you are alive, [1]but you are [e]dead.

2 'Wake up, and strengthen the things that remain, which were about to die; for I have not found your deeds completed in the sight of My God.

3 'So [a]remember [1]what you have received and heard; and keep *it*, and [a]repent. Therefore if you do not wake up, [a]I will come [b]like a thief, and you will not know at [c]what hour I will come to you.

4 'But you have a few [1a]people in [b]Sardis who have not [c]soiled their garments; and they will walk with Me [d]in white, for they are worthy.

5 '[a]He who overcomes will thus be clothed in [b]white garments; and I will not [c]erase his name from the book of life, and [d]I will confess his name before My Father and before His angels.

6 '[a]He who has an ear, let him hear what the Spirit says to the churches.'

Message to Philadelphia

7 ¶ "And to the angel of the church in [a]Philadelphia write:

¶ [b]He who is holy, [c]who is true, who has [d]the key of David, who opens and no one will shut, and who shuts and no one opens, says this:

8 ¶ '[a]I know your [1]deeds. Behold, I have put before you [b]an open door which no one can shut, because you have a little power, and have kept My word, and [c]have not denied My name.

9 'Behold, I [1]will cause *those* of [a]the synagogue of Satan, who say that they are Jews and are not, but lie—I will make them [b]come and bow down [2]at your feet, and *make them* know that [c]I have loved you.

10 'Because you have [a]kept the word of [b]My [1]perseverance, [c]I also will keep you from the hour of [2d]testing, that *hour* which is about to come upon the whole

---

13 [a]Matt 4:10; Rev 2:24 [b]1 Tim 5:8; Rev 14:12 [c]Acts 22:20; Rev 1:5 [d]Rev 2:10 [e]Rev 2:9
14 [a]Rev 2:20 [b]Num 31:16; 2 Pet 2:15 [c]Num 25:1f; Acts 15:29; 1 Cor 10:20; Rev 2:20
15 [a]Rev 2:6
16 [a]Rev 2:5 [b]Rev 22:7 [c]2 Thess 2:8; Rev 1:16
17 [a]Rev 2:7 [b]Ex 16:33; John 6:49f [c]Is 56:5 [d]Rev 14:3
18 [1]Lit *His eyes* [a]Rev 1:11 [b]Matt 4:3 [c]Rev 1:14f
19 [1]Or *steadfastness* [2]Lit *last deeds* [3]Lit *the first* [a]Rev 2:2
20 [a]Rev 2:14 [b]1 Kin 16:31; 2 Kin 9:7 [c]Acts 15:29; 1 Cor 10:20; Rev 2:14
21 [a]Rom 2:4; 2 Pet 3:9 [b]Rom 2:5; Rev 9:20f
22 [1]Lit *into* [2]One early ms reads *their* [a]Rev 17:2
23 [1]Lit *death* [2]Lit *kidneys,* i.e. inner man [a]Ps 7:9; Jer 11:20; Matt 16:27; Luke 16:15; Acts 1:24; Rom 8:27 [b]Ps 62:12
24 [a]Rev 2:18 [b]1 Cor 2:10 [c]Acts 15:28
25 [a]Rev 3:11 [b]John 21:22
26 [1]Or *Gentiles* [a]Rev 2:7 [b]Matt 10:22; Heb 3:6 [c]Ps 2:8; Rev 3:21
27 [1]Lit *shepherd* [a]Ps 2:9; Rev 12:5 [b]Is 30:14; Jer 19:11
28 [a]1 John 3:2; Rev 22:16
29 [a]Rev 2:7
3:1 [1]Lit *and* [a]Rev 1:11 [b]Rev 1:4 [c]Rev 1:16 [d]Rev 2:2 [e]1 Tim 5:6
3 [1]Lit *how* [a]Rev 2:5 [b]1 Thess 5:2; 2 Pet 3:10; Rev 16:15 [c]Matt 24:43; Luke 12:39f
4 [1]Lit *names* [a]Rev 11:13 [b]Rev 1:11 [c]Jude 23 [d]Eccl 9:8; Rev 3:5
5 [a]Rev 2:7 [b]Rev 3:4 [c]Ex 32:32f; Ps 69:28; Luke 10:20; Rev 13:8 [d]Matt 10:32; Luke 12:8
6 [a]Rev 2:7
7 [a]Rev 1:11 [b]Rev 6:10 [c]1 John 5:20; Rev 3:14 [d]Job 12:14; Is 22:22; Matt 16:19; Rev 1:18
8 [1]Or *deeds (behold...shut), that you have* [a]Rev 3:1 [b]Acts 14:27 [c]Rev 2:13
9 [1]Lit *give* [2]Lit *before* [a]Rev 2:9 [b]Is 45:14 [c]Is 43:4; John 17:23
10 [1]Or *steadfastness* [2]Or *temptation* [a]John 17:6; Rev 3:8 [b]Rev 1:9 [c]2 Tim 2:12; 2 Pet 2:9 [d]Rev 2:10

[3e]world, to [4]test [f]those who dwell on the earth.

11 '[a]I am coming quickly; [b]hold fast what you have, so that no one will take your [c]crown.

12 '[a]He who overcomes, I will make him a [b]pillar in the temple of My God, and he will not go out from it anymore; and I will write on him the [c]name of My God, and [d]the name of the city of My God, [e]the new Jerusalem, which comes down out of heaven from My God, and My [f]new name.

13 '[a]He who has an ear, let him hear what the Spirit says to the churches.'

Message to Laodicea

14 ¶ "To the angel of the church in [a]Laodicea write:

¶ [b]The Amen, [c]the faithful and true Witness, [d]the [1]Beginning of the creation of God, says this:

15 ¶ '[a]I know your deeds, that you are neither cold nor hot; [b]I wish that you were cold or hot.

16 'So because you are lukewarm, and neither hot nor cold, I will [1]spit you out of My mouth.

17 'Because you say, "[a]I am rich, and have become wealthy, and have need of nothing," and you do not know that you are wretched and miserable and poor and blind and naked,

18 I advise you to [a]buy from Me [b]gold refined by fire so that you may become rich, and [c]white garments so that you may clothe yourself, and *that* [d]the shame of your nakedness will not be revealed; and eye salve to anoint your eyes so that you may see.

19 '[a]Those whom I love, I reprove and discipline; therefore be zealous and [b]repent.

20 'Behold, I stand [a]at the door and [b]knock; if anyone hears My voice and opens the door, [c]I will come in to him and will dine with him, and he with Me.

21 '[a]He who overcomes, I will grant to him [b]to sit down with Me on My throne, as [c]I also overcame and sat down with My Father on His throne.

22 '[a]He who has an ear, let him hear what the Spirit says to the churches.' "

Scene in Heaven

4 After [a]these things I looked, and behold, [b]a door *standing* open in heaven, and the first voice which I had heard, [c]like *the sound* of a trumpet speaking with me, said, "[d]Come up here, and I will [e]show you what must take place after these things."

2 Immediately I was [1a]in the Spirit; and behold, [b]a throne was standing in heaven, and [c]One sitting on the throne.

3 And He who was sitting *was* like a [a]jasper stone and a [b]sardius in appearance; and *there was* a [1c]rainbow around the throne, like an [d]emerald in appearance.

4 [a]Around the throne *were* [b]twenty-four thrones; and upon the thrones *I saw* [c]twenty-four elders [d]sitting, clothed in [e]white garments, and [f]golden crowns on their heads.

The Throne and Worship of the Creator

5 Out from the throne come [a]flashes of lightning and sounds and peals of thunder. And *there were* [b]seven lamps of fire burning before the throne, which are [c]the seven Spirits of God;

6 and before the throne *there was something* like a [a]sea of glass, like crystal; and in the [1]center and [b]around the throne, [c]four living creatures [d]full of eyes in front and behind.

7 [a]The first creature *was* like a lion, and the second creature like a calf, and the third creature had a face like that of a man, and the fourth creature *was* like a flying eagle.

8 And the [a]four living creatures, each one of them having [b]six wings, are [c]full of eyes around and within; and [d]day and night [1]they do not cease to say,

"[e]HOLY, HOLY, HOLY *is* THE [f]LORD
GOD, THE ALMIGHTY, [g]WHO WAS
AND WHO IS AND WHO [2]IS TO
COME."

9 And when the living creatures give glory and honor and thanks to Him who [a]sits on the throne, to [b]Him who lives forever and ever,

10 the [a]twenty-four elders will [b]fall down before Him who [c]sits on the throne, and will worship [d]Him who lives forever and ever, and will cast their [e]crowns before the throne, saying,

11 "[a]Worthy are You, our Lord and
our God, to receive glory and
honor and power; for You [b]created all things, and because of Your
will they [1]existed, and were created."

The Book with Seven Seals

5 I saw [1]in the right hand of Him who [a]sat on the throne a [2b]book written inside and on the back, [c]sealed up with seven seals.

2 And I saw a [a]strong angel proclaiming with a loud voice, "Who is wor-

10 [3]Lit *inhabited earth* [4]Or *tempt* [e]Matt 24:14; Rev 16:14 [f]Rev 6:10 **11** [a]Rev 1:3 [b]Rev 2:25 [c]Rev 2:10 **12** [a]Rev 3:5 [b]1 Kin 7:21; Jer 1:18; Gal 2:9 [c]Rev 14:1 [d]Ezek 48:35; Rev 21:2 [e]Gal 4:26; Heb 13:14; Rev 21:2 [f]Is 62:2; Rev 2:17 **13** [a]Rev 3:6 **14** [1]I.e. Origin or Source [a]Rev 1:11 [b]2 Cor 1:20 [c]Rev 1:5 [d]Gen 49:3; Deut 21:17; Prov 8:22; John 1:3; Col 1:18; Rev 21:6 **15** [a]Rev 3:1 [b]Rom 12:11 **16** [1]Lit *vomit* **17** [a]Hos 12:8; Zech 11:5; Matt 5:3; 1 Cor 4:8 **18** [a]Is 55:1; Matt 13:44 [b]1 Pet 1:7 [c]Rev 3:4 [d]Rev 16:15 **19** [a]Prov 3:12; 1 Cor 11:32; Heb 12:6 [b]Rev 2:5 **20** [a]Matt 24:33; James 5:9 [b]Luke 12:36; John 10:3 [c]John 14:23 **21** [a]Rev 2:7 [b]Matt 19:28; 2 Tim 2:12; Rev 2:26 [c]John 16:33; Rev 5:5 **22** [a]Rev 2:7 **4:1** [a]Rev 1:12ff [b]Ezek 1:1; Rev 19:11 [c]Rev 1:10 [d]Rev 11:12 [e]Rev 1:19 **2** [1]Or *in spirit* [a]Rev 1:10 [b]1 Kin 22:19; Is 6:1; Ezek 1:26; Dan 7:9; Rev 4:9f [c]Rev 4:9 **3** [1]Or *halo* [a]Rev 21:11 [b]Rev 21:20 [c]Ezek 1:28; Rev 10:1 [d]Rev 21:19 **4** [a]Rev 4:6 [b]Rev 11:16 [c]Rev 4:10 [d]Matt 19:28; Rev 20:4 [e]Rev 3:18 [f]Rev 4:10 **5** [a]Ex 19:16; Rev 8:5 [b]Ex 25:37; Zech 4:2 [c]Rev 1:4 **6** [1]Lit *middle of the throne and around* [a]Ezek 1:22; Rev 15:2 [b]Rev 4:4 [c]Ezek 1:5; Rev 4:8f [d]Ezek 1:18 **7** [a]Ezek 1:10 **8** [1]Lit *they have no rest, saying,* [2]Or *is coming* [a]Ezek 1:5; Rev 4:6 [b]Is 6:2 [c]Ezek 1:18 [d]Rev 14:11 [e]Is 6:3 [f]Rev 1:8 [g]Rev 1:4 **9** [a]Ps 47:8; Is 6:1; Rev 4:2 [b]Deut 32:40; Dan 4:34; Rev 10:6 **10** [a]Rev 4:4 [b]Rev 5:8 [c]Ps 47:8; Is 6:1; Rev 4:2 [d]Deut 32:40; Dan 4:34 [e]Rev 4:4 **11** [1]Lit *were* [a]Rev 1:6 [b]Acts 14:15; Rev 10:6 **5:1** [1]Lit *upon* [2]Or *scroll* [a]Rev 4:9 [b]Ezek 2:9 [c]Is 29:11; Dan 12:4 **2** [a]Rev 10:1

thy to open the [1]book and to break its seals?"

3 And no one [a]in heaven or on the earth or under the earth was able to open the [1]book or to look into it.

4 Then I *began* to weep greatly because no one was found worthy to open the [1]book or to look into it;

5 and one of the elders *said to me, "Stop weeping; behold, the [a]Lion that is [b]from the tribe of Judah, the [c]Root of David, has overcome so as to open the [1]book and its seven seals."

6 ¶ And I saw [1]between the throne (with the four living creatures) and [a]the elders a [b]Lamb standing, as if [c]slain, having seven [d]horns and [e]seven eyes, which are [f]the seven Spirits of God, sent out into all the earth.

7 And He came and took [a]the book out of the right hand of Him who [a]sat on the throne.

8 When He had taken the [1]book, the [a]four living creatures and the [b]twenty-four elders [c]fell down before the [d]Lamb, each one holding a [e]harp and [f]golden bowls full of incense, which are the [g]prayers of the [2]saints.

9 And they *sang a [a]new song, saying,

"[b]Worthy are You to take the [1]book and to break its seals; for You were [c]slain, and [d]purchased for God with Your blood *men* from [e]every tribe and tongue and people and nation.

10 "You have made them *to be* a [a]kingdom and [a]priests to our God; and they will [b]reign upon the earth."

Angels Exalt the Lamb

11 ¶ Then I looked, and I heard the voice of many angels [a]around the throne and the [b]living creatures and the [c]elders; and the number of them was [d]myriads of myriads, and thousands of thousands,

12 saying with a loud voice,

"[a]Worthy is the [b]Lamb that was [b]slain to receive power and riches and wisdom and might and honor and glory and blessing."

13 And [a]every created thing which is in heaven and on the earth and under the earth and on the sea, and all things in them, I heard saying,

"To Him who [b]sits on the throne, and to the [c]Lamb, [d]*be* blessing and honor and glory and dominion forever and ever."

14 And the [a]four living creatures kept

2 [1]Or *scroll*
3 [1]Or *scroll* [a]Phil 2:10; Rev 5:13
4 [1]Or *scroll*
5 [1]Or *scroll* [a]Gen 49:9 [b]Heb 7:14 [c]Is 11:1; Rom 15:12; Rev 22:16
6 [1]Lit *in the middle of the throne and of the four living creatures, and in the middle of the elders* [a]Rev 4:4 [b]John 1:29; Rev 5:8 [c]Rev 5:9 [d]Dan 8:3f [e]Zech 3:9 [f]Rev 1:4
7 [a]Rev 5:1
8 [1]Or *scroll* [2]Or *holy ones* [a]Rev 4:6 [b]Rev 4:4 [c]Rev 4:10 [d]John 1:29; Rev 5:6 [e]Rev 14:2 [f]Rev 15:7 [g]Ps 141:2; Rev 8:3f
9 [1]Or *scroll* [a]Ps 33:3; Is 42:10; Rev 14:3 [b]Rev 4:11 [c]Rev 5:6 [d]1 Cor 6:20; Rev 14:3f [e]Dan 3:4; Rev 7:9
10 [a]Rev 1:6 [b]Rev 3:21
11 [a]Rev 4:4 [b]Rev 4:6 [c]Rev 4:4 [d]Dan 7:10; Heb 12:22; Jude 14; Rev 9:16
12 [a]Rev 1:6 [b]John 1:29; Rev 5:6
13 [a]Phil 2:10; Rev 5:3 [b]Rev 5:1 [c]John 1:29; Rev 5:6 [d]Rom 11:36; Rev 1:6
14 [a]Rev 4:6 [b]1 Cor 14:16; Rev 7:12 [c]Rev 4:4 [d]Rev 4:10
6:1 [1]One early ms reads *and see* [a]John 1:29; Rev 5:6 [b]Rev 5:1 [c]Rev 4:6 [d]Rev 14:2
2 [a]Zech 1:8; Rev 19:11 [b]Zech 6:11; Rev 9:7 [c]Rev 3:21
3 [1]One early ms reads *and see* [a]Rev 4:7
4 [a]Zech 1:8 [b]Matt 10:34
5 [1]One early ms reads *and see* [a]Rev 4:7 [b]Zech 6:2 [c]Ezek 4:16
6 [1]Gr *choenix*; i.e. a dry measure almost equal to a qt [2]The denarius was equivalent to a day's wages [a]Rev 4:6f [b]Rev 7:3
7 [1]One early ms reads *and see* [a]Rev 4:7
8 [1]Or *sickly pale* [2]Or *death* [a]Zech 6:3 [b]Prov 5:5; Hos 13:14; Matt 11:23; Rev 1:18 [c]Jer 14:12; Ezek 5:12
9 [a]Ex 29:12; Lev 4:7; John 16:2 [b]Rev 14:18 [c]Rev 20:4 [d]Rev 1:2 [e]Rev 12:17
10 [1]Or *Master*

saying, "[b]Amen." And the [c]elders [d]fell down and worshiped.

The Book Opened
The First Seal—The False Christ

6 Then I saw when the [a]Lamb broke one of the [b]seven seals, and I heard one of the [c]four living creatures saying as with a [d]voice of thunder, "Come[1]."

2 I looked, and behold, a [a]white horse, and he who sat on it had a bow; and [b]a crown was given to him, and he went out [c]conquering and to conquer.

The Second Seal—War

3 ¶ When He broke the second seal, I heard the [a]second living creature saying, "Come[1]."

4 And another, [a]a red horse, went out; and to him who sat on it, it was granted to [b]take peace from the earth, and that *men* would slay one another; and a great sword was given to him.

The Third Seal—Famine

5 ¶ When He broke the third seal, I heard the [a]third living creature saying, "Come[1]." I looked, and behold, a [b]black horse; and he who sat on it had a [c]pair of scales in his hand.

6 And I heard *something* like a voice in the center of the [a]four living creatures saying, "A [1]quart of wheat for a [2]denarius, and three [1]quarts of barley for a [2]denarius; and [b]do not damage the oil and the wine."

The Fourth Seal—Death

7 ¶ When the Lamb broke the fourth seal, I heard the voice of the [a]fourth living creature saying, "Come[1]."

8 I looked, and behold, an [1a]ashen horse; and he who sat on it had the name [b]Death; and [b]Hades was following with him. Authority was given to them over a fourth of the earth, [c]to kill with sword and with famine and with [2]pestilence and by the wild beasts of the earth.

The Fifth Seal—Martyrs

9 ¶ When the Lamb broke the fifth seal, I saw [a]underneath the [b]altar the [c]souls of those who had been slain [d]because of the word of God, and because of the [e]testimony which they had maintained;

10 and they cried out with a loud voice, saying, "[a]How long, O [1b]Lord, [c]holy and true, [2]will You refrain from [d]judging and avenging our blood on [e]those who dwell on the earth?"

[2]Lit *do You not judge and avenge* [a]Zech 1:12 [b]Luke 2:29; 2 Pet 2:1 [c]Rev 3:7 [d]Deut 32:43; Ps 79:10; Luke 18:7; Rev 19:2 [e]Rev 3:10

11 And [a]there was given to each of them a white robe; and they were told that they should [b]rest for a little while longer, [c]until *the number of* their fellow servants and their brethren who were to be killed even as they had been, would be [d]completed also.

The Sixth Seal—Terror

12 ¶ I looked when He broke the sixth seal, and there was a great [a]earthquake; and the [b]sun became black as [c]sackcloth *made* of hair, and the whole moon became like blood;

13 and [a]the stars of the sky fell to the earth, [b]as a fig tree casts its unripe figs when shaken by a great wind.

14 [a]The sky was split apart like a scroll when it is rolled up, and [b]every mountain and island were moved out of their places.

15 Then [a]the kings of the earth and the great men and the [1]commanders and the rich and the strong and every slave and free man hid themselves in the caves and among the rocks of the mountains;

16 and they *[a]said to the mountains and to the rocks, "Fall on us and hide us from the [1]presence of Him [b]who sits on the throne, and from the [c]wrath of the Lamb;

17 for [a]the great day of their wrath has come, and [b]who is able to stand?"

An Interlude

7 After this I saw [a]four angels standing at the [b]four corners of the earth, holding back [c]the four winds of the earth, [d]so that no wind would blow on the earth or on the sea or on any tree.

2 And I saw another angel ascending [a]from the rising of the sun, having the [b]seal of [c]the living God; and he cried out with a loud voice to the [d]four angels to whom it was granted to harm the earth and the sea,

3 saying, "[a]Do not harm the earth or the sea or the trees until we have [b]sealed the bond-servants of our God on their [c]foreheads."

A Remnant of Israel—144,000

4 ¶ And I heard the [a]number of those who were sealed, [b]one hundred and forty-four thousand sealed from every tribe of the sons of Israel:

5 from the tribe of Judah, twelve thousand *were* sealed, from the tribe of Reuben twelve thousand, from the tribe of Gad twelve thousand,

6 from the tribe of Asher twelve thousand, from the tribe of Naphtali twelve thousand, from the tribe of Manasseh twelve thousand,

7 from the tribe of Simeon twelve thousand, from the tribe of Levi twelve thousand, from the tribe of Issachar twelve thousand,

8 from the tribe of Zebulun twelve thousand, from the tribe of Joseph twelve thousand, from the tribe of Benjamin, twelve thousand *were* sealed.

A Multitude from the Tribulation

9 ¶ After these things I looked, and behold, a great multitude which no one could count, from [a]every nation and *all* tribes and peoples and tongues, standing [b]before the throne and [c]before the Lamb, clothed in [d]white robes, and [e]palm branches *were* in their hands;

10 and they cry out with a loud voice, saying,

¶ "[a]Salvation to our God [b]who sits on the throne, and to the Lamb."

11 And all the angels were standing [a]around the throne and *around* [a]the elders and the [b]four living creatures; and they [c]fell on their faces before the throne and worshiped God,

12 saying,

¶ "[a]Amen, [b]blessing and glory and wisdom and thanksgiving and honor and power and might, *be* to our God forever and ever. [a]Amen."

13 ¶ Then one of the elders [a]answered, saying to me, "These who are clothed in the [b]white robes, who are they, and where have they come from?"

14 I [1]said to him, "My lord, you know." And he said to me, "These are the ones who come out of the [a]great tribulation, and they have [b]washed their robes and made them [c]white in the [d]blood of the Lamb.

15 "For this reason, they are [a]before the throne of God; and they [b]serve Him day and night in His [1c]temple; and [d]He who sits on the throne will spread His [e]tabernacle over them.

16 "[a]They will hunger no longer, nor thirst anymore; nor will the sun [1]beat down on them, nor any heat;

17 for the Lamb in the center of the throne will be their [a]shepherd, and will guide them to springs of the [1b]water of life; and [c]God will wipe every tear from their eyes."

The Seventh Seal—the Trumpets

8 When the Lamb broke the [a]seventh seal, there was silence in heaven for about half an hour.

2 And I saw [a]the seven angels who

---

11 [a]Rev 3:4 [b]2 Thess 1:7; Heb 4:10; Rev 14:13 [c]Heb 11:40 [d]Acts 20:24; 2 Tim 4:7
12 [a]Matt 24:7; Rev 8:5 [b]Is 13:10; Joel 2:10; Matt 24:29; Mark 13:24 [c]Is 50:3; Matt 11:21
13 [a]Matt 24:29; Mark 13:25; Rev 8:10 [b]Is 34:4
14 [a]Is 34:4; 2 Pet 3:10; Rev 20:11 [b]Is 54:10; Jer 4:24; Ezek 38:20; Nah 1:5; Rev 16:20
15 [1]I.e. chiliarchs, in command of one thousand troops [a]Is 2:10f; Rev 19:18
16 [1]Lit *face* [a]Hos 10:8; Luke 23:30; Rev 9:6 [b]Rev 4:9 [c]Mark 3:5
17 [a]Is 63:4; Jer 30:7; Joel 1:15; Zeph 1:14f; Rev 16:14 [b]Ps 76:7; Nah 1:6; Mal 3:2; Luke 21:36
7:1 [a]Rev 9:14 [b]Is 11:12; Ezek 7:2; Rev 20:8 [c]Jer 49:36; Dan 7:2; Zech 6:5; Matt 24:31 [d]Rev 7:3
2 [a]Is 41:2 [b]Rev 7:3 [c]Matt 16:16 [d]Rev 9:14
3 [a]Rev 6:6 [b]John 3:33; Rev 7:3-8 [c]Ezek 9:4; Rev 13:16
4 [a]Rev 9:16 [b]Rev 14:1
9 [a]Rev 5:9 [b]Rev 7:15 [c]Rev 22:3 [d]Rev 6:11 [e]Lev 23:40
10 [a]Ps 3:8; Rev 12:10 [b]Rev 22:3
11 [a]Rev 4:4 [b]Rev 4:6 [c]Rev 4:10
12 [a]Rev 5:14 [b]Rev 5:12
13 [a]Acts 3:12 [b]Rev 7:9
14 [1]Lit *have said* [a]Dan 12:1; Matt 24:21; Mark 13:19 [b]Zech 3:3-5; Rev 22:14 [c]Rev 6:11 [d]Heb 9:14; 1 John 1:7
15 [1]Or *sanctuary* [a]Rev 7:9 [b]Rev 4:8f [c]Rev 11:19 [d]Rev 4:9 [e]Lev 26:11; Ezek 37:27; John 1:14; Rev 21:3
16 [1]Lit *fall* [a]Ps 121:5f; Is 49:10
17 [1]Lit *waters* [a]Ps 23:1f; Matt 2:6; John 10:11 [b]John 4:14; Rev 21:6 [c]Is 25:8; Matt 5:4; Rev 21:4
8:1 [a]Rev 5:1
2 [a]Rev 1:4

stand before God, and seven [b]trumpets were given to them.

3 ¶ [a]Another angel came and stood at the [b]altar, holding a [c]golden censer; and much [d]incense was given to him, so that he might [1]add it to the [d]prayers of all the [2]saints on the [e]golden altar which was before the throne.

4 And [a]the smoke of the incense, [1]with the prayers of the [2]saints, went up before God out of the angel's hand.

5 Then the angel [1]took the censer and [a]filled it with the fire of the altar, and [b]threw it to the earth; and there followed [c]peals of thunder and sounds and flashes of lightning and an [d]earthquake.

6 ¶ [a]And the seven angels who had the seven trumpets prepared themselves to sound them.

7 ¶ The first sounded, and there came [a]hail and fire, mixed with blood, and they were thrown to the earth; and [b]a third of the earth was burned up, and [b]a third of the [c]trees were burned up, and all the green [c]grass was burned up.

8 ¶ The second angel sounded, and *something* like a great [a]mountain burning with fire was thrown into the sea; and [b]a third of the [c]sea became blood,

9 and [a]a third of the creatures which were in the sea [1]and had life, died; and a third of the [b]ships were destroyed.

10 ¶ The third angel sounded, and a great star [a]fell from heaven, burning like a torch, and it fell on a [b]third of the rivers and on the [c]springs of waters.

11 The name of the star is called Wormwood; and a [a]third of the waters became [b]wormwood, and many men died from the waters, because they were made bitter.

12 ¶ The fourth angel sounded, and a [a]third of the [b]sun and a third of the [b]moon and a [a]third of the [b]stars were struck, so that a [a]third of them would be darkened and the day would not shine for a [a]third of it, and the night in the same way.

13 ¶ Then I looked, and I heard [1]an eagle flying in [a]midheaven, saying with a loud voice, "[b]Woe, woe, woe to [c]those who dwell on the earth, because of the remaining blasts of the trumpet of the [d]three angels who are about to sound!"

The Fifth Trumpet—the Bottomless Pit

9 Then the [a]fifth angel sounded, and I saw a [b]star from heaven which had fallen to the earth; and the [c]key of the [1d]bottomless pit was given to him.

2 He opened the [1]bottomless pit, and [a]smoke went up out of the pit, like the smoke of a great furnace; and [b]the sun and the air were darkened by the smoke of the pit.

3 Then out of the smoke came [a]locusts [1]upon the earth, and power was given them, as the [b]scorpions of the earth have power.

4 They were told not to [a]hurt the [b]grass of the earth, nor any green thing, nor any tree, but only the men who do not have the [c]seal of God on their foreheads.

5 And [1]they were not permitted to kill [2]anyone, but to torment for [a]five months; and their torment was like the torment of a [b]scorpion when it [3]stings a man.

6 And in those days [a]men will seek death and will not find it; they will long to die, and death flees from them.

7 ¶ The [1a]appearance of the locusts was like horses prepared for battle; and on their heads appeared to be crowns like gold, and their faces were like the faces of men.

8 They had hair like the hair of women, and their [a]teeth were like *the teeth* of lions.

9 They had breastplates like breastplates of iron; and the [a]sound of their wings was like the sound of chariots, of many horses rushing to battle.

10 They have tails like [a]scorpions, and stings; and in their [b]tails is their power to hurt men for [c]five months.

11 They have as king over them, the angel of the [a]abyss; his name in [b]Hebrew is [1c]Abaddon, and in the Greek he has the name [2]Apollyon.

12 ¶ [a]The first woe is past; behold, two woes are still coming after these things.

The Sixth Trumpet—Army from the East

13 ¶ Then the sixth angel sounded, and I heard [1]a voice from the [2]four [a]horns of the [b]golden altar which is before God,

14 one saying to the sixth angel who had the trumpet, "Release the [a]four angels who are bound at the [b]great river Euphrates."

15 And the four angels, who had been prepared for the hour and day and month and year, were [a]released, so that they would kill a [b]third of [1]mankind.

16 The number of the armies of the horsemen was [a]two hundred million; [b]I heard the number of them.

---

2 [b]1 Cor 15:52; 1 Thess 4:16 **3** [1]Lit *give* [2]Or *holy ones* [a]Rev 7:2 [b]Amos 9:1; Rev 6:9 [c]Heb 9:4 [d]Ex 30:1; Rev 5:8 [e]Ex 30:3; Num 4:11; Rev 8:5 **4** [1]Or *for* [2]V 3, note 2 [a]Ps 141:2 **5** [1]Lit *has taken* [a]Lev 16:12 [b]Ezek 10:2 [c]Ex 19:16; Rev 4:5 [d]Rev 6:12 **6** [a]Rev 8:2 **7** [a]Ex 9:23ff; Is 28:2; Ezek 38:22; Joel 2:30 [b]Zech 13:8; Rev 8:7-12 [c]Rev 9:4 **8** [a]Jer 51:25 [b]Zech 13:8; Rev 8:7-12 [c]Ex 7:17ff; Rev 11:6 **9** [1]Lit *the ones having* [a]Zech 13:8; Rev 8:7-12 [b]Is 2:16 **10** [a]Is 14:12; Rev 6:13 [b]Zech 13:8; Rev 8:7-12 [c]Rev 14:7 **11** [a]Zech 13:8; Rev 8:7-12 [b]Jer 9:15 **12** [a]Zech 13:8; Rev 8:7-12 [b]Ex 10:21ff; Is 13:10; Ezek 32:7; Joel 2:10; Rev 6:12f **13** [1]Lit *one eagle* [a]Rev 14:6 [b]Rev 9:12 [c]Rev 3:10 [d]Rev 8:2 **9:1** [1]Lit *shaft of the abyss* [a]Rev 8:2 [b]Rev 8:10 [c]Rev 1:18 [d]Luke 8:31; Rev 9:2 **2** [1]V 1, note 1 [a]Gen 19:28; Ex 19:18 [b]Joel 2:2 **3** [1]Lit *into* [a]Ex 10:12-15; Rev 9:7 [b]2 Chr 10:11; Ezek 2:6; Rev 9:5 **4** [a]Rev 6:6 [b]Rev 8:7 [c]Ezek 9:4; Rev 7:2 **5** [1]Lit *it was given to them* [2]Lit *them* [3]Lit *strikes* [a]Rev 9:10 [b]2 Chr 10:11; Ezek 2:6; Rev 9:3 **6** [a]Job 3:21; Jer 8:3; Rev 6:16 **7** [1]Lit *likenesses* [a]Joel 2:4 **8** [a]Joel 1:6 **9** [a]Jer 47:3; Joel 2:5 **10** [a]2 Chr 10:11; Ezek 2:6; Rev 9:3 [b]Rev 9:19 [c]Rev 9:5 **11** [1]I.e. destruction [2]I.e. destroyer [a]Luke 8:31; Rev 9:1 [b]John 5:2; Rev 16:16 [c]Job 26:6; Ps 88:11 mg; Prov 15:11 **12** [a]Rev 8:13 **13** [1]Lit *one voice* [2]Two early mss do not contain *four* [a]Ex 30:2f [b]Rev 8:3 **14** [a]Rev 7:1 [b]Gen 15:18; Deut 1:7; Josh 1:4; Rev 16:12 **15** [1]Gr *anthropoi* [a]Rev 20:7 [b]Rev 8:7 **16** [a]Rev 5:11 [b]Rev 7:4

17 And [1]this is how I saw [a]in the vision the horses and those who sat on them: *the riders* had breastplates *the color* of fire and of hyacinth and of [2b]brimstone; and the heads of the horses are like the heads of lions; and [c]out of their mouths proceed fire and smoke and [2b]brimstone.

18 A [a]third of [1]mankind was killed by these three plagues, by the [b]fire and the smoke and the [2]brimstone which proceeded out of their mouths.

19 For the power of the horses is in their mouths and in their tails; for their tails are like serpents and have heads, and with them they do harm.

20 ¶ The rest of [1]mankind, who were not killed by these plagues, [a]did not repent of [b]the works of their hands, so as not to [c]worship demons, and [d]the idols of gold and of silver and of brass and of stone and of wood, which can neither see nor hear nor walk;

21 and they [a]did not repent of their murders nor of their [b]sorceries nor of their [c]immorality nor of their thefts.

The Angel and the Little Book

10 I saw another [a]strong angel [b]coming down out of heaven, clothed with a cloud; and the [c]rainbow was upon his head, and [d]his face was like the sun, and his [e]feet like pillars of fire;

2 and he had in his hand a [a]little book which was open. He placed [b]his right foot on the sea and his left on the land;

3 and he cried out with a loud voice, [a]as when a lion roars; and when he had cried out, the [b]seven peals of thunder [1]uttered their voices.

4 When the seven peals of thunder had spoken, [a]I was about to write; and I [b]heard a voice from heaven saying, "[c]Seal up the things which the seven peals of thunder have spoken and do not write them."

5 Then the angel whom I saw standing on the sea and on the land [a]lifted up his right hand to heaven,

6 [a]and swore by [b]Him who lives forever and ever, [c]WHO CREATED HEAVEN AND THE THINGS IN IT, AND THE EARTH AND THE THINGS IN IT, AND THE SEA AND THE THINGS IN IT, that [d]there will be delay no longer,

7 but in the days of the voice of the [a]seventh angel, when he is about to sound, then [b]the mystery of God is finished, as He [1]preached to His servants the prophets.

8 ¶ Then [a]the voice which I heard from heaven, *I heard* again speaking with me, and saying, "Go, take [b]the [1]book which is open in the hand of the angel who [b]stands on the sea and on the land."

9 So I went to the angel, telling him to give me the little book. And he *said to me, "[a]Take it and eat it; it will make your stomach bitter, but in your mouth it will be sweet as honey."

10 I took the little book out of the angel's hand and ate it, and in my mouth it was sweet as honey; and when I had eaten it, my stomach was made bitter.

11 And [a]they *said to me, "You must [b]prophesy again concerning [c]many peoples and nations and tongues and [d]kings."

The Two Witnesses

11 Then there was given me a [1a]measuring rod like a staff; [2]and [b]someone said, "Get up and measure the [3]temple of God and the altar, and those who worship in it.

2 "[1]Leave out the [a]court which is outside the [2]temple and do not measure it, for [b]it has been given to the nations; and they will [b]tread under foot [c]the holy city for [d]forty-two months.

3 "And I will grant *authority* to my two [a]witnesses, and they will prophesy for [b]twelve hundred and sixty days, clothed in [c]sackcloth."

4 These are the [a]two olive trees and the two lampstands that stand before the Lord of the earth.

5 And if anyone wants to harm them, [a]fire flows out of their mouth and devours their enemies; so if anyone wants to harm them, [b]he must be killed in this way.

6 These have the power to [a]shut up the sky, so that rain will not fall during [b]the days of their prophesying; and they have power over the waters to [c]turn them into blood, and [d]to strike the earth with every plague, as often as they desire.

7 ¶ When they have finished their testimony, [a]the beast that comes up out of the [b]abyss will [c]make war with them, and overcome them and kill them.

8 And their dead bodies *will lie* in the street of the [a]great city which [1]mystically is called [b]Sodom and [c]Egypt, where also their Lord was crucified.

9 Those from [a]the peoples and tribes and tongues and nations *will* look at their dead [1]bodies for three and a half days, and [2b]will not permit their dead bodies to be laid in a tomb.

10 And [a]those who dwell on the earth *will* rejoice over them and celebrate; and they will [b]send gifts to one another, because these two prophets tormented [a]those who dwell on the earth.

17 [1]Lit *thus I saw* [2]I.e. burning sulphur [a]Dan 8:2 [b]Rev 9:18 [c]Rev 11:5
18 [1]Gr *anthropoi* [2]I.e. burning sulphur [a]Rev 8:7 [b]Rev 9:17
20 [1]Gr *anthropoi* [a]Rev 2:21 [b]Deut 4:28; Jer 1:16; Mic 5:13; Acts 7:41 [c]1 Cor 10:20 [d]Ps 115:4-7; Dan 5:23
21 [a]Rev 9:20 [b]Is 47:9; Rev 18:23 [c]Rev 17:2
10:1 [a]Rev 5:2 [b]Rev 18:1 [c]Rev 4:3 [d]Matt 17:2; Rev 1:16 [e]Rev 1:15
2 [a]Rev 5:1 [b]Rev 10:5
3 [1]Or *spoke* [a]Is 31:4; Hos 11:10 [b]Ps 29:3-9; Rev 4:5
4 [a]Rev 1:11 [b]Rev 10:8 [c]Dan 8:26; Rev 22:10
5 [a]Deut 32:40; Dan 12:7
6 [a]Gen 14:22; Ex 6:8; Num 14:30; Ezek 20:5 [b]Rev 4:9 [c]Ex 20:11; Rev 4:11 [d]Rev 6:11
7 [1]Lit *preached the gospel* [a]Rev 11:15 [b]Amos 3:7; Rom 16:25
8 [1]Or *scroll* [a]Rev 10:4 [b]Rev 10:2
9 [a]Jer 15:16; Ezek 2:8
11 [a]Rev 11:1 [b]Ezek 37:4 [c]Rev 5:9 [d]Rev 17:10
11:1 [1]Lit *reed* [2]Lit *saying* [3]Or *sanctuary* [a]Ezek 40:3-42:20; Zech 2:1; Rev 21:15f [b]Rev 10:11
2 [1]Lit *throw out* [2]Or *sanctuary* [a]Ezek 40:17 [b]Luke 21:24 [c]Is 52:1; Matt 4:5; Rev 21:2 [d]Dan 7:25; Rev 12:6
3 [a]Rev 1:5 [b]Dan 7:25; Rev 12:6 [c]Gen 37:34; 2 Sam 3:31; 1 Kin 21:27; 2 Kin 19:1f; Neh 9:1; Esth 4:1; Ps 69:11; Joel 1:13; Jon 3:5f
4 [a]Ps 52:8; Jer 11:16; Zech 4:3
5 [a]2 Kin 1:10-12; Jer 5:14; Rev 9:17f [b]Num 16:29
6 [a]1 Kin 17:1; Luke 4:25 [b]Rev 11:3 [c]Ex 7:17ff; Rev 8:8 [d]1 Sam 4:8
7 [a]Rev 13:1ff [b]Rev 9:1 [c]Dan 7:21; Rev 13:7
8 [1]Lit *spiritually* [a]Rev 14:8 [b]Is 1:9; Jer 23:14; Ezek 16:46 [c]Ezek 23:3
9 [1]Lit *body* [2]Lit *do not permit* [a]Rev 5:9 [b]1 Kin 13:22; Ps 79:2f
10 [a]Rev 3:10 [b]Neh 8:10; Esth 9:19

11 ¶ But after the three and a half
days, [a]the breath of life from God came
into them, and they stood on their feet;
and great fear fell upon those who were
watching them.
12 And they heard a loud voice from
heaven saying to them, "[a]Come up
here." Then they [b]went up into heaven
in the cloud, and their enemies watched
them.
13 And in that hour there was a great
[a]earthquake, and a tenth of the city fell;
[1]seven thousand people were killed in
the earthquake, and the rest were terrified and [b]gave glory to the [c]God of
heaven.
14 ¶ The second [a]woe is past; behold,
the third woe is coming quickly.

The Seventh Trumpet—Christ's Reign Foreseen

15 ¶ Then the [a]seventh angel sounded; and there were [b]loud voices in heav-
en, saying,
¶ "[c]The kingdom of the world has become *the kingdom* of our Lord and of
[d]His [1]Christ; and [e]He will reign forever
and ever."
16 And the twenty-four elders, who
[a]sit on their thrones before God, [b]fell on
their faces and worshiped God,
17 saying,
¶ "We give You thanks, [a]O Lord God,
the Almighty, who are and who were,
because You have taken Your great power
and have begun to [b]reign.
18 "And [a]the nations were enraged,
and [b]Your wrath came, and [c]the time
came for the dead to be judged, and *the
time* to [1]reward Your [d]bond-servants
the prophets and the [2]saints and those
who fear Your name, [e]the small and the
great, and to destroy those who destroy
the earth."
19 ¶ And [a]the [1]temple of God which
is in heaven was opened; and [b]the ark of
His covenant appeared in His [1]temple,
and there were flashes of [c]lightning and
sounds and peals of thunder and an earthquake and a [d]great [2]hailstorm.

The Woman, Israel

12 A great [a]sign appeared [b]in heav-
en: [c]a woman [d]clothed with the
sun, and the moon under her feet, and on
her head a crown of twelve stars;
2 and she was with child; and she
*[a]cried out, being in labor and in pain to
give birth.

The Red Dragon, Satan

3 Then [a]another sign appeared in
heaven: and behold, a great red [b]dragon
having [c]seven heads and [d]ten horns,
and on his heads *were* [e]seven diadems.
4 And his tail *swept away a [a]third
of the stars of heaven and [b]threw them
to the earth. And the [c]dragon stood before the woman who was about to give
birth, so that when she gave birth [d]he
might devour her child.

The Male Child, Christ

5 And [a]she gave birth to a son, a
male *child,* who is to [1][b]rule all the [2]na-
tions with a rod of iron; and her child was
[c]caught up to God and to His throne.
6 Then the woman fled into the wilderness where she *had a place prepared
by God, so that there [1]she would be
nourished for [a]one thousand two hundred and sixty days.

The Angel, Michael

7 ¶ And there was war in heaven,
[a]Michael and his angels waging war with
the [b]dragon. The dragon and [c]his angels
waged war,
8 and they were not strong enough,
and there was no longer a place found for
them in heaven.
9 And the great [a]dragon was thrown
down, the [b]serpent of old who is called
the devil and [c]Satan, who [d]deceives the
whole [1]world; he was [e]thrown down to
the earth, and his angels were thrown
down with him.
10 Then I heard [a]a loud voice in heav-
en, saying,
¶ "Now the [b]salvation, and the power,
and the [a]kingdom of our God and the
authority of His Christ have come, for
the [c]accuser of our brethren has been
thrown down, he who accuses them before our God day and night.
11 "And they [a]overcame him because
of [b]the blood of the Lamb and because of
[c]the word of their testimony, and they
[d]did not love their life even [1]when faced
with death.
12 "For this reason, [a]rejoice, O heavens and [b]you who [1]dwell in them.
[c]Woe to the earth and the sea, because [d]the devil has come down to
you, having great wrath, knowing that he
has *only* [e]a short time."
13 ¶ And when the [a]dragon saw that
he was thrown down to the earth, he
persecuted [b]the woman who gave birth
to the male *child.*
14 But the [a]two wings of the great
eagle were given to the woman, so that
she could fly [b]into the wilderness to her
place, where she *was nourished for [c]a
time and times and half a time, from the
[1]presence of the serpent.
15 And the [a]serpent [1]poured water
like a river out of his mouth after the

11 [a]Ezek 37:5
12 [a]Rev 4:1 [b]2 Kin 2:11; Acts 1:9
13 [1]Lit *names of people, seven thousand* [a]Rev 6:12 [b]John 9:24; Rev 14:7 [c]Rev 16:11
14 [a]Rev 8:13
15 [1]I.e. Messiah [a]Rev 8:2 [b]Rev 16:17 [c]Rev 12:10 [d]Ps 2:2; Acts 4:26 [e]Ex 15:18; Dan 2:44; Luke 1:33
16 [a]Matt 19:28; Rev 4:4 [b]Rev 4:10
17 [a]Rev 1:8 [b]Rev 19:6
18 [1]Lit *give the reward to* [2]Or *holy ones* [a]Ps 2:1 [b]Ps 2:5 [c]Dan 7:10; Rev 20:12 [d]Rev 10:7 [e]Ps 115:13; Rev 13:16
19 [1]Or *sanctuary* [2]Lit *hail* [a]Rev 4:1 [b]Heb 9:4 [c]Rev 4:5 [d]Rev 16:21
12:1 [a]Matt 24:30; Rev 12:3 [b]Rev 11:19 [c]Gal 4:26 [d]Ps 104:2; Song 6:10
2 [a]Is 26:17; Mic 4:9f
3 [a]Rev 12:1 [b]Is 27:1; Rev 12:4 [c]Rev 13:1 [d]Dan 7:7; Rev 13:1 [e]Rev 13:1
4 [a]Rev 8:7 [b]Dan 8:10 [c]Is 27:1; Rev 12:3 [d]Matt 2:16
5 [1]Or *shepherd* [2]Or *Gentiles* [a]Is 66:7 [b]Ps 2:9; Rev 2:27 [c]2 Cor 12:2ff
6 [1]Lit *they would nourish her for* [a]Rev 11:3
7 [a]Dan 10:13; Jude 9 [b]Rev 12:3 [c]Matt 25:41
9 [1]Lit *inhabited earth* [a]Rev 12:3 [b]Gen 3:1; 2 Cor 11:3; Rev 12:15 [c]Matt 4:10 [d]Rev 13:14 [e]Luke 10:18; John 12:31
10 [a]Rev 11:15 [b]Rev 7:10 [c]Job 1:11; Zech 3:1; Luke 22:31; 1 Pet 5:8
11 [1]Lit *to death* [a]John 16:33; 1 John 2:13; Rev 15:2 [b]Rev 7:14 [c]Rev 6:9 [d]Luke 14:26; Rev 2:10
12 [1]Or *tabernacle* [a]Ps 96:11; Is 44:23; Rev 18:20 [b]Rev 13:6 [c]Rev 8:13 [d]Rev 12:9 [e]Rev 10:6
13 [a]Rev 12:3 [b]Rev 12:5
14 [1]Lit *face* [a]Ex 19:4; Deut 32:11; Is 40:31 [b]Rev 12:6 [c]Dan 7:25
15 [1]Lit *threw* [a]Gen 3:1; 2 Cor 11:3; Rev 12:9

woman, so that he might cause her to be
swept away with the flood.
16 [1]But the earth helped the woman,
and the earth opened its mouth and
drank up the river which the dragon
[2]poured out of his mouth.
17 So the dragon was enraged with the
woman, and went off to [a]make war with
the rest of her [1b]children, who [c]keep
the commandments of God and [d]hold to
the testimony of Jesus.

The Beast from the Sea

13 And the dragon stood on the sand
of the [1]seashore.
¶ Then I saw a [a]beast coming up out of
the sea, having [b]ten horns and [b]seven
heads, and on his horns *were* [c]ten diadems, and on his heads *were* [d]blasphe-
mous names.
2 And the beast which I saw was
[a]like a leopard, and his feet were like
those of [b]a bear, and his mouth like the
mouth of [c]a lion. And the [d]dragon gave
him his power and his [e]throne and great
authority.
3 *I saw* one of his heads as if it had
been [1]slain, and his [a]fatal wound was
healed. And the whole earth [b]was
amazed *and followed* after the beast;
4 they worshiped the [a]dragon because he [a]gave his authority to the beast;
and they worshiped the beast, saying,
"[b]Who is like the beast, and who is able
to wage war with him?"
5 There was given to him a mouth
[a]speaking [1]arrogant words and blasphemies, and authority to act for [b]forty-two
months was given to him.
6 And he opened his mouth in blasphemies against God, to blaspheme His
name and His tabernacle, *that is,* [a]those
who [1]dwell in heaven.
7 ¶ It was also given to him to [a]make
war with the [1]saints and to overcome
them, and authority over [b]every tribe
and people and tongue and nation was
given to him.
8 All who [a]dwell on the earth will
worship him, *everyone* [b]whose name
has not been [1]written [c]from the foundation of the world in the [d]book of life of
[e]the Lamb who has been slain.
9 [a]If anyone has an ear, let him hear.
10 [a]If anyone [1]*is destined* for captivity, to captivity he goes; [b]if anyone kills
with the sword, with the sword he must
be killed. Here is [c]the [2]perseverance
and the faith of the [3]saints.

The Beast from the Earth

11 ¶ Then [a]I saw another beast coming up out of the earth; and he had [b]two
horns like a lamb and he spoke as a
[c]dragon.
12 He [a]exercises all the authority of
the first beast [1b]in his presence. And he
makes [c]the earth and those who dwell in
it to [d]worship the first beast, whose [e]fa-
tal wound was healed.
13 He [a]performs great signs, so that
he even makes [b]fire come down out of
heaven to the earth in the presence of
men.
14 And he [a]deceives [b]those who
dwell on the earth because of [c]the signs
which it was given him to perform [1d]in
the presence of the beast, telling those
who dwell on the earth to make an image
to the beast who *had the [e]wound of the
sword and has come to life.
15 And it was given to him to give
breath to the image of the beast, so that
the image of the beast would even
[1]speak and cause [a]as many as do not
[b]worship the image of the beast to be
killed.
16 And he causes all, [a]the small and
the great, and the rich and the poor, and
the free men and the slaves, [1]to be given
a [b]mark on their right hand or on their
forehead,
17 and *he provides* that no one will be
able to buy or to sell, except the one who
has the [a]mark, *either* [b]the name of the
beast or [c]the number of his name.
18 [a]Here is wisdom. Let him who has
understanding calculate the number of
the beast, for the number is that [b]of a
man; and his number is [1]six hundred
and sixty-six.

The Lamb and the 144,000 on Mount Zion

14 Then I looked, and behold, [a]the
Lamb *was* standing on [b]Mount
Zion, and with Him [c]one hundred and
forty-four thousand, having [d]His name
and the [d]name of His Father written [e]on
their foreheads.
2 And I heard a voice from heaven,
like [a]the sound of many waters and like
the [b]sound of loud thunder, and the
voice which I heard *was* like *the sound* of
[c]harpists playing on their harps.
3 And they [1]*sang [a]a new song before the throne and before the [b]four living creatures and the [c]elders; and [d]no
one could learn the song except the [e]one
hundred and forty-four thousand who
had been [a]purchased from the earth.
4 [a]These are the ones who have not
been defiled with women, for they [1]have
kept themselves chaste. These *are* the

16 [1]Lit *And* [2]Lit *threw*
17 [1]Lit *seed* [a]Rev 11:7 [b]Gen 3:15 [c]1 John 2:3; Rev 14:12 [d]Rev 1:2
13:1 [1]Lit *sea* [a]Dan 7:3; Rev 11:7 [b]Rev 12:3 [c]Rev 12:3 [d]Dan 7:8; Rev 17:3
2 [a]Dan 7:6; Hos 13:7f [b]Dan 7:5 [c]Dan 7:4 [d]Rev 12:3 [e]Rev 2:13
3 [1]Lit *slaughtered to death* [a]Rev 13:12 [b]Rev 17:8
4 [a]Rev 12:3 [b]Ex 15:11; Is 46:5; Rev 18:18
5 [1]Lit *great things* [a]Dan 7:8; 2 Thess 2:3f [b]Rev 11:2
6 [1]Or *tabernacle* [a]Rev 7:15
7 [1]Or *holy ones* [a]Dan 7:21; Rev 11:7 [b]Rev 5:9
8 [1]Or *written in the book...slain from the foundation of the world* [a]Rev 3:10 [b]Rev 3:5 [c]Matt 25:34; Rev 17:8 [d]Ps 69:28 [e]Rev 5:6
9 [a]Rev 2:7
10 [1]Or leads *into captivity* [2]Or *steadfastness* [3]Or *holy ones* [a]Is 33:1; Jer 15:2 [b]Gen 9:6; Matt 26:52; Rev 11:18 [c]Heb 6:12; Rev 14:12
11 [a]Rev 13:1 [b]Dan 8:3 [c]Rev 13:4
12 [1]Or *by his authority* [a]Rev 13:4 [b]Rev 13:14 [c]Rev 13:8 [d]Rev 13:15 [e]Rev 13:3
13 [a]Matt 24:24; Rev 16:14 [b]1 Kin 18:38; Luke 9:54; Rev 11:5
14 [1]Or *by the authority of* [a]Rev 12:9 [b]Rev 13:8 [c]2 Thess 2:9f [d]Rev 13:12 [e]Rev 13:3
15 [1]One early ms reads *speak, and he will cause* [a]Dan 3:3ff [b]Rev 13:12
16 [1]Lit *causes all,...that they give them a mark* [a]Rev 11:18 [b]Gal 6:17; Rev 7:3
17 [a]Gal 6:17; Rev 7:3 [b]Rev 14:11 [c]Rev 15:2
18 [1]One early ms reads 616 [a]Rev 17:9 [b]Rev 21:17
14:1 [a]Rev 5:6 [b]Ps 2:6; Heb 12:22 [c]Rev 7:4 [d]Rev 3:12 [e]Ezek 9:4; Rev 7:3
2 [a]Rev 1:15 [b]Rev 6:1 [c]Rev 5:8
3 [1]Two early mss read *sing something like a new song* [a]Rev 5:9 [b]Rev 4:6 [c]Rev 4:4 [d]Rev 2:17 [e]Rev 7:4
4 [1]Lit *are chaste men* [a]Matt 19:12; 2 Cor 11:2; Eph 5:27; Rev 3:4

ones who [b]follow the Lamb wherever He goes. These have been [c]purchased from among men [d]as first fruits to God and to the Lamb.

5 And [a]no lie was found in their mouth; they are [b]blameless.

Vision of the Angel with the Gospel

6 ¶ And I saw another angel flying in [a]midheaven, having [b]an eternal gospel to preach to [c]those who [1]live on the earth, and to [d]every nation and tribe and tongue and people;

7 and he said with a loud voice, "[a]Fear God, and [b]give Him glory, because the hour of His judgment has come; worship Him who [c]made the heaven and the earth and sea and [d]springs of waters."

8 ¶ And another angel, a second one, followed, saying, "[1a]Fallen, fallen is [b]Babylon the great, she who has [c]made all the nations drink of the [d]wine of the [2]passion of her immorality."

Doom for Worshipers of the Beast

9 ¶ Then another angel, a third one, followed them, saying with a loud voice, "If anyone [a]worships the beast and his [b]image, and receives a [c]mark on his forehead or on his hand,

10 he also will drink of the [a]wine of the wrath of God, which is mixed [1]in full strength [b]in the cup of His anger; and he will be tormented with [c]fire and [2]brimstone in the presence of the [d]holy angels and in the presence of the Lamb.

11 "And the [a]smoke of their torment goes up forever and ever; [b]they have no rest day and night, those who [c]worship the beast and his [c]image, and [1]whoever receives the [d]mark of his name."

12 Here is [a]the [1]perseverance of the [2]saints who [b]keep the commandments of God and [3c]their faith in Jesus.

13 ¶ And I heard a voice from heaven, saying, "Write, '[a]Blessed are the dead who [b]die in the Lord from now on!' " "Yes," [c]says the Spirit, "so that they may [d]rest from their labors, for their [e]deeds follow with them."

The Reapers

14 ¶ Then I looked, and behold, a [a]white cloud, and sitting on the cloud *was* one [b]like [1]a son of man, having a golden [c]crown on His head and a sharp sickle in His hand.

15 And another angel [a]came out of the [1]temple, crying out with a loud voice to Him who sat on the cloud, "[2b]Put in your sickle and reap, for the hour to reap has come, because the [c]harvest of the earth [3]is ripe."

16 Then He who sat on the cloud [1]swung His sickle over the earth, and the earth was reaped.

17 ¶ And another angel [a]came out of the [1]temple which is in heaven, and he also had a sharp sickle.

18 Then another angel, [a]the one who has power over fire, came out from [b]the altar; and he called with a loud voice to him who had the sharp sickle, saying, "[1c]Put in your sharp sickle and gather the clusters [2]from the vine of the earth, [d]because her grapes are ripe."

19 So the angel [1]swung his sickle to the earth and gathered *the clusters from* the vine of the earth, and threw them into [a]the great wine press of the wrath of God.

20 And [a]the wine press was trodden [b]outside the city, and [c]blood came out from the wine press, up to the horses' bridles, [1]for a distance of [2]two hundred miles.

A Scene of Heaven

15 Then I saw [a]another sign in heaven, great and marvelous, [b]seven angels who had [c]seven plagues, *which are* [d]the last, because in them the wrath of God is finished.

2 ¶ And I saw something like a [a]sea of glass mixed with fire, and those who had [b]been victorious [1]over the [c]beast and [d]his image and the [e]number of his name, standing on the [a]sea of glass, holding [f]harps of God.

3 And they *sang the [a]song of Moses, [b]the bond-servant of God, and the [c]song of the Lamb, saying,

¶ "[d]Great and marvelous are
Your works,
[e]O Lord God, the Almighty;
Righteous and true are Your
ways,
[f]King of the [1]nations!
4 "[a]Who will not fear, O Lord, and
glorify Your name?
For You alone are holy;
For [b]ALL THE NATIONS WILL COME
AND WORSHIP BEFORE YOU,
FOR YOUR [1c]RIGHTEOUS ACTS HAVE
BEEN REVEALED."

5 ¶ After these things I looked, and [a]the [1]temple of the [b]tabernacle of testimony in heaven was opened,

6 and the [a]seven angels who had the seven plagues [b]came out of the [1]temple, clothed in [2]linen, clean *and* bright, and

4 [b]Rev 3:4 [c]Rev 5:9 [d]Heb 12:23; James 1:18
5 [a]Ps 32:2; Zeph 3:13; Mal 2:6; John 1:47; 1 Pet 2:22 [b]Heb 9:14; 1 Pet 1:19; Jude 24
6 [1]Lit *sit* [a]Rev 8:13 [b]1 Pet 1:25; Rev 10:7 [c]Rev 3:10 [d]Rev 5:9
7 [a]Rev 15:4 [b]Rev 11:13 [c]Rev 4:11 [d]Rev 8:10
8 [1]Lit *Babylon... fell, fell, she who* [2]Or *wrath* [a]Is 21:9; Jer 51:8; Rev 18:2 [b]Dan 4:30; Rev 16:19 [c]Jer 51:7 [d]Rev 17:2
9 [a]Rev 13:12 [b]Rev 13:14f [c]Rev 13:16
10 [1]Lit *unmixed*; in ancient times wine was usually diluted with water [2]I.e. burning sulphur [a]Is 51:17; Jer 25:15f; Rev 16:19 [b]Ps 75:8; Rev 18:6 [c]Gen 19:24; Ezek 38:22; 2 Thess 1:7; Rev 19:20 [d]Mark 8:38
11 [1]Lit *if anyone* [a]Is 34:8-10; Rev 18:9 [b]Rev 4:8 [c]Rev 13:12 [d]Rev 13:17
12 [1]Or *steadfastness* [2]Or *holy ones* [3]Lit *the faith of* [a]Rev 13:10 [b]Rev 12:17 [c]Rev 2:13
13 [a]Rev 20:6 [b]1 Cor 15:18; 1 Thess 4:16 [c]Rev 2:7 [d]Heb 4:9ff; Rev 6:11 [e]1 Tim 5:25
14 [1]Or *the Son of Man* [a]Matt 17:5 [b]Dan 7:13; Rev 1:13 [c]Ps 21:3; Rev 6:2
15 [1]Or *sanctuary* [2]Lit *Send forth* [3]Lit *has become dry* [a]Rev 11:19 [b]Joel 3:13; Mark 4:29; Rev 14:18 [c]Jer 51:33; Matt 13:39-41
16 [1]Lit *cast*
17 [1]Or *sanctuary* [a]Rev 11:19
18 [1]Lit *Send forth* [2]Lit *of* [a]Rev 16:8 [b]Rev 6:9 [c]Joel 3:13; Mark 4:29; Rev 14:15 [d]Joel 3:13
19 [1]Lit *cast* [a]Is 63:2f; Rev 19:15
20 [1]Lit *from* [2]Lit *sixteen hundred stadia*; a stadion was approx 600 ft [a]Is 63:3; Lam 1:15; Rev 19:15 [b]Heb 13:12; Rev 11:8 [c]Gen 49:11; Deut 32:14
15:1 [a]Rev 12:1 [b]Rev 15:6-8 [c]Lev 26:21 [d]Rev 9:20
2 [1]Lit *from* [a]Rev

4:6 [b]Rev 12:11 [c]Rev 13:1 [d]Rev 13:14f [e]Rev 13:17 [f]Rev 5:8 3 [1]Two early mss read *ages* [a]Ex 15:1ff [b]Josh 22:5; Heb 3:5 [c]Rev 5:9f [d]Deut 32:3f; Ps 111:2 [e]Hos 14:9; Rev 1:8 [f]1 Tim 1:17 4 [1]Or *judgments* [a]Jer 10:7; Rev 14:7 [b]Ps 86:9; Is 66:23 [c]Rev 19:8 5 [1]Or *sanctuary* [a]Rev 11:19 [b]Ex 38:21; Num 1:50; Heb 8:5; Rev 13:6 6 [1]Or *sanctuary* [2]One early mss reads *stone* [a]Rev 15:1 [b]Rev 14:15

[c]girded around their chests with golden
sashes.
7 Then one of the [a]four living creatures gave to the [b]seven angels seven
[c]golden bowls full of the [d]wrath of God,
who [e]lives forever and ever.
8 And the [1]temple was filled with
[a]smoke from the glory of God and from
His power; and no one was able to enter
the [1]temple until the seven plagues of
the seven angels were finished.

Six Bowls of Wrath

16 Then I heard a loud voice from
[a]the [1]temple, saying to the
[b]seven angels, "Go and [c]pour out [2]on
the earth the seven bowls of the wrath of
God."
2 ¶ So the first *angel* went and
poured out his bowl [1a]on the earth; and
it became a loathsome and malignant
[b]sore on the [2]people [c]who had the
mark of the beast and who worshiped his
image.
3 ¶ The second *angel* poured out his
bowl [a]into the sea, and it became blood
like *that* of a dead man; and every living
[1]thing in the sea died.
4 ¶ Then the third *angel* poured out
his bowl into the [a]rivers and the springs
of waters; and they [b]became blood.
5 And I heard the angel of the waters
saying, "[a]Righteous are You, [b]who are
and who were, O [c]Holy One, because
You [d]judged these things;
6 for they poured out [a]the blood of
saints and prophets, and You have giv-
en them [b]blood to drink. They [1]de-
serve it."
7 And I heard [a]the altar saying, "Yes,
O [b]Lord God, the Almighty, [c]true and
righteous are Your judgments."
8 ¶ The fourth *angel* poured out his
bowl upon [a]the sun, [b]and it was given to
it to scorch men with fire.
9 Men were scorched with [1]fierce
heat; and they [a]blasphemed the name
of God who has the power over these
plagues, and they [b]did not repent so as to
[c]give Him glory.
10 ¶ Then the fifth *angel* poured out
his bowl on the [a]throne of the beast, and
his kingdom became [b]darkened; and
they gnawed their tongues because of
pain,
11 and they [a]blasphemed the [b]God of
heaven because of their pains and their
[c]sores; and they [d]did not repent of their
deeds.
12 ¶ The sixth *angel* poured out his
bowl on the [a]great river, the Euphrates;
and [b]its water was dried up, so that [c]the
way would be prepared for the kings
[d]from the [1]east.

Armageddon

13 And I saw *coming* out of the mouth
of the [a]dragon and out of the mouth of
the [b]beast and out of the mouth of the
[c]false prophet, three [d]unclean spirits
like [e]frogs;
14 for they are [a]spirits of demons,
[b]performing signs, which go out to the
kings of the [c]whole [1]world, to [d]gather
them together for the war of the [e]great
day of God, the Almighty.
15 ("Behold, [a]I am coming like a
thief. [b]Blessed is the one who stays
awake and keeps his clothes, [c]so that he
will not walk about naked and men will
not see his shame.")
16 And they [a]gathered them together
to the place which [b]in Hebrew is called
[1c]Har-Magedon.

Seventh Bowl of Wrath

17 ¶ Then the seventh *angel* poured
out his bowl upon [a]the air, and a [b]loud
voice came out of the [1c]temple from the
throne, saying, "[d]It is done."
18 And there were flashes of [a]light-
ning and sounds and peals of thunder;
and there was [b]a great earthquake,
[c]such as there had not been since man
came to be upon the earth, so great an
earthquake *was it, and* so mighty.
19 [a]The great city was split into three
parts, and the cities of the [1]nations fell.
[b]Babylon the great was [c]remembered
before God, to give her [d]the cup of the
wine of [2]His fierce wrath.
20 And [a]every island fled away, and
the mountains were not found.
21 And [a]huge [1]hailstones, about
[2]one hundred pounds each, *came down
from heaven upon men; and men [b]blas-
phemed God because of the [c]plague of
the hail, because its plague *was extremely [3]severe.

The Doom of Babylon

17 [a]Then one of the [b]seven angels
who had the [c]seven bowls came
and spoke with me, saying, "Come here,
I will show you [d]the judgment of the
[e]great harlot who [f]sits on many waters,
2 with whom [a]the kings of the earth
committed *acts of* immorality, and
[b]those who dwell on the earth were
[c]made drunk with the wine of her immorality."
3 And [a]he carried me away [1b]in the
Spirit [c]into a wilderness; and I saw a
woman sitting on a [d]scarlet beast, full of

6 [c]Rev 1:13
7 [a]Rev 4:6 [b]Rev 15:1 [c]Rev 5:8 [d]Rev 14:10 [e]Rev 4:9
8 [1]Or *sanctuary* [a]Ex 19:18; Lev 16:2; 1 Kin 8:10f; 2 Chr 5:13f; Is 6:4
16:1 [1]Or *sanctuary* [2]Lit *into* [a]Rev 11:19 [b]Rev 15:1 [c]Ps 79:6; Jer 10:25; Ezek 22:31; Zeph 3:8; Rev 16:2ff
2 [1]Lit *into* [2]Gr *anthropoi* [a]Rev 8:7 [b]Ex 9:9-11; Deut 28:35; Rev 16:11 [c]Rev 13:15-17
3 [1]Lit *soul* [a]Ex 7:17-21; Rev 8:8f
4 [a]Rev 8:10 [b]Ex 7:17-20; Ps 78:44; Rev 11:6
5 [a]John 17:25 [b]Rev 11:17 [c]Rev 15:4 [d]Rev 6:10
6 [1]Lit *are worthy* [a]Rev 17:6 [b]Is 49:26; Luke 11:49-51
7 [a]Rev 6:9 [b]Rev 1:8 [c]Rev 15:3
8 [a]Rev 6:12 [b]Rev 14:18
9 [1]Lit *great* [a]Rev 16:11 [b]Rev 2:21 [c]Rev 11:13
10 [a]Rev 13:2 [b]Ex 10:21f; Is 8:22; Rev 8:12
11 [a]Rev 16:9 [b]Rev 11:13 [c]Rev 16:2 [d]Rev 2:21
12 [1]Lit *rising of the sun* [a]Rev 9:14 [b]Is 11:15f; Jer 51:36 [c]Is 41:2 [d]Rev 7:2
13 [a]Rev 12:3 [b]Rev 13:1 [c]Rev 13:11 [d]Rev 18:2 [e]Ex 8:6
14 [1]Lit *inhabited earth* [a]1 Tim 4:1 [b]Rev 13:13 [c]Rev 3:10 [d]1 Kin 22:21-23; Rev 17:14 [e]Rev 6:17
15 [a]Matt 24:43f; Luke 12:39f; Rev 3:3 [b]Luke 12:37 [c]Rev 3:18
16 [1]Two early mss read *Armagedon* [a]Rev 19:19 [b]Rev 9:11 [c]Judg 5:19; 2 Kin 23:29f; 2 Chr 35:22; Zech 12:11
17 [1]Or *sanctuary* [a]Eph 2:2 [b]Rev 11:15 [c]Rev 14:15 [d]Rev 10:6
18 [a]Rev 4:5 [b]Rev 6:12 [c]Dan 12:1; Matt 24:21
19 [1]Or *Gentiles* [2]Lit *wrath of His anger* [a]Rev 11:8 [b]Rev 14:8 [c]Rev 18:5 [d]Rev 14:10
20 [a]Rev 6:14
21 [1]Lit *hail* [2]Lit *the weight of a talent* [3]Lit *great* [a]Rev 8:7 [b]Rev 16:9 [c]Ex 9:18-25
17:1 [a]Rev 1:1 [b]Rev 15:1 [c]Rev 15:7 [d]Rev 16:19 [e]Is 1:21; Jer 2:20; Nah 3:4; Rev 17:5 [f]Jer 51:13; Rev 17:15
2 [a]Rev 2:22 [b]Rev 3:10 [c]Rev 14:8 **3** [1]Or *in spirit* [a]Rev 21:10 [b]Rev 1:10 [c]Rev 12:6 [d]Matt 27:28; Rev 18:12

[e]blasphemous names, having [f]seven heads and ten horns.

4 The woman [a]was clothed in purple and scarlet, and [1]adorned with gold and precious [2]stones and pearls, having in her hand [b]a gold cup full of abominations and of the unclean things of her immorality,

5 and on her forehead a name *was* written, a [a]mystery, "[b]BABYLON THE GREAT, THE MOTHER OF HARLOTS AND OF [c]THE ABOMINATIONS OF THE EARTH."

6 And I saw the woman drunk with [a]the blood of the [1]saints, and with the blood of the witnesses of Jesus. When I saw her, I wondered [2]greatly.

7 And the angel said to me, "Why [1]do you wonder? I will tell you the [a]mystery of the woman and of the beast that carries her, which has the [b]seven heads and the ten horns.

8 ¶ "[a]The beast that you saw [b]was, and is not, and is about to [c]come up out of the [d]abyss and [1e]go to destruction. And [f]those who dwell on the earth, [g]whose name has not been written in the book of life [h]from the foundation of the world, will [i]wonder when they see the beast, that he was and is not and will come.

9 "[a]Here is the mind which has wisdom. The [b]seven heads are seven mountains on which the woman sits,

10 and they are seven [a]kings; five have fallen, one is, the other has not yet come; and when he comes, he must remain a little while.

11 "The beast which [a]was and is not, is himself also an eighth and is *one* of the seven, and he [b]goes to destruction.

12 "The [a]ten horns which you saw are ten kings who have not yet received a kingdom, but they receive authority as kings with the beast [b]for one hour.

13 "These have [a]one [1]purpose, and they give their power and authority to the beast.

Victory for the Lamb

14 "These will wage [a]war against the Lamb, and the Lamb will [b]overcome them, because He is [c]Lord of lords and [c]King of kings, and [d]those who are with Him *are the* [e]called and chosen and faithful."

15 ¶ And he *said to me, "The [a]waters which you saw where the harlot sits, are [b]peoples and multitudes and nations and tongues.

16 "And the [a]ten horns which you saw, and the beast, these will hate the harlot and will make her [b]desolate and [c]naked, and will [d]eat her flesh and will [e]burn her up with fire.

17 "For [a]God has put it in their hearts to execute His [1]purpose [2]by [b]having a common purpose, and by giving their kingdom to the beast, until the [c]words of God will be fulfilled.

18 "The woman whom you saw is [a]the great city, which [1]reigns over the kings of the earth."

Babylon Is Fallen

18 After these things I saw another [a]angel [b]coming down from heaven, having great authority, and the earth was [c]illumined with his glory.

2 And he cried out with a mighty voice, saying, "[1a]Fallen, fallen is Babylon the great! She [b]has become a dwelling place of demons and a [2]prison of every [c]unclean spirit, and a [2]prison of every unclean and hateful bird.

3 "For all the nations [1]have drunk of the [a]wine of the [2]passion of her immorality, and [b]the kings of the earth have committed *acts of* immorality with her, and the [c]merchants of the earth have become rich by the [3]wealth of her [4d]sensuality."

4 ¶ I heard another voice from heaven, saying, "[a]Come out of her, my people, so that you will not participate in her sins and receive of her plagues;

5 for her sins have [1a]piled up as high as heaven, and God has [b]remembered her iniquities.

6 "[a]Pay her back even as she has paid, and [1]give back *to her* double according to her deeds; in the [b]cup which she has mixed, mix twice as much for her.

7 "[a]To the degree that she glorified herself and [b]lived [1]sensuously, to the same degree give her torment and mourning; for she says in her heart, '[c]I SIT *as* A QUEEN AND I AM NOT A WIDOW, and will never see mourning.'

8 "For this reason [a]in one day her plagues will come, [1]pestilence and mourning and famine, and she will be [b]burned up with fire; for the Lord God who judges her [c]is strong.

Lament for Babylon

9 ¶ "And [a]the kings of the earth, who committed *acts of* immorality and [b]lived [1]sensuously with her, will [c]weep and lament over her when they [d]see the smoke of her burning,

10 [a]standing at a distance because of the fear of her torment, saying, '[b]Woe,

3 [e]Rev 13:1 [f]Rev 12:3
4 [1]Lit *gilded* [2]Lit *stone* [a]Ezek 28:13; Rev 18:12 [b]Jer 51:7; Rev 18:6
5 [a]2 Thess 2:7; Rev 1:20 [b]Rev 14:8 [c]Rev 17:2
6 [1]Or *holy ones* [2]Lit *with great wonder* [a]Rev 16:6
7 [1]Lit *have you wondered* [a]2 Thess 2:7; Rev 1:20 [b]Rev 17:3
8 [1]One early ms reads *is going* [a]Dan 7:7 [b]Rev 13:3 [c]Rev 11:7 [d]Rev 9:1 [e]Rev 13:10 [f]Rev 3:10 [g]Ps 69:28; Rev 3:5 [h]Matt 25:34; Rev 13:8 [i]Rev 13:3
9 [a]Rev 13:18 [b]Rev 17:3
10 [a]Rev 10:11
11 [a]Rev 13:3 [b]Rev 13:10
12 [a]Dan 7:24; Rev 12:3 [b]Rev 18:10
13 [1]Or *mind* [a]Rev 17:17
14 [a]Rev 16:14 [b]Rev 3:21 [c]1 Tim 6:15; Rev 19:16 [d]Rev 2:10f [e]Matt 22:14
15 [a]Is 8:7; Jer 47:2; Rev 17:1 [b]Rev 5:9
16 [a]Rev 17:12 [b]Rev 18:17 [c]Ezek 16:37 [d]Rev 19:18 [e]Rev 18:8
17 [1]Or *mind* [2]Lit *even to do one mind and to give* [a]2 Cor 8:16 [b]Rev 17:13 [c]Rev 10:7
18 [1]Lit *has a kingdom* [a]Rev 11:8
18:1 [a]Rev 17:1 [b]Rev 10:1 [c]Ezek 43:2
2 [1]Lit *Babylon...fell, fell* [2]Or *haunt* [a]Is 21:9; Jer 51:8; Rev 14:8 [b]Is 13:21f; Jer 50:39; Zeph 2:14f [c]Rev 16:13
3 [1]Two early ancient mss read *have fallen by* [2]Lit *wrath* [3]Lit *power* [4]Or *luxury* [a]Jer 51:7; Rev 14:8 [b]Rev 17:2 [c]Ezek 27:9-25; Rev 18:11 [d]1 Tim 5:11; Rev 18:7
4 [a]Is 52:11; Jer 50:8; 2 Cor 6:17
5 [1]Lit *joined together* [a]Jer 51:9 [b]Rev 16:19
6 [1]Lit *double* to her [a]Ps 137:8; Jer 50:15 [b]Rev 17:4
7 [1]Or *luxuriously* [a]Ezek 28:2-8 [b]1 Tim 5:11; Rev 18:3 [c]Is 47:7f; Zeph 2:15

8 [1]Lit *death* [a]Is 47:9; Jer 50:31f; Rev 18:10 [b]Rev 17:16 [c]Jer 50:34; Rev 11:17f **9** [1]Or *luxuriously* [a]Rev 17:2 [b]1 Tim 5:11; Rev 18:3 [c]Ezek 26:16f [d]Rev 14:11 **10** [a]Rev 18:15 [b]Rev 18:16

woe, [c]the great city, Babylon, the strong
city! For in [d]one hour your judgment has
come.'
11 ¶ "And the [a]merchants of the
earth [b]weep and mourn over her, because no one buys their cargoes any
more—
12 cargoes of [a]gold and silver and precious [1]stones and pearls and fine linen
and purple and silk and scarlet, and every
kind of citron wood and every article of
ivory and every article *made* from very
costly wood and [2]bronze and iron and
marble,
13 and cinnamon and [1]spice and incense and perfume and frankincense and
wine and olive oil and fine flour and
wheat and cattle and sheep, and *cargoes*
of horses and chariots and [2]slaves and
[3a]human lives.
14 "The fruit [1]you long for has gone
from you, and all things that were luxurious and splendid have passed away from
you and *men* will no longer find them.
15 "The [a]merchants of [b]these things,
who became rich from her, will [c]stand at
a distance because of the fear of her torment, weeping and mourning,
16 saying, '[a]Woe, woe, [b]the great
city, she who [c]was clothed in fine linen
and purple and scarlet, and [1]adorned
with gold and precious [2]stones and
pearls;
17 for in [a]one hour such great wealth
has been laid [b]waste!' And [c]every ship-
master and every [1]passenger and sailor,
and as many as make their living by the
sea, [a]stood at a distance,
18 and were [a]crying out as they [b]saw
the smoke of her burning, saying, '[c]What
city is like [d]the great city?'
19 "And they threw [a]dust on their
heads and were crying out, weeping and
mourning, saying, '[b]Woe, woe, the great
city, in which all who had ships at sea
[c]became rich by her [1]wealth, for in
[b]one hour she has been laid [d]waste!'
20 "[a]Rejoice over her, O heaven, and
you [1]saints and [b]apostles and prophets,
because [c]God has [2]pronounced judgment for you against her."
21 ¶ Then [1]a [a]strong angel [b]took up
a stone like a great millstone and threw it
into the sea, saying, "So will Babylon,
[c]the great city, be thrown down with
violence, and [d]will not be found any
longer.
22 "And [a]the sound of harpists and
musicians and flute-players and trumpeters will not be heard in you any longer;
and no craftsman of any craft will be
found in you any longer; and the [b]sound
of a mill will not be heard in you any
longer;
23 and the light of a lamp will not
shine in you any longer; and the [a]voice
of the bridegroom and bride will not be
heard in you any longer; for your [b]mer-
chants were the great men of the earth,
because all the nations were deceived
[c]by your sorcery.
24 "And in her was found the [a]blood of
prophets and of [1]saints and of [b]all who
have been slain on the earth."

The Fourfold Hallelujah

19 After these things I heard something like a [a]loud voice of a great
multitude in heaven, saying,
¶ "[b]Hallelujah! [c]Salvation and [d]glory
and power belong to our God;
2 [a]BECAUSE HIS [b]JUDGMENTS ARE
[c]TRUE AND RIGHTEOUS; for He has judged
the [d]great harlot who was corrupting the
earth with her immorality, and HE HAS
[e]AVENGED THE BLOOD OF HIS BOND-
SERVANTS [1]ON HER."
3 And a second time they said,
"[a]Hallelujah! [b]HER SMOKE RISES UP FOREV-
ER AND EVER."
4 And the [a]twenty-four elders and
the [b]four living creatures [c]fell down and
worshiped God who sits on the throne
saying, "[d]Amen. [e]Hallelujah!"
5 And a voice came from the throne,
saying,
¶ "[a]Give praise to our God, all you His
bond-servants, [b]you who fear Him, the
small and the great."
6 Then I heard *something* like
[a]the voice of a great multitude and like
[b]the sound of many waters and like the
[c]sound of mighty peals of thunder, saying,
¶ "[a]Hallelujah! For the [d]Lord our
God, the Almighty, reigns.

Marriage of the Lamb

7 "Let us rejoice and be glad and [a]give
the glory to Him, for [b]the marriage of the
Lamb has come and His [1c]bride has
made herself ready."
8 It was given to her to clothe herself
in [a]fine linen, bright *and* clean; for the
fine linen is the [b]righteous acts of the
[1]saints.
9 ¶ Then [a]he *said to me, "[b]Write,
'[c]Blessed are those who are invited to
the marriage supper of the Lamb.' " And
he *said to me, "[d]These are true words
of God."
10 Then [a]I fell at his feet to worship
him. [b]But he *said to me, "Do not do
that; I am a [c]fellow servant of yours and
your brethren who [d]hold the testimony

10 [c]Rev 11:8 [d]Rev 17:12
11 [a]Ezek 27:9-25; Rev 18:3 [b]Ezek 27:27-34
12 [1]Lit *stone* [2]Or *brass* [a]Ezek 27:12-22; Rev 17:4
13 [1]Gr *amomon* [2]Lit *bodies* [3]Lit *souls of people* (Gr *anthropoi*) [a]1 Chr 5:21; Ezek 27:13; 1 Tim 1:10
14 [1]Lit *of your soul's desire*
15 [a]Rev 18:3 [b]Rev 18:12 [c]Rev 18:10
16 [1]Lit *gilded* [2]Lit *stone and pearl* [a]Rev 18:10 [b]Rev 18:10 [c]Rev 17:4
17 [1]Lit *one who sails to a place* [a]Rev 18:10 [b]Rev 17:16 [c]Ezek 27:28f
18 [a]Ezek 27:30 [b]Rev 18:9 [c]Ezek 27:32; Rev 13:4 [d]Rev 18:10
19 [1]Lit *costliness* [a]Josh 7:6; Job 2:12; Lam 2:10 [b]Rev 18:10 [c]Rev 18:3 [d]Rev 17:16
20 [1]Or *holy ones* [2]Lit *judged your judgment of her* [a]Jer 51:48; Rev 12:12 [b]Luke 11:49f [c]Rev 6:10
21 [1]Lit *One* [a]Rev 5:2 [b]Jer 51:63f [c]Rev 18:10 [d]Ezek 26:21
22 [a]Is 24:8; Ezek 26:13; Matt 9:23 [b]Eccl 12:4; Jer 25:10
23 [a]Jer 7:34 [b]Is 23:8; Rev 6:15 [c]Nah 3:4; Rev 9:21
24 [1]Or *holy ones* [a]Rev 16:6 [b]Matt 23:35
19:1 [a]Jer 51:48; Rev 11:15 [b]Ps 104:35; Rev 19:3 [c]Rev 7:10 [d]Rev 4:11
2 [1]Lit *from her hand* [a]Ps 19:9 [b]Rev 6:10 [c]Rev 16:7 [d]Rev 17:1 [e]Deut 32:43; 2 Kin 9:7; Rev 16:6
3 [a]Ps 104:35; Rev 19:1 [b]Is 34:10; Rev 14:11
4 [a]Rev 4:4 [b]Rev 4:6 [c]Rev 4:10 [d]Ps 106:48; Rev 5:14 [e]Ps 104:35; Rev 19:3
5 [a]Ps 22:23 [b]Rev 11:18
6 [a]Jer 51:48; Rev 11:15 [b]Ezek 1:24; Rev 1:15 [c]Rev 6:1 [d]Ps 93:1; Rev 1:8
7 [1]Lit *wife* [a]Rev 11:13 [b]Matt 22:2; Luke 12:36; John 3:29; Eph 5:23; Rev 19:9 [c]Matt 1:20; Rev 21:2

8 [1]Or *holy ones* [a]Rev 15:6 [b]Rev 15:4 9 [a]Rev 17:1 [b]Rev 1:19 [c]Matt 22:2f; Luke 14:15 [d]Rev 17:17 10 [a]Rev 22:8 [b]Acts 10:26; Rev 22:9 [c]Rev 1:1f [d]Rev 12:17

of Jesus; worship God. For the testimony
of Jesus is the spirit of prophecy."

The Coming of Christ

11 ¶ And I saw [a]heaven opened, and
behold, a [b]white horse, and He who sat
on it *is* called [c]Faithful and True, and
in [d]righteousness He judges and wages
war.
12 His [a]eyes *are* a flame of fire, and on
His head *are* many [b]diadems; and He has
a [c]name written *on Him* which no one
knows except Himself.
13 *He is* clothed with a [a]robe dipped
in blood, and His name is called [b]The
Word of God.
14 And the armies which are in heav-
en, clothed in [a]fine linen, [b]white *and*
clean, were following Him on white
horses.
15 [a]From His mouth comes a sharp
sword, so that [b]with it He may strike
down the nations, and He will [1c]rule
them with a rod of iron; and [d]He treads
the [2]wine press of the fierce wrath of
God, the Almighty.
16 And on His robe and on His thigh
He has [a]a name written, "[b]KING OF
KINGS, AND LORD OF LORDS."
17 ¶ Then I saw [1]an angel standing in
the sun, and he cried out with a loud
voice, saying to [a]all the birds which fly in
[b]midheaven, "[c]Come, assemble for the
great supper of God,
18 so that you may [a]eat the flesh of
kings and the flesh of [1]commanders and
the flesh of mighty men and the flesh of
horses and of those who sit on them and
the flesh of all men, [b]both free men and
slaves, and [c]small and great."
19 ¶ And I saw [a]the beast and [b]the
kings of the earth and their armies assembled to make war against Him who [c]sat
on the horse and against His army.

Doom of the Beast and False Prophet

20 And the beast was seized, and with
him the [a]false prophet who [b]performed
the signs [1c]in his presence, by which he
[d]deceived those who had received the
[e]mark of the beast and those who [f]wor-
shiped his image; these two were thrown
alive into the [g]lake of [h]fire which burns
with [2]brimstone.
21 And the rest were killed with the
sword which [a]came from the mouth of
Him who [b]sat on the horse, and [c]all the
birds were filled with their flesh.

Satan Bound

20 Then I saw [a]an angel coming
down from heaven, holding the
[b]key of the abyss and a great chain [1]in
his hand.
2 And he laid hold of the [a]dragon,
the serpent of old, who is the devil and
Satan, and [b]bound him for a thousand
years;
3 and he threw him into the [a]abyss,
and shut *it* and [b]sealed *it* over him, so
that he would [c]not deceive the nations
any longer, until the thousand years were
completed; after these things he must be
released for a short time.
4 ¶ Then I saw [a]thrones, and [b]they
sat on them, and [c]judgment was given to
them. And I *saw* [d]the souls of those who
had been beheaded because of [1]their
[e]testimony of Jesus and because of the
word of God, and those who had not
[f]worshiped the beast or his image, and
had not received the [g]mark on their forehead and on their hand; and they [h]came
to life and [i]reigned with Christ for a
thousand years.
5 The rest of the dead did not come to
life until the thousand years were completed. [a]This is the first resurrection.
6 [a]Blessed and holy is the one who
has a part in the first resurrection; over
these the [b]second death has no power,
but they will be [c]priests of God and of
Christ and will [d]reign with Him for a
thousand years.

Satan Freed, Doomed

7 ¶ When the thousand years are
completed, Satan will be [a]released from
his prison,
8 and will come out to [a]deceive the
nations which are in the [b]four corners of
the earth, [c]Gog and Magog, to [d]gather
them together for the war; the number of
them is like the [e]sand of the [1]seashore.
9 And they [a]came up on the [1]broad
plain of the earth and surrounded the
[b]camp of the [2]saints and the [c]beloved
city, and [d]fire came down from heaven
and devoured them.
10 And [a]the devil who [a]deceived
them was thrown into the [b]lake of fire
and [1]brimstone, where the [c]beast and
the [c]false prophet are also; and they will
be [d]tormented day and night forever and
ever.

Judgment at the Throne of God

11 ¶ Then I saw a great white [a]throne
and Him who sat upon it, from whose
[1]presence [b]earth and heaven fled away,
and [c]no place was found for them.
12 And I saw the dead, the [a]great and
the small, standing before the throne,

11 [a]Ezek 1:1; John 1:51; Rev 4:1 [b]Rev 6:2 [c]Rev 3:14 [d]Ps 96:13; Is 11:4
12 [a]Dan 10:6; Rev 1:14 [b]Rev 6:2 [c]Rev 2:17
13 [a]Is 63:3 [b]John 1:1
14 [a]Rev 19:8 [b]Rev 3:4
15 [1]Or *shepherd* [2]Lit *wine press of the wine of the wrath of God's anger* [a]Rev 1:16 [b]Is 11:4; 2 Thess 2:8 [c]Ps 2:9; Rev 2:27 [d]Is 63:3; Joel 3:13; Rev 14:19
16 [a]Rev 2:17 [b]Rev 17:14
17 [1]Lit *one* [a]Rev 19:21 [b]Rev 8:13 [c]1 Sam 17:44; Jer 12:9; Ezek 39:17
18 [1]I.e. chiliarchs, in command of one thousand troops [a]Ezek 39:18-20 [b]Rev 6:15 [c]Rev 11:18
19 [a]Rev 11:7 [b]Rev 16:14 [c]Rev 19:11
20 [1]Or *by his authority* [2]I.e. burning sulphur [a]Rev 16:13 [b]Rev 13:13 [c]Rev 13:12 [d]Rev 13:14 [e]Rev 13:16f [f]Rev 13:12 [g]Rev 20:10 [h]Is 30:33; Dan 7:11; Rev 14:10
21 [a]Rev 19:15 [b]Rev 19:11 [c]Rev 19:17
20:1 [1]Lit *upon* [a]Rev 10:1 [b]Rev 1:18
2 [a]Gen 3:1; Rev 12:9 [b]Is 24:22; 2 Pet 2:4; Jude 6
3 [a]Rev 20:1 [b]Dan 6:17; Matt 27:66 [c]Rev 12:9
4 [1]Lit *the* [a]Dan 7:9 [b]Matt 19:28; Rev 3:21 [c]Dan 7:22; 1 Cor 6:2 [d]Rev 6:9 [e]Rev 1:9 [f]Rev 13:12 [g]Rev 13:16f [h]John 14:19 [i]Rev 3:21
5 [a]Luke 14:14; Phil 3:11; 1 Thess 4:16
6 [a]Rev 14:13 [b]Rev 2:11 [c]Rev 1:6 [d]Rev 3:21
7 [a]Rev 20:2f
8 [1]Lit *sea* [a]Rev 12:9 [b]Ezek 7:2; Rev 7:1 [c]Ezek 38:2 [d]Rev 16:14 [e]Heb 11:12
9 [1]Lit *breadth of the earth* [2]Or *holy ones* [a]Ezek 38:9 [b]Deut 23:14 [c]Ps 87:2 [d]Ezek 38:22; Rev 13:13
10 [1]I.e. burning sulphur [a]Rev 20:2f [b]Rev 19:20 [c]Rev 16:13 [d]Rev 14:10f
11 [1]Lit *face* [a]Rev 4:2 [b]Rev 6:14 [c]Dan 2:35; Rev 12:8 **12** [a]Rev 11:18

and [1b]books were opened; and another [2]book was opened, which is [c]*the book* of life; and the dead [d]were judged from the things which were written in the [1]books, [e]according to their deeds.

13 And the sea gave up the dead which were in it, and [a]death and Hades [b]gave up the dead which were in them; and they were judged, every one *of them* [c]according to their deeds.

14 Then [a]death and Hades were thrown into [b]the lake of fire. This is the [c]second death, the lake of fire.

15 And if [1]anyone's name was not found written in [a]the book of life, he was thrown into the lake of fire.

The New Heaven and Earth

21 Then I saw [a]a new heaven and a new earth; for [b]the first heaven and the first earth passed away, and there is no longer *any* sea.

2 And I saw [a]the holy city, [b]new Jerusalem, [c]coming down out of heaven from God, [d]made ready as a bride adorned for her husband.

3 And I heard a loud voice from the throne, saying, "Behold, [a]the tabernacle of God is among men, and He will [1b]dwell among them, and they shall be His people, and God Himself will be among them,[2]

4 and He will [a]wipe away every tear from their eyes; and [b]there will no longer be *any* death; [c]there will no longer be *any* mourning, or crying, or pain; [d]the first things have passed away."

5 ¶ And [a]He who sits on the throne said, "Behold, I am [b]making all things new." And He *said, "Write, for [c]these words are faithful and true."

6 Then He said to me, "[1a]It is done. I am the [b]Alpha and the Omega, the beginning and the end. [c]I will give to the one who thirsts from the spring of the [d]water of life without cost.

7 "[a]He who overcomes will inherit these things, and [b]I will be his God and he will be My son.

8 "[a]But for the cowardly and [1]unbelieving and abominable and murderers and immoral persons and sorcerers and idolaters and all liars, their part *will be* in [b]the lake that burns with fire and [2]brimstone, which is the [c]second death."

9 ¶ [a]Then one of the seven angels who had the [b]seven bowls [1]full of the [c]seven last plagues came and spoke with me, saying, "[a]Come here, I will show you the [d]bride, the wife of the Lamb."

The New Jerusalem

10 And [a]he carried me away [1b]in the Spirit to a great and high mountain, and showed me [c]the holy city, Jerusalem, coming down out of heaven from God,

11 having [a]the glory of God. Her [1]brilliance was like a very costly stone, as a [b]stone of [c]crystal-clear jasper.

12 [1]It had a great and high wall, [1a]with twelve [b]gates, and at the gates twelve angels; and names *were* written on them, which are *the names* of the twelve tribes of the sons of Israel.

13 *There were* three gates on the east and three gates on the north and three gates on the south and three gates on the west.

14 And the wall of the city had [a]twelve foundation stones, and on them *were* the twelve names of the [b]twelve apostles of the Lamb.

15 ¶ The one who spoke with me had a [1]gold measuring [a]rod to measure the city, and its [b]gates and its wall.

16 The city is laid out as a square, and its length is as great as the width; and he measured the city with the [1]rod, [2]fifteen hundred miles; its length and width and height are equal.

17 And he measured its wall, [1]seventy-two yards, *according to* [a]human [2]measurements, which are *also* [b]angelic *measurements.*

18 The material of the wall was [a]jasper; and the city was [b]pure gold, like [1]clear [c]glass.

19 [a]The foundation stones of the city wall were adorned with every kind of precious stone. The first foundation stone was [b]jasper; the second, sapphire; the third, chalcedony; the fourth, [c]emerald;

20 the fifth, sardonyx; the sixth, [a]sardius; the seventh, chrysolite; the eighth, beryl; the ninth, topaz; the tenth, chrysoprase; the eleventh, jacinth; the twelfth, amethyst.

21 And the twelve [a]gates were twelve [b]pearls; each one of the gates was a single pearl. And the street of the city was [c]pure gold, like transparent [d]glass.

22 ¶ I saw [a]no [1]temple in it, for the [b]Lord God the Almighty and the [c]Lamb are its [1]temple.

23 And the city [a]has no need of the sun or of the moon to shine on it, for [b]the glory of God has illumined it, and its lamp *is* the [c]Lamb.

24 [a]The nations will walk by its light, and the [b]kings of the earth [1]will bring their glory into it.

25 In the daytime (for [a]there will be

12 [1]Or *scrolls* [2]Or *scroll* [b]Dan 7:10 [c]Rev 3:5 [d]Rev 11:18 [e]Matt 16:27; Rev 2:23
13 [a]1 Cor 15:26; Rev 1:18 [b]Is 26:19 [c]Matt 16:27; Rev 2:23
14 [a]1 Cor 15:26; Rev 1:18 [b]Rev 19:20 [c]Rev 20:6
15 [1]Lit *anyone was* [a]Rev 3:5
21:1 [a]Is 65:17; 2 Pet 3:13 [b]2 Pet 3:10; Rev 20:11
2 [a]Is 52:1; Rev 11:2 [b]Rev 3:12 [c]Heb 11:10; Rev 21:10 [d]Is 61:10; Rev 19:7
3 [1]Or *tabernacle* [2]One early ms reads, and be *their God* [a]Lev 26:11f; Ezek 37:27; Heb 8:2; Rev 7:15 [b]John 14:23; 2 Cor 6:16
4 [a]Is 25:8; Rev 7:17 [b]1 Cor 15:26; Rev 20:14 [c]Is 35:10 [d]2 Cor 5:17; Heb 12:27
5 [a]Rev 4:9 [b]2 Cor 5:17; Heb 12:27 [c]Rev 19:9
6 [1]Lit *They are* [a]Rev 10:6 [b]Rev 1:8 [c]Is 55:1; John 4:10; Rev 7:17 [d]Rev 7:17
7 [a]Rev 2:7 [b]2 Sam 7:14; Ps 89:26f; 2 Cor 6:16; Rev 21:3
8 [1]Or *untrustworthy* [2]I.e. burning sulphur [a]1 Cor 6:9; Gal 5:19-21; Rev 9:21 [b]Rev 19:20 [c]Rev 2:11
9 [1]Lit *who were full* [a]Rev 17:1 [b]Rev 15:7 [c]Rev 15:1 [d]Rev 19:7
10 [1]Or *in spirit* [a]Ezek 40:2; Rev 17:3 [b]Rev 1:10 [c]Rev 21:2
11 [1]Lit *luminary* [a]Is 60:1f; Ezek 43:2; Rev 15:8 [b]Rev 4:3 [c]Rev 4:6
12 [1]Lit *having* [a]Ezek 48:31-34 [b]Rev 21:15
14 [a]Heb 11:10 [b]Acts 1:26
15 [1]Lit *measure, a gold reed* [a]Ezek 40:3; Rev 11:1 [b]Rev 21:12
16 [1]Lit *reed* [2]Lit *twelve thousand stadia*; a stadion was approx 600 ft
17 [1]Lit *one hundred forty-four cubits* [2]Lit *measure* [a]Deut 3:11; Rev 13:18 [b]Rev 21:9
18 [1]Lit *pure* [a]Rev 21:11 [b]Rev 21:21 [c]Rev 4:6
19 [a]Ex 28:17-20; Is 54:11f; Ezek 28:13 [b]Rev 21:11 [c]Rev 4:3 **20** [a]Rev 4:3 **21** [a]Rev 21:12 [b]Rev 17:4 [c]Rev 21:18 [d]Rev 4:6 **22** [1]Or *sanctuary* [a]Matt 24:2; John 4:21 [b]Rev 1:8 [c]Rev 5:6 **23** [a]Is 24:23; Rev 21:25 [b]Rev 21:11 [c]Rev 5:6 **24** [1]Lit *bring* [a]Is 60:3 [b]Ps 72:10f; Is 49:23; Rev 21:26 **25** [a]Zech 14:7; Rev 21:23

no night there) [b]its gates [c]will never be
closed;
26 and [a]they will bring the glory and
the honor of the nations into it;
27 and [a]nothing unclean, and no one
who practices abomination and lying,
shall ever come into it, but only those
[1]whose names are [b]written in the
Lamb's book of life.

The River and the Tree of Life

22 Then [a]he showed me a [b]river
of the [c]water of life, [1]clear [d]as
crystal, coming from the throne of God
and of [2]the Lamb,
2 in the middle of [a]its street. [b]On
either side of the river was [c]the tree of
life, bearing twelve [1]*kinds of* fruit, yielding
its fruit every month; and the leaves
of the tree were for the healing of the
nations.
3 [a]There will no longer be any curse;
and [b]the throne of God and of the Lamb
will be in it, and His bond-servants will
[c]serve Him;
4 they will [a]see His face, and His
[b]name *will be* on their [c]foreheads.
5 And [a]there will no longer be *any*
night; and they [1]will not have need [b]of
the light of a lamp nor the light of the sun,
because the Lord God will illumine them;
and they will [c]reign forever and ever.
6 ¶ And [a]he said to me, "[b]These
words are faithful and true"; and the
Lord, the [c]God of the spirits of the
prophets, [d]sent His angel to show to His
bond-servants the things which must
soon take place.
7 ¶ "And behold, [a]I am coming
quickly. [b]Blessed is he who [1]heeds [c]the
words of the prophecy of this book."
8 ¶ [a]I, John, am the one who heard
and saw these things. And when I heard
and saw, [b]I fell down to worship at the
feet of the angel who showed me these
things.
9 But [a]he *said to me, "Do not do
that. I am a [b]fellow servant of yours and
of your brethren the prophets and of
those who [1]heed the words of [c]this
book. Worship God."

The Final Message

10 ¶ And he *said to me, "[a]Do not
seal up [b]the words of the prophecy of
this book, [c]for the time is near.
11 "[a]Let the one who does wrong, still
do wrong; and the one who is filthy, still
be filthy; and let the one who is righteous,
still practice righteousness; and
the one who is holy, still keep himself
holy."
12 ¶ "Behold, [a]I am coming quickly,
and My [b]reward *is* with Me, [c]to render
to every man [1]according to what he has
done.
13 "I am the [a]Alpha and the Omega,
[b]the first and the last, [c]the beginning
and the end."
14 ¶ Blessed are those who [a]wash
their robes, so that they may have the
right to [b]the tree of life, and may [c]enter
by the [d]gates into the city.
15 [a]Outside are the [b]dogs and the
sorcerers and the immoral persons and
the murderers and the idolaters, and
everyone who loves and practices lying.
16 ¶ "[a]I, Jesus, have sent [b]My angel
to testify to you these things [1c]for the
churches. I am [d]the root and the
[e]descendant of David, the bright [f]morning
star."
17 ¶ The [a]Spirit and the [b]bride say,
"Come." And let the one who hears say,
"Come." And [c]let the one who is thirsty
come; let the one who wishes take the
[d]water of life without cost.
18 ¶ I testify to everyone who hears
[a]the words of the prophecy of this book:
if anyone [b]adds to them, God will add to
him [c]the plagues which are written in
[a]this book;
19 and if anyone [a]takes away from the
[b]words of the book of this prophecy, God
will take away his part from [c]the tree of
life and [1]from the holy city, [d]which are
written in this book.
20 ¶ He who [a]testifies to these things
says, "Yes, [b]I am coming quickly."
Amen. [c]Come, Lord Jesus.
21 ¶ [a]The grace of the Lord Jesus be
with [1]all. Amen.

25 [b]Rev 21:12 [c]Is 60:11 **26** [a]Ps 72:10f; Is 49:23 **27** [1]Lit *who have been* [a]Is 52:1; Ezek 44:9; Zech 14:21; Rev 22:14f [b]Rev 3:5 **22:1** [1]Lit *bright* [2]Or *the Lamb. In the middle of its street, and on either side of the river, was* [a]Rev 1:1 [b]Ps 46:4; Ezek 47:1 [c]Zech 14:8; Rev 7:17 [d]Rev 4:6 **2** [1]Or *crops of fruit* [a]Rev 21:21 [b]Ezek 47:12 [c]Gen 2:9; Rev 2:7 **3** [a]Zech 14:11 [b]Rev 21:3 [c]Rev 7:15 **4** [a]Ps 17:15; Matt 5:8 [b]Rev 14:1 [c]Rev 7:3 **5** [1]Lit *do not have* [a]Zech 14:7; Rev 21:25 [b]Is 60:19; Rev 21:23 [c]Dan 7:18; Matt 19:28; Rom 5:17; Rev 20:4 **6** [a]Rev 1:1 [b]Rev 19:9 [c]1 Cor 14:32; Heb 12:9 [d]Rev 1:1 **7** [1]Lit *keeps* [a]Rev 1:3 [b]Rev 1:3 [c]Rev 1:11 **8** [a]Rev 1:1 [b]Rev 19:10 **9** [1]Lit *keep* [a]Rev 19:10 [b]Rev 1:1 [c]Rev 1:11 **10** [a]Dan 8:26; Rev 10:4 [b]Rev 1:11 [c]Rev 1:3 **11** [a]Ezek 3:27; Dan 12:10 **12** [1]Lit *as his work is* [a]Rev 22:7 [b]Is 40:10 [c]Ps 28:4; Jer 17:10; Matt 16:27; Rev 2:23 **13** [a]Rev 1:8 [b]Is 44:6; Rev 1:17 [c]Rev 21:6 **14** [a]Rev 7:14 [b]Gen 2:9; Rev 22:2 [c]Rev 21:27 [d]Rev 21:12 **15** [a]Matt 8:12; 1 Cor 6:9f; Gal 5:19ff; Rev 21:8 [b]Deut 23:18; Matt 7:6; Phil 3:2 **16** [1]Or *concerning* [a]Rev 1:1 [b]Rev 1:1 [c]Rev 1:4 [d]Rev 5:5 [e]Matt 1:1 [f]Matt 2:2; Rev 2:28 **17** [a]Rev 2:7 [b]Rev 21:2 [c]Is 55:1; Rev 21:6 [d]Rev 7:17 **18** [a]Rev 22:7 [b]Deut 4:2; Prov 30:6 [c]Rev 15:6-16:21 **19** [1]Lit *out of* [a]Deut 4:2; Prov 30:6 [b]Rev 22:7 [c]Rev 22:2 [d]Rev 21:10-22:5 **20** [a]Rev 1:2 [b]Rev 22:7 [c]1 Cor 16:22 **21** [1]One early ms reads *the saints* [a]Rom 16:20

The New American Standard

CONCORDANCE

to the Old and New Testaments

A collection of the principal common words with their most widely used examples in text and lesser usages in reference. Related words, or synonyms follow the key word. The key word is abbreviated in the text to its first letter, e.g., " accept" is "a." Variants add suffixes or prefixes, e.g., "accepted" appears as "a-ed."

Book Abbreviations

Genesis	Gen
Exodus	Ex
Leviticus	Lev
Numbers	Num
Deuteronomy	Deut
Joshua	Josh
Judges	Judg
Ruth	Ruth
1 Samuel	1 Sam
2 Samuel	2 Sam
1 Kings	1 Kin
2 Kings	2 Kin
1 Chronicles	1 Chr
2 Chronicles	2 Chr
Ezra	Ezra
Nehemiah	Neh
Esther	Esth
Job	Job
Psalms	Ps
Proverbs	Prov
Ecclesiastes	Eccl
Song of Solomon	Song
Isaiah	Is
Jeremiah	Jer
Lamentations	Lam
Ezekiel	Ezek
Daniel	Dan
Hosea	Hos
Joel	Joel
Amos	Amos
Obadiah	Obad
Jonah	Jon
Micah	Mic
Nahum	Nah
Habakkuk	Hab
Zephaniah	Zeph
Haggai	Hag
Zechariah	Zech
Malachi	Mal
Matthew	Matt
Mark	Mark
Luke	Luke
John	John
Acts	Acts
Romans	Rom
1 Corinthians	1 Cor
2 Corinthians	2 Cor
Galatians	Gal
Ephesians	Eph
Philippians	Phil
Colossians	Col
1 Thessalonians	1 Thess
2 Thessalonians	2 Thess
1 Timothy	1 Tim
2 Timothy	2 Tim
Titus	Titus
Philemon	Philem
Hebrews	Heb
James	James
1 Peter	1 Pet
2 Peter	2 Pet
1 John	1 John
2 John	2 John
3 John	3 John
Jude	Jude
Revelation	Rev

A

AARON
brother of Moses Ex 4:14
spokesman for Moses Ex 4:28; 7:1-2
as priest Ex 28:1; 29:44
rod of Num 17:8; Heb 9:4
critical of Moses Num 12:1
death Deut 10:6

ABBA *father*
A! Father Mark 14:36
we cry out, **A!** Rom 8:15

ABEL
son of Adam Gen 4:2
shepherd Gen 4:2
favored by God Gen 4:4
slain by Cain Gen 4:8
called righteous Matt 23:35

ABIHU
son of Aaron Ex 6:23
priest Ex 28:1
disobeyed God Lev 10:1
judged by God Lev 10:2

ABIJAH
1 *son of Samuel* 1 Sam 8:2
2 *son of Jeroboam* 1 Kin 14:1
3 *son of Becher* 1 Chr 7:8
4 *line of Eleazar* 1 Chr 24:10
5 *king of Judah* 2 Chr 12:16
6 *Hezekiah's mother* 2 Chr 29:1
7 *priest* Neh 10:7; 12:4

ABIMELECH
1 *king of Gerar* Gen 20:1-18
2 *king of Gerar* Gen 26:1ff
3 *king of Shechem* Judg 9:1ff
4 *priest* 1 Chr 18:16
5 *Psalm title* Ps 34

ABNER
Saul's commander 1 Sam 17:55
loyal to David 2 Sam 3:12ff
killed by Joab 2 Sam 3:27
mourned by David 2 Sam 3:32

ABRAHAM
covenant Gen 17:1-8
promise of Isaac Gen 17:19
asked the Lord Gen 18:22ff
offers Isaac Gen 22:9,10
death Gen 25:8
righteousness of Rom 4:3-9

ABSALOM
son of David 2 Sam 13:1
his revolt 2 Sam 15:1,2
popular 2 Sam 15:6
slain by Joab 2 Sam 18:15

ABSTAIN *refrain from*
a from wine Num 6:3
a-ing from foods 1 Tim 4:3
a from wickedness 2 Tim 2:19
a from fleshly lusts 1 Pet 2:11

ABUSE (n) *insulting speech*
hurling **a** at Him Matt 27:39
was hurling **a** Luke 23:39

ABUSE (v) *hurt, molest*
a-d her all night Judg 19:25
uncircumcised...**a** me 1 Chr 10:4

ABUSIVE *filthy, vulgar*
a speech from your Col 3:8
strife, **a** language 1 Tim 6:4

ACCEPT *receive*
a the work of Deut 33:11
a good from God Job 2:10
the LORD **a-ed** Job Job 42:9
a-ed no chastening Jer 2:30
hear the word and **a** Mark 4:20
God has **a-ed** him Rom 14:3
a one another Rom 15:7

ACCOUNT (n) *reckoning*
the **a** of the heavens Gen 2:4
On whose **a** *has* this Jon 1:8
settled **a-s** with Matt 25:19
who will give an **a** Heb 13:17

ACCOUNT (v) *reckon*
do not **a** *this* sin Num 12:11
I am **a-ed** wicked Job 9:29
You have taken **a** of Ps 56:8
are **a-ed** as nothing Dan 4:35

ACCUSATION *charge of wrong*
wrote an **a** against Ezra 4:6
find a ground of **a** Dan 6:4
What **a** do you John 18:29
a against my nation Acts 28:19
Do not receive an **a** 1 Tim 5:19

ACCUSE *testify against*
a-d his brother Deut 19:18
a-s you in judgment Is 54:17
He was being **a-d** Matt 27:12
a-ing...vehemently Luke 23:10
a you before the John 5:45
alternately **a-ing** Rom 2:15
not **a-d** of dissipation Titus 1:6
unjustly **a-ing** us 3 John 10

ACHAIA
province of Greece Acts 18:12; Rom 15:26; 1 Cor 16:15

ACHAN
stole from Jericho Josh 7:1
executed by people Josh 7:25

ACQUIT *declare innocent*
not **a** me of my guilt Job 10:14
A me of hidden *faults* Ps 19:12
You will not be **a-ted** Jer 49:12

ADAM
1 *first man* Gen 2:20
fall of man Gen 3:6,7
type of Christ Rom 5:14
compared to Jesus 1 Cor 15:22
2 *site in Jordan Valley* Josh 3:16

ADAR
twelfth month of Hebrew calendar Ezra 6:15
Purim observed Esth 3:7; 9:19ff

ADMINISTRATION
a of the province Dan 3:12
healings, helps, **a-s** 1 Cor 12:28
in our **a** of this 2 Cor 8:20
a of the mystery Eph 3:9

ADMONISH *warn*
prophets...had **a-ed** Neh 9:26
How shall I **a** you Lam 2:13
not cease to **a** each Acts 20:31
able also to **a** one Rom 15:14
a-ing one another Col 3:16
a the unruly 1 Thess 5:14
a him as a brother 2 Thess 3:15

ADONIJAH
1 *son of David* 2 Sam 3:4
aspired to throne 1 Kin 1:5ff
pardoned 1 Kin 1:52ff
executed 1 Kin 2:25
2 *Levite* 2 Chr 17:8
3 *of the restoration* Neh 10:16

ADOPTION *acceptance*
spirit of **a** as sons Rom 8:15
to whom belongs...**a** Rom 9:4
receive the **a** as sons Gal 4:5
predestined us to **a** Eph 1:5

ADORN *array, clothe*
A yourself with Job 40:10
as a bride **a-s** herself Is 61:10
a-ed with beautiful Luke 21:5
women to **a** 1 Tim 2:9
a the doctrine of God Titus 2:10

a-ed with gold Rev 17:4
as a bride **a-ed** Rev 21:2

ADULTERER
a and the adulteress Lev 20:10
eye of the a waits Job 24:15
associate with **a-s** Ps 50:18
a-s, nor effeminate 1 Cor 6:9
a-s God will judge Heb 13:4

ADULTERESS
a shall surely be Lev 20:10
a who flatters with Prov 2:16
mouth of an a Prov 22:14
You a wife, who Ezek 16:32
they are **a-es** Ezek 23:45
shall be called an a Rom 7:3

ADULTERY
shall not commit a Ex 20:14
man who commits a Lev 20:10
a-ies of faithless Jer 3:8
worn out by **a-ies** Ezek 23:43
committed a with her Matt 5:28
woman commits a Matt 5:32
Do not commit a Luke 18:20
eyes full of a 2 Pet 2:14

ADVICE *counsel*
forsook the a 1 Kin 12:13
a of the young 2 Chr 10:14
a of the cunning Job 5:13
they took his a Acts 5:40
have followed my a Acts 27:21

ADVISER *counselor*
with his a Ahuzzath Gen 26:26
Pharaoh's wisest **a-s** Is 19:11

ADVOCATE *defender, witness*
my a is on high Job 16:19
A with the Father 1 John 2:1

AFFECTION *devotion, love*
set His a to love Deut 10:15
in your own **a-s** 2 Cor 6:12
a of Christ Jesus Phil 1:8
fond an a for you 1 Thess 2:8

AFFLICTION *oppression*
my a and the toil Gen 31:42
the land of my a Gen 41:52
the bread of a Deut 16:3
LORD saw the a 2 Kin 14:26
You saw the a Neh 9:9
afflicted in their a Job 36:15
Look upon my a Ps 25:18
a severe a Eccl 6:2
a or persecution Mark 4:17
healed of her a Mark 5:29
a-s await me Acts 20:23
out of much a 2 Cor 2:4
great ordeal of a 2 Cor 8:2
to suffer a 1 Thess 3:4

AGRIPPA
1 *Herod Agrippa I* see **HEROD**
2 *Herod Agrippa II* see **HEROD**

AHAB
1 *king of Israel* 1 Kin 16:28
son of Omri 1 Kin 16:29
married Jezebel 1 Kin 16:31
idolater 1 Kin 16:33
2 *false prophet* Jer 29:21,22

AHASUERUS
1 *Persian king, Xerxes I* Ezra 4:6; Book of Esther
2 *father of Darius the Mede* Dan 9:1

AHAZ
1 *son of Jotham* 2 Kin 15:38
king of Judah 2 Kin 16:2
2 *line of Jonathan* 1 Chr 8:35

AHIJAH / AHIAH
1 *prophet of Shiloh* 1 Kin 14:2
2 *of Issachar* 1 Kin 15:27
3 *son of Jerahmeel* 1 Chr 2:25
4 *the Pelonite* 1 Chr 11:36
5 *under Nehemiah* Neh 10:26

AI
place near Bethel Gen 12:8
defeat of Israelites Josh 7:5
captured Josh 8:23,29

AIJALON
1 *city of refuge* Josh 10:12
Levitical city Josh 21:24
2 *valley* Josh 19:42
3 *Zebulunite town* Judg 12:12

ALABASTER *whitish stone*
stones and a 1 Chr 29:2
pillars of a Song 5:15
brought an a vial Luke 7:37

ALEXANDER
1 *son of Simon of Cyrene* Mark 15:21
2 *of priestly family* Acts 4:6
3 *Ephesian Jew* Acts 19:33
4 *apostate teacher* 1 Tim 1:20
5 *enemy of Paul* 2 Tim 4:14

ALEXANDRIAN
1 *of Alexandria* Acts 6:9
2 *ship* Acts 27:6; 28:11
3 *Apollos* Acts 18:24

ALPHA
first letter of Gr. alphabet Rev 1:8
title of Jesus Christ Rev 21:6
expresses eternalness of God Rev 22:13

ALTAR *place of sacrifice*
offerings on the a Gen 8:20
Moses built an a Ex 17:15
fire on the a Lev 6:9
Gideon built an a Judg 6:24
erect an a to 2 Sam 24:18
go to the a of God Ps 43:4
a-s may become waste Ezek 6:6
offering at the a Matt 5:23
a that sanctifies Matt 23:19
golden a of incense Heb 9:4
we have an a Heb 13:10
horns of the golden a Rev 9:13

AMASA
1 *son of Abigail* 1 Chr 2:17
Absalom's commander 2 Sam 17:25
pardoned 2 Sam 19:13
2 *an Ephraimite* 2 Chr 28:12

AMAZIAH
1 *king of Judah* 2 Kin 12:21
son of Joash 2 Kin 14:1
2 *a Simeonite* 1 Chr 4:34
3 *son of Hilkiah* 1 Chr 6:45
4 *a priest of Bethel* Amos 7:10

AMBASSADOR *envoy*
a-s of peace weep Is 33:7
a-s for Christ 2 Cor 5:20
an a in chains Eph 6:20

AMEN *so be it*
people shall say, A Deut 27:16
the LORD forever! A Ps 89:52
glory forever…A Phil 4:20
the A, the faithful Rev 3:14
A. Come, Lord Jesus Rev 22:20

AMMONITES
tribes E of Jordan Gen 19:38
defeated Israel Judg 3:13
hired Arameans 2 Sam 10:6
fought against Judah 2 Kin 24:2

AMNON
1 *eldest son of David* 2 Sam 3:2
raped his sister 2 Sam 13:2ff
ordered killed 2 Sam 13:28
2 *line of Judah* 1 Chr 4:20

AMON
1 *Ahab's governor* 1 Kin 22:26
2 *king of Judah* 2 Kin 21:18-26
3 *of the Nethinims* Neh 7:59
4 *Egyptian deity* Jer 46:25
AMORITES
tribe on both sides of Jordan Gen 15:16; Ex 34:11; Deut 1:27; Judg 11:23; Amos 2:9
AMOS
prophet to Israel Book of Amos
AMRAM
1 *father of Moses* Ex 6:18-20; 1 Chr 23:13
2 *son of Bani* Ezra 10:34
ANAK / ANAKIM
pre-Israelite tribe of Palestine Num 13:22-33
giants Deut 2:10; Josh 14:15
ANCHOR
they weighed **a** Acts 27:13
they cast four **a-s** Acts 27:29
an **a** of the soul Heb 6:19
ANDREW
fisherman Matt 4:18
brother of Peter Matt 4:18
receives Jesus John 1:40-42
apostle Luke 6:14
ANGEL *divine messenger*
send His **a** before Gen 24:7
a-s...were ascending Gen 28:12
an **a** to Jerusalem 1 Chr 21:15
bread of **a-s** Ps 78:25
Praise Him, all His **a-s** Ps 148:2
a of His presence Is 63:9
a who was speaking Zech 4:4
command His **a-s** Matt 4:6
a Gabriel was sent Luke 1:26
they are like **a-s** Luke 20:36
two **a-s** in white John 20:12
like the face of an **a** Acts 6:15
as an **a** of light 2 Cor 11:14
worship of the **a-s** Col 2:18
entertained **a-s** Heb 13:2
God did not spare **a-s** 2 Pet 2:4
a of the church Rev 2:1
ANGEL OF THE LORD
a called to Abraham Gen 22:15
a took his stand Num 22:22
I have seen the **a** Judg 6:22
a said to Elijah 2 Kin 1:3
a destroying 1 Chr 21:12
a encamps around those Ps 34:7
a admonished Joshua Zech 3:6
a commanded him Matt 1:24
a appeared to Joseph Matt 2:13
a...opened the gates Acts 5:19
ANOINT (v) *sprinkle oil upon*
a them and ordain Ex 28:41
a Aaron and his sons Ex 30:30
LORD **a-ed** you king 1 Sam 15:17
a-ed my head with oil Ps 23:5
a the most holy *place* Dan 9:24
has **a-ed** My body Mark 14:8
did not **a** My head Luke 7:46
and **a-ed** my eyes John 9:11
a-ed...feet of Jesus John 12:3
a-ed Him...Holy Spirit Acts 10:38
a-ing him with oil James 5:14
ANOINTED (adj) *consecrated*
if the **a** priest sins Lev 4:3
not touch My **a** 1 Chr 16:22
a cherub who Ezek 28:14
the two **a** ones Zech 4:14
ANOINTED (n) *consecrated one*
walk before My **a** 1 Sam 2:35
he is the LORD's **a** 1 Sam 24:10
against His **A** Ps 2:2
ANOINTING (adj) *consecration*
spices for the **a** oil Ex 25:6
shall be a holy **a** oil Ex 30:31
for the LORD's **a** oil Lev 10:7
ANOINTING (n) *consecration*
a will qualify them Ex 40:15
a from the Holy 1 John 2:20
His **a** teaches you 1 John 2:27
ANTICHRIST *foe of Christ*
a-s have appeared 1 John 2:18
This is the **a** 1 John 2:22
the *spirit* of the **a** 1 John 4:3
deceiver and the **a** 2 John 7
ANTIOCH
1 *city in Syria* Acts 6:5; 11:19,26
2 *city in Galatia* Acts 13:14; 14:19
APOLLOS
Alexandrian Jew Acts 18:24
taught at Ephesus Acts 18:24
taught at Corinth 1 Cor 3:4,6
APOSTASY *faithlessness*
a-ies are numerous Jer 5:6
Turned away in...**a** Jer 8:5
I will heal their **a** Hos 14:4
unless the **a** comes 2 Thess 2:3
APOSTLE *sent with authority*
the twelve **a-s** Matt 10:2
named as **a-s** Luke 6:13
called *as* an **a** Rom 1:1
an **a** of Gentiles Rom 11:13
not fit to be called an **a** 1 Cor 15:9
men are false **a-s** 2 Cor 11:13
He gave some *as* **a-s** Eph 4:11
Jesus, the **A** and Heb 3:1
a-s of the Lamb Rev 21:14
APPLE *fruit*
as the **a** of the eye Ps 17:8
Like **a-s** of gold Prov 25:11
Refresh me with **a-s** Song 2:5
touches the **a** of His Zech 2:8
AQUILA
a native of Pontus Acts 18:2
Corinthian Christian Acts 18:18
co-worker with Paul Rom 16:3
ARAB
1 *town in Judah* Josh 15:52
2 *ethnic identity* 1 Kin 10:15; Neh 2:19; Is 13:20
ARABAH
1 *desert steppe* Is 35:1,6; Jer 52:7
2 *Jordan rift valley* Deut 1:1; Josh 3:17
3 *Dead Sea* Josh 3:16; 2 Kin 14:25
ARABIA
land SE of Israel / Judah Is 21:13; Ezek 30:5; Gal 1:17; 4:25
ARAM
1 *son of Shem* Gen 10:22,23
2 *line of Asher* 1 Chr 7:34
3 *ancestor of Jesus, shortened to Ram* Ruth 4:19; Matt 1:3; Luke 3:33
4 *Syria and N Mesopotamia* Num 23:7; 1 Kin 11:25; 2 Kin 13:19; Is 7:8
ARAMAIC
Semitic language 2 Kin 18:26; Ezra 4:7; Is 36:11; Dan 2:4
ARAMEANS
tribes of Aram 2 Sam 8:5; 1 Kin 20:20; 2 Kin 24:2
ARARAT
kingdom and mountain range in Armenia Gen 8:4; 2 Kin 19:37; Jer 51:27
ARAUNAH
Jebusite owner of threshing floor on Mt. Moriah 2 Sam 24:16,18
David purchases threshing floor for altar and later temple 2 Sam 24:23,24
see also **ORNAN**

ARCHANGEL
voice of *the* a 1 Thess 4:16
But Michael the a Jude 9
ARIEL
1 *a Moabite* 2 Sam 23:20; 1 Chr 11:22
2 *applied to Jerusalem* Is 29:1ff
3 *sent by Ezra* Ezra 8:16
ARISE *rise, stand*
A, walk about the Gen 13:17
Abraham **arose** early Gen 19:27
will a and play Deut 31:16
you have **a-n** early 1 Sam 29:10
arose and tore his robe Job 1:20
when God **a-s** Job 31:14
A, O LORD; save me Ps 3:7
Though war **a** Ps 27:3
A, my darling Song 2:13
a-n *anyone* greater Matt 11:11
false prophets will a Matt 24:11
arose from the dead Acts 10:41
a from the dead Eph 5:14
ARK *chest, vessel*
a of gopher wood Gen 6:14
into the a to Noah Gen 7:9
a of acacia wood Ex 37:1
a of the covenant Josh 4:7
Noah entered the **a** Matt 24:38
a of His covenant Rev 11:19
ARM (v) *mobilize*
A men from among Num 31:3
a-ed for battle Num 32:29
a-ed with iron 2 Sam 23:7
a yourselves also 1 Pet 4:1
ARTAXERXES
Persian king Ezra 4:7,8; 7:1,12; Neh 2:1; 5:14
ARTEMIS
Greek goddess Acts 19:24ff
ASA
1 *king of Judah* 1 Kin 15:8-24; 2 Chr 14:8-15
2 *a Levite* 1 Chr 9:16
ASCEND *go up*
a into the hill Ps 24:3
If I **a** to heaven Ps 139:8
Who has **a-ed** into Prov 30:4
breath of man **a-s** Eccl 3:21
has **a-ed** into heaven John 3:13
Son of Man **a-ing** John 6:62
a-ed to the Father John 20:17
who **a-ed** far above Eph 4:10
ASCENT *hill, rise*
by the a of Heres Judg 8:13
a of the…Olives 2 Sam 15:30
Song of **A-s** Ps 120-134
ASH
but dust and **a-es** Gen 18:27
from the **a** heap 1 Sam 2:8
a-es on her head 2 Sam 13:19
a-es were poured 1 Kin 13:5
proverbs of **a-es** Job 13:12
repent in dust and **a-es** Job 42:6
garland instead of **a-es** Is 61:3
roll in **a-es** Jer 6:26
sackcloth and **a-es** Luke 10:13
a-es of a heifer Heb 9:13
ASHDOD
Philistine city Josh 15:47; 1 Sam 5:1,6; Amos 1:8
ASHER
1 *eighth son of Jacob* Gen 35:26; 49:20
2 *tribe of Israel* Num 1:41; 13:13; Rev 7:6
3 *town in hill country* Josh 17:7
ASHERAH
Canaanite goddess and symbol Deut 16:21; Judg 6:25
Asherim (pl) 1 Kin 14:15; Mic 5:14
Asheroth (pl) Judg 3:7; 2 Chr 19:3

ASHKELON
Philistine city Judg 1:18; 2 Sam 1:20; Jer 47:5; Zeph 2:4
ASHTORETH
1 *Near Eastern goddess* 1 Kin 11:5,33; 2 Kin 23:13
Ashtaroth (pl) Judg 2:13; 1 Sam 7:4; 31:10
2 *town of Bashan in E Manasseh* Deut 1:4; Josh 13:12
ASIA
Roman province of Asia Minor Acts 6:9; Rom 16:5; Rev 1:4
ATHENS
leading Greek city Acts 17:15ff
ATONEMENT *expiation*
by which **a** was made Ex 29:33
shall make a for him Lev 4:35
a before the LORD Lev 14:31
how can I make **a** 2 Sam 21:3
make **a** for iniquity Dan 9:24
AUGUSTUS
name of Caesar Octavianus Luke 2:1
see **CAESAR**
AZARIAH
1 *ancestor of Samuel* 1 Chr 6:36
2 *official of Solomon* 1 Kin 4:2
3 *son of Nathan* 1 Kin 4:5
4 *prophet* 2 Chr 15:1-8
5 *two sons of king Jehoshaphat* 2 Chr 21:2
6 *king of Judah*, also **Uzziah** 2 Kin 15:1; 2 Chr 26:1
7 *high priest* 1 Chr 6:10
8 *family of Merari* 2 Chr 29:12
9 *son of Hilkiah* 1 Chr 6:13,14
10 *original name of Abed-nego* Dan 1:7
the name of twelve other individuals in the OT

B

BAAL
1 *Canaanite god(s)* Num 22:41; Judg 6:25; 1 Kin 18:40
2 *line of Reuben* 1 Chr 5:5
3 *personal name* 1 Chr 8:30
4 *place name* 1 Chr 4:33
BAAL-ZEBUB
god of Ekron 2 Kin 1:2,16
see also **BEELZEBUL**
BAASHA
king of Israel 1 Kin 15:16,32
BABEL *a city*
founded by Nimrod Gen 10:10; 11:9
later called Babylon
BABY *infant*
woe…who are nursing **b-ies** Matt 24:19
b leaped…her womb Luke 1:41
b wrapped in cloths Luke 2:12
b as He lay Luke 2:16
like newborn **b-ies** 1 Pet 2:2
BABYLON *city*
1 *on the Euphrates* 2 Kin 17:24; Jer 20:4; Ezek 29:18; Dan 4:29
2 *symbolic of godlessness* Rev 14:8; 17:5
BALAAM
diviner Num 22:5-31; 23:5; Josh 13:22; Rev 2:14
BALAK
king of Moab Num 22:4; Mic 6:5
BAPTISM *symbolic washing*
Sadducees coming…**b** Matt 3:7
b of repentance Mark 1:4
b with which I am Mark 10:38
with the **b** of John Luke 7:29
a **b** to undergo Luke 12:50
through **b** into death Rom 6:4
one faith, one **b** Eph 4:5
buried with Him in **b** Col 2:12

BAPTIZE *symbolic washing*
b...Holy Spirit Matt 3:11
tax collectors...**b-d** Luke 3:12
Jesus was also **b-d** Luke 3:21
sent me to **b** in water John 1:33
b-ing more disciples John 4:1
b-d with the Holy Acts 1:5
each of you be **b-d** Acts 2:38
he got up and was **b-d** Acts 9:18
household...been **b-d** Acts 16:15
John **b-d** with the Acts 19:4
b-d into Christ Jesus Rom 6:3
b-d into Moses 1 Cor 10:2
b-d into one body 1 Cor 12:13
b-d for the dead 1 Cor 15:29

BARABBAS
robber Matt 27:16; Luke 23:18
released by Pilate Matt 27:26

BARBARIAN *non-Hellenic*
obligation...to **b-s** Rom 1:14
who speaks a **b** 1 Cor 14:11
b, Scythian, slave Col 3:11

BARNABAS
Cyprian by birth Acts 4:36
introduced Paul Acts 9:27
co-worker with Paul Acts 13:2,7
separated from Paul Acts 15:39

BARREN *childless, sterile*
Sarai was **b** Gen 11:30
but Rachel was **b** Gen 29:31
wrongs the **b** woman Job 24:21
Shout...O **b** one Is 54:1
Blessed are the **b** Luke 23:29

BARSABBAS
1 *Apostolic candidate, also called Joseph and Justus* Acts 1:23
2 *colleague of Paul, also called Judas* Acts 15:22

BARTHOLOMEW
apostle Matt 10:3; Luke 6:14; Acts 1:13

BARTIMAEUS
healed by Jesus Mark 10:46

BARUCH
1 *scribe* Jer 36:26; 43:6
2 *priest* Neh 3:20
3 *a Judean* Neh 11:5

BASEMATH
1 *Esau's wife* Gen 26:34
2 *daughter of Solomon* 1 Kin 4:15

BASHAN
land E of Jordan Num 21:33; Josh 13:11; Is 2:13

BATHSHEBA
wife of Uriah 2 Sam 11:3
taken by David 2 Sam 11:4
wife of David 2 Sam 11:27
mother of Solomon 2 Sam 12:24

BEELZEBUL
NT prince of the demons Matt 12:27; Luke 11:15
see also **BAAL-ZEBUB**

BEERSHEBA
well / town in Negev Gen 21:31; Judg 20:1
home of Abraham Gen 22:19
home of Isaac Gen 26:23

BEGOTTEN (adj) *born one*
b from the Father John 1:14
the only **b** God John 1:18
gave His only **b** Son John 3:16
only **b** Son of God John 3:18
offering...only **b** Heb 11:17
sent His only **b** Son 1 John 4:9

BEHEMOTH
hippopotamus Job 40:15

BEL
Babylonian god, related to Baal Jer 50:2; 51:44

BELA
1 *king of Edom* Gen 36:32
2 *son of Benjamin* Gen 46:21; 1 Chr 8:1
3 *a Reubenite* 1 Chr 5:8
4 *city of the plain near the Dead Sea* Gen 14:2,8
also **ZOAR**

BELSHAZZAR
ruler of Babylon Dan 5:1; 7:1

BELTESHAZZAR
Daniel's Babylonian name Dan 1:7; 2:26; 5:12; 10:1

BENAIAH
1 *son of Jehoiada* 2 Sam 8:18
captain of David 2 Sam 23:23
2 *Levitical singer* 1 Chr 15:18,20
3 *a priest* 1 Chr 15:24; 16:5
the name of nine other individuals in the OT

BEN-HADAD
1 *Ben-hadad I* 1 Kin 15:18-21
2 *Ben-hadad II* 1 Kin 20
3 *Ben-hadad III* 2 Kin 8:7-15; 13:22

BENJAMIN
1 *son of Jacob* Gen 35:18
2 *tribe* Num 2:22
3 *of clan of Jediael* 1 Chr 7:10
4 *of the restoration* Neh 3:23

BEREA
city in Macedonia visited by Paul Acts 17:10,13

BERODACH-BALADAN
king of Babylon 2 Kin 20:12
see also **MERODACH-BALADAN**

BETHANY
1 *E of Jerusalem* Matt 21:17
home of Mary, Martha and Lazarus John 11:1,18
2 *where John baptized* John 1:28

BETHEL
town in Benjamin Gen 12:8
N of Jerusalem Josh 8:17

BETHESDA
pool in Jerusalem John 5:2

BETH-HORON
1 *famous battle site*
pass NW of Jerusalem Josh 10:10,11
2 *two towns at both ends of mountain pass* Josh 16:3,5

BETHLEHEM
1 *town S of Jerusalem* Gen 35:19
home of Ruth and Boaz Ruth 4:11
birthplace of Jesus Matt 2:1
2 *Zebulunite village* Josh 19:15

BETHPHAGE
village on the Mount of Olives Matt 21:1; Mark 11:1

BETHSAIDA
village on Sea of Galilee Mark 8:22; Luke 9:10
home of Philip, Andrew and Peter John 1:44

BETH-SHAN/BETH-SHEAN
city at junction of Jezreel and Jordan valleys Josh 17:11; 1 Kin 4:12; 1 Chr 7:29

BETH-SHEMESH
1 *city of Judah* Josh 15:10
2 *Issachar border city* Josh 19:22
3 *city of Naphtali* Josh 19:38

BETRAY *break faith, disloyal*
do not **b** the fugitive Is 16:3
wine **b-s** the haughty Hab 2:5
b Him to you Matt 26:15
how to **b** Him Mark 14:11
one...will **b** Me Mark 14:18
Judas, are you **b-ing** Luke 22:48

BETROTH *promise to wed*
You shall **b** a wife Deut 28:30
I will **b** you to Me Hos 2:19
Mary had been **b-ed** Matt 1:18
I **b-ed** you to one 2 Cor 11:2

BEZALEL
1 *architect of tabernacle* Ex 31:1ff
2 *Israelite* Ezra 10:30
BEZER
1 *son of Zophah* 1 Chr 7:37
2 *city of refuge* Josh 20:8
BILDAD
one of Job's friends Job 2:11; 18:1; 42:9
BILHAH
1 *Rachel's servant* Gen 29:29
Jacob's concubine Gen 30:3,4
2 *Simeonite town* 1 Chr 4:29
BIRD *fowl*
let **b-s** fly above Gen 1:20
eat any clean **b** Deut 14:20
b-s of the heavens Ps 8:8
Flee *as* a **b** to Ps 11:1
snare of a **b** catcher Hos 9:8
b-s...*have* nests Luke 9:58
BIRTHDAY *day of birth*
was Pharaoh's **b** Gen 40:20
Herod's **b** came Matt 14:6
his **b**...banquet Mark 6:21
BIRTHRIGHT *firstborn rights*
First sell me your **b** Gen 25:31
He took away my **b** Gen 27:36
sold his own **b** Heb 12:16
BITHYNIA
territory on the Bosporus in Asia Minor Acts 16:7; 1 Pet 1:1
BLASPHEME *curse*
enemies...to **b** 2 Sam 12:14
name is continually **b-d** Is 52:5
This *fellow* **b-s** Matt 9:3
b-s...Holy Spirit Mark 3:29
force them to **b** Acts 26:11
name of God is **b-d** Rom 2:24
taught not to **b** 1 Tim 1:20
b-d the God of Rev 16:11
BLASPHEMY *cursing, profanity*
b against the Spirit Matt 12:31
b-ies they utter Mark 3:28
You...heard the **b** Mark 14:64
man...speaks **b-ies** Luke 5:21
stone You...for **b** John 10:33
words and **b-ies** Rev 13:5
BLESS (v) *bestow favor or praise*
God **b-ed** the...day Gen 2:3
I will greatly **b** you Gen 22:17
LORD **b-ed** the sabbath Ex 20:11
and **b** Your inheritance Ps 28:9
LORD will **b** His people Ps 29:11
B the LORD Ps 103:2
generous will be **b-ed** Prov 22:9
who **b-es** his friend Prov 27:14
rise up and **b** her Prov 31:28
b-ed of My Father Matt 25:34
He **b-ed** *the food* Mark 6:41
b...who curse you Luke 6:28
while He was **b-ing** Luke 24:51
you are **b-ed** if you John 13:17
B...who persecute Rom 12:14
we **b** *our* Lord James 3:9
BLESSED (adj) *favored, happy*
b be God Most High Gen 14:20
B are you, O Israel Deut 33:29
B be the name of Job 1:21
How **b** is the man Ps 127:5
b...who finds wisdom Prov 3:13
nations will call you **b** Mal 3:12
B are the poor in Matt 5:3
B are the gentle Matt 5:5
B *is* the...kingdom Mark 11:10
B *are* you among women Luke 1:42
more **b** to give Acts 20:35
looking for...**b** hope Titus 2:13
BLESSING (n) *God's favor*
you shall be a **b** Gen 12:2
taken away your **b** Gen 27:35
a **b** and a curse Deut 11:26
curse into a **b** Neh 13:2
b of the LORD be upon Ps 129:8
showers of **b** Ezek 34:26
pour out for you a **b** Mal 3:10
fullness of the **b** Rom 15:29
cup of **b** which we 1 Cor 10:16
inherit a **b** 1 Pet 3:9
honor and glory and **b** Rev 5:12
BLIND (adj) *sightless*
misleads a **b** *person* Deut 27:18
To open **b** eyes Is 42:7
b...guides a **b** man Matt 15:14
b beggar *named* Mark 10:46
b man was sitting Luke 18:35
I was **b**, now I see John 9:25
BLIND (n) *without sight*
block before the **b** Lev 19:14
I was eyes to the **b** Job 29:15
the **b** receive sight Matt 11:5
a guide to the **b** Rom 2:19
BLIND (v) *make sightless*
b-s the clear-sighted Ex 23:8
bribe to **b** my eyes 1 Sam 12:3
has **b-ed** the minds 2 Cor 4:4
darkness has **b-ed** 1 John 2:11
BLOOD
Whoever sheds man's **b** Gen 9:6
bridegroom of **b** Ex 4:25
b shall be a sign Ex 12:13
not eat...any **b** Lev 3:17
land is filled with **b** Ezek 9:9
b did not reveal Matt 16:17
covenant in My **b** Luke 22:20
sweat...drops of **b** Luke 22:44
drinks My **b** abides John 6:56
Field of **B** Acts 1:19
the moon into **b** Acts 2:20
justified by His **b** Rom 5:9
sharing in the **b** 1 Cor 10:16
redemption...His **b** Eph 1:7
cleansed with **b** Heb 9:22
b, as of a lamb 1 Pet 1:19
the sea became **b** Rev 8:8
b of the saints Rev 17:6
BLOODGUILTINESS
no **b** on his account Ex 22:2
b is upon them Lev 20:11
b shall be forgiven Deut 21:8
Deliver me from **b** Ps 51:14
BLOODSHED *killing, murder*
abhors the man of **b** Ps 5:6
Men of **b** hate Prov 29:10
the **b** of Jerusalem Is 4:4
give you over to **b** Ezek 35:6
b follows **b** Hos 4:2
BOANERGES
name of James and John Mark 3:17
BOAZ
1 *husband of Ruth* Ruth 4:13
grandfather of David Ruth 4:17ff
2 *temple pillar* 2 Chr 3:17
BODY *corpse, flesh*
b cleaves to the earth Ps 44:25
lamp of the **b** Matt 6:22
perfume on My **b** Matt 26:12
this is My **b** Mark 14:22
did not find His **b** Luke 24:23
b of sin...done away Rom 6:6
redemption of our **b** Rom 8:23

present your **b-ies** Rom 12:1
b-ies are members 1 Cor 6:15
b is a temple 1 Cor 6:19
you are Christ's **b** 1 Cor 12:27
b to be burned 1 Cor 13:3
absent from the **b** 2 Cor 5:8
one **b** and one Spirit Eph 4:4
building up of the **b** Eph 4:12
wives as…own **b-ies** Eph 5:28
transform the **b** Phil 3:21
b be preserved 1 Thess 5:23
bore…sins in His **b** 1 Pet 2:24

BOIL (n) *sore, swelling*
When…has a **b** Lev 13:18
b-s of Egypt Deut 28:27
smote Job with sore **b-s** Job 2:7

BOIL (v) *cook, heat*
not **b** a young goat in its Ex 34:26
we **b-ed** my son 2 Kin 6:29
fire causes water to **b** Is 64:2
b the guilt offering Ezek 46:20

BONDAGE *servitude, slavery*
Israel sighed…**b** Ex 2:23
the **b** of iniquity Acts 8:23
sold into **b** to sin Rom 7:14

BOND-SERVANT *servant, slave*
b-s of…Most High Acts 16:17
Paul, a **b** of Christ Rom 1:1
ourselves as your **b-s** 2 Cor 4:5
b…be quarrelsome 2 Tim 2:24
b of God…apostle Titus 1:1
His **b-s**…serve Him Rev 22:3

BONDSLAVE *servant, slave*
state of His **b** Luke 1:48
a **b** of Jesus Christ Col 4:12
Urge **b-s** to be subject Titus 2:9
use it as **b-s** of God 1 Pet 2:16

BOOK OF LIFE
God's book with names of righteous Ps 69:28; Phil 4:3; Rev 13:8; 17:8; 20:15

BORN *brought into life*
man is **b** for trouble Job 5:7
mountains were **b** Ps 90:2
child will be **b** to us Is 9:6
land be **b** in one day Is 66:8
b King of the Jews Matt 2:2
those **b** of women Luke 7:28
b not of blood John 1:13
unless one is **b** again John 3:3
b of the Spirit John 3:6
to one untimely **b** 1 Cor 15:8
b…to a living hope 1 Pet 1:3
loves is **b** of God 1 John 4:7

BORROW *use temporarily*
if a man **b-s** *anything* Ex 22:14
you shall not **b** Deut 28:12
b-s and does not pay Ps 37:21
wants to **b** from you Matt 5:42

BREAD *food*
eat unleavened **b** Ex 12:20
rain **b** from heaven Ex 16:4
He will bless your **b** Ex 23:25
b of the Presence Ex 25:30
not live by **b** alone Deut 8:3
ravens brought…**b** 1 Kin 17:6
b of heaven Ps 105:40
satisfy…with **b** Ps 132:15
b *eaten* in secret Prov 9:17
eat the **b** of idleness Prov 31:27
Cast your **b**…waters Eccl 11:1
not live on **b** alone Matt 4:4
Give us…daily **b** Matt 6:11
gives you the true **b** John 6:32
I am the **b** of life John 6:35

BREATH *air, spirit, wind*
the **b** of life Gen 2:7
days are *but* a **b** Job 7:16
man is a mere **b** Ps 39:11
b came into them Ezek 37:10
give **b** to the image Rev 13:15

BRIDE *newlywed*
as a **b** adorns herself Is 61:10
the voice of the **b** Jer 7:34
b out of her *bridal* Joel 2:16
He who has the **b** John 3:29
b…of the Lamb Rev 21:9

BRIDEGROOM *newlywed*
a **b** of blood to me Ex 4:25
As a **b** decks himself Is 61:10
voice of the **b** Jer 7:34
attendants of the **b** Matt 9:15
out to meet the **b** Matt 25:1

BROTHER *male relative*
Am I my **b-'s** Gen 4:9
b-s were jealous Gen 37:11
b-s may redeem Lev 25:48
b-s to dwell together Ps 133:1
b is born for Prov 17:17
closer than a **b** Prov 18:24
b-s of a poor man Prov 19:7
reconciled to your **b** Matt 5:24
B will betray **b** Matt 10:21
behold, His…**b-s** Matt 12:46
not forgive his **b** Matt 18:35
My **b** and sister Mark 3:35
b of yours was dead Luke 15:32
left…wife or **b-s** Luke 18:29
not even His **b-s** John 7:5
b will rise again John 11:23
b goes to law with **b** 1 Cor 6:6
my **b** to stumble 1 Cor 8:13
yet hates his **b** 1 John 2:9

BROTHERHOOD
the covenant of **b** Amos 1:9
love the **b**, fear God 1 Pet 2:17

BULRUSH *marsh plant*
b in a single day Is 9:14
b-es by the Nile Is 19:7
palm branch or **b** Is 19:15

BURIAL *interment*
give me a **b** site Gen 23:4
even have a *proper* **b** Eccl 6:3
to prepare Me for **b** Matt 26:12
b custom of the Jews John 19:40

C

CAESAR
1 *Roman emperor* Matt 22:17,21; Mark 12:14; John 19:12
2 *Augustus* Luke 2:1
3 *Tiberius* Luke 3:1; John 19:12
4 *Claudius* Acts 11:28; 17:7; 18:2
5 *Nero* Acts 25:12; 26:32; Phil 4:22

CAESAREA
Roman coastal city Acts 8:40; 10:1; 21:16; 25:4

CAESAREA PHILIPPI
city at base of Mt. Hermon Matt 16:13; Mark 8:27

CAIAPHAS
high priest Matt 26:57; Luke 3:2; John 11:49ff; Acts 4:6

CAIN
son of Adam Gen 4:1
tiller of the ground Gen 4:2
killed his brother Gen 4:8
marked by sign Gen 4:15

CALEB
1 *aide to Moses* Num 13:30
son of Jephunneh Num 32:12

received Hebron Josh 14:13
2 *son of Hezron* 1 Chr 2:18

CALL *address, summon, name*
God c-ed the light day Gen 1:5
c upon the name Gen 4:26
c-s up the dead Deut 18:11
LORD was c-ing…boy 1 Sam 3:8
c-ed fine gold my trust Job 31:24
c upon the LORD Ps 18:3
those who c evil good Is 5:20
c His name Immanuel Is 7:14
You shall c Me Jer 3:19
who is c-ed the Messiah Matt 1:16
to c the righteous Matt 9:13
c-s his own sheep John 10:3
c Me Teacher and John 13:13
God has not c-ed 1 Thess 4:7
c-s…a prophetess Rev 2:20

CALLING *summoning*
the c of assemblies Is 1:13
the c of God Rom 11:29
For consider your c 1 Cor 1:26
with a holy c 2 Tim 1:9
His c and choosing 2 Pet 1:10

CAMEL *animal*
dismounted…the c Gen 24:64
his wives upon c-s Gen 31:17
a garment of c's hair Matt 3:4
c…eye of a needle Matt 19:24
clothed with c's hair Mark 1:6

CANAAN
1 *son of Ham* Gen 9:18,25
2 *Syro-Palestine* Gen 13:12; 42:5; Ex 16:35; Ps 105:11
3 *language (Hebrew)* Is 19:18
see also **HEBREW**
see also **JUDEAN**

CAPERNAUM
city on Sea of Galilee Matt 4:13; Luke 4:23; John 6:24,59

CAPITAL *top part of column*
height of the other c 1 Kin 7:16
c on the top of each 2 Chr 3:15
c-s…were on top 2 Chr 4:12

CARAVAN *expedition*
a c of Ishmaelites Gen 37:25
The c-s of Tema Job 6:19
O c-s of Dedanites Is 21:13

CARCASS *corpse*
down upon the c-es Gen 15:11
one who touches…c Lev 11:39
c-es will be food Deut 28:26
c of the lion Judg 14:8
c-es of their…idols Jer 16:18

CARMEL
1 *range of hills* 1 Kin 18:42; 2 Kin 4:25; Jer 46:18
2 *town in Judah* 1 Sam 15:12; 25:5,40

CARPENTER *craftsman*
c-s and stonemasons 2 Sam 5:11
to the masons and c-s Ezra 3:7
this the c-'s son Matt 13:55
c, the son of Mary Mark 6:3

CEDAR *tree, wood*
with the c wood Lev 14:6
c-s beside the waters Num 24:6
all the c-s of Lebanon Is 2:13
the height of c-s Amos 2:9

CELEBRATE *rejoice*
may c a feast to Me Ex 5:1
you shall c it in Lev 23:41
C the Passover 2 Kin 23:21
all Israel were c-ing 1 Chr 13:8
to c *the feast* 2 Chr 30:23
David…c-ing 1 Chr 15:29
c with my friends Luke 15:29

CENSUS *population roll*
c of…congregation Num 1:2
number of the c 1 Chr 21:5
c which…David 2 Chr 2:17
the first c taken Luke 2:2
in the days of the c Acts 5:37

CENTURION *captain*
Jesus said to the c Matt 8:13
summoning the c Mark 15:44
soldiers and c-s Acts 21:32
gave orders to the c Acts 24:23

CEPHAS
apostle Peter John 1:42; 1 Cor 1:12; 15:5; Gal 2:11

CHAFF *husk*
consumes them as c Ex 15:7
c which the wind drives Ps 1:4
make the hills like c Is 41:15
c from the summer Dan 2:35
burn up the c Matt 3:12

CHALDEANS
inhabitants of Chaldea Gen 11:28; 2 Kin 24:2; Job 1:17; Jer 24:5; Dan 5:11; Hab 1:6

CHARIOT *wagon*
Joseph prepared…c Gen 46:29
appeared a c of fire 2 Kin 2:11
Some *boast* in c-s Ps 20:7
c-s of God are myriads Ps 68:17
Your c-s of salvation Hab 3:8
I will cut off the c Zech 9:10
and sitting in his c Acts 8:28

CHARITY *alms*
give that…as c Luke 11:41
and give to c Luke 12:33
deeds of…c Acts 9:36

CHASTE *pure*
c…behavior 1 Pet 3:2
kept themselves c Rev 14:4

CHASTEN *discipline*
Man is also c-ed Job 33:19
Nor c me in Your wrath Ps 6:1
c-ed every morning Ps 73:14
who c-s the nations Ps 94:10

CHASTISE *punish*
You have c-d me Jer 31:18
I will c all of them Hos 5:2

CHEBAR
river in Babylonia Ezek 3:15; 10:15

CHEMOSH
god of Moab Judg 11:24; 1 Kin 11:7; Jer 48:13

CHERETHITES
1 *tribe on Philistine plain* 1 Sam 30:14; Ezek 25:16; Zeph 2:5
2 *David's bodyguards* 2 Sam 8:18; 15:18; 1 Kin 1:38; 1 Chr 18:17

CHERUB *celestial being*
He rode on a c 2 Sam 22:11
one c…ten cubits 1 Kin 6:26
c stretched out his Ezek 10:7

CHERUBIM *plural of cherub*
He stationed the c Gen 3:24
c had *their* wings Ex 37:9
enthroned *above*…c 2 Sam 6:2
c appeared to have Ezek 10:8

CHILD
c grew…weaned Gen 21:8
Train up a c in Prov 22:6
discipline from the c Prov 23:13
c will be born to us Is 9:6
with c by the Holy Matt 1:18
take the C and His Matt 2:13
He called a c to Matt 18:2

saying, **C**, arise Luke 8:54
a woman with c 1 Thess 5:3

CHINNERETH / CHINNEROTH
1 *lake* Num 34:11; Josh 12:3
also **Sea of Galilee**
also **Lake of Gennesaret**
also **Sea of Tiberias**
2 *city of Naphtali* Deut 3:17; Josh 19:35
3 *plain near Galilee* Josh 11:2; 1 Kin 15:20

CHISLEV
ninth month of Hebrew calendar Neh 1:1; Zech 7:1

CHRIST *Messiah*
birth of Jesus **C** was Matt 1:18
C would suffer and Luke 24:46
both Lord and **C** Acts 2:36
fellow heirs with **C** Rom 8:17
are one body in **C** Rom 12:5
preach **C** crucified 1 Cor 1:23
judgment seat of **C** 2 Cor 5:10
ambassadors for **C** 2 Cor 5:20
faith in **C** Jesus Gal 2:16
as sons through Jesus **C** Eph 1:5
to live is **C** Phil 1:21
C, who is our life Col 3:4
dead in **C** will 1 Thess 4:16
coming of…**C** 2 Thess 2:1
C…high priest Heb 9:11
Advocate…Jesus **C** 1 John 2:1
with **C** for a thousand Rev 20:4

CHRISTIAN *follower of Christ*
first called **C-s** in Acts 11:26
me to become a **C** Acts 26:28
suffers as a **C** 1 Pet 4:16

CHRONICLES *book of register*
1 *of kings of Israel* 1 Kin 14:19; 15:31; 2 Kin 14:28; 15:26
2 *of kings of Judah* 1 Kin 14:29; 15:23; 2 Kin 15:36; 24:5
3 *of kings of Media / Persia* Esth 10:2

CHURCH *a called-out assembly*
I will build my **c** Matt 16:18
tell it to the **c** Matt 18:17
shepherd the **c** Acts 20:28
c-es of the Gentiles Rom 16:4
together as a **c** 1 Cor 11:18
woman…speak in **c** 1 Cor 14:35
to the **c-es** of Judea Gal 1:22
Christ…head of the **c** Eph 5:23
persecutor of the **c** Phil 3:6
c of the living God 1 Tim 3:15
Spirit says to the **c-es** Rev 2:11

CILICIA
region in SE Asia Minor Acts 15:41; 21:39; 27:5

CIRCUMCISE *be pure* or *cut off*
every male…be **c-d** Gen 17:10
Abraham **c-d** his son Gen 21:4
So **c** your heart Deut 10:16
God will **c**…heart Deut 30:6
C yourselves…LORD Jer 4:4
came to **c** the child Luke 1:59
c-d the eighth day Phil 3:5

CIRCUMCISION *act of purity*
because of the **c** Ex 4:26
c is…of the heart Rom 2:29
if you receive **c** Gal 5:2
if I still preach **c** Gal 5:11
we are the *true* **c** Phil 3:3
c made without hands Col 2:11
those of the **c** Titus 1:10

CISTERN *reservoir*
a **c** collecting water Lev 11:36
water from your…**c** Prov 5:15
wheel at the **c** is Eccl 12:6
prophet from the **c** Jer 38:10

CITADEL *fortress*
c of the king's 1 Kin 16:18
c of Susa Esth 2:3
in the **c** of Susa Dan 8:2
c-s of Jerusalem Amos 2:5
Proclaim on the **c-s** Amos 3:9
tramples on our **c-s** Mic 5:5

CLAUDIA
Roman Christian 2 Tim 4:21

COAST
c of the Great Sea Josh 9:1
along the **c** of Asia Acts 27:2

COASTLAND
inhabitants of this **c** Is 20:6
to the **c-s** of Kittim Jer 2:10
c-s shake at the Ezek 26:15
c-s of the nations Zeph 2:11

COBRA *snake*
deadly poison of **c-s** Deut 32:33
To the venom of **c-s** Job 20:14
tread upon the…**c** Ps 91:13

COLT *foal*
camels and their **c-s** Gen 32:15
Even on a **c** Zech 9:9
and a **c** with her Matt 21:2
on a donkey's **c** John 12:15

COMMANDMENT *instruction*
and keep My **c-s** Ex 20:6
the Ten **C-s** Ex 34:28
and keep His **c-s** Josh 22:5
c of the LORD is pure Ps 19:8
the **c** of your father Prov 6:20
which is the great **c** Matt 22:36
A new **c** I give John 13:34
will keep My **c-s** John 14:15
I have kept…**c-s** John 15:10
not writing a new **c** 1 John 2:7
keep the **c-s** of God Rev 14:12

CONCEIVE *become pregnant*
Sarah **c-d** and bore a Gen 21:2
c-d all this people Num 11:12
sin my mother **c-d** me Ps 51:5
she **c-d** and gave birth Is 8:3
when lust has **c-d** James 1:15

CONCUBINE *secondary wife*
Ephraim…took a **c** Judg 19:1
Now Saul had a **c** 2 Sam 3:7
king left ten **c-s** 2 Sam 15:16
three hundred **c-s** 1 Kin 11:3
in charge of the **c-s** Esth 2:14

CONDUCT (n) *behavior*
queen's **c**…known Esth 1:17
turn…*from his* **c** Job 33:17
who are upright in **c** Ps 37:14
sensual **c** of…men 2 Pet 2:7
holy **c** and godliness 2 Pet 3:11

CONDUCT (v) *behave*
c-s himself arrogantly Job 15:25
c…same spirit 2 Cor 12:18
C…with wisdom Col 4:5
c yourselves in fear 1 Pet 1:17

CONFESS *acknowledge*
that he shall **c** Lev 5:5
c-ing the sins of Neh 1:6
c my transgressions Ps 32:5
c-es Me before men Matt 10:32
c-ing their sins Mark 1:5
c with your mouth Rom 10:9
If we **c** our sins 1 John 1:9
I will **c** his name Rev 3:5

CONFRONT *challenge, face*
snares of death **c-ed** 2 Sam 22:6
Days of affliction **c** Job 30:27
Arise, O LORD, **c** him Ps 17:13
the elders **c-ed** *Him* Luke 20:1

CONGREGATION *assembly*
all the c of Israel — Ex 12:3
c shall stone him — Num 15:35
strife of the c — Num 27:14
Bless God in the c-s — Ps 68:26
c of the godly ones — Ps 149:1
the c of the disciples — Acts 6:2
In the midst of the c — Heb 2:12
CONSCIENCE *moral obligation*
David's c bothered — 1 Sam 24:5
always a blameless c — Acts 24:16
also for c' sake — Rom 13:5
their c being weak is — 1 Cor 8:7
faith with a clear c — 1 Tim 3:9
seared in their own c — 1 Tim 4:2
keep a good c — 1 Pet 3:16
CONSECRATE (v) *sanctify*
sons of Israel c — Ex 28:38
garments shall be c-d — Ex 29:21
c it and all its — Ex 40:9
C yourselves — Lev 11:44
c the fiftieth year — Lev 25:10
c-s his house as holy — Lev 27:14
he shall c his head — Num 6:11
C yourselves — Josh 3:5
have c-d this house — 1 Kin 9:3
CONSECRATED (adj) *sanctified*
touch any c thing — Lev 12:4
c people…LORD — Deut 26:19
there is c bread — 1 Sam 21:4
c ones were purer — Lam 4:7
ate the c bread — Matt 12:4
CONSPIRACY *plot, scheme*
the c was strong — 2 Sam 15:12
found c in Hoshea — 2 Kin 17:4
from the c-ies of man — Ps 31:20
CONSPIRE *plot against*
have c-d against me — 1 Sam 22:8
c-d against my — 2 Kin 10:9
c together against — Ps 83:3
Amos…c-d against — Amos 7:10
CONSTELLATION *stars*
a c in its season — Job 38:32
c-s Will not flash — Is 13:10
CONTRIBUTE *give*
Josiah c-d to the — 2 Chr 35:7
c yearly one third — Neh 10:32
c-ing to their support — Luke 8:3
c-ing to…the saints — Rom 12:13
CONTRIBUTION *gift, offering*
to raise a c for Me — Ex 25:2
as a c to the LORD — Lev 7:14
c-s, the first fruits — Neh 12:44
a c for the poor — Rom 15:26
liberality of your c — 2 Cor 9:13
CONTROL (v) *rule, subdue*
he c-led himself and — Gen 43:31
Joseph could not c — Gen 45:1
Haman c-led himself — Esth 5:10
CONTROVERSY *dispute*
wise man has a c — Prov 29:9
LORD has a c with the — Jer 25:31
avoid foolish c-ies — Titus 3:9
CONVOCATION *conclave*
sabbath…a holy c — Lev 23:3
shall have a holy c — Num 29:7
CORBAN *offering*
C (that is…) — Mark 7:11
CORNELIUS
centurion, believer — Acts 10:1ff
CORNER *angle, intersection*
the chief c *stone* — Ps 118:22
lurks by every c — Prov 7:12
on the street c-s — Matt 6:5
the chief c *stone* — Mark 12:10
four c-s of the earth — Rev 7:1
CORNERSTONE *support stone*
who laid its c — Job 38:6
the c of her tribes — Is 19:13
costly c *for* the — Is 28:16
From them…the c — Zech 10:4
COUNCIL *assembly*
not enter into their c — Gen 49:6
the c of the holy ones — Ps 89:7
the c of My people — Ezek 13:9
to their c *chamber* — Luke 22:66
conferred with his c — Acts 25:12
COUNCIL
Sanhedrin — Matt 26:59
Jewish governing body — Mark 15:1,43; Luke 23:50
COUNSEL (n) *advice, opinion*
I will give you c — Ex 18:19
Take c and speak up — Judg 19:30
To Him belong c — Job 12:13
not walk in the c — Ps 1:1
Listen to c and — Prov 19:20
the c of His will — Eph 1:11
COUNSEL (v) *advise*
he has c-ed rebellion — Deut 13:5
I c that all Israel — 2 Sam 17:11
How do you c *me* — 1 Kin 12:6
c you with My eye — Ps 32:8
COUNSELOR *adviser*
the king and his c-s — Ezra 7:15
c-s walk barefoot — Job 12:17
abundance of c-s — Prov 11:14
Wonderful C, Mighty — Is 9:6
who became His c — Rom 11:34
COVENANT *agreement*
establish My c — Gen 6:18
for a sign of a c — Gen 9:13
for an everlasting c — Gen 17:13
ark of the c — Num 10:33
My c of peace — Num 25:12
book of the c — 2 Kin 23:2
Remember His c — 1 Chr 16:15
who keep His c — Ps 103:18
I will make a new c — Jer 31:31
forsake the holy c — Dan 11:30
a c with Assyria — Hos 12:1
the blood of *My* c — Zech 9:11
cup…is the new c — Luke 22:20
c which God made — Acts 3:25
this is My c with — Rom 11:27
servants of a new c — 2 Cor 3:6
strangers to the c-s — Eph 2:12
guarantee…better c — Heb 7:22
blood of the…c — Heb 13:20
ark of His c — Rev 11:19
CREATION
beginning of c — Mark 10:6
preach…to all c — Mark 16:15
whole c groans — Rom 8:22
beginning of c — 2 Pet 3:4
CREATOR *Maker*
Remember…your C — Eccl 12:1
The C of Israel — Is 43:15
rather than the C — Rom 1:25
to a faithful C — 1 Pet 4:19
CREATURE *created being*
every living c that — Gen 1:21
winged c will make — Eccl 10:20
and crawling c-s — Rom 1:23
in Christ…new c — 2 Cor 5:17
as c-s of instinct — 2 Pet 2:12
CREDITOR *lender*
not to act as a c to — Ex 22:25
every c shall release — Deut 15:2

Let the **c** seize all Ps 109:11
My **c-s** did I sell you Is 50:1
CRIMSON *deep red*
purple, **c** and violet 2 Chr 2:7
like **c**...be like wool Is 1:18
CROSS (n) *execution device*
take his **c** and Matt 10:38
down from the **c** Matt 27:40
to bear His **c** Mark 15:21
take up his **c** daily Luke 9:23
standing by the **c** John 19:25
hanging Him on a **c** Acts 5:30
c of Christ would 1 Cor 1:17
word of the **c** is 1 Cor 1:18
boast, except in the **c** Gal 6:14
even death on a **c** Phil 2:8
enemies of the **c** Phil 3:18
blood of His **c** Col 1:20
endured the **c** Heb 12:2
CROSS (v) *pass over*
you **c** the Jordan Deut 12:10
c-ed opposite Jericho Josh 3:16
kept **c-ing** the ford 2 Sam 19:18
Jesus had **c-ed** over Mark 5:21
c-ing over to Acts 21:2
CROWN (n) *royal emblem* or *top*
on the **c** of the head Gen 49:26
the **c** of their king 2 Sam 12:30
he set the royal **c** Esth 2:17
wife is the **c** of Prov 12:4
gray head is a **c** Prov 16:31
c of the drunkards Is 28:3
a **c** of thorns Matt 27:29
receive the **c** of life James 1:12
c-s before the throne Rev 4:10
golden **c** on His head Rev 14:14
CROWN (v) *to place crown on*
c him with glory Ps 8:5
Who **c-s** you with Ps 103:4
head **c-s** you like Song 7:5
c-ed him with glory Heb 2:7
CRUCIFY *to execute on a cross*
scourge and **c** *Him* Matt 20:19
C Him Matt 27:22
Jesus...been **c-ied** Matt 28:5
c your King John 19:15
Paul was not **c-ied** 1 Cor 1:13
preach Christ **c-ied** 1 Cor 1:23
not have **c-ied** the 1 Cor 2:8
c-ied with Christ Gal 2:20
world...**c-ied** to me Gal 6:14
their Lord was **c-ied** Rev 11:8
CRYSTAL *glass*
awesome gleam of **c** Ezek 1:22
sea of glass, like **c** Rev 4:6
water...clear as **c** Rev 22:1
CUBIT *linear measure*
ark three hundred **c-s** Gen 6:15
length was nine **c-s** Deut 3:11
gallows fifty **c-s** high Esth 5:14
the altar by **c-s** Ezek 43:13
CULT *religious ritual*
be a **c** prostitute Deut 23:17
male **c** prostitutes 1 Kin 14:24
male **c** prostitutes 2 Kin 23:7
CURE *heal*
c him of his leprosy 2 Kin 5:3
c you of your wound Hos 5:13
they could not **c** him Matt 17:16
that...time He **c-d** Luke 7:21
CYMBAL *musical instrument*
castanets and **c-s** 2 Sam 6:5
loud-sounding **c-s** 1 Chr 15:16
with loud **c-s** Ps 150:5
or a clanging **c** 1 Cor 13:1

CYPRESS *tree*
cedar and **c** timber 1 Kin 5:10
c and algum timber 2 Chr 2:8
Our rafters, **c-es** Song 1:17
Wail, O **c**, for the Zech 11:2
CYPRUS
Mediterranean island Is 23:1; Acts 11:19; 15:39; 21:16
see also **KITTIM**
CYRENE
NW African port Mark 15:21; Luke 23:26; Acts 2:10; 11:20
CYRUS
king of Persia 2 Chr 36:22; Is 45:1
decreed to rebuild Temple Ezra 1:1; 5:13

D

DAGON
god of Philistines Judg 16:23; 1 Sam 5:4; 1 Chr 10:10
DAMASCUS
city of Aram (Syria) Gen 14:15; 2 Kin 5:12; Acts 9:3,27; 26:20
DAN
1 *son of Jacob* Gen 30:6; 49:16
2 *tribal area* Josh 19:40; Judg 18:2
3 *city in N Palestine* Josh 19:47
DANIEL
1 *son of David and Abigail* 1 Chr 3:1
2 *priest* Ezra 8:2
3 *prophet* Ezek 14:14; Dan 1:6
see also **BELTESHAZZAR**
DARIUS
1 *Darius the Mede* Dan 5:31
2 *Darius I* Ezra 4:5; Hag 1:1
3 *Darius II* Neh 12:22
DARK *dim, shadow*
not in **d** sayings Num 12:8
d places of the land Ps 74:20
live in a **d** land Is 9:2
it was still **d** John 20:1
shining in a **d** place 2 Pet 1:19
DARKNESS *gloom, shadow*
blind...gropes in **d** Deut 28:29
are silenced in **d** 1 Sam 2:9
illumines my **d** 2 Sam 22:29
that stalks in **d** Ps 91:6
those who dwelt in **d** Ps 107:10
as light excels **d** Eccl 2:13
people who walk in **d** Is 9:2
light will rise in **d** Is 58:10
into the outer **d** Matt 22:13
those who sit in **d** Luke 1:79
men loved the **d** John 3:19
turn from **d** to light Acts 26:18
has light with **d** 2 Cor 6:14
unfruitful deeds of **d** Eph 5:11
in Him there is no **d** 1 John 1:5
brother is in the **d** 1 John 2:9
DAVID
anointed 1 Sam 16:13
killed Goliath 1 Sam 17:50
fled from Saul 1 Sam 19:18
spared Saul 1 Sam 26:9
king of Judah and Israel 2 Sam 2:4; 5:3
covenant with God 2 Sam 7:8
death 1 Kin 2:10
DAWN (n) *daylight*
at the approach of **d** Judg 19:25
caused the **d** to know Job 38:12
rise before **d** and Ps 119:147
wings of the **d** Ps 139:9
As the **d** is spread Joel 2:2
DAWN (v) *become light*
the day began to **d** Judg 19:26

when morning **d-s** Ps 46:5
a Light **d-ed** Matt 4:16
d toward the first Matt 28:1
until the day **d-s** 2 Pet 1:19

DAY *light*
God called the light **d** Gen 1:5
come on a festive **d** 1 Sam 25:8
d…LORD has made Ps 118:24
what a **d** may bring Prov 27:1
d-s of your youth Eccl 12:1
a **d** of reckoning Is 2:12
d of the LORD is near Is 13:6
has despised the **d** Zech 4:10
the **d** of His coming Mal 3:2
Give us this **d** Matt 6:11
raise…the last **d** John 6:39
judge…the last **d** John 12:48
the **d** of salvation 2 Cor 6:2
perfect it until the **d** Phil 1:6
d of the Lord 1 Thess 5:2
d is like a thousand 2 Pet 3:8
tormented **d**…night Rev 20:10

DAY OF ATONEMENT
month is the **d** Lev 23:27
for it is a **d** Lev 23:28

DEACONS *officer, server*
overseers and **d** Phil 1:1
D likewise *must be* 1 Tim 3:8
let them serve as **d** 1 Tim 3:10
D must be husbands 1 Tim 3:12
served well as **d** 1 Tim 3:13

DEAD *without life*
you are a **d** man Gen 20:3
near to a **d** person Num 6:6
dealt with the **d** Ruth 1:8
forgotten as a **d** man Ps 31:12
d do not praise Ps 115:17
better than a **d** lion Eccl 9:4
Your **d** will live Is 26:19
not weep for the **d** Jer 22:10
rising from the **d** Mark 9:10
d will hear the John 5:25
resurrection of the **d** Acts 23:6
d in your trespasses Eph 2:1
firstborn from the **d** Col 1:18
living and the **d** 2 Tim 4:1
repentance…**d** works Heb 6:1
to those who are **d** 1 Pet 4:6
I was **d**…I am alive Rev 1:18
Hades gave up the **d** Rev 20:13

DEAF *without hearing*
makes *him* mute or **d** Ex 4:11
not curse a **d** man Lev 19:14
Like a **d** cobra Ps 58:4
the **d** will hear Is 29:18
and *the* **d** hear Matt 11:5
the **d** to hear Mark 7:37
d and mute spirit Mark 9:25

DEATH *cessation of life*
d of the upright Num 23:10
d encompassed me 2 Sam 22:5
d for his own sin 2 Chr 25:4
D rather than my pains Job 7:15
no mention of You in **d** Ps 6:5
cords of **d** encompassed Ps 18:4
the shadow of **d** Ps 23:4
escapes from **d** Ps 68:20
doomed to **d** Ps 102:20
d of His godly ones Ps 116:15
who hate me love **d** Prov 8:36
love is as strong as **d** Song 8:6
He will swallow up **d** Is 25:8
D cannot praise You Is 38:18
no pleasure in the **d** Ezek 18:32
d is better to me Jon 4:3
is to be put to **d** Matt 15:4
will not taste **d** Matt 16:28
to the point of **d** Mark 14:34
passed out of **d** John 5:24
he will never see **d** John 8:51
sickness is not to end in **d** John 11:4
the agony of **d** Acts 2:24
d by hanging Him Acts 10:39
d reigned from Adam Rom 5:14
wages of sin is **d** Rom 6:23
the law of sin and of **d** Rom 8:2
proclaim…Lord's **d** 1 Cor 11:26
d, where…victory 1 Cor 15:55
even **d** on a cross Phil 2:8
He might taste **d** Heb 2:9
it brings forth **d** James 1:15
passed out of **d** 1 John 3:14
Be faithful until **d** Rev 2:10
had the name **D** Rev 6:8
second **d**…no power Rev 20:6

DEBORAH
1 *nurse of Rebekah* Gen 35:8
2 *prophetess, judge* Judg 4:4ff

DEBT *obligation*
and pay your **d** 2 Kin 4:7
exaction of every **d** Neh 10:31
guarantors for **d-s** Prov 22:26
forgive us our **d-s** Matt 6:12

DEBTOR *borrower*
restores to the **d** Ezek 18:7
forgiven our **d-s** Matt 6:12
had two **d-s** Luke 7:41
his master's **d-s** Luke 16:5

DECEASED *dead*
wife of the **d** shall Deut 25:5
the widow of the **d** Ruth 4:5
the name of the **d** Ruth 4:10
the sister of the **d** John 11:39

DECEIT *deception, falsehood, guile*
full of curses and **d** Ps 10:7
in whose spirit…no **d** Ps 32:2
your tongue frames **d** Ps 50:19
D is in the heart Prov 12:20
he lays up **d** Prov 26:24
Offspring of **d** Is 57:4
houses are full of **d** Jer 5:27
house of Israel…**d** Hos 11:12
d, sensuality, envy Mark 7:22
in whom…is no **d** John 1:47
full of envy…**d** Rom 1:29
the lusts of **d** Eph 4:22
all malice and all **d** 1 Pet 2:1
nor was any **d** found 1 Pet 2:22
lips from speaking **d** 1 Pet 3:10

DECEIVE *cheat, mislead*
have you **d-d** me Gen 29:25
Jacob **d-d** Laban Gen 31:20
d-s his companion Lev 6:2
both stolen and **d-d** Josh 7:11
Do not **d** me 2 Kin 4:28
who **d-s** his neighbor Prov 26:19
Do not **d** yourselves Jer 37:9
your heart has **d-d** you Obad 3
they keep **d-ing** Rom 3:13
Let no one **d** you Eph 5:6
d-ing and being **d-d** 2 Tim 3:13

DECEIVER *liar*
as a **d** in his sight Gen 27:12
as **d-s** and yet true 2 Cor 6:8
d and the antichrist 2 John 7

DECEPTION *falsehood*
their mind prepares **d** Job 15:35
the hills are a **d** Jer 3:23
last **d** will be worse Matt 27:64

philosophy and empty **d** Col 2:8
reveling in their **d-s** 2 Pet 2:13
DEFRAUD *deprive, wrong*
whom have I **d-ed** 1 Sam 12:3
To **d** a man Lam 3:36
Do not **d** Mark 10:19
no one keep **d-ing** Col 2:18
DEITY *God, gods*
of strange **d-ies** Acts 17:18
fullness of **D** dwells Col 2:9
DELILAH
Philistine woman Judg 16:4
enticed Samson Judg 16:6-20
DELIVERANCE *salvation*
by a great **d** Gen 45:7
given this great **d** Judg 15:18
with songs of **d** Ps 32:7
a God of **d-s** Ps 68:20
d through...prayers Phil 1:19
DELIVERER *savior*
the LORD raised up a **d** Judg 3:9
gave them **d-s** Neh 9:27
my fortress and my **d** Ps 18:2
d-s...ascend Mount Obad 21
D...come from Zion Rom 11:26
DEMETRIUS
1 *Ephesian smith* Acts 19:24,38
2 *a Christian* 3 John 12
DEMON *devil*
sacrificed to **d-s** Deut 32:17
daughters to the **d-s** Ps 106:37
after the **d** was cast Matt 9:33
sacrifice to **d-s** 1 Cor 10:20
d-s also believe James 2:19
not to worship **d-s** Rev 9:20
DEMONIACS *possessed ones*
d, epileptics Matt 4:24
what had happened to the **d** Matt 8:33
DEMON-POSSESSED
many who were **d** Matt 8:16
a mute, **d** man Matt 9:32
to the **d** man Mark 5:16
sayings of one **d** John 10:21
DEN *abode*
remains in its **d** Job 37:8
From the **d-s** of lions Song 4:8
the viper's **d** Is 11:8
cast into the lions' **d** Dan 6:7
it a robbers' **d** Mark 11:17
DENARIUS
Roman silver coin Matt 20:2,9
a day's wage Luke 20:24
Denarii *(pl)* John 6:7; 12:5
DEPORTATION *exile*
after the **d** to Matt 1:12
to the **d** to Babylon Matt 1:17
DEPUTY *proconsul*
he was the only **d** 1 Kin 4:19
Solomon's...**d-ies** 1 Kin 5:16
a **d** was king 1 Kin 22:47
DESCEND *go down*
angels of God...**d-ing** Gen 28:12
His glory will not **d** Ps 49:17
breath of...**d-s** Eccl 3:21
will **d** to Hades Matt 11:23
Spirit **d-ing**...dove John 1:32
d into the abyss Rom 10:7
who **d-ed**...ascended Eph 4:10
DESCENDANT *seed, offering*
your **d-s** I will give Gen 12:7
will raise up your **d** 2 Sam 7:12
His **d-s** shall endure Ps 89:36
So shall your **d-s** be Rom 4:18
you are Abraham's **d-s** Gal 3:29

to the **d** of Abraham Heb 2:16
and the **d** of David Rev 22:16
DESECRATE *defile*
d the sanctuary Dan 11:31
tried to **d** the temple Acts 24:6
DESERT (n) *wilderness*
d plains of Jericho Josh 5:10
grieved Him in the **d** Ps 78:40
better to live in a **d** Prov 21:19
in the **d** a highway Is 40:3
Rivers in the **d** Is 43:19
like a bush in the **d** Jer 17:6
he lived in the **d-s** Luke 1:80
DESERT (v) *abandon, forsake*
d-ed to the king 2 Kin 25:11
who had **d-ed** them Acts 15:38
so quickly **d-ing** Him Gal 1:6
but all **d-ed** me 2 Tim 4:16
I will never **d** you Heb 13:5
DESERVE *earn, merit*
with him as he **d-d** Judg 9:16
done this **d-s** to die 2 Sam 12:5
He **d-s** death Matt 26:66
receiving what we **d** Luke 23:41
DESIRE (v) *crave, wish*
your heart **d-s** Deut 14:26
as much as you **d** 1 Sam 2:16
I **d** to argue with God Job 13:3
You **d** truth Ps 51:6
not **d** his delicacies Prov 23:3
all that my eyes **d-d** Eccl 2:10
righteous men **d-d** Matt 13:17
d the greater gifts 1 Cor 12:31
d...a good showing Gal 6:12
d a better *country* Heb 11:16
DEVIL *demon, Satan*
tempted by the **d** Matt 4:1
one of you is a **d** John 6:70
you son of the **d** Acts 13:10
firm against...the **d** Eph 6:11
render powerless...**d** Heb 2:14
serpent...the **d** Rev 12:9
d...into the lake Rev 20:10
DIAMOND *jewel*
a sapphire and a **d** Ex 28:18
With a **d** point Jer 17:1
DIE *decease, expire*
you will surely **d** Gen 2:17
not eat...which **d-s** Deut 14:21
Where you **d**, I will **d** Ruth 1:17
Curse God and **d** Job 2:9
even wise men **d** Ps 49:10
fools **d** for lack of Prov 10:21
and the fool alike **d** Eccl 2:16
soul who sins will **d** Ezek 18:4
to **d** with You Matt 26:35
child has not **d-d** Mark 5:39
live even if he **d-s** John 11:25
grain of wheat...**d-s** John 12:24
she fell sick and **d-d** Acts 9:37
d-d for the ungodly Rom 5:6
we who **d-d** to sin Rom 6:2
for whom Christ **d-d** Rom 14:15
I **d** daily 1 Cor 15:31
I **d-d** to the Law Gal 2:19
to **d** is gain Phil 1:21
Jesus **d-d** and rose 1 Thess 4:14
to **d** once and after Heb 9:27
these **d-d** in faith Heb 11:13
who **d** in the Lord Rev 14:13
DINAH
daughter of Jacob Gen 34:1,
raped by Shechem Gen 34:2,
DINNER *meal*
I have prepared...**d** Matt 22:4

because of…**d** guests Mark 6:26
was giving a big **d** Luke 14:16

DISCIPLE *student, learner*
to listen as a **d** Is 50:4
His twelve **d-s** Matt 10:1
d is not above his Matt 10:24
d-s rebuked them Matt 19:13
d-s left Him…fled Matt 26:56
make **d-s** of all Matt 28:19
Your **d-s** do not fast Mark 2:18
Passover…My **d-s** Mark 14:14
gaze toward His **d-s** Luke 6:20
he cannot be My **d** Luke 14:26
d-s believed in Him John 2:11
His **d-s** withdrew John 6:66
wash the **d-s'** feet John 13:5
d whom He loved John 19:26
d-s were first called Acts 11:26

DISEASE *sickness*
none of the **d-s** on you Ex 15:26
harmful **d-s** of Egypt Deut 7:15
d-d in his feet 2 Chr 16:12
d-d…not healed Ezek 34:4
heals all your **d-s** Ps 103:3
various **d-s** and pains Matt 4:24
power…to heal **d-s** Luke 9:1

DISHONEST *untruthful*
those who hate **d** gain Ex 18:21
order to get **d** gain Ezek 22:27
cheat with **d** scales Amos 8:5

DISHONOR (v) *disgrace, shame*
who **d-s** his father Deut 27:16
be ashamed and **d-ed** Ps 35:4
and you **d** Me John 8:49
bodies would be **d-ed** Rom 1:24
do you **d** God Rom 2:23

DISOBEDIENCE *rebellion*
the one man's **d** Rom 5:19
in the sons of **d** Eph 2:2
d received a just Heb 2:2
same example of **d** Heb 4:11

DIVINE (adj) *pertaining to deity*
in whom…**d** spirit Gen 41:38
I see a **d** being 1 Sam 28:13
D Nature…gold Acts 17:29
power and **d** nature Rom 1:20
is the **d** response Rom 11:4

DIVINE (v) *practice divination*
d-d that the LORD Gen 30:27
they **d** lies for you Ezek 21:29
d-ing lies for them Ezek 22:28
prophets **d** for money Mic 3:11

DIVINER *seer*
called for the…**d-s** 1 Sam 6:2
The **d** and the elder Is 3:2
your **d-s** deceive you Jer 29:8
d-s will be embarrassed Mic 3:7
d-s see lying visions Zech 10:2

DIVORCE (n) *separation*
a certificate of **d** Deut 24:1
given her a writ of **d** Jer 3:8
For I hate **d** Mal 2:16

DIVORCE (v) *separate*
he cannot **d** her Deut 22:19
husband **d-s** his wife Jer 3:1
man to **d** his wife Matt 19:3
Whoever **d-s** his Mark 10:11

DOCTRINE *teaching*
Teaching as **d-s** the Matt 15:9
every wind of **d** Eph 4:14
to teach strange **d-s** 1 Tim 1:3
to exhort in sound **d** Titus 1:9

DONKEY *ass*
a wild **d** of a man Gen 16:12
Balaam…to the **d** Num 22:29
the foal of a **d** Zech 9:9
you will find a **d** Matt 21:2
and mounted on a **d** Matt 21:5
a mute **d**, speaking 2 Pet 2:16

DOVE *bird*
he sent out a **d** Gen 8:8
had wings like a **d** Ps 55:6
eyes are *like* **d-s** Song 1:15
descending as a **d** Matt 3:16
descending as a **d** John 1:32
selling the **d-s** John 2:16

DRACHMA
Greek silver coin Neh 7:70-72; Matt 17:24

DRAGON *monster, serpent*
d who *lives* in the sea Is 27:1
Who pierced the **d** Is 51:9
d stood before the Rev 12:4
he laid hold of the **d** Rev 20:2

DREAM (n) *vision*
had a **d**, and behold Gen 28:12
man was relating a **d** Judg 7:13
flies away like a **d** Job 20:8
like a **d**, a vision Is 29:7
visions and **d-s** Dan 1:17
to Joseph in a **d** Matt 2:13

DREAM (v) *see a vision*
asleep and **d-ed** Gen 41:5
like those who **d** Ps 126:1
when a hungry man **d-s** Is 29:8
Your old men will **d** Joel 2:28

DRINK (n) *refreshment*
gave the lad a **d** Gen 21:19
or wine, or strong **d** Deut 14:26
to desire strong **d** Prov 31:4
gave Me *something* to **d** Matt 25:35
My blood is true **d** John 6:55
thirsty, give him a **d** Rom 12:20

DRINK (v)
he **drank** of the wine Gen 9:21
Do not **d** wine Lev 10:9
d from the brook 1 Kin 17:6
they all **drank** from Mark 14:23
after **d-ing** old *wine* Luke 5:39
who eats and **d-s** 1 Cor 11:29
ground that **d-s** the Heb 6:7

DRUNK *intoxicated*
arrows **d** with blood Deut 32:42
d, but not with wine Is 29:9
made…**d** in My wrath Is 63:6
not get **d** with wine Eph 5:18
I saw the woman **d** Rev 17:6

DRUNKARD *intoxicated person*
a glutton and a **d** Deut 21:20
song of the **d-s** Ps 69:12
Awake, **d-s**, and weep Joel 1:5
a reviler, or a **d** 1 Cor 5:11

DUST *dirt, earth*
God formed man of **d** Gen 2:7
And **d** you will eat Gen 3:14
the poor from the **d** 1 Sam 2:8
repent in **d** and ashes Job 42:6
d before the wind Ps 18:42
Will the **d** praise You Ps 30:9
You who lie in the **d** Is 26:19
shake the **d** off Matt 10:14
the **d** of your city Luke 10:11
d on their heads Rev 18:19

E

EAGLE *bird*
bore you on **e-s'** wings Ex 19:4
the **e** swoops down Deut 28:49
swifter than **e-s** 2 Sam 1:23
with wings like **e-s** Is 40:31

the face of an **e** Ezek 1:10
was like a flying **e** Rev 4:7

EARTH *land, world*
God created the…**e** Gen 1:1
Judge of all the **e** Gen 18:25
the **e** is the LORD'S Ex 9:29
way of all the **e** Josh 23:14
His stand on the **e** Job 19:25
foundation of the **e** Job 38:4
saints…in the **e** Ps 16:3
the shields of the **e** Ps 47:9
gave birth to the **e** Ps 90:2
He established the **e** Ps 104:5
wisdom founded…**e** Prov 3:19
the **e** remains forever Eccl 1:4
made the **e** tremble Is 14:16
the circle of the **e** Is 40:22
the ends of the **e** Is 45:22
the **e** is My footstool Is 66:1
e shone with His Ezek 43:2
make the **e** dark Amos 8:9
e will be devoured Zeph 3:8
shall inherit the **e** Matt 5:5
you bind on **e** Matt 16:19
on **e** peace among Luke 2:14
glorified…on the **e** John 17:4
man is from the **e** 1 Cor 15:47
heavens and a new **e** 2 Pet 3:13
e and heaven fled Rev 20:11

EARTHQUAKE *temblor*
LORD *was* not…**e** 1 Kin 19:11
punished with…**e** Is 29:6
be famines and **e-s** Matt 24:7
will be great **e-s** Luke 21:11
there was a great **e** Rev 6:12
killed in the **e** Rev 11:13

EAST *direction of compass*
spread out…to the **e** Gen 28:14
directed an **e** wind Ex 10:13
sons of the **e** were Judg 7:12
men of the **e** Job 1:3
With the **e** wind You Ps 48:7
offspring from the **e** Is 43:5
faces toward the **e** Ezek 8:16
Jerusalem on the **e** Zech 14:4
saw His star in the **e** Matt 2:2
lightning…the **e** Matt 24:27
kings from the **e** Rev 16:12

EBAL
1 *son of Shobal* Gen 36:23
2 *son of Joktan* 1 Chr 1:22
also Obal Gen 10:28
3 *mountain near Shechem* Deut 11:29

EBENEZER
a memorial stone 1 Sam 7:12

EBER
1 *line of Shem* Gen 10:21-24
progenitor of Jocktanide Arabs Gen 10:25-30
progenitor of Hebrews Gen 11:16ff
2 *a Gadite* 1 Chr 5:13
3 *son of Elpaal* 1 Chr 8:12
4 *son of Shashak* 1 Chr 8:22
5 *priest* Neh 12:20
see also **HEBER**

EDEN
1 *garden of God* Gen 2:15; Is 51:3
2 *city area* 2 Kin 19:12; Ezek 27:23
3 *son of Joah* 2 Chr 29:12

EDOM
1 *name of Esau* Gen 25:30
2 *Edomites* Num 20:18,20
3 *region or country* Gen 32:3; Judg 11:17
see also **SEIR**

EGYPT
country in NE Africa Gen 12:10; 37:25
source of food Gen 42:1,2
on the Nile Ex 4:19; 7:5
conflict with Moses Ex 7:8ff
scene of Passover Ex 12:1-36

EHUD
1 *left-handed Benjamite judge of Israel* Judg 3:15,21
2 *son of Bilhan* 1 Chr 7:10
3 *progenitor of clan* 1 Chr 8:6

ELAH
1 *Edomite* Gen 36:41
2 *valley SW of Jerusalem* 1 Sam 17:2
3 *father of Shimei* 1 Kin 4:18
4 *king of Israel* 1 Kin 16:8-10
5 *father of Hoshea* 2 Kin 15:30
6 *son of Caleb* 1 Chr 4:15
7 *son of Uzzi* 1 Chr 9:8

ELAM
1 *son of Shem* Gen 10:22
2 *son of Shashak* 1 Chr 8:24
3 *Korahite Levite* 1 Chr 26:3
4 *head of restoration family* Ezra 2:7; Neh 7:12
5 *head of restoration family* Ezra 2:31; Neh 7:34
6 *chief of people* Neh 10:14
7 *priest* Neh 12:42
8 *region E of Babylonia* Is 21:2; Dan 8:2

ELATH / ELOTH *city*
at Gulf of Aqabah 2 Kin 14:22
near Ezion-geber

ELDER *aged, older*
words of her **e** son Gen 27:42
the **e-s** of Israel Ex 17:6
sits among the **e-s** Prov 31:23
Assemble the **e-s** Joel 2:16
tradition of the **e-s** Matt 15:2
chief priests and **e-s** Matt 27:12
scribes…**e-s** came Mark 11:27
Council of **e-s** of Luke 22:66
e-s of the church Acts 20:17
I saw twenty-four **e-s** Rev 4:4

ELEAZAR
1 *son of Aaron* Ex 6:23
high priest Num 20:25-28
2 *son of Abinadab* 1 Sam 7:1
3 *son of Dodo* 2 Sam 23:9
4 *a Levite* 1 Chr 23:22
5 *son of Phinehas* Ezra 8:33
6 *son of Parosh* Ezra 10:18-25
7 *priest* Neh 12:42
8 *ancestor of Jesus* Matt 1:15

ELI
high priest 1 Sam 1:9; 2:12; 3:6; 4:18

ELIAKIM
1 *son of Hilkiah* 2 Kin 18:18; 19:2
2 *son of Josiah* 2 Kin 23:34
3 *priest* Neh 12:41
4 *ancestor of Jesus* Matt 1:13
5 *ancestor of Jesus* Luke 3:30,31

ELIEZER
1 *Abraham's servant* Gen 15:2
2 *son of Moses* 1 Chr 23:15
3 *son of Becher* 1 Chr 7:8
4 *priest* 1 Chr 15:24
5 *son of Zichri* 1 Chr 27:16
6 *a prophet* 2 Chr 20:37
7 *served under Ezra* Ezra 8:16
8 *son of Jeshua* Ezra 10:18
9 *Levite* Ezra 10:23
10 *son of Harim* Ezra 10:31
11 *ancestor of Jesus* Luke 3:29

ELIHU
1 *son of Tohu* 1 Sam 1:1
2 *Manassite captain* 1 Chr 12:20
3 *temple gatekeeper* 1 Chr 26:1

4 *officer of Judah* 1 Chr 27:18
5 *one of Job's friends* Job 32:17

ELIJAH
1 *prophet* 1 Kin 17:1
aided by widow 1 Kin 17:8ff
revived child 1 Kin 17:23
defeats prophets 1 Kin 18:20ff
flees Jezebel 1 Kin 19:4-8
chooses Elisha 1 Kin 19:19-21
taken up 2 Kin 2:1-11
2 *Benjamite* 1 Chr 8:27
3 *son of Harim* Ezra 10:21
4 *son of Elam* Ezra 10:26

ELISHA
prophet 2 Kin 6:12
called 1 Kin 19:19-21
Elijah's successor 2 Kin 2:1ff
miracle of oil 2 Kin 4:1-7
revived child 2 Kin 4:8-37
death 2 Kin 13:20

ELIZABETH
mother of John the Baptist Luke 1:7,13,41,57

ELUL
sixth month of Hebrew calendar Neh 6:15

ELYMAS
magician Acts 13:8
see also **BAR-JESUS**

EMERALD *precious stone*
ruby, topaz and **e** Ex 28:17
throne, like an **e** Rev 4:3

EMMAUS
village by Jerusalem Luke 24:13

ENCOURAGE *strengthen*
charge Joshua and **e** Deut 3:28
e-d him in God 1 Sam 23:16
e them in the work Ezra 6:22
Paul was **e-ing** them Acts 27:33
e one another 1 Thess 5:11
e the young women Titus 2:4

ENEMY *foe*
delivered your **e-ies** Gen 14:20
Your **e-ies** perish Judg 5:31
a man finds his **e** 1 Sam 24:19
consider me Your **e** Job 13:24
make the **e**...cease Ps 8:2
presence of my **e-ies** Ps 23:5
e has persecuted my Ps 143:3
If your **e** is hungry Prov 25:21
kisses of an **e** Prov 27:6
love your **e-ies**, and Matt 5:44
e-ies with each other Luke 23:12
e of all righteousness Acts 13:10
e is hungry, feed Rom 12:20
e...be abolished 1 Cor 15:26
an **e** of God James 4:4

ENGEDI
spring and town near Dead Sea 1 Sam 23:29; 24:1; Song 1:14

ENOCH
1 *son of Cain* Gen 4:17
2 *city* Gen 4:17
3 *Methuselah's father* Gen 5:22
walked with God Gen 5:24

EPHAH
1 *bushel, measure of capacity* Lev 5:11; Num 5:15
2 *son of Midian* Gen 25:4; 1 Chr 1:33
3 *Caleb's concubine* 1 Chr 2:46
4 *son of Jahdai* 1 Chr 2:47

EPHESUS
city of Asia Minor Acts 18:19; 1 Cor 16:8; Rev 1:11; 2:1

EPHOD
1 *priestly garment* Ex 28:6; 1 Sam 23:9; 2 Sam 6:14
2 *father of Hanniel* Num 34:23

EPHRAIM
1 *son of Joseph* Gen 41:52; 48:17
2 *tribe* Josh 16:5; Judg 7:24
3 *northern kingdom* Is 7:2-17; Hos 4:17; 9:3-17
4 *city* 2 Sam 13:23; John 11:54

EPHRATH(AH)
1 *Bethlehem* Gen 35:19; 48:7; Ruth 4:11; Mic 5:2
2 *wife of Caleb* 1 Chr 2:19,50
3 *territory* Ps 132:6

EPICUREAN
a Greek philosophy Acts 17:18

EPOCHS *ages, seasons*
the times and the **e** Dan 2:21
to know times or **e** Acts 1:7

ESARHADDON
Assyrian king 2 Kin 19:37; Ezra 4:2; Is 37:38

ESAU
son of Isaac Gen 25:25
twin of Jacob Gen 25:26
skillful hunter Gen 25:27
sold birthright Gen 25:34
despised Jacob Gen 27:41
reconciled with Jacob Gen 33:4

ESTHER
Hebrew name Hadassah
cousin of Mordecai Esth 2:7
Persian queen Esth 2:16-18

ETERNAL *everlasting*
e God is a dwelling Deut 33:27
E Father, Prince of Is 9:6
An **e** decree Jer 5:22
cast into the **e** fire Matt 18:8
guilty of an **e** sin Mark 3:29
to inherit **e** life Luke 10:25
He may give **e** life John 17:2
gift of God is **e** life Rom 6:23
e weight of glory 2 Cor 4:17
with the **e** purpose Eph 3:11
Now to the King **e** 1 Tim 1:17
source of **e** salvation Heb 5:9
through the **e** Spirit Heb 9:14
kept in **e** bonds Jude 6
an **e** gospel to preach Rev 14:6

ETERNITY *perpetuity*
set **e** in their heart Eccl 3:11
from **e** I am He Is 43:13
Jesus from all **e** 2 Tim 1:9
to the day of **e** 2 Pet 3:18

ETHIOPIA
NE African country Esth 1:1; Ps 68:31; Nah 3:9; Zeph 3:10

EUNUCH *chamberlain official*
seven **e-s** who served Esth 1:10
Nor let the **e** say Is 56:3
children, and *the* **e-s** Jer 41:16
made **e-s** by men Matt 19:12
an Ethiopian **e** Acts 8:27

EUPHRATES
river of Mesopotamia Gen 2:14; Jer 13:5; 46:10; Rev 9:14; 16:12

EVANGELIST *proclaimer*
house of Philip the **e** Acts 21:8
and some *as* **e-s** Eph 4:11
do the work of an **e** 2 Tim 4:5

EVE
first woman Gen 2:22
wife of Adam Gen 2:23
deceived by serpent Gen 3:1-7
named by Adam Gen 3:20

EVERLASTING *eternal*
e covenant between Gen 9:16
the LORD, the E God Gen 21:33
are the e arms Deut 33:27
e to e, You are God Ps 90:2
lovingkindness is e Ps 106:1
From e I was Prov 8:23
The E God, the LORD Is 40:28
e name which will Is 56:5
LORD for an e light Is 60:20
loved you with an e Jer 31:3
EVIDENCE *facts, testimony*
the e of witnesses Num 35:30
on the e of two Deut 19:15
not able to give e Ezra 2:59
and giving e Acts 17:3
EVIL *bad, wicked, wrong*
man's heart is e Gen 8:21
keep...from every e Deut 23:9
discern good and e 2 Sam 14:17
rebellious and e city Ezra 4:12
I fear no e Ps 23:4
repay me e for good Ps 35:12
turn away from e Prov 3:7
run rapidly to e Prov 6:18
returns e for good Prov 17:13
taken away from e Is 57:1
committed two e-s Jer 2:13
deliver us from e Matt 6:13
what e has He Matt 27:23
If you then, being e Luke 11:13
who does e hates the John 3:20
Never...e for e Rom 12:17
love of money is...e 1 Tim 6:10
tongue...restless e James 3:8
EVIL-MERODACH
king of Babylon 2 Kin 25:27; Jer 52:31
EWE *female sheep*
seven e lambs Gen 21:28
e lamb without Lev 14:10
poor man's e lamb 2 Sam 12:4
e-s with suckling Ps 78:71
like a flock of e-s Song 6:6
EXODUS *departure*
e of...Israel Heb 11:22
EXPANSE *firmament, vastness*
e of the heavens Gen 1:20
e of the waters Job 37:10
in His mighty e Ps 150:1
from above the e Ezek 1:25
EZRA
priest Ezra 7:1-5
scribe Ezra 7:6
sent by king Ezra 7:14,21
brought exiles Ezra 8:1-14
Nehemiah's colleague Neh 8:2-6

F

FACE *countenance*
sweat of your f You Gen 3:19
Abram fell on his f Gen 17:3
speak to Moses f to f Ex 33:11
skin of his f shone Ex 34:30
make His f shine Num 6:25
hide Your f from me Ps 13:1
Who seek Your f Ps 24:6
His f to shine upon us Ps 67:1
f of Your anointed Ps 84:9
makes a cheerful f Prov 15:13
set My f against you Jer 44:11
had the f of an eagle Ezek 1:10
Each...had four f-s Ezek 10:21
fast...wash your f Matt 6:17
they spat in His f Matt 26:67
like the f of an angel Acts 6:15
natural f in a mirror James 1:23
His f was like the sun Rev 1:16
FAITH *believe, trust*
because you broke f Deut 32:51
Will you have f Job 39:12
Who keeps f forever Ps 146:6
will live by his f Hab 2:4
Seeing their f, Jesus Matt 9:2
f the size of a mustard seed Matt 17:20
Your f has saved you Luke 7:50
Increase our f Luke 17:5
your f may not fail Luke 22:32
man full of f Acts 6:5
of f to the Gentiles Acts 14:27
sanctified by f in Me Acts 26:18
justified by f Rom 5:1
f...from hearing Rom 10:17
if I have all f 1 Cor 13:2
your f also is vain 1 Cor 15:14
we walk by f 2 Cor 5:7
live by f in the Son Gal 2:20
saved through f Eph 2:8
one Lord, one f Eph 4:5
joy in the f Phil 1:25
stability of your f Col 2:5
breastplate of f 1 Thess 5:8
for not all have f 2 Thess 3:2
fall away from the f 1 Tim 4:1
conduct, love, f 1 Tim 4:12
they upset the f 2 Tim 2:18
sound in the f Titus 1:13
showing all good f Titus 2:10
full assurance of f Heb 10:22
By f Enoch was taken Heb 11:5
perfecter of f Heb 12:2
ask in f James 1:6
prayer offered in f James 5:15
power of God...f 1 Pet 1:5
the f of the saints Rev 13:10
FAITHFUL *loyal, trustworthy*
the f God, who keeps Deut 7:9
raise...a f priest 1 Sam 2:35
heart f before You Neh 9:8
LORD preserves the f Ps 31:23
commandments...f Ps 119:86
the LORD who is f Is 49:7
Well done...f Matt 25:23
God is f 1 Cor 1:9
F is He who calls 1 Thess 5:24
He considered me f 1 Tim 1:12
entrust...to f men 2 Tim 2:2
souls to a f Creator 1 Pet 4:19
He is f...to forgive 1 John 1:9
Be f until death Rev 2:10
called F and True Rev 19:11
FAITHFULNESS *loyalty*
kindness and f Gen 47:29
A God of f Deut 32:4
make known Your f Ps 89:1
f to all generations Ps 100:5
and mercy and f Matt 23:23
nullify the f of God Rom 3:3
kindness, goodness, f Gal 5:22
FAITHLESS *unbelieving*
what f Israel did Jer 3:6
O f daughter Jer 31:22
Their heart is f Hos 10:2
If we are f 2 Tim 2:13
FAMILY *household, relatives*
f-ies from the ark Gen 8:19
all the f-ies of Gen 12:3
f may redeem him Lev 25:49
f-ies of the Levites Num 3:20
my f is the least Judg 6:15
f-ies like a flock Ps 107:41

God of all the f-ies Jer 31:1
f-ies of the earth Amos 3:2
every f in heaven Eph 3:15
upsetting whole f-ies Titus 1:11

FAST (n) *food abstinence*
Proclaim a f 1 Kin 21:9
you call this a f Is 58:5
Consecrate a f Joel 1:14
f was already over Acts 27:9

FAST (v) *abstain from food*
and David f-ed 2 Sam 12:16
maidens also will f Esth 4:16
you f for contention Is 58:4
had f-ed forty days Matt 4:2
whenever you f Matt 6:16
disciples do not f Mark 2:18
I f twice a week Luke 18:12
had f-ed and prayed Acts 13:3

FASTING *food abstinence*
times of f Esth 9:31
weak from f Ps 109:24
noticed…when they are f Matt 6:16
by prayer and f Matt 17:21
Pharisees were f Mark 2:18

FATE *destiny*
appalled at his f Job 18:20
one f befalls them Eccl 2:14
f for the righteous Eccl 9:2
one f for all men Eccl 9:3

FATHER *God* or *parent*
leave his f…mother Gen 2:24
f of a multitude Gen 17:4
Honor your f Ex 20:12
who strikes his f Ex 21:15
iniquity of the f-s Deut 5:9
Is not He your F Deut 32:6
your f-'s instruction Prov 1:8
son makes a f glad Prov 10:1
Eternal F, Prince of Is 9:6
all have one f Mal 2:10
F who sees…in secret Matt 6:4
Our F who is in Matt 6:9
does the will of My F Matt 7:21
in My F-'s kingdom Matt 26:29
in the glory of His F Mark 8:38
be in my F-'s *house* Luke 2:49
F, hallowed be Your Luke 11:2
F, forgive them Luke 23:34
begotten from the F John 1:14
my F-'s house a John 2:16
F…testifies John 8:18
the f of lies John 8:44
I and the F are one John 10:30
In my F-'s house are John 14:2
F is the vinedresser John 15:1
ask the F for John 16:23
I ascend to My F John 20:17
one God and F of all Eph 4:6

FATHER-IN-LAW
she sent to her f Gen 38:25
returned to Jethro his f Ex 4:18
his f, the girl's Judg 19:4
f of Caiaphas John 18:13

FATHERLESS *orphan*
father of the f Ps 68:5
He supports the f Ps 146:9
fields of the f Prov 23:10
f and the widow Ezek 22:7

FATLING *young lamb* or *kid*
sacrificed…a f 2 Sam 6:13
f-s…in abundance 1 Kin 1:19
f-s of Bashan Ezek 39:18

FEAR (n) *awe, dread, reverence*
no f of God in Gen 20:11
f of the LORD is clean Ps 19:9
f…is the beginning Ps 111:10
afraid of sudden f Prov 3:25
f…prolongs life Prov 10:27
f of man brings a Prov 29:25
they cried out in f Matt 14:26
guards shook for f Matt 28:4
men fainting from f Luke 21:26
for f of the Jews John 7:13
no f of God before Rom 3:18
in weakness and in f 1 Cor 2:3
knowing the f of the 2 Cor 5:11
with f and trembling Eph 6:5
through f of death Heb 2:15
love casts out f 1 John 4:18

FEAR (v) *be afraid, revere*
the midwives f-ed God Ex 1:21
Moses said…Do not f Ex 14:13
may learn to f Me Deut 4:10
not f other gods 2 Kin 17:37
I f no evil Ps 23:4
Whom shall I f Ps 27:1
not f evil tidings Ps 112:7
who f-s the LORD Prov 31:30
Rather, f God Eccl 5:7
Take courage, f not Is 35:4
Do not f, for I am Is 41:10
will f and tremble Jer 33:9
do not f them Matt 10:26
f-ed the crowd Matt 14:5
who did not f God Luke 18:2
slavery leading to f Rom 8:15
I f for you Gal 4:11
let us f if Heb 4:1

FEARFUL *terrifying*
it is a f thing Ex 34:10
were f and amazed Luke 8:25
will be f *of sinning* 1 Tim 5:20

FELIX
Roman procurator Acts 23:26; 24:25; 25:14

FELLOWSHIP *companionship*
had sweet f together Ps 55:14
f…Holy Spirit 2 Cor 13:14
right hand of f Gal 2:9
f of His sufferings Phil 3:10
f is with the Father 1 John 1:3
f with one another 1 John 1:7

FEMALE *girl, woman*
and f He created Gen 1:27
a f slave Ex 21:7
f from the flock Lev 5:6
likeness of male or f Deut 4:16
neither male nor f Gal 3:28

FESTUS, PORCIUS
Roman procurator of Judea Acts 24:27; 25:14,23; 26:25

FIERY *burning*
LORD sent f serpents Num 21:6
with f heat Deut 28:22
His arrows f shafts Ps 7:13
f ordeal among you 1 Pet 4:12

FIG *fruit*
they sewed f leaves Gen 3:7
But the f tree said Judg 9:11
a piece of f cake 1 Sam 30:12
nor f-s from thistles Matt 7:16
the f tree withered Matt 21:19
f-s from thorns Luke 6:44
under the f tree John 1:48
Can a f tree James 3:12

FIRE *burning or flame*
the f and the knife Gen 22:6
bush…burning with f Ex 3:2
pillar of f by night Ex 13:21
offered strange f Num 3:4
f of the LORD fell 1 Kin 18:38

a chariot of f 2 Kin 2:11
jealousy burn like f Ps 79:5
Israel will become a f Is 10:17
Is not My word like f Jer 23:29
the Holy Spirit and f Matt 3:11
with unquenchable f Matt 3:12
tongues as of f Acts 2:3
lake that burns with f Rev 21:8
FIRSTBORN *oldest*
Sidon, his f Gen 10:15
the f bore a son Gen 19:37
I am Esau your f Gen 27:19
LORD killed every f Ex 13:15
birth to her f son Luke 2:7
church of the f Heb 12:23
f of the dead Rev 1:5
FISH
rule over the f Gen 1:26
Their f stink Is 50:2
a great f to swallow Jon 1:17
loaves and two f Matt 14:17
snake instead of a f Luke 11:11
net *full* of f John 21:8
FISHERMEN *fishers*
f will lament Is 19:8
for they were f Matt 4:18
the f had gotten out Luke 5:2
FISHERS *fishermen*
make you f of men Matt 4:19
become f of men Mark 1:17
FLAMING *burning*
the f sword Gen 3:24
f fire by night Is 4:5
eyes were like f Dan 10:6
angels in f fire 2 Thess 1:7
FLEECE *wool*
put a f of wool Judg 6:37
dry only on the f Judg 6:39
warmed with the f Job 31:20
FLESH *body, meat*
f of my f Gen 2:23
shall become one f Gen 2:24
from my f I shall see Job 19:26
heart and my f sing Ps 84:2
All f is grass Is 40:6
the f is weak Matt 26:41
spirit…not have f Luke 24:39
the Word became f John 1:14
born of the f is f John 3:6
who eats My f John 6:56
children of the f Rom 9:8
thorn in the f 2 Cor 12:7
desires of the f Eph 2:3
polluted by the f Jude 23
filled with their f Rev 19:21
FLESHLY *carnal*
not in f wisdom 2 Cor 1:12
His f body Col 1:22
abstain from f lusts 1 Pet 2:11
FLOCK *goats, sheep*
a keeper of f-s Gen 4:2
water their father's f Ex 2:16
Your people like a f Ps 77:20
He will tend His f Is 40:11
scattered My f Jer 23:2
over their f by night Luke 2:8
will become one f John 10:16
f of God among you 1 Pet 5:2
FLOOD *overflowing of water*
I am bringing the f Gen 6:17
f came upon the earth Gen 7:17
end…with a f Dan 9:26
the f-s came Matt 7:25
f…destroyed Luke 17:27
FLUTE *musical instrument*
tambourine, f, and 1 Sam 10:5
playing on f-s 1 Kin 1:40
the f or on the harp 1 Cor 14:7
musicians…**f-players** Rev 18:22
FOAL *colt*
ties *his* f to the vine Gen 49:11
f of a wild donkey Job 11:12
f of a beast of burden Matt 21:5
FOE *enemy*
before your f-s 1 Chr 21:12
A f and an enemy Esth 7:6
iniquity of my f-s Ps 49:5
the evil to my f-s Ps 54:5
avenge…His f-s Jer 46:10
FOOD *bread, meat*
shall be f for you Gen 1:29
tree was good for f Gen 3:6
in giving them f Ruth 1:6
tears have been my f Ps 42:3
it is deceptive f Prov 23:3
his f was locusts Matt 3:4
life more than f Matt 6:25
f is to do the will John 4:34
My flesh is true f John 6:55
milk…not solid f 1 Cor 3:2
FOOL *unwise person*
The f has said in his Ps 14:1
F-s despise wisdom Prov 1:7
too exalted for a f Prov 24:7
f multiplies words Eccl 10:14
The prophet is a f Hos 9:7
says, You f Matt 5:22
f-s and blind men Matt 23:17
wise, they became **f-s** Rom 1:22
f-s for Christ's sake 1 Cor 4:10
FOOLISH *silly, unwise*
O f and unwise Deut 32:6
a f son is a grief Prov 10:1
False and f *visions* Lam 2:14
Woe to the f Ezek 13:3
f took their lamps Matt 25:3
O f men and slow Luke 24:25
he must become f 1 Cor 3:18
You f Galatians Gal 3:1
do not be f Eph 5:17
FOOLISHNESS *folly*
The naive inherit f Prov 14:18
folly of fools is f Prov 14:24
mouth is speaking f Is 9:17
f of God is wiser 1 Cor 1:25
is f before God 1 Cor 3:19
FORBID *prohibit*
if her father should f Num 30:5
f-ding to pay taxes Luke 23:2
do not f to speak 1 Cor 14:39
men who f marriage 1 Tim 4:3
he f-s those who 3 John 10
FOREFATHER *ancestor*
iniquity of their f-s Lev 26:40
Your first f sinned Is 43:27
I swore to your f-s Jer 11:5
Abraham, our f Rom 4:1
the way my f-s did 2 Tim 1:3
FOREIGNER *alien, stranger*
no f is to eat of it Ex 12:43
sell it to a f Deut 14:21
charge…a f Deut 23:20
since I am a f Ruth 2:10
a f in their sight Job 19:15
f-s entered his gate Obad 11
FORGIVE *pardon*
f the transgression Gen 50:17
f their sin Ex 32:32
f our sins Ps 79:9

not f their iniquity Jer 18:23
f us our debts Matt 6:12
authority…to f sins Matt 9:6
f-gave him the debt Matt 18:27
can f sins but God Mark 2:7
he who is **f-n** little Luke 7:47
Father, f them Luke 23:34
whom you f 2 Cor 2:10
f-ing each other Eph 4:32
f-n us all our Col 2:13
righteous to f us 1 John 1:9

FORGIVENESS *pardon*
a God of f Neh 9:17
there is f with You Ps 130:4
poured out…for f Matt 26:28
repentance for f Luke 24:47
receives f of sins Acts 10:43
f of our trespasses Eph 1:7
the f of sins Col 1:14
there is no f Heb 9:22

FORNICATION
f-s, thefts, false Matt 15:19
were not born of f John 8:41
strangled and from f Acts 15:29

FORNICATORS
neither f, nor 1 Cor 6:9
f…God will judge Heb 13:4

FOX *small animal*
three hundred **f-es** Judg 15:4
f-es that are ruining Song 2:15
like **f-es** among ruins Ezek 13:4
The **f-es** have holes Matt 8:20
Go and tell that f Luke 13:32

FRANKINCENSE *spice*
spices with pure f Ex 30:34
f and the spices 1 Chr 9:29
trees of f Song 4:14
gold, f, and myrrh Matt 2:11

FRIEND *companion, comrade*
man speaks to his f Ex 33:11
f-s are my scoffers Job 16:20
loved ones and my **f-s** Ps 38:11
my familiar f Ps 55:13
A f loves at all Prov 17:17
Wealth adds…**f-s** Prov 19:4
who blesses his f Prov 27:14
confidence in a f Mic 7:5
f of tax collectors Matt 11:19
F, your sins are Luke 5:20
f of the bridegroom John 3:29
his life for his **f-s** John 15:13
You are My **f-s**, if John 15:14

FRIENDSHIP
the f of God Job 29:4
f with the world James 4:4

FROGS
smite…with f Ex 8:2
f which destroyed Ps 78:45
land swarmed with f Ps 105:30
unclean spirits like f Rev 16:13

FRUIT *growth, produce*
f trees…bearing f Gen 1:11
she took from its f Gen 3:6
the f of the womb Gen 30:2
offering of first **f-s** Lev 2:12
its f in its season Ps 1:3
yield f in old age Ps 92:14
eat its choice **f-s** Song 4:16
eaten the f of lies Hos 10:13
know…by their **f-s** Matt 7:16
bad tree bears bad f Matt 7:17
f for life eternal John 4:36
the f of the Spirit Gal 5:22
f in every good work Col 1:10

G

GABRIEL
angel of high rank Dan 8:16; 9:21; Luke 1:19,26

GAD
1 *son of Jacob* Gen 30:11; 35:26
2 *tribe of* Num 1:25; 2:14
3 *valley* 2 Sam 24:5
4 *seer, prophet* 2 Sam 24:11,18

GAIUS
1 *Macedonian* Acts 19:29
2 *companion of Paul* Acts 20:4
3 *Corinthian believer* 1 Cor 1:14
4 *addressee of 3 John* 3 John 1

GALATIA
Roman province in Asia Minor 1 Cor 16:1; 2 Tim 4:10

GALE *storm*
dust before a g Is 17:13
a fierce g of wind Mark 4:37

GALILEE
1 *district in N Palestine* Josh 21:32; 1 Kin 9:11; Matt 2:22; Acts 10:37
2 *Sea of* Matt 4:18; Mark 7:31
also **Sea of Chinnereth**
also **Lake of Gennesaret**
also **Sea of Tiberias**

GAMALIEL
1 *head of tribe* Num 2:20; 7:54
2 *Pharisee* Acts 5:34; 22:3

GARDEN *planted area*
God walking in the g Gen 3:8
from the g of Eden Gen 3:23
Make my g breathe Song 4:16
plant **g-s**, and eat Jer 29:5
tabernacle like a g Lam 2:6
in the g with Him John 18:26
the g a new tomb John 19:41

GAZA
Philistine city Gen 10:19; Judg 16:1; Jer 47:5

GAZELLE *animal*
swift as the **g-s** 1 Chr 12:8
a g Or a young stag Song 2:17
like a hunted g Is 13:14

GEDERAH
1 *town of Judah* Josh 15:36
2 *town of Benjamin* 1 Chr 12:4

GEHAZI
servant of Elisha 2 Kin 4:12; 5:20; 8:4

GENNESARET
1 *lake* Luke 5:1
also **Sea of Chinnereth**
also **Sea of Galilee**
also **Sea of Tiberias**
2 *land or district* Matt 14:34; Mark 6:53

GENTILES *foreigners, non-Jews*
Galilee of the **G** Matt 4:15
hand Him over to the **G** Matt 20:19
revelation to the **G** Luke 2:32
Why did the **G** rage Acts 4:25
salvation…to the **G** Rom 11:11
preach…among the **G** Gal 1:16

GERIZIM
mountain near Shechem Deut 11:29; Josh 8:33

GERSHOM
1 *son of Moses* Ex 2:22; 18:3
2 *son of Levi* 1 Chr 6:16,43
3 *line of Phinehas* Ezra 8:2

GETHSEMANE
garden on Mount of Olives Matt 26:36; Mark 14:32

GIANT
were born to the g 2 Sam 21:22
from the **g-s** 1 Chr 20:6

GIBEAH
1 *village in Judah* Josh 15:57

2 *in Ephraim* Josh 24:33
3 *town of Benjamin* 1 Sam 10:26; 13:2; 2 Sam 23:29

GIBEON
town in Benjamin Josh 9:3,17; 1 Kin 3:5; 1 Chr 8:29

GIDEON
son of Joash Judg 6:11,36
judge Judg 8:4-21

GIHON
1 *river of Eden* Gen 2:13
2 *Jerusalem spring* 2 Chr 32:30

GILBOA
mountain 2 Sam 1:6
where Saul died 2 Sam 21:12

GILEAD
1 *son of Machir* Num 36:1
2 *descendant of Gad* 1 Chr 5:14
3 *father of Jephthah* Judg 11:1
4 *land E of Jordan* Num 32:29
5 *mountain* Judg 7:3
6 *city* Hos 6:8

GILGAL
1 *in Arabah* Deut 11:30
2 *encampment in Jordan Valley* Josh 5:9; 1 Sam 7:16
near Jericho Josh 5:8,10
3 *in N Judah* Josh 15:7
4 *in Galilee* Josh 12:23
5 *village near Bethel* 2 Kin 2:1

GIRL *maiden*
the g and consult Gen 24:57
sold a g for wine Joel 3:3
boys and g-s playing Zech 8:5
the g has not died Matt 9:24

GLORIFY *honor, worship*
g Your name forever Ps 86:12
Let the LORD be g-ied Is 66:5
g your Father Matt 5:16
shepherds...g-ing Luke 2:20
Jesus...not yet g-ied John 7:39
Father, g Your name John 12:28
God is g-ied in Him John 13:31
were all g-ing God Acts 4:21
Gentiles to g God Rom 15:9
g God in your body 1 Cor 6:20
did not g Himself Heb 5:5

GLORIOUS *exalted, great*
g name be blessed Neh 9:5
G things are spoken Ps 87:3
resting place will be g Is 11:10
the law great and g Is 42:21
g gospel of...God 1 Tim 1:11

GLORY (n) *honor, splendor*
show me Your g Ex 33:18
while My g is passing Ex 33:22
Tell of His g 1 Chr 16:24
King of g may come Ps 24:7
exchanged their g Ps 106:20
earth is full of His g Is 6:3
their g into shame Hos 4:7
Solomon in all his g Matt 6:29
g of the Lord shone Luke 2:9
G...in the highest Luke 2:14
He comes in His g Luke 9:26
do not seek My g John 8:50
short of the g of God Rom 3:23
all to the g of God 1 Cor 10:31
eternal weight of g 2 Cor 4:17
body of His g Phil 3:21
crowned Him with g Heb 2:7
unfading crown of g 1 Pet 5:4

GLORY (v) *exalt*
And g in Your praise 1 Chr 16:35
G in His holy name Ps 105:3

in Him they will g Jer 4:2
I...have reason to g Phil 2:16

GLUTTON *excessive eater*
g...come to poverty Prov 23:21
a companion of g-s Prov 28:7
evil beasts, lazy g-s Titus 1:12

GOAT *animal*
a young g from the flock Gen 38:17
curtains of g-s' *hair* Ex 26:7
not boil a young g...milk Ex 34:26
g for a sin offering Num 15:27
prepare a young g for you Judg 13:15
quilt of g-s' *hair* 1 Sam 19:13
g *had* a...horn Dan 8:5
shaggy g *represents* Dan 8:21
sheep from the g-s Matt 25:32
never given me a young g Luke 15:29
blood of g-s...bulls Heb 9:13

GOD *Deity, Eternal One*
In the beginning G Gen 1:1
G formed man of dust Gen 2:7
G sent him out Gen 3:23
G gave to Abraham Gen 28:4
tablets were G-'s work Ex 32:16
G is my...fortress 2 Sam 22:33
G of my salvation Ps 18:46
In G...put my trust Ps 56:4
Search me, O G Ps 139:23
word of G is tested Prov 30:5
servant of the living G Dan 6:20
I am G and not man Hos 11:9
Will a man rob G Mal 3:8
G descending...dove Matt 3:16
they shall see G Matt 5:8
What...G has joined Matt 19:6
kingdom of G is at Mark 1:15
My G, why have Mark 15:34
You the Son of G Luke 22:70
the Word was G John 1:1
No one has seen G John 1:18
the Lamb of G John 1:29
G so loved the world John 3:16
G is spirit John 4:24
voice of...Son of G John 5:25
obey G rather than Acts 5:29
judgment of G Rom 2:2
bear fruit for G Rom 7:4
we are children of G Rom 8:16
are a temple of G 1 Cor 3:16
full armor of G Eph 6:11
one G...one mediator 1 Tim 2:5
is inspired by G 2 Tim 3:16
word of G is...sharper Heb 4:12
impossible...G to lie Heb 6:18
G is love 1 John 4:8
great supper of G Rev 19:17

GOD *false deity, idols*
no other g-s before Me Ex 20:3
New g-s were chosen Judg 5:8
cast their g-s into Is 37:19
bowed...to other g-s Jer 22:9
no other g who is Dan 3:29
The voice of a g Acts 12:22
g-s...become like Acts 14:11
the g of this world 2 Cor 4:4

GODDESS *female deity*
Ashtoreth the g of 1 Kin 11:5
great g Artemis Acts 19:27
blasphemers of...g Acts 19:37

GODLESS *pagan, without God*
hope of the g will Job 8:13
joy of...g momentary Job 20:5
g man destroys his Prov 11:9
hands of g men Acts 2:23
become of the g 1 Pet 4:18

GODLINESS *holiness*
in all g and dignity 1 Tim 2:2
the mystery of g 1 Tim 3:16
g is profitable 1 Tim 4:8
to a form of g 2 Tim 3:5
g, brotherly kindness 2 Pet 1:7
GODLY *holy*
keeps…His g ones 1 Sam 2:9
g man ceases to be Ps 12:1
not forsake His g ones Ps 37:28
and g sincerity 2 Cor 1:12
to live g in Christ 2 Tim 3:12
rescue the g from 2 Pet 2:9
GOG
1 *a Reubenite* 1 Chr 5:4
2 *prince of Meshech and Tubal* Ezek 38:2
3 *symbol of godless nations* Rev 20:8
see also MAGOG
GOLAN
city of refuge Josh 21:27
a Levitical city 1 Chr 6:71
GOLD *precious metal*
g of that land is good Gen 2:12
mercy seat of pure g Ex 25:17
Almighty…be your g Job 22:25
more desirable than g Ps 19:10
refine them like g Mal 3:3
to Him gifts of g Matt 2:11
Do not acquire g Matt 10:9
Divine Nature…g Acts 17:29
coveted no…g Acts 20:33
city was pure g Rev 21:18
GOLDSMITH *gold craftsman*
g-s and…merchants Neh 3:32
g, and he makes it Is 46:6
GOLGOTHA
site of Crucifixion Matt 27:33; Mark 15:22; John 19:17
GOLIATH
Philistine giant 1 Sam 17:4,23; 21:9; 1 Chr 20:5
GOMER
1 *son of Japheth* Gen 10:2
2 *group of people* Ezek 38:6
3 *wife of Hosea* Hos 1:3
GOMORRAH
city of Jordan plain Gen 10:19; 14:10; 19:24
probably S of Dead Sea Is 13:19; 2 Pet 2:6
GOSHEN
1 *district of Egypt in Nile Delta* Gen 45:10; 47:6,27
2 *S Judah region* Josh 10:41
3 *town in Judah* Josh 15:51
GOSPEL *good news*
proclaiming the g of Matt 4:23
preach the g to all Mark 16:15
not ashamed of the g Rom 1:16
if our g is veiled 2 Cor 4:3
or a different g 2 Cor 11:4
distort the g of Christ Gal 1:7
g of your salvation Eph 1:13
g of peace Eph 6:15
defense of the g Phil 1:16
the hope of the g Col 1:23
eternal g to preach Rev 14:6
GOVERNMENT *authority, rule*
g…on His shoulders Is 9:6
be no end to…*His* g Is 9:7
GOVERNOR *ruler*
not offer it to your g Mal 1:8
brought before g-s Matt 10:18
g was quite amazed Matt 27:14
Pilate was g of Judea Luke 3:1
g over Egypt Acts 7:10
GRACE *benevolence, favor*
G is poured upon Your Ps 45:2
g to the afflicted Prov 3:34
g of God was upon Luke 2:40
full of g and truth John 1:14
g abounded…more Rom 5:20
g of our Lord Jesus Rom 16:20
My g is sufficient 2 Cor 12:9
by g you have been Eph 2:8
justified by His g Titus 3:7
to the throne of g Heb 4:16
g to the humble James 4:6
GRACIOUS *kind*
God be g to you Gen 43:29
g to whom I will be Ex 33:19
a g and…God Neh 9:31
Be g to me, O LORD Ps 6:2
and g, Slow to anger Ps 86:15
g to a poor man Prov 19:17
be g to…remnant Amos 5:15
GRANDCHILDREN
G are the crown of Prov 17:6
widow has…or g 1 Tim 5:4
GRANDDAUGHTER
g-s, and all his Gen 46:7
g of Omri king of 2 Kin 8:26
GRANDSON
g might fear the LORD Deut 6:2
sons and thirty g-s Judg 12:14
master's g shall eat 2 Sam 9:10
GRAPE *fruit*
nor eat…dried g-s Num 6:3
of g-s you drank Deut 32:14
when the g harvest is Is 24:13
G-s are not gathered Matt 7:16
g-s from a briar Luke 6:44
GREED *excessive desire*
caught by *their*…g Prov 11:6
every form of g Luke 12:15
wickedness, g, evil Rom 1:29
a pretext for g 1 Thess 2:5
a heart trained in g 2 Pet 2:14
GREEDY *craving*
had g desires Num 11:4
g man curses Ps 10:3
Everyone is g for Jer 6:13
GREEKS
people of Greece Joel 3:6; Acts 16:1,3; Rom 1:16; 1 Cor 12:13
GUARDIAN *overseer*
g-s of *the children* 2 Kin 10:1
under g-s and Gal 4:2
G of your souls 1 Pet 2:25
GUILT *offence*
be free from g Num 5:31
according to his g Deut 25:2
charge me with a g 2 Sam 3:8
our g has grown Ezra 9:6
land is full of g Jer 51:5
must bear their g Hos 10:2
I find no g in Him John 18:38
GUILTY *charged* or *condemned*
he sins and becomes g Lev 6:4
murderer…g of Num 35:31
as one who is g 2 Sam 14:13
g by the blood Ezek 22:4
g of an eternal sin Mark 3:29
has become g of all James 2:10

H

HABOR
river in Mesopotamia 2 Kin 17:6; 18:11; 1 Chr 5:26
HADAD
1 *son of Ishmael* Gen 25:15; 1 Chr 1:30
2 *king of Edom, son of Bedad* Gen 36:35,36; 1 Chr 1:46,47

3 *king of Edom* Gen 36:39; 1 Chr 1:50,51
4 *Edomite prince* 1 Kin 11:14ff
HADASSAH
Esther's Hebrew name Esth 2:7
HADES *hell, place of dead*
will descend to **H** Matt 11:23
in **H** he lifted up Luke 16:23
abandoned to **H** Acts 2:31
see also **HELL** *and* **SHEOL**
HAGAR
Sarah's handmaiden Gen 16:1
Abraham's slave wife Gen 16:3
mother of Ishmael Gen 16:15
HAGGITH
David's wife 2 Sam 3:4
mother of Adonijah 1 Kin 1:11
HAIL (n) *pieces of ice*
rained **h** on the land Ex 9:23
storehouses of the **h** Job 38:22
gave them **h** for rain Ps 105:32
plague of the **h** Rev 16:21
HAILSTONES *pieces of ice*
who died from the **h** Josh 10:11
H and coals of fire Ps 18:13
you, O **h**, will fall Ezek 13:11
h…one hundred Rev 16:21
HALLELUJAH *praise Yahweh*
H! Salvation and Rev 19:1
H! Her smoke rises Rev 19:3
Amen. **H** Rev 19:4
H! For the Lord our Rev 19:6
HALLOWED *consecrated, holy*
H be Your name Matt 6:9
HAM
1 *son of Noah* Gen 5:32; 9:18
2 *city* Gen 14:5
3 *poetic name for Egypt* Ps 105:27; 106:22
HAMAN
Persian prime minister
son of Hammedatha Esth 3:1
HAMATH
city in Aram 2 Kin 23:33; 25:21
HAMON-GOG
valley where army of Gog is defeated
Ezek 39:11,15
HANANIAH
1 *son of Zerubbabel* 1 Chr 3:19
2 *son of Shashak* 1 Chr 8:24
3 *musician* 1 Chr 25:4,23
4 *in Uzziah's army* 2 Chr 26:11
5 *repaired wall* Neh 3:30
6 *overseer of palace* Neh 7:2
7 *false prophet* Jer 28:15
8 *Shadrach* Dan 1:6,7
name of six other individuals
HANNAH
mother of Samuel 1 Sam 2:21
HAPPY *blessed, joyful*
Leah said, **H** am I Gen 30:13
h…man whom God Job 5:17
h…who keeps the Prov 29:18
HARAN
1 *brother of Abraham* Gen 11:27
father of Lot Gen 11:31
2 *Gershonite Levite* 1 Chr 23:9
3 *Mesopotamian city* Gen 11:32; 27:43
HARLOT *prostitute*
thought she *was* a **h** Gen 38:15
the hire of a **h** Deut 23:18
h whose name was Josh 2:1
Dressed as a **h** Prov 7:10
city has become a **h** Is 1:21
also played the **h** Ezek 16:26
Traded a boy for a **h** Joel 3:3
Mother of **H-s** Rev 17:5

HAR-MAGEDON
hill of Megiddo Rev 16:16
see also **MEGIDDO**
HARP *musical instrument*
my **h** is turned to Job 30:31
praises…with a **h** Ps 33:2
Awake, **h** and lyre Ps 57:8
gaiety of the **h** ceases Is 24:8
each one holding a **h** Rev 5:8
holding **h-s** of God Rev 15:2
HARVEST *reap and gather*
Seedtime and **h** Gen 8:22
fruits of the wheat **h** Ex 34:22
you reap your **h** Deut 24:19
he who sleeps in **h** Prov 10:5
snow…time of **h** Prov 25:13
like rain in **h** Prov 26:1
the gladness of **h** Is 9:3
time of **h** will come Jer 51:33
Lord of the **h** Matt 9:38
h is the end of the Matt 13:39
fields…white for **h** John 4:35
h of the earth is Rev 14:15
HAVILAH
1 *second son of Cush* Gen 10:7
2 *son of Joktan* Gen 10:29; 1 Chr 1:23
3 *region encompassed by one of Eden's rivers*
Gen 2:11
4 *area in W Arabia* Gen 25:18
HAZAEL
anointed by Elijah 1 Kin 19:15
killed Ben-hadad 2 Kin 8:15
Aramaic king 2 Kin 8:15; 9:14
defeated Israel 2 Kin 10:32
HAZOR
1 *Canaanite city in N Palestine* Josh 11:1
2 *town of the Negev* Josh 15:23
3 *Benjamite city* Neh 11:33
4 *desert kingdom* Jer 49:33
HEAL *make well, restore*
will **h** their land 2 Chr 7:14
h-s the brokenhearted Ps 147:3
a time to **h** Eccl 3:3
H me, O LORD Jer 17:14
will **h** their apostasy Hos 14:4
h-ed all who were Matt 8:16
H *the* sick, raise Matt 10:8
h him on…Sabbath Mark 3:2
Physician, **h** yourself Luke 4:23
you may be **h-ed** James 5:16
fatal wound was **h-ed** Rev 13:3
HEALING *health, wholeness*
be **h** to your body Prov 3:8
h to the bones Prov 16:24
sorrow is beyond **h** Jer 8:18
There is no **h** for Jer 46:11
their leaves for **h** Ezek 47:12
h every kind of Matt 4:23
gifts of **h** 1 Cor 12:9
h of the nations Rev 22:2
HEALTH *soundness, wholeness*
no **h** in my bones Ps 38:3
restore you to **h** Jer 30:17
and be in good **h** 3 John 2
HEART *mind* or *seat of emotions*
intent of man's **h** is Gen 8:21
I will harden his **h** Ex 4:21
great searchings of **h** Judg 5:16
LORD looks at the **h** 1 Sam 16:7
fool has said in his **h** Ps 14:1
meditation of my **h** Ps 19:14
My **h** is like wax Ps 22:14
in me a clean **h** Ps 51:10
and a contrite **h** Ps 51:17
Your word…in my **h** Ps 119:11

Deceit is in the **h** Prov 12:20
A joyful **h** is good Prov 17:22
to a troubled **h** Prov 25:20
bribe corrupts the **h** Eccl 7:7
a new **h** and a new Ezek 18:31
uncircumcised in **h** Ezek 44:7
are the pure in **h** Matt 5:8
adultery…in his **h** Matt 5:28
and humble in **h** Matt 11:29
h is far…from Me Matt 15:8
pondering…in her **h** Luke 2:19
pierced to the **h** Acts 2:37
cleansing their **h-s** Acts 15:9
who searches the **h-s** Rom 8:27
tablets of human **h-s** 2 Cor 3:3
not lose **h** in doing Gal 6:9
melody with your **h** Eph 5:19
intentions of the **h** Heb 4:12
deceives his *own* **h** James 1:26

HEAVEN *place of God* or *sky*
God created the **h-s** Gen 1:1
rain bread from **h** Ex 16:4
shut up the **h-s** Deut 11:17
thunder in the **h-s** 1 Sam 2:10
fire came…from **h** 2 Kin 1:14
make windows in **h** 2 Kin 7:2
walks…vault of **h** Job 22:14
I consider Your **h-s** Ps 8:3
h and earth praise Ps 69:34
fixed patterns of **h** Jer 33:25
lights in the **h-s** Ezek 32:8
open…windows of **h** Mal 3:10
kingdom of **h** is at Matt 3:2
voice out of the **h-s** Matt 3:17
reward in **h** is great Matt 5:12
Father who is in **h** Matt 6:9
shall have been loosed in **h** Matt 16:19
great signs from **h** Luke 21:11
Him go into **h** Acts 1:11
no…name under **h** Acts 4:12
up to the third **h** 2 Cor 12:2
citizenship is in **h** Phil 3:20
there was war in **h** Rev 12:7
new **h** and a new Rev 21:1

HEAVENLY *related to God*
h Father is perfect Matt 5:48
h Father knows that Matt 6:32
h host praising God Luke 2:13
I tell you **h** things John 3:12
Him in the **h** *places* Eph 2:6
partakers of a **h** Heb 3:1
shadow of the **h** Heb 8:5

HEAVY *burdensome, hard to lift*
Moses' hands were **h** Ex 17:12
servitude was **h** on Neh 5:18
h drinkers of wine Prov 23:20
A stone is **h** Prov 27:3
Jerusalem a **h** stone Zech 12:3
eyes were very **h** Mark 14:40

HEBER
1 *son of Beriah* Gen 46:17
2 *husband of Jael* Judg 4:17
3 *son of Mered* 1 Chr 4:18
4 *son of Elpaal* 1 Chr 8:17
see also **EBER**

HEBREW(S)
1 *people* Gen 14:13; Ex 1:15; 9:13; Jon 1:9
2 *language* John 19:17; Acts 22:2; 26:14
see also **JUDEAN**
see also **CANAAN**

HEBRON
1 *site of Sarah's death* Gen 23:2
visited by spies Num 13:22
destroyed Josh 10:37
city of refuge Josh 20:7
residence of David 2 Sam 2:1
2 *son of Kohath* Ex 6:18
3 *son of Mareshah* 1 Chr 2:42

HEIFER *young cow*
unblemished red **h** Num 19:2
plowed with my **h** Judg 14:18
Egypt is a pretty **h** Jer 46:20
Like a stubborn **h** Hos 4:16

HEIR *person who inherits*
in my house is my **h** Gen 15:3
has he no **h-s** Jer 49:1
h-s also, **h-s** of God Rom 8:17
an **h** through God Gal 4:7
h-s of the kingdom James 2:5

HELIOPOLIS
ancient Egyptian city Jer 43:13
also **ON**

HELL *place of dead*
go into the fiery **h** Matt 5:22
soul and body in **h** Matt 10:28
to be cast into **h** Mark 9:47
set on fire by **h** James 3:6
cast them into **h** 2 Pet 2:4
see also **HADES** *and* **SHEOL**

HELP (n) *assistance, relief*
h is not within me Job 6:13
He is our **h** and our Ps 33:20
present **h** in trouble Ps 46:1
I cried for **h** Jon 2:2
gifts of…**h-s** 1 Cor 12:28

HELP (v) *aid, assist*
h-ing the Hebrew Ex 1:16
the LORD **h-ed** David 2 Sam 8:6
whence shall my **h** Ps 121:1
I will **h** you Is 41:13
Lord, **h** me Matt 15:25
h my unbelief Mark 9:24
must **h** the weak Acts 20:35
Spirit also **h-s** our Rom 8:26
earth **h-ed** the Rev 12:16

HEPHZIBAH
Manasseh's mother 2 Kin 21:1
Hezekiah's wife 2 Kin 21:3

HERB *dried plant*
bread and bitter **h-s** Ex 12:8
fade like the green **h** Ps 37:2
h-s of…mountains Prov 27:25
sweet-scented **h-s** Song 5:13

HERD *cattle, flock*
firstborn of your **h** Deut 12:6
h, or flock taste a Jon 3:7
h of many swine Matt 8:30

HERMES
1 *Greek god* Acts 14:12
2 *Roman Christian* Rom 16:14

HERMON
mountain region in N Palestine Josh 11:17; Ps 42:6; 133:3
N boundary of Promised Land Deut 3:8

HEROD
1 **Herod the Great**
king of Judea, Samaria, Ituraea and Traconitis Matt 2:1
ruled during Jesus' birth Matt 2:1ff
2 **Herod Archelaus**
son of Herod the Great Matt 2:22
governor of Ituraea and Traconitis
3 **Herod Antipas**
son of Herod the Great Matt 14:1
tetrarch of Galilee and Perea Luke 3:1
ruled during Jesus' ministry Luke 13:31; 23:7,8,11
executed John the Baptist Matt 14:10; Mark 6:27
4 **Herod Philip I**

son of Herod the Great Mark 6:17
5 **Herod Philip II**
son of Herod the Great Luke 3:1
tetrarch of Ituraea and Traconitis
6 **Herod Agrippa I**
grandson of Herod the Great Acts 12:1
king of Judea and Samaria
persecuted the early church Acts 12:2-23
7 **Herod Agrippa II**
son of Agrippa I Acts 25:13
tetrarch of Tiberias, Abila and Traconitis
heard Paul's testimony Acts 25:23ff; 26:1ff

HERODIANS
influential Jews favoring Herod Matt 22:16; Mark 3:6

HERODIAS
wife of Herod Antipas Matt 14:3; Mark 6:17
requested head of John the Baptist Matt 14:8; Mark 6:24

HETH
1 *son of Canaan* Gen 10:15
2 *Hebrew eponym for Hittites* Gen 23:10

HEZEKIAH
king of Judah 2 Kin 18:1
reformer 2 Kin 18:4
warrior 2 Kin 18:7,8
builder 2 Kin 20:20

HIGH PRIEST
first in hierarchy Ex 27:21
under Aaron Ex 28:1,2
enters Holy of Holies Ex 28:29,30; Heb 9:7
head of Sanhedrin Matt 26:57; Acts 5:21
Jesus as High Priest Heb 3:1; 5:5-9

HILKIAH
1 *father of Eliakim* 2 Kin 18:18
2 *high priest* 2 Kin 22:4-14
3 *Merarite Levite* 1 Chr 6:45
4 *son of Hosah* 1 Chr 26:11
5 *was with Ezra* Neh 8:4
6 *returned from exile* Neh 12:7

HINNOM
1 *valley SW of Jerusalem* Josh 15:8; Neh 11:30
2 *person for whom valley named* 2 Kin 23:10; Jer 7:31

HIRAM / HURAM
1 *king of Tyre* 1 Kin 5:1ff; 2 Chr 2:3,11
2 *skilled craftsman* 1 Kin 7:14; 2 Chr 4:11

HITTITES
1 *people in Palestine in patriarchal age* Gen 15:20; 49:29
2 *inhabitants of Aram during Israelite monarchy* 2 Kin 7:6; 2 Chr 8:7

HIVITES
people dispossessed by the Israelites Ex 23:28; Josh 3:10; 2 Sam 24:7

HOLINESS *sacredness*
majestic in **h** Ex 15:11
H befits Your house Ps 93:5
the Highway of **H** Is 35:8
without blame in **h** 1 Thess 3:13
we may share His **h** Heb 12:10

HOLY *sacred, sanctified*
standing is **h** ground Ex 3:5
sabbath…keep it **h** Ex 20:8
you are a **h** people Deut 7:6
ten thousand **h** ones Deut 33:2
h like the LORD 1 Sam 2:2
Worship…**h** array 1 Chr 16:29
His **h** dwelling 2 Chr 30:27
Jerusalem, the **h** city Neh 11:1
Zion, My **h** mountain Ps 2:6
to His **h** land Ps 78:54
bless His **h** name Ps 145:21
H, **H**, **H**, is the LORD Is 6:3
the **H** One of Israel Is 30:15
what is **h** to dogs Matt 7:6
righteous and **h** man Mark 6:20
the **H** One of God Luke 4:34
in the **h** Scriptures Rom 1:2
and **h** sacrifice Rom 12:1
with a **h** kiss Rom 16:16
h both in body 1 Cor 7:34
lifting up **h** hands 1 Tim 2:8
with a **h** calling 2 Tim 1:9
I saw the **h** city Rev 21:2

HOLY OF HOLIES
most holy place in the Tabernacle / Temple Ex 26:33,34; 2 Chr 3:8

HOLY SPIRIT
Third Person of the Godhead Matt 28:19; 2 Cor 13:14
Helper John 14:16,26
Giver of gifts Rom 12:6-8; 1 Cor 12:8-11
fruit of the Spirit Gal 5:22

HOMAGE *act of reverence*
my people shall do **h** Gen 41:40
did **h** to the LORD 1 Chr 29:20
and paid **h** to Haman Esth 3:2
did **h** to Daniel Dan 2:46

HOMER *measure of capacity*
a **h** of barley Lev 27:16
a **h** of seed Is 5:10
from a **h** of wheat Ezek 45:13

HOMOSEXUALS
effeminate, nor **h** 1 Cor 6:9
immoral men and **h** 1 Tim 1:10

HONEST *respectable, truthful*
we are **h** men Gen 42:11
painful are **h** words Job 6:25
an **h** and good heart Luke 8:15

HONEY *sweetness*
with milk and **h** Ex 3:8
swarm of bees and **h** Judg 14:8
is sweeter than **h** Judg 14:18
sweet as **h** in my Ezek 3:3
locusts and wild **h** Matt 3:4

HOREB
another name for Mount Sinai Ex 3:1; Deut 4:10; Ps 106:19

HORITES
inhabitants of Mount Seir in Edom Gen 14:6; 36:29

HORSE *animal*
bites the **h**-'s heels Gen 49:17
h-s and chariots of 2 Kin 6:17
A **h** is a false hope Ps 33:17
whip is for the **h** Prov 26:3
slaves *riding* on **h**-s Eccl 10:7
behold, a black **h** Rev 6:5

HORSEMEN *cavalry, horse rider*
Pharaoh, his **h** and Ex 14:9
chariots and **h** 1 Kin 10:26
h riding on Ezek 23:12
H charging, Swords Nah 3:3
armies of the **h** Rev 9:16

HOSANNA *acclamation of praise*
H to the Son of Matt 21:9
H in the highest Mark 11:10
H! Blessed is He John 12:13

HOSHEA
1 *name of Joshua* Num 13:8,16
2 *king of Israel* 2 Kin 15:30; 17:6
3 *Ephraim's officer* 1 Chr 27:20
4 *signer of covenant* Neh 10:23

HULDAH
a Hebrew prophetess 2 Kin 22:14; 2 Chr 34:22

HUMAN *mankind, person*
the life of any **h** Lev 24:17
guilt of **h** blood Prov 28:17

they had **h** form Ezek 1:5
tablets of **h** hearts 2 Cor 3:3

HUR
1 *helped Moses and Aaron* Ex 17:12; 24:14
2 *Bezalel's grandfather* Ex 31:2
3 *king of Midian* Num 31:8
4 *father of Rephaiah* Neh 3:9

HURAM
a Benjamite 1 Chr 8:5
see also **HIRAM / HURAM**

HUSBAND *family head, spouse*
desire…your **h** Gen 3:16
honor to their **h-s** Esth 1:20
crown of her **h** Prov 12:4
is loved by *her* **h** Hos 3:1
divorces her **h** and Mark 10:12
have had five **h-s** John 4:18
if her **h** dies Rom 7:2
have her own **h** 1 Cor 7:2
unbelieving **h** is 1 Cor 7:14
h is the head of Eph 5:23
H-s, love your wives Eph 5:25
h-s of…one wife 1 Tim 3:12
adorned for her **h** Rev 21:2

HYSSOP *fragrant plant*
bunch of **h** and dip it Ex 12:22
scarlet string and **h** Lev 14:4
Purify me with **h** Ps 51:7
upon *a branch of* **h** John 19:29

I

I AM
related to name of God in Hebrew
I WHO I Ex 3:14
I has sent me Ex 3:14
I the LORD Ex 6:2
I the LORD your God Lev 19:3
I the first Is 44:6
I the Son of God Matt 27:43
Jesus said, I Mark 14:62
believe that I *He* John 8:24
will know that I *He* John 8:28
before Abraham…I John 8:58
believe that I *He* John 13:19
I the Alpha and Rev 1:8
I the first and Rev 1:17

ICHABOD
1 *son of Phinehas* 1 Sam 4:19,20
grandson of Eli 1 Sam 14:3
2 *name commemorates departed glory from Israel* 1 Sam 4:21,22

IDOL *false deity, image*
not make…an **i** Ex 20:4
Do not turn to **i-s** Lev 19:4
who makes an **i** or Deut 27:15
the gods…are **i-s** Ps 96:5
who blesses an **i** Is 66:3
abstain from…**i-s** Acts 15:20
guard…from **i-s** 1 John 5:21

IDOLATRY *idol worship*
flee from **i** 1 Cor 10:14
i, sorcery, enmities Gal 5:20
and abominable **i-ies** 1 Pet 4:3

ILL *unhealthy, sick*
woman who is **i** Lev 15:33
became mortally **i** Is 38:1
lunatic and is…**i** Matt 17:15
healed many…**i** Mark 1:34

ILLEGITIMATE *bastard*
No one of **i** birth Deut 23:2
borne **i** children Hos 5:7
you are **i** children Heb 12:8

ILLUMINE *light up*
God **i-s** my darkness Ps 18:28
fire to **i** by night Ps 105:39

glory of God has **i-d** Rev 21:23
God will **i** them Rev 22:5

IMMANUEL
1 *son born to a virgin* Is 7:14
a sign to King Ahaz Is 8:8
2 *title of Jesus* Matt 1:23

IMMORAL *lewd, unchaste*
with **i** people 1 Cor 5:9
the **i** man sins 1 Cor 6:18
i men…liars 1 Tim 1:10
i or godless person Heb 12:16
and **i** persons Rev 21:8

IMMORALITY *immoral acts*
no **i** in your midst Lev 20:14
except for **i** Matt 19:9
Flee **i** 1 Cor 6:18
abstain from…**i** 1 Thess 4:3
the wine of her **i** Rev 17:2

IMMORTALITY *everlasting life*
must put on **i** 1 Cor 15:53
alone possesses **i** 1 Tim 6:16
life and **i** to light 2 Tim 1:10

IMPURE *unclean*
her **i** discharge Lev 15:25
eating…with **i** hands Mark 7:2
no immoral or **i** person Eph 5:5

IMPURITY *uncleanness*
menstrual **i** for seven Lev 15:19
i-ies of the sons of Lev 16:19
the **i** of the nations Ezra 6:21
as slaves to **i** Rom 6:19
of **i** with greediness Eph 4:19

INCENSE *fragrant substance*
burn fragrant **i** on Ex 30:7
i as an offering Lev 2:16
gold pans, full of **i** Num 7:86
My altar, to burn **i** 1 Sam 2:28
i on the high places 2 Kin 14:4
i before the LORD 1 Chr 23:13
golden altar of **i** Heb 9:4
the smoke of the **i** Rev 8:4

INCEST *illicit sexual relations*
they…committed **i** Lev 20:12

INFANT *child*
carries a nursing **i** Num 11:12
an **i** *who lives* Is 65:20
tongue of the **i** Lam 4:4
the mouth of **i-s** Matt 21:16
as to **i-s** in Christ 1 Cor 3:1

INFINITE *unlimited*
His understanding is **i** Ps 147:5

INJUSTICE *inequity, unfairness*
do no **i** in judgment Lev 19:15
A God…without **i** Deut 32:4
there **i** on my tongue Job 6:30
They devise **i-s** Ps 64:6
is no **i** with God Rom 9:14

INN *lodge for travelers*
no room…in the **i** Luke 2:7
brought him to…**i** Luke 10:34

INSANE *mad*
a demon and is **i** John 10:20
I speak as if **i** 2 Cor 11:23

INSECTS
swarms of **i** on you Ex 8:21
all other winged **i** Lev 11:23

INSPIRED *stimulated*
the love we **i** in you 2 Cor 8:7
All Scripture is **i** 2 Tim 3:16

INTERMARRY
I with us Gen 34:9
shall not **i** with Deut 7:3
i with the peoples Ezra 9:14

INTIMATE *close*
my **i** friends have Job 19:14

i with the upright Prov 3:32
separates i friends Prov 16:28

ISAAC
birth, son of Abraham Gen 21:3
offered for sacrifice Gen 22:2
took Rebekah as wife Gen 24
father of twins Gen 25:26
blessed Jacob Gen 27:1-40

ISAIAH
prophet of Judah Is 1:1
son of Amoz 2 Kin 19:2
called Is 6:8ff
under four kings Is 1:1

ISCARIOT
geographical identity of Judas Mark 3:19; John 12:4; 13:26

ISHMAEL
1 *son of Abraham* Gen 16:11; 17:18; 25:17
2 *son of Nethaniah* 2 Kin 25:23
3 *line of Jonathan* 1 Chr 8:38; 9:44
4 *Zebadiah's father* 2 Chr 19:11
5 *son of Jehohanan* 2 Chr 23:1
6 *son of Pashhur* Ezra 10:22

ISRAEL
1 *Jacob* Gen 32:28-32; 35:10; 37:3
2 *line of Jacob* Gen 34:7
tribal nation Ex 1:7; 4:22; Num 10:29
3 *united kingdom* 1 Sam 15:35; 1 Kin 4:1
4 *northern kingdom* 1 Kin 14:19; 15:9; 2 Kin 10:29
5 *under Roman rule* Luke 2:32; John 1:49; Rom 9:6

ISSACHAR
1 *son of Jacob* Gen 30:18; 49:14
2 *tribe* Num 1:29; Josh 21:28; Rev 7:7
3 *Levite* 1 Chr 26:5

ITURAEA
region N of Palestine Luke 3:1
tetrarchy of Herod Philip II

IVORY *elephant tusk*
a great throne of i 1 Kin 10:18
silver, i and apes 2 Chr 9:21
Out of i palaces Ps 45:8
every article of i Rev 18:12

J

JABAL
son of Lamech Gen 4:20
father of herders

JABBOK
tributary of Jordan Gen 32:22; Num 21:24; Josh 12:2; Judg 11:13,22

JACKALS *wild dogs*
j in their…palaces Is 13:22
ruins, A haunt of j Jer 9:11
a lament like the j Mic 1:8

JACOB
1 *son of Isaac* Gen 25:26
brother of Esau Gen 25:27
obtained birthright Gen 25:33
fled to Aram Gen 28:5,6
marriage Gen 29:1ff
wrestled angel Gen 32:24ff
name changed Gen 35:9,10
went down to Egypt Gen 46:4ff
death and burial Gen 49:28ff
2 *father of Joseph* Matt 1:15,16

JAIL *place of confinement*
put him into the j Gen 39:20
in j in the house Jer 37:15
put them in…j Acts 5:18

JAILER *warden*
sight of the chief j Gen 39:21
chief j did not Gen 39:23
the j to guard them Acts 16:23

JAIRUS
ruler of synagogue Mark 5:22; Luke 8:41

JAMES
1 *son of Zebedee* Matt 4:21
brother of John Matt 10:2
called as apostle Matt 10:2ff
martyred Acts 12:2
2 *son of Alphaeus* Matt 10:3
called as apostle Matt 10:3ff
3 *brother of Jesus* Matt 13:55; Mark 6:3
church leader Acts 12:17; 15:13
4 *Judas's father* Luke 6:16

JASHAR
book quoted in Bible Josh 10:13; 2 Sam 1:18

JASPER *precious stone*
fourth row…a j Ex 28:20
the onyx, and the j Ezek 28:13
was like a j stone Rev 4:3
of crystal-clear j Rev 21:11

JAVAN
Hebrew word for Greeks or Greece Gen 10:2,4; 1 Chr 1:5,7; Is 66:19; Ezek 27:13,19

JAVELIN *spear*
Stretch out the j Josh 8:18
j *slung* between his 1 Sam 17:6
flashing spear and j Job 39:23
seize *their*…j Jer 50:42

JAWBONE
j of a donkey Judg 15:15
threw the j from Judg 15:17

JEALOUS *envious, zealous*
brothers were j of Gen 37:11
your God, am a j God Ex 20:5
whose name is J, is Ex 34:14
j with My jealousy Num 25:11
He is a j God Josh 24:19
j and avenging God Nah 1:2
j for Jerusalem Zech 1:14
Jews, becoming j Acts 17:5
I will make you j Rom 10:19
love is kind…not j 1 Cor 13:4

JEBUS
Jerusalem Judg 19:10,11; 1 Chr 11:4,5

JEBUSITES
clan or tribe Gen 10:16
inhabitants of Jebus Ex 3:8,17; Josh 15:63; 2 Sam 24:16,18; Ezra 9:1; Zech 9:7

JECONIAH
variant of Jehoiachin's name 1 Chr 3:16,17; Esth 2:6

JEHOAHAZ
1 *son of Jehu* 2 Kin 10:35
king of Israel 2 Kin 13:1ff
2 *son of Josiah* 2 Kin 23:30-34
king of Judah 2 Kin 23:30
see also SHALLUM 1 Chr 3:15
3 *son of Jehoram* 2 Chr 21:17
also Ahaziah 2 Chr 22:1ff

JEHOASH
1 *king of Judah* 2 Kin 11:21
son of Ahaziah 2 Kin 12:1-18
2 *king of Israel* 2 Kin 13:10
son of Jehoahaz 2 Kin 13:25; 14:13

JEHOIACHIN
son of Jehoiakim 2 Kin 24:6
king of Judah 2 Kin 24:8-15; 2 Chr 36:8,9; Jer 52:31,33

JEHOIADA
1 *father of Benaiah* 2 Sam 8:18
priest 1 Chr 27:5
2 *son of Benaiah* 1 Chr 27:34
3 *high priest* 2 Kin 11:4,9
4 *priest* Jer 29:26

JEHOIAKIM
son of King Josiah 2 Kin 23:34; 2 Chr 36:4

king of Judah 2 Kin 23:36; 2 Chr 36:5; Jer 22:18; Dan 1:2
father of Jehoiachin 2 Kin 24:6

JEHORAM
1 *son of Ahab* 2 Kin 3:1
king of Israel 2 Kin 3:6
2 *priest* 2 Chr 17:8
3 *Jehoshaphat's son* 2 Kin 8:16
king of Judah 2 Kin 8:25,29
see also JORAM

JEHOSHAPHAT
1 *son of Ahilud* 2 Sam 8:16
2 *son of Paruah* 1 Kin 4:17
3 *son of Asa* 1 Kin 15:24
king of Judah 1 Kin 22:2-51; 2 Chr 17:1-12
4 *father of Jehu* 2 Kin 9:2,14
5 *wadi E of Jerusalem* Joel 3:2,12

JEHU
1 *prophet, son of Hanani* 1 Kin 16:1,7,12; 2 Chr 19:2
2 *king of Israel* 1 Kin 19:16; 2 Kin 9:14,30; 2 Chr 22:7
3 *man of Judah* 1 Chr 2:38
4 *Simeonite* 1 Chr 4:35
5 *Benjamite* 1 Chr 12:3

JEREMIAH
1 *lived in Libnah* 2 Kin 23:31
2 *man of Manasseh* 1 Chr 5:24
3 *three individuals who joined David* 1 Chr 12:4,10,13
4 *prophet* Jer 1:1
called Jer 1:2-10
put in stocks Jer 20:2,3
life threatened Jer 26
put in prison Jer 32:2; 37:13ff
taken to Egypt Jer 43:1-6
5 *son of Habazziniah* Jer 35:3
6 *priest* Neh 10:2
7 *priest from Babylon* Neh 12:1

ERICHO
city in Jordan Valley Josh 3:16
N of Dead Sea Josh 6:1; 1 Kin 16:34; Luke 18:35

EROBOAM
1 *Solomon's warrior* 1 Kin 11:28
first king of N Kingdom 1 Kin 12:26,27; 2 Chr 10:13
made golden calves 1 Kin 12:28
2 *son of Joash* 2 Kin 14:27
king of Israel 2 Kin 14:28,29

ERUSALEM
city called Salem Gen 14:18
city called Jebus Judg 1:21; 19:10
David's capital 2 Sam 5:5,6
capital of united kingdom 1 Kin 2:36; 11:42
site of temple 1 Kin 6:2; 8:6,12
destroyed by Babylonians Jer 52:12-14
rebuilt by remnant Neh 2:11-20; 12:27
city of Roman period Matt 2:1,3; 21:1,10; Luke 13:34; Acts 11:2,22
new Jerusalem Rev 3:12; 21:2,10

ESHUA
1 *line of Aaron* 1 Chr 24:11
2 *under Kore* 2 Chr 31:15
3 *high priest* Ezra 3:2; Neh 7:7
4 *of Pahath-moab* Ezra 2:6; Neh 7:11
5 *part of remnant* Ezra 2:40; Neh 7:43
6 *aided Ezra* Neh 8:7
7 *village in Judah* Neh 11:26
see also JOSHUA

ESHURUN
poetic name for Israel Deut 32:15; 33:5,26; Is 44:2

ESSE
father of David 1 Sam 16:1,8; 2 Sam 20:1; 1 Kin 12:16; 1 Chr 2:12,13

JESUS
1 *name of the Lord* Matt 1:21; Luke 1:31
birth in Bethlehem Matt 1:18-25; Luke 2:1-7
youth in Nazareth Matt 2:19ff
baptized Matt 3:13ff; Mark 1:9ff; Luke 3:21; John 1:31ff
tempted Matt 4:1-11; Mark 1:12; Luke 4:1ff
called disciples Matt 4:18ff; Mark 1:16ff; Luke 5:1ff
transfigured Matt 17:1ff; Mark 9:2ff; Luke 9:28ff
triumphal entry to Jerusalem Matt 21:1ff; Mark 11:1ff; Luke 19:29ff
crucified Matt 27:31ff; Mark 15:20ff; Luke 23:26ff; John 19:16ff
resurrected Christ Matt 28:1ff; Mark 16:1ff; Luke 24:13ff; John 20:11ff
ascended to the Father Mark 16:19; Luke 24:50ff; Acts 1:9ff
2 *Jewish Christian called Justus* Col 4:11

JETHRO
priest of Midian Ex 3:1
Moses' father-in-law Ex 4:18; 18:1-12

JEW(S)
originally an inhabitant of Judah, a Judean 2 Kin 16:6
Judean shortened to Jew during exile 2 Kin 25:25
synonym for Hebrew Ezra 4:12,23; Neh 4:1,2; Esth 4:3,7; Jer 34:9
later term for all Israelites in the land and in Diaspora Matt 27:11; Mark 7:3; Luke 23:51; John 4:9; Acts 22:3; Rom 3:1; Gal 3:28; Rev 2:9

JEWEL *precious stone*
precious than j-s Prov 3:15
better than j-s Prov 8:11
adorns…her j-s Is 61:10
the J of *his* kingdom Dan 11:20

JEZEBEL
1 *wife of Ahab* 1 Kin 21:5ff; 2 Kin 9:7ff
2 *woman at Thyatira* Rev 2:20

JEZREEL
1 *valley and plain* Josh 17:16; Judg 6:33; Hos 1:5
2 *fortified town* Josh 19:18; 1 Kin 18:45; 2 Kin 8:29; 9:30
3 *descendant of Etam* 1 Chr 4:3
4 *son of Hosea* Hos 1:4

JOAB
1 *son of Zeruiah* 2 Sam 8:16
David's nephew 2 Sam 17:25
David's commander 2 Sam 20:23; 1 Chr 11:6
2 *son of Seraiah* 1 Chr 4:14
3 *father of those returning from captivity* Ezra 2:6; 8:9; Neh 7:11

JOASH
1 *father of Gideon* Judg 6:11,31
2 *son of Ahab* 1 Kin 22:26; 2 Chr 18:25
3 *son of Ahaziah* 2 Kin 11:2
king of Judah 2 Chr 24:1-4
4 *son of Jehoahaz* 2 Kin 13:9
king of Israel 2 Kin 13:25
5 *line of Shelah* 1 Chr 4:22
6 *son of Becher* 1 Chr 7:8
7 *a Benjamite* 1 Chr 12:3
8 *official of David* 1 Chr 27:28

JOB *occupation*
workmen…j to j 2 Chr 34:13

JOEL
1 *son of Samuel* 1 Sam 8:2
2 *line of Simeon* 1 Chr 4:35
3 *line of Reuben* 1 Chr 5:4
4 *chief of Gadites* 1 Chr 5:12
5 *ancestor of Samuel* 1 Chr 6:36
6 *son of Izrahiah* 1 Chr 7:3
7 *brother of Nathan* 1 Chr 11:38

8 *Gershonite Levite* 1 Chr 15:7; 26:22
9 *son of Pedaiah* 1 Chr 27:20
10 *Kohathite Levite* 2 Chr 29:12
11 *son of Nebo* Ezra 10:43
12 *son of Zichri* Neh 11:9
13 *prophet* Joel 1:1; Acts 2:16

JOHN
1 *father of Peter* John 1:42
2 *the Baptist* Matt 3:1
baptizing Matt 3:13
beheaded Mark 6:25
birth foretold Luke 1:13
son of Zacharias Luke 1:57ff
praised by Jesus Luke 7:28
preached John 1:15
3 *the apostle* Matt 10:2
called by Jesus Matt 4:21
Sons of Thunder Mark 3:17
inner circle Matt 17:1
request refused Mark 10:35ff
assigned the care of Mary John 19:26,27
with Peter Acts 3:1,3
4 *Jewish leader* Acts 4:6
5 *Mark, evangelist* Acts 12:12,25

JOIN *bring together, couple*
j-ed to his wife Gen 2:24
do not **j** your hand Ex 23:1
j field to field Is 5:8
j...in hypocrisy Dan 11:34
God...**j-ed** together Matt 19:6
j-ed him...believed Acts 17:34
shall be **j-ed** to his wife Eph 5:31
j...*me* in suffering 2 Tim 1:8

JONATHAN
1 *son of Gershom* Judg 18:30
2 *son of King Saul* 1 Sam 13:16; 14:49
friend of David 1 Sam 18:1
3 *son of Abiathar* 2 Sam 15:36
4 *son of Shimei* 2 Sam 21:21
5 *son of Jada* 1 Chr 2:32
6 *son of Shagee* 1 Chr 11:34
7 *official of David* 1 Chr 27:25
8 *David's uncle* 1 Chr 27:32

JOPPA
seaport W of Jerusalem 2 Chr 2:16; Ezra 3:7; Jon 1:3; Acts 9:36

JORAM
1 *son of Toi* 2 Sam 8:10
2 *son of Ahab* 2 Kin 8:16
king of Israel 2 Kin 8:25
3 *line of Eliezer* 1 Chr 26:25
4 *son of Jehoshaphat* Matt 1:8
king of Judah
see also **JEHORAM**

JORDAN
1 *river in Palestine* Gen 32:10; Josh 3:17; Judg 8:4; 2 Kin 5:10; Matt 3:6
2 *valley* Gen 13:10,11

JOSEPH
1 *son of Jacob* Gen 30:23,24
sold by brothers Gen 37:28
put in prison Gen 40:3
prime minister Gen 41:41
revealed himself Gen 45:4
death Gen 50:26
2 *father of spy* Num 13:7ff
3 *son of Asaph* 1 Chr 25:9
4 *son of Bani* Ezra 10:42
5 *son of Shebaniah* Neh 12:14
6 *husband of Mary* Matt 1:18; 2:13; Luke 2:16; John 6:42
7 *brother of Jesus* Matt 13:55
see also **JOSES**
8 *brother of James the Less* Matt 27:56
see also **JOSES**
9 *of Arimathea* Matt 27:57ff
in Sanhedrin (Council) Mark 15:43
disciple of Jesus John 19:38
provided tomb Matt 27:57
10 *ancestor of Jesus* Luke 3:24
11 *ancestor of Jesus* Luke 3:30
12 *surname Barsabbas* Acts 1:23
13 *Barnabas* Acts 4:36

JOSES
1 *brother of James the Less* Mark 15:40
see also **JOSEPH**
2 *brother of Jesus* Mark 6:3
see also **JOSEPH**

JOSHUA
1 *Moses' successor* Deut 31:23
attended Moses Num 11:28
chosen by God Num 27:18
encouraged by God Josh 1:1-9
charged Israel Josh 23:1ff
death Josh 24:29
2 *of Beth-shemesh* 1 Sam 6:14
3 *governor* 2 Kin 23:8
4 *high priest* Hag 1:1,12; Zech 3:1ff
see also **JESHUA**

JOSIAH
1 *son of Amon* 2 Kin 21:24
king of Judah 2 Kin 21:26
removed false worship 2 Kin 23:19,24; 2 Chr 34:33
responded to the Law 2 Chr 34:15-28
2 *son of Zephaniah* Zech 6:10

JOTHAM
1 *son of Gideon* Judg 9:5ff
2 *king of Judah* 2 Kin 15:5
son of Uzziah 2 Chr 27:2
3 *line of Caleb* 1 Chr 2:47

JUDAH
1 *son of Jacob* Gen 29:35; 37:26; 44:14; 49:8,10
2 *tribe* Num 1:27; Judg 1:8; 2 Sam 2:4; 1 Kin 12:20
3 *border city* Josh 19:34
4 *S kingdom* 1 Kin 14:21; 1 Chr 9:1; Ps 60:7; Jer 20:4
5 *relative of Kadmiel* Ezra 2:40
6 *urged by Ezra to put away foreign wife* Ezra 10:23
7 *Benjamite* Neh 11:9
8 *Levite who returned from captivity* Neh 12:8
9 *participant in wall dedication* Neh 12:34
10 *musician* Neh 12:36

JUDAISM *Jewish way of life*
manner of life in **J** Gal 1:13
advancing in **J** Gal 1:14

JUDAS
1 *Iscariot* Matt 10:4
used by Satan Luke 22:3
son of Simon John 6:71
treasurer John 13:29
betrayed Jesus John 18:2
2 *Jesus' brother* Matt 13:55; Mark 6:3
3 *apostle* Luke 6:16; Acts 1:13
4 *Judas of Galilee* Acts 5:37
5 *of Damascus* Acts 9:11
6 *Barsabbas* Acts 15:22,27

JUDE
brother of Jesus Matt 13:55; Mark 6:3
brother of James Jude 1

JUDEA
Roman province in Palestine based on earlier Judah Matt 2:1; Mark 1:5; Luke 2:4; John 11:7

JUDEAN
language (Hebrew) 2 Kin 18:26,28; Is 36:11,13
see also **CANAAN**
see also **HEBREW**

JUDGE (n) *leader*
J of all the earth Gen 18:25
prince or a j over us Ex 2:14
LORD was with the j Judg 2:18
For God Himself is j Ps 50:6
unrighteous j said Luke 18:6
one Lawgiver and J James 4:12

JUDGE (v) *pass judgment*
LORD j between you Gen 16:5
Moses sat to j the Ex 18:13
LORD will j…earth 1 Sam 2:10
coming to j the earth Ps 98:9
He will j the poor Is 11:4
Do not j…will not be j-d Matt 7:1
Son…world to j John 3:17
Law…not j a man John 7:51
not come to j the John 12:47
able to j…thoughts Heb 4:12
adulterers God will j Heb 13:4

JUDGMENT *condemnation*
I will execute j-s Ex 12:12
partiality in j Deut 1:17
let j be executed Ezra 7:26
will not stand in the j Ps 1:5
in the day of j Matt 10:15
j, that the light John 3:19
resurrection of j John 5:29
My j is just John 5:30
after this *comes* j Heb 9:27
incur a stricter j James 3:1
not fall under j James 5:12
kept for the day of j 2 Pet 3:7
j of the great day Jude 6
to execute j upon all Jude 15
His j-s are true Rev 19:2

JUTTAH
Levitical city in Judah Josh 15:55; 21:16

K

KADESH / KADESH-BARNEA
desert oasis in Negev Gen 14:7
Israelite encampment Num 13:26; 33:37

KEDESH
1 *city in S Judah* Josh 15:23
2 *city of Issachar* 1 Chr 6:72
3 *city of Naphtali* Josh 12:22
4 *city of refuge, in Galilee* Josh 20:7

KENITE(S)
Canaanite tribe Gen 15:19; Num 24:21
tribe of metal-workers Judg 4:11; 1 Sam 15:6

KENIZZITE
Canaanite tribe in S Palestine and Edom Gen 15:19; Num 32:12; Josh 14:14

KETURAH
second wife of Abraham Gen 25:1,4; 1 Chr 1:32,33

KIDRON
brook and valley between Jerusalem and Mount of Olives 2 Sam 15:23; 2 Kin 23:6; 2 Chr 29:16; John 18:1

KILL *take life*
for Cain k-ed him Gen 4:25
k-ed every firstborn Ex 13:15
who k-s a man shall Lev 24:21
LORD k-s and makes 1 Sam 2:6
Am I God, to k 2 Kin 5:7
jealousy k-s the simple Job 5:2
he k-s the innocent Ps 10:8
A time to k Eccl 3:3
unable to k the Matt 10:28
k-ed, and be raised Luke 9:22
do you seek to k Me John 7:19
Get up, Peter, k and Acts 10:13
the letter k-s, but 2 Cor 3:6
who k their father 1 Tim 1:9
k a third of mankind Rev 9:15

KING *monarch, regent*
the k-'s highway Num 20:17
no k in Israel Judg 17:6
appoint a k for us 1 Sam 8:5
anointed David k 2 Sam 5:3
my K and my God Ps 5:2
The LORD is K forever Ps 10:16
Who is the k of glory Ps 24:8
will shatter k-s Ps 110:5
By me k-s reign Prov 8:15
He will…before k-s Prov 22:29
The Creator…your K Is 43:15
O K of the nations Jer 10:7
born K of the Jews Matt 2:2
Are You the K of Matt 27:11
your K is coming John 12:15
no k but Caesar John 19:15
K of k-s and Lord 1 Tim 6:15
God, honor the k 1 Pet 2:17

KINGDOM *domain, monarchy*
his k was Babel Gen 10:10
to Me a k of priests Ex 19:6
tear the k from 1 Kin 11:11
will establish his k 1 Chr 28:7
the k is the LORD's Ps 22:28
Sing to God, O k-s Ps 68:32
an everlasting k Ps 145:13
k against k Is 19:2
k of heaven is at Matt 3:2
showed Him…k-s Matt 4:8
Your k come Matt 6:10
sons of the k Matt 13:38
keys of the k Matt 16:19
in My Father's k Matt 26:29
enter the k of God Mark 10:24
to give you the k Luke 12:32
cannot see the k of John 3:3
preaching the k Acts 28:31
k of His beloved Son Col 1:13
to His heavenly k 2 Tim 4:18
faith conquered k-s Heb 11:33
heirs of the k James 2:5

KINSMAN *relative*
of my master's k Gen 24:48
he took his k-men Gen 31:23
a man has no k Lev 25:26
Naomi had a k of her Ruth 2:1
k-men stand afar off Ps 38:11
Herodion, my k Rom 16:11

KIRIATHAIM
1 *Reubenite city* Num 32:37; Josh 13:19
2 *Levitical city* 1 Chr 6:76

KIRIATH-ARBA
old name of Hebron Gen 23:2; Josh 14:15; 15:13,54; Judg 1:10
city of refuge Josh 20:7

KIRIATH-JEARIM
Gibeonite town Josh 9:17; Judg 18:12; Jer 26:20
location of ark of covenant 1 Sam 6:21; 7:1,2; 2 Chr 1:4

KISHON
battle scene Judg 4:7
river Judg 4:13; 5:21
priests of Baal slain on its bank 1 Kin 18:40

KITTIM
1 *grandson of Japheth* Gen 10:4; 1 Chr 1:7
2 *island of Cyprus* Num 24:24; Jer 2:10; Dan 11:30

KOR *measure of capacity*
k-s of fine flour 1 Kin 4:22
20,000 k-s of barley 2 Chr 2:10
100 k-s of wheat Ezra 7:22
a bath from *each* k Ezek 45:14

KORAH
1 *son of Esau* Gen 36:5
2 *opposed Moses* Num 16:8,16
3 *son of Hebron* 1 Chr 2:43
4 *a Kohathite* 1 Chr 6:37

L

LABAN
1 *Abraham's kinsman* Gen 24:29
Rachel's father Gen 29:10,16
2 *place in the desert* Deut 1:1

LACHISH
city in Judah Josh 10:3; 2 Kin 14:19; 2 Chr 32:9

LAISH
1 *a Benjamite* 1 Sam 25:44; 2 Sam 3:15
2 *place in N Palestine later called Dan* Judg 18:27,29

LAMB *young sheep*
l for the burnt Gen 22:7
shall redeem with a l Ex 34:20
l without defect Lev 14:10
will dwell with the l Is 11:6
l…led to slaughter Is 53:7
wolf and the l will Is 65:25
send you out as l-s Luke 10:3
Behold, the L of God John 1:29
Tend My l-s John 21:15
l before its shearer Acts 8:32
Worthy is the L Rev 5:12
blood of the L Rev 12:11

LAMP *light*
You are my l 2 Sam 22:29
l-s of pure gold 2 Chr 4:20
his l goes out Job 18:6
Your word is a l Ps 119:105
commandment is a l Prov 6:23
l of the body Matt 6:22
l-s are going out Matt 25:8
l-s in the upper room Acts 20:8
l shining in a dark 2 Pet 1:19
seven l-s of fire Rev 4:5

LAMPSTAND *candlestick*
l of pure gold Ex 25:31
and a chair and a l 2 Kin 4:10
puts it on a l Luke 8:16
will remove your l Rev 2:5

LAODICEA
city in Asia Minor Col 2:1
location of early church Col 4:15; Rev 1:11; 3:14

LAPIS LAZULI *precious stone*
polishing *was* like l Lam 4:7
like l in appearance Ezek 1:26
the jasper; The l Ezek 28:13

LATIN
language of the Roman Empire
one of three languages written on Jesus' cross John 19:20

LAW *scripture, statute*
tablets with the l Ex 24:12
Moses wrote this l Deut 31:9
found the…l 2 Kin 22:8
walk in My l 2 Chr 6:16
l…is perfect Ps 19:7
I delight in Your l Ps 119:70
abolish the L or the Matt 5:17
Our L…not judge John 7:51
by that l He ought John 19:7
by a l of faith Rom 3:27
L brings…wrath Rom 4:15
not under l Rom 6:14
Is the L sin Rom 7:7
the L is holy Rom 7:12
L…become our tutor Gal 3:24
thereby fulfill the l Gal 6:2
L…nothing perfect Heb 7:19

LAWFUL *legal, right*
not l for him to eat Matt 12:4
Is it l to heal Matt 12:10
l…man to divorce Mark 10:2
All things are l 1 Cor 6:12

LAWGIVER *lawmaker*
The LORD is our l Is 33:22
one L and Judge James 4:12

LAWLESS *illegal, without law*
l one will be 2 Thess 2:8
are l and rebellious 1 Tim 1:9
from every l deed Titus 2:14

LAWYER *interpreter of law*
a l, asked Him *a* Matt 22:35
One of the l-s said Luke 11:45
Woe to you l-s Luke 11:52

LAYMAN *non-ecclesiastic*
l shall not eat *them* Ex 29:33
married to a l Lev 22:12
l who comes near Num 3:10

LAZARUS
1 *beggar* Luke 16:20-25
2 *brother of Mary and Martha* John 11:1,2,5,11,43

LAZY *idle, slothful*
Because they are l Ex 5:8
You are l, *very* l Ex 5:17
You wicked, l slave Matt 25:26
beasts, l gluttons Titus 1:12

LEAH
wife of Jacob Gen 29:23,30
mother of Reuben, Simeon, Levi and Judah Gen 29:32-35

LEAVEN *yeast*
no l found in your Ex 12:19
not be baked with l Lev 6:17
seven days no l shall Deut 16:4
heaven is like l Matt 13:33
little l leavens the 1 Cor 5:6

LEBANON
mountain range N of Israel Josh 9:1; Judg 3:3; 1 Kin 5:6
showing God's greatness Ps 29:6
symbol of prosperity Ps 92:12

LEND *loan*
l-ing them money Neh 5:10
l-s…on interest Ezek 18:13
l, expecting nothing Luke 6:35
l me three loaves Luke 11:5

LENDER *loaner*
becomes the l-'s slave Prov 22:7
l like the borrower Is 24:2

LEPER *one having leprosy*
As for the l Lev 13:45
King Uzziah…a l 2 Chr 26:21
a l came to Him Matt 8:2
cleanse *the* l-s Matt 10:8
home of Simon the l Mark 14:3

LEPROSY *infectious disease*
of l on the skin Lev 13:2
mark of l on a Lev 14:34
an infection of l Deut 24:8
cure him of his l 2 Kin 5:3
his l was cleansed Matt 8:3

LEVI
1 *son of Jacob* Gen 34:25
2 *tribe* Num 1:49; Rev 7:7
3 *two ancestors of Jesus* Luke 3:24,29
4 *apostle* Mark 2:14; Luke 5:27,29

LEVIATHAN
symbolic monster of the deep Job 3:8; Ps 104:26; Is 27:1

LEVITES
descendants of Levi Ex 6:19,25
charged with the care of the sanctuary Num 1:50; 3:41

LIAR *one telling lies*
who...prove me a l Job 24:25
a poor man than a l Prov 19:22
I will be a l like John 8:55
hypocrisy of l-s 1 Tim 4:2
we make Him a l 1 John 1:10

LIBNAH
1 *place in wilderness* Num 33:21
2 *Canaanite city* Josh 10:29; 2 Kin 23:31
a Levitical city 1 Chr 6:57

LIE (n) *false statement*
speak l-s go astray Ps 58:3
tells l-s will perish Prov 19:9
prophesy a l to you Jer 27:10
the father of l-s John 8:44
truth of God for a l Rom 1:25
no l is of the truth 1 John 2:21

LIE (v) *make false statement*
nor l to one another Lev 19:11
l-d to Him with their Ps 78:36
l-d about the LORD Jer 5:12
l to the Holy Spirit Acts 5:3
not l to one another Col 3:9
impossible...God to l Heb 6:18

LIGHT *brightness, lamp*
Let there be l Gen 1:3
Israel had l in Ex 10:23
l of the wicked Job 18:5
LORD is my l Ps 27:1
And a l to my path Ps 119:105
like the l of dawn Prov 4:18
walk in the l of the Is 2:5
your l has come Is 60:1
stars for l by night Jer 31:35
the l of the world Matt 5:14
body will be full of l Matt 6:22
L of revelation to Luke 2:32
There was the true l John 1:9
I am the L John 8:12
while you have...L John 12:35
l of the gospel 2 Cor 4:4
walk as children of L Eph 5:8
Father of l-s James 1:17
if we walk in the L 1 John 1:7

LION *wild animal*
Judah is a l-'s whelp Gen 49:9
a l or a bear 1 Sam 17:34
hunt me like a l Job 10:16
tear my soul like a l Ps 7:2
are bold as a l Prov 28:1
cast into the l-s' Dan 6:16
like a roaring l 1 Pet 5:8

LIPS *part of mouth*
My l will praise Ps 63:3
With her flattering l Prov 7:21
Your l, *my* bride Song 4:11
a man of unclean l Is 6:5
honors Me with...l Matt 15:8

LIQUOR *alcoholic drink*
concerning wine and l Mic 2:11
drink no wine or l Luke 1:15

LOAF *portion of bread*
gave him a l of bread Jer 37:21
asks for a l Matt 7:9
five **l-ves** and two Matt 14:17

LOAN *something lent*
your neighbor a l Deut 24:10
rich with l-s Hab 2:6

LOCUST *grasshopper*
wind brought the l-s Ex 10:13
you may eat: the l Lev 11:22
come in like l-s Judg 6:5
leap like the l Job 39:20
l-s have no king Prov 30:27
like the swarming l Nah 3:17
food was l-s and wild Matt 3:4

LOINS *lower back*
with your l girded Ex 12:11
Gird up your l 2 Kin 4:29
l are full of anguish Is 21:3
having girded your l Eph 6:14

LONELY *alone, isolated*
I am l and afflicted Ps 25:16
makes a home for the l Ps 68:6
How l sits the city Lam 1:1

LORD *personal name of God*
Old Testament
Different Hebrew words are translated as Lord
LORD *(Yahweh)* Gen 4:1; Ex 3:2,15; Ps 23:1; Is 40:31; Ezek 11:23
Lord GOD *(Adonai Yahweh)* Gen 15:2; 2 Sam 7:18,19; Is 1:24; Ezek 28:6; Hab 3:19
LORD God *(Yahweh Elohim)* Gen 2:4; Ps 59:5; 68:18; Jer 15:16; Jon 1:9
Lord *(Adonai)* Gen 18:27; Ex 4:10; Josh 3:11; Ps 68:19; Mic 4:13
LORD GOD *(Yah Yahweh)* Is 12:2
New Testament
Different Greek words are translated as Lord
Lord *(Kyrios, refers to either the Father or the Son)* Matt 1:20; John 11:2; Acts 5:19; 2 Cor 5:6; 1 Thess 4:16
Lord *(Despotes, refers to the Father)* Luke 2:29; Acts 4:24; Rev 6:10
Lord God *(Kyrios Theos, refers to either the Father or the Son)* Luke 1:32; Rev 1:8; 11:17; 16:7; 18:8
Lord Jesus *(Kyrios Iesous)* Mark 16:19; Luke 24:3; Acts 4:33; 7:59
Lord Jesus Christ *(Kyrios Iesous Christos)* Acts 15:26; Rom 1:7; 5:1; 1 Cor 1:10; Eph 1:2,3; 1 Thess 5:9; James 2:1

LORD *human master, ruler*
Hear us, my l Gen 23:6
not my l be angry Gen 31:35
Moses, my l Num 11:28
l-s of...Philistines Judg 16:27
counsel of my l Ezra 10:3
l-s of the nations Is 16:8
his l commanded Matt 18:25
write to my l Acts 25:26

LOVE (n) *compassion, devotion*
l covers all Prov 10:12
in unchanging l Mic 7:18
l will grow cold Matt 24:12
abide in My l John 15:10
Greater l has no one John 15:13
demonstrates His...l Rom 5:8
separate us from...l Rom 8:39
l edifies 1 Cor 8:1
l is kind 1 Cor 13:4
Pursue l 1 Cor 14:1
l of Christ controls 2 Cor 5:14
through l serve one Gal 5:13
fruit...is l Gal 5:22
speaking...truth in l Eph 4:15
l of money is a root 1 Tim 6:10
for l is from God 1 John 4:7
God is l 1 John 4:16
l casts out fear 1 John 4:18
have left your first l Rev 2:4

LOVE (v)
who l Me and keep My Ex 20:6
l your neighbor as Lev 19:18
l the LORD your God Deut 6:5
the LORD **l-d** Israel 1 Kin 10:9

I l Your testimonies Ps 119:119
LORD l-s He reproves Prov 3:12
friend l-s at all Prov 17:17
Do not l sleep Prov 20:13
A time to l Eccl 3:8
Hate evil, l good Amos 5:15
do not l perjury Zech 8:17
l your enemies Matt 5:44
l to stand and pray Matt 6:5
God so l-d the world John 3:16
you l one another John 13:34
l-s a cheerful giver 2 Cor 9:7
Husbands, l…wives Eph 5:25
Do not l the world 1 John 2:15
whom I l, I reprove Rev 3:19

LOVERS *one who desires, loves*
l have been crushed Jer 22:20
I called to my l Lam 1:19
the hands of your l Ezek 16:39
I will go after my l Hos 2:5
l of pleasure…l of 2 Tim 3:4

LOVINGKINDNESS *compassion*
His l is upon Israel Ezra 3:11
abundant in l and Ps 86:15
sing of the l of the Ps 89:1
By l and truth Prov 16:6
with everlasting l Is 54:8

LUKE
associate of Paul 2 Tim 4:11; Philem 24
author of Luke and Acts Luke 1:1; Acts 1:1
physician Col 4:14

LUST *sexual desire*
looks at…woman with l Matt 5:28
from youthful l-s 2 Tim 2:22
You l and do not James 4:2
l of the eyes 1 John 2:16

LYDIA
1 *seller of purple dyes and goods* Acts 16:14,40
2 *region on the W coast of Asia Minor* Jer 46:9

LYING (adj) *false*
with a l tongue Ps 109:2
hatred *has* l lips Prov 10:18
l pen of the scribes Jer 8:8
and l divination Ezek 13:6

LYRE *stringed instrument*
play the l and pipe Gen 4:21
prophesy with l-s 1 Chr 25:1
Awake, harp and l Ps 57:8

M

MACHPELAH
cave near Hebron Gen 23:17,19
Sarah's burial place Gen 23:19
Abraham buried there Gen 25:9
burial place of Jacob, Isaac, Rebekah, and Leah Gen 49:29ff; 50:13

MAD *insane*
makes a wise man m Eccl 7:7
nations are going m Jer 51:7

MADMAN *insane person*
behaving as a m 1 Sam 21:14
m who prophesies Jer 29:26

MAGDALENE
Mary Matt 27:56,61
from village of Magdala Mark 15:40,47; John 20:1,18

MAGI
wise men from Persia who visited Jesus, Mary, and Joseph Matt 2:1,7,16

MAGIC *sorcery*
practicing m Acts 8:9
who practiced m Acts 19:19

MAGICIAN *sorcerer, wizard*
called for…m-s Gen 41:8
the m-s of Egypt Ex 7:11
of any m, conjurer or Dan 2:10
found a m Acts 13:6

MAGISTRATE
appear before the m Luke 12:58
to the chief m-s Acts 16:20

MAGNIFY *extol, praise*
name…be m-ied 2 Sam 7:26
You m him Job 7:17
O m the LORD with me Ps 34:3
have m-ied Your word Ps 138:2
Jesus was…m-ied Acts 19:17
I m my ministry Rom 11:13

MAGOG
1 *son of Japheth* 1 Chr 1:5
2 *region in Asia Minor or further N ruled by Gog* Ezek 38:2; 39:6
see also GOG

MAHANAIM
city in Trans-Jordan Josh 13:26,30
city of refuge Josh 21:38
Levitical city 1 Chr 6:80

MAJESTY *grandeur*
Around God is…m Job 37:22
He is clothed with m Ps 93:1
The m of our God Is 35:2
right hand of the M Heb 1:3
revile angelic m-ies Jude 8

MAKER *creator*
Where is God my M Job 35:10
kneel before…our M Ps 95:6
M of heaven and Ps 115:15
I, the LORD, am the m Is 44:24

MALCHUS
servant whose ear was cut off by Peter John 18:10

MALE
m and female He Gen 1:27
lamb…unblemished m Ex 12:5
likeness of m or Deut 4:16
slew…m children Matt 2:16
made…m and female Matt 19:4
neither m nor female Gal 3:28

MAMRE
1 *Abraham's dwelling place near Hebron* Gen 13:18
2 *Amorite chieftain* Gen 14:24

MAN *male*
make m in Our image Gen 1:26
God formed m of dust Gen 2:7
Elisha the m of God 2 Kin 5:8
m is born for trouble Job 5:7
blessed is the m Ps 1:1
m is a mere breath Ps 39:11
righteous m hates Prov 13:5
Will a m rob God Mal 3:8
light…before men Matt 5:16
fishers of men Mark 1:17
Sabbath…for m Mark 2:27
rich m to enter Mark 10:25
what is a m profited Luke 9:25
a m, sent from God John 1:6
How can a m be born John 3:4
a m of Macedonia Acts 16:9
through one m sin Rom 5:12
as is common to m 1 Cor 10:13
when I became a m 1 Cor 13:11
m…leave his father Eph 5:31

MANASSEH
1 *son of Joseph* Gen 41:51; 46:20
2 *tribe and area* Num 13:11; Josh 17:1
3 *king of Judah* 2 Kin 21:1,11
4 *Pahath-moab's son* Ezra 10:30
5 *son of Hashum* Ezra 10:33

MANDRAKES *love fruit*
found m in the field Gen 30:14
m…fragrance Song 7:13

MANGER *feeding trough*
spend...at your **m** Job 39:9
the **m** is clean Prov 14:4
laid Him in a **m** Luke 2:7
MANKIND *the human race*
God...dwell with **m** 2 Chr 6:18
All **m** is stupid Jer 51:17
His love for **m** Titus 3:4
kill a third of **m** Rev 9:15
MANNA *food of the desert*
Israel named it **m** Ex 16:31
m was like coriander Num 11:7
m ceased on the day Josh 5:12
He rained down **m** Ps 78:24
Our fathers ate the **m** John 6:31
MARDUK
chief Babylonian god Jer 50:2
MARESHAH
1 *father of Hebron* 1 Chr 2:42
2 *son of Laadah* 1 Chr 4:21
3 *town in Judah* 2 Chr 11:5-8
MARK *sign, spot*
make any tattoo **m-s** Lev 19:28
m on the foreheads Ezek 9:4
m on his forehead Rev 14:9
m of the beast Rev 19:20
MARK, JOHN
author of Gospel of Mark
accompanied Paul and Barnabas Acts 13:5; 15:37
cousin of Barnabas Col 4:10
MARRIAGE *wedlock*
a **m** alliance with 1 Kin 3:1
nor are given in **m** Matt 22:30
M *is to be held* in honor Heb 13:4
m supper of the Lamb Rev 19:9
MARRY *join in wedlock*
m-ied foreign wives Ezra 10:10
m-ies a divorced Matt 5:32
better not to **m** Matt 19:10
neither **m** nor are Mark 12:25
m-ied woman is bound Rom 7:2
better to **m** than to 1 Cor 7:9
MARTHA
sister of Lazarus and Mary John 11:1,5
MARY
1 *mother of Jesus* Matt 1:16
2 *Mary Magdalene* Matt 27:56; Mark 15:40
3 *mother of James and Joseph* Matt 27:56; Mark 16:1
4 *sister of Martha and Lazarus* John 11:1
5 *mother of Mark* Acts 12:12
6 *wife of Clopas* John 19:25
7 *Roman believer* Rom 16:6
MASTER *lord, ruler*
God of...**m** Abraham Gen 24:12
m shall pierce his ear Ex 21:6
can serve two **m-s** Matt 6:24
death no longer is **m** Rom 6:9
sin shall not be **m** Rom 6:14
obedient to...your **m-s** Eph 6:5
a **M** in heaven Col 4:1
MATTHEW
tax-gatherer Matt 9:9; 10:3
apostle Matt 10:3; Luke 6:15; Acts 1:13
MATTHIAS
replaced Judas Acts 1:23,26
MEDE(S)
ancient Indo-Europeans of NW Iran Dan 5:31; 11:1
MEDIA
country of the Medes Ezra 6:2; Esth 1:18; Is 21:2
MEDIATOR *intermediary*
by the agency of a **m** Gal 3:19
one **m**...between God 1 Tim 2:5
Jesus...**m** of a new Heb 12:24

MEDITATE *ponder*
Isaac went out to **m** Gen 24:63
His law he **m-s** day Ps 1:2
M in your heart Ps 4:4
I **m** on You in the Ps 63:6
MEDITATION *deep reflection*
m...Be acceptable Ps 19:14
m be pleasing to Him Ps 104:34
my **m** all the day Ps 119:97
MEDIUM *summons spirits*
not turn to **m-s** or Lev 19:31
m...be put to death Lev 20:27
a **m**, or a spiritist Deut 18:11
woman who is a **m** 1 Sam 28:7
will resort to...**m-s** Is 19:3
MEEKNESS *gentleness*
cause of truth and **m** Ps 45:4
m and...of Christ 2 Cor 10:1
MEGIDDO
strategic city between Manasseh and Issachar Josh 12:21; 2 Kin 9:27
plain in Jezreel Valley 2 Chr 35:22; Zech 12:11
see also **HAR-MAGEDON**
MELCHIZEDEK
1 *king of Salem* Gen 14:18,19
priest Ps 110:4
2 *type of undying priesthood* Heb 5:6,10; 6:20; 7:1ff
MEMPHIS
city in Egypt Is 19:13; Jer 46:19; Ezek 30:13
MENSTRUAL
m impurity for seven Lev 15:19
a woman during...**m** Ezek 18:6
MENSTRUATION
in the days of her **m** Lev 12:2
like her bed at **m** Lev 15:26
MERCHANT *buyer / seller*
m-s procured *them* 1 Kin 10:28
m of the peoples Ezek 27:3
A **m**, in whose hands Hos 12:7
m seeking...pearls Matt 13:45
m-s of the earth Rev 18:3
MERCIFUL *compassionate*
God **m** and gracious Ps 86:15
The LORD is...and **m** Ps 145:8
The **m** man...good Prov 11:17
Blessed are the **m** Matt 5:7
as your Father is **m** Luke 6:36
m to me, the sinner Luke 18:13
MERCY *compassion*
Great are Your **m-ies** Ps 119:156
in His **m** He redeemed Is 63:9
m to *the* poor Dan 4:27
the orphan finds **m** Hos 14:3
they shall receive **m** Matt 5:7
tender **m** of our God Luke 1:78
m on whom I have **m** Rom 9:15
by the **m-ies** of God Rom 12:1
God, being rich in **m** Eph 2:4
MERCY SEAT *covering over ark*
a **m** of pure gold Ex 25:17
put the **m** on the ark Ex 26:34
in front of the **m** Ex 30:6
sprinkle it on the **m** Lev 16:15
overshadowing the **m** Heb 9:5
MERODACH-BALADAN
king of Babylon Is 39:1
see also **BERODACH-BALADAN**
MESHA
1 *territorial boundary in Arabia* Gen 10:30
2 *Moabite king* 2 Kin 3:4
3 *man of Judah* 1 Chr 2:42
4 *a Benjamite* 1 Chr 8:9

MESOPOTAMIA
land of Tigris and Euphrates Rivers Deut 23:4; Judg 3:8; 1 Chr 19:6; Acts 7:2
MESSAGE *communication*
m from God for you Judg 3:20
m…with authority Luke 4:32
m and my preaching 1 Cor 2:4
the **m** of truth Eph 1:13
m we have heard 1 John 1:5
MESSIAH
anointed one Dan 9:25,26; John 1:41; 4:25
Greek: Christ
METHUSELAH
son of Enoch Gen 5:21
grandfather of Noah Gen 5:25ff
MICAH
1 *an Ephraimite* Judg 17:1
2 *line of Reuben* 1 Chr 5:5
3 *father of Abdon* 2 Chr 34:20
4 *prophet* Jer 26:18; Mic 1:1
name of several other people
MICAIAH
1 *prophet* 1 Kin 22:8-26
2 *father of Achbor* 2 Kin 22:12
3 *wife of Rehoboam* 2 Chr 13:2
4 *under Jehoshaphat* 2 Chr 17:7
5 *line of Asaph* Neh 12:35
6 *under Nehemiah* Neh 12:41
7 *son of Gemariah* Jer 36:11
MICHAEL
1 *an archangel* Dan 10:21; 12:1; Jude 9; Rev 12:7
2 *Jehoshaphat's son* 2 Chr 21:2
prince of Judah
3 *army captain* 1 Chr 12:20
4 *line of Gershom* 1 Chr 6:40
name of seven other people
MIDHEAVEN *directly overhead*
eagle flying in **m** Rev 8:13
angel flying in **m** Rev 14:6
birds which fly in **m** Rev 19:17
MIDIAN
1 *a son of Abraham* Gen 25:1,2
2 *land SE of Canaan in desert* Ex 2:15; Num 31:8; Judg 8:28
MIDIANITES
people of Midian Gen 37:36; Num 31:2; Judg 7:7
MIDWIFE *aids childbirth*
m…tied a scarlet Gen 38:28
before the **m** can get Ex 1:19
MIGDOL
1 *Israelite camp near Red Sea* Ex 14:2; Num 33:7
2 *town in Egypt* Jer 44:1
MILCOM
god of Ammonites 1 Kin 11:5,33; 2 Kin 23:13; Zeph 1:5
see also MOLECH
MILLO
1 *fort near Shechem* *Beth-millo* Judg 9:6,20
2 *fortress in Jerusalem* 2 Sam 5:9; 1 Kin 9:15,24; 1 Chr 11:8; 2 Chr 32:5
MILLSTONE *grinding stone*
upper **m** in pledge Deut 24:6
woman threw…**m** Judg 9:53
m hung around Matt 18:6
stone like a great **m** Rev 18:21
MINA
measure of gold or silver coin 1 Kin 10:17; Ezra 2:69; Neh 7:71; Luke 19:13ff
MINISTER (n) *one who serves*
m-s before the ark 1 Chr 16:4
spoken of *as* **m-s** Is 61:6
a **m** and a witness Acts 26:16
a **m** of Christ Jesus Rom 15:16
is Christ then a **m** Gal 2:17
I was made a **m** Eph 3:7
faithful **m** in the Eph 6:21
His **m-s** a flame of Heb 1:7
a **m** in the sanctuary Heb 8:2
MINISTER (v) *give help, serve*
to **m** as priest to Me Ex 28:1
the boy **m-ed** to 1 Sam 2:11
not stand to **m** 1 Kin 8:11
to the LORD, To **m** Is 56:6
angels were **m-ing** Mark 1:13
follow Him and **m** Mark 15:41
MINISTRY *service*
He began His **m** Luke 3:23
to the **m** of the word Acts 6:4
m of the Spirit 2 Cor 3:8
m of reconciliation 2 Cor 5:18
fulfill your **m** 2 Tim 4:5
a more excellent **m** Heb 8:6
MIRACLE *supernatural event*
Work a **m** Ex 7:9
I will perform **m-s** Ex 34:10
m-s had occurred Matt 11:21
He could do no **m** Mark 6:5
perform a **m** in My Mark 9:39
this **m** of healing Acts 4:22
works **m-s** among you Gal 3:5
wonders and…**m-s** Heb 2:4
MIRE *mud*
cast me into the **m** Job 30:1
Deliver me from the **m** Ps 69:1
wallowing in the **m** 2 Pet 2:22
MIRIAM
1 *sister of Moses and Aaron* Ex 15:20; Num 12:4,10; 20:
2 *line of Ezrah* 1 Chr 4:1
MISCARRIAGE *aborted fetus*
so that she has a **m** Ex 21:2
m-s of a woman Ps 58:
MISHAEL
1 *of family of Kohath* Ex 6:22; Lev 10:
2 *associate of Ezra* Neh 8:
3 *Daniel's friend* Dan 1:6,7,11,19; 2:1
see also MESHACH
MISLEAD *lead astray*
m-s a blind *person* Deut 27:1
m-led My people Ezek 13:1
that no one **m-s** you Mark 13:
m-ing our nation Luke 23:
MISTREAT *treat badly, wrong*
not **m**…the stranger Jer 22:
slaves…**m-ed** them Matt 22:
pray for…who **m** Luke 6:2
mocked and **m-ed** Luke 18:3
m and to stone them Acts 14:
MISTRESS *woman in charge*
her **m** was despised Gen 16:
m of the house 1 Kin 17:1
the maid like her **m** Is 24:
the **m** of sorceries Nah 3:
MIZPAH / MIZPEH
1 *heap of stones* Gen 31:4
2 *near Mt. Hermon* Josh 11:
3 *village in Judah* Josh 15:3
4 *Benjamite town* Josh 18:2
5 *town in Gilead* Judg 10:1
6 *Moabite town* 1 Sam 22:
MIZRAIM
1 *son of Ham* Gen 10
father of nations Gen 10:1
2 *Heb. for Egypt* 1 Chr 1:8,1
MOAB
1 *son of Lot* Gen 19:3
2 *country E of the Dead Sea* Ex 15:15; Josh 24:; Ruth 1:2; 2 Kin 3:7; Ps 60:8; Jer 48

MOLECH
god of the Ammonites Lev 18:21; 1 Kin 11:7; Jer 32:35
see also MILCOM
MOLTEN *cast metal*
made it into a **m** calf Ex 32:4
make…no **m** gods Ex 34:17
destroy…**m** images Num 33:52
capitals of **m** bronze 1 Kin 7:16
his **m** images are Jer 10:14
MONEY *currency*
take double *the* **m** Gen 43:12
not sell her for **m** Deut 21:14
time to receive **m** 2 Kin 5:26
loves **m** will not be Eccl 5:10
no **m** in their belt Mark 6:8
m in the bank Luke 19:23
love of **m** is a root 1 Tim 6:10
MONSTER *enormous animal*
created…sea **m-s** Gen 1:21
sea, or the sea **m** Job 7:12
sea **m-s** in the waters Ps 74:13
belly of the sea **m** Matt 12:40
MORALS *principles*
Bad…good **m** 1 Cor 15:33
MORDECAI
1 *returned from exile with Zerubbabel* Ezra 2:2
2 *Esther's cousin* Esth 2:7; 3:2; 9:20; 10:3
MORIAH
land / mountain where Abraham offered Isaac Gen 22:2
threshing floor of Araunah (Ornan) 2 Sam 24:18
site of Temple 2 Chr 3:1
MOSES
birth Ex 2:1-3
in Pharaoh's care Ex 2:5-10
killed an Egyptian Ex 2:11,12
exiled Ex 2:15
called by God Ex 3:1-22
opposed Pharaoh Ex 5:11
crossed Red Sea Ex 14
Ten Commandments Ex 20:1-18
saw Canaan Deut 3:23ff; 34:1ff
death Deut 31:14; 34:5
MOTH *insect*
crushed before the **m** Job 4:19
The **m** will eat them Is 50:9
like a **m** to Ephraim Hos 5:12
m and rust destroy Matt 6:19
MOTHER
leave…and his **m** Gen 2:24
m of all *the* living Gen 3:20
Honor…and your **m** Ex 20:12
a grief to his **m** Prov 10:1
Contend with your **m** Hos 2:2
When His **m** Mary Matt 1:18
Take…and His **m** Matt 2:13
Who is My **m** Matt 12:48
Honor your…**m** Matt 19:19
Behold, your **m** John 19:27
MOTHER-IN-LAW
who lies with his **m** Deut 27:23
Orpah kissed her **m** Ruth 1:14
m lying sick in bed Matt 8:14
MOUNTAIN
sacrifice on the **m** Gen 31:54
from His holy **m** Ps 3:4
lift up…to the **m-s** Ps 121:1
lovely on the **m-s** Is 52:7
eat at the **m** shrines Ezek 18:6
m-s will melt Mic 1:4
the **m** will move Zech 14:4
m-s, Fall on us Luke 23:30
withdrew…to the **m** John 6:15
faith…remove **m-s** 1 Cor 13:2

MULE *animal*
mounted his **m** 2 Sam 13:29
Absalom…on *his* **m** 2 Sam 18:9
ride on the king's **m** 1 Kin 1:44
war horses and **m-s** Ezek 27:14
MURDER *premeditated killing*
You shall not **m** Ex 20:13
Whoever commits **m** Matt 5:21
m-ed the prophets Matt 23:31
full of envy, **m** Rom 1:29
MURDERER *killer*
m shall be put to Num 35:30
m from…beginning John 8:44
this man is a **m** Acts 28:4
no **m** has eternal 1 John 3:15
MUSTARD *type of plant*
kingdom…like a **m** Matt 13:31
faith the size of a **m** seed Matt 17:20
It is like a **m** seed Luke 13:19
MUZZLE *gag*
shall not **m** the ox Deut 25:4
guard…as with a **m** Ps 39:1
MYRRH *spice*
aromatic gum…**m** Gen 43:11
Dripping with…**m** Song 5:13
frankincense and **m** Matt 2:11
mixture of **m** and John 19:39
MYRTLE *type of plant*
the **m**, and the olive Is 41:19
among the **m** trees Zech 1:11
MYSTERY *hidden truth, secret*
no **m** baffles you Dan 4:9
God's wisdom in a **m** 1 Cor 2:7
know all **m-ies** 1 Cor 13:2
into the **m** of Christ Eph 3:4
the **m** of the gospel Eph 6:19
the **m** of the faith 1 Tim 3:9
MYTHS *fables*
to pay attention to **m** 1 Tim 1:4
will turn aside to **m** 2 Tim 4:4
attention to Jewish **m** Titus 1:14

N

NADAB
1 *son of Aaron* Ex 6:23
2 *king of Israel* 1 Kin 14:20
3 *son of Shammai* 1 Chr 2:28
4 *son of Jehiel* 1 Chr 8:29,30
NAHOR
1 *Abram's grandfather* Gen 11:24ff
2 *brother of Abram* Gen 11:27; 22:23
3 *city in N Mesopotamia* Gen 24:10
NAILED (v) *attached*
you **n** to a cross Acts 2:23
n it to the cross Col 2:14
NAILS (n) *finger ends* or *pins*
and trim her **n** Deut 21:12
fasten it with **n** Jer 10:4
imprint of the **n** John 20:25
NAKED *unclothed*
n and…not ashamed Gen 2:25
n I shall return there Job 1:21
n…you clothed Me Matt 25:36
NAOMI
woman of Bethlehem Ruth 1:1
Ruth's mother-in-law Ruth 1:4,6
NAPHTALI
1 *son of Jacob* Gen 30:8
2 *tribe / district* Num 13:14; 1 Chr 2:2; Rev 7:6
NARD *fragrant ointment*
henna with **n** plants Song 4:13
perfume of pure **n** John 12:3
NATHAN
1 *a son of David* 2 Sam 5:14; Luke 3:31
2 *prophet* 2 Sam 7:2; 12:1ff

3 *son of Attai* 1 Chr 2:36
4 *helped Ezra* Ezra 8:16,17
name of several other individuals

NATHANAEL
disciple of Jesus John 1:49

NATION *government, people*
make you a great **n** Gen 12:2
priests and a holy **n** Ex 19:6
scatter…the **n-s** Lev 26:33
the **n-s** in an uproar Ps 2:1
n-s…fear the name Ps 102:15
N will not lift up sword Is 2:4
sprinkle many **n-s** Is 52:15
glory among the **n-s** Is 66:19
n…rise against **n** Matt 24:7
n not perish John 11:50
men, from every **n** Acts 2:5
tongue…people and **n** Rev 5:9

NAZARENE
1 *of Nazareth* John 18:7
2 *follower of Jesus* Acts 24:5

NAZARETH
town of Galilee Matt 2:23
home of Joseph, Mary, and Jesus Luke 4:16; John 1:45

NAZIRITE
1 *one consecrated to God* Num 6:2,19,20
2 *religious vow* Judg 13:5,7; Amos 2:11,12

NEBO
1 *Moabite town* Num 32:38
2 *mountain where Moses viewed promised land* Deut 32:49; 34:1
3 *Babylonian god* Is 46:1
4 *town W of Jordan* Ezra 2:29; Neh 7:33
5 *Jew whose sons married foreign wives* Ezra 10:43

NEBUCHADNEZZAR
king of Babylon 2 Kin 24:1,10
captured Judah 1 Chr 6:15; Ezra 2:1

NEBUZARADAN
Babylonian commander responsible for destruction of Jerusalem and the Temple 2 Kin 25:8ff; Jer 39:9,10

NEGEV
S desert region Gen 12:9; Judg 1:9; Jer 32:44; Zech 7:7

NEGLECT *disregard, ignore*
You **n-ed** the Rock Deut 32:18
who **n-s** discipline Prov 15:32
n so great a salvation Heb 2:3
n to show hospitality Heb 13:2
do not **n** doing good Heb 13:16

NEHEMIAH
1 *Jewish exile* Ezra 2:2; Neh 7:7
2 *son of Azbuk* Neh 3:16
3 *son of Hacaliah* Neh 1:1
rebuilt walls Neh 3:1ff
governor of Jerusalem Neh 8:9

NEIGHBOR *one living nearby*
not covet…**n-'s** wife Ex 20:17
shall love your **n** Lev 19:18
make your **n-s** drink Hab 2:15
love your **n** and Matt 5:43
And who is my **n** Luke 10:29
love your **n** as Gal 5:14

NEPHILIM
people of great stature Gen 6:4; Num 13:33

NICODEMUS
Pharisee John 3:1,4,9
in Sanhedrin John 7:50; 19:39

NIGHT *darkness*
darkness He called **n** Gen 1:5
pillar of fire by **n** Ex 13:21
meditate…day and **n** Josh 1:8
make **n** into day Job 17:12
The terror by **n** Ps 91:5
At **n** my soul longs Is 26:9
over their flock by **n** Luke 2:8
a thief in the **n** 1 Thess 5:2
tormented day and **n** Rev 20:10

NIMROD
son of Cush Gen 10:8
a mighty hunter Gen 10:9
ruler of Shinar Gen 10:10

NINEVEH
capital of Assyria 2 Kin 19:36
visited by Jonah Jon 1:1ff

NISAN
first month of the Hebrew calendar Neh 2:1; Esth 3:7

NOAH
1 *son of Lamech* Gen 5:28,29
father of Shem, Ham, Japheth Gen 5:32
built an ark Gen 6:14-22
saved from Flood Gen 6:9; 7:15; 8:1; 8:13
promised by God Gen 9:9-17
2 *daughter of Zelophehad* Num 26:33; 27:1; 36:11

NOBLE *lofty* or *renowned one*
king's most **n** princes Esth 6:9
speak **n** things Prov 8:6
all the **n-s** of Judah Jer 39:6

NOBLEMAN *of high rank*
the house of the **n** Job 21:28
A **n** went to Luke 19:12

NOMADS *desert wanderers*
n of the desert bow Ps 72:9

NORTH *direction of compass*
stretches out the **n** Job 26:7
Zion *in* the far **n** Ps 48:2
king of the **N** will Dan 11:13
three gates on the **n** Rev 21:13

O

OAK *type of tree*
by the **o-s** of Mamre Gen 13:18
the diviners' **o** Judg 9:37
o-s of righteousness Is 61:3
strong as the **o-s** Amos 2:9

OBADIAH
1 *in Ahab's court* 1 Kin 18:3f
2 *Gadite warrior* 1 Chr 12:8,9
3 *sent to teach* 2 Chr 17:7
4 *Levite, of Merari* 2 Chr 34:12
5 *son of Jehiel* Ezra 8:9
6 *signer of covenant* Neh 10:1,5
7 *prophet* Obad 1
name of five other Old Testament people

OBED
1 *son of Ruth / Boaz* Ruth 4:1[illegible]
ancestor of Jesus Matt 1:5; Luke 3:3[illegible]
2 *son of Ephlal* 1 Chr 2:3[illegible]
3 *warrior* 1 Chr 11:26,4[illegible]
4 *temple gatekeeper* 1 Chr 26:1,[illegible]
5 *father of Azariah* 2 Chr 23:[illegible]

OBEDIENCE *submission*
the **o** of the peoples Gen 49:1[illegible]
pretend **o** to me 2 Sam 22:4[illegible]
the **o** of the One Rom 5:1[illegible]
leading to **o** of faith Rom 16:2[illegible]
in **o** to the truth 1 Pet 1:2[illegible]

OBEY *follow commands, orders*
have **o-ed** My voice Gen 22:1[illegible]
o My voice and keep Ex 19:[illegible]
o the LORD your God Deut 27:1[illegible]
to **o** is better than 1 Sam 15:2[illegible]
O-ing…His word Ps 103:2[illegible]
and the sea **o** Him Matt 8:2[illegible]
o God rather than Acts 5:2[illegible]
o your parents Eph 6:[illegible]

O your leaders Heb 13:17
to o Jesus Christ 1 Pet 1:2

OBLIGATION *duty*
o toward the LORD Num 32:22
for his daily o-s 2 Chr 31:16
under o, not to the Rom 8:12
o to keep the…Law Gal 5:3

ODIOUS *offensive*
o in Pharaoh's sight Ex 5:21
o to the Philistines 1 Sam 13:4

OFFERING (n) *contribution*
freewill o to the LORD Ex 35:29
o of first fruits Lev 2:12
your worthless o-s Is 1:13
presenting your o Matt 5:23
any o for sin Heb 10:18

OFFERINGS
1 **Burnt Offering** Gen 22:13; Lev 1:17
2 **Drink Offering** Phil 2:17; 2 Tim 4:6
also Libation
3 **Freewill Offering** Ex 35:29; Lev 7:16
4 **Grain Offering** Lev 9:4; Josh 22:29
also Meal Offering
5 **Guilt Offering** Lev 5:6; Num 6:12
6 **Heave Offering** Ex 29:27,28
7 **Libation Offering** Num 6:15,17; 28:9,10
also Drink Offering
8 **Meal Offering** 2 Kin 16:15; Ps 40:6
also Grain Offering
9 **Ordination Offering** Lev 8:28,31
10 **Peace Offering** Lev 4:31; Num 6:14
11 **Sin Offering** Ex 29:14; Ezek 46:20
12 **Thank Offering** 2 Chr 33:16; Jer 33:11
13 **Votive Offering** Deut 12:26; 23:18
14 **Wave Offering** Lev 14:12; Num 18:18

OFFSPRING *descendants*
o in place of Abel Gen 4:25
bring forth o from Is 65:9

OG
Amorite king Num 21:33; Deut 3:4; Josh 12:4

OIL
o for lighting Ex 25:6
anointed my head…o Ps 23:5
the o of joy Ps 45:7
words…softer than o Ps 55:21
prudent took o in Matt 25:4
not anoint…with o Luke 7:46

OLIVE *tree* or *fruit*
freshly picked o leaf Gen 8:11
land of o oil and Deut 8:8
cherubim of o wood 1 Kin 6:23
children like o plants Ps 128:3

OLIVES, MOUNT OF
mountain E of Jerusalem 2 Sam 15:30; Zech 14:4; Matt 24:3; Mark 11:1
place where Jesus prayed Matt 26:30; Luke 22:39-41

OMEGA
last letter of Gr. alphabet Rev 1:8
title of Jesus Christ Rev 21:6
expresses eternalness of God Rev 22:13

OMEN *foretells a future event*
who interprets o-s Deut 18:10
took this as an o 1 Kin 20:33

OMER *dry measure*
take an o apiece Ex 16:16
o is a tenth of an Ex 16:36

OMRI
1 *king of Israel* 1 Kin 16:22ff
2 *a Benjamite* 1 Chr 7:8
3 *line of Perez* 1 Chr 9:4
4 *son of Michael* 1 Chr 27:18

ONYX *precious stone*
bdellium and the o Gen 2:12
o, and the jasper Ezek 28:13

OPHEL
citadel on S slope of Temple Mount in Jerusalem 2 Chr 27:3; 33:14; Neh 3:27
home of temple servants (Nethinim) Neh 3:26; 11:21

OPPOSE *contend, resist*
o the Prince of Dan 8:25
o-d the ordinance of Rom 13:2
men also o the truth 2 Tim 3:8
God is o-d to the James 4:6

OPPOSITION *hostility*
you…know My o Num 14:34
these are in o Gal 5:17
gospel…much o 1 Thess 2:2

ORACLE *revelation*
The o of Balaam Num 24:3
o concerning Babylon Is 13:1
the o of the LORD Jer 23:33
and misleading o-s Lam 2:14
entrusted with the o-s Rom 3:2

ORDAIN *invest, set apart*
anoint…and o them Ex 28:41
o Aaron and his sons Ex 29:9
o-ed His covenant Ps 111:9
law as o-ed by angels Acts 7:53

ORNAN
Jebusite owner of threshing floor on Mount Moriah 1 Chr 21:15,18
sells threshing floor to David for altar and temple 1 Chr 21:25,28

ORPHAN *fatherless child*
not afflict any…o Ex 22:22
justice for the o Deut 10:18
helper of the o Ps 10:14
may plunder the o-s Is 10:2
Leave…o-s behind Jer 49:11
visit o-s and widows James 1:27

OX *bull used as draft animal*
oxen and donkeys Gen 12:16
servant or his o Ex 20:17
horns of the wild **oxen** Ps 22:21
An o knows its owner Is 1:3
not muzzle the o 1 Tim 5:18

P

PADDAN-ARAM
NW Mesopotamia Gen 25:20
home of Laban Gen 28:5
birthplace of most of Jacob's sons Gen 35:26

PALACE *royal residence*
build…royal p 2 Chr 2:12
to the king's p Esth 2:8
Out of ivory p-s Ps 45:8
A p of strangers Is 25:2
luxury…royal p-s Luke 7:25

PALM *type of tree*
the city of p trees Deut 34:3
flourish like the p Ps 92:12
branches of the p John 12:13

PAPYRUS *reed plant*
p…without a marsh Job 8:11
Even in p vessels Is 18:2

PARABLE *story for illustration*
speak a p to Ezek 17:2
p of the sower Matt 13:18
heard His p-s Matt 21:45
p from the fig tree Mark 13:28
spoke by way of a p Luke 8:4

PARADISE
abode of the righteous dead Luke 23:43; 2 Cor 12:4; Rev 2:7
see also **ABRAHAM'S BOSOM**

PARALYTIC
said to the p, Get up Matt 9:6
p, carried by four Mark 2:3

PARAN
wilderness area in Sinai Gen 21:21; Num 13:3
place of Israelite wanderings and encampments Num 12:16
mountain in Sinai Deut 33:2

PARDON *forgive, release*
he will not **p** your Ex 23:21
May the…LORD **p** 2 Chr 30:18
O LORD, **P** my iniquity Ps 25:11
He will abundantly **p** Is 55:7
p, and you will be Luke 6:37

PARENTS *father and mother*
rise up against **p** Matt 10:21
left house or…**p** Luke 18:29
evil, disobedient to **p** Rom 1:30
Children, obey your **p** Eph 6:1
disobedient to **p** 2 Tim 3:2

PASSOVER
Israel's firstborn protected from the plague of death prior to the exodus from Egypt Ex 12:1-30
Feast commemorating Israelite exodus and protection from death Ex 12:42,43; Lev 23:5; Num 9:2,12,14; Matt 26:2,18; John 19:14; Acts 12:4
see also **FEASTS**

PASTORS *shepherds of people*
and some *as* **p** Eph 4:11

PATIENCE *endurance*
try the **p** of men Is 7:13
in **p**, in kindness 2 Cor 6:6
love, joy, peace, **p** Gal 5:22
exhort, with great **p** 2 Tim 4:2
endure it with **p** 1 Pet 2:20

PATRIARCH *father of clan*
regarding the **p** David Acts 2:29
the twelve **p-s** Acts 7:8
Abraham, the **p**, gave Heb 7:4

PAUL
heritage Acts 21:39; 22:3; Phil 3:5
persecuted believers Acts 7:58; 8:1,3; 9:1,2; 1 Cor 15:9
conversion and call Acts 9:1-19
name changed Acts 13:9
Jerusalem council Acts 15:2-6
missionary journeys Acts 13:1ff; 15:36ff; 18:23ff
apostolic defense Acts 11:5ff; Gal 1:13ff
arrest and imprisonment Acts 21:33; 22:24-28:31
defense Acts 22:1ff; 24:10ff; 25:10,11; 26:2ff
final journey to Rome Acts 27,28
see also **SAUL**

PAY *give what is due*
thief…**p** double Ex 22:7
p You my vows Ps 66:13
P back what you Matt 18:28
Never **p** back evil Rom 12:17
p the penalty 2 Thess 1:9

PEACE *calmness, tranquility*
grant **p** in the land Lev 26:6
made **p** with David 1 Chr 19:19
Seek **p**, and pursue Ps 34:14
for the **p** of Jerusalem Ps 122:6
all her paths are **p** Prov 3:17
a time for **p** Eccl 3:8
Prince of **P** Is 9:6
p…like a river Is 66:12
have withdrawn My **p** Jer 16:5
not come to bring **p** Matt 10:34
on earth **p** among Luke 2:14
P I leave with you John 14:27
we have **p** with God Rom 5:1
love, joy, **p** Gal 5:22
He Himself is our **p** Eph 2:14
gospel of **p** Eph 6:15
p of God…surpasses Phil 4:7
p through the blood Col 1:20
take **p** from the earth Rev 6:4

PEACEMAKERS
Blessed are the **p** Matt 5:9

PEARL *precious gem*
wisdom is above…**p-s** Job 28:18
p-s before swine Matt 7:6
one **p** of great value Matt 13:46

PENIEL
where Jacob wrestled with God Gen 32:30
see also **PENUEL**

PENTECOST
Jewish feast held 50 days after Passover Acts 20:16; 1 Cor 16:8
coming of the Holy Spirit Acts 2:1
see also **FEASTS**

PENUEL
1 *tower destroyed* Judg 8:17
rebuilt 1 Kin 12:25
see also **PENIEL**
2 *father of Gedor* 1 Chr 4:4
3 *son of Shashak* 1 Chr 8:25

PEOPLE *group, nation*
they are one **p** Gen 11:6
Let My **p** go Ex 5:1
You are an obstinate **p** Ex 33:5
blessed above all **p-s** Deut 7:14
Forgive Your **p** Israel Deut 21:8
LORD loves His **p** 2 Chr 2:11
p who are called by 2 Chr 7:14
restores His captive **p** Ps 14:7
We are His **p** Ps 100:3
LORD will judge His **p** Ps 135:14
p are unrestrained Prov 29:18
p whom I formed Is 43:21
do **p** say that I am Mark 8:27
they feared the **p** Luke 20:19
die for the **p** John 11:50
not rejected His **p** Rom 11:2
every tribe and **p** Rev 13:7

PERFUME *fragrant oil*
and **p** make the heart Prov 27:9
instead of sweet **p** Is 3:24
p on My body Matt 26:12
anointed…with **p** Luke 7:46
prepared…**p-s** Luke 23:56

PERSECUTE *afflict, oppress*
Why do you **p** me Job 19:22
has **p-d** my soul Ps 143:3
pray for those who **p** Matt 5:44
p you in one city Matt 10:23
why are you **p-ing** Me Acts 9:4
used to **p** the church Gal 1:13

PERSECUTION *oppression*
p arises because of Mark 4:17
p began against the Acts 8:1
a **p** against Paul Acts 13:50
distress, or **p**, or Rom 8:35

PERSEVERANCE *persistence*
by **p** in doing good Rom 2:7
tribulation brings…**p** Rom 5:3
for your **p** and faith 2 Thess 1:4
p of the saints Rev 14:12

PESTILENCE *epidemic, plague*
LORD sent a **p** 2 Sam 24:15
sword, famine, and **p** Jer 27:13
p and mourning and Rev 18:8

PETER
heritage and occupation Matt 4:18; John 1:42,44
called by Jesus Matt 1:17; Mark 3:16; Luke 5:1ff
names: Cephas, Simon Matt 4:18; Mark 3:16; John 1:42; Acts 15:14
walked on water Matt 14:28ff
confessed Jesus as Messiah Matt 16:16; Luke 9:20

on mount of Transfiguration Matt 17:1ff; Mark 9:2ff
denied Jesus Matt 26:70; Mark 14:70; Luke 22:58
at Pentecost Acts 2
apostle of Christ Gal 2:8; 1 Pet 1:1; 2 Pet 1:1

PHARAOH *title of Egyptian kings*
1 **Pharaoh,** *time of Abraham* Gen 12:15ff
2 **Pharaoh,** *time of Joseph* Gen 37:36; 39:1-50:26
3 **Pharaoh,** *during oppression* Ex 1:8-2:23
4 **Pharaoh,** *during the Exodus* Ex 5:1-12:41
5 **Pharaoh,** *father of Bithiah* 1 Chr 4:17
6 **Pharaoh,** *time of David* 1 Kin 11:14ff
7 **Pharaoh,** *whose daughter married Solomon* 1 Kin 3:1; 7:8; 9:16
8 **Shishak,** *time of Rehoboam* 1 Kin 14:25,26
9 **So,** *time of Hoshea* 2 Kin 17:4
10 **Tirhakah,** *time of Hezekiah* 2 Kin 19:9; Is 37:9
11 **Neco,** *slew Josiah* 2 Kin 23:29,33,34
12 **Hophra,** *subject of prophecy* Jer 44:30

PHARISEES
Jewish religious party Matt 3:7; 23:13; Mark 2:18; 7:3; Luke 11:42; 16:14; John 3:1; 11:47

PHILIP
1 *Herod Philip I, son of Herod the Great* Mark 6:17
2 *Herod Philip II, son of Herod the Great* Luke 3:1
3 *Philip the apostle* Matt 10:3; Mark 3:18; Luke 6:14; John 1:43ff; Acts 1:13
4 *Philip the evangelist* Acts 6:5; 8:5,29; 21:8

PHILIPPI
Macedonian city Acts 16:12; 20:6

PHILISTIA
coastal area of SW Palestine Ex 15:14; Ps 60:8; 83:7; Joel 3:4

PHINEHAS
1 *grandson of Aaron* Num 25:7; 31:6; Judg 20:28
2 *son of Eli* 1 Sam 1:3; 4:4,11
3 *father of a priest* Ezra 8:33

PHOEBE
Cenchrea (Corinth) deaconess commended by Paul Rom 16:1

PHOENICIA
coastal land N of land of Israel Acts 11:19; 21:2
visited by Paul Acts 15:3

PHYLACTERIES *prayer bands*
as **p** on your forehead Ex 13:16
they broaden their **p** Matt 23:5
see also FRONTALS

PHYSICIAN
all worthless **p-s** Job 13:4
healthy who need a **p** Matt 9:12
P, heal yourself Luke 4:23
Luke, the beloved **p** Col 4:14

PILATE, PONTIUS
Roman governor of Judea Matt 27:2; Luke 3:1
presided at Jesus' trial Matt 27:11ff; Mark 15:2ff; Luke 23:1ff; John 18:28-38
warned by his wife Matt 27:19
orders Jesus' crucifixion Matt 27:24ff; Mark 15:15; Luke 23:24,25; John 19:15,16

PILLAR *column* or *memorial*
became a **p** of salt Gen 19:26
p of fire by night Ex 13:21
set up…a **p** 2 Sam 18:18
hewn…her seven **p-s** Prov 9:1
feet like **p-s** of fire Rev 10:1

PILOT *steersman*
sailors, and your **p-s** Ezek 27:27
the **p** and…captain Acts 27:11
inclination of the **p** James 3:4

PITHOM
Egyptian storage city built by Hebrew slaves Ex 1:11

PLAGUE *contagious disease*
no **p** will befall you Ex 12:13
Remove Your **p** from Ps 39:10
p of the hail Rev 16:21
the seven last **p-s** Rev 21:9

PLEASURE *gratification*
old, shall I have **p** Gen 18:12
p in His people Ps 149:4
He who loves **p** *will* Prov 21:17
work for *His* good **p** Phil 2:13
lovers of **p** rather 2 Tim 3:4
passing **p-s** of sin Heb 11:25

PLEDGE *promise*
cloak as a **p** Ex 22:26
those who give **p-s** Prov 22:26
the Spirit as a **p** 2 Cor 5:5
p of our inheritance Eph 1:14

PLUMB LINE *vertical line*
the **p** of emptiness Is 34:11
p In the midst of My Amos 7:8
when they see the **p** Zech 4:10

POISON *lethal substance*
P…under their lips Ps 140:3
given us **p-ed** water Jer 8:14
turned justice into **p** Amos 6:12

POLL-TAX *income and head tax*
collect customs or **p** Matt 17:25
give a **p** to Caesar Matt 22:17

POMEGRANATE *fruit*
golden bell and a **p** Ex 28:34
p-s of blue and purple Ex 39:24
juice of my **p-s** Song 8:2
the fig tree, the **p** Hag 2:19

POOR *impoverished, needy*
p will never cease Deut 15:11
raises the **p** from the 1 Sam 2:8
or you will become **p** Prov 20:13
not rob the **p** Prov 22:22
are the **p** in spirit Matt 5:3
a **p** widow came Mark 12:42
you always have the **p** Mark 14:7
sake He became **p** 2 Cor 8:9
not God choose the **p** James 2:5

POVERTY *destitution, want*
glutton…come to **p** Prov 23:21
neither **p** nor riches Prov 30:8
through His **p** might 2 Cor 8:9

POWER *authority, strength*
to show you My **p** Ex 9:16
from the **p** of Sheol Ps 49:15
the **p** of His works Ps 111:6
p of the tongue Prov 18:21
the **p** of the sword Jer 18:21
Not by might nor…**p** Zech 4:6
Yours is…the **p** Matt 6:13
the right hand of **p** Mark 14:62
clothed with **p** from Luke 24:49
you will receive **p** Acts 1:8
gospel…**p** of God Rom 1:16
the **p** of our Lord 1 Cor 5:4
p of sin is the law 1 Cor 15:56
p of Christ…dwell 2 Cor 12:9
prince of the **p** of Eph 2:2
p of His resurrection Phil 3:10
timidity, but of **p** 2 Tim 1:7
by the word of His **p** Heb 1:3
quenched the **p** of Heb 11:34
p-s…been subjected 1 Pet 3:22

POWERLESS *without strength*
p before this great 2 Chr 20:12
He might render **p** Heb 2:14

PRAETORIAN / PRAETORIUM *guard* or *palace*
1 *Imperial palace guards in Rome* Phil 1:13

2 *Pontius Pilate's palace in Jerusalem* Matt 27:27; Mark 15:16; John 18:28,33
3 *Herod's palace at Caesarea* Acts 23:35

PRAISE (n) *acclamation, honor*
offering of **p** Lev 19:24
sing **p-s** to Him 1 Chr 16:9
songs of **p**...hymns Neh 12:46
From You...my **p** Ps 22:25
sound His **p** abroad Ps 66:8
makes Jerusalem a **p** Is 62:7
his **p** is not from men Rom 2:29
anything worthy of **p** Phil 4:8
a sacrifice of **p** Heb 13:15
Give **p** to our God Rev 19:5

PRAISE (v) *extol, glorify*
I will **p** Him Ex 15:2
greatly to be **p-d** 1 Chr 16:25
Will the dust **p** You Ps 30:9
My lips will **p** You Ps 63:3
heavens will **p** Your Ps 89:5
P Him, sun and moon Ps 148:3
P Him with trumpet Ps 150:3
Death cannot **p** You Is 38:18
I **p** You, Father Matt 11:25
heavenly host **p-ing** Luke 2:13
disciples began to **p** Luke 19:37
leaping and **p-ing** God Acts 3:8

PRAY *ask, worship*
Abraham **p-ed** to Gen 20:17
For this boy I **p-ed** 1 Sam 1:27
found *courage* to **p** 1 Chr 17:25
For to You I **p** Ps 5:2
P for...Jerusalem Ps 122:6
p to a god who cannot Is 45:20
We earnestly **p** Jon 1:14
p for...persecute Matt 5:44
by Himself to **p** Matt 14:23
p and ask, believe Mark 11:24
until I have **p-ed** Mark 14:32
Lord, teach us to **p** Luke 11:1
they ought to **p** Luke 18:1
I have **p-ed** for you Luke 22:32
p-ed with fasting Acts 14:23
if I **p** in a tongue 1 Cor 14:14
p without ceasing 1 Thess 5:17
p for one another James 5:16
p-ing in the...Spirit Jude 20

PRAYER
I have heard your **p** 2 Chr 7:12
And my **p** is pure Job 16:17
LORD receives my **p** Ps 6:9
Give ear to my **p** Ps 55:1
p of the righteous Prov 15:29
joyful in My house of **p** Is 56:7
ask in **p**, believing Matt 21:22
you make long **p-s** Matt 23:14
whole night in **p** Luke 6:12
My house...of **p** Luke 19:46
devoting...to **p** Acts 1:14
offering **p** with joy Phil 1:4
but in everything by **p** Phil 4:6
p-s...not be hindered 1 Pet 3:7
p-s of the saints Rev 5:8

PREACH *exhort, proclaim*
Jesus began to **p** Matt 4:17
as you go, **p** Matt 10:7
teach and **p** in their Matt 11:1
p-ing...repentance Mark 1:4
p the gospel to all Mark 16:15
p the kingdom of Luke 4:43
he **p-ed** Jesus to him Acts 8:35
p...the good news Acts 13:32
How will they **p** Rom 10:15
we **p** Christ crucified 1 Cor 1:23
He...**p-ed** peace Eph 2:17
p the word 2 Tim 4:2

PREACHER *one who proclaims*
hear without a **p** Rom 10:14
appointed a **p** and an 1 Tim 2:7
Noah, a **p** of 2 Pet 2:5

PRECEPTS *commandments*
All His **p** are sure Ps 111:7
meditate on Your **p** Ps 119:15
as doctrines the **p** of Matt 15:9

PREDESTINED *foreordained*
purpose **p** to occur Acts 4:28
foreknew, He also **p** Rom 8:29
God **p** before the ages 1 Cor 2:7
p us to adoption Eph 1:5
p according to His Eph 1:11

PREEMINENT *foremost*
P in dignity Gen 49:3

PREFECTS *Persian officials*
shatter governors...**p** Jer 51:23
the satraps, the **p** Dan 3:3

PREGNANT *with child*
womb of...**p** woman Eccl 11:5
And her womb ever **p** Jer 20:17
ripped open...**p** Amos 1:13
Elizabeth...became **p** Luke 1:24

PRIEST *intermediary*
a **p** of God Most Gen 14:18
a kingdom of **p-s** Ex 19:6
Aaron's sons, the **p-s** Lev 1:5
if the anointed **p** sins Lev 4:3
p...make atonement Lev 4:31
without a teaching **p** 2 Chr 15:3
You are a **p** forever Ps 110:4
all the chief **p-s** Matt 2:4
show yourself to the **p** Matt 8:4
faithful high **p** Heb 2:17
have a great high **p** Heb 4:14
You are a **p** forever Heb 5:6

PRIESTHOOD *office of priest*
for a perpetual **p** Ex 40:15
have defiled the **p** Neh 13:29
His **p** permanently Heb 7:24
royal **p**, a holy nation 1 Pet 2:9

PRINCE *ruler*
Who made you a **p** Ex 2:14
p-s of the tribes 1 Chr 29:6
contempt upon **p-s** Ps 107:40
Do not trust in **p-s** Ps 146:3
Father, **P** of Peace Is 9:6
p-s will rule justly Is 32:1
to death the **P** of life Acts 3:15
p of...the air Eph 2:2

PRISON *jail*
Put this man in **p** 1 Kin 22:27
my soul out of **p** Ps 142:7
beheaded in the **p** Matt 14:10
I was in **p**, and Matt 25:36
opened...the **p** Acts 5:19
spirits *now* in **p** 1 Pet 3:19

PRISONER *one who is confined*
sets the **p-s** free Ps 146:7
a notorious **p** Matt 27:16
p of the law of sin Rom 7:23
Paul, a **p** of Christ Philem 1

PROFIT (v) *reap an advantage*
p...my destruction Job 30:13
what does it **p** a Mark 8:36
the flesh **p-s** nothing John 6:63
it **p-s** me nothing 1 Cor 13:3

PROMISE (n) *agreement, pledge*
p of the Holy Spirit Acts 2:33
the **p** made by God Acts 26:6
the **p** is nullified Rom 4:14
children of the **p** Rom 9:8

commandment…a **p** Eph 6:2
heirs of the **p** Heb 6:17
precious…**p-s** 2 Pet 1:4
the **p** of His coming 2 Pet 3:4

PROMISED *made an agreement*
land which He had **p** Deut 9:28
p to keep Your words Ps 119:57
p long ages ago Titus 1:2
He who **p** is faithful Heb 10:23

PROPHECY *proclamation*
seal up vision and **p** Dan 9:24
p…fulfilled Matt 13:14
have *the gift of* **p** 1 Cor 13:2
no **p**…of human will 2 Pet 1:21
the spirit of **p** Rev 19:10

PROPHESY *predict, proclaim*
to **p** with lyres 1 Chr 25:1
he never **p-ies** good 2 Chr 18:7
p-ing…false vision Jer 14:14
P over these bones Ezek 37:4
sons and…will **p** Joel 2:28
did we…**p** in Your Matt 7:22
P to us…Christ Matt 26:68
speaking…**p-ing** Acts 19:6
who **p-ies** edifies 1 Cor 14:4

PROPHET *spokesman for God*
Aaron shall be your **p** Ex 7:1
a **p** or a dreamer Deut 13:1
I will raise up a **p** Deut 18:18
p in your place 1 Kin 19:16
summon all…**p-s** 2 Kin 10:19
vision of…the **p** 2 Chr 32:32
Woe…foolish **p-s** Ezek 13:3
written by the **p** Matt 2:5
persecuted the **p-s** Matt 5:12
Beware…false **p-s** Matt 7:15
He…receives a **p** Matt 10:41
the **p** Jesus Matt 21:11
false **p-s**…arise Mark 13:22
p of the Most High Luke 1:76
great **p** has arisen Luke 7:16
Are you the **P** John 1:21
reading Isaiah the **p** Acts 8:30
a Jewish false **p** Acts 13:6
All are not **p-s** 1 Cor 12:29
and some *as* **p-s** Eph 4:11
beast and…false **p** Rev 20:10

PROPHETESS *speaker for God*
Miriam the **p** Ex 15:20
Deborah, a **p** Judg 4:4
there was a **p**, Anna Luke 2:36
calls herself a **p** Rev 2:20

PROPHETIC *predictive*
not…**p** utterances 1 Thess 5:20
p word…sure 2 Pet 1:19

PROPITIATION *atonement*
a **p** in His blood Rom 3:25
p for the sins Heb 2:17
He himself is the **p** 1 John 2:2
p for our sins 1 John 4:10

PROSTITUTE *harlot*
Where…temple **p** Gen 38:21
male cult **p-s** in the 1 Kin 14:24
an adulterer and a **p** Is 57:3
to a **p** is one body 1 Cor 6:16

PROTECT *guard, shield*
The LORD will **p** him Ps 41:2
LORD **p-s** the strangers Ps 146:9
LORD…**p** Jerusalem Is 31:5
He will…**p** you 2 Thess 3:3
p-ed by the power of 1 Pet 1:5

PROVINCE *district* or *territory*
rulers of the **p-s** 1 Kin 20:17
holiday for the **p-s** Esth 2:18
whole **p** of Babylon Dan 2:48
arrived in the **p** Acts 25:1

PUNISH *chastise, penalize*
p them for their sin Ex 32:34
and are **p-ed** for it Prov 22:3
p the world for its Is 13:11
will **p** your iniquity Lam 4:22
p Him and release Luke 23:16
I **p-ed** them often Acts 26:11
p all disobedience 2 Cor 10:6

PUNISHMENT *penalty*
My **p** is too great Gen 4:13
p of the sword Job 19:29
fear involves **p** 1 John 4:18
the **p** of eternal fire Jude 7

PURIM
Jewish festival Esth 9:26ff

PURPLE *color*
a veil of blue and **p** Ex 26:31
Those reared in **p** Lam 4:5
clothed Daniel with **p** Dan 5:29
dressed Him…**p** Mark 15:17
a seller of **p** fabrics Acts 16:14
clothed in **p** and Rev 17:4

Q

QUAIL *type of bird*
q-s came up and Ex 16:13
q from the sea Num 11:31

QUARREL (n) *altercation*
if men have a **q** Ex 21:18
So abandon the **q** Prov 17:14
are **q-s** among you 1 Cor 1:11
the source of **q-s** James 4:1

QUARREL (v) *contend, fight*
did not **q** over it Gen 26:22
Why do you **q** with me Ex 17:2
any fool will **q** Prov 20:3
those who **q** with you Is 41:12

QUEEN *female sovereign*
when the **q** of Sheba 1 Kin 10:1
king saw Esther the **q** Esth 5:2
The **q** of kingdoms Is 47:5
The **Q** *of the* South Matt 12:42
Candace, **q** of the Acts 8:27

QUIVER *case for holding arrows*
your **q** and your bow Gen 27:3
man whose **q** is full Ps 127:5
hidden Me in His **q** Is 49:2
q is like an open grave Jer 5:16
fill the **q-s** Jer 51:11

R

RAAMSES / RAMESES
where Joseph settled Gen 47:11
Egyptian storage-city built by Hebrew slaves Ex 1:11
origin of exodus Ex 12:37; Num 33:3,5

RABBI / RABBONI
respectful form of address Matt 23:7; 26:25; Mark 10:51
master, teacher John 1:49; 6:25; 11:8; 20:16

RACE (n) *nation, people*
r has intermingled Ezra 9:2
mongrel **r** will dwell Zech 9:6
advantage of our **r** Acts 7:19
you are a chosen **r** 1 Pet 2:9

RACHEL
Jacob's wife Gen 29:18,28
mother of Joseph and Benjamin Gen 30:25; 35:24; 46:19

RADIANCE *brightness*
a **r** around Him Ezek 1:27
His **r** is like Hab 3:4
r of His glory Heb 1:3

RAHAB
1 *harlot in Jericho* Josh 2:1
assisted spies Josh 2:4-7
family spared Josh 2:13,14; 6:22,23
ancestor of Jesus Matt 1:5
example of faith Heb 11:31; James 2:25
2 *symbolic for sea monster* Job 9:13; 26:12; Ps 89:10
3 *symbolic for Egypt* Ps 87:4; Is 30:7

RAINBOW *colored arc in sky*
appearance of the **r** Ezek 1:28
a **r** around the throne Rev 4:3
r was upon his head Rev 10:1

RAISIN *dried grapes*
clusters of **r-s** 2 Sam 16:1
Sustain me with **r** Song 2:5
and love **r** cakes Hos 3:1

RAM *male sheep*
Abraham...took the **r** Gen 22:13
a **r** without defect Lev 5:15
the **r** of atonement Num 5:8
r which had two horns Dan 8:3

RAMAH
1 *city of Naphtali* Josh 19:36
2 *town of Asher* Josh 19:29
3 *town of Benjamin* Josh 18:25; Judg 4:5; 19:13
4 *town in the Negev* Josh 19:8
5 *town in Gilead* 2 Kin 8:28,29; 2 Chr 22:5,6

RAMPART *bulwark, siege*
and **r-s** for security Is 26:1
Whose **r** *was* the sea Nah 3:8
station myself on the **r** Hab 2:1

RAVEN *type of bird*
he sent out a **r** Gen 8:7
young **r-s** which cry Ps 147:9
Consider the **r-s** Luke 12:24

RAVINE *gorge*
settle on the steep **r-s** Is 7:19
smooth *stones* of the **r** Is 57:6
Every **r** will be filled Luke 3:5

REALM *area, kingdom*
ruler over the **r** of Dan 4:17
kingdom is not...**r** John 18:36

REAPER *harvester*
after the **r-s** Ruth 2:3
will overtake the **r** Amos 9:13
the **r-s** are angels Matt 13:39

REBEKAH
wife of Isaac Gen 24:67; 26:8
mother of Esau and Jacob Gen 25:21ff

REBEL (n) *rebellious one*
Your rulers are **r-s** Is 1:23
called a **r** from birth Is 48:8
their princes are **r-s** Hos 9:15

REBEL (v) *revolt*
not **r** against the Num 14:9
r-led against...words Ps 107:11
r-led against Me Ezek 20:21

REBELLION *insurrection*
he has counseled **r** Deut 13:5
I know your **r** Deut 31:27
r is as the sin of 1 Sam 15:23
my **r** and my sin Job 13:23
children of **r** Is 57:4

RECEIVE *encounter, take*
The LORD **r-s** my prayer Ps 6:9
r me to glory Ps 73:24
man **r-s** a bribe Prov 17:23
Freely you **r-d** Matt 10:8
who **r-s** you **r-s** Me Matt 10:40
the blind **r** sight Matt 11:5
ask...you will **r** Matt 21:22
r-d up into heaven Mark 16:19
This man **r-s** sinners Luke 15:2
as many as **r-d** Him John 1:12
r you to Myself John 14:3
R the Holy Spirit John 20:22
you will **r** power Acts 1:8
to give than to **r** Acts 20:35
one **r-s** the prize 1 Cor 9:24
r the crown of life James 1:12
whatever...ask we **r** 1 John 3:22
r-d the mark of Rev 19:20

RECKONED *accounted for*
r it to him as Gen 15:6
r among the nations Num 23:9
r...as righteousness James 2:23

RECONCILE *bring together*
r-d to your brother Matt 5:24
be **r-d** to God 2 Cor 5:20
r them both in one Eph 2:16
r all...to Himself Col 1:20

RECONCILIATION
now received the **r** Rom 5:11
the **r** of the world Rom 11:15
the ministry of **r** 2 Cor 5:18
the word of **r** 2 Cor 5:19

RED *color*
first came forth **r** Gen 25:25
water...**r** as blood 2 Kin 3:22
they are **r** like crimson Is 1:18
the sky is **r** Matt 16:2
a great **r** dragon Rev 12:3

RED SEA
Hebrew: Sea of Reeds Ex 10:19
body of water between Egypt and Sinai Ex 13:18
Ps 106:9; Jer 49:2

REDEEM *buy back*
I will also **r** you Ex 6:
family may **r** him Lev 25:4
wish to **r** the field Lev 27:1
I will **r** *it* Ruth 4:
God will **r** my soul Ps 49:1
He will **r** Israel Ps 130:
Christ **r-ed** us Gal 3:1
He might **r** those Gal 4:

REDEEMER *one who buys back*
left you without a **r** Ruth 4:1
know that my **R** lives Job 19:2
my rock and my **R** Ps 19:1
your **R** is the Holy Is 41:1
our Father, Our **R** Is 63:1
Their **R** is strong Jer 50:3

REDEMPTION *deliverance*
r of the land Lev 25:2
have my right of **r** Ruth 4:
r of his soul is Ps 49:
r is drawing near Luke 21:2
r...in Christ Jesus Rom 3:2
r of our body Rom 8:2
r through His blood Eph 1:
in whom we have **r** Col 1:1
obtained eternal **r** Heb 9:1

REED *tall marsh grass*
set *it* among the **r-s** Ex 2
bruised **r** He will Is 42
the **r**...to beat Him Matt 27:3
and put it on a **r** Matt 27:

REFUGE *protection, shelter*
in whom I take **r** 2 Sam 22
God is our **r** Ps 46
r in the LORD Ps 118
the **r** of lies Is 28:
r in...distress Jer 16:
who have taken **r** Heb 6:

REGION *area*
r of the Jordan Josh 22:
the **r-s** of Galilee Matt 2:
to the **r** of Judea Mark 10
same **r**...shepherds Luke 2

REGISTER *enroll, record*
r…people of Israel 2 Sam 24:4
to r for the census Luke 2:3

REHOBOAM
son of Solomon 1 Kin 11:43
king of Judah 1 Kin 12:16ff; 2 Chr 11:1ff

REJOICE *be glad*
r before the LORD Lev 23:40
R, O nations Deut 32:43
I r in Your salvation 1 Sam 2:1
let the earth r 1 Chr 16:31
my soul shall r Ps 35:9
king will r in God Ps 63:11
Let us r and be glad Ps 118:24
I r at Your word Ps 119:162
R, young man Eccl 11:9
God will r over you Is 62:5
r-d exceedingly Matt 2:10
r at his birth Luke 1:14
crowd was r-ing Luke 13:17
you would have r-d John 14:28
r-ing in hope Rom 12:12
yet always r-ing 2 Cor 6:10
R in the Lord Phil 4:4
I r in my sufferings Col 1:24
r, O heavens Rev 12:12

ELATIONS *sexual intercourse*
r with his wife Eve Gen 4:1
had no r with a man Judg 11:39
we may have r with Judg 19:22
had r with Hannah 1 Sam 1:19

ELIGION *system of belief*
about their own r Acts 25:19
sect of our r Acts 26:5
pure and undefiled r James 1:27

ELIGIOUS *devout, pious*
r in all respects Acts 17:22
thinks…to be r James 1:26

EMEMBRANCE *memory*
Your r, O LORD Ps 135:13
Put Me in r Is 43:26
a book of r was Mal 3:16
do this in r of Me Luke 22:19
in r of Me 1 Cor 11:25

EPAY *pay back*
you thus r the LORD Deut 32:6
so God has **repaid** Judg 1:7
LORD r the evildoer 2 Sam 3:39
repaid me evil for Ps 109:5
r their iniquity Jer 16:18
He will fully r Jer 51:56
s Mine, I will r Rom 12:19
no one r-s…evil 1 Thess 5:15

EPENT *change mind*
that He should r Num 23:19
r in dust and ashes Job 42:6
have refused to r Jer 5:3
R, for the kingdom Matt 3:2
-ed long ago in Matt 11:21
and believe Mark 1:15
one sinner who r-s Luke 15:7
R…be baptized Acts 2:38
all…should r Acts 17:30
and turn to God Acts 26:20

EPENTANCE *penitence*
with water for r Matt 3:11
baptism of r Mark 1:4
for forgiveness Luke 24:47
appropriate to r Acts 26:20
without regret 2 Cor 7:10
from dead works Heb 6:1
o come to r 2 Pet 3:9

EPHAIM
pre-Israelite people of Palestine Gen 14:5; 15:20
people of large stature
2 *valley near Jerusalem* Josh 15:8; 2 Sam 23:13

REPROACH (n) *dishonor*
taken away my r Gen 30:23
a r on all Israel 1 Sam 11:2
I have become a r Ps 31:11
with dishonor…r Prov 18:3
not fear the r of Is 51:7
the r of Christ Heb 11:26

REPROACH (v) *accuse, rebuke*
to r the living God 2 Kin 19:4
My heart does not r Job 27:6
foolish man r-es You Ps 74:22
enemies have r-ed me Ps 102:8
He r-ed them for Mark 16:14

REPROOF *correction, rebuke*
spurned all my r Prov 1:30
regards r is sensible Prov 15:5
who hates r will Prov 15:10
and r give wisdom Prov 29:15
for teaching, for r 2 Tim 3:16

REPTILE *snake*
and the sand r Lev 11:30
r-s of the earth Mic 7:17
r-s and creatures James 3:7

RESURRECTION
who say…no r Matt 22:23
r of the righteous Luke 14:14
being sons of the r Luke 20:36
r of judgment John 5:29
the r and the life John 11:25
r of the dead Acts 24:21
if there is no r 1 Cor 15:13
power of His r Phil 3:10
hope through the r 1 Pet 1:3
This is the first r Rev 20:5

RETRIBUTION *punishment*
days of r have come Hos 9:7
stumbling block…r Rom 11:9
dealing out r to 2 Thess 1:8

REUBEN
1 *son of Jacob / Leah* Gen 29:32
2 *tribe* Ex 6:14; Num 1:21

REVELATION *divine disclosure*
a r to Your servant 2 Sam 7:27
the r ended Dan 7:28
r to the Gentiles Luke 2:32
r of…judgment Rom 2:5
the r of the mystery Rom 16:25
awaiting…the r 1 Cor 1:7
through a r of Jesus Gal 1:12
by r…made known Eph 3:3
The R of Jesus Rev 1:1

REVENGE *vengeance*
take our r on him Jer 20:10
Never take…r Rom 12:19

RIB *bone*
took one of his r-s Gen 2:21
r-s *were* in its mouth Dan 7:5

RICH (adj) *wealthy*
Abram was very r Gen 13:2
LORD makes poor…r 1 Sam 2:7
not a r man boast Jer 9:23
woe to you who are r Luke 6:24
a r man Luke 16:1
being r in mercy Eph 2:4
r in good works 1 Tim 6:18

RICH (n) *wealthy*
r shall not pay more Ex 30:15
the r above the poor Job 34:19
r among the people Ps 45:12
The r and the poor Prov 22:2

RICHES *wealth*
R do not profit Prov 11:4
who trusts in his r Prov 11:28

neither poverty nor **r** Prov 30:8
choked with…**r** Luke 8:14
abounding in **r** Rom 10:12
r of His grace Eph 1:7
r of Christ Eph 3:8
His **r** in glory Phil 4:19
uncertainty of **r** 1 Tim 6:17
Your **r** have rotted James 5:2

RIGHTEOUS (adj) *virtuous*
Noah was a **r** man Gen 6:9
LORD is the **r** one Ex 9:27
You are more **r** 1 Sam 24:17
God is a **r** judge Ps 7:11
A **r** man hates Prov 13:5
for David a **r** Branch Jer 23:5
LORD our God is **r** Dan 9:14
ninety-nine **r** Luke 15:7
coming of the **R** One Acts 7:52
r *man* shall live by Rom 1:17
none **r**, not even one Rom 3:10
many will be made **r** Rom 5:19
prayer of a **r** man James 5:16

RIGHTEOUS (n) *moral one*
assembly of the **r** Ps 1:5
LORD tests the **r** Ps 11:5
LORD loves the **r** Ps 146:8
the paths of the **r** Prov 2:20
the **r** will flourish Prov 11:28
joy for the **r** Prov 21:15
way of the **r** is Is 26:7
they sell the **r** for Amos 2:6
sends rain on *the* **r** Matt 5:45
r into eternal life Matt 25:46

RIGHTEOUSNESS
reckoned it…as **r** Gen 15:6
will repay…his **r** 1 Sam 26:23
I put on **r** Job 29:14
in the paths of **r** Ps 23:3
judge the world in **r** Ps 96:13
declare His **r** Ps 97:6
His **r** endures forever Ps 111:3
R exalts a nation Prov 14:34
clouds pour down **r** Is 45:8
wrapped me with…**r** Is 61:10
The LORD our **r** Jer 23:6
to rain **r** on you Hos 10:12
to fulfill all **r** Matt 3:15
and thirst for **r** Matt 5:6
kingdom and His **r** Matt 6:33
you enemy of all **r** Acts 13:10
through one act of **r** Rom 5:18
breastplate of **r** Eph 6:14
pursue **r**, faith 2 Tim 2:22
the crown of **r** 2 Tim 4:8
peaceful fruit of **r** Heb 12:11
not achieve the **r** James 1:20
suffer for…**r** 1 Pet 3:14

RIMMON
1 *a Benjamite* 2 Sam 4:2
2 *Aramean deity* 2 Kin 5:18
3 *town in Simeon* Josh 19:1,7
4 *city of Zebulun* Josh 19:13
5 *rock of* Judg 20:45; 21:13

RING *jewelry, ornament*
make four gold **r-s** Ex 25:26
took his signet **r** Esth 3:10
As a **r** of gold Prov 11:22
finger **r-s**, nose **r-s** Is 3:21

RIVER
r flowed out of Eden Gen 2:10
the **r** Euphrates Josh 1:4
r of Your delights Ps 36:8
He changes **r-s** into Ps 107:33
the **r-s** of Babylon Ps 137:1
A place of **r-s** and Is 33:21
r-s in the desert Is 43:20
peace…like a **r** Is 66:12
tears…like a **r** Lam 2:18
baptized…Jordan **R** Mark 1:5
r-s of living water John 7:38
r of the water of life Rev 22:1

ROD *staff, stick*
fresh **r-s** of poplar Gen 30:37
r of Aaron Num 17:8
break them with a **r** Ps 2:9
Your **r** and Your staff Ps 23:4
who withholds his **r** Prov 13:24
The **r** of discipline Prov 22:15
r of My anger Is 10:5
rule them with a **r** Rev 19:15

ROME
Italian city Acts 2:10
Roman Empire capital Acts 18:2
Paul held there Acts 28:14,16

ROOSTER *bird*
The strutting **r** Prov 30:31
before a **r** crows Matt 26:34
r will not crow John 13:38

ROSE (n) *flower*
I am the **r** of Sharon Song 2:1

RULER *king, monarch*
Joseph was the **r** Gen 42:6
nor curse a **r** Ex 22:28
no chief…or **r** Prov 6:7
your **r-s** have fled Is 22:3
Most High is **r** Dan 4:32
come forth a **R** Matt 2:6
r of the demons Matt 9:34
r-s of the Gentiles Mark 10:42
the **r** of this world John 12:31
Who made you a **r** Acts 7:27
be subject to **r-s** Titus 3:1

RUSHES *marshy plant*
Can the **r** grow Job 8:11
reeds and **r** will rot Is 19:6

RUTH
Moabitess Ruth 1:4
Naomi's daughter-in-law Ruth 1:14ff
married Boaz Ruth 4:13
in Messianic line Matt 1:5

S

SABAOTH
Lord of Sabaoth is same as Lord of Hosts
Rom 9:29; James 5:4

see also **HOST**

SABBATH *day of rest*
Remember the **s** day Ex 20:8
LORD blessed the **s** day Ex 20:11
keep My **s-s** and Lev 26:2
Observe the **s** day Deut 5:12
new moon nor **s** 2 Kin 4:23
call the **s** a delight Is 58:13
My **s-s** to be a sign Ezek 20:12
is Lord of the **S** Matt 12:8
S was made for man Mark 2:27
to do good…on the **S** Mark 3:4
the cross on the **S** John 19:31
a **S** day's journey Acts 1:12
are read every **S** Acts 13:27
S rest for the people Heb 4:9

SABBATICAL YEAR
seventh year of rest Lev 25:5

SACKCLOTH *coarse cloth*
put **s** on his loins Gen 37:34
gird on **s** and lament 2 Sam 3:31
put on **s** and ashes Esth 4:1
sewed **s** over my skin Job 16:15
with fasting, **s**, and Dan 9:3
sun became black as **s** Rev 6:12

SACRED *consecrated, holy*
took all the s things 2 Kin 12:18
perform s services 1 Cor 9:13
known…s writings 2 Tim 3:15
table and the s bread Heb 9:2

SACRIFICE (n) *offering of a life*
Jacob offered a s Gen 31:54
a Passover s to Ex 12:27
s-s of righteousness Ps 4:5
The s of the wicked Prov 15:8
loyalty rather than s Hos 6:6
compassion…not s Matt 9:13
a s to the idol Acts 7:41
a living and holy s Rom 12:1
an acceptable s Phil 4:18
by the s of Himself Heb 9:26
s-s God is pleased Heb 13:16
offer up spiritual s-s 1 Pet 2:5

SACRIFICE (v) *offer a life*
we may s to the Lord Ex 5:3
s on it your burnt Ex 20:24
when you s a sacrifice Lev 22:29
they s-d to the LORD Judg 2:5
even s-d their sons Ps 106:37
s-ing to the Baals Hos 11:2
lamb had to be s-d Luke 22:7
they s to demons 1 Cor 10:20

SADDUCEES
Jewish religious party Matt 3:7; 16:11,12; Mark 12:18; Acts 5:17; 23:6-8

SAINTS *ones faithful to God*
s…in the earth Ps 16:3
the s of the Highest Dan 7:22
s…fallen asleep Matt 27:52
lock up…s in prisons Acts 26:10
intercedes for the s Rom 8:27
s will judge the 1 Cor 6:2
citizens with the s Eph 2:19
perseverance of the s Rev 14:12

SALEM
Jerusalem Gen 14:18; Ps 76:2; Heb 7:1,2

SALOME
1 *wife of Zebedee* Mark 15:40
mother of James and John at open tomb Mark 16:1
2 *daughter of Herodias* Matt 14:6ff; Mark 6:22-26

SALT *preservative*
became a pillar of s Gen 19:26
and sowed it with s Judg 9:45
be eaten without s Job 6:6
the s of the earth Matt 5:13
seasoned with s Col 4:6
can s water produce James 3:12

SALT SEA
the Dead Sea Gen 14:3; Num 34:3; Deut 3:17; Josh 15:2

SALT, VALLEY OF
S of Dead Sea 2 Sam 8:13; 2 Chr 25:11

SALVATION *deliverance*
For Your s I wait Gen 49:18
He has become my s Ex 15:2
scorned…his s Deut 32:15
S belongs to the LORD Ps 3:8
my light and my s Ps 27:1
lift up the cup of s Ps 116:13
My s will be forever Is 51:6
helmet of s on His Is 59:17
S is from the LORD Jon 2:9
eyes have seen Your s Luke 2:30
s in no one else Acts 4:12
power of God for s Rom 1:16
now is the day of s 2 Cor 6:2
take the helmet of s Eph 6:17
work out your s with Phil 2:12
s through our Lord 1 Thess 5:9
that leads to s 2 Tim 3:15
who will inherit s Heb 1:14
neglect so great a s Heb 2:3
S to our God who Rev 7:10

SAMARIA
1 *capital of N kingdom* 1 Kin 16:24; 2 Chr 18:9
2 *another name for N kingdom* 1 Kin 13:32; 2 Kin 17:24; Hos 8:5; Amos 3:9; Obad 19
3 *region of central hill country* John 4:4-7; Acts 8:1ff

SAMSON
a Hebrew judge Judg 13:24
weak in character Judg 14:1ff
slave of passion Judg 16:1ff
great strength Judg 16:5,12

SAMUEL
son of Elkanah and Hannah 1 Sam 1:20
dedicated to God 1 Sam 1:21ff
called by God 1 Sam 3:1-18
judge 1 Sam 7:15-17
opposed monarchy 1 Sam 8:6
anointed Saul 1 Sam 10:1
anointed David 1 Sam 16:12
death 1 Sam 25:1

SANCTIFICATION *holiness*
resulting in s Rom 6:22
righteousness and s 1 Cor 1:30
will of God, your s 1 Thess 4:3
s by the Spirit 2 Thess 2:13
s without which no Heb 12:14

SANCTIFY *set apart to God*
S to Me every Ex 13:2
the LORD who s-ies Lev 22:32
They will s My name Is 29:23
will s the Holy One Is 29:23
S My sabbaths Ezek 20:20
S them in the truth John 17:17
s-ied by the…Spirit Rom 15:16
husband is s-ied 1 Cor 7:14
s Christ as Lord 1 Pet 3:15

SANCTUARY *place of worship*
construct a s for Me Ex 25:8
revere My s Lev 19:30
utensils of the s 1 Chr 9:29
into the s of God Ps 73:17
Praise God in His s Ps 150:1
beautify…My s Is 60:13
a minister in the s Heb 8:2

SAPPHIRE *precious stone*
a s and a diamond Ex 28:18
Inlaid with s-s Song 5:14
foundations…in s-s Is 54:11

SARAH / SARAI
wife of Abraham Gen 11:29
barren Gen 11:30
beautiful Gen 12:11
gave birth to Isaac Gen 21:2,3
death Gen 23:2

SATAN
Titles:
Abaddon Rev 9:11
accuser Ps 109:6; Rev 12:10
adversary 1 Pet 5:8
Apollyon Rev 9:11
Beelzebul Matt 10:25; Mark 3:22
Belial 2 Cor 6:15
deceiver of the world Rev 12:9
devil Matt 4:1,5; 25:41; John 6:70; 13:2; Eph 4:27; 6:11; 1 Tim 3:6,7; Heb 2:14; 1 Pet 5:8; Rev 2:10; 20:2,10
dragon Rev 12:9
enemy Matt 13:28,39
evil one Matt 13:19,38; John 17:15; Eph 6:16; 1 John 2:13,14; 5:18,19
father of lies John 8:44

god of this world 2 Cor 4:4
liar John 8:44
murderer John 8:44
prince of the power of the air Eph 2:2
ruler of the demons Matt 9:34; Mark 3:22
ruler of this world John 12:31; 14:30; 16:11
serpent of old Rev 12:9

SATISFY *be content*
eat and not be **s-ied** Lev 26:26
s-ied their desire Ps 78:30
steals To s himself Prov 6:30
Nor will he be **s-ied** Prov 6:35
hunger is not **s-ied** Is 29:8
to s the crowd Mark 15:15

SATRAPS *Persian officials*
to the king's s Ezra 8:36
the s, the governors Esth 8:9
commissioners and s Dan 6:4

SAUL
1 *son of Kish* 1 Sam 9:1,2
anointed 1 Sam 10:1ff
first king 1 Sam 11:15
rejected as king 1 Sam 15:11ff
jealous of David 1 Sam 18:6ff
death 1 Sam 31:4ff
2 *apostle Paul,* see **PAUL**

SAVE *deliver, rescue*
s-d by the LORD Deut 33:29
S with Your right hand Ps 60:5
He will s you Prov 20:22
Turn to Me, and be **s-d** Is 45:22
s you from afar Jer 30:10
he will s his life Ezek 18:27
will s His people Matt 1:21
wishes to s his life Matt 16:25
Son…has come to s Matt 18:11
faith has **s-d** you Luke 7:50
world might be **s-d** John 3:17
Father, s Me from John 12:27
by which we…be **s-d** Acts 4:12
be **s-d** by His life Rom 5:10
will s your husband 1 Cor 7:16
Jesus came…to s 1 Tim 1:15
One who is able to s James 4:12
the righteous is **s-d** 1 Pet 4:18

SAVIOR *one who saves*
My s, You 2 Sam 22:3
forgot God their S Ps 106:21
send them a S and a Is 19:20
no s besides Me Is 43:11
righteous God and a S Is 45:21
S, who is Christ Luke 2:11
the S of the world John 4:42
as a Prince and a S Acts 5:31
S of all men 1 Tim 4:10
appearing of our S 2 Tim 1:10
our great God and S Titus 2:13
kingdom of our…S 2 Pet 1:11

SCARLET *bright red*
tied a s *thread* Gen 38:28
s thread…window Josh 2:18
lips are like a s Song 4:3
sins are as s Is 1:18
put a s robe on Him Matt 27:28

SCEPTER *symbol of authority*
s shall not depart Gen 49:10
s…rise from Israel Num 24:17
A s of uprightness Ps 45:6
The s of rulers Is 14:5
s of His kingdom Heb 1:8

SCORPION *poisonous spider*
serpents and s-s Deut 8:15
discipline…with s-s 1 Kin 12:11
tread on…s-s Luke 10:19

not give him a s Luke 11:12
s-s…have power Rev 9:3

SCRIBE *copier, writer*
and Sheva was s 2 Sam 20:25
then the king's s 2 Chr 24:11
Ezra the s stood Neh 8:4
lying pen of the s-s Jer 8:8
chief priests and s-s Matt 2:4
and not as the s-s Mark 1:22
Where is the s 1 Cor 1:20

SCRIPTURE
understanding…S-s Matt 22:29
fulfill…S-s Mark 14:49
S has been fulfilled Luke 4:21
You search the S-s John 5:39
S cannot be broken John 10:35
mighty in the **S-s** Acts 18:24
what does the S say Rom 4:3
S is inspired by God 2 Tim 3:16

SCROLL *parchment*
these curses on a s Num 5:23
Take a s and write Jer 36:2
eat this s, and go Ezek 3:1
like a s…rolled Rev 6:14

SEA *body of salt water*
waters He called s-s Gen 1:10
s, or the s monster Job 7:1
founded it upon the s-s Ps 24:2
to the s in ships Ps 107:23
the waters cover the s Is 11:9
rebukes the s and Nah 1:4
walking on the s Matt 14:2
s *began* to be stirred John 6:1
dangers on the s 2 Cor 11:2
s of glass, like crystal Rev 4:

SEACOAST *seashore*
remnant of the s Ezek 25:1
inhabitants of the s Zeph 2:
s will be pastures Zeph 2:

SEAL (n) *mark, stamp*
Your s and your cord Gen 38:1
the engravings of a s Ex 28:2
the s of perfection Ezek 28:1
testimony has set his s John 3:3
s of God on their Rev 9:

SEAL (v) *mark, secure*
s-ed…his seal 1 Kin 21:
s *it*…king's signet Esth 8:
a spring **s-ed** up Song 4:1
to s up vision Dan 9:2
s up the book until Dan 12:

SEASHORE *sea coast*
sand that is on the s Josh 11:
the s in abundance 1 Kin 4:2
the dragon stood on…s Rev 13:

SEASON *time of the year*
rains in their s Lev 26:
grain in its s Job 5:2
its fruit in its s Ps 1:
in s *and* out of s 2 Tim 4:

SEED *descendant* or *plant*
sow your s uselessly Lev 26:1
establish your s Ps 89:
O s of Abraham Ps 105:
s to the sower Is 55:1
like a mustard s Matt 13:3
went out to sow his s Luke 8
s is the word of God Luke 8:1
s which is perishable 1 Pet 1:2
His s abides in him 1 John 3

SELA
rock city in Edom Judg 1:36; Is 16:1; 42:
also **Joktheel** 2 Kin 14
later known as Petra

SELAH
musical or liturgical sign Ps 3:2,4,8; 20:3; 60:4; 81:7; Hab 3:3,9,13

SELF-CONTROL
s and the judgment Acts 24:25
your lack of s 1 Cor 7:5
gentleness, s Gal 5:23
without s, brutal 2 Tim 3:3
in *your* knowledge, s 2 Pet 1:6

SENATE
Sanhedrin Acts 5:21
see also **COUNCIL**

SERAPHIM
celestial beings Is 6:2,6

SERPENT *snake*
s was more crafty Gen 3:1
they turned into s-s Ex 7:12
viper and flying s Is 30:6
be shrewd as s-s Matt 10:16
will pick up s-s Mark 16:18
Moses lifted up the s John 3:14

ERVANT *helper, slave*
s of s-s He shall be Gen 9:25
Your s is listening 1 Sam 3:9
to shine upon Your s Ps 31:16
s-s of a new covenant 2 Cor 3:6
they s-s of Christ 2 Cor 11:23
s of Christ Jesus 1 Tim 4:6

EVEN *number*
Jacob served s years Gen 29:20
For s women…one man Is 4:1
will be s weeks Dan 9:25
s other spirits more Matt 12:45
forgive…s times Matt 18:21
John to the s churches Rev 1:4
s golden lampstands Rev 1:12

EXUAL
not in s promiscuity Rom 13:13
from s immorality 1 Thess 4:3

HALLUM
1 *king of Israel* 2 Kin 15:8-15
2 *Huldah's husband* 2 Kin 22:14
3 *son of Josiah* 1 Chr 3:15
king of Judah 2 Kin 23:31-33
called **JEHOAHAZ** 2 Kin 23:30
4 *gatekeeper* 1 Chr 9:17
5 *son of Zadok* 1 Chr 6:12
6 *time of Nehemiah* Neh 3:12
name of nine other men

HARON
coastal plain in central Israel Is 33:9; 65:10

HEAF *bundle of grain stalks*
s-ves in the field Gen 37:7
s of the first fruits Lev 23:10
among the s-ves Ruth 2:15

HEBAT
eleventh month of Hebrew calendar Zech 1:7

HECHEM
1 *city in Ephraim hill country* Gen 12:6; 33:18; 1 Chr 7:28
city of refuge Josh 20:7
2 *son of Hamor* Gen 34:2
3 *line of Manasseh* Num 26:31
4 *son of Shemida* 1 Chr 7:19

HEEP *animal*
Rachel came with…s Gen 29:9
not be like s Num 27:17
the fleece of my s Job 31:20
s of His pasture Ps 100:3
All of us like s Is 53:6
a s that is silent Is 53:7
will care for My s Ezek 34:12
lost s of…Israel Matt 10:6
s from the goats Matt 25:32
my s which was lost Luke 15:6
His life for the s John 10:11
s hear My voice John 10:27
Tend My s John 21:17
Shepherd of the s Heb 13:20

SHEEPFOLDS *enclosure*
s for the flocks 2 Chr 32:28
lie down among the s Ps 68:13
took him from the s Ps 78:70

SHEEPSKINS *coverings*
they went about in s Heb 11:37

SHEOL
place of the dead Gen 37:35; Job 7:9; Ps 49:15; Prov 15:11; Is 38:10; Ezek 32:27; Hab 2:5
see also **HADES** *and* **HELL**

SHEPHERD (n)
sheep…have no s Num 27:17
The LORD is my s Ps 23:1
Like a s He Is 40:11
s-s after My own heart Jer 3:15
for lack of a s Ezek 34:5
raise up a s Zech 11:16
sheep without a s Matt 9:36
strike down the s Matt 26:31
s-s…in the fields Luke 2:8
I am the good s John 10:11
the great S Heb 13:20
the Chief S 1 Pet 5:4

SHEPHERD (v)
s My people 2 Sam 5:2
s My people Matt 2:6
S My sheep John 21:16
to s the church Acts 20:28
s the flock of God 1 Pet 5:2

SHIBBOLETH
test word for identification Judg 12:6

SHIELD *protection*
Abram, I am a s Gen 15:1
He is a s to all 2 Sam 22:31
My s is with God Ps 7:10
faithfulness is a s Ps 91:4
the s of faith Eph 6:16

SHILOH
1 *Messianic title* Gen 49:10
2 *town N of Bethel* Josh 18:1
site of tabernacle Judg 18:31

SHINE *be radiant, glow*
his face **shone** Ex 34:29
His face s on you Num 6:25
Your face to s *upon us* Ps 80:3
light s before men Matt 5:16
s-s in the darkness John 1:5
lamp s-ing in a dark 2 Pet 1:19
Light is…s-ing 1 John 2:8

SHRINE *object of worship*
built yourself a s Ezek 16:24
tear down your s-s Ezek 16:39
who made silver s-s Acts 19:24

SIBBOLETH
test word for identification Judg 12:6

SICK *unwell*
strengthen the s Ezek 34:16
lying s with a fever Mark 1:30
Lazarus was s John 11:2
anyone among you s James 5:14

SICKLE *cutting tool*
who wields the s Jer 50:16
sharp s in His hand Rev 14:14
Put in your s Rev 14:15

SICKNESS *illness*
remove from you…s Deut 7:15
every kind of s Matt 4:23
authority over…s Matt 10:1
s is not to end in death John 11:4

SIDON
1 *son of Canaan* Gen 10:15; 1 Chr 1:13
2 *Phoenician port* Gen 10:19; Is 23:4; Ezek 28:22

SIGN *indication* or *wonder*
a s for Cain Gen 4:15
s of the covenant Gen 9:12
this shall be the s Ex 3:12
blood shall be a s Ex 12:13
His s-s in Egypt Ps 78:43
Ask a s for yourself Is 7:11
an everlasting s Is 55:13
a s from You Matt 12:38
s of Your coming Matt 24:3
show s-s and Mark 13:22
s-s in sun and moon Luke 21:25
beginning of *His* s-s John 2:11
s of circumcision Rom 4:11
Jews ask for s-s 1 Cor 1:22
tongues are for a s 1 Cor 14:22
s-s…false wonders 2 Thess 2:9

SIGNET *seal*
examine…whose s Gen 38:25
engravings of a s Ex 39:14
s rings of his nobles Dan 6:17

SILAS
co-worker with Paul Acts 15:22,32,40; 16:19,25; 17:4,10,14
also **Silvanus**

SILOAM
1 *tower in Jerusalem* Luke 13:4
2 *water pool in Jerusalem* John 9:7,11

SILVER *precious metal*
rich in…s Gen 13:2
took no plunder in s Judg 5:19
as s is refined Ps 66:10
in settings of s Prov 25:11
s has become dross Is 1:22
The s is Mine Hag 2:8
not acquire…s Matt 10:9
thirty pieces of s Matt 26:15

SIMEON
1 *son of Jacob* Gen 29:33
2 *tribe* Num 1:23; Rev 7:7
3 *devout Jew* Luke 2:25
4 *ancestor of Jesus* Luke 3:30
5 *Christian prophet* Acts 13:1
6 *Simon Peter* Acts 15:14

SIMON
1 *apostle* Matt 4:18; Mark 1:16
see also **PETER**
2 *the Zealot* Matt 10:4; Mark 3:18; Luke 6:15
3 *brother of Jesus* Matt 13:55; Mark 6:3
4 *leper* Matt 26:6; Mark 14:3
5 *a Pharisee* Luke 7:40,43
6 *of Cyrene* Matt 27:32
carried Jesus' cross Mark 15:21; Luke 23:26
7 *father of Judas* John 6:71; 13:2
8 *Magus* Acts 8:9,13,18
sorcerer
9 *the tanner* Acts 9:43; 10:6,32

SIN (n) *transgression*
please forgive my s Ex 10:17
atonement for your s Ex 32:30
purification from s Num 19:9
s will find you out Num 32:23
s of divination 1 Sam 15:23
the s-s of my youth Ps 25:7
s my mother conceived Ps 51:5
Fools mock at s Prov 14:9
bore the s of many Is 53:12
s-s of her prophets Lam 4:13
an eternal s Mark 3:29
forgive us our s-s Luke 11:4
takes away the s John 1:29
wash away your s-s Acts 22:16
wages of s is death Rom 6:23
died for our s-s 1 Cor 15:3
Him who knew no s 2 Cor 5:21
pleasures of s Heb 11:25
confess your s-s James 5:16
a multitude of s-s James 5:20
confess our s-s 1 John 1:9
s is lawlessness 1 John 3:4

SIN (v) *transgress*
When a leader s-s Lev 4:22
s against the LORD 1 Sam 14:34
Job did not s Job 1:22
s against You Ps 119:11
Father, I have **s-ned** Luke 15:18
s no more John 8:11
all have **s-ned** Rom 3:23
that you may not s 1 John 2:1

SIN
1 *wilderness in Sinai* Ex 16:1; Num 33:11,12
2 *Egyptian city* Ezek 30:15,16

SINAI
1 *mountain* Ex 19:11; Lev 26:46; Num 28:6
where Law received Ex 31:18; 34:29
see also **HOREB**
2 *desert wilderness* Ex 16:1; 19:1; Num 1:19; 9:5

SINFUL *wicked*
a brood of s men Num 32:14
s generation Mark 8:38
I am a s man Luke 5:8
likeness of s flesh Rom 8:3

SINNER *wrongdoer*
He instructs s-s Ps 25:8
if s-s entice you Prov 1:10
Adversity…s-s Prov 13:21
one s destroys much Eccl 9:18
a friend of…s-s Matt 11:19
one s who repents Luke 15:7
merciful to me…s Luke 18:13
God…not hear s-s John 9:31
while we were yet s-s Rom 5:8
came…to save s-s 1 Tim 1:15

SISERA
1 *Canaanite warrior* Judg 4:2f
2 *class of Nethinim* Ezra 2:53; Neh 7:55

SISTER
She is my s Gen 12:19
We have a little s Song 8:8
a s called Mary Luke 10:39
commend…our s Rom 16:1
younger women…s-s 1 Tim 5:2

SIVAN
third month of Hebrew calendar Esth 8:9

SKY *heavens*
sun stopped in…s Josh 10:1
the s grew black 1 Kin 18:4
witness in the s Ps 89:3
s will be rolled up Is 34:4
for the s is red Matt 16:2
will appear in the s Matt 24:3
s was shut up Luke 4:2
gazing…into the s Acts 1:1
s was split apart Rev 6:1

SLAVERY *servitude*
from the house of s Ex 13:
ransomed you from…s Mic 6:
received a spirit of s Rom 8:1
to a yoke of s Gal 5:

SLAY *destroy, kill*
knife to s his son Gen 22:1
s-s the foolish Job 5:
Though He s me Job 13:1
Evil…s the wicked Ps 34:2

s her with thirst — Hos 2:3
Lamb that was **slain** — Rev 5:12

SLEEP (n) *rest*
caused a deep s — Gen 2:21
Do not love s — Prov 20:13
a spirit of deep s — Is 29:10
s fled from him — Dan 6:18
overcome by s — Acts 20:9

SLEEP (v) *slumber*
why do You s — Ps 44:23
neither slumber nor s — Ps 121:4
who s-s in harvest — Prov 10:5
found them **s-ing** — Matt 26:43
we will not all s — 1 Cor 15:51

SLUMBER *sleep*
s in their beds — Job 33:15
He...will not s — Ps 121:3
None s-s or sleeps — Is 5:27
Dreamers...love to s — Is 56:10

SNAKE *serpent*
horned s in the path — Gen 49:17
a s bites him — Amos 5:19
s instead of a fish — Luke 11:11

SNOW *ice flakes*
storehouses of the s — Job 38:22
be whiter than s — Ps 51:7
He gives s like wool — Ps 147:16
Like s in summer — Prov 26:1
as white as s — Matt 28:3

SOBER *serious, temperate*
words of s truth — Acts 26:25
be alert and s — 1 Thess 5:6
Be of s *spirit* — 1 Pet 5:8

SODOM
city S of Dead Sea — Gen 10:19
home of Lot — Gen 19:1,4
destroyed by God — Gen 19:24

SODOMITE
one guilty of unnatural sexual practices — 1 Kin 22:46

SOIL *earth, ground*
first fruits of your s — Ex 23:19
he loved the s — 2 Chr 26:10
fell into the good s — Mark 4:8
produce of the s — James 5:7

SOJOURN *visit temporarily*
S in this land — Gen 26:3
stranger s-s with you — Ex 12:48
s...land of Moab — Ruth 1:1

SOJOURNER
s in a foreign land — Ex 2:22
are s-s before You — 1 Chr 29:15
oppressed the s — Ezek 22:29

SOLOMON
1 *son of David* — 2 Sam 12:24
king of Israel — 1 Kin 1:43
ruled wisely — 1 Kin 4:29,34
built the Temple — 1 Kin 6:2; 9:1
international fame — 1 Kin 10:1
ruled foolishly — 1 Kin 11:6
death — 1 Kin 11:43
2 *Song of Solomon*
also Song of Songs

SON *male descendant*
the s-s of Noah — Gen 9:18
Take...your only s — Gen 22:2
O Absalom, my s — 2 Sam 18:33
to be a s to Me — 1 Chr 28:6
s-s of God shouted — Job 38:7
You are My S — Ps 2:7
wise s makes a — Prov 10:1
Discipline your s — Prov 19:18
bear a s...Immanuel — Is 7:14
Egypt I called My s — Hos 11:1
she gave birth to a S — Matt 1:25
This is My beloved S — Matt 3:17
the carpenter's s — Matt 13:55
I am the S of God — Matt 27:43
S of Man...suffer — Mark 8:31
her firstborn s — Luke 2:7
If You are the S — Luke 4:3
man had two s-s — Luke 15:11
only begotten S — John 3:16
S also gives life — John 5:21
become s-s of Light — John 12:36
sending His own S — Rom 8:3
image of His S — Rom 8:29
not spare His own S — Rom 8:32
fellowship with His S — 1 Cor 1:9
if a s, then an heir — Gal 4:7
shall be a S to Me — Heb 1:5
abide in the S — 1 John 2:24
He who has the S — 1 John 5:12

SON-IN-LAW
the s of the Timnite — Judg 15:6
be the king's s — 1 Sam 18:18
s of Sanballat — Neh 13:28

SON OF GOD
Messianic title indicating deity of Jesus Christ — Matt 4:3; 8:29; 16:16; Mark 1:20; 3:11; 14:61; Luke 1:35; John 3:13; 11:27; Acts 8:37

SON OF MAN
Messianic title of Jesus Christ — Matt 8:20; 9:6; Mark 2:10; 10:33; Luke 12:10; 18:31; John 6:27; 13:31

SORCERER *witch*
interprets...or a s — Deut 18:10
witness against the s-s — Mal 3:5
immoral persons...s-s — Rev 21:8

SORCERY *witchcraft*
practiced s — 2 Chr 33:6
idolatry, s, enmities — Gal 5:20
deceived by your s — Rev 18:23

SORDID *filthy*
fond of s gain — 1 Tim 3:8
the sake of s gain — Titus 1:11
not for s gain — 1 Pet 5:2

SOUL *life, spirit*
her s was departing — Gen 35:18
humble your s-s — Lev 16:29
poured out my s — 1 Sam 1:15
not abandon my s — Ps 16:10
He restores my s — Ps 23:3
my s pants for You — Ps 42:1
Bless...LORD, O my s — Ps 103:1
who is wise wins s-s — Prov 11:30
s who sins will die — Ezek 18:4
unable to kill the s — Matt 10:28
exchange for his s — Matt 16:26
My s is...grieved — Matt 26:38
and forfeit his s — Mark 8:36
My s exalts the Lord — Luke 1:46
your s is required — Luke 12:20
one heart and s — Acts 4:32
an anchor of the s — Heb 6:19
able to save your s-s — James 1:21
save his s from — James 5:20
war against the s — 1 Pet 2:11

SOVEREIGNTY *authority*
His s rules over all — Ps 103:19
s from Damascus — Is 17:3
s will be uprooted — Dan 11:4

SOW *plant, spread*
you may s the land — Gen 47:23
s your seed uselessly — Lev 26:16
who s in tears — Ps 126:5
who s-s iniquity will — Prov 22:8
they s the wind — Hos 8:7
birds...do not s — Matt 6:26

s good seed Matt 13:27
s-ed spiritual things 1 Cor 9:11
whatever a man s-s Gal 6:7

SOWER *planter*
seed to the s Is 55:10
s went out to sow Matt 13:3
s sows the word Mark 4:14

SPEAR *weapon*
leaning on his s 2 Sam 1:6
s-s into pruning hooks Is 2:4
pruning hooks into s-s Joel 3:10
pierced…with a s John 19:34

SPICE
s and the oil Ex 35:28
mix in the s-s Ezek 24:10
prepared s-s and Luke 23:56
wrappings with…s-s John 19:40

SPIES (n) *clandestine persons*
we are not s Gen 42:31
two men as s Josh 2:1
David sent out s 1 Sam 26:4
welcomed the s Heb 11:31

SPIRIT
S rested upon them Num 11:26
God sent an evil s Judg 9:23
My s is broken Job 17:1
renew a steadfast s Ps 51:10
my s grows faint Ps 77:3
a haughty s before Prov 16:18
the S lifted me up Ezek 3:14
his s was troubled Dan 2:1
four s-s of heaven Zech 6:5
are the poor in s Matt 5:3
authority over…s-s Matt 10:1
put My S upon Him Matt 12:18
blasphemy…the S Matt 12:31
yielded up *His* s Matt 27:50
S like a dove Mark 1:10
s…not have flesh Luke 24:39
born of…the S John 3:5
worship in s and John 4:24
gave up His s John 19:30
pour forth of My S Acts 2:17
Jesus, receive my s Acts 7:59
power of the S Rom 15:19
taught by the s 1 Cor 2:13
pray with the s 1 Cor 14:15
walk by the S Gal 5:16
fruit of the S is love Gal 5:22
one body and one S Eph 4:4
be filled with the S Eph 5:18
sword of the S Eph 6:17
not quench the S 1 Thess 5:19
division of soul and s Heb 4:12
the s-s *now* in prison 1 Pet 3:19
S who testifies 1 John 5:6
see also **HOLY SPIRIT**

SPIRIT OF GOD
the S was moving Gen 1:2
S came upon him 1 Sam 10:10
a vision by the S Ezek 11:24
S descending as a Matt 3:16
being led by the S Rom 8:14
S dwells in you 1 Cor 3:16
worship in the S Phil 3:3
see also **HOLY SPIRIT**

SPIRIT OF THE LORD
S came upon him Judg 3:10
S departed from 1 Sam 16:14
S gave them rest Is 63:14
filled with…the S Mic 3:8
S is upon Me Luke 4:18
see also **HOLY SPIRIT**

SPIRITUAL *of the spirit*
the Law is s Rom 7:14
s service of worship Rom 12:1
raised a s body 1 Cor 15:44
with every s blessing Eph 1:3
hymns and s songs Eph 5:19
offer up s sacrifices 1 Pet 2:5

SPIT
began to s at Him Mark 14:65
and s upon Luke 18:32
He **spat** on…ground John 9:6
I will s you out Rev 3:16

SPRING (adj) *period, season*
has been no s rain Jer 3:3
Like the s rain Hos 6:3
s crop began to sprout Amos 7:1

SPRING (n) *water source*
went down to the s Gen 24:16
twelve s-s of water Ex 15:27
stop all s-s of water 2 Kin 3:19
s-s of the deep…fixed Prov 8:28
the s-s of salvation Is 12:3
s of the water of life Rev 21:6

SPRING (v) *jump, leap*
S up, O well Num 21:17
Truth s-s from the Ps 85:11
s-**ing** up to eternal John 4:14

SPRINKLE *scatter*
take its blood and s Ex 29:16
s some of the blood Lev 4:6
s *it* seven times Lev 4:17
s some of the oil Lev 14:16

STAFF *rod*
s of God in his hand Ex 4:20
Your s, they comfort Ps 23:4
or sandals, or a s Matt 10:10
a mere s; no bread Mark 6:8

STANDARD *banner* or *rule*
set up their own s-s Ps 74:4
set up My s Is 49:22
s of the Law Acts 22:12
s of sound words 2 Tim 1:13

STAR *heavenly body*
He made the s-s Gen 1:16
s shall come forth Num 24:17
morning s-s sang Job 38:7
s of the morning Is 14:12
s-s for light by night Jer 31:35
His s in the east Matt 2:2
morning s arises 2 Pet 1:19
wandering s-s Jude 13
s fell from heaven Rev 8:10
the bright morning s Rev 22:16

STEWARDSHIP *responsibility*
a s entrusted to me 1 Cor 9:17
s of God's grace Eph 3:2

STOMACH *part of body*
s will be satisfied Prov 18:20
s of the fish Jon 1:17
Food is for the s 1 Cor 6:13
s was made bitter Rev 10:10

STORK *bird*
the s, the heron Lev 11:19
the s in the sky Jer 8:7
wings of a s Zech 5:9

STORM *tempest, whirlwind*
A refuge from the s Is 25:4
will come like a s Ezek 38:9
a great s on the sea Jon 1:4
mists driven by a s 2 Pet 2:17

STRENGTH *force, power*
no longer yield its s Gen 4:12
The LORD is my s Ex 15:2
was no s in him 1 Sam 28:20
My s is dried up Ps 22:15
The LORD is my s Ps 28:7
s in time of trouble Ps 37:39

God is our refuge...s Ps 46:1
s of my salvation Ps 140:7
your s to women Prov 31:3
s to the weary Is 40:29
Strangers devour his s Hos 7:9
with all your s Mark 12:30
s which God supplies 1 Pet 4:11
sun shining in its s Rev 1:16

STRENGTHEN *make strong*
please s me Judg 16:28
David **s-ed** himself 1 Sam 30:6
s-ed weak hands Job 4:3
s the feeble Is 35:3
s the sick Ezek 34:16
s your brothers Luke 22:32
s-ed in the faith Acts 16:5
Him who **s-s** me Phil 4:13
s-ed with all power Col 1:11
s your hearts 2 Thess 2:17
who has **s-ed** me 1 Tim 1:12

SUBMISSIVE *yielding*
Servants, be s 1 Pet 2:18
s to...husbands 1 Pet 3:5

SUBMIT *yield to*
Foreigners s to me Ps 18:44
s yourself to decrees Col 2:20
S therefore to God James 4:7

SUCCESS *accomplishment*
grant me s today Gen 24:12
hands cannot attain s Job 5:12
Daniel enjoyed s Dan 6:28

SUMMER *season*
fever heat of s Ps 32:4
You have made s Ps 74:17
Like snow in s Prov 26:1
know that s is near Matt 24:32

SUMMIT *peak, top*
Like the s of Lebanon Jer 22:6
hide on the s Amos 9:3

SUN *heavenly body*
when the s grew hot Ex 16:21
the s stood still Josh 10:13
chariots of the s 2 Kin 23:11
God is a s Ps 84:11
s will not smite Ps 121:6
s to rule by day Ps 136:8
new under the s Eccl 1:9
s go down at noon Amos 8:9
shine forth as the s Matt 13:43
signs in s Luke 21:25
not let the s go down Eph 4:26
clothed with the s Rev 12:1

SUNRISE *appearance of sun*
toward the s Num 3:38
Jordan toward the s Josh 1:15

SUNSET
Passover...at s Deut 16:6
dawn and the s shout Ps 65:8

SUNSHINE
Through s after rain 2 Sam 23:4
dazzling heat in the s Is 18:4

SUPPER *meal*
made Him a s John 12:2
eat the Lord's S 1 Cor 11:20
marriage s of the Rev 19:9
the great s of God Rev 19:17

SURRENDER *yield*
s me into his hand 1 Sam 23:11
How can I s you Hos 11:8

SUSA
a Persian capital city Neh 1:1; Esth 1:2,5; 3:15; 9:15

SUSTAIN *provide for*
land could not s Gen 13:6
LORD **s-s** the righteous Ps 37:17
He will s you Ps 55:22
S...with raisin cakes Song 2:5

SWINE *pig*
gold in a s-'s snout Prov 11:22
Who eat s-'s flesh Is 65:4
your pearls before s Matt 7:6
Send us into the s Mark 5:12

SWORD *weapon with blade*
flaming s...turned Gen 3:24
by your s you shall Gen 27:40
the s will bereave Deut 32:25
A s for the LORD Judg 7:20
s devour forever 2 Sam 2:26
fell on his s 1 Chr 10:5
tongue a sharp s Ps 57:4
as a two-edged s Prov 5:4
teeth are *like* s-s Prov 30:14
s against nation Is 2:4
the power of the s Jer 18:21
abolish...the s Hos 2:18
s-s into plowshares Mic 4:3
perish by the s Matt 26:52
s of the Spirit Eph 6:17
than any two-edged s Heb 4:12
s of My mouth Rev 2:16

SYCAMORE *tree*
olive and s trees 1 Chr 27:28
plentiful as s-s 2 Chr 1:15
grower of s figs Amos 7:14
climbed up into a s Luke 19:4

SYNAGOGUE *assembly*
pray in the s-s Matt 6:5
He went into their s Matt 12:9
flogged in *the* s-s Mark 13:9
chief seats in...s-s Luke 20:46
outcasts from the s John 16:2
taught in s-s John 18:20
reasoning in the s Acts 17:17
but are a s of Satan Rev 2:9

T

TABERNACLE *assembly and area for sacrificial worship*
dwelling place of God among the Israelites Ex 25:8
construction directed by God Ex 25:9
contained Ark of the Covenant Ex 25:10
other descriptive names of the tabernacle:
house of the LORD Ex 23:19; 34:26; Deut 23:18
tabernacle of the house of God 1 Chr 6:48
tabernacle of the tent of meeting Ex 39:40; 40:6,29
tabernacle of the testimony Ex 38:21; Num 1:50,53
tent of meeting Ex 29:32; 30:26; 38:30; 38:43; 40:2,6,7

TABLET *writing surface*
give you the stone **t-s** Ex 24:12
t-s of the testimony Ex 31:18
the t of their heart Jer 17:1
t-s of human hearts 2 Cor 3:3

TABOR
1 *mountain* Judg 4:6,12
2 *city in Zebulun* 1 Chr 6:77
3 *oak in Benjamin* 1 Sam 10:3

TALENT
measure of weight Ex 38:27; 2 Sam 12:30; 1 Chr 20:2
measure of money 1 Kin 20:39; Matt 18:24; 25:15,25

TAMAR
1 *Judah's daughter-in-law* Gen 38:6ff
2 *daughter of David* 2 Sam 13:1

3 *daughter of Absalom* 2 Sam 14:27
4 *town near the Dead Sea* 1 Kin 9:18; Ezek 47:19; 48:28

TAMARISK *tree*
a t tree at Beersheba Gen 21:33
under the t tree 1 Sam 22:6

TAMBOURINE
accompanied by...t Is 5:12
gaiety of t-s ceases Is 24:8

TARES *weeds*
t among the wheat Matt 13:25
gather up the t Matt 13:30
parable of the t Matt 13:36

TARSHISH
1 *lineage of Japheth* Gen 10:4
2 *ships of* 1 Kin 10:22; 22:48; 2 Chr 9:21; Ps 48:7
3 *line of Benjamin* 1 Chr 7:6-10
4 *Persian official* Esth 1:14
5 *city* Is 66:19; Jon 1:3

TASKMASTERS *overseers*
appointed t over them Ex 1:11
Pharaoh commanded...t Ex 5:6

TAX *charge, tribute*
a t for the LORD Num 31:28
money for the king's t Neh 5:4
sitting in the t collector's booth Matt 9:9
pay t-es to Caesar Luke 20:22
t to whom t *is due* Rom 13:7

TAX COLLECTOR *tax gatherer*
t-s do the same Matt 5:46
many t-s and sinners Matt 9:10
Matthew the t Matt 10:3
a friend of t-s Matt 11:19
he was a chief t Luke 19:2

TEACH *instruct*
t you what...to say Ex 4:12
t them the good way 1 Kin 8:36
Can anyone t God Job 21:22
T me Your paths Ps 25:4
T me to do Your will Ps 143:10
would He t knowledge Is 28:9
He...*began* to t them Matt 5:2
t-ing...in parables Mark 4:2
Lord, t us to pray Luke 11:1
Spirit will t you Luke 12:12
He will t you all John 14:26
t strange doctrines 1 Tim 1:3
allow a woman to t 1 Tim 2:12
she t-es and leads Rev 2:20

TEACHER *instructor*
will behold your T Is 30:20
T, I will follow You Matt 8:19
not above his t Matt 10:24
why trouble the T Mark 5:35
the t of Israel John 3:10
call Me T and Lord John 13:13
t of the immature Rom 2:20
as pastors and t-s Eph 4:11
t of the Gentiles 1 Tim 2:7
false t-s among you 2 Pet 2:1

TEACHING (n) *instruction*
t drop as the rain Deut 32:2
your mother's t Prov 1:8
amazed at His t Matt 7:28
My t is not Mine John 7:16
contrary to sound t 1 Tim 1:10

TEBETH
name of the tenth month in Hebrew calendar Esth 2:16

TEL-ABIB
place in Babylonia
Jewish exiles located there Ezek 3:15

TEMPLE *structure for worship*
doorpost of the t 1 Sam 1:9
t is not for man 1 Chr 29:1
LORD is in His holy t Ps 11:4
meditate in His t Ps 27:4
t of the LORD Jer 7:4
pinnacle of the t Matt 4:5
will destroy this t Mark 14:58
veil of the t Luke 23:45
Destroy this t, and John 2:19
you are a t of God 1 Cor 3:16
t of the Holy Spirit 1 Cor 6:19
his seat in the t 2 Thess 2:4
the Lamb, are its t Rev 21:22

TEMPT *test, try*
And t-ed God in the Ps 106:14
being t-ed by Satan Mark 1:13
so that Satan will not t you 1 Cor 7:5
t-ed beyond what 1 Cor 10:13
Himself does not t James 1:13

TEMPTATION *testing, trial*
not lead us into t Matt 6:13
not enter into t Matt 26:41
time of t fall away Luke 8:13
t has overtaken you 1 Cor 10:13
the godly from t 2 Pet 2:9

TEN *number*
T Commandments Deut 10:4
it had t horns Dan 7:7
has the t talents Matt 25:28

TENT OF MEETING
perhaps the same as the Tabernacle or at certain periods a separate meeting place Ex 33:7
Lev 1:1; Num 7:5; Josh 18:1

TERAPHIM
household gods, idols 2 Kin 23:24; Zech 10:2

TERRITORY *country, land*
smite your whole t Ex 8:2
God enlarges your t Deut 19:8
t of...inheritance Josh 19:10
possess the t Obad 1

TEST (n) *trial*
put God to the t Ps 78:18
put Him to the t Luke 10:25
you fail the t 2 Cor 13:5

TEST (v) *try*
God t-ed Abraham Gen 22:1
Why do you t the LORD Ex 17:2
she came to t him 1 Kin 10:1
T my mind and my Ps 26:2
word of God is t-ed Prov 30:5
Spirit...to the t Acts 5:9
fire itself will t 1 Cor 3:13
t the spirits to see 1 John 4:1

TESTIFY *give witness*
nor shall you t Ex 23:2
them t against him 1 Kin 21:10
I will t against you Ps 50:7
our sins t against us Is 59:12
John t-ied John 1:15
John t-ied John 1:32
Jesus Himself t-ied John 4:44
If I *alone* t John 5:31
t about Me John 15:26
you *will* t John 15:27
Spirit...t-ies Rom 8:16
three that t 1 John 5:7

TESTIMONY *witness*
into the ark the t Ex 25:16
two tablets of the t Ex 31:18
t of the LORD is sure Ps 19:7
t-ies are righteous Ps 119:144
Bind up the t Is 8:16
t to all the nations Matt 24:14
t against Jesus Matt 26:59
My t is true John 8:14
t of two men is true John 8:17

t concerning Christ 1 Cor 1:6
ashamed of the t 2 Tim 1:8
This t is true Titus 1:13
t of God is greater 1 John 5:9

TETRARCH
governor of a region Matt 14:1; Luke 3:1,19; Acts 13:1

THANK (v) *express gratitude*
my song I shall t Him Ps 28:7
God, I t You Luke 18:11
I t my God always 1 Cor 1:4

THANKS (n) *gratitude*
give t to the LORD 1 Chr 16:7
It is good to give t Ps 92:1
giving t, He broke Matt 15:36
a cup and given t Matt 26:27
But t be to God Rom 6:17
not cease giving t Eph 1:16
always to give t 2 Thess 1:3

THANKSGIVING *gratitude*
the sacrifice of t Lev 7:12
with the voice of t Ps 26:7
His presence with t Ps 95:2
supplication with t Phil 4:6
t and honor and Rev 7:12

THEFT *robbery*
be sold for his t Ex 22:3
t-s, murders Mark 7:21

THIRD *number*
morning, a t day Gen 1:13
raised…the t day Matt 16:21
raised on the t day 1 Cor 15:4
to the t heaven 2 Cor 12:2

THORN *sharp point*
Both t-s and thistles Gen 3:18
as t-s in your sides Num 33:55
as a hedge of t-s Prov 15:19
lily among the t-s Song 2:2
have reaped t-s Jer 12:13
fell among the t-s Matt 13:7
a crown of t-s Matt 27:29
a burning t bush Acts 7:30
t in the flesh 2 Cor 12:7

THREE *number*
Job's t friends Job 2:11
or t have gathered Matt 18:20
deny Me t times Matt 26:34
t days I will raise John 2:19

THRONE *seat of sovereign*
sitting on His t 1 Kin 22:19
LORD'S t is in heaven Ps 11:4
Your t is established Ps 93:2
it is the t of God Matt 5:34
sit upon twelve t-s Matt 19:28
Your t…is forever Heb 1:8
to the t of grace Heb 4:16
a great white t Rev 20:11

THUMMIM
kept in high priest's breastplate for determining will of God Ex 28:30; Lev 8:8; Deut 33:8; Ezra 2:63; Neh 7:65

TIBERIUS
Roman emperor Luke 3:1
see also **CAESAR**

TIDINGS *information, news*
t of His salvation 1 Chr 16:23
not fear evil t Ps 112:7

TILLER *cultivator*
Cain was a t Gen 4:2
a t of the ground Zech 13:5

TIMOTHY
companion of Paul Acts 17:15; 18:5; Phil 1:1; Col 1:1; Heb 13:23

TIRZAH
1 *daughter of Zelophehad* Num 26:33; 27:1; 36:11
2 *royal Canaanite city* 1 Kin 14:17; 2 Kin 15:14

TITHE (n) *tenth*
all the t of the land Lev 27:30
a t of the t Num 18:26
the t of your grain Deut 12:17
t into the storehouse Mal 3:10
t-s of all that I get Luke 18:12
mortal men receive t-s Heb 7:8

TITHE (v) *pay a tithe*
shall surely t all Deut 14:22
you t mint and dill Matt 23:23

TITUS
co-worker with Paul 2 Cor 2:13; 8:23; Gal 2:1

TOMB *grave, sepulchre*
from womb to t Job 10:19
you have hewn a t Is 22:16
like whitewashed t-s Matt 23:27
laid Him in a t Mark 15:46
Lazarus out of the t John 12:17
outside the t John 20:11

TONGUE *speech, talk*
speech and slow of t Ex 4:10
flatter with their t Ps 5:9
their t a sharp sword Ps 57:4
a lying t Prov 6:17
t of the wise Prov 12:18
soft t breaks…bone Prov 25:15
His t is like…fire Is 30:27
t is a deadly arrow Jer 9:8
impediment of his t Mark 7:35
and his t *loosed* Luke 1:64
no one…tame the t James 3:8

TONGUE *language*
speak with new t-s Mark 16:17
speak with other t-s Acts 2:4
t-s of men…angels 1 Cor 13:1
if I pray in a t 1 Cor 14:14
every tribe and t Rev 5:9

TOOTH
teeth white from Gen 49:12
eye for eye, t for t Ex 21:24
and a t for a t Matt 5:38

TOPAZ *precious stone*
ruby, t, and emerald Ex 39:10
t of Ethiopia Job 28:19
the ninth, t Rev 21:20

TOWER *fortress structure*
t whose top *will reach* Gen 11:4
Count her t-s Ps 48:12
name…strong t Prov 18:10
and built a t Matt 21:33

TRADITION *custom*
sake of your t Matt 15:3
hold to the t of men Mark 7:8
hold…to the t-s 1 Cor 11:2
my ancestral t-s Gal 1:14

TRANCE *daze, dream*
he fell into a t Acts 10:10
in a t I saw a vision Acts 11:5
fell into a t Acts 22:17

TRANSGRESS *break, overstep*
you t the covenant Josh 23:16
rulers also t-ed Jer 2:8
they t-ed laws Is 24:5

TRANSGRESSION *trespass, sin*
forgives iniquity, t Ex 34:7
I am pure, without t Job 33:9
I know my t-s Ps 51:3
removed our t-s from Ps 103:12
love covers all t-s Prov 10:12
pierced…for our t-s Is 53:5

not forgive your **t-s** Matt 6:15
dead in our **t-s** Eph 2:5
TRANSGRESSOR *sinner*
teach **t-s** Your ways Ps 51:13
numbered with the **t-s** Is 53:12
a **t** of the law James 2:11
TRANSLATED
t and read before me Ezra 4:18
Immanuel…**t** means Matt 1:23
Golgotha, which is **t** Mark 15:22
Messiah…**t** means John 1:41
TRAVAIL *intense pain*
t-ed nor given birth Is 23:4
TREASURE (v) *value greatly*
I have **t-d** the words Job 23:12
Your word I have **t-d** Ps 119:11
t my commandments Prov 7:1
TREE *woody plant*
fruit **t-s**…bearing Gen 1:11
t of life Gen 2:9
gave me from the **t** Gen 3:12
hang him on a **t** Deut 21:22
said to the olive **t** Judg 9:8
t *firmly* planted Ps 1:3
she is a **t** of life Prov 3:18
Beneath the apple **t** Song 8:5
like a **t** planted by Jer 17:8
under his fig **t** Mic 4:4
good **t** bears good Matt 7:17
the fig **t** withered Matt 21:19
a sycamore **t** Luke 19:4
autumn **t-s** without Jude 12
eat of the **t** of life Rev 2:7
TRESPASS *fault, sin*
Saul died for his **t** 1 Chr 10:13
caught in any **t** Gal 6:1
dead in your **t-es** Eph 2:1
TRIAL *testing*
if we are on **t** today Acts 4:9
which was a **t** to you Gal 4:14
perseveres under **t** James 1:12
TRIBE *common ancestry*
twelve **t-s** of Israel Gen 49:28
a man of each **t** Num 1:4
t-s of the LORD Ps 122:4
judging…twelve **t-s** Luke 22:30
men from every **t** Rev 5:9
TRIBULATION *affliction*
will be a great **t** Matt 24:21
world you have **t** John 16:33
exult in our **t-s** Rom 5:3
my **t-s** on your behalf Eph 3:13
out of the great **t** Rev 7:14
TRUE *actual, real, reliable*
gets a **t** reward Prov 11:18
There was the **t** light John 1:9
gives you…**t** bread John 6:32
let God be found **t** Rom 3:4
signs of a **t** apostle 2 Cor 12:12
This testimony is **t** Titus 1:13
t grace of God 1 Pet 5:12
faithful and **t** Witness Rev 3:14
TRUMPET *wind instrument*
t-s of rams' horns Josh 6:6
t-s…empty pitchers Judg 7:16
Praise Him with **t** Ps 150:3
do not sound a **t** Matt 6:2
at the last **t** 1 Cor 15:52
voice like…a **t** Rev 1:10
TRUST (n) *confidence, hope*
whose **t** a spider's web Job 8:14
In God…put my **t** Ps 56:11
put My **t** in Him Heb 2:13
TRUST (v) *commit to*
t in the LORD Ps 4:5
Than to **t** in man Ps 118:8
t-s in his riches Prov 11:28
not **t** in a neighbor Mic 7:5
not **t** in ourselves 2 Cor 1:9
TRUTH *genuineness, honesty*
walk before Me in **t** 1 Kin 2:4
speaks **t** in his heart Ps 15:2
Your word is **t** Ps 119:160
Buy **t**, and do not Prov 23:23
judge with **t** Zech 8:16
full of grace and **t** John 1:14
worship in…**t** John 4:24
t will make you free John 8:32
the way, and the **t** John 14:6
exchanged the **t** of Rom 1:25
t of the gospel Gal 2:5
speaking the **t** in love Eph 4:15
the word of **t** 2 Tim 2:15
the **t** is not in us 1 John 1:8
TUMULT *disturbance*
t of the peoples Ps 65:7
A sound of **t** Is 13:4
t of waters Jer 51:16
TUNIC *cloak, garment*
a varicolored **t** Gen 37:3
the holy linen **t** Lev 16:4
TURBAN *headdress*
a **t** of fine linen Ex 28:39
justice was like…a **t** Job 29:14
Remove the **t** Ezek 21:26
TURTLEDOVE *bird*
t for a sin offering Lev 12:6
the voice of the **t** Song 2:12
TWELVE *number*
t tribes of Israel Gen 49:28
summoned His **t** Matt 10:1
t legions of angels Matt 26:53
when He became **t** Luke 2:42
a crown of **t** stars Rev 12:1
TWILIGHT *darkness, dusk*
lamb…offer at **t** Ex 29:39
waits for the **t** Job 24:15
midday as in the **t** Is 59:10
TWINKLING *flicker*
in the **t** of an eye 1 Cor 15:52
TWINS *pair, two*
t in her womb Gen 25:24
T of a gazelle Song 4:5
TWO-EDGED *with two edges*
than any **t** sword Heb 4:12
His mouth…**t** sword Rev 1:16
TYRE
Phoenician seaport Josh 19:29; Ezek 27:3; Matt 15:21; Acts 21:3

U

UGLY *unsightly*
u and gaunt cows Gen 41:4
seven lean…**u** cows Gen 41:27
UNBELIEF *lack of faith*
wondered at their **u** Mark 6:6
help my **u** Mark 9:24
continue in their **u** Rom 11:23
UNBELIEVER *non-believer*
a place with the **u-s** Luke 12:46
wife who is an **u** 1 Cor 7:12
ungifted men or **u-s** 1 Cor 14:23
bound…with **u-s** 2 Cor 6:14
worse than an **u** 1 Tim 5:8
UNFAITHFUL
u to her husband Num 5:27
very **u** to the LORD 2 Chr 28:19
u to our God Ezra 10:2
UNFAITHFULNESS *faithless*
u…they committed Lev 26:40

to Babylon for their **u** 1 Chr 9:1
the **u** of the exiles Ezra 9:4
UNFRUITFUL *not productive*
the land is **u** 2 Kin 2:19
my mind is **u** 1 Cor 14:14
u deeds of darkness Eph 5:11
UNGODLY *sinful, wicked*
who justifies the **u** Rom 4:5
Christ died for the **u** Rom 5:6
destruction of **u** men 2 Pet 3:7
their own **u** lusts Jude 18
UNHOLY *not holy*
no *longer* consider **u** Acts 10:15
for the **u** and profane 1 Tim 1:9
UNITED *joined, union*
u as one man Judg 20:11
become **u** with *Him* Rom 6:5
love, **u** in spirit Phil 2:2
not **u** by faith Heb 4:2
UNJUST *unfair*
u man is abominable Prov 29:27
For God is not **u** Heb 6:10
the just for *the* **u** 1 Pet 3:18
UNLEAVENED *non-fermented*
and baked **u** bread Gen 19:3
you shall eat **u** bread Ex 12:15
first day of **U** Bread Matt 26:17
you are *in fact* **u** 1 Cor 5:7
UNRIGHTEOUS *evil, wicked*
u man his thoughts Is 55:7
rain on…*the* **u** Matt 5:45
u in a…little thing Luke 16:10
God…is not **u** Rom 3:5
u will not inherit 1 Cor 6:9
u under punishment 2 Pet 2:9
UNRIGHTEOUSNESS *evil*
have no part in **u** 2 Chr 19:7
no **u** in Him Ps 92:15
not rejoice in **u** 1 Cor 13:6
cleanse us from all **u** 1 John 1:9
All **u** is sin 1 John 5:17
URIAH
1 *husband of Bathsheba* 2 Sam 11:3; 12:9
2 *priest under Ezra* Neh 8:4
3 *priest under Ahaz* Is 8:2
also Urijah 2 Kin 16:10ff
4 *time of Jeremiah* Jer 26:20
URIM
kept in high priest's breastplate for determining the will of God Ex 28:30; Lev 8:8; Num 27:21
USURY *interest*
leave off this **u** Neh 5:10
by interest and **u** Prov 28:8

V

VAIN *empty* or *profane*
name of…God in **v** Ex 20:7
devising a **v** thing Ps 2:1
labor in **v** who build Ps 127:1
our preaching is **v** 1 Cor 15:14
VALIANT *brave, strong*
these…**v** warriors Judg 20:46
be a **v** man for me 1 Sam 18:17
even all the **v** men 1 Chr 28:1
He drags off the **v** Job 24:22
VALLEY *ravine*
v of the Jordan Gen 13:10
the **v** of Aijalon Josh 10:12
v of the shadow of Ps 23:4
The lily of the **v-s** Song 2:1
v of the dead bodies Jer 31:40
v…full of bones Ezek 37:1
the **v** of decision Joel 3:14

VANITY *futility, pride*
will reap **v** Prov 22:8
V of **v-ies**! All is **v** Eccl 1:2
arrogant *words* of **v** 2 Pet 2:18
VEGETABLE *plant*
like a **v** garden Deut 11:10
Better…dish of **v-s** Prov 15:17
weak eats **v-s** *only* Rom 14:2
VEGETATION *plant life*
earth brought forth **v** Gen 1:12
ate up all **v** Ps 105:35
wither all their **v** Is 42:15
VEIL *cover, curtain*
a **v** over his face Ex 34:33
v of the sanctuary Lev 4:6
Remove your **v** Is 47:2
v of the temple Matt 27:51
enters within the **v** Heb 6:19
VENGEANCE *revenge*
not take **v** Lev 19:18
V is Mine Deut 32:35
God…executes **v** 2 Sam 22:48
LORD takes **v** on His Nah 1:2
V is Mine, I will Heb 10:30
VESSEL *utensil*
Go, borrow **v-s** 2 Kin 4:3
I am like a broken **v** Ps 31:12
v-s of wrath Rom 9:22
treasure in…**v-s** 2 Cor 4:7
be a **v** for honor 2 Tim 2:21
v-s of the potter Rev 2:27
VICTORIOUS *triumphant*
A **v** warrior Zeph 3:17
v over the beast Rev 15:2
VICTORY *triumph*
LORD brought…**v** 2 Sam 23:10
had given **v** to Aram 2 Kin 5:1
the glory and the **v** 1 Chr 29:11
gained the **v** for Him Ps 98:1
v belongs to…LORD Prov 21:31
He leads justice to **v** Matt 12:20
swallowed up in **v** 1 Cor 15:54
v that has overcome 1 John 5:4
VILLAGE *small town*
land of unwalled **v-s** Ezek 38:11
Go into the **v** Matt 21:2
entered a **v** Luke 10:38
VINE *stem of plant*
trees said to the **v** Judg 9:12
every man…his **v** 1 Kin 4:25
like a fruitful **v** Ps 128:3
the **v-s** in blossom Song 2:13
mother was like a **v** Ezek 19:10
Israel is a luxuriant **v** Hos 10:1
The **v** dries up Joel 1:12
fruit of the **v** Matt 26:29
I am the true **v** John 15:1
VINEGAR *sour liquid*
he shall drink no **v** Num 6:3
bread in the **v** Ruth 2:14
gave me **v** to drink Ps 69:21
Like **v** to the teeth Prov 10:26
VINEYARD *grapevines*
Noah…planted a **v** Gen 9:20
Nor…glean your **v** Lev 19:10
Hewn cisterns, **v-s** Neh 9:25
shelter in a **v** Is 1:8
ruined My **v** Jer 12:10
laborers for his **v** Matt 20:1
Who plants a **v** 1 Cor 9:7
VIPER *snake*
v-'s tongue slays him Job 20:16
hand on the **v-'s** den Is 11:8
v and flying serpent Is 30:6
You brood of **v-s** Matt 3:7

VIRGIN *unmarried maiden*
very beautiful, a v Gen 24:16
if a man seduces a v Ex 22:16
could I gaze at a v Job 31:1
the v will rejoice Jer 31:13
v shall be with child Matt 1:23
kept her a v Matt 1:25
comparable to ten v-s Matt 25:1
v-'s name was Mary Luke 1:27
if a v marries 1 Cor 7:28
VOW *solemn promise*
Jacob made a v Gen 28:20
v of a Nazirite Num 6:2
I shall pay my v-s Ps 22:25
not make false v-s Matt 5:33
he was keeping a v Acts 18:18
VULTURE *bird*
not eat…the v Deut 14:12
the v-s will gather Matt 24:28
the v-s will be gathered Luke 17:37

W

WAFER *thin cake of bread*
w-s with honey Ex 16:31
one unleavened w Num 6:19
WAGE *salary*
God has given…w-s Gen 30:18
w-s of the righteous Prov 10:16
w is not credited Rom 4:4
the w-s of sin Rom 6:23
worthy of his w-s 1 Tim 5:18
WANDER *roam*
w in the wilderness Num 32:13
I would w far away Ps 55:7
w…Your statutes Ps 119:118
people w like sheep Zech 10:2
w-ed…the faith 1 Tim 6:10
w-ing stars, for whom Jude 13
WANDERER *roamer*
a w on the earth Gen 4:12
an exile and a w Is 49:21
w-s among…nations Hos 9:17
WAR *battle, conflict*
when they see w Ex 13:17
sound of w in…camp Ex 32:17
land…rest from w Josh 11:23
He makes w-s to cease Ps 46:9
the weapons of w Ps 76:3
A time for w Eccl 3:8
will they learn w Is 2:4
w-s…rumors of w-s Matt 24:6
w against the law Rom 7:23
w in your members James 4:1
w against the soul 1 Pet 2:11
judges and wages w Rev 19:11
WATER (n) *flood, liquid*
moving over…the w-s Gen 1:2
flood of w came Gen 7:6
w-s *were like* a wall Ex 14:22
w of bitterness Num 5:18
the clouds dripped w Judg 5:4
W wears away stones Job 14:19
poured out like w Ps 22:14
beside quiet w-s Ps 23:2
Stolen w is sweet Prov 9:17
bread on the…w-s Eccl 11:1
come to the w-s Is 55:1
fountain of living w-s Jer 2:13
eyes run…with w Lam 1:16
knees…*like* w Ezek 7:17
baptize you with w Matt 3:11
a cup of cold w Matt 10:42
walked on the w Matt 14:29
no w for My feet Luke 7:44
one is born of w John 3:5
given you living w John 4:10
John baptized with w Acts 1:5
of w with the word Eph 5:26
formed out of w 2 Pet 3:5
by w and blood 1 John 5:6
sound of many w-s Rev 19:6
WATER (v) *make moist*
to w the garden Gen 2:10
I will w your camels Gen 24:46
w their father's flock Ex 2:16
that w the earth Ps 72:6
Apollos w-ed 1 Cor 3:6
WAVES *billows*
w of death 2 Sam 22:5
tramples down the w Job 9:8
Your w have rolled Ps 42:7
w were breaking Mark 4:37
wild w of the sea Jude 13
WAX *paraffin*
My heart is like w Ps 22:1
Like w before the fire Mic 1:
WAY *manner* or *path*
guard the w Gen 3:2
all His w-s are just Deut 32:
blameless…His w 2 Sam 22:3
from your evil w-s 2 Kin 17:1
joy of His w Job 8:1
w of the righteous Ps 1:
Commit your w to Ps 37:
your w-s acknowledge Prov 3:
is the w of death Prov 14:1
Clear the w Is 40:
w of the wicked Jer 12:
Make ready the w Matt 3:
Pray…in this w Matt 6:
w is broad that leads Matt 7:1
teach…w of God Mark 12:1
into the w of peace Luke 1:7
I am the w John 14:
belonging to the W Acts 9:
the w of salvation Acts 16:1
unfathomable…w-s Rom 11:3
the w of escape 1 Cor 10:1
new and living w Heb 10:2
the w of the truth 2 Pet 2:
WEAK *feeble*
I will become w Judg 16:1
Rescue the w Ps 82:
but the flesh is w Matt 26:4
must help the w Acts 20:3
who is w in faith Rom 14:
God…chosen the w 1 Cor 1:2
WEALTH *riches*
power to make w Deut 8:1
a man of great w Ruth 2:
who trust in their w Ps 49:
Honor…from your w Prov 3:
W adds many friends Prov 19:
A w of salvation Is 33:
the w of all nations Hag 2:
serve God and w Matt 6:2
deceitfulness of w Matt 13:2
w of their liberality 2 Cor 8:
rich by her w Rev 18:1
WEAPON *armament*
girded on his w-s Deut 1:4
flee from the iron w Job 20:2
turn back the w-s Jer 21:
w-s of righteousness 2 Cor 6:
WEDDING *marriage*
had no w songs Ps 78:6
day of his w Song 3:1
come to the w feast Matt 22:
a w in Cana John 2:

WEEK *period of time*	
Complete the w of	Gen 29:27
Seventy w-s	Dan 9:24
first *day* of the w	Matt 28:1
I fast twice a w	Luke 18:12
WEST *direction*	
very strong w wind	Ex 10:19
east is from the w	Ps 103:12
gather you from the w	Is 43:5
WHEAT *grain*	
days of w harvest	Gen 30:14
first fruits of the w	Ex 34:22
plant w in rows	Is 28:25
gather His w into	Matt 3:12
to sift you like w	Luke 22:31
unless a grain of w	John 12:24
WHIRLWIND	
take...Elijah by a w	2 Kin 2:1
comes like a w	Prov 1:27
chariots like the w	Jer 4:13
they reap the w	Hos 8:7
WHITE *color*	
teeth w from milk	Gen 49:12
w of an egg	Job 6:6
be as w as snow	Is 1:18
make one hair w	Matt 5:36
clothing *became* w	Luke 9:29
fields...w for harvest	John 4:35
clothed in w robes	Rev 7:9
WHITEWASHED *wall covering*	
like w tombs	Matt 23:27
you w wall	Acts 23:3
WICK *candle thread*	
extinguished like a w	Is 43:17
a smoldering w	Matt 12:20
WICKED *evil, ungodly*	
condemn the w	Deut 25:1
w ones are silenced	1 Sam 2:9
counsel of the w	Ps 1:1
the w spurned God	Ps 10:13
The w strut about	Ps 12:8
devises w plans	Prov 6:18
When a w man dies	Prov 11:7
no peace for the w	Is 48:22
turn from his w way	Jon 3:8
taking...some w men	Acts 17:5
righteous and the w	Acts 24:15
WICKEDNESS *evil*	
w of man was great	Gen 6:5
If I regard w	Ps 66:18
eat the bread of w	Prov 4:17
inclines toward w	Is 32:6
w of My people	Jer 7:12
You have plowed w	Hos 10:13
repent of this w	Acts 8:22
spiritual *forces* of w	Eph 6:12
WIDOW *husband dead*	
Remain a w	Gen 38:11
not afflict any w	Ex 22:22
sent w-s away empty	Job 22:9
judge for the w-s	Ps 68:5
Plead for the w	Is 1:17
devour w-s' houses	Matt 23:14
w put in more	Mark 12:43
Honor w-s	1 Tim 5:3
visit orphans...w-s	James 1:27
WIFE *married woman*	
joined to his w	Gen 2:24
man and his w hid	Gen 3:8
shall not covet...w	Ex 20:17
w of your youth	Prov 5:18
An excellent w	Prov 31:10
who divorces his w	Matt 5:32
Remember Lot's w	Luke 17:32
have his own w	1 Cor 7:2
head of the w	Eph 5:23
husband of one w	1 Tim 3:2
w-ves, be submissive	1 Pet 3:1
w of the Lamb	Rev 21:9
WILDERNESS *barren area*	
water in the w	Gen 16:7
journey into the w	Ex 5:3
to die in the w	Ex 14:11
forty years in the w	Deut 29:5
pastures of the w	Ps 65:12
roadway in the w	Is 43:19
Have I been a w	Jer 2:31
preaching in the w	Matt 3:1
into the w...tempted	Matt 4:1
crying in the w	Mark 1:3
manna in the w	John 6:31
WIND	
caused a w to pass	Gen 8:1
scorched by...w	Gen 41:27
will inherit w	Prov 11:29
prophets are *as* w	Jer 5:13
they sow the w	Hos 8:7
reed shaken by...w	Matt 11:7
w and the sea obey	Mark 4:41
He...rebuked the w	Luke 8:24
violent, rushing w	Acts 2:2
every w of doctrine	Eph 4:14
driven by strong w-s	James 3:4
WINDOW *opening*	
enter through the w-s	Joel 2:9
open...w-s of heaven	Mal 3:10
sitting on the w sill	Acts 20:9
basket through a w	2 Cor 11:33
WINE *strong drink*	
eyes...dull from w	Gen 49:12
Do not drink w	Lev 10:9
overflow with new w	Prov 3:10
W is a mocker	Prov 20:1
love is better than w	Song 1:2
new w into old	Matt 9:17
gave Him w to	Matt 27:34
made the water w	John 4:46
full of sweet w	Acts 2:13
not get drunk with w	Eph 5:18
not addicted to w	1 Tim 3:3
WINESKINS *animal skin bag*	
These w...were new	Josh 9:13
Like new w	Job 32:19
wine into fresh w	Matt 9:17
WINGS	
bore you on eagles' w	Ex 19:4
He spread His w	Deut 32:11
under whose w	Ruth 2:12
under His w...refuge	Ps 91:4
with w like eagles	Is 40:31
healing in its w	Mal 4:2
chicks under her w	Matt 23:37
WINTER *season*	
And summer and w	Gen 8:22
the w is past	Song 2:11
even spend the w	1 Cor 16:6
WITHER *dry up*	
its leaf does not w	Ps 1:3
w...like the grass	Ps 37:2
earth mourns *and* w-s	Is 24:4
the leaf will w	Jer 8:13
whose hand was w-ed	Mark 3:1
the fig tree w-ed	Mark 11:20
WITNESS (n) *testimony*	
This heap is a w	Gen 31:48
is w between us	Judg 11:10
my w is in heaven	Job 16:19
a w to the LORD	Is 19:20
He came as a w	John 1:7
you shall be My w-es	Acts 1:8

For God is my **w** Phil 1:8
Christ, the faithful **w** Rev 1:5

WITNESS (v) *testify*
not bear false **w** Ex 20:16
w against you today Deut 4:26

WOLF *animal*
w will dwell with Is 11:6
the midst of **w-ves** Matt 10:16
w snatches them John 10:12

WOMAN *female, lady*
She shall be called **W** Gen 2:23
w...not wear man's Deut 22:5
a **w** of excellence Ruth 3:11
Man...born of **w** Job 14:1
gracious **w** attains Prov 11:16
a contentious **w** Prov 25:24
like a **w** in labor Is 42:14
looks at a **w** with lust Matt 5:28
w-en...grinding Matt 24:41
Blessed...among **w-en** Luke 1:42
W, behold, your son John 19:26
not to touch a **w** 1 Cor 7:1
w is the glory of 1 Cor 11:7
w to speak in 1 Cor 14:35
His Son, born of a **w** Gal 4:4
w clothed with...sun Rev 12:1

WOMB
nations...in your **w** Gen 25:23
LORD...closed her **w** 1 Sam 1:5
from **w** to tomb Job 10:19
formed you from the **w** Is 44:2
baby leaped in...**w** Luke 1:41

WONDER *marvel, sign*
consider the **w-s** of Job 37:14
tell of all Your **w-s** Ps 9:1
His **w-s** in the deep Ps 107:24
w-s in the sky Joel 2:30
were filled with **w** Acts 3:10

WORD *message, speech*
to the **w** of Moses Lev 10:7
declare to you the **w** Deut 5:5
Joshua wrote...**w-s** Josh 24:26
proclaim the **w** of 1 Sam 9:27
Your **w**...confirmed 2 Chr 6:17
no limit to windy **w-s** Job 16:3
w-s of my mouth Ps 19:14
Your **w** is a lamp Ps 119:105
harsh **w** stirs up Prov 15:1
w of God is tested Prov 30:5
despised the **w** Is 5:24
w-s of a sealed book Is 29:11
speak My **w** in truth Jer 23:28
conceal these **w-s** Dan 12:4
every **w** that proceeds Matt 4:4
these **w-s** of Mine Matt 7:24
sower sows the **w** Mark 4:14
the **W** was God John 1:1
the **W** became flesh John 1:14
w-s of eternal life John 6:68
continue in My **w** John 8:31
glorifying the **w** Acts 13:48
too deep for **w-s** Rom 8:26
hearing by the **w** Rom 10:17
the **w** of the cross 1 Cor 1:18
fulfilled in one **w** Gal 5:14
no unwholesome **w** Eph 4:29
sanctified by...**w** 1 Tim 4:5
the **w** of truth 2 Tim 2:15
the faithful **w** Titus 1:9
w of God is living Heb 4:12
doers of the **w** James 1:22
pure milk of the **w** 1 Pet 2:2
the **W** of Life 1 John 1:1
The **W** of God Rev 19:13

WORK (v) *perform, produce*
has **w-ed** with God 1 Sam 14:45
those who **w** iniquity Ps 28:3
Who...**w-s** wonders Ps 72:18
not **w** for the food John 6:27
w together for good Rom 8:28
So death **w-s** in us 2 Cor 4:12
w out your salvation Phil 2:12
anyone is not willing to **w** 2 Thess 3:10

WORLD *earth, humanity*
foundations of...**w** 2 Sam 22:16
He will judge the **w** Ps 9:8
first dust of the **w** Prov 8:26
the light of the **w** Matt 5:14
the field is the **w** Matt 13:38
Go into all the **w** Mark 16:15
gains the whole **w** Luke 9:25
God so loved the **w** John 3:16
Savior of the **w** John 4:42
w cannot hate you John 7:7
the Light of the **w** John 8:12
overcome the **w** John 16:33
have upset the **w** Acts 17:6
sin entered...the **w** Rom 5:12
reconciling the **w** 2 Cor 5:19
unstained by the **w** James 1:27
flood upon the **w** 2 Pet 2:5
Do not love the **w** 1 John 2:15

WORLDLY *earthly*
w fables fit only 1 Tim 4:7
avoid **w**...chatter 2 Tim 2:16

WORM *creeping animal*
But I am a **w** Ps 22:6
w-s are your covering Is 14:11
God appointed a **w** Jon 4:7
their **w** does not die Mark 9:48
he was eaten by **w-s** Acts 12:23

WORMWOOD
1 *a bitter plant* Deut 29:18
2 *used figuratively* Prov 5:4; Amos 6:12; Rev 8:11

WORSHIP *bow, revere*
not **w** any other god Ex 34:14
you shall **w** Him Deut 6:13
W the LORD Ps 2:11
earth will **w** You Ps 66:4
in vain do they **w** Matt 15:9
w in spirit and truth John 4:24
w in the Spirit Phil 3:3
w Him who lives Rev 4:10
who **w** the beast Rev 14:11

WORTHLESS *useless*
all **w** physicians Job 13:4
w man digs up evil Prov 16:27
your **w** offerings Is 1:13
your faith is **w** 1 Cor 15:17
w for any good Titus 1:16
man's religion is **w** James 1:26

WORTHY *having merit*
sin **w** of death Deut 21:22
w of his support Matt 10:10
is not **w** of Me Matt 10:37
is **w** of his wages Luke 10:7
manner **w** of the Rom 16:2
w of the gospel Phil 1:27
world was not **w** Heb 11:38
W is the Lamb Rev 5:12

Y

YAHWEH *see* **YHWH** *and* **LORD**

YEAR *period, time*
atonement...every **y** Lev 16:34
fiftieth **y**...jubilee Lev 25:1
the **y** of remission Deut 15:9
crowned the **y** with Ps 65:11
length of...**y-s** Prov 3:2

favorable y of the LORD Is 61:2
thirty y-s of age Luke 3:23
y of the LORD Luke 4:19
priest *enters,* once a y Heb 9:7
sacrifices…y by y Heb 10:1
y-s like one day 2 Pet 3:8
reign…thousand y-s Rev 20:6

YHWH
Hebrew tetragrammaton for name of God, probably pronounced Yahweh
Derived from Hebrew verb meaning "to be"
Translated usually as LORD
see also **LORD**
see also introductory material to NASB

YOUNG *early age, youth*
he sent y men Ex 24:5
or two y pigeons Lev 15:29
glory of y men is Prov 20:29
y men stumble Is 40:30
like a y lion Hos 5:14
finding a y donkey John 12:14
y men…visions Acts 2:17
urge the y men Titus 2:6

YOUTH *young*
evil from his y Gen 8:21
fresher than in y Job 33:25
the sins of my y Ps 25:7
confidence from my y Ps 71:5
your y is renewed Ps 103:5
the wife of your y Prov 5:18
y-s grow weary Is 40:30
the reproach of my y Jer 31:19
life from my y up Acts 26:4

Z

ZEALOT
member of radical Jewish nationalist party
Matt 10:4; Mark 3:18; Luke 6:15; Acts 1:13

ZEBULUN
1 *son of Jacob* Gen 30:20
2 *tribe* Num 34:25; Josh 21:34
3 *territory of the tribe, located in N Palestine* Josh 19:27; Judg 12:12; Is 9:1; Ezek 48:27

ZECHARIAH
1 *son of Jeiel* 1 Chr 9:35-37
2 *priest with ark* 1 Chr 15:24
3 *son of Isshiah* 1 Chr 24:25
4 *father of Iddo* 1 Chr 27:21
5 *son of Benaiah* 2 Chr 20:14
6 *son of Jehoshaphat* 2 Chr 21:2
7 *son of Jehoida* 2 Chr 24:20
8 *prophet* 2 Chr 26:5
9 *priest under Ezra* Neh 12:41
10 *minor prophet* Zech 1:1

ZEPHANIAH
1 *priest* 2 Kin 25:18
2 *Kohathite Levite* 1 Chr 6:36
3 *minor prophet* Zeph 1:1
4 *father of Josiah* Zech 6:10

ZERUBBABEL
line of David 1 Chr 3:1-19
helped rebuild temple Ezra 3:8

ZIN
wilderness in Negev Num 13:21; Deut 32:51; Josh 15:1,3

ZION
1 *hill / City of David which is Jerusalem* 2 Sam 5:7; 1 Chr 11:5
2 *after Temple built, name extended to top of hill, Mount Zion* Is 8:18; 18:7; Mic 4:7
3 *applied to all of Jerusalem as city spreads* 2 Kin 19:21; Ps 69:35; Is 1:8
4 *used in the corporate sense for the people and land* Ps 97:8; 149:2; Is 3:16; 8:14; 59:20; Joel 2:23; Zech 9:9; Rom 9:33; 1 Pet 2:3
5 *used eschatologically for heavenly Jerusalem* Is 60:14; Heb 12:22; Rev 14:1

ZIPPORAH
wife of Moses Ex 2:21; 4:25

ZIV
name of the second month in Hebrew calendar 1 Kin 6:1,37

Promises
from the Bible

GOD'S PROMISE OF:

Love—Psalm 89:38; Isaiah 54:10; Jeremiah 31:3–4a; Matthew 10:30–31; John 3:16; 15:9,13; 1 John 4:9

Forgiveness—2 Chronicles 7:14; Psalm 103:8–12; Jeremiah 31:34; Luke 15:3–7; Acts 10:43; Ephesians 1:7; 1 John 1:9

Salvation—Psalm 37:39–40; Isaiah 25:9; Matthew 1:21; Acts 16:31; Ephesians 2:8; Hebrews 7:25

The Holy Spirit—Joel 2:29; Luke 11:13; John 14:16–17; Acts 2:38; Romans 8:11

Everlasting Life—Job 19:25–27; John 6:40; 10:28; 1 Corinthians 15:51–52; 1 Thessalonians 4:17

Peace—Psalm 29:11; Isaiah 26:3; John 14:27; Romans 5:1–2; Ephesians 2:14; 2 Thessalonians 3:16

Joy—Psalm 16:11; 90:14; John 15:10–11; 16:22; Romans 16:13; 1 Peter 1:8

Freedom—Psalm 119:32; 146:7; John 8:34–36; Romans 6:6,14,20–22; 2 Corinthians 3:17; Revelation 1:5

Growth—Psalm 92:12, 14; 2 Corinthians 3:18; Ephesians 4:14–15; Philippians 1:6; 2 Peter 1:3–4

Encouragement—Psalm 10:17; Jeremiah 29:11; 1 Thessalonians 5:23; 2 Thessalonians 2:16–17; Hebrews 6:10; 1 Peter 2:9

Excellence—Joshua 1:7; Proverbs 16:3; Matthew 20:26–28; John 14:12; 15:15–16; 2 Corinthians 3:5–6

Strength—Psalm 73:25–26; Isaiah 40:29,31; 1 Corinthians 1:8; Ephesians 3:20; 2 Thessalonians 3:3; 1 Peter 5:10

Blessing—Psalm 128:5–6; Ezekiel 34:26; John 1:16; 10:10; Romans 8:28; Ephesians 1:3

His Presence—Joshua 1:5; Psalm 46:1,7; Matthew 18:20; 28:20; John 6:37; Romans 8:38–39

Answered Prayer—Psalm 65:2,5; Matthew 7:7–11; 21:22; 1 Peter 3:12; 1 John 5:14–15

Christ's Return—John 14:2–3; Acts 1:11; 1 Thessalonians 4:16–17; Revelation 1:7

GOD'S PROMISE WHEN YOU:

Feel Guilty—2 Samuel 14:14; Psalm 130:3–4; Romans 8:1–2; 1 Corinthians 6:11; Ephesians 3:12; Hebrews 10:22–23

Feel Dejected—Psalm 130:7; Isaiah 65:24; Matthew 11:28–30; Romans 8:26–27; Hebrews 4:16; James 4:8,10

Feel Despair—Psalm 119:116; Isaiah 57:15; Jeremiah 32:17; Hebrews 10:35

Are Disappointed—Psalm 22:4–5; Isaiah 49:23; Matthew 19:25–26; Mark 9:21–24; John 15:7; Ephesians 3:20

Are Depressed—Deuteronomy 31:8; Psalm 34:18; Isaiah 49:13–15; Romans 5:5

Are Persecuted—Genesis 50:20; Psalm 37:1–2; Matthew 5:10–12; 2 Corinthians 4:8–12; 2 Timothy 1:11–12; 1 Peter 3:13–14

Are Anxious—Psalm 55:22; Isaiah 41:13; Matthew 6:25; 11:28–29; Philippians 4:6–7; 1 Peter 5:7

Are Filled With Longing—Psalm 37:4; 84:11; 103:5; Luke 12:29–31

Are Sick—Psalm 23:4; 73:26; Isaiah 57:18; Matthew 8:16–17; John 16:33; Romans 8:37–39; James 5:14–15

Are Impatient—Psalm 27:13–14; 37:7,9; Romans 2:7; 1 Timothy 1:16; Hebrews 6:12; 1 Peter 3:9

Are Confused—Psalm 32:8; Isaiah 42:16; John 8:12; 14:27; 1 Corinthians 2:15–16; James 1:5

Are Tempted—Job 23:10–11; 1 Corinthians 10:13; Hebrews 2:18; 4:15–16; James 1:2–4,13–14; 1 Peter 5:8–10

Are Weak—Psalm 72:13; Isaiah 41:10; Romans 8:26; 1 Corinthians 1:7–9; 2 Corinthians 4:7–9; 12:9–10

Are Afraid—Psalm 4:8; 23:4; Isaiah 35:4; Romans 8:37–39; 2 Corinthians 1:10; 2 Timothy 1:7; Hebrews 13:6
Obey—Exodus 14:23; Matthew 16:27; John 8:31–32; 14:21,23; James 1:25
Are In Need—Isaiah 58:11; John 6:35; 2 Corinthians 9:10–11; Ephesians 3:20–21; Philippians 4:19
Grieve—Psalm 119:50,76–77; Jeremiah 31:13; Matthew 5:4; John 16:20–22; 1 Thessalonians 4:13–14; Revelation 21:3–4
Suffer—Psalm 34:19; Nahum 1:7; John 16:33; Romans 8:16–17; 1 Peter 2:20–21; 4:12–13
Fail—Joshua 1:9; Romans 3:23–24; 5:8; Hebrews 10:36; 1 John 1:8–9
Doubt—Psalm 34:22; John 3:18; 11:25–26; Romans 4:5; 1 John 4:15–16

Perspectives

from the Bible

WHAT TO READ WHEN:

The Future Seems Hopeless—Isaiah 54:1–7; Lamentations 3:19–24; 1 Corinthians 15:20–28; 1 Peter 1:1–9; 5:10–11; Revelation 11:15–19

Seeking God's Direction—1 Kings 3:1–14; Proverbs 2:1–6; Romans 12:1–3; Ephesians 5:15–17; Colossians 1:9–14; James 1:5–8

You Need Comfort—Isaiah 12; 40:1–11; Jeremiah 31:10–13; 2 Corinthians 1:3–7; 7:6–13

Others Disagree With You—Matthew 7:1–5; Romans 12:9–21; 14:1—15:7; 2 Corinthians 5:11–21

The World Seems Enticing—Genesis 3:1–7; Ecclesiastes 2:1–11; 2 Corinthians 6:14—7:1; James 1:26–27; 4:4–10; 1 John 2:15–17

You Need Assurance of Salvation—Psalm 91:14–16; Micah 7:18–20; John 3:14–21; 11:25–26; Acts 16:31–34; 1 John 5:9–13

Others Have Sinned Against You—Genesis 33:1–4; 50:15–20; Matthew 6:14–15; 18:21–35; Colossians 3:12–14; James 2:12–13

You Are Tempted to Be Bitter—Psalm 38:7–9; Proverbs 16:32; 1 Corinthians 13; Ephesians 4:29—5:2; Hebrews 12:14–15

You Are Tempted to Neglect Public Worship—Exodus 20:8–11; Psalm 95:1–7; Acts 2:42–47; Hebrews 10:19–25

Your Faith Needs Strengthening—Genesis 15:1–6; Proverbs 3:5–9; Romans 5:1–11; 1 Corinthians 9:24–27; Hebrews 10:19–25, 35–39; 11:1—12:13

You Need to Control Your Tongue—Psalm 39:1; Proverbs 10:18–20; Matthew 15:1–20; James 3:1–12

You Are Prone to Judge Others—Matthew 7:1–5; 1 Corinthians 4:1–5; James 2:1–13; 4:11–12

You Have Been Cheated—Genesis 33:1–4; Matthew 18:15–17; 1 Corinthians 6:1–8; James 5:1–8

Things Are Going Well—Job 31:24–28; Proverbs 15:27; Luke 12:13–21; 1 Timothy 6:3–19; Hebrews 13:5; James 2:1–17

You Wonder About Your Spiritual Gifts—Romans 12:3–8; 1 Corinthians 1:4–9; 12:1—14:25; 1 Peter 4:7–11

You Are Starting a New Job—1 Kings 3:1–4; Proverbs 10:4–5; Matthew 5:13–16; Romans 12:1–2; Galatians 5:13–26; Ephesians 1:3–14

You Are in a Position of Responsibility—1 Kings 11:5–7; Proverbs 3:21–27; Mark 10:35–45; Luke 7:1–10; 1 Corinthians 16:13–14; Galatians 6:9–10

You Are Establishing a New Home—Genesis 2:19–25; Ecclesiastes 9:7–10; Ephesians 5:22—6:4; Colossians 3:18–21; 1 Peter 3:1–7

You Have Been Quarreling—Genesis 13:5–11; Psalm 133; 1 Corinthians 3; Ephesians 4:1–6; 4:15—5:2; 2 Timothy 2:14–26; James 4:1–12

You Are Challenged by Dark Forces—Joshua 1:6–9; Psalm 56:1–4; Romans 8:38–39; 2 Corinthians 4:7–18; Ephesians 6:10–18; 2 Timothy 4:6–7

You Are Jealous—Numbers 12:1–15; 16:1–35; Galatians 5:13–15, 19–21; James 3:13–18

You Struggle With Laziness—Proverbs 6:6–11; 10:4–5; Ephesians 5:15–16; Philippians 2:12–13; 1 Thessalonians 4:1–12; 2 Thessalonians 3:6–15

You Struggle With Lust—Deuteronomy 22:22–4; 2 Samuel 11:1—12:14; Matthew 5:27–30; Romans 7:7–25; 13:8–14; James 1:13–18

You Are Angry—Genesis 4:1–12; Psalm 4:4; Matthew 5:21–22; 18:21–35; Ephesians 4:25—5:2; James 1:19–21

You Desire Revenge—Deuteronomy 32:34–35; Psalm 94:1; Proverbs 25:21–22; Matthew 5:38–42; Romans 12:17–21; 1 Thessalonians 5:12–15; 1 Peter 3:8–14

You Are Proud—Proverbs 8:12–14; Matthew 25:34–40; Mark 10:35–45; Romans 12:3; Philippians 2:1–11

You Struggle With Addiction—Psalm 18:28–36; Proverbs 23:29–35; Romans 6:1–23; 12:1–2; 1 Corinthians 6:12–20; Philippians 3:17—4:1
You Are Greedy—Psalm 62:1–2,10; Ecclesiastes 2:1–11; Luke 12:13–21; 2 Corinthians 9:6–15; Ephesians 5:3–7; 1 John 3:16–18
You Desire to Learn How to Pray—2 Chronicles 6:13–42; 20:5–12; Matthew 6:5–15; Mark 11:22–25; Luke 18:9–14; Philippians 4:4–7
You Struggle With Apathy—Numbers 25:10–13; Ecclesiastes 9:10; Matthew 25:1–13; Luke 12:35–48; 1 Thessalonians 5:1–11; Revelation 3:1–6,14–22

WHAT THE BIBLE SAYS ABOUT:

Adultery—Exodus 20:14; Leviticus 20:10; Deuteronomy 22:22–24; Matthew 5:27–32; Galatians 5:13–26; Ephesians 4:17—5:3
Ambition—1 Kings 3:5–12; Haggai 1:2–8; Matthew 16:21–27; Mark 9:33–37; 10:35–45; Philippians 2:1–4
Anger—Genesis 4:1–12; Psalm 4:4; 38:7–9; Proverbs 16:32; Matthew 5:21–26; Ephesians 4:25—5:2; James 1:19–27
Anxiety—Psalm 94:17–19; Ecclesiastes 22–25; Luke 12:22–34; Philippians 4:4–9; Hebrews 13:5–6
Atonement—Leviticus 16:2–34; Isaiah 6:1–7; Romans 3:21–26; 2 Corinthians 5:14–21; Hebrews 9; 1 Peter 2:22–25
Baptism—Matthew 3:1–12; 28:16–20; Romans 6:1–5
Bible Reading—Nehemiah 8:1–6; Psalm 1; 2 Timothy 3:14–17; Hebrews 4:12; James 1:19–27
Blood of Christ—Matthew 26:27–29; Hebrews 9:11–28
Body of Christ—Mark 14:22–24; 1 Corinthians 12:12–31; Hebrews 2:14–18
Celibacy—Matthew 19:4–12; 1 Corinthians 7:32–40; 1 Timothy 4:1–5
Children—Psalm 78:1–7; 127; 128; Matthew 18:1–9; Mark 10:13–16; Ephesians 6:1–4
Compassion—Psalm 103:8–12; 116:5–6; Micah 6:8; John 11:17–44; 2 Corinthians 1:3–7; 1 John 3:11–24
Conversion—Deuteronomy 4:30–31; 2 Chronicles 7:14; Ezekiel 18:30–32; John 3:1–21; 2 Corinthians 5:17–19; Ephesians 2:1–10
Creation—Genesis 1—2; Psalm 8; 19; 104; Romans 1:18–23; 8:18–27; Colossians 1:15–17
Cross—Mark 8:31—9:1; Luke 23:26–49
Death—Psalm 116:15–16; Isaiah 57:1–2; John 12:23–26; Romans 6:1–23; 1 Corinthians 15
Discipleship—Luke 14:25–34; John 15:1–17; 21:15–19
Discipline—Proverbs 3:11–12; 13:24; 1 Corinthians 11:27–32; Hebrews 12:1–13; Revelation 3:19
Divorce—Deuteronomy 24:1–4; Malachi 2:13–16; Matthew 19:1–12; Mark 10:2–12; 1 Corinthians 7:10–16
Eternal Life—Job 19:25–27; Psalm 23; Matthew 19:16–30; John 3:1–21; Romans 6:15–23
Faith—Genesis 15:1–6; Psalm 119:65–72; Proverbs 3:5–6; Matthew 6:25–34; Romans 3:21—5:11; Hebrews 11
Freedom—John 8:31–41; Romans 8:1–17; Galatians 4:21—5:26
Friendship—Proverbs 17:17; 27:6; Ecclesiastes 4:9–12; John 14:23—15:17; Colossians 3:12–17; 1 John 1:1–7
Giving—Deuteronomy 15:7–11; Proverbs 3:9; Malachi 3:10–12; Matthew 6:1–4; 2 Corinthians 8—9
Grace—Psalm 86; 103; Micah 7:18–20; Luke 15:11–31; Romans 5; Ephesians 2
Greed—1 Kings 21:1–22; Proverbs 15:27; Luke 12:13–21; 1 Timothy 6:3–10; James 5:1–6
Happiness—Psalm 33; Isaiah 12; 52:7–10; Matthew 5:1–12; John 13:1–17; Philippians 4:4–9
Heaven—1 Kings 8:23–30; Isaiah 65:17–25; Matthew 6:19–24; 25:31–46; Philippians 3:12—4:1; Revelation 21
Holy Spirit—Isaiah 61:1–3; Joel 2:28–32; John 14:15–31; 16:5–16; Acts 2; Romans 8:1–17

Homosexuality—Leviticus 18:22; 20:13; Romans 1:18–32; 1 Corinthians 6:9–11; 1 Timothy 1:9–11
Hope—Psalm 42; 130; Romans 5:1–11; Colossians 1:3–27; 1 Peter 1:3–9
Hospitality—Genesis 18:1–8; 2 Samuel 9:1–7; Luke 14:12–14; Romans 12:13; 1 Peter 4:9
Hypocrisy—1 Samuel 12:1–23; Isaiah 1:10–15; Zechariah 7:2–14; Matthew 6:1–24; 23; James 1:22–27
Joy—Isaiah 12; 52:7–10; Luke 15; James 1:2–18; 1 Peter 4:12–19
Justification—Genesis 15:1–6; Isaiah 53; Romans 3:21–31; 4:1—5:11; Galatians 2:15–21
Loneliness—1 Kings 19:1–18; Psalm 41; Matthew 26:36–46; 2 Timothy 4:16–18
Lord's Supper—Luke 22:7–23; John 13; 1 Corinthians 11:17–34
Love—Leviticus 19:18,34; Deuteronomy 6:1–5; Song of Solomon 1—2; Mark 12:28–34; 1 Corinthians 13; 1 John 4:7–21
Marriage—Genesis 2:19–25; Ecclesiastes 9:7–10; Matthew 19:1–12; 1 Corinthians 7; Ephesians 5:22–33
Peace—Numbers 6:24–26; Psalm 122; Isaiah 9:2–7; John 14:25–27; Romans 5:1–11; Ephesians 2:14–18; Philippians 4:4–9
Poor—Deuteronomy 15:1–11; Isaiah 58:1–9; Amos 5:11–15; Matthew 25:31–46; Luke 1:39–56; James 2:1–13
Profanity—Exodus 20:7; Leviticus 24:10–16; Proverbs 30:10–14; Ephesians 4:29–32; James 3:1–12
Reconciliation—Genesis 33:1–4; 50:15–21; Matthew 5:23–26; 2 Corinthians 5:11—6:2; Ephesians 2:11–22
Repentance—Deuteronomy 4:30–31; 2 Chronicles 7:14; Ezekiel 18:30–32; Matthew 4:12–17; Luke 18:9–14; Acts 2:38–41
Resurrection—Job 19:23–27; Psalm 16; Daniel 12:1–4; Matthew 27:57—28:20; 1 Corinthians 15
Revenge—Deuteronomy 32:34–35; Psalm 94:1; Proverbs 25:21–22; Matthew 5:38–47; Romans 12:17–21
Reward—Leviticus 26:3–39; Psalm 19:1–11; Isaiah 61:8–11; Matthew 5:3–12; Mark 10:29–31; 1 Corinthians 3:10–15
Salvation—Exodus 15:1–18; Psalm 62; Isaiah 59:15–20; Luke 19:1–10; Acts 16:16–34; Ephesians 2:1–10
Sanctification—2 Corinthians 7:1; 1 Thessalonians 5:23; 2 Peter 1:3–11
Second Coming—Matthew 24; John 14:1–4; 1 Corinthians 15:12–28; 1 Thessalonians 4:13—5:11
Stewardship—1 Chronicles 29:1–9; Matthew 25:14–30; Luke 12:35–48
Suffering—Deuteronomy 8:1–5; Job 1—2; Psalm 77; Isaiah 53; Romans 8:12–17; 1 Peter 3:8–22; 4:12–19
Unity—Psalm 133; John 17; Ephesians 4:1–16

Guarantee

Zondervan Publishing House guarantees leather Bibles unconditionally against manufacturing defects for a lifetime and hardcover and softcover Bibles for four years. This guarantee does not apply to normal wear. Contact Zondervan Customer Service, 800-727-1309, for replacement instructions.

Care

We suggest loosening the binding of your new Bible by gently pressing on a small section of pages at a time from the center. To ensure against breakage of the spine, it is best not to bend the cover backward around the spine or to carry study notes, church bulletins, pens, and the like, inside the cover. Because a felt-tipped marker will "bleed" through the pages, we recommend use of a ball-point pen or pencil to underline favorite passages. Your Bible should not be exposed to excessive heat, cold or humidity. Protecting the gold or silver edges of the paper from moisture will avoid spotting, streaking or fading.

WORLD OF THE PATRIARCHS

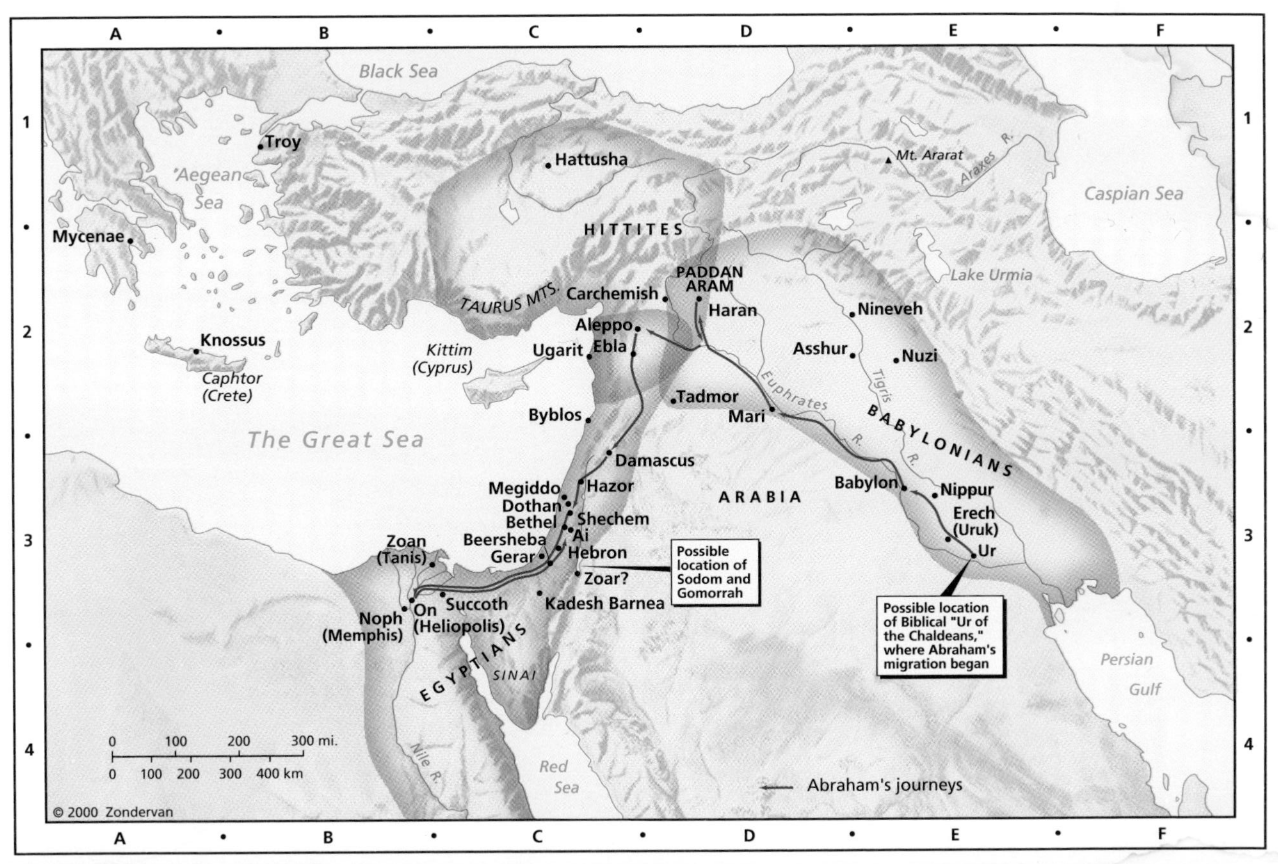

EXODUS AND CONQUEST OF CANAAN

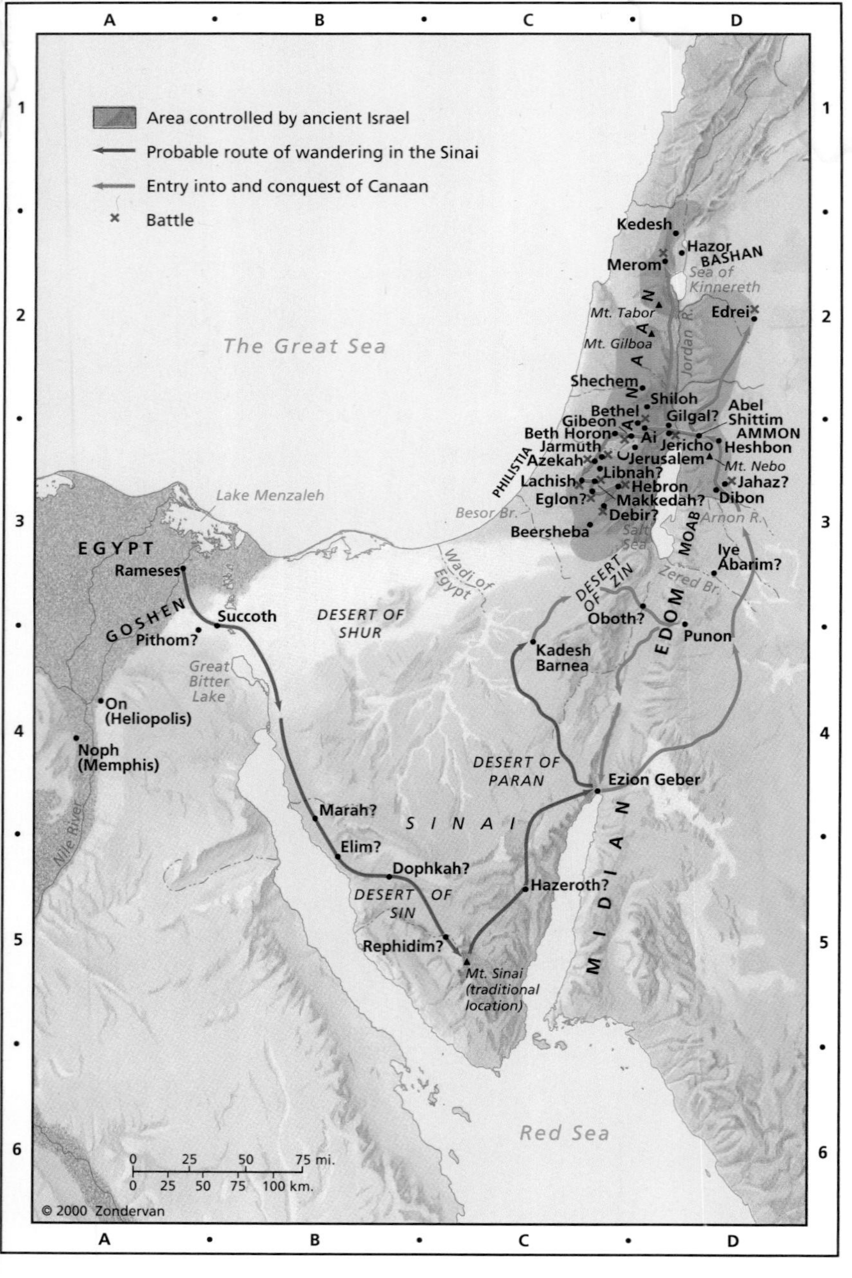

LAND OF THE TWELVE TRIBES

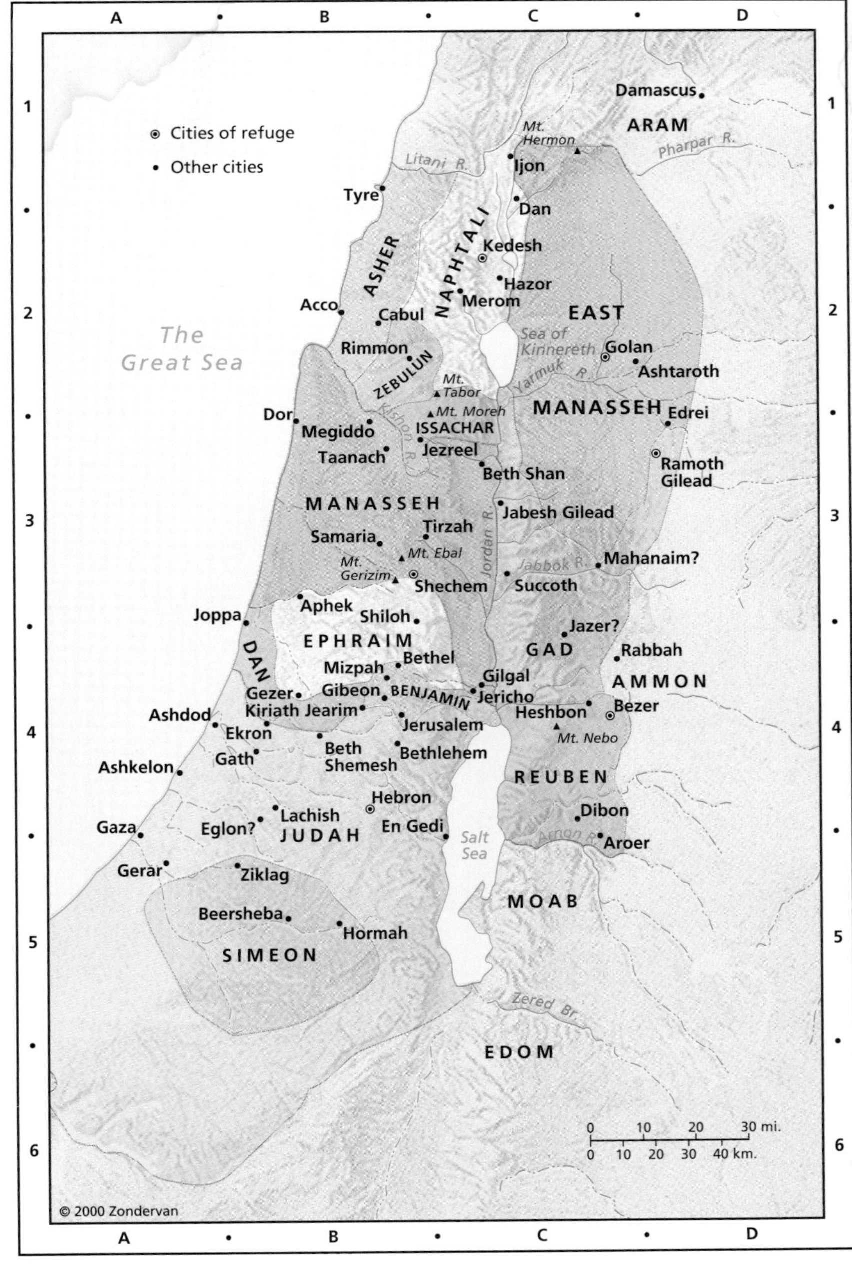

KINGDOM OF DAVID AND SOLOMON

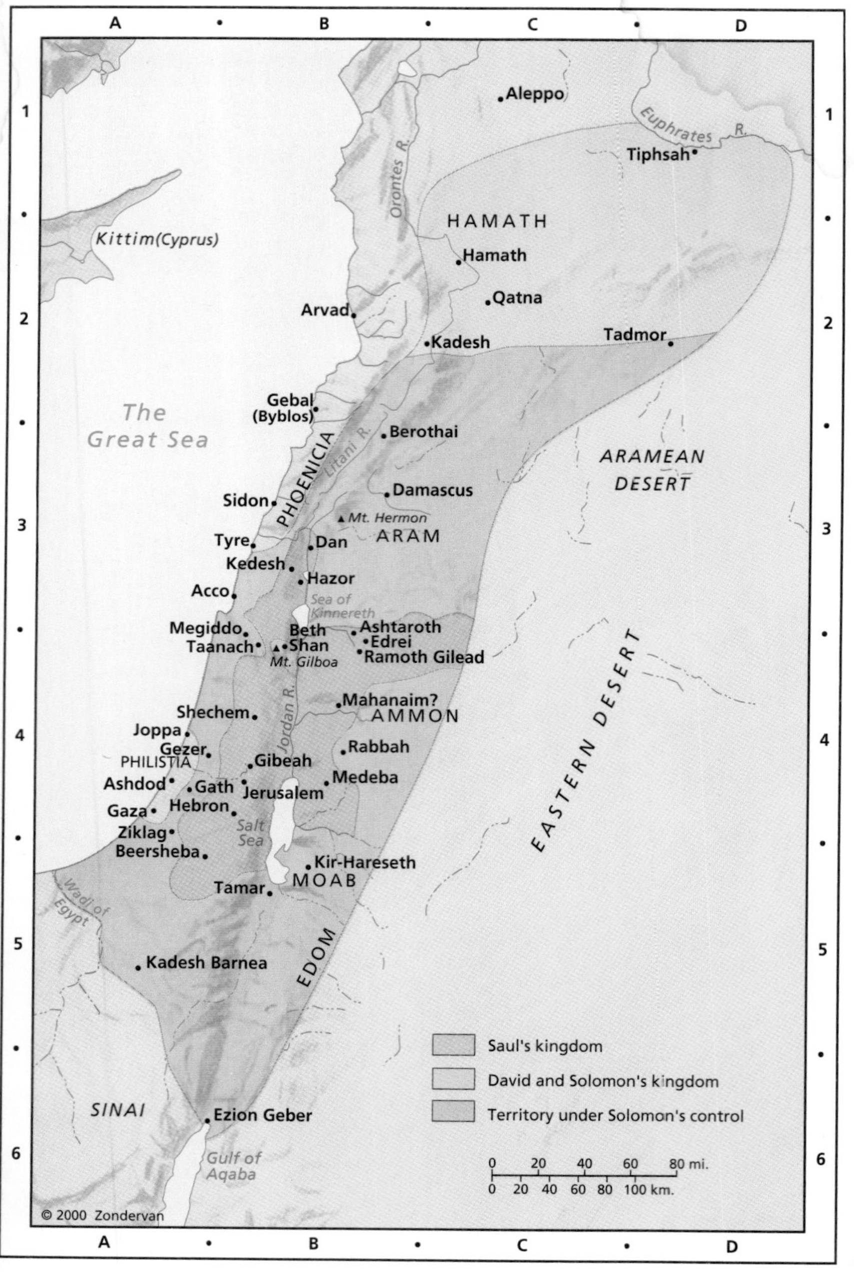
A
B
C
D
1
2
3
4
5
6
Aleppo
Euphrates R.
Tiphsah
Orontes R.
HAMATH
Kittim (Cyprus)
Hamath
Qatna
Arvad
Tadmor
Kadesh
The Great Sea
Gebal (Byblos)
Berothai
PHOENICIA
Litani R.
ARAMEAN DESERT
Sidon
Damascus
Mt. Hermon
Tyre
Dan
ARAM
Kedesh
Hazor
Acco
Sea of Kinnereth
Megiddo
Beth Shan
Ashtaroth
Taanach
Edrei
Mt. Gilboa
Ramoth Gilead
EASTERN DESERT
Jordan R.
Mahanaim?
Shechem
AMMON
Joppa
Gezer
Rabbah
PHILISTIA
Gibeah
Ashdod
Gath
Medeba
Jerusalem
Gaza
Hebron
Salt Sea
Ziklag
Beersheba
Kir-Hareseth
Wadi of Egypt
Tamar
MOAB
EDOM
Kadesh Barnea
Saul's kingdom
David and Solomon's kingdom
Territory under Solomon's control
SINAI
Ezion Geber
Gulf of Aqaba
0 20 40 60 80 mi.
0 20 40 60 80 100 km.
© 2000 Zondervan

JESUS' MINISTRY

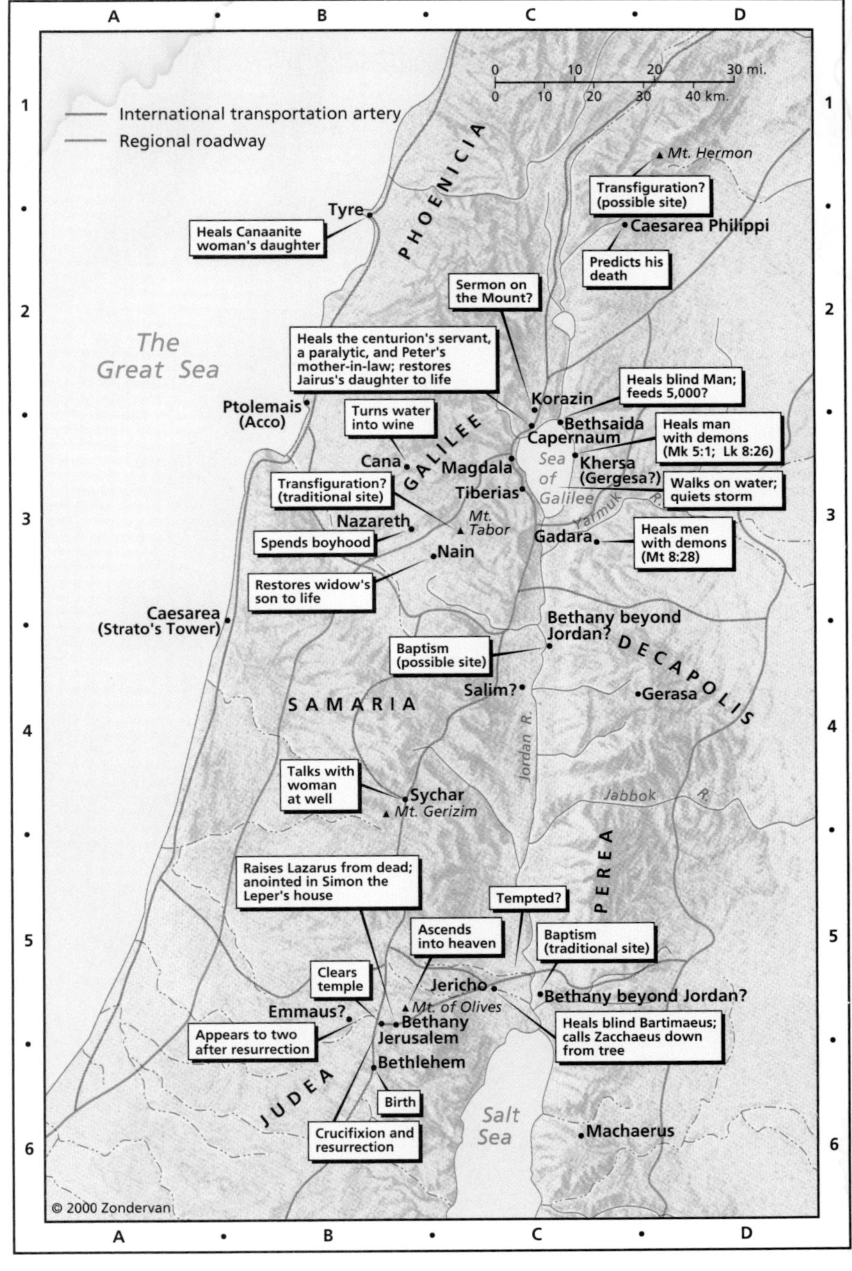

A
B
C
D
1
2
3
4
5
6
0
10
20
30 mi.
0
10
20
30
40 km.
International transportation artery
Regional roadway
PHOENICIA
Mt. Hermon
Transfiguration? (possible site)
Tyre
Heals Canaanite woman's daughter
Caesarea Philippi
Predicts his death
Sermon on the Mount?
The Great Sea
Heals the centurion's servant, a paralytic, and Peter's mother-in-law; restores Jairus's daughter to life
Heals blind Man; feeds 5,000?
Korazin
Ptolemais (Acco)
Turns water into wine
Bethsaida
Capernaum
Heals man with demons (Mk 5:1; Lk 8:26)
GALILEE
Cana
Magdala
Sea of Galilee
Khersa (Gergesa?)
Transfiguration? (traditional site)
Tiberias
Walks on water; quiets storm
Yarmuk R.
Nazareth
Mt. Tabor
Spends boyhood
Gadara
Heals men with demons (Mt 8:28)
Nain
Restores widow's son to life
Caesarea (Strato's Tower)
Bethany beyond Jordan?
DECAPOLIS
Baptism (possible site)
Salim?
Gerasa
SAMARIA
Jordan R.
Talks with woman at well
Sychar
Mt. Gerizim
Jabbok R.
PEREA
Raises Lazarus from dead; anointed in Simon the Leper's house
Tempted?
Ascends into heaven
Baptism (traditional site)
Clears temple
Jericho
Bethany beyond Jordan?
Mt. of Olives
Emmaus?
Bethany
Jerusalem
Appears to two after resurrection
Heals blind Bartimaeus; calls Zacchaeus down from tree
Bethlehem
JUDEA
Birth
Salt Sea
Machaerus
Crucifixion and resurrection

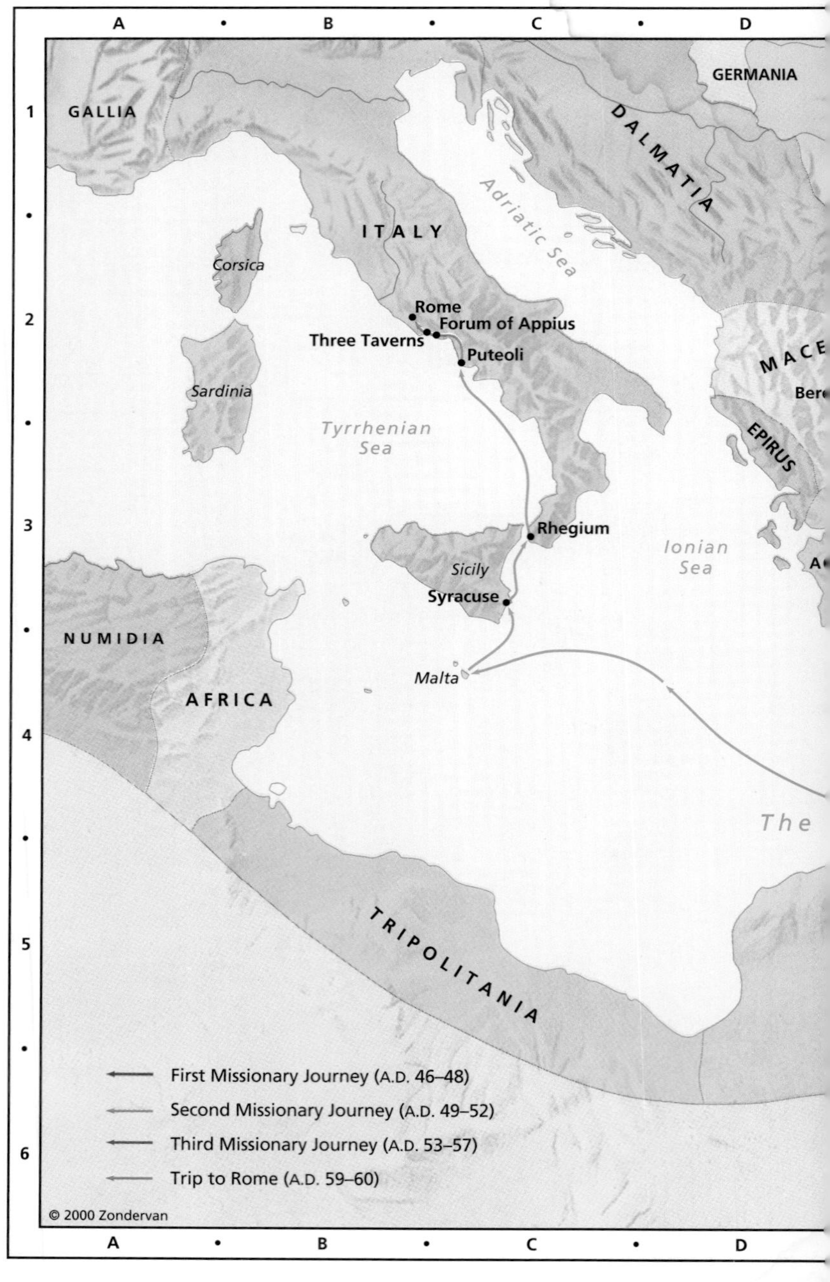
A
B
C
D
1
2
3
4
5
6
GERMANIA
GALLIA
DALMATIA
Adriatic Sea
ITALY
Corsica
Rome
Forum of Appius
Three Taverns
Puteoli
Sardinia
Tyrrhenian Sea
Rhegium
Ionian Sea
Sicily
Syracuse
Malta
NUMIDIA
AFRICA
TRIPOLITANIA
EPIRUS
First Missionary Journey (A.D. 46–48)
Second Missionary Journey (A.D. 49–52)
Third Missionary Journey (A.D. 53–57)
Trip to Rome (A.D. 59–60)
© 2000 Zondervan

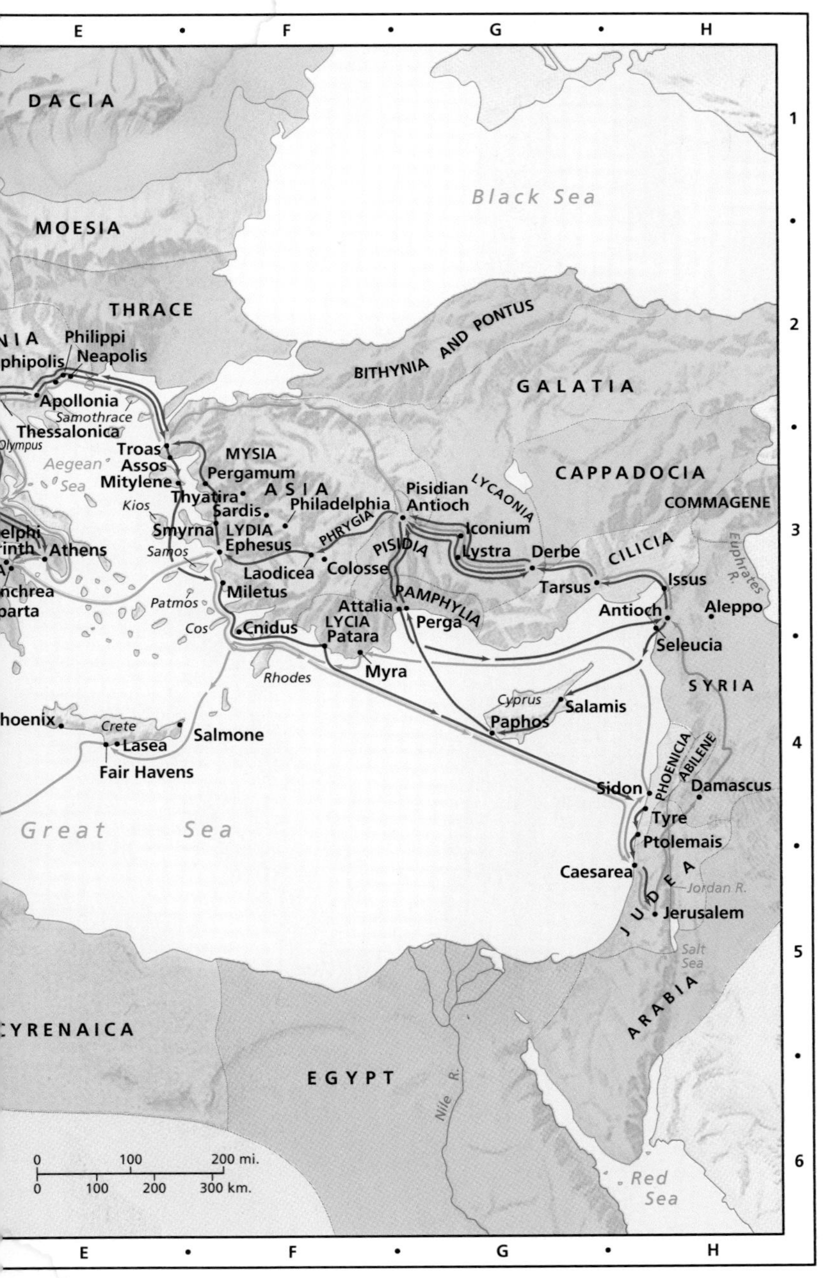
E
F
G
H
1
2
3
4
5
6
DACIA
MOESIA
THRACE
Philippi
Neapolis
Apollonia
Samothrace
Thessalonica
Olympus
Troas
Assos
Aegean Sea
Mitylene
MYSIA
Pergamum
Thyatira
ASIA
Kios
Sardis
Philadelphia
Smyrna
LYDIA
Athens
Samos
Ephesus
PHRYGIA
Laodicea
Colosse
Miletus
Patmos
Cos
Cnidus
Rhodes
Crete
Lasea
Fair Havens
Salmone
Great Sea
Black Sea
BITHYNIA AND PONTUS
GALATIA
CAPPADOCIA
COMMAGENE
LYCAONIA
Pisidian Antioch
PISIDIA
Iconium
Lystra
Derbe
CILICIA
Tarsus
Issus
Euphrates R.
Aleppo
Antioch
Seleucia
Attalia
PAMPHYLIA
Perga
LYCIA
Patara
Myra
SYRIA
Cyprus
Salamis
Paphos
PHOENICIA
ABILENE
Sidon
Damascus
Tyre
Ptolemais
Caesarea
JUDEA
Jordan R.
Jerusalem
Salt Sea
ARABIA
EGYPT
Nile R.
Red Sea
0
100
200 mi.
0
100
200
300 km.

JERUSALEM IN THE TIME OF JESUS

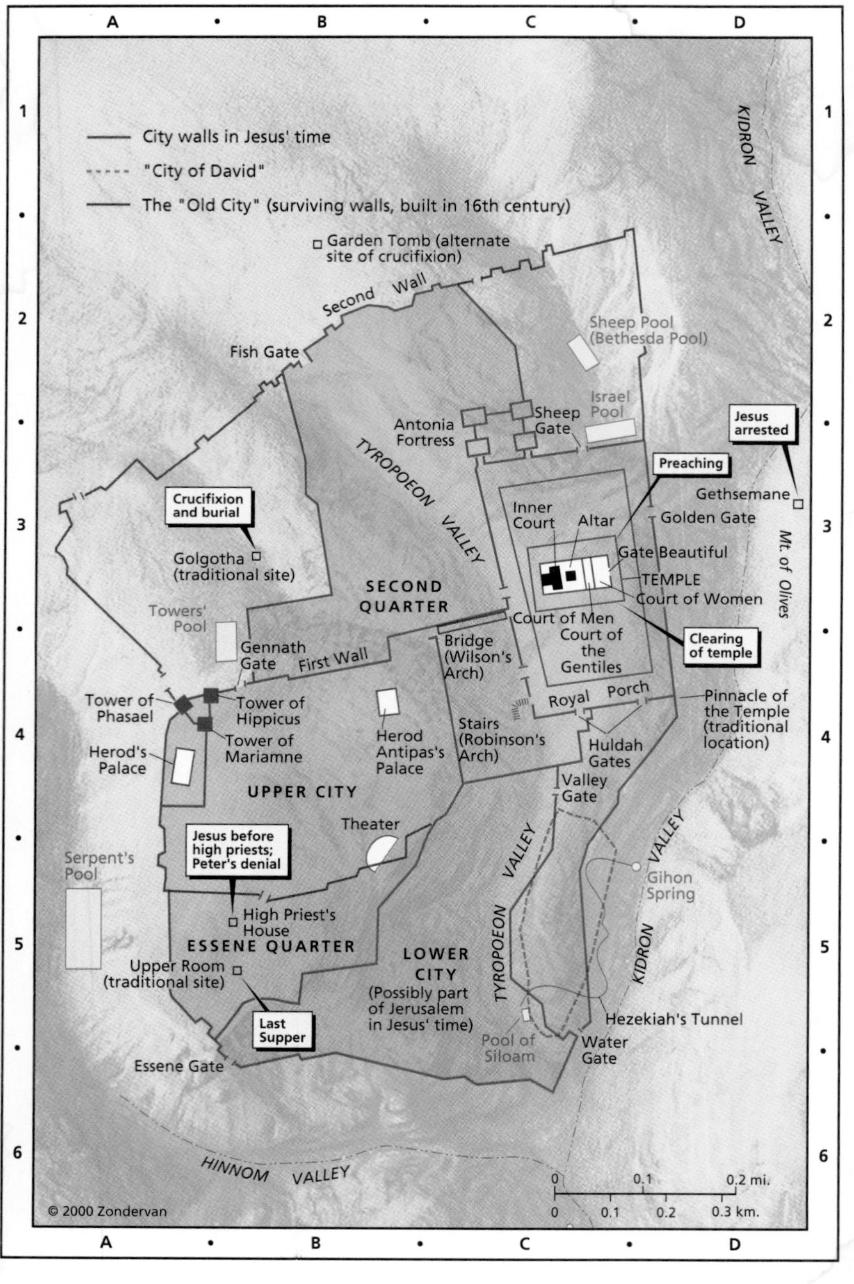

City walls in Jesus' time
"City of David"
The "Old City" (surviving walls, built in 16th century)
Garden Tomb (alternate site of crucifixion)
Second Wall
Fish Gate
Sheep Pool (Bethesda Pool)
Israel Pool
Antonia Fortress
Sheep Gate
Jesus arrested
Preaching
Gethsemane
KIDRON VALLEY
TYROPOEON VALLEY
Crucifixion and burial
Golgotha (traditional site)
Inner Court
Altar
Golden Gate
Gate Beautiful
TEMPLE
Court of Women
Mt. of Olives
SECOND QUARTER
Towers' Pool
Court of Men
Court of the Gentiles
Clearing of temple
Gennath Gate
First Wall
Bridge (Wilson's Arch)
Royal Porch
Pinnacle of the Temple (traditional location)
Tower of Phasael
Tower of Hippicus
Tower of Mariamne
Herod's Palace
Herod Antipas's Palace
Stairs (Robinson's Arch)
Huldah Gates
Valley Gate
UPPER CITY
Theater
Jesus before high priests; Peter's denial
Serpent's Pool
Gihon Spring
High Priest's House
ESSENE QUARTER
LOWER CITY (Possibly part of Jerusalem in Jesus' time)
Upper Room (traditional site)
Last Supper
Hezekiah's Tunnel
Pool of Siloam
Water Gate
Essene Gate
HINNOM VALLEY
0 0.1 0.2 mi.
0 0.1 0.2 0.3 km.
A B C D
1 2 3 4 5 6